22^{00}

HARRAP'S
New Standard

FRENCH AND ENGLISH
DICTIONARY

VOLUME TWO

FRENCH—ENGLISH

J—Z

PRINCIPAL
SUB-EDITORS

Vivien Flynn, B.A.
Christine Fontan, *Licenciée-ès-Lettres*
Muriel Holland Smith
Elizabeth A. Strick, M.A.

PRINCIPAL COLLABORATORS AND TECHNICAL ADVISERS

Jean Bétesta
Dr Reginal Bowen
Marcel Ferlin, 1888–1970
Michel Ginguay
Roland Ginguay
Professor Lewis C. Harmer

HARRAP'S
New Standard
FRENCH AND ENGLISH DICTIONARY

by

J. E. MANSION, M.A.

Revised and Edited by

R. P. L. LEDÉSERT, *Licencié-ès-Lettres, Licencié en Droit,*

and

MARGARET LEDÉSERT, M.A.

VOLUME TWO
FRENCH—ENGLISH
J—Z

HARRAP
LONDON AND PARIS
1981

Published in Great Britain
by GEORGE G. HARRAP & Co. LTD.
182 High Holborn, London WC1V 7AX
Ninth impression: 1981

© *George G. Harrap & Co. Ltd. 1934, 1972*

ISBN 0 245-50973-9

Text set in 7 pt Monotype Times New Roman, printed by photolithography,
and bound in Great Britain at The Pitman Press, Bath

Pronunciation

THE symbols used are those of the International Phonetic Association, and the pronunciation given is the one used most frequently by educated Frenchmen. It is sometimes different from that given in previous editions of the dictionary, as allowance has been made for the evolution of the pronunciation from one generation to another. A few points, however, call for special explanation:

1. Although the accent on the letter *e* (é, è, ê) frequently indicates the pronunciation [e, ɛ, ɛː], this is not automatically so, as the proximity of certain sounds may modify the pronunciation. This modification has been represented, where it is most marked, by the nearest phonetic symbol available. Moreover, as unaccented vowels are always less closed or less open than those in a tonic position, [e] and [ɛ] are often reduced to an intermediate sound which is less closed than [e] and less open than [ɛ]. It has not, however, been considered desirable to show this intermediate sound.

2. The endings *-ation*, *-assion* have in general been represented as [asjɔ̃], though there is a modern tendency, particularly in some parts of France, for the pronunciation [ɑsjɔ̃] to be gaining ground in certain words.

3. Certain final syllables have been indicated as long [ː], notably before a final [j], [r], [v], [z] or [ʒ], and when a nasalized vowel is followed by a pronounced consonant. The user should note that in the table of phonetic symbols vowels followed by the lengthening sign have not been listed separately, though for each vowel, where applicable, examples of the lengthened syllable have been included. The half-length sign [ˑ], denoting a half lengthening within a phonetic group, has not been used at all, as it was felt that such discrimination, liable to give rise to a certain amount of controversy, would be out of place in a dictionary that is not primarily phonetic.

4. For the ending *-aille* the pronunciations [aːj] and [ɑːj] are both current; though in general the pronunciation [ɑːj] is associated with words that are pejorative in meaning, this is not always the case, and the user will note a certain number of words which are in no way pejorative for which we have considered that the pronunciation [ɑːj] is the more current.

5. The pronunciation of the unvoiced final *r* and *l* after a consonant has been given as [r̥] and [l̥], as in *mètre* [mɛtr̥] and *table* [tabl̥].

6. The pronunciation [œ̃] to represent *un* has been used throughout, despite the growing tendency, especially in some parts of France, for the pronunciation [ɛ̃] to be used in words such as *lundi* or *Verdun*.

7. The tonic accent is not indicated, but it may be assumed to fall, however slightly, on the last sounded syllable of a word, when that word is considered alone, apart from a word group. It should, however, be borne in mind that the tonic accent is much less pronounced in French than in English.

Prononciation

Les signes employés pour figurer la prononciation sont ceux de *l'Association phonétique internationale*.

La prononciation figurée est, dans chaque cas, la prononciation la plus courante chez les Français instruits. Elle est parfois différente de celle notée dans nos précédentes éditions; la prononciation française, comme la prononciation anglaise, évolue au cours des générations; nous avons autant que possible tenu compte de cette évolution.

Nous nous permettons d'attirer l'attention sur quelques particularités:

1. Il ne faut pas oublier que si dans un *e* accentué (é, è, ê) l'accent, dans beaucoup de cas, indique la prononciation [e, ɛ, ɛ:], il n'en est pas toujours ainsi, car le voisinage de certains sons peut modifier cette prononciation. Nous avons noté cette modification, lorsqu'elle est patente, par le signe le plus approchant. D'autre part, les voyelles en position atone étant toujours moins fermées ou moins ouvertes qu'en position tonique, [e] ou [ɛ] sont souvent réduits à un son intermédiaire. Nous avons jugé superflu de noter spécialement cet *e* intermédiaire.

2. Pour les terminaisons *-ation, -assion* nous avons dans la plupart des cas choisi la prononciation [asjɔ̃]. Il faut cependant remarquer que la prononciation [ɑsjɔ̃] a une tendance à se répandre dans certaines régions, surtout pour certains mots.

3. Nous avons indiqué comme longues [:] certaines syllabes finales, notamment celles qui se terminent en [j], [r], [v], [z], ou [ʒ] et celles dans lesquelles une voyelle nasale est suivie par une consonne prononcée. Dans la table des symboles phonétiques nous n'avons pas indiqué séparément les voyelles courtes et les voyelles longues ([i], [i:], [a], [a:], etc.) mais pour chaque voyelle où cela est nécessaire nous avons donné des exemples de syllabes courtes et longues. Nous n'avons pas considéré comme utile l'introduction du symbole ['] qui se réfère à une voyelle demi-longue, car une distinction si minutieuse n'est pas à sa place dans un dictionnaire qui n'est pas primordialement un dictionnaire phonétique.

4. La terminaison *-aille* peut se prononcer ou [a:j] ou [ɑ:j]; en général la prononciation [ɑ:j] est associée aux mots qui ont un sens péjoratif, mais ceci n'est pas toujours le cas, et l'usager remarquera un certain nombre de mots avec la terminaison [ɑ:j] dont le sens n'est aucunement péjoratif.

5. La prononciation de l'*r* ou de l'*l* final atone qui suit une consonne, comme dans des mots comme *mètre* ou *table*, est représentée par [ɹ] et [l̩]: [mɛtɹ], [tɑbl̩].

6. Nous avons maintenu partout la figuration [œ̃] pour la graphie *un*; il faut cependant noter que la prononciation [ɛ̃] pour [œ̃] dans des mots comme *lundi, Verdun*, tend à se répandre, surtout dans certaines régions.

7. Nous n'avons pas noté l'accent tonique. L'accent *normal* (qu'il faut distinguer de l'accent *d'insistance*) porte, dans le mot isolé ,sur la dernière syllabe (ou l'avant-dernière si la dernière comporte un *e* muet); mais il ne faut pas oublier que l'accent tonique est moins prononcé en français qu'en anglais.

Phonetic Symbols

VOWELS

[i] vite [vit]; signe [siɲ]; rire [riːr]; fille [fiːj]; Moïse [mɔiːz]; ami [ami]; sortie [sɔrti].

[e] été [ete]; donner, donné [dɔne]; légal [legal]; saisir [seziːr].

[ɛ] elle [ɛl]; très [trɛ]; parquet [parkɛ]; forêt [fɔrɛ]; mais [mɛ]; terre [tɛːr]; pèse [pɛːz]; rêve [rɛːv]; paire [pɛːr]; père [pɛːr].

[a] absent [absɑ̃]; chat [ʃa]; tache [taʃ]; toit [twa]; couramment [kuramɑ̃]; phare [faːr]; lave [laːv]; noir [nwaːr]; courage [kuraːʒ].

[ɑ] pas [pɑ]; âgé [ɑʒe]; âge [ɑːʒ]; tâche [tɑʃ]; sable [sɑbl̩].

[ɔ] donner [dɔne]; Paul [pɔl]; album [albɔm]; fort [fɔːr]; éloge [elɔːʒ].

[o] dos [do]; impôt [ɛ̃po]; chaud [ʃo]; chapeau [ʃapo]; saumoneau [somono]; rose [roːz]; sauge [soːʒ].

[u] tout [tu]; goût [gu]; goutte [gut]; août [u]; cour [kuːr]; loup [lu]; louve [luːv].

[y] cru [kry]; crû [kry]; ciguë [sigy]; punir [pyniːr]; mur [myːr]; mûr [myːr]; gageure [gaʒyːr]; muse [myːz].

[ø] feu [fø]; nœud [nø]; heureux [œrø]; heureuse [œrøːz].

[œ] seul [sœl]; jeune [ʒœn]; œuf [œf]; cueillir [kœjiːr]; fleurir [flœriːr]; sœur [sœːr]; feuille [fœːj].

[ə]* le [lə]; ce [sə]; entremets [ɑ̃trəmɛ]; vendredi [vɑ̃drədi].

[ɛ̃] vin [vɛ̃]; plein [plɛ̃]; main [mɛ̃]; chien [ʃjɛ̃]; examen [egzamɛ̃]; syntaxe [sɛ̃taks]; impair [ɛ̃pɛːr]; faim [fɛ̃]; thym [tɛ̃]; prince [prɛ̃ːs]; plainte [plɛ̃ːt]; teindre [tɛ̃ːdr̩].

[ɑ̃] enfant [ɑ̃fɑ̃]; tambour [tɑ̃buːr]; temps [tɑ̃]; tant [tɑ̃]; tante [tɑ̃ːt]; paon [pɑ̃]; danse [dɑ̃ːs]; centre [sɑ̃ːtr̩]; exempt [egzɑ̃]; exempte [egzɑ̃ːt]; ample [ɑ̃ːpl̩]; branche [brɑ̃ːʃ].

[ɔ̃] mon [mɔ̃]; plomb [plɔ̃]; fronton [frɔ̃tɔ̃]; long [lɔ̃]; longe [lɔ̃ːʒ]; honte [ɔ̃ːt]; nombre [nɔ̃ːbr̩]; compte [kɔ̃ːt]; comte [kɔ̃ːt].

[œ̃] un [œ̃]; lundi [lœ̃di]; Verdun [vɛrdœ̃]; parfum [parfœ̃]; humble [œ̃ːbl̩]; lunch [lœ̃ːʃ].

CONSONANTS

[p] pain [pɛ̃]; frapper [frape]; tape [tap].

[b] beau [bo]; abbé [abe]; robe [rɔb].

[m] mon [mɔ̃]; aimer [ɛme]; madame [madam]; flamme [flam]; prisme [prism]; immatériel [im(m)aterjɛl].

[f] feu [fø]; effet [efɛ]; bref [brɛf]; phrase [fraːz]; Joseph [ʒozɛf].

[v] voir [vwaːr]; vie [vi]; wagon [vagɔ̃]; neuf heures [nœvœːr].

[t] table [tabl̩]; tête [tɛt]; nette [nɛt]; grand homme [grɑ̃tɔm]; théâtre [teɑːtr̩].

[d] donner [dɔne]; addition [adisjɔ̃]; sud [syd].

[n] né [ne]; animal [animal]; canne [kan]; amen [amɛn]; automne [otɔn]; penniforme [pɛn(n)ifɔrm].

[s] sou [su]; assassin [asasɛ̃]; tasse [tɑːs]; rébus [rebys]; prisme [prism]; cire [siːr]; leçon [ləsɔ̃]; scène [sɛn]; six [sis]; soixante [swasɑ̃ːt]; Bruxelles [brysɛl]; déhiscence [deis(s)ɑːs].

[z] cousin [kuzɛ̃]; les enfants [lezɑ̃fɑ̃]; vas-y [vazi]; zéro [zero]; deuxième [døzjɛm].

[l] lait [lɛ]; aile [ɛl]; facile [fasil]; aller [ale]; balle [bal]; illusion [il(l)yzjɔ̃].

[l̩] table [tabl̩]; sensible [sɑ̃sibl̩] hièble [jɛbl̩]; faible [fɛbl̩]; double [dubl̩]; noble [nɔbl̩].

[ʃ] chose [ʃoːz]; chercher [ʃɛrʃe]; schisme [ʃism].

[ʒ] Jean [ʒɑ̃]; gilet [ʒilɛ]; manger [mɑ̃ʒe]; âge [ɑːʒ]; changeable [ʃɑ̃ʒabl̩].

[k] camp [kɑ̃]; képi [kepi]; bifteck [biftɛk]; coq [kɔk]; quatre [katr̩]; queue- [kø]; écho [eko]; chrétien [kretjɛ̃]; physique [fizik].

[g] garde [gard]; agrandir [agrɑ̃diːr]; aggraver [agrave]; guerre [gɛːr]; gui [gi]; second [səgɔ̃]; agnostique [agnɔstik]; gneiss [gnɛs]; grammaire [gram(m)ɛːr].

[ɲ] campagne [kɑ̃paɲ]; poignet [pwaɲɛ]; gnaf [ɲaf].

[ŋ] (in words of foreign origin) parking [parkiŋ]; smoking [smɔkiŋ].

[r] rare [raːr]; chariot [ʃarjo]; arbre [arbr̩]; marron [marɔ̃]; ménorrhée [menore]; rhume [rym]; sentir [sɑ̃tiːr]; irréparable [ir(r)eparabl̩].

[r̩] être [ɛːtr̩]; marbre [marbr̩]; neutre [nøtr̩]; notre [nɔtr̩]; moudre [mudr̩]; sabre [sɑːbr̩].

[ks] accident [aksidɑ̃]; exception [ɛksɛpsjɔ̃]; action [aksjɔ̃]; (la lettre) x [iks]; xénophobe [ksenɔfɔb]; xylophone [ksilɔfɔn].

[gz] exister [egziste]; examen [egzamɛ̃]; xanthéine [gzɑ̃tein].

SEMI-CONSONANTS

[j] yacht [jɔt]; yeux [jø]; yougoslave [jugɔslaːv]; yucca [juka]; piano [pjano]; mioche [mjɔʃ]; ration [rasjɔ̃]; voyager [vwajaʒe]; fauteuil [fotœːj]; travail [travaːj]; travailler [travaje]; ensoleillé [ɑ̃sɔleje]; œillade [œjad]; feuille [fœːj]; cahier [kaje]; levier [ləvje]; lévrier [levrije].

[w] ouate [wat]; ouest [wɛst]; oui [wi]; jouer [ʒwe]; noir [nwaːr]; loin [lwɛ̃]; pingouin [pɛ̃gwɛ̃]; (also in words of foreign origin) water-closet [watɛrklɔzɛt]; wattage [wataːʒ]; whist [wist]; wellingtonia [wɛliŋtɔnja].

[ɥ] muet [mɥe]; huit [ɥit]; luire [lɥiːr]; aiguille [ɛgɥiːj]; distribuer [distribɥe].

---

* The symbol (ə) (in brackets) indicates that the 'mute' e is pronounced in careful speech but not in rapid speech.

Abbreviations Used in the Dictionary
Abréviations Utilisées dans le Dictionnaire

A:	archaism; ancient; in former use	désuet
a., adj.	adjective	adjectif
abbr.	abbreviation	abréviation
abs.	absolutely; absolute use	emploi absolu
Ac:	acoustics	acoustique
acc.	accusative	accusatif
Adm:	administration; civil service	administration
adv.	adverb	adverbe
adv.phr.	adverbial phrase	locution adverbiale
Aer:	aeronautics	aéronautique
Agr:	agriculture	agriculture
A.Hist:	ancient history	histoire ancienne
Alch:	alchemy	alchimie
Alg:	algebra	algèbre
Algae:	algae	algues
Amph:	Amphibia	amphibiens
Anat:	anatomy	anatomy
Ann:	Annelida, worms	annelés
Ant:	antiquity, antiquities	antiquité
Anthr:	anthropology	anthropologie
Ap:	apiculture	apiculture
approx:	approximately	sens approché
Ar:	arithmetic	arithmétique
Arach:	Arachnida	arachnides
Arb:	arboriculture	arboriculture; sylviculture
Arch:	architecture	architecture
Archeol:	archaeology	archéologie
Arm:	armour	armure
Arms:	arms; armaments	armes; armements
art.	article	article
Art:	art	beaux-arts
Artil:	artillery	artillerie
Astr:	astronomy	astronomie
Astrol:	astrology	astrologie
Astro-Ph:	astrophysics	astrophysique
Atom.Ph:	atomic physics	sciences atomiques
attrib.	attributive	attributif
Austr.	Australia; Australian	Australie; australien
Aut:	motoring; automobile industry	automobilisme; industrie automobile
aux.	auxiliary	auxiliaire
Av:	aviation; aircraft	aviation; avions
B:	Bible; biblical	Bible; biblique
Bac:	bacteriology	bactériologie
Bak:	baking	boulangerie
Ball:	ballistics	ballistique
Bank:	banking	opérations de banque
Belg:	Belgium; Belgian	Belgique; belge
B.Hist:	Bible history	histoire sainte
Bib:	bibliography	bibliographie
Bill:	billiards	jeu de billard
Bio-Ch:	biochemistry	biochimie
Biol:	biology	biologie
Bookb:	bookbinding	reliure
Book-k:	book-keeping	comptabilité
Bootm:	boot and shoe industry	cordonnerie; industrie de la chaussure
Bot:	botany	botanique
Box:	boxing	boxe
Breed:	breeding	élevage
Brew:	brewing	brasserie
Brickm:	brickmaking	briqueterie
card.a.	cardinal adjective	adjectif cardinal
Cards:	card games	jeu de cartes
Carp:	carpentry	charpenterie; menuiserie du bâtiment
Cav:	cavalry	cavalerie
Cer:	ceramics	céramique
cf.	refer to	conferatur
Ch:	chemistry	chimie
Chess:	chess	jeu d'échecs
Chr:	chronology	chronologie
Cin:	cinema	cinéma
Civ:	civilization	civilisation
Civ.E:	civil engineering	génie civil
Cl:	classical: Greek or Roman antiquity	classique; antiquité grecque ou romaine
Clockm:	clock and watch making	horlogerie
Coel:	Coelenterata	cœlentérés
cogn.acc.	cognate accusative	accusatif de l'objet interne
Cokem:	cokemaking	industrie du coke
coll.	collective	collectif
Com:	commerce; business term	(terme du) commerce
comb.fm.	combining form	forme de combinaison
Comest:	comestibles, food	comestibles
comp.	comparative	comparatif
Conch:	conchology	conchyliologie
condit.	conditional	conditionnel
conj.	conjunction	conjonction
conj. like	conjugated like	se conjuge comme
Const:	construction, building industry	industrie du bâtiment
Coop:	cooperage	tonnellerie
Corr:	correspondence, letters	correspondance, lettres
Cost:	costume; clothing	costume; habillement
cp.	compare	comparer
Cr:	cricket	cricket
Crust:	Crustacea	crustacés
Cryst:	crystallography	cristallographie
Cu:	culinary; cooking	culinaire; cuisine
Cust:	customs	douane
Cy:	cycles; cycling	bicyclettes; cyclisme
Danc:	dancing	danse
dat.	dative	datif
def.	(i) definitive; (ii) defective (verb)	(i) défini; (ii) (verbe) défectif
dem.	demonstrative	démonstratif
Dent:	dentistry	art dentaire
Dial:	dialectal	dialectal
dim.	diminutive	diminutif
Dipl:	diplomacy; diplomatic	diplomatie; diplomatique
Dist:	distilling	distillation
Dom.Ec:	domestic economy; household equipment	économie domestique; ménage
Draw:	drawing	dessin
Dressm:	dressmaking	couture (mode)
Dy:	dyeing	teinture

Abbreviations Used in the Dictionary

Dyn:	dynamics	dynamique	*inv.*	invariable	invariable
			Iron:	ironic(ally)	ironique(ment)
E.	east	est			
E:	engineering	industries mécaniques	*Jap:*	Japanese	japonais
Ecc:	ecclesiastical	église et clergé	*Jew:*	Jewish	juif, juive
Echin:	Echinodermata	échinodermes	*Jewel:*	jewellery	bijouterie
e.g.	for example	par exemple	*Join:*	joinery	menuiserie
El:	electricity; electrical	électricité; électrique	*Journ:*	journalism; journalistic	journalisme; style journa-listique
El.Ch:	electrochemistry	électrochimie			
Elcs:	electronics	électronique	*Jur:*	jurisprudence; legal term	droit; terme de palais
El.E:	electrical engineering	électrotechnique			
Eng:	England; English	Angleterre; anglais, britannique	*Knitting:*	knitting	tricot
Engr:	engraving	gravure	*Lacem:*	lacemaking	dentellerie
Ent:	entomology	entomologie	*Lap:*	lapidary arts	arts lapidaires; taillerie
Equit:	equitation	équitation	*Laund:*	laundering	blanchissage
esp.	especially	surtout	*Leath:*	leatherwork	travail du cuir
etc.	et cetera	et cætera	*Leg:*	legislation	législation
Eth:	ethics	morale	*Ling:*	linguistics; language	linguistique; langue
Ethn:	ethnology	ethnologie	*Lit:*	literary use; literature; literary	forme littéraire; littérature; littéraire
Exp:	explosives	explosifs			
			Lith:	lithography	lithographie
f.	feminine	féminin	*Locksm:*	locksmithery	serrurerie
F:	colloquial(ism)	familier; style de la conversation	*Log:*	logic	logique
			Lt.	Latin	latin
Farr:	farriery	maréchalerie			
Fb:	(Association) football	football	*m.*	masculine	masculin
Fenc:	fencing	escrime	*Magn:*	magnetism	magnétisme
Ferns:	ferns	fougères	*Mapm:*	mapmaking	cartographie
Fin:	finance	finances	*Matchm:*	match industry	industrie des allumettes
Fish:	fishing	pêche	*Mch:*	machines; machinery	machines; machines à vapeur
For:	forestry	forêts			
Fort:	fortification	fortification	*Mch.Tls:*	machine tools	machines-outils
Fr.	France; French	France; français	*Meas:*	weights and measures	poids et mesures
Fr.C:	French Canadian	canadien français	*Mec:*	mechanics	mécanique
fu.	future	futur	*Mec.E:*	mechanical engineering	industries mécaniques
Fuel:	fuel	combustibles	*Med:*	medicine; illnesses	médecine; maladies
Fung:	fungi	champignons	*Metall:*	metallurgy	métallurgie
Furn:	furniture	mobilier	*Metalw:*	metalworking	travail des métaux
			Metaph:	metaphysics	métaphysique
Games:	games	jeux	*Meteor:*	meteorology	météorologie
Gaming:	gaming; gambling	le jeu; jeux d'argent	*Mil:*	military; army	militaire; armée de terre
Gasm:	gasmaking	industrie du gaz	*Mill:*	milling	meunerie
Geog:	geography	géographie	*Min:*	mining and quarrying	exploitation des mines et carrières
Geol:	geology	géologie			
Geom:	geometry	géométrie	*Miner:*	mineralogy	minéralogie
ger.	gerund	gérondif	*M.Ins:*	marine insurance	assurance maritime
Glassm:	glassmaking	verrerie	*Moll:*	molluscs	mollusques
Gr.	Greek	grec	*Moss:*	mosses and lichens	muscinées
Gr.Alph:	Greek alphabet	alphabet grec	*Mount:*	mountaineering	alpinisme
Gr.Ant:	Greek antiquity	antiquité grecque	*Mth:*	mathematics	mathématiques
Gr.Civ:	Greek civilization	civilisation grecque	*Mus:*	music	musique
Gr.Hist:	Greek history	histoire grecque	*Myr:*	Myriapoda	myriapodes
Gram:	grammar	grammaire	*Myth:*	mythology; myths and legends	mythologie; mythes et légendes
Gym:	gymnastics	gymnastique			
			n.		nous
Hairdr:	hairdressing	coiffure	*N.*	north	nord
Harn:	harness; saddlery	sellerie; harnais	*N.Arch:*	naval architecture	architecture navale
Hatm:	hatmaking	chapellerie	*Nat.Hist:*	natural history	histoire naturelle
Her:	heraldry	blason	*Nau:*	nautical	terme de marine
Hist:	history; historical	histoire; historique	*Nav:*	navigation	navigation
Hor:	horology	horométrie	*Navy:*	Navy	marine militaire
Hort:	horticulture	horticulture	*Needlew:*	needlework	couture (travaux d'aiguille)
Hum:	humorous	humoristique	*neg.*	negative	négatif
Husb:	animal husbandry	élevage	*neut.*	neuter	neutre
Hyd:	hydraulics; hydrostatics	hydraulique; hydrostatique	*nom.*	nominative	nominatif
Hyg:	hygiene; sanitation	hygiène; installations sanitaires	*Num:*	numismatics	numismatique
			num.a.	numeral adjective	adjectif numéral
i.	intransitive	intransitif			
I.C.E:	internal combustion engines	moteurs à combustion interne	*O:*	obsolescent	vieilli
			Obst:	obstetrics	obstétrique
Ich:	ichthyology; fish	ichtyologie; poissons	*Oc:*	oceanography	océanographie
Ill:	illuminants; lighting	illuminants; éclairage	*occ.*	occasionally	parfois
imp.	imperative	impératif	*onomat.*	onomatopoeia	onomatopée
impers.	impersonal	impersonnel	*Opt:*	optics	optique
ind.	indicative	indicatif	*Orn:*	ornithology; birds	ornithologie; oiseaux
Ind:	industry; industrial	industrie; industriel	*Ost:*	ostreiculture; oysters	ostréiculture; huîtres
indef.	indefinite	indéfini			
ind.tr.	indirectly transitive	transitif avec régime indirect	*p.*	(i) past; (ii) participle	(i) passé; (ii) participe
			P:	uneducated speech; slang	expression populaire; argot
inf.	infinitive	infinitif	*Paint:*	painting trade	peinture en bâtiment
Ins:	insurance	assurance	*Pal:*	paleography	paléographie
int.	interjection	interjection	*Paleont:*	paleontology	paléontologie
Internat:	international	international	*Paperm:*	papermaking	fabrication du papier
interr.	interrogative	interrogatif			

Abbreviations Used in the Dictionary

Abbr.	English	Français
Parl:	parliament	parlement
Path:	pathology	pathologie
p.d.	imperfect, *past descriptive* (tense)	imparfait (de l'indicatif), passé descriptif
Pej:	pejorative	péjoratif
perf.	perfect (tense)	passé composé
pers.	person(s); personal	personne(s); personnel
p.h.	past historic, past definite (tense)	passé historique, passé simple
Ph:	physics	physique
Pharm:	pharmacy	pharmacie
Ph.Geog:	physical geography	géographie physique
Phil:	philosophy	philosophie
Phot:	photography	photographie
Phot.Engr:	photo-engraving; process work	procédés photomécaniques; photogravure
phr.	phrase	locution
Phren:	phrenology	phrénologie
Pisc:	pisciculture	pisciculture
pl.	plural	pluriel
Plumb:	plumbing	plomberie
P.N:	public notice	affichage; avis au public
Poet:	poetical	poétique
Pol:	politics; political	politique
Pol.Ec:	political economy, economics	économie politique
poss.	possessive	possessif
Post:	postal services	postes et télécommunications
p.p.	past participle	participe passé
pr.	present (tense)	présent (de l'indicatif)
pref.	prefix	préfixe
Prehist:	prehistory	préhistoire
prep.	preposition	préposition
prep.phr.	prepositional phrase	locution prépositive
Pr.n.	proper name	nom propre
pron.	pronoun	pronom
Pros:	prosody	prosodie; métrique
Prot:	Protozoa	protozoaires
Prov:	proverb	proverbe
pr.p.	present participle	participe présent
Psy:	psychology	psychologie
Psychics:	psychics	métapsychisme
Publ:	publishing	édition
Pyr:	pyrotechnics	pyrotechnie
qch.		quelque chose
qn		quelqu'un
q.v.	which see	se reporter à ce mot
Rac:	racing	courses
Rad.-A:	radioactivity	radioactivité
Rail:	railways, railroads	chemins de fer
R.C.Ch:	Roman Catholic Church	Église catholique
Rec:	tape *recorders*; record players	magnétophones; tourne-disques
rel.	relative	relatif
Rel:	religion(s)	religion(s)
Rel.H:	religious history	histoire des religions
Rept:	reptiles	reptiles
Rh:	rhetoric	rhétorique
Rom:	Roman	romain, romaine
Ropem:	ropemaking	corderie
Row:	rowing	aviron
R.t.m:	registered trade mark	marque déposée
Rubberm:	rubber manufacture	industrie du caoutchouc
Rugby Fb:	Rugby (football)	le rugby
Russ:	Russian	russe
S.	south	sud
s., sb.	substantive, noun	substantif, nom
s.a.	see also	voir
Sch:	schools and universities; students' (slang, etc.)	université; écoles; (argot, etc.) scolaire
Scot:	Scotland; Scottish	Écosse; écossais
Scouting:	Scout and Guide Movements	scoutisme
Sculp:	sculpture	sculpture
Ser:	sericulture	sériciculture
sg.	singular	singulier
Ski:	skiing	le ski
Sm.a:	small arms	armes portatives
s.o.	someone	
Soapm:	soapmaking	savonnerie
Soc.H:	social history	histoire sociale
Sp:	sport	sport
Space:	astronautics; space travel	astronautique; voyages interplanétaires
Spong:	sponges	spongiaires
St.Exch:	Stock Exchange	terme de Bourse
sth.	something	
Stonew:	stoneworking	taille de la pierre
sub.	subjunctive	subjonctif
suff.	suffix	suffixe
Sug.-R:	sugar refining	raffinerie du sucre
sup.	superlative	superlatif
Surg:	surgery	chirurgie
Surv:	surveying	géodésie et levé de plans
Swim:	swimming	natation
Sw.Fr:	Swiss French	mot utilisé en Suisse
Switz:	Switzerland	la Suisse
Tail:	tailoring	mode masculine
Tan:	tanning	tannage des cuirs
Tchn:	technical	terme technique, terme de métier
Telecom:	telecommunications	télécommunications
Ten:	tennis	tennis
Ter:	teratology	tératologie
Tex:	textiles, textile industry	industries textiles
Tg:	telegraphy	télégraphie
Th:	theatre; theatrical	théâtre
Theol:	theology	théologie
thg	thing(s)	
Tls:	tools	outils
Toil:	toilet; make up	toilette; maquillage
Torp:	torpedoes	torpilles
Town P:	town planning	urbanisme
Toys:	toys	jouets
Tp:	telephony	téléphonie
tr.	transitive	transitif
Trans:	transport	transports
Trig:	trigonometry	trigonométrie
Turb:	turbines	turbines
Turf:	turf, horse racing	turf
T.V:	television	télévision
Typ:	typography	typographie
Typew:	typing; typewriters	dactylographie; machines à écrire
U.S:	United States; American	États-Unis; américain
usu.	usually	d'ordinaire
v.	verb	verbe
v.		vous
V:	vulgar; not in polite use	trivial
Veh:	vehicles	véhicules
Ven:	venery; hunting	la chasse
Vet:	veterinary science	art vétérinaire
v.i.	intransitive verb	verbe intransitif
v.ind.tr.	indirectly transitive verb	verbe transitif indirect
Vit:	viticulture	viticulture
voc.	vocative	vocatif
v.pr.	pronominal verb	verbe pronominal
v.tr.	transitive verb	verbe transitif
W.	west	ouest
Wine-m:	wine making	l'industrie du vin
Woodw:	woodworking	menuiserie
Wr:	wrestling	la lutte
W.Tel:	wireless telegraphy and telephony; radio	téléphonie et télégraphie sans fil; radio
W.Tg:	wireless telegraphy	télégraphie sans fil
W.Tp:	wireless telephony	téléphonie sans fil
Y:	yachting	yachting
Z:	zoology; mammals	zoologie; mammifères
=	nearest equivalent (of an institution, an office, etc., when systems vary in the different countries)	équivalent le plus proche (d'un terme désignant une institution, une charge, etc., dans les cas où les systèmes varient dans les différents pays)

J

J, j [ʒi], s.m. the letter J, j; Tp: **J comme Joseph, J for Jack**; Mil: etc: **le jour J**, D-day; F: **les J. 3**, (i) O: teenagers; (ii) juvenile delinquents; (during the 1939-45 war, coupons allowing a special ration to young people were marked J3).

j' [ʒ], pers.pron. = JE; used before a verb beginning with a vowel or h "mute"; also before en, y.

jà [ʒa], adv. A: **1.** = DÉJÀ. **2.** in sooth.

jab [ʒab], s.m. Box: jab.

jabiru [ʒabiry], s.m. Orn: jabiru.

jablage [ʒabla:ʒ], s.m. Coop: crozing (of barrel stave).

jable [ʒabl̩], s.m. Coop: (i) croze, (ii) chimb (of barrel).

jabler [ʒable], v.tr. Coop: to croze (barrel stave).

jablière [ʒablijɛ:r], s.f., **jabloir** [ʒablwa:r], s.m., **jabloire** [ʒablwa:r], s.f. Tls: Coop: croze.

jaborandi [ʒaborɑ̃di], s.m. Bot: Pharm: jaborandi.

jaborosa [ʒaborɔza], s.m. Bot: jaborosa.

jabot [ʒabo], s.m. **1.** crop (of bird); Vet: **j. œsophagien**, partial ectasis of the oesophagus; **faire j.; enfler, gonfler, le j.**, (i) (of pigeon) to pout, (ii) F: (of pers.) to swell with importance, to give oneself airs, to strut; F: **se remplir le j.**, to fill one's belly. **2.** Cost: frill, ruffle, jabot.

jabotage [ʒabota:ʒ], s.m. F: jabbering, chatter.

jaboter [ʒabɔte], v.i. **1.** (of bird) to gobble. **2.** F: to jabber, chatter.

jaboteur, -euse [ʒabɔtœːr, -øːz], s. F: chatterer, jabberer.

jaboticaba [ʒabɔtikaba], s.m. Bot: jaboticaba.

jabotière [ʒabɔtjɛːr], s.f. **1.** lace for frills. **2.** Orn: guinea goose.

jacamar [ʒakamaːr], s.m. Orn: jacamar.

jacana [ʒakana], s.m. Orn: jacana.

jacanidés [ʒakanide], s.m.pl. Orn: Jacanidae.

jacapucayo [ʒakapykajo], s.m. Bot: lecythis ollaria; **noix de j.**, sapucaia nut.

jacaranda [ʒakarɑ̃da], s.m. Bot: jacaranda.

jacaré [ʒakare], s.m. Rept: jacare.

jacarini [ʒakarini], s.m. Orn: jacarini.

jacassage [ʒakasa:ʒ], s.m. **jacassement** [ʒakasmɑ̃], s.m. = JACASSERIE.

jacasse [ʒakas], s.f. (a) Orn: F: magpie; (b) F: (of woman) chatterbox.

jacasser [ʒakase], v.i. (of magpie) to chatter; F: (of pers.) to chatter, jabber, U.S: to yak, to yakkety-yak; F: **assez jacassé**, cut it out.

jacasserie [ʒakas(ə)ri], s.f. F: chatter, idle talk, U.S: yak; **des jacasseries sans fin**, endless gossip.

jacasseur, -euse [ʒakasœːr, -øːz], s. F: chatterer; gossip.

jacée [ʒase], s.f. Bot: **1.** brown radiant knapweed. **2. petite j.**, wild pansy.

jacent [ʒasɑ̃], a. Jur: A: unclaimed (land, estate); (land) in abeyance.

jachère [ʒaʃɛːr], s.f. Agr: unploughed land, fallow; **champ en j.**, fallow field; **mettre la terre en j.**, to lay land fallow.

jachérer [ʒaʃere], v.tr. (je jachère, n. jachérons; je jachérerai) Agr: to plough up (fallow land); to fallow (land).

jacinthe [ʒasɛ̃ːt], s.f. **1.** Bot: hyacinth; **j. sauvage, des bois**, wild hyacinth, bluebell. **2.** Miner: jacinth.

Jaciste [ʒasist], a. & s.m. & f. (from the abbreviation J.A.C. = **Jeunesse agricole catholique**) belonging to, member of, the J.A.C.

jack [ʒak], s.m. El: Tp: etc: jack; **j. de jonction, de liaison**, spring jack; **j. d'écoute**, listening jack;

j. de manipulation, key jack; **j. de renvoi**, transfer jack.

jackass [ʒakas], s.f. Nau: jackass bark, brig.

jacksonien, -ienne [ʒaksɔnjɛ̃, -jɛn], a. Med: **épilepsie jacksonienne**, Jacksonian epilepsy, Bravais-Jackson epilepsy.

Jacob [ʒakɔb], Pr.n.m. Jacob; **l'échelle de J.**, Jacob's ladder; F: **bâton de J.**, (i) Astr: Orion's belt; (ii) Bot: yellow asphodel.

jacobée [ʒakɔbe], s.f. Bot: jacobaea.

jacobien, -ienne [ʒakɔbjɛ̃], s.m. Mth: Jacobian (determinant).

jacobin, -ine [ʒakɔbɛ̃, -in], s. **1.** Ecc: Dominican friar, nun. **2.** Fr.Hist: (1789): Jacobin (i.e. member of a political club that met in an old couvent de jacobins); a. **doctrines jacobines**, Jacobin, Jacobinic(al), revolutionary, doctrines. **3.** Orn: (a) s.m. jacobin (pigeon); (b) s.f. jacobine, (i) saddleback crow, hooded crow; (ii) jacobin (humming-bird). **4.** s.f. **jacobine** (in S. of Fr.) roof window.

jacobinia [ʒakɔbinja], s.m. Bot: jacobinia.

jacobinisme [ʒakɔbinism], s.m. Jacobinism.

jacobite [ʒakɔbit], a. & s.m. Jacobite: (i) Ecc.Hist: Syrian Monophysite; (ii) Eng.Hist: adherent of James II.

jacobsite [ʒakɔbsit], s.f. Miner: jacobsite.

jacobus [ʒakɔbys], s.m. A.Num: Jacobus.

jaconas [ʒakɔna], s.m. jaconet (muslin).

jaco(t) [ʒakɔ], s.m. = JACQUOT.

jacquard [ʒakaːr], s.m. or f. Tex: Jacquard loom; **à la j.**, Jacquard woven; a. **tissu j.**, Jacquard cloth; **(chandail, tricot) j.**, woollen sweater in the Jacquard style.

jacquardé [ʒakarde], a. **étoffe jacquardée**, cloth woven on a Jacquard loom; **métier j.**, Jacquard loom.

jacque [ʒak], s.f. = JAQUE².

Jacqueline [ʒaklin]. **1.** Pr.n.f. Jacqueline. **2.** s.f. = toby jug.

jacquemart [ʒakmaːr], s.m. = JAQUEMART.

jacquerie [ʒakri], s.f. Fr.Hist: Jacquerie (peasant rising; primarily that of 1358).

jacquerotte [ʒakrɔt], s.f. Bot: heath pea, tuberous pea.

Jacques [ʒɑːk], Pr.n.m. (a) James; Lit.Hist: **J. de Voragine**, Jacobus a Voragine; (b) **Maître J.**, factotum; Jack-of-all-trades; (c) Hist: **J. (Bonhomme)**, the French peasant; F: **faire le J.**, (i) to act in a stupid manner, to act dumb; (ii) to try to be funny.

jacquet [ʒakɛ], s.m. **1.** (a) backgammon; (b) backgammon board. **2.** Dial: squirrel.

jacquier [ʒakje], s.m. Bot: = JAQUIER.

Jacquot [ʒako]. **1.** Pr.n.m. F: = Jim, Jimmy. **2.** s.m. West African grey parrot, F: Poll (parrot), Polly.

jactance [ʒaktɑ̃ːs], s.f. **1.** boastfulness, boasting, bragging; **discours plein de j.**, boastful speech; **parler avec j.**, to speak boastfully. **2.** boast, piece of brag. **3.** P: talk; **il a de la j.**, he's got the gift of the gab. **4.** A.Jur: provocation.

jact(it)ation [ʒakt(it)asjɔ̃], s.f. Med: jact(it)ation.

jacter [ʒakte], v.i. P: to speak, talk, spout.

jacteur, -euse [ʒaktœːr, -øːz], F: (a) a. garrulous; (b) s. chatterbox.

jaculatoire [ʒakylatwaːr], a. **1.** Theol: ejaculatory; **oraison j.**, ejaculatory prayer. **2.** Hyd: (of fountain) spurting.

jade [ʒad], s.m. Miner: jade(-stone); nephrite; **j. de Saussure, j. tenace**, saussurite.

jadéite [ʒadeit], s.f. Miner: jadeite.

jadien, -ienne [ʒadjɛ̃, -jɛn], a. like jade; containing jade.

jadis [ʒadis], adv. Lit: (a) formerly, once, of old; **dans Florence j., vivait un médecin**, in Florence there lived a doctor; **les chevaliers de j.**, the knights of old; Hum: **un col j. blanc**, a collar that had once been white; (b) attrib. **le temps j.**, the olden days; **au temps j.**, in the olden days, in the days of old; **contes du temps j.**, tales of long ago.

jadot [ʒado], s.m. Bak: ring-shaped dough mould.

Jaël [ʒael], Pr.n.f. B.Hist: Jael.

jaffe [ʒaf], s.f. Mil: P: (a) soup; (b) meal.

jaghernath [ʒagɛrnat], Pr.n.m. Juggernaut.

jagré [ʒagre], s.m. Sug.-R: jaggery.

jaguar [ʒagwaːr], s.m. Z: jaguar.

jaguarondi, jaguarundi [ʒagwarɔ̃di], s.m. Z: jaguarondi, jaguarundi.

Jahel [ʒael], Pr.n.f. = JAËL.

Jahvé [ʒave], Pr.n.m. B.Lit: Yahweh.

jaïet [ʒaje], s.m. A: = JAIS.

jaillir [ʒajiːr], v.i. (a) to spring (up); to shoot forth; (of water) to gush (forth), to spout up, out, to squirt (out); (of blood) to spurt; (of sparks) to fly; (of light) to flash; **les larmes étaient prêtes à j.**, he, she, was on the point of bursting into tears; **les larmes jaillirent de ses yeux**, tears gushed, welled, from her eyes; **les flammes jaillissaient de la fenêtre**, the flames were shooting out of the window; **faire j. des étincelles d'une pierre à fusil**, to strike sparks from a flint; El: **faire j. une étincelle**, to produce a spark; **faire j. un arc**, to arc; (b) la vérité jaillira de l'apparente injustice, the truth will spring from the apparent injustice; **idée qui jaillit à la lumière**, idea that springs to light.

jaillissant [ʒajisɑ̃], a. gushing, spouting, spurting; flying (sparks); **puits j.**, (mineral oil) gusher; Geol: **nappe jaillissante**, artesian layer; **source jaillissante**, spouting, gushing, upwelling, spring.

jaillissement [ʒajismɑ̃], s.m. gush(ing), spouting spurt(ing); springing (out, forth); **j. d'éloquence**, burst of eloquence; El: **j. d'étincelles**, flash across (between terminals), arcing over (between carbons); sparking; Petroleum Ind: **j. (d'un puits de pétrole)**, (oil well) blowing; Geol: **j. de lave**, spatter cone.

jaïn(a) [ʒain(a)], s.m. & f. Rel: Jain(a).

jaïnisme [ʒainism], s.m. Rel: Jainism.

Jaïr(e) [ʒaiːr], Pr.n.m. B: Jairus.

jais [ʒɛ], s.m. Miner: jet; **j. artificiel**, imitation jet; (i) black onyx, (ii) jet-glass; **noir comme (du) j., noir (de) j.**, jet-black.

jalap [ʒalap], s.m. Bot: Pharm: jalap.

jale [ʒal], s.f. (a) Vit: tub; (b) A.Meas: = gallon.

jaler [ʒale], v.tr. Nau: to stock (anchor).

jalet [ʒalɛ], s.m. A.Arms: pebble (thrown with a stone-bow).

jal(l)ais [ʒalɛ], s.m., **jal(l)ois** [ʒalwa], s.m. A: (i) about fifteen litres; (ii) about fifteen ares.

jalon [ʒalɔ̃], s.m. (a) (surveyor's) staff; (range-)pole; stake, rod; marker, sighting mark; Surv: **j. gradué**, graduated rod; **poser, planter, des jalons (dans une science, etc.)**, to show, to pave, the way; to blaze a trail; **poser les jalons de son travail**, to establish the main heads of one's work; F: **suggérer des jalons à un témoin**, to prompt a witness; (b) landmark; milestone; (c) Mil: **j. de pointage, de repérage**, (i) Artil: aiming post; (ii) firing peg (of machine gun).

jalon-mire [ʒalɔ̃miːr], *s.m. Surv:* target levelling-rod; *pl. jalons-mires.*

jalonnage [ʒalɔnaːʒ], *s.m.*, **jalonnement** [ʒalɔnmɑ̃], *s.m.* marking out; marking off; *Surv:* laying out a line, staking(-out), pegging (-out, -off); *Mil:* placing of markers (at drill); **j. de l'avance ennemie par les éléments de couverture,** screening of the enemy advance by the covering troops; *Mil.Av:* **bombes de jalonnement,** target flares.

jalonner [ʒalɔne], *v.tr. Surv:* to lay out, stake out, mark out (line, piece of ground, etc.); to peg (out) (claim); *Av:* to mark out, stake out (landing strip); *Mil:* to screen (the enemy advance); *Mil:* **j. une direction,** to take up points (in marching); *Tp:* **j. une ligne,** to mark out positions for telegraph poles; **ils ont jalonné la route à ceux qui suivront,** they have shown the way to, blazed the trail for, their successors; **événements qui jalonnent la vie de qn,** events that stand out as landmarks, milestones, in s.o.'s life.

jalonnette [ʒalɔnɛt], *s.f. Surv:* measuring pole (for determining depth of excavations).

jalonneur [ʒalɔnœːr], *s.m.* marker. **1.** *Surv:* staff-man, leader. **2.** *Mil:* marker (at drill).

jalousé [ʒaluze], *a.* latticed, screened (window).

jalousement [ʒaluzmɑ̃], *adv.* jealously.

jalouser [ʒaluze], *v.tr.* to envy (s.o.); to be jealous of (s.o.).

jalousie [ʒaluzi], *s.f.* **1.** jealousy; **j. de métier,** professional jealousy; **exciter la j. de qn,** to arouse s.o.'s jealousy, s.o.'s envy; **avoir de la j. contre qn,** to be jealous, envious, of s.o.; **la sombre j.,** the green-eyed monster. **2.** (*a*) (lattice-work) screen; (*b*) Venetian blind, sun blind; **ruban à j.,** ladder tape; (*c*) Venetian shutter (of organ swell-box); Venetian swell. **3.** *Bot:* sweet william; **j. des jardins,** rose campion.

jalousie-store [ʒaluzistɔːr], *s.f.* (slatted) roller-blind; *pl. jalousies-stores.*

jaloux, -ouse [ʒalu, -uːz], *a.* **1.** jealous; (*a*) **j. de qn,** jealous of s.o.; **j. du succès d'autrui,** jealous of another's success; **j. que quelqu'un ne l'éclipsât,** jealous lest some one should put him in the shade; **observer qn d'un œil j.,** to keep a jealous, a watchful, eye on s.o.; (*b*) zealous, careful; **surveiller qn avec un soin j.,** to keep a jealous watch over s.o.; **j. de faire qch.,** anxious, desirous, to do sth.; **j. de sa réputation,** careful of one's reputation; jealous of, for, one's good name. **2.** *A:* (*causing anxiety*) unsafe; **voiture jalouse,** rickety carriage; *Mil:* **endroit j.,** exposed position; *Nau:* **barque jalouse,** crank(y), top-heavy, boat.

jalpaïte [ʒalpait], *s.f. Miner:* jalpaite.

jamaïquain, -aine [ʒamaikɛ̃, -ɛn], *a. & s. Geog:* Jamaican.

Jamaïque (la) [laʒamaik]. **1.** *Pr.n.f. Geog:* Jamaica. **2.** *s.m. Dy:* Jamaica wood.

jamais [ʒamɛ], *adv.* **1.** ever; **plus cher que j.,** dearer than ever; **s'il revenait j., si j. il revenait, il ne voudrait pas le croire,** if ever he came back he would not believe it; **avez-vous j. entendu chose pareille?** did you ever hear such a thing? **c'est moins que j. le moment de . . .,** it is less than ever the time to . . .; **je lis rarement, pour ne pas dire j.,** I read seldom, if ever; *adv.phr.* **à j., pour jamais,** for ever; **à tout j.,** for ever and ever, for evermore. **2.** (*with neg. expressed or understood*) never; **je ne l'ai j. vu,** I have never seen him; **j. homme ne fut plus admiré,** never was a man more admired; **ça n'avait pas l'air de lui être j. venu à l'esprit,** it never seemed to have occurred to him; **sans j. y avoir pensé,** without ever having thought of it; **c'est le cas ou j.,** now or never; **on n'en avait encore j. entendu parler,** it had never been heard of before; **on ne le voit presque j.,** one hardly ever sees him; **on ne le verra plus j., j. plus,** we shall never see him again; **plus j. nous n'entendrons sa voix,** we shall never hear his voice again; **avez-vous j. été à Rome?—j.,** were you ever in Rome?—never; **j. de la vie!** (i) never! out of the question! *F:* not on your life! no fear! good gracious, no! (ii) (*expressing incredulity*) *P:* a likely story! *Prov:* **mieux vaut tard que j.,** better late than never. **3.** *s.m.* **au grand j.!** never, never! **j., au grand j., je n'admettrai cela,** never shall I admit it; *F:* **au lendemain de j., trois jours après j.,** never; when pigs begin to fly.

jambage [ʒɑ̃baːʒ], *s.m.* **1.** *Const:* (*a*) jamb (post), (side)post (of door, window, etc.); jamb, side, cheek (of fireplace); (*b*) foundation wall; sub-structure. **2.** leg, standard (of crane, etc.). **3.** down stroke (of written letter); *Sch:* **faire des j.,** to make pothooks. **4.** *Ven:* skin covering the legs (of an animal).

jambardé [ʒɑ̃barde], *a. A.Arm:* greaved.

jambart [ʒɑ̃baːr], *s.m. A.Arm:* greave.

jambe [ʒɑ̃ːb], *s.f.* **1.** leg (of person, animal); **j. artificielle, j. de bois,** artificial, wooden, leg; **jambes d'un pantalon,** trouser legs; **j. deçà, j. delà,** astride, astraddle; **avoir de bonnes jambes,** to be a good walker; **il a des jambes de cerf,** he can go on running for ever; **jeune homme aux longues jambes,** long-legged youth; *Hist:* **Édouard Longues-jambes,** Edward Longshanks; **il s'enfuit, se sauva, à toutes jambes,** he ran off as fast as his legs could carry him, at full speed; he scampered away; *occ.* he ran for his life; *F:* **prendre ses jambes à son cou,** to take to one's heels, to show a clean pair of heels; **jouer des jambes,** to leg it; **la peur lui donna des jambes,** fear lent him wings; **il se met dans vos jambes,** he gets under your feet; he gets in your way; *F:* **tenir la j. à qn,** to buttonhole s.o.; **tirer dans les jambes de qn,** (i) to fire low (in duel, etc.), (ii) *F:* to play a dirty trick on s.o.; *O:* **jeter un chat aux jambes de qn,** to put an obstacle in s.o.'s way; **par-dessous la j.,** without care or exertion; **travail fait par-dessous la j.,** scamped work; **traiter qn par-dessous la j.,** to treat s.o. with contempt, in an offhand manner; **faire la belle j.,** to strut about; to show off; **c'est ça qui me fera une belle j.!** a (fat) lot of good that will do me! *Prov:* **il faut faire le pas selon la j.,** you must cut your coat according to your cloth; **avoir les jambes rompues,** to feel one's legs giving way under one, to be worn out, done up, knocked up; **ça ne va que d'une j.,** things aren't going too well; **couper, casser, bras et jambes à qn,** to cut the ground from under s.o.'s feet; to take the wind out of s.o.'s sails; **avoir tant de kilomètres dans les jambes,** (i) to have walked so many miles; (ii) to feel weary after walking so many miles; (*of horse, etc.*) **chercher sa cinquième j.,** to drop from exhaustion; **n'avoir plus de jambes,** to be tired out, exhausted; **je n'ai plus mes jambes de vingt ans,** I'm not as young as I was; *Box: Fb:* **jeu de jambes,** footwork; *Cr:* **j. touchée,** leg bye; *s.a.* PASSER II, 2, RENTRER I, 2; TRAÎNER 1. **2.** (*a*) stem (of a glass); (*b*) *pl.* legs (of compasses, dividers); (*c*) **j. de force,** *Const:* strut, prop, brace; *Aut:* stay (rod), torque rod; **jambes de force en croix,** diagonal members; (*d*) stone pier (in brickwork); **j. d'encoignure,** stone corner; (*e*) *N.Arch:* **j. de hune,** futtock shroud; (*f*) *Av:* leg (of landing gear); **j. à amortisseur hydraulique, j. oléopneumatique,** oleo-leg, oleo-strut; (*g*) *Nau:* **(nœud de) j. de chien,** sheepshank. **3.** *Bot: Agr:* **j. noire,** black leg.

jambé [ʒɑ̃be], *a. A: used in* **bien, mal, j.,** with shapely, unshapely, legs; **femme bien jambée,** woman with a well-turned leg.

jambette [ʒɑ̃bɛt], *s.f.* **1.** (*a*) *A: or Hum:* small leg; **donner la j. à qn,** to trip s.o. up; (*b*) *Com:* sable fur of inferior quality. **2.** (*a*) *Const:* stanchion; (upright) prop; **j. de comble,** purlin post; (*b*) *N.Arch:* (i) timber head; (ii) **jambettes de voûte,** stern timbers; (iii) **j. de pavois,** bulwark stay. **3.** *Dial:* clasp knife, pocket knife.

jambier, -ière [ʒɑ̃bje, -jɛːr]. **1.** *a. Anat:* tibial (muscle, etc.). **2.** *s.m.* (butcher's) gambrel. **3.** *s.f.* **jambière;** (*a*) *A.Arm:* greave; (*b*) *Surg:* elastic stocking; (*c*) *pl. Mil:* (infantry) leggings; *Sp: etc:* (cyclist's) mackintosh leggings, overall leggings, seatless trousers; *Cr:* pads, leg guards; *Fb:* shin guards.

jambon [ʒɑ̃bɔ̃], *s.m.* **1.** (*a*) ham; **œufs au j.,** ham and eggs; **papier j.,** greaseproof paper; **j. de pays, de montagne,** raw, cured, ham; (*b*) *P:* thigh. **2.** *Bot:* *F:* **j. des jardiniers,** common evening primrose.

jambonneau, -eaux [ʒɑ̃bɔno], *s.m.* **1.** knuckle of ham. **2.** foreleg ham; hand of pork. **3.** *Moll:* *F:* fan-mussel; pinna; pen-shell.

jamboree [dʒambəri; ʒambɔre, -i], *s.m.* (boy scouts') jamboree.

jambose [ʒɑ̃boːz], *s.f.*, **jambosier** [ʒɑ̃bozje], *s.m.* *Bot:* roseapple tree, jambosa.

jambot [ʒɑ̃bo], *s.m.* (*in Belgium*) miner's mate, butty.

jamesonite [ʒamsɔnit], *s.f. Miner:* jamesonite; feather ore.

jan [ʒɑ̃], *s.m.* **1.** *Games:* (*trictrac*) each of the two tables. **2.** *Bot:* gorse.

jangada [ʒɑ̃gada], *s.m. Nau:* jangada.

janissaire [ʒanisɛːr], *s.m.* janissary, janizary.

janot [ʒano], *s.m. O: F:* (= JEANNOT) simpleton, silly Billy; **j. tête-en-l'air,** jay-walker.

janoterie [ʒanɔtri], *s.f. O:* **1.** silliness, simplicity. **2.** silly, ingenuous, remark.

janotisme [ʒanɔtism], *s.m.* **1.** = JANOTERIE 1. **2.** *Gram:* amphibology.

jansénisme [ʒɑ̃senism], *s.m.* **1.** *Rel.H:* Jansenism. **2.** *A:* austerity.

janséniste [ʒɑ̃senist], *a. & s.* **1.** *Rel.H:* (*a*) Jansenist; (*b*) *F:* austere moralist; **à la j.,** austerely. **2.** *Bookb:* **reliure j.,** plain binding.

jante [ʒɑ̃ːt], *s.f.* felloe, felly (of wheel); rim (of cycle or car wheel, of pulley); *Aut:* **j. amovible,** detachable rim; **j. à base creuse,** well-base rim; **j. à rebord,** beaded rim; **j. à talon,** clincher rim; **rendement à la j.,** horse-power at road wheels, actual efficiency; *Cy:* **j. en bois,** sprint.

jantier [ʒɑ̃tje], *s.m.*, **jantière** [ʒɑ̃tjɛːr], *s.f.* felloe assembling tool, machine.

jantille [ʒɑ̃tiːj], *s.f.* paddle (of water-wheel).

Janus [ʒanyːs], *Pr.n.m. Rom.Myth:* Janus; *Lit:* *Hum:* janitor (of a house, prison, etc.).

janvier [ʒɑ̃vje]. **1.** *s.m.* January; **en j.,** in January; **au mois de j.,** in the month of January; **le premier, le sept, j.,** (on) January (the) first, (the) seventh; (on) the first, the seventh, of January; *F:* **c'est le soleil de j.,** he's a feeble sort of chap. **2.** *Pr.n.m. Ecc.Hist:* (Saint) Januarius.

Japhet [ʒafɛt], *Pr.n.m. B.Hist:* Japhet(h).

japhétique [ʒafetik], *a. Ethn: etc:* Japhetic; Aryan.

Japon [ʒapɔ̃]. **1.** *Pr.n.m. Geog:* Japan; **au J.,** in, to, Japan; **l'ambassadeur du J.,** the Japanese ambassador; **papier J.,** Japanese vellum; *Bot:* **vernis du J.,** varnish tree, lacquer tree, tree of heaven. **2.** *s.m.* Japan(ese) porcelain; fine porcelain.

japonais, -aise [ʒapɔnɛ, -ɛːz]. **1.** *a. & s.* Japanese. **2.** *s.m. Ling:* Japanese. **3.** *a.* **vernis j.,** japan.

japonaiserie [ʒapɔnɛzri], *s.f.*, **japonerie** [ʒapɔnri], *s.f.* **1.** craze for Japanese curios. **2.** article of Japanese art; *pl.* Japanese curios.

japonique [ʒapɔnik], *a. Ch:* japonic (acid).

japonisant, -ante [ʒapɔnizɑ̃, -ɑ̃ːt], *s.* **1.** friend of Japan. **2.** amateur of Japanese antiques, works of art; lover of things Japanese. **3.** student of the Japanese language.

japonisme [ʒapɔnism], *s.m.* japonism.

japoniste [ʒapɔnist], *s.* collector of Japanese objets d'art.

japonner [ʒapɔne], *v.tr. Cer:* to give (porcelain) a second firing.

jappement [ʒapmɑ̃], *s.m.* yelp(ing), yap(ping) (of dog).

japper [ʒape], *v.i.* (*of dog*) to yelp, yap.

jappeur, -euse [ʒapœːr, -øːz], *a. & s.* yelping, yapping (dog, etc.).

japyx [ʒapiks], *s.m. Ent:* japyx.

jaque[1] [ʒak], *s.m.* jack(-fruit).

jaque[2], *s.f. A:* jerkin, jack(-coat).

jaqueline [ʒaklin], *s.f.* = toby jug.

jaquemart [ʒakmaːr], *s.m.* (*a*) Jack(-o'-the-clock) (striking the hours in old town clocks); (*b*) toy version of Jack-o'-the-clock.

jaquet [ʒakɛ], *s.m. Orn:* jack-snipe.

jaquette[1] [ʒakɛt], *s.f.* **1.** (*a*) (man's) morning coat, *U.S:* cutaway; *P:* **il est de la j.,** he's a homosexual, a queer; (*b*) (woman's) jacket; (*c*) *A:* (child's) frock; (*d*) *Fr.C:* nightdress. **2.** *Artil:* jacket; cradle of gun. **3.** *Bookb:* dust jacket, dust cover, dust wrapper. **4.** *Tchn:* jacket, case, casing (of boiler, etc.).

jaquette[2], *s.f. Dial:* magpie.

jaquier [ʒakje], *s.m. Bot:* bread-fruit (tree); **j. de Malaisie,** jack (tree), jack-fruit (tree).

jar[1] [ʒaːr], **jard** [ʒaːr], *s.m. Dial:* gravel bank (in the Loire).

jar[2], *s.m. P:* = JARS[2].

jardang [ʒardɑ̃], *s.m. Geol:* yardang.

jarde[1] [ʒard], *s.f. Vet:* bog spavin.

jarde[2], *s.f.* flaw (in diamond).

jardin [ʒardɛ̃], *s.m.* **1.** garden; **j. potager,** kitchen garden; **j. d'agrément,** pleasure garden; **j. à l'anglaise,** landscape garden; **l'art de dessiner les jardins,** landscape gardening; **j. des plantes,** botanical garden; **j. sec,** herbarium; **j. d'hiver,** winter garden; **j. alpin,** rock garden; **j. japonais,** miniature Japanese garden; **cultiver son j.,** to lead a calm and peaceful life; **j. de curé,** small mixed garden; **jeter des pierres dans le j. de qn,** to attack s.o., to throw stones at s.o.; **jardins ouvriers,** allotments; *Adm:* **j. familial,** subsistence plot; *Ven:* **donner le j. à l'oiseau,** to put a falcon in the open air; *Sch:* **j. d'enfants,** kindergarten; *Th:* **côté j.,** prompt side, P.S.; *s.a.* ACCLIMATATION. **2.** *N.Arch:* **j. des tambours,** paddle-box sponson.

jardinage [ʒardinaːʒ], *s.m.* **1.** (*a*) gardening; **instruments de j.,** garden(ing) tools; (*b*) *A:* garden produce; (*c*) *A:* garden plot. **2.** *For:* selection felling; planting up after thinning. **3.** flaw (in diamond).

jardinatoire [ʒardinatwa:r], *a. For:* **coupe j.,** selection felling.

jardiner [ʒardine]. **1.** *v.i.* to garden. **2.** *v.tr.* (*a*) *For:* to plant up (wood) after thinning; (*b*) *F:* to criticize, run down (s.o.); (*c*) *Ven:* **j. l'oiseau,** to put a falcon in the open air.

jardinet [ʒardinɛ], *s.m.* **1.** small garden. **2.** *Ven:* (special arrangement of branches as a) trap. **3.** *Fish:* compartment (on deck of a fishing-boat) for barrelling herrings.

jardineux, -euse [ʒardinø, -ø:z], *a. Lap:* dark, misty, cloudy (stone); **une émeraude jardineuse,** a cloudy emerald.

jardinier, -ière [ʒardinje, -jɛ:r]. **1.** *a.* **plantes jardinières,** garden plants; *For:* **exploitation jardinière,** selection felling. **2.** *s.* gardener; **j. fleuriste,** flower grower; **j. maraîcher,** market gardener; vegetable grower; **j. paysagiste,** landscape gardener; **j. pépiniériste,** nurseryman (who cultivates trees only); *F:* **j. trois branches,** flower, fruit and vegetable grower; **j. quatre branches,** grower of flowers, fruit, vegetables and greenhouse plants. **3.** *s.f.* **jardinière:** (*a*) (i) flower stand, window-box; (ii) jardinière; (*b*) bottle stand (in bar); (*c*) *Cu:* **jardinière (de légumes),** jardinière; macédoine of vegetables; **bœuf à la jardinière,** beef with mixed vegetables; (*d*) market-gardener's cart; spring cart; (*e*) pruning saw; (*f*) *Ent:* ground-beetle; (*g*) *Sch:* **jardinière d'enfants,** kindergarten mistress; **jardinière de neige,** children's ski instructress. **4.** *s.m. Orn:* ortolan.

jardiniste [ʒardinist], *s.m. A:* landscape gardener.

jardon [ʒardɔ̃], *s.m. Vet:* bog spavin.

jargon[1] [ʒargɔ̃], *s.m.* (*a*) jargon; **le j. du palais,** the jargon of the law-courts, legal jargon; **j. journalistique,** journalese; (*b*) cant, slang; (*c*) (foreign) language, *F:* lingo.

jargon[2], *s.m. Miner:* jargon, jargoon.

jargonelle [ʒargɔnɛl], *s.f.* jargonelle pear.

jargonnant [ʒargɔnɑ̃], *a.* incomprehensible to all but the initiated.

jargonner [ʒargɔne], *v.* **1.** *v.i.* to talk jargon, to talk incomprehensibly. **2.** *v.tr.* to talk professional jargon, etc.; *F:* **j. médical,** to talk medical jargon.

jargonneur, -euse [ʒargɔnœ:r, -ø:z], *s.* person who talks jargon; jargonist.

Jarnac [ʒarnak]. **1.** *Pr.n.m. used in* **coup de J.,** treacherous stroke, stab in the back, low trick (*in the sixteenth century Guy de Jarnac hamstrung an opponent in a duel*). **2.** *s.m. A:* poniard, dirk.

jarnacais, -aise [ʒarnakɛ, -ɛ:z], *a. & s. Geog:* (native) of Jarnac.

jarnicoton [ʒarnikɔtɔ̃], *int. Dial: A:* = JARNIDIEU.

jarni(dieu) [ʒarni(djø)], *int. Dial: A:* (*softened form of* **je renie Dieu**) zounds, 'sdeath.

jarosite [ʒarɔzit], *s.f. Miner:* jarosite.

jarosse [ʒarɔs], *s.f.*, **jarousse** [ʒarus], *s.f. Bot:* lesser chickpea.

jarovisation [ʒarɔvizasjɔ̃], *s.f. Agr:* vernalization (of wheat).

jarrah [ʒara], *s.m. Bot:* jarrah; *Com:* **bois de j.,** jarrah wood.

jarre[1] [ʒa:r], *s.f.* (large glazed) earthenware jar; **j. électrique,** Leyden jar.

jarre[2], *s.m. Dial:* gravel bank (in the Loire).

jarre[3], *s.m. Tex:* kemp (in wool); *Furs:* overhair, guard hair.

jarré [ʒare], *a. Tex:* **laine jarrée,** kempy wool.

jarret [ʒarɛ], *s.m.* **1.** bend of the knee, popliteal space, ham (in man); hock, hough (of horse, etc.); (*of horse*) **avoir les jarrets bien évidés,** to have well-shaped hocks; **tendre les jarrets,** to brace the knees; *F:* **tendre le j.,** to make a leg; **s'avancer le j. tendu,** (i) (*of courtier*) to advance making a leg, (ii) (*of fencer, etc.*) to advance on his toes; **plier le j.,** to bend the knee; **avoir le j. solide, avoir du j.,** to be strong on one's legs, to have a good pair of legs; **couper les jarrets à un cheval,** to hamstring a horse. **2.** *Cu:* knuckle (of veal); shin (of beef). **3.** (*a*) *Arch:* unevenness, bulge, break of outline (in curve of arch, etc.); (*b*) elbow, knee-joint (of pipe).

jarreté [ʒarte], *a.* **1.** gartered. **2.** (*a*) (*of horse*) close-hocked; (*b*) (*of dancer*) with legs turned in. **3.** *Arch:* protruding, bulging (outline of a curve).

jarretelle [ʒartɛl], *s.f.* (sock or stocking) suspender, *U.S:* garter.

jarreter [ʒarte], *v.* (**je jarrette** [ʒart], **nous jarretons; je jarretterai** [ʒartəre]) **1.** *v.tr.* (*a*) (*rare*) to put garters on (s.o.); to garter (stocking); (*b*) *Arb:* to strip (tree) of its side branches. **2.** *v.i. Arch:* (*of curve, of vault, etc.*) to show an uneven, bulging, outline; to bulge.

se jarreter, (*rare*) to put on, wear, one's garters.

jarretière [ʒartjɛ:r], *s.f.* **1.** garter; **Ordre de la J.,** Order of the Garter. **2.** (*a*) picketing rope; (*b*) sling (for guns); (*c*) tug-of-war rope; **lutte à la j.,** tug of war; (*d*) *Nau:* gasket; (*e*) *Tp: Tg:* connecting wire; jumper; (*f*) *Av: etc:* bonding (strip). **3.** *Ich:* scabbard-fish.

jarrettes [ʒarɛt], *s.f.pl.* socks; *Com:* half-hose.

jarreux, -euse [ʒarø, -ø:z], *a. Tex:* (*of wool*) kempy.

jarron [ʒarɔ̃], *s.m.* small jar.

jars[1] [ʒa:r], *s.m.* gander.

jars[2], *s.m. O:* (thieves', etc.) slang; **dévider le j.,** to talk slang; **il entend le j.,** he's a crafty devil.

jars[3], *s.m. Tex:* kemp (in wool).

jas [ʒɑ], *s.m.* **1.** *Nau:* stock (of anchor); **sans j.,** stockless. **2.** (*in Provence*) shepherd's hut.

jasement [ʒɑzmɑ̃], *s.m. A:* chattering, chatter.

jaser [ʒɑze], *v.i.* (*a*) to chatter (**de,** about); to gossip; (*esp. of children*) to babble; **j. comme une pie (borgne),** to talk nineteen to the dozen, to chatter like a magpie; **tout le monde en jase,** it's the talk of the place; **faire j. les gens,** to set tongues wagging; (*b*) to blab; to tell tales; **quelqu'un a jasé,** some one has been talking (indiscreetly); **faire j. qn,** to make s.o. talk, *F:* to pump s.o.

jaseran [ʒazrɑ̃], *s.m.* (*a*) shirt, coat, of mail; (*b*) gold chain (from which locket is suspended).

jaserie [ʒɑzri], *s.f.* (*a*) chatter; tittle-tattle; (*esp. of children*) babble; (*b*) blabbing; tale-bearing.

jaseur, -euse [ʒɑzœ:r, -ø:z]. **1.** *a.* talkative; **cours d'eau j.,** babbling brook. **2.** *s.* (*a*) chatterbox; tattler; gossip; (*b*) blabber, tale-bearer. **3.** *s.m. Orn:* waxwing; **j. (de Bohême, boréal),** Bohemian waxwing.

jasione [ʒazjɔn], *s.f. Bot:* jasione.

jasmin [ʒasmɛ̃], *s.m. Bot:* jasmine, jessamine; **j. du Cap,** Cape jasmin; **j. de Virginie, j. trompette,** trumpet creeper; **j. en arbre,** mock orange; **j. d'hiver,** winter jasmine.

jasmone [ʒasmɔn], *s.f. Ch:* jasmone.

Jason [ʒazɔ̃], *Pr.n.m. Myth:* Jason.

jaspagate [ʒaspagat], *s.f. Lap:* agate jasper.

jaspage [ʒaspa:ʒ], *s.m. Bookb:* (*a*) marbling; (*b*) sprinkling.

jaspe [ʒasp], *s.m.* **1.** *Miner:* jasper; **j. noir,** touchstone; **j. sanguin,** bloodstone. **2.** *Bookb:* (*a*) marbling; (*b*) sprinkling.

jaspe-opale [ʒaspɔpal], *s.m. Miner:* jasp-opal, jasper-opal.

jasper [ʒaspe], *v.tr. Tchn:* to marble, mottle; to mottle-finish (tools, etc.); *Bookb:* (i) to marble; (ii) to sprinkle (edges); **papier jaspé,** marbled paper.

jaspeur [ʒaspœ:r], *s.m. Bookb:* **j. sur tranches,** marbler.

jaspiner [ʒaspine], *v.i. P:* to chatter.

jaspineur, -euse [ʒaspinœ:r, -ø:z]. *P:* **1.** *s.* chatterbox. **2.** *a.* chattering.

jaspure [ʒaspy:r], *s.f. Bookb:* (*a*) marbling; (*b*) sprinkling.

jasse [ʒɑs], *s.f.* open cowshed for protection against the heat.

jasserie [ʒɑs(ə)ri], *s.f. Dial:* (*in Auvergne*) mountain farm where cheese is made.

jassidés [ʒaside], *s.m.pl. Ent:* Jassidae.

jassus [ʒasy:s], *s.m. Ent:* jassid; leafhopper.

jatte [ʒat], *s.f.* **1.** bowl; (milk-)pan; basin; pancheon. **2.** *Bookb:* wooden bowl for glue.

jattée [ʒate], *s.f.* bowlful; panful (of milk).

jauge [ʒo:ʒ], *s.f.* **1.** (*a*) gauge; (standard of) measure, capacity (of cask, etc.); (*b*) *Nau:* tonnage, burden (of ship); **j. ancienne,** builders' old measurement; **j. brute,** gross register(ed) tonnage; **j. nette,** net register(ed) tonnage; **j. sous le pont,** under-deck tonnage; **j. officielle, j. de douane, j. de registre,** register(ed) tonnage; **j. de course,** standard measurement (of racing craft). **2.** (*a*) *Tchn:* gauge; **j. à tige,** gauging rod; *Aut:* dipstick; **j. enregistreuse,** recording gauge; *Aut:* **j. de carter,** dipstick; *Aut: etc:* **j. à essence,** petrol gauge; *Ph: Elcs:* **j. du vide,** vacuum gauge; **j. bêta,** beta-absorption gauge; **j. à ionisation, j. thermionique,** ionization gauge; (*b*) *Mec.E: etc:* gauge, templet; **j. étalon,** standard gauge; **j. à coulisse,** cal(l)iper gauge; **j. micrométrique,** vernier cal(l)iper; **j. de pas,** screw-pitch gauge; **j. pour fil métallique, j. à fil,** wire gauge; **j. de Paris,** French wire gauge; **j. annulaire,** ring gauge; **j. pour tôles** (i) **(épaisses),** plate gauge, (ii) **(minces),** sheet (metal) gauge; *Civ.E: Mec:* **j. de contrainte,** strain gauge; (*c*) *Mch:* **j. de vapeur,** steam gauge; **j. de pression,** pressure gauge; **robinet de j.,** gauge cock; (*d*) **bas de j. fine,** fine gauge stockings; **bas de grosse j.,** heavy gauge stockings. **3.** *Hort:* trench (in digging, for young trees, etc.); **mettre en j.,** to heel in (seedling, etc.).

jaugeage [ʒoʒa:ʒ], *s.m.* gauging, measuring, measurement.

jauger [ʒoʒe], *v.tr.* (**je jaugeai(s); n. jaugeons**) **1.** (*a*) to gauge, measure, the capacity of (cask, etc.); **j. un navire,** to measure the tonnage of a ship; **j. un homme,** to size up a man; (*b*) to gauge, to measure, the output of (pump, well, etc.). **2.** *Nau:* (*of ship*) (*a*) **j. 300 tonneaux,** to be of 300 tons burden; **pétrolier qui jauge quarante mille tonneaux,** forty thousand ton tanker; (*b*) **j. deux mètres d'eau,** to draw six feet of water.

jaugeur [ʒoʒœ:r], *s.m.* **1.** (*pers.*) gauger. **2.** (*instrument*) gauge.

jaumière [ʒomjɛ:r], *s.f. N.Arch:* rudder trunk, hole, tube.

jaunâtre [ʒonɑ:tr̥], *a.* yellowish; sallow (complexion).

jaune [ʒo:n]. **1.** (*a*) *a.* yellow; **les races jaunes,** the yellow races; **j. comme un coing, comme un citron,** yellow as a guinea, a lemon; **colère j.,** violent rage; **chaussures jaunes,** brown shoes; *Med:* **fièvre j.,** yellow fever; *Geog:* **la mer J.,** the Yellow Sea; *Adm:* **livre j.** = Blue Book; **feu, lumière j.,** amber light; *Tex:* **toile j.,** unbleached calico; *Anat:* **ligaments jaunes,** supraspinous ligaments; (*b*) *a.inv.* **des gants j. paille,** straw-yellow gloves; **j. citron,** lemon-yellow; **j. serin,** canary-yellow. **2.** *adv.* **rire j.,** to give a sickly smile, to force a laugh; **les cierges brûlaient j.,** the candles were burning with a yellow flame; **voir j.,** to be morose, to see everything with a jaundiced eye. **3.** *s.m.* (*a*) yellow (colour); **j. d'ocre,** yellow ochre; **j. de chrome,** chrome-yellow; **j. de cadmium,** cadmium yellow; *A: F:* **sa femme le peint en j.,** his wife is unfaithful; (*b*) **j. d'œuf,** yolk (of egg); (*c*) *Ind: F:* strike breaker, blackleg, scab; (*d*) *Bot:* **j. d'eau,** water lily.

jauneau, -eaux [ʒono], *s.m. Bot:* lesser celandine.

jaunet, -ette [ʒonɛ, -ɛt]. **1.** *a. F:* yellowish. **2.** *s.m.* (*a*) *A: F:* gold coin; (*b*) *Bot:* **j. d'eau,** yellow water lily.

jauni, -ie [ʒoni], *a.* yellowed by age, sun, etc.; faded; bleached (grass); **doigts jaunis par la nicotine,** tobacco-stained fingers.

jaunir [ʒoni:r], *v.* **1.** *v.tr.* (*a*) to colour (sth.) yellow; (*b*) *Bot: F:* **herbe à j.,** (i) dyer's green weed; (ii) yellow weed. **2.** *v.i.* to become, grow, turn, yellow; to fade; to yellow (with age, etc.).

jaunissage [ʒonisa:ʒ], *s.m.* touching-up of gilt work.

jaunissant [ʒonisɑ̃], *a.* yellowing, turning yellow; **blés jaunissants,** ripening corn.

jaunisse [ʒonis], *s.f.* **1.** *Med:* jaundice; **il en ferait, en aurait fait, une j.,** he would be, would have been, mad with jealousy, green with envy. **2.** **j. des arbres, de la vigne, etc.,** the yellows.

jaunissement [ʒonismɑ̃], *s.m.* yellowing; ripening (of corn).

Java[1] [ʒava], *Pr.n. Geog:* Java; **habiter à J.,** to live in Java.

java[2], *s.f.* (*a*) *Danc:* Javanaise; (*b*) *P:* **faire la j.,** to go on the spree.

javanais, -aise [ʒavanɛ, -ɛ:z], *a. & s.* **1.** *Geog:* Javanese. **2.** *s.m.* a form of cant popular under the Second Empire (*to every syllable was added* **av** *or* **va** (**jeudi** *becoming* **javeudavi**); *the resulting sentence was intelligible only to the initiated*) **c'est du j.,** it's double Dutch. **3.** *s.f. Danc:* **javanaise,** Javanaise.

javart [ʒava:r], *s.m.* (*a*) *Vet:* ulcerous sore (on horse's pastern); *A:* quitter; (*b*) *Bot:* chestnut canker, blight.

javeau, -eaux [ʒavo], *s.m.* sand-bank, silt deposit.

Javel [ʒavɛl], *s.m.* **eau de J.,** Javel water, bleach and disinfectant.

javelage[1] [ʒavla:ʒ], *s.m. Agr:* laying (of corn) in swaths.

javelage[2], *s.m. Dy:* bleaching (with potassium chloride).

javelé [ʒavle], *a. Agr:* **avoine javelée,** oats that have rotted in the swath.

javeler[1] [ʒavle], *v.* (**je javelle, n. javelons; je javellerai**) **1.** *v.tr. Agr:* to lay (corn) in swaths. **2.** *v.i.* (*of reaped corn*) to turn yellow.

javeler[2], *v.tr. Dy:* to bleach (with potassium chloride).

javeleur, -euse [ʒavlœ:r, -ø:z], *Agr:* (*a*) *s.m. & f.* (*pers.*) swath layer, harvester; (*b*) *s.f.* (*machine*) **javeleuse,** harvester.

javeline[1] [ʒavlin], *s.f.* javelin.

javeline[2], *s.f. Agr:* small swath, bundle (of corn, etc.).

javelle[1] [ʒavɛl], *s.f.* **1.** *Agr:* swath, loose sheaf. **2.** bundle (of vine twigs, hop poles, etc.); heap of roughly cut slates; (*of barrel, etc.*) **tomber en j.,** to drop to pieces. **3.** heap (of salt, in salt pans).

javelle[2], *s.f. F:* **eau de j.,** Javel water, bleach and disinfectant; **passer à la j.,** to wash in a solution of Javel water.

javellisation [ʒavelizasjɔ̃], *s.f. Hyg:* chlorination.

javelliser [ʒavelize], *v.tr. Hyg:* to chlorinate.

javelot [ʒavlo], *s.m.* **1.** *A.Arms: Sp:* javelin. **2.** *Rept:* sand snake.

javelotte [ʒavlɔt], *s.f.* anvil bed.

javotte [ʒavɔt], *s.f.* **1.** *F: A:* chattering woman, gossip. **2.** anvil bed.

javotter [ʒavɔte], *v.i. A:* to chatter, gossip.

jayet [ʒajɛ], *s.m. Miner: A:* jade.

jayotype [ʒajɔtip], *s.m. Hatm:* graduated circle for measuring the size of the head.

jazz [dʒaːz], *s.m.* jazz; *U.S:* hot music.

jazz-band [dʒazbɑ̃ːd], *s.m.* jazz band; *pl. jazz-bands.*

jazzman [dʒazman], *s.m. Mus:* jazz musician; *pl. jazzmen.*

je, *before a vowel sound (and in colloquial speech often before a consonant also)* **j'** [ʒ(ə)], *pers.pron. nom.* I. **1.** *(unstressed)* **je vois,** I see; **j'ai,** I have; **j'en ai,** I have some; **que vois-je** [vwaːʒ]? what do I see? **puissé-je** [pɥisɛːʒ] . . ., may I . . .; **aussi lui ai-je écrit** [ɛʒekri], so I wrote to him; *P:* **j'sais pas,** I don't know. **2.** *(stressed* [ʒə]) *Jur:* **je, soussigné . . .,** I, the undersigned . . .. **3.** *Dial: P: (with pl.vb. but either sg. or pl. in meaning)* **j'avons fini,** I've done, we've done; **j'en avions assez,** I, we, had enough of it; *the interrog. is* **j'avons-t-i fini?** have we done?

Jean [ʒɑ̃], *Pr.n.m.* (*a*) John; **(saint) J.-Baptiste** [batist], (St) John the Baptist; *F: (of child)* **comme un petit saint J.,** naked; *F: (of boy)* **il fait son petit saint J.,** he's on his best behaviour, he is acting the little cherub; **la Saint-J.,** Midsummer Day; *Bot: F:* **herbe de la Saint J.,** St John's wort; *F:* **un J. fait tout,** a Jack-of-all-trades; *A:* **J. Potage, J. Farine** = Jack Pudding; *Hist:* **J. sans Terre,** John Lackland; **J. des vignes,** stupid man; (*b*) *occ.* = GROS-JEAN.

Jean-Bart [ʒɑ̃baːr], *s.m.inv. A.Cost:* (little boy's) sailor-hat.

Jean-doré [ʒɑ̃dɔre], *s.m.inv. Ich: F:* (John) Dory.

jean-fesse [ʒɑ̃fɛs], **jean-foutre** [ʒɑ̃futr̥], *s.m.inv. F:* unreliable fellow.

jean-jean [ʒɑ̃ʒɑ̃], *s.m.inv. F:* stupid person, fool, dope.

Jean-le-blanc [ʒɑ̃ləblɑ̃], *s.m.inv. Orn: F:* short-toed eagle.

Jeanne [ʒɑ(ː)n, ʒan], *Pr.n.f.* Jane, Joan, Jean; **Jeanne Seymour,** Jane Seymour; **la Papesse J.,** Pope Joan; **J. d'Arc,** Joan of Arc; **cheveux à la J. d'Arc,** bobbed hair with a fringe.

Jeanneton [ʒantɔ̃]. **1.** *Pr.n.f.* Jenny. **2.** *s.f. F:* (rough-mannered) servant girl (in an inn).

Jeannette [ʒanɛt]. **1.** *Pr.n.f.* Jenny, Janet. **2.** *s.f.* (*a*) small gold cross (worn by peasants); (*b*) sleeve-board; (*c*) (botanist's) vasculum; (*d*) *Bot:* **j. jaune,** daffodil; **j. blanche,** pheasant's eye. **3.** *s.f. Scouting:* Brownie.

Jeannot [ʒano]. **1.** *Pr.n.m. F:* Johnny, Jack; *F:* **J. lapin,** bunny(rabbit). **2.** *s.m. F:* (*a*) cuckold; (*b*) simpleton.

jeannotterie [ʒanɔtri], *s.f.* = JANOTERIE.

jéciste [ʒesist], *a. & s.m. & f. (from the abbreviation* **J.E.C.** = **Jeunesse Étudiante Catholique**), belonging to, member of, the Students' Catholic Association.

jeep [(d)ʒip], *s.f. Aut:* jeep.

jefferisite [ʒɛferizit], *s.f. Miner:* jefferisite.

jeffersonite [ʒɛfɛrsɔnit], *s.f. Miner:* jeffersonite.

Jehanne [ʒan], *Pr.n.f. A:* = JEANNE.

Jehosaphat [ʒeɔzafat], *Pr.n.m. B.Hist:* Jehoshaphat.

Jéhovah [ʒeɔva], *Pr.n.m.* Jehovah, Yahweh; **J. Sabaoth,** the Lord of the Sabaoth.

jéhovisme [ʒeɔvism], *s.m.* Yahwism.

jéhoviste [ʒeɔvist], *a. B.Hist:* Jehovistic.

Jéhu [ʒey], *Pr.n.m. B.Hist:* Jehu.

jéjuno-iléon [ʒeʒynɔileɔ̃], *s.m. Anat:* jejunoileum; *pl. jéjuno-iléons.*

jéjunostomie [ʒeʒynɔstɔmi], *s.f. Surg:* jejunostomy.

jéjunum [ʒeʒynɔm], *s.m. Anat:* jejunum.

je-m'en-fichisme [ʒmɑ̃fiʃism], *s.m., F:* **je-m'en-foutisme** [ʒmɑ̃futism], *s.m. P:* couldn't-care-less attitude.

je-m'en-fichiste [ʒmɑ̃fiʃist], *s.m. & f., F:* **je-m'en-foutiste** [ʒmɑ̃futist], *s.m. & f. P:* person who doesn't care a hang about anything or anybody.

je-ne-sais-quoi, je ne sais quoi [ʒənsɛkwa], *s.m.,* **un-je-ne-s.-q.,** an indescribable something; **il y a un je-ne-s.-q. qui ne me plaît pas,** there is something about it I don't like.

jennérien, -ienne [ʒɛnerjɛ̃, -jɛːn], *a. Med:* Jennerian; **vaccin j.,** Jennerian, smallpox, vaccine; **vaccination jennérienne,** vaccination (against smallpox).

jenny [ʒɛni], *s.f. Tex:* spinning-jenny.

Jephté [ʒɛfte], *Pr.n.m. B.Hist:* Jephthah.

jérémiade [ʒeremjad], *s.f.* jeremiad, lamentation, doleful story; **assez de jérémiades!** that's enough whining! stop complaining!

Jérémie [ʒeremi], *Pr.n.m.* (*a*) *B.Hist:* Jeremiah; (*b*) Jeremiah; Jeremy.

Jerez [keres]. **1.** *Pr.n. Geog:* Jerez. **2.** *s.m.* sherry.

Jéricho [ʒeriko], *Pr.n.m. Geog:* Jericho; *Bot:* **rose de J.,** rose of Jericho.

Jéroboam [ʒerɔbɔam]. **1.** *Pr.n.m.* Jeroboam. **2.** *s.m.* jeroboam (of champagne, holding six litres).

Jérôme [ʒeroːm], *Pr.n.m.* Jerome.

jérose [ʒeroːz], *s.f. Bot:* rose of Jericho.

jérosolymitain, -aine [ʒerozolimitɛ̃, -ɛn], *a. & s.* Hierosolymitan, Hierosolymite; (inhabitant, native) of Jerusalem.

jerricane, *s.f.,* **jerrycan,** *s.m.,* **jerry-can,** *s.m.* (*pl. jerry-cans*) [ʒerikan], jerrycan.

Jersey [ʒɛrzɛ]. **1.** *Pr.n.m. Geog:* (Island of) Jersey; *Husb:* **vache de J.,** Jersey cow. **2.** *s.m. Cost:* jersey. **3.** *s.m. Tex:* jersey; **j. de laine,** wool jersey; **j. de soie,** silk jersey; *Knitting:* **point (de) j.,** stocking stitch.

jersiais, -aise [ʒɛrzjɛ, -ɛːz], *a. & s.* (native, inhabitant) of Jersey; **(vache) jersiaise,** Jersey cow; **bœuf j.,** Jersey bull.

Jérusalem [ʒeryzalɛm], *Pr.n. Geog:* Jerusalem.

je-sais-tout [ʒ(ə)sɛtu], *a. & s.m.inv.* know-all.

Jessé [ʒɛse], *Pr.n.m. B.Hist:* Jesse; **arbre de J.,** Jesse tree, tree of Jesse, Jesse.

jésuite [ʒezɥit], *s.m.* (*a*) *Ecc:* Jesuit; (*b*) *Pej: F:* hypocrite.

jésuitesse [ʒezɥitɛs], *s.f. A:* nun of the Saint-Omer community.

jésuitière [ʒezɥitjɛːr], *s.f. Pej:* Jesuit house, institution.

jésuitique [ʒezɥitik], *a.* **1.** *Ecc:* jesuitic(al). **2.** *Pej:* jesuitic(al); plausible, specious. **3.** *Arch:* **fenêtre j.,** one-way glass.

jésuitiquement [ʒezɥitikmɑ̃], *adv. Pej:* jesuitically.

jésuitiser [ʒezɥitize], *v.i. Pej:* to act hypocritically.

jésuitisme [ʒezɥitism], *s.m.* (*a*) Jesuitism; (*b*) *Pej:* Jesuitry; hypocrisy.

Jésus [ʒezy]. **1.** (*a*) *Pr.n.m.* Jesus; **J.-Christ,** Jesus Christ; **en l'an 44 avant J.-C.,** in the year 44 B.C.; *Ecc:* **la compagnie de J.,** the Society of Jesus; **l'Enfant J.,** the Infant Jesus, the Christ-Child; *Art:* the Bambino; (*b*) *s.m.* **un j.,** (i) a statue of the Christ Child; (ii) *F:* a small baby; **mon j.,** my little pet. **2.** *a.m. & s.m. Typ:* **(papier) j.,** (*approx.*) super-royal, long royal (paper); **grand j.,** (*approx.*) imperial. **3.** *s.m.* (type of) large (cooked) sausage. **4.** *int: F:* Christ!

jet[1] [ʒɛ], *s.m.* **1.** (*a*) throwing, casting; throw, cast (of net, stone, dice, etc.); **à un j. de pierre de . . .,** within a stone's throw of . . .; *Fish:* **j. de filet,** (i) cast (of a net); (ii) haul; **poissons pris d'un seul j.,** fish taken at a single cast; **j. en arrière (du lancer),** back cast; *Art: Lit:* **premier j.,** first sketch, rough outline; rough draft (of novel); **du premier j.,** at the first attempt; **force de j.,** impetus; **armes de j.,** missiles, projectiles; *Box:* **j. de l'éponge,** (act of) throwing in the sponge; (*b*) *Metall:* cast, casting; **couler qch. d'un seul j.,** to cast sth. in one piece; **faire qch. d'un seul j.,** to do sth. at one go, at one sitting; (*c*) *Nau:* **ancre à j.,** kedge anchor; *Jur:* **j. (de marchandises) à la mer, pardessus bord,** jettison(ing), throwing overboard (of cargo); (*d*) *Civ.E:* **j. de fossé,** (i) throwing up of earth from trench; (ii) earth thrown up. **2.** (*a*) jet, gush, stream (of liquid); spurt (of blood); flash, ray (of light); **j. de vapeur,** steam jet; blast of steam; **j. plein,** solid stream; **j. d'incendie,** jet of water from a fire hose; **j. d'eau,** (i) jet of water, fountain; (ii) jet-nozzle (of hose-pipe); (iii) *Const:* watertight moulding, weather board, drip moulding, flashing-moulding (of windows); **appareil à j. d'air comprimé,** compressed air spray apparatus; **j. de flamme,** (i) burst of flame; (ii) blowpipe flame; *Min:* **perforation par j. abrasif,** abrasive jetting; *Metalw: etc:* **j. de sable,** sand blast; **à j. continu,** in one continuous stream; *F:* **parler à j. continu,** to spout; **débiter des sottises à j. continu,** to spout nonsense; (*b*) *Bot:* **j. (d'un arbre),** young shoot; **j. d'osier,** osier spear; **elle est tout d'un j.,** she is tall and slender. **3.** (*a*) jet (of nozzle, etc.); spout (of pump, watering can, etc.); **j. de gaz,** gas jet; **j. à pomme,** rose (of watering can, etc.); **ouvrir le robinet à petit j.,** to set the tap at a trickle, to turn on a trickle of water; (*b*) *Metall:* **j. de coulée,** casting hole, jet, gate, runner, sprue. **4.** *Nau: Jur:* jetsam; *Com:* **bois de j.,** driftwood. **5.** *Ven:* jess (for falcon). **6.** *Ap:* cast, after-swarm (of bees).

jet[2] [dʒɛt], *s.m. Av: F:* jet (aircraft).

jetable [ʒ(ə)tabl̥], *a.* disposable (nappies, bags, etc.).

jetage [ʒ(ə)taːʒ], *s.m.* **1.** (action of) throwing (logs into the river). **2.** *Vet:* running at the nostrils, gleet (of glanderous horse).

jeté [ʒ(ə)te], *s.m.* (*a*) *Danc:* jeté; (*b*) *Knitting:* (wool) over, (wool) forward; **j. simple, j. double,** make one, make two; (*c*) *(weight lifting)* **j. à deux bras (de l'haltère),** two-hands jerk; **épaulé j.,** clean and jerk; (*d*) **j. de table,** (table-)runner; **j. de lit,** bedspread.

jetée [ʒ(ə)te], *s.f.* **1.** jetty, pier; **j. promenade,** (seaside) pier; **j. d'accostage,** discharging jetty; **droits de j.,** pier dues, pierage. **2.** (= BRISE-LAMES) breakwater. **3.** *Civ.E:* layer of grit (on road).

jeter [ʒəte, ʃte], *v.tr.* **(je jette, n. jetons; je jetterai)** to throw, fling, cast; to throw away; **j. qch. de côté,** to toss sth. aside; **j. une balle, une pierre,** to throw, toss, a ball; to throw a stone; **j. le foin sur la charrette,** to pitch the hay on to the cart; **j. son argent par la fenêtre,** to throw one's money down the drain, to play ducks and drakes with one's money; **j. qch. à la tête de qn,** (i) to throw sth. at s.o.'s head; (ii) *F:* to foist sth. on s.o.; **j. qch. au nez, à la face, à la figure, de qn,** to throw sth. in s.o.'s face, teeth; **j. des reproches à la tête de qn,** to hurl reproaches at s.o.; **j. de l'eau au visage de qn,** to splash water in s.o.'s face; **les baigneurs se jettent de l'eau,** the bathers are splashing each other; **j. un filet,** to cast a net; **j. bas qch., j. qch. à terre, par terre,** to throw sth. down; **j. bas une idole,** to hurl down an idol; **j. qn à bas de sa bicyclette,** to throw s.o. off his bicycle; *Mch:* **j. bas les feux,** to draw, to put out, the fires; **j. loin qch.,** to fling sth. away; **j. ses armes,** to throw down one's arms; to throw away one's weapons; **jetez cette cigarette,** throw away that cigarette; *adj.phr.* **à j.,** (i) to be thrown away; (ii) disposable (dust-bag, baby's nappy, etc.); **j. son bien,** to waste one's substance; *A:* **j. au sort,** to cast lots; **j. un sort à qn,** to cast a spell on s.o.; *F:* **elle m'a jeté un sort,** she turned my head, she captivated me; **les dés sont jetés, le sort en est jeté,** the die is cast; **j. des étincelles,** to emit sparks; **j. une flamme claire,** to burn clear; **j. un cri, des menaces,** to utter a cry, threats; **j. un soupir,** to heave a sigh; **j. un regard sur qn,** to cast a glance at s.o.; **j. une ombre,** to cast a shadow; **j. qn dans l'embarras,** to throw s.o. into confusion; **j. qn en prison,** to throw, cast, s.o. into prison; **j. qn à la porte,** to bundle s.o. out of the house; to throw s.o. out; *O:* **j. sa colère,** to vent one's wrath; **j. des racines,** to throw out roots; to strike (root); **j. une lettre à la poste,** to drop a letter in the post(-box); **j. les fondements d'un édifice,** to lay the foundations of a building; **j. un pont sur une rivière,** to throw a bridge over a river; *Mil:* **j. des hommes dans une place,** to throw troops into a place; **navires jetés à la côte par la tempête,** ships driven ashore by the storm; **l'ulcère jette du pus,** the ulcer is discharging (pus); *Ap:* **abeilles qui vont j. (un essaim),** bees about to swarm; *Metall:* **j. (une statue, etc.) en fonte,** to cast (a statue, etc.); *Nau:* **j. le plomb, la sonde,** to heave the lead; **j. l'ancre,** to cast anchor; **(faire) j. qch. à la mer, par-dessus bord,** to jettison sth.; **objets jetés à la mer,** jetsam; **j. l'éponge,** to throw in, up, the sponge; *F: Hum:* **n'en jetez plus (la cour est pleine),** that's more than enough; *s.a.* BOMBE 1, CHIEN 1, LOCH, PIERRE[1].

se jeter. **se j. par la fenêtre,** to throw oneself out of the window; **se j. à l'eau,** (i) to jump into the water; (ii) to take the plunge; (iii) to drown oneself; **se j. à l'eau pour sauver qn,** to plunge into the water, to jump in, in order to save s.o.; **se j. à bas de son lit,** to jump out of bed; **se j. sur qn,** to fall upon s.o., to attack s.o.; **se j. dans la discussion,** to throw oneself into the discussion; to plunge into the debate; **se j. sur le cou, au cou, de qn,** to fall on s.o.'s neck; *F:* **se j. dans qn,** to run right into s.o.; **la Loire se jette dans l'Atlantique,** the Loire flows into the Atlantic; **cours d'eau qui se jette dans la Seine,** stream that flows into the Seine; *Nau: (of ship)* **se j. sur . . .,** to run aground on . . ..

jeteur, -euse [ʒətœːr, -øːz], *s.* thrower; caster (of dice, etc.); *now used only in:* **jeteur, -euse de sort,** (i) person who casts spells on people, things; (ii) *F:* spellbinder.

jeton [ʒətɔ̃, ʃtɔ̃], *s.m.* (*a*) *Cards: etc:* counter; chip; *Num: A:* (trade) token; *F:* **un faux j.,** (i) an unreliable customer; (ii) a hypocrite; *F:* **vieux j.,** old man, woman; (*b*) **j. de présence,** tally, token (issued as voucher for attendance at meeting); director's fees; **toucher ses jetons,** to hand in one's checks, to draw one's fees, to cash in; *Ind:* **j. d'outils,** tool check; (*c*) *Ap:* **j. d'abeilles,** swarm; (*d*) *P:* punch, blow; (*e*) *P:* **avoir les jetons,** to have the jitters.

jet-stream [ʒɛtstrim], *s.m. Meteor:* jet(-)stream; *pl. jet-streams.*

jettatura [ʒɛttatura], *s.f.*, **jettature** [ʒɛttatyːr], *s.f.* evil eye.

jette-feu [ʒɛtfø], *s.m.inv. Mch:* drop-grate.

jette-sable [ʒɛtsɑːbl̩], *s.m.inv.* sand-box (of locomotive, etc.).

jettice [ʒɛtis], *a.f. Tex:* (*of kempy wool*) wasted.

jeu, jeux [ʒø], *s.m.* **1.** (*a*) play, sport; **jouer à un j.,** to play a game; **j. bruyant,** noisy game; **salle de jeux,** playroom; **j. de mots,** play on words, pun; **j. d'esprit,** witticism (*s.a.* 2 (*a*)); **j. de main,** horseplay, rough-and-tumble; *Prov:* **j. de main(s), j. de vilain; j. de pied(s), j. de charretier,** (let us have) no horseplay! **jeux de la fortune,** tricks of fortune; **j. de la nature,** freak (of nature); **c'est un j. d'enfant,** it's child's play; **se faire (un) j. de qch., de faire qch.,** to make light of sth., of doing sth.; to make nothing of doing sth.; **se faire un j. de la douleur d'autrui,** to make fun of someone's suffering; **ils se faisaient un j. de le tourmenter,** they made a sport of baiting him; **être le j. de la Fortune,** to be the plaything of Fortune; **par un j. de la Fortune . . .,** through a freak of chance . . .; (*b*) (manner of) playing; acting (of actor); execution, playing (of musician); **j. muet,** dumb show; **jeux de scène,** stage business; **jeux de physionomie,** play of features; **j'admire son j.,** I admire his playing; **j. brillant,** brilliant execution; **il a un j. remarquable,** (i) he plays a remarkable game; (ii) his execution is remarkable; (iii) his acting is remarkable; **vieux-j.,** old-fashioned. **2.** (*a*) **jeux d'adresse,** games of skill; **jeux olympiques,** Olympic games; **le j. de tennis,** (lawn) tennis; **le j. de paume,** (court) tennis; **jeux de société, petits jeux,** parlour games, forfeit games; **j. des métiers,** happy families; **jeux d'esprit,** intellectual pastimes (acrostics, etc.); **jeux de hasard,** games of chance; **jeux d'argent,** gambling (games); **terrain de jeux,** sports ground; **ce n'est pas de j., cela passe le j.,** that's not fair, *F:* that's not cricket; **c'est de bon j., c'est le j.,** it's quite fair, fair play; **jouer beau j., jouer le j.,** to play the game, to play fair; **où en est le j.?** what's the score? **on aurait beau j. de, à, répondre,** it would be quite easy to answer that; *Games:* **(déclaré) hors-j.,** out; *Bill:* **j. livré à l'adversaire,** leave; **livrer du j. à son adversaire,** to give one's opponent a leave; *Tchn:* **théorie des jeux rectangulaires,** game theory; *Prov:* **à beau j. beau retour,** one good turn deserves another; *Cards:* **avoir beau j., avoir du j.,** to have a good hand; *F:* **vous avez beau j.,** now's your chance; **il a bien joué son j.,** he played his cards well; **il a fait mon j.,** he played into my hands; **jouer bon j. bon argent,** (i) to play a straight game; (ii) to mean business; **y aller bon j. bon argent,** to come, go, straight to the point; *Ten:* **j. et partie,** game and set; **j., set et partie,** game set and match; **j. blanc,** love game; *Fb:* (i) **hors-j.,** off side; (ii) **ballon hors-j.,** ball out of play; **rester juste en deçà de la limite du hors-j.,** to remain just on side; **en j.,** in play; **mettre la balle en j.,** to bring the ball into play; (*Hockey*) to bully off; *s.a.* ENGAGEMENT 3, FRANC² 2, REMETTRE 1, REMISE 1; (*b*) (*place*) **j. de cricket,** cricket ground; **j. de tennis,** (lawn-)tennis courts; **j. de boules,** (*in Fr.*) bowling ground, (*in Eng.*) bowling green; **j. de quilles,** skittle alley. **3.** set; **j. d'échecs, de dominos,** set of chessmen, of dominoes; pack of dominoes; **j. de cartes,** pack of cards; **j. d'avirons,** set of oars; *Mec.E:* **j. de coussinets,** set of brasses; *Metall:* **j. de cylindres,** train of rolls; **j. de voiles,** suit of sails; **j. de fiches,** card-index; **j. de croquet,** croquet set; *Mus:* **j. d'orgue,** (i) (organ) stop; (ii) draw-stop, stop-key; **j. d'outils,** set, assortment, string (of tools); **en jeux complets,** (tools, etc.) in sets; *Nau:* **j. complet de connaissements,** complete set of bills of lading; *Elcs:* **j. d'essai,** test deck (of computer). **4.** (*a*) gaming, gambling, play; card playing; dicing; **maison de j.,** gaming house; **salle de j.,** gaming room; **perdre au j.,** to lose at play, to have gaming losses; **perdre une fortune au j.,** to gamble away a fortune; **se ruiner au j.,** to ruin oneself gambling; *Jur:* **invoquer l'exception de j.,** to plead the Gaming Act; **dettes de j.,** gambling debts, gaming debts; **table de j.,** gaming table, card table; **jouer gros j.,** to play for high stakes, to play high; **jouer un j. d'enfer,** to plunge recklessly; **faites votre j., vos jeux!** put down your stakes! **les jeux sont faits,** (i) (*at roulette*) the stakes are down, les jeux sont faits; (ii) the die is cast; the chips are down; **se mettre du j.,** to take a hand; **mettre qch. au j.,** to stake sth.; **mettre tout en j.,** (i) to stake one's all; (ii) to leave no stone unturned, to bring every influence to bear; **son honneur est en j.,** his honour is at stake; **mettre l'honneur de qn en j.,** to call s.o.'s honour in(to) question; **les intérêts en j.,** the interests at issue, at stake; **les questions en j.,** the questions involved, implied, at issue; **le j. ne, n'en, vaut pas la chandelle,** the game isn't worth the candle; **jouer double j.,** to play a double game; to run with the hare and hunt with the hounds; **faire le j., de l'adversaire,** to play into the enemy's hands; **jouer un j. dangereux,** to play a dangerous game; to play with edged tools; **cacher son j.,** to hide one's cards, to play an underhand game; **montrer son j.,** to show one's cards; to play above-board; **jouer le grand j.,** to do everything in one's power; *F:* **faire à qn le grand j.,** to give s.o. the works; (*b*) *St.Exch:* speculating; **j. sur les reports,** speculating in contangoes. **5.** (*activity, action*) **les forces en j.,** the forces at work, involved; **par le j. de cette loi,** through the action of this law; **mettre qch. en j.,** to set sth. in action, to bring, call, sth. into play, into action; **d'autres forces entrent en j.,** other forces come into play; **j. d'une pompe,** play, working, of a pump; **j. d'un piston,** length of stroke of a piston; **j. de lumière,** play of light; *Th:* **jeux de lumière,** lighting effects; **j. d'éventails,** fluttering, flirting, of fans; **le j. de la pensée,** the processes of thought; **j. d'une serrure,** action of a lock; *Mec.E:* **en j.,** in gear. **6.** *Mec.E:* (*a*) **j. (utile),** clearance, play, free motion; **j. admissible, j. permis,** admissible, permissible, play; **j. axial, j. en bout, j. longitudional,** end play, end clearance; **j. latéral,** side play, side clearance; **j. à fond de course, à fond de dents, à fond de filet,** bottom clearance; **j. de palier,** bearing clearance; **j. de fonctionnement,** running clearance; *I.C.E:* **j. aux queues des soupapes,** valve clearance; **donner du j. à un organe,** to give play to a part, to give a part clearance; to ease, slacken, a part; **laisser du j.,** to leave play; **reprendre le j.,** to remove play; **appareil à mesurer le(s) jeu(x),** clearance gauge, clearance meter; (*b*) **j. (nuisible),** looseness, play, slack; (back)lash (of gear); **trop de j.,** too much play; **prendre du j.,** to work free, loose; **rattraper le j.,** to take up the slack, the wear; (*c*) *Av:* gap.

jeu-concours [ʒøkɔ̃kuːr], *s.m. W.Tel: T.V: etc:* quiz; *pl. jeux-concours.*

jeudi [ʒødi], *s.m.* (*a*) Thursday; **j. saint,** Maundy Thursday; **j. gras,** Thursday before Shrove Tuesday; *F:* **la semaine des quatre jeudis,** when two Sundays come in one week (*i.e.* never); when pigs begin to fly; **vous risquez d'attendre jusqu'à la semaine des quatre jeudis,** I'm afraid you'll wait till the cows come home; (*b*) *Geog:* **l'île de J.,** Thursday Island.

jeun (à) [aʒœ̃], *adj.phr.* **1.** fasting; **boire à j.,** to drink on an empty stomach; *Med:* **à prendre le matin à j.,** to be taken on an empty stomach. **2.** sober.

jeune [ʒœn]. **1.** *a.* (*a*) young; juvenile; youthful; **homme j.,** man still young, youngish man; **j. homme,** *pl. jeunes gens, occ. jeunes hommes,* young man; **venez ici, j. homme,** come here, young man, come here, my lad; **un j. homme encore au lycée,** a youth still at school; *F:* **une femme plus très j.,** a not-so-young woman; a woman who is not so young as she was; *F:* **son j. homme,** her young man, her boy friend; **elle dînait avec un petit j. homme,** she was dining with some young man (or other); **j. personne,** young lady; **j. fille,** girl; young woman; **jeunes gens,** (i) young people; (ii) young men; **j. aveugle,** blind boy, girl; **un j. Français, un j. Anglais,** a French boy, an English boy; **une j. Indienne,** an Indian girl; **une j. servante,** a servant girl; **j. détenu,** juvenile offender (in approved school, etc.); young prisoner; **le j. âge,** youth; **dans son j. âge,** in his young(er) days; **j. d'esprit,** young in mind; **esprit qui est resté j.,** mind that has stayed young; **j. visage, visage j.,** youthful, young-looking, face; **chapeau coiffant j.,** youthful hat; (*b*) younger; **mon j. frère,** my younger brother; **je suis plus j. que lui de quatre ans,** I am four years younger than he is; **Pline le J.,** Pliny the Younger; **M. Martin J.,** Mr Martin junior; young Mr Martin; (*c*) **vin j.,** new wine. **2.** *s.* (*a*) **les jeunes,** young people; the younger generation; **les jeunes et les moins jeunes,** the young and the not so young; (*b*) young animal; **un animal et ses jeunes,** an animal and its young.

jeûne [ʒøːn], *s.m.* (*a*) fast; **observer un j. rigoureux,** to observe a rigorous fast; **rompre le j.,** (i) to break one's fast; (ii) *Ecc:* to break the rule of fasting; **j. des amusements,** fast from amusements; (*b*) fasting; **jour de j.,** (i) day of fasting; (ii) *Ecc:* fast day.

jeunement [ʒœnmɑ̃], *adv.* **1.** *A:* like a young man or woman; youthfully. **2.** *Ven:* **un dix cors j.,** a stag just turned five years.

jeûner [ʒøne], *v.i.* (*a*) to fast (**de,** from); **j. au pain et à l'eau,** to take nothing but bread and water; (*b*) *F:* to forego, be deprived of, the pleasures of life.

jeunesse [ʒœnɛs], *s.f.* **1.** (*a*) youth; boyhood, girlhood; **je le connais de j.,** I have known him from my youth; **dans sa première j.,** in (his, her) early youth; **la toute première j.,** earliest youth; infancy; **ne pas être de la première j.,** not to be in the first flush of youth; *F:* to be getting on; **erreurs, péchés, de j.,** errors of youth, youthful indiscretions; **si j. savait!** if youth but knew! **œuvres de j.,** juvenilia; *Prov:* **j. est difficile à passer,** youth has its growing pains; **la j. revient de loin,** when one is young there is always hope; **il faut que j. se passe,** youth will have its way, its fling; boys will be boys; **organismes de j.,** youth organizations; (*b*) youthfulness, juvenility (of appearance, etc.); **avoir un air de j.,** to look young; (*c*) newness (of wine); (*d*) *coll.* **livres pour la j.,** juveniles, children's books; **la j. du village,** the youth of the village. **2.** *F:* girl.

jeunet, -ette [ʒœnɛ, -ɛt], *F:* **1.** *a.* (*a*) youngish; (*b*) quite young. **2.** *s.* **un petit j.,** a mere boy.

Jeune-Turc, -Turque [ʒœntyrk], *s. Pol:* (*a*) young Turk, member of the Young-Turkey party; (*b*) member of the avant-garde of a political party; *pl. Jeunes Turcs, Turques.*

Jeune-Turquie [ʒœntyrki], *s.f. Pol:* Young-Turkey party.

jeûneur, -euse [ʒønœːr, -øːz], *s.* one who fasts; faster.

jeunot, -otte [ʒœno, -ɔt], *a. & s. F:* **1.** young; youngish; on the young side; **il est j. pour travailler dur,** he's a bit young for hard work. **2.** youngster; **c'est une jeunotte, l'institutrice du village,** the village schoolmistress is quite a young girl.

jeu-pari [ʒøpari], *s.m.inv. Jur:* gaming and wagering.

Jézabel [ʒezabɛl], *Pr.n.f. B.Hist:* Jezebel.

ji [ʒi], *adv. O: P:* yes.

jig [ʒig], *s.m. Min:* jig (for crushing ore).

jigger [ʒigɛːr], *s.m. W.Tel:* jigger, oscillation transformer.

jingo [dʒingo], *s.m. Hist.Pol:* jingo, jingoist.

jingoïsm [dʒingoism], *s.m. Hist: Pol:* jingoism.

jiu-jitsu [dʒydʒitsy, ʒjuʒitsy], *s.m.inv. Sp:* jiu-jitsu, ju-jutsu.

jive [dʒaiːv], *s.m. Danc:* jive; **faire du j.,** to jive.

Joad [ʒɔad], *Pr.n.m. B.Hist:* Joad.

joaillerie [ʒɔɑjri], *s.f.* **1.** jeweller's business. **2.** jewellery.

joaillier, -ière [ʒɔɑje, jɛːr], *s.* jeweller.

Joas [ʒɔas], *Pr.n.m. B.Hist:* Joash, Jehoash.

job¹ [ʒɔb], *s.m. P:* **1.** *A:* = JOBARD. **2.** *F:* **monter le j. à qn,** to pull s.o.'s leg; to work s.o. up **(contre,** against); **se monter le j.,** to get excited; to imagine things; *Th:* **battre le j.,** to get muddled in one's part.

Job², *Pr.n.m. B.Hist:* Job; **pauvre comme J.,** as poor as Job.

job³, *s.m. F:* job, task.

jobard, -arde [ʒɔbaːr, -ard], *F:* **1.** *a.* stupid, naïve. **2.** *s.* person easily taken in (by beggars, etc.); easy prey; *F:* easy mark; mug, sucker, *U.S:* patsy.

jobarder [ʒɔbarde], *v.tr. F:* to dupe (s.o.); to take (s.o.) in.

jobarderie [ʒɔbard(ə)ri], *s.f.*, **jobardise** [ʒɔbardiːz], *s.f. F:* **1.** gullibility; **c'est de la j.,** *F:* it's a mug's game. **2.** piece of misplaced philanthropy; **commettre une j.,** to allow oneself to be fooled, to be taken in.

jocasse [ʒɔkas], *s.f. Orn: F:* fieldfare.

Jocaste [ʒɔkast], *Pr.n.f. Gr.Lit:* Jocasta.

jociste [ʒɔsist], *a. & s.m. & f.* (*from the abbreviation* **J.O.C.** = **Jeunesse Ouvrière Catholique**), belonging to, member of, the Young Worker's Catholic Association.

jockey [ʒɔkɛ], *s.m.* **1.** (*a*) jockey; (*b*) outrider; (*c*) *A:* groom; (*d*) *attrib. F:* **régime j.,** starvation diet. **2.** dumb jockey (used in horse training).

jocko [ʒɔko], *s.m.* **1.** *Z: F: O:* (*a*) orang-utan; (*b*) chimpanzee. **2.** *P:* baker; **pain j.,** small French loaf.

Joconde (la) [laʒɔkɔ̃:d], *Pr.n.f. Hist. of Art:* Mona Lisa; la Gioconda.

jocosité [ʒɔkozite], *s.f.* jocoseness, jocosity, mirthfulness.

jocothérapie [ʒɔkɔterapi], *s.f. Med:* play therapy.

jocrisse [ʒɔkris], *s.m.* **1.** stupid servant. **2.** (*a*) fool, simpleton; (*b*) henpecked husband; (from the character in old farces).

jocrisserie [ʒɔkrisri], *s.f.* **1.** stupidity, gullibility. **2.** piece of stupidity.

jodhpurs [ʒɔdpœ:r], *s.m.pl.* **1.** jodhpurs. **2.** jodhpur boots, shoes.

jodler [jɔdle], *v.i. Mus:* to yodel, *U.S:* to warble.

jodleur, -euse [jɔdlœ:r, -ø:z], *s. Mus:* yodeller.

jogglinage [ʒɔglina:ʒ], *s.m. N.Arch:* joggling.

joggliner [ʒɔgline], *v.tr. N.Arch:* to joggle.

johannique [ʒɔanik], *a. Theol:* Johannine (writings, etc.).

johannite [ʒɔanit], *s.m. Miner:* johannite.

joie [ʒwa], *s.f.* **1.** joy; delight; gladness, glee; **plein de j.,** full of joy; in high spirits; **sauter de j.,** to leap for joy; **ne pas se posséder de j.,** to be beside oneself with joy; **à ma grande j., on me permit . . .,** to my great joy, to my great delight, I was allowed . . .; **cette nouvelle me remplit de j., me transporta de j., me mit au comble de la j.,** I was overjoyed at the news; **c'est une grande j. qu'il nous revienne,** it is a great joy to us that he is coming back; **visage rayonnant de j.,** face beaming with joy; **respirer la, être en, j.,** to be full of joy, to be joyful; **accepter avec j.,** to accept joyfully, gladly; **les joies et les plaisirs de ce monde,** the joys of life; **faire la j. de qn,** (i) to be s.o.'s joy; (ii) to make s.o. happy; **se faire une j. de servir qn,** to delight, to take a delight, in serving s.o.; **feu de j.,** bonfire; **j. de vivre,** joy of living, joie de vivre; high spirits; exhilaration; **je suis tout à la j. de vous revoir,** I'm overjoyed at seeing you; **il se faisait une j. de vous voir,** he was looking forward to seeing you; **avoir le cœur à la j.,** to feel happy; *adv.phr.* **à cœur j.,** to one's heart's content; **s'en donner à cœur j.,** to enjoy oneself to the full, to have one's fling. **2.** (*a*) mirth, merriment; **la j. bruyante des convives,** the noisy enjoyment of the guests; the expansive gaiety of the guests; (*b*) **aimer la j.,** to be fond of pleasure; **fille de j.,** prostitute.

joignant [ʒwaɲɑ̃], *A:* **1.** *a.* **maison joignante à la mienne,** house adjoining mine, next door to mine. **2.** *prep.* **maison (tout) j. la mienne,** house adjoining mine.

joigneur [ʒwaɲœ:r], *s.m. Tail: Leath:* joiner.

joindre [ʒwɛ̃:dr], *v.tr.* (*pr.p.* **joignant;** *p.p.* **joint;** *pr.ind.* **je joins, il joint, n. joignons, ils joignent;** *p.d.* **je joignais;** *p.h.* **je joignis;** *fu.* **je joindrai**) **1.** to join; (*a*) to bring together; **j. les mains,** to clasp, join, fold, one's hands; **joignons nos efforts,** let us unite our efforts; **j. (un tube, etc.) à chaud,** to weld (a tube, etc.); **j. deux mots,** to join two words; **j. les deux bouts,** to make both ends meet; (*b*) to add (à, to); **le bon sens joint à l'intelligence,** common sense combined with, coupled with, intelligence; **j. le geste à la parole,** to suit the action to the word; **j. l'utile à l'agréable,** to combine business with pleasure; **j. sa voix aux protestations,** to join in the protests; **j. une pièce à un mémoire,** to annex a document to a statement; **j. l'arrogance à, avec, l'imprudence,** to add arrogance to imprudence; *Com: etc:* **l'échantillon joint à votre lettre,** the sample attached to your letter; (*c*) **j. son régiment, son navire,** to join one's regiment, one's ship; (*d*) (= REJOINDRE) to meet, join (s.o.); **je vous joindrai à . . .,** I shall meet, join, you at . . .; **comment puis-je vous j.?** how can I get in touch with you? *Tp:* **j'ai téléphoné, mais je n'ai pas réussi à le j.,** I phoned but couldn't get him, get in(to) touch with him. **2.** to adjoin; **notre maison joint la sienne,** our house is next to his. **3.** *v.i.* to meet, fit; **fenêtre qui joint mal,** window that does not shut tight; **ces planches ne joignent pas,** these boards do not meet; these boards gape.

se joindre. **1.** to join, unite; **se j. à, avec, qn pour faire qch.,** to join s.o., to join with s.o., in doing sth.; **se j. à la conversation,** to join in the conversation; **voulez-vous vous j. à nous?** would you like to join us? **2.** to adjoin; **les deux maisons se joignent,** the two houses adjoin, are contiguous. **3.** (*of animals*) to mate.

joint [ʒwɛ̃]. **1.** *a.* joined, united; **pieds joints,** feet close together; **saut à pieds joints,** standing jump; *F:* **sauter à pieds joints sur qn,** (i) to ride rough-shod over s.o.; (ii) to come down on s.o. like a ton of bricks; **à mains jointes,** with clasped hands; **implorer qn à mains jointes,** to implore s.o. earnestly; *Corr:* **pièces jointes,** enclosures; *conj.phr:* **j. (à ce) que,** besides which, added to which; *s.a.* CI-JOINT. **2.** *s.m.* (*a*) joint, join; **j. de l'épaule,** shoulder joint; *F:* **trouver le j.,** to hit upon the right plan, to find a way; **trouver le j. pour faire qch.,** to discover the trick, the dodge, for doing sth.; **j. de tuyaux en toile,** hose coupling; *Const: etc:* **j. abouté, en about, carré, plat,** butt joint; **j. biseauté,** scarf joint; **j. de recouvrement, j. à clin,** (i) *N.Arch:* lap joint; (ii) *Metalw:* (over)lap joint, overlapping joint, step joint, bolted joint, **j. d'étanchéité,** gasket; seal; *N. Arch:* butt joint, flush joint; **j. étanche,** (water-)tight joint; **j. hermétique,** hermetic seal, vacuum seal; **j. union,** union joint; *Mec.E: etc:* **j. articulé, j. en charnière,** knuckle(-joint); **j. universel, j. brisé, j. de Cardan,** universal Cardan coupling; **j. de Cardan à croisillons,** cross-pin Cardan joint; **j. plein,** blind flange; blind, blank, dead, end; **j. de réglage,** calibrated spacer; **j. de Hooke,** Hooke's joint, coupling; **j. sphérique, à rotule, à boulet, double,** ball(-and-socket) joint; **j. glissant,** expansion joint; **boîte de j. glissant,** expansion gland; **j. à vis, j. vissé,** screw joint; **j. à franc-bord,** butt joint; **j. à brides,** flange joint; **j. au carton d'amiante,** asbestos joint; **j. sec,** face-to-face joint; *El.E:* **j. par torsade,** twisted joint; *N.Arch:* **j. rivé,** crack asbestos; (*b*) (i) *Geol:* joint, line of jointing; diaclase; **j. de cisaillement,** shear joint; **j. parallèle à l'inclinaison,** joint dip; (ii) *Const:* **joints d'un mur,** jointing of a wall; (*c*) *Mch:* packing (of piston, gland); **j. de presse-étoupe,** packing gasket, ring; *I.C.E:* **j. de culasse, j. à l'amiante,** gasket; *Elcs:* **j. de guide d'ondes,** wave-guide gasket; (*d*) *Metalw: etc:* seam (of boiler, etc.); **j. sans épaisseur,** ridgeless seam; *s.a.* SURÉPAISSER; (*e*) **j. à la thermite,** thermite weld, bond; (*f*) *Petroleum Ind:* **j. bitumineux préparé,** bituminous expansion joint; **j. sans lut, sec,** self-sealing joint; **j. torique,** O-ring, doughnut ring.

jointage [ʒwɛ̃ta:ʒ], *s.m.* **1.** *Coop:* bevelling (of edges of staves). **2.** assembling (of sheets to form plywood).

jointé [ʒwɛ̃te], *a.* jointed.

jointement [ʒwɛ̃tmɑ̃], *s.m.* **1.** joining; formation of a joint. **2.** *Const:* (*a*) jointing; pointing; (*b*) grouting. **3.** *Coop:* bevel profile (of staves).

jointer [ʒwɛ̃te], *v.tr.* to assemble and bond (sheets to form plywood).

jointeuse [ʒwɛ̃tø:z], *s.f. Carp:* (*machine*) beveller.

jointif, -ive [ʒwɛ̃tif, -i:v], *a. Const:* **1.** joined, placed edge to edge, contiguous, jointed; *N. Arch:* **vaigrage j.,** close ceiling. **2. pièces (de tuyau, etc.) jointives,** make-up pieces.

jointoiement [ʒwɛ̃twamɑ̃], *s.m. Const:* **1.** pointing, jointing (of wall, etc.). **2. j. au mortier liquide,** grouting.

jointoyer [ʒwɛ̃twaje], *v.tr.* (**je jointoie, n. jointoyons; je jointoierai**) *Const:* **1.** to point, joint (wall, etc.). **2.** to grout.

jointoyeur [zwɛ̃twajœ:r], *s.m. Const:* **1.** mason who points walls. **2.** groutman.

jointure [ʒwɛ̃ty:r], *s.f.* (*a*) *Anat: Tchn:* joint, join; **j. du genou,** knee joint; **les jointures des doigts,** the knuckles; **j. de cheval,** (i) fetlock joint, (ii) pastern, of horse; **entre les jointures de la cuirasse,** between the joints of the harness; (*b*) *A:* **n'avoir point de jointures,** to be entirely unbending.

joinvillais, -aise [ʒwɛ̃vilɛ, -ɛ:z], *a. & s. Geog:* (native, inhabitant) of Joinville-le-Pont.

joinvillois, -oise [ʒwɛ̃vilwa, -wa:z], *a. & s. Geog:* (native, inhabitant) of Joinville (in Haute-Marne).

jojo [ʒɔʒo], *a. & s. F:* **1.** pretty, good-looking. **2. c'est un affreux j.,** he's a noisy (little) brat.

joker [ʒɔkɛ:r], *s.m. Cards:* joker.

joli [ʒɔli], *a.* pretty; good-looking (girl); nice; **jolie comme un cœur, jolie à croquer,** sweetly pretty, pretty as a picture; **de jolis yeux,** fine eyes; **dire de jolies choses,** to say pleasant, agreeable, things; **il a une jolie fortune,** he has a tidy fortune; **jolie brise,** fresh breeze; *Iron:* **voilà une jolie conduite!** that's a nice way to behave! **vous êtes un j. personnage!** you're a nice sort of chap! *P:* **ce n'est pas j. j.,** that's a poor show; *F:* **faire le j. cœur,** to put on airs and graces; *s.m.* **c'est du j. de me parler comme ça,** that's a nice way to talk to me! **le j. de l'affaire c'est que . . .,** the beauty of the thing, the best of it, is that . . .; **voilà du j.!** here's a nice mess! a pretty state of things!

joliesse [ʒɔljɛs], *s.f.* prettiness, delicacy (of sth.).

joliet, -ette [ʒɔljɛ, -ɛt], *a.* (*used mainly in f.*) rather pretty, attractive.

joliment [ʒɔlimɑ̃], *adv.* **1.** prettily, nicely, finely; **c'est j. dit!** that's neatly put. **2.** (*intensive*) *F:* **j. amusant,** very amusing, awfully funny; **il danse j. bien,** he's a frightfully good dancer; **vous avez j. raison,** you're jolly well right; **je suis j. content,** I'm awfully, frightfully, pleased; I'm jolly glad, **elle est j. laide,** she's pretty ugly; **on s'est j. amusé(s),** we had a marvellous time.

Jonas [ʒɔnas], *Pr.n.m. B.Hist:* Jonah.

jonc [ʒɔ̃], *s.m.* **1.** (*a*) *Bot:* rush; **j. fleuri,** flowering rush; **j. glauque,** hard rush; **j. odorant,** sweet calamus, sweet rush ((i) sweet flag, (ii) lemon grass, camel's hay); **j. à balais,** reed; **j. des chaisiers,** bulrush; **j. marin,** whin, furze; (*b*) **j. d'Inde,** rattan; **(canne de) j.,** Malacca cane; rattan (walking stick). **2.** (*a*) keeper (ring); retaining ring; plain ring; (*b*) *Fr.C:* wedding ring; (*c*) *P:* (i) gold; (ii) money, dough. **3.** *Aut:* nailing strip.

joncacées [ʒɔ̃kase], *s.f.pl. Bot:* Juncaceae.

joncaille [ʒɔ̃ka:j], *s.f. P:* **1.** money. **2.** gold. **3.** jewels.

joncer [ʒɔ̃se], *v.tr.* (**je jonçai(s); n. jonçons**) to rush the bottom of (chair).

jonchaie [ʒɔ̃ʃɛ], *s.f.* **1.** plantation of rushes; rush bed. **2.** cane plantation, brake.

jonchée [ʒɔ̃ʃe], *s.f.* **1.** strewing (of branches, flowers, etc.); **faire une j. de fleurs,** to strew flowers; **une j. de roseaux, de morts, recouvrait le sol,** the ground was strewn with rushes, with dead. **2.** (soft white) cheese (made in rush basket).

jonchement [ʒɔ̃ʃmɑ̃], *s.m.* strewing, scattering (of flowers, etc.).

joncher [ʒɔ̃ʃe], *v.tr.* to strew; **j. la terre de fleurs,** to strew, *Lit:* to bestrew, the ground with flowers; **les débris de la statue jonchaient le pavé,** fragments of the statue lay strewn about the pavement; **champ jonché de cadavres,** field strewn with corpses; **plancher jonché de débris,** floor strewn, littered, with rubbish; **des journaux jonchaient la table,** newspapers littered the table.

joncheraie [ʒɔ̃ʃ(ə)rɛ], *s.f.* **1.** plantation of rushes, rush bed. **2.** rushes floating (on lake, pond, etc.).

jonchets [ʒɔ̃ʃɛ], *s.m.pl. Games:* spillikins, jack-straws.

jonciforme [ʒɔ̃sifɔrm], *a.* rush-like.

jonction [ʒɔ̃ksjɔ̃], *s.f.* **1.** junction, joining; *Jur:* joinder; *Mus:* blending (of vocal registers); **j. de deux routes,** meeting of two roads; **point de j.,** junction point; **canal de j.,** junction canal; *Tchn:* **tuyau de j.,** joint pipe; *Rail:* **gare de j.,** junction (station); **voie de j.,** cross-over; *Mil:* (*of troops*) **opérer une j.,** to join forces, to come together; *Jur:* **j. d'instances,** joinder, consolidation of actions. **2.** *El:* connector; *Mec.E:* **j. (d'un bec, d'une conduite de vapeur),** nipple. **3.** docking (of two spacecraft).

jonglage [ʒɔ̃gla:ʒ], *s.m.* (art and technique of) juggling.

jongler [ʒɔ̃gle], *v.i.* to juggle; **j. avec des rimes, des difficultés,** to juggle with rhymes, difficulties.

jonglerie [ʒɔ̃gləri], *s.f.* **1.** juggling, jugglery. **2.** trickery, imposture; trick.

jongleur [ʒɔ̃glœ:r], *s.m.* **1.** *A:* jongleur; (mediaeval) entertainer; tumbler. **2.** juggler. **3.** (*with f.* **jongleuse**) trickster, charlatan.

jonque [ʒɔ̃:k], *s.f. Nau:* (Chinese) junk.

jonquille [ʒɔ̃ki:j]. **1.** *s.f. Bot:* (*a*) jonquil; (*b*) daffodil. **2.** *a.inv. & s.m.* jonquil (colour); pale yellow.

Joppé [ʒɔpe], *Pr.n. B.Geog:* Joppa.

Jordanie [ʒɔrdani], *Pr.n.f. Geog:* Jordan.

jordanien, -ienne [ʒɔrdanjɛ̃, -jɛn]. **1.** *a. Geog:* Jordanian. **2.** *s.* Jordanian; native, inhabitant, of Jordan.

Jordonne [ʒɔrdɔn], *Pr.n.* **(= j'ordonne)** *F:* **c'est un monsieur, une madame, J.,** he's, she's, bossy.

jordonner [ʒɔrdɔne], *v.tr. F:* to boss (s.o., people) about.

Josabeth [ʒozabɛt], *Pr.n.f. B.Hist:* Jehosheba.

Josaphat [ʒozafat], *Pr.n.m. B.Geog:* **la vallée de J.,** the Valley of Jehoshaphat.

Joseph [ʒozɛf]. **1.** *Pr.n.m. B.Hist: etc:* Joseph. **2.** *s.m. F:* self-righteous, smug, young man; a real Joseph. **3.** *a.m. & s.m.* **(papier) j.,** fine transparent filter paper.

Josèphe [ʒozɛf], *Pr.n.m. Gr.Lit:* Josephus.

Joséphine [ʒozefin]. **1.** *Pr.n.f.* Josephine; *A: F:* **faire sa Joséphine,** to be goody-goody. **2.** *s.f. Mil: P:* bayonet.

joséphinite [ʒozefinit], *s.f. Miner:* Josephinite.
joséphisme [ʒozefism], *s.m. Hist:* Josephism.
joséphiste [ʒozefist], *a. & s.m. & f.* Josephist.
Josias [ʒozjɑːs], *Pr.n.m. B.Hist:* Josias, Josiah.
Josué [ʒozɥe], *Pr.n.m. B.Hist:* Joshua.
jottereau, -aux [ʒɔtro], *s.m. usu. pl. Nau:* cheek(s), hound(s) (of mast).
jouable [ʒwabl̩], *a.* **1.** *Th: Mus: etc:* playable. **2.** *Sp:* (*of ground*) playable, fit for play.
jouail [ʒwaːj], *s.m. Nau:* stock of anchor.
jouailler [ʒwaje], *v.i. F:* **1.** to play for small stakes. **2.** to strum (on the piano), to scrape (on the fiddle).
joual [ʒwal], *s.m. Fr.C:* French Canadian dialect.
joualle [ʒwal], *s.f. Vit:* **vignes plantées à, en, joualles,** vines planted in widely spaced rows (to allow for a catch crop).
joubarbe [ʒubarb], *s.f. Bot:* sempervivum, *F:* houseleek, Jupiter's beard; **petite j.,** white stonecrop.
joue [ʒu], *s.f.* **1.** cheek (of person, horse); **donner sur la j. à, de, qn,** to slap s.o.'s face; **avoir de bonnes joues, des joues rebondies,** to have rosy cheeks; to look healthy; **danser j. contre j.,** to dance cheek to cheek; **tendre, présenter, l'autre j.,** to turn the other cheek; **mettre, tenir, coucher, qn en j.,** to aim (with a gun) at s.o.; *Mil: A:* **j.!** present! *P:* **se caler les joues,** to eat a square meal; to have a good blow out. **2.** side (of armchair, etc.); cheek (of bearing, pulley-block, mortise, etc.); flange (of wheel); web (of girder, etc.); **les joues (d'un violon),** the two sides of the peg box (of a violin); **j. de manivelle,** crank-web; *I.C.E:* **joues de vilebrequin,** crankshaft flanges; *Nau:* **j. de vache,** cheek-block; *Rail:* **j. de croisement,** guard-rail (of points); *Aut:* **j. d'aile,** wing flange. **3.** *N.Arch:* **les joues,** the bows; **à grosses joues,** bluff-bowed.
jouée [ʒwe], *s.f.* **1.** *Arch:* (*a*) reveal (of window); (*b*) side (of dormer window). **2.** *Carp:* thickness (of wood over a tenon); *pl.* cheeks (of mortise).
jouer [ʒwe], *v.* to play. **I.** *v.i.* **1.** (*a*) **j. avec qn, avec qch.,** to play with s.o., with sth.; **j. avec sa chaîne de montre,** to toy, fiddle, with one's watch-chain; **j. avec ses lunettes,** to play, fidget, with one's glasses; **j. sur les mots,** to play upon words; **je l'ai dit pour j.,** I said it for fun; **j. avec sa santé,** to trifle with one's health; (*b*) **j. à qch.,** to play at sth.; **j. aux soldats, aux Indiens,** to play (at) soldiers, Red Indians; **les enfants jouaient à traverser la rue en courant,** the children were playing at running across the street; **ne jouez pas avec l'eau, les enfants!** don't play with water, children! **j. à la marchande, au ménage,** to play at keeping shop, at keeping house; **j. à l'innocent,** to play the innocent; **j. au cricket, aux cartes, au billard,** to play cricket, cards, billiards; **j. au golf,** to play golf; **il joue bien aux cartes, au billard,** he plays a good game of cards, of billiards; **j. à qui perd gagne,** to win a Pyrrhic victory, to win the war and lose the peace; *F:* **j. à la fille de l'air,** to be very elusive, an elusive character; **c'est à qui de j.?** whose turn is it to play? (*at chess, etc.*) whose move is it? (*at billiards, etc.*) whose stroke is it? (*c*) **j. de qch.,** to bring sth. into action; to make play with sth.; **j. de malheur,** to be unlucky; **j. du piano, de la harpe,** to play the piano, the harp; **l'orchestre commença à j.,** the orchestra began to play; **j. de l'éventail,** to flutter one's fan; **j. des coudes,** to elbow one's way (through a crowd); **j. des dents,** to munch away. **2.** (*a*) to gamble; **j. aux courses,** to back horses, to play the horses; *Prov:* **qui a joué, jouera,** once a gambler always a gambler; (*b*) *Fin:* to speculate, operate; to play the market; **j. à la hausse,** to gamble, speculate, on a rise in prices; to bull the market; **j. à la baisse,** to speculate on a fall in prices; to bear the market; **j. sur les mines,** to speculate in mining securities. **3.** (*a*) to come into play, to work, to act; **mécanisme qui joue, qui ne joue pas,** mechanism that works, that will not work; **le tiroir ne joue pas bien,** the drawer does not run well; **clef qui ne joue pas bien,** key that is hard to turn; **les eaux joueront dimanche,** the fountains will play on Sunday; **faire j. qch.,** to bring sth. into play; to set sth. in motion; **faire j. ses muscles,** to flex one's muscles; **faire j. les eaux,** to set the fountains playing, to turn on the fountains; **faire j. une mine,** to spring, touch off, a mine; **faire j. un ressort,** to work, touch, release, a spring; **faire j. la gâchette,** to squeeze the trigger (of gun); **faire j. la culasse d'un fusil,** to work the bolt of a rifle; **il faisait j. la monnaie dans sa poche,** he was jingling the money in his pocket; *A: El:* **faire j. les fusibles,** to blow the fuses; (*b*) to be, become, operative, to operate; **l'augmentation des salaires joue depuis le 1er janvier,** the rise in salaries has been operative since January 1; (*c*) (*of wood*) to warp; to shrink or swell; (*d*) (*of part*) to fit loosely, to have too much play.
II. **jouer,** *v.tr.* **1.** (*a*) to stake; **j. cinq francs,** to stake five francs; **j. gros jeu,** to play for high stakes; to play high; **j. le jeu,** to play ball; **j. sa tête,** to risk one's neck; *s.a.* CARTE 2, TOUR; (*b*) *Turf:* to back (horse); **j. un cheval gagnant,** (i) to back a horse to win, for a win; (ii) to back a winner; **j. un cheval placé,** (i) to back a horse for a place; (ii) to back a placed horse; **j. perdant,** to back to lose. **2.** (*a*) to play; *Games:* **j. une carte, un pion,** to play a card, a pawn; *Cards:* **j. trèfle,** (i) to play clubs, (ii) to lead clubs; **bien j. ses cartes,** to play one's cards well; *Chess: etc:* **j. une pièce,** to move a piece! (*b*) *Mus:* **j. un air au piano, sur la flûte,** to play a tune on the piano, on the flute; *Th:* **j. une comédie,** to act, play, perform, a comedy; **la pièce s'est jouée cent fois,** the play has been acted a hundred times, has had a run of a hundred performances; **que joue-t-on, qu'est-ce qui se joue, actuellement?** what are they playing, what is on, at present? **j. un rôle, j. Hamlet,** to act a part; to play Hamlet; **elle va j. dans "Comme il vous plaira,"** she is to appear in "As you like it"; **ce soir je joue un rôle de gendarme,** tonight I'm going on as a gendarme; **j. un rôle dans une affaire,** to play a part in a matter; **j. la surprise,** to affect, feign, surprise, to pretend to be surprised; *P:* **en j. un air,** to decamp, to skedaddle; *F:* **j. les durs, les martyrs,** to play, act the tough guy, the martyr; **j. l'idéaliste,** to play the idealist. **3.** to trick, fool, make a fool of (s.o.).
se jouer. 1. to play (about, around); **faire qch. en se jouant,** to make child's play of sth., to do sth. without (any) difficulty. **2. se j. de qn,** to trifle with s.o.; **vous vous jouez de moi,** you are trifling with me, making game of me; **se j. de toutes les convenances,** to throw propriety to the winds; **3.** *Lit:* **se j. à qn,** to venture to confront s.o., to stand up to s.o.
jouet[1] [ʒwɛ], *s.m.* (child's) toy, plaything; **être le j. de la fortune, des vents,** to be the sport of fortune, of every wind; **être le j. d'une illusion,** to be the victim of an illusion, of fancy.
jouet[2], *s.m. N.Arch: etc:* fishplate, washer (plate).
jouette [ʒwɛt], *s.f.* **1.** shallow rabbit-hole. **2.** *Ven:* (*of dog*) **rapporter à la j.,** to retrieve in a playful way.
joueur, -euse [ʒwœːr, -øːz], *s.* **1.** (*a*) player (of game); **j. de golf, de boules, de cricket, de football,** golfer, bowler, cricketer, footballer; **j. aux cartes,** card-player; **être beau j.,** to be a sport, a good loser; **être mauvais j.,** to be a bad loser; **c'est un rude j.,** (i) he's a good player; (ii) he's a keen sportsman; (iii) he knows how to handle things; *a.* **enfant j.,** child fond of playing; (*b*) performer, player (on an instrument); **j. de trombone,** trombone player; **j. de cornemuse,** piper; (*c*) actor; **joueurs d'une farce,** actors in a farce. **2.** (*a*) gambler, gamester; *a.* given to gambling, fond of gambling; (*b*) *St.Exch:* speculator, operator; **j. à la hausse,** bull; **j. à la baisse,** bear.
joufflu [ʒufly], *a.* **1.** chubby-cheeked, with fat cheeks; **anges joufflus,** chubby-cheeked cherubs; **des Amours joufflus,** chubby little Cupids. **2.** *Nau:* bluff-bowed (ship).
joufflure [ʒuflyːr], *s.f.* chubby cheeks; roundness of cheeks, face.
joug [ʒu(g)], *s.m.* **1.** yoke; **mettre les bœufs au j.,** to yoke the oxen; **subir le j. d'une passion,** to be under the sway of a passion; *Rom.Hist:* **faire passer une armée sous le j.,** to send an army under the yoke; **courber un peuple sous le j.,** to bend a people under the yoke; **secouer le j., s'affranchir du j.,** to throw off the yoke. **2.** (*a*) beam (of balance); (*b*) yoke, cross-head (of engine).
jouguet [ʒugɛ], *s.m.* single head yoke.
jouière [ʒujɛːr], *s.f. Hyd.E:* wing-wall (of lock).
jouir [ʒwiːr], *v.i.* to enjoy; (*a*) **j. de la vie, d'un bon dîner,** to enjoy life, a good dinner; **je n'ai pas eu le temps de j. de mes invités,** I have had no time to enjoy the company of my guests; **j. de faire qch.,** to delight in doing sth.; (*b*) **j. de toutes ses facultés,** to be in full possession of all one's faculties; **j. d'une bonne réputation,** to have a good reputation; **j. d'une bonne santé,** to enjoy good health; to be blessed with good health; **j. du privilège de faire qch.,** to have the exclusive right to do sth., to enjoy the privilege of doing sth.; **j. de la faveur de qn,** to be in high favour with s.o.; (*c*) *abs.* **gens qui ne pensent qu'à j., qui ne vivent que pour j.,** people who think only of enjoyment, who live only for enjoyment; *Iron: F:* **on lui a arraché une dent; ça l'a fait j.,** he had a tooth out; he must have enjoyed that! (*d*) *abs. P:* (= *to have an orgasm*) to come.
jouissance [ʒwisɑ̃ːs], *s.f.* **1.** enjoyment; (*a*) **jouissances des sens,** sensual enjoyment; **le travail est une j. pour lui,** work is a delight, a pleasure, to him; (*b*) possession, tenure; *Jur:* **j. en commun (d'un bien),** communal tenure; **trouble de j.,** disturbance of possession; **avoir la j. de certains droits,** to enjoy certain rights; **avoir la j. d'un navire,** to have a ship at one's disposal, to have the use of a ship; **entrer en j. de ses biens,** to enter into possession of one's property; **maison à vendre avec j. immédiate,** house for sale with immediate possession, with vacant possession; (*of accommodation*) **avec j. de la cuisine,** with use of kitchen; **j. de passage,** right of way; *Min:* way-leave. **2.** *Fin:* right to interest, dividends; **date de j. (de bons du Trésor, etc.),** date from which interest begins to run; **action de j.,** redeemed share that continues to participate in dividends.
jouissant [ʒwisɑ̃], *a.* in possession (**de,** of); enjoying.
jouisseur, -euse [ʒwisœːr, -øːz]. **1.** *s.* pleasure-seeker; sensualist. **2.** *a.* pleasure-seeking; sensual.
joujou, -oux, *occ.* **-ous** [ʒuʒu], *s.m.* (*child's word*) (*a*) toy, plaything; (*b*) **faire j. avec une poupée,** to play with a doll.
joule [ʒul], *s.m. El: Ph:* joule.
jour [ʒuːr], *s.m.* day. **1.** (day)light; (*a*) **la naissance, le point, la pointe, du j.,** daybreak; **le petit j.,** the morning twilight; **se lever avant le j., au petit j.,** to rise before daylight; **éveiller qn au j.,** to rouse s.o. at daybreak; **au grand j., en plein j.,** (i) in broad, full, daylight; (ii) publicly; **rentrer au grand j.,** to come home in broad daylight, *F:* to come home with the milk; **craindre le grand j.,** to shun (i) the light of day, (ii) publicity; **il fait (tout à fait) j.,** it is (quite) light; **il fait grand j.,** it is broad daylight; **il fait à peine j.,** it is hardly light; **demain il fera j.,** to morrow is another day; **le j. se faisait dans mon esprit,** I was beginning to understand, to see daylight; it was beginning to dawn on me; *Poet:* **l'astre du j.,** the sun, the daystar; **voyager le j., de j.,** to travel by day(light); **travailler j. et nuit,** to work day and night; **bombardement de j.,** daylight bombing; *Min:* **travail au j.,** work at the surface, work above ground; **ouvriers du j.,** surface workers; **ils sont le j. et la nuit,** they are as different, as like, as chalk and cheese; (*b*) **mettre au j. un enfant, donner le j. à un enfant,** to give birth to a child, to bear a child; **elle avait mis au j. trois enfants,** she had given birth to three children; **mise au j. d'un enfant,** giving birth to a child; *Lit:* **j'ai vu le j. à Paris,** I first saw the light, I was born, in Paris; **l'auteur de mes jours,** the author of my being, my father; *Lit:* **attenter aux jours de qn,** to make an attempt on s.o.'s life; **mettre qch. à j., au j.,** to bring sth. to light; to publish (a fact); **mise au j. d'un mystère,** bringing to light, elucidation of a mystery; (*c*) lighting; **j. d'atelier,** studio lighting; **chambre qui prend j. sur la cour,** room that looks out on to the courtyard; *Const:* **j. zénithal,** light coming from above, from the roof of a building; **vous êtes dans mon j., vous me prenez mon j., vous me cachez le j.,** you're in my light; **jeter le j. sur une affaire, dans une affaire,** to throw light on a subject; **voir qch. sous un j. nouveau, sous son vrai j.,** to see sth. in a new light, in its true light; **se montrer sous son vrai j.,** to show oneself in one's true colours; **présenter une affaire sous un j. défavorable, favorable,** to present a matter in an unfavourable, favourable, light; to paint sth. in dark, bright, colours. **2.** (*a*) aperture, opening; clearance (between bars, etc.); **pratiquer un j. dans un mur,** to make, cut, an opening, a hole, in a wall; **jours d'un bâtiment,** apertures of a building; **il y a des jours entre les planches,** there are gaps, chinks, between the planks; **j. de l'escalier,** well (of staircase); **voir j. (dans une affaire),** to see daylight (in a matter); *Jur:* **droit de vues et de jours,** ancient lights; **percer (qch.) à j.,** (i) to bore, to go, right through (sth.); (ii) to see through (plan, etc.), to penetrate (a design); **percer (qn) à j.,** to find s.o. out; (*b*) *Needlew:* **garniture, bas, à jours,** open-work trimming, stockings; **ourlet à j.,** hemstitched hem; **j. échelle,** ladder hemstitch; (*c*) **se faire j.,** to make a way for oneself; (*of thg*) to appear; **la vérité se fait j. dans son**

esprit, the truth is dawning on him; he is waking up to the truth; **idée qui se fait j.,** idea that is coming to the front; *Prov:* **tôt ou tard la vérité se fait j.,** truth will out. **3.** (*period of time, point in time*) (*a*) **j. sidéral,** sidereal day; **j. apparent,** apparent day; **j. solaire,** solar (apparent) day; *Jur:* **j. civil,** civil day; **j. pair, impair,** even, odd, date; **huit jours,** a week; **quinze jours,** a fortnight; **donner ses huit jours à un domestique,** to give a servant a week's notice; *P: esp. Mil:* **on lui a flanqué quatre jours,** he got four days (C.B.); **j. franc, j. plein,** clear day; **préavis de dix jours francs,** ten clear days' notice; **c'est à un j. de voyage,** it's a day's journey (away); **trois jours d'approvisionnement,** three days' supply; **quel j. (du mois) sommes-nous?** what is the date (today)? **quel j. (de la semaine) sommes-nous?** what day (of the week) is it (today)? *Prov:* **les jours se suivent et ne se ressemblent pas,** who knows what tomorrow holds? *Prov:* **à chaque j. suffit sa peine,** sufficient unto the day is the evil thereof; (*b*) **ce j.,** today; *Jur:* **ce j. d'hui,** this day; **ce j. entre tous,** this day of all days; **intérêts à ce j.,** interest to date; **je l'ai vu l'autre j.,** I saw him the other day; **un j. ou l'autre,** some time or other; **d'un j. à l'autre, de j. en j.,** from day to day; **nous l'attendons d'un j. à l'autre,** we are expecting him any day; **du j. au lendemain,** (i) soon, (ii) at a moment's notice, (iii) overnight; **la chose n'a été sue que ces jours-ci,** it is only lately that the matter has been known; (*past*) **un j. je me promenais . . .,** one day I was walking . . .; (*future*) **un j. je vous le dirai,** some day I will tell you; **tous les jours,** every day; **mes habits de tous les jours,** my everyday clothes; **mon parapluie de tous les jours,** my second-best umbrella; **il y a six ans j. pour j.,** six years ago to the (very) day, to a day; **l'an dernier à pareil j.,** a year (ago) today; this day last year; **vivre au j. le j.,** to live from day to day, from hand to mouth; **affrètement au j. le j.,** spot chartering; *Fin:* **prêts au j. le j.,** money at call, call money; **mettre (une liste, etc.) à j.,** to bring (a list, etc.) up to date; to update; **mise à j.,** updating; *Com:* **tenir les livres à j.,** to keep the books up to date; **mettre son journal à j.,** to write up one's diary; **tenir qn à j.,** to keep s.o. posted; *F:* **à un de ces jours!** I'll be seeing you! so long! (*c*) *Mil: etc:* **service de j.,** day duty; **officier de j.,** officer of the day; **être (de service) de j.,** to be on duty for 24 hours; **j. de présence, d'absence,** day on duty, off duty; (*d*) **le j. de l'An,** New Year's Day; **le j. de Pâques,** Easter Sunday, Easter Day; *Mil:* **le j. J,** D Day; *O:* **quel est votre j.?** which is your at-home day? *F:* (*of woman*) **avoir ses jours,** to have the curse; *Nau: Jur:* **jours de planche,** lay days; *Jur:* **j. utile,** lawful day; *Adm:* **j. férié** = Bank holiday; **jours d'orage,** stormy days; **j. d'été,** summer's day; **prendre un j., fixer un j., pour qch.,** to appoint a day, to make an appointment, for sth.; *Prov:* **bon j., bonne œuvre,** better the day better the deed; (*e*) **de nos jours,** in the present time, in this day and age, these days, in these times, now, nowadays; *Com:* **les prix du j.,** ruling prices; **les jours de l'individualisme sont révolus,** the day of individualism has gone; **les hommes d'État du j.,** the statesmen of the day; **l'homme du j.,** the man of the moment; **le journal du j.,** today's paper; (*in restaurant*) **plat du j.,** (special) dish of the day, *F:* today's special; **vieux jours,** old age; **abréger ses jours,** to shorten one's life; **être dans ses bons jours,** to be in good form, in good fettle; (*of athlete, etc.*) **il n'était pas dans un de ses meilleurs jours,** it was one of his off days; **je l'ai connue dans ses beaux jours,** I knew her in her prime; **mes beaux jours sont passés,** I've had my day; *Lit:* **leur beauté n'est que d'un j.,** their beauty is ephemeral, is but for one day.

Jourdain [ʒurdɛ̃], *Pr.n.m. Geog:* Jordan.

journal, -aux [ʒurnal, -o], *s.m.* **1.** journal, diary, record; *Book-k:* **(livre) j.,** account book; **j. des achats,** purchase book; **j. des ventes,** sales book; **tenir un j.,** to keep a diary; **j. intime,** private diary; **l'auteur du j.,** the diarist; *Com: Fin:* **j. originaire,** book of original entry; **j. des transferts,** transfer register; *Ind:* **j. de travail d'une usine,** log book of a factory; *Nau:* **j. de navigation,** log book (at sea); **j. timbré,** official log book (kept by the captain of Fr. ship); **j. de bord,** (i) (mate's) log book, (ii) log book in harbour; **le j. nautique,** the ship's log book; **porter les événements au j.,** to write up the log; *Mil:* **j. d'écoute,** log of a listening post. **2.** newspaper, journal; periodical; *attrib.* **papier j.,** (i) newsprint; (ii) old newspaper; **le j. d'aujourd'hui,** today's paper; *F:* **je de concierge,** popular (news)paper; **j. d'entreprise,** company's (technical and professional) magazine, *U.S:* house organ; **j. de mode,** fashion paper; **j. officiel,** official gazette; **j. savant,** learned periodical; **les journaux,** the Press; **marchand de journaux,** (i) newsagent; (ii) (news)paper seller; newsboy; **c'est au j.,** it's in the paper; **style des journaux,** journalese; **j. lumineux,** electric newspaper; *W.Tel: Cin: T.V:* **j. parlé, filmé, télévisé,** the news, newscast; **rédacteur de j. parlé,** newscaster. **3.** *A: Dial: Agr:* (*amount of land that can be ploughed in one day*) = acre.

journalier, -ière [ʒurnalje, -jɛːr]. **1.** *a.* (*a*) daily (task, etc.); everyday (occurrence); (*b*) *A:* variable, uncertain, changeable; **humeur journalière,** mood that changes from day to day. **2.** *s.m.* (*a*) day labourer, journeyman; (*b*) *Aut: etc:* **(totalisateur) j.,** trip-recorder (of speedometer).

journaliser [ʒurnalize]. **1.** *v.i. A:* to write for the papers, to be a journalist. **2.** *v.tr. Com:* to journalize; to book (entry) in the journal.

journalisme [ʒurnalism], *s.m.* journalism; **l'influence du j.,** the influence of the Press; **faire du j.,** to write for the papers.

journaliste [ʒurnalist], *s.m. & f.* **1.** journalist, pressman; reporter; **j. aux armées,** war correspondent; **style de j.,** journalese; **j. informateur,** police-news reporter. **2.** press compositor. **3.** *Book-k:* journalizer.

journalistique [ʒurnalistik], *a.* journalistic; **style j.,** journalese.

journée [ʒurne], *s.f.* **1.** (*a*) day(time); **pendant la j.,** in the daytime; during the day; **toute la j., à longueur de j.,** all day(long), the whole day; **je travaillais à longueur de journées,** I worked for days on end; **dans la j.,** in the course of the day; **j. de travail,** (i) day's work, (ii) working day; shift; (*of shop*) **faire la j. continue,** to remain open at lunch time; **il ne fait rien de la j.,** he does nothing all day long; **il a fait une j. de soleil,** it has been a sunny day; (*b*) *Adm:* (civil) day (from midnight to midnight). **2.** (*events of the day*) (*a*) day's work; **faire une bonne j.,** to do a good day's work; **travailler à la j.,** to work by the day; **homme de j.,** (day-)labourer; **femme de j.,** charwoman, daily help, *F:* daily; (*of charwoman*) **aller en j., faire des journées,** to go out charring, *F:* to oblige; **nous avons une femme à la j.,** we have a daily (help); (*b*) day's wages; (*c*) day's march; **voyager à petites journées,** to travel by easy, short, stages; **à grandes journées,** by forced marches; (*d*) historic day; day of battle; **les journées de Juillet (1830),** the 27th, 28th, 29th of July, 1830; **la j. des Dupes (1630),** the Day of Dupes; **la j. d'Austerlitz,** the day, battle, of Austerlitz; **j. sanglante,** day of carnage; bloody battle; **gagner la j.,** to win the day; **la j. fut perdue,** the day, the battle, was lost.

journellement [ʒurnɛlmɑ̃], *adv.* daily, every day; **tournure employée j.,** expression in daily use.

journoyer [ʒurnwaje], *v.i.* **(je journoie, n. journoyons; je journoierai)** *O:* to kill time.

joute [ʒut], *s.f.* **1.** *A.Sp:* joust, tilt, tilting. **2.** contest; *Fr.C:* game, match; **j. de coqs,** cock fight; **j. oratoire,** contest in eloquence; *Sp:* **j. sur l'eau, j. lyonnaise, j. aquatique,** water tournament.

jouter [ʒute], *v.i.* **1.** (*a*) *A.Sp:* to joust, tilt; (*b*) to take part in a water tournament. **2.** (*of cocks, etc.*) to fight; **faire j. des coqs,** to arrange a cock fight; to set cocks fighting; to pit cocks. **3. j. avec qn,** to argue, struggle, cross swords, with s.o.

jouteur [ʒutœːr], *s.m.* **1.** *A.Sp:* jouster, tilter. **2. un rude j.,** a formidable opponent, antagonist.

joûtir [ʒutiːr], *v.i.* (*of fruit*) to ripen (under glass); **mettre j. des nèfles,** to lay out medlars to ripen.

jouvence [ʒuvɑ̃ːs], *s.f. A:* youthfulness, youth; *Myth: Lit:* **la Fontaine de J.,** the Fountain of Youth.

jouvenceau, -eaux [ʒuvɑ̃so], *s.m. A: & Hum:* stripling, youth, lad.

jouvencelle [ʒuvɑ̃sɛl], *s.f. A: & Hum:* maiden, damsel, lass.

jouxte [ʒukst], *prep. A. & Jur:* **1.** contiguous to (the church, etc.). **2.** in conformity with (original copy).

jouxter [ʒukste], *v.tr. A: & Lit:* to be contiguous to (sth.); **sa chambre jouxtait la mienne,** his room was next to mine.

jovial, -aux [ʒɔvjal, -o], *a.* jovial, jolly, merry; breezy; **figure joviale,** jolly face; **rire j.,** hearty, good-natured, laugh.

jovialement [ʒɔvjalmɑ̃], *adv.* jovially, merrily.

jovialité [ʒɔvjalite], *s.f.* joviality, jollity; breeziness; **la grosse j. de Dickens,** Dickens's jovial, hearty, humour.

Jovien[1] [ʒɔvjɛ̃], *Pr.n.m. Rom.Hist:* Jovian, Jovianus.

jovien[2], **-ienne** [ʒɔvjɛ̃, -jɛn], *a. Astr:* Jovian (system, satellite).

jovinien, -ienne [ʒɔvinjɛ̃, -jɛn], *a. & s.* (native, inhabitant) of Joigny.

joyau, -aux [ʒwajo], *s.m.* jewel; (*the usual word is* **bijou,** *but*) **les joyaux de la Couronne,** the Crown jewels, the regalia; **c'est le plus beau j. de ma collection,** it is the brightest jewel in my collection; *Jur:* **bagues et joyaux,** personal trinkets of the bride (that do not fall into the estate on the death of the husband); **le Mont Saint-Michel, j. de l'art médiéval,** Mont Saint-Michel, a jewel of mediaeval art.

joyeusement [ʒwajøzmɑ̃], *adv.* joyously, joyfully, gladly.

joyeuseté [ʒwajøzte], *s.f. F:* joke; light-hearted, amusing, action; **dire des joyeusetés,** to make jokes; to tell funny stories; **joyeusetés de bouffon,** buffoonery.

joyeux, -euse [ʒwajø, -øːz]. **1.** *a.* (*a*) merry, mirthful, joyous; **j. Noël!** a merry Christmas! **le j. mois de mai,** the merry month of May; **j. et gai,** blithe and gay; **mine joyeuse,** cheerful, happy, expression; **le cœur j.,** with a light heart; **bande joyeuse,** joyful, happy, party (of children, etc.); **être j. que qch. soit arrivé, de ce que qch. est arrivé,** to be glad that sth. has happened; **joyeuse nouvelle,** good news; (*b*) **mener joyeuse vie,** to lead a life of pleasure. **2.** *s.m. Mil: P: A:* soldier serving in the *bataillon d'Afrique, q.v. under* BATAILLON; **les j.** = *le bataillon d'Afrique.*

Jubal [ʒybal], *Pr.n.m. B.Hist:* Jubal.

jubarte [ʒybart], *s.f. Z:* humpbacked whale.

jubé [ʒybe], *s.m. Ecc.Arch:* rood screen; rood loft; jube.

jubéa [ʒybea], *s.m. Bot:* coquito.

jubilaire [ʒybilɛːr], *a.* **année j.,** jubilee year; **fêtes jubilaires,** jubilee celebrations; **docteur j.,** doctor of fifty years' standing.

jubilant [ʒybilɑ̃], *a. F:* jubilant.

Jubilate Deo [ʒybilate deo], *s.m.inv. Ecc:* Jubilate.

jubilation [ʒybilasjɔ̃], *s.f. F:* jubilation.

jubilé [ʒybile], *s.m.* jubilee; **célébrer son j.,** to celebrate one's jubilee, fifty years of office, one's golden wedding.

jubiler [ʒybile], *v.i. F:* (*a*) to exult, jubilate; to be delighted; (*b*) to gloat.

juché [ʒyʃe], *a.* **1.** (*of fowls*) gone to roost. **2. cheval j.,** horse up on its toes.

juchée [ʒyʃe], *s.f.* pheasants' roost(ing place).

jucher [ʒyʃe]. **1.** *v.i.* (*of birds*) to go to roost; to perch; *F:* **où juchez-vous?** where do you hang out? **2.** *v.tr.* **j. un tableau sur un mur,** to hang a picture high up on the wall, *F:* to sky a picture; **on m'avait juché au dernier étage,** they had perched me at the top of the house.

se jucher. 1. (*of fowls*) to go to roost; **se j. sur une branche,** to perch upon a branch. **2. se j. sur un haut tabouret, sur une branche,** to perch oneself on a high stool, on a branch; **pitre juché sur des échasses,** clown perched on stilts.

juchoir [ʒyʃwaːr], *s.m.* (*a*) *Husb:* perch (for fowls); roosting place; hen roost; (*b*) rabbit fattening hutch.

Juda [ʒyda], *Pr.n.m. B.Hist:* Judah.

judaïque [ʒydaik], *a.* Judaic (law, etc.); Jewish (history, etc.).

judaïquement [ʒydaikmɑ̃], *adv.* Judaically.

judaïsant, -ante [ʒydaizɑ̃, -ɑːt]. **1.** *a.* Judaizing **2.** *s.* Judaist, Judaizer.

judaïser [ʒydaize], *v.i.* to Judaize.

judaïsme [ʒydaism], *s.m.* Judaism.

Judas [ʒyda]. **1.** *Pr.n.m. B.Hist:* Judas (Iscariot); *F:* **poil de J.,** red hair, Judas-coloured hair; *F:* **bran de Judas, marques de J.,** freckles; **baiser de J.,** Judas kiss. **2.** *s.m.* (*a*) traitor, betrayer; (*b*) Judas (hole, trap); spy hole (in door).

Jude [ʒyd], *Pr.n.m. B.Hist:* **J. frère de Jacques,** Judas, brother of James; Jude.

Judée [ʒyde], *Pr.n.f. B.Hist:* Judaea; *Miner:* **bitume de J.,** Jew's pitch; **arbre de J.,** Judas tree.

judelle [ʒydɛl], *s.f. Orn:* coot.

judéo-allemand, -ande [ʒydeɔalmɑ̃, -ɑ̃ːd], *a. & s.m. Ling:* Yiddish; *pl. judéo-allemands.*

judéo-christianisme [ʒydeɔkristjanism], *s.m. Rel.H:* Judeo-Christianity.

judéo-espagnol [ʒydeɔɛspaɲɔl]. **1.** *a.* of, pertaining to, Spanish Jews. **2.** *s.m. Ling:* Judeo-Spanish; *pl. judéo-espagnol(e)s.*

judicatoire [ʒydikatwaːr], *s.m. Jur:* judicatory.

judicature [ʒydikatyːr], *s.f.* **1.** judicature. **2.** *Hist:* judgeship.

judiciaire [ʒydisjɛːr]. 1. *a.* (*a*) judicial, legal; **enquête j.,** judicial inquiry; **frais judiciaires,** legal charges (in an action); **erreur j.,** miscarriage of justice; **employer les voies judiciaires,** to have recourse to the law; **vente j.,** sale by order of the court; **poursuites judiciaires,** (i) proceedings; (ii) prosecution; *A:* **combat j.,** judicial combat, trial by combat; wager of battle; (*b*) **le pouvoir j.,** (i) judiciary power, judicial power; (ii) the Bench; **fonctionnaires de l'ordre j.,** officials of the judiciary; **éloquence j.,** forensic eloquence; *Journ:* **nouvelles judiciaires,** law reports. 2. *s.f. A:* (sound) judgment.

judiciairement [ʒydisjɛrmɑ̃], *adv.* judicially.

judicieusement [ʒydisjøzmɑ̃], *adv.* judiciously; discerningly.

judicieux, -euse [ʒydisjø, -øːz], *a.* judicious, sensible, well-advised (person, action); discerning; **peu j.,** injudicious, indiscreet (person); ill-advised (speech, etc.).

Judith [ʒydit], *Pr.n.f. B.Hist:* Judith.

judo [ʒydo], *s.m.* judo.

judoka [ʒydɔka], *s.m. & f.* judoka.

juène [ʒɥɛn], *s.m. Ich:* chub.

jugal, -aux [ʒygal, -o], *a. Anat:* jugal; **os j.,** cheekbone.

juge [ʒyːʒ], *s.m.* 1. (*a*) *Jur:* judge; **j. d'instruction,** examining magistrate; **j. d'instance,** *A:* **j. de paix,** (i) conciliation magistrate (in commercial cases); (ii) police-court magistrate = Justice of the Peace; **j. de fond, de fait,** judge whose sole function is to arrive at the facts of the case; **j. rapporteur,** judge in charge of legal enquiry; **j. commissaire,** judge sitting in bankruptcy case; **j. des référés,** judge sitting in chambers to deal provisionally with matters of special urgency; **j. au tribunal de commerce,** (tradesman acting as) judge in commercial court; **les juges,** the Bench; **être nommé j.,** to be appointed judge; (*in Engl.*) to be raised to the Bench; **je vous en fais j.,** I appeal to you; **être j. et partie,** to be judge in your case; (*b*) *B.Lit:* judge; **le livre des Juges, les Juges,** the Book of Judges; Judges; (*c*) *Games:* umpire; *Turf:* judge; **j. de touche,** *Fb:* linesman; *Rugby Fb:* touch-judge. 2. *occ. f.* **être bon j. de qch., en matière de qch.,** to be a good judge of sth.; **il, elle, est bon j. en matière de musique,** he, she, is a good judge of music; **nos sens sont des juges trompeurs,** our senses are poor judges.

jugeable [ʒyʒabl̩], *a.* subject to a legal decision.

juge-assesseur [ʒyʒasɛsœːr], *s.m.* associate judge; *pl. juges-assesseurs.*

jugement [ʒyʒmɑ̃], *s.m.* judg(e)ment. 1. *Jur:* (*a*) trial (of case); **le tribunal est en j.,** the court is sitting; **mettre, faire passer, qn en j.,** to bring s.o. to trial, to bring s.o. up for trial; **mise en j.,** arraignment; **passer en j.,** to be brought up for trial, to stand one's trial; **j. contradictoire,** judgment after trial; **j. par défaut,** judgment by default; **le (jour du) j. dernier,** the Last Judgment, Judgment Day, doomsday; **jusqu'au dernier j.,** until the crack of doom; (*b*) decision, award; (*in criminal cases*) sentence; **prononcer un j.,** to pass judgment, to adjudicate; **rendre un j. arbitral,** to make an award; **j. exécutoire,** enforceable judgment; **j. exécutoire par provision,** judgment provisionally enforceable; **j. provisoire,** decree nisi; **j. définitif,** decree absolute; **j. déclaratif de faillite,** adjudication in bankruptcy; **j. en dernier ressort,** final decision; (*c*) (*in the middle ages*) **le j. de Dieu,** the ordeal. 2. opinion, estimation; **au j. de bien des gens,** in the judgment, opinion, view, of many people; **porter un j. sur un poème,** to pass judgment, give an opinion, on a poem; **suspendre son j.,** to suspend judgment; **pas de j. hâtif!** don't jump to conclusions! **j. de valeur,** value judgment. 3. discernment, discrimination; **montrer du j.,** to show sound judgment, good sense, good understanding; **il aurait dû faire preuve de plus de j.,** he ought to have known better, to have had more sense; **erreur de j.,** error of, in, judgment; **avoir perdu le j.,** to be out of one's senses.

jugeot(t)e [ʒyʒɔt], *s.f. F:* common sense, *F:* gumption, nous; **avoir de la j.,** to know what's what.

juger [ʒyʒe]. I. *v.tr.* (**je jugeai(s); n. jugeons**) to judge. 1. (*a*) *Jur:* **j. un procès,** to try, judge, a case; **j. un accusé,** (i) to sit in judgment on a prisoner, to try a prisoner; (ii) to pass sentence, pass judgment, on a prisoner; **j. une réclamation, un différend,** to adjudicate, adjudge, a claim, to decide a dispute; **j. par défaut,** to deliver judgment by default; **chose jugée,** *res judicata;* (*b*) *abs.* to adjudicate (**entre,** between); (*c*) **j. un livre,** to pass judgment on, to criticize, a book; **il juge bien la musique,** he is a good judge of music; **j. la situation,** to take in the situation; **j. mal qn,** to be mistaken in one's judgment of s.o.; **mal j. qn,** to misjudge s.o.; **un homme se juge par ses actions,** a man is judged by his actions; **ce n'est pas à moi de le j.,** it is not for me to judge, pass judgment on, him; **j. qch. sur qch.,** to judge sth. by sth. else; (*d*) *Ven:* **j. la bête,** to recognize the quarry by its traces. 2. (*a*) to think, believe; to be of opinion; **je juge que vous devez le faire,** I think you ought to do it; **je ne juge pas bon que vous le fassiez,** I don't think you ought to do it; **que jugez-vous que je doive faire?** what do you think I ought to do? **on le jugeait fou,** people, everybody, thought he was mad; **le médecin le juge un homme perdu,** the doctor considers his case hopeless; **j. à propos, nécessaire, de faire qch., que qch. se fasse,** to think, deem, it proper, advisable, necessary, to do sth., that sth. should be done; **je jugeai qu'il était américain,** I put him down as, for, an American, I thought he was an American; (*b*) **j. de qch.,** to judge sth.; **j. de qn, de qch.,** to form an opinion of s.o., of sth.; **j. de la qualité de qch.,** to assess the quality of sth.; **jugez de ma surprise, jugez quelle fut ma surprise,** imagine my surprise; **j. des gens d'après, par, sur, les apparences,** to judge people by, from, appearances, to take people at their face value; **à en j. par . . .,** to judge by . . ., judging by . . .; **autant que j'en puis, puisse, j.,** to the best of my judgment; **je vous laisse à j. si j'ai tort ou raison,** I leave it to you to judge whether I am right or wrong; **à vous d'en j.,** it's up to you to draw your own conclusions.

II. **juger, jugé,** *s.m.* **faire qch. au j.,** to do sth. by guesswork; **tirer au j.,** to fire at a venture; to fire blind.

jugerie [ʒyʒ(ə)ri], *s.f. A.Jur:* judgeship.

jugeur, -euse [ʒyʒœːr, -øːz], *s. Pej:* self-appointed judge, hasty judge.

juglandacées [ʒyglɑ̃dase], *s.f.pl. Bot:* Juglandaceae.

juglans [ʒyglɑ̃ːs], *s.m. Bot:* juglans; *F:* walnut tree.

jugoslave [jygɔslaːv], *a. & s. A: Geog:* Jugoslav.

jugulaire [ʒygylɛːr]. 1. *a. & s.f.* jugular (vein). 2. *s.f.* chin strap, (of helmet); **fausse j.,** ornamental, dummy, chin strap. 3. *s.m.pl. Ich:* **les jugulaires,** the Jugulares.

juguler [ʒygyle], *v.tr.* 1. (*a*) *A:* to jugulate; to cut (s.o.'s) throat; to strangle, throttle (s.o.); (*b*) *Med:* to jugulate (disease); **j. une révolte,** to suppress, stifle, a revolt; **il avait toujours été jugulé par sa mère,** he had always been repressed by his mother. 2. *A:* to bore (s.o.).

juif, juive [ʒɥif, ʒɥiːv]. 1. *a.* Jewish (custom, quarter, calendar, etc.); Jew (moneylender, etc.). 2. *s.* (*a*) Jew, *f.* Jewess; **le Juif errant,** the Wandering Jew; (*b*) *O: F: Pej:* (i) moneylender; (ii) miser; (iii) moneygrubber; (*c*) *F:* **le petit j.,** the funny bone.

juillet [ʒɥijɛ], *s.m.* July; **en j.,** in July; **au mois de j.,** in the month of July; **le premier, le sept, j.,** (on) the first, the seventh, of July, (on) July (the) first, (the) seventh; **le quatorze j.,** the fourteenth of July, Bastille Day.

juin [ʒɥɛ̃], *s.m.* June; **en j.,** in June; **au mois de j.,** in the month of June; **le premier, le sept, j.,** (on) the first, the seventh, of June, (on) June (the) first, (the) seventh.

juiverie [ʒɥivri], *s.f.* 1. (*a*) jewry, ghetto; (*b*) *coll. Pej:* the Jews, Jewry. 2. *O: F: Pej:* usury, sharp practice; **il m'a fait une j.,** he cheated me.

jujube [ʒyʒyb]. 1. *s.f. Bot:* jujube (fruit). 2. *s.m. Pharm:* jujube (lozenge).

jujubier [ʒyʒybje], *s.m. Bot:* jujube (tree).

juke-box [(d)ʒykbɔks], *s.m.* juke-box.

julep [ʒylɛp], *s.m. Pharm:* julep.

Jules [ʒyl]. 1. *Pr.n.m.* Julius. 2. *s.m. P:* (*a*) chamber pot, jerry; (*b*) latrine pail. 3. *s.m. P:* (*a*) man friend; (*b*) **mon j.,** my husband, my old man; (*c*) pimp.

julibrissin, julibrizzin [ʒylibrisɛ̃, -zɛ̃], *s.m. Bot:* (Constantinople) acacia, silk tree.

Julie [ʒyli], *Pr.n.f.* Julia, Julie; *A: F:* **faire sa J.,** to be goody-goody.

Julien[1] [ʒyljɛ̃], *Pr.n.m.* Julian.

julien[2], **-ienne**[1] [ʒyljɛ̃, -jɛn], *a.* Julian; *Chr:* **année julienne,** Julian year.

juliénite [ʒyljenit], *s.f. Miner:* julienite.

Julienne[2]. 1. *Pr.n.f.* Juliana; Gillian. 2. *s.f.* (*a*) *Bot:* rocket, dame's violet; **j. de Mahon,** Virginia(n) stock; (*b*) **(potage à la) j.,** julienne (soup); (*c*) packet of mixed vegetables (for soup); (*d*) *Ich:* ling.

Juliette [ʒyljɛt], *Pr.n.f.* Juliet.

Julot [ʒylo], *s.m. P:* (*a*) fancy man; (*b*) pimp.

jumbo [ʒœ̃bo], *s.m. Min: U.S:* jumbo.

jumeau, -elle, -eaux [ʒymo, -ɛl, -o]. I. 1. *a. & s.* twin; (*a*) **frères jumeaux, sœurs jumelles,** twin brothers, twin sisters; twins; **vrais jumeaux,** identical twins; **faux jumeaux,** fraternal twins; **trois jumeaux,** triplets; **quatre jumeaux,** quadruplets; (*b*) **lits jumeaux,** twin beds; **maisons, villas, jumelles,** semi-detached houses; **vapeur à hélices jumelles,** twin-screw steamer; **machine à vapeur jumelle,** duplex steam-engine; (*c*) (*of apples, cherries*) double. 2. *s.m. Anat:* gemellus muscle.

II. *s.f.pl.* **jumelles** (*occ. used in sing.*) 1. *Opt:* binoculars; **jumelles prismatiques, à prismes,** prism binoculars; **jumelles de théâtre,** opera-glasses; **jumelles de campagne,** field glass(es); **jumelles grand-angulaires,** wide-angle field glass. 2. (*a*) *Mec.E:* cheeks, side pieces; guide poles (of pile driver); cheeks (of lathe); cheek stones (of gutter); *Nau:* fishes (of mast); **poutre assemblée à jumelles,** fished beam; (*b*) *Veh:* (spring-)shackles; (*c*) *Her:* gemels; (*d*) *Cost:* **jumelles de manchettes,** cuff links; (*e*) *Av:* **jumelle de liaison,** connecting twin yoke.

jumelage [ʒymlaːʒ], *s.m.* 1. coupling, pairing; overlapping (for strength). 2. (*a*) twinning (of towns); (*b*) *Mil:* twinning (of guns, etc.).

jumelé [ʒymle], *a.* arranged in pairs, coupled; **textes jumelés,** bilingual texts; **maison jumelée,** semi-detached house; **villes jumelées,** twinned towns; *Aut:* **pneus jumelés,** twin tyres; dual tyres; *Tg:* **poteaux jumelés,** double pole; *Mec: etc:* **orifices jumelés,** siamesed ports; *Turf:* **pari j.,** forecast (of the first two horses).

jumeler [ʒymle], *v.tr.* (**je jumelle, n. jumelons; je jumellerai**) 1. (*a*) to pair; to arrange in pairs; to twin (towns); (*b*) to fix (beams, etc.) longitudinally together. 2. to strengthen by means of cheeks or side pieces; to fish (mast, beam, etc.).

jument [ʒymɑ̃], *s.f.* mare; **j. poulinière,** brood mare.

jumenterie [ʒymɑ̃t(ə)ri], *s.f.* 1. stud (farm) (for mares); **j. de trait,** draught-horse stud (farm). 2. breeding stock (of mares).

jumentés [ʒymɑ̃te], *s.m.pl. Z:* Equidae.

jumper[1] [(d)ʒœmpœːr], *s.m. Equit:* (show-)jumper.

jumper[2], *s.m. Cost: F:* (*a*) **jupe, robe, j.,** *Fr.C:* **j.,** pinafore dress, *U.S:* jumper; (*b*) sweater, jumper.

jumping [ʒœmpiŋ], *s.m. Equit:* (show-)jumping.

jungle [ʒɔ̃ːgl̩, ʒœ̃ːgl̩], *s.f.* jungle; *Med:* **fièvre des jungles,** jungle fever; **l'appel de la j.,** the call of the wild; **la loi de la j.,** the law of the jungle.

junior [ʒynjɔːr], *s.m. Sp:* junior.

juniperus [ʒyniperys], *s.m. Bot:* juniper (tree).

junker [junkɛːr], *s.m.* 1. *Hist:* Junker. 2. narrow-minded, reactionary aristocrat; Junker.

Junon [ʒynɔ̃], *Pr.n.f. Myth:* Juno.

junonien, -ienne [ʒynɔnjɛ̃, -jɛn], *a.* Junonian, Junoesque.

junte [ʒœ̃ːt, ʒɔ̃ːt], *s.f.* 1. *Hist: Pol:* junta. 2. junto, junta, clique, cabal.

jupe [ʒyp], *s.f.* 1. (woman's) skirt; **j. de dessous,** (i) petticoat, (ii) slip; *Dressm:* **j. en forme, j. à godets, évasée,** flared skirt; **j. cloche,** bell skirt; **j. portefeuille,** wrap-over skirt; **j. jumper,** pinafore dress; *F:* **pendu aux jupes de sa mère,** tied to his mother's apron strings; *F:* **une assemblée de jupes,** a hen party. 2. skirt (of frock-coat, etc.). 3. *I.C.E:* **j. du piston,** skirt of the piston; **j. (d'un hovercraft, d'un naviplane),** skirt (of hovercraft); **j. segmentée,** segmented skirt (of hovercraft); **j. rigide,** rigid sidewall (of hovercraft); **appareil à j. rigide,** sidewaller; **dispositif, vérin, de levage de la j.,** skirt-retraction system, jack.

jupe-culotte [ʒypkylɔt], *s.f.* divided skirt, culotte; *pl. jupes-culottes.*

jupette [ʒypɛt], *s.f.* little skirt.

jupier, -ière [ʒupje, -jɛːr], *s. & a.* skirt maker; skirt hand.

Jupin [ʒypɛ̃], *Pr.n.m. A: F:* Jupiter.

Jupiter [ʒypitɛːr], *Pr.n.m.* 1. *Myth:* Jupiter, Jove; *Astr:* Jupiter; **les traits de J.,** Jove's thunderbolts; *Const:* **(assemblage à) trait de J.,** (skew) scarf joint; *F:* **il se croit sorti de la cuisse de J.,** he thinks he's the cat's whiskers. 2. *Cin: etc:* **lampe J.,** Jupiter lamp.

jupitérien, -ienne [ʒypiterjɛ̃, -jɛn], *a.* Jovian.

jupon [ʒypɔ̃], *s.m.* 1. (*a*) petticoat, underskirt, half slip, waist slip; *F:* **il est toujours dans les jupons de sa mère,** he's always hanging on to his mother's apron strings; (*b*) *P:* woman, girl, *P:* skirt; **courir le j.,** to run after women, to chase the girls. 2. *Scot:* kilt. 3. *A.Cost:* (*in the 17th cent.*) petticoat-breeches. 4. *Furn:* **j. (de lit),** (bed) valance.

juponné, -ée [ʒypɔne], *a.* **1.** *O:* wearing petticoats. **2.** *Dressm:* (skirt, dress) with a (full) petticoat attached. **3.** *P:* drunk.

juponner [ʒypɔne], *v.tr.* to dress (s.o.) up, in a petticoat.

se juponner, to put on one's petticoat, slip.

Jura [ʒyra]. **1.** *Pr.n.m. Geog:* **le J.,** the Jura (Mountains). **2.** *s.m. Geol:* (*a*) *A:* Jurassic; (*b*) **j. blanc,** upper Jurassic, Malm; **j. brun,** middle Jurassic, Dogger; **j. noir,** lower Jurassic, Lias.

jurable [ʒyrabl̩], *a. A.Jur:* (fief) for which allegiance had to be sworn to the suzerain.

jurançon [ʒyrɑ̃sɔ̃], *s.m.* (*also* **vin de Jurançon**) Jurançon wine (of the Pau region).

jurançonnais, -aise [ʒyrɑ̃sɔnɛ, -ɛːz], *a. & s. Geog:* (native, inhabitant) of Jurançon.

jurande [ʒyrɑ̃ːd], *s.f. A:* guild-mastership, wardenship.

jurassien, -ienne [ʒyrasjɛ̃, -jɛn], *a. & s. Geog:* (native, inhabitant) of the Jura (region or department); *Geol:* **relief j.,** Jurassic relief.

jurassique [ʒyrasik], *a. & s.m. Geol:* Jurassic; *s.m.* **j. moyen,** Dogger, middle Jurassic; **j. supérieur,** Malm, upper Jurassic; **j. inférieur,** Lias, lower Jurassic.

jurat [ʒyra], *s.m. Hist:* (*in S. of Fr., esp. in Bordeaux*) jurat, alderman.

juratoire [ʒyratwaːr], *a.* juratory (obligation); **caution j.,** guarantee given on oath.

juré [ʒyre]. **1.** *a.* sworn; **ennemi j. de qn,** sworn enemy of s.o.; **expert j.,** sworn expert; **traducteur j.,** sworn translator. **2.** *s.m.* juryman, juror; **les jurés,** the jury; **messieurs les jurés,** gentleman of the jury; **liste des jurés,** jury panel.

jurée [ʒyre], *s.f. A.Jur:* oath.

jurement [ʒyrmɑ̃], *s.m. A:* (profane) swearing; oath; **faire, proférer, des jurements,** to curse and swear.

jurer [ʒyre], *v.tr.* to swear. **1. j. sa foi,** (i) to swear by one's honour, to pledge one's word; (ii) *A:* to plight one's troth (**à,** to); *Ecc:* **Dieu en vain tu ne jureras,** thou shalt not take the name of the Lord thy God in vain; **j. le ciel,** to call heaven to witness; **il rompit la paix par lui jurée,** he broke the peace he had sworn; *abs.* **j. sur la Bible,** to swear on the Bible; **il ne jure que par son gérant,** he swears by his manager. **2.** (*to promise*) **j. la fidélité à qn,** to swear, vow, fidelity to s.o.; **faire j. le secret à qn,** to swear s.o. to secrecy; **j. de faire qch.,** to swear to do sth.; **j. de se venger,** to swear revenge; **vous m'avez juré de m'aimer toujours,** you swore, vowed, to love me for ever; **j'ai juré que je le perdrais,** I have sworn to ruin him. **3.** (*to assert*) **je le jure sur mon âme,** I swear it on my (soul and) conscience; **je vous jure que c'est vrai,** on my Bible oath, it is the truth; **j. ses grands dieux que . . .,** to swear by all the gods, by all that is sacred, that . . .; **on eût juré entendre des cris,** we could have sworn that we heard shouts; **j'en jurerais,** I would swear to it; *Prov:* **il ne faut (jamais) j. de rien,** one can never be sure of anything; you never can tell. **4.** *abs.* (*a*) to swear (profanely); to curse; *F:* **j. comme un charretier (embourbé), comme un païen,** to swear like a bargee, like a trooper; **j. comme un démon, comme tous les diables,** to swear like blazes; **il y a de quoi faire j. un saint,** it's enough to make a saint swear; (*b*) (*of colours, etc.*) to clash, jar (**avec,** with); **couleurs qui jurent ensemble,** colours that swear, clash; *A:* **violon qui jure,** scratchy fiddle.

jureur [ʒyrœːr], *s.m.* **1.** *Jur:* swearer. **2.** (profane) swearer.

juridiction [ʒyridiksjɔ̃], *s.f.* jurisdiction; **question tombant sous la j. de . . .,** matter within the jurisdiction of . . .; **soumis à la j. de . . .,** under the jurisdiction of . . .; **cela n'est pas dans ma j.,** that's not within my province, not in my line.

juridictionnalisation [ʒyridiksjɔnalizasjɔ̃], *s.f. F:* giving control of a situation over to jurisdiction.

juridictionnel, -elle [ʒyridiksjɔnɛl], *a.* jurisdictional.

juridictionnellement [ʒyridiksjɔnɛlmɑ̃], *adv.* jurisdictionally.

juridique [ʒyridik], *a.* juridical, judicial; legal (tie, claim, etc.); **conseiller j.,** legal adviser (to a government, etc.); **assassinat j.,** judicial murder; **frais juridiques,** lawyer's fees, legal charges (in a transaction).

juridiquement [ʒyridikmɑ̃], *adv.* juridically, judicially, legally.

juridisme [ʒyridism], *s.m. often Pej:* legalism.

jurisconsulte [ʒyriskɔ̃sylt], *s.m.* jurisconsult; jurist; legal expert; **j. en droit coutumier,** common lawyer.

jurisprudence [ʒyrisprydɑ̃ːs], *s.f.* **1.** jurisprudence. **2.** (*a*) statute law, case law; **recueil de j.,** casebook. **3.** holding of the courts (on a question); the precedents (of a case).

jurisprudentiel, -elle [ʒyrisprydɑ̃sjɛl], *a.* jurisprudential.

juriste [ʒyrist], *s.m.* jurist; legal writer.

juron [ʒyrɔ̃], *s.m.* (profane) oath, *F:* swear-word; **lâcher, pousser, un j.,** to let fly, rap out, an oath.

jury [ʒyri], *s.m.* **1.** *Jur:* jury; (*a*) **dresser la liste du j.,** to empanel the jury; **chef du j.,** foreman of the jury; **membre du j.,** juryman, juror; (*b*) (*in Engl.*) **j. d'accusation,** Grand Jury; **j. de jugement, petit j.,** trial jury, petty jury, common jury. **2.** selection committee (*e.g.* for the *Salon*); **j. d'une exposition d'horticulture,** judges at a flower show; **j. d'examen,** examining board, board of examiners; **membre du j.** (i) (**dans un concours de musique, etc.**), adjudicator; (ii) (**à une exposition, etc.**), judge; (iii) *Sch:* awarder; examiner.

jus [ʒy], *s.m.* **1.** juice; **j. de fruit,** fruit juice; *F:* **le j. de la treille,** the juice of the grape; wine; **plein de j.,** juicy; *F:* **c'est j. vert et verjus,** it is six of one and half a dozen of the other; *F:* **j. de coude,** elbow grease; *F:* **y mettre du j.,** to put some vim into it; *F:* **un Anglais pur j.,** a hundred per cent Englishman, a typical Englishman. **2.** *Cu:* juice (of meat); gravy; **arroser de j. (un rôti, etc.),** to baste (a roast, etc.); *F:* **cuire, mijoter, dans son j.,** to stew in one's own juice. **3.** *Leath:* = JUSÉE. **4.** *P:* (*a*) (dirty) water; **il est tombé dans le j.,** he fell in; (*b*) coffee; **j. de chique, de chaussette,** watery coffee; **c'est clair comme du j. de chique,** it's as clear as mud; *Mil:* **aller au j.,** (i) to go for coffee, (ii) *A:* to go over the top; (*c*) petrol, *F:* juice, *U.S:* gas; (*d*) electric current, *F:* juice; (*e*) publisher's blurb; *Journ:* **faire un j.,** to write a paper; (*f*) long speech; **faire un j.,** to spout (at length); (*g*) *O:* elegance, smartness; **il a du j.,** he's quite the toff; **jeter du j.,** to make an impression; to look classy, swell; (*h*) **ça vaut le j.,** it's worth it, worth while. **5.** *Art:* glaze; **passer un tableau au j.,** to glaze a painting.

jusant [ʒyzɑ̃], *s.m.* ebb (tide); **direction du j.,** set of the ebb; **étale du j.,** slack of the ebb.

jusée [ʒyze], *s.f. Leath:* tan(ning) liquor, ooze, pickle; **j. colorante,** dyeing liquor; **fosse à j.,** leach.

jusqu'auboutisme [ʒyskobutism], *s.m.* whole-hoggism, going the whole hog, policy of the whole-hogger.

jusqu'auboutiste [ʒyskobutist], *s.m. & f. Pol: etc: F:* **1.** whole-hogger. **2.** diehard, last-ditcher.

jusque [ʒysk(ə)], *prep.* **1.** as far as, up to; **jusqu'ici,** thus far, so far; **venez jusqu'ici,** come over here; **j.-là** [ʒyskəla], thus far, up to that point; **jusqu'ici, j.-là, c'est très bien,** so far so good; **jusqu'où?** how far? **jusqu'où va le parc?** how far does the park extend? **depuis Londres jusqu'à Paris,** all the way from London to Paris; **jusqu'au bout (de la rue, etc.),** as far as, up to, the end (of the street, etc.); **monter jusqu'à moins de cent mètres du sommet,** to climb to within one hundred metres of the summit; **pousser la hardiesse jusqu'à la témérité,** to carry daring to the point of rashness; **les lexicographes sont honnêtes jusqu'à la naïveté,** lexicographers are honest to the point of naïvety; **jusqu'à un certain point,** up to a certain point; **aller jusqu'à faire qch.,** to go so far as to do sth.; **il irait jusqu'au crime,** he would go the length of committing a crime; **jusqu'à la cruauté,** to the point of cruelty; **j. devant les murs,** up to the very walls; **j. chez lui,** up to his very door; **la jupe descend jusqu'au genou,** the skirt reaches to the knee; **rougir jusqu'aux oreilles,** to blush right up to the ears; **son amitié ne va pas jusqu'à la bourse,** his friendship stops short of his purse; **plaisanter j. sur l'échafaud,** to jest even on the scaffold; **compter jusqu'à dix,** to count up to ten; **défendre son pays jusqu'à la mort,** to defend one's country to the death; **ils furent tués jusqu'au dernier,** they were killed to a man; **jusqu'à concurrence de 5000 francs,** (up) to the amount of 5000 francs; *Post:* **jusqu'à 250 gr.,** not over, not exceeding, 250 gr. **2.** (*a*) till, until; **attendez jusqu'après les vacances,** wait till after the holidays; **suspendre les séances jusqu'après les vacances,** to adjourn over the holidays; **jusqu'ici,** till, until, up to, now; to date, up to the present time, as yet; **rumeurs jusqu'ici sans crédit,** rumours hitherto uncredited; **j.-là, jusqu'alors,** until then; **jusqu'à présent,** up to now, hitherto; **jusqu'à hier, à midi, à dix heures,** until, up to, yesterday, midday, ten o'clock; **jusqu'(à) aujourd'hui,** until today; **jusqu'à fin mai,** up to the end of May; **jusqu'à quel âge avez-vous vécu en France?** up to what age did you live in France? **je m'en souviendrai jusqu'à mon dernier jour,** I shall remember it to my dying day; **jusqu'au jour que . . ., jusqu'au jour où . . ., jusqu'au moment que, où . . .,** (i) until such time as . . .; (ii) until the time when . . .; **il courut jusqu'à tomber épuisé,** he ran until he fell exhausted; (*b*) **si nous remontons jusqu'en 1800,** if we go as far back as (the year) 1800. **3.** (*intensive*) (*a*) **il sait jusqu'à nos pensées,** he knows our very thoughts; **un style grandiose jusqu'à l'emphase,** a grand and even grandiloquent style; **jusqu'à mon père était indigné,** even my father was indignant; **on en donne jusqu'à mille francs,** people give as much as a thousand francs for it; **jusqu'à dix personnes l'ont vu,** as many as ten people saw it; **il est venu des foules j. de Leeds,** crowds came from as far away as Leeds, all the way from Leeds; **il mangea l'oie jusqu'aux os,** he ate the goose bones and all; **j'ai oublié jusqu'à son existence,** I have forgotten his very existence; **ils mangèrent jusqu'à leurs souliers,** they ate their very boots, they even ate their boots; **noter jusqu'aux moindres détails,** to make a note of the smallest details; **il n'y a pas, il n'est pas, jusqu'aux petits enfants qui ne sachent cela,** babes in arms know that; (*b*) **il se montra sévère jusqu'à mériter le reproche d'être cruel,** he was severe to the point of cruelty; **il nous a aimés jusqu'à mourir pour nous,** he so loved us that he even died for us. **4.** *conj.phr.* **jusqu'à ce que,** *usu.* + *sub.*, till, until; **jusqu'à ce que les portes soient fermées,** till the doors are shut; *A: & Dial:* **jusqu'à tant que** *occ.*, **jusqu'à temps que = jusqu'à ce que.**

jusques [ʒyskə(z)], *prep.* (*a*) *A: & Lit:* **j. à quand, ô Catilina . . .!** how long, Catiline . . .! **percé j. au fond du cœur . . .,** pierced to the very heart . . .; (*b*) **j. et y compris . . .,** up to and including . . ..

jusquiame [ʒyskjam], *s.f. Bot:* henbane.

jussiée [ʒysje], *s.f. Bot:* primrose willow.

jussif, -ive [ʒysif, -iːv], *s. & a. Gram:* jussive, imperative.

jussion [ʒysjɔ̃], *s.f. Hist:* **lettres de j.,** jussive letter, peremptory order (from the king).

Just(e) [ʒyst], *Pr.n.m.* Justus.

justaucorps [ʒystokɔːr], *s.m.* **1.** *A.Cost:* justaucorps, jerkin. **2.** *Danc:* leotard.

juste [ʒyst]. **1.** *a.* just, right, fair; (*a*) **j. sentence,** just sentence; **j. punition de ses méfaits,** just, appropriate, punishment for his misdeeds; **principe j.,** right principle; **esprit j.,** just, fair, mind; **un protecteur, j. appréciateur des arts,** a protector who knows how to appreciate art; **traitement j.,** fair play, just treatment; **j. colère,** legitimate, righteous, anger; **j. orgueil,** proper pride; **rien de plus j.,** nothing could be fairer; *s.* **le j. et l'injuste,** right and wrong; (*b*) **magistrat j.,** just, upright, judge; **être j. à, envers, pour, qn,** to give s.o. his due, to be just to s.o.; **vous n'êtes pas j. vis-à-vis de vous-même,** you are not being fair to yourself; **je suis obligé, pour être j., de . . .,** I am bound in justice to . . .; **j. ciel!** heavens above! *s.* **les justes et les repentis,** the just, the righteous, and the repentant; **dormir du sommeil du j.,** to sleep the sleep of the just. **2.** *a.* right, exact, accurate; (*a*) **quelle est l'heure j.?** what exactly is the time? **le mot j.,** the mot juste, the proper expression, the exact word, the right word; **raisonnement j.,** sound reasoning; **avoir l'oreille j.,** to have a good ear (for music); **ce piano n'est pas j.,** this piano is out of tune; **chiffres justes,** right, correct, figures; **se faire une idée j. de la situation,** to form a true estimate of the situation; **s'en tenir à un j. milieu,** to stick to a happy medium; **votre réponse n'est pas j.,** you have got the answer wrong; **la prédiction se trouva être j.,** the prediction chanced, turned out, to be right; **mesure j.,** full measure; **balance j.,** accurate scales; **ma montre est j.,** my watch is right; **arriver à l'heure j.,** to arrive on the dot, on the stroke; **c'est j.,** that's so! that's right! quite so! **rien de plus j.,** you are perfectly right; *Mus:* **quarte j.,** perfect fourth; (*b*) **ration bien j.,** very scanty, bare, allowance; **poids bien j.,** scant weight; **chaussures trop justes,** tight shoes; **vis j.,** tight screw; **vêtement (bien) j.,** tightfitting, skimpy, garment; **c'est bien j.,** there is barely enough (food, etc.) to go round; *F:* **ç'a été j.!** it was a tight squeeze! **c'est tout j. s'il ne m'a pas frappé,** he was within an ace of striking me; **c'est tout j. s'il sait lire,** he can barely read, it's as much as he can do to read; **il ne manque jamais son train, mais c'est tout j.,** he never misses his train, but he cuts it fine; *Com:* **au plus j. prix,** at rock-bottom price. **3.** *adv.* (*a*) rightly; **parler j.,** to speak to the point; **frapper j.,** (i) to strike home, to strike an accurate blow; (ii) to make, effect, a hit; (iii) to hit the nail on the head; **trait, critique, qui frappe j.,** shrewd thrust, criticism; **chanter j.,** to sing in tune, to sing true; **sonner j.,** to ring true; **voir j.,** to take a right view of things; **tomber j.,** to come, to happen, at the right moment; (b) exactly, precisely, just; **arriver à dix heures j.,** to arrive on the stroke of ten, at ten o'clock sharp; **j. au milieu,** right, plumb, in the centre); **j. à temps,** just in time, in the nick of time; **c'est j. l'homme qu'il nous faut,** he's exactly the man, he is the very man, we want; **c'est j. ce qu'il faut,** it's the very thing; **la terre se trouve j. au nord,** the land lies directly to the north; (c) barely, just; **n'avoir que j. le temps,** to have barely time, to have just (enough) time, to have no time to spare; **vous avez tout j. le temps,** you haven't a moment to spare; **échapper tout j.,** to escape by the skin of one's teeth; **il échappa tout j. à la mort,** he barely, narrowly, escaped death. 4. *adv.phr.* **je ne sais pas au j. si . . .,** I do not exactly know whether . . .; **je ne saurais dire au j.,** I cannot rightly say; **comme de j.,** of course; as it should be; as is only fair, only just; *Com:* **prix de revient calculé au plus j.,** strict cost price.

justement [ʒystəmɑ̃], *adv.* 1. justly, rightly, properly, deservedly. 2. precisely, exactly, just; **c'est j. ce que je disais,** that's just, precisely, what I was saying; **j. ce soir-là il avait rendez-vous,** it so happened he had an appointment that evening; **voici j. la lettre que j'attendais,** here is the very letter I was waiting for.

juste-milieu [ʒystmiljø], *s.m.inv. Pol: etc:* middle course, juste-milieu.

justesse [ʒystɛs], *s.f.* 1. exactness, correctness, precision, accuracy; **j. d'une vis,** exact fit of a screw; **j. d'une prédiction,** accuracy of a prediction; **j. d'une opinion,** soundness of an opinion; **j. d'une expression,** aptness appropriateness, of an expression; **raisonner avec j.,** to argue soundly, rightly; **j. du tir,** accuracy of fire; **j. de la voix,** accuracy of intonation; **j. de l'oreille,** accuracy of ear; **chanter avec j.,** to sing true, in tune, correctly. 2. (arriver) de j., (to arrive) just in time, to cut it fine; *Turf:* **gagner de j.,** to win on the post; *Sp:* **victoire de j.,** narrow victory.

justice [ʒystis], *s.f.* 1. justice; (a) **la j. de ma cause,** the justice, justness, equity, of my cause; **la j. la plus élémentaire nous oblige à reconnaître que . . .,** it is only simple justice to admit that . . .; **c'est j. que** + *sub.,* it is only right, fair, that . . .; **il est de toute j. de l'entendre,** it is only fair to give him a hearing; **en toute j.,** by rights; **reconnaître, en toute j., que . . .,** to acknowledge, in all fairness, that . . .; **je ne peux pas, en toute j., lui permettre de payer,** I cannot, in all fairness, allow him to pay; **avec j.,** justly, deservedly; **faire j. à qn,** (i) to do justice to s.o.; (ii) to deal with s.o. according to his deserts; **faire j. à un coupable,** to deal with a culprit; **ce n'est que j.,** it is only just; **ce qui n'est que j.,** which is only fair, as is only fair;

se faire j., (i) (*of murderer*) to commit suicide; (ii) to get one's revenge, to take the law into one's own hands; **se faire j. à soi-même,** to take the law into one's own hands; **faire j. de qn,** to treat s.o. as he deserves; **faire j. de qch.,** to put an end to the myth of sth.; **rendre j. à qn,** to do s.o. justice; **rendre j. au zèle de qn,** to give s.o. credit for his zeal; *F:* **des cheveux raides comme la j.,** hair straight as a yard of pump water; (b) **demander j. à qn,** to seek redress from s.o., at the hands of s.o. 2. law, legal proceedings; **la j. militaire, maritime,** Service's Legal Arm; **Palais de J.,** Law Courts; **gens de j.,** (i) officers of the law, of the court, (ii) lawyers; **la j. suivit son cours,** the law had its way; **action en j.,** action at law; **aller, plaider, en j., recourir à la j.,** to go to law; **citer qn en j.,** to go to law with s.o.; **poursuivre qn en j.,** to institute legal proceedings against s.o.; to take action against s.o.

justicia [ʒystisja], *s.m. Bot: Pharm:* justicia.

justiciabilité [ʒystisjabilite], *s.f.* justiciability.

justiciable [ʒystisjabl]. 1. a. **j. d'un tribunal,** justiciable to, in, a court; amenable to (the jurisdiction of) a court; **j. des tribunaux militaires,** subject to military law; **cette question n'est pas j. des règles ordinaires,** this question is not amenable to ordinary rules; **un auteur est j. de la critique,** an author is open to criticism; *Med:* **cas j. d'un certain traitement,** case to which a certain treatment is applicable, in which a certain treatment is indicated. 2. *s.* (a) justiciable (**de,** of); **c'est un de mes justiciables,** he comes under my jurisdiction; (b) the ordinary man (in the eyes of the law).

justicier¹ [ʒystisje], *v.tr.* (*p.d. & pr.sub.* n. **justicions,** v. **justiciiez**) *A:* 1. to subject (criminal) to corporal punishment. 2. to execute (criminal).

justicier², -ière [ʒystisje, -jɛːr]. 1. *s.* (a) lover of justice; (b) administrator of justice, justiciary; **j. de la mode,** arbiter of fashion; (c) *A:* justicer, judge. 2. *a.* retributive (punishment).

justifiable [ʒystifjabl], *a.* justifiable, warrantable.

justifiant [ʒystifjɑ̃], *a. Theol:* justifying (faith, grace).

justificateur, -trice [ʒystifikatœːr, -tris]. 1. *a.* justificatory, justifying. 2. *s.* justifier.

justificatif, -ive [ʒystifikatif, -iːv], *a.* justificatory, justificative; **pièce justificative,** *s.m.* (i) *Com:* voucher, voucher copy; (ii) *Jur:* document in proof; relevant paper.

justification [ʒystifikasjɔ̃], *s.f.* 1. justification, vindication; *Theol:* justification. 2. proof (of fact, of identity). 3. *Typ:* (a) justification (of lines); (b) type area; **petite j.,** narrow measure.

justifié [ʒystifje], *a.* 1. (a) justified, justifiable (action); **peu j.,** hardly justifiable; unwarranted; (b) **être j. à faire qch.,** to be justified in doing sth. 2. *Jur:* **préjudice j.,** proved damages.

justifier [ʒystifje], *v.tr.* (*p.d. & pr.sub.* n. **justifiions,** v. **justifiiez**) 1. (a) to justify, vindicate (s.o.'s conduct, etc.); to warrant (action, expenditure); **la fin justifie les moyens,** the end justifies the means; **j. qn d'une imputation,** to clear s.o. of, from, an imputation; **votre maladie ne vous**

justifie pas de rester à la maison, your illness is no excuse for staying at home; (b) *Theol:* to justify (sinners). 2. to prove, give proof of, make good (assertion, etc.); **je suis prêt à j. que je suis son fils,** I am ready to prove that I am his son; **le plaignant a justifié ne pas pouvoir trouver de logement,** the complainant proved that he could find no accommodation. 3. *Typ:* to justify, adjust (line of type or length of column). 4. *v.ind.tr. Jur:* **j. de ses mouvements,** to give a satisfactory account of one's movements; to account for one's movements; **j. de son identité,** to prove one's identity; to give satisfactory proof of one's identity; **j. de sa bonne foi,** to prove one's good faith.

se justifier, to clear oneself, to vindicate one's character; to justify oneself.

Justin¹ [ʒystɛ̃], *Pr.n.m.* Justin.

justin², *s.m. Dial:* (*Brittany*) tight-fitting bodice.

Justine [ʒystin], *Pr.n.f.* Justina, Justine.

Justinien [ʒystinjɛ̃]. 1. *Pr.n.m. Rom.Hist:* Justinian. 2. *a.* **le Code J.,** the Justinian Code.

jutage [ʒytaːʒ], *s.m. Ind:* introduction of hot juice into tins of fruit or vegetables.

jute¹ [ʒyt], *Hist:* 1. *a.* Jutish. 2. *s.m.pl.* **les Jutes,** the Jutes.

jute², *s.m. Tex:* jute; **sac en j.,** gunny bag; **toile de j.,** crash.

juter [ʒyte], *v.i.* (a) to be juicy; **pêche qui jute,** juicy peach; **rôti qui jute,** juicy joint, dripping joint; *F:* **pipe qui jute,** pipe that dribbles; (b) *P:* to speechify.

juteux, -euse [ʒytø, -øːz]. 1. *a.* (a) juicy; **la plante reste juteuse,** the plant retains its sap; (b) *P: O:* smart, tarted up; (c) *P:* **affaire juteuse,** juicy bit of business. 2. *s.m. Mil: P:* (company) sergeant-major.

jutlandais, -aise [ʒytlɑ̃dɛ, -ɛːz], *a. & s. Geog:* 1. *a.* Jutlandish; **vache jutlandaise,** Jutland cow. 2. *s.* Jutlander.

Juvénal [ʒyvenal], *Pr.n.m. Lt.Lit:* Juvenal.

juvénat [ʒyvena], *s.m. Ecc:* (*in certain orders*) juvenate.

juvénile [ʒyvenil], *a.* (a) juvenile; youthful (ardour, etc.); *Jur:* **délinquence j.,** juvenile delinquency; (b) *Geol:* juvenile, magmatic (water).

juvénilement [ʒyvenilmɑ̃], *adv.* youthfully, juvenilely.

juvenilia [ʒyvenilja], *s.m.pl. Lit:* juvenilia.

juvénilité [ʒyvenilite], *s.f.* juvenility, youthfulness.

juxtalinéaire [ʒykstalineɛːr], *a.* **traduction j.,** juxtalinear translation; text and translation arranged in parallel columns.

juxta-médullaire [ʒykstamedylɛːr], *a. Anat:* juxtamedullary; *pl. juxta-médullaires.*

juxtaposable [ʒykstapozabl], *a.* that can be placed side by side; **mobilier à éléments juxtaposables,** unit furniture.

juxtaposer [ʒykstapoze], *v.tr.* to place side by side, to juxtapose.

se juxtaposer, (*of molecules, etc.*) to come together.

juxtaposition [ʒykstapozisjɔ̃], *s.f.* juxtaposition.

jy [ʒi], *adv. P: O:* = OUI.

K

K, k [kɑ], *s.m.* (the letter) K, k; *Tp:* **K comme Kléber,** K for King; *Ph:* échelle K. (= Kelvin), Kelvin, absolute, scale (of temperatures); 288° K, 288° K, 288° A.

Ka'aba, Ka'ba, Kaaba [kaaba], *s.f. Rel.H:* the Kaaba.

kabbale [kabal], *s.f. Jew.Rel.H:* cab(b)ala.

Kaboul [kabul], *Pr.n. Geog:* Kabul.

kabyle [kabil]. **1.** *a. & s. Ethn:* Kabyle. **2.** *s.m. Ling:* le k., Kabyle.

Kabylie [kabili], *Pr.n.f. Geog:* (la Grande, Petite) K., (Great, Lesser) Kabylia.

Kâchan [kaʃã], *Pr.n. Geog:* Kashan.

Kachgar [kaʃgaːr], *Pr.n. Geog:* Kashgar.

kaddisch [kadiʃ], *s.m. Jew.Rel:* Kaddish.

kagou [kagu], *s.m. Orn:* kagu.

kaïnite [kainit], *s.f. Miner:* kainite.

kaïnosite [kainɔzit], *s.f. Miner:* kainosite.

kaïr [kaiːr], *s.m.* coir, coconut fibre.

kaire [kɛːr], *s.m. Nau:* coir rope.

Kairouan [kɛrwã], *Pr.n. Geog:* Kairwan.

kaiser [kɛzɛːr], *s.m.* kaiser.

kaiserlick [kezɛrlik], *s.m. Hist: F:* (during Fr. Revolution) (a) Austrian, German, soldier; (b) French émigré.

kakatoès [kakatɔɛs], *s.m. Orn:* cockatoo.

kakémono [kakemɔnɔ], *s.m. Jap.Art:* kakemono; Japanese wall picture.

kakerlak, kakerlat [kakɛrla], *s.m. Ent:* cockroach, blackbeetle.

kaki¹ [kaki], *s.m. & a.inv. Dy:* khaki, *U.S:* olive-drab.

kaki², *s.m. Bot:* (Chinese) persimmon.

kala-azar [kalaazar], *s.m. Med:* kala azar, visceral leishmaniasis; **k.-a. méditerranéen,** leishmania infantium, mediterranea.

kalanchoe [kalãkoe], *s.m. Bot:* kalanchoe.

kaléidoscope [kaleidɔskɔp], *s.m.* kaleidoscope.

kaléidoscopique [kaleidɔskɔpik], *a.* kaleidoscopic.

kali [kali], *s.m.* (a) *Bot:* kali, glasswort, prickly saltwort; (b) *Ch:* kali, potash.

kaliborite [kalibɔrit], *s.f. Miner:* kaliborite.

kalinite [kalinit], *s.f. Miner:* kalinite.

kaliophilite [kaljɔfilit], *s.f. Miner:* kaliophilite.

kalium [kaljɔm], *s.m. A.Ch:* potassium.

kalmie [kalmi], *s.f. Bot:* kalmia; **k. à larges feuilles,** mountain-laurel, American laurel, calico bush; **k. à feuilles étroites,** sheep laurel.

kalmouk, -ouke [kalmuk]. **1.** *a. & s. Ethn:* Kalmuck. **2.** *s.m. Ling:* le k., Kalmuck.

kâlong [kalɔ̃(g)], *s.m. Z:* kalong, Malaysian roussette.

Kamakoura [kamakura], *Pr.n. Geog:* Kamakura.

kamala [kamala], *s.m.* **1.** *Bot:* kamala (tree). **2.** *Dy/Pharm:* kamala, kamela, kamila.

kamarézite [kamarezit], *s.f. Miner:* kamarezite.

kame [kam], *s.m. Geol:* kame.

kamichi [kamiʃi], *s.m. Orn:* kamichi, horned screamer.

kamikaze [kamikaze], *s.m. Japanese Hist:* kamikaze.

Kamtchadales [kamtʃadal], *s.m.pl. Geog:* (natives, inhabitants) of Kamchatka.

Kamtchatka [kamtʃatka], *Pr.n. Geog:* Kamchatka.

kan¹ [kã], *s.m.* (Eastern potentate) khan.

kan², *s.m.* (in the Orient) rest house, caravanserai, khan.

kanaster [kanastɛːr], *s.m.* canaster (for tobacco).

kangourou [kãguru], *s.m. Z:* kangaroo; **k. de rochers,** wallaby; *Geog:* **île des Kangourous,** Kangaroo Island.

kansanien [kãsanjɛ̃], *s.m. Geol:* kansan.

Kan-Sou [kãsu], *Pr.n.m. Geog:* Kansu.

Kan-tcheou [kãtʃeu], *Pr.n.f. Geog:* Kanchow.

kantien, -ienne [kãtjɛ̃, -jɛn], *a. Phil:* Kantian.

kantisme [kãtism], *s.m. Phil:* Kantianism, Kantism.

kantiste [kãtist], *Phil:* **1.** *a.* Kantian, Kantist. **2.** *s.* Kantist.

kaolin [kaɔlɛ̃], *s.m.* kaolin, porcelain clay, china clay.

kaolinique [kaɔlinik], *a.* kaolinic.

kaolinisation [kaɔlinizasjɔ̃], *s.f.* kaolinization (of feldspar, etc.).

kaoliniser [kaɔlinize], *v.tr.* to kaolinize.

kaolinite [kaɔlinit], *s.f. Miner:* kaolinite.

kaon [kaɔ̃], *s.m. Atom.Ph:* kaon.

kaori [kaɔri], *s.m. Bot:* kaori, kauri.

kapok [kapɔk], *s.m. Com:* kapok.

kapokier [kapɔkje], *s.m. Bot:* kapok tree.

kappa [kap(p)a], *s.m. Gr.Alph:* kappa.

karacul, karakul [karakyl], *s.m. Husb:* caracul, karakul (sheep).

karagan [karagã], *s.m. Z:* karagan, corsak.

karatas [karatas], **karata** [karata], *s.m. Bot: Tex:* karatas, *F:* silk grass.

karaté [karate], *s.m. Sp:* karate.

karbau [karbo], *s.m. Z:* carabao; water buffalo.

karité [karite], *s.m. Bot:* karite, shea(-tree); **beurre de k.,** karite nut butter, shea butter.

karma [karma], *s.m. Buddhist Rel:* karma.

Karman [karmã], *s.m. Av:* K. (de raccordement), wing fillet, fin fillet.

Karnatic (le) [lǝkarnatik], *Pr.n.m. Hist:* the Carnatic.

Karpat(h)es [karpat], *Pr.n.m.pl. Geog:* the Carpathians.

karri [kari], *s.m. Bot:* karri.

karst [karst], *s.m. Geol:* karst.

karsténite [karstenit], *s.f. Miner:* anhydrite.

karstique [karstik], *a. Geog:* karstic; karst (country).

kart [kart], *s.m. Sp: Aut:* (go-)kart.

karting [kartiŋ], *s.m. Sp: Aut:* (go-)kart racing, karting; **faire du k.,** to go (in for) karting.

kary [kari], *s.m. Cu:* **1.** curry powder. **2.** (chicken, etc.) curry.

karyokinèse [karjɔkinɛːz], *s.f. Biol:* karyokinesis, mitosis.

karyomère [karjɔmɛːr], **karyomérite** [karjɔmerit], *s.m. Biol:* karyomere, karyomerite.

karyotype [karjɔtip], *s.m. Biol:* karyotype.

kasba(h) [kazba], *s.f.* kasba.

kascher, kasher [kaʃɛːr], *a.inv. Jew.Rel:* kosher.

kasolite [kasɔlit], *s.f. Miner:* kasolite.

kassite [kasit]. **1.** *a. & s. A.Geog:* Kassite. **2.** *s.m. Ling:* the Elamite language, Kassite.

Katanga [katãga], *Pr.n.m. Geog:* Katanga.

katangais, -aise [katãgɛ, -ɛːz], *a.* Katangan.

katathermomètre [katatɛrmɔmɛtr], *s.m.* katathermometer.

kauri [kɔri], *s.m. Bot:* **1.** kauri(pine). **2.** kauri gum.

kaurite [korit], *s.f. Ch:* (synthetic) kauri resin (used for sticking plywood).

kava, kawa [kava], *s.f.* kava ((i) shrub, (ii) drink).

kayac, kayak [kajak], *s.m.* kayak.

kayakiste [kajakist], *s.m. & f.* kayaker.

kea [kea], *s.m. Orn:* kea (parrot).

kebâb [kebab], *s.m. Cu:* kebab.

kébir [kebiːr], (a) *a. P:* large, big; (b) *s.m. Mil: P:* general.

keepsake [kipsɛk], *s.m. A:* **1.** (young lady's) autograph album, keepsake.

kéfir [kefiːr], *s.m.* (drink) kefir, kephir.

kelp [kɛlp], *s.m.* **1.** *Ind:* kelp ash. **2.** floating seaweed (of the Southern hemisphere).

kelt [kɛlt], *s.m. Ich:* kelt.

kempite [kɛmpit], *s.f. Miner:* kempite.

kennedya [kenedja], *s.m. Bot:* kennedya.

kénotoxine [kenotɔksin], *s.f. Physiol:* kenotoxin.

kénotron [kenotrɔ̃], *s.m. El:* kenotron.

kentia [kɛntja], *s.m. Bot:* kentia.

kentrolite [kɛtrɔlit], *s.f. Miner:* kentrolite.

kentrophylle [kɛtrɔfil], *s.m. Bot:* safflower.

Kenya [kenja], *Pr.n.m. Geog:* Kenya.

képhyr [kefiːr], *s.m.* (drink) kefir, kephir.

képi [kepi], *s.m.* kepi, peaked cap.

képlérien, -ienne [keplerjɛ̃, -jɛn], *a. Astr:* Keplerian.

kérabau [kerabo], *s.m. Z:* carabao, water-buffalo.

kéraphylleux, -euse [kerafilø, -øz], *a. Vet:* horny (tumour, etc.).

kéraphyllocèle [kerafilɔsɛl], *s.f. Vet:* keraphyllocele.

kératectomie [keratɛktɔmi], *s.f. Opt.Surg:* keratectomy.

kératerpéton [keratɛrpetɔ̃], *s.m. Paleont:* keraterpeton.

kératine [keratin], *s.f. Physiol: Ch:* keratin, ceratin.

kératinique [keratinik], *a.* keratinous, ceratinous.

kératinisation [keratinizasjɔ̃], *s.f.* keratinization.

kératinisé [keratinize], *a.* keratinized, keratosed; (become) horny.

kératique [keratik], *a.* (a) (of sponge) keratose; (b) **porphyre k.,** hornstone porphyry; (c) *Physiol:* keratic, keratose; **réaction k.,** keratic reaction.

kératite [keratit], *s.f. Med:* keratitis, inflammation of the cornea.

kératocône [keratokoːn], *s.m. Med:* keratoconus.

kérato-conjonctivite [keratokɔ̃jɔ̃ktivit], *s.f. Med:* keratoconjunctivitis, *occ.* cerato-conjunctivitis.

kératodermie [keratɔdɛrmi], *s.f. Med:* keratodermia, ceratodermia.

kératogène [keratɔʒɛn], *a. Physiol:* ceratogenous, keratogenous.

kératoïde [keratɔid], *a. Physiol:* ceratoid, keratoid; horny.

kératolyse [keratɔliːz], *s.f. Med:* keratolysis.

kératomalacie [keratɔmalasi], *s.f. Med:* keratomalacia.

kératomycose [keratɔmikoːz], *s.f. Med:* keratomycosis.

kératoplastie [keratɔplasti], *s.f. Surg:* keratoplasty, corneal grafting.

kératoscope [keratɔskɔp], *s.m. Med:* keratoscope.

kératoscopie [keratɔskɔpi], *s.f. Med:* keratoscopy.

kératose [keratoːz], *s.f. Med: Vet:* keratosis; **k. pilaire,** keratosis pilaris, keratosis suprafollicularis.

kératotomie [keratɔtɔmi], *s.f. Surg:* keratotomy; **faire une k.,** to couch a cataract.

kerma [kɛrma], *s.m. Atom.Ph:* kerma.

kermès [kɛrmɛs], *s.m.* **1.** *Ent:* (al)kermes; **k. de la vigne,** vine scale. **2.** *Bot:* **chêne k.,** kermes oak. **3.** *Pharm: etc:* **k. minéral,** kermes mineral, amorphous sulphide of antimony, red antimony; kermesite.

kermésite [kɛrmezit], *s.f. Miner:* kermesite, red antimony, kermes mineral.

kermesse [kɛrmɛs], *s.f.* (*a*) (Flemish) kermis; village fair; (*b*) painting, picture, of a *kermesse*; (*c*) (charity) fête.

kérogène [kerɔʒɛn], *s.m. Geol:* kerogen.

kérosène [kerɔzɛn], *s.m.*, **kérosine** [kerɔzin], *s.f.* paraffin (oil), *U.S:* kerosene; *Av:* **k. aviation,** kerosene; *Ch:* **k. chloré,** keryl.

kerria [kɛrja], *s.m.*, **kerrie** [kɛri], *s.f. Bot:* kerria.

kérygmatique [kerigmatik], *a. Theol:* kerygmatic.

kérygme [kerigm], *s.m. Theol:* kerygma.

ketch [kɛtʃ], *s.m. Nau:* ketch.

ketmie [kɛtmi], *s.f. Bot:* ketmia; **k. comestible,** gumbo; **k. rose de Chine,** shoeflower; **k. à chanvre,** brown Indian hemp; ambary.

Ketsia [kɛtsja], *Pr.n.f. B.Hist:* Kezia(h).

kétupa [ketypa], **kétupu** [ketypy], *s.m. Orn:* ketupa, fish owl.

keuper [kœpɔːr], *a. & s.m. Geol:* Keuper.

keynésien, -ienne [kenezjɛ̃, -jɛn], *a. & s. Pol.Ec:* Keynesian.

khâgne [kaːɲ], *s.f. Sch: P:* = CAGNE[2].

khâgneux, -euse [kaɲø, -øːz], *s. Sch: P:* = CAGNEUX 2.

Khaïber [kaibɛːr], *Pr.n. Geog:* **la Passe de K., le K.,** the Khyber Pass.

khaki [kaki], *s.m. & a.inv. Tex:* khaki; *U.S:* olive drab.

khalife [kalif], *s.m.* caliph.

khalifat [kalifa], *s.m.* caliphate.

khamsin [kamzin], *s.m. Meteor:* khamsin.

khan [kɑ̃], *s.m.* khan.

khanat [kana], *s.m.* khanate.

Kharbin(e) [karbin], *Pr.n.m. Geog:* Harbin.

kharidjite [kari(d)ʒit], *a. & s. Muslim Rel:* Kharijite.

Khartoum [kartum], *Pr.n.m. Geog:* Khartum.

khédiv(i)al, -aux [kediv(j)al, -o], *a.* khediv(i)al.

khédiv(i)at [kediv(j)a], *s.m.* khediv(i)ate.

khédive [kediːv], *s.m.* khedive.

khi [ki], *s.m. Gr.Alph:* chi.

khmer, khmère [kmɛ(ː)r]. **1.** *a. & s. Geog:* Khmer, Kmer. **2.** *s.m. Ling:* **le k.,** K(h)mer.

khôl [koːl], *s.m. Toil:* kohl.

Khorassan [kɔrasɑ̃], *Pr.n.m. Geog:* Khoras(s)an.

kiang [kjɑ̃g], *s.m. Z:* hemione, kiang, wild ass.

Kiang-sou [kjɑ̃gsu], *Pr.n.m. Geog:* Kiang-su.

Kiao-Tchéou [kjaotʃeu], *Pr.n.m. Geog:* Kiaochow.

kibbouts, kibboutz [kibuts], *s.m. Pol.Ec:* kibbutz; *pl. kibboutsim, kibboutzim.*

kichenotte [kiʃ(ə)nɔt], *s.f.* traditional women's head-dress from Saintonge.

kick(-starter) [kik(startœːr)], *s.m. Motor Cy:* kick starter.

kidnappage [kidnapaːʒ], *s.m.* kidnapping.

kidnapper [kidnape], *v.tr. F:* (*a*) to kidnap; (*b*) to pinch, steal.

kidnappeur, -euse [kidnapœːr, -øːz], *s. F:* kidnapper.

kidnapping [kidnapiŋ], *s.m. F:* kidnapping.

kieselguhr [kizɛlguːr], *s.m. Miner:* kieselguhr; infusorial earth.

kiesérite [kiezerit], *s.f. Miner:* kieserite.

kievien, -ienne [kjevjɛ̃, -jɛn], *a. & s.* Kievan; *Hist:* **Russie kievienne,** Kievan Russia.

kif [kif], *s.m.* cannabis.

kif-kif [kifkif], *a.inv. P:* same, likewise; **c'est k.-k. (bourricot),** *s.m.* **c'est du kif,** it's all one, it's six of one and half a dozen of the other, it's as broad as it's long.

kiki [kiki], *s.m. P:* neck, throat; **serrer le k. à qn,** to throttle s.o.

kil [kil], *s.m. P:* **un k. de rouge,** a litre of wine.

killinite [kilinit], *s.f. Miner:* killinite.

kilo- [kilɔ], *pref.* kilo-; **kiloampère,** kiloampère.

kilo [kilo], *s.m. F:* (= **kilogramme**), kilo.

kiloampère [kilɔɑ̃pɛːr], *s.m. El:* kiloampere.

kilocalorie [kilɔkalɔri], *s.f. Ph:* kilo(gram) calorie, large calorie.

kilocycle [kilɔsikl], *s.m. Ph: El.E:* kilocycle.

kiloerg [kilɔɛrg], *s.m. Ph.Meas:* kilerg.

kilogramme [kilɔgram], *s.m. Meas:* kilogram(me) (= 2.2 lbs).

kilogrammètre [kilɔgrammɛtr], *s.m. Med:* kilogrammeter, kilogrammetre.

kilohertz [kilɔɛrtz], *El:* kilocycle.

kilojoule [kilɔʒul], *s.m. Meas:* kilojoule.

kilolitre [kilɔlitr], *s.m. Meas:* kilolitre.

kilométrage [kilɔmetraːʒ], *s.m.* **1.** (*a*) measuring (of road, etc.) in kilometres; (*b*) marking off (of road) with kilometre stones. **2.** length in kilometres, mileage.

kilomètre [kilɔmɛtr], *s.m. Meas:* kilometre (= 0.624 mile); *Rail: Adm:* **voyageurs kilomètres,** passenger kilometres; **tonnes-kilomètres marchandises,** ton kilometres.

kilomètre-passager [kilɔmɛtrpasaʒe], *s.m. Adm: Av:* passenger-kilometre; *pl. kilomètres-passagers.*

kilométrer [kilɔmetre], *v.tr.* (**je kilomètre, n. kilométrons; je kilométrerai**) (*a*) to measure (road, etc.) in kilometres; (*b*) to mark off (road) with kilometre stones (= milestones).

kilomètre-voyageur [kilɔmɛtrvwajaʒœːr], *s.m. Adm:* passenger-kilometre; *pl. kilomètres-voyageurs.*

kilométrique [kilɔmetrik], *a.* kilometric(al); **borne k.,** kilometre stone (= milestone); *Aut:* **indemnité k.** = mileage allowance.

kilotonne [kilɔtɔn], *s.f. Meas:* kiloton.

kilovolt [kilɔvɔlt], *s.m. El:* kilovolt.

kilovoltampère [kilɔvɔltɑ̃pɛːr], *s.m. El:* kilovolt-ampere; *pl. kilovolts-ampères.*

kilowatt [kilɔwat], *s.m. El:* kilowatt.

kilowattheure [kilɔwatœːr], *s.m. El:* kilowatt-hour.

kilt [kilt], *s.m. Scot: Cost:* kilt.

kimberlite [kɛ̃bɛrlit], *s.f. Geol: Min:* kimberlite.

kimmeridgien [kimeridʒjɛ̃], *a. & s.m. Geol:* Kimmeridgian.

kimono [kimɔno], *s.m. Cost:* kimono; **manche k.,** kimono sleeve.

kinase [kinɑːz], *s.f. Bio-Ch:* kinase.

kinescope [kinɛskɔp], *s.m. T.V:* kinescope.

kinésie [kinezi], *s.f.* kinesis.

kinésimètre [kinezimɛtr], *s.m. Med:* kinesi(o)-meter.

kinésique [kinezik], *a. Med:* kinesthetic, kinaesthetic.

kinésithérapeute [kineziterapøt], *a. & s. Med:* kinesitherapist, kinesipathist.

kinésithérapie [kineziterapi], *s.f. Med:* kinesitherapy, kinesipathy.

kinesthésie [kinɛstezi], *s.f.* kinesthesia, kinesthesis.

kinesthésique [kinɛstezik], *a. Med:* kinesthetic, kinaesthetic.

kinétographe [kinetɔgraf], *s.m. Cin:* kinetograph.

kinétoscope [kinetɔskɔp], *s.m. Cin:* kinetoscope.

king-charles [kiŋʃarl], *s.m.inv.* King Charles spaniel.

kinkajou [kɛ̃kaʒu], *s.m. Z:* kinkajou, honey bear.

kino [kino], *s.m. Pharm: etc:* kino; **k. du Bengale,** kino, Bengal kino, butea gum.

kinoplasma [kinoplasma], *s.m. Biol:* kinoplasm.

kinostermidés [kinɔstɛrmide], *s.m.pl. Rept:* Kinostermidae.

kiosque [kjɔsk], *s.m.* **1.** (*a*) kiosk (in public park, etc.); **k. de, à, musique,** bandstand; **k. de jardin,** summerhouse; (*b*) newspaper stall, flower stall; **k. à journaux,** newspaper kiosk. **2.** *Nau:* (*a*) house; **k. de la barre,** wheel-house; **k. de veille, de navigation,** pilot house, chart house, room; (*b*) conning tower (of submarine). **3.** *El.E:* **k. de transformation,** transformer box, tower.

kip [kip], *s.m.* Cambodian piastre.

kirghize, kirghise [kirgiːz], *a. & s.m.inv. Ethn:* Kirghiz, Khirghiz.

kirsch [kirʃ], *s.m.* kirsch.

kitool, kit(t)ul [kitɔl], *s.m. Tex:* kittul, kitool.

kiwi [kiwi], *s.m.* (*a*) *Orn:* kiwi, apteryx; (*b*) *Sp:* (*member of New Zealand rugby team*) Kiwi.

klaprothite [klaprɔtit], *s.f. Miner:* klaprothite, klaprotholite.

klakson, Klaxon [klaksɔn, -ɔ̃], *s.m. Aut: R.t.m:* Klaxon, horn, hooter; *Nau: etc:* **K. d'alarme,** alarm rattler.

klaxonner [klaksɔne], *v.i. & tr. Aut:* to hoot, to sound one's horn, to honk; *F:* **il m'a klaxonné,** he hooted at me.

klaubage [klobaːʒ], *s.m. Min:* bucking, cobbing, sorting.

klauber [klobe], *v.tr. Min:* to buck, to cob, to sort.

klebs [klɛb(s)], *s.m. P:* dog, tyke.

klecksographie [klɛksɔgrafi], *s.f. Psy:* ink-blot test.

klephte [klɛft], *s.m.* klepht, (Greek) brigand.

klepper [klepœːr], *s.m. Breed:* klepper.

kleptomane [klɛptɔman], *a. & s.* kleptomaniac.

kleptomanie [klɛptɔmani], *s.f.* kleptomania.

klik [klik], *s.m. Ling:* click.

klippe [klip], *s.m. Geol:* klippe, outlier.

klukia [klykja], *s.m. Paleo-Bot:* klukia.

klydonographe [klidɔnɔgraf], *s.m. R.t.m: El:* Klydonograph.

klystron [klistrɔ̃], *s.m. Elcs:* klystron; **k. à glissement,** drift-tube klystron; **k. fonctionnant en sous tension, en sustension,** underbunching, overbunching, klystron.

knautia [knotja], *s.m. Bot:* knautia.

knébélite [knebelit], *s.f. Miner:* knebelite.

knickerbockers [knikœrbɔkœːr], **knicker(s)** [knikœːr(z)], *s.m.pl. Cost:* plus-fours.

knobben [knobən], *s.m. Bot: Com:* knopper.

knock-out [knɔkut, nɔkaut], *Box:* **1.** *a.inv.* **mettre (qn) k.-o.,** to knock (s.o.) out; **être k.-o.,** to be knocked out. **2.** *s.m.* knock-out.

knockouter [(k)nɔk(ɑ)ute], *v.tr. Box:* to knock out (opponent).

knopite [knɔpit], *s.f. Miner:* knopite.

knoppern [knɔpɛrn], *s.m. Bot: Com:* knopper.

Knossos [(k)nɔsɔs], *Pr.n.m. A.Geog:* Cnossus, Cnossos, Knossos.

knout [knut], *s.m.* **1.** knout, Russian scourge. **2.** (*punishment*) knout.

knouter [knute], *v.tr.* to knout.

knoxvillite [knɔksvilit], *s.f. Miner:* knoxvillite, magnesiocopiapite.

koa [kɔa], *s.m. Bot:* koa (acacia).

koala [kɔala], *s.m. Z:* koala.

kob [kɔb], **kobus** [kɔbyːs], *s.m. Z:* kobus; water antelope, water buck; **k. singsing,** singsing, (West African) water antelope, water buck.

kobellite [kɔbɛlit], *s.f. Miner:* kobellite.

kobez [kɔbɛːz], *s.m. Orn:* **faucon k.,** red-footed falcon.

kobold [kɔbɔld], *s.m. Myth:* kobold.

kœchlinite [køʃlinit], *s.f. Miner:* koechlinite.

kogia [kɔʒja], *s.m. Z:* kogia; pygmy sperm whale.

kohol [kɔɔl], *s.m. Toil:* kohl.

kola [kɔla], *s.m. Bot:* cola, kola; **noix de k.,** cola nut, kola nut, goora nut.

kolatier [kɔlatje], *s.m. Bot:* cola, kola, tree.

kolback [kɔlbak], *s.m. Mil.Cost:* colback.

kolinski [kɔlɛ̃ski], *s.m. Com:* (*Fur*) kolinsky; Russian mink or polecat.

kolkhose, kolkhoz(e) [kɔlkoːz], *s.m.* kolkhoz, collective farm.

kolkhozien, -ienne [kɔlkozjɛ̃, -jɛn], *a. & s.* **1.** *s.* kolkhoznik, member of a collective farm. **2.** *a.* pertaining to a kolkhoz; **production kolkhozienne,** kolkhoz output.

kombé [kɔ̃be], *s.m. Pharm:* strophanthus.

kominform [kɔminfɔrm], *s.m. Pol.Hist:* cominform.

komintern [kɔmintɛrn], *s.m. Pol.Hist:* comintern.

kommandatur [kɔmɑ̃datyːr], *s.f. German Mil. Adm:* kommandatura, kommandantur.

kommando [kɔmɑ̃do], *s.m.* prisoner-of-war camp in Germany (1939-1945).

Komsomol [kɔmsɔmɔl], *s.m. Pol:* Komsomol, Comsomol.

konel [kɔnɛl], *s.m.* konel metal.

koninckite [kɔnɛ̃kit], *s.f. Miner:* koninckite.

kope(c)k [kɔpɛk], *s.m. Num:* copeck, kopec(k); *F:* **ne plus avoir un k. (en poche),** to be broke.

kopje [kɔpʒe], *s.m. Geol:* kopje.

koppa [kɔpa], *s.m. A.Gr.Alph:* koppa.

koppite [kɔpit], *s.f. Miner:* koppite.

Koran (le) [ləkɔrɑ̃], *Pr.n.m.* the Koran.

Kordofan (le) [ləkɔrdɔfɑ̃], *Pr.n.m. Geog:* the Kordofan (region).

koré [kɔre], *s.f. Gr.Art:* kore.

koréite [kɔreit], *s.f. Miner:* agalmatolite.

korfball [kɔrfbɑl], *s.m. Sp:* Dutch basketball.

kornélite [kɔrnelit], *s.f. Miner:* kornelite.

kornérupine [kɔrnerypin], *s.f. Miner:* kornerupine.

korrigan, -ane [kɔrigɑ̃, -an], *s.* (*in Brittany*) goblin, evil sprite.

koto [kɔto], *s.m. Mus:* koto.

köttigite [køtiʒit], *s.f. Miner:* köttigite, koettigite.

koudou [kudu], *s.m. Z:* kudu; **grand k.,** greater kudu.

kouffa [kufa], *s.m. Nau:* gufa, goofah.

koufique [kufik], *a. & s. Pal:* Cufic.

koukri [kukri], *s.m.* kukri, Gurkha knife.

koulak [kulak], *s.m.* kulak (rich Russian peasant).

Koumassi [kumasi], *Pr.n. Geog:* Kumasi.

koumis(s), koumys [kumis], *s.m.* koumiss, kumiss.

koumquat [kumkwat], *s.m. Bot:* cumquat, kumquat.

kouprey [kuprɛ], *s.m. Z:* **k. du Cambodge,** kouprey, Cambodian forest ox.

kourgane [kurgaːn], *s.m. Archeol:* kurgan.

Kourile [kuril], *Geog:* **1.** *a.* **les îles Kouriles,** the Kuril(e) Islands. **2.** *s.* Kurile, Kurilian.

Kouro-sivo (le) [ləkurosivo], *Pr.n.m. Oc:* the Japan current, the Japan stream, the Kuroshiwo.

kourtka [kurtka], *s.m. A.Mil: Cost:* jacket worn by lancers.

Koush [kuʃ], *Pr.n.m. B.Hist: A.Geog:* Cush, Kush.

kraâl [kraːl], *s.m.* kraal.

krach [krak], *s.m.* (financial) crash, smash (*esp.* of a bank); **il a perdu tout ce qu'il possédait dans le k. de sa banque,** he lost everything when his bank went smash.

krachena [krakena], *s.m.* Algerian tobacco.

kraft [kraft], *s.m. Paperm:* kraft.

kraken [kraken], *s.m. Myth:* kraken.

krameria [kramerja], *s.m.*, **kramérie** [krameri], *s.f. Bot:* krameria; rhatany.

kraps, kreps [kraps, krɛps], *s.m. Games:* craps.

krarupisation [krarypizasjɔ̃], *s.f. Tp: Tg:* Krarup, continuous, loading.

kraton [kratɔ̃], *s.m.* palace of Javanese or Madurese prince.

kraurosis [krorosis], *s.m. Path:* kraurosis.

Krause [kraus], *Pr.n. Anat:* **corpuscules de K.,** Krause's corpuscles.

krausite [krosit], *s.f. Miner:* krausite.

krémersite [kremɛrsit], *s.f. Miner:* kremersite.

Kremlin (le) [ləkrɛmlɛ̃], *s.m.* the Kremlin.

kremlinologie [kremlinɔlɔʒi], *s.f.* kremlinology.

kremlinologiste [kremlinɔlɔʒist], *s.m. & f.* kremlinologist.

krennérite [krenerit], *s.f. Miner:* krennerite.

kriegspiel [krigspil], *s.m. Mil:* kriegspiel, war game.

krill [kril], *s.m. Z:* krill.

Krishna, Kri(t)chna [kri(t)ʃna], *Pr.n.m. Rel:* Krishna.

kriss [kris], *s.m.* kris, Malay dagger.

kröhnkite [krønkit], *s.f. Miner:* kroehnkite.

kronprinz [krɔnprints], *s.m.* Crown Prince (of Prussia).

Krupp [krup], *Pr.n. Metall:* **maladie de K.,** temper brittleness.

kryokonite [krijɔkɔnit], *s.f. Geol:* kryokonite.

krypton [kriptɔ̃], *s.m. Ch:* krypton.

ksar [ksaːr], *s.m. (in North Africa)* fortress; fortified village; *pl. ksour* [ksur].

ksi [ksi], *s.m. Gr.Alph:* ksi.

ksouriens [ksurjɛ̃], *s.m.pl.* inhabitants of a *ksar.*

ku-dzu [kudzu], *s.m.inv. Bot:* kudzu (vine).

kummel [kymɛl], *s.m.* kümmel (liqueur).

kumquat [kymkwat], *s.m. Bot:* kumquat, cumquat.

kupferblende [kupfɛrblɛːd], *s.f. Miner:* copperblende.

kupfernickel [kupfɛrnikɛl], *s.m.* kupfernickel, niccolite.

Kupffer [kypfɛr], *Pr.n. Anat:* **cellules de K.,** Kupffer cells.

Kurde [kyrd]. **1.** *s.m. & f. Ethn:* Kurd. **2.** *a.* Kurdish. **3.** *s.m. Ling:* Kurdish.

Kurdistan [kyrdistɑ̃], *Pr.n.m. Geog:* Kurdistan.

kurtosis [kyrtozis], *s.m. (statistics)* kurtosis.

kwas [kvas], *s.m.* kvass (beer).

kyaniser [kjanize], *v.tr.* to kyanize.

kybistétère [kibisteːr], *s.m. Gr.Ant:* kubistetic dancer, acrobat.

kylix [kiliks], *s.f. Gr.Ant:* kylix.

kymographe [kimɔgraf], *s.m. Med: etc:* kymograph.

kymographie [kimɔgrafi], *s.f. Med: etc:* kymography.

kymomètre [kimɔmɛtr̩], *s.m. Med: etc:* sphygmomanometer.

kymrique [kimrik], *a. & s.m. Ethn: Ling:* Cymric; Welsh.

kyriale [kirjal], *s.m. Ecc.Mus:* kyrial(l)e.

kyrie [kirje], *s.m. Ecc:* Kyrie (eleison).

kyrielle [kirjɛl], *s.f.* **1.** *A:* litany. **2.** *F:* rigmarole, long string (of words, etc.); **toute une k. de noms, d'enfants,** a whole string of names, of children. **3.** *Pros: A:* kyrielle.

kyriologique [kirjɔlɔʒik], *a.* **écriture k.,** curiologic, kyriologic, writing.

kyste [kist], *s.m. Med:* cyst; **k. synovial,** ganglion; **k. branchial,** branchial cyst; **k. dermoïde,** dermoid cyst; **k. épithélial,** epithelial cyst; **k. mucoïde, k. muqueux,** mucous cyst; **k. intraosseux,** bone cyst; *Dent:* **k. dentaire, d'origine dentaire,** dental, odontogenic, cyst.

kysteux, kystique [kistø, kistik], *a. Med:* cystic.

kystitome [kistitɔm], *s.m. Opt.Surg:* cystotome.

kystitomie [kistitɔmi], *s.f. Opt.Surg:* cystotomy.

L

L, l [ɛl], *s.m. or f.* (the letter) L, l; *Tp:* L. comme Louis, L for Lucy; *Phon:* l. mouillé(e), liquid l, palatal(ized) l; (*final* l, *if silent, is not subject to liaison*; un gentil enfant [ʒɑ̃tiɑ̃fɑ̃].)

l', la¹ [la], *def. article & pron. f.* See LE¹,².

la², *s.m.inv. Mus:* **1.** (a) (the note) A; morceau en la, piece in A; donner le la à l'orchestre, to give the A to the orchestra; les huit premières lignes donnent le la du livre, the first eight lines set the tone of the book; (b) the A string (of violin, etc.). **2.** la (in the fixed do system).

là [la], *adv.* **1.** (*of place*) there; (a) je l'ai rencontré là, I met him there; là où vous êtes, where you are; une dame qui était là, a lady who was there, who was present; quand il n'est pas là, when he isn't there, when he is away; *F:* est-ce que le patron est là? is the boss in? les choses en sont là, this is the state of things at the moment; les choses en sont là que . . ., matters are at such a point that . . .; en êtes-vous là avec lui? have you got that far with him? sa maladie en est-elle là? is his illness as bad as that? has his illness reached that point? à cinq pas de là se tenait . . ., five paces away stood . . .; *F:* ôtez-vous de là! get out of there! get out of that! passez par là, go that way; si je n'étais pas là vous mourriez de faim, if it weren't for me you would die of hunger; là en bas, down there; ce n'est pas là que je vise, that's not what I'm after; il va falloir en passer par là, we'll have to go through all that; *F:* elle a trente-cinq ans, par-là, she is thirty-five or thereabouts; elle est triste, mais de là à se jeter à l'eau . . ., she's unhappy, but she won't drown herself yet, but not to the point of drowning herself yet; (= ici) il est là, he is here; *F:* viens là! come here! (b) (*emphatic use*) c'est là la question, that is the question; c'est là qu'il demeure, that is where he lives; que dites-vous là? what's that you're saying? ce, cette, etc. . . .-là, *see* CE¹ 1, CE² 5; celui-là, celle-là, *see* CELUI 4; (c) *F:* pour la pêche je suis (un peu) là, when it comes to fishing I know what I'm talking about, what I'm doing; comme menteur il est un peu là! he's a pretty good liar! en fait de tours de cartes il est un peu là! he's some conjuror! elle est un peu là, (i) she makes her presence felt; (ii) she takes up a lot of room, she's no sylph; (d) là où . . ., when, whereas; il a dit là où il aurait dû dire non, he said yes when he should have said no. **2.** (*of time*) then; d'ici là, between now and then; in the meantime; à quelques jours de là, some days after (that); a few days later; *O:* dès là, (i) at once, (ii) from that time onwards. **3.** (= cela) qu'entendez-vous par là? what do you mean by that? il faut le tirer de là, we must get him out of that; de là dépendent vos destins, your fate hinges on that; il suit de là que . . ., it follows from that, therefrom, that . . .; on l'avait roulé, de là sa fureur, he had been swindled, hence his rage; ce n'est pas un méchant homme, loin de là, he is not a bad man, far from it; *A:* je n'ai rien à dire là-contre, I have nothing to say against it, I have no objection (to it). **4.** *int.* (a) là! voilà qui est fait, there now! that's done; là, là! ne vous inquiétez point, there now, don't you worry; (*to child*) là, là! there, there; (b) moderately; est-il riche?—là, là! is he rich?—so so! fairly; là! ne vous pressez pas, gently! don't hurry; (c) oh là là! (i) oh dear! (ii) (*jeeringly*) look at him!

look at her! (d) *Ven:* là, là! hark away! hark forward! hark back!

laager [lagɛːr], *s.m. Hist:* (in S. Africa) laager; former (des wagons) en l., mettre (des gens) en l., to laager (wag(g)ons, people); (*of pers.*) se mettre en l., to laager.

lab¹ [lab], *s.m. Bio-Ch:* labenzyme.

lab², *s.m. F:* lab(oratory).

labadens [labadɛ̃ːs], *s.m. F:* **1.** *A:* (type of) cramming schoolmaster. **2.** *Lit:* old schoolfellow; (*from the Pensionnat Labadens, in Labiche's L'Affaire de la rue de Lourcine*).

labadisme [labadism], *s.m. Rel.H:* Labadism.

labadiste [labadist], *a. & s. Rel.H:* Labadist.

labanotation [labanɔtasjɔ̃], *s.f. Danc:* labanotation.

labarum [labarɔm], *s.m. Hist:* labarum.

là-bas [labɑ], *adv.* over there; regardez ce nuage là-b., look at that cloud over there; par là-b. en France, over, somewhere, in France; le voilà là-b., there he is over there.

labbe [lab], *s.m. Orn:* skua; l. à longue queue, long-tailed, Buffon's, skua; l. cataracte, grand l., great skua, *U.S:* skua; l. parasite, Arctic skua, *U.S:* Arctic jaeger; l. pomarin, pomarine skua, *U.S:* pomarine jaeger.

labdacisme [labdasism], *s.m. Ling:* lambdacism.

labdanum [labdanɔm], *s.m. Ch:* labdanum.

label [labɛl], *s.m. Com:* (a) trade-union mark, label (on manufactured article *esp.* on published work); (b) label, seal of approval; l. de qualité, quality label. **2.** trade-union list of approved retailers.

labelle [labɛl], *s.m.* **1.** *Bot:* label(lum), lip (of orchids). **2.** *Conch:* (of certain shells) lip. **3.** *Ent:* labium, lip.

labéo [labeo], *s.m. Ich:* bearded barbel.

labeur [labœːr], *s.m.* **1.** labour, toil, hard work. **2.** *Typ:* bookwork; imprimerie de l., book printing works. **3.** (= LABOUR); cheval de l., plough-horse; terre en l., ploughed land.

labeurier [labœrje], *s.m. Typ:* (book) compositor.

labferment [labfɛrmɑ̃], *s.m. Bio-Ch:* labenzyme.

labiacées [labjase], *s.f.pl. Bot:* Labiatae.

labial, -ale, -iaux [labjal, -jo], *a.* labial (muscle, etc.); *Ling:* consonne labiale, *s.f.* labiale, lip consonant, labial; voyelle labiale, rounded, labial, vowel; lecture labiale, lip-reading.

labialisation [labjalizasjɔ̃], *s.f. Ling:* labialization.

labialiser [labjalize], *v.tr. Ling:* to labialize.

labidognathes [labidɔgnat], *s.m.pl. Arach:* Labidognatha.

labidure [labidyːr], *s.f. Ent:* large nocturnal earwig.

labie [labi], *s.f. Ent:* small earwig.

labié [labje], *a. Bot:* labiate, lipped.

labiées [labje], *s.f.pl. Bot: A:* Labiatae.

labile [labil], *a.* **1.** *Biol: Ch: Med:* labile, unstable. **2.** untrustworthy (memory).

labilité [labilite], *s.f. Biol: Ch:* lability.

labiodental, -ale, -aux [labjɔdɑ̃tal, -o], *Ling: a.* labiodental; *s.f.* labiodentale, labiodental (consonant).

labio-glosso-pharyngé [labjɔglɔsofarɛ̃ʒe], *a. Med:* paralysie l.-g.-pharyngée, labioglossopharyngeal paralysis.

labionasal, -ale, -aux [labjɔnazal, -o], *a. Ling:* labionasal.

labiopalatal, -ale, -aux [labjɔpalatal, -o], *a. Ling:* labiopalatal.

labiovélaire [labjɔvelɛːr], *a. & s.f. Ling:* labiovelar.

labium [labjɔm], *s.m. Ent:* labium.

labo¹ [labo], *s.m. F:* lab(oratory).

labo², *s.m. Dressm:* canvas lining.

laborantin, -ine [labɔrɑ̃tɛ̃, -in], *s.* laboratory assistant.

laboratoire [labɔratwaːr], *s.m.* **1.** *Ch: etc:* laboratory; l. de recherche, research laboratory; l. industriel, technical laboratory; l. d'essai, testing laboratory, plant; essayé, éprouvé, en l., laboratory-tested; chercheur de l., (scientific) research worker; l. de langues, language laboratory; *Civ.E:* route l., experimental road; *Atom.Ph:* l. nucléaire, nuclear research laboratory; l. de haute activité, radioactif, *F:* chaud, highly radioactive, *F:* hot, laboratory; l. non-radioactif, non-radioactive, *F:* cold, laboratory; l. d'analyses (médicales), pathology laboratory, *F:* path. lab.; l. bactériologique, bacteriological laboratory; l. de prothèse dentaire, dental laboratory; *Phot:* l. obscur, darkroom. **2.** *Metall:* hearth, chamber (of furnace).

laborieusement [labɔrjøzmɑ̃], *adv.* laboriously; gagner l. sa vie, son pain, vivre l., to work hard for a living.

laborieux, -euse [labɔrjø, -øːz], *a.* **1.** arduous, hard (work, etc.); laboured (diction, etc.); digestion laborieuse, sluggish digestion; mets d'une digestion laborieuse, dish hard to digest; accouchement l., difficult confinement; plaisanterie laborieuse, laboured joke. **2.** (*of pers.*) laborious, hard-working; les classes laborieuses, the working classes.

labour [labuːr], *s.m.* (a) tilling, tillage; *esp.* ploughing; l. à la bêche, digging; donner un l. à un champ, to plough a field; chevaux de l., plough horses; (b) terres de l., les labours, ploughed land.

labourable [laburabl], *a.* arable, tillable (land); plough(land).

labourage [laburaːʒ], *s.m.* (a) tilling, *esp.* ploughing; (b) arable land.

labourer [labure], **1.** *v.tr.* (a) to till, *esp.* to plough, *U.S:* to plow (land); l. à la bêche, to dig; commencer à l., to break ground; pré que les taupes ont labouré, meadow ploughed up, churned up, by moles; les canons ont labouré ce champ, the guns have ploughed up this field; (b) *Nau:* l. le fond, (i) (*of ship*) to graze the bottom; (ii) (*of anchor*) to drag; (c) se l. le visage, to lacerate one's face; visage labouré de rides, face furrowed with wrinkles. **2.** *v.i. A:* to labour, toil.

laboureur [laburœːr], *s.m. Agr:* **1.** *A:* farmer. **2.** farm labourer, agricultural labourer; *esp.* ploughman, *U.S:* plowman.

laboureuse [laburøːz], *s.f.* **1.** *Agr:* motor cultivator. **2.** *Ent: F:* mole-cricket.

Labrador [labradɔːr]. **1.** *Pr.n.m. Geog:* Labrador; courant du L., Labrador current. **2.** *s.m. Miner:* = LABRADORITE. **3.** chien du L., *s.m.* un l., Labrador (retriever).

labradorite [labradɔrit], *s.f. Miner:* labradorite, Labrador feldspar.

labre [lɑːbr], *s.m.* **1.** *Nat.Hist:* labrum, lip. **2.** *Ich:* labrus, wrasse; l. (des coraux), puddingwife; l. commun, ballan wrasse.

labret [labrɛ], *s.m.* labret.

labridés [labride], *s.m.pl. Ich:* Labridae, the wrasses.

labroïde [labrɔid], *a. & s.m. Ich:* labroid.

labrusca [labryska], *s.m. Vit:* labrusca vine, wild vine, *vitis labrusca.*

laburne [labyrn], **laburnum** [labyrnɔm], *s.m. Bot:* laburnum.

labyrinthe [labirɛ̃:t], *s.m.* **1.** (*a*) labyrinth, maze; (*b*) *Psy:* **test des labyrinthes,** maze test; **technique des labyrinthes,** maze learning. **2.** *Anat:* labyrinth (of the ear). **3.** *Arch:* labyrinth. **4.** *Mec.E:* **(joint) l.,** labyrinth (packing), high-pressure end (of turbine).

labyrinthiformes [labirɛ̃tifɔrm], *s.m.pl. Ich:* Labyrinthici.

labyrinthique [labirɛ̃tik], *a.* labyrinthian, labyrinthine.

labyrinthite [labirɛ̃tit], *s.f. Med:* labyrinthitis.

labyrinthodontes [labirɛ̃tɔdɔ̃:t], *s.m.pl. Paleont:* Labyrinthodontia.

labyrinthule [labirɛ̃tyl], *s.f. Biol:* Labyrinthula.

lac [lak], *s.m.* (*a*) *Geog:* lake; **l. volcanique,** lake of volcanic origin; **l. de cratère,** crater lake; **l. tectonique,** tectonic lake; **l. glaciaire,** lake of glacial origin; **l. de barrage,** barrier lake; **l. de cirque,** tarn; **l. en forme de croissant,** oxbow lake; **l. salé,** salt lake; **l. asséché,** dry lake; **les lacs de l'Écosse,** the lochs of Scotland, the Scottish lochs; **le l. Léman,** the lake of Geneva; **le l. Baïkal,** Lake Baikal; **le l. Trasimène,** Lake Trasimene; *F:* (*of pers.*) **être dans le l.,** to be in the soup; to be in a hopeless fix; *F:* (*of project, etc.*) **tomber dans le l.,** to fizzle out; to come to grief; (*b*) *Anat:* **l. lacrymal,** lachrymal sac; **lacs sanguins,** venous sinuses.

laçage [lasa:ʒ], *s.m.* lacing (up) (of shoes, etc.).

laccase [laka:z], *s.f. Ch:* laccase.

laccifère [laksifɛ:r], *a. Bot:* lac-bearing, -producing.

laccol [lakɔl], *s.m. Ch:* laccol.

laccolite, laccolithe [lakɔlit], *s.f. Geol:* laccolite, laccolith.

lac-dye [lakdaj], *s.m. Dy:* lacdye.

lacé [lase], *s.m.* chain of prisms (of chandelier).

Lacédémone [lasedemɔn], *Pr.n.f. A.Geog:* Lacedaemon, Sparta.

lacédémonien, -ienne [lasedemɔnjɛ̃, -jɛn], *a. & s.* Lacedaemonian.

lacement [lasmɑ̃], *s.m.* lacing (up) (of shoes, etc.).

lacer [lase], *v.tr.* **(je laçai(s); n. laçons) 1.** (*a*) to lace (up) (shoe, etc.); *Nau:* **l. une bonnette à une voile,** to lace a bonnet to a sail; **corset qui se lace sur le côté,** corset that laces at the side; (*b*) **l. un filet,** to make a net, to net; (*c*) *Nau:* to belay (rope). **2.** (*of dog*) to cover, line (bitch).

se lacer, to lace up one's shoes, etc.; *A:* (*of woman*) to lace oneself in, up.

lacérable [laserabl̩], *a.* lacerable.

lacération [laserasjɔ̃], *s.f.* laceration. **1.** tearing, lacerating, slashing; defacing (of poster, etc.); mauling (by wild beast). **2.** tear, jagged wound.

lacéré [lasere], *a.* (*a*) lacerated; torn to shreds; (*b*) *Bot:* lacerate (leaf).

lacérer [lasere], *v.tr.* **(je lacère, n. lacérons; je lacérerai)** to tear, lacerate, maul; to tear, slash (sth.) to pieces; to deface (poster).

laceret [las(ə)rɛ], *s.m.* **1.** *Tls:* small auger; spoon auger. **2.** screw-eye.

lacerie [las(ə)ri], *s.f.* fine open-work basketry, wickerwork.

laceron [las(ə)rɔ̃], *s.m. Bot:* = LAITERON 1.

lacertidés [lasɛrtide], *s.m.pl. Rept:* Lacertidae, the Old World lizards.

lacertien [lasɛrtjɛ̃], *a. & s.m. Rept:* lacertian, lacertilian; *s.m.pl.* **lacertiens,** Lacertilia.

lacertiforme [lasɛrtifɔrm], *a.* lacertiform, lacertian; lizard-like.

lacertiliens [lasɛrtiljɛ̃], *s.m.pl. Rept:* Lacertilia.

lacet [lasɛ], *s.m.* **1.** (*a*) lace (of shoe, etc.); bootlace, shoelace; *Nau:* lacing (of sail); **chaussures à lacets,** lace-up shoes; (*b*) **mouvement de l.,** (i) *Rail:* swaying, rocking (of carriages); hammering (of engine), (ii) *Av:* yaw(ing); **angle de l.,** angle of yaw; **axe des lacets,** yaw axis; **moment de l.,** yawing moment; **plan de l.,** yawing plane; **amplitude de l.,** yaw rate; **amortisseur de l.,** yaw damper; *Rail:* **dispositif anti-l.,** stabilizing device; (*c*) *Needlw:* **l. de broderie,** embroidery braid; **dentelle au l.,** imitation lacework; (*d*) gold and silver lacework. **2.** hairpin bend (in road); **sentier en lacets,** winding, twisting, path; zigzag path; **la route fait un l. dangereux à . . .,** there is a dangerous hairpin bend at . . .; **les lacets de la route,** the windings of the road. **3.** (*a*) noose, springe, snare (for rabbits, etc.); *pl.* toils; **prendre un lapin au l.,** to snare a rabbit; **tendre un l.,** to set a snare; **tendre des lacets à qn,** to lay traps for s.o.; **pris dans ses propres lacets,** caught in his own snare; hoist with his own petard; (*b*) *Mil:* wire-loop entanglement; (*c*) (Turkish) bowstring (as instrument of execution); **étrangler qn avec un l.,** to bowstring s.o.; (*d*) (cowboy's) bolas. **4.** pin (of hinge). **5.** *Algae:* **l. de mer,** sea whipcord. **6.** *Med:* **signe du l.,** Rumpel-Leede sign (in scarlet fever).

laceur, -euse [lasœ:r, -ø:z], *s.* net-maker, netter.

lâchage [lɑʃa:ʒ], *s.m.* **1.** releasing (of bomb from aircraft, etc). **2.** *F:* dropping, shedding (of acquaintance); jilting (of lover, fiancé(e)).

lâche [lɑ:ʃ], *a.* **1.** (*a*) loose, slack (spring, knot, etc.); loosely fitting (garment); lax (discipline); woolly, slipshod, careless, (style); *A:* **il a le ventre l.,** his bowels are loose; (*b*) *A:* slack, indolent; **être l. au travail,** to be slack at one's work. **2.** (*a*) cowardly; *s.m. & f.* coward; (*b*) low, despicable.

lâché [lɑʃe], *a.* slovenly, slipshod (work, style).

lâchement¹ [lɑʃmɑ̃], *adv.* **1.** *A:* (*a*) loosely, slackly; (*b*) indolently, slackly. **2.** in a cowardly manner.

lâchement², *s.m.* releasing, slackening (of rope, etc.); giving up (of situation, etc.); freeing, letting loose (of animal, etc.).

lachenalia [laʃnalja], *s.m. Bot:* lachenalia.

lâcher [lɑʃe]. **I. 1.** *v.tr.* to release; (*a*) to slacken, loosen (spring, etc.); **l. la détente (d'un fusil),** to release, pull, the trigger (of gun); **l. un coup de fusil à qn,** to fire at s.o.; **l. une bordée,** to fire, let fly, a broadside; **l. un coup de pied à qn,** to let fly at s.o. with one's foot; **l. une écluse,** to open a lock; *Aut:* **l. le frein,** to release the brake; *Aut:* **l. brusquement la pédale d'embrayage,** to let out the clutch (pedal) abruptly; *A:* **l. le ventre,** to relax the bowels; *A:* **l. un robinet,** to turn on a tap; *s.a.* BRIDE 1; (*b*) to let go; to leave go of (sth.); to drop (sth.); *Av:* to release (bomb); to drop (parachutist); **lâchez-moi!** let me go! (*of bird*) **l. sa proie,** to drop its prey; **il ne lâcha pas la corde,** he retained his hold on the rope; *F:* **l. un emploi, un travail,** to throw up, chuck (in), a job; **l. la politique,** to drop politics; **l. pied,** to give ground, to give way; (*of troops*) to break, to take to flight; **l. prise,** (i) to let go; to lose one's hold; (ii) to give in; *F:* **l. qn,** (i) to drop s.o., s.o.'s acquaintance; (ii) to leave s.o. in the lurch; **l. un parti,** to break away from a party; *F:* **l. des sous, les l.,** to fork out; **il les lâche avec un élastique,** you have to drag the money out of him; (*c*) to set free (prisoner, bird, etc.); to let (animal) loose; **l. un chien,** to unleash a dog; to let a dog loose; *Ven:* to slip a dog; **l. le chien contre qn,** to set the dog on s.o.; **l. les eaux d'une écluse,** to let the water out of a lock; *Mch:* **l. la vapeur,** to blow off steam; *F:* **l. un juron,** to let out, rap out, an oath; **l. un secret,** to blurt out, let out, a secret; *P:* **l. le paquet,** to spill the beans; **l. des gros mots,** to use bad language; *F:* **l. de l'eau,** *P:* **l. les écluses,** to make water; *F:* **l. un vent,** to break wind. **2.** *v.i.* (*a*) to get loose; (*of spring, etc.*) to slacken; (*of rope*) to slip; (*of gun*) to go off; **fer qui lâche,** loose horseshoe; **mes freins ont brusquement lâché,** my brakes suddenly failed, gave out; **mes nerfs lâchèrent,** my nerve went, I lost my nerve; (*b*) to give up.

II. lâcher, *s.m.* **1.** release (of pigeons, etc.). **2.** *Av:* (pilot's) first solo flight.

se lâcher. 1. to become slack. **2.** *Lit:* (*of pers.*) to let oneself go, to throw off all restraint; to speak too freely.

Lachésis [lakezis]. **1.** *Pr.n.f. Gr.Myth:* Lachesis. **2.** *s.m. Rept:* Lachesis, genus of American pit vipers. **3.** *Moll:* chauvitia.

lâcheté [lɑʃte], *s.f.* **1.** *A:* laziness, slackness. **2.** (*a*) cowardice, cowardliness; (*b*) piece of, act of, cowardice. **3.** (*a*) despicableness; baseness; (*b*) low, despicable, action; **encore une l.!** another piece of treachery!

lâcheur, -euse [lɑʃœ:r, -ø:z], *s. F:* fickle, unreliable, person; *F:* funk, quitter; **on ne voit plus votre ami, c'est un l.,** we haven't seen your friend for a long time; he's deserted us.

lacinia [lasinja], **lacinie** [lasini], *s.f.* **1.** *Bot:* lacinia, slash (in leaf, etc.). **2.** *Z:* lacinia.

lacinié [lasinje], *a. Nat.Hist:* laciniate(d); jagged, slashed (petals, leaves).

lacinien, -ienne [lasinjɛ̃, -jɛn], *a.* **1.** *A.Geog:* relating to Cape Colonna. **2.** *Myth:* agnomen of Hera.

lacinifolié [lasinifɔlje], *a. Bot:* laciniate-leaved.

laciniure [lasinjy:r], *s.f. Bot:* laciniation.

Lacinion [lasinjɔ̃], *Pr.n. A.Geog:* **cap L.,** Cape Colonna.

lacinule [lasinyl], *s.f. Bot:* lacinula.

lacinulé [lasinyle], *a. Nat.Hist:* lacinulate.

lacis [lasi], *s.m.* (*a*) network (of nerves, trenches, wire, etc.); **l. de ruelles,** network of back streets; (*b*) *Lacem:* lacis.

lack [lak], *s.m.* lac, lakh (of rupees).

lacmoïde [lakmɔid], *s.m. Ch:* lackmoid, lacmoid.

lacon [lakɔ̃], *s.m. Fr.C:* small lake.

laconicum [lakɔnikɔm], *s.m. Rom.Ant:* laconicum, sudatorium, sweating room.

Laconie [lakɔni], *Pr.n.f. A.Geog:* Laconia.

laconien, -ienne [lakɔnjɛ̃, -jɛn], *a. & s.* Laconian.

laconique [lakɔnik], *a.* laconic; (man) of few words.

laconiquement [lakɔnikmɑ̃], *adv.* laconically.

laconisme [lakɔnism], *s.m.* **1.** lacon(ic)ism, brevity. **2.** *A.Gr.Hist:* laconism.

là-contre [lakɔ̃:tr̥], *adv.* to the contrary.

lacrimatoire, lacrymatoire [lakrimatwa:r], *a. & s.m. Archeol:* **(urne) l.,** lachrymatory (vase); tear (-bottle).

lacrymal, -aux [lakrimal, -o], *a.* lachrymal; tear (gland, etc.); **conduit l.,** tear duct; **sac l.,** lachrymal sac, tear sac.

lacrymogène [lakrimɔʒɛn], *a.* tear-exciting; **gaz l.,** lachrymatory gas, tear gas; **grenade l.,** tear bomb.

lacs [lɑ], *s.m.* **1.** knotted cord; **lacs d'amour,** love knot; **l. d'amour (en 8 couché),** true-love(r's) knot. **2.** (*a*) noose, snare, springe (for trapping animals); **tendre des l. à qn,** to set traps for s.o.; **pris dans le(s) l.,** caught in the toils; **tomber dans le l.,** to fall into the trap; (*b*) *Vet:* long rope (i) for throwing a horse to the ground in order to operate, (ii) to aid the extraction of the foetus of a large animal.

lactaire [laktɛ:r]. **1.** *a.* lactary; lacteous. **2.** *s.m. Fung:* lactarius; **l. délicieux,** saffron milk cap.

lactalbumine [laktalbymin], *s.f. Ch:* lactalbumen.

lactame [laktam], *s.f. Ch:* lactam.

Lactance [laktɑ̃:s], *Pr.n.m. Ecc.Lit:* Lactantius.

lactarium [laktarjɔm], *s.m. Med:* milk bank.

lactase [lakta:z], *s.f. Ch:* lactase.

lactate [laktat], *s.m. Ch:* lactate.

lactation [laktasjɔ̃], *s.f.* **1.** *Physiol:* lactation. **2.** suckling, nursing.

lacté [lakte], *a.* **1.** lacteous, milky; **diète lactée, régime l.,** milk diet; **fièvre lactée,** milk fever, lacteal fever; lactation tetany; *Bot:* **plante lactée,** lactescent plant; *Astr:* **la Voie lactée,** the Milky Way. **2.** *Anat:* lacteal (duct, etc.); **vaisseaux lactés,** lacteal vessels, lacteals.

lactéal, -aux [lakteal, -o], *a.* **dents lactéales,** milk teeth.

lactescence [laktɛs(s)ɑ̃:s], *s.f.* lactescence, milkiness.

lactescent [laktɛs(s)ɑ̃], *a.* **1.** lactescent (plant, etc.). **2.** milky, milk-white.

lacticémie [laktisemi], *s.f. Path:* lactiacidemia.

lactide [laktid], *s.m. Ch:* lactide.

lactifère [laktifɛ:r], *a.* lactiferous, milk-bearing (gland, plant, etc.); lacteal (duct).

lactiflore [laktiflɔ:r], *a.* bearing milky white flowers.

lactifuge [laktify:ʒ], *s.m. Med:* lactifuge.

lactime [laktim], *s.f. Ch:* lactim.

lactique [laktik], *a. Ch:* lactic (acid).

lactobacille [laktɔbasil], *s.m. Bac:* lactobacillus.

lacto-densimètre [laktɔdɑ̃simɛtr̥], *s.m.,* **lactomètre** [laktɔmɛtr̥], *s.m.* lactodensimeter, (ga)lactometer, milk gauge; *pl. lacto-densimètres.*

lactoduc [laktɔdyk], *s.m. Sw.Fr:* (*in Valais*) pipeline for conveying milk from the mountain pastures to the dairy where cheese is made.

lactofermentation [laktɔfɛrmɑ̃tasjɔ̃], *s.f.* lactic fermentation.

lactoflavine [laktɔflavin], *s.f. Ch:* lactoflavin, riboflavin(e).

lactoglobuline [laktɔglɔbylin], *s.f.* lactoglobulin.

lactone [laktɔn], *s.f. Ch:* lactone.

lactonique [laktɔnik], *a.* lactonic.

lactonisation [laktɔnizasjɔ̃], *s.f. Ch:* lactonization.

lactonitrile [laktɔnitril], *s.m. Ch:* lactonitrile.

lactoscope [laktɔskɔp], *s.m.* lactoscope.

lactose [lakto:z], *s.f. Ch:* lactose, sugar of milk.

lactosé [laktoze], *a.* to which lactose has been added.

lactosérum [laktɔserɔm], *s.m.* whey.

lactosurie [laktɔzyri], *s.f. Obst:* lactosuria.

lactucarium [laktykarjɔm], *s.m. Pharm:* lactucarium.

lacturique [laktyrik], *a. Ch:* **acide l.,** lactic acid.

lacuna [lakyna], *s.f. Moll:* lacuna.

lacunaire [lakynɛːr], *a. & s.* **1.** *a.* (*a*) lacunar(y); *Path:* **image l.,** filling defect; (*b*) *Physiol:* **système l.,** system of sinuses, of cavities; (*c*) **documentation l.,** incomplete documentation. **2.** *s. Med:* old patient suffering from *lacuna cerebri.*

lacunar [lakynaːr], *s.m. Arch:* lacunar.

lacune [lakyn], *s.f.* **1.** lacuna, gap, hiatus (in text, etc.); break (in succession, etc.); blank (in memory, etc.); **combler les lacunes de son éducation,** to fill in the gaps, the blanks, in one's education. **2.** (*a*) *Biol: Miner:* lacuna; gap; non-sequence; *Bot:* air cell; (*b*) *Atom.Ph:* vacancy (of electron, etc.). **3.** *Moll:* = LACUNA.

lacuneux, -euse [lakynø, -øːz], *a.* lacunose, lacunate, lacunary, full of gaps.

lacunidés [lakynide], *s.m.pl. Moll:* Lacunidae.

laçure [lasyːr], *s.f.* **1.** *A.Cost:* laced part of bodice. **2.** lacing (of shoes, etc.).

lacustre [lakystr̥]. **1.** *a.* lacustrine (animal, etc.); lacustrian (dwelling, etc.); **habitation, cité, l.,** lake dwelling, pile dwelling. **2.** *s.* lacustrian, lake dweller, pile dweller.

lad [lad], *s.m.* stable boy (in racing stable).

ladanifère [ladanifɛːr], *a. Bot: Ch:* labdanum-bearing, ladanum-bearing.

ladanum [ladanɔm], *s.m. Bot: Ch:* labdanum, ladanum.

là-dedans [lad(ə)dɑ̃], *adv.* in there; inside, in it, in this; *F:* **il y a qch. là-d.,** he, she, is no fool.

là-dehors [ladəɔːr], *adv.* outside.

là-dessous [latsu], *adv.* under that, under there, underneath.

là-dessus [latsy], *adv.* on that, on it; **asseyez-vous l.-d.,** sit down on that; **tout le monde est d'accord l.-d.,** everybody is agreed about that; **l.-d. il est parti,** thereupon he went away; **nous reviendrons là-d.,** we shall return to this (later); **rien à dire là-d.,** no comment.

ladin [ladɛ̃], *s.m. Ling:* ladin.

Ladislas [ladislas], *Pr.n.m.* Ladislaus.

ladre [lɑːdr̥]. **1.** *a.* (*a*) *A:* leprous; (*b*) *A:* niggardly, mean, stingy; (*c*) *Vet:* measly, measled (pig or pork). **2.** *s. A:* (*f.* **ladresse** [lɑdrɛs]) (*a*) leper; (*b*) niggard, churl, skinflint; **un vieux l.,** an old screw. **3.** *s.m. Vet:* (*a*) **tache de l.,** bare patch (on horse's nose, etc.); **cheval qui a du l. aux naseaux,** horse with bare patch on its nose; (*b*) horse showing bare patches.

ladrerie [lɑdrəri], *s.f.* **1.** *A:* (*a*) leprosy; (*b*) lazar-house. **1.** *A:* meanness, stinginess. **3.** *Vet:* measles (of pigs).

ladure [ladyːr], *s.f.* small circular piece of land between salt pans.

laelia [lelja], *s.m. Bot:* laelia.

Laërce [laɛrs], *Pr.n.m.* Laertius.

Laërte [laɛrt], *Pr.n.m.* Laertes.

lagan [lagɑ̃], *s.m. Nau: Jur:* lagan, ligan.

lagena [laʒena], **lagène** [laʒɛːn], *s.f.* **1.** *Prot:* Lagena. **2.** *Orn: Rept:* lagena.

lagenaria [laʒenarja], *s.m. Bot:* Lagenaria.

lagéniforme [laʒenifɔrm], *a. Nat.Hist:* lageniform, bottle-shaped, flask-shaped.

lagenophora [laʒenɔfɔra], *s.m. Bot:* lagenophora.

lagénostoma [laʒenɔstɔma], *s.m. Paleont: Bot:* lagenostoma.

lagerstrœmia [lagɛrstrømja], *s.m. Bot:* lagerstroemia.

lagetta [lagɛta], *s.m. Bot:* lagetta; lacebark tree.

Lagides [laʒid], *Pr.n.m.pl. Hist:* the Ptolemies.

lagidium [laʒidjɔm], *s.m.inv. Z:* lagidium.

lagomorphes [lagɔmɔrf], *s.m.pl. Z:* Lagomorpha.

lagon [lagɔ̃], *s.m. Geog:* lagoon.

lagopède [lagɔpɛd], *s.m. Orn:* lagopus; **l. d'Écosse,** red grouse; **l. des saules,** willow grouse, *U.S:* willow ptarmigan; **l. muet, des Alpes,** ptarmigan, *U.S:* rock ptarmigan.

lagophtalmie [lagɔftalmi], *s.f. Med:* lagophthalmos, lagophthalmus.

lagorcheste(s) [lagɔrkɛst(ɛs)], *s.m. Z:* (genus of) Lagorchestes, hare wallabies.

lagostome [lagɔstɔm], **lagostomus** [lagɔstɔmys], *s.m. Z:* lagostomus.

lagostomidés [lagɔstɔmide], *s.m.pl. Z:* Lagostomus family, Chinchillidae.

lagotis [lagɔtis], *s.m.inv. Z:* lagidium, mountain viscacha.

lagotriche [lagɔtriʃ], **lagothrix** [lagɔtriks], *s.m. Z:* lagothrix.

lagre [lagr̥], *s.m. Glassm:* glass-plate used in making window panes.

laguis [lagi], *s.m. Nau:* running bowline.

lagunaire [lagynɛːr], *a.* lagoonal, relating to a lagoon.

lagune [lagyn], *s.f.* **l. (vive),** lagoon (in the Adriatic, etc.); **l. à marée,** tidal lagoon; **l. morte,** salt-water lake.

lagurus [lagyryːs], *s.m. Bot:* lagurus, hare's tail grass.

lahar [laar], *s.m. Geol:* lehar.

là-haut [lao], *adv.* up there; **est-ce qu'il y a quelqu'un l.-h.?** is there anyone up there? upstairs? **grâce qui vient de l.-h.,** blessing that comes from above, from on high, from Heaven.

lai[1] [lɛ], *s.m. Lit: Pros:* lay (in eight-foot verse).

lai[2]. **1.** *a.* **frère l., sœur laie,** lay-brother, -sister. **2.** *s.m.* layman.

laïc [laik], *a.m. & s.m.* = LAÏQUE.

laïcat [laika], *s.m.* laity.

laîche [lɛʃ], *s.f. Bot:* sedge.

laïcisation [laisizasjɔ̃], *s.f.* laicization, secularization.

laïciser [laisize], *v.tr.* to laicize, secularize (school, etc.).

laïcisme [laisism], *s.m.* laicism.

laïcité [laisite], *s.f.* secularity (of schools, etc.).

laid [lɛ]. **1.** *a.* (*a*) ugly; unsightly; (*of face*) plain, *U.S:* homely; *F:* **l. comme les sept péchés capitaux, comme un pou, comme un singe, comme un démon, à faire peur,** as ugly as sin; *s.a.* AMOUR 1; (*b*) unseemly; unhandsome; mean, shabby, low-down (action, etc.); (*to child*) **il est l. de mentir,** it's very naughty to tell lies; (*c*) *P:* (*of child*) **faire l. à qn,** to make (nasty) faces at s.o. **2.** *s.* (*a*) plain(-faced), *U.S:* homely, person; **c'est une belle laide,** she is very striking, though not good-looking; she's one of those attractively ugly people; (*b*) *F:* **oh, le l.! la laide!** what a naughty boy, naughty girl! (*c*) **le l. et le beau,** the ugly and the beautiful; **la haine du l.,** hatred of ugliness; **il l'a épousée pour son argent, c'est là le l. de l'affaire,** the unpleasant thing about it is that he married her for her money.

laidasse [lɛdas], *s.f. O: F:* ill-favoured woman.

laidement [lɛdmɑ̃], *adv.* **1. il pleurait l.,** he was crying in an unsightly way. **2.** in an unseemly manner, shabbily, meanly.

laideron [lɛdrɔ̃], *s.m. A:* **laideronne** [lɛdrɔn], *s.f.* ugly, plain, *U.S:* homely, woman or girl, *F:* a fright; **un petit l.,** *A:* **une petite laideron,** a plain Jane, an ugly duckling; *a.* **une petite princesse laideronne,** a plain little princess.

laideur [lɛdœːr], *s.f.* **1.** ugliness, unsightliness; plainness, *U.S:* homeliness (of features); **la l. du vice, du péché,** the ugliness of vice, of sin; **la l. de ces bâtiments,** the unsightliness of these buildings; **d'une l. épouvantable,** frighteningly ugly. **2.** unseemliness, meanness, shabbiness (of conduct, etc.).

laidir [lɛdiːr], *v.tr. & i. A:* = ENLAIDIR.

laie[1] [lɛ], *s.f.* (wild) sow.

laie[2], *s.f. For:* ride; **l. sommière,** major ride.

laie[3], *s.f. Tls: Stonew:* bush hammer.

laie[4], *s.f. Mus:* wind trunk (of organ).

lainage [lɛnaːʒ], *s.m.* **1.** (*a*) fleece (of sheep); (*b*) woollen article; *pl.* woollen goods, woollens; *Cost:* **mets ton l.,** put on your woolly. **2.** *Tex:* teaseling, teazling, raising, napping.

laine [lɛn], *s.f.* **1.** wool; **bêtes à l.,** woolly-coated animals; **l. basse, basse l.,** short wool; **l. haute, haute l.,** long wool; **l. mère, l. prime,** picklock wool; **l. bâtarde,** wether (wool); **l. cuisse,** breech, livery, wool; **l. morte,** (i) sliped wool, slipe; (ii) skin wool; **l. lavée à dos,** fleece-washed wool; **l. lavée à chaud,** scoured wool; **l. cardée,** carding wool; **l. renaissance,** reworked, reclaimed, wool; shoddy; **pure l.,** pure wool; *Fr.C: F:* **une Canadienne pure l.,** a typical Canadian; **l. peignée,** worsted; **l. filée,** yarn; **l. à tricoter,** knitting wool; **l. perlée,** crochet wool; **l. de tapisserie,** *A:* **de Berlin,** embroidery wool, *A:* Berlin wool; **bas de l.,** (i) woollen stockings; (ii) *F:* savings; **étoffe de l.,** woollen cloth; **tapis de haute l.,** thick-pile carpet; *F:* **manger la l. sur le dos à qn,** to fleece s.o.; to eat s.o. out of house and home; **se laisser manger, tondre, la l. sur le dos,** to be easy-going, to allow oneself to be fleeced; **aller chercher de la l. et revenir tondu,** to go for wool and come home shorn; *Prov:* **à la l. on connaît la brebis,** by their fruits ye shall know them; *A:* **jambes de l.,** weak, groggy, legs. **2.** (*a*) wool, woolly hair (of negroes); (*b*) *Bot: Ent:* wool, tomentum; (*c*) **l. de bois,** wood fibre, wood wool; fine shavings (for packing); **l. de verre,** glass wool; fibre-glass.

lainé [lɛne], *a.* woolly; **mouton bien l.,** sheep with a thick fleece.

lainer [lɛne]. I. *v.tr. Tex:* to tease, teasel, teazle, raise, nap (cloth).

II. **lainer,** *s.m. Tex:* nap (of cloth).

lainerie [lɛnri], *s.f.* **1.** (*a*) manufacture of woollens; (*b*) woollen mill; (*c*) woollen goods, woollens; (*d*) wool shop. **2.** sheep-shearing shed, ground.

lainette [lɛnɛt], *s.f. Tex:* wool waste.

laineur, -euse[1] [lɛnœːr, -øːz], *Tex:* **1.** *s.* teaseler, teazler, napper. **2.** *s.f.* **laineuse,** napping machine, gig (mill). **3.** *s.f. Ent: F:* **laineuse,** woolly bear (caterpillar).

laineux, -euse[2] [lɛnø, -øːz], *a.* (*a*) fleecy (cloth, etc.); woolly (sheep, hair, etc.); (*b*) *Bot: Ent:* woolly, tomentose.

lainier, -ière [lɛnje, -jɛːr]. **1.** *a.* wool(len) (trade, etc.); **l'industrie lainière,** the wool industry. **2.** *s.* (*a*) wool merchant; (*b*) woollen-goods manufacturer; (*c*) worker in a woollen mill; wool worker.

laïque [laik]. **1.** *a.* laic; lay (dress, etc.); secular (education, etc.); **école l.,** = (non-religious) state school. **2.** *s.* layman, laywoman; **les laïques,** the laity. **3.** *s.f. F:* **la l.** = the State primary school.

lais [lɛ], *s.m.* **1.** *For:* staddle. **2.** (*a*) *Geol:* **l. (de rivière),** alluvium; (*b*) *Jur:* **les l. (et relais) de la mer,** the foreshore.

Laïs [lais], *Pr.n.f.* **1.** *Gr.Hist:* Lais. **2.** *s.f. A: Lit:* courtesan.

laisse[1] [lɛs], *s.f.* **1.** (*a*) leash, lead; *Ven:* slip; **tenir un chien en l.,** to keep a dog on a lead, on the leash; *F:* **mener, tenir, qn en l.,** to keep s.o. in leading-strings; to keep a tight hand on s.o.; **sa mère le tient en l.,** his mother keeps him tied to her apron-strings; (*b*) **l. de chiens,** pair, brace, of dogs (on a leash). **2.** *Cost:* hat guard. **3.** *Clockm:* stop work.

laisse[2], *s.f.* **1.** *Pros:* laisse. **2.** (*a*) beach (of shore); foreshore; **l. de haute, basse, mer,** high-water, low-water mark; (*b*) *usu. pl.* wrack; (*c*) (river) alluvium.

laissé [lɛse, lese], *s.m. Typ:* out.

laissées [lɛse, lese], *s.f.pl. Ven:* droppings (of boars and wolves).

laissé-pour-compte [lɛsepurkɔ̃ːt, le-], *s.m.* (*a*) *Com:* returned or rejected article; tailor's misfit; (*b*) (i) unwanted article, white elephant; (ii) (*pers.*) unwanted person; misfit; *pl. laissés-pour-compte.*

laisser [lɛse, lese], *v.tr.* **1.** to let, allow; **il le laissa partir,** he let him go, allowed him to go; **je les ai laissés dire,** *occ.* **laissé dire,** I let them talk (away); **laissez dire,** let them talk (as they like); **je me le suis laissé dire,** that's what I was told; **elle se laissa embrasser,** she allowed herself to be kissed, she let him (or her) kiss her; **ils se sont laissé filouter,** they let themselves be swindled; **je ne me laisserai pas abuser,** I am not going to be cheated; **le toit laissait entrer la pluie,** the roof let the rain in; **l. voir qch.,** to reveal sth.; **l. voir son mécontentement,** to show one's displeasure, disapproval; **l. tomber qch.,** to drop sth.; **l. tout aller,** to let things go their own way, to let things slide; *Nau:* **laissez arriver!** bear up! **laissez aller!** (i) lower away! (ii) way enough! (iii) *Sp:* let's go! *Nau:* **laisse courir!** way enough! **laissez les avirons dans l'eau!** trail! **se l. aller,** to let oneself go, to get into slovenly ways, habits; to become slack; **se l. aller, tomber, dans un fauteuil,** to loll in, sink into, an armchair; **se l. aller aux larmes, au pessimisme,** to give way to tears, to pessimism; to drift into pessimism; **se l. aller à rire, à sourire,** to go so far as to laugh, to smile; *F:* **laissez-moi rire!** don't make me laugh! **ne vous laissez pas aller comme ça!** pull yourself together! *F:* (*of woman*) **se l. aller avec qn,** to compromise oneself with s.o.; *F:* **ce fruit se laisse manger,** this fruit is very good to eat, *F:* asks to be eaten; **ce vin se laisse boire,** this wine is very drinkable, very palatable; **le public lit les livres qui se laissent lire facilement,** the public reads books that are easy to read; **se l. emporter à, par, la colère,** to give way to anger; to let one's temper get the better of one; **se l. guider par l'expérience,** to let oneself be guided by experience; **l. sécher la peinture,** to let the paint dry; **l. prendre aux blessés un peu d'exercice, l. les blessés prendre un peu d'exercice,** to let the wounded take a little exercise; **l. la loi suivre son cours,** to let the law take its course; **ils nous laissaient venir,** they waited for us to make a move; **la politique du l. venir,** the wait-and-see policy; **laissez-les, -leur, boire un verre de vin,** let them have a glass of wine; **je vous le laisse raconter, je vous laisse le raconter,** I will let you tell it; **il les a laissé(s) se ruiner,** he let them ruin themselves; **l. faire,** to let things alone; **laissez-le faire!** leave it to him! let him get on with it; **laissez faire au temps, laissez faire le temps,** leave it to time; **laissons faire aux dieux,** let us leave it in the hands of the gods; *F:* **l. courir,** drop it; **il se laissa faire,** (i) he allowed himself to be led; (ii) he offered no resistance, *F:* **he didn't kick;**

vous n'iriez pas si on me laissait faire, you would not go if I had my way; **on ne le laissa pas approcher de la Reine,** he was denied access to the Queen; **vous n'allez pas me l. dîner tout seul?** you aren't going to leave me to have my dinner all by myself? 2. (*a*) to leave (s.o., sth., somewhere); **l. sa valise à la consigne,** to leave one's case at the left-luggage office; **l. qn derrière soi,** to leave s.o. behind; **allons, je vous laisse,** well, I'm going, I'm off; (*of train*) **l. des voyageurs à . . .,** to set passengers down at . . .; **l. une veuve et trois enfants,** to leave a widow and three children; **vin qui laisse un goût désagréable,** wine that leaves a nasty taste in the mouth; **partir sans l. d'adresse,** to go away without leaving one's address; to disappear without trace; **l. qch. de côté,** to leave sth. out; to put sth. aside; **il a laissé son travail de côté pour vous voir,** he put his work aside in order to see you; **l. là qn,** to leave s.o. in the lurch; **l. là qch.,** to give up doing sth., to throw up (a job); **elle y laissa la vie,** it cost her her life; **c'est à prendre ou à l.,** take it or leave it; (*b*) (i) to leave, keep (s.o., sth., in a certain state); **l. la fenêtre ouverte,** to leave, keep, the window open; **l. une page en blanc,** to leave a blank page; **l. qn à la porte,** to keep s.o. waiting at the door; **l. qn dans l'embarras,** to leave s.o. in difficulties; **je vous laisse libre d'agir,** I leave you free to act; **nous l'avions laissé pour mort,** we had left him for dead; (ii) to leave (s.o., sth., alone); **laissez-moi, je vous prie!** please leave me alone, *F:* let me be; *F:* **laissez-moi tranquille!** leave me in peace! **laissez-moi donc avec vos conseils!** you can keep your advice! **laissons cela jusqu'à demain,** we will leave that, let that stand over, until tomorrow; **l. les détails,** to pass over, leave out, the details; **laissez donc!** (please) don't bother! don't worry! (iii) **vous pouvez nous l.,** you may leave us, you may go; (*c*) **l. qch. à qn;** (i) **laissez-lui son secret,** let him keep his secret; **l. la vie à qn,** to spare s.o.'s life; **cela nous laisse le temps de . . .,** that leaves us time to . . .; (ii) **l. à qn un héritage,** to leave s.o. a legacy; **laissez-moi vos clefs,** leave me, let me have, your keys; **je vous le laisserai à bon compte,** I will let you have it cheap; **je vous le laisserai pour 100 francs,** you may have it for 100 francs; **l. qch. aux soins de qn,** to leave sth. to s.o.'s care, to entrust s.o. with sth.; (*d*) **je vous laisse à penser notre bonheur,** you can imagine how happy we are, were; **cela laisse (beaucoup) à désirer,** it leaves much to be desired; (*e*) **ne pas l. de faire qch.,** not to fail to do sth.; **il ne laissera pas d'y aller,** he will not fail to go; **on ne peut l. d'admirer ce travail,** one can't help admiring this work; **cela ne laisse pas de m'inquiéter,** I feel anxious all the same, nevertheless; **ça ne laissa pas de m'amuser,** I couldn't help being rather amused at it; (*f*) to leave, abandon (s.o., sth.); **elle a laissé son mari,** she has left her husband, *F:* has walked out on her husband.

laisser-aller [lɛseale, le-], *s.m.inv.* **1.** unconstraint, free-and-easiness; abandon. **2.** carelessness, slovenliness (of attire, etc.).

laisser-courre [lɛsekuːr, le-], *s.m.inv. Ven:* laying-on of the pack.

laisser-faire [lɛsefɛːr, le-], *s.m.* non-interference, laissez-faire; **politique de l.-f.,** policy of inaction, of drift; laisser-faire policy.

laissez-passer [lɛsepɑse, le-], *s.m.inv.* pass, permit; *Dipl:* laissez-passer; *Cust:* transire; *Rail:* platform ticket; *Nau:* sea pass, sea letter.

lait [lɛ], *s.m.* milk; **1. l. chaud,** (i) new milk, (ii) hot milk; **l. entier,** whole milk; **l. écrémé,** skimmed, skim, milk; **l. cru certifié** = tuberculin-tested milk, T.T. milk; **l. homogénéisé,** homogenized milk; **l. battu, de beurre,** buttermilk; **petit l., l. clair,** whey; **l. concentré (sucré),** condensed milk; **l. concentré (non sucré),** evaporated milk; **l. en poudre,** dried milk; **l. emprésuré, aromatisé,** (flavoured) junket; **l. gélifié,** milk jelly, jellied milk; **l. frappé,** chilled milk; **l. cru,** raw milk; **l. caillé,** curd, curdled milk; **l. au rhum,** milk punch; **au l.,** with milk; **café au l.,** white coffee; *Cu:* **l. de poule,** egg flip, egg nog; **vache à l.,** (i) milch cow; (ii) *F: (pers.)* mug, sucker, milch cow; **boîte à l.,** (domestic) milk can; *P:* **les boîtes-à-l.,** the breasts; **pot à l.,** milk jug; **dents de l.,** milk teeth, first teeth; *Med:* **fièvre de l.,** milk fever; **frère, sœur, de l.,** foster-brother, -sister; **cochon de l., veau de l.,** sucking pig, sucking calf; **se mettre au l.,** to go on (to) a milk diet; **avoir sucé avec le l. une doctrine, une opinion,** to have been brought up in a doctrine, in an opinion; *s.a.* BOIRE I, 1, SOUPE 1, SUCRE. **2.** (*a*) **l. de coco,** coconut milk; (*b*) **l. de chaux,** milk of lime, whitewash; *Const:* **l. de ciment,** grout, cement wash; *Paperm:* **l. de colle,** white size; (*c*) *Pharm:* **l. d'amandes,** milk of almonds, almond milk; *Toil:* **l. virginal,** benzoin skin lotion. **3.** *Bot:* **l. d'âne,** hogweed, milkweed, sow thistle; **l. battu,** fumitory; **l. de couleuvre,** cypress spurge; **l. Sainte-Marie,** milk thistle; **herbe au l.,** (i) milkwort; (ii) euphorbia.

laitage [lɛtaːʒ], *s.m.* (*a*) dairy produce; (*b*) *pl.* home-made milk or cheese dishes; **vivre de laitages,** to live on milk foods, on a milk diet.

laitance [lɛtɑ̃ːs], *s.f.*, **laite** [lɛt], *s.f.* **1.** *Ich:* milt; *Cu:* soft roe. **2.** *Const:* **l. de ciment,** cement grout.

laité [lɛte, lete], *a.* soft-roed (fish).

laitée [lɛte, lete], *s.f.* litter (of bitch-hound).

laiterie [lɛtri], *s.f.* **1.** dairy; creamery. **2.** (*a*) dairying, dairy work; (*b*) dairy farming.

laiteron [lɛtrɔ̃], *s.m.* **1.** *Bot:* sow thistle, milk weed, hogweed; **l. des champs,** corn sow thistle; **l. épineux,** spiny sow thistle. **2.** yearling (colt).

laiteux[1], -euse [lɛtø, -øːz], *a.* **1.** *Med:* lacteal, milk-(disorder, etc.). **2.** lacteous, milky. **3.** milk-like, milky; **aspect l. d'un liquide,** milkiness of a liquid; **pierre laiteuse,** milk white stone, gem.

laiteux[2], -euse, *a.* milky (oyster, etc.).

laitier[1], -ière [lɛtje, -jɛːr, le-]. **1.** *a.* **l'industrie laitière,** the milk industry; dairying; **coopérative laitière,** co-operative dairies; **produits laitiers,** dairy produce; **ferme laitière,** dairy farm; **beurre l.,** dairy butter; **vache laitière,** milch cow; *pl.* dairy cattle; **(vache) bonne, mauvaise, laitière,** good, bad, milker. **2.** *s.* (*a*) milkman; milk woman, milkmaid; (*b*) dairyman; dairy woman, dairymaid. **3.** *s.m. Bot:* milkwort. **4.** *s.f. O:* **laitière,** milk cart.

laitier[2], *s.m. Metall: etc:* dross, slag; cinders (of iron furnace); **l. basique,** basic slag; *Geol:* **l. des volcans,** vitreous lava.

laiton [lɛtɔ̃], *s.m.* brass; **fil de l.,** brass wire; **vis en l.,** brass screw; **l. en feuilles, l. laminé,** latten brass.

laitonnage [lɛtɔnaːʒ], *s.m. Metall:* brass plating.

laitonner [lɛtɔne], *v.tr.* **1.** to make a brass wire frame for (a hat). **2.** *Metall:* to plate, cover (sth.) with brass, to brass-plate.

laitue [lɛty, le-], *s.f.* lettuce; *Sw.Fr:* cos lettuce; **l. pommée,** cabbage lettuce; **l. romaine,** cos lettuce; **l. des murs, des murailles,** wall lettuce; **l. scarole,** broad-leaved chicory; *Algae:* **l. de mer,** sea lettuce, ulva.

laïus [lajyːs], *s.m. F:* speech, lecture; *F:* **faire, piquer, un l.,** to make a speech; to hold forth; **ce n'est que du l.,** it's just talk, waffle.

laïusser [lajyse], *v.i. F:* to make a speech; *F:* to spout, speechify; to hold forth.

laïusseur [lajysœːr], *s.m. F:* great talker; speechifier, spouter.

laize [lɛːz], *s.f. Tex:* **1.** (*a*) width (of cloth); (*b*) difference between nominal and actual width. **2.** *Nau:* cloth (for sail-making); **voile de tant de laizes,** sail of so many cloths.

lakh [lak], *s.m. Num:* lac, lakh (of rupees).

lakiste [lakist], *a. & s. Lit:* (*a*) *a.* in the style of the Lake School of poetry, Lakist; (*b*) *s.m.* Lakist, one of the Lake Poets.

lallation [lalasjɔ̃], *s.f.* **1.** *Ling:* lallation. **2.** *Psy:* lalling, lallation.

lama[1] [lama], *s.m.* (Buddhist) lama; **le Grand L.,** the Grand Lama.

lama[2], *s.m. Z:* llama; *Tex:* llama (cloth).

lamage [lamaːʒ], *s.m. Metall:* facing, spot facing.

lamaïsme [lamaism], *s.m. Rel:* Lamaism.

lamaïste [lamaist], *s.m. Rel:* Lamaist.

lamanage [lamanaːʒ], *s.m. Nau:* (river, harbour) piloting; inshore pilotage.

lamaneur [lamanœːr], *s.m.* (river, harbour) pilot; inshore pilot; branch pilot.

lamantin [lamɑ̃tɛ̃], *s.m. Z:* manatee, sea-cow.

lamarckisme [lamarkism], *s.m.* Lamarckism.

lamartinien, -ienne [lamartinjɛ̃, -jɛn]. **1.** *a.* in the style of Lamartine. **2.** *s.* imitator, follower, of Lamartine.

lamaserie [lamazri], *s.f.* lamasery, lama monastery.

lamballais, -aise [lɑ̃balɛ, -ɛːz], *a. & s. Geog:* (native, inhabitant) of Lamballe.

lambda [lɑ̃bda], *s.m.* **1.** *Gr.Alph:* lambda. **2.** *Anat:* lambda.

lambdacisme [lɑ̃bdasism], *s.m. Ling:* lambdacism.

lambdatique [lɑ̃bdatik], *a. Anat:* **os l.,** epactal; wormian bone.

lambdoïde [lɑ̃bdɔid], *a. Anat:* lambdoid(al) (suture).

lambeau, -eaux [lɑ̃bo], *s.m.* **1.** (*a*) scrap, bit, shred (of cloth, knowledge, flesh, etc.); **vêtements en lambeaux,** clothes in rags, in tatters; (*of garment*) **s'en aller en lambeaux,** to go, fall, to pieces; **ma robe tombe en lambeaux,** my dress is worn to rags, falling to pieces, falling off my back; **mettre qch. en lambeaux,** to tear sth. to shreds, to rags; **se disputer les lambeaux d'une succession,** to fight like vultures over a succession; (*b*) *Geol:* **l. de recouvrement,** outlier. **2.** *Surg:* **l. (cutané),** (skin) flap.

lambel [lɑ̃bɛl], *s.m. Her:* label.

lambert [lɑ̃bɛːr], *s.m. Opt:* lambert; **loi de Lambert,** Lambert's law.

lambic(k) [lɑ̃bik], *s.m.* a strong Belgian beer.

lambin, -ine [lɑ̃bɛ̃, -in], *F:* **1.** *a.* dawdling, slow. **2.** *s.* dawdler, slowcoach.

lambinage [lɑ̃binaːʒ], *s.m. F:* dawdling.

lambiner [lɑ̃bine], *v.i. F:* to dawdle; to take all one's time; to mess about, to potter.

lambis [lɑ̃bi], *s.m. Moll:* lambis.

lamblia [lɑ̃blia], *s.m. Path:* lamblia, giardia.

lambliase [lɑ̃bliaːz], *s.f. Path:* lambliasis, giardasis.

lambourde [lɑ̃burd], *s.f.* **1.** *Arb:* fruit-shoot. **2.** *Const:* (*a*) wall plate, beam bearing; (*b*) bridging joist; **l. de parquet,** sleeper; bearing joist (of flooring). **3.** soft, chalky, stone.

lambrequin [lɑ̃brəkɛ̃], *s.m.* **1.** *Her:* mantling (of helmet, etc.); lambrequin. **2.** (*a*) *Furn:* valance, lambrequin, pelmet; (*b*) publicity strip on shop blind.

lambris [lɑ̃bri], *s.m. Const:* **1.** panelling, wainscoting (in wood); casing, lining (in marble, etc.) (of wall); **l. de hauteur,** wainscot, panelling; **l. d'appui,** dado. **2.** (*a*) plasterwork of attic ceiling, of partition; (*b*) (panelled) ceiling; *Lit:* **né sous des l. dorés,** born in marble halls, in the purple; **l. sacrés,** church; *Poet:* **les célestes l.,** the vault of heaven.

lambrissage [lɑ̃brisaːʒ], *s.m.*, **lambrissure** [lɑ̃brisyːr], *s.f. Const:* wainscoting, panelling, lining (of room).

lambrisser [lɑ̃brise], *v.tr. Const:* **1.** to wainscot, panel, line (room, etc.); **salle lambrissée de chêne,** room panelled, dadoed, in oak; **plafond lambrissé,** panelled ceiling. **2.** to plaster (*esp.* lean-to walls of attic); **mansarde lambrissée,** attic.

lambrotte [lɑ̃brɔt], *s.f. Vit:* thin bunch of grapes.

lambruche [lɑ̃bryʃ], *s.f.*, **lambrusque** [lɑ̃brysk], *s.f. Lit:* wild vine.

lame [lam], *s.f.* **1.** (*a*) lamina, thin plate, strip (of metal, etc.); web (of saw, etc.); leaf (of spring); floorboard (of strip flooring); slide (for microscope); *Needlew:* foil, tinsel; *El:* plate (of condenser, of accumulator); segment (of commutator); *Miner: etc:* section; **l. de platine,** platinum foil; **l. de jalousie,** slat of a Venetian blind; *Sm.a:* **l. chargeur,** loading clip, charger; **pierre qui se partage en lames,** stone that splits, that cleaves; *El:* **interrupteur à lames,** knife switch; (*b*) blade (of sword, knife, razor, etc.); **canif à deux lames,** double-bladed knife; **couteau à l. crantée,** knife with a serrated edge; **c'est une fine l.,** (i) he's a fine swordsman; (ii) he, she, is very sharp-witted; **visage en l. de couteau,** hatchet face; **la l. use le fourreau,** the mind is wearing out the body; *Mec.E:* **l. d'aléseuse,** boring tool, cutter; **l. (de faucheuse),** (machine-)knife; *Aut: A:* **carrosserie en l. de couteau,** razor-edge body; (*c*) *Num:* fillet (of gold, silver); (*d*) *Tex:* leaf; *pl.* heddles (of loom); (*e*) *Bot:* lamina; blade (of leaf); (*f*) *Orn:* vane, web (of feather); (*g*) *Moll:* **l. de sabre,** razor clam; (*h*) **l. d'eau,** (i) sheet of water; (ii) flat jet of water; (iii) *Mch:* water-space (in boiler). **2.** wave; *Poet:* billow; **l. de fond,** (i) ground-swell; (ii) tidal wave; **l. de houle,** roller, surge; **filer arrière à la l.,** to run before the sea; **recevoir une l.,** to be struck by a sea; **crête, creux, de l.,** crest, trough, of a sea; **debout à la l.,** head on to the sea; **en travers de la l.,** in the trough of the sea; **recevoir la l. par le travers,** to keep broadside on to the sea; **entre deux lames,** in a trough between two waves. **3.** *Anat:* lamina; **l. criblée,** lamina cribrosa; **l. perpendiculaire,** lamina perpendicularis; **l. spirale,** lamina spiralis; **l. vertébrale,** lamina of vertebral arch.

lamé [lame]. **1.** *a.* **l. d'argent, d'or,** spangled, worked, with silver, with gold. **2.** *s.m.* **l. (d')or,** gold lamé, gold spangles; **l. d'argent,** silver lamé, silver spangles.

lame-fusible [lamfyzibl], *s.f. El:* fuse strip; *pl. lames-fusibles.*

lamellaire [lamɛl(l)ɛːr], *a.* **1.** *Miner: etc:* lamellar, lamellate, foliated. **2.** *El:* **noyau l.,** laminated core (of transformer). **3.** *s.f.pl. Z:* **lamellaires,** Lamellariidae.

lamellariidés [lamɛl(l)aride], *s.m.pl. Z:* Lamellariidae.
lamellation [lamɛl(l)asjɔ̃], *s.f.* lamellation.
lamelle [lamɛl], *s.f.* (*a*) lamella, lamination; lamina (of slate, etc.); thin sheet, plate (of iron, etc.); scale, flake (of mica, etc.); **l. de jalousie,** blind-slat; *W.Tel:* **l. (de condensateur variable),** vane; (*b*) *Sm.a:* leaf (of sight); (*c*) (microscope) slide; **l. (portant une préparation microscopique),** object slide.
lamellé [lamɛl(l)e], **lamelleux, -euse** [lamɛ(l)lø, -ø:z], *a.* lamellate(d) (fungus, etc.); foliated, fissile (slate, etc.); flaky, scaly.
lamellibranche [lamɛl(l)ibrɑ̃:ʃ], *Moll:* **1.** *a.* lamellibranchiate. **2.** *s.m.* lamellibranch; *pl.* **lamellibranches,** Lamellibranchia.
lamellicorne [lamɛl(l)ikɔrn], *a.* & *s.m. Ent:* lamellicorn.
lamelliforme [lamɛl(l)ifɔrm], *a.* lamelliform, lamellar; flaky.
lamellirostre [lamɛl(l)rɔstr̥], *a.* & *s.* **1.** *a. Z:* lamellirostral. **2.** *s.m.pl. Orn:* **lamellirostres,** Lamellirostres.
lamentable [lamɑ̃tabl̥], *a.* **1.** lamentable, deplorable (accident, etc.); pitiful, pitiable (fate, etc.). **2.** mournful (voice, etc.). **3.** (*of result, etc.*) lamentable, feeble, pitiable; shockingly bad; **orateur l.,** pitiful speaker; **il s'est montré l.,** he put up a very poor show.
lamentablement [lamɑ̃tabləmɑ̃], *adv.* lamentably.
lamentation [lamɑ̃tasjɔ̃], *s.f.* lamentation. **1.** (be)wailing. **2.** lament; **cri de l.,** wail; **le mur des Lamentations,** the Wailing Wall (in Jerusalem); *F:* **pourquoi ces lamentations?** what's all the complaining, moaning, about?
lamenter [lamɑ̃te]. **1.** *v.pr.* & *A: v.i.* to lament; *Lit:* to wail; (*of crocodile*) to whimper; **se l. sur son sort,** to bewail, bemoan, one's lot; **se l. de son ignorance,** to deplore, regret, one's ignorance. **2.** *v.tr. A:* **il lamentait une chanson bachique,** he was wailing out a drinking-song.
lamer [lame], *v.tr.* **1.** to spangle. **2.** *Tchn:* to spot-face.
lame-ressort [lamrəsɔ:r], *s.f.* flat spring; *pl. lames-ressorts.*
lamette [lamɛt], *s.f.* **1.** small plate, strip (of metal, etc.). **2.** small blade.
lamiacées [lamjase], *s.f.pl. Bot:* Lamiaceae.
lamiaque [lamjak], *a.* & *s. Geog:* Lamian; *Gr. Hist:* **la guerre l.,** the Lamian War.
lamie [lami], *s.f.* **1.** *Myth:* lamia. **2.** *Ich:* lamna; **l. long-nez,** porbeagle, mackerel shark.
lamier[1] [lamje], *s.m.* **1.** tinsel maker; worker in lamé. **2.** *Tex:* (*a*) harness fixer; (*b*) heddle maker.
lamier[2], *s.m. Bot:* dead-nettle; archangel; **l. pourpre,** red archangel.
lamifié [lamifje], *a.* & *s.m.* laminated (plastic, glass, etc.).
laminage [lamina:ʒ], *s.m.* **1.** (*a*) laminating, rolling, flatt(en)ing (of metal, etc.); calendering, plate-glazing (of paper); (*b*) *Mch:* throttling (of steam); (*c*) wire-drawing. **2.** (*a*) *Mch: Metalw:* lamination, rolled strip; **l. des brames,** slabbing; **usine de l.,** strip mill; (*b*) *Geol:* lamination.
laminagraphie [laminagrafi], *s.f. Tchn:* laminagraphy, laminography.
laminaire [laminɛ:r]. **1.** *a.* laminar; flaky, scaly; *Ph:* **régime l.,** laminar flow. **2.** *s.f.* (*a*) *Algae:* laminaria, sea-tangle; oarweed; **l. à tige souple,** flexible-stemmed oarweed; **l. en ruban,** ribbon oar-weed; **l. bulbeuse,** Saccorhiza (genus); (*b*) *Surg:* sea-tangle tent.
laminariales [laminarjal], *s.f.pl. Algae:* Laminariales.
laminé [lamine]. **1.** *a.* laminate(d). **2.** *s.m.* (i) rolled iron; (ii) laminate, laminated plastic.
laminectomie [laminɛktɔmi], *s.f. Surg:* laminectomy.
laminer [lamine], *v.tr.* **1.** to laminate, flat(ten), roll (metal); to calender, plate-glaze (paper); **tôle laminée,** rolled sheet iron; **plomb laminé,** sheet lead; **le cuivre se lamine à chaud ou à froid,** copper can be hot or cold rolled. **2.** *Mch:* to throttle (the steam).
laminerie [laminri], *s.f. Metalw:* flatting mill, rolling mill.
lamineur [laminœ:r], *a.* & *s.m.* **1.** *Metalw:* roller, mill-hand, laminator. **2.** *Paperm:* calenderer, plate-glazer. **3.** *a.* laminating.
lamineux, -euse [laminø, -ø:z], *a.* laminous, laminose; scaly; *Anat: A:* **tissu l.,** cellular tissue.
laminiforme [laminifɔrm], *a.* laminiform.
laminoir [laminwa:r], *s.m.* **1.** *Metalw:* (*a*) flatting mill, rolling mill; **l. de finissage,** finishing rolls; **l. à tubes,** tube mill; **l. à profilés, pour fers profilés,** section mill, shape-rolling mill; **travailler un métal au l.,** to roll a metal; *F:* **faire passer qn au l.,** to put s.o. through the mill; (*b*) roller (of mill). **2.** *Paperm:* rolling press, calendering machine, plate-glazing machine; **l. pour faux filigranage,** embossing calender.
laminosiopte [laminɔziɔpt], *s.m. Ent:* Laminosioptes.
lamium [lamjɔm], *s.m. Bot:* lamium.
lamna [lamna], *s.m. Ich:* lamna.
lamnidés [lamnide], *s.m.pl. Ich:* Lamnidae.
Lamourette [lamurɛt], *Pr.n.m.* **baiser L.,** short-lived peace; **échanger le baiser L.,** to effect a temporary reconciliation (*from the kisses of peace that Lamourette moved the different factions of the Legislative Assembly to exchange in 1792*).
lampadaire [lɑ̃padɛ:r], *s.m. Furn:* **1.** standard lamp; **pied de l.,** lampstand. **2.** candelabrum.
lampant [lɑ̃pɑ̃], *a.* illuminating, refined (oil); **huile lampante,** lamp oil, illuminating oil; *s.a.* PÉTROLE.
lampadite [lɑ̃padit], *s.f. Miner:* lampadite.
lampas[1] [lɑ̃pɑ(:s)], *s.m. Vet:* lampas.
lampas[2], *s.m. Tex:* lampas.
lampassé [lɑ̃pase], *a. Her:* **l. de gueules,** langued gules.
lampe [lɑ̃:p], *s.f.* lamp. **1.** (*a*) **l. à huile,** oil lamp, paraffin lamp; **l. à modérateur,** moderator lamp; **l. d'Argand,** Argand lamp; *Min:* **l. de sécurité, de sûreté,** safety lamp; **l. de mineur,** miner's lamp; **l. de Davy,** Davy lamp; **à (la lumière de) la l.,** by lamplight, in the lamplight; **faire les lampes,** to do, trim, the lamps; **remplir, garnir, entretenir, une l.,** to replenish a lamp; *P:* **s'en mettre plein la l.,** to have a good blowout; *Lit:* **mettre la l. sous le boisseau,** to hide one's light under a bushel; *s.a.* HUILE 1, SENTIR 2; (*b*) **l. à incandescence,** incandescent lamp; **l. à atmosphère gazeuse,** gas-filled lamp; **l. à arc,** arc lamp; **l. à vapeur de mercure,** mercury-vapour lamp; **l. au krypton, au néon,** krypton, neon, lamp; **l. à rayons ultra-violets,** ultra-violet lamp; **l. infra-rouge,** infra-red lamp; **l. à baïonnette,** bulb with bayonet socket; **l. à vis,** screw-in bulb; (*c*) **l. de table, portative,** table lamp; **l. de travail, de bureau,** reading lamp; **l. sur pied,** standard lamp; **l. de chevet,** bedside lamp; **l. de poche,** electric torch, (pocket) torch, flashlight; **l. de tableau,** panel lamp (of instrument), switchboard lamp (of power plant); *Aut:* **l. de bord, de tablier,** dashboard light; **l. route, l. foyer,** focusing headlamp; **l. code,** regulation lamp; **lampes satellites,** side lights; *Cin:* **l. à luminescence, à lueur,** discharge lamp, glow lamp; **enregistrement par l. à lueur,** glow-lamp recording (of sound); *Phot:* **l. éclair,** flashlight; *Med:* **l. d'opération,** operating light; **l. frontale,** head lamp; *Dent:* **l. de bouche,** mouth lamp; *s.a.* TÉMOIN 3. **2.** *Elcs:* **l. valve,** (radio) valve; tube; **l. à vide,** vacuum-valve, electron valve, thermionic valve; **l. de faible consommation,** dull emitter; **l. de puissance, l. émettrice, l. génératrice,** power-valve, -tube; **l. amplificatrice,** amplifying valve; **émetteur à lampes,** tube transmitter, valve transmitter; **l. molle,** gassy valve, soft valve; *s.a.* DÉTECTEUR, OSCILLATEUR 1, TRIODE. **3. l. à alcool,** spirit lamp, spirit stove; **l. à souder,** brazing lamp, blow torch.
lampée [lɑ̃pe], *s.f. F:* draught (of water, wine, etc.); **vider un verre d'une l.,** to empty a glass at one gulp.
lamper[1] [lɑ̃pe], *v.tr. F:* to swig, toss off, gulp down (drink).
lamper[2], *v.i.* (*of sea*) to phosphoresce, to grow phosphorescent.
lamperon [lɑ̃prɔ̃], *s.m.* **1.** (oil) container (of lamp). **2.** wick holder.
lampe-tempête [lɑ̃ptɑ̃pɛ:t], *s.f.* storm lantern, hurricane lamp; *pl. lampes-tempêtes.*
lampette [lɑ̃pɛt], *s.f. Bot:* **1.** ragged Robin. **2.** corn cockle.
lampion [lɑ̃pjɔ̃], *s.m.* **1.** (*a*) fairylight (for illuminations); lampion; *F:* **"les lampions!"** rhythmical call or stamping of feet (♪ ♪ ♩ ♪ ♪ ♩), to denote impatience, *e.g.* when the curtain is late in going up; (*b*) Chinese lantern; (*c*) *Fr.C:* (*in church*) votive light. **2.** *F:* cocked hat.
lampiste [lɑ̃pist], *s.m.* & *f.* **1.** lamp maker; lamp seller. **2.** (*a*) *A:* lamp trimmer, lamplighter; lampman; (*b*) *F:* underling, scapegoat, *U.S:* fall guy; **punir le l.,** to blame the cat; **s'en prendre au l.,** to bully one's subordinate(s); **t'en prends pas au l.,** don't shoot the driver.
lampisterie [lɑ̃pistəri], *s.f.* **1.** lamp-making, lamp works. **2.** *Rail: etc:* lamp room, lamp cabin, lamp locker.
lampon [lɑ̃pɔ̃], *s.m. A:* drinking song.
lampotte [lɑ̃pɔt], *s.f. Conch:* limpet.
lampourde [lɑ̃purd], *s.f. Bot:* xanthium, *F:* burweed.
lampresse [lɑ̃prɛs], *s.f. Fish:* (*in Loire estuary*) lamprey net.
lamprillon [lɑ̃prijɔ̃], *s.m. Ich:* larval lamprey.
lamprocère [lɑ̃prɔsɛ:r], *s.m. Ent:* (South American) lampyrid.
lamproie [lɑ̃prwɑ], *s.f. Ich:* lamprey; **l. d'alose, l. fluviatile,** river lamprey, lampern; **petite l.,** sand pride; **l. marine,** sea lamprey.
lamprophyre [lɑ̃prɔfi:r], *s.f. Miner:* lamprophyre.
lamproyon [lɑ̃prwɑjɔ̃], *s.m.* = LAMPRILLON.
lampsane [lɑ̃psan], *s.f. Bot:* lapsana, *F:* nipplewort.
lampyre [lɑ̃pi:r], *s.m. Ent:* lampyris, firefly, glowworm.
lampyridés [lɑ̃piride], *s.m.pl. Ent:* Lampyridae, the lampyrids.
lanarkia [lanarkja], *s.m. Paleont:* Lanarkia.
lanarkite [lanarkit], *s.f. Miner:* lanarkite.
lançage [lɑ̃sa:ʒ], *s.m.* **1.** launching (of ship, of scheme). **2.** *Civ.E:* driving in a pile with a monitor.
Lancastre [lɑ̃kastr̥], *Pr.n.m. Geog:* Lancaster; **le comté de L.,** Lancashire.
lancastrien, -enne [lɑ̃kastriɛ̃, -ɛn], *a.* & *s. Geog:* Lancastrian.
lance [lɑ̃:s], *s.f.* **1.** (*a*) spear; **percer un animal d'un coup de l.,** to spear an animal; **fer de l.,** (i) spearhead; (ii) *Rept:* bushmaster, fer-delance; *Bot:* **en fer de l.,** lanceolate; (*b*) lance; **l. courtoise, mousse, gracieuse,** blunt or coronal lance (used in tournaments); **l. à outrance,** sharp-point lance; **rompre une l. avec qn,** to break a lance with s.o.; to cross swords with s.o.; **rompre une l. pour qn,** to take up the cudgels for s.o.; **baisser la l.,** to acknowledge defeat; (*c*) (*whaling*) spear. **2.** (*a*) **l. à feu,** (i) *A.Artil:* port-fire; (ii) *Mch:* slice bar; (*b*) spike (on railing, etc.); (*c*) **l. d'arrosage, l. à eau,** water hose nozzle; **l. d'incendie,** fire hose nozzle; *Hyd.E: Min:* **l. hydraulique,** monitor. **3.** *Hist:* **l. fournie,** lance (= man-at-arms with his retinue). **4.** *Bot:* **l. de Christ,** gipsywort.
lancé[1] [lɑ̃se], *a.* **1. train l. à toute vapeur,** train going at full speed; **voiture lancée à toute vitesse,** car going all out, flat out, at top speed; *Sp:* **départ l.,** flying start; **le voilà l.,** (i) now he has got a start (in life, in his profession); (ii) *F:* now he's off on his pet subject; **après le champagne j'étais un peu l.,** after the champagne I got a bit chatty, my tongue was wagging; **il est éloquent une fois l.,** he is eloquent once he gets going. **2. actrice lancée,** actress who has made her name, who has made a hit; **jeune homme l.,** young man who is in the swim, who has achieved (social) success, *F:* who has made it.
lancé[2], *s.m.* **1.** *Ven:* (*a*) starting (of quarry); (*b*) **sonner le l.,** to sound the view halloo. **2. avec un brusque l. de l'avant bras,** with a flick of the forearm.
lance-amarre [lɑ̃sama:r], *s.m.* line-throwing apparatus, gun; *pl. lance-amarres.*
lance-bombes [lɑ̃sbɔ̃:b], *a.* & *s.m.inv.* **1.** *Artil:* bomb thrower, projector; **l.-b. fumigène,** smoke-bomb thrower. **2.** *Av:* **(appareil) l.-b.,** bomb-releasing apparatus, bomb-dropping gear; bomb rack; **commande de l.-b.,** bomb release.
lancée [lɑ̃se], *s.f.* **1.** (*a*) momentum, impetus; **continuer sur sa l.,** to keep moving by one's own momentum; **couper les moteurs et laisser un avion, un véhicule spatial, se mouvoir sur sa l.,** to cut the engines and allow an aircraft, a spacecraft, to coast; **la voiture continua sur sa l.,** the car continued under its own impetus; (*b*) = LANCEMENT, 1; **lâcher un bateau à la l.,** to let a boat run with the stream. **2.** *pl.* throbbing; shooting pains.
lance-flammes [lɑ̃sflam], *s.m.inv. Mil:* flame projector; flame thrower.
lance-fusée, lance-fusées [lɑ̃sfyze], *s.m.* (*a*) (i) *Pyr:* pyrotechnic projector; (ii) signal flare, signal rocket, projector; **pistolet l.-f.,** Very (light) pistol; (*b*) *Mil: Ball:* rocket launcher, rocket gun; *pl. lance-fusées.*
lance-grenades [lɑ̃sgrənad], *s.m.inv.* (*a*) *Mil:* grenade thrower, launcher; **l.-g. à fusil,** rifle grenade launcher; (*b*) *Navy:* **l.-g. sous-marines,** depth-charge thrower.
lancéiforme [lɑ̃seifɔrm], *a.* = LANCIFORME.
lancelet [lɑ̃slɛ], *s.m. Ich:* lancelet.
lancement [lɑ̃smɑ̃], *s.m.* **1.** throwing, flinging; *F:* shying (of stone, etc.); emission (of jet of steam); *Sp:* (*baseball*) pitching; pitch; **l. du javelot,** throwing the javelin; **l. du poids,** putting the weight, shot put; **l. du disque,** discus throwing;

l. du marteau, throwing the hammer; *Navy:* **tube de l.,** torpedo-tube; **à portée de l.,** within torpedo range. **2.** (*a*) *Ball: etc:* launching, delivery (of missile, rocket); dropping, releasing (of bomb, parachute); throwing, launching (of grenade); catapulting (of aircraft, etc.); sending, taking, (of glider) into the air; sending up (of balloon); *Av: etc:* **dispositif de l. aéroporté,** airborne launcher; **l. de messages au sol,** dropping of messages; **viseur de l.,** bomb sight (of bomber); *Ball:* **rampe de l.,** rocket launcher; **tour de l.,** (rocket) gantry; **plate-forme, socle, de l.,** launching pad; **chariot de l.,** starting cradle (on board ship); (*b*) *Nau:* launching (of ship); **cale de l.,** slip(way); **l. en long,** end launching; **l. en travers,** side launching; **l. sur flanc, sur double coulisse,** double-way launching; **l. sur quille, sur savate,** single-way launching; (*c*) *Mec.E:* starting (up) (of engine); *Av:* swinging (of propeller); **l. par inertie,** inertia starting device; *El:* **l. du courant,** closure of current; (*d*) *Com:* floating, launching (of company); launching, bringing out (of an actress, a painter); *Mil:* launching (of an attack); *Com:* **l. d'une campagne publicitaire,** launching of a publicity campaign; **prix de l.,** introductory offer, price.

lance-mines [lɑ̃smin], *s.m.inv. Mil:* mine thrower.

lancéolé [lɑ̃seɔle], *a. Bot:* lanceolate, spear-shaped, lance-shaped; *Arch:* **gothique l.** = decorated Gothic.

lance-pierre [lɑ̃spjɛːr], *s.m.* catapult; *pl. lance-pierres.*

lancer [lɑ̃se]. I. *v.tr.* **(je lançai(s); n. lançons) 1.** to throw, fling, cast, hurl; *F:* to shy (stone, etc.); to shoot (an arrow); to send up (a rocket); **l. deux sous à qn,** to throw a penny to s.o.; **l. des pierres à, contre, qn,** to throw, *F:* chuck, stones at s.o.; **l. des bombes,** to throw bombs; (*of aircraft*) to drop bombs; **l. un avion,** to catapult a plane; **l. une torpille,** to fire a torpedo; **l. un jet de vapeur,** to emit a jet of steam; **l. de la fumée,** to puff out smoke; **l. de l'eau sur qch.,** to play water on sth.; **l. des étincelles,** to shoot out sparks; **l. un corps à la mer,** to heave a body overboard; *Fish:* **l. la ligne,** to cast; **l. qch. en l'air,** to toss sth. into the air; **l. un coup à qn,** to aim a blow at s.o.; to deal s.o. a blow; **l. un coup d'œil à qn,** to dart a glance at s.o.; **l. un mandat d'amener contre qn,** to issue a warrant against s.o.; **l. une proclamation,** to issue, launch, a proclamation; **l. un juron,** to let out an oath; **l. une accusation,** to level an accusation; **l. une plaisanterie,** to crack a joke; *abs. F:* **ça me lance,** it gives me stabbing pains; (*b*) *Sp:* **l. un ballon,** to throw a ball; *abs.* (*at baseball*) **l.,** to pitch; **l. le disque, le javelot,** to throw the discus, the javelin; **l. le poids,** to put the shot. **2.** to start, set, (s.o., sth.) going; (*a*) **l. un cheval,** to start a horse off at full gallop; **il lança son cheval contre nous,** he rode straight at us; **l. un chien contre qn,** to set a dog on s.o.; **l. les chiens contre le taureau,** to bait the bull (with the dogs); **l. une division sur, à, l'ennemi,** to throw a division against the enemy; **si vous le lancez sur ce sujet il ne tarira pas,** if you start him on this subject he will never stop; *Ven:* **l. un cerf, un sanglier, etc.,** to start a stag, a (wild) boar, etc.; (*b*) to launch (ship, scheme, attack); to deliver (attack); to release (bomb, parachute); to send up (balloon); to float, promote (company); to bring out (actress, etc.); to initiate, launch, set (fashion); *El:* to switch on (current); *Aut:* **l. le moteur,** to start (up) the engine; *Av:* **l. l'hélice,** to swing the propeller; **l. une marchandise,** to put an article on the market, to launch a (new) product; **l. une enquête sur une question,** to launch an inquiry; **l. une souscription,** to start a fund; **l. qn (dans les affaires, etc.),** to give s.o. a start, to set s.o. up (in business, etc.); to give s.o. a start; **je suis lancé dans une grosse affaire,** *F:* I'm on to something big; **l. une théorie,** to set forth, advance, put up, a theory; **l. un appel de grève,** to put out a strike call. **3.** *abs. Nau:* **l. dans le vent,** to broach to.

II. **lancer,** *s.m.* (*a*) release (of pigeons, bombs, etc.); (*b*) *Fish:* **pêche au l.,** (i) casting, (ii) spinning; **pêcher au l.,** (i) to cast, (ii) to spin (for fish); **canne à l.,** spinning-rod; **l. arrière, avant, roulé, sous la main,** back, forward, switch, underhand, cast; (*c*) *Wr:* throw; *Sp:* **l. du javelot, du disque,** throwing the javelin, the discus; **l. du poids,** shot put; (*d*) *Ven:* starting (of quarry).

se lancer, se l. en avant, to rush, dash, shoot, forward; (*of dogs*) **se l. contre le taureau,** to bait the bull; **se l. à la poursuite de qn,** to dash off in pursuit of s.o.; **se l. dans qch.,** to tackle sth,; **se l. dans des détails, dans une description, dans la politique, dans les affaires,** to launch out into detail, into a description, into politics, into business; **il s'est lancé dans la photographie,** he has taken up photography; **se l. dans la dépense,** to launch into expenditure; **se l. (à fond) dans une description de qch.,** to plunge (headlong) into a description of sth.; *F:* **il se lance!** he's being a bit ambitious!

lanceron [lɑ̃s(ə)rɔ̃], *s.m. Ich:* pikelet.

lance-roquettes [lɑ̃srɔkɛt], *s.m.inv. Mil:* rocket launcher.

lance-satellite [lɑ̃ssatɛlit], *s.m.* satellite launcher; *pl. lance-satellites.*

lance-torpille [lɑ̃stɔrpiːj], *a. & s.m. Navy:* **(tube) l.-t.,** torpedo tube; *pl. lance-torpilles.*

lancette [lɑ̃sɛt], *s.f.* **1.** (*a*) *Surg:* lancet; **ouvrir un abcès avec une l.,** to lance an abscess; (*b*) (print-)trimming knife or nib. **2.** *Arch:* **(arc à) l.,** lancet arch; **(fenêtre en) l.,** lancet window.

lanceur, -euse [lɑ̃sœːr, -øːz], *s.* **1.** (*a*) thrower; *Cr:* bowler; (*at baseball*) pitcher; *Mil:* **l. de grenades,** (i) (*pers.*) grenade thrower, grenadier; (ii) (*thg*) grenade launcher; (*b*) *Ball: etc:* launcher (of satellite, spacecraft, etc.); **l. d'appoint, l. auxiliaire,** booster. **2.** promoter, floater (of company, etc.); initiator (of fashion); **l. d'affaires,** business promoter.

lancewood [lanswud], *s.m.* (*a*) *Bot:* lancewood tree; (*b*) *Com:* lancewood.

lanche [lɑ̃ʃ], *s.f. Nau:* lancha, lanchara.

lancier [lɑ̃sje], *s.m.* **1.** *Mil:* lancer. **2. (quadrille des) lanciers,** lancers; **danser les lanciers,** to dance a set of lancers.

lancière [lɑ̃sjɛːr], *a. Hyd.E:* **vanne l.,** gate (of water-wheel).

lanciforme [lɑ̃sifɔrm], *a.* lanciform, lance-shaped, lanced, spear-shaped.

lancinant [lɑ̃sinɑ̃], *a.* lancinating, shooting, throbbing (pain), obsessing (tune, idea, etc.); *P:* boring.

lancination [lɑ̃sinasjɔ̃], *s.f.* shooting (of pain); throbbing (of finger, etc.).

lanciner [lɑ̃sine]. **1.** *v.i.* (*of pain*) to shoot; (*of finger, etc.*) to throb. **2.** *v.tr.* (*a*) to harass, trouble; **ce problème me lancine,** this problem is harassing me, getting me down; (*b*) *P:* to bore (s.o.).

lançoir [lɑ̃swaːr], *s.m.* (*a*) mill gate (of water mill); (*b*) *For:* timber shoot.

lançon [lɑ̃sɔ̃], *s.m. Ich:* sand launce, sand eel, grig.

landais, -aise [lɑ̃dɛ, -ɛːz], *a. & s. Geog:* (native, inhabitant) of the Landes; **course de vaches landaises,** corrida in which the animal is not killed.

landau, -aus [lɑ̃do], *s.m.* (*a*) *Veh:* landau; (*b*) baby carriage; pram.

landaulet [lɑ̃dolɛ], *s.m.,* **landaulette** [lɑ̃dolɛt], *s.f. Aut: A:* landaulet(te).

lande [lɑ̃ːd], *s.f.* sandy moor; heath, heathland; waste; *U.S:* barren.

landerira, landerirette [lɑ̃dərira, lɑ̃dərirɛt, lɑ̃de-] (*burden of old songs*) = fol-de-rol (derido, folderol-deray).

Landerneau [lɑ̃dɛrno], *Pr.n.* (*small town near Brest, in Brittany*) **cela fera du bruit dans L.,** that will upset the apple-cart; that'll make the yokels sit up.

landeux, -euse [lɑ̃dø, -øːz], *a.* moor-like, heath-like.

landgrave [lɑ̃(d)graːv], (*a*) *s.m.* landgrave; (*b*) *s.f.* landgravine, wife of a landgrave.

landgraviat [lɑ̃(d)gravja], *s.m.* landgraviate.

landgravine [lɑ̃(d)gravin], *s.f.* landgravine.

landier[1] [lɑ̃dje], *s.m.* andiron, fire dog.

landier[2], *s.m. Bot: F:* (= AJONC) furze, gorse.

landit [lɑ̃di], *s.m.* = LENDIT.

landole [lɑ̃dɔl], *s.f. Ich:* flying fish.

landolphie [lɑ̃dɔlfi], *s.f. Bot:* landolphia; Congo rubber plant.

laneret [lanrɛ], *s.m. Ven:* lanneret (falcon).

langage [lɑ̃gaːʒ], *s.m.* language. **1.** speech (*of the individual, as opposed to the common language of a whole people*; *cp.* LANGUE 3); **correction du l.,** correctness of speech, of language; **l. violent,** strong language; **brusquerie de l.,** abruptness of speech; **tenir un l. aimable, grossier, à qn,** to speak amiably, rudely, to s.o.; **vous tenez là un étrange l.,** that is a strange way to talk; **ils tiennent tous le même l.,** they all say the same thing; *F:* **changer de l.,** to change one's tune; **beau l., l. fleuri,** flowery, high-falutin(g), language; **en voilà un l.!** that's no way to talk! **connu, en l. ordinaire, sous le nom de . . .,** known in common parlance as . . .; **en l. de pratique . . .,** in legal parlance . . .; **surveillez votre l.!** watch your language! **parler le l. de la raison,** to talk common sense; **troubles du l.,** speech disorder, defective speech. **2. le l. des fleurs,** the language of flowers; **ayez recours au l. des fleurs,** say it with flowers; **les langages par signes,** sign languages; **les animaux ont-ils un l.?** have animals a language? **l. chiffré, l. secret,** secret language, text, cipher, code; **l. convenu,** conventional language; **l. clair,** clear, plain, language, text; (*computers*) **l. symbolique,** symbolic language; **l. source, d'origine,** source language; **l. généré, objet,** target language; **l. synthétique,** computer-independent language; **l. d'assemblage,** assembly language.

langage-machine [lɑ̃gaʒmaʃin], *s.m.* computer language, machine language; *pl. langages-machine.*

langagier, -ière [lɑ̃gaʒje, -jɛːr], *a.* linguistic.

langaha [lagaa], *s.m. Rept:* (Madagascan) langaha.

langbanite [lɑ̃gbanit], *s.f. Miner:* langbanite.

langbeinite [lɑ̃gbenit], *s.f. Miner:* langbeinite.

lange[1] [lɑːʒ], *s.m.* **1.** *pl. A.Cost:* **langes,** swaddling clothes; *now used in:* **bébé en langes** = babe in arms; **science encore en ses langes,** science still in its infancy. **2.** baby's napkin.

Lange[2], *Pr.n. Med:* **réaction de L.,** Lange's colloidal-gold test.

langer [lɑ̃ʒe], *v.tr. A:* **(je langeai(s); n. langeons)** to wrap a baby in swaddling clothes.

Langhans [lɑ̃gɑ̃(s)], *Pr.n. Anat:* **cellules de L.,** Langhans' layer.

langite [lɑ̃ʒit], *s.f. Miner:* langite.

langognais, -aise [lɑ̃gɔɲɛ, -ɛːz], *a. & s. Geog:* (native, inhabitant) of Langogne.

langoureusement [lɑ̃gurøzmɑ̃], *adv.* languorously, languidly, languishingly.

langoureux, -euse [lɑ̃gurø, -øːz], *a.* languid, languorous; **amant l.,** languishing lover.

langouste [lɑ̃gust], *s.f. Crust:* spiny, rock, lobster; sea crayfish, crawfish.

langoustier, -ière [lɑ̃gustje, -jɛːr], (*a*) *s.m. & f.* lobster net; (*b*) *s.m.* lobster boat.

langoustine [lɑ̃gustin], *s.f. Crust:* (*a*) Norway lobster; (*b*) Dublin bay prawn; *Com: Cu: pl.* scampi.

langouti [lɑ̃guti], *s.m. Cost:* langooty.

langrayen [lɑ̃grajɛ̃], *s.m. Orn:* swallow shrike.

langrois, -oise [lɑ̃grwa, -waːz], *a. & s.* (native, inhabitant) of Langres.

languard [lɑ̃gaːr], *s.m. Orn:* wryneck.

langue [lɑ̃ːg], *s.f.* **1.** (*a*) tongue; **tirer la l.,** (i) to put out, stick out, one's tongue **(à qn,** at s.o.); (ii) (*of dog*) to hang out its tongue; (iii) *F:* (*of pers.*) to be near the end of one's tether; (iv) to have one's tongue hanging out (for sth.); *F:* **tirer la l. d'un pied de long,** to be in desperate circumstances, up against it; **faire tirer la l. à qn,** to keep s.o. waiting; **montrez-moi votre l.,** show me, put out, your tongue; **avoir la l. liée,** to be tongue-tied; **délier la l. à qn,** to loosen s.o.'s tongue; **avoir la l. déliée, bien pendue, bien affilée,** to have a ready tongue, *F:* the gift of the gab; **avoir la l. trop longue,** to be unable to hold one's tongue; **tenir sa l.,** to hold one's tongue; **gouverner sa l.,** to keep a watch on one's tongue; **je l'avais sur le bout de la l.,** I had it on the tip of my tongue; **coup de l.,** (i) click (of the tongue); tonguing (on wind instrument); (ii) lick; (iii) cutting remark; *Prov:* **coup de l. est pire que coup de lance,** the tongue is sharper than any sword; **faire aller les langues,** to set people's tongues wagging; **jeter, donner, sa l. au chat,** (*with reference to riddle, etc.*) to give it up; **quelle l.!** what a chatterbox! **mauvaise l.,** backbiter, mischief maker, scandalmonger; **se mordre la l. d'avoir parlé,** *F:* **s'en mordre la l.,** to regret bitterly having spoken; *Prov:* **beau parler n'écorche point la l.,** civility costs nothing; **prendre l.,** (i) to establish contact, to start preliminary conversations; (ii) to open up a conversation, *F:* to break the ice; *F:* **avoir un cheveu sur la l.,** to lisp, to have a lisp; *s.a.* AVALER 3, POCHE 1; (*b*) *Anat:* **l. bifide,** bifid, cleft, tongue; *Med:* **l. de bœuf, l. pellagre,** pellagrous, beefy, tongue; *Med: Vet:* **l. noire,** black tongue; *Vet:* **l. bleue,** blue tongue; *Med:* **langue scrotale,** scrotal, furrowed, tongue; **l. pâteuse,** coated tongue; **langue noire villeuse,** (black) villous, hairy, tongue; (*c*) *Cu:* **l. de bœuf,** ox tongue; (*d*) *Moll:* foot (of bivalve). **2.** (*a*) **langues de feu,** tongues of flame; (*b*) **l. de terre,** spit of land, neck of land, tongue of land; gore; (*c*) *Nau:* **l. de toile,** gore (of sail); (*d*) pointer, index, tongue, needle (of a balance). **3.** language (of a people); **l. maternelle, l. mère,** mother tongue; **langues étrangères,** foreign languages; **l. morte,** dead language; **professeur de langues**

vivantes, modern-language master, mistress; **avoir le don des langues,** to be a good linguist; **écrire une belle l.,** to have a good style; to write beautiful English, French, etc.; **peuples, pays, de l. anglaise,** English-speaking people, countries; **minorités de l.,** linguistic minorities; *Sch: Ling:* **l. de départ,** source language; **l. d'arrivée,** target language; *F:* **l. verte,** slang; **l. du barreau,** legal jargon.

langué [lɑ̃ge], *a. Her:* **l. de gueules,** langued gules.

langue-de-bœuf [lɑ̃gdəbœf], *s.f.* **1.** *A.Arms:* langue de bœuf. **2.** *Fung:* fistulina, beefsteak fungus. **3.** *Tls:* (heart-shaped) trowel; *pl. langues-de-bœuf.*

langue-de-carpe [lɑ̃gdəkarp], *s.f.* **1.** cold chisel. **2.** *Dent:* elevator; *pl. langues-de-carpe.*

langue-de-carpette [lɑ̃gdəkarpɛt], *s.f.* locksmith's graver; *pl. langues-de-carpette.*

langue-de-cerf [lɑ̃gdəsɛːr], *s.f. Bot:* hart's tongue, scolopendrium; *pl. langues-de-cerf.*

langue-de-chat [lɑ̃gdəʃa], *s.f.* **1.** *Cu:* (flat) finger biscuit; langue-de-chat; *Tls:* (engraver's) narrow-bladed graver, burin. **2.** *Ich:* variegated sole; *pl. langues-de-chat.*

langue-de-chien [lɑ̃gdəʃjɛ̃], *s.f. Bot:* hound's tongue; *pl. langues-de-chien.*

langue-de-serpent [lɑ̃gdəsɛrpɑ̃], *s.f.* **1.** *Bot:* adder's tongue. **2.** *A:* (*for tasting food in case of poison*) adder's tongue; *pl. langues-de-serpent.*

langue-de-vache [lɑ̃gdəvaʃ], *s.f.* (type of) anvil; *pl. langues-de-vache.*

languedocien, -ienne [lɑ̃gdəsjɛ̃, -jɛn], *a. & s. Geog:* (native, inhabitant) of Languedoc; Languedocian.

langueter [lɑ̃gəte], *v.tr.* (**je languette, n. languetons; je languetterai**) to tongue (edge of board, etc.).

languette [lɑ̃gɛt], *s.f.* small tongue (of wood, metal, land, etc.); tab; strip (of tinfoil, etc.); tongue (of shoe); *Const:* withe (between flues); *Carp:* feather; *Mec.E:* feather (key), spline (*e.g.* locking wheel hub to shaft); pointer, index, tongue, needle (of balance); *Mus:* (*in organ*) tongue (for the reed); languet (of flue pipe); **l. de fermeture,** small latch; *Carp:* **l. rapportée,** loose tongue, slipped tongue; **assemblage à rainure et l.,** tongue and groove (joint); *El:* **contact à l.,** snap contact; *s.a.* RAPPORTÉ 2.

langueur [lɑ̃gœːr], *s.f.* **1.** languor, languidness; listlessness; **l. du commerce,** dullness, flatness, of trade; *A:* **(maladie de) l.,** decline. **2.** languishment; **regard plein de l.,** languishing look.

langueyer [lɑ̃geje], *v.tr.* **1.** *Vet:* to examine the tongue of (a pig). **2.** *Mus:* to tongue (an organ pipe).

langueyeur [lɑ̃gejœːr], *s.m. A.Vet:* examiner of pigs' tongues (in markets).

languide [lɑ̃gid], *a. Lit:* languid.

languier [lɑ̃gje], *s.m. Cu:* smoked pig's tongue and throat.

languir [lɑ̃giːr], *v.i.* to languish, pine; to waste away; (*of plant*) to wilt; **pendant les années qu'il avait langui en prison,** during the years when he had languished in prison; **l. d'amour,** to be lovesick; **l. d'ennui,** to yawn one's life away; **l. dans la solitude,** to mope in solitude; **l. de misère,** to languish in misery; **l. pour qn, qch.,** to long, pine, yearn, for s.o., sth.; **l. après qch.,** to weary for sth.; to languish after, for, sth.; **ne nous faites pas l.,** don't keep us on tenterhooks; **je languis d'avoir de vos nouvelles,** I am dying for news of you; **la conversation languit,** the conversation flags; **ne pas laisser l. la conversation,** to keep the conversation alive; to keep the ball rolling; **les affaires languissent,** business is slack, dull; *Th:* **l'action languit,** the action drags.

se languir, *Dial:* to be bored.

languissamment [lɑ̃gisamɑ̃], *adv.* **1.** languidly. **2.** languishingly.

languissant [lɑ̃gisɑ̃], *a.* **1.** languid, listless; **style l.,** nerveless style; **conversation languissante,** lagging, dragging, conversation; **intérêt l.,** unsustained, languishing, interest; *Com:* **marché l.,** dull, flat, market. **2.** languishing (eyes, look); **l. d'amour,** pining away from love.

langur [lɑ̃gyːr], *s.m. Z:* langur (monkey), leaf monkey; **l. à nez retroussé,** snub-nosed monkey.

laniaire [lanjɛːr], *a. & s.f. Z:* laniary (teeth).

lanice[1] [lanis], *a.f.* **bourre l.,** flock of wool.

lanice[2], *s.m. Ann:* sand-mason worm.

lanier [lanje], *s.m. Ven:* lanner (falcon).

lanière [lanjɛːr], *s.f.* **1.** (*a*) thin strip of material; *esp.* thin strap; thong; (leather) lace; lash (of whip); **drapeau réduit en lanières,** flag reduced to ribbons; (*b*) hair-cloth (for friction); (*c*) **l. de cuir (pour affûter les rasoirs),** belt strop (for razors). **2.** *Her:* (= BANDE) bend.

lanifère [lanifɛːr], *a.* laniferous, wool-bearing.

laniflore [laniflɔːr], *a. Bot:* laniflorous.

lanigère [laniʒɛːr], *a.* lanigerous, wool-bearing; **puceron l.,** woolly aphis.

laniidés [laniide], *s.m.pl. Orn:* Laniidae; the shrikes.

lanista [lanista], *s.m. Rom.Ant:* lanista.

lanius [lanjys], *s.m. Orn:* lanius, shrike.

lanlaire [lɑ̃lɛːr] (*burden of old songs*) *F:* **envoyer qn faire l.,** to send s.o. packing, to Jericho.

lannionais, -aise [lanjɔnɛ, -ɛːz], *a. & s. Geog:* (native, inhabitant) of Lannion.

lanoléine [lanɔlein], **lanoline** [lanɔlin], *s.f.* lanoline.

lansfordite [lɑ̃sfɔrdit], *s.f. Miner:* lansfordite.

lansquenet [lɑ̃skənɛ], *s.m.* (*a*) *Hist:* lansquenet, German foot-soldier (16th century); (*b*) *Cards:* lansquenet.

lansquenette [lɑ̃skənɛt], *s.f. Hist:* short sword worn by the lansquenets (16th century).

lansquine [lɑ̃skin], *s.f. P:* (*a*) rain; (*b*) water.

lansquiner [lɑ̃skine], *v.i. P:* (*a*) to rain; (*b*) to piss.

lantana [lɑ̃tana], **lantanier** [lɑ̃tanje], *s.m. Bot:* lantana.

lanterne [lɑ̃tɛrn], *s.f.* **1.** (*a*) lantern; **l. sourde,** dark lantern, bull's-eye lantern; **l. vénitienne,** Chinese lantern; **l. magique,** magic lantern; **l. à projections,** projector; *A:* **l. de tempête,** hurricane lamp, tornado lamp; **homme aux joues en l.,** lantern-jawed man; *F:* **oublier d'allumer, d'éclairer, sa l.,** to forget the most important thing (with reference to Florian's fable *Le Singe qui montre la l. magique*); **éclairer sa l.,** to explain one's point; *A:* **dire des lanternes,** to say foolish things, to talk rubbish; *s.a.* VESSIE 1; (*b*) **l. de signalisation,** signalling lamp; *O:* **l. de voiture, de bicyclette,** carriage-lamp, cycle-lamp; *O: Aut:* **l. à feu blanc,** side-light; **l. à feu rouge, l. arrière,** tail-light; *Sp:* **la l. rouge,** the last man in the race; *F:* **être la l. rouge,** to win the donkey race, to come last; *Sch:* to be bottom of the class; (*c*) *A:* **l. de rue,** street-lamp; *Fr.Hist:* (*during the Revolution*) **à la l.!** string him up! (*d*) *P:* (i) window; (ii) belly; **se taper sur la l.,** to be hungry. **2.** (*a*) *Arch:* lantern (light, turret); **l. des morts,** graveyard lantern; turret; light column; (*b*) *Ecc: etc:* (screened off) box, pew, gallery; (*c*) *Ph:* balance case; (*d*) *Mec.E:* **(roue à) l.,** lantern (wheel), trundle (wheel), wallower (wheel); **l. à billes,** ball cage; **l. (de serrage),** turnbuckle; (*e*) *Mch:* **tiroir à l.,** gridiron valve; (*f*) *pl. N.Arch:* pintle scores (of rudder); (*g*) *Echin:* **l. d'Aristote,** Aristotle's lantern.

lanterne-applique [lɑ̃tɛrnaplik], *s.f.* bracket lamp; *pl. lanternes-appliques.*

lanterneau, -eaux [lɑ̃tɛrno], *s.m.* **1.** *Arch:* skylight (over staircase); lantern (light). **2.** *Rail: U.S:* monitor roof; turret.

lanterner [lɑ̃tɛrne], *F:* **1.** *v.i.* to trifle; to dilly-dally; to trifle away one's time; to hum and ha(w). **2.** *v.tr.* (*a*) to shilly-shally with (s.o.); to put (s.o.) off; (*b*) to bother, importune (s.o.); (*c*) *A:* to hang (s.o. on a lamp-post).

lanternerie [lɑ̃tɛrn(ə)ri], *s.f.* *A:* (*a*) trifling, frivoling, dilly-dallying, shilly-shallying; (*b*) idle talk, frivolity.

lanterne-tempête [lɑ̃tɛrntɑ̃pɛːt], *s.f.* hurricane lamp; *pl. lanternes-tempêtes.*

lanternier[1], **-ière** [lɑ̃tɛrnje, -jɛːr], *s. F: A:* frivoller, trifler, dilly-dallier, shilly-shallier.

lanternier[2], **-ière,** *s.* **1.** (*a*) lantern maker; (*b*) *A:* lamplighter. **2.** *P:* brothel keeper; *f.* madam.

lanternon [lɑ̃tɛrnɔ̃], *s.m.* = LANTERNEAU.

lanthane [lɑ̃tan], *s.m. Ch:* lanthanum.

lanthanide [lɑ̃tanid], *s.m. Ch:* lanthanide.

lanthanite [lɑ̃tanit], *s.f. Miner:* lanthanite.

lantiponnage [lɑ̃tipɔnaːʒ], *s.m. F:* idle, frivolous, talk.

lantiponner [lɑ̃tipɔne], *v.i.* to talk in an idle, frivolous, way.

lantur(e)lu [lɑ̃tyrly], *int. burden of old songs, now used in the meanings:* **1.** you don't catch me! I'm not having any! nonsense! **2.** wait and see!

lanugineux, -euse [lanyʒinø, -øːz], *a. Bot: etc:* lanuginous, downy.

lanugo [lanygo], *s.m. Biol:* lanugo.

Laodamie [laɔdami], *Pr.n.f. Myth:* Laodamia.

Laodicée [laɔdise], *Pr.n.f. A.Geog:* Laodicea.

laodicéen, -éenne [laɔdiseɛ̃, -eɛn], *a. & s.* Laodicean.

Laomédon [laɔmedɔ̃], *Pr.n.m. Gr.Myth:* Laomedon.

laonnois, -oise [lanwa, -waːz], *a. & s. Geog:* (native, inhabitant) of Laon [lɑ̃].

Laos [laɔs], *Pr.n.m. Geog:* Laos.

laotien, -ienne [laɔsjɛ̃, -jɛn], *a. & s. Geog:* Laotian.

lapacho [lapaʃo], *s.m. Bot:* lapacho.

La Palice, La Palisse [lapalis], *Pr.n.m. F:* **vérité de (monsieur de) La P.,** self-evident truth, obvious remark, truism (*from an old song*).

lapalissade [lapalisad], *s.f.* = **vérité de La Palice.**

laparocèle [laparɔsɛl], *s.f. Med:* laparocele.

laparoscopie [laparɔskɔpi], *s.f. Med:* laparoscopy.

laparotomie [laparɔtɔmi], *s.f. Surg:* laparotomy.

lapement [lapmɑ̃], *s.m.* lapping (up) (of milk, etc.).

laper [lape], *v.tr. & i.* (*of dog, cat, etc.*) to lap (up) (water, milk, etc.).

lapereau, -eaux [lapro], *s.m.* young rabbit.

lapeyrousia [laperuzja], *s.m. Bot:* lapeyrousia.

laphygma [lafigma], *s.m. Ent:* laphygma.

lapiaz [lapjaːz], *s.m. Geol:* lapiaz, lapiés.

lapicide [lapisid], *s.m.* (*pers.*) lapidary.

lapidaire [lapidɛːr]. **1.** *a.* lapidary (inscription, style, etc.); concise (style); **phrase l.,** pithy expression. **2.** *s.m.* (*a*) lapidary; (*b*) lapidary's mill.

lapidateur, -trice [lapidatœːr, -tris], *s.* **1.** stoner. **2.** *pl.* vilifiers, insulters.

lapidation [lapidasjɔ̃], *s.f.* lapidation, stoning.

lapider [lapide], *v.tr.* to lapidate; to stone (s.o.) to death; **l. un chien,** to throw stones at a dog; **l. qn de reproches,** to hurl reproaches at s.o.; **l. qn dans les journaux,** to abuse s.o. in the papers.

lapideur [lapidœːr], *s.m.* (optical) grinder.

lapidification [lapidifikasjɔ̃], *s.f.* lapidification, petrification.

lapidifier [lapidifje], *v.tr.* to lapidify, petrify.

se lapidifier, to petrify, to turn into stone.

lapié, lapiez [lapje], *s.m. Geol: usu. pl.* lapiés, lapiaz.

lapiésation [lapjezasjɔ̃], *s.f. Geol:* lapiésation.

lapilleux, -euse [lapijø, -øːz], *a.* gritty (pear, etc.).

lapilli [lapili], *s.m.pl. Geol:* lapilli.

lapilliforme [lapilifɔrm], *a. Geol:* lapilliform.

lapin, -ine [lapɛ̃, -in], *s.* **1.** rabbit, *f.* doe (of tame rabbit); *cf.* HASE; **l. mâle,** buck rabbit; **l. de garenne,** wild rabbit; **l. domestique, de clapier,** *F.* **l. de choux,** tame rabbit; **l. russe,** albino rabbit; *Com:* **peau de l.,** cony (skin); *F:* **l. de gouttière,** cat; *P:* **poser un l. à qn,** (i) to stand s.o. up; to fail to turn up; (ii) to bilk (restaurant); *F:* **un drôle de l.,** a queer customer; *F:* **un chaud l.,** a don Juan, a (regular) Casanova; *F:* **c'est un rude l., un fier l.,** (i) he's cunning, astute; (ii) he's got plenty of pluck; **se sauver comme un l.,** to turn tail (and run); **coup du l.,** (i) rabbit punch; (ii) *Med:* whiplash injury; *F:* **faire le coup du l. à qn,** to kill s.o. treacherously; *A: F:* **aller, être, en l.,** to sit beside the driver, the chauffeur; *F:* **une (mère) lapine,** a woman with lots of children; *F:* **mon petit l.,** my dear; darling. **2.** *Z:* (*a*) **l. d'Allemagne,** suslik; **l. d'Amérique,** agouti; **l. d'Aroe,** filander kangaroo; **l. de Norvège,** lemming; (*b*) *P: O:* **l. (ferré),** horse.

lapiner [lapine], *v.i.* (*of rabbit*) to litter.

lapinière [lapinjɛːr], *s.f.* **1.** rabbit hutch. **2.** rabbit warren.

lapinisme [lapinism], *s.m. F: Pej:* excessive fecundity (in woman).

lapis [lapis], *s.m.,* **lapis-lazuli** [lapislazyli], *s.m. inv. Miner:* lapis lazuli; *a.inv.* **robe l.-l.,** bright blue dress.

Lapithes [lapit], *s.m.pl. Myth:* Lapithae.

Laplace [laplas], *Pr.n. Mth:* **équation de L.,** Laplace's equation.

laplacien, -ienne [laplasjɛ̃, -jɛn], *a. & s.m. Mth:* **1.** *a.* Laplacian. **2.** *s.m.* Laplacian operator, Laplacian. **3.** *s.m. Atom.Ph:* buckling (of reactor); **l. géométrique,** geometric buckling; **l. matériel, l.-matière,** material buckling.

lapon, -one [lapɔ̃, -ɔn], *Geog: Ethn:* **1.** *a.* Lappish, Lapp. **2.** *s.* Lapp, Laplander. **3.** *s.m. Ling:* **le l.,** Lappish, Lapp.

Laponie [lapɔni], *Pr.n.f. Geog:* Lapland.

laportea [lapɔrtea], *s.m. Bot:* laportea.

lappa [lapa], *s.m. Bot:* lappa, burdock.

lapping [lapiŋ], *s.m. Mec.E:* lapping.

laps[1] [laps], *s.m. used only in* **un l. de temps,** a lapse, space, of time.

laps[2], *a. used only in Ecc:* **être l. et relaps,** *f.* **être lapse et relapse,** to have relapsed into a former heresy.

lapsana [lapsana], *s.m. Bot:* lapsana, nipplewort.

lapsi [lapsi], *s.m.pl. Ecc:* the lapsed.

lapsus [lapsyːs], *s.m. Lt:* slip, mistake, lapse; **l. linguae,** slip, lapse, of the tongue; *lapsus linguae*; **l. calami,** slip of the pen; **l. de mémoire,** lapse of memory.

laptot [lapto], *s.m.* **1.** *A:* Senegalese serving in the French armed forces. **2.** (*in Africa*) (*a*) paddler (in a pirogue); bargee. (*b*) (*in African ports*) docker.

laquage [laka:ʒ], *s.m.* **1.** (*action*) lacquering. **2.** lacquered surface. **3.** *Med:* **l. (du sang),** hemolysis.

laquais [lakɛ], *s.m.* lackey, footman; *Pej: F:* flunkey; **petit l.,** buttons; *Lit:* **âme de l.,** servile nature, cringing nature; *F:* **mentir comme un l.,** to lie like a trooper; **être insolent comme un l.,** to have the cheek of the devil.

laque [lak]. **1.** *s.f.* (*a*) lac; **gomme l., l. en écailles,** shellac, gum lac; **l. en grains,** seed lac; (*b*) *Paint:* lake; **l. carminée,** crimson lake; **l. jaune,** yellow lake; **l. de garance,** madder lake; (*c*) *Hairdr:* lacquer, hair spray; (*d*) *Aut:* cellulose lacquer, *F:* dope. **2.** *s.m.* lacquer; **de l., en l.,** lacquered; **l. de Chine,** japan; **je peux vous montrer un beau l., de beaux laques,** I can show you some fine lacquer ware.

laqué [lake], *a.* **1.** japanned, lacquered (ware). **2.** *Med:* **sang l.,** laky, laked, blood. **3. cheveux laqués,** lacquered, brilliantined, hair.

Laquedives [lakdi:v], *Pr.n. Geog:* les (îles) **L.,** the Laccadive Islands.

laquer [lake], *v.tr.* (*a*) to lacquer, to japan; (*b*) to enamel; **meubles laqués de blanc,** white-enamelled furniture; (*c*) *Aut: etc:* to paint, to spray, (a car, etc.) with cellulose lacquer.

laquet [lakɛ], *s.m.* (*in the Pyrenees*) small lake.

laqueur [lakœ:r], *s.m.* lacquerer, japanner.

laqueux, -euse [lakø, -ø:z], *a.* **1.** lake (tint, etc.). **2.** lacquer-like.

laquier [lakje], *s.m.* lac-bearing tree, lac tree.

laraire [larɛ:r], *s.m.* *Rom.Ant:* lararium; *pl.* lararia.

laramien, -ienne [laramjɛ̃, -jɛn], *a.* *Geol:* **plissement l.,** Laramide orogeny, mountain-building movement.

larbin [larbɛ̃], *s.m. F:* *usu. Pej:* (= LAQUAIS, VALET) flunkey.

larcin [larsɛ̃], *s.m.* **1.** (*a*) *Jur:* larceny; (petty) theft; (piece of) pilfering; (*b*) **l. littéraire,** plagiarism. **2.** stolen article, goods; *Poet: A:* **doux l.,** stolen kiss.

lard [la:r], *s.m.* **1.** (*a*) back-fat, flare (*esp.* of pig); *F:* **faire du l.,** to grow stout; **être gras à l.,** to be as fat as a pig; *P:* **rentrer dans le l. à qn,** to go for s.o.; (*b*) (*esp. with reference to Eng. cookery*) bacon; **flèche de l.,** flitch of bacon; **petit l., l. maigre,** streaky bacon; **gros l., l. gras,** fat bacon; **omelette au l.,** bacon omelette; *P:* (*of pers.*) **gros l.,** big fat slob; **tête de l.,** pig-headed person; (*c*) *Fr.C:* **l. salé,** salt pork; (*d*) **l. de baleine,** blubber. **2.** *Cu:* larding bacon, lardon. **3. pierre de l.,** soapstone, steatite.

lardacé [lardase], *a.* lardaceous; *Med:* **tissu l.,** amyloid tissue, lardaceous tissue.

lardage [larda:ʒ], *s.m.* **1.** (*a*) *Cu:* larding (of piece of meat); (*b*) *Av: A:* **l. des toiles,** stitching on of the wing coverings. **2.** *Nau:* thrum. **3.** *Fung:* spawning of mushrooms, planting of mushroom spawn.

lardé [larde], *a.* (*a*) (*of joint*) larded; (*b*) streaked; *Geol:* interbedded (**de,** with); (*c*) *Typ:* **composition lardée,** mixed matter, mixed composition.

larder [larde], *v.tr.* **1.** (*a*) to lard (piece of meat); **aiguille à l.,** larding needle; **l. qn,** to run through, to pink, s.o.; **l. qn de coups de couteau,** to stab s.o. (all over) with a knife; **l. qn de ridicule,** to cover s.o. with ridicule; **l. ses écrits de citations,** to (inter)lard, sprinkle, one's writings with quotations; *Cards:* **l. une carte,** to slip in a marked card; (*b*) *Av: A:* to stitch on (the wing coverings); (*c*) *Horse Rac:* to spur on (a horse) savagely. **2.** (*a*) *Const:* to stud (beam, etc.) with nails (before plastering); (*b*) *Nau:* to thrum, pad (a mat, etc.).

larderasse [lardəras], *s.f.* *Nau:* rombowline.

larderellite [lardərelit], *s.f.* *Miner:* larderellite.

lardier [lardjɛ], *s.m.* *Dom.Ec: O: Dial:* larder.

lardite [lardit], *s.f.* *Miner:* steatite.

lardoire [lardwa:r], *s.f.* **1.** *Cu:* larding needle, pin. **2.** *Civ.E:* shoe (of pile). **3.** *F:* sword.

lardon [lardɔ̃], *s.m.* **1.** (*a*) *Cu:* piece of larding bacon, lardon, lardoon, piece of diced bacon; (*b*) jibe, cutting remark; (*c*) *Cards:* marked card. **2.** *Metalw:* plug (concealing defect in casting); *Mec.E:* **l. d'ajustage,** packing strip. **3.** *P:* baby, brat.

lardonner [lardɔne], *v.tr.* **1.** to cut (bacon) into strips, into lardons, lardoons. **2.** *O: F:* to jibe at (s.o.); to satirize (s.o.).

lare [la:r], *s.m.* *Rom.Ant:* household god; lar; *esp. pl.* **dieux lares,** lares; *Lit:* **transporter ailleurs ses lares et pénates,** to remove with one's Lares and Penates, with all one's belongings; **abandonner ses lares,** to desert one's home.

largable [largabl], *a.* *Av:* (*of container, equipment*), droppable, releasable; **réservoir, siège, l.,** drop tank, drop seat.

largage [larga:ʒ], *s.m.* (*a*) *Av:* dropping (of personnel, supplies, equipment); dropping, releasing (of bomb); **point de l.,** (i) drop point (of personnel, supplies, equipment); (ii) bomb-release point; **zone de l.,** dropping area, drop(ping) zone; **dispositif de l. des bombes,** bomb-release mechanism; **ligne de l. des bombes,** bomb-release line; (*b*) *Nau:* letting go (of mooring); unfurling (of sail).

large [larʒ]. **1.** *a.* (*a*) broad, wide; **l. d'épaules,** broad-shouldered; **chapeau à larges bords,** broad-brimmed hat; **route l. de dix mètres,** road ten metres wide; **vêtements larges,** loose-fitting clothes; (*of garment*) **trop l.,** too wide, too full; **il me faut des souliers larges,** (i) I need broad-fitting shoes; (ii) I want easy-fitting shoes; **on lui a donné une l. marge,** he has been given plenty of scope; **avoir la main l.,** to be generous, liberal, with one's money; **d'un geste l.,** with a broad, sweeping, gesture; **conscience l.,** accommodating conscience; **critique à l'esprit l.,** broad-minded critic; **au sens le plus l. du mot,** in the most liberal, the widest, sense of the word; **terme employé dans un sens très l.,** term used (i) in a broad sense, (ii) in its broadest sense; **être l. en affaires, avec ses domestiques,** to be generous, free, liberal, in business, with one's servants; **avoir l'esprit l.,** to be broad-minded; *Art:* **style l.,** broad, bold, free, style; *adv.* **peindre l.,** to paint boldly, broadly; **calculer l.,** to allow a good margin for error; *Rac:* **prendre le tournant l.,** to take the turning wide; **roses larges épanouies,** roses in full bloom; **portes larges ouvertes,** wide-open doors; **mener la vie l.,** to spend freely; *s.a.* MENER 3; (*b*) large, big, ample; **faire de larges concessions,** to make big concessions; **prendre une l. part dans la direction,** to take a large share in the management; **de larges ressources,** ample resources; **de larges pouvoirs,** extensive powers. **2.** *s.m.* (*a*) room, space; **donner du l. à qn,** to give s.o. elbow room; **vous êtes au l. ici,** you have plenty of room here; *F:* **être au l.,** to be well off; (*b*) *Nau:* open sea; **au grand l.,** on the high seas; **navigation au l.,** high-seas navigation; **brise du l.,** sea breeze; **prendre le l., tirer au l.,** (i) to stand out to sea, to put to sea; (ii) *F:* to decamp, to beat it; **porter au l., mettre le cap au l.,** to stand out to sea; **gagner le l.,** to get an offing; **tenir le l.,** to keep an offing; **se tenir au l.,** to keep out at sea; **pousser au l.,** to push off, to shove off (boat); **au large,** (i) in the offing, (ii) (*to small boat*) pay off! keep away! keep off! **passer au large d'un navire,** to give a ship a wide berth; **au l. de Cherbourg,** off Cherbourg; **trop au l.,** too far from the shore; (*c*) breadth; **route qui a dix mètres de l.,** road ten metres broad; **en l.,** broadwise; breadthways, breadthwise; **se promener de long en l.,** to walk up and down, to and fro; **il parcourut la pièce de long en l., en long et en l.,** he walked up and down the room; **il examina la question en long et en l.,** he went into all sides of the question; **au long et au l.,** far and wide.

largement [larʒəmɑ̃], *adv.* (*a*) broadly, widely; **envisager une question l.,** to look at a question broad-mindedly; **services l. rétribués,** highly-paid services; **opinion l. répandue,** widely held opinion; *Art:* **peindre l.,** to paint in a free, broad, style; (*b*) amply; **avoir l. de quoi vivre,** to have ample means; **avoir l. le temps,** to have plenty of time; **avoir l. dépassé la quarantaine,** to be well over forty; *F:* **il en a eu l. (assez),** he's had (more than) enough.

largesse [larʒɛs], *s.f.* **1.** liberality (**envers,** towards); **avec l.,** generously. **2.** *A. & Hum:* bounty, largess(e); **faire l.,** to make handsome presents; **combler qn de largesses,** to overwhelm s.o. with (generous) gifts; (*of guest*) **faire ses largesses,** to tip the servants (before leaving).

larget [larʒɛ], *s.m.* *Metalw:* billet (of metal).

largeur [larʒœ:r], *s.f.* (*a*) breadth, width; span (of arch); gauge (of railway track); *Tex:* **étoffe grande l.,** double-width cloth; **avoir trois mètres de l.,** to be three metres wide; **en l., dans la l.,** widthwise, breadthwise; **distance en l.,** distance across; **l. de vues, d'esprit,** broadness of outlook, of mind; *F:* **dans les grandes largeurs,** in a big way; (*b*) *Nau:* breadth, beam (of ship); **l. au fort, l. hors tout,** extreme breadth; **l. hors membrures,** moulded breadth; **l. de jauge,** tonnage breadth; (*of sail*) **se déchirer dans toute sa l.,** to tear from luff to leach; (*c*) *Elcs:* **l. de bande,** band width (of radar, etc.); **l. de bande de fréquence,** frequency-band width; **l. d'impulsion,** pulse width; *T.V:* **l. de bande autorisée,** standard broadcast channel; **commande de l. d'image,** width control; (*d*) *Ph: Atom.Ph:* **l. d'énergie,** energy width; **l. de niveau,** level width; **l. de maille,** mesh spacing; (*e*) *Mec.E:* **l. sur pans,** width across flats; **l. de la dent (d'un engrenage),** width of tooth; **l. de l'intervalle (entre les dents),** width of space.

larghetto [largɛtto], *adv. & s.m.* *Mus:* larghetto.

largo [largo], *adv. & s.m.* *Mus:* largo.

largonji [largɔ̃ʒi], *s.m.* *P: A:* variety of slang in which words were altered by substituting l for the first letter and adding the original first letter and é, em, i, oque, etc. to the end.

largue [larg], *a.* *Nau:* **1.** (*of rope, etc.*) loose, slack. **2.** (*of wind*) large, free; **naviguer vent l.,** *s.m.*, **avoir du l.,** to sail free, large; to sail off the wind; to run free; **vent grand l.,** quartering wind, wind on the quarter.

larguer [large], *v.tr.* **1.** *Nau:* (*a*) to let go, loose (rope); **l. l'amarre,** to cast off, slip, the mooring rope; **largué!** all gone! *Av:* **l. un réservoir, etc.,** to release, drop, get rid of, a tank, etc.; **l. une bombe,** to release a bomb; *P:* **tu devrais l. cette môme,** you should drop, chuck, that girl; (*b*) to let out, loose out, unfurl (sail); **l. un ris,** to shake out a reef. **2.** (*a*) to blow off, let off (steam); (*b*) to release (balloon). **3.** *v.i.* *Nau:* (*of seams*) to start, to gape.

laridés [laride], *s.m.pl.* *Orn:* Laridae; the gulls.

larie [lari], *s.f.* *Ent:* laria, bruchus.

larigot [larigo], *s.m.* *Mus:* (*a*) *A:* flageolet; (*b*) larigot (stop of organ).

Larisse [laris], *Pr.n.f.* *Geog:* Larissa.

larme [larm], *s.f.* tear. **1. ses yeux se mouillèrent de larmes,** tears came, rose, started, welled, (in)to her eyes; **ses yeux étaient mouillés de larmes,** her eyes were wet, suffused, with tears; **fondre en larmes,** to burst into tears; to break down; **elle eut une crise de larmes,** she burst into tears, she broke into a flood of tears; **verser des larmes de joie,** to shed tears of joy; **pleurer à chaudes larmes,** to weep copiously, bitterly; **avoir les larmes aux yeux,** to have tears in one's eyes; **les larmes me vinrent aux yeux,** tears came to my eyes; **faire venir des larmes aux yeux de qn,** to bring tears to s.o.'s eyes; **elle s'endormit dans les larmes,** she cried, wept, sobbed, herself to sleep; **elle était (tout) en larmes,** she was in tears; **voix mouillée de larmes,** tearful voice; **avec des larmes dans la voix,** in a tearful voice; **au bord des larmes,** on the verge of tears; **avoir le don des larmes,** to be able to weep at will; *F:* **le faire aux larmes,** to turn on the taps; **avoir la l. facile, avoir toujours la l. à l'œil,** to be easily moved to tears; **il a ri (jusqu')aux larmes,** he laughed till he cried, till the tears came; *F:* **y aller de sa (petite) l.,** to shed a (perfunctory) tear; **larmes de commande, de crocodile,** crocodile tears; *Lit:* **mêler ses larmes à celles de qn,** to share s.o.'s sorrow; *F:* **prendre une l. de rhum dans son café,** to take just a drop of rum in one's coffee. **2. larmes de résine,** resin tears; *Geol:* **larmes du Vésuve,** volcanic bombs; *Ph:* **l. batavique,** Prince Rupert's drop.

larme-de-Job [larmdəʒɔb], *s.f.*, **larme-du-Christ** [larmdykrist], *s.f.* *Bot:* Job's tears; *pl. larmes-de-Job, larmes-du-Christ.*

larmier [larmje], *s.m.* **1.** *Anat:* (*a*) inner canthus; corner (of the eye); (*b*) tear bag (of deer); (*c*) temple (of horse). **2.** *Arch:* drip (stone), label; gutter overhang; hood, weather, moulding.

larmière [larmjɛ:r], *s.f.* tear bag (of deer).

larmille [larmi:j], *s.f.* *Bot:* Job's tears.

larmoiement [larmwamɑ̃], *s.m.* *Med:* lachrymation, watering, weeping (of the eyes).

Larmor [larmɔ:r], *Pr.n.* *Ph:* **théorème de L.,** Larmor's theorem.

larmoyant [larmwajɑ̃], *a.* **1.** (*a*) weeping, tearful; **voix larmoyante,** tearful voice; (*b*) *Med:* **yeux larmoyants,** watering eyes. **2.** *Pej:* lachrymose, doleful, snivelling, maudlin (voice, etc.); soppy (sentimentality); **histoire larmoyante,** sob story, *F:* tear jerker; **comédie larmoyante,** sentimental domestic drama (of the XVIIIth century).

larmoyer [larmwaje], *v.* (**je larmoie, n. larmoyons; je larmoierai**) **1.** *v.i.* (*of the eyes*) to water. **2.** *v.i. Pej:* to weep, to shed tears, to snivel. **3.** *v.tr.* **l. un rôle,** to speak a part in a tearful, whining, voice.

larmoyeur, -euse [larmwajœ:r, -ø:z], *Pej:* (*a*) *a.* snivelling; (*b*) *s.* sniveller.

larnax [larnaks], *s.m.* *Gr.Ant:* larnax.

larnite [larnit], *s.f.* *Miner:* larnite.

larra [lara], *s.m.* *Ent:* larra.

larron, -onnesse, *occ.* **-onne** [larɔ̃, -ɔnɛs, -ɔn], *s.* **1.** (*a*) *A:* robber, thief; *B:* **le bon, le mauvais, l.,** the penitent, the impenitent, thief; *Lit:* **l. d'amour, d'honneur,** seducer; **au l.!** stop thief! *F:* **s'entendre, s'accorder, comme larrons en foire,** to be as thick as thieves; *s.a.* OCCASION 1, PIE[1] 1; (*b*) thief (in candle). **2.** *Geog: A:* **les îles des Larrons,** the Mariana Islands, *A:* the Ladrones. **3.** (*a*) *Typ:* bite (in the paper); (*b*) *Bookb:* dog's ear (not cut). **4.** *Hyd.E:* small drainage canal.
larronner [larɔne], *v.tr. & i. A:* to filch, pilfer.
larsénite [larsenit], *s.f. Miner:* larsenite.
larvaire [larvɛːr], *a.* (*a*) larval; (*b*) immature (work).
larve [larv], *s.f.* **1.** *Rom.Ant:* ghost, spectre, larva. **2.** (*a*) *Biol:* larva; grub (of insect); (*b*) *F:* spineless person, wet.
larvé [larve], *a.* (*a*) *Med:* larval, larvated, masked (fever, etc.); (*b*) insidious; **dictature larvée,** masked dictatorship.
larvicide [larvisid], *s.m. Agr:* larvicide, larvacide.
larvicole [larvikɔl], *a.* larvicolous (parasite).
larviforme [larvifɔrm], *a. Biol:* larviform, larva-shaped.
larvipare [larvipaːr], *a. Ent:* larviparous.
larvivore [larvivɔːr], *a. Nat.Hist:* larvivorous.
larvule [larvyl], *s.f. Ent:* larvule.
laryngal, -ale, -aux [larɛ̃gal, -o], *a. & s.f. Ling:* laryngeal.
laryngé [larɛ̃ʒe], *a.* laryngeal (artery, phthisis, etc.); **spasme l.,** laryngospasmus.
laryngectomie [larɛ̃ʒɛktɔmi], *s.f. Surg:* laryngectomy.
laryngectomisé, -ée [larɛ̃ʒɛktɔmize], *s. Med:* laryngectomee.
laryngien, -ienne [larɛ̃ʒjɛ̃, -jɛn], *a.* laryngeal (cavity, *Surg:* tube).
laryngite [larɛ̃ʒit], *s.f. Med:* laryngitis; **l. striduleuse,** false croup; **l. diphtérique,** diphtheritic, membranous, laryngitis.
laryngocèle [larɛ̃gɔsɛl], *s.f. Med:* laryngocele.
laryngofissure [larɛ̃gɔfisyːr], *s.f. Surg:* laryngo(-)fissure.
laryngologie [larɛ̃gɔlɔʒi], *s.f.* laryngology; treatise, work, on laryngology.
laryngologiste [larɛ̃gɔlɔʒist], **laryngologue** [larɛ̃gɔlɔg], *s.m. & f. Med:* laryngologist.
laryngonécrose [larɛ̃gɔnekroːz], *s.f. Med:* necrosis of the cartilage of the larynx.
laryngophone [larɛ̃gɔfɔn], *s.m.* laryngophone, throat microphone.
laryngoplégie [larɛ̃gɔpleʒi], *s.f. Med:* laryngoplegia, laryngoparalysis.
laryngoscope [larɛ̃gɔskɔp], *s.m. Surg:* laryngoscope.
laryngoscopie [larɛ̃gɔskɔpi], *s.f. Surg:* laryngoscopy.
laryngospasme [larɛ̃gɔspasm], *s.m. Med:* laryngopasmus, laryngospasm.
laryngotome [larɛ̃gɔtɔm], *s.m. Surg:* laryngotome.
laryngotomie [larɛ̃gɔtɔmi], *s.f. Surg:* laryngotomy.
laryngo-trachéal, -aux [larɛ̃gɔtrakeal, -o], *a. Anat:* laryngotracheal.
laryngo-trachéite [larɛ̃gɔtrakeit], *s.f. Med:* laryngotracheitis.
laryngo-trachéotomie [larɛ̃gɔtrakeɔtɔmi], *s.f. Surg:* laryngotracheotomy; *pl. laryngo-trachéotomies.*
larynx [larɛ̃ks], *s.m.* larynx.
las[1] [lɑ(ːs)], *int. A:* alack! alas!
las[2], lasse [lɑ, lɑːs], *a.* tired, weary; **être l. de qch.,** to be (sick and) tired of sth.; **ma main était lasse d'écrire,** my hand was tired of writing; **être l. de marcher,** to be tired of walking; **de guerre lasse . . .,** for the sake of peace and quiet.
las[3] [lɑːs], *s.m.* **1.** *Agr:* mow (of barn). **2.** *Tchn:* salt-maker's wooden shovel.
lascar [laskaːr], *s.m.* **1.** lascar. **2.** *P:* (fine, clever, lazy, etc.) fellow; **c'est un l.,** he's a fine specimen; **sacrés lascars, va!** you're a fine bunch! **c'est un drôle de l.,** he's a funny chap.
lascif, -ive [lasif, -iːv], *a.* lascivious; sensual, voluptuous; lewd.
lascivement [lasivmɑ̃], *adv.* lasciviously, voluptuously, lewdly.
lasciveté [lasivte], *s.f.* lasciviousness, lewdness, lust.
laser [lazɛːr], *s.m. & a.* (*abbr. for Light Amplification by Stimulated Emission of Radiations*) *Atom.Ph:* laser; *Tchn:* **usinage par l.,** modelling, cutting of plates, etc. by means of a laser beam.
lasérothérapie [lazerɔterapi], *s.f. Med:* laser therapy.
lasiocampe [lazjɔkɑ̃ːp], *s.m. Ent:* egger; **l. du chêne,** oak-egger (moth).
lasiocampides [lazjɔkɑ̃pid], *s.m.pl. Ent:* Lasiocampidae, lasiocampids.
lasius [lazjyːs], *s.m. Ent:* lasius.
lasque [lask], *s.m. Miner:* diamond of inferior quality.
lassant [lɑsɑ̃], *a.* tiring, wearying, tedious.
lasser[1] [lɑse], *v.tr.* to tire, weary; **l. la patience de qn,** to exhaust s.o.'s patience, to tire s.o. out; *Lit:* **tout passe, tout casse, tout lasse,** all is vanity and vexation of spirit.
se lasser, to become, grow, get, tired or weary; **to tire; se l. de qn, de qch.,** to get tired of s.o., of sth.; **se l. de faire qch.,** to get tired of doing sth.; **on ne se lasse pas de l'écouter,** one is never tired of listening to him; **se l. à faire qch.,** to tire oneself out doing sth.
lasser[2] [lase], *v.tr.* (*rare*) to lasso (an animal).
lassitude [lɑsityd], *s.f.* lassitude, tiredness, weariness.
lasso [laso], *s.m.* lasso; **prendre un cheval au l.,** to lasso a horse.
last(e) [last], *s.m. A.Meas:* last (of wool, malt, etc.).
lastex [lastɛks], *s.m. R.t.m:* Lastex.
lasting [lastiŋ], *s.m. Tex:* lasting(s).
latakié, latakieh [latakje], *s.m.* Latakia (tobacco).
latania [latanja], **latanier** [latanje], *s.m. Bot:* latania; **l. de Bourbon,** Bourbon palm.
latence [latɑ̃ːs], *s.f.* latency; *Psy:* **période de l.,** latency period; **temps de l.,** reaction time.
latent [latɑ̃], *a.* latent (disease, *Phot:* image, etc.); hidden, concealed; *Ph:* **chaleur latente,** latent heat; état l., latency.
latéral, -aux [lateral, -o], *a.* lateral; **rue, nef, latérale,** side street, cross street; side aisle; **entrée latérale,** side entrance; **étuder un problème d'une manière latérale,** to study a problem from a side angle; *Nau:* **soutes latérales,** side bunkers; *Navy:* **tourelle latérale,** wing turret; *a. & s.f. Ling:* **(consonne) latérale,** lateral, side, divided, consonant; *Bot:* **bourgeon l.,** lateral bud; lateral; *Ich:* **ligne latérale,** lateral line.
latéralement [lateralmɑ̃], *adv.* laterally; on, at, the side.
latéralisation [lateralizasjɔ̃], *s.f. Psy:* lateralization.
latéralisé [lateralize], *a. Psy: Med:* lateralized.
latéralité [lateralite], *s.f. Psy:* laterality.
latériflore [lateriflɔːr], *a.* laterifloral.
latérigrade [laterigrad], *a. & s.m. Nat.Hist:* laterigrade.
latérite [laterit], *s.f. Min:* laterite.
latéritique [lateritik], *a. Geol:* lateritic.
latéritisation [lateritizasjɔ̃], *s.f. Geol:* laterization; laterite formation.
latérodorsal, -aux [laterɔdɔrsal, -o], *a. Anat:* laterodorsal.
latéroflexion [laterɔflɛksjɔ̃], *s.f. Obst:* lateroflexion.
latéroposition [laterɔpozisjɔ̃], *s.f.*, **latéroversion** [laterɔvɛrsjɔ̃], *s.f. Obst:* lateroposition.
latéro-ventral, -aux [laterɔvɑ̃tral, -o], *a. Anat:* lateroventral.
latès [latɛs], *s.m. Ich:* Lates.
latex [latɛks], *s.m. Bot: Ind:* latex.
lathyrisme [latirism], *s.m. Med:* lathyrism.
lathyrus [latiryːs], *s.m. Bot:* lathyrus.
latial, -aux [lasjal, -o], *a. Rom.Hist:* Latian.
laticifère [latisifɛːr], *Bot:* **1.** *a.* laticiferous, latex-bearing. **2.** *s.m.* laticiferous element, cell.
laticlave [latiklaːv], *s.m. Rom.Ant:* laticlave.
latif [latif], *s.m. Gram:* lative (case).
latifolié [latifɔlje], *a. Bot:* latifoliate, broad-leaved.
latifundium, *pl.* **-ia** [latifɔ̃djɔm, -ja], *s.m.* (*esp. in Italy & Latin America*) latifundium, great landed estate.
latin, -ine [latɛ̃, -in]. **1.** *a.* (*a*) Latin (people, etc.); *Sch:* **thème l.,** Latin composition, prose; **dissertation latine,** essay in Latin; **le Quartier L.,** the Latin Quarter; *Ecc:* **l'Église latine,** the Latin, Western, Church; **Amérique latine,** Latin America; *s.* **les Latins,** the Latin races; (*b*) *Nau:* **voile latine,** lateen sail. **2.** *s.m. Ling:* Latin; **l. classique,** classical Latin; **l. de la décadence,** late Latin; **bas l.,** low Latin; **l. de cuisine,** dog Latin; **c'est du l. pour moi,** that's all Greek to me; **être au bout de son l.,** to be at the end of one's tether, at one's wits' end; **j'y perds mon l.,** I can't make head or tail of it; I'm all at sea.
latinisant, -ante [latinizɑ̃, -ɑ̃ːt]. **1.** *a. & s.m. & f. R.C.Ch:* (follower) of the Latin rite (in a country of Eastern rite). **2.** *s.m. & f.* Latinist, Latin scholar.
latinisation [latinizasjɔ̃], *s.f.* Latinization.
latiniser [latinize], *v.tr. & i.* to Latinize.
latinisme [latinism], *s.m.* Latinism, Latin idiom.
latiniste [latinist], *s.m. & f.* Latinist, Latin scholar.
latinité [latinite], *s.f.* Latinity.
latino-américain [latinɔamerikɛ̃], *a. Geog:* Latin-American; *pl. latino-américain(e)s.*
latirostres [latirɔstr], *s.m.pl. Orn: A:* Latirostres.
latitude [latityd], *s.f.* latitude. **1.** scope, freedom; **avoir toute l. pour agir,** to have free scope, full discretion, to act; **laisser trop de l. à qn,** to allow s.o. too much latitude, scope, *F:* rope. **2.** *Geog:* (*a*) **l. géographique, l. terrestre, l. vraie,** geographical, normal, true, latitude; **l. méridienne,** meridian latitude; **l. circumméridienne,** exmeridian latitude; **l. moyenne,** mid-latitude, middle latitude; **l. estimée, l. par l'estime,** latitude by dead reckoning; **l. observée,** latitude by observation; **être par, sous, telle ou telle l.,** to be in such and such a latitude; **l. nord, sud,** latitude North, South; **par 30° (de) l. nord,** in latitude 30° North; *Nau:* **faire une l. par la polaire,** to find the latitude by the pole star; (*b*) *pl.* latitudes, regions; **la flore des hautes latitudes,** the high-latitude flora.
latitudinaire [latitydinɛːr], *a. & s.*, **latitudinarien, -ienne** [latitydinarjɛ̃, -ɛn], *a. & s. Rel.H:* latitudinarian.
latitudinal, -aux [latitydinal, -o], *a. N.Arch:* athwartship (plan, section); **dans le sens l.,** athwartship.
latitudinarisme [latitydinarism], *s.m. Rel.H:* latitudinarianism.
latomies [latɔmi], *s.f.pl. Rom. & Gr.Ant:* lautumiae, stone quarries (*esp.* in Syracuse).
Latone [latɔn], *Pr.n.f. Myth:* Latona, Leto.
latosol [latɔsɔl], *s.m. Geol:* latosol.
Latran [latrɑ̃], *Pr.n.m.* Lateran; **le palais de L.,** the Lateran Palace; **la basilique de L., Saint-Jean de L.,** Saint John Lateran, the Lateran church; *Ecc.Hist:* **les Conciles de L.,** the Lateran Councils.
latrie [latri], *s.f. Theol: used in the phr.* **(culte de) l.,** latria; **accorder à qn, à qch., un culte de l.,** to worship s.o., sth.
latrines [latrin], *s.f.pl.* latrines, privies; *Mil: F:* rear(s); *Nau:* head(s).
latrodecte [latrɔdɛkt], **latrodectus** [latrɔdɛktyːs], *s.m. Arach:* Latrodectus; *F:* black widow.
lattage [lataːʒ], *s.m.* **1.** lathing (of wall, etc.); *Mch:* lagging (of cylinder, etc.). **2.** *N.Arch:* diagonal trussing.
latte [lat], *s.f.* **1.** lath, batten, slat; (*a*) **l. jointive,** partition lath; **l. volige,** slate lath, roof batten; *Nau:* **l. de hune,** futtock plate; *Com:* **fer en lattes,** slat iron; (*b*) **l. d'Arlequin,** Harlequin's lath, bat. **2.** *A:* straight (heavy cavalry) sword. **3.** *P: usu. pl.* shoes.
latté [late], *s.m.* core board.
latter [late], *v.tr.* **1.** to lath; to batten; *Mch:* to lag (cylinder, etc.); **cloison lattée et plâtrée,** lath-and-plaster partition. **2.** *N.Arch:* to truss (ship).
lattis [lati], *s.m.* lathing, lath work; **plancher en l.,** grating floor.
Latvie [latvi], *Pr.n.f. Geog:* Latvia.
latvien, -ienne [latvjɛ̃, -jɛn], *a. & s.* Latvian.
lauan [luɑ̃], *s.m.* lauan (wood).
laubanite [lobanit], *s.f. Miner:* laubanite.
lauda [loda], *s.f. Mus:* (i) *Ecc:* laud; (ii) hymn of praise.
laudanisé [lodanize], *a. Pharm:* containing laudanum.
laudanum [lodanɔm], *s.m.* laudanum; *F: A:* **donner du l. à qn,** to lull s.o. with fair words, to soft-sawder s.o.
laudateur, -trice [lodatœːr, -tris], *s.* laudator, lauder, praiser.
laudatif, -ive [lodatif, -iːv], *a.* laudatory, lauding, praising.
laudes [loːd], *s.f.pl. Ecc:* laud(e)s.
laudinien, -ienne [lodinjɛ̃, -jɛn], *a. & s.* (native, inhabitant) of Saint-Lo.
laumonite [lɔmɔnit], **laumontite** [lɔmɔ̃tit], *s.f. Miner:* laumonite, laumontite.
lauracé [lɔrase], *Bot:* **1.** *a.* lauraceous. **2.** *s.f.pl.* **lauracées,** Lauraceae.
Laure [lɔːr], *Pr.n.f.* Laura.
lauré [lɔre], *a. Num:* laureate (bust, head).
lauréat, -ate [lɔrea, -at], *a. & s.* laureate, prize-winner, prizeman; **l. d'un concours,** (prize)-winner of a competition; **les lauréats du prix Nobel,** the Nobel prizewinners; **poète l.,** poet laureate.
laurelle [lɔrɛl], *s.f. Bot:* oleander.
Laurent [lɔrɑ̃], *Pr.n.m.* Lawrence; Laurence; *Hist:* **L. le magnifique,** Lorenzo the Magnificent; **être sur le gril comme Saint L.,** to be in a critical situation; to be tortured (by indecision, anxiety, etc.).
Laurentides (les) [lɛlɔrɑ̃tid], *s.m.pl. Geog:* **the** Laurentide Mountains, the Laurentides.
laurentien [lɔrɑ̃sjɛ̃], *a. & s.m. Geol:* Laurentian.

lauréole [lɔreɔl], *s.f. Bot:* daphne, mezereon.

laurier [lɔrje], *s.m. Bot:* laurel; **l. commun, d'Apollon, des poètes,** noble laurel, bay laurel, sweet bay; **l. amandier,** cherry laurel, cherry bay; **l. des bois,** spurge laurel; **l. des marais,** great laurel; *Cu:* **feuille de l.,** bay leaf; **couronne de lauriers,** laurel wreath; bays; **couronné, ceint, de lauriers,** crowned with laurel(s), laurelled; **cueillir, moissonner, des lauriers,** to reap, win, laurels, glory; **se reposer sur ses lauriers, à l'ombre de ses lauriers,** to rest on one's laurels; **s'endormir sur ses lauriers,** to rest on one's oars.

laurier-cerise [lɔrjesriːz], *s.m. Bot:* cherry-laurel, cherry-bay; *pl. lauriers-cerise(s).*

laurier-rose [lɔrjeroːz], *s.m. Bot:* common oleander, rose laurel, rose bay; *pl. lauriers-rose(s).*

laurier-sauce [lɔrjesoːs], *s.m. Bot: Cu:* bay laurel; *pl. lauriers-sauce.*

laurier-thym, -tin [lɔrjetɛ̃], *s.m. Bot:* laurustinus, laurustine; *pl. lauriers-thym, -tin.*

laurier-tulipier [lɔrjetylipje], *s.m. Bot:* magnolia grandiflora; evergreen magnolia; laurel magnolia, *U.S:* bull bay; *pl. lauriers-tulipiers.*

laurifolié [lɔrifɔlje], *a. Bot:* laurel-leaved; laurel-like; resembling laurels.

laurinoxylon [lɔrinɔksilɔ̃], *s.m. Paleont:* laurinoxylon.

laurionite [lɔrjɔnit], *s.f. Miner:* laurionite.

laurique [lɔrik], *a. Ch:* lauric (acid).

laurite [lɔrit], *s.f. Miner:* laurite.

laurose [lɔroːz], *s.m.* = LAURIER-ROSE.

lausannois, -oise [lozanwa, -waːz], *a. & s. Geog:* (native, inhabitant) of Lausanne.

lautarite [lɔtarit], *s.f. Miner:* lautarite.

lauze [loːz], *s.f. (in the S. of Fr.)* (*a*) roofing stone; (*b*) flat paving stone.

lavabilité [lavabilite], *s.f.* washability.

lavable [lavabl̩], *a.* washable; **garanti l.,** guaranteed to wash, guaranteed washable.

lavabo [lavabo], *s.m.* **1.** *Ecc:* lavabo ((i) ritual, (ii) towel). **2.** *Hyg:* (*a*) wash basin, lavatory basin; *Com:* wash-hand basin; (*b*) *A.Furn:* washstand. **3.** (*place for washing*) (*a*) lavatory (in schools, etc.); **les lavabos,** the lavatories, the wash-room; (*b*) *Min:* pit-head baths.

lavage [lavaːʒ], *s.m.* **1.** washing (of pots, linen, mineral ores, etc.); scrubbing (of gas); *Med:* lavage; *A.Artil:* sponging (of gun); **l. à grande eau,** swilling (of floor, etc.); **couleurs qui s'en vont au l.,** colours that come out in the wash; *Min:* **produits de l.,** washings; *Petroleum Ind: Min: etc:* **l. au crible,** jigger work; **l. de la carotte,** core flushing; **l. (des graviers),** panning; *Geol:* **terre de l.,** alluvium; *St.Exch:* **l. des titres,** fraudulent conversion of stocks; *A:* **faire un l. de ses biens,** to sell off one's possessions; *F:* **l. de cerveau,** brainwashing; *F:* **l. de tête,** dressing down. **2.** = LAVASSE.

La Vallière, lavallière [lavaljɛːr], *s.f.* **1. (cravate) lavallière,** loosely tied bow. **2. maroquin La Vallière,** russet-coloured morocco.

lavallois, -oise [lavalwa, -waːz], *a. & s. Geog:* (native, inhabitant) of Laval.

lavande [lavɑ̃ːd], *s.f.* **1.** *Bot:* lavender; **l. vraie, femelle,** (true) lavender; **l. aspic, commune, mâle, officinale, grande l.,** French lavender; spike; **l. de mer,** statice, sea pink, (sea-)thrift, sea lavender; **eau de l.,** lavender water; **eau de l. blanche, ambrée,** clear, amber, lavender water; **bleu l.,** lavender blue. **2.** *Cin:* **copie l.,** lavender print; **(pellicule) l.,** duplicating positive.

lavanderaie [lavɑ̃d(ə)rɛ], **lavanderie**[1] [lavɑ̃d(ə)ri], *s.f.* lavender field, plantation.

lavanderie[2], *s.f. (rare)* wash-house; laundry.

lavandière[1] [lavɑ̃djɛːr], *s.f.* **1.** washerwoman; laundress. **2.** *Orn:* wagtail; **l. jaune,** grey wagtail; **l. grise,** white wagtail.

lavandière[2], *s.f.* lavender field, plantation.

lavandin [lavɑ̃dɛ̃], *s.m. Bot:* lavandin; hybrid lavender.

lavanga [lavɑ̃ga], *s.m. Bot:* lavanga.

lavaret [lavarɛ], *s.m. Ich:* lavaret, pollan.

lavasse [lavas], *s.f.* **1.** *O:* torrential rain. **2.** *F:* = skilly; *F:* cat-lap, hogwash, dishwater; **du café! c'est de la l.!** coffee! it's just dishwater!

lavatère [lavatɛːr], *s.f. Bot:* lavatera; **l. en arbre,** tree mallow.

lavatory [lavatɔri], *s.m.* **1.** public lavatory (and convenience). **2.** *A:* barber's shop (with lavatory attached).

lave [laːv], *s.f.* **1.** (*a*) *Geol:* lava; **l. vitreuse,** vitreous lava; (*b*) *Geog:* **l. torrentielle,** mud spate. **2.** = LAUZE.

lavé [lave], *a.* **1.** (*a*) washed out; **couleur lavée,** faint, washed-out, colour; **bleu l.,** light blue; *Equit:* **cheval bai lavé,** light bay horse; **robe lavée,** light bay coat (of horse); (*b*) *P:* cleaned out, (stony) broke. **2. non l.,** unwashed (coal, etc.).

lave-bouteilles [lavbutɛːj], *s.m.inv.* bottle-washer.

lave-dos [lavdo], *s.m.inv. Toil:* back brush.

lavedu [lavdy], *s.m. P:* sucker, mug; clot, dope.

lavée [lave], *s.f.* amount (of wool, ore, etc.) washed at one time; washing (of wool, ore, etc.).

lave-glace [lavglas], *s.m. Aut:* windscreen washer; *U.S:* windshield washer; *pl. lave-glaces.*

lave-mains [lavmɛ̃], *s.m.inv. Ecc:* lavabo.

lavement [lavmɑ̃], *s.m.* **1.** *B: Ecc:* washing (of the Disciples' feet, of the priest's hands). **2.** (*a*) *Med:* (rectal) injection; enema; (*b*) *P: (pers.)* bore.

lavenite [lav(ə)nit], *s.f. Miner:* lavenite.

lave-pieds [lavpje], *s.m.inv.* foot bath.

lave-pinceaux [lavpɛ̃so], *s.m.inv.* brush washer.

lave-pont [lavpɔ̃], *s.m.* deck scrub; *pl. lave-ponts.*

laver [lave], *v.tr.* **1.** to wash; (*a*) **l. qch. à l'eau froide,** to wash sth. in cold water; **se l.,** to wash (oneself), to have a wash; *P:* **allez vous l.!** scram! *F:* **se l. le bout du nez,** to give oneself a cat's lick, a lick and a promise; **se l. les dents,** to clean one's teeth; **se l. la tête,** to wash one's hair; *F:* **l. la tête à qn,** to haul s.o. over the coals; to give s.o. a good dressing-down; to tear s.o. off a strip; **se l. les mains,** to wash one's hands; **l. à la brosse,** to scrub; **machine à l.,** washing machine; **l. la vaisselle,** to wash up; **machine à l. la vaisselle,** washing-up machine, dishwasher; **tissu qui ne se lave pas,** material that won't wash; **l. une souillure,** to wash out a stain; **l. qn d'une souillure,** to clear s.o.'s name; **l. une insulte dans le sang,** to wash out an insult in blood; **l. qn d'une accusation,** to clear s.o. from an accusation; **l. une plaie,** to bathe a wound; *Fin: F:* **l. un chèque,** to forge a cheque (by altering it); *P: A:* **l. sa montre,** to sell one's watch; **l. ses effets,** to sell off one's goods and chattels; *s.a.* LINGE 1; (*b*) *Ch:* **l. un gaz,** to scrub a gas; *Nau:* **l. un ballast,** to wash out a tank; (*c*) **l. un dessin,** to wash a drawing; (*d*) *(of stream)* **l. un pré,** to flow alongside a meadow. **2.** *Carp:* to trim up (roughly dressed timber).

lavé-repassé [laverəpɑse], *a.inv.* non-iron, wash-and-wear.

laverie [lavri], *s.f.* (*a*) *Ind:* washing plant, washery; (*b*) scullery; washing-place; (*c*) **l. automatique,** (modern) laundry; launderette.

lave-tête [lavtɛːt], *s.m.inv.* shampoo basin.

lavette [lavɛt], *s.f.* **1.** (*a*) (dish-)mop; saucepan brush; **l. métallique,** scrubber, scourer; (*b*) dish cloth; (*c*) *P:* spineless person, *F:* drip. **2.** *P:* tongue.

laveur, -euse [lavœːr, -øːz], *s.* **1.** *(pers.)* washer; scrubber (of gas); **laveuse de linge,** washerwoman; **laveur, -euse de vaisselle,** washer-up; *U.S:* dishwasher; **l. de bouteilles,** bottle-washer; **l. d'or,** gold-washer. **2.** (*a*) *a. Ch:* **flacon l.,** scrubber, washing-bottle (for gases); (*b*) *s.m. Gasm: Ind:* scrubber, scrubbing-column; *Petroleum Ind: Ch:* **l. à barbotage,** bubble scrubber. **3.** *s.f.* **laveuse mécanique,** (laundry) washing machine; *Fr.C:* **laveuse ((à) vaisselle),** dishwasher, washing-up machine.

lave-vaisselle [lavvɛsɛl], *s.m.inv.* dishwasher; **l.-v. automatique,** automatic dishwasher, washing-up machine.

Lavinie [lavini], *Pr.n.f. Lt.Lit:* Lavinia.

lavis [lavi], *s.m.* **1.** washing, tinting (of drawing). **2.** (*a*) wash tint; (*b*) **(épure au) l.,** wash drawing, tinted drawing.

lavogne [lavɔɲ], *s.f. Geol: (in the Causses)* pond (in a doline).

lavoir [lavwaːr], *s.m.* **1.** (*a*) **l. (public),** (public) wash-house; (*b*) washing and rinsing board by river-side; (*c*) **l. de cuisine,** scullery. **2.** (*a*) *Ind:* washing machine; (*b*) *Min:* buddle. **3.** *Artil: A:* cleaning-rod.

lavure [lavyːr], *s.f.* **1.** (*a*) dirty water; **l. (de vaisselle),** (kitchen) swill, dishwater; (*b*) insipid, watery, soup. **2.** *pl.* metal turnings and filings; sweepings (of goldsmith's shop).

lawrencite [lɔrɑ̃sit], *s.f. Miner:* lawrencite.

lawsonite [lɔsɔnit], *s.f. Miner:* lawsonite.

laxatif, -ive [laksatif, -iːv], *a. & s.m. Med:* laxative, aperient.

laxisme [laksism], *s.m. Phil:* laxism.

laxiste [laksist], *s. Phil:* laxist.

laxité [laksite], *s.f.* laxity, relaxed state (of ligament, etc.); slackness (of a rope).

layage [lɛjaːʒ], *s.m. Stonew:* bush hammering.

laye [lɛ], *s.f. Tls: Stonew:* bush hammer.

layer[1] [lɛje], *v.tr.* **(je laie, je laye, n. layons; je laierai, je layerai) 1.** to trace, open up, a path through (forest); to blaze a trail through (forest). **2.** to blaze (the trees to be left in a cutting).

layer[2], *v.tr. Stonew:* to tool, tooth (a stone); to bush-hammer.

layet(t)erie [lɛjɛtri], *s.f. A:* packing-case making, box-making.

layetier [lɛjtje], *s.m.*, **layetier-emballeur** [lɛjtjeɑ̃balœːr], *s.m. A:* packing-case maker, box-maker; *pl. layetiers-emballeurs.*

layette [lɛjɛt], *s.f.* **1.** *A:* (*a*) small drawer, box; (*b*) packing-case. **2.** set of baby-linen; layette.

layeur [lɛjœːr], *s.m.* forester (in charge of tracing or cutting cross-rides in forests, etc.).

layon [lɛjɔ̃], *s.m.* **1.** tailboard (of cart). **2.** *For: Ven:* cross ride; minor ride; service path.

Lazare [lazaːr], *Pr.n.m.* Lazarus.

lazaret [lazarɛ], *s.m. Med:* (*a*) *A:* lazaret(to); lazar-house; (*b*) *Vet:* = quarantine kennels; *Nau: etc:* quarantine station.

lazarist [lazarist], *s.m.* lazarist (priest).

lazaro [lazaro], *s.m. P:* prison; *P:* jug, nick, clink.

lazulite [lazylit], *s.m. Miner:* blue spar.

lazzi [lazi, ladzi], *s.m.pl. (used occ. as s.sg. with pl.* **lazzis). 1.** *Th: A:* **scène de l.,** scene of pantomime, knock-about scene. **2.** (*a*) piece of buffoonery; (*b*) jeers, hooting, cat calls.

le[1], **la, les** [lə, la, le, lɛ], *def.art.* (**le** *and* **la** *are elided to* **l'** *before a vowel or* **h 'mute'**; **le** *and* **les** *contract with* **à, de,** *into* **au, aux; du, des**) the. **1.** *(particularizing the noun or pron.)* (*a*) **ouvrez la porte,** open the door; **il est venu la semaine dernière,** he came last week; **j'apprends le français,** I am learning French; **la province a perdu le quart, le tiers, de ses habitants,** the province has lost a quarter, a third, of its inhabitants; **l'île est située entre les 30e et 32e degrés de longitude est,** the island lies between longitudes 30° and 32° east; **l'un . . . l'autre,** (the) one . . . the other; **mon livre et le tien,** my books and yours; **les amis qui me restent sont tous pauvres,** the friends I have left (to me) are all poor; **je suis né le matin du 5 mai,** I was born on the morning of the 5th of May; **il est arrivé le lundi 12,** he arrived on Monday the 12th; (*b*) **la France,** France; **l'Afrique,** Africa; **le Mont Blanc,** Mont Blanc; **les Alpes,** the Alps; **la Seine,** the Seine; **le Rhône,** the Rhone; **le Ciel,** Heaven; **le Purgatoire,** Purgatory; **l'Enfer,** Hell; (*c*) **l'empereur Guillaume,** the Emperor William; **le poète Keats,** the poet Keats; **le patriarche Nikon,** the patriarch Nikon; **le roi Édouard,** King Edward; **le colonel Chabot,** Colonel Chabot; **le cardinal Richelieu,** Cardinal Richelieu; **le petit Robert,** little Robert; **la mère l'Oie,** Mother Goose; *P: (in market, etc.)* **eh, la (petite) mère?** well, mum, missus (what can I get you?) *often Pej:* **la Thénardier,** the Thénardier woman; (*d*) *(with certain Italian names, certain French actresses)* **l'Arioste,** Ariosto; **le Dante,** Dante; **le Tasse,** Tasso; **la Champmeslé,** Champmeslé; **la "Jérusalem délivrée" du Tasse,** Tasso's "Jerusalem Delivered"; (*e*) *(as an inherent part of many place-names that were originally substantives)* **Le Havre, La Rochelle, La Ferté-Milon; Le Caire,** Cairo; **La Mecque,** Mecca; **je reviens du Havre,** I am just back from le Havre; **je me rends au Caire,** I am going to Cairo; (*f*) *(as an inherent part of many family names; the article is always capitalized)* **le peintre Le Brun, l'économiste Le Play, le fabuliste La Fontaine;** *(the article is never contracted)* **les tableaux de Le Brun,** Le Brun's pictures; **les œuvres de Le Play,** the works of Le Play; (*g*) *(with most feast days)* **la Toussaint,** All Saints' Day; **la Fête-Dieu,** Corpus Christi; *F:* **à la Noël,** at Christmas; (*h*) *(often with parts of the body in the oblique cases)* **j'ai mal à la gorge,** I have a sore throat; **il a la bouche grande,** he has a large mouth; **elle a les yeux bleus,** she has blue eyes; **hausser les épaules,** to shrug one's shoulders; **elle ferma les yeux,** she closed her eyes; **il s'est pincé le doigt,** he pinched his finger; **je lui ai tiré les oreilles,** I pulled his ears for him; **ils étaient là, le chapeau sur la tête,** there they stood, with their hats on their heads; *(or in the nominative, with the pers. referred to in the dative)* **les yeux leur cuisaient,** their eyes were smarting; **la gorge me fait mal,** my throat is sore; **il a fallu couper la jambe à deux des victimes,** two of the wounded have had to have a leg amputated. **2.** *(forming superlatives)* (*a*) **dès les temps les plus anciens,** from the earliest times; **le meilleur vin de sa cave,** the best wine in his cellar; **le meilleur des mondes,** the best of (all) worlds; **mon amie la plus intime,** my most intimate friend; **c'est elle qui est la plus heureuse,** she is (the) happiest (one); (*b*) (*in the neuter*) (i) (*with adverbs*) **c'est elle qui travaille le mieux,** she's the one who works best; (ii) (*when there is an absolute superlative*); **c'est lorsqu'elle est seule qu'elle est le plus heureuse,** she is happiest when she is by herself; **c'est là qu'elle était le moins malheureuse,** that was where she felt least unhappy. **3.** (*generalizing the noun*) **le chien est le meilleur ami de l'homme,** the dog is man's best friend; **je préfère le café au thé,** I prefer coffee to tea. **4.** (*distributive use*) **trois fois l'an,** three times a year; **cinq francs la livre,** five francs a pound; **il vient le jeudi,** he comes on Thursdays, every Thursday. **5.** (*in addition to the constructions shown in* 1 (*h*) *and* 4 *above*, **le** *is often rendered by the indef. art. in Eng.*; *thus*) (*a*) (*particularizing*) **j'ai le droit de vivre,** I have a right to live; **ils sont du même âge,** they are of an age; **faire deux choses à la fois,** to do two things at a time; **donner l'exemple,** to set an example; **demander le divorce,** to sue for a divorce; **la belle excuse!** a fine excuse (indeed)! (*b*) (*generalizing*) **au petit trot,** at a slow trot; **il n'a pas le sou,** he hasn't a penny; **le calme plat précède souvent la tempête,** a dead calm often precedes a storm; **avoir le dédain de qn,** to have a feeling of contempt for s.o. **6.** *partitive* **du, de la, des;** *see* DE III; NOTE **le** *is used in the menus of some restaurants, with an affectation of grandiloquence*; *e.g.* **le Poulet au vin, la Bombe glacée, = poulet au vin, bombe glacée.**

le², **la, les,** *pers.pron., unstressed, attached to the verb or its adjuncts.* **1.** (*replacing sb.*) him, her, it, them; (*a*) **je vous le, la, présenterai,** I will introduce him, her, to you; **je ne le lui ai pas donné,** I did not give it to him; **l'en avez-vous débarrassé?** did you relieve him of it? **êtes-vous les parents de cet enfant?—nous les sommes,** are you the parents of this child?—we are; **est-ce qu'il n'est pas encore quatre heures?—mais si, il les est,** it isn't four o'clock yet, is it?—yes, it is; **les voilà!** there they are! **ne l'abîmez pas!** don't spoil it! (*b*) (*following the vb.*) **donnez-le-lui,** give it to him; (*in stressed position*) **prenez-le** [lə], take it; **regardez-les,** look at them; **donne-le à ton frère** [dɔnləatɔ̃frɛːr], give it to your brother. **2.** *neut. pron.* **le;** (*a*) (*replacing an adj. or a sb. used as an adj.*) **malheureux, je l'étais certainement,** unhappy, I certainly was; **son frère est médecin, il voudrait l'être aussi,** his brother is a doctor, he would like to be one too; **êtes-vous mère?—je le suis,** are you a mother?—I am; (*referring to a p.p. only implied*) **excusez-moi, Madame—vous l'êtes, monsieur,** excuse me, madam—certainly, sir; (*b*) (*replacing a clause*) (i) so; **il me l'a dit,** he told me so; **on me l'a dit,** I was told so; **le train est-il parti?—je le crois,** has the train gone?—I think so; **elle est donc vraiment malade?—il le semble,** is she really ill then?—so it seems; (ii) **il est plus riche que vous (ne) le pensez,** he is richer than you think (he is); **vous le devriez,** you ought to. **3.** *for idiomatic uses, such as* **l'emporter sur qn, on ne la lui fait pas,** *see* BOUCLER 1, CÉDER 1, CONNAÎTRE 1, COULER 1, CREVER 1, EMPORTER 4, FAIRE IV. 3, FERMER 1, FOULER 2, LÂCHER 1, METTRE 1, PRENDRE I 1.

lé [le], *s.m.* **1.** *Tex:* width, breadth (of cloth); *Const:* strip of wallpaper; *Dressm:* **jupe à lés,** gored skirt; **jupe à quatre lés,** four-gore skirt. **2.** towpath.

leader [lidœːr], *s.m. F:* (*a*) *Pol:* leader; (*b*) *Journ:* leader, editorial; (*c*) *Av:* (i) leading aircraft (in a formation); (ii) leading pilot; (*d*) *Sp:* (i) captain of a team; (ii) leading runner (in a race).

leadership [lidœrʃip], *s.m. F:* leadership.

leadhillite [lɛdilit], *s.f. Miner:* leadhillite.

Léandre [leɑ̃ːdr], *Pr.n.m.* **1.** *Gr.Myth:* Leander. **2.** *Th:* type of the elegant fop.

lebachia [lebakja], *s.m. Paleont:* Lebachia.

lebel [ləbɛl], *s.m. Sm.a:* Lebel rifle (*from name of inventor*).

lecanium [ləkanjɔm], *s.m. Ent:* lecanium, soft scale.

lecanore [lekanɔːr], **lecanora** [lekanɔra], *s.m. Bot:* lecanora.

léchage [leʃaːʒ], *s.m.* licking; **surface de l.,** air surface (of radiator, etc.); *F:* **l. de vitrines,** window-shopping.

lèche¹ [lɛʃ], *s.f. F:* thin slice (of bread, meat); **l. de beurre,** pat of butter.

lèche², *s.f. P:* **faire (de) la l. à qn,** to suck up to s.o.; to toady to s.o.

léché [leʃe], *a.* **1.** licked; *s.a.* OURS 1. **2. travail, style, trop l.,** over-polished, over-finished, finicking, work, style.

lèche-bottes [lɛʃbɔt], *s.m.inv. P:* bootlicker.

lèche-cul [lɛʃky], *s.m.inv. V:* arse-crawler; *U.S:* ass-licker.

lèche-doigts (à) [alɛʃdwa], *adv.phr.* in small quantity; **il n'y en avait qu'à l.-d.,** there was only just enough to taste.

lèchefrite [lɛʃfrit], *s.f. Cu:* dripping pan, grease pan.

lèchement [lɛʃmɑ̃], *s.m.* licking.

lécher [leʃe], *v.tr.* (**je lèche, n. léchons; je lécherai**) **1.** to lick; **les chiens venaient me l. la main,** the dogs would come and lick my hand; **le chat lécha tout le lait répandu,** the cat licked up all the spilt milk; **se l. les doigts,** to lick one's fingers; *F:* **il s'en léchait les doigts, les pouces, les babines,** he smacked his lips, licked his chops, over it; **l. un timbre, une enveloppe,** to lick a stamp, an envelope; *F:* **l. les vitrines,** to go window-shopping; **l. la cuiller,** to lick the spoon (clean); **l. les bottes, les pieds, les genoux, de qn,** to lick s.o.'s boots; to toady to s.o.; to suck up to s.o.; **l. la poussière,** to be humiliated, to bite the dust; **l. les murs,** to hug the wall; **surface léchée par les flammes,** surface licked by the flames; *Lit:* **l. l'ours,** to draw out proceedings with endless formalities. **2.** to over-polish, over-finish (work, style). **3.** *abs. F:* **se l.,** (*of two persons*) to kiss.

lècherie [lɛʃri], *s.f.* (*a*) *F:* greed; (*b*) (*rare*) obsequious flattery.

léchette [leʃɛt], *s.f. F:* small slice, shaving (of bread, meat, etc.).

lécheur, -euse [leʃœːr, -øːz], *s.* **1.** (*a*) gourmand; (*b*) *F:* free loader, sponger. **2.** *Pej:* perfectionist. **3.** *P:* (*a*) inveterate (i) hugger, (ii) kisser; (*b*) toady, lickspittle, *F:* creep; **l. de bottes,** bootlicker, *U.S:* apple polisher. **4.** *a.m.* (*of insect*) proboscidate.

lèche-vitrine(s) [lɛʃvitrin], *s.m. no pl. F:* window shopping; **faire du l.-v.,** to go window shopping.

lecidia [lesidja], *s.m. Bot:* lecidia.

lécithe [lesit], *s.m. Biol:* vitellus.

lécithine [lesitin], *s.f. Ch:* lecithin.

leçon [ləsɔ̃], *s.f.* **1.** (*a*) reading (of a manuscript, etc.), *Lit:* version (of an event); **bonne l.,** true reading; **les leçons du manuscrit non retenues sont données au bas de la page,** manuscript readings not retained are given in footnotes; (*b*) *Ecc:* lesson (at Matins and Evensong). **2.** *Sch: etc:* (*a*) lesson; *A:* **l. de choses,** object lesson; **faire à la classe une l. de physique,** to give the class a lesson in physics; **leçons particulières,** private lessons; **prendre des leçons particulières,** to be coached; **il donne des leçons particulières,** he does tutoring; he is a private coach; **prendre des leçons de français,** to take lessons in French; **leçons de chant,** singing lessons; **donner une l. à qn,** (i) to give s.o. a lesson, (ii) to teach s.o. a lesson; **donner à qn une l. de politesse,** to teach s.o. manners; **que cela vous serve de l.,** let that be a lesson, a warning, to you; **j'espère qu'il aura retenu la l.,** I hope he's learnt his lesson; **les leçons de l'expérience,** the lessons, teachings, of experience; **faire la l. à qn,** (i) to prime, drill s.o. (in what he has to say or do); (ii) to dictate to s.o.; (iii) to lecture s.o.; **on lui a fait la l.,** he's been coached in what he should say; (*b*) *Sch:* prep, homework (to be learnt); *O:* **faire réciter les leçons,** to hear the lessons.

lecontite [ləkɔ̃tit], *s.f. Miner:* lecontite.

lecteur, -trice [lɛktœːr, -tris], *s.* **1.** (*a*) reader; **le public des lecteurs,** the reading public; *s.a.* AVIS 2; (*b*) *Typ: Publ:* (proof, publisher's) reader; (*c*) *Mus:* **être bon l.,** to be a good sight reader. **2.** (*a*) reader aloud; *Hist:* **lectrice de la Reine,** reader to the Queen; (*b*) foreign (language) assistant (in university); (*c*) *R.C.Ch:* lector. **3.** *s.m.* (*a*) *Phot:* retouching desk; (*b*) *Elcs:* reader (of data processor, magnetic tape, etc.); *Rec:* **l. (phonographique),** pick-up; *Cin: etc:* **l. de son, l. phonique,** sound reproducer, sound reproducing unit, sound pick-up; **l. optique,** optical sound reproducer; *Atom.Ph:* **l. de charge,** charger reader.

lecteur-perforateur, *s.m.* (*computers*) read punch unit.

lectionnaire [lɛksjɔnɛːr], *s.m. Ecc:* lectionary.

lectisterne [lɛktistɛrn], *s.m. Rom.Ant:* lectisternium.

lectorat [lɛktɔra], *s.m.* (foreign) assistantship (in a university).

lectrin [lɛktrɛ̃], *s.m. A:* (*a*) lectern; (*b*) praying-desk.

lectuarisme [lɛktyarism], *s.m. Med:* the obsession of wanting to lie down.

lecture [lɛktyːr], *s.f.* reading; (*a*) **enseigner la l. à qn,** to teach s.o. to read; **s'initier à une langue par la l.,** to get to know a language by reading; **commencer la l. d'un livre,** to begin to read a book; **il était plongé dans la l. du "Figaro,"** he was plunged in his "Figaro"; **livre d'une l. agréable,** book that makes pleasant reading; **cabinet de l.,** (i) (*also* **salle de l.**), reading room, news room (of library); (ii) lending library; **livre en l.,** book "out"; **il a de la l.,** (i) *F:* he is well read; (ii) he has plenty to read; **adonné à la l.,** fond of reading; bookish; *O:* **personne sans l., qui n'a aucune l.,** ill-read person; **prendre l. d'un contrat,** to read through, make oneself acquainted with the terms of, a contract; **à la l., ces discours n'intéressent guère,** in cold print these speeches are not very interesting; *Mus:* **l. à vue,** sight reading; (*b*) **l. à haute voix,** reading aloud; **faire la l. à qn,** to read aloud to s.o.; **entendre l. d'un testament,** to hear a will read; **donner l. de l'ordre du jour,** to read out the agenda; *Pol:* **projet repoussé en deuxième l.,** bill rejected at the second reading; (*c*) **l. des cartes,** map reading; **l. sur les lèvres,** lip reading; *Tg:* **l. au son,** sound reading; (*d*) *Elcs: E:* reading (of data); read-out (of tape recorder); reception, reproduction (of sound); **l. directe,** direct reading; *Ph: etc:* **faire la l. des instruments de contrôle,** *F:* **faire des lectures,** to take readings; **(instrument) à l. directe,** direct-reading (instrument); **(instrument) à l. automatique,** self-reading (instrument); *Av:* **appareil, instrument, à l. tête haute, tête basse,** head-up, head-down, display instrument; **origine des lectures,** zero; (*radar*) **l. automatique de la distance,** automatic range tracking; (*computers*) **l. arrière,** reverse reading; **l. avec éclatement,** scatter read; **l. de marques,** mark sensing; **l. optique de marques,** mark scanning; (*e*) *Cin:* **l. sonore (d'un film),** reproduction (of a sound film); sound pick-up; *Rec:* **bras de l.,** pick-up arm; **tête de l.,** head of pick-up; **pointe de l.,** stylus; **l. sonore,** play-back (of tape recorder).

lécythe [lesit], *s.m. Cl.Archeol:* lecythus.

lécythidacées [lesitidase], *s.f.pl. Bot:* Lecythidaceae.

lécythis [lesitis], *s.m. Bot:* lecythis.

Léda [leda], *Pr.n.f. Gr.Myth:* Leda.

ledit, ladite, *pl.* **lesdits, lesdites** [lədi, ladit, ledi, ledit], *a.* (*with* **le** *and* **les** *the contractions are as shown under* LE¹; **audit, auxdit(e)s, dudit, desdit(e)s**) *Jur:* the aforesaid, *F:* the said (Dupont, etc.).

lédonien, -ienne [ledɔnjɛ̃, -jɛn], *a. & s. Geog:* (native, inhabitant) of Lons-le-Saunier.

lèdre [lɛdr], *s.f. Ent:* ledra; leafhopper.

ledum [ledɔm], *s.m. Bot:* ledum.

leea [lia], *s.m. Bot:* water vine.

leersia [leɛrsja], *s.f. Bot:* leersia.

lefaucheux [ləfoʃø], *s.m.* Lefaucheux (breech-loading) sporting gun (*from name of gunsmith Casimir Lefaucheux, 1802-1852*).

légal, -aux [legal, -o], *a.* **1.** (*a*) legal; statutory; **fête légale,** legal holiday, statutory holiday; **avoir recours aux moyens légaux,** to have recourse to the law; to institute legal proceedings; **par voies légales,** by legal process; **assassinat l.,** judicial murder; **médecine légale,** forensic medicine; *Fin:* **taux l.,** legal rate of interest; **le pays l.,** the electorate (as opposed to the non-voting population); (*b*) *Lit:* law-abiding, loyal. **2.** *Theol:* legal, in accordance with the law of Moses.

légalement [legalmɑ̃], *adv.* legally, lawfully.

légalisation [legalizasjɔ̃], *s.f.* authentication, certification (of signature, etc., by an official).

légaliser [legalize], *v.tr.* **1.** to legalize (holiday, custom, etc.). **2.** to attest, certify, authenticate (signature, etc.); **déclaration légalisée,** duly attested declaration.

légalisme [legalism], *s.m.* legalism.

légaliste [legalist], *a. & s.m.* **1.** *a.* legalistic. **2.** *s.m.* legalist.

légalité [legalite], *s.f.* (*a*) legality, lawfulness; **rester dans la l.,** to keep within the law; (*b*) *Lit:* loyalty.

légat [lega], *s.m. Ecc: Rom.Ant:* legate; **le l. du Pape,** the Papal Legate; **l. a latere** [alatere], legate *a latere*; **légats-nés du Saint-Siège,** *legati nati.*

légataire [legatɛːr], *s. Jur:* legatee, devisee, heir; **l. universel,** universal, sole, legatee; **l. à titre universel,** residuary legatee; **l. à titre particulier,** specific legatee; **l. d'une propriété,** heir to an estate; **l. de qn,** heir of s.o.

légatine [legatin], *s.f. Tex:* legatine.

légation [legasjɔ̃], *s.f. Pol: Ecc:* **1.** legation (staff or building. **2.** legateship. **3.** *usu. pl. Hist:* **légations,** provinces, legations (of Papal States). **4.** *Lit:* mission.

legato [legato], *adv. & s.m. Mus:* legato, slur.
légatoire [legatwa:r], *a. Rom.Ant:* **province l.,** province of a legate.
lège [lɛ:ʒ], *a. (of ship)* light; **tirant d'eau l.,** light draught.
légendaire [leʒɑ̃dɛ:r]. **1.** *a.* (*a*) legendary (story, etc.); (*b*) epic (combat, etc.). **2.** *s.m.* legendary (writer or book).
légende [leʒɑ̃:d], *s.f.* **1.** legend; **la L. dorée,** the Golden Legend, the Lives of the Saints; **le domaine de la l.,** the region of fable; **entrer dans la l.,** to become a legend; **la l. veut que . . .,** legend has it that . . .. **2.** (*a*) inscription, legend (on coin, etc.); (*b*) caption, legend (of drawing, etc.); *Typ:* underline; (*c*) list of references; key, *esp. U.S:* legend (to diagram, etc.); list of conventional signs (on map, etc.); (*d*) *Lit:* long and tedious recital of uninteresting facts; (*e*) *Mus:* légende.
légendé [leʒɑ̃de], *a.* bearing a legend; *Navy:* **ruban l.,** cap ribbon.
légender [leʒɑ̃de], *v.tr.* to caption (map, illustration, etc.).
léger, -ère [leʒe, -ɛ:r], *a.* **1.** (*a*) light (weight, clothes, troops, cavalry, artillery, food, etc.); (*of coin*) light, below the legal weight; **l. à la course,** light, fleet, of foot; **Achille au pied l.,** swift-foot(ed) Achilles; **j'entendis son pas l.,** I heard his, her, light footstep; **d'un cœur l.,** with a light heart; **avoir le cœur l.,** to be light-hearted; **avoir le sommeil l.,** to be a light sleeper; **avoir la main légère,** to be (i) gentle, kind, (ii) quick, clever, with one's hands, (iii) light-fingered, (iv) quick to chastise; **joug l.,** light yoke; **avoir la langue légère,** to talk inconsiderately; **être l. d'argent,** to have a light purse; **cœur l. de reconnaissance,** heart not overburdened with gratitude; **avoir la plume légère, le style l.,** to write with a light touch; **conduite légère,** (i) flighty conduct, (ii) fickle conduct; **femme légère,** fast woman; **propos légers,** (i) frivolous, idle, talk; (ii) slightly improper, free, talk; **coup l.,** tap, touch; *Aut:* **un l. coup de frein,** a touch on the brake; **repas l.,** light meal; (*b*) slight (pain, mistake, etc.); light, gentle (breeze); mild (tobacco, beer); weak (tea, coffee); faint (sound, tint, etc.); **il y a un l. mieux,** there is a slight improvement; he is a shade better; **faire un l. geste,** to make a slight gesture; **perte légère,** trivial loss. **2.** *adv.phr.* **à la légère,** (i) lightly; (ii) without due consideration; **vêtu à la légère,** lightly, scantily, dressed; **prendre un engagement à la légère,** to commit oneself without due reflection, rashly, unthinkingly; **traiter une affaire à la légère,** (i) to make light of sth.; (ii) to deal with a matter without due consideration; **conclure à la légère,** to jump to conclusions. **2.** *s.m.pl. Const:* **légers,** light plaster work, partitions, etc.
légèrement [leʒɛrmɑ̃], *adv.* **1.** (*a*) lightly (dressed, armed, etc.); **passer l. sur les endroits difficiles,** to glide over the difficult passages; **courir l.,** to run nimbly; **parler l.,** to talk lightly; **souper l.,** to take a light supper; (*b*) slightly (wounded, etc.); (*c*) **il parut l. surpris,** he seemed a bit taken aback; **il est l. pointilleux,** he is rather touchy; **tournez l. à gauche,** turn slightly to the left; **eau l. radioactive,** water with low radioactive content. **2. agir l.,** to act without due consideration; **traiter qch. l.,** to make light of sth.; **ne croyez pas trop l. ce qu'il dit,** don't be too ready to believe what he says.
légèreté [leʒɛrte], *s.f.* **1.** (*a*) lightness (of gas, etc.); nimbleness, agility (of dancer, etc.); **l. de main,** lightness of touch (of doctor, etc.); **l. de plume, de style,** lightness of touch (in writing); **l. de pinceau,** lightness of touch (in painting); (*b*) slightness, trivial nature (of injury, etc.); mildness (of beer, etc.); weakness (of tea, etc.). **2.** (*a*) levity; flightiness (of conduct); (*b*) fickleness.
légérite [leʒerit], *s.f. Const:* anti-corrosive coat.
léger-vêtu [leʒevety], *a. Lit:* lightly clad; **des nymphes léger-vêtues,** lightly clad nymphs.
leggings, leggins [lɛginz, -ŋz], *s.m.pl.* leggings.
leghorn [legɔrn], *s.m.* Leghorn (fowl).
légiférer [leʒifere], *v.i.* **(je légifère, n. légiférons; je légiférerai)** to legislate (sur, on).
légion [leʒjɔ̃], *s.f.* legion; **la L. étrangère,** the Foreign Legion; **la L. d'honneur,** the Legion of Honour; **l. de moucherons,** host, swarm, of gnats; *B:* **je m'appelle L.,** my name is Legion; *F:* **ils sont l. ceux qui se conduisent ainsi,** there are many who behave like that.
légionnaire [leʒjɔnɛ:r], *a. & s.m.* **1.** (*a*) *Rom. & Fr.Hist:* legionary (soldier); (*b*) (soldier) of the Foreign Legion. **2.** (member) of the Legion of Honour.
législateur, -trice [leʒislatœ:r, -tris]. **1.** *s.* legislator, lawgiver. **2.** *a.* **roi l.,** law-making king; **puissance législatrice,** legislative power.
législatif, -ive [leʒislatif, -i:v], *a.* legislative; (*a*) *Fr.Hist:* **l'Assemblée législative,** the Legislative Assembly; (*b*) **élection législative,** parliamentary election; **le pouvoir l.,** the legislature; *s.f.pl. F:* **les législatives,** parliamentary elections; (*c*) *s.m.* **le l. et l'exécutif,** the legislative and the executive.
législation [leʒislasjɔ̃], *s.f.* (*a*) legislation, lawgiving; **l. nationale,** internal legislation; (*b*) (set of) laws; **l. criminelle,** criminal law; **la l. industrielle** = the Factory Acts; **l. du travail,** labour laws; **modifier la l. en vigueur,** to modify the laws in force.
législativement [leʒislativmɑ̃], *adv.* legislatively.
législature [leʒislaty:r], *s.f.* **1.** legislature, legislative body. **2.** period during which a legislative body functions.
légiste [leʒist], *s.m.* legist, jurist; **médecin l.,** forensic pathologist; **expert l.,** forensic scientist.
légitimaire [leʒitimɛ:r], *a. Jur:* (*of portion in parent's estate*) fixed, secured, by law (to each child).
légitimation [leʒitimasjɔ̃], *s.f.* **1.** legitimation (of child). **2.** (*a*) official recognition (of delegate, title, etc.); (*b*) submission of credentials; **verser une somme à qn contre l.,** to pay s.o. a sum upon submission of proof of identity.
légitime [leʒitim], *a.* **1.** legitimate, lawful (child, wife, authority); **propriétaire l.,** legal owner; **héritier l.,** heir-at-law, rightful heir. **2.** (*a*) justifiable, rightful (demand, anger, etc.); legitimate (reasoning, deduction); well-founded (fears, etc.); *Jur:* **l. défense,** self-defence; (*b*) sound (deduction, inference). **3.** *s.f. A: Jur:* portion to which a child is entitled in his parents' estate. **4.** *P:* **ma l.,** my wife, my missus.
légitimé [leʒitime], *a. & s.* legitim(at)ized (child).
légitimement [leʒitimmɑ̃], *adv.* legitimately, lawfully, justifiably, rightfully, reasonably.
légitimer [leʒitime], *v.tr.* **1.** to legitimate, legitimatize (child, etc.). **2.** to justify (action, claim, etc.). **3.** to grant recognition to (delegate, etc.); to recognize (title).
légitimisme [leʒitimism], *s.m. Fr.Hist:* legitimism; adherence to the elder branch of the Bourbon dynasty.
légitimiste [leʒitimist], *a. & s. Fr. & Spanish Pol:* legitimist.
légitimité [leʒitimite], *s.f.* **1.** legitimacy (of child, of title of sovereign, of deduction). **2.** lawfulness (of measure, etc.).
legs [lɛ, lɛg], *s.m.* legacy, bequest; **l. de charité,** charitable bequest; **faire un l. à qn,** to leave a legacy to s.o.; **hériter d'un l.,** to come into a legacy; *O: F:* **coureur de l.,** legacy hunter; **l. (à titre) particulier,** specific bequest; **l. à titre universel,** residue of the estate; **l. de residuo,** life interest in a bequest; **l. universel,** universal bequest; **le l. du passé,** the legacy of the past.
léguer [lege], *v.tr.* **(je lègue, n. léguons; je léguerai)** to bequeath, leave (personalty); to devise (realty) **(à qn,** to s.o.); **le siècle dernier nous a légué plusieurs découvertes précieuses,** the last century bequeathed to us a number of valuable discoveries.
légume [legym], *s.* **1.** *s.m.* (*a*) vegetable; *Cu:* **légumes verts,** greens; **légumes secs,** dried vegetables (beans, peas, lentils, etc.); **légumes déshydratés,** (machine-processed) dehydrated vegetables; **régime de légumes,** vegetable diet; (*b*) *Bot:* legume(n), pod. **2.** *P:* **gros l.,** *s.f.* **grosse l.,** important person, big shot; **les grosses légumes,** the top brass; **être, dans, parmi les (grosses) légumes,** to be one of the top brass.
légumier, -ière [legymje, -jɛ:r], *a.* **1.** of, pertaining to, vegetables; **jardin l.,** vegetable garden. **2.** *s.m.* vegetable dish. **3.** *s.m.* (*in Belgium*) greengrocer.
légumine [legymin], *s.f. Ch:* legumin.
légumineux, -euse [legyminø, -ø:z], *Bot:* **1.** *a.* leguminous. **2.** *s.f.* **légumineuse,** leguminous plant; *pl.* **légumineuses,** Leguminosae.
légumiste [legymist], *s.* **1.** vegetable gardener. **2.** *occ.* vegetarian.
lehm [lɛm], *s.m. Geol:* limon; *Agr:* loam.
leibnizianisme [lɛbnitsjanism], *s.m. Phil:* Leibnitzianism.
leibnizien, -ienne [lɛbnitsjɛ̃, -jɛn], *a. & s. Phil:* Leibnitzian.
leio- [lejɔ], *pref.* leio-, lio-.
leiomyome [lejɔmjo:m], *s.m. Med:* leiomyoma.
leiomysarcome [lejɔmisarko:m], *s.m. Med:* leiomyosarcoma.
leiothrix [lejɔtriks], *s.m. Orn:* leiothrix.
leipoa [lepɔa], *s.m. Orn:* leipoa.
Leipzig [lɛpsik], *Pr.n. Geog:* Leipzig.
leipzigois, -oise [lɛpsikwa, -wa:z], *a. & s. Geog:* (native, inhabitant) of Leipzig.
leishmanie [lɛʃmani], *s.f. Prot:* leishmania.
leishmanide [lɛʃmanid], *s.f. Med:* post-kala-azar dermal leishmaniasis; leishmanioid disease.
leishmaniose [lɛʃmanjo:z], *s.f. Med:* leishmaniosis, leishmaniasis.
leitmotif, leitmotiv [laitmɔtif], *s.m. Mus:* leitmotif, leitmotiv; **l. musical,** theme song; *F:* **c'est toujours le même l. avec lui,** he's always harping on the same theme, thing.
leitneria [laitnerja], *s.m. Bot:* leitneria.
Lélie [leli], *Pr.n.f.* Laelia, Lelia.
lem [lɛm], *s.m. F:* lunar module.
Léman [lemɑ̃], *Pr.n.m. Geog:* **le lac L.,** the lake of Geneva, Lake Geneva.
lémanique [lemanik], *a.* of, relating to, Lake Geneva.
lemme [lɛm], *s.m. Log: Mth:* lemma.
lemming [lɛmiŋ], *s.m. Z:* lemming.
lemna [lɛmna], *s.f.,* **lemne** [lɛmn], *s.f. Bot:* lemna, duckweed.
lemnacées [lɛmnase], *s.f.pl. Bot:* Lemnaceae.
lemnien, -ienne [lɛmnjɛ̃, -jɛn], *a. & s. Geog:* Lemnian; *Miner: A.Med:* **terre lemnienne,** Lemnian earth, Lemnian bole.
lemniscate [lɛmniskat], *s.f. Geom:* lemniscate.
lemnisque [lɛmnisk], *s.m. Rom.Ant: Pal:* lemniscus.
lémonange [lemɔnɑ̃:ʒ], *s.m.* hybrid resulting from the crossing of lemon and orange trees.
lémoniidés [lemɔniide], *s.m.pl. Ent:* Lemoniidae.
lémonime [lemɔnim], *s.m. Bot:* limon.
lémonol [lemɔnɔl], *s.m. Ch: A:* geraniol.
lémur(e) [lemy:r], *s.m. Z:* lemur; **l. catta,** ring-tailed lemur.
lémures [lemy:r], *s.m.pl. Rom.Ant:* lemures; spirits of the dead.
lémuridés [lemyride], *s.m.pl. Z:* Lemuridae.
lémurien, -ienne [lemyrjɛ̃, -jɛn]. *Z:* **1.** *a. & s.m.* lemurian. **2.** *s.m.pl.* **lémuriens,** Lemuridae, lemurs; **lémuriens inférieurs,** mouse lemurs.
lémuries [lemyri], *s.f.pl. Rom.Ant:* Lemuria.
lendemain [lɑ̃dmɛ̃], *s.m.* next day; **le l. de la bataille,** the day after the battle; **le l. matin,** the next morning, the morning after; **songer au l.,** to think of the morrow, of the future; **du jour au l. il devint célèbre,** he became famous overnight; **au l. de,** (on) the day following; shortly after; **des succès sans lendemains,** short-lived successes; *F:* **le l. de cuite, de bombe,** the morning after the night before.
lendit [lɑ̃di], *s.m. A:* **1.** fair (held near Paris in June). **2.** fees paid to the schoolmasters on this occasion. **3.** (*in Paris*) **l. scolaire,** inter(-)schools athletics meetings.
lendore [lɑ̃dɔ:r], *s.m. & f. F: A:* slowcoach, sleepy-head.
lénéennes [leneɛn], *s.f.pl. Gr.Ant:* lenaea.
lénifiant [lenifjɑ̃], *a. Med: etc:* assuaging, soothing, lenitive.
lénifier [lenifje], *v.tr.* (*pr.sub. & p.d.* **n. lénifiions, v. lénifiiez**) *Med:* to assuage, soothe, alleviate.
Lénine [lenin], *Pr.n.* Lenin.
Léningrad [leningrad], *Pr.n.m. Geog:* Leningrad.
léninisme [leninism], *s.m. Pol:* Leninism.
léniniste [leninist], *a. & s. Pol:* Leninist.
lénitif, -ive [lenitif, -i:v], *a.* **1.** lenitive, palliative, soothing. **2.** *s.m. Med:* lenitive.
lénition [lenisjɔ̃], *s.f. Ling:* lenition.
lensois, -oise [lɑ̃swa, -wa:z], *a. & s.* (native, inhabitant) of Lens [lɑ̃:s].
lent, lente[1] [lɑ̃, lɑ̃:t], *a.* (*a*) slow (movement, poison, etc.); **les heures étaient bien lentes le dimanche,** time hung heavy on Sundays; **mort lente,** lingering death; **être l. à faire qch.,** to be slow to do sth.; **l. à agir,** slow to act, slow in action; **l. à répondre,** slow in answering; **l. à croire,** slow of belief; **l. à la colère,** slow to anger; **avoir la parole lente,** to be slow of speech; **l. d'esprit,** slow of comprehension; *Med:* **pouls l. permanent,** Adams-Stokes syndrome; (*b*) *Exp:* slow-burning (powder); (*c*) (ship) slow in tacking, slack in stays.
lente[2], *s.f.* nit; egg (of louse).
lentement [lɑ̃tmɑ̃], *adv.* slowly; **ruisseau qui coule l.,** slow-flowing stream; **il parlait toujours l.,** he was a slow speaker, always spoke slowly; *Nau:* **avant l.!** slow ahead! **l. la machine!** ease the engines!
lenteur [lɑ̃tœ:r], *s.f.* **1.** slowness; **mettre de la l. à faire qch.,** to be slow in doing sth.; **avec l.,** (i) slowly; (ii) with due deliberation; **l. à répondre,** (i) slowness to answer; (ii) dilatoriness, remissness, in answering; (iii) deliberation in answering. **2.** *pl.* slow ways, progress; slowness of

action; **excusez mes lenteurs,** please forgive me for being so slow; **les lenteurs de l'administration,** the delays, dilatoriness, of government departments, of officialdom.

lentibulariacées [lɑ̃tibylarjase], *s.f.pl. Bot:* Lentibulariaceae.

lenticelle [lɑ̃tisɛl], *s.f. Bot:* lenticel.

lenticellé [lɑ̃tisɛl(l)e], *a. Bot:* lenticellate.

lenticulaire [lɑ̃tikylɛːr], **lenticulé** [lɑ̃tikyle], *a. Anat: etc:* lenticular, lentiform, lens-shaped; **trame lenticulaire,** lenticular screen.

lenticule [lɑ̃tikyl], *s.f. Bot:* duckweed.

lentiforme [lɑ̃tifɔrm], *a.* lentiform, lenticular.

lentigineux, -euse [lɑ̃tiʒinø, -øːz], *a.* lentiginous; freckled.

lentigo [lɑ̃tigo], *s.m. Med:* lentigo, freckles.

lentille [lɑ̃tiːj], *s.f.* **1.** *Bot:* (*a*) *Cu:* lentil; *B.Lit:* **plat de lentilles,** (Esau's) mess of pottage; (*b*) **l. d'eau,** lemna, duckweed. **2.** bob, ball (of pendulum). **3.** *Opt:* (*a*) (spectacle) lens; single lens; **l. cornéenne,** corneal, contact, lens; **l. convergente,** converging lens; **l. divergente,** diverging, deflecting, lens; **l. plan-concave,** plano-concave lens; **l. plan-convexe,** plano-convex lens; **l. plan-convexe à court foyer,** bull's-eye lens; **l. à échelons,** Fresnel lens (of light-house); (*b*) component (of photographic lens, etc.); **objectif à quatre lentilles,** four-component lens; (*c*) *Anat: F:* crystalline lens (of eye); (*d*) **l. électronique,** electron lens; (*e*) **l. allongée de minerai,** pod; **l. de roche,** sill; **l. de minerai,** lenticular body. **4.** *Nau:* bull's eye; deck light. **5.** freckle.

lentillon [lɑ̃tijɔ̃], *s.m. Bot:* (variety of) small red lentil.

lentiprisme [lɑ̃tiprism], *s.m. Opt:* prismatic lens.

lentisque [lɑ̃tisk], *s.m. Bot:* lentiscus, lentisk, mastic tree.

lento [lɛnto], *adv. & s.m. Mus:* lento.

Léon [leɔ̃], *Pr.n.m.* **1.** Leo, Leon. **2.** *Geog:* Leon.

léonais, -aise [leɔnɛ, -ɛːz]. **1.** *a. & s. Geog:* (*a*) (native, inhabitant) of (i) the pays de Léon (in Brittany), (ii) Saint-Pol-de-Léon; (*b*) (native, inhabitant) of Leon (Spain); Leonese. **2.** *s.m.* the pays de Léon (Brittany). **3.** *s.m. Ling:* (*a*) Breton dialect (of the Pays de Léon); (*b*) Leonese.

léonard[1], **-arde** [leɔnaːr, -ard], *a. & s. Geog:* (native, inhabitant) of (i) the pays de Léon, (ii) Saint-Pol-de-Léon.

Léonard[2] [leɔnaːr], *Pr.n.m.* Leonard; **L. de Vinci** [vɛ̃si], Leonardo da Vinci.

Léonce [leɔ̃ːs], *Pr.n.m.* Leontius.

Léonidas [leɔnidɑːs], *Pr.n.m. Gr.Hist:* Leonidas.

Léonide [leɔnid], *s.f. Astr:* Leonid.

Léonie [leɔni], *Pr.n.f.* Leonie.

léonin[1] [leɔnɛ̃], *a.* leonine, lion-like; **part léonine,** lion's share; *Jur:* **contrat l.,** leonine convention; unconscionable bargain.

léonin[2], *a. Pros:* Leonine; **vers léonins,** Leonine verse, Leonines; **rimes léonines,** Leonine rhymes.

léonite [leɔnit], *s.f. Miner:* leonite.

Léonore [leɔnɔːr], *Pr.n.f.* Leonora.

léonotis [leɔnɔtis], *s.m. Bot:* leonotis, lion's ear.

léontiasis [leɔ̃tjazis], *s.f. Med:* leontiasis.

léontice [leɔ̃tis], *s.f. Bot:* leontice, lion's leaf.

léontine [leɔ̃tin], *s.f.* lady's double watch chain.

léontocéphale [leɔ̃tɔsefal], *a. & s.m. or f.* lion-headed (divinity).

léontodon [leɔ̃tɔdɔ̃], *s.m. Bot:* leontodon; lion's tooth; hawkbit.

léontopodium [leɔ̃tɔpɔdjɔm], *s.m. Bot:* leontopodium.

léonure [leɔnyːr], **leonurus** [leɔnyryːs], *s.m. Bot:* leonurus, motherwort.

léopard [leɔpaːr], *s.m.* (*a*) *Z: Her:* leopard; **l. femelle,** leopardess; **l. des neiges,** snow leopard; mountain panther; ounce; **l. de mer,** sea leopard, leopard seal; (*b*) *Mil:* **tenue l.,** (camouflaged) combat clothing; (*c*) *Const:* (flecked) reddish-grey Belgian marble with dash of grey and black.

léopardé [leɔparde], *a.* (*a*) *Her:* (lion) passant gardant, leopardé; (*b*) (*of animal*) spotted like a leopard.

Léopold [leɔpɔl(d)], *Pr.n.m.* Leopold.

léopoldinia [leɔpɔldinja], *s.m. Bot:* leopoldinia.

léopoldite [leɔpɔldit], *s.f. Miner:* leopoldite.

Léopoldville [leɔpɔldvil], *Pr.n. Geog:* Leopoldville.

léotard [leɔtaːr], *s.m. Cost:* leotard.

lépadogastre [lepadɔgastr̥], *s.m. Ich:* lepadogaster, (Cornish) sucker, sucking fish.

Lépante [lepɑ̃ːt], *Pr.n. Geog:* Lepanto.

lépas [lepɑːs], *s.m. Moll:* lepas, goose mussel, goose barnacle.

lépidagathis [lepidagatis], *s.m. Bot:* lepidagathis.

Lépide [lepid], *Pr.n.m. Rom.Hist:* Lepidus.

lépidine [lepidin], *s.m. Ch:* lepidine.

lépidium [lepidjɔm], *s.m. Bot:* lepidium.

lépidochromie [lepidɔkrɔmi], *s.f.* the art of making a transfer of butterflies onto paper or china and of fixing the image with natural colours.

lépidocrocite [lepidɔcrɔsit], *s.f. Miner:* lepidocrocite.

lépidodendracées [lepidɔdɛ̃drase], *s.f.pl. Paleont:* Lepidodendraceae.

lépidodendron [lepidɔdɛ̃drɔ̃], *s.m. Paleont:* lepidodendron.

lépidolit(h)e [lepidɔlit], *s.m. Miner:* lepidolite.

lépidomélane [lepidɔmelan], *s.m. Miner:* lepidomelane.

lépidope [lepidɔp], *s.m. Ich:* scabbard fish, garter fish.

lépidophloios [lepidɔflɔjɔs], *s.m. Paleont:* lepidophloios.

lépidophylle [lepidɔfil], *a.* lepidophyllous.

lépidophyllum [lepidɔfilɔm], *s.m. Bot:* lepidophyllum.

lépidoptère [lepidɔptɛːr], *Ent:* **1.** *a.* lepidopterous. **2.** *s.m.* lepidopteran; *pl.* **lépidoptères,** Lepidoptera.

lépidoptériste [lepidɔpterist], *s.m.* lepidopterist.

lépidoptérologie [lepidɔpterɔlɔʒi], *s.f.* lepidopterology.

lepidosaphes [lepidɔsafɛs], *s.m. Ent:* lepidosaphes.

lépidosirène [lepidɔsirɛn], *s.m. Ich:* lepidosiren.

lépidostée [lepidɔste], *s.m. Ich:* gar pike.

lépidostrobus [lepidɔstrɔbyːs], *s.m. Paleont:* lepidostrobus.

lépidurus [lepidyryːs], *s.m. Crust:* lepidurus.

lépilemur, lépilémure [lepilemyːr], *s.m. Z:* sportive lemur.

lépiote [lepjɔt], *s.f. Fung:* lepiota, parasol mushroom.

lépisme [lepism], *s.m. Ent:* lepisma, *F:* bristle-tail, silver fish, silver lady; **l. myrmécophile,** myrmecophilous bristle-tail.

lépismidés [lepismide], *s.m.pl. Ent:* Lepismidae.

léporide [lepɔrid], *s.m.* (*a*) leporide; (*b*) Belgian hare.

léporides [lepɔrid], **léporidés** [lepɔride], *s.m.pl. Z:* Leporidae.

lépospondyles [lepɔspɔ̃dil], *s.m.pl. Paleont:* Lepospondyli.

lépothrix [lepɔtriks], *s.m. Med:* lepothrix, trichomycosis nodosa.

lèpre [lɛpr̥], *s.f. Med:* leprosy; **l. maculeuse,** spotted leprosy; **l. tuberculeuse,** nodular leprosy; **l. anesthésique,** anaesthetic leprosy; *Bot:* **l. des olives,** gloeosporiose (of olives).

lépreux, -euse [leprø, -øːz], *a. & s.* **1.** *a.* (*a*) *Med:* leprous; (*b*) peeling, scaly, dilapidated (wall). **2.** *s.* leper.

lépride [leprid], *s.f. Med:* leprid.

léprome [leproːm], *s.m. Med:* leproma.

léproserie [leprozri], *s.f.* leper hospital, leprosarium; *A:* lazar-house.

lepte [lɛpt], *s.m. Arach:* leptus; **l. automnal,** harvest bug, harvest mite.

lept(i)- [lɛpt(i)-], *pref.* lept-, lepto-.

leptidés [lɛptide], *s.m.pl. Ent:* Leptidae.

leptis [lɛptis], *s.m. Ent:* snipe fly.

leptite [lɛptit], *s.f. Miner:* leptite.

lepto- [lɛpt(ɔ)], *pref.* lept(o).

leptobos [lɛptɔbɔs], *s.m. Paleont:* leptobos.

leptocardien [lɛptɔkardjɛ̃], *s.m. Biol:* leptocardian.

leptocéphale [lɛptɔsefal], *Ich:* (*a*) *a.* leptocephalic; (*b*) *s.m.* leptocephalus.

leptocurtique [lɛptɔkyrtik], *a.* (*statistics*) leptokurtic.

leptodactyle [lɛptɔdaktil], *Z: Orn:* **1.** *a.* leptodactylous. **2.** *s.m.* leptodactyl.

leptodactylidés [lɛptɔdaktilide], *s.m.pl. Amph:* Leptodactylidae.

leptodore, leptodora [lɛptɔdɔːr, lɛptɔdɔra], *s.f. Crust:* leptodora.

leptolépidés [lɛptɔlepide], *s.m.pl. Paleont:* Leptolepidae.

leptolepis [lɛptɔlepis], *s.m. Paleont:* leptolepis.

leptome [lɛptɔːm], *s.m. Bot:* leptome.

leptoméningite [lɛptɔmenɛ̃ʒit], *s.f. Med:* leptomeningitis.

leptoméryx [lɛptɔmeriks], *s.m. Paleont:* leptomeryx.

leptomonas [lɛptɔmɔnas], *s.m. Prot:* leptomonas.

lepton [lɛptɔ̃], *s.m.* **1.** *A.Meas: A.Num:* lepton. **2.** *Moll:* lepton, coin shell. **3.** *Atom.Ph:* lepton.

leptonique [lɛptɔnik], *a. Atom.Ph:* lepton (number).

leptoprosope [lɛptɔprɔzɔp], *Anthr:* (*a*) *a.* leptoprosopic; (*b*) *s.m. & f.* leptoprosope.

leptoprosopie [lɛptɔprɔzɔpi], *s.f. Anthr:* leptoprosopy.

leptorhin [lɛptɔrɛ̃], *a.* leptorrhine.

leptorhinie [lɛptɔrini], *s.f. Anthr:* leptorrhiny.

leptorhinien, -ienne [lɛptɔrinjɛ̃, -jɛn], *Anthr:* (*a*) *a.* leptorrhinic, leptorrhinian; (*b*) *s.* leptorrhin(ian).

leptosome [lɛptɔzɔm], *Anthr:* (*a*) *a.* leptosome, leptosomic, leptosomatic; (*b*) *s.m. & f.* leptosome.

leptosomie [lɛptɔzɔmi], *s.f. Anthr:* ectomorphy.

leptospermum [lɛptɔspɛrmɔm], *s.m. Bot:* leptospermum.

leptospire [lɛptɔspiːr], *s.m. Prot:* leptospira.

leptospirose [lɛptɔspiroːz], *s.f. Med: Vet:* leptospirosis.

leptosporangiées [lɛptɔspɔrɑ̃ʒje], *s.f.pl. Bot:* Leptosporangiatae.

leptostracés [lɛptɔstrase], *s.m.pl. Crust:* Leptostraca.

leptotène [lɛptɔtɛn], *a. Biol:* leptotene.

leptothrix [lɛptɔtriks], *s.m. Bac:* leptothrix.

leptotyphlopidés [lɛptɔtiflɔpide], *s.m.pl. Rept:* Leptotyphlopidae.

lepture [lɛptyːr], *s.m. Ent:* leptura.

leptynite [lɛptinit], *s.f. Geol:* leptynite.

leptynolite [lɛptinɔlit], *s.f. Geol:* leptynolite.

lequel, laquelle, lesquels, lesquelles [ləkɛl, lakɛl, lekɛl], *pron.* (*contracted with* **à** *and* **de** *to* **auquel, auxquel(le)s, duquel, desquel(le)s**) **1.** *rel.pron.* who, whom; which; (*a*) (*of thgs after prep.*) **le champ dans lequel je me promène,** the field in which I am walking; **les adresses auxquelles il devait m'écrire,** the addresses at which he was to write to me; **décision par laquelle . . .,** decision whereby . . .; (*b*) (*of pers.*) (i) (*stressed after a pause, in official language*) **ont comparu trois témoins, lesquels ont déclaré . . .,** three witnesses appeared, who averred . . .; (ii) (*used in preference to* **qui** *after* **entre, parmi,** *and often after* **avec**) **les deux officiers entre lesquels elle était assise,** the two officers between whom she was seated; **la dame avec laquelle elle était sortie,** the lady with whom she had gone out; (iii) (*occ. with other preps.*) **mon frère, au domicile duquel je suis allé,** my brother, to whose house I have been; **la dame chez laquelle je l'ai rencontrée,** the lady at whose house I met her; (*c*) (*of pers. or thg to avoid ambiguity*) **le père de cette jeune fille, lequel est très riche,** the girl's father, who is very rich; **il épousa une sœur de Colin, laquelle le rendit très heureux,** he married one of Colin's sisters, who made him very happy; **la reliure du livre, laquelle s'en allait en morceaux,** the binding of the book, which binding was falling to pieces; (*d*) (*adjectival*) **je me plaindrai au colonel, lequel colonel, soit dit en passant, est mon cousin,** I shall complain to the colonel, who by the way is my cousin; **voici cent francs, laquelle somme vous était due par mon père,** here are a hundred francs, a sum which my father owed you; **il écrira peut-être, auquel cas . . .,** perhaps he will write, in which case. . . . **2.** *interr.pron.* which (one)? **elle est assise sur une chaise—sur laquelle?** she is sitting on a chair—(on) which one? **lequel de ces chapeaux préférez-vous?** which of these hats do you prefer? **lequel d'entre nous?** which one of us? **lequel d'entre vous n'eût pas fait de même?** which (one) of you would not have done the same? **auquel des enfants a-t-il parlé?** to which of the children did he speak? **lesquels préférez-vous?** which do you prefer?

lerche [lɛrʃ], *adv. P:* **il n'y avait pas l. de crème sur le gâteau,** there wasn't much cream on the cake.

Lerne [lɛrn], *Pr.n. A.Geog:* **le marais de L.,** the Lerna Marsh; **l'hydre de L.,** the Lernaean hydra.

lernée [lɛrne], *s.f. Crust:* lern(a)ean; (*genus*) Lernaea.

lérot [lero], *s.m. Z:* lerot, garden dormouse.

lès [lɛ, le], *prep.* (*occurs only in place names*) near(-by); **Plessis-lès-Tours,** Plessis near Tours.

Lesbie [lɛsbi], *Pr.n.f. Lt.Lit:* Lesbia.

lesbien, -ienne [lɛsbjɛ̃, -jɛn]. **1.** *a. & s. Geog:* Lesbian. **2.** *s.f.* **lesbienne,** lesbian.

lèse [lɛːz], *a.f.* (*attached to the noun by a hyphen*) injured; **crime de lèse-société, de lèse-humanité,** outrage against society, against humanity.

lèse-majesté [lɛzmaʒɛste], *s.f. Jur:* high treason, lese-majesty.

léser [leze], *v.tr.* (**je lèse, n. lésons; je léserai**) (*a*) to wrong (s.o.); to wound, injure (s.o., s.o.'s pride, etc.); *Jur:* **l. les droits de qn,** to encroach upon s.o.'s rights; **la partie lésée,** the injured party; (*b*) (*of action*) to prove injurious to, to endanger (s.o.'s interests, etc.); (*c*) **le coup a lésé un nerf, le poumon droit,** the blow has injured a nerve, the right lung.

lésine [lezin], *s.f. O:* stinginess, niggardliness, close-fistedness.

lésiner [lezine], *v.i.* to be stingy, close-fisted; to haggle (**sur**, over); to be penny wise; **ne lésinez pas sur la nourriture,** don't stint yourself on food.

lésinerie [lezinri], *s.f. O:* **1.** stingy act; piece of stinginess. **2.** = LÉSINE.

lésineur, -euse [lezinœ:r, -ø:z]; *O:* **1.** *a.* close-fisted, niggardly, stingy; penny-wise. **2.** *s.* (old) hunks; niggard.

lésion [lezjɔ̃], *s.f.* (*a*) injury, hurt; *Med:* lesion; **l. du tissu, des tissus, l. tissulaire,** tissue lesion; (*b*) *Jur:* injury, wrong; **contrat où il y a l.,** burdensome contract.

lésionnaire [lezjɔnɛ:r], *a. Jur:* prejudicial.

lésionnel [lezjɔnɛl], *a. Med:* **troubles lésionnels,** organic disease.

lespedeza [lɛspedeza], *s.m. Bot:* lespedeza.

lessivable [lesivabl̩], *a.* (wallpaper, material, etc.) that can be washed (with detergent, etc.); washable.

lessivage [lesiva:ʒ], *s.m.* **1.** (*a*) washing (of household linen); *F:* **l. de crâne,** brainwashing; (*b*) *F: A:* heavy loss (at cards, etc.). **2.** (*a*) cleaning (of boilers, etc.); steaming out (of tanks in a tanker); (*b*) *Paperm:* boiling; (*c*) *Geol: Min: etc:* leaching.

lessive [lesi:v], *s.f.* **1.** lye; detergent; **l. de soude, de potasse,** caustic soda; **acheter un paquet de l.,** to buy a packet of detergent, of washing powder; *s.a.* ÂNE 1. **2.** (household) washing; (*a*) wash; **faire la l.,** to do the washing; **envoyer qch. à la l.,** to send sth. to the wash; **jour de l.,** washing day; **blanc de l.,** clean (garment, etc.); fresh from the wash; (*b*) soiled linen (going to the wash); (*c*) articles washed; **étendre la l.,** to hang out the washing; **faire une l. de Gascon,** to turn the table cloth (instead of laying a new one); (*d*) *F: O:* heavy loss (at cards, etc.); (*e*) *esp. Pol:* purge; clean-up; **gouvernement qui promet une l. générale,** government that promises a general clean-up.

lessivé [lesive], *a.* (*a*) *Geol:* leached (soil, horizon); (*b*) *P:* (*of pers.*) exhausted, washed out.

lessiver [lesive], *v.tr.* **1.** (*a*) *O:* to wash, boil (linen, etc. in lye, detergent); (*b*) to scrub, wash over (floor, etc. with detergent); to clean (boiler, etc.); **l. les citernes (d'un pétrolier),** to steam out the tanks (in a tanker); **l. le bois peint,** to wash down the paint (with washing-soda); *F:* **l. la tête à qn,** to haul s.o. over the coals. **2.** (*a*) *Ch:* to lixiviate (ashes); (*b*) *Geol: Min: etc:* to leach. **3.** (*a*) *P: O:* **l. sa montre,** to sell, flog, one's watch; to turn one's watch into money; (*b*) *P:* (*at cards, etc.*) **se faire l.,** to be cleaned out; (*of pers.*) **être lessivé,** (i) to be washed out; (ii) to be out of the running.

lessiveur, -euse [lesivœ:r, -ø:z], *s.* **1.** *A:* washer, washerwoman. **2.** *s.f.* **lessiveuse,** copper, boiler. **3.** *s.m. Paperm:* boiler.

lessiviel, -ielle [lesivjɛl, -jɛl], *a.* **produits lessiviels,** detergents.

lest [lɛst], *s.m.* no *pl.* **1.** ballast (of ship, balloon, etc.); **navire sur l.,** ship in ballast (trim); **l. liquide, l. d'eau,** water ballast; **l. en gueuses,** kentledge; **l. volant,** shifting ballast; **faire son l.,** to take in ballast; *Nau:* **partir, retourner, sur son l.,** to sail, return, in ballast; **jeter du l.,** to discharge ballast; (ii) to make sacrifices (in order to attain one's end); **homme qui a besoin de l.,** man who lacks ballast. **2.** weights, sinkers (of fishing net). **3.** *Husb:* food with bulk but little nutritional value.

lestage [lɛsta:ʒ], *s.m.* ballasting (of ship, etc.).

leste [lɛst], *a.* **1.** light; nimble, agile (person, animal); smart, brisk (motion); **maman avait la main l.,** I got many a slap from my mother; mother was always ready to give one a spanking. **2.** (*a*) *a. O:* unceremonious, unscrupulous (behaviour); sharp (practice); **je trouve le procédé un peu l.!** that's a bit thick! (*b*) **être l. dans ses discours,** to be free, broad, in one's conversation; **roman l.,** spicy novel; **anecdotes lestes,** naughty stories. **3.** *A. & Lit:* elegant (dress).

lestement [lɛstəmɑ̃], *adv.* **1.** lightly; nimbly; smartly, briskly. **2.** (*a*) *O:* unscrupulously; (*b*) **plaisanter un peu l.,** to make irreverent remarks, rather naughty jokes.

lester [lɛste], *v.tr.* **1.** to ballast (ship, balloon); *F:* **se l. l'estomac,** to have a good feed, a good drink. **2.** to weight (fishing net, etc.); *Aer:* **message lesté,** weighted message.

se lester, *F:* (*of pers.*) to tuck in, have a good feed.

lesteur [lɛstœ:r], *s.m. Nau:* **1.** ballast man. **2.** ballast lighter.

lestobiose [lɛstɔbjo:z], *s.f. Biol:* lestobiosis.

lestodon [lɛstɔdɔ̃], *s.m. Paleont:* lestodon.

let [lɛt], *a. Ten:* let.

lét(h)al, -aux [letal, -o], *a. Biol: Med:* lethal; **gène, facteur, l.,** lethal gene, factor; *Atom.Ph:* **dose lét(h)ale,** lethal dose.

lét(h)alité [letalite], *s.f. Med:* lethality; **tables de l.,** mortality tables; **l. due aux radiations,** radiation lethality.

letchi [lɛtʃi], *s.m. Bot:* = LITCHI.

Lètes [lɛt], *s.m.pl. Rom.Hist:* Laeti.

léthargie [letarʒi], *s.f.* (*a*) *Med:* state of suspended animation; catalepsy; coma; **l. hypnotique,** hypnotic trance; (*b*) lethargy; inactivity; **il faudrait le sortir de sa l.,** he needs rousing, stirring up; (*c*) (*of animal*) **passer l'hiver en état de l.,** to hibernate.

léthargique [letarʒik], *a.* (*a*) *Med:* **sommeil l.,** comatose sleep; **encéphalite l.,** lethargic encephalitis, sleeping sickness; (*b*) lethargic(al); **gouvernement l.,** dilatory government; *F:* **discours l.,** speech that sends you to sleep; *s.* **un, une, l.,** a lethargic person.

Léthé [lete], *Pr.n.m. Myth:* (the river) Lethe; *Poet:* **les eaux du L.,** the Lethean waters, the Lethean springs.

léthifère [letifɛ:r], *a.* lethiferous, deadly (juice, etc.); lethal (weapon); death-dealing (device).

léthisimulation [letisimylasjɔ̃], *s.f. Biol:* feigning of death (by animals).

lethocerus [letɔsery:s], *s.m. Ent:* lethocerus.

lethrinidés [letrinide], *s.m.pl. Ich:* Lethrinidae, the lethrinids.

lètique [letik], *a. Rom.Hist:* Laetic.

lette [lɛt], *s.m.*, **lettique** [lɛt(t)ik], *s.m. Ling:* Lettic, Lettish.

letton, -onne [lɛtɔ̃, -ɔn]. **1.** *a. & s.* (*a*) *Ethn:* Lett, Lettonian; (*b*) *Geog:* Latvian. **2.** *s.m. Ling:* Lettic, lettish.

Lettonie [lɛtɔni], *Pr.n.f. Geog:* Latvia.

lettonien, -ienne [lɛtɔnjɛ̃, -jɛn], *a.* Lett, Lettonian.

lettrage [lɛtra:ʒ], *s.m.* lettering.

lettre [lɛtr̥], *s.f.* **1.** letter (of the alphabet); *Typ:* **l. moulée,** printed letter; **l. de deux-points,** drop letter; **l. accentuée,** primed letter; **dessin de lettres,** lettering; *Mapm:* **l. du quadrillage,** grid letter; **écrire qch. en toutes lettres,** to write sth. out in full; **écrire une somme en (toutes) lettres,** to write an amount in words (not in figures); *s.a.* CINQ, SOT 2. **2. selon la l. de la loi,** according to the letter of the law; **à la l., au pied de la l.,** to the letter, literally; **traduire à la l.,** to translate literally, word for word; **exécuter un ordre à la l.,** to carry out an order to the letter; **il prend les choses à la l.,** he is a literalist, he takes everything literally; **cela est vrai à la l.,** it is literally true; **rester l. morte,** to remain a dead letter; **ajouter à la l.,** to interpret what has been said in a wider, broader, sense; to embroider; **dans sa pensée et dans sa l.,** in its essence and its form; *Engr:* **épreuve avant la l.,** proof before letter, proof engraving; **estampe après la l.,** (i) open letter proof; (ii) second state proof; **avant la l.,** in advance, premature, before his, (her, etc.) time; *s.a.* AIDER 2. **3.** (*a*) letter; epistle; missive; *Adm: Jur:* **l. missive,** (postal) communication; *Post:* **l. close,** sealed letter; **l. collective,** official circular; **l. recommandée,** registered letter; **l. taxée, l. avec surtaxe,** surcharged letter; **l. renvoyée à l'expéditeur, faisant retour à l'expéditeur,** returned letter; **l. (par) exprès,** express letter; **l. type, l. passe-partout,** set-form letter; **l. de, au, rebut,** dead letter, unclaimed letter; *Journ:* **l. ouverte,** open letter; **l. de rappel,** (i) *Com:* (letter of) reminder, follow-up letter; (ii) *Pol:* letter of recall (of ambassador, etc.); **dès que je recevrai une l. de lui,** as soon as I hear from him, get a letter from him; **c'est l. close pour moi,** it is a mystery, a sealed book, to me; **cela a passé comme une l. à la poste,** it went down easily, without any difficulty; (*b*) **l. de grâce,** reprieve; **l. de mission,** detached-service warrant; **lettres de patentes,** letters patent; **lettres de noblesse,** letters patent of nobility; **lettres de naturalisation,** naturalization papers; *Hist:* **lettres de représailles, de marque,** letters of marque and reprisal; *Bank: Com:* **l. de crédit,** letter of credit; **l. de crédit circulaire,** circular letter of credit, circular note; *s.a.* CHANGE 1, CRÉANCE 2, GAGE 1 (*c*); **l. de voiture,** waybill, consignment note; **l. de port aérien,** air waybill; *Nau:* **l. de mer,** certificate of registry, clearance certificate, ship's papers. **4.** *pl.* (*a*) literature, letters; humanities; **homme, femme, de lettres,** man, woman, of letters; **avoir des lettres,** to be well-read; **la république des lettres,** the republic of letters; *Sch:* **faculté des lettres,** faculty of arts; **élève fort en lettres,** pupil strong on the arts side, in arts subjects; *F:* **faire des lettres,** to study arts subjects; (*b*) *A:* **les lettres saintes,** Holy Writ. **5.** *Bot:* **bois de lettres,** *s.m.* **l. moucheté,** leopard wood, letter wood.

lettré [lɛtre]. **1.** *a.* lettered, well-read, literate (person); **le public l.,** the book-reading public. **2.** *s.m.* scholar; well-read man.

lettre-avion [lɛtravjɔ̃], *s.f.* air letter; *pl. lettres-avion.*

lettrine [lɛtrin], *s.f. Typ:* **1.** reference letter, superior letter. **2.** (ornamental) capital, head letter, initial letter (introducing a new chapter, etc.).

lettrisé [lɛtrize], *a.m.* **vers lettrisés,** verse in which all the words begin with the same letter.

leu[1] [lø], *s.m. Num:* (Romanian) leu; *pl. lei.*

leu[2], *s.m. A:* wolf; *used only in the adv.phr.* **à la queue leu leu,** (i) in single file, in Indian file, one after another; (ii) helter-skelter; (iii) *Aut: etc:* nose-to-tail.

leuc(o)- [løk(ɔ)], *pref.* leuc(o), leuk(o)-.

Leucade [løkad], *Pr.n. Geog:* Leucadia; **le Promontoire de L.,** the Leucadian Promontory.

leucæna [løsena], *s.m. Bot:* leucaena.

leucanie [løkani], *s.f. Ent:* leucania.

leucanthème [løkɑ̃tɛm], **leucanthemum** [løkɑ̃temɔm], *s.m. Bot:* white oxeye.

leucaurine [løkorin], *s.f. Ch:* leucorine.

leucémide [løsemid], *s.f. Med:* leuk(a)emid.

leucémie [løsemi], *s.f. Med:* leuk(a)emia, leuc(h)aemia, leucocythaemia.

leucémique [løsemik], *Med:* (*a*) *a.* leuk(a)emic; (*b*) *s.m. & f.* leuk(a)emia sufferer.

leucine [løsin], *s.f. Bio-Ch:* leucine.

Leucippe [løsip], *Pr.n.m. Gr.Phil:* Leucippus.

leucite [løsit], *s.m.* **1.** *Miner:* leucite. **2.** *Bot:* leucite, leucoplast.

leucitite [løsitit], *s.f. Miner:* leucitite.

leucobase [løkɔba:z], *s.f. Bio-Ch:* leuco base.

leucoblaste [løkɔblast], *s.m. Biol:* leucoblast, leukoblast.

leucoblastique [løkɔblastik], *a. Biol:* leucoblastic.

leucoblastose [løkɔblasto:z], *s.f. Med:* leucoblastosis.

leucobryum [løkɔbrijɔm], *s.m. Moss:* leucobryum.

leucochalcite [løkɔkalsit], *s.f. Miner:* leucochalcite.

leucocrate [løkɔkrat], *a. Geol:* leucocratic.

leucocytaire [løkɔsitɛ:r], *a. Med:* leucocytic.

leucocyte [løkɔsit], *s.m. Physiol:* leucocyte, white blood corpuscle.

leucocythémie [løkɔsitemi], *s.f.* = LEUCÉMIE.

leucocytogénèse [løkɔsitɔʒenɛ:z], *s.f. Biol: Med:* leucocytogenesis.

leucocytolyse [løkɔsitɔli:z], *s.f. Biol: Med:* leucocytolysis.

leucocytolysine [løkɔsitɔlizin], *s.f. Path:* leucocytolysin.

leucocytose [løkɔsito:z], *s.f. Med:* leucocytosis.

leucodérivé [løkɔderive], *s.m. Bio-Ch:* leuco base.

leucoderme [løkɔdɛrm], *a.* **1.** *Ethn:* white-skinned. **2.** *Med:* leucodermic.

leucodermie [løkɔdɛrmi], *s.f. Med:* leucoderma, leucodermia.

leuco-encéphalite [løkɔɑ̃sefalit], *s.f. Med:* leucoencephalitis, leukoencephalitis.

leucogénèse [løkɔʒenɛ:z], *s.f. Biol:* leucocytogenesis.

leucokératose [løkɔkerato:z], *s.f. Med:* leucokeratosis, leucoplakia.

leucomaïne [løkɔmain], *s.f. Bio-Ch:* leucomaine.

leucome [løko:m], *s.m. Med:* leucoma, albugo.

leucomélanodermie [løkɔmelanɔdɛrmi], *s.f. Med:* leucoderm(i)a.

leucomyélite [løkɔmjelit], *s.f. Med:* leucomyelitis.

leuconostoc [løkɔnɔstɔk], *s.m. Bac:* leuconostoc.

leuconychie [løkɔniki], *s.f. Path:* leuconychia.

leucopédèse [løkɔpedɛ:z], *s.f. Physiol:* leucopedesis.

leucopénie [løkɔpeni], *s.f. Med:* leucopenia.

leucopénique [løkɔpenik], *a.* leucopenic.

leucophane [løkɔfan], *s.m. Miner:* leucophane, leucophanite.

leucophlegmasie [løkɔflɛgmazi], *s.f. Med:* phlegmasia dolens; *F:* white-leg, milk-leg; anasarca.

leucoplasie [løkɔplazi], *s.f. Med:* leucoplakia, leucoplasia.

leucoplaste [løkɔplast], *s.m. Biol:* leucoplast(id), leucoplast.

leucopoïèse [løkɔpɔjɛ:z], *s.f. Med:* leucopoiesis, leucocytopoiesis.

leucopyrite [løkɔpirit], *s.f. Miner:* leucopyrite.

leucorrhée [løkɔre], *s.f. Med:* leucorrhoea, *F:* whites.

leucorrhéique [løkɔreik], *a.* leucorrhoeal; *s.f.* person suffering from leucorrhoea.

leucose [løkoːz], *s.f. Med: Vet:* leucosis.

leucosine [løkɔzin], *s.f. Biol:* leucosin.

leucosphénite [løkɔsfenit], *s.f. Miner:* leucosphenite.

leucothoé [løkɔtɔe], *s.f. Bot:* leucothoe.

leucotomie [løkɔtɔmi], *s.f. Surg:* leucotomy, lobotomy.

leucotoxique [løkɔtɔksik], *a. Med:* leucotoxic.

leucoxène [løkɔksɛn], *s.m. Miner:* leucoxene.

Leuctres [løktr̥], *Pr.n. A.Geog:* Leuctra.

leude [løːd], *s.m. Hist:* leud, feudatory, feudal vassal.

leur[1] [lœ(ː)r]. **1.** *poss.a.* [lœr]; their; **leur oncle et leur tante,** their uncle and (their) aunt; **un(e) de leurs ami(e)s,** a friend of theirs, one of their friends; **leur propre fils,** their own son; **leurs père et mère,** their father and mother. **2.** (*a*) *poss.pron.* **le leur** [lœːr], **la leur, les leurs,** theirs; **j'ai écrit à mes amis et aux leurs,** I wrote to my friends and to theirs; **notre maison a plus de chambres que la leur,** our house has more rooms than theirs; (*b*) *s.m.* (i) their own (property, etc.); *A:* **si vous trouvez quelque chose du leur,** if you find anything of theirs; **ils n'y mettent pas du leur,** they don't pull their weight, they don't do their share; (ii) their own (friends, followers, etc.); **ils sont reniés par les leurs,** they are disowned by their own (people); **je m'intéresse à eux et aux leurs,** I am interested in them and in theirs; (iii) *F:* **ils continuent à faire des leurs,** they go on playing their old tricks; **ils ont encore fait des leurs,** they have been up to their old tricks again.

leur[2]. *See* LUI[1].

leurre [lœːr], *s.m.* (*a*) lure (for hawks); (*b*) decoy (for birds); (artificial) bait, lure (for fish); (*c*) bait, allurement, enticement; **cette annonce n'est qu'un l.,** the advertisement is only a catch, a take-in; (*d*) *Mil.Av:* chaff, window (to interfere with enemy's radar).

leurrer [lœre, lø-], *v.tr.* (*a*) to lure (hawk, etc.); (*b*) to bait (fish); to decoy (bird); (*c*) to allure, entice (s.o.); **se l. d'illusions,** to delude oneself; **se l. d'un espoir,** to delude, deceive oneself with, to indulge in, a fond hope; **il se laisse facilement l.,** he is easily taken in.

lev [lɛv], *s.m. Num:* (Bulgarian) lev; *pl. leva.*

levade [ləvad], *s.f. Dial:* hill pasture.

levage [ləvaːʒ], *s.m.* **1.** (*a*) lifting (up), hoisting, raising; *Rail:* lifting (for major overhaul of locomotive); **câble de l.,** hoisting cable; **cric de l.,** lifting jack; **l. (sur cric),** jacking up; **hauteur de l. (d'une grue),** lift (of a crane); **puissance de l.,** lifting power (of a crane); (*b*) levying (of taxes, etc.); (*c*) *P:* picking up (of man or woman in the street, etc.). **2.** (*a*) rising (of dough, etc.); (*b*) blistering off (of chromium plate). **3.** *Vit:* (*in Médoc*) propping up of vines.

levain [ləvɛ̃], *s.m.* leaven; **l. de bière,** barm, yeast; **poudre l.,** baking powder; **pain sans l.,** unleavened bread; *B:* **se défaire du vieux l. (du péché),** to purge out the old leaven; **un l. de révolte, de haine,** a leaven of revolt, of hate.

levalloisien, -ienne [ləvalwazjɛ̃, -jɛn]. **1.** *a. & s.m. Prehist:* Levalloisian (period). **2.** *a. & s.* (native, inhabitant) of Levallois-Perret.

levant [ləvɑ̃]. **1.** *a.m.* **soleil l.,** (i) rising sun, (ii) rising power or fame. **2.** *s.m.* (*a*) **le levant,** the east; (*b*) *Geog:* **le Levant,** the Levant; *Hist:* **la Compagnie du L.,** the Levant Company; *Furn:* **tapis, toiles, du Levant,** oriental carpets, materials; (*c*) *Meteor:* levante(r) (wind); (*d*) Turkish, oriental, tobacco.

levantin, -ine [ləvɑ̃tɛ̃, -in]. **1.** *a. & s. Geog:* Levantine, Levant. **2.** *s.m. Nau:* levanter (gale). **3.** *s.f. Tex:* **levantine,** Levantine, Levantine silk.

lève [lɛːv], *s.f.* **1.** *Mec.E:* (*a*) cam (of stamping-mill, etc.); wiper; (*b*) tappet. **2.** *Games:* mall.

levé [ləve]. **1.** *a.* (*a*) raised (hand, standard); **s'avancer, répondre, la tête levée, le front l.,** to come forward, to answer, with head erect, resolutely, boldly, proudly; **il avait le bras l.,** his arm was raised; **main levée,** with raised hand; **voter à main levée,** to vote by a show of hands; **dessin à main levée,** (i) freehand drawing; (ii) sketch; **dessiner à main levée,** to draw freehand; **courbe dessinée à main levée,** freehand curve; **pierre levée,** standing stone, menhir; *s.a.* PIED 1; (*b*) **blé l.,** wheat spearing; **pâte bien levée,** well raised dough, dough that has risen well; (*c*) (*of pers.*) up, out of bed; (*of sun, etc.*) up; **je suis l. de bonne heure,** I am up early; **elle était levée, mais pas encore descendue,** she was up but not yet down; **rester l. à attendre qn,** to wait up for s.o.; **la lune était levée,** the moon was up; (*d*) *Surv:* surveyed; **cours d'eau non l.,** unsurveyed river. **2.** *s.m.* (*a*) **voter par assis et l.,** to give one's vote by rising or remaining seated; (*b*) *Surv:* **l. d'un terrain, d'une côte,** plan, survey, of a piece of land, of a coast; **l. du canevas,** skeleton survey; **l. d'ensemble,** general survey; **l. terrestre,** ground survey; **l. à la planchette,** plane-table survey; **l. aérophotogrammétrique, l. aérien,** air survey, aerial survey; **l. cadastral,** property survey(ing); **l. à la boussole,** compass survey, sketch; **l. à la stadia,** stadia surveying; **l. d'exploration, de reconnaissance,** exploratory survey; **l. par cheminement,** survey, plotting, by successive stations; **l. par renseignements,** survey, sketch, made from information received; **l. de mémoire,** map, sketch, made from memory; **faire le l. d'un terrain,** to survey a piece of ground; (*c*) *Mus:* up beat.

lève-cadre [lɛvkadr̥], *s.m. Ap:* frame lifter; *pl. lève-cadre(s).*

levée [ləve], *s.f.* **1.** (*a*) raising, lifting; lifting up (of shields, etc.); *Nau:* weighing (of anchor); **câble de l.,** lift wire; *s.a.* CORPS 2; (*b*) raising (of siege); striking (of camp); lifting (of embargo); cancellation (of arrest); closing, adjourning (of meeting); **l. de quarantaine,** lifting of quarantine; *s.a.* BOUCLIER 1, ÉCROU[1]; (*c*) removal (of dressings, etc.); breaking (of seals); cutting off (of length of cloth from a web); (*d*) collecting, gathering (of crops, etc.); levy(ing) (of troops, taxes); *Post:* collection (of letters); clearing (of letter boxes); **la l. est faite,** the box has been cleared; *Mil:* **l. en masse,** levy in mass, en masse; *Fin:* **l. des actions,** taking (up) (of stock); **l. d'une prime,** exercise of an option. **2.** (*a*) spearing (of corn); (*b*) rising (of court, etc.); (*c*) *Nau:* **l. de la mer,** rough sea, sea way; **l. de la lame,** surge, swell; (*d*) *Mch:* (up) stroke, travel (of piston); lift (of cam, of valve). **3.** (*a*) embankment, sea wall; dyke, levee; **l. de terre,** earth bank; *Ph.Geog:* **l. de galets,** shingle spit; (*b*) *Mec.E:* cam, cog, lifter, wiper; (*c*) *Cards:* trick; **faire une l.,** to take a trick; **levées manquantes,** under tricks; **la l. supplémentaire,** the odd trick. **4.** *Cu:* **l. d'agneau,** lamb's pluck.

lève-gazon [lɛvgɑzɔ̃], *s.m.inv.* turfing iron.

lève-glace(s) [lɛvglas], *s.m.inv. Aut:* window raiser; winder.

lève-nez [lɛvne], *s.m.inv. Nau:* tricing line.

lever [ləve]. **I.** *v.tr.* (**je lève, n. levons; je lèverai**) to raise. **1.** (*a*) to lift (up), to hold up; **l. les épaules,** to shrug one's shoulders; **l. un doigt pour commander le silence,** to hold up a finger to enforce silence; *A:* **j'en lève la main,** I swear to it; **l. la main sur qn,** to raise, lift, one's hand against s.o.; **l. les bras au ciel (dans un geste d'étonnement),** to throw up one's hands (in astonishment); **l. la tête,** (i) to hold up one's head; (ii) to raise one's head, to look up; *Mil:* **levez la tête!** chin(s) up! **l. les yeux,** to look up; **l. les yeux vers qn,** to look up at s.o.; **l. les yeux au ciel,** to raise, cast up, one's eyes to heaven, heavenwards; **il ne leva pas les yeux de (sur) son livre,** he never took his eyes off his book; **l. le store, la glace,** to pull up, draw up, the blind, the (carriage) window; **l. le pont-levis,** to raise the drawbridge, to draw up the bridge; **l. l'ancre,** to weigh anchor; *Ven:* **l. le gibier,** to put up, flush, the birds; **l. un lièvre,** to start a hare; *P:* (*of prostitute*) **l. un homme,** to pick up a man; *P:* (*of man*) **l. une femme,** to pick up a woman; to seduce a woman; (*b*) to set upright; **l. un étendard,** to raise a standard; **l. boutique,** to set up in business; to open a shop; (*c*) to raise (siege, interdict); to strike (camp); to cancel (arrest); to close, adjourn (meeting); **l. une saisie,** to lift, raise, an embargo; **l. une quarantaine,** to lift a quarantine; **la séance a été levée à trois heures,** the meeting (i) was adjourned, (ii) was closed at three o'clock; (*d*) **l. un complet sur une pièce d'étoffe,** to cut off a suit-length from a piece of material; **l. un morceau sur une dinde,** to carve a slice off a turkey; (*e*) **l. une difficulté,** to remove a difficulty; **l. tous les doutes,** to remove all doubts; **l. les scellés,** to break, remove, the seals; **l. une sentinelle,** to withdraw a sentry; *Med:* **l. un spasme,** to eliminate a spasm; *Surg:* **l. l'appareil,** to remove, take off the bandages. **2.** to collect, gather (crops); to lift (potatoes, etc.); to raise, levy (troops); to levy (tax); *Cards:* **l. les cartes,** to pick up a trick; *Post:* **l. les lettres,** to collect the letters; **l. une boîte,** to clear a letterbox; *Fin:* **l. des actions,** to take up stock; **l. une option, une prime,** to take up, exercise, an option. **3.** **l. un plan,** to make, draw, get out, a plan; *Surv:* **l. les courbes de niveau,** to contour, to plot the contours. **4.** *v.i.* (*a*) (*of plants*) to shoot; (*b*) (*of dough*) to rise; **faire l. la pâte,** to raise the dough; (*c*) **la mer lève,** the sea is getting up; (*d*) (*of chromium plating*) to blister off.

II. **lever,** *s.m.* **1.** (*a*) rising; getting up (from bed); *A: Sch:* **le tambour du l.,** the getting-up drum; (*b*) levee (of sovereign, etc.); (*c*) **l. du soleil,** sunrise; **l. du jour,** daybreak. **2.** *Th:* **l. du rideau,** rise of the curtain; **un l. de rideau en un acte,** a one-act curtain-raiser; *F:* **en l. de rideau,** as a curtain-raiser, to start with. **3.** = LEVÉ 2. **4.** *Mil:* **l. des couleurs,** (hoisting the) colours.

se lever, to rise; to get up; (*a*) to stand up; **levez-vous,** stand up, get up; **à son entrée nous nous levâmes,** when he appeared we rose to our feet; **se l. brusquement,** to start up; **il se leva vivement,** he sprang to his feet; **se l. de son siège,** to rise from one's seat, to get up off one's seat; **se l. de table,** to leave the table; **se l. pour, contre, une résolution,** to vote for, against, a resolution; (*b*) to get up (from bed); to rise (early, late); **se l. de bon matin,** to get up early; **je me lève de bonne heure,** I am an early riser, I get up early; *F:* **se l. du pied gauche,** to get out of bed on the wrong side; **faire l. qn,** (i) to rouse s.o. (from his sleep, etc.); (ii) to make s.o. get up, stand up; (*c*) **le jour se lève,** day is breaking, is dawning; **nous avons vu le soleil se l.,** we saw the sun rise; **le vent se lève,** the wind is rising, is getting up, is springing up; **le temps se lève,** the weather is clearing; **le mauvais temps se lève sans s'annoncer en montagne,** bad weather comes on without warning in the mountains; (*d*) *Ven:* (*of game*) to rise; **faire l. une perdrix, un lièvre,** to flush, put up, a partridge, to start a hare.

lève-rail(s) [lɛvraːj], *s.m.inv. Tls:* rail-jack.

lève-roue(s) [lɛvru], *s.m.inv. A: Veh:* wheel jack.

lève-soupape(s) [lɛvsupap], *s.m.inv. Tls: I.C.E:* valve spring compressor, valve lifter.

lève-tôt [lɛvto], *s.m.inv. F:* early riser.

leveur [ləvœr], *s.m. Rail:* member of a lifting gang; *Typ:* **l. de lettres,** compositor.

Lévi [levi], *Pr.n.m.* Levi.

Léviathan [leviatɑ̃], *s.m.* Leviathan.

levier [ləvje], *s.m.* **1.** (*a*) *Ph: Mec:* lever; **l. du premier, du second, du troisième, genre,** lever of the first, of the second, of the third, kind; **bras de l.,** (i) lever arm; (ii) leverage; **rapport des bras de l., force de l.,** leverage; **effet, mouvement, de l.,** leverage movement; **point d'appui de l.,** fulcrum; *Row:* **l. de l'aviron,** leverage of the oar; (*b*) *Tls:* crowbar, lever; **l. à dresser,** straightening bar; **l. à griffe, à pince,** pinch bar, claw lever; **soulever, ouvrir, forcer, qch. avec un l.,** to prize, prise, lever, sth. up, open, out; **faire l. sur qch.,** to lever, prize, prise, against sth. **2.** lever, handle; (*a*) *Mec.E:* **l. à main,** hand lever; **l. articulé, l. à bascule,** toggle lever; **l. à rotule,** ball lever; **l. à cliquet,** pawl lever; **l. oscillant, l. à mouvement latéral,** rocking lever; **l. coudé, l. d'équerre, l. à renvoi,** bent lever, angle lever, bell-crank lever; **l. à poignée,** handle lever; **poignée à l.,** lever handle; **l. de commande,** actuating lever, control lever; **l. de commande à main,** manual lever; **s'emparer des leviers de commande d'un parti,** to get hold of the party machine; **l. de manœuvre,** (i) operating lever, handle; (ii) operating control; **l. de blocage, de serrage, de verrouillage,** clamping, locking, lever or handle; lock; **l. de frein,** brake lever; **l. d'embrayage, d'enclenchement, d'engagement,** coupling, engaging, meshing, lever; **l. de débrayage, de déclenchement, de dégagement,** disengaging, releasing, lever handle; release lever, handle; throw-out lever, handle; (*b*) *Mch: Veh:* **l. de mise en marche,** starting lever; **l. de changement, de renversement, de marche; l. de renvoi,** reversing, reverse, lever; *Aut:* **l. de frein à main,** hand-brake lever; **l. des vitesses,** gear lever; change-speed lever; **l. de cric,** jack handle; (*c*) *Civ.E: etc:* **l. de pompe,** (i) pump handle, (ii) *Nau: etc:* pump brake (worked by gang of men); **l. d'une chèvre,** handspike of a winch; (*d*) *Rail:* **l. de manœuvre (d'une aiguille),** point lever; **l. à contrepoids,** tumble-point; **appui de l.,** lever skid; (*e*) *El.E:* **l. inverseur (de courant),** reversing key; **l. de rupteur,** breaker arm; (*f*) *Sm.a: etc:* **l. d'armement,** arming, cocking, lever; **l. de culasse (mobile),** bolt handle, lever; *Av:* **l. de lance-bombes,** bomb-dropping, bomb-releasing, lever, gear; *Navy:* **l. de prise d'air,** starting lever (of torpedo).

lévigation [levigasjɔ̃], *s.f. Pharm:* levigation.

léviger [leviʒe], *v.tr.* (**je lévigeai(s); n. lévigeons**) *Pharm:* to levigate.

lévirat [levira], *s.m. Jew.Rel:* levirate.

lévirostres [levirɔstr̥], *s.m.pl. Orn: A:* Levirostres.

levis [ləvi], *a.m. See* PONT-LEVIS.

levisticum [levistikəm], *s.m. Bot: Pharm:* levisticum.

lévitation [levitasjɔ̃], *s.f. Psychics:* levitation.

lévite [levit]. **1.** *s.m.* (*a*) *B:* levite; (*b*) *Poet:* priest, cleric. **2.** *s.f. A.Cost:* (*a*) (man's) long and warm indoor gown; dressing-gown; (*b*) long frock-coat.

lévitique [levitik]. **1.** *a.* levitical. **2.** *s.m. B:* **le L.,** (the book of) Leviticus.

lévoglucosane [levoglykɔzan], *s.m. Ch:* levoglucosan.

lévogyre [levɔʒiːr], *a. Ch:* l(a)evogyrous, l(a)evogyrate (crystal, etc.); **composé l.,** laevo-compound.

levraut [ləvro], *s.m.* leveret; young hare.

lèvre [lɛːvr̥], *s.f.* **1.** lip; **il avait un cigare aux lèvres,** he had a cigar between his lips; **tremper ses lèvres dans un verre,** to set, put, one's lips to a glass; **j'ai le mot sur le bord des lèvres,** I have the word on the tip of my tongue; **avoir la mort sur les lèvres,** to be at death's door; *s.a.* CŒUR 2; **du bout des lèvres,** in a forced, artificial, manner; **rire du bout des lèvres,** to force a laugh; **un rire du bout des lèvres,** a forced laugh; **féliciter qn du bout des lèvres,** to force out a few words of congratulation, to congratulate s.o. grudgingly; **manger du bout des lèvres,** to nibble, pick at, one's food; **son rire ne passe pas les lèvres,** his laughter is always forced, is never genuine; **sourire du bout des lèvres,** to give a faint smile; **il le dit des lèvres, mais le cœur n'y est pas,** he pays lip service; **pincer les lèvres,** to prim (up) one's mouth; to purse, screw up, one's lips; **se mordre les lèvres (pour ne pas rire),** to bite one's lips (in order not to laugh); *s.a.* DESSERRER, SUSPENDU 1. **2.** (*a*) rim (of crater); *Geol:* wall (of fault); **l. soulevée,** upthrow side (of fault); **l. affaissée,** downthrow side; (*b*) lip (of wound); (*c*) *Bot:* lip, labium (of labiate corolla); *pl. Anat:* labia (of vulva); **grandes lèvres,** labia majora; **petites lèvres,** labia minora; nymphae.

levreteau, -eaux [ləvrəto], *s.m.* young unweaned hare.

levrette [ləvrɛt], *s.f.* **1.** greyhound (bitch); **l. de salon,** Italian greyhound. **2.** *Tls:* multiblade scraper (used by roughcasters).

levretté [ləvrɛte], *a.* **ventre l.,** greyhound belly (of horse).

levretter [ləvrɛte], *v.i.* **1.** (*of rabbit, hare*) to litter. **2.** *Const:* to roughcast a building using a *levrette*.

lévrier [levrije], *s.m.* **1.** greyhound; **l. irlandais, d'Irlande,** Irish wolf hound; **l. persan, arabe,** Arabian gazelle hound; **l. afghan,** Afghan hound; **l. d'Écosse,** deerhound; **l. russe,** borzoi; **l. bâtard,** lurcher; **courses de lévriers,** greyhound racing. **2.** *F:* police spy, *F:* sleuthhound.

lévrière [levrijɛːr], *s.f. Cu:* oval terrine (used for hare, etc. pâté).

levron [ləvrɔ̃], *s.m.* **1.** young greyhound, sapling. **2.** Italian greyhound.

levronne [ləvrɔn], *s.f.* young greyhound bitch.

lévulique [levylik], *a. Ch:* **acide l.,** levulinic acid.

lévulose [levyloːz], *s.f.* in *Ch: usu. s.m.* l(a)evulose, *F:* fruit sugar.

lévulosurique [levylɔzyrik], *a. Path:* **syndrome l.,** levulosuria accompanied by a state of depression.

lévulosurie [levylɔzyri], *s.f. Med:* levulosuria.

levurage [ləvyraːʒ], *s.m. Brew:* addition of brewer's yeast to activate fermentation.

levure [ləvyːr], *s.f.* **1.** yeast; **l. de bière,** barm; brewer's yeast; **l. artificielle,** baking powder. **2.** (*in Jura*) propping up of vines. **3.** *Cu:* rind and trimmings from bacon.

levurer [ləvyre], *v.tr.* to add yeast, barm, to (beer, etc.).

levurier [ləvyrje], *s.m.* yeast manufacturer.

levyne [levin], *s.f. Miner:* levyne, levynite.

lewisite [levizit], *s.f.* **1.** *Miner:* lewisite. **2.** *Ch:* lewisite.

lexème [lɛksɛːm], *s.m. Ling:* lexeme.

lexical, -aux [lɛksikal, -o], *a.* lexical.

lexicalisation [lɛksikalizasjɔ̃], *s.f.* lexiconizing.

lexicaliser [lɛksikalize], *v.tr.* to lexiconize.

lexicographe [lɛksikɔgraf], *s.m. & f.* lexicographer.

lexicographie [lɛksikɔgrafi], *s.f.* lexicography.

lexicographique [lɛksikɔgrafik], *a.* lexicographical.

lexicologie [lɛksikɔlɔʒi], *s.f.* **1.** lexicology. **2.** *Gram:* accidence.

lexicologique [lɛksikɔlɔʒik], *a.* lexicological; *Ling:* **champ l.,** area of meaning.

lexicologue [lɛksikɔlɔg], *s.m. & f.* lexicologist.

lexicométrie [lɛksikɔmetri], *s.f.*, **lexico-statistique** [lɛksikɔstatistik], *s.f. Ling:* lexicostatistics, glottochronology.

lexigraphie [lɛksigrafi], *s.f.* lexigraphy.

lexique [lɛksik]. **1.** *s.m.* (*a*) lexicon; (*b*) small dictionary; glossary; vocabulary (at end of book, etc.); (*c*) vocabulary (of a language). **2.** *a.* lexical.

lexovien, -ienne [lɛksɔvjɛ̃, -jɛn], *a. & s. Geog:* (native, inhabitant) of Lisieux.

Leyde [lɛd], *Pr.n.f. Geog:* Leyden; *El:* **bouteille de L.,** Leyden jar.

ley-farming [lɛfarmiŋ], *s.m. Agr:* ley farming.

lez [le], *prep.* = LÈS.

lézard [lezaːr], *s.m.* (*a*) lizard; **l. des murailles,** wall lizard; **l. à collerette,** frilled lizard; **l. vivipare,** common lizard; **l. des souches,** sand-lizard; **l. de mer,** sea iguana; **l. de mangrove,** mangrove lizard; **l. marin des Galapagos,** Galapagos sea iguana; **l. à collier australien,** Australian frilled lizard; **l. épineux vert végétal,** leaf-green spiny-tailed lizard; **l. pomme-de-pin,** Australian shingleback, pine-cone lizard; **l. à barbe (australien),** Australian bearded lizard; **l. ocellé,** eyed lizard; **l. nocturne,** desert night lizard; **les lézards (de l'Ancien Monde),** Lacertidae; **se chauffer au soleil comme un l., faire le l.,** to bask in the sun; to sunbathe; to sun oneself; (*b*) idler, lounger.

lézarde [lezard], *s.f.* **1.** split, crevice, cranny, crack, chink (in wall, plaster, etc.). **2.** *Furn:* gimp. **3.** *Typ:* river of white (down page). **4.** *Geol:* crack; **l. de tassement,** settling crack.

lézardé [lezarde], *a.* (*of wall, plaster*) cracked, full of cracks; crannied.

lézarder [lezarde]. **1.** *v.tr.* to crack, split (plaster, etc.). **2.** *v.i. F:* (*a*) to bask in the sun; to sun oneself; **l. sur le sable,** to sunbathe on the sands; (*b*) to idle, lounge, loaf.

se lézarder, (*of wall*) to crack, split.

lézignannais, -aise [leziɲanɛ, -ɛːz], *a. & s. Geog:* (native, inhabitant) of Lézignan.

Lhassa [lasa], *Pr.n.m. Geog:* Lhasa.

Lia [lja], *Pr.n.f. B.Hist:* Leah.

liage [ljaːʒ], *s.m.* **1.** tying, binding, fastening, roping. **2.** *Tex:* the process of weaving. **3.** *Exp:* mixing of ingredients (in manufacture of gun powder).

liais[1] [ljɛ], *s.m. Miner: Const:* hard limestone.

liais[2], *s.m. Tex:* heddle bar.

liaison [ljɛzɔ̃], *s.f.* **1.** (*a*) joining, binding, connection; *Const:* (i) bonding (of bricks, etc.); (ii) mortar, cement; *Mus:* (i) slur; (ii) tie, ligature, bind; (iii) syncopation; **l. entre deux lettres,** joining stroke between two letters; *Av:* **poutre de l.,** tail outrigger; *Const:* **en l.,** bonded; **perdre la l.,** to break joint; **l. à sec,** bonding (of stones, etc.) without use of mortar; (*b*) *Ch:* bond, linkage; **l. simple, multiple,** simple, multiple bond; **l. semi-polaire, l. de coordination,** semi-polar, coordinate, bond; **l. de covalence,** covalent bond; **l. métallique,** metallic bond; **l. électrovalente,** ionic bond; (*c*) *Ling:* sounding of final consonant before initial vowel sound; linking (of words), liaison; **faire la l. (entre deux mots),** to link (two words); to make the liaison; (*d*) *Cu:* thickening (of sauce); (*e*) *Mil:* liaison, intercommunications; **réseau de liaisons,** liaison net; **détachement de l.,** liaison detachment; **être en l. avec . . .,** to be in touch with . . .; **se mettre en l. avec . . .,** to establish liaison, to get into touch, with . . .; **perdre la l.,** to lose touch; *Navy:* **bâtiment de l.,** linking ship; *s.a.* AGENT 2, OFFICIER 2. (*f*) *Tg: Tp:* **l. descendante,** down link; **l. montante,** up link; (*g*) (*computers*) **l. de base,** basic linkage; **l. hertzienne,** radio link; **l. multivoie,** multichannel link. **2.** (*a*) intimacy, intimate relationship; **l. d'affaires,** business connection; **travailler en l. avec qn,** to work in conjunction with s.o.; (*b*) (illicit) intimacy; liaison.

liaisonner [ljɛzɔne], *v.tr. Const:* **1.** to bond (stones, etc.). **2.** to grout, point (stonework); to bind (stonework) with mortar.

liane [ljan], *s.f. Bot:* liana, (tropical) creeper; **l. à scie,** supplejack; **l. à serpents,** snakeweed, bistort.

liant [ljɑ̃]. **1.** *a.* (*a*) winning, good-natured, responsive; **il est l. avec tout le monde,** he readily makes friends with everybody; he is a good mixer; **caractère l.,** nature quick to make friends; **peu l.,** stand-offish; (*b*) flexible, pliant, springy (rod, etc.); tough (metal); easily worked (dough, etc.); *s.a.* SABLE[1] 1. **2.** *s.m.* (*a*) engaging manner, responsiveness, good-nature, amiability; **avoir du l.,** to have an engaging manner; (*b*) flexibility, pliability, springiness. **3.** *s.m. Civ.E:* binding material (of road); binder; *Const: Paint:* binding material, vehicle (of paint); *Petroleum Ind:* binder, bond, binding agent.

liard[1] [ljaːr], *s.m.* (*a*) *Num: A:* liard, half-farthing; *F:* **il n'a pas un (rouge) l.,** he hasn't a halfpenny, *F:* a red cent; **couper un l. en deux, en quatre,** to be very stingy; *Geol:* **pierre à liards,** nummulitic limestone; (*b*) *Cu:* (potato) crisp.

liard[2], *s.m. Bot:* black poplar.

liarder [ljarde], *v.i. O: F:* **1.** to haggle over every halfpenny, to look twice at every penny. **2.** to pinch and scrape.

liardeur, -euse [ljardœːr, -øːz], *s. O: F:* **1.** haggler. **2.** screw, scrape-penny.

lias [ljɑ(ːs)], *s.m. Geol:* lias.

liasique [ljazik], **liassique** [liasik], *a. Geol:* lias(s)ic.

liasse [ljas], *s.f.* bundle, packet (of letters, etc.); wad (of banknotes); file (of papers); *Com: etc:* multipart forms, paper, set, stationery; **mettre des documents en l.,** (i) to bundle, (ii) to file, documents.

liasthénie [liasteni], *s.f. Med:* asthenia of the unstriped muscles.

libage [libaːʒ], *s.m. Const:* **1.** rubble. **2.** bastard ashlar, rough ashlar.

Liban [libɑ̃], *Pr.n.m. Geog:* Lebanon.

libanais, -aise [libanɛ, -ɛːz], *a. & s.* Lebanese.

libation [libasjɔ̃], *s.f.* (*a*) *Ant:* libation; drink-offering; (*b*) *F:* **faire d'amples libations, des libations copieuses,** to indulge in a drinking bout; to drink immoderately, like a fish; **leurs libations leur firent bientôt oublier leur querelle,** they soon drowned their quarrel.

libeccio [libetʃjo], *s.m. Meteor:* libeccio.

libelle [libɛl], *s.m.* **1.** lampoon, scurrilous satire. **2.** *Jur:* libel.

libellé [libɛl(l)e], *s.m.* **1.** drawing up, writing, wording (of document, etc.). **2.** wording, terms used (in document). **3.** *Com:* trade description.

libeller [libɛl(l)e], *v.tr.* to draw up, word (document, etc.); to sign and date (sketch, etc.); **l. un chèque,** to draw, fill in, a cheque; **l. un chèque au nom de qn,** to make out, to write out, a cheque to s.o.; **bons libellés en francs,** bonds made payable in francs; **télégramme libellé comme suit . . .,** telegram worded as follows . . ., that reads as follows . . .

libelliste [libɛl(l)ist], *s.m.* lampoonist, scurrilous satirist.

libellule [libɛl(l)yl], *s.f. Ent:* dragonfly, flying adder, adder fly.

libellulides [libɛl(l)ylid], *s.f.pl. Ent:* Libellulidae.

liber [libɛːr], *s.m. Bot:* liber, inner bark, bast, phloem.

libérable [liberabl̥], (*a*) *a. & s.m. Mil:* (*pers.*) who can be demobbed; **congé l.,** demob leave; (*b*) *a. Tchn:* releasable.

libéral, -ale, -aux [liberal, -o], *a.* **1.** liberal; (*a*) broad, wide (education, etc.); **il exerce une profession libérale,** he's a professional man; **les arts libéraux,** the liberal arts; (*b*) generous; open-handed; **être l. envers, pour, qn,** to be liberal to, towards, s.o.; **il a été très l. de conseils,** he was very free with his advice, very generous with his advice. **2.** *a. & s. Pol:* liberal; **le parti l., les libéraux,** the Liberal party, the liberals.

libéralement [liberalmɑ̃], *adv.* liberally, generously, open-handedly.

libéralisation [liberalizasjɔ̃], *s.f.* liberalization.

libéraliser [liberalize], *v.tr.* to liberalize.

libéralisme [liberalism], *s.m. Pol: Theol: Com:* liberalism.

libéralité [liberalite], *s.f.* liberality. **1.** (*a*) breadth, broadness (of outlook, etc.); (*b*) generosity; open-handedness. **2.** act of liberality; gift; **faire des libéralités à qn,** to give liberally, freely, to s.o.; **il s'est appauvri par ses libéralités,** he has impoverished himself by his generosity.

libérateur, -trice [liberatœːr, -tris]. **1.** *a.* liberating. **2.** *s.* (*a*) liberator, deliverer; (*b*) rescuer.

libération [liberasjɔ̃], *s.f.* **1.** (*a*) liberation, freeing, releasing; discharge (of prisoner, etc.); *Mil:* discharge (of soldier) to the reserve; **l. définitive,** final discharge; **l. conditionnelle,** release (of prisoner) on licence, *F:* on ticket of leave; *Pol. Hist:* **Anniversaire de la L.,** Liberation Day; (*b*) payment in full, discharge; **l. d'une dette,** discharging, redeeming, of a debt; **l. d'une action,** paying up of a share; **l. à la répartition,** payment in full on allotment; (*c*) *Aer:* (*spacecraft*) **l. de l'attraction terrestre,** escape; **vitesse de l.,** escape velocity, parabolic velocity; (*d*) *Ph:* **l. d'énergie,** release of energy; **l. d'énergie Wigner,** Wigner release; (*e*) (*computers*) de-allocation; (*f*) **l. de biens,** release of property. **2.** *F:* certificate of discharge.

libératoire [liberatwa:r], *a.* **monnaie l.,** legal tender (currency); (*of money*) **avoir force l.,** to be legal tender.

libéré [libere]. **1.** *a. Fin:* (fully) paid-up (share); **non l.,** partly paid-up. **2.** *s.m.* discharged soldier, prisoner; **l. conditionnellement,** ticket-of-leave man.

libérer [libere], *v.tr.* **(je libère, n. libérons; je libérerai)** (*a*) to liberate, release; to set (s.o.) free; to discharge (prisoner, debtor); **son retour avait libéré toute l'hostilité dormante,** his return had unleashed all the dormant hostility; *Jur:* **l. un garant,** to discharge a surety; *Mil:* **l. un homme,** to exempt a man from military service; **l. un soldat,** to discharge a soldier (to the reserve); (*b*) to free (s.o., an institution, etc., of debt, etc.); **titre de 1000 francs libéré de 750 francs,** 1000 franc share of which 750 francs are paid (up).

se libérer, (*a*) to free oneself; **se l. de toute prévention,** to free, rid, oneself of all prejudice, bias; **se l. des entraves de l'étiquette,** to break away from the restraints of etiquette; **se l. (d'une dette),** to redeem, liquidate, a debt; (*b*) **se l. pour deux jours,** to arrange to take two days off.

Libéria (le) [ləliberja], *Pr.n.m. Geog:* Liberia.

libérien[1], **-ienne** [liberjɛ̃, -jɛn], *a.* & *s. Geog:* Liberian.

libérien[2], **-ienne,** *a. Bot:* pertaining to the phloem or bast (of a tree); bast, liber (cell).

libéro-ligneux, -euse [liberoliɲø, -ø:z], *a. Bot:* wood-and-bast.

libertaire [libɛrtɛ:r], *a.* & *s. Pol:* libertarian.

liberté [libɛrte], *s.f.* **1.** liberty, freedom; (*a*) **animaux en l.,** animals at liberty; **obtenir sa l.,** to secure one's liberty; **mettre qn en l.,** to set s.o. free; to liberate s.o.; **être mis en l.,** to be allowed to go free; **mettre en l. l'inculpé,** to discharge the accused; **pourquoi est-il en l.?** why is he at large? **l'hydrogène est mis en l. à la cathode,** hydrogen is released, comes off, at the cathode; **mise en l.,** (i) liberation, freeing, release (of prisoner); (ii) release (of gas); *Jur:* **(mise en) l. provisoire, sous caution,** bail; **accorder la l. provisoire à qn (sous, moyennant, caution),** to let s.o. out on bail; to admit s.o. to bail; **rejeter la demande de l. provisoire,** to refuse bail; *Jur:* **la l. civile,** the liberty of the subject; **la Statue de la L.,** the Statue of Liberty; **avoir pleine l. d'action,** (i) to have full liberty of action; (ii) (*of engine part*) to have free play; **donner à qn une l. d'action en rapport avec ses capacités,** to give s.o. scope for his abilities; **l. de conscience, de la presse,** liberty, freedom, of conscience, of the press; **l. d'expression,** freedom of expression, freedom of speech; **l. de croyance,** freedom of belief; **l. du culte,** freedom of worship; **l. d'opinion,** freedom of thought; **l. d'association,** freedom of association; **l. de réunion,** freedom of assembly; **l. du commerce,** freedom of trade; **l. d'allures,** unconventionality; **parler avec l., en toute l.,** to speak freely, without restraint; **prendre la l. de faire qch.,** to take leave to do sth.; **prendre la l. de parler à qn,** to take the liberty of speaking to s.o.; to make so bold (as) to speak to s.o.; **si je puis prendre une telle l. . . .,** if I may be so bold . . .; **avez-vous jamais quelques moments de l.?—jamais, je révise le Standard Dictionary,** are you ever free for a few minutes?—never, I'm revising the Standard Dictionary; **c'est demain mon jour de l.,** to-morrow is my free day, my day off; *Mch:* **l. du piston, du cylindre,** clearance of the piston; *Equit:* **l. de langue,** port (of bit); **avoir l. de manœuvre,** (i) *Nau:* to have a roving commission; (ii) to have full liberty of action; (*b*) **il fait tout avec l. et grâce,** he is free and graceful in all his actions; *Art:* **l. de crayon, de pinceau,** breadth, boldness, of touch. **2. prendre des libertés avec qn,** to take liberties, make free, make bold, with s.o.

liberticide[1] [libɛrtisid], *a.* & *s.* liberticide.

liberticide[2], *s.m.* (crime of) liberticide.

libertin, -ine [libɛrtɛ̃, -in]. **1.** *a.* (*a*) *A:* free-thinking; (*b*) licentious, dissolute; (*c*) wayward, freakish (imagination). **2.** *s.* (*a*) *A:* free-thinker; (*b*) libertine, rake.

libertinage [libɛrtina:ʒ], *s.m.* libertinage; (*a*) *A:* free-thinking; (*b*) licentious ways; dissolute ways; libertinism.

libertiner [libɛrtine], *v.i.* **1.** to go one's own way, to go off the beaten track. **2.** to act the libertine; **l. avec une femme,** to trifle, act the Don Juan, with a woman.

libertinisme [libɛrtinism], *s.m.* libertinism.

liberty ship [libœrtiʃip], *s.m. N.Arch:* liberty ship.

libéthénite [libetenit], *s.f. Miner:* libethenite.

libidineux, -euse [libidinø, -ø:z], *a.* libidinous, lustful, lewd.

libidinosité [libidinozite], *s.f.* lustfulness, lewdness; libidinousness.

libido [libido], *s.f. Psy:* libido.

libitinaire [libitinɛ:r], *s.m. Rom.Ant:* undertaker.

libocèdre [libosɛdr̥], *s.m. Bot:* libocedrus.

libournais, -laise [liburnɛ, -ɛ:z], *a.* & *s.* (native, inhabitant) of Libourne.

libra [libra], *s.f.* **1.** *Ant.Meas:* libra. **2.** *Astr:* Libra.

libraire [librɛ:r], *s.m.* & *f.* **1.** *A:* copyist (of manuscripts, books). **2.** bookseller; *Rail:* bookstall attendant.

libraire-éditeur [librɛreditœ:r], *s.m.* publisher and bookseller; *pl. libraires-éditeurs.*

libraire-imprimeur [librɛrɛ̃primœ:r], *s.m.* printer and bookseller; *pl. libraires-imprimeurs.*

librairie [librɛri, -eri], *s.f.* (*a*) book trade, bookselling; **inédit en l.,** not published in book form; **ouvrages en l.,** published books; **succès de l.,** best-seller; (*b*) bookshop; **l. de neuf et d'occasion,** new and secondhand bookseller; (*c*) publishing house; (*d*) *Com:* **l. en caisse,** books packed in cases; (*e*) *Hist:* library; **maître de la l.,** librarian to the King.

libration [librasjɔ̃], *s.f.* swing(ing); *Astr:* libration.

libre [libr̥], *a.* free. **1.** (*a*) **homme né l. dans un pays l.,** man born free in a free country; **traduction l.,** free translation; **vers libres,** free verse; **je suis l. de onze heures à midi,** I am disengaged between eleven and twelve; (*to porter, taxi driver*) **êtes-vous l.?** are you free? **quand je suis l.,** when I am off duty; **avez-vous un homme de l.?** have you a man available? **être l. de faire qch.,** to be free to do sth.; **nous sommes libres de courir dans le jardin,** we have the run of the garden; **laisser qn l. d'agir,** to leave s.o. a free hand; **vous êtes l. de le faire, l. à vous de le faire,** you are quite free, at liberty, to do it; **l. à vous d'essayer,** you are welcome to try; **l. à vous de dire que . . .,** it is all very well for you to say that . . .; **je suis l. de mes mouvements,** I am free to do what I please; **je suis l. de mon temps,** my time is my own; **l. arbitre,** free will; **l. parole,** free speech; **l. penseur,** free-thinker; **l. pensée,** free-thinking, free thought; **l'homme est l.,** man is a free agent; **école l.,** independent (catholic) school; **il vaudrait mieux laisser chaque pays l. de déterminer comme il l'entend le mode de recensement des accidents,** the method of recording accidents can best be left to the discretion of each country; *Sch:* **composition l.,** free composition; *Geol:* **méandre l.,** free meander; *s.a.* ENTRÉE 2, PRATIQUE[2] 6; (*b*) **l. de préjugés,** free from prejudice; **l. de soucis,** free from care, carefree; **si j'avais l'esprit l. . . .,** if I were free from care, from preoccupation . . .; *s.a.* INSCRIPTION; (*c*) **allure l.,** easy bearing; **jeune fille d'allures libres,** (i) fast girl; (ii) girl with free and easy manner; **conversation l.,** free, broad, conversation; **tenir des propos un peu libres,** to talk rather broadly; (*d*) **jeune fille à la taille l.,** well set up, supple, young woman; *Art:* **avoir la main l.,** to draw or paint boldly, broadly; **pinceau l.,** bold brush. **2.** (*a*) clear, open (space, road, etc.); vacant, unoccupied, unengaged (table, seat); **avoir du temps de l.,** to have some time free, some spare time, some time to spare; **on m'a donné un jour l.,** I have been given a day off; **avoir le ventre l.,** to have one's bowels free of food; **la mer est l.,** the sea is clear of ice; **toute cette région est l.,** all this region is clear of the enemy; *Fb:* **avoir le champ l. devant soi,** to have an open field; *F:* **le champ est l.,** the coast is clear; *Rail:* **voie l.,** line clear; *Tp:* **pas l.,** line engaged, *U.S:* line busy; (*taxi sign*) **libre,** for hire; **il faut faire cette expérience à l'air l.,** this experiment must be carried out in the open air; **navire avec ses cales libres,** ship with clear holds; **l. possession,** vacant possession; (*b*) *Mec.E:* disengaged, running free, out of gear; *Cy:* **roue l.,** free wheel; **faire roue l.,** to free-wheel; **descendre une côte en roue l.,** to free-wheel down a hill. **3.** *Ent:* (*of chrysalis*) exarate. **4.** *Bot:* **calice l.,** free central calix; **amande l.,** freestone.

libre-échange [libreʃɑ̃:ʒ], *s.m. Pol.Ec:* free trade; **zone de l.-é.,** free-trade area.

libre-échangisme [libreʃɑ̃ʒism], *s.m.inv.* free-trade policy.

libre-échangiste [libreʃɑ̃ʒist], *s.m.* free-trader; **politique l.-é.,** free-trade policy; *pl. libre-échangistes.*

librement [librəmɑ̃], *adv.* freely, unrestrainedly; (*a*) **droit de passer l. les frontières (à l'aller et au retour),** right of free entry (and return); **usez l. de mes livres,** make free use of my books; **je puis user l. de sa bibliothèque,** I have the run of his library; (*b*) **se conduire l.,** to behave in a free and easy manner; **se conduire, parler, trop l.,** to be over-free (in conduct or speech); to lack restraint.

libre-service [librəsɛrvis], *s.m.* self-service; **magasin, restaurant, l.-s.,** self-service store, restaurant; *pl. libres-services.*

librettiste [librɛt(t)ist], *s.m. Th:* librettist.

libretto [librɛt(t)o], *s.m.* libretto, *F:* book (of an opera); *pl. libretti, librettos.*

Liburnie [libyrni], *Pr.n.f. A.Geog:* Liburnia.

liburnien, -ienne [libyrnjɛ̃, -jɛn], *a.* & *s. Geog:* Liburnian.

Libye [libi], *Pr.n.f.* **1.** *Geog:* Libya. **2. le désert de L.,** the Libyan Desert.

libyen, -enne [libjɛ̃, -jɛn], *a.* & *s. Geog:* Libyan.

libyque [libik], *a.* & *s.m.* & *f. Geog:* Libyan.

libythéides [libiteid], *s.m.pl. Ent:* Libytheidae, the snout butterflies.

licaria [likarja], *s.m. Bot:* licaria.

licaréol [likareol], *s.m. Ch:* linalool, licareol.

lice[1] [lis], *s.f.* **1.** (*a*) *A:* lists; **entrer en l. contre qn,** (i) to enter the lists against s.o., (ii) *F:* to try a fall with s.o., to have a tilt at s.o.; (*b*) white fence along a race track; (*c*) crossbar of a jump. **2.** (*a*) = LISSE[1]; (*b*) handrail of wooden bridge. **3.** *Com:* string holding goods, parcels, together.

lice[2], *s.f. Ven:* hound bitch.

lice[3], *s.f. Tex:* **1.** heddles. **2.** warp; **tapisserie de haute l., de basse l.,** high-warp, low-warp, tapestry.

licence [lisɑ̃:s], *s.f.* licence. **1.** (*a*) leave, permission; *Adm:* **l. pour vendre qch.,** licence to sell sth.; **l. de débitant,** liquor licence; licence to sell beer, wines and spirits; **détenteur d'une l.,** licensee; **l. de fabrication,** manufacturing licence; **fabriqué sous l.,** made under licence; **l. d'importation, d'exportation,** import, export licence; (*b*) *Sp:* registration card, licence; (*c*) *Sch:* bachelor's degree; **l. ès lettres, ès sciences en droit,** bachelor's degree in arts, in science, in law; (*in Scot:*) = Master's degree in arts, in science, in law; **passer sa l.,** to take one's degree, to graduate. **2.** (*a*) licence, abuse of liberty; **l. poétique,** poetic licence; **prendre des licences avec qn,** to take liberties with s.o.; (*b*) licentiousness.

licencié, -ée [lisɑ̃sje], *s.* **1. l. ès lettres, l. ès sciences, l. en droit,** bachelor, (*in Scot.*) master, of arts, of science, of law; **être reçu l.,** to graduate, to receive one's degree. **2.** licensee, licence-holder. **3.** *a. Fr.C:* licensed (to sell beer, etc.).

licenciement [lisɑ̃simɑ̃], *s.m.* disbanding (of troops); discharge, dismissal, laying off, (of workmen); sending home (of schoolchildren).

licencier [lisɑ̃sje], *v.tr.* (*pr.sub.* & *p.d.* **n. licenciions, v. licenciiez**) to disband (troops); to lay off, discharge (workmen); to send home (schoolchildren).

se licencier, *A:* **1.** to pass the bounds of discretion. **2. se l. à faire qch.,** to make so bold as to do sth.

licencieusement [lisɑ̃sjøzmɑ̃], *adv.* licentiously.

licencieux, -euse [lisɑ̃sjø, -ø:z], *a.* licentious, ribald.

licet [lisɛt], *s.m. A:* permit, leave.

lichade [liʃad], *s.f. P: O:* guzzle.

lichard [liʃa:r], *s.m. P:* tippler.

liche [liʃ], *s.f. O:* spree.

lichen [likɛn], *s.m.* (*a*) *Bot:* lichen; **l. d'Islande,** Iceland moss; **couvert de l.,** lichened; **l. filamenteux, l. chevelu,** hairy lichen; (*b*) *Med:* lichen; **l. plan,** lichen planus.

lichéneux, -euse [likenø, -ø:z], *a.* lichenous.

lichénification [likenifikasjɔ̃], *s.f. Med:* lichenification.

lichénine [likenin], *s.f. Bio-Ch:* lichenin.

lichénique [likenik], *a. Bot:* lichenous.

lichénoïde [likenɔid], *a. Med:* lichenoid.

licher [liʃe], *v.tr. P:* **1.** to lick. **2.** (*a*) to drink up (tot of spirits, etc.); (*b*) *abs.* to drink, to tipple.

licherie [liʃ(ə)ri], *s.f. P:* (action of) guzzling and drinking greedily.

lichette [liʃɛt], *s.f. P:* small slice, shaving (of bread, meat, etc.).

licheur, -euse [liʃœ:r, -ø:z], *s. P:* tippler.

liciet [lisjɛ], *s.m. Bot:* = LYCIET.

licitation [lisitasjɔ̃], *s.f. Jur:* sale by auction in one lot of property held *indivisum.*

licitatoire [lisitatwa:r], *a. Jur:* **contrat l.,** agreement (between joint owners) to sell property held *indivisum.*

licite [lisit], *a.* licit, lawful, permissible.

licitement [lisitmɑ̃], *adv.* licitly, lawfully, permissibly.

liciter [lisite], *v.tr. Jur:* to sell by auction (property held *indivisum*).

licol [likɔl], *s.m. Harn:* halter; stable head-stall.

licorne [likɔrn], *s.f.* **1.** *Myth: Her:* unicorn. **2.** *Z: F:* **l. de mer,** sea unicorn, narwhal, unicorn fish. **3.** *Astr:* **la L.,** Monoceros; the Unicorn.

licou [liku], *s.m.* = LICOL.

licteur [liktœ:r], *s.m. Rom.Ant:* lictor.

lido [lido], *s.m.* (*a*) *Geog:* sand bar; (*b*) lido.

lie[1] [li], *a.f. A:* joyous; **faire chère l.,** to live well.

lie[2], *s.f.* (*a*) dregs; **boire le calice jusqu'à la l.,** to drain the cup (of sorrow, etc.) to the dregs; **l. de vin,** (i) lees of wine (in cask); (ii) *a.inv.* purplish red, lie-de-vin; (*b*) **la l. du peuple,** the scum, dregs, of the populace.

lié [lje], *a.* **1.** bound; **être l. par ses engagements,** **avoir les mains liées,** to have one's hands tied; **pieds et poings liés,** bound hand and foot; **avoir la langue liée,** to be tongue-tied. **2. être (très) l. avec qn,** to be (great) friends, intimately acquainted, with s.o.; **être liés d'une étroite amitié,** to be bound together by a close friendship. **3.** *Mus:* **notes liées,** (i) tied, (ii) syncopated, notes; **l. coulant,** slurred. **4.** *Cards: etc:* **jouer une partie liée,** to play the best (out) of three (games); **avoir partie liée avec qn,** to be in league with s.o. **5.** *Pal:* **lettres liées,** letters connected by a line.

liebenerite [lib(ə)nerit], *s.f. Miner:* liebenerite.

liebig [libig], *s.m.* beef extract.

liebigite [libiʒit], *s.f. Miner:* liebigite.

Liechtenstein [liʃtənʃtain], *Pr.n.m. Geog:* Lichtenstein.

lie-de-vin [lidvɛ̃], *a. & s.m.inv.* wine colour(ed).

liège [ljɛ:ʒ], *s.m.* **1.** *Bot:* cork oak. **2.** (*a*) cork; **cigarettes à bouts de l.,** cork-tipped cigarettes; (*b*) *Fish:* cork, float. **3.** *Miner:* **l. fossile, de montagne,** mountain flax, mountain cork.

liégeois, -oise [ljeʒwa, -wa:z], *a. & s. Geog:* (native, inhabitant) of Liège; *Cu:* **café l.,** iced coffee topped with Chantilly cream.

liéger [ljeʒe], *v.tr.* (**je liégeai(s); n. liégeons**) to put floats on (fishing net, etc.); to buoy (a net).

liégeux, -euse [ljeʒø, -ø:z], *a.* cork-like, corky (bark, etc.).

liement [limɑ̃], *s.m.* binding.

lien [ljɛ̃], *s.m.* **1.** tie, bond; **rompre ses liens,** to burst one's bonds, one's fetters, one's shackles; **liens du sang,** ties of blood; **l. de parenté,** family relationship; **mes liens de famille,** my family ties; **l. d'amitié,** bond of friendship; **liens religieux,** monastic, religious, vows. **2.** (*a*) *Carp:* diagonal brace, tie; *Mec.E:* (metal) strap, band; (*b*) **l. de fagot, de gerbe,** withe, bond; *Prov:* **mieux vaut le l. que la paille,** the coat is better than the wearer.

lientérie [ljɑ̃teri], *s.f. Med:* lientery.

lientérique [ljɑ̃terik], *a. Med:* lienteric.

lier [lje], *v.tr.* (*pr.sub. & p.d.* **n. liions, v. liiez**) **1.** (*a*) to bind, fasten, tie, tie up; **l. qch. avec une corde,** to bind sth. with a rope; **l. les pieds et les mains à qn,** to bind s.o. hand and foot; **l. qn à un poteau,** to tie s.o. to a stake; **l. les lacets de ses souliers,** to tie, knot, one's shoelaces; **l. qn par un engagement,** to bind s.o. (to do sth.); **contrat qui lie qn,** agreement binding (up)on s.o.; **ce contrat vous lie,** you are bound by this agreement; **l'intérêt nous lie,** we have common interests; **pierres liées avec du ciment,** stones bound together with cement; **l. des idées,** to connect, link, ideas; **questions liées à une transaction,** considerations in connection with, questions involved in, a transaction; **l. deux lettres,** to join (up) two letters; **l. deux mots,** to link two words (in pronunciation); to sound the liaison; **le t de "et" ne se lie pas,** the t of "*et*" is always silent; *Mus:* **l. deux notes,** (i) to slur, (ii) to tie, two notes; *Fenc:* **l. le fer,** to bind one's blade round the adversary's; (*b*) *Cu:* **l. une sauce,** to thicken, give body to, a sauce. **2. l. connaissance avec qn,** to strike up an acquaintance with s.o.; **l. conversation avec qn,** to start a, enter into, conversation with s.o.

se lier. 1. se l. (d'amitié) avec, à, qn, to form, strike up, a friendship with s.o., to become intimate with s.o.; **je me suis lié d'amitié avec son père,** I have made friends with his father. **2.** (*a*) *Cu:* (*of sauces, etc.*) to thicken; (*b*) (*of gravel, etc.*) to bind.

lierne [ljɛrn], *s.f.* **1.** *Const: etc:* inter-tie. **2.** *Arch:* lierne rib; ridge rib. **3.** floor plank (of boat).

lierre [ljɛ:r], *s.m.* **1.** ivy; **couvert de l.,** covered with ivy, ivy-clad, ivy-mantled. **2. l. terrestre, rampant,** ground ivy.

liesse [ljɛs], *s.f. A:* jollity, gaiety; *now used only in expressions like:* **la ville était en l.,** the town was given up to rejoicing; it was a gala occasion.

lieu[1], **-eux** [ljø], *s.m.* **1.** place; (*a*) locality, spot; **l. dit** = LIEUDIT; **mettre qch. en l. sûr,** to put sth. in a safe place; *F:* **mettre qn en l. sûr,** to lock s.o. up; **en tout l., en tous lieux,** everywhere; **en aucun l.,** nowhere; **en quelque l. que ce soit,** wherever it be; **les lieux de ses premiers exploits,** the scenes of his early exploits; **un haut l.,** a shrine; **en haut l.,** in high circles, in high places; **amis en haut l.,** friends in high places, influential friends; **je tiens ce renseignement de bon l.,** I have this information from a good source; **le l. du sinistre,** the scene of the disaster; **j'étais sur le l., sur les lieux,** I was on the spot; **il fut arrêté dans un mauvais l.,** he was arrested in an evil haunt; **l. de passage,** thoroughfare; **l. de rendez-vous,** meeting place, rendezvous; **les gens du l.,** the local people, the locals; **l. public,** a public place; **ouvriers habitant loin du l. de leur travail,** workers who live a long way from their work; **en (tout) premier l.,** in the first instance, in the first place, first of all, first and foremost, firstly; **en troisième l.,** in the third place, thirdly; **en dernier l.,** last of all, lastly; **il est tout d'abord Irlandais, et critique en second l.,** he is an Irishman first, and then a critic; **nous en parlerons en son temps et l.,** we shall speak of it at the proper time and place; (*b*) *pl.* house, premises; *Jur:* **sur ces lieux,** on the premises, at the spot; **la police est sur les lieux,** the police are on the spot; **avant de quitter ces lieux,** before I leave this place, before I leave here; *s.a.* VIDER 1; (*c*) *pl. F:* **lieux (d'aisances),** (i) privy, (ii) latrines; **lieux payants,** public lavatories; *A:* **lieux à l'anglaise,** water closet. **2.** (*a*) **avoir l.,** to take place; **quand le mariage aura-t-il l.?** when will the marriage take place, *F:* come off? **la réunion aura l. à . . .,** the meeting will be held at . . .; **la correspondance qui a eu l. entre nous,** the correspondence that has passed between us; (*b*) ground(s), cause; **il y a (tout) l., j'ai l., de supposer que + *ind.*,** there is, I have, (good) ground, (every) reason, for supposing that . . .; **il y a l. d'attendre,** it would be advisable to wait; it would be (as) well to wait; **s'il y a l. de réunir le comité,** if a meeting of the committee is necessary; **je vous écrirai s'il y a l.,** I shall write to you if there is any occasion, if need be, should occasion **arise;** **il y aurait l. de . . .,** there is a case for . . .; **donner l. à des désagréments,** to give rise to trouble; **action qui pourrait donner l. à des critiques,** action which could give rise to criticism; **tout donne l. de croire que . . .,** everything leads one, us, to believe that . . ., leads to the belief that . . .; **son retour a donné l. à une réunion de famille,** his return was the occasion for a family gathering; *s.a.* CRAINDRE; (*c*) (*function*) **tenir l. de qch.,** to take the place of, stand instead of, sth.; **la caisse nous tenait l. de table,** the box served us as a table; **elle lui a tenu l. de mère,** she has been a mother to him; *Adm:* **en l. et place de qn,** in s.o.'s stead; *prep. phr.* **au l. de,** instead of, in lieu of; **au l. de son frère,** instead of his brother, in his brother's stead; **au l. de détails arides, il nous a donné . . .,** in place of dry details, he gave us . . .; **au lieu d'être satisfait,** instead of being satisfied; *conj. phr.* **au l. que + *ind.*,** whereas; **je suis bergère, au l. qu'elle est fille de roi,** I am a shepherdess, while, whereas, she is a king's daughter; **au l. que + *sub.*,** instead of + *ger.*; **au l. que nous y ayons gagné quelque chose,** instead of our having profited by it. **3.** *Geom:* locus. **4. l. commun,** commonplace.

lieu[2], **-eus,** *s.m. Ich:* **l. (jaune),** pollack; **l. noir,** coalfish, *F:* coalie; *Com:* coalfish, green pollack.

lieudit, lieu-dit [ljødi], *s.m.* (named) place; **ce n'est pas un hameau, c'est un l.,** it's not a hamlet, it's just a place; **le l. Pré du Moulin,** (the place called) Mill Field; *pl. lieuxdits, lieux-dits.*

lieue [ljø], *s.f.* league (= 4 kilometres); **deux lieues** = five miles; **l. marine,** $5\frac{1}{2}$ kilometres; **à une petite l. d'ici,** barely a league from here; **être à mille lieues de croire qch.,** to be far, miles, from believing sth.; **j'étais à mille lieues de penser que . . .,** I should never have dreamt that . . .; **les bottes de sept lieues de l'ogre,** the ogre's seven-league boots; **l. d'Angleterre,** mile; *F:* **ça se voit à une, d'une l.,** it's obvious a mile off, you can see it a mile off; *F:* **il sent d'une l. son docteur,** you can tell he's a doctor a mile off; *F:* **être à cent lieues de la conversation,** to be miles away.

lieur, -euse [ljœ:r, -ø:z]. **1.** *s.* binder (of sheaves, etc.). **2.** *s.f. Agr:* **lieuse,** (mechanical) sheaf-binder. **3.** *s.f. Ent:* **(chenilles) lieuses,** leaf rollers.

lieutenance [ljøtnɑ̃:s], *s.f. Lit:* lieutenancy.

lieutenant [ljøtnɑ̃], *s.m.* (*a*) *Mil: etc:* lieutenant; *Navy:* **l. de vaisseau,** lieutenant; *Av:* **l. (aviateur),** flying officer; (*b*) (*Mercantile Marine*) mate; **premier l.,** second mate; (*c*) **l. de port,** deputy harbour-master; (*d*) *F:* **il n'est que le l. de sa femme,** he always has to ask his wife's permission; it's his wife who wears the trousers.

lieutenant-colonel [ljøtnɑ̃kɔlɔnɛl], *s.m. Mil:* lieutenant-colonel; *Av:* wing-commander; *pl. lieutenants-colonels.*

lièvre [ljɛ:vr], *s.m.* **1.** (*a*) *Z:* hare; **l. des armoisiées,** sage hare, sage rabbit; **l. des neiges,** arctic, polar, hare; **l. patagon,** Patagonian hare, Salinas con(e)y, mara; **l. américain,** snowshoe hare; **l. variable,** varying hare; **l. de l'Himalaya,** Himalayan woolly hare; **l. de Filchner,** Filchner's tolai hare; **lever un l.,** to start a hare; *F:* **c'est vous qui avez levé le l.,** you started it; **c'est là que gît le l.,** that's the crucial point; **prendre le l. au gîte,** to catch s.o. napping; **courir deux lièvres à la fois,** to try to do two things at once; **nous courons le même l.,** we are both after the same thing; **mémoire de l.,** memory like a sieve; *s.a.* CERVELLE 1, DORMIR 1, GÉSIR; (*b*) *Sp:* pace-maker; (*c*) *Moll: F:* **l. marin,** sea-hare, aplysia, tethys. **2.** *P:* woman of easy morals.

lièvre-sauteur [ljɛvr(ə)sotœ:r], *s.m. Z:* jumping hare, springhaas; *pl. lièvres-sauteurs.*

lièvreteau, -eaux [ljɛvr(ə)to], *s.m. Z:* young unweaned hare.

liévrite [ljevrit], *s.f. Miner:* lievrite, ilvaite.

lift [lift], *s.m.* **1.** *A:* lift, *U.S:* elevator. **2.** *A:* lift attendant. **3.** *Sp:* top spin.

lifter [lifte], *v.tr. Ten:* to put top spin on (the ball); **il joue très lifté,** he uses a lot of top spin (in his game).

liftier, -ière [liftje, -jɛ:r], *s.* lift attendant, *U.S:* elevator operator.

lifting [liftiŋ], *s.m.* face lift.

ligament [ligamɑ̃], *s.m. Anat: Moll:* ligament.

ligamenteux, -euse [ligamɑ̃tø, -ø:z], *a.* ligamentous, ligamentary.

ligamentopexie [ligamɑ̃tɔpɛksi], *s.f. Obst:* ligamentopexy, ligamentopexis.

ligature [ligaty:r], *s.f.* **1.** tying, binding; whipping (of fishing-rod, rope, etc.); **fil de l.,** binding wire. **2.** (*a*) *Mus:* tie; (*b*) *El.E: Nau: etc:* splice (in wire, cable); (*c*) *Surg: Typ:* ligature; **faire une l.,** to ligature, ligate. **3.** (*Psychics*) ligature.

ligaturer [ligatyre], *v.tr.* to bind, whip, splice; to tie (sth.) up; *Surg:* to ligature, ligate, tie (artery, etc.); **maladie des ligaturés,** disorder following the ligature of main arteries.

lige [li:ʒ], *a. A:* liege; **homme l.,** liege man.

ligérien, -ienne [liʒerjɛ̃, -jɛn], *a. Geog:* of the Loire valley.

ligie [liʒi], *s.f. Crust:* ligia, wharf-monkey.

lignage[1] [liɲa:ʒ], *s.m. A:* lineage, descent; **demoiselle de haut l.,** maiden of high degree.

lignage[2], *s.m. Fish:* float (for lines).

lignage[3], *s.m.* chalk-lining, lining off (of timber); alignment (of line-shafting).

lignage[4], *s.m. Typ:* lin(e)age (of a page, etc.).

lignager [liɲaʒe], *a.m. & s.m. Jur:* lineal (relative).

lignard [liɲa:r], *s.m. F:* **1.** *A:* soldier of the line; **les lignards,** the infantry. **2.** *Journ:* penny-a-liner. **3.** *F:* maintenance and repair worker on high-tension electric lines, lineman, linesman.

ligne [liɲ], *s.f.* line. **1.** (*a*) cord; **planter des arbres à la l.,** to plant trees straight by using a line, a cord; **l. de pêche,** fishing line; **l. de fond,** ground line; **pêche à la l. de fond,** bottom fishing; *Nau:* **l. de loch,** log line; **l. de sonde,** lead line, sounding line; **l. d'amarrage,** lashing; **l. de mouillage,** anchor cable path and gear; (*b*) **ligne droite,** straight line; **l. brisée,** jagged line; *Mth:* **la l. des x, des y, des z,** the x, y, z, axis (for coordinates); **tracer une l.,** to draw a line; **prolonger une l.,** to produce a line; **les lignes de la main,** the lines of the hand; **la l. de vie,** the line of life, the life line; *Mus:* **l. additionnelle, ajoutée, postiche, supplémentaire,** ledger line; *Fb:* **l. de touche,** touch line; **la l. des vingt-deux mètres,** the twenty-five; *Ten:* **l. de fond,** base line; **l. médiane,** centre line; **l. de côté de service,** side service-line; *Paperm:* **lignes d'eaux transversales,** chain lines, chain marks; *T.V:* **définition de 625 lignes d'exploration,** definition of 625 lines; *Geol:* **l. isoséiste, isosiste,** isoseismal line; *Aut: Adm:* **l. jaune** = white line, *U.S:* yellow line; **l. rouge** = yellow (no-parking) line; (*c*) (out)line; **la l. du nez, les lignes de la bouche,** the line, contour, of the nose, the lines of the mouth; **fermeté, pureté, des lignes,** boldness, purity, of line (in picture); **l. élégante d'une voiture,** good lines of a car; **auto qui a de la l.,** car with clean lines; **grandes lignes d'une œuvre,** broad, general, outline of a work; **les grandes lignes du projet,** the major principles upon which the project is, was, based; **garder sa l., soigner sa l.,** (*of women*) to keep one's figure, (*of men*) to keep, to watch, one's waistline; **avoir de la l., avoir la l.,** to look smart, elegant; (*d*) *Nau:* **l. de flottaison,** water-line (of ship); **l. de charge,** load line; **l. de flottaison en charge,** load water line; **l. de foi,** lubber's line; (*of ship*) **être dans ses lignes d'eau,** to be on an even keel; *Ph:* **l. de force,** line of force; *Opt:* **l. visuelle,** line of sight; *Sm.a: Artil:* **l. de visée, de mire,** line of sight; **l. de tir, de départ,** line of fire; line of departure; *Nau:* **la l. (équatoriale),** the line, the Equator; **passer la l.,** to cross the line; **l. de tuyauterie,** run of pipes; **l. de conduite,** line of conduct; **suivre la l. du devoir, de l'honneur,** to follow the path of duty, of honour; **l. généalogique,** genealogical line; **descendre en l. directe de . . .,** to be lineally descended from . . .; **c'est la l. paternelle qui a hérité,** it was the father's side that inherited; *s.a.* FOI 2; (*e*) **l. de maisons,** row of houses; **enfants assis en l.,** children seated in a row; **se mettre en l.,** (i) to line up, to draw up in a line; (ii) *F:* to come up to the scratch; **en première l.,** in the first place, first and foremost; **question qui vient en première l.,** question of primary importance; *adj.phr:* **hors l.,** out of the common; unrivalled, outstanding, incomparable (artist, etc.); **son talent n'est pas hors l.,** his talent is nothing out of the ordinary; *F:* **c'est bien dans sa l.!** that's just him! **sur toute la l.,** all along the line; *s.a.* COMPTE; (*f*) **l. d'écriture,** line of writing; **lignes laissées en blanc,** lines left blank; **écris-moi deux lignes,** drop me a line; **lire entre les lignes,** to read between the lines; **aller à la l.,** to begin a new paragraph; (*in dictating*) **à la l.,** new paragraph, next line, "indent"; **journaliste à la l.,** penny-a-liner; *s.a.* TIRER I, 1; (*g*) narrow cutting through wood; service path. **2.** *Mil:* (*a*) **l. d'avant-postes,** outpost line, *A:* picket line; **l. de contact,** line of contact, front line; **l. d'arrêt,** holding line; **l. de retranchements,** line of intrenchments; **les lignes,** the lines; **l. de débouché, de départ (de l'attaque),** start line, jumping-off line; **lignes de communication,** (i) communication lines; (ii) communication trenches; (*b*) **l. de soldats,** line of soldiers; *A:* **bataillon, vaisseaux, en l.,** battalion, ships, in line; **l. de bataille,** line of battle, battle-line; **infanterie de l.,** line infantry, infantry of the line; **cavalerie de l.,** cavalry of the line; **le 20e régiment de l.,** the 20th regiment of the line; *Navy: A:* **vaisseau de l.,** ship of the line. **3.** (*a*) **l. de chemin de fer,** railway line; **grande l.,** main line, trunk line; **l. à voie simple, unique,** single-track line; **l. à voie double, à double voie,** double-track line, twin-track railway; **l. de tramways,** tram-line; **l. de paquebots, l. maritime,** steamship line; **l. d'autobus,** bus service; (*b*) *Av:* flight; **pilote de l.,** airline pilot; **les voyageurs pour Bruxelles l. A doivent se présenter au guichet 20,** passengers for flight A to Brussels are to report at counter 20; (*c*) **l. télégraphique,** telegraph line; *Tp:* **l. partagée,** shared line, party line; **êtes-vous encore en l.?** are you still there? are you holding? *Tp: Pol:* **la l. rouge,** the hot line (*U.S.A. to Kremlin*); **la l. verte,** the hot line (*Élysée to Kremlin*); *El:* **les fils de l.,** the mains; **l. aérienne,** overhead power line; **l. souterraine,** underground power line, buried line.

ligné [liɲe], *a. Bot: etc:* lineate, lined.

ligne-bloc [liɲblɔk], *s.f. Typ:* type-bar, slug; *pl. lignes-blocs.*

lignée [liɲe], *s.f.* issue, (line of) descendants; **de bonne l. puritaine,** of good puritan stock; **chien de bonne l.,** pedigree dog; *Biol:* **colonies en l. pure,** cloned colonies.

ligner [liɲe], *v.tr.* **1.** to chalk-line, line off (timber). **2.** (*of stag*) to cover, line (the doe).

lignerolle [liɲrɔl], *s.f. Nau:* small twine.

lignette [liɲɛt], *s.f.* (*a*) twine (for netting); (*b*) light fishing line.

ligneul [liɲœl], *s.m.* **1.** *Bootm:* shoemaker's end, wax end. **2.** *Const:* wall plate.

ligneux, -euse [liɲø, -øːz]. **1.** *a.* ligneous, woody. **2.** *s. Sug.-R:* bagasse, cane trash.

lignicole [liɲikɔl], *a.* lignicolous, xylophilous.

lignifère [liɲifɛːr], *a.* ligniferous.

lignification [liɲifikasjɔ̃], *s.f.* lignification.

lignifier [liɲifje], *v.tr.* to lignify; to turn (sth.) into wood.

se lignifier, (*of tissue, etc.*) to lignify; to turn into wood; to become woody.

ligniforme [liɲifɔrm], *a.* ligniform.

lignine [liɲin], *s.f. Bot: Ch:* lignin.

lignite [liɲit], *s.m. Miner:* lignite.

ligniteux, -euse [liɲitø, -øːz], *a.* resembling lignite; lignitic.

lignitifère [liɲitifɛːr], *a. Geol:* lignitiferous.

lignocérique [liɲɔserik], *a. Ch:* lignoceric.

lignomètre [liɲɔmɛtr̥], *s.m. Typ:* type scale.

lignosité [liɲozite], *s.f.* woodiness.

ligot [ligo], *s.m.* **1.** bundle of firelighters. **2.** *P:* garter.

ligotage [ligɔtaːʒ], *s.m.* binding, tying up (of person).

ligoter [ligɔte], *v.tr.* to bind (s.o.) hand and foot; to tie (s.o.) up; to lash (thgs) together; **sa peur de la foule le ligote,** his fear of crowds holds him back.

ligroïne [ligrɔin], *s.f. Ch:* ligroin(e).

ligue [lig], *s.f.* (*a*) league, confederacy; *Hist:* **la (Sainte-)L.,** the (Catholic) League; (*b*) *F:* faction.

liguer [lige], *v.tr.* to league, bond (nations, etc.) together; **être ligué avec qn,** to be in league with s.o.

se liguer, to league, to form a league (**avec, contre,** with, against); *abs.* to league together.

ligueur, -euse [ligœːr, -øːz], *s.* (*a*) *Hist:* leaguer, member of the *Sainte-Ligue*; (*b*) member of a league, a confederacy, a faction.

ligulaire [ligylɛːr], *s.f.,* **ligularia** [ligylarja], *s.m. Bot:* ligularia, leopard plant.

ligule [ligyl], *s.f. Bot:* ligula, ligule, strap.

ligulé [ligyle], *a. Bot:* ligulate.

liguliflore [ligyliflɔːr], *a. & s. Bot:* **1.** *a.* liguliflorous. **2.** *s.f.pl.* **liguliflores,** Ligularia, Liguliflorae.

ligure [ligyːr], *s.m.* **1.** *Ling:* Ligurian. **2.** *Hist: pl.* **les Ligures,** Ligures, Ligurians.

Ligurie [ligyri], *Pr.n.f. Geog:* Liguria.

ligurien, -ienne [ligyrjɛ̃, -jɛn], *a. & s. Geog:* Ligurian; *s.m. Ling:* Ligurian.

ligurite [ligyrit], *s.f. Miner:* ligurite.

ligustique [ligystik], *s.m. Bot:* ligusticum, levisticum.

ligustrum [ligystrɔm], *s.m. Bot:* ligustrum, *F:* privet.

liguus [ligyys], *s.m. Moll:* liguus.

lilas [lila]. **1.** *s.m. Bot:* lilac. **2.** *a.inv.* lilac (-coloured).

liliacé [liljase], *Bot:* **1.** *a.* liliaceous, lily-like. **2.** *s.f.pl.* **liliacées,** Liliaceae.

lilial, -iaux [liljal, -jo], *a.* (*m.pl. form usu. avoided*) lily-like, lily-white; lilied (complexion, etc.).

liliales [liljal], **liliiflores** [liliiflɔːr], *s.f.pl. Bot:* Liliales, Liliiflorae.

lillerois, -oise [lilɔrwa, -waːz], *a. & s. Geog:* (native, inhabitant) of Lillers [lilɛːr].

lillianite [liljanit], *s.f. Miner:* lillianite.

lilliputien, -ienne [lilipysjɛ̃, -jɛn], *a. & s.* Lilliputian.

lillois, -oise [lilwa, -waːz], *a. & s. Geog:* (native, inhabitant) of Lille.

Lima [lima], *Pr.n.m. Geog:* Lima.

limace [limas], *s.f.* **1.** (*a*) *Moll:* slug; *P:* **c'est une vraie l.,** he's so slow; (*b*) *Ich:* **l. de mer,** snail-fish. **2.** *Hyd.E:* Archimedean screw. **3.** *P:* shirt.

limacelle [limasɛl], *s.f. Moll:* limacel, limacelle.

limacien, -ienne [limasjɛ̃, -jɛn], *a. Moll:* limaceous, limacine.

limaciform [limasifɔrm], *a.* limaciform.

limacodidés [limakɔdide], *s.m.pl. Ent:* Limacodidae.

limaçon [limasɔ̃], *s.m.* **1.** *Moll:* (*a*) snail; **escalier en l.,** spiral staircase; (*b*) **l. de mer,** periwinkle. **2.** (*a*) road with winding turns; (*b*) *Anat:* cochlea (of the ear); (*c*) *Clockm:* snail-wheel; (*d*) = LIMACE 2; (*e*) *Mth:* **l. de Pascal,** limaçon.

limaçonnage [limasɔnaːʒ], *s.m. Tail:* shine (on cloth caused by ironing).

limaçonnière [limasɔnjɛːr], *s.f.* edible snail farm.

limage [limaːʒ], *s.m.* filing.

limaille [limaːj], *s.f.* filings; **l. de fer,** iron filings.

liman [limɑ̃], *s.m. Geog:* liman, (freshwater) lagoon (at river-mouth, *esp.* in the Black Sea).

limande [limɑ̃ːd], *s.f.* **1.** (*a*) *Ich:* limanda, dab; **fausse l.,** scald fish, megrim; **l. salope,** megrim; *P:* (*of woman*) **plate comme une l.,** as flat as a pancake; *F:* **faire la l.,** to be obsequious; (*b*) *A: P:* slap (in the face). **2.** (*a*) *Carp:* graving piece (let into defective timber); (*b*) *Min:* sheeting (of gallery). **3.** (*carpenter's, mason's, etc.*) straight-edge. **4.** *Nau:* parcelling (of rope).

limander [limɑ̃de], *v.tr.* **1.** (*a*) to apply a graving piece to (timber); (*b*) *Min:* to sheet (gallery). *Nau:* to parcel (rope, etc.).

limba [lɛ̃ba], *s.m. Bot:* limba.

limbaire [lɛ̃bɛːr], *a. Bot:* pertaining to a limb; limb (surface, etc.).

limbe [lɛ̃ːb], *s.m.* **1.** *Bot: Mth:* limb; *Astr:* rim, edge (of the sun, etc.); *Bot:* lamina (of leaf); *Anat:* limbus; **l. de la conjonctive,** limbus corneae. **2.** (*a*) *Theol:* **les Limbes,** limbo; (*b*) **être dans les limbes,** (i) *A:* to be in one's second childhood; (ii) to be wool-gathering.

limbifère [lɛ̃bifɛːr], *a. Bot:* limbate.

limbique [lɛ̃bik], *a. Anat:* limbic (lobe of the brain).

Limbourg [lɛ̃buːr], *Pr.n. Geog:* Limburg.

limburgite [lɛ̃byrʒit], *s.f. Geol:* limburgite.

lime[1] [lim], *s.f.* **1.** *Tls:* file; **l. triangulaire,** three-square file; **l. à champs lisses,** safe-edge file; **l. à couteau,** knife file, slitting file; **l. à barrettes, à biseau,** cant file; **grosse l., l. grosse, l. d'Allemagne,** coarse, rough, file; rasp; **l. douce,** smooth file; **l. demi-douce,** middle-cut, second-cut, file; **l. sourde,** dead-smooth file; **l. demi-ronde,** half-round file; **l. queue de rat,** rat tail, rat-tailed file; **l. à taille simple,** float; *Toil:* **l. à ongles,** nail file; **l. de carton, d'émeri,** emery board; **fabricant de limes,** file-cutter; **travail à la l.,** file work; **aiguiser un outil à la l.,** to file up a tool; **enlever une saillie à la l.,** to file off a projection; **donner un coup de l. à qch.,** to touch sth. up with a file; to give sth. a touch up with a file; **donner le dernier coup de l. à un ouvrage,** to put the finishing touches to a piece of work; *O:* **c'est une l. sourde,** he's a deep old file. **2.** *Moll:* lima.

lime[2], *s.f. Bot:* (sweet) lime.

lime-bois [limbwa], *s.m.inv. Ent:* wood-eater.

liménitide [limenitid], *s.m. Ent:* Limenitis; the emperor and admiral butterflies.

limequat [lim(ə)kwa], *s.m. Bot:* limequat.

limer [lime], *v.tr.* to file; to file up; to file off; to file down; **l. des vers, son style,** to polish verses, one's style; **vêtement limé,** garment shiny with wear.

limette [limɛt], *s.f. Bot:* (sweet) lime.

limettier [limɛtje], *s.m. Bot:* (sweet) lime (tree).

limeur, -euse [limœːr, -øːz], *s.* **1.** filer. **2.** *s.f.* **limeuse,** filing machine; shaping-machine.

limicole [limikɔl], *a. & s.m.* **1.** *a.* limicolous. **2.** *s.m.pl. Orn:* **limicoles,** Limicolae.

limidés [limide], *s.m.pl. Moll:* Limidae.

limier [limje], *s.m.* bloodhound; sleuthhound; *Ven:* **valet de l.,** harbourer; *F:* **les limiers de la police,** the police sleuthhounds; the detective force; the sleuths.

liminaire [liminɛːr], *a.* **1.** *Typ:* **pièces liminaires,** preliminary pages, *F:* prelims. **2.** **épître l.,** prefatory letter; foreword.

liminal, -aux [liminal, -o], *a. Psy:* liminal.

limitable [limitabl̥], *a.* limitable.

limitateur [limitatœːr], *s.m.* limiter, limiting device; *Ac:* **l. de bruit,** noise limiter; *El:* **l. de charge,** charge-limiting, load-limiting, device; **l. de courant,** current limiter; **l. de tension,** circuit breaker; *Mec.E:* **l. d'emballement, l. de vitesse,** speed limiter; **l. de course,** stroke limiter; **l. d'avance,** feed limiter.

limitatif, -ive [limitatif, -iːv], *a.* limitary, limiting, restrictive; **article l.,** limiting clause; *Jur:* **énumération limitative,** limitative enumeration.

limitation [limitasjɔ̃], *s.f.* **1.** limitation, restriction; **limitations imposées à l'action d'une administration,** limitations imposed on an administration; **l. des naissances,** birth control, family planning; **l. des salaires,** wage restraint; **l. de vitesse,** speed limit; **voie sans l. de vitesse,** unrestricted road; *Com: Ind:* **l. de la production en fonction de la demande,** supply and demand ratio. **2.** marking off (of ground).

limite [limit], *s.f.* **1.** (*a*) boundary (of country, field, etc.); limit (of s.o.'s power, etc.); limitation; **l. d'état,** frontier line; **marquer les limites du terrain,** to mark out the ground; **l. d'âge,** age limit; **fixer, imposer, des limites à l'autorité de qn,** to set bounds to s.o.'s authority; **sortir des limites de son droit,** to go beyond, to exceed, one's rights; **atteindre la l. d'âge,** to reach, attain, the age limit; **franchir, dépasser, les limites,** to pass all bounds; **tenez-vous dans les limites de 1000 francs,** keep to a limit of 1000 francs; **mettre une l., des limites, à . . .,** to set a limit, limits, to . . .; **dans les limites où les circonstances le permettent,** so far as circumstances permit; **les dernières limites de l'espace,** the ultimate bounds of space; **à la dernière l. de l'exaspération,** exasperated beyond measure; **à**

la l. de ses forces, completely exhausted; **sans limites,** unbounded, limitless; **la vanité humaine n'a pas de limites,** human vanity has no bounds; **il y a l. à tout,** there's a limit to everything; one must draw the line somewhere; **c'est à la l.,** it's a borderline case; **il n'y a pas de l. clairement définie entre maturité et sénilité,** there is no clear-cut dividing line between maturity and senility; *Med: etc:* **l. inférieure,** threshold (of pain, etc.); *Sp:* **limites du jeu,** boundary(-lines); *Cr:* **hors l.,** out of one's crease; (*on mountain*) **l. des arbres,** tree limit, line, timber line; (*b*) *Mec:* **l. d'élasticité, l. élastique,** elastic(-stress) limit, yield stress; **l. de résistance,** strength limit, yield limit or point; **l. de rupture, l. critique de résistance,** breaking(-down) point; **l. de stabilité,** range of stability; **l. de fatigue,** stress limit; **l. d'endurance,** fatigue limit; (*c*) *Elcs:* **l. des fréquences audibles,** pitch limit; **l. de détection (électromagnétique, etc.),** maximum range (of radiolocation, etc.); (*d*) *Av:* **limites d'utilisation,** operating limitations. **2. cas l.,** borderline case; **angle l.,** (i) *Artil:* limiting angle (of fire); (ii) *Opt:* critical angle; **vitesse l.,** maximum speed; *Civ.E:* **charge l. d'un pont,** weight capacity of a bridge; *Mth:* **valeur l.,** ultimate, limiting, value (of an expression); **méthode des limites,** method of limits; **date l.,** latest date, deadline.

limité [limite], *a.* limited, restricted (number of seats, etc.); **télégramme l.,** telegram upon which a late fee is levied for priority of transmission.

limiter [limite], *v.tr.* **1.** to bound, to mark the bounds of (countries, etc.). **2.** to limit; to set bounds, limits, to (s.o.'s power, rights, etc.); **se l. à . . .,** to limit, restrict oneself to . . ..

limiteur [limitœːr], *s.m. El: Elcs:* limiting device, (current) limiter; *Mec.E:* regulator, governor; **l. de vitesse,** speed-limiting device; **l. d'emballement, de vitesse,** overspeed limiter (of turbine); *Hyd.E:* **l. de niveau d'eau,** water-level regulator, water-level valve.

limitrophe [limitrɔf], *a.* limitrophe, adjacent (**de,** to); abutting (**de,** on); bordering (**de,** on); **être l. d'un autre pays,** to border on another country; **pays l.,** borderland; *T.V:* **zone l.,** fringe area.

limivore [limivɔːr], *a. Z:* limivorous.

limma [lima], *s.m. Mus:* limma.

limnanthe [limnɑ̃ːt], *s.m. Bot:* limnanthes.

limnée [limne], *s.f. Moll:* lymnaea.

limnéidés [limneide], *s.m.pl. Moll:* lymnaeidae.

limnétique [limnetik], *a. Biol:* limnetic.

limnigraphe [limnigraf], *s.m.* limnograph.

limnimètre [limnimɛtr̥], *s.m.* limnimetre, limnometre.

limnique [limnik], *a. Min: Geol:* limnic; **sédiments limniques,** lake deposits.

limnite [limnit], *s.f. Miner:* limnite, bog iron ore.

limnivore [limnivɔːr], *a. Z:* limnivorous.

limnobiologie [limnɔbjɔlɔʒi], *s.f.* biological study of lakes.

limnobios [limnɔbjɔs], *s.m. Biol:* plant and animal life of lakes and marshes.

limnodrome [limnɔdroːm], *s.m. Orn:* **1. gris,** red-breasted snipe, *U.S:* dowitcher.

limnologie [limnɔlɔʒi], *s.f.* limnology.

limnopithèque [limnɔpitɛk], *s.m. Paleont:* limnopithecus.

limnoplancton [limnɔplɑ̃ktɔ̃], *s.m. Biol:* limnoplankton.

limnoscelis [limnɔselis], *s.m. Rept:* limnoscelis.

limogeage [limɔʒaːʒ], *s.m.* (*a*) superseding (of general, etc.); (*b*) dismissal.

limoger [limɔʒe], *v.tr. F:* (*a*) to supersede (general, etc.), to give (s.o.) his bowler hat; (*b*) to dismiss (s.o.).

Limoges [limɔːʒ], *Pr.n. Geog:* Limoges; **porcelaine, émaux, de L.,** Limoges (porcelain), Limoges enamels.

limon[1] [limɔ̃], *s.m.* (*a*) mud, silt, alluvium (on river banks, etc.); *Lit:* **il se croit d'un autre l. que nous,** he thinks he is of a different clay from ours; **le l. du vice,** the slough of vice; (*b*) *Geol:* limon; **l. fin,** loess.

limon[2], *s.m.* **1.** *Veh:* shaft, thill. **2.** *Const:* stringboard, stringer (of staircase); **faux l.,** wall-string.

limon[3], *s.m. Bot:* sour lime.

limonade [limɔnad], *s.f.* **1.** lemonade; **l. non gazeuse,** lemon squash, still lemonade; **l. sèche,** lemonade powder; *P:* **tomber dans la l.,** to fall upon evil days; **être dans la l.,** to keep a small pub. **2.** *pl.* mineral waters; minerals, soft drinks.

limonadier, -ière [limɔnadje, -jɛːr], *s.* **1.** *occ.* dealer in lemonade, in mineral waters, in soft drinks; *U.S:* soda-fountain keeper. **2.** *more usu.* keeper of a bar, of a small pub. **3.** *Jur:* victualler.

limonage [limɔnaːʒ], *s.m. Agr:* enriching (of the soil) with loam.

limonaire [limɔnɛːr], *s.m.* barrel-organ.

limonène [limɔnɛn], *s.m. Ch:* limonene.

limoner [limɔne], *v.tr. Cu:* to clean, scale (fish by scalding); to wash and remove membrane (of brains).

limoneux, -euse [limɔnø, -øːz], *a.* **1.** (*of water, etc.*) muddy, charged with mud. **2.** (*of plant*) growing in mud; bog(-plant). **3.** *Geol:* alluvial.

limonier[1] [limɔnje], *s.m.* shaft horse, thill horse; wheeler.

limonier[2], *s.m. Bot:* sour-lime tree.

limonière [limɔnjɛːr], *s.f. Veh:* **1.** pair of shafts; *A.Artil:* **affût à l.,** galloper carriage. **2.** shaft-draught vehicle; four-wheeled dray.

limonite [limɔnit], *s.f. Miner:* limonite, brown iron ore; bog iron ore.

limonium [limɔnjɔm], *s.m. Bot:* limonium, sea lavender.

limoselle [limɔzɛl], *s.f. Bot:* limosella; mudwort.

limosinage [limɔzinaːʒ], *s.m. Const:* rubble work, rough masonry.

limousin, -ine [limuzɛ̃, -in]. **1.** *a. & s. Geog:* (native, inhabitant) (i) of Limoges, (ii) of the province of Limousin. **2.** *s.m. A:* stonemason. **3.** *s.f.* **limousine,** (*a*) *A:* (carter's) rough woollen greatcoat or cloak; (*b*) *Aut: A:* limousine; *Fr.C:* saloon, *U.S:* sedan.

limousinage [limuzinaːʒ], *s.m.* = LIMOSINAGE.

limousiner [limuzine], *v.tr. Const:* to build (wall, etc.) in rubble work.

limpide [lɛ̃pid], *a.* limpid, clear, transparent (quartz, water, etc.); clear (style).

limpidité [lɛ̃pidite], *s.f.* limpidity, limpidness; clarity, clearness.

limule [limyl], *s.m. Crust:* (East Indian) king crab, sea louse.

limure [limyːr], *s.f.* **1.** *A:* filing. **2.** *pl.* filings.

lin [lɛ̃], *s.m.* **1.** flax; **graine de l.,** linseed; **huile de l.,** linseed oil; **farine de l.,** linseed meal; *Bot:* **l. sauvage,** toadflax; **l. purgatif,** purging flax; **l. des marais,** moor grass, cotton grass; **l. bâtard,** camelina, false flax; *a.inv.* **bleu de l.,** flax-blue. **2.** *Tex:* **(tissu de) l.,** linen; **fil de l.,** linen thread, yarn; *a.inv.* **(couleur) gris de l.,** (natural) linen colour.

linacé [linase], *Bot:* **1.** *a.* linaceous. **2.** *s.f.pl.* **linacées,** Linaceae, the flax family.

linaigrette [linɛgrɛt], *s.f. Bot:* cotton grass; **l. à larges feuilles,** broad-leaved cotton grass.

linaire [linɛːr], *s.f. Bot:* linaria, *F:* toadflax, butter-and-eggs; **l. cymbalaire,** ivy-leaved toadflax.

linaloé [linalɔe], *s.m. Bot:* linaloe; **essence de l.,** linaloe oil.

linalol [linalɔl], *s.m. Ch: Bot:* linalo(o)l.

linarite [linarit], *s.f. Miner:* linarite.

linceul [lɛ̃sœl], *s.m.* **1.** *A:* sheet (for bed). **2.** winding-sheet, shroud; **envelopper un corps d'un l.,** to shroud a corpse; **les champs sous leur l. de neige,** the fields shrouded in snow, under their shroud of snow; **le plus riche n'emporte qu'un l.,** we can carry nothing out of this world.

linçoir [lɛ̃swaːr], *s.m. Const:* trimmer, trimming joist.

lindane [lɛ̃dan], *s.m. Ch:* lindane.

lindackérite [lɛ̃dakerit], *s.f. Miner:* lindackerite.

lindera [lɛ̃dera], *s.m. Bot:* lindera.

Lindor[1] [lɛ̃dɔːr], *Pr.n.m. Th:* typical Spanish serenader (*from Almaviva's disguise in Beaumarchais' Le Barbier de Séville*).

lindor[2], *s.m. Cards:* (*a*) seven of diamonds (in game of Pope Joan); (*b*) Pope Joan.

linéaire [lineɛːr], *a.* linear (equation, leaf, etc.); **mesures linéaires,** linear measures; **fonction l.,** linear function; **dessin l.,** geometrical drawing, machine drawing; **traduction l.,** line for line translation; **récit l.,** direct, straightforward, narrative.

linéairement [lineɛrmɑ̃], *adv.* in a straight line; linearly.

linéal, -aux [lineal, -o], *a.* lineal (descent, heir, etc.).

linéalement [linealmɑ̃], *adv.* lineally (descended).

linéament [lineamɑ̃], *s.m.* lineament, feature (of face); **linéaments d'un discours,** brief outline, main features, of a speech.

linéarité [linearite], *s.f.* (*computers*) **erreur de l.,** linearity error.

linéature [lineatyːr], *s.f.* **1.** outline (of face, features, etc.). **2.** *Phot.Engr:* **l. de la trame,** ruling of the screen. **3.** *T.V:* line system, (television) lines.

liner [lainœːr], *s.m. Nau: F:* liner.

linette [linɛt], *s.f.* linseed, flax seed.

lineus [lineys], *s.m. Ann:* lineus.

linge [lɛ̃ːʒ], *s.m.* **1.** (made-up) linen, calico; **l. de table, de lit,** table linen, bed linen; **(gros) l. de maison,** household linen; **l. de cuisine, d'office,** kitchen cloths; **l. de corps, de dessous,** underwear, underlinen; *F:* **il faut laver son l. sale en famille,** don't wash your dirty linen in public; **corde à (étendre le) l.,** clothesline; *P:* **avoir du l.,** to be well off, to be well dressed; **du beau l.,** (*of woman*) a good-looker. **2.** piece of linen, of calico; **essuyer qch. avec un l.,** to wipe sth. with a cloth; **tête enveloppée de linges,** head swathed in bandages; *s.a.* BLANC 1, 2.

lingé [lɛ̃ʒe], *a. Dial:* provided with linen.

linger, -ère [lɛ̃ʒe, -ɛːr], *s.* **1.** linen-draper. **2.** *s.f.* **lingère,** (*a*) linen maid; (*b*) sewing maid (in boarding school, etc.).

lingerie [lɛ̃ʒri], *s.f.* **1.** (*a*) *Com:* linen drapery; (*b*) underclothing, linen; **l. pour dames,** (women's) underwear, lingerie; **vente de l.,** white sale. **2.** linen room.

lingot [lɛ̃go], *s.m.* **1.** *Metall:* ingot; **l. d'or,** gold bar, ingot; *Fin:* **or, argent, en lingots,** bullion. **2.** *Sm.a: Typ:* slug.

lingotage [lɛ̃gɔtaːʒ], *s.m. Metall:* teeming.

lingoter [lɛ̃gɔte], *v.tr. Metall:* to teem.

lingotière [lɛ̃gɔtjɛːr], *s.f. Metall:* ingot mould.

lingual, -aux [lɛ̃gwal, -o]. **1.** *a. Anat: Ling:* lingual (nerve, consonant, etc.); tongue (consonant). **2.** *s.f. Ling:* **linguale,** lingual.

linguatule [lɛ̃gwatyl], *s.f. Arach:* linguatula, tongue worm.

linguatulose [lɛ̃gwatyloːz], *s.f. Vet:* linguatulosis.

lingue[1] [lɛ̃ːg], *s.f. Ich:* ling.

lingue[2], *s.m. P: O:* knife.

linguet [lɛ̃gɛ], *s.m. Nau: Mec.E:* pawl, catch.

linguiforme [lɛ̃gɥifɔrm], *a.* linguiform, tongue-shaped.

linguiste [lɛ̃gɥist], *s.m. & f.* linguist.

linguistique [lɛ̃gɥistik]. **1.** *a.* linguistic. **2.** *s.f.* linguistics; **l. structurale,** structural linguistics.

linguistiquement [lɛ̃gɥistikmɑ̃], *adv.* linguistically.

lingulaire [lɛ̃gylɛːr], **lingulé** [lɛ̃gyle], *a. Bot:* lingulate.

lingulelle [lɛ̃gylɛl], *s.f. Paleont:* lingula.

linguodental, -ale, -aux [lɛ̃gwɔdɑ̃tal, -o]. **1.** *a.* linguodental (consonant). **2.** *s.f.* **linguodentale,** linguodental.

linier, -ière [linje, -jɛːr]. **1.** *a.* pertaining to linen, to flax; **industrie linière,** linen industry. **2.** *s.f.* **linière,** flax field.

liniment [linimɑ̃], *s.m. Med:* liniment.

linite [linit], *s.f. Med:* linitis.

links [liŋks], *s.m.pl.* golf course, (golf) links.

Linné [lin(n)e], *Pr.n.m.* Linnaeus.

linnée [lin(n)e], *s.f. Bot:* linnaea, twin flower.

linnéen, -enne [linneɛ̃, -ɛn], *a.* Linn(a)ean (classification).

linnéite [lin(n)eit], *s.f. Miner:* linnaeite, linneite.

linnéon [lin(n)eɔ̃], *s.m.* linneon, macrospecies.

lino[1] [lino], *s.m. F:* (*a*) (= LINOLEUM) lino; (*b*) linocut.

lino[2], *F:* (*a*) *s.f.* = LINOTYPE; (*b*) *s.m. & f.* = LINOTYPISTE.

linognatus [linɔgnatyːs], *s.m. Ent:* linognathus.

linoléique [linɔleik], *a. Ch:* linoleic (acid).

linoléum [linɔleɔm], *s.m.* **l. (incrusté),** linoleum; **l. imprimé,** (floor) oilcloth; *Engr:* **gravure sur l.,** linocut.

linon [linɔ̃], *s.m. Tex:* **1.** lawn; **l. mercerisé,** mercerized lawn. **2.** buckram.

linot [lino], *s.m.* = LINOTTE.

linotte [linɔt], *s.f. Orn:* **l. (mélodieuse),** linnet; **l. à bec jaune, l. montagnarde,** twite; *F:* **tête de l.,** empty-headed, feather-brained, person; *P:* **siffler la linotte,** (i) to tipple; (ii) to prime an accomplice; (iii) to be in quod.

Linotype [linɔtip], *s.f. R.t.m: Typ:* Linotype (machine).

linotypie [linɔtipi], *s.f. Typ:* setting by Linotype.

linotypiste [linɔtipist], *s.m. & f.* linotypist, Linotype operator.

linsang [lɛ̃sɑ̃ːg], *s.m. Z:* linsang; **l. à bandes,** banded linsang; **l. tacheté,** spotted linsang.

linsoir [lɛ̃swaːr], *s.m. Const:* trimmer, trimming joist.

linteau, -eaux [lɛ̃to], *s.m. Const:* **1.** lintel; **à l.,** lintelled. **2. l. de baie,** breastsummer, bressummer.

lion, -onne [ljɔ̃, -ɔn], *s.* **1.** (*a*) lion, *f.* lioness; **hardi comme un l.,** as bold as a lion; **homme au cœur de l.,** lion-hearted man; *B:* **Daniel dans la fosse aux lions,** Daniel in the lions' den; **la part du l.,** the lion's share; **se faire la part du l.,** to keep, take, the lion's share; *Lit:* **c'est l'âne couvert de la peau du l.,** it's the ass in the lion's skin; *F:* **avoir mangé,** *P:* **bouffé, du l.,** to be on the rampage; *s.a.* CHIEN 1, GRIFFE[1] 1, ONGLE 1; (*b*) **l. d'Amérique, du Pérou,** American lion; puma, cougar; (*c*) **l. marin, l. de mer,** sea-lion. **2.** *A: or Lit:* (*a*) celebrity of the day, (literary) lion; (*b*) (*Parisian slang*) **une lionne,** a fashionable woman. **3.** *Astr:* **le L.,** Leo. **4.** *Geog:* **le golfe du L.,** the Gulf of Lions.

lionceau, -eaux [ljɔ̃so], *s.m.* **1.** lion's cub or whelp; *F: A: Lit:* young dandy. **2.** *Her:* lioncel.

liondent [ljɔ̃dɑ̃], *s.m. Bot:* **l. à tige nue,** common hawkbit; **l. hispide,** rough hawkbit; **l. d'automne,** smooth hawkbit.

lionnerie [lijɔn(ə)ri], *s.f. A: Lit:* lionism.

liparéen, -enne [lipareɛ̃, -ɛn], *a. & s. Geog:* (native, inhabitant) of the Lipari Islands.

liparidés [liparide], *s.m.pl. Ent:* Liparidae, the tussock moths.

liparis [liparis], *s.m.* **1.** *Ich:* sea snail. **2.** *Ent:* tussock moth; **l. cul-doré,** brown-tail moth. **3.** *Bot:* liparis.

liparite [liparit], *s.f. Miner:* liparite, rhyolite.

lipase [lipɑːz], *s.f. Ch:* lipase.

lipémie [lipemi], *s.f. Bio-Ch:* lipid content (of the blood).

lipeure [lipœːr], *s.m. Ent:* lipeurus.

lipide [lipid], *s.m. Bio-Ch:* lipid.

lipidique [lipidik], *a. Bio-Ch:* lipidic.

lipidogramme [lipidɔgram], *s.m. Med:* graph showing the different ratios of lipoproteins (in an organic liquid) separated by means of electrophoresis.

lipochrome [lipɔkroːm], *s.m. Bio-Ch:* lipochrome.

lipodystrophie [lipɔdistrɔfi], *s.f. Med:* lipodystrophy; **l. progressive,** progressive lipodystrophy.

lipogénèse [lipɔʒenɛːz], *s.f. Biol:* lipogenesis.

lipogramme [lipɔgram], *s.m. Lit:* lipogram.

lipoïde [lipɔid], *a. & s.m.* lipoid.

lipoïdique [lipɔidik], *a.* lipoidic.

lipolyse [lipɔliːz], *s.f. Biol:* lypolysis.

lipolytique [lipɔlitik], *a. Biol:* lipolytic.

lipomateux, -euse [lipɔmatø, -øːz], *a. Med:* lipomatous.

lipomatose [lipɔmatoːz], *s.f. Med:* lipomatosis.

lipome [lipom], *s.m. Med:* lipoma.

lipophile [lipɔfil], *a. Ch:* lipophilic, lipophile.

lipophilie [lipɔfili], *s.f.* lipophilia.

lipoprotéine [lipɔprɔtein], *s.f. Bio-Ch:* lipoprotein.

liposoluble [lipɔsɔlybl], *a. Ch:* liposoluble, fat-soluble, oil-soluble.

lipothymie [lipɔtimi], *s.f. Med:* lipothymia, lipothymy; faint(ing).

lipothymique [lipɔtimik], *a. Med:* lipothymic.

lipotrope [lipɔtrɔp], *a. Bio-Ch:* lipotropic, lipotrophic.

lipovaccin [lipɔvaksɛ̃], *s.m. Med: etc:* lipovaccine.

lipoxydase [lipɔksidaːz], *s.f. Ch:* lipoxydase.

lippe [lip], *s.f.* thick (lower) lip; blubber lip; **faire sa, la, l.,** to pout.

lippée [lipe], *s.f. A:* mouthful; **franche l.,** good tuck-in at someone's else's expense; **courir la l.,** to try to get a free meal out of somebody; to sponge on one's friends.

lippu [lipy], *a.* (*a*) thick-lipped; blubber-lipped; (*b*) thick, blubber (lip).

lipurie [lipyri], *s.f. Med:* lipuria.

liquater [likwate], *v.tr. Metall:* to liquate (copper and lead, etc.).

liquation [likwasjɔ̃], *s.f. Metall:* liquation.

liquéfacteur [likefaktœːr], *s.m. Gasm:* condenser.

liquéfaction [likefaksjɔ̃], *s.f.* liquefaction (*esp.* of a gas).

liquéfiable [likefjabl], *a.* liquefiable (gas).

liquéfiant [likefjɑ̃], (*a*) *a.* liquefactive; (*b*) *s.m.* liquefacient.

liquéfier [likefje], *v.tr.* (*pr.sub. & p.d.* **n. liquéfiions, v. liquéfiiez**) to liquefy; to reduce (gas, etc.) to the liquid state.

liquescence [likɛs(s)ɑ̃s, likɥɛ-], *s.f. Ch:* liquescence.

liquescent [likɛs(s)ɑ̃, likyɛ-], *a.* liquescent.

liquette [likɛt], *s.f. P:* shirt.

liqueur [likœːr], *s.f.* **1.** (*a*) liquor, drink; **liqueurs fortes,** strong drink; *A:* **liqueurs fraîches,** refreshing drinks; *Fr.C:* **l. douce,** soft drink; (*b*) **l. (de dessert),** liqueur; **vin de l.,** dessert wine; **l. de dames,** very sweet liqueur. **2.** *Ch:* liquid, solution; **l. titrée,** standard solution; **l. de Fowler,** Fowler's liquor; **l.-mère,** (i) *Ch:* mother liquid or liquor; (ii) *Atom.Ph:* feed.

liquidable [likidabl], *a.* ready for selling off.

liquidambar [likidɑ̃baːr], *s.m. Bot:* liquidambar; **l. styraciflua,** sweet gum (tree).

liquidateur, -trice [likidatœːr, -tris], *s.* **1.** *Jur:* liquidator. **2.** *Fin:* **l. officiel,** official assignee (on the Stock Exchange).

liquidatif, -ive [likidatif, -iːv], *a. Jur:* pertaining to liquidation; **acte l. de société,** winding-up resolution, order.

liquidation [likidasjɔ̃], *s.f.* **1.** liquidation; (*a*) **l. judiciaire,** winding up (of estate, company, etc.); **faire une l.,** to wind up a business; **entrer en l.,** to go into liquidation; (*b*) clearing (of accounts); *St.Exch:* settlement; **chambre de l.,** (bankers') clearing house; *St.Exch:* **jour de la l.,** account day, settling day; **l. courante, prochaine,** current a/c., next a/c. **2.** *Com:* selling off; clearance sale. **3.** *Soapm:* fitting.

liquide [likid]. **1.** *a.* liquid; (*a*) **poix l.,** liquid pitch; **air l.,** liquid air; (*b*) *Ling:* **consonne l.,** liquid consonant; (*c*) *Fin:* **dette l.,** liquid debt; **argent l.,** ready money, available cash; (*d*) *Lit:* **l'élément l.,** water; **la plaine l.,** the sea. **2.** *s.m.* (*a*) liquid, fluid; **mesures pour les liquides,** fluid measures; **élément à un l.,** single-fluid cell; *Com:* **liquides,** wet goods; *Aut: etc:* **l. pour freins,** brake fluid; **l. réfrigérant,** freezing, refrigerating, liquid; **l. de refroidissement,** coolant; **l. antigel,** antifreeze liquid; **l. antigivrant,** anti-icing fluid; (*b*) *F:* drink (*i.e.* beer, wine, etc.); (*c*) *Med:* **l. pleural,** pleural effusion. **3.** *s.f.* **liquide,** liquid consonant; liquid.

liquidé [likide], *s.m.* insolvent debtor (whose affairs are being settled).

liquider [likide], *v.tr.* **1.** to liquidate; (*a*) to wind up (a business); (*b*) *abs.* to go into liquidation; (*c*) to clear, settle (account); to close (transaction); to settle (a deal); **l. son passé,** to wipe out one's past; *F:* **l. qn,** to liquidate s.o. **2.** to realize (one's fortune, etc.); to sell off (one's stable, etc.); *Com:* **l. des marchandises,** to clear out goods; to have a clearance sale of goods.

se liquider, to clear oneself of debt (**avec qn,** with s.o.).

liquidien, -ienne [likidjɛ̃, -jɛn], *a. Med:* liquid, of a watery nature, consistency; **épanchement l. de la plèvre,** watery pleural effusion.

liquidité [likidite], *s.f.* liquidity; *Fin:* liquidity; *pl.* **liquidités,** liquid assets.

liquoreux, -euse [likɔrø, -øːz], *a.* liqueur-like (wine, etc.); (*wine*) still, sweet and soft; **vapeurs liquoreuses,** dizziness caused by drinking too much alcohol.

liquoriste [likɔrist], *s.m.* wine and spirit merchant.

lire[1] [liːr], *v.tr.* (*pr.p.* **lisant;** *p.p.* **lu;** *pr.ind.* **je lis, il lit;** *p.d.* **je lisais;** *p.h.* **je lus;** *fu.* **je lirai**) to read. **1. l. tout haut, à haute voix,** to read aloud; **l. tout bas, des yeux,** to read to oneself; **apprendre à l.,** to learn to read; **l. une carte,** to map-read; **l. qch. dans un livre,** to read sth. (i) in a book, (ii) (aloud) out of a book; **j'ai lu quelque part que . . .,** I have read somewhere, seen it stated, that . . .; **l. de la musique,** to read music; **l. à vue,** to read (music) at sight; to sight-read; *Typ:* **l. des épreuves,** to proof-read; (*in errata*) **lisez . . .,** read . . .; **ce passage peut être lu différemment,** this passage can be interpreted in different ways; **sur l'anneau se lisent ces paroles . . .,** on the ring one can read these words . . .; **ouvrage qui se laisse l.,** readable book; **l. pour s'endormir,** to read oneself to sleep; **le public qui lit,** the (book-)reading public; **avoir beaucoup lu,** to be well read; **l. dans la pensée de qn, dans la main de qn, dans l'avenir,** to read s.o.'s thoughts, s.o.'s hand, the future; **je lis en lui comme dans un livre ouvert,** I can read him like an open book; **je le lis dans vos yeux,** I can read it in your eyes; **cela se lit sur votre visage,** one can read it on your face; **la peur se lisait sur tous les visages,** fear was written on every face; *Tp:* **un numéro se lit de la façon suivante: 628.08.71, (six cent vingt huit, zéro huit, soixante et onze),** a telephone number must be read, given, as follows: 628.08.71; *Corr:* **dans l'attente de vous l.,** hoping to hear from you; *s.a.* POUCE 1. **2. l. une communication,** to read out, give out, a notice. **3.** *Tex:* to read in, read off (dobbie card).

lire[2], *s.f. Num:* lira.

liriodendron [lirjɔdɛ̃drɔ̃], *s.m. Bot:* liriodendron.

liriope [lirjɔp], *s.m. Bot:* liriope.

liroconite [lirɔkɔnit], *s.f. Miner:* liroconite.

liron [lirɔ̃], *s.m. Z:* lerot, garden dormouse.

lis [lis], *s.m.* (*a*) lily; **l. blanc,** white lily, Madonna lily; **l. orangé,** orange lily; **l. tigré,** tiger lily; **l. du Mexique,** Mexican lily; **l. des marais,** sweet calamus, sweet flag, sweet rush; **l. de Saint-Jacques,** amaryllis belladonna, belladonna lily; **l. des vallées, de mai,** lily of the valley; **l. d'eau, l. des étangs, l. jaune,** yellow pond-lily, water lily; **l. du Japon,** Guernsey lily; **teint de l.,** lily-white complexion; (*b*) *Her:* **fleur de l.** [flœrdəli(s)], fleur-de-lis; *Hist:* **marqué d'une fleur de l.,** (criminal) branded with a fleur-de-lis; (*c*) *A. Num.* lis.

lisable [lizabl], *a.* readable, interesting; **le livre n'est pas l.,** the book is unreadable.

lisage[1] [lizaːʒ], *s.m. Tex:* reading in, off (of dobbie cards).

lisage[2], *s.m. Civ.E:* compaction.

Lisbonne [lizbɔn], *Pr.n.f. Geog:* Lisbon.

lisbonnin, -ine [lizbɔnɛ̃, -in], *a. & s. Geog:* (native, inhabitant) of Lisbon.

lise[1] [liːz], *s.f.* quicksand.

Lise[2], *Pr.n.f. F:* Eliza, Lizzie.

lise[3], *s.m. Tex:* dye stick.

liser [lize], *v.tr. Tex: Dy:* to stir (skeins of silk round on the dye sticks).

liserage [lizraːʒ], *s.m.,* **lisérage** [lizeraːʒ], *s.m.* ornamental edging (round embroidery).

liseré [liz(ə)re], **lisèré** [lizere]. **1.** *a.* (*a*) edged; bordered (handkerchief, flower); (*b*) piped (skirt). **2.** *s.m. Needlew:* (*a*) border, edge, edging (of ribbon, handkerchief); *Phot:* **l. blanc,** white edge, margin (of print); (*b*) piping, binding (of skirt); (*c*) *Mapm:* hatching.

liserer [liz(ə)re], **lisérer** [lizere], *v.tr.* (**je lisère, n. liserons** *or* **n. lisérons; je lisèrerai**) *Needlew:* (*a*) to border, edge; to sew an edging on (sth.); (*b*) to pipe; to trim (sth.) with piping.

liseron [lizrɔ̃], *s.m.,* **liset** [lizɛ], *s.m. Bot:* bindweed, convolvulus; **liseron des champs,** (small) bindweed, field bindweed, wild convolvulus; **l. des haies,** bear's-bind, bearbine; **liseron tricolore,** three-coloured bindweed; **liseron pourpre,** morning glory.

Lisette[1] [lizɛt], *Pr.n.f. F:* Lizzie, Eliza; *Lit:* gay, light-hearted, work girl (of popular songs); *Th:* **jouer les Lisettes,** to take the witty soubrette parts.

lisette[2], *s.f. Ent: eumolpus vitis,* common vine grub.

lisette[3], *s.f.* child's table knife.

liseur, -euse [lizœːr, -øːz]. **1.** (*a*) *a.* given to reading, fond of reading; **le public l.,** the reading public; (*b*) *s.* **c'est un l.,** he is a reading man, a great reader. **2.** *s.* **l. de pensées, d'âmes,** thought-reader; *Tex:* **l. de dessins,** reader in, reader off. **3.** *s.f.* **liseuse,** (*a*) book-marker and paper-knife combined; (*b*) book wrapper, (dust) cover, (dust) jacket; (*c*) book rest, reading stand; (*d*) reading lamp; (*e*) (lady's) bed jacket. **4.** *s.m. Mil: etc:* map holder.

lisibilité [lizibilite], *s.f.* legibility.

lisible [lizibl], *a.* **1.** legible (writing, etc.); **sa lettre n'est pas l.,** his letter is illegible. **2.** readable; worth reading; **cela n'est pas l.,** it's unreadable.

lisiblement [lizibləmɑ̃], *adv.* legibly.

lisier [lizje], *s.m. Sw.Fr:* liquid manure.

lisière [lizjɛːr], *s.f.* **1.** (*a*) selvedge, selvage, list (of cloth); **articles à l.,** knit goods; **chaussons de l.,** list slippers; (*b*) *A:* (child's) leading-strings; **tenir qn en l.,** to keep s.o. in leading-strings; **marcher sans lisières,** to need no guidance, to show initiative. **2.** edge, border (of field); skirt (of forest, etc.).

liskéardite [liskeardit], *s.f. Miner:* liskeardite.

lisoir [lizwaːr], *s.m. Rail: Veh:* bolster, transom; transom frame; *Artil:* pintle transom, pintle frame.

lisotter [lizɔte], *v.tr. O: F:* to read off and on; to glance through (papers, etc.).

lissage[1] [lisaːʒ], *s.m.* smoothing, polishing (of stone, etc.); sleeking (of leather); glazing (of paper, *Exp:* of grains of powder, etc.); burnishing (of metals); (*statistics*) smoothing (of time series, etc.).

lissage[2], *s.m. N.Arch:* **1.** fixing of the rails, ribbands, or strakes (in ship). **2.** *coll:* rails, ribbands.

Lissajous [lisaʒu], *Pr.n. Ph:* **courbes de L.,** Lissajous figures, curves.

lisse[1] [lis], *s.f. N.Arch:* **1.** (*a*) ribband (of the hull); rail, strake; longitudinal girder; **l. de fond,** bottom longitudinal; **l. latérale, de muraille,** side longitudinal; **l. de pont,** deck longitudinal; **lisses de l'avant,** harpings; (*b*) hand-rail (of the bulwarks); **l. de couronnement,** taffrail; (*c*) *Av:* stringer. **2.** *pl.* lines (of ship, as laid down on plan); **lisses de fort, d'ouverture,** breadth lines.

lisse[2], *s.f. Tex:* **1.** heddle. **2.** warp.

lisse[3], **1.** *a.* smooth, glossy, polished; **peau l.,** smooth skin; **cheveux lisses,** sleek hair; *Aut:* **pneu l.,** smooth, bald, tyre; **fusil à canon l., à âme l.,** smoothbore gun; *Anat:* **muscles lisses,** unstriped muscles. **2.** *s.m.* smoothness, polish. **3.** *s.f.* = LISSOIR.

lissé [lise]. **1.** *a.* smooth, polished. **2.** *s.m.* (*a*) smoothness, polish, gloss; (*b*) *Cu:* (*sugar boiling*) **petit l.,** thread stage; **grand l.,** pearl stage.

lisseau, -eaux [liso], *s.m.* ball of thread, of string.

lisser [lise], *v.tr.* to smooth, gloss, polish (stone, etc.); to sleek, slick (leather); to glaze (paper, etc.); to burnish (metal); *Dial: Laund:* to iron; (*of bird*) **se l. les plumes,** to preen its feathers; *Cu:* **l. des amandes,** to sugar almonds; *Civ.E:* **l. le macadam, l'asphalte,** to smooth the asphalt.
se lisser, to become smooth; **se l. par frottement,** to wear smooth.
lisseron [lisrɔ̃], *s.m. N.Arch:* small rail.
lissette [lisɛt], *s.f. Leath: etc:* smoothing iron, plane.
lisseur, -euse [lisœːr, -øːz], *s.* **1.** smoother, polisher, glazer, burnisher. **2.** *s.f.* **lisseuse;** (*a*) *Laund: Dial:* ironer; (*b*) smoothing machine.
lissoir [liswaːr], *s.m. Tls:* smoother, smoothing tool; polishing iron; slick (chisel); sleeker, slicker; **l. à congé,** fillet stick.
lissotriche, -trique [lisɔtrik], *a. Anthr:* lissotrichous, leiotrichous (races).
lissure [lisyːr], *s.f.* smoothing, polishing, glazing, sleeking.
listage [listaːʒ], *s.m. Adm: Elcs:* (*computers*) listing; **bande de l.,** listing tape (of computer).
liste[1] [list], *s.f.* list, roll, register; *Mil:* roster; *Nau:* **l. d'embarquement,** ship's book; **son nom se trouve sur la l.,** his name is in the list, on the roll; **l. officielle de taux,** schedule of charges; **listes électorales,** register (of voters); **la l. civile,** the Civil List; **l. du jury,** panel of jury; **l. noire,** black list; **l. d'envoi, des abonnés,** mailing list; **l. de mariage,** wedding list; **l. de contrôle, l. de vérification,** check list; (*for computer*) **l. d'assemblage,** assembly list; **l. directe,** pop-up, push-up, list; **l. refoulée,** push-down list; **dresser, faire, une l.,** to draw up a list; *Jur:* **dresser la l. du jury,** to empanel a jury; **grossir la l.,** to swell the numbers; **venir en tête de l. (dans une élection),** to head the poll; *s.a.* SCRUTIN 1.
liste[2], *s.f.* (*of horse*) list.
listeau, -eaux [listo], *s.m.*, **listel, -eaux** [listɛl, -o], *s.m.*, **liston** [listɔ̃], *s.m.* **1.** (*a*) *Arch: etc:* listel, fillet, plain moulding; stria (between flutings); (*b*) *Carp:* batten. **2.** (*a*) *Num:* rim, edge-ring (of coin); (*b*) *Her:* scroll. **3.** *N.Arch:* (*a*) sheer-rail; (*b*) rubbing strake.
lister [liste], *v.tr.* (*of computers, etc.*) to list.
listeuse [listøːz], *s.f.* lister (of computer).
lit [li], *s.m.* **1.** bed; (*a*) **l. pour une personne,** single bed; **l. pour deux personnes, grand l.,** double bed; **lits jumeaux,** twin beds; **l. clos,** box bed; **l. de camp,** (i) camp bed; (ii) plank bed; **l. de sangle,** camp bed, trestle bed; **l. pliant, escamotable,** folding bed; **lits superposés,** bunks; **l. à colonnes,** four-poster; **l. de coin,** bed specially built to be put in the corner of a room; **l. de milieu,** ordinary bed, as opposed to *lit de coin*; **l. d'ami,** spare bed; **l. d'enfant, à galerie,** crib, cot; **l. de repos,** couch, day bed, rest bed, divan; **mettre un enfant au l.,** to put a child to bed; **se mettre au l.,** to get into bed; **prendre qn au saut du l., au sortir du l.,** to pay a visit to s.o. in the early hours of the morning; **prendre le l.,** to go to bed (on account of illness); to take to one's bed; **être au l., garder le l.,** to be, stay, in bed (*usu.* through illness); to be laid up; **cloué au l.,** bedridden; **sauter à bas du l.,** to jump, to spring, out of bed; **faire les lits,** to make the beds; **faire l. à part,** to sleep apart; **chambre à un l., à deux lits,** single-, double-bedded room; **leur dortoir était une mansarde à trois lits,** their dormitory was a three-bed attic; **le l. conjugal, matrimonial,** the marriage bed; **enfant du second l.,** child of the second bed, of the second marriage; **enfant d'un autre l.,** stepchild; **être sur son l. de mort,** to be on one's death bed; **mourir dans son l.,** to die of natural causes; **aveu fait au l. de mort,** death-bed confession; **l. de douleur,** bed of sickness; *Prov:* **comme on fait son l., on se couche,** as you make your bed so you must lie on it; *s.a.* PARADE[1] 3; (*b*) **bois de l.,** bedstead; **l. de fer,** iron bedstead. **2.** (*a*) **l. de plume,** (i) feather bed; (ii) *F:* comfortable situation, cushy job; *Fr.Hist:* **l. de justice,** *lit de justice,* bed of justice; (*b*) *Ven:* (stag's) harbour, lair; (hare's) form. **3.** (*a*) bed, layer (of mortar, clay, planks, etc.); *Hyd.E:* **l. de filtrage,** filter-bed; *Mch: etc:* **l. de pose,** seating (of engine, etc.); *Metall:* **l. de fusion,** burden, charge; (*b*) bed (of river, etc.); **l. majeur (d'un fleuve),** flood plain; *Hyd:* **l. majeur, mineur,** high-water, mean-water, bed. **4.** (*a*) set (of the tide, etc.); **être dans le l. de la marée,** to be in the tideway; *Nau:* **dans le l. du vent,** in the wind's eye; **s'effacer dans le l. du vent,** to come up into the wind; (*b*) (*in quarrying, etc.*) **l. de la pierre,** (i) cleaving-grain of the stone; (ii) lie of the stone.
litanie [litani], *s.f.* (*a*) *pl.* litany; **litanies de la Sainte Vierge,** litany of the Blessed Virgin; (*b*) *sg. F:* rigmarole, rambling story; long list of complaints; **réciter toujours la même l.,** to harp, keep harping, upon one string.
lit-armoire [liarmwaːr], *s.m.* box bed; *pl. lits-armoires.*
lit-cage [likaːʒ], *s.m.* folding bedstead; *F: Av:* **l.-c. volant,** flying bedstead; *pl. lits-cages.*
lit-canapé [likanape], *s.m.* bed settee, settee bed; *pl. lits-canapés.*
litchi, li-tchi [litʃi], *s.m. Bot:* litchi; **l. chevelu,** rambutan.
lit-divan [lidivɑ̃], *s.m.* divan (bed); *pl. lits-divans.*
liteau[1], **-eaux** [lito], *s.m.* **1.** *Const:* batten, rail, ribband. **2.** *Tex:* (coloured) band, stripe (on table linen, etc.).
liteau[2], *s.m. Ven:* haunt (of wolves during the day).
litée [lite], *s.f.* litter (of animals).
liter [lite], *v.tr.* **1.** to put (herrings, etc.) into layers in a barrel. **2.** to furnish (wall) with a rail (to support shelf, etc.).
literie [litri], *s.f.* bedding; bed linen.
lit-fauteuil [lifotœːj], *s.m.* chair bed; *pl. lits-fauteuils.*
litham [litam], *s.m. Cost:* litham.
litharge [litarʒ], *s.f. Ch: Ind:* litharge.
lithargé [litarʒe], **lithargyré** [litarʒire], *a. A:* (alcohol, wine, etc.) containing litharge.
lithectomie [litɛktɔmi], *s.f. Surg:* lithectomy.
lithergol [litɛrgɔl], *s.m.* rocket propellant.
lithiase [litjɑːz], *s.f.*, **lithiasie** [litjɑzi], *s.f. Med:* lithiasis.
lithiasique [litjɑzik], *Med:* **1.** *a.* relative to lithiasis. **2.** *a. & s.* (patient) suffering from lithiasis.
lithidionite [litidjɔnit], *s.f. Miner:* lithidionite.
lithié [litje], *a. Ch:* containing lithium.
lithine [litin], *s.f. Ch:* lithia.
lithiné [litine], *a.* containing lithia; **eau lithinée,** lithia water.
lithinifère [litinifɛːr], *a. Ch:* containing lithia.
lithiophilite [litjɔfilit], *s.f. Miner:* lithiophilite.
lithiophorite [litjɔfɔrit], *s.f. Miner:* lithiophorite.
lithium [litjɔm], *s.m. Ch:* lithium.
litho- [litɔ], *pref.* litho-.
litho [lito], *s.f. F:* litho(graphy).
lithobie [litɔbi], *s.f. Myr:* lithobius.
lithochromatographie [litɔkrɔmatɔgrafi], *s.f.* chromolithography.
lithochromatographique [litɔkrɔmatɔgrafik], *a.* chromolithographic.
lithoclase [litɔklɑːz], *s.f. Geol:* crack (in the earth's surface); rock fracture.
lithocolle [litɔkɔl], *s.f.* (diamond-cutter's) cement.
lithocrâne [litɔkrɑːn], *s.m. Z: lithocranius walleri,* gerenuk.
lithodome [litɔdɔm], *s.m. Moll:* lithophaga, lithodomus.
lithogène [litɔʒɛn], *a. Geol: Med: Nat.Hist:* lithogenous.
lithogénèse [litɔʒenɛːz], *s.f. Geol:* lithogenesis.
lithogénie [litɔʒeni], *s.f. Med:* lithogenesis.
lithoglyphie [litɔglifi], *s.f.* lithoglyptics, engraving on stones.
lithographe [litɔgraf], *s.m.* lithographer; **imprimeur l.,** lithographic printer.
lithographie [litɔgrafi], *s.f.* **1.** lithography. **2.** lithograph. **3.** lithographic printing works.
lithographier [litɔgrafje], *v.tr.* (*p.d. & pr.sub.* **n. lithographiions, v. lithographiiez**) to lithograph.
lithographique [litɔgrafik], *a.* lithographic; **crayon l.,** lithographic crayon; **calcaire l.,** lithographic limestone; **machine l. plate,** flat-bed litho machine; **machine rotative l. directe,** direct rotary machine.
lithoïde [litɔid], *a. Nat.Hist:* lithoid(al).
lithologie [litɔlɔʒi], *s.f. Geol: Med:* lithology.
lithologique [litɔlɔʒik], *a. Geol:* lithological.
lithomarge [litɔmarʒ], *s.f. Miner:* lithomarge.
lithopédion [litɔpedjɔ̃], *s.m. Obst:* lithop(a)edion.
lithophage [litɔfaːʒ], *a. Z:* lithophagous (molluscs).
lithophanie [litɔfani], *s.f. Cer:* lithophane.
lithophile [litɔfil], *a. Bot:* lithophilous.
lithophyse [litɔfiːz], *s.f. Miner:* lithophysa.
lithophyte [litɔfit], *s.m. Coel:* lithophyte.
lithopone [litɔpɔn], *s.m. Ind:* lithopone.
lithosides [litɔzid], *s.m.pl. Ent:* Lithosiidae, the lithosiid moths.
lithosie [litɔzi], *s.f. Ent:* lithosia.
lithosol [litɔsɔl], *s.m. Geol:* lithosol.
lithospermum [litɔspɛrmɔm], *s.m. Bot:* lithospermum.
lithosphère [litɔsfɛːr], *s.f. Geol:* lithosphere.
lithothamnion [litɔtamniɔ̃], *s.m. Algae:* lithothamnion.
lithotome [litɔtɔm, -toːm], *s.m. Surg:* lithotome, cystotome.
lithotomie [litɔtɔmi], *s.f. Surg:* lithotomy; operation for stone; *Lap:* the cutting of precious stones.
lithotriteur [litɔtritœːr], *s.m. Surg:* lithotriptor, lithotrite.
lithotritie [litɔtrisi], *s.f. Surg:* lithotrity.
lithotypographie [litɔtipɔgrafi], *s.f. Typ:* lithotypy.
lithoxyle [litɔksil], *s.m. Miner:* lithoxyl(e), lithoxylite, petrified wood.
Lithuanie [litɥani], *Pr.n.f. Geog:* Lithuania.
lithuanien, -ienne [litɥanjɛ̃, -jɛn], *a. & s. Geog:* Lithuanian.
litière [litjɛːr], *s.f.* **1.** (stable) litter; **l. de feuilles,** leaf litter; **faire la l. d'un cheval,** to bed down, litter down, a horse; **cheval sur la l.,** sick horse; **faire l. de l'honneur de qn,** to trample s.o.'s reputation under foot; **faire l. de certaines conventions,** to throw certain conventions to the winds. **2.** litter, palanquin; **être porté en l.,** to be carried in a litter.
litigant [litigɑ̃], *a. Jur: A:* litigant (party).
litige [litiːʒ], *s.m.* litigation; dispute at law; suit; **objet du l., en l.,** (i) subject of the action; (ii) bone of contention; **cas en l.,** case at issue, under dispute, in question, in litigation; **la frontière en l.,** the debatable frontier; **matière à l.,** issuable matter.
litigieux, -euse [litiʒjø, -øːz], *a.* litigious; (*a*) disputable at law; (*b*) contentious (spirit, etc.).
litispendance [litispɑ̃dɑ̃ːs], *s.f. Jur: A:* pendency (of case).
litopternes [litɔptɛrn], *s.m.pl. Z:* litopterna.
litorne [litɔrn], *s.f. Orn:* fieldfare.
litote [litɔt], *s.f. Rh:* litotes; understatement.
litre[1] [litr̥], *s.f. Her:* litre (as hatchment); mourning band.
litre[2], *s.m.* (*a*) *Meas:* litre (1000 cubic cm. = about 1¾ pints); **vin au l.,** wine on draught; *Aut:* (*Petrol consumption*) **dix litres aux cent kilomètres** = thirty miles to the gallon; (*b*) litre bottle; (*c*) *P:* a litre of wine.
litron [litrɔ̃], *s.m.* (*a*) *A.Meas:* = 0·813 litres; (*b*) *P:* a litre of wine.
lit-salon [lisalɔ̃], *s.m. Rail:* first-class sleeping car; *pl. lits-salons.*
littéraire [literɛːr]. **1.** *a.* literary; **salon l.,** literary salon; **agent l.,** literary agent; *s.a.* PROPRIÉTÉ 1. **2.** *s.m. & f.* arts man, woman; **c'est plutôt un l.,** his talents are literary (rather than scientific).
littérairement [literɛrmɑ̃], *adv.* literarily.
littéral, -aux [literal, -o], *a.* **1.** literal (translation, etc.); **remarques littérales,** textual notes (on a work); *Alg:* **coefficient l.,** literal coefficient. **2. grec l.,** literary Greek, classical Greek. **3.** *Jur:* **preuve littérale,** evidence in writing, documentary evidence.
littéralement [literalmɑ̃], *adv.* (*a*) literally; **traduire l.,** to make a literal translation; (*b*) *F:* utterly, absolutely; **il m'épouvante l.,** he positively terrifies me.
littéralisme [literalism], *s.m.* literalism (in art, etc.).
littéraliste [literalist], *a.* literalistic.
littéralité [literalite], *s.f.* literality, literalness.
littérarité [literarite], *s.f.* literary value (of book, etc.).
littérateur [literatœːr], *s.m.* literary man, man of letters, littérateur.
littérature [literatyːr], *s.f.* literature; **l. d'imagination,** fiction; **l. d'évasion,** escapist literature; **c'est de la l.,** it's artificial, lacking in depth, insincere.
littéromanie [literɔmani], *s.f.* mania for writing.
Little [litl̥], *Pr.n. Psy:* **maladie de Little,** Little's disease, Little's paralysis.
littoral, -aux [litɔral, -o]. **1.** *a.* littoral, coastal (region, etc.); **la zone littorale (des rivages marins),** the laminarian zone (of coastal waters). **2.** *s.m.* coast line, littoral; **le l. de la France,** the French coast(line), seaboard; **le l. de la Mer Rouge,** the shores of the Red Sea, the Red Sea littoral.
littorine [litɔrin], *s.f. Moll:* Lit(t)orina, *F:* periwinkle.
littorinidés [litɔrinide], *s.m.pl. Moll:* Lit(t)orinidae.
Littre [litr̥], *Pr.n. Anat:* **glandes de L.,** Littre's glands.
littrite [litrit], *s.f. Med:* littreitis, littritis.
Lituanie [litɥani], *Pr.n.f. Geog:* Lithuania.
lituanien, -ienne [litɥanjɛ̃, -jɛn], *a. & s. Geog:* Lithuanian.
lituole [litɥɔl], *s.f. Prot:* lituola.
lituolidés [litɥɔlide], *s.m.pl. Prot:* Lituolidae.
liturge [lityrʒ], *s.m. Gr.Ant:* liturgist.
liturgie [lityrʒi], *s.f. Ecc:* liturgy.

liturgique [lityrʒik], *a.* liturgical.

liturgiste [lityrʒist], *s.m.* liturgist.

liure [ljyːr], *s.f.* **1.** lashing (of load on cart, etc.). **2.** *Nau:* gammoning, frapping; **faire la l., les liures, du beaupré,** to gammon the bowsprit.

livarde [livard], *s.f.* **1.** *Nau:* sprit; **voile à l.,** spritsail. **2.** *Ropem:* (i) thick string used in the process of cable twisting; (ii) soft rope used for rubbing a cable-laid rope to polish it.

livarot [livaro], *s.m.* Livarot cheese (made in Calvados).

livèche [livɛʃ], *s.f. Bot:* common, Italian, lovage.

livedo [livedo], *s.f. Med:* livedo.

liveingite [livɛ̃ʒit], *s.f. Miner:* liveingite.

liverpoolien, -ienne [livɛrpuljɛ̃, -jɛn], *a. & s. Geog:* Liverpudlian.

livet [livɛ], *s.m. N.Arch:* **l. de pont,** beam line, deck line.

livide [livid], *a.* (*a*) livid; ghastly (pale); *s.m.* **le l. de son teint,** the ghastly pallor of his complexion; (*b*) *A:* blackish blue, leaden.

lividité [lividite], *s.f.* lividity, lividness; ghastliness; *Med:* **lividités cadavériques,** livor mortis, cadaveric lividity, post-mortem lividity.

Livie [livi], *Pr.n.f. Rom.Hist:* Livia.

living(-room) [liviŋ(rum)], *s.m.* living room.

livingstonite [liviŋstɔnit], *s.f. Miner:* livingston(e)ite.

livistona [livistɔna], *s.m. Bot:* livistona, Chinese fan-palm.

livon [livɔ̃], *s.m. Hyd.E:* waste weir.

Livonie [livɔni], *Pr.n.f. Hist:* Livonia.

livonien, -ienne [livɔnjɛ̃, -jɛn], *a. & s. Hist:* Livonian.

livournais, -aise [livurnɛ, -ɛːz], **livournien, -ienne** [livurnjɛ̃, -jɛn], *a. & s. Geog:* (native, inhabitant) of Leghorn.

Livourne [livurn], *Pr.n. Geog:* Leghorn.

livrable [livrabl̩], *a.* (*a*) *Com: Fin:* deliverable; (*b*) *Com:* ready for delivery.

livraison [livrɛzɔ̃], *s.f.* **1.** delivery (of goods, shares, etc.); **l. franco,** free delivery, delivered free; **payable à l.,** payable on delivery; **l. contre espèces,** cash on delivery; **payer sur l.,** to pay on delivery; **faire l. de qch.,** to deliver sth.; **prendre l. de qch.,** to take delivery of sth.; **défaut de l.,** non-delivery; **voiture de l.,** delivery van; *P.N: Com:* **l. à domicile,** goods delivered at any address, we deliver; **conditions de l.,** delivery terms; *Nau:* **l. sous palan,** overside delivery; *Fin:* **livraisons à terme,** future deliveries, futures. **2.** part, instalment (of book published in parts); **prendre un ouvrage par livraisons,** to take a work in parts.

livrancier [livrɑ̃sje], *s.m.* **1.** deliverer (of goods, shares, etc.). **2.** contractor for supplies.

livre[1] [liːvr̥], *s.f.* pound. **1.** (*weight*) **vendre qch. à la l.,** to sell sth. by the pound; *A:* **canon lançant un projectile de douze livres,** twelve-pounder. **2.** (*money*) (*a*) **l. sterling,** pound sterling; (*b*) *A:* (= FRANC); **dix mille livres de rente,** private income of ten thousand francs a year; *A:* **l. tournois,** franc (minted at Tours) of 20 sous; **l. parisis,** franc (minted at Paris) of 25 sous.

livre[2], *s.m.* book; (*a*) **l'industrie du l.,** the book trade; *Publ:* **livres de fonds,** books belonging to the publisher's goodwill; **l. en feuilles,** book in sheets, in quires; **l. relié,** bound book; **l. de classe,** school book; **l. de prix,** prize book; **l. d'images,** picture book; **livres pour la jeunesse,** books for young people, *Com:* juveniles; *Sch:* **l. de lecture,** reader; **l. à succès, à fort tirage, à forte vente,** best-seller; *Pol:* **l. blanc, jaune** = Blue Book; **l. de poche,** (i) pocket book; (ii) paperback; **livres d'église,** church books; sacred books; *F:* **parler comme un l.,** to talk like a book; **traduire un passage, jouer un morceau, à l. ouvert,** to translate a passage, play a piece, at sight; **après cela il faut fermer le l.,** after that there is nothing more to be said; (*b*) *A:* **l. de raison,** (i) record book, register (of a district); (ii) family record book = family Bible; **l. d'or,** visitors' book; **l. de bord,** (i) *Nau:* ship's book, ship's register, (ii) *Av:* flight log book; (*c*) **l. de comptabilité,** account book; **l. de paie,** wage book; *Com:* **l. journal,** journal, day book; **tenir les livres,** to keep the accounts; **tenue des livres,** book-keeping; **teneur de livres,** book-keeper; *Turf:* **l. de paris,** betting book; **faire un l.,** to make a book; (*d*) book (of work divided into books); **les livres de l'Ancien Testament,** the books of the Old Testament.

livrée [livre], *s.f.* **1.** (*a*) livery; **grande l.,** full livery; **valet en l.,** servant in livery, liveried servant, livery servant; **sans l.,** out of livery; **porter la l.,** to be a liveried servant, a lackey; **porter la l. de qn,** (i) to be in s.o.'s service, (ii) *F:* to be a follower of s.o.; (*b*) *coll. A:* the servants, domestics; the livery. **2.** *Ven:* coat (of horse, deer, etc.); plumage (of certain birds); colour pattern (of insect). **3.** *Ent: F:* lackey moth.

livre-journal [livr(ə)ʒurnal], *s.m. Adm: Com:* journal, day book; *pl. livres-journaux.*

livrer [livre], *v.tr.* **1.** (*a*) to deliver, surrender; to give (s.o., sth.) up; **l. une ville aux assiégeants,** to surrender a town to the besiegers; **l. qn aux mains de l'ennemi,** to deliver s.o. into the hands of the enemy; **l. qn à la justice,** to deliver, hand over, s.o. to justice; **l. qn à la mort,** to consign s.o. to the scaffold; **l. un corps à la tombe,** to commit a body to the grave; **livré à l'oubli,** consigned to oblivion; **livré à soi-même,** left to oneself; **l. un canot au courant,** to let a boat drift with the current; **l. un poste à l'ennemi,** to give up a post to the enemy; **l. un secret,** to betray a secret; **l. ses secrets à qn,** to confide one's secrets to s.o.; **des pâturages livrés à la charrue,** grassland put under the plough; **ce coup leur livra le village,** this move put them in possession of the village; **l. passage (à),** to leave the way open (to); *Ven:* **l. le cerf aux chiens,** to lay the hounds on the stag; (*b*) **l. un assaut à l'ennemi,** to deliver an attack on the enemy; **l. bataille (à, with);** to join battle (à, with); to give battle (à, to); **la lutte qui se livre dans son cœur,** the struggle taking place within his heart; **après avoir livré trois batailles . . .,** after fighting three battles . . .; **l. bataille pour qn,** to take up the cudgels on s.o.'s behalf, to take up s.o.'s cause. **2.** to deliver (goods, etc.); **on livre le pain dans la matinée,** the bread is brought round in the (course of the) morning; *St.Exch:* **vente à l.,** sale for delivery; time-bargain; *v.i. F: Com:* **si vous voulez être livré,** if you want goods delivered (to you); *Com:* **livré avec batterie,** complete with battery.

se livrer. **1. se l. à la justice,** to surrender to justice; to give oneself up; **se l. à qn,** to confide in s.o.; to put oneself in s.o.'s hands. **2.** (*a*) **se l. à un vice,** to indulge in, surrender to, a vice; **se l. à la boisson,** (i) to take to drink; (ii) to be a heavy drinker; **livré à la boisson,** addicted to drink; **se l. à la joie,** to give oneself up to rejoicing; **se l. au désespoir,** to give way to despair; **se l. à des excès,** to break out (into excesses); **se l. à l'étude, à une profession,** to devote oneself to study, to a profession; **se l. à un trafic,** to traffic in sth.; **se l. à de longs calculs,** to plunge (oneself) into long calculations; **se l. à une enquête,** to hold an inquiry; (*b*) (*of woman*) to surrender to a man. **3.** to reveal oneself, one's ideas, etc.; **c'est la pièce où l'auteur s'est le plus livré,** this is the play in which the author has revealed himself most fully.

livresque [livrɛsk], *a.* (*a*) acquired from books; **science l., connaissances livresques,** book learning; (*b*) **esprit l.,** bookish mind.

livret [livrɛ], *s.m.* **1.** small book, booklet; *Rail:* (local) timetable; **l. d'un musée,** handbook of, guide to, a museum; **l. de banque,** pass-book; **l. de Caisse d'Épargne,** savings-bank book; *Adm:* **l. de famille,** booklet delivered by mayor to married couple, for registration of births and deaths; *Mil: Navy:* **l. matricule,** conduct book; (soldier's) record; service certificate; **l. individuel, militaire,** service record; *Sch:* **l. scolaire,** school record; *Av: etc:* **l. moteur,** engine log book. **2.** *Mus:* libretto, book (of opera). **3.** fold (in the third stomach of a ruminant).

livret-police [livrɛpɔlis], *s.m. Ins:* policy (in book form); *pl. livrets-polices.*

livret-portefeuille [livrɛpɔrtəfœːj], *s.m.* savings-bank book; *pl. livrets-portefeuilles.*

livreur, -euse [livrœːr, -øːz]. **1.** *s.* (*a*) deliveryman; roundsman; (*b*) carman, van driver. **2.** *s.f.* **livreuse,** delivery van.

lixiviable [liksivjabl̩], *a. Atom.Ph: etc:* leachable.

lixiviation [liksivjasjɔ̃], *s.f.* lixiviation; leaching; percolation; **extraire par l.,** to leach out.

lixivier [liksivje], *v.tr.* to lixiviate; to leach.

llano [ljano], *s.m. Geog:* llano, (South American) savanna(h).

lloyd [lɔjd], *s.m. M.Ins:* (*a*) (any) association of marine brokers and underwriters; (*b*) **le Lloyd('s) anglais,** Lloyd's.

loader [lodœːr], *s.m. Const:* (mechanical) loader.

loa-loa [loaloa], *s.m. Ann:* loa.

lob [lɔb], *s.m. Ten:* lob.

lobaire [lɔbɛːr], *a. Nat.Hist:* lobate; lobar.

lobby [lɔbi], *s.m. Pol: etc:* lobby; **ils représentent un l. puissant,** they constitute a powerful lobby, pressure group; *pl. lobbies.*

lobe [lɔb], *s.m.* **1.** lobe (of ear, liver, leaf, etc.); flap (of ear). **2.** *Arch:* foil.

lobé [lɔbe], *a.* (*a*) *Nat.Hist:* lobed, lobate (leaf, etc.); (*b*) *P:* good-looking.

lobectomie [lɔbɛktɔmi], *s.f. Surg:* lobectomy.

lobéliacées [lɔbeljase], *s.f.pl. Bot:* Lobeliaceae, the lobelia family.

lobélie [lɔbeli], *s.f. Bot:* lobelia.

lobéline [lɔbelin], *s.f. Pharm:* lobeline.

lober [lɔbe], *v.tr. Ten: Fb:* **1.** to lob (ball). **2.** to play a lob against (one's opponent); **se faire l.,** (to allow one's return) to be lobbed.

lobiole [lɔbjɔl], *s.f. Bot:* lobiole.

lobiophase [lɔbjɔfaːz], *s.m. Orn:* Bulwer's pheasant.

lobipède [lɔbipɛd], *s.m. Orn:* lobefoot, lobiped, northern phalarope.

lobite [lɔbit], *s.f. Med:* lobitis.

lobopode [lɔbɔpɔd], *s.m. Biol:* lobopodium, lobopod.

lobosa [lɔbɔza], *s.m.pl. Prot:* lobosa.

lobotomie [lɔbɔtɔmi], *s.f. Surg:* lobotomy; leucotomy.

lobulaire [lɔbylɛːr], *a.* lobular.

lobule [lɔbyl], *s.m. Anat:* lobule; *Bot:* lobelet.

lobulé [lɔbyle], **lobuleux, -euse** [lɔbylø, -øːz], *a.* lobulate, lobulous.

lob-volée [lɔbvɔle], *s.m. Ten:* lob volley; *pl. lobs-volées.*

local, -aux [lɔkal, -o]. **1.** *a.* local (authority, etc.); *Med:* local, topical (disease, remedy); **anesthésie locale,** local anaesthetic; **bonne mémoire locale,** gift of locality; **couleur locale,** local colour; *Rail:* **ligne d'intérêt l.,** branch line, local line. **2.** *s.m.* (*a*) premises; building; room; **locaux insalubres,** insanitary buildings; buildings unfit for human habitation; **l. d'habitation,** dwelling; residential unit; *Adm:* accommodation unit; **locaux commerciaux,** business premises; **vaste l. pour le commerce,** large business premises; **l. professionnel,** premises used for professional purposes; **taxe sur les locaux loués meublés,** tax on property rented furnished; (*b*) *Nau:* **locaux affectés au personnel du bord,** crew's quarters; *Mil:* **locaux disciplinaires,** guard house; (*c*) *Fb:* **les locaux,** the home side; **les arrières locaux,** the home backs; (*d*) *Fr.C: Tp:* extension.

localement [lɔkalmɑ̃], *adv.* locally.

localisateur [lɔkalizatœːr], *s.m.* **1.** *X Rays:* localizing apparatus. **2.** *Tchn: Petroleum Ind:* locator; **l. de canalisations en place,** electronic pipe locator, underground line locator.

localisation [lɔkalizasjɔ̃], *s.f.* **1.** localization; *Med:* **l. cérébrale,** cerebral localization; *Biol:* **localisations germinales,** embryological, germinal, localizations. **2.** *Psy:* locality.

localiser [lɔkalize], *v.tr.* **1.** to localize (epidemic, conflagration, etc.). **2.** to locate, to pin-point (hidden artillery, leak, etc.). **3.** to position, to place in position.

se localiser. **1.** to fix one's residence, settle down (in a place). **2.** (*of disease, etc.*) to become localized.

localisme [lɔkalism], *s.m.* localism.

localité [lɔkalite], *s.f.* (*a*) locality, place, spot; **l. malsaine,** unwholesome district, spot; (*b*) *Paint:* local touch.

locataire [lɔkatɛːr], *s.m. & f.* **1.** tenant, occupier (of property); *Jur:* lessee, leaseholder. **2.** lodger. **3.** hirer, renter (of equipment, etc.). **4.** *Ent: lepinotus inquilinus.*

locateur, -trice [lɔkatœːr, -tris], *s.* lessor.

locatif[1], **-ive** [lɔkatif, -iːv], *a.* **1.** concerning the renting or letting of premises; **valeur locative,** rental (value); **impôts locatifs** = rates; **prix l.,** rent; **réparations locatives,** repairs incumbent upon the tenant; **risques locatifs,** tenant's risks. **2. appartement l.,** rented flat.

locatif[2], **-ive,** *a. & s.m. Gram:* locative (case).

location [lɔkasjɔ̃], *s.f.* (*a*) (i) hiring; (ii) letting out on hire (of boat, etc.); **donner qch. en l.,** to hire sth. out, to let sth. out on hire; **prendre qch. en l.,** to hire sth., to take sth. on hire, to rent sth.; **l. de voitures sans chauffeur,** self-drive cars for hire; (*b*) (i) renting, tenancy; (ii) letting (of house, etc.); *Jur:* location; **agent de l.,** house agent; **(prix de) l.,** rent; **faire une l. à Paris pour un mois,** to take a flat, etc. in Paris for a month; (*c*) *Th: etc:* booking (of seats); **(bureau de) l.,** box office, booking office; **la l. est ouverte de dix heures à huit heures,** seats can be booked from ten to eight; (*d*) *P.N:* **l. de livres,** books on loan; lending library.

location-vente [lɔkasjɔ̃vɑ̃ːt], *s.f.* (type of) hire purchase; *pl. locations-ventes.*

locatis [lɔkati], *s.m. A: F:* **1.** (*a*) hack, hired horse; (*b*) hired vehicle. **2.** furnished room; apartments, *F:* diggings, digs.

locator [lɔkatɔːr], *s.m. Tchn:* locator.

locelle [lɔsɛl], *s.f. Bot:* locellus.

loch [lɔk], *s.m. Nau:* (ship's) log; **l. à main,** hand log; **l. enregistreur, à hélice,** patent log; **ligne de l.,** log line; **touret de l.,** log reel; **bateau de l.,** log ship; **jeter, filer, le l.,** to heave, to stream, the log; **livre de l.,** log.

lochague [lɔʃag], *s.m. Gr.Ant:* lochage.

loche [lɔʃ], *s.f.* **1.** *Ich:* loach; **l. franche,** common loach; **l. épineuse, de rivière,** spined loach, groundling; **l. de mer,** rockling; **l. d'étang,** thunder fish, weather fish. **2.** *Moll:* grey slug.

locher [lɔʃe]. **1.** *v.i. F:* (*of horseshoe*) to be loose; *F:* **il y a quelque fer qui loche,** there's something wrong somewhere, a screw loose somewhere; **il a toujours quelque fer qui loche,** he always has some little trouble. **2.** *v.tr. Dial:* to shake (fruit tree, etc.). **3.** *v.tr. Fish:* to fix (live bait on to a hook).

lochial, -aux [lɔʃjal, -o], *a.* (*rare*) *Obst:* lochial.

lochies [lɔʃi], *s.f.pl. Obst:* lochia, cleansings.

lochomètre [lɔkɔmɛtr], *s.m. Nau:* logometer.

lochos, lokhos [lɔkɔs], *s.m. Gr.Ant:* lochus.

lockisme [lɔkism], *s.m. Phil:* Lockeanism, Lockianism.

lockiste [lɔkist], *s. Phil:* Lockean, Lockian.

lock-out [lɔk(a)ut], *s.m.inv. Ind:* lockout.

lock(-)outer [lɔk(a)ute], *v.tr. Ind:* to lock out (the personnel).

locman [lɔkmɑ̃], *s.m. Nau:* river pilot; harbour pilot; inshore pilot; branch pilot.

loco¹ [loko], *adv. Com:* loco; **prix l.,** loco price.

loco² [loko], *s.f. F:* (= LOCOMOTIVE) engine.

locobatteuse [lɔkɔbatøːz], *s.f. A: Agr:* steam-thresher.

locomobile [lɔkɔmɔbil]. **1.** *a.* capable of being moved from place to place; locomotive; **grue l.,** travelling crane. **2.** *s.f.* (transportable) steam-engine.

locomoteur, -trice [lɔkɔmɔtœːr, -tris]. **1.** *a.* locomotor(y) (organ, etc.); *Med:* **ataxie locomotrice progressive,** locomotor ataxia, ataxy. **2.** *s.m.* locomotor. **3.** *s.f. Rail:* **locomotrice,** electric engine.

locomotif, -ive [lɔkɔmɔtif, -iːv]. **1.** *a.* (*a*) *A:* transportable (engine, etc.); (*b*) locomotive, self-propelling; **grue locomotive,** travelling crane; (*c*) *Physiol:* locomotive (organs, faculty); **troubles locomotifs,** disorder affecting the locomotory organs, locomotor disorder. **2.** *s.f.* **locomotive,** (*a*) *Rail:* locomotive, engine; **locomotive tender,** tank engine; **train avec deux locomotives en tête,** double-headed train; **locomotive (à moteur) diesel-électrique,** diesel-electric locomotive; (*b*) **locomotive routière,** traction engine.

locomotion [lɔkɔmosjɔ̃], *s.f.* locomotion; **de quels moyens de l. disposez-vous?** what means of transport have you?

locomotivité [lɔkɔmɔtivite], *s.f. Physiol:* locomotivity.

locotracteur [lɔkɔtraktœːr], *s.m.* light railway motor tractor; power trolley.

Locres [lɔkr], *Pr.n. A.Geog:* Locri Epizephyrii.

Locride [lɔkrid], *Pr.n.f. A.Geog:* Locris.

locrien, -ienne [lɔkrijɛ̃, -jɛn], *a. & s. A.Geog:* Locrian.

loculaire [lɔkylɛːr], *a. Bot:* locular.

locule [lɔkyl], *s.f. A: Nat.Hist:* loculus.

loculé [lɔkyle], **loculeux, -euse** [lɔkylø, -øːz], *a. Bot:* loculate(d); loculose.

loculicide [lɔkylisid], *a. Bot:* loculicidal (dehiscence, etc.).

locus [lɔkyːs], *s.m. Biol:* locus (of a chromosome).

locuste [lɔkyst], *s.f. Ent:* locust.

locustelle [lɔkystɛl], *s.f. Orn:* **l. tachetée,** grasshopper warbler; **l. fluviatile,** river warbler; **l. luscinioïde,** Savi's warbler; **l. fasciée,** Gray's grasshopper warbler; **l. lancéolée,** lanceolated, Temminck's, grasshopper warbler; **l. de Pallas,** Pallas's grasshopper warbler.

locuteur, -trice [lɔkytœːr, -tris], *s. Ling:* speaker.

locution [lɔkysjɔ̃], *s.f.* expression, phrase; **l. vicieuse,** incorrect, faulty, expression; *Gram:* **l. adverbiale, prépositive,** adverbial, prepositional, phrase.

loddigésie [lɔdiʒezi], *s.m. Orn:* loddigesia.

loden [lɔdɛn], *s.m. Tex:* loden cloth.

lodévois, -oise [lɔdevwa, -waːz], *a. & s. Geog:* (native, inhabitant) of Lodève.

lodicule [lɔdikyl], *s.f. Bot:* lodicule, lodicula (of grass flower).

lodier [lɔdje], *s.m. A:* (*a*) quilt; (*b*) *A.Cost:* loosely fitting surcoat.

lods [lo], *s.m. A.Jur:* permission, authorization.

lœllingite [lølɛ̃ʒit], *s.f. Miner:* loellingite, löllingite.

lœss [løs], *s.m. Geol:* loess.

lœwéite [løveit], *s.f. Miner:* loeweite.

lof [lɔf], *s.m. Nau:* **1.** windward side (of ship); **venir, aller, au l.,** to sail into the wind; **revenir au l.,** (i) to come back into the wind, (ii) *F:* to give in, to knuckle under; **virer l. pour l.,** to wear. **2.** (*a*) luff, weather-leech (of sail); (*b*) *pl.* tacks and sheets (of sail).

lof(f)er [lɔfe], *v.i. Nau:* to luff; **lofe tout!** hard a-lee!

log [lɔg], *s.m.* **1.** *Mth: F:* log. **2.** *Petroleum Ind:* log.

loganiacées [lɔganjase], *s.f.pl. Bot:* Loganiaceae.

logarithme [lɔgaritm], *s.m.* logarithm; **l. dans la base *e* d'un nombre,** logarithm of a number to the base *e*; **l. décimal, l. vulgaire,** decimal, common, logarithm; **l. naturel, l. népérien,** Napierian logarithm; **l. à cinq décimales,** five-figure, five-place, logarithm; **table de logarithmes,** table of logarithms, *F:* log table.

logarithmique [lɔgaritmik]. **1.** *a.* logarithmic (scale, etc.). **2.** *s.f.* logarithmic (curve).

logate, logathe [lɔgat], *s.f. Cu:* **gigot à la l.,** larded leg of mutton cooked very slowly.

logatome [lɔgatɔm], *s.m. Ac:* logatom.

loge [lɔːʒ], *s.f.* **1.** hut, cabin; (gardener's, porter's, freemasons') lodge; (dog's) kennel; (wild animal's) cage (in menagerie); booth (at fair); (lunatic's, hermit's) cell. **2.** *Th:* (*a*) box; **l. d'avant-scène,** stage box; **première l.,** first-tier box; *F:* **être aux premières loges,** to have a full view (of sth.); to have a front seat; (*b*) **loges des artistes,** artists' dressing-rooms. **3.** *Art: Mus:* **entrer en l. pour le prix de Rome,** to compete for the *Prix de Rome* (each competitor occupying a separate room or cell). **4.** *El.Rail:* (driver's) cabin. **5.** *Arch:* loggia, stanza. **6.** *Bot:* loculus, locule, theca, cell; lith (of orange); *Conch:* chamber; **l. initiale,** first chamber, protoconch; **l. dernière,** body chamber; **coquillage à loges,** chambered shell.

logé [lɔʒe], *a. Com:* non-returnable.

logeabilité [lɔʒabilite], *s.f.* **l. (d'un appartement, d'une voiture),** spaciousness (of a flat, car); habitability.

logeable [lɔʒabl̩], *a.* **1.** (*of house*) tenantable, fit for occupation. **2.** *Aut:* **carrosserie l.,** comfortable body.

logement [lɔʒmɑ̃], *s.m.* **1.** lodging, housing (of people); quartering, billeting (of troops); stabling (of horses, etc.); **le problème du l.,** the housing problem; **la crise du l.,** the housing shortage; *Mil: etc:* **indemnité de l.,** living-out allowance; board-wages. **2.** (*a*) accommodation; lodgings; *F:* digs; **nous manquons de l. pour tant de monde,** we lack accommodation for so many people; **l. garni, meublé,** furnished apartment(s); **misérable l.,** shabby digs, quarters; **prendre l. quelque part,** to go and live, to take rooms, somewhere; **le l. et la nourriture,** board and lodging; **chercher un l. pour la nuit,** to look for a night's lodging; (*b*) self-contained flat, flatlet; (*c*) *Mil:* quarters; (*in private house*) billet; *Nau:* berth; **billet de l.,** billeting order; (*d*) *Mil: A:* **effectuer un l. dans les lignes de l'ennemi,** to effect a lodgment in the enemy lines. **3.** *Com:* packing, container (of goods). **4.** *El.E:* bedding (of cable); *Mec.E:* (i) seating (of machine part); housing (of shaft); well; (ii) recess; **l. de clef,** cotter slot, keyway, spline; **l. de vis,** screw hole.

logement-foyer [lɔʒmɑ̃fwaje], *s.m.* = old people's home; *pl. logements-foyers.*

loger [lɔʒe], *v.* (**je logeai(s); n. logeons**). **1.** *v.i.* to lodge, live; (*of troops*) to be quartered, billeted; **l. à un hôtel,** to put up, stay, at a hotel; **l. en garni,** to be in lodgings; *F:* to live in digs; *s.a.* ENSEIGNE 1; **l. chez l'habitant,** (i) *Mil:* to go into billets; (ii) to have bed and breakfast; **l. à la belle étoile,** to sleep in the open. **2.** *v.tr.* (*a*) to lodge, accommodate, house (s.o.); to quarter, billet (troops); to stable (horses); **l. un ami pour la nuit,** to put up a friend for the night; *A:* (**ici**) **on loge à pied et à cheval,** good accommodation for man and beast; **vin logé,** wine in the wood; (*b*) to place, to put; **l. une balle dans la cible,** to plant a shot on the target; **je ne sais où l. mes livres,** I don't know where to put my books; *Mec.E:* **l. l'arbre dans les paliers,** to set the shaft in its bearings; *El:* **l. les fils,** to bed the wires.

se loger. **1.** (*a*) to go into lodgings; to take lodgings; **nous avons trouvé à nous l.,** we have found accommodation; (*b*) to build a house or to find a suitable house. **2.** (*a*) **mon ballon s'est logé sur le toit,** my ball has stuck on the roof; (*b*) **le soupçon se logea dans son cœur,** suspicion became firmly fixed in his mind; **la balle se logea dans le mur,** the bullet embedded itself in the wall; *A:* **les troupes se logèrent sur le flanc de l'ennemi,** the troops lodged themselves on the enemy's flank.

logette [lɔʒɛt], *s.f.* small lodge, small cell; *Th:* small box.

logeur, -euse [lɔʒœːr, -øːz], *s.* (*a*) landlord, landlady (of furnished apartments); **logeurs et logés,** householders and lodgers; (*b*) owner, manager(-ess) of lodging house; lodging-house keeper; (*c*) **l. de chevaux,** stable keeper; (*d*) occupier on whom soldier is billeted.

loggia [lɔdʒja], *s.f. Arch:* loggia.

logging [lɔgiŋ], *s.m. Petroleum Ind:* logging.

logicien, -ienne [lɔʒisjɛ̃, -jɛn], *s.* logician.

logicisme [lɔʒisism], *s.m. Phil:* logicism.

logiciste [lɔʒisist], *s.* logicist.

logique [lɔʒik]. **1.** *a.* logical; **régime, menu, l.,** reasoned diet, menu; **il est l. qu'il reprenne son bien,** it is only logical that he should take back his own; *Gram:* **analyse l.,** analysis (of sentence); **être l. avec soi-même,** to be consistent. **2.** *s.f.* logic; **en toute, en bonne, l.,** logically.

logiquement [lɔʒikmɑ̃], *adv.* logically.

logis [lɔʒi], *s.m.* (*a*) home, house, dwelling; **garder le l.,** to stay in; to stay at home; **être confiné au l.,** to be confined to the house; **l. déserté par la mère,** home deserted by the mother; **corps de l.,** main (portion of) building; *s.a.* FOU 2; (*b*) (temporary) lodgings; *A:* **bon l. à pied et à cheval,** good accommodation for man and beast; *s.a.* MARÉCHAL 3; (*c*) inn.

logiste [lɔʒist], *s.m. Art: Mus:* competitor for the *Prix de Rome*; *cf.* LOGE 3.

logisticien, -ienne [lɔʒistisjɛ̃, -jɛn], *s. Phil:* logistician.

logistique [lɔʒistik]. **1.** *a.* logistic. **2.** *s.f.* (i) *Mil: etc:* logistics; (ii) *Phil:* logistic.

logoclonie [lɔgɔklɔni], *s.f. Psy:* logoclonia.

logographe [lɔgɔgraf], *s.m.* **1.** *Gr.Ant:* logographer. **2.** *A.Ac:* a forerunner of the oscillograph.

logogriphe [lɔgɔgrif], *s.m.* logogriph; word puzzle.

logomachie [lɔgɔmaʃi], *s.f.* logomachy, battle of words.

logomachique [lɔgɔmaʃik], *a.* logomachic(al).

logopédie [lɔgɔpedi], *s.f.* logopedics.

logorrhée [lɔgɔre], *s.f. Med:* logorrhea, logomania.

logos [lɔgɔs], *s.m. Theol:* logos, the Word.

logotype [lɔgɔtip], *s.m. Typ:* logotype.

loi¹ [lwa], *s.f.* **1.** (*a*) law; **homme de l.,** man of law, lawyer, legal practitioner; **consulter un homme de l.,** to take legal advice; **usage qui a passé en l.,** custom that has become law; **tomber sous le coup de la l.,** to come under the law; **être jugé selon les lois,** to be brought to a legal trial; **appliquer la l.,** to put the law in force; to carry out the law; **la l. de Moïse,** the law of Moses; **la l. des nations,** the law of nations, *jus gentium*; **faire, avoir force de, l.,** to have the force of law; **c'est lui qui fait la l., sa parole fait l., a force de l.; c'est la l., et les prophètes,** his word is law; **faire la l. à qn,** to lay down the law, to dictate, to s.o.; **se faire une l. de faire qch.,** to make a rule, a point, of doing sth.; **c'est à eux de recevoir la l.,** it is for them to submit; **subir la l. de qn,** to be ruled by s.o., to be under s.o.'s thumb; **l. du bâton,** government by violence, club law; **force est restée à la l.,** the law prevailed; **hors la l.,** outlawed; **mettre qn hors la l.,** to outlaw s.o.; **mise hors la l.,** outlawry; *s.a.* NÉCESSITÉ 1, REPRÉSENTANT 2; (*b*) law, enactment, statute; **projet de l., l. proposée (émanant du gouvernement), proposition de l. (émanant de l'initiative d'un membre du Parlement),** bill; **l. (votée),** act (of Parliament); **l. Bérenger** = First Offender's Act. **2.** law (of nature, etc.); **les lois de la pesanteur,** the laws of gravity; **loi de Grimm,** Grimm's law; **l. organique,** organic law; **l. de la diffusion du typhus,** laws governing the spread of typhus; **les lois du jeu,** the rules of the game.

loi² [lwa], *s.f.* sterling standard (*for minting of coins*).

loi-cadre [lwakɑdr], *s.f.* outline law (to be completed by decrees); *pl. lois-cadres.*

loi-programme [lwaprɔgram], *s.f. Fin: Pol:* law enforced for a certain period, in stages; *pl. lois-programmes.*

loin [lwɛ̃], *adv.* far; **plus l.,** farther (on); further; **moins l.,** less far. **1.** (*of place*) (*a*) **est-ce l. d'ici?** is it far from here? **la poste est l.,** the post office is a long way off; **fusil qui porte l.,** gun that carries far; **aller très l.,** to go far afield, farther afield; **jeune homme qui ira l.,** young man who will go a long way, who will go far, who will succeed; **un pays très l.,** a distant country; **être**

l. de la terre, to be far from land; **l. l'un de l'autre,** far from each other, far from one another; **l. derrière lui,** far, way, behind him; *Prov:* **l. des yeux, l. du cœur,** out of sight, out of mind; **il y a l. d'ici à Paris,** it's a long way to Paris; **il y a l. de Paris à Rome,** it's a long way from Paris to Rome; *Prov:* **il y a l. de la coupe aux lèvres,** there's many a slip 'twixt (the) cup and (the) lip; **rejeter bien l. une proposition,** to dismiss a proposal with scorn, to scorn a proposal; **être l. de faire qch.,** to be far from doing sth.; **c'est l. d'être complet,** it's a long way from being complete, it's far from complete; **ne pas être l. d'une découverte,** to be on the brink of a discovery; **l. de moi l'idée de vous influencer,** far be it from me to put pressure on you; **je ne suis pas mécontent, (bien) l. de là,** I am not ill-pleased, far from it, anything but; **vous allez trop l.,** you are going, carrying things, too far; **je ne pensais pas que vous iriez aussi l.,** I did not believe that you would go to such lengths; **l. du but,** wide of the mark; *conj.phr.* **l. qu'il se repente de sa conduite, il en est fier,** far from being sorry for his conduct, he is proud of it; *s.a.* COMPTE, DOUCEMENT; (*b*) **de l.,** by far; **il est de l. le plus intelligent,** he is by far the most intelligent; **il est de l. plus intelligent que moi,** he is far more intelligent than I am, he is more intelligent that I am by a long chalk; **admirer qn de l.,** to admire s.o. at a distance, from afar; (*c*) **je l'ai reconnu de l.,** I recognized him from a distance, from a long way off; **j'aperçus de l. un cerf,** I caught a distant sight of a stag; **ils sont parents, mais de l.,** they are only distantly related; *s.m.* **tout-à-fait au l.,** in the far distance; **apercevoir qn au l.,** to see s.o. a long way away, in the distance; **le parfum se répandit au l.,** the scent spread (over a large area); **sa renommée s'étendait au l.,** his fame had spread abroad; *conj.phr.* **du plus l. qu'il les voit,** as soon as he sees them; *s.a.* REVENIR 3. **2.** (*of time*) (*a*) **famille qui remonte bien l.,** family that goes a long way back; **circonstances que le lecteur trouvera détaillées plus l.,** circumstances that the reader will find detailed later; **nous reviendrons là-dessus plus l.,** we shall refer to this again elsewhere; **il ne devait pas être l. de midi,** it must have been getting on for noon, for twelve (o'clock); **ce jour est encore l.,** that day is still distant; *conj.phr.* **(d')aussi l. qu'il me souvienne,** as far back as I remember; (*b*) **prévoir les choses de l.,** to see things a long time beforehand, a long time ahead; *adv. phr.* **de l. en l.,** at long intervals, now and then; *conj.phr.* **du plus l. dont je me souviens, dont je me souvienne, qu'il me souvienne,** as far back as I remember.

lointain [lwɛ̃tɛ̃]. **1.** *a.* distant, remote, far off (country, period, etc.); **mes souvenirs les plus lointains,** my earliest recollections; **des causes lointaines,** remote causes; **des jours lointains,** far-off days, far-away days; **dans un avenir l.,** in a distant, remote, future; **avoir un air l.,** to have a far-away look. **2.** *s.m.* distance; **dans le l.,** in the distance, in the background; **les lointains de la vallée,** the far reaches of the valley; **je les découvris dans le l.,** I caught sight of them far off, from afar; *Art:* **les lointains,** the distances (of a picture); *Th:* **le l.,** up stage.

lointainement [lwɛ̃tɛnmɑ̃], *adv.* in a remote way.

lointaineté [lwɛ̃tɛnte], *s.f. A:* remoteness.

loir [lwa:r], *s.m. Z:* dormouse, loir; **l. gris,** fat, edible, dormouse; **dormir comme un l.,** to sleep like a log.

loirot [lwaro], *s.m. Z: Dial:* garden dormouse.

loisible [lwazibl], *a.* permissible, optional; **il lui est l. de refuser,** it is open to him to refuse; he is free, he is entitled, to refuse; **s'il ne vous est pas l. de venir,** if it is not convenient for you to come.

loisir [lwazi:r], *s.m.* leisure; **les loisirs,** spare-time activities; *F:* **le monde des loisirs,** the leisured world; *A:* **être de l.,** to be free, at leisure; **avoir des loisirs,** to have some spare time; **prendre des loisirs,** to enjoy some leisure; to take some time off; **dans mes heures de l., pendant mes loisirs,** in my leisure hours, in my spare time; **examiner qch. à l.,** to examine sth. at leisure; **faites-le à (votre) l.,** do it at your leisure, at your convenience; **je n'ai pas le l. d'un long entretien,** I have no time for a long conversation; **ne pas avoir le l. de respirer,** not to have time to breathe.

lokoum [lɔkum], *s.m.* Turkish delight.

loligo [lɔligo], *s.m. Moll:* Loligo, *F:* squid.

lollard [lɔla:r], *s.m. Ecc.Hist:* Lollard.

lollardisme [lɔlardism], *s.m. Ecc.Hist:* Lollardry, Lollardy, Lollardism.

lolo [lolo], *s.m.* (*a*) *F:* (*child's word*) milk; (*b*) *P:* **les lolos,** the breasts.

lombago [lɔ̃bago], *s.m. Med:* lumbago.

lombaire [lɔ̃bɛ:r], *a. Anat:* lumbar.

lombard, -arde [lɔ̃ba:r, -ard], *a. & s.* (*a*) *Geog: etc:* Lombard; *Arch:* **bandes lombardes,** Lombard bands, pilaster strip, arched corbel table; (*b*) *s.m. A:* usurer; *s.m.pl. Mediev.Hist:* The Lombard Bankers; (*c*) *s.f. Meteor:* **lombarde,** strong easterly wind.

Lombardie [lɔ̃bardi], *Pr.n.f. Geog:* Lombardy.

lombardique [lɔ̃bardik], *a.* Lombardic (alphabet, etc.).

lombarthrie [lɔ̃bartri], **lombarthrose** [lɔ̃bartro:z], *s.f. Med:* spondylosis lumbalis.

lombes [lɔ̃:b], *s.m.pl. Anat:* lumbar region; loins; *occ. sg.* **le lombe droit,** the right loin.

lombo-sacralgie [lɔ̃bɔsakralʒi], *s.f. Med:* sacrolumbar, lumbo-sacral, pain; *pl. lombo-sacralgies.*

lombo-sacré [lɔ̃bɔsakre], *a. Anat:* sacrolumbar, lumbo-sacral; *pl. lombo-sacré(e)s.*

lombostat [lɔ̃bɔsta], *s.m. Surg:* orthopaedic lumbo-sacral corset.

lombotomie [lɔ̃bɔtɔmi], *s.f. Surg:* incision into the lumbar region.

lombric [lɔ̃brik], *s.m. Ann:* **1.** lumbricus; earthworm. **2.** (*intestinal parasite*) ascaris.

lombrical, -aux [lɔ̃brikal, -o], *a. & s.m.* lumbrical (muscle).

lombriciforme [lɔ̃brisifɔrm], *a.* lumbriciform, vermiform.

lombricoïde [lɔ̃brikɔid], *a.* lumbricoid.

lombricose [lɔ̃briko:z], *s.f. Med:* lumbricosis.

lombricule [lɔ̃brikyl], *s.m. Ann:* lumbriculus.

lomentacé [lɔmɑ̃tase], *a. Bot:* lomentaceous.

lompe [lɔ̃:p], *s.f. Ich:* lump(-fish), lump-sucker; sea-owl.

lonchite [lɔ̃ʃit], *s.f. Bot:* holly-fern.

lonchocarpe [lɔ̃kɔkarp], *s.m. Bot:* lonchocarpus.

londonien, -ienne [lɔ̃dɔnjɛ̃, -jɛn]. **1.** *a.* of, pertaining to, London; **les brouillards londoniens,** London fogs. **2.** *s.* Londoner; **un vrai L. de Londres,** a Londoner born and bred.

Londres [lɔ̃:dr̥], *Pr.n.m. or f. Geog:* London; **je serai à L. mardi,** I shall be in London, *F:* in town, on Tuesday; **le grand L.,** greater London.

londrès [lɔ̃drɛs], *s.m.* Havana cigar.

long, longue [lɔ̃, lɔ̃:g]. **1.** *a.* long; (*a*) (*of space*) **un jardin plus l. que large,** a garden longer than it is wide; **ruban l. de cinq mètres,** ribbon five metres long; **avoir le nez l.,** to be long-nosed; *F:* **avoir le nez trop l.,** to be (too) nosy; *I.C.E:* **moteur à longue course,** long-stroke engine; **prendre le chemin le plus l., prendre au plus l.,** to go the longest way (round); **vue longue,** long sight; **avoir la vue longue,** (i) to be long-sighted; (ii) to have foresight; *Artil:* **coup l.,** "over"; **mer longue,** long sea; *s.a.* DENT 1, BRAS 1; (*b*) (*of time*; *cf. also the note to* PROLONGÉ); **un l. hiver** [lɔ̃givɛ:r], a long, protracted, winter; **avoir un l. entretien avec qn,** to have a long talk with s.o.; **longue vie,** long life; **discours un peu l.,** somewhat lengthy speech; **longue histoire,** long-drawn-out story; **l. comme un jour sans pain,** (i) interminable; (ii) (*of pers.*) long and lanky; **trouver le temps l.,** to find time heavy on one's hands; to get bored; **les jours me semblent (bien) longs,** time seems to be dragging (on); **l. de vingt-huit jours,** twenty-eight days long, lasting twenty-eight days; **je ne serai pas l.,** I won't be long; **l. soupir,** long-drawn sigh; **l. espoir,** long-cherished hope; **travail l. à faire** [lɔ̃afɛ:r], slow work; **être l. à faire qch.,** to take a long time to do sth.; to be slow in doing sth.; **ce serait beaucoup trop l. de vous le dire, à vous raconter,** it would take much too long to tell you; **il s'en sortira, mais ce sera l.,** he'll recover but it'll take a long time; **elle fut longue à s'en remettre,** she was a long time getting over it; **arbres longs à pousser,** trees of slow growth; **relations de longues années,** connection of long standing; **bail à longue échéance,** long lease; *Com:* **papiers à longue échéance,** *F:* **papiers longs,** long-dated bills; **disque (microsillon) de longue durée,** long-playing record; *adv.phr.* **à la longue,** in course of time, in the long run, in the end; **à la longue il vous deviendra sympathique,** you will get to like him (in time); *s.a.* FEU I, 3; (*c*) *Cu:* **sauce longue,** thin sauce. **2.** *s.m.* length; (*a*) (*of space*) **table qui a deux mètres de l.,** table two metres long, two metres in length; **en l., de l.,** lengthwise; (*of bricks, etc.*) stretcherwise; **de l. en large,** up and down, to and fro; **expliquer qch. en l. et en large,** to explain sth. in great detail; **au l. et au large,** far and wide; **étendu de tout son l., tout de son l.,** stretched (out) at full length; **tout le l. du rivage,** all along the bank; **tomber de tout son l.,** to fall flat on one's face; **le l. de la pente,** (all the way) down the slope; **il se promenait au bord du ruisseau; il y avait des arbres tout du l.,** he walked beside the stream; there were trees all along it; **raconter qch. (tout) au l.,** *F:* **tout au l. de l'aune,** to tell, to relate sth. at full length; **le l. de,** along, alongside; **s'amarrer le l. d'un navire,** to moor alongside a ship; **se faufiler le l. du mur,** to creep along the wall; **se laisser couler le l. du mur,** to slide down the wall; **se hisser le l. du mur,** to hoist oneself up the wall; *P:* **avoir les côtes en l.,** to be extremely lazy or tired; (*b*) (*of time*) **tout au l., tout le l., du jour, de la semaine, de l'année,** (i) all day long, throughout the week, the year; (ii) day in day out, week in week out, year in year out; **tout au l. de,** throughout; **tirer de l. une affaire,** to drag out, spin out, a matter; (*c*) *adv.* (*of amount*) **inutile d'en dire plus l.,** I need say no more, there's no need to say any more; **regard qui en dit l.,** look which speaks volumes; meaning, telling, eloquent, look; **ses traits tirés en disaient l. sur ses souffrances,** his drawn face told the tale of his sufferings; ces **meurtrissures en disent l.,** these bruises tell their own story; **cette action en dit l. sur . . .,** this action speaks volumes for . . .; **je ne cherche pas à en savoir plus l.,** I don't want to know any more; **je n'en sais pas plus l. que vous,** I am no wiser than you about it, I don't know any more about it than you (do); **je n'en sais pas plus l. pour cela,** I am not any the wiser, I am none the wiser; **il en sait l. sur votre compte,** he knows quite a lot about you; **enfant qui en sait déjà l.,** precocious, sophisticated, child. **3.** *s.f.* **longue** (*a*) *Pros:* long syllable; *A:* **observer les longues et les brèves,** to be most meticulous, to dot every i and cross every t; *A:* **en savoir les longues et les brèves,** to be well up in the subject; (*b*) *Cards:* **la plus haute carte de sa longue,** the highest card of one's longest suit; **attaquer dans sa longue,** to lead from one's long suit; (*c*) *Hist. of Mus:* long.

longailles [lɔ̃gɑ:j], *s.f.pl. Coop:* staves (of barrel).

longanier [lɔ̃ganje], *s.m. Bot:* longan.

longanimité [lɔ̃ganimite], *s.f.* long-suffering, forbearance.

long-atout [lɔ̃atu], *s.m. Cards:* thirteenth trump; **avoir l.-a.,** (i) to hold the odd trump; (ii) to be long in trumps.

long-courrier [lɔ̃kurje], *a. & s.m. Nau:* **1.** ocean-going (ship); ocean liner; *Av:* long-distance, long-range (aircraft). **2.** deep-sea (sailor); captain (of a liner); *pl. long-courriers.*

longe[1] [lɔ̃:ʒ], *s.f. Harn:* (*a*) leading rein, head rope, halter, tether; (*b*) lunging rein, lunge, longe; **trotter, faire travailler, un cheval à la l.,** to lunge a horse; (*c*) thong (of whip); (*d*) picket(ing) rope; *F:* **marcher sur sa l.,** to get into a fix, to get tied up.

longe[2], *s.f. Cu:* loin (of veal or venison).

longer [lɔ̃ʒe], *v.tr.* (**je longeai(s); n. longeons**) to pass, go, along (road, etc.); **la route longe un bois,** the road runs along the edge of a wood; the road skirts a wood; **l. la côte, le mur,** to hug the coast, the wall; **l. un navire,** to follow a route parallel to that of another vessel.

longeron [lɔ̃ʒrɔ̃], *s.m.* **1.** *Civ.E:* stringer, longitudinal girder; beam, member (of bridge, etc.); *Const:* **l. de faîtage,** ridge bar. **2.** (*a*) *Aut:* side member, side-sill (of frame); **faux longerons,** sub-frame; **châssis à longerons coudés,** inswept frame; (*b*) *Rail:* sideframe. **3.** *Av:* longeron; spar (of wing); **l.-caisson,** box spar; **l. en "U,"** channel-type spar; **l. d'assemblage, de réunion,** tail boom; **l.-support,** outrigger; **ferrure de l.,** spar fitting; **semelle de l.,** spar cap.

longévital, -aux [lɔ̃ʒevital, -o], *a. A:* long-lived; *A:* longevous, longaevous.

longévité [lɔ̃ʒevite], *s.f.* longevity, long life; (*Statistics*) life-span; *Mec.E:* operating life, service life (of equipment); **matériel à l. élevée,** long-life equipment.

longicaude [lɔ̃ʒiko:d], *a. Z:* longicaudate, long-tailed.

longicaule [lɔ̃ʒiko:l], *a. Bot:* longicauline, long-stemmed.

longicorne [lɔ̃ʒikɔrn], *a. & s.m. Ent:* longicorn.

longière [lɔ̃ʒjɛ:r], *s.f. Dom.Ec: A:* long strip of table-linen laid round edge of table to serve as communal napkin.

longifolié [lɔ̃ʒifɔlje], *a. Bot:* long-leaved.

longiligne [lɔ̃ʒiliɲ], *a. Z. Anat:* long-limbed.

longimane [lɔ̃ʒiman], *a. Z:* longimanous, long-handed.

longimétrie [lɔ̃ʒimetri], *s.f. Mth:* science of long-distance measurement.

Longin [lɔ̃ʒɛ̃], *Pr.n.m. Gr.Hist:* Longinus.

longipède [lɔ̃ʒipɛd], *a. Z:* longipedate, long-footed.
longipenne [lɔ̃ʒipɛn], *a. Orn:* longipennate, long-winged.
longirostre [lɔ̃ʒirɔstr]. **1.** *a. Orn:* longirostral, long-billed. **2.** *s.m.* longiroster.
longis [lɔ̃ʒi], *s.m. N.Arch:* girder, beam (between deck houses).
longistyle [lɔ̃ʒistil], *a. Bot:* long-styled, pin-eyed (flowers).
longitude [lɔ̃ʒityd], *s.f. Geog:* longitude; **l. estimée,** longitude by dead reckoning; **par 10° (de) l. ouest; sous, par, la l. de 10° ouest,** in (the) longitude (of) 10° west; **Bureau des longitudes,** central astronomical office.
longitudinal, -aux [lɔ̃ʒitydinal, -o], *a.* longitudinal, lengthwise; *Nau:* fore-and-aft; **axe l. (d'un navire),** (ship's) centre line; *Mec.E:* **jeu l.,** end play.
longitudinalement [lɔ̃ʒitydinalmɑ̃], *adv.* longitudinally, lengthwise.
long-jointé, -ée [lɔ̃ʒwɛ̃te], *a.* long-pasterned (horse); *pl. long-jointé(e)s.*
long-nez [lɔ̃ne], *s.m.inv. Z:* proboscis monkey (of Borneo).
longovicien, -ienne [lɔ̃gɔvisjɛ̃, -jɛn], *a. & s.* (native, inhabitant) of Longwy.
long-pan [lɔ̃pɑ̃], *s.m.* long side (of roof); *pl. longs-pans.*
longrine [lɔ̃grin], *s.f.* (*a*) *Const:* longitudinal beam, girder, member; **l. de faîtage,** ridge-bar; (*b*) *N.Arch:* groundway; **l. (de lancement),** slips; (*c*) *Rail:* longitudinal sleeper.
longtemps [lɔ̃tɑ̃]. **1.** *adv.* long; a long time; **attendre l.,** to wait for a long time; **cela ne pouvait durer l.,** it could not last long; **ça ne va plus durer l. maintenant, (et nous pourrons nous marier),** it won't be long now (before we can get married); **être l. à faire qch.,** to be a long time (i) doing sth., (ii) before one does sth.; **il a été l. sans rien faire,** for a long time he did nothing, he had nothing to do; **on a été l. à reconnaître, avant de reconnaître, ces faits,** it was a long time before these facts were acknowledged; **rester trop l.,** to stay too long; to stay beyond one's time. **2.** *s.m.* **il y a l.,** long ago, a long time ago, a long while ago; **il n'y a pas l.,** not long ago; **il y a l. qu'il est mort,** he has been dead (for) a long time; **il y a l. que je ne l'ai vu,** it is a long time since I saw him; **mettre l. à faire qch.,** to be a long time doing sth.; **cela existe depuis l.,** it has existed for a long time; **nécessité reconnue depuis l.,** necessity long recognized; **avant l.,** before long, ere long; **pas avant l.,** not for a long while; **de l.,** for a long time; **cela ne se fera pas de l.,** it will not happen for a long time to come; **de l. on ne verra son pareil,** it will be long before we see his like again; **je n'en ai pas pour l.,** (i) it won't take me long; (ii) I haven't much longer to live; **pendant l. on le crut mort,** for a long time he was thought to be dead.
longuement [lɔ̃gmɑ̃], *adv.* **1.** for a long time; *A:* **vivre l.,** to live long; *B:* **afin de vivre l.,** that thy days may be long. **2.** (*a*) **manger l.,** to eat slowly, deliberately; (*b*) **il la regarda l.,** he gazed earnestly at her. **3. plaider l. une cause,** to argue a case lengthily, at great length; **s'étendre l. sur un sujet,** to expatiate on a subject; **il faut entrer plus l. dans le détail,** you must go more fully into details; **s'étendre trop l. sur les détails,** to dwell at too great length on details; **causer l. avec qn,** to have a long talk with s.o.
longue-paume [lɔ̃gpoːm], *s.f.* open-air tennis (the forerunner of lawn tennis).
longuerine [lɔ̃grin], *s.f.* = LONGRINE.
longuet, -ette [lɔ̃gɛ, -ɛt]. **1.** *a. F:* (*a*) rather long, longish (book, time, etc.); on the long side; (*b*) slender. **2.** *s.m.* **longuet,** bread stick.
longueur [lɔ̃gœːr], *s.f.* length. **1. l. totale, l. hors tout,** length over all, overall length; **l. des lignes d'un réseau,** mileage of a railway system; **le canal est praticable aux gros chalands dans toute sa l.,** the canal will take heavy barges throughout its length; **mesures de l.,** linear measures; **jardin qui a cent mètres de l., une l. de cent mètres,** garden a hundred metres long; **couper qch. en l., dans le sens de la l.,** to cut sth. lengthwise; **tirer un discours en l.,** to spin out a speech; (*of lawsuit, etc.*) **traîner, tirer, en l.,** to drag (on); **à l. de journée, de semaine, d'année,** throughout the day, week, year; **à l. de journées, de semaines, d'années,** for days, weeks, years, on end; *Pros:* **signe de l.,** mark of length; *s.a.* ONDE 3. **2. les longueurs de la justice,** the law's delays; **roman où il y a des longueurs,** novel with tedious passages; **cette scène fait l.,** this scene drags, slows down the action. **3.** (*a*) *Row: Turf:* **mener, gagner, par une, d'une, l.,** to lead, win, by a length; (*b*) *Ten: Cr:* **conserver une bonne l. de balle,** to keep a good length.
longue-vue [lɔ̃gvy], *s.f.* telescope, field glass; *pl. longues-vues.*
longulite [lɔ̃gylit], *s.f. Miner:* longulite.
lonicera [lɔnisera], *s.m. Bot:* lonicera, honeysuckle.
longwall [lɔŋwɔl], *a. & s.m. Min:* longwall (system).
looch [lɔk], *s.m. Pharm:* soothing emulsion (to be sipped).
loofa, loofah [lufa], *s.m.* (*a*) *Bot:* loofah, sponge cucumber, sponge gourd, towel gourd; (*b*) *Toil:* loofah.
looping [lupiŋ], *s.m. Av:* **faire un l.,** to loop (the loop); **l. à l'envers,** bunt.
lope [lɔp], *s.f.,* **lopette** [lɔpɛt], *s.f. P:* (*a*) rotter; (*b*) homosexual, pansy.
lophiodon [lɔfjɔdɔ̃], *s.m. Paleont:* lophiodon.
lophiomyinés [lofjɔmiine], *s.m.pl. Z:* the Lophiomys family.
lophiomys [lɔfjɔmis], *s.m. Z:* lophiomys.
lophobranche [lɔfɔbrɑ̃ːʃ]. **1.** *a. & s.m. Ich:* lophobranch, lophobranchiate. **2.** *s.m.pl.* **lophobranches,** Lophobranchii; Syngnathidae.
lophophore [lɔfɔfɔːr], *s.m. Orn:* lophophorus; monal pheasant; *pl.* the Monals.
lophophytie [lɔfɔfiti], *s.f. Vet:* lophophytosis, favus of fowls.
lophornis [lɔfɔrnis], *s.m. Orn:* lophornis, coquette.
lophotriche [lɔfɔtriʃ], *s.m. Biol:* lophotrichate bacillus.
lophure [lɔfyːr], *s.m. Orn:* lophura, fireback.
lophyre [lɔfiːr], *s.m. Ent:* saw fly.
lopin [lɔpɛ̃], *s.m.* **1.** (*a*) *A:* portion, bit, piece (of bread, meat, etc.); (*b*) **l. de terre,** piece, patch, plot, of ground; allotment. **2.** *Metall:* bloom, billet.
loquace [lɔkwas, -kas], *a.* loquacious, talkative; garrulous (old person).
loquacement [lɔkwasmɑ̃, -kasmɑ̃], *adv.* loquaciously, talkatively.
loquacité [lɔkwasite, -kasite], *s.f.* **1.** loquacity, loquaciousness, talkativeness; garrulity. **2.** *Med:* logorrhea.
loque [lɔk], *s.f.* **1.** rag; *pl. P:* clothes; **être en loques,** to be in rags, in tatters; **ses vêtements tombent en loques,** his clothes are falling to pieces, are worn to rags; *F:* (*of pers.*) **être comme une l.,** to be worn out, absolutely limp; to feel like a rag. **2.** *Bot: F:* woody nightshade, bittersweet. **3.** *Ap:* foul-brood.
loqué [lɔke], *a. P:* dressed, togged up.
loquedu [lɔkdy], *P:* (*a*) *a.* worthless; (*b*) *s.m.* good-for-nothing; (*c*) dangerous fellow, bastard.
loquèle [lɔkɥɛl], *s.f. A:* flow of language; **avoir de la l.,** to have the gift of the gab.
loquer [lɔke], *v.tr. P:* to dress.
loquet[1] [lɔkɛ], *s.m.* **1.** latch (of door); **fermer la porte au l.,** *F:* **tirer le l.,** to latch the door; **porte fermée au l.,** door on the latch. **2.** locking device; **couteau à l.,** clasp knife.
loquet[2], *s.m.* **1.** tuft (of bristles in a brush). **2.** *Tex:* livery wool.
loqueteau, -eaux [lɔkto], *s.m.* small latch, catch (for shutter, etc.).
loqueter [lɔkte], *v.* (**je loquette, n. loquetons; je loquetterai**) *A:* **1.** *v.i.* to rattle the latch of the door. **2.** *v.tr.* to tear (sth.) into shreds.
loqueteux, -euse [lɔktø, -øːz]. **1.** *a.* in rags, in tatters, ragged. **2.** *s.* ragamuffin, tatterdemalion.
loquette [lɔkɛt], *s.f.* **1.** *A:* bit, scrap (of bread, etc.). **2.** *Tex:* roll of carded wool. **3.** *Ich: F:* viviparous blenny.
loqueux, -euse [lɔko, -øːz], *a. Ap:* suffering from foul-brood.
loran [lɔrɑ̃], *s.m. Av: Nau:* loran (Long Range Aid to Navigation).
lorandite [lɔrɑ̃dit], *s.f. Miner:* lorandite.
loranskite [lɔrɑ̃skit], *s.f. Miner:* loranskite.
loranthacées [lɔrɑ̃tase], *s.f.pl. Bot:* Loranthaceae.
lord [lɔːr], *s.m.* (British) lord; **la Chambre des lords,** the House of Lords; **lord de l'Amirauté, de la mer,** First Lord of the Admiralty, First Sea Lord.
lord-lieutenant [lɔrljøtnɑ̃], *s.m.* Lord Lieutenant; *pl. lords-lieutenants.*
lord-maire [lɔrmɛːr], *s.m.* Lord Mayor (of London, etc.); *pl. lords-maires.*
lordose [lɔrdoːz], *s.f. Med:* lordosis.
lordosique [lɔrdozik], *a. Med:* lordosic.
Lorentz [lɔrɛnts], *Pr.n. Ph:* **contraction de L.,** (Lorentz-)Fitzgerald contraction; **équations, formules, transformation, de L.,** Lorentz transformation.
Lorette [lɔrɛt]. **1.** *Pr.n.f. Geog:* Loret(t)o. **2.** *s.f. Lit:* woman of easy virtue; lorette (*from the quarter of Paris in which the church of Notre-Dame de Lorette stands*).
lorettoïte [lɔrɛtɔit], *s.f. Miner:* lorettoite.
lorgnade [lɔrɲad], *s.f. A:* (*a*) sidelong glance; (*b*) ogle; **lancer des lorgnades à qn,** to ogle s.o.
lorgnement [lɔrɲəmɑ̃], *s.m.* glancing, ogling.
lorgner [lɔrɲe]. **1.** *v.tr.* (*a*) to cast a sidelong glance at (sth.); **l. une dot, une place,** to have one's eye on an heiress, on a post; (*b*) to ogle, to make eyes at (s.o.); to leer at (s.o.); (*c*) to stare at (s.o., sth.) through a lorgnette or through opera-glasses. **2.** *v.i. A:* to squint.
lorgnerie [lɔrɲ(ə)ri], *s.f. A:* ogle, ogling.
lorgnette [lɔrɲɛt], *s.f.* (pair of) opera glasses; (small) field glasses; **regarder, voir, les choses par le petit bout de la l.,** (*rare*) **par le gros bout de la l.,** to magnify, minimize, events.
lorgneur -euse [lɔrɲœːr, -øːz], *s.* ogler.
lorgnon [lɔrɲɔ̃], *s.m.* (*a*) pince-nez, eyeglasses; (*b*) (handled) lorgnette; (*c*) *A:* monocle.
lori [lɔri], *s.m. Orn:* lory.
loricaire [lɔrikɛːr], *a. & s.f. Ich:* loricarian.
lorientais, -aise [lɔrjɑ̃tɛ, -ɛːz], *a. & s.* (native, inhabitant) of Lorient.
loriot [lɔrjo], *s.m. Orn:* oriole; **l. (d'Europe),** golden oriole.
lorique [lɔrik], *s.f. Nat.Hist:* lorica.
loriqué [lɔrike], *a. Nat.Hist:* loricate(d).
loris [lɔris], *s.m. Z:* loris; **l. grêle, de l'Inde,** slender loris.
lorisidés [lɔriside], *s.m.pl. Z:* Lorisidae.
lorrain, -aine [lɔrɛ̃, -ɛn]. **1.** *a.* Lorrainese; from, of, Lorraine. **2.** *s.* (*a*) Lorrainer, (inhabitant, native) of Lorraine; (*b*) **le L.,** (the painter) Claude Gellée. **3.** *Pr.n.f. Geog:* **la Lorraine,** Lorraine.
lorry [lɔri], *s.m. Rail:* (platelayer's) trolley, lorry.
lors [lɔːr], *adv.* **1.** *A:* = ALORS. **2.** *still used in combination as follows:* (*a*) **depuis l.,** from that time, ever since then; *F:* **pour l. . . .,** so . . . then . . ., to go on with my story . . .; *s.a.* DÈS; (*b*) **l. . . . que,** (= LORSQUE) when; **l. même que nous sommes heureux,** even when we are happy; **l. même que nous serions heureux,** even if, even though, we were happy; **l. donc qu'il arriva,** thus when he arrived; *prep.phr.* **l. de sa naissance, de son mariage,** at the time of his birth, of his marriage; when he was born, married; **l. de sa majorité,** on his majority; **l. de la remise de la lettre,** on delivery of the letter.
lorsque [lɔrsk(ə)], *conj.* (*becomes* **lorsqu'** *before* **il(s), elle(s), on, en, un(e)**) (at the time, moment) when; **l. j'entrai,** when I entered, on my entering; **ce ne fut que l. . . .,** it was not until . . .; **lorsque arriva le printemps . . .,** when spring came . . .; **lorsqu'il sera parti . . .,** when he has gone; *s.a.* LORS 2.
lorum [lɔrɔm], *s.m. Ap: Orn: Arach:* lorum.
los [lo], *s.m. A: Lit:* renown; praise.
losange [lɔzɑ̃ːʒ], *s.m.* **1.** (*a*) *Her:* lozenge; **en l.,** diamond-shaped; (*b*) *Rail:* warning signal (in the form of a lozenge); (*c*) *Mus:* black lozenge-shaped semibreve (used in plain song). **2.** *Geom:* rhomb(us).
losangé [lɔzɑ̃ʒe], *a. Her:* lozengy.
losanger [lɔzɑ̃ʒe], *v.tr.* to divide into lozenges.
lose [loːz], *s.f.* roofing stone.
lot[1] [lo], *s.m.* **1.** (*a*) share (of estate); portion, lot; **avoir son lot de tourments,** to have one's share of worries; **la pauvreté fut son lot,** poverty was his lot, fate; (*b*) prize (at a lottery); **gros l.,** first prize; *F:* jackpot; **gagner le gros l.,** (i) to draw the first prize; (ii) *F:* to strike it lucky; *Fin:* **emprunt à lots,** lottery loan; **tirage à lots,** prize-drawing; *s.a.* OBLIGATION 3, VALEUR 2; (*c*) *P:* (*of girl*) **un beau petit l.,** a bit of all right, a nice bit of goods. **2.** lot, parcel (of goods); batch (of goods, people, etc.); **lot d'envoi,** consignment; *Metall:* **l. en réception,** batch for testing.
Lot[2] [lɔt], *Pr.n.m. B.Hist:* Lot.
lote [lɔt], *s.f. Ich:* = LOTTE.
loterie [lɔtri], *s.f.* (*a*) lottery; **c'est une l.,** it's (merely) a matter of chance; **la vie, le mariage, est une l.,** life, marriage, is a lottery; (*b*) raffle, draw; **mettre une montre en l.,** to raffle a watch; (*c*) (*in fair*) tombola booth.
Loth [lɔt], *Pr.n.m. B.Hist:* Lot.
Lothaire [lɔtɛːr], *Pr.n.m.* Lothair.
Lotharingie [lɔtarɛ̃ʒi], *Pr.n.f. A.Geog:* Lotharingia, Lorraine.
lotharingien, -ienne [lɔtarɛ̃ʒjɛ̃, -jɛn], *a. & s. Geol:* Lotharingian.
lotier [lɔtje], *s.m. Bot:* lotus, bird's-foot trefoil; sweet clover.

lotière [lɔtjɛːr], *s.f. Agr:* meadow planted with sweet clover.

lotiforme [lɔtifɔrm], *a.* lotus-like.

lotion [losjɔ̃], *s.f.* **1.** (*a*) *Med: A:* washing, bathing (of wound); sponging; (*b*) *Ch: Ind:* washing (of precipitate, etc.). **2.** *Pharm:* lotion; *Hairdr:* **l. pour mise en plis,** setting lotion.

lotionner [losjɔne], *v.tr.* (*a*) *Med:* to wash, bathe (wound, etc.); to sponge; (*b*) *Hairdr:* to set (hair) with a lotion.

lotir [lɔtiːr], *v.tr.* **1.** (*a*) to divide (sth.) into lots, into batches; **l. une propriété,** to parcel out an estate; (*b*) *Com:* to sort (out) (hides, grain, etc.); to parcel out (goods); (*c*) *Min:* to sample (ores to be assayed). **2. l. qn de qch.,** to allot sth. to s.o.; **être bien loti,** to be well provided for; to have one's fair share; to be favoured by fortune; to be well off; **mal loti,** badly off, poorly off.

lotissage [lɔtisaːʒ], *s.m. Miner:* sampling (of ores).

lotissement [lɔtismɑ̃], *s.m.* **1.** (*a*) dividing (of goods, etc.) into lots; parcelling out; sorting (of hides, etc.); (*b*) making up (of various objects) into sets; (*c*) allotment, apportionment (of estate, of articles to be drawn by lot); (*d*) development (of building land); (*e*) *Mil:* **l. des munitions,** division of munitions into standardized units for issue and transport. **2.** (*a*) building plot; (*b*) housing estate.

lotisseur [lɔtisœːr], *s.m.* **1.** person in charge of dividing goods into lots. **2.** *Surv:* developer, speculative builder.

loto [lɔto, lo-], *s.m. Games:* **1.** lotto; housey-housey, house; *F:* **yeux en boules de l.,** goggle-eyes. **2.** lotto set.

Lotophages [lɔtɔfaːʒ], *s.m.pl. Gr.Myth:* Lotophagi, Lotus-eaters.

lotos [lɔtɔs], *s.m.* = LOTUS.

lotte [lɔt], *s.f. Ich:* burbot, eel pout; lote; **l. de mer,** lophius, angler.

lotus [lɔtyːs], *s.m.* **1.** *Bot:* (*a*) lotus; **l. sacré,** Indian lotus, water lotus; (*b*) lotus-tree. **2.** *Gr.Myth:* Lotus; **manger du l.,** to live in a state of dreamy content; **mangeur de l.,** lotus-eater. **3.** *Egyptian Arch:* lotus-patterned moulding.

louable [lwabl̩], *a.* laudable, praiseworthy, creditable; commendable; **elle est l. d'avoir persévéré,** one must praise her, she is to be commended, for having persevered.

louablement [lwabləmɑ̃], *adv.* (*rare*) laudably, praiseworthily, commendably.

louage [lwaːʒ], *s.m.* **1.** letting out, hiring out; **donner qch. en, à, l.,** to let sth. out on hire, to hire sth. out; (*of farm hand, etc.*) **se donner en, à, l.,** to engage oneself (for the season), *U.S:* to hire oneself out. **2.** hiring, hire (of labour, horses, etc.); chartering (of aircraft); **prendre qch. à l.,** to hire sth.; to take sth. on hire, *U.S:* to rent sth.; *Adm:* **voiture de l.,** hackney carriage; **auto, bicyclette, de l.,** hired car, bicycle; **cheval de l.,** hack; **avion de l.,** charter aircraft.

louageur [lwaʒœːr], *s.m.* jobmaster.

louange [lwɑ̃ːʒ], *s.f.* praise; laudation; commendation; eulogy, *esp.* adulatory praise; *cf.* ÉLOGE; **chanter, entonner, les louanges de qn,** to laud s.o. to the skies; to sing s.o.'s praises; **chanter ses propres louanges,** to blow one's own trumpet, horn; **ce fut un concert de louanges,** there was a chorus of praise; **combler qn de louanges,** to heap praise on s.o.; **dire qch. à la l. de qn,** to say sth. in praise of s.o.; **s'attirer les louanges de . . .,** to be praised by . . .; **c'est à sa l.,** it's to his credit.

louanger [lwɑ̃ʒe], *v.tr.* to praise (s.o.) fulsomely; *F:* to butter (s.o.) up.

louangeur, -euse [lwɑ̃ʒœːr, -øːz]. **1.** *a.* (*a*) adulatory, laudatory (poem, etc.); **comme critique il n'est pas l.,** as a critic he is chary of praise; (*b*) flattering. **2.** *s.* (*a*) adulator, praiser, lauder; (*b*) flatterer.

loubette [lubɛt], *s.f. Const:* lewis, lewisson.

loucedé (en) [ɑ̃lusde], *adv.phr. P:* on the quiet.

louchard[1], -arde [luʃaːr, -ard], *s. F:* person with a squint.

louchard[2], *s.m. Const:* building stone (found in the Vienne).

louche[1] [luʃ], *a.* **1.** cross-eyed, squint-eyed (person); **yeux louches,** eyes that squint; **il est l. de l'œil gauche,** he has a squint in his left eye. **2.** (*a*) ambiguous (expression, etc.); *s.m.* **phrase où il y a du l.,** sentence that is not clear; (*b*) shady, suspicious (house, conduct, character, etc.); shifty (person); dubious, equivocal; **cela me paraît l.,** it looks suspicious, *F:* fishy, to me; *s.m.* **il y a du l. dans cette affaire,** there's something shady in the business; **il n'y a rien de l. là-dedans,** it is all fair and above-board; **individu aux allures louches,** shady-looking customer; (*c*) cloudy (wine, pearl, etc.); (*d*) *s.m. Ch:* clouds; light precipitate.

louche[2], *s.f.* **1.** (*a*) (soup) ladle; (*b*) basting spoon; (*c*) *P:* hand, flipper. **2.** *Agr:* (manure) shovel, scoop. **3.** *Mec.E:* (*a*) reamer, broach; (*b*) countersink bit.

louchement [luʃmɑ̃], *s.m.* squint(ing).

loucher [luʃe], *v.i.* to squint; to be cross-eyed; **l. de l'œil gauche,** to have a cast in the left eye; **avoir une tendance à l.,** to have a cast in one's eye; *F:* **faire l. qn de jalousie,** to turn s.o. green with envy; *F:* **l. vers, dans la direction de, sur, qch.,** to cast longing eyes at, a sidelong glance at, sth.

loucherbème, loucherbem [luʃebɛm], *s.m. P:* butcher.

loucherie [luʃri], *s.f.* strabismus, squint(ing).

louchet [luʃɛ], *s.m.* **1.** (*a*) peat spade, draining spade; (*b*) whaling spade. **2.** bucket (of dredger).

loucheur, -euse [luʃœːr, -øːz], *s.* squinter; cross-eyed, squint-eyed, person.

louchir [luʃiːr], *v.i.* (*of liquid*) to turn cloudy.

louchon, -onne [luʃɔ̃, -ɔn], *s. P:* **1.** cross-eyed person; squint-eyes. **2. la louchonne,** the moon.

loudéacien, -ienne [ludeasjɛ̃, -jɛn], *a. & s. Geog:* (native, inhabitant) of Loudéac.

loudunais, -aise [ludynɛ, -ɛːz], *a. & s. Geog:* (native, inhabitant) of Loudun.

louée [lue], *s.f. A:* statute fair.

louer[1] [lwe, lue], *v.tr.* **1.** (*a*) to hire out, let (out) (**à,** to); **maison à l.,** house to let; **l. une ferme à bail,** to lease out a farm; (*b*) (*of farmhand*) **se l. pour la saison,** to engage oneself for the season. **2.** to hire (horse, etc.); to rent (house, etc.) (**à,** from); to take on (seasonal workers); **l. une maison pour la saison,** to take a house for the season; **l. une place d'avance,** to reserve, book, a seat (in advance); *Rail:* **compartiment loué,** reserved compartment; *Th:* **tout est loué,** all seats are booked; (*on seat*) **loué,** reserved.

louer[2], *v.tr.* to praise; to commend; **l. qn de, pour, qch.,** to praise s.o. for sth.; **l. qn de, pour, avoir fait, qch.,** to praise s.o. for doing sth.; **loué de tous,** praised by all; **Dieu soit loué!** God be praised! praise be to God! **le ciel en soit loué!** thank Heaven (for that)! **je sais peu l.,** I am not given to praise.

se louer, se l. de qch., to be pleased, well satisfied, with sth.; **se l. d'avoir fait qch.,** to congratulate oneself upon having done sth.; **je me loue de vous avoir rencontré sur mon chemin,** I, bless my stars, thank my lucky stars, that I came across you; **je n'ai qu'à me l. de lui, de sa conduite,** I have nothing but praise for him, for his conduct; **j'eus à me l. de mon professeur,** I was fortunate in my teacher.

loueur[1], -euse [lwœːr, lu-, -øːz], *s.* hirer out; letter; renter out; **l. de bicyclettes,** hirer out of bicycles; **l. de bateaux,** boat keeper; **l. de chevaux, de voitures,** jobmaster, livery-stable keeper; **loueuse de chambres garnies,** landlady (who lets furnished rooms).

loueur[2], -euse, *s. A:* praiser.

louf [luf], *F:* = LOUFOQUE.

louffa, loufah [lufa], *s.m.* = LUFFA.

louf(f)iat [lufja], *s.m.* **1.** *P:* (*a*) coarse, unmannerly, fellow; boor; (*b*) waiter (in a café). **2.** *Nau: F:* lieutenant.

loufoque [lufɔk], (*a*) *a. F:* cracked, loony, a little touched, dippy, barmy; (*b*) *s. F:* crank, crackpot, *U.S:* screwball.

loufoquerie [lufɔkri], *s.f. F:* (*a*) eccentricity; barminess, craziness; (*b*) crackbrained action.

louftingue [luftɛ̃ːg], *a. P:* = LOUFOQUE.

lougre [lugr], *s.m. Nau:* lugger.

louhannais, -aise [luanɛ, -ɛːz], *a. & s. Geog:* (native, inhabitant) of Louhans.

Louis [lwi, lui]. **1.** *Pr.n.m.* Lewis; Louis; **un mobilier L. Quinze,** a Louis-Quinze set of furniture. **2.** *s.m. Num: A:* **louis (d'or),** twenty-franc piece; *Prov:* **on n'est pas louis-d'or,** you can't please everybody.

Louise [lwiːz], *Pr.n.f.* Louisa, Louise.

louise-bonne [lwizbɔn], *s.f. Hort:* type of pear; *pl. louises-bonnes.*

louisette [lwizɛt], *s.f. Hist: F:* the guillotine.

louisianais, -aise [lwizjanɛ, -ɛːz], *a. & s. Geog:* (native, inhabitant) of Louisiana.

Louisiane [lwizjan], *Pr.n.f. Geog:* Louisiana.

louis-philippard, -arde [lwifilipaːr, -ard], *a. Pej:* pertaining to the reign of Louis Philippe.

louis-quatorzien, -ienne [lwikatɔrzjɛ̃, -jɛn], *a. F:* pertaining to the reign of Louis XIV.

loulou, -outte [lulu, -ut], *s. F:* **1.** dear, darling. **2. l. de Poméranie,** Pomeranian (dog), *F:* pom.

loup[1] [lu], *s.m.* **1.** (*a*) wolf; **l. à crinière,** maned wolf, dog; **crier au l.,** to cry wolf; **marcher à pas de l.,** to walk stealthily; to creep along, steal along; **monter, descendre, entrer, sortir, à pas de l.,** to steal up, down, in, out; **avoir une faim de l.,** to be ravenously hungry, as hungry as a hunter, as a horse; **il fait un froid de l.,** it's bitterly cold; **se jeter, se fourrer, dans la gueule du l.,** to jump, rush, into the lion's mouth; **tenir le l. par les oreilles,** to have, hold, the wolf by the ears; to be in a fix; **il est connu comme le l. blanc,** he is known to everybody; he is known everywhere; **donner la brebis à garder au l.; enfermer le l. dans la bergerie,** to set the fox to keep the geese; **avoir vu le l.,** (i) to know a thing or two; (ii) (*of girl*) to have lost her virginity; *Prov:* **quand on parle du l. on en voit la queue,** talk of the devil and he will appear; talk of angels and you will hear the flutter of their wings; **les loups ne se mangent pas entre eux,** there is honour among thieves; dog doesn't eat dog; **le grand méchant l.,** the big, bad wolf; *F:* (*to man or woman*) **mon petit l. mon gros l.,** my darling, my pet; *Bot: F:* **herbe à loups,** wolf's bane, monk's hood; *s.a.* BREBIS 2, CHIEN 1, HERBE 4, HURLER 1; (*b*) *Z: F:* **l. peint,** painted hyena; (*c*) **l. de mer,** (i) *Ich:* sea perch, sea dace; (ii) *F:* old salt, sea-dog, jack tar; **vieux l. de mer,** old tarry-breeks; (*d*) *St.Exch: F:* premium hunter, stag. **2.** *F:* (*a*) flaw (in timber, etc.); mistake committed in working wood; *Ind:* defect; (*b*) error, miscalculation; (*c*) *Ind: Com: F:* white elephant; (*d*) *Th:* fluff, fluffed entrance. **3.** (*a*) black velvet mask (worn at a masked ball); (*b*) *Mil:* face mask (of gas mask). **4.** (*a*) crow bar; (*b*) nail wrench; (*c*) *Tex:* wood-breaker, willow, will(e)y. **5.** *Metall:* bear, salamander, shadrach.

Loup[2], *Pr.n.m. Ecc.Hist:* (Saint) Loup.

loupage [lupaːʒ], *s.m. F:* (*a*) bungling; (*b*) bungled work.

loup-cerve [lusɛrv], *s.f. Z:* she-lynx; *pl. loups-cerves.*

loup-cervier [lusɛrvje], *s.m.* (*a*) *Z:* lynx; (*b*) *F:* profiteer, shark; *pl. loups-cerviers.*

loupe[1] [lup], *s.f.* **1.** (*a*) *Med:* wen; (*b*) excrescence, knobby growth, gnarl (on tree); **l. d'orme,** elm bur; (*c*) hump (of camel). **2.** *Metall:* bloom; **four à loupes,** bloomery furnace. **3.** lens, magnifying glass; **l. de mise au point,** focusing glass, magnifier; **l. de tisserand,** weaver's glass; **scruter (un document) à la l.,** to go through (a document) with a fine tooth-comb. **4.** *Lap:* **l. de rubis, de saphir,** flawed, imperfect, ruby, sapphire.

loupe[2], *s.f. F:* (*a*) *A:* laziness, slackness; (*b*) bungling, botching; defect (in manufacture, etc.).

loupé [lupe], *F:* (*a*) *a.* defective; spoilt, bungled (work); (*b*) *s.m.* slip, mistake; defect (in manufacture, etc.).

louper [lupe]. **1.** *v.i. F:* (*a*) *A:* to be slack, lazy; (*b*) **ça n'a pas loupé,** that didn't miss; that hit the mark. **2.** *v.tr. F:* to botch, bungle (piece of work); to make a botch of (piece of work); to miss (one's turn, opportunity, train); to fail (exam); *Ind:* **pièce loupée,** defective piece; *Av:* **l. son atterrissage,** to crash; *Th:* **l. son entrée,** to fluff one's entrance; *P:* **pas besoin de s'en faire, c'est loupé,** don't get het up, you've had it.

loupeur, -euse[1] [lupœːr, -øːz], *s. F:* **1.** *A:* idler, slacker. **2.** bungler, botcher.

loupeux, -euse[2] [lupø, -øːz], *a.* knobby; (*a*) covered with wens; (*b*) (*of trees*) gnarled.

loup-garou [lugaru], *s.m.* **1.** (*a*) *Myth:* wer(e)-wolf; (*b*) bogey, bugaboo. **2.** recluse, bear; *a. inv. A:* **il a l'accueil l.-g.,** he has a gruff, bearish, manner; *pl. loups-garous.*

loupiau [lupjo], *s.m.,* **loupiot, -iote[1]** [lupjo, -jɔt], *s.m. & f. F:* small child, urchin, brat, kid.

loupiote[2], *s.f. F:* small light, lamp.

Louqsor [luksɔːr], *Pr.n. Geog:* Luxor.

lourd, -ourde [luːr, -urd]. **1.** *a.* (*a*) heavy (load, sleep, food, etc.); unwieldy (load); heavily-built, ungainly (person); **poids l.,** (i) heavy weight; (ii) *Veh:* heavy lorry; **cric pour poids l.,** heavy-duty jack; **carburant l.,** heavy fuel; **terrain l.,** heavy ground; **lourde responsabilité,** heavy responsibility; **faire une lourde chute,** to fall heavily; **avancer, entrer, sortir, monter, d'un pas l.,** to lumber along, in, out, up; **à la main lourde,** heavy-handed; **avoir la main lourde,** to be heavy-handed; **avoir le sommeil l.,** to be a heavy sleeper; **j'ai la tête lourde,** my head feels heavy, I feel headachy; **avoir une allure lourde,** to slouch; **l'affaire est lourde pour lui,** the business is rather too much for him; *N.Arch:* **formes lourdes,** full lines; *adv.* **peser l.,** to weigh heavy;

péchés qui pèsent l. sur la conscience, sins that lie heavy on the conscience; (*b*) clumsy, awkward (action, etc.); dull (mind, speech); dull-witted, stupid (person); **avoir l'esprit l., l'intelligence lourde,** to be slow of comprehension, dull-witted; (*c*) **lourde erreur,** serious mistake; **lourde bévue,** gross blunder; **lourde perte,** heavy, severe, loss; (*d*) **incident l. de conséquences,** incident fraught with consequences; **silence l. de menaces,** ominous silence; (*e*) close, sultry, muggy, (weather); drowsy (afternoon); **il fait l.,** it is very close, sultry, muggy; (*f*) *F:* **il n'en reste pas l.,** there isn't much left, there aren't many left; **je ne suis pas payé l., je ne gagne pas l.,** I'm not paid much; **je n'en fais pas l.,** I don't exactly overwork. **2.** *s.f. P:* **lourde,** door; **boucler la lourde,** to shut the door; **casser la lourde,** to burgle, to break in.

lourdais, -aise [lurdɛ, -ɛ:z], *a. & s.* (native, inhabitant) of Lourdes.

lourdaud, -aude [lurdo, -o:d]. **1.** *a.* (*a*) loutish (fellow); lumpish, awkward, clumsy (fellow or girl); (*b*) dull-witted, thick-headed. **2.** *s.* (*a*) lout; lumpish fellow, clod; lump (of a girl); (*b*) dullard, thickhead, blockhead.

lourdée [lurde], *s.f. Vet:* staggers, sturdy, gid, goggles.

lourdement [lurdəmɑ̃], *adv.* (*a*) heavily, awkwardly, clumsily; **l. chargé,** heavily laden; **tomber l.,** to fall heavily; **laisser tomber l. qch.,** *F:* to plonk sth. down; **s'exprimer l.,** to express oneself ponderously; **les charrettes s'avancent l.,** the carts lumber along; (*b*) **se tromper l.,** to make a serious mistake.

lourder [lurde], *v.tr. P:* to shut (a door).

lourderie [lurdəri], *s.f. A:* **1.** loutishness, lumpishness; dullness. **2.** gross blunder. **3.** *Vet:* = LOURDÉE.

lourdeur¹ [lurdœ:r], *s.f.* heaviness (of burden, of style, etc.); ponderousness (of style); clumsiness, unwieldiness, awkwardness, ungainliness; dullness (of intellect); severity (of a loss); weight (of a responsibility); sultriness, closeness, (of the weather); **avoir des lourdeurs de tête,** to have fits of drowsiness, of slight headache.

lourdeur², *s.m. P:* burglar.

lourdingue [lurdɛ̃g], *a. P:* (*a*) stupid, dull-witted; (*b*) heavy; **c'est plutôt l. à trimballer,** it's rather heavy to carry.

loure [lu:r], *s.f. A:* **1.** (Normandy) bagpipe. **2.** slow dance in ¾ or ⁶⁄₄ time.

louré [lure], *a. Mus:* slurred, legato.

lourer [lure], *v.tr. Mus:* to play (passage) legato with first note of each bar strongly marked; to drone out (tune).

lousdé (en) [ɑ̃lusde], *adv.phr. P:* on the quiet.

lousse¹ [lus], *s.f. Coop:* auger.

lousse², *s.f.,* **lousseau, -eaux** [luso], *s.m.,* **loussec** [lusɛk], *s.m.,* **lousset** [lusɛ], *s.m.* bilge channel (in bottom of boat).

loustic [lustik], *s.m. F:* joker; barrack-room humorist; **c'est un drôle de l.,** he's a queer fish.

loutre [lutr̥], *s.f.* **1.** *Z:* (*a*) otter; **casquette de l.,** otter-skin cap; (*b*) **l. de mer, l. marine,** sea otter; (*c*) **l. marsupiale,** aquatic opposum, yapo(c)k; (*d*) **l. d'Amérique,** nutria. **2.** *Com:* **(peau de) l.,** sealskin; **fourrure genre l.,** coney seal.

loutreur [lutrœ:r], **loutrier** [lutrije], *s.m.* otter hunter, trapper.

loutrophore [lutrɔfɔ:r], *s.m. Gr.Ant:* loutrophoros.

louvaniste [luvanist], *a. & s.* (native, inhabitant) of Louvain.

louvard, louvart [luva:r], *s.m.,* **louvat** [luva], *s.m.* (weaned) wolf cub.

louve [lu:v], *s.f.* **1.** (*a*) *Z:* she-wolf; (*b*) *A:* wanton; (*c*) **les fils de la Louve,** the Freemasons. **2.** (*a*) *Const: etc:* lewis, lewisson; (*b*) *Const:* **l. à pinces,** (hoisting) scissors. **3.** *N.Arch:* rudder-case, -trunk.

louvelle [luvɛl], *s.f. N.Arch:* **bordé en l.,** carvel-built.

louver¹ [luve], *v.tr.* to lewis (a stone).

louver², *v.tr.* to coil (down) (rope).

louvet, -ette [luvɛ, -ɛt], *a. & s.m.* (*of horse*) yellow-dun, wolf-colour, *U.S:* clay-bank.

louvetage [luvta:ʒ], *s.m. Tex:* willowing (of wool).

louveteau, -eaux [luvto], *s.m.* **1.** (*a*) *Z: Scouting:* wolf cub; (*b*) freemason's son. **2.** *Const:* lewis; wedge (of lewis).

louveter¹ [luvte], *v.i.* **(elle louvette; elle louvettera)** (*of wolf*) to whelp.

louveter², *v.tr. Tex:* to break, willow, will(e)y (wool).

louveterie [luvtri], *s.f.* (*a*) all the paraphernalia of a wolf-destroying battue; wolf-hunting train; (*b*) wolf-hunting; *Hist:* **lieutenant de l.,** official responsible for the extermination of wolves and other vermin; master of the wolf-hunt; (*c*) headquarters of the wolf-hunt.

louveteur [luvtœ:r], *s.m. Tex:* willower.

louvetier [luvtje], *s.m. Hist:* master of the wolf-hunt (in a royal household).

louviers [luvje], *s.m. Tex:* cloth (made at Louviers).

louvoiement [luvwamɑ̃], *s.m.,* **louvoyage** [luvwaja:ʒ], *s.m. Nau:* tacking; beating to windward.

louvoyant [luvwajɑ̃], *a. Tchn:* **piston à mouvement l.,** reciprocating and rotating piston.

louvoyer [luvwaje], *v.i.* **(je louvoie, n. louvoyons; je louvoierai)** (*a*) *Nau:* to tack, to beat about; to beat to windward; **l. à petits bords,** to take short tacks; **l. vers la terre,** to beat up; **le chemin louvoyait parmi les rocs,** the path wound around the rocks; **elle louvoyait, incapable de se décider,** she kept wavering, unable to make up her mind; (*b*) to scheme, manœuvre (to attain one's end).

louvre [lu:vr̥], *s.m. A:* Royal Palace; **le (Palais du) L.,** the Louvre (in Paris).

Louxor [luksɔ:r], *Pr.n. Geog:* Luxor.

lovage [lɔva:ʒ], *s.m. Nau:* **1.** coiling (of rope). **2.** coil (of rope).

love [lɔ:v], *s.f. Tchn:* block of soap.

lovéite [lɔveit], *s.f. Miner:* loewite.

lover [lɔve], *v.tr.* to coil (down) (rope); **l. à contre,** to coil down (a rope) anticlockwise; **l. en galette,** to coil down (a rope) to form a Flemish coil.

se lover, (*of snake, etc.*) to coil up; **vipère lovée,** coiled adder.

lovérien, -ienne [lɔverjɛ̃, -jɛn], *a. & s. Geog:* (native, inhabitant) of Louviers.

loveur [lɔvœ:r], *s.m.* coiler (of ropes).

loxoclase [lɔksɔkla:z], *s.f. Miner:* loxoclase.

loxodonte [lɔksɔdɔ̃:t], *a. Z:* loxodont(ous).

loxodromie [lɔksɔdrɔmi], *s.f. Nau:* **1.** loxodromic curve, rhumb line. **2.** loxodromics.

loxodromique [lɔksɔdrɔmik]. **1.** *a. Nau:* loxodromic; **navigation l.,** loxodromic sailing, sailing by the rhumb line, plane sailing, Mercator's sailing, oblique sailing. **2.** *s.f.* loxodromic curve.

loxolophodon [lɔksɔlɔfɔdɔ̃], *s.m. Paleont:* loxolophodont.

loxomma [lɔksɔma], *s.m. Amph:* loxomma.

loyal, -aux [lwajal, -o], *a.* **1.** honest, fair, straight (-forward), sincere, frank (person, answer, etc.); *F:* on the level; *U.S: F:* white; **être l. en affaires,** to be upright, straightforward, in business; **il est toujours l. en affaires,** he is always straight in business; he always gives you a square deal; **jeu l.,** fair play; *Com: A:* **marchandises d'une bonne qualité loyale,** genuine goods; **valeur loyale et marchande,** fair market value; *Jur:* **compte rendu l. et exact,** true and faithful report; **bon et l. inventaire,** true and accurate inventory; **loyaux coûts,** (purchaser's) contract costs. **2.** loyal, faithful (servant, heart); true, staunch, (friend). **3. Monsieur Loyal,** (stereotype) ringmaster. **4.** *Equit:* **cheval l.,** docile horse; **bouche loyale,** light mouth.

loyalement [lwajalmɑ̃], *adv.* **1.** honestly, fairly, straightforwardly; *F:* on the square; **jouer l.,** to play the game, to play fair; **agir l.,** to behave honourably. **2.** loyally, faithfully.

loyalisme [lwajalism], *s.m.* **1.** loyalty (to the Crown, etc.); **déclaration de l. à qn,** declaration of loyalty to s.o. **2.** *Pol:* loyalism.

loyaliste [lwajalist], *a. & s.m. Eng.Hist:* loyalist.

loyauté [lwajote], *s.f.* **1.** honesty, straightforwardness, uprightness, fairness; **manque de l.,** (i) dishonesty; (ii) unfairness; **au mépris de toute l.,** with gross unfairness. **2.** loyalty, fidelity **(envers,** to); *Geog:* **les îles L.,** Loyalty Islands.

loyer [lwaje], *s.m.* **1.** rent, rental; **prendre une maison à l.,** to rent a house; **donner à l.,** to let; **l. nominal,** peppercorn rent; **gros l.,** heavy rent, big rent; **le montant des loyers,** the rent roll; **devoir trois mois de l.,** to owe three months' rent; *s.a.* BAIL. **2.** *A:* (*a*) reward; (*b*) (servant's) wages. **3.** *Bank:* **le l. de l'argent,** the rates for money on loan, the price of money.

loyoliste [lɔjɔlist], *s.m. Ecc.Hist:* Loyolite, Jesuit.

lozange [lɔzɑ̃:ʒ], *s.m.* = LOSANGE.

lozans [lɔzɑ̃], *s.m.pl. Cu:* shredded pasta used in soup, etc.

lozérien, -ienne [lɔzerjɛ̃, -jɛn], *a. & s. Geog:* (native, inhabitant) of the Lozère region.

lubeckois, -oise [lybɛkwa, -wa:z], *a. & s. Geog:* (native, inhabitant) of Lubeck.

luberne [lybɛrn], *s.f. A:* (*a*) panther; (*b*) panther fur.

lubie [lybi], *s.f.* whim, fad, freak; **vieille dame qui a des lubies,** faddy old lady; **encore une de ses lubies!** another of his fads, ideas!

lubricité [lybrisite], *s.f.* lubricity, lewdness, lust.

lubrifiant [lybrifjɑ̃]. **1.** *a.* lubricating. **2.** *s.m.* lubricant; lubricating oil; *U.S: F:* lube.

lubrificateur, -trice [lybrifikatœ:r, -tris], (*a*) *a.* lubricating, lubricant; (*b*) *s.m.* lubricant.

lubrification [lybrifikasjɔ̃], *s.f.* lubrication, greasing; **l. par jet,** flood lubrication; **l. à compte-gouttes,** drip-feed lubrication; **l. par barbottage,** splash lubrication; **l. sous pression,** pressure, force-feed, lubrication.

lubrifier [lybrifje], *v.tr.* (*pr.sub. & p.d.* **n. lubrifiions, v. lubrifiiez)** to lubricate; to grease, to oil (machinery); *Physiol:* **la synovie lubrifie les articulations,** synovia lubricates the joints.

lubrique [lybrik], *a.* libidinous, lustful, lewd.

lubriquement [lybrik(ə)mɑ̃], *adv.* libidinously, lustfully, lewdly.

Luc [lyk], *Pr.n.m.* Luke.

Lucain [lykɛ̃], *Pr.n. Lt.Lit:* Lucan.

lucane [lykan], *s.m. Ent:* lucanus, stag beetle.

Lucanie [lykani], *Pr.n.f. A.Geog:* Lucania.

lucanien, -ienne [lykanjɛ̃, -jɛn], *a. & s. A.Geog:* Lucanian.

lucarne [lykarn], *s.f. Arch:* (*a*) dormer window, attic window, gable window; (*b*) skylight; light; (*c*) *Opt:* aperture diaphragm; **l. d'entrée, de sortie,** large, small, absolute aperture; (*d*) *Fb:* **"lucarne,"** upper corner (of goal-posts).

lucarnon [lykarnɔ̃], *s.m. Arch:* small dormer window.

Lucayes (les) [lelyka:j], *Pr.n.f.pl. Geog:* the Bahama Islands, the Bahamas.

Luce [lys], *Pr.n.f.* Luce, Lucy.

lucernaire¹ [lysɛrnɛ:r], *s.m.* **1.** *Ecc: A:* lucernarium. **2.** *Rom.Ant:* access shaft to the catacombs.

lucernaire², *s.f. Coel:* lucernaria.

lucernaridés [lysɛrnaride], *s.m.pl. Coel:* Stauromedusae; Lucernariida, Lucernariidea.

lucernois, -oise [lysɛrnwa, -wa:z], *a. & s. Geog:* (native, inhabitant) of Lucerne.

lucernule [lysɛrnyl], *s.f. Ent:* South American lampyrid.

luchage [lyʃa:ʒ], *s.m. Tex:* lustring (of lace).

luche [ly:ʃ], *s.f. Tex:* lustring tool (for lace).

lucher [lyʃe], *v.tr.* to lustre (lace).

lucianesque [lysjanɛsk], *a. Gr.Phil:* Lucianic.

lucide [lysid], *a.* lucid, clear (mind); clear-headed (person); *Med:* lucid (interval); *Psychics:* **somnambule l.,** clairvoyant(e).

lucidement [lysidmɑ̃], *adv.* lucidly, clearly.

lucidité [lysidite], *s.f.* **1.** lucidity, clearness; **fou qui a des intervalles de l.,** madman who has lucid intervals, intervals of sanity. **2.** *Psychics:* clairvoyance.

Lucie [lysi], *Pr.n.f.* Lucia, Lucy.

Lucien [lysjɛ̃], *Pr.n.m. Gr.Lit:* Lucian.

Lucifer [lysifɛ:r]. **1.** *Pr.n.m.* Lucifer; (*a*) morning star; (*b*) Satan. **2.** *s.m. Orn:* lucifer humming bird.

luciférianisme [lysiferjanism], *s.m. Rel.H:* (*a*) theory and practices of the Luciferian schism; (*b*) Satanism.

lucifériens [lysiferjɛ̃], *s.m.pl. Rel.H:* (*a*) Luciferians; (*b*) Satanists.

luciférine [lysiferin], *s.f. Bio-Ch:* luciferin.

lucifuge [lysify:ʒ]. **1.** *a.* lucifugous (insect, etc.). **2.** *s.m. Ent: reticulitermes lucifugus,* lucifugous termite.

lucilie [lysili], *s.f. Ent:* lucilia, *esp.* green-bottle, blowfly.

lucimètre [lysimɛtr̥], *s.m. Opt:* lucimeter.

Lucine [lysin]. **1.** *Pr.n.f. Rom.Myth:* Lucina. **2.** *s.f. Moll:* lucinoid; (*genus*) Lucina.

lucinidés [lysinide], *s.m.pl. Moll:* lucinidae.

luciole [lysjɔl], *s.f.* **1.** *Ent:* luciola, firefly, glow-worm, *U.S:* firebug. **2.** *Com:* artificial straw (made of Cellophane and grass-cloth).

lucite [lysit], *s.f. Med:* burn (from X rays, electricity, etc.).

Luçon [lysɔ̃], *Pr.n. Geog:* **1.** Luzon (in the Philippines). **2.** Luçon (in Vendée).

luçonnais, -aise [lysɔnɛ, -ɛ:z], *a. & s. Geog:* (native, inhabitant) of Luçon.

Lucques [lyk], *Pr.n. Geog:* Lucca.

lucquois, -oise [lykwa, -wa:z], *a. & s. Geog:* Lucchese.

lucratif, -ive [lykratif, -i:v], *a.* lucrative, profitable, paying; **(association) sans but l.,** non-profit-making (association); *Jur:* **dans un but l.,** for pecuniary gain.

lucrativement [lykrativmɑ̃], *adv.* lucratively, profitably.

lucre [lykr̥], *s.m. Pej:* lucre, profit; **faire qch. par amour du l.,** to do sth. for filthy lucre.

Lucrèce [lykrɛs]. **1.** *Pr.n.m. Lt.Lit:* Lucretius. **2.** *Pr.n.f. Rom.Hist:* Lucretia. **3.** *s.f. Pej:* **c'est une L.,** she's a prude.
lucule [lykyl], *s.f. Astr:* lucule.
lucullus [lykylys], *s.m.* gourmet, epicure.
lucuma [lykyma], *s.m. Bot:* lucuma.
luddisme [lydism], *s.m. Eng.Hist:* Luddism.
luddite [lydit], *a. & s.m.* Luddite.
ludien [lydjɛ̃], *a. & s.m. Geol:* Ludian.
ludion [lydjɔ̃], *s.m. Ph:* Cartesian diver; *F:* bottle-imp.
ludique [lydik], *a.* relating to (*Olympian, etc.*) games; *Psy:* ludic (activity, etc.).
ludisme [lydism], *s.m. Psy:* ludic behaviour.
ludlamite [lydlamit], *s.f. Miner:* ludlamite.
ludothérapie [lydəterapi], *s.f. Psy:* play therapy.
ludovicien, -ienne [lydəvisjɛ̃, -jɛn], *a. Hist:* relating to Louis.
ludwigite [lydviʒit], *s.f. Miner:* ludwigite.
luette [lyɛt], *s.f. Anat:* uvula.
lueur [lɥœːr], *s.f.* **1.** gleam, glimmer (of light, hope, etc.); **les premières lueurs de l'aube,** the first rays, glimmer(ings), of dawn; **à la l. des étoiles,** by starlight; **l. crue,** glare. **2. l. momentanée,** flash; **l. d'un coup de feu,** flash of a shot; **jeter une l.,** to flash; **tirer de qn une l. d'intelligence,** to strike a spark out of s.o.
luffa [lyfa], *s.m.* (*a*) *Bot:* sponge cucumber, sponge gourd, loofah, towel gourd; (*b*) *Toil:* vegetable sponge, loofah.
luge [lyːʒ], *s.f.* luge, Swiss toboggan.
lugeage [lyʒaːʒ], *s.m. Sp:* tobogganing.
lugeon[1] [lyʒɔ̃], *s.m. Veh:* skid(-pan) (for wheels); drag shoe.
Lugeon[2], *Pr.n.m. Hyd.E:* **essai de L.,** Lugeon (permeability) test.
luger [lyʒe], *v.i.* (**je lugeai(s); n. lugeons**) to luge, to toboggan.
lugeur, -euse [lyʒœːr, -øːz], *s. Sp:* luger, tobogganer.
lugol [lygəl], *s.m. Pharm:* Lugol's solution.
lugubre [lygybr], *a.* **1.** lugubrious, dismal, gloomy, doleful, mournful. **2.** ominous, dire (news, forebodings, etc.).
lugubrement [lygybrəmɑ̃], *adv.* **1.** lugubriously, dismally, dolefully. **2.** ominously.
lui[1], *pl.* **leur** [lɥi, lœ(ː)r], *pers.pron. m. & f.* (to) him, her, it, them; (*a*) (*unstressed, attached to the verb or its adjuncts*) **je le lui donne,** I give it (to) him, (to) her; **je lui en donne,** I give him some, I give her some; **donnez-lui-en,** give him some; **cette maison leur appartient,** this house belongs to them; **je lui trouve mauvaise mine,** I think he, she, looks ill; **il vient de lui mourir un vieux parent,** he has just lost an old relative; **il leur jeta une pierre,** he threw a stone at them; (*b*) (*stressed in imp.*) **donnez-le-lui,** give it him; **montrez-le-leur,** show it to them.
lui[2], *pl.* **eux** [lɥi, ø], *stressed pers.pron. m.* (*a*) (*subject*) he, it, they; **c'est lui,** it is he, *F:* it's him; that's him; **ce sont eux,** *F:* **c'est eux,** it is they; *F:* it's them; **lui et sa femme étaient là,** he and his wife were there; **lui, il a raison; il a raison, lui; c'est lui qui a raison,** as for him, he's right; he's the one who is right; **mais lui ne t'aime pas,** but he doesn't like you; **il est plus grand qu'eux,** he is taller than they are; **c'est lui-même qui me l'a dit,** he told me so himself; **eux deux, eux tous,** the two of them, all (every one) of them; (*b*) (*object*) him, it, them; **j'accuse son frère et lui,** I accuse him and his brother; **lui, je le connais; je le connais, lui,** him, (yes) I know him; I know him of old; **vous l'avez ruiné, lui qui a été si bon pour vous,** you have ruined him who was so good to you; **je n'ai vu que lui,** I have seen only him; **elle m'a présenté à lui,** she introduced me to him; **ce livre est à lui, à eux,** this book is his, is theirs, **marchez devant eux,** walk in front of them; **il acheta un cheval et bâtit une écurie pour lui,** he bought a horse and built a stable for it; **eux deux, eux tous,** the two of them, all (every-one) of them; **je me rappelle une remarque de lui,** I remember a remark of his; (*c*) (*refl.*) him(self), it(self), them(selves); **il les rassembla autour de lui,** he gathered them round him; **ils ne pensent qu'à eux,** they think of nobody but themselves; **chacun d'eux travaille pour lui-même,** each of them works for himself.
Luidia [lɥidja], *s.m. Echin:* Luidia; *F:* the mud-stars.
lui-même [lɥimɛːm], *pers.pron. See* LUI[2] *and* MÊME 1 (*c*).
luire [lɥiːr], *v.i.* (*pr.p.* **luisant;** *p.p.* **lui** (*no f.*); *pr.ind.* **il luit, ils luisent;** *p.h.* **il luit, ils luirent,** *occ.* **il luisit;** *fu.* **il luira**) to shine; **le soleil luit,** the sun is shining; **son couteau luisait dans l'ombre,** his knife gleamed in the dark; **mon nez luit,** my nose is shiny; **le jour luit,** day is breaking; **un nouveau jour (nous) luit,** a new day is dawning (for us); **les étoiles luisent dans le ciel,** the stars are glimmering in the sky; **les charbons luisent dans la pièce remplie d'ombre,** the embers are glowing in the dark room.
luisance [lɥizɑ̃ːs], *s.f. Lit:* shininess, gloss, lustre; gleam; **l. des cheveux,** sheen on the hair.
luisant, -ante [lɥizɑ̃, -ɑ̃ːt]. **1.** *a.* shining, bright (star, metal, etc.); shiny, glossy (surface, etc.); gleaming (eyes, etc.); **front l. de sueur,** forehead glistening with perspiration; **manteau l. d'usure,** coat shiny with wear; **ver l.,** glow-worm; *Arb:* **à écorce luisante,** silver-barked. **2.** *s.m.* (*a*) shine, gloss, sheen; (*b*) *pl. P:* patent leather shoes; (*c*) *P:* the sun. **3.** *s.f. Astr:* **luisante,** brightest star (of a constellation).
Lulle [lyl], *Pr.n.m. Rel.H:* Lully; **Raymond L.,** Raymond Lully.
lullisme [lylism], *s.m. Theol:* Lullian philosophy.
lulliste [lylist], *s.m. Rel.H:* Lullian, Lullist, Lullianist.
lulu [lyly], *s.m. Orn: F:* **(alouette) l.,** woodlark.
lumachelle [lymaʃɛl], *s.f. Miner:* lumachel(le).
lumbago [lɔ̃bago], *s.m. Med:* lumbago.
lumen [lymɛn], *s.m. Ph.Meas:* lumen.
lumen-heure [lymɛnœːr], *s.f. Ph.Meas:* lumen-hour.
lumière [lymjɛːr], *s.f.* **1.** light; **l. du gaz, du jour, du soleil,** gaslight, daylight, sunlight; **la l. de la lune éclairait la chambre,** the moonlight shone into the room; **l. oxhydrique,** limelight; **l. électrique,** electric light; *Phot:* **l. ambiante,** available light; *Th:* **lumières de la rampe,** limelights; **couper la l.,** to turn off the light; to black out; **remettre la l.,** to put the light on again; **donner de la l.,** to turn on the light; **ce tissu craint la l.,** this material fades; *Ph:* **l. blanche,** white light; **l. noire,** ultra-violet radiations; **l. sélective,** yellow light (without any blue or violet, as used for cars, lighthouses); **bain de l.,** light bath; **à la l. de la lune,** by moonlight; **lire à la l. d'une bougie,** to read by the light of a candle, by candlelight; *Lit:* **voir la l.,** to see the light of day, to be born; **apportez de la l.,** bring in a light; **mettre qch. en l.,** (i) to bring sth. to light; (ii) to bring sth. forward, under the public eye; **mettre en l. les défauts de . . .,** to bring out the faults of . . .; **porter la l. dans un sujet,** to throw light on a subject; **je ne puis vous donner aucune l. sur ce sujet,** I can cast no light on this matter; **faire la l. sur une affaire,** to clear up a business; **la l. se faisait en mon esprit,** I was beginning to understand, to see (a) light; **dépêches secrètes qui ne supporteraient pas la l.,** secret dispatches that would not bear the light of day; **les lumières de la raison,** the light of reason; (*of person*) **l'une des lumières de la science,** one of the leading lights in science; *F:* **ce n'est pas une l.,** he's not very bright; **difficultés au-dessus de mes lumières,** difficulties beyond my understanding; **avoir recours aux lumières des spécialistes,** to have recourse to the superior knowledge of specialists; **la Ville L.,** the City of Light; Paris; *A:* **foyer de lumières,** seat of learning; **le progrès des lumières,** the advance of knowledge; enlightenment; **le siècle des lumières,** the Age of Enlightenment; **un siècle de lumières,** an age of enlightenment; *Sp:* **l'habit de l.,** the bullfighter's costume; *Art:* **hautes lumières,** highlights; *Astr:* **année (de) l.,** light year; **l. cendrée (de la lune),** earth light, earth shine. **2.** aperture (of sighting vane); *A:* priming-hole, vent (of gun); *Carp:* mouth (of plane); *Mec.E:* oil hole (of bearing); *I.C.E:* slot (in sleeve or in piston wall of sleeve-valve engine); *Mch:* **l. de cylindre,** cylinder port; **l. d'échappement,** exhaust port.
lumignon [lymiɲɔ̃], *s.m.* **1.** snuff (of candle). **2.** candle end. **3.** dim light.
luminade [lyminad], *s.f. used only in the phr.* **pêche à la l.,** torch fishing, torching.
luminaire [lyminɛːr], *s.m.* (*a*) luminary, light; star, sun; (*b*) *Coll.* lights, lighting (at church ceremony, evening party, etc.); *Ecc:* **frais de l.,** lighting expenses.
luminance [lyminɑ̃ːs], *s.f. Opt:* luminance, brightness; *T.V:* **signal de l.,** luminance signal.
luminariste [lyminarist], *s.m. Art:* luminarist, painter who works in high lights.
lumination [lyminasjɔ̃], *s.f. Phot:* illumination.
luminescence [lyminɛs(s)ɑ̃ːs], *s.f.* luminescence; **éclairage par l.,** neon lighting; *El: etc:* **l. résiduelle,** post-luminescence; **tension de l. (d'une cellule photo-électrique),** blue-glow voltage.
luminescent [lyminɛs(s)ɑ̃], *a.* luminescent, (self-) luminous; **éclairage l.,** neon lighting.
lumineusement [lyminøzmɑ̃], *adv.* luminously; brightly.
lumineux, -euse [lyminø, -øːz], *a.* luminous (body, sea, mind); **pouvoir l. d'une lampe,** candle-power of a lamp; **yeux l.,** bright eyes; **idée lumineuse,** brilliant idea, bright idea, brainwave; **cadran l.,** luminous dial; *Ph:* **onde lumineuse,** light wave; *T.V:* **tache, bande, lumineuse,** light spot, strip; *Biol:* **organe l.,** phosphorescent, luminous, organ.
luminifère [lyminifɛːr], *a.* luminiferous.
luministe [lyminist], *s.m. Art:* luminist, luminarist.
luminogène [lyminəʒɛn], *s.m. Ph:* light generating element.
luminophore [lyminəfəːr], *s.m.* **1.** *Nat.Hist:* any being with luminescent organs. **2.** *Elcs:* luminophore, luminescent material.
luminosité [lyminozite], *s.f.* **1.** luminosity, luminousness, brightness; sheen; *T.V:* **dispositif de réglage de la l.,** brightness control; *Opt:* **coefficient de l.,** luminosity factor; **la puissance de l. du peintre,** the painter's mastery of light effects. **2.** patch of light.
Lumitype [lymitip], *s.f. R.t.m: Typ:* Lumitype.
lumme [lym], *s.m. Orn:* black-throated diver.
lump [lɔ̃p], *s.m. Ich:* lump (fish), lump sucker; sea-owl.
lunaire [lynɛːr]. **1.** *a.* (*a*) lunar, (month, caustic, mountain, etc.); **paysage l.,** moonscape; **pays l.,** moonlit country; **cycle l.,** metonic, lunar, cycle; **année l.,** lunar year; **année l. embolismique,** embolismic year; **cadran l.,** lunar dial; **mois l. synodique,** synodic(al) month; **mois l. sidéral,** sidereal month; **fusée l.,** moon rocket; **piéton l.,** moonwalker; **germes lunaires,** moonbugs; **secousse l.,** moonquake; **Institut, Laboratoire, de chimie l.,** Lunar Receiving Laboratory; (*b*) moon-shaped; **visage l.,** moonface; **jeune homme à visage l.,** moonfaced young man; (*c*) visionary; **il a un esprit l.,** he has the mind of a dreamer. **2.** *s.f. Bot:* lunaria, *F:* honesty, satin flower, satin pod, moonwort. **3.** *s.m. Ent:* luna moth.
lunaison [lynɛzɔ̃], *s.f. Astr:* lunation, synodic(al) month.
lunatique [lynatik], *a. & s.* **1.** whimsical, capricious, temperamental, (person). **2.** *B.Lit:* lunatic. **3.** *Vet:* **œil l.,** moon-eye (of horse); moon blindness; **cheval l.,** moon-eyed, moon-blind, horse.
lunaute [lynoːt], *s.m.* lunarnaut.
lunch [lœːʃ], *s.m.* (*a*) (wedding, etc.) reception; buffet meal; (*b*) light meal, snack; *pl. lunches, lunchs.*
luncher [lœ̃ʃe], *v.i.* (*a*) to attend a (buffet) reception; (*b*) to have a light meal, a snack.
lundi [lœ̃di], *s.m.* Monday; **le l. gras,** Shrove Monday; **le l. de Pâques,** Easter Monday; **chômer le l.,** *F:* **faire le l., fêter la Saint-L.,** to take Monday off; *A:* to keep Saint Monday; **faire l.,** to take the day off.
lundiste [lœ̃dist], *s.m. Journ:* critic who writes the Monday article (*usu.* literary criticism).
lune [lyn], *s.f.* **1.** (*a*) moon; **se poser sur la l.,** to land on the moon; **pleine l.,** full moon; **nouvelle l.,** new moon; **l. des moissons,** harvest moon; **l'homme de la l.,** the man in the moon; **clair de l.,** moonlight; **à la clarté de la l.,** by moonlight; **se promener au clair de l.,** to go for a walk in the moonlight; **coucher à l'enseigne de la l.,** to sleep in the open; **nuit sans l.,** moonless night; **être le clair de l. de qn, de qch.,** to be a pale reflection of s.o., of sth.; **paysage éclairé par la l.,** moonlit landscape; **l. rousse,** (i) April moon; (ii) *F:* period of domestic bickerings; **l. de miel,** honeymoon; **leur mariage fut une l. de miel sans fin,** their marriage was an endless honeymoon; **les vieilles lunes, les lunes d'autrefois,** (i) the good old days, the remote past; (ii) out-of-date ideas; *F:* **une vieille l.,** an old fogey; *F:* **aller où vont, s'en aller rejoindre, les vieilles lunes,** to disappear, to be forgotten; **ce sont de vieilles lunes,** all that's old hat; **vouloir prendre la l. entre ses dents,** to attempt the impossible; **demander la l.,** to ask for the moon (and the stars), to cry for the moon; **promettre la l.,** to promise the moon (and stars); **faire voir la l. à qn en plein midi,** to lead s.o. up the garden path; to fool s.o.; *A:* **faire un trou à la l.,** to shoot the moon, do a moonlight flit; (*of banker*) to abscond; *F:* **être dans la l.,** to be starry-eyed, miles away, in the clouds; to be wool-gathering; **tomber de la l.,** not to know what's going on; to look blank; *F:* **être bête comme la l.,** to be completely stupid; **avoir (un quartier de) la l. dans la tête,** to be loony; *s.a.* ABOYER 1; (*b*) **les lunes de Saturne,** the moons of Saturn; (*c*) *Poet:* month, moon; (*d*) moonlight. **2.** (*a*)

crescent-shaped object or aperture; **en forme de l.,** lunate, moon-shaped, crescent-shaped; (*b*) *F:* (i) moonface; **avoir une figure, un visage, de pleine l.,** to be moonfaced; (ii) *P:* posterior, bum. **3.** vagary, caprice, whim; **avoir des lunes,** to have moods, to be moody; **il est dans une bonne l., dans une mauvaise l.,** he is in one of his good moods, in one of his bad moods. **4.** (*a*) *Bot:* **l. d'eau,** white water-lily; (*b*) *Ich:* **poisson (de) l.,** sunfish; (*c*) *Lap:* **pierre de l.,** moonstone. **5.** *Alch:* silver; *s.a.* CORNÉ 2.

luné [lyne], *a.* **1.** lunate, crescent-shaped; luniform. **2.** *F:* **être bien, mal, l.,** to be in a good, bad, mood; **esprits mal lunés,** ill-disposed people.

lunelle [lynɛl], *s.f. Moll:* lunule.

lunetier, -ière [lyntje, -jɛːr], *s. & a.* **1.** *s.* spectacle-maker; optician; *f.* spectacle-maker's wife. **2.** *a.* **industrie lunetière,** spectacle industry. **3.** *s.f. Bot:* **lunetière,** biscutella; buckler mustard.

lunette [lynɛt], *s.f.* **1. l. d'approche,** (refracting) telescope, field glass; *Surv:* **l. viseur,** *Artil:* **l. de pointage,** sighting telescope; *Surv:* **coup de l.,** observation, sight; *Artil: etc:* **l. de pointage continu,** tracking telescope; **l. astronomique,** astronomical telescope; **l. de navigation astronomique,** astro-navigation telescope; **l. méridienne,** transit telescope; **l. coudée,** elbow telescope, broken telescope; **l. terrestre, de Galilée,** Galilean telescope. **2.** *pl.* (*a*) **(paire de) lunettes,** (pair of) spectacles; **mettre, chausser, ses lunettes,** to put on one's glasses; *F:* **mettez (donc) vos lunettes,** you'd better look properly; **porter (des) lunettes,** to wear spectacles; **chacun voit avec ses lunettes,** we all see through our own spectacles; *F:* **nez à lunettes,** long nose; **lunettes de protection, (de soudeur),** etc., goggles; **lunettes d'alpiniste, de glacier, pour le ski,** snow goggles; **lunettes fumées, noires, solaires, de soleil,** sun glasses, dark glasses; **serpent à lunettes,** spectacled snake, Indian cobra; (*b*) *Harn:* blinkers, blinders. **3.** *Cu:* merrythought, wishbone (of fowl). **4.** (*a*) *Arch: Fort:* lunette; (*b*) lunette (of guillotine); *P:* **mettre la tête à la l.,** to be guillotined. **5.** (*a*) seat (of w.c. pan); (*b*) rim of watch (in which glass is set); (*c*) *Rail:* cab-window (of locomotive); *pl.* cab-spectacles; *Aut:* **l. arrière,** rear window; **l. enveloppante, panoramique,** wrap round rear window; (*d*) *Mec.E:* (screw-cutting) die; (*e*) **l. (fixe) d'un tour,** back rest, steady rest, of a lathe; **l. (de tour) à suivre,** following steady rest; follow rest; (*f*) *N.Arch:* shaft hole (of propeller-post).

lunetté [lynɛte], *a. Z:* spectacled (bear, cobra, etc.).

lunetterie [lynɛtri], *s.f.* (i) making of spectacles, of optical instruments; (ii) spectacle industry.

lunetteux, -euse [lynɛtø, -øːz], *a. F: & Pej:* bespectacled.

lunettier, -ière [lynɛtje, -jɛːr], *s.* = LUNETIER, -IÈRE.

lunévillois, -oise [lynevilwa, -waːz], *a. & s.* (native, inhabitant) of Lunéville.

lunifère [lynifɛːr], *a. Bot: etc:* bearing lunate markings.

luni-solaire [lynisɔlɛːr], *a.* lunisolar (year, etc.); *pl. luni-solaires.*

lunulaire [lynylɛːr], *a.* lunular, lunulate.

lunularia [lynylarja], *s.f. Bot:* lunularia.

lunule [lynyl], *s.f.* **1.** *Geom:* lunule, lunula. **2.** *Anat:* lunule, lunula, (half-)moon (of finger nail). **3.** *Rom.Ant:* crescent-shaped ivory ornament (on patrician's shoes), lunula. **4.** *Ent: Moll:* lunule.

lunulé [lynyle], *a.* lunulate(d).

lunulite [lynylit], **lunulites** [lynylitɛs], *s.m. Prot:* lunulite; (*genus*) Lunulites.

lunure [lynyːr], *s.f.* lunate, crescent-shaped defect in wood.

lupa [lypa], *s.f. Crust:* lupa.

lupanar [lypanaːr], *s.m.* brothel.

lupercales [lypɛrkal], *s.f.pl. Rom.Ant:* Lupercalia.

lupétidine [lypetidin], *s.f. Ch:* lupetidine.

lupin[1] [lypɛ̃], *s.m. Bot:* lupin.

lupin[2], *a.* lupine; wolfish.

lupinelle [lypinɛl], *s.f. Bot:* **1.** clover. **2.** sainfoin.

lupinose [lypinoːz], *s.f. Vet:* lupinosis.

lupique [lypik], *a. Med:* lupous.

lupoïde [lypɔid], *a. Med:* lupiform, lupoid.

lupome [lypoːm], *s.m. Med:* lupoma.

lupulin [lypylɛ̃], *s.m. Bot: Brew:* lupulin.

lupuline [lypylin], *s.f.* **1.** *Bot:* (*a*) = LUPULIN; (*b*) black medic, nonesuch. **2.** *Ch:* lupulin.

lupus [lypys], *s.m. Med:* lupus; **l. érythémateux,** lupus erythematosus; **l. tuberculeux,** lupus vulgaris.

lurette [lyrɛt], *s.f. F:* (*corruption of* **l'heurette,** *dimin. of* **heure**) *used only in* **il y a belle l.,** a long time ago, ages ago.

luride [lyrid], *a. Med:* lurid, sallow (skin).

luridité [lyridite], *s.f. Med:* sallowness.

luron[1], **-onne** [lyrɔ̃, -ɔn], *s.m. F:* (*a*) *m.* jolly chap; strapping fellow; **c'est un l.,** he's quite a lad! **c'est un gai l., un joyeux l.,** he's a gay dog; he's one of the boys; (*b*) *f.* (i) strapping girl; (ii) tomboy; **c'est une luronne,** she's not at all shy.

luron[2], **-onne,** *a. & s. Geog:* (native, inhabitant) of Lure.

Lusace [lyzas], *Pr.n.f. Geog:* Lusatia.

lusacien, -ienne [lyzasjɛ̃, -jɛn], *a. Geog:* Lusatian.

luscinia [lysinja], *s.m. Orn:* luscinia, nightingale.

lusciniole [lysinjɔl], *s.f. Orn:* **l. à moustaches,** moustached warbler.

Lusiades (les) [lelyzjad], *Pr.n.f. Portuguese Lit:* the Lusiad.

lusin [lyzɛ̃], *s.m. Nau:* houseline, marline.

lusitain, -aine [lyzitɛ̃, -ɛn], *a. & s. A.Geog:* Lusitanian.

Lusitanie [lyzitani], *Pr.n.f. A.Geog:* Lusitania.

lusitanien, -ienne [lyzitanjɛ̃, -jɛn]. **1.** *a. & s. A.Geog:* Lusitanian. **2.** *s.m. Geol:* Lusitanian; English Corallian.

lusol [lyzɔl], *s.m.* commercial benzine.

lussatite [lysatit], *s.f. Miner:* lussatite.

lustrage [lystraːʒ], *s.m.* **1.** glossing, glazing, lustring (of cloth, etc.); polishing (of glass). **2.** shininess (due to wear).

lustral, -aux [lystral, -o], *a. Rom.Ant:* lustral (water, days).

lustration [lystrasjɔ̃], *s.f. Rom.Ant:* lustration.

lustre[1] [lystr̥], *s.m.* **1.** (*a*) lustre, polish, gloss, glaze (of silk, etc.); *Cer:* **l. irisé,** transmutation glaze; (*b*) *Lit:* renown, splendour; **ajouter un nouveau l. à sa gloire,** to add fresh lustre to one's glory; **servir de l. au talent de qn,** to set off s.o.'s talent. **2.** chandelier; **l. électrique,** (electric) chandelier.

lustre[2], *s.m. Lit: Poet:* lustrum, lustre, period of five years.

lustré [lystre], *a.* glazed; glossy; **le poil lustré du chat,** the cat's glossy coat; **toile lustrée,** glazed cloth; **étoffe lustrée par l'usure,** cloth shiny with wear; *Geol:* **schistes lustrés,** mica schists.

lustrer [lystre], *v.tr.* to glaze, gloss, polish (up), lustre (leather, etc.).

lustrerie [lystr(ə)ri], *s.f. Ind:* chandelier factory.

lustreur [lystrœːr], *s.m. Tex:* lusterer.

lustreuse [lystrøːz], *s.f.* (*machine*) floor polisher.

lustrine [lystrin], *s.f. Tex:* **1.** (silk) lustrine, lustring, lutestring. **2.** cotton lustre, linenette; **manchettes de l.,** oversleeves.

lustroir [lystrwaːr], *s.m.* (*a*) polisher (for glass, mirrors); (*b*) *Glassm:* felt pad for polishing mirrors (as after treatment).

lustucru [lystykry], *s.m.* (*a*) *A: F:* (? = **l'eusses-tu cru**) simpleton; (*b*) **(le père) L.,** bogey-man (*as a threat to children*).

lut [lyt], *s.m. Cer: Ind:* lute, luting, cement.

lutage [lytaːʒ], *s.m. Tchn:* lute, luting; sealing with luting.

lutation [lytasjɔ̃], *s.f.* luting (of joint, etc.).

Lutèce [lytɛs], *Pr.n.f. A.Geog:* Lutetia (Roman name of Paris).

lutécien, lutétien, -ienne [lytesjɛ̃, -jɛn], *a. & s.* Lutetian.

lutécium [lytesjɔm], *s.m. Ch:* lutecium.

lutéine [lytein], *s.f. Biol: Ch:* lutein.

lutéinisation [lyteinizasjɔ̃], *s.f. Biol: Physiol:* luteinization.

lutéocobaltique [lyteɔkɔbaltik], *a. Ch:* luteo-cobaltic (chloride, etc.).

lutéol [lyteɔl], *s.m. Ch:* chemical indicator which turns bright yellow with alkalis and colourless with acids.

luter [lyte], *v.tr.* to lute; to seal with luting; *Cu:* to seal (a dish with a flour and water paste).

lutétien [lytesjɛ̃], *a. & s.m. Geol:* Lutetian.

lutévain, -aine [lytevɛ̃, -ɛn], *a. & s. Geog:* (native, inhabitant) of Lodève.

luth [lyt], *s.m. Mus:* lute; **joueur de l.,** lutist, lute player; *Lit:* (*of poet*) **prendre son l.,** to start composing; *s.a.* TORTUE.

luthé [lyte], *a.* transposed for, accompanied by, the lute.

luthéranisme [lyteranism], *s.m. Rel.H:* Lutheranism.

lutherie [lytri], *s.f. Mus:* (*a*) stringed-instrument industry, trade; (*b*) *Coll.* stringed instruments; (*c*) stringed-instrument shop.

luthérien, -ienne [lyterjɛ̃, -jɛn], *a. & s. Rel.H:* Lutheran.

luthier [lytje], *s.m.* (*a*) stringed-instrument maker, violin maker; (*b*) seller of stringed instruments.

luthiste [lytist], *s.m. Mus:* lutist, lute player.

lutidine [lytidin], *s.f. Ch:* lutidine.

lutidique [lytidik], *a. Ch:* **acide l.,** lutidinic acid.

lutin, -ine [lytɛ̃, -in]. **1.** *s.m.* (*a*) mischievous sprite, imp, elf, brownie, goblin; (*b*) *F:* (*of child*) imp. **2.** *a.* mischievous, impish, roguish, elfish; **l'œil, un air, l.,** a mischievous glance, a saucy look.

lutiner [lytine]. **1.** *v.tr.* to tease, plague, torment (s.o.); **l. les bonnes,** to make free with, to tease, the servant girls. **2.** *v.i.* to play the imp.

lutinerie [lytinri], *s.f.* **1.** impishness, mischievousness. **2.** impish trick or prank.

lutjan [lytjɑ̃], *s.m. Ich:* lutjanus; *F:* snapper.

lutjanides [lytjanid], **lutjanidés** [lytjanide], *s.m.pl. Ich:* Lutjanidae, Lutianidae.

lutraire [lytrɛːr], *s.m. Moll:* common otter-shell.

lutrin [lytrɛ̃], *s.m.* (*a*) *Ecc:* lectern; choir singing-desk; (*b*) *Ecc: Coll.* the succentors; **chanter au l.,** to sing bass in the choir; (*c*) *Fr.C:* reading stand, music stand.

lutrinés [lytrine], *s.m.pl. Z:* the otters.

lutte [lyt], *s.f.* **1.** wrestling; **l. gréco-romaine,** Graeco-Roman wrestling; **l. libre,** freestyle wrestling; **assaut de l.,** wrestling bout. **2.** (*a*) contest, fight, struggle, tussle; **l. entre deux personnes,** contest between two people; **entrer en l. avec qn,** to join battle with s.o.; to come into collision with s.o.; to come to grips with s.o.; **soutenir une l. inégale,** to fight against odds; **les partis en l.,** the contending parties; **luttes parlementaires,** parliamentary clashes; **soutenir une l. opiniâtre contre qn,** to carry on a stubborn fight against s.o.; **l. à mort,** life and death struggle; fight to the death; **l. contre la maladie,** disease prevention, control; fight against disease; **l. contre l'alcoolisme,** campaign against alcoholism; **l. pour la vie,** (i) struggle for life; (ii) natural selection; **la l. des intérêts et du devoir,** the struggle, conflict, between (self-)interest and duty; *adv.phr.* **de haute,** *Lit:* **de vive, l.,** by force, by sheer fighting; by force of arms; **remporter un prix de haute l.,** to carry off a prize in an open competition; **trophée remporté de haute l.,** hard-won trophy; **de bonne l.,** fair(ly), above-board; **c'est de bonne l.,** it's quite fair; *Sp:* **l. à la corde de traction,** tug-of-war; (*b*) strife; **politique de l.,** policy of strife; **la l. des classes,** the class struggle, class warfare. **3.** *Husb:* mating (of sheep).

lutter [lyte], *v.i.* **1.** to wrestle **(avec, contre,** with). **2.** to struggle, contend, fight, compete **(contre,** with, against); **l. contre la maladie,** to fight against disease; to combat disease; **l. contre le vent,** to battle with the wind; **l. contre les vagues,** to buffet (with, against) the waves; **l. contre l'incendie,** to battle with the fire; **l. contre un abus,** to make a stand against an abuse; **l. de vitesse avec qn,** to race s.o.; **l. à qui fera qch.,** to vie (with one another) in doing sth.; **elles luttent de beauté,** they try to outdo each other in beauty; *s.a.* PIED 1. **3.** (*of ram*) to tup, cover, the ewe.

lutteur, -euse [lytœːr, -øːz], *s.* **1.** wrestler. **2.** fighter (for a cause, against fate).

lux [lyks], *s.m. Ph.Meas:* lux (unit of intensity of illumination).

luxation [lyksasjɔ̃], *s.f. Med: Vet:* luxation, dislocation (of joint); *Dent:* **l. dentaire,** luxated tooth; *Med:* **l. congénitale de la hanche,** *luxatio coxae congenita;* congenital dislocation of the hip; **l. du cristallin,** luxation of the globe.

luxe [lyks], *s.m.* luxury; (*a*) **vivre dans le l.,** to live in luxury; **gros l.,** ostentation, vulgar display of wealth; **étaler tout son l.,** to flaunt one's wealth; **c'est du luxe,** that is quite unnecessary, a mere luxury; **l. de pacotille,** shoddy kind of luxury; **je me suis acheté un manteau; ce n'était pas du l.,** I bought myself a coat; it was a necessity, not a luxury; **je me suis payé le l. de le lui dire,** I gave myself the pleasure of telling him so; **se payer le l. d'un cigare,** to indulge in the luxury of a cigar; **c'est un l. que nous nous sommes offert,** we indulged ourselves, did ourselves well; **le l. discret de sa toilette,** the unostentatious expensiveness of her dress; **livre imprimé avec l.,** sumptuously printed book; **articles de l.,** luxury articles; **cabine, édition, de l.,** de luxe cabin, edition; **train de l.,** first-class and Pullman train; **taxe de l.,** luxury tax; (*b*) abundance, profusion, superfluity (of food, etc.); **l. de précautions,** extravagant precautions; **le l. de la végétation,** the luxuriance of the vegetation.

Luxembourg [lyksɑ̃buːr], *Pr.n.m.* **1.** *Geog:* (*a*) (Grand Duchy of) Luxemburg; (*b*) Luxembourg (in Belgium). **2. le L.,** the Luxembourg (palace and gardens in Paris).

luxembourgeois, -oise [lyksɑ̃burʒwa, -waːz], *a.* *& s. Geog:* (native, inhabitant) of Luxemburg; Luxemburger.

luxer [lykse], *v.tr.* to luxate, dislocate (joint, etc.); **se l. le genou,** to put one's knee out (of joint).

luxmètre [lyksmɛtr̩], *s.m. Opt:* lux-meter.

luxovien, -ienne [lyksɔvjɛ̃, -jɛn], *a. & s. Geog:* (native, inhabitant) of Luxeuil.

luxueusement [lyksɥøzmɑ̃], *a.* luxuriously, sumptuously.

luxueux, -euse [lyksɥø, -øːz], *a.* luxurious; rich (dress); sumptuous (feast).

luxure [lyksyːr], *s.f.* lewdness, lechery, lust.

luxuriance [lyksyrjɑ̃ːs], *s.f.* luxuriance.

luxuriant [lyksyrjɑ̃], *a.* luxuriant (vegetation, etc.); **une chevelure luxuriante,** a magnificent head of hair; **style l.,** over-ornate style.

luxurieusement [lyksyrjøzmɑ̃], *adv.* lecherously, lewdly, lustfully.

luxurieux, -euse [lyksyrjø, -øːz], *a.* lecherous, lewd, lustful.

luzerne [lyzɛrn], *s.f. Bot: Agr:* lucern(e), purple medic; alfalfa; **l. en faux,** sickle medic, yellow medic; **l. houblon,** black medic, hop medic, nonesuch.

luzernière [lyzɛrnjɛːr], *s.f. Agr:* lucern(e) field.

luzien, -ienne [lyzjɛ̃, -jɛn], *a. & s. Geog:* (native, inhabitant) of Saint-Jean-de-Luz.

luzule [lyzyl], *s.f. Bot:* **l. des champs,** sweet bent.

lycanthrope [likɑ̃trɔp], *s.m. Med:* lycanthrope.

lycanthropie [likɑ̃trɔpi], *s.f. Med:* lycanthropy.

lycaon [likaɔ̃], *s.m. Z:* lycaon, Cape hunting dog, painted hyena.

Lycaonie [likaɔni], *Pr.n.f. A.Geog:* Lycaonia.

lycaonien, -ienne [likaɔnjɛ̃, -jɛn], *a. & s. A.Geog:* Lycaonian.

lycée [lise], *s.m.* 1. le L., (a) *Gr.Ant:* the Lyceum; (b) *Fr.Hist:* the Lycée (where La Harpe lectured in the 18th century). 2. = grammar, high, school; **l. technique** = college of technology.

lycéen, -éenne [liseɛ̃, -een], *a. & s.* 1. *Gr.Ant:* pertaining to the Lyceum. 2. *Sch:* (a) *a.* pertaining to a *lycée*; (b) *s.* = grammar-school, high-school, pupil.

lycène [lisɛn], *s.f. Ent:* lycaena; common blue (butterfly).

lycénidés [lisenide], *s.m.pl. Ent:* Lycaenidae, the lycaenids.

lychnide [liknid], *s.f.,* **lychnis** [liknis], *s.m. Bot:* lychnis, campion; **l. diurne,** red campion; **l. des prés,** ragged robin.

lychnite [liknit], *s.f.* (white) Parian marble.

Lycie [lisi], *Pr.n.f. A.Geog:* Lycia.

lycien, -ienne [lisjɛ̃, -jɛn], *a. & s. A.Geog:* Lycian.

lyciet [lisjɛ], *s.m. Bot:* box thorn.

lycodon [likɔdɔ̃], *s.m. Rept:* lycodon.

lycomèdes [likɔmedɛs], *s.m. Ent:* lycomedes.

lycope [likɔp], *s.m. Bot:* lycopus, gipsywort, water-horehound.

lycopène [likɔpɛn], *s.m. Bio-Ch:* lycopene.

lycoperdon [likɔpɛrdɔ̃], *s.m. Fung:* lycoperdon; *F:* puff-ball.

lycopode [likɔpɔd], *s.m. Bot:* lycopod(ium); **l. en massue,** club-moss; *Pharm: etc:* **poudre de l.,** lycopodium (powder) *F:* vegetable brimstone.

lycopodiacées [likɔpɔdjase], *s.f.pl. Bot:* Lycopodiaceae.

lycopodiales [likɔpɔdjal], *s.f.pl. Bot:* Lycopodiales.

lycopodinées [likɔpɔdine], *s.f.pl. Bot:* Lycopodineae.

lycopside [likɔpsid], *s.f.,* **lycopsis** [likɔpsis], *s.m. Bot:* lycopsis; **l. des champs,** field bugloss.

lycopus [likɔpyːs], *s.m. Bot:* lycopus; water horehound; bugleweed.

lycose [likoːz], *s.f. Arach:* lycosid; wolf spider.

lycosidés [likɔzide], *s.m.pl. Arach:* Lycosidae.

lycte [likt], *s.m. Ent:* lyctid; powder-post beetle.

Lycurgue [likyrg], *Pr.n.m. Gr.Hist:* Lycurgus.

lyddite [lidit], *s.f. Exp:* lyddite.

Lydie [lidi], *Pr.n.f. A.Geog: etc:* Lydia.

lydien, -ienne [lidjɛ̃, -jɛn], 1. *a. & s. A.Geog: Mus:* Lydian. 2. *s.f. Miner:* **lydienne,** Lydian stone, touchstone.

lydite [lidit], *s.f. Miner:* Lydian stone, touchstone.

lygaeus [ligeyːs], *s.m. Ent:* lygaeid.

lygée [liʒe], *s.f. Bot:* lygeum, esparto grass.

lygéidés [liʒeide], *s.m.pl. Ent:* Lygaeidae.

lygie [liʒi], *s.f. Crust:* common sea(-)slater.

lyginopteris [liʒinɔpteris], *s.f. Paleont: Bot:* Lyginopteris.

lygodium [ligɔdjɔm], *s.m. Bot:* lygodium; climbing fern.

lygosome [ligɔzom], *s.m. Rept:* lygosoma.

lygus [ligys], *s.m. Ent:* lygus bug.

lymantri(i)dés [limɑ̃tri(i)de], *s.m.pl. Ent:* Lymantriidae, the lymantriids.

lymphadénectomie [lɛ̃fadenɛktɔmi], *s.f. Surg:* lymphadenectomy; excision of a lymph gland.

lymphadénie [lɛ̃fadeni], *s.f. Med:* lymphadenia.

lymphadénite [lɛ̃fadenit], *s.f. Med:* lymphadenitis.

lymphadénome [lɛ̃fadeno:m], *s.m. Med:* lymphadenoma.

lymphangiectasie [lɛ̃fɑ̃ʒjɛktazi], *s.f. Med:* lymphangiectasis, lymphangiectasia.

lymphangiome [lɛ̃fɑ̃ʒjo:m], *s.m. Med:* lymphangioma.

lymphangite [lɛ̃fɑ̃ʒit], *s.f. Med:* lymphangitis; *Vet:* **l. ulcéreuse,** ulcerative lymphangitis.

lymphatique [lɛ̃fatik], *Physiol:* 1. *a. & s.* lymphatic (gland, subject). 2. *s.m.* lymphatic (duct).

lymphatisme [lɛ̃fatism], *s.m. Med:* lymphatism.

lymphatite [lɛ̃fatit], *s.f. Med:* lymphatitis.

lymphe [lɛ̃f], *s.f.* 1. (a) *Physiol:* lymph; (b) *A.Bot:* sap, *A:* lymph. 2. *Med:* **l. de Koch,** tuberculin.

lymphoblaste [lɛ̃fɔblast], *s.m. Biol:* lymphoblast.

lymphocèle [lɛ̃fɔsɛl], *s.m. Path:* lymphocele, lymphocyst.

lymphocyte [lɛ̃fɔsit], *s.m. Physiol:* lymphocyte.

lymphocytémie [lɛ̃fɔsitemi], *s.f. Med:* lymphocythaemia.

lymphocytogénèse [lɛ̃fɔsitɔʒenɛːz], *s.f. Physiol:* lymphocytopoiesis, lymphocytogenesis.

lymphocytose [lɛ̃fɔsitoːz], *s.f. Med:* lymphocytosis.

lymphogène [lɛ̃fɔʒɛn], *a. Physiol:* lymphogenic, lymphogenous.

lymphogénèse [lɛ̃fɔʒenɛːz], *s.f. Physiol:* lymphogenesis.

lymphogranulomatose [lɛ̃fɔgranylɔmatoːz], *s.f. Med:* lymphogranulomatosis; **l. bénigne,** benign lymphogranulomatosis, sarcoidosis; **l. maligne,** Hodgkin's disease.

lymphographie [lɛ̃fɔgrafi], *s.f. Med:* lymphography, lymphangiography.

lymphoïde [lɛ̃fɔid], *a. Anat:* lymphoid (cells, tissue).

lymphome [lɛ̃foːm], *s. Med:* lymphoma.

lymphopoïèse [lɛ̃fɔpɔjɛːz], *s.f. Physiol:* lymphopoiesis.

lymphoréticulose [lɛ̃fɔretikyloːz], *s.f. Med:* lymphoreticulosis, *F:* cat scratch fever.

lymphosarcome [lɛ̃fɔsarkoːm], *s.m. Med:* lymphosarcoma.

Lyncée [lɛse], *Pr.n.m. Gr.Myth:* Lynceus.

Lynch [lɛ̃ːʃ], *Pr.n.m.* **loi de L.,** lynch law.

lynchage [lɛ̃ʃaːʒ], *s.m.* lynching.

lyncher [lɛ̃ʃe], *v.tr.* to lynch.

lyncodon [lɛ̃kɔdɔ̃], *s.m. Z:* **l. de Patagonie,** Patagonian polecat.

lynx [lɛ̃ːks], *s.m.* lynx; **l. des marais,** jungle cat; **aux yeux de l.,** lynx-eyed; **avoir des yeux de l.,** to be sharp-sighted.

lyocyte [ljɔsit], *s.m. Biol:* lyo-enzyme.

Lyon [ljɔ̃], *Pr.n. Geog:* Lyon(s).

lyonnais, -aise [ljɔnɛ, -ɛːz], *a. & s. Geog:* (native, inhabitant) of Lyon(s); Lyonese.

lyophile [ljɔfil], *a.* lyophilic.

lyophilisation [ljɔfilizasjɔ̃], *s.f.* freeze-drying, lyophilization.

lyophiliser [ljɔfilize], *v.tr.* to freeze-dry, to lyophilize.

lyophobe [ljɔfɔb], *a.* lyophobic.

lypémanie [lipemani], *s.f.* lypemania.

lyre [liːr], *s.f.* 1. *Mus:* lyre; *Lit:* poetic talent; poetry; **ajouter une corde à sa l.,** to add a string to one's lute; **toute la l.,** the whole range (of poetic emotion, etc.). 2. *Astr:* Lyra. 3. *Orn:* (oiseau-)l., lyre bird. 4. (a) *Mec.E:* quadrant (-plate) (of lathe); (b) stirrup (of rowlock); (c) **l. de dilatation,** loop (in a circuit, etc.); **l. de raccordement,** connecting pipe, loop.

lyré [lire], *a. Nat.Hist:* lyrate.

lyre-carillon [lirkarijɔ̃], *s.f. Mus:* Jingling Johnny; *pl.* lyres-carillons.

lyre-guitare [lirgitaːr], *s.f. Mus:* lyre-guitar; *pl.* lyres-guitares.

lyriforme [liriform], *a.* lyriform.

lyrique [lirik], 1. (a) *a.* lyric(al) (poem, etc.); **poète l.,** lyric poet; *Pros:* **coupe l.,** lyric caesura; **drame l.,** œuvre l., lyric drama, opera; (b) **théâtre l.,** opera house; **faire une carrière l.,** to take up a career as a singer. 2. *s.m.* (a) lyricism; (b) lyric poetry; (c) lyric poet.

lyrisme [lirism], *s.m.* 1. lyricism. 2. poetic enthusiasm. 3. *F:* excessive enthusiasm, gush.

lyriste [lirist], *s.m.* lyrist; lyricist.

lyrure [liryːr], *s.m. Orn:* lyrurus; **l. des bouleaux,** blackcock; (femelle) grey hen.

lys [lis], *s.m. A:* = LIS.

Lysandre [lizɑ̃:dr̩], *Pr.n.m. Gr.Hist:* Lysander.

lysat [liza], *s.m. Biol:* lysate.

lyse [liːz], *s.f. Biol:* lysis.

lyser [lize], *v.tr. Biol:* (of lysin) to lyse, dissolve (cell).

lysergique [lizɛrʒik], *a.* **acide l.** (synthétique diéthylamine), lysergic acid diethylamide (L.S.D.)

lysidine [lizidin], *s.f. Ch:* lysidine.

lysigène [liziʒɛn], *a. Biol:* lysigenous, lysigenic.

lysimachie [lizimaki], *s.f.,* **lysimaque**[1] [lizimak], *s.f. Bot:* loose(-)strife, yellow pimpernel; **l. nummulaire,** moneywort, herb-twopence, creeping jenny.

Lysimaque[2], *Pr.n.m. A.Hist:* Lysimachus.

lysimètre [lizimɛtr̩], *s.m.* lysimeter.

lysine [lizin], *s.f. Bio-Ch:* lysin.

Lysippe [lizip], *Pr.n.m. Gr.Art:* Lysippus.

lysis [lizis], *s.m. Med:* lysis.

lysol [lizɔl], *s.m. Pharm:* lysol.

lysosome [lizozo:m], *s.m. Biol:* lysosoma, corpuscles capable of destroying the cytoplasm.

lysotype [lizotip], *s.m. Bac:* phage typing.

lysotypie [lizotipi], *s.f. Bac:* phage typing; **l. entérique,** enteric phage typing.

lysozyme [lizozim], *s.m. Biol:* lysozyme.

lysse [lis], *s.f.* lyssa; sub-lingual lesion.

lyssophobie [lisɔfɔbi], *s.f. Biol:* lyssophobia.

lythracées [litrase], **lythrariées** [litrarje], *s.f.pl. Bot:* Lythraceae.

lythrum [litrɔm], *s.m. Bot:* lythrum.

lytique [litik], *a. Biol:* lytic (action, serum, etc.).

lytta [lita], *s.m. Ent:* lytta, cantharis.

lyxose [liksoːz], *s.m. Ch:* lyxose.

M

M, m [εm], *s.m. or f.* (the letter) M, m; *Tp:* M comme Marcel, M for Mary.

m'. 1. *See* ME. 2. *A: poss.a.f.* = **ma**; **m'amie**, my dear.

ma [ma], *poss.a.f. See* MON.

maboul, -oule [mabul], *P:* 1. *a.* mad, cracked, nuts, dippy, bats. 2. *s.* loony, idiot.

maboulisme [mabulism], *s.m. P:* madness, battiness, dippiness.

mac [mak], *s.m. P:* pimp.

macab [makab], *s.m. P:* corpse, stiff.

macabre [makɑ:bṛ, -ka-], *a.* (*a*) *Art:* **danse m.**, dance of Death, danse macabre; (*b*) macabre; gruesome (discovery); ghoulish, grim (humour, etc.).

macabrement [makabṛəmɑ̃, -ka-], *adv.* gruesomely; ghoulishly; grimly.

macache [makaʃ], *int. P:* (*expresses negation or refusal*) not likely! nothing doing! no fear! **m. les permissions!** no (bloody) leave (and that's final)!

macadam [makadam], *s.m.* 1. macadam; **m. au goudron**, tar macadam; **m. à l'eau**, waterbound macadam. 2. macadamized road.

macadam-ciment [makadamsimɑ̃], *s.m.* cement-bound macadam; *pl.* **macadams-ciments**.

macadamisage [makadamiza:ʒ], *s.m.*, **macadamisation** [makadamizasjɔ̃], *s.f.* macadamization, macadamizing (of roads).

macadamiser [makadamize], *v.tr.* to macadamize (road).

Macaire [makɛ:r], *Pr.n.m.* 1. *Ecc.Hist:* Macarius. 2. (Robert) M., type of the bold and adroit highwayman or villain (*in* "*l'Auberge des Adrets,*" 1823).

macaque [makak], *s.m.* 1. *Z:* macaque; **m. silène**, lion-tailed monkey; **m. rhésus**, bandar, rhesus (monkey). 2. *Ent:* (*ver*) m., macaco worm, torcel. 3. *F:* exceedingly ugly person; *P:* **espèce de m.!** you great baboon!

macareux [makarø], *s.m. Orn:* **m.** (moine), puffin, *F:* sea parrot; **m. huppé**, crested auklet; **m. starik**, paroquet auklet.

macaron [makarɔ̃], *s.m.* 1. (*a*) *Cu:* macaroon; (*b*) *pl. Hairdr:* coils (over the ears), *F:* earphones. 2. (*a*) *Mec: etc:* boss; (*b*) (hat) peg; (*c*) *Cost: etc:* (round-shaped) motif, ornamental button; (*d*) *Nau:* support for wash-strakes; (*e*) *F:* rosette (of a decoration); (*f*) badge (on official car). 3. *P:* blow, biff.

macaroné [makarɔne], *a. Cu:* macaroon (paste).

macaronée [makarɔne], *s.f. Lit:* macaronic verse; *pl.* **macaronées**, macaronics.

macaroni [makarɔni], *s.m.* 1. *Cu:* macaroni; *pl.* **manger des macaronis**, to eat macaroni. 2. *P: Pej:* Italian; *P:* wop. 3. *F:* involved, rambling, speech.

macaronique [makarɔnik], *a.* (*a*) *Lit:* macaronic (verse); (*b*) *F:* **latin m.**, dog Latin; **texte m.**, rambling text.

macaronisme [makarɔnism], *s.m.* macaronicism; macaronic writing.

macaroniste [makarɔnist], *s.m.&f.* macaronic poet.

Macassar [makasa:r]. 1. *Pr.n. Geog:* Macassar; **huile de M.**, macassar (oil). 2. *s.m. Bot:* macassar (ebony).

macchab [makab], *s.m. P:* corpse, stiff.

Macchabée [makabe]. 1. *Pr.n.m. B.Hist:* Maccabaeus; **les Macchabées**, the Maccabees. 2. *s.m. P:* corpse (*esp.* of a drowned person); *P:* stiff.

macchabéen, -enne [makabeɛ̃, -ɛn], *a. B.Hist:* Maccabean.

Macédoine [masedwan]. 1. *Pr.n.f. Geog:* Macedonia; *A.Geog:* Macedon. 2. *s.f.* (*a*) *Cu:* **m. de fruits**, fruit salad; **m. de légumes**, macedoine of vegetables; (*b*) medley, miscellany (of literary extracts, etc.); *Pej:* hotchpotch, farrago.

macédonien, -ienne [masedɔnjɛ̃, -jɛn], *a. & s. Geog: Hist:* Macedonian.

macérateur [maseratœ:r]. 1. *a.m.* macerative, steeping (agent). 2. *s.m.* bowl, vessel, used for maceration.

macération [maserasjɔ̃], *s.f.* maceration. 1. steeping, soaking. 2. mortifying of the flesh (by fasting, etc.).

macérer [masere], (je **macère**, n. **macérons**; je **macérerai**) to macerate. 1. *v.tr.* to steep, soak. 2. *v.tr.* to mortify (the flesh, etc.). 3. *v.i.* **faire m. des oignons dans le vinaigre**, to steep onions in vinegar.

se macérer, to mortify one's flesh.

macérien, -ienne [maserjɛ̃, -jɛn], *a. & s. Geog:* (native, inhabitant) of Mézières.

maceron [masrɔ̃], *s.m. Bot:* horse parsley.

macfarlane [makfarlan], *s.m. A.Cost:* Inverness cape.

Mach [mak, maʃ], *s.m.* (*Aerodynamics*) (nombre de) M., Mach, Mach number.

machaon [makaɔ̃], *s.m. Ent:* swallow-tail butterfly.

mâche[1] [mɑ:ʃ], *s.f. Bot:* corn salad, lamb's lettuce.

mâche[2], *s.f.* mash (for horses, etc.).

mâché [maʃe], *a.* 1. (*a*) worn, fretted, galled (rope, etc.); **plaie mâchée**, jagged, ragged, wound; (*b*) **balle mâchée**, nicked bullet. 2. pulped; **papier m.**, papier mâché; *F:* **figure de papier m.**, pale, washed-out, face.

mâche-bouchon(s) [maʃbuʃɔ̃], *s.m.inv.* cork squeezer.

machecol [maʃkɔl], **machecollie** [maʃkɔli], **machecoule** [maʃkul], **mâchecoulis** [maʃkuli], *s.m. A.Fort:* machicolation.

mâchefer [maʃfɛ:r], *s.m.* 1. clinker, scoria, slag (from furnace). 2. dross (of molten lead).

mâchelier, -ière [maʃəlje, -jɛ:r], 1. *a. Anat:* masticatory (muscle). 2. *a. & s.f.* (**dent**) **mâchelière**, molar (tooth), grinder; *esp.* **dents mâchelières**, masticatory teeth (of ruminants).

mâchement [maʃmɑ̃], *s.m.* chewing, mastication.

mâcher [maʃe], *v.tr.* (*a*) to chew, masticate; to munch (biscuit, etc.); (*of animal*) to champ (fodder); (*of horse*) **m. le mors**, *F:* (*of pers.*) **m. son frein**, to champ the bit; *F:* **m. à vide**, (i) to chew with nothing in one's mouth; (ii) to live on day-dreams; *F:* **m. de haut**, to eat without appetite; **je ne vais pas lui m. mes mots**, I shan't mince words with him; **m. les morceaux, la besogne, à qn**, to break the back of the work for s.o.; **se m. le cœur**, to eat one's heart out; (*b*) (*of blunt tool, etc.*) **m. le bois**, to chew up the wood.

mâchérode [makerɔd], *s.m. Paleont:* machaerodus, sabre-toothed lion, tiger; sabre-tooth.

machette [maʃɛt], *s.f.* machete.

mâcheur, -euse [maʃœ:r, -ø:z], *s.* chewer (of tobacco, etc.); *P:* **un terrible m.**, a tremendous eater; *P:* a great guzzler.

Machiavel [makjavɛl], *Pr.n.m.* Machiavelli.

machiavélique [makjavelik], *a.* Machiavellian.

machiavéliquement [makjavelikmɑ̃], *adv.* in a Machiavellian manner.

machiavélisme [makjavelism], *s.m.* Machiavellism.

machiavéliste [makjavelist], *s.m. & f.* Machiavellist.

mâchicoulis [maʃikuli], *s.m. A.Fort:* machicolation; **porte à m.**, machicolated gateway.

machile [maʃil], **machilis** [makilis], *s.m. Ent:* machilis, bristle tail.

machilidés [makilide], *s.m.pl. Ent:* Machilidae.

mâchiller [maʃije], *v.tr.* to half-chew (food); to chew (cigar).

machin [maʃɛ̃], *s. F:* 1. monsieur, madame, M., Mr, Mrs, what's his (her) name, what d'ye call him (her), Thingumbob. 2. *s.m.* thing(amy); **passe-moi le m.**, pass me the what's its name; **qu'est-ce que c'est que ce m.-là?** what's that gadget?

machinal, -aux [maʃinal, -o], *a.* mechanical, unconscious, involuntary (action, etc.); **réaction machinale**, automatic, instinctive, reaction; **geste m.**, involuntary gesture.

machinalement [maʃinalmɑ̃], *adv,* mechanically, unconsciously; instinctively; automatically.

machinateur, -trice [maʃinatœ:r, -tris], *s.* machinator, hatcher (of plot, etc.); **m. d'intrigues**, schemer.

machination [maʃinasjɔ̃], *s.f.* machination, plot, intrigue; *pl.* scheming; **déjouer une m.**, to defeat, frustrate, a plot.

machine [maʃin], *s.f.* 1. machine; (*a*) *Dom.Ec:* **m. à coudre**, sewing machine; **m. à laver**, washing machine; **m. à laver la vaisselle**, washing-up machine, dishwasher; **m. à repasser**, ironing machine; **m. à couper le pain**, bread slicer; **m. à éplucher les légumes, les pommes de terre**, vegetable peeler, potato peeler; **m. à hacher la viande**, (meat) mincer; **m. à glace**, ice machine, freezer; (*b*) *Com: etc:* **m. de bureau**, office machine; **m. à écrire**, typewriter; **écrire une lettre à la m.**, to type a letter; **écrit à la m.**, typed, typewritten; **écriture à la m.**, typing; *F:* **trois pages de m.**, three typewritten pages; **m. à dicter**, dictating machine; **m. à calculer**, calculating machine; computer; **m. comptable**, accounting machine; **m. électronique**, electronic machine; **m. à calculer électronique**, electronic, automatic, computer; **m. à calculer à analogie**, analogic, analog(ue), computer; **m. à calculer arithmétique, numérique**, digital computer; **m. à additionner, à soustraire, à multiplier**, adding, subtracting, multiplying, machine; **m. à apprendre, à enseigner**, teaching machine; **m. à sous**, (i) slot machine; (ii) fruit machine; one-armed bandit; (*c*) *Ind: etc:* (i) **les machines**, the machinery; **les grosses machines**, the heavy plant; **le siècle de la m., des machines**, the machine age; **m. pneumatique**, air pump; **m. à vent**, blower; (ii) *Mec.E: Metalw: etc:* **atelier des machines**, machine shop; **m. à affûter**, sharpening machine, sharpener, grinder; **m. à affûter les outils**, tool sharpener, grinder; **m. à border, à rabattre**, flanging machine, flanger; **m. à river**, rivet(t)ing machine, rivet(t)er; **m. à cingler**, shingling machine; shingler, squeezer; **m. à forger**, forging press; **m. à boudiner**, extruding machine; **m. à cisailler**, shearing machine, shears; **m. à étamper**, stamping machine; **m. à cintrer, à plier**, bending machine, bender; **m. à mouler**, moulding machine; **m. à mouler en coquille**, die-casting machine; **m. à souder**, welding machine; **m. à tréfiler**, wire-drawing machine; **m. à**

étirer, drawing frame; *Mch.-Tls:* **m. à aléser,** boring machine, fine borer; **m. à brocher,** broaching machine; **m. à canneler, à rainer,** grooving machine; groove-cutting, keyway-cutting, machine; **m. à chantourner, à découper,** fret-cutting machine; **m. à tarauder,** screwing, tapping, machine; **m. à ébarber,** burring, trimming, machine; **m. à planer, à raboter,** planing, planishing, machine, planer; **m. à surfacer, à dégauchir,** surfacing machine, surfacer; **m. à fraiser,** milling machine, shaper; **m. à décolleter, à fileter,** screw-cutting machine; threading machine; **m. à roder,** lapping machine; **finir à la m.,** to machine finish; **tailler à la m.,** to machine cut; **travail exécuté, fait, à la m.,** machine work; **travailler le métal à la m.,** to machine metal; **fait à la m.,** machine-made, *esp.* turned (on the lathe); (iii) *Typ:* **m. à imprimer,** printing machine; **m. offset,** offset machine; **m. à reproduire (les plans, etc.),** (blueprint, etc.) copying machine; **m. à reports,** transferring machine; **m. rotative,** rotary machine; **m. en blanc,** single-cylinder machine; **m. à retiration,** perfecting press; **m. à composer,** type-setting machine, type-setter; **m. à graver,** etching machine; **atelier des machines,** press, machine, room; **conducteur de m.,** machine minder, press man; **passer les feuilles dans la m.,** to run sheets through the machine; (iv) *Min: etc:* **m. de hissage, d'extraction,** winding engine; hoist(ing engine); **m. d'épuisement,** pumping engine; (v) *Nau:* **m. à mâter,** shears, sheer hulk; (vi) *Civ.E:* **m. à battre, à enfoncer, les pieux,** pile driver; **m. à déblayer,** excavator; **m. à damer pour remblayage,** backfill tamper; **m. à broyer, à concasser,** crushing machine, crusher; *Rail:* **m. à poser les rails,** rail-laying machine; (*d*) **machines agricoles,** agricultural machinery; **m. à battre,** threshing machine; (*e*) = (*vehicle, bicycle, motor cycle or occ. car*) machine; *A.Aer:* **m. volante,** flying machine; *Cy:* **m. de route, routière,** roadster (bicycle); **m. de course,** racing bicycle; **monter sur sa m.,** to mount, get on, one's machine (*i.e.* bicycle, motor cycle); **c'est une belle m.!** she's a nice machine! (*f*) *F:* thing, gadget; **qu'est-ce que c'est que cette m.-là?** what's that contraption? what's that (gadget) for? (*g*) *Th:* **pièce à machines,** play with stage effects; **c'est une m. épatante,** it's a wonderful production, a great show; (*h*) *A:* **m. de guerre,** engine of war; **m. infernale,** (i) *A:* infernal machine; (ii) booby trap; (*i*) (i) *A:* **la m. de l'homme,** the human organism; (ii) *Pej:* (*of pers.*) automaton; **c'est une m. à fabriquer de l'argent,** he's just a money-making machine; (*j*) (i) *A:* **la m. ronde,** the earth; (ii) **la m. administrative, gouvernementale,** administrative, government, machinery; the wheels of government; (*k*) (i) *A:* work of genius; (ii) *Art:* **une grande m.,** a large, pretentious painting. 2. engine; (*a*) **m. motrice,** prime mover; **m. (dynamo-)électrique,** (dynamo-)electric engine; **m. hydraulique,** hydraulic engine; **m. à combustion interne,** internal combustion engine; **m. à gaz,** gas engine; **m. à air chaud,** hot-air engine; **m. à pétrole,** oil engine; **m. à vapeur,** steam engine; **m. à turbine,** turbine engine; **m. turbo-alternative,** turbo-reciprocating engine; **m. à condensation, sans condensation,** condensing, non-condensing, engine; **m. frigorifique,** refrigerating engine; **m. à balancier,** beam engine, lever engine; **m. à simple, double, effet,** single-acting, double-acting engine; **m. alternative,** reciprocating engine; **m. compound, à cylindres accouplés,** compound engine; **m. marine,** marine engine; **m. à double expansion, à double détente,** compound engine; **m. à triple détente,** triple-expansion engine; **m. auxiliaire,** donkey engine; (*b*) (i) *Rail:* locomotive; **m. tender,** tank engine; **m. de manœuvre,** shunting engine; **m. de renfort,** bank engine, banker; **m. de secours, de réserve,** helper (engine); **m. pilote,** pilot engine; **m. électrique, Diesel,** electric, Diesel, locomotive, engine; (ii) **m. routière,** traction engine; (*c*) *Nau:* **la m.,** (i) the engine room; (ii) the engine-room staff; **salle, chambre, des machines,** engine room; **stopper les machines,** to cut off the engines; **faire m. arrière,** to reverse the engine; *F:* to back down, to back-pedal. 3. *El:* dynamo; **m. alternative,** alternating-current dynamo; **m. à courant(s) continu(s),** direct-current dynamo.

machine-outil [maʃinuti], *s.f.* machine tool; *pl. machines-outils.*

machiner [maʃine], *v.tr.* 1. to scheme, plot, machinate, contrive; **affaire machinée d'avance,** put-up job; **ce n'était pas trop mal machiné,** that was quite well thought out. 2. *A:* to supply (sth.), fit (sth.) up, with mechanical contrivances.

machinerie [maʃinri], *s.f.* 1. machine construction. 2. (*a*) *coll.* machinery; *Ind:* plant; (*b*) (i) *Ind:* machine shop; (ii) *Nau:* engine room; (*c*) **la m. de la guerre,** the machinery of war.

machinette [maʃinɛt], *s.f.* (*rare*) *F:* small contrivance; *F:* gadget.

machine-transfert [maʃintrɑ̃sfɛːr], *s.f. Elcs:* transfer-machine; *pl. machines-transferts.*

machineur, -euse [maʃinœːr, -øːz], *s.* = MACHINATEUR.

machinique [maʃinik], *a.* mechanical; **la civilisation m.,** the machine age.

machiniser [maʃinize], *v.tr.* to reduce (s.o.) to a mere machine; to make a drudge of (s.o.).

machinisme [maʃinism], *s.m.* 1. *A.Phil:* mechanism. 2. (*a*) *Pol.Ec:* mechanization (of agriculture, industry); (*b*) *Pol:* machinism.

machiniste [maʃinist], *s.m.* 1. *A:* machinist, designer of machines. 2. (*a*) machinist; machine operator; (*b*) driver (of bus, electric train, etc.); (*c*) *Civ.E:* **m. d'extracteur,** hoistman. 3. *Th:* scene shifter, stage hand; **chef m.,** stage setter.

machmètre [makmɛtr, maʃ-], *s.m. Aer:* machmeter.

mâchoire [mɑʃwaːr], *s.f.* 1. (*a*) jaw (of person, animal); **m. supérieure, inférieure,** upper, lower, jaw; **la m., les mâchoires,** the jaws; **homme à la m. allongée,** lantern-jawed man; *F:* **jouer, travailler, de la m., des mâchoires,** to eat with (an) appetite; *F:* **bâiller à se décrocher, se démantibuler, la m.,** to yawn one's head off; (*b*) jawbone. 2. *Mec.E:* **mâchoires d'un étau,** jaws, chaps, chops, of a vice; **mâchoires d'un mandrin,** jaws, grip, of a chuck; **m. à tendre,** draw vice; **m. à tordre,** twisting vice; **m. d'une poulie,** flange of a pulley; **m. mobile de clef à molette,** sliding jaw of a wrench; **m. de serrage,** clamp, gripping jaw; **m. dentelée, striée,** meshing jaw; **fixer par une m.,** to clamp; *Nau:* **m. de corne,** throat, jaw, of a gaff; *Aut:* **mâchoires du frein,** brake shoes.

mâchon [mɑʃɔ̃], *s.m. P:* big feed, blowout, tuck-in.

mâchonnement [mɑʃɔnmɑ̃], *s.m.* 1. chewing. 2. muttering, mumbling.

mâchonner [mɑʃɔne], *v.tr.* 1. to chew (food) with difficulty; to munch; to chew (cigar); (*of horse*) to champ (the bit); **m. son crayon,** to bite (the end of) one's pencil. 2. to mutter (threats, etc.); to mumble (prayer); **m. des injures,** to swear under one's breath. 3. *Art: F:* to draw with hazy outlines.

mâchonneur, -euse [mɑʃɔnœːr, -øːz], *s.* mumbler.

mâchouillement [mɑʃujmɑ̃], *s.m. F:* chewing sound.

mâchouiller [mɑʃuje], *v.tr. F:* to chew away at (sth.).

mâchure [mɑʃyːr], *s.f.* 1. flaw (in pile of velvet, in nap of cloth). 2. bruise (on pear, flesh, etc.); *pl.* crushed edges (of wound).

mâchurer[1] [mɑʃyre], *v.tr.* to soil, dirty; *Typ:* to smudge, mackle, blur (sheet); *Prov:* **le chaudron mâchure la poêle,** it's the pot calling the kettle black.

mâchurer[2], *v.tr.* 1. to bruise; *Mec.E:* to dent, bruise (metal part in the vice). 2. to reduce (handkerchief, etc.) to pulp.

mâchuron [mɑʃyrɔ̃], *s.m. Dial:* smut (of soot on the face, etc.).

macis [masi], *s.m. Bot: Cu:* mace.

mackintosh [makintɔʃ], *s.m. A:* 1. mackintosh. 2. waterproof sheet.

mackintoshite [makintɔʃit], *s.f. Miner:* mackintoshite.

maclage [maklaːʒ], *s.m. Glassm:* mixing, stirring.

macle[1] [makl], *s.f.* 1. *Fish:* wide-meshed net. 2. (*a*) *Miner:* macle, chiastolite, cross-stone; (*b*) *Cryst:* macle, twin(ned) crystal; **m. par accolement,** contact twin; **m. par entre-croisement,** interpenetrant twin; **m. polysynthétique,** repeated twinning. 3. *Her:* mascle, lozenge voided.

macle[2], *s.f. Bot:* water caltrop; water chestnut.

maclé [makle], *a. Cryst:* macled, hemitrope, twinned (crystal).

macler[1] [makle], *v.i. & pr. Cryst:* to twin.

macler[2], *v.tr. Glassm:* to mix, stir (glass).

maçon [masɔ̃, mɑ-], *s.m.* 1. (*a*) mason; **m. en briques,** bricklayer; *F: O:* **soupe de m.,** thick soup (like mortar); (*b*) (free)mason; (*c*) *F: A:* clumsy workman, bungler, poor hand. 2. (*a*) *Moll:* top shell; (*b*) *Ann:* **m. des sables,** sand mason worm. 3. *a. f.* **maçonne** [masɔn] (*a*) *Ent:* **abeille maçonne,** mason bee; potter bee; **fourmi maçonne,** mason ant; (*b*) *Orn:* **pic m.,** nuthatch.

mâcon [mɑkɔ̃], *s.m.* (also **vin de M.**) Mâcon (wine).

maconite [makɔnit], *s.f. Miner:* maconite.

maçonnage [masɔnaːʒ, mɑ-], *s.m.* mason's work; bricklaying.

mâconnais, -aise [mɑkɔnɛ, -ɛːz], *a. & s.* (native, inhabitant) of (i) Mâcon, (ii) the Mâconnais (region).

maçonner [masɔne, mɑ-], *v.tr.* 1. (*a*) to build (wall, etc.); (*b*) to mason (wall); to face (wall, etc.) with stone; (*c*) to wall up, brick up (door, etc.); (*d*) (*of bee, ant, etc.*) to build. 2. to construct, (i) solidly, (ii) roughly; **phrases rudement maçonnées,** sentences roughly strung together.

maçonnerie [masɔnri, mɑ-], *s.f.* 1. masonry; stonework; bricklaying; **m. brute en blocage, en blocaille, en moellons,** rubble-work; **m. en liaison,** coursed masonry; **m. de brique,** brickwork; **m. de béton,** concrete masonry. 2. freemasonry.

maçonnique [masɔnik, mɑ-], *a.* masonic (lodge, etc.).

macouba [makuba], *s.m.* maccaboy, maccabaw (tobacco, snuff).

macquage [makaːʒ], *s.m.* 1. *Tex:* braking (of hemp, flax). 2. *Metall:* squeezing (of bloom).

macque [mak], *s.f. Tex:* brake (for flax or hemp).

macquer [make], *v.tr.* 1. *Tex:* to brake (flax, hemp). 2. *Metall:* to squeeze (bloom); **machine à m.,** squeezer.

macquoir [makwaːr], *s.m. Tex:* brake (for flax or hemp).

macramé [makrame], *s.m. Needlew:* macramé, knotted-bar work.

macre [makr], *s.f. Bot:* water caltrop; **m. (nageante),** water chestnut, saligot.

macreuse [makrøːz], *s.f.* 1. *Orn:* scoter (duck); **m. noire,** common scoter; **m. à lunettes,** surf scoter; **m. brune, double m.,** velvet scoter, *U.S:* white-winged scoter; *F:* **avoir du sang de m.,** to be (very) cool and collected. 2. *Cu:* blade-bone of beef.

macro- [makrɔ, -o], *pref.* macro-.

Macrobe [makrɔb], *Pr.n.m. Lt.Lit:* Macrobius.

macrobien, -ienne [makrɔbjɛ̃, -jɛn]. 1. *a.* macrobian, long-lived. 2. *s.m.pl. Myth:* Macrobians.

macrobiote [makrɔbjɔt], *s.m. Z:* macrobiotus.

macrobiotique [makrɔbjɔtik], *s.f.* macrobiotics.

macrobite [makrɔbit], *s.m. Biol:* macrobiotic, long-lived, person.

macrocéphale [makrɔsefal], *a. Z: Med:* macrocephalic, macrocephalous, large-headed.

macrocéphalie [makrɔsefali], *s.f.* macrocephaly.

macrocheilie [makrɔkeli], *s.f. Anthr:* macroch(e)ilia.

macrochéire [makrɔkeiːr], *s.m. Crust:* macrocheira.

macrochète [makrɔkɛt], *s.m. Ent:* macrochaeta.

macrochirie [makrɔkiri], *s.f. Med:* macroch(e)iria.

macrocosme [makrɔkɔsm], *s.m.* macrocosm.

macrocyste [makrɔsist], *s.m. Bot:* macrocyst.

macrocystis [makrɔsistis], *s.m. Algae:* macrocystis.

macrocyte [makrɔsit], *s.m. Med:* macrocyte.

macrodactyle [makrɔdaktil], *a. Z:* macrodactyl, macrodactylous.

macrodactylie [makrɔdaktili], *s.f.* macrodactyly.

macroéconomie [makrɔekɔnɔmi], *s.f.* macroeconomics.

macroéconomique [makrɔekɔnɔmik], *a.* macroeconomic.

macroergate [makrɔɛrgat], *a. Ent:* **ouvrière m.,** macr(o)ergate.

macroévolution [makrɔevɔlysjɔ̃], *s.f.* macroevolution.

macrogamète [makrɔgamɛt], *s.m. Biol:* macrogamete.

macrogamétocyte [makrɔgametɔsit], **macrogamonte** [makrɔgamɔ̃ːt], *s.m. Prot:* macrogametocyte.

macrogénitosomie [makrɔʒenitɔzɔmi], *s.f. Med:* macrogenitosomia.

macroglobuline [makrɔglɔbylin], *s.f. Bio-Ch:* macroglobulin.

macroglobulinémie [makrɔglɔbylinemi], *s.f. Med:* macroglobulin(a)emia.

macroglosse [makrɔglɔs], *s.m.* 1. *Ent:* hawk moth; (*genus*) macroglossa. 2. *Z:* fruit bat.

macroglossie [makrɔglɔsi], *s.f. Med:* macroglossia.

macrographie [makrɔgrafi], *s.f.* macrography.

macrographique [makrɔgrafik], *a.* macrographic.

macrolépidoptères [makrɔlepidɔptɛːr], *s.m.pl. Ent:* Macrolepidoptera.

macrolymphocyte [makrɔlɛ̃fɔsit], *s.m. Physiol:* macrolymphocyte.

macromélie [makrɔmeli], *s.f. Med:* macromelia.

macromère [makrɔmɛːr], *s.m. Z:* macromere.

macromoléculaire [makrɔmɔlekylɛːr], *a.* macromolecular.

macromolécule [makrɔmɔlekyl], *s.f. Ch:* macromolecule.
macronucléus [makrɔnykleyːs], *s.m. Prot:* macronucleus.
macronus [makrɔnyːs], *s.m. Orn:* (Malayan) tit babbler.
macrophage [makrɔfaːʒ], *Biol: Physiol:* **1.** *a.* macrophagic. **2.** *s.m.* macrophage; histiocyte.
macrophotographie [makrɔfɔtɔgrafi], *s.f.* (*a*) macrophotography, photomacrography; (*b*) enlargement; photomacrograph, macrophotograph.
macropode [makrɔpɔd]. **1.** *a. Nat.Hist:* macropodous. **2.** *s.m. Ich:* paradise fish.
macropodidés [makrɔpɔdide], *s.m.pl. Z:* Macropodidae.
macropodie [makrɔpɔdi], *s.f. Med:* macropodia.
macroporosité [makrɔpɔrozite], *s.f.* macroporosity.
macroptère [makrɔptɛːr], *a. Ich: Orn:* macropterous.
macroramphe [makrɔrɑ̃ːf], *s.m. Orn:* (Canadian) red-breasted snipe, robin snipe, dowitcher.
macrorhine [makrɔrin], *s.m. Z:* macrorhinus; elephant seal.
macroscélide [makrɔs(s)elid], *s.m. Z:* elephant shrew(-mouse).
macroscélidés [makrɔs(s)elide], *s.m.pl. Z:* Macroscelididae.
macroscopique [makrɔskɔpik], *a.* macroscopic.
macroséisme [makrɔseism], *s.m. Geol:* macroseism.
macrosismique [makrɔsismik], *a. Geol:* macroseismic.
macroskélie [makrɔskeli], *s.f. Med:* macroscelia.
macrosomie [makrɔzɔmi], *s.f. Med:* macrosomia.
macrosporange [makrɔspɔrɑ̃ːʒ], *s.m. Bot:* macrosporangium.
macrospore [makrɔspɔːr], *s.f. Bot:* macrospore.
macrosporophylle [makrɔspɔrɔfil], *s.m. Bot:* macrosporophyl(l), megasporophyll, pistil.
macrostomie [makrɔstɔmi], *s.f. Med:* macrostomia.
macrostructure [makrɔstryktyːr], *s.f.* macrostructure.
macrothérium [makrɔterjɔm], *s.m. Paleont:* macrotherium.
macroule [makrul], *s.f. Orn:* **(foulque) m.,** coot.
macroure [makruːr]. **1.** *a.* macrurous, long-tailed. **2.** *s.m.* (*a*) *Ich:* macrurus, rat-tail; (*b*) *Crust:* macruran.
macrozamia [makrɔzamja], *s.m. Bot:* macrozamia.
macruridés [makryride], *s.m.pl. Ich:* Macruridae.
macula [makyla], *s.f. Anat:* **m. (lutea),** macula (lutea).
maculage [makylaːʒ], *s.m.*, **maculation** [makylasjɔ̃], *s.f.* **1.** (*a*) *Lit:* soiling, staining; (*b*) *Typ:* mackling; setting off. **2.** (*a*) *Lit:* stain, spot; (*b*) *Typ:* offset, set-off; mackle; **m. du cadrat,** square mark.
maculature [makylatyːr], *s.f. Typ:* **1.** mackle; spoilt sheet. **2.** waste sheets (used as packing, etc.); waste.
macule [makyl], *s.f.* **1.** (*a*) *A. & Lit:* stain, spot, blemish; **sans m.,** immaculate, spotless, without blemish; (*b*) *Astr:* macula, sun spot; (*c*) *Med:* macula, macule. **2.** *Typ:* waste sheet (used for packing or protective interleaving).
maculé [makyle], *a.* (*a*) *Z: etc:* spotted; (*b*) foxed (engraving, etc.); (*c*) *Typ:* smudged.
maculer [makyle]. **1.** *v.tr. Lit:* to stain, maculate, spot; *Typ:* (i) to set off, offset; (ii) to mackle, blur. **2.** *v.i. & pr.* (*of paper*) to mackle, blur; (*of engraving*) to fox.
maculeux, -euse [makylø, -øːz], *a. Med:* macular.
maculicole [makylikɔl], *a. Fung:* maculicole.
Madagascar [madagaskaːr], *Pr.n.m. Geog:* Madagascar.
madame, *pl.* **mesdames** [madam, medam, mɛ-], *s.f.* **1.** (*a*) (*attached to a name, a title, etc.*) (i) **Madame, Mme, Martin,** Mrs Martin; **Mesdames, Mmes, Martin,** the Mrs Martin; **Madame, Mme, la Colonelle X,** Mrs X, wife of Colonel X; **Madame Veuve X,** Mrs X, widow of (the late) (David) X; (ii) (*not rendered in English*) **madame la marquise, la comtesse, de . . .,** the Marchioness, the Countess, of . . .; **Madame la comtesse, etc.,** her ladyship; **je voudrais parler à madame la directrice,** I would like to speak to the manageress, to the headmistress; **comment va madame votre mère?** how is your mother? (*b*) (*used alone*) (*pl.* **ces dames**) **voici le chapeau de madame,** here is Mrs X's hat; **madame vous demande,** Mrs X, (*of titled lady*) Lady X, is asking for you; *F:* (*in servants' language*) the mistress, her ladyship, is asking for you; **ces dames n'y sont pas,** the ladies are not at home; (*name unknown, e.g. in shop*) **madame se plaint que . . .,** the lady, this lady, madam, complains that . . .; *Hum:* **et m. d'entrer,** in walked her ladyship; **et ces dames d'entrer,** in walked their ladyships. **2.** (*a*) (*in address, more extensively used than in English*) (*pl.* **mesdames,** *occ.* **ces dames**) madam, ma'am, (*to titled lady*) your ladyship; **non, madame,** no, (madam); **entrez, mesdames,** come in, ladies; **madame est servie,** dinner is served, madam; **que prendront ces dames?** what can I offer you, ladies? (*b*) (*in letter writing*) (i) (*to stranger*) **Madame** (always written in full), (Dear) Madam; **Mesdames,** Mesdames; (ii) (*implying previous acquaintance and some friendship*) **chère Madame,** Dear Mrs X. **3.** *F:* (*often with pl.* **madames**) lady; **jouer à la m.,** to put on airs; *A:* **une riche madame,** a rich lady; **il peint des belles madames,** he paints fine ladies. **4.** *Fr.Hist:* (*title of the King's eldest daughter, of the wife of the Dauphin, of the wife of* MONSIEUR, *q.v.*) Madame.
madapol(l)am [madapɔlam], *s.m.* madapol(l)am, fine calico.
madarosis [madarɔzis], *s.f. Med:* madarosis.
madécasse [madekas], *a. & s. A.Geog:* Malagasy, Madagascan.
madéfaction [madefaksjɔ̃], *s.f.* moistening, damping, wetting.
madéfier [madefje], *v.tr.* (*p.d. & pr.sub.* **n. madéfiions, v. madéfiiez**) to moisten, damp, wet (cement, etc.).
Madeleine [madlɛn]. **1.** *Pr.n.f.* (*a*) *B.Hist:* Magdalen(e); **une M. repentante, repentie,** a reformed prostitute, a Magdalen; *F:* **pleurer comme une M.,** to weep copiously, bitterly; (*b*) Madel(e)ine. **2.** *s.f.* (*a*) Magdalen pear; (*b*) *Cu:* madeleine.
Madelon [madlɔ̃], *Pr.n.f.* (*dim. of Madeleine*) Magda, Maddy.
madelonnette [madlɔnɛt], *s.f. A:* **1.** inmate of a Magdalen(e) asylum; **maison des Madelonnettes,** Magdelen(e) asylum. **2.** Madelonnette (nun).
mademoiselle, *pl.* **mesdemoiselles** [madmwazɛl, medmwazɛl, mɛ-], *s.f.* **1.** (*a*) Miss; **Mademoiselle, Mlle, Martin,** Miss Martin; **Mesdemoiselles Martin,** the Misses Martin; **voici le chapeau de m.,** here is Miss X's hat; (*b*) (*not rendered in English*) **voici m. la directrice,** here is the manageress, the headmistress; **comment va m. votre cousine?** how is your cousin? **2.** (*a*) (*in address*) **bonjour m.,** good morning, Miss X; (*to child, name unknown*) good morning, my dear; (*in shop, etc.*), *used only to child or very young woman*) **merci m.,** thank you, miss; (*b*) (*pl.* **ces demoiselles**) **mademoiselle est servie,** dinner is served, madam; **que prendront ces demoiselles?** what can I offer you, ladies? **mademoiselle vous demande,** Miss X is asking for you; **ces demoiselles n'y sont pas,** the young ladies are not at home; (*name unknown, e.g. in shop*) **Mademoiselle se plaint que . . .,** the, this, young lady, complains that . . .; (*c*) (*in letter writing*) (i) (*to stranger*) **Mademoiselle** (*always written in full*) (Dear) Madam; **Mesdemoiselles,** Mesdames; (ii) (*implying previous acquaintance and some friendship*) **chère Mademoiselle,** Dear Miss X. **3.** *Fr.Hist:* (*title of the eldest daughter of* MONSIEUR, *q.v.*) Mademoiselle.
Madère [madɛːr]. **1.** *Pr.n. Geog:* Madeira. **2.** *s.m.* (also **vin de M.**) Madeira (wine).
madérien, -ienne [maderjɛ̃, -jɛn], **madérois, -oise** [maderwa, -waːz], *a. & s. Geog:* Madeiran.
madi [madi], *s.m.*, **madia** [madja], *s.m.*, **madie** [madi], *s.f. Bot:* madia, tarweed; **huile de m.,** madia oil.
Madian [madjɑ̃], *Pr.n.m.* **1.** *B.Geog:* (the land of) Midian. **2.** Midian (son of Abraham).
madianite [madjanit], *a. & s. B.Hist:* Midianite.
madicole [madikɔl], *a.* (*of fauna*) living in rock pools.
madone [madɔn], *s.f.* madonna.
madrague [madrag], *s.f. Fish:* mandrague, madrague, tunny net.
madragueur [madragœːr], *s.m.* fisherman (who uses a *madrague*).
Madras [madrɑːs]. **1.** *Pr.n. Geog:* Madras. **2.** *s.m. Tex:* (*a*) Madras; (*b*) **(foulard de) m.,** knotted head scarf, madras.
madré [madre, mɑ-], *a.* **1.** veined, mottled (wood, porcelain, etc.); **savon m.,** mottled soap; **érable m.,** bird's eye maple; figured, curled, maple. **2.** sly, crafty, wily; *s.* sly fox; **c'est un vieux m.,** he's an old fox, an old hand at the game.
madréporaires [madrepɔrɛːr], *s.m.pl. Coel:* Madreporaria, the stony corals.
madrépore [madrepɔːr], *s.m. Coel:* madrepore.
madréporien, -ienne [madrepɔrjɛ̃, -jɛn], **madréporique** [madrepɔrik], *a.* madreporic; **île madréporique,** coral island; *Echin:* **plaque madréporique,** madreporite.
madréporite [madrepɔrit], *s.f. Echin:* madreporite (of shield urchin).
madrier [madrije], *s.m.* **1.** (*a*) (piece of) timber; beam; thick board, plank; (*b*) *Tchn:* plank 3½" thick. **2.** chess (of pontoon bridge). **3.** *A.Mil:* madrier.
madrières [madrijɛːr], *s.f.pl.* speckles, spots.
madriette [madrijɛt], *s.f. Bot:* aconite, monkshood.
madrigal, -aux [madrigal, -o], *s.m.* **1.** *Lit: Mus:* madrigal. **2.** flowery speech, compliment.
madrigalesque [madrigalɛsk], *a.* madrigalesque.
madrigalique [madrigalik], *a.* madrigalian.
madrigaliser [madrigalize]. **1.** *v.tr.* to write madrigals to (s.o.); to pay flowery compliments to (s.o.). **2.** *v.i.* to write madrigals; to make pretty speeches.
madrilène [madrilɛn], *a. & s. Geog:* of Madrid; Madrilenian.
madrin [madrɛ̃], *s.m. A:* wooden drinking vessel.
madrure [madryːr, mɑ-], *s.f.* mottle (on wood, etc.); spot (on animal fur); *pl.* speckles (of bird's feathers).
Maelström (le) [ləmalstrøːm, -strɔm], *Pr.n.m. Geog:* the Maelstrom.
maërl [maɛrl, mɛrl], *s.m. Agr:* Breton ameliorant (sand, shell and seaweed mixture).
maestoso [maɛstozo], *adv. Mus:* maestoso.
maestria [maɛstrija], *s.f. Art:* masterliness (of execution); **exécuter un morceau, conduire une auto, avec m.,** to play a piece, drive a car, in a masterly manner.
maëstrichtien [mɑstriksjɛ̃, mae-], *a. & s.m. Geol:* upper Senonian.
maëstrichtois, -oise [maestriktwa, mɑ-, -waːz], *a. & s. Geog:* (native, inhabitant) of Maëstricht [mɑstrik, maestrikt].
maestro [maɛstro], *s.m. Mus:* maestro; *pl. maestros.*
Mae West [mewɛst], *s.f. Av: O:* Mae West; *pl. Mae Wests.*
maffia, mafia [mafja], *s.f.* maffia, mafia.
mafflé [mafle], **maf(f)lu** [mafly], *a. F: O:* with bulging cheeks; heavy-jowled.
magasin [magazɛ̃], *s.m.* **1.** (*a*) shop, *U.S:* store; **grand m.,** department store; **m. à libre service,** self-service store; **m. à succursales multiples,** chain store; **chaîne de magasins,** chain of shops; **tenir un m.,** to keep a shop, to be a shopkeeper; **employé(e) de m.,** shop assistant; **courir les magasins,** *F:* **faire les magasins,** to go from shop to shop, to do, go, the round of the shops; (*b*) store, warehouse; **petit m. à outils,** tool store, *U.S:* crib; **marchand en m.,** warehouseman (= wholesaler); **avoir qch. en m.,** to have sth. in stock; **garçon de m.,** warehouseman, storeman; **marchandises en m.,** stock in hand; **magasins généraux,** bonded warehouse(s); *Nau:* **m. de l'arsenal,** warehouse, store, of the arsenal; (*c*) *Mil:* **m. à poudre,** powder magazine; **m. d'armes,** armoury; **m. du corps,** regimental store. **2.** (*a*) magazine (of rifle, camera, *Cin:* of projector); **m. débiteur,** supply magazine; **m. récepteur,** take-up magazine; (*b*) **m. d'alimentation,** card hopper (of computer); **m. de réception,** card stacker. **3.** *A:* magazine, periodical.
magasinage [magazinaːʒ], *s.m.* **1.** warehousing, storing (of goods). **2.** **(droits de) m.,** warehouse dues; storage (charges); *Rail:* demurrage (charges). **3.** *Fr.C:* **faire du m.,** to go shopping.
magasiner [magazine], *v.i. Fr.C:* to go shopping.
magasinier [magazinje], *s.m.* **1.** warehouseman, stock keeper, storekeeper, storeman. **2.** *Com:* stock book.
magazine [magazin], *s.m.* (illustrated) magazine, periodical.
magdalénien, -ienne [magdalenjɛ̃, -jɛn], *a. & s.m. Prehist:* Magdalenian.
Magdebourg [magdəbuːr], *Pr.n. Geog:* Magdeburg.
mage [maːʒ], *s.m.* (*a*) Magus; **les trois Mages,** (i) *B.Hist:* the Three Magi, the Three Wise Men; (ii) *Astr:* Orion's belt; (*b*) seer.
Magellan [maʒɛl(l)ɑ̃], *Pr.n.* **1.** *Geog:* **détroit de M.,** Straits of Magellan. **2.** *Astr:* **nuages de M.,** Magellanic clouds; **petit nuage de M.,** nubecula minor; **grand nuage de M.,** nubecula major.
magellanique [maʒɛl(l)anik], *a.* Magellanic; *Astr:* **nuée m.,** Magellanic cloud, nubecula.
magenta [maʒɛ̃ta], *s.m. & a.inv.* magenta (colour).
Maghreb (le) [ləmagrɛb], **Maghrib (le)** [ləmagrib], *Pr.n.m. Geog:* the Maghrib, Maghreb (Morocco, Algeria and Tunisia).

maghrebin, -ine [magrɛbɛ̃, -in], *a. & s. Geog:* Maugrabin, Mograbin; North African.

maghzen [makzɛn], *s.m. Hist:* maghzen, makhzen, Moroccan administration (under the French protectorate).

magicien, -ienne [maʒisjɛ̃, -jɛn], *s.* magician; wizard, sorcerer; *f.* sorceress; *a.* **son pinceau m.,** the magic touch of his brush, his magic skill with the brush.

magie [maʒi], *s.f.* magic, wizardry; **m. noire,** black magic, the black art; **m. blanche,** white magic; **la m. des mots, de son sourire,** the magic of words, of her smile; **comme par m.,** as if by magic.

magique [maʒik], *a.* magic(al); **baguette m.,** magic wand; **lanterne m.,** magic lantern; **carré m.,** magic square.

magiquement [maʒikmɑ̃], *adv.* magically; preternaturally, supernaturally.

magisme [maʒism], *s.m.* Mag(ian)ism.

magiste [maʒist], *s.m. & f.* Magian.

magister [maʒistɛːr], *s.m.* **1.** *A:* pedagogue; (village) schoolmaster. **2.** *Pej:* pedant.

magistère [maʒistɛːr], *s.m.* **1.** *A: Alch:* magisterium, magistery. **2.** *R.C.Ch:* magisterium. **3.** **exercer un m.,** to exercise authoritative power.

magistral, -aux [maʒistral, -o], *a.* **1.** (*a*) magisterial, authoritative; *F:* pompous (tone, opinion, etc.); masterful (manner); (*b*) masterly (work, etc.); *F:* **infliger une volée magistrale à qn,** to give s.o. a colossal, sound, thrashing. **2.** *Fort:* magistral (line, gallery). **3.** (*of medicine*) prepared according to prescription; magistral.

magistralement [maʒistralmɑ̃], *adv.* **1.** magisterially, authoritatively. **2.** in a masterly manner.

magistrat [maʒistra], *s.m.* **1.** magistrate; judge; **le premier m. de la République,** the President of the Republic; **le premier m. de la ville,** the Mayor; **il est m.,** he sits on the Bench; **m. inspecteur,** visiting magistrate. **2.** *coll. A:* the magistracy.

magistrature [maʒistratyːr], *s.f.* magistrature. **1.** magistrateship. **2.** magistracy; **la m. assise,** the judges, the Bench; **la m. debout,** the (body of) public prosecutors; **entrer dans la m.,** to be appointed judge or public prosecutor.

maglemosien, -ienne [magləmozjɛ̃, -jɛn], *a. Prehist:* Maglemosian.

magma [magma], *s.m. Ch: Geol:* magma; **m. primaire,** parental magma.

magmatique [magmatik], *a. Geol:* magmatic (rock, water).

magnalium [magnaljɔm], *s.m. Metall:* magnalium.

magnan [maɲɑ̃], *s.m. Dial:* (*Provence*) silkworm.

magnanage [maɲanaːʒ], *s.m.* silkworm breeding, sericulture.

magnanarelle [maɲanarɛl], *s.f. Dial:* (*Provence*) (woman) silkworm breeder.

magnanerie [maɲanri], *s.f.* **1.** silkworm rearing-house; cocoonery, magnanerie. **2.** silkworm breeding; sericulture.

magnanier, -ière [maɲanje, -jɛːr], *s.* silkworm breeder; sericulturist.

magnanime [maɲanim], *a.* magnanimous, noble-minded; generous; noble, lofty (thought, etc.).

magnanimement [maɲanimmɑ̃], *adv.* magnanimously; generously; nobly.

magnanimité [maɲanimite], *s.f.* magnanimity; generosity; nobility (of character).

magnat [magna, -ɲa], *s.m.* **1.** *Hist:* magnate, grandee (of Poland, Hungary). **2.** magnate (of industry, etc.), *F:* tycoon.

magnéferrite [maɲefɛrit], *s.f. Miner:* magnoferrite, magnesioferrite.

magner (se) [s(ə)maɲe], *v.pr. P:* to get a move on; **magne-toi!** get cracking!

magnes [maɲ], *s.f.pl. P:* **faire des m.,** (i) to put on airs; (ii) to make difficulties, to kick up a fuss.

magnésie [maɲezi], *s.f.* **1.** *Ch: Pharm:* magnesia, magnesium oxide. **2. m. des peintres,** manganese oxide. **3.** *Pharm:* (= MAGNÉSIUM) **sulfate de m.,** Epsom salts.

magnésien, -ienne [maɲezjɛ̃, -jɛn], *a.* magnesian; **grenat m.,** pyrope.

magnésifère [maɲezifɛːr], *a.* magnesiferous.

magnésioferrite [maɲezjɔfɛrit], *s.f. Miner:* magnesioferrite.

magnésique [maɲezik], *a. Geol: etc:* magnesic (rock, etc.); **lumière m.,** magnesium light.

magnésite [maɲezit], *s.f. Miner:* **1.** magnesite. **2.** meerschaum.

magnésium [maɲezjɔm], *s.m. Ch:* magnesium; *Phot:* **lampe au m.,** flash lamp; **éclair de m.,** flash, magnesium light.

magnétimètre [maɲetimɛtr̥], *s.m.* magnetometer, magnetimeter.

magnétique [maɲetik], *a. Ph:* magnetic (field, flux, attraction, pole, etc.); *Mec.E:* magnetic (clutch, brake, etc.); **déperdition m.,** magnetic decay; **traction m.,** magnetic pull; *Av: etc:* **cap m.,** magnetic heading; **volant m.,** flywheel magneto; **acier m.,** magnet steel; **enveloppe, gaine, m.,** magneto sheath.

magnétiquement [maɲetikmɑ̃], *adv.* magnetically.

magnétisable [maɲetizabl̥], *a.* magnetizable.

magnétisant, -ante [maɲetizɑ̃, -ɑ̃ːt]. **1.** *a.* (*a*) magnetizing; (*b*) mesmerizing. **2.** *s.m.* (*a*) magnetizer; (*b*) mesmerizer.

magnétisation [maɲetizasjɔ̃], *s.f.* **1.** magnetization, magnetizing. **2.** mesmerizing.

magnétiser [maɲetize], *v.tr.* **1.** to magnetize (iron, etc.). **2.** to magnetize, mesmerize, hypnotize; **auditoire magnétisé,** spellbound audience.

magnétiseur, -euse [maɲetizœːr, -øːz], *s.* (*pers.*) magnetizer, mesmerizer, hypnotizer.

magnétisme [maɲetism], *s.m.* **1.** *Ph:* magnetism; **m. rémanent,** residual magnetism; **m. terrestre,** terrestrial magnetism. **2.** (*a*) **m. animal,** animal magnetism; mesmerism; (*b*) **m. personnel,** personal magnetism.

magnétite [maɲetit], *s.f. Miner:* magnetite, lodestone.

magnétite-olivinite [maɲetitɔlivinit], *s.f. Miner:* magnetite-olivinite.

magnéto [maɲeto], *s.f. I.C.E:* magneto; **m. à haute tension,** high-tension magneto; **m. à avance automatique, fixe,** automatic-lead, fixed-lead, magneto; **m. à avance réglable, variable,** adjustable-lead magneto; **m. de démarrage, de départ,** magneto booster; **support de m.,** magneto block.

magnétocalorique [maɲetɔkalɔrik], *a.* magneto-caloric.

magnétochimie [maɲetɔʃimi], *s.f.* magneto-chemistry.

magnétodynamique [maɲetɔdinamik]. **1.** *a.* magnetodynamic. **2.** *s.f.* magnetodynamics; **m. des fluides,** magnetohydrodynamics.

magnéto-électrique [maɲetɔelɛktrik], *a. Ph:* magneto-electric; *pl. magnéto-électriques.*

magnétogramme [maɲetɔgram], *s.m.* magnetogram; magnetic map.

magnétographe [maɲetɔgraf], *s.m.* magnetograph.

magnétohydrodynamique [maɲetɔidrɔdinamik], *s.f.* magnetohydrodynamics.

magnétomètre [maɲetɔmɛtr̥], *s.m. Ph:* magnetometer; **m. aéroporté,** airborne magnetometer, *F:* bird; **m. à noyau saturable,** saturable magnetometer.

magnétométrie [maɲetɔmetri], *s.f. Geol:* magnetometry.

magnétométrique [maɲetɔmetrik], *a. Geol:* magnetometric; magnetic (method of oil-prospecting).

magnétomoteur, -trice [maɲetɔmɔtœːr, -tris], *a.* magnetomotive; **force magnétomotrice,** magnetomotive force, magnetic potential.

magnéton [maɲetɔ̃], *s.m. Atom.Ph:* magneton.

magnéto-optique [maɲetɔɔptik]. **1.** *a.* magneto-optic(al). **2.** *s.f.* magneto-optics; *pl. magnéto-optiques.*

magnétophone [maɲetɔfɔn], *s.m.* tape recorder.

magnétophonique [maɲetɔfɔnik], *a.* **enregistrement m.,** tape recording.

magnétoplumbite [maɲetɔplœ̃bit], *s.f. Miner:* magnetoplumbite.

magnétopyrite [maɲetɔpirit], *s.f. Miner:* magnetic pyrites, pyrrhotite.

magnétorésistance [maɲetɔrezistɑ̃ːs], *s.f.* magneto resistance.

magnétoscope [maɲetɔskɔp], *s.m.* video tape recorder, magnetoscope.

magnétoscopie [maɲetɔskɔpi], *s.f.* video tape recording.

magnétosphère [maɲetɔsfɛːr], *s.f.* magnetosphere.

magnétostatique [maɲetɔstatik], *a.* magnetostatic.

magnétostricteur [maɲetɔstriktœːr], *s.m. Elcs:* magnetostriction transmitter-receiver.

magnétostrictif, -ive [maɲetɔstriktif, -iːv], *a. Ph:* magnetostrictive.

magnétostriction [maɲetɔstriksjɔ̃], *s.f. Ph:* magnetostriction.

magnétothèque [maɲetɔtɛk], *s.f.* tape (recording) library.

magnétothérapie [maɲetɔterapi], *s.f. Med:* magnetotherapy.

magnétron [maɲetrɔ̃], *s.m. Elcs:* magnetron; **m. à anode fendue,** split-anode magnetron; **m. à cavités,** cavity magnetron; **m. à plusieurs secteurs,** multi-segment magnetron.

magnette [maɲɛt], *s.f. Ph: A:* magnet.

magnificat [magnifikat, maɲifika], *s.m. Ecc:* magnificat; *F:* **le m. est plus long que les vêpres,** your slip's showing.

magnificence [maɲifisɑ̃ːs], *s.f.* **1.** magnificence, splendour; sumptuousness. **2.** *Lit:* munificence; extravagant liberality; **prince ruiné par ses magnificences,** prince ruined by his open-handed sumptuousness, by his lavishness.

magnifier [magnifje, maɲifje], *v.tr.* (*p.d. & pr.sub.* **n. magnifiions, v. magnifiiez**) (*a*) to magnify, glorify (God); (*b*) to magnify, idealize.

magnifique [maɲifik], *a.* **1.** (*a*) magnificent, splendid, grand (palace, spectacle, etc.); sumptuous (meal); (*of child*) bonny; **récolte m.,** bumper crop; **découverte m.,** remarkable discovery; **situation m.,** wonderful job; *F:* **vous êtes m.!** you're the limit! (*b*) grandiloquent, pompous (tone); (*c*) high-resounding (promises). **2.** *A:* liberal, open-handed (prince, etc.); lavish of princely gifts.

magnifiquement [maɲifikmɑ̃], *adv.* magnificently, grandly; sumptuously; wonderfully.

magnitude [magnityd], *s.f.* (*a*) *Astr:* magnitude (of star); **m. absolue,** absolute magnitude; **m. apparente,** apparent magnitude; **de la m. 4,** of the fourth magnitude; (*b*) magnitude (of earthquake).

magnochromite [maɲɔkrɔmit], *s.f. Miner:* magnochromite.

magnoferrite [maɲɔfɛrit], *s.f. Miner:* magnoferrite.

magnolia [maɲɔlja, -gn-], *s.m.* **1.** *Bot:* magnolia (flower or tree); **m. grandiflora,** evergreen magnolia, laurel magnolia, bull-bay. **2.** *Metall:* magnolia(-metal).

magnoliacées [maɲɔljase, -gn-], *s.f.pl. Bot:* Magnoliaceae.

magnolier [maɲɔlje, -gn-], *s.m. Bot:* magnolia (-tree); **m. (en) parasol,** umbrella-tree.

magnum [magnɔm], *s.m.* magnum (of champagne).

magot[1] [mago], *s.m. F:* hoard (of money); savings, *F:* pile; **il a un joli m.,** he's got a nice bit put by.

magot[2], *s.m.* **1.** barbary ape, pigmy ape; macaque, magot. **2.** (*a*) Chinese grotesque porcelain figure; magot; (*b*) *F: O:* (*with f.* **magotte**) ugly person; scarecrow; *F:* fright.

magyar, -are [maʒjaːr], *a. & s. Ethn:* Magyar.

magyarisation [maʒjarizasjɔ̃], *s.f.* Magyarization.

magyariser [maʒjarize], *v.tr.* to Magyarize.

mahaleb [maalɛb], *s.m. Bot:* mahaleb (cherry).

maharajah [maaraʒa], *s.m.* maharaja(h).

maharani [maarani], *s.f.* maharani, maharanee.

mahaseer [maasiːr], *s.m. Ich:* mahseer.

mahatma [maatma], *s.m.* mahatma, saint.

mahdi [madi], *s.m.* Mahdi.

mahdisme [madism], *s.m.* Mahdism.

mahdiste [madist], *a. & s.m. & f.* Mahdist.

mah-jong [maʒɔ̃g], *s.m. Games:* mah-jong(g).

Mahomet [maɔmɛ], *Pr.n.m.* Mohammed, Mahomet.

mahométan, -ane [maɔmetɑ̃, -an], *a. & s. O:* Mohammedan, Mahometan, Moslem.

mahométisme [maɔmetism], *s.m. O:* Mohammedanism, Mahometanism, Moslemism.

Mahon [maɔ̃], *Pr.n.m. A:* Mahound, Mahomet.

mahonais, -aise [maɔnɛ, -ɛːz], *a. & s.* (native, inhabitant) of Port Mahon.

mahonia [maɔnja], *s.m. Bot:* mahonia; **m. (à feuilles de houx),** Oregon grape.

mahonne [maɔn], *s.f. Nau:* (*S. of Fr.*) barge.

mahous(s), mahousse [maus], *a. P:* (*a*) huge, enormous, tremendous, whacking great; (*b*) tremendously strong; (*c*) slap-up, stupendous.

mahout [mau], *s.m.* mahout, elephant driver.

mahratte [marat]. **1.** *Ethn: a. & s.m. & f.* Mahratta. **2.** *s.m. Ling:* Mahratti, Mahratta.

mai [mɛ], *s.m.* **1.** May; **en m.,** in May; **au mois de m.,** in the month of May; **le premier, le sept, m.,** (on) the first, the seventh, of May; (on) May (the) first, (the) seventh; **au, dans le, mois de m. suivant,** in the following May; **le premier m.,** May day. **2.** maypole; **planter un m.,** to set up a maypole.

maïa [maja], *s.m. Crust:* maia, spider crab.

maïanthème [majɑ̃tɛ(ː)m], *s.m. Bot:* maianthemum.

maie [mɛ], *s.f.* **1.** kneading trough. **2.** bread bin. **3.** flour bin.

maïeur [majœːr], *s.m.* **1.** *A:* mayor. **2.** *Dial:* (*in Belgium*) mayor (of village).

maïeutique [majøtik], *s.f. Phil:* maieutics.

maigre[1] [mɛgr̥]. **1.** *a.* (*a*) thin, skinny, lean (person, animal); *F:* **m. comme un clou, comme un hareng saur, comme un squelette,** as thin as a lath, as a rake; **homme grand et m.,** *s.* **un grand m.,** a tall, thin man; *s.* **c'est une fausse m.,** she's not as thin as she looks; (*b*) lean (meat, coal, limestone, etc.); meagre (fare); scanty (vegetation, etc.); small (crop); unfertile, poor (land, etc.); straggling (beard); **fromage m.,** skim-milk cheese; **m. filet d'eau,** thin trickle of water; **m. repas,** scanty, frugal, meal; **repas m.,** meatless meal (on abstinence days); **jour m.,** *s.m.* **maigre,** day of abstinence; *Nau: A:* banian-day; **faire m.,** to abstain (from meat); **de maigres appointements,** a poor salary; **m. bagage de latin,** scanty knowledge of Latin; **travailler sur un sujet m.,** to be at work on a meagre, barren, subject; **se décider sur de maigres raisons,** to make up one's mind on poor grounds; **faire m. chère, m. visage, m. réception, à qn,** to show s.o. meagre hospitality, to give s.o. a poor reception; **cela me fit un m. plaisir,** I was not over-pleased; **c'est une m. consolation,** it's a poor consolation; **n'avoir qu'une m. chance de succès,** to have but a poor chance of success; **style m.,** meagre, thin, bald, style; *Art:* **pinceau, crayon, m.,** meagre brush, pencil; *adv.* **peindre, dessiner, m.,** to lack breadth of brush, of pencil; to paint, draw, thin; *Nau:* **eau m., m. eau,** shallow water. **2.** *s.m.* (*a*) lean (part of meat); **voulez-vous du gras ou du m.?** will you have fat or lean? (*b*) *pl.* shallows (of river, etc.).

maigre², *s.m. Ich:* meagre, bar.

maigrelet, -ette [mɛgrəlɛ, -ɛt], *a.* thin, slight (person).

maigrement [mɛgrəmɑ̃], *adv.* meagrely; poorly, scantily; **m. satisfait,** not very well satisfied; **traiter m. ses invités,** to offer one's guests, poor, meagre, hospitality.

maigreur [mɛgrœːr], *s.f.* **1.** (*a*) thinness, leanness (of person, animal); (*b*) emaciation; **homme d'une m. extrême,** (i) man of extremely spare build; (ii) man greatly emaciated. **2.** (*a*) poorness, meagreness, scantiness (of a meal, etc.); baldness (of style); *Art:* thinness (of brush or pencil); (*b*) **m. du terrain,** meagreness, poorness, of the land.

maigrichon, -onne [mɛgriʃɔ̃, -ɔn], **maigriot, -otte** [mɛgrijo, -ɔt], *a. F:* thin, skinny (urchin, etc.).

maigrir [mɛgriːr, me-]. **1.** *v.i.* to grow thin, lean; to lose flesh; **j'ai maigri de dix kilos,** I have lost ten kilos. **2.** *v.tr.* (*a*) (*of illness*) to make (s.o.) thin(ner); (*b*) (*of garment*) to make (s.o.) look thin(ner); (*c*) to thin (piece of wood, etc.).

mail [maːj], *s.m.* **1.** (*a*) *A:* mall (game, club, or alley); (*b*) avenue, promenade. **2.** sledge-hammer; maul.

mail-coach [mɛlkoːtʃ], *s.m. A.Veh:* four-in-hand; tally-ho coach; *pl. mail-coaches.*

maillage¹ [mɑjaːʒ, ma-], *s.m.* **1.** *Tex:* braking (of flax). **2.** (*a*) meshing, meshes, mesh-work (of net, lattice, etc.); (*b*) *El: Elcs:* grid(mesh) (of network); *Av: etc:* **guidage par radio-m.,** grid guidance.

maillage², *s.m. Min:* (*N.Fr.*) airway.

maillage³, *s.m. Metall:* hot working.

maille¹ [mɑːj], *s.f.* **1.** (*a*) stitch (in knitting, crochet, etc.); **m. à l'endroit,** plain (stitch); **m. à l'envers,** purl (stitch); **m. à côte,** stocking stitch; **m. jersey,** plain knitting; **m. coulée,** run (caused by dropped stitch or broken thread); **m. qui file,** ladder (in stocking); (*b*) link (of chain); **m. à étai, m. étançonnée,** stud link; **m. sans étai,** studless link; **m. courante, m. ordinaire,** (i) common link; (ii) *Nau:* commercial link (of anchor cable); **m. amovible, m. démontable,** detachable link, patent link; **m. brisée,** split link; **m. ouverte,** open link; **m. à talon,** link and stud; (*c*) *Arm:* (chain-)mail; **cotte de mailles,** coat of mail; (*d*) *Tex:* mail (of heddle twine). **2.** (*a*) mesh (of net, lattice, etc.); **à mailles fines,** close-meshed; **filet à larges mailles,** wide-mesh net; (*b*) *Aut: Adm:* parking space; (*c*) *El: Elcs:* mesh (of grid, of network); *Av: etc:* **guidage par radio-mailles,** grid guidance; (*d*) *N.Arch:* timber and space (in frame); frame space; **les mailles,** the bilges. **3.** (*a*) speckle, spot (on partridge feather, etc.); (*b*) (*on the eye*) albugo, leucoma; (*c*) bud (of vine, melon). **4.** star shake (in timber); **débit sur m.,** sawing (of timber) radially.

maille², *s.f.* two-handed mallet.

maille³, *s.f.* **1.** *Num: A:* mail; *F:* **il n'a ni sou ni m.,** he hasn't a penny to bless himself with; **avoir m. à partir avec qn,** to have a bone to pick with s.o. **2.** *A:* **ne . . . m.,** not anything (at all); **de nouveauté dans mon fait il n'est m.,** in my tale there is nothing new.

maillé [mɑje], *a.* **1.** mailed (knight, etc.). **2.** (*of fish, etc.*) netted, caught in a net. **3.** (*a*) (*of partridge, etc.*) speckled; *hence* (*b*) full-grown. **4.** star-shaked (timber). **5.** leaded (window). **6.** reticulated, retiform; *El:* **réseau m.,** grid (network). **7.** (*in Champagne*) **terre maillée,** clay(ey) soil.

maillechor(t) [mɑjʃɔːr, ma-], *s.m.* German silver, nickel silver.

mailler¹ [mɑje, ma-], *v.tr. & i.* **1.** *v.tr.* (*a*) to net (a purse, etc.); (*b*) to make (sth.) in lattice work; (*c*) *Vit:* **m. un treillage,** to trellis vines. **2.** *v.tr.* (*a*) to shackle (two chains); (*b*) *Nau:* to lace (one sail to another). **3.** *v.i.* (*a*) (*of vine, etc.*) to bud; (*b*) (*of partridge, etc.*) to become speckled. **4.** *v.i. Fish:* (*a*) **filet qui maille,** net with a mesh suitable for the size of the fish to be caught; (*b*) **poisson qui maille,** fish that gets caught in the net.

se mailler. 1. (*of partridge, etc.*) to become speckled, to assume adult plumage, to attain full growth. **2.** (*of fish*) to be caught in the net.

mailler² [mɑje, ma-], *v.tr.* to mallet; to beat with a mallet; *Tex:* to brake (hemp, flax).

maillerie [mɑjəri, ma-], *s.f. Tex:* braking mill (for hemp).

maillet [majɛ], *s.m.* **1.** (*a*) *Tls:* mallet, maul; beetle; **m. à fourrer,** serving mallet; **m. à calfat,** caulking mallet; (*b*) polo stick; (*c*) croquet mallet. **2.** *Ich:* hammer-head (shark).

mailletage [majtaːʒ], *s.m. A.Nau:* studding, clouting (of hull).

mailleter [majte], *v.tr.* (**je maillette, n. mailletons; je mailletterai**) *A.Nau:* to stud, clout, fill (hull of ship).

mailleton [majtɔ̃], *s.m.* **1.** *Hort: O:* (i) bud; (ii) cutting (of the current year). **2.** tie (to attach vine).

maillochage [mɑjɔʃaːʒ, ma-], *s.m. Hort:* crushing of base (of a cutting to encourage formation of roots).

mailloche [majɔʃ], *s.f.* **1.** beetle; large mallet, maul; **m. à fourrer,** serving mallet; **battre qch. à coups de m.,** to beetle sth. **2.** bass drumstick.

maillocheur [majɔʃœːr], *s.m.* (*pers.*) leather beater.

maillole [mɑjɔl, ma-], *s.f. Hort:* (i) bud, (ii) cutting (of the year).

maillon [mɑjɔ̃, ma-], *s.m.* **1.** (*a*) link (of a chain); *Mec.E:* **m. d'attache,** clevis; **m. de connexion, de raccord,** connecting link, connector; **m. d'emerillon,** shackle; **m. tournant,** swivel; (*of pers.*) **être le m. d'une chaîne,** to be a link in the chain; *s.a.* ÉTALINGURE; (*b*) *Tex:* mail (of heddle-twine); (*c*) *W.Tel:* **m. isolateur,** shell insulator. **2.** *Nau:* (*length of chain of 30 metres*) shackle.

maillot¹ [majo], *s.m.* (*a*) *A:* (infant's) swaddling-band; (*b*) swaddling clothes; **enfant encore au m.,** baby not yet "shortened"; (*c*) *Med:* (wet, dry) pack(ing).

maillot², *s.m.* (*a*) *Th: etc:* tights; **m. couleur chair,** fleshings; (*b*) **m. de bain,** bathing costume, bathing suit, swimsuit; (*c*) *Sp:* (football) jersey; (running, boxing, rowing) vest, singlet; (*Tour de France*) **le m. jaune,** (yellow jersey worn by) the race leader; **le m. vert,** (green jersey worn by) the leader on points classification; (*d*) **m. de corps,** (man's) vest, *U.S:* undervest, undershirt.

maillotin¹ [majɔtɛ̃], *s.m.* (*a*) *A.Arms:* war hammer; (*b*) *pl. Hist:* Maillotins (insurgent Parisians, 1382).

maillotin², *s.m. Agr:* (type of) olive-press.

maillure [majyːr, mɑ-], *s.f.* **1.** *Orn:* speckles (on plumage). **2.** star shaking (in timber).

main [mɛ̃], *s.f.* **1.** hand; (*a*) **se laver les mains,** to wash one's hands; **se laver les mains de qch.,** to wash one's hands of sth.; **une m. lave l'autre,** they all work in with one another, they all help each other; **soin des mains,** manicure; **se faire les mains,** to give oneself a manicure; **se faire faire les mains,** to have a manicure; **faire les mains à qn,** to give s.o. a manicure; **la froide m. de la mort,** the cold hand of death; **donner la m. à qn,** (i) to take s.o.'s hand, to lead s.o. by the hand; (ii) to shake hands with s.o.; (iii) to help s.o.; to favour s.o.; **ils se donnèrent la m. pour traverser la rivière,** they joined hands to cross the river; **donner la m.,** (i) to consent; (ii) to give in, to throw up the sponge; **se donner la m.,** (i) to shake hands; (ii) (*of two armies*) to effect a junction; **donner sa m. à qn,** (i) to shake hands with s.o.; (ii) (*of woman*) to give one's hand in marriage to s.o.; **demander la m. d'une jeune fille,** to ask for a girl in marriage; **je lui ai serré la m.,** I shook hands with him; **elle me reprit sa m.,** she drew back her hand; **elle me reprit la m.,** she took my hand again; **faire qch. de la m. droite, de la m. gauche,** to do sth. right-handed, left-handed; **mariage de la m. gauche,** left-handed marriage; ((i) morganatic marriage, (ii) illicit union); **de marchand en marchand il n'y a que la m.,** an honest man's word is as good as his bond; **mettre, porter, la m. à son chapeau,** to touch one's hat to s.o.; **porter la m. sur qn,** to lay hands on s.o.; to strike s.o.; **je n'en mettrais pas la m. au feu,** I shouldn't like to swear to it; **sac à m.,** handbag; **en venir aux mains,** to come to blows, to grips; to begin to fight; **lever la m. sur qn,** to raise one's hand against s.o.; to strike s.o.; **ne pas y aller de m. morte,** (i) to put one's back into it; to go hard at it; (ii) to make an all-out attack; **homme de m.,** (i) man of action; (ii) bully; thug; **faire m. basse sur qch.,** to lay hands on sth.; to help oneself to sth.; **faire m. basse sur une ville,** to pillage, loot, a town; **haut les mains!** hands up! **à bas les mains!** hands off! **sous la m.,** within reach; near at hand; **avoir tout sous la m.,** to have everything ready to hand; **faire qch. sous la m.,** to do sth. in an underhand way; **affaire conclue sous la m.,** hole-and-corner deal; *Mil:* **coup de m.,** raid, sudden attack, surprise attack; **donner un coup de m. à qn, prêter la m. à qn,** to lend s.o. a (helping) hand; *F:* **passer la m. dans le dos, dans les cheveux, à qn,** to butter s.o. up; **faire des pieds et des mains pour faire qch.,** to move heaven and earth to do sth.; **avoir la m. chaude,** to have a run of luck (at a game); **avoir le cœur sur la m.,** to be very generous; to be open-handed; *s.a.* LÉGER 1, NU 1; REVERS 1; (*b*) (*hand used for gripping sth.*) **prendre qch. dans les mains,** to take sth. in one's hands; **il a des mains de beurre,** he's a butterfingers; **prendre un plateau, son courage, à deux mains,** to take a tray, one's courage, in both hands; **épée à deux mains,** two-handed sword; **il signa le contrat des deux mains,** he signed the contract eagerly; **donner de l'argent à pleine(s) main(s),** to hand out money lavishly; **semer l'argent à pleines mains,** to scatter money broadcast; **avoir de l'atout plein les mains,** to have a handful of trumps; **avoir, tenir, une canne à la m.,** to have a stick in one's hand; **qui leur a mis des armes aux mains?** who put weapons into their hands? **avoir, tenir, qch. dans la m.,** to have, hold, sth. in one's hand; **avoir sans cesse l'argent à la m.,** to be constantly paying up, *F:* shelling out; **argent en main(s),** money in hand; **pièces en mains il écrasa ses adversaires,** documents in hand he crushed his opponents; **outil bien en main(s), bien à la m.,** handy, easily handled, tool; **ne lui laissez pas ce couteau entre les mains,** don't leave that knife in his hands; **tenir le succès entre ses mains,** to have success within one's grasp; **mon sort est entre vos mains,** my fate is in your hands; **passer aux mains de . . .,** to pass, fall, into the hands of . . .; **tomber entre les mains, aux mains, de l'ennemi,** to fall into the enemy's hands; **être en bonnes mains,** to be in good hands, in safe keeping; **prendre une affaire en m.,** to take a matter in hand; to take up a matter; **mettre la m. sur qn,** to lay hands on s.o.; *F:* to collar s.o.; **mettre la m. sur qch.,** to lay hands on, take possession of, sth.; to grab sth.; **mettre la m. sur les meilleures places,** to grab the best seats; **je ne peux pas mettre la m. sur sa lettre,** I can't put my hand on his letter; *Nau:* **gagner un navire m. sur m.,** to make up on a ship hand over hand; **recevoir qch. des mains de qn,** to receive sth. at the hands of s.o.; *A: & Dial:* **bonne m.,** gratuity, tip; **acheter qch. de première, seconde, m.,** to buy sth. (at) first hand, secondhand; **article de seconde m.,** secondhand article; *Com: Aut:* **une première m.,** a car that has had only one owner; **renseignements de première, de seconde, m.,** first-hand information, information at second hand; **ouvrage de première m.,** work compiled from first-hand knowledge; **mesures de seconde m.,** measures of secondary importance, that must yield precedence to others; **je tiens cela de bonne(s) main(s),** I have it on good authority; **de m. en m.,** from hand to hand; **payer de la m. à la m.,** to hand over the money direct (without receipt or other formality); *A:* **faire sa m.,** to feather one's nest; (*c*) (*hand for making, executing, sth.*) **faire, fabriquer, qch. à la m.,** to do, make, sth. by hand; **fait à la m.,** hand-made; *F: A:* **chose faite à la m.,** put-up job; **papier (fait) à la m.,** hand-made paper; **scie à m.,** handsaw; **chargement d'un fourneau à la m.,** hand-stoking of a furnace; **dire adieu de la m. à qn,** to wave s.o. goodbye; **faire qch. par ses mains, de sa m.,** to do sth. with one's own hands; **écrire une lettre de sa propre m.,** to write a letter in one's own hand; **il écrit de la m. gauche,** he writes with his left hand; **notes en marge écrites à la m.,** handwritten marginal notes; **vers frappés de m. de maître,** verses turned by a master hand; **mettre la m. à l'œuvre,** to put one's hand to the plough; to get down to the job; **mettre la m. à la pâte,** to lend a hand; **mettre la m. à la plume,** to put pen to paper; **mettre la dernière m. à qch.,** to give, put, the finishing touches to sth.; **tenir la m. à qch.,** to make sure that sth. is done; **se faire la m.,** to learn how to handle a tool, etc.; to get one's hand in; to acquire the knack of sth.; **s'entretenir la m.,** to keep one's hand in; **il a perdu la m.,** he's out of practice; **il a vite attrapé le coup de m.,** he soon got the knack, the hang, of it; **j'ai perdu le coup de m. pour donner les cartes,** I've got out of the way of, lost the knack of, dealing; *Hort:* **avoir la bonne m.,** to have green fingers; **dessin à m. levée,** freehand drawing; *Dressm:* **petite m.,** apprentice, junior assistant; **première m.,** chief assistant; *s.a.* TOUR³ 3; (*d*) *Equit:* **m. de la bride,** bridle hand, left hand; **rendre la m. à son cheval,** to give one's horse its head; *Av:* **rendre la m.,** to ease the stick; **cheval à toute m., de m., mené en m.,** led horse; **cheval à toute m.,** horse for riding or driving; **homme à toute m.,** man ready to do anything; handyman; **un homme à toute m. chez lui,** a very handy man about the house; **cheval, armée, bien en m., bien dans la m.,** horse, army, well in hand, under control; **tenir qch. bien en m.,** to have a firm grip on sth.; *Aut:* **il a sa voiture bien en m.,** he has the feel of his car; **tenez-vous en m.,** control yourself; **faire sentir sa m. à un cheval, à qn; tenir la m., soutenir la m., tenir la m. haute, à un cheval, à qn,** to keep a horse, s.o., in hand; to ride with a high hand; to make one's authority felt, to make s.o. feel one's authority; **tenir la m. à l'observation d'une règle,** to enforce (the observance of) a rule; **être sous la m. de qn,** to be under s.o.'s thumb; **agir de haute m.,** to act with a high hand, in a high-handed way; **avoir la haute m. sur . . .,** to have supreme control over . . .; **avoir la haute m. dans une maison,** to be the ruling spirit in a firm, *F:* to rule the roost; **il faut avoir la haute m.,** we must keep the upper hand; **gagner haut la m.,** (i) *Turf:* to win in a canter, (ii) to win easily, hands down; **passer (un examen) haut la m.,** to pass with flying colours; (*e*) *adv.phr.* **de longue m.,** for a long time (past); **ami de longue m.,** friend of long standing. 2. (*a*) hand(writing); **avoir une belle m.,** to have a fine hand, to write well; (*b*) *Com:* **m. courante,** rough book; **m. courante de caisse,** counter cash-book; **m. courante de sorties, de dépenses,** paid-cash book. 3. *Cards:* (*a*) hand; **avoir une m. longue, courte,** to have a long, short, suit in trumps, to be long, short, in trumps; (*b*) deal; **avoir la m.,** to have the deal; **passer la m.,** (i) (*Baccarat, etc.*) to pass the deal; (ii) to stand aside; to give someone else a chance; (*c*) lead; **avoir la m.,** to have the lead. 4. (*something for holding, picking up, sth.*) (*a*) (grocer's, etc.) scoop; (*b*) **mains de caoutchouc,** rubber gloves; (*c*) handle (of drawer, etc.); (*d*) hook (of well chain); (*e*) *Aut:* **m. de ressort,** dumb iron, spring carrier arm; **mains avant, arrière,** front, back, dumb irons; front, rear, spring carriers. 5. *Paperm:* **m. de papier,** (**25 feuilles**), approx. = quire of paper (24 sheets); *s.a.* PASSE 5. 6. *Tex. etc:* feel, hand, (of cloth, etc.); *Paperm:* **papier qui a de la m.,** paper with some substance, that handles easily; **papier qui a la m. très élevée,** paper that bulks high. 7. **m. courante, m. coulante,** handrail (of stair); hand rope; side rail (of locomotive). 8. **m. de fer;** (*a*) hand-hold (on wall, etc.); (*b*) hanging clamp, hanger (of spring, etc.); (*c*) handled hook (of rag-pickers, etc.). 9. gang of workers.

mainate [mɛnat], *s.m. Orn:* grackle; **m. religieux,** mina, myna(h).

main-d'œuvre [mɛ̃dœːvr], *s.f.* 1. labour; manpower; **m.-d'œ. à bon marché,** cheap labour; **m.-d'œ. spécialisée,** semi-skilled labour; **m. d'œ. qualifiée,** skilled labour; **rareté de m.-d'œ.,** shortage of labour; **embaucher de la m.-d'œ.,** to take on hands. 2. cost of labour; **matériel et m.-d'œ.,** material and labour. 3. workmanship; *pl. mains-d'œuvre.*

main-forte [mɛ̃fɔrt], *s.f. no pl.* help, assistance (to authority or of authority); *used only with* **demander, donner, prêter, quérir; prêter m.-f. à la justice,** to give assistance to the law; to support law and order; **prêter m.-f. à un agent,** to come to the help of a policeman; *A:* **demander, quérir, m.-f.,** to call out the watch, the soldiery.

mainlevée [mɛ̃lve], *s.f. Jur:* **m. de saisie,** replevin; restoration of goods (taken in distraint); cancellation of garnishee order; **m. d'opposition à mariage,** withdrawal of opposition to marriage; *Ecc:* **m. d'interdit,** removal of interdict; **donner m. de saisie,** to grant replevin; **donner m. d'opposition,** to withdraw one's opposition.

mainmettre [mɛ̃mɛtr], *v.tr.* (*conj. like* METTRE) *Jur: A:* to manumit, free (slave).

mainmise [mɛ̃miːz], *s.f.* 1. *Jur: A:* manumission; freeing (of bondman). 2. seizure (**sur,** of); (*a*) distraint (upon property); (*b*) **m. sur un État,** annexation of a State; (*c*) **m. économique, linguistique,** economic, linguistic, stranglehold.

mainmortable [mɛ̃mɔrtabl̩], *a. Jur:* subject to mortmain.

mainmorte [mɛ̃mɔrt], *s.f. Jur:* mortmain; **biens de m.,** property in mortmain.

maint [mɛ̃]. 1. *a.* many (a . . .); **m. auteur,** many an author; **maintes et maintes fois, à maintes reprises, en mainte (et mainte) occasion,** time and again; **les maints raffinements de l'oisiveté,** the many refinements of a life of leisure. 2. *indef.pron.* **maint(s) d'entre eux,** many of them; **maintes des personnes qui . . .,** many of those who . . ..

maintenage [mɛ̃tnaːʒ], *s.m. Min:* supporting (of steeply sloping gallery) with timber-work.

maintenance [mɛ̃tnɑ̃ːs], *s.f.* 1. *A:* maintaining (of law and order, etc.). 2. (*a*) *Mil:* keeping up to strength (of unit and equipment); (*b*) *Ind: etc:* (i) maintenance (service); **m. périodique,** routine maintenance; *Mil:* **m. de campagne, de combat,** field, combat, maintenance; **m. du premier, du deuxième degré,** first-line, second-line, maintenance; (ii) spare parts service.

maintenant [mɛ̃tnɑ̃], *adv.* (*a*) now; **vous devriez être prêt m.,** you ought to be ready by now; **qu'est-ce que nous allons faire m.?** what shall we do now? what shall we do next? **à vous m.,** your turn next; **m. que la vie est chère,** now that the cost of living is high; *F:* **oh! m.,** come now! (*b*) **la pluie tombait m.,** the rain was falling now; (*c*) **dès m.,** (i) from now onwards; (ii) even now; (**à partir de**) **m. il cessera de le faire,** from now onwards, in future, he'll stop doing it; (*d*) **voilà ce que je vous conseille; m. vous ferez ce que vous voudrez,** that's my advice; but of course you'll do as you like.

maintenir [mɛ̃tniːr], *v.tr.* (*conj. like* TENIR) to maintain. 1. (*a*) to keep (sth.) in position; **colonnes qui maintiennent la voûte,** columns that keep up, support, the roof; **flotteurs qui maintiennent qch. à la surface,** floats that keep sth. on the surface; **les digues maintiennent le fleuve dans son lit,** the dykes maintain, hold back, the river in its bed; (*b*) **m. la foule,** to hold back the crowd; **m. son cheval,** to keep one's horse under control; **m. à grand-peine un malade agité,** to have great difficulty in holding down a violent patient; **il est difficile de m. ces étudiants dans la carrière de l'enseignement,** it is difficult to keep these students to the teaching profession; (*c*) **m. qn debout,** to hold s.o. up, to keep s.o. on his feet; **m. qn en prison,** to keep s.o. in prison. 2. (*a*) to uphold, keep (the law, peace, discipline, one's opinions, etc.); to adhere to (an opinion); to abide by (a decision); **m. sa réputation,** to keep up one's reputation; **m. sa position,** to hold one's own; (*b*) **m. qn dans ses fonctions,** to maintain s.o. in office; **m. une vitesse de 80 kilomètres à l'heure,** to keep up a speed of 80 kilometres an hour; (*c*) **je maintiens que c'est faux,** I maintain that it is untrue; **maintenez-vous vos accusations?** do you persist in your accusations?

se maintenir. 1. (*a*) to remain, to last; **murs qui se maintiennent bien,** walls that last well; (*b*) (*of casting-mould, etc.*) to hold together. 2. to hold on; **se m. dans les bonnes grâces de qn,** to keep in favour with s.o.; **tâchons de nous m. dans la voie moyenne,** let us try to keep to a middle course; **se m. contre les attaques de l'ennemi,** to hold one's own, to hold one's ground, against the enemy; **le malade se maintient,** the patient is holding his own; **les prix se maintiennent (en hausse),** prices are keeping up; *St.Exch:* **ces actions se maintiennent à . . .,** these shares remain firm at . . .; *F:* **comment ça va?—on se maintient,** how are things?—jogging along. 3. to be maintained, to continue; **cela ne peut pas se m. longtemps,** it cannot last long; **le temps se maintient,** the weather is holding; **l'amélioration enregistrée se maintient,** the improvement is being maintained; **le temps se maintient au beau,** the weather remains fine.

maintenon [mɛ̃tnɔ̃], *s.m. A:* small cross (as worn on necklace by Mme de Maintenon).

maintenue [mɛ̃tny], *s.f. Jur:* confirmation in possession (of voidable estate, etc.).

maintien [mɛ̃tjɛ̃], *s.m.* 1. maintenance, upholding, keeping (of order, of the law, etc.). 2. bearing, carriage, deportment; **leçons de m.,** lessons in deportment; **avoir un m. grave,** to carry oneself seriously, solemnly; **il n'a pas de m.,** he's awkward; **perdre son m.,** to lose countenance; **faire qch. pour se donner un m.,** to do sth. to keep oneself in countenance.

maïolique [majɔlik], *s.f. Cer:* majolica.

mairain [mɛrɛ̃], *s.m.* = MERRAIN.

maire [mɛːr], *s.m.* mayor; **exercice des fonctions de m., temps d'exercice des fonctions de m.,** mayoralty; *F:* **être passé devant le m.,** to be married; *Hist:* **les maires du palais,** the mayors of the Palace.

mairesse [mɛrɛs], *s.f.* (*a*) *F: usu. Hum:* mayoress; (*b*) *O:* (woman) mayor.

mairie [mɛri, me-], *s.f.* 1. (*a*) mayoralty, office of mayor; (*b*) mayoralty, term of office of mayor. 2. local administration; **être employé de m.,** to work in local government service. 3. town hall, municipal buildings.

mais [mɛ]. 1. *adv.* (*a*) *A:* more; *still so used in* **n'en pouvoir m.,** (i) to be exhausted, at the end of one's tether; (ii) to be too disconcerted to protest; (*b*) (*emphatic*) **m. oui!** of course! oh yes! why, certainly! **m. si!** I tell you, yes! but it is (true, etc.); **m. non!** not at all! **il ne craint rien, m. rien!** he is afraid of nothing, absolutely nothing! **il a parlé très bien, m. très bien,** he spoke very well, very well indeed; **m. qu'avez-vous donc?** but what's the matter? **m. c'est que c'est vrai!** but it's true! but then it's true; **ah m.!** I say! look here! **m. enfin!** well really! 2. *conj.* but; **famille riche m. honnête,** rich but honest family; **je vais t'attendre, m. ne sois pas longtemps,** I'll wait for you, but don't be long; **non seulement . . ., m. aussi, m. encore . . .,** not only . . ., but also . . .; *s.* **il y a un m.,** there is one objection, criticism, to be made; **il n'y a pas de m.,** there's no but about it.

maïs [mais], *s.m.* 1. maize, Indian corn, *U.S:* corn; **farine de m.,** cornflour; *Fr.C:* **flocons de m.,** cornflakes; **grains de m. grillés,** popcorn. 2. *Bot:* **m. d'eau,** water maize, victoria regia.

maïserie [maiz(ə)ri], *s.f.* corn mill.

maison [mɛzɔ̃], *s.f.* 1. (*a*) house; **m. de maître,** gentleman's residence; **m. de banlieue,** suburban house; **maisons doubles,** semi-detached houses; **m. de ville,** town house; **m. de campagne,** house in the country; **m. de plaisance,** holiday, week-end, house; **m. de chasse,** hunting lodge, box; **m. de rapport,** (block of) flats, apartment house; **m. garnie,** (house let in) furnished apartments; **m. d'habitation,** dwelling house; **m. de ferme,** farm-house; **m. de poupée,** doll's house; **la M. Blanche,** the White House; **la politique de la M. Blanche,** White House policy, American government policy; *Prov:* **les maisons empêchent de voir la ville,** you can't see the wood for the trees; **faire des demandes par-dessus les maisons,** to make exorbitant demands, to ask for the moon; (*b*) home; **à la m.,** at home; **retournons à la m.,** let's go home; **garder la m.,** to stay at home, in (-doors); **faire sa m.,** to set up house; **avoir m. montée,** to have set up house, to have a home (of one's own); **dépenses de la m.,** household expenses; **tenir la m.,** to keep house; **tenir m.,** to entertain (formally); **tenir m. ouverte,** to keep open house; **m. accueillante,** friendly, hospitable, house; **c'est la m. du bon Dieu,** it's a most hospitable house; **trouver m. nette,** to find the house empty; **cela a eu lieu dans la m.,** it happened indoors; **il porte des pantoufles dans la m.,** he wears slippers indoors; **w.c. dans la m.,** indoor sanitation; **adduction des eaux potables de m.,** domestic water supply; (*c*) **gens de m.,** domestic servants, domestic staff; **elle a vingt ans de m.,** she has been in service for twenty years; (*d*) **la m. de Dieu,** the house of God; (*e*) *Astrol:* house, mansion. 2. (*building used for a specific purpose*) (*a*) *A: or regional:* **m. de ville, m. commune,** town hall; municipal buildings; *Jur:* **m. centrale, m. de force, de détention,** prison; **m. d'arrêt, de dépôt; m. de justice,** prison (for prisoners awaiting trial); **m. de correction,** (i) prison (where short sentences are served); (ii) *A:* reformatory (school); **m. de redressement, m. (d'éducation) surveillée,** approved school; (*b*) **m. mortuaire,** (i) house where s.o. has died; (ii) mortuary (chapel); (*c*) **m. de santé,** (i) nursing home; (ii) home for the insane, mental hospital; **m. de repos, de convalescence,** rest home; convalescent home; **m. de retraite,** old people's home; **m. du marin, du soldat** = N.A.A.F.I.; **m. de la culture,** cultural centre; **m. de la jeunesse,** youth centre; youth club; **m. d'éducation,** educational establishment; (*d*) **m. de jeux,** (licensed) gaming establishment; gaming club;

m. close, m. de tolérance, m. de passe, m. publique, brothel; (*e*) **m. (de commerce),** firm; business house; **m. de gros,** wholesale firm; **il a une grosse m.,** he's in a big way of business; **les traditions de la m.,** the traditions of the firm, house traditions; **m. mère,** (i) head office; (ii) *Ecc:* mother house; (*in restaurant, etc.*) **spécialité de la m.,** house speciality, *F:* house special; **j'en ai assez de cette m.!** I've had enough of this firm, *F:* of this show! **3.** (*a*) family; **le fils et la fille de la m.,** the son and daughter of the house; **faire la jeune fille de la m.,** to pass, hand round, the snacks (at cocktail party, etc.); **il est de bonne m.,** he comes from a good family; **ami de la m.,** friend of the family; **être de la m.,** to be one of the family; (*b*) dynasty; **la m. des Bourbons,** the House of Bourbon; (*c*) household, staff; **la m. du Roi,** the Royal Household; **m. militaire d'un souverain, d'un président,** sovereign's, president's, military household; **gens de m.,** servants; **faire m. nette,** to make a clean sweep (of all servants, employees); **faire m. neuve,** to engage a new staff. **4.** *attrib.* (*a*) *Com: etc:* **genre, style, m.,** house style, firm's style; (*on menu*) **pâté m.,** home-made pâté, pâté maison; (*b*) *P:* slap-up; extraordinarily good; **ça, c'est m.!** that's the goods! **c'était un chou m.,** it was a monstrous, huge, cabbage.

maisonnage [mɛzɔnaːʒ], *s.m.* building timber, constructional timber.

maisonnée [mɛzɔne], *s.f. F:* household, family; **toute la m.,** all the family.

maisonnette [mɛzɔnɛt], *s.f.* small house, cottage; **m. du garde,** gatekeeper's lodge; **m. de passage à niveau,** level-crossing keeper's house.

maistrance [mɛstrɑ̃ːs], *s.f.* (*a*) petty officers (of the navy); (*b*) *A:* dockyard staff.

maitlandite [mɛtlɑ̃dit], *s.f. Miner:* maitlandite.

maître, -esse [mɛːtr̥, mɛtrɛs], *s.* **1.** (*a*) master, *f.* mistress; **c'est moi le m., la maîtresse, ici,** I am master, mistress, here; **le m., la maîtresse, de maison,** the master, the mistress, of the house; **je veux être m. chez moi,** I will be master in my own house; **chauffeur de m.,** private chauffeur; **je suis m. de mon temps,** my time is my own; **Rome, la maîtresse du monde,** Rome, the mistress of the world; **parler à qn en m.,** to speak authoritatively to s.o.; **être m. de la situation,** to be master of the situation; **être m. absolu de faire qch.,** to be entirely free to do sth.; **si j'étais le m.,** if I were master, if I were free, if I had my way; *F:* **faire le m.,** to lord it; **trouver son m.,** to meet one's master; *Games:* to be outplayed; **être m., maîtresse, de soi(-même),** to be master, mistress, of oneself; to have one's feelings under control, under command; **ne pas être m. de ses actes,** to have no control over one's actions; to be quite irresponsible; **être m. de son cheval, de sa voiture,** to have one's horse, one's car, well in hand; **les freins cessèrent de fonctionner et le conducteur ne fut plus m. de sa voiture,** the brakes failed and the car went out of control; **le mécanicien n'était plus m. du train,** the driver had lost control of the train; **navire qui n'est pas m. de sa manœuvre,** ship out of control; **devenir, se rendre, m., maîtresse, de qch.,** (i) to become the owner of sth., to take possession of sth.; (ii) to master sth.; **se rendre m. de la conversation,** to take the lead in the conversation; **avec de l'argent on est m. du monde,** with money a man commands the world; **il est toujours m. de son auditoire,** he always commands the attention of his audience; *Com:* **être m. du marché,** to command the market; **rester m. du champ de bataille,** to remain master of the field, in possession of the field; *Prov:* **tel m., tel valet,** like master, like man; (*b*) **m., maîtresse, d'école,** primary school teacher; **m. d'internat** = housemaster; **m. assistant** = assistant lecturer (at university); **m. de danse,** dancing master; **m. d'escrime,** *A:* **d'armes,** fencing master; **m. de chapelle,** choirmaster; (*c*) skilled tradesman (working on his own account); **m. charpentier, m. maçon,** master carpenter, master mason; **main de m.,** master hand; **c'est fait de main de m.,** it is a masterpiece; **coup de m.,** master stroke; **être passé m. en qch.,** to be a past master in sth., of sth., at doing sth.; **passé m. en fait d'ironie,** past master of irony; **il est passé m. en photographie,** he's a first-class photographer; (*d*) works owner; **m. de carrière,** quarry-master; **m. de forges,** ironmaster; (*e*) employee in charge; **m. d'œuvre,** (i) foreman; (ii) prime contractor; **m. clerc,** (lawyer's) managing clerk; *Min:* **m. mineur,** overman; *Petroleum Ind:* **m. sondeur,** foreman driller; *A:* **m., maîtresse, de poste,** postmaster, postmistress; (*f*) *Navy:* petty officer first class; **second m.,** petty officer second class; **premier m.,** chief petty officer; **m. principal,** senior chief petty officer; **m. d'équipage,** boatswain; **m. mécanicien,** chief engine-room artificer; **le m. du navire,** the master of the ship; **m. au cabotage,** master of a coasting vessel; (*g*) **m. d'hôtel,** (i) major-domo, butler; (ii) head waiter; (iii) *Nau:* chief steward; (iv) *Navy:* officers' steward; *Cu:* **sauce (à la) m. d'hôtel,** maître d'hôtel sauce (melted butter with parsley and lemon juice); (*h*) *A.Mil:* cavalry trooper; (*i*) master (of an art); **les grands maîtres (de la peinture, etc.),** the great masters (of painting, etc.); **déjà il écrit en m.,** his writing is already that of a master; **m. chanteur,** blackmailer; (*j*) (i) *Jur:* (*title given to barristers, solicitors*) Maître; (ii) *A: F:* **M. François,** good Master Francis; (iii) *Sch: A:* **m. ès arts** = Master of Arts. **2.** *N.Arch:* midships; **demi-coupe au m.,** half-midship section. **3.** *attrib.* (*a*) **m. homme, maîtresse femme,** capable, managing, man, woman; *F:* **m. sot,** utter fool; **m. filou,** arrant scoundrel; **m. chou,** champion cabbage; (*b*) chief, principal, main; **maîtresse poutre, m. bau,** main girder, main beam; **cheville maîtresse, pièce maîtresse,** king pin; *Geol:* **m. filon,** mother lode; **lame maîtresse d'un ressort,** main leaf of a spring; **branche maîtresse d'un cours d'eau,** main stream of a river; **un des maîtres buts de ma vie,** one of the main, chief, objects of my life; **idée maîtresse d'un ouvrage,** governing idea of a work; **les deux maîtresses conditions du succès,** the two main conditions of success; *Games: Elcs:* (*data processing*) **carte maîtresse,** master card; *Nau:* **maîtresse ancre,** best bower anchor; *N.Arch:* **maîtresse varangue,** midship floor. **4.** *s.f.* **maîtresse,** mistress (= kept woman).

maître-à-danser [mɛtradɑ̃se], *s.m. Tls:* (pair of) callipers, calliper compasses; *pl. maîtres-à-danser.*

maître-autel [mɛtrotɛl], *s.m. Ecc:* high altar; *pl. maîtres-autels.*

maître(-)couple [mɛtrəkupl̥], *s.m. N.Arch:* midship(s) frame; *A.Aer:* **diamètre au m.-c.,** diameter amidships (of dirigible); *pl. maîtres(-) couples.*

maître-mot [mɛtrəmo], *s.m.* master word; *pl. maîtres-mots.*

maître-nageur [mɛtr(ə)naʒœːr], *s.m.* (*a*) swimming instructor; (*b*) lifeguard; *pl. maîtres-nageurs.*

maître-queux [mɛtr(ə)kø], *s.m.* chef; *pl. maîtres-queux.*

maître-ressort [mɛtrərəsɔːr], *s.m.* driving spring; *pl. maîtres-ressorts.*

maîtresse [mɛtrɛs], *s.f. See* MAÎTRE.

maître-timonier [mɛtrətimɔnje], *s.m. Navy:* yeoman of the signals; *pl. maîtres-timoniers.*

maîtrisable [mɛtrizabl̥, me-], *a.* that can be mastered; controllable.

maîtrise [mɛtriːz, me-], *s.f.* **1.** (*a*) mastership; *A:* **m. des eaux et forêts,** superintendence of waterways and forests; *Sch:* **m. de conférences,** lectureship; **m. (ès lettres,** *A:* **ès arts)** = Master of Arts degree; (*b*) choir mastership (of cathedral); (*c*) (i) choir school, music school (attached to cathedral); (ii) choir (of cathedral, etc.); (*d*) *Ind:* supervisory staff; **agent de m.,** foreman. **2.** (*a*) mastery (of one's passions, etc.); **m. de soi, m. personnelle,** self-control, self-mastery; **m. des mers,** command of the seas; (*b*) mastery (in a profession, of an art, etc.); **sa m. du violon,** his mastery of the violin.

maîtriser [mɛtrize, me-], *v.tr.* to master (a horse, etc.); to subdue (a fire, etc.); to get (fire, etc.) under control; to curb, bridle (passion); **m. une épidémie,** to control an epidemic; **m. une rébellion,** to quell, crush, a rebellion; **il a fallu quatre hommes pour le m.,** it took four men to overpower him; **m. son envie de rire,** to keep a solemn face; **m. son effroi,** to get the better of, to overcome, one's fears; **m. une voie d'eau,** to stop a leak.

se maîtriser, to control oneself; **ne pas savoir se m.,** to have no self-control.

maja [maʒa], *s.f. Crust:* maia, maja, spider crab.

majesté [maʒɛste], *s.f.* majesty. **1.** (*a*) **la m. du peuple romain,** the majesty of the Roman people; **la m. du trône,** the majesty of the throne; **Dieu dans toute sa m.,** God in all His majesty; (*b*) *Hist:* **sa M. Très Chrétienne,** His Most Christian Majesty (the King of France); **sa M. Catholique,** His Most Catholic Majesty (the King of Spain); **Sa M. Impériale,** His Imperial Majesty; (*c*) **Sa M. le Roi, la Reine,** His Majesty the King, Her Majesty the Queen; **leurs Majestés,** their Majesties; **votre Majesté,** your Majesty; (*d*) *Gram:* **le pluriel de m.,** the royal "we." **2.** (*a*) stateliness; dignity; **allures pleines de m.,** majestic, stately, bearing; (*b*) grandeur (of style, of landscape).

majestueusement [maʒɛstɥøzmɑ̃], *adv.* majestically.

majestueux, -euse [maʒɛstɥø, -øːz], *a.* (*a*) majestic, stately, dignified (bearing, etc.); imposing (figure); (*b*) **château m.,** stately, imposing, majestic, castle; **paysage m.,** magnificent landscape.

majeur, -eure [maʒœːr], *a.* (*a*) major, greater; **la majeure partie de qch.,** the greater part, the bulk, of sth.; **la majeure partie du temps il ne fait rien,** most of the time he does nothing; **en majeure partie,** for the most part; **le doigt m.,** *s.* **le m.,** the second finger; *Log:* **prémisse majeure,** major premise; *Nau:* **les mâts majeurs,** the main masts; *Geog:* **le lac M.,** Lake Maggiore; *Ecc:* **les ordres majeurs,** the major, greater, holy, sacred orders; *Ecc.Hist:* **Jacques le M.,** James the Greater; (*b*) **affaire majeure,** well-established business; **raison majeure de qch.,** chief reason for sth.; **refuser son assentiment pour des raisons majeures,** to refuse one's consent for imperative reasons; **être absent pour raison majeure,** to be unavoidably absent; **cas de force majeure,** case of absolute necessity, of force majeure; (*c*) *Jur:* major, of full age; *s.* major; **devenir m.,** to attain one's majority, to come of age; (*d*) *Mus:* major (mode, scale, etc.); **tierce m.,** major third; **concerto en sol bémol m.,** concerto in G flat major; (*e*) *Cards:* **(couleur) majeure,** major suit; **tierce majeure,** tierce major.

majidés [maʒide], *s.m.pl. Crust:* Majidae, the spider crabs.

majolique [maʒɔlik], *s.f. Cer:* majolica.

ma-jong [maʒɔ̃g], *s.m. Games:* mah-jong(g).

major [maʒɔːr], *s.m.* **1.** (*a*) *Mil:* regimental adjutant (with administrative duties); chief of staff (of a Commander-in-Chief in the field); **m. de garnison,** garrison adjutant, assistant to town major; **m. du camp,** camp commandant; (*b*) *Navy:* vice-chief (of naval staff); **m. général,** assistant to the admiral superintendent of a dockyard; (*c*) *Mil: Navy: A:* **(médecin) m.,** medical officer; (*d*) *s.f. F:* **la m.,** the matron. **2.** *Sch:* **sortir m. (d'une grande école)** = to leave (a university, etc.) head of the list.

majoral, -aux [maʒɔral, -o], *s.m. Dial:* (*Provence*) **1.** chief herdsman. **2.** member of the committee of a *félibrige* meeting.

majorat [maʒɔra], *s.m. Jur: A:* entailed property, estate in tail, majorat.

majoraté [maʒɔrate], *a. Jur:* entailed (estate).

majoration [maʒɔrasjɔ̃], *s.f.* **1.** (*a*) over-estimation, overvaluation (of assets, etc.); (*b*) additional charge (on bill); **frapper un immeuble d'une m. de cinq pour cent,** to put five per cent on to the valuation of a building. **2.** (*a*) increase (in price); (*b*) increased allowance; **majorations de pension,** supplementary allowances; *Adm:* **m. pour enfants (ajoutée à une pension),** child bounty; (*c*) *Adm:* **m. d'anciennete,** advance in seniority.

majorcain, -aine [maʒɔrkɛ̃, -ɛn], *a. & s. Geog:* Majorcan.

majordome [maʒɔrdɔm], *s.m.* (*a*) major-domo; steward; (*b*) *Hist:* mayor of the palace.

majorer [maʒɔre], *v.tr.* **1.** to overestimate, overvalue (assets, etc.). **2.** to make an additional charge on (bill); **majoré de notre commission de 10%,** to which we have added our commission of 10%; **m. une facture de 10%,** to put 10% on an invoice. **3.** to raise, put up, increase, the price of (sth.).

majorette [maʒɔrɛt], *s.f. U.S:* (drum-)majorette.

majoritaire [maʒɔritɛːr]. **1.** *a.* of, pertaining to, a majority; **vote m.,** majority vote; **scrutin m.,** election by an increased majority; **parti m.,** majority party. **2.** *a. & s.m. & f. Fin:* majority (shareholder).

majoritard [maʒɔritaːr], *s.m. A: F:* member of Parliament who always votes with the majority.

majorité [maʒɔrite], *s.f.* **1.** majority; **la m. de la nation,** the majority, greater part, of the nation; **les hommes en m.,** most men, the majority, of men; **emporter la m.,** to secure a majority, to carry a vote; **décision prise à la m. (des voix),** decision taken by a majority; **la m. est favorable, défavorable,** the ayes, the noes, have it; **élu à la m. de dix,** elected by a majority of ten; **faible m.,** narrow majority; **être en m., avoir la m.,** to be in a, in the, majority; **nous sommes en m. opposés à ce système,** most of us are opposed to this system; **m. absolue,** absolute majority; **m. relative,** relative majority, *U.S:* plurality; **dans la m. des cas,** in most cases. **2.** *Jur:* majority, coming of age; **atteindre sa m.,** to attain one's majority, to come of age. **3.** (*a*) *Mil:* majority; (*b*) *Navy:* (i) admiral-superintendent's office; (ii) officers' quarters; **officier de la m.,** staff officer.

Majorque [maʒɔrk], *Pr.n.f. Geog:* Majorca.

majorquin, -ine [maʒɔrkɛ̃, -in], *a. & s. Geog:* Majorcan.

majuscule [maʒyskyl], *a. & s.f.* (large) capital (letter); *Typ:* large cap; *Pal:* majuscule; **majuscules d'imprimerie,** block capitals; **écrire un mot avec une m.,** to capitalize a word, to write a word with a capital (letter).

makarov [makarɔf], *s.m. Nau:* **(paillet) m.,** collision mat (*from the name of the inventor*).

makémono [makemɔno], *s.m. Art:* makimono.

maki [maki], *s.m. Z:* **1.** lemur, macaco; **m. catta,** ring-tailed lemur. **2.** Madagascar cat.

mal[1] [mal], *a. A:* = MAUVAIS; *still used in the phrs.* **bon an, m. an,** year in, year out; **bon gré, m. gré,** willy-nilly.

mal[2], **maux** [mal, mo], *s.m.* **1** evil; (*a*) hurt, harm; **faire du m.,** to do harm; **faire du m. à qn,** to do s.o. harm, to injure, to hurt, s.o.; **il fait plus de bruit que de m.,** his bark is worse than his bite; **il n'a eu aucun m.,** he was quite unhurt; **je suis sûr qu'il lui arrivera du m.,** I am sure he will come to harm; **s'en tirer sans aucun m.,** to escape uninjured, unhurt, unscathed, none the worse; **vouloir du m. à qn,** to wish s.o. evil; **je ne lui veux pas de m.,** I mean him no harm; **le m. qu'il m'a fait subir,** the wrongs which I have suffered at his hands; **cela fera plus de m. que de bien,** it will do more harm than good; **réparer le m.,** to undo the mischief; **souffrir de grands maux,** to suffer great ills; **raconter ses maux,** to tell one's troubles; **entre deux maux il faut choisir le moindre; de deux maux il faut éviter le pire,** of two evils one must choose the lesser; **il n'y a pas de m. à cela,** there is no harm in that; **il n'y aurait pas de m. à lui écrire, cela ne ferait pas de m. de lui écrire,** it would do no harm to write to him! **il n'y a pas grand m.!** there's no great harm done! **m. lui en a pris,** he has had cause to regret it; (*b*) **dire du m. de qn,** to speak ill of s.o., to abuse s.o., to run s.o. down; **dire du m. de qch.,** to speak badly, ill, of sth.; **changement en m.,** change for the worse; **prendre qch. en m.,** to take sth. the wrong way; to take offence at sth.; **tourner qch. en m.,** to put the worst interpretation on sth., to distort the meaning of sth.; **mener les affaires à m.,** to mismanage matters; (*c*) wrong (doing); **le bien et le m.,** right and wrong, good and evil; **rendre le bien pour le m.,** to return good for evil; **le roi ne peut pas faire le m.,** the king can do no wrong; **il ne songe pas à m.,** he doesn't mean any harm; *Ecc:* **délivre-nous du m.,** deliver us from evil; **induire, pousser, qn à m.,** to lead s.o. astray; **penser à m.,** to have evil intentions; **cet enfant a le génie du m.,** this child has a genius for doing wrong; **mettre (qn) à m.,** (i) to hurt s.o. badly; (ii) to lead (s.o.) astray; (iii) to seduce (a woman). **2.** (*a*) disorder; malady, disease; ailment; sickness; pain, ache; **m. de Pott,** Pott's disease; **être atteint d'un m. incurable,** to suffer from an incurable disease; **quel est votre m.?** what is your complaint? what is wrong with you? **attraper, prendre (du) m.,** to catch a complaint; *esp.* **vous allez prendre du m.,** you'll catch your death of cold; **les petits maux de l'enfance,** childish ailments; **m. de tête,** headache; **fréquents maux de tête,** frequent headaches; **m. de dents,** toothache; **m. de cœur,** sickness, nausea; **avoir m. à l'estomac,** to have stomach ache; **m. de gorge,** sore throat; **m. de mer,** seasickness; **avoir le m. de mer,** to be seasick; **m. de l'air, d'avion,** air sickness; **m. de voiture, de la route,** car sickness; **m. du rail,** train sickness; **m. des montagnes,** mountain sickness; **m. des rayons,** radiation sickness; *Lit:* **m. du siècle,** world weariness; **haut m., m. caduc,** *A:* **m. sacré,** epilepsy; *A:* falling sickness; **tomber du haut m.,** to have an epileptic fit; **m. blanc,** gathering, sore; *esp.* gathered finger; *O:* **m. d'aventure,** whitlow; **m. de reins,** lumbago; **avoir m. à la tête, aux dents, à la gorge,** to have a headache, toothache, a sore throat; **avoir m. au doigt, au pied,** to have a bad finger, foot; **on se cogne toujours où l'on a m.,** once always knocks oneself on a sore place; **vous me faites (du) m.,** you're hurting me; **mes os me font m.,** my bones ache; **tous les membres me font m.,** I am aching in every limb; **mon genou commençait à me faire m.,** my knee was getting painful; **serrant les dents à se faire m.,** clenching one's teeth until it hurts; **spectacle qui fait m.,** painful sight; **avoir le m. du pays,** to be homesick; *A:* **femme en m. d'enfant,** woman in labour, in travail; *F:* **journaliste en m. de copie,** journalist casting about for copy; **être en m. de qch.,** to be badly in need of sth.; **être en m. de faire qch.,** to be desperately anxious to do sth.; (*b*) pains, trouble; **non sans m.,** not without trouble, without difficulty; **se donner du m. pour faire qch.,** to take pains to do sth.; **se donner du m. pour contenter qn,** to be at pains to satisfy s.o.; **avoir du m. à faire qch.,** to have difficulty in doing sth.; to find it difficult to do sth.; to be hard put to it to do sth.; **il a eu bien du m. à vous quitter,** he found it very hard to leave you; **il eut du m. à en venir à bout,** he had a job to manage it; **j'en ai eu du m. pour le ravoir!** I had a job, a lot of trouble, to get it back! it was a job getting it back; **mon dîner a du m. à passer,** my dinner won't go down; *F:* **sans se faire de m.,** without over-exerting oneself, without taking too much trouble, without breaking one's back.

mal[3], *adv.* **1.** (*a*) badly, ill; **m. se conduire, se m. conduire, se conduire m.,** to behave badly; **les choses tournent m.,** things are turning out badly; **m. à l'aise,** ill at ease; **vous avez m. agi,** you did wrong, you acted badly; **biens m. acquis,** ill-gotten gains; **travail m. fait,** badly done work, botched work, a botch; **vous avez m. mené l'affaire,** you have made a botch of the business; **faire qch. tant bien que m.,** to do sth. after a fashion; **les choses ont l'air d'aller m.,** things seem to be in a bad way; **aller de m. en pis,** to go from bad to worse; **bien ou m., nous y parviendrons,** we shall manage it somehow or other; **s'y m. prendre,** to go the wrong way about it; **m. choisir,** to choose wrongly; **m. adresser une lettre,** to address a letter wrongly; **m. conseiller qn,** to misadvise s.o.; **on voit m. d'ici,** you can't see well from here; **on voit m. comment . . .,** it's difficult, not easy, to see how . . .; **vous êtes m. informé,** you are ill-informed; **vous me jugez m.,** you misjudge me; **il a très m. pris la chose,** he took it very badly, *F:* he cut up very rough; **il a m. pris ce que je lui ai dit,** he took what I said to him badly, the wrong way; **vous ne trouvez pas m. que je corrige vos fautes?** you do not mind, object to, my correcting your mistakes? **vous ne feriez peut-être pas m. de . . .,** it wouldn't be a bad plan, thing, to . . .; (*b*) **aller, se porter, m.,** to be ill, in bad health; **il va plus m. aujourd'hui,** he is worse to-day; **je ne vais ni bien ni m.,** I am only so so; **comment allez-vous?—pas m.! pas trop m.!** how are you?—not so bad! pretty well! **être au plus m.,** to be dangerously ill, at death's door; **elle est, elle va, très m.,** she is very low, in a very bad way; *F:* **pas m. (de qch.),** a fair amount (of sth.); **il (n')y en a pas m.,** there are a good many, a good few, quite a lot; **il a pas m. d'argent,** he has a good deal of money; **il a pas m. du charlatan,** he's more than a bit of a quack; **cela m'a pris pas m. de temps,** it took me quite a time; **pas m. de gens s'en doutent,** a good many people suspect it; **j'ai pas m. envie de rester,** I have a good mind to stay; **nous sommes pas m. à dîner ce soir,** we are rather a lot for dinner this evening. **2.** (*with adj. function*) (*a*) not right; **vous savez ce qui est bien et ce qui est m.,** you know the difference between right and wrong; **cela est m.,** it is not right, it is wicked; **c'est très m. à lui,** (i) that's too bad of him; (ii) that's very unkind of him; (*b*) uncomfortable, badly off; **on est très m. dans ce lit,** this is a very uncomfortable bed; **nous ne sommes pas m. ici,** we are quite comfortable, not at all badly off, here; **être m. dans ses affaires,** to be in a bad way of business; (*c*) **ils sont m. ensemble,** they are on bad terms (with each other); (*d*) (*of health*) **se sentir m.,** to feel ill, sick, faint; **se trouver m.,** to faint; (*e*) *F:* **pas m.,** of good appearance, quality, etc.; **ce tableau n'est pas m.,** this picture is quite good; **ce n'est pas m.,** it's not badly done; **ce n'était pas m. du tout,** it wasn't at all bad; **elle n'est pas m.,** (i) she's quite good-looking; (ii) she's quite presentable.

mal- [mal], *pref.* **1.** mal-. **2.** mis-, dis-. **3.** un-. **4.** ill-.

malabar [malabaːr], *P:* (*a*) *a.* strapping, *F:* beefy; (*b*) *s.m.* strapping, *F:* beefy, fellow.

malabare [malabaːr], *a. & s. Geog:* (native, inhabitant) of Malabar.

malac [malak], *s.m.* **m., étain de M.,** Malacca tin.

Malacca [malaka], *Pr.n. Geog:* (*a*) Malacca; (*b*) the Malay Peninsula; (*c*) **détroit de M.,** Malacca Straits.

Malachie [malaki], *Pr.n.m. B.Hist:* Malachi.

malachite [malakit], *s.f. Miner:* malachite.

malacia [malasja], **malacie** [malasi], *s.f. Med:* malacia.

malacobdelle [malakɔbdɛl], *s.f. Ann:* malacobdella.

malacoderme [malakɔdɛrm], *Ent:* **1.** *a.* malacoderm, malacodermatous. **2.** *s.m.* malacoderm; *pl.* (*family*) Malacodermidae.

malacolite [malakɔlit], *s.f. Miner:* malacolite.

malacologie [malakɔlɔʒi], *s.f.* malacology.

malacologiste [malakɔlɔʒist], *s.m. & f.* malacologist.

malacon [malakɔ̃], *s.m. Miner:* malakon, malacon.

malacophile [malakɔfil], *a. & s.f. Bot:* malacophilous (plant).

malacopodes [malakɔpɔd], *s.m.pl. Z:* Malacopoda.

malacoptérygien, -ienne [malakɔpteriʒjɛ̃, -jɛn], *a.* and *s. Ich:* malacopterygian.

malacosoma [malakɔzɔma], *s.m.,* **malacosome** [malakɔzom], *s.m. Ent:* malacosoma; tent caterpillar.

malacostracé [malakɔstrase], *a. & s. Crust:* malacostracan; *pl.* **malacostracés,** Malacostraca.

malacozoaire [malakɔzɔɛːr], *A:* **1.** *a.* malacozoic. **2.** *s.m.pl.* Malacozoa.

malade [malad]. **1.** *a.* (*a*) ill, sick, poorly, unwell; diseased; **être m.,** to be ill, poorly; **il est plus m. que vous,** he is more ill than you, he is worse than you are; **dent m.,** (i) aching tooth; (ii) carious, decaying, tooth; **yeux malades,** sore eyes; **jambe m.,** bad leg; **j'ai l'estomac m.,** my stomach is out of order; **tomber m.,** to fall ill, to be taken ill; **il est m. de la fièvre typhoïde,** he is ill, down, with typhoid; *F:* **il a été m. comme un chien,** he was as sick as a dog; **être m. de fatigue,** to be ill from exhaustion; **être m. d'inquiétude,** to be ill with anxiety; **il en est m.,** he is really upset about it; **m. à mourir,** sick unto death, dying; **m. d'esprit et de corps,** diseased in body and mind; **être m. du cœur, de l'estomac,** to have heart trouble, stomach trouble; *F:* **vous voilà bien m.!** poor fellow! poor you! **est bien m. qui en meurt,** it's not so dangerous as all that; **plante m.,** diseased, sickly, plant; **vin m.,** diseased wine; **livre bien m.,** badly battered book; **industrie m.,** industry in a bad way; **esprit m.,** disordered, unhealthy, mind; *Mil: etc:* **se faire porter m.,** to report sick; (*b*) *P:* mad, crazy, off one's head; **t'es pas m.?** are you off your rocker? **2.** *s.* sick person, invalid; *Med:* patient; case; **un grand m.,** a person who is very seriously ill; **un m. de la poitrine,** a t.b. patient; **les malades,** the sick; **chambre de, des malade(s),** sickroom; **avez-vous des malades à bord?** is there any sickness on board? *Mil: etc:* **rôle des malades,** sick list; **faire le malade,** to malinger; *Navy:* **poste des malades,** sick bay.

maladie [maladi], *s.f.* (*a*) illness, sickness, disease, disorder, complaint, malady; **m. de l'enfance,** child's complaint, childish ailment; **faire une m.,** to be ill; *F:* **il en fait une m.,** he's very upset about it; he's making a song and dance about it; **faire une longue m.,** to have a long illness; **m. grave,** severe illness; **il a fait une grosse m. l'année dernière,** he was seriously ill last year; **pour cause de m., par suite de m.,** through illness; **mourir de m.,** to die of disease; **m. générale,** systemic disease; **m. par carence,** deficiency disease; **m. de la peau, cutanée,** skin disease; **m. des camps,** camp fever; typhus; **m. de foie, de cœur,** liver complaint, heart complaint; **m. bleue,** blue disease; cyanosis; **m. mentale,** mental illness; **m. de Parkinson,** Parkinson's disease; **m. du sommeil,** sleeping sickness; **m. professionnelle,** occupational disease; **m. du pays,** homesickness; **congé de m.,** sick leave; **bénéficier de l'assurance m.,** to draw sickness benefit; *F:* **avoir la m. des grandeurs,** to suffer from delusions of grandeur; (*b*) **maladies des plantes, des vins,** diseases of plants, of wines; **m. des pommes de terre,** potato disease, potato rot; **m. des ormes,** elm disease; (*c*) *Vet:* **m. des chiens, m. du jeune âge, m. de Carré,** distemper; **m. d'Aujesky,** bulbar paralysis; **m. de Borna,** Borna disease (of horse).

maladif, -ive [maladif, -iːv], *a.* sickly; **curiosité maladive,** morbid, unhealthy, curiosity.

maladivement [maladivmɑ̃], *adv.* morbidly.

maladministration [maladministrasjɔ̃], *s.f.* maladministration.

maladrerie [maladrəri], *s.f. A:* leper-house, lazar-house.

maladresse [maladrɛs], *s.f.* **1.** (*a*) clumsiness, awkwardness; unhandiness; (*b*) tactlessness. **2.** blunder; **commettre une m.,** to make a blunder, to blunder.

maladroit, -oite [maladrwɑ, -wɑːt; -a, -at]. **1.** *a.* (*a*) unskilful, clumsy, awkward, unhandy (person); clumsy, maladroit (compliment, etc.); **il a la main maladroite, il est m. de ses mains,** he's all (fingers and) thumbs, his fingers are all thumbs; (*b*) blundering; tactless. **2.** *s.* (*a*) awkward, clumsy, person; (*b*) blunderer, tactless person.

maladroitement [maladrwɑtmɑ̃, -a-], *adv.* (*a*) clumsily, awkwardly; (*b*) tactlessly, in a blundering fashion.

Malaga [malaga]. **1.** *Pr.n. Geog:* Malaga. **2.** *s.m.* (*also* **vin de M.**) Malaga (wine).

malaguette [malagɛt], *s.f.* malaguetta pepper, grains of paradise.

malaire [malɛːr], *a. Anat:* malar; **os m.,** malar bone, cheek bone.

malai, -aie, malais, -aise[1] [malɛ, -ɛːz], *a. & s. Ethn: Geog: Ling:* Malay(an); Malaysian; **la péninsule, la presqu'île, malaise,** the Malay peninsula.

malaise[2] [malɛːz], *s.m.* **1.** uneasiness, discomfort, malaise; **sentiment de m.,** (i) uneasy feeling, (ii) sickish feeling; **se sentir du m. dans tout son corps,** to feel queer all over; **m. chez les habitants,** unrest among the inhabitants. **2.** indisposition, fit of faintness; **avoir un m.,** to become indisposed, to feel faint. **3.** *A:* **être dans le m.,** to be in straitened circumstances.

malaisé [maleze], *a.* **1.** difficult; **chemin m.,** difficult, arduous, road; **il est m. de faire cela,** it is not easy to do that; **chose malaisée à faire,** thing difficult to do. **2.** *A:* poor, in straitened circumstances.

malaisément [malezemɑ̃], *adv.* with difficulty. **1.** arduously. **2.** unwillingly.

Malaisie [malezi], *Pr.n.f. Geog:* **1.** the Malay Archipelago. **2.** Malaya.

malakoffois, -oise [malakɔfwa, -waːz], *a. & s. Geog:* (native, inhabitant) of Malakoff.

malakon [malakɔ̃], *s.m. Miner:* malakon, malacon.

malandre [malɑ̃ːdr̥], *s.f.* **1.** rotten knot, defect (in wood); **bois sans malandres,** clean wood. **2.** *Vet:* malanders, mallenders.

malandreux, -euse [malɑ̃drø, -øːz], *a.* **1.** (*of wood*) rotten at the knots. **2.** *Vet:* (*of horse*) malandered.

malandrin [malɑ̃drɛ̃], *s.m.* **1.** *Hist:* (*in the 14th century*) disbanded mercenary (preying on the people). **2.** *A. & Lit:* brigand, robber, highwayman; marauder.

malappris, -ise [malapri, -iːz]. **1.** *a.* uncouth, ill-bred. **2.** *s.* ill-bred person; lout; **c'est le fait d'un m. de . . .,** only an ill-bred person would . . .; **c'est une malapprise,** she has no manners.

malaptérure [malapteryːr], *s.m. Ich:* malapterurus; thunderfish, electric catfish, raad.

malard [malaːr], *s.m.* wild drake; mallard.

malaria [malarja], *s.f. Med:* malaria.

malariathérapie [malarjaterapi], *s.f. Med:* malariatherapy.

malarique [malarik], *a. & s.m. & f.* malarial.

malarmat [malarma], *s.m. Ich:* armed gurnard; sea robin.

malart [malaːr], *s.m.* = MALARD.

malate [malat], *s.m. Ch:* malate.

malavisé, -ée [malavize]. **1.** *a.* ill-advised, blundering (act); tactless (remark); unwise, injudicious (person, etc.); **c'est être m. que de donner des conseils à qui n'en demande point,** it is tactless, ill-advised, to give advice when none is asked for; **il a été m. de le refuser,** he was unwise to refuse it. **2.** *s.* blunderer; tactless person; foolish person.

Malawi [malawi], *Pr.n.m. Geog:* Malawi.

malaxage [malaksaːʒ], *s.m.* **1.** malaxation; kneading (of dough, etc.); working (of butter); mixing (of cement); pugging (of clay). **2.** massage.

malaxer [malakse], *v.tr.* **1.** to malaxate (pills); to knead (dough etc.); to work (butter); to mix (cement); to pug (clay). **2.** to massage (limb, etc.).

malaxeur [malaksœːr], *s.m.* malaxator, malaxating machine; mixer, mixing machine; *Ind:* butter worker; *Civ.E: etc:* **m. à ciment, à mortier,** mortar mixer; **m. à palettes,** pug mill; **broyeur m.,** mixing mill.

malayo-polynésien, -ienne [malɛjopɔlinezjɛ̃, -jɛn], *a. & s.* **1.** *Ethn:* Malayo-Polynesian. **2.** *Ling:* Austronesian.

Malaysia [malɛzja], *Pr.n.f. Geog:* Malaysia.

malbâti, -ie [malbɑti], *a. & s.* misshapen (person).

malchance [malʃɑ̃ːs], *s.f.* **1.** bad luck, ill luck; **par m.,** as ill luck would have it, by mischance; **être poursuivi par la m.,** to be dogged by ill luck; to be up against it. **2.** mishap, misfortune.

malchanceux, -euse [malʃɑ̃sø, -øːz], *a.* unfortunate, unlucky.

malcolmie [malkɔlmi], *s.f. Bot:* Virginia(n) stock.

malcommode [malkɔmɔd], *a.* inconvenient; awkward; unpractical, not practical; **c'est un homme bien m.,** he's a very difficult man (to handle); **vêtements malcommodes pour la campagne,** clothes not practical for country wear.

malcontent [malkɔ̃tɑ̃]. **1.** *a. A:* dissatisfied. **2.** *s.m.pl. Fr.Hist:* **les Malcontents,** the Malcontents (*c.* 1573); *A:* **cheveux à la malcontent,** close-cropped hair.

maldisant [maldizɑ̃], *a. A:* slanderous; backbiting.

Maldives [maldiːv], *Pr.n. Geog:* **les îles M.,** the Maldive Islands.

maldonite [maldɔnit], *s.f. Miner:* maldonite.

maldonne [maldɔn], *s.f.* **1.** *Cards:* misdeal; **faire m.,** to misdeal. **2.** mistake; misunderstanding; *Com:* error in forwarding, in delivery; **leur amitié avait pour base une m.,** their friendship was founded on a misunderstanding; *F:* **il y a m.,** there's a mistake somewhere; someone's got the wrong end of the stick.

maldonner [maldɔne], *v.i.* **1.** *Cards:* to misdeal. **2.** *Com:* to make an error in delivery, in forwarding.

mâle [mɑːl], *a. & s.m.* **1.** male (person, flower, etc.); cock (bird); buck (rabbit, antelope, etc.); dog (fox, wolf); bull (elephant, etc.); (*of animals*) he-; **un ours m.,** a he-bear; **un âne m.,** a jackass, jack; **héritier m.,** male heir; **elle accoucha d'un enfant m.,** she gave birth to a son, to a boy; **l'enfant est un m.,** it's a boy; **un beau m.,** a fine specimen of manhood, *F:* a real he-man. **2.** (*a*) **courage m., m. courage,** manly courage; **voix m.,** manly voice; **style m.,** virile style; **m. éloquence,** virile eloquence; *Art:* **touche m.,** masculine, virile, touch; (*b*) *Nau:* **mer m.,** heavy sea; **bâtiment m.,** ship that rides the waves well. **3.** *Mec.E:* **vis m.,** male screw; **bout m. d'un tuyau,** spigot end of a pipe, pipe spigot; *El:* **fiche m.,** plug.

malebête [malbɛːt], *s.f.* **1.** *A:* evil, dangerous, beast, person. **2.** caulker's hammer-axe.

malebouche [malbuʃ], *s.f. A:* **1.** slander, backbiting. **2.** slanderer, backbiter.

malechance [malʃɑ̃ːs], *s.f.* = MALCHANCE.

malédiction [malediksjɔ̃], *s.f.* (*a*) *Lit:* malediction, curse; **être sous le coup d'une m.,** to be under a curse; **appeler les malédictions du ciel sur qn,** to call down curses from heaven upon s.o.; **vouer qn à la m. publique,** to hold s.o. up to public execration; **encourir les malédictions de ses sujets,** to be cursed by one's subjects; (*b*) misfortune (to which one seems fated); **depuis son enfance il vit sous la m. de la guerre,** since his childhood he has been living under the threat of war; (*c*) *int.* **m.! il m'a échappé,** curse it! he has escaped me.

maléfice [malefis], *s.m.* malefice, evil spell.

maléficié [malefisje], *a.* (*a*) *A. & Lit:* bewitched, under a spell; (*b*) *A:* ill.

maléfique [malefik], *a.* maleficent; malefic (star, etc.); evil (influence); **né sous une étoile m.,** born under an unlucky star.

malefortune [malfɔrtyn], *s.f. A:* misfortune, mishap.

mal-égal [malegal], *s.m.inv. Metall:* inequality (in surface of forging, etc.).

maléique [maleik], *a. Ch:* maleic (acid).

malékites [malekit], *s.m.pl. Jur:* Malekites, Malikites.

malembouché [malɑ̃buʃe], *a. P:* foul-mouthed.

malemort [malmɔːr], *s.f. A:* foul death; **mourir de m.,** to come to a tragic end; to die a violent death; **vouloir m. aux critiques,** to be death on critics.

malencontre [malɑ̃kɔ̃ːtr̥], *s.f. A. & Lit:* misfortune, mishap, unfortunate occurrence; **il vous arrivera m.,** you will meet with some misfortune; **par m.,** unfortunately.

malencontreusement [malɑ̃kɔ̃trøzmɑ̃], *adv.* unfortunately, unhappily, unluckily.

malencontreux, -euse [malɑ̃kɔ̃trø, -øːz], *a.* **1.** (*a*) ill-timed, awkward, unfortunate (event, etc.); **jour m.,** unlucky day; **remarque malencontreuse,** unfortunate remark; (*b*) (*person, etc.*) of ill omen. **2.** (*a*) unlucky, unfortunate (person); (*b*) tiresome (person).

malendurant [malɑ̃dyrɑ̃], *a. A:* impatient, short-tempered, testy.

mal-en-pattes [malɑ̃pat], *s.m.inv. F:* **c'est un m.-en-p.,** he's a clumsy type, his fingers are all thumbs.

mal-en-point [malɑ̃pwɛ̃], *adj.phr.* in a bad way; in an unfortunate situation; in a poor state of health.

malentendant [malɑ̃tɑ̃dɑ̃], *a. & s.m.* (partially) deaf (person); hard of hearing.

malentendu [malɑ̃tɑ̃dy], *s.m.* misunderstanding, misapprehension; **par un m. . . .,** through a misunderstanding . . .; **je suis sûr qu'il y a m.,** I am sure there is a misunderstanding.

malentente [malɑ̃tɑ̃ːt], *s.f.* dissension, disagreement.

malepeste [malpɛst], *A:* **1.** *s.f.* **la m. soit de lui!** plague take him! a pox on him! **2.** *int.* zounds! the devil!

malesherbia [mal(ə)zɛrbja], *s.f. Bot:* malesherbia.

malesherbiacées [mal(ə)zɛrbjase], *s.f.pl. Bot:* Malesherbiaceae.

malestan [malɛstɑ̃], *s.m.* (*a*) barrel for pickling sardines (in brine); (*b*) sardine pickled in brine.

malêtre, mal-être [malɛtr̥], *s.m.* no *pl. A:* **1.** feeling of discomfort, (physical) uneasiness. **2.** discomfort, straitened circumstances.

malevole [malvɔl], **malévole** [malevɔl], *a. A:* malevolent.

malfaçon [malfasɔ̃], *s.f.* **1.** bad work(manship); defect. **2.** illicit profit, cheating; malpractice.

malfaire [malfɛːr], *v.i.* (*used only in the inf.*) to do evil, wrong.

malfaisance [malfəzɑ̃ːs], *s.f.* **1.** maleficence, evil-mindedness. **2.** *Jur:* malfeasance.

malfaisant [malfəzɑ̃], *a.* (*a*) evil-minded (person); bad (influence); pernicious (ideas); (*b*) *Jur:* malfeasant; (*c*) *O:* noxious, harmful (food, etc.).

malfait [malfɛ], *a. A:* badly made; misshapen; **esprit m.,** warped mind.

malfaiteur, -trice [malfɛtœːr, -tris], *s.* malefactor; criminal; wrong-doer; offender.

malfamé [malfame], *a. O:* (*now usu.* **mal famé**) with a bad reputation; (*of pers.*) notorious; (*of place*) disreputable.

malfend [malfɑ̃], *a. & s.m.* **(bois) m.,** timber that does not split well.

malfil [malfil], *s.m.* raw ivory.

malformation [malfɔrmasjɔ̃], *s.f.* malformation; **m. congénitale,** congenital malformation.

malfrat [malfra], *s.m. P:* (*a*) doubtful, shady, character; (*b*) tough.

malgache [malgaʃ]. **1.** *a. & s.m. & f. Geog:* Malagasy; Madagascan; **la République M.,** the Malagasy Republic. **2.** *s.m. Ling:* Malagasy.

malgracieusement [malgrasjøzmɑ̃], *adv. A:* ungraciously, impolitely, rudely; with a bad, ill, grace.

malgracieux, -ieuse [malgrasjø, -jøːz], *a.* (*a*) ungracious, churlish, rude; (*b*) inelegant, clumsy.

malgré [malgre], *prep.* **1.** in spite of, notwithstanding; **m. tout ce que j'ai pu dire,** in spite of all I could say; **faire qch. m. un ordre,** to do sth. in spite of an order; **m. cela, m. tout,** for all that, nevertheless; yet; in spite of everything; **m. tout son talent il était peu connu,** with all his talent he was little known; **m. sa fortune,** in spite of his wealth, for all his wealth; **je l'ai fait m. moi,** I did it against my will. **2.** *conj.phr.* **m. que** + *sub.* (*a*) **m. que vous en ayez,** in spite of all you may say, do; **m. que j'en aie,** in spite of myself; however distasteful; (*b*) although; **m. que je le déteste je l'aiderai,** although I hate him I'll help him.

malhabile [malabil], *a.* unskilful; clumsy, awkward; **m. aux affaires,** poor at business, unbusinesslike; **m. à la flatterie,** untutored in the art of flattery; **il est m. à mentir,** he's a poor liar, unaccustomed, unused, to lying.

malhabilement [malabilmɑ̃], *adv.* unskilfully, clumsily, awkwardly.

malhabileté [malabilte], *s.f.* (*rare*) lack of skill, of experience; clumsiness, awkwardness.

malherbe [malɛrb], *s.f. Bot:* **1.** plumbago. **2.** daphne mezereon.

malheur [malœːr], *s.m.* **1.** (*a*) misfortune; calamity; (serious) accident; **il lui est arrivé un m.,** he has met with an accident; **il n'est pas arrivé un m., je l'espère,** I hope nothing is wrong; I hope nothing terrible has happened; **un m. est si vite arrivé!** accidents happen so quickly! **un m. n'arrive, ne vient, jamais seul,** misfortunes never come singly; **en cas de m.,** should an accident happen; if something goes wrong; **ils ont eu des malheurs,** they have known misfortune; they have been through difficult times; **quel m.!** what a tragedy! *Iron:* **le grand m.!** how dreadful! what's all the fuss about? what about it? **le m. est que . . .,** the unfortunate thing is that . . .; *Prov:* **à quelque chose m. est bon,** it's an ill wind that blows nobody any good; every cloud has a silver lining; (*b*) *F:* **faire un m.,** (i) to do something desperate; (ii) to commit murder; **se faire un m.,** to commit suicide; **s'il entre ici je fais un m.!** if he comes in here I'll (i) do something desperate, (ii) kill him, (iii) kill myself. **2.** (*a*) misfortune, unhappiness; **bonheur et m.,** happiness and sorrow; **enfant qui fait le m. de ses parents,** child who brings sorrow to his parents; **c'est cela qui a fait son m.,** that is what has caused his misfortune, his unhappiness; **le m. des uns fait le bonheur des autres,** one man's joy is another man's sorrow; **le m. de notre temps,** the misfortunes of our times; **c'est dans le m. qu'on connaît ses vrais amis,** a friend in need is a friend indeed; (*b*) affliction; **la surdité est un grand m.,** deafness is a great affliction. **3.** (*a*) bad luck; **oiseau de m.,** bird of ill omen; **quel m.!** what a pity! what bad luck! **quel m. que je ne l'aie pas su,** what a pity I didn't know (about it); **je le connais pour mon m.,** unfortunately, unluckily, for me I know him; I know him to my cost; **porter m. à qn,** to bring s.o. bad luck; **en ce jour de m.,** on this ill-fated, unlucky, day; **il a pour son m. un tempérament violent,** he is cursed with a violent temper; **ceux qui ont le m. d'avoir affaire à lui,** those who are unfortunate, unlucky, enough to have to deal with him; **jouer de m., être en m.,** to be unlucky; **c'est jouer de m.,** it's most unfortunate; *F:* **ces lettres de m.!** these blasted letters! (*b*) **m. à eux!** woe betide them! curse them! *int.* **m.!** hell!

malheure [malœːr], *s.f. A:* (*a*) **aller à la m.,** to fall into misfortune; to fall upon evil days; (*b*) **par m.,** by misfortune; unfortunately.

malheureusement [malœrøzmɑ̃], *adv.* **1.** unfortunately, unhappily, unluckily; **au cas où m. cet événement se produirait,** in that unfortunate event; **il est m. parti,** unfortunately he has left. **2. mourir m.,** to die miserably, to die a miserable death.

malheureux, -euse [malœrø, -øːz], *a.* (*a*) unfortunate, unhappy, wretched (person, business, etc.), poor, badly off (person), sad, miserable (countenance, etc.); **mémoire malheureuse,** defective memory; *s.* **secourir les m.,** to help the unfortunate, the poor; **le m.! la malheureuse!** poor man! poor woman! **m.!** wretched man! wretch! **m. comme les pierres,** (i) wretched, utterly miserable; (ii) in wretched poverty, absolutely penniless; (*b*) unlucky; *Prov:* **heureux au jeu m. en amour,** lucky at cards unlucky in love; **né sous une étoile malheureuse,** born under an unlucky star; **un jour m.,** an ill-starred, unlucky, day; **entreprise malheureuse,** ill-starred adventure; **Ilion la malheureuse,** Ilium the ill-fated; **candidat m.,** unsuccessful candidate; **c'est bien m. pour vous!** it's hard lines on you! **il est bien m. que +** *sub.*, it is very unfortunate, a great pity, that . . .; *s.* **les m. de la vie,** the unsuccessful in life; **avoir la main malheureuse,** (i) to be unlucky; (ii) to be clumsy, awkward, with one's hands, to be always breaking things; **le voilà enfin, ce n'est pas m.!** here he comes at last, and a good job too! (*c*) paltry, wretched; **une malheureuse pièce de cinq francs,** a miserable, beggarly, paltry, five-franc piece; **vous me faites des histoires pour douze m. francs!** you are making all this fuss for a mere twelve francs!

malhonnête [malɔnɛt], *a.* (*a*) dishonest; **un m. homme,** a dishonest man; **financier m.,** financial crook; swindler; **engager un procès m.,** to engage in a dishonest lawsuit; *Cards:* **joueur m.,** cheat; (*b*) rude, impolite; **un homme m.,** a rude man; **comme vous êtes m.!** how impolite, uncivil, you are! (*c*) *A:* indecent (gesture); improper.

malhonnêtement [malɔnɛtmɑ̃], *adv.* (*a*) dishonestly; (*b*) rudely, impolitely; (*c*) *A:* indecently, improperly.

malhonnêteté [malɔnɛtte], *s.f.* **1.** (*a*) dishonesty; (*b*) dishonest action, piece of dishonesty. **2.** (*a*) *O:* rudeness, impoliteness, incivility; (*b*) rude remark; piece of incivility; **c'est assez de malhonnêtetés!** that's enough of, I'll have no more of, your abuse! **3.** *A:* indecency.

Mali (le) [ləmali], *Pr.n.m. Geog:* Mali.

malice [malis], *s.f.* **1.** (*a*) malice, maliciousness, spitefulness; **c'est de la m. noire,** it is rank malice on his part; **ne pas voir, entendre, m., à qch.,** (i) to see no harm in sth.; (ii) to mean no harm by sth.; **il ne faut pas y voir m.,** you mustn't think he meant anything; (*b*) mischievousness, naughtiness. **2.** (*a*) *O:* smart remark; dig (at s.o.), *A:* quip; **dire des malices à qn,** to chaff s.o.; (*b*) trick, prank; **faire une m. à qn,** to play a trick on s.o.; **une m. bien innocente,** a harmless joke, trick; **la m. est cousue de fil blanc,** any child can see through that trick; (*c*) **sac à m.,** conjuror's deep pocket; bag of tricks; *F:* **avoir un nouvel expédient dans son sac à m.,** to have another card up one's sleeve; (*of pers.*) **c'est un sac à m.,** he's always got something else up his sleeve; he's always got a second string to his bow; **la belle m.!** there's nothing very clever in that!

malicieusement [malisjøzmɑ̃], *adv.* **1.** *A:* maliciously, spitefully. **2.** (*a*) mischievously; naughtily; (*b*) by way of a joke; in a mocking manner.

malicieux, -ieuse [malisjø, -jøːz], *a.* **1.** *A:* malicious, spiteful; *still so used in* **cheval m.,** unreliable horse. **2.** (*a*) mischievous; naughty; **petit m.!** you little imp, devil! (*b*) ironic, mocking (smile); joking, bantering (remark); **avoir un esprit vif et m.,** to have a quick, witty, mind; to be full of quick repartee.

malien, -ienne [maljɛ̃, -jɛn]. **1.** *a.* Mali; of, relating to, (the Republic of) Mali. **2.** *s.* native, inhabitant of Mali.

malignement [maliɲmɑ̃], *adv.* **1.** malignantly, spitefully. **2.** mischievously, slyly.

malignité [maliɲite], *s.f.* **1.** (*a*) malignity, malignancy, spite(fulness); (*b*) malignancy, malignity (of disease). **2.** piece of spite, *F:* dirty trick.

malin, -igne [malɛ̃, -iɲ], *a.* **1.** (*a*) *A:* malignant, evil(-minded), wicked; (*b*) **l'esprit m.,** *s.* **le m.,** the devil, Satan; *Astrol:* **astre m.,** malign star, unlucky star; (*c*) malicious (pleasure, etc.); (*d*) *Med:* malignant (tumour, etc.). **2.** (*a*) shrewd, cunning, sharp, *F:* all there; **il est plus m. que ça,** he knows better; **m. comme un singe,** as artful as a cart-load of monkeys; **vous vous croyez m.,** you think you're very clever; **elle n'est pas bien maligne,** *F:* **maline,** she's not very, *F:* all that, bright; **bien m. qui le trouvera!** it will take a smart one to find that! **il serait plus m. d'attendre sa réponse,** we'd do better to wait for his reply; **ce n'était pas très m.,** that wasn't very bright, was it? *F:* **ce n'est pas bien m., un enfant saurait le faire,** it's not very difficult, a child could do it; *Iron:* **c'est m.!** that *is* clever of you! **air m.,** sly, knowing, look; **sourire m.,** knowing smile; (*b*) *s.* **c'est un m.,** (i) he has his wits about him; *F:* he knows what's what, he knows a thing or two, there are no flies on him; (ii) he thinks he knows all the answers; (iii) he's a trickster, *F:* a wide boy; **un petit m.,** a smart Aleck; **une petite maligne,** (i) a sly little piece; (ii) a little imp; *Prov:* **à m. m. et demi,** diamond cut diamond; **faire le m.,** to try to be smart; **il veut faire le m. avec sa nouvelle voiture,** he wants to swank with his new car.

maline [malin], *s.f.* spring tide.

Malines [malin]. **1.** *Pr.n.f. Geog:* Malines, Mechlin. **2.** *s.f.* Mechlin lace.

malingre [malɛ̃ːgr], *a.* sickly, puny; fragile.

malinofskite, malinowskite [malinɔfskit], *s.f. Miner:* malinowskite.

malinois, -oise [malinwa, -waːz]. **1.** *a.* & *s. Geog:* (native, inhabitant) of Malines, of Mechlin. **2.** *s.m. Husb:* **malinois,** Belgian sheep-dog.

malintentionné, -ée [malɛ̃tɑ̃sjɔne], *a.* & *s.* ill-intentioned, spiteful (person) (**envers,** towards).

malique [malik], *a. Ch:* malic (acid).

malitorne [malitɔrn], *A:* **1.** *a.* loutish, clumsy, awkward. **2.** (*a*) *s.m.* lout; (*b*) *s.f.* slut.

mal-jugé [malʒyʒe], *s.m. no pl. Jur:* miscarriage of justice.

mallard [malaːr], *s.m.* small grindstone.

mallardite [malardit], *s.f. Miner:* mallardite.

malle [mal], *s.f.* **1.** (*a*) trunk, box; **m. de tôle,** tin trunk; **m. (de) paquebot, m. (de) cabine,** cabin trunk; **m. bombée,** Saratoga trunk; **faire sa malle, ses malles,** (i) to pack (one's trunk); (ii) to get ready to leave; (iii) *F:* to be at death's door; *F:* **vous pouvez faire votre m.,** you can pack your bags; you'd better clear out; *F:* **(se) faire la m.,** to do a moonlight flit; **défaire sa m.,** to unpack; *P:* **boucler sa m.,** to die, to peg out, to kick the bucket; *P:* **ferme ta m.!** shut up! (*b*) *Aut:* boot, *U.S:* trunk; (*c*) *A:* (pedlar's) pack; *F:* **porter sa m.,** to have a hump, to be hunch-backed. **2.** (*a*) *A:* mailbag (hung to horse's saddle); (*b*) *A.Veh:* mail-coach; (*c*) *A.Nau:* mail-boat; *Rail:* **la m. des Indes,** the Indian mail; (*d*) *Fr.C:* mail, post.

malléabilisation [mal(l)eabilizasjɔ̃], *s.f. Metall:* malleabilization.

malléabiliser [mal(l)eabilize], *v.tr. Metall:* to malleabl(e)ize.

malléabilité [mal(l)eabilite], *s.f.* malleability (of (metal); pliability (of disposition).

malléable [mal(l)eabl], *a.* (*a*) malleable (metal, etc.); (*b*) plastic, soft, pliable, malleable (nature).

malléaire [maleɛːr], **malléal, -aux** [maleal, -o], *a. Anat:* malleal, mallear.

malle-armoire [malarmwaːr], *s.f.* wardrobe trunk; *pl. malles-armoires.*

malléer [mal(l)ee], *v.tr.* to hammer out (metal).

malléination [maleinasjɔ̃], *s.f. Vet:* malleinization.

malléine [malein], *s.f. Vet:* mallein.

malléiner [maleine], *v.tr. Vet:* to mallein(ize).

malléolaire [mal(l)eɔlɛːr], *a. Anat:* malleolar.

malléole [mal(l)eɔl], *s.f. Anat:* malleolus.

malle-poste [malpɔst], *s.f. A.Veh:* mail(-coach); *pl. malles-poste(s).*

maller [male], *v.tr. Fr.C:* to post (a letter, etc.).

malleterie [maltri], *s.f.* trunk manufacture.

malletier, -ière [maltje, -jɛːr], *s.* bag and trunk maker.

mallette [malɛt], *s.f.* **1.** small (suit)case; overnight case; attaché case; **m. garnie,** dressing case; **m. à disques, m. porte-disques,** record case; **m. de camping,** picnic basket, case; **2.** *Bot:* shepherd's purse.

mal-logé, -ée [mallɔʒe], *s.* badly-housed person; *pl. mal-logé(e)s.*

mallophages [mal(l)ɔfaːʒ], *s.m.pl. Ent:* Mallophaga.

malm [malm], *s.m. Geol:* malm.

malmenage [malmənaːʒ], *s.m.* mishandling, misuse (of delicate instrument, etc.).

malmener [malməne], *v.tr.* (*conj. like* MENER) (*a*) to maltreat, ill-treat, ill-use, mishandle, misuse; to manhandle (s.o.), to handle (s.o.) severely, to knock (s.o.) about; to give (s.o.) a rough handling; to bully (s.o.); (*b*) to abuse, *F:* slate (s.o.).

malmignate [malmiɲat], *s.f. Arach:* malmignatte.

malnutrition [malnytrisjɔ̃], *s.f.* malnutrition.

malocclusion [malɔklysjɔ̃], *s.f. Dent:* malocclusion.

malodorant [malɔdɔrɑ̃], *a.* evil-smelling, malodorous, smelly, stinking.

malon [malɔ̃], *s.m.* (*in S. of Fr.*) paving-brick.

malot [malo], *s.m. F:* horse fly.

malotru, -ue [malɔtry]. **1.** *a.* (*a*) coarse, vulgar, ill-bred; uncouth; (*b*) *A:* (i) ugly; misshapen; (ii) ill, out of sorts. **2.** *s.m.* boor; uncouth person.

malouin, -ine [malwɛ̃, -in], *a.* & *s. Geog:* **1.** (native, inhabitant) of Saint-Malo. **2. les (îles) Malouines,** the Falkland Islands; **la mer des Malouines,** the Falkland Sea.

malpeigné, -ée [malpɛɲe]. **1.** *a.* unkempt, tousled, untidy (hair, person). **2.** *s.* sloven; *f.* slut, slattern.

Malpighi [malpigi], *Pr.n.* Malpighi; *Anat:* **(corpuscules, etc.) de M.,** Malpighian (corpuscles, etc.).

malpighiacées [malpigjase], *s.f.pl. Bot:* Malpighiaceae.

malpighie [malpigi], *s.f. Bot:* malpighia.

malplaisant [malplɛzɑ̃], *a.* unpleasant, displeasing.

malpoli [malpɔli], *a. F:* impolite.

malposition [malpɔzisjɔ̃], *s.f. Obst: Dent:* malposition; **dents en m.,** malposed teeth.

malpropre [malprɔpr], *a.* **1.** *A:* **être m. à qch., à faire qch.,** to be ill-fitted for sth., ill-fitted to do sth. **2.** (*a*) dirty, grubby (hands, etc.); slovenly, untidy (appearance, etc.); (*b*) poorly done, slovenly, slapdash (work); (*c*) *F:* smutty (story, etc.); dirty, unsavoury (business, conduct).

malproprement [malprɔprəmɑ̃], *adv.* dirtily; **in a** slovenly manner.

malpropreté [malprɔprəte], *s.f.* **1.** (*a*) dirtiness, grubbiness, slovenliness; **la m. occasionne des maladies,** dirt breeds disease; (*b*) indecency, smuttiness (of story); unsavouriness, dirtiness (of business, conduct). **2.** *pl.* (*a*) **malpropretés retenues par le tamis,** dirt retained by the strainer; (*b*) **raconter des malpropretés,** to tell smutty stories; **dire des malpropretés,** to talk smut.

malsain [malsɛ̃], *a.* **1.** (*a*) unhealthy (person, climate); (*b*) *Nau:* dangerous (coast). **2.** unwholesome (food); unwholesome, pernicious (literature, etc.).

malséance [malseɑ̃ːs], *s.f.* unseemliness, indecorousness.

malséant [malseɑ̃], *a.* unseemly, indecorous; unbecoming (**à,** to).

malsonnant [malsɔnɑ̃], *a.* offensive (to the ear); objectionable.

malt [malt], *s.m. Brew:* malt; **convertir l'orge en m.,** to malt the barley.

maltage [maltaːʒ], *s.m. Brew:* malting.

maltais, -aise [maltɛ, -ɛːz], *a.* & *s. Geog:* Maltese; *Z:* **chien m.,** Maltese, bichon.

maltalent [maltalɑ̃], *s.m. A:* ill will; animosity.

maltase [maltɑːz], *s.f. Ch:* maltase.

Malte [malt], *Pr.n.f. Geog:* Malta; **fièvre de M.,** Malta fever; *Mec.E: etc:* **croix de M.,** Maltese cross; *Cin:* star-wheel; *Mec.E:* **entraînement par croix de M.,** Geneva(-cross) movement, Geneva motion.

malter [malte], *v.tr. Brew:* to malt (barley); *Com:* **lait malté,** malted milk.

malterie [malt(ə)ri], *s.f.* **1.** malt house. **2.** malting.

malteur [maltœːr], *s.m.* maltster, maltman.

malthe [malt], *s.f. Miner:* maltha, mineral tar.

malthènes [maltɛn], *s.m.pl. Ch:* malthenes.

malthusianiser [maltyzjanize], *v.i. F:* to practise contraception.

malthusianisme [maltyzjanism], *s.m.* (*a*) Malthusianism; (*b*) (practice of) contraception; neo-Malthusianism; (*c*) **m. économique,** planned restriction of production.

malthusien, -ienne [maltyzjɛ̃, -jɛn], *a. & s.* Malthusian.

maltose [maltoːz], *s.m. Ch: Ind:* maltose.

maltôte [maltoːt], *s.f. A:* **1.** (*a*) *Fr.Hist:* tax levied by Philip the Fair; (*b*) maletolt, maletot(e); extortionate or illegal tax. **2.** (*a*) tax-collecting; (*b*) *coll.* the tax collectors.

maltôtier [maltotje], *s.m. A:* **1.** extortioner, extortionist. **2.** tax collector.

maltraitement [maltrɛtmɑ̃], *s.m.* ill-treatment.

maltraiter [maltrete, -tre-], *v.tr.* to maltreat, ill-treat, ill-use; to treat (s.o.) badly (by word or deed); to handle (s.o.) roughly; *F:* to manhandle (s.o.); to batter (s.o.) about; **m. qn pour lui faire faire qch.,** to bully s.o. into doing sth.; **régiment maltraité dans le combat,** regiment that suffered severely, that was badly cut up, in the battle.

malure [malyːr], *s.m. Orn:* malurine; Australian warbler.

malvacé [malvase], *Bot:* **1.** *a.* malvaceous. **2.** *s.f.pl.* **malvacées,** Malvaceae, *F:* mallows.

malvé [malve], *a. Bot:* malvaceous.

malveillamment [malvɛjamɑ̃], *adv.* malevolently, with ill will; spitefully.

malveillance [malvɛjɑ̃ːs], *s.f.* (*a*) malevolence, ill will (**pour, envers,** to, towards); **agir par m.,** to act out of spite; **avec m.,** malevolently, spitefully; (*b*) foul play.

malveillant [malvɛjɑ̃], *a.* (*a*) malevolent, ill-willed; malicious; **se montrer m. pour qn,** to show ill will towards s.o.; **regarder qn d'un œil m.,** to look unkindly at, on, s.o.; to look askance at s.o.; to look at s.o. with a malevolent eye; *s.* **c'est un m. qui vous a dit cela,** some ill-disposed, spiteful, person told you that; (*b*) spiteful (remark).

malvenant [malvənɑ̃], *a.* unthrifty (tree, etc.).

malvenu [malvəny], *a. Lit:* ill-advised, utterly in the wrong; **vous êtes m. à critiquer,** you are the last one who ought to criticize; **il est m. à se plaindre,** he has no right to complain.

malversation [malvɛrsasjɔ̃], *s.f.* malversation, embezzlement, malpractice, breach of trust; malfeasance.

malverser [malvɛrse], *v.i. A:* to be guilty of malversation, of malpractices.

Malvoisie [malvwazi]. **1.** *Pr.n.f. Geog:* Malvasia, Monemvasia. **2.** *s.m. or f. Vit:* (*also* **vin de M.**) malmsey (wine); **m. de Samos,** Samos (wine); **m. de Madère,** madeira.

mamamouchi [mamamuʃi], *s.m.* Grand Panjandrum; (title bestowed on M. Jourdain in Molière's *Bourgeois Gentilhomme*).

maman [mamɑ̃, mɑ̃mɑ̃], *s.f.* (*a*) (*form of address*) mummy, mam(m)a, *P:* mum; **oui, m.,** yes, mummy; (*b*) **ta m. t'appelle,** mummy's calling you; **il va se plaindre à sa m.,** he goes and whines to his mummy; **les mamans sont assises à regarder,** the mothers sit and look on; *F:* **grosse m.,** portly matron; (*c*) **la m.,** the mother of the family; **jouer à la m.,** to play mothers (and fathers).

mamba [mɑ̃ba], *s.m. Rept:* mamba.

mambo [mɑ̃mbo], *s.f. Danc:* mambo.

mame [mam], *s.f. P:* ma'am, mum; **M. X,** Mrs X.

mamelé [mamle], *a. Z:* (*rare*) mammate.

mamellaire [mamɛl(l)ɛːr], *a. Anat:* mammary.

mamelle [mamɛl], *s.f.* **1.** *Anat:* mamma; breast (of woman, *A:* of man); udder (of animal); **enfant à la m.,** (i) child at the breast; (ii) baby, young child; *Lit:* **labourage et pâturage sont les deux mamelles de l'État,** tillage and pasturage are the mother's milk of the State; *F: O:* **il n'a rien sous la m. gauche,** he has no heart. **2.** *occ. F:* teat; dug (of animal). **3.** *Bot: F:* **arbre aux mamelles,** mammee; **herbe aux mamelles,** nipplewort.

mamelliforme [mamɛl(l)ifɔrm], *a.* mammiform.

mamelon [mamlɔ̃], *s.m.* **1.** *Anat:* mamilla; (*a*) nipple, teat, pap (of woman); (*b*) dug, teat (of animal). **2.** (*small excrescence*) (*a*) *Anat:* papilla (of the tongue); (*b*) *Geog:* mamelon, rounded hillock, knoll. **3.** *Mec.E:* (*a*) boss, swell; (*b*) gudgeon (on axle, for rudder, etc.); (*c*) nipple (for lubrication, of hinge, etc.).

mamelonné [mamlɔne], *a.* mamillate(d); **plaine mamelonnée de collines,** plain covered with rounded hillocks.

mamelonner [mamlɔne], *v.tr. Const:* to cover with protuberances; **coupoles qui mamelonnent un toit,** cupolas that protrude from a roof.

mamelouk, mameluk [mamluk, -lyk], *s.m. Hist:* mameluke.

mamelu [mamly], *a. P:* (man or woman) with strongly marked breasts; **une grosse mamelue,** a stout and big-bubbed woman.

mamertin, -ine [mamɛrtɛ̃, -in], *a. & s. Geog:* (native, inhabitant) of Mamers [mamɛrs].

m'amie [mami], *s.f. A: F:* my dear.

mamillaire [mamil(l)ɛːr]. **1.** *a. Anat:* mamillary. **2.** *s.f. Bot:* nipple cactus.

mamilloplastie [mamil(l)ɔplasti], *s.f. Surg:* mamilloplasty.

mammaire [mam(m)ɛːr], *a. Anat:* mammary (gland, etc.); **sillon m.,** cleavage.

mammalogie [mam(m)alɔʒi], mammalogy, therology.

mammalogique [mam(m)alɔʒik], *a.* mammalogical.

mammalogiste [mam(m)alɔʒist], *s.m. & f.* mammalogist.

mammea [mam(m)ea], *s.m.,* **mammée** [mam(m)e], *s.f. Bot:* **m. (américaine),** mammee.

mammectomie [mam(m)ɛktɔmi], *s.f. Surg:* mastectomy, mammectomy.

mammifère [mam(m)ifɛːr]. **1.** *a.* mammalian. **2.** *s.m.* mammal; **les mammifères,** the Mammalia, the mammals.

mammiforme [mam(m)ifɔrm], *a.* mammiform.

mammite [mam(m)it], *s.f. Med:* mammitis, mastitis.

mammographie [mam(m)ɔgrafi], *s.f. Med:* X-ray examination of the breast.

mammoplastie [mam(m)ɔplasti], *s.f. Surg:* mastoplasty.

Mammon [mamɔ̃], *Pr.n.m.* Mammon; **adorateur de M.,** worshipper of Mammon; mammonite.

mammouth [mamut], *s.m.* mammoth.

m'amour, mamour [mamuːr], *s.m.* **1.** my love, my dear, darling. **2.** *pl.* fondling, caressing; *F:* **faire des mamours à qn,** to caress, fondle, s.o.

mam'selle, mam'zelle [mamzɛl], *s.f. F:* = MADEMOISELLE.

Man[1] [mɑ̃], *Pr.n.f. Geog:* **l'île de M.,** the Isle of Man; *Z:* **chat de l'île de M.,** Manx cat.

man[2], *s.m. Ent: F:* grub (of cockchafer).

manade [manad], *s.f.* (*S. of Fr. esp. Camargue*) herd of cattle or horses.

manadier [manadje], *s.m.* (*in Camargue*) cattle dealer.

manager [manadʒœːr, -ɛːr], *s.m. F: Ind: Cin: Sp:* manager.

manakin [manakɛ̃], *s.m. Orn:* man(n)ikin, manakin.

manant [manɑ̃], *s.m.* **1.** *Hist:* boor, villager. **2.** (*a*) yokel; *but more usu.* (*b*) churl, boor; lout.

Manassé [manase], *Pr.n.m. B.Hist:* Manasseh.

manceau, -elle [mɑ̃so, -ɛl], *a. & s.* **1.** *Geog:* (native, inhabitant) (i) of the Maine region, (ii) of Le Mans. **2.** *s.f. Harn:* **mancelle,** tug chain, pole chain.

mancenille [mɑ̃sniːj], *s.f. Bot:* manchineel apple.

mancenillier [mɑ̃snije], *s.m. Bot:* manchineel (tree).

manche[1] [mɑ̃ːʃ], *s.f.* **1.** (*a*) sleeve; **être en manches de chemise,** to be in one's shirt sleeves; *A:* **manches à gigot,** leg-of-mutton sleeves; **robe à manches, sans manches,** sleeved, sleeveless, dress; **fausses manches, manches de travail, en lustrine,** oversleeves; **relever, retrousser, ses manches,** to roll up one's sleeves; **retroussons nos manches,** let's get down to work; **mettre qch. dans sa m.,** (i) to put sth. up one's sleeve; (ii) to get hold of, lay hands on, sth.; **garder (qn, qch.) dans sa m.,** to keep (s.o., sth.) in reserve; **avoir qn dans sa m.,** to have s.o. at one's disposal; *F:* in one's pocket; **être dans la m. de qn,** (i) to be at s.o.'s disposal; (ii) to be under s.o.'s protection; **tirer qn par la m.,** (i) to pull s.o. by the sleeve, to tug at s.o.'s sleeve; (ii) to attract s.o.'s attention; (iii) to prevent s.o. from leaving; (iv) to coax, entice, s.o.; **se faire tirer par la m.,** to do sth. with reluctance; to be persuaded into doing sth.; *F:* **ça, c'est une autre paire de manches,** that's another matter, another story, another pair of shoes, another cup of tea; **avoir la m. large,** to be easy-going, broadminded; (*b*) *Tchn:* **m. à eau, m. en toile,** (canvas) hose pipe; **m. à incendie,** fire hose; **m. à air,** *A:* **m. à vent,** (i) (canvas) wind sail; (ii) air shaft, air intake, ventilator; *Nau:* air scoop; (iii) *Av:* wind sock; *Mec.E:* **m. d'aspiration,** suction sleeve; **m. d'aspiration d'air,** air duct; **m. à charbon,** coal shoot; **m. à ordures,** rubbish, *U.S:* garbage, shoot, chute; **m. à escarbilles,** ash shoot; *Nau:* **m. de cale, de chaufferie,** hold, stokehold, ventilator; **m. de dalot,** scupper hose. **2.** *Sp: etc:* (i) heat; (ii) round; (iii) *Ten:* set; (iv) *Cards:* hand (played); single game; **nous sommes m. à m.,** we're even; we're game all; we're neck and neck; **nous avons chacun une m., il faut jouer la belle,** we're one all, we must play the deciding game, set, etc.; **il a remporté la première m. dans la partie diplomatique,** he won the first round in the diplomatic game, struggle. **3.** *F:* (*a*) **faire la m.,** to beg; to go round with the hat; (*b*) *coll.* **la m.,** beggars; (*c*) *A:* **(bonne) m.,** tip, gratuity. **4.** *Geog:* **la M.,** the English Channel.

manche[2], *s.m.* **1.** (*a*) handle (of hammer, knife, saucepan, etc.); stilt (of plough); haft (of dagger, etc.); stock (of whip); helve (of axe, etc.); neck (of violin, etc.); **savoir son m.,** to know one's positions (on the violin, etc.); **m. à balai,** (i) broomstick; (ii) *Av: F:* control stick, column, *F:* joystick; *Av:* **m. au ventre,** stick full back; **tirer sur le m.,** to ease the stick back; **m. de couteau,** knife handle; **couteau à m. d'ivoire,** ivory-handled knife; **m. à gigot, de gigot,** leg-of-mutton holder (for carving); **m. d'un gigot,** knuckle (of a leg of mutton); **jeter le m. après la cognée,** to give up in sheer despair; **il ne faut pas jeter le m. après la cognée,** never say die; *F:* **être du côté du m.,** to be on the strongest, the winning, side; to take sides with the winner; *F:* **dormir, s'endormir, sur le m.,** to do nothing; to idle one's time away; *F:* **branler dans le m.,** to be in a shaky, sticky, position; *P:* **tomber sur un m.,** to come up against a difficulty, an obstacle; to meet with a snag; (*b*) *P:* idiot, clot; **c'est un m.,** he's a nit, a clot; **raisonner comme un m.,** to reason in a cockeyed fashion; **se débrouiller, s'y prendre, comme un m.,** to go about things in a fat-headed, idiotic, ham-handed, way. **2.** *Moll:* **m. de couteau,** razor clam, razor shell.

Manche[3] **(la),** *Pr.n.f. Geog:* La Mancha (Spain); *s.a.* MANCHE[1] 4.

manché [mɑ̃ʃe], *s.m. Nau:* Indian (i) fishing boat, (ii) coasting steamer.

mancheron[1] [mɑ̃ʃrɔ̃], *s.m. Dressm:* (*a*) short sleeve; (*b*) cuff.

mancheron[2], *s.m.* handle, stilt (of plough).

manchette [mɑ̃ʃɛt], *s.f.* **1.** (*a*) cuff; wristband; **manchettes à revers,** gauntlet cuffs; **m. de dentelles,** lace ruffle; **m. mousquetaire,** double cuff, turn-back cuff (of shirt); *F:* **mettre des manchettes pour faire qch.,** to make elaborate preparations, to make a fuss, before doing sth.; (*b*) gauntlet (of glove); (*c*) oversleeve, cuff protector; (*d*) *pl. F:* handcuffs; (*e*) *F:* head (on beer); (*f*) *Wr:* (i) foul; (ii) (*all-in wrestling*) forearm smash; (*g*) **coup de m.,** (i) *Fenc:* slash on the sword wrist; (ii) *Wr:* forearm blow on the chin. **2.** *Surg:* flap (of amputated limb). **3.** (*a*) headline (of newspaper); **tenir la m. (des journaux),** to get into the headlines; (*b*) *Typ:* shoulder note; side note, marginal note. **4.** *Nau:* lizard.

manchon [mɑ̃ʃɔ̃], *s.m.* **1.** (*a*) muff; (*b*) *Mil:* **m. de képi,** cap cover; (*c*) *Mil:* white cap band (worn by troops on one side in manœuvres). **2.** *Tchn:* (*a*) sleeve, muff (for axle, rod, tube, etc.); bush(ing) (of bearing, pipe, etc.); quill (of shaft, etc.); socket (for pivot, tool, etc.); **m. d'accouplement, de raccord(ement), d'attache,** (i) *Mec.E:* coupling sleeve, connecting sleeve; (coupling) muff; coupling box; (ii) *Tp:* jointing sleeve; **accouplement à m.,** sleeve, muff, box, coupling; **m. pour tuyau,** pipe coupling, connection; *El:* **m. de raccordement, de jonction,** coupling, junction, box; **m. de fixation,** adapter; **m. de graissage,** oil sleeve; **m. de réchauffage,** heating muff; **m. coulissant,** sliding sleeve; **m. entraîneur,** driving sleeve; **m. guide,** guide bush; **m. taraudé, fileté,** sleeve nut; *Mch-Tls:* **m. pour foret,** drill sleeve, socket; *Min:* **m. vissé,** tool joint; (*b*) *Aut: etc:* **m. d'embrayage,** coupling, clutch; **m. à friction,** friction coupling, clutch; **m. à plateaux,** flange, plate, coupling or clutch; (*c*) casing, jacket; **m. de refroidissement,** cooling jacket (of machine-gun, pipe, etc.); **m. intérieur (de cylindre),** cylinder liner; *Artil:* **m. (de renfort) de canon,** barrel jacket, outer case; *Nau:* **m. d'écubier,** hawse pipe; **m. de capelage,** mast funnel; **m. de puits aux chaînes,** chain pipe; **m.**

de cimentation, baffle collar; (*d*) *Av:* cuff (of propeller blade); *Aer:* neck (of balloon); *Aer:* **m. de remplissage,** filler neck; (*e*) *Ten:* **m. pour raquette,** grip. **3.** *Ill:* (gas-)mantle; *Atom.Ph: Ill:* **m. incandescent, m. à incandescence,** incandescent mantle.

manchonner [mɑ̃ʃɔne], *v.tr.* to couple (parts) together by a sleeve coupling, by a box coupling.

manchot, -ote [mɑ̃ʃo, -ɔt], *a. & s.* **1.** one-armed, one-handed (person); **il est m. du bras gauche,** he has lost his left arm (or hand); *F:* **il n'est pas m.,** (i) he's clever with his hands; (ii) he's very capable, he knows how to set about things. **2.** *s.m. Orn:* penguin; **m. empereur,** emperor penguin; **m. royal,** king penguin; **m. d'Adélie,** Adelie penguin; **m. sauteur,** crested penguin, rock hopper.

mancienne [mɑ̃sjɛn], *s.f. Bot:* wayfaring tree.

mancoliste [mɑ̃kɔlist], *s.f.* want list (of philatelist, etc.).

mandant [mɑ̃dɑ̃], *s.m.* **1.** mandator; *Jur:* principal (in transaction); employer. **2.** *pl. Pol:* **le député et ses mandants,** the member and his constituents, and his constituency.

mandarin, -ine [mɑ̃darɛ̃, -in]. **1.** *s.m.* (*a*) *A: Chinese Adm:* mandarin; (*b*) intellectual; *Pej:* pedant; (*c*) (*grotesque figure*) (nodding) mandarin; (*d*) *Orn:* **canard m.,** mandarin duck. **2.** *a.* mandarin; *Ling:* **la langue mandarine,** *s.* **le m.,** mandarin. **3.** *s.f.* **mandarine,** mandarin(e), tangerine (orange).

mandarinat [mɑ̃darina], *s.m.* **1.** (*a*) *A. Chinese Adm:* mandarinate, (i) function of mandarin; (ii) the mandarins (as a body); (*b*) *coll. usu. Pej:* the intellectuals; the pedants. **2.** system of competitive examinations for administrative posts.

mandarinier [mɑ̃darinje], *s.m.* mandarin (orange) tree, tangerine (orange) tree.

mandarinisme [mɑ̃darinism], *s.m.* (*a*) system of competitive examinations for (i) *A:* the mandarinate; (ii) any administrative post; (*b*) mandarinism; blind faith in competitive examinations as a method of promotion.

mandat [mɑ̃da], *s.m.* **1.** (*a*) mandate; commission; terms of reference (of committee); **attribuer un m. à une puissance,** to confer a mandate on a power; **m. international,** international mandate; *Hist:* **le m. sur la Palestine,** the mandate for Palestine; **les territoires sous m.,** the mandated territories; (*b*) **m. de député,** member's (electoral) mandate; **fonctionnaire sans m.,** unauthorized official; **vote par mandats,** card vote; (*c*) *Jur:* power of attorney; proxy; act of procuration, of agency. **2.** warrant; (*a*) *Jur:* **m. de perquisition,** search warrant; **m. d'arrêt,** warrant for arrest; **m. d'amener,** order to offender or witness to appear (enforceable through arrest); **m. de comparution,** summons (to appear); **lancer un m.,** to issue a warrant; **m. de dépôt,** committal (of prisoner); (*b*) *Fin:* **m. du Trésor,** Treasury warrant. **3.** (*a*) order (to pay); money order; draft; **m. sur la Banque de France,** order on the Bank of France; (*b*) *Post:* **m. (de) poste, m. postal** = postal order; **m. international, sur l'étranger,** foreign, international, money order; **m. télégraphique,** telegraph(ic) money order.

mandataire [mɑ̃datɛːr], *s.m. & f.* **1.** mandatory (of electors, etc.). **2.** proxy (at meeting); representative. **3.** *Jur:* authorized agent; attorney; assignee; **m. général,** general agent; *Com:* **m. aux Halles,** inside broker (at the *Halles* in Paris). **4.** trustee.

mandat-carte [mɑ̃dakart], *s.m. Post:* postal order, money order (in postcard form); *pl. mandats-cartes.*

mandat-contributions [mɑ̃dakɔ̃tribysjɔ̃], *s.m. Post:* (special) money order (for paying income tax, etc.); *pl. mandats-contributions.*

mandatement [mɑ̃datmɑ̃], *s.m.* **1.** (action of) commissioning, sending (a representative, etc.). **2.** (action of) paying by means of a money order.

mandater [mɑ̃date], *v.tr.* **1.** to elect, send, commission (representative, etc.); **m. un député pour faire voter une loi,** to give a member a mandate to support a bill. **2. m. des frais,** to pay expenses by money order, by draft.

mandat-lettre [mɑ̃dalɛtr̥], *s.m. Post:* = postal order, money order (in the form of a letter card); *pl. mandats-lettres.*

mandat-poste [mɑ̃dapɔst], *s.m. Post:* = postal order, money order; *pl. mandats-poste.*

mandchou, -oue [mɑ̃tʃu, mɑ̃ʃ-]. **1.** *a. & s. Ethn:* Manchu, Manchurian; *Hist:* **l'État mandchou,** Manchukuo, Manchuria. **2.** *s.m. Ling:* Manchu. **3.** *a. Z:* **chien m.,** chow; *pl. mandchoux, mandchous.*

Mandchoukouo [mɑ̃tʃukuo, mɑ̃ʃ-], *Pr.n.m. Geog:* Manchukuo.

Mandchourie [mɑ̃tʃuri, mɑ̃ʃ-], *Pr.n.f. Geog:* Manchuria.

mandement [mɑ̃dmɑ̃], *s.m.* **1.** *A:* mandate, mandamus; order; instructions (of superior to inferior). **2.** *Ecc:* pastoral letter.

mander [mɑ̃de], *v.tr.* **1.** *A:* (*a*) **m. une nouvelle à qn,** to send news (by letter) to s.o.; (*b*) *Journ:* **on mande de . . .,** it is reported from . . .; **on nous mande que l'équipe arrivera demain,** we have word that the team will arrive tomorrow. **2.** *A:* to instruct; to send word to (s.o.); **m. à qn de faire qch.,** to instruct s.o. to do sth.; **m. qu'on fasse préparer une chambre,** to send word, send orders, that a room be made ready. **3.** *O: & Lit:* to summon (s.o. to attend); to send for (subordinate); *Jur:* to summon (witness, etc.) to appear; **m. qn d'urgence,** to send for s.o. urgently.

mandibulaire [mɑ̃dibylɛːr], *a.* mandibular.

mandibule [mɑ̃dibyl], *s.f. Z:* mandible.

mandibulé [mɑ̃dibyle], *a.* mandibulate.

mandille [mɑ̃diːj], **mandole** [mɑ̃dɔl], *s.f. A.Mus:* mandola, mandora.

mandoline [mɑ̃dɔlin], *s.f.* **1.** *Mus:* mandoline. **2.** *Cu:* mandolin(e), vegetable slicer or shredder.

mandoliniste [mɑ̃dɔlinist], *s.m. & f.* mandolin player, mandolinist.

mandore [mɑ̃dɔːr], *s.f. A.Mus:* mandola, mandora.

mandorle [mɑ̃dɔrl̥], *s.f. Art:* mandorla.

mandragore [mɑ̃dragɔːr], *s.f. Bot:* mandragora, mandrake.

mandre [mɑ̃dr̥], *s.f.* (*in Eastern Church*) (*a*) monastery; (*b*) anchorite's grotto, cell.

mandrill [mɑ̃driːj], *s.m. Z:* mandrill.

mandrin[1] [mɑ̃drɛ̃], *s.m.* **1.** *Mec.E:* (*a*) mandrel (of lathe); **m. de fraisage,** cutter arbor, cutter spindle; (*b*) chuck, face plate (of lathe); **m. à commande pneumatique,** pneumatic chuck; **m. à griffes,** claw chuck, dog chuck; **m. à mâchoires, à mordaches, à mors,** jaw chuck; **m. à trois mordaches, à trois mors,** three-jaw chuck; **m. à pointes,** fork, prong, spur, chuck; **m. à vis,** bell, screw, chuck; **m. à quatre vis,** four-screw bell chuck; **m. de serrage,** clamp chuck; **m. porte-foret,** drill chuck; (*c*) **m. de vilebrequin,** pad of a brace. **2.** *Metalw:* (*a*) mandrel, swage; (*Riveting*) **m. d'abattage,** holding-up hammer; dolly; snap tool; (*b*) punch; (*Riveting*) drift; (*c*) tube beader; expander. **3.** *Exp:* tamping iron, bar.

mandrin[2], *s.m.* bandit, ruffian (from Mandrin, a bandit executed in 1755).

mandrinage [mɑ̃drinaːʒ], *s.m. Mec.E:* **1.** chucking (of work on the lathe). **2.** drifting (of holes). **3.** swaging (of iron). **4.** expanding, beading (of boiler tube).

mandriner [mɑ̃drine], *v.tr.* **1.** to chuck (work on the lathe). **2.** to drift (rivet holes). **3.** to swage (iron). **4.** to expand, bead, open out (pipe, tube, etc.).

mandrineur [mɑ̃drinœːr], *s.m. Mec.E:* (*pers.*) (*a*) chucker; (*b*) drifter; (*c*) swager.

mandrite [mɑ̃drit], *s.m.* (*in Eastern church*) (*a*) monk; (*b*) anchorite.

manducation [mɑ̃dykasjɔ̃], *s.f.* (*a*) mastication; (*b*) *Ecc:* manducation (of the Eucharist, of the Paschal Lamb).

Mané, Thécel, Pharès [mane tesɛl farɛs], *B:* mene, tekel, upharsin.

manéage [maneaːʒ], *s.m. Nau:* unpaid overtime work (loading or unloading).

manécanterie [manekɑ̃tri], *s.f.* choir school (attached to a church).

manège [manɛːʒ], *s.m.* **1.** (*a*) horsemanship, riding; riding-school equitation; manege; **maître de m.,** riding master; ringmaster (of circus); (*b*) training, breaking (in) (of a horse); (*c*) (i) **(salle de) m.,** riding school; manege; **m. découvert,** open-air riding school; (ii) (*in circus*) ring; (*d*) **m. (de chevaux de bois),** merry-go-round, round about. **2.** wile, stratagem, trick; **je connais bien ses manèges,** I know his little goings on, his little tricks; **j'observais leur m.,** I was watching their little game; I noticed how they were carrying on; *A:* **réussir à force de m.,** to succeed by dint of intrigue. **3.** *A:* horse-gear, horse-driven mill (for threshing, etc.); *Min:* whim(-gin); **m. à plan incliné,** (horse) treadmill.

manéger [maneʒe], *v.* (**je manège, n. manégeons; je manégeai(s); je manégerai**) **1.** *v.tr.* to train, to break (in) (horse). **2.** *v.i. O:* **m. de l'éventail,** to play, flirt, with one's fan; to flirt one's fan.

mânes [mɑːn], *s.m.pl. Rom.Ant:* manes, shades, spirits (of the departed).

manet [manɛ], *s.m. Fish:* entangling net, gill net.

maneton [mantɔ̃], *s.m. Mec.E:* **1.** crank pin (of crankshaft); *Aut: etc:* **m. (de vilebrequin),** throw. **2.** handle (of hand crank).

manette [manɛt], *s.f.* **1.** (*a*) handle, hand lever; *Aut:* **m. des gaz,** throttle lever; **m. d'avance à l'allumage,** ignition (advance-)lever; **m. du frein,** trigger of the hand brake; *El:* **m. de contact,** contact finger; (*b*) switch; key; (*c*) *Nau:* spoke (of the wheel). **2.** *Hort:* trowel.

manezingue [manzɛ̃ːg], *s.m. P: O:* (*a*) = publican, pub keeper; (*b*) = pub.

mangabey [mɑ̃gabɛ], *s.m. Z:* mangabey.

manganapatite [mɑ̃ganapatit], *s.f. Miner:* manganapatite.

manganate [mɑ̃ganat], *s.m. Ch:* manganate.

manganépidote [mɑ̃ganepidɔt], *s.f. Miner:* manganese epidote, piedmontite.

manganèse [mɑ̃ganɛːz], *s.m.* manganese; **acier au m.,** manganese steel.

manganésé [mɑ̃ganeze], *a. Ch:* containing manganese.

manganésien, -ienne [mɑ̃ganezjɛ̃, -jɛn], *a. Ch:* manganesian.

manganésifère [mɑ̃ganezifɛːr], *a.* manganiferous.

manganeux, -euse [mɑ̃ganø, -øːz], *a. Ch:* manganous.

manganine [mɑ̃ganin], *s.f. Metall:* manganin.

manganique [mɑ̃ganik], *a. Ch:* manganic.

manganisme [mɑ̃ganism], *s.m.* manganese poisoning.

manganite [mɑ̃ganit], *s.f.* **1.** *Ch:* manganite. **2.** *Miner:* manganite, grey manganese ore.

manganocalcite [mɑ̃ganɔkalsit], *s.f. Miner:* manganocalcite.

manganophyllite [mɑ̃ganɔfilit], *s.f. Miner:* manganophyllite.

manganosite [mɑ̃ganɔzit], *s.f. Miner:* manganosite.

manganostibite [mɑ̃ganɔstibit], *s.f. Miner:* manganostibite.

manganotantalite [mɑ̃ganɔtɑ̃talit], *s.f. Miner:* manganotantalite.

manganspath [mɑ̃ganspat], *s.m. Miner:* manganese spar, rhodochrosite.

mangeable [mɑ̃ʒabl̥], *a.* edible; **aliments à peine mangeables,** food that is hardly eatable, edible.

mangeaille [mɑ̃ʒɑːj], *s.f.* **1.** (soft) food; feed (for fowls, domestic animals). **2.** *F:* food, grub.

mangeant [mɑ̃ʒɑ̃], *a. A:* **être bien mangeant,** to be in good eating trim; to be blessed with a good appetite.

mange-boutou [mɑ̃ʒbutu], **mange-maillols** [mɑ̃ʒmajɔl], *s.m.inv. Ent: F: Dial:* grub of the long-horned beetle.

mangement [mɑ̃ʒmɑ̃], *s.m. F:* eating away (**de,** of); eating into (sth.); corrosion.

mange-mil [mɑ̃ʒmil], *s.m.inv. Orn: F:* **m.-m. africain,** red-tailed quelea.

mangeoire [mɑ̃ʒwaːr], *s.f.* **1.** manger. **2.** feeding trough.

mangeot(t)er [mɑ̃ʒɔte], *v.tr.* (*a*) to peck at (one's food); (*b*) to keep nibbling at (food).

manger [mɑ̃ʒe]. **I.** *v.tr.* (**je mangeai(s); n. mangeons**) **1.** (*a*) to eat; **il a tout mangé,** he's eaten (up) everything; **il mange de tout,** he'll eat anything; **mange ta soupe,** drink (up) your soup; *F:* **ça peut se m.,** that's quite good (to eat); *F:* **on en mangerait,** isn't it delicious, lovely! *pred.* **m. son pain sec,** to eat dry bread; **m. dans une assiette,** to eat out of, off, a plate; **m. dans l'argenterie,** to eat off plate, silver; **mangeons à la cuisine,** let's just eat, have a snack, in the kitchen; **les oiseaux lui mangent dans la main,** the birds eat, feed, out of his hand; **le fromage se mange avec du pain,** cheese is eaten with bread; **salle à m.,** dining room; **m. au restaurant,** (i) to have one's meals in a restaurant; (ii) to go out to a restaurant for a meal; **donner à m. à qn,** to give s.o. sth. to eat; to offer s.o. a meal; **donner à m. aux poules, aux chevaux,** to feed the chicken(s), the horses; *F:* **donner à m. aux poissons,** to be seasick, to feed the fishes; **voulez-vous à m.? voulez-vous m. qch.?** would you like sth. to eat? **m. avec grand appétit,** to eat heartily; *F:* **m. comme quatre, comme un ogre, comme un chancre,** to eat like a horse; **m. à son appétit, à sa faim,** to eat one's fill; **nous avons bien mangé** we ate very well; we had a very good meal; **restaurant où l'on mange bien,** restaurant where one eats well, where the cooking is good; restaurant with a reputation for good food, good cooking; **m. à se rendre malade,** to eat oneself sick; **bon à m.,** good to eat; *F:* **être bête à m. du foin,** to be completely stupid, as stupid as they make them; *F:* **il y a à boire et à m.,** (i) this soup, sauce, is on the thick side; (ii) it's not altogether bad; it's like the curate's egg; **m. son pain blanc**

le premier, to start with the best, the easiest, part of a job; **m. du curé,** to be violently anti-clerical, to be a priest-hater; *F:* **on ne vous mangera pas,** (don't be afraid) they won't eat you; *s.a.* BLÉ 1, DENT 1, LÈVRE 1; (*b*) **la rouille mange l'acier,** rust eats into steel; **mangé des vers,** wormeaten; **mangé par les, aux, mites,** motheaten; **m. le chemin,** to eat up the miles; **chemin mangé d'herbes,** path overgrown with weeds; **tête mangée de poux,** head alive with lice; **chaudière qui mange beaucoup de charbon,** boiler that devours coal; **m. ses mots,** (i) to mumble, to speak indistinctly; (ii) to clip one's words; **l'e muet se mange devant une voyelle,** e mute is elided before a vowel; *F:* **m. la consigne,** to forget one's orders; *F:* **m. qn des yeux,** to devour s.o. with one's eyes; **m. qn de caresses,** to smother s.o. with caresses, *F:* to slobber over (a child); **n'allez pas me m.!** don't snap my head off! **il avait l'air de vouloir me m.,** he looked ferociously at me; *P:* **m. le morceau,** (i) to own up (to a crime), to make a clean breast of it; (ii) to turn informer, to split, to squeal; (iii) to let out a secret; *F:* **m. de la prison,** to do time, to do a stretch; (*c*) **m. son argent,** to squander, *F:* blue, one's money; **m. le dernier sou à qn,** to eat s.o. out of house and home. **2.** *Nau:* (*a*) to gall, fret (rope); (*b*) (*of ship*) **être mangé par la mer,** to be buffeted by the sea. **3.** *Nau:* **m. le vent à un navire,** to blanket, wrong, a ship.

II. **manger,** *s.m.* (*a*) eating; **en perdre le boire et le m.,** to be completely absorbed in sth.; (*b*) food; (*of medicine*) **à prendre après m.,** to be taken after meals, after food.

mangerie [mɑ̃ʒri], *s.f. F:* **1.** (*a*) gorging, guzzling; (*b*) gorge, guzzle, blowout. **2.** *A:* (*a*) extortion (of taxes, etc.); (*b*) devouring (of one race by another, etc.).

mange(-)tout [mɑ̃ʒtu], *s.m.inv.* **1.** *Hort:* (*a*) sugar pea, *U.S:* string pea; (*b*) French bean, *U.S:* string bean. **2.** *F:* squanderer, spendthrift.

mangeur, -euse [mɑ̃ʒœːr, -øːz], *s.* (*a*) eater; **petit m.,** small eater; **gros m.,** large eater, good trencherman; **c'est un gros m.,** he's got a huge appetite; **m. de pommes,** Norman; **m. de rosbif,** Englishman; (*b*) **m. (d'argent),** spendthrift; (*c*) **m. de curés,** violent anticlerical; **m. de livres,** bookworm; **m. de kilomètres,** speed merchant; *Nau:* **m. d'écoute,** old salt; (*d*) *Orn: F:* **m. de noyaux,** grosbeak; **m. de poivre,** toucan; (*e*) *Z:* **m. d'hommes,** man-eating tiger, man-eater; **m. de fourmis,** (i) anteater; (ii) great anteater; (iii) guinea-pig.

mangeure [mɑ̃ʒyːr], *s.f.* **1.** place nibbled, eaten (by insects, mice); **étoffe criblée de mangeures,** motheaten cloth, cloth riddled with moth. **2.** food, feeding place of (i) wild boar, (ii) wolf.

mangle [mɑ̃ːgl̩], *s.f. Bot:* (*a*) mangrove fruit; (*b*) mangrove (tree); **forêt de mangles,** mangrove swamp.

manglier [mɑ̃glije], *s.m. Bot:* mangrove (tree), mangle; **écorce de m.,** mangle bark, mangrove bark.

mangonneau, -eaux [mɑ̃gɔno], *s.m. A.Arms:* mangonel.

mangoustan [mɑ̃gustɑ̃], *s.m. Bot:* mangosteen (fruit).

mangoustanier [mɑ̃gustanje], *s.m. Bot:* mangosteen (tree).

mangouste[1] [mɑ̃gust], *s.f. Bot:* mangosteen (fruit).

mangouste[2], *s.f. Z:* mongoose; **m. zébrée,** striped mongoose; **m. crabière,** crab-eating mongoose; **m. des marais,** marsh mongoose.

mangrove [mɑ̃grɔv], *s.f.* mangrove swamp.

mangue[1] [mɑ̃ːg], *s.f. Bot:* mango (fruit).

mangue[2], *s.f. Z:* mangue.

manguier [mɑ̃gje], *s.m. Bot:* mango (tree); **m. du Gabon,** oba, (African) bread tree.

maniabilité [manjabilite], *s.f.* **1.** handiness (of tool, ship, etc.). **2.** controllability, manœuvrability (of aircraft, etc.); handling ability (of vehicle, machine, etc.). **3.** *Civ.E:* workability (of concrete).

maniable [manjabl̩], *a.* manageable, easy to handle, to control; controllable, manœuvrable (aircraft, etc.); **caractère m.,** tractable nature; **langue m.,** flexible language; **drap, cuir, m.,** workable cloth, leather; **cordage m.,** supple rope; **outil, vaisseau, m.,** handy tool, ship; **peu m.,** unhandy (tool, ship); awkward (tool); **fer m.,** easily wrought iron; *Nau:* **temps, mer, m.,** moderate weather, moderate sea; **mer peu m.,** rough sea; **brise m.,** commanding breeze.

maniacal, -aux [manjakal, -o], *a.* maniacal.

maniaco-dépressif, -ive [manjakɔdeprɛsif, -iːv], *a.* **psychose maniaco-dépressive,** manio-depressive psychosis; *pl. maniaco-dépressifs, -ives.*

maniant [manjɑ̃], *a.* (*of cloth*) having a soft feel, soft to the touch, pleasant to the hand.

maniaque [manjak], *a. & s.* **1.** maniac, raving mad(man, -woman). **2.** finical, finicky, faddy (person); *s.* fuss-pot, crank; **m. de la perfection,** perfectionist.

maniaquerie [manjakri], *s.f. F:* **1.** finicalness, faddiness. **2.** (*a*) mania; fad; (*b*) *pl.* fads.

maniaquement [manjakmɑ̃], *adv.* in a fussy, finicky, manner.

manichéen, -éenne [maniʃeɛ̃, -eɛn, -ik-], *a. & s. Rel.H:* Manich(a)ean; *s.* Manichee.

manichéisme [maniʃeism, -ik-], *s.m. Rel.H:* Manich(a)eism.

manicle [manikl̩], *s.f.* = MANIQUE.

manic(h)ordion [manikɔrdjɔ̃], **manicorde** [manikɔrd], *s.m. A.Mus:* manichord(on).

manicure [manikyːr], *s.m. & f. A:* manicurist.

manidés [manide], *s.m.pl. Z:* Manidae.

manie [mani], *s.f.* (*a*) *Med: A:* mental derangement; (*b*) *Med:* mania, obsession; **m. de la persécution,** persecution mania; (*c*) mania; craze; (inveterate) habit; idiosyncrasy; **avoir la m. de la propreté,** to be obsessed with the idea of cleanliness; **avoir la m. des tableaux,** to be mad on pictures, to have a craze for pictures; **il a la m. d'écrire,** he's an inveterate writer, he's for ever writing, scribbling; **il a la m. de bricoler,** he's always doing some odd job or other; he can't stop doing (little) odd jobs; **il a ses petites manies,** he's full of (little) fads; **ses manies de célibataire,** his bachelor habits, ways; **la m. lui prit de . . .,** he became obsessed with the idea of. . . .

maniement [manimɑ̃], *s.m.* **1.** (*a*) feeling, handling (of cloth, etc.); (*b*) management, handling (of tools, business, people, etc.); conduct (of affairs); **recouvrer le m. de ses membres,** to recover the use of one's limbs; **le m. des armes,** the handling of arms; *Mil:* **m. d'armes,** drill; arms' manual; **m. du fusil,** rifle drill manual; rifle drill; **m. du sabre,** sword drill; **m. des deniers publics,** handling, care, of public money; **caisse qui a un m. considérable,** counting-house that handles a lot of money. **2.** *pl. Husb:* points (on fatstock, for checking their condition).

manier [manje]. I. *v.tr.* (*p.d. & pr.sub.* **n. maniions, v. maniiez**) **1.** to feel (cloth, etc.); to handle (tool, rope, etc.); *Fb:* **ballon manié,** hand ball. **2.** to handle (affair); to wield (sword, pen); to handle, manage, control (horse, machine, business, people); to handle (ship); **cheval qui se manie bien,** horse easy to handle; **m. les avirons,** to ply, pull, the oars; **savoir m. la parole,** to know how to handle words; *Cu:* **m. du beurre et de la farine,** to rub the butter into the flour; *Const:* **m. la toiture,** to repair the roof; *Civ.E:* **m. le pavage,** to repave; to relay the paving.

II. **manier,** *s.m.* feel (of cloth); **juger au m.,** to judge by the feel.

manière [manjɛːr], *s.f.* **1.** (*a*) manner, way; **m. de faire qch.,** way, manner, of doing sth.; **m. d'être,** state, condition; **c'est sa m. d'être,** that's the sort of man he is; **ce n'est pas ma m. à moi,** that's not my way of doing things; **laissez-moi faire à ma m.,** let me do it my own way; **il est heureux à sa m.,** he is happy in his own way; **tout homme a sa m. de voir, de penser,** every man has his own way of looking at things; **s'y prendre de la bonne m.,** to set about it the right way; **d'une m. adroite,** in a skilful manner, skilfully; (*of doctor*) **avoir une bonne m. professionnelle,** to have a good bedside manner; **de cette m.,** thus, in this way; *F:* **tancer qn de la belle m.,** to give s.o. a good dressing-down, to put s.o. in his place; **de m. ou d'autre, d'une m. ou d'une autre,** somehow or other, by some means or other, by hook or by crook; **commission constituée de la m. suivante,** commission set up on the following lines; **par, en, m. de consolation,** by way of consolation; **en quelque m.,** in a way; *F:* **c'est une m. d'artiste,** he is by way of being an artist; he's a sort of artist; **d'une m. générale,** generally speaking; **d'aucune m.,** under no circumstances; **de toute m.,** in any case; **feu établi de m. à projeter un rayon,** light so constructed as to throw a beam; **je me suis renseigné sur la m. d'envoyer un mandat,** I enquired how to send a postal order; *conj.phr.* **de la m. que,** as; **si les choses se sont passées de la m. que vous dites,** if things happened as you say; *conj.phr.* **de m. que** ((i) + *ind. indicating result,* (ii) + *sub. indicating purpose*), so that; **il a agi de m. que tout le monde a été content,** he acted in such a way that everyone was pleased; **agissez de m. qu'on n'en sache rien,** act so that nobody knows anything about it; *conj.phr.* **de m. à ce que le lecteur ne se méprenne point,** so that the reader should not misunderstand; *prep.phr.* **ne buvez pas de m. à vous faire enivrer,** don't drink so much that you get drunk; **agir de m. à se faire du mal,** to act in such a way that one hurts oneself, that one does oneself harm; (*b*) *Gram:* **adverbe de m.,** adverb of manner; (*c*) *Art: Lit:* manner, style; mannerism, **tableau à la m. de Degas,** painting after the manner of Degas; **cela ressemble à du Verdi de la première m.,** it sounds rather like Verdi in his early manner. **2.** (*a*) *pl.* manners; **avoir de bonnes, de belles, manières,** to be well-mannered; **avoir de mauvaises manières,** to be ill-mannered; (*to child*) **n'oublie pas tes bonnes manières,** don't forget your manners; (*b*) *F:* **faire des manières,** (i) to be affected; (ii) to pretend reluctance; **il ne fit pas de manières pour accepter,** he made no bones about accepting; he accepted without having to be asked twice; *F:* **trêve de manières!** stop beating about the bush! get down to it! get it out!

maniéré [manjere], *a.* **1.** affected (person, behaviour, etc.). **2.** *Art: Lit:* mannered (style).

maniérer [manjere], *v.tr.* (**je manière, n. maniérons; je maniérerai**) *Art: Lit:* **m. son style,** to introduce mannerisms into one's style, one's art.

maniérisme [manjerism], *s.m.* **1.** *Art: Lit:* mannerism. **2.** affectation, affectedness.

maniériste [manjerist], *s.m. & f. Art: Lit:* mannerist.

manieur, -euse [manjœːr, -øːz], *s.* handler, manager, controller (of men, business, etc.); *esp. Pej:* **m. d'argent,** (i) financier; (ii) (shady) company promoter.

manif [manif], *s.f. P:* (= *manifestation*) demo.

manifestant, -ante [manifestɑ̃, -ɑ̃ːt], *s. Pol: etc:* demonstrator.

manifestation [manifɛstasjɔ̃], *s.f.* (*a*) manifestation (of feeling, etc.); **m. de sympathie,** celebration (on occasion of promotion, retirement, etc.); (*b*) **première m. d'une épidémie,** outbreak of an epidemic; *Min:* **m. de pétrole,** occurrence of oil; (*c*) *Theol:* revelation; (*d*) (political) demonstration; **m. collective,** mass demonstration; (*e*) **m. sportive,** sporting event.

manifeste[1] [manifɛst], *a.* **1.** manifest, evident, patent, obvious, clear, plain (truth, etc.); palpable (error). **2.** *Jur:* overt (act).

manifeste[2], *s.m.* **1.** manifesto, proclamation. **2.** *Nau:* **m. du chargement,** ship's manifest; **m. d'entrée, de sortie,** inward, outward, manifest.

manifestement [manifestəmɑ̃], *adv.* **1.** manifestly, obviously, patently, visibly, clearly, plainly; palpably; **son témoignage est m. faux,** his evidence is clearly false. **2.** *Jur:* overtly.

manifester [manifeste], *v.tr.* **1.** to manifest, reveal; to evince (opinion); **m. sa joie, sa douleur,** to express, show, one's joy, one's grief; to give vent to one's grief; **m. de la confusion,** to show, exhibit, confusion; **m. sa volonté,** make one's wishes clear; **il ne manifesta en aucune façon avoir rien entendu,** he gave no sign of having heard anything. **2.** *abs.* to make a public demonstration, to demonstrate.

se manifester, to appear; **le démon se manifesta sous l'apparence de . . .,** the demon appeared to him in the guise, the form, of . . .; **leur impatience se manifestait par de bruyantes interruptions,** their impatience showed itself in loud interruptions; *Tp:* **lorsque la téléphoniste se manifeste,** when the operator answers; **il ne s'est pas encore manifesté,** he hasn't got in touch with me yet.

manifold [manifɔld], *s.m.* duplicate book.

manigance [manigɑ̃ːs], *s.f. F:* (*a*) intrigue, piece of wire-pulling; **il y a quelque m. sous roche,** there's some underhand work going on; (*b*) *pl.* underhand practices, meddling; *Pol:* gerrymandering.

manigancer [manigɑ̃se], *v.tr.* (**je manigançai(s); n. manigançons**) *F:* to scheme, to plot; to work (sth.) underhand; **voilà donc ce que vous manigancez!** so that's your little game! **qu'est-ce qu'ils manigancent?** what are they up to? **il se manigance quelque chose,** there's dirty work afoot; **m. une élection,** to rig an election.

maniguette [manigɛt], *s.f.* malaguetta pepper, grains of paradise.

manillage [manijaːʒ], *s.m.* shackling (of chains).

Manille[1] [maniːj]. **1.** *Pr.n. Geog:* Manilla; **chanvre de M.,** Manil(l)a hemp. **2.** *s.m.* (*a*) Manil(l)a (cheroot); (*b*) Manil(l)a straw hat. **3.** *s.f.* Manil(l)a rope.

manille[2], *s.f. Cards:* (*a*) manille (in games of manille, ombre, etc.); (*b*) (French game of) manille.

manille[3], *s.f.* **1.** (*a*) manilla, anklet; (*b*) *A:* (convict's) shackle. **2.** shackle, connecting link (of chain); **m. d'assemblage, d'ajust, de jonction,** connecting, joiner, shackle; **m. d'extrémité,** end shackle; **m. à vis forme D,** screwed D shackle; **m. à vis forme lyre,** screwed harp shackle; **m. d'affourche, d'affourchage,** joggle shackle; **m. de corps mort,** rocking shackle.

maniller[1] [manije], *v.tr.* to shackle (chains).

maniller[2], *v.i. Cards:* to play manille.

manillon [manijɔ̃], *s.m. Cards:* ace (at manille).

maniluve [manilyːv], *s.m. Med: A:* manuluvium, hand bath.

manîment [manimɑ̃], *s.m. A:* = MANIEMENT.

manioc [manjɔk], *s.m. Bot:* manioc, cassava.

manipulaire [manipylɛːr]. *Rom.Mil:* **1.** *a.* manipular (standard, etc.). **2.** *s.m.* manipular.

manipulateur, -trice [manipylatœːr, -tris], *s.* **1.** (*a*) manipulator; operator; handler (of money, goods, etc.); *Bank:* cashier, teller; **m. de laboratoire,** laboratory assistant; **m. radiographe,** radiographer; (*b*) conjuror. **2.** *s.m.* (*a*) *Mec.E: Atom.Ph:* manipulator; **m. à distance,** remote(-control) manipulator; **m. asservi,** master-slave manipulator; **m. sous eau,** underwater manipulator; (*b*) *Tg:* (signalling, sending) key; *W.Tel: etc:* **m. automatique,** automatic sender.

manipulation [manipylasjɔ̃], *s.f.* **1.** (*a*) manipulation; handling; **m. brutale,** rough handling; (*b*) *Tg: W.Tel:* keying; **table de m.,** operating table; **vitesse de m.,** keying speed; **m. par relais, par tube,** relay, tube, keying; (*c*) *Med:* manipulation. **2.** *Sch: pl.* practical work (*esp.* in chemistry, physics); **cahier de manipulations,** practical notebook. **3.** conjuring.

manipule [manipyl], *s.m.* **1.** *Rom.Ant: Ecc:* maniple. **2.** *Pharm:* handful (of herbs).

manipuler [manipyle], *v.tr.* **1.** to manipulate; to handle (apparatus, etc.); *Tg:* to operate; **m. avec soin,** handle with care; **m. les fils d'une marionnette,** to pull the puppet strings. **2.** *Pej:* to manipulate (accounts, business deal); to rig (election); to manœuvre (sth.). **3.** *abs. Sch:* to carry out experiments, do practical work (in chemistry, etc.).

manipuleur, -euse [manipylœːr, -øːz], *s. F: Pej:* wire-puller; gerrymanderer.

manique [manik], *s.f.* **1.** *Rom.Ant:* manica. **2.** (*a*) (workman's) protective gloves; hand-leather (of shoemaker, etc.); **homme de la m.,** cobbler; (*b*) (*Archery*) brace. **3.** *A:* trade, profession.

manitou [manitu], *s.m.* **1.** Manitou (of American Indians). **2.** *F:* **(grand) m.,** big boss, big shot; **être le m. de l'affaire,** to run, boss, the show.

maniveau, -eaux [manivo], *s.m.* display basket, tray (for fruit, etc.); punnet.

manivelle [manivɛl], *s.f. Mec.E:* **1.** (*a*) crank; **m. à plateau, plateau m.,** disc crank, wheel crank; **arbre à une seule m., à deux manivelles,** single-throw, double-throw, crankshaft; **bras de m.,** crank arm; **course de m.,** crank throw; (*b*) pedal crank (of bicycle). **2.** crank (handle); *Aut:* starting handle, *F:* handle; **démarrer, mettre (le moteur) en marche, à la m.,** to crank up the engine, to start the engine by hand; **m. (de manœuvre) de la glace latérale,** window hand crank; *Artil: etc:* **m. de pointage,** elevating crank, handle; *Cin: F:* **donner le premier tour de m.,** to start shooting.

manjac, manjak [mɑ̃ʒak], *s.m. Miner:* manjak (bitumen).

manne[1] [man], *s.f.* **1.** *B:* manna. **2.** *Pharm:* **m. du frêne,** manna; **m. en larmes,** manna in tears; **m. en sortes,** manna in sorts.

manne[2], *s.f.* basket, hamper, crate; **m. à charbon,** coal basket; *Min:* corf; **m. à lessive,** washing basket; **m. d'enfant,** baby's wicker cradle; bassinet; **m. à marée,** fishwife's creel.

mannée [mane], *s.f.* basketful, hamperful.

manne-lichen [manlikɛn], *s.f. Moss:* manna lichen; *pl. manne-lichens.*

mannequin[1] [mankɛ̃], *s.m.* small hamper; wicker crate.

mannequin[2], *s.m.* **1.** (anatomical) manikin. **2.** (*a*) *Art:* lay figure; *F:* **c'est un m.,** he's a mere puppet; (*b*) *Tail: Dressm:* dummy; dress stand; **cette robe est juste votre m.,** this dress is just your size; (*c*) *Agr:* scarecrow. **3.** mannequin; model; **m. de cabine,** permanent mannequin; **m. volant,** free-lance mannequin.

mannequiné [mankine], *a. Art:* stiff, lifeless (figure, etc.).

mannequiner [mankine], *v.tr. Art:* to pose (figures) in a stiff, unnatural, position.

mannette [manɛt], *s.f.* small crate.

mannezingue [manzɛ̃ːg], *s.m. P: O:* (*a*) = publican, pub keeper; (*b*) = pub.

mannide [manid], *s.m. Ch:* mannide.

mannipare [manipaːr], *a. Ent:* manniferous.

mannitane [manitan], *s.m. Ch:* mannitan.

mannite [manit], *s.f.,* **mannitol** [manitɔl], *s.m. Ch:* mannite, mannitol, manna-sugar.

mannonique [manɔnik], *a. Ch:* mannonic.

mannoze [manoːz], *s.m. Ch:* mannose.

manodétendeur [manɔdetɑ̃dœːr], *s.m. Tchn:* (pressure) reducing valve.

manœuvrabilité [manœvrabilite], *s.f.* manœuvrability.

manœuvrable [manœvrabl̥], *a.* manœuvrable; manageable.

manœuvrant [manœvrɑ̃], *a.* (*of ship*) under way, able to steer; **navire bien m.,** ship easy to manœuvre, easy to handle.

manœuvre [manœːvr̥]. **1.** *s.f.* (*a*) working, managing, driving (of machine, etc.); **m. à bras,** working by hand; **tringle de m.,** control rod, operating rod; **poste de m.,** control station; *Nau:* **m. des ancres,** working of the anchors; **fausse m.,** false manœuvre, error of judgement, mistake (in handling piece of machinery, etc.); *Av:* **chariot de m.,** docking trolley; *Tp:* **signal de m.,** dialling tone; (*b*) *Nau:* handling, manœuvring (of ship); seamanship; **maître de m.,** boatswain; **navire qui n'est pas maître de sa m.,** ship not under command, not under control; *Navy:* **officier de m.,** officer of the deck; *Aut: etc:* **tableau de m.,** instrument panel; (*c*) *Mil: Navy:* (i) drill, exercise; **champ, terrain, de manœuvres,** drill ground; (ii) tactical exercise, manœuvre; **manœuvres de garnison,** garrison field day; **grandes manœuvres,** army manœuvres; **troupes en m.,** troops on manœuvres; **m. à double action,** two-sided manœuvre; **m. avec tir réel,** firing manœuvres; **m. de nuit,** night training; **m. sur la carte,** map manœuvre; **manœuvres aériennes,** air manœuvres; **critique de la m.,** post mortem, *U.S:* critique; **réglement de m.,** drill regulations; *Navy:* **manœuvres d'escadre,** fleet manœuvres; (*d*) *Mil: Navy:* movement, action; **m. de débordement,** outflanking movement; **m. d'encerclement,** encircling movement; **m. de flanc,** flanking action; **pivot de m.,** pivot of manœuvre; **liberté de m.,** freedom of action, of manœuvre; (*e*) *Rail:* shunting, marshalling (of trains); **locomotive de m.,** shunting engine, *U.S:* switching engine, switcher; **voie de m.,** shunting track; *U.S:* switching track; **m. au lancé,** fly shunting; **m. par (la) gravité,** shunting by gravitation; **équipe de m.,** shunting gang; **gare de m.,** sorting, siding, depot; (*f*) *Pej:* scheme, manœuvre, intrigue; **m. électorale,** vote-catching manœuvre; **c'est une fausse m. de sa part,** it's a false manœuvre, a wrong move, on his part; (*g*) *pl.* scheming; *Jur:* **manœuvres frauduleuses,** swindling; *Jur: Med:* **avortement provoqué par manœuvres criminelles,** illegal abortion; *Jur:* **manœuvres captatoires,** undue influence (upon testator). **2.** *s.f. Nau:* rope; **manœuvres,** rigging; **manœuvres dormantes,** standing rigging; **manœuvres courantes,** running rigging; *A.Aer:* **m. de retenue,** guy (for handling airship). **3.** *s.m.* (*a*) **m. (ordinaire),** unskilled labourer, unskilled worker; **m. spécialisé,** skilled worker; **m. de force,** heavy worker; **travail de m.,** manual labour; unskilled work; (*b*) *Pej:* hack (writer, artist); **ce n'est qu'un m.,** he's only a hack; (*c*) assistant (for literary, artistic, work).

manœuvrer [manœvre]. **1.** *v.tr.* (*a*) to work, operate, control (machine, pump, gun, etc.); to actuate (control mechanism); to shift (lever); **appareil facile à m.,** apparatus that works easily; (*b*) to manœuvre, handle (ship); **m. les voiles,** to work, handle, the sails; (*c*) *Rail:* to shunt; to marshal (trucks); (*d*) *Fish:* to play. **2.** *v.i.* (*a*) *Mil: Nau:* to manœuvre; **faire m. une armée, une flotte,** to manœuvre an army, a fleet; (*b*) to contrive, manœuvre, scheme.

manœuvrier, -ière [manœvrije, -ijɛːr]. **1.** *a.* (*a*) *Mil:* skilful in manœuvres; (*of troops*) highly trained; (*b*) *Nau:* clever, capable (seaman); **dextérité, habileté, manœuvrière,** skill in handling (*esp.* boat, ship); (*c*) *Nau:* handy (ship); easy to handle. **2.** *s.m.* (*a*) tactician; (*b*) expert seaman; (*c*) skilful (public) speaker; clever politician.

manographe [manɔgraf], *s.m. Tchn:* manograph.

manoir [manwaːr], *s.m.* (*a*) (feudal) manor; (*b*) country seat, manor house, country house; (*c*) *A:* (any) dwelling-house; **changer de m.,** to move one's place of residence; (*d*) *Poet: A:* **le m. sombre, le m. de Pluton,** the nether regions, the underworld; **le m. liquide,** the ocean.

manomètre [manɔmɛtr̥], *s.m.* manometer, pressure gauge; **m. étalon,** standard, master, pressure gauge; **m. à vapeur,** steam (pressure) gauge; **m. à plaque, à membrane,** diaphragm pressure gauge; **m. différentiel,** differential pressure gauge; **m enregistreur,** manograph; recording gauge; **m. de Bourdon,** Bourdon tube; *Aut:* **m. (de pression) d'huile,** oil (pressure) gauge.

manométrie [manɔmetri], *s.f. Ph:* manometry.

manométrique [manɔmetrik], *a. Ph:* manometric(al); **hauteur m.,** head of water.

manoque [manɔk], *s.f.* **1.** hank (of rope). **2.** hand (of tobacco leaves); plug (of tobacco).

manoquer [manɔke], *v.tr.* to put (tobacco) in hands, plugs.

manoscain, -aine, manosquin, -ine [manɔskɛ̃, -ɛn, -in], *a. & s. Geog:* (native, inhabitant) of Manosque.

manostat [manɔsta], *s.m. El:* manostat.

manoul [manul], *s.m. Z:* manul.

manouvrier, -ère [manuvrije, -ɛːr], *s. A:* day labourer; woman employed by the day.

manquant, -ante [mɑ̃kɑ̃, -ɑ̃ːt]. **1.** *a.* (*a*) missing, absent; (*b*) wanting, lacking; (*c*) *Com:* out of stock. **2.** *s.* (*a*) absentee; (*b*) *Mil: etc:* **les manquants,** the missing. **3.** *s.m.* deficiency; *Cust:* ullage; *Com:* **les manquants,** (the) shortages; **éviter des manquants dans la marchandise,** to prevent short delivery.

manque [mɑ̃ːk], *s.m.* **1.** lack, want; deficiency; shortage; **m. de place,** lack of space; **m. de respect,** lack of respect; disrespect (**envers,** to); **m. de cœur,** heartlessness; **m. de parole,** breach of faith; **je ne lui pardonne pas son m. de parole,** I can't forgive him for breaking his word; **m. de convenances,** breach of good manners; **m. de poids,** deficiency in weight, short weight; **m. à l'embarquement,** short-shipped (goods); **m. à la livraison,** short delivery; **dix kilos de m.,** ten kilos short; **suppléer à un m.,** to make good a deficiency; *Com:* **m. d'affaires,** slackness; slack market; *Com: Jur:* **m. à gagner,** (i) lost opportunity of doing business; (ii) slack period, period with no returns; (*of pers.*) **être de m.,** to be missing, absent; *prep.phr.* **(par) m. de,** for lack of, for want of (foresight, etc.); **m. de chance!** bad luck (for you, him)! **2.** (*a*) *Bill:* **m. de touche, m. à toucher,** miss; (*b*) *Equit:* slip, stumble (of horse); (*c*) *Typ:* defect (in printing); (*d*) *P:* **à la m.** (= RATÉ), feeble, poor; dud; **artiste à la m.,** would-be artist, dud artist; **c'est un . . . à la m.,** he is a wash-out, a dud, as a . . .. **3.** *A:* = MANQUEMENT.

manqué [mɑ̃ke], *a.* **1.** missed (opportunity, etc.); unsuccessful, abortive (attempt, etc.); **coup m.,** (i) miss, *F:* boss shot; (ii) failure; **vie manquée,** wasted life; **vêtement m.,** spoilt garment, misfit; *Ind:* **pièce manquée,** wastrel, waster. **2.** *F:* **c'est un médecin m.,** he ought to have been a doctor; **c'est un garçon m.,** she ought to have been a boy; she's a regular tomboy.

manquement [mɑ̃kmɑ̃], *s.m.* **1.** *A:* lack, want (of faith, etc.). **2.** failure, shortcoming, omission, lapse; **m. de mémoire,** lapse of memory; **m. à une règle,** violation of a rule; **m. à la discipline,** breach, infraction, of discipline, departure from discipline; **m. au devoir,** lapse from duty; **m. à l'amitié,** breach of friendship; **m. à l'appel,** failure to answer one's name, absence from roll-call; **m. aux devoirs de la profession,** unprofessional conduct.

manquer [mɑ̃ke]. I. *v.i.* **1.** (*a*) **m. de qch.,** to lack, want, be short of, sth.; **on ne manquait pas d'eau,** we were not short of water; there was no lack of water; we found no lack of water; **m. de sucre,** to be out, to have run short, of sugar; **je manque d'argent,** I am short of money; *Com:* **m. de disponibilités,** to be pressed for funds; **m. de politesse, de patience,** to be lacking in politeness, in patience; **m. de courage,** to lack courage; **m. de tout,** to be destitute (of everything); **m. de savoir-vivre,** to be wanting in manners; not to know how to behave; **ne m. de rien,** to lack nothing; (*b*) **m. de faire qch.,** narrowly to miss doing sth.; **il a manqué (de) tomber,** he nearly fell; **l'auto a manqué capoter,** the car was within an ace of turning completely over; (*c*) *impers.* **il s'en manque de beaucoup,** far from it; **il s'en est manqué de beaucoup qu'il gagnât la partie,** he was far from winning the match; **il s'en est manqué de peu qu'il ne gagnât la partie,** he very nearly won the match. **2.** to fail; (*a*) to be missing, lacking, deficient; **les vivres commencement à m.,** provisions are beginning to run short, to give out; **m. en magasin,** to be out of stock; **les mots me manquent pour exprimer . . .,** I am at a loss for words to express . . .; I have no words to express . . .; **la place me manque pour vous en écrire davantage,** I have no room to write more; *impers.* **il ne manque pas de candidats,** there is no lack of candidates; **il ne manquait plus que cela!** *F:* **(il ne) manquait plus que ça!** that's the last straw! that crowns all! **il ne manquerait plus que cela,** that would be the crowning mistake, the crowning offence, the last straw; **il manque quelques pages,** there are a few pages missing; **il n'en manque qu'une,** there is only one missing; **il lui manque un bras,** he has lost an arm; **il me manque dix francs,** I am ten francs short; **il manque 50 grammes au poids,** the weight is 50 grammes short; **remarquer qu'il manque de l'argent, un prisonnier,** to miss money, a prisoner; to notice that there is money, a prisoner, missing; (*b*) to give way; **le cœur lui manqua,** his heart failed him; **la respiration commençait à me m.,** I was beginning to have difficulty in breathing; **prenez garde que le pied ne vous manque,** take care you don't miss your footing; **la planche manqua sous nos pieds, nous manqua sous les pieds,** the plank gave way under our feet; **la maison commençait à m. par les fondements,** the foundations of the house were giving way; (*c*) (*of pers.*) to be absent, missing; **m. à l'appel,** to be absent from roll-call; **m. à un rendez-vous,** to fail to keep an appointment; **m. à qn,** to be missed by s.o.; **comme tu nous manques!** how we miss you! **si votre père venait à vous m.,** if your father should be taken (from you); (*d*) to fall short; **m. à son devoir,** to fall short of, to fail in, to shirk, one's duty; **m. à sa parole,** to break one's word; to go back on one's word; **ne manquez pas à votre promesse, à votre parole,** don't break your promise, your word; don't disappoint me; **m. à l'amitié,** to fail to help a friend; to let a friend down; **m. à la politesse,** to commit a breach of (good) manners; to be impolite, rude; **il n'a pas manqué à sa destinée,** he did not fail to accomplish his destiny; **m. à la consigne,** to disregard orders; **m. à une règle,** to violate a rule; **m. à qn,** (i) to fail in one's duty to s.o., (ii) to be disrespectful to s.o.; **se m. à soi-même,** to do sth. derogatory to one's position, to do sth. infra dig; *Bill:* **m. de touche,** to miss; *abs.* **le fusil manqua,** the gun missed fire; **le projet, le coup, a manqué,** the plan, the attempt, proved a failure, miscarried; **le mariage a manqué,** the marriage didn't come off; (*e*) (i) **m. à, de, faire qch.,** to fail, omit, to do sth.; **ne manquez pas de retenir vos places,** don't fail to book your seats; **ne manquez pas de nous écrire,** be sure to write to us, mind you write to us; **je n'y manquerai pas,** I shall not fail to do so; **personne ne peut m. d'avoir observé . . .,** no one can fail to have noticed . . .; **cela ne pouvait m. d'arriver,** it was bound to happen; (ii) to fail (in one's endeavour) to do sth.; *Nau:* **m. à virer,** to miss stays; **l'obus manqua à éclater,** the shell failed to explode, was a dud; (*f*) *Com:* to fail in business, go bankrupt.

II. **manquer,** *v.tr.* **1.** (*a*) to miss (target, train, etc.); **j'ai manqué le train de trois minutes,** I missed the train by three minutes; **m. une occasion,** to lose, miss, let slip, an opportunity; to let an opportunity go by; **m. un mariage, une affaire,** to miss one's chance of getting married, of doing business; **m. son coup,** (i) to miss one's aim; to strike, shoot, wide of the mark; to miss one's blow, one's stroke, one's shot; (ii) to make an abortive attempt; to fail; **il ne manque jamais son coup,** (i) he never misses, he is a dead shot; (ii) he never fails; **il l'a manqué belle,** (i) he missed a splendid chance, (ii) he had a narrow escape; *Golf: etc:* **m. un coup,** to fluff a shot; (*b*) **il ne manque jamais une première,** he never fails to attend, never misses, a first night; **pourquoi avez-vous manqué l'office?** why weren't you at church? why did you miss church? **2. m. sa vie,** to wreck one's life; **m. un tableau,** to make a failure of, to spoil, a picture.

manrèse [mɑ̃rɛːz], *s.m. Ecc:* retreat.

mansard [mɑ̃saːr], *s.m. Orn: F:* wood pigeon.

mansarde [mɑ̃sard], *s.f. Arch:* **1.** (*a*) **toit, comble, en m.,** mansard roof, curb roof; (*b*) **(fenêtre en) m.,** garret window, dormer window. **2.** attic, garret.

mansardé [mɑ̃sarde], *a.* mansard-roofed; **étage m.,** attic storey; **chambre mansardée,** attic; room with sloping ceiling.

mansart [mɑ̃saːr], *s.m. Orn: F:* wood pigeon.

manse [mɑ̃ːs], *s.m. Hist:* messuage; small manor.

mansion [mɑ̃sjɔ̃], *s.f.* **1.** *Rom.Ant:* post house, rest house, stage. **2.** *A.Th:* mansion. **3.** *Astr:* mansion (of the heavens).

mansuétude [mɑ̃sɥetyd], *s.f. Lit:* goodness (of heart); indulgence.

mantais, -aise [mɑ̃tɛ, -ɛːz], *a. & s.* (native, inhabitant) of Mantes (-la-Jolie).

mante[1] [mɑ̃ːt], *s.f. A.Cost:* (*a*) (woman's) cloak, mantle; (*b*) mourning veil.

mante[2], *s.f.* **1.** *Ent:* mantis; **m. religieuse,** praying mantis. **2.** (*a*) *Crust:* **m. de mer,** mantis shrimp, squill (fish); (*b*) *Ich:* manta ray, devil fish.

manteau, -eaux [mɑ̃to], *s.m.* **1.** (*a*) (i) cloak; (ii) (over)coat; *Mil:* greatcoat; **m. d'hiver,** winter coat; **m. de pluie,** raincoat; *A.Ecc.Cost:* **petit m.,** (abbé's) short cloak; *Th: A:* **jouer les manteaux,** to play serious, elderly, parts; *El.E:* **enroulement en m.,** barrel winding; **m. de neige,** mantle of snow; **avancer sous le m. de la nuit,** to advance under the cover of darkness; **sous le m. de la religion,** under the cover of religion; (*b*) *Z:* saddle (of dog, etc.); *Orn:* **goéland à m. gris,** grey-backed gull; (*c*) mantle (of mollusc); (*d*) *Geog:* **m. superficiel,** mantle; regolith; (*e*) *Her:* mantling, mantle. **2.** (*a*) **m. de cheminée,** mantelpiece; **faire qch. sous le m. (de la cheminée),** to do sth. clandestinely, secretly, sub rosa; (*b*) *Th:* **m. d'Arlequin,** proscenium arch. **3.** *Metall:* (*a*) casing, outer mould; (*b*) shell, mantle (of mould). **4.** *Bot:* **m. royal,** columbine.

mantelé [mɑ̃tle], *a.* **1.** *Orn:* hooded (crow). **2.** *Z:* saddled. **3.** *Her:* mantellé, mantled.

mantelet [mɑ̃tlɛ], *s.m.* **1.** *Cost:* (*a*) *Ecc:* mantelletta; (*b*) (woman's) short cape; **m. de fourrure,** fur cape; *Bot: F:* **m. de dame,** lady's mantle. **2.** (*a*) *Harn:* (cart) saddle, pad; (*b*) *A.Veh:* carriage apron. **3.** (*a*) *A.Mil:* mantlet; embrasure shutter; (*b*) *Nau:* port lid, dead light; **m. d'écubier,** hawse flap.

mantelure [mɑ̃tlyːr], *s.f. Z:* saddle (of dog).

mantevillois, -oise [mɑ̃tvilwa, -waːz], *a. & s. Geog:* (native, inhabitant) of Mantes-la-Ville.

mantidés [mɑ̃tide], *s.m.pl. Ent:* Mantidae.

mantille [mɑ̃tiːj], *s.f. Cost:* mantilla.

Mantinée [mɑ̃tine], *Pr.n.f. A.Geog:* Mantinea.

mantique [mɑ̃tik], *s.f.* divination, soothsaying.

mantispe [mɑ̃tisp], *s.f. Ent:* mantispid.

mantisse [mɑ̃tis], *s.f. Mth:* mantissa (of logarithm).

mantouan, -ane [mɑ̃twɑ̃, -an], *a. & s. Geog:* Mantuan.

Mantoue [mɑ̃tu], *Pr.n. Geog:* Mantua.

Manuce [manys], *Pr.n.m. Typ.Hist:* Manutius, Manuzio.

manucode [manykɔd], *s.m. Orn:* **m. royal,** king bird of paradise.

manucodie [manykɔdi], **manucodia** [manykɔdja], *s.m. Orn:* manucodia.

manucure [manykyːr], *s.m. & f.* manicurist, manicure; **trousse de m.,** manicure set.

manucuré [manykyre], *a.* manicured.

manuel, -elle [manɥɛl]. **1.** (*a*) *a.* manual (labour, etc.); **habileté manuelle,** manual dexterity; handiness; (*b*) *s.m.* manual worker, *U.S:* blue collar. **2.** *s.m.* manual, handbook; text book (of a subject); **m. d'entretien,** maintenance instruction book.

manuélin [manɥelɛ̃], *a. Arch:* Manoeline.

manuellement [manɥɛlmɑ̃], *adv.* **1.** manually, with the hands; **travailler m.,** to do manual work; to work with one's hands. **2.** by hand.

manufacturable [manyfaktyrabl̩], *a.* manufacturable.

manufacture [manyfaktyːr], *s.f.* **1.** *A:* (*a*) manufacture, making; (*b*) manufactured article. **2.** *O:* factory; (textile, iron) mill; works; *still used in* **m. de porcelaines de Sèvres, de tapisseries des Gobelins, etc.,** Sèvres porcelain factory, Gobelins tapestry works, etc.

manufacturé [manyfaktyre], *a.* manufactured; factory-made.

manufacturer [manyfaktyre], *v.tr.* to manufacture.

manufacturier, -ière [manyfaktyrje, -jɛːr]. **1.** *a.* manufacturing (town, etc.). **2.** *s.* manufacturer; factory owner; factory manager.

manul [manyl], *s.m. Z:* manul.

manuluve [manylyːv], *s.m. Med: A:* manuluvium, hand bath.

manumission [manymisjɔ̃], *s.f.* manumission; freeing (of slave).

manuscrit [manyskri], *a. & s.m.* manuscript; **lettre manuscrite,** handwritten letter; **m. dactylographié,** typescript; **les Manuscrits de la mer Morte,** the Dead Sea scrolls.

manutention [manytɑ̃sjɔ̃], *s.f.* **1.** *A:* management, administration (of public money, business, etc.). **2.** (*a*) handling (of stores, materials, etc.); **appareils de m.,** handling machines, handling equipment; **appareils, dispositifs, de m. à distance,** remote-handling equipment; (*b*) working up (of tobacco). **3.** *Mil: Navy: A:* (*a*) storekeeping; (*b*) storehouse; stores; (*c*) bakery.

manutentionnaire [manytɑ̃sjɔnɛːr], *s.m. & f. Ind: etc:* warehouseman; handler; packer.

manutentionner [manytɑ̃sjɔne], *v.tr.* **1.** (*a*) to handle, manhandle (stores, materials); (*b*) to work up (tobacco). **2.** *Mil: Navy: A:* (*a*) to store; (*b*) to bake.

manuterge [manytɛrʒ], *s.m. Ecc:* (*R.C.Ch:*) manutergium.

maoïsme [maɔism], *s.m. Pol:* Maoism.

maoïste [maɔist], *a. & s.m. & f. Pol:* Maoist.

maori, -ie [maɔri], *a. & s. Ethn:* Maori; *s.m. Ling:* **le m.,** Maori.

maous, maousse [maus], *a. P:* (*a*) huge, enormous, tremendous, whacking great; (*b*) tremendously strong; (*c*) slap-up, stupendous.

mappe [map], *s.f.* sheet of squared paper (with latitude and longitude network for drawing maps).

mappemonde [mapmɔ̃ːd], *s.f.* map of the world in two hemispheres; **m. céleste,** map of the heavens, planisphere.

maque [mak], *s.m. Z:* Madagascar cat, lemur, macaco.

maqueraison [makrɛzɔ̃], *s.f. Fish:* mackerel-fishing season.

maquereau[1], **-eaux** [makro], *s.m. Ich:* mackerel; **m. bâtard,** scad, horse mackerel; **m. serpent,** snake mackerel.

maquereau[2], **-elle, -eaux, -elles** [makro, -ɛl], *s. P:* pimp, procurer; *f.* procuress; madame.

maquereautage [makrotaːʒ], *s.m. P:* pimping.

maquereautier [makrotje], *s.m. Fish:* mackerel boat.

maquerellage [makrɛlaːʒ], *s.m. P:* pimping.

maquette [makɛt], *s.f.* **1.** (*a*) *Sculp:* clay model; (*b*) *Art:* small figure (for arranging groups, etc.); (*c*) *Th:* model (of a stage setting); *Cin: T.V:* diorama; (*d*) *Publ:* (i) dummy (of book); (ii) lay-out (of page, etc.); (*e*) *Ind:* mock-up; (*f*) *Cin: etc:* miniature, model; **prise de vues avec maquettes,** miniature work, model work; (*g*) scale model; **m. (pour l'enseignement),** demonstration model; (*h*) *Dent:* **m. de cire,** wax model, pattern (of denture); **m. dentée,** wax-model denture. **2.** (*a*) *Metall:* bloom; (*b*) (*gun making*) skelp.

maquettiste [makɛtist], *s.m. & f.* model maker.

maquignon, -onne [makiɲɔ̃, -ɔn], *s.* (*the f. form is rare*) **1.** horse dealer, (horse) coper. **2.** *Pej:* (*a*) (shady) horse dealer, cattle dealer; (*b*) slick agent, go-between, horse trader.

maquignonnage [makiɲɔnaːʒ], *s.m.* **1.** (*a*) horse dealing; (*b*) horse faking; bishoping. **2.** sharp practice, tricky dealing, jobbery, horse-trading.

maquignonner [makiɲɔne], *v.tr.* **1.** to fake up, bishop (horse). **2.** to arrange (business, etc.) by sharp, tricky, practices; **affaire maquignonnée,** put-up job; horse trade.

maquillage [makijaːʒ], *s.m.* **1.** (*a*) making up (of one's face); disguising (of stolen car); (*b*) *Toil: Th: etc:* make-up. **2.** *Phot:* working up (of a negative). **3.** forging, faking; fiddling.

maquille [makiːj], *s.f.* marking (of playing cards).

maquiller [makije], *v.tr.* (*a*) to make up (face); (*b*) *Phot:* to work up (negative); (*c*) to get up, fake up (picture, etc.); *F:* to overface (a basket of apples, etc.); **m. un chèque,** to forge a cheque; **m. une voiture volée,** to disguise a stolen car; **m. la comptabilité,** to fiddle the accounts; **m. la vérité,** to distort the truth; (*d*) *Min:* **m. un puits, une mine,** to salt a well, a mine; (*e*) to mark (playing cards); (*f*) *abs. Mil: P:* to sham sick.

se maquiller, to make up (one's face).

maquilleur[1], **-euse** [makijœːr, -øːz], *s.* (*a*) *Th:* maker-up; make-up man; (*b*) faker-up (of stolen car); (*c*) forger, cheat; fiddler (of accounts).

maquilleur[2], *s.m. Fish:* mackerel boat.

maquis [maki], *s.m.* (*a*) *Geog:* maquis, (Mediterranean) scrub, brush; (*b*) *Pol:* (*esp. 1939-45 war*) maquis, underground forces; **le maquis norvégien,** the Norwegian underground forces; **prendre le m.,** to go underground, to take to the maquis; (*c*) **le m. de la procédure,** the jungle (growth) of legal procedure.

maquisard [makizaːr], *s.m.* (*1939-45 war*); man of the maquis, maquisard.

mara [mara], *s.m. Z:* mara, Patagonian hare, Salinas con(e)y.

marabout [marabu], *s.m.* **1.** (*a*) marabout (priest or shrine); (*b*) *F: A:* ugly, misshapen man; figure of fun. **2.** (*a*) *A:* (round-bodied) jug; (*b*) *Dial: F:* (*in Algeria*) bell tent. **3.** (*a*) *Orn:* marabou (stork); **m. des Indes,** adjutant bird; (*b*) marabou (feathers). **4.** *Tex:* marabou (silk).

maraîchage [marɛʃa:ʒ], *s.m.* market gardening, *U.S:* truck gardening, truck farming.

maraîcher, -aîchère [mareʃe, -ɛʃɛ:r]. **1.** *a.* (*a*) pertaining to marshland; (*b*) **industrie maraîchère,** market-gardening (industry), *U.S:* truck farming, truck gardening; **jardin m.,** market garden, *U.S:* truck garden, truck farm; **produits maraîchers,** market-garden produce, *U.S:* truck. **2.** *s.* market gardener, *U.S:* truck gardener, truck farmer.

maraîchin, -ine [marɛʃɛ̃, -in], *a. & s. Geog:* (native, inhabitant) of the Marais (of Poitou or Brittany).

marais [marɛ], *s.m.* **1.** (*a*) marsh(land); bog, fen; water-meadow land; swamp, morass; **m. tourbeux,** peat bog; **gaz des m.,** marsh gas; (*b*) **m. salant,** salt-marsh; (*c*) *Pr.n.m. Geog:* **le M.,** (i) the Marais (in the Deux-Sèvres); (ii) the Marais (old quarter of Paris); (*d*) slough (of political life, etc.). **2.** market garden.

marantacées [marɑ̃tase], *s.f.pl. Bot:* Marantaceae.

marante [marɑ̃:t], *s.f. Bot:* maranta; arrowroot.

marasme[1] [marasm], *s.m.* (*a*) *Med:* marasmus, wasting; tabes; (*b*) **les affaires sont dans le m.,** business is in a state of stagnation, in a bad way; **le m. des affaires,** the stagnation, slackness, of business, the slump in business; **commerce dans le m.,** stagnating business; (*c*) depression (of mind).

marasme[2], *s.m. Fung:* marasmius.

marasque [marask], *s.f.* marasca (cherry).

marasquin [maraskɛ̃], *s.m.* maraschino (liqueur).

Marathon [maratɔ̃]. **1.** *Pr.n. A.Geog:* Marathon. **2.** *s.m. Sp:* marathon (race); long-distance race; **m. de danse,** dancing marathon; **m. oratoire,** marathon speech; **m. diplomatique,** diplomatic marathon.

marathonien, -ienne [maratɔnjɛ̃, -jɛn], *a. & s. A.Geog:* Marathonian.

marâtre [marɑ:tr̥], *s.f.* (unnatural, cruel) stepmother, mother; (*of woman*) **être une m. pour qn,** to treat s.o. harshly, unkindly; to be unkind to s.o.; **la nature est m. en ces climats,** nature is harsh, unkind, in this part of the world.

marattiacées [maratjase], *s.f.pl. Bot:* Marattiaceae.

marattiales [maratjal], *s.f.pl. Bot:* Marattiales.

maraud, -aude[1] [maro, -o:d], *s. A:* villain, rascal, rogue; *f.* wench, hussy.

maraudage [maroda:ʒ], *s.m. Jur:* petty thieving (of fruit from trees, of standing crops).

maraudaille [marodɑ:j], *s.f. A:* **1.** troop of marauders. **2.** (the) riff-raff; rag, tag and bobtail.

maraude[2] [maro:d], *s.f.* (*a*) marauding, plundering; **aller à la m.,** to go looting, marauding; **soldats en m.,** soldiers on the loot; (*b*) filching, pilfering, petty thieving (from orchards, etc.); (*c*) cruising (of taxi); **taxi en m.,** cruising taxi.

marauder [marode]. **1.** *v.i.* (*a*) to maraud, plunder; (*b*) to filch, thieve (*esp.* from market gardens, orchards, etc.); (*c*) (*of taxi*) to cruise (in search of fares). **2.** *v.tr.* **m. des fruits dans les vergers,** to raid orchards.

maraudeur, -euse [marodœ:r, -ø:z], *s.* (*a*) marauder, plunderer; (*b*) filcher, petty thief; (*c*) *a.* **taxi, chauffeur, m.,** cruising taxi, taxi driver; **loup m.,** prowling wolf.

maravédis [maravedi(s)], *s.m.* (*a*) *A.Num:* maravedi (of Spain); (*b*) **je n'ai pas un m.,** I haven't a brass farthing.

marayon [marɛjɔ̃], *s.m.* salt-pan worker (sharing profits with landlord).

marbre [marbr̥], *s.m.* **1.** (*a*) marble; **m. de Carrare,** Carrara marble; **m. tacheté,** clouded marble; **cœur de m.,** cold heart, stony heart; **être en m.,** to be as cold as marble, to be stony-hearted; (*b*) marble (statue, etc.); **collection de marbres,** collection of marbles; **les marbres d'Elgin,** the Elgin marbles; (*c*) marble top (of mantelpiece, etc.). **2.** *Bookb:* marbling (of book edges). **3.** (*a*) slab (of stone or metal, for grinding colours, etc.); (*b*) *Mec.E:* surface plate, face plate; table (of comparator). **4.** *Typ:* (*a*) imposing stone; (*b*) bed (of press), press stone; **livre en m., sur le m.,** book in type; *Journ:* **matière restée sur le m.,** matter crowded out. **5.** *Nau:* **m. de la roue du gouvernail,** barrel of the steering wheel.

marbré, -ée [marbre]. **1.** *a.* marbled; (i) mottled; (ii) veined; **savon m.,** mottled soap; *Bookb:* **peau marbrée,** mottled skin; **livre m. sur tranche, à tranches marbrées,** marble-edged book. **2.** *s.m.* (*a*) *Geol:* calc-spar (of Pyrenees); (*b*) *Rept:* marblet. **3.** *s.f. Ich:* **marbrée,** lamprey.

marbrer [marbre], *v.tr. Bookb: etc:* to marble; to mottle, to vein; **joues marbrées par les larmes,** tear-stained face; **le froid marbre la peau,** the cold mottles, blotches the skin; **les nuages qui marbrent le ciel,** the clouds that mottle the sky.

marbrerie [marbrəri], *s.f.* **1.** (*a*) marble working, marble cutting; (*b*) marble work. **2.** marble-mason's yard.

marbreur, -euse [marbrœ:r, -ø:z], *s. Bookb:* marbler.

marbrier, -ère [marbrije, -ijɛ:r]. **1.** *a.* marble (industry, etc.). **2.** *s.m.* (*a*) marble mason; monumental mason; (*b*) dealer in marble; (*c*) *Paint:* grainer. **3.** *s.f.* **marbrière,** marble quarry.

marbrure [marbry:r], *s.f.* **1.** marbling, veining. **2.** mottling (of the skin).

marc[1] [ma:r], *s.m.* **1.** *A.Meas:* mark; *Jur:* **m. le franc,** pro rata repartition (of assets); **au m. le franc,** pro rata. **2.** [mark] *Num:* (German) mark.

marc[2] [ma:r], *s.m.* **1.** (*a*) marc (of grapes, olives, etc.), murc, murk, rape(s) (of grapes); **m. de pommes,** pomace; (*b*) **eau de vie de m.,** white brandy (distilled from marc); marc (brandy). **2.** **m. de café, de thé,** coffee grounds, grouts (used) tea leaves; **faire le m. de café** = to tell fortunes from a teacup.

Marc[3] [mark], *Pr.n.m.* Mark, Marcus; **M. Antoine,** Mark Antony; **l'évangile selon saint M.,** the Gospel according to Saint Mark, St Mark's gospel.

marcassin [markasɛ̃], *s.m.* young wild boar.

marcassite [markasit], *s.f. Miner:* marcasite, white iron pyrites.

Marc(-)Aurèle [markɔrɛl], *Pr.n.m. Rom.Hist:* Marcus Aurelius; **Pensées de M. A.,** Meditations of Marcus Aurelius.

marceau, -eaux [marso], *s.m. Bot:* sallow, goat willow.

Marcel [marsɛl], *Pr.n.m.* (*a*) Marcel; (*b*) *Rel.H:* Marcellus; **Saint M. l'Acémète,** Marcellus the Righteous.

marceline [marsəlin], *s.f. Miner: Tex:* marceline.

Marcelle [marsɛl], *Pr.n.f.* Marcella.

marcellianisme [marsɛljanism], *s.m. Rel.H:* Marcellianism.

Marcellin [marsəlɛ̃], *Pr.n.m. Rel.H:* Marcellinus.

marcescence [marsɛs(s)ɑ̃:s], *s.f. Bot:* marcescence, withering.

marcescent [marsɛs(s)ɑ̃], *a. Bot:* marcescent, withering; (**organe**) **m.,** sub-persistent (organ).

marchage [marʃa:ʒ], *s.m.* **1.** *A:* walking, tramping. **2.** kneading (of clay by treading).

marchand, -ande [marʃɑ̃, -ɑ̃:d]. **1.** *s.* (*a*) (*rarely used in modern Fr. without qualification*) dealer, merchant; shopkeeper; tradesman, tradeswoman; *pl.* tradespeople; **m. en détail,** retailer; **m. en gros,** wholesaler, wholesale dealer; **m. de vins en gros,** wholesale wine merchant; *O:* **m. de vin** = publican; **m. de chevaux, de tableaux,** horse dealer, picture dealer; **m. de fromage,** cheesemonger; **m. de poisson,** fishmonger; **m. de tabac,** tobacconist; **m. de grains,** corn chandler; **m. ambulant,** travelling salesman; **m. des quatre saisons,** costermonger; barrow boy; **m. d'habits,** *F:* **m. de puces,** old-clothes man, dealer; *Pej:* **m. de canons,** armaments magnate; **m. de biens,** estate agent; *F:* **m. de soupe,** (i) keeper of a poor restaurant; (ii) headmaster of a sub-standard private school; **ce n'est qu'un m. de soupe,** he's only interested in making a profit; *F:* **m. de participes,** schoolmaster; *F:* **marchande de plaisir, d'amour,** prostitute, tart; *F:* **être le mauvais m. de qch.,** to have made a bad speculation; to have done badly out of sth.; to be the loser by sth.; *s.a.* SABLE[1] 1; (*b*) *A:* buyer, customer; (*at auction*) bidder; **ne pas trouver m.,** to find no buyers, no bidders. **2.** *a.* (*a*) commercial; **denrées marchandes,** saleable, marketable, goods; **prix m.,** market price; **valeur marchande,** commercial value; **procédé peu m.,** unbusiness-like behaviour; (*b*) **ville marchande,** commercial town; **quartier m.,** shopping centre; commercial centre; (*c*) **marine marchande,** merchant navy; **navire m.,** merchant vessel, cargo ship.

marchandage [marʃɑ̃da:ʒ], *s.m.* (*a*) bargaining, haggling; *Pej:* **m. électoral,** electoral bargaining; (*b*) *Ind: Jur:* (illegal) sub-contracting of labour (under which the workman receives less than a fair wage).

marchandailler [marʃɑ̃dɑje], *v.tr. O:* to haggle over the price of (trifling things).

marchandailleur, -euse [marʃɑ̃dɑjœ:r, -ø:z], *s. O: F:* petty haggler.

marchander [marʃɑ̃de], *v.tr.* **1.** (*a*) **m. qch. avec qn,** to haggle, bargain, with s.o. over sth.; **m. qn,** to haggle over the price with s.o., to beat s.o. down; **se faire m.,** to invite haggling; **m. sur le prix de qch.,** to beat down the price of sth.; **m. la conscience de qn,** to make tempting offers to s.o.; to try to buy s.o.'s conscience; (*b*) **m. les éloges à qn,** to grudge one's praise; to praise s.o. grudgingly; **il ne marchande pas sa peine,** he does not grudge his efforts, he spares no pains; **ne pas m. sa vie,** to hold one's life of little account; **m. à agir,** to hesitate to act, to boggle at, about, doing sth.; **faire qch. sans m.,** to do sth. without hesitation; to make no bones about doing sth. **2.** to job (contract); to sub-contract (job).

marchandeur, -euse [marʃɑ̃dœ:r, -ø:z], *s.* **1.** haggler, bargainer. **2.** *Ind:* sub-contractor of labour.

marchandise [marʃɑ̃di:z], *s.f.* merchandise, goods, wares, commodities; stock-in-trade; *Nau:* **marchandises diverses,** general cargo; **train de marchandises,** goods train, *U.S:* freight train; **m. en magasin,** stock in hand; **vanter, étaler, faire valoir, sa m.,** (i) to boost one's wares; (ii) *F:* to make the most of oneself; (*of attractive woman*) to show off one's goods; *s.a.* MÉTIER 1.

marchant [marʃɑ̃], *a.* moving, on the move; *Mil:* **aile marchante,** outer flank (of wheeling movement); leading wing.

marchantiales [marʃɑ̃tjal], *s.f.pl. Bot:* Marchantiales.

marchantie [marʃɑ̃ti], *s.f. Bot:* marchantia.

marche[1] [marʃ], *s.f.* **1.** march, border, boundary, frontier. **2.** march land, borderland.

marche[2], *s.f.* **1.** (*a*) (i) step, stair (of stairs); (ii) tread (of step); **m. de départ,** curtail step (of staircase); **m. d'angle,** corner stair; **marches tournantes, marches dansantes,** winders; **marches carrées, marches droites,** flyers; **la m. du bas,** the bottom stair, step; **les marches du trône,** the steps of the throne; (*b*) (i) treadle (of loom, lathe, etc.); (ii) pedal (of pedal-board of organ); (iii) tread (of pedal-board pedal of organ); (*c*) *Ven:* track, hoofmark (of animal). **2.** (*a*) walk, walking; **aimer la m.,** to be fond of walking; **la m. est le meilleur des exercices,** walking is the best exercise; **chaussures de m.,** walking shoes; **avoir une m. gracieuse,** to have a graceful walk; **ralentir sa m.,** to slacken one's pace; **continuer sa m.,** to walk on; **continuer sa pénible m.,** to plod on; **se mettre en m.,** to set out, start off, march off, move off; **deux heures de m.,** two hours' walk(ing); **il n'y a qu'une heure de m.,** it is only an hour's walk, it is within an hour's walking distance; **arrêter la m. des sauterelles,** to arrest the progress, the advance, of the locusts; (*b*) march; (i) *Mil:* **m. militaire,** route march; **colonne en m.,** column on the march; **ordres de m.,** marching orders; **mettre les troupes en m.,** to set the troops in motion; **se mettre en m.,** to march off; **ouvrir la m.,** to lead the way; **fermer la m.,** to bring up the rear; **gagner une m. sur l'ennemi,** to steal a march on the enemy; (ii) *Mus:* **jouer une m.,** to play a march; **m. nuptiale, funèbre,** wedding march, dead march; **m. militaire,** military march. **3.** (*a*) running (of trains, etc.); sailing (of ships); **mettre en m. un service,** to start, run, a service; **mise en m. d'un service,** running of a service; **jours de mise en m.,** days when a train is run; **modifier la m. des trains,** to alter the running, the working, of the trains; to alter the timetable; (*b*) **en m.,** in motion; **m. avant,** (i) forward motion; (ii) headway (of ship); **m. arrière,** (i) backward motion; *Mec: Cin:* reverse motion; (ii) backing (of train); reversing, backing (of car); sternway (of ship); **entrer dans le garage en m. arrière,** to back, reverse, into the garage; **navire en m.,** ship under way; **navire de m.,** fast ship; **tramway en m.,** moving tram; *Cin:* **m.** (**du film**), motion. **4.** (*a*) running, going, working (of machine, etc.); **être en m.,** (i) (*of machine*) to be going, running; (ii) (*of furnace*) to be in blast; **(re)mettre une machine en m.,** to (re)start an engine, to set an engine going; **en état de m.,** in working order; **mettre l'interrupteur sur m.,** to switch on (the engine, etc.); **mise sur m.,** switching on; (*of machine*) **se mettre en m.,** to start; **mettre en m. un projecteur,** to switch on a searchlight; *Av:* **mettre en m. à l'hélice,** to swing the propeller; **m. au ralenti, à vide,** idling, idle motion; **bonne m. d'une exploitation,** smooth running of an undertaking; (*b*) course (of stars, events, etc.); march (of events, time); progress (of time, malady, etc.); **m. à suivre,** course to be followed, to adopt; procedure; **indiquez-moi la m. à suivre,** tell me how to proceed, to set about it; (*c*) **m. d'un poème, d'un ouvrage,** progress, course, progression of ideas, in a poem, a literary work; **les principes qui guident la m. de**

la pensée humaine, the principles that guide the working, the processes, progress, trend, of human thought; (*d*) rate (of speed, of progress); **m. (diurne) d'un chronomètre,** daily rate of a chronometer; (*e*) *Chess:* manner of moving (of a piece); **la m. du cavalier,** the knight's move; (*f*) *Mus:* **m. harmonique,** harmonic progression; **m. des accords,** sequence of chords.

marché [marʃe], *s.m.* **1.** (*a*) dealing, buying; **m. noir, parallèle,** black market; **m. gris,** semi-black market, grey market; **faire son m.,** to do one's shopping; **faire le m. d'autrui,** (i) to do someone else's shopping; (ii) to act on someone else's behalf; **être en m. avec qn pour qch.,** to be negotiating with s.o. about sth.; (*b*) deal, bargain, contract; **faire, conclure, un m.,** to strike a bargain; **faire m. de qch. avec qn,** to bargain for sth. with s.o.; **faire, passer, (un) m. avec qn pour un travail,** to contract, to make, sign, a contract, with s.o. for a piece of work; **m. de fourniture,** supply contract; **c'est m. fait,** it's a bargain; *F:* done! **cela n'est pas dans notre m.,** I didn't bargain for that; **m. conclu reste conclu; on ne revient pas sur un m.,** a bargain is a bargain; **c'est un m. de dupes,** we've been cheated, *F:* had; we've made a bad bargain; **mettre à qn le m. en main,** to call upon s.o. to say yes or no; to invite s.o. to take it or leave it; *F:* **boire le vin du m.,** to wet a bargain; **c'est m. donné,** that's giving it away; **par-dessus le m.,** into the bargain, thrown in; *Fin:* **m. au comptant,** cash transaction; **m. à terme,** time bargain; *s.a.* PRIME² 1; (*c*) **bon m.,** cheapness (de, of); **avoir qch. à très bon m.,** to have, get, sth. very cheap; to get a great bargain; **acheter, vendre, qch. à bon m.,** to buy, sell, sth. cheaply, at a cheap rate, cheap; **à meilleur m.,** more cheaply, cheaper; **articles bon m.,** low-priced, cheap, goods; bargains; **faire bon m. des conseils de qn,** to hold s.o.'s advice cheap, to care little for s.o.'s advice; **faire bon m. de sa vie,** to hold one's life of little account; **il fait bon m. de la douleur physique,** he makes little of physical pain; **avoir bon m. de qn, de qch.,** to make short work of s.o., sth.; **vous en êtes quitte, vous vous en êtes tiré, à bon m.,** you are well out of it, you have got off lightly. **2.** market; (*a*) **jour de m.,** market day; **m. aux fleurs, à la volaille,** flower, poultry, market; **m. en plein vent, en plein air,** open-air market; **m. couvert,** covered market, market hall; *Jur:* **m. public,** market overt; *F:* **m. aux puces,** flea market; **aller au m.,** to go to market; **cours du m.,** market price; *F:* **courir sur le m. de qn,** to try to cut s.o. out; **lancer un article sur le m.,** to market an article; **article qui n'a pas de m.,** article for which there is no sale; **il n'existe pas de m. pour ces titres,** these shares cannot be realized; *Pol. Ec:* **m. commun,** common market; **étude de m.,** market research; **étude des marchés,** marketing, market research; *St.Exch:* **le m. officiel, en Bourse,** the Ring; **m. hors cote,** curbstone market; (*b*) (state of the) market; **m. ferme,** steady, strong, firm, market; **m. instable,** sensitive market; **le m. est nul,** there's nothing doing.

marche(-)palier [marʃpalje], *s.f. Const:* top step (of staircase); *pl. marches(-)paliers.*

marchepied [marʃəpje], *s.m.* **1.** (*a*) steps (of altar, to the throne, etc.); **sa position n'est qu'un m.,** his position is merely a stepping stone; (*b*) *Veh:* footboard; *Aut:* running-board; (*c*) tail-board (of wag(g)on); (*d*) *Row:* stretcher; (*e*) pair of steps, step-ladder; (*f*) *Nau:* foot-rope, horse (of a yard, of bowsprit); **m. de bout de vergue,** Flemish horse. **2.** (*a*) footpath (along canal or river, opposite towpath); (*b*) towpath, towing path.

marcher [marʃe]. I. *v.i.* **1.** (*a*) to tread; **m. sur le pied à qn,** (i) to tread on s.o.'s foot, on s.o.'s toes; (ii) to offend s.o., to tread on s.o.'s corns; **ne marchez pas sur les pelouses,** keep off the grass; **m. sur les traces, sur les pas, de qn,** to follow, tread, in s.o.'s footsteps; **m. sur les talons de qn,** to tread on s.o.'s heels; *s.a.* HERBE 1; (*b*) *v.tr.* to tread (sth. under foot); to knead, tread (clay); to full (cloth). **2.** (*a*) to walk, go; **il ne marche pas encore,** (the child) isn't walking yet; **il peut m. seul,** (i) (*of child*) he's able to walk, has learnt to walk, by himself; (ii) he's quite able to look after himself; *Mil:* **blessé qui marche, qui peut m.,** walking case; **il boite en marchant,** he's limping; he's got a limp; **une façon de m. à lui propre,** his own particular way of walking; **m. à quatre pattes,** to walk on all fours; *F:* **m. à la dix heures dix,** to walk with one's feet turned out, *F:* with one's feet at a quarter to three; **m. vers qn, qch.,** to walk towards s.o., sth.; **m. sur qn,** to walk quickly towards s.o.; **m. avec qn,** (i) to walk with, accompany, s.o.; (ii) to agree with s.o.; **deux choses qui marchent toujours ensemble,** two things that always go together; *s.a.* PAIR 1; **m. après qn,** to walk behind s.o., in s.o.'s footsteps; **m. devant qn,** to walk in front of s.o.; to prepare the way for s.o.; **l'État marche à la ruine,** the State is heading for ruin; *with cogn. acc.* **m. deux pas en avant,** to walk, step, two paces forward; (*b*) *F:* to obey orders, to conform to a plan; **il marchera,** he'll do as he's told; he won't jib; **(je ne) marche pas!** nothing doing! **je ne marche pas à moins de 1000 francs,** nothing doing under 1000 francs; **faire m. qn,** (i) to order s.o. about; (ii) to deceive, fool, s.o., to lead s.o. up the garden path; to pull s.o.'s leg; **je lui ai raconté une histoire et elle a marché,** I told her a tale and she swallowed it, fell for it; (*c*) *Mil: etc:* to march; **en avant, marche!** quick march! **m. à l'ennemi,** to advance, move, against the enemy; **m. à la victoire,** to advance to victory; **m. en tête,** to lead the van; **il avait marché sous La Fayette,** he had served under La Fayette; **m. au canon,** to make for the sound of guns. **3.** (*a*) (*of trains, etc.*) to move, travel, go; (*of ships*) to sail, steam; to steer (**à l'est,** for the east); (*of plans, etc.*) to proceed, progress; **la table marche sur des roulettes,** the table goes, runs, on wheels; (*of ship, etc.*) **m. à toute allure, à toute vitesse,** to proceed, steam, at full speed; **le temps marche,** time goes on; **les affaires marchent,** business is brisk; **les affaires ne marchent plus,** business is at a standstill, is slack; **faire m. la maison,** to run the house; **faire m. le feu,** to make the fire burn, to look after the fire; **cela fait m. le commerce,** it's good for trade; **c'est lui qui fait m. l'affaire,** he runs the show; **est-ce que ça marche?** are you getting along, going on, all right? **ça ne marche pas si mal,** we are doing not so badly; **depuis une huitaine ça marchait ainsi,** things had been going on like this for a week; **comment cela a-t-il marché?** how did you get on? **la répétition a bien, mal, marché,** the rehearsal went well, badly; (*b*) (*of machine*) to work, run, go; **ma montre ne marche plus; je ne peux pas la faire m.,** my watch has stopped, is out of order; I can't get it to go; **machine qui marche à la vapeur,** machine that is worked, driven, that goes, by steam; **m. à vide, au ralenti,** to (run) idle; **m. à plein, à pleine puissance,** to run full load; **rasoir électrique marchant sur tous courants,** electric razor that works on all voltages; **faire m. le tourne-disques,** to put on the record player; **sa langue marchait sans arrêt,** her tongue ran on without stopping; she couldn't stop talking.

II. **marcher,** *s.m. A:* **1.** (*a*) walking (as exercise); (*b*) walk, gait; **reconnaître qn à son m.,** to recognize s.o. by his walk; (*c*) ground (walked on); **c'est un m. très rude,** it is very heavy going. **2.** *Sp:* (*netball, basket ball*) running with the ball.

marcheur, -euse [marʃœːr, -øːz]. **1.** *s.* (*a*) walker; **bon m.,** good walker; (*of horse*) good goer; (*b*) *Pej:* **vieux m.,** old rake; lady-killer. **2.** *a.* **animaux marcheurs,** walking animals; **navire bon m.,** fast ship. **3.** *s.f.* **marcheuse,** (*a*) *Th:* walker-on; figurante (in ballet); (*b*) street walker, prostitute.

marchiennois, -oise [marʃjɛnwa, -waːz], *a. & s. Geog:* (native, inhabitant) of Marchiennes.

marchite [marʃit], *s.f. Miner:* marchite.

Marcien [marsjɛ̃], *Pr.n.m. Hist:* Marcianus.

Marcomans [markɔmɑ̃], *s.m.pl. Hist:* Marcomanni.

marconigramme [markɔnigram], *s.m. A: Tg:* marconigram.

marcottage [markɔtaːʒ], *s.m. Hort:* layering.

marcotte [markɔt], *s.f. Hort:* **1.** layer. **2.** runner, sucker.

marcotter [markɔte], *v.tr. Hort:* to layer.

mardi [mardi], *s.m.* Tuesday; **m. gras,** Shrove Tuesday; *F:* (*to oddly dressed person*) **ce n'est pas m. gras aujourd'hui,** what on earth have you got on? it's not fancy dress!

Mardochée [mardɔʃe], *Pr.n.m. B.Hist:* Mordecai.

mare¹ [maːr], *s.f.* (stagnant) pool; pond; (*on rocky coast*) rock pool; **m. artificielle,** dew pond; **m. de sang,** pool of blood; *F:* **la m. aux harengs,** the Herring Pond, the Atlantic.

mare², *adv.* = MARRE.

maréage [mareaːʒ], *s.m. Nau: A:* contract (with sailor) for the run.

maréca [mareka], *s.m. Orn:* mareca; widgeon.

marécage [marekaːʒ], *s.m.* (*a*) fen, marshland; (*b*) bog, slough, swamp.

marécageux, -euse [marekaʒø, -øːz], *a.* boggy, marshy, swampy.

marécanite [marekanit], *s.f. Miner:* marekanite.

maréchal, -aux [mareʃal, -o], *s.m.* **1.** farrier, shoeing smith. **2.** marshal (of royal household, etc.). **3.** *Mil:* (*a*) **m. (de France),** field-marshal; *s.a.* BATON 1; (*b*) **m. des logis,** sergeant (in mounted arms); **m. des logis chef,** senior sergeant; (*c*) *A:* **m. de camp,** brigadier.

maréchalat [mareʃala], *s.m.* marshalship.

maréchale [mareʃal]. **1.** *s.f.* wife of field-marshal; *Toil:* **poudre à la m.,** scented hair powder. **2.** *a.f.* **houille m.,** forge coal.

maréchalerie [mareʃalri], *s.f.* horse-shoeing, farriery; **atelier de m.,** smithy, forge.

maréchal-ferrant [mareʃalferɑ̃], *s.m.* farrier; shoeing smith; *pl. maréchaux-ferrants.*

maréchaussée [mareʃose], *s.f. Hist:* **1.** = Marshalsea. **2.** (*a*) corps of mounted constabulary; (*b*) *Iron:* the *gendarmerie,* the police.

marée [mare], *s.f.* **1.** tide; **m. haute,** high water, high tide; **m. basse,** low water, low tide; **m. montante,** rising, flowing, tide; flood tide; **m. descendante,** falling tide, ebb tide; **grande m., m. de syzygie,** spring tide; **m. bâtarde, m. de quadrature,** neap tide; **renversement, changement, de m.,** turning of the tide; **la m. change,** the tide is on the turn; **mer sans m.,** tideless sea; **fleuve à m.,** tidal river; *Nau:* **faire m.,** to tide; **faire double m.,** to work double tides; **contre vent et m.,** (i) against wind and tide; (ii) in spite of all opposition; **avoir vent et m.,** to be favoured by circumstances, to have everything in one's favour; **port à m., de m.,** tidal harbour; **partir à la m.,** to go out with the tide; **une m. humaine,** a flood of people; *F:* **m. noire,** oil slick; *Prov:* **la m. n'attend personne,** time and tide wait for no man. **2.** fresh (seawater) fish; **train de m.,** fish train; **arriver comme m. en carême,** to arrive just at the right moment, in the nick of time; to be a godsend; **arriver comme m. après carême,** to turn up when everything is over; to arrive a day after the fair.

marégramme [maregram], *s.m. Oc:* marigram.

marégraphe [maregraf], *s.m. Oc:* marigraph; self-registering tide gauge.

marékanite [marekanit], *s.f. Miner:* marekanite.

marelle [marɛl], *s.f. Games:* hopscotch.

marémètre [maremɛtr], *s.m. Oc:* maregraph, marigraph.

maremmatique [marɛmatik], *a.* **fièvre m.,** malaria.

maremme [marɛm], *s.f.* coastal fen, maremma; *Geog:* **la M.,** the Maremma.

marémoteur, -trice [maremɔtœːr, -tris], *a.* tidal (power); **usine marémotrice,** tidal power station.

marène [marɛn], *s.f. Ich:* whitefish.

Marengo [marɛ̃go]. **1.** *Pr.n.m. Geog:* Marengo; *Cu:* **poulet (à la) M.,** chicken Marengo. **2.** *a.inv. & s.m.inv. Tex:* speckled-brown; pepper-and-salt.

marennais, -aise [marɛnɛ, -ɛːz], *a. & s. Geog:* (native, inhabitant) of Marennes.

marennes [marɛn], *s.f.* Marenne oyster.

marennine [marɛnin], *s.f.* marennin.

maréographe [mareɔgraf], *s.m.,* **maréomètre** [mareɔmɛtr], *s.m. Oc:* maregraph, marigraph.

marèque [marɛk], *s.m. Orn:* wi(d)geon.

maresque [marɛsk], *a. Dial:* (*N.Fr.*) marshy.

mareyage [marɛjaːʒ], *s.m.* (the) fish trade.

mareyeur, -euse [marɛjœːr, -øːz]. **1.** (wholesale) fishmonger. **2.** fish porter.

marfil [marfil], *s.m.* raw ivory.

margarate [margarat], *s.m. Ch:* margarate.

margarine [margarin], *s.f.* **1.** *Com:* margarine. **2.** *Ch: A:* margarin.

margarinier [margarinje], *s.m.* margarine manufacturer.

margarique [margarik], *a. Ch:* margaric (acid).

margarite [margarit], *s.f. Miner:* margarite, pearl mica.

margarodes [margarɔdɛs], *s.m. Ent:* margarodes.

margarodite [margarɔdit], *s.f. Miner:* margarodite.

margarosanite [margarozanit], *s.f. Miner:* margarosanite.

margay [margɛ], *s.m. Z:* margay.

marge [marʒ], *s.f.* **1.** (*a*) border, edge (of ditch, road, etc.); *Const: Adm:* **m. d'isolement,** curtilage (of building); **m. de reculement,** unbuilt space between building and road; **en m. de,** (i) arising out of; in connection with; (ii) outside; apart from; **en m. de l'histoire,** a footnote to history; **vivre en m. (de la société),** (i) to lead a quiet life; (ii) to live on the fringe of society; **homme en m.,** outsider; **faire de la médecine en m. de la faculté,** to practise medicine without being qualified; (*b*) margin (of book); **m.**

supérieure, head, top, margin; m. inférieure, tail, bottom, margin; m. de fond, back, inner, margin; fausse m., faulty margin; écrire qch. en m., to write sth. in the margin; note en m., marginal note; *Typ:* illustrations à marges perdues, bled-off illustrations; *Typewr:* curseur, régulateur, de m., marginal stop; (c) *Typ:* (i) tympan sheet; (ii) feed; m. à deux feuilles, m. en double, twin-sheet feed; table de m., feed board; (d) *Oc:* m. continentale, continental shelf. 2. (a) m. de liberté, margin of liberty; m. de réflexion, time for thought, time to think; m. de sécurité, safety margin; m. d'erreur, margin of error; *Ind:* m. de tolérance, tolerance (margin); *Mec.E: etc:* m. de puissance, margin, range, of power; capacity; *Fin:* appel de m., call for additional cover; laisser une bonne m. pour les déchets, to make a generous allowance for waste; accorder de la m. à qn, to allow s.o. some margin, some latitude; avoir de la m., to have plenty of margin; to have time enough (and to spare); to have sufficient means, enough scope; cela nous laisse de la m. pour manœuvrer, that leaves us (i) room, (ii) scope, to manœuvre; (b) *Ind: Com:* m. bénéficiaire, profit margin; m. commerciale, gross profit.

margelle [marʒɛl], *s.f.* curb(stone), lip (of a well).

marger [marʒe], *v.tr.* (je margeai(s); n. margeons) 1. *Typ:* to lay on, feed, stroke in (the paper). 2. *Engr:* m. la planche avec du blanc d'Espagne, to edge the plate with chalk. 3. page margée d'annotations au crayon, page with (numerous) pencil notes in the margin.

margeur, -euse [marʒœːr, -øːz], *s.* 1. *Typ:* layer-on, stroker-in, feeder. 2. *s.m.* (a) m. à friction, à succion, friction feeder; suction feeder; (b) *Typewr:* marginal stop.

marginal, -aux [marʒinal, -o], *a.* 1. (a) marginal (note, etc.); (b) *Geog:* fringing (reef); (c) marginal (preoccupations, conscience, etc.); (d) *Nat.Hist:* marginal; *Bot:* placentation marginale, marginal placentation. 2. *Pol.Ec:* marginal; *s.m.pl.* les marginaux, the fringe; coût, prix, m., marginal cost, price; utilité, marginale, marginal utility; entreprise marginale, firm with only a marginal profit.

marginé [marʒine], *a. Nat.Hist:* marginate(d), margined.

marginer [marʒine], *v.tr.* to annotate (book) in the margin; to write in the margin of (page, etc.).

margis [marʒi], *s.m. Mil: P:* (= maréchal des logis) sarge.

Margot [margo]. 1. *Pr.n.f.* Margot, Madge, Maggie. 2. *s.f.* (a) *F:* magpie; (b) *P: A:* (i) chatterbox; (ii) trollop.

margota [margɔta], *s.m.*, **margotas** [margɔtɑːs], *s.m.* (open) canal barge; lighter.

margotin [margɔtɛ̃], *s.m.* bundle of firewood.

margoton [margɔtɔ̃], *s.f. F: A:* woman of easy virtue; trollop.

margouillat [marguja], *s.m. Rept:* (West African) grey lizard, agama.

margouillet [margujɛ], *s.m. Nau:* fairlead; (bull's eye) truck; lizard.

margouillis [marguji], *s.m. F:* slush, slime, mud; mess; mettre qn dans le m., to put s.o. in a hole, in a fix.

margoulette [margulɛt], *s.f. P:* mouth, jaw, mug; casser la m. à qn, to smash s.o.'s face in; to bash s.o.'s face.

margoulin [margulɛ̃], *s.m. F:* 1. *St.Exch:* petty speculator; small man. 2. (a) dishonest tradesman, shopkeeper; (b) black marketeer. 3. blackmailer. 4. poor workman; bungler.

margousier [marguzje], *s.m. Bot:* margosa, bead tree, pride of India.

margrave [margraːv], *Hist:* 1. *s.m.* margrave. 2. *s.f.* margravine.

margravial, -aux [margravjal, -o], *a. Hist:* margravial.

margraviat [margravja], *s.m. Hist:* margraviate.

margravine [margravin], *s.f. Hist:* margravine.

Marguerite [margərit]. 1. *Pr.n.f.* Margaret, Marguerite. 2. *s.f.* (a) *A: & B:* pearl; jeter des marguerites aux pourceaux, to cast pearls before swine; (b) *Bot:* (petite) m., daisy; grande m., m. des champs, ox-eye daisy, marguerite; m. dorée, yellow ox-eye, yellow bottle, corn marigold; m. de la Saint-Michel, d'automne, Michaelmas daisy; *F:* effeuiller la m., to play "she loves me, she loves me not"; (c) *Leath:* graining board; (d) *Nau: A:* messenger chain, deck tackle (to assist in weighing anchor, etc.); (e) *Mil.Av:* dispersal area.

marguillage [margijaːʒ], *s.m. coll.* churchwardens (of a parish).

marguillerie [margijri], *s.f.* 1. office of churchwarden, churchwardenship. 2. church records.

marguillier [margije], *s.m.* churchwarden.

mari [mari], *s.m.* husband.

Maria [marja], *Pr.n.f.* Maria.

mariable [marjabl̩], *a.* marriageable.

mariage [marjaːʒ], *s.m.* 1. marriage; (a) wedlock, matrimony; leur m. a été heureux, theirs was a happy marriage; leur m. est en ruines, their marriage is on the rocks; (b) wedding; m. d'amour, d'inclination, love match; faire un m. d'amour, to marry for love; m. de raison, de convenance, marriage of convenience; m. d'argent, d'intérêt, money marriage; m. religieux, wedding (in church); m. civil, civil marriage (before mayor, = marriage before registrar); m. mixte, mixed marriage (between catholic and non-catholic); acte de m., marriage certificate; prendre qn en m., to marry s.o.; demande en m., proposal of marriage; faire la demande en m., (i) to propose (marriage to a lady); (ii) to make formal proposals of marriage on behalf of one's son (to the parents of the lady); il revint le jour de notre m., he came back on our wedding day; leur première année de m., the first year of their married life; enfant né hors du m., child born out of wedlock, *F:* born on the wrong side of the blanket; liste de m., wedding list. 2. *A:* marriage portion. 3. joining, uniting; (a) le m. de l'esprit et de la beauté, the combination, association, of wit and beauty; heureux m. de mots, happy combination of worlds; m. de deux couleurs, blending of two colours; (b) *Nau:* marrying (of two ropes).

marial, -aux [marjal, -o], *a. Theol:* Marian.

marialite [marialit], *s.f. Miner:* marialite.

marianisme [marjanism], *s.m. Rel.H:* Marianism; devotion to the Virgin Mary.

mariannais, -aise [marjanɛ, -ɛːz], *a. & s. Geog:* (native, inhabitant) of the Marianas Islands.

Marianne [marjan], *Pr.n.f.* 1. Marian(ne); *Geog:* les îles Mariannes, the Marianas Islands. 2. *F:* the (French) Republic; travailler pour M., to be expecting a baby.

Marie [mari], *Pr.n.f.* Mary, Maria, Marie; la Vierge M., the Virgin Mary; Sainte M. Majeure, (the church of) Santa Maria Maggiore; Sainte Marie l'Égyptienne, St Mary the Egyptian.

marié, -ée [marje], *a. & s.* 1. married (person); nouveau m., nouvelle mariée, (i) newly-married man, woman; (ii) bridegroom; *f.* bride; nouveaux mariés, (i) newly-married couple; (ii) bride and bridegroom; vieux mariés, old couple; couple who have been married a long time; *F:* la mariée est trop belle, it's too good to be true; se plaindre que la mariée est trop belle, (i) to complain about a good bargain; (ii) not to know how lucky one is; oncle non m., tante non mariée, unmarried uncle, aunt; bachelor uncle, maiden aunt. 2. *s.m.* bridegroom, *s.f.* bride (about to be married); robe de mariée, wedding dress; couronne de mariée, bridal wreath. 3. *Pros:* rimes mariées, alternate masculine and feminine couplets.

Marie-Chantal [mariʃɑ̃tal], *Pr.n.f.* c'est une M.-C., she's a rich, empty-headed little snob, a Mayfair nitwit.

marie-couche-toi-là [marikuʃtwala], *s.f.inv. P:* woman of easy virtue; *P:* easy lay.

marie-graillon [marigrajɔ̃], *s.f.inv. P:* slut.

Marie-Louise [marilwiːz]. 1. *Pr.n.f.* Maria Louisa. 2. *s.f.* coloured border on picture (inside frame); coloured border on poster. 3. *s.m. or f. Mil: P:* un (or une) m.-l., an angel-face; *pl. maries-louises.*

marier [marje], *v.tr.* (*p.d. & pr.sub.* n. mariions, v. mariiez) 1. to marry; (a) (*of priest, etc.*) to unite (man and woman) in wedlock, to join in marriage; (b) to give (one's daughter, etc.) in marriage; to find a husband, a wife, for (s.o.); fille à m., marriageable daughter. 2. (a) to join, unite; m. des couleurs, to blend colours; (b) *Nau:* m. des cordages, to marry ropes; (c) *Ap:* m. des ruches, to transfer bees from one hive to another.

se marier, (a) to marry, to get married; se m. avec qn, to marry s.o.; ils se marient entre eux, they intermarry; elle est d'âge à se m., she is of a marriageable age; il, elle, ne s'était pas marié(e), he, she, had remained single; (b) (*of colour, etc.*) se m. avec qch., to go with sth., to harmonize with sth.; voix qui se marient heureusement, voices that blend, harmonize.

marie-salope [marisalɔp], *s.f. F:* 1. (a) slut; (b) prostitute. 2. (a) (dredger's) mud barge; hopper (barge); (b) mud dredger; (c) *Mil: P:* field kitchen; *pl. maries-salopes.*

marieur, -ieuse [marjœːr, -jøːz], *s.* matchmaker.

Marignan[1] [mariɲɑ̃], *Pr.n. Geog:* Marignano.

marignan[2], *s.m. Bot:* aubergine.

marigot [marigo], *s.m.* (*in tropical regions*) (a) marigot, backwater (of river); (b) low-lying area subject to flooding in the rainy season; (c) *Fish:* aller, courir, au m., to moor in a quiet spot abounding in fish.

marihuana [marihɥana], **marijuana** [mariʒɥana], *s.f.* marihuana, *F:* pot; cigarette de m., marihuana cigarette, *F:* reefer.

marikina [marikina], *s.m. Z:* marikina, silky tamarin.

marin, -ine[1] [marɛ̃, -in]. 1. *a.* marine (plant, engine, etc.); carte marine, sea chart; mille m., nautical mile; dieu m., sea god; plante marine, sea plant; faune, flore, marine, marine fauna, flora; costume m., sailor suit; avoir le pied marin, to have found one's sea legs; to be a good sailor. 2. *s.m.* (a) seafaring man (officer or seaman); mariner; peuple de marins, seafaring nation; (b) sailor; m. de commerce, merchant sailor, seaman; m. de l'État, de la Marine nationale, naval rating; se faire m., to go to sea; *F:* m. d'eau douce, landlubber; swab. 3. *s.m.* (*in Languedoc, etc.*) moist wind from the south-east.

marinade [marinad], *s.f.* pickle; (a) brine, souse; (b) *Cu:* marinade; m. de chevreuil, soused venison; (c) *pl. Fr.C:* marinades, pickles.

marinage [marinaːʒ], *s.m.* (a) pickling, salting (of food); (b) *Cu:* marinading, sousing (of mackerel, etc.).

marine[2] [marin], *s.f.* 1. (a) *A:* sea-front; (b) *Art:* seascape, seapiece. 2. seamanship, the art of navigation; terme de m., nautical term. 3. the sea service; la m. marchande, the merchant service, navy, the mercantile marine; la m. de guerre, la m. militaire, the Navy, the naval forces; officier de m., naval officer; les troupes de m., the French Marines; infanterie de m., naval infantry, marines; artillerie de m., marine artillery; soldat de m., soldier serving in the marine infantry or artillery; le Ministère de la M. = the Admiralty (Division of the Ministry of Defence); Ministre de la M., Minister for the Navy, = First Lord of the Admiralty, = *U.S:* Secretary for the Navy. 4. sentir la m., avoir un goût de m., to smell, taste, of the sea. 5. *a.inv.* navy-blue, navy; un costume m., a navy-blue suit.

mariné[1] [marine], *a.* 1. sea-damaged (goods). 2. *Cu:* soused, pickled; harengs marinés, soused herrings; bœuf m., salt beef.

mariné[2], *a. Her:* marined.

mariner [marine]. 1. *v.tr.* to pickle; (a) to salt; (b) *Cu:* to marinade, to marinate, to souse (mackerel, etc.). 2. *v.i.* en train de m., in pickle.

maringot(t)e [marɛ̃gɔt], *s.f.* 1. spring cart. 2. caravan (of strolling players, gipsies, etc.).

maringouin [marɛ̃gwɛ̃], *s.m. Ent:* (*in tropical America, Canada*) mosquito; sand fly.

marinier, -ière [marinje, -jɛːr]. 1. *a.* (a) marine, naval; officier m., petty officer; (b) *Civ.E:* arche marinière, navigation arch (of bridge). 2. *s.m.* waterman, bargeman, bargee. 3. *s.f.* marinière, (a) *Swimming:* side stroke; (b) *Cost:* (women's) (i) sailor blouse; (ii) teeshirt; (c) *Cu:* moules (à la) marinière, moules marinière.

marinisme [marinism], *s.m. Lit.Hist:* Marinism.

mariniste [marinist], *s.m. & f.* 1. *Lit.Hist:* Marinist. 2. *Art:* seascape painter.

mariol, mariolle[1] [marjɔl], *P:* (a) *a. O:* cunning, clever, smart; (b) *s.m.* faire le m., to show off.

mariolâtre [marjɔlɑːtr̥], *Theol:* 1. *a.* Mariolatrous. 2. *s.m. & f.* Mariolater.

mariolâtrie [marjɔlɑtri], *s.f. Theol:* Mariolatry.

mariol(l)e[2] [marjɔl], *s.f. A:* (a) medallion, statuette, of the Virgin; (b) statuette of a saint.

mariologie [marjɔlɔʒi], *s.f. Theol:* Mariology.

Marion [marjɔ̃], *Pr.n.f.* Marion, Marian.

marionite [marjɔnit], *s.f. Miner:* hydrozincite.

marionnette [marjɔnɛt], *s.f.* 1. (a) m. (à gaine), (glove) puppet; m. (à fil), marionette, puppet; (théâtre de) marionnettes, puppet theatre; spectacle de marionnettes, marionette, puppet, show; joueur, montreur, de marionnettes, puppet player, puppeteer; faire jouer les grandes marionnettes, to pull every possible string (to attain one's ends); (b) (*pers.*) (i) puppet, tool; (ii) stiff, awkward person. 2. *Nau:* ninepin block.

marionnettiste [marjɔnɛtist], *s.m. & f.* puppeteer.

Mariotte [marjɔt], *Pr.n. Ph:* la loi de M., Boyle's law; flacon, vase, de M., Mariotte's bottle, flask.

mariposite [maripɔzit], *s.f. Miner:* mariposite.

marisque [marisk], *s.f.* 1. (variety of) large fig. 2. *Med:* marisca, haemorrhoidal tumour.

mariste [marist], *a. & s.m. Ecc:* Marist (father).

marital, -aux [marital, -o], *a.* marital; *Jur:* **autorisation maritale,** husband's authorization.

maritalement [maritalmɑ̃], *adv.* maritally; **vivre m.,** to live together as husband and wife; to cohabit.

maritime [maritim], *a.* maritime (navigation, plant, province, etc.); **droit, législation, m.,** maritime law; **les grandes puissances maritimes,** the great maritime powers; *Geog:* **les (Provinces) Maritimes,** the Maritime Provinces, the Maritimes; **ville m.,** seaboard town, seaside town; **commerce m.,** sea-borne trade; **mouvement m.,** movement of shipping; *Journ:* shipping intelligence; **assurance m.,** marine insurance; **courtier m.,** shipbroker; **agent m.,** shipping agent; **arsenal m.,** naval dockyard; **navire affecté à la navigation m.,** sea-going vessel; *Rail:* **gare m.,** harbour station; *s.a.* INSCRIPTION 1.

maritorne [maritɔrn], *s.f.* sloven, slut.

marivaudage [marivodaːʒ], *s.m.* (*a*) *Lit:* artificiality of language; affectation of style; (*b*) delicate, witty, repartee.

marivauder [marivode], *v.i.* (*a*) *A: Lit:* to write in the style of Marivaux; (*b*) to engage in delicate, witty, repartee.

marjolaine [marʒɔlɛn], *s.f. Bot:* (sweet) marjoram; **m. bâtarde,** lady's slipper.

mark [mark], *s.m. Num:* (German) mark.

marketing [markətiŋ], *s.m. F: Com:* marketing.

markhor [markɔːr], *s.m. Z:* markhor.

marle [marl], *s.m. P:* bully.

marler [marle], *v.tr. Agr:* to marl (soil).

marli [marli], *s.m.* marli. **1.** *A:* fine gauze. **2.** raised rim (of plate); **filet au m.,** coloured border (on plate).

marlou [marlu], *s.m. P:* **1.** procurer, pimp. **2.** good-for-nothing.

marlychois, -oise [marliʃwa, -waːz], *a. & s. Geog:* (native, inhabitant) of Marly(-le-Roi).

marmaille [marmɑːj], *s.f. coll. F:* children; **la m. sortait de l'école,** the kids were coming out of school; **rue pleine de m.,** street swarming with noisy little brats; **donner à manger à toute la m.,** to feed the whole brood.

marmailleux, -euse [marmɑjø, -øːz], *a. F:* full of, swarming with, children, brats.

marmandais, -aise [marmɑ̃dɛ, -ɛːz], *a. & s. Geog:* (native, inhabitant) of Marmande.

Marmara [marmara], *Pr.n. Geog:* **la mer de M.,** the Sea of Marmora.

marmatite [marmatit], *s.f. Miner:* marmatite.

marmelade [marməlad], *s.f.* (*a*) compote (of fruit); **m. de pommes,** (i) stewed apples; (ii) apple purée; (*b*) **viande en m.,** meat cooked to shreds; *F:* **mettre qn en m.,** to make mincemeat of s.o.; to pound s.o. to a jelly; (*c*) *F:* mess, hash; **la ville est en m.,** the town is a frightful mess, a shambles (as a result of air raids, etc.); **être dans la m.,** to be in the soup.

marmenteau, -eaux [marmɑ̃to], *a. & s.m. Jur:* **(arbre) m., (bois) marmenteaux,** full-grown, ornamental tree(s) (forming part of the amenities of an estate, and not to be cut down).

marmitage [marmitaːʒ], *s.m. Mil: P:* bombardment with heavy shells; shelling.

marmite [marmit], *s.f.* **1.** (*a*) (i) (cooking) pot, (stew)pan; (ii) potful, panful; **m. à conserves,** preserving pan; **m. à vapeur,** steamer; **m. étuve (à double compartiment),** double cooker; **m. à pression, m. autoclave,** pressure cooker; *Tchn:* **m. de Papin,** Papin's digester; **m. à brai,** pitch pot, kettle; **m. suédoise, norvégienne,** hay box; **écumer la m.,** (i) to skim the pot; (ii) *F:* to cadge, sponge; **faire bouillir la m.,** to keep the pot boiling; *F:* **casser la m.,** to quarrel with one's bread and butter; **nez en pied de m.,** bulbous nose; *s.a.* GRAISSER 1; (*b*) *Mil:* dixy, camp kettle; **m. individuelle,** mess tin; (*c*) *P: A:* prostitute (*esp.* when living with a pimp). **2.** *Mil: P:* heavy shell. **3.** *Geol:* **m. de géants,** pothole; giant's kettle. **4.** *Bot:* **m. de singe,** monkey pot.

marmitée [marmite], *s.f.* potful, panful.

marmiter [marmite], *v.tr. Mil: P:* to bombard (place) with heavy shells; to shell (trenches, etc.).

marmiteux, -euse [marmitø, -øːz], *a. & s.* poor, miserable (wretch).

marmiton [marmitɔ̃], *s.m.* (*a*) *A:* scullion; (*b*) cook's boy; pastry cook's errand boy.

marmitonner [marmitɔne], *v.i. F:* to do the kitchenmaid's work.

marmolite [marmɔlit], *s.f. Miner:* marmolite.

marmonner [marmɔne], *v.tr.* to mumble, mutter.

marmoréen, -enne [marmɔreɛ̃, -ɛn], *a.* marmoreal, marmorean; **blancheur marmoréenne,** marble whiteness; **d'une pâleur marmoréenne,** as white as marble.

marmoriforme [marmɔrifɔrm], *a.* marble-like.

marmorisation [marmɔrizasjɔ̃], *s.f. Geol:* marmarization, marmorization.

marmoriser [marmɔrize], *v.tr. Geol:* to marmarize, marmorize, to metamorphose into marble.

marmot [marmo], *s.m.* **1.** *F:* (small) boy, brat, urchin; *pl.* children, brats (of either sex). **2.** *A:* (*a*) monkey; (*b*) grotesque figure (*esp.* as door knocker); *hence* **croquer le m.,** to be kept waiting; to cool one's heels.

marmottage [marmɔtaːʒ], *s.m.* **1.** mumbling, muttering. **2.** mumble, mutter.

marmotte [marmɔt], *s.f.* **1.** *Z:* marmot; **m. canadienne,** whistler; **m. d'Amérique,** woodchuck, groundhog; **dormir comme une m.,** to sleep like a log. **2.** headscarf (tied over the forehead). **3.** (commercial traveller's) sample case. **4.** *Nau: A:* match-tub.

marmottement [marmɔtmɑ̃], *s.m.* muttering, mumbling.

marmotter [marmɔte], *v.tr.* to mumble, mutter.

marmotteur, -euse [marmɔtœːr, -øːz], *s.* mumbler, mutterer.

marmouset [marmuzɛ], *s.m.* (*a*) quaint figure (in ivory, china); grotesque; (*b*) *F:* (i) little chap; brat, nipper; (ii) little runt (of a man); (*c*) *Dial:* (= OUISTITI) marmoset; (*d*) firedog (with grotesque head).

marmouton [marmutɔ̃], *s.m. Civ.E:* pile driver.

marnage[1] [marnaːʒ], *s.m. Agr:* marling (of soil).

marnage[2], *s.m. Nau:* range, rise (of the tide); tide level (on a given day).

marne [marn], *s.f.* **1.** *Geol: Agr:* marl. **2. m. à foulon,** fuller's earth.

marner[1] [marne], *v.tr. Agr:* to marl (soil).

marner[2], *v.i.* **1.** *Nau:* (*of the tide*) to flow, rise; **ici la mer marne de trois mètres,** here the range of the tide is ten feet, there is a rise of and fall of the tide of ten feet. **2.** *P:* to work hard, to slog.

marneron [marnərɔ̃], *s.m.* worker in a marl pit.

marneur [marnœːr], *s.m.* (*pers.*) (*a*) *Agr:* marl spreader; (*b*) worker in a marl pit.

marneux, -euse [marnø, -øːz], *a.* marly (soil).

marnière [marnjɛːr], *s.f.* marl pit.

marnon [marnɔ̃], *s.m. Agr:* heap of marl (for spreading on fields).

Maroc (le) [ləmarɔk], *Pr.n.m. Geog:* Morocco; **au M.,** in Morocco; **se rendre au M.,** to go to Morocco.

marocain, -aine [marɔkɛ̃, -ɛn], *a. & s. Geog:* Moroccan; *Tex:* **crêpe m.,** marocain.

maroilles [marwal], *s.m.* Maroilles cheese.

marommais, -aise [marɔmɛ, -ɛːz], *a. & s. Geog:* (native, inhabitant) of Maromme.

maronite [marɔnit], *a. & s. Ecc.Hist:* Maronite.

maronnant [marɔnɑ̃], *a. F:* annoying; **que c'est m.!** how rotten! what a bind!

maronner [marɔne], *v.i. F:* to growl; to grumble; to be annoyed, furious; (*with cogn. acc.*) **m. des jurons,** to mutter, growl out, oaths; **faire m. qn,** to get s.o.'s back up.

maroquin[1] [marɔkɛ̃], *s.m.* (*a*) morocco (leather); **papier m.,** morocco paper, leather paper; (*b*) minister's portfolio; **il a fini par obtenir un m.,** he was finally made a minister.

maroquin[2], *s.m. Nau:* triatic stay; span.

maroquinage [marɔkinaːʒ], *s.m.* morocco-leather tanning, dressing.

maroquiner [marɔkine], *v.tr. Leath:* (*a*) to make (skin) into morocco (leather); (*b*) to give a morocco finish to (leather, paper).

maroquinerie [marɔkinri], *s.f.* **1.** (*a*) morocco-leather tanning, dressing; leather working; (*b*) morocco-leather tannery. **2.** *Com:* (*a*) morocco-leather goods; (*b*) fancy leather work; (*c*) (fancy) leather shop.

maroquinier [marɔkinje], *s.m.* (*a*) morocco-leather dresser, tanner; leather worker; (*b*) leather-paper maker; (*c*) dealer in fancy leather goods; **chez le m.,** at the leather shop.

marotisme [marɔtism], *s.m. Lit:* archaism of style, after the manner of Marot.

marotte [marɔt], *s.f.* **1.** (*a*) (court fool's) bauble; cap and bells; (*b*) (milliner's, hairdresser's) dummy head. **2.** fad; hobby; **chacun a sa m.,** everyone has a bee in his bonnet, his own pet hobby; **le jardin est sa m.,** the garden's his baby; **flatter la m. de qn,** to play up to s.o.

marouette [marwɛt], *s.f. Orn:* crake; **m. poussin,** little crake; **m. ponctuée,** spotted crake; **m. de Baillon,** Baillon's crake; **m. de la Caroline,** sora rail, Carolina crake.

marouflage [maruflaːʒ], *s.m.* (*a*) *Art: etc:* cloth backing; (*b*) taping.

maroufle[1] [marufl], *s.m. A:* rogue, scoundrel; low individual.

maroufle[2], *s.f.* strong paste (for re-mounting pictures).

maroufler [marufle], *v.tr.* **1.** (*a*) to re-mount (painted picture) on a new foundation; to strengthen (panelling, etc.) with a canvas backing; (*b*) **m. une couture,** to tape a seam; **bande à m.,** taping, tape. **2.** to prime, size (canvas).

maroute [marut], *s.f. Bot:* stinking camomile, May weed, dog fennel.

marprime [marprim], *s.f. Nau:* sailmaker's awl.

marquage [markaːʒ], *s.m.* marking; *Radar, etc:* plotting.

marquant [markɑ̃], *a.* **1.** prominent, outstanding (incident, personage, etc.); **homme m.,** man of note; *F:* big man; *Lit:* **passages marquants,** highlights; purple passages. **2.** *Cards:* **carte marquante,** *s.f.* **marquante,** card that counts.

marque[1] [mark], *s.f.* **1.** mark; (*a*) **m. d'identité,** identification mark; **m. d'immatriculation,** registration mark; *Av:* **m. de nationalité,** nationality mark, badge; *Mil:* **marques distinctives de commandement,** insignia, marks, of command; **marques distinctives des véhicules,** vehicle markings; *Jur:* **m. distinctive,** earmark; **m. de fabrique, de commerce,** trade mark, brand; **produits de m.,** branded goods; **m. courante,** standard make; **m. déposée,** registered trade mark; **j'ai eu des voitures de trois marques,** I have had three makes of car, cars of three different makes; **bicyclette de première m.,** bicycle of the best make; **m. de distributeur,** distributor's brand name; **bonne m. de cigares,** good brand of cigars; **vin de m.,** (i) wine of a well-known brand; (ii) choice, vintage, wine; **personnage de m.,** person of distinction; distinguished, prominent, person; **m. typographique,** (publisher's, printer's) colophon; **m. de la douane,** customs stamp; *Dom.Ec:* **m. à linge,** name tape, name tab; **m. de l'État,** government stamp, = broad arrow; *Navy:* **la m. de l'amiral,** the admiral's flag; **mettre sa m. sur un document,** to make one's mark on a document; **m. au crayon, à la plume, à la craie,** pencil mark, pen mark, chalk mark; **blessure qui laisse une m.,** wound that leaves its mark; **marques d'un coup,** marks of a blow; *Mec.E:* **m. de dent (d'engrenage),** gear streak; *F:* **faire porter ses marques à qn,** to leave one's mark on s.o.; *A:* (*of criminal, etc.*) **porter la m.,** to be branded; **m. de haute noblesse,** stamp of nobility; **porter la m. du génie,** to bear the stamp of genius; **l'auteur a imprimé sa m. sur cette œuvre,** the author has set his own imprint on this work; **marques d'amitié, de respect,** tokens of friendship, of respect; **recevoir des marques de respect, de faveur, de qn,** to receive marks of respect, of favour, from s.o.; *Mil:* **marques extérieures de respect,** military courtesy; **m. des temps,** sign of the times; **m. du beau temps,** sign, indication, of good weather; (*b*) *Com:* price marked in letters; private mark, cipher; **taux de m.,** mark-up rate; (*c*) mark (on horse's tooth); mark of mouth; (*d*) star, blaze (on horse's forehead); (*e*) *Rugby Fb:* **faire une m.,** to make a mark. **2.** marking tool, branding iron, marker. **3.** (*a*) *Com:* tally; (*b*) *Games:* counting board; scoreboard; marker; (*c*) *Games:* score; (*at bridge*) score below line; **tenir la m.,** to keep the score; *Sp:* **à vos marques! prêts? partez!** on the mark! on your marks! get set! go! (*d*) *Games:* counter. **4.** *A:* badge, *pl.* insignia (of office, etc.).

marque[2], *s.f.* **1.** *A:* reprisals. **2.** *Jur: Hist:* **lettres de m.,** letters of marque (and reprisal).

marqué [marke], *a.* **1.** (*a*) marked (card, etc.); **être né m.,** to be born with a birthmark; **être m.,** to have a lined, furrowed, face; *Th:* **rôle m.,** elderly part; (*b*) *Adm: Jur:* **papier m.,** stamped paper; (*c*) *Pej:* **c'est un homme m.,** he is a marked man; (*d*) *Atom.Ph:* **corps m.,** tracer (element); **atome m.,** labelled atom. **2.** marked, decided, unmistakable (difference, etc.); pronounced, decided (features, opinions, taste, etc.); distinct (inclination, etc.); **d'une manière marquée,** pointedly; **avoir pour qn des attentions marquées,** to show s.o. marked attention. **3. au jour m.,** on the appointed day.

marque-mal [markmal], *s.m.inv. O: F:* suspicious, shady-looking, individual; man of unprepossessing appearance.

marquer [marke]. **1.** *v.tr.* to mark; (*a*) to leave, put, a mark on (sth.); **m. du linge,** to mark linen; *Com:* **prix marqué,** (i) catalogue price, list price, (ii) price marked in plain figures; **papier à lettre marqué à son adresse,** notepaper stamped with one's address; *Com: Ind:* **m. une caisse, un ballot,** to stencil a box, a bale; **figure marquée par, de, la petite vérole,** face marked, pitted, with smallpox, pock-marked face; **m. un criminel,** to brand a criminal; *F:* **m. qn, qch., du sceau de l'infamie,** to brand s.o., sth., with infamy; **m. un arbre,** to blaze a tree; **projet marqué d'un certain idéalisme,** scheme bearing the stamp of, characterized by, a certain idealism; *Rail: etc:* **m. sa place,** to leave one's hat, etc., on a seat (to show that it is taken); (*b*) to record, note; to make a note of, jot down (sth.); **m. ses dépenses,** to keep a record of, mark down, write down, one's expenses; **m. l'heure d'un rendez-vous,** to note down the time of an appointment; **m. l'endroit où l'on a cessé de lire,** to mark one's place (in a book); *Games:* **m. un adversaire,** to mark a man; **m. un adversaire de deux points,** to be two up; **m. un but,** to score a goal; *abs.* **réussir à m.,** to score; **m. les points,** to keep the score; **m. trente points,** to score thirty; **ne m. aucun point,** to fail to score; **en français moderne le subjonctif marque des points après cette conjonction,** in modern French the use of the subjunctive after this conjunction is gaining ground; (*c*) to indicate, show; **l'horloge marque l'heure,** the clock tells the time; **la pendule marque dix heures,** the clock says, points to, ten o'clock; **le thermomètre marque 25°,** the thermometer shows, registers, 25°; the thermometer stands at 25°; **ruisseau qui marque la limite d'une propriété,** stream that marks the boundary of an estate; **m. ses sentiments,** to show one's feelings; **m. le temps avec son bâton,** to beat time with one's baton; **m. le pas,** to mark time; **m. un rythme,** to beat out a rhythm; **m. la mélodie,** to emphasize the melody; **habit qui marque bien la taille,** coat that shows off the figure; **cheval qui marque,** horse with mark of mouth; **il marque son âge,** he shows his age; **il marque plus que son âge,** he looks older than he really is; **m. à qn son estime,** to give s.o. proof, a token, of one's esteem; **il nous a marqué que tout allait bien,** he let us know, informed us, wrote to tell us, that all was well; (*d*) to determine, ascertain (scientific fact, etc.). **2.** *v.i.* (*a*) **crayon qui ne marque pas,** pencil that won't write; (*b*) to stand out, make a mark; to cut a conspicuous figure; **notre famille n'a jamais marqué,** our family has never been remarkable, never made its mark; **événement qui marque,** outstanding event; **aucun événement ne marqua dans sa vie,** there were no outstanding events in his life; *F:* **m. mal,** to be of dubious, unprepossessing, appearance; to give a bad impression; (*c*) *Nau:* **(faire) m. un pavillon, un signal,** to dip a flag, a signal.

marque-repère [markrəpɛːr], *s.f.* point of reference, fiducial mark, line-up mark; *Mec.E:* index mark (on part); *pl. marques-repères.*

marquésan, -anne [markesɑ̃, -an], *a. & s. Geog:* Marquesan.

marqueté [markəte], *a.* **1.** *Nat.Hist:* tessellated; spotted. **2.** *Furn: etc:* inlaid. **3.** *Her:* speckled; checky.

marqueter [markəte], *v.tr.* **(je marquette, n. marquetons; je marquetterai) 1.** to spot, speckle (fur, imitation tiger-skin, etc.). **2.** to inlay (table, etc.).

marqueterie [markətri, -kɛ-], *s.f.* **1.** inlaid work, marquetry. **2.** patchwork, piecemeal literary composition, etc..

marqueteur [markətœːr], *s.m.* worker in marquetry; inlayer.

marqueur, -euse [markœːr, -øːz]. **1.** *s.* marker; (*a*) stamper, brander; stenciller (of boxes, bales, etc.); (*b*) scorer (at games); *Fb: etc:* **m. de but,** scorer (of goal); (*c*) tally keeper; (radar) plotter. **2.** *s.m.* (*a*) *Ten:* **m. à chaux,** court-marking machine; court marker; (*b*) *Needlew:* **m. de plis,** (sewing-machine) tucker, tuck creaser, tuck folder; (*c*) *Mil.Av:* marker bomb, target indicator bomb; (*d*) **m. à feutre,** felt (marker) pen. **3.** *s.f. Ind:* **marqueuse,** stamper, stamping machine (for bars of chocolate, soap, etc.). **4.** *a. Atom.Ph:* **élément m.,** tracer (element).

marquis [marki], *s.m.* (*a*) marquis, marquess; (*b*) *Th:* (*17th cent.*) aristocratic fop; (*c*) *Pej:* person who apes an aristocratic manner; *F:* **M. de Carabas,** person who boasts of the lands he possesses.

marquisat [markiza], *s.m.* marquisate.

marquise [markiːz], *s.f.* **1.** marchioness. **2.** (*a*) awning (on pleasure boat, etc.); (*b*) (overhanging) shelter; canopy; glass porch; carriage awning (of hotel, etc.); *Rail: etc:* umbrella roof; (*c*) *Nau:* mizzen topmast staysail. **3.** (*a*) marquise (ring); (*b*) marquise sunshade. **4.** *Hort:* marquise pear. **5.** *Cu:* champagne cup; wine cup.

Marquises [markiːz], *Pr.n.f.pl. Geog:* **les îles M.,** the Marquesas (Islands).

marquisien, -ienne [markizjɛ̃, -jɛn], *a. & s. Geog:* Marquesan.

marquoir [markwaːr], *s.m.* **1.** tailor's marking tool. **2.** *Needlew:* sample letter on canvas for linen embroidery.

marraine [marɛn], *s.f.* (*a*) godmother; sponsor (at baptism); (*b*) *F:* aunt; **m. de guerre,** self-constituted godmother, correspondent (of soldier at the front); (*c*) presenter (of débutante); (*d*) christener (of bell, ship, etc.).

Marrakech [marakɛʃ], *Pr.n. Geog:* Marrakesh.

marrant [marɑ̃], *a. P:* (*a*) (screamingly) funny, side-splitting; (*b*) odd, strange, funny, queer; **vous êtes m., vous, alors!** you're the limit! **il n'est pas m.,** he's wet; he's as dull as ditchwater.

marre [maːr], *adv. P:* **avoir m. de qch., de qn,** to be fed up with, to have had enough of, to be bored stiff with, sth., s.o.; **j'en ai m.!** I've had about enough, I'm fed (up) to the (back) teeth; **(il) y en a m.!** that's enough! **et puis, un point, c'est m.!** and that's all there is to it! enough said! and that's that!

marrer (se) [səmare], *v.pr. P:* to split one's sides (with) laughing; to have a good time; **tu me fais m.,** you make me laugh.

marri [mari], *a. A:* sad, sorry, grieved.

marron[1] [mɑrɔ̃, ma-], *s.m.* **1.** (*a*) (large edible) chestnut; **marchand de marrons,** chestnut seller; **tirer les marrons du feu pour qn,** to be s.o.'s cat's paw; **marrons glacés,** candied chestnuts, marrons glacés; *P:* **coller un m. sur la figure de qn,** to give s.o. a biff in the face; **je lui ai flanqué un m.,** I fetched him one, landed him one; (*b*) **m. d'Inde,** horse chestnut. **2.** *pl.* lumps (in badly kneaded dough, etc.). **3.** *A:* large curl (tied up with ribbon). **4. m. de service, de ronde,** token, tally, deposited by sentry or watchman on his rounds. **5.** *Pyr:* maroon. **6.** *Cin:* master positive. **7.** *a.inv. & s.m.* chestnut (colour); maroon; **chaussures m.,** tan, light brown, shoes. **8.** *P:* (*a*) *a.inv.* **être (fait) m.,** (i) to be arrested, nabbed; (ii) to be taken in, had; (*b*) *s.m.* victim, sucker.

marron[2], -onne [mɑrɔ̃, -ɔn, ma-], *a.* **1. nègre m.,** *s.* **marron,** maroon, runaway negro slave; **animal m.,** animal that has run wild, *F:* gone bush. **2.** unlicensed (trader, etc.); unqualified (doctor); *Sp:* **amateur m.,** pseudo-amateur, sham amateur. **3.** *s.m.* (*a*) book printed clandestinely; (*b*) stencil (plate).

marronnage[1] [mɑrɔnaːʒ, ma-], *s.m.* **1.** *Hist:* running away (of slaves). **2.** *Fin:* jobbing, outside broking. **3.** clandestine printing.

marronnage[2], *s.m. Civ.E:* cracks (in a road surface).

marronnant [mɑrɔnɑ̃, ma-], *a. P:* tiresome; boring.

marronner[1] [mɑrɔne, ma-], *v.i.* **1.** *Hist:* (*of runaway slave*) to live in hiding. **2.** to carry on a trade, profession, without legal qualification; *St.Exch:* to job.

marronner[2], *v.i. F:* to grouse, to grumble.

marronnier [mɑrɔnje, ma-], *s.m.* chestnut tree; **m. d'Inde,** horse-chestnut tree; **m. à fleurs rouges,** *U.S:* red buckeye.

marrube [maryb], *s.m. Bot:* marrubium, *F:* hoarhound, horehound; **m. aquatique,** gipsy wort.

Mars [mars]. **1.** *Pr.n.m. Myth: Astr:* Mars; **Champ de M.,** (i) *Rom.Ant:* Campus Martius, (ii) *Mil:* parade ground; **la planète M.,** the planet Mars. **2.** *s.m.* (*a*) March; **en m.,** in March; **au mois de m.,** in the month of March; **le premier, le sept, m.,** (on) the first, the seventh, of March, (on) March (the) first, (the) seventh; **blé de m.,** *pl.* **les mars,** spring wheat; **bière de m.,** March beer, March ale; **arriver comme m. en carême,** (i) to come round as regularly as clockwork, (ii) (*through confusion with* **marée**) to arrive at an opportune moment, in the nick of time; **cela arrivera comme m. en carême,** it's bound to happen; (*b*) *Ent:* **grand m.,** purple emperor (butterfly).

marsage [marsaːʒ], *s.m. Dial:* spring sowing (of cereals).

marsala [marsala], *s.m.* (*also* **vin de Marsala**) Marsala (wine).

marsaule [marsoːl], **marsault, marsaux, marseau** [marso], *s.m. Bot:* sallow, goat willow.

marseillais, -aise [marsɛjɛ, -ɛːz], *a. & s. Geog:* Marseillais, -aise; *Cu:* **une recette marseillaise,** a Marseilles recipe; *Mus:* **la Marseillaise,** the Marseillaise.

Marseille [marsɛːj], *Pr.n. Geog:* Marseille(s); *F:* **il est bien de M.,** he's a great one for telling tall stories.

marshite [marʃit], *s.f. Miner:* marshite.

marsouin [marswɛ̃], *s.m.* **1.** (*a*) *Z:* porpoise; (*b*) *A:* scruffy, disreputable, man; (*c*) *Mil: F: A:* (i) marine; (ii) colonial infantry soldier. **2.** (*a*) *Nau:* forecastle awning; (*b*) *N.Arch:* **m. arrière,** sternson; **m. avant,** stemson.

marsouinage [marswinaːʒ], *s.m. Av: Nau:* porpoising.

marsouiner [marswine], *v.i. Av: Nau:* to porpoise.

marsupial, -iaux [marsypjal, -jo], *a. & s.m. Z:* marsupial; *s.m.pl.* **marsupiaux,** Marsupiala, Metatheria.

marsupialisation [marsypjalizasjɔ̃], *s.f. Surg:* marsupialization.

marsupialiser [marsypjalize], *v.tr. Surg:* to marsupialize.

marsupium [marsypjɔm], *s.m.* **1.** *Z:* marsupium, (ventral) pouch. **2.** *Anat:* pecten.

martagon [martagɔ̃], *s.m. Bot:* martagon (lily).

marte [mart], *s.f.* = MARTRE.

marteau, -eaux [marto], *s.m.* **1.** (*a*) hammer; **m. à panne fendue,** claw hammer; **m. à deux mains, à frapper devant,** sledgehammer; about sledge; **m. à bascule, à soulèvement,** trip hammer; tilt hammer; **m. à emboutir,** chasing hammer; **m. à piquer,** scaling hammer; *Civ.E:* **m. pneumatique,** pneumatic drill; **marteaux, etc., pneumatiques,** pneumatic tools; *Civ.E: Min:* **m. perforateur,** hammer drill; *Min:* **m. piqueur,** pneumatic pick; **m. de scheidage,** cobbing hammer; *Metalw:* **m. de mécanicien, à panne boule, à panne sphérique,** ball-peen hammer; **m. riveur,** riveting hammer; rivet gun; *Stonew:* **m. à boucharder,** bush hammer; **dressé au m.,** hammer-dressed; *Tex:* **m. à face cannelée (pour briser le lin),** bott hammer; *Bookb:* **m. à endosser,** backing hammer; **travailler le fer au m.,** to hammer iron; **coup de m.,** hammer stroke, stroke of the hammer; **enfoncer un clou à coups de m.,** to hammer in a nail; **façonner qch. à coups de m.,** to hammer sth. into shape; **étendre un métal sous le m.,** to hammer out metal; **être entre l'enclume et le m.,** to be in a dilemma, to be between the devil and the deep blue sea; (*b*) *A.Arms:* **m. d'armes,** martel-de-fer; (*c*) *Ph:* **m. d'eau,** water hammer; (*d*) *Sp:* **lancement du m.,** throwing the hammer; (*e*) (auctioneer's) hammer; gavel; **passer sous le m.,** to come under the hammer; (*f*) (door) knocker; striker (of gong, clock); *Mus:* (i) hammer (of piano); (ii) tuning hammer; **coup de m.,** knock at the door; *F:* **graisser le m.,** to tip the doorman, the porter; (*g*) *Anat:* malleus, hammer (of the ear); *A.Hairdr:* **perruque à marteaux,** bob wig. **2.** (*a*) *Ich:* hammerhead (shark); (*b*) *Moll:* hammer shell; hammer oyster. **3.** *a. F:* **il est un peu m.,** he isn't all there, he's a bit cracked; **devenir m.,** to go round the bend, up the wall.

marteau-pilon [martopilɔ̃], *s.m. Metall:* power hammer; forging press; *F:* **se servir d'un m.-p. pour enfoncer un clou,** to use a sledgehammer to crack a nut; *pl. marteaux-pilons.*

marteau-piolet [martopjɔlɛ], *s.m. Mount:* piton hammer; *pl. marteaux-piolets.*

martégal, -ale, -aux [martegal, -o], *a. & s. Geog:* (native, inhabitant) of Martigues.

martel [martɛl], *s.m.* (*a*) *A:* hammer; (*b*) **se mettre m. en tête,** to be uneasy in one's mind; to be anxious; to worry; **mettre m. en tête à qn,** to cause s.o. uneasiness, anxiety.

martelage [martəlaːʒ], *s.m.* **1.** hammering. **2.** *For:* (*a*) marking (of trees); (*b*) (forester's) mark (on tree); blaze.

martelé [martəle], *a.* **1.** hammer-wrought; hammered; **argent m.,** beaten silver; repoussé work. **2. style m.,** laboured style (of writing). **3.** *Mus:* martellato. **4.** *Ven:* **voix martelée,** yelp (of hounds).

martèlement [martɛlmɑ̃], *s.m.* (*a*) hammering; (*b*) **un m. de bottes sur le pavé,** a clanking, clanging, of boots on the cobbles.

marteler [martəle], *v.tr.* **(je martèle, n. martelons; je martèlerai) 1.** (*a*) to hammer; *Metalw:* **m. à froid,** to cold-hammer; (*b*) **il lui martelait la figure à coups de poing,** he was hammering away at his face with his fists; **idée qui lui martelait la cervelle,** idea that was tormenting him, that kept hammering in his brain; (*c*) **m. ses mots,** to speak each word emphatically; to hammer out one's words. **2.** *For:* to mark, blaze (trees).

martelet [martəlɛ], *s.m.* small hammer, *esp.* slater's hammer.

marteleur [martəlœːr], *s.m.* hammersmith, hammerman.

martellement [martɛlmɑ̃], *s.m. A:* = MARTÈLEMENT.

martellerie [martɛlri], *s.f.* hammering shop (of forge); forging shop.
martello [martɛlo], *s.m.* martello tower.
martelures [martəlyːr], *s.f.pl. Metalw:* hammer-scales.
martensite [martɛ̃zit], *s.f. Metall:* martensite.
Marthe [mart], *Pr.n.f.* Martha.
martial, -aux [marsjal, -o], *a.* 1. (*a*) martial; warlike; soldierly (bearing, etc.); **discours m.**, warlike speech; (*b*) **loi martiale**, martial law; **code m.**, articles of war; **cour martiale**, court martial. 2. (*a*) *Ch: A:* chalybeate, martial; **pyrite martiale**, iron pyrites; (*b*) *Med:* **carence martiale**, iron deficiency.
martialement [marsjalmɑ̃], *adv.* martially; in a warlike manner; in a soldierly manner.
martien, -ienne [marsjɛ̃, -jɛn]. 1. (*a*) *Astr: a.* Martian; **observation martienne**, observation of Mars; (*b*) *s.* (*hypothetical inhabitant of Mars*) Martian. 2. *a. & s. Astrol:* Martian; *a.* Martial (influence).
martigais, -aise [martigɛ, -ɛːz], *a. & s. Geog:* (native, inhabitant) of Martigues.
Martin [martɛ̃]. 1. *Pr.n.m.* (*a*) Martin; (*b*) (*name given to a donkey*) = Neddy; *Prov:* **il y a à la foire plus d'un âne qui s'appelle M.**, there are more Jacks than one at the fair; (*c*) **ours M.**, Bruin; Teddy Bear; (*d*) *A:* = MARTIN-BÂTON. 2. *s.m. Orn:* **m. rose**, rose starling, crested starling, pastor; **M. roselin**, rose-coloured starling, rose-coloured pastor. 3. *s.m. Tchn:* sander.
martin-bâton [martɛ̃batɔ̃], *s.m. F: A:* 1. man armed with a stick, with a cudgel. 2. stick, cudgel; *pl. martins-bâtons.*
martin-chasseur [martɛ̃ʃasœːr], *s.m. Orn:* wood kingfisher; *pl. martins-chasseurs.*
martiné [martine], *s.m. Metall:* (small) forging.
martiner [martine], *v.tr. Metall:* to tilt, hammer (iron, etc.).
martinet[1] [martinɛ], *s.m.* 1. *Metall:* tilt hammer, trip hammer, drop stamp. 2. (*a*) *A:* cat(-o'-nine-tails); (*b*) strap (for beating child); (*c*) clothes beater. 3. flat candlestick. 4. *Nau:* (*a*) peak halyard; (*b*) boom span, topping lift; **m. du mât de charge**, derrick span.
martinet[2], *s.m. Orn:* **m. (noir)**, swift; **m. alpin, à ventre blanc**, alpine swift; **m. pâle**, pallid swift; **m. à dos blanc**, white-rumped swift; **m. épineux**, needle-tailed swift; **m. houppé de l'Inde**, Indian crested swift; **m. des palmes**, palm swift; **naucler m.**, American swallow-tailed kite.
martineur [martinœːr], *s.m. Metall:* (tilt-)hammer-man, tilter.
martingale [martɛ̃gal], *s.f.* 1. (*a*) *Harn:* martingale; **fausse m.**, half martingale; (*b*) *Nau:* martingale (guying down jib boom); (*c*) *Mil:* bayonet frog; (*d*) *Mil:* pouch flap; (*e*) *Cost:* half belt (of greatcoat, sports coat, etc.). 2. (*Gaming*) martingale.
martingaler [martɛ̃gale], *v.i.* (*Gaming*) to martingale.
martiniquais, -aise [martinikɛ, -ɛːz], *a. & s. Geog:* (native, inhabitant) of Martinique.
Martinique [martinik]. 1. *Pr.n.f. Geog:* **la M.**, Martinique. 2. *s.m.* (i) coffee, (ii) rum, from Martinique.
martin-pêcheur [martɛ̃pɛʃœːr], *s.m. Orn:* (*a*) kingfisher; (*b*) **m.-p. géant, d'Australie**, laughing jackass, kookaburra; *pl. martins-pêcheurs.*
martite [martit], *s.f. Miner:* martite.
martre [martr̥], *s.f. Z:* marten; **m. des pins**, pine marten; **m. asiatique à gorge jaune**, Asiatic yellow-throated marten; **m. zibeline**, sable; **m. du Canada**, mink; **m. des palmiers**, palm cat, civet; **manteau en m.**, marten fur coat; **prendre m. pour renard**, to be taken in by appearances.
martyr, -yre[1] [martiːr], *s.* 1. martyr; *R.C.Ch:* **commun des martyrs**, common of martyrs; **être du commun des martyrs**, to be an insignificant person, a nobody; *a.* **un peuple m.**, a martyred people; **mourir m. pour une cause**, to die a martyr in, to, a cause; **les martyrs de la science**, martyrs in the cause of science; **prendre, se donner, des airs de m.**, to take on a martyred expression, look. 2. *s.m. Nau:* chafing block, chafing gear; skid.
martyre[2], *s.m.* (*a*) martyrdom; **souffrir le m.**, to suffer martyrdom; (*b*) **dent qui fait souffrir le m.**, agonizing toothache; **mettre qn au m.**, to torture s.o.; **toute sa vie fut un m.**, his whole life was sheer martyrdom, sheer torture.
martyriser [martirize], *v.tr.* 1. to martyr (s.o. on account of his faith). 2. to martyrize, torture; to make a martyr of (s.o.).
martyrium [martirjɔm], *s.m. Ecc:* martyry, shrine.
martyrologe [martirɔlɔːʒ], *s.m.* (*list of martyrs*) martyrology.
martyrologie [martirɔlɔʒi], *s.f.* (*history of martyrs*) martyrology.
martyrologique [martirɔlɔʒik], *a.* martyrological.
martyrologiste [martirɔlɔʒist], *s.m. & f.* martyrologist.
marxisant, -ante [marksizɑ̃, -ɑ̃ːt], *a. & s.m. & f.* (person) with Marxist leanings.
marxisme [marksism], *s.m.* Marxism.
marxiste [marksist]. 1. *a.* Marxian, Marxist. 2. *s.m. & f.* Marxist.
maryland [marilɑ̃], *s.m.* Maryland tobacco.
mas [mɑ(ːs)], *s.m. Dial:* (*S. of Fr.*) farmhouse; farm.
mascagnine [maskaɲin], *s.f. Miner:* mascagnine, mascagnite.
mascara [maskara], *s.m. Toil:* mascara.
mascarade [maskarad], *s.f.* masquerade.
mascaret [maskarɛ], *s.m.* bore, tidal wave (in estuary).
Mascarille [maskariːj], *s.m. Th:* (type of) impudent valet (from the plays of Molière).
mascaron [maskarɔ̃], *s.m. Arch:* mask, grotesque mask (on keystone of arch, etc.); mascaron.
Mascate [maskat], *Pr.n. Geog:* Muscat.
mascotte [maskɔt], *s.f.* mascot; charm; *Sp: F:* **terrain m.**, lucky ground.
masculin [maskylɛ̃]. 1. *a.* (*a*) male; **enfant du sexe m.**, male child; **ligne masculine**, male line (of descent); **population masculine**, male population; (*b*) masculine, mannish (woman). 2. *a. & s.m. Gram:* masculine (gender); **ce mot est du m.**, this word is masculine; **adjectif au m.**, adjective in the masculine; *Pros:* **rimes masculines**, masculine rhymes.
masculiniser [maskylinize], *v.tr.* 1. (*a*) *Biol:* to masculinize; (*b*) **mode qui masculinise les femmes**, fashion that makes women look mannish. 2. *Gram:* to give (word) the masculine gender.
masculinité [maskylinite], *s.f.* masculinity; *A.Jur:* **privilège de m.**, descent in the male line.
maser [mazɛːr], *s.m. Atom.Ph:* maser.
mash [maʃ], *s.m. Husb:* (bran) mash; *pl. mashes.*
maskelynite [maskɛlinit], *s.f. Miner:* maskelynite.
maskinongé [maskinɔ̃ʒe], *s.m. Ich: Fr.C:* muskelunge, ugly fish.
masochisme [mazɔʃism], *s.m. Psy:* masochism.
masochiste [mazɔʃist], *s.m. & f. Psy:* masochist.
masonite [mazɔnit], *s.f. Miner:* masonite.
masquage [maskaːʒ], *s.m.* 1. (*before spray-painting*) masking, shielding (of a surface). 2. *Psy:* camouflage.
masque[1] [mask], *s.m.* 1. mask; (*a*) **m. de velours noir**, black velvet mask; **masques nègres**, (ceremonial) negro masks; *Hist:* **l'homme au m. de fer, le m. de fer**, the man in the iron mask; **lever, ôter, son m.**, to take off one's mask; **ôter, arracher, le m. à qn**, to unmask s.o.; **lever le m.**, to throw off the mask, to throw off all disguise; **sa piété n'est qu'un m.**, his piety is only a blind; (*b*) *A:* masked person, *A:* mask(er); (*c*) (protective) mask; **m. à gaz**, gas mask, respirator; **m. respiratoire**, breathing apparatus; **m. à oxygène**, oxygen mask; **m. d'inhalation**, inhalation mask; **m. pour anesthésie générale**, anaesthetic mask; **m. de chirurgien**, operating mask; **m. sous-marin**, (skin diver's) mask; **m. d'escrime**, (fencing) mask; *Metall: etc:* **m. protecteur, m. de protection**, protective mask; face shield; **m. d'apiculteur**, beekeeper's mask; (*d*) *Toil:* **m. (anti-rides, hydratant, facial, etc.)**, face pack; (*e*) **m. mortuaire**, death mask; (*f*) (expression of the) face; features; **il a le m. mobile**, he has mobile features; (*g*) *Bot:* **fleurs en m.**, masked, personate, flowers; (*h*) *Ent:* mask (of dragonfly nymph). 2. (*a*) *Th:* masque; (*b*) masquerader, masker, mummer. 3. protection, cover; *Artil:* shield, hood (of gun); *T.V:* shadow mask; *Nau:* smoke sail; *Civ.E:* panel filling; **m. d'étanchéité**, cut-off. 5. *Cin:* vignette.
masque[2], *s.f.* 1. *A:* hag, harridan. 2. **petite m.**, little minx, hussy.
masqué [maske], *a.* 1. masked (person, animal); **bal m.**, masked ball; *Vit:* **bouteille (de vin) masquée**, bottle in which the wine is clear and the deposit adheres to the bottle. 2. concealed; *Aut:* **virage m.**, concealed turning, blind corner; *Mil:* **batterie masquée**, screened, concealed, battery; *Nau:* **voile masquée**, sail aback; **m. partout**, all aback.
masquer [maske], *v.tr.* to mask. 1. (*a*) to put a mask on (s.o.); **se m.**, to put on a mask, to mask one's face; (*b*) *Typ: etc:* to mask (portion of type, of block); (*c*) to hide, screen, conceal (sth.); *Cu:* to mask; *Paint:* (*when using spray gun*) to mask, shield (a surface); **m. qch. à qn**, to conceal sth. from s.o.; **m. une fenêtre**, to blind a window; **m. une odeur**, to disguise a smell; *Mil:* **m. une batterie**, to conceal a battery; **m. ses batteries**, to conceal one's intentions; *Nau:* **m. les feux**, to cover, obscure, the navigation lights; **naviguer à feux masqués, avec tous les feux masqués**, to steam without lights, with all lights obscured; (*d*) *Mil:* **m. le feu de ses propres batteries**, to mask the fire of one's own batteries; *Navy:* (*of ships*) **se m. les uns les autres**, to interfere with each other's fire. 2. *Nau:* to back (sail); **être masqué**, *v.i.* **masquer**, to be caught aback, taken aback.
massacrant, -ante [masakrɑ̃, -ɑ̃ːt], *a.* **être d'une humeur massacrante**, to be in a filthy, vile, temper; *F:* to be like a bear with a sore head.
massacre [masakr̥], *s.m.* 1. (*a*) massacre, slaughter; *F:* butchery; **faire un grand m. de gibier**, to make a great slaughter of game; **m. d'un rôti**, hacking up of a joint; **m. d'un morceau de musique**, murdering of a piece of music; (*b*) **jeu de m.** = Aunt Sally; *F:* **il a une tête de m.**, he's got a face you'd like to punch. 2. *A:* = MASSACREUR 2. 3. *Ven:* head and antlers (of stag); horns (of antelope); *Her:* massacre; attire (of stag).
massacrer [masakre], *v.tr.* 1. to massacre, butcher, slaughter; **m. le gibier**, to make havoc among the game. 2. *F:* to bungle, spoil, make a hash of (work); to murder, massacre (music, a language); to ruin (clothes); to hack up, mangle (the turkey, etc.). 3. *Ten:* **m. un lob**, to kill, smash, a lob.
massacreur, -euse [masakrœːr, -øːz], *s.* 1. massacrer, slaughterer. 2. *F:* bungler, spoiler (of work murderer (of music, etc.).
massage [masaːʒ], *s.m.* (*a*) massage; **m. facial**, facial massage; (*b*) rubbing down (of horse).
Massaliote [masaljɔt], *A.Geog:* 1. *a.* Massalian. 2. *s.* Massaliot.
Massaouah [masawa], *Pr.n. Geog:* Massawa.
masse[1] [mas], *s.f.* 1. mass; (*a*) **m. dure, solide**, hard, solid, mass; **une m. de neige se détacha**, a mass of snow broke away; **se prendre en m.**, to solidify, coagulate; **tomber, s'affaisser, s'écrouler, comme une m.**, to fall like a log; **m. d'air froid**, mass of cold air; *Geol:* **m. charriée**, overthrust block; **grande m. d'eau**, (i) great mass of (falling) water; (ii) great body of water (forming a lake, etc.); **taillé, sculpté, dans la m.**, carved from the block; **colonnade qui allège la m. d'un édifice**, colonnade that lightens the mass, bulk, of a building; *Surv:* **plan de m.**, overall plan; **réunir une m. de documents**, to collect a whole mass, pile, of documents; *F:* **il va nous arriver une grande m. de marchandises**, we are going to get a whole mass of goods delivered; (*b*) *Mil:* mass formation; **m. de manœuvre**, main striking force; (*c*) *Mec:* mass (of moving body); **m. d'équilibrage**, balance weight; *Ph:* **m. critique, subcritique**, critical, sub-critical, mass; **m. spécifique**, density; **m. atomique**, atomic mass; **m. molaire, moléculaire**, molecular mass; **loi d'action de m.**, law of mass action; *Ch:* **nombre de m.**, mass number; (*d*) weight (of machine); (*e*) mass, crowd, body (of people); *Pej:* **la m.**, the mob; **émouvoir les masses**, to move the masses; the mob; **psychologie des masses**, mass psychology; *Jur:* **m. des créanciers**, general body of creditors; **la (grande) m. de**, the majority of; **la m. des mots français provient du latin**, the majority of French words come from Latin; *F:* **il n'y en a pas des masses**, there aren't an awful lot; (*f*) **en m.**, (i) in a body; (ii) as a whole; **nous étions présents en m.**, we turned out in full force; **ils se soulevèrent en m.**, they rose in a body; **exécutions en m.**, mass, wholesale, executions; **avoir des livres en m.**, to have a huge quantity, a whole mass, of books; **marchandises en m.**, goods in bulk; **il faut voir les choses en m.**, one should consider things as a whole. 2. (*a*) *Fin:* fund, stock; **la m. monétaire**, the (total amount of) money in circulation; *Jur:* **m. des biens (de la faillite)**, (bankrupt's) total estate; assets; **m. passive**, liabilities; **m. active**, assets; **m. de recours**, emergency fund; (*b*) common fund (of an art studio); *Mil:* company funds; **m. d'habillement**, clothing fund; (*c*) (prisoner's) earnings (handed to him on liberation); (*d*) *Games: A:* stake. 3. *El:* earth (constituted by frame of machine); **m. polaire**, pole piece; **mettre le courant à la m.**, to earth the current; **mis à la m.**, earthed; **mise à la m.**, earthing.
masse[2], *s.f.* 1. sledge-hammer, maul; **m. en bois**, beetle; *F:* (*in restaurant*) **coup de m.**, fleecing. 2. (*a*) *A.Arms:* **m. d'armes**, mace; (*b*) (ceremonial) mace; (*c*) butt (of billiard cue). 3. *Bot:* **m. d'eau**, bulrush, reed mace.

massé[1] [mase], *s.m. Metall:* sponge (produced in Catalan forge).

massé[2], *s.m. Bill:* massé (shot); **faire un m.,** to play a massé (shot).

massé[3], *a.* forming a compact mass; **une foule massée sur la place,** a crowd of people packed, massed, in the square.

masseau, -eaux [maso], *s.m. Metall:* shingled bloom.

masse-cuite [maskɥit], *s.f. Sug.R:* massecuite; *pl. masses-cuites.*

masselet [maslɛ], *s.m. Metall:* small bloom.

masselotte [maslɔt], *s.f.* **1.** *Metall:* deadhead (of casting); sullage piece, (feed-)head, sprue, runner. **2.** *Mec.E:* fly-weight; inertia block (of fuse, etc.).

massepain [maspɛ̃], *s.m.* marzipan cake, biscuit.

masser[1] [mase]. **1.** *v.tr.* (*a*) to mass (soldiers, crowds, etc.); (*b*) *Art:* to group (figures, etc.); *abs.* **peintre qui masse bien,** painter who has a (good) sense of grouping, of arrangement. **2.** *v.i. P: A:* to work hard.

se masser, to mass; to form a crowd; to gather in masses.

masser[2], *v.tr.* (*a*) to massage; (*b*) to rub down (horse).

masser[3], *v.tr. Bill:* **m. une bille,** to play a massé (shot).

masséter [masetɛ:r], *a.m. & s.m. Anat:* masseter (muscle).

massétérin [maseterɛ̃], *a. Anat:* masseteric.

massette [masɛt], *s.f.* **1.** (*a*) (stonemason's) two-handed hammer; (*b*) *Leath:* scraper. **2.** *Bot:* bulrush, reed mace, cat's-tail, cattail, typha.

masseur[1], **-euse** [masœ:r, -ø:z], *s. Med:* masseur, *f.* masseuse.

masseur[2], *s.m. Metalw:* hammerman.

massicot[1] [masiko], *s.m. Ch: Ind:* massicot, yellow lead.

massicot[2], *s.m. Bookb: etc:* guillotine, trimmer.

massicotage [masikɔta:ʒ], *s.m. Bookb:* guillotining.

massicoter [masikɔte], *v.tr. Bookb: etc:* to guillotine.

massier[1], **-ière** [masje, -jɛ:r], *s.* treasurer; student in charge (in Fr. art studio).

massier[2], *s.m.* mace-bearer, macer; beadle.

massif, -ive [masif, -i:v]. **1.** *a.* (*a*) massive, bulky; gross, dull, material (mind, etc.); **statue massive,** massive statue; (*b*) **argent m.,** solid silver; **meubles en acajou m.,** solid mahogany furniture; (*c*) **action massive contre l'ennemi,** mass attack against the enemy; **aide immédiate et massive,** immediate and substantial help; **manifestation massive,** large-scale, mass, demonstration; **bombardement m.,** large-scale air raid; **quantités massives,** huge, large, quantities; *Com:* **ventes massives,** heavy sales. **2.** *s.m.* (*a*) solid mass (of masonry, etc.); **m. d'une culée,** body of a pier; (*b*) clump (of shrubs, trees, etc.); bed, massif (of rose trees, etc.); (*c*) *Geog:* massif, mountain mass; *Geol:* **m. intrusif,** intrusion; (*d*) *Nau:* dead wood.

massique [masik], *a. Ph:* pertaining to the mass; *Mec.E:* **puissance m.,** power-to-weight ratio (of engine); power per unit of mass.

massiquot [masiko], *s.m. Bookb:* guillotine, trimmer.

massivement [masivmɑ̃], *adv.* massively; ponderously; heavily; **danser m.,** to dance like an elephant; **un monument m. construit,** a monument built on massive, solid, lines; **voter m. pour un candidat,** to vote in large numbers for a candidate.

massiveté [masivte], *s.f.* massiveness.

massoque [masɔk], *s.f. Metall:* slab (half-bloom).

massorah [masɔra], *s.f.,* **massore** [masɔ:r], *s.f. Hebrew Lit:* mas(s)ora(h).

massorète [masɔrɛt], *s.m. Hebrew Lit:* mas(s)orete, mas(s)orite.

massorétique [masɔretik], *a. Hebrew Lit:* masoretic.

massothérapie [masɔterapi], *s.f.* massotherapy.

Massouah [masua], *Pr.n. Geog:* Massawa.

massue [masy], *s.f.* (*a*) club, bludgeon; **coup de m.,** (i) bludgeon stroke, (ii) staggering blow, crushing news, *F:* bombshell; **ce fut un coup de m.,** the news, etc., stunned us, was a great blow; **argument (coup de) m.,** decisive, sledgehammer, argument; *Ent:* **antenne en m.,** antenna ending in a knob or club; capitate antenna; (*b*) *pl.* Indian clubs; (*c*) mace; (*d*) *Bot:* spadix; *F:* **herbe aux massues,** club moss.

mastaba [mastaba], *s.m. Egyptian Archeol:* mastaba, square Egyptian tomb.

mastacembelidés [mastasɑ̃bəlide], *s.m.pl. Ich:* Mastacembalidae.

mastic [mastik], *s.m.* **1.** mastic (resin). **2.** (*a*) cement, mastic, compound; **m. à vitres,** (glazier's) putty; **m. d'étanchéité, m. pour joints,** sealing compound; **m. de fer, à limailles,** iron cement; *Woodw: etc:* **m. à reboucher,** stopping-out wax; beaumontag(u)e; badigeon; *Metall:* **m. de fonte,** beaumontag(u)e; *a.inv.* **couleur m.,** putty-coloured; (*b*) *Dent:* filling, stopping; (*c*) *Aut: Cy:* **m. pour enveloppes,** tyre cement; (*d*) *Hort:* **m. à greffer,** grafting wax. **3.** *P:* (*a*) thick soup; (*b*) muddle, mess; *Typ:* (accidental) transposition of matter; pie.

masticage [mastika:ʒ], *s.m.* cementing, puttying, stopping; *Dent:* filling, stopping.

masticateur, -trice [mastikatœ:r, -tris]. **1.** *a.* masticatory (organ, etc.). **2.** *s.m.* masticator (animal or instrument).

mastication [mastikasjɔ̃], *s.f.* mastication, masticating; chewing.

masticatoire [mastikatwa:r]. **1.** *a.* masticatory. **2.** *s.m. Pharm:* masticatory.

mastiff [mastif], *s.m. Z:* mastiff.

mastiquer[1] [mastike], *v.tr.* to cement; to fill in (cracks, etc.) with cement; to putty (window); to stop (hole); *Dent:* to fill, stop (teeth); *Tls:* **couteau à m.,** putty knife.

mastiquer[2], *v.tr.* to masticate; to chew.

mastite [mastit], *s.f. Med:* mastitis.

mastoc [mastɔk], *F:* **1.** *s.m.* heavy, lumpish, person; lump of a chap. **2.** *a.inv.* **construction m.,** clumsy construction.

mastocyte [mastɔsit], *s.m. Biol:* mastocyte.

mastodonsaurus [mastɔdɔ̃sɔrys], *s.m. Paleont:* mastodonsaurus.

mastodonte [mastɔdɔ̃:t], *s.m.* **1.** *Paleont:* mastodon. **2.** *F:* (*a*) **les mastodontes de la route,** road monsters; juggernauts; mammoth lorries, buses, etc.; (*b*) (*pers.*) colossus.

mastodynie [mastɔdini], *s.f. Med:* mastodynia.

mastoïde [mastɔid], *a. Anat:* mastoid (bone, etc.); **apophyse m.,** mastoid process, mastoid.

mastoïdectomie [mastɔidɛktɔmi], *s.f. Surg:* mastoidectomy.

mastoïdien, -ienne [mastɔidjɛ̃, -jɛn], *a. Anat:* mastoidean.

mastoïdite [mastɔidit], *s.f. Med:* mastoiditis, inflammation of the mastoid, *F:* mastoids.

mastoïdo-huméral, -aux [mastɔidɔymeral, -o], *a. Z:* mastoido-humeral.

mastopexie [mastɔpɛksi], *s.f. Surg:* mastopexy.

mastroquet [mastrɔkɛ], *s.m. P: O:* (*a*) publican, keeper of a pub; (*b*) bar, pub.

masturbation [mastyrbasjɔ̃], *s.f.* masturbation.

masturber [mastyrbe], *v.tr.* to masturbate.

se masturber, to masturbate.

m'as-tu-vu [matyvy], *s.m.inv. F:* **1.** swanking actor. **2.** lover of publicity; swank, show-off.

masure [mazy:r], *s.f.* tumbledown cottage; hovel, shanty.

Masurie [mazyri], *Pr.n.f. Geog:* Masuria.

masurien, -ienne [mazyrjɛ̃, -jɛn], *a. Geog:* **les lacs masuriens,** the Masurian Lakes.

masurium [mazyrjɔm], *s.m. Hist. of Ch:* masurium.

mat[1] [mat], *a.* mat(t), unpolished, dull (metal); **couleur mate,** lustreless, dead, flat, dull, colour; **teint m.,** mat(t) complexion; **son m.,** dull, dead, sound; thud; **pâte mate,** heavy dough; **pain m.,** doughy bread; **papier m.,** matt paper; *Phot:* **bromure m.,** rough bromide print; *adv.* **sonner m.,** to give a dull, dead, sound.

mat[2] [mat]. **1.** *a.inv. Chess:* checkmated; **être m.,** to be the loser; **faire qn m., échec et m.,** to win a decisive victory over s.o. **2.** *s.m.* (check)mate; **donner le m. à son adversaire,** to checkmate one's opponent; **faire (échec et) m. en trois coups,** to mate in three; **être sous le m.,** to be in danger of being checkmated.

mât [mɑ], *s.m.* mast; pole; (*a*) *Nau:* **grand m.,** (i) mainmast; (ii) *F:* captain (of liner); **m. d'artimon,** mizzen mast; **m. de misaine,** foremast; **bas m.,** lower mast; **m. de hune,** top mast; **m. de beaupré,** bowsprit; **m. de charge,** cargo boom; **m. de fortune,** jury mast; **m. à pible,** pole mast; **m. bipode, tripode,** bipod, tripod, mast; **m. à portique,** goalpost mast; **m. de pavillon arrière,** flagstaff, ensign staff; **m. de pavillon avant,** jackstaff; **navire à trois mâts,** three-masted ship, three-master; **m. d'une pièce,** single-tree mast; **m. d'assemblage,** built mast; **m. rabattable,** lowering mast; **m. croisillonné, m. treillis,** lattice mast; **mâts jumelés,** twin masts; **bout de m.,** spar; **aller à m. et à corde,** to go under bare poles; **voiles sur le m.,** sails aback; *Navy:* **m. militaire,** military mast; (*b*) **m. de tente,** tent pole; **m. de cocagne,** greasy pole; **m. de pavoisement,** Venetian mast; (*c*) *Av:* strut; (*d*) *Rail:* **m. de signaux, m. sémaphorique,** signal post, signal mast; (*e*) *Min:* **m. de forage,** drilling mast.

Matabélé, -ée [matabele], *s. Ethn:* Matabele.

matador [matadɔ:r], *s.m.* **1.** matador. **2.** *A: F:* bigwig, big pot; magnate. **3.** *Games:* matador(e) (game of dominoes).

mataf [mataf], *s.m. P:* sailor.

matage [mata:ʒ], *s.m.* **1.** matting (of gilt, etc.). **2.** (*a*) *Metalw:* caulking, hammering (of boiler seams), peening; (*b*) *Mec.E: etc:* hammering, battering, bruising (of parts).

mâtage [mɑta:ʒ], *s.m. Nau:* shipping of the lower masts; masting.

matagot [matago], *s.m. Nau:* parrel.

matamata [matamata], *s.f. Rept:* matamata (turtle).

matamore[1] [matamɔ:r], *s.m.* braggart; swash-buckler; **faire le m.,** to bully, to hector.

matamore[2], *s.m.* **1.** *Hist:* (Arab) dungeon. **2.** *Agr:* underground silo.

matassé [matase], *s.m. Tex:* (*a*) **(soie en) m.,** thrown silk; (*b*) raw cotton.

matassin [matasɛ̃], *s.m.* (*a*) *A.Danc:* matachin(e); (*b*) buffoon.

match [matʃ], *s.m.* **1.** *Sp:* match; *Wr:* contest; **m. de football,** football match; **m. d'aviron,** boat race; **m. prévu,** fixture; *Fb:* **m. de championnat (professionnel),** league match; **faire m. nul,** to tie; *Wr:* **m. à quatre, par équipes,** tag match; *Ten:* **balle de m.,** match point; *Box:* **m. en 10 reprises,** 10 round match; *s.a.* ALLER II 1, RETOUR 4. **2.** struggle; *pl. matchs, matches* [matʃ].

matcher [matʃe]. **1.** *v.tr.* to match (*e.g.* one boxer against another). **2.** *v.i.* **m. contre une équipe adverse,** to play a match with another team.

mate [mat], *s.f.* **1.** swindling. **2.** *A:* **enfant, suppôt, de la m.,** swindler.

maté [mate], *s.m.* Paraguay tea, maté.

matefaim [matfɛ̃], *s.m. Cu:* thick pancake.

matelas [matlɑ, -a], *s.m.* (*a*) (overlay) mattress; **m. de mousse,** foam-rubber mattress; **m. pneumatique, de camping,** inflatable mattress; **m. d'eau,** water bed; **toile à m.,** ticking; **la toile du m.,** the tick; **retourner le m.,** to turn the mattress, the bed; **mon portefeuille fit m. et amortit le coup,** my wallet acted as a cushion and softened the blow; (*b*) *A:* padding (of carriage); (*c*) *Fort:* earth layer, filling; *Const:* **m. d'air,** air space; *Mch:* **m. de vapeur,** steam cushion; *Civ.E:* **macadam sur m. de sable,** macadam bedded on sand; **m. d'isolation,** insulation blanket; (*d*) *N.Arch:* backing (of armour plates); (*e*) *P:* wad of banknotes; well-filled wallet; **avoir le m.,** to be rolling (in it).

matelassé [matlase], *a. & s.m. Tex:* (*a*) matelassé (cloth); (*b*) quilted (material).

matelasser [matlase], *v.tr.* to pad, quilt, stuff, cushion (chair, etc.); *Fort:* to cover, fill, with earth; **chambre matelassée,** padded room; **porte matelassée,** baize door.

se matelasser, to wrap (oneself) up well.

matelassier, -ière [matlasje, -jɛ:r], *s.* **1.** mattress maker. **2.** mattress carder.

matelassure [matlasy:r], *s.f.* (*a*) padding, stuffing (of mattress, saddle, etc.); (*b*) *N.Arch:* backing (of armour plates).

matelot [matlo], *s.m.* **1.** sailor, seaman; **m. de, à, l'État,** seaman in the navy, *F:* bluejacket; **m. (breveté) de première classe,** leading seaman; **m. de deuxième classe,** able seaman; **m. de troisième classe,** ordinary seaman; **m. de pont,** deck hand; **servir comme simple m.,** to sail before the mast. **2.** *Nau:* (*a*) **mon m.,** my shipmate (who shares my hammock watch and watch about); (*b*) consort (ship); **m. d'avant, d'arrière,** next ship ahead, next astern. **3.** *Cost: A:* (child's) sailor suit.

matelotage [matlɔta:ʒ], *s.m.* (*a*) seamanship; (*b*) sailor's pay; (*c*) *A:* comradeship (between sailors).

matelote [matlɔt], *s.f.* **1.** sailor's wife. **2.** *A:* sailor's dance, matelote (approx. = hornpipe). **3.** *adv.phr.* **à la m.,** sailor-fashion; *Cu:* **poisson à la m.,** *s.f.* **m.,** fish stew (with wine, onions and herbs); matelote.

mâtement [mɑtmɑ̃], *s.m.* = MÂTAGE.

mater[1] [mate], *v.tr.* **1.** to mat(t), dull (metals, etc.). **2.** (*a*) to caulk, hammer (boiler seams, etc.); to burr (bolt, etc.); (*b*) *Mec.E:* to hammer, batter, bruise (working parts). **3.** *Bak:* to work (dough) into a compact state.

mater[2], *v.tr.* (*a*) *Chess:* to (check)mate; (*b*) **m. qn,** to subdue s.o.; to tame s.o.; to bring s.o. to heel; **m. l'orgueil de qn,** to humble, bring down, s.o.'s pride; **il n'était pas encore maté,** he had still some fight in him; **son mari l'avait matée,** her husband had broken her in.

mâter [mɑte], *v.tr.* (*a*) to mast (ship), to set up the lower masts of (ship); **mâté en frégate,** masted with a rake; **mâté en chandelier,** upright-masted; **machine à m.,** masting shears; **m. les mâts de charge,** to rig the booms; (*b*) **m. les avirons,** to toss oars; (*c*) to up-end (boat, etc.); **canot mâté debout par une lame,** boat up-ended by a sea.

mâtereau, -eaux [mɑtro], *s.m.* (*a*) *Nau:* small mast, hand mast, spar, staff; (*g*) *Carp:* kingpost.

matérialisation [materjalizasjɔ̃], *s.f.* materialization, materializing.

matérialisé [materjalize], *a. Adm:* **voie matérialisée** = section of a road delimited by a white line.

matérialiser [materjalize], *v.tr.* (*a*) to materialize; (*b*) **m. un projet,** to bring a plan into being.

se matérialiser, to materialize; *F:* to appear.

matérialisme [materjalism], *s.m.* materialism.

matérialiste [materjalist]. **1.** *a.* materialistic. **2.** *s.m. & f.* materialist.

matérialité [materjalite], *s.f.* materiality.

matériau [materjo], *s.m. Civ.E: Const: Ind:* (building, constructional) material; **le m. d'une pièce,** the material for a play; (back formation from *matériaux*).

matériaux [materjo], *s.m.pl. Civ.E: Const:* materials; **m. composites,** composite materials; **m. de construction,** building materials; **rassembler les m. pour l'histoire d'un règne,** to collect material for the history of a reign; *Geol:* **m. d'origine,** parent materials; **m. de transport glaciaire,** glacial drift; **m. triturés,** rock flour; **m. détritiques,** debris, detritus.

matériel, -elle [materjɛl]. **1.** *a.* (*a*) material, physical (body); *Mec:* **point m.,** physical point; (*b*) materialistic, gross, sensual (pleasures, mind, etc.); (*c*) **porte trop matérielle,** door that is too substantially, heavily, built; (*d*) **la vie matérielle,** the necessities of life; living; **besoins matériels,** bodily needs; (*e*) *Jur:* **dommages matériels,** damage to property. **2.** *s.m.* equipment; material; appliances; stock in trade; plant (of factory); (*a*) **m. de l'artiste,** artists' materials; **m. de campement, de camping,** camping equipment; **m. agricole,** farm equipment, machinery; farm implements; **m. d'école, m. scolaire,** school equipment; *Ind: etc:* **m. de série,** production equipment; **m. lourd,** heavy equipment, plant; **m. fixe,** fixed equipment, stationary plant; **m. mobile,** portable equipment, loose plant; **main d'œuvre et m.,** labour and material; (*b*) *Rail:* **m. de chemin de fer, m. ferroviaire,** railway material, plant; **m. fixe,** permanent way; **m. roulant,** rolling stock; **m. de traction,** hauling stock; **m. vide,** empty rolling stock, empties; (*c*) *Mil:* **Service du M.,** = Royal Army Ordnance Corps (R.A.O.C.), *U.S:* Ordnance Corps; **unité du M.,** ordnance unit; **m. réglementaire,** service, standard, equipment; **m. de guerre,** war equipment, material; **m. de soutien logistique,** (logistical) support equipment; **m. d'instruction,** training equipment, training aids; **m. consommable,** consumable, expendable, equipment or stores; **m. non consommable,** non-expendable equipment or stores; **m. en excédent,** surplus equipment, property; **m. hors service (H.S.),** unserviceable equipment, property; **m. d'artillerie,** artillery equipment, material; ordnance material; **m. du génie,** engineer equipment, stores; **m. des transmissions,** signal equipment, *U.S:* communication equipment; **m. de guerre chimique, matériel "Z,"** chemical-warfare equipment; (*d*) *Elcs:* hardware. **3.** *s.f. F:* **la matérielle,** the wherewithal; the needful; **cela leur assurera la matérielle,** that will bring them in the needful, will keep the pot boiling, the wolf from the door.

matériellement [materjɛlmɑ̃], *adv.* (*a*) materially; **avoir de quoi vivre m.,** to have enough for one's material needs, enough to live on; **chose m. impossible,** thing impossible in point of fact, thing physically impossible, physical impossibility; (*b*) materialistically; sensually.

maternage [matɛrnaːʒ], *s.m.* mothering (of child).

maternel, -elle [matɛrnɛl], *a.* maternal. **1.** motherly (care, etc.); **école maternelle,** *s.f.* **maternelle,** nursery school. **2.** (*a*) **aïeul m.,** maternal grandfather; (*b*) **langue maternelle,** mother tongue, native tongue; **avoir pour langue maternelle le français,** to speak French as one's mother tongue.

maternellement [matɛrnɛlmɑ̃], *adv.* maternally; in a motherly fashion.

materniser [matɛrnize], *v.tr.* to give (milk) the composition, qualities, of mother's milk.

maternité [matɛrnite], *s.f.* **1.** (*a*) maternity, motherhood; **m. divine,** virgin birth; **pousser la m. jusqu'au fanatisme,** to carry one's duties as a mother to the point of fanaticism; *Adm:* **allocation de m.,** maternity grant; (*b*) **elle a été fatiguée par ses maternités successives,** she was exhausted by a succession of confinements. **2.** (*a*) maternity hospital; **service de la m.,** maternity ward; (*b*) school of midwifery.

mateur [matœːr], *s.m. Metalw:* scarfer.

mât-grue [magry], *s.m.* mast-crane; *pl. mâts-grues.*

math(s) [mat], *s.f.pl. Sch: F:* maths; **il est fort en m.,** he's good at maths; **m. élém** [matelɛm] = A Level maths; **m. sup** [matsyp], **m. spé** [matspe] maths classes preparing for the entrance exam to the *grandes écoles*; **m. géné** [matʒene], first-year university course in maths.

mathématicien, -ienne [matematisjɛ̃, -jɛn], *s.* mathematician.

mathématique [matematik]. **1.** *a.* mathematical; **précision m.,** mathematical precision; *F:* **c'est m.,** it's inevitable. **2.** *s.f. usu. pl.* **mathématiques,** mathematics; **mathématiques pures, appliquées,** pure, applied, mathematics; **instruments de mathématiques,** mathematical instruments; *Sch:* **mathématiques élémentaires** = A Level mathematics; **mathématiques supérieures, mathématiques spéciales,** first-year, second-year, mathematics course preparing for the entrance examination to one of the *grandes écoles*; **mathématiques générales,** first-year university mathematics course (taken by science students); **mathématiques modernes,** modern mathematics.

mathématiquement [matematikmɑ̃], *adv.* mathematically; **cela devait m. arriver,** it was inevitable, bound to happen.

mathématiser [matematize], *v.tr.* **m. une question,** to mathematize, to apply mathematical concepts to a question, to deal with a question in terms of mathematics.

matheux, -euse [matø, -øːz], *s. F:* keen mathematician, maths fiend.

Mathieu [matjø], *Pr.n.m.* = MATTHIEU.

Mathilde [matild], *Pr.n.f.* Matilda; Maud.

Mathurin [matyrɛ̃]. **1.** *Pr.n.m.* Mathelin, Mathurin (patron saint of idiots and fools); *A:* **colique de Saint-M.,** malady of St Mathurin, folly, stupidity. **2.** *s.m. Ecc.Hist:* Mathurin (friar). **3.** *s.m. Nau: F: O:* Jack Tar.

Mathusalem [matyzalɛm]. **1.** *Pr.n.m. B.Hist:* Methuselah. **2.** *s.m.* jeroboam (of champagne).

matière [matjɛːr], *s.f.* **1.** (*a*) matter; **m. inanimée,** inanimate matter; (*b*) *Phil: etc:* substance; **être enfoncé dans la m.,** to be engrossed in material things. **2.** matter, material, substance; (*a*) *Ph: Ch:* **m. organique, inorganique,** organic, inorganic, matter; **m. cosmique, m. interstellaire,** cosmic dust; **m. en suspension (dans l'eau, etc.),** suspended matter (in water, etc.); *Atom.Ph:* **m. active,** active material; **m. nucléaire,** nuclear matter; **m. radioactive,** radioactive material; **m. hautement radioactive, m. chaude,** highly radioactive, hot, material; **m. appauvrie, enrichie,** impoverished, enriched, material; **m. fertile,** fertile material, breeder material; **m. (non-)régénératrice,** (non-)breeding material; (*b*) *Anat:* **m. grise,** grey matter (of the brain); *F:* **il a de la m. grise,** he's intelligent, clever, bright; *Med:* **matières fécales,** faeces, stools, excreta; **m. purulente,** pus, matter; (*c*) *Ind:* **matière(s) première(s),** raw material(s); **m. brute,** unprocessed material; **m. d'apport,** additive, addition agent; **m. de remplissage,** filler, filling-material, fillings; **m. obturatrice,** sealing material, compound; **m. absorbante,** absorbent material; **m. colorante,** colouring matter, dye; **m. filtrante,** filter material; **m. spongieuse,** foam material, spongy material; **matière(s) plastique(s),** plastic(s); **m. synthétique,** synthetic material; (*d*) **matières grasses,** fats; **m. grasse,** fat; oily, greasy, substance; butterfat (of dairy products); **la teneur du lait en m. grasse,** the butterfat content of milk; (*e*) *Fin:* **matières d'or et d'argent,** bullion; *Typ:* **vieille m.,** battered or worn type, *F:* metal. **3.** (*a*) subject (of speech, etc.); topic, theme (for discussion, for an essay); (school) subject; **table des matières,** (table of) contents (of book); **la m. à lecture (d'un journal),** the reading matter (of a newspaper); **entrer en m.,** to broach the subject; to begin (one's speech); **entrée en m.,** introduction, preamble; **versé dans une m.,** well up in a subject; **fournir m. à de longues discussions,** to provide material for long discussions; **il n'y a pas m. à rire,** there is nothing to laugh about, it's no laughing matter; **m. à controverse, à réflexion,** food for controversy, for thought; **m. à procès,** grounds, cause, case, for litigation; **être bon juge en m. de musique,** to be a good judge of music; **tolérance en m. de religion,** toleration in religious matters; **en m. de mode ce sont les sots qui font la loi,** in matters of fashion, fools lay down the law; (*b*) *Jur:* (i) **matières sommaires,** summary matters; (ii) **m. d'un crime,** gravamen of a charge; (*c*) *Adm:* **m. imposable,** taxable object.

Matignon [matiɲɔ̃], *Pr.n.m.* **l'hôtel M.,** the Prime Minister's residence.

matildite [matildit], *s.f. Miner:* matildite.

matin [matɛ̃]. **1.** *s.m.* morning, *Poet:* morn; **je l'ai vu ce m.,** I saw him this morning; **j'appris la nouvelle le m. de mon mariage,** I heard the news on my wedding morning; **travailler du m. au soir,** to work from morning to night; to work morning, noon and night; **dire ses prières m. et soir,** to say one's prayers night and morning; **quatre heures du m.,** four o'clock in the morning, 4 a.m.; **au matin,** in the morning, the next morning; **le jeudi deux au m.,** on the morning of Thursday the second; **c'est le m. que je travaille le mieux,** I work best in the morning(s); **que faites-vous le m.?** what do you do in the morning, of a morning? **demain m.,** tomorrow morning; **tous les lundis m.,** every Monday morning; **de grand, bon, m.; le m. de bonne heure,** early in the morning, in the early morning; **il était grand m.,** it was very early (in the day); **rentrer au petit m.,** *F:* to come home with the milk; **un de ces (quatre) matins, un beau m.,** one of these (fine) days; *Prov:* **heure du m., heure du gain,** the early bird catches the worm. **2.** *adv.* in the morning, early; **se lever très m.,** to get up very early; *Prov:* **à qui se lève m. Dieu aide et prête la main,** the early bird catches the worm.

mâtin [mɑtɛ̃], *s.m.* **1.** (*a*) mastiff; (*b*) large mongrel; watchdog. **2.** *F:* (*a*) *A:* sly, disagreeable, person; (*b*) (*with f.* **mâtine** [mɑtin]) mischievous, boisterous, person; **petite mâtine!** you young monkey! **la mâtine nous a trompés,** the little wretch has had us. **3.** *int. F:* good heavens! **mille milles à l'heure! m.!** a thousand miles an hour! some speed!

matinal, -aux [matinal, -o], *a.* **1.** morning (breeze, etc.); **à cette heure matinale,** at this early hour; **promenade matinale,** early morning walk; *Bot:* **fleur matinale,** matutinal flower. **2.** (*of pers.*) early rising; **comme tu es m. aujourd'hui!** you're up very early this morning! *s.* **c'est un m.,** he is an early riser.

matinalement [matinalmɑ̃], *adv.* early (in the morning).

mâtiné [mɑtine], *a.* (*a*) (*of dog*) mongrel, cross-bred; **terrier m. de lévrier,** terrier crossed with a greyhound; (*b*) **il parle un français m. d'espagnol,** he speaks a mixture of French and Spanish.

mâtineau, -eaux [mɑtino], *s.m.* **1.** mastiff pup. **2.** young mongrel, mongrel pup.

matinée [matine], *s.f.* **1.** morning; **travailler toute la m.,** to work all the morning; **dans la m.,** in the course of the morning; **belle m. de printemps,** fine spring morning; **à onze heures de la m.,** at eleven in the morning; **je l'ai vu hier dans la m.,** I saw him yesterday morning; **c'était par une froide m. d'hiver,** it was on a cold winter morning; **je ne l'ai pas vu de toute la m.,** I haven't seen him all morning; *F:* **faire la grasse m.,** to sleep late in the morning, to stay in bed late, to have a lie in. **2.** *Th: etc:* matinée. **3.** *Cost: A:* (woman's) wrapper (worn in the mornings).

mâtiner [mɑtine], *v.tr.* **1.** (*of dog*) to cover, line (bitch of a different breed). **2.** *F: A:* to abuse, slang (s.o.).

matines [matin], *s.f.pl. Ecc:* matins; **la cloche sonnait m.,** the bell was ringing for matins.

matineux, -euse [matinø, -øːz], *O:* **1.** *a.* early rising. **2.** *s.* (habitual) early riser, *F:* early bird.

matinier, -ière [matinje, -jɛːr], *a. A:* of the morning; *still used occ. in* **l'étoile matinière,** the morning star.

matir [matiːr], *v.tr.* = MATER[1] 1, 2.

matité [matite], *s.f.* (*a*) deadness, dullness (of sound, etc.); *Med:* **m. pleurale, m. à la base du poumon,** dullness at the base of the lungs; (*b*) mattness (of colour).

matlockite [matlɔkit], *s.f. Miner:* matlockite.

matoir [matwaːr], *s.m.* **1.** matting tool. **2.** *Metalw:* caulking chisel. **3.** riveting hammer.

matois, -oise [matwa, -waːz]. **1.** *a.* sly, cunning, crafty. **2.** *s.* sly, crafty, person; **c'est un fin m.,** he's a sly character, a cunning type.

matoisement [matwazmɑ̃], *adv.* slyly, cunningly, craftily.

matoiserie [matwazri], *s.f. A:* (*a*) slyness, cunning, craftiness; (*b*) trick, wile, dodge.

matolin [matɔlɛ̃], *s.m.* (**vernis**) **m.**, mat(t) varnish; *Phot:* retouching medium.

matou [matu], *s.m.* **1.** tom cat. **2.** *F:* **c'est un vilain m.**, he's an unpleasant customer.

matraquage [matrakaːʒ], *s.m.* bludgeoning; rough-handling.

matraque [matrak], *s.f.* bludgeon, (knotted) club, *U.S:* blackjack; **m. en caoutchouc,** rubber truncheon; *F:* **coup de m.,** barefaced overcharging (in restaurant).

matraquer [matrake], *v.tr.* to bludgeon (s.o.); to treat (s.o.) roughly.

matras[1] [matrɑ], *s.m. A.Arms:* quarrel (for crossbow).

matras[2], *s.m. Ch:* matrass, bolt-head, receiver.

matriarcal, -aux [matriarkal, -o], *a.* matriarchal.

matriarcat [matriarka], *s.m.* matriarchate, matriarchy.

matriçage [matrisaːʒ], *s.m. Metalw:* (*a*) dieing (out), die stamping; coining; **forgeage par m.,** die forging; **m. extrusion,** cored forging; (*b*) swaging.

matricaire [matrikɛːr], *s.f. Bot:* feverfew; **m. camomille,** wild camomile.

matrice [matris], *s.f.* **1.** matrix; (*a*) *Anat:* (i) uterus, womb; (ii) matrix (of hair, nail); **m. cervicale,** cervical matrix; (*b*) *Metalw:* (i) die, former; (ii) bottom tool, bolster; (iii) mould; **m. à estamper,** stamping die; **m. d'emboutissage,** pressing die; **m. d'étirage,** drawing die; **m.-type,** master die; **coulé en m.,** die cast; (*c*) *Typ:* type mould; (*d*) *Rec:* **m. de disques, m. de réserve,** matrix, mother record; (*e*) *Mth: Elcs:* matrix; **m. positive, négative,** positive, negative, matrix; **m. carrée,** square matrix; **m. de base,** basis; **m. inverse,** inverse matrix; **m. singulière, m. non inversible,** singular matrix; **m. régulière, m. inversible,** non-singular matrix; **inversion de m.,** matrix inversion (of computer). **2.** *Meas:* standard. **3.** *Adm:* original (of register of taxes). **4.** *a.f.* (*a*) *Dy:* **couleurs matrices,** primary colours (black, white, blue, yellow, red); (*b*) **langue m.,** mother tongue; **église m.,** mother church.

matricer [matrise], *v.tr.* (*a*) to die (out), to stamp (metal); **pièce matricée,** (i) stamping, stamped out part; (ii) drop forging; **moulage matricé,** die-cast moulding; (*b*) to swage.

matricide[1] [matrisid]. **1.** *s.m. & f.* matricide, one who murders his, her, mother. **2.** *a.* matricidal.

matricide[2], *s.m.* (crime of) matricide.

matriciel, -elle [matrisjɛl], *a.* **1.** *Fin:* pertaining to the register from which the direct taxation assessments are compiled. **2.** *Mth: etc:* matric(al); **équation matricielle,** matric equation; **analyse matricielle,** matrix analysis; *Elcs:* **mémoire à sélection matricielle,** matrix storage, matric store (of computer).

matriclan [matriklɑ̃], *s.m. Ethn:* matriclan.

matriculaire [matrikylɛːr]. **1.** *a.* pertaining to registration or enrolment; *Mil: Navy:* **feuille m.,** history sheet. **2.** *s.* registered person, *esp.* enrolled soldier or sailor.

matricule [matrikyl]. **1.** *s.f.* (*a*) roll, register, list (of members, etc.); *Mil:* regimental roll; (*b*) inscription, registration; enrolling, enrolment; (*c*) registration certificate; *s.a.* LIVRET 1. **2. numéro m.,** *s.m.* **matricule,** (regimental or administrative) number; **prenez son m.!** take his number! **numéro m. d'un fusil,** number of a rifle; *Mil: P:* **ça va barder pour ton m.,** you've got it coming to you.

matriculer [matrikyle], *v.tr.* **1.** to enter (s.o.'s) name on a register; to enrol (soldier, sailor). **2.** to mark (soldier's kit, etc.) with his regimental number; to stamp the number on (car engine, etc.).

matrilinéaire [matrilineɛːr], *a.* *Ethn:* matrilinear.

matrilocal, -aux [matrilɔkal, -o], *a.* *Ethn:* matrilocal.

matrimonial, -iaux [matrimɔnjal, -jo], *a.* matrimonial (agency, etc.); *Jur:* **régime m.,** marriage contract.

matrimonialement [matrimɔnjalmɑ̃], *adv.* matrimonially; **conjoindre m.,** to join in matrimony.

matrocline [matrɔklin], *a.* *Biol:* matroclinous, matroclinic.

matronal, -aux [matrɔnal, -o], *a.* matronal; matronly.

matrone [matrɔn], *s.f.* **1.** matron; *Pej:* **vieille m.,** (fat) old hag. **2.** (*a*) *A:* midwife; (*b*) woman illegally established as midwife; (*c*) abortionist.

matronyme [matrɔnim], *s.m.* matronymic.

matte [mat], *s.f. Metall:* matte, coarse metal; **m. blanche de cuivre,** white metal, regulus.

matteau, -eaux [mato], *s.m.* hank (of raw silk).

Matthieu [matjø], *Pr.n.m.* Matthew.

matthiole [matjɔl], *s.f. Bot:* mat(t)hiola, stock.

maturatif, -ive [matyratif, -iːv], *Med:* **1.** *a.* maturative. **2.** *s.m.* maturant, maturative.

maturateur [matyratœːr], *s.m. Ap:* vat (for honey).

maturation [matyrasjɔ̃], *s.f.* (*a*) *Biol: Psy:* maturation; ripening (of fruit); *Med:* maturation (of abscess); **la m. de son talent,** the maturing of his talent; (*b*) *Ind: etc:* maturing (of tobacco); **cave de m. des fromages,** cellar for ripening, maturing, cheese; *Phot:* **m. de l'émulsion,** digestion of the emulsion.

mature [matyːr], *a.* (*of fish*) ready to spawn, ripe.

mâture [matyːr], *s.f. Nau:* **1.** (art of) masting. **2.** (*a*) masts; masts and spars; **dans la m.,** aloft; (*b*) mast-house; (*c*) timber suitable for masts. **3.** mast crane, sheer-legs, sheers; **m. flottante,** sheer hulk.

maturément [matyremɑ̃], *adv.* with, after, mature consideration; maturely.

maturer [matyre], *v.tr.* **1.** to mature (tobacco). **2.** *Metall:* to refine (ore).

maturité [matyrite], *s.f.* (*a*) maturity, ripeness (of fruit, abscess, etc.); **arriver à m.,** to come to maturity; (*b*) **l'œuvre de sa m.,** the work of his maturity; **avec m.,** after mature consideration; **projet exposé avant m.,** plan publicised before it is ready; **le défaut de m. de ces projets,** the immaturity of these plans; (*c*) *Geog:* **topographie arrivée à l'état de m.,** mature landscape; (*d*) *Sw.Fr: Sch:* = General Certificate of Education.

matutinal, -aux [matytinal, -o], *a.* (*a*) *A. & Lit:* matutinal; **toux matutinale,** (early) morning cough; (*b*) *Ecc:* pertaining to matins.

maubèche [mobɛʃ], *s.f. Orn:* sandpiper; **m. violette,** redleg(s); **grande m.,** knot; robin snipe; **petite m.,** sea lark, summer snipe.

maubeugeois, -oise [mobøʒwa, -waːz], *a. & s.* *Geog:* (native, inhabitant) of Maubeuge.

maudire [modiːr], *v.tr.* (*pr.p.* **maudissant;** *p.p.* **maudit;** *pr.ind.* **je maudis, n. maudissons, v. maudissez, ils maudissent;** *pr.sub.* **je maudisse;** *p.d.* **je maudissais;** *p.h.* **je maudis;** *fu.* **je maudirai**) to curse, to call down curses upon (s.o., sth.); to anathematize; **m. le mauvais temps,** to grumble about, curse, the weather.

maudissable [modisabḷ], *a.* damnable, detestable.

maudit [modi]. **1.** *a.* (*a*) (ac)cursed (crime, etc.); **m. soit le jour où . . .,** cursed be the day when . . .; *A:* **m. soit le coquin!** hang the fellow! confound the fellow! (*b*) **quel m. temps!** what filthy, damnable, execrable, weather! **2.** *s.* **le M.,** the Devil, the Evil One; **les maudits,** the accursed, the damned.

maugère [moʒɛːr], *s.f. Nau:* pump leather, hose leather; **m. de dalot, de pompe,** scupper leather, pump leather.

maugré [mogre], *prep. A:* = MALGRÉ.

maugrebleu [mogrəblø], **maugrébleu** [mogreblø], *int. F: O:* for the love of heaven!

maugréer [mogree], *v.i.* to curse, fume; to grumble, to grouse (**après, contre,** about, at).

maurandie [morɑ̃di], *s.f. Bot:* maurandia.

Maure [moːr], *Ethn: Geog:* **1.** *s.m.* (*a*) Moor; (*b*) **tête de M.,** (i) *Her:* Moor's head; (ii) *Cu: F:* Dutch cheese. **2.** *a.m.* Moorish.

maurelle [morɛl], *s.f. Bot:* turnsole.

mauresque [morɛsk], *Ethn: Geog: etc:* **1.** (*a*) *a.f.* Moorish (woman, etc.); (*b*) *a.* Moorish (architecture, design). **2.** *s.f.* (*a*) Moorish woman; (*b*) moresque (pattern); (*c*) *Cost:* pair of loosely fitting Eastern trousers.

Maurice [moris], *Pr.n.m.* Maurice; *Geog:* **l'île M.,** Mauritius.

mauricien, -ienne [morisjɛ̃, -jɛn], *a. & s.* *Geog:* (native, inhabitant) of Mauritius.

Mauritanie [moritani], *Pr.n.f. Geog:* Mauritania; **la république islamique de M.,** the Islamic Republic of Mauritania.

mauritanien, -ienne [moritanjɛ̃, -jɛn], *a. & s.* *Geog:* Mauritanian.

mauser [mozeːr], *s.m. Sm.a:* (*a*) Mauser (rifle); (*b*) automatic pistol.

Mausole [mozɔl], *Pr.n.m. Hist:* Mausolus.

mausolée [mozɔle], *s.m.* mausoleum.

maussade [mosad], *a.* (*a*) surly, sullen, glum; peevish; grumpy, disgruntled; **d'un ton m.,** irritably; **il est m. comme tout! he's like a bear with a sore head;** (*b*) **temps m.,** dull, gloomy, weather; **livre m.,** depressing book; **une grande maison m.,** a large, gloomy house.

maussadement [mosadmɑ̃], *adv.* sullenly, surlily, grumpily; peevishly, irritably.

maussaderie [mosadri], *s.f.* sullenness, peevishness; gloominess.

mauvais [mɔvɛ], *a.* (*a*) evil (thought); ill (omen); wicked (person); bad (son); **mauvaise action,** bad action; wrong; **de plus en plus m.,** worse and worse; **le plus m.,** the worst; **avoir l'air m.,** (i) to look evil-minded; (ii) to look fierce, vicious; **regarder qn d'un air m.,** to give s.o. a black look; **de m. bruits courent sur son compte,** there are unpleasant rumours abroad about him; **avoir de m. desseins,** to be bent on mischief; **c'est un m. cœur,** he's no good, *F:* he's a bad egg; **c'est un m. sujet, un m. garçon,** he's a bad lot; **ce n'est pas un m. homme,** he is not a bad-hearted man; **il a une mauvaise réputation,** he has a bad reputation, he is in bad repute; **son m. ange,** his evil genius; **né sous une mauvaise étoile,** born under an unlucky star; **le m. œil,** the evil eye; (*b*) ill-natured (**pour,** towards); **c'est une mauvaise langue,** she has a vicious tongue, she's a gossip, a scandalmonger; *F:* **ne sois pas si mauvais(e)!** don't be so horrible, so mean! *s.a.* TÊTE 2; (*c*) nasty, displeasing, unpleasant; **mauvaise haleine,** bad breath; **m. pas,** dangerous situation; **comment sortir de ce m. pas?** how are we to get out of this fix? **m. temps,** bad weather; **mer mauvaise,** rough sea; **trouver qch. m.,** to dislike sth.; **trouve-t-il m. ce que j'ai fait?** does he disapprove of what I have done? **trouver m. que qn fasse qch.,** to disapprove of, take exception to, s.o.'s doing sth.; *F:* **je la trouve mauvaise,** that's a poor joke! it isn't at all funny! **prendre qch. en mauvaise part,** to take sth. in bad part, to take offence at sth., to take sth. unkindly; *adv.* **sentir m.,** to smell (bad), to stink; **il fait m. être pauvre,** it is wretched to be poor; **il fait m.,** the weather is bad; (*d*) **m. pour la santé, pour la digestion,** bad for the health, the digestion; (*e*) imperfect, poor, inadequate; **assez m., plutôt m.,** not very good, none too good, rather bad; **mauvaise qualité de qch.,** badness of sth.; **de mauvaise qualité,** of poor quality, inferior; (*of ores, etc.*) low grade; **avoir m. air,** (i) to look ill; (ii) to have a poor appearance; **mauvaise santé,** bad, poor, health; **mauvaise hygiène,** faulty hygiene; **avoir mauvaise vue,** to have bad eyesight; **m. estomac,** weak stomach; **il a fait une mauvaise bronchite,** he's had a bad, nasty, attack of bronchitis; **m. peintre,** poor painter; **faire de mauvaises affaires,** to be doing badly (in business); **m. marché,** bad bargain; **écrire en m. français,** to write in bad, poor, French; **parler en m. français,** to speak bad, broken, French; to speak French badly; *El:* **m. conducteur,** poor conductor; *Mec.E:* **m. fonctionnement,** defective working; crankiness; **m. roman,** bad, poor, novel; **m. frein,** defective brake; *F:* **il ne me faudrait que dix mille m. francs pour me remettre d'aplomb,** I want only a miserable ten thousand francs to get straight; (*f*) wrong, due to a mistake; **c'est la mauvaise clef,** it is the wrong key; **venir dans un m. moment,** to come at an inconvenient time, at the wrong time, at an awkward moment; **rire au m. endroit,** to laugh in the wrong place; **mauvaise mesure,** short measure; **tenir qch. par le m. bout,** (i) to hold sth. by the wrong end; (ii) *F:* to get the wrong end of the stick.

mauvaiseté [movɛzte], *s.f. A:* ill nature (of criticism, etc.).

mauve[1] [moːv]. **1.** *s.f. Bot:* mallow; **grande m.,** tree mallow. **2.** *a. & s.m.* mauve.

mauve[2], *s.f. Orn: Dial:* seagull.

mauvéine [movein], *s.f. Ch: Dy:* mauvein(e).

mauviette [movjɛt], *s.f.* (*a*) *Cu:* lark (in season); *F:* **elle mange comme une m.,** she doesn't eat enough to keep a sparrow alive; (*b*) *F:* slight, frail, person; **une petite m.,** a little slip of a girl.

mauvis [movi], *s.m. Orn:* redwing.

Maxence [maksɑ̃ːs]. **1.** *Pr.n.m.* Maxentius. **2.** *Pr.n.f.* Maxentia.

maxi [maksi], *s.m. or f. Cost: F:* maxi (coat, skirt).

maxillaire [maksil(l)ɛːr], *a. Anat:* maxillary; **os m.,** jawbone, maxilla.

maxille [maksiːj], *s.f. Ent: Crust:* maxilla.

maxillipède [maksil(l)ipɛd], *s.m. Arach: Crust:* maxilliped(e).

maxillite [maksil(l)it], *s.f. Med: Vet:* inflammation of the maxillary gland.

maxillule [maksil(l)yl], *s.f. Ent: Crust:* maxillula.

maximal, -aux [maksimal, -o], *a.* **1.** maximum (effect, etc.). **2.** maximal.

maximaliser [maksimalize], *v.tr.* to maximize.

maximalisme [maksimalism], *s.m. Pol.Hist:* maximalism.

maximaliste [maksimalist], *a. & s.m. & f. Pol. Hist:* maximalist; *Russ.Hist:* Bolshevik.

Maxime[1] [maksim], *Pr.n.m.* Maximus.

maxime[2], *s.f.* 1. maxim; **prendre qch. pour m.,** to take sth. as a maxim; **il tenait pour m. que l'on doit . . .,** it was a maxim of his that one ought to . . .. 2. *Mus:* maxim, maxima.

maximer [maksime], *v.tr.* to make a maxim of sth.

Maximilien [maksimiljɛ̃], *Pr.n.m.* Maximilian.

maximiser [maksimize], *v.tr.* to maximize.

maximum [maksimɔm], maximum. 1. *s.m.* **m. de rendement,** highest efficiency, maximum efficiency; **au m.,** to the maximum; to the highest degree; **porter la production au m.,** to raise production to a maximum; **courir le m. de risques,** to run the maximum of risks; **être condamné au m. de la peine,** to be condemned to the maximum punishment; **faire rendre son m. à un cheval, à un coureur, à un navire,** to extend a horse, a runner, a ship; **thermomètre à maxima,** maximum thermometer; *El:* **m. d'intensité et minimum de tension,** overload and undervoltage; *pl. maximums, (esp. for scientific terms) maxima.* 2. *a. often inv. in sing. but f.* **maxima** *(inv. in pl.) also used; m.pl.* **maximums** *or* **maxima; rendement m.,** maximum, peak, output; **pression m., pression maxima,** maximum pressure; **les vitesses maxima,** the maximum speeds; **nos chances seront maxima,** we shall have the best possible chance of success.

Maxwell [makswɛl]. 1. *Pr.n. El:* **loi de M.,** Maxwell's rule, law. 2. *s.m. El.Meas:* maxwell.

maya[1] [maja], *a. & s. Ethn:* Maya(n).

maya[2], *s.f.* 1. *Hindu Rel:* maya. 2. *Phil:* maya; illusion.

mayday [mede], *inv. Av: Nau: W.Tp:* mayday (*usu.* preceded by S.O.S.).

mayen [majɛn], *s.m. (in Switz.)* Alpine chalet (on summer high pastures).

mayençais, -aise [majɑ̃sɛ, -ɛːz], *a. & s. Geog:* (native, inhabitant) of Mainz.

Mayence [majɑ̃ːs], *Pr.n.f. Geog:* Mainz.

mayennais, -aise [majɛnɛ, -ɛːz], *a. & s. Geog:* (native, inhabitant) of Mayenne.

mayonnaise [majɔnɛːz], *s.f. Cu:* mayonnaise.

mazagran [mazagrɑ̃], *s.m. (a)* glass of coffee; *(b)* china tumbler (in form of stemmed glass for serving coffee).

mazamétain, -aine [mazametɛ̃, -ɛn], **mazamétois, -oise** [mazametwa, -waːz], *a. & s. Geog:* (native, inhabitant) of Mazamet.

Mazandéran [mazɑ̃derɑ̃], *Pr.n. Geog:* Mazandaran.

mazapilite [mazapilit], *s.f. Miner:* mazapilite.

mazarinade [mazarinad], *s.f. Hist:* lampoon (on Cardinal Mazarin).

mazdéisme [mazdeism], *s.m. Rel.H:* Mazdaism.

mazéage [mɑzeaːʒ], *s.m. Metall:* refining (of pig iron).

mazer [mɑze], *v.tr. Metall:* to refine (pig iron).

mazerie [mɑzri], *s.f. Metall:* finery.

mazet [mɑzɛ], *s.m. Dial: (S.Fr.)* small farmhouse.

mazetier [maztje], *s.m. Dial: (S.Fr.)* farmer.

mazette [mɑzɛt, ma-], *s.f. F:* 1. *A:* poor horse; screw, jade. 2. *(a) O:* duffer (at a game, etc.), *F:* rabbit; *(b)* spineless person. 3. *int. (expressing astonishment, admiration)* well! heavens!

mazout [mazu(t)], *s.m.* fuel oil (for ships, locomotives, etc.); **chauffage central au m.,** oil-fired central heating.

mazoutage [mazutaːʒ], *s.m. Nau:* refuelling.

mazouter [mazute]. 1. *v.i. Nau:* to refuel. 2. *v.tr.* to foul (beach); to oil (bird).

mazouteur [mazutœːr], *s.m. Nau:* refuelling tanker.

mazurka [mazyrka], *s.f.* mazurka.

me, *before a vowel sound* **m'** [m(ə)], *pers.pron., unstressed, attached to the verb or its adjuncts; (a) (acc.)* me; **il m'aime,** he loves me; **me voici,** here I am; *(b) (dat.)* (to) me; **il m'a écrit,** he wrote to me; **il me l'a dit,** he told me so; **on me l'a dit,** I was told so; **donnez-m'en,** give me some; **il faut tout me dire, il faut me tout dire,** you must tell me everything; *(c) (with pr.vbs.)* myself; **je me lave,** I wash myself; **je me dis que . . .,** I said to myself that . . .; *with many vbs.* **me** *is not rendered into English; see* S'EN ALLER, SE BATTRE, SE DÉPÊCHER, etc.

mé-, més-, mes- [me, mez, mɛs], *pref.* mis-, dis-; **mésalliance,** misalliance; **mécontent,** displeased; **méjuger,** to misjudge.

mea-culpa [meakylpa], *s.m.inv.* **faire, dire, son m.-c.,** to confess one's sins.

Méandre [meɑ̃ːdr̥]. 1. *Pr.n.m. A.Geog:* **le M.,** the (river) Meander. 2. *s.m. (a)* meander (of river); winding (of road); *Geog:* **m. encaissé,** incised meander; **m. recoupé,** cut-off meander; **m. divagant,** flood-plain meander; **la rivière fait des méandres à travers la plaine,** the river meanders through the plain; *(b)* **les méandres de la politique,** the tortuous paths of politics; **il est difficile de suivre les méandres de sa pensée,** it is difficult to follow the intricate pattern, the ins and outs, of his thoughts; *(c)* Greek key pattern; zigzag design.

méandrine [meɑ̃drin], *s.f. Coel:* m(a)éandra, meandrina, m(a)eandrine coral.

méat [mea], *s.m. Anat: Bot:* meatus; *Bot:* **m. intercellulaire,** intercellular space.

méatotome [meatɔtɔm], *s.m. Surg:* meatotome.

méatotomie [meatɔtɔmi], *s.f. Surg:* meatotomy.

mec [mɛk], *s.m. P: (a)* tough guy; **m. à la redresse,** thug; *(b)* pimp; *(c)* bloke, type; **c'est un drôle de m.,** he's an odd customer; **vilain m.,** nasty type; **petit m.,** little twerp; **c'est un bon m.,** he's a nice guy; **le m. des mecs,** God.

mécanicien, -ienne [mekanisjɛ̃, -jɛn]. 1. *s.m.* **(ouvrier) m.,** mechanic; *(a)* **m. d'automobile,** *F:* **m. auto,** motor mechanic; **m. de garage,** garage mechanic; **il répare sa voiture lui-même; il est bon m.,** he does his own car repairs; he's a good mechanic; **m. électricien,** electrical mechanic; **m. radio,** radio mechanic; **m. (de) radar,** radar mechanic; *Dent:* **m. dentiste,** dental mechanic, dental (laboratory) technician; *(b) Nau:* (marine) engineer; *Navy:* engine-room artificer; **chef m.,** chief engineer; **m. (chef) de quart,** watch engineer, *U.S:* assistant engineer; **officier m.,** *Av: Navy:* engineer officer; *Mil.Trans:* motor officer; *Nau:* engineer; *Nau:* **officier m. en second,** second engineer, *U.S:* first assistant engineer; *Nau:* **m. de garantie,** guarantee engineer; *Av:* **m. d'aviation, m. d'avion,** air(craft) mechanic; **m. de moteur d'avion,** aero-engine mechanic; *Civ.Av:* **m. de bord,** *Mil.Av:* **m. navigant,** flight engineer, operational engineer; **m. de piste,** aircraft engineer; **les mécaniciens de piste,** the ground crew; *(c)* **ingénieur m.,** mechanical engineer; **m. constructeur,** mechanician; *(d) Rail:* engine driver, *U.S:* engineer; motorman, engineman (of rail car, etc.); machineman, machinist, operator (of machine, etc.); **m. de groupe électrogène,** generator operator. 2. *s.f.* **mécanicienne,** machinist; sewing-woman (in factory).

mécanicité [mekanisite], *s.f.* mechanicalism.

mécanique [mekanik]. 1. *a.* mechanical; *(a) Mec:* **effet m.,** mechanical advantage; **effort m.,** stress; **propriétés mécaniques,** mechanical properties; **rendement m.,** mechanical efficiency; *(b) Mec.E: Ind:* **à commande m.,** mechanically driven, operated; **dispositif m.,** mechanical contrivance; **les constructions mécaniques,** mechanical engineering; **atelier(s) de constructions mécaniques,** engineering works; **les industries mécaniques,** engineering industries; *(c)* machine-made (lace, tiles, carpets, etc.); *(d) Physiol:* mechanical (action, reflex). 2. *s.f.* **mécanique,** *(a)* (science of) mechanics; **m. appliquée,** applied mechanics; **m. céleste,** celestial mechanics, gravitational astronomy; **m. matricielle,** matrix mechanics; **m. ondulatoire,** wave mechanics; **phénomène de m. ondulatoire,** wave-mechanical phenomenon; **m. rationnelle,** theoretic mechanics, pure mechanics; **m. quantique,** quantum mechanics; **problème de m. quantique,** quantum-mechanical problem; *(b) Mec.E: Ind:* engineering; **m. générale,** general engineering; **m. de précision,** precision engineering; **m. navale,** marine, naval, engineering; *(c)* mechanism, piece of machinery; action (of musical instrument); *O:* **fait à la m.,** machine-made; **m. du piano, de l'orgue,** piano action, organ action; *F:* **remonter la m.,** to buck s.o. up; *(d)* technical skill (in an art, etc.); **la m. du piano, de l'accordéon,** piano, accordion, technique.

mécaniquement [mekanikmɑ̃], *adv.* mechanically; like a machine.

mécanisation [mekanizasjɔ̃], *s.f.* mechanization.

mécanisé [mekanize], *a.* mechanized.

mécaniser [mekanize], *v.tr.* 1. to mechanize; **le travail à la chaîne mécanise l'ouvrier,** working on the assembly line turns a worker into a machine, an automaton. 2. *P: A:* to torment, bait (s.o.).

mécaniseur [mekanizœːr], *s.m. P: A:* teaser, tormentor.

mécanisme [mekanism], *s.m.* 1. mechanism, machinery, (operating) gear; *(a) Mec.E:* **m. de commande, m. d'entraînement, m. moteur,** drive mechanism; **m. de manœuvre, m. de fonctionnement,** operating mechanism, working mechanism; **m. de renversement (de marche),** reversing gear (of machine), change gear (of lathe); **m. de renvoi,** counter gearing, counter shafting; bell-crank linkage; **m. de distribution,** distribution gear, distributing mechanism; **m. de sécurité,** safety gear, safety mechanism; **m. enregistreur,** recording system; *Mch.-Tls:* **m. d'avance,** feed mechanism; *Civ.E:* **m. de treuil,** crab machinery, crab gear; *Aut: etc:* **m. de direction,** steering gear, mechanism; *Av:* **m. d'intégration,** integrator mechanism; *(b)* **m. d'horlogerie,** clockwork (mechanism); **mû par un m. d'horlogerie,** clockwork(-driven); **m. d'une montre,** works of a watch; *(c) Artil: Sm.a:* **m. d'alimentation,** feed mechanism; **m. de détente, m. de mise de feu,** firing mechanism; **m. de pointage en direction,** traversing gear, mechanism; **m. de pointage en hauteur,** elevating gear or mechanism; *Artil:* **m. d'extrapolation automatique,** automatic prediction mechanism; *(d)* **m. administratif,** administrative machinery; **le corps humain est un m. délicat,** the human body is a delicate piece of machinery, of mechanism. 2. working; technique; **le m. du violon,** the technique of violin playing. 3. *(a)* structure (of a language); *(b)* (grammatical) construction; **c'est un m. typiquement français,** this is a typically French construction. 4. *Phil: etc:* mechanism, mechanicalism; method; **m. déductif, inductif,** deductive, inductive, method.

mécaniste [mekanist], *Phil: (a) a.* mechanistic; *(b) s.m. & f.* mechanist.

mécanistique [mekanistik], *a. Phil:* mechanistic.

mécano [mekano], *s.m. F:* mechanic.

mécanographe [mekanɔgraf], *s.m. & f.* 1. *A:* multicopier. 2. *A:* multicopying machine maker. 3. junior programmer (for computer); accounting-machine operator; punched-card machine operator.

mécanographie [mekanɔgrafi], *s.f.* 1. *A:* multicopying. 2. *A:* multicopying industry, business. 3. *(a)* use of machinery, *esp.* of punched-card machines, in office work; data processing; *(b)* data-processing department, tabulating department; computer section.

mécanographique [mekanɔgrafik], *a.* **service m.,** data processing department; computer department, section; **atelier m.,** data-preparation department, punch-card shop; **carte m.,** tab(ulating) card, punch(ed) card; **installation m.,** tabulating equipment; data-processing equipment; **comptabilité m.,** machine, automatic, accounting; computer accounting; **document m.,** computer record; **données mécanographiques,** computer-stored data; **état m.,** printed report; computer (output) report; computer-prepared, computer-produced, report; **fiche m.,** punch(ed) card; **fichier m.,** punch(ed)-card file; computer file; **imprimé m.,** data-processing form; computer form, tab form; **matériel m. (classique à cartes perforées),** (conventional) punch(ed)-card equipment.

mécanographiquement [mekanɔgrafikmɑ̃], *adv.* by mechanical means; by (a) computer; **état établi m.,** machine-produced report; computer-produced report.

mécanothérapie [mekanɔterapi], *s.f.* mechanotherapy.

mécénat [mesena], *s.m.* patronage; **l'état entreprend le m. des beaux arts,** art is under the patronage of the state.

Mécène [mesɛn]. 1. *Pr.n.m. Lt.Lit:* Maecenas. 2. *s.m.* patron (of art, letters); Maecenas.

méchage [meʃaːʒ], *s.m.* 1. matching, fumigating (of casks). 2. *Med:* tenting (of wound).

méchamment [meʃamɑ̃], *adv.* 1. wickedly; naughtily, mischievously. 2. spitefully, maliciously, ill-naturedly, unkindly, nastily; viciously.

méchanceté [meʃɑ̃ste], *s.f.* 1. *A:* poorness, mediocrity. 2. spitefulness, malice; cruelty, unkindness; ill-naturedness; viciousness; **faire qch. par m.,** to do sth. out of spite; **c'est de la pure m.,** it's sheer spite; **rire sans m.,** good-natured laughter, laughter untinged by malice. 3. spiteful action, remark; **quelle m.!** what a spiteful, ill-natured, thing to say, to do! **m. gratuite,** gratuitous piece of spite; **il leur a dit de petites méchancetés,** he made spiteful remarks at them; he made nasty little digs at them.

méchant, -ante [meʃɑ̃, -ɑ̃ːt], *a.* 1. *(a) A:* miserable, wretched, poor, sorry (dwelling, orator, etc.); **un m. écrivain,** a poor writer; **m. cheval,** sorry steed; **méchante robe de soie,** shabby silk gown; *(b)* **un m. billet de cent francs,** a paltry hundred-franc note; **une méchante égratignure,** a slight, paltry, scratch; **méchante excuse,** lame excuse;

(*c*) **une méchante affaire,** an unpleasant, disagreeable, business; **être de méchante humeur,** to be in a (bad) temper. 2. (*a*) spiteful, malicious, ill-intentioned, cruel, unkind (person); **m. comme un âne rouge, comme un diable, comme la gale,** as spiteful as hell; **il est plus bête que m.,** he's stupid rather than spiteful, than cruel; (*b*) naughty, mischievous (child); **petite méchante!** you naughty, wicked, little girl! **si tu es m. tu iras te coucher,** if you're naughty you'll be put to bed; (*c*) savage, vicious, bad-tempered (animal); **le chien est-il m.?** does the dog bite? *P.N:* **chien m.,** beware of the dog; **le fils du patron est m.,** the manager's son is vicious; (*d*) spiteful (expression, etc.); cruel (smile); spiteful, unkind (action); (*e*) *F:* **ce n'est pas bien m.,** there's no harm in it. 3. *s.* (*a*) *B:* **les méchants,** the wicked; (*b*) **faire le m.,** (i) to fly into a temper, a rage; (ii) to threaten s.o.; (iii) to protest violently.

mèche[1] [mɛʃ], *s.f.* 1. (*a*) wick (of candle, lamp); tinder (of tinder box); **couper la m.,** to trim the wick; (*b*) match (for firing explosives, for fumigating cask); touch, fuse (of mine); *Min:* cord; **m. lente,** safety fuse; *F:* **vendre la m.,** to give the show away, let the cat out of the bag, spill the beans, blow the gaff; **découvrir, éventer, la m.,** to uncover the plot. 2. (*a*) cracker, *U.S:* snapper (of whip); **stimuler son cheval de la m. de son fouet,** to give one's horse a flick of the whip; (*b*) lock (of hair); wisp (of wool, etc.); *Hairdr:* **m. postiche,** hair piece; toupet; (*c*) *Surg:* tent; **introduire une m. dans une plaie,** to tent a wound; (*d*) *Tex:* rove; **m. de préparation,** roving, sliver; **faire la m.,** to rove the slivers; (*e*) **m. d'archet,** hair of (violin) bow. 3. (*a*) core, heart (of cable, etc.); *El.E:* **charbon à m.,** cored carbon; (*b*) *Nau:* main-piece (of rudder); spindle (of capstan); **m. de treuil,** winding barrel of winch. 4. *Tls:* (*a*) bit, drill; **m. anglaise, m. de centrage, m. à trois pointes,** centre-bit, centre drill; **m. à cuiller, à louche,** spoon bit, shell bit; **m. à deux tranches,** double-cutting drill; **m. circulaire, cercle cutter; m. en hélice, en spirale, m. hélicoïdale, m. américaine,** twist bit, twist drill; auger bit; **m. universelle,** expanding bit; (*b*) *Carp:* auger, gimlet; (*c*) *Carp:* **m. de rabot,** plane iron.

mèche[2], *s.f.inv.* (*a*) *P:* **il n'y a pas m.,** it's quite impossible, there's not the ghost of a chance; (*b*) *F:* **être de m. avec qn,** to be in collusion, in league, with s.o., to be hand in glove with s.o., *U.S:* to be in cahoots with s.o.; (*c*) *F:* **et m.,** and a bit more; **il est midi et m.,** it's gone twelve.

mèche-cuiller [mɛʃkɥijɛːr], *s.f. Tls:* shell bit, spoon bit; *pl. mèches-cuillers.*

méchef [meʃɛf], *s.m. A:* misadventure, mischance.

mécher [meʃe], *v.tr.* (**je mèche, n. méchons; je mécherai**) 1. to match, fumigate (cask). 2. *Surg:* to tent (wound).

mécheux, -euse [meʃø, -øːz], *a.* (*of wool, etc.*) wispy.

méchoir [meʃwaːr], *v.impers.* (**il méchoit; il méchut; il mécherra**) *A:* to fall out ill, to mischance.

méchoui [meʃwi], *s.m.* (*in N.Africa*) = barbecue; whole lamb roasted on a spit.

mechta [meʃta], *s.f.* (*in Algeria, Tunisia*) hamlet.

Mecklembourg [mɛklɛ̃buːr], *Pr.n.m. Geog:* Mecklenburg.

mecklembourgeois, -oise [mɛklɛ̃burʒwa, -waːz], *Geog:* 1. *a.* of Mecklenburg. 2. *s.* Mecklenburger.

mécompte [mekɔ̃ːt], *s.m.* 1. miscalculation, miscount; error, mistake, in reckoning; **m. de chronologie,** error in chronology. 2. mistaken judgment; disappointment; **il a eu un grave m.,** he was greatly disappointed; he has been badly let down.

mécompter [mekɔ̃te], *v.i.* (*of clock*) to strike the wrong hour.

se mécompter. *A:* (*a*) to make a miscalculation; to find oneself mistaken; (*b*) to be disappointed, to suffer a disappointment.

méconate [mekɔnat], *s.m. Ch:* meconate.

méconduire [mekɔ̃dɥiːr], *v.tr.* (*conj. like* CONDUIRE) *A:* to mislead; to lead (s.o.) astray.

méconial, -aux [mekɔnjal, -o], *a. Physiol:* meconioid.

méconine [mekɔnin], *s.f. Ch:* meconin.

méconique [mekɔnik], *a. Ch:* meconic.

méconium [mekɔnjɔm], *s.m. Physiol:* meconium.

méconnaissable [mekɔnɛsabl], *a.* hardly recognizable, unrecognizable; altered beyond recognition.

méconnaissance [mekɔnɛsɑ̃ːs], *s.f.* (*a*) failure to recognize, to appreciate (s.o.'s talent, etc.); misappreciation; **m. des faits,** misreading of the facts; **m. de ses obligations,** ignoring of one's obligations; (*b*) disavowal, repudiation (of an action, etc.); (*c*) ingratitude.

méconnaître [mekɔnɛːtr̥], *v.tr.* (*conj. like* CONNAÎTRE) to fail to recognize; (*a*) *A:* not to know (s.o.) again; (*b*) not to appreciate (s.o.'s talent, etc.); to belittle (plan, etc.); to disregard (duty); **m. ses propres intérêts,** fail to look after one's own interests; **m. les faits,** to ignore the facts; **je ne méconnais pas les faits,** I fully realize, appreciate, the facts; **je ne méconnais pas vos services,** I fully appreciate all you have done; **je ne peux pas m. qu'il y ait des gens aussi intelligents que moi,** I cannot ignore the fact that there are people as intelligent as myself; (*c*) *O:* to disown, repudiate.

se méconnaître. 1. to underestimate oneself, one's worth. 2. to forget oneself, one's position; not to know one's place.

méconnu [mekɔny], *a.* unrecognized, unappreciated (talent, etc.); misunderstood; **un homme fort m.,** a much misunderstood man.

méconopsis [mekɔnɔpsis], *s.m. Bot:* meconopsis, blue poppy.

mécontent, -ente [mekɔ̃tɑ̃, -ɑ̃ːt]. 1. *a.* discontented, dissatisfied (**de,** with); **être m. de son sort,** to be dissatisfied with one's lot; **il est m. de ce que vous avez dit,** he is annoyed, displeased, with what you said; **il est m. que vous ne soyez pas venu,** he is annoyed that you didn't come; **il avait un nouveau pardessus dont il n'était pas m.,** he had a new overcoat with which he was quite pleased. 2. *s.* dissatisfied person; malcontent; *Pol:* **ce parti a rassemblé tous les mécontents,** this party, has gathered together all the malcontents, all the grumblers.

mécontentement [mekɔ̃tɑ̃tmɑ̃], *s.m.* dissatisfaction (**de,** with); displeasure (**de,** at); *Pol: etc:* grumbling, disaffection; **marquer son m.,** to show, express, one's dissatisfaction, one's annoyance; **avoir du m. de la conduite de qn,** to be dissatisfied with s.o.'s conduct; **sujet, motif, de m.,** cause for dissatisfaction, for complaint.

mécontenter [mekɔ̃tɑ̃te], *v.tr.* to dissatisfy, displease, annoy (s.o.); to cause (s.o.) dissatisfaction.

mécoptères [mekɔptɛːr], *s.m.pl. Ent:* Mecoptera, the scorpion flies.

mécoptéroïdes [mekɔpterɔid], *s.m.pl. Ent:* Mecopteroidea.

Mecque (la) [lamɛk], *Pr.n.f. Geog:* Mecca.

mecquois, -oise [mɛkwa, -waːz], *a. & s. Geog:* (native, inhabitant) of Mecca, Meccan.

mécréance [mekreɑ̃ːs], *s.f. A. & Lit:* 1. misbelief, heterodoxy. 2. unbelief.

mécréant, -ante [mekreɑ̃, -ɑ̃ːt]. 1. *a.* (*a*) *O:* misbelieving, heterodox; (*b*) unbelievin g. 2. *s.* (*a*) *O:* misbeliever; (*b*) unbeliever, infidel; (*c*) *F: A:* miscreant, wretch.

mécroire [mekrwaːr], *v.tr.* (*conj. like* CROIRE) *A:* to have no belief, no faith, in.

médaille [medaːj], *s.f.* 1. medal; *Mil:* **m. commémorative,** campaign medal; **le revers de la m.,** (i) the reverse of the medal; (ii) the other side, the dark side, of the picture; the seamy side (of the business); *Prov:* **chaque m. a son revers,** every rose has its thorn; **tourner la m.,** to look at, consider, the other side; *F:* **recevoir une m. en carton,** *occ.* **en chocolat,** to get a putty medal; (*to child*) **si tu es sage tu auras une m. en chocolat,** if you're good I'll give you a surprise, I'll give you sth. nice. 2. (porter's, hawker's) (official) badge. 3. *Arch:* medallion. 4. *Bot:* **m. (de Judas),** honesty, white satin, satin flower.

médaillé, -ée [medaje]. 1. *a.* holding a medal; decorated. 2. *s.* holder of a medal; medallist; medal winner, prize winner; **les médaillés du travail,** workers with long-service medals.

médailler [medaje], *v.tr.* 1. to award a medal to (s.o.), to decorate (soldier, etc.). 2. *Adm:* to issue a (licence) badge to (hawker, etc.).

médailleur [medajœːr], *s.m.* medal maker, medallist; die sinker.

médaillier [medaje], *s.m.* 1. medal cabinet. 2. collection of medals (in cabinet).

médailliste [medajist], *s.m.* 1. *A:* collector of medals. 2. = MÉDAILLEUR.

médaillon [medajɔ̃], *s.m.* 1. (*a*) medallion; (*b*) *Journ: etc:* inset; **portrait en, dans le, m.,** inset portrait (in corner of larger illustration); (*c*) *Arch:* medallion; *Furn:* **chaise m.,** oval back chair; (*d*) pat (of butter); médaillon (of foie gras).

mède [mɛd], *A.Geog:* 1. *a.* Median. 2. *s.m. & f.* Mede.

médecin [metsɛ̃, medsɛ̃], *s.m.* doctor; physician; **femme m.,** woman doctor; **m. de médecine générale, m. généraliste,** general practitioner, G.P., *U.S:* generalist; **m. homéopathe,** homeopathist; **m. consultant,** consulting physician, consultant; **m. nez-gorge-oreilles,** ear, nose and throat specialist; **m. de famille,** family doctor; **m. de quartier,** local practitioner; **m. du travail,** factory, works, doctor; **m. conventionné,** contract doctor; *Mil:* contract surgeon; *Adm:* **m. du service de la santé, du service d'hygiène,** medical officer of health; **m. légiste,** forensic pathologist; **m. militaire,** army medical officer, M.O.; *Mil:* **m. chef,** senior surgeon, *U.S:* chief surgeon; **m. de bord,** ship's doctor; **m. de papier,** official medical instructions issued to a ship carrying no doctor; *Sw.Fr:* **m. dentiste,** dental surgeon; **consulter un m.,** to consult a doctor, to take medical advice; **quel est votre m. (traitant)?** who is your doctor? **le temps est un grand m.,** time is a great healer; **après la mort le m.,** that's shutting the stable door after the horse has gone; **m. marron,** quack, charlatan; **m. de l'âme,** (father) confessor.

médecine [metsin, medsin], *s.f.* 1. (*a*) (art of) medicine; **docteur en m.,** doctor of medicine, M.D.; **étudiant en m.,** medical student; **école de m.,** medical school; **livres de m.,** medical books; **pratiquer, exercer, la m.,** to practise medicine; **m. légale,** forensic medicine, medical jurisprudence; **m. du travail,** industrial medicine; **m. opératoire,** surgery; **m. physique,** physical therapy; **m. sociale,** social medicine; **m. de l'air,** aviation medicine, *U.S:* aeromedicine; **m. de l'espace,** space medicine; **m. atomique, nucléaire,** nuclear medicine; **m. radiologique,** radiological medicine; **m. vétérinaire,** veterinary treatment; (*b*) the medical profession; *Hum:* **mourir traité en règle par la m.,** to die fortified by the attentions of the Faculty. 2. *A:* (dose of) medicine; **m. noire,** black draught; **prendre (une) m.,** to take a dose of medicine, of physic; **m. de cheval,** horse-draught; drench; *F:* **avaler la, sa, m.,** (i) to take one's gruel, one's punishment; (ii) to give in, to knuckle under; **administrer une m. à qn, à un cheval,** to physic s.o., to drench a horse; **il ne faut pas prendre la m. en plusieurs verres,** it's best to get it over.

médeciner [metsine, medsine], *v.tr. F: O:* to dose (s.o.).

Médée [mede], *Pr.n.f. Gr.Myth:* Medea.

médéen, -enne [medeɛ̃, -ɛn], *a. & s. Geog:* (native, inhabitant) of Médéa (in Algeria).

médersa [medɛrsa], *s.f.* Moslem college.

médial, -ale, -aux [medjal, -o], *Ling:* 1. *a.* medial (letter). 2. *s.f.* **médiale,** medial; medial letter; (*in statistics*) median, mean.

médialement [medjalmɑ̃], *adv.* medially.

médian, -iane [medjɑ̃, -jan]. 1. *a.* median (nerve, etc.); medial (line of the body); *Geom:* **ligne médiane,** median (line); *Hairdr:* **raie médiane,** parting in the middle; *Fb:* **ligne médiane,** half-way line; *s.a.* BANDE[1] 1. 2. *s.m.* (*in statistics*) median. 3. *s.f.* **médiane,** (*a*) *Ling:* mid vowel; (*b*) **médiane d'une distribution,** median of a distribution; (*c*) *Geom:* median (line); (*d*) *Fr.C. Civ.E:* central reservation; *N.Am:* **mediane.**

médianique [medjanik], *a. Psychics:* mediumistic.

médianito [medjanito], *s.m. A:* small cigar, *F:* whiff.

médianoche [medjanɔʃ], *s.m.* (*a*) *A:* midnight meal (to break a fast); (*b*) (midnight) banquet.

médiante [medjɑ̃ːt], *s.f. Mus:* mediant; mi (of movable Do system).

médiastin [medjastɛ̃], *Anat:* 1. *s.m.* mediastinum. 2. *a.* mediastinal.

médiastinal, -aux [medjastinal, -o], *a. Med:* mediastinal (inflammation, etc.).

médiastinite [medjastinit], *s.f. Med:* mediastinitis.

médiastinotomie [medjastinɔtɔmi], *s.f. Surg:* mediastinotomy.

médiat [medja], *a. Phil: Jur:* mediate (cause, etc.).

médiatement [medjatmɑ̃], *adv. Phil: Jur:* mediately.

médiateur, -trice [medjatœːr, -tris]. 1. *a.* mediating, mediatory, mediative. 2. *s.* mediator (**entre . . . et . . .,** between . . . and . . .); intermediary; *f. occ.* mediatress, mediatrix; **m. de la paix,** peacemaker. 3. *s.f. Geom:* **médiatrice,** mid-perpendicular.

médiation [medjasjɔ̃], *s.f.* 1. mediation. 2. (*a*) *Astrol:* midday; (*b*) *Astr:* southing (of star).

médiatisation [medjatizasjɔ̃], *s.f. Hist:* mediatization (of a prince, a state).

médiatiser [medjatize], *v.tr. Hist:* to mediatize (a state).

médiator [medjatɔːr], *s.m. Mus:* plectrum.

médical, -aux [medikal, -o], *a.* medical (properties of plants, etc.); *Med:* **matière médicale,** materia medica; **le corps m.,** the medical profession, (the) doctors; **visite médicale,** medical examination; **examen m.** (**complet**), check-up; **gymnastique médicale,** medical gymnastics, corrective, remedial, exercises; **certificat m.,** medical certificate; **auxiliaires médicaux,** ancillary medical personnel.

médicalement [medikalmɑ̃], *adv.* medically.

médicament [medikamɑ̃], *s.m.* medicament, medicine; **coffre aux médicaments,** medicine chest.

médicamentaire [medikamɑ̃tɛːr], *a.* medicamental, medicamentary.

médicamentation [medikamɑ̃tasjɔ̃], *s.f.* medication, medical treatment.

médicamenter [medikamɑ̃te], *v.tr.* to give (s.o.) medicine; to dose (s.o.).

se médicamenter, to dose oneself, to take medicine.

médicamenteux, -euse [medikamɑ̃tø, -øːz], *a.* **1.** medicinal. **2.** medicamentous, caused by a medicine; **éruption médicamenteuse,** medicinal rash.

médicastre [medikastr̥], *s.m.* quack (doctor), medicaster.

médicat [medika], *s.m.* **1.** competitive examination for qualified doctors to enter the hospital service. **2.** the doctors attached to hospitals.

médicateur, -trice [medikatœːr, -tris]. **1.** *a.* medicative, curative, healing (power of nature, etc.). **2.** *s.* healer.

médication [medikasjɔ̃], *s.f.* medication, medical treatment (of disease).

médicéen, -enne [mediseɛ̃, -ɛn], *a. Italian Hist:* Medicean.

médicinal, -aux [medisinal, -o], *a.* medicinal.

médicinier [medisinje], *s.m. Bot:* oil tree.

Médicis [medisis], *s.m.pl. Hist:* Medici (family); **Catherine de M.,** Catherine de Medici; **les M.,** the Medici.

médico-chirurgical, -aux [medikoʃiryrʒikal, -o], *a.* medico-surgical.

médico-légal, -aux [medikolegal, -o], *a.* medico-legal, forensic.

médico-social, -aux [medikososjal, -o], *a.* medico-social.

Médie [medi], *Pr.n.f. A.Geog:* Media.

médiéval, -aux [medjeval, -o], *a.* medi(a)eval.

médiévisme [medjevism], *s.m.* medi(a)evalism.

médiéviste [medjevist], *s.m. & f.* medi(a)evalist.

médifixe [medifiks], *a. Bot:* medifixed.

médina [medina], *s.f.* (*esp. in Morocco*) medina, native quarter (of town).

Médine [medin], *Pr.n. Geog:* Medina.

médiocarpien, -ienne [medjokarpjɛ̃, -jɛn], *a. Anat:* mediocarpal.

médiocratie [medjokrasi], *s.f.* (*a*) government by the middle classes; (*b*) power in the hands of mediocrity.

médiocre [medjokr̥]. **1.** *a.* (*a*) *A:* medium, middling (size, etc.); (*b*) mediocre; indifferent (work); feeble (performance); second-rate, moderate (ability, etc.); **individu de m. apparence,** shabby-looking individual; **vin m.,** poor wine; **tenir qn en m. estime,** to have no great opinion of s.o. **2.** *s.m.* **travail qui ne s'élève jamais au-dessus du m.,** work that never rises above mediocrity; **au-dessous du m.,** substantially below average, third-rate.

médiocrement [medjokrəmɑ̃], *adv.* indifferently, poorly; **m. riche,** not very rich; **m. satisfait,** not very well pleased; *F:* **et nous n'en sommes pas m. fiers!** and aren't we proud of it!

médiocrité [medjokrite], *s.f.* **1.** mediocrity (of talent, means, mind); **vivre dans la m.,** to live (i) undistinguished, (ii) on a bare competency. **2. applaudi par les médiocrités,** praised by the mediocre, the undistinguished, by small minds; **ministère composé de médiocrités,** ministry of second-raters.

médio-dorsal, -aux [medjodorsal, -o], *a. Anat:* medio-dorsal.

médionner [medjone], *v.tr.* to take the average, the mid-point, the mean, of (sth.).

médiopalatal, -ale, -aux [medjopalatal, -o], *a. & s.f. Ling:* mediopalatal.

médiopassif [medjopasif], *a. & s.m. Gram:* mediopassive.

médiotarsienne [medjotarsjɛn], *a.f. Anat:* mediotarsal (articulation).

médique [medik], *a. A.Hist:* Median.

médire [mediːr], *v.i.* (*conj. like* DIRE, *except pr.ind. and imp.* **médisez**) **m. de qn,** to speak ill of s.o.; to slander s.o.; to run s.o. down.

médisance [medizɑ̃ːs], *s.f.* **1.** slander, backbiting, scandalmongering; **être victime de la m.,** to be a victim of slander. **2.** piece of slander; **dire des médisances,** to talk scandal, to say ill-natured things.

médisant, -ante [medizɑ̃, -ɑ̃ːt]. **1.** *a.* slanderous, backbiting, scandalmongering. **2.** *s.* slanderer, backbiter, scandalmonger.

méditatif, -ive [meditatif, -iːv], *a.* **1.** meditating, meditative; **contempler qch. d'un air m.,** to gaze meditatively at sth.; *s.* **c'est un m.,** he's always lost in the clouds. **2.** *Gram:* **verbes méditatifs,** desiderative verbs.

méditation [meditasjɔ̃], *s.f.* meditation; musing; **plongé dans la m.,** in a brown study; lost in thought; *Ecc:* **faire la m.,** to give oneself up to meditation, to meditate.

méditer [medite]. **1.** *v.i.* to meditate, to muse; **m. sur un problème,** to think over a problem; **m. sur la mort,** to meditate on, ponder over, death; **passer une heure à m.,** to spend an hour in thought; *F:* **qu'est-ce qu'il peut bien m.?** what can he be thinking up, plotting? **2.** *v.tr.* to contemplate (a journey, etc.); to think of (sth.); to have (sth.) in mind; **m. la mort,** to contemplate suicide; **projet bien médité,** well-thought-out-plan; **m. de faire qch.,** to be thinking of doing sth.; to contemplate doing sth., to plan to do sth.

méditerrané [mediterane], *a.* (*a*) *A:* mediterranean, inland, land-locked (sea, etc.); (*b*) **la (mer) Méditerranée,** the Mediterranean (Sea).

méditerranéen, -enne [mediteraneɛ̃, -ɛn], *a.* Mediterranean; **climat m.,** Mediterranean climate.

médium [medjɔm], *s.m.* **1.** (*a*) *A:* compromise; (*b*) *Mus:* middle register (of the voice). **2.** *Psychics:* medium. **3.** *Paint:* medium.

médiumnique [medjɔmnik], *a. Psychics:* mediumistic; **fraudes médiumniques,** fraud on the part of the medium.

médiumnité [medjɔmnite], *s.f. Psychics:* mediumism.

médius [medjyːs], *s.m.* middle finger.

médoc [medɔk], *s.m.* (*also* **vin de M.**) Medoc (claret).

médocain, -aine [medɔkɛ̃, -ɛn], **médoquin, -ine** [medɔkɛ̃, -in], *a. & s.* (native, inhabitant) of the Médoc.

Médor [medɔːr], *Pr.n.m.* (*name commonly given to dogs*) = Rover, Fido.

médullaire [medyl(l)ɛːr], *a. Anat: Bot:* medullary (tube, ray, etc.); *Arb:* **rayon m.,** pith ray.

médulle [medyl], *s.f. Bot:* medulla, pith.

médulleux, -euse [medyl(l)ø, -øːz], *a. Bot:* medullated, medullary.

médullite [medyl(l)it], *s.f. Med:* medullitis.

médusaire [medyzɛːr], *a. & s.m. Coel:* medusan.

Méduse [medyːz]. **1.** *Pr.n.f. Gr.Myth:* Medusa; *F:* **c'est la tête de M.,** it's paralysing. **2.** *s.f. Coel:* medusa, jellyfish.

méduser [medyze], *v.tr. F:* to petrify; to paralyse, stupefy.

meeting [mitiŋ], *s.m. Pol: Sp: etc:* meeting; rally; **m. d'aviation,** air display.

méfaire [mefɛːr], *v.i.* (*used only in inf.*) *A:* to do ill; to do wrong.

méfait [mefɛ], *s.m.* misdeed; malpractice; **méfaits d'un orage,** damage caused by a storm; **se déclarer l'auteur du m.,** to own up to the deed.

méfiance [mefjɑ̃ːs], *s.f.* distrust, mistrust; **avoir de la m. envers, à l'égard de, qn,** to distrust s.o.; **regarder qn avec m.,** to look at s.o. distrustfully, suspiciously; to look askance at s.o.; *Prov:* **m. est mère de sûreté,** safety first!

méfiant [mefjɑ̃], *a.* distrustful, mistrustful, suspicious (**à l'égard de, à l'endroit de,** of); **d'un air m.,** distrustfully, suspiciously.

méfier (se) [səmefje], *v.pr.* (*p.d. & pr.sub.* **n.n. méfiions, v.v. méfiiez**) (*a*) **se m. de qn,** to distrust, mistrust, s.o.; **méfiez-vous des voleurs,** beware of pickpockets; (*b*) *abs.* to be on one's guard.

méforme [meform], *s.f. Sp:* poor form, condition; **être en m.,** to be off form.

még(a) [meg(a)], *pref.* meg(a)-.

mégabarye [megabari], *s.f. Ph.Meas:* megabarye.

mégacaryocyte [megakarjɔsit], *s.m. Physiol:* megakaryocyte, megacaryocyte.

mégacéros [megaserɔs], *s.m. Paleont:* megaloceros, megaceros.

mégachile [megakil], *s.f. Ent:* megachile; leaf-cutter (bee), leaf-cutting bee.

mégachiroptères [megakirɔptɛːr], *s.m.pl. Z:* Megachiroptera, the large fruit bats, the flying foxes.

mégacôlon [megakolɔ̃], *s.m. Med:* megacolon.

mégacycle [megasikl], *s.m. El.Meas:* megacycle.

mégaderme [megadɛrm], *s.m. Z:* big-eared bat.

mégadermidés [megadɛrmide], *s.m.pl. Z:* Megadermatidae, Megadermidae.

mégadyne [megadin], *s.f. Mec.Meas:* megadyne.

méga-électron-volt [megaelɛktrɔ̃vɔlt], *s.m. Ph:* mega-electron-volt; *pl. méga-électrons-volts.*

mégafarad [megafarad], *s.m. El.Meas:* megafarad.

mégagraphe [megagraf], *s.m. E:* enlarging board.

mégahertz [megaɛrtz], *s.m. El.Meas:* megacycle.

mégajoule [megaʒul], *s.m. El.Meas:* megajoule.

mégalithe [megalit], *s.m.* megalith.

mégalithique [megalitik], *a.* megalithic (monument).

mégalo- [megalo], *pref.* megalo-; **mégalomanie,** megalomania.

mégaloblaste [megaloblast], *s.m. Physiol:* megaloblast.

mégaloblastique [megaloblastik], *a.* megaloblastic.

mégalocéphale [megalosefal], *a. & s.* megalocephalic; megalocephalous (individual).

mégalocéphalie [megalosefali], *s.f.* megalocephaly.

mégalocornée [megalokɔrne], *s.f. Physiol:* megalocornea.

mégalocyte [megalosit], *s.m. Physiol:* megalocyte.

mégalocytose [megalositoːz], *s.f. Med:* megalocytosis.

mégalodon [megalodɔ̃], *s.m. Paleont:* megalodon.

mégalomane [megaloman], *a. & s.m. & f.* megalomaniac.

mégalomanie [megalomani], *s.f.* megalomania.

mégalonyx [megaloniks], *s.m. Paleont:* Megalonyx.

mégalope [megalɔp], *s.f. Crust:* megalops.

mégalophtalmie [megalɔftalmi], *s.f. Med:* megalophthalmus.

mégalopolis [megalɔpɔlis], *s.f.* megalopolis.

mégalopsie [megalɔpsi], *s.f. Med:* megalopsia.

mégaloptères [megalɔptɛːr], *s.m.pl. Ent:* Megaloptera.

mégalopygides [megalɔpiʒid], *s.m.pl. Ent:* Megalopygidae, the flannel moths.

mégalosaure [megalosoːr], *s.m. Paleont:* megalosaurus.

méganisoptères [meganizɔptɛːr], *s.m.pl. Ent: Paleont:* Meganisoptera.

mégaphone [megafɔn], *s.m.* megaphone.

mégaphyton [megafitɔ̃], *s.m. Paleont:* megaphyton.

mégapode [megapɔd], *s.m. Orn:* megapod(e), mound bird, mound builder, brush turkey.

mégapodidés [megapɔdide], *s.m.pl. Orn:* Megapodiidae.

mégaptère [megaptɛːr], *s.f. Z:* hump-backed whale, humpback, hump whale.

mégarde (par) [parmegard], *adv.phr.* inadvertently, through carelessness; accidentally; unawares.

Mégare [megaːr], *Pr.n.f. Geog:* Megara.

mégarhine [megarin], *s.m. Ent:* megarhinus.

Mégaride [megarid], *Pr.n.f. A.Geog:* Megaris.

mégarien, -ienne [megarjɛ̃, -jɛn], *a. & s. A.Geog:* Megarian.

mégarique [megarik], *a. Phil:* Megarian, Megaric (school); Eristic (school).

mégascope [megaskɔp], *s.m. A.Opt:* megascope.

mégasécoptères [megasekɔptɛːr], *s.m.pl. Ent: Paleont:* Megasecoptera.

mégasème [megazɛm], *a. Anthr:* megaseme.

mégasome [megazoːm], *s.m. Ent:* Megasoma; elephant beetle.

mégasporange [megasporɑ̃ːʒ], *s.m. Bot:* megasporangium.

mégaspore [megaspɔːr], *s.m. Bot:* megaspore.

mégathérium [megaterjɔm], *s.m. Paleont:* megatherium.

mégatherme [megatɛrm], *s.f. Bot:* megatherm.

mégathymides [megatimid], *s.m.pl. Ent:* Megathymidae.

mégatonne [megatɔn], *s.f. Exp:* megaton.

méga-uretère [megayrətɛːr], *s.m. Med:* megaloureter.

mégavolt [megavɔlt], *s.m. El.Meas:* megavolt.

mégavoltampère [megavɔltɑ̃pɛːr], *s.m. El.Meas:* megavoltampere.

mégawatt [megawat], *s.m. El.Meas:* megawatt.

Mégère [meʒɛːr]. **1.** *Pr.n.f. Gr.Myth:* Megaera. **2.** *s.f.* shrew, termagant; **la Mégère apprivoisée,** the Taming of the Shrew.

mégerg [megɛrg], *s.m. Mec.Meas:* megerg, megaerg.

megévan, -ane [məʒevɑ̃, -an], *a. & s. Geog:* (native, inhabitant) of Megève.

Méghara [megara], *Pr.n.f. Geog:* Megara.

mégie [meʒi], *s.f. Tan:* tawing; **passer une peau en m.,** to taw a skin.

mégir [meʒiːr], *v.tr.*, **mégisser** [meʒise], *v.tr.* to taw, dress (light skins).

mégis [meʒi]. **1.** *s.m. Tan:* alum steep. **2.** *a.m.* **cuir m.**, tawed leather, white leather, whit-leather.

mégisserie [meʒisri], *s.f.* **1.** tawing, dressing (of light skins). **2.** tawery.

mégissier [meʒisje], *s.m. Tan:* tawer.

mégohm [megoːm], *s.m. El.Meas:* megohm.

mégohmmètre [megommɛtr̥], *s.m. El:* megohmmeter.

mégot [mego], *s.m. P:* fag-end (of cigarette); stump, butt (of cigar); cigarette end; cigar end.

mégotage [megɔtaːʒ], *s.m. P:* (*a*) scrimping, skimping; (*b*) small-time activities.

mégot(t)er [megɔte], *v.i. P:* (*a*) to collect cigarette ends; (*b*) to scrimp, to skimp; to live meanly; **ne pas m. sur qch.**, not to be mean, stingy, with sth.; (*c*) to be a small-time operator.

mégot(t)eur [megɔtœːr], **mégot(t)ier** [megɔtje], **mégot(t)eux** [megɔtø], *s.m. P:* (*a*) collector of cigar-ends, of fag-ends; (*b*) skinflint; (*c*) small-time operator.

méhalla [meala], *s.f.* (*in N. Africa*) **1.** desert camping place. **2.** column of troops.

méhari [meari], *s.m.* fast dromedary, racing camel, mehari, heiri(e); *pl. méhara, méharis.*

méhariste [mearist], *s.m.* dromedarist; cameleer; meharist; *Mil:* **compagnie de méharistes,** camel corps; camelry.

meilleur, -eure [mɛjœːr], *a.* **1.** (*comp. of* BON) better; **rendre qch. m.,** to improve sth.; **devenir m.,** to grow better, to improve; **il est m. de s'en passer,** it is better to do without it; **les femmes sont meilleures ou pires que les hommes,** women are either better or worse than men; **trouver un m. emploi,** to find a better job; **je ne connais rien de m.,** I know nothing better, I don't know anything better; **les choses prennent une meilleure tournure,** things are taking a turn for the better; **de meilleure heure,** earlier; **m. marché,** cheaper; (*b*) *adv.* **il fait m.,** the weather is better; **il fait m. ici,** it is better, pleasanter, milder, here; **cette rose sent m. que celle-là,** this rose has a better scent than that one. **2.** (*sup. of* BON) **le m., la meilleure,** (i) the best (of several); (ii) the better (of two); (*a*) **le m. moyen de faire qch.,** the best, the most effective, way of doing sth.; **c'est celui-là le m.,** it's, he's, the best, the pick of the bunch; **le m. homme qui soit,** the best of men; **les meilleurs postes,** the best jobs; **il accapare les meilleures affaires,** he keeps all the plums for himself; **avec la meilleure volonté du monde,** with the best will in the world; *Sp:* **battre son m. temps,** to beat one's previous best; *Corr:* **je vous adresse mes vœux les meilleurs, mes meilleurs vœux,** with all good wishes, with best wishes; (*b*) *s.* **même les meilleurs renoncent,** even the best give up; **que le m. gagne,** may the best man win; **nous avons bu de son m.,** we drank of his best; **du m. de mon cœur,** with all my heart; **pour le m. et pour le pire,** for better, for worse; **donner le m. de soi-même,** to give of one's best; **le m. c'est de s'en aller,** it is best, better, to go (away); *Sp:* **jouer au m. de trois,** to play the best of three; **prendre le m. sur son adversaire,** to get the better of one's opponent.

méionite [mejɔnit], *s.f. Miner:* meionite.

méiose [mejoːz], *s.f. Biol:* meiosis.

meistre [mɛstr̥], *s.m. A.Nau:* = MESTRE.

méjuger [meʒyʒe], *v.tr.* (*conj. like* JUGER) to misjudge; **on le méjugerait sur sa mine,** his appearance belies him.

mékhithariste [mekitarist], *s.m. Ecc:* Mechitarist (monk).

Mékong [mekɔ̃ːg], *Pr.n.m. Geog:* the (river) Mekong.

mélaconite [melakɔnit], *s.f. Miner:* melaconite.

melæna [melena], *s.m. Med:* melaena, black vomit.

mélamine [melamin], *s.f. Ch:* melamine.

mélampsoracées [melɑ̃psɔrase], *s.f.pl. Fung:* Melampsoraceae.

mélampyre [melɑ̃piːr], *s.m. Bot:* melampyrum, cow-wheat.

mélancolie [melɑ̃kɔli], *s.f.* **1.** melancholy, dejection, mournfulness; **m. byronienne,** Byronic gloom; *F:* **ne pas engendrer la mélancolie,** to be always cheerful. **2.** *Med:* melancholia.

mélancolieux, -euse [melɑ̃kɔljø, -øːz], *a. A: F:* given to melancholy; tinged with melancholy.

mélancolique [melɑ̃kɔlik], *a.* **1.** melancholy, dejected, gloomy, mournful. **2.** *Med:* melancholic.

mélancoliquement [melɑ̃kɔlikmɑ̃], *adv.* melancholically; mournfully, gloomily.

mélancoliser [melɑ̃kɔlize], *v.i.* to be melancholy.

mélanellidés [melanɛlide], *s.m.pl. Moll:* Melanellidae.

Mélanésie [melanezi], *Pr.n.f. Geog:* Melanesia.

mélanésien, -ienne [melanezjɛ̃, -jɛn], *a. & s. Geog:* Melanesian.

mélange [melɑ̃ːʒ], *s.m.* **1.** mixing; blending (of tea, etc.); crossing (of breeds); mingling; *Cards:* shuffling; *W.Tel: T.V:* mixing; *I.C.E:* **chambre de m.,** mixing chamber; *Cin:* **appareil de m.,** mixing apparatus (of recording studio). **2.** mixture; blend (of tea, etc.); intermixture (of breeds, etc.); mix (of cement, etc.); compound; **sans mélange,** unmixed, unalloyed, unadulterated; *I.C.E:* **m. explosif, détonant,** explosive mixture; *Civ.E:* **m. de ciment et de gasoil,** diesel (oil) cement; *Ch:* **m. à point d'ébullition constant, azéotropique,** constant boiling mixture. **3. m. de toutes sortes de gens,** medley of all kinds of people; (*in catalogue*) **mélanges,** miscellaneous; **auteur de mélanges,** miscellanist.

mélangé [melɑ̃ʒe], *a.* mixed (society, breed); motley (crowd); *Tex:* **drap m., étoffe mélangée,** mixture, union (of wool and cotton).

mélange-maître [melɑ̃ʒmɛtr̥], *s.m.* masterbatch; *pl. mélanges-maîtres.*

mélangeoir [melɑ̃ʒwaːr], *s.m.* mixing receptacle.

mélanger [melɑ̃ʒe], *v.tr.* (**je mélangeai(s); n. mélangeons**) to mix; to mingle; to blend (teas, wines, etc.); *F:* **m. tous les dossiers, toutes les fiches,** to mix up all the files, all the cards.

se mélanger, (*of liquids, etc.*) to mix, to mingle, to blend.

mélangeur [melɑ̃ʒœːr], *s.m.*, **mélangeuse** [melɑ̃ʒøːz], *s.f.* mixer, mixing-machine; *Cin:* **mélangeur de sons,** mixing panel; mixer.

Mélanie [melani], *Pr.n.f.* Melania, Melanie.

mélaniidés [melaniide], *s.m.pl. Moll:* Melaniidae.

mélanine [melanin], *s.f. Bio-Ch:* melanin.

mélanique [melanik], *a.* (*a*) *Biol:* melanistic; (*b*) *Med:* melanose (tumour, etc.).

mélanisation [melanizasjɔ̃], *s.f. Geol:* melanization.

mélanisme [melanism], *s.m. Physiol. etc:* melanism.

mélanite [melanit], *s.f. Miner:* melanite.

mélanoblaste [melanɔblast], *s.m. Biol:* melanoblast.

mélanocarcinome [melanɔkarsinoːm, -ɔm], *s.m. Med:* melanocarcinoma.

mélanocérite [melanɔserit], *s.f. Miner:* melanocerite.

mélanochroïte [melanɔkrɔit], *s.f. Miner:* melanochroite.

mélanocrate [melanɔkrat], *a. Geol:* **roche m.,** melanocrate.

mélanocyte [melanɔsit], *s.m. Biol:* melanocyte.

mélanoderme [melanɔdɛrm], *a. Anthr:* melanodermic, dark-skinned.

mélanodermie [melanɔdɛrmi], *s.f. Med:* melanoderm(i)a.

mélanoïde [melanɔid], *a. Med:* melanoid (tumour).

mélanome [melanoːm, -ɔm], *s.m. Med:* melanoma.

mélanophore [melanɔfɔːr], *s.f. Biol:* melanophore.

mélanorrhœa [melanɔrea], *s.m. Bot:* melanorrhoea, black varnish tree.

mélanosarcome [melanɔsarkoːm, -ɔm], *s.m. Med:* melanosarcoma.

mélanose [melanoːz], *s.f. Med:* melanosis; black degeneration.

mélanostibiane [melanɔstibjan], *s.f. Miner:* melanostibian.

mélanote [melanɔt], *s.m. Ent:* melanotus.

mélanotékite [melanɔtekit], *s.f. Miner:* melanotekite.

mélantérie [melɑ̃teri], **mélantérite** [melɑ̃terit], *s.f. Miner:* melanterite.

mélanurie [melanyri], *s.f. Med:* melanuria.

mélaphyre [melafiːr], *s.m. Miner:* melaphyre.

mélasse [melas], *s.f.* molasses, treacle; **m. raffinée,** golden syrup; *P:* **être dans la m.,** (i) to be in a fix, in the soup; (ii) to be penniless, broke.

mélassigène [melasiʒɛn], *a.* melassigenic.

mélastomacées [melastɔmase], *s.f.pl. Bot:* Melastomaceae.

melchior [mɛlʃjɔːr], *s.m. Metall:* German silver, nickel silver.

Melchisédech [mɛlkisedɛk], *Pr.n.m. B.Lit:* Melchisedec, Melchizedek.

melchite [mɛlkit], *s.m. Rel.H:* Melchite.

meldien, -ienne [mɛldjɛ̃, -jɛn], **meldois, -oise** [mɛldwa, -waːz], *a. & s. Geog:* (native, inhabitant) of Meaux.

mêlé [mele], *a.* **1.** mixed (feelings, company); mingled (colours); **race de sang m.,** mixed race. **2.** tangled (skein, hair, etc.); tousled (hair); involved (business, estate); *F:* **avoir la langue mêlée, les dents mêlées,** to speak thickly (when intoxicated).

Méléagre [meleagr̥], *Pr.n.m. Gr.Myth:* Meleager.

méléagriculteur [meleagrikyltœːr], *s.m.* guinea-fowl breeder, producer.

méléagride [meleagrid], *a. Bot:* **fritillaire m.,** snake's head fritillary.

méléagrine [meleagrin], *s.f.* **1.** *Moll:* pearl oyster. **2.** *Orn:* guinea fowl.

mêlécasse [melekɑːs], **mêlé-cass(is)** [melekas(is)], *s.m.* black-currant syrup and water mixed with cognac or vermouth; **voix de m.(-)c.,** husky voice (of a drunkard).

mêlée [mele], *s.f.* (*a*) conflict, fray, mêlée; (*b*) *F:* scuffle, tussle, free fight, free-for-all, rough-and-tumble; **m. générale,** battle-royal; (*c*) scramble; (*d*) *Rugby Fb:* scrum; **m. ouverte,** loose scrum; **m. fermée,** tight scrum.

mêlement [mɛlmɑ̃], *s.m.* mixing, mingling, blending.

mêler [mele], *v.tr.* to mix, mingle, blend; (*a*) **m. qch. à, avec, qch.,** to mix sth. with sth.; **m. l'utile à l'agréable,** to combine the useful with the pleasant; **joie mêlée de tristesse,** joy (not un)tinged with sadness; **il mêle toujours son mot à la conversation; il mêle partout son mot,** he is always putting his word in; **il est mêlé à tout,** he has a finger in every pie; **m. son vin d'eau,** to mix water with one's wine; **m. un bol de punch,** to brew a bowl of punch; (*b*) to put out of order, to throw into confusion, to tangle; **m. ses papiers,** to mix up, jumble up, muddle, one's papers; **m. les cartes, le jeu,** to shuffle the cards, the pack; *F:* **vous avez bien mêlé les cartes!** a nice tangle, a nice mess, you've made of it! **m. une serrure,** to jam, *F:* mess up, a lock; (*c*) **m. qn à, dans, qch.,** to mix s.o. up, to implicate s.o., involve s.o., in sth.; **m. qn à la conversation,** to bring s.o. into the conversation; **il est mêlé dans une mauvaise affaire,** he is mixed up in, involved in, a bad business.

se mêler, to mix, mingle, blend; **se m. à la foule,** to mingle with, lose oneself in, the crowd; **se m. au cortège,** to join the procession; **se m. à la conversation,** to take part in the conversation, *F:* to chip in; **se m. de qch.,** to take a hand in sth.; **mêlez-vous de ce qui vous regarde,** *F:* **de quoi je me mêle!** mind your own business; what's it to you? **ce n'est pas à moi de m'en m.,** it's not for me to interfere; *F:* **le diable s'en mêle!** the devil's in it! **ne vous en mêlez pas,** let it alone; **se m. de politique,** to dabble in politics; **ne pas se m. de politique,** to keep aloof from, have nothing to do with, politics.

mêle-tout [mɛltu], *s.inv. F:* busybody, buttinsky.

mélette [melɛt], *s.f. Ich: F:* sprat.

mélèze [melɛːz], *s.m.* larch (tree, wood); **m. d'Amérique,** tamarack.

mélézin [melezɛ̃], *s.m. For:* larch plantation (with trees widely spaced to allow for pasture).

mélézitose [melezitoːz], *s.m. Ch:* melezitose.

mélia [melja], *s.f. Bot:* melia, bead tree.

méliacées [meljase], *s.f.pl. Bot:* Meliaceae.

mélianthe [meljɑ̃ːt], *s.m. Bot:* melianthus; (Cape) honey flower.

mélianthacées [meljɑ̃tase], *s.f.pl. Bot:* Melianthaceae.

Mélibée [melibe], *Pr.n.m. Lt.Lit:* Meliboeus.

mélibiose [melibjoːz], *s.m. Ch:* melibiose.

mélicérique [meliserik], *a.* meliceric, melicerous.

mélicoque [melikɔk], *s.m. Bot:* melicocca, *F:* honey-berry.

mélicrat [melikra], *s.m.* mead.

mélie [meli], *s.f. Bot:* melia; bead tree.

mélien, -ienne [meljɛ̃, -jɛn], *a. & s.* (native, inhabitant) of Milo, Milian.

méliérat [meliera], *s.m.* mead.

mélil(l)ite [melilit], *s.f. Miner:* melilite.

mélilot [melilo], *s.m. Bot:* melilot, *F:* sweet clover.

méli-mélo [melimelo], *s.m. F:* jumble (of facts, etc.); hotchpotch; medley (of people, etc.); clutter (of furniture, etc.); *pl. mélis-mélos.*

mélinet [melinɛ], *s.m. Bot:* honeywort.

mélinite [melinit], *s.f. Geol: Expl:* melinite.

mélinophane [melinɔfan], *s.f. Miner:* meliphanite.

méliorati f, -ive [meljɔratif, -iːv], *a. & s.m. Ling:* meliorative.

mélioration [meljɔrasjɔ̃], *s.f.* **1.** *Jur: A:* improvement (of one's property, etc.). **2.** *Ling:* melioration.

méliorisme [meljɔrism], *s.m. Phil:* meliorism.

mélioriste [meljɔrist], *a. & s.m. & f. Phil:* meliorist.

méliphage [melifaːʒ], *s.m. Orn:* honey-eater; **m. à gorge blanche,** white-throated honey-eater (of New Guinea).

méliphagidés [melifaʒide], *s.m.pl. Orn:* Meliphagidae, the honey-eaters.

mélipone [melipɔn], *s.f. Ent:* melipona; stingless bee.

mélique[1] [melik], *a. Gr.Lit:* melic (poetry).

mélique[2], *s.f. Bot:* melica, melic (grass).

mélisse [melis], *s.f. Bot:* melissa, balm; **m. officinale,** (common lemon) balm; **m. sauvage,** melittis; *Pharm:* **eau de m.,** melissa cordial.

mélitée [melite], *s.f. Ent:* melitaea; **m. artémise,** greasy fritillary.

mélitte [melit], *s.f. Bot:* melittis.

méliturie [melityri], *s.f. Med:* melituria, saccharine diabetes, diabetes mellitus.

melkite [mɛlkit], *a. & s.m. & f. Rel.H:* Melchite.

mellier [mɛlje], *s.m. Z:* psalterium, omasum, third stomach (of ruminant).

mellifère [mɛl(l)ifɛːr]. **1.** *a.* melliferous, honey-bearing. **2.** *s.m.pl. Ent:* **mellifères,** Mellifera, honey-bees.

mellification [mɛl(l)ifikasjɔ̃], *s.f. Ent:* mellification, honeymaking.

mellifique [mɛl(l)ifik], *a.* mellific, honey-making.

melliflue [mɛl(l)ifly], *a.* mellifluous, honeyed, sugary (eloquence, words, etc.).

mellifluité [mɛl(l)iflyite], *s.f.* mellifluence; honeyed flow of eloquence.

mellite [mɛl(l)it], *s.m.* **1.** *Miner:* mellite. **2.** *Pharm:* honey preparation; **m. de borax,** borax honey.

mellivore [mɛl(l)ivɔːr], *a. Z:* mellivorous, honey-eating.

mellois, -oise [mɛlwa, -waːz], *a. & s. Geog:* (native, inhabitant) of Melle.

mélo [melo], *s.m. F:* melodrama.

mélocacte [melɔkakt], *s.m.*, **mélocactus** [melɔkaktyːs], *s.m. Bot:* melocactus, melon cactus, pope's head.

mélodie [melɔdi], *s.f.* **1.** melody, tune. **2.** melodiousness (of style, verse, etc.).

mélodieusement [melɔdjøzmɑ̃], *adv.* melodiously.

mélodieux, -ieuse [melɔdjø, -jøːz], *a.* melodious.

mélodion [melɔdjɔ̃], *s.m. A.Mus:* melodeon, melodion.

mélodique [melɔdik], *a. Mus:* melodic (progression, etc.).

mélodiste [melɔdist], *s.m.* **1.** melody writer. **2.** melodist (as opposed to harmonist).

mélodramatique [melɔdramatik], *a.* melodramatic.

mélodramatiser [melɔdramatize], *v.tr.* to melodramatize.

mélodramaturge [melɔdramatyrʒ], *s.m.* melodramatist.

mélodrame [melɔdram], *s.m.* melodrama; **auteur de mélodrames,** melodramatist.

mélodunois, -oise [melɔdynwa, -waːz], *a. & s. Geog:* (native, inhabitant) of Melun.

méloé [melɔe], *s.m. Ent:* meloe; meloid (beetle); oil beetle.

mélographe [melɔgraf], *s.m. Mus:* melograph.

méloïdes [melɔid], *s.m.pl. Ent:* Meloidae.

mélolonthe [melɔlɔ̃ːt], *s.m. Ent:* melolonthid; *pl.* **mélolonthes,** Melolonthidae.

mélolonthoïde [melɔlɔ̃tɔid], *a. Ent:* melolonthoid.

mélomane [melɔman], *a. & s.* melomaniac; music-lover; **être m.,** to be music-mad; **le Tout-Paris m.,** all musical Paris.

mélomanie [melɔmani], *s.f.* melomania, passion for music.

melon [məlɔ̃], *s.m.* **1.** *Bot:* melon; **m. d'eau,** water melon. **2.** *(a) P: A:* simpleton, muff, fathead; *(b)* freshman (at Saint-Cyr). **3. (chapeau) m.,** bowler (hat), *U.S:* derby. **4.** *Z: F:* melon (on sperm-whale's head).

mélongène [melɔ̃ʒɛn], *s.f. Bot:* aubergine, egg plant.

mélonite [melɔnit], *s.f. Miner:* melonite.

melonites [məlɔnit], *s.m. Paleont:* Melonites.

melonnière [məlɔnjɛːr], *s.f.* melon bed.

mélopée [melɔpe], *s.f. Mus:* **1.** art of recitative. **2.** *(a)* chant, recitative; *(b)* singsong.

mélophage [melɔfaːʒ], *s.m. Ent:* sheep tick.

mélophobe [melɔfɔb]. **1.** *a.* music-hating. **2.** *s.* music hater.

méloplastie [melɔplasti], *s.f. Surg:* meloplasty.

mélote [melɔt], *s.f. Tan:* pelt.

Melpomène [mɛlpɔmɛn], *Pr.n.f. Gr.Myth:* Melpomene.

melunois, -oise [məlynwa, -waːz], **melunais, -aise** [məlynɛ, -ɛːz], *a. & s. Geog:* (native, inhabitant) of Melun.

mélurse [melyrs], *s.m. Z:* sloth bear.

Mélusine [melyzin]. **1.** *Pr.n.f. Myth:* Melusina; *F: (of woman)* **pousser des cris de M.,** to scream, to screech. **2.** *s.f. R.t.m:* long-haired felt.

mémarchure [memarʃyːr], *s.f. Vet: A:* wrench, sprain (of horse's leg).

membracide [mɑ̃brasid], *s.m. Ent:* membracid, tree-hopper.

membracidés [mɑ̃braside], *s.m.pl. Ent:* Membracidae.

membrane [mɑ̃bran], *s.f.* **1.** *(a) Anat: Bot: etc:* membrane; **m. muqueuse,** mucous membrane; **m. cellulaire,** cell membrane; *Z:* **m. clignotante, nictitante,** nictitating membrane (of bird, etc.); haw (of horse); *Med:* **fausse m.,** false membrane (in diphtheria); *(b) Z:* web (of web-footed bird); *(c) Ind: etc:* **m. poreuse,** porous membrane, diaphragm; **m. gonflable,** vapour dome, conical roof (of tank). **2.** *Tp:* diaphragm; **m. de charbon,** carbon diaphragm; *Rec:* **m. du diaphragme,** diaphragm of the sound-box.

membrané [mɑ̃brane], *a. (a)* membranous; membraned; *(b)* webbed (fingers, toes).

membraneux, -euse [mɑ̃branø, -øːz], *a.* membranous (tissue, etc.).

membraniforme [mɑ̃branifɔrm], *a.* membraniform.

membranipore [mɑ̃branipɔːr], *s.m. Prot:* membranipora; *F:* sea-mat.

membraniporidés [mɑ̃branipɔride], *s.m.pl. Prot:* Membraniporidae.

membranule [mɑ̃branyl], *s.f. Anat:* membranula, small membrane.

membre [mɑ̃ːbr̥], *s.m.* member. **1.** *(a)* limb (of the body); **les membres inférieurs,** the lower limbs; **m. viril,** membrum virile, penis; *F:* **se saigner aux quatre membres,** to work oneself to the bone; *(b)* **devenir m. d'une société,** to become a member of an association; to join an association; **m. actif,** active member; **m. honoraire (d'une société, d'un cercle),** honorary member (of an association, of a club); **les membres de la famille,** the members of the family; **m. du Parlement,** member of Parliament; *A:* **m. de Jésus-Christ,** member of Christ. **2.** constituent part; *(a) Hist:* **les membres de l'Empire britannique,** the members of the British Empire; **les membres de la phrase,** the members of the sentence; *Arch:* **membres de la façade,** members of the facade; *Mth:* **premier, second, m. d'une équation,** left-hand, right-hand, side of an equation; *(b) N.Arch:* rib, timber (of ship); **m. de remplissage,** filling timber.

membré [mɑ̃bre], *a.* **1.** *used only with an adv.* limbed; **cheval bien m.,** well-limbed horse; **homme fortement m.,** strong-limbed man. **2.** *Her:* membered (bird).

membrer [mɑ̃bre], *v.i. O: F:* to work hard; to slog away.

membrette [mɑ̃brɛt], *s.f. Arch:* alette (of arch, etc.).

membrière [mɑ̃brijɛːr], *s.f. Const:* element (of framework).

membru [mɑ̃bry], *a.* big-limbed, strong-limbed.

membrure [mɑ̃bryːr], *s.f.* **1.** *(a) coll.* limbs; **homme à forte m.,** strong-limbed man, powerfully built man; *(b)* frame(work) (of building, of panelling, etc.); *(c) N.Arch:* frame, rib; **les membrures,** the ribs; **l'ensemble des membrures,** the framing; **m. cintrée,** curved frame; **m. dévoyée,** cant frame; **m. en profilé,** section frame; **m. renforcée,** deep frame; **m. renversée,** reverse frame; **m. transversale,** athwart rib; **écartement des membrures,** frame spacing; **déplacement, largeur, hors membrures,** moulded displacement, breadth; *(d) Av:* member. **2.** *Civ.E:* boom, flange (of web girder); **m. tendue,** tension flange; **m. comprimée,** compression flange.

même [mɛːm]. **1.** *a. (a)* same; **une seule et m. chose,** one and the same thing; **ils sont du m. âge,** they're the same age; they're of an age; **deux plantes de m. espèce,** two plants of the same species; **de mêmes causes produisent de mêmes effets,** similar causes produce similar effects; **ce m. jour,** the same day; **tous assis à une m. table,** all seated, sitting, round the same table; **tous rassemblés en un m. lieu,** all gathered in one spot, in the same place; **nous avons les mêmes opinions,** we have the same opinions; we see eye to eye; **les deux concepts sont mêmes,** the two concepts are identical; **en m. temps,** at the same time; *pron.* **elle est toujours la m.,** she's always the same; *pron.neut.* **cela revient au m.,** it comes, amounts, to the same thing; it's all one; it's as broad as it's long; *Mus:* **à la m.,** tempo primo; *(b) (following the noun)* very; **aujourd'hui m.,** this very day; **il habite ici m.,** he lives in this very place, in this very house; **les enfants mêmes le savaient,** the very children knew of it; even the children knew it; **c'est cela m.,** that's the very thing; **donner les chiffres mêmes,** to give the actual figures; **il est mort il y a un an ce soir m.,** he died a year ago this very night; *(c)* self; **elle est la bonté m.,** she is kindness itself; **moi-m.,** myself; **toi-m.,** yourself; **lui-m.,** himself, itself; **elle-m.,** herself, itself; **soi-m.,** oneself; **nous-m.,** ourself; **nous-mêmes,** ourselves; **vous-m.,** yourself; **vous-mêmes,** yourselves; **eux-mêmes, elles-mêmes,** themselves; **je conduis moi-m.,** I drive (the car) myself; **il l'a fait lui-m.,** he did it himself; **voyez vous-même,** see for yourself; **faire qch. de soi-m.,** to do sth. of one's own accord; **ces questions se posent d'elles-mêmes,** these questions crop up of themselves; **la chose n'est pas mauvaise en elle-m.,** the thing is not bad in itself, per se; **ne parler que de soi-m.,** to speak only of oneself; **un autre lui-m.,** a second self; **c'était l'Empereur lui-m.,** it was the Emperor himself; **c'était un autre moi-m.,** he was my other self. **2.** *adv.* even; **aimer m. ses ennemis,** to love even one's enemies; **je le pense et m. j'en suis sûr,** I think so; in fact I am sure of it; **je n'ai pas m. le prix de mon voyage,** I haven't even enough to pay my fare; **il ne manquait pas m. une virgule,** not so much as a comma was missing; **m. si je le savais, m. si je le pouvais,** even if I knew, even if I could; *P:* **je l'avais prévenue, m. que je lui avais écrit;** I told her; I even wrote to her, *s.a.* QUAND 1. **3.** *(a) adv.phr.* **de même,** in the same way; likewise; **faire de m.,** to do likewise; to do the same; to follow suit; **il en est de m. des autres,** so it is with the others; **il en est de m. pour lui,** the same holds true, holds good, for him; **il va à peu près de m.,** he is much about the same; *(b) conj.phr.* **de m. que,** (just) as, like; **j'ai pensé de m. que vous,** I thought like you, the same as you; **de m. que** + *ind.* . . . **de m.** + *ind.* . . . , (just) as . . . so (also) . . .; *(c) adv.phr.* (i) **tout de m.,** all the same, for all that; **je l'aime tout de m.,** I like him nevertheless, all the same; **mais tout de m.!** hang it all! **ah, tout de m., le voilà!** at last, here he is! (ii) **c'est, il en est, tout de m.,** it is all the same. **4.** *prep. & adv.phr.* **à m.,** *(a)* **boire à m. la bouteille,** to drink straight out of the bottle; **des maisons bâties à m. le trottoir,** houses built flush with the pavement; **couché à m. le sable,** lying on the bare sand; **tout cela se passait à m. la rue,** all this took place right in the street; **escalier taillé à m. la pierre,** steps cut out of the solid rock; **il portait cette ceinture à m. la peau,** he wore this belt next his skin; **il porte son argent à m. sa poche,** he carries his money loose in his pocket; **il prit un abricot et mordit à m.,** he took an apricot and bit into it; *(b)* **être à m. de faire qch.,** to be able to do sth.; to have it in one's power, to be in a position, to do sth.; **il n'est pas à m. de faire le voyage,** he is not equal to, up to, making the journey; **je ne suis pas à m. de faire quoi que ce soit,** I'm not in a position to do anything; **cela me met à m. de le faire,** that enables me, puts me in a position, to do it.

mémé [meme], *s.f. F:* grandma(ma), granny, nana.

mêmement [mɛmmɑ̃], *adv. A:* **1.** even. **2.** especially. **3.** likewise, the same; **il en est m. des autres,** so it is with the others.

mémento [memɛ̃to], *s.m.* **1.** *(a)* memorandum, note; **bloc m.,** scribbling block; *(b)* memento, reminder. **2.** *(a)* notebook, memorandum book; *(b) Sch:* **m. de chimie, d'histoire,** revision notes in chemistry, in history. **3.** *Ecc: (R.C. Liturgy)* memento.

mémento-mori [memɛ̃tomɔri], *s.m.* memento mori, death's-head.

mémère [memɛːr], *s.f. F:* **1.** *(child's language)* grandma(ma), granny, nana. **2. à sa m.,** mummy's; **un beau chien-chien à sa m.,** mummy's (dear) little doggie-woggie, petsy-wetsy. **3.** *Pej:* (blousy) middle-aged woman; **et si tu avais vu arriver la grosse m.,** and if you'd seen the old girl stumping in.

mémo [memo], *s.m. F:* memo.

mémoire[1] [memwaːr], *s.f.* memory; *(a)* **je n'ai pas la m. des noms,** I have no memory for names; **la m. des lieux,** the bump of locality; **si j'ai bonne m.,** if I remember rightly, if my memory is correct; **mon peu de m.,** the shortness of my memory, *F:* **m. de lièvre,** memory like a sieve; *F:* **m. de cheval,** excellent memory; **lui, il a une m. de cheval,** he's like the elephant, he never forgets; **sa m. baisse,** his memory is failing; *(b)* recollection, remembrance; **perdre la m. de qch.,** to forget sth.; **garder la m. de qch.,** to keep sth. in mind; **avoir m. de qch.,** to remember sth.; **cela m'est sorti de la m.,** it slipped, escaped, my memory; it went out of my head; **j'ai eu un trou, une lacune, de m.,** my mind went blank;

l'incident s'est gravé dans ma m., this incident has stuck in my memory; **gravé dans la m.**, well-remembered; **se mettre qch. en m.**, to commit sth. to memory; **se remettre qch. en m.**, to refresh one's memory of sth.; **rappeler qch. à la m. de qn**, to remind s.o. of sth.; **je vais lui rafraîchir la m.**, I'll send him a reminder; I'll jog his memory; **mentionné pour m.**, mentioned as a reminder; **réciter, jouer, qch. de m.**, to recite, play, sth. from memory; **de m. d'homme**, within living memory; **jamais de m. d'homme**, never within living memory; **de m. d'homme on n'a jamais vu cela**, this has never been seen within living memory; **en m. de qn, à la m. de qn**, (monument, etc.) in memory of s.o., to the memory of s.o.; *Ecc:* **faire m. d'un saint**, to commemorate a saint; *Lit:* **le Temple de M.**, the House of Fame; (*c*) *Elcs:* (*of computer*) storage, memory, store; **m. centrale**, core; **m. à noyau**, core store; **m. à tores magnétiques**, core storage; **position de m.**, core storage location, position; **unité de m. à tores**, core storage unit; **m. à disques**, disc storage; **m. tampon**, buffer storage, buffer store; **m. de travail**, working storage; **m. dynamique**, dynamic memory; **m. externe, auxiliaire**, external memory; external storage, store; secondary storage; **m. rapide**, high speed memory; **m. interne**, internal memory; internal storage, store; **m. à accès sélectif, aléatoire, direct**, random access storage, random access memory; **m. à accès séquentiel**, sequential access storage; **mise en m.**, storage, storing; **mettre, introduire, en m.**, to read in; **extraire, sortir, de la m.**, to read out; **m. fixe, m. morte**, read-only storage, store.

mémoire², *s.m.* **1.** (*a*) memorial; *Jur:* (written) statement (of case); report; **m. descriptif (d'une invention)**, specifications (of patent); (*b*) memoir, paper, dissertation, thesis. **2.** (contractor's) account; memorandum (of costs); **présenter un m.**, to send a detailed account (of costs). **3.** *pl.* (*a*) (historical) memoirs; (*b*) memorials, transactions (of learned society, etc.).

mémorable [memɔrabl̥], *a.* memorable, noteworthy; eventful (year); **le jour m. du grand incendie**, the never-to-be-forgotten day of the great fire; *Gr.Lit:* **les (Entretiens) Mémorables**, The Memorabilia (of Xenophon).

mémorablement [memɔrabləmɑ̃], *adv.* memorably.

mémorandum [memɔrɑ̃dɔm], *s.m.* **1.** memorandum, note; *Adm: Mil: Navy:* orders (in brief); *Navy:* **m. de combat**, battle orders. **2.** notebook.

mémoratif, -ive [memɔratif, -iːv]. **1.** *a.* (*a*) memorative, memorial (faculty, etc.); (*b*) *A:* **être m. de qch.**, to be mindful of sth. **2.** *s.m.* **cela me servira de m.**, this will be a reminder to me.

mémorial, -iaux [memɔrjal, -jo], *s.m.* **1.** (*a*) memorial; memoirs (*e.g.* of Napoleon); (*b*) (*title of certain periodicals*) **le M. diplomatique**, the Diplomatic Gazette. **2.** *Com:* waste book, day book.

mémorialiste [memɔrjalist], *s.m.* memorialist.

mémorisation [memɔrizasjɔ̃], *s.f.* (*a*) memorizing; (*b*) *Elcs:* (*computers*) storage, storing; **zone de m.**, storage area; **tore de m.**, storage core.

mémoriser [memɔrize], *v.tr.* & *i.* (*a*) to memorize (sth.); to commit (sth.) to memory; (*b*) (*of computer*) to store.

memphite [mɛ̃fit], *A.Geog:* **1.** *a.* Memphian, Memphitic. **2.** *s.* Memphian, Memphite.

menable [mənabl̥], *a.* amenable, tractable.

menaçant [mənasɑ̃], *a.* menacing, threatening (attitude, etc.); forbidding (look, etc.); lowering (look, sky).

ménaccanite [menakanit], *s.f.* *Miner:* menaccanite.

menace [mənas], *s.f.* threat, menace; *pl.* *Jur:* intimidation; **lettre de menaces**, threatening letter; **faire faire qch. à qn à force de menaces**, to bully s.o. into doing sth.; **arracher qch. à qn par des menaces**, to get sth. out of s.o. by threats; **menaces en l'air**, empty threats, idle threats; **menaces de part et d'autre**, threats and counterthreats; **silence lourd de menaces**, ominous silence; **menaces de guerre**, sabre-rattling; **la m. sur l'Italie**, the threat to Italy.

menacer [mənase], *v.tr.* (**je menaçai(s); n. menaçons**) to threaten, menace; (*a*) **m. qn du doigt, du poing**, to shake one's finger, one's fist, at s.o.; **un grand danger vous menace**, a great danger is hanging over you, over your head; **m. qn d'un procès**, to threaten s.o. with legal proceedings; **menacé de la fièvre**, threatened with, in danger of, fever; **m. de faire qch.**, to threaten to do sth.; **il menaça de le renvoyer**, he threatened him with dismissal; (*b*) **m. ruine**, to be in danger of falling; **empire qui menace ruine**, tottering, crumbling, empire; **le temps menace la neige**, it looks like snow; (*c*) *abs.* **la tempête menace**, a storm is threatening, is brewing.

ménade [menad], *s.f.* *Gr.Myth:* maenad, bacchante.

menage [mənaːʒ], *s.m.* leading (of horse, etc.); driving (of car).

ménage [menaːʒ], *s.m.* **1.** (*a*) housekeeping; domestic arrangements; establishment; **faire m. avec qn**, to keep house with s.o.; **entrer en m.**, to set up house; **m. de garçon**, bachelor's establishment; **jouer au m.**, to play at keeping house; **tenir le m. de qn**, to keep house for s.o.; **elle met son argent dans le m.**, she contributes to the household expenses; **pain de m.**, large (home-made) loaf; **liqueurs de m.**, home-made liqueurs; **bière de m.**, home-brewed beer; **toile de m.**, homespun linen; **il a un m. en ville**, he keeps a separate establishment (for a mistress); (*b*) housework; household duties; **faire le m.**, (i) to do the housework; (ii) *Games:* to shuffle the dominoes; *Fr.C:* **le grand m.**, spring cleaning; **faire des ménages**, to go out charring; **femme de m.**, charwoman, daily help, *F:* daily; (*c*) home; **les affaires du m.**, household matters. **2.** household goods; **acheter un m. complet**, to buy a full set of furniture; to equip one's house; **m. de poupée**, set of doll's furniture; **se monter en m.**, to furnish one's house. **3.** household, family; (*a*) **jeune ménage**, young (married) couple; **ils font un bon m.**, they are a happily married couple; **"on demande un m. recommandable,"** "reliable couple wanted"; *Jur:* **le m. Dupont**, the man Dupont and his wife; **hospice des ménages**, home for aged couples; **m. à trois**, (matrimonial) triangle; **faux m.**, couple living together; **se mettre en m.**, to set up house; to enter upon married life; (*b*) **faire bon, mauvais, m. (ensemble)**, to live, get on, happily, unhappily, together; **ils font bon m.**, they get on well together; **le desservant fait mauvais m. avec le maire**, the parish priest is at loggerheads with the mayor, does not get on with the mayor. **4.** *A:* (*a*) thrift; **vivre de m.**, to live thriftily; (*b*) management, administration; handling of public affairs, of finance; **le grand m. de Colbert**, Colbert's great administration.

ménagement [menaʒmɑ̃], *s.m.* **1.** care; caution, circumspection; consideration; **avoir des ménagements pour qn**, to treat s.o. with consideration; to have regard for s.o., for s.o.'s feelings; **faire qch. avec ménagement(s)**, to do sth. with great caution, cautiously, tactfully; **parler sans ménagement(s)**, to speak bluntly. **2.** *A:* management (of house, of servants, etc.; of heating, ventilation, etc.).

ménager¹ [menaʒe], *v.tr.* (**je ménageai(s); n. ménageons**) **1.** to save; to be sparing of (sth.); to use (sth.) economically; (*a*) **m. ses ressources**, to husband one's resources; **savoir m. les sous**, to make a penny go a long way; **m. sa santé**, to take care of one's health; **m. l'étoffe**, to make the most of a piece of cloth; **m. son cheval**, to spare, nurse, one's horse; *Prov:* **qui veut aller loin ménage sa monture**, slow and steady wins the race; **m. qn**, to treat s.o. with consideration; to humour s.o.; to deal tactfully, gently, with s.o.; *F:* to handle s.o. with kid gloves; **ne le ménagez pas**, don't spare him; **m. ses pas**, to save one's legs; **m. le temps**, to plan, make the best use of, one's time; **transition ménagée (de . . . à . . .)**, gradual transition (from . . . to . . .); *s.a.* CHÈVRE 1; (*b*) to use (words) with circumspection, with tact; **sans m. ses termes, ses paroles**, without mincing one's words. **2.** to contrive, arrange; (*a*) **m. à qn l'occasion de faire qch.**, to arrange, make, provide, an opportunity for s.o. to do sth.; **m. que qch. se fasse**, to arrange for sth. to be done; **m. une réconciliation entre deux ennemis**, to bring about a reconciliation between two enemies; **m. les intérêts de qn**, to look after s.o.'s interests; **m. une surprise à qn**, to prepare a surprise for s.o.; **je lui ménage une surprise**, I've (got) a surprise (in store) for him; **m. avec beaucoup d'habileté les effets de scène**, to manage the stage effects with great skill; **bien m. un terrain**, to make the most of a piece of ground; (*b*) **m. une ouverture pour les fils**, to make an opening for the wires; **m. de la place pour un accumulateur**, to allow space for a battery; **m. un escalier dans l'épaisseur des murs**, to contrive a staircase within the thickness of the walls; **m. une sortie**, to provide an exit. **3.** *A:* to administer, manage.

se ménager, to spare oneself, to take care of oneself; *F:* not to overdo it; **il ne se ménage pas**, he does not spare himself; **il se ménage un peu trop**, he tends to coddle himself.

ménager², -ère [menaʒe, -ɛːr]. **1.** *a.* (*a*) connected with the house; **travaux ménagers**, housework; **arts ménagers**, domestic arts; **appareils ménagers**, household equipment; domestic equipment, appliances; **enseignement m.**, domestic science; **eau ménagère**, water for domestic use; **eaux ménagères**, waste water, slop-water, slops; **Salon des Arts Ménagers** = Ideal Home Exhibition, *U.S:* Home Show; (*b*) housewifely (virtues, etc.); (*c*) thrifty, sparing, economical; *s.* **être bon m. du temps**, to know how to make the most of one's time; **être m. de ses éloges**, to be chary, sparing, of praise. **2.** *s.f.* **ménagère**, (*a*) housewife; **elle est bonne ménagère**, she's a good housekeeper; *P: O:* **la ménagère**, the wife, the missus; (*b*) *Furn:* (i) cruet stand; (ii) canteen of cutlery, cutlery cabinet.

ménagerie [menaʒri], *s.f.* menagerie; *F:* **c'est une vraie m. que cette maison**, this house is a perfect zoo, menagerie (with cats, dogs, etc.).

Menaï [mənai], *Pr.n. Geog:* **le détroit de M.**, the Menai Strait.

Ménandre [menɑ̃ːdr̥], *Pr.n.m. Gr.Lit:* Menander.

menant [mənɑ̃], *a.* *Mec.E:* driving; **brin m.**, driving side (of belt).

ménarche [menarʃ], *s.m.* *Physiol:* menarche.

mendaïte [mɑ̃dait], *a.* & *s.m.* & *f.* *Rel:* Mandaean.

mendélévium [mɑ̃delevjɔm], *s.m.* *Ch:* mendelevium.

mendélien, -ienne [mɛ̃deljɛ̃, -jɛn], *a.* *Biol:* Mendelian.

mendélisme [mɛ̃delism], *s.m.* Mendelism.

mendiant, -ante [mɑ̃djɑ̃, -ɑ̃ːt]. **1.** *a.* mendicant, begging (friar, order, etc.). **2.** *s.* mendicant; beggar; **les quatre mendiants**, (i) *Ecc.Hist:* the four mendicant orders, (ii) *F:* almonds, raisins, nuts and figs (served as dessert).

mendicité [mɑ̃disite], *s.f.* (*a*) mendicity, mendicancy, begging; *A:* **dépôt de m.**, workhouse; **réduit à la m.**, reduced to beggary; (*b*) (community of) beggars.

mendier [mɑ̃dje], *v.* (*p.d.* & *pr.sub.* **n. mendiions, v. mendiiez**) **1.** *v.i.* to beg; **faire son chemin jusqu'à Paris en mendiant**, to beg one's way to Paris. **2.** *v.tr.* (*a*) **m. son pain**, to beg (for) one's bread; (*b*) **m. des suffrages**, to canvass votes.

mendigo(t), -ote [mɑ̃digo, -ɔt], *s.* *P:* beggar.

mendigoter [mɑ̃digɔte], *v.tr.* & *i.* *P:* to beg.

mendipite [mɑ̃dipit], *s.f.* *Miner:* mendipite.

mendois, -oise [mɑ̃dwa, -waːz], *a.* & *s.* (native, inhabitant) of Mende.

mendole [mɑ̃dɔl], *s.f.* *Ich:* picarel; any small fish of the Maenidae family.

mendozite [mɑ̃dɔzit], *s.f.* *Miner:* mendozite.

meneau, -eaux [məno], *s.m.* *Arch:* **m. vertical**, mullion; **m. horizontal**, transom.

Ménechmes (les) [lemenɛkm]. **1.** *Pr.n.m.pl.* *Lt. Lit:* the Menaechmi (of Plautus). **2.** *s.m.* **un ménechme**, a double, a counterpart (of s.o.).

menée [məne], *s.f.* **1.** *Ven:* track; **chasser m.**, to follow the track. **2.** underhand manœuvre, intrigue; *pl.* schemings (of political party, etc.); meddling; **menées communistes**, communist plots; **menées anti-nationales**, anti-national activities; **déjouer les menées de qn**, to thwart s.o., to outwit s.o.

méneghinite [meneginit], *s.f.* *Miner:* meneghinite.

menehouldien, -ienne [mənuldjɛ̃, -jɛn], *a.* & *s.* *Geog:* (native, inhabitant) of Sainte-Menehould [sɛ̃tmənu].

Ménélas [menelɑːs], *Pr.n.m. Gr.Lit:* Menelaus.

ménémère [menemɛːr], *s.m.* *Arach:* jumping spider.

mener [m(ə)ne], *v.tr.* (**je mène, n. menons; je mènerai**) **1.** to lead; (*a*) to conduct; **m. qn à sa chambre**, to conduct, take, s.o. to his room; **il menait avec lui une suite nombreuse**, he brought a large retinue with him; **m. qn voir qch.**, to take s.o. to see sth.; *Danc: A:* **m. une dame**, to partner a lady; *Geom:* **m. une ligne entre deux points**, to draw a line between two points; (*b*) to be, go, ahead (of); **m. la danse**, to lead the dance; **m. le deuil**, to be chief mourner; *Games:* **la France mène la Belgique par 2 à 1**, France is leading Belgium by 2 to 1; *abs.* **m. par huit points**, to lead by eight points; (*c*) **chemin qui mène à la ville**, road that leads to the town; **cela ne mène à rien**, this leads (us) nowhere; **la flatterie ne vous mènera à rien**, flattery wil get you nowhere; **la modestie ne vous mènera pas loin**, modesty will not carry you far; **cela nous mène à croire que . . .**, that leads us to believe that . . .; (*d*) to control, manage (children, etc.); **il va comme on le mène,**

he is easily led; **mari mené par sa femme,** henpecked husband; **on ne le mène pas comme on veut,** he won't be driven; **mener son personnel au doigt et à l'œil,** to have one's staff well trained; **il mène tout (le monde) à la maison,** he bosses everything, everybody, at home; *s.a.* NEZ 1. **2.** to drive (horse); to steer (boat); **m. trois chevaux de front,** to drive three horses abreast; **cheval facile à m.,** horse light in hand; **m. plusieurs choses de front,** to have several irons in the fire, several things on at once; *s.a.* TRAIN 2; *Mec.E:* **roue menée,** driven wheel, follower. **3.** to manage, conduct (business, etc.); **mener qch. à fin,** to bring sth. to an end; **m. qch. à bonne fin, à bien,** to bring sth. to a successful issue, conclusion; to carry through, carry out (mission, etc.); to work out (plan); **qui va m. les négociations?** who will conduct the negotiations? **m. une vie triste,** to lead a sad life; **m. une campagne contre qn,** to conduct a campaign against s.o.; **c'est lui qui mène le mouvement,** he is the leader of the movement; *F:* **ne pas en m. large,** to be in a tight corner; **je n'en menais pas large,** my heart was in my boots.

ménesse [menɛs], *s.f. P:* woman, skirt.

ménestrandie [menɛstrɑ̃di], *s.f.* **1.** *Mus: A:* the art of playing musical instruments. **2.** *A.Mus:* (kind of) trumpet.

ménestrandise [menɛstrɑ̃di:z], *s.f. coll. A:* minstrelsy.

ménestrel [menɛstrɛl], *s.m. A:* minstrel; gleeman.

ménétrier [menetrije], *s.m.* **1.** (strolling) fiddler, village musician. **2.** *A:* gleeman.

meneur, -euse [m(ə)nœ:r, -ø:z], *s.* (*a*) leader (of blind man, etc.); *Pol:* **m. du parti,** party leader; **m. du jeu,** (i) moving spirit; (ii) *W.Tel: T.V: etc:* question master, quiz master; *Husb:* **poule meneuse,** brooder (hen); *A:* **m. de nourrices,** (i) baby-farmer's agent; (ii) recruiter of wet-nurses for registry office; (*b*) ringleader (of revolt, etc.); agitator; (*c*) **m. de bœufs,** cattle drover; **m. d'ours,** bear leader.

menhaden [menadɛ̃], *s.m. Ich:* menhaden, *U.S:* mossbunker, pogy.

menhir [meni:r], *s.m. Archeol:* menhir, standing stone.

méniane [menjan], *s.f. Ital.Arch:* balcony, veranda.

ménianthe [menjɑ̃:t], *s.m. Bot:* menyanthes, buckbean.

Ménière [menjɛ:r], *Pr.n. Med:* **maladie, syndrome, de M.,** Ménière's disease, syndrome.

ménil [meni], *s.m. A:* (*a*) small country house, small farm; (*b*) hamlet.

ménilite [menilit], *s.f. Miner:* menilite.

menin, -ine [mənɛ̃, -in], *s. Fr. & Span.Hist:* young nobleman, noblewoman, attached as companion to a prince or princess of the blood.

méninge [menɛ̃:ʒ], *s.f. Anat:* meninx; **les trois méninges,** the three meninges; *F:* **se creuser les méninges,** to rack one's brains; **il ne s'abîme, ne se fatigue, pas les méninges,** he doesn't exactly overwork, he doesn't overtax his brains.

méningé [menɛ̃ʒe], *a. Anat:* meningeal (artery, etc.).

méningette [menɛ̃ʒɛt], *s.f. Anat:* pia mater.

méningiome [menɛ̃ʒjo:m], *s.m. Med:* meningioma.

méningisme [menɛ̃ʒism], *s.m. Med:* meningism(us).

méningite [menɛ̃ʒit], *s.f. Med:* meningitis; **m. cérébro-spinale,** cerebro-spinal meningitis.

méningitique [menɛ̃ʒitik], *a.* meningitic.

méningocèle [menɛgosɛl], *s.f. Med:* meningocele.

méningococcémie [menɛ̃gɔkɔksemi], *s.f.*, **méningococcie** [menɛ̃gɔkɔksi], *s.f. Med:* meningococc(a)emia.

méningocoque [menɛ̃gɔkɔk], *s.m. Bac:* meningococcus.

méningo-encéphalite [menɛ̃goɑ̃sefalit], *s.f. Med:* meningoencephalitis; *pl. méningo-encéphalites.*

méningo-myélite [menɛ̃gɔmjelit], *s.f. Med:* meningomyelitis; *pl. méningo-myélites.*

méningorragie [menɛ̃gɔraʒi], *s.f. Med:* meningorrhagia.

Ménippe [menip], *Pr.n.m. Gr.Lit:* Menippus.

méniscite [menisit], *s.f. Med:* meniscitis.

ménispermacé [menispɛrmase], *Bot:* **1.** *a.* menispermaceous. **2.** *s.f.pl.* **ménispermacées,** Menispermaceae.

ménisperme [menispɛrm], *s.m. Bot:* menisperm, moonseed.

ménisque [menisk], *s.m.* meniscus; *Anat:* **m. articulaire,** articular disc.

Mennonite [mɛnɔnit], *a. & s.m. & f. Rel.H:* Mennonite.

ménologe [menɔlɔ:ʒ], *s.m. Gr.Church:* menology, martyrology.

Ménomène [menɔmɛn], *s.m. & f. Ethn:* Menominee (Indian).

ménopause [menɔpo:z], *s.f. Physiol:* menopause.

ménorragie [menɔraʒi], *s.f. Med:* menorrhagia.

ménorragique [menɔraʒik], *a. Med:* menorrhagic.

ménorrhée [menɔre], *s.f. Med:* menorrhoea, menstrual flow.

ménostase [menɔstɑ:z], *s.f. Med:* menostasis.

menotte [mənɔt], *s.f.* **1.** (*a*) (child's) little hand; (*b*) handle (of winch, etc.). **2.** (*a*) *pl.* handcuffs; manacles; **mettre les menottes à qn,** to handcuff s.o.; **menottes aux mains,** handcuffed; (*b*) *Mec.E: Veh:* link, shackle (of shaft, spring, etc.).

menotter [mənɔte], *v.tr.* to handcuff (**à, avec, qn,** to, with, s.o.).

mensale [mɑ̃sal], *s.f.* (*palmistry*) mensal line, heart line.

mense [mɑ̃:s], *s.f. Ecc.Jur:* revenue, income (*esp.* of an abbot).

mensole [mɑ̃sɔl], *s.f. Arch: A:* keystone (of arch).

mensonge [mɑ̃sɔ̃:ʒ], *s.m.* (*a*) lie, untruth, falsehood; **faire, dire, un m.,** to tell a lie, a story; **petit m.,** fib; **m. pieux,** *Theol:* **m. officieux,** white lie; **gros m.,** out-and-out lie; whopper; *Hum:* **c'est vrai, ce gros m.?** you're kidding! oh, yeah! **l'habitude du m.,** mendacity; (*b*) error, fallacy, delusion; **tout n'est que m.,** all is vanity.

mensonger, -ère [mɑ̃sɔ̃ʒe, -ɛ:r], *a.* lying, untrue, mendacious (story); deceitful, false (look); vain, illusory (hope, pleasure).

mensongèrement [mɑ̃sɔ̃ʒɛrmɑ̃], *adv.* falsely, untruthfully, mendaciously.

menstruation [mɑ̃stryasjɔ̃], *s.f. Physiol:* menstruation.

menstrue [mɑ̃stry]. **1.** *s.m. Ch: A:* (= DISSOLVANT) solvent, menstruum. **2.** *s.f.pl. Physiol:* menstrua, menses, (monthly) periods.

menstruel, -elle [mɑ̃stryɛl], *a. Physiol:* menstrual (flow).

mensualisation [mɑ̃sɥalizasjɔ̃], *s.f.* paying (of workers) by the month.

mensualiser [mɑ̃sɥalize], *v.tr.* to pay (workers) by the month.

mensualité [mɑ̃sɥalite], *s.f.* (*a*) monthly nature (of payments, etc.); (*b*) monthly payment, remittance; **payer par mensualités,** to pay by monthly instalments.

mensuel, -elle [mɑ̃sɥɛl]. **1.** *a.* monthly; **publication mensuelle,** monthly publication. **2.** (*a*) *s.m.* monthly magazine; (*b*) *s.m. & f.* employee, worker, paid by the month.

mensuellement [mɑ̃sɥɛlmɑ̃], *adv.* monthly, each month, every month.

mensurabilité [mɑ̃syrabilite], *s.f.* mensurability.

mensurable [mɑ̃syrabl̩], *a.* mensurable, measurable.

mensuration [mɑ̃syrasjɔ̃], *s.f.* measurement. **1.** measuring, *Geom:* mensuration. **2.** *Anthr:* **prendre les mensurations de qn,** to take s.o.'s measurements; *F:* (*of a woman*) **mensurations,** vital statistics.

mensurer [mɑ̃syre], *v.tr.* to measure (size and weight).

mentagre [mɑ̃tagr̩], *s.f. Med:* sycosis, barber's itch.

mental[1], -ale, -aux [mɑ̃tal, -o]. **1.** *a.* mental (arithmetic, disease, reservation, etc.); **aliénation mentale,** mental alienation, insanity; **les débiles mentaux,** the mentally deficient. **2.** *s.* mental patient.

mental[2], -aux, *a. Anat: Z:* mental (angle).

mentalement [mɑ̃talmɑ̃], *adv.* mentally.

mentalité [mɑ̃talite], *s.f.* mentality. **1. enfant à petite m.,** mentally retarded child. **2.** mental habit (of a nation, etc.); turn of mind (of person); *F:* **avoir une sale m.,** to have an unpleasant, an unhealthy, outlook.

menterie [mɑ̃tri], *s.f. F:* fib, story.

menteur, -euse [mɑ̃tœ:r, -ø:z]. **1.** *a.* (*a*) lying, mendacious, fibbing, story-telling (person); given to lying; (*b*) false, deceptive (appearance). **2.** *s.* liar, fibber, story-teller.

menteusement [mɑ̃tøzmɑ̃], *adv.* lyingly, mendaciously; falsely.

menthadiène [mɑ̃tadjɛn], *s.m. Ch:* menthadiene.

menthanol [mɑ̃tanɔl], *s.m. Ch:* menthanol.

menthanone [mɑ̃tanon], *s.f. Ch:* menthanone.

menthe [mɑ̃:t], *s.f. Bot:* mint; **m. verte,** spearmint, garden mint; **m. aquatique, m. sauvage,** horse mint; **m. anglaise, poivrée,** peppermint; **pastilles de m.,** peppermint lozenges, peppermints.

menthe-coq [mɑ̃tkɔk], *s.f. Bot:* costmary, alecost; *pl. menthes-coqs.*

menthène [mɑ̃tɛn], *s.m. Ch:* menthene.

menthénone [mɑ̃tenɔn], *s.f. Ch:* menthenone.

menthol [mɛ̃tɔl], *s.m. Ch: Pharm:* menthol; peppermint camphor.

mentholé [mɛ̃tɔle], **mentholique** [mɛ̃tɔlik], *a. Pharm:* mentholated; containing menthol.

menthone [mɑ̃tɔn], *s.f. Ch:* menthone.

menthyle [mɑ̃til], *s.m. Ch:* menthyl.

mention [mɑ̃sjɔ̃], *s.f.* (*a*) mention; **faire m. de qn, de qch.,** to make mention of, to refer to, to mention, s.o., sth.; *Sch:* **reçu avec m.,** passed with distinction; **il a été reçu, mais sans m.,** he got a (bare) pass; (*b*) *Post:* endorsement (on envelope, etc.); **m. "inconnu,"** endorsed "not known"; (*on form, etc.*) **à la m. "couleur des yeux,"** at, under the heading, "colour of eyes"; **mentions de service,** service instructions (on telegram, etc.); **mentions du cachet d'oblitération,** particulars on the postmark; **revêtu de la m. "fragile,"** marked "breakable"; *Publ:* **m. de réserve,** *Journ:* **m. d'interdiction,** copyright notice; (*c*) *Adm: Com:* reference (at head of letter).

mentionner [mɑ̃sjɔne], *v.tr.* to mention; to make mention of (s.o., sth.) **m. "fragile,"** to mark "breakable"; **mentionné ci-dessous,** undermentioned; **mentionné ci-dessus,** abovementioned, aforesaid.

mentir [mɑ̃ti:r], *v.i.* (*pr.p.* **mentant;** *p.p.* **menti;** *pr.ind.* **je mens, tu mens, il ment, n. mentons, v. mentez, ils mentent;** *p.d.* **je mentais;** *p.h.* **je mentis;** *fu.* **je mentirai**) to lie, to tell lies, untruths; **m. à qn,** to lie to s.o.; **à ne point m.,** to tell the truth; **sans m.!** on my honour! *Sch:* honour bright! **il en a menti!** he is a liar! *A:* **il en a menti par la gorge!** he lies in his throat! **faire m. qn,** to catch s.o. out; **faire m. un proverbe,** to belie, falsify, a proverb.

menton[1] [mɑ̃tɔ̃], *s.m.* chin; **double m., menton à deux étages,** double chin; **m. de, en, galoche,** undershot jaw; nutcracker chin; **m. effacé,** receding chin; **avoir de l'eau jusqu'au m.,** to be up to the chin, the neck, in water; *F:* **en avoir jusqu'au m.,** to be fed up to the (back) teeth; *F:* **s'en mettre jusqu'au m.,** to have a good feed, a good tuck in; to fill oneself up to the neck; **le m. dans le creux de la main,** with one's chin cupped in one's hand; **relever le m. à qn,** to chuck s.o. under the chin.

Menton[2], *Pr.n. Geog:* Menton(e).

mentonnais, -aise [mɑ̃tɔnɛ, -ɛ:z], *a. & s.* (native, inhabitant) of Menton(e).

mentonnet [mɑ̃tɔnɛ], *s.m.* (*a*) catch (of latch, etc.); stop (on moving part of machine); (*b*) *Mec.E:* tappet, cam, wiper; *I.C.E:* **m. lubrificateur,** oil dipper (of big end), scoop, splasher; (*c*) *Rail:* flange (of wheel); (*d*) lug; cocking piece (of revolver, etc.); ear (of bomb); kick (of penknife blade).

mentonnier, -ière [mɑ̃tɔnje, -jɛ:r]. **1.** *a. Anat:* mental, genial; **trou m.,** mental foramen. **2.** *s.f.* **mentonnière,** (*a*) *Arm:* chinpiece (of helmet); (*b*) (bonnet) string; *Mil:* check strap, chain; *Surg:* chin bandage; (*c*) *Mus:* chin rest (of violin).

Mentor [mɛ̃tɔ:r]. **1.** *Pr.n.m. Gr.Lit:* Mentor. **2.** *s.m. Lit:* mentor; guide, philosopher and friend.

menu [məny]. **1.** *a.* small; (*a*) fine (grass, gravel, etc.); slender, slim, slight (figure); tiny, little (fragment); **m. plomb,** small shot, bird shot; **menue monnaie,** small change; **m. bétail,** small(er) livestock; **m. bois,** brushwood; *Her:* **menue pièce,** subordinary; (*b*) trifling (incident, etc.); **menues réparations,** minor repairs; **menus détails,** small, minute, details; full particulars; **menus frais,** (i) petty expenses; (ii) pocket-money; **donner à qn tant pour ses menus plaisirs,** to give s.o. so much (as) pocket-money; **le m. peuple,** the poorer classes; **menus propos,** small talk. **2.** *adv.* small, fine; **hacher m.,** (i) to chop (meat, etc.) up small; to mince (sth.); (ii) *F:* to make mincemeat of (s.o.); **il pleuvait dru et m.,** the rain came down in a steady drizzle; **trotter dru et m.,** to walk with short quick steps, to trip along; **écrire m.,** to write small. **3.** *s.m.* (*a*) small fragments; **m. du charbon, menus de houille,** small (coal); slack; (*b*) **raconter qch. par le m.,** to relate sth. in detail; (*c*) menu, bill of fare (of a meal).

menuaille [mənɥɑ:j], *s.f. A:* quantity of trifling, rubbishy, things; *Fish:* small fry; **payer qn en m.,** to pay s.o. with small change.

menuchon [mənyʃɔ̃], *s.m. Bot: F:* scarlet pimpernel.

menuet [mənɥɛ], *s.m.* minuet.

menuisage [mənɥiza:ʒ], *s.m.* cutting down (of timber) to the required size.

menuisaille [mənɥiza:j], *s.f.* **1.** *Fish:* small fry. **2.** *Sm.a:* small shot, dust shot.

menuise [mənɥiːz], *s.f.* 1. = MENUISAILLE. 2. twigs, sticks (of wood).

menuiser [mənɥize], *v.tr.* 1. to cut down, plane down (timber to required size). 2. *abs.* to do joiner's work, woodwork.

menuiserie [mənɥizri], *s.f.* 1. joinery, woodwork; **grosse m.**, carpentry. 2. joinery, woodwork finishings (of house, etc.). 3. joiner's shop.

menuisier, -ière [mənɥizje, -jɛːr]. 1. *a.* **ouvrier m.**, joiner; *Ent:* **abeille menuisière**, carpenter bee. 2. *s.m.* joiner; (light) carpenter; **m. en meubles**, cabinet-maker; **m. en bâtiments**, carpenter.

ménure [menyːr], *s.m. Orn:* menura, lyre bird.

ménuridés [menyride], *s.m.pl. Orn:* Menuridae, the lyre birds.

menu-vair [mənyvɛːr], *s.m.* squirrel (fur), miniver.

ményanthe [menjɑ̃ːt], *s.m. Bot:* menyanthes, buckbean.

Méphistophélès [mefistɔfelɛs], *F:* **Méphisto** [mefisto], *Pr.n.m.* Mephistopheles.

méphistophélique [mefistɔfelik], *a.* Mephistophelian, Mephistophelean.

méphite [mefit], *s.f. Ch: A:* mephitic gas.

méphitique [mefitik], *a.* mephitic, foul, noxious, noisome.

méphitiser [mefitize], *v.tr.* to make foul; to vitiate (air).

méphitisme [mefitism], *s.m.* (*a*) mephitism; (*b*) mephitis, stench.

méplat [mepla]. 1. *a.* (*a*) flat; *Const:* (*of joist*) flat-laid; **fer m.**, flat bar-iron; **bois m.**, wood in planks; *El:* **conducteur m.**, strap-braided conductor; (*b*) *Art:* **lignes méplates**, lines showing up the different planes (of the face, etc.). 2. *s.m.* (*a*) flat part; flattening, flat lug, flatted end; ledge (of rock); **former des méplats à l'extrémité d'une tige**, to flatten the end of a rod; (*b*) *Art:* **méplats du visage**, planes that build up the face; **méplats hardis**, boldly chiselled features.

méprendre (se) [səmeprɑ̃ːdr], *v.pr.* (*conj. like* PRENDRE) to be mistaken, to make a mistake (**sur, quant à**, about, regarding); **se m. sur un motif**, to mistake, misjudge, a motive; **il n'y a pas à s'y m.**, there can be no mistake about it; there is no mistaking it; **c'est son frère à s'y m.**, he is the very image of his brother; **il imitait le maître à s'y m.**, he could give a life-like imitation of the master; he could imitate the master to the life; **de manière (à ce) que le lecteur ne se méprenne point**, so that the reader should not misunderstand.

mépris [mepri], *s.m.* 1. contempt, scorn; **m. des richesses**, contempt for, scorn of, wealth; **subir le m. de qn**, to incur s.o.'s contempt; **tenir qn en m.**, to hold s.o. in contempt, to despise s.o.; **avoir un souverain m. pour qn**, to hold s.o. in supreme contempt; **tomber dans le m.**, to fall into disrepute; **faire m. de qch.**, to despise sth.; **c'est un objet de m. pour ses collègues**, his colleagues despise him; *A:* **être à m. (à qn)**, to be held in contempt, to be despised (by s.o.); **au, en, m. de qch.**, in contempt of sth.; **agir au m. de la loi, du bons sens**, to act in defiance of the law, of common sense; **avec m.**, scornfully, contemptuously; **regarder ses semblables avec m.**, to look down on one's fellow-beings; **repousser un conseil avec m.**, to pooh-pooh a piece of advice; **sourire de m.**, contemptuous smile; *Prov:* **la familiarité engendre le m.**, familiarity breeds contempt. 2. *pl. A:* marks of contempt; sneers, disparaging remarks.

méprisable [meprizabḷ], *a.* contemptible, despicable.

méprisablement [meprizabl(ə)mɑ̃], *adv.* contemptibly, despicably.

méprisant [meprizɑ̃], *a.* contemptuous, scornful.

méprise [mepriːz], *s.f.* mistake, misapprehension; **par m.**, by mistake; inadvertently; **commettre une lourde m.**, to make a bad mistake; *F:* to put one's foot in it; to make a bad break.

mépriser [meprize], *v.tr.* to despise, scorn; to hold (s.o., sth.) in contempt; **méprisé de, par, qn**, despised by s.o.; **m. qn d'avoir fait qch.**, to despise s.o. for doing sth.; **m. les dangers**, to disregard, scoff at, make light of, dangers.

mépriseur, -euse [meprizœːr, -øːz], *a. & s.* contemptuous (person).

mer [mɛːr], *s.f.* sea; (*a*) **la haute m., la grande m., la m. libre**, the open sea, the high seas; **en haute m., en pleine m.**, on the high seas, out at sea; **navire de (haute) m.**, sea-going ship; **m. intérieure, m. fermée**, enclosed sea, inland sea, landlocked sea; *F:* **m. d'huile**, sea as smooth as a millpond; **d'une m. à l'autre**, from coast to coast; **au bord de la m.**, at the seaside; **il est parti à la m.**, he has gone to the seaside; **il est parti en m.**, he has gone to sea; **l'air de la mer**, the sea air; **mal de m.**, seasickness; **avoir le mal de m.**, to be seasick; **homme, gens, de m.**, seaman, seamen; seafaring man, men; **mer debout**, head sea; **grosse m.**, heavy sea; **m. dure, mauvaise**, rough sea; **m. du fond**, ground swell; **il y a de la m., la m. est grosse**, the sea is running high; there is a heavy sea; **m. à contre vent**, counter sea; **essuyer un coup de m.**, to be struck by a heavy sea; **tomber à la m.**, to fall into the sea, overboard; **une lame le jeta à la m.**, a wave swept him overboard; **un homme à la m.!** man overboard! **un mât fut emporté par la m.**, a mast went by the board; **sur m.**, afloat; **servir sur m.**, to serve afloat, to serve at sea; **voyage sur m.**, sea voyage; **prendre la m.**, to set sail, to sail, to put (out) to sea; **envoyer un navire en m.**, to send a ship to sea; **mettre une embarcation à la m.**, to get out, lower, a boat; (se) **mettre à la m.**, to put to sea; **tenir la m.**, (i) to keep the sea, to remain at sea; (ii) to hold the seas, to rule the waves; **navire qui tient bien la m.**, ship that behaves well in a seaway; **chercher qn par m. et par terre**, to look up hill and down dale for s.o.; **porter de l'eau à la m.**, to carry coals to Newcastle; *F:* **ce n'est pas la m. à boire**, it's quite easy; **une goutte d'eau dans la m.**, a drop in the ocean, the bucket; (*b*) tide; **m. haute, pleine m.**, high tide; **basse m.**, low tide; **la m. monte, descend**, the tide is rising, falling, is coming in, going out; **grandes mers**, spring tides; (*c*) **une m. de sable**, a vast expanse, an ocean, of sand; **une m. de sang**, a sea of blood; **m. de glace**, glacier (surface).

méralgie [meralʒi], *s.f. Med:* meralgia.

mercanette [mɛrkanɛt], *s.f. Orn:* teal.

mercanti [mɛrkɑ̃ti], *s.m.* 1. (*a*) (oriental) bazaar-keeper; (*b*) *Mil: A:* sutler, hawker, camp-follower. 2. *Pej:* low-class profiteer; shark; **mercantis de guerre**, war profiteers.

mercantile [mɛrkɑ̃til], *a.* 1. mercantile (operation, etc.); commercial. 2. *Pej:* **esprit m.**, grabbing, money-making, mentality.

mercantilisme [mɛrkɑ̃tilism], *s.m.* 1. *Pol.Ec:* mercantilism. 2. *Pej:* commercialism; money-grubbing.

mercantiliste [mɛrkɑ̃tilist]. 1. *a.* mercantile, commercial; mercantilist. 2. *s.m. & f.* mercantilist, advocate of mercantilism.

mercantille [mɛrkɑ̃tiːj], *s.f. A:* petty trading, business in a small way; **faire la m.**, to go in for petty trading.

mercaptal [mɛrkaptal], *s.m. Ch:* mercaptal.

mercaptan [mɛrkaptɑ̃], *s.m. Ch:* mercaptan.

mercaptide [mɛrkaptid], *s.m. Ch:* mercaptide.

mercaptomérine [mɛrkaptɔmerin], *s.f. Ch:* mercaptomerin.

mercédaires [mɛrsedɛːr], *s.m.pl. Ecc:* Mercedarians.

mercenaire [mɛrsənɛːr]. 1. *a.* mercenary. 2 *s.m.* (*a*) *A:* hireling; (*b*) *Mil:* mercenary; (*c*) **travailler comme un m.**, to work hard for next to nothing; to get little reward for one's pains.

mercenarisme [mɛrsənarism], *s.m.* mercenariness.

mercerie [mɛrsəri], *s.f.* 1. drapery, haberdashery, *U.S:* notions. 2. (*a*) (small) draper's shop; (*in store*) haberdashery counter, department; (*b*) *A:* pedlar's small wares; **il a plu sur sa m.**, his business is in a bad way.

mercerisage [mɛrsərizaːʒ], *s.m. Tex:* mercerizing, mercerization.

merceriser [mɛrsərize], *v.tr. Tex:* to mercerize; **coton mercerisé**, mercerized cotton.

mercerisette [mɛrsərizɛt], *s.f. Tex:* mercerized sateen.

merceriseuse [mɛrsərizøːz], *s.f. Tex:* (*machine*) mercerizer.

merci [mɛrsi]. 1. *s.f.* (*a*) *A:* favour; **Dieu m.**, by the favour of God; thank God; (*b*) *A:* pleasure, discretion; **à merci**, at pleasure; *A:* **se rendre à m.**, to surrender unconditionally; (*c*) mercy; **être à la m. de qn**, to be at s.o.'s mercy; **se mettre à la m. de qn**, to place oneself in s.o.'s power; **implorer m.**, to beg (for) mercy; **crier m.**, to cry quarter; **accorder m. à qn**, to give s.o. quarter; **sans m.**, merciless(ly), pitiless(ly), ruthless(ly); *int. A:* **m. de moi! m. de ma vie!** mercy me! (*d*) *Hist:* **l'ordre de Notre-Dame de la M.**, the Order of Our Lady of Ransom. 2. *adv.* (*a*) thank you; **m. bien, beaucoup**, many thanks, thank you very much; **m. de, pour, votre offre**, thank you for your offer; **mille fois m., m. mille fois**, very many thanks; (*b*) no thank you; **prenez-vous du thé?—merci! (non!)** will you have some tea?—no, thank you! 3. *s.m.* **adresser un cordial m. à qn**, to thank s.o. heartily; **elle me dit un joli m.**, she thanked me in a charming manner; *usu. Iron:* **grand m.!** many thanks! no thank you!

Mercie [mɛrsi], *Pr.n.f. Hist:* Mercia.

mercien, -ienne [mɛrsjɛ̃, -jɛn], *a. & s. Hist:* Mercian.

mercier, -ière [mɛrsje, -jɛːr], *s.* 1. haberdasher; (small-scale) draper. 2. *A:* pedlar of small wares; *Prov:* **à petit m. petit panier**, don't bite off more than you can chew.

mercredi [mɛrkrədi], *s.m.* Wednesday; **le m. des Cendres**, Ash Wednesday.

mercuration [mɛrkyrasjɔ̃], *s.f. Ch:* mercuration.

Mercure [mɛrkyːr]. 1. (*a*) *Pr.n.m. Myth: Astr:* Mercury; (*b*) *s.m. F: A:* **un m.**, a go-between. 2. *s.m. Ch:* mercury; *Pharm:* **m. précipité blanc**, ammoniated mercury; white precipitate; **m. doux**, calomel; **lampe à vapeur de m.**, mercury-vapour lamp; *P:* **avoir du m. aux fesses**, to have ants in one's pants.

mercureux, -euse [mɛrkyrø, -øːz], *a. Ch:* mercurous.

mercuriale[1] [mɛrkyrjal], *s.f. Bot:* (*a*) **m. annuelle**, garden mercury; (*b*) **m. vivace**, dog's mercury.

mercuriale[2], *s.f.* 1. *Hist:* meeting of the Courts of Justice on the first Wednesday after the vacation. 2. (*a*) *A:* speech made at the re-opening of the Courts of Justice; (*b*) reprimand, dressing down; *A:* **m. entre deux draps**, curtain lecture.

mercuriale[3], *s.f.* market price-list, market prices (of corn, etc.).

mercurialiser [mɛrkyrjalize], *v.tr. Med:* to mercurialize.

mercurialisme [mɛrkyrjalism], *s.m. Med:* mercurialism, mercurial poisoning.

mercuriel, -ielle [mɛrkyrjɛl], *a. Pharm:* mercurial (ointment, etc.).

mercurifère [mɛrkyrifɛːr], *a. Miner:* containing mercury, mercury-bearing.

mercurique [mɛrkyrik], *a. Ch:* mercuric (salt, etc.).

Mercurochrome [mɛrkyrɔkrom], *s.m. Pharm: R.t.m:* Mercurochrome.

mercurophylline [mɛrkyrɔfilin], *s.f. Pharm:* mercurophylline.

merdaille [mɛrdɑːj], *s.f.coll. P:* 1. dirty brats, raga-muffins. 2. riff-raff; scum; rag, tag and bobtail.

merdaillon [mɛrdajɔ̃], *s.m. P.* 1. dirty brat, street arab. 2. little squit of a man; little stinker.

merde [mɛrd], *s.f. P:* (*not used in polite conversation*) 1. (*a*) excrement, shit, dung; (*b*) *Bot:* **m. du diable**, asafoetida; (*c*) *a.inv.* **m. d'oie** [mɛrdwa], yellowish-green, sickly green; (*d*) (*of pers.*) **être dans la m.**, to be in a hell of a fix; to be up to the bloody neck in it. 2. (*a*) (*pers.*) **(grosse, grossière) m.**, turd, bugger; **il fait sa m., ne se prend pas pour une, de la, m., ne se croit pas de la m.**, he's got a bloody high opinion of himself; he's bloody snooty; (*b*) (*thg*) crap. 3. *int.* (*a*) **m. (alors)! et puis m.! m. et contre-m.! m. de m.!** damn and blast it! bloody hell! bugger it! (*b*) **m.! ce qu'elle est belle!** cor! Christ! she's a smasher, a corker! (*c*) **m. à la puissance treize!** bloody good luck!

merdeux, -euse [mɛrdø, -øːz], *P:* (*not used in polite conversation*) 1. *a.* (*of linen, etc.*) soiled with faeces; filthy, shitty; (*of pers.*) **c'est un bâton m.**, he's bloody impossible, the bloody end. 2. *s.* (*pers.*) (*a*) dirty swine; bugger; *f.* dirty bitch; (*b*) **un petit m.**, a little whipper-snapper, a little squirt, a little stinker.

merdicole [mɛrdikɔl], *a. Ent:* stercoricolous.

merdier [mɛrdje], *s.m. P:* **je suis dans un sacré m.**, I'm in a bloody mess, hole, in the shit.

merdivore [mɛrdivɔːr], *a.* coprophagous, scatophagous, stercovorous, dung-eating.

merdoie [mɛrdwa], *a.inv.* yellowish-green, sickly green, gosling green.

merdoyer [mɛrdwaje], *v.i.* (**je merdoie, n. merdoyons; je merdoierai**) *P:* to get all tangled up (in one's speech); *Sch:* to dry up, to get stuck.

mère[1] [mɛːr], *s.f.* mother. 1. (*a*) **être m. de six enfants**, to be the mother of six children; **elle est m. de famille**, she is the mother of a family; **frère, sœur, de m.**, uterine brother, sister; half-brother, -sister; **enfants sans m.**, motherless children; **m. nourrice**, wet nurse, foster-mother; **m. célibataire**, unmarried mother; **la fête des mères** = Mothering Sunday, Mother's Day; *A:* **m. des compagnons**, landlady who mothered the itinerant members of trade guilds; (*b*) *Z:* dam; *Husb:* **m. poule**, mother hen; **m. artificielle**, artificial mother, incubator; *F:* (*of woman*) **c'est une m. poule**, she's a real mother hen; (*c*) **ma mère n'est pas là**, (my) mother isn't in; **oui, ma m.**, (i) *A:* yes, mother; (ii) *Ecc:* yes, Mother (Ursula, etc.); **rappelez-moi au bon souvenir de (madame) votre mère**, please remember me to your mother; (*d*) *F:* **la m. Martin**, old Mrs Martin, old mother Martin; *P:* **et dites donc, la petite m.!** well, missus, mum, ducks! (*e*) *Ecc:*

m. abbesse, abbess, mother superior (of convent); **la m. Ursule,** Mother Ursula. **2.** (*source, origin*) (*a*) **la Grèce, m. des arts,** Greece, mother of the arts; **m. de vinaigre,** mother of vinegar; **l'oisiveté est la m. de tous les vices,** idleness is the source, the root, of all evil; (*b*) (i) *Art: Cer:* mould, matrix (for plaster casts, etc.); (ii) *Mec.E:* die (of screw-thread). **3.** *attrib.* (*a*) **la Reine M.,** the Queen Mother; (*b*) **langue m.,** mother language (of other languages); **m. branche,** main branch (of tree or stream); **idée m.,** original, main, governing, idea (of work, etc.); **perle m., m. perle,** pearl oyster; *Biol:* **cellule m.,** mother cell; *Cryst:* **eau m.,** mother liquor; *Hort:* **pied m.,** stool; *Geol:* **roche m.,** matrix, gangue; parent rock; *Rec:* **bande m.,** master tape; *Com:* **maison m.,** parent, main, establishment.

mère², *a.f.* pure. **1. vin de la m. goutte,** wine from the first pressing. **2. m. laine,** mother wool.

méreau, -eaux [mero], *s.m.* **1.** quoit, disc (used in the game of hopscotch). **2.** *A:* counter, tally, token; attendance voucher.

mère-grand [mɛrgrɑ̃], *s.f. F: A:* grandmam(m)a; *pl. mères-grand.*

mère-gueuse [mɛrgøːz], *s.f. Metall:* sow (channel); *pl. mères-gueuses.*

mérelle [merɛl], *s.f. Games:* hopscotch.

mérenchyme [merɑ̃ʃim], *s.m. Bot:* merenchyma.

mère-patrie [mɛrpatri], *s.f.* mother country; parent state (of colonies), metropolis; *pl. mères-patries.*

mère-pipi [mɛrpipi], *s.f. P:* lavatory attendant; *pl. mères-pipi.*

mérétrice [meretris], *s.f. Moll:* meretrix.

merganser [mɛrgɑ̃sɛːr], *s.m. Orn:* merganser, goosander.

merguez [mɛrgɛːz], *s.f. Cu:* merguez.

mergule [mɛrgyl], *s.m. Orn:* **m. nain,** little auk, *U.S:* dovekie.

méricarpe [merikarp], *s.m. Bot:* mericarp.

méridien, -ienne [meridjɛ̃, -jɛn]. **1.** *a.* (*a*) meridian, meridional (line, altitude, etc.); **distance zénithale méridionale,** meridional zenith distance; (*b*) **chaleur méridienne,** midday heat; **ombre méridienne,** shadow at noon; *Astr:* **lunette méridienne,** transit instrument; **cercle m.,** transit (circle). **2.** *s.m.* meridian; **m. géographique, magnétique, céleste,** geographic, magnetic, celestial, meridian; **m.-origine,** standard, prime, meridian; **m. zéro,** zero meridian; **sous le m. de vingt degrés à l'ouest de Greenwich,** twenty degrees West of Greenwich; (*of star*) **passer le m.,** to transit; (*in N. hemisphere*) to south; (*in S. hemisphere*) to north; **passage au m.,** southing; northing; **passage inférieur au m.,** lower transit; **passage supérieur au m.,** upper transit, culmination. **3.** *s.f.* **méridienne,** (*a*) (i) meridian line; (ii) meridian altitude; (*b*) (i) midday siesta, nap; (ii) couch, sofa.

méridional, -ale, -aux [meridjɔnal, -o]. **1.** *a.* (*a*) meridional (distance, etc.); (*b*) south(ern); **transept m.,** south transept; **les pays méridionaux de l'Europe,** the southern countries of Europe. **2.** *s.* southerner; meridional (*esp.* of France).

mérièdre [merjɛdr], *a. Cryst:* merohedral, merohedric.

mériédrie [merjedri], *s.f. Cryst:* merohedrism.

meringue [mərɛ̃ːg], *s.f. Cu:* meringue.

meringuer [mərɛ̃ge], *v.tr. Cu:* **1.** to enclose (sweet, etc.) in a meringue shell. **2. pommes meringuées,** apple snow.

mérinos [merinoːs], *s.m.* (*a*) merino (sheep, cloth, etc.); *P:* **laisser pisser le m.,** to let things take their normal course; to wait until the moment is ripe; (*b*) *a.inv.* **brebis m.,** merino ewe.

mérione [merjɔn], *s.m. Z:* jird.

merise [məriːz], *s.f. Bot:* wild cherry, gean, merry; **m. de Virginie,** choke cherry.

merisier [mərizje], *s.m. Bot:* wild cherry (tree), gean (tree), merry (tree); **m. à grappes,** bird cherry; **pipe en m.,** cherry-wood pipe.

méristèle [meristɛl], *s.f. Bot:* meristele.

méristème [meristɛm], *s.m. Bot:* meristem.

méritant [meritɑ̃], *a.* meritorious, deserving; **peu m.,** undeserving.

mérite [merit], *s.m.* merit; (*a*) worth; **une œuvre de peu de m.,** a work of little merit, value; **chose de peu de m.,** thing of little worth, value; **être récompensé selon ses mérites,** to be rewarded according to one's merits, to meet with one's deserts; **s'attribuer le m. de qch.,** to take the glory, the credit, for sth.; **se faire un grand m. de qch.,** to take great credit to oneself for sth.; **il faut dire à son m. que . . .,** it must be said to his credit, in his favour, that . . .; **par ordre de m.,** in order of merit; *Adm:* **le M. agricole,** decoration awarded to prominent farmers, etc., by the Ministry of Agriculture; *Theol:* **les mérites du Christ,** the righteousness of Christ; (*b*) excellence, talent; **homme de m.,** man of talent, of ability.

mériter [merite], *v.tr.* **1.** to deserve, merit; **il mérite notre estime,** he deserves our esteem; **il n'a que ce qu'il mérite,** he has got what he deserves; it serves him right; **bien m. de la patrie,** to deserve well of one's country; **livre qui mérite d'être lu,** book worth reading; **cela mérite réflexion, examen,** it is worth thinking over, examining; **cela mérite d'être vu, entendu,** it is worth seeing, hearing; **il mérite qu'on fasse quelque chose pour lui,** he deserves to have something done on his behalf. **2. voilà ce qui lui a mérité cette faveur,** this is what earned him, entitled him to, this favour. **3.** *A:* to require; **cette nouvelle mérite confirmation,** the news requires confirmation.

mérithalle [merital], *s.m. Bot:* merithal(lus), internode.

méritoire [meritwaːr], *a.* meritorious, deserving, praiseworthy.

méritoirement [meritwarmɑ̃], *adv.* meritoriously, deservingly.

merl [mɛrl], *s.m. Agr: Hort:* = MAËRL.

merlan [mɛrlɑ̃], *s.m.* **1.** *Ich:* whiting; **m. bleu,** mackerel; **m. jaune,** pollack; *F:* **faire des yeux de m. frit,** (i) to roll one's eyes heavenwards; (ii) to gaze ecstatically (at s.o.). **2.** *P: A:* hairdresser.

merle [mɛrl], *s.m. Orn:* **1.** (*a*) **m. (noir),** blackbird; (*b*) **m. bleu,** blue rock thrush; **m. doré,** White's, golden mountain, thrush; **m. solitaire,** Pallas's thrush; **m. rose,** rose-coloured starling, rose-coloured pastor; **m. orange** (Indian) orange-headed ground thrush; **m. obscur,** eyebrowed, dark, thrush; **m. de roche,** rock thrush; **m. brun,** dusky thrush; **m. sibérien,** Siberian thrush; **m. migrateur,** American robin; **m. blanc,** (i) white crow; (ii) rara avis; *s.a.* GRIVE 1; (*c*) *F:* **jaser comme un m.,** to chatter like a magpie; **c'est un fin m.,** he's a cunning type, specimen; **vilain m.,** *Iron:* **beau m.,** ugly type; nasty piece of work; *Iron:* fine specimen. **2. m. d'eau,** water ouzel, dipper; **m. à plastron, à collier,** ring ouzel.

merleau, -eaux [mɛrlo], *s.m. Orn:* young blackbird.

merlette [mɛrlɛt], *s.f.* **1.** *Orn:* hen blackbird. **2.** *Her:* martlet.

merlin¹ [mɛrlɛ̃], *s.m.* **1.** *Nau:* marline; small stuff. **2.** *P:* leg, shank.

merlin², *s.m.* axe, cleaver, cleaving axe; *Arb:* felling axe; (butcher's) poleaxe.

Merlin³, *Pr.n.m. Lit:* Merlin.

merliner [mɛrline], *v.tr.* to marl (rope).

merlon [mɛrlɔ̃], *s.m.* (*a*) *Fort:* merlon, *A:* cop; (*b*) *Tchn:* barricade; earthwork; revetment.

merlonner [mɛrlɔne], *v.tr.* to surround (building) with earthworks, to barricade.

merlu(s) [mɛrly], *s.m. Ich:* hake.

merluche [mɛrlyʃ], *s.f.* **1.** *Ich:* hake. **2.** *Cu:* dried (unsalted) cod, stockfish.

méro- [merɔ], *comb.fm. Biol: Med: etc:* mero-.

méroblastique [merɔblastik], *a. Biol:* meroblastic.

mérocèle [merɔsɛl], *s.f. Med:* merocele.

mérocrine [merɔkrin], *a. Physiol:* merocrine (gland).

mérocyte [merɔsit], *s.m. Biol:* merocyte.

mérogonie [merɔgɔni], *s.f. Biol:* merogony.

méromorphe [merɔmɔrf], *a. Med:* meromorphic.

méropidés [merɔpide], *s.m.pl. Orn:* Meropidae, the bee-eaters.

mérostomes [merɔstom], *s.m.pl. Crust:* Merostomata.

mérotomie [merɔtɔmi], *s.f. Biol:* merotomy.

mérou [meru], *s.m. Ich:* **m. (brun),** grouper; **m. des Basques,** stonebass, wreckfish; **m. rouge,** red hind, cabrilla.

Mérovée [merɔve], *Pr.n.m. Hist:* Merovaeus, Mervig.

mérovingien, -ienne [merɔvɛ̃ʒjɛ̃, -jɛn], *a. & s. Hist:* Merovingian.

mérozoïte [merɔzɔit], *s.m. Biol:* merozoite.

merrain [mɛrɛ̃], *s.m.* **1.** cask wood, stave wood; wood for cooperage. **2.** *Ven:* beam (of deer's antlers).

Mersebourg [mɛrsəbuːr], *Pr.n.m. Geog:* Merseburg.

mérule [meryl], *s.f. Fung:* merulius, house fungus.

mérulé [meryle], *a.* (*of timber*) attacked by wet rot.

merveille [mɛrvɛːj], *s.f.* marvel, wonder; **les sept merveilles du monde,** the seven wonders of the world; **une m. d'un jour,** a nine days' wonder; **faire m., faire des merveilles,** to work, do, perform, wonders, work marvels; **cela fait m. ici,** it looks, does, just right, wonderfully, here; **crier m.,** to exclaim in admiration; **dire m. de qn,** to speak in glowing terms of s.o.; **c'était m. de le voir,** it was wonderful to see him; **m. qu'il ne se soit pas tué!** it was a marvel that he wasn't killed! **les Aventures d'Alice au pays des Merveilles,** Alice's Adventures in Wonderland; *Bot:* **m. du Pérou,** marvel of Peru, *U.S:* pretty-by-night; *adv.phr.* **à m.,** excellently; **cette robe vous va à m.,** this dress suits you wonderfully, down to the ground; **se porter à m.,** to be in excellent health, in the best of health; **il a réussi à m.,** he succeeded admirably, he was wonderfully successful; **il réussit à m.,** *F:* he is doing splendidly; **ça marche à m.,** we, you, etc., are getting on famously; **ce chèque tombe à m.,** this cheque is most welcome, most opportune.

merveilleusement [mɛrvɛjøzmɑ̃], *adv.* wonderfully, marvellously.

merveilleux, -euse [mɛrvɛjø, -øːz]. **1.** *a.* marvellous, wonderful; **il fait des affaires merveilleuses,** he is doing marvellously, doing amazingly well; **elle est vraiment merveilleuse,** she is wonderful, just splendid; *s.m.* **je ne crois pas au m.,** I don't believe in miracles. **2.** *s. Hist:* (= INCROYABLE) ultra-fashionable man, woman (of the Directoire period); fop; merveilleux, merveilleuse.

merychippus [merikipys], *s.m. Paleont:* Merychippus.

mérycisme [merisism], *s.m.* merycism.

merycopotamus [merikɔpɔtamys], *s.m. Paleont:* Merycopotamus.

mesa [mesa], *s.f.* **1.** *Geog:* mesa. **2.** *Elcs:* **transistor m.,** mesa transistor.

mésaconique [mezakɔnik], *a. Ch:* mesaconic.

mésaise [mezɛːz], *s.m. A:* uneasiness, discomfort.

mésalliance [mezaljɑ̃ːs], *s.f.* unsuitable alliance (*esp.* by marriage); mésalliance, misalliance; **faire une m.,** to marry beneath one.

mésallier [mezalje], *v.tr.* (*p.d. & pr.sub.* **n. mésalliions, v. mésalliiez**) to misally; to contract a mésalliance for (s.o.).

se mésallier, to marry beneath one.

mésange [mezɑ̃ːʒ], *s.f. Orn:* tit(mouse); **m. azurée,** azure tit(mouse); **m. bleue,** bluetit; **m. boréale,** willow tit; **m. charbonnière,** great tit; **m. huppée,** crested tit; **m. laponne,** Siberian tit; **m. à moustaches,** bearded tit; **m. lugubre,** sombre tit; **m. noire,** coal tit; **m. à longue queue,** long-tailed tit; **m. rémiz,** penduline tit.

mésangeai [mezɑ̃ʒɛ], *s.m. Orn:* **m. imitateur, de malheur,** Siberian jay.

mésangère [mezɑ̃ʒɛːr], *s.f. Orn:* great tit(mouse), tomtit, oxeye.

mésangette [mezɑ̃ʒɛt], *s.f.* bird trap.

mésarriver [mezarive], *v.impers. A:* to turn out ill.

mésartérite [mezarterit], *s.f. Med:* mesarteritis.

mésaticéphale [mezatisefal], *a. Anthr:* mesaticephalic, mesaticephalous.

mésaticéphalie [mezatisefali], *s.f. Anthr:* mesaticephaly, mesaticephalism.

mésavenant [mezavənɑ̃], *a. A:* unseemly; unpleasant, displeasing.

mésavenir [mesavniːr], *v.impers.* (*conj. like* VENIR) *A:* to turn out unfortunately.

mésaventure [mezavɑ̃tyːr], *s.f.* misadventure, mishap, mischance.

mescal [mɛskal], *s.m.* **1.** mescal (drink). **2.** *Bot:* mescal buttons.

mescaline [mɛskalin], *s.f. Ch:* mescalin.

mésédifier [mezedifje], *v.tr.* (*conj. like* ÉDIFIER) *A:* to scandalize, shock (s.o.).

mésembryanthème [mezɑ̃brijɑ̃tɛm], *s.m. Bot:* mesembryanthemum, fig marigold; **m. cristallin,** ice plant.

mésembryanthémacées [mezɑ̃brijɑ̃temase], **mésembryanthémées** [mezɑ̃brijɑ̃teme], *s.f.pl. Bot:* Mesembryanthemaceae, Arizoaceae.

mésemploi [mezɑ̃plwa], *s.m.* misuse.

mésemployer [mezɑ̃plwaje], *v.tr.* (*conj. like* EMPLOYER) to misuse.

mésencéphale [mezɑ̃sefal], *s.m. Anat:* mesencephalon.

mésencéphalique [mezɑ̃sefalik], *a. Anat:* mesencephalic.

mésenchyme [mezɑ̃ʃim], *s.m. Biol:* mesenchyma.

mésentente [mezɑ̃tɑ̃ːt], *s.f.* misunderstanding, disagreement.

mésentère [mezɑ̃tɛːr], *s.m. Anat:* mesentery.

mésentérique [mezɑ̃terik], *a. & s.f. Anat:* mesenteric.

mésentérite [mezɑ̃terit], *s.f. Med:* mesenteritis.

mésestimation [mezɛstimasjɔ̃], *s.f.* underestimation, underrating, undervaluing.

mésestime [mezɛstim], *s.f.* lack of esteem; **tenir qn en m.,** to have a poor opinion of s.o.; **encourir la m. de qn,** to fall in s.o.'s opinion.

mésestimer [mezɛstime], *v.tr.* 1. to underestimate, undervalue, underrate. 2. to have a poor opinion of (s.o.).

mésidine [mezidin], *s.f. Ch:* mesidine.

Mésie [mezi], *Pr.n.f. A.Geog:* Moesia.

mésien, -ienne [mezjɛ̃, -jɛn], *a. & s. A.Geog:* Moesian.

mésintelligence [mezɛ̃tɛliʒɑ̃:s], *s.f.* disagreement; **être en m. avec qn,** to be at variance, on bad terms, at loggerheads, with s.o.

mésinterprétation [mezɛ̃tɛrpretasjɔ̃], *s.f.* misinterpretation.

mésinterpréter [mezɛ̃tɛrprete], *v.tr.* (*conj. like* INTERPRÉTER) to misinterpret, misconstrue.

mésique [mezik], *a. Atom.Ph:* mesonic, meson.

mésitine [mezitin], *s.f. Miner:* mesitine, mesitite.

mésityle [mezitil], *s.m. Ch:* mesityl.

mésitylène [mezitilɛn], *s.m. Ch:* mesitylene.

meslier [melje], *s.m.* 1. *Bot: A:* medlar tree. 2. *Vit:* white grape of the Orléans region yielding beverage wines.

mesmérien, -ienne [mɛsmerjɛ̃, -jɛn]. 1. *a.* mesmerian, mesmeric. 2. *s. A:* mesmerist, mesmerite.

mesmérique [mɛsmerik], *a.* = MESMÉRIEN 1.

mesmérisme [mɛsmerism], *s.m.* mesmerism.

mesmériste [mɛsmerist], *s.m. & f.* mesmerist.

mesnil [meni], *s.m. A:* small farm; small country house.

méso- [mezɔ], *pref.* meso-.

mésoblaste [mezɔblast], *s.m. Biol:* mesoblast, mesoderm.

mésocarpe [mezɔkarp]. 1. *s.m. Bot:* mesocarp. 2. *s.f. Algae:* mesocarpus.

mésocéphale [mezɔsefal]. 1. *s.m. Anat:* mesocephalon. 2. *Anthr:* (*a*) *a.* mesocephalic; (*b*) *s.m. & f.* mesocephal.

mésocéphalie [mezɔsefali], *s.f. Anthr:* mesocephaly.

mésocéphalique [mezɔsefalik], *a.* mesocephalic.

mésocœliaque [mezɔseljak], *a. Anat:* mesocoelic.

mésocôlon [mezɔkolɔ̃], *s.m. Anat:* mesocolon.

mésocotyle [mezɔkɔtil], *s.m. Bot:* mesocotyl.

mésocrétacé [mezɔkretase], *a. & s.m. Geol:* middle Cretaceous.

mésocurtique [mezɔkyrtik], *a.* (*statistics*) mesokurtic.

mésoderme [mezɔdɛrm], *s.m. Biol: Moss:* mesoderm.

mésodermique [mezɔdɛrmik], *a.* mesodermic, mesodermal.

mésodévonien, -ienne [mezɔdevɔnjɛ̃, -jɛn], *a. & s.m. Geol:* Mesodevonian, Mesodevonic, middle-Devonian.

mésœnatidés [mezenatide], *s.m.pl. Orn:* Mesoenatidae.

mésoffrir [mezɔfri:r], *v.i.* make too small an offer.

mésogastre [mezɔgastr], *s.m. Anat:* mesogaster.

mésogastrique [mezɔgastrik], *a. Anat:* mesogastric.

mésogastropodes [mezɔgastrɔpɔd], *s.m.pl. Moll:* Mesogastropoda.

mésoglée [mezɔgle], *s.f. Coel: Spong:* mesogl(o)ea.

mésohippus [mezɔipy:s], *s.m. Paleont:* Mesohippus.

mésolabe [mezɔlab], *s.m. A.Mth:* mesolabe.

mésole [mezɔl], *s.m. Miner:* mesole.

mésolite [mezɔlit], *s.f. Miner:* mesolite.

mésolithique [mezɔlitik], *Prehist:* 1. *a.* Mesolithic. 2. *s.m.* Mesolithic (era).

mésologie [mezɔlɔʒi], *s.f. Biol:* mesology.

mésologique [mezɔlɔʒik], *a. Biol:* mesologic(al).

mésomère [mezɔmɛ:r], *a. Ch:* mesomeric.

mésomérie [mezɔmeri], *s.f. Ch:* mesomerism.

mésomorphe [mezɔmɔrf]. 1. *a.* mesomorphic. 2. *s.m. & f.* mesomorph.

mésomorphisme [mezɔmɔrfism], *s.m.* mesomorphy, mesomorphism.

mésomyodés [mezɔmjɔde], *s.m.pl. Orn:* Mesomyodi.

méson [mezɔ̃], *s.m. Atom.Ph:* meson; **m. mu,** mu meson, muon; **m. pi,** pi meson, pion; **m. K,** K meson, kaon.

mésonéphros [mezɔnefrɔs], *s.m. Biol: Anat:* mesonephros.

mésonotum [mezɔnɔtɔm], *s.m. Ent:* mesonotum.

mesonyx [mezɔniks], *s.m. Paleont:* mesonyx.

mésopause [mezɔpo:z], *s.f. Meteor:* mesopause.

mésophile [mezɔfil], *a. Bac:* mesophile.

mésophragmatique [mezɔfragmatik], *a. Z:* mesophragmal.

mésophragme [mezɔfragm], *s.m. Z:* mesophragm(a).

mésophylle [mezɔfil], *s.m. Bot:* mesophyll(um).

mésophyllien, -ienne [mezɔfiljɛ̃, -jɛn], *a. Bot:* mesophyllic, mesophyllous.

mésophyte [mezɔfit], *Bot:* 1. *a.* mesophytic. 2. *s.f.* mesophyte.

mésoplodon [mezɔplɔdɔ̃], *s.m. Z:* mesoplodon.

Mésopotamie [mezɔpɔtami], *Pr.n.f. Geog:* Mesopotamia.

mésopotamien, -ienne [mezɔpɔtamjɛ̃, -jɛn], *a. & s. Geog:* Mesopotamian.

mésorhinien, -ienne [mezɔrinjɛ̃, -jɛn], *a. & s. Anthr:* mesor(r)hinian.

mesosaurus [mezɔzɔrys], *s.m. Paleont: Rept:* mesosaur.

mésoscaphe [mezɔskaf], *s.m.* mesoscaph.

mésosème [mezɔzɛm], *a. Anthr:* mesoseme.

mésosoma [mezɔzɔma], *s.m. Z:* mesosoma.

mésosphère [mezɔsfɛ:r], *s.f. Meteor:* mesosphere.

mésosternal, -aux [mezɔstɛrnal, -o], *a. Anat: Ent:* mesosternal.

mésosternum [mezɔstɛrnɔm], *s.m. Anat: Ent:* mesosternum.

mésostomatidés [mezɔstɔmatide], *s.m.pl. Ann:* Mesostomatidae.

mésostome [mezɔstom], *s.m. Ann:* mesostomid.

mésotartrique [mezɔtartrik], *a. Ch:* mesotartaric (acid).

mésoténiales [mezɔtenjal], *s.f.pl. Algae:* Mesoteniales.

mésothéliome [mezɔteljom], *s.m. Med:* mesothelioma.

mésothélium [mezɔteljɔm], *s.m. Anat:* mesothelium.

mésothérium [mezɔteriɔm], *s.m. Palaeont:* mesotherium.

mésothermal, -aux [mezɔtɛrmal, -o], *a.* mesothermal.

mésotherme [mezɔtɛrm], *Bot:* 1. *a.* mesothermal. 2. *s.f.* mesotherm.

mésothoracique [mezɔtɔrasik], *a.* mesothoracic.

mésothorax [mezɔtɔraks], *s.m. Anat: Ent:* mesothorax.

mésoton [mezɔtɔ̃], **mésotron** [mezɔtrɔ̃], *s.m. Atom.Ph:* mesoton, mesotron.

mésotype [mezɔtip], *s.f. Miner:* mesotype.

mésoxalique [mezɔksalik], *a. Ch:* mesoxalic.

mésozoaire [mezɔzɔɛ:r], *s.m. Z:* mesozoon.

mésozoïque [mezɔzɔik], *a. Geol:* mesozoic.

mésozone [mezɔzo:n], *s.f. Geol:* mesozone.

mesquin [mɛskɛ̃], *a.* (*a*) mean, shabby (dwelling, policy, appearance); paltry, petty (excuse, etc.); **c'est très m. de sa part,** it is very mean of him; (*b*) mean, niggardly, stingy (person).

mesquinement [mɛskinmɑ̃], *adv.* (*a*) meanly, shabbily; pettily, in a petty manner; (*b*) meanly, stingily.

mesquinerie [mɛskinri], *s.f.* 1. meanness; (*a*) pettiness, paltriness; (*b*) niggardliness; **il est d'une rare m.,** he's incredibly mean. 2. shabby, mean, action; piece of meanness.

mess [mɛs], *s.m. Mil:* (officers' or N.C.O.s') mess.

message [mesa:ʒ, mɛ-], *s.m.* message; official communication; **m. radio (télégraphique),** radio message; **m. téléphone, téléphonique,** message by telephone, telephone(d) message; **m. lancé d'avion,** dropped message; **m. lesté,** weighted message; *Av: Nau:* **m. météo(rologique),** weather message; *Nau: etc:* **m. de détresse,** distress message, distress signal; *Tp: Tg:* **m. de service,** service message; **m. en transit,** through message; **carnet de messages,** message book; **m. chiffré, m. en code,** code message, message in code, cipher message; **m. en clair,** message in clear; **m. ordinaire,** routine message; **m. urgent,** priority message, urgent message; **m. extrême urgent,** emergency message; **m. immédiat, m. "flash,"** **m. en priorité absolue,** flash message; **m. différé,** deferred message; **m. mal acheminé,** misrouted, missent, message; **dépôt des messages,** handing in of messages; **remise des messages,** delivery of messages; *Mil:* **centre de régulation des messages,** message centre.

messager, -ère [mesaʒe, -ɛ:r, mɛ-], *s.* 1. (*a*) messenger; **m. d'État** = King's, Queen's, messenger; (diplomatic) courier; **m. de malheur,** bearer of bad news; *Lit:* **m. du printemps,** harbinger of spring; *a.* **pigeon m.,** carrier pigeon; (*b*) *s.m.* carrier. 2. *s.m. A:* (*a*) carrier's cart; (*b*) stage-coach. 3. *a. Biol:* **A.R.N. m.,** messenger R.N.A.

messagerie [mesaʒri, mɛ-], *s.f.* carrying trade; **service de messageries,** parcel post, parcel delivery; **messageries maritimes,** (i) sea transport of goods, (ii) shipping line; **bureau de(s) messageries,** (i) *A:* stage-coach office; (ii) shipping office; (iii) *Rail:* parcels office; *Rail:* **expédier qch. comme m.,** to forward sth. by passenger train.

messagiste [mesaʒist, mɛ-], *s.m.* carrier.

messalien, -ienne [mesaljɛ̃, -jɛn, mɛ-], *a. & s. Rel.H:* Messalian, Massalian, Euchite, Adelphian.

Messaline [mesalin, mɛ-]. 1. *Pr.n.f. Rom.Hist:* Messalina. 2. *s.f.* dissolute woman.

messe [mɛs], *s.f.* (*a*) *Ecc:* mass; **m. haute, solennelle, grande m., m. chantée,** high mass, sung mass; **m. basse, petite m.,** low mass; **m. des morts, des trépassés, de requiem,** requiem mass; **célébrer, dire, la m.,** to celebrate, say, mass; *F:* **dire des messes basses,** to speak in an undertone; **livre de m.,** mass book, missal; **vin de m.,** communion wine; *A:* **m. sèche,** *missa sicca,* dry mass; *Mus:* **composer une m.,** to compose a mass; (*b*) **m. noire,** black mass.

messéance [meseɑ̃:s, mɛ-], *s.f. A. & Lit:* unseemliness, impropriety (of conduct).

messéant [meseɑ̃, mɛ-], *a. A. & Lit:* (*a*) unbecoming (à, to); (*b*) unseemly, improper (words, dress, behaviour, etc.).

messelite [mɛsɛlit], *s.f. Miner:* messelite.

Messène [mesɛn, -mɛ-], *Pr.n.f. Geog:* Messene.

Messénie [meseni, mɛ-], *Pr.n.f. Geog:* Messenia.

messénien, -ienne [mesenjɛ̃, -jɛn, mɛ-], *a. & s. Geog:* Messenian.

messeoir [meswa:r, mɛ-], *v.ind.tr., def.* (*pr.p.* **messeyant;** *p.p. is lacking; pr.ind.* **il messied, ils messeyent;** *pr.sub.* **il messeye;** *p.d.* **il messeyait;** *p.h. is lacking; fu.* **il messiéra**) *A. & Lit:* to be unbecoming, unseemly; to misbecome; **il lui messied de . . .,** it ill becomes him to . . ..

messer [mɛsɛ:r], *s.m. A: Hum:* Messire; **M. Loup,** Sir Wolf; **M. Gaster,** the stomach, the inner man.

messianique [mesjanik, mɛ-], *a.* Messianic (tradition, etc.).

messianisme [mesjanism, mɛ-], *s.m.* Messianism.

messianiste [mesjanist, mɛ-], *s.m. & f.* believer in Messianism, in a Messiah.

messicole [mesikɔl, mɛ-], *a. Bot:* cornfield, *U.S:* grainland (plant).

Messidor [mesidɔ:r, mɛ-], *s.m.* tenth month of the French Republican calendar (June July).

Messie [mesi, mɛ-], *Pr.n.m.* (*a*) *B:* Messiah; (*b*) *F:* **attendre qn comme le M.,** to await s.o. impatiently.

messier [mesje, mɛ-], *s.m. A:* official crop watcher; assistant bailiff.

messieurs-dames [msjødam], *s.m.pl. F:* (*used by shopkeeper, etc., often not translated*) **bonjour, au-revoir, m.-d.,** good morning sir, madam; **entrez, m.-d.,** come in, Sir, come in, Ma'am; come in, ladies and gentlemen.

messin, -ine[1] [mɛsɛ̃, -in], *a. & s. Geog:* (native, inhabitant) of Metz.

Messine[2] [mɛsin], *Pr.n.f. Geog:* Messina; **détroit de M.,** Strait of Messina.

messinois, -oise [mɛsinwa, -wa:z], *a. & s. Geog:* Messinese.

messire [mesi:r, mɛ-], *s.m. A:* (*a*) (*title of honour*) Sir; (*b*) (*mode of address of priests, lawyers, doctors, etc.*) **M. Jean Froissart,** Master Jean Froissart.

mestome [mɛsto:m], *s.m. Bot:* mestome.

mestre [mɛstr], *s.* 1. *Mil: A:* **m. de camp,** (i) *s.m.* colonel; (ii) *s.f.* first company (of regiment). 2. *s.m. Nau:* (**arbre de**) **m.,** mainmast (of lateen-rigged ship); **voile de m.,** mainsail.

mesurable [məzyrabl], *a.* measurable, mensurable.

mesurage [məzyra:ʒ], *s.m.* 1. measuring, measurement (of cloth, land, etc.); *Adm:* **bureau de mesurage,** office of weights and measures. 2. (surveyor's dimensioned) plan (of piece of land).

mesure [məzy:r], *s.f.* measure. 1. (*a*) (act of) measurement, measuring; **m. des distances,** range measurement, ranging; **m. du temps, de la chaleur,** measurement of time, of heat; **m. du rayonnement, des radiations,** radiation measurement; **m. astronomique,** astronomical determination; *Mec.E:* **m. entre axes, entre pointes,** measurement between centres; *Civ.E:* **m. dans œuvre, hors d'œuvre,** inside, outside, measurement; **appareil, instrument, de m.,** measuring apparatus, instrument; meter; **appareil de m. électronique,** thermionic instrument; **relevé de m.,** measurement reading; (*b*) measure(ment), extent; **prendre les mesures de qn,** to take s.o.'s measurements, to measure s.o.; **prendre la m. de qn,** to size s.o. up; **complet fait sur mesure(s),** suit made to measure, to order; bespoke suit; **donner sa m.,** to show one's capacity, to show what one is made of, what one is capable of; **être à la m. de qn, de qch.,** to measure up to s.o., to sth.; **dans une certaine m.,** in some degree, to a certain extent; **dans une large m.,** mainly; to a large extent; **dans la m. où,** insofar as; **dans quelle m. . . .?** to what extent . . .? **je vous aiderai dans la m. de mes forces, du possible,** I shall help you as far as I can, as far as possible, to the best of my ability; **dans la m. où cela m'est possible,** as far as lies within my power; **si c'est dans la m. du possible,** if it lies within the bounds of possibility; **dépasser la m. de l'esprit de qn,** to be beyond s.o.'s intelligence, understanding; **sans m. avec . . .,** out of all proportion to . . .; *adv.phr.* **à m.,** in proportion; successively, one by one; **je fais mes comptes et vérifie les chiffres à m.,** I make up my accounts and check the figures as I go along; *s.a.* FUR; *conj.phr.* **à m. que,** (in proportion) as; **à m. que je reculais, il s'avançait,** as (fast as) I retreated he advanced; **à m. que le travail prendra de l'extension,** as the work increases; (*c*) action, measure, step; **m. contraignante,** forcible measure; **m. disciplinaire,** disciplinary action; **m. de défense,** defence measure; **m. de sécurité,** security measure, safety precaution; **par m. d'hygiène,** as a hygienic measure; **mesures à prendre en cas de . . .,** action, measures, steps, to be taken in case of . . .; **mesures à prendre en cas de panne (de l'appareil, du véhicule, etc.),** breakdown procedure; **prendre des mesures,** to take action, to adopt measures; **prendre des mesures pour faire qch.,** to take measures, steps, to do sth., to make arrangements for doing sth.; **j'ai pris des mesures pour que tout se fasse en ordre,** I have taken steps to ensure that everything shall be done in an orderly fashion; **prendre des mesures contre qch.,** to make provision against sth.; **prendre ses mesures,** to make one's arrangements (**pour, pour que,** in order to, in order that); **bien prendre ses mesures,** to take all due measures; **supprimer qch. par m. d'économie,** to do away with sth. as a measure of economy; **les demi-mesures ne servent à rien,** half-measures are no use; **rompre les mesures de qn,** to upset s.o.'s plans. **2.** (*a*) *Mth:* **commune m.,** common measure; (*b*) *Mth: Ph:* gauge, standard; **m. de capacité,** measure of capacity; **m. de capacité pour les liquides,** liquid measure; **m. (de capacité) pour les grains, pour les matières sèches,** corn measure, dry measure; **m. de longueur,** measure of length, linear measure; **m. de poids, m. pondérale,** weight (measure); **m. de pression,** pression measure; **m. de surface, de superficie,** square measure; **m. de volume,** cubic measure; **poids et mesures,** weights and measures; **m. comble,** heaped-up measure; **m. rase,** strike measure, bare measure; (*c*) **m. en ruban,** tape measure; (*d*) (*quantity measured out*) **verser une m. de vin, de rhum, à qn,** to pour s.o. out a measure of wine, of rum; **faites-moi bonne m.,** give me good measure. **3.** (*a*) required size, amount; **pièces qui ne sont pas de m.,** pieces that are not the right size, that are not to size; **garder la m.,** to keep within bounds, to be temperate (in one's language, etc.); **dépasser la m.,** (i) to overstep the mark; (ii) to overdo it; **cela passe, dépasse, la m.,** that exceeds all bounds, that's the limit; **ne garder aucune m., oublier toute m.,** to fling aside all restraint, to go beyond all bounds, to lose all sense of proportion; **ne pas garder de m. avec qn,** not to mince one's words with s.o.; **ambition sans m.,** unbounded ambition; *s.a.* OUTRE[2] 1; (*b*) *Fenc:* measure, reach, distance; **être hors de m.,** to be out of measure; **être en m. de faire qch.,** to be in a position, to have the power, to do sth.; to be able to do sth.; to be prepared to do sth.; **je ne suis pas en m. de . . .,** I am not able to . . .; I am unable to . . .. **4.** (*a*) *Mus:* (i) bar; **les premières mesures du morceau,** the first bars of the piece; (ii) time, *A:* measure; **m. à quatre temps,** quadruple time, common time; **m. à deux-quatre,** two-four time, duple measure; **battre la m.,** to beat time; **en m.,** in strict time; **jouer, danser, en m.,** to play, dance, in time; **aller en m.,** to keep time; **à la m.,** a tempo; (*b*) **nager en m.,** to keep stroke (in rowing). **5.** *Pros:* metre (of verse), measure.

mesuré [məzyre], *a.* measured, regular (tread, etc.); temperate, moderate, restrained, guarded (language, etc.); **langage peu m.,** unrestrained, unguarded, language.

mesure-étalon [məzyretalɔ̃], *s.f.* standard measure; *pl. mesures-etalons.*

mesurément [məzyremɑ̃], *adv.* moderately, with due measure, with moderation; temperately.

mesurer [məzyre], *v.tr.* **1.** (*a*) to measure (dimensions, quantity); to measure out (corn, etc.); to measure up (wood, land); to measure off (cloth, etc.); to measure out (tennis court); **m. une distance au pas,** to pace out a distance; *Cust:* **m. le contenu d'une caisse de thé,** to bulk a chest of tea; (*of tailor*) **m. un client,** to take a customer's measurement; **m. qn des yeux,** to eye s.o. up and down; **m. des vers,** to scan verses; *F:* **m. le tapis, le sol, la terre,** to measure one's length; (*b*) (*of pers.*) **m. deux mètres,** to be two metres, over six foot, tall; **colonne qui mesure dix mètres,** column ten metres high; (*c*) **m. la nourriture à qn,** to ration s.o.'s food; to grudge s.o. his food; to keep s.o. on short commons; **on me mesure le feu et la lumière,** they keep me short of fire and light; **lucarne qui mesure le jour,** garret-window that scarcely lets the light through. **2.** (*a*) to calculate, to use judgment in (sth.); to weigh (one's words, etc.); to size (s.o., sth.) up; **m. sa dépense sur ses profits,** to cut one's coat according to one's cloth; **on pouvait m. à leur anxiété la gravité de la situation,** the gravity of the situation could be judged by their anxiety; **m. la distance à la vue,** to judge, estimate, gauge, distance by sight; **m. une influence,** to estimate an influence; **m. ses paroles,** to curb, bridle, one's tongue; to weigh one's words; *Prov:* **à brebis tondue Dieu mesure le vent,** God tempers the wind to the shorn lamb; (*b*) **m. le châtiment à l'offense,** to make the punishment fit the crime.

se mesurer avec, à, qn, to try, measure, one's strength against s.o.; to measure, pit, oneself against s.o.; to try conclusions with s.o.; **vous n'êtes pas de force, de taille, à vous m. avec lui,** you are no match for him; **Jacob se mesurant avec, à, l'ange,** Jacob wrestling with the angel; *F:* **il se mesure à Dieu,** he thinks no small beer of himself.

mesureur, -euse [məzyrœːr, -øːz]. **1.** *s.m.* measurer (man or machine); *Jur:* **m. juré,** wharfinger; **m. de pression,** pressure-gauge; *El.E:* **m. de courant,** current-meter; *Ch:* **(tube) m.,** measuring cylinder. **2.** *s.f.* **mesureuse,** measurer (woman or machine).

mésusage [mezyzaːʒ], *s.m. A:* misuse.

mésuser [mezyze], *v.ind.tr.* **1. m. de son bien,** to misuse one's wealth. **2. m. de son pouvoir,** to abuse one's power.

Méta [meta], *s.m. Ch: R.t.m:* Meta.

méta- [meta], *pref.* meta-.

métaarsénieux [metaarsenjø], *a.m. Ch:* metarsenious (acid).

métaarsénite [metaarsenit], *s.m. Ch:* metarsenite.

métabase [metabɑːz], *s.f. Med:* metabasis.

métabiose [metabjoːz], *s.f. Biol:* metabiosis.

métabisulfite [metabisylfit], *s.m. Ch:* metabisulphite.

métaboles [metabɔl], *s.m.pl. Ent:* Metabola.

métabolique [metabɔlik], *a. Biol: Z:* metabolic.

métabolisme [metabɔlism], *s.m. Biol:* metabolism; **m. lipidique, protidique,** fat, protein, metabolism; **m. basal,** basal metabolism.

métabolite [metabɔlit], *s.m. Biol:* metabolite; metabolic waste.

métaborate [metabɔrat], *s.m. Ch:* metaborate.

métaborique [metabɔrik], *a. Ch:* metaboric (acid).

métabrushite [metabryʃit], *s.f. Miner:* metabrushite.

métacarpe [metakarp], *s.m. Anat:* metacarpus.

métacarpien, -ienne [metakarpjɛ̃, -jɛn], *a. & s.m. Anat:* metacarpal.

métacarpo-phalangien, -ienne [metakarpɔfalɑ̃ʒjɛ̃, -jɛn], *a. Anat:* metacarpo-phalangeal.

métacentre [metasɑ̃ːtr], *s.m. Hyd: N.Arch: Av:* metacentre.

métacentrique [metasɑ̃trik], *a.* metacentric (curve, etc.).

métachromasie [metakrɔmazi], *s.f. Biol:* metachromasia, metachromasy.

métachromatique [metakrɔmatik], *a. Biol:* metachromatic.

métachromatisme [metakrɔmatism], *s.m. Biol:* metachromatism.

métacinnabre [metasinabr], *s.m.* **métacinnabarite** [metasinabarit], *s.f. Miner:* metacinnabar, metacinnabarite.

métacrylique [metakrilik], *a. Ch:* methacrylic.

métadyne [metadin], *s.f. El:* metadyne.

métagalaxie [metagalaksi], *s.f. Astr:* metagalaxy.

métagénèse [metaʒenɛːz], *s.f. Biol:* metagenesis.

métagénésique [metaʒenezik], *a. Biol:* metagenetic.

métagéométrie [metaʒeɔmetri], *s.f.* metageometry.

métagnomie [metagnɔmi], *s.f.* metagnomy.

métairie [meteri, -tɛ-], *s.f.* metairie, farm (held on share-cropping agreement).

métal, -aux [metal, -o], *s.m.* **1.** metal; (*a*) **métaux précieux,** precious, noble, metals; **métaux vils,** base metals; **m. amalgamé,** amalgam; **m. antifriction, m. blanc,** babbit, white metal, antifriction metal; **garnir de m. antifriction, de m. blanc,** to babbitt; **m. (blanc) d'Alger,** German silver; **m. (blanc) anglais,** Britannia metal; **m. de cloche,** bell metal; **m. oxydé,** oxidized steel; *Com:* gunmetal; **m. d'apport,** filler (metal); **m. déployé,** expanded metal; **m. en feuilles,** sheet metal; **m. en feuilles très minces,** metal foil; **métaux de construction,** structural metals; (*b*) *Typ:* **copier sur m.,** to print down (on metal plate); **coucher le m.,** to coat upon the metal; **salle de copie sur m.,** metal-printing room. **2.** *Fin:* **m. en barres,** bullion.

métal-carbonyle [metalkarbɔnil], *s.m. Ch:* metal carbonyl.

métaldéhyde [metaldeid], *s.f. Ch:* metaldehyde.

métalepse [metalɛps], *s.f. Rh:* metalepsis.

métalimnion [metalimnjɔ̃], *s.m. Oc: etc:* metalimnion, thermocline.

métallation [metal(l)asjɔ̃], *s.f. Ch:* metallation.

métallescent [metal(l)ɛs(s)ɑ̃], *a.* metallescent.

métallifère [metal(l)ifɛːr], *a.* metalliferous; metal-bearing; *Geog:* **les monts Métallifères,** the Erzgebirge.

métalliforme [metal(l)ifɔrm], *a.* metalliform, metal-like.

métallin [metal(l)ɛ̃], *a.* metalline, metallic.

métallique [metal(l)ik], *a.* metallic; **câble m.,** wire rope; **plume m.,** steel pen; **rendre un son m.,** to clang; **bruit m.,** clang; *Fin: A:* **réserve m.,** metallic reserve, bullion reserve, gold reserve; *Med:* **colique m.,** painter's colic; *Geog:* **les monts Métalliques,** the Erzgebirge.

métallisation [metal(l)izasjɔ̃], *s.f.* **1.** metallization; converting (of ore, etc.) into metal. **2.** metallizing, metal-coating, plating (with metal); **m. par projection,** metal spraying. **3.** *Phot:* bronzing (of print, negative). **4.** *Av:* bonding.

métalliseur [metal(l)izœːr]. **1.** *a.* **pistolet m.,** metal spray. **2.** *s.m.* (*pers.*) metal sprayer.

métalliser [metal(l)ize], *v.tr.* **1.** to metallize; to convert (oxide, etc.) into metal; **peinture métallisée,** metallic paint. **2.** to cover with metal; to plate; to metal (plaster cast, etc.); **m. au pistolet, par projection,** to spray with metal.

se métalliser, *Phot:* (*of print or negative*) to bronze.

métallo [metal(l)o], *s.m. F:* metal-worker.

métallochimie [metal(l)ɔʃimi], metallurgical chemistry; chemistry of metals.

métallochromie [metal(l)ɔkrɔmi], *s.f.* metallochromy.

métallogénèse [metal(l)ɔʒenɛːz], *s.f. Geol:* metallogenesis.

métallogénie [metal(l)ɔʒeni], *s.f. Geol:* metallogeny.

métallographe [metal(l)ɔgraf], *s.m. & f.* metallographer, metallographist.

métallographie [metal(l)ɔgrafi], *s.f.* metallography.

métallographique [metal(l)ɔgrafik], *a.* metallographic.

métalloïde [metal(l)ɔid]. **1.** *a.* metalloid, metal-like. **2.** *s.m. Ch:* metalloid.

métalloïdique [metal(l)ɔidik], *a. Ch:* metalloid(al).

métalloplastique [metal(l)ɔplastik], *a.* **joint m.,** copper-asbestos gasket.

métalloscope [metal(l)ɔskɔp], *s.m.* metalloscope; magnetic crack detector.

métallurgie [metal(l)yrʒi], *s.f.* metallurgy; **m. par voie ignée,** pyrometallurgy; **m. des poudres,** powder metallurgy.

métallurgique [metal(l)yrʒik], *a.* metallurgic(al); **usine m.,** metallurgical plant, metal works, *esp.* ironworks.

métallurgiquement [metal(l)yrʒikmɑ̃], *adv.* metallurgically.

métallurgiste [metal(l)yrʒist], *s.m.* metallurgist; (*a*) ironmaster; (*b*) metal-worker; (*c*) smelter.

métalogique [metalɔʒik], *a.* metalogical.

métamère [metamɛːr]. **1.** *a. Ch:* metameric. **2.** *s.m. Z:* metamere, somite.

métamérie [metameri], *s.f. Biol: Ch:* metamerism, metamery.

métamérique [metamerik], *a.* (*of embryo*) metamerized.

métamérisation [metamerizasjɔ̃], *s.f. Biol:* metamerization.

métamérisé [metamerize], *a. Biol:* metamerized, divided into metameres.

métamicte [metamikt], *a. Atom.Ph:* metamict.

métamorphique [metamɔrfik], *a. Geol:* metamorphic.

métamorphiser [metamɔrfize], *v.tr. Geol:* to metamorphize.
métamorphisme [metamɔrfism], *s.m. Geol:* metamorphism.
métamorphopsie [metamɔrfɔpsi], *s.f. Med:* metamorphopsia, metamorphopsy.
métamorphosable [metamɔrfozabl̩], *a.* metamorphosable, transformable.
métamorphose [metamɔrfoːz], *s.f.* metamorphosis, transformation; **subir une complète m.,** to undergo a complete metamorphosis.
métamorphoser [metamɔrfoze], *v.tr.* to metamorphose, transform; **m. une bonne d'enfants en étoile de cinéma,** to turn a nursemaid into a film star; **les malheurs l'ont métamorphosé,** his sufferings have completely changed him.
se métamorphoser, to change completely; to metamorphose.
metamynodon [metaminɔdɔ̃], *s.m. Paleont:* Metamynodon.
métanéphros [metanefrɔs], *s.m. Biol: Anat:* metanephros.
métaphase [metafɑːz], *s.f. Biol:* metaphase.
métaphénylène-diamine [metafenilɛndjamin], *s.f. Ch:* metaphenylenediamene.
métaphonie [metafɔni], *s.f. Ling:* vowel mutation; metaphony; umlaut.
métaphore [metafɔːr], *s.f.* metaphor; figure of speech; image; **m. disparate, incohérente,** mixed metaphor; **s'exprimer par métaphores,** to speak in metaphors.
métaphorique [metafɔrik], *a.* metaphorical; figurative.
métaphoriquement [metafɔrikmɑ̃], *adv.* metaphorically; figuratively.
métaphoriser [metafɔrize], *v.tr.* **1.** to write, say, (sth.) metaphorically. **2.** *abs.* to speak in metaphors, in images.
métaphoriste [metafɔrist], *s.m. & f.* metaphorist.
métaphosphate [metafɔsfat], *s.m. Ch:* metaphosphate.
métaphosphorique [metafɔsfɔrik], *a.* metaphosphoric.
métaphrase [metafrɑːz], *s.f.* metaphrase.
métaphraste [metafrast], *s.m.* metaphrast.
métaphrastique [metafrastik], *a.* metaphrastic; word-for-word, literal (translation).
métaphyse [metafiːz], *s.f. Anat:* metaphysis.
métaphysicien, -ienne [metafizisjɛ̃, -jɛn], *s.* metaphysician.
métaphysique [metafizik]. **1.** *a.* metaphysical; abstract, abstruse. **2.** *s.f.* metaphysics.
métaphysiquement [metafizikmɑ̃], *adv.* metaphysically.
métaphysiquer [metafizike], *v.i. F:* to metaphysicize; to lose oneself in abstractions.
métaphyte [metafit], *s.m. Bot:* metaphyte.
métaplasie [metaplazi], *s.f. Med:* metaplasia.
métaplasme [metaplasm], *s.m. A.Gram: Biol:* metaplasm.
métapsychique [metapsiʃik]. **1.** *a.* metapsychic(al). **2.** *s.f.* metapsychology; metapsychics.
métapsychiste [metapsiʃist], *s.m. & f.* metapsychist.
métapsychologie [metapsikɔlɔʒi], *s.f.* metapsychology.
métargon [metargɔ̃], *s.m. Ch:* metargon.
métaséquoia [metasekɔja], *s.m. Bot: Paleont:* metasequoia.
métasilicique [metasilisik], *a. Ch:* metasilicic (acid).
métasoma [metazoma], *s.m. Z:* metasoma.
métasomatose [metasɔmatoːz], *s.f. Geol:* metasomatism, metasomatosis.
métastable [metastabl̩], *a. Ch:* metastable.
métastannique [metastanik], *a. Ch:* metastannic (acid).
métastase [metastɑːz], *s.f.* metastasis.
métastatique [metastatik], *a.* metastatic.
métasternal, -aux [metatɛrnal, -o], *a. Ent:* metasternal.
métasternum [matastɛrnɔm], *s.m. Ent:* metasternum.
métastibnite [metastibnit], *s.f. Miner:* metastibnite.
métatarsalgie [metatarsalʒi], *s.f. Med:* metatarsalgia.
métatarse [metatars], *s.m. Anat:* metatarsus.
métatarsien, -ienne [metatarsjɛ̃, -jɛn], *a. & s.m.* metatarsal.
métathériens [metaterjɛ̃], *s.m.pl. Z:* Metatheria.
métathèse [metatɛːz], *s.f. Ling: Surg: Phil:* metathesis.
métathoracique [metatɔrasik], *a. Ent:* metathoracic.
métathorax [metatɔraks], *s.m. Ent:* metathorax.
métatypie [metatipi], *s.f. Biol:* mutation of type.
Métaure (le) [ləmetoːr], *Pr.n.m. A.Geog:* the (river) Metaurus.
métavoltine [metavɔltin], *s.f. Miner:* metavoltine.
métaxite [metaksit], *s.f. Miner:* metaxite.
métayage [metɛjaːʒ], *s.m. Agr:* métayage, share-cropping.
métayer, -ère [metɛje, -ɛːr], *s.m. & f. Agr:* métayer, share-cropper; *s.f.* **métayère,** (i) (woman) share-cropper; (ii) share-cropper's wife.
métazoaire [metazɔɛːr], *Biol:* **1.** *a.* metazoan, metazoic. **2.** *s.m.* metazoon; *pl.* **métazoaires,** Metazoa.
méteil [metɛːj], *s.m. Agr:* (mixed crop of) wheat and rye; *Dial:* maslin.
métel [metɛl], *s.m. Bot:* metel.
métempirique [metɑ̃pirik], *a.* metempiric(al).
métempsyc(h)ose [metɑ̃psikoːz], *s.f.* metempsychosis, transmigration of souls.
métempsyc(h)osiste [metɑ̃psikozist], *s.m. & f.* believer in metempsychosis.
métencéphale [metɑ̃sefal], *s.m. Anat:* metencephalon.
métensomatose [metɑ̃sɔmatoːz], *s.f.* metensomatosis.
météo [meteo], *F:* **1.** *s.f.* (*a*) weather report; (*b*) (= **bureau central de météorologie**) the meteorological office, the weather centre. **2.** *s.m.* (*pers.*) meteorologist, *F:* weather man.
météore [meteoːr], *s.m.* meteor; **météores aériens, aqueux, ignés,** aerial, aqueous, igneous, meteors; *F:* **c'est un véritable m.,** he comes in like a thunderbolt.
météorique [meteɔrik], *a.* meteoric (phenomenon, iron, career, etc.).
météorisation [meteɔrizasjɔ̃], *s.f. Med:* meteorism, distension (of stomach); flatulence; *Vet:* hoove, hoven, bloat.
météorisé [meteɔrize], *a.* (*of sheep, etc.*) hoven, blown, bloated.
météoriser [meteɔrize], *v.tr. Med:* to distend; to make (abdomen) flatulent; *Vet:* to hove, bloat (sheep, cattle).
météorisme [meteɔrism], *s.m. Med:* meteorism; flatulence.
météorite [meteɔrit], *s.m. or f.* **1.** meteorite. **2.** meteorolite, meteoroïd; (*space travel*) **plaquette de détection de météorites,** meteorite detector plate.
météoritique [meteɔritik], *a.* meteoritic.
météorographe [meteɔrɔgraf], *s.m. Meteor:* meteorograph.
météorologie [meteɔrɔlɔʒi], *s.f.* meteorology, **le bureau central de m.** = the meteorological office.
météorologique [meteɔrɔlɔʒik], *a.* meteorological; **bulletin m.,** weather report, weather forecast; **station m.,** meteorological station, weather station; **frégate, navire, m.,** weather ship; **l'office national m. (l'O.N.M.)** = the central forecasting office.
météorologiste [meteɔrɔlɔʒist], *s.m. & f.*, **météorologue** [meteɔrɔlɔg], *s.m. & f.* meteorologist.
métèque [metɛk], *s.m.* (*a*) *Gr.Ant:* metic; (*b*) *F: Pej:* foreigner; dago; wop; wog.
méthacrylique [metakrilik], *a. Ch:* methacrylic (acid).
méthane [metan], *s.m. Ch:* methane.
méthanier [metanje], *s.m. Nau:* methane tanker.
méthanique [metanik], *a. Ch:* methane, pertaining to the methane series.
méthanisation [metanizasjɔ̃], *s.f.* methanization.
méthanoduc [metanɔdyk], *s.m.* methane, gas, pipeline.
méthanol [metanɔl], *s.m. Ch:* methanol.
méthémalbumine [metemalbymin], *s.f. Bio-Ch:* methaemalbumin.
méthémoglobine [metemɔglɔbin], *s.f. Bio-Ch:* methaemoglobin.
méthémoglobinémie [metemɔglɔbinemi], *s.f. Med:* methaemoglobinaemia.
méthionine [metjɔnin], *s.f. Bio-Ch:* methionine.
méthionique [metjɔnik], *a. Ch:* methionic.
méthode[1] [metɔd], *s.f.* **1.** method, system; way; **m. pour faire qch.,** method of doing sth.; **m. expérimentale,** experimental method; **m. empirique,** trial and error method; **m. d'essai normalisée,** standard testing method; **m. de classement,** filing system; **m. d'exploitation,** method of working, method of operation; **m. de contrôle,** monitoring technique; **m. opératoire,** (i) *Tchn:* procedure; (ii) *Surg:* operative method; *Ind:* **ingénieur des méthodes,** industrial engineer, methods engineer; **elle a sa m.,** she has her own way of doing things; **il a beaucoup de m.,** he is very methodical; **faire qch. avec m.,** to do sth. methodically, systematically; **absence de m.,** lack of method, unmethodicalness; **travailler sans m.,** to work without method, without system; **lectures sans m.,** desultory reading. **2.** primer, grammar; **il a publié une m. de français,** he has published a course in French; **m. de piano,** piano tutor.
Méthode[2], *Pr.n.m. Ecc.Hist:* Methodius.
méthodique [metɔdik], *a.* methodical, systematic; *s.a.* CATALOGUE.
méthodiquement [metɔdikmɑ̃], *adv.* methodically, systematically.
méthodisme [metɔdism], *s.m. Rel:* Methodism.
méthodiste [metɔdist], *a. & s.m. & f. Rel:* Methodist.
méthodologie [metɔdɔlɔʒi], *s.f.* methodology.
méthodologique [metɔdɔlɔʒik], *a.* methodological.
méthoxyle [metɔksil], *s.m. Ch:* methoxyl.
méthylal [metilal], *s.m. Ch:* methylal.
méthylamine [metilamin], *s.f. Ch:* methylamine.
méthylaniline [metilanilin], *s.f. Ch:* methylaniline.
méthylate [metilat], *s.m. Ch:* methylate.
méthylation [metilasjɔ̃], *s.f.* methylation.
méthylbenzène [metilbɛ̃zɛn], *s.m. Ch:* methyl benzene.
méthylcellulose [metilsɛlyloːz], *s.f.* methyl cellulose.
méthyle [metil], *s.m. Ch:* methyl.
méthylène [metilɛn], *s.m. Ch:* methylene; **bleu de m.,** methylene blue.
méthyler [metile], *v.tr. Ch:* to methylate.
méthyléthylcétone [metiletilsetɔn], *s.f. Ch:* methyl ethyl ketone.
méthylique [metilik], *a.* methyl(ic); **alcool m.,** methyl alcohol.
méthylisobutylcétone [metilizɔbytilsetɔn], *s.f. Ch:* methyl isobutyl ketone.
méthylorange [metilɔrɑ̃ːʒ], *s.m. Ch:* methyl orange.
méthylpentose [metilpɛ̃toːz], *s.m. Ch:* methylpentose.
méthylpropane [metilprɔpan], *s.m. Ch:* methylpropane.
méthylrouge [metilruːʒ], *s.m. Ch:* methyl red.
méticuleusement [metikyløzmɑ̃], *adv.* meticulously, scrupulously; punctiliously.
méticuleux, -euse [metikylø, -øːz], *a.* meticulous, punctilious (person, care, civility); scrupulously careful (person); **par trop m.,** over-scrupulous, over-particular.
méticulosité [metikylozite], *s.f.* meticulousness; meticulosity; over-carefulness; punctiliousness.
métier [metje], *s.m.* **1.** (*a*) trade, profession, craft, occupation, business; **quel est votre m.?** what do you do (for a living)? what's your job, your profession? **le m. des armes, le m. militaire,** the profession of arms; **École Nationale des Ingénieurs des Arts et Métiers,** *F:* **les Arts et Métiers,** establishment of university level for training engineers; **gens de m.,** experts; professionals; **terme de m.,** technical term; **argot de m.,** trade, technical, jargon; **armée de m.,** professional army; **risques de m.,** occupational hazards; **exercer, faire, un m.,** to carry on a trade, a profession; **apprenez-lui un m.,** teach him a trade; **il est charpentier de m.,** he is a carpenter by trade; **il apprend le m. de charpentier,** he is learning carpentering, carpentry; **le m. de tailleur,** tailoring; **ils sont du m.,** they belong to the trade; **cela n'est pas (de) mon m.,** that's not in my line; **il n'a pas le cœur au m.,** he has no heart in his occupation, job; *F:* **vous faites là un vilain m.!** that's a dirty game you're playing! **faites votre m.!** mind your own business! **faire m. de sa religion,** to make a business of one's religion; *Lit:* **faire m. et marchandise de mensonges,** to deal in lies; **tours de m.,** tricks of the trade; **je lui ai joué un tour de mon m.,** I had him properly; **parler m.,** to talk shop; *F:* **quel m.!** what a life! **corps de m.,** corporation; g(u)ild; trade association; **chacun son m.,** everyone to his trade; (*b*) craftsmanship; **peintre, sculpteur, qui a du m.,** painter, sculptor, of sound technique; **il a du m.,** he knows what he's doing, *F:* he's on the ball; **il manque encore de m.,** he still lacks experience; (*of boxer*) he still lacks ring-craft. **2.** *Tex:* (*a*) **m. à tisser,** loom; **m. à main,** hand loom; **m. mécanique,** power loom; **fait au m.,** woven; **avoir un ouvrage sur le m.,** to have a piece of work in hand, on the stocks; (*b*) **m. à filer,** spinning frame; **m. continu,** continuous-spinning frame; throstle (frame); (*c*) **m. à tapisserie,** tapestry frame; **m. à broder,** tambour frame.

métis, -isse [meti, -is]. **1.** *a.* (*a*) half-bred, cross-bred; mongrel (dog); **plante métisse,** hybrid plant; *Ling:* **son m.,** mixed sound (*e.g.* [y, œ]); (*b*) *Metall:* **fer m.,** red-short iron; (*c*) *Tex:* **toile métisse,** linen-cotton mixture. **2.** *s.* half-caste; half-breed; mestizo, *f.* mestiza; mongrel (dog, etc.).

métisation [metizasjɔ̃], *s.f.* cross-breeding (*esp.* of sheep).

métissage [metisa:ʒ], *s.m.* cross-breeding.

métisser [metise], *v.tr.* to cross (breeds).

métol [metɔl], *s.m. Phot: R.t.m:* Metol.

métonien, -ienne [metɔnjɛ̃, -jɛn], **métonique** [metɔnik], *a. Astr:* metonic (cycle, etc.).

métonymie [metɔnimi], *s.f.* metonymy.

métonymique [metɔnimik], *a.* metonymic(al).

métope [metɔp], *s.f. Arch:* metope.

métopique [metɔpik], *a. Anat:* metopic; **suture m.,** metopic suture.

métoposcopie [metɔpɔskɔpi], *s.f.* metoposcopy.

métoquinone [metɔkinɔn], *s.f. Phot:* metoquinone.

métrage [metra:ʒ], *s.m.* **1.** (*a*) measuring, measure(ment); (*b*) *Civ.E: Const:* quantity surveying. **2.** (*a*) (metric) length; *Cin:* footage, length (of film); **long m.,** full-length film, feature film; **court m.,** short; *Com:* **quel m. désirez-vous?** how many metres do you want? (*b*) metric area; (*c*) metric volume.

métralgie [metralʒi], *s.f. Med:* metralgia.

mètre[1] [mɛtr̥], *s.m. Pros:* metre.

mètre[2], *s.m.* **1.** *Meas:* metre (= 3·281 ft); **m. courant,** linear metre, running metre; **m. carré, cube,** square, cubic, metre. **2.** (*a*) (metre) rule; **m. pliant,** folding rule; **m. à ruban,** tape-measure; (*b*) = yardstick; **je ne l'ai pas mesuré au m.,** I didn't measure it with a yardstick.

métré [metre], *s.m. Const:* (*a*) measurement(s) (of building land, etc.); quantity survey; (*b*) bill of quantities.

mètre-kilogramme [mɛtrəkilɔgram], *s.m. Mec. Meas:* kilogram(me)-metre; *pl. mètres-kilogrammes.*

métrer [metre], *v.tr.* (**je mètre, n. métrons; je métrerai**) **1.** to measure (by the metre). **2.** *Civ.E: Const:* to survey (for quantities, for amount of work done).

métreur [metrœ:r], *s.m.* **m. (vérificateur),** quantity surveyor.

métricien, -ienne [metrisjɛ̃, -jɛn], *s. Pros:* metrician, metrist.

métrique[1] [metrik]. **1.** *a. Pros:* metric(al). **2.** *s.f.* prosody, metrics.

métrique[2], *a.* metric; **le système m.,** the metric system.

métrite [metrit], *s.f. Med:* metritis.

métro (le) [ləmetro], *s.m. F:* the metro, the underground (railway), *U.S: Scot:* the subway; **le m. de Londres,** the tube.

métrologie [metrɔlɔʒi], *s.f.* metrology.

métrologique [metrɔlɔʒik], *a.* metrological.

métrologiste [metrɔlɔʒist], *s.m. & f.* metrologist.

métromane [metrɔman], *s.m. & f.* (*rare*) metromaniac.

métromanie [metrɔmani], *s.f.* metromania.

métronome [metrɔnɔm], *s.m. Mus:* metronome.

métronomique [metrɔnɔmik], *a. Mus:* metronomic (indication of tempo).

métropole [metrɔpɔl], *s.f.* metropolis; (*a*) capital; (*b*) parent state, mother country (of colony); (*c*) see (of archbishop); *a.* **église m.,** metropolitan church.

métropolitain [metrɔpɔlitɛ̃], *a.* **1.** metropolitan; **chemin de fer m.,** *s.m.* **le M.,** the Underground (railway); **police métropolitaine,** metropolitan police. **2. armée métropolitaine,** home army; **bâtiment m.,** ship for service in home waters. **3.** *Ecc:* (*a*) metropolitan (church, etc.); archiepiscopal; (*b*) *s.m.* metropolitan; archbishop.

métropolite [metrɔpɔlit], *s.m. Gr. Orthodox Church:* metropolitan.

métrorragie [metrɔraʒi], *s.f. Med:* metrorrhagia.

métrorragique [metrɔraʒik], *a. Med:* metrorrhagic.

métrosidère [metrɔside:r], **metrosideros** [metrɔsiderɔs], *s.m. Bot:* Metrosideros.

metroxylon [metrɔksilɔ̃], *s.m. Bot:* Metroxylon.

mets [mɛ], *s.m.* (article of prepared) food; dish (of food).

mettable [mɛtabl̥], *a.* (*of clothes, etc.*) wearable; **ma robe n'est pas m.,** my dress isn't fit to wear.

mettage [mɛta:ʒ], *s.m.* (*a*) putting, placing; setting (of stones, etc.); (*b*) *Ind:* **m. en couleur,** colouring, staining.

metteur, -euse [mɛtœ:r, -ø:z], *s.* setter, layer; **m. en œuvre,** (i) setter, mounter (of scientific instrument, of jewellery); (ii) promoter (of peace, etc.); *Rail:* **m. de rails,** platelayer; **m. en scène,** (i) *Th:* producer; (ii) *Cin:* director; *W.Tel:* **m. en ondes,** producer; *s.a.* PAGE[1].

mettre [mɛtr̥], *v.tr.* (*pr.p.* **mettant;** *p.p.* **mis;** *pr.ind.* **je mets, tu mets, il met, n. mettons, v. mettez, ils mettent;** *p.d.* **je mettais;** *p.h.* **je mis;** *fu.* **je mettrai**) **1.** (*a*) to put, lay, place, set; **mettez tout cela par terre,** put all that on the floor; **mettez-le dans le coin,** put it in the corner; **m. la nappe sur la table, m. la table, m. le couvert,** to lay the table; **m. la main sur qn,** to lay hands on s.o.; *O:* **m. des cartes chez qn,** to leave cards on s.o.; **m. un manche à un balai,** to fit a handle to a broom; **m. une pièce à un pantalon,** to patch a pair of trousers; **m. une annonce dans les journaux,** to put an advertisement in the (news)papers; **m. son œil au trou de la serrure,** to put one's eye to the keyhole; **m. une sentinelle à une porte,** to post a sentry at a door; *P:* **qu'est-ce qu'on s'est mis (derrière le paletot)!** what pigs we've made of ourselves! what a blow-out (we've had)! *Aut:* **m. le bras avant de stopper,** to put out one's arm, to signal, before stopping; **m. qn à la porte,** (i) to turn s.o. out (of doors); (ii) to dismiss, sack, s.o.; **je vais vous m. à votre porte,** I'll see you home; **m. des enfants au collège,** to send children to school; **m. un enfant au lit,** to put a child to bed; *Nau:* **être mis sur un écueil,** to be carried on to a reef; *Mus:* (*organ*) **mettez . . .,** draw . . . (stop); **m. les volets,** to put up the shutters; (*gaming*) **m. un enjeu, une somme,** to lay a stake, a sum; **m. le tout pour le tout,** to stake one's all, to risk everything, on one throw; *abs.* **m. sur le mauvais cheval,** to back the wrong horse; **m. une balle dans la cible,** to hit the target; *abs.* **m. dans le blanc,** to get a bull's eye, a bull; **qu'est-ce qui vous a mis cela dans la tête?** what put that into your head? **il me met dans toutes ses affaires, dans tous ses secrets,** he tells me all his business, I share all his secrets; **je l'ai mis sur la question du mariage,** I got him talking about marriage; *s.a.* BAS II. 2, DEDANS 1, TOMBEAU; (*b*) to put, devote; **j'y mettrai tous mes soins,** I will give the matter my full attention; **il a mis de la modération dans ses paroles,** he spoke guardedly, he was guarded in what he said; **m. sa confiance en qn,** to put one's trust in s.o.; **m. le feu à qch.,** to set fire to sth., to set sth. on fire; **m. le siège à une ville,** to lay siege to a town; **m. du temps à faire qch.,** to take time over sth.; **j'ai mis deux ans à, pour, faire cela,** I took, it took me, two years to do that; **m. cinq cents francs à un bibelot,** to spend five hundred francs on a knick-knack; **je ne peux pas y m. tant que cela,** I can't afford as much as that; **m. sur qn,** to outbid s.o., to make a higher bid (at an auction); *F:* **mets-en, mets-y, un coup,** put a bit of energy into it; give it everything you've got; (*c*) to put on (one's clothes); **qu'est-ce que je vais m.?** what shall I wear? **mettez votre robe bleue,** put on your blue dress; **je n'ai rien à me m.,** I haven't a thing to wear; *F:* **je n'ai plus une nippe à me m.,** I haven't a rag to my back; **ne plus m.,** to leave off (a garment); **il avait mis toutes ses médailles,** he was wearing, *F:* sporting, all his medals; **j'ai du mal à m. mes souliers,** I find it difficult to get my shoes on; **m. ses gants,** to put on one's gloves; *Box: F:* **les m. avec qn,** to have a bout with s.o.; *A:* **allons, mettez!** do put your hat on! (*d*) *P:* **il s'agit de les m.!** (i) we'd better scram, run for it; (ii) we must hurry up; **est-ce-qu'on se les met?** isn't it time we got going? (*e*) **m. sécher du linge, m. du linge à sécher,** to put the washing out to dry; **m. égoutter la vaisselle,** to put the dishes to drain in the rack; **m. chauffer de l'eau,** to put some water on to heat, to put the kettle on; **quand on le met à causer,** if once you start him talking. **2.** to set, put (in a condition); **m. une machine en mouvement,** to set a machine going; *F:* **m. la radio plus fort,** to turn up the radio; **m. en vente une maison,** to put a house up for sale; **m. des vers en musique,** to set verse to music; **m. du latin en français,** to translate Latin into French; **m. une terre en blé,** to plant a field with corn; to put a field under corn; **m. son argent en fonds de terre, en viager,** to invest one's money in real estate, in an annuity; **m. qn à la torture,** to put, subject, s.o. to torture; *s.a.* JOUR 1, MORT [1] 1, [2] 1, NET 2, POINT[1] 3, PRIX 1, SEC 3; **m. qn en retard,** to make s.o. late; **m. qn dans la misère,** to reduce s.o. to poverty; *s.a.* RAISON 2; *Nau:* **m. une voile au vent,** to hoist, set, a sail; *abs.* **m. à la voile,** to set sail; *P:* **m. les voiles,** to make oneself scarce; *Ven:* **m. sur pied, m. debout, un renard, etc.,** to draw a fox, etc. **3.** (*a*) to admit, grant; **mettons que vous ayez raison,** say that you are right; suppose, granted, you are right; put it that you are right; **mettons cent francs,** let's say a hundred francs; we'll call it a hundred francs; (*b*) **mettez que je n'ai rien dit,** consider that unsaid; I withdraw that remark; *F:* come back all I said.

se mettre. 1. (*a*) to go, get; **se m. derrière un arbre,** to get behind a tree; **se m. à la fenêtre,** to go to the window; **se m. au lit,** to go to bed; **se m. contre un mur,** to stand, lean, against a wall; **mettez-vous auprès du feu,** sit by the fire; **je ne savais où me mettre,** (i) I didn't know where to stand (or sit); (ii) I didn't know where to put myself; *Nau:* **se m. à, sur, une manœuvre,** (i) to man a rope; (ii) to tail, tally, on a rope; **se m. au service de qn,** to enter s.o.'s service; **se m. d'une société,** to join a company, an association; *F:* **se m. avec qn, se m. ensemble,** to take up with s.o. (of the opposite sex); **ils se sont mis ensemble,** they are living together; (*b*) to begin, to set about (sth.); **se m. à une tâche,** to attack a job; **se m. à l'œuvre, au travail,** to set, fall, to work; **il est temps de s'y m.,** it is time to set about it; **je ne peux pas m'y m. à présent,** I can't do it, start on it, just now; **elle sait se m. au ménage bien mieux que moi,** she gets down to doing the housework better than I do; **il s'y est mis de bonne heure,** he had an early training; (*of tree*) **se m. à fruit,** to begin to fruit; **se m. dans la politique,** to go in for, to take up, politics; **l'épouvante se mit partout,** terror spread everywhere; **le feu s'est mis chez nous,** our house caught fire; (*c*) **se m. à faire qch.,** to set about doing sth.; to begin to do sth.; **se m. à rire,** to begin to laugh, to start laughing; **elle se mit à pleurer,** she started to cry, she burst into tears; **se m. à chanter,** to burst into song; **se m. à flamber,** to burst, break, into flame; **ils se mirent à manger,** they started eating; **se m. à parler de qn,** to come to talk of s.o.; **il s'est mis à boire,** he has taken to drink; **il se mit à écrire,** (i) he began to write; (ii) he took to writing (as a profession); **il se mit à faire du théâtre, du tennis,** he took to the stage, to tennis; **quand le vent se met à souffler,** when the wind starts blowing; *impers.* **il se mit à pleuvoir,** it began to rain; the rain set in; it came on to rain. **2.** to dress; **se m. à la mode, simplement,** to dress fashionably, simply; **se m. en smoking,** to put on a dinner jacket; **être bien, mal, mis,** to be well, badly, dressed; **il est mis à faire peur,** he's dressed like a scarecrow; *s.a.* TRENTE[1]. **3.** (*to put oneself in a condition*) **se m. en rage,** to get into a rage; **se m. en route,** to start off, to start on one's way; **se m. au pas,** (i) to fall into step; (ii) to subside into a walk (after running); **le cheval se mit au trot, au galop,** the horse broke into a trot, into a gallop; *s.a.* FRAIS[2], QUATRE, RAISON 2; *P:* **des cigares! il se met bien, votre ami!** cigars! your friend does himself well. **4. le temps se met au beau,** the weather is turning out fine; **le temps se met à la pluie,** rain is setting in; **dans l'après-midi le temps s'est mis au beau, à la pluie,** the afternoon turned out fine, rainy.

méture [mety:r], *s.f.* maize bread, *U.S:* corn bread.

Metz [mɛs], *Pr.n. Geog:* Metz.

meublant [mœblɑ̃], *a.* **1.** (*of fabric, etc.*) fit for furnishing; **ornements meublants,** ornaments that help to furnish, that help to make, a home. **2.** *Jur:* **meubles meublants,** movables (as opposed to fixtures); (household) furniture.

meuble [mœbl̥]. **1.** *a.* (*a*) movable; *Jur:* **biens meubles,** *s.m.* **meubles,** movables, personal estate, chattels, personalty; (*b*) (*of stones, etc.*) uncemented; *Agr:* **terre m.,** light, running, soil; loose ground. **2.** *s.m.* (*a*) piece of furniture; *pl.* furniture; **meubles en tube,** tubular furniture; **meubles en bois courbé,** bentwood furniture; **être dans ses meubles,** to have one's own furniture, to have set up house, to have a home of one's own; **mettre qn dans ses meubles,** to furnish a house, a flat, for s.o.; **m. de famille,** heirloom; *s.a.* SAUVER; (*b*) suite of furniture; **m. de salon,** drawing-room suite; (*c*) *A:* commodity; **la vertu sans l'argent n'est qu'un m. inutile,** virtue without money is a useless commodity; (*d*) *pl. Her:* charges (on shield).

meublé [mœble]. **1.** *a.* furnished (room, etc.); **non m.,** unfurnished; **appartement m.,** furnished flat; **maison meublée,** (house let out in) furnished apartments; **maison bien meublée,** well-appointed, well-furnished, house; **pièce pauvrement meublée,** barely, poorly, furnished room; **Monsieur Thomas est richement m.,** Mr Thomas's home is beautifully furnished; **cave bien meublée,** well-stocked cellar; *F:* **bouche bien meublée,** fine set of teeth; **mémoire bien meublée de faits,** memory well stocked with facts; **tête**

bien meublée, well-informed mind; *s.a.* HÔTEL. **2.** *s.m.* furnished apartment(s); **tenir un m.,** to let lodgings; **habiter en m.,** to live in lodgings.

meuble-classeur [mœbləklɑsœːr], *s.m.* filing cabinet; *pl. meubles-classeurs.*

meubler [mœble], *v.tr.* to furnish (room); to stock (farm, cellar, memory) (**de,** with); *abs.* **rideaux qui meublent bien,** curtains that furnish a room well; **m. une maison de neuf,** to refurnish a house; **m. sa tête de choses inutiles,** to fill one's head with useless things; **m. la conversation,** to stimulate the conversation; **m. un silence,** to fill a gap in the conversation; **il y eut un silence qu'il meubla en allumant une cigarette,** he filled the silence that had fallen by lighting a cigarette; **m. ses loisirs,** to occupy one's leisure hours, one's free time.

se meubler, to furnish one's room, one's home.

meudonais, -aise [mødɔnɛ, -ɛːz], *a. & s.* (native, inhabitant) of Meudon.

meuglement [møgləmɑ̃], *s.m.* (*a*) lowing, mooing (of cow); (*b*) moaning (of ship's siren, etc.).

meugler [møgle]. **1.** *v.i.* (*of cow*) to low, to moo. **2.** *v.tr.* (*of crowd, etc.*) to bellow out (slogans, etc.).

meuh [mø], *int.* moo!

meulage [mølaːʒ], *s.m.* grinding (down) (*e.g.* of lens); **m. à la machine,** machine grinding; **m. à la main,** off-hand grinding.

meulanais, -aise [mølanɛ, -ɛːz], *a. & s. Geog:* (native, inhabitant) of Meulan.

meulard [mølaːr], *s.m.* large grindstone.

meularde [mølard], *s.f.* (medium-sized) grindstone.

meulardeau, -eaux [mølardo], *s.m.* (tool-grinder's) grindstone.

meule [møːl], *s.f.* **1.** (*a*) millstone; **m. gisante, de dessous,** nether millstone, bedder, bedstone; **m. courante,** runner; (*b*) grinding wheel; **m. en émeri, en carborundum,** emery wheel, carborundum wheel; **m. à affûter, à aiguiser,** (i) grindstone, grinding wheel; (ii) grinding machine, grinder; **m. à polir, à buffler,** polishing wheel, buffing wheel; **m. à gros grain, à grain fin,** coarse-grained, fine-grained, wheel; **m. à rectifier,** tru(e)ing-wheel; **m. d'ébarbage,** rough-grinding wheel; (*c*) **m. de fromage,** round cheese; **une m. de gruyère,** a gruyère cheese. **2.** (*a*) stack, rick (of hay, etc.); (charcoal) stack or pile; clamp (of bricks); **mettre le foin en m.,** to stack, rick, the hay; **mise en m.,** stacking; **m. de foin,** haystack, hayrick; (*b*) *Hort:* hotbed; **m. à champignons,** mushroom bed; (*c*) manure heap. **3.** *Ven:* burr (of deer's antler).

meuleau, -eaux [mølo], *s.m.* (medium-sized) grindstone.

meuler [møle], *v.tr.* to grind (chisel, casting, etc.); to grind (down) (lens, etc.); **acier meulé,** ground steel; *Tls:* **machine à m.,** grinding machine; **tour à m.,** emery grinder.

meulerie [mølri], *s.f.* millstone factory; grindstone factory.

meuleton [møltɔ̃], *s.m.* (*a*) (small) grindstone; (*b*) *Paperm:* pulping machine (for pulping old paper).

meulette [mølɛt], *s.f.* **1.** (*a*) small haystack; (*b*) shock, stook (of corn, etc.); **mettre les gerbes en meulettes,** to shock, stook, the sheaves; **m. de foin,** haycock. **2.** *Fish:* stomach (of cod).

meulier, -ière [mølje, -jɛːr]. **1.** *a.* pertaining to millstones or grindstones; **pierre meulière,** *s.f.* **meulière; grès meulier,** millstone grit, grindstone grit, burr(stone), millstone. **2.** *s.m.* millstone maker, grindstone maker. **3.** *s.f.* **meulière,** millstone quarry.

meuliérisation [møljerizasjɔ̃], *s.f.* formation of millstone.

meullarde [mølard], *s.f.* = MEULARDE.

meullardeau, -eaux [mølardo], *s.m.* = MEULARDEAU.

meulon [mølɔ̃], *s.m.* = MEULETTE 1.

méum [meɔm], *s.m. Bot:* meum, baldmoney, spicknel.

meunerie [mønri], *s.f.* **1.** (flour-)milling. **2.** milling trade; the millers.

meunier, -ière [mønje, -jɛːr]. **1.** *s.m.* (*a*) miller; **garçon m.,** mill-hand; **escalier de m.,** very steep and narrow flight of steps; (*b*) *F:* cockroach; (*c*) *Ich:* (i) miller's thumb; (ii) chub. **2.** *s.f.* **meunière,** (*a*) (i) miller's wife, (ii) woman owner of a flour mill; (*b*) *Orn:* (i) long-tailed tit; (ii) hooded crow, saddleback crow. **3.** *a.* flour-milling (plant, process, etc.). **4.** *a. Cu:* **truite, sole, meunière,** trout, sole, fried in butter and garnished with parsley.

meurt-de-faim [mœrdəfɛ̃], **meurt-la-faim** [mœrlafɛ̃], *s.m.inv. F:* down-and-out; **salaire de m.-de-f.,** starvation wage.

meurt-de-soif [mœrdəswaf], *s.m.inv. F:* toper, thirsty fish.

meurtre [mœrtr̥], *s.m.* (*a*) *Jur:* voluntary manslaughter; (*b*) murder, killing; **au m.!** murder! **commettre un m.,** to commit murder; **c'est un m. de retoucher ces tableaux,** it is a shame, a crime, rank vandalism, downright vandalism, downright murder, to touch up these pictures; **il crie au m. à tout propos,** he is for ever fussing about nothing, for ever crying blue murder.

meurtrier, -ère [mœrtrije, -ɛːr]. **1.** *a.* (*a*) (*used only of things*) murderous (war); deadly (weapon, etc.); **l'imprudence rend la route meurtrière,** rash driving turns roads into death traps; (*b*) (*of pers.*) who has committed a murderous assault; guilty of murder; *Lit:* **de Jézabel la fille meurtrière,** Jezebel's blood-stained daughter. **2.** *s.* murderer, *f.* murderess. **3.** *s.f. Fort:* **meurtrière,** loophole.

meurtri [mœrtri], *a.* bruised (arm, fruit, etc.); **visage m.,** (i) battered face; (ii) ravaged face; **avoir les pieds meurtris,** to be footsore, to have aching feet; **avoir le cœur m.,** to be sad (at heart); **être tout m.,** to be black and blue all over.

meurtrir [mœrtriːr], *v.tr.* **1.** *A:* to murder, slaughter. **2.** to bruise (one's arm, fruit, etc.); **m. qn de coups,** to beat s.o. black and blue. **3.** to supple (leather).

meurtrissure [mœrtrisyːr], *s.f.* bruise.

Meuse [møːz], *Pr.n.f. Geog:* (the river) Meuse, Maas.

meusien, -ienne [møzjɛ̃, -jɛn], *a. & s.* (native, inhabitant) of the Department of Meuse or of the Meuse valley.

meute [møːt], *s.f.* **1.** (*a*) *Ven:* pack (of staghounds, etc.); (*b*) crowd, mob, pack, (of people in pursuit); **chef de m.,** ringleader. **2.** decoy bird.

mévendre [mevɑ̃ːdr̥], *v.tr. A:* to sell (sth.) at a loss; to sacrifice (goods).

mévente [mevɑ̃ːt], *s.f.* **1.** sale (of goods) at a loss, at a sacrifice. **2.** slump, stagnation (of business); **m. des vins,** slump in wines.

mexicain, -aine [mɛksikɛ̃, -ɛn], *a. & s. Geog:* Mexican.

Mexico [mɛksiko], *Pr.n. Geog:* Mexico (City).

Mexique (le) [ləmɛksik], *Pr.n.m. Geog:* Mexico (State).

meyerhofférite [mejɛrɔferit], *s.f. Miner:* meyerhofferite.

mézail [mɛzaːj], *s.m. A.Arm:* mesail, vizor.

mezcal [mɛzkal], *s.m.* mescal, mezcal.

mézéréon [mezereɔ̃], *s.m. Bot:* mezereon, mezereum.

méziérois, -oise [mezjerwa, -waːz], *a. & s. Geog:* (native, inhabitant) of Mézières.

mézig, mézigue [mezig], *pron. P:* myself.

mezzanine [mɛdzanin], *s.f. & m. Arch:* **1.** mezzanine (floor). **2.** mezzanine window.

mezza voce [mɛdzavɔtʃe], *adv.phr.* mezza voce, in a low tone, voice.

mezzo [mɛdzo], *Mus:* **1.** *adv.* mezzo. **2.** *s.m. F:* mezzo-soprano.

mezzo forte [mɛdzofɔrte], *adv. Mus:* mezzo forte.

mezzo-soprano [mɛdzosɔprano], *s.m. Mus:* mezzo-soprano (voice); *pl. mezzo-sopranos.*

mezzo-tinto [mɛdzotinto], *s.m.inv. Engr:* mezzotint.

mi[1] [mi], *adv.* (*a*) half, mid, semi-; **paupières mi-closes,** half-closed eyelids; **acier mi-doux, mi-dur,** semi-mild, semi-hard, steel; **la mi-avril, -mai, etc.,** mid-April, -May, etc.; **mi-quadrupède, mi-poisson,** half quadruped, half fish; **à mi-hauteur,** half-way up, down; **cloison à mi-hauteur,** half-partition; **à mi-jambe,** half-way up the legs; **avoir de l'eau jusqu'à mi-jambe,** to stand up to the calves in water; **louer une voiture à mi-frais,** to go halves in the expense of hiring a car; **faire qch. mi de gré mi de force,** to do sth. half willingly half under compulsion; (*b*) in half; *Her:* **écu mi-coupé,** shield divided down the centre; NOTE: *the more common compounds are entered in their alphabetical place.*

mi[2], *s.m.inv. Mus:* **1.** (*a*) (*the note*) E; **morceau en mi,** piece in E; (*b*) first string, E string (of violin). **2.** mi (in the Fixed Do system).

miacis [mjasis], *s.m. Paleont:* miacis.

miam-miam [mjam mjam], *int. F:* yum-yum!

miaou [mjau], *s.m.* miaow, mew; (*of cat*) **faire m.,** to mew.

mi-août [miu], *s.f.inv.* mid-August; **à la mi-a.,** in the middle of August.

miargyrite [mjarʒirit], *s.f. Miner:* miargyrite.

miasmatique [mjasmatik], *a.* miasmic, miasmatic, miasmal, noxious (exhalation, etc.).

miasme [mjasm], *s.m.* miasma.

miastor [mjastɔːr], *s.m. Ent:* miastor.

miaulard [mjolaːr], *s.m.,* **miaule** [mjol], *s.m. Orn: F:* seamew.

miaulement [mjolmɑ̃], *s.m.* **1.** (*a*) mewing, miaowing; caterwauling; whining. **2.** (*a*) mew; (*b*) *pl. F:* (*of pers.*) cat calls.

miauler [mjole], *v.i.* to mew, miaow; to caterwaul; to whine.

miauleur, -euse [mjolœːr, -øːz]. **1.** *a.* mewing, miaowing (cat). **2.** *s.m. Orn: F:* seamew.

mi-bas [mibɑ], *s.m.inv.* half-hose; knee-length stocking, sock.

mi-bis [mibi], *a.* **1.** second-quality (bread, flour). **2.** half-bleached (linen, thread).

mi-bois (à) [amibwɑ], *adv.phr. Carp:* **assemblage à mi-b.,** halved joint, halving, scarf joint, half-lap joint.

mica [mika], *s.m. Miner:* mica.

micacé [mikase], *a. Miner:* micaceous.

micanite [mikanit], *s.f. El:* micanite.

mi-carême [mikarɛm], *s.f.* mid-Lent; **(dimanche de) la mi-c.,** mid-Lent (Sunday); *pl. mi-carêmes.*

micaschiste [mikaʃist], *s.m. Miner:* mica schist.

micellaire [misɛl(l)ɛːr], *a. Ph:* micellar.

micelle [misɛl], *s.f. Ph: Ch:* micelle, micella.

mi-chaussette [miʃosɛt], *s.f.* short sock, ankle sock; *pl. mi-chaussettes.*

miche [miʃ], *s.f.* (*a*) round loaf; cob (of bread); (*b*) *pl. P:* buttocks.

miché [miʃe], *s.m. P:* (*a*) the mug who pays (for woman's favours); sucker; (*b*) dude.

Michée [miʃe], *Pr.n.m. B.Hist:* Micah.

Michel [miʃɛl]. **1.** *Pr.n.m.* Michael; **la Saint-M.,** Michaelmas. **2.** *s.m. Com:* **gros m.,** plantain (banana).

Michel-Ange [mikɛlɑ̃ːʒ], *Pr.n.m.* Michelangelo.

michelang(el)esque [mikɛlɑ̃ʒ(el)ɛsk], *a. Art:* Michaelangelesque.

Micheline [miʃlin], *s.f. Rail:* rail car (invented and equipped by the Michelin Tyre Company).

mi-chemin (à) [amiʃmɛ̃], *adv.phr.* halfway; **à mi-c. entre Blois et Tours,** half way between Blois and Tours; **à mi-c. de Paris,** half way to Paris; **maison à mi-c.,** halfway house; **elle marcha jusqu'à mi-c. de l'allée,** she walked half way along the path.

michet [miʃɛ], **micheton** [miʃtɔ̃], *s.m. P:* (*a*) the mug who pays (for woman's favours); sucker; (*b*) dude.

Michler [miʃlɛːr], *Pr.n. Ch:* **cétone de M.,** Michler's ketone.

michon [miʃɔ̃], *s.m.* hunk, hunch (of bread).

mi-clos [miklo], *a.* half-shut (eyes, shutters, etc.); *pl. mi-clos(es).*

micmac [mikmak], *s.m. F:* underhand intrigue, scheming; **il y a un m., du m., là-dedans,** it's a put-up job; there's something fishy about it.

micocoule [mikɔkul], *s.f. Bot:* hackberry.

micocoulier [mikɔkulje], *s.m. Bot:* nettle tree; **m. (occidental),** hackberry (tree); **m. (de Provence),** lotus (tree).

micoine [mikwan], *s.f. Fr.C:* wooden spoon.

mi-corps (à) [amikɔːr], *adv.phr.* to the waist; **portrait à mi.-c.,** half-length portrait; **saisi à mi-c.,** caught round the waist; **être penché à mi-c. à la fenêtre,** to be leaning half out of the window.

mi-côte (à) [amikoːt], *adv.phr:* halfway up, down, the hill.

mi-course (à) [amikurs], *adv.phr. Rac:* at the halfway post.

micraster [mikrastɛːr], *s.m. Paleont:* micraster.

micro [mikro], *s.m. F:* microphone, *F:* mike; *W.Tel:* **parler au m.,** to speak, give a talk, on the radio.

micro- [mikrɔ, -o], *pref.* micro-.

microampère [mikrɔɑ̃pɛːr], *s.m. El:* microampere.

microampèremètre [mikrɔɑ̃pɛrmɛtr̥], *s.m. El:* microammeter.

microanalyse [mikrɔanaliːz], *s.f. Ch:* microanalysis.

microanalyste [mikrɔanalist], *s.m. & f.* microanalyst.

microbalance [mikrɔbalɑ̃ːs], *s.f. Ph:* microbalance.

microbe [mikrɔb], *s.m.* microbe; *F:* germ, bug; *F:* **attraper un m.,** to catch a bug.

microbicide [mikrɔbisid]. **1.** *a.* microbicidal, germ-killing. **2.** *s.m.* microbicide, germ-killer.

microbien, -ienne [mikrɔbjɛ̃, -jɛn], *a.* microbial, microbic (disease, etc.).

microbiologie [mikrɔbjɔlɔʒi], *s.f.* microbiology.

microbiologique [mikrɔbjɔlɔʒik], *a.* microbiological.

microbique [mikrɔbik], *a.* microbic, microbial.

microbisme [mikrɔbism], *s.m. Med:* microbism, microbial infection (of the body).

microbus [mikrɔbys], *s.m.* minibus.

microcalorimètre [mikrɔkalɔrimɛtr], s.m. Ph: microcalorimeter.

microcalorimétrie [mikrɔkalɔrimetri], s.f. Ph: microcalorimetry.

microcalorimétrique [mikrɔkalɔrimetrik], a. Ph: microcalorimetric.

microcapsule [mikrɔkapsyl], s.f. Biol: Tchn: microcapsule; miniature capsule.

microcèbe [mikrɔsɛb], s.m. Z: microcebus, dwarf lemur.

microcéphale [mikrɔsefal]. 1. a. microcephalous, microcephalic, small-headed. 2. s. microcephalic.

microcéphalie [mikrɔsefali], s.f. microcephaly.

microchimie [mikrɔʃimi], s.f. microchemistry.

microchimique [mikrɔʃimik], a. microchemical; analyse m., microchemical analysis.

microchiroptères [mikrɔkirɔptɛr], s.m.pl. Microchiroptera, the insectivorous bats.

microchirurgie [mikrɔʃiryrʒi], s.f. micrurgy, micro-dissection.

microcinématographe [mikrɔsinematɔgraf], s.m. micro cine-camera.

microcinématographie [mikrɔsinematɔgrafi], s.f. microcinematography, cinemicrography, cinephotomicography, microkinematography.

microcinématographique [mikrɔsinematɔgrafik], a. microcinematographic.

microcircuit [mikrɔsirkɥi], s.m. Elcs: microcircuit.

microclimat [mikrɔklima], s.m. Meteor: microclimate.

microclimatique [mikrɔklimatik], a. microclimatic.

microclimatologie [mikrɔklimatɔlɔʒi], s.f. microclimatology.

microcline [mikrɔklin], s.f. Miner: microcline.

micrococcus [mikrɔkɔk(k)ys], s.m., **microcoque** [mikrɔkɔk], s.m. Bac: micrococcus.

micro(-)contact [mikrɔkɔ̃takt], s.m. microswitch; pl. micro(-)contacts.

microcopie [mikrɔkɔpi], s.f. Phot: microcopy.

micro-cornée [mikrɔkɔrne], s.f. micro-cornea; pl. micro-cornées.

micro-cornéen, -éenne [mikrɔkɔrneɛ̃, -ɛɛn], a. Opt: micro-corneal.

microcosme [mikrɔkɔsm], s.m. microcosm.

microcosmique [mikrɔkɔsmik], a. microcosmic.

microcosmus [mikrɔkɔsmys], s.m. microcosmus, F: edible sea-squirt.

micro-cravate [mikrɔkravat], s.m. F: miniature microphone (hidden under one's tie, etc.); pl. micro-cravates.

microcristal, -aux [mikrɔkristal, -o], s.m. microcrystal.

microcristallin [mikrɔkristalɛ̃], a. Miner: microcrystalline.

microcurie [mikrɔkyri], s.m. Ph.Meas: microcurie.

microcyte [mikrɔsit], s.m. Physiol: microcyte.

microdactyle [mikrɔdaktil], a. microdactylous.

microdactylie [mikrɔdaktili], s.f. microdactylia.

microdissection [mikrɔdis(s)ɛksjɔ̃], s.f. microdissection.

micro-économie [mikrɔekɔnɔmi], s.f. microeconomics.

micro-électronique [mikrɔelɛktrɔnik], s.f. Elcs: micro-electronics.

micro-électrophorèse [mikrɔelɛktrɔfɔrɛːz], s.f. micro-electrophoresis.

microencapsulation [mikrɔɑ̃kapsylasjɔ̃], s.f. Biol: Tchn: micro-encapsulation.

microévolution [mikrɔevɔlysjɔ̃], s.f. micro-evolution.

microfaciès [mikrɔfasjes], s.m. Geol: microfacies.

microfarad [mikrɔfarad], s.m. El.Meas: microfarad.

microfaune [mikrɔfoːn], s.f. Z: microfauna.

microfibrille [mikrɔfibriːj], s.f. Ch: Biol: microfibril(la).

microfelsite [mikrɔfɛlsit], s.f. Miner: microfelsite.

microfiche [mikrɔfiʃ], s.f. Phot: microfiche.

microfilm [mikrɔfilm], s.m. Phot: microfilm.

microfilmage [mikrɔfilmaːʒ], s.m. microfilming.

microfilmer [mikrɔfilme], v.tr. Phot: to microfilm.

microfissure [mikrɔfis(s)yːr], s.f. microscopic fissure, crack.

microfossile [mikrɔfɔsil], s.m. microfossil.

microgamète [mikrɔgamɛt], s.m. Biol: microgamete.

microgamétocyte [mikrɔgametɔsit], s.m. Biol: microgametocyte.

microgastre [mikrɔgastr], s.m. Ent: microgaster.

microglossie [mikrɔglɔsi], s.f. Med: microglossia.

micrognathie [mikrɔgnati], s.f. Anthr: micrognathia.

microgranit(e) [mikrɔgranit], s.m. microgranite.

micrographe [mikrɔgraf], s.m. micrograph; micropantograph.

micrographie [mikrɔgrafi], s.f. micrography.

micrographique [mikrɔgrafik], a. micrographic.

microgrenu [mikrɔgrɔny], a. microgranular.

microgyrie [mikrɔʒiri], s.f. microgyria.

microhenry [mikrɔɑ̃ri], s.m. El.Meas: microhenry.

microhm [mikroːm], s.m. El.Meas: microhm.

microhmmètre [mikrom(m)ɛtr], s.m. El: microhm-meter.

microhylidés [mikrɔilide], s.m.pl. Amph: Microhylidae, F: the narrow-mouth(ed) toads.

microlecteur [mikrɔlɛktœːr], s.m., **microliseuse** [mikrɔlizøːz], s.f. microreader.

microlépidoptères [mikrɔlepidɔptɛːr], s.m.pl. Ent: Microlepidoptera.

microlite [mikrɔlit]. 1. s.m. Cryst: microcrystal; microlite. 2. s.f. Miner: microlite.

microlitique [mikrɔlitik], a. Geol: microlitic.

micrologie [mikrɔlɔʒi], s.f. micrology.

micrologique [mikrɔlɔʒik], a. micrological.

micromammifère [mikrɔmam(m)ifɛːr], s.m. Z: small mammal.

micromanipulateur [mikrɔmanipylatœːr], s.m. micromanipulator.

micromanipulation [mikrɔmanipylasjɔ̃], s.f. micromanipulation.

micromélie [mikrɔmeli], s.f. Med: micromelia.

micromélien, -ienne [mikrɔmeljɛ̃, -jɛn], a. Med: micromelic.

micromère [mikrɔmɛːr], s.m. Biol: micromere.

micromérisme [mikrɔmerism], s.m. micromerism.

micrométallographie [mikrɔmetal(l)ɔgrafi], s.f. micrometallography.

micrométéorite [mikrɔmeteɔrit], s.f. micrometeorite.

microméthode [mikrɔmetɔd], s.f. Ph: Ch: micromethod.

micromètre [mikrɔmɛtr], s.m. micrometer.

micrométrie [mikrɔmetri], s.f. micrometry.

micrométrique [mikrɔmetrik], a. micrometric(al); vis m., micrometer screw.

micromillimètre [mikrɔmilimɛtr], s.m. Meas: micromillimetre.

micro-module [mikrɔmɔdyl], s.m. Elcs: micromodule; pl. micro-modules.

micro-moteur [mikrɔmɔtœːr], s.m. micro engine; pl. micro-moteurs.

micromycète [mikrɔmiset], s.m. Fung: micromycete.

micron [mikrɔ̃], s.m. Meas: micromillimeter, micron.

Micronésie [mikrɔnezi], Pr.n.f. Geog: Micronesia.

micronésien, -ienne [mikrɔnezjɛ̃, -jɛn], a. & s. Geog: Micronesian.

micronucleus [mikrɔnykleys], s.m. micronucleus.

micro-objectif [mikrɔɔbʒɛktif], s.m. 1. photomicrographic object-glass. 2. microscope object-lens; pl. micro-objectifs.

micro-onde [mikrɔɔ̃ːd], s.f. W.Tel: etc: microwave; pl. micro-ondes.

micro-organisme [mikrɔɔrganism], s.m. micro-organism; pl. micro-organismes.

micropaléontologie [mikrɔpaleɔ̃tɔlɔʒi], s.f. micropaleontology.

microphage [mikrɔfaːʒ], (a) a. microphagous; (b) s.f. microphage.

microphone [mikrɔfɔn]. 1. a. microphonous. 2. s.m. (a) Ph: microphone; (b) Tp: etc: microphone, transmitter, mouthpiece (of telephone); m. à granules de charbon, carbon-granule microphone; m. à grenaille, granular microphone; m. à barrette de charbon, carbon-stick microphone; (c) Elcs: W.Tel: microphone; m. antivibrateur, anti-noise microphone; m. condensateur, condenser microphone; m. de bouche, F: m. moustache, lip microphone, F: lip mike; m. électrodynamique, moving-coil microphone; m. espion, m. caché, detectophone, F: bug; m. sans diaphragme, m. statique, diaphragmless microphone; Cin: etc: m. mobile, following microphone; m. directionnel, directional microphone; m. à concentrateur parabolique, parabolic-horn microphone.

microphonique [mikrɔfɔnik], a. microphonic.

microphotographie [mikrɔfɔtɔgrafi], s.f. 1. microphotography. 2. microphotograph, microcopy.

microphotographique [mikrɔfɔtɔgrafik], a. microphotographic; lettre m., airgraph.

microphotomètre [mikrɔfɔtɔmɛtr], s. microphotometer.

microphtalmie [mikrɔftalmi], s.f. microphthalmia.

microphylle [mikrɔfil], a. Bot: microphyllous.

microphysique [mikrɔfizik], s.f. microphysics.

micropodidés [mikrɔpɔdide], s.m.pl. Orn: Micropodidae.

micropodiformes [mikrɔpɔdifɔrm], s.m.pl. Orn: Micropodiformes.

micropoint [mikrɔpwɛ̃], s.m. microdot.

microporosité [mikrɔpɔrɔzite], s.f. microporosity.

microprogrammation [mikrɔprɔgramasjɔ̃], s.f. Elcs: microprogramming, microcoding.

microprogramme [mikrɔprɔgram], s.m. Elcs: microprogram(me).

microprogrammer [mikrɔprɔgrame], v.tr. Elcs: to microprogram(me).

micropsie [mikrɔpsi], s.f. Med: micropsia, micropsy.

microptère [mikrɔptɛːr], a. Orn: Ent: micropterous.

microptérygides [mikrɔpteriʒid], **microptérygidés** [mikrɔpteriʒide], s.m.pl. Ent: Micropterygidae, micropterygids.

micropyle [mikrɔpil], s.m. Biol: Bot: micropyle.

microradiographie [mikrɔradjɔgrafi], s.f. microradiography.

microscope [mikrɔskɔp], s.m. microscope; m. simple, composé, binoculaire, simple, compound, binocular, microscope; m. électronique, electron microscope; m. à champ émissif, field emission microscope; m. optique, photonique, light microscope; visible au m., visible under the microscope.

microscopie [mikrɔskɔpi], s.f. microscopy.

microscopique [mikrɔskɔpik], a. microscopic.

microscopiste [mikrɔskɔpist], s.m. & f. microscopist.

microseconde [mikrɔsəgɔ̃ːd], s.f. Meas: microsecond.

microséisme [mikrɔseism], s.m. microseism.

microséismique [mikrɔseismik], a. microseismic.

micros(é)ismographe [mikrɔs(e)ismɔgraf], s.m., **micros(é)ismographie** [mikrɔs(e)ismɔgrafi], s.f. microseismograph.

microsillon [mikrɔsijɔ̃], s.m. Rec: 1. microgroove. 2. (disque) m., long-playing record, F: L.P.

microsociologie [mikrɔsɔsjɔlɔʒi], s.f. microsociology.

microsomatie [mikrɔzɔmati], s.f. Med: microsomia.

microsome [mikrɔzoːm], s.m. Biol: microsome.

microsomie [mikrɔzɔmi], s.f. Med: microsomia.

microsommite [mikrɔsɔmit], s.f. Miner: microsommite.

microspectroscope [mikrɔspɛktrɔskɔp], s.m. microspectroscope.

microsporange [mikrɔspɔrɑ̃ːʒ], s.m. Bot: microsporange, microsporangium.

microspore [mikrɔspɔːr], s.f. Bot: microspore.

microsporidies [mikrɔspɔridi], s.f.pl. Prot: Microsporidia, Microsporidiida, microsporidians.

microsporie [mikrɔspɔri], s.f. Med: microsporiasis.

microsporon [mikrɔspɔrɔ̃], **microsporum** [mikrɔspɔrɔm], s.m. Med: microspore, microsporon.

microsporophylle [mikrɔspɔrɔfil], s.m. Bot: microsporophyll, stamen.

microstome [mikrɔstɔm]. 1. a. microstomous. 2. s.m. Ich: microstome.

microstructure [mikrɔstryktyːr], s.f. microstructure.

microtasimètre [mikrɔtazimɛtr], s.m. Ph: microtasimeter.

microtéléphone [mikrɔtelefɔn], s.m. microtelephone.

microtherme [mikrɔtɛrm], Bot: 1. a. microthermic. 2. s.f. microtherm.

microthermie [mikrɔtɛrmi], s.f. Ph.Meas: gram-calorie, small calorie.

microtinés [mikrɔtine], s.m.pl. Z: Microtinae.

microtome [mikrɔtɔm], s.m. microtome.

microtron [mikrɔtrɔ̃], s.m. Atom.Ph: microtron.

microvolt [mikrɔvɔlt], s.m. El.Meas: microvolt.

microwatt [mikrɔwat], s.m. El.Meas: microwatt.

microzoaire [mikrɔzɔɛːr], s.m. Biol: microzoarian, microzoan, microzoon.

microzyma [mikrɔzima], s.m. Biol: microzyme, microzyma.

micrurgie [mikryrʒi], s.f. micrurgy.

miction [miksjɔ̃], s.f. urination.

micturition [miktyrisjɔ̃], s.f. Med: micturition.

midi¹ [midi], s.m. no pl. 1. (a) midday, noon, twelve o'clock; m. apparent local, local apparent noon; m. vrai local, local true noon; m. moyen local, local mean noon; il est m., it is twelve o'clock; arriver sur le m., F: sur les m., to arrive about noon; arriver sur le coup de m., to arrive on the stroke of twelve; avant m., ante meridiem, a.m.; before noon; après m., post meridium, p.m.; after twelve (noon); m. et demi, half-past twelve; le soleil de m., the midday sun, en plein m., (i) in broad daylight, (ii) in the full light of day; F: faire voir à qn des étoiles en

plein m., to lead s.o. up the garden path; to have s.o. on; **chercher m. à quatorze heures**, to look for difficulties where there are none; to miss the obvious; **ne pas voir clair en plein m.**, to be blind to the obvious, to blink the facts; *P:* **c'est m. (sonné)**, that's that! you've, we've, had it; (*b*) **être au m. de la vie**, to be in the prime of life. **2.** (*a*) south; **vent du m.**, south wind; **exposition au m.**, southerly exposure, south aspect; **chambre au m.**, room facing south; (*b*) southern part (of country); *esp.* **le M. (de la France)**, the South of France.

midi[2], *s.f. Cost: F:* midi (skirt, etc.).

midinette [midinɛt], *s.f. F:* young milliner; young dressmaker.

mi-distance [midistɑ̃:s], *s.f.* middle distance; **à mi-d.**, halfway; *pl. mi-distances.*

mi-drisse (à) [amidris], *adv.phr. Nau:* **pavillon à mi-d.**, flag at the dip.

midship [midʃip], *s.m. F:* midshipman.

mie[1] [mi], *s.f.* **1.** crumb (of loaf, as opposed to crust); **pain avec beaucoup de m.**, crumby bread; *P:* **à la m. de pain**, not worth a damn; *P:* **m. de pain mécanique**, lice, livestock. **2.** *A:* (*a*) = MIETTE; (*b*) *adv. still used as a lit. mannerism in* **ne . . . m.** (= **ne . . . point**), not at all; **je n'en veux m.**, I will have none of it; **il ne chanta m.**, he didn't sing a note.

mie[2], *s.f.* (= AMIE) *used only with* **ma, ta, sa**; (*a*) **ma m.** (= *A:* **m'amie**), my pet; darling, sweetheart; my love; (*b*) *F:* girl friend; mistress.

miel [mjɛl], *s.m.* honey; **rayon, gâteau, gaufre, de m.**, honeycomb; **m. vierge, de goutte**, virgin honey, white honey; **m. rosat**, rose honey; **elle était tout sucre et tout m.**, she was all sugar and honey; **paroles de m.**, honeyed words; **faire son m. de qch.**, to turn sth. to advantage; **lune de m.**, honeymoon; *P:* **m.!** blast! damn!

miélaison [mjelɛzɔ̃], *s.f.* honey time, honey season, honey flow.

miélat [mjela], *s.m.*, **miellat** [mjela], *s.m.* honeydew.

miellé [mjele], *a.* **1.** (*a*) honeyed, sweetened with honey; (*b*) honey-coloured (flower, etc.). **2.** = MIELLEUX.

miellée [mjele], *s.f.*, **miellure** [mjely:r], *s.f.* honeydew.

mielleusement [mjɛløzmɑ̃], *adv.* blandly, with honeyed words, in a sugary manner.

mielleux, -euse [mjɛlø, -ø:z], *a.* **1. goût m.**, taste of honey. **2.** *Pej:* honeyed, sugary (speech, etc.); bland (smile); soapy, smooth-tongued, mealymouthed, soft-spoken (person).

mien, mienne [mjɛ̃, mjɛn]. **1.** *occ. poss. a.* mine; **un mien ami**, a friend of mine. **2. le mien, la mienne, les miens, les miennes**, mine; (*a*) *poss. pron.* **je pris ses mains dans les deux miennes**, I took her hands in both of mine; **un de vos amis et des miens**, a friend of yours and mine; **il donna des cadeaux à ses frères et aux miens**, he gave presents to his brothers and mine; (*b*) *s.m.* (i) my own (property, etc.); mine; **le m. et le tien**, mine and thine; **tels sont les faits, je n'y mets rien du m.**, such are the facts, I am not adding anything of my own (invention); (ii) *s.m.pl.* my own (friends, followers, etc.); **j'ai été renié par les miens**, I have been disowned by my own people, by my own folk; **les deux miens, miennes**, my two (friends, children, books, etc.); (*c*) *s.f.pl.* **on dit que j'ai encore fait des miennes**, they say I've been up to my old tricks again.

miersite [mjɛrzit], *s.f. Miner:* miersite.

miette [mjɛt], *s.f.* (*a*) crumb (of broken bread); (*b*) morsel, scrap; **il n'en a pas laissé une m.**, he didn't leave a crumb; he ate every bit; **mettre un vase en miettes**, to smash a vase to atoms, *F:* to smithereens; **vivre des miettes d'une fortune**, to live on the (scant) remains of a fortune; (*c*) *pl. Husb:* **miettes**, crumbles.

mieux [mjø], *adv.* **1.** *comp.* better; (*a*) (i) **il faut m. les surveiller, les m. surveiller**, you must watch them more closely; **vous pouvez décider m. que personne**, you know best; **pouvez-vous faire m. que cela?** can you better that? can you go one better? **vous feriez m. de m'écouter**, you would do better to, had better, listen to me; **vous auriez m. fait de ne rien dire**, it would have been better not to have said anything; **afin de m. faire qch.**, in order to do sth. better; **il vaudrait m. le faire**, it would be better to do it; *Prov:* **m. vaut tard que jamais**, better late than never; **ça va m.**, things are improving; **pour m. dire**, to be more exact; or rather; **pour ne pas dire m., pour ne pas m. dire**, to say the least of it; **de m. en m.**, better and better; **m. encore . . .**, better still . . .; *adv.phr.* **(faire qch.) à qui m. m.**, to vie with one another (in doing sth.); **tous travaillaient à qui m. m.**, all worked their hardest; **ils criaient à qui m. m.**, it was a case of who could shout loudest; they shouted loudly, lustily; **tant m.!** so much the better! that's all to the good; *Iron:* **de m. en m., non seulement tu as déja oublié de couper l'eau, mais tu as laissé le gaz ouvert**, better and better, to improve matters, not only have you forgotten to turn off the water, but you've left the gas on; (ii) **il va m.**, he's (feeling) better; (*b*) (*with adj. function*) (i) **c'est on ne peut m.**, it couldn't be better; **ce qui est m., qui m. est . . .**, what is better . . ., better still . . .; **il n'y a rien de m.**, that is the best there is; (ii) **vous serez m. dans ce fauteuil**, you will be more comfortable in this armchair; (iii) **il est m.**, he is (feeling) better; (iv) **il est m. que son frère**, he is better-looking, more prepossessing, than his brother; (*c*) *s.m.* (i) **le m. est l'ennemi du bien**, leave well alone; **faute de m.**, for want of, for lack of, failing, something better; **elle ressemble à sa mère, mais en m.**, she is very like her mother, but better-looking; **je ne demande pas m.!** I shall be delighted (to do so, to have it so); **je ne demande pas m. que de . . .**, I am only too willing to . . .; **j'avais espéré m.**, I had hoped for better things; **vous ne trouverez pas m. comme hôtel**, you won't find a better hotel; *Cards:* **faire une levée de m.**, to take one (trick) over; (ii) *Med: etc:* **un m., du m.**, a change for the better; **il y a un léger m.**, there is a slight improvement; (*of patient*) he is a little better, a shade better. **2.** *sup.* **le m.**, (the) best; (*a*) **la femme le m. habillée de Paris**, the best-dressed woman in Paris; **savoir ce qui convient le m. à qn**, to know what is best for s.o.; **il s'en est acquitté le m. du monde**, nobody could have done it better; (*b*) (*with adj. function*) (i) **ce qu'il y a de m. à faire, c'est de . . .**, the best course to take, the best thing to do, is to . . .; **c'est tout ce qu'il y a de m.**, there is absolutely nothing better; (ii) **être le m. du monde avec qn**, to be on the best of terms, on excellent terms, with s.o.; (iii) **c'était la m. des trois sœurs**, she was the best-looking of the three sisters; (*c*) *s.m.* **faire, agir, pour le m.**, to act for the best; **le m. serait de . . .**, the best plan would be to . . .; **(en mettant les choses) au m., cela vous rapportera . . .**, at best it will bring you in . . .; **faire qch. au m.**, to do sth. as well as one can; *St.Exch:* **exécuter un ordre au m.**, to execute an order at best; **fabriquer au m.**, to manufacture under the best conditions; **agir au m. des intérêts de qn**, to act in the best interests of s.o.; **faire qch. de son m.**, to do sth. to the best of one's ability; **faire de son m.**, to do one's best; to put one's best foot foremost; **je la consolai de mon m.**, I comforted her as well as I could, I did my best to comfort her; **je vous aiderai de mon m.**, I will help you all I can; **être au m. avec qn**, to be on the best of terms, on excellent terms, with s.o.; **ils s'entendent du m. qui soit**, they are on the best possible terms; **le cheval est du m. de sa forme**, the horse is at the top of its form; (*d*) *A. & Lit:* **il chante des m.**, he sings extremely well.

mieux-être [mjøzɛtr̥], *s.m. no pl.* improved condition, situation; greater degree of comfort; improved status.

mièvre [mjɛ:vr̥], *a.* (*a*) fragile, delicate (child, etc.); (*b*) finical, affected (style, etc.).

mièvrement [mjɛvrəmɑ̃], *adv.* finically, affectedly.

mièvrerie [mjɛvrəri], *s.f.*, **mièvreté** [mjɛvrəte], *s.f.* **1.** (*a*) fragility, delicateness; (*b*) finicalness, affectation (of style, etc.). **2.** *A:* roguish prank.

mi-fer (à) [amifɛ:r], *adv.phr. Metalw:* **assemblage à mi-f.**, lap joint; **assembler à mi-f.**, to lap-joint.

mi-fini [mifini], *a. Ind: etc:* semi-finished (product); *pl. mi-fini(e)s.*

mi-fixe [mifiks], *a.* semi-portable (boiler, etc.); *pl. mi-fixes.*

mi-fort [mifɔ:r], *s.m.* middle of (sword) blade.

mi-fruit [mifrɥi], *s.m.* half-share of the produce (of farm under *métayage*); *pl. mi-fruits.*

migmatite [migmatit], *s.f. Geol:* migmatite, injection gneiss.

mignard [miɲa:r], *a.* (*a*) *A:* dainty, delicate, caressing; (*b*) affected, mincing, simpering (person, manner); pretty-pretty.

mignardement [miɲardəmɑ̃], *adv.* (*a*) *A:* daintily, delicately; (*b*) affectedly, mincingly.

mignarder [miɲarde], *v.tr.* (*a*) *A:* to pat, caress, fondle (child, etc.); (*b*) **m. son style**, to be finical (in one's style).

mignardise [miɲardi:z], *s.f.* **1.** (*a*) *A:* daintiness, delicacy; caressing ways; (*b*) affectation; mincing manner; (*c*) *Art: Lit:* finicalness; affectation (of style, etc.). **2.** *Bot:* garden pink.

mignon, -onne [miɲɔ̃, -ɔn]. **1.** *a.* dainty, tiny, delicate (person, painting, etc.); **est-elle mignonne!** isn't she sweet! isn't she a darling! *Iron:* **ça va être m.!** that *will* be nice! **son péché m.**, his pet vice, his particular weakness; *A:* **argent m.**, spare cash, pocket-money. **2.** *s.* (*a*) pet, darling, favourite; **ma mignonne**, my dear; (*b*) *A:* minion. **3.** *s.f. Typ:* **mignonne**, minion; seven-point type.

mignonnement [miɲɔnmɑ̃], *adv.* daintily, delicately, prettily.

mignonnet, -ette [miɲɔnɛ, -ɛt]. **1** *a.* tiny, dainty (person, etc.). **2.** *s.* **mignonnet** *or* **mignonnette**; *Bot:* (*a*) *A:* mignonette; (*b*) London pride; (*c*) wild succory; (*d*) clover. **3.** *s.f.* **mignonnette**; (*a*) mignonette lace; (*b*) coarse-ground pepper.

mignoter [miɲɔte], *v.tr. O:* to fondle, caress, make much of (child, etc.); to pet (child).

se mignoter, to titivate (oneself).

migraine [migrɛn], *s.f.* migraine, *Med:* hemicrania.

migraineux, -euse [migrɛnø, -ø:z], *a. & s. Med:* (person) subject to, suffering from, migraine; migrainous.

migrant, -ante [migrɑ̃, -ɑ̃:t], *a. & s.* migrant.

migrateur, -trice [migratœ:r, -tris], *a.* migrating, migratory (bird, etc.); migrant (people); *Biol:* **cellule migratrice**, migratory cell.

migration [migrasjɔ̃], *s.f.* (*a*) migration; *Pol.Ec:* **migrations alternantes**, commuting; (*b*) *Ch:* **m. des ions**, ion migration, drift; (*c*) *Geol:* migration (of humus in the soil, of oil, etc. through porous layers).

migratoire [migratwa:r], *a.* migratory (movement, etc.).

migrer [migre], *v.i.* to migrate.

mihrab [mirab], *s.m.* mihrab (of mosque).

mi-jambe (à) [amiʒɑ̃:b], *adv.phr.* halfway up the leg; **avoir de l'eau jusqu'à mi-j.**, to be up to the calves in water.

mijaurée [miʒɔre], *s.f.* conceited, affected, *F:* stuck-up, woman.

mijoter [miʒɔte]. **1.** *v.tr.* (*a*) *Cu:* to stew (sth.) slowly; to let (sth.) simmer; to keep (sth.) simmering; **m. un projet**, to nurse a scheme, to turn a scheme over in one's mind; *F:* **m. un complot**, to hatch a plot; **je sais qu'il se mijote quelque chose**, I know there's something in the wind; **je me demande ce qui se mijote**, I wonder what's up, what's in the wind, what's brewing; (*b*) **m. un enfant**, to coddle a child. **2.** *v.i.* to simmer, stew; **idées qui mijotent dans l'esprit**, ideas that one turns over in one's mind.

se mijoter, *F:* to coddle oneself.

mikado [mikado], *s.m.* Mikado.

mil[1] [mil], *s.m. Gym:* Indian club.

mil[2] [mil], *a.* (*used only in writing out dates A.D.*) thousand; **l'an mil neuf cent quatre-vingt-un**, the year nineteen hundred and eighty-one.

mil[3] [mi:j], *s.m. Bot:* millet.

milady [miledi], *s.f.* **1.** (*title*) My Lady. **2.** *F:* **une m.**, a titled (English) lady; *pl. miladys.*

milage [mila:ʒ], *s.m. Fr.C:* mileage; distance in miles.

mi-laine [milɛn], *s.m. Tex:* half-wool cloth; union (cloth).

Milan[1] [milɑ̃], *Pr.n. Geog:* Milan.

milan[2] [milɑ̃], *s.m.* **1.** *Ich:* red gurnard. **2.** *Orn:* **m. (royal)**, kite; **m. noir**, black kite.

milanais, -aise [milanɛ, -ɛ:z], *a. & s.* **1.** *Geog:* Milanese. **2.** *s.f. Dressm:* **milanaise**, gimp.

milandre [milɑ̃:dr̥], *s.m. Ich:* tope, dogfish.

milaneau, -eaux [milano], *s.m. Orn:* young kite.

milarite [milarit], *s.f. Miner:* milarite.

mildew, mildiou [mildju], *s.m. Vit:* mildew, brown rot; **atteint de m.**, mildewed, mildewy.

mildiousé [mildjuze], *a. Vit:* mildewed (vine, etc.); mildewy.

milésiaque [milezjak], **milésien, -ienne** [milezjɛ̃, -jɛn], *a. & s. A.Geog:* Milesian.

Milet [milɛ], *Pr.n.m. A.Geog:* Miletus.

miliaire [miljɛ:r]. **1.** *a.* resembling millet-seed; *Med:* miliary (gland, tubercle, fever, etc.). **2.** *s.f. Med:* miliary fever, miliaria, prickly heat.

milice [milis], *s.f.* **1.** *A:* (*a*) the art of war; warfare; (*b*) military expedition, campaign. **2.** (*a*) *A:* army, host; *Lit:* **les milices célestes**, the heavenly hosts; (*b*) militia.

milicien [milisjɛ̃], *s.m.* militiaman.

milieu, -ieux [miljø], *s.m.* **1.** middle, midst; **au m. de**, amid(st); **inaperçu au m. de la foule**, unseen in the midst of the crowd; **assise au m. de ses enfants**, seated among her children; **au beau m. de la rue**, right in the middle of the street; **frappé au beau m. du front**, struck right on the forehead; **s'arrêter au (beau) m. de sa carrière**, to stop in mid-career; **au m. du navire**, amidships; **le navire s'ouvrit par le m.**, the boat parted amidships; **au m. du courant,** in mid-stream; **au m. des plaisirs,** in the midst of pleasure; **au m. de la place,** in the centre of the square; **au m. de la forêt,** in the heart of the forest; **le m. du jour,** midday; **m. du siècle,** middle of the century; **au m. de l'été, de l'hiver, du jour, de la nuit,** in the height of summer, in the depth of winter, at (full) noon, at dead of night; **vers le m. du mois,** about the middle of the month; **mettez ce livre sur le rayon du m.,** put this book on the middle shelf; **assis à la table du m.,** seated at the middle table; **cheval du m.,** centre-horse (of team); *Hist:* **l'Empire, le Royaume, du M.,** the Middle Empire, the Middle Kingdom (*i.e.* China); *Geom:* **le m. d'une droite,** the middle point of a straight line; *a.* **les points milieux,** the middle points. **2.** (*a*) *Ph:* medium; **l'air est le m. dans lequel nous vivons,** the air is the medium in which we live; **m. diffusant,** scattering medium; **m. gazeux,** gaseous medium; **m. réfringent,** refracting medium; *Atom.Ph:* **m. actif, m. multiqlicateur,** active core; *Biol:* **m. de culture,** culture medium; (*b*) milieu, environment; surroundings; (social) sphere, circle; walk of life; **les invités représentaient tous les milieux politiques,** the guests were drawn from every political milieu; **les différents milieux,** the different social classes; **je n'appartiens pas à leur m.,** I don't belong to their set, circle; **les milieux autorisés,** responsible quarters; **les milieux bien informés,** well-informed people, quarters; *Ind: etc:* **en m. réel,** in the field; **essai en m. réel,** field trial; **dans des conditions de m. réel,** under field conditions; *Mil:* **m. opérationnel,** operational environment; (*c*) **le m., les gens du m.,** the underworld. **3.** middle course, mean; **il n'y a pas de m.,** there is no middle course; **le juste m.,** the happy medium; **politique du juste m.,** middle-of-the-road policy; **tenir le m. entre . . . et . . .,** to be something between . . . and . . .; to steer a middle course between . . . and . . ..

militaire [militɛːr]. **1.** *a.* (*a*) military (authority, discipline, etc.); **service m.,** military service; **l'Annuaire m.** = the Army List; **camion m.,** army lorry, *U.S:* truck; **allure m.,** military bearing; **prendre l'attitude m.,** to stand to attention; **à huit heures, heure m.,** at eight o'clock sharp; (*b*) **la marine m.,** the Navy; **aviation m.,** military aviation; **port m.,** naval port; **champ d'aviation m.,** military airfield; *s.a.* CODE 1. **2.** *s.m.* (*a*) military man; soldier; **m. du contingent** = National Serviceman; **ancien m.,** ex-serviceman; **les militaires,** the military, the armed forces; **les militaires de tous grades,** all ranks; (*b*) military life; the army (as a profession); **passer du civil au m.,** to leave civilian life for the army.

militairement [militɛrmɑ̃], *adv.* militarily. **1.** (*a*) in a soldierly manner, in a soldierlike manner; **saluer m.,** to give a military salute; (*b*) with military, stringent, discipline; **il fait marcher ses employés m.,** he is a regular martinet. **2. occuper une ville m.,** to occupy a town militarily, by force of arms.

militant, -ante [militɑ̃, -ɑ̃ːt]. **1.** *a.* militant (church, etc.); **politique militante,** (i) strong policy, policy of action; (ii) fighting policy, aggressive policy. **2.** *s.* militant; **m. d'une idée,** fighter for an idea; **les militants d'un parti,** the fighting wing of a party.

militantisme [militɑ̃tism], *s.m.* militancy.

militarisation [militarizasjɔ̃], *s.f.* militarization.

militariser [militarize], *v.tr.* (*a*) to militarize (a nation, etc.); **zone militarisée,** militarized zone; (*b*) to give (civilian) (temporary) military status; (*c*) to impress (workmen, etc.) into military service.

militarisme [militarism], *s.m.* militarism.

militariste [militarist], *a.* & *s.m.* & *f.* militarist.

militer [milite], *v.i.* (*a*) *A:* to go to war; (*b*) to militate (**pour, en faveur de,** in favour of); **faits qui militent contre l'accusé,** facts that militate, tell, go, against the prisoner; **cela milite en sa faveur,** that tells in his favour.

milk-bar [milkbar], *s.m.* milk bar; *pl. milk-bars.*

millade [mijad], *s.f.* maize or millet gruel.

millage [milaːʒ], *s.m. Fr.C:* mileage.

millavois, -oise [mijavwa, -waːz], *a.* & *s. Geog:* (native, inhabitant) of Millau [mijo].

mille[1] [mil]. **1.** *num.a.inv.* & *s.m.inv.* (*a*) thousand; **m. hommes,** a thousand men; **trois cent m. hommes,** three hundred thousand men; **plusieurs m. habitants,** several thousand inhabitants; **ils moururent par centaines de m.,** they died in hundreds of thousands; **quelque m. soldats,** about a thousand soldiers; **quelques m. soldats,** some thousands of soldiers; **m. un,** a thousand and one; *but* **Les M. et une Nuits,** the Arabian Nights; *Hist:* **l'an mille,** the year one thousand; *c.f.* MIL[2]; (*b*) countless, many; **c'est m. fois dommage,** it's a thousand pities; **je vous l'ai dit m. fois,** I've told you a thousand times, times without number; **les m. et un détails,** the thousand and one details, the countless details; **j'étais à m. lieues de supposer que . . .,** I should never have dreamt that . . .; **il a des m. et des cents,** he has tons of money, pots of money. **2.** *s.m.* (*a*) **un m. de briques,** a thousand bricks; **un m. de houille,** a ton of coal; (*b*) **mettre dans le m.,** (i) to make a "thousand" throw (at the game of *tonneau*); (*darts*) to hit the bull's eye; (ii) *F:* to be successful, to come out top; *F:* **en plein dans le m.!** you've hit it!

mille[2], *s.m.* mile; **vingt milles,** twenty miles; **m. marin, nautique,** (French) sea mile (= 0.992 British nautical mile).

millée [mije], *s.f.* millet gruel.

mille(-)feuille [milfœːj], *s.f.* **1.** *Bot:* milfoil, yarrow; **m. aquatique,** water violet; *pl. mille-feuilles.* **2.** *Cu:* millefeuille, *U.S:* napoleon.

millefiori [milfjɔri], *s.m.inv.* millefiori (glassware).

mille-fleurs [milflœːr], *s.f.inv. Toil:* millefleurs.

millénaire [mil(l)enɛːr]. **1.** *a.* millennial, millenary. **2.** *s.m.* (*a*) (aggregate of) one thousand; (*b*) thousand years; millenary, millennium. **3.** *s.m.* & *f. Rel.H:* millenarian, chiliast.

millénarisme [mil(l)enarism], *s.m. Rel.H:* millenarianism, milleniarism, chiliasm.

millénariste [mil(l)enarist], *s.m.* millenarist, millenarian.

millénium [mil(l)enjɔm], *s.m.* millenium.

mille-pattes [milpat], **mille-pieds** [milpje], *s.m. inv. Myr:* millepede.

mille(-)pertuis [milpɛrtɥi], *s.m.inv. Bot:* St John's wort; **m.-p. velu,** Aaron's beard.

millépore [mil(l)epɔːr], *s.m. Coel:* millepore.

mille-raies [milrɛ], *s.m.inv. Tex:* very finely striped material; **velours m.-r.,** needlecord.

millerandage [milrɑ̃daːʒ], *s.m. Vit:* partial failure of the grape harvest.

millérite [milerit], *s.f. Miner:* millerite.

millésime [mil(l)ezim], *s.m.* (*a*) date (on coin, etc.); **pièce au m. de . . .,** coin dated . . .; (*b*) *Ind:* year of manufacture; *Vit:* year, vintage.

millésimer [milezime], *v.tr. Vit:* to date (vintage wine bottles).

millesimo [mil(l)ɛzimo], *adv.* in the thousandth place.

millet [mijɛ], *s.m.* **1.** *Bot:* millet; wood millet grass; **m. long,** canary grass; **grand m.,** sorghum, sorg(h); **(grains de) m.,** birdseed, canary seed; *F:* **c'est un grain de m. dans la gueule d'un âne,** it's no more than a peanut to an elephant. **2.** *Med:* miliary eruption, millet-seed rash.

milli- [mil(l)i], *pref.* milli-.

milliaire [miljɛːr], *a.* milliary, marking a mile; *Rom.Ant:* **borne, pierre, m.,** milliary (column).

milliampère [mil(l)iɑ̃pɛːr], *s.m. El.Meas:* milliampere.

milliampèremètre [mil(l)iɑ̃pɛrmɛtr̥], *s.m.* milliammeter.

milliard [miljaːr], *s.m.* milliard, *U.S:* billion.

milliardaire [miljardɛːr], *a.* & *s.m.* & *f.* multi-millionaire, *U.S:* billionaire.

milliardième [miljardjɛm], *num. a.* & *s.m.* one thousand millionth, *U.S:* billionth (part).

milliasse [miljas], *s.f.* (*a*) *A:* a million millions, *U.S:* trillion; (*b*) *F:* enormous quantity, sum (of money); millions and millions.

millibar [mil(l)ibaːr], *s.m. Meteor.Meas:* millibar.

millicurie [mil(l)ikyri], *s.m. Meas:* millicurie.

millième [miljɛm]. **1.** *num. a.* & *s.m.* thousandth. **2.** *s.m. Bookb:* bulk (in millimetres). **3.** *s.m. Artil:* millieme, mil (of angular measure).

milliéquivalent [mil(l)iekivalɑ̃], *s.m.* milliequivalent.

millier [milje], *s.m.* (about a) thousand; a thousand or so; **des milliers de personnes,** thousands of people; **ils viennent par milliers,** they come in thousands; **des milliers de milliers,** thousands upon thousands.

milligrade [mil(l)igrad], *s.m. Angular Meas:* milligrade.

milligramme [mil(l)igram], *s.m.* milligram(me).

millihenry [mil(l)iɑ̃ri], *s.m. El.Meas:* millihenry.

millilitre [mil(l)ilitr̥], *s.m.* millilitre.

millimètre [mil(l)imɛtr̥], *s.m.* millimetre.

millimétrique [mil(l)imetrik], *a.* **échelle m.,** millimetre scale; **papier m.,** scale paper, graph paper.

millimicron [mil(l)imikrɔ̃], *s.m. Ph.Meas:* millimicron.

million [miljɔ̃], *s.m.* million; **un m. d'hommes,** a million men, one million men; **quatre millions d'hommes,** four million men; **riche à millions,** worth millions.

millionième [miljɔnjɛm], *num. a.* & *s.m.* millionth.

millionnaire [miljɔnɛːr], *a.* & *s.* millionaire; **plusieurs fois m.,** multi-millionaire.

milliröntgen [mil(l)irœntgɛn], *s.m.* milliroentgen.

millithermie [mil(l)itɛrmi], *s.f.* large, great, major, calorie; kilogram(me) calorie.

millivolt [mil(l)ivɔlt], *s.m. El.Meas:* millivolt.

millivoltmètre [mil(l)ivɔltmɛtr̥], *s.m.* millivoltmeter.

milliwatt [mil(l)iwat], *s.m. El.Meas:* milliwatt.

Milo [milo], *Pr.n. Geog:* Melos, Milo; **la Vénus de M.,** the Venus of Milo.

Milon [milɔ̃], *Pr.n.m. Gr.Hist:* Milo.

milord [milɔːr], *s.m.* **1.** (*in address*) my Lord. **2.** (*a*) (English) nobleman; (*b*) *F:* immensely wealthy man. **3.** *A.Veh:* Victoria.

milouin [milwɛ̃], *s.m. Orn:* pochard.

milouinan [milwinɑ̃], *s.m. Orn:* scaup (duck).

mi-lourd [miluːr], *a.* & *s.m. Box:* **(poids) mi-l.,** light heavyweight; cruiser weight; *pl. mi-lourds.*

milreis [milreis], *s.m. A.Num:* milreis.

Miltiade [milsjad], *Pr.n.m. Gr.Hist:* Miltiades.

miltonien, -ienne [miltɔnjɛ̃, -jɛn], *a. Lit:* Miltonian, Miltonic.

mimallonides [mimalɔnid], *s.m.pl. Ent:* Mimallonidae.

mi-marée [mimare], *s.f.* half-tide; **bassin accessible à mi-m.,** half-tide basin.

mi-mât (à) [amimɑ], *adv.phr.* (flag, etc.) at half mast; **mettre les couleurs à m.-m.,** to half-mast the colours.

mime [mim]. **1.** *s.m. Gr.* & *Lt.Th:* (*a*) mime; (*b*) (actor in) mime. **2.** *s.m.* **l'art du m.,** the art of miming. **3.** *s.m.* & *f.* (*pers.*) (*a*) mime; actor who depends on miming, on gestures; **elle fut plutôt une m. tragique,** her miming, her gestures, conveyed a somewhat tragic impression; (*b*) mimic.

mimer [mime], *v.tr.* **1.** to mime; **m. une scène,** to mime a scene, to act a scene in dumb show; **m. un signal,** to signal by gesture; **m. sa joie, sa douleur,** to express one's joy, one's sorrow, in dumb show. **2.** to mimic, to ape (s.o.).

mimèse [mimɛːz], *s.f. Rh:* mimesis.

mimétèse [mimetɛːz], *s.f. Miner:* mimetite, mimetene.

mimétique [mimetik], *a.* mimetic; imitative.

mimétisme [mimetism], *s.m. Z:* mimesis; mimicry (in animals).

mimétite [mimetit], *s.f. Miner:* mimetite.

mimeux, -euse [mimø, -øːz], *Bot:* **1.** *a.* sensitive (plant). **2.** *s.f.* **mimeuse pudique,** sensitive plant, mimosa pudica.

mimi [mimi]. **1.** *s.m.* (*a*) (*child's language*) pussy; (*b*) *F:* **mon petit m.,** darling; my pet; (*c*) (*to child*) **fais un gros m. à ta maman,** give mummy a nice big kiss. **2.** *s.f.* (*from Murger's "Scènes de la Vie de Bohème"*) (type of) light-hearted shop-girl.

mimïambes [mimiɑ̃ːb], *s.m.pl. A.Pros:* mimiambics.

mimidés [mimide], *s.m.pl. Orn:* Mimidae.

mimique [mimik]. **1.** *a.* (*a*) mimic; **langage m.,** (i) sign language; (ii) mime, dumb show; (*b*) *Z:* mimetic. **2.** *s.f.* (*a*) mimic art, mimicry; (*b*) dumb show.

mimmation [mimasjɔ̃], *s.f. Ling:* mimmation.

mimodrame [mimɔdram], *s.m. Th:* mimodrama, mime, dumb-show performance.

mimographe [mimɔgraf], *s.m. A:* mime writer, mimographer.

mimologie [mimɔlɔʒi], *s.f.* mimicry; (theatrical) impersonation.

mimosa [mimoza], *s.m. Bot:* mimosa.

mimosacées [mimozase], *s.f.pl. Bot:* Mimosaceae.

mimosées [mimoze], *s.f.pl. Bot:* Mimoseae.

mi-mot (à) [amimo], *adv.phr. F:* **comprendre à mi-m.,** (i) to take a hint; (ii) to catch on (to what was said).

mi-moyen [mimwajɛ̃], *a.* & *s.m. Box:* **(poids) mi-m.,** welter-weight (boxer); *pl. mi-moyens.*

mimule [mimyl], **mimulus** [mimylys], *s.m. Bot:* mimulus, monkey-flower.

mimusops [mimyzɔps], *s.m. Bot:* Mimusops.

minable [minabl̥], *a.* **1.** mineable (fort, etc.). **2.** *F:* shabby, seedy-looking (person); shabby, pitiable (appearance, furniture, etc.); **sa conférence a été m.,** his lecture was poor beyond belief; **un salaire m.,** a mere pittance (of a wage); *s.* **un tas de minables,** a seedy lot.

minahouet [minawɛ], *s.m. Nau:* serving-board.

minaret [minarɛ], *s.m.* minaret.

minasragrite [minasragrit], *s.f. Miner:* minasragrite.

minauder [minode], *v.i.* to simper, smirk; **en minaudant,** with a simper, a smirk.

minauderie [minodri], *s.f.* **1.** simpering, smirking. **2.** *pl.* simpering manner.

minaudier, -ière [minodje, -jɛːr]. **1.** *a. & s.* simpering, smirking, affected (person). **2.** *s.f.* **minaudière,** (powder) compact.

minbar [minbaːr], *s.m.* mimbar (of mosque).

mince [mɛ̃ːs]. **1** *a.* thin (board, cloth, etc.); slender, slight, slim (person); **m. revenu,** slender, small, scanty, income; **minces arguments,** poor, feeble, thin, arguments; **savoir m.,** slight, shallow, knowledge; **homme de m. étoffe, m. personnage,** man of little importance; nonentity; **aux minces lèvres,** thin-lipped; *s.* **c'était un grand m.,** he was a tall spare man. **2.** *int. P:* **m. de pluie!** what a downpour! that's *some* rain! **m. alors!** well! just fancy that! my word! good heavens! **3.** *adv.* **peindre m.,** to paint thinly, in thin layers.

mincement [mɛ̃smɑ̃], *adv.* thinly (clad, etc.); **m. payé,** badly paid.

mincer [mɛ̃se], *v.tr.* (**je minçai(s); n. minçons**) *Cu:* to mince; to shred.

minceur [mɛ̃sœːr], *s.f.* (*a*) thinness; (*of pers.*) slenderness, slimness; (*b*) scantiness (of income, etc.).

mincir [mɛ̃siːr], *v.i. F:* to slim; **cette manie de m.,** this slimming craze.

Mincopies (les) [lemɛ̃kɔpi], *s.m.pl. Ethn:* the Andamans, the Andamanners.

mine[1] [min], *s.f.* **1.** mine; (*a*) **m. de houille, de charbon,** coal mine; colliery; **m. d'or,** gold mine; **m. de plomb,** lead mine; **m. de sel,** salt mine; **m. de sel gemme,** rock-salt mine; **m. à ciel ouvert,** surface, open-cast, mine; **propriétaire de m.,** mine owner; **directeur de m.,** mine manager; **inspecteur des mines,** mine inspector, mine viewer; **exploitation des mines,** mining; **exploiter une m.,** to work a mine; **explosif de m.,** mining explosive; (*b*) **une m. de sagesse,** a storehouse of wisdom, **une m. de renseignements, de faits,** a mine of information. **2.** (*a*) *A:* ore; **m. de fer,** iron ore; (*b*) **m. de plomb,** graphite, blacklead; **passer le poêle à la m. de plomb,** to blacklead the stove; **m. anglaise,** red lead; **m. douce,** zinc blende; **m. d'étain,** tin stone; **m. (de crayon),** (pencil) lead. **3.** *Exp: Civ.E: Mil:* **coup de m.,** blast, shot; **cartouche de m.,** blasting cartridge; **ouvrir la roche à coups de m.,** to blast the rock; **faire jouer une m., tirer un coup de m.,** to fire a blast, a mine; *Min: etc:* **exploitation à la m.,** blasting; *P.N:* **attention aux coups de m.!** beware of blasting; danger, blasting. **4.** *Mil: Navy:* mine; **m. de fond, m. dormante,** ground mine; **m. flottante,** floating mine; **m. dérivante,** drifting mine; **m. sous-marine,** submarine mine; **m. à mouillage par tube,** tube-type mine; **m. à orin,** moored mine; **m. à dépression,** pressure mine; **m. de contact,** contact mine; **m. à influence,** influence mine; **m. acoustique,** acoustic mine; **m. magnétique,** magnetic mine; **m. télécommandée,** radio-controlled mine; **m. télécommandée de la côte,** coast-controlled mine; **armer une m.,** to arm a mine, to make a mine live; **m. amorcée,** activated mine; **poser, mouiller, une m.,** to lay a mine; **pose, mouillage, de mines,** mine laying; **mouilleur de mines,** minelayer; **poseur de mines,** mineplanter; **champ de mines,** minefield; **établir un champ de mines,** to lay, plant, a minefield; **ménager un passage libre dans un champ de mines,** to leave a lane in a minefield; **déblayer un champ de mines,** to clear a minefield; **enlèvement des mines,** mine clearance; **relever une m.,** to pick up, lift, a mine; **détecteur de mines,** mine detector; **neutralisateur de mine(s),** mine sterilizer; **désarmer, neutraliser, une m.,** to disarm a mine; **sauter sur une m.,** to be blown up by a mine; *Mil:* **m. terrestre,** land mine; **m. antichar,** anti-tank mine; **m. antipersonnel,** anti-personnel mine; **m. atomique,** atomic demolition mine; **m. bondissante,** bounding mine; **ceinture de mines,** mine belt; *Mil.Av:* **m. aérienne,** aerial mine.

mine[2], *s.f.* **1.** (*general appearance*) (*a*) *A:* **avoir belle m., avoir de la m.,** to be good-looking; **de bonne m.,** well-favoured; **homme de bonne m.,** man of prepossessing appearance; **individu de mauvaise m., de méchante m.,** shady-looking individual; individual of unprepossessing appearance; **il est de mauvaise m.,** he's an ill-looking fellow; **il a la m. d'un fripon,** he looks a rogue, a rascal; (*b*) **juger les gens sur la m.,** to judge people by appearances; **vous avez la m. d'avoir mal dormi,** you look as though you had slept badly; **plat qui a bonne m.,** appetising dish; dish that looks good; **il ne paie pas de m.,** his appearance goes against him; he isn't much to look at; **ça ne paie pas de m.,** it doesn't look anything much; it isn't much to look at; (*c*) **faire m. d'être fâché,** to pretend to be angry; to look as though one is angry; **j'ai fait m. de vouloir le battre,** I made as if to strike him; **il a fait m. de me suivre,** he made as if to follow me; he pretended to follow me; **il m'a fait m. de me taire,** he signalled to me to be quiet; **avoir m. de (vouloir) faire qch.,** to look like doing sth., to look as if one were going to do sth.; (*d*) *F: Iron:* **nous avons bonne m. maintenant!** we *do* look silly! *don't* we look fools! **on aura bonne m. si on débarque chez eux sans les prévenir!** we *shall* look bright if we land on them without warning! *P:* **m. de rien,** as if nothing had happened; casually; **tâche de le cuisiner un peu, m. de rien,** try and pump him a bit, without letting him see that you're doing it. **2.** (*facial expression*) (*a*) (*of health*) **avoir bonne m., mauvaise m.,** to look well, ill; **vous avez mauvaise m.,** you don't look very well, very fit; you're not looking up to the mark; **vous avez meilleure m.,** you're looking better; **il a une (sale) m.,** he *does* look ill; **avoir une m. de papier mâché, de déterré,** to look terribly ill; (*b*) **m. boudeuse,** sulky expression; **avoir la m. longue, allongée,** to have a long face, a miserable expression; **faire une m. de dix pieds de long,** to make a face as long as a fiddle; **faire triste m.,** to look disappointed; **faire la m.,** to look sulky; **faire la m. à qn,** to scowl at s.o.; **faire bonne m. à qn,** to greet s.o. with a welcome, pleasantly, with a smile; **faire mauvaise, grise, m. à qn,** to give s.o. a poor welcome; **faire froide m. à qn,** to greet, receive, s.o. coldly; **faire une laide m.,** to scowl, to look black; **faire une m. niaise,** to put on a vacant look; **faire bonne m. à mauvais jeu,** to smile in the face of adversity; to keep smiling; to grin and bear it; to put a good face on it; (*c*) *pl.* **petites mines gracieuses d'un bébé,** graceful little gestures, expressions, of a baby; *Pej:* **faire des mines,** (i) *A:* to grimace; (ii) to simper, to look affected; **les mines d'une coquette,** the affectations of a flirt.

mine[3], *s.f. A.Gr.Meas. & Num:* mina.

miné [mine], *a. Mil: etc:* mined; *P.N:* **danger! terrain m.,** danger! beware of mines.

mine-piège [minpjɛːʒ], *s.f.* booby-trap; *pl. mines-pièges.*

miner [mine], *v.tr.* to mine, undermine (fortress, etc.); **la mer mine les falaises,** the sea is undermining the cliffs, is eating the cliffs away; **la fièvre l'a miné,** fever has undermined his health; **l'inquiétude a miné sa santé,** anxiety has preyed upon his health; **miné par l'envie,** eaten up, consumed, with envy.

se miner, to waste away; **se m. à attendre des nouvelles,** to pine for, after, news.

minerai [minrɛ], *s.m. Min:* ore; **m. pauvre,** low-grade ore; **m. riche,** high-grade ore, rich ore; **m. de fer,** iron ore; **m. de fer argileux,** band clay, clay ironstone; **m. de fer charbonneux,** black band; **m. métallique,** metalliferous ore; **m. non-métallique,** non-metallic ore.

minéral, -aux [mineral, -o]. **1.** *a.* mineral; (*a*) **le règne m.,** the mineral kingdom; **chimie minérale,** inorganic chemistry; **huile minérale,** mineral oil; (*b*) **eau minérale,** mineral water(s), table water, spa water; **source minérale,** mineral spring; spa. **2.** *s.m.* mineral.

minéralier [mineralje], *s.m. Nau:* ore ship.

minéralisable [mineralizabl̩], *a.* mineralizable.

minéralisateur, -trice [mineralizatœːr, -tris], *Ch: etc:* **1.** *a.* mineralizing (agent). **2.** *s.m.* mineralizer; mineralizing element.

minéralisation [mineralizasjɔ̃], *s.f.* mineralization.

minéralisé [mineralize], *a. Geol:* mineral-bearing; rich in minerals.

minéraliser [mineralize], *v.tr.* **1.** *Metall:* to mineralize; *Agr:* to enrich (soil) with minerals. **2.** to mineralize (table water). **3.** *Ch:* to ash.

minéralogie [mineralɔʒi], *s.f.* mineralogy.

minéralogique [mineralɔʒik], *a.* **1.** mineralogical. **2.** *Adm:* **numéro m.,** registration number (of car); **plaque m.,** number plate (of car).

minéralogiste [mineralɔʒist], **minéralogue** [mineralɔg], *s.m. & f.* mineralogist.

minerie [minri], *s.f.* rock-salt mine.

minerval, -aux [minɛrval, -o]. **1.** *a.* Minervan; **culte m.,** worship, cult, of Minerva. **2.** *s.m. Rom.Ant: Belg: Sch:* minerval.

Minerve [minɛrv]. **1.** *Pr.n.m. Myth:* Minerva; *Lit:* **rimer malgré M.,** to write uninspired verse, to write *invita Minerva.* **2.** *s.f.* (*a*) *Typ: R.t.m:* Minerva (jobbing machine); cropper; (*b*) *F: A:* **avoir de la m.,** to have brains, sense, a good head. **3.** *s.f. Surg:* brace for neck and spinal injuries.

minervien, -ienne [minɛrvjɛ̃, -jɛn], *a. Rom.Ant:* Minervan.

minerviste [minɛrvist], *s.m. & f. Typ:* typesetter (on Minerva machine).

minestrone [minɛstrɔn], *s.m. Cu:* minestrone.

minet, -ette[1] [minɛ, -ɛt]. **1.** *s. F:* (*a*) pussy; (*b*) **mon m., ma minette,** my pet, my darling; (*c*) fashionable, sophisticated, young man, young woman; (*d*) *m.pl.* **des minets,** fluff (under furniture). **3.** *s.f. Bot:* **minette,** black medic, hop medic, hop trefoil, nonesuch.

minette[2], *s.f.* minette (iron ore).

mineur[1], **-euse** [minœːr, -øːz]. **1.** *a.* (*a*) *Ent:* burrowing (insect); **larve mineuse,** miner; (*b*) **ouvrier m.,** miner. **2.** *s.m.* (*a*) miner; **m. de houille,** coal miner, collier; **m. de fond,** underground worker; (*b*) *Mil:* sapper.

mineur[2], **-eure** [minœːr]. **1.** *a.* (*a*) minor, lesser; **l'Asie Mineure,** Asia Minor; *Ecc:* **les ordres mineurs,** the minor orders; **frère m.,** Minorite; (*b*) *Jur:* under age; (*c*) *Mus:* minor (scale, interval, etc.); **tierce mineure,** minor third; **sonate en ut m.,** sonata in C minor; (*d*) *Cards:* **couleur mineure,** minor suit. **2.** *s.* minor, *Jur:* infant; **plaider l'incapacité en tant que m.,** to plead infancy; **mineurs délinquants,** juvenile delinquents. **3.** *s.m. Mus:* minor key; **en m.,** in a minor key. **4.** *s.f. Log:* **mineure,** minor premise; assumption.

mineur-artificier [minœrartifisje], **mineur-boutefeu** [minœrbutfø], *s.m. Min:* shot-firer, blaster; *pl. mineurs-artificiers, mineurs-boutefeux.*

mineur-perforateur [minœrpɛrfɔratœːr], *s.m. Min:* shot-hole driller; *pl. mineurs-perforateurs.*

Mingrélie [mɛ̃greli], *Pr.n. Geog: A:* Mingrelia.

mingrélien, -ienne [mɛ̃greljɛ̃, -jɛn], *a. & s. Geog:* Mingrelian.

mini [mini], *s.f.* **1.** *Aut: R.t.m:* mini. **2.** *Cost: F:* mini (skirt).

miniature [minjatyːr], *s.f.* (*a*) illuminated letter, illumination (on manuscript); (*b*) miniature; **peintre de miniatures,** miniature painter, miniaturist; (*c*) *adv.phr:* **en m.,** in miniature, on a small scale; **c'était un Paris en m.,** it was Paris in miniature; **notre étang était un lac en m.,** our pond was a miniature lake; *attrib.* **golf m.,** miniature golf; **jardin m.,** miniature garden; **poste de radio m.,** miniature radio set; **yacht m.,** model yacht; (*d*) **une m. de . . .,** a small-scale, miniature, model of . . .; **les jardiniers japonais savent, d'un arbre qui normalement aurait 30 mètres de haut, faire une m. d'à peine 15 centimètres,** Japanese gardeners know how to produce, from a tree normally 30 metres high, a miniature of barely 15 centimetres; (*of woman*) **c'est une m.,** she's a (tiny) little slip of a thing.

miniaturé [minjatyre], *a.* (*a*) (*of manuscript*) illuminated; (*b*) **portrait m.,** miniature portrait.

miniaturisation [minjatyrizasjɔ̃], *s.f.* miniaturization.

miniaturiser [minjatyrize], *v.tr.* to miniaturize; to reduce to a very small scale; **m. les postes de radio par les transistors,** to miniaturize radio sets by the use of transistors.

miniaturiste [minjatyrist], *s.m. & f.* miniaturist, miniature painter.

minibasket [minibaskɛt], *s.m. Games:* miniature basket-ball (for children).

minibus [minibyːs], *s.m.* minibus.

minier, -ière [minje, -jɛːr]. **1.** *a.* mining (industry, district, etc.). **2.** *s.f.* **minière,** (*a*) *A:* mine; mineral **deposit;** (*b*) surface, open-cast, mine.

mini(-)jupe [miniʒyp], *s.f.* miniskirt; *pl. mini(-)jupes.*

minima (a) [aminima], *Lt.adv.phr. Jur:* **appel a m.,** appeal by the Public Prosecutor against the leniency of a sentence.

minimal, -aux [minimal, -o], *a.* minimal (effect).

minimaliser [minimalize], *v.tr.* to minimize.

minimaliste [minimalist], *s.m. & f. Pol:* minimalist; *Russ.Hist:* Menshevik.

minime [minim]. **1.** *a.* small, tiny; **perte m.,** trivial loss; **d'une valeur m.,** of trifling value. **2.** *s.m. Ecc.Hist:* Minim. **3.** *s.f. Mus:* minim (in plainsong). **4.** *s.m. & f. Sp:* young player, young athlete (13-15 years of age).

minimiser [minimize], *v.tr.* to minimize; to reduce (sth.) to the minimum.

minimisme [minimism], *s.m. Theol:* minimism.

minimité [minimite], *s.f.* smallness, tininess.

minimum [minimɔm], minimum. 1. *s.m.* **m. de vitesse,** minimum speed; **réduire les frais au m.,** to reduce expenses to a minimum; *Pol.Ec:* **m. vital,** minimum living wage; **les minimums de densité,** the minimum densities; **thermomètre à minima,** minimum thermometer; *pl. minima, minimums.* 2. *a.* (*usu. inv., but f.* **minima** *and pl.* **minima** *or* **minimums** *are often found*); **la largeur, les largeurs, minimum, minima,** the minimum width(s); **prix minimum,** reserve price (at auction); **quantité minimum,** minimal amount; *Mth:* **valeur minima,** minimum value, minimal value; *El:* **charge m. (d'un générateur),** base load; *F:* **un maillot de bain m.,** an abbreviated swimsuit; a bikini. 3. *adv.phr.* **au m.,** as a minimum; at least; **un homme a besoin, au m., de six mètres cubes d'air par heure,** a man needs as a minimim, a minimum of, six cubic metres of air an hour.

minioptère [minjɔptɛːr], *s.m. Z:* long-fingered bat.

ministère [ministɛːr], *s.m.* 1. (*a*) agency; **user du m. de qn,** to make use of s.o.'s services; **par le m. de,** through; (*b*) *Ecc:* **m. des autels, le saint m.,** the ministry; **m. de la prédication, de la parole,** ministry of the Gospel. 2. *Adm:* ministry; (*a*) office; **entrer au m.,** to take office; **être appelé à un m.,** to be called to office; to be called to a Secretaryship of State; (*b*) **former un m.,** to form a ministry, a government, (*in Engl.*) a cabinet; (*c*) Government department; **le M. des Affaires étrangères** = the Foreign Office; **M. de l'Intérieur** = Home Office; **M. du Commerce** = Board of Trade; **Ministère des Travaux publics** = Ministry of Works; **Ministère de la Guerre** = War Office, War Department; **M. de l'Éducation nationale,** *A:* **M. de l'Instruction publique** = Department of Education and Science, *A:* Ministry of Education; *F:* **ce n'est pas de mon m.,** it's not within my province; (*d*) *Jur:* **le Ministère public,** the (Department of the) Public Prosecutor; the prosecuting magistrate.

ministériel, -ielle [ministerjɛl]. 1. *a.* ministerial; **journal m.,** newspaper that supports the Government, Government organ; **commission ministérielle,** departmental committee; **crise ministérielle,** cabinet crisis; *Jur:* **officier m.,** law official (*i.e.* **avoué, huissier,** *or* **notaire**). 2. *s.m. Pol:* ministerialist.

ministériellement [ministerjɛlmɑ̃], *adv.* ministerially.

ministrable [ministrabl̩], *Pol: F:* (*a*) *a.* likely to become a minister; (*b*) *s.m. & f.* a likely choice as minister.

ministrant [ministrɑ̃], *a.* ministering (angel, etc.); **chirurgie ministrante,** minor surgery.

ministre [ministr̩], *s.m.* 1. (*a*) *A. & Lit:* servant, agent (of God, of prince, etc.); (*b*) *Ecc:* (Protestant) minister; clergyman. 2. *Adm:* (*a*) Minister; Secretary of State; **Premier m.,** Prime Minister; **M. des Affaires Étrangères,** Foreign Secretary; **M. de l'Intérieur** = Home Secretary; **M. du Commerce** = President of the Board of Trade; **M. des Finances,** Minister of Finance, = Chancellor of the Exchequer, = *U.S:* Secretary of the Treasury; **M. de la Guerre,** Secretary of State for War; **M. de l'Air,** Air Minister; **M. de la Justice** = (i) the Lord (High) Chancellor; (ii) *U.S:* Attorney-general; **M. des Travaux publics** = minister of Works; **papier m.,** petition paper, = official foolscap; (*b*) **m. plénipotentiaire,** minister plenipotentiary (**auprès de,** to).

minium [minjɔm], *s.m. Ch:* minium; red oxide of lead; *Com:* red lead; **m. de fer,** ferric oxide.

minoen, -enne [minɔɛ̃, -ɛn], *a. & s. Archeol:* Minoan.

minois [minwa], *s.m.* (*a*) *A:* face, countenance; (*b*) (pretty) face (of child, young woman); **son joli m.,** her pretty little face.

minon [minɔ̃], *s.m.* 1. *F:* pussy. 2. *Bot: Dial: O:* catkin, pussy willow. 3. *F:* fluff.

minorant [minɔrɑ̃], *s.m. Mth:* minor, subdeterminant.

minoratif, -ive [minɔratif, -iːv], *a. & s.m. Med: A:* laxative.

minoration [minɔrasjɔ̃], *s.f.* decrease.

minoré [minɔre], *s.m. Ecc:* clerk in minor orders.

minorer [minɔre], *v.tr.* to undervalue; to underestimate; to decrease the importance of (sth.).

minoritaire [minɔritɛːr], (*a*) *a.* of, pertaining to, a minority; **parti m.,** minority party; (*b*) *s.m. & f.* member of a minority.

minorite [minɔrit], *s.m. Ecc:* Minorite.

minorité [minɔrite], *s.f.* minority. 1. nonage; *Jur:* infancy; **appuyer sa défense sur sa m.,** to plead infancy. 2. **être en minorité,** to be in the, in a, minority; **mettre en minorité,** to defeat; **le gouvernement a été mis en m. au parlement,** the government was defeated in parliament; **les minorités ont leurs droits,** minorities have their rights.

Minorque [minɔrk], *Pr.n. Geog:* Minorca.

minorquin, -ine [minɔrkɛ̃, -in], *a. & s. Geog:* Minorcan.

minot[1] [mino], *s.m.* 1. minot (old measure of about 39 litres); **nous ne mangerons pas un m. de sel ensemble,** we shan't be together for long. 2. hard-wheat flour (used for cattle feed). 3. *Dial: F:* (*S.Fr.*) kid, brat.

minot[2], *s.m. A.Nau:* bumpkin.

Minotaure (le) [ləminɔtɔːr], *Pr.n.m. Myth:* the Minotaur.

minoterie [minɔtri], *s.f.* 1. (large) flour mill. 2. flour-milling.

minotier [minɔtje], *s.m.* (flour)miller; owner of a flour mill.

Minquiers (les) [lemɛ̃kje], *Pr.n. Geog:* the Minkies.

Minturnes [mɛ̃tyrn], *Pr.n.f.pl. A.Geog:* Minturnae.

minuit [minɥi], *s.m.* midnight; twelve o'clock (at night); **m. et demi,** half-past twelve at night; **sur le m.,** *F:* **sur les m.,** about midnight; **sur le coup de m.,** on the stroke of midnight; **vers les m.,** towards midnight; **messe de m.,** midnight mass; **soleil de m.,** midnight sun.

mi-nuit [minɥi], *s.f.* middle of the night.

minus [minyːs], *s.m. F:* half-wit, moron, clot.

minuscule [minyskyl], *a.* (*a*) small, tiny, minute; **un salon m.,** a tiny drawing-room; **réformes minuscules,** petty reforms; (*b*) **lettre m.,** *s.f.* **minuscule,** small letter; *Typ:* lower-case letter; *Pal:* minuscule; **édition m.,** miniature edition.

minus habens [minysabɛ̃ːs], *s.m.inv. F:* half-wit, moron, clot; **c'est un m. h.,** he's not very bright, he's a bit of a clot.

minutage [minytaːʒ], *s.m.* 1. *Mil: Th: etc:* timing. 2. drafting (of document).

minutaire [minytɛːr], *a.* (*of document*) in draft (form).

minute [minyt], *s.f.* 1. (*a*) minute (of hour, degree); **je suis à vous dans une m.,** I'll be with you in a minute, a moment; **d'une m. à l'autre,** any minute; **faire qch. à la m.,** to do sth. at a minute's notice, a moment's notice; **vous êtes à la m.,** you're punctual to the, a, minute; **réparations à la m.,** repairs while you wait; *P.N: Com:* **talon m.,** heels (repaired) while you wait; **la m. de vérité,** the moment of truth; **avoir cinq minutes à soi,** to have five minutes to oneself; to have five minutes to spare; **il ne perd pas une minute,** he never wastes a second; *F:* **m. (papillon)!** just a minute! hold on! *s.a.* ENTRECÔTE; (*b*) **m. centésimale,** centesimal minute. 2. (*a*) *A:* small hand(writing); (*b*) minute, draft (of contract, etc.); **faire la m. d'un acte,** to draft an act; *Mapm:* **m. (cartographique),** draft map; (*c*) record (of deed, of judgment).

minuté [minyte], *a.* timed; **horaire m.,** (i) tight schedule; (ii) detailed schedule.

minuter [minyte], *v.tr.* 1. (*a*) to minute, draw up, draft (agreement, etc.); (*b*) to record, enter (deed, judgment). 2. *A:* to purpose, contemplate (an action). 3. to time; **sa journée est soigneusement minutée,** his day is carefully planned; his day is run on a tight schedule; **mon temps est très minuté,** I work to a very tight schedule; **il sait se m.,** he knows how to plan his time, how to work to a schedule.

minuterie [minytri], *s.f.* 1. (*a*) *Clockm: etc:* motion-work, train of wheels; (*b*) **m. d'enregistrement,** counting mechanism (of meter). 2. (*a*) timer, timing mechanism; counting train (of meter); automatic time-switch (for light on stairs, etc.); (*b*) *Dom.Ec:* timer.

minuteur [minytœːr], *s.m. Dom.Ec:* timer.

minutie [minysi], *s.f.* 1. (*a*) minute detail, trifle; (*b*) *pl.* minutiae. 2. meticulousness; attention to minute detail; minuteness; **faire qch. avec m.,** to do sth. meticulously, very carefully.

minutier [minytje], *s.m.* 1. (lawyer's) minute book. 2. (lawyer's) filing cabinet.

minutieusement [minysjøzmɑ̃], *adv.* thoroughly, scrupulously, minutely; meticulously; **examiner m. une affaire,** to go closely into a matter, to go into a matter meticulously.

minutieux, -ieuse [minysjø, -jøːz], *a.* scrupulously careful, meticulous (person); close, thorough, meticulous, searching, minute, detailed (inspection, etc.); **examen m.,** searching examination; **travail m.,** meticulous work.

mi-occlusive [miɔklyziv], *s.f. Ling:* affricate (consonant); *pl. mi-occlusives.*

miocène [mjɔsɛn], *a. & s.m. Geol:* Miocene.

mioche [mjɔʃ], *s.m. & f. F:* small child, mite, kiddie; **bande de mioches,** band of little urchins, of tiny tots.

mi-ouvré [miuvre], *a. Ind:* semi-manufactured; *pl. mi-ouvré(e)s.*

mi-parti [miparti], *a.* (*a*) equally divided (opinions, etc.); halved; (*b*) parti-coloured; **robe mi-partie de blanc et de noir,** dress half black and half white; (*c*) *Her:* party per pale; *pl. mi-parti(e)s.*

mi-partition [mipartisjɔ̃], *s.f.* halving; equal division.

mi-pente (à) [amipɑ̃ːt], *adv.phr.* halfway up or down the hill.

miquelet [miklɛ], *s.m. Hist:* miquelet; (*a*) *A:* Spanish brigand of the Pyrenees; (*b*) irregular Spanish soldier.

mirabelle [mirabɛl], *s.f.* mirabelle plum.

mirabellier [mirabɛlje], *s.m.* mirabelle plum tree.

mirabilis [mirabilis], *s.m. Bot:* mirabilis; *F:* four o'clock; **m. jalapa,** mirabilis jalapa, *F:* marvel of Peru, *U.S:* pretty-by-night.

mirabilite [mirabilit], *s.f. Miner:* mirabilite.

miracle [mirɑːkl̩], *s.m.* 1. miracle; **faire, opérer, un m.,** to perform, work, accomplish, a miracle; **faiseur de miracles,** miracle worker; **cela tient du m.,** it's miraculous; **m. d'architecture,** marvel, miracle, of architecture; **fait à m.,** marvellously well done; **échapper comme par m.,** to have a miraculous escape, a hairbreadth escape; to escape by a hair's breadth; **par m.,** for a wonder; **c'est (un) m. que** + *sub.*, it is a miracle that . . .; **crier (au) m.,** to go into raptures; **il n'y a pas de quoi crier (au) m.,** there's nothing marvellous about it, *F:* it's nothing to rave about. 2. *Lit. Hist:* miracle (play). 3. *a.inv. F:* **produit m.,** wonder product.

miraculé, -ée [mirakyle], *a. & s.* miraculously healed, saved (person); (person) cured, saved by a miracle.

miraculeusement [mirakyløzmɑ̃], *adv.* miraculously; by a miracle; **elle est m. belle,** she's marvellously beautiful.

miraculeux, -euse [mirakylø, -øːz], *a.* (*a*) miraculous; *B:* **la pêche miraculeuse,** the miraculous draught of fishes; **la grotte miraculeuse de Lourdes,** the miraculous grotto at Lourdes; (*b*) **remède m.,** miraculous, marvellous, cure; wonder drug; **il n'y a rien de m. dans sa réussite,** there's nothing miraculous, wonderful, about his success.

mirador [miradɔːr], *s.m.* 1. mirador, belvedere. 2. *Mil:* observation post (in tree, etc.). 3. (traffic policeman's) raised platform; rostrum. 4. watch-tower (of prison camp).

mirage[1] [miraːʒ], *s.m.* (*a*) mirage; (*b*) *Nau:* looming; (*c*) *fata Morgana*; (*d*) *Mil.Av:* Mirage fighter-bomber.

mirage[2], *s.m. Tchn:* candling (of eggs); **lampe de m.,** candling lamp.

mirbane [mirban], *s.f.* **(essence de) m.,** oil of mirbane; nitrobenzene.

mire[1] [miːr], *s.f.* 1. sighting, aiming (of firearm); **ligne de m.,** line of sight; *Artil:* **angle de m.,** angle of sight; *Sm.a:* **m. de nuit,** gloaming sight; **point de m.,** aim; **point de m. de tous les yeux,** target for criticism; *A:* **prendre sa m.,** to take aim. 2. (*a*) sighting mark; *T.V:* test pattern; **m. électronique,** electronic pattern; (*b*) surveyor's pole, (levelling-) staff, rod; **m. à voyant,** target levelling-rod; **m. à coulisse,** sliding staff; **m. de nivellement,** levelling pole; **m. graduée,** levelling rule; (*c*) foresight (of rifle), bead; *s.a.* CRAN[1] 1.

mire[2], *s.m. A:* doctor, apothecary.

mire[3], *s.f.* boar's tusk.

mire-jalon [mirʒalɔ̃], *s.m. Surv:* target levelling-rod; *pl. mires-jalons.*

mire-œufs [mirø], *s.m.inv.* candling apparatus, candling lamp (for eggs).

mirepoix [mirpwa], *s.m. Cu:* Mirepoix (garnish).

mirer [mire], *v.tr.* 1. (*a*) *O:* to aim at, take aim at (sth.); **m. une dot, une place,** to have one's eye on a dowry, on a situation; (*b*) *Surv:* to take a sight on (sth.); (*c*) *P:* to look (closely) at; **appelez-la, que je la mire de près,** call her, so that I can get a good look at her. 2. **m. un œuf,** to candle an egg; **m. du drap,** to look at a piece of material against the light. 3. *Lit:* to reflect; **Venise mire son front dans ses eaux,** the outline of Venice is reflected, mirrored, in her waters.

se mirer, *Lit:* to look at, admire, oneself (in mirror, etc.); **les arbres se mirent dans l'eau,** the trees are mirrored, are reflected, in the water; **se m. dans ses plumes,** to preen oneself; *A:* **se m. dans son ouvrage,** to look upon one's work with complacency.

mirette [mirɛt], *s.f.* **1.** *Bot:* Venus's looking-glass. **2.** *Const:* (mason's) jointer. **3.** *pl. P:* eyes, *P:* optics, peepers.

mireur, -euse [mirœːr, -øːz], *s.* candler (of eggs).

mirifique [mirifik], *a. F:* wonderful, mirific.

mirifiquement [mirifikmɑ̃], *adv. F:* wonderfully.

mirliflor(e) [mirliflɔːr], *s.m. Hist: F:* dandy, exquisite (of the reign of Louis XVI).

mirlipot [mirlipo], *s.m. Cu:* sage tea, infusion of sage.

mirliton [mirlitɔ̃], *s.m.* **1.** eunuch flute, mirliton, kazoo; **vers de m.,** vulgar doggerel, trashy verse. **2.** *Cu:* cream horn. **3.** *Hist: F:* shako (as worn by the troops of the First Republic). **4.** *Rail: Aut:* banded signals (indicating proximity of level crossing, exit to motorway, hidden lights signal, etc.).

mirmidon [mirmidɔ̃], *s.m.* myrmidon.

mirmillon [mirmijɔ̃], *s.m. Ant:* myrmillo.

mirobolant [mirɔbɔlɑ̃], *a. F:* wonderful, prodigious; astounding, staggering (news, etc.); **gains mirobolants,** staggering, stupendous, profits.

mirobolé [mirɔbɔle], *a. O: P:* astonished, flabbergasted, knocked all of a heap.

miroir [mirwaːr], *s.m.* **1.** (*a*) mirror, looking glass; **m. à main,** hand mirror, hand glass; **m. à barbe,** shaving mirror; **m. déformant,** distorting mirror; **m. à facettes,** facet mirror, segmented mirror; **m. (pliant) à trois faces,** triple mirror; *Med:* **m. frontal,** head mirror; *Opt:* **m. concave, convexe,** concave, convex, mirror; **m. parabolique,** parabolic mirror; *Atom.Ph:* **m. magnétique,** magnetic mirror; **m. ardent,** burning mirror; *Av:* **m. d'appontage,** landing mirror (on aircraft carrier); **m. à, aux, alouettes,** (i) *Ven:* lark mirror; twirl; (ii) a snare (and a delusion); **image en m.,** mirror image; **écriture en m.,** mirror writing; *Med:* **paroles en m.,** inversion of syllables, of words (in speaking); *Geol:* **m. de faille,** slickenside; (*b*) **m. d'eau,** ornamental pond, lake, *Lit:* **le m. azuré du lac,** the azure mirror of the lake; *Lit:* **les yeux sont les miroirs de l'âme,** the eyes are the mirrors of the soul; (*c*) *Bot: F:* **m. de Vénus,** Venus's looking glass. **2.** *Cu:* **œufs au m.,** fried eggs. **3.** (*a*) speculum (on wing of bird or insect); eye, ocellus (on peacock's feather); **cheval à m.,** dappled horse; (*b*) *For:* blaze (on tree to be felled). **4.** *Ent: F:* skipper (moth).

miroitant [mirwatɑ̃], *a.* flashing, glistening (armour, etc.); shimmering (lake, etc.); sparkling (jewel); **les rues mouillées et miroitantes,** the wet and glistening streets.

miroité [mirwate], *a.* dappled bay (horse).

miroitement [mirwatmɑ̃], *s.m.* flashing (of lark mirror, etc.); gleam, glisten(ing) (of polished surface); sheen, shimmer.

miroiter [mirwate], *v.i.* to flash; to gleam, glisten; (*of lake, etc.*) to shimmer; (*of jewel*) to sparkle; **les lumières miroitent dans l'eau,** the lights sparkle, glint, in the water; **faire m. l'avenir aux yeux de qn,** to lure s.o. with bright prospects; to hold out bright prospects to s.o.

miroiterie [mirwatri], *s.f.* **1.** (*a*) mirror manufacture; (*b*) mirror trade. **2.** mirror factory.

miroitier, -ière [mirwatje, -jɛːr], *s.* **1.** cutter, silverer, or mounter of mirrors. **2.** dealer in mirrors.

mironton [mirɔ̃tɔ̃], *a. & s.m. F:* queer, odd (type); **un drôle de m.,** a queer cuss.

mironton mirontaine [mirɔ̃tɔ̃mirɔ̃tɛn], burden of some old songs, *e.g.* of "Malbrouk."

miroton [mirɔtɔ̃], *s.m. Cu:* (*a*) hash of beef served with onions; (*b*) **m. de fruits,** stewed fruit.

mirouetté [mirwɛte], *a. A:* = MIROITÉ.

miroutte [mirut], *a.* (*of dark bay horse*) dappled (with lighter colour).

mirtil [mirtil], *s.m.,* **mirtille** [mirtil, mirtiːj], *s.f. Bot:* = MYRTILLE.

misaine [mizɛn], *s.f. Nau:* **(voile de) m.,** (square) foresail; **m. goélette,** fore trysail; **mât de m.,** foremast.

misanthrope [mizɑ̃trɔp]. **1.** *s.m.* misanthropist, misanthrope. **2.** *a.* misanthropic(al) (disposition).

misanthropie [mizɑ̃trɔpi], *s.f.* misanthropy.

misanthropique [mizɑ̃trɔpik], *a.* misanthropic(al).

miscellanées [misɛl(l)ane], *s.f.pl. Lit:* miscellany, miscellanea.

mischmétal [miʃmetal], *s.m.* misch metal.

mischna (la) [lamiʃna], *s.f. Rel.H:* the Mishna(h).

miscibilité [mis(s)ibilite], *s.f.* miscibility.

miscible [mis(s)ibl], *a.* miscible, that can be mixed (avec, with).

mise [miːz], *s.f.* **1.** (*a*) (*putting of sth. in a place*) **m. en place (de qch.),** placing, positioning (of sth.), putting (of sth.) in its place; setting (of boiler, etc.); **m. à la poste,** posting; **m. à l'eau,** launching (of a ship); **m. en bouteilles,** bottling (of wine, etc.); **m. à terre,** (i) landing (of goods); (ii) *El:* earthing, *U.S:* grounding (of current); **m. au tombeau,** entombment; **m. bas,** (i) *Z:* dropping (of young); littering; calving (of cow); lambing (of ewe); farrowing (of sow); kittening (of cat); (ii) *Z:* litter; (iii) *A:* cast-off clothing; (*b*) (*setting, putting, of sth. into a condition, a state*) **m. en pratique d'une maxime,** carrying out, practical application, of a maxim; **m. en jeu de forces,** bringing of forces into play; **m. en musique d'un poème,** setting of a poem to music; **m. à jour,** bringing to light; elucidation (of a mystery); **m. en route,** starting (up); getting under way; *Psy:* **effet de m. en route,** warming up; **m. en garde,** warning, caution; *Com:* **m. en vente,** bringing (of product) on to the market; launching (of new product); publication (of book); **m. à mort,** killing, kill, *Ven:* mort; **m. en eau (d'un barrage),** filling (of a reservoir); *Typ:* **m. en pages,** page-setting; **m. en feu,** firing (of furnace, etc.); *Ball: Space:* **m. à feu,** firing (of rocket); **m. en marche,** starting (of engine, etc.); *Metalw:* **m. en forme à chaud, à froid,** hot, cold, working; *Gram:* **m. en relief,** emphasis; *W.Tel: etc:* **m. en ondes,** production; staging coordination; *Haird:* **m. en plis,** setting; **shampooing et m. en plis,** shampoo and set; **m. en liberté,** releasing, release; **m. en retraite,** pensioning, retiring (on a pension); **demander sa m. à la retraite,** to apply to be retired on a pension; **m. en circulation,** putting (of money) into circulation; **m. à nu de ses pensées,** laying bare of one's thoughts; (*c*) **être de m.,** (i) *A:* (*of money*) to be in circulation; (ii) (*of clothes*) to be in the fashion; to be worn; (iii) (*of pers.*) to be presentable; **un smoking sera de m.,** a dinner jacket may be worn, will be acceptable; **la familiarité n'est pas de m.,** familiarity is (quite) out of place; **au volant d'une voiture de sport un melon n'est pas de m.,** when driving a sports car a bowler hat isn't the thing. **2.** dress, attire; **soigner sa m.,** to dress with care; to be well dressed, carefully dressed; **m. irréprochable,** faultless dress, attire; **elle est simple dans sa m.,** she dresses simply, unostentatiously. **3.** (*a*) *Gaming: Cards:* staking; stake; bet; **doubler sa m.,** to double one's stake, one's bet; *Turf:* **la technique de la m.,** the art of betting, of laying and taking odds; (*b*) bid (at auction sale); **m. à prix,** reserve price; (*c*) *Fin: Com:* **m. hors,** (i) disbursement (of money); (ii) sum advanced; **m. de fonds,** putting up of money, of capital; **fournir, faire, une m. de fonds,** to put up some capital; **sans grande m. de fonds,** without any great outlay; **m. sociale,** working capital (of company); **m. d'un associé,** partner's holding (in a business); *s.a.* METTRE, *and, for phrases not given above, the other noun of the phrase.*

mi-sel (à) [amisɛl], *adj.phr.* partly salted (meat, etc.).

Misène [mizɛn], *Pr.n.m.* **1.** *Lt.Lit:* Misenus. **2.** *Geog:* **le cap M.,** Cape Miseno; *Rom.Hist:* Cape Misenum.

misénite [mizenit], *s.f. Miner:* misenite.

miser [mize], *v.tr.* (*a*) to stake (**sur, on**); **m. vingt francs,** to stake, lay, twenty francs; **m. sur un cheval,** to back a horse; **m. sur les deux tableaux,** to try to have it both ways, to play for safety; **m. sur le mauvais tableau,** to back a loser; *F:* **on ne peut pas m. là-dessus,** you can't count on it; (*b*) to speculate, bank (on a rise, etc.); (*c*) (*at auction sale*) to bid.

misérabilisme [mizerabilism], *s.m. Phil: Lit: Art:* miserabilism.

misérabiliste [mizerabilist], *a.* **peinture m.,** miserabilist painting.

misérable [mizerabl]. **1.** *a.* (*a*) (*after s.*) poor, wretched, miserable; **quartier m.,** poverty-stricken district; **mener une existence m.,** to lead a wretched life; (*b*) (*before s.*) wretched, miserable, worthless; **une m. querelle,** a wretched quarrel; **un m. salaire,** a wretchedly low wage; a mere pittance (of a wage); **pour un m. franc,** for a paltry, wretched, franc; (*c*) (*before s.*) despicable, mean (action, etc.); **un m. acte de vengeance,** a mean (act of) revenge. **2.** *s.m. & f.* (*a*) *O:* poor wretch; person in poor circumstances; (*b*) scoundrel, wretch; **un m. capable de tout,** a scoundrel capable of (doing) anything; *F:* **ah, petit(e) m.!** you little wretch!

misérablement [mizerabləmɑ̃], *adv.* miserably; wretchedly; **mourir m.,** to die abandoned, in (abject) poverty; **vivre m.,** to eke out a wretched existence.

misère [mizɛːr], *s.f.* **1.** misery; (*a*) *Lit:* **vallée de m.,** vale of woe, vale of tears; **manger le pain de m.,** to eat the bread of affliction; **reprendre le collier de m,** to go back to drudgery, to the treadmill; **vous savez la m. des temps,** you know what hard times we are living through; (*b*) trouble, misfortune; **les misères de la guerre,** the distress caused by war; **misères domestiques,** domestic worries; **lit de m.,** (i) bed of sickness; (ii) childbed; **faire des misères à qn,** to tease s.o. unmercifully. **2.** extreme poverty, destitution; **dans la m.,** poverty-stricken; **tomber dans la m.,** to fall into distress; to come to want; **mourir de m.,** to die of want; **réduire qn à la m.,** to reduce s.o. to destitution; **dames réduites à la m.,** distressed gentlewomen; **avoir un air de m.,** to look poverty-stricken; **crier m.,** to plead poverty; **vêtements qui crient m.,** shabby, threadbare, garments; **maison qui crie m.,** dilapidated house; **ils sont presque dans la m.,** they are very badly off; **pour parer à la m.,** to keep the wolf from the door. **3.** *F:* trifle; **cent francs? une m.!** a hundred francs? a mere nothing! **4.** *Cards:* misère.

misérer [mizere], *v.i.* (**je misère, n. misérons; je misérerai**) *A: F:* to live in poverty, in penury.

miserere, miséréré [mizerere], *s.m.inv. Ecc: Mus:* miserere; *Med: A:* **colique de m.,** iliac passion.

miséreux, -euse [mizerø, -øːz], *a. & s.* **1.** poverty-stricken, destitute (person); **secourir les m.,** to help the poor; **cabane à l'air m.,** wretched hovel. **2.** shabby-genteel; seedy-looking (person).

miséricorde [mizerikɔrd], *s.f.* **1.** mercy, mercifulness; **crier m.,** to cry, beg, for mercy; **se remettre à la m. de qn,** to throw oneself on s.o.'s mercy; **être à la m. de qn,** to be at s.o.'s mercy; **faire m. à qn,** to be merciful to s.o.; **la m. infinie de Dieu,** the infinite mercy of God; **à tout péché miséricorde,** no sin but should find mercy; *Nau: A:* **ancre de m.,** sheet anchor. **2.** *Ecc: Art:* misericord, miserere (on under side of tilt-up seat in choir stall). **3.** *A:* misericord(e) (dagger). **4.** *int.* heavens above! heaven help us!

miséricordieusement [mizerikɔrdjøzmɑ̃], *adv.* mercifully.

miséricordieux, -ieuse [mizerikɔrdjø, -jøːz], *a. & s.* merciful (**envers,** to); *B:* **bienheureux sont les m.,** blessed are the merciful.

mishnaïque [miʃnaik], *a. Rel:* Mishnaic.

mis(o)- [miz(ɔ)], *pref.* mis(o)-.

misogame [mizɔgam], *s.m. & f.* misogamist.

misogamie [mizɔgami], *s.f.* misogamy.

misogyne [mizɔʒin]. **1.** *a.* misogynous. **2.** *s.m. & f.* misogynist, woman-hater.

misogynie [mizɔʒini], *s.f.* misogyny.

misologie [mizɔlɔʒi], *s.f.* misology.

misologue [mizɔlɔg], *s.m.* misologist.

misonéisme [mizɔneism], *s.m.* misoneism.

misonéiste [mizɔneist]. **1.** *a.* misoneistic. **2.** *s.m. & f.* misoneist; **m. endurci,** determined opponent of new-fangled ideas.

mi-souverain [misuvrɛ̃], *a.m.* **état mi-s.,** protectorate; semi-sovereign state; *pl. mi-souverains.*

mispickel [mispikɛl], *s.m. Miner:* mispickel, arsenical pyrites.

miss [mis], *s.f. F:* (*a*) *A:* (English) governess; (*b*) beauty queen; **parmi toutes ces m. il ne se trouvera qu'une Miss Monde,** among all these beauty queens there will be only one Miss World; *pl. miss, misses.*

missel [misɛl], *s.m. Ecc:* missal; (altar) mass book.

missile [misil], *s.m.* guided missile; **m. balistique de moyenne portée,** intermediate range ballistic missile; **m. intercontinental,** intercontinental ballistic missile; **m. à tête chercheuse,** homing missile; **m. antimissile,** anti-missile missile; **m. antifusée(s),** anti-ballistic missile (A.B.M.); **m. à têtes, à ogives, multiples,** multiple-warhead missile, *U.S:* multiple independently targeted re-entry vehicle.

missiologie [misjɔlɔʒi], *s.f. Ecc:* missiology.

mission [misjɔ̃], *s.f.* mission. **1.** (*a*) commission; **avoir m. de faire qch.,** to be commissioned to do sth.; **prêcher sans m.,** to speak, act, without authority; **ministre en m. spéciale à Paris,** minister on (a) special mission to Paris; **m. diplomatique, économique,** diplomatic, economic, mission; **m. scientifique,** scientific expedition; **partir en m. au pôle nord,** to go on an expedition to the North Pole; *Mil:* **en m.,** on detached service; **m. de combat,** battle task, mission; **m. de reconnaissance,** reconnaissance mission, *Av:* sortie, flight; **en m. de reconnaissance,** on reconnaissance duty; **m. principale, secondaire,** primary, secondary, mission; **m. générale, particulière,** general, special, mission; **répartition des missions,** distribution, allotment, of tasks, of missions; **attribuer une m. à qn, à une unité,** to assign a mission, a task, to s.o., to a unit; **effectuer une m.,** to carry out, execute, a mission, a task; **m. accomplie,** mission accomplished; (*b*) *Ecc:* **missions étrangères,** foreign missions; **faire des dons aux missions,** to give to the missions; (*c*) function; task; rôle; **la m. de l'université est d'enseigner et de promouvoir la recherche,** the aim, function, of the university is to teach and to promote research; **la m. de l'art n'est pas de copier la nature,** the rôle of art is not to copy nature; **se donner pour m. de faire qch.,** to set oneself the task of doing sth.; **il a failli dans sa m.,** he failed in his mission; he did not achieve his aim. 2. *Ecc:* mission station; missionary field. 3. *coll.* envoys; delegation, mission; **faire partie de la m.,** to be a member of the delegation.

missionnaire [misjɔnɛːr], *Ecc:* 1. *s.m.* missionary. 2. *a.* **œuvre, esprit, m.,** missionary work, spirit.

missionnariat [misjɔnarja], *s.m.* (*functions of a missionary*) mission.

Mississipi (le) [ləmisisipi], *Pr.n.m. Geog:* the (river) Mississippi.

mississipien, -ienne [misisipjɛ̃, -jɛn], *a. & s.m. Geog: Geol:* Mississipian.

missive [misiːv]. 1. *a.f. A. & Jur:* **lettre m.,** letter missive. 2. *s.f.* missive; letter.

missourien, -ienne [misurjɛ̃, -jɛn], *a. & s.* (*a*) *Geog:* Missourian; (*b*) *Geol:* Missourian, upper Middle Pennsylvanian.

mistelle [mistɛl], *s.f. Com:* (*a*) wine made of unfermented grape juice blended with alcohol; (*b*) basis wine.

mistenflûte [mistɑ̃flyt], *s.m. A: F:* thingumbob, what's-his-name.

misti [misti], *s.m. Cards: F:* = MISTIGRI 2.

mistigri [mistigri], *s.m.* 1. *F:* puss; grimalkin. 2. *Cards:* (*at trente et un, etc.*) knave of clubs; pam.

mistoufle [mistufl], *s.f.* 1. *P:* poverty; **être dans la m.,** to be hard up, cleaned out. 2. *F:* **faire des mistoufles à qn,** to annoy, tease, plague, s.o.

mistoufler [mistufle], *v.tr. F:* to annoy, tease, plague (s.o.).

mistral [mistral], *s.m.* (*a*) *Meteor:* (*S.E.Fr.*) mistral; (*b*) *Rail:* crack express train.

mistron [mistrɔ̃], *s.m. Cards: P:* trente et un.

mitaine[1] [mitɛn], *s.f.* (*a*) mitten; *F:* **y aller avec des mitaines,** to set to work with great caution, with kid gloves; **dire qch. sans mitaines,** to blurt sth. out; to tell sth. bluntly; **je n'ai pas pris de mitaines pour le lui dire,** I didn't mince matters with him; *Box: F:* **mettre les mitaines,** to put on the gloves, *F:* the mitts; (*b*) *Fr.C:* (protestant) church; (*c*) *Com:* damaged beaver skin.

mitaine[2]. *See* MITON[4].

mitan [mitɑ̃], *s.m. Dial:* middle, centre; **au m. de la place,** in the centre of the square.

mitard [mitaːr], *s.m. P:* (*a*) disciplinary cell (in prison), cooler; (*b*) **faire du m.,** to lie low.

mitarder [mitarde], *v.tr. P:* **se faire m.,** to get put in the cooler.

mite [mit], *s.f.* 1. mite, acarid; **m. du fromage,** cheese mite; **fromage plein de mites,** cheese alive with mites. 2. (*a*) moth worm; (*b*) clothes moth; **fourrure rongée, mangée, des mites,** motheaten fur.

mité [mite], *a.* motheaten.

mitelle [mitɛl], *s.f.* 1. *Bot:* mitella, mitre wort, bishop's cap. 2. *Surg:* mitella.

mi-temps [mitɑ̃]. 1. *s.f.inv. Fb: etc:* (*a*) **la m.-t.,** half-time; interval; (*b*) **la première, seconde, m.-t.,** the first, second, half. 2. *adv.phr.* **emploi à mi-t.,** part-time employment.

miter (se) [səmite], *v.pr.* to become motheaten.

mi-terme (à) [amitɛrm], *adv.phr.* 1. half way through (the term, the period); **accoucher à m.-t.,** to miscarry half way through pregnancy. 2. on half-quarter day.

miteusement [mitøzmɑ̃], *adv. F:* shabbily (dressed).

miteux, -euse [mitø, -øːz], *a.* 1. *A:* blear(y)-eyed. 2. *F:* (*a*) shabby, disreputable (clothes); dilapidated, tatty (furniture); shabbily-dressed, seedy-looking (person); **hôtel m.,** poor-looking, third-rate, hotel; **dans un état m.,** in a pitiable state; **laboratoire un peu m.,** poorly-equipped laboratory; (*b*) *s.* shabby, down-at-heel, person; **ce n'est pas un endroit pour des m. comme nous,** it's not a place for poor, shabby, types like us.

Mithra(s) [mitra, mitraːs], *Pr.n.m. Rel.H:* Mithra(s).

mithracisme [mitrasism], **mithriacisme** [mitrjasism], *s.m.* Mithraism.

mithriaque [mitrijak], *a.* Mithraic.

Mithridate [mitridat]. 1. *Pr.n.m. Hist:* Mithridates, Mithradates. 2. *s.m. A.Pharm:* mithridate, antidote; *F: A:* **vendeur de m.,** charlatan, quack.

mithridatique [mitridatik], *a. Hist:* Mithridatic.

mithridatisation [mitridatizasjɔ̃], *s.f. Med:* mithridatising.

mithridatiser [mitridatize], *v.tr.* to mithridatize, to immunize (against poison, by giving gradually increasing doses).

mithridatisme [mitridatism], *s.m.* mithridatism, immunity from poison.

mitigation [mitigasjɔ̃], *s.f.* mitigation.

mitigé [mitiʒe], *a.* mitigated, modified; **morale mitigée,** lax morals; *Jur:* **peine mitigée,** reduced sentence.

mitigeant [mitiʒɑ̃], *a.* mitigating, modifying.

mitiger [mitiʒe], *v.tr.* (**je mitigeai(s); n. mitigeons**) 1. to mitigate (pain, penalty); to modify (penalty). 2. to relax (rule, law).

mitigeur [mitiʒœːr], *s.m. Dom.Ec:* **m. de douche,** shower mixer, mixing valve; tap with temperature control.

mitis [mitis], *s.m. A:* puss (in la Fontaine's fables).

mitochondrie [mitɔkɔ̃dri], *s.f. Biol:* mitochondrion.

mi-toile (en) [ɑ̃mitwal], *adv.phr. Bookb:* in half-cloth.

miton[1] [mitɔ̃], *s.m. A:* woollen wristlet; *A:* muffetee.

miton[2], *s.m. F:* crumb (of the loaf).

miton[3], *s.m. F:* puss, pussy.

miton[4], *found in* **m. mitaine** (*originally burden of old songs*), *and used in the phr.:* **onguent m. mitaine,** innocuous (and worthless) salve; **explications m. mitaine,** *F:* eyewash.

mitonnage [mitɔnaːʒ], *s.m. Cu:* bread soup.

mitonner [mitɔne]. 1. *v.tr.* (*a*) *Cu:* to let (bread) boil to pulp (in the soup); to let (the soup) simmer; (*b*) to concoct (sth. special); **m. un projet,** to nurse, prepare quietly, a project; **qu'est-ce qui se mitonne?** what's brewing? what's in the wind? (*c*) to coddle, pamper (child, etc.); **homme qu'il faut m.,** man who must be humoured. 2. *v.i.* (*of soup, etc.*) to simmer.

mitonnerie [mitɔnri], *s.f. F:* humouring, wheedling.

mitose [mitoːz], *s.f. Biol:* mitosis.

mitotique [mitɔtik], *a.* mitotic.

mitouflets [mituflɛ], *s.m.pl. P:* gloves.

mitouissan [mitwisɑ̃], *s.m. Orn:* scaup (duck).

mitoyen, -yenne [mitwajɛ̃, -jɛn], *a.* 1. intermediate (space); **mur m.,** party wall; **cloison mitoyenne,** dividing wall (between two rooms); *Mil:* **route mitoyenne,** road common to two sectors, to both sectors; **puits m.,** well common to two houses; *A:* **prendre le parti m.,** to take the middle course. 2. *s.f. Z:* **mitoyenne,** central incisor (of horse, cow, sheep).

mitoyenneté [mitwajɛnte], *s.f.* joint ownership (of party wall, hedge, ditch, etc.); joint use (of a well, etc.).

mitraillade [mitrɑjad, -aja-], *s.f.* (*a*) *A:* discharge of case-shot, of grapeshot, *Nau:* of langrage; (*b*) machine-gunning, machine-gun fire.

mitraillage [mitrɑjaːʒ, -aja-], *s.m.* 1. machine-gunning. 2. *Geol:* corrosion (by waves).

mitraille [mitrɑːj], *s.f.* 1. (*a*) *A:* **m. de fer,** scrap-iron; (*b*) *A.Mil:* case-shot, canister-shot, grape-shot; *Nau:* langrage; **boîte à m.,** canister; **tirer à m.,** to fire case-shot; (*c*) hail of bullets. 2. *F:* copper coinage, coppers.

mitrailler [mitrɑje], *v.tr.* (*a*) *Mil:* to machine-gun; to pepper, rake, (enemy's troops, etc.) (i) *A:* with grapeshot, (ii) with machine-gun fire; (*b*) **m. qn (de questions),** to fire questions at s.o., to pepper s.o. with questions; *F:* **les photographes mitraillent les délégués,** the photographers are taking shots of the delegates.

mitraillette [mitrɑjɛt, -aj-], *s.f.* sub-machine-gun; **m. sten,** sten gun.

mitrailleur [mitrɑjœːr, -aj-], *s.m.* 1. *Mil:* machine-gunner; **m. guetteur,** gunner-observer; *Mil.Av:* **m. d'avion,** air gunner; **m. avant,** front gunner; **m. arrière,** rear gunner; *a.* **fusil m.,** Bren gun. 2. *A: F:* butcher of the people (always ready to quell a riot with grape-shot).

mitrailleuse [mitrɑjøːz, -aj-], *s.f. Mil:* 1. *A:* mitrailleuse (*esp.* multiple-barrelled gun of 1870). 2. machine-gun; **mitrailleuses jumelées,** twin machine-guns; **groupe de mitrailleuses,** machine-gun section; **section de mitrailleuses,** machine-gun platoon; **mettre la m. sur son affût,** to mount, set up, the gun; **enlever la m. de son affût,** to dismount the gun; *Mil.Av:* **m. d'aviation, d'avion,** aircraft machine-gun; **m. avant,** front machine-gun; **m. arrière,** aft, rear, machine-gun; **m. d'aile,** wing machine-gun.

mitral, -ale, -aux [mitral, -o]. 1. *a.* mitral (valve of the heart, etc.). 2. *s. Med:* person suffering from a diseased mitral valve.

mitre [mitr], *s.f.* 1. (*a*) mitre (of bishop, etc.); (*b*) *A:* (baker's) paper cap. 2. (*a*) chimney pot; (*b*) chimney cowl; **m. à tête mobile,** gyrating cowl; chimney jack. 3. bolster (of table knife). 4. *Moll:* mitre shell. 5. *A: P:* prison, clink.

mitré [mitre], *a.* 1. mitred (abbot). 2. *A: P:* in prison; jugged.

mitriforme [mitrifɔrm], *a. Nat.Hist:* mitriform.

mitron [mitrɔ̃], *s.m.* 1. *A:* (baker's) paper cap. 2. baker's assistant. 3. *Const:* chimney-cowl seating.

mitte [mit], *s.f. F:* 1. ammoniacal exhalation (from cesspool). 2. sewerman's ophthalmia.

mive [miːv], *s.f.* **m. de coing,** quince jelly.

mi-vent [mivɑ̃], *s.m.inv.* fruit tree stunted by being in an exposed position.

mi-vitesse (à) [amivitɛs], *adv.phr.* at half-speed.

mi-voix (à) [amivwa], *adv.* in an undertone, under one's breath, in a subdued voice.

mixage [miksaːʒ], *s.m. Cin: etc:* mixing (of sounds).

mixe(u)r [miksœːr], *s.m. Dom.Ec:* 1. mixer. 2. liquidizer.

mixite [miksit], *s.f. Miner:* mixite.

mixité [miksite], *s.f. Sch:* co-education.

mixosaurus [miksɔsɔryːs], *s.m. Paleont:* Mixosaurus.

mixte [mikst], *a.* 1. mixed (race, bathing, etc.); composite; **école m.,** co-educational, mixed, school; *Ecc:* **mariage m.,** mixed marriage (between catholic and non-catholic); **commission m.,** joint commission; *Jur:* **action m.,** mixed action; *Nau:* **navire m.,** composite ship (of wood and steel); **pont m.,** steel and reinforced concrete bridge; *Geol:* **cône m.,** composite cone; *Ling:* **son m.,** mixed sound; *s.m. Ten:* **m. double,** mixed doubles. 2. serving a double purpose; *Rail:* **train m.,** composite train (goods and passengers); **wagon, voiture, m.,** carriage with compartments of different classes, composite coach; **billet m.,** combined rail and road ticket; **pont m.,** road and rail bridge.

mixtiligne [mikstiliɲ], *a.* mixtilineal, mixtilinear.

mixtion [miksjɔ̃], *s.f.* 1. compounding (of drugs, etc.). 2. (*a*) *Pharm:* mixture; (*b*) gold-size, mordant, mixtion.

mixtionner [miksjɔne], *v.tr.* to compound (drug).

mixture [mikstyːr], *s.f.* (*a*) mixture (*esp.* of drugs); **m. frigorifique,** freezing mixture; *F: Pej:* **ce n'est pas du café, c'est une affreuse m.,** it's not coffee, it's a horrible mixture; (*b*) *Mus:* **jeu de m.,** mixture stop, furniture stop (of organ); (*c*) *Agr:* mixture of grains (for sowing).

mnémonique [mnemɔnik]. 1. *a.* mnemonic. 2. *s.f.* mnemonics.

mnémoniser [mnemɔnize], *v.tr.* to mnemonize; to remember (sth.) by mnemonic methods; to memorize.

mnémotechnicien, -ienne [mnemɔtɛknisjɛ̃, -jɛn], *s.* mnemotechnist; mnemonist.

mnémotechnie [mnemɔtɛkni], *s.f.* mnemonics, mnemotechny.

mnémotechnique [mnemɔtɛknik]. 1. *a.* mnemotechnic. 2. *s.f.* mnemotechny, mnemonics.

moabite [moabit], *a. & s. B.Hist:* Moabite.

mobile [mɔbil]. 1. *a.* (*a*) mobile, movable; **fête m.,** movable feast; (*b*) unstable, inconstant, changeable, fickle (nature); restless, excitable (population); **physionomie m.,** mobile features; (*c*) detachable; **objectif m.,** detachable lens, screw-on lens; **album à feuilles mobiles,** loose-leaf album; *Typ:* **caractères mobiles,** movable type; (*d*) moving (body, target, etc.); shifting, changing (expression, etc.); sliding (poppet of lathe, etc.); **organes mobiles,** sliding, working, parts; *Fr.C:* **escalier m.,** moving staircase, escalator; *I.C.E: etc:* **axe m.,** floating gudgeon-pin; *Med:* **rein m.,** floating kidney; *Mil:* **colonne m.,** flying column; *Fr.Hist:* **garde m.,** militia (of 1848, of 1868-71); **La Garde M., la Gendarmerie M.,** the Mobile Guard = security (state) police; **un garde, un gendarme, m.,** a member of the *Garde Mobile*, the *Gendarmerie Mobile*. 2. *s.m.* (*a*) moving body, body in motion; (*b*) driving power; (i) (*of pers.*) **premier m. dans un complot,** prime mover in a plot; originator of a plot; (ii) incitement; **m. d'un crime,** motive of a crime; **cette passion était le m. de tous ses actes,** every action of his was prompted by this passion; **la gloire est un puissant m. de toutes les grandes âmes,** fame is a powerful spur to all great souls; **m. d'achat,** buying impulse; *A.Astr & F:* **le premier m.,** the *primum mobile* (*c*) *Art:* mobile. 3. *s.m. Hist:*

les mobiles de 1870, the 1870 militia, the militiamen of 1870.

mobiliaire [mɔbiljɛːr], *a. Jur: A:* = MOBILIER 1.

mobilier, -ière [mɔbilje, -jɛːr]. **1.** *a. Jur:* movable, personal; **action mobilière,** personal action; **biens mobiliers,** personal estate, chattels, personalty, *Scot:* movables; **saisie mobilière,** distraint on furniture; **héritier m.,** heir to personal estate; *Fin:* **valeurs mobilières,** stocks and shares; transferable securities. **2.** *s.m.* (*a*) furniture; (*b*) set, suite, of furniture; **m. de salon,** drawing-room suite.

mobilisable [mɔbilizabl̩], *a.* mobilizable (troops, real estate); (capital) that can be made available.

mobilisation [mɔbilizasjɔ̃], *s.f.* mobilization (of troops, of real estate); liquidation, liberation (of capital); realization (of war indemnity, etc.).

mobilisé [mɔbilize]. **1.** *a.* mobilized, called up. **2.** *s.m.* serviceman; **anciens mobilisés,** ex-servicemen.

mobiliser [mɔbilize], *v.tr.* (*a*) to mobilize (troops, real estate); to call out, call up (reservist); to liberate (capital); to set (money) free; (*b*) **m. tous ses amis,** to round up all one's friends; **m. toute son énergie,** to summon up all one's strength.

mobilisme [mɔbilism], *s.m.* (the) use of movable-frame hives.

mobilité [mɔbilite], *s.f.* **1.** mobility, movableness (of body); mobility (of features); *Pol.Ec:* **m. sociale,** social mobility; **taux de m.,** migration rate. **2.** changeableness, instability (of character). **3.** *Ph:* **m. d'un ion,** ion mobility.

Möbius[1] [mœbjyːs], *Pr.n. Mth:* **ruban de M.,** Möbius band, strip.

Möbius[2], *Pr.n. Med:* **maladie de M.,** Möbius's disease, ophthalmoplegic migraine.

moblot [mɔblo], *s.m. Fr.Hist: F:* militiaman (of 1870).

Mobylette [mɔbilɛt], *s.f. R.t.m:* (*often used for a*) light motor cycle.

mocassin [mɔkasɛ̃], *s.m.* **1.** *Cost:* mocassin; *pl.* **mocassins,** casuals, casual shoes, *U.S:* loafers. **2.** *Rept:* **m. d'eau,** cottonmouth, water moccasin.

moche[1] [mɔʃ], *s.f. Tex:* package, moche (of spun silk).

moche[2], *a. F:* rotten, lousy (conduct, etc.); poor, shoddy (work); ugly, misbegotten (individual); dowdy, badly-dressed (woman); **elle est m. comme un pou, m. à pleurer,** she's as ugly as sin; **la pluie pendant les vacances, c'est m.,** it's lousy having rain in the holidays; **c'est m. ce qu'il a fait,** that's a dirty trick.

mocheté [mɔʃte], *s.f. F:* (*a*) (*of woman*) **quelle m.,** what a hag; what an ugly mug; (*b*) (*of thgs*) **ce complet! a-t-on jamais vu une m. pareille?** have you ever seen such a lousy suit?

moco [mɔko], *s.m. Nau: P:* Provençal; native of Toulon, of Marseille(s).

mococo [mɔkɔko], *s.m. Z:* macaco.

modal, -aux [mɔdal, -o]. **1.** *a. Jur: Log: Mus:* modal. **2.** *s.f.* **modale,** (*a*) *Log:* modal proposition; (*b*) *Mus:* modal note (major or minor third or sixth).

modalité [mɔdalite]. **1.** *Phil:* modality. **2.** *Ecc. Mus:* (*a*) mode; (*b*) modality. **3.** *pl.* ways and means; *Jur:* (restrictive) clauses; **modalités d'une entente,** lines on which an understanding can be reached; **modalités d'application,** mode of application; **modalités d'utilisation, de mise en œuvre,** operating conditions; **modalités de paiement,** methods of payment; *Fin:* **modalités d'une émission,** terms and conditions of an issue; **les modalités de cette opération,** the procedure for doing this, the way in which this is to be done.

mode[1] [mɔd], *s.f.* **1.** fashion; (*a*) **vivre à sa m.,** to live according to one's own fancy, in one's own way; (*b*) **amener la m. de faire qch.,** to bring in the fashion of doing sth.; **mener la m.,** to set the fashion; **lancer la m. de qch., mettre qch. à la m.,** to bring sth. into fashion; **la m. s'établit de . . .,** it is becoming the custom, the fashion, to . . .; **être de m., à la m.,** to be in fashion, in vogue; **cela n'est plus de m.,** it is no longer the fashion, in fashion; **devenir à la m.,** to come into fashion; **passer de m.,** to go out of fashion; **la redingote a passé de m.,** the frock-coat has gone out; **passé de m.,** out of fashion, out of date; **à l'ancienne m.,** in the old style; **Noël à l'ancienne m.,** old-fashioned Christmas (celebrations); **à la dernière m.,** in the latest, newest, fashion; in the height of fashion; **robe à la m.,** fashionable dress; **lingerie dans tous les coloris m.,** lingerie in all the leading shades; **suivre la m.,** (i) to follow the fashion; (ii) to be in the swim; *Com:* **la haute m.,** the fashion trade; **le thé dansant était à la m., la m. était au thé dansant,** thé dansant was fashionable, all the rage; **à la mode de . . .,** after the style, manner, of . . .; *s.a.* BŒUF 2. **2.** *pl. Com:* (*a*) ladies' dresses; fashions; **gravures de modes,** fashion plates; (*b*) **(articles de) modes,** millinery; **magasin de modes,** milliner's shop.

mode[2], *s.m.* **1.** *Log:* mode, mood. **2.** *Gram:* mood. **3.** *Mus:* (*a*) mode (in plainsong); (*b*) (major, minor) mode or mood. **4. il était impossible de parler de son cas sur le m. raisonnable,** it was impossible to talk reasonably about his case. **5.** method, mode (of education, of demonstration, of use, etc.); **m. d'emploi,** directions for use; method of using; **m. d'emploi de la règle à calcul,** operation of the slide rule; **m. de fonctionnement,** mode of operation; **m. de vie,** mode, way, of life.

modelage [mɔdlaːʒ], *s.m.* modelling (in clay, etc.); *Metall:* **m. mécanique,** pattern making.

modèle [mɔdɛl]. **1.** *s.m.* (*a*) model, pattern; **m. de chèque, de lettre de change,** form of wording for a cheque, for a bill of exchange; **m. de broderie,** sampler; **m. d'écriture,** handwriting copy; calligraph; **machines toutes bâties, établies, sur le même m.,** machines all built to one pattern, on the same lines; **m. déposé,** registered pattern; **m. réduit, à petite échelle,** scale model; **m. réduit de yacht,** model yacht; **construction de modèles réduits,** model making; **constructeur de modèles réduits d'avions,** aero-modeller; *Dent:* **m. de cire, de plâtre,** wax model, plaster model; *Ind: etc:* **m. de démonstration,** demonstration model; **m. périmé,** obsolete type; *Mil:* **m. réglementaire,** regulation pattern; **prendre qn pour m., prendre m. sur qn,** to take s.o. as one's model, as one's pattern; to take a leaf out of s.o.'s book; *s.a.* GENRE 3; **il est le m. des pères,** he is a model father; **m. de vertu,** paragon of virtue; (*b*) *Mec.E:* template; *Metall:* pattern (of casting); *Cost:* model gown, hat; (*c*) *Com: etc:* (*article*) **grand, petit, m.,** large-, small-size (article); (*d*) *Typ:* subject, copy; **m. à teintes continues,** continuous tone subject; **m. de trait,** line subject; **porte-m.,** copy-board, copyholder. **2.** *s.m.* (artist's) model; **il a épousé un de ses modèles,** he married one of his models; **figure dessinée d'après le m.,** figure drawn from the model; **servir de m. à un artiste,** to sit for an artist, to model for an artist. **3.** *a.* **un époux m.,** a model, exemplary, husband; **écolier m.,** model pupil; **échantillon m.,** standard sample.

modelé [mɔdle], *s.m.* (*a*) *Art:* relief; (*b*) *Mapm:* representation of hill features (on maps); hill shading; (*c*) *Geog:* surface relief.

modeler [mɔdle], *v.tr.* **(je modèle, n. modelons; je modèlerai)** to model; (*a*) to mould (clay, etc.); **m. la destinée de qn,** to shape s.o.'s destiny; (*b*) to make a model, a pattern, of (figure, casting).

se modeler sur qn, to take s.o. as a pattern; to copy s.o.; to model one's conduct on that of s.o.

modèlerie [mɔdɛlri], *s.f. Metall:* pattern making.

modeleur [mɔdlœːr], *s.m.* modeller; *Metall:* pattern maker.

modélisme [mɔdelism], *s.m.* model making.

modéliste [mɔdelist], **modelliste** [mɔdɛlist], *s.m. & f.* (*a*) model maker; (*b*) dress designer; (*c*) pattern maker.

modem [mɔdɛm], *s.m. Elcs:* modem.

modénais, -aise [mɔdenɛ, -ɛːz], *a. & s. Geog:* Modenese.

modénature [mɔdenatyːr], *s.f. Arch:* (proportions and) outline (of building).

Modène [mɔdɛn], *Pr.n.f. Geog:* Modena.

moder [mɔdɛːr], *s.m. Geol:* moder.

modérantisme [mɔderɑ̃tism], *s.m.* **1.** *Fr.Hist:* moderantism (during the Revolution). **2.** *Pol:* moderate opinions.

modérantiste [mɔderɑ̃tist], *s.m. & f.* **1.** *Fr.Hist:* moderantist. **2.** *Pol:* person of moderate opinions, moderate.

modérateur, -trice [mɔderatœːr, -tris]. **1.** *a.* moderating, restraining. **2.** *s.* moderator, restrainer. **3.** *s.m. Mec.E: etc:* regulator, governor (of engine, etc.); *El:* damper (of magnetic needle); *Atom.Ph:* moderator; **m. de neutrons,** neutron moderator; **lampe à m.,** moderator lamp; **m. de son,** volume control (of gramophone, of radio); *Phot:* **m. du voile chimique,** restrainer (in developing solution); *Const:* **m. de pression,** pressure regulator; *Med:* **m. de l'appétit,** appetite reducer.

modération [mɔderasjɔ̃], *s.f.* **1.** moderation, restraint; temperateness; **avec m.,** temperately, with moderation. **2. m. de prix,** reduction in price; **m. de peine,** mitigation of penalty; **apporter les modérations à un impôt,** to reduce a tax; **demande en m. d'impôt,** request for diminution of taxes, of rates.

moderato [mɔderato], *adv. Mus:* moderato.

modéré, -ée [mɔdere]. **1.** *a.* (*a*) moderate; conservative; temperate (person); reasonable (price, etc.); **allure modérée,** moderate, steady, pace; **acclamations modérées,** subdued cheers; *Iron:* mild cheers; **selon des estimations modérées,** according to conservative estimates; **m. dans ses désirs,** reasonable, moderate, in one's desires; (*b*) **m. envers qn,** moderate in one's demands on s.o.; (*c*) *Pol:* moderate (party, views). **2.** *s. Pol:* conservative; person of moderate opinions, moderate.

modérément [mɔderemɑ̃], *adv.* moderately, in moderation, temperately.

modérer [mɔdere], *v.tr.* **(je modère, n. modérons; je modérerai) 1.** (*a*) to moderate, restrain, temper, check (passions, etc.); to regulate (machine, etc.); **m. son impatience,** to curb one's impatience; **m. ses dépenses,** to reduce one's expenses; **m. la vitesse d'une machine,** to reduce the speed of a machine; (*b*) *El:* to damp (magnetic needle). **2.** to reduce (price, etc.); to mitigate (penalty).

se modérer. 1. to control oneself; to keep cool, calm; to calm down. **2.** (*of wind, etc.*) to abate, to subside; **le temps s'est modéré,** the storm has died down, has abated.

moderne [mɔdɛrn], *a.* modern (times, writer, etc.); **enseignement m.,** modern side (in schools); **maison m.,** modern, up-to-date, house; *Hist:* **époque m.,** post-mediæval period (1453-1789); *s.* **les anciens et les modernes,** the ancients and the moderns; *adv.phr.* **à la moderne,** in the modern style.

modernisation [mɔdɛrnizasjɔ̃], *s.f.* modernization, modernizing.

moderniser [mɔdɛrnize], *v.tr.* to modernize; **se m.,** to be, become, modern; to bring oneself up to date.

modernisme [mɔdɛrnism], *s.m.* modernism.

moderniste [mɔdɛrnist], (*a*) *a.* modernist; modernistic; (*b*) *s.m. & f.* modernist.

modernité [mɔdɛrnite], *s.f.* modernity, modernness; up-to-dateness.

modern style [mɔdɛrnstil], *s.m. & a. Art:* art nouveau.

modeste [mɔdɛst], *a.* **1.** *A:* moderate; **courroux m.,** moderate, mild, anger. **2.** simple, unpretentious; **robe m.,** simple dress; **avoir un train de vie m.,** to live quietly, in an unostentatious, unpretentious, way; **être m. dans ses prétentions,** to be modest, moderate, in one's claims; **gens modestes,** people with modest, small, incomes; **être d'une origine m.,** to be of humble origin; **un hôtel m.,** a small hotel; an unpretentious hotel; **un m. affluent de la Seine,** a small tributary of the Seine. **3.** modest; **femme m., qui n'a pas la vanité de vouloir être admirée,** a modest woman, not vain enough to want to be admired; **avoir le succès m.,** to be modest about one's achievements; *s.* **ne faites pas le m.,** don't be (so) modest.

modestement [mɔdɛstəmɑ̃], *adv.* **1.** simply; unpretentiously; **vivre m.,** to live in a small way. **2.** modestly, with modesty.

modestie [mɔdɛsti], *s.f.* **1.** *A:* (*a*) moderation; (*b*) unpretentiousness. **2.** modesty; **elle est d'une m. naturelle charmante,** she has charming natural modesty; **fausse m.,** false modesty; **la m. est son moindre défaut,** he doesn't hide his light under a bushel; *Gram:* **le pluriel de m.** = the editorial we. **3.** *A.Cost:* modesty.

modicité [mɔdisite], *s.f.* moderateness, slenderness (of means, etc.); lowness, reasonableness (of price).

modifiable [mɔdifjabl̩], *a.* modifiable, alterable.

modifiant [mɔdifjɑ̃], *a.* modifying (influence, etc.).

modificateur, -trice [mɔdifikatœːr, -tris]. **1.** *a.* modifying, modificatory; *Biol:* **gène m.,** modifier. **2.** *s.* modifier. **3.** *s.m. Mec.E:* engaging or disengaging gear; **m. instantané,** trip gear. **4.** *s.m. Biol:* modifier, modifying factor.

modificatif, -ive [mɔdifikatif, -iːv]. **1.** *a.* modifying, qualifying (clause, etc.); modal (verb). **2.** *s.m. Gram:* modifier, qualifier.

modification [mɔdifikasjɔ̃], *s.f.* modification, alteration; **apporter, faire, une m. à qch.,** to make an alteration in sth.; to modify sth., to amend (a plan); **modifications de frontière,** frontier changes, modifications; **petite m.,** slight alteration; **programme sauf modifications,** timetable subject to alteration.

modifier [mɔdifje], *v.tr.* (*p.d. & pr.sub.* **n. modifiions, v. modifiiez) 1.** to modify (statement, penalty); to modify, alter, change (plan, arrangement, etc.); *Book-k:* to rectify (an entry); *Nau:* **m. la route,** to alter course. **2.** *Gram:* **to qualify, modify (the verb).**

se modifier, to change, alter, to undergo changes; **les plans se sont modifiés au fur et à mesure**, the plans were changed as we went along.

modillon [mɔdijɔ̃], *s.m. Arch:* modillion; bracket; corbel; *Civ.E:* cantilever.

modiola [mɔdjɔla], **modiole** [mɔdjɔl], *s.f. Moll:* horse mussel; (*genus*) Modiolus, Modiola.

modique [mɔdik], *a.* moderate, reasonable (cost, charge, etc.); slender (income, means).

modiquement [mɔdikmɑ̃], *adv.* at a low price; at small cost.

modiste [mɔdist], *s.m. & f.* milliner, modiste; **chez la m.**, at the hat shop, at the milliner's.

modulaire [mɔdylɛːr], *a. Arch: Mth: Mec.E:* modular; **construction m.**, modular construction.

modulant [mɔdylɑ̃], *Mus:* **1.** *a.* modulatory. **2.** *s.m.* modulant.

modulateur, -trice [mɔdylatœːr, -tris]. **1.** *a. Mus:* modulating (voice); *El:* modulating (current); *Elcs:* **étage m.**, modulator stage; **lampe modulatrice**, modulator tube. **2.** *s.m. El: Elcs:* modulator; **m. à réactance**, reactance modulator; **m. à lampe**, vacuum-tube modulator.

modulateur-démodulateur [mɔdylatœrdemɔdylatœːr], *s.m. Elcs:* modulator-demodulator.

modulation [mɔdylasjɔ̃], *s.f.* **1.** *Mus:* modulation, transition. **2.** modulation, inflexion (of the voice); **voix aux modulations câlines**, voice with caressing inflexions. **3.** *Elcs: W.Tel: etc:* modulation; **m. à courant constant**, constant-current modulation; **m. dans l'anode, dans la cathode, dans la grille**, anode, cathode, grid, modulation; **m. d'amplitude**, amplitude modulation; **m. de fréquence**, frequency modulation; **m. de phase**, phase modulation; **m. par impulsions**, pulse modulation; **m. par impulsions codées, M.I.C.**, pulse code modulation, P.C.M.; **m. parasite**, spurious modulation; **bandes de m.**, side bands; **lampe, tube, de m.**, modulating tube.

module [mɔdyl], *s.m.* **1.** (*a*) *Arch: Hyd: Num:* module; (*b*) standard, unit; **le mètre est le m. des longueurs**, the metre is the standard of length; *F:* **cigarettes gros m.**, king-sized cigarettes. **2.** *Mth: Mec:* modulus; **m. d'élasticité**, modulus of elasticity; Young's modulus; *Civ.E:* **m. de finesse, m. Braines**, coefficient of fineness (of grinding cement). **3.** module; **m. de service**, service module (of spacecraft); **m. (d'excursion) lunaire**, lunar (excursion) module; **m. de commande**, command module.

moduler [mɔdyle]. **1.** *v.tr.* (*a*) to modulate (one's voice, *Ph: etc:* amplitude, etc.); *W.Tel: Cin:* **puissance modulée, watts modulés**, modulated output power; **m. en impulsions**, to pulse; **modulé en amplitude**, amplitude-modulated, A.M.; **modulé en fréquence**, frequency-modulated, F.M.; *Cin:* **parties modulées de la bande photophonique**, modulated parts of the sound track; (*b*) to modify. **2.** *v.i. Mus:* to modulate.

modus vivendi [mɔdysvivɛ̃di], *s.m.inv. in pl.* (*from Lt.*) *modus vivendi*, working agreement.

moelle [mwal], *s.f.* **1.** marrow (of bone); *Anat:* medulla; **os à m.**, marrow bone; **il n'a pas de m. dans les os**, he has no backbone; **Anglais jusqu'à la m. des os**, English to the backbone; **glacé jusqu'à la m. (des os)**, frozen to the bone, to the marrow; **ils sont corrompus jusqu'à la m. des os**, they are rotten to the core; *F:* **sucer qn jusqu'à la m.**, to suck s.o. dry; **extraire la m. d'un livre**, to get the meat out of a book; *Anat:* **m. allongée**, *medulla oblongata;* **m. épinière**, spinal cord. **2.** *Bot:* pith.

moelleusement [mwaløzmɑ̃], *adv.* softly, luxuriously; mellowly.

moelleux, -euse [mwalø, -øːz], *a.* **1.** (*a*) marrowy (bone); (*b*) *Bot:* pithy. **2.** (*a*) soft, velvety (to the touch); mellow (wine, voice, light); easy (motion); **tapis m.**, soft, springy, carpet; **couche moelleuse**, luxurious, downy, couch; **couleur moelleuse**, soft colour; (*b*) *s.m.* softness (of colour); mellowness (of voice, etc.); ease (of motion); **donner du m. à un tableau, à la voix**, to soften a painting, to mellow the voice.

moellon [mwalɔ̃], *s.m.* **1.** quarry stone; *Const:* **m. brut**, rubble (stone), moellon; **m. d'appareil**, ashlar; **maçonnerie en moellons bruts**, random ashlar-work; **m. de roche**, rock rubble. **2.** stone wall.

moellon(n)age [mwalɔnaːʒ], *s.m. Const:* **1.** (*a*) rubble work; (*b*) ashlar work. **2.** production of ashlar.

moellon(n)ier [mwalɔnje], *s.m.* stonecutter.

moère [mwɛːr], *s.f. Dial:* (*Flanders*) polder.

mœurs [mœrs, mœːr], *s.f.pl.* (i) morals, (ii) manners (of people); customs (of country, epoch, etc.); habits (of animals); **bonnes m.**, morality; **avoir de bonnes m., avoir des m.**, to have high principles, to be of good moral character; **certificat de bonne vie et m.**, certificate of good character; **la brigade (de la police) des m.**, the public morals brigade (of the police); the vice squad; **gens sans m.**, unprincipled people; **fille de m. faciles**, woman of easy virtue; **m. spéciales**, homosexual practices; **c'est passé, entré, dans les m.**, it has become a custom, it has come to stay; *Prov:* **les mauvaises compagnies corrompent les bonnes m.**, evil communications corrupt good manners; **autres temps autres m.**, other times other ways.

mofette [mɔfɛt], *s.f.* **1.** (*a*) *Geol:* mofette; (*b*) *Min: A:* choke damp; **m. inflammable**, fire-damp. **2.** *Z:* skunk.

Mogol [mɔgɔl], *s.m. Hist:* **le grand M.**, the (Grand, Great) Mogul.

mohair [mɔɛːr], *s.m. Tex:* mohair.

mohatra [mɔatra], *a. & s.m. Jur: A:* **contrat m.**, mohatra; illegal loan disguised as a sale.

mohawkite [mɔokit], *s.f. Miner:* mohawkite.

Mohr [moːr], *Pr.n. Ch:* **sel de M.**, Mohr's salt.

Mohs [mɔs], *Pr.n. Miner:* **échelle de M.**, Mohs' scale.

mohur [mɔyːr], *s.m. A.Num:* mohur (of India).

moi [mwa]. **1.** *stressed pers.pron.* (*a*) (*subject*) I; **c'est m.**, it is I, *F:* it's me; **vous et m. nous irons ensemble**, you and I will go together; **il est plus âgé que m.**, he is older than I (am); **elle est invitée et m. aussi**, she is invited and so am I; **m. je veux bien; je veux bien, m.**, personally, for my part, I am willing; **je l'ai fait m.-même**, I did it myself; **m. qui vous parle**, I myself; **ce n'est pas m. qui en rirais**, I'm not the one to scoff at it; (*b*) (*object*) me; **il accuse mon frère et m.**, he accuses my brother and me; **il n'aime que m.**, he loves me alone; **vous me soupçonnez, m.!** do you suspect (even) me! **il me hait, m. qui ai été si bon pour lui**, he hates me who have been so good to him; **avec m.**, with me; **venez à m.**, come to me; **à m.!** help! **de vous à m.**, between you and me; **ce livre est à m.**, this book is mine, belongs to me; **un ami à m.**, a friend of mine; one of my friends; **ces vers ne sont pas de m.**, the verses are not mine; **une bagatelle, mais qui est de m.**, a small thing, but my own! (*c*) (*after imp.*) (i) (*acc.*) **laissez-m. tranquille**, leave me alone; (ii) (*dat.*) **donnez-le-m.**, give it (to) me; **écrivez-m.**, write to me; (*ethical dat., usu. untranslated*) **faites-m. taire ces gens-là!** tell these people to hold their tongues; *P:* **donnez-leur-m. sur les oreilles!** just you warm their ears for them! **2.** *s.m.* ego, self; **immolation du m.**, self-sacrifice; **culte du m.**, egoism; **le m. est haïssable**, egotism is hateful; **c'était un autre m.(-même)**, he was my other self.

moïdore [mɔidɔːr], *s.f. A.Num:* moidore.

moie [mwa], *s.f.* **1.** stack, mow (of hay, etc.). **2.** sand-heap.

moignet [mwaɲɛ], *s.m. Orn:* long-tailed tit.

moignon [mwaɲɔ̃], *s.m.* stump (of amputated limb, crowned tooth, sawn-off branch, etc.); *Av:* **m. de dérive**, fin stub; **le manchot a des moignons au lieu d'ailes**, the penguin has flippers instead of wings.

moilleron [mwajjrɔ̃], *s.m. Const:* damp-proofing coat, waterproof skin (applied to walls).

moi-même [mwamɛm], *pers.pron. See* MOI *and* MÊME 1 (*c*).

moinaille [mwanɑːj], *s.f. coll. F: Pej:* monkery, monkdom, monkhood.

moindre [mwɛ̃ːdr], *a.* **1.** *comp.* less(er); **m. prix**, lower price; **quantité m.**, smaller quantity; **question de m. importance**, question of less(er) importance, of minor importance; **les gens moindres que soi**, people of less importance, less important, than oneself; **ils étaient plus que rois, ils sont moindres qu'esclaves**, they were more than kings, they are less than slaves; *s.* **choisir le m. de deux maux**, to choose the lesser of two evils. **2.** *sup.* **le, la, m.**, the least; **le m. bruit l'effraye**, the least noise frightens him; **pas la m. chance (de succès)**, not the slightest, remotest, faintest, chance (of success); *F:* not a ghost of a chance; *P:* not an earthly; **raconter jusqu'aux moindres détails**, to relate even the smallest, the most trifling, details; **certains hommes, et non des moindres**, some men, and not the least important; **c'est la m. des choses**, it's nothing; it's the least I can do; **il ne lui a pas dit le m. mot**, he didn't say a word to him; **je ne lui ai pas fait le m. reproche**, I didn't reproach him in the slightest, in the least; **c'est là son m. défaut**, that's certainly not one of his shortcomings; **le m. souffle fait tomber les feuilles mortes**, the merest (breath (of wind) makes the dead leaves fall; **le dernier, mais non le m.**, last but not least; *s.* **le m. d'entre nous**, the least of us; *Mth:* **méthode des moindres carrés**, method of least squares.

moindrement [mwɛ̃drəmɑ̃], *adv.* (*usu. with a neg.*) less; **je ne suis pas m. atteint que vous**, I am just as badly hit as you are; **le m.**, least; **sans être le m. intéressé**, without being in the least interested.

moine [mwan], *s.m.* **1.** monk, friar; (*a*) **se faire m.**, to take the cowl; **gras comme un m.**, as fat as a priest; *Prov:* **l'habit ne fait pas le m.**, it is not the cowl that makes the monk; **pour un m. l'abbaye ne chôme pas**, no one is indispensable; he'll never be missed; *A:* **m. bourru**, hobgoblin, bugaboo; (*b*) *Ich:* monk fish, angel fish; (*c*) *Z:* monk seal; (*d*) *Orn:* (**vautour**) **m.**, cinereous vulture; (*e*) *Ent: F:* (i) soldier beetle; (ii) gypsy moth. **2.** (*a*) bed warmer; (*b*) hot-water bottle. **3.** *Metall:* blister (on iron, etc.). **4.** *N.Arch:* pin maul. **5.** *Nau:* long(-burning) light. **6.** *Typ:* friar.

moineau, -eaux [mwano], *s.m.* **1.** (*a*) *Orn:* sparrow; **m. domestique, m. franc**, house sparrow, *U.S:* English sparrow; **m. friquet**, tree sparrow; **m. soulcie**, rock sparrow; **m. cisalpin**, Italian sparrow; **m. espagnol**, Spanish sparrow; **m. de Java**, Java sparrow; **manger comme un m.**, to eat next to nothing, to eat like a bird; *F:* **c'est un drôle de m.**, he's a queer bird, a queer customer; *P:* **c'est un vilain m., un sale m.**, he's a bad egg, a heel; *F:* **c'est un épouvantail aux moineaux**, he's, she's, an absolute scarecrow; he's, she's, enough to frighten the birds; *F:* **tirer, brûler, user, sa poudre aux moineaux**, (i) to waste one's shot, one's efforts; (ii) to spend recklessly; **s'abattre (sur qch.) comme une volée de moineaux**, to come down (on sth.) like a pack of wolves; *Com:* **têtes de m.**, nuts (of coal); (*b*) *Ich:* **m. de mer**, plaice. **2.** *A.Fort:* moineau.

moinelle [mwanɛl], *s.f. Orn:* hen sparrow.

moinerie [mwanri], *s.f. Pej: F:* **1.** = MOINAILLE. **2.** monastery, friary.

moinesse [mwanɛs], *s.f. Pej: A:* nun.

moinillon [mwanijɔ̃], *s.m. F:* young monk; shaveling.

moinotin [mwanɔtɛ̃], *s.m. Orn:* coal tit.

moins [mwɛ̃]. **1.** *adv.* (*a*) *comp.* less; **je gagne m. que vous**, I earn less than you; **si je l'eusse aimé m., si je l'eusse m. aimé**, if I had loved him less; **m. encore**, still less, even less; **elle est m. jolie que sa sœur**, she is less pretty than, not so pretty as, her sister; **l'aîné est très intelligent, le cadet l'est m.**, the elder boy is very clever, the younger is less so; **beaucoup m. long**, much shorter; **m. d'argent**, less money, not so much money; **m. d'hommes, d'occasions**, fewer men, not so many opportunities; **bien qu'estropié il n'en est pas m. actif**, though lame he is none the less active; **il n'en fait que m. de travail**, he does that much less, even less, work; **plus on le punit m. il travaille**, the more he is punished the less he works; **il travaille de m. en m.**, he is working less and less; **m. on en parle mieux cela vaut**, the less said about it the better; **m. de dix francs**, less than ten francs; **il a m. de trente ans**, he is less than thirty; **les m. de trente ans**, people under thirty, the under-thirties; **les jeunes et les m. jeunes**, the young and the not so young; **je n'en attendais pas m. de vous**, I expected no less from you; **nous avançâmes jusqu'à m. d'un kilomètre de l'ennemi**, we advanced to within a kilometre of the enemy; *F:* **la lettre était signée de X, pas m.!** the letter was signed by X, no less! **il a trois voitures, pas m.!** he has three cars, no less! **en m. de dix minutes**, in less than ten minutes; **je reviens en m. d'un instant**, I shall be back in half a second, before you can say Jack Robinson; **en m. de rien**, in less than no time; **vous allez vous ruiner en m. de rien**, you'll be ruined before you know where you are; **en m. de deux**, in no time; **en m. de temps qu'il ne faut, n'en faut, pour le dire**, in less time than it takes to tell; **je peux le faire en deux fois m. de temps**, I can do it in half the time; **vendre qch. à m. du prix de revient**, to sell sth. at less than cost price; **je ne peux pas vous le laisser à m.**, I can't let you have it for less; **dix francs de m.**, (i) ten francs less; (ii) ten francs short, too little; **quand j'avais vingt ans de m.**, when I was twenty years younger; **une bouche de m. à nourrir**, one mouth less; to feed; **cela lui a coûté mille livres, rien de m.**, it cost him a thousand, not a penny less; *F:* it cost him a cool thousand; **il y a eu 20% de visiteurs de m., en m., que l'année dernière**, there were 20% fewer visitors than last year; *prep.phr.* **à m. de**, without, barring; **à m. d'accidents**, barring accidents; **à m. de folie il acceptera,** unless he is mad he will accept; **je ne le ferai pas à m. d'être payé,** I won't do it without being paid; **à m. d'avis contraire,** unless I hear to the contrary; **à m. (que) de l'insulter je ne puis parler plus fortement,** short of insulting him I cannot speak more strongly; **vous arriverez trop tard à m. de partir sur le champ,** you will be too late unless you start at once; *conj.phr.* **à moins que** + *sub.*, unless; **il ne fera rien à m. que vous (ne) l'ordonniez,** he will do nothing unless you order it; **rien m. que** (*ambiguous*), (i) anything but; (ii) nothing less than; **il n'est (rien) m. que fou,** he is anything but mad; **ce n'est rien m. qu'un héros,** (i) he is nothing less than a hero; (ii) he is anything but a hero; **ce n'est rien (de) m. qu'un miracle,** it is nothing short of a miracle; **non m. que,** as well as; quite as much as; **il mérite des éloges, non m. que son frère,** he deserves praise quite as much as his brother; (*b*) *sup.* **le m.,** least; **les élèves les m. appliqués,** the least industrious pupils; **le m. de gens possible,** the smallest possible number of people; **les m. rares de mes bijoux,** the least rare of my jewels; **pas le m. du monde,** not in the least (degree); by no means; not in the slightest; *F:* not a bit of it; *s.* **c'est (bien) le m. (qu'il puisse faire),** it is the least he can do; *adv.phr.* **du m.,** at least, that is to say, at all events; **il est de retour, du m. on l'affirme,** he is back, at least so it is said; **au m.,** at least (= not less than); **avoir 100.000 francs de rentes (tout) au m., à tout le m., pour le m.,** to have 100,000 francs a year at (the very) least; **il conviendrait tout le moins de . . .,** it would at least be advisable to . . .; **il est au m. aussi riche que vous,** he is every bit as rich as you; **tout au m. auriez-vous dû m'avertir,** you should at least have warned me; **pour le moins,** at (the very) least, lowest; nothing less than, to say the least of it, nothing short of; *F:* **tu as fait ton travail, au m.?** you have done your work, haven't you? I hope, I can take it, you've done your work? **vous compterez cela en m.,** you may deduct that; **je m'en tirai avec un œil en m.,** I got out of it minus an eye. **2.** (*a*) *prep.* minus, less; **une heure m. cinq,** five minutes to one; **six m. quatre égale deux,** six minus four equals two; **toutes les qualités m. la patience,** all the virtues except patience; **il fait m. 10 (degrés),** it's minus 10(°C); *P:* **il était m. une, m. deux, m. cinq,** that was a near thing; we've, you've, just made it; we've, you've, had a narrow escape; *Ten:* **m. quinze à rien,** owe fifteen, love; (*b*) *s.m. Mth:* minus sign; *Typ:* dash.

moins-perçu [mwɛ̃pɛrsy], *s.m. Adm:* credit (due to soldier, etc.); amount not drawn; *pl. moins-perçus.*

moins-value [mwɛ̃valy], *s.f.* depreciation; diminution, drop, in value; **actions qui se trouvent en m.-v., qui ont enregistré une m.-v.,** shares that stand at a discount, that show a depreciation, shares that have dropped; *pl. moins-values.*

moirage [mwaraːʒ], *s.m.* watering (of fabrics); mottling (of metals); *Phot:* crêpe marking; *Typ:* cross-hatching (as a defect in half-tone work).

moire [mwaːr], *s.f.* (*a*) *Tex:* moire; watered material; **m. de soie,** watered silk; (*b*) watered effect, watering.

moiré [mware]. **1.** *a. Tex:* watered, moiré (silk, etc.). **2.** *s.m.* (*a*) = MOIRURE; (*b*) **m. métallique,** crystal tinplate, *moiré métallique.*

moirer [mware], *v.tr.* **1.** *Tex:* to water, to moiré (silk, etc.). **2.** to mottle, to moiré (metal).

moirure [mwaryːr], *s.f.* watered effect; moiré; *T.V:* shot-silk effect.

mois [mwɑ], *s.m.* **1.** month; (*a*) **le m. de Marie,** the Month of Mary; **on ne mange les huîtres que pendant les m. en r.,** you eat oysters only when there is an r in the month; **m. en cours,** current month; **le onze du m. prochain,** the eleventh of next month, *Com:* proximo; **du m. dernier,** of last month, *Com:* ultimo; **de ce m.,** of this month; *Com:* instant; **au m. d'août,** in (the month of August); **c'est le combien du m. aujourd'hui?** what day of the month is it? **louer qch. au m.,** to hire, rent, sth. by the month; **devoir trois m. de loyer,** to owe a quarter's rent; **cent francs par m.,** a hundred francs a month; *Com:* **payer m. par m.,** to pay in monthly instalments; *Fin:* **papier à trois m. (d'échéance),** bill at three months; **un bébé de treize m.,** a thirteen-month-old baby; (*b*) month's wages, salary; **toucher son m.,** to draw one's pay; *F:* **treizième m.,** Christmas bonus; (*c*) *pl. F:* (= MENSTRUES) monthlies, (monthly) periods. **2.** *Astr:* **m. solaire,** solar month; **m. lunaire,** lunar month; **m. civil, commun,** calendar month.

Moïse [mɔiːz]. **1.** *Pr.n.m. B.Hist:* Moses; *Bot: F:* **arbre de M.,** evergreen thorn, Egyptian thorn. **2.** *s.m.* wicker cradle; Moses basket; basket cot; bassinet(te); **m. de toile,** carrycot, baby carrier.

moise [mwaːz], *s.f. Carp:* cross piece, binding piece, tie, tie beam, brace (of framework, etc.); nogging piece (of brick partition); *Hyd.E: etc:* wale piece (of piling); **m. en écharpe,** diagonal brace, tie.

moiser [mwaze], *v.tr. Carp:* to brace, tie (frame); to (cross-)strut.

moisi [mwazi]. **1.** *a.* mouldy, mildewy (bread, etc.); musty, fusty (taste, smell, etc.). **2.** *s.m.* mould, mildew; **sentir le m.,** to smell musty, fusty; **goût de m.,** musty taste.

moisir [mwaziːr]. **1.** *v.tr.* to mildew; to make (sth.) mouldy. **2.** *v.i. & pr.* to mildew; to go mouldy; *F:* **m. dans un bureau,** to moulder, to vegetate, in an office.

moisissure [mwazisyːr], *s.f.* **1.** *Agr: Hort:* mildew; mould. **2.** mouldiness, mustiness.

moissagais, -aise [mwasagɛ, -ɛːz], *a. & s.* (native, inhabitant) of Moissac.

moissanite [mwasanit], *s.f. Miner:* moissanite.

moissine [mwasin], *s.f.* bunch of grapes with leaves attached.

moisson [mwasɔ̃], *s.f.* **1.** (*a*) harvest(ing) (of cereals); **faire la m.,** to harvest; (*b*) harvest time. **2.** (cereal) crop; **rentrer la m.,** to gather in the crops; **faire une m. de lauriers,** to win laurels; **m. de souvenirs,** (rich) harvest of memories; **faire une m. d'idées,** to gather ideas.

moissonnage [mwasɔnaːʒ], *s.m.* harvesting; reaping.

moissonner [mwasɔne], *v.tr.* **1.** to reap, (corn, field, etc.); to harvest, gather (cereal) crops); **m. des lauriers,** to win laurels, glory; *B:* **comme tu sèmeras, tu moissonneras,** whatsoever a man soweth, that shall he also reap. **2.** *Lit:* **être moissonné dans la fleur de l'âge, de ses jours,** to be cut off in the prime of life, in one's prime; **la tempête a tout moissonné,** the storm swept everything away, devastated everything; **la guerre moissonne la vie humaine,** war mows down, carries away, human life.

moissonneur, -euse [mwasɔnœːr, -øːz], *s.* **1.** (*pers.*) harvester, reaper. **2.** *s.f.* **moissonneuse,** reaping machine, reaper. **3.** *s.m. Orn: F:* rook. **4.** *s.f. Ent: F:* **moissonneuse,** harvester ant.

moissonneuse-batteuse [mwasɔnøzbatøːz], *s.f.* combine (harvester); *pl. moissonneuses-batteuses.*

moissonneuse-lieuse [mwasɔnøzljøːz], *s.f.* reaper-binder; *pl. moissonneuses-lieuses.*

moite [mwat], *a.* **1.** moist (brow, hand); **(froid et) m.,** clammy; **chaleur m.,** moist, damp, *F:* muggy, heat; *Art:* **couleurs moites,** moist colours. **2.** *F: A:* flabby, limp; nerveless.

moiteur [mwatœːr], *s.f.* moistness (of hands, etc.); *Med:* **entrer en m.,** to break into perspiration; **m. froide,** clamminess.

moitié [mwatje]. **1.** *s.f.* half; **quelle est la m. de douze?** what is half of twelve? **perdre la m. de son argent,** to lose half one's money; **une bonne m. des employés est malade, sont malades,** a good half, fully half, of the employees are ill; **la m. du temps, il n'est pas là,** half the time he isn't there; **la bouteille était à m.,** the bottle was half full; the bottle was half empty; **couper qch. par (la) m.,** to cut something in half; **partagé en deux moitiés,** divided into two halves; *Prov:* **à m. fait qui commence bien,** well begun is half done; **vendre qch. à m. prix,** to sell sth. at half price; **s'arrêter à m. chemin,** to stop half way; **nous sommes plus d'à m. chemin (du village),** we are more than half way (to the village), we are well on (towards the village); *F:* **vers la m. du mois,** about the middle of the month; **l'obus avait dû tomber à la m. de la rue,** the shell must have fallen half way up, down, the street; **la gare est m. moins loin,** the station is half as far; **m. plus,** half as much again; **la gare est m. plus loin,** the station is half as far again; **plus grand de m.,** (i) half as large again; (ii) *occ.* twice as large; **réduit de m.,** reduced by half; **il n'est pas de m. si redoutable qu'on le pense,** he is not half so formidable as people think; **m.-m.,** fifty-fifty; **se mettre de m. avec qn dans qch.,** to go halves with s.o. in sth.; to go fifty-fifty with s.o.; **il a proposé de faire de m. avec moi,** he offered to go halves with me; **être de m. avec qn,** to share and share alike; **partager la différence par la m.,** to meet s.o. half way; *F:* **sans m. ni demi,** without restriction; *F:* **ma (chère) m.,** my better half; *adv.phr.* **à m.,** half; **à m. mort,** half-dead; **à m. cuit,** half-cooked, half-done; **faire les choses à m., par m.,** to half-do things, to do things by halves; *F:* **il ne fait pas les choses à m.,** he doesn't do things by halves; *F:* **ça ne va qu'à m.,** I'm not too good; I'm only so so; *Jur:* **cheptel à m.,** cheptel by moiety. **2.** *adv.* half, partly; **m. riant, m. pleurant,** half laughing, half crying; **m. railleur, m. sérieux,** half mocking, half serious; **m. l'un, m. l'autre,** half and half; **m. distraction, m. myopie, je n'avais rien remarqué,** what with being absentminded and shortsighted, I hadn't noticed anything.

moitir [mwatiːr], *v.tr.* to moisten (the skin); to make (sth.) damp, clammy.

Moka [mɔka]. **1.** *Pr.n. Geog:* Mocha. **2.** *s.m.* (*a*) mocha (coffee); **cuillère à m.,** (small) coffee spoon; (*b*) *Cu:* mocha cake.

mol. *See* MOU.

molaire[1] [mɔlɛːr], *a. & s.f.* molar (tooth).

molaire[2], *a. Ph: etc:* pertaining to mass or matter; molar (concretion, etc.), molal; **physique m.,** molar physics.

môlaire [molɛːr], *a. Obst:* **grossesse m.,** molar pregnancy.

molard [mɔlaːr], *s,m. P:* spit, gob.

molarité [mɔlarite], *s.f. Ch:* molarity, molar concentration.

molasse [mɔlas], *s.f. Geol:* molasse; sandstone.

moldave [mɔldaːv], *a. & s. Geog:* Moldavian.

Moldavie [mɔldavi], *Pr.n.f. Geog:* Moldavia.

moldavique [mɔldavik], *a.* Moldavian.

moldavite [mɔldavit], *s.f. Miner:* moldavite.

mole [mɔl], *s.f. Ch.Meas:* mole, mol.

môle[1] [moːl], *s.m.* (*a*) mole; (harbour) breakwater; (*b*) pier.

môle[2], *s.f. Obst:* mola, mole.

môle[3], *s.f. Ich:* sunfish.

moléculaire [mɔlekylɛːr], *a.* molecular; **masse, poids, m.,** molecular weight; **concentration m.,** molecular concentration; **attraction m.,** molecular attraction.

molécule [mɔlekyl], *s.f.* molecule.

molécule-gramme [mɔlekylgram], *s.f. Ph.Meas:* gramme-molecule; gramme-molecular weight; *pl. molécules-grammes.*

molène [mɔlɛn], *s.f. Bot:* mullein; **m. commune,** great mullein, Aaron's rod; **m. blattaire,** moth mullein.

moler [mɔle], *v.i. Dial:* (*S. of Fr.*) to sail before the wind.

moleskine, molesquine [mɔlɛskin], *s.f.* **1.** *Tex: A:* moleskin. **2.** imitation leather; (enamelled) American cloth.

molestation [mɔlɛstasjɔ̃], *s.f.* molestation.

molester [mɔlɛste], *v.tr.* (*a*) to molest; (*b*) *O:* to subject (s.o.) to annoyance.

molet(t)age [mɔltaːʒ, -ɛt-], *s.m. Metalw: etc:* milling, knurling.

molet(t)er [mɔlte, -ɛt-], *v.tr.* (**je molette, m. moletons; je moletterai**) to mill, knurl; **bord, cercle, moleté,** milled edge, ring.

molets [mɔlɛ], *s.m.pl.* boggy, swampy, ground; quag(mire).

molette [mɔlɛt], *s.f.* **1.** small pestle; muller (for colours). **2.** (*a*) serrated, embossed, roller or wheel; wheel (of lighter); *Metalw:* knurling tool; **soudure à molettes,** seam welding; **m. d'éperon,** rowel of a spur; **m. métrique,** map meter, map measurer; **clef à m.,** adjustable spanner, clyburn (spanner), *U.S:* monkey wrench; *Tg:* **m. d'encrage,** inking-roller, inker; **appareil à m.,** ink-writer; (*b*) cutting wheel (for glass, wallpaper, etc.); *Phot:* trimmer (for prints); (*c*) *Hort:* grass edging-iron; (*d*) *Min:* (winding) pulley; (*e*) *Ropem:* whirl; (*f*) *Her:* mullet. **3.** *Vet:* windgall.

molgule [mɔlgyl], *s.f. Z:* Molgula.

moliéresque [mɔljerɛsk], *a.* (*a*) relating to, of, Molière; (*b*) Moliéresque, in the manner of Molière.

moliériste [mɔljerist], *s.m. & f.* Molière specialist.

molimen [mɔlimɛn], *s.m. Med:* molimen.

molinie [mɔlini], *s.f. Bot:* molinia coerulea, flying bent.

molinisme [mɔlinism], *s.m. Ecc.Hist:* Molinism.

moliniste [mɔlinist], *a. & s.m. & f. Ecc.Hist:* Molinist.

molinosisme [mɔlinɔzism], *s.m. Ecc.Hist:* Molinism (of Molinos), Quietism.

molinosiste [mɔlinɔzist], *s.m. & f. Ecc.Hist:* (*follower of Molinos*) Molinist, Quietist.

mollah [mɔlla], *s.m.* mullah.

mollasse[1] [mɔlas], *a.* (*a*) soft, flabby (flesh, etc.); (cloth, etc.) lacking in body; (*b*) slow, apathetic, indolent (pers,); spineless (character); *s.* **un, une, grand(e) m.,** a big lump of a fellow, of a woman.

mollasse[2], *s.f. Geol:* molasse; sandstone.

mollasserie [mɔlasri], *s.f.* flabbiness, softness (of body); spinelessness (of character).

mollasson, -onne [mɔlasɔ̃, -ɔn], *a.* & *s.* flabby, soft, spineless (person); **comme elle est mollassonne cette fille!** what a great soft flabby lump she is!

molle¹ [mɔl], *s.f.* bundle of split osiers.

molle², *s.f. Ich:* sea tench (of the Mediterranean).

molle³. *See* MOU.

mollé [mɔle], *s.m. Bot:* pepper tree.

mollement [mɔlmɑ̃], *adv.* (*a*) softly; **m. assis sur le gazon,** softly cushioned on the grass; **tomber m.,** to flop down (gently); (*b*) slackly, feebly; **travailler m.,** to work indolently, without vigour, in a spineless manner; **vivre m.,** to live effeminately.

mollesse [mɔlɛs], *s.f.* (*a*) softness (of cushion, of ground); flabbiness (of flesh, muscle); (*b*) want of vigour; slackness, flabbiness, lifelessness, spinelessness (of person, character); flabbiness, woolliness (of style); **la m. de son prédécesseur,** the laxity, slackness, of his predecessor; **sans m.,** briskly, smartly; (*c*) indolence, effeminacy (of life); **vivre dans la m.,** to lead a life of ease and luxury.

mollet¹, -ette [mɔlɛ, -ɛt]. **1.** *a.* moderately soft; softish; **avoir les pieds mollets,** to have tender feet; **pain m.,** (soft) milk roll; **œuf m.,** soft-boiled egg; **crabe m.,** soft(-shelled) crab. **2.** *s.m.* calf (of leg); *F:* **avoir des mollets de coq,** to have legs like match sticks, to have spindle-shanks; **aux mollets de coq,** spindle-shanked.

mollet², *s.m. Ich:* lumpfish, lumpsucker.

molleterie [mɔltri], *s.f. Bootm:* light sole-leather.

molletière [mɔltjɛːr], *a.* & *s.f.* (*a*) *A.Mil.Cost:* **(bandes) molletières,** puttees; (*b*) **m: cycliste,** anklet.

molleton [mɔltɔ̃], *s.m.* **1.** *Tex:* (*a*) soft thick flannel, cotton; duffel; **m. à drapeaux,** bunting; (*b*) swansdown, swanskin. **2.** table felt.

molletonner [mɔltɔne], *v.tr.* **1.** to raise the nap of (cloth); to nap. **2.** to line (cloak, etc.) with swansdown.

molletonné [mɔltɔne], *a.* **1.** (*of cloth*) with raised nap. **2.** lined with swansdown; **m. de neige,** under a blanket of snow.

molletonneux, -euse [mɔltɔnø, -øːz], *a.* soft, cosy; **doublure molletonneuse,** cosy, warm, lining.

mollienisie [mɔljenizi], *s.f. Ich:* mollienisia.

mollifier [mɔlifje], *v.tr.* (*a*) to soften; (*b*) to mollify.

mollir [mɔliːr]. **1.** *v.i,* (*a*) to soften; to become soft; (*b*) (*of rope, effort, etc.*) to slacken, to slack off; (*of wind*) to die down, to abate; (*of tide*) to slacken; (*of gunfire*) to slow down; **les troupes mollissaient,** the troops were giving ground; **mes jambes mollissent,** my legs are giving way beneath me; *Com:* **le blé mollit,** (the price of) corn is getting easier, is easing off, is sagging. **2.** *v.tr. Nau:* to slacken, ease, slack off (rope); to ease (helm); *abs. Row:* to shorten the stroke.

mollisol [mɔlisɔl], *s.m. Geog:* (*in tundra*) surface layer (which thaws in summer above permafrost).

mollissement [mɔlismɑ̃], *s.m. F:* relaxation, relaxing.

mollo(-mollo) [mɔlo(mɔlo)], **mollot** [mɔlo], *adv. P:* **(vas-y) m.!** (take it) easy!

molluscoïde [mɔlyskɔid]. **1.** *a.* molluscoid. **2.** *s.m.pl. O:* **molluscoïdes,** Molluscoid(e)a.

molluscum [mɔlyskɔm], *s.m. Med:* molluscum.

mollusque [mɔlysk], *s.m.* **1.** mollusc; *pl.* **mollusques,** Mollusca; **les mollusques céphalopodes,** the squids. **2.** *F:* (*pers.*) drip.

moloch [mɔlɔk], *s.m. Rept:* **m. (épineux),** moloch, thorny devil.

molosse [mɔlɔs]. **1.** *a.* & *s. A.Geog:* Molossian. **2.** *s.m.* (*a*) watchdog; mastiff; (*b*) *Z:* mastiff bat; bulldog bat; molossus. **3.** *s.m. A.Pros:* Molussus.

molossidés [mɔlɔside], *s.m.pl. Z:* Molossidae, the bulldog bats.

molossique [mɔlɔsik], *a. A.Pros:* molossic.

molothre [mɔlɔtr̥], *s.m. Orn:* cowbird; **m. à ailes baies,** bay-winged cowbird; **m. bruyant,** screaming cowbird; **m. des troupeaux,** North American cowbird.

molucelle [mɔlysɛl], *s.f. Bot:* black horehound, stinking horehound.

moluque [mɔlyk], *s.f. Bot:* molucca balm; **m. odorante,** shell flower.

Moluques (les) [lemɔlyk], *Pr.n.f.pl. Geog:* the Moluccas, the Spice Islands.

moluquois, -oise [mɔlykwa, -waːz], *a.* & *s. Geog:* Moluccan.

molure [mɔlyːr], *s.m. Rept:* Indian python.

molusson [mɔlysɔ̃], *s.m.* small barge, canal boat.

molve [mɔlv], *s.f. Ich:* ling.

moly [mɔli], *s.m.* (*a*) *Bot:* wild garlic, moly; (*b*) *Myth:* moly.

molybdate [mɔlibdat], *s.m. Ch:* molybdate.

molybdène [mɔlibdɛn], *s.m. Miner:* (*a*) molybdenum; (*b*) *A:* plumbago, graphite.

molybdénite [mɔlibdenit], *s.f. Miner:* molybdenite.

molybdénocre [mɔlibdenɔkr̥], *s.f. Miner:* molybdic ochre.

molybdine [mɔlibdin], *s.f. Miner:* molybdite.

molybdique [mɔlibdik], *a. Ch:* molybdic (acid).

molybdomancie [mɔlibdɔmɑ̃si], *s.f. Gr.Ant:* molybdomancy.

molybdoménite [mɔlibdɔmenit], *s.f. Miner:* molybdomenite.

molybdophyllite [mɔlibdɔfilit], *s.f. Miner:* molybdophyllite.

molybdoscheelite [mɔlibdɔʃɛlit], *s.f. Miner:* powellite.

molysite [mɔlizit], *s.f. Miner:* molysite.

molyte [mɔlit], *s.m. Ent:* tussock moth.

momasser [mɔmase], *v.tr. Vit:* to disbud.

mombin [mɔ̃bɛ̃], *s.m. Bot:* mombin.

mombrescia [mɔ̃bresja], *s.f. Bot:* montbretia.

môme [mom]. **1.** *s.m.* & *f. F:* kid, brat, youngster; *a. P:* **il est encore tout m.,** he's still just a kid; **y en a de tout mômes,** there's some real small ones. **2.** *s.f. P:* (*a*) dame, skirt; **c'est une jolie m.,** she's a fine bit of goods; (*b*) mistress; (gangster's) moll.

moment [mɔmɑ̃], *s.m.* **1.** (*a*) moment; **choisir son m.,** to choose one's time; **le m. venu,** when the time had come; **je vous écrirai le m. venu,** you'll hear from me at the proper time; **le m. psychologique,** the psychological moment; **pas un m. d'hésitation,** not a moment's hesitation; **attendre le bon m.,** to bide one's time; **j'étais étudiant à ce m.-là,** I was s student then, in those days; **l'état des affaires à ce m.-là,** the state of affairs at that time; **à ce m.(-là) je l'aurais tué,** at that moment I could have killed him; **histoire racontée au m. des liqueurs** = story told over the port; **à un m. donné,** at one time; **c'est le bon m. pour . . .,** now is the time to . . .; it's the right moment for . . .; **c'est le m. ou jamais,** it's (a case of) now or never; *Iron:* **c'est bien le m. de jouer!** it's a fine time to play! **un m.!** one moment! wait (a bit)! **il est là en, à, ce m.,** he is there at the moment, this moment, (just) now, at present; **je suis à vous dans un m.,** I shall be at your disposal in a moment; **il ne me faut rien pour le m.,** I don't need anything at the moment; **rien de plus pour le m.,** nothing more for the moment, for the time being; **sur le m. je ne sus que faire,** for a moment I was at a loss; **j'ai répondu sur le m.,** I answered on the spur of the moment; **arriver au bon m.,** to arrive in the nick of time; **arriver dans un mauvais m.,** to arrive at a bad time, at an awkward moment; **passer un bon m.,** to enjoy oneself; **par moments,** at times, now and again; **dans mes moments perdus,** in my spare moments; **cela peut arriver d'un m. à l'autre,** it may happen any minute; **à tout m., à tous moments,** constantly, at every turn; **au m. donné,** at the appointed time; **le m. culminant du drame,** the culminating point of the drama; **tâchez de le prendre dans un de ses bons moments,** try to catch him in one of his good moods; **au m. de partir,** just as I, he, etc., was starting, was on the point of starting; **au m. où je suis entré,** *A:* **au m. que je suis entré,** when, just as, I came in; the moment I came in; **jusqu'au m. où . . .,** until . . ., until such time as . . .; **il faut attendre jusqu'au m. où les affaires seront meilleures,** we must wait until (such time as) business is better; *conj.phr.* **du m. que . . .,** (i) from the moment when . . .; (ii) seeing that . . .; **du m. que je l'aperçus,** as soon as I saw him, directly I saw him; **du m. qu'il refuse il n'y a plus rien à faire,** since, seeing that, he refuses, there is nothing more to be done; (*b*) stage; **à quel m. de son développement?** at what stage of his development? **2.** *Mec:* moment (of force, of couple); **m. d'inertie,** moment of inertia; **m. de flexion,** bending moment; **m. de torsion,** torsional, twisting, moment; **m. cinétique, angulaire,** angular momentum.

momentané [mɔmɑ̃tane], *a.* momentary (effort, etc.); temporary (absence); **vision momentanée de qch.,** glimpse of sth.

momentanément [mɔmɑ̃tanemɑ̃], *adv.* momentarily; temporarily; **il disparut m.,** he disappeared for a moment.

momerie [mɔmri], *s.f.* **1.** *A:* mummery; masquerade. **2.** affected mannerisms; insincerity.

mômerie [momri], *s.f.* (*a*) *coll. F:* kids, youngsters; (*b*) kid stuff.

momie [mɔmi], *s.f.* **1.** (*a*) mummy; (*b*) *F:* (i) thin, skinny, person; **c'est une vraie m.,** he's, she's, nothing but a bag of bones; (ii) old fog(e)y, old fossil; (iii) sluggard, sleepyhead. **2.** *A:* (*a*) *Art:* mummy (pigment); (*b*) *a. Miner:* **baume m.,** maltha.

momification [mɔmifikasjɔ̃], *s.f.* mummification.

momifier [mɔmifje], *v.tr.* (*p.d.* & *p.sub.* **n. momifiions, v. momifiiez**) to mummify.

se momifier. **1.** to become mummified. **2.** *F:* (*a*) to waste away to skin and bone; (*b*) to become rooted in antiquated ideas; to fossilize.

mômignard, -arde [momiɲar, -ard], *s. P:* little kid, brat.

môminette [mominɛt], *s.f. P:* **1.** little girl. **2.** (glass of) absinthe.

momordique [mɔmɔrdik], *s.f. Bot:* **m. balsamique,** balsam apple.

Momos [mɔmɔs], *Pr.n.m.*, **Momus** [mɔmys], *Pr.n.m. Gr.Myth:* Momus.

momot [mɔmo], *s.m. Orn:* mo(t)mot; (*genus*) Momotus.

momotidés [mɔmɔtide], *s.m.pl. Orn:* Momotidae.

mon, ma, mes [mɔ̃, ma, me, mɛ], *poss.a.* (**mon** *is used instead of* **ma** *before f. words beginning with vowel or h "mute."*) my; **mon ami, mon amie,** my friend; **mon meilleur ami, ma meilleure amie,** my best friend; **je l'ai traité comme mon propre fils,** I treated him like my own son; **c'est mon affaire à moi,** that's my (own) business; **un de mes amis,** a friend of mine; **mon père et ma mère, mes père et mère,** my father and mother; **il est mon roi et maître,** he is my king and master; **oui, mon oncle,** yes, uncle; (*used in the army, but not in the navy, in addressing superiors*) **non, mon colonel,** no, sir.

monacal, -aux [mɔnakal, -o], *a. usu. Pej:* monac(h)al, monkish, monastic.

monacanthe [mɔnakɑ̃ːt]. **1.** *a. Z:* monacanthid, monacanthous. **2.** *s.m. Ich:* monacanthid.

monachisme [mɔnakism, -ʃism], *s.m.* monachism, monkhood, monasticism.

monaco [mɔnako], *s.m.* (*a*) *A.Num:* silver coin (of Monaco); (*b*) copper coinage (of Monaco); (*c*) *pl. P:* **monacos,** money, cash, dough.

monadaire [mɔnadɛːr], *a. Phil:* monadic.

monade [mɔnad], *s.f. Phil: Biol: Ch:* monad.

monadelphe [mɔnadɛlf], *a. Bot:* monadelphous; **plante m.,** monadelph.

monadelphie [mɔnadɛlfi], *s.f. A.Bot:* monadelphia.

monadisme [mɔnadism], *s.m. Phil:* monadism.

monadiste [mɔnadist], *Phil.Hist:* (*a*) *a.* monadistic; (*b*) *s.m.* & *f.* adherent of monadism.

monadologie [mɔnadɔlɔʒi], *s.f. Phil:* monadology.

monandre [mɔnɑ̃ːdr̥], *a. Bot:* monandrous; **plante m.,** monander.

monandrie [mɔnɑ̃dri], *s.f.* **1.** *A.Bot:* monandria. **2.** *Anthr:* monandry.

monanthe [mɔnɑ̃ːt], *a. Bot:* monanthous, one-flowered.

monanthère [mɔnɑ̃tɛːr], *a. Bot:* having one anther.

monarchie [mɔnarʃi], *s.f.* monarchy; **m. absolue,** absolute monarchy; **m. constitutionnelle,** constitutional monarchy.

monarchique [mɔnarʃik], *a.* monarchic(al).

monarchiser [mɔnarʃize], *v.tr.* to monarchize (nation).

monarchisme [mɔnarʃism], *s.m. Pol:* monarchism.

monarchiste [mɔnarʃist], *a.* & *s.m.* & *f.* monarchist (party, etc.).

monarde [mɔnard], *s.f. Bot:* monarda.

monarque [mɔnark], *s.m.* **1.** monarch. **2.** *Ent:* monarch butterfly. **3.** *Orn:* fly-catcher (of Oceania).

monastère [mɔnastɛːr], *s.m.* monastery; convent.

monastique [mɔnastik], *a.* monastic.

monastiquement [mɔnastikmɑ̃], *adv.* monastically.

monaural, -aux [mɔnɔral, -o], *a. Ac:* monaural.

monaut [mɔno], *a.m.* & *s.m.* one-eared (rabbit, horse, dog, etc.).

monazite [mɔnazit], *s.f. Miner:* monazite.

monbin [mɔ̃bɛ̃], *s.m. Bot:* mombin.

monceau, -eaux [mɔ̃so], *s.m.* heap, pile (of stones, gold, bodies, etc.); **des monceaux d'erreurs,** vast quantities of mistakes.

mondain, -aine [mɔ̃dɛ̃, -ɛn], *a.* **1.** mundane, worldly, earthly (pleasures, etc.); worldly-minded (person); *s.* worldling. **2.** of society; fashionable (resort, etc.); **réunion mondaine,** society gathering; **assister à toutes les grandes réunions mondaines,** to attend all the fashionable gatherings; **petit carnet de la vie mondaine,** diary of social events; **être trop m.,** to think too much of society, of fashion; *s.* **un mondain,** a man about town; **une mondaine,** a society woman.

mondanité [mɔ̃danite], *s.f.* **1.** mundaneness, worldliness, worldy-mindedness, mundanity. **2.** *pl.* social events; *Journ:* society news.

monde¹ [mɔ̃d], *s.m.* **1.** world; **le m. entier,** the whole world; **dans le m. entier,** all the world over; *Geog:* **le Nouveau M.,** the New World; **l'Ancien M.,** the Old World; *Pol:* **le tiers m.,** the third world; **en ce bas m.,** in this world we live in; **le m. est petit,** it's a small world; **mettre qn, qch., au m.,** to bring s.o., sth., into the world; to give birth to s.o., sth.; **elle mit au m. un fils,** she gave birth to a son; **venir au m.,** to come into the world, to be born; **être au m.,** to be in the land of the living; **être seul au m.,** to be alone in the world; **depuis que je suis au m.,** (i) since I was born, since my birth; (ii) in all my born days; **il est encore de ce m.,** he is still alive, still in the land of the living; **depuis que le m. est m.,** since the beginning of things; **pour rien au m., pas pour tout au m.,** not for the world, not for worlds, not on any account; **je ne le ferais pour rien au m.,** I wouldn't do it on any account, at any price, for the life of me, for love or money; **faire tout au m. pour obtenir qch.,** to do everything possible to get sth.; **personne au m.,** no man alive; **un des meilleurs hommes du m.,** one of the best men living; **l'homme le plus fier du m.,** the proudest man alive; **le plus simplement du m.,** in the simplest possible way; **être le mieux du m. avec qn,** to be on the best of terms with s.o.; **vieux comme le m.,** (as) old as the hills; **il revient du bout du m.,** he is just back from the ends of the earth; **jusqu'au bout du m.,** to the world's end; **c'est tout au bout du m.,** it's at the back of beyond; *F:* **de quel m. venez-vous?** where have you been all this time (that you heard nothing about it)? **la justice n'est pas de ce m.,** justice is not of this world; **ainsi va le m.,** such is the way of the world; **dans l'autre m.,** in the next world, in the hereafter; *F:* **expédier qn dans l'autre m.,** to send s.o. to kingdom come; **elle entendait des voix de l'autre m.,** she heard unearthly voices, voices from beyond. **2.** (*a*) **le (beau) m.,** (fashionable) society; **aller (beaucoup) dans le m.,** to go out a great deal; to move in fashionable circles; **homme du m.,** society man; man of the world; *A:* **savoir son m.,** avoir du m., to be accustomed to move in polite circles; to have a certain polish, savoir-faire; (*b*) milieu; **le m. savant,** the world of science; **le m. de la haute finance,** the financial world, financial circles; **le m. du cinéma,** the film world; **le m. des courses,** the racing set; **je ne suis pas de leur m.,** I'm not in their set; **dans ce m.-là on ne peut pas se défendre de boire,** in that crowd, set, you simply can't get out of drinking; **il faut de tout pour faire un m.,** it takes all sorts to make a world. **3.** people; (*a*) **rue pleine de m.,** street full of people; **peu de m., pas grand m.,** not many people, not a large crowd; **avoir du m. à dîner,** to have people to dinner; **on ne voit pas grand m. ici,** we don't see many people here; **visitors are few; s'il vient du m., dites d'attendre,** if anybody comes tell them to wait; **il connaît son m.,** he knows the people he has to deal with; *s.a.* SE MOQUER; **tout le m.,** everybody, everyone; **comme tout le m.,** like other people; **il ne peut rien faire comme tout le m.,** he has to be different (from everyone else); **tout le m. l'aime,** he is a universal favourite; *F:* **tout le m. et son père,** the whole world and his wife, all and sundry; **on ne peut pas contenter tout le m. et son père,** one cannot please everybody; **Monsieur Tout-le-M.,** Mr Everyman; the man-in-the-street; (*b*) family; **comment va tout votre m.?** how are all your people, all your family? **votre petit m. va bien?** are the children all right? (*c*) servants, men, hands; **congédier tout son m.,** to dismiss all one's people, one's servants, one's staff, one's hands; *Nau:* **mettre du m. à un navire,** to man a ship; **manquer de m.,** to be short-handed. **4.** *Her:* mound, orb. **5.** *Astr:* world; **mondes morts du système solaire,** dead worlds of the solar system.

monde², *a. B:* **les animaux mondes et immondes,** clean and unclean animals.

mondé [mɔ̃de], *a.* **orge m.,** (i) hulled barley; (ii) barley water.

monder [mɔ̃de], *v.tr.* to clean (grain, etc.) of impurities; to hull (barley, etc.); to blanch (almonds); to stone (raisins).

mondial, -iaux [mɔ̃djal, -jo], *a.* covering the whole world; world-wide (crisis, etc.); **la première, deuxième guerre mondiale,** the First, Second, World War, World War One, Two; **guerre mondiale,** global warfare.

mondialement [mɔ̃djalmɑ̃], *adv.* throughout the world, universally; **marque de voitures m. connue,** a make of cars famous all over the world, of world-wide reputation.

mondialiser [mɔ̃djalize], to make world-wide.

mondification [mɔ̃difikasjɔ̃], *s.f.* cleansing (of wound, etc.).

mondifier [mɔ̃difje], *v.tr.* (*p.d. & pr.sub.* n. **mondifiions,** v. **mondifiiez**) *Med:* to cleanse (wound, etc.).

mondrain [mɔ̃drɛ̃], *s.m.* (*a*) hillock (in plain); (*b*) sandhill.

monégasque [monegask], *a. & s.m. & f. Geog:* Monegasque, Monacan.

monel [monɛl], *s.m. Metall: R.t.m:* Monel metal.

monème [monɛm], *s.m. Ling:* moneme.

monère [monɛːr], *s.f. Prot:* moneron.

monergol [monɛrgɔl], *s.m.* monopropellant.

monétaire [monetɛːr], *a.* monetary; **réforme m.,** monetary reform; **système m. d'un pays,** coinage of a country; **unité m. d'un pays,** currency of a country; **questions monétaires,** (i) questions of currency; (ii) questions of finance; **le marché m.,** the money market; **presse m.,** minting press.

monétisation [monetizasjɔ̃], *s.f.* monetization; minting.

monétiser [monetize], *v.tr.* to monetize; to mint.

monétite [monetit], *s.f. Miner:* monetite.

mongol, -ole [mɔ̃gɔl]. **1.** *a. & s. Ethn:* Mongol, Mongolian; **les invasions mongoles,** the Mongol invasions. **2.** *s.m. Ling:* Mongolian. **3.** *a. Med:* **enfant m.,** mongol (child).

Mongolie [mɔ̃gɔli]. **1.** *Pr.n.f. Geog:* Mongolia; **la République populaire de M.,** the Mongolian People's Republic; **la M. intérieure, extérieure,** Inner, Outer, Mongolia. **2.** *s.f. Com:* goat (fur).

mongolien, -ienne [mɔ̃gɔljɛ̃, -jɛn], *a.* **1.** *Geog:* Mongolian. **2.** *Med:* mongol, mongolian.

mongolique [mɔ̃gɔlik], *a.* **1.** *Ethn:* Mongolian. **2.** *Med:* **tache m.,** Mongolian spot.

mongolisme [mɔ̃gɔlism], *s.m. Med:* mongolism.

mongoloïde [mɔ̃gɔlɔid], *a. Ethn:* mongoloid.

monheimite [monemit], *s.f. Miner:* monheimite.

monial, -iaux [monjal, -jo]. **1.** *a. A:* = MONACAL. **2.** *s.m.* recluse. **3.** *s.f.* **moniale,** enclosed nun.

monilia [monilja], *s.m. Fung:* monilia.

moniliforme [moniliform], *a. Anat:* moniliform.

moniliose [moniljoːz], *s.f. Fung:* monilia disease, brown rot (of fruit).

monimiacées [monimjase], *s.f.pl. Bot:* Monimiaceae.

monimolite [monimolit], *s.f. Miner:* monimolite.

Monique [monik], *Pr.n.f.* Monica.

monisme [monism], *s.m. Phil:* monism.

moniste [monist], *Phil:* **1.** *a.* monistic. **2.** *s.m. & f.* monist.

monistique [monistik], *a.* monistic.

moniteur, -trice [monitœːr, -tris], *s.* **1.** *A:* adviser. **2.** *Sch: etc:* (*a*) *A:* monitor; (*b*) instructor, *f.* instructress; *Sp:* coach; **m. d'éducation physique,** gym instructor; **m. de natation,** swimming instructor; **m. de ski,** ski(ing) instructor; **m. de conduite, d'auto-école,** driving instructor; **monitrice d'enseignement ménager,** domestic science mistress; (*c*) assistant (in holiday camp). **3.** *attrib.* **programme m.,** monitor(ing) programme (of computer). **4.** *Atom.Ph:* monitor; **m. atmosphérique,** air monitor; **m. de radioprotection,** health monitor; **m. de rupture de gaine,** burst-can monitor, *U.S:* failed element monitor.

monition [monisjɔ̃], *s.f. Ecc:* monition.

monitoire [monitwaːr], *Ecc:* **1.** *a.* monitory (letter, etc.). **2.** *s.m.* monitory letter; monitory.

monitor [monitɔr], *s.m.* **1.** *Navy: A:* monitor. **2.** *Rept:* monitor. **3.** *Civ.E:* monitor(-nozzle), giant.

monitorat [monitora], *s.m.* instructor's profession.

monitorial, -iaux [monitorjal, -jo], *a. Ecc:* monitorial, monitory.

monitoring [monitoriŋ], *s.m. W.Tel:* monitoring.

monnaie [monɛ], *s.f.* **1.** money; **pièce de m.,** coin; **m. légale,** legal tender; currency; **m. de mise,** current money; **m. blanche,** silver (coins); **m. forte,** hard currency; **m. faible,** soft currency; **m. scripturale,** paper currency, money; **fausse m.,** spurious, counterfeit, coinage; **m. de compte,** money of account (*e.g.* guinea); **frapper la m.,** to coin, mint, money; **battre m.,** (i) to coin, mint, money; (ii) *F:* to raise the wind, to fill one's pockets; **hôtel de la M., hôtel des Monnaies, la M.** = the Mint; *F:* **payer qn en m. de singe,** to let s.o. whistle for his money, to bilk s.o. **2.** change; **petite m.,** *occ.* **menue m.,** petty cash, small change; **donner la m. de mille francs,** to give change for a thousand-franc note; **rendre à qn la m. de sa pièce,** to pay s.o. (back) in his

own coin. **3.** *Bot:* **m. du pape,** honesty, satin flower.

monnayage [monɛjaːʒ], *s.m.* (*a*) minting, coining; (*b*) (frais de) m., mintage; **droit de m.,** brassage; seigniorage.

monnayer [monɛje], *v.tr.* (je **monnaie,** je **monnaye;** je **monnaierai,** je **monnayerai**) **1.** to coin, mint (money). **2.** (*a*) to cash; (*b*) *F:* to cash in on; **m. son influence,** to cash in on one's influence.

monnayère [monɛjɛːr], *s.f. Bot:* (*a*) moneywort; (*b*) penny-cress.

monnayeur, -euse [monɛjœːr, -øːz]. **1.** *s.m.* coiner, minter; **faux m.,** coiner, counterfeiter. **2.** *a.* **presse monnayeuse,** minting press.

mono- [monɔ, -o], *pref.* mon(o)-; single-; one-; uni-.

mono [monɔ], *a. F:* monaural, mono (record, etc.).

monoacide [monɔasid], *Ch:* **1.** *a.* monoacid(ic). **2.** *s.m.* monoacid, monacid.

monoamide [monɔamid], *s.m. Ch:* monoamid(e).

monoarthrite [monɔartrit], *s.f. Med:* localized arthritis.

monoarticulaire [monɔartikylɛːr], *a. Med: Anat:* monarticular.

monoatomique [monɔatomik], *a. Ch:* monatomic.

monoaxe [monɔaks], *a. Spong:* monaxon(ic).

monoaxifère [monɔaksifɛːr], *a. Cryst:* monaxial.

monobase [monɔbaːz]. **1.** *a.* (*a*) *Cryst:* monobasal; (*b*) *Bot:* monobasic. **2.** *s.f. Ch:* monobase.

monobasique [monɔbazik], *a. Ch:* monobasic.

monobloc [monɔblɔk]. **1.** *a.inv.* (of cylinders, etc.) monobloc; cast, pressed, made, in one piece; solid-forged; cast solid; *I.C.E:* block (engine). **2.** *s.m.* monobloc.

monobranche [monɔbrɑ̃ːʃ], *a.* single-spoke (steering wheel).

monocâble [monɔkabl], *a. & s.m.* monocable (telpher railway).

monocalcique [monɔkalsik], *a. Ch:* monocalcium.

monocamér(al)isme [monɔkamer(al)ism], *s.m.* unicameral political system, unicameralism.

monocarpe [monɔkarp], *a. Bot:* monocarpous.

monocarpien, -ienne [monɔkarpjɛ̃, -jɛn], *a.* **monocarpique** [monɔkarpik], *a. Bot:* monocarpic, monocarpian.

monocéphale [monɔsefal], *a. Bot:* monocephalous.

monochlamydées [monɔklamide], *s.f.pl. Bot:* Monochlamydeae.

monochloré [monɔklore], *a. Ch:* monochlorinated.

monochromateur [monɔkromatœːr], *s.m. Opt:* monochromator.

monochromatique [monɔkromatik], *a.* monochromatic.

monochrome [monɔkroːm]. **1.** *a.* monochromic, monochromous, monochrome. **2.** *s.m.* monochrome.

monochromie [monɔkromi], *s.f.* (*a*) monochromy; (*b*) monochrome (painting).

monocle [monɔkl]. **1.** *a. A:* monoculous, monocular, one-eyed. **2.** *s.m.* monocle; (single) eyeglass.

monoclinal, -aux [monɔklinal, -o], *a. Geol:* monoclinal; **pli m.,** monoclinal fold.

monocline [monɔklin], *a. Bot:* monoclinous.

monoclinique [monɔklinik], *a. Cryst:* monoclinic.

monocoque [monɔkɔk], *s.m. Av:* monocoque; *Aut:* monoshell; **carrosserie m.,** integral all-steel welded body, monopiece body.

monocorde [monɔkɔrd]. **1.** *a.* (*a*) *Mus:* single-stringed (instrument); (*b*) *F:* monotonous. **2.** *s.m.* (*a*) *Ph:* monochord, sonometer; (*b*) *A.Mus:* monochord.

monocotylé [monɔkotile]. **1.** *a. Bot:* monocotyledonous. **2.** *s.m.pl. Moll:* monocotylés, Monocotylea.

monocotylédone [monɔkotiledɔn], *Bot:* **1.** *a.* monocotyledonous. **2.** *s.f.* monocotyledon; *pl.* **monocotylédones,** Monocotyledones.

monocratie [monɔkrasi], *s.f.* monocracy, autocracy.

monocristal, -aux [monɔkristal, -o], *Cryst:* monocristal.

monoculaire [monɔkylɛːr], *a.* monocular (field-glass, vision, etc.); **cécité m.,** blindness in one eye.

monoculture [monɔkyltyːr], *s.f. Agr:* monoculture.

monocycle [monɔsikl], *s.m. Cy:* monocycle, unicycle.

monocyclique [monɔsiklik], *a. Ch: Biol:* monocyclic.

monocylindrique [monɔsilɛ̃drik], *a. Aut: etc:* single-cylinder, one-cylinder (engine).

monocyte [monɔsit], *s.m. Biol:* monocyte.

monodactyle [monɔdaktil], *a. Z:* monodactylous.

monodelphe [mɔnɔdɛlf], Z: 1. a. monodelphian, monodelphic. 2. s.m. monodelph; pl. **monodelphes**, Monodelphes, Eutheria.

monodelphien, -ienne [mɔnɔdɛlfjɛ̃, -jɛn], a. Z: monodelphian.

monodermique [mɔnɔdɛrmik], a. monodermic.

monodie [mɔnɔdi], s.f. Gr.Lit: monody.

monodique [mɔnɔdik], a. monodic (song).

monodisque [mɔnɔdisk], a. Aut: single-plate (clutch).

monodrome [mɔnɔdroːm], a. Mth: monodromic.

monœcie [mɔnesi], s.f. Bot: 1. monoecism. 2. monoecian; pl. A: monœcies, Monoecia.

monœcique [mɔnesik], a. monoecious.

monoénergétique [mɔnɔenɛrʒetik], a. Atom.Ph: monoenergic.

monoéthylénique [mɔnɔetilenik], a. Ch: monoethylenic (acid).

monofamille [mɔnɔfamiːj], a.inv. maison m., one-family house, U.S: single.

monofil [mɔnɔfil], a. single-thread (nylon, etc.).

monogame [mɔnɔgam], 1. a. monogamous. 2. s.m. & f. monogamist.

monogamie [mɔnɔgami], s.f. Anthr: monogamy.

monogamique [mɔnɔgamik], a. monogamic.

monogamiste [mɔnɔgamist], s.m. & f. monogamist.

monogène [mɔnɔʒɛn], a. (a) Biol: monogenic, monogenetic; (b) Mth: monogenic.

monogenèse [mɔnɔʒənɛːz], s.f. Biol: monogenesis.

monogénésique [mɔnɔʒenezik], a. Biol: Geol: monogenic, monogenetic.

monogénie [mɔnɔʒeni], s.f. Biol: monogenesis, asexual reproduction.

monogénique [mɔnɔʒenik], a. Geol: monogenic, monogenetic.

monogénisme [mɔnɔʒenism], s.m. monogenism.

monogéniste [mɔnɔʒenist], s.m. & f. monogenist.

monoglotte [mɔnɔglɔt], a. monoglot, unilingual.

monogonie [mɔnɔgɔni], s.f. Biol: monogony.

monogrammatique [mɔnɔgram(m)atik], a. monogrammatic.

monogramme [mɔnɔgram], s.m. monogram; initials (for sewing on garment).

monographe [mɔnɔgraf], 1. s.m. monographer. 2. a. monographic (publication, etc.).

monographie [mɔnɔgrafi], s.f. monograph.

monographique [mɔnɔgrafik], a. monographic(al).

monograptidés [mɔnɔgraptide], s.m.pl. Paleont: Monograptidae.

monogyne [mɔnɔʒin], a. A.Bot: monogynous; plante m., monogyn; plantes monogynes, monogynia.

monogynie [mɔnɔʒini], s.f. Bot: Ent: monogyny.

monohybride [mɔnɔibrid], s.m. Biol: monohybrid.

monohydrate [mɔnɔidrat], s.m. monohydrate.

monohydraté [mɔnɔidrate], a. Ch: monohydrated.

monohydrique [mɔnɔidrik], a. Ch: monohydric.

monoïde [mɔnɔid], a. & s.m. Mth: monoid.

monoïdéisme [mɔnɔideism], s.m. Psy: Med: monoideism.

monoïdéiste [mɔnɔideist], a. monoideic, monoideistic.

monoïque [mɔnɔik], a. Bot: monoecious.

monolingue [mɔnɔlɛ̃ːg], a. & s. monolingual.

monolithe [mɔnɔlit], 1. a. monolithic; Pol: état m., totalitarian, monolithic, state. 2. s.m. monolith. 3. a. Psy: Pol: single unit whose members think alike.

monolithique [mɔnɔlitik], a. 1. monolithic. 2. Psy: Pol: (group, party, whose members are) thinking alike, monolithic.

monolithisme [mɔnɔlitism], s.m. Pol: monolithism.

monologue [mɔnɔlɔg], s.m. monologue, soliloquy.

monologuer [mɔnɔlɔge], v.i. (a) to soliloquize; to talk to oneself; to monologize; (b) F: to monopolize the conversation.

monologueur [mɔnɔlɔgœːr], s.m. (a) monolog(u)ist, soliloquist, soliloquizer; (b) F: monopolizer of the conversation.

monomane [mɔnɔman], **monomaniaque** [mɔnɔmanjak]. 1. a. monomaniac(al); être m. de qch., to have sth. on the brain. 2. s. monomaniac; person of one idea.

monomanie [mɔnɔmani], s.f. monomania, obsession.

monôme [mɔnoːm], s.m. 1. Alg: monomial, single term. 2. parade (of students) through the streets in single file; (student) rag.

monomère [mɔnɔmɛːr], Ch: 1. a. monomeric. 2. s.m. monomer.

monométallisme [mɔnɔmetalism], s.m. Pol.Ec: monometallism.

monométalliste [mɔnɔmetalist]. 1. a. monometallic (currency, etc.). 2. s.m. Pol.Ec: monometallist.

monomètre [mɔnɔmɛtr]. 1. a. monometric(al) (verse). 2. s.m. Pros: monometer.

monométrique [mɔnɔmetrik], a. monometric(al).

monomoléculaire [mɔnɔmɔlekylɛːr], a. Ph: etc: mono(-)molecular.

monomoteur [mɔnɔmɔtœːr], a.m. & s.m. single-engined (aircraft).

monomyaires [mɔnɔmjɛːr], s.m.pl. Moll: Monomyaria.

mononucléaire [mɔnɔnyklɛːr], a. Biol: mononuclear, uninuclear.

mononucléose [mɔnɔnykleoːz], s.f. Med: mononucleosis; m. infectieuse, glandular fever.

monopétale [mɔnɔpetal], a. Bot: monopetalous, unipetalous.

monophage [mɔnɔfaːʒ], a. Z: monophagous.

monophasé [mɔnɔfaze], a. El.E: monophase, monophasic, single-phase, uniphase (current); s.m. m. de traction, single-phase traction current.

monophasique [mɔnɔfazik], a. Psy: monophasic.

monophonie [mɔnɔfɔni], s.f. Ac: monophony.

monophonique [mɔnɔfɔnik], a. Ac: monophonic, monophonous, monaural.

monophtalme [mɔnɔftalm], a. monophthalmic.

monophtalmie [mɔnɔftalmi], s.f. monophthalmia.

monophtongaison [mɔnɔftɔ̃gɛzɔ̃], s.f. Ling: monophthongization.

monophtongue [mɔnɔftɔ̃ːg], s.f. Ling: monophthong.

monophylétique [mɔnɔfiletik], a. monophyletic; developed from a single stock.

monophylétisme [mɔnɔfiletism], s.m. Biol: monophyleticism.

monophylle [mɔnɔfil], a. Bot: monophyllous, unifoliate.

monophyodonte [mɔnɔfjɔdɔ̃t], s.m. Z: monophyodont.

monophysisme [mɔnɔfizism], s.m. Rel.H: monophysism, monophysitism.

monophysite [mɔnɔfizit], a. & s.m. Rel.H: monophysite.

monophyte [mɔnɔfit], a. Bot: monophytic.

monoplace [mɔnɔplas], a. & s.m. or f. single-seater (car, aircraft, etc.).

monoplan [mɔnɔplɑ̃], a. & s.m. Av: monoplane.

monoplastide [mɔnɔplastid], s.m. Biol: monoplast(id).

monoplégie [mɔnɔpleʒi], s.f. Med: monoplegia.

monopode [mɔnɔpɔd]. 1. a. monopode, monopodous, one-footed; Bot: monopodial. 2. s.m. (a) Ter: monopode; (b) Bot: monopodium.

monopole [mɔnɔpɔl], s.m. monopoly; avoir le m. de qch., to have the monopoly of sth.; avoir le m. de faire qch., to have the monopoly of doing sth.; m. d'État, State monopoly; Com: Fin: m. des prix, price ring.

monopoleur, -euse [mɔnɔpɔlœːr, -øːz]. 1. a. monopolist(ic). 2. s. monopolist.

monopolisateur, -trice [mɔnɔpɔlizatœːr, -tris]. 1. a. monopolistic (tendency, etc.). 2. s. monopolizer; Com: monopolist.

monopolisation [mɔnɔpɔlizasjɔ̃], s.f. monopolization.

monopoliser [mɔnɔpɔlize], v.tr. to monopolize; to have the monopoly of (sth.).

monopolistique [mɔnɔpɔlistik], a. monopolistic; contrôle m., monopoly control.

monopoulie [mɔnɔpuli], a. single-pulley.

monoptère¹ [mɔnɔptɛːr], a. Arch: monopteral; temple m., monopteros.

monoptère², a. Orn: Ich: monopteral; having one wing, one fin.

monorail [mɔnɔrɑːj], a. & s.m. monorail.

monorchide [mɔnɔrkid]. 1. a. (a) Physiol: monorchid; (b) Husb: etc: cheval, taureau, bélier, m., rig, ridgel. 2. s.m. Physiol: monorchis; pl. -ides.

monorchidie [mɔnɔrkidi], s.f. Physiol: monorchism.

monoréfringent [mɔnɔrefrɛ̃ʒɑ̃], a. Ph: monorefringent; Ph: Cryst: optically isotropic.

monorime [mɔnɔrim], Pros: 1. a. monorhyme(d), monorime(d). 2. s.m. monorhyme, monorime.

monoroue [mɔnɔru], a. single-wheeled.

monosaccharide [mɔnɔsakarid], s.m. Ch: monosaccharide.

monoscope [mɔnɔskɔp], s.m. T.V: monoscope.

monosépale [mɔnɔsepal], a. Bot: monosepalous, unisepalous.

monosoc [mɔnɔsɔk], s.m. Agr: single plough.

monosomique [mɔnɔsɔmik], a. & s.m. Biol: monosomic, monosome.

monosome [mɔnɔzom], **monosomien** [mɔnɔzɔmjɛ̃], s.m. Ter: two-headed monster.

monosperme [mɔnɔspɛrm], a. Bot: monospermous.

monosporé [mɔnɔspɔre], a. Bot: monosporous.

monostable [mɔnɔstabl], a. Elcs: monostable.

monostélie [mɔnɔsteli], s.f. Bot: monostely.

monostiche [mɔnɔstik], s.m. Pros: monostich.

monostique [mɔnɔstik]. 1. a. & s.m. Pros: monostich. 2. a. Cryst: monostichous.

monostome [mɔnɔstɔm], Ann: 1. a. monostome, monostomatous. 2. s.m. monostome.

monostyle [mɔnɔstil], a. 1. Bot: monostylous, monostylic. 2. Arch: colonne m., single-shafted column.

monosubstitué [mɔnɔsypstitɥe], a. Ch: monosubstituted.

monosyllabe [mɔnɔsil(l)ab]. 1. a. monosyllabic. 2. s.m. monosyllable; parler par monosyllabes, to speak in monosyllables.

monosyllabique [mɔnɔsil(l)abik], a. monosyllabic.

monosyllabisme [mɔnɔsil(l)abism], s.m. Ling: monosyllabism.

monothalame [mɔnɔtalam], a. monothalamous.

monothéisme [mɔnɔteism], s.m. monotheism.

monothéiste [mɔnɔteist]. 1. a. monotheist(ic). 2. s.m. & f. monotheist.

monothéistique [mɔnɔteistik], a. monotheistic.

monothélisme [mɔnɔtelism], s.m. Rel.H: Monothelitism.

monothélite [mɔnɔtelit], Rel.H: 1. a. Monothelitic. 2. s.m. & f. Monothelite.

monotone [mɔnɔtɔn], a. 1. monotonous (speech, etc.); humdrum, dull (life). 2. Mth: monotonic.

monotonement [mɔnɔtɔnmɑ̃], adv. monotonously.

monotonie [mɔnɔtɔni], s.f. 1. monotony; sameness; existence d'une m. endormante, humdrum existence. 2. Elcs: (computers) string; rupture de m., string break; constitution de m., string building.

monotrace [mɔnɔtras], a. Av: train (d'atterrissage) m., bicycle gear.

monotrème [mɔnɔtrɛm], Z: 1. a. monotreme. 2. s.m. monotreme; les monotrèmes, Monotremata, monotremes.

monotriche [mɔnɔtriʃ], s.m. monotrichous bacterium.

monotriglyphe [mɔnɔtriglif], Arch: 1. a. monotriglyphic. 2. s.m. monotriglyph.

monotropacées [mɔnɔtrɔpase], s.f.pl. Bot: Monotropaceae.

monotrope [mɔnɔtrɔp], s.m. Bot: monotropa.

monotype [mɔnɔtip]. 1. a. (a) Bot: Z: etc: monotypic(al), monotypal, monotypous; (b) a. & s.m. Sp: (voiliers) monotypes, one-design sailing boats. 2. s.f. Typ: R.t.m: Monotype) machine).

monovalence [mɔnɔvalɑ̃ːs], s.f. Ch: monovalency, monovalence; univalency, univalence.

monovalent [mɔnɔvalɑ̃], a. Ch: monovalent; univalent.

monovalve [mɔnɔvalv], a. single-valve (machine, etc.).

monoxène [mɔnɔksɛn], a. Biol: monoxenous.

monozygote [mɔnɔzigɔt], a. Biol: monovular; monozygotic, monozygous; jumeaux monozygotes, identical twins.

Monroe, Monroë [mɔ̃ro(e)], Pr.n.m. la doctrine de M., the Monroe doctrine.

monseigneur [mɔ̃sɛɲœːr], s.m. 1. (title of dignity) (a) (referring to prince) His Royal Highness; (to cardinal) his Eminence; (to duke, archbishop) his Grace; (to bishop) his Lordship; monseigneur, Mgr, l'évêque de . . ., the Lord Bishop of . . .; pl. nosseigneurs; (b) (as mode of address to prince) Your Royal Highness; (to cardinal) your Eminence; (to duke, archbishop) your Grace; (to bishop) my Lord (Bishop), your Lordship; (to Papal prelate) Monsignor; pl. messeigneurs. 2. F: (burglar's) jemmy; pl. des monseigneurs.

monsieur, pl. **messieurs** [m(ə)sjø, mesjø], s.m. 1. (a) (attached to name, title) (i) M. Robert Martin, Mr Robert Martin; Messieurs Martin et Cie, Messrs Martin and Co.; (ii) (not rendered in English) m. le duc, le comte, de . . ., the Duke, the Earl, of . . .; m. le duc, m. le comte, his Grace, his Lordship; m. le président du conseil, the President of the Council; m. le juge, (in police court) his Worship, (in higher courts) his Lordship, (in county court) his Honour; m. le colonel m'a dit que . . ., the colonel told me that . . .; comment va monsieur votre oncle? how is your uncle? (b) (to distinguish between father and son, etc.) M. Robert (Martin), Mr Robert; (used by servants of small boy) M. Robert, Master Robert; (c) (used alone) voici le chapeau de m., here is Mr X's hat; m. n'est pas là, est sorti, Mr X is out; (to child) dis ton nom à m., tell the gentleman, this gentleman, your name; dis ton nom aux messieurs, à ces messieurs, tell the gentlemen your name. 2. (a) (in address, more extensively used than in English) sir; (to titled gentleman) your Grace, your Lordship, etc.; oui, monsieur, yes (, sir); bonsoir, messieurs good night, gentlemen; m. a sonné? did you ring, sir? **que prendront ces messieurs?** what will you have, gentlemen? **m. le président,** Mr President; **m. le juge,** your Worship, your Lordship, your Honour; my Lord; **m. le maire,** Mr Mayor; (*b*) (*in letter writing*) (i) (*to stranger*) **Monsieur** (*always written in full*), (Dear) Sir; (ii) (*frequently, where appropriate*) **Monsieur et cher Confrère, Monsieur et cher Collègue,** Dear (Mr) X; (iii) (*implying previous acquaintance*) **cher M.,** Dear Mr X. 3. (gentle)man; **le m. qui vient de sortir,** the gentleman who has just gone out; **deux messieurs que je ne connais pas,** two men whom I do not know; **c'est un m. très convenable,** he's quite a gentleman; **c'est un m.,** he's quite a bigwig; *F:* **faire le gros m.,** to act big; **paysan devenu m.,** peasant who has got on in the world; *Iron:* **mon petit m.,** young fellow my lad; **c'est un vilain m.,** he's a bad lot, a nasty piece of work; *Hum:* **et m. d'entrer,** in walked his Lordship; **et ces messieurs d'entrer,** in walked their Lordships. 4. *Fr.Hist:* title given to King's eldest brother.

monsignor(e) [mɔ̃siɲɔr(e)], *s.m. Ecc. title:* Monsignor.

monstrance [mɔ̃strɑ̃:s], *s.f. Ecc: R.C.Ch:* monstrance.

monstre [mɔ̃:str̥]. 1. *s.m.* (*a*) *Ter:* monster, abortion, monstrosity; (*b*) *Myth: etc:* monster; **les monstres marins,** the monsters of the deep; *F:* **se faire des monstres de tout,** to make mountains out of molehills; (*c*) **m. d'ingratitude, de cruauté,** monster of ingratitude, of cruelty; **ces monstres d'hommes,** those brutes of men; those monsters; (*d*) *F:* **cet enfant est un petit m.,** that child's a little devil; **vous voilà, petit monstre!** is that you, you little monster! 2. *a. F:* huge; colossal; monster (demonstration); prodigious (display); **un dîner m.,** a huge meal.

monstrueusement [mɔ̃stryøzmɑ̃], *adv.* monstrously; colossally.

monstrueux, -euse [mɔ̃stryø, -ø:z], *a.* monstrous. 1. unnatural; **ombre monstrueuse,** monstrous shadow. 2. huge, colossal. 3. shocking, dreadful; **il est m. que cela soit permis!** it is monstrous that such a thing should be allowed!

monstruosité [mɔ̃stryozite], *s.f.* 1. monstrousness (of crime, etc.). 2. monstrosity.

mont [mɔ̃], *s.m.* 1. mount, mountain; (*a*) **le m. Sinaï,** Mount Sinai; **les monts Pyrénées,** the Pyrenees (mountains); **les monts Alleghanys,** the Alleghany Mountains; **par monts et par vaux,** up hill and down dale; **être toujours par monts et par vaux,** to be always on the move; *F:* **promettre monts et merveilles à qn,** to promise s.o. the earth; (*b*) *A:* **les monts,** the Alps; **passer les monts,** to cross the Alps. 2. (*a*) *Anat:* **m. de Vénus,** mons Veneris; (*b*) (*Palmistry*) mount.

montage [mɔ̃ta:ʒ], *s.m.* 1. (*a*) taking up, carrying up, hoisting (of building materials, etc.); (*b*) rising up; boiling up (of liquids). 2. installation; fitment; fixture; setting (of jewel, of specimen, of a scene); mounting (of photograph, fishhook, gun, etc.); fitting (on) (of tyre); fitting up, erecting, assembling (of apparatus); fitting out (of workshop, etc.); hanging (of door); casting on (of switches); pitching (of tent); *Fish:* dressing (of fly); *Cin:* (i) montage; editing; (ii) dubbing (of sound track); **carton de m.,** mount (of photograph, etc.). 3. *El:* (*a*) connecting up; wiring; **schéma de m.,** wiring diagram; layout (of radio set, etc.); (*b*) (system of) wiring; **m. à trois fils,** three-wire system of distribution; **m. en circuit fermé,** closed circuit arrangement; **m. en dérivation,** shunt connection; **m. (en) série,** series connection; **m. des piles,** cell arrangement; **m. en triangle,** delta connection; **m. en étoile,** Y connection. 4. (*a*) *Ind: Mec.E:* assembling, assembly; mounting; **(appareil, gabarit, de) montage,** (assembly) jig, assembling gauge; assembly gauge; **banc de m.,** assembly bench; **chaîne de m.,** assembly line; **m. à la chaîne,** continuous assembly; production line-up; **plan de m.,** assembly drawing; **atelier, hall, de m.,** assembly hall; **m. du moteur,** assembling of engine; **m. du moteur sur bâti,** mounting of engine on framework; **m. antivibrations,** anti-vibration mounting; (*b*) *Phot:* **m. de photographies (aériennes, etc.),** (photo-)mosaic assembly; (*c*) *Typ:* patching-up (in photolithography, photogravure, etc.); **m. par transparence,** shining-up.

montagnard, -arde [mɔ̃taɲa:r, -ard]. 1. *a.* mountain, highland (people, etc.). 2. *s.* (*a*) mountain dweller; highlander; (*b*) *Fr.Hist:* member of the *Montagne.*

montagne [mɔ̃taɲ], *s.f.* 1. (*a*) mountain; *B:* **le sermon sur la m.,** the Sermon on the Mount; **les vagues se dressaient comme des montagnes,** the waves rose mountain-high; **se faire une m., des montagnes,** to make mountains out of molehills; **c'est la m. qui accouche d'une souris,** what a lot of fuss for nothing; **il ferait battre des montagnes,** he makes trouble wherever he goes; **si la m. ne vient pas à nous il faut aller à elle,** if the mountain won't come to Mahomet, Mahomet must go to the mountain; (*b*) mountain region, zone; **passer ses vacances à la m.,** to spend one's holiday in the mountains; (*in the tropics*) **passer l'été dans une station de m.,** to spend the summer in a hill station; **son médecin lui a conseillé la m.,** his doctor advised a mountain climate, a stay in the mountains; **m. à vaches,** (i) mountain pasture; (ii) *Mount: Pej:* easy climb; **secours en m.,** mountain rescue; (*c*) **m. de glace,** iceberg; **une m. de choux,** a mountain, huge pile, of cabbages; (*d*) **montagnes russes,** scenic railway, switchback, roller-coaster. 2. *Fr.Hist:* (*during the Revolution*) **la Montagne,** the extremist party (who occupied seats in the higher part of the House); the Mountain.

montagnette [mɔ̃taɲɛt], *s.f.* (*a*) *F:* small mountain; (*b*) (*in the Alps*) (spring, autumn) mid-altitude pasture.

montagneux, -euse [mɔ̃taɲø, -ø:z], *a.* mountainous.

montaison [mɔ̃tɛzɔ̃], *s.f.* 1. boiling up (of milk, etc.). 2. (*a*) season during which salmon migrate up river; (*b*) ascent from sea to river, run-up (of salmon).

montalbanais, -aise [mɔ̃talbanɛ, -ɛ:z], *a. & s. Geog:* (native, inhabitant) of Montauban.

montanisme [mɔ̃tanism], *s.m. Rel.H:* Montanism.

montaniste [mɔ̃tanist], *a. & s.m. & f. Rel.H:* Montanist.

montant [mɔ̃tɑ̃]. 1. *a.* (*a*) rising, ascending, uphill (slope, etc.); **chemin m.,** uphill road; **marée montante,** rising tide, flowing tide; flood tide; **robe montante,** high-necked dress; **col m.,** stand-up collar; **épaules montantes,** high shoulders; *Mus:* **gamme montante,** ascending scale; *Const:* **joint m.,** upright, vertical, joint; *Rail:* **train m.,** (i) down train; (ii) up train; *Mch:* **course montante,** up stroke (of piston); *Hyd.E: etc:* **tube m.,** uptake pipe; stand-pipe; riser; (*b*) *Mil:* **garde montante,** new guard, relieving guard. 2. *s.m.* (*a*) upright (of ladder, etc.); leg (of trestle, of tripod stand); column, pillar, vertical standard (in machine); pole (of tent); stile (of door, window); post (of gate); cheek (of window); riser (of stair); *Nau:* stanchion; **m. de tente,** awning stanchion; **m. de réverbère,** lamp post, lamp standard; *Av:* **m. de cellule,** interplane strut; *Civ.E:* **m. de sonnette,** guide post of the monkey; *Harn:* **m. de la bride,** cheek strap of the bridle; *Fb:* **les montants,** the goal-posts; (*b*) (*sum*) total amount (of account); proceeds (of sale, etc.); **j'ignore le m. de mes dettes,** I do not know what my debts amount to; **acheter et vendre de gros montants de marchandises,** to buy and sell on a large scale; (*c*) striking nature (of pers., thg); high flavour, tang (of mustard, etc.); **vin qui a du m.,** wine that goes to the head, heady wine; **femme qui a du m.,** striking woman; (*d*) flow(ing), rising (of tide).

montargois, -oise [mɔ̃targwa, -wa:z], *a. & s. Geog:* (native, inhabitant) of Montargis.

montbardois, -oise [mɔ̃bardwa, -wa:z], *a. & s. Geog:* (native, inhabitant) of Montbard.

montbéliardais, -aise [mɔ̃beljardɛ, -ɛ:z], *a. & s. Geog:* (native, inhabitant) of Montbéliard.

Mont-Blanc (le) [ləmɔ̃blɑ̃], *Pr.n.m.* 1. *Geog:* Mont Blanc. 2. *s.m. Cu:* Mont Blanc.

montbrétie [mɔ̃bresi], *s.f. Bot:* montbretia.

montbrisonnais, -aise [mɔ̃brizɔnɛ, -ɛ:z], *a. & s. Geog:* (native, inhabitant) of Montbrison.

Mont-Cassin (le) [ləmɔ̃kasɛ̃], *Pr.n.m. Geog:* Monte Casssino.

montcellien, -ienne [mɔ̃sɛljɛ̃, -jɛn], *a. & s. Geog:* (native, inhabitant) of Montceau-les-Mines.

mont-de-piété [mɔ̃d(ə)pjete], *s.m. A:* (*now* **crédit municipal**) pawnshop; **mettre qch. au m.-de-p.,** to pawn, *F:* pop, sth.; **retirer qch. du m.-de-p.,** to take sth. out of pawn; *pl. monts-de-piété.*

montdidérien, -ienne [mɔ̃diderjɛ̃, -jɛn], *a. & s. Geog:* (native, inhabitant) of Montdidier.

monte [mɔ̃:t], *s.f.* 1. rising, mounting; **mouvement de m. et baisse,** up and down movement, rising and falling movement. 2. *Breed:* (*a*) covering (of mare); (*b*) breeding season, mating season (of domestic animals). 3. *Turf:* (*a*) mounting (of horse); **jockey qui a eu trois montes dans la journée,** jockey who has ridden three times, who has had three mounts, during the day; **partants et montes probables,** probable starters and jockeys; (*b*) (method of) riding, horsemanship; **avoir une m. adroite,** to be a clever rider; **m. à l'obstacle,** obstacle riding; jumping.

monté [mɔ̃te], *a.* 1. mounted (soldier, etc.); **cavalier bien, mal, m.,** well, badly, mounted rider. 2. (*a*) **m. en couleur,** high in colour; (*b*) *F:* **il était m., il avait la tête montée,** he was worked up, his blood was up; **avoir la tête montée contre qn,** to be worked up against s.o. 3. set (jewel); mounted (gun, etc.); equipped, fitted, appointed (ship, house, army, etc.); **photographies non montées,** unmounted photographs; **pièce mal montée,** badly produced play; **maison bien montée,** (i) well-furnished house; (ii) well-stocked establishment; **cave, boutique, bien montée,** well-stocked cellar, shop; **il est mieux m.,** (*of shopkeeper*) he has a better, more varied, stock; *F:* **coup m.,** plot; *F:* put-up job; frame-up.

montebrasite [mɔ̃tbrazit], *s.f. Miner:* montebrasite.

monte-carliste [mɔ̃tekarlist], *a. & s.m. & f.* (native, inhabitant) of Monte Carlo.

monte-charge [mɔ̃tʃarʒ], *s.m.inv.* hoist, goods lift, *U.S:* elevator; *Nav:* lift (of aircraft carrier); *Ind:* **m.-c. à godets,** skip hoist; **m.-c. de haut-fourneau,** furnace hoist.

monte-courroie [mɔ̃tkurwɑ, -a], *s.m.inv. Mec.E:* belt-slipper, belt-shifter.

montée [mɔ̃te], *s.f.* 1. rise; (*a*) rising; **mouvement de m.,** up motion; **m. de la crème, de la sève,** rising of the cream to the surface, rising of the sap; **la m. de l'eau,** the rising of the tide; *Mch: I.C.E:* **m. du piston,** up stroke of the piston; *Hyd.E: etc:* **tuyau de m.,** uptake pipe, riser; (*in reservoir*) **m. des eaux,** inflow; (*b*) uphill pull, climb; *Aut: Av:* **essai de m.,** climbing test; **vitesse en m.,** climbing speed, speed on a gradient; **m. à la verticale (après décollage ou piqué),** zooming; **puissance de m.,** ascending power; (*c*) *Ski:* **m. en ciseaux, en pas de canard,** herring-bone; **m. en diagonale,** diagonal uphill traverse; **m. en escalier,** side-stepping; (*d*) **m. au pouvoir,** rise to power. 2. (*a*) ascent, gradient, upgrade, acclivity, slope (up); **ménager une m. en pente douce,** to make a way up on a gradual slope; (*b*) step (of stair); (*c*) *Arch:* height (of arch, etc.).

monte-en-l'air [mɔ̃tɑ̃lɛ:r], *s.m.inv. F:* cat burglar.

monte-fûts [mɔ̃tfy], *s.m.inv.* barrel hoist.

monte-glace [mɔ̃tglas], *s.m.inv. Aut:* window winder, opener.

monte-jus [mɔ̃tʒy], *s.m.inv. Petroleum Ind:* monte-jus, suction and forcing apparatus.

monte-matériaux [mɔ̃tmaterjo], *s.m.inv. Const:* (rope-pulley) hoist, lift.

monténégrin, -ine [mɔ̃tenegrɛ̃, -in], *a. & s. Geog:* Montenegrin.

Monténégro [mɔ̃tenegro], *Pr.n.m. Geog:* Montenegro.

monte-pente [mɔ̃tpɑ̃:t], *s.m.* ski lift; *pl. monte-pentes.*

monte-plats [mɔ̃tpla], *s.m.inv.* (*in restaurant*) service lift; service hoist, plate hoist.

monter [mɔ̃te]. I. *v.i.* (*the aux. is usu.* **être,** *occ.* **avoir; il est monté chez moi, sur le trône, en voiture, en grade; nous avons monté à l'assaut).** 1. (*a*) to climb (up), mount, ascend; to go upstairs; (*of bird*) to soar; *Av:* to climb; **m. en avion,** to go up in an aircraft, a plane; **m. à, sur, un arbre,** to climb (up) a tree; **m. dans un arbre,** to get, climb, into a tree; **m. à une échelle,** to climb up a ladder; **m. en haut d'une colline,** to climb, go up, (right) to the top of a hill; **m. au second étage,** to go up to the second floor; **m. en boitant, en courant, en soufflant,** to limp up, to run up, to pant up; **m. en toute hâte,** to hasten up; **m. péniblement,** to toil up; **m. se coucher,** to go (up) to bed; **faire m. qn,** to call, ask, show, s.o. up(stairs); **inviter qn à m.,** to ask s.o. to step up, to ask s.o. to come upstairs; **montez chez moi,** come up to my room(s); *Mil:* **m. en ligne,** to go up the line; **m. à l'assaut,** *F:* to go over the top; *Ten:* **m. au filet,** to come, go, up to the net; *Nau:* **faire m. un homme,** to order a man up on deck; **faire m. tous les hommes,** to order all hands on deck; (*b*) to climb, get, on, into (sth.); **m. sur une chaise,** to get on to a chair; **m. en chaire,** to go into the pulpit; **m. sur un cheval,** to get on a horse, to mount a horse; **m. à cheval,** (i) to mount; (ii) to ride; **montez-vous (à cheval)?** do you ride? **monté sur un superbe cheval,** riding on a magnificent horse; **m. à poil, à cru, à dos,** to ride bareback; **m. à califourchon,** to ride astride; **m. en amazone,** to ride side-saddle; **cheval qui se monte en dame,**

horse broken to side-saddle; *F:* **monter sur ses grands chevaux,** to get on one's high horse; **m. en auto, en voiture,** to get into a car; **m. dans un train,** to get into, on, a train; to board a train; **m. sur un navire, m. à bord,** to go on board (ship); **faire m. qn,** to help s.o. in(to) (a car, a train), on (to a train), up (a staircase); **faire m. qn (en voiture) avec soi,** to give s.o. a lift; **est-il jamais monté en avion?** has he ever flown, been in a plane? **m. sur la scène, sur les planches,** to go on the stage. **2.** *(a) (of balloon, of the sun, etc.)* to rise; *(of prices, barometer, etc.)* to rise, to go up; *(of tide)* to flow, to rise, to make; *(of aircraft),* to rise; to nose up; **les eaux montent en pression,** the waters are gathering head; **les frais montent,** the costs are mounting up; **la somme monte à cent francs,** the total amounts, comes, to a hundred francs; **frais montant à mille francs,** expenses amounting to, expenses to the tune of, one thousand francs; **les enchères ont monté à cent mille francs,** the bidding went up to a hundred thousand francs; **faire m. les prix,** to raise prices; to send prices up; **empêcher les prix de m.,** to keep prices down; **laisser m. un compte,** (i) to allow an account to run up; (ii) to run up an account; **vin qui monte au cerveau,** wine that goes to the head; **le sang lui monte à la tête,** the blood rushes to his head; **faire m. le rouge au visage à qn,** to bring a blush to s.o.'s cheek; **les larmes lui montent aux yeux,** tears rise to her eyes; tears well up in her eyes; **faire m. les larmes aux yeux de qn,** to bring tears to s.o.'s eyes; **le lait monte,** the milk is boiling up, boiling over; *F:* **m. comme une soupe au lait,** to flare up in a moment, *F:* to go off the deep end (easily); **la colère qui montait en lui,** his rising anger; **son ton montait à mesure qu'il voyait s'allonger les visages,** his voice rose as he saw their faces lengthening; *s.a.* GRAINE 1; *(b) (of road, etc.)* to climb; *(of stairs)* **m. droit,** to fly; **m. en tournant,** to wind; **la rue va en montant,** the street climbs; *(c) (of pers., etc.)* **m. dans l'estime de qn,** to rise in s.o.'s estimation; **m. en faveur,** to rise in favour; **m. au grade de colonel,** to rise to the rank of colonel; **faire m. qn dans l'estime de qn,** to raise s.o. in s.o.'s estimation; **faire m. les actions de qn,** to raise s.o.'s stock; *F:* **faire m. qn,** to get a rise out of s.o.

II. **monter,** *v.tr.* **1.** to mount; *(a)* to climb (up), go up, come up (hill, stairs, etc.); *Nau:* **m. la coupée,** to go, come, up the gangway; **m. un fleuve,** to go, sail, steam, up a river; **si vous saviez les escaliers qu'on a monté!** if you knew how many stairs we climbed! *(b) Mil:* **m. la garde, sa faction,** (i) to mount guard; (ii) to go on guard; *(c)* to ride (horse); *Turf:* **Comet monté par Jones,** Comet ridden by Jones; Comet, Jones up; **quels chevaux a-t-il montés?** what horses has he ridden? *(d) Breed: (of male animal)* to cover, serve (mare, etc.). **2.** *Nau: (a)* to command (ship); *(b)* to man (boat). **3.** *(a)* to raise, carry up, take up, haul up; **m. du grain dans le grenier,** to carry, take, grain up into the loft; **m. du vin de la cave,** to fetch, bring up, wine from the cellar; **faire m. son souper à sa chambre,** to have one's supper brought up to one's room; **vous me monterez une tasse de thé à sept heures,** please bring me a cup of tea at seven; **m. la mèche d'une lampe,** to turn up a lamp; **m. le gaz,** to turn up the gas; **m. un piano d'un quart de ton,** to raise (the pitch of) a piano by a quarter-tone; *(b) F:* **se m. la tête,** *occ.* **le cou,** to get excited; **m. la tête à qn,** to work on s.o.'s feelings; **m. (la tête à) qn contre qn,** to set s.o. against s.o.; **on vous a monté la tête contre moi,** someone has been setting you against me; you've been listening to someone. **4.** *(a)* to set, mount (jewel); to mount (photo, fishhook, gun, etc.); to fit (on) (tyre); to set up, fit up, erect, install (apparatus, etc.); to hang (door); to fit out, equip (workshop, etc.); **m. un papillon en spécimen,** to mount a butterfly; **m. une machine,** to assemble, erect, a machine; **m. un décor,** to set a scene; **monté sur roulements à billes,** mounted on ball bearings; *Veh: etc:* **monté sur ressorts,** hung on springs; *Nau:* **m. l'hélice, le gouvernail,** to ship the screw, the rudder; *Rail: etc:* **m. les couchettes,** to rig up the beds; **m. une robe,** to make up a dress; **se m. en ménage,** to set up house; **m. un magasin,** to set up, open, a shop; **m. une pièce de théâtre,** to stage a play; **m. un film,** to edit a film; **m. un complot, un coup,** to hatch a plot; to plan a burglary, etc.; *F:* **m. le coup,** *occ.* **le cou, à qn,** to deceive s.o., to take s.o. in; *Knitting:* **m. les mailles,** to cast on (the stitches); **m. un violon,** to string a violin; *Fish:* **m. une mouche,** to tie, to dub, dress, a fly; *s.a.* BATEAU 1; *(b) El:* to connect up, wire up (batteries, etc.); **m. en série, en parallèle,** to connect up in series, in parallel. **5.** *Cu:* **m. une sauce,** to thicken, give body to, a sauce.

se monter. 1. to amount; **frais qui se montent à des milliers de francs,** expenses that mount up to thousands of francs; **à combien se monte tout cela?** how much does all this add up to, come out at? **la note se monte à mille francs,** the bill amounts, adds up, to a thousand francs. **2.** to equip oneself, fit oneself out (**en,** with); **se m. en linge,** to lay in a good stock of linen. **3.** *F:* to lose one's temper, to fly off the handle.

monterelais, -aise [mɔ̃trəlɛ, -ɛːz], *a. & s. Geog:* (native, inhabitant) of Montereau.

monte-sacs [mɔ̃tsak], *s.m.inv.* sack hoist, lift.

montessorien, -ienne [mɔ̃tɛsɔrjɛ̃, -jɛn], *a. Sch:* Montessori (method).

monteur, -euse [mɔ̃tœːr, -øːz], *s.* setter (of jewels); mounter (of pictures, etc.); producer (of play); *Cin:* editor, cutter; *Mec.E: El: etc.* fitter, assembler; erector, *U.S:* installer; *Av:* rigger; **m. de derrick,** rig builder; **m. de grosses pièces,** major assembler; **m. d'affaires,** business promoter; **m. de farces,** practical joker.

monteur-électricien [mɔ̃tœrelɛktrisjɛ̃], *s.m.* electrician; *pl. monteurs-électriciens.*

montévidéen, -enne [mɔ̃tevideɛ̃, -ɛn], *a. & s. Geog:* (native, inhabitant) of Montevideo.

monte-voiture [mɔ̃tvwatyːr], *s.m. Aut:* car hoist; *pl. monte-voitures.*

montgolfière [mɔ̃gɔlfjɛːr], *s.f. A:* montgolfier (balloon); fire-balloon, hot-air balloon.

monticellite [mɔ̃tisɛlit], *s.f. Miner:* monticellite.

monticole [mɔ̃tikɔl]. **1.** *a.* mountain (plant, etc.). **2.** *s.m. Orn:* **m. bleu,** blue rock thrush; **m. de roche,** rock thrush.

monticule [mɔ̃tikyl], *s.m. (a)* hillock, monticule; *(b)* hummock (of ice).

montien [mɔ̃tjɛ̃], *a. & s.m. Geol:* Montian.

montilien, -ienne [mɔ̃tiljɛ̃, -jɛn], *a. & s. Geog:* (native, inhabitant) of Montélimar.

mont-joie [mɔ̃ʒwa], *s.f.* **1.** cairn, heap of stones; *A:* montjoy(e); *pl. monts-joie.* **2.** *Hist:* (*also* **Montjoie**) (French) war banner; *A:* (*war cry of the French armies*) **M.-j. Saint-Denis!** montjoy(e)!

montluçonnais, -aise [mɔ̃lysɔnɛ, -ɛːz], *a. & s. Geog:* (native, inhabitant) of Montluçon.

montmartrois, -oise [mɔ̃martrwa, -waːz], *a. & s.* (native, inhabitant) of the Montmartre district (of Paris).

montmartrite [mɔ̃martrit], *s.f. Miner:* montmartrite.

montmorencéen, -éenne [mɔ̃mɔrɑ̃seɛ̃, -eɛn], **montmorencien, -ienne** [mɔ̃mɔrɑ̃sjɛ̃, -jɛn], *a. & s. Geog:* (native, inhabitant) of Montmorency.

montmorillonite [mɔ̃mɔrijɔnit], *s.f. Miner:* montmorillonite.

montmorillonnais, -aise [mɔ̃mɔrijɔnɛ, -ɛːz], *a. & s. Geog:* (native, inhabitant) of Montmorillon.

montoir [mɔ̃twaːr], *s.m.* mounting block, horse block; **cheval difficile, vert, au m.,** horse hard to mount; **côté (du) m.,** near side (of horse); **côté hors (du) m.,** off side; **pied du m.,** near foreleg (of (horse).

montois, -oise [mɔ̃twa, -waːz], *a. & s. Geog:* (native, inhabitant) of (i) Mons, (ii) Mont-de-Marsan, (iii) the Mont Saint-Michel.

montpelliérain, -aine [mɔ̃pɛljerɛ̃, -ɛn], *a. & s. Geog:* (native, inhabitant) of Montpellier.

montrable [mɔ̃trabl], *a.* fit to be seen; presentable; visible.

montre [mɔ̃ːtr], *s.f.* **1.** *(a)* show, display; **faire m. d'un grand courage,** to display great courage; **faire m. de sa richesse,** to show off, display, flaunt, one's wealth; **faire m. d'un cheval, faire passer un cheval à la m.,** to put a horse through its paces; **la m. des blés est belle,** the crops look well, are shaping well; **faire qch. pour la m.,** to do sth. merely for show; *(b) Mil: A:* (i) muster, parade; pay parade; (ii) month's pay; *F:* **il peut passer à la m.,** he'll pass muster, he'll pass in a crowd; *(c)* (i) shop window, display window; **mettre qch. en m.,** to put sth. in the window, on show; (ii) show case; (iii) show pipes (of organ); **m. parlante,** speaking front; *(d)* sample; **acheter du blé sur m.,** to buy wheat from a sample. **2.** *(a)* watch; **m. (de poignet),** (wrist) watch; **m. à guichet,** half hunter; **m. à double boîtier, à recouvrement,** hunter; **m. à répétition,** repeater (watch); **m. à remontoir,** keyless watch; **m. marine, de bord,** ship's chronometer; *Nau: A:* **officier des montres,** navigating officer; **regarder à sa m.,** to look at one's watch; **à ma m. il est midi,** by my watch it is midday; **cela lui a pris dix minutes m. en main,** it took him ten minutes by the clock; **nous serons là dans trente minutes m. en main,** we shall be there in half an hour to the second, *F:* to the tick; **course contre la m.,** (i) *Sp:* timed race; race against the clock, the watch; (ii) race against time; *(b) Ind: Av: etc:* **m. de Seger,** Seger cone.

Montréal [mɔ̃real], *Pr.n. Geog:* Montreal.

montréalais, -aise [mɔ̃realɛ, -ɛːz], *Geog:* **1.** *a.* of Montreal. **2,** *s.* Montrealer.

montre-bracelet [mɔ̃trəbraslɛ], *s.f.* wrist watch; *pl. montres-bracelets.*

montre-chevalet [mɔ̃trəʃ(ə)valɛ], *s.f.* bedside clock; *pl. montres-chevalet.*

montrer [mɔ̃tre], *v.tr.* to show; *(a)* to display, exhibit; **rire qui montre de belles dents,** laugh that displays a fine set of teeth; **il a montré un grand courage,** he showed, displayed, great courage; **il ne voulut pas m. son émotion,** he tried not to betray his emotion; **ces lettres nous le montrent plein de bonté,** in these letters he shows himself full of kindness; **il n'y montre jamais le nez,** he never shows his face there; **m. les talons,** to show a clean pair of heels; *(b)* to point out; **m. qch. du doigt,** to point sth. out (with one's finger); **m. qn du, au, doigt,** to point s.o. out (with one's finger), *esp.* to point the finger of scorn at s.o.; **m. le chemin à qn,** to show s.o. the way; **m. la ville à qn,** to show s.o. round the town; *(c)* **montrer à qn à faire qch.,** to show, teach, s.o. how to do sth.; **elle me montra à coudre,** she showed me how to sew; she taught me to sew; **montrez-moi comment faire,** show me how to do it.

se montrer, *(a)* **se m. au bon moment,** to appear at the right moment; **se m. à la fenêtre,** to appear at the window; **il ne se montrera plus ici,** he will not show his face here again; **il ne s'est pas montré (à la cérémonie),** he failed to put in an appearance; **il ne se montre jamais quand elle reçoit,** he never shows up at her parties; **le soleil se montra tout à coup,** the sun suddenly appeared; *(b)* **des taches brunes se montrent sur la peau,** brown marks appear, can be seen, on the skin; **ici la main de l'homme se montre partout,** in this the hand of man is everywhere visible; *(c)* **il faut vous m.,** you must assert yourself, assert your authority; *(d)* **il se montra prudent,** he showed prudence; **il s'est montré bon prophète,** he proved a good prophet; **il s'est montré très gentil,** he turned out to be very friendly; **il s'est montré excellent chef d'équipe,** he made an excellent captain; **il s'est montré très brave,** he displayed great courage; **il s'est montré assommant,** (i) he proved an awful bore; (ii) he made a nuisance of himself; **se m. mûr pour le commandement,** to show oneself ready for command.

montreuillois, -oise [mɔ̃trœjwa, -waːz], *a. & s. Geog:* (native, inhabitant) of Montreuil (-sur-Mer).

montreur, -euse [mɔ̃trœːr, -øːz], *s.* showman, -woman (at fair, etc.); **m. de bêtes féroces,** exhibitor of wild beasts; **m. d'ours,** bear leader.

montreusien, -ienne [mɔ̃trøzjɛ̃, -jɛn], *a. & s. Geog:* (native, inhabitant) of Montreux.

Mont Rose (le) [ləmɔ̃roːz], *Pr.n.m. Geog:* Monte Rosa.

montrougien, -ienne [mɔ̃ruʒjɛ̃, -jɛn], *a. & s. Geog:* (native, inhabitant) of Montrouge.

montroydite [mɔ̃trɔidit], *s.f. Miner:* montroydite.

montueux, -euse [mɔ̃tɥø, -øːz], *a.* mountainous; **rue montueuse,** steep street.

montuosité [mɔ̃tɥozite], *s.f.* hilliness; unevenness (of country).

monture [mɔ̃tyːr], *s.f.* **1.** *(horse, etc.)* mount; (saddle) horse. **2.** *(a) occ.* (= MONTAGE) mounting; fitting up; assembling (of machinery, etc.); *(b)* setting (of stone); mount(ing) (of picture, fan, etc.); mounting (of fishhook, etc.); frame (of saw, umbrella, spectacles, etc.); strings (of violin, etc.); stock (of gun, pistol); handle, guard, etc. (of sword); attachment (of mudguard, etc.); *Fish:* **montures,** tackle; **m. de store à rouleau,** roller-blind fittings; *Opt:* **m. d'objectif,** lens mounting; **lunettes à m. d'écaille,** tortoiseshell-rimmed glasses; **lunettes sans m.,** rimless spectacles; *Phot: Cin:* **m. normale,** flange mount) of lens); *(c)* stock and equipment (of farm); *Nau:* (i) equipment; (ii) cargo (of ship).

monument [mɔnymɑ̃], *s.m.* **1.** monument, memorial; **m. funéraire,** monument (over a tomb); **entrepreneur de monuments funéraires,** monumental mason; **le dictionnaire Harrap sera notre m.,** Harrap's Dictionary will be our tombstone; **m. aux morts (de la guerre),** war memorial. **2.** public, historic, building; **m. historique,** classified historic(al) monument; **montrer à qn**

les monuments de la ville, to show s.o. the sights of the town. 3. *F:* **cette armoire est un m.,** it's an enormous cupboard; **un nez qui est un vrai m.,** an outsize nose; **c'est un m. de bêtise,** for sheer stupidity it takes some beating.

monumental, -aux [mɔnymɑ̃tal, -o], *a.* (*a*) monumental; (*b*) *F:* huge, colossal; **nez m.,** outsize nose; **elle est d'une bêtise monumentale,** she's incredibly, fantastically, stupid.

monumentalité [mɔnymɑ̃talite], *s.f.* monumental nature, proportions.

monzonite [mɔ̃zɔnit], *s.f. Miner:* monzonite.

moquable [mɔkabl̩], *a.* foolish, ridiculous.

moque[1] [mɔk], *s.f.* 1. *Nau:* bull's-eye (sheaveless block); heart; **m. à rouet,** clump(-block). 2. *Cu:* (*in Belg:*) (type of) dumpling.

moque[2], *s.f.* (*in Normandy*) earthenware bowl (used for cider); mug; *Nau:* container, vessel.

moquer [mɔke], *v.tr. A:* to mock, make fun of, ridicule (s.o., sth.); to deride, *A:* to jeer (s.o.); *A:* **se faire m.,** to get laughed at.

se moquer. se m. de qn, de qch., to mock, make fun of, make game of, make sport of, laugh at, s.o., sth.; to poke fun at s.o., to deride s.o.; to jeer at s.o., at sth.; **on ne peut pas se m. de lui,** you can't make fun of him; he is not to be trifled with; **vous vous moquez (d'en demander cent francs)!** you're joking, you're not serious (when you ask a hundred francs for it)! **se faire m. de soi,** to make oneself look ridiculous, to get laughed at, to make a fool of oneself; **il se moque du tiers comme du quart,** he doesn't care (a damn) for anybody or anything; **se m. des convenances,** not to care (a damn) for convention; **je m'en moque comme de l'an quarante, comme de ma première chemise, comme de ma première culotte, comme de colin-tampon, comme un poisson d'une pomme; je m'en moque absolument,** I don't care a bit, two hoots, a brass farthing, a damn, a tinker's cuss; **vous vous moquez du monde!** you're joking! **c'est se m. du monde! c'est se m. des gens!** it's the height of impertinence! it's a piece of damned cheek! **il se moque bien de passer pour un idiot,** he doesn't give a damn if people think he's a fool; **je me moque qu'elle parte ou non,** I don't care a damn whether she goes or not; she can go for all I care.

moquerie [mɔkri], *s.f.* (*a*) mockery, scoffing; ridicule, derision; **faire des compliments à qn par m.,** to compliment s.o. with one's tongue in one's cheek; (*b*) piece of mockery; **c'est une m. que de parler ainsi,** it's absurd, ridiculous, to talk like that.

moquette[1] [mɔkɛt], *s.f.* decoy bird.

moquette[2], *s.f. Tex:* moquette; (*a*) velvet-pile upholstery fabric; (*b*) **m. de Bruxelles,** Brussels carpet.

moquette[3], *s.f. Ven:* droppings (of deer).

moqueur, -euse [mɔkœːr, -øːz]. 1. *a.* (*a*) mocking, scoffing; **rires moqueurs,** derisive laughter; (*b*) given to mockery; facetious. 2. *s.* (*a*) mocker, scoffer, derider; (*b*) practical joker. 3. *s.m. Orn:* mockingbird.

moqueusement [mɔkøzmɑ̃], *adv.* (*a*) mockingly, derisively; (*b*) facetiously.

mor [mɔːr], *s.m. Geol:* mor.

moracées [mɔrase], **morées** [mɔre], *s.f.pl. Bot:* Moraceae, the fig family.

morailles [mɔrɑːj], *s.f.pl.* 1. *Farr: Vet:* barnacles. 2. *Glassm:* tongs.

moraillon [mɔrɑjɔ̃], *s.m.* hasp, clasp (of lock).

moraine[1] [mɔrɛn], *s.f. Geol:* moraine; **m. frontale, latérale, médiane,** terminal moraine, lateral moraine, medial moraine.

moraine[2], *s.f.* dead wool.

morainique [mɔrenik], *a. Geol:* morainic, morainal.

moral, -aux [mɔral, -o]. 1. *a.* (*a*) moral (person, play, etc.); ethical (philosophy, etc.); **science morale,** moral science; ethics; **conte m.,** story with a moral; (*b*) mental, intellectual, moral; **facultés morales,** faculties of the mind; **courage m.,** moral courage; **maladie morale,** mental disease; **victoire morale,** moral victory; **certitude morale,** moral certainty; *s.a.* PERSONNALITÉ 1, PERSONNE 1. 2. *s.m.* (*a*) (state of) mind; **relever, remonter, le m. de, à, qn,** to raise s.o.'s spirits; to cheer s.o. up; **m. d'une armée, d'une école,** morale of an army, of a school; **son m. est bas,** his spirits are low; *F:* **aujourd'hui elle n'a pas le m**, her spirits are low today; *P:* **avoir le m. à zéro,** to be down in the dumps; (*b*) moral nature; **Molière a observé profondément le m. de l'homme,** Molière made a profound study of human nature; **son m. dévoyé,** his warped nature.

morale [mɔral], *s.f.* 1. (*a*) morals; **contraire à la m.,** immoral; (*b*) ethics; moral science; **m. professionnelle,** business ethics; *F:* **faire de la m. à qn,** to read s.o. a lecture; to lecture s.o.; **pas de m.!** none of your moralizing! spare me, us, the lecture! *Sch:* **m. pratique, m. en action,** stories for character training. 2. moral (of fable, story).

moralement [mɔralmɑ̃], *adv.* morally. 1. uprightly. 2. **m. obligé de faire qch.,** in honour bound to do sth., morally bound to do sth. 3. **m. parlant,** morally speaking, to all intents and purposes.

moralisant [mɔralizɑ̃], *a.* moralizing.

moralisateur, -trice [mɔralizatœːr, -tris]. 1. *a.* (*a*) moralizing (person); (*b*) elevating, edifying (principles). 2. *s.* moralizer.

moralisation [mɔralizasjɔ̃], *s.f.* moralization; raising the moral standard (of community).

moraliser [mɔralize]. 1. *v.i.* to moralize. 2. *v.tr.* (*a*) to improve the moral standard of; (*b*) *F:* to lecture, sermonize (s.o.).

moraliseur, -euse [mɔralizœːr, -øːz], *s. F:* moralizer, sermonizer.

moralisme [mɔralism], *s.m.* moralism.

moraliste [mɔralist]. 1. *s.m. & f.* (*a*) moralist; (*b*) *F:* sermonizer. 2. *a.* moralist(ic).

moralité [mɔralite], *s.f.* 1. (*a*) morality, (good) moral conduct; **certificat de m.,** good-conduct certificate; reference, character; (*b*) morals; **homme sans m.,** man without morals; **commerçant d'une m. douteuse,** tradesman of doubtful honesty. 2. moral lesson; moral (of story). 3. *Lit.Hist:* morality (play).

morasse [mɔras], *s.f. Typ:* brush-proof (of newspaper).

moratoire [mɔratwaːr]. 1. *a. Jur:* moratory (agreement, etc.); (payment) delayed by agreement; **intérêts moratoires,** interest on overdue payments. 2. *s.m.* moratorium.

moratorié [mɔratɔrje], *a.* (bill, etc.) for which a moratorium has been granted.

moratorium [mɔratɔrjɔm], *s.m. Jur:* moratorium.

morave [mɔraːv], *a. & s. Geog:* Moravian; *Rel. H:* **Frères moraves,** Moravian Brethren, United Brethren.

Moravie [mɔravi], *Pr.n.f. Geog:* Moravia.

morbide [mɔrbid], *a.* 1. morbid; sick (humour); **processus m.,** disease process. 2. *Art:* soft, delicate (flesh tints).

morbidement [mɔrbidmɑ̃], *adv.* morbidly.

morbidesse [mɔrbidɛs], *s.f.* 1. *Art:* morbidezza; delicacy of flesh tints. 2. languid and graceful ease (of pose, manners).

morbidité [mɔrbidite], *s.f.* 1. morbidity, morbidness. 2. morbidity, sickness ratio (of community).

morbifique [mɔrbifik], *a. A:* morbific, morbiferous (microbe, etc.).

morbihannais, -aise [mɔrbianɛ, -ɛːz], *a. & s. Geog:* (native, inhabitant) of the department of Morbihan.

morbilleux, -euse [mɔrbijø, -øːz], *a. Med:* morbillous; pertaining to measles; **éruption morbilleuse,** measles rash.

morbilliforme [mɔrbijifɔrm], *a. Med:* morbilliform.

morbleu [mɔrblø], *int. A:* 'sdeath! zounds!

morceau, -eaux [mɔrso], *s.m.* 1. (*a*) morsel, piece (of food); **m. friand,** dainty morsel; **m. de choix,** choice morsel; **morceaux de prince,** sumptuous fare; **aimer les bons morceaux,** to like good things (to eat); *F:* **manger un morceau,** to have a bit of sth.; to have a bite; to have a snack; **ne faire qu'un m. de qch.,** to make one mouthful of sth.; **s'ôter les morceaux de la bouche,** to stint oneself (for others); *F:* **gober le m.,** to swallow the bait; **mâcher les morceaux à qn,** to spoonfeed s.o.; **compter les morceaux à qn,** to keep s.o. on short commons, to stint s.o.; **il a les morceaux taillés,** he can just scrape along; **m. honteux,** last piece (left on the dish); **je l'ai acheté pour un m. de pain,** I bought it for next to nothing, for a mere song; *F:* **emporter le m.,** (i) to be very trenchant, cutting; (ii) to win (in deal, etc.); *F:* **lâcher le m.,** to split, to squeal; *P:* **casser le m. à qn,** to tell s.o. the whole (unpleasant) story; *s.a.* AVALER 3; (*b*) **m. de rôti,** cut off the joint; **bas morceaux,** cheap cuts (of meat). 2. piece (of soap, cloth, poetry, music, land, etc.); bit (of wood, etc.); scrap, fragment (of paper, etc.); lump (of sugar, etc.); **beau m. d'architecture,** fine piece of architecture; **sucre en morceaux,** lump sugar; **m. à quatre voix,** four-part song; *O:* **ma fille va vous jouer son m.,** my daughter must play you her piece; **mettre qch. en morceaux,** to pull sth. to pieces, to bits; to break, cut, sth. up; **assembler les morceaux d'un vase brisé,** to piece a broken vase together; **s'en aller en morceaux, tomber en morceaux,** to fall to pieces; to be falling to pieces; *F:* **un m. de femme,** a slip of a woman; **fait de pièces et de morceaux,** made of bits and pieces; *Lit: Sch:* **morceaux choisis,** selected verses, passages; extracts.

morcelable [mɔrsəlabl̩], *a.* that can be divided, cut up.

morceler [mɔrsəle], *v.tr.* **(je morcelle, n. morcelons; je morcellerai)** to cut (sth.) up into small pieces; **m. une propriété,** (i) to break up an estate; (ii) to parcel out an estate; **m. un pays,** to carve up a country.

morcellement [mɔrsɛlmɑ̃], *s.m.* breaking up, parcelling out, cutting up (of estate, etc.); *Surg:* morcellation (of myoma, etc.); **m. des terres,** parcelling out, division, of land into small holdings.

mordache [mɔrdaʃ], *s.f. Tls:* clam(p), claw (of vice); chuck; jaw, clip, grip, dog (of chuck).

mordacité [mɔrdasite], *s.f.* 1. corrosiveness (of acid). 2. mordancy, causticity, mordacity (of critic, etc.).

mordançage [mɔrdɑ̃saːʒ], *s.m. Dy:* mordanting; *Phot:* **(virage par) m.,** mordant toning.

mordancer [mɔrdɑ̃se], *v.tr.* **(je mordançai(s); n. mordançons)** *Dy: etc:* to mordant.

mordâne [mɔrdɑːn], *s.m. Carp:* tusk (of tenon).

mordant [mɔrdɑ̃]. 1. *a.* (*a*) (*of acid*) corrosive; corroding; **lime mordante,** sharp file, file that has plenty of bite; (*b*) mordant, biting, caustic, pungent, scathing (wit, speech, etc.); **répondre d'un ton m.,** to answer caustically; (*c*) penetrating, piercing (sound). 2. *s.m.* (*a*) (i) corrosiveness (of acid); bite (of file, etc.); (ii) mordancy, pungency, causticity, (of wit, etc.); keenness, dash, punch (of troops, etc.); (*b*) *Dy: etc:* mordant; (*c*) gold size; (*d*) *Mus:* mordent.

mordelle [mɔrdɛl], *s.f. Ent:* mordellid.

mordellidés [mɔrdɛlide], *s.m.pl. Ent:* Mordellidae.

mordénite [mɔrdenit], *s.f. Miner:* mordenite.

mordeur, -euse [mɔrdœːr, -øːz]. 1. (*a*) *s.* biter; (*b*) *s.m.* fish that bites. 2. *a.* biting (horse, fish, etc.).

mordicant [mɔrdikɑ̃], *a.* stinging; prickly.

mordicus [mɔrdikys], *adv. F:* stoutly, with tooth and nail; **nier qch m.,** to deny sth. stoutly, doggedly; **défendre m. son opinion,** to stick to one's guns.

mordienne [mɔrdjɛn], *A:* 1. *int.* 'sdeath! zounds! 2. *adv.phr.* **à la grosse m.,** (i) bluntly, without beating about the bush; (ii) without ceremony.

mordieu [mɔrdjø], *int. A:* 'sdeath! zounds!

mordillage [mɔrdijaːʒ], *s.m.* nibbling.

mordiller [mɔrdije], **mordillonner** [mɔrdijɔne], 1. *v.tr.* to nibble; **m. le coin de son mouchoir,** to suck the corner of one's handkerchief. 2. *v.i.* (*of puppy, etc.*) to pretend to bite.

mordillure [mɔrdijyːr], *s.f.* 1. nibble; trace of nibbling. 2. nibbling.

mordoré [mɔrdɔre], *a. & s.m.* reddish brown, bronze (colour); **souliers mordorés,** bronze shoes.

mordorer [mɔrdɔre], *v.tr.* to bronze (leather, etc.).

mordorure [mɔrdɔryːr], *s.f.* bronze finish (on leather, etc.).

mordre [mɔrdr̩], *v.tr. & ind.tr.* 1. to bite; (*a*) **le chien le mordit à la jambe,** the dog bit him in the leg; **le chien a essayé de me m.,** the dog snapped at me; *F:* **quel chien l'a mordu?** what's bitten him? **se m. la langue,** to bite one's tongue; **se m. la langue d'avoir parlé,** to regret bitterly having spoken; **il s'en mord les pouces, les lèvres,** he bitterly regrets it; **se m. les lèvres (pour ne pas rire),** to bite one's lips (in order not to laugh); **se m. les poings d'impatience,** to gnaw one's knuckles with impatience; *s.a.* DOIGT 1; *Poet:* **m. la poussière, la terre,** to bite the dust, the ground; (*of horse*) **m. son frein,** to champ the bit; **vis qui mord le bois,** screw that bites into the wood; (*b*) **lime, vis, qui mord,** file, screw, that bites, that has a good bite; **l'ancre ne mord pas,** the anchor does not bite, does not hold, does not grip; **acide qui mord (sur) les métaux,** acid that bites, acts on, metals; **ses cheveux mordent sur le front,** she wears her hair low on her forehead; **m. à, dans, une pomme,** to bite into, take a bite out of, an apple; *Sp:* **m. la ligne,** (i) (*athletics*) to have one's foot over the starting line; (ii) *Ten:* to foot-fault; **m. sur qch.,** to encroach upon sth.; *Aut:* **m. sur la ligne jaune** = to go over the white line; **m. à l'appât, m. à l'hameçon,** to swallow the bait; **m. à la grappe,** to jump at the offer; **m. au travail,** to get one's teeth into the work; *F:* **il mord au latin,** he's shaping well at Latin, he's taking to Latin; **je ne mords pas au latin,** I can't do Latin, I'm no good at Latin; **je ne peux pas y m., it's beyond**

my reach, beyond me; *Journ:* **article qui ne mord pas,** article without any bite, any vigour; *F:* **une fois mordu, vous continuez à collectionner,** once the bug bites you, you have to go on collecting; **sa théorie n'a pas mordu,** his theory didn't take on, catch on; *Fish:* **ça mord,** I've got a bite, a nibble; *F:* **ça mord?** any luck? (*c*) (*of cog wheels*) to catch, engage. **2.** *Engr:* **m. une planche, faire m. une planche,** to etch a plate.

mords [mɔːr], *s.m.* **1.** = MORS 1 (*a*). **2.** *Ind:* salt pan.

mordu, -e [mɔrdy], *F:* (*a*) *a.* mad; **m. du cinéma,** mad on, crazy about, the cinema; (*b*) *s.* fan; **c'est un m. du bridge,** he's a bridge fiend.

more [mɔːr], *a.* Moorish; *s.m. & f.* Moor; **gris de M.,** dark grey; clerical grey; **(cheval) cap de M.,** black-pointed roan; *Cu:* **tête de M.,** (round, red-skinned) Dutch cheese.

moreau, -elle[1], -eaux [mɔro, -ɛl, -o]. **1.** *a. & s.* black (horse, mare). **2.** *s.m.* nosebag.

Morée (la) [lamɔre], *Pr.n.f. Geog:* Morea.

moreen [mɔrin], *s.f. Tex: A:* moreen.

morelle[2] [mɔrɛl], *s.f.* **1.** *Bot:* (*a*) nightshade, morel; **m. noire,** black nightshade, petty morel; **m. douce-amère,** woody nightshade, bitter-sweet; **m. toxique,** deadly nightshade; (*b*) **m. comestible,** aubergine. **2.** *Orn: F:* coot.

morène [mɔrɛn], *s.f. Bot: F:* frog bit.

morénosite [mɔrenɔzit], *s.f. Miner:* morenosite.

moréote [mɔreɔt], *a. & s. Geog:* (native, inhabitant) of Morea, Moreote.

moresque [mɔrɛsk], *a.* Moorish.

morézien, -ienne [mɔrezjɛ̃, -jɛn], *a. & s.* (native, inhabitant) of Morez.

morfil[1] [mɔrfil], *s.m.* wire edge (on tool).

morfil[2], *s.m.* raw ivory.

morfiler [mɔrfile], *v.tr.* to remove the wire-edge from (tool); *Tls:* **pierre à m.,** hone; oilstone.

morfondre [mɔrfɔ̃dr̥], *v.tr. A:* (*of wind, etc.*) to freeze (s.o.); to chill (s.o.) to the bone.

se morfondre, (*a*) to be bored to death (**à faire qch., en faisant qch.,** doing sth.); **se m. en mélancolie,** to mope; (*b*) **se m. à la porte de qn,** to stand waiting at s.o.'s door; **se m. dans l'antichambre,** to kick, cool, one's heels in the hall.

morfondu [mɔrfɔ̃dy], *a.* **1.** *Ser:* (*of silkworm's eggs*) infertile. **2.** *Nau:* **cordage m.,** relaid rope. **3.** (*of pers.*) (*a*) gloomy; *F:* browned-off; (*b*) *A:* frozen (with cold).

morfondure [mɔrfɔ̃dyːr], *s.f.* nasal catarrh (of horse).

morganatique [mɔrganatik], *a.* morganatic.

morganatiquement [mɔrganatikmɑ̃], *a.* morganatically.

Morgane [mɔrgan], *Pr.n.f. Mediev.Lit:* **la Fée M., M. la Fée,** Fata Morgana, Morgan le Fay.

morgeline [mɔrʒəlin], *s.f. Bot:* **1.** scarlet pimpernel. **2.** chickweed.

morgue [mɔrg], *s.f.* **1.** pride, haughtiness, arrogance, standoffishness; *A:* **faire la m. (à qn),** to defy (s.o.). **2.** (*a*) *A:* search room (at a prison); (*b*) mortuary, morgue.

morgué [mɔrge], **morguenne** [mɔrgɛn], **morguienne** [mɔrgjɛn], *int. A: Dial:* 'sdeath! zounds!

morguer [mɔrge], *v.tr. A:* to brave, dare, defy; to snap one's fingers in the face of (s.o.).

moribond, -onde [mɔribɔ̃, -ɔ̃ːd]. **1.** *a.* moribund, dying, at death's door. **2.** *s.* person at the point of death; **les morts et les moribonds,** the dead and the dying.

moricaud, -aude [mɔriko, -oːd]. **1.** *a. F:* dark-skinned, dusky, swarthy. **2.** *s. Pej:* nigger.

morigéner [mɔriʒene], *v.tr.* (**je morigène, n. morigénons; je morigénerai**) **1.** *A:* to instil good manners into (s.o.). **2.** *F:* to lecture (s.o.); to take (s.o.) to task; to talk seriously to (s.o.); to give (s.o.) a good talking to, (**d'avoir fait qch.,** for doing sth.).

morille [mɔriːj], *s.f.* **1.** *Fung: Cu:* morel. **2.** *pl. Orn:* jewing (of domestic pigeon).

morillon [mɔrijɔ̃], *s.m.* **1.** *Vit:* morillon. **2.** *Orn:* tufted duck. **3.** *pl. Lap:* small rough emeralds.

morin [mɔrɛ̃], *s.m. Ch:* morin.

morindine [mɔrɛ̃din], *s.f. Ch:* morindin.

morine [mɔrin], *s.f.* = MORAINE[2].

morio [mɔrjo], *s.m. Ent:* Camberwell beauty (butterfly).

morion[1] [mɔrjɔ̃], *s.m. A.Arm:* morion.

morion[2], *s.m. Miner: A:* morion (quartz).

morisque [mɔrisk], *a. Spanish Hist:* Mudejar.

morlaisien, -ienne [mɔrlɛzjɛ̃, -jɛn], *a. & s. Geog:* (native, inhabitant) of Morlaix.

mormon, -on(n)e [mɔrmɔ̃, -ɔn]. **1.** *s.* Mormon; latter-day Saint. **2.** *a.* Mormon (Church, etc.). **3.** *s.m. Orn: F:* puffin.

mormonisme [mɔrmɔnism], *s.m.* Mormonism.

mormyre [mɔrmiːr], *s.m. Ich:* mormyrid; (*genus*) Mormyrus.

mormyridés [mɔrmiride], *s.m.pl. Ich:* Mormyridae.

morne[1] [mɔrn], *a.* dejected (person, etc.); gloomy (silence); dull (colour, weather, etc.); bleak, dreary, dismal, cheerless (outlook, existence, etc.); **l'aspect m. de ces montagnes,** the bleakness of these mountains.

morne[2], *s.f. A.Arms:* coronal (of tilting-lance); morne.

morne[3], *s.m.* (*in West Indies*) bluff, hillock.

morné[1] [mɔrne], *a.* **1.** (*of tilting-lance*) blunted, harmless. **2.** *Her:* disarmed (lion, etc.); (lion) morné.

morné[2], *a.* (*of meat*) tainted.

mornement [mɔrnəmɑ̃], *adv.* gloomily, dejectedly, dismally, cheerlessly.

mornifle [mɔrnifl], *s.f. F:* **1.** backhanded blow, backhander (in the face). **2.** jibe, dig (at s.o.).

morose[1] [mɔroːz], *a.* morose, moody, surly (person); gloomy, forbidding (building, etc.); **gens au visage m.,** sour-faced people.

morose[2], *a. Theol:* **délectation m.,** morose delectation.

morosité [mɔrozite], *s.f.* moroseness, moodiness, surliness; gloominess.

moro(-)sphinx [mɔrɔsfɛ̃ːks], *s.m.inv. Ent:* humming-bird hawk-moth.

moroxite [mɔrɔksit], *s.f. Miner:* moroxite.

morphal(ou) [mɔrfal(u)], *s.m. P:* greedy-guts, pig, glutton.

morphaler (se) [səmɔrfale], *v.pr. P:* to stuff, gorge, cram, oneself.

Morphée[1] [mɔrfe], *Pr.n.m. Myth:* Morpheus; **dans les bras de M.,** in the arms of Morpheus.

morphée[2], *s.f. Med:* morphea.

morphéique [mɔrfeik], *a. Psy: Med:* morphetic.

morphématique [mɔrfematik], *a. Ling:* morphemic.

morphème [mɔrfɛm], *s.m. Ling:* morpheme.

morphides [mɔrfid], *s.m.pl. Ent:* Morphoidae.

morphine [mɔrfin], *s.f.* morphia, morphine.

morphinisme [mɔrfinism], *s.m. Med:* morphinism.

morphinomane [mɔrfinɔman], *a. & s.m. & f.* morphi(n)o-maniac; morphia addict.

morphinomanie [mɔrfinɔmani], *s.f.* morphi(n)omania; the morphia habit.

morpho [mɔrfo], *s.m. Ent:* morpho.

morphogène [mɔrfɔʒɛn], *a. Physiol:* morphogenic, morphogenetic.

morphogénèse [mɔrfɔʒenɛːz], *s.f. Biol:* morphogenesis.

morphogénétique [mɔrfɔʒenetik], *a. Biol:* morphogenetic (hormones, etc.).

morphologie [mɔrfɔlɔʒi], *s.f. Biol: Ling:* morphology; *Gram:* accidence.

morphologique [mɔrfɔlɔʒik], *a.* morphological.

morphologiquement [mɔrfɔlɔʒikmɑ̃], *adv.* morphologically.

morphologue [mɔrfɔlɔg], *s.m. & f.* morphologist.

morphométrie [mɔrfɔmetri], *s.f.* morphometry.

morphophonologie [mɔrfɔfɔnɔlɔʒi], *s.f. Ling:* morphophonemics.

morphose [mɔrfoːz], *s.f. Biol:* morphosis.

morphotropie [mɔrfɔtrɔpi], *s.f.* morphotropism, morphotropy.

morphotropique [mɔrfɔtrɔpik], *a.* morphotropic.

morpion [mɔrpjɔ̃], *s.m.* **1.** *F:* crab(-louse). **2.** *P:* brat. **3.** *Games: F:* = noughts and crosses, *U.S:* tick tack toe.

morpionner [mɔrpjɔne], *v.tr.* to tack (rivet).

morrène [mɔrɛn], *s.f. Bot:* frogbit.

morrude [mɔryd], *s.m. Ich:* long-finned gurnard.

mors [mɔːr], *s.m.* **1.** (*a*) *Tls:* jaw, chap, chop (of vice); bit (of smith's tongs); **m. de serrage,** holding jaw; (*b*) *Bookb:* joint; (*c*) *Ecc.Cost:* morse (of cope). **2.** *Harn:* bit; **m. de bride,** curb bit, bridle bit; **m. de bridon, de filet,** snaffle; **m. à canon brisé,** jointed bit; **ronger son m.,** (*of horse, F: of pers.*) to champ the bit; **prendre le m. aux dents,** (i) (*of horse*) to take the bit in its teeth; to bolt; (ii) *F:* (*of pers.*) to take the bit between one's teeth; **hocher le m. à un cheval,** to jerk a horse's bridle; to urge on a horse; *F:* **hocher le m. à qn,** to shake s.o. up. **3.** *Bot:* **m. du diable,** devil's-bit scabious; **m. de grenouille,** frogbit.

morse[1] [mɔrs], *s.m. Z:* walrus.

Morse[2], *Pr.n.m. Tg:* Morse (alphabet, etc.).

morsure [mɔrsyːr], *s.f.* **1.** bite; **morsures de la gelée,** frostbite. **2.** *Engr:* biting, etching; **m. en creux,** intaglio etching; deep etching; **profondeur de m.,** depth of erosion; **solution de m. en creux,** deep etching solution; **bac, cuve, de m.,** etching trough.

mort[1], morte [mɔːr, mɔrt]. **1.** *a.* (*a*) dead (person, leaf, language, colour, etc.); **m. et enterré,** dead and buried, dead and gone; **il est m.,** he is dead; **m. et bien m.,** as dead as a doornail; **c'est un homme m.,** he is done for; he is a dead man; *Prov:* **morte la bête, m. le venin,** dead men tell no tales; **battre qn à le laisser pour m.,** to thrash s.o. within an inch of his life; **plus m. que vif,** half-dead with fright; almost ready to die with fear; more dead than alive; **cœur m. à l'affection,** heart dead to affection; **un petit trou à moitié m.,** a dead(-and)-alive little hole (of a place); *Com:* **marché m.,** dead market; **le marché est m.,** there is absolutely nothing doing; *Sp:* **ballon m.,** dead ball; ball out of play; *Geog:* **la mer Morte,** the Dead Sea; **arbre m. en cime,** stag-headed tree; *F:* **elle est morte,** let's call it a day; (*b*) **argent m.,** money lying idle, bringing in no interest; **temps m.,** time wasted, idle period (in a movement); *Metalw:* cool time; **rester lettre morte,** to remain a dead letter; *Mec.E:* **poids m.,** dead weight; *Mch:* **point m.,** (i) centre (of piston stroke); (ii) neutral position (of lever, etc.); (iii) *Aut:* neutral gear; *Aut:* **mettre le levier au point m.,** to put the (gear) lever into neutral; *Mch:* **mettre le registre au point m.,** to shut off steam; *F:* **la conférence est arrivée à un point m.,** the conference has come to a standstill, to a deadlock; *N.Arch:* **œuvres mortes,** dead works; *s.a.* BOUT 2, ESPACE 1; (*c*) **eau morte,** still, stagnant, water; *Art:* **nature morte,** still life; (*d*) **balle morte,** spent bullet. **2.** *s.* dead person; deceased; **les morts,** the dead, the departed; *Ecc:* **jour, fête, des Morts,** All Souls' day; **l'office des morts,** the burial service; **la cloche des morts,** the funeral bell; *Prov:* **les morts ont toujours tort,** the dead are always in the wrong; **faire le m.,** (i) to sham dead; (ii) *F:* to lie low (and say nothing); **tête de m.,** (i) death's head, skull; (ii) *Cu: F:* (round, red-skinned) Dutch cheese; (iii) *Bot: F:* snapdragon; *Ent:* **sphinx tête de m.,** death's head hawk moth; *Jur:* **le m. saisit le vif, le vif chasse le m.,** the estate is vested in the heir the moment the owner dies; *Aut: F:* **la place du m.,** the front passenger seat. **3.** *s.m. Cards:* dummy; **faire le m.,** to be dummy.

mort[2], *s.f.* **1.** (*a*) death; **pâle comme la m.,** as pale as death; **nombre de morts,** number of lives lost; **il n'y a pas eu m. d'homme,** (i) there was no taking of life; (ii) there was no loss of life; **mettre qn à m.,** to put s.o. to death; **condamner qn à m.,** to condemn, *Jur:* sentence, s.o. to death; **sentence, arrêt, de m.,** death sentence, sentence of death; *Jur:* **m. civile,** civil death; **à m. les traîtres!** death to the traitors! **à m. les capitalistes!** to hell with the capitalists! *P:* **m. aux vaches!** down with the cops! **blessé à m.,** mortally wounded; **lutte à la m.,** struggle to the death; **torturer qn à m.,** to torture s.o. to death; **travailler à m.,** to work oneself to death; **boire à m.,** to drink oneself to death; **se soûler à m.,** to get dead drunk; *F:* **freiner à m.,** to jam on the brakes; **se donner la m.,** to take one's own life, to commit suicide; **vous aller attraper la m.!** you'll catch your death (of cold, etc.)! **vous courez à la m.,** you're going to certain death; **mur, ravin, de la m.,** wall of death; *F:* **ce n'est pas la m. (d'un homme),** it's not all that difficult; **faire une bonne m.,** to die well; **mourir de sa belle m.,** to die a natural death; to die in one's bed; **trouver la m. dans une entreprise,** to meet, find, one's death in an enterprise; **être entre la vie et la m.,** to hover between life and death; **être à l'article de la m., à deux doigts de la mort; avoir la mort entre ses dents, sur les lèvres,** to be on the verge of death, at death's door; **arracher qn à la m.,** to snatch s.o. from the jaws of death; **à la m. de son père il rentra en France,** on his father's death he returned to France; **à sa m. la propriété lui appartenait,** at (the time of) his death, he was the owner of the estate; **haïr qn à m.,** to hate s.o. like poison, like death; **ennemis à m.,** moral enemies; deadly enemies; **fatigué à m.,** tired to death; *Lit:* **la m. d'Arthur,** the Morte d'Arthur; **sommeil de m.,** deathlike sleep; **silence de m.,** dead silence, deathlike hush; **il avait la m. dans l'âme,** he was sick at heart; **souffrir m. et passion,** to suffer agonies; **je m'en souviendrai jusqu'à la m.,** I shall remember it until my dying day; **germes de m. (dans une société, etc.),** seeds of decay; **à la vie, à la m.,** for ever; **c'est entre nous à la vie, à la m.,** we are friends for life; *Prov:* **après la m. le médecin,** that's shutting, bolting, the stable door after the horse has gone; **le monopole est la m. de l'industrie,** monopoly is the ruin of industry; (*b*) **nul ne peut tromper la M.,** no one can cheat Death. **2.** *Bot:* **m. aux chiens,** meadow saffron; **m. au(x) loup(s),** wolf's bane; **m. aux poules,** henbane; **m. aux vaches,** celery-leaved crow-foot.

mortadelle [mɔrtadɛl], *s.f. Cu:* mortadella.
mortaisage [mɔrtɛzaːʒ], *s.m.* mortising, slotting.
mortaise [mɔrtɛːz], *s.f.* slot; (*a*) *Carp:* mortise; **assemblage à tenon et à m.,** (tenon and) mortise joint; **assemblé à m.,** mortised; (*b*) sheave hole (of block); (*c*) **m. de clavette,** keyway; *Nau:* **m. de cabestan,** capstan-bar hole.
mortaiser [mɔrtɛze], *v.tr.* to slot, mortise; **machine à m.,** mortising machine, slotting machine.
mortaiseur, -euse [mɔrtɛzœːr, -øːz]. **1.** *a.* mortising, slotting (tool, etc.). **2.** *s.f.* **mortaiseuse,** mortising machine, slotting machine.
mortalité [mɔrtalite], *s.f.* mortality. **1.** mortal nature. **2.** death rate; **m. infantile,** infant mortality; *Ins:* **tables de m.,** mortality tables, expectation of life tables, actuaries' tables.
mort-aux-rats [mɔrora], *s.f.inv.* rat poison.
mort-bois [mɔrbwɑ], *s.m. For:* underwood, brushwood; undesirable tree, shrub; *pl.* forest weeds; *pl. morts-bois.*
mort-Dieu [mɔrdjø], *int. A:* **(par la) m.-D!** 'sdeath!
morte-eau [mɔrto], *s.f.* neap tide(s); neaps; *pl. mortes-eaux.*
mortel, -elle [mɔrtɛl], *a.* mortal; (*a*) destined to die; *s.* **un m., une mortelle,** a mortal; (*b*) fatal (wound, accident, etc.); **coup m.,** mortal blow, death blow; **rayon m.,** death ray; **il fit une chute mortelle de 100 mètres,** he fell 100 metres to his death; (*c*) *F:* deadly dull; **ennui m.,** unrelieved boredom; **je l'ai attendu deux mortelles heures,** I waited two mortal, solid, hours for him; (*d*) deadly (hatred, sin, enemy, etc.); **d'une pâleur mortelle,** deadly pale, deadly-white; **ennemi m.,** mortal enemy; **poison m.,** deadly poison.
mortellement [mɔrtɛlmɑ̃], *adv.* (*a*) mortally, fatally (wounded, etc.); **pécher m.,** to commit a mortal sin; (*b*) *F:* **s'ennuyer m.,** to be bored to death; **m. ennuyeux,** deadly dull; (*c*) **m. offensé,** mortally offended.
mortellerie [mɔrtɛlri], *s.f.* cement-stone milling.
mortellier [mɔrtɛlje], *s.m.* workman in charge of a cement mill.
morte-paye [mɔrtəpɛ], *s.f. A:* **1.** *Mil:* soldier on reserve with full pay. **2.** pensioner (on estate, etc.). **3.** *pl.* defaulting taxpayers, ratepayers; *pl. mortes-payes.*
morte-saison [mɔrt(ə)sɛzɔ̃], *s.f. Com: etc:* dead season, slack season, off season; **c'est la m.-s.,** there's nothing going on, nothing doing, at present; *pl. mortes-saisons.*
mort-gage [mɔrgaːʒ], *s.m. Jur: A:* chattel mortgage; *pl. morts-gages.*
morticole [mɔrtikɔl], *s.m. A: F:* doctor, sawbones; (from L. Daudet's novel *Les Morticoles*).
mortier [mɔrtje], *s.m.* **1.** mortar; (*a*) **pilon et m.,** pestle and mortar; (*b*) *Artil:* **m. de tranchée,** trench mortar; mine thrower; (*c*) *Fr.Hist:* cap, mortier (worn by High-Court presidents, etc.). **2.** *Const:* **m. ordinaire,** lime mortar; **m. gras,** rich mortar; **m. maigre,** lean mortar; **m. à prise lente,** slow-setting mortar, slow-hardening mortar; **m. hydraulique,** hydraulic cement, hydraulic mortar; **m. liquide, clair,** grout(ing); **m. de terre,** cob(-mortar); **planche à m.,** mortar board; **bâti à chaux et à m.,** strongly put together; built to last for ever.
mortifère [mɔrtifɛːr], *a.* mortiferous, death-dealing.
mortifiant [mɔrtifjɑ̃], *a.* mortifying.
mortification [mɔrtifikasjɔ̃], *s.f.* **1.** (*a*) *Med:* mortification, gangrene, necrosis; (*b*) **m. corporelle,** mortification of the body; **m. des passions,** mortification, chastening, of the passions; (*c*) mortification, humiliation. **2.** *Cu:* hanging (of game, etc.).
mortifié [mɔrtifje], *a.* **1.** mortified, humiliated. **2.** *Med:* (*occ.*) gangrened.
mortifier [mɔrtifje], *v.tr.* (*p.d. & pr.sub.* **n. mortifions, v. mortifiiez**) **1.** (*a*) to gangrene, to necrotize; to cause (limb, etc.) to mortify; (*b*) *Cu:* to hang (game, etc.). **2.** (*a*) to mortify (one's passions, body, etc.); (*b*) to mortify (s.o.); to hurt (s.o.'s) feelings.
se mortifier. **1.** *Med:* to mortify; to gangrene. **2.** (*of game, etc.*) to become tender (with hanging).
mortinaissance [mɔrtinɛsɑ̃ːs], *s.f.* stillbirth.
mortinatalité [mɔrtinatalite], *s.f.* rate of stillbirths.
mort-né, -née [mɔrne], *a. & s.* stillborn (child, etc.); *Tan:* **peau d'animal m.-n.,** slink skin; **projet m.-n.,** abortive plan, plan foredoomed to failure; *pl. mort-nés, -nées.*
mort-terrain, *s.m.,* **morts-terrains,** *s.m.pl.* [mɔrtɛrɛ̃], *Min:* dead ground; barren measures; **morts-terrains de recouvrement,** overburden.
mortuaire [mɔrtɥɛːr], *a.* mortuary (urn, etc.); of death, of burial; **drap m.,** pall; **acte, extrait, m.,** death certificate; **registre m.,** register of deaths; **avis m.,** announcement of death (in papers, etc.); **la maison m.,** the house of the deceased; **lit m.,** bed on which the body lies in state; **chambre m.,** death chamber; **dépôt m.,** mortuary; *Ecc: A:* **droit m.,** corse-present; mortuary.
morue [mɔry], *s.f.* **1.** *Ich:* cod; *Cu:* **m. fraîche,** fresh cod; **m. salée, sèche,** salt cod; **huile de foie de m.,** cod-liver oil. **2.** *P: A:* prostitute.
morula [mɔryla], *s.f. Biol:* morula.
morun [mɔrœ̃], *s.m. Ich:* morun (sturgeon), beluga, Caspian white sturgeon.
morutier [mɔrytje], *s.m.,* **moruyer** [mɔryje], *s.m.* **1.** cod-fishing boat; banker. **2.** cod-fisher(man).
morvandais, -aise [mɔrvɑ̃dɛ, -ɛːz], **morvandeau, -elle, -eaux** [mɔrvɑ̃do, -ɛl], **morvandiau, -ale, -aux** [mɔrvɑ̃djo, -al], **morvandiot, -ote** [mɔrvɑ̃djo, -ɔt], *a. & s. Geog:* (native, inhabitant) of the Morvan (region).
morve [mɔrv], *s.f.* **1.** *Vet:* glanders; **m. chronique,** farcy. **2.** nasal mucus; **enfants avec la m. au nez,** children with runny noses. **3.** *Hort:* rot (of lettuce, etc.).
morver [mɔrve], *v.i. Hort:* (*of lettuce, etc.*) to get the rot.
morveux, -euse [mɔrvø, -øːz]. **1.** *a.* (*a*) *Vet:* glandered; (*b*) *F:* snotty(-nosed); with a runny nose; *Prov:* **qui se sent m. se mouche,** if the cap fits wear it; **les morveux veulent moucher les autres,** it's like Satan reproving sin. **2.** *s.* (*a*) *F:* (young) child; (*b*) *F:* raw, green, youngster; **un petit m.,** a young puppy.
mos [mɔs], *s.m. Elcs:* most.
mosaïque[1] [mɔzaik], *a. B.Hist:* Mosaic (law, etc.).
mosaïque[2]. **1.** *s.f.* (*a*) *Art: etc:* mosaic; **dallage en, de, m.,** mosaic flooring; (*b*) *T.V:* mosaic; **m. photoélectrique,** photoelectric mosaic; (*c*) *Hort:* mosaic disease, (leaf) mosaic; **m. du tabac,** tobacco mosaic virus; **m. des tomates,** tomato mosaic virus. **2.** *a.* **reliure m.,** inlay; inlaid leather; *Phot:* **film en trichrome à réseau m.,** mosaic-screen film.
mosaïsme [mɔzaism], *s.m. Rel.H:* Mosaism.
mosaïste [mɔzaist], *a. & s. Art:* mosaicist, worker in mosaic.
mosandrite [mɔzɑ̃drit], *s.f. Miner:* mosandrite.
mosasaure [mɔzasɔːr], **mosasaurus** [mɔzasɔrys], *s.m. Paleont:* mosasaurid; (*genus*) Mosasaurus.
mosasauriens [mɔzasɔrjɛ̃], *s.m.pl. Paleont:* Mosasauri, Mosasauria.
moscatelle [mɔskatɛl], **moscatelline** [mɔskatɛlin], *s.f. Bot:* (tuberous) moschatel.
moschifère [mɔskifɛːr], *a.* moschiferous.
Moscou [mɔsku], *Pr.n. Geog:* Moscow.
moscouade [mɔskwad], *s.f. Sug.-R:* muscorado.
moscoutaire [mɔskutɛːr], *Pej:* **1.** *a.* (government, etc.) of Moscow; communist. **2.** *s.m. & f. F:* **un, une, m.,** a Bolshie, a Commie.
Moscova (la) [lamɔskɔva], *Pr.n.f. Geog:* the (river) Moskva.
moscovade [mɔskɔvad], *s.f. Sug.-R:* muscovado.
Moscovie [mɔskɔvi], *Pr.n.f. Geog: A:* Muscovy.
moscovite [mɔskɔvit], *a. & s. Geog:* Muscovite.
mosellan, -ane [mɔzɛl(l)ɑ̃, -an], *a. & s. Geog:* (native, inhabitant) of the Moselle region.
mosette [mɔzɛt], *s.f. Ecc.Cost:* moz(z)etta.
Moskova [mɔskɔva], *Pr.n.f. Geog:* the (river) Moskva.
mosquée [mɔske], *s.f.* mosque.
moss [mɔs], *s.m. F: A:* large glass or pot of beer.
mossieu [mɔsjø], *s.m. F: Hum:* = MONSIEUR.
Mossoul [mɔsul], *Pr.n. Geog:* Mosul.
most [mɔst], *s.m. Elcs:* metal oxide silicon transistor, most.
mot [mo], *s.m.* **1.** word; **répéter qch. m. pour m.,** to repeat sth. word for word; **traduire m. à m.** [motamo], **faire du m. à m.,** to translate word for word; **faire le m. à m. d'une phrase,** to construe a sentence; to translate a sentence literally; **prendre qn au m.,** to take s.o. at his word; **sans m. dire, sans dire m.,** without (saying) a word; **il me regarda sans m. dire,** he looked dumbly at me; **qui ne dit m. consent,** silence gives consent; **ne pas souffler, sonner, m. de qch.,** not to breathe a word about sth.; **ne plus dire m., ne plus souffler m.,** to subside into silence, *F:* to shut up; **dire deux mots à qn,** to have a word with s.o.; *F:* **dire deux mots à un pâté,** to tuck into a pâté; **dire, glisser, un m. pour qn,** to put in a word for s.o.; **avoir des mots avec qn,** to have words, to quarrel, with s.o.; **vous avez dit le m.!** you've hit it! **avoir le dernier m.,** to have the last word; **c'est mon dernier m.,** that's my final offer; **le dernier m. du confort,** the last word in comfort; **ignorer le premier m. de la chimie,** not to know the first word, the first thing, about chemistry; **je ne sais pas un m. d'algèbre,** I don't know a thing about algebra; **à ces mots . . .,** (i) so saying . . .; (ii) at these words . . .; **en d'autres mots,** in other words; **en un m., en peu de mots, en quelques mots,** briefly, in a word, in a nutshell; **pour vous dire la chose en deux mots, en trois mots,** (to put it) briefly; **pour dire la chose en deux mots comme en dix; en un m. comme en cent, comme en mille,** the long and the short of it is (that); in a nutshell; briefly; **au bas m.,** at the lowest estimate, the lowest figure; **gros m.,** coarse expression; swear word; *F:* **le m. de Cambronne,** *i.e.* MERDE, *q.v.* **grands mots,** fine words; **le m. de l'énigme,** the key to the enigma; **voilà le fin m. de l'affaire!** so that's what's at the bottom of it! **il faut que j'en sache le fin m.,** I must get to the bottom of it; **avoir le m. de l'affaire,** to be in the secret, in the know; **le grand m. est lâché,** the cat's out of the bag; **faire comprendre qch. à qn à mots couverts,** to give s.o. a hint of sth.; **donner le m. à qn,** to give s.o. his cue; **ils se sont donné le m.,** they are acting in collusion; it's a put-up job; **on s'est donné le m.,** the word has gone round; *Mil:* **m. de ralliement,** password; **m. d'ordre,** (i) countersign; (ii) shibboleth; key-note (of policy); **ce parti reste fidèle à ses mots d'ordre,** the party remains faithful to its watchword; **l'humanité attend toujours le m. d'ordre de la pensée française,** humanity always takes its cue from French thought; **mots croisés,** crossword (puzzle); **mots carrés,** word-square; *Tg:* **m. (télégraphique) convenu,** code word; **envoyer un (petit) m. à qn, écrire un m. à qn,** to drop s.o. a line; **j'ai reçu un m. de lui,** I had a line, a few lines, from him; **dire un m. à qn,** to speak to, have a word with, s.o.; **j'aurais un m. à vous dire,** I want a word with you; **j'ai besoin de lui dire un m.,** I want a word with him; **laissez-moi dire un m.,** let me get a word in; let me have my say; **avoir son m. à dire,** to have sth. to say; to have a contribution to make; **se permettre un m.,** to make a remark; **placer un m., dire son m.,** to put in a word; to have one's say; to make one's contribution; **je n'ai pu placer un m.,** I couldn't get a word in edgeways; **chacun lui lança son m.,** everyone had a fling, a dig, at him; **tranchons le m., vous refusez,** to put it bluntly, you refuse; **et puis il a eu ce m.,** and then he came out with this remark; **il a toujours le m. pour rire,** he's always ready with a joke; **m. historique,** historic remark, memorable saying; **bon m.,** witty remark, *F:* wisecrack; **faire des mots,** to be witty; **jeu de mots,** play on words; **jouer sur les mots,** to play on words; *Elcs:* (*computers*) **machine (à) mots,** word machine; **mémoire organisée par mots,** word-organized store, storage; **m. de commande,** control word; **m. d'index, m. d'information,** index, information, word; **m. instruction,** instruction word; **m. d'état, m. qualificatif,** status word; **drapeau m.,** word mark; **séparateur de mots,** word separator. **2.** *Her:* motto.
motacillidés [mɔtasilide], *s.m.pl. Orn:* Motacillidae, the wagtails and pipits.
motard [mɔtaːr], *s.m. F:* (*a*) motor-cyclist; (*b*) motor-cycle policeman; **m. (de la route)** = courtesy cop, speed cop; **m. d'escorte,** motor-cycle outrider.
mot-clé [mokle], *s.m.* key word; *pl. mots-clé(s).*
motel [mɔtɛl], *s.m.* motel.
motelle [mɔtɛl], *s.f. Ich:* rockling.
motet [mɔtɛ], *s.m. Mus:* motet.
moteur, -trice [mɔtœːr, -tris]. **1.** *a.* (*a*) motive, propulsive, driving (power, etc.); **arbre m.,** driving shaft, main shaft; *Mec.E:* **unité motrice,** power unit; **couple m.,** (motor) torque; **force motrice,** driving force; *Cy:* **roue motrice,** back wheel; **voiture à roues avant motrices,** car with front-wheel drive; **véhicule à quatre roues motrices,** vehicle with four-wheel drive; **l'appareil m.,** (i) *Ind: etc:* the driving machinery; (ii) *Nau:* the propelling machinery, the engines; **véhicule à traction motrice,** motor vehicle; **fourniture de force motrice,** supply of power; *I.C.E:* **temps m.,** power stroke; (*b*) *Anat:* motor(y) (nerve, muscle); motorial (excitement). **2.** *s.m.* (*a*) mover; (i) *A. & Lit:* **Dieu le souverain m. de la nature,** God the sovereign mover of nature; (ii) prime mover (of an enterprise, etc.); instigator (of a plot); (*b*) *Mec.E:* motor, engine; motor element (of mechanical contrivance); **m. à air chaud,** hot-air engine; **m. à air comprimé,** compressed-air engine, pneumatic engine; **m. à vapeur,** steam engine; **m. à vent,** wind engine, windmill; **m. hydraulique,** hydraulic

engine; **m. thermique,** thermal engine, heat engine; **m. auxiliaire,** auxiliary engine, booster; **m. démultiplié, m. à réducteurs,** geared engine; **m. non démultiplié, m. sans démultiplication,** direct-drive engine; **commandé, entraîné, mû, par m.,** motor(-driven), power(-driven); **à plusieurs moteurs, à moteurs multiples,** multi-engine(d); **m. de voiture, d'automobile, d'auto,** car engine; *U.S:* automobile engine; **m. d'avion, d'aviation,** aero-engine; **m. marin,** marine engine; **m. hors-bord,** outboard motor, **m. de lancement,** starting engine; *Cin:* **appareil (de prise de vues) à m.,** motor(-driven) camera; *I.C.E:* **m. à combustion interne, m. à explosion,** internal combustion engine; **m. Diesel,** Diesel engine; **m. à gaz,** gas engine; **m. à gaz pauvre,** producer-gas engine; **m. à essence,** petrol engine, *U.S:* gas engine; **m. à pétrole,** oil engine; **m. à pistons,** piston engine; **m. à deux, à quatre, temps,** two-stroke, four-stroke, engine; **m. (à cylindres) en ligne,** in-line engine; **m. (à cylindres) en étoile,** radial engine; **m. (à cylindres) en "V,"** V-type engine; **m. carré,** square engine; **m. droit,** upright engine; **m. inversé,** inverted engine; **m. à injection,** injection engine; **m. à soupapes,** valve engine; **m. à soupapes en tête,** valve-in-head engine; **m. à soupapes latérales,** side-valve engine; **m. à arbre à cames en tête,** overhead-valve engine; **m. sans soupape,** valve-less engine, sleeve-valve engine; **m. à refroidissement par liquide,** fluid-cooled engine; **m. à refroidissement par air,** air-cooled engine; **m. à réaction,** jet engine; **m. fixe,** stationary engine; **m. rotatif,** rotary engine, whirlwind engine; **m. électrique,** electric motor; **m. à courant alternatif, à courant continu,** alternating-current, direct-current, motor; **m. à induction,** induction motor; **m. à excitation composée, m. composé,** compensated-winding motor; **m. à excitation en dérivation, m. shunt,** shunt-wound motor; **m. (à excitation en) série,** series-wound motor; **m. à collecteur,** commutator motor; **m. universel,** universal motor; **m. linéaire,** linear motor; **m. atomique, m. nucléaire,** nuclear engine; **m. (de véhicule) spatial,** space(craft) engine; **m. à arc,** arc-jet engine; **m. à photons,** photon engine; **m. à plasma,** plasma engine; **m. ionique,** ion engine; **m. d'apogée,** apogee motor. **3.** *s.f. Rail:* **motrice,** (electric, Diesel) motor carriage.

moteur-fusée [mɔtœrfyze], *s.m.* rocket engine; *pl. moteurs-fusées.*

motif, -ive [mɔtif, -iːv]. **1.** *a.* motive (cause, etc.). **2.** *s.m.* (*a*) motive, incentive, reason; **nos motifs d'espérance,** our reasons for hope; **m. de mécontentement,** cause, grounds, for discontent; **il cherche des motifs à leur mécontentement,** he is looking for reasons for their discontent; **avoir m. à faire qch.; avoir un m. pour, de, faire qch.,** to have a motive in doing sth.; **pour des motifs de bonté,** from considerations of kindness; *F:* **courtiser qn pour le bon m.,** to court s.o. with honourable intentions, with marriage in view; **soupçons sans m.,** groundless suspicions; **insulte sans m.,** gratuitous insult; **insulter qn sans m.,** to insult s.o. gratuitously; *Jur:* **motifs d'un jugement,** grounds upon which a judgment has been delivered; (*b*) *Mil: Jur:* charge; **porter le m.,** to put on a charge; (*c*) (i) *Art:* motif; **m. de paysage,** subject for a landscape sketch; (ii) *Needlew:* design, pattern, motif (for embroidery, etc.); *Dressm:* ornament, trimming; **m. perlé,** bead trimming; (iii) *Mus:* theme, motto, figure.

motilité [mɔtilite], *s.f.* motility, motivity.

motion [mosjɔ̃], *s.f.* **1.** *A:* motion (of the limbs, etc.). **2.** motion, proposal; **faire une m.,** to propose, bring forward, a motion; to move a proposal; **faire adopter une m.,** to carry a motion; **la m. fut adoptée,** the motion was carried; **m. de censure,** motion of censure; **présenter une motion,** to table a motion.

motionnaire [mɔsjɔnɛːr], *s.m. & f.* mover of a proposal; proposer of a motion.

motionnel, -elle [mɔsjɔnɛl], *a. Ph:* motional.

motionner [mɔsjɔne], *v.i.* to propose a motion; to move a proposal.

motival, -aux [mɔtival, -o], *a. Jur:* **clause motivale,** clause expressing the reasons, the grounds, for a decision.

motivation [mɔtivasjɔ̃], *s.f. Psy: etc:* motivation; *Pol.Ec:* **études de m.,** motivational research.

motivé [mɔtive], *a.* **1. sentence arbitrale motivée,** award stating the reasons on which it is based. **2.** justified; **refus m.,** justifiable refusal; **opinion motivée,** considered opinion; **non m.,** unjustified, unwarranted; *Jur:* **décision motivée,** decision based on the evidence of reason; well-founded decision; **avis m.,** counsel's opinion.

motiver [mɔtive], *v.tr.* **1.** to state the reason for (refusal, etc.); **les juges sont obligés de m. leurs jugements,** judges are bound to give the grounds for their judgments; **m. une décision sur qch.,** to base a decision on sth. **2.** (*a*) to motive, motivate (an action); **m. les entrées et les sorties dans une pièce de théâtre,** to motivate the entrances and exits in a play; (*b*) to justify, warrant, be the motive for (sth.); **la situation motive des craintes,** the situation gives cause for apprehension; **les circonstances qui ont motivé son retour,** the circumstances to which his return was due; **action qui a motivé des critiques,** action that led to criticism.

moto [moto], *s.f. F:* motor cycle, motor bike; **je suis venu à, en, m.,** I came on my, by, motor bike.

moto-aviette [mɔtoavjɛt], *s.f. A:* light aircraft with low-powered engine; *pl. moto-aviettes.*

motobatteuse [mɔtɔbatøːz], *s.f. Agr:* motor thresher; mechanical thresher.

motobrouette [mɔtɔbruɛt], *s.f. Veh: Civ.E: etc:* dumper.

motocar [mɔtɔkaːr], *s.m. Aut: Adm:* miniature car, baby car.

motociste [mɔtɔsist], *s.m.* motor cycle dealer, repairer.

motocompresseur [mɔtɔkɔ̃prɛsœːr], *s.m.* compressor unit, (air) compressor.

motocross [mɔtɔkrɔs], *s.m. Sp:* (*a*) motor-cycle scramble; moto-cross; (*b*) rough riding.

motoculteur [mɔtɔkyltœːr], *s.m. Agr:* (power-driven) cultivator.

motoculture [mɔtɔkyltyːr], *s.f.* mechanized farming.

motocyclable [mɔtɔsiklabl̩], *a. Adm:* (track) suitable for motor cycles.

motocycle [mɔtɔsikl̩], *s.m. Adm:* motor bicycle.

motocyclette [mɔtɔsiklɛt], *s.f.* motor cycle, *F:* motor bike.

motocycliste [mɔtɔsiklist], *s.m.* motor cyclist; *Mil:* dispatch-rider.

motofaucheuse [mɔtɔfoʃøːz], *s.f.* motor scythe.

motogodille [mɔtɔgɔdiːj], *s.f.* outboard motor.

motolaveur [mɔtɔlavœːr], *s.m.* washing-up machine.

motomodèle [mɔtɔmɔdɛl], *s.m.* motorized model aircraft.

motonautique [mɔtɔnotik], *a.* **sport m.,** motor-boating.

motonautisme [mɔtɔnotism], *s.m.* motor-boating.

motoneurone [mɔtɔnørɔn], *s.m.* motor neuron.

motoplaneur [mɔtɔplanœːr], *s.m. Av:* glider equipped with an auxiliary engine.

motopompe [mɔtɔpɔ̃ːp], *s.f.* (movable) motor-driven pump.

motopropulseur [mɔtɔprɔpylsœːr], *a. & s.m.* **(groupe) m.,** power unit.

motorisation [mɔtɔrizasjɔ̃], *s.f.* motorization, mechanization.

motorisé [mɔtɔrise], *a.* fitted with a motor, motorized; *F:* **vous êtes m.?** have you got a car? are you mobile?

motoriser [mɔtɔrize], *v.tr.* to motorize; to mechanize.

motoriste [mɔtɔrist], *s.m.* motor mechanic.

motoscie [mɔtɔsi], *s.f.* motor saw.

mototracteur [mɔtɔtraktœːr], *s.m.* motor tractor.

mot-outil [mouti], *s.m. Ling:* form word, link word; *pl. mots-outils.*

motoviticulture [mɔtɔvitikyltyːr], *s.f.* motorized viticulture.

mot-phrase [mofrɑːz], *s.m. Ling:* sentence word; *pl. mots-phrases.*

mot-piège [mopjɛːʒ], *s.m.* deceptive cognate; *pl. mots-pièges.*

motrice. *See* MOTEUR.

motricité [mɔtrisite], *s.f. Biol:* motivity; *Psy:* motricity, motor function.

mot-souche [mosuʃ], *s.m. Typ:* catchword (in catalogue, etc.); *pl. mots-souche(s).*

mottage [mɔtaːʒ], *s.m.* (*of cement*) binding capacity.

motte [mɔt], *s.f.* **1.** mound (of windmill, etc.); *Archeol:* motte; **m. de taupe,** molehill. **2.** clod, lump (of earth); *Hort:* ball (left on roots of tree); **m. de gazon,** sod, turf; **m. de tourbe,** turf of peat, block of peat; **m. à brûler,** (i) sod of peat; (ii) briquette (of spent tan, olive marc, etc.); **m. de beurre,** pat, block, of butter; *For:* **plantation en mottes,** ball planting.

motteau, -eaux [mɔto], *s.m.* islet in river (formed of clods of earth and branches).

motter [mɔte], *v.tr.* to throw clods of earth at, to clod (sheep, etc.).

se motter, *Ven:* (*of partridge, etc.*) to take cover behind a clod.

mottereau, -eaux [mɔtro], *s.m. Orn:* sand martin.

motteux [mɔtø], *s.m. Orn: Dial:* wheatear, white tail, stonechat; *s.a.* TRAQUET[1] 2.

motton [mɔtɔ̃], *s.m.* lump (in porridge, etc.).

mottramite [mɔtramit], *s.f. Miner:* mottramite.

motu proprio [mɔtyprɔprio], *Lt.adv.phr.* (to act, etc.) on one's own initiative, of one's own accord.

motus [mɔtys], *int.* mum's the word! don't say a word! keep it dark!

mou[1], mol, *f.* **molle** [mu, mɔl]. **1.** *a.* (*the masc. form* **mol** *is used before vowel or h "mute" in the word group*) soft (wax, tyre, etc.); slack (rope, belt); weak, lifeless, soft, flabby, languid, spiritless, *F:* spineless (person); flabby, flaccid (flesh, hand); dull, flat (wine); woolly, flabby, limp (style); feeble (attempt); lax (government); gentle, light (breeze); calm (sea); soft, close, muggy (weather); *Rad.-A:* **rayons mous,** soft rays; **fromage m.,** soft cheese; *Art:* **pinceau m., touche molle,** brush lacking in vigour; **homme m. au travail,** man who is slack, indolent, at his work; **m., mol, au toucher,** soft to the touch; **reposant sur un mol (et doux) oreiller,** resting on a (soft and) downy pillow; *F:* **pâte molle, cire molle,** person you can twist round your little finger; *F:* **m. comme une chiffe, comme une chique,** as limp as a rag. **2.** *s.m.* (*a*) slack (of rope, belt, etc.); slab (of sail); slackness (of gear, etc.); **donner du m. à un cordage,** to slack off, slacken, ease, a rope; **prendre, faire rendre, le m.,** to take in the slack; (*of rope*) **prendre du m.,** to slacken; *s.a.* EMBRAQUER; (*b*) *F:* **c'est un m.,** he's (completely) spineless; (*c*) *P:* **bourrer le m. à qn,** to stuff s.o. up (with lies); to pull a fast one over on s.o.; **rentrer dans le m. à qn,** to go for s.o., to give s.o. a (good) bashing.

mou[2], *s.m.* (*a*) lights, lungs (of slaughtered animal); **acheter du m. pour le chat,** to buy some lights for the cat; (*b*) *P:* **les mous,** the lungs.

mouchage [muʃaːʒ], *s.m.* **1.** nose blowing, blowing one's nose. **2.** snuffing (of candles).

moucharabieh [muʃarabje], *s.m.* moucharaby.

mouchard [muʃaːr], *s.m. F:* (*a*) informer; police spy; stool pigeon; *Sch:* sneak; (*b*) detective; (*c*) spy hole (in door); (*d*) mechanical speed check (on trains and lorries); (*e*) time clock, watchman's clock; (*f*) *Av:* observation plane, snooper; **m. radioactif,** snooperscope.

mouchardage [muʃardaːʒ], *s.m. F:* spying, sneaking; **m. électronique,** telephone tapping.

moucharder [muʃarde], *v.tr. F:* (*a*) to spy on (s.o.); *abs.* to spy; (*b*) to denounce (s.o.).

mouche [muʃ], *s.f.* **1.** fly; **m. commune,** house fly; **m. à viande,** blowfly; bluebottle; **m. dorée (de la viande),** greenbottle, blowfly; **m. noire,** black fly; **m. du vinaigre,** vinegar fly; **m. des chevaux,** horsefly, bot fly; **m. à chien, m. araignée,** tick; **m. d'Espagne,** Spanish fly, blistering fly; **m. à feu,** firefly; **m. à miel,** honey bee; **m. de la Saint-Jean, de la Saint-Marc,** bibio; **m. à scie,** sawfly; **m. glossine, m. tsé-tsé,** tsetse fly; **piqué des mouches,** flyblown; **on mourait comme des mouches,** they were dying like flies; **faire d'une m. un éléphant,** to make a mountain out of a molehill; **on aurait entendu voler une m.,** you could have heard a pin drop; **prendre la m.,** to fly into a temper, to take offence; **quelle m. vous prend? quelle m. vous pique?** what's the matter with you? what's bitten you? *F:* **c'est une fine m.,** he's a sharp customer, a crafty little so and so; **il ne ferait pas de mal à une m.,** he wouldn't hurt a fly; *P:* **tuer les mouches au vol, à quinze pas,** to have foul breath; *Fish:* **m. mouillée,** wet fly; **m. noyée,** wet, sunk, fly; **m. à saumon,** salmon fly; **pêche à la m. sèche, flottante.** dry-fly fishing; **pêche à la m. noyée,** wet-fly fishing; **fabricant, monteur, de mouches artificielles,** fly maker; *Box:* **poids m.,** flyweight; *s.a.* GOBER, PATTE 1. **2.** (*a*) spot, speck; stain (on garment, etc.); *Bill:* spot (for red ball, etc.); *Cost: A:* patch (on face); beauty spot; *Med:* **mouches volantes,** muscae volitantes, *F:* floating specks (before the eyes); (*b*) tuft of hair (on lower lip); chin tuft; (*c*) bull's eye (of target); **faire m.,** to hit the bull's eye; to get, score, a bull; **faire m. six fois,** to get, score, six bulls; (*d*) catch (of clasp knife); **couteau à m.,** clasp knife (with lock back); (*e*) *Fenc:* covering of foil button; button (on sword); (*f*) *Tls:* point (of drill). **3. m. d'escadre,** (i) *Navy:* dispatch boat; (ii) *Navy:* scout; *Av:* air scout. **4.** *P: O:* = MOUCHARD.

moucher[1] [muʃe], *v.tr.* **1.** (*a*) to wipe (child's, etc.) nose; **mouche ton nez,** (i) wipe, blow, your nose; (ii) *P:* mind your own business; (*b*) **m. du sang,** to bleed at the nose (when blowing it); (*c*) *F:* to put (s.o.) in his place; to snub (s.o.); to tell (s.o.) off; to sit on (s.o.); **il a été mouché de la**

belle façon, he got properly snubbed. **2.** (*a*) to snuff (candle); (*b*) to cut the frayed end off (rope); to trim, to square up, the end of (piece of wood). **3.** *P:* to beat (s.o.) up. **4** *v.i. Fish:* (*of trout*) to rise to the bait.

se moucher, to wipe, blow, one's nose; *F:* **il ne se mouche pas du pied,** (i) he thinks no small beer of himself; he does things in great style; (ii) *A:* he's a smart chap, he's no fool; **ne pas avoir le temps de se m.,** to be on the go the whole time; *P:* **je m'en mouche,** I don't care a damn; *s.a.* MORVEUX 2.

moucher[2], *v.tr. A:* = MOUCHARDER.

moucherie [muʃri], *s.f.* wiping of one's nose; nose-blowing.

moucherolle [muʃrɔl], *s.f. Orn:* flycatcher.

moucheron[1] [muʃrɔ̃], *s.m.* **1.** gnat, midge; *s.a.* CHAMEAU 1. **2.** *F:* (*occ. f.* **moucheronne**) brat, urchin, kid.

moucheron[2], *s.m.* snuff (of candle).

moucheronnage [muʃrɔna:ʒ], *s.m.* rising (of fish to the surface).

moucheronner [muʃrɔne], *v.i.* (*of fish*) to leap at flies, to be on the rise.

mouchet [muʃɛ], *s.m. Orn:* hedge sparrow, dunnock, chanter.

moucheté [muʃte], *a.* spotty, speckled, flecked; **cheval m.,** flea-bitten horse; **chat m.,** tabby cat; **blé m.,** smutty wheat; *Leath:* **chamois m.,** mottled chamois; **acajou m.,** bird's eye mahogany.

moucheter [muʃte], *v.tr.* (**je mouchette, n. mouchetons; je mouchetterai**) **1.** to spot, speckle; **la mer se mouchetait d'écume,** the sea was flecked with foam; **mer mouchetée d'écume,** foam-flecked sea. **2.** (*a*) **m. un fleuret,** to cover the button of a foil; **m. une épée,** to put a button on a sword; to button a sword; (*b*) *Nau:* to mouse (hook).

mouchetis [muʃti], *s.m. Const:* (type of) rough-rendering (for outside walls).

mouchette [muʃɛt], *s.f.* **1.** *pl.* (pair of) snuffers. **2.** (*a*) *Arch:* outer fillet (of drip moulding, of label), (*b*) *Carp:* moulding plane. **3.** (*a*) *Husb:* nose ring (for pig, etc.); (*b*) *pl. Vet:* barnacles.

moucheture [muʃty:r], *s.f.* spot, speck, speckle, fleck; **mouchetures d'hermine,** ermine tails.

moucheur, -euse [muʃœ:r, -ø:z], *s.* **1.** *Th: A:* candle-snuffer. **2.** *A: F:* inveterate nose-blower. **3.** *Fish:* fly fisher.

mouchoir [muʃwa:r], *s.m.* **1. m. (de poche),** (pocket) handkerchief; **m. fin,** cambric handkerchief; **m. (de cou),** scarf; **m. (de tête),** head scarf; *P:* **le m. d'Adam,** one's fingers; **jardin grand comme un m. (de poche),** garden the size of a pocket handkerchief; **se garer dans un m.,** to park in a space no bigger than a pocket handkerchief; (*of car, etc.*) **manœuvrer dans un m. de poche,** to turn on a sixpence; *Sp:* **arriver dans un m.,** to arrive all in a bunch; to make a close finish.

mouchure [muʃy:r], *s.f.* **1.** nasal mucus. **2.** (*a*) snuff (of candle); (*b*) fag-end (cut off rope); *Carp:* waste end (cut off board).

moudir [mudi:r], *s.m. Turkish Adm:* mudir.

moudre [mudr̩], *v.tr.* (*pr.p.* **moulant**; *p.p.* **moulu**; *pr.ind.* **je mouds, il moud, n. moulons, ils moulent**; *pr.sub.* **je moule**; *p.d.* **je moulais**; *p.h.* **je moulus**; *fu.* **je moudrai**) to grind, mill (corn, etc.); to grind (coffee); **m. en grosse,** to grind (corn) by the low, flat, process; **m. un air,** to grind out a tune (on barrel organ); **m. qn de coups,** to rain blows on s.o., to give s.o. a good thrashing; **moulu de coups,** black and blue; **m. du vent,** to waste one's time on a futile piece of work.

moue [mu], *s.f.* pout; **faire la m.,** to purse one's lips, to pout, to look sulky; **faire une vilaine m.,** to pull a face; to look black; **il a fait la m. à notre proposition,** he didn't enthuse over our proposal.

mouette [mwɛt], *s.f. Orn:* gull; **m. rieuse,** black-headed gull; **m. brune,** lesser black-backed gull; **m. argentée,** herring gull; **m. tridactyle,** kittiwake; **m. de Bonaparte,** Bonaparte's gull; **m. de Ross,** Ross's gull; **m. de Sabine,** Sabine's gull; **m. sénateur,** ivory gull; **m. pygmée,** little gull; **m. mélanocéphale,** Mediterranean gull.

mouf(f)ette [mufɛt], *s.f. Z:* skunk.

mouflage [mufla:ʒ], *s.m. Tchn:* reeving; **m. à quatre, à six, brins,** four-, six-, line reeving.

mouflard, -arde [mufla:r, -ard], *s.* fat-cheeked, round-faced, heavy-jowled, person.

moufle[1] [mufl̩], *s.f. or m.* **1.** *s.f.* (*glove without fingers*) mitten; *El.E:* wiring glove. **2.** *Mec.E:* (*a*) pulley-block (with several sheaves), tackle-block; (*b*) (= PALAN) (block and) tackle; purchase; (*c*) trolley (on ropeway). **3.** *Const:* tie (bar), clamp.

moufle[2], *s.m.* (*in Ch: often f.*) *Ch: Cer:* muffle; **(four à) moufle,** muffle furnace.

mouflé [mufle], *a.* **poulie mouflée,** single pulley in a tackle.

moufler[1] [mufle], *v.tr.* **1.** *Const:* to tie (walls). **2.** *Tchn:* **m. un câble,** to reeve a cable.

moufler[2], *v.tr.* to put (enamel ware, pottery, etc.) in a muffle furnace.

mouflet, -ette [muflɛ, -ɛt], *s. F:* kid, brat.

mouflette [muflɛt], *s.f.* **1.** *Mec.E:* differential block. **2.** *Veh:* pole tip, shaft tip.

mouflon [muflɔ̃], *s.m. Z:* moufflon, wild sheep; **m. à manchettes,** maned, ruffled, moufflon; **m. d'Amérique, du Canada, des Rocheuses,** big horn.

mougeotte [muʒɔt], *s.f.* private letterbox.

mouillabilité [mujabilite], *s.f. Ph: Ch:* absorptivity, absorptive power.

mouillable [mujabl̩], *a. Ph: Ch:* absorbing, absorbent (surface, etc.).

mouillade [mujad], *s.m. Ind:* moistening, damping (of tobacco leaves).

mouillage [muja:ʒ], *s.m.* **1.** (*a*) moistening, damping; (*b*) (fraudulent) watering (of wine); (*c*) *Ph: Ch:* absorption; (*d*) *Fin:* watering down (of capital). **2.** *Nau:* (*a*) casting anchor, anchoring; **poste de m.,** anchoring berth; (*b*) laying, mooring (of mine); putting down (of buoy). **3.** anchorage, mooring ground; **être au m.,** to ride at anchor; **prendre son m.,** to anchor; **changer de m.,** to change berth; **droits de m.,** mooring dues; berthage, keelage; **m. forain,** open berth.

mouillance [mujɑ̃:s], *s.f. Ch: Ph:* absorptivity.

mouillant [mujɑ̃]. **1.** *a. Tchn: Ind:* softening, dampening (chemicals, agents, etc.); *Ch: Ph:* absorptive. **2.** *s.m. Tex: Tan: etc:* softener, damp(en)er.

mouille [mu:j], *s.f.* **1.** (*a*) pool (in a river); (*b*) section of a river (*esp.* the Loire) bordering the bank. **2.** depression formed by running water. **3.** meadow spring. **4.** damage by water to goods in transit; damp marks. **5.** moistening, damping.

mouillé [muje], *a.* **1.** (*a*) moist, damp, wet; **joues mouillées de larmes,** cheeks wet with tears; **m. à tordre,** wringing wet, soaking wet; **m. jusqu'aux os,** wet to the skin, wet through; *Nau:* **surface mouillée,** wetted surface (of ship); **voix mouillée,** voice charged with emotion; *F:* (*pers.*) **poule mouillée,** wet, drip; *F:* **il est m. dans cette affaire,** he's involved in this business; he's in it up to the neck; (*b*) **vin (etc.) m.,** watered-down wine (etc.); (*c*) **il fait m.,** it's wet, it's raining; **mois m.,** rainy month. **2.** *Nau:* (*of ship*) (lying) at anchor; moored. **3.** *Ling:* palatalized (consonant).

mouille-bouche [mujbuʃ], *s.f.inv.* juicy pear; *esp.* bergamot pear.

mouille-étiquettes [mujetikɛt], *s.m.inv.* (stamp and envelope) damper.

mouillement [mujmɑ̃], *s.m.* **1.** moistening, damping; *Cu:* basting. **2.** *Ling:* palatalization.

mouiller [muje], *v.tr.* **1.** (*a*) to wet, moisten, damp; *Cu:* to baste; to add a liquid; **m. un ragoût avec du vin,** to cook a stew in wine; **m. du linge,** (i) to steep, soak, linen; (ii) to damp, sprinkle, linen (for ironing); **se m. les pieds,** to get one's feet wet; **se faire m. en rentrant,** to get wet coming home; *P:* **en m.,** to talk nineteen to the dozen; (*b*) to dilute; **m. du vin,** to water down wine; **m. le lait,** to water the milk; (*c*) *F:* **il mouille,** it's raining. **2.** *Nau:* (*a*) **m. l'ancre,** to cast, drop, anchor; **m. un navire,** to bring a ship to anchor, to anchor a ship; *abs.* to anchor; to lie at anchor; (*b*) *abs.* **m. au large,** to bring up, to anchor, in the open sea; **m. par l'arrière,** to anchor by the stern; **mouillez!** let go (the anchor)! (*c*) to lay, launch (mine); to moor (mine, *Ven:* decoy); to put down (buoy). **3.** *Ling:* to palatalize (consonant). **4.** *v.i. P:* to be afraid; **les m.,** to funk it; **quand j'ai sauté en parachute j'ai drôlement mouillé,** when I parachuted down I was in a blue funk. **5.** *v.i. Ph:* (*capillarity*) **le liquide mouille, ne mouille pas,** the liquid is elevated, depressed.

se mouiller, (*a*) to become wet; (*of pers.*) to get wet; (*of eyes*) to water; **ses yeux se mouillèrent,** the tears came to his eyes; (*b*) *F:* to stick one's neck out; **il ne veut pas se m.,** he doesn't want to take any risks, to get mixed up in the business.

mouillère [mujɛ:r], *s.f.* wet, boggy, patch (in field).

mouillette [mujɛt], *s.f.* **1.** *Cu:* sippet; finger (of bread, etc.). **2.** *El:* moving contact (of mercury interrupter). **3.** sprinkling brush.

mouilleur, -euse[1] [mujœ:r, -ø:z], *s.* **1.** (*a*) one who wets or waters sth.; **m. de lait,** dairyman who waters his milk; (*b*) *Navy:* **m. de mines, de filets,** minelayer, net layer; **m. de mines côtier,** coastal minelayer; **m. de mines d'escadre,** fleet minelayer; **sous-marin m. de mines,** submarine minelayer; **avion m. de mines,** mine-laying aircraft. **2.** *s.m.* (*a*) moistener, damper (for stamps, etc.); *Metalw:* sprinkler, swab; (*b*) *Nau:* tumbler (of anchor), trip stopper, anchor tripper.

mouilleux, -euse[2] [mujø, -ø:z]. **1.** *a.* damp, wet (ground). **2.** *s.f. Paperm: etc:* **mouilleuse,** humidifier.

mouilloir [mujwa:r], *s.m. Tex: etc:* water pot (for moistening the fingers).

mouillure [mujy:r], *s.f.* **1.** wetting; *Typ:* damping, wetting; *Agr:* (light) watering. **2.** damp mark, stain. **3.** *Ling:* palatality, palatalization, (of consonant).

mouise [mwi:z], *s.f. P:* poverty; **être dans la m.,** to be in great straits, hard up.

moujik [muʒik], *s.m.* moujik.

moujingue [muʒɛ̃:g], *s.m. P:* (*a*) child, kid, brat; (*b*) **tricoter le m.,** to bring about an abortion.

Moukden [mukdɛn], *Pr.n. Geog:* Mukden.

moukère [mukɛ:r], *s.f. P:* (*a*) woman; (*b*) mistress; (*c*) prostitute, tart.

moulage[1] [mula:ʒ], *s.m.* **1.** grinding, milling (of corn). **2.** grinding machinery (of mill).

moulage[2], *s.m.* **1.** casting, moulding; *Metall:* founding (of iron); **m. en coquille,** chilled casting, die casting; **m. par enrobage,** investment casting; **m. par injection,** injection moulding; **m. par pression,** compression moulding; **m. en terre,** loam casting; **m. à noyau,** hollow casting; **m. à cire perdue,** (i) *Art:* cire-perdue, lost wax, process; (ii) *Metall:* waste wax casting. **2.** (*thing cast*) **m. au plâtre, en plâtre,** (i) plaster cast; (ii) *Const:* plaster moulding.

moule[1] [mul], *s.m.* **1.** mould; (*a*) *Metall: Art:* matrix; **m. à gelée,** jelly mould; **m. à balles,** bullet mould; **m. à beurre,** butter print; **m. à fromage,** cheese tub; **m. de bouton,** button mould; *Metall:* **m. à fonte,** casting mould; **m. en fonte,** chill (mould); *Glassm:* **m. mesureur,** parison mould; *A:* **jeter qch. en m.,** to cast sth.; *F:* **cela ne se jette pas en m.,** it's more easily said than done; **ils ont tous été jetés dans le même m.,** they are all cast in the same mould; they are all exactly alike; **jeune femme faite au m.,** exquisitely proportioned young woman; **jambes faites au m.,** shapely legs; *F:* **le m. en est brisé, cassé, perdu, on a cassé le m.,** we shan't see his, her, its, like again; (*b*) *Geol:* **m. externe,** mould (of fossil); **m. interne,** cast. **2.** (net maker's) net pin.

moule[2], *s.f.* **1.** *Moll:* mussel; **m. d'étang,** freshwater mussel. **2.** *P:* (*pers.*) (*a*) drip, wet; (*b*) fool, idiot.

moulé [mule], *a.* cast, moulded; **acier m.,** moulded steel, cast steel; **statue de plâtre m.,** plaster cast; **pain m.,** tin(ned) loaf; *F:* **bien m.,** shapely, well-proportioned; **homme bien m.,** man with a good figure; *F:* **c'est m.!** it fits you like a glove! **écriture moulée,** copperplate handwriting; **lettres moulées,** *s.m.* **moulé,** block letters.

moule-beurre [mulbœ:r], *s.m.inv.* butter print.

mouler [mule], *v.tr.* (*a*) to cast (statue in liquid material); to found (iron); (*b*) to mould (statue, etc., in plastic material); *F:* **robe qui moule la taille,** tightly fitting dress; dress that clings to the figure; **se m. sur qn,** to model oneself on s.o.

mouleur [mulœ:r], *s.m.* caster, moulder.

moulier, -ière[1] [mulje, -jɛ:r]. **1.** *a.* mussel (industry, etc.). **2.** *s.f.* **moulière,** mussel bed.

moulière[2], *s.f.* **1.** boggy ground. **2.** soft streak (in oil-stone).

moulin [mulɛ̃], *s.m.* **1.** mill; (*a*) **m. à farine,** flour mill; **m. à vent,** windmill; **m. à toit tournant,** smock mill; **m. à corps tournant,** post mill; *F:* **se battre contre des moulins à vent,** to fight windmills, to tilt at windmills (like Don Quixote); **m. à eau,** water-mill; **roue de m.,** millwheel; **constructeur de moulins,** millwright; **faire venir l'eau au m.,** to bring grist to the mill; (*of young woman*) **jeter son bonnet par dessus les moulins,** to throw propriety to the winds; *F:* **on y entre comme dans un m.,** anybody can go in; (*b*) **m. à minerai,** ore crusher; **m. à huile,** oil crusher; *Min:* **m. à bocards,** stamp mill; **m. à cylindres,** (crushing) rolls; **m. à scie,** saw-mill; (*c*) **m. à poivre,** pepper mill; **m. à légumes,** food, vegetable, mill; **m. à café,** (i) coffee mill; (ii) *Mil: P:* machine gun; **m. à prières,** prayer wheel; *F:* **m. à paroles,** (i) tongue; (ii) chatterbox; windbag; (*d*) *Aut: Av: F:* engine; **j'ai fait refaire le m. à 80.000 km.,** I had the engine overhauled at 80,000 km. **2.** *Geol:* pothole (in glacier).

moulinage [mulina:ʒ], *s.m.* **1.** grinding, milling. **2.** *Tex:* throwing (of silk).

mouliner [muline], *v.tr.* **1.** (*a*) *Tex:* to throw (silk); (*b*) *Fish:* to reel in (the line). **2.** *A:* (*of insect, worm*) to eat into (wood). **3.** *Tan:* **m. les peaux,** to paddle the skins. **4.** (*a*) to crush (olives); (*b*) *F:* **m. des légumes,** to pass vegetables through the mill; (*c*) *abs. Cy: F:* to pedal away; (*d*) *abs. F:* to chatter.

moulinet [mulinɛ], *s.m.* **1.** (*a*) winch; *Ropem:* **m. à bitord,** spunyarn winch; (*b*) *Fish:* reel; **m. à cliquet,** click reel; (*c*) rack-lashing or racking stick; (*d*) child's paper windmill; (*e*) **m. à musique,** toy musical box. **2.** turnstile. **3.** (*a*) *Ind:* paddle (wheel); **m. à tanner,** tanning paddle; (*b*) *Hyd.E:* current meter. **4.** (*a*) *Fenc:* moulinet; **faire des moulinets (avec sa canne),** to twirl one's stick (about one's head); to flourish one's stick; (*b*) *Danc:* moulinet. **5.** *Crust:* **m. gastrique,** (lobster's) triturating apparatus; gastric mill; lady. **6.** *Av:* **hélice tournant en m.,** windmilling propeller.

Moulinette [mulinɛt], *s.f. Dom.Ec: R.t.m:* Moulinette, vegetable shredder.

moulineur, -euse [mulinœːr, -øːz], *s.* **1.** *s.m. Min:* putter, trammer. **2.** *Tex:* (silk) throwster, thrower.

moulinier, -ière [mulinje, -jɛːr], *s.* **1.** *Tex:* (silk) thrower. **2.** *s.m.* owner, manager, of an oil mill.

moulinois, -oise [mulinwa, -waːz], *a. & s. Geog:* (native, inhabitant) of Moulins.

moulon [mulɔ̃], *s.m. A:* heap.

moult [mult], *adv. A. & Hum:* much, greatly.

moulu [muly], *a.* (*a*) ground, powdered; **or m.,** ormulu; (*b*) *F:* (i) dead-beat, fagged out; (ii) aching all over.

moulurage [mulyraːʒ], *s.m. Carp: Ind:* profiling; moulding.

mouluration [mulyrasjɔ̃], *s.f.* design of mouldings.

moulure [mulyːr], *s.f. Arch: Carp:* (ornamental) moulding; profile; profiling; **rabot à moulures,** moulding plane.

moulurer [mulyre], *v.tr.* to cut a moulding on (sth.); to profile; **machine à m.,** moulding machine; **profils moulurés,** mouldings.

moumout, -oute [mumu, -ut], *s.* **1.** *O:* (*nursery language*) pussy, kitty. **2.** *s.f. P:* wig, toupet.

mourant, -ante [murɑ̃, -ɑ̃ːt]. **1.** *a.* (*a*) dying (person, embers, etc.); **voix mourante,** (i) dying voice; (ii) faint, trailing, voice; **d'une voix mourante,** faintly, in a faint voice; **regarder qn avec des yeux mourants,** to look at s.o. with languishing eyes; **bleu m.,** pale blue; (*b*) *F:* screamingly funny; killing; (*c*) *F:* exasperating; maddening. **2.** *s.* dying man, woman; **les mourants,** the dying.

mourir [muriːr], *v.i.* (*pr.p.* **mourant;** *p.p.* **mort;** *pr.ind.* **je meurs, il meurt, n. mourons, ils meurent;** *pr.sub.* **je meure, nous mourions;** *p.d.* **je mourais;** *p.h.* **il mourut;** *fu.* **je mourrai** [murre]; *the aux. is* **être**) (*a*) to die; **bien m.,** (i) to die in the faith, to die well; (ii) to meet death calmly, without flinching; **il est mort hier,** he died yesterday; **il y a cinq ans qu'il est mort,** it is five years since he died; **si vous veniez à m.,** if anything happened to you; **m. de faim,** (i) to die of starvation; (ii) *F:* to be starving; **m. de mort naturelle, m. de sa belle mort,** to die a natural death; to die in one's bed; **m. de mort violente,** to die a violent death; *F:* **il m'a fait le coup de m.,** he died on me; **elle l'aimait à en m.,** she was desperately in love with him; **m. avant l'âge,** to die before one's time; to come to an untimely end; **m. à la peine, à la tâche,** to die in harness; **au moment de m.,** when about to die; in the hour of death; **on ne sait pas comment il mourut,** we do not know how he died; **m. martyr pour une cause,** to die a martyr in a cause; *A:* **je veux m. si ce n'est pas vrai,** may I die if it is not true; **il mourut glorieusement,** he died a glorious death; **faire m. qn,** (i) to put s.o. to death; (ii) *F:* to worry s.o. to death; **faire m. qn de froid,** to give s.o. his death of cold; *F:* **il me fera m.,** he will be the death of me; **je mourais de peur,** I was frightened to death; **toutes ces inquiétudes me font m.,** all this anxiety is killing me; **vous me faites m. d'impatience,** you are killing me with suspense; I'm dying to know; **faire m. qn à petit feu,** to keep s.o. on tenterhooks; *Lit: A:* **je meurs pour Isabelle,** I am dying for love of Isabel; **la presse était à m.,** we were nearly crushed to death; **ennuyer qn à m.,** to bore s.o. to death; **m. d'envie de faire qch.,** to be dying to do sth.; **je mourais d'envie de le lui dire,** I was dying, bursting, to tell him; **je mourais de rire,** I nearly died laughing; **c'est à m. de rire,** it's simply killing; (*b*) to die away, out; *Min:* (*of seam*) to peter out; **laisser m. le feu,** to let the fire die out; *Mus:* **en mourant,** morendo; **le son s'en va en mourant,** the sound is dying away; **voix qui meurt à la fin de chaque phrase,** voice that dies away, trails off, at the end of each sentence.

se mourir, (*a*) to be dying; (*thus used only in the pres. and p.d. of the indicative*); **je sens que je me meurs,** I feel that I am dying; (*b*) to die away, die out; to fade (away); **la lampe se mourait,** the lamp was giving out.

Mourmane [murman], *Pr.n. Geog:* **côte M.,** Murmansk coast.

Mourmansk [murmɑ̃sk], *Pr.n. Geog:* Murmansk.

mouron [murɔ̃], *s.m.* **1.** *Bot:* **m. rouge, des champs, faux m.,** scarlet pimpernel; **m. blanc, m. des oiseaux,** chickweed; **m. des fontaines,** water blinks, water chickweed, blinking chickweed; **m. d'eau,** water pimpernel, brookweed. **2.** *P:* hair; **ne plus avoir de m. sur la cage,** to be as bald as a coot; **se faire du m.,** to worry oneself stiff; to get in a stew.

mourre [muːr], *s.f. Games:* mor(r)a.

mouscaille [muskɑːj], *s.f. P:* **être dans la m.,** to be in a mess, in a fix, in the soup; to be up to the neck in it.

mousmé(e) [musme], *s.f.* (*a*) mousmee, Japanese waitress; (*b*) *P:* woman, skirt.

mousquet [muskɛ], *s.m. A:* musket; **à (une) portée de m.,** within musket shot.

mousquetade [muskətad], *s.f. A:* **1.** musket shot. **2.** volley (of musket shots).

mousquetaire [muskətɛːr], *s.m. A:* musketeer; **gants (à la) m.,** gauntlet gloves; **poignets, manchettes, m.,** double cuff (of shirt sleeve).

mousqueter [muskəte], *v.tr.* (**je mousquète, n. mousquetons; je mousquèterai**) *A:* to fire a musket at (s.o.).

mousqueterie [muskətri, -kɛ-], *s.f.* musketry; **feu de m.,** rifle fire.

mousqueton [muskətɔ̃], *s.m.* **1.** (*a*) *A:* musketoon, blunderbuss; (*b*) *Mil: A:* artillery carbine; (*c*) *Mil:* cavalry magazine rifle. **2.** snap (hook).

moussaillon [musajɔ̃], *s.m. F:* young ship's boy.

moussant [musɑ̃]. **1.** *a.* frothing, foaming. **2.** *s.m. Ch:* frother, froth flotation agent. **3.** *s.f. P:* **moussante,** beer, ale.

mousse[1] [mus], *s.f.* **1.** moss; **couvert de m.,** moss-grown; **m. d'azur,** eritrichium; **m. perlée d'Irlande,** pearl moss, carrageen; **m. de chêne,** plum-tree evernia; **m. terrestre,** walking fern; **étendu sur un lit de m.,** lying on a mossy bed; *Prov:* **pierre qui roule n'amasse pas m.,** a rolling stone gathers no moss; **vert m.,** moss green. **2.** (*a*) froth, foam (of beer, sea, etc.); head (on glass of beer); lather (of soap); *P:* **se faire de la m.,** to fret, to worry; *s.a.* EXTINCTEUR; (*b*) *Cu:* mousse. **3.** *Ch:* **m. de platine,** platinum sponge. **4. m. de plastique,** foam plastic, plastic foam, expanded plastic; **m. de latex microporeuse,** microfoam rubber; *attrib.* **caoutchouc m.,** foam rubber. **5.** *Knitting:* **point m.,** moss stitch.

mousse[2], *s.m.* **1.** ship's boy, *A:* cabin boy; **m. de pont,** deck boy. **2.** *Const:* mate.

mousse[3], *a.* blunt (knife blade, point, etc.); **ciseaux mousses,** blunt-pointed scissors; *A:* **à l'esprit m.,** dull-witted; *Z:* **chèvre m.,** hornless goat.

mousseau, -eaux [muso], *a.m.* **pain m.,** finest wheaten bread.

mousseline [muslin], *s.f.* **1.** *Tex:* (*a*) muslin; **m. forte,** foundation muslin; **m. de soie,** chiffon; (*b*) *Bookb:* mull. **2.** (*a*) **(verre) m.,** muslin glass; mousseline; (*b*) **gâteau m.,** sponge cake; (*c*) **pommes (de terre) m.,** creamed potatoes; **sauce m.,** mousseline sauce.

mousselinette [muslinɛt], *s.f. Tex:* fine muslin.

mousser [muse], *v.i.* to froth, foam; (*of soapy water*) to lather; (*of wine*) to sparkle, to effervesce, *F:* to fizz; *F:* (*of pers.*) to foam with rage; **faire m. qn,** (i) *F:* to build s.o. up, to crack s.o. up; (ii) *P:* to make s.o. lose his temper, flare up; *F:* **faire m. qch.,** to boost sth., to crack sth. up; to boast about sth.; **se faire m. au détriment d'un collègue,** to score at a colleague's expense; **faire m. de la crème,** to whip, whisk, cream.

mousseron [musrɔ̃], *s.m.* edible mushroom; *esp.* St George's agaric; **faux m.,** fairy-ring agaric; fairy-ring mushroom; champignon.

mousseux, -euse [musø, -øːz], *a.* **1.** mossy; **rose mousseuse,** moss rose; **agate mousseuse,** moss agate. **2.** (*a*) frothy, foaming; (*b*) *a. & s.m.* sparkling (wine); **une bouteille de m.,** a bottle of sparkling wine; **vin non m.,** still wine.

moussoir [muswaːr], *s.m. Cu:* whisk; egg beater.

mousson [musɔ̃], *s.f.* monsoon; **m. d'été,** summer, wet, monsoon; **m. d'hiver,** winter, dry, monsoon.

moussot [muso], *a.m.* **pain m.,** finest wheaten bread.

moussu [musy], *a.* mossy; moss-grown (wall, etc.); **rose moussue,** moss rose.

moustac [mustak], *s.m. Z:* moustache (monkey).

moustache [mustaʃ], *s.f.* **1.** (*a*) **la m., les moustaches,** moustache; **m. courte,** short, clipped, moustache; **m. à la gauloise,** walrus moustache; **m. en brosse,** toothbrush moustache; *A:* **brûler la m. à qn,** to fire point blank at s.o.; *F: A:* **vieille m.,** old soldier; (*b*) whiskers (of cat, etc.); (*c*) *F:* bow wave (of ship). **2.** *pl.* (*a*) *Nau:* back-ropes (of martingale); gob lines; (*b*) *Av:* slots, guide-vanes, (leading edge) flaps (for modifying airflow); (*c*) *Cryst:* whiskers.

moustachu [mustaʃy], *a.* moustached; wearing a heavy moustache.

moustérien[1], **-ienne** [musterjɛ̃, -jɛn], **moustiérien, -ienne** [mustjerjɛ̃, -jɛn], *a. & s.m. Prehist:* Mousterian.

moustérien[2], **-ienne,** *a. & s. Geog:* (native, inhabitant) of Moutiers.

moustille [mustiːj], *s.f.* sparkle (of wine).

moustiquaire [mustikɛːr], *s.f.* mosquito net; **tulle, gaze, à m.,** mosquito netting.

moustique [mustik], *s.m.* **1.** *Ent:* (*a*) mosquito; (*b*) gnat; sand fly. **2.** *P:* kid, brat.

moût [mu], *s.m.* (*a*) must (of grapes); wort (of beer); (*b*) unfermented wine.

moutard [mutaːr], *s.m. F:* small boy, kid, brat; *pl.* **les moutards,** the kids (without distinction of sex).

moutarde [mutard], *s.f.* **1.** mustard; (*a*) **graine de m.,** mustard seed; **champ de m.,** mustard field; **m. blanche,** white mustard; (*b*) **farine de m.,** (flour of) mustard; *F:* **c'est de la m. après dîner,** it's too late to be of any use; it's a day after the fair; *F:* **s'amuser à la m.,** to waste one's time on trifles; *F:* **la m. lui est montée au nez,** he lost his temper, he flared up; he went off the deep end; *s.a.* PESANT 2. **2.** *attrib.* **jaune m.,** mustard yellow, mustard(-coloured); **gaz m.,** mustard gas.

moutardelle [mutardɛl], *s.f.* (type of) horse-radish.

moutardier [mutardje], *s.m.* **1.** mustard maker, seller; *so used in the phr. F:* **il se croit le premier m. du pape,** he thinks no small beer of himself; he's grown too big for his boots. **2.** mustard pot.

moutardin [mutardɛ̃], *s.m.,* **moutardon** [mutardɔ̃], *s.m. Bot:* charlock, wild mustard.

moutier [mutje], *s.m. A. & Dial:* (*still used in place names*) monastery, church.

moutiérain, -aine [mutjerɛ̃, -ɛn], *a. & s. Geog:* (native, inhabitant) of Moûtiers (Savoie)

mouton [mutɔ̃], *s.m.* **1.** (*a*) sheep; **élevage de moutons,** sheep raising; **éleveur de moutons,** sheep farmer, breeder; **doux comme un m.,** as gentle as a lamb; (*of pers.*) **frisé comme un m.,** (very) curly-haired; **revenons à nos moutons,** let's get back to the subject, come back to the point; **se laisser égorger comme un m.,** to let oneself be (i) led to the slaughter; (ii) fleeced; **c'est un m. à cinq pattes,** he's a rare bird; **chercher le m. à cinq pattes,** to look for the impossible; *Equit:* **saut de m.,** buck, bucking (of horse); *s.a.* SAUT-DE-MOUTON; *Games:* **faire le m.,** to make a back (at leapfrog); (*b*) *Husb:* wether; *Cu:* mutton; **ragoût de m.,** mutton stew; *Husb:* **m. d'un an,** wether hog; (*c*) **peau de m.,** sheepskin; wool fell; **reliure en m.,** sheep-skin binding; *Bookb:* **m. scié,** skiver; *Com:* **m. doré,** beaver lamb; *Cost:* **manteau doublé de m.,** coat with a sheepskin lining; (*d*) sheep(-like person); **ce sont de vrais moutons de Panurge,** they just follow each other like sheep, they're like a flock of sheep; **c'est un m. enragé,** he's calm enough normally, but when he loses his temper, look out for squalls! (*e*) *F:* (*in prisons*) (police) spy; (*f*) *pl. Nau:* white horses, foam (on waves); (*g*) *pl. F:* fluff (under bed, etc.), *U.S:* house moss, kittens. **2.** (*a*) *Civ.E: etc:* ram, monkey (of pile driver); head (of beetle, rammer); tup (of steam hammer); drop hammer; (*b*) stock (of church bell); (*c*) *Nau:* belfry. **3.** *Orn: F:* **m. du Cap,** albatross. **4.** *a.* (*f.* **moutonne**) (*a*) *A:* **l'espèce moutonne,** the sheep family; (*b*) ovine, sheep-like (nature, placidity); **il n'y a pas plus m. que lui,** I've never met such a sheep-like person.

moutonnage [mutɔnaːʒ], *s.m. Civ.E:* (action of) ramming, pile driving.

moutonnaille [mutɔnɑːj], *s.f. F: Pej: A:* (*of people*) flock of sheep.

moutonnant [mutɔnɑ̃], *a.* (*of the sea*) covered with, beginning to show, white horses; foam-flecked.

moutonné [mutɔne], *a.* fleecy (cloud, sky, etc.); **mer moutonnée,** sea with white horses; foam-flecked, frothy, sea; **tête moutonnée,** extremely curly, frizzy, head of hair; *Geol:* **roche moutonnée,** roche moutonnée.

moutonnement [mutɔnmɑ̃], *s.m.* **1.** *A:* frizzing (of hair, etc.). **2.** (*of the sea*) breaking into white horses; frothing.

moutonner [mutɔne]. **1.** *v.tr.* (*a*) *A:* to frizz, curl (hair, etc.); (*b*) *F:* to spy on, inform against (prisoner). **2.** *v.i.* (*of the sea*) to break into white horses; to froth.

se moutonner, (*of sky*) to become covered with fleecy clouds.

moutonnerie [mutɔnri], *s.f. F:* sheep-like stupidity.

moutonneux, -euse [mutɔnø, -øːz], *a.* **1.** (*of the sea*) foam-flecked; covered with white horses; frothy. **2.** (*of the sky*) fleecy.

moutonnier, -ière [mutɔnje, -jɛːr]. **1.** *a.* (*a*) ovine; **la race moutonnière,** the sheep family; **profile m.,** ovine, sheep-like, profile; *Nau:* **cargo m.,** sheep carrier; (*b*) *F:* sheep-like (crowd, etc.). **2.** *s.m.* (wholesale) butcher (specializing in mutton).

mouture [mutyːr], *s.f.* **1.** grinding, milling (of corn); **m. en grosse,** low, flat, milling process. **2.** milling dues; multure; **tirer d'un sac deux moutures,** to get double profit out of sth. **3.** *Agr:* **(blé) m.,** maslin. **4.** *Journ: etc: F:* **(nouvelle, seconde) m.,** recast version, rehash (of article, etc.).

mouvaison [muvɛzɔ̃], *s.f. Vit:* first spring hoeing (of vineyard).

mouvance [muvɑ̃ːs], *s.f.* **1.** *A: Jur:* subinfeudation. **2.** *Phil:* mobility.

mouvant [muvɑ̃], *a.* **1.** *A:* actuating (force, etc.). **2.** moving; mobile; unstable, fickle, changeable (mind, etc.); **sable m.,** drift sand; **sables mouvants,** shifting sands; quicksand; **terrain m.,** loose, shifting, ground. **3.** *Jur: A:* (*of fief*) subinfeudated (**de,** to); under the jurisdiction (of).

mouvement [muvmɑ̃], *s.m.* **1.** (*a*) movement; motion; gesture; **m. en avant, en arrière,** forward, backward, movement; **rester sans m.,** to stand motionless, stock still; **faire un m.,** to move; **je n'osais pas faire un m.,** I was afraid to move; **il aime le m.,** he likes going about, around; he's fond of change; he can't stay still; **répondre d'un m. de tête,** to answer (i) with a shake of the head; (ii) with a nod; **mettre qch. en m., imprimer un m. à qch.,** to put, set, sth. in motion; to bring sth. into action; to set (machinery) going; to start (engine); **se mettre en m.,** to start off, move off; to get on the move, to get going; **se donner du m.,** (i) to bustle about; to exert oneself; (ii) to take exercise; **être toujours en m.,** to be always on the move; **le m. d'une grande ville,** the bustle, activity, of a large town; **petite ville sans m.,** lifeless, dull, little town; *Fin:* **m. d'espèces,** cash transaction; **m. de l'argent,** circulation of money; *Mus:* (i) **presser, ralentir, le m.,** to quicken the time, to slow the time; (ii) **m. contraire, oblique,** contrary, oblique, motion; (iii) **symphonie à trois mouvements,** symphony in three movements; (*b*) *Mec: Mec.E:* **m. simple, composé,** simple, compound, motion; **m. acquis,** impressed motion; **m. alternatif,** reciprocating, alternating, motion; **à m. alternatif,** reciprocating; **m. curviligne,** curvilinear motion, motion in a curve; **m. de bascule, m. basculaire,** seesaw motion, balancing motion; tipping movement; tilting; **m. de rotation, m. rotatif,** rotary, rotational, motion; spinning motion; **m. de translation,** motion, movement, of translation; translatory movement; **m. hélicoïdal,** helicoid motion, spiral motion; **m. orbital, m. orbitaire,** orbital motion; **m. perpétuel,** perpetual motion; *F:* (*of child, etc.*) **c'est le, un, m. perpétuel,** he is never still; **m. rectiligne,** rectilinear motion, straight-line motion; **m. rectiligne uniformément accéléré,** uniformly accelerated rectilinear motion; **m. sinusoïdal,** harmonic motion; **m. vibratoire,** vibratory motion; **quantité de m.,** (linear) momentum (mv), impulse; *Mch:* **m. du piston,** stroke of the piston; **pièces en m.,** moving parts (of machine); *Ph:* **m. relatif de la terre et de l'éther,** ether drift; (*c*) *Mil: etc:* **m. d'ensemble,** co-ordinated, simultaneous, movement; **exécuter un m.,** to go through, perform, a movement; **exécuter un m. en décomposant,** to go through a movement in detail; **m. tactique, stratégique,** tactical, strategic, movement; **m. de troupes,** troup movement; **troupes en m.,** troops on the move; **m. en terrain varié,** cross-country movement; **faire m. sur, en direction de, Paris,** to move towards, make for, advance on, march on, Paris; **le feu et le m.,** fire and movement; **guerre de m.,** mobile warfare, war of movement; **m. de repli, m. rétrograde,** retrograde movement, withdrawal; **m. débordant,** outflanking movement; **m. tournant,** turning movement; **m. en tenaille,** pincer movement; **m. par camion(s),** movement by lorry, *U.S:* by truck; **m. par voie de terre,** movement by road, by land; **m. par voie ferrée,** movement by rail; **m. par voie d'eau,** movement by water; **m. par voie maritime, par mer,** movement by sea; **m. par voie aérienne, par air,** movement by air. **2.** (*a*) change, modification; **m. des idées,** change of ideas; **m. de terrain,** (i) undulation, break in (the flat surface of) a plain; (ii) landslip; *Geog:* **m. négatif, m. positif,** relative fall, relative rise (in sea level); **m. du marché,** market fluctuations; **m. de personnel,** staff changes; **il n'y a pas de m. dans la magistrature,** there are no changes on the bench; *Pol.Ec:* **m. séculaire des prix,** secular trend of prices; **le m. des naissances, de la natalité,** the trend of the birth rate; *F:* **être dans le m.,** to be in the swim; to be up-to-date; to be with it; **suivre le m.,** to follow suit; to follow the crowd; (*b*) impulse; **premier m.,** first impulse; **elle a le premier m. désagréable,** she is always inclined to be disagreeable at first; **il eut un m. d'éloquence,** he had a burst of eloquence; **m. d'humeur,** outburst of temper, of petulance; **il eut un m. de répulsion,** a wave of repulsion swept over him; **faire qch. de son propre m.,** to do sth. of one's own accord, *motu proprio*; **avoir un bon m.,** to act on a kindly impulse; **j'apprécie votre bon m.,** I appreciate your kind thought; **allons, un bon m.!** come on, be a sport! (*c*) agitation, emotion; **m. de plaisir,** thrill, flutter, of pleasure; **il eut un m. de surprise,** he gave a start of surprise; **dans un m. de colère,** in a fit of anger; **m. populaire,** popular movement; (*d*) line(s) (of drapery, etc.). **3.** traffic (on road, in port, etc.); *Rail:* **mouvements des trains,** train arrivals and departures; **chef de m.,** traffic manager; *Journ:* **mouvements des navires,** shipping intelligence. **4.** works, action, movement (of clock, etc.); **m. d'horlogerie,** clockwork; **à m. à billes,** mounted on ball bearings; **m. de sonnette,** bell-crank lever; *Rail:* **m. d'une locomotive,** engine of a locomotive.

mouvementé [muvmɑ̃te], *a.* **1.** animated, lively (discussion, etc.); thrilling (voyage, etc.); full of incident; **une partie mouvementée,** an exciting game; **ville, rue, mouvementée,** busy town, street; **vie mouvementée,** (i) eventful life; (ii) life of ups and downs; **carrière mouvementée,** chequered career; **époque mouvementée,** stirring times. **2. terrain m.,** undulating ground.

mouvementer [muvmɑ̃te], *v.tr.* to enliven, animate (discussion, etc.); *Th:* to liven up (the action); **collines qui mouvementent la plaine,** hills that break the monotony of the plain.

mouver [muve], *v.tr.* **1.** *Hort:* to loosen, turn over (soil). **2.** *Cu:* to stir (sauce, etc.).

mouvette [muvɛt], *s.f.* (*a*) *Cu:* wooden spoon; (*b*) spatula.

mouvoir[1] [muvwaːr], *v.tr.* (*pr.p.* **mouvant;** *p.p.* **mû, mue;** *pr.ind.* **je meus, il meut, n. mouvons, ils meuvent;** *pr.sub.* **je meuve, n. mouvions, ils meuvent;** *p.h.* **je mus** (*rare*); *fu.* **je mouvrai**) **1.** (*little used to-day in this sense, the usu. vbs. being* **remuer, bouger**) to move (chair, one's head, etc.); **m. qch. de sa place,** to move sth. from its place. **2.** to drive, actuate (machine, etc.); to propel (ship, etc.); **machine mue à la main,** machine driven, worked, by hand; **navire mû à la vapeur,** ship propelled by steam; **mû par turbine,** turbine-driven; **mû par courroie,** belt-driven; **mû par la colère, par l'intérêt,** moved by anger, prompted by interest; **mû par un sentiment de pitié,** prompted by a feeling of pity. **3.** *Jur: A:* (*of fief*) to be subinfeudated (**de,** to).

se mouvoir, to move, stir; **il ne pouvait pas se m. de son fauteuil,** he could not get out of his armchair; **faire mouvoir qch.,** to set sth. going, in motion.

mouvoir[2], *s.m.* (wooden) spatula.

moviola [mɔvjɔla], *s.f. Cin:* moviola.

moxa [mɔksa], *s.m. Med:* moxa.

moye [mwa], *s.f.* soft vein (in quarry stone).

moyen[1], **-enne** [mwajɛ̃, -ɛn]. **1.** *a.* (*a*) middle; **la classe moyenne, les classes moyennes,** the middle class(es); **personne d'un âge m.,** middle-aged person; **le m. âge** [mwajɛnɑːʒ], the middle ages; **coutumes du m. âge,** medi(a)eval customs; *Sch:* **cours m.,** intermediate course (in French, etc.); *Gram:* **voix moyenne,** middle voice; *Box:* **poids m.,** middle weight; (*b*) average, mean (pressure, speed, level, price, etc.); **le Français, l'Anglais, etc., m.,** the average Frenchman, Englishman, etc.; the man in the street; **le lecteur m.,** the average reader; **intelligence moyenne,** average intelligence; **température moyenne annuelle,** mean annual temperature; **temps m. de réaction,** mean reaction time; *Log:* **m. terme,** middle term; *St.Exch:* **cours m.,** middle price; *Mth:* **termes moyens, les moyens,** means (of ratio); **prendre un m. terme,** to take a middle course; (*c*) medium (quality, etc.); **de taille, de grandeur, moyenne,** medium-sized, middle-sized; **homme de taille moyenne,** man of average height; **petites et moyennes entreprises,** small and medium-sized undertakings; **capacité moyenne,** middling, average, capacity; **louer une maison dans les prix moyens,** to lease a house at a moderate rent. **2.** *s.m.* (*a*) *Mth:* mean (of progression); **m. arithmétique,** arithmetical mean; **m. géométrique,** geometrical mean; (*b*) **écrire en m.,** to write an average hand (neither large nor small). **3.** *s.f.* **moyenne;** (*a*) *Mth:* **m. proportionnelle,** geometrical mean; (*b*) average; **m. pondérée,** weighted average; **les recettes donnent une m. de mille francs par jour,** receipts average a thousand francs a day; **établir la m. (des pertes, etc.),** to average (the losses, etc.); (*in scientific work, etc.*) **faire la m. des lectures,** to average the readings taken; **en m.,** on an average; *St.Exch:* **faire une m.,** to average; **faiseur de m.,** averager; *Aut:* **m. (horaire),** average (speed); (*c*) *Sch:* pass mark; **travail au-dessus, au-dessous, de la m.,** work above, below, average; **avoir la m. à l'examen,** to have a pass mark.

moyen[2], *s.m.* **1.** means; (*a*) **un nouveau m. de transport,** a new means of transport; **le journal comme m. de réclame,** the newspaper as a vehicle, medium, for advertising; **moyens de masse, d'action sur les masses,** mass media; *Ind:* **moyens de production,** capital goods; *Prov:* **la fin justifie les moyens,** the end justifies the means; **par tous les moyens, bons ou mauvais,** by fair means or foul; **employer les grands moyens,** to take extreme measures; **ce n'est pas le m. de le faire consentir,** that is not the way to get him to consent; **c'est le meilleur m. de, pour, le retrouver,** that is the best way to find it again; **au m., par le m., de qch.,** by means of sth.; **par le m. de qn,** through (the instrumentality of) s.o.; **y a-t-il m. de le faire?** is it possible to do it? is there any means of doing it? **il n'y a pas m.,** it can't be done; it's impossible; **il n'y a pas m. de le nier,** there is no denying it; **le m. d'y aller?** how does one, do we, get there? **le m. qu'on sorte par un temps pareil!** how could one go out in such weather! **trouver (le) m. de faire qch.,** to find a means, a way, to contrive, manage, to do sth.; **dès que je trouverai le m. de faire mieux,** as soon as I see my way to something better; **il a trouvé le m. de se faire recaler à l'oral,** he managed to fail the oral; **s'arranger pour trouver m. de faire qch.,** to make shift to do sth.; **inventer un m. de s'échapper,** to invent a plan of escape; **les moyens manquent pour mettre cette loi en vigueur,** there is no machinery to make this law effective; **par aucun m. on ne peut le faire,** it is in no way possible, completely impossible, to do it; **moyens temporaires,** temporary devices; **faire qch. par ses propres moyens,** to do sth. with one's own resources, on one's own; **arriver par ses propres moyens,** to get there under one's own steam; **avec les moyens du bord,** with the means at one's disposal; **quels moyens avait-il employés pour réussir?** how did he manage to do it, to pull it off? **voies et moyens,** ways and means; **si vous en avez le m.,** if you can; if you can manage it; **dans la (pleine) mesure de mes moyens,** to the best, to the utmost, of my ability; **morceau (de musique) qui n'est pas dans mes moyens,** piece that is not within my range, within my scope; **enfant qui a des moyens,** bright, talented, child; **homme sans moyens,** man of no resource; *Nau:* **navire avarié qui continue son chemin par ses seuls moyens,** damaged ship continuing its course under its own steam; **enlever les moyens à qn,** to upset, disconcert, s.o.; to cramp s.o.'s style; (*b*) **vivre au-dessus de ses moyens,** to live beyond one's means; **il a largement les moyens de faire construire,** he can well afford to build; **je n'en ai pas les moyens,** it does not lie within my means; I can't afford it; **je ne sais pas si ses moyens le lui permettraient,** I don't know if he can afford it; **chacun donne selon ses moyens,** each one gives according to his means; (*c*) *Mil: etc:* **moyens de maintenance,** maintenance resources; **moyens demandés, exigés, nécessaires, requis (pour accomplir une tâche),** requirements (for performing a task); **répartition des moyens,** allocation, distribution, of resources. **2.** *Jur:* grounds put forward for a claim.

moyenâgeux, -euse [mwajɛnɑʒø, -øːz], *a.* (*a*) medi(a)eval; (*b*) old fashioned; **procédés m.,** outdated processes.

moyenâgiste [mwajɛnɑʒist], *s.m. & f.* mediaevalist.

moyen-courrier [mwajɛ̃kurje], *a. & s.m. Av:* medium-range (aircraft); *pl. moyens-courriers.*

moyennant [mwajɛnɑ̃], *prep.* on (a certain) condition; **louer qch. m. quinze francs par jour,** to hire sth. for, at (a charge of), fifteen francs a day; **faire qch. m. finance,** to do sth. for a consideration; **le manuscrit lui fut adjugé m. 2000 fr.,** the manuscript was knocked down to him for 2000 fr.; **m. paiement de dix francs,** on payment of ten francs; **vous vous rétablirez m. quelques précautions,** you will get better provided you take a few precautions; **m. quoi,** in return for which, in consideration of which; **m. que** + *fu. ind. or* + *sub.*, provided that . . ..

moyennement [mwajɛnmɑ̃], *adv.* **1.** moderately, fairly; mildly (interested); **m. vite,** quite, fairly, quickly; **travailler m.,** to work fairly well. **2.** *A:* on an average, on the average.

moyenner [mwajɛne], *v.tr.* (*a*) *A:* to bring (sth.) about; (*b*) *F:* **il n'y a pas moyen de m.,** it can't be done.

Moyen-Orient [mwajɛ̃nɔrjɑ̃], *Pr.n.m. Geog:* the Middle East.

moyer [mwaje], *v.tr.* (*conj. like* ABOYER) to saw (an ashlar) along the soft vein.

moyette [mwajɛt], *s.f. Agr:* shock (of corn); **mettre le blé en moyettes,** to shock (up) the corn.

moyetter [mwajete], *v.tr. Agr:* to shock (up) (corn).

moyeu[1], -eux [mwajø], *s.m.* **1.** nave, (pipe) box (of cart wheel, etc.); boss (of fly wheel, propeller, etc.); hub (of bicycle wheel); *Cy:* **m. à changement de vitesse,** gear-change hub. **2.** *A:* yolk (of egg).

moyeu[2], -eux, *s.m. Dial:* preserved plum.

mozabite [mɔzabit], *a. & s. Geog: Ling:* Mozabite.

mozarabe [mɔzarab], *Spanish Hist:* **1.** *a.* Mozarabic. **2.** *s.* Mozarab.

mozarabique [mɔzarabik], *a.* Mozarabic.

mozette [mɔzɛt], *s.f. Ecc.Cost:* moz(z)etta.

m'sieu [msjø], *s.m. P:* = MONSIEUR.

mu [my], *s.m. Gr.Alph: Ph.Meas:* mu.

mû. *See* MOUVOIR.

muabilité [mɥabilite], *s.f. A: & Lit:* mutability, instability.

muable [mɥabl̩], *a. A. & Lit:* changeable, mutable; unstable; fickle.

muance [mɥɑ̃ːs], *s.f.* **1.** *Mus: A:* mutation. **2.** *O:* breaking (of voice at puberty).

muche [myʃ], *s.f. F: Dial:* hiding place.

muche-pot (à) [amyʃpo], *adv.phr. Dial: A:* **1. vendre de la boisson à m.-p.,** to shebeen. *hence* **2.** secretly, stealthily.

mucher [myʃe], *v.tr. F: Dial:* to hide.

muciforme [mysifɔrm], *a.* muciform.

mucigène [mysiʒɛn], *s.m. Bio-Ch:* mucigen.

mucilage [mysilaːʒ], *s.m.* mucilage; gum.

mucilagineux, -euse [mysilaʒinø, -øːz], *a.* mucilaginous, viscous.

mucine [mysin], *s.f. Ch:* mucin.

muckite [mykit], *s.f. Miner:* muckite.

mucocèle [mykɔsɛl], *s.f. Med:* mucocele.

mucoïde [mykɔid], *s.m. Bio-Ch:* mucoid.

mucoïtine-sulfurique [mykɔitinsylfyrik], *a.* mucoitin-sulphuric (acid).

muconique [mykɔnik], *a.* muconic (acid).

muco-purulent [mykɔpyrylɑ̃], *a. Med:* mucopurulent; *pl. muco-purulent(e)s.*

muco-pus [mykɔpy], *s.m.inv. Med:* mucopus.

mucor [mykɔːr], *s.m. Fung:* mucor.

mucoracées [mykɔrase], *s.f.pl. Fung:* Mucoraceae.

mucorales [mykɔral], *s.f.pl. Fung:* Mucorales.

mucosité [mykozite], *s.f. Physiol:* mucus, mucosity.

mucre [mykr̥], *a. Dial:* damp; mouldy.

mucron [mykrɔ̃], *s.m. Bot:* mucro, terminal point.

mucroné [mykrɔne], *a. Bot:* mucronate(d).

mucus [mykys], *s.m. Physiol:* mucus.

mudar [mydaːr], *s.m. Bot: Pharm:* mudar.

mudéjar, -jare [mydeʒaːr], *a. & s. Spanish Hist:* Mudejar.

mue[1] [my], *s.f.* **1.** (*a*) moulting (of birds); shedding or casting of the coat, of the skin, of the antlers (of animals); sloughing (of reptiles); instar; ecdysis (of insects, etc.); **serin en m.,** moulting canary; (*b*) season of moulting, etc.; moulting time; (*c*) feathers moulted; antlers, etc., shed; slough (of snakes). **2.** breaking of the voice (at puberty). **3.** mew (for hawks); coop (for poultry); **mettre des poules en m.,** to coop up hens.

mue[2], *a.f. used only in* **rage m.,** mute rabies, dumb rabies.

mué [mɥe], *a.* **oiseau m.,** bird that has moulted; **voix muée,** voice that has broken (at puberty).

muer [mɥe]. **1.** *v.tr.* (*a*) *A:* to change (**en,** into); (*b*) (*still current in*) **le cerf mue sa tête,** the stag casts its antlers. **2.** *v.i.* (*a*) (*of bird*) to moult; (*of animal*) to shed or cast its coat, its antlers; (*of reptile*) to slough; to cast its skin; (*b*) (*of voice*) to break (at puberty).

se muer (en), to be transformed; to change (oneself) (into); **ces ouvriers se muent en véritables artistes,** these workmen are becoming real artists.

muet, -ette[1] [mɥɛ, -ɛt]. **1.** *a.* dumb, mute; (*a*) unable to speak, speechless; **m. de naissance,** born dumb; **la stupeur me rendit m.,** I was struck dumb with astonishment; **j'écoutais, m. d'étonnement,** I listened in mute astonishment; **m. de colère,** speechless with anger; (*b*) unwilling to speak, silent; **rester m.,** to remain silent; **rester m. devant le tribunal,** to stand mute before the court; **m. comme un poisson, comme une carpe,** (as) dumb, mute, as a fish; **m. comme la tombe,** (as) silent as the grave; (*c*) without word or sound; **douleur muette,** silent sorrow; **jeu m.,** dumb show; *Th:* **rôle m.,** silent part; **personnage m.,** mute; *Cin:* **le cinéma m.,** silent films; **prière muette,** mute appeal; *adv.phr.* **à la muette,** without speaking, by gestures; **carte muette,** blank map; *Gram:* **lettre muette,** silent letter; *Fr.Gram:* **h muet(te),** mute h; *Ling:* **consonne muette,** unvoiced consonant. **2.** *s.* (*a*) dumb person, mute; (*b*) *s.m.* (sultan's) mute; (*c*) *s.m. Cin:* silent film. **3** *s.f.* (*a*) *Gram:* **muette,** mute letter, unsounded letter; (*b*) **la grande m.,** the army.

muette[2], *s.f.* **1.** *Ven: A:* mew. **2.** hunting box.

muettement [mɥɛtmɑ̃], *adv.* mutely; without uttering a word; silently.

muézin, muezzin [mɥezɛ̃], *s.m.* muezzin.

muffée [myfe], *s.f. P: O:* **1.** skinful (of drink); **avoir, prendre, une m.,** to be, get, dead drunk. **2.** (*large quantity*) **y en a une m.,** there's a lot of it, any amount of it.

mufle [myfl̩], *s.m.* **1.** muffle; (hairless part of) muzzle (of ox, bison, etc.); nose, *F:* snout (of lion, etc.). **2.** *P:* (*a*) face, mug; (*b*) boor; **il a une vraie tête de m.,** he has a coarse face. **3.** *Bot: F:* **m. de veau, de bœuf,** antirrhinum, snapdragon.

mufleau, -eaux [myflo], *s.m. Bot:* antirrhinum, snapdragon.

muflée [myfle], *s.f. P:* = MUFFÉE.

muflerie [myfləri], *s.f. F:* **1.** boorishness; **la m. humaine,** the rottenness of mankind. **2.** low-down trick.

muflier [myflije], *s.m. Bot:* antirrhinum, snapdragon; **m. bâtard,** linaria, *F:* toadflax, butter-and-eggs.

mufti [myfti], *s.m. Moslem Rel:* mufti.

muge [myːʒ], *s.m. Ich:* mullet; **m. capiton,** common grey mullet; **m. à grosse tête,** striped mullet.

mugilidés [myʒilide], *s.m.pl. Ich:* Mugilidae.

mugir [myʒiːr], *v.i.* (*a*) (*of cow*) to low; (*of bull*) to bellow; (*of pers.*) **il mugissait de fureur,** he was bellowing with anger; (*b*) (*of sea, wind*) to roar; to boom; to moan; (*of wind*) to howl; (*c*) (*of siren*) to wail.

mugissant [myʒisɑ̃], *a.* (*a*) lowing (cow); bellowing (bull); (*b*) roaring, booming, moaning (sea, wind); howling (wind); (*c*) wailing (siren).

mugissement [myʒismɑ̃], *s.m.* (*a*) lowing (of cow); bellowing (of bull); (*b*) roaring, booming, moaning (of sea, wind); howling (of wind); (*c*) wailing (of siren).

muguet [mygɛ], *s.m.* **1.** *Bot:* lily of the valley; **petit m.,** woodruff. **2.** *A:* gallant, dandy. **3.** *Med:* thrush.

mugueter [myg(ə)te], *v.tr.* (**je muguette, n. muguetons; je muguetterai**) *A:* to make love, to flirt with (s.o.); *abs.* to flirt, to philander.

muid [mɥi], *s.m. A:* large barrel; hogshead (of wine).

mulasse [mylas], *s.f.* young mule.

mulasserie [mylasri], *s.f.* mule breeding.

mulassier, -ière [mylasje, -jɛːr], **mulatier, -ière** [mylatije, -jɛːr]. **1.** *a.* pertaining to mule breeding; **jument mulassière,** mule-breeding mare; **l'industrie mulassière,** mule breeding. **2.** *s.m.* breeder of mules.

mulâtre [mylɑːtr̥]. **1.** *a.* mulatto, half-caste. **2.** *s.* (*f.* **mulâtre** *or* **mulâtresse** [mylɑtrɛs]) mulatto, *f. occ.* mulattress.

mulcter [mylkte], *v.tr. Jur: A:* to mulct, fine; **on le mulcta de cinq cents francs,** he was mulcted of five hundred francs; he was fined five hundred francs.

mule[1] [myl], *s.f.* (*a*) (she) mule; *s.a.* FERRER 1, TÊTU 1; (*b*) **m. électrique,** electric tractor, mule.

mule[2], *s.f.* **1.** (*slipper*) mule; *Ecc:* **la m. du Pape,** the Pope's slipper; **baiser la m. du Pape,** to kiss the Pope's toe. **2.** chilblain on the heel; kibe. **3.** *Vet:* **m. traversière, m. traversine,** cracked heel (of horse).

mule-jenny [mylʒeni], *s.f. A.Tex:* mule(-jenny); *pl. mule(s)-jennys.*

mulet[1] [mylɛ], *s.m.* **1.** (he-)mule; **m. de cacolet,** pack mule (for carrying wounded); *F: A:* **garder le m.,** to be kept waiting; to kick one's heels (at the door, etc.); *F:* **chargé comme un m.,** loaded like a donkey; *F:* **têtu comme un m.,** as stubborn as a mule. **2.** *Nau:* iron truss (of yard).

mulet[2], *s.m. Ich:* grey mullet; **m. de mer,** striped mullet.

muleta [myleta], *s.f.* (matador's) muleta.

muletier, -ière [myltje, -jɛːr]. **1.** *a.* suitable for mules; **chemin m.,** mule track; **équipage m.,** mule train. **2.** *s.m.* mule driver, muleteer.

muletières [myltjɛːr], *s.f.pl. Fish:* mullet net.

muleton, -onne [myltɔ̃, -ɔn], *s.* young mule.

mulette[1] [mylɛt], *s.f. Moll:* unio, freshwater mussel.

mulette[2], *s.f. Ven:* gizzard (of bird of prey).

Mulhouse [myluːz], *Pr.n. Geog:* Mulhouse.

mulhousien, -ienne [myluzjɛ̃, -jɛn], *a. & s. Geog:* (native, inhabitant) of Mulhouse.

mulier [mylje], *s.m. Fish:* = MULETIÈRES.

mull [myl], *s.m. Geol:* mull.

mulle [myl], *s.m. Ich:* mullet; **m. barbu,** red mullet, surmullet.

mullite [mylit], *s.f. Miner:* mullite.

mulot [mylo], *s.m.* field mouse.

mulsion [mylsjɔ̃], *s.f.* milking (of cows, etc.).

multangulaire [myltɑ̃gylɛːr], *a.* multangular, multiangular.

multi- [mylti], *pref.* multi-.

multiadresse [myltiadrɛs], *a.* (*computers*) **instruction m.,** multiple address code, multi-address instruction.

multiarticulé [myltiartikyle], *a. Z:* multi-articulate.

multibande [myltibɑ̃ːd], *a.* (*of computer*) **imprimante m.,** multiple tape lister.

multibobine [myltibɔbin], *a.* (*of computer*) **fichier m.,** multiple reel file.

multibranche [myltibrɑ̃ːʃ], *a.* multi-branched; multibranchiate.

multibroche [myltibrɔʃ], *a.* multipin, multispindle.

multicalcul [myltikalkyl], *s.m.* multi computing.

multicalculateur [myltikalkylatœːr], *s.m.* multi-computer, multi processor.

multicanal, -aux [myltikanal, -o], *a. Elcs: T.V:* multi-channel.

multicapsulaire [myltikapsylɛːr], *a. Bot:* multi-capsulate, multicapsular.

multicaule [myltikoːl], *a. Bot:* many-stemmed; multicauline.

multicellulaire [myltisɛlylɛːr], *a.* multicellular.

multicolore [myltikɔlɔːr], *a.* multicoloured, many-coloured.

multicopiste [myltikɔpist], *a.* **carnet m.,** duplicating book.

multiconversion [myltikɔ̃vɛrsjɔ̃], *s.f. Elcs:* (*computers*) multi-way conversion.

multicoque [myltikɔk], *a. & s.m. N.Arch:* multi-hull.

multicouche [myltikuʃ], *a.* multi-layer; having many coats (of paint, etc.).

multicuspidé [myltikyspide], *a. Bot:* multi-cuspid(ate).

multidestinataire [myltidɛstinatɛːr], *a. Elcs:* (*computers*) **message m.,** multi-address message.

multidigité [myltidiʒite], *a.* multidigitate.

multidimensionnel, -elle [myltidimɑ̃sjɔnɛl], *a.* multidimensional.

multifichier [myltifiʃje], *a.inv.* (*of computer*) **bobine m.,** multi-file reel; **bande m.,** multi-file tape.

multifide [myltifid], *a. Nat.Hist:* multifid(ous).

multifilaire [myltifilɛːr], *a. O: El:* multi-wire (aerial, etc.).

multiflore [myltiflɔːr], *a. Bot:* multiflorous, many-flowered.

multiforme [myltifɔrm], *a.* multiform; many-sided (truth, etc.).

multigrade [myltigrad], *a. Aut:* multigrade (oil).

multilatéral, -aux [myltilateral, -o], *a.* multilateral; **désarmement m.,** multilateral disarmament; *Mil:* **force multilatérale,** multilateral force.

multilatère [myltilatɛːr], *a. Geom: A:* multilateral, many-sided.

multiligne [myltiliɲ], *a.* multiple-line.

multilinéaire [myltilinɛ:r], *a.* multilinear.

multilobé [myltilɔbe], *a.* multilobular, multilobate(d).

multiloculaire [myltilɔkylɛ:r], *a.* multilocular, multiloculate(d).

multimillionnaire [myltimiljɔnɛ:r], *a. & s.m. & f.* multimillionaire.

multimoteur, -trice [myltimɔtœ:r, -tris], *a. Av:* multi-engined.

multinervé [myltinɛrve], *a. Bot:* multinervose, multinervate.

multipare [myltipa:r], *a.* multiparous.

multiparité [myltiparite], *s.f.* multiparity.

multiparti(te) [myltiparti(t)], *a.* multipartite.

multiperforé [myltipɛrfɔre], *a.* multiperforate.

multipétalé [myltipetale], *a.* multipetalous.

multiphasé [myltifaze], *a. El:* multiphase, polyphase.

multiphasique [myltifazik], *a.* multiphase.

multiplace [myltiplas], (a) *s.m. Av: A:* m. de combat, multiseat fighter; (b) *a. Furn:* canapé m., sofa for several people.

multiplan [myltiplã], *a. & s.m. Av:* multiplane.

multiple [myltipl]. 1. *a.* multiple, manifold; multifarious (duties, etc.); à usages multiples, multi-purpose; perceuse à forets multiples, gang driller; *Typewr:* papier à copies multiples, manifold paper; maison à succursales multiples, multiple store, chain store; *Aut:* trompe à sons multiples, multitone horn; *El:* enroulement à couches multiples, multilayer winding; fiche, prise, m., multiple plug; (of computer) mémoire à bandes multiples, multitape memory; carte à usages multiples, multiple-use card. 2. *s.m.* (a) multiple; le plus petit commun m., P.P.C.M., the lowest common multiple, the L.C.M.; (b) multiple jack-panel.

multiplex [myltiplɛks], *a.inv.* multiplex (telegraphy, etc.).

multiplexage [myltiplɛksa:ʒ], *s.m. Elcs:* multiplexing.

multiplexer [myltiplɛkse], *v.tr.* to multiplex.

multiplexeur [myltiplɛksœ:r], *s.m.* (a) multiplex radio transmitter; (b) (computers) multiplexor; *a.* canal m., multiplex channel.

multipliable [myltiplijabl], *a.* multipli(c)able.

multipliant [myltiplijã]. 1. *a.* multiplying. 2. *s.m. Opt:* multiplying-glass.

multiplicande [myltiplikã:d], *s.m. Mth:* multiplicand.

multiplicateur, -trice [myltiplikatœ:r, -tris]. 1. *a.* multiplying; engrenage m., step-up gear. 2. *s.m. Mth: El:* multiplier; *Aut:* m. de dépression, vacuum booster; (of computer) m. analogique, numérique, analog(ue), digital, multiplier.

multiplicatif, -ive [myltiplikatif, -i:v], *a.* multiplicative, multiplying.

multiplication [myltiplikasjɔ̃], *s.f.* 1. multiplication; (a) table de m., multiplication table; (b) la m. des crimes, the increase in crime; la m. du genre humain, the multiplication of the human species; *B:* la m. des pains, the miracle of the loaves and fishes. 2. *Mec.E:* gear (ratio); step-up, stepdown (of gear); changement de m., change of gear; grande, petite, m., high, low, gear; *Mec:* m. du levier, advantage of a lever; leverage.

multiplicité [myltiplisite], *s.f.* multiplicity (of gods, laws, etc.); multifariousness (of duties, etc.); *Mth:* m. vectorielle, vector manifold.

multiplié [myltiplije], *a.* multiplied, multiple; manifold, multifarious.

multiplier [myltiplije], *v.tr. & i.* (p.d. & pr.sub. n. multipliions, v. multipliez) 1. to multiply (par, by); m. par deux, trois, quatre, to multiply by two, three, four; to double, treble, quadruple; il faut ·m. les contacts, we must step up the contacts. 2. *Mec.E:* m. la vitesse de révolution, to gear up.
se multiplier, (a) to multiply; ses efforts se multipliaient, his efforts increased (substantially); ses visites se multiplient, his visits are becoming more frequent; les crimes se multiplient, crime is on the increase; (b) to be here, there, and everywhere, to be in half a dozen places at once; *Th:* to take several parts; se m. pour servir qn, to exert oneself to the utmost, to do one's utmost, to help s.o.; se m. en tentatives, to make repeated attempts.

multiplieuse [myltiplijø:z], *s.f.* automatic folding machine (for letters, circulars).

multipolaire [myltipɔlɛ:r], *a. El: Biol:* multipolar.

multiprogrammation [myltiprɔgramasjɔ̃], *s.f.* (of computer) multiprogramming; exploitation en m., multiprogram(me) working.

multipropriété [myltiprɔprijete], *s.f.* multiple ownership (of house).

multiséculaire [myltisekylɛ:r], *a.* centuries old.

multisoc [myltisɔk], *s.m.* multiple plough, gang plough.

multiterminal, -aux [myltitɛrminal, -o], *s.m.* multiterminal.

multitraitement [myltitrɛtmã], *s.m. Elcs:* (computers) multiprocessing.

multitube [myltityb], *a. Artil:* canon m., multibarrelled gun.

multituberculés [myltitybɛrkyle], *s.m.pl. Paleont:* Multituberculata.

multitubulaire [myltitybylɛ:r], *a. Mch:* multitubular, water-tube (boiler).

multitude [myltityd], *s.f.* multitude (de, of); crowd; faire appel à la m., to appeal to the multitude, to the crowd; on se plaint de la m. des livres, people complain of the multiplicity of books; il reçoit une m. de lettres, he gets shoals of letters.

multivalve [myltivalv], *Moll:* 1. *a.* multivalvular, multivalve. 2. *s.m.* multivalve.

multivarié [myltivarje], *a. Psy:* analyse multivariée, multivariate analysis.

multi-vitamine [myltivitamin], *s.f.* multi-vitamin; *pl.* multi-vitamines.

munichisme [myniʃism], *s.m. Pol.Hist:* Munich spirit, appeasement.

munichois, -oise [mynikwa, -wa:z]. 1. *a. & s. Geog:* (native, inhabitant) of Munich. 2. *s. Pol. Hist:* F: appeaser.

municipal, -aux [mynisipal, -o], *a.* municipal; conseil m., town council; local council; loi municipale, by-law; la Garde municipale, the military police (of Paris); un garde m., *s.* un municipal, a member of the Paris military police.

municipalement [mynisipalmã], *adv.* municipally.

municipalisation [mynisipalizasjɔ̃], *s.f.* municipalization.

municipaliser [mynisipalize], *v.tr.* to municipalize.

municipalisme [mynisipalism], *s.m.* municipalism.

municipalité [mynisipalite], *s.f.* municipality; (a) local administrative area, (b) municipal corporation; local council; (c) town hall.

municipe [mynisip], *s.m. Rom.Ant:* municipium.

munificence [mynifisã:s], *s.f. Lit:* munificence; avec m., munificently.

munificent [mynifisã], *a. Lit:* munificent.

munir [myni:r], *v.tr.* to furnish, supply, fit, equip, provide (de, with); m. une place, to provision, to store, a stronghold; m. sa canne d'un bout de fer, to fit a ferrule on to one's stick; se m. de provisions, to provide oneself with food; se m. de patience, to have patience; to possess one's soul in patience; *Ecc:* muni des sacrements de l'Église, fortified with the rites of the Church.

munition [mynisjɔ̃], *s.f.* 1. (i) munitioning, (ii) provisioning (of an army); pain de m., ration bread; chaussures, chemise, de m., issue boots, shirt; *A:* fusil de m., regulation rifle. 2. *pl.* (a) munitions (de guerre), munitions of war, ammunition; munitions à blanc, blank ammunition; munitions d'exercice, (target) practice ammunition; munitions d'instruction, training ammunition; munitions de guerre, pour tir réel, live ammunition; munitions réglementaires, service ammunition; commencer à manquer de munitions, to run short of ammunition; caisse à munitions, ammunition chest, container; parc à munitions, ammunition park; (b) stores, supplies; munitions de bouche, provisions; (c) *B:* ville de munitions, treasure city.

munitionnaire [mynisjɔnɛ:r], *s.m. Mil.Hist:* commissary; supply officer.

munitionner [mynisjɔne], *v.tr.* (i) to munition, (ii) to furnish (army) with supplies.

munster [mœ̃stɛ:r], *s.m.* Munster (cheese).

muntjac, muntjak [mœ̃tʒak], *s.m. Z:* muntjac, muntjak; barking deer.

muon [myɔ̃], *s.m. Atom.Ph:* muon.

muphti [myfti], *s.m.* = MUFTI.

muqueux, -euse [mykø, -ø:z]. 1. *a.* mucous (membrane, etc.); bactéries muqueuses, slime bacteria; croissance des bactéries muqueuses, sliming; *Med: A:* fièvre muqueuse, paratyphoid. 2. *s.f.* muqueuse, mucosa, mucous membrane; muqueuse de revêtement, lining mucosa.

mur [my:r], *s.m.* wall; m. de soutènement, supporting wall, breast wall; m. de clôture, enclosing wall; m. d'enceinte, surrounding wall; m. d'appui, low wall, wall only breast-high; m. de culée, abutment wall (of bridge); entourer un verger de murs, to wall in an orchard; le mur d'Adrien, Hadrian's Wall; *Hist:* le m. de Berlin, the Berlin wall; murs d'une ville, town walls; l'ennemi est dans nos murs, the enemy is within our walls;

maison aux murs en briques, brick-walled house; m. de refend, internal partition (wall), cross wall; m. mitoyen, party wall; les tableaux qui pendent au m., the pictures that hang on the wall; gros murs, main walls; ne laisser que les quatre murs, to leave only the bare walls, the four walls, standing; *F:* entre quatre murs, in prison, quod; battre les murs, to stagger from side to side of the road; mettre qn au pied du m., (i) to drive s.o. into a corner; (ii) to demand a "yes" or "no" from s.o.; poussé au pied du m., with his back to the wall; donner de la tête contre un m., se battre la tête contre un m., to run one's head against a brick wall; *F:* il y a de quoi se taper la tête contre les murs, it's enough to drive you mad; *F:* se heurter contre un m., to come up against a blank wall; se heurter à un m. d'incompréhension, to come up against a wall, a barrier, of incomprehension; il s'est trouvé au pied du m. sans échelle, he failed for lack of foresight; he came unprepared; *Fenc:* parer au m., to remain entirely on the defensive; to stonewall; tirer au m., to fence against an opponent who opposes an impenetrable defence; *Prov:* les murs ont des oreilles, walls have ears; *Ph:* m. cosmique, cosmic wall; *Aer:* m. de chaleur, heat barrier, thermal barrier; m. sonique, m. du son, sound barrier; sonic wall; franchir le m. du son, to break the sound barrier; faire le m., (i) *Fb: etc:* to form a defensive wall; (ii) *F:* to slip out, to do a bunk; *Mil:* to go over the wall.

mûr [my:r], *a.* ripe (fruit, abscess, etc.); mellow (wine, etc.); mature (age, mind, etc.); couple m., middle-aged couple; après mûre réflexion, after close, mature, consideration; advisedly; être m. pour qch., to be just fit, ready, for sth.; *F:* habit m., coat that has done its time, seen better days; *P:* il est mûr, he's drunk, mellow, a bit high.

murage [myra:ʒ], *s.m.* 1. walling (in); walling up, bricking up, blocking up (of door, window). 2. masonry, setting (of boiler, etc.).

mûraie [myrɛ], *s.f.* mulberry plantation.

muraille [myra:j], *s.f.* 1. (a) high defensive wall; la Grande M. de Chine, the Great Wall of China; les murailles de la ville, the town walls; m. de glace, ice barrier; couleur (de) m., grey; (b) entre quatre murailles, (i) in an empty room; between four bare walls; (ii) *F:* in prison, in quod. 2. (a) side (of ship); navire à murailles droites, wall-sided ship; *N.Arch:* bordé de m., side plating; virure de m., side strake; (b) wall (of horse's hoof).

muraillement [myrajmã], *s.m.* walling.

murailler [myraje], *v.tr.* to wall (sides of well, etc.).

muraillon [myrajɔ̃], *s.m.* (field boundary) dry (-stone) wall, dry dyke.

mural, -aux [myral, -o], *a.* mural; peintures murales, mural paintings, wall paintings; *Rom. Ant:* couronne murale, mural crown; *Astr:* cercle m., mural circle; pendule murale, wall clock; carte murale, wall map; console murale, wall bracket; tableau m., wall chart; *El:* tableau de distribution m., switchboard.

murchisonite [myrʃisɔnit], *s.f. Miner:* murchisonite.

Murcie [myrsi], *Pr.n.f. Geog:* Murcia.

murcien, -ienne [myrsjɛ̃, -jɛn], *a. & s. Geog:* (native, inhabitant) of Murcia.

mûre [my:r], *s.f.* (a) mulberry; (b) m. sauvage, de ronce, blackberry, brambleberry; m. des haies, m. bleue, dewberry.

mureau, -eaux [myro], *s.m.* low wall.

mûrement [myrmã], *adv.* with mature consideration; étudier m. une question, to study a question closely, exhaustively, with (mature) deliberation; après avoir m. réfléchi, after careful consideration.

murène [myrɛn], *s.f. Ich:* muraena; moray.

murer [myre], *v.tr.* to wall in (town, etc.); to wall up, block up, brick up (doorway, etc.); m. qn dans une cave, to wall s.o. up in a cellar; *O:* m. sa fille, to shut up one's daughter in a nunnery.

muret [myrɛ], *s.m.* low wall; dry stone wall.

mûreraie [myrɔrɛ], *s.f.* mulberry plantation.

muretain, -aine [myrtɛ̃, -ɛn], *a. & s. Geog:* (native, inhabitant) of Muret.

murette [myrɛt], *s.f.* (a) low wall; dry stone wall; (b) curb (of well).

mureux, -euse [myrø, -ø:z], *a. Const:* pierre mureuse, building stone.

murex [myrɛks], *s.m. Moll:* murex, *F:* sting winkle.

murexide [myrɛksid], *s.f. Ch:* murexide.

muriate [myrjat], *s.m. A.Ch:* muriate; (a) chloride; (b) hydrochloride.

muriaté [myrjate], *a. Ch: A:* muriated.

muriatique [myrjatik], *a. A.Ch:* muriatic, hydrochloric (acid).
muricidés [myriside], *s.m.pl. Moll:* Muricidae.
muriculé [myrikyle], *a. Bot:* muriculate.
muridés [myride], *s.m.pl. Z:* Muridae.
mûrier [myrje], *s.m. Bot:* (*a*) mulberry (tree, bush); **m. à papier, de Chine,** paper mulberry; (*b*) **m. sauvage,** bramble, blackberry bush.
mûriforme [myrifɔrm], *a. Med:* muriform.
murin [myrɛ̃], *a. Z:* murine.
murinés [myrine], *s.m.pl. Z:* Murinae.
muriqué [myrike], *a. Nat.Hist:* muricate.
mûrir [myriːr]. **1.** *v.tr.* to ripen, mature; **m. un abcès,** to bring an abscess to a head; **m. une question,** to think out a question thoroughly; to give a question mature deliberation; to thrash out a question; **projet mûri,** well thought out plan. **2.** *v.i. & occ. pr.* to ripen; to mature; to come to maturity; (*of fruit*) to grow ripe; (*of abscess*) to come to a head; (*of wine*) to mellow; **laisser m. une affaire,** to let a matter wait until a favourable outcome is likely.
mûrissant [myrisɑ̃], *a.* ripening; maturing.
mûrisserie [myrisri], *s.f.* ripening depot (for fruit).
murmel [myrmɛl], *s.m. Z:* bobac, bobak.
murmurant [myrmyrɑ̃], *a.* murmuring; **ruisseau m.,** babbling brook.
murmurateur, -trice [myrmyratœːr, -tris], *A:* **1.** *a.* murmuring, muttering. **2.** *s.* murmurer.
murmure [myrmyːr], *s.m.* (*a*) murmur, murmuring; **m. d'un ruisseau,** babbling of a brook; **un m. de voix,** a hum of voices; *Med:* **m. cardiaque,** cardiac murmur; (*b*) **sans hésitation ni m.,** unquestioningly.
murmurer [myrmyre], *v.tr. & i.* to murmur. **1.** to grumble, to complain; **m. de qch.,** to murmur at sth.; **m. de se voir négligé,** to grumble at being neglected; **m. entre ses dents,** to mutter. **2. m. un secret à l'oreille de qn,** to murmur, whisper, a secret in s.o.'s ear; **m. une prière,** to breathe a prayer; **vent qui murmure dans le feuillage,** wind sighing among the leaves; **le ruisseau coule en murmurant,** the stream babbles over the stones.
murois, -oise [myrwa, -waːz], *a. & s. Geog:* (native, inhabitant) of La Mure.
muromontite [myrɔmɔ̃tit], *s.f. Miner:* muromontite.
mûron [myrɔ̃], *s.m.* **1.** blackberry. **2.** wild raspberry.
murrhe [myːr], *s.f. Rom.Ant:* murra, murrha.
murrhin [myr(r)ɛ̃], *a. & s.m.* murrhine (glass).
mur-rideau [myrrido], *s.m. Arch:* curtain-wall; *pl. murs-rideaux.*
musacées [myzase], *s.f.pl. Bot:* Musaceae.
Musagète [myzaʒɛt], *a.m. Gr.Ant: Myth:* (Apollo) Musagetes.
musaraigne [myzarɛɲ], *s.f.* shrew mouse.
musard, -arde [myzaːr, -ard]. **1.** *a.* dawdling, idling. **2.** *s.* dawdler, idler, trifler.
musarder [myzarde], *v.i.* to idle; to waste one's time.
musarderie [myzard(ə)ri], **musardise** [myzardiːz], *s.f.* dawdling, idling, hanging about.
musc [mysk], *s.m.* **1.** (*a*) musk; (*b*) **m. artificiel,** artificial musk (resin or coal-tar product). **2.** *Z:* musk deer; **couleur (de) m.,** musk-coloured. **3.** *Bot:* **herbe au m.,** musk mallow.
muscade [myskad], *s.f.* **1. (noix) m.,** nutmeg; **fleur de m.,** mace. **2.** conjuror's vanishing ball or pea; **passez m.!** hey presto!
muscadelle [myskadɛl], *s.f. Hort:* musk pear.
muscadet [myskadɛ], *s.m.* white wine from the lower Loire valley.
muscadier [myskadje], *s.m. Bot:* nutmeg tree.
muscadin [myskadɛ̃], *A:* **1.** *s.m.* (*a*) musk pastille or lozenge; (*b*) dandy, fop; (*first applied to the Royalists in 1793*). **2.** *a.* (*f.* **muscadine** [myskadin]), foppish.
muscardin [myskardɛ̃], *s.m.* dormouse, hazel mouse.
muscardine [myskardin], *s.f. Ser:* muscardine, calcino; silkworm rot.
muscari [myskari], *s.m. Bot:* grape hyacinth.
muscarine [myskarin], *s.f. Ch:* muscarine.
muscat [myska], *a. & s.m.* **1.** *Vit:* muscat; **(raisin) m.,** muscat grape, muscadine grape; **(vin) m.,** muscat wine, muscatel. **2.** musk pear.
muscicapidés [mysikapide], *s.m.pl. Orn:* Muscicapidae, the flycatchers.
muscicole [mysikɔl], *a. Nat.Hist:* muscicole, muscicolous.
muscidés [myside], *s.m.pl. Ent:* Muscidae, *F:* flesh flies.
muscinées [mysine], *s.f.pl. Bot:* mosses.

muscle [myskḷ], *s.m.* muscle; *Anat:* **m. strié, lisse,** striated, smooth, muscle; *F:* **avoir du m.,** to have plenty of beef, plenty of brawn; **être tout nerfs et muscles,** to be all thew and sinew.
musclé [myskle], *a.* **1.** muscular; sinewy, brawny (arm); **il est bien m.,** he has well-developed muscles, he's very muscular; **peu m.,** slight (man). **2.** *Art:* muscled; with well-marked muscles.
muscler [myskle], *v.tr.* to develop the muscles of (one's limbs).
muscoïde [myskɔid], *a.* muscoid.
muscologie [myskɔlɔʒi], *s.f. Bot:* muscology.
muscovite [myskɔvit], *s.f. Miner:* muscovite.
musculaire [myskylɛːr], *a.* muscular (system, tissue, strength, contraction); **fibre m.,** muscle fibre.
muscularité [myskylarite], *s.f.* muscularity.
musculation [myskylasjɔ̃], *s.f. Anat:* musculation.
musculature [myskylatyːr], *s.f. Anat: Aer:* musculature, musculation.
musculeux, -euse [myskylø, -øːz], *a.* muscular, brawny, well-developed (person, arm, etc.); *F:* beefy (person).
musculo-cutané [myskylɔkytane], *a. & s. Anat:* musculocutaneous (nerve); *pl. musculo-cutané(e)s.*
musculosité [myskylozite], *s.f.* muscularity.
muse[1] [myːz], *s.f.* muse; (*a*) *Myth:* **les neuf muses,** the nine muses; (*b*) *Lit:* poetry; poetic inspiration; **invoquer sa m.,** to call on one's muse.
muse[2], *s.f. Ven:* onset of the rut (of deer).
museau, -eaux [myzo], *s.m.* **1.** (*a*) muzzle, snout (of animal); (*b*) *F:* **joli petit m.,** nice little face, mug; **se poudrer le m.,** to powder one's face, one's nose; **vilain m.,** ugly mug. **2.** fore-edge of the web (of a key).
musée[1] [myze], *s.m.* (*a*) museum; **m. de figures de cire,** wax-works; (*b*) **m. de peinture, d'objets d'art,** picture gallery, art gallery; *P:* **le m. des refroidis,** the mortuary, the morgue.
Musée[2], *Pr.n.m. Gr.Lit: Myth:* Musaeus.
musées [myze], *s.f.pl. Bot:* Musaceae.
museler [myzle], *v.tr.* (**je muselle, n. muselons; je musellerai**) **1.** to muzzle (dog, *F:* the press, etc.). **2.** to gag (s.o.); *F:* **m. qn,** to make s.o. hold his tongue; **muselé par la peur,** dumb with fear.
muselet [myzlɛ], *s.m.* cork wire, cork wiring (of bottle of wine).
museletage [myzlətaːʒ], *s.m.* (*action of*) wiring (of cork of bottle).
museleter [myzləte], *v.tr.* (**je muselette, n. museletons; je museletterai**) to wire (corks).
museletteuse [myzlɛtøːz], **museleuse** [myzəløːz], *s.f.* cork-wiring machine.
muselière [myzəljɛːr], *s.f.* (strap or wire) muzzle; **mettre une m. à un chien,** to muzzle a dog.
musellement [myzɛlmɑ̃], *s.m.* muzzling (of animal, *F:* of person, of newspaper).
muséographie [myzeɔgrafi], *s.f.* museography.
muséologie [myzeɔlɔʒi], *s.f.* museology.
muséologique [myzeɔlɔʒik], *a.* museological.
muséologue [myzeɔlɔg], *s.m.* museologist.
muser [myze], *v.i. O: & Lit:* to idle, dawdle; to moon about; to saunter; to frivol, to trifle; to fritter away one's time; *Prov:* **qui refuse, muse; tel refuse qui après muse,** he that will not when he may, when he will he shall have nay.
muserie [myzri], *s.f. A:* trifling, idling.
muserol(l)e [myzrɔl], *s.f. Harn:* nose-band.
musette[1] [myzɛt], *s.f.* **1.** *Mus: A:* musette (of the (bag)-pipe type); *Mus: Danc:* musette; (*nowadays*) *F:* **orchestre m.,** band with accordions; **bal m.,** popular dance hall (with accordion band). **2.** (*a*) **m.(-mangeoire),** (horse's) nose-bag; (*b*) *A:* (schoolboy's) satchel; *Mil: etc:* haversack; **m. de pansement,** medical haversack; *P:* **il a reçu une râclée qui n'était pas dans une m., il en a pris plein sa m.,** he got a rare thrashing.
musette[2], *s.f. Z:* common shrew.
muséum [myzeɔm], *s.m.* natural history museum.
museur, -euse [myzœːr, -øːz], *s. A:* trifler, idler.
musical, -aux [myzikal, -o], *a.* musical (sound, evening, scale, etc.); **l'art m.,** the art of music; **avoir l'oreille musicale,** to have an ear for music, a musical ear; *Aut:* **avertisseur à tonalité musicale,** musical horn.
musicalement [myzikalmɑ̃], *adv.* musically.
musicalité [myzikalite], *s.f.* musicality; musical quality.
music-hall [myzikal], *s.m.* music hall; **numéros de m.-h.,** variety turns; *pl. music-halls.*
musicien, -ienne [myzisjɛ̃, -jɛn], *a. & s.* **1.** musician; **elle est bonne musicienne,** (i) she is very musical; (ii) she is a good player; **je ne suis pas du tout musicien(ne),** I am not at all musical; **oreille musicienne,** musical ear, good ear for music; *Poet:* **les musiciens des bois,** the songsters of the woods. **2.** *Mil: etc:* bandsman; member of the band, of the orchestra; performer; **un orchestre de deux, trois, musiciens,** a two-piece, three-piece band.
musicographe [myzikɔgraf]. **1.** *s.m. & f.* musicographer. **2.** *s.m.* machine for writing music.
musicographie [myzikɔgrafi], *s.f.* musicography.
musicographique [myzikɔgrafik], *a.* musicographic.
musicologie [muzikɔlɔʒi], *s.f.* musicology.
musicologue [mysikɔlɔg], *s.m. & f.* musicologist.
musicomane [myzikɔman], *s.m. & f.* music lover.
musicomanie [myzikɔmani], *s.f.* love of music.
musicothérapie [myzikɔterapi], *s.f.* musicotherapy.
musique [myzik], *s.f.* **1.** (*a*) music; **aimer la m.,** to love music, to be musical; **mettre des paroles en m.,** to set words to music; **instrument de m.,** musical instrument; **boîte à m.,** musical box. **m. de chambre,** chamber music; **m. d'orchestre,** orchestral music; **m. instrumentale,** instrumental music; **m. religieuse, sacrée,** sacred music; **m. d'ambiance, de fond,** background music; **la m. pour une pièce,** the incidental music for a play; **m. de genre,** programme music; **travail en m.,** music while you work; *F:* **m. de chats,** caterwauling; **ils faisaient une m. enragée,** they were making an awful din; **voulez-vous nous faire un peu de m.?** won't you play for us? **faire de la m.,** (i) to make music; to have a musical evening; (ii) to go in for music; (iii) *P:* to kick up a dust, a shindy; **ses parents ont fait une m. énorme,** her parents made an awful fuss about it; *F:* **c'est une autre m.,** that's another matter, another cup of tea; *s.a.* RÉGLÉ; (*b*) *P:* blackmail; (*c*) *P:* blarney; **ah! je connais la m.,** I'm up to all the tricks. **2.** band; **m. du régiment,** regimental band; **m. de la ville,** town band, municipal band; **chef de m.,** bandmaster.
musiquer [myzike], *A:* **1.** *v.tr.* to set (libretto, etc.) to music. **2.** *v.i.* to make music.
musiquette [myzikɛt], *s.f.* (*a*) *F: Pej:* amateur music, music of sorts; cheap music; (*b*) **m. publicitaire,** signature tune (of band).
musoir [myzwaːr], *s.m.* **1.** pierhead, jetty head. **2. m. d'une écluse,** wing wall of a lock.
musophagidés [myzɔfaʒide], *s.m.pl. Orn:* Musophagidae, the touracos.
musqué [myske], *a.* **1.** (*a*) musky; scented with musk; **rose musquée, rosier m.,** musk rose; **poire musquée,** musk pear; **paroles musquées,** flattering, honeyed, words; (*b*) affected, effeminate (poet, style, etc.). **2. bœuf m.,** musk ox; **rat m.,** musk rat, musquash; **canard m.,** musk duck, Muscovy duck; **chat m.,** civet (cat).
musquer [myske], *v.tr.* to scent with musk.
musse-pot (à) [amyspo], *adv.phr. A:* = À MUCHE-POT.
musser (se) [səmyse], *v.tr. A:* to hide.
mussif [mysif], *a.m.* **or m.,** mosaic gold, disulphide of tin.
mussipontain, -aine [mysipɔ̃tɛ̃, -ɛn], **mussipontin, -ine** [mysipɔ̃tɛ̃, -in], *a. & s. Geog:* (native, inhabitant) of Pont-à-Mousson.
mussitation [mysitasjɔ̃], *s.f. Med:* mussitation.
mustang [mystɑ̃g], *s.m.* mustang.
mustélidés [mystelide], *s.m.pl. Z:* Mustelidae.
musulman, -ane [myzylmɑ̃, -an], *a. & s.* Mohammedan, Moslem.
mutabilité [mytabilite], *s.f.* **1.** mutability. **2.** *Jur:* alienability.
mutable [mytabḷ], *a.* **1.** changeable, mutable. **2.** *Jur:* alienable.
mutacisme [mytasism], *s.m.* **1.** *Ling:* mytacism, mutacism. **2.** *Psy:* mutism.
mutage [mytaːʒ], *s.m.* mutage (of wine).
mutagène [mytaʒɛn], *a.* **agent m.,** mutagen.
mutant, -ante [mytɑ̃, ɑ̃ːt], *a. & s. Biol:* mutant.
mutation [mytasjɔ̃], *s.f.* (*a*) change, alteration; *Mus: Biol:* mutation; *Biol:* saltation; **m. dirigée,** controlled mutation; **jeux de m.,** mutation stops (of organ); *Ling:* **m. vocalique,** (vowel) gradation; (*b*) *Jur:* change of ownership; transfer (of property); **impôt sur les mutations,** tax on (real estate) transfers; **m. entre vifs,** conveyance (of property) *inter vivos*; **m. par décès,** transfer by death; *s.a.* DROIT[2] 2; (*c*) transfer (of personnel, *Fb:* of players); (*d*) *Mus:* shift(ing) (in violin playing).
mutationnisme [mytasjɔnism], *s.m. Biol:* mutationism.
mutationniste [mytasjɔnist], *Biol:* **1.** *a.* mutationist (theory). **2.** *s.m. & f.* mutationist, believer in mutationism.
muter[1] [myte], *v.tr.* to mute (wine).

muter[2], *v.tr. Adm: Mil: etc:* to transfer (civil servant, officer, etc.).

mutilant [mytilɑ̃], *a.* disfiguring, maiming (operation, etc.).

mutilateur, -trice [mytilatœːr, -tris], *s.* mutilator; (*a*) maimer; (*b*) defacer.

mutilation [mytilasjɔ̃], *s.f.* (*a*) mutilation, maiming (of person); **m. volontaire,** self-mutilation; (*b*) defacement (of a statue, etc.); mutilation (of book, statue, etc.).

mutilé, -ée [mytile], *a. & s.* mutilated, maimed (person); **mutilés de guerre,** disabled ex-servicemen; **grand m.,** badly-disabled ex-serviceman; **m. du travail,** disabled worker; **il est m. du bras,** he has lost an arm; **m. de la face,** disfigured.

mutiler [mytile], *v.tr.* (*a*) to mutilate, maim (s.o.); **m. qn au visage,** to disfigure s.o.; (*b*) to deface (statue, etc.); to mutilate (book, statue, etc.); **comédie mutilée par la censure,** play cut about by the censor.

mutille [mytiːj], *s.f. Ent:* velvet ant; mutillid.

mutin, -ine [mytɛ̃, -in], *a. & s.* **1.** (*a*) *A:* insubordinate (soldier, etc.); disobedient, unruly, unbiddable (child); **faire le m.,** to be refractory; (*b*) full of fun; saucy, cheeky (child). **2.** *s.m.* mutineer.

mutiné [mytine]. **1.** *a.* rebellious, riotous (people); mutinous (troops). **2.** *s.m.* mutineer.

mutinement [mytinmɑ̃], *s.m.* mutiny.

mutiner [mytine], *v.tr. A:* to incite (s.o.) to rebellion.

se mutiner, to rise in revolt; (*of troops*) to mutiny; (*of children*) to be disobedient, unruly.

mutinerie [mytinri], *s.f.* **1.** (*a*) unruliness, disobedience (of children); (*b*) *O:* roguishness, sauciness. **2.** rebellion (of people); mutiny (of troops).

mutisme [mytism], *s.m.* dumbness, muteness; **réduire qn au m.,** to silence s.o.; **se renfermer dans le m.,** to maintain a stubborn silence.

mutité [mytite], *s.f.* (*a*) *Med:* mutism; (*b*) **la m. des évangiles sur la jeunesse du Christ,** the silence of the gospels on the subject of the youth of Christ.

mutoscope [mytɔskɔp], *s.m. A:* mutoscope.

mutualisation [mytɥalizasjɔ̃], *s.f.* mutualization.

mutualisme [mytɥalism], *s.m. Biol: Pol.Ec:* mutualism.

mutualiste [mytɥalist], *s.m. & f.* **1.** member of a mutual benefit society, of a mutual insurance company, of a friendly society. **2.** *Pol.Ec:* mutualist.

mutualité [mytɥalite], *s.f.* **1.** mutuality, reciprocity. **2.** mutual insurance; **société de m.,** friendly society; **m. agricole,** = *U.S.* farmers' mutual.

mutuel, -elle [mytɥɛl]. **1.** *a.* mutual (consent, service, insurance, etc.); **enseignement m.,** mutual improvement; **société de secours mutuels,** mutual benefit society, friendly society; **pari m.,** *s.m. F:* **le m.** = totalizator (betting), *F:* the tote. **2.** *s.f.* **mutuelle,** mutual insurance company; friendly society.

mutuellement [mytɥɛlmɑ̃], *adv.* mutually, reciprocally.

mutuellisme [mytɥelism], *s.m. Pol.Ec: A:* mutualism.

mutuelliste [mytɥelist], *s.m. & f. Pol.Ec: A:* mutualist.

mutulaire [mytylɛːr], *a. Arch:* mutulary.

mutule [mytyl], *s.f. Arch:* mutule (of Doric order).

myalgie [mialʒi], *s.f. Med:* myalgia.

myasthénie [miasteni], *s.f. Med:* myasthenia.

myatonie [miatɔni], *s.f. Med:* myatony.

myatrophie [miatrɔfi], *s.f. Med:* myatrophy.

mycélium [miseljɔm], *s.m.,* **mycélion** [miseljɔ̃], *s.m. Fung:* mycelium.

mycélien, -ienne [miseljɛ̃, -jɛn], *a.* mycelial, mycelian.

Mycènes [misɛn], *Pr.n. A.Geog:* Mycenae.

mycénien, -ienne [misenjɛ̃, -jɛn], *a. & s. A.Geog:* Mycenaean.

mycète [misɛt], *s.m.* **1.** *Bot:* fungus, mushroom. **2.** *Z:* howling monkey.

mycétologie [misetɔlɔʒi], *s.f.* mycetology.

mycétome [misetoːm], *s.m. Med:* mycetoma.

mycétophage [misetɔfaːʒ], *a. Ent:* mycetophagous, fungivorous.

mycétophile [misetɔfil], *a. & s.f. Ent:* mycetophilid.

mycétozoaires [misetɔzɔɛːr], *s.m.pl. Prot:* mycetozoa.

myciculteur [misikyltœːr], *s.m.* mushroom grower.

myciculture [misikyltyːr], *s.f.* mushroom growing.

mycobactériées [mikɔbakterje], *s.f.pl.* Mycobacteriaceae.

mycocécidie [mikɔsesidi], *s.f. Bot:* mycocecidium.

mycoderme [mikɔdɛrm], *s.m. Fung:* mycoderm(a).

mycodermique [mikɔdɛrmik], *a. Fung:* mycodermic, mycodermatoid.

mycologie [mikɔlɔʒi], *s.f. Bot:* myc(et)ology, fungology.

mycologique [mikɔlɔʒik], *a. Bot:* mycologic(al).

mycologue [mikɔlɔg], *s.m.* mycologist, fungologist.

mycophage [mikɔfaːʒ]. **1.** *a. Z:* mycophagous. **2.** *s.* mycophagist.

mycor(r)hize [mikɔriːz], *s.f. Fung:* mycorrhiza.

mycose [mikoːz], *s.f. Med:* mycosis.

mycosis [mikɔzis], *s.m. Med:* **m. fongoïde,** mycosis fungoides.

mycotête [mikɔtɛt], *s.f. Fung:* swelling on the mycelium.

myctophidés, myctophides [miktɔfide, -fid], *s.m.pl. Ich:* Myctophidae; myctophids.

mydriase [midrjaːz], *s.f. Med:* mydriasis.

mydriatique [midrjatik], *a. & s.m.* mydriatic.

mye [mi], *s.f. Moll:* gaper (shell), old maid, *U.S:* soft (shell) clam.

myélémie [mjelemi], *s.f. Med:* myelemia.

myélencéphale [mjelɑ̃sefal], *s.m. Anat:* myelencephalon.

myéline [mjelin], *s.f. Anat:* myelin(e), medullary sheath.

myélinique [mjelinik], *a.* myelinic.

myélite [mjelit], *s.f. Med:* myelitis.

myéloblaste [mjelɔblast], *s.m. Med:* myeloblast.

myélocèle [mjelɔsɛl], *s.f. Med:* myelocele.

myélocystocèle [mjelɔsistɔsɛl], *s.f. Med:* myelocystocele.

myélocyte [mjelɔsit], *s.m. Med:* myelocyte.

myélocytémie [mjelɔsitemi], *s.f. Med:* myelemia.

myélogène [mjelɔʒɛn], *a. Med:* myelogenous.

myéloïde [mjelɔid], *a.* myeloid.

myélome [mjeloːm], *s.m. Med:* myeloma.

myélo-méningite [mjelɔmenɛ̃ʒit], *s.f. Med:* myelomeningitis, spinal meningitis.

myélopathie [mjelɔpati], *s.f.* myelopathy

myélophtisie [mjelɔftizi], *s.f. Med:* myelophthisis.

myéloplaxe [mjelɔplaks], *s.m. Anat:* myeloplax.

myélosarcome [mjelɔsarkɔm], *s.m. Med:* myelosarcoma.

mygale [migal], *s.f. Arach:* mygale, trap-door spider; **m. aviculaire,** bird-eating spider, bird spider.

myiase [mi(j)aːz], *s.f. Med:* my(i)asis.

myliobatidés [miljɔbatide], *s.m.pl. Ich:* Myliobatidae.

mylonite [milɔnit], *s.f. Miner:* mylonite.

mymarides [mimarid], *s.m.pl. Ent:* Mymaridae.

myo- [mjɔ-], *pref.* myo-.

myoblaste [mjɔblast], *s.m. Physiol:* myoblast.

myocarde [mjɔkard], *s.m. Anat:* myocardium; *s.a.* INFARCTUS.

myocardite [mjɔkardit], *s.f. Med:* myocarditis.

myocastor [mjɔkastɔːr], *s.m. Z:* myopotamus, myocastor.

myoclonie [mjɔklɔni], *s.f. Med:* myoclonus.

myodynamie [mjɔdinami], *s.f.* myodynamia.

myodynie [mjɔdini], *s.f. Med:* myalgia, muscular rheumatism.

myoélectrique [mjɔelɛktrik], *a.* myoelectric.

myogène [mjɔʒɛn], *a.* myogenetic.

myogénie [mjɔʒeni], *s.f.* myogenesis.

myoglobine [mjɔglɔbin], *s.f. Bio-Ch:* myoglobin, myoh(a)emoglobin.

myoglobinurie [mjɔglɔbinyri], *s.f. Vet:* myoglobinuria.

myogramme [mjɔgram], *s.m. Med:* myogram.

myographe [mjɔgraf], *s.m. Med:* **1.** myograph. **2.** myographist.

myographie [mjɔgrafi], *s.f.* myography.

myographique [mjɔgrafik], *a.* myographic(al).

myokinétique [mjɔkinetik], *a.* myokinetic.

myolemme [mjɔlɛm], *s.m. Anat:* myolemma.

myologie [mjɔlɔʒi], *s.f. Anat:* myology.

myologique [mjɔlɔʒik], *a. Anat:* myological.

myologiste [mjɔlɔʒist], *s.m. & f.* myologist.

myome [mjoːm], *s.m. Med:* myoma.

myomère [mjɔmɛːr], *s.m. usu. pl. Anat:* myomere, muscle segment.

myomorphes [mjɔmɔrf], *s.m.pl. Z:* (*suborder*) Myomorpha.

myoœdème [mjɔødɛm], *s.m. Med:* myoedema.

myopathie [mjɔpati], *s.f. Med:* myopathy.

myopathique [mjɔpatik], *a. Med:* myopathic.

myope [mjɔp]. **1.** *a.* myopic, near-sighted, short-sighted; **m. comme une taupe,** as blind as a bat. **2.** *s.m. & f.* myope; near-sighted, short-sighted, person.

myopie [mjɔpi], *s.f. Med:* myopia, short-sightedness.

myopique [mjɔpik], *a.* myopic, relating to myopia.

myoplastie [mjɔplasti], *s.f. Surg:* myoplasty.

myopotame [mjɔpɔtam], *s.m. Z:* myopotamus, myocastor; **m. coypou,** coypu.

myorraphie [mjɔrafi], *s.f. Surg:* myorrhaphy.

myosclérose [mjɔskleroːz], *s.f. Med:* myosclerosis.

myose [mjoːz], *s.f.,* **myosis** [mjɔzis], *s.m. Med:* myosis, miosis.

myosite [mjɔzit], *s.f. Med:* myositis.

myosotis [mjɔzɔtis], *s.m. Bot:* myosotis, mouse ear, scorpion grass; **m. des marais,** forget(-)me(-)not.

myospalax [mjɔspalaks], *s.m. Z:* zokor.

myosure [mjɔzyːr], *s.m. Bot:* mouse-tail.

myothérapie [mjɔterapi], *s.f. Med:* myofunctional therapy.

myotique [mjɔtik], *a. Med:* myotic.

myotome [mjɔtɔm], *s.m. Anat:* myotome.

myotomie [mjɔtɔmi], *s.f. Surg:* myotomy.

myotonie [mjɔtɔni], *s.f. Anat: Med:* myotonia.

myotonique [mjɔtɔnik], *a.* myotonic.

myoxidés [mjɔkside], *s.m.pl. Z:* Myoxidae.

myrcène [mirsɛn], *s.m. Ch:* myrcene.

myria [mirja], *pref.* myria-.

myriade [mirjad], *s.f.* myriad; **des myriades de fourmis,** myriads of ants, swarms of ants.

myriagramme [mirjagram], *s.m.* myriagram(me).

myriamètre [mirjamɛtr̥], *s.m.* myriameter.

myriapode [mirjapɔd], *Z:* **1.** *a.* myriapodous. **2.** *s.m.* myriapod, myripod; *pl.* **myriapodes,** Myriapoda; centipedes and millipedes.

myrica [mirika], *s.m. Bot:* myrica; **cire de m.,** myrtle wax.

myricacées [mirikase], *s.f.pl. Bot:* Myricaceae.

myriophylle [mirjɔfil], *s.m. Bot:* myriophyllum; *F:* water milfoil.

myristine [miristin], *s.f. Ch:* myristin(e).

myristique [miristik], *a. Ch:* myristic (acid).

myrmécobiidés [mirmekɔbiide], *s.m.pl. Z:* Myrmecobiidae, the marsupial anteaters.

myrmécologie [mirmekɔlɔʒi], *s.f. Ent:* myrmecology.

myrmécologique [mirmekɔlɔʒik], *a. Ent:* myrmecological.

myrmécologiste [mirmekɔlɔʒist], *s.m. Ent:* myrmecologist.

myrmécophage [mirmekɔfaːʒ], *Z:* **1.** *a.* myrmecophagous, ant-eating. **2.** *s.m.* anteater.

myrmécophagidés [mirmekɔfaʒide], *s.m.pl. Z:* Myrmecophagidae, the anteaters.

myrmécophile [mirmekɔfil], *a. & s.m. Ent:* myrmecophile; **les pucerons sont myrmécophiles,** greenfly are myrmecophilous.

myrmécophilie [miːrmekɔfili], *s.f. Nat.Hist:* myrmecophily.

myrmécophyte [mirmekɔfit], *s.m. Bot:* myrmecophyte.

Myrmidons [mirmidɔ̃], *s.m.pl. Gr.Myth:* Myrmidons; *F: A:* **un myrmidon,** a little whipper-snapper of a man.

myrobolan [mirɔbɔlɑ̃], *s.m.* **1.** *Bot:* myrobalan. **2. prunier m.,** myrobalan plum (tree).

myronique [mirɔnik], *a.* myronic.

myrosine [mirɔzin], *s.f. Ch:* myrosin.

myroxylon [mirɔksilɔ̃], *s.m. Bot:* myroxylon.

myrrhe [miːr], *s.f.* myrrh.

myrrhé [mir(r)e], *a.* perfumed with myrrh.

myrrhide [mir(r)id], *s.f.,* **myrrhis** [mirris], *s.m. Bot:* myrrhis; **myrrhide odorante,** sweet cicely; myrrh.

myrsinacées [mirsinase], *s.f.pl. Bot:* Myrsinaceae.

myrtacé [mirtase], *Bot:* **1.** *a.* myrtaceous. **2.** *s.f.pl.* **myrtacées,** Myrtaceae, myrtles.

myrte [mirt], *s.m. Bot:* myrtle; **m. des marais, m. bâtard,** sweet gale, bog myrtle, Dutch myrtle.

myrtiforme [mirtifɔrm], *a.* myrtiform.

myrtille [mirtiːj, -til], *s.f. Bot:* bilberry, whortleberry, whinberry, *U.S:* huckleberry.

mysidacés [misidase], *s.m.pl. Crust:* Mysidacea.

myside [misid], **mysis** [misis], *s.m. Crust:* mysid; (*genus*) Mysis.

Mysie [mizi], *Pr.n.f. A.Geog:* Mysia.

mysien, -ienne [mizjɛ̃, -jɛn], *a. & s. A.Geog:* Mysian.

mystagogie [mistagɔʒi], *s.f. Gr.Ant:* mystagogy.

mystagogue [mistagɔg], *s.m. Gr.Ant:* mystagogue.

mystère [mistɛːr], *s.m.* **1.** (*a*) *A.Rel: Theol:* mystery; **les mystères d'Éleusis,** the Eleusinian mysteries; (*b*) **on n'a jamais pénétré ce m.,** this mystery has never been fathomed; **se conduire avec m., mettre du m. dans sa conduite,** to act, behave, mysteriously; **je n'y entends pas m.,** I see nothing mysterious, unusual, about it; **faire grand m. d'un événement,** to be very reticent, secretive, about an event; **je n'en fais pas m.,** I make no mystery, no secret, of it; **les mystères de la politique,** the mysteries, secrets, of politics;

la clef du m., the key to the mystery; **m. qu'il ne se soit pas tué,** I can't understand how he wasn't killed. **2** *Lit.Hist:* mystery (play); **m. de la Passion,** Passion play. **3.** *Mil.Av: Pr.n.* **M.,** (French) supersonic fighter.

mystérieusement [misterjøzmã], *adv.* mysteriously.

mystérieux, -euse [misterjø, -ø:z], *a.* mysterious; enigmatical; uncanny; *s.m.* le m. séduit toujours les hommes, men are always attracted by the mysterious.

mysticètes [mistisɛt], *s.m.pl. Z:* Mysticeti.

mysticisme [mistisism], *s.m.* mysticism.

mysticité [mistisite], *s.f.* mysticity.

mystifiable [mistifjab], *a.* mystifiable, dupable, gullible.

mystificateur, -trice [mistifikatœ:r, -tris]. **1.** *a.* mystifying. **2.** *s.* hoaxer; mystifier.

mystification [mistifikasjõ], *s.f.* (*a*) mystification; (*b*) hoax, practical joke.

mystifier [mistifje], *v.tr.* (*p.d. & pr.sub.* **n. mystifiions, v. mystifiiez**) (*a*) to mystify; (*b*) to hoax, fool (s.o.); to play a practical joke on (s.o.); to make a fool of (s.o.); to have (s.o.) on; to pull (s.o.'s) leg; to take a rise out of (s.o.); **m. le public,** to deceive, bamboozle, the public; **m. un adversaire,** to keep an opponent guessing; *Fb:* to trick, outwit, an opponent.

mystique [mistik]. **1** *a.* mystic(al); *Jur:* testament m., mystic will, sealed will. **2.** *s.m. & f.* mystic. **3.** *s.f.* mystical theology. **4.** *s.f.* mystique.

mystiquement [mistikmã], *adv.* mystically.

mytacisme [mitasism], *s.m. Ling:* mytacism.

mythe [mit], *s.m.* (*a*) myth, legend; (*b*) (*imaginary thg*) **la justice est-elle un m.?** is justice a myth?

mythique [mitik], *a.* mythical.

mythographe [mitograf], *s.m.* mythographer.

mythographie [mitografi], *s.f.* mythography.

mythologie [mitolɔʒi], *s.f.* mythology.

mythologique [mitolɔʒik], *a.* mythological.

mythologiquement [mitolɔʒikmã], *adv.* mythologically.

mythologiste [mitolɔʒist], *s.m. & f.* **mythologue** [mitolɔg], *s.m. & f.* mythologist.

mythomane [mitoman], *a. & s.m. & f.* mythomaniac; pathological liar.

mythomaniaque [mitomanjak], *a.* mythomaniac.

mythomanie [mitomani], *s.f.* mythomania.

mytilacés [mitilase], *s.m.pl. Moll:* Mytilacea.

Mytilène [mitilɛn], *Pr.n. Geog:* Mytilene.

mytilénien, -ienne [mitilenjɛ̃, -jɛn], *a. & s. Geog:* (native, inhabitant) of Mytilene.

mytilicole [mitilikɔl], *a.* pertaining to mussel breeding; **parc m.,** mussel bed.

mytiliculteur [mitilikyltœ:r], *s.m.* mussel breeder.

mytiliculture [mitilikylty:r], *s.f.* mussel breeding.

mytilidés [mitilide], *s.m.pl. Moll:* Mytilidae.

mytilotoxine [mitilɔtɔksin], *s.f. Ch:* mytilotoxine.

myure [mijy:r], *a. Med:* myurous; **pouls m.,** myurous, progressively sinking, pulse.

myxa [miksa], *s.f. Orn:* myxa.

myxamibe [miksamib], *s.f. Biol:* myxamoeba.

myxine [miksin], *s.f. Ich:* myxine, hagfish.

myxoamibe [miksɔamib], *s.f. Biol:* myxamoeba.

myxobactérie [miksɔbakteri], *s.f.* myxobacterium.

myxochondrome [miksɔkõdrɔm], *s.m. Med:* myxochondroma.

myxœdème [miksedɛm], *s.m.* myx(o)edema.

myxœdémateux, -euse [miksedematø, -ø:z], *Med:* **1.** *a.* myx(o)edematous. **2.** *s.* sufferer from myx(o)edema.

myxofibrome [miksɔfibro:m], *s.m. Med:* myxofibroma.

myxoïde [miksɔid], *a.* myxoid.

myxomateux, -euse [miksɔmatø, -ø:z], *a.* myxomatous.

myxomatose [miksɔmato:z], *s.f.* myxomatosis.

myxome [mikso:m], *s.m. Med:* myxoma.

myxomycètes [miksɔmisɛt], *s.m.pl. Fung:* myxomycetes.

myxomyome [miksɔmjo:m], *s.m. Med:* myxomyoma.

myxorrhée [miksɔre], *s.f. Med:* myxorrhea.

myxosarcome [miksɔsarko:m], *s.m. Med:* myxosarcoma.

myxosporidies [miksɔspɔridi], *s.f.pl. Prot:* Myxosporidia.

myzostomes [mizɔsto:m], *s.m.pl. Ann:* Myzostomata.

Mzabi [mzabi], *s.m.,* **Mzabite** [mzabit], *s.m. & f. Geog:* Mozabite.

N

N, n [ɛn], *s.m. & f.* (the letter) N, n; *Mth. & F:* à la nième puissance, to the nth (power); *F:* c'est la nième fois que je vous le dis, I'm telling you for the unpteenth time; *Biol:* N, N; *Typ:* n; *Ph. Meas:* N., newton (N); *Ph:* rayons n., n rays; *Tp:* N comme Nicolas, N for Nellie.

n'. *See* NE.

na [na], *int. F:* (a) (= là!) there now! (b) (emphatic and defiant conclusion to a statement, *esp.* on the part of little girls) j'irai pas, na! I'm not going, so there! and that's that!

nabab [nabab], **nabob** [nabɔb], *s.m.* nabob.

nababie [nababi], *s.f.* (a) rank of nabob; (b) territory governed by a nabob.

nabat(h)éen, -enne [nabateɛ̃, -ɛn], *a. & s. Hist:* Nabataean.

nabi [nabi], *s.m.* (Hebrew) prophet.

nabla [nabla], *s.m.* 1. *Mus:* nabla. 2. *Mth:* (opérateur) n., del, nabla.

nable [nabl], *s.m. Nau:* 1. plug-hole (of small boat). 2. (bouchon tampon, vis, (de)) n., (boat) plug; nables des ballasts, ballast-tank plugs.

nabot, -ote [nabo, -ɔt]. 1. *s.* dwarf, midget; *m.* manikin. 2. *a.* dwarfish, tiny (person).

Nabuchodonosor [nabykɔdɔnɔzɔːr], *Pr.n.m. B. Hist:* Nebuchadnezzar, Nebuchadrezzar.

nacarat [nakara]. 1. *s.m. & a.inv.* nacarat, orange-red. 2. *s.m.* nacarat (crape).

nacelle [nasɛl], *s.f.* 1. skiff, wherry, dinghy; *Mil:* pontoon-boat. 2. (a) *Aer:* basket, nacelle, car (of balloon); nacelle, gondola (of airship); *Av:* nacelle, pod; réacteurs installés en nacelles sous la voilure, engines installed in underwing pods; *Mil.Av:* n.-canon, gun-pod; (b) car (of transporter-bridge); (c) body (of perambulator). 3. *Arch:* scotia. 4. *Bot:* = CARÈNE. 5. (weighing) scoop. 6. *Ch:* n. de porcelaine, etc., porcelain, etc., boat.

nacre [nakr], *s.f.* mother of pearl.

nacré [nakre]. 1. *a.* nacreous, pearly (lustre, etc.). 2. *s.m.* sheen. 3. *s.m. Ent: F:* petit n., Queen of Spain fritillary.

nacrer [nakre], *v.tr.* to give a pearly lustre to (beads, etc.).

nacrite [nakrit], *s.f. Miner:* nacrite.

nacroculture [nakrɔkylty:r], *s.f.* mother-of-pearl culture.

nacrure [nakry:r], *s.f.* pearly quality.

nactage [nakta:ʒ], *s.m. A.Tex:* process of removing impurities from fine materials by hand.

nacteur [naktœːr], *a.m. Tex:* peigne n., comb of rectilinear combing machine.

nadir [nadiːr], *s.m. Astr:* nadir.

nadiral, -aux [nadiral, -o], *a. Astr:* nadiral.

nadorite [nadɔrit], *s.f. Miner:* nadorite.

nævo-carcinome [nevokarsinoːm], *s.m. Med:* melanoma, nevocarcinoma, melanocarcinoma; *pl.* nævo-carcinomes.

nævus [nevys], *s.m.* naevus, birth-mark, mole; *Med:* n. vasculaire, angioma, vascular naevus; n. pigmentaire, pigmented naevus, pigmented mole; *pl. nævi.*

naga[1] [naga], *s.m.inv. Myth:* naga.

naga[2], *s.m. Ling:* naga.

nagaïka [nagaika], *s.f.* nagaika.

nagari [nagari], *s.f. & a. Ling:* Nagari.

nage [na:ʒ], *s.f.* 1. rowing, sculling; *Nau:* pulling; banc de n., thwart; barre de n., foot rest; cadence de n., rate of striking; chef de nage, stroke(sman), stroke oarsman; donner la n., to row stroke, pull stroke; to set the stroke;

exercice de n., rowing drill, boat-work; n. à culer, backing; n. en couple, double-sculling; n. en pointe, rowing; *Lit:* se mettre en n., to start rowing. 2. (a) (in certain phrases) swimming; se jeter, se mettre, à la n., to start to swim; to start swimming; to leap into the water; il faut nous mettre à la n., nous sauver à la n., we must swim for it; it's sink or swim; passer, traverser, une rivière à la n., to swim across a river; faire traverser son cheval à la n., to swim one's horse across (a river, etc.); *F:* être (tout), se mettre, en n., to be bathed in perspiration; (b) stroke (in swimming); n. (à l') indienne, over-arm stroke; n. en grenouille, breast stroke; n. sur le dos, backstroke; n. debout, treading water; n. libre, freestyle; course en n. libre, freestyle relay; le 220 mètres (en) n. libre, the 220 freestyle; 4 × 100 mètres quatre nages, 400 metre medley relay.

nageant [naʒɑ̃], *a. Bot:* floating (water-lily leaves, etc.); *Her:* naiant.

nagée [naʒe], *s.f. O:* stroke; stroke's length (in swimming or rowing).

nagement [naʒmɑ̃], *s.m. A:* swimming (of fishes, etc.).

nageoire [naʒwaːr], *s.f.* 1. (a) fin (of fish); paddle, flipper (of whale, etc.); n. ventrale, anale, abdominal fin, anal fin; n. caudale, tail flukes; (b) *P:* (i) (side-)whisker; (ii) arm (of pers.), *F:* fin, flipper. 2. bladder, float (to support swimmer); *Av:* float; stabilizing sponson; *Av: etc.* hydrovane, hydrofoil; n. porteuse, stubwing. 3. float (to prevent liquid splashing).

nageoter [naʒɔte], *v.i. F:* to swim badly, with difficulty.

nager [naʒe], *v.i.* (je nageais, n. nageons) 1. *Nau:* to row, to pull; to scull (double); nagez ensemble, pull together! keep stroke! nagez partout! give way! pull away! n. en arrière, à culer, à scier, to back water; n. plat, to feather; n. à, en, couple, to double-scull; n. en pointe, to row; n. à tribord, to row to starboard; n. à bâbord, to row to port; n. à l'embellie, to take advantage of a smooth in sea; n. à sec, to proceed along a narrow space by pushing on the banks or on the bed with the oars; (cf. non-nautical RAMER). 2. to swim; (a) n. à l'indienne, to use the over-arm stroke; n. debout, to tread water; (with cogn. acc.) n. la brasse, to swim the breaststroke; je nageais dans la direction du rivage, I swam, struck out, for the shore; n. à la chien, to dog-paddle; *F:* n. comme un poisson, comme un phoque, to swim like a fish; il nage comme un chien de plomb, comme une meule de moulin, comme un caillou, he swims like a brick, a stone; he can't swim a stroke; n. en pleine eau, dans les grandes eaux, (i) to swim in deep water; (ii) to live in style; (iii) to take one's pleasure, to indulge oneself; n. entre deux eaux, (i) to swim under water; (ii) to trim, to run with the hare and hunt with the hounds; n. contre le courant, à contre-courant, (i) to swim against the current; (ii) to struggle against the current, against circumstances, against fate; *F:* il sait n., he knows the ropes; (b) (to float on or be submerged in liquid); le bois nage sur l'eau, wood floats on water; légumes qui nagent dans le beurre, vegetables swimming in butter; je nage dans cette robe, I'm swimming in this dress; *F:* je nage complètement, I'm (all) at sea; n. dans son sang, to welter in one's blood; n. dans l'abondance, dans l'opulence, to be rolling in

money; to have one's bread buttered on both sides; n. dans la joie, to be overjoyed; son regard nageait dans le vague, his eyes had a far-away look.

nageret [naʒrɛ], *s.m.* duck-shooting punt.

nageur, -euse [naʒœːr, -øːz]. 1. *a.* swimming (bird, animal). 2. *s.* (a) swimmer; n. de combat, frogman; maître n., swimming instructor or supervisor (at swimming pools, baths, etc.); (b) *Nau:* oarsman, rower; n. de l'arrière, stroke; n. de l'avant, bow(-oar); *cf.* non-nautical RAMEUR. 3. *pl. Crust:* nageurs, Natantia.

Nagpour [nagpuːr], *Pr.n.m. Geog:* Nagpur.

naguère [nagɛːr], *adv.* (Poet: also naguères) not long since, a short time ago, but lately; *A:* erstwhile; il était riche n., he was well off not so very long ago.

nagyagite [naʒijaʒit], *s.f. Miner:* nagyagite; foliated tellurium.

nahaïka [naaika], *s.f.* nagaika.

nahor [naɔr], *s.m. Z:* nahoor, bhar(h)al.

Naïadacées [najadase], *s.f.pl.,* **Naïadées** [najade], *s.f.pl. Bot: Algae:* Naiadaceae.

naïade [najad], *s.f.* 1. naiad, water-nymph; *F:* graceful swimmer; *Iron:* bathing beauty. 2. *Bot: Moll:* naiad.

naïf, -ïve [naif, -iːv], *a.* 1. artless, ingenuous, unaffected, naive, naïve; les grâces naïves de l'enfance, the artless graces of childhood; avoir un air n., to look innocent, artless; style n., unaffected style; *Art:* l'art naïf, naïve art; les naïfs, the naïves; *s.m.* le naïf, (depiction of) nature without artifice (in Lit. or Art). 2. simpleminded, credulous, guileless, unsophisticated, *F:* green; *s.* quel n.! what a simpleton! 3. *A:* original, natural (candour, colour, etc.). 4. *Jewel:* naif.

nain, naine [nɛ̃, nɛn]. 1. *s.* dwarf; *F:* midget, pygmy; *Cards:* jouer au N. jaune, to play (at) Pope Joan; *Astr:* naine blanche, white dwarf. 2. *a.* (a) dwarf(ish); palmier n., dwarf palm-tree; capucine naine, Tom-Thumb nasturtium; *Astr:* étoiles naines, dwarf stars; (b) œuf n., yolkless egg; (c) *Rail:* signal n., ground, dwarf, signal, tommy dodd.

naïs [nais], *s.f. Ann:* nais.

naissain [nɛsɛ̃], *s.m.* (oyster-, mussel-)brood; spat; seed-oysters.

naissance [nɛsɑ̃s], *s.f.* 1. birth; (a) sourd de n., deaf from birth, born deaf; jour, fête, anniversaire, de n., birthday; lieu de n., birthplace; donner n. à un enfant, to give birth to a child; *Adm:* nombre des naissances, birth rate; acte de n., extrait de n., birth certificate; n. avant terme, premature birth; naissances différées, postponed births; *Adm:* récupération des naissances, "making up" of births; *s.a.* CONTRÔLE 4, DÉCLARATION; (b) descent, extraction; de n. obscure, sans n., of low birth, of low extraction; base-born; être de haute n., to be high-born; par droit de n., by right of birth; être allemand de n., to be German-born; un gentilhomme de n., a gentleman born; famille de n., patrician family; *Prov:* la n. ne fait pas la noblesse, handsome is that handsome does; (c) la n. du printemps, the birth of spring; la n. du jour, dawn; the break of day; donner n. à une rumeur, to give rise to a rumour; prendre n., (of rumour, etc.) to originate, arise, come into being, spring up. 2. (place where sth. begins) root (of plant, tongue, nail, spinal cord, etc.); source (of river); *Arch:* spring (of pillar, arch); **ligne de n.,** springing line; **la Loire prend n. au Mont Gerbier-de-Jonc,** the Loire has its source in the Mont Gerbier-de-Jonc; **cicatrice à la n. des cheveux,** scar just where the hair begins; **point de n.,** point of origin.

naissant [nɛsɑ̃], *a.* (*a*) new-born; dawning (day); budding (love); nascent (beauty, charms); **bourgeon n.,** newly-formed bud; **à l'aube naissante,** at break of day; **une intimité naissante,** a newborn, dawning, intimacy; **barbe naissante,** incipient beard; **cheveux naissants,** (i) loose flowing hair; (ii) hair curled in ringlets; **tête naissante,** newly shaved downy head; **perruque naissante,** wig imitation of *cheveux naissants*; *Ph:* **rouge n.,** nascent red, black; *Ch:* **à l'état naissant,** nascent; (*b*) *Her:* naissant.

naître [nɛtr], *v.i.* (*pr.p.* **naissant**; *p.p.* **né, née**; *pr.ind.* **je nais, il naît, n. naissons, ils naissent**; *pr.sub.* **je naisse, n. naissions**; *p.d.* **je naissais**; *p.h.* **je naquis**; *fu.* **je naîtrai**; *the aux. is* être) (*a*) to be born, to come into the world; **il naquit, est né, en 1880,** he was born in 1880; **enfant, poussin, qui vient de n.,** newly-born child, newly-hatched chick; **n. aveugle, pauvre,** to be born blind, poor; **né de parents pauvres,** born of poor parents; **né pour la peine,** born to trouble; *impers.* **il naît dans cette ville cent enfants par mois,** in this town a hundred children are born every month; **encore à n.,** as yet unborn; **enfant à n.,** child unborn; **deux enfants lui étaient nés d'un premier mariage,** his first wife had borne him two children; **être bien, mal, né,** to be well-, low-born; *F:* **être né pour qch.,** to be cut out for sth.; *Lit:* **être nés l'un pour l'autre,** to be made for one another; **n. à la vie politique,** (i) to become conscious of politics; (ii) to embark on one's political career; **l'ordinateur est le dernier né de . . .,** the computer is the latest addition to . . .; **il est né poète, peintre,** he is a born poet, a born painter; **les ennemis-nés de la liberté,** the born enemies of liberty; **je l'ai vu n.,** I have known him from his birth, from a baby; **ce pays vit n. l'éloquence,** this country saw the birth of eloquence; **Marie Dupont, née Lapointe,** Marie Dupont, maiden name Lapointe, née Lapointe; *A. or Lit:* **qui est-elle née?** what was her maiden name? **infortunes nées de la guerre,** misfortunes born of the war; *F:* **je ne suis pas né d'hier,** I was not born yesterday; *s.a.* COIFFÉ 1; **être innocent comme l'enfant qui vient de naître,** to be as innocent as a babe; (*b*) (*of hopes, fears, etc.*) to be born, to (a)rise, to spring up; **faire n.,** to give birth to, give rise to, raise, breed, awaken (hope, anxiety, suspicion); to arouse, occasion (suspicion); to give birth to (idea); to give rise to (rumour); **faire n. un sourire,** to provoke, call forth, a smile; **faire n. une difficulté,** to cause a difficulty; **faire n. le mépris,** to breed contempt; **c'est le désir qui fait n. la pensée,** the wish is father to the thought; **cela me fit n. l'idée de voyager,** that gave me the idea of travelling; (*c*) (*of vegetation, etc.*) to begin to grow, to spring up, come up; **les feuilles naissent au printemps,** leaves appear, come, in spring; (*d*) (*of river, race, project, etc.*) to originate, (a)rise; to spring into existence; **le paquebot naissait du brouillard,** the steamer loomed out of the fog; **n. sous les pas de . . .,** to come in abundance to . . .; **les plaisirs naissent sous les pas des riches,** the pleasures of life come to the rich.

naïvement [naivmɑ̃], *adv.* artlessly, ingenuously; guilelessly, naively; **je m'imaginais n. que . . .,** I fondly imagined that . . .; *Lit: A:* **ressembler n. à ses parents,** to have a natural resemblance to one's parents.

naïveté [naivte], *s.f.* **1.** (*a*) artlessness, simplicity, ingenuousness, naïvety; (*b*) *F:* greenness, guilelessness; **avoir la n. de s'imaginer que . . .,** to be so simple, so green, as to imagine that . . . . **2.** artless, ingenuous, remark; **dire une n.,** to say something silly.

naja [naʒa], *s.m. Rept:* naja, cobra, hooded snake.

nakrite [nakrit], *s.f. Miner:* nakrite.

nama [nama], *s.m. Ling:* Nama.

namaz [namaːz], *s.m. Rel:* namaz.

namurien [namyrjɛ̃], *a. & s.m. Geol:* Namurian.

namurois, -oise [namyrwa, -waːz], *a. & s. Geog:* (native, inhabitant) of Namur.

nana [nana], *s.f. P:* woman.

nanan [nanɑ̃, nɑ̃nɑ̃], *s.m. F:* (*in the nursery*) something nice (to eat); **c'est du n.!** yum-yum!

nancéen, -enne [nɑ̃seɛ̃, -ɛn], **nancéien, -ienne** (nɑ̃sejɛ̃, -jɛn], *a. & s. Geog:* (native, inhabitant) of Nancy.

nancéique [nɑ̃seik], *a. A: Ch:* lactic (acid).

nandinie [nɑ̃dini], *s.f. Z:* spotted palm(-) civet.

nandou [nɑ̃du], *s.m. Orn:* nandu, rhea.

Nanette [nanɛt], *Pr.n.f.* Nanette, Nancy.

naniser [nanize], *v.tr.* to dwarf (plant).

nanisme [nanism], *s.m.* dwarfism, nanism; *Bot:* dwarfing, nanism.

Nankin [nɑ̃kɛ̃]. **1.** *Pr.n. Geog:* Nanking. **2.** (*a*) *s.m. Tex:* nankeen; (*b*) *a.inv.* (buff) yellow, nankeen.

nano- [nanɔ], *comb.fm. Meas:* nano-.

nanocéphale [nanɔsefal]. **1.** *a.* nanocephalous, nanocephalic. **2.** *s.* nanocephalus.

nanocéphalie [nanɔsefali], *s.f. Med:* nanocephalia, nanocephaly.

nanocorme [nanɔkɔrm], *s.m. Med:* nanocormus.

nanocormie [nanɔkɔrmi], *s.f. Med:* nanocormia.

nanomèle [nanɔmɛl], *Med:* **1.** *a.* nanomelous. **2.** *s.* nanomelus.

nanomélie [nanɔmeli], *s.f. Med:* nanomelia.

nanoseconde [nanɔsəgɔ̃ːd], *s.f. Meas:* nanosecond; ns, nsec.

nanosome [nanɔzoːm], *s.m. Med:* nanosomus.

nanosomie [nanɔzomi], *s.f. Med:* nanosomia.

Nansen [nɑ̃sɛn], *Pr.n.m. Adm:* **passeport N.,** Nansen passport.

nansouk [nɑ̃zu(k)], *s.m. Tex:* nainsook.

nant [nɑ̃], *s.m. Dial:* torrent (in the Jura and Savoy regions).

nantais, -aise [nɑ̃tɛ, -ɛːz]. **1.** *a. & s. Geog:* (native, inhabitant) of Nantes. **2.** *s.m. Cu:* small almond cake.

nanterrois, -oise [nɑ̃tɛrwa, -waːz], *a. & s. Geog:* (native, inhabitant) of Nanterre.

nanti [nɑ̃ti], *a.* provided for; **bien n.,** well endowed; **mal n.,** underprivileged; *F:* **être bien mal nanti,** to have a bad wife, husband; *s.* **les nantis,** the rich; **les nantis et les non nantis,** the haves and the have-nots.

nantir [nɑ̃tiːr], *v.tr.* (*a*) *Jur:* to give security to, to secure (creditor); **être nanti de gages,** to be in possession of, secured by, pledges; **il veut qu'on le nantisse,** he wants a security; **se n. des effets d'une succession,** to secure an inheritance by taking possession; **n. un prêteur par hypothèque,** to secure a lender by a mortgage; *A.Jur:* **n. une hypothèque,** to register a mortgage; (*b*) *F:* **n. qn de qch.,** to provide s.o. with sth.; **se n. d'un parapluie,** to provide, arm, oneself with an umbrella.

nantissement [nɑ̃tismɑ̃], *s.m. Jur: Com:* **1.** hypothecation, pledging, bailment. **2.** pledge, collateral security, cover; *A:* mortgage; **droit de n.,** lien on goods; **déposer des titres en n.,** to hypothecate securities; to lodge stock as security, as cover.

nantokite [nɑ̃tɔkit], *s.f. Miner:* nantokite.

nanzouk [nɑ̃zuk], *s.m. Tex:* nainsook.

naos [naɔs], *s.m. Gr.Ant:* naos.

napalm [napalm], *s.m.* napalm; **bombe au n.,** napalm bomb.

napée [nape], *s.f. Myth:* nymph of the meadows and copses.

napel [napɛl], *s.m. Bot:* monk's-hood, wolf's-bane.

naphta [nafta], *s.m. Ch:* naphtha.

naphtacène [naftasɛn], *s.m. Ch:* naphthacene.

naphtalène-sulfonique [naftalɛnsylfɔnik], *a. Ch:* naphthalene-sulfonic (acid).

naphtalénique [naftalenik], *a. Ch:* naphthalenic.

naphtaline [naftalin], *s.f.,* **naphtalène** [naftalɛn], *s.m. Ch: Com:* naphthalene, naphthaline; **n. blanche en boules,** white naphthalene in balls; *F:* moth-balls.

naphte [naft], *s.m. Ind:* (*a*) naphtha, mineral oil; **n. de pétrole,** petroleum naphtha; **n. de première distillation,** virgin naphtha, straight run naphtha; **n. minéral, natif,** petroleum; (*b*) **n. de goudron,** coal-tar naphtha; **n. de schiste,** shale naphtha.

naphtéine [naftein], *s.f. Miner:* naphthein, naphthine.

naphténate [naftenat], *s.m. Ch:* naphthenate.

naphtènes [naftɛn], *s.m.pl. Ch:* naphthenes.

naphténique [naftenik], *a. Ch:* naphthenic.

naphtoïque [naftɔik], *a. Ch:* naphthoic (acid).

naphtol [naftɔl], *s.m. Ch: Pharm:* naphthol.

naphtoquinone [naftɔkinɔn], *s.f. Ch:* naphthoquinone, naphthaquinone.

naphtylamine [naftilamin], *s.f. Ch:* naphthylamine.

naphtyle [naftil], *s.m. Ch:* naphthyl.

naphtylène [naftilɛn], *s.m. Ch:* naphthylene.

napiforme [napifɔrm], *a. Bot:* napiform.

Naples [napl], *Pr.n.m. Geog:* Naples.

Napoléon [napɔleɔ̃]. **1.** *Pr.n.m.* Napoleon. **2.** *s.m. A:* twenty-franc piece (bearing the effigy of Napoleon I).

napoléonien, -ienne [napɔleɔnjɛ̃, -jɛn]. **1.** *a.* Napoleonic; **les guerres napoléoniennes,** the Napoleonic wars. **2.** *s. Pol:* Napoleonist.

napoléonisme [napɔleɔnism], *s.m. Pol:* Napoleonism.

napoléonite [napɔleɔnit], *s.f. Geol:* napoleonite.

napolitain, -aine [napɔlitɛ̃, -ɛn]. **1.** *a. & s. Geog:* Neapolitan; *Pharm:* **onguent n.,** mercurial ointment, blue ointment; **tranche, glace, napolitaine,** Neapolitan ice(cream), cassata; *Mus:* **sixte napolitaine,** Neapolitan sixth. **2.** *s.f. Mus:* **napolitaine,** (kind of) barrel-organ.

nappage [napaːʒ], *s.m.* **1.** table linen; napery. **2.** (act of) pouring sauce over a dish, a cake, etc.

nappe [nap], *s.f.* **1.** (*a*) tablecloth; **mettre, ôter, la n.,** to lay, remove, the cloth; *F:* **trouver la n. mise,** to marry a fortune; (*b*) cloth, cover; *Ecc:* **n. de communion,** communion cloth; **n. d'autel,** altar cloth; (*c*) *Ven:* (stag's) skin (on which the quarry is laid for the hounds). **2.** sheet (of ice, fire, lead, petroleum); *Mth:* nappe (of hyperboloid); **n. d'eau,** (i) sheet of water; (ii) waterfall of a weir; (iii) underground water-level; **n. d'écume,** sheet of foam; **n. de mazout,** oil slick; *Geol:* **n. éruptive,** lava flow; **n. de gaz naturel,** layer, sheet, of natural gas; **n. pétrolifère,** oil layer; **n. de recouvrement,** recumbent fold; **n. aquifère,** water table; **n. d'eau souterraine,** water-bearing bed; **n. de charriage, de chevauchement,** overthrust nappe; **nappes chevauchantes,** overlapping folds; **n. phréatique,** phreatic, underground, water; *Av:* **n. tourbillonnaire,** vortex sheet; *s.a.* ÉCLAIR 1. **3.** clap net (for small birds). **4.** *Tex:* fleece.

napper [nape], *v.tr.* **1.** to cover with a cloth. **2.** *Cu:* to coat; **n. un mets d'une sauce,** to pour a sauce over a dish.

napperon [naprɔ̃], *s.m.* (*a*) cloth; **n. de plateau,** tray cloth; **petit n.,** doily; **n. (individuel),** place mat, table mat; (*b*) slip, napkin (to protect table cloth); (*c*) tea cloth.

nappeuse [napøːz], *s.f. Tex:* fleecing machine.

napu [napy], *s.m. Z:* napu.

naqui-s, -t, etc. *See* NAÎTRE.

narbonnais, -aise [narbɔnɛ, -ɛːz]. **1.** *a. & s. Geog:* (native, inhabitant) of Narbonne. **2.** *s.f. A. Hist:* **Narbonnaise,** Gallia Narbonensis.

narcéine [narsein], *s.f. Ch:* narceine.

Narcisse [narsis]. **1.** *Pr.n.m.* Narcissus. **2.** *s.m. Bot:* narcissus; **n. sauvage, des bois, des prés,** daffodil; **n. des poètes,** pheasant's-eye; poet's narcissus; **anémone à fleur de n.,** narcissus-flowered wind-flower.

narcissisme [narsisism], *s.m. Psy:* narcissism, auto-eroticism.

narcissique [narsisik], *a. Psy:* narcissic (instinct, etc.).

narco-analyse [narkɔanaliːz], *s.f. Psy:* narco-analysis, narcolysis; *pl. narco-analyses.*

narcolepsie [narkɔlɛpsi], *s.f. Med:* narcolepsy.

narcoleptique [narkɔlɛptik], *s. & a. Med:* narcoleptic.

narcomanie [narkɔmani], *s.f.* drug mania.

narcose [narkoːz], *s.f. Med:* narcosis; (*diving*) nitrogen narcosis; *Fish:* **n. galvanique,** torpor in fish induced by electric current.

narcosynthèse [narkɔsɛ̃tɛːz], *s.f. Psy:* narcosynthesis.

narcothérapie [narkɔterapi], *s.f. Med:* narcotherapy.

narcotine [narkɔtin], *s.f. Ch:* narcotin(e).

narcotique [narkɔtik], *a. & s.m. Med:* narcotic; *s.m.* opiate; **faire prendre un n. à qn, administrer un n. à qn,** to drug s.o.; **écrivain au style n.,** author who sends you to sleep.

narcotiser [narkɔtize], *v.tr. Med:* to narcotize; *F:* to drug, dope.

narcotisme [narkɔtism], *s.m. Med:* narcotism; **n. des nègres,** sleeping-sickness.

nard [naːr], *s.m. Bot: Pharm:* spikenard, nard; *Bot:* **n. raide,** mat-grass, white bent, wire bent; **n. sauvage,** asarabacca; **n. de montange,** setwall; **n. celtique,** celtic spikenard; **n. indien,** Indian nard, ancient spikenard.

narghilé, narghileh [nargile], *s.m.* narghile, hookah.

nargue [narg], *s.f. A: used esp. in* **faire n. à qn, à qch.; dire n. de qn, de qch.,** to snap one's fingers at s.o., at sth.; **n. de, pour** (qn, qch.)! a fig for (s.o., sth.)! **n. du chagrin!** away with care! **la n. parisienne,** Parisian off handedness, flippancy.

narguer [narge], *v.tr.* to flout, *F:* to cheek (s.o.); to set (s.o.) at defiance; to defy (s.o.); to snap one's fingers at (s.o.).

narguilé [nargile], *s.m.* narghile, hookah.

narine [narin], *s.f.* 1. *Anat:* nostril (of man, horse, ox); **se remplir les narines d'air frais,** to sniff in the fresh air; *Vet:* **fausse n.,** false nostril; 2. snifting-hole (of pump).
narquois, -oise [narkwa, -wa:z]. 1. *a.* (*a*) *A:* sly, cunning; (*b*) quizzing, bantering (tone, smile). 2. *s.m.* (*a*) *Mil: A:* deserter living as a tramp; (*b*) *A:* language of tramps; *F:* **parler n.,** to speak the jargon (of the gang).
narquoisement [narkwazmɑ̃], *adv.* 1. *A:* slyly. 2. banteringly, quizzingly.
narquoiserie [narkwazri], *s.f.* 1. bantering nature (of answer, etc.); **la n. de son visage,** the cynical amusement depicted on his face. 2. piece of banter, of quizzing.
narrateur, -trice [nar(r)atœ:r, -tris], *s.* narrator, relater, teller (of story); **l'historien n. de ces faits,** the historian who relates these facts.
narratif, -ive [nar(r)atif, -i:v], *a.* narrative; *Jur:* **procès-verbal n. du fait,** report setting forth all the facts (of the misdemeanour).
narration [nar(r)asjɔ̃], *s.f.* 1. narrating, narration; *Gram:* **présent de n.,** historic present; *Lt. & Fr. Gram:* **infinitif de n.,** historic infinitive. 2. (*a*) narrative, account (of event); (*b*) *Sch:* reproduction of a story (as an exercise in composition). 3. *Rh:* exposé of facts preceding conclusion.
narré [nare], *s.m. O:* recital, account; **faire le n. de qch.,** to narrate, give an account of, some happening.
narrer [nare], *v.tr.* to narrate, relate (*esp.* in a lively way); **n. avoir fait qch.,** to tell how one did sth., to tell of having done sth.; (*the usu. vb. is* RACONTER).
narsarsukite [narsarsykit], *s.f. Miner:* narsarsukite.
narthecium [nartesjɔm], *s.m. Bot:* narthecium.
narthex [narteks], *s.m. Arch:* narthex.
narval [narval], *s.m. Z:* narwhal, unicorn-whale, unicorn-fish; *pl. narvals.*
nasal, -aux [nazal, -o]. 1. *a. Anat: Ling:* nasal (bone, sound); *Anthr:* **indice n.,** nasal index; **point n.,** nasion. 2. *s.m. Arm:* nasal (of helmet). 3. *s.f. Ling:* **nasale,** nasal.
nasalement [nazalmɑ̃], *adv.* nasally, *F:* with a twang.
nasalisation [nazalizasjɔ̃], *s.f. Ling:* nasalization.
nasaliser [nazalize], *v.tr. Ling:* to nasalize (sound).
nasalité [nazalite], *s.f.* nasality, *F:* twang.
nasard [naza:r]. 1. *a. F:* = NASILLARD. 2. *s.m. Mus:* nasard.
nasarde [nazard], *s.f.* fillip, rap, flip, on the nose; *F: A:* **recevoir des nasardes,** to be scoffed at, mocked at, made game of; **essuyer une n.,** to receive a rebuff, a snub.
nasarder [nazarde], *v.tr.* 1. to rap (s.o.) on the nose. 2. *A:* to scoff, jeer, at (s.o.).
nase[1] [na:z], *s.m. Ich:* beaked carp, nose-carp.
nase[2], *s.m. Dial: P:* nose.
naseau, -eaux [nazo], *s.m.* (orifice of) nostril (of horse, ox); *F:* **les naseaux,** the nose, nostrils; *A:* **fendeur de naseaux,** braggart, bully.
nasicorne [nazikɔrn], *a.* nasicorn.
nasière [nazjɛ:r], *s.f. Husb:* nose-ring.
nasillard [nazija:r], *a.* nasal; **ton n.,** (i) (nasal) twang; (ii) snuffle; **parler d'une voix nasillarde,** to talk through one's nose, with a twang; **le hautbois n.,** the reedy oboe.
nasillement [nazijmɑ̃], *s.m.* 1. speaking through one's nose; snuffling. 2. (nasal) twang.
nasiller [nazije]. 1. *v.i.* (*a*) to speak through one's nose, to snuffle; to have a nasal twang; (*b*) (*of boar*) to root; (*of dog*) to follow the scent nose to ground. 2. *v.tr. F:* **un prêtre qui nasille la messe,** a priest who bleats through the mass.
nasilleur, -euse [nazijœ:r, -ø:z], *s.* person who speaks through his, her, nose, who speaks with a twang; snuffler.
nasillonner [nazijɔne], *v.i.* = NASILLER.
nasion [nazjɔ̃], *s.m. Anthr:* nasion.
nasique [nazik], *s.m. Z:* proboscis monkey; nose-ape.
nasitor(t) [nazitɔr], *s.m. Bot:* garden cress, golden cress.
naso-labial, -iale, -iaux [nazɔlabjal, -jo], *a. Anat:* nasolabial.
nasonite [nazɔnit], *s.f. Miner:* nasonite.
nasonné [nazɔne], *a. Med:* having a nasal quality (as in rhinolalia aperta).
nasonnement [nazɔnmɑ̃], *s.m.* nasal voice, twang; *Med:* open rhinolalia, rhinolalia aperta.
naso-palatin, -ine [nazɔpalatɛ̃, -in], *a. Anat:* nasopalatine; *pl. naso-palatins, -ines.*
naso-pharyngien, -ienne [nazɔfarɛ̃ʒjɛ̃, -jɛn], *a. Anat:* nasopharyngeal; **adénomes naso-pharyngiens,** adenoids; *pl. naso-pharyngiens, -iennes.*
naso-pharynx [nazɔfarɛ̃:ks], *s.m.inv.* nasopharynx.
nasse [nas], *s.f.* 1. bow net, eel pot, lobster pot; hoop net (for birds); trap (for rats); *F:* **être, tomber, dans la n.,** to be in a fix, to fall into a trap. 2. *Moll:* netted dog whelk.
nasselle [nasɛl], *s.f. Fish:* small net made of reeds.
nastie [nasti], *s.f. Bot:* nastic movement (in plants).
nasturce [nastyrs], *s.m. Bot:* nasturtium, water-cress.
nasua [nazya], *s.m. Z:* nasua.
natal[1], **-als** [natal], *a.* (*very rarely used in the plural*) native (country); **ville natale,** birthplace; **respirer l'air n.,** to breathe one's native air; **mon pays n.,** my native land; **ma maison natale,** the house where I was born.
Natal[2] **(le),** *Pr.n. Geog:* Natal.
natalice [natalis], *s.f. A.Rel:* natale, natalis.
nataliste [natalist], *a.* favouring an increasing birthrate.
natalité [natalite], *s.f.* birthrate; **restriction, réglementation, de la n.,** birthcontrol.
natation [natasjɔ̃], *s.f.* swimming; **ceinture de n.,** swimming-belt; **école de n.,** swimming-baths, bathing place.
natatoire [natatwa:r], *a. Z:* natatory, natatorial (organ, membrane); *Ich:* **vessie n.,** swim(ming)-bladder, air-bladder; sound.
nates [natɛs], *s.m.pl. Anat:* nates (of the brain).
Nathan [natɑ̃], *Pr.n.m.* Nathan.
Nathanael [natanaɛl], *Pr.n.m.* Nathaniel.
natice [natis], *s.f. Moll:* natica.
naticidés [natiside], *s.m.pl. Moll:* Naticidae.
natif, -ive [natif, -i:v]. 1. *a.* native; (*a*) **être n. d'un endroit,** to be a native of a place; **je suis n. de Londres,** I am London born; (*b*) *Miner: etc:* native, virgin; **argent n.,** native silver; **or à l'état n.,** free gold; (*c*) natural, inborn; **bon sens n.,** mother wit. 2. *s.m. & f.* native.
nation [nasjɔ̃], *s.f.* 1. nation; *Nau:* **pavillon de n.,** national flag; **les Nations Unies,** the United Nations; *A: Sch:* **les quatre nations de l'Université,** the four nations of the University; *s.a.* SOCIÉTÉ 2. 2. *pl. B.Hist:* **les Nations,** the Nations, the Gentiles; the Heathen.
national, -le -aux [nasjɔnal, -o]. 1. *a.* national; **la dette nationale,** the National Debt; **billets nationaux,** inland notes; *War Adm: A:* **la chaussure nationale,** utility footwear; *s.a.* GARDE[2] 4, ROUTE 1. 2. *s.m.pl.* **nationaux,** nationals (of a country). 3. *s.f.* (*a*) **nationale,** main road, = "A" road; (*b*) **la Nationale,** the National Library (in Paris).
nationalement [nasjɔnalmɑ̃], *adv.* nationally.
nationalisation [nasjɔnalizasjɔ̃], *s.f.* nationalization.
nationaliser [nasjɔnalize], *v.tr.* to nationalize.
se nationaliser, to become nationalized.
nationalisme [nasjɔnalism], *s.m. Pol:* nationalism.
nationaliste [nasjɔnalist]. 1. *s.m. Pol:* nationalist. 2. *a.* (*a*) nationalist; **la Chine n.,** Nationalist China; (*b*) nationalistic.
nationalité [nasjɔnalite], *s.f.* 1. nationality; citizenship; *Adm:* national status; **prendre la n. britannique,** to take British nationality; *Nau:* **acte de n.,** (ship's) certificate of registry. 2. nation.
national-socialisme [nasjɔnalsɔsjalism], *s.m. Pol: Hist:* National Socialism.
national(e)-socialiste [nasjɔnalsɔsjalist], *a. & s.m. & f. Pol: Hist:* National Socialist; *pl. nationaux-socialistes, nationales-socialistes.*
nativement [nativmɑ̃], *adv.* 1. natively. 2. innately, naturally.
nativisme [nativism], *s.m. Psy:* nativism.
nativiste [nativist], *Psy:* 1. *a.* nativistic. 2. *s.m. & f.* nativist.
nativité [nativite], *s.f.* 1. *Ecc: Astrol:* nativity. 2. *A:* = NAISSANCE.
natrémie [natremi], *s.f.* normal amount of sodium in the blood.
natrite [natrit], *s.f. Miner:* natron, native soda.
natrium [natriɔm], *s.m. A:* sodium, natrium.
natrocalcite [natrɔkalsit], *s.f. Miner:* natrochalcite.
natrojarosite [natrɔʒarɔzit], *s.f. Miner:* natrojarosite.
natrolite [natrɔlit], *s.f. Miner:* natrolite.
natron [natrɔ̃], **natrum** [natrɔm], *s.m. Miner:* natron, native soda.
natronalun [natronalœ̃], *s.m. Miner:* mendozite.
natroné [natrɔne], *a.* containing natron.
nattage [nata:ʒ], *s.m.* 1. plaiting (of straw, hair, etc.). 2. *Nau:* (i) chafing-mat, fender; (ii) protection (of sth.) with a chafing-mat.
natte [nat], *s.f.* 1. mat, matting (of rush, straw); **n. de Chine,** Indian matting. 2. plait, braid (of hair, of gold, or silver thread, etc.); **porter des nattes (dans le dos),** to wear one's hair in plaits; **porter une n.,** *F:* to wear a pigtail. 3. *Bot:* **bois de nattes,** mat-wood tree.
natter [nate], *v.tr.* 1. to cover (room, wall) with mats. 2. to plait, braid (hair, straw, etc.); **tissu natté,** basket-weave material; *Knitting:* **point natté,** cable-stitch.
nattier[1], **-ière** [natje, -jɛ:r]. 1. *s.* straw-, rush-mat maker. 2. *s.m. Bot:* mat-wood tree.
nattier[2], *a.* (*from the painter*) **bleu n.,** light blue, Nattier blue.
naturalisation [natyralizasjɔ̃], *s.f.* 1. *Adm: etc:* naturalization; **déclaration de n.,** letters of naturalization. 2. (*a*) **n. d'animaux,** taxidermy; (*b*) preservation, mounting (of botanical specimen, etc.). 3. naturalizing, acclimatizing (of plant or animal).
naturalisé, -ée [natyralize]. 1. *a.* naturalized. 2. *s.* naturalized subject, citizen.
naturaliser [natyralize], *v.tr.* 1. *Adm: etc:* to naturalize; **se faire n. (britannique),** to take out (British) naturalization papers. 2. (*a*) to mount, stuff, set up (animal); (*b*) to preserve, mount (botanical specimen). 3. to naturalize, acclimatize (plant, animal).
naturalisme [natyralism], *s.m. Lit: Art: etc:* naturalism.
naturaliste [natyralist]. 1. *s.m. & f.* (*a*) *Z: Bot: Lit: Art:* naturalist; (*b*) taxidermist. 2. *a.* naturalistic.
naturalité [natyralite], *s.f.* 1. *O:* naturalness. 2. *A:* naturalization.
nature [naty:r], *s.f.* 1. nature; **les lois de la n.,** the laws of nature; **crime contre n.,** crime against nature; **à l'état de n.,** in a state of nature; in the natural state; **laisser faire la n.,** to let nature take its course; **plus grand que n.,** larger than life; **peindre d'après n.,** to paint from nature, from life; **n. morte,** still life (painting); **perdu dans la n.,** far away from civilization; *F:* **il s'est perdu, il a disparu, dans la n.,** he's vanished into thin air; *F: Aut:* **partir dans la n., se retrouver dans la n.,** to run, smash, into a wall, tree, bank, etc.; *F:* **envoyer, expédier, qn dans la n.,** to send s.o. packing; *F:* **lâcher qn dans la n.,** to let s.o. have his head; *F:* **c'est une (vraie) force de la n.,** he's as strong as a bull, he has the strength of a giant. 2. (*a*) nature, kind, constitution, character; **n. humaine, divine, de qch.,** human, divine, nature of sth.; **n. du climat, du sol,** nature of the climate, of the soil; **tout traité, de quelque n. qu'il soit,** every treaty of whatsoever character, of any character whatever; **faits de n. à nous étonner,** astonishing facts, facts calculated to astonish (us); **il est de, dans, la n. de l'homme de . . .,** it is man's nature to . . ., it comes natural for a man to . . .; **ce n'est pas dans sa n.,** it's not in his nature; **aliments de n. à vous faire du mal,** food likely to do you harm; **des articles de toute n.,** all kinds of articles; (*b*) nature, character, disposition, temperament; **être d'une n. douce,** to be of a gentle disposition; **il est timide de n., il est d'une n. timide,** he's naturally shy, he's shy by nature; **il est gai de sa n.,** he's naturally cheerful; **il tient cela de sa n.,** it is in his nature, it comes naturally to him; **par n.,** by nature; **il est envieux par n.,** he is envious by nature, he has an envious nature; **c'est une bonne n.,** he is of a kindly disposition; he's a kindly (sort of) man; *F:* **c'est une n.,** he's a real personality; *F:* **c'est une petite n.,** he's a weakly sort of person. 3. kind; **payer en n.,** to pay in kind; **réparations en n.,** reparations in kind. 4. *a.inv.* (*a*) *Cu: etc:* plain; **bœuf, pommes (de terre), n.,** boiled beef, potatoes; **café n.,** black coffee; **champagne n.,** still champagne; (*b*) natural; **son jeu est tout à fait n.,** his acting is absolutely natural, true to life; *F:* **peindre n.,** to paint naturalistically, (absolutely) true to life; *F:* **ça fera plus n.,** that'll look more natural; (*c*) **grandeur n.,** full scale, life-size(d); (*d*) *F:* open, frank; (*e*) *F:* gullible, easily taken in. 5. *adj.phr.* **contre n.,** unnatural; anti-natural. 6. *adv. P:* naturally, of course.
naturel, -elle [natyrɛl]. 1. *a.* natural; (*a*) **histoire naturelle,** natural history; **droit n.,** natural law; **mort naturelle,** death from natural causes; natural death; **enfant n.,** natural, illegitimate, child; **penchant n.,** natural inclination; **les parties naturelles,** the genitals, the private parts; **de grandeur naturelle,** life-size(d); **je trouve n. que** + *sub.*, I find it reasonable that (s.o. should do sth.); **mais c'est tout n.,** (but) it was a pleasure, *U.S:* you're welcome; (*b*) **esprit n.,** native wit;

don n., natural, innate, gift; **il lui est n. d'écrire en vers**, it comes natural to him to write in verse; (*c*) **personne naturelle**, natural, unaffected, person; **réponse naturelle**, simple, straightforward, answer; **langage n.**, unstudied language; **alcool n.**, raw spirit; **vin n.**, straight, unfortified, wine; *Cu:* **huile naturelle**, virgin oil; **soie naturelle**, pure, real, silk; (*d*) *Mus:* **(note) naturelle**, natural; **tons naturels**, natural keys; (*e*) *Mth:* **nombre entier n.**, whole number; (*f*) **ordre n.**, direct order. **2.** *s.m.* (*a*) native (of country); **parler l'anglais comme un n.**, to speak English like a native; (*b*) nature, character, disposition; **avoir un heureux n.**, to have a happy disposition; **enfant d'un bon n.**, child of a nice disposition; *Prov:* **chassez le n., il revient au galop**, what's bred in the bone will come out in the flesh; (*c*) **se conduire avec n.**, to behave naturally; (*d*) *adv.phr.* **au naturel**, (i) **voir les choses au n.**, to see things as they are; *Art: Lit:* **peindre qch. au n.**, to paint sth. to the life, realistically; (ii) *Cu:* = NATURE 4; (iii) *Her:* **lion au n.**, lion proper.

naturellement [natyrɛlmɑ̃], *adv.* naturally. **1.** by nature; by birth. **2.** without affectation; unaffectedly; **répondre n.**, to answer naturally. **3.** of course; **vous lui avez répondu?—naturellement**, you answered him?—of course (I did); naturally; **n. que je viendrai!** of course I'll come! **on l'attaqua et n. il riposta**, he was attacked, and naturally hit back. **4.** *Lit:* frankly, sincerely.

naturisme [natyrism], *s.m.* **1.** *Lit: Art: Phil:* naturism. **2.** naturism, nudism.

naturiste [natyrist]. **1.** *s.m. & f.* (*a*) *Lit: Phil: Art: etc:* naturist; (*b*) naturist, nudist. **2.** *a.* naturistic.

naucore [nokɔːr], *s.f. Ent:* naucorid; water creeper.

naufrage [nofraːʒ, nɔ-], *s.m.* (ship)wreck; **faire n.**, to be shipwrecked; **faire n. au port**, (i) to be shipwrecked in sight of the harbour; (ii) to fail with one's goal in sight; **périr dans un n.**, to be lost at sea; **échapper au n.**, to be saved from the wreck; **le n. de mes espérances**, the shattering of my hopes.

naufragé, -ée [nofraʒe, nɔ-]. **1.** *a.* (ship)wrecked; castaway (crew). **2.** *s.* shipwrecked man, woman; castaway.

naufrager [nofraʒe, nɔ-], *v.i.* (**je naufrageai(s); n. naufrageons**) (*a*) to be (ship)wrecked, to suffer shipwreck; (*b*) to cause a shipwreck; to wreck (deliberately).

naufrageur, -euse [nofraʒœːr, nɔ-, -øːz], *s.* wrecker; **X a été le n. de l'Empire**, X dealt the deathblow to the Empire.

naulage [nolaːʒ], *s.m. Nau:* **1.** freighting. **2.** (cost of) freight.

naumachie [nomaʃi], *s.f. Rom.Ant:* naumachy.

naumannite [nomanit], *s.f. Miner:* naumannite.

naupathie [nopati], *s.f. Med:* seasickness.

Nauplie [nopli], *Pr.n.f. Geog:* Nauplia, Nauplion.

nauplius [noplіys], *s.m. Crust:* nauplius.

nauséabond [nozeabɔ̃], *a.* nauseous, nauseating, foul, sickening (smell, etc.); evil-smelling; stinking; repugnant, disgusting; **l'insipidité la plus nauséabonde**, the most nauseating, revolting, insipidity.

nausée [noze], *s.f.* (*a*) nausea; **avoir la n., des nausées**, to feel squeamish, sick; **donner des nausées à qn**, to nauseate s.o.; **odeur qui donne la n.**, smell that makes one's gorge rise; nauseating smell; (*b*) disgust; **son air protecteur me donne la n.**, his patronizing manner makes me sick.

nauséeux, -euse [nozeø, -øːz], *a.* (*a*) nauseating, nauseous; **odeur nauséeuse**, nauseating smell, smell that makes one feel sick; (*b*) loathsome, nauseating (hypocrisy, etc.).

naute [noːt], *s.m.* **1.** *Poet:* sailor, mariner. **2.** *A:* **nautes parisiens**, (corporation of) boatmen of the Seine.

nautile [notil], *s.m.* **1.** *A:* (inflated) life-belt. **2.** *Moll:* nautilus.

nautique [notik], *a.* nautical (term, instrument, etc.); **sports nautiques**, aquatic sports; **ski n.**, water skiing; **club n.**, nautical club; sailing club; rowing club, boat club; **carte n.**, (sea) chart; **qualités nautiques d'un navire**, sailing qualities of a ship.

nautiquement [notikmɑ̃], *adv.* nautically.

nautisme [notism], *s.m. Sp:* sailing.

nautonier [notɔnje], *s.m. A. & Poet:* pilot, mariner; **le n. des enfers**, the boatman of the underworld.

nautophone [notɔfɔn], *s.m. Nau:* fog signal.

naval, -ale, -als [naval], *a.* naval; nautical; **termes navals**, nautical terms; **armée navale**, fleet, naval force; **combat n., bataille navale**, naval engagement; sea battle; **architecture navale**, naval architecture; **construction navale**, shipbuilding; **chantier n., chantier de construction navale**, shipyard, shipbuilding yard; **station navale**, naval station; **base navale**, naval base; **base navale de réparations**, naval repair base; **attaché n.**, naval attaché; **l'École navale**, the Naval College; *s.f.* **entrer à Navale**, to enter the Naval College; **faire (l'École) Navale**, to be at the Naval College; *Rom.Ant:* **couronne navale**, naval crown.

navarin[1] [navarɛ̃], *s.m. Cu:* mutton stew (with potatoes and turnips); haricot mutton.

Navarin[2], *Pr.n. Geog:* Navarino.

navarque [navark], *s.m. Gr.Ant:* navarch.

navarrais, -aise [navarɛ, -ɛːz], **navarrin, -ine** [navarrɛ̃, -in], *a. & s. Geog:* Navarrese; **race navarrine**, Béarn stock (of horses).

Navarre [navaːr], *Pr.n.f. Geog:* Navarre, Navarra; *Hist:* **le royaume de N.**, the kingdom of Navarre; *F:* **les polices de France et de N. sont à sa recherche**, all the police in creation are after him.

nave[1] [naːv], *s.m. A:* (*S.Fr.*) ship.

nave[2], *s.m. P:* **(fleur de) n.**, idiot, clot.

navée [nave], *s.f.* (*a*) *A:* boatload, boatful; (*b*) *Dial:* (*Normandy*) load of salted fish.

navet [navɛ], *s.m.* **1.** (*a*) turnip; **n. long**, tankard turnip; **n. de Suède**, swede; *P: A:* **des navets!** I'm not having any! nothing doing! **il a du sang de n.**, (i) *F:* he's anaemic; (ii) *P:* he's got no guts; *P:* **le champ de navets**, the cemetery; (*b*) *Bot: F:* **n. du diable**, bryony. **2.** *P:* idiot, clot. **3.** *F:* (*of book*) dud; (*of picture*) daub; (*of film, etc.*) tripe; (*of play*) pure ham.

navette[1] [navɛt], *s.f.* **1.** incense boat; incense box. **2.** (*a*) shuttle; **faire la n., entre deux endroits**, (*of vehicle*) to ply between two places; (*of pers.*) (i) to run backwards and forwards, to and fro, (ii) to commute; **navettes fréquentes entre la gare et la ville**, frequent (shuttle) service between station and town; **ligne de chemin de fer exploitée en n.**, (railway) line over which a shuttle service is run; *St.Exch:* **faire la n.**, to job in bills; (*b*) netting needle. **3.** pig of lead. **4.** *Nau:* sister block.

navette[2], *s.f. Bot:* rape; **(huile de) n.**, rape (seed) oil, colza oil.

navicert [navisɛːr], *s.m.* navicert.

naviculaire [navikylɛːr], *a. Anat: etc:* navicular (bone, etc.); *Vet:* **maladie n.**, navicular disease, navicularthritis.

navigabilité [navigabilite], *s.f.* **1.** navigability (of river, etc.). **2.** **(état de) n.**, seaworthiness (of ship); airworthiness (of aircraft); **en (bon) état de n.**, seaworthy; airworthy; **certificat de n.**, certificate of seaworthiness, of airworthiness.

navigable [navigabl̩], *a.* **1.** navigable (canal, river); **eaux navigables**, navigable waters; **espace (aérien) n.**, navigable airspace; **non n.**, non-navigable, unnavigable. **2.** seaworthy; airworthy.

navigant [navigɑ̃], *a.* sailing (fleet, etc.); **personnel n.**, *s.m.pl.* **les navigants**, (i) *Navy: Nau:* seagoing personnel; (ii) *Av:* flying personnel; aircrew.

navigateur [navigatœːr]. **1.** *s.m.* (*a*) navigator (of ship, aircraft, spacecraft, etc.); *attrib.* **officier n.**, navigating officer, navigation officer, navigator; (*b*) seaman; (*c*) navigator, seafaring man; *Hist:* **Henri le N.**, Henry the Navigator; *O:* **il est grand n.**, he's very fond of sea travel; he's a great sailor. **2.** *a.m.* **peuple n.**, seafaring people.

navigation [navigasjɔ̃], *s.f.* navigation, sailing; shipping; **n. astronomique**, celestial, astronomical, navigation or sailing; astronavigation; **n. au radar**, radar-monitored navigation or sailing; **n. loxodromique**, loxodromic navigation, sailing; loxodromics; Mercator's sailing; **n. orthodromique, n. sur arc de grand cercle**, orthodromic navigation, sailing; great-circle navigation, sailing; **n. à voile**, sailing; **n. par radio, par T.S.F.**, radio navigation; **système automatique de n.**, automatic navigation system; **appareils de n.**, navigational equipment; **instrument de n.**, navigational instrument; **officier de n.**, navigation officer, navigating officer; *U.S:* navigator; **n. à l'estime**, dead reckoning; **n. au cabotage, n. côtière**, coastal, coasting, navigation; home trade; **n. au long cours, n. hauturière**, deep-sea navigation, high-seas navigation, ocean navigation, foreign navigation, foreign trade; **n. intérieure, n. fluviale**, inland navigation; **n. de plaisance**, yachting; **n. sur un parallèle**, parallel sailing; **n. en collision**, collision course; **n. fautive**, improper navigation; **école de n. (de la marine marchande)**, nautical school; **compagnie de n. (maritime)**, shipping company; **compagnie de n. à vapeur**, steamship navigation company; **routes de n. (maritime)**, shipping routes, lanes; **dangereux pour la n.**, dangerous to shipping; **terme de n.**, nautical term; **permis de n.**, ship's passport, sea-letter; **journal de n.**, log (book); *Av:* **n. aérienne**, air navigation, aerial navigation; **n. à vue, n. observée**, contact flying; **n. aux instruments**, instrument flying; **aides à la n.**, navigation(al) aids; **compagnie de n. aérienne**, airline; *Ball: Space:* **n. spatiale, n. interplanétaire**, space navigation, astronautics; *Hist:* **Acte de n.**, Navigation Act; *s.a.* CABINE.

naviguer [navige]. **1.** *v.i.* (*a*) to sail, navigate; **n. au commerce**, to be in the merchant service; **n. au cabotage**, to be in the coasting trade; **n. au long cours**, to be in the foreign trade; **n. sur, dans, les mers**, *with cogn. acc.* **n. les mers**, to navigate, sail, the seas; **n. près de la terre**, to sail, steer, along the land; to hug the land; (*of ship*) **n. à l'aventure**, to tramp; **il a beaucoup navigué**, he's knocked about the world; *F:* **il sait n.**, he knows the ropes; (*b*) **navire qui navigue bien, mal**, ship that behaves well, ill, at sea. **2.** *v.tr.* to navigate (ship, aircraft).

naviplane [naviplan], *s.m.* hovercraft.

navire [naviːr], *s.m.* **1.** ship, vessel; **n. à voiles**, sailing ship; **n. à vapeur**, steamship, steamer; **n. à moteur**, motor ship; **n. à turbines à gaz**, gas-turbine ship; **n. à propulsion nucléaire**, nuclear-powered ship; **n. à ailes portantes**, hydrofoil (vessel); **n. école, n. d'application**, training ship; **n. frère, n. jumeau**, sister ship, twin ship; **navire à trois superstructures**, three-island ship; **n. de commerce, n. marchand**, merchantman, merchant ship, vessel; trading ship, vessel; trader; **n. de commerce armé (en guerre)**, armed merchantman; **n. (de commerce) armé en croiseur auxiliaire**, auxiliary cruiser; **n. à passagers, à voyageurs**, passenger ship, vessel; passenger boat; **n. de charge**, cargo boat, vessel, freighter; **n. mixte**, cargo and passenger ship; **n. de plaisance**, pleasure boat, vessel; yacht; **n. de pêche**, fishing vessel; **n. de croisière**, cruising ship; **n. de mer**, sea-going ship; **n. au long cours, n. long courrier, n. de haute mer, n. hauturier**, foreign-going ship, ocean-going ship; ocean liner; **n. au cabotage, n. côtier**, coasting ship, vessel; coaster; **n. de ligne (régulière), n. régulier**, liner; **n. bananier**, banana boat; **n. baleinier**, whaling ship, whale factory ship, whaler; *U.S:* whale catcher, chaser; **n. butanier**, gas carrier, gas tanker; **n. méthanier**, methane carrier, liquefied (petroleum) gas tanker; **n. céréalier**, grain carrier; **n. minéralier, n. transport de minerai**, ore carrier; **n. pétrolier**, (oil) tanker; **n. charbonnier**, coal ship, collier; **n. asphaltier**, asphalt tanker; **n. harenguier**, herring boat; **n. moutonnier**, sheep carrier; **n. porte-remorques**, trailer ship; **n. porte-chars**, tank-carrying ship; **n. météorologique**, weather ship; **n. brise-glaces**, ice-breaker; **n. porte-cadres, n. porte-containers**, container ship; lift-on lift-off ship; **n. porte-véhicules, à manutention horizontale**, vehicle cargo ship, trailer ship; roll-on roll-off, drive-on drive-off, ship; **n. frigorifique**, refrigerated ship, vessel; refrigerator ship, vessel; cold-storage ship, vessel; reefer; **n. de guerre**, warship, *A:* man-of-war; **n. de combat**, battleship; **n. de surface**, surface ship; **n. de commandement (tactique)**, (tactical) command ship; **n. aménagé, converti, en porte-avions**, converted aircraft carrier; **n. porte-hélicoptères**, helicopter carrier; **n. de barrage**, boom-defence vessel, boom-working vessel; **n. de débarquement**, landing ship; **n. de débarquement de chars**, tank landing craft; **n. espion**, spy vessel, intelligence ship; **navire amiral**, flagship; **n. auxiliaire (de la flotte)**, (fleet) auxiliary, naval auxiliary; **n. câblier**, cable-(laying) ship; **n. de recherche océanographique**, oceanographic research ship; **n. hydrographe**, survey(ing) ship; **n. météo(rologique)**, weather ship, *U.S:* ocean station vessel; **n. de soutien logistique**, logistic ship, maintenance ship, support ship; **n. magasin**, store ship; **n. ravitailleur**, supply ship, replenishment ship; **armer un n.**, to fit out, equip, man, a ship; **désarmer un n.**, to lay up a ship; **mettre un n. en chantier, sur cale**, to lay down a ship; **mettre un n. à la mer**, to set a ship afloat; **lancer un n.**, to launch a ship; **mettre un n. à la côte**, to run a ship aground; **les navires dans le port**, the shipping in the harbour; "**Navire!**" "Ship ahoy!" **2.** *A:* **n. aérien**, airship.

navire-atelier [naviratəlje], *s.m.* repair ship, floating workshop; *pl. navires-ateliers.*

navire-citerne [navirsitɛrn], *s.m. Nau:* tanker; *pl. navires-citernes.*

navire-école [navirekɔl], *s.m.* training ship; *pl. navires-écoles.*

navire-gigogne [navirʒigɔɲ], *s.m.* mother ship (for seaplanes); *pl. navires-gigognes.*

navire-hôpital [navirɔpital], *s.m. Nau:* hospital ship; *pl. navires-hôpitaux.*

navire-jumeau [navirʒymo], *s.m.* sister ship; *pl. navires-jumeaux.*

navire-météo [navirmeteo], *s.m.* weathership; *pl. navires-météo.*

navire-transport [navirtrɑ̃spɔːr], *s.m.* (naval) storeship; *pl. navires-transports.*

navire-usine [naviryzin], *s.m.* (whale) factory ship; *pl. navires-usines.*

navrance [nɑvrɑ̃ːs], *s.f. A:* heart-soreness; despair.

navrant [nɑvrɑ̃], *a.* heart-rending, heartbreaking; harrowing; agonizing; that goes to one's heart; annoying.

navré [nɑvre], *a.* heartbroken (person); woe-begone (expression); cut to the heart; **avoir le cœur n., être n., de qch.,** to be deeply grieved, brokenhearted, at sth.; **je suis n. de l'apprendre,** I am truly, dreadfully, terribly, sorry to hear it; **j'ai le cœur n. de penser que . . .,** it cuts me to the very heart, to the quick, to think that . . .; **je suis n. qu'il ait échoué,** I am heartbroken, terribly upset, that he has failed.

navrement [nɑvrəmɑ̃], *s.m. Lit:* anguished grief; despair; **dans un n. sauvage,** in wild anguish.

navrer [nɑvre], *v.tr.* **1.** *A:* to wound. **2.** to grieve (s.o.) deeply; to break (s.o.'s) heart; to cut (s.o.) to the heart; **spectacle qui me navra,** sight that went to my heart; **cela me navre le cœur de penser que . . .,** it cuts me to the (very) heart, it upsets me beyond belief, to think that . . ..

naz [naːz], *s.m. Dial: P:* nose.

nazairien, -ienne [nazɛrjɛ̃, -jɛn], *a. & s. Geog:* (native, inhabitant) of Saint-Nazaire.

nazaréen, -enne [nazareɛ̃, -ɛn], *a. & s. B.Hist:* Nazarene; *s.* Nazarite; *Art:* **l'école nazaréenne,** the Nazarene school.

nazi, -e [nazi], *a. & s. Hist: Pol:* Nazi.

nazifier [nazifje], *v.tr.* (*pr.sub. & p.d.* **n. nazifiions, v. nazifiiez**) *Hist: Pol:* to nazify.

naziréen, -enne [nazireɛ̃, -ɛn], *a. & s. B.Hist:* Nazarite.

nazisme [nazism], *s.m. Hist: Pol:* Nazism.

ne, n' [n(ə)], *neg.adv.* not. **1.** *for the use of* **ne** (i) *strengthened by* **pas, point, goutte, mie, mot,** or (ii) *in conjunction with* **ni, guère, nullement, aucunement, jamais, plus; aucun, nul, personne, rien; que (ne . . . que),** *see these words.* **2.** used alone (*i.e. with omission of* **pas**), *chiefly in literary or academic style, with* **cesser, oser, pouvoir, savoir, importer,** *and often as an archaism or a mannerism with other verbs;* **il ne cesse de parler,** he is for ever talking; **je n'ose lui parler,** I dare not speak to him; **je ne puis vous le promettre,** I cannot promise you that; **je ne sais que faire,** I don't know what to do; **je ne sais s'il viendra,** I don't know if he will come; **je ne saurais vous le dire,** I cannot tell you; *always used without* **pas** *in the phr.* **n'importe,** never mind, it doesn't matter. **3.** *in the following constructions:* (*a*) **qui ne connaît cette œuvre célèbre?** who does not know that famous work? **que ne ferait-il pour vous?** what would he not do for you? **lequel d'entre vous ne se souvient de . . .?** who among you can fail to remember . . .? (*b*) **je n'ai d'autre désir que celui de vous plaire,** I have no other desire than to please you; (*c*) **il n'est pas si stupide qu'il ne vous comprenne,** he is not so stupid that he fails to understand you; (*d*) **si je ne me trompe . . .,** unless I am mistaken . . .; **s'il n'était venu à mon secours . . .,** if he had not come to my help . . .; (*e*) **voilà, il y a, six mois que je ne l'ai vu,** it is now six months since I saw him; I have not seen him for six months; (*f*) **il n'y a personne à qui il ne se soit adressé,** there is no one to whom he did not apply; (*g*) **il n'eut garde d'y aller,** he took good care not to go; **à dieu ne plaise!** God forbid! **qu'à cela ne tienne!** by all means! don't let that make any difference! **je n'ai que faire de votre aide,** I don't need your help. **4.** *used optionally in literary or academic style with a vague negative connotation;* (*a*) (*expressions of fear*) **je crains qu'il (ne) prenne froid,** I am afraid he may catch cold, of his catching cold, *F:* of him catching cold; **j'ai peur qu'on (ne) me voie,** I am afraid some one might see me, of being seen; **de crainte qu'on (ne) me voie,** for fear some one may see me; (*b*) **évitez, prenez garde, qu'on (ne) vous voie,** avoid being seen, take care not to be seen; **j'empêcherai qu'il (ne) vienne,** I shall prevent him coming; **peu s'en fallut qu'il (ne) tombât,** he nearly fell; **à moins qu'on (ne) vous appelle,** unless they call you; **avant que l'heure (ne) sonne,** before the hour strikes; (*c*) (*comparison*) **il est plus vigoureux qu'il (ne) paraît,** he is stronger than he looks; **il agit autrement qu'il ne parle,** he acts otherwise than he speaks; his actions belie his words.

né [ne], *a.* born; **c'est un conteur né,** he's a born storyteller.

Néandert(h)al [neɑ̃dɛrtal], *Pr.n. Geog:* Neanderthal; *Anthr:* **l'homme de N.,** Neanderthal man.

néandert(h)alien, -ienne [neɑ̃dɛrtaljɛ̃, -jɛn], *a. & s. Anthr:* Neandert(h)al, Neandert(h)alian.

néandert(h)aloïde [neɑ̃dɛrtaloid], *a. Anthr:* Neanderthaloid.

néanmoins [neɑ̃mwɛ̃], *adv.* nevertheless, none the less; for all that; yet; still; **il la néglige, et n. elle l'aime,** he neglects her, and yet she loves him; *A:* **ce n., c'est le meilleur des hommes,** for all that, he is the best of men.

néant [neɑ̃], *s.m.* **1.** nothingness, nought, naught; **sortir du n.,** to rise from obscurity; *A:* **un homme de n.,** a man of naught; **le n. des grandeurs humaines,** the emptiness of human greatness; **rentrer dans un éternel n.,** to return to everlasting nothingness; **réduire qch. à n.,** to reduce sth. to nothing, to nought; to annihilate sth.; *Jur:* **mettre une appellation à n.,** to dismiss an appeal. **2.** *Adm:* **n.,** (*on income-tax return, etc.*) "none"; (*on report-sheet, etc.*), "nothing to report," "nil"; *F:* **qu'a-t-il fait aujourd'hui?—N.!** what has he done to-day?—nothing at all! *s.a.* ÉTAT 2.

néapolitain, -aine [neapɔlitɛ̃, -ɛn], *a. & s. Geog:* Napolitan.

néarctique [nearktik], *a. Z: etc:* nearctic.

Néarque [neark], *Pr.n.m. A.Hist:* Nearchus.

néarthrose [neartroːz], *s.f. Med:* nearthrosis.

nébalie [nebali], *s.f. Crust:* nebalia.

nèble [nɛbl], *s.m. or f. Dial:* fog, mist.

nébride [nebrid], *s.f. Gr.Ant:* nebris.

nébrie [nebri], *s.f. Ent:* Nebria.

nébulaire [nebylɛːr], *a. Astr:* nebular.

nébule [nebyl], *s.f. Arch:* nebule.

nébulé [nebyle], *a. Her:* nebuly.

nébuleusement [nebyløzmɑ̃], *adv.* nebulously, obscurely.

nébuleux, -euse [nebylø, -øːz]. **1.** *a.* nebulous; (*a*) cloudy, hazy, misty (sky, view); (*b*) turbid, cloudy (liquor, crystal); (*c*) gloomy, clouded (brow); (*d*) unintelligible, obscure (writer, theory). **2.** *s.f.* **nébuleuse,** (*a*) *Astr:* nebula; (*b*) *Psy:* cluster.

nébulisation [nebylizasjɔ̃], *s.f. Med:* **n. nasale,** use of a nasal spray.

nébuliseur [nebylizœːr], *s.m. Med:* (nasal) spray.

nébulium [nebyljɔm], *s.m. Ch:* nebulium.

nébulosité [nebylozite], *s.f.* **1.** (*a*) nebulosity, nebulousness, haziness; *Meteor:* **forte n.,** heavy cloud cover; (*b*) obscurity, haziness (of ideas, writing). **2.** patch of mist, of haze.

nécessaire [nesesɛːr]. **1.** *a.* necessary, needful; requisite (information, etc.); *Log:* necessary; **la chose est devenue n.,** the thing has become a necessity; **n. à, pour, qch., qn,** necessary, indispensable, for sth., s.o.; **n. pour faire qch.,** necessary, indispensable, for doing sth.; **choses qu'il est n. de savoir,** things which one should know; **se rendre n. à qn,** to make oneself indispensable to s.o.; **avoir l'argent n.,** to have the money required; *s.* **faire le n.,** to play the busybody; to fuss round s.o.; **il n'est pas n. de . . .,** there is no need to . . .; **est-il n. que je +** *sub.*? is it necessary that I should . . .? is it necessary for me to . . .? **c'est une enquête n. à reprendre,** this enquiry should be taken up again; **peu n.,** needless, unnecessary. **2.** *s.m.* (*a*) necessities, necessaries, the needful, the indispensable; **le strict n.,** bare necessities; **je me suis borné au strict n.,** I did not go beyond what was strictly necessary; **se refuser le n.,** to deny oneself the necessities of life; **faire le n.,** to do what is necessary; to do the needful; (*b*) outfit, kit (of some sort); **n. à ouvrage,** (i) work box, work basket; (ii) housewife; **n. de fumeur,** smoker's set; **n. de réparation,** repair kit; **n. de toilette,** dressing case, toilet case; **n. de maquillage,** vanity case; **n. de couture,** sewing outfit; **n. de nettoyage,** cleaning kit; (*c*) *Lit:* servant, domestic; *Lit:* indispensable person.

nécessairement [nesesɛrmɑ̃], *adv.* **1.** necessarily, of necessity; **il faut n. manger pour vivre,** we must needs eat to live. **2.** inevitably, infallibly.

nécessarien [nesesarjɛ̃], *s.m. Rel.H:* necessitarian, necessarian; **doctrine des nécessariens,** necessitarianism.

nécessitant [nesesitɑ̃], *a.* (*a*) *Theol:* necessitating (grace, action); (*b*) *F:* **de nécessité nécessitante,** of absolute necessity.

nécessité [nesesite], *s.f.* necessity. **1. la dure n. me force à . . .,** dire necessity compels me to . . .; **de n., de toute n.,** necessarily, of necessity; **il est de toute n. de (faire qch.),** it is essential to (do sth.); **il est de toute n. qu'il vienne,** it is imperative that he should come; he simply must come; **être dans la n. de faire qch.,** to be compelled, forced, to do sth.; **ce voyage est une n.,** this journey is a matter of necessity; **mettre qn dans la n. de faire qch.,** to make it necessary for s.o. to do sth.; to compel, constrain, s.o. to do sth.; **quelle n. y avait-il de faire cela?** what need was there for doing that? **faire qch. par n., être réduit à la n. de faire qch.,** to do sth., out of necessity, to be compelled to do sth.; **faire de n. vertu,** to make a virtue of necessity; **vous comprenez la n. de votre retour,** you understand the necessity for your return; **agir sans n.,** to act unnecessarily; *Prov:* **n. est mère d'industrie, d'invention,** necessity is the mother of invention; **n. n'a point de loi,** necessity knows no law. **2.** (*a*) need, want; **les nécessités de la vie,** the necessities of life; **la musique est une n. de mon existence,** music is the breath of life to me, I could not live without music; **objets de première n., de toute n.,** indispensable articles; **denrées de première n.,** essential foodstuffs; staple commodities; **les nécessités du cas,** the demands of the case; **selon les nécessités,** as circumstances (may) require; **c'est une n.,** it's a must; **chalet de n.,** public convenience; *F:* **faire ses nécessités,** to relieve nature; *Num:* **monnaies de n.,** necessity money; *Jur:* **état de n.,** situation of sudden and urgent necessity; (*b*) necessitousness; **être dans la n.,** to be in need, in necessity, in straitened circumstances.

nécessiter [nesesite], *v.tr.* **1.** to require, demand, necessitate, entail (sth.); **cela nécessitera des négociations,** this will entail negotiations. **2.** *A:* **n. qn à, de, faire qch.,** to oblige, force, s.o. to do sth.

nécessiteux, -euse [nesesitø, -øːz], *a.* needy, in want, necessitous; *s.* **les nécessiteux,** the needy, the destitute.

neck [nɛk], *s.m. Geol:* (volcanic) neck.

nécro- [nekrɔ], *pref.* necr(o)-.

nécrobacillose [nekrɔbasil(l)oːz], *s.f. Vet:* necrobacillosis.

nécrobie [nekrɔbi], *s.f. Ent:* necrobia; scavenger-beetle.

nécrobiose [nekrɔbjoːz], *s.f. Med:* necrobiosis.

nécrobiotique [nekrɔbjɔtik], *a. Med:* necrobiotic.

nécrode [nekrɔd], *s.m. Ent:* necrodes.

nécrogène [nekrɔʒɛn], *a. Bot:* necrogenic, necrogenous.

nécrolâtrie [nekrolɑtri], *s.f.* necrolatry, ancestor worship.

nécrologe [nekrɔlɔːʒ], *s.m.* necrology, obituary list, death roll.

nécrologie [nekrɔlɔʒi], *s.f.* necrology, obituary notice; *Journ:* deaths.

nécrologique [nekrɔlɔʒik], *a.* necrological; **notice n.,** obituary notice.

nécrologue [nekrɔlɔg], *s.m.* necrologist, necrographer.

nécromancie [nekrɔmɑ̃si], *s.f.* necromancy.

nécromancien, -ienne [nekrɔmɑ̃sjɛ̃, -jɛn], *s.* necromancer.

nécromant [nekrɔmɑ̃], *s.m. A:* necromancer.

nécrophage [nekrɔfaːʒ], *a. Z:* necrophagous.

nécrophile [nekrɔfil], *Med:* (*a*) *a.* necrophilic, necrophiliac; (*b*) *s.* necrophile, necrophilic.

nécrophilie [nekrɔfili], *s.f. Med:* necrophily, necrophilia.

nécrophobe [nekrɔfɔb], *a. Med:* necrophobic.

nécrophobie [nekrɔfɔbi], *s.f. Med:* necrophobia.

nécrophobique [nekrɔfɔbik], *a. Med:* necrophobic.

nécrophore [nekrɔfɔːr], *s.m. Ent:* carrion beetle, necrophore; scavenger, burying, beetle.

nécropole [nekrɔpɔl], *s.f.* necropolis.

nécropsie [nekrɔpsi], *s.f. Med:* necropsy.

nécropsique [nekrɔpsik], *a. Med:* necroscopic.

nécrose [nekroːz], *s.f.* **1.** *Med:* necrosis (of bone, etc.); **n. phosphorée,** phosphorus necrosis, *F:* phossy jaw. **2.** *Bot:* canker (in wood).

nécroser [nekroze], *v.tr.* **1.** *Med:* to cause necrosis in (bone). **2.** *Bot:* to canker.

se nécroser. 1. *Med:* to necrose, to necrotize. **2.** *Bot:* to become cankered.

nécrosique [nekrozik], **nécrotique** [nekrɔtik], *a. Med:* necrotic.

nécrospermie [nekrɔspɛrmi], *s.f. Med:* necrospermia.

nectaire [nɛktɛːr], *s.m. Bot:* nectary, honey-cup.

nectandra [nɛktɑ̃dra], *s.m. Bot:* nectandra.
nectar [nɛktaːr], *s.m. Myth: Bot:* nectar.
nectaré [nɛktare], *a.* nectareous, nectarine.
nectarien, -ienne [nɛktarjɛ̃, -jɛn], *a. Bot:* 1. nectarous, nectar-like. 2. nectariferous, nectar-bearing.
nectarifère [nɛktarifɛːr], *a. Bot:* nectariferous.
nectarine [nɛktarin], *s.f. Hort:* nectarine.
nectarinie [nɛktarini], *s.f. Orn:* sugar-bird.
nectarinidés [nɛktarinide], *s.m.pl.* **nectariniidés** [nɛktariniide], *s.m.pl. Orn:* Nectariniidae.
nectarivore [nɛktarivɔːr], *Orn:* 1. *a.* nectarivorous. 2. *s.m. pl.* Nectariniidae, the nectar eaters.
necton [nɛktɔ̃], *s.m. Z:* necton, nekton.
nectria [nɛktrja], *s.m. Fung:* nectria.
necture [nɛktyːr], *s.m. Z:* necturus.
néerlandais, -aise [neɛrlɑ̃dɛ, -ɛːz], *Geog:* 1. *a.* of the Netherlands, Dutch; **le Gouvernement n.,** the Dutch Government. 2. *s.* Netherlander; Dutchman, Dutchwoman.
nef [nɛf], *s.f.* 1. (*a*) nave (of church); **n. latérale,** aisle; (*b*) **n. de montage,** erecting hall, bay. 2. *A. & Poet:* ship; *Lit.Hist:* **la N. des Fous,** the Ship of Fools; *Hist:* **la Blanche N.,** the White Ship. 3. *Furn:* **n. de table,** nef.
néfaste [nefast], *a.* 1. luckless, ill-omened, baneful; **guerre n.,** ill-fated war; **jour n.,** (i) *Rom.Ant:* day of mourning, *dies non*; (ii) ill-fated day, black-letter day; ill-starred, evil day; **influence n.,** baleful, baneful, pernicious, influence; **mesure n.,** measure attended by evil consequences; **cet incendie ne fut pas si n.,** this fire was not a bad thing. 2. **aliment n. aux dyspeptiques,** food that is bad for, disastrous to, dyspeptic subjects.
nèfle [nɛfl̩], *s.f.* medlar (fruit); **n. du Japon,** loquat; *F:* **avoir qch. pour des nèfles,** to get sth. dirt cheap; *P:* **des nèfles!** no fear! certainly not! nothing doing!
néflier [neflije], *s.m. Bot:* medlar (tree); **n. du Japon,** loquat (tree).
négateur, -trice [negatœːr, -tris]. 1. *a.* denying. 2. *s.* denier; **les négateurs de la Providence,** those who deny Providence.
négatif, -ive [negatif, -iːv]. 1. *a.* negative (answer, proposition, quantity, electricity); **avoir voix négative,** to have a negative voice, the power of veto; *Phot:* **épreuve négative,** *s.m.* **négatif,** negative; **dessin n.,** blueprint; *Med:* **examen n.,** negative result; negative test. 2. *s.f.* **négative,** negative; **soutenir la négative,** to argue in the negative; to speak against the motion; to maintain, uphold, the negative; **je réponds par la négative,** my answer is no; my answer is in the negative; **se tenir sur la négative,** to maintain a negative attitude; **dites-moi si vous pouvez venir demain; dans la n. je vous attendrai dans huit jours,** tell me if you can come tomorrow; if not I will expect you next week.
négation [negasjɔ̃], *s.f.* 1. negation, denial (of a fact, etc.); *Med:* **délire de la n.,** Cotard's syndrome. 2. *Gram:* negative; **deux négations valent une affirmation,** two negatives make an affirmative.
négatité [negatite], *s.f. Phil:* negativeness.
négativement [negativmɑ̃], *adv.* negatively; **répondre n.,** to answer in the negative.
négativisme [negativism], *s.m. Phil:* negativism.
négativité [negativite], *s.f.* negativity.
négatogène [negatɔʒɛn], *a. Atom.Ph:* emitting negatons.
négatoire [negatwaːr], *a.* negatory (formula, action, etc.).
négaton [negatɔ̃], *s.m. Atom.Ph:* negaton, negatron.
négatoscope [negatɔskɔp], *s.m. Med:* negatoscope.
négligé [negliʒe]. 1. *a.* (*a*) neglected (opportunity, etc.); **épouse négligée,** neglected wife; **un rhume n. peut dégénérer en bronchite,** a neglected cold may develop into bronchitis; (*b*) careless, slovenly (dress, appearance); **intérieur n.,** badly-kept, neglected, house; **style n.,** slipshod style. 2. *s.m.* (*a*) carelessness (in one's appearance); slovenliness; **le n. de sa tenue a choqué tout le monde,** everyone was shocked by his slovenly appearance; (*b*) *Cost:* négligé(e).
négligeable [negliʒabl̩], *a.* negligible; **considérer un danger n.,** to treat a danger as negligible, to disregard a danger; **un groupe de gens dont les moyens ne sont pas négligeables,** a group of people of not inconsiderable means; *Mth:* **quantité n.,** negligible quantity; **considérer, traiter, qn comme quantité n.,** to treat s.o. as if he weren't there; to disregard s.o., s.o.'s opinions; **elle le jugeait n.,** she considered him insignificant, a negligible quantity.
négligemment [negliʒamɑ̃], *adv.* 1. negligently, carelessly. 2. casually, nonchalantly.
négligence [negliʒɑ̃ːs], *s.f.* 1. (*a*) negligence; neglect (of s.o., of duty); carelessness, lack of care; **n. à faire qch.,** (i) carelessness in doing sth.; (ii) neglecting to do sth.; (*b*) *Jur:* **n. grave, grosse n.,** gross negligence; **n. coupable, criminelle,** criminal negligence. 2. (*a*) piece of negligence; **négligences de style,** negligences of style; (*b*) oversight; **par n.,** through an oversight.
négligent [negliʒɑ̃], *a.* 1. negligent, careless, neglectful (**de,** of); **être n. à faire qch.,** to be careless, remiss, in doing sth.; *s.* **les négligents,** careless people. 2. indifferent, casual; **d'un air n.,** carelessly, casually, nonchalantly.
négliger [negliʒe], *v.tr.* (**je négligeai(s); n. négligeons**) 1. (*a*) to neglect (sth.); **n. sa santé, ses devoirs,** to neglect one's health, one's duty; **n. sa personne, se n.,** to be careless about one's appearance; to neglect oneself; **n. la syntaxe,** to be careless about syntax; (*b*) **n. de** + *inf.*, to neglect to do sth.; to fail to do sth.; to leave sth. undone; **il a négligé de frapper à la porte,** he didn't (bother to) knock; **vous ne négligerez pas de vous vêtir chaudement,** you'll not forget to put on warm clothes, will you? (*c*) to neglect (s.o., one's children). 2. (*a*) to disregard (advice, etc.); *Mth:* **n. les décimales,** to disregard the decimals; to work to the nearest whole number; (*b*) **ne rien n. pour . . .,** to leave no stone unturned (in order) to . . .; **il ne faut pas n. cette occasion,** you mustn't miss this opportunity, let this opportunity go by.
négoce [negɔs], *s.m.* 1. trade, trading, business; **faire le n.,** to trade; **suivre le n.,** to go into, to be in, business; **le petit, le haut, n.,** small, big, business. 2. (unscrupulous) traffic(king); **vous faites là un vilain n.,** that's a dirty business you're engaged in.
négociabilité [negɔsjabilite], *s.f. Com:* negotiability.
négociable [negɔsjabl̩], *a. Com:* negotiable, transferable (bond, bill, cheque); **n. en banque,** bankable; **valeur n.,** market value.
négociant, -ante [negɔsjɑ̃, -ɑ̃ːt], *s.* (wholesale) merchant; trader; dealer; **n. en gros,** wholesaler; **n. en blés, en vins,** corn, wine, merchant.
négociateur, -trice [negɔsjatœːr, -tris]. 1. *s.* (*a*) negotiator *f.* negotiatrix; (of treaty, etc.); (*b*) middleman, intermediary. 2. *s.* transactor (of deal). 3. *a.* **groupement n.,** bargaining unit.
négociation [negɔsjasjɔ̃], *s.f.* 1. negotiation, negotiating (of treaty, bill); *Mil:* parley; **en n.,** under negotiation, in treaty; **par voie de négociations,** by negotiation; **engager, entamer, des négociations,** to enter into negotiations; to parley; **des négociations sont en cours,** negotiations are proceeding; **qui va mener les négociations?** who will conduct the negotiations? **n. d'un effet,** negotiation of a bill. 2. transaction; **négociations de Bourse,** Stock Exchange transactions.
négocier [negɔsje], *v.* (*p.d. & pr.sub.* **n. négociions, v. négociiez**) 1. *v.i. A:* to trade, traffic (**en,** in); to negotiate. 2. *v.tr.* (*a*) to negotiate (loan, bill, treaty, marriage, etc.); (*b*) to place (loan); (*c*) *Aut:* **n. un virage,** to negotiate a bend.
négondo [negɔ̃do], *s.m. Arb:* box elder.
négous [negus], *s.m.,* **négoush** [neguʃ], *s.m.* Negus (of Abyssinia).
nègre, négresse [nɛgr, negrɛs]. 1. *s.* (*a*) *occ. Pej:* negro, *f.* negress; black; **n. blanc,** albino negro; **la traite des Nègres,** the slave trade; **parler petit n.,** to talk pidgin (English, etc.); *s.a.* TÊTE-DE-NÈGRE, TRAVAILLER 2; (*b*) *F:* drudge; stooge; ghost (of literary man); devil (of barrister); do-all (in studio, etc.); **il me faut un n.,** I want s.o. to do all the donkey work; (*c*) *P:* flea; (*d*) *Soapm:* nigre; (*e*) *s.f. P:* **négresse,** bottle of red wine; **étouffer, éventrer, éternuer sur, une négresse,** to drink a bottle of wine; (*f*) *s.m. Tchn:* (*for lifting logs*) nigger. 2. *a.* (*f.* **nègre**) (*a*) **la race n.,** the negro race; (*b*) *a.inv.* nigger (-brown); *F:* **propos n. blanc,** double talk.
Nègrepont [nɛgrəpɔ̃], *Pr.n.m. Geog:* Negropont.
négrerie [negrəri], **nègrerie** [nɛgrəri], *s.f.* 1. *A:* slave compound, barracoon. 2. negro quarters.
négrier [negrije]. 1. *s.m.* (*a*) slave trader; (*b*) slave ship. 2. *a.m.* **bâtiment n.,** slave ship; **centre n.,** slave centre.
négrifier [negrifje], *v.tr.* to make negro.
négrille [negriːj], *s.m. Ethn:* negrillo.
négrillon, -onne [negrijɔ̃, -ɔn], *s. occ. Pej:* (little) nigger boy, girl; negrillo; *F:* piccaninny.
négrite [negrit], *s.f. Hist: A:* little black girl.
négrito [negrito], *s.m. Ethn:* negrito.
négritude [negrityd], *s.f.* (*a*) state of being a negro; (*b*) negro life; negro culture; negro cultural and spiritual values.
négro-africain, -aine [negrɔafrikɛ̃, -ɛn], *a.* **les langues négro-africaines,** Negro-African.
négroïde [negrɔid], *a. Ethn:* negroid(al).
négrophile [negrɔfil], *s.m. & f.* negrophil(e).
négundo [negɔ̃do], *s.m. Arb:* box elder.
négus [negys], *s.m.* Negus (of Abyssinia).
Néhémie [neemi], *Pr.n.m. B.Hist:* Nehemiah.
neige [nɛːʒ], *s.f.* snow; **la saison des neiges,** the snowy season; **train de n.,** winter-sports train; **neiges éternelles, perpétuelles, permanentes,** perpetual snow; **limite des neiges éternelles, persistantes,** snow line; **il tombe de la n.,** it is snowing; **rafale de n.,** snow flurry; blizzard; **amas de n.,** snowdrift; **être bloqué par la n.,** to be snowed up, snowbound; **n. fondue,** (i) sleet; (ii) slush; **boule de n.,** snowball; **histoire qui fait boule de n.,** story that grows as it spreads, that snowballs; **faire un bonhomme de n.,** to make a snowman; *A: F:* **chose de n.,** passing, ephemeral, matter; **homme de n.,** man of no substance; **cheveux, barbe, sein, de n.,** snowy hair, beard, breast; **blanc, comme (la) n.,** (i) snow-white; (ii) innocent; *s.a.* ANTAN, BLANC I 3, CLASSE 2, FONTE[1] 1, VACANCE 2; **des mains de n.,** snowy white hands; *Cu:* **blancs d'œufs battus en n.,** whites of eggs beaten stiff; **monter les blancs en n.,** to beat the whites until stiff; **œufs à la n.,** floating islands; *Ind:* **n. carbonique,** (carbonic acid) snow, carbon-dioxide snow, dry ice; *Ch:* **n. d'antimoine,** antimony trioxide; (*b*) *Art:* snowscape; (*c*) *P:* cocaine, *P:* snow, coke.
neigeoter [neʒɔte], *v.impers.* to snow slightly; **il neigeotait,** now and again a few snowflakes fell.
neiger [neʒe], *v.impers.* (**il neigeait**) to snow; **il neige beaucoup au Canada,** it snows a lot in Canada; *F:* **il a neigé sur la tête,** he's got white hair; *v.i.* **les fleurs des pommiers neigent sur les allées,** the apple blossom snows down on the walks.
neigeux, -euse [neʒø, -øːz], *a.* 1. snowy (peak, weather); snow-covered (roof, etc.). 2. snow-white, snowy.
nélombo, nélumbo [nelɔ̃bo], *s.m. Bot:* Egyptian lotus, Nile lily, nelumbium, nelumbo.
Nelson [nɛlsɔn]. 1. *Pr.n.* Nelson; *Med:* **test de N., réaction de N.,** treponemal immobilization test. 2. *s.m. Wr:* nelson; **double n.,** double, full, nelson.
néma- [nema], *pref.* nem-, nema-, nemo-.
némalion [nemaljɔ̃], *s.m. Algae:* nemalion.
némalionales [nemaljɔnal], *s.f.pl. Algae:* Nemalionales.
némalite [nemalit], *s.f. Miner:* nemalite.
némate [nemat], *s.m. Ent:* nematus.
némathelminthe [nematɛlmɛ̃ːt], *s.m. Ann:* nemathelminth.
nématique [nematik], *a. Ph:* nematic.
némato- [nematɔ], *pref.* nemato-, nem(a)-, nemo-.
nématoblaste [nematɔblast], *s.m. Biol:* nematoblast.
nématocécidie [nematɔsesidi], *s.f. Bot:* gall caused by a nematode.
nématocères [nematɔsɛːr], *s.m.pl. Ent:* Nematocera.
nématocyste [nematɔsist], *s.m. Biol:* nematocyst.
nématode [nematɔd], *s.m. Ann:* nematode, thread worm.
nématoïde [nematɔid], *a.* nematoid.
nématophores [nematɔfɔːr], *s.m.pl. Coel:* Nematophora.
Némée [neme], *Pr.n.f. A.Geog:* Nemea; **le lion de N.,** the Nemean lion.
néméen, -enne [nemeɛ̃, -ɛn], *a. & s. A.Geog:* Nemean.
néméobie [nemeɔbi], *s.m. Ent:* Duke of Burgundy butterfly.
néméophile [nemeɔfil], *s.f. Ent:* nemeophila.
némerte [nemɛrt], *s.f.,* **nemertes** [nemɛrtɛs], *s.m. Ann:* nemertine; **les némertes,** the Nemertea.
némertien [nemɛrsjɛ̃], *s.m. Ann:* nemertean, nemertine.
nemesia [nemezja], *s.m. Bot:* nemesia.
Némésis [nemezis], *Pr.n.f. Myth:* Nemesis.
nemestrinus [nemɛstrinyːs], *s.m. Z:* pig-tailed macaque.
némobie [nemɔbi], *s.m. Z:* nemobius.
némocères [nemɔsɛːr], *s.m.pl. Ent:* Nematocera.
némophila [nemɔfila], *s.m. Bot:* nemophila.
némoptère [nemɔptɛːr], *s.m. Lep:* nemopterid.
némoral, -aux [nemɔral, -o], *a. Lit:* nemoral, of the woods.
némoréen, -éenne [nemɔreɛ̃, -ɛn], *a. Rom.Ant:* nemoral.
nemorhædus [nemɔredyːs], *s.m. Z:* Nemorhaedus.

némoricole [nemɔrikɔl], *a. Orn:* nemoricole, nemoricoline, nemoricolous.

né-mort, *f.* **née-morte** [nemɔːr, nemɔrt], *a.* still-born; *pl. né(e)s-mort(e)s.*

ne m'oubliez pas [nɔmublijepɑ], *s.m.inv. Bot: F:* forget-me-not.

némoure [nemuːr], *s.f.,* **nemura** [nemyrɑ], *s.m. Ent:* nemourid.

nemourien, -ienne [nɔmurjɛ̃, -jɛn], *a. & s. Geog:* (native, inhabitant) of Nemours.

Nemrod [nɛmrɔd], *Pr.n.m. B.Hist:* Nimrod.

néné [nene], *s.m. P:* breast, *P:* tit; **des nénés de chez Michelin,** falsies.

nénies [neni], *s.f.pl. Gr. & Rom.Ant:* n(a)eniae.

nenni [nani], **nennida** [nanida]. **1.** *adv. A:* (a) not he! (b) nay! not I! **2.** *s.m. A:* refusal.

nénufar, nénuphar [nenyfaːr], *s.m. Bot:* nenuphar, water lily; **n. des étangs, n. jaune,** yellow pond lily, spatter dock.

néo- [neo, neo], *pref.* neo-.

néoarsphénamine [neoarsfenamin], *s.f. Pharm:* neoarsphenamine.

néo-babylonien, -ienne [neobabilɔnjɛ̃, -jɛn], *a.* neo-Babylonian.

néobaleine [neobalɛn], *s.f. Z:* neobalaena.

neobisium [neobizjɔm], *s.m. Arach:* neobisium.

néo-calédonien, -ienne [neokaledɔnjɛ̃, -jɛn], *a. & s. Geog:* New Caledonian; *pl. néo-calédoniens, -iennes.*

néocastrien, -ienne [neokastriɛ̃,-jɛn], *a. & s. Geog:* (native, inhabitant) of Neufchâteau.

néo-catholicisme [neokatɔlisism], *s.m.* Neo-Catholicism.

néo-catholique [neokatɔlik], *a.* Neo-Catholic; *pl. néo-catholiques.*

néo-celtique [neosɛltik], *a.* Neo-Celtic; *pl. néo-celtiques.*

neoceratodus [neoseratɔdys], *s.m. Ich:* neo-ceratodus.

néo-chrétien, -ienne [neokretjɛ̃, -jɛn], *a.* Neo-Christian; *pl. néo-chrétiens, -iennes.*

néo-christianisme [neokristjanism], *s.m.inv.* Neo-Christianity.

néo-classicisme [neoklasisism], *s.m.* neo-classicism.

néo-classique [neoklasik], *a.* neo-classic(al); *pl. néo-classiques.*

néo-colonialisme [neokɔlɔnjalism], *s.m. Pol:* neocolonialism.

néo-colonialiste [neokɔlɔnjalist], *s.* neocolonialist; *pl. néo-colonialistes.*

néocomien, -ienne [neokɔmjɛ̃, -jɛn], *a. & s.m. Geol:* Neocomian.

néo-confucianisme [neokɔ̃fysjanism], *s.m.* Neo-Confucianism.

néocorat [neokɔra], *s.m. Gr.Ant:* office and title of neocorus.

néocore [neokɔːr], *s.m. Gr.Ant:* neocorus.

néo-criticisme [neokritisism], *s.m. Phil:* neocriticism.

néo-criticiste [neokritisist], (a) *a.* relating to neocriticism; (b) *s.* adherent of neocriticism; *pl. néo-criticistes.*

néo-culture [neokyltyːr], *s.f. Agr:* modern farming techniques.

néocyanite [neosjanit], *s.f. Miner:* lithidionite.

néocyte [neɔsit], *s.m. Biol:* neocyte.

néo-darwinien, -ienne [neodarwinjɛ̃, -jɛn], *a.* Neo-Darwinian; *pl. néo-darwiniens, -iennes.*

néo-darwinisme [neodarwinism], *s.m. Biol:* Neo-Darwinism.

néo-darwiniste [neodarwinist], (a) *a.* Neo-Darwinian; (b) *s.m. & f.* Neo-Darwinist; *pl. néo-darwinistes.*

néodyme [neodim], *s.m. Ch:* neodymium.

néo-fascisme [neofasism], *s.m. Pol:* neofascism; *pl. néo-fascismes.*

néo-fasciste [neofasist], *a. & s.m. & f.* neofascist; *pl. néo-fascistes.*

néo-formation [neofɔrmasjɔ̃], *s.f. Biol:* neo-formation; *pl. néo-formations.*

néo-gallois, -oise [neogalwa, -waːz], *a. & s. Geog:* (native, inhabitant) of New South Wales. *s.* New South Welshman, -woman.

néogène [neoʒɛn], *a. & s.m. Geol:* Neocene, Neo-gene.

néo-gothique [neogɔtik], *Arch:* **1.** *a.* neo-gothic. **2.** *s.m.* neo-gothic (style); *pl. néo-gothiques.*

néographe [neograf], *s.m. & f.* spelling reformer.

néographie [neografi], *s.f.* new, reformed, spelling.

néographisme [neografism], *s.m.* spelling reform.

néo-grec, *f.* **néo-grecque** [neogrɛk], *a.* Neo-Greek; modern Greek (literature, language); *pl. néo-grecs, -grecques.*

néo-guinéen, -enne [neogineɛ̃, -ɛn], *a. & s. Geog:* New Guinean; *pl. néo-guinéens, -ennes.*

néo-hébreu [neoebrø], *s.m.* Neo-Hebrew; *pl. néo-hébreux.*

néo-hébridais, -aise [neoebridɛ, -ɛːz], *a. & s. Geog:* (native, inhabitant) of the New Hebrides (Islands); *pl. néo-hébridais, -aises.*

néo-hégélianisme [neoeʒeljanism], *s.m.inv. Phil:* Neo-Hegelianism.

néo-hégélien, -ienne [neoeʒeljɛ̃, -jɛn], *a. & s. Phil:* Neo-Hegelian; *pl. néo-hégéliens, -iennes.*

néo-hellénisme [neoɛl(l)enism], *s.m.* Neo-Hellen-ism.

néo-impressionnisme [neoɛ̃prɛsjɔnism], *s.m.inv. Art:* neo-impressionism.

néo-impressionniste [neoɛ̃prɛsjɔnist], *a. & s.m. & f., Art:* neo-impressionist; *pl. néo-impression-nistes.*

néo-kantien, -ienne [neokɑ̃tjɛ̃, -jɛn], *a. & s. Phil:* Neo-Kantian; *pl. néo-kantiens, -iennes.*

néo-kantisme [neokɑ̃tism], *s.m. Phil:* Neo-Kantianism.

néo-lamarckien, -ienne [neolamarkjɛ̃, -jɛn], *a. & s. Biol:* Neo-Lamarckian; *pl. néo-lamarckiens, -iennes.*

néo-lamarckisme [neolamarkism], *s.m. Biol:* Neo-Lamarckism.

néo-latin [neolatɛ̃], *a.* Neo-Latin; **langues néo-latines,** romance languages.

néo-libéralisme [neoliberalism], *s.m. Pol:* neo-liberalism.

néolithique [neolitik]. **1.** *a.* Neolithic. **2.** *s.m.* **le n.,** the Neolithic (Age). **3.** *s.m. & f.* Neolithic man, woman.

néolocal, -aux [neɔlɔkal, -o], *a. Ethn:* neolocal.

néologie [neolɔʒi], *s.f.* neology.

néologique [neolɔʒik], *a.* neological.

néologisme [neolɔʒism], *s.m.* neologism.

néologiste [neolɔʒist], *s.m.,* **néologue** [neolɔg], *s.m.* neologist, neologian.

néo-malthusianisme [neomaltyzjanism], *s.m.* Neo-Malthusianism.

néo-malthusien, -ienne [neomaltyzjɛ̃, -jɛn], *a.* Neo-Malthusian; *pl. néo-malthusiens, -iennes.*

néoménie [neomeni], *s.f. Gr. & Jew.Ant:* neo-menia.

néomycine [neomisin], *s.f. Pharm:* neomycin.

néon [neɔ̃], *s.m. Ch:* neon; **tube, lampe, au n.,** neon tube; neon lamp; neon light; **enseigne au n.,** neon sign.

néo-natal [neonatal], *a. Med:* neonatal; *pl. néo-natal(e)s.*

néophobie [neofɔbi], *s.f.* neophobia.

néophron [neofrɔ̃], *s.m. Orn:* neophron.

néophyte [neofit], *s.m.* (a) neophyte; (b) beginner, tyro.

néoplasie [neoplazi], *s.f. Med:* neoplasia.

néoplasique [neoplazik], *a. Med:* neoplastic; **infiltration n.,** infiltration neoplasm, infiltrating neoplasm.

néoplasme [neoplasm], *s.m. Med:* neoplasm.

néo-plasticisme [neoplastisism], *s.m. Art:* neo-plasticism.

néoplastie [neoplasti], *s.f. Surg:* autoplasty, neo-plasty, plastic surgery.

néoplastique [neoplastik], *a. Med:* neoplastic.

néo-platonicien, -ienne [neoplatonisjɛ̃, -jɛn]. **1.** *a.* Neo-Platonic. **2.** *s.* Neo-Platonist.

néo-platonisme [neoplatɔnism], *s.m.* Neo-Platonism.

néo-positivisme [neopozitivism], *s.m. Phil:* neo-positivism, logical positivism.

néo-positiviste [neopozitivist], *Phil:* (a) *a.* neo-positivist, neopositivistic; (b) *s.m. & f.* neo-positivist; *pl. néo-positivistes.*

néoprène [neoprɛn], *s.m. R.t.m:* Neoprene.

néoptères [neoptɛːr], *s.m.pl. Ent:* Neoptera.

Néoptolème [neoptɔlɛm], *Pr.n.m. Gr.Lit: Hist:* Neoptolemus.

néo-pythagoricien, -ienne [neopitagɔrisjɛ̃, -jɛn], *a. & s. Phil:* Neo-Pythagorean; *pl. néo-pytha-goriciens, -iennes.*

néo-pythagorisme [neopitagɔrism], *s.m. Phil:* Neo-Pythagoreanism.

néo-réalisme [neorealism], *s.m.* neo-realism.

néo-réaliste [neorealist], (a) *a.* neo-realist, neo-realistic; (b) *s.m. & f.* neo-realist; *pl. néo-réalistes.*

néo-romantique [neorɔmɑ̃tik], *a. & s.m. & f.* neo-romantic; *pl. néo-romantiques.*

néo-romantisme [neorɔmɑ̃tism], *s.m.* neo-roman-ticism.

néo-scolastique [neoskɔlastik], (a) *a.* neo-scholas-tic; (b) *s.f.* neo-scholasticism; *pl. néo-scolas-tiques.*

néostigmine [neostigmin], *s.f. Pharm:* neostig-mine.

néostomie [neostɔmi] *s.f. Surg:* neostomy.

néo-syriaque [neosirjak]. *s.m. Ling:* Neo-Syriac; *pl. néo-syriaques.*

néotantalite [neotɑ̃talit], *s.f. Miner:* neotan-talite.

néotène [neotɛn], *s.m. Biol:* neotenic species.

néoténie [neoteni], *s.f. Biol:* neoteny, neoteinia.

néoténique [neotenik], *a. Biol:* neotenic, neoten-ous.

néo-thomisme [neotɔmism], *s.m. Rel:* Neo-Thomism.

néo-thomiste [neotɔmist], *Rel:* (a) *a.* Neo-Thomist(ic); (b) *s.m. & f.* Neo-Thomist; *pl. néo-thomistes.*

néotome [neotɔm], *s.m. Z:* neotoma.

néotraginés [neotraʒine], *s.m.pl. Z:* Neotraginae.

néotrague [neotrag], *s.m. Z:* royal antelope.

néotremata [neotremata], *s.m.pl. Z:* Neotremata.

neottia [neotja], *s.m.,* **néottie** [neoti], *s.f. Bot:* bird's nest orchid, neottia.

néo-vitalisme [neovitalism], *s.m.* neo-vitalism.

néovolcanique [neovɔlkanik], *a. Geol: A:* neo-volcanic.

néo-zélandais, -aise [neozelɑ̃dɛ, -ɛːz]. **1.** *a. Geog:* New Zealand (government, butter, etc.). **2.** *s.* New Zealander; *pl. néo-zélandais, -aises.*

néozoïque [neozoik], *Geol:* **1.** *a.* Neozoic. **2.** *s.m.* Neozoic (age).

Népal, Népaul [nepal], *Pr.n.m. Geog:* Nepal.

népalais, -aise [nepalɛ, -ɛːz], *a. & s. Geog:* Nepalese.

nèpe [nɛp], *s.f. Ent:* nepa, water scorpion.

népenthe [nepɛ̃t], *s.m.,* **népenthès** [nepɛ̃tɛs], *s.m.* **1.** *Gr.Lit:* nepenthe(s). **2.** *Bot:* pitcher-plant, nepenthe.

néper [nepeːr], *s.m. Ph:* neper.

népérien, -ienne [neperjɛ̃, -jɛn], *a. Mth:* Napierian (logarithms).

népermètre [nepɛrmɛtr], *s.m.* hypsometer.

nepeta [nepeta], *s.f. Bot:* nepeta.

néphalisme [nefalism], *s.m.* nephalism, teetotal-ism.

néphaliste [nefalist], *s.m. & f.* nephalist, tee-totaller.

néphélé- [nefele], **néphél(o)-** [nefɛl(o)], *pref.* nephel(o)-.

néphélémétrie [nefelemetri], *s.f. Ph:* nephelo-metry.

néphéline [nefelin], *s.f. Miner:* nephelite, nephel-ine.

néphélinique [nefelinik], *a. Miner:* nephelinic.

néphélinite [nefelinit], *s.f. Geol:* nephelinite.

néphélion [nefeljɔ̃], *s.m. Med:* nubecula.

néphélococcygie [nefelɔkɔksiʒi], *s.f. Gr.Lit:* cloud-cuckoo-land.

néphéloïde [nefelɔid], *a.* cloudy, cloud-like.

néphélomètre [nefelɔmɛtr], *s.m. Ph:* nephelo-meter.

néphélométrie [nefelɔmetri] *s.f. Ph:* nephelo-metry.

néphile [nefil], *s.f. Arach:* nephila.

néphoscope [nefɔskɔp], *s.m. Meteor:* nepho-scope.

néphralgie [nefralʒi], *s.f. Med:* nephralgia.

néphralgique [nefralʒik], *a. Med:* nephralgic.

néphrectomie [nefrɛktɔmi], *s.f. Surg:* nephrec-tomy.

néphrectomiser [nefrɛktɔmize], *v.tr. Surg:* to do, perform, a nephrectomy on (s.o.).

néphrétique [nefretik], *occ.* **néphritique** [nefritik]. **1.** *Med:* (a) *a.* nephritic, renal (pain, colic); (b) *s.* sufferer from nephritis; nephritic. **2.** *s.m. Med:* nephritic (remedy). **3.** *s.f. Miner:* = NÉPHRITE 2.

néphridies [nefridi], *s.f. Ent: Ann:* nephridium.

néphrite [nefrit], *s.f.* **1.** *Med:* nephritis; **n. chronique,** Bright's disease. **2.** *Miner:* nephrite, jade, greenstone.

néphro- [nefro], *pref.* nephro-.

néphrocyte [nefrosit], *s.m. Biol:* nephrocyte.

néphrolepis [nefrolɛpis], *s.m. Bot:* nephrolepis.

néphrolithe [nefrolit], *s.m. Med:* (rare) nephrolith.

néphrolithiase [nefrolitjaːz], *s.f. Med:* nephroli-thiasis.

néphrolithotomie [nefrolitotɔmi], *s.f. Surg:* nephrolithotomy.

néphrologie [nefrolɔʒi], *s.f. Med:* nephrology.

néphrologique [nefrolɔʒik], *a. Med:* relating to nephrology.

néphrolyse [nefroliːz], *s.f. Surg:* nephrolysis.

néphron [nefrɔ̃], *s.m. Anat:* nephron.

néphropathie [nefropati], *s.f. Med:* nephro-pathy.

néphropexie [nefropɛksi], *s.f. Surg:* nephropexy.

néphrops [nefrɔps], *s.m. Crust:* nephrops.

néphroptose [nefroptoːz], *s.f. Med:* nephroptosis, floating kidney.

néphrorragie [nefrɔraʒi], *s.f. Med:* nephrorrhagia.

néphrorraphie [nefrɔrafi], *s.f. Med:* nephrorrhaphy.

néphrosclérose [nefroskleroːz], *s.f. Med:* nephrosclerosis.

néphrose [nefroːz], *s.f. Med:* nephrosis.

néphrostomie [nefrɔstɔmi], *s.f. Surg:* nephrostomy.

néphrostomiser [nefrɔstɔmize], *v.tr. Surg:* to do, perform, a nephrostomy on (s.o.).

néphrotique [nefrɔtik], *a. Med:* nephrotic.

néphrotome [nefrɔtɔm], *s.m. Anat:* nephrotome.

néphrotomie [nefrɔtɔmi], *s.f. Surg:* nephrotomy.

néphrotoxine [nefrɔtɔksin], *s.f.* nephrotoxin.

néphro-urétérectomie [nefrɔyreterɛktɔmi], *s.f. Surg:* nephro-ureterectomy.

népidés [nepide], *s.m.pl. Ent:* Nepidae.

népotisme [nepɔtism], *s.m.* nepotism.

népouite [nepuit], *s.f. Miner:* nepouite.

nepticulides [nɛptikylid], *s.m.pl. Ent:* Nepticulidae, the nepticulid moths.

Neptune [nɛptyn]. 1. *Pr.n.m. Myth: Astr:* Neptune. 2. *s.m.* (*a*) *Nau: A:* collection of sea charts; marine atlas; (*b*) lock chamber (of canal).

neptunien, -ienne [nɛptynjɛ̃, -jɛn], *Geol:* (*a*) *a.* neptunian; (*b*) *s.m. & f.* neptunist, neptunian.

neptunisme [nɛptynism], *s.m. A.Geol:* neptunism.

neptunite [nɛptynit], *s.f. Miner:* neptunite.

neptunium [nɛptynjɔm], *s.m. Ch:* neptunium.

néracais, -aise [nerake, -ɛːz], *a. & s. Geog:* (native, inhabitant) of Nérac.

Nérée [nere], *Pr.n.m. Myth:* Nereus.

néréide [nereid], *s.f.* 1. *Myth:* Nereid, sea nymph. 2. *Ann:* nereid.

néréidés [nereide], **néréidiens** [nereidjɛ̃], *s.m.pl. Ann:* Nereides, the ragworms.

néréis [nereis], *s.m. Ann:* nereid.

nerf [nɛːr], *s.m.* 1. (*a*) *Anat:* nerve; **maladie de nerfs,** nervous complaint; **le n. optique** [nɛrfɔptik], the optic nerve; **n. moteur oculaire commun,** oculomotor nerve; **n. moteur oculaire externe,** abducens nerve; **n. spinal,** spinal nerve; (*b*) **attaque de nerfs,** (fit of) hysterics; **avoir une attaque, une crise, de nerfs,** to go into hysterics; **cela faillit lui donner une attaque de nerfs,** it almost sent her into hysterics, *F:* into fits; *F:* **il a les nerfs agacés, à vif, en boule, à fleur de peau,** his nerves are on edge; *F:* he's a bit jumpy; **porter, donner, taper, sur les nerfs à qn,** to get, jar, on s.o.'s nerves; **cela lui portait, donnait,** *F:* **tapait, sur les nerfs,** it exasperated her; it got on her nerves; **elle est un peu sur les nerfs aujourd'hui,** she is a bit on edge to-day; **je suis à bout de nerfs,** my nerves are frayed; **elle a ses nerfs aujourd'hui,** she has got a fit of nerves today; she is in a tantrum again today; **c'est un paquet de nerfs,** he, she, is a bundle of nerves; **être, vivre, sur les nerfs,** to live on one's nerves; **le bruit continuel me met les nerfs à vif,** the constant noise frays my nerves; **avoir les nerfs à toute épreuve,** to have cast-iron nerves; **passer ses nerfs sur qn, sur qch.,** to take out, work out, one's irritation on s.o., sth.; *s.a.* GUERRE 1. 2. *F:* (*in sing. always* [nɛrf] *at the end of the word-group*) sinew, tendon, ligament; **nerfs d'acier,** nerves of steel; *P:* **mets-y du n.** [nɛrf]! put some guts into it! **le n. de la guerre,** the sinews of war; **caractère sans n.,** weak, nerveless, character; **manquer de n.,** to lack energy, stamina; **avoir du n.,** to be vigorous, energetic; **n. de bœuf** [nɛrdəbœf], (i) leader of bull's neck; bull's pizzle; (ii) (as weapon) bull's pizzle; life-preserver; black-jack; cosh. 3. (*a*) *Bookb:* band, cord, slip; (*b*) *Arch:* rib, fillet (of groin); (*c*) *Min:* horse (in the seam); (*d*) *Metall:* fibre. 4. *Ven:* penis (of stag).

nerférer (se) [sənɛrfere], *v.pr.* (**il se nerfère; il se nerférera**) (*of horse*) to overreach.

nerf-férure [nɛrferyːr], *s.m. Vet:* cut (through overreaching); overreach; *pl. nerfs-férures.*

nerf-foulure [nɛrfulyːr], *s.f. Vet:* sprain, sprained ankle; *pl. nerfs-foulures.*

nérine [nerin], *s.f. Bot:* nerine, Guernsey lily.

nérite [nerit], *s.f. Moll:* nerita.

néritidés [neritide], *s.m.pl. Moll:* Neritidae.

néritine [neritin], *s.f. Moll:* neritina.

néritique [neritik], *a. Oc:* neritic, relating to the coastal belt; (**zone**) **n.,** neritic zone.

nerium [nerjɔm], *s.m. Bot:* nerium.

néroli [nerɔli], *s.m. Perfumes:* neroli, orange-flower essential oil.

Néron [nerɔ̃], *Pr.n.m. Rom.Hist:* Nero; *s.a.* FERMOIR[2].

néronien, -ienne [nerɔnjɛ̃, -jɛn], *a.* Neronian.

néronisme [nerɔnism], *s.m.* sophisticated cruelty (as practised by Nero).

nerprun [nɛrprœ̃], *s.m. Bot:* buckthorn.

nerval, -aux [nɛrval, -o], *a.* 1. *Anat: etc:* nerval, neural. 2. nerve (medicine); neurotic (drug).

nervation [nɛrvasjɔ̃], *s.f. Bot: etc:* nervation.

nervé [nɛrve], *a. Bot:* nervate, nervose.

nerver [nɛrve], *v.tr.* to stiffen; (*a*) to back (panel, etc.) with strips of canvas, etc.; (*b*) to put a flange on (sth.); (*c*) to cord (saddlery); to put bands on (book).

nerveusement [nɛrvøzmɑ̃], *adv.* 1. energetically. 2. impatiently, irritably; *F:* nervily; **manier n. sa chaîne de montre,** to fiddle with one's watch-chain; **rire n.,** to laugh hysterically.

nerveux, -euse [nɛrvø, -øːz], *a.* 1. nervous (system, disease, etc.); **centre n.,** nerve centre; **ganglion n.,** nerve-knot; **prostration, dépression, nerveuse,** nervous breakdown; **maladie nerveuse fonctionnelle,** functional nervous disease; **maladie nerveuse organique,** organic nervous disease. 2. (*a*) sinewy, wiry (arm, body); *F:* vigorous, virile, terse (style, etc.); *s.a.* SEC 2; **vin n.,** wine that preserves its quality well; **moteur n.,** engine with a good pick-up; responsive engine; **salle de spectacle nerveuse,** responsive audience; (*b*) (leaf) with well-marked ribs, veins, nerves; (*c*) **fer n.,** fibrous iron. 3. (*a*) excitable, highly-strung; *F:* nervy (person); skittish (horse); (*b*) *F:* fidgety; **elle est nerveuse aujourd'hui,** she is on edge, she is nervy, today; **rire n.,** hysterical laugh; (*c*) *s.* nervy person.

nervi [nɛrvi], *s.m. F:* gangster.

Nerviens [nɛrvjɛ̃], *s.m.pl. Hist:* Nervii.

nervifolié [nɛrvifɔlje], *a. Bot:* ribbed (leaf).

nervin [nɛrvɛ̃], *a. & s.m. Pharm:* nervine.

nervisme [nɛrvism], *s.m. Med:* (theory of) nervosism.

nervosisme [nɛrvozism], *s.m. Med:* nervosism; nervous diathesis; nervous predisposition.

nervosité [nɛrvozite], *s.f.* irritability, state of nerves, edginess; **calmer les nervosités de qn,** calm s.o. down.

nervo-tabès [nɛrvɔtabɛs], *s.m. Med:* nervotabes.

nervulation [nɛrvylasjɔ̃], *s.f. Ent:* venation (of an insect's wings).

nervule [nɛrvyl], *s.f. Nat.Hist:* nervule.

nervurage [nɛrvyraːz], *s.m. Mec.E:* ribbing.

nervure [nɛrvyːr], *s.f.* (*a*) nervure, rib, vein (of leaf, insect-wing); (*b*) branch (of mountain-group); (*c*) flange, rib (on casting, etc.); gill (of radiator, etc.); **couvercle à nervures,** ribbed cover (of steamchest, etc.); *Mec.E:* **n. de renfort, de renforcement,** stiffening rib; *I.C.E:* **nervures du piston,** ribs of the piston; **carter à nervures,** stiffened crank-case; **n. de refroidissement,** cooling flange, fin; (*d*) rib, fillet (of groin, ship, etc.); *Arch:* **voûte à nervures,** ribbed vault; **plafond à nervures,** filleted ceiling; (*e*) *Carp:* batten; (*f*) *Av:* rib; **n. forte,** main rib; (*g*) *Bookb:* rib, raised band (on back of book); (*h*) *Dressm:* **nervures,** piping (of garment); braiding; pin-tucks; (*i*) *Nau:* whelp (of capstan).

nervuré [nɛrvyre], *a. Mec.E: Nat.Hist:* ribbed.

nervure-guide [nɛrvyrgid], *s.f. Mec.E:* guide rib; *pl. nervures-guides.*

nervurer [nɛrvyre], *v.tr. Mec.E:* to rib.

nescience [nɛs(s)jɑ̃ːs], *s.f.* nescience, state of ignorance.

nescient [nɛs(s)jɑ̃], *a.* nescient, ignorant.

neslois, -oise [nɛlwa, -waːz], *a. & s. Geog:* (native, inhabitant) of Nesle.

nésocie [nezɔsi], **nesokia** [nezɔkja], *s.m. Z:* nesokia.

nesodon [nezɔdɔ̃], *s.m. Paleont:* nesodon.

nésomyinés [nezɔmiine], *s.m.pl. Z:* Nesomyinae.

nésotrague [nezɔtrag], *s.m. Z:* Nesotragus.

nesquehonite [nɛskeɔnit], *s.f. Miner:* nesquehonite.

n'est-ce pas [nɛspɑ], *adv.phr.* (*inviting assent*) **vous venez, n'est-ce pas?** you are coming, aren't you? **vous viendrez, n'est -ce pas?** you will come, won't you? **vous ne venez pas, n'est-ce pas?** you are not coming, are you? **il en a, n'est-ce pas?** he has some, hasn't he? **vous lui avez parlé n'est-ce pas?** you spoke to him, didn't you? **oui, n'est-ce pas?** yes, of course! **non, n'est-ce pas?** I shouldn't think so! **il n'en vend pas, n'est-ce pas?** he doesn't sell any, does he? **n'est-ce pas qu'il a de la chance?** isn't he lucky?

neste [nɛst], *s.m. or f.* torrent (in Pyrenees).

nesticus [nɛstikys], *s.m. Arach:* nesticus.

Nestor[1] [nɛstɔːr], *Pr.n.m. Gr.Lit:* Nestor.

nestor[2], *s.m. Orn:* kea.

nestorianisme [nɛstɔrjanism], *Rel.H:* Nestorianism.

nestorien, -ienne [nɛstɔrjɛ̃, -jɛn], *a. & s. Rel.H:* Nestorian.

Nestorius [nɛstɔrjys], *Pr.n.m. Rel.H:* Nestorius.

net, nette[1] [nɛt], *a.* 1. clean, spotless (plate, etc.); flawless (stone); pure, unadulterated (rice, etc.); clear, sound (conscience); *F:* slick (performance); *F:* **j'ai les mains nettes,** my hands are clean; I had nothing to do with it; **faire les plats nets,** to leave nothing in the dishes; *F:* to lick the platter clean; **son cas n'est pas net,** his case is not above suspicion; **ma conscience est nette de tout reproche,** my conscience is clear of all reproach; **n. d'impôt,** tax paid, tax free; **rente nette de tout impôt,** (stock yielding) income free of tax; **cassure nette,** clean break; **bois net,** clean wood, wood free from knots; **maison nette comme un sou neuf,** house as clean as a new pin; **faire place nette,** to remove oneself and all one's belongings; *Gaming:* **faire tapis net,** to clear the board; *s.a.* CŒUR 2, MAISON 3, SAIN. 2. (*a*) clear (sight, idea, style); distinct (print); plain (answer); **avoir la vision nette,** to be clear-sighted; **avoir une nette vision de l'avenir,** to have a clear vision of the future; **division nette,** clear-cut division; **contours nets,** sharp outlines; **écriture nette,** fair hand; *Phot: etc:* **image nette,** sharp image; **voilà qui est net!** that's a plain enough answer! that settles it! *s.m.* **mettre une lettre, un devoir, au net,** to make, write, a fair copy of a letter, of an exercise; *Sch:* **cahier de net,** fair-copy book; (*b*) **poids, prix, net,** net weight, price; **bénéfice net,** net, clear, profit; **recettes nettes,** net receipts. 3. *adv.* (*a*) plainly, flatly, outright; **parler net,** to speak plainly; **je vous dis tout net ce que je pense,** I tell you bluntly what I think; I do not mince matters; **refuser qch. (tout) net,** to refuse sth. point-blank; to give a flat refusal; **je refusai net,** I flatly refused; **il fut tué net,** he was killed outright, on the spot; **s'arrêter net,** to stop dead; to come to a dead stop; **se casser net,** to break off clean; to snap (in two); (*b*) clearly, distinctly; **voir net,** (i) to see distinctly; (ii) to be clear-headed; (*c*) **cela m'a rapporté cent francs net,** it brought me a clear hundred francs; I cleared a hundred francs.

netball [nɛtbɔl], *s.m. Sp:* netball.

netsuké [nɛtsyke], *s.m.inv.* netsuke.

nettapus [nɛtapyːs], *s.m. Orn:* nettapus.

nette[2], *s.f. Orn:* **n. rousse,** red-crested pochard.

nettement [nɛtmɑ̃], *adv.* 1. (*a*) cleanly; (*b*) clearly, distinctly; **profil n. découpé,** clear-cut, sharp-cut, profile; **journal n. révolutionnaire,** distinctly, markedly, revolutionary paper; **innocence n. établie,** innocence clearly proved; **partagé n. en deux classes,** sharply divided into two classes; **ce livre est n. pacifiste,** this book is definitely pacifist. 2. plainly, flatly; **parler n.,** to speak plainly; **il me dit n. que . . .,** he told me flatly, straight out, that. . . .

netteté [nɛt(ə)te], *s.f.* 1. cleanness (of mirror, wound, break); cleanliness (of body); *F:* slickness (of performance); **écrit avec n.,** neatly written. 2. (*a*) clearness (of water, thought, style); distinctness (of vision, of object); sharpness (of image, etc.); vividness (of memory); **d'une n. admirable,** wonderfully clear; (*b*) flatness (of refusal).

nettoie-becs [nɛtwabɛk], *s.m.inv.* probe, pricker (for acetylene jet, etc.).

nettoie-bouteilles [nɛtwabutɛːj], *s.m.inv.* bottle-washer.

nettoie-glaces [nɛtwaglas], *s.m.inv. in pl.* window-cleaner, mop.

nettoiement [nɛtwamɑ̃], *s.m.* (*a*) cleaning, clearing (of ground); (*b*) cleaning, scouring, screening (of grain, etc.); **service de n.,** refuse collection, *U.S:* garbage service.

nettoie-pipes [nɛtwapip], *s.m.inv.* smoker's combination (metal).

nettoyable [nɛtwajabl], *a.* cleanable; **filtre n. en marche,** clean-in-service strainer.

nettoyage [nɛtwajaːʒ], *s.m.* 1. cleaning; **n. à sec,** dry cleaning; **n. par le vide,** vacuum cleaning; *Petroleum Ind: etc:* **n. au chalumeau,** flame priming; **faire le n.,** to clean up; **le grand n.,** the spring-cleaning; **le n. de la semaine,** the weekly clean-up; *Mil:* **n. des tranchées,** clearing of the trenches, mopping-up; **opérations de n.,** mopping-up operations. 2. = NETTOIEMENT. 3. (act of) cleaning out.

nettoyant [nɛtwajɑ̃], *a. Agr:* **culture nettoyante,** cleaning crop.

nettoyer [nɛtwaje], *v.tr.* (**je nettoie, nous nettoyons; je nettoierai**) (*a*) to clean (room, clothes, pen, child); to scour (pan, deck); to swab (deck); to wash out (bottle, etc.); to clean, scour, screen (corn); to gin (cotton); to pickle (metal); to blow out (cylinder); **n. à grande eau,** to swill over; **n. une pièce à fond,** to turn out a room; **n.**

qch. avec **une brosse,** to brush sth. clean; **se n. les dents,** to clean one's teeth; **n. à sec,** to dry-clean; **appareil à n.,** cleaner; *Art:* **n. les contours,** to clean up the lines; (*b*) *F:* (*of burglar, thief*) **n. une maison,** to strip a house bare; **n. un homme,** to rifle a man's pockets; (*c*) **n. (un endroit) de brigands, etc.,** to rid (a place) of thieves, etc.; *Mil:* **n. les tranchées,** to clear the trenches (of remaining enemy, after attack); *F:* to mop up; (*d*) *F:* **il est rentré du club nettoyé (à sec),** he came home from the club cleaned out; (*e*) *F:* (*of disease, etc.*) to kill, carry off (s.o.); to wipe out (population).

nettoyeur, -euse [nɛtwajœːr, -øːz]. **1.** *a.* cleaning (apparatus, etc.). **2.** *s.* cleaner; *Ind:* scrubber; **n. de vitres,** window-cleaner; *Mil:* **n. de tranchée,** trench mopper-up; *Mch:* **n. de chaudières,** scurfer. **3.** *s.f.* **nettoyeuse,** cleaning machine, cleaner.

neuchâtelois, -oise [nøʃatəlwa, -waːz], *a. & s. Geog:* (native, inhabitant) of Neuchâtel.

neuf[1], *num.a.inv. & s.m.inv.* nine. **1.** *card. a.* (at the end of the word-group [nœf]; before **ans** and **heures** [nœv]; otherwise before vowel sounds [nœf]; before a noun or adj. beginning with a consonant *usu.* [nœ], often [nœf]) **j'en ai n.** [nœf], I have nine; **il a n. ans** [nœvɑ̃], he is nine years old; **n. élèves** [nœfeleːv], nine pupils; **n. francs** [nœfrɑ̃], nine francs; **les n. Muses,** [lenœfmyːz], the nine Muses; **n. petits enfants** [nœ(f)p(e)tizɑ̃fɑ̃], nine little children; **à n. heures** [nœvœːr], at nine o'clock; **n. et demi** [nœfedmi], nine and a half; **n. ou dix** [nœfudis], nine or ten. **2.** ordinal uses, etc.; (always [nœf]) **le n. mai** [lənœfmɛ], the ninth of May; **le n. avril** [lənœfavril], the ninth of April; **Louis N.,** Louis the Ninth; **le numéro n.,** number nine; **deux neufs,** two nines; *Ar:* **faire la preuve par n.,** to cast out the nines, *F:* quick check; **le n. de carreau,** the nine of diamonds, *F:* **je m'en fiche comme de l'an n.,** I don't care a rap, a hoot.

neuf[2], **neuve** [nœf nœːv], new. **1.** *a.* (*a*) (shop-) new (garment, etc.); new (thought, subject); *Num: Philately:* mint, unused; *Com:* **à l'état (de) n.,** in new condition, as new, unsoiled; (*of medal, book*) in mint state; **état n. absolu,** absolutely as new; **presque à l'état de n.,** very little the worse for wear; (almost) as good as new; **regarder qch. d'un œil n.,** to take a fresh view of sth.; *s.a.* BATTANT I. 2, FLAMBANT 1, MAISON 3; (*b*) **prés d'herbe neuve,** meadows of new grass; **pays n.,** new country; **la curiosité neuve d'un enfant,** a child's newly awakened curiosity; **jeune homme bien n.,** a very raw, green, young man; **n. aux affaires,** new to business; **n. dans son métier,** new to his trade; inexperienced; (*c*) *F:* **qu'est-ce qu'il y a de n.?** what is the news? **il n'y a rien de n.,** there is nothing new; there is no news. **2.** *s.m.* **habillé de n.,** *A. & Hum:* **de n. vêtu,** dressed in new clothes; *F:* in a new rig-out; **meublé de n.,** newly furnished; **trouver du n.,** to find sth. new; **faire du n. avec du vieux,** to make sth. new out of sth. old; **il y a du n.,** I have news for you; *adv.phr.* **à n.,** (i) anew; **écrire qch. à n.,** to write sth. out again; **refaire un mur à n.,** to rebuild a wall; (ii) **remettre qch. à n.,** to make sth. like new, as good as new; to recondition, renovate, sth.; to do sth. up; to refurbish (furniture, etc.).

neufchâtel [nøʃatɛl], *s.m. Cu:* (bung-shaped) cheese from Neufchâtel-en-Bray.

neufchâtelois, -oise [nøʃatəlwa, -waːz], *a. & s. Geog:* (native, inhabitant) of (i) Neufchâtel (Switz.); (ii) Neufchâtel-en-Bray.

neuf-huit [nœfɥit], *s.m.inv. Mus:* **1.** nine-eight time. **2.** piece in nine-eight time.

neuf-trous [nœ(f)tru], *s.m.inv. Golf:* nine-hole course.

neume [nøːm], *s.m. A.Mus:* neum(e).

neur(o)- [nør(ɔ)], *pref:* neur(o)-.

neural, -aux [nøral, -o], *a. Anat:* neural (cavity, etc.).

neurasthénie [nørasteni], *s.f. Med:* neurasthenia.

neurasthénique [nørastenik], *a. & s. Med:* neurasthenic.

neurine [nørin], *s.f. Ch:* neurine.

neuro- [nørɔ], *pref.* neuro-.

neuro-arthritisme [nørɔartritism], *s.m. Med:* neuroarthritism.

neuroblaste [nørɔblast], *s.m. Anat:* neuroblast.

neurochirurgie [nørɔʃiryrʒi], *s.f. Surg:* neurosurgery.

neurochirurgien, -ienne [nørɔʃiryrʒjɛ̃, -jɛn], *s. Surg:* neurosurgeon.

neurocirculatoire [nørɔsirkylatwaːr], *a. Med:* neurocirculatory.

neurocrinie [nørɔkrini], *s.f. Physiol:* neurocriny.

neurodermatose [nørɔdɛrmatoːz], *s.f. Med:* neurodermatitis.

neuro-épithélium [nørɔepiteljɔm], *s.m. Anat:* neuro-epithelium.

neurofibrille [nørɔfibril], *s.m. Anat:* neurofibril.

neurofibromatose [nørɔfibrɔmatoːz], *s.f. Med:* neurofibromatosis.

neurogène [nørɔʒɛn], *a. Med:* neurogenic.

neurogénèse [nørɔʒenɛːz], *s.f.* neurogenesis.

neurogliome [nørɔgljɔm], *s.m. Med:* neuroglioma.

neurokératine [nørɔkeratin], *s.f. Bio-Ch:* neurokeratin.

neuroleptique [nørɔlɛptik], *Med:* **1.** *a.* nerve sedative. **2.** *s.m.* nerve sedative; neuroleptic.

neurologie [nørɔlɔʒi], *s.f. Med:* neurology.

neurologique [nørɔlɔʒik], *a. Med:* neurological.

neurologiste [nørɔlɔʒist], **neurologue** [nørɔlɔg], *s.m. & f. Med:* nerve specialist, neurologist.

neurolymphomatose [nørɔlɛ̃fɔmatoːz], *s.f. Vet:* neurolymphomatosis.

neurolyse [nørɔliːz], *s.f. Med:* neurolysis.

neurome [nøroːm], *s.m. Med:* neuroma.

neuromusculaire [nørɔmyskylɛːr], *a.* neuromuscular.

neuromyélite [nørɔmjelit], *s.f. Opt:* **n. optique,** neuromyelitis optica.

neuronal, -aux [nørɔnal, -o], *a.* neuronal.

neurone [nørɔn, -oːn], *Physiol:* neuron.

neuronique [nørɔnik], *a.* neuronic.

neuronophage [nørɔnɔfaːʒ], *s.m. Anat:* neuronophag(e).

neuropathie [nørɔpati], *s.f. Med:* neuropathy.

neuropathologie [nørɔpatɔlɔʒi], *s.f.* neuropathology.

neurophile [nørɔfil], *a. Med:* neurophile, neurophilic.

neurophysiologie [nørɔfizjɔlɔʒi], *s.f. Med: Physiol:* neurophysiology.

neuroplégique [nørɔpleʒik], *Med:* **1.** *a.* neuroplegic. **2.** *s.m.* neuroplegic substance.

neuropsychiatre [nørɔpsikjaːtr], *s.m. & f. Med: Psy:* neuropsychiatrist.

neuropsychiatrie [nørɔpsikjatri], *s.f. Med: Psy:* neuropsychiatry.

neuropsychiatrique [nørɔpsikjatrik], *a.* neuropsychiatric.

neuropsychique [nørɔpsiʃik], *a. Med: Psy:* neuropsychic.

neuropsychologie [nørɔpsikɔlɔʒi], *s.f. Med: Psy:* neuropsychology.

neuropsychologique [nørɔpsikɔlɔʒik], *a. Med: Psy:* neuropsychologic(al).

neuroptéridées [nørɔpteride], *s.f.pl. Paleont:* Neuropterideae.

neuropteris [nørɔpteris], *s.m. Paleont:* neuropteris.

neurorétinite [nørɔretinit], *s.f. Med:* neuroretinitis.

neurorraphie [nørɔrafi], *s.f. Med:* neurorrhaphy.

neurosécrétion [nørɔsekresjɔ̃], *s.f.* neurosecretion.

neurosome [nørɔzoːm], *s.m. Anat:* neurosome.

neurotique [nørɔtik], *a. Med:* neurotic.

neurotisation [nørɔtizasjɔ̃], *s.f. Physiol:* neurotization.

neurotomie [nørɔtɔmi], *s.f. Surg: Vet:* neurotomy.

neurotoxine [nørɔtɔksin], *s.f.* neurotoxin.

neurotrope [nørɔtrɔp], **neurotropique** [nørɔtrɔpik], *a. Med:* neurotropic.

neurotropisme [nørɔtrɔpism], *s.m. Med:* neurotropism, neurotropy.

neurovégétatif, -ive [nørɔveʒetatif, -iːv], *a. Med:* neurovegetative.

neuro-viscéral, -aux [nørɔviseral, -o], *a.* neurovisceral.

neurula [nøryla], *s.f. Biol:* neurula.

neuston [nøstɔ̃], *s.m. Biol:* neuston.

Neustrie [nøstri], *Pr.n.f. A.Geog:* Neustria.

neustrien, -enne [nøstriɛ̃, -ɛn], *a. & s. Hist:* Neustrian.

neutralement [nøtralmɑ̃], *adv. Gram: etc:* neutrally.

neutralisant [nøtralizɑ̃], *Ch:* **1.** *a.* neutralizing. **2.** *s.m.* neutralizing agent.

neutralisation [nøtralizasjɔ̃], *s.f.* neutralization, neutralizing (of country, acid, etc.); *Petroleum Ind:* **indice de n.,** neutralization number.

neutraliser [nøtralize], *v.tr.* to neutralize (effort, country, acid, etc.); to compensate (torque reaction, etc.); *F:* to render harmless.

se neutraliser, (i) to become neutralized; (ii) to neutralize one another.

neutralisme [nøtralism], *s.m. Pol:* neutralism, non-alignment.

neutraliste [nøtralist], *a. & s.m. & f.* neutralist; **les pays neutralistes,** the uncommitted countries.

neutralité [nøtralite], *s.f.* **1.** neutrality (of umpire, country); **n. armée,** armed neutrality; **garder la n.,** to remain neutral; **sortir de la n.,** to take sides; **violation de la n.,** breach of neutrality. **2.** *Ch:* neutral state, neutrality (of substance); adiaphoria.

neutre [nøːtr̥], *a.* **1.** neuter; (*a*) *Gram:* **pronom n.,** neuter pronoun; *s.m.* **adjectif au n.,** adjective in the neuter; (*b*) *Bot:* **fleur n.,** neuter, asexual, sexless, flower; *Ent:* **abeille n.,** neuter bee, working bee. **2.** neutral (tint, power, flag; *Ch:* substance); *El.E:* **fil n.,** equalizing, neutral, conductor; **lunettes à verres neutres,** spectacles with plain glass; *Mil:* **la zone n.,** no-man's land; **rester n.,** to remain neutral; **je resterai tout à fait n.,** I'll be quite non-committal; *s.m.* **droits des neutres,** rights of neutrals; *Geol:* **roche n.,** neutral rock.

neutretto [nøtrɛto], *s.m. Atom.Ph:* neutretto.

neutrinien, -ienne [nøtrinjɛ̃, -jɛn], **neutrinique** [nøtrinik], *a. Atom.Ph:* pertaining to the neutrino.

neutrino [nøtrino], *s.m. Atom.Ph:* neutrino.

neutrino-astronomie [nøtrinɔastrɔnɔmi], *s.f.* that part of astronomy which deals with neutrinos.

neutrodyne [nøtrɔdin], *s.m. R.t.m: W.Tel:* Neutrodyne.

neutrodyner [nøtrɔdine], *v.tr.* to apply the principle of the Neutrodyne apparatus.

neutrographie [nøtrɔgrafi], *s.f.* photograph taken by means of a neutron beam.

neutrographier [nøtrɔgrafje], *v.tr.* to photograph by means of a neutron beam.

neutron [nøtrɔ̃], *s.m. Atom.Ph:* neutron; **n. de fission,** fission neutron; **n. à basse, de faible, énergie,** low-energy neutron; **n. de grande énergie,** high-energy neutron; **n. différé, retardé,** delayed neutron; **n. immédiat, instantané, prompt,** prompt neutron; **fraction, taux, de neutrons différés, de neutrons prompts,** delayed-neutron, prompt-neutron, fraction; **n. lent, rapide,** slow, fast, neutron; **n. froid, subthermique,** cold neutron; **n. thermique,** thermal neutron; **n. vagabond, n. erratique,** stray neutron; **n. vierge, non vierge,** virgin, non-virgin, neutron; **faisceau, pinceau, de neutrons,** neutron beam; **densité, nombre volumique, des neutrons,** neutron density; **fuite de(s) neutrons,** neutron escape, leakage.

neutronique [nøtrɔnik], *Atom.Ph:* *a.* relating to neutrons; *s.f.* study of neutrons.

neutropénie [nøtrɔpeni], *s.f. Med:* neutropenia.

neutrophile [nøtrɔfil], *a. Med:* neutrophil(e), neutrophilic.

neutrophilie [nøtrɔfili], *s.f. Med:* neutrophilia.

neuvage [nøvaːʒ], *s.m.* trial period of a new ship.

neuvain [nœvɛ̃], *s.m. Pros:* nine-line stanza.

neuvaine [nœvɛn], *s.f. Ecc:* novena, neuvaine.

neuve. *See* NEUF[2].

neuvième [nœvjɛm]. **1.** *num. a. & s.* ninth. **2.** *s.m.* ninth (part). **3.** *s.f.* (*a*) *Mus:* ninth; (*b*) (*in Fr.*) first form (of junior school).

neuvièmement [nœvjɛmmɑ̃], *adv.* ninthly.

ne varietur [nevarjetyːr], *a.inv.* not to be departed from; definitive (edition, form of return, etc.).

névé [neve], *s.m. Geol:* névé, firn.

névéen, -enne [neveɛ̃, -ɛn], *a. Geol:* **région névéenne,** (i) snow region; (ii) névé region.

neveu, -eux [nəvø], *s.m.* **1.** nephew; *F:* **n. à la mode de Bretagne,** first cousin once removed. **2.** *pl. A:* **nos neveux,** our descendants; posterity; our children's children. **3.** *Hist:* title given by the emperor of the Holy Roman Empire to the temporal electors.

névr(o)- [nevr(ɔ)], *pref.* neur(o)-.

névragmie [nevragmi], *s.f. Physiol:* neuragmia.

névralgie [nevralʒi], *s.f.* neuralgia.

névralgique [nevralʒik], *a.* neuralgic; *F:* **point n.,** trouble spot.

névraxe [nevraks], *s.m. Anat:* central nervous system, cerebrospinal axis, *A:* neuraxis.

névraxite [nevraksit], *s.f. Med:* neuraxitis.

névrectomie [nevrɛktɔmi], *s.f. Surg:* neurectomy.

névrilème [nevrilɛm], *s.m. Anat:* neurilemma.

névrine [nevrin], *s.f. Ch:* neurine.

névrite [nevrite], *s.f.* neuritis.

névritique [nevritik], *a. Med:* neuritic.

névro- [nevrɔ], *pref.* neuro-.

névrodermite [nevrɔdɛrmit], *s.f. Med:* neurodermatitis.

névrogène [nevrɔʒɛn], *a.* neurogenic.

névroglie [nevrɔgli], *s.f. Anat:* neuroglia.

névroglique [nevrɔglik], *a. Med:* neurogliac, neurogliar, neuroglial.

névrokératine [nevrɔkeratin], *s.f. Bio-Ch:* neurokeratin.

névrologie [nevrɔlɔʒi], *s.f. Med:* neurology.

névrologique [nevrɔlɔʒik], *a.* neurological.

névrome [nevrom], *s.m. Med:* neuroma.
névropathe [nevrɔpat], *s.m. & f.* neuropath.
névropathie [nevrɔpati], *s.f. Med:* neuropathy.
névropathique [nevrɔpatik], *a. Med:* neuropathic.
névropathologie [nevrɔpatɔlɔʒi], *s.f.* neuropathology.
névroptère [nevrɔptɛːr], *Ent:* **1.** *a. & s.m.* neuropteran. **2.** *s.m.pl.* **névroptères,** neuroptera.
névroptéridées [nevrɔpteride], *s.f. pl. Paleont:* Neuropterideae.
nevropteris [nevrɔpteris], *s.m. Paleont:* neuropteris.
névroptéroïdes [nevrɔpterɔid], *s.m.pl. Ent:* Neuropteroidea.
névrose [nevroːz], *s.f. Med:* neurosis.
névrosé, -ée [nevroze], *a. & s. Med:* neurotic, neurasthenic (patient).
névrosique [nevrozik], *a. Med:* neurotic.
névrosisme [nevrozism], *s.m. Med:* nervous diathesis; nervous predisposition.
névrotique [nevrɔtik], *a. Med:* neurotic (drug).
névrotomie [nevrɔtɔmi], *s.f.* neurotomy.
newberyite [njuberiit], *s.f. Miner:* newberyite.
new-look [njuluk], *s.m. Com: Pol: etc:* new look.
newmaniste [njumanist]. **1.** *a.* relating to Newmanism. **2.** *s.* Newmanite.
newton [njutɔn], *s.m. Ph:* newton.
newtonianisme [njutɔnjanism, nø-], *s.m.* Newtonianism.
newtonien, -ienne [njutɔnjɛ̃, nø-, -jɛn], *a. & s.* Newtonian.
newtonisme [njutɔnism, nø-], *s.m.* = NEWTONIANISME.
newyorkais, -aise [njujɔrkɛ, nœj-, -ɛːz]. **1.** *a.* of New York. **2.** *s.* New-Yorker.
nez [ne], *s.m.* **1.** nose; (*a*) **avoir le nez bouché,** to be blocked up; **voilà un beau n. à porter lunettes!** a fine nose for a pair of spectacles! **parler, chanter, du n.,** to speak, sing, through one's nose; *F:* **s'arracher le n. pour faire dépit à son visage,** to cut off one's nose to spite one's face; **mener, conduire, qn par le bout du n.,** to lead s.o. by the nose, to push s.o. around, to twist s.o. round one's little finger; **un pauvre homme que sa femme mène par le bout du n.,** a poor hen-pecked husband; **fourrer son n. partout,** to poke, thrust, one's nose into everything; **fourrer le n. dans,** to pry into; **baisser le n.,** to look ashamed; **ça lui pendait au n.,** he had it coming to him; **cela lui pend au n.,** *A:* **autant lui en pend au n.,** it, the same thing, may very well happen to him any day, *F:* he's due for it; **qui sait ce qui nous pend au n.?** who knows what's in store for us? **ton n. remue! ton n. branle!** you're telling a lie! you're fibbing! **faire un pied de n. à qn,** to cock a snook at s.o.; *F: A:* **avoir un pied de n.,** to look crestfallen; *P:* **je l'ai dans le n.,** I can't stand him; **tordre le n. sur qch.,** to turn up one's nose at sth.; *P:* **si on te pressait le n. il en sortirait du lait,** you're still wet behind the ears; **se piquer le nez,** to get drunk; **avoir un coup dans le n.,** to be drunk; **avoir un verre dans le n.,** to be a bit squiffy; **cela se voit comme le n. au milieu du visage,** that's as plain as the nose on my face, as plain as a pikestaff; **allonger le n., avoir le n. long,** *F:* **(en) faire un n.,** to pull a long face; **cela te passera sous le n.,** that'll be just beyond your grasp; **tirer les vers du n.,** to invite confidences; **il ne voit pas plus loin que le bout de son n.,** he can't see beyond the end of his nose; (*of horse*) **porter le n. au vent,** to star-gaze; *F:* **se promener le n. au vent,** to be on the lookout for opportunities; *F:* **n. à n.,** face to face; (*of ships, motor cars, etc.*) **se rencontrer n. à n.,** to meet head on; **montrer son n., le bout de son n., quelque part,** to show one's face somewhere; **il ne met jamais le n. à la fenêtre,** he never shows his face at the window; **regardez donc quel n. il fait,** do look at the face he's pulling; **avoir le n. dans son livre,** to have one's nose in a book; **regarder qn sous le n.,** to look defiantly at s.o.; **faire, dire, qch., au n. (et à la barbe) de qn,** to do sth. under s.o.'s very nose; to say sth. to s.o.'s face; **fermer la porte au n. de qn,** to shut the door in s.o.'s face; **jeter qch. au n. de qn,** (i) to throw sth. in s.o.'s face; (ii) to throw sth. in s.o.'s teeth; **rire au n. de qn,** to laugh in s.o.'s face; **on lui a ri au n.,** they simply laughed at him; **faire qch. à vue de n.,** to do sth. (i) at first sight, (ii) in a rough and ready way; **à vue de n. cela vaut vingt francs,** at a rough estimate it is worth twenty francs; **cela n'est pas pour ton n.,** that's not for you, *F:* for the likes of you; **se casser le n. contre qn,** to knock up against s.o.; **se casser le n.,** (i) to find the door closed, to find nobody at home; (ii) to come a cropper; (*of two persons*) **se manger, se bouffer, le n.,** to quarrel; *s.a.* LAVER 1, MARMITE 1, PIQUER 2, SAIGNER 1; (*b*) sense of smell; (*of dogs*) scent; **avoir bon n., le n. fin,** (i) to be keen-scented; to have a good nose, a keen sense of smell; (ii) *F:* to be shrewd, far-seeing; **chien qui a du n.,** dog that has good scent; **vous avez eu bon n. en achetant . . .,** you were well inspired to buy . . .; **avoir le n. creux,** to be shrewd, far-seeing; **avoir le n. dur,** to have a poor sense of smell. **2.** *Tchn:* (*nose-shaped object*) (*a*) *Nau: Av: Aer:* nose, bow, head (of ship, dirigible); nose (of aircraft); *Nau:* **navire sur le n.,** ship (down) by the head, down by the bow(s); ship trimmed by the head; **mettre le n. dans la lame, dans la plume, piquer du n.,** to dive into it, into the seas; to nose-dive; *Av:* **cône de n.,** nose cone; **lourd du n.,** nose-, bow-, heavy; **lourdeur dans le n.,** nose-heavy, bow-heavy, condition; nose, bow, heaviness; **roulette de n.,** nose-wheel; **logement de roulette de n.,** nose-gear well; (*of aircraft*) **lever le n.,** to nose-lift; **piquer du n.,** to nose-dive, to nose-down; (*b*) nosing (of step); (*c*) nose-piece (of engine); *Tchn:* **n. de raccord,** nose-piece, stud-union, stud-coupling; (*d*) nose (of spindle); (*e*) lug (of flat tile, of cotter); (*f*) (*of spacecraft*) nozzle; (*g*) *Geog:* head, nose, ness; (*h*) *Bot:* **n. coupé,** St. Anthony's nut.
Nez-percé [nepɛrse], *s.m. Ethn:* pierced-nose Indian; *pl. Nez-percés.*
ni [ni], *conj.* (**ne** is either expressed or implied) nor, or; (*a*) **ni moi (non plus),** nor I (either), neither do, did, shall, I; **jamais Mlle Dupont ni sa sœur n'étaient sorties seules,** never had Mlle Dupont or her sister gone out alone; **il arriva sans argent ni bagages,** he arrived without money or luggage; **il ne semble pas l'avoir laissé ici ni chez lui,** he does not appear to have left it here or at home; (*b*) **il ne mange ni ne boit,** he neither eats nor drinks; **je ne l'aime ni ne l'aime pas,** I neither like nor dislike her; **il est parti sans manger ni boire,** he went off without (either) eating or drinking; (*c*) **ni . . ., ni,** neither . . . nor; **ni Pierre ni Henri ne sont** (*occ.* **n'est**) **là,** neither Peter nor Henry is there; **je n'ai ni femme ni enfant ni amis,** I have neither wife nor child nor friends; **il ne veut ni manger ni boire,** he will neither eat nor drink; **ni l'un ni l'autre ne l'a vu,** neither (of them) saw it; **ni d'un côté ni de l'autre,** on neither side; **ce n'est ni plus ni moins qu'un crime,** it is neither more nor less than a crime; NOTE: **ni** *seldom introduces a clause,* "I will not apologize, nor will I admit that I am wrong" *is best translated* **"Je ne ferai pas d'excuses et je n'admets pas non plus que j'aie tort."**
niable [njabl̩], *a.* deniable; *Jur:* traversable.
niacine [njasin], *s.f. Pharm:* niacin.
Niagara (le) [lənjagara], *Pr.n.m. Geog:* the (river) Niagara; **les chutes du N.,** the Niagara Falls.
niais, -aise [njɛ, -ɛːz]. **1.** *a.* (*a*) simple, foolish (person, answer, air); inane (smile); **il n'est pas si n. qu'il en a l'air,** he isn't so soft, isn't such a fool, isn't so green, as he looks; **je ne suis pas assez n. pour . . .,** I know better than to . . .; **rire n.,** vacuous laugh; (*b*) *Falconry: A:* nyas, eyas, unfledged. **2.** *s.* fool, simpleton; **c'est un n. de Sologne,** he pretends to be silly (in order to dupe others), he's not such a fool as he makes himself out to be; **faire le n.,** to act the simpleton; **elle fait la niaise,** she pretends to know nothing; **petite niaise!** you little silly! *Th:* **jouer les niais,** to play the part of the fool.
niaisement [njɛzmɑ̃], *adv.* foolishly, in a silly manner; **rire n.,** to laugh like a fool; to give a silly, vacuous, laugh.
niaiser [njeze], *v.i.* to fool away one's time; to play the fool.
niaiserie [njɛz(ə)ri], *s.f.* **1.** silliness, foolishness. **2. dire des niaiseries,** to talk nonsense; to make silly, vacuous, remarks.
niaouli [njauli], *s.m. Bot:* niaouli.
nib [nib], *adv. & pron.inv. P:* = **pas, rien; n. de n.,** nothing at all; sweet Fanny Adams, not a sausage; **n. de braise,** no money.
niblick [niblik], *s.m. Golf:* niblick.
Nicaise [nikɛːz]. **1.** *Pr.n.m. Ecc.Hist:* Nicasius. **2.** *s.m. F:* = NICODÈME 2.
nicandre [nikɑ̃dr̥], *s.f.,* **nicandra** [nikɑ̃dra], *s.m. Bot:* Nicandra.
nicaraguayen, -enne [nikaragwajɛ̃, -ɛn], *a. & s. Geog:* Nicaraguan.
niccolite [nikɔlit], *s.f. Miner:* niccolite.
niccolo [nikɔlo], *s.m. Miner:* nic(c)olo.
nicdouille [nikduːj], *s.m.* simpleton.
nice [nis], *a. A:* simple, foolish.
Nicée [nise], *Pr.n.f. A.Geog:* Nicaea; **les conciles de Nicée,** the Nicene Councils; *Theol:* **le symbole de Nicée,** the Nicene Creed.
nicéen, -enne [niseɛ̃, -ɛn], *a.* Nicene.
niche[1] [niʃ], *s.f.* **1.** (*a*) niche, nook, recess, alcove (in wall, room, trench-parapet, etc.); **n. de jardin,** arbour; *Civ.E: Min: etc:* **n. de refuge,** refuge-hole (in tunnel); (*b*) *Geol:* alcove; **n. de rongement glaciaire,** ice-scour notch; (*c*) *Biol:* **n. écologique,** biotope. **2. n. à chien,** dog-kennel.
niche[2], *s.f. F:* trick, prank; **faire une n. à qn,** to play a trick, a practical joke, on s.o.
niche-abri [niʃabri], *s.f. Mil:* (1914-18) dug-out; *pl. niches-abris.*
nichée [niʃe], *s.f.* nest(ful) of birds); brood (of ducklings; *F:* of children); litter (of mice, puppies).
nicher [niʃe]. **1.** *v.i.* (*a*) (*of bird*) to build a nest, to nest; (*b*) *F:* to live, dwell; **où nichez-vous?** *F:* where do you hang out? **2.** *v.tr.* to put, lodge (in a nest or niche); to niche; **statue nichée dans une embrasure,** statue placed, set, in a recess.
se nicher, (*a*) (*of bird*) **se n. dans un arbre,** to build its nest in a tree; **couvée nichée dans les branches,** brood nested, nesting, among the branches; **maisonnette nichée dans un bois,** cottage nestling in a wood, lying half-hidden in a wood; *F:* **je ne sais où (aller) me nicher,** I don't know where to find a house, lodgings, somewhere to live; *F:* **où la vertu va-t-elle se n.?** who could expect to find virtue there? (*b*) to ensconce oneself (**dans,** in); **niché dans un fauteuil,** ensconced in an armchair.
nichet [niʃɛ], *s.m. Husb:* nest-egg.
nicheur, -euse [niʃœːz]. **1.** *a.* nest-building, nesting (bird). **2.** *s m. Husb:* nest with a nest-egg.
nichoir [niʃwaːr], *s.m. Husb:* breeding-cage, -coop, nesting-box.
nichon [niʃɔ̃], *s.m. P:* breast, *P:* tit; *P:* **faux nichons,** falsies.
nickel [nikɛl], *s.m.* **1.** (*a*) nickel; *s.a.* ACIER 1; (*b*) nickel fitting. **2.** *a. P:* **c'est drôlement n.,** it's spick and span; that's great.
nickelage [niklaːʒ], *s.m.* nickelling, nickel-plating.
nickel-carbonyle [nikɛlkarbɔnil], *s.m. Ch:* nickel-carbonyl; *pl. nickels-carbonyles.*
nickelé [nikle], *a.* nickelled; nickel-plated; *F:* **avoir les pieds nickelés,** to refuse to agree to sth.; *F:* to sit tight, to refuse to budge.
nickeler [nikle], *v.tr.* (**je nickelle, n. nickelons; je nickellerai**) to nickel; to nickel-plate.
nickelgymnite [nikɛlʒimnit], *s.f. Miner:* nickel gymnite.
nickélifère [nikelifɛːr], *a. Miner:* nickel-bearing, nickeliferous.
nickéline [nikelin], *s.f. Miner:* niccolite, kupfernickel.
nickélique [nikelik], *a.* nickelic.
nickelure [niklyːr], *s.f.* nickelling.
nicobar [nikɔbaːr], *s.m. Orn:* Nicobar pigeon.
nicobarais, -aise [nikɔbarɛ, -ɛːz]. **1.** *a. & s. Geog:* Nicobarese. **2.** *s.m. Ling:* Nicobarese.
Nicodème [nikɔdɛːm]. **1.** *Pr.n.m. B.Hist:* Nicodemus. **2.** *s.m. F:* ninny; simpleton, simple Simon.
niçois, -oise [niswa, -waːz]. **1.** *a. & s. Geog:* (native, inhabitant) of Nice; *Cu:* **salade niçoise,** raw vegetable salad with anchovies and hard-boiled eggs. **2.** *s.m. Ling:* Provençal dialect spoken in Nice.
nicol [nikɔl], *s.m. Opt:* Nicol (prism).
nicolaïsme [nikɔlaism], *s.m. Rel.H:* doctrine of the Nicolaitans.
nicolaïte [nikɔlait], *s.m. Rel.H:* Nicolaitan.
Nicolas [nikɔla]. **1.** *Pr.n.m.* Nicholas. **2.** *s.m. F:* = NICODÈME 2.
Nicolet [nikɔlɛ], *Pr.n.m. A:* **c'est de plus en plus fort, comme chez N.,** they go one better every day; (as at Nicolet's theatre in the 18th century).
Nicolette [nikɔlɛt], *Pr.n.f.* Nicolette.
Nicomède [nikɔmɛd], *Pr.n.m. A.Hist:* Nicomedes.
nicotéine [nikɔtein], *s.f. Ch:* nicotein.
nicotiane [nikɔsjan], *s.f. Bot:* nicotiana.
nicotine [nikɔtin], *s.f. Ch:* nicotine.
nicotinique [nikɔtinik], *a. Ch:* nicotinic.
nicotiniser [nikɔtinize], *v.tr.* to nicotinize.
nicotinisme [nikɔtinism], *s.m. Med:* nicotinism.
nicotique [nikɔtik], *a.* nicotian.
nictation [niktasjɔ̃], *s.f.,* **nictitation** [niktitasjɔ̃], *s.f.* nictation, nictitation.
nicter [nikte], *v.i.* (*of horse*) to nict(it)ate.
nictitant [niktitɑ̃], *a. Z: etc:* nictitating (membrane, eyelid).
nid [ni], *s.m.* **1.** nest (of bird, mouse, ant, etc.); **n. d'ange,** baby's sleeping bag; **faire, façonner, un n.,** to build a nest; *F:* **trouver le n. vide,** to find the bird flown; **pondre au n. de qn,** to have an affair with s.o. else's wife; **trouver la pie au n.,** (i) to find exactly what one is looking for, to

have a lucky find; (ii) *Iron:* to discover a mare's-nest; **mettre une poule au n.**, to set a hen; *Prov:* **petit à petit l'oiseau fait son n.**, little and often fills the purse, little strokes fell great oaks; **à tout oiseau son n. est beau,** home is home, be it never so homely; *F:* **écraser une révolte au n.**, to nip a rising in the bud, to crush a revolt at birth; **n. de brigands,** robbers' den, robbers' retreat; **n. à rats,** (i) rat's nest; (ii) *F:* poky little room, wretched hole of a place; **n. à poussière,** dust-trap; *s.a.* ABEILLE. **2.** *Mil:* (*a*) **n. de mitrailleuses,** nest of machine-guns; (*b*) **n. à bombes, à obus,** dangerous spot; (*c*) **n. de pie,** (i) *Fort: A:* lodgement in an outwork; (ii) *Nau:* crow's nest; **n. de poule,** pot-hole (in road); *Navy:* **n. de sous-marins,** submarine pen; *s.a.* CORBEAU 2. **3.** *Min:* pocket (of ore).

nidation [nidasjɔ̃], *s.f. Physiol:* nidation, implantation.

nid-d'abeilles [nidabɛːj], *s.m. Tex:* honeycomb; *pl. nids-d'abeilles.*

nid-de-pie [nid(ə)pi], *s.m.* **1.** *Fort: A:* lodgement in an outwork. **2.** *Nau:* crow's nest; *pl. nids-de-pie.*

nid-de-poule [nid(ə)pul], *s.m.* pothole (in road); *pl. nids-de-poule.*

nidicole [nidikɔl], *a. Orn:* nidicolous; altricial.

nidificateur, -trice [nidifikatœːr, -tris], (*a*) *a.* nest-building; (*b*) *s.* nest builder.

nidification [nidifikasjɔ̃], *s.f.* nidification, nest-building.

nidifier [nidifje], *v.i.* to nidify; to build a nest.

nidifuge [nidifyːʒ], *a. Orn:* nidifugous, precocial.

nidoreux, -euse [nidɔrø, -øːz], *a.* foul-smelling, fetid; which smells of rotten eggs, of hydrogen sulphide.

nid-trappe [nitrap], *m. Husb:* trap-nest (of hen-house); *pl. nids-trappes.*

nièce [njɛs], *s.f.* niece; **n. à la mode de Bretagne,** first cousin once removed.

niellage [njɛlaːʒ], *s.m.* **1.** inlaying with niello; niello-work. **2.** inlaid enamel-work.

nielle[1] [njɛl], *s.f. Agr:* ear-cockle; *F:* smut, blight (of wheat).

nielle[2], *s.f. Bot:* **n. des blés,** corn-cockle.

nielle[3], *s.m. Metalw:* niello, inlaid enamel-work.

nieller[1] [njele], *v.tr. Agr:* to smut, to blight; **blé niellé,** blighted corn.

nieller[2], *v.tr.* to inlay with niello; **sabre niellé,** nielloed sword.

nielleur [njɛlœːr], *s.m.* niellist, niello-worker.

niellure[1] [njelyːr], *s.f. Agr:* blighting (of cereals, etc.).

niellure[2], *s.f.* niello-work.

nième [enjɛm], *a. & s.m. F:* nth; **je te le dis pour la n. fois,** I'm telling you for the nth, umpteenth, time.

nier [nje], *v.tr.* (*p.d. & pr.sub.* **n. niions, v. niiez**) (*a*) to deny; **n. un fait,** to deny, *Jur:* to traverse, a fact; *abs.* **l'accusé nie,** the accused denies the charge, pleads not guilty; **n. une vérité,** to deny a truth; **n. Dieu,** to deny God; **je nie l'avoir vu,** I deny having seen him; *A:* **n. d'avoir fait qch.,** to deny having done sth.; *B:* **et Sara nia d'avoir ri,** then Sarah denied, saying, I laughed not; (*still frequent in the neg.*) **il ne nia pas d'avoir trempé dans le meurtre,** he did not deny having had a hand in the murder; **je nie qu'il m'ait vu,** I deny that he saw me; **je ne nie pas que nous avons des intérêts en commun, que nous (n')ayons des intérêts en commun,** I do not deny that we have common interests; **il n'y a pas à le n.,** there is no denying it, *F:* no getting away from it; **on ne saurait n. que . . .,** there can be no denying that . . .; **les lettres qu'il avait nié avoir reçues,** the letters that he had denied having received; (*b*) **n. une dette,** to repudiate a debt.

nière [njɛːr], *s.m. P:* chap; **bon n.,** bon viveur.

nietzschéen, -enne [nitʃeɛ̃, -ɛn], *a. Phil:* Nietzschean.

nietzsch(é)isme [nitʃ(e)ism], *s.m. Phil:* Nietzschism.

nifé [nife], *s.m. Geol:* nife.

nigaud, -aude [nigo, -oːd]. **1.** (*a*) *s.* simpleton, booby, fool, *F:* fat-head, mutt, clot, *f.* silly girl; **c'est un n.,** he can't say boo to a goose; **quel n.!** what an ass! **mon grand n. de fils,** my big fool of a son; (*b*) *a.* **elle est un peu nigaude,** she's rather silly, simple. **2.** *s.m.* (*a*) *Orn:* booby, gannet; (*b*) *Cards:* Russian patience.

nigauder [nigode], *v.i. O: F:* to play the fool, to trifle.

nigauderie [nigodri], *s.f. O: F:* **1.** stupidity, simplicity; **être d'une incroyable n.,** to be incredibly simple, green. **2.** piece of stupidity; **commettre une n.,** to do a silly thing, to put one's foot in it.

nigelle [niʒɛl], *s.f. Bot:* nigella, fennel-flower, love-in-a-mist, devil-in-the-bush.

Niger (le) [ləniʒɛːr], *Pr.n.m. Geog:* (*a*) the (river) Niger; (*b*) (*state*) Niger.

Nigéria [niʒerja], *Pr.n.f. or m. Geog:* Nigeria; **au N.,** in Nigeria.

Nigérian, -iane [niʒerjɑ̃, -jan], *a. & s.* Nigerian.

Nigérien, -ienne [niʒerjɛ̃, -jɛn], *a. & s.* (native, inhabitant) of the Niger republic.

nigrescent [nigrɛs(s)ɑ̃], *a.* nigrescent.

nigrine [nigrin], *s.f. Miner:* nigrine.

nigrite [nigrit], *s.f. El.E:* nigrite.

Nigritie [nigrisi], *Pr.n. A: Geog:* Nigritia, the Sudan.

nigritique [nigritik], *a. Ethn:* Nigritic.

nigrosine [nigrɔzin], *s.f. Ch:* nigrosin(e).

niguedouille [nigduːj]. **1.** *s.m. & f.* idiot, imbecile. **2.** *a.* idiotic.

nihilisme [niilism], *s.m. Phil: Pol:* nihilism.

nihiliste [niilist]. **1.** *a.* nihilist(ic). **2.** *s.* nihilist.

Nil (le) [lənil], (*a*) *Pr.n.m. Geog:* the (river) Nile; (*b*) *adj.phr.inv. Ch:* **bleu de N.,** Nile-blue; **(vert de) N.,** eau-de-nil.

nilgau(t) [nilgo], *s.m. Z:* nylghau, nilgau, nilgai; blue bull; *pl. nilgau(t)s.*

nille [niːj], *s.f.* **1.** loose handle (of crank, tool, etc.). **2.** tendril (of vine).

nilomètre [nilɔmɛtr̥], *s.m.*, **niloscope** [nilɔskɔp], *s.m.* nilometer.

nilotique [nilɔtik], *a. Geog:* nilotic (race, mud, etc.).

nilpotent [nilpɔtɑ̃], *a. Mth:* nilpotent.

nimbe [nɛ̃ːb], *s.m.* nimbus, halo, glory (in paintings, etc.).

nimbé [nɛ̃be], *a.* haloed, nimbused (head, etc.).

nimber [nɛ̃be], *v.tr.* to halo (head, etc.); to create the illusion of a halo around; to suffuse (**de,** with).

nimbo-stratus [nɛ̃bɔstratys], *s.m.inv. Meteor:* nimbo-stratus.

nimbus [nɛ̃bys], *s.m. Meteor:* nimbus; rain-cloud.

Nimègue [nimɛg], *Pr.n.f. Geog:* Nijmegen.

nîmois, -oise [nimwa, -waːz], *a. & s. Geog:* (native, inhabitant) of Nîmes.

ninas [ninas], *s.m.inv.* small cigar, whiff.

Ninette [ninɛt], *Pr.n.f.* (*Dim. of Ninon*) Ninon.

n-i-ni [ɛnini], *a.inv. used only in F:* **n-i-ni,** c'est **fini,** (i) that's an end to that; (ii) it's all over between us.

Ninive [niniːv], *Pr.n.f. A.Geog:* Nineveh.

ninivite [ninivit], *a. & s.* Ninevite.

Ninon [ninɔ̃], *Pr.n.f. Hist:* Ninon (de Lenclos); **cheveux à la N.,** bobbed hair.

Niobé [njɔbe], *Pr.n.f. Myth:* Niobe.

niobium [njɔbjɔm], *s.m. Ch:* columbium, niobium.

niortais, -aise [njɔrtɛ, -ɛːz], *a. & s. Geog:* (native, inhabitant) of Niort.

Niphon [nifɔ̃], *Pr.n.m. Geog:* Nippon.

nippe [nip], *s.f. normally used in the pl. F:* **1.** *A:* garments. **2.** togs, rig out; **je n'ai plus une n. à me mettre,** I haven't a rag to my back.

nipple [nipl̥], *s.m. Tchn:* nipple.

nipper [nipe], *v.tr. F:* to fit (s.o.) out; to rig (s.o.) out; **personne bien nippée,** person well supplied with clothes, well rigged out.

se nipper, (*a*) to fit or rig oneself out; (*b*) to buy a trousseau.

nippon, -one [nipɔ̃, -ɔn]. **1.** *Pr.n.m. Geog:* **Nippon,** Nippon. **2.** *a. & s.* Nipponese, Japanese.

nique [nik], *s.f. used only in F:* **faire la n. à qn,** to make a long nose at s.o.; to cock a snook at s.o.; *A:* **faire la n. à qch.,** to despise sth.; to treat (riches, fame, etc.) with contempt; to snap one's fingers at sth.

niquedouille [nikduːj], *a. & s.m. & f.* = NIGUEDOUILLE.

niquetage [niktaːʒ], *s.m.* = ANGLAISAGE.

niqueter [nikte], *v.tr.* = ANGLAISER 1.

nirvâna, nirvana [nirvana], *s.m.* nirvana, nirwana, (Buddhist) state of beatitude; *Psy:* **principe de n.,** nirvana principle.

nirvanisme [nirvanism], *s.m.* cult of nirvana.

nisetru [nizetry], *s.m. Ich:* nisetru (sturgeon).

nitescence [nitɛs(s)ɑ̃ːs], *s.f.* lustre, dazzling, brightness.

nitouche [nituʃ], *s.f. F:* **sainte n.,** little hypocrite; **jouer les saintes n.,** to play the hypocrite; **c'est une sainte n., elle fait la sainte n.,** butter wouldn't melt in her mouth; **un petit air de sainte n.,** a demure look.

nitraniline [nitranilin], *s.f. Ch:* nitroaniline.

nitrant [nitrɑ̃], *a. Ch:* nitriding.

nitratation [nitratasjɔ̃], *s.f. Ch: Agr:* conversion (in the soil) of nitrites into nitrates.

nitrate [nitrat], *s.m. Ch:* nitrate; **n. d'argent,** silver nitrate; **n. de potassium,** potassium nitrate, nitre.

nitraté [nitrate], *a. Ch:* nitrated.

nitrater [nitrate], *v.tr. Ch:* to nitrate.

nitratier, -ière [nitratje, -jɛːr], *a.* pertaining to nitrates; **exploitation nitratière,** exploitation of nitrate fields; *St.Exch:* **(valeurs) nitratières,** nitrate shares; nitrates.

nitratine [nitratin], *s.f. Miner:* nitratine.

nitration [nitrasjɔ̃], *s.f. Ch:* nitration.

nitre [nitr̥], *s.m.* nitre, saltpetre.

nitré [nitre], *a. Ch:* nitrated; **composé n.,** nitro-compound.

nitreux, -euse [nitrø, -øːz], *a. Ch:* nitrous (acid, soil, etc.).

nitrière [nitrijɛːr], *s.f.* **1.** nitrebed, saltpetrebed. **2.** nitreworks.

nitrifiant [nitrifjɑ̃], *a. Ch:* nitrifying.

nitrification [nitrifikasjɔ̃], *s.f. Ch:* nitrification.

nitrifier [nitrifje], *v.tr. Ch:* to nitrify.

se nitrifier, to nitrify; to turn into nitre, become nitrous.

nitrile [nitril], *s.m. Ch:* nitril(e).

nitrique [nitrik], *a. Ch:* nitric (acid).

nitrite [nitrit], *s.m. Ch:* nitrite.

nitro- [nitrɔ], *comb.fm. Ch:* nitro-(compound).

nitro-alcane [nitrɔalkan], *s.m. Ch:* nitroparaffin.

nitrobacter [nitrɔbaktɛːr], *s.m.*, **nitrobactérie** [nitrɔbakteri], *s.f. Biol:* nitrobacter; nitric bacterium; nitrobacteria.

nitrobaryte [nitrɔbarit], *s.f. Miner:* nitrobaryte.

nitrobenzène [nitrɔbɛ̃zɛn], *s.m.*, **nitrobenzine** [nitrɔbɛ̃zin], *s.f. Ch:* nitrobenzine; *Com:* mirbane, oil of mirbane.

nitrocalcite [nitrɔkalsit], *s.f. Miner:* nitrocalcite.

nitrocellulose [nitrɔsɛlyloːz], *s.f. Exp:* nitrocellulose.

nitrocellulosique [nitrɔsɛlylɔzik], *a.* nitrocellulosic.

nitrochloroforme [nitrɔklɔrɔfɔrm], *s.m. Ch:* nitrochloroform.

nitrocoton [nitrɔkɔtɔ̃], *s.m. Exp: A:* gun-cotton.

nitrogélatine [nitrɔʒelatin], *s.f. Exp:* gelatine dynamite.

nitrogène [nitrɔʒɛn], *s.m. A:* (= AZOTE) nitrogen.

nitroglycérine [nitrɔgliserin], *s.f. Exp:* nitroglycerine.

nitrométhane [nitrɔmetan], *s.m. Ch:* nitromethane.

nitromètre [nitrɔmɛtr̥], *s.m.* nitrometer.

nitronaphtalène [nitrɔnaftalɛn], *s.m. Ch:* nitronaphthalene.

nitronium [nitrɔnjɔm], *s.m. Ch:* nitronium.

nitroparaffine [nitrɔparafin], *s.f. Ch:* nitroparaffin.

nitrophénol [nitrɔfenɔl], *s.m. Ch:* nitrophenol.

nitrophile [nitrɔfil], *a. Bot:* nitrophytic; nitrophilous; **plante n.,** nitrophyte.

nitrosate [nitrɔzat], *s.m. Ch:* nitrosate.

nitrosation [nitrɔzasjɔ̃], *s.f. Ch:* nitrosation.

nitrosite [nitrɔzit], *s.m. Ch:* nitrosite.

nitrosomonas [nitrɔzɔmɔnas], *s.m.* nitrosomonas.

nitrotoluène [nitrɔtɔlɥɛn], *s.m. Ch:* nitrotoluene.

nitruration [nitryrasjɔ̃], *s.f. Ch:* nitriding, nitridation; *s.a.* ACIER.

nitrure [nitryːr], *s.m. Ch:* nitride.

nitruré [nitryre], *Ch: Ind:* **1.** *a.* nitrided. **2.** *s.m.* nitride.

nitrurer [nitryre], *v.tr.* to nitride.

nitryle [nitril], *s.m. Ch:* nitroxyl, nitryl.

nival, -aux [nival, -o], *a.* nival.

nivation [nivasjɔ̃], *s.f. Geol:* nivation; **niche de n.,** nivation cirque.

nive [niːv], *s.f. Dial:* (*in Pyrenees*) torrent.

nivéal, -aux [niveal, -o], *a.* winter-flowering (plant).

niveau, -eaux [nivo], *s.m.* level. **1.** (*instrument*) (*a*) clinometer; **n. à bulle d'air,** air, spirit, level; **n. d'eau,** water-level; **n. de maçon, à plomb,** mason's level, vertical level, plumb level, plumb rule; *Surv:* **n. à lunette,** surveyor's level; *Rail:* **n. de poseur de rails, de poseur de voies,** platelayer's, track-layer's, level; *Phot:* **viseur à n.,** view finder and level combined; (*b*) *Mch: etc:* gauge level; **n. d'eau,** water gauge; **n. d'huile,** oil gauge; *Aut:* **n. d'essence,** petrol gauge. **2.** (*a*) *Ph:* **n. de bruit,** noise level; **n. (d'intensité) sonore, n. du son,** sound level; **n. d'énergie, n. énergétique,** energy level; **n. d'énergie nul,** zero-energy level; **baisse, hausse, de n.,** drop, rise, of level; (*b*) *Surv: etc:* **le n. de l'eau, de la mer,** the level of the water, of the sea; water, sea, level; **pression au n. de la mer,** sea-level pressure; **n. moyen de la mer,** mean sea-level; **n. des basses, des hautes, eaux,** low-water, high-water, mark; **le n. des eaux monte,** the waters are gathering head; **être de n.,** to be level; **nous sommes à n. de Grenoble,** we are on a level with Grenoble, at the same altitude as Grenoble; *Geol:* **n. minéralisé,** ore horizon; **n.**

parfait, à franc n., dead level; **n. de référence,** (i) *Surv:* datum level; (ii) *Civ.E: Mec.E:* reference level; *s.a.* COURBE 2; (c) *Civ.E: etc:* **n. des remblais,** formation-level; **n. de retenue,** top-water level (of dam); *Min:* **premier, deuxième, troisième, etc., n.,** first, second, third, etc., level; **n. profond,** deep level; **voie de n.,** level; *Const:* **immeuble à dix niveaux,** ten-floor building; **tranchée de n.,** level cutting; **mettre qch. de niveau, à niveau,** to level sth., to bring sth. to a level; **mise à n.,** levelling; *El:* **ramener l'électrolyte (de l'accu) à n.,** to top up the battery; *Nau:* **navire de n.,** boat on an even keel; *Rail:* **passage à n.,** level crossing, *U.S:* grade crossing; **passage à n. non gardé,** unattended level crossing; (d) *Mec.E:* **n. de réglage,** trueing up level; **cales de n.,** levelling lugs; **enregistreur de n.,** level recorder; **indicateur de n.,** level gauge, indicator; *Mch:* **indicateur de n. d'eau, tube de n.,** water gauge, gauge glass; **régulateur de n.,** level regulator; *Aut: etc:* **alimenté par différence de n.,** gravity-fed (carburettor, etc.); (e) *Elcs:* **n. accepteur, n. donneur,** acceptor, donor, level; *W.Tel:* **n. de réception, de transmission,** receiving, transmission, level; (f) **n. de bien-être, de vie,** standard of comfort, of living; **n. de vie élevé,** high standard of living; **n. des études,** academic level, standard; **un n. élevé de capacité intellectuelle,** a high level, high standard, high plane, of intelligence; **être au n. de qch., de qn, être de n. avec qch., avec qn,** to be on a level with sth., with s.o.; to be on a par with sth., s.o.; **se mettre, s'élever, au n. de qn,** to put oneself on a level with s.o., to rise to the level of s.o.

nivéen, -enne [niveɛ̃, -ɛn], *a.* niveous, snow-like, snowy.

nivelage [niv(ə)laːʒ], *s.m.* levelling (of ground, etc.); *Civ.E:* grading (of road, canal).

niveler [nivle], *v.tr.* (**je nivelle, n. nivelons; je nivellerai**) 1. to take the level of, to survey, contour (ground); to bone. 2. (a) to level, to even up (ground, ranks, fortunes); **n. par le bas, au plus bas,** to level down; **n. au plus haut,** to level up; (b) *Civ.E:* to grade (road, canal); (c) to line up, true up (engine, etc.).

se niveler, to become level, to settle (down); **les fortunes tendent à se n. par les partages,** fortunes tend to become equalized through the breaking up of estates.

nivelette [nivlɛt], *s.f. Civ.E:* boning rod.

niveleur, -euse [nivlœːr, -øːz]. 1. *a.* levelling. 2. *s.* (*pers.*) leveller. 3. *s.m. Agr:* small harrow. 4. *s.f. Civ.E:* niveleuse, grader.

nivellement [nivɛlmɑ̃], *s.m.* 1. *Surv:* levelling, contouring; **n. barométrique,** barometric levelling; **n. de précision,** precise levelling; **instrument de n.,** levelling instrument; **mire de n.,** levelling staff; **repère de n.,** bench mark. 2. levelling (of ground, ranks, etc.).

nivéole [niveɔl], *s.f. Bot:* snow-flake.

nivernais, -aise [nivɛrnɛ, -ɛːz]. 1. *a. & s. Geog:* (native, inhabitant) of Nevers. 2. *s.m.* **le Nivernais,** province of old France with capital Nevers. 3. *s.f. Cu:* **nivernaise,** carrot garnishing.

nivernichon, -onne [nivɛrniʃɔ̃, -ɔn], *a.* of Nevers.

niverolle [niv(ə)rɔl], *s.f. Orn:* **n. des Alpes,** snow finch.

nivet [nivɛ], *s.m.* (a) offal; (b) *F:* bribe (in business); secret commission.

niviforme [nivifɔrm], *a.* niveous, snow-like.

nivomètre [nivɔmɛtr], *s.m.* snow gauge.

nivométrique [nivɔmetrik], *a.* **sondage n.,** snow surveying.

nivôse [nivoːz], *s.m. Fr.Hist:* fourth month of Fr. Republican calendar (Dec.-Jan.)

nivosité [nivɔzite], *s.f.* snowiness.

nix(e) [niks], *s.f. Myth:* nix(ie).

nizam [nizam], *s.m.* nizam.

nizeré [niz(ə)re], *s.m.* essence of white roses (from Tunis).

nô [no], *s.m. Th:* (*Japanese*) no, noh, nogaku.

nobélite [nɔbelit], *s.f. Exp: A:* dynamite.

nobélium [nɔbeljɔm], *s.m. Ch:* nobelium.

nobiliaire [nɔbiljɛːr], *a.* nobiliary (rank, etc.); **la particule n.,** the nobiliary particle (i.e. de); **almanach n.,** *s.m.* **nobiliaire,** Peerage(-book, -list).

noblaillon [nɔblɑjɔ̃], *s.m. Pej:* member of decayed nobility.

noble [nɔbl]. 1. *a.* noble; (a) **être n. de race,** to be of noble descent, of noble birth; **famille n.,** noble family; (b) stately, lofty (air, demeanour); *Th:* **père n.,** heavy father; *s.a.* ART 1; (c) high-minded, lofty (soul, etc.); (d) *A:* **les parties nobles,** the genitals. 2. *s.* noble(man), noblewoman; **les nobles,** the nobles, the nobility. 3. *s.m. Num: A:* **n. (à la rose),** (rose-)noble.

noblement [nɔbləmɑ̃], *adv.* 1. nobly. 2. *A:* as a noble; **tenir n. une terre,** to hold an estate in fief, in fee.

noble-épine [nɔblepin], *s.f. Bot:* hawthorn.

noblesse [nɔblɛs], *s.f.* 1. nobility; (a) noble birth; **sa (haute) n. par sa mère,** his noble birth, high lineage, on his mother's side; **famille de vieille n.,** patrician family; *Prov:* **n. oblige,** the nobly born must nobly do; noblesse oblige; **n. vient de vertu,** handsome is that handsome does; *s.a.* DÉROGER; (b) **famille de n. récente,** family recently ennobled; *s.a.* LETTRE 3; (c) *coll.* **la haute et la petite n.,** the nobility and gentry; **la n. d'épée,** the old nobility; **elle voulait se marier dans la n.,** she wanted to marry into the nobility; *F:* she wanted to marry a title; *s.a.* ROBE 1. 2. nobility, nobleness (of style, heart, behaviour).

nobliau, -aux [nɔblijo], *s.m.* = NOBLAILLON.

noc [nɔk], *s.m.* 1. culvert, conduit. 2. = NOCHÈRE 1.

noce [nɔs], *s.f.* 1. (a) wedding; wedding festivities; **être de n.,** to be (a guest) at a wedding; (b) wedding party; (c) *pl. A:* marriage, nuptials; *the pl. is still usual in such phrases as* **repas de noces,** wedding breakfast; **nuit de noces,** wedding night; **voyage de noces,** honeymoon trip; **partir en voyage de noces,** to leave for the honeymoon; **robe de voyage de noces,** going-away dress; **noces d'argent, de vermeil, d'or, de diamant,** silver, ruby, golden, diamond, wedding; **épouser qn en secondes noces,** to marry for the second time; **il l'avait épousée en secondes noces,** she was his second wife. 2. *F:* (a) **faire la n.,** to be, go, on the spree, on a binge, to live it up, to have one's fling; **usé par la n.,** worn out with riotous living, by dissipation; (b) **il n'avait jamais été à pareille n.,** (i) he was having the time of his life; (ii) *Iron:* he had never seen such a mix-up, such an unholy mess; **je n'étais pas à la n.,** I was having a bad time, I was feeling very uncomfortable.

nocer [nɔse], *v.i. F:* (**je noçai(s); n. noçons**) 1. to feast. 2. (a) to go on the binge, spree; (b) to live fast.

noceur, -euse [nɔsœːr, -øːz], *s. F:* (a) reveller, roisterer; (b) fast liver; dissipated man or woman; *m.* gay dog.

nocher [nɔʃe], *s.m. Poet:* pilot, boatman; **le farouche n. du Styx,** the grim ferryman of the Styx.

nochère [nɔʃɛːr], *s.f.* 1. (wooden) gutter (under eaves). 2. leaded roof-light.

nociceptif, -ive [nɔsisɛptif, -iːv], *a. Med:* noxious.

nocif, -ive [nɔsif, -iːv], *a.* injurious, harmful, hurtful, noxious, nocuous (à, to).

nocivité [nɔsivite], *s.f.* noxiousness; harmfulness.

noctambule [nɔktɑ̃byl]. 1. *a.* noctambulant, noctambulous. 2. *s.* (a) *A:* somnambulist, sleep-walker; **il est n.,** he walks in his sleep; (b) *F:* night-bird, fly-by-night.

noctambulisme [nɔktɑ̃bylism], *s.m.* (a) *A:* noctambulism, somnambulism, sleep-walking; (b) *F:* going out on the tiles.

noctiflore [nɔktiflɔːr], *a. Bot:* noctiflorous.

noctilionidés [nɔktiljɔnide], *s.m.pl. Z:* Noctilionidae.

noctiluque [nɔktilyk], *s.f. Prot:* noctiluca.

noctoviseur [nɔktɔvizœːr], *s.m. Nau:* night finder.

noctuelle [nɔktɥɛl], *s.f. Ent:* noctua, noctuid, owlet-moth; **n. piniperde, du pin,** pine-beauty; **n. du coton,** cotton-moth.

noctuides [nɔktɥid], *s.m.pl. Ent:* Noctuid family (of moths).

noctuoidea [nɔktyɔidea], *s.m.pl.,* **noctuoïdes** [nɔktyɔid], *s.m.pl. Ent:* Noctuoidea.

noctule [nɔktyl], *s.f. Z:* noctule (bat).

nocturne [nɔktyrn]. 1. *a.* nocturnal (visit, animal); *Bot:* night-flowering; **attaque n.,** night attack; **évasion n.,** escape by night; **dans le silence n.,** in the silence of the night; *Jur:* **tapage n.,** disorder by night. 2. *s.m.* (a) *Ecc:* nocturn; (b) *Art: Mus:* nocturne, night-piece; (c) *Sp:* **match (disputé) en n.,** evening game. 3. *s.m.pl. Orn:* **nocturnes,** nocturnal birds of prey, nocturnals, night-birds.

nocturnement [nɔktyrnəmɑ̃], *adv.* by night.

nocuite [nɔkɥite], *s.f.* noxiousness.

nodal, -aux [nɔdal, -o], *a. Opt: Ph:* nodal (point, line).

noddi [nɔdi], *s.m. Orn:* **n. (niais),** noddy.

nodosité [nɔdozite], *s.f.* 1. nodosity (in plant, body). 2. node, nodule (on tree trunk, on gouty hand).

nodulaire [nɔdylɛːr]. 1. *a.* nodular (concretion, etc.); noduled; *Geol:* **filon n.,** ball-vein. 2. *s.f. Algae:* nostoc, star-jelly, witches'-butter.

nodule [nɔdyl], *s.m. Geol: Med: etc:* nodule, small node.

noduleux, -euse [nɔdylø, -øːz], *a.* nodulous (limestone, etc.).

nodus [nɔdys], *s.m. Med:* node.

noe [no], *s.f. Dial:* tidal pool.

Noé [nɔe], *Pr.n.m. B.Hist:* Noah.

noégénèse [nɔeʒenɛːz], *s.f. Psy:* noegenesis.

Noël [nɔɛl], *s.m.* 1. Christmas; Christmas-tide; yule(tide); **à la (fête de) N., à N.,** at Christmas; **le jour de N.,** Christmas day; **la nuit, la veillée, de N.,** Christmas Eve; **bûche de N.,** yule log; **arbre de N.,** (i) Christmas tree; (ii) *Min:* control manifold, Christmas tree; **carte de N.,** Christmas card; **le Bonhomme N., le Père N.,** Father Christmas, Santa Claus; **sabot de N.** = Christmas stocking; **le petit N.,** the Christ Child; **faire N. à la campagne,** to spend, celebrate, Christmas in the country; *A:* **crier N.,** to shout Nowel. 2. (a) **un n.,** a Christmas carol; (b) Christmas present.

Noémi [nɔemi], *Pr.n.f.* Naomi.

noèse [nɔɛːz], *s.f. Phil:* noesis.

nœud [nø], *s.m.* 1. (a) knot; *Nau:* hitch; bend; **n. de bec d'oiseau,** slip-knot; **n. de drisse, de bonnette,** studding-sail bend; **n. coulant,** (i) slip-knot, running knot; (ii) noose; **n. de grappin, n. d'ancre,** fisherman's bend, anchor bend; **n. droit, plat,** reef knot; **n. mal fait, de ménagère, de soldat,** granny('s bend, knot); **n. de passe,** wall knot; **n. d'ajut, de vache,** carrick bend; **n. de bois,** timber hitch; **corde à nœuds,** knotted rope; **faire, former, serrer, un n.,** to make, tie, a knot; **faire un n. à son mouchoir,** to tie a knot in one's handkerchief; **défaire un n.,** to undo, untie, a knot; **faire son n. de cravate,** to knot one's tie; **les nœuds de l'amitié, du mariage,** the bonds, ties, of friendship, of marriage; **trancher le n. gordien,** to cut the Gordian knot; *s.a.* ANGUILLE 1, BOULINE, PÊCHEUR 1; (b) coil (of snake); (c) *Lit:* **le n. d'une pièce,** the crux, knot, of a play; **le n. de la question,** the crux of the matter; (d) *Cost:* bow; **faire un n.,** to tie a bow; **n. de ruban,** bow of ribbon; **n. papillon,** bow-tie; **n. régate,** sailor's knot; *Scouting:* **n. de foulard,** woggle; **n. de diamants,** diamond cluster; *Mil: A:* **n. d'épaule,** shoulder-knot. 2. *Astr: Mth: Ph:* node (of orbit, curve, oscillation); *El: W.Tel:* **n. de potentiel, de tension,** potential node (in circuit, in aerial). 3. (a) knot, knur(l) (in timber); **n. tombant,** loose knot; (b) node, joint, knot (in stem of grass, etc.); (c) *Tex:* burl; (d) **n. de la gorge,** Adam's apple; **rire qui ne passe pas le n. de la gorge,** forced laugh; (e) *A:* **n. du doigt,** knuckle; (f) *F:* = NODUS. 4. (a) (*on roads*) **n. de communications,** centre of communication; **n. routier,** (important) road junction; *Rail:* **n. ferroviaire, n. de voies ferrées,** railway junction; *Mil:* **n. de tranchées,** (important) trench junction; (b) *Anat:* **n. vital,** vital centre (of medulla oblongata); **n. sinusal de Keith et Flack,** pace-maker (of the heart); (c) *Mec.E:* **n. de jonction,** butt-joint. 5. *Nau.Meas:* knot; **filer, faire, tant de nœuds,** to make, steam, do, so many knots; *s.a.* FILER I. 2.

nogentais, -aise [nɔʒɑ̃tɛ, -ɛːz], *a. & s. Geog:* (native, inhabitant) of Nogent-le-Rotrou, of Nogent-sur-Marne, of Nogent-sur-Seine.

noir, noire [nwaːr]. 1. *a.* black; (a) **robe noire,** black dress; **n. comme l'ébène, comme de l'encre,** as black as ebony, inky-black, coal-black; **n. comme du jais,** jet-black; **n. comme poix,** pitch-black; **n. comme une taupe,** black as sin, as a crow; **des yeux noirs,** dark eyes, jet-black eyes; *A:* **les esclaves noirs,** black ivory; **race noire,** negro race; **rendre qch. n.,** to blacken sth.; *Ven:* **bête noire,** wild boar; *Geog:* **la mer Noire,** the Black Sea; **la forêt Noire,** the Black Forest; *Art:* **dessiner au crayon n.,** to work in black and white; *s.a.* BEURRE 1, GRAVURE 1, POINT[1] 5, VIANDE 2; (b) dark, swarthy (skin, complexion); *F:* **être tout n. de coups,** to be black and blue; (c) dark (night, dungeon); gloomy (weather, thoughts); **il fait déjà n.,** it is dark already; **il faisait n. comme dans un four, il faisait nuit noire,** it was pitch dark, it was a pitch-black night; *Phot:* **chambre noire,** (i) camera obscura; (ii) camera (body); (iii) dark room; **avoir des idées noires,** to be down in the dumps, to have the blues; **les noirs chagrins, les noirs soucis,** overwhelming grief, worries; **être d'une humeur noire,** (i) to feel depressed, to have a fit of the blues; (ii) to be in a temper; **humour n.,** macabre, grim, humour; **ma bête noire,** my pet aversion; **misère noire,** dire poverty; *Th:* **four n.,** complete flop; *F:* **série noire,** series, chapter, of accidents, run of ill-luck; *adv.* **voir n.,** to see the gloomy side of everything; **regarder n.,** to scowl; (d) dirty, grimy, black (hands, nails, linen); *Petroleum*

Ind: **produit n.,** black oil; (*e*) base, black (ingratitude); wicked (calumny); heinous (crime); foul (deed); black (magic); **liste noire,** black list; **marché n.,** black market; *Pol:* **caisse noire,** bribery fund; *U.S:* boodle; **nourrir de noirs desseins,** to nurture evil intentions; **n. ou blanc il est digne de pitié,** guilty or innocent, he is to be pitied; *Prov:* **le diable n'est pas si n. qu'on le dit,** the devil is not as black as he's painted; **il n'est pas aussi diable qu'il est n.,** he's not as black as he's painted; **c'est de la malice noire,** it's rank malice on his part; (*f*) *P:* dead drunk. **2.** *s.* black man, woman; *Ethn: & Pej:* negro, negress; *A:* **traite des Noirs,** slave trade, black ivory trade. **3.** *s.m.* black; (*a*) **hommes d'un n. d'ébène,** men as black as ebony; **n. bleu,** blue-black; **cheveux d'un n. de corbeau,** raven-black hair; **cheveux (d'un) n. de jais, n. bleu,** jet-black hair, blue-black hair; **carte en n.,** black and white postcard; *F:* **mettre du n. sur du blanc,** to write, scribble; **c'était écrit n. sur blanc,** it was there in black and white; **voir tout en n.,** to take a gloomy view of everything, to look at the dark side of everything; **il ne faut pas voir les choses trop en n.,** we must not look too much on the dark side of things; we must not take too gloomy a view of things; **broyer du n.,** to be in the dumps, to be low-spirited, to have the blues, a fit of the blues; **un broyeur de n.,** a dismal Jemmy; *Prov:* **deux noirs ne font pas un blanc,** two blacks don't make a white; two wrongs don't make a right; **aller, passer, du blanc au n.,** to go from one extreme to the other; **ces tableaux ont poussé au n.,** these pictures have darkened (with time); **pousser au n.,** to present, to paint, a gloomy picture; **tableau poussé au n.,** gloomy picture; *s.a.* POT 1; (*b*) black (clothes); **être vêtu (tout) de n., être en n.,** to be dressed (all) in black, to be in mourning; **prendre, quitter, le n.,** to go into, out of, mourning; **elle porte toujours du n.,** she always wears black; (*c*) bull's eye (of target); *F:* **mettre dans le n.,** to hit the mark; (*d*) **les noirs d'une gravure,** the shadows of an engraving; *Phot:* **les grands noirs,** (i) the high lights (of a plate); (ii) the deep shadows (of a print); (*e*) **avoir des noirs,** to have bruises; to be black and blue; (*f*) *Tchn:* **n. animal,** bone black, animal black; char; **n. d'ivoire, de velours,** ivory black; **n. d'Allemagne,** Frankfort black; **n. à fourneaux,** grate polish; **n. de fumée, de lampe,** smoky black, lamp black; **passer (du cuir, etc.) au n. de fumée,** to lamp black (leather, etc.); **n. de Chine,** India(n) ink; **n. de la seiche,** cuttle-fish's ink; **n. de fumée, de pétrole, de carbone,** carbon black; (*g*) *Agr:* smut (of cereals); (*h*) *P:* **petit n.,** (cup of) black coffee; *F:* small black; (*i*) *Typ:* **en n.,** Clarendon; (*j*) **le n.,** the dark; **l'enfant a peur du n., dans le n.,** the child is afraid of the dark; (*k*) (*at roulette*) **le n.,** the black. **4.** *s.f.* **noire;** (*a*) (*at roulette*) **jouer sur la noire,** to stake, play, on the black; **série à la noire,** series, chapter, of accidents, run of ill-luck; (*b*) (*in balloting*) black ball; (*c*) *Mus:* crotchet; (*d*) *F:* **il est dans ses noires,** he's in one of his black moods.

noirâtre [nwarɑːtr̥], *a.* blackish, darkish.

noiraud, -aude [nwaro, -oːd], *a. & s.* swarthy (man, woman).

noirceur [nwarsœːr], *s.f.* **1.** blackness (of ink, etc.); darkness, gloominess (of weather, etc.); baseness (of soul); heinousness, foulness (of crime); **d'une n. d'ébène,** ebony-black. **2.** black spot; smudge; smut (on the face, etc.). **3.** atrocity, base action. **4. dire des noirceurs de qn,** to cast aspersions on s.o., to slander s.o.; to vilify s.o.

noircir [nwarsiːr]. **1.** *v.i.* to grow, become, turn, black or dark; to darken; (*of potatoes, etc.*) to go black. **2.** *v.tr.* (*a*) to blacken; to make (sth.) black; *Tchn:* to blackwash; **le soleil noircit le teint,** the sun tans the complexion; **bois noirci,** ebonized wood; **se n. le visage,** to black one's face; **se n. la barbe,** to dye one's beard black; *F:* **n. du papier,** to scribble; (*b*) to smut, grime, sully (sth.); **n. la réputation de qn,** to blacken s.o.'s character; **il se noircit à plaisir,** he makes himself out worse than he is; (*c*) to darken, throw a gloom over (the sky, the mind, etc.); **il ne faut pas n. la situation,** we must not paint things blacker than they are; *F:* **n. le tableau,** to take a gloomy view of things.

se noircir, to grow black, dark; **cela s'est noirci à la fumée,** it has blackened in the smoke; **le ciel se noircit,** the sky is getting dark, overcast.

noircissage [nwarsisaːʒ], *s.m. Leath:* burnishing.

noircissement [nwarsismɑ̃], *s.m.* **1.** (*a*) (action of) blackening; *Tchn:* blackwashing; (*b*) blackening (of s.o.'s character). **2.** darkening; *Phot:* **tirage par n. direct,** daylight printing.

noircisseur, -euse [nwarsisœːr, -øːz], *s. Tchn:* dyer in black; *F:* **n. de papier,** scribbler, quill-driver.

noircissure [nwarsisyːr], *s.f.* black spot, smudge.

noiré [nware], *s.m.* smut (on the face, etc.).

noirement [nwarmɑ̃], *adv.* foully, perfidiously.

noirien [nwarjɛ̃], *s.m.,* **noirin** [nwarɛ̃], *s.m. Vit:* Burgundy black grape or vine.

noirmoutrin, -ine [nwarmutrɛ̃, -in], *a. & s. Geog:* (native, inhabitant) of Noirmoutier.

noise [nwaːz], *s.f. A:* quarrelling; *now used only in* **chercher n. à qn,** to try to pick a quarrel with s.o.; *F:* to go for s.o., to pick on s.o.; **chercher n. à tout le monde,** to trail one's coat; **on me cherche n. à tout propos,** people are always finding fault with me.

noiseraie [nwazrɛ], *s.f.* (*a*) hazelnut plantation; (*b*) walnut plantation.

noisetier [nwaztje], *s.m.* hazel tree, hazel bush.

noisette [nwazɛt]. **1.** *s.f. Bot:* (*a*) hazel nut; **aller aux noisettes,** to go nutting; (*b*) **n. de terre = noix de terre;** (*c*) *Cu:* **n. de beurre,** knob of butter; **n. de chevreuil, d'agneau,** thick round venison, lamb, cutlet from the fillet. **2.** *a.inv.* **étoffe n.,** hazel, nut-brown, material; **yeux couleur (de) n.,** hazel eyes. **3.** *s.pl.* **noisettes,** coal nuts, fuel nuts.

noix [nwɑ], *s.f.* **1.** walnut; **coquille de n.,** walnut-shell; **huile de n.,** (wal)nut oil; *s.a.* COQUILLE 3. **2.** nut; (*a*) **n. d'Amérique, du Brésil,** Brazil nut, Para-nut, cream-nut (of various regions); **n. cendrée,** butter-nut; **n. d'arec,** betel nut, areca nut; **n. de Banda, n. muscade,** nutmeg; **n. de coco, d'Inde,** coconut; **n. d'acajou,** cashew nut; **n. des Barbades,** Barbados nut; **n. vomique,** nux vomica; **n. de terre,** pig nut, groundnut, earth nut, pea nut; *s.a.* GALLE; (*b*) *P:* head, nut; (*c*) *P:* **à la n.,** useless, *P:* lousy; **excuses à la n. (de coco),** worthless excuses; **travail à la n.,** lousy piece of work; (*d*) *P:* **vieille n.,** old chap, old pal; (*e*) *a.inv. P:* **ce que tu es n.!** you are hopeless! **3.** *Cu:* **n. de gigot,** pope's eye (in leg of mutton); **n. de jambon, de côtelette,** similar juicy morsel in ham, cutlet; **n. de veau,** kernel of veal; **n. de beurre,** knob of butter; *s.a.* GÎTE[1] 3. **4.** *Tchn:* (*a*) tumbler (of gun lock); (*b*) sprocket (of chain wheel); grinder (of coffee mill, etc.); (*c*) cam-wheel; (*d*) plug (of cock); (*e*) cable drum, drum-head (of capstan, winch); (*f*) *Carp:* (i) half-round groove; (ii) half-round tongue; (iii) grooving-plane; (*g*) *Nau:* **les noix du mât de hune,** the hounds; (*h*) *Tex:* whorl (of spindle); (*i*) rule-joint (of folding rule).

nolage [nɔlaːʒ], *s.m.,* **nolis** [nɔli], *s.m. Com:* (Mediterranean ports) **1.** freighting (of ships), affreightment. **2.** (cost of) freight.

noli-me-tangere [nɔlimetɑ̃ʒere], *s.m. Bot:* balsamine, garden balsam, yellow balsam, impatiens; *F:* jumping-betty, touch-me-not.

nolisateur [nɔlizatœːr], *s.m. Com: A:* freighter, charterer (of ship).

nolisement [nɔlizmɑ̃], *s.m. Com: A:* freighting, chartering; **acte de n.,** charter-party.

noliser [nɔlize], *v.tr. Com: A:* to freight, to charter and load (ship).

noliseur [nɔlizœːr], *s.m. Com: A:* freighter, charterer (of ship).

nom [nɔ̃], *s.m.* **1.** name; (*a*) **quel est votre n.?** what is your name? **un homme du n. de Pierre,** a man of the name of Peter; a man called Peter; **elle avait n. Philis,** her name was Phyllis; **de son vrai n. il s'appelle Dupont,** his real name is Dupont; **n. de famille,** surname; **n. de baptême, petit n.,** Christian name; **comment s'appelle-t-il de son petit n.?** what is his Christian name? **n. de jeune fille,** maiden name; *Adm:* name at birth; **n. de femme mariée, de mariage,** married name; **porter le n. de qn,** to be named, called, after s.o; **donner le n. de qn à qn,** to name, call, s.o. after s.o.; **il a le même n. que moi,** he is my namesake; **n. d'emprunt,** assumed name; **n. de guerre,** stage-name; assumed name; (journalist's) pen-name; **nom de plume** (*more usu.* PSEUDONYME), (author's) pen name, nom de plume; **n. de théâtre,** stage-name; **n. de voyage,** name assumed when travelling; **attribuer un faux n. à qn,** to miscall s.o.; **voyager sous un faux n.,** to travel under an alias; **on le connaissait sous le n. de Leduc,** he went by the name of Leduc, he was known by the name of Leduc; *Jur:* **erreur de n.,** misnomer; **noms de villes, de fleuves,** names of towns, of rivers; **n. et prénoms,** full name; **il se pare du n. de philosophe,** he calls himself, styles himself, a philosopher; *F:* **appeler les choses par leur n.,** to call a spade a spade; **mieux vaut nommer les choses par leur n.,** it is best to speak plainly; it is no use beating about the bush; **changements auxquels, par un n. fort mal choisi, on donne le n. de progrès,** changes which, by a great misnomer, are called progress; **quelqu'un dont je tairai le n.,** someone who shall be nameless; **impolitesse qui n'a pas de n.,** rudeness beyond words; **désordre sans n.,** unspeakable confusion; **ça n'a pas de n.!** it is unspeakable! **je le ferai ou j'y perdrai mon n.,** I'll do it or my name isn't (Jones); **n. de n.! n. d'une pipe! n. d'un chien! n. d'un tonnerre! n. d'un petit bonhomme!** *euphemisms for* **n. de Dieu,** for heavens' sake; *Com:* **n. déposé,** registered (trade) name; *s.a.* CHARNIÈRE 1; (*b*) **porter un beau, grand, n.,** to bear a great name; **se faire un grand n.,** to win fame, renown; to make, achieve, a name, a reputation, for oneself; (*c*) *adv.phr.* **de n.,** by name, in name; **n'être maître que de n.,** to be master in name only; **ne connaître qn que de n.,** to know s.o. only by name, by reputation; **au n. de la loi,** in the name of the law; **au n. du Père, du Fils,** in the name of the Father, the Son; **faire une proposition au n. de qn,** to make a proposal for s.o., on behalf of s.o.; **fait en mon n.,** done on my behalf, by my authority; **parlant en mon n. et au n. de M. X,** speaking for myself and in the name of Mr X; on behalf of Mr X and myself; **je ne parle pas en mon n.,** I am not speaking for myself; *s.a.* PRIVÉ 1. **2.** *Gram:* noun, substantive; **n. commun,** common noun; **n. propre,** proper name, proper noun.

noma [nɔma], *s.f. Med:* noma.

nomade [nɔmad]. **1.** *a.* nomadic (life); wandering (tribe); migratory (game); roving (instinct). **2.** *s.m.pl.* **nomades,** wandering tribes, wanderers, nomads; *P.N:* **stationnement interdit aux nomades,** no gypsies. **3.** *s.f Ent:* wasp-bee.

nomaderie [nɔmadri], *s.f.* wandering.

nomadisation [nɔmadizasjɔ̃], *s.f.* nomadization.

nomadiser [nɔmadize], *v.i. & tr.* to nomadize.

nomadisme [nɔmadism], *s.m.* nomadism.

no-man's land [nomanslɑ̃ːd], *s.m.* no man's land.

nomarque [nɔmark], *s.m. A.Hist:* nomarch (in Egypt).

nombrable [nɔ̃brabl̥], *a.* numerable, countable.

nombrant [nɔ̃brɑ̃], *a. used only in Mth:* **nombre n.,** abstract number.

nombre [nɔ̃ːbr̥], *s.m.* number. **1.** (*a*) *Ar: Ch: etc:* number, digit; **n. pair, impair, premier,** even, odd, prime, number; **n. entier,** whole number, integral number, integer; **n. aléatoire,** random number or digit; **n. pseudo-aléatoire,** pseudo-random number; **n. amiable,** amicable number; *Atom.Ph:* **n. atomique,** atomic number; **n. de masse,** mass number; **nombres magiques,** magic numbers; **n. quantique,** quantum number; *Ph:* **n. d'onde,** wave number; **la théorie des nombres,** the number theory; **la loi des grands nombres,** the law of numbers; *Pol.Ec:* **n. index,** index number; *Book-k:* **n. rouge,** red product; *Ecc:* **n. d'or,** golden number; *Nau:* **n. d'armement,** equipment number, numeral; (*b*) **n. de . . ., bon n. de . . ., un certain n. de. . ., un assez grand n. de . . .,** a number of, a good many . . .; **dans la foule il y avait un n. respectable, un assez grand n., de ses partisans,** among the crowd was a fair sprinkling of his supporters; **bon n. de gens l'ont vu,** a good many people saw him; **le plus grand n. est de cet avis,** the greater number are of this opinion; **auteur cher à un n. croissant de lecteurs,** author popular with more and more readers; **un grand n., un petit n., d'entre nous,** many, few, of us; **ceux, en petit n., qui . . .,** those, not very many, who . . .; **le grand n. de mes occupations, de mes amis,** my multifarious duties, my many friends; **nous étions en n. égal,** we were in equal numbers; **ils ont vaincu par le n.,** they conquered by force of numbers; **surpasser en n.,** to outnumber; **succomber sous le n.,** to succumb to odds, to numbers; to be overpowered by numbers; **la victoire de dépend pas du n.,** victory does not depend on numbers; **le n. suffisant, voulu (de membres),** the (full) quorum (at meeting); **ne pas être en n.,** not to have a quorum; **sans n.,** countless, numberless; without number; **n. de mots,** wordage; **prendre le n. des articles,** to count the goods; **tout fait n.,** every little helps; **venez pour faire n.,** come and help to make up an audience, *F:* and help to make a crowd; **en n. écrasant,** by an overwhelming majority; **la population s'élève au n. de 10.000,** the population amounts to 10,000; **ils sont au n. de huit,** they are eight in number; **ils s'engagèrent au n. de 10.000,** as many as 10,000 volunteered; **il**

est au n., du n., des élus, he is one of the elect; he is among the elect; **mettre, compter, qn au n. de ses intimes,** to number s.o. among one's friends; **du n., dans le n., se trouvaient plusieurs étrangers,** among them were several strangers; **à n. égal nous serions les plus forts,** given equal numbers we should be the stronger; *B:* **Le Livre des Nombres,** the Book of Numbers. **2.** *Gram:* (*a*) number; (*b*) **nom de n.,** numeral. **3. phrase qui a du n.,** well-balanced sentence.

nombrer [nɔ̃bre], *v.tr.* to number, reckon, count; *B:* **trop riche pour pouvoir n. ses troupeaux,** too rich to tell the tale of his flocks.

nombreux, -euse [nɔ̃brø, -øːz], *a.* **1.** (*a*) numerous (army, competitors); **pendant de nombreuses générations,** for many generations; **de n. clients nous écrivent que . . .,** many customers write to us that . . .; **une famille nombreuse,** a large family; **peu n.,** few (in number); **réunion peu nombreuse,** small party; **nous sommes peu n.,** we are very few, there are very few of us, we are a small party; **demain nous serons encore moins n.,** to-morrow, we shall be still fewer, even fewer; **auditoire peu n.,** thin house; **ils étaient si n. que,** they were in such numbers that; **ils viennent de plus en plus n.,** they are coming in ever increasing numbers; **les n. événements de cette journée,** the crowded events of that day; (*b*) multifarious, manifold (occupations, duties, etc.). **2.** *Lit:* harmonious, rhythmical, well-balanced (style, prose).

nombril [nɔ̃bri], *s.m.* **1.** (*a*) *Anat:* navel; *F:* **il se prend pour le n. du monde,** he thinks he's God's gift to mankind; **il ne s'intéresse qu'à son n.,** he is only interested in himself; (*b*) *Bot:* hilum; (*c*) *Her:* nombril, navel (of escutcheon). **2.** *Bot:* **n. de Vénus,** navelwort, pennywort.

nome [noːm], *s.m. A.Hist:* nome, nomos (of Egypt).

nomenclateur, -trice [nɔmɑ̃klatœːr, -tris]. **1.** *s.* nomenclator. **2.** *s.m. Lit:* classified list.

nomenclature [nɔmɑ̃klatyːr], *s.f.* **1.** nomenclature. **2.** *Com: Ind:* parts list; catalogue; schedule; **n. de constitution,** (i) specification (of an engine); (ii) parts schedule; **numéro de n.,** catalogue number, inventory number.

nominal, -aux [nɔminal, -o]. **1.** *a.* nominal; (*a*) **appel n.,** roll-call, call-over; **faire l'appel n.,** (i) to call over (assembly); (ii) to array (jury); **voter par appel n.,** to vote by call-over; *Psy:* **échelle nominale,** nominal scale; (*b*) nominal (price, horse-power, authority); *Fin:* **valeur nominale,** face value (of bill, etc.); *Mec.E:* **force en chevaux nominaux,** nominal horse-power; *El:* **courant n.,** rated current (of machine, etc.). **2.** *s.m.* (*a*) *Phil: A:* = NOMINALISTE 1; (*b*) *Gram:* demonstrative, indefinite, personal or possessive pronoun.

nominalement [nɔminalmɑ̃], *adv.* nominally. **1. désigner qn n.,** to refer to s.o. by name. **2. cela n'existe que n.,** it exists in name only.

nominalisation [nɔminalizasjɔ̃], *s.f. Ling:* nominalization.

nominaliser [nɔminalize], *v.tr. Ling:* to nominalize.

nominalisme [nɔminalism], *s.m. Phil:* nominalism.

nominaliste [nɔminalist], *Phil:* **1.** *s.m.* nominalist. **2.** *a.* nominalistic.

nominataire [nɔminatɛːr], *s.m. Ecc: A:* nominee (to a living).

nominateur [nɔminatœːr], *s.m.* nominator (**à,** to); presenter, patron (of living, etc.).

nominatif, -ive [nɔminatif, -iːv]. **1.** *a.* **état n.,** list of names; nominal roll; **carte nominative,** (invitation, membership, etc.) card bearing the holder's name; personal, individual, card; *Fin:* **titres nominatifs,** registered securities; scrip; *s.m. Fin:* **dividende de tant au n.,** dividend of so much on registered securities. **2.** *a. & s.m. Gram:* (*a*) nominative (case); **substantif au n.,** substantive in the nominative (case); (*b*) subject.

nomination [nɔminasjɔ̃], *s.f.* **1.** nomination (for an appointment); **poste à la n. du ministre,** post in the gift of the Minister. **2.** appointment; **recevoir sa n.,** to be appointed (**à un poste,** to a post); **n. d'un officier,** commissioning of an officer; **n. à un grade supérieur,** promotion; (*of officer*) **sa n. a paru la semaine dernière,** he was gazetted last week. **3.** *Sch:* **il a eu deux nominations,** he's been commended twice in the prize list, honours list.

nominativement [nɔminativmɑ̃], *adv.* by name; **il fut sommé n. de répondre,** he was called upon by name to answer.

nommément [nɔmemɑ̃], *adv.* **1.** (*a*) namely, to wit; (*b*) especially; **l'influence du climat et n. celle de l'humidité,** the influence of climate and in particular of moisture. **2. mentionner qn n.,** to mention s.o. by name.

nommer [nɔme], *v.tr.* **1.** (*a*) to name; to give a name to (s.o., sth.); (*b*) **n. qn qch.,** to name, call, s.o. sth.; **on le nomma Jean,** they named him John; **on nomme aumôniers les prêtres attachés à un régiment,** priests attached to a regiment are called, styled, chaplains; *Jur:* **le nommé Dupont,** (i) a man of the name of Dupont; (ii) the man Dupont, the so-called Dupont. **2.** (*a*) to name, to mention by name; **il ne nomma personne,** he mentioned no names; **un homme que je ne nommerai pas,** a man who shall be nameless; **je nomme . . .,** namely . . ., I refer to . . .; **on ne la nomme jamais chez nous,** her name is never mentioned in our house; (*b*) **n. un jour,** to appoint a day; **à jour nommé,** on the appointed day; *s.a.* POINT[1] 3. **3.** (*a*) to appoint, name (s.o. to an office or post); to commission (officer); **être nommé au grade de . . .,** to be promoted to the rank of . . .; **n. qn à un poste,** to nominate s.o. to, for, a post; **n. qn gouverneur d'une forteresse,** to appoint s.o. (as) governor of a fortress; **faire n. qn à un poste,** to obtain s.o.'s appointment to a post; **n. qn son héritier,** to appoint s.o. one's heir; (*b*) *Pol: etc:* to return, elect (s.o.).

se nommer. 1. to state one's name; **sans se n.,** without giving his name. **2.** to be called, named; **comment vous nommez-vous?** what is your name?

nomogramme [nɔmɔgram], *s.m. Mth:* nomogram, nomograph, alignment chart, graph.

nomographe [nɔmɔgraf], *s.m.* nomographer.

nomographie [nɔmɔgrafi], *s.f.* **1.** nomography. **2.** *Mth:* nomogram; graph of parallel lines.

nomographique [nɔmɔgrafik], *a. Mth:* nomographical (table).

nomothète [nɔmɔtɛt], *s.m. Gr.Hist:* nomothete; law-giver.

non [nɔ̃], *adv.* (*no "liaison" with a following word*) no; *A. & Lit:* nay; not. **1. vient-il?—non,** is he coming?—no(, he's not, he isn't); **fumez-vous?—non,** do you smoke?—no(, I don't); **répondrez-vous?—non!** will you answer?—no, I won't; **oui ou non?** yes or no? **répondre par oui ou non,** to answer yes or no; **viendra-t-il oui ou non?—je dis que non,** Will he come or not?—I say no, I say he won't; **comment non?** how could it be otherwise, how could it have been otherwise? **c'est dégoûtant, non?** isn't it disgusting? **mais non! dame non! mon Dieu non! que non!** oh dear, no! no indeed! **non pas!** not so! not at all! **non, je vous en prie,** please don't! **je pense que non,** I think not; **j'ai peur que non,** I fear not; **je parie que non,** I bet it isn't; **je voudrais que non,** I wish it weren't so; **faire signe que non,** to shake one's head; **il est respecté mais non pas aimé,** he is respected but not loved; **qu'il vienne ou non . . .,** whether he comes or not . . .; **non pas même en France,** not even in France; **non (pas) que je le craigne,** not that I fear him; **non que je ne vous plaigne,** not but that I pity you; not that I don't pity you; *s.a.* MOINS 1, OUI 1, PAS[2] 1, PLUS 1; *s.m.inv.* **répondre par un non,** to answer in the negative; **vingt oui et trente non,** twenty ayes and thirty noes; **les non l'emportent,** the noes have it; **il se fâche pour un oui, pour un non,** he flares up at the least thing; *s.a.* OUI 2. **2. il a commencé comme boueur.—non!** he started as a dustman.—indeed! **3. non loin de la ville,** not far from the town; **non sans raison,** not without reason; **non seulement . . ., mais encore . . .,** not only . . ., but also . . .; **leçon non sue,** lesson not known; **mine non encore exploitée,** mine not yet worked. **4.** (*in compound words*) non-, in-, un-; *e.g.* **non-comparution,** non-appearance; **pacte de non-agression,** non-aggression pact; **non-cohésif,** incohesive; **non-vérifié,** unverified; **non-classé,** unclassified. **5.** *s.m.* (*computers*) not.

non-acceptation [nɔ̃aksɛptasjɔ̃, nɔn-], *s.f. Com:* non-acceptance (of bill); refusal (of goods).

non-achèvement [nɔ̃aʃɛvmɑ̃, nɔn-], *s.m.* non-completion.

non-activité [nɔ̃aktivite, nɔn-], *s.f.* non-activity; *Mil:* **mettre un officier en n.-a.,** to put an officer on half-pay; **mise en n.-a.,** (i) suspension; (ii) placing (of officer) on half-pay; *s.a.* SOLDE[1].

nonagénaire [nɔnaʒenɛːr], *a. & s.* nonagenarian.

nonagésime [nɔnaʒezim], *a. Astr:* nonagesimal (degree, point).

nonagone [nɔnagɔn], *s.m. Mth:* nonagon.

non-agression [nɔ̃agrɛsjɔ̃, nɔn-], *s.f.* non-aggression.

non-alcoolisé [nɔ̃alkɔlize, nɔn-], *a.* non-alcoholic; *pl. non-alcoolisé(e)s.*

non-aligné [nɔ̃aliɲe, nɔn-], *a. Pol:* non-aligned, uncommitted; *s.* **les non-alignés,** the non-aligned countries.

non-alignement [nɔ̃aliɲmɑ̃, nɔn-], *s.m. Pol:* non-alignment.

nonane [nɔnan], *s.m. Ch:* nonane.

nonante [nɔnɑ̃ːt], *num.a. & s.m.inv. Dial:* (*Switz., Belg., S. of Fr. and Canada*), ninety.

nonantième [nɔnɑ̃tjɛm], *num.a. Dial:* (*Switz., Belg., S. of Fr. and Canada*), ninetieth.

non-arrivée [nɔ̃arive, nɔn-], *s.f.* non-arrival.

non-assistance [nɔ̃asistɑ̃ːs, nɔn-], *s.f. Jur:* non-assistance; **n.-a. à personne en danger,** failure to assist s.o. in danger.

non-belligérance [nɔ̃bɛl(l)iʒɛrɑ̃ːs], *s.f.* non-belligerency.

non-casse [nɔ̃kɑːs], *s.f. Av:* **prime de n.-c.,** no-accident bonus.

nonce [nɔ̃ːs], *s.m.* nuncio; **n. du Pape,** Papal Nuncio.

nonchalamment [nɔ̃ʃalamɑ̃], *adv.* nonchalantly, unconcernedly, listlessly; **n. étendu sur une chaise,** lolling on a chair; **marcher n.,** to saunter along; **s'appuyer n. au mur,** to lounge against the wall.

nonchalance [nɔ̃ʃalɑ̃ːs], *s.f.* nonchalance, unconcern; listlessness, indolence; **faire qch. avec n.,** to do sth. listlessly, unconcernedly; **par n.,** out of nonchalance.

nonchalant [nɔ̃ʃalɑ̃], *a.* nonchalant, unconcerned; listless, indolent; *Lit:* **n. du terme où finiront mes jours,** indifferent as to when my days may end.

nonchaloir [nɔ̃ʃalwaːr], *s.m. A:* indifference, apathy.

nonciature [nɔ̃sjatyːr], *s.f.* **1.** nunciature. **2.** nuncio's residence.

non-collant [nɔ̃kɔlɑ̃], *a.* non-caking (coal); *pl. non-collant(e)s.*

non-combattant [nɔ̃kɔ̃batɑ̃], *a. & s.m.* non-combatant; *A:* **les non-combattants à la suite de l'armée,** the camp-followers, the hangers-on; *pl. non-combattants.*

non-comparant [nɔ̃kɔ̃parɑ̃], *s. Jur:* defaulter; *pl. non-comparant(e)s.*

non-conciliation [nɔ̃kɔ̃siljasjɔ̃], *s.f. Jur:* refusal to settle out of Court.

non-conducteur, -trice [nɔ̃kɔ̃dyktœːr, -tris], *Ph:* **1.** non-conducting. **2.** *s.m.* non-conductor; *pl. non-conducteurs, -trices.*

non-conformisme [nɔ̃kɔ̃fɔrmism], *s.m.* nonconformity.

non-conformiste [nɔ̃kɔ̃fɔrmist]. **1.** *a.* (*a*) *Ecc:* non-conforming, nonconformist; (*b*) unconventional; (*c*) unethical. **2.** *s.* nonconformist; *pl. non-conformistes.*

non-conformité [nɔ̃kɔ̃fɔrmite], *s.f.* nonconformity.

non-conscience [nɔ̃kɔ̃sjɑ̃ːs], *s.f.* unconsciousness (**de,** of).

non-contradiction [nɔ̃kɔ̃tradiksjɔ̃], *s.f. Phil:* non-contradiction.

non-croyant, -ante [nɔ̃krwajɑ̃, -ɑ̃ːt], *s. Rel:* unbeliever; *pl. non-croyants, -antes.*

non-dépassement [nɔ̃depasmɑ̃], *s.m. Fin:* not exceeding (a limit).

non-directivisme [nɔ̃dirɛktivism], *s.m. Psy:* non-directive therapy.

non-disponibilité [nɔ̃dispɔnibilite], *s.f.* non-availability, unavailability (of men, supplies, etc.).

non-disponible [nɔ̃dispɔnibl̩], *a.* non-available, unavailable (men, supplies, etc.); *pl. non-disponibles.*

non-dissémination [nɔ̃diseminasjɔ̃], *s.f.* non-dissemination (of nuclear weapons).

non-dosé [nɔ̃doze], *a. Ch: etc:* undetermined (quantity); *pl. non-dosés.*

none [nɔn], *s.f.* **1.** *Rom.Ant:* (*a*) ninth hour (3 p.m.); (*b*) *pl.* nones (ninth day before the ides). **2.** *Ecc:* nones.

non-endommagé [nɔ̃ɑ̃dɔmaʒe, nɔn-], *a.* undamaged, sound; *pl. non-endommagés.*

non-engagement [nɔ̃ɑ̃gaʒmɑ̃, nɔn-], *s.m. Pol:* neutralism; non-alignment.

non-étanche [nɔ̃etɑ̃ːʃ, nɔn-], *a.* leaky (washer, etc.); *pl. non-étanches.*

non-être [nɔ̃ɛːtr̥, nɔnɛtr̥], *s.m. no pl. Phil:* non-entity, non-existence.

nonetto [nɔnetto], *s.m. Mus:* nonet.

non-euclidien, -ienne [nɔ̃øklidjɛ̃, -jɛn, nɔn-], *a.* non-Euclidean (geometry).

non-exécution [nɔnegzekysjɔ̃, nɔn-], *s.f.* non-fulfilment (of agreement, etc.); non-performance.

non-existant [nɔ̃egzistɑ̃, nɔn-], *a.* non-existent; *pl. non-existants.*

non-existence [nɔ̃egzistɑ̃:s, nɔn-], *s.f.* non-existence.

non-ferreux, -euse [nɔ̃ferø, -ø:z], *a.* non-ferrous; *pl. non-ferreux, -euses.*

non-fonctionnement [nɔ̃fɔ̃ksjɔnmɑ̃], *s.m. Tchn:* failure, failure to operate.

non-grisouteux, -euse [nɔ̃grizutø, -ø:z], *a. Min:* sweet; *pl. non-grisouteux, -euses.*

non-identifiable [nɔ̃idɑ̃tifjabl̥, nɔn-], *a. Adm:* unidentifiable, faceless; *pl. non-identifiables.*

nonidi [nɔnidi], *s.m. Fr.Hist:* (Republican calendar) ninth day of the decade.

non-ingérence [nɔ̃ɛ̃ʒerɑ̃:s, nɔn-], *s.f.* non-interference.

non-inscrit [nɔ̃ɛ̃skri, nɔn-], *s.m. Pol:* independent; *pl. non-inscrits.*

non-intervention [nɔ̃ɛ̃tɛrvɑ̃sjɔ̃, nɔn-], *s.f. Pol:* non-intervention, non-interference.

non-interventionnisme [nɔ̃ɛ̃tɛrvɑ̃sjɔnism, nɔn-], *s.m.* non-intervention.

non-interventionniste [nɔ̃ɛ̃tɛrvɑ̃sjɔnist, nɔn-], *a. & s. Pol:* non-interventionist; *pl. non-interventionnistes.*

non-isolé [nɔ̃izɔle, nɔn-], *a. El: etc:* uninsulated; *pl. non-isolés.*

non-jouissance [nɔ̃ʒwisɑ̃:s], *s.f. Jur:* prevention of possession.

non-jureurs [nɔ̃ʒyrœ:r], *s.m.pl. Hist:* non-jurors.

non-lieu [nɔ̃ljø], *s.m. Jur:* no true bill, no ground for prosecution; **ordonnance de n.-l.,** nonsuit; **rendre une ordonnance de n.-l.,** to refuse to order a prosecution, to nonsuit (s.o.); to dismiss the charge; to throw out the bill; **bénéficier d'une ordonnance de n.-l.,** to be discharged; *pl. non-lieux.*

non-livraison [nɔ̃livrɛzɔ̃], *s.f. Com:* non-delivery (of goods).

non-métallique [nɔ̃metalik], *a.* non-metallic; *pl. non-métalliques.*

non-moi [nɔ̃mwa], *s.m. Phil:* non-ego, not-I.

nonnain [nɔnɛ̃], *s.f. A. & F:* (young) nun; **ouvrage de n.,** lace made in *béguinages.*

nonne [nɔn], *s.f.* **1.** nun. **2.** *Geol:* earth-pillar. **3.** *Ent:* winter nun, moth.

non-négociable [nɔ̃negɔsjabl̥], *a. Com:* unnegotiable (cheque, etc.); *pl. non-négociables.*

nonnerie [nɔnri], *s.f. F: Pej:* nunnery.

nonnette [nɔnɛt], *s.f.* **1.** *F:* young, little, nun. **2.** small cake of iced gingerbread. **3.** *Orn:* titmouse, *pl.* titmice; tomtit; **n. cendrée,** marsh tit(mouse).

nonobstant [nɔnɔpstɑ̃]. **1.** *prep. A:* notwithstanding; *Jur:* **n. toute clause contraire,** notwithstanding any clause to the contrary; **ce n.,** this notwithstanding. **2.** *adv.* nevertheless, notwithstanding.

non-ouvré [nɔ̃uvre, nɔnuvre], *a.* unworked, unwrought (metal); uncut (fabric); *pl. non-ouvré(e)s.*

non-paiement [nɔ̃pɛmɑ̃], *s.m. Com:* non-payment.

nonpareil, -eille [nɔ̃parɛ:j]. **1.** *a.* peerless, matchless (beauty, etc.); unparalleled (patience, courage, etc.). **2.** *s.m. Orn:* nonpareil. **3.** *s.f.* **nonpareille,** (*a*) nonesuch (apple, etc.); nonpareil; (*b*) (confectioner's) fancy ribbon; (*c*) small sugar almond, nonpareil; (*d*) *Typ:* six-point type, nonpareil; *A:* **grosse nonpareille,** 96-point type.

non-payement [nɔ̃pɛ(j)mɑ̃], *s.m. Com: O:* non-payment.

non-pesanteur [nɔ̃pəzɑ̃tœ:r], *s.f.* weightlessness.

non-porteur [nɔ̃pɔrtœ:r], *a. Av:* non-lifting; *pl. non-porteurs.*

non-présentation [nɔ̃presɑ̃tasjɔ̃], *s.f.* **n.-p. d'enfant,** concealment of birth.

non-prolifération [nɔ̃prɔliferasjɔ̃], *s.f.* non-proliferation; **traité de n.-p.,** non-proliferation treaty.

non-réception [nɔ̃resepsjɔ̃], *s.f.* non-reception; *Com:* non-delivery (of goods).

non-recevable [nɔ̃r(ə)səvabl̥], *a. Jur:* **demandeur n.-r. dans son action,** petitioner declared to have no right of action; *pl. non-recevables.*

non-recevoir [nɔ̃r(ə)səvwa:r], *s.m. Jur:* **fin de n.-r.,** refusal; **opposer une fin de n.-r. (à une réclamation, etc.),** to put in a plea in bar (of a claim, etc.); to traverse (a claim).

non-reconduction [nɔ̃rəkɔ̃dyksjɔ̃], *s.f. Adm:* failure to renew (a contract, a treaty).

non-récupérable [nɔ̃rekyperabl̥], *a.* expendable; *pl. non-récupérables.*

non-remise [nɔ̃r(ə)mi:z], *s.f.* non-delivery (of letter).

non-réponse [nɔ̃repɔ̃:s], *s.f.* lack of answer; **en cas de n.-r. . . .,** if no reply is received . . ..

non-résidence [nɔ̃rezidɑ̃:s], *s.f.* non-residence.

non-résident [nɔ̃rezidɑ̃], *a.* non-resident (priest, etc.); *pl. non-résidents.*

non-respect [nɔ̃rɛspɛ], *s.m.* failure to observe (halt sign, etc.).

non-retour [nɔ̃r(ə)tu:r], *s.m.* **point de n.-r.,** point of no return; *Hyd.E: etc:* **clapet de n.-r.,** non-return valve.

non-réussite [nɔ̃reysit], *s.f.* failure, unsuccess(fulness), non-success; miscarriage (of plan); *pl. non-réussites.*

non-salarié, -e [nɔ̃salarje], *s.* non wage-earning person; *pl. non-salariés, -ées.*

non-sens [nɔ̃sɑ̃:s], *s.m.inv.* meaningless sentence, translation, or action; **cette phrase est un n.-s.,** this sentence conveys no meaning.

non-spécialiste [nɔ̃spesjalist], *s.m. & f.* non-specialist; *pl. non-spécialistes.*

non-succès [nɔ̃syksɛ], *s.m.inv.* non-success, failure.

non-syndiqué, -ée [nɔ̃sɛ̃dike], *Ind:* **1.** *a.* non-union (workman). **2.** *s.* non-unionist; *pl. non-syndiqués, -ées.*

non-tarifé [nɔ̃tarife], *a.* duty-free; *pl. non-tarifés.*

non-tissé [nɔ̃tise], *a. & s.m. Tex:* non-woven (material); *pl. non-tissés.*

nontronite [nɔ̃trɔnit], *s.f. Miner:* nontronite.

nontronnais, -aise [nɔ̃trɔnɛ, -ɛ:z], *a. & s. Geog:* (native, inhabitant) of Nontron.

nonuple [nɔnypl̥], *a.* ninefold; *s.m.* **au nonuple,** ninefold.

non-usage [nɔ̃yza:ʒ, non-], *s.m.* disuse; *Jur:* non-user.

non-utilisation [nɔ̃ytilizasjɔ̃, nɔn-], *s.f.* non-utilization.

non-valable [nɔ̃valabl̥], *a.* **1.** *Jur:* invalid (clause, etc.). **2.** (*of ticket, etc.*) not valid, invalid; *pl. non-valables.*

non-valeur [nɔ̃valœ:r], *s.f.* **1.** object of no value; *Com: Fin:* (i) bad debt; (ii) worthless security; (iii) non-productive land, etc.; *Adm:* **fonds de n.-v.,** provision for possible deficit (in Budget estimates). **2.** (*a*) inefficient, purely decorative, employee or member of staff; *F:* passenger; **c'est une n.-v.,** he's no use, no good; (*b*) *Mil:* non-effective; person not on the strength. **3.** unproductiveness; **terres en n.-v.,** unproductive land; *pl. non-valeurs.*

non-valide [nɔ̃valid], *a. Mil: Navy:* non-effective (man, rating); *pl. non-valides.*

non-vente [nɔ̃vɑ̃:t], *s.f. Com:* no sale.

non-viabilité [nɔ̃vjabilite], *s.f.* non-viability (of new-born child).

non-viable [nɔ̃vjabl̥], *a. Med:* non-viable; *pl. non-viables.*

non-violence [nɔ̃vjɔlɑ̃:s], *s.f.* non-violence.

non-violent, -ente [nɔ̃vjɔlɑ̃, -ɑ̃:t], (*a*) *s.* advocate of non-violence; (*b*) *a.* non-violent; *pl. non-violents, -entes.*

non-voisé [nɔ̃vwaze], *a. Ling:* unvoiced; **voyelle non-voisée,** unvoiced vowel; *pl. non-voisés, -ées.*

nonyle [nɔnil], *s.m. Ch:* nonyl.

noogénèse [nɔɔgenɛ:z], *s.f. Psy:* noegenesis.

nopal, -als [nɔpal], *s.m. Bot:* nopal; cochineal cactus, cochineal fig; Indian fig.

nopalerie [nɔpalri], *s.f.*, **nopalière** [nɔpaljɛ:r], *s.f.* nopalry.

nope [nɔp], *s.f. Tex:* burl.

noper [nɔpe], *v.tr. Tex:* to burl (cloth).

nopeuse [nɔpø:z], *s.f. Tex:* burler, dresser of cloth.

noquet [nɔkɛ], *s.m. Plumb:* flashing, gutter-lead.

noradrénaline [nɔradrenalin], *s.f. Ch:* noradrenalin.

norberte [nɔrbɛrt], *s.f.* small black plum.

nord [nɔ:r], *s.m.* no *pl.* **1.** north; **n. vrai, n. géographique,** true north; **le n. de la France,** the north of France; **au nord, dans le nord,** in the North; **le vent est au n.,** the wind is in the north; **au nord de,** (to the) north, northwards, of (country, etc.); **borné au n. par,** bounded on the north by; **maison exposée au n.,** house facing north; **exposition au n.,** northerly aspect; **il habite quelque part dans le n.,** he lives somewhere in the north (of Paris, of France, of Europe); **vers le n.,** northward; **du n.,** of the north; from the north; northern (province); northerly (wind); **du n. au midi** = from Land's End to John o'Groats; **l'Étoile du n.,** the North Star; **le vent du n.,** the north wind; **du côté du n. l'hôtel regarde le lac,** on the north side, to the north, the hotel overlooks the lake; **la mer du N.,** the North Sea; **le Canal du Nord,** the North Channel; **l'Amérique du N.,** North America; **l'Irlande du N.,** Northern Ireland; **le Grand N.,** the frozen North; **le Grand N., Canadien,** Canadian Far North; *Nau:* **chemin n. (d'un navire),** northing (of a ship); *F:* **perdre le n.** (i) to lose one's bearings, to be all at sea; (ii) to lose one's head, to get confused; *Nau:* **n.-quart-n.-est,** north by east; **n.-quart-n.-ouest,** north by west; *Mapm:* **n. du quadrillage,** grid north; **gisement par rapport au n. du quadrillage,** grid bearing. **2.** *Nau:* **le n.,** the north wind. **3.** *a.inv.* north (side, latitude, etc.); northern (part of country, latitude, etc.); **le Pôle N.,** the North pole; **le Cap N.,** the North Cape.

nord-africain, -aine [nɔrafrikɛ̃, -ɛn], *a. & s.* North-African, *esp.* Algerian; *pl. nord-africains, -aines.*

nord-américain, -aine [nɔramerikɛ̃, -ɛn], *a. & s.* North-American; *pl. nord-américains, -aines.*

nord-coréen, -enne [nɔrkɔreɛ̃, -ɛn], *a. & s.* North-Korean; *pl. nord-coréens, -ennes.*

nordé [nɔr(d)e], *s.m. Nau:* = NORD-EST.

nord-est [nɔr(d)ɛst, *Nau:* nɔrde], *s.m.* **1.** north-east; *Geog:* **le Passage du N.-E.,** the North-East Passage; *Nau:* **n.-e.-quart-est,** north-east by east; **n.-e.-quart-nord,** north-east by north. **2.** north-east wind, north-easter, *F:* nor'easter. **3.** *a.inv.* north-east(ern).

nordester [nɔrdɛste], *v.i. Nau:* (*of wind*) to veer to the north-east.

nordique [nɔrdik]. **1.** *a.* Norse, Scandinavian; Nordic. **2.** *s.m.* Norse (language).

nordir [nɔrdi:r], *v.i. Nau:* (*of the wind*) to veer north(ward).

nordiste [nɔrdist]. **1.** *a. & s.m. Hist.* (*U.S.A.*): northerner. **2.** *a. Sp:* northern; **clubs nordistes,** northern clubs.

nord-nord-est [nɔrnɔr(d)ɛst], *s.m. & a.inv.* north-north-east.

nord-nord-ouest [nɔrnɔr(d)wɛst], *s.m. & a.inv.* north-north-west.

nord-ouest [nɔr(d)wɛst, *Nau:* nɔrwɛ, nɔrwa], *s.m.* **1.** north-west; *Geog:* **le Passage du N.-O.,** the North-West Passage; *Nau:* **n.-o.-quart-ouest,** north-west by west; **n.-o.-quart-nord,** north-west by north. **2.** north-west wind, north-wester, *F:* nor'wester. **3.** *a.inv.* north-west(ern).

nord-ouester [nɔr(d)wɛste], *v.i. Nau:* (*of wind*) to veer to the north-west.

nord-vietnamien, -enne [nɔrvjɛtnamjɛ̃, -ɛn], *a. & s.* North-Vietnamese; *pl. nord-vietnamiens, -iennes.*

noria [nɔrja], *s.f.* **1.** chain-pump, bucket-chain, noria, Persian wheel. **2.** noria conveyor hoist; bucket-conveyor, -elevator.

norite [nɔrit], *s.f. Geol:* norite.

normal, -aux [nɔrmal, -o]. **1.** *a.* (*a*) normal (state, course, speed); **être dans son état n.,** to be in one's usual health; **le bureau n'était pas dans son état n.,** the office was not in its normal state; **c'est tout à fait n. que,** it's only natural that; **école normale,** teachers' training college, college of education; **l'École normale supérieure,** *s.f. F:* **Normale,** selective college of university level preparing students for the higher posts in teaching and other professions; (*b*) standard; **poids n.,** standard weight; **échantillon n.,** average sample; *Rail:* **écartement n.,** standard gauge (of track); **aux cotes normales,** of standard dimensions; **vitesse normale,** rated speed; *Phot:* **émulsion normale,** ordinary emulsion; (*c*) *Geom:* perpendicular, normal (**à,** to). **2.** *s.f.* **normale;** (*a*) *Geom:* perpendicular, normal; (*b*) **température au-dessus de la normale,** temperature above (the) normal; *Golf:* **normale du parcours,** standard scratch score; par for the course; *O:* bogey; **jouer contre la normale,** to play against the course, against bogey.

normalement [nɔrmalmɑ̃], *adv.* **1.** normally; in the ordinary course (of things). **2.** *Geom:* perpendicularly, normally (**à,** to).

normalien, -ienne [nɔrmaljɛ̃, -jɛn], *s.* (*a*) student, former student, at a training college, at a college of education; (*b*) student, former student, at the *École normale supérieure.*

normalisateur [nɔrmalizatœ:r], *s.m. El:* **n. d'impulsions,** pulse equalizer.

normalisation [nɔrmalizasjɔ̃], *s.f.* normalization, standardization; *Tchn:* normalizing, annealing.

normaliser [nɔrmalize], *v.tr.* to normalize; to standardize.

normalité [nɔrmalite], *s.f.* normality.

normand, -ande [nɔrmɑ̃, -ɑ̃:d], *a. & s.* **1.** Norman; of Normandy; *F:* shrewd; **les Iles anglo-normandes,** the Channel Islands; *Cu:* **sauce normande,** gravy made of cream and mushrooms; *F:* **réponse normande,** non-committal, pawky, answer; **répondre en N.,** to give an evasive, equivocal, answer; **c'est un fin N.,** he is a shrewd, canny, fellow; **à N. N. et demi,** set a thief to catch a thief. **2.** *Hist:* (*a*) **les Normands,** the Norsemen, the Northmen; (*b*) **la conquête**

normande, the Norman conquest. **3.** *s.f.* **normande:** *(a) Typ:* clarendon; *(b)* single-furrow plough.

Normandie [nɔrmɑ̃di], *Pr.n.f. Geog:* Normandy.

normannique [nɔrmanik], *a. & s.m. Hist: Ling:* **1.** Norse. **2.** *occ.* Anglo-Norman.

normatif, -ive [nɔrmatif, -iːv], *a.* normative.

normativité [nɔrmativite], *s.f.* normalcy.

norme [nɔrm], *s.f.* **1.** *Phil: etc:* norm, standard; **n. de conduite,** rule of conduct; **qui échappe à la n.,** abnormal; **ramener les aberrants à la n. sociale,** to bring back the stray sheep to the (social) fold. **2.** *Ind: Com: etc:* standard, (standard) specification; **normes françaises (N.F.)** = British Standards.

normé [nɔrme], *a.* normed.

normoblaste [nɔrmɔblast], *s.m. Physiol:* normoblast.

normocyte [nɔrmɔsit], *s.m. Physiol:* normocyte.

normographe [nɔrmɔgraf], *s.f.* stencil.

normographie [nɔrmɔgrafi], *s.f.* stencilling.

Norne [nɔrn], *Pr.n.f. Myth:* Norn, Norna.

norois[1]**, norrois, -oise** [nɔrwa, -waːz]. **1.** *a. & s. A:* Norman. **2.** *s.m. Ling:* Norse.

norois[2]**, noroît,** *s.m.* north-west wind, north-wester, *F:* nor'wester.

noropianique [nɔrɔpjanik], *a. Ch:* noropianic (acid).

norrain [nɔrɛ̃], *a. Ling:* Norwegian.

norroy [nɔrwa], *s.m. Her:* norroy.

norse [nɔrs], *s.m. Ling:* Norse (of the Orkneys, Shetlands, etc.).

northumbrien, -enne [nɔrtœbriɛ̃, -ɛn], *a. & s. Ling: Geog:* Northumbrian.

northupite [nɔrtypit], *s.f. Miner:* northupite.

nortier [nɔrtje], *s.m. Dial:* (in N. of Fr.) cattle-breeder.

Norvège [nɔrvɛːʒ], *Pr.n.f. Geog:* Norway.

norvégien, -ienne [nɔrveʒjɛ̃, -jɛn]. **1.** *a. & s.* Norwegian. **2.** *s.m. Ling:* Norwegian. **3.** *s.f.* **norvégienne,** round-stemmed rowing-boat (of Norwegian type). **4.** *Dom.Ec:* **marmite norvégienne,** hay-box; *Cu:* **omelette norvégienne,** omelette with ice-cream and served with burning brandy.

nos [no], *poss.a. See* NOTRE.

nosema [nɔzema], *s.m. Ap:* nosema disease.

nosogénie [nɔzɔʒeni], *s.f. Med:* nosogeny.

nosographe [nɔzɔgraf], *s.m.* nosologist.

nosographie [nɔzɔgrafi], *s.f.* nosography.

nosologie [nɔzɔlɔʒi], *s.f.* nosology.

nosologique [nɔzɔlɔʒik], *a.* nosological.

nosologiste [nɔzɔlɔʒist], *s.m. & f.* nosologist.

nosseigneurs [nosɛɲœːr], *s.m.pl. See* MONSEIGNEUR.

nostalgie [nɔstalʒi], *s.f. (a) Med:* nostalgia; *(b) F:* home-sickness; **avoir la n. du foyer,** to pine for, sigh for, long for, yearn after, home; **n. de la mer,** hankering after the sea.

nostalgique [nɔstalʒik], *a. (a)* nostalgic; *(b)* home-sick; *(c) s.* nostalgic person.

nostalgiquement [nɔstalʒikmɑ̃], *adv.* nostalgically.

nostoc [nɔstɔk], *s.m. Algae:* nostoc, star-jelly, witches'-butter.

nostomanie [nɔstɔmani], *s.f. Psy:* nostomania.

nostras [nɔstras], *a.m. Med:* **choléra n.,** endemic cholera.

nota [nɔta], *s.m.inv.* marginal note, foot-note; **n. bene, N.B.** [nɔtabene], please note.

notabilité [nɔtabilite], *s.f.* notability. **1.** notableness. **2.** person of distinction, of note; **les notabilités du commerce,** outstanding names in the commercial world.

notable [nɔtabl], *a.* notable. **1.** worthy of note, considerable; **une fraction n. du pays,** a considerable section of the country; **sans variation n.,** without appreciable change. **2.** eminent, distinguished (person); *s.m.* person of distinction, of influence, of standing; **les notables,** the leading citizens; *Fr.Hist:* **Assemblée de notables,** Assembly of Notables.

notablement [nɔtabləmɑ̃], *adv.* notably; appreciably.

notage [nɔtaːʒ], *s.m. Com:* recording (of an order).

notaire [nɔtɛːr], *s.m.* **1.** *Jur:* notary (executes authentic deeds; deals with sales of real estate, with successions, with marriage contracts); *Scot:* notary public; **par-devant n.,** before a notary; **le n. y a passé, on ne peut plus s'en dédire,** it is a legal agreement, there is no going back on it; *F:* **c'est comme si le n. y avait passé,** his word is as good as his bond. **2.** *Ecc:* **n. apostolique,** apostolical notary.

notairesse [nɔtɛrɛs], *s.f.,* **notaresse** [nɔtarɛs], *s.f. F:* wife of the notary.

notamment [nɔtamɑ̃], *adv. (a)* notably; more particularly; especially, in particular; *(b)* among others . . ..

notarial, -aux [nɔtarjal, -o], *a.* notarial (function, etc.).

notariat [nɔtarja], *s.m.* **1.** the profession of notary. **2.** the body of notaries.

notarié [nɔtarje], *a. Jur: See* ACTE 2.

notation [nɔtasjɔ̃], *s.f. (a)* notation; **n. algébrique, musicale,** algebraic, musical, notation; *(b) Sch:* marking (of work); *(c) Com:* trade code.

note [nɔt], *s.f.* **1.** *(a)* note, memorandum, memo, minute; **n. d'avis,** advice note; **n. de débit, de crédit,** debit note, credit note; **prendre des notes sur une feuille de papier,** to take down notes on a piece of paper; **jeter quelques notes sur le papier,** to jot down a few notes; **prononcer un discours en s'aidant de notes,** to speak from notes; *Sch:* **notes de cours,** lecture notes; **prendre n. de qch., prendre qch. en n.,** to note sth.; to take, make, a note of sth.; to make a memorandum of sth., to jot sth. down; **prendre n. d'une commande,** to book an order; **prendre bonne n. de qch.,** to take due note of sth.; **nous prenons bonne n. de . . .,** we duly note . . .; **prenez-en bonne n.!** bear that in mind! **garder n. de qch.,** to keep a note of sth.; *(b)* statement; *Const:* **n. de cubage,** statement of measurement; **n. volante,** ephemeral minute; **n. de service,** minute. **2.** annotation; **n. en bas de page, n. au bas de la page,** foot-note; **n. marginale,** marginal note, side-note. **3.** *(a)* notice; **faire passer une n. dans les journaux,** to have a notice put in the papers; **n. favorable sur un livre,** favourable notice, favourable appreciation, of a book; *(b)* note; **remettez-moi une n. de l'affaire,** let me have a note on the matter; **n. diplomatique,** diplomatic note; *Dipl:* **notes de la même teneur,** identic notes. **4.** *Sch: etc:* mark; **bonne, mauvaise, n.,** good, bad, mark; **notes trimestrielles,** (end-of-term) report; **notes d'examen,** examination marks; **les bonnes notes d'un employé, d'un officier,** an employee's, officer's, good record. **5.** *Mus:* note; **les sept notes de la gamme,** the seven notes of the scale; **faire une fausse n.,** to play or sing a false note; **donner la n.,** (i) to sound the key-note, strike the note, give the lead (to singers, etc.); (ii) *F:* to call the tune, to give the lead, to set the fashion; *F:* **chanter sur une autre n., changer de n.,** to alter one's tone, change one's tune; **cela change la n.,** that alters the matter, that makes a difference; **forcer la n.,** (i) to exaggerate; (ii) to overdo it; **discours dans la n. voulue,** speech that strikes the right note; **votre chapeau n'est pas tout à fait dans la n.,** your hat doesn't exactly suit the occasion; **une n. d'originalité,** a touch, note, of originality. **6.** *(repute)* **un homme de n.,** a man of note. **7.** bill, account, invoice; **faut-il le porter sur la n.?** shall I charge it on the bill? **régler une n.,** to settle an account; **payer la n.,** *F:* to foot the bill.

noté [nɔte], *a.* **homme mal n.,** man of bad reputation; *Adm:* **être bien, mal, n.,** to have a good, bad, record; **être mal n. de, par, qn,** to be in s.o.'s black books; **il est mal n. de +** *inf.,* it is considered very bad to; **personne notée,** person on the black list.

noter [nɔte], *v.tr.* **1.** to note; to take notice of (sth.); **chose à n.,** thing worthy of notice; **cela est à n.,** that is worth remembering; **il sied de n. que,** it is worthy of note that; **il est à n. que,** it should be noted, observed, that; **n. les paroles de qu,** to mark s.o.'s words; **notez bien!** note! mind you! **notez bien ce que je vous dis,** mark my words; **avez-vous noté l'heure?** did you note, notice, the time? *s.a.* INFAMIE 1. **2.** *(a)* to put down, jot down (sth.); to take, make, a note or memorandum of (sth.); to keep track of (sth.); **n. la consommation de combustible,** to keep track of the fuel consumption; **veuillez n. votre réclamation ci-dessous,** please state your claim below; **n. une conversation,** to take minutes of a conversation; *(b)* **n. un passage d'un trait,** to mark a passage in red, with a red line; *(c) Sch:* to mark (work). **3.** *Mus:* **n. un air,** to write out, write down, take down, a tune.

noteur [nɔtœːr], *s.m. Mus: (rare)* music copier.

notice [nɔtis], *s.f.* **1.** notice, account; **une courte n. sur qch., qn,** a short account of, report on, sth., s.o.; **publier une n. dans un journal,** to advertise, publish, a notice in a paper. **2. n. d'un livre,** review of a book. **3.** book(let), handbook, manual; instructions, directions; **n. d'emploi,** (i) directions for use; (ii) instruction-book; **n. explicative,** leaflet (giving directions for use); **n. de fonctionnement,** operating instructions, operating manual; **n. technique,** technical instructions, technical handbook; data sheet; **n. provisoire,** tentative instructions, tentative manual; **n. publicitaire,** (i) advertising brochure; (ii) advertisement (in newspaper).

notification [nɔtifikasjɔ̃], *s.f.* notification, notice, intimation; **recevoir n. de qch.,** to be notified of sth.

notificatif, -ive [nɔtifikatif, -iːv], *a.* **lettre notificative,** letter of notification.

notifier [nɔtifje], *v.tr. (p.d. & pr.sub.* **n. notifiions, v. notifiiez)** **n. qch. à qn,** to notify s.o. of sth.; to intimate sth. to s.o.; **n. son consentement,** to signify one's consent; **on lui notifia qu'il eût à déménager dans les vingt-quatre heures,** he received notice to quit within twenty-four hours.

notion [nosjɔ̃], *s.f.* notion, idea; **la n. du bien et du mal,** the notion of good and evil; **je n'ai aucune n. de ce qu'il veut dire,** I haven't the faintest notion of what he means; **perdre la n. du temps, des dates, de la réalité,** to lose count of time, to forget the date, to lose all sense of reality; *(in vocabulary, etc.)* **n. absente,** no corresponding concept, concept does not exist; **il a des notions de chimie,** he has a smattering of chemistry.

notionnel, -elle [nosjɔnɛl], *a. Ling:* notional; **champ n.,** area of meaning.

notoc(h)orde [nɔtɔkɔrd], *s.f. Biol:* notochord.

notodontides [nɔtɔdɔ̃tid], *s.m.pl. Ent:* Notodontidae, the puss moths, etc.

notoire [nɔtwaːr], *a.* well-known (fact); (fact) of common knowledge; manifest (injustice); **il est n. que . . .,** *(with evil imputation)* it is notorious, is known to all, that . . .; *Jur: A:* **soit n. à tous que . . .,** be it known to all men that . . ..

notoirement [nɔtwarmɑ̃], *adv. (a)* manifestly; *(b)* notoriously.

notonecte [nɔtɔnɛkt], *s.m. Ent:* backswimmer, water-boatman, *U.S:* boat bug.

notoptère [nɔtɔptɛːr], *s.m. Ich:* notopterid (fish); *F:* feather-back.

notoptères [nɔtɔptɛːr], *s.m.pl. Ent:* Notoptera.

notoriété [nɔtɔrjete], *s.f.* **1.** notoriety, notoriousness (of fact); repute (of person); **il est de n. publique que,** it is a matter of common knowledge, it is notorious, that; **avoir de la n.,** to be well-known, to have a (good or bad) reputation. **2.** *Jur:* **acte de n.,** identity certificate (with declaration by seven witnesses); attested affidavit (in proof of death, etc.); **n. de droit,** proof by documentary evidence; **n. de fait,** proof by the evidence of witnesses.

notornis [nɔtɔrnis], *s.m. Orn:* notornis, takahe.

notorycte [nɔtɔrikt], *s.m. Z:* notoryctid.

notoryctidés [nɔtɔriktide], *s.m.pl. Z:* Notoryctidae.

notothénides [nɔtɔtenid], **notothénidés** [nɔtɔtenide], *s.m.pl. Ich:* Nototheniidae.

notre, nos [nɔtr, no], *poss.a.* our; **n. maison et n. jardin,** our house and garden; **nos frères et sœurs,** our brothers and sisters; **nos père et mère,** our father and mother; **n. meilleur ami,** our best friend; *Com:* **de n. place,** in this town; *F:* **voilà n. homme,** (i) that's the man for us; (ii) that's the man we are looking for.

nôtre [noːtr]. **1.** *poss.a.* ours; **sa maison est n.,** his house is ours; **provinces redevenues nôtres,** provinces that have become ours again. **2. le nôtre, la nôtre, les nôtres;** *(a) poss.pron.* ours, our own; **il préfère vos tableaux aux nôtres,** he prefers your pictures to ours; **les deux nôtres,** our two; *(b) s.m.* (i) our own (property, etc.); **nous défendons le n.,** we defend our own; (ii) *pl.* our own (friends, followers, etc.); **aidons les nôtres,** let us help our own (people), our own folk; **est-il des nôtres?** is he one of us? **vous serez des nôtres, n'est-ce pas?** you will join us, join our party, won't you? *(c) s.f.pl. F:* **nous avons bien fait des nôtres,** we have played quite a few tricks of our own.

Notre-Dame [nɔtrədam], *s.f.* **1.** *Ecc:* Our Lady; **la fête de N-D.,** the feast of the Assumption. **2.** (the church of) Notre-Dame (name borne by many churches in France).

notule [nɔtyl], *s.f.* minute, short note, summary.

nouage [nwaːʒ, nu-], *s.m.* **1.** *Tex:* knotting, tying, joining. **2.** knitting (of bone).

nouaison [nwɛzɔ̃, nu-]. *Bot:* first stage in the formation of the fruit.

nouba [nuba], *s.f.* **1.** Algerian military band. **2.** *P:* **faire la n.,** to go on a spree, to paint the town red.

noue[1] [nu], *s.f. Agr:* marshy meadow, water-meadow.

noue[2], *s.f. Const: (a)* valley (of roof); *(b)* **(arêtier de) n.,** valley-rafter, -piece; *(c)* gutter-tile, gutter-lead, flashing.

noué [nwe, nue], *a.* 1. *Med:* (*a*) rickety (child); *F:* esprit n., stunted mind, intelligence; (*b*) articulations nouées, stiff, anchylosed, joints; goutte nouée, chronic gout. 2. *Needlew:* point n., lock-stitch (made by sewing machine). 3. fruit n., fertilized fruit, fruit that has set; set; chienne nouée, bitch in pup.

nouement [numɑ̃], *s.m.* = NOUAGE.

nouer [nwe, nue], *v.tr.* 1. (*a*) to tie, knot; n. qch. serré, to knot sth. tightly, to make a tight knot; n. ses cheveux, se n. les cheveux, to tie up one's hair; n. qch. dans qch., to tie up sth. in sth.; (*b*) *Dressm:* to catch (up); noué souple, loosely caught, loosely tied; (*c*) *F:* n. la gorge d'émotion, to bring a lump to the throat. 2. l'âge lui a noué les membres, age has stiffened his joints. 3. n. conversation avec qn, to enter into conversation with s.o.; n. des relations avec qn, to establish relations with s.o.; *s.a.* AMITIÉ 1. 4. n. l'intrigue (d'une pièce, d'un roman), to bring the plot, the action (of a play, novel) to a head; pièce bien nouée, well-knit play. 5. *v.i.* (*of fruit*) to set, knit.

se nouer. 1. (*a*) (*of cord, thread*) to become knotted; to kink; (*b*) (*of the bowels*) to become twisted. 2. se n. à qch., to fasten, cling, to sth.; le lierre se noue à l'arbre, ivy clings to the tree. 3. *Med:* (*a*) (*of child*) to become rickety; (*b*) (*of joints*) to become anchylosed; to knot; (*c*) (*of broken bone*) to knit; (*d*) (*of muscles*) to stiffen. 4. (*of fruit*) to set, knit.

nouet [nwɛ, nuɛ], *s.m. Cu:* small linen bag for infusions.

noueur, -euse [nwœːr, nuœːr, -øːz], *s.* tier, knotter.

noueux, -euse [nwø, nuø, -øːz], *a.* 1. knotty (string, wood); gnarled (stem, hands). 2. *Med:* anchylosed, knotted (joints, etc.); rhumatisme n., rheumatoid arthritis, arthritis deformans, nodose rheumatism, osseous rheumatism.

nougat [nuga], *s.m.* 1. nougat. 2. *Husb:* nut-oil cake (for cattle). 3. *pl. P:* feet.

nougénèse [nuʒenɛːz], *s.f. Psy:* noegenesis.

nouille [nuːj]. 1. *s.f. normally used in the pl. Cu:* (ribbon) noodle(s). 2. (*in sg.*) *a. & s.f. P:* c'est une n., he's, she's, a drip, a wet; he's, she's, got no guts; quelle n.! what a drip! ce que tu peux être n.! how wet can you get? *F:* style n., spineless style, wishy-washy style.

nouillettes [nujɛt], *s.f.pl. Cu:* small noodles.

noulet [nulɛ], *s.m. Const:* valley gutter.

noumène [numɛn], *s.m. Phil:* noumenon.

nouménie [numeni], *s.f. Gr. & Jew.Ant:* neomenia.

nounou [nunu], *s.f. F:* (*in the nursery*) nanny.

nounours [nunurs], *s.m.* (*child's language*) teddy bear.

nourrain [nurɛ̃], *s.m.* 1. *Pisc:* fry, young fish. 2. *Husb:* young pig.

nourri [nuri], *a.* 1. (*a*) nourished, fed; bien n., well-fed (person); brawny (limbs); mal n., ill-fed, underfed; (*b*) n. des auteurs classiques, steeped in, brought up on, the classics; rapport n. de faits, report well furnished with facts. 2. rich, copious (style); broad, firm (line in drawing); full (tone, sound); thick-laid (paint); acclamations nourries, warm, hearty, prolonged, sustained, acclamations or applause; discussion nourrie, heated debate, lively discussion; *Mil:* feu n., brisk, heavy, well-directed, well-sustained, fire; entretenir un feu n. contre l'ennemi, *F:* to blaze away at the enemy; *Cu:* gigot n. d'ail, leg of mutton well seasoned with garlic; *Nau:* vent n., temps n., feeding gale; *Typ:* caractère n., large thick type.

nourrice [nuris], *s.f.* 1. (wet-)nurse; n. sèche, dry-nurse; conte de n., nursery tale; mère qui est n., nursing mother; la Sicile était la n. de Rome, Rome was fed by Sicily; la mémoire est la n. du génie, genius is fostered by memory; *s.a.* ÉPINGLE 1, MÈRE[1] 1. 2. (wet-)nursing; mettre, prendre, un enfant en n., to put out, take in, a child to nurse; mise en n., fosterage; avoir été changé en n., to have been changed in the cradle; enfant changé en n., changeling; mois de n., suckling-time; *F:* elle a vingt-neuf ans et les mois de n., she is twenty-nine and a bit! 3. *Tchn:* (*a*) auxiliary tank, service-tank; *Aut: Av:* n. d'alimentation d'essence, feed-tank; dash-tank; n. d'huile, oil-feed; (*b*) feed-pipe, -pump; (*c*) *Aut:* spare can (of petrol). 4. *Moll: F:* salpa.

nourricerie [nurisri], *s.f.* 1. *Pej:* baby farm. 2. stock-farm. 3. silk-worm farm.

nourricier, -ière [nurisje, -jɛːr]. 1. *a.* nutritious, nutritive (juices, etc.). 2. *s.m.* (père) nourricier, foster-father; *s.f.* (mère) nourricière, foster-mother. 3. *s.f. Hyd.E:* nourricière, feeder.

nourrir [nuriːr], *v.tr.* to nourish. 1. (*a*) to suckle, nurse (infant); n. un enfant au biberon, to bring up a child by hand, on the bottle; (*b*) to bring up, nurture, rear (children, etc.); to fatten (cattle); nourri dans la misère, nurtured, reared, in poverty; il faut n. les enfants de la vérité, children must be nurtured on truth. 2. (*a*) to feed (people, animals, the fire) (de, avec, with, on); n. qn, to keep, maintain, s.o.; n. sa famille, to maintain one's family; n. des employés, des élèves, to board workers, pupils; la poésie ne nourrit pas son homme, poetry doesn't make a man's living, there's no living to be had from poetry, poetry doesn't earn one's bread and butter; c'est un travail qui nourrit son homme, it's a job that brings in the money; j'ai dix francs par jour et nourri, I get ten francs a day and my keep; cinq cents francs par mois logé et nourri, five hundred francs a month with board and lodging; (*of pasture*) n. de nombreux moutons, to carry a great many sheep; lectures qui nourrissent l'esprit, reading that improves, feeds, the mind; (*b*) *Art:* n. le trait, to give breadth to the line, to the stroke; *Mus:* n. le son, to give fullness, body, volume, to the tone; *El.E:* n. le filament, to flash the filament (of lamp). 3. to foster (plants, hatred); to harbour (thoughts); to cherish, harbour, entertain (hope); n. l'espoir que . . ., to indulge the hope that . . .; n. un sentiment d'injustice, to labour under a sense of injustice; n. des doutes sur qch., to entertain doubts about sth.; n. des intentions hostiles contre qn, to have hostile intentions towards s.o. 4. *abs.* le lait nourrit, milk is nourishing, nutritious; cela nourrit trop, it is too nourishing.

se nourrir. 1. se n. de lait, to live, subsist, on milk; *F:* se n. de rien, avec rien, to eat next to nothing. 2. to keep oneself.

nourrissage [nurisaːʒ], *s.m.* 1. rearing; feeding (of cattle); nourishing (of crystal, etc.). 2. *A: El.E:* flashing (of filament).

nourrissant [nurisɑ̃], *a.* nourishing, nutritive, nutritious; satisfying; rich, substantial (food).

nourrisseur [nurisœːr], *s.m.* 1. *Husb:* (*a*) stock-raiser; (*b*) cow-keeper, dairyman. 2. *Tchn:* feed-roll (of various machines).

nourrisson [nurisɔ̃], *s.m. A:* **nourrissonne** [nurisɔn], *s.f.* 1. baby at the breast; infant. 2. nurs(e)ling, foster-child, nurse-child.

nourriture [nurityːr], *s.f.* 1. (*a*) feeding, suckling (of infant); (*b*) *Husb:* feeding, rearing (of cattle); (*c*) n. de l'esprit, nurture of the mind; *Prov:* n. passe nature, nurture is stronger than nature. 2. food, nourishment, sustenance; provender (for cattle); priver qn de n., to starve s.o.; il ne gagne pas sa n., he isn't worth his keep, his salt; n. de l'esprit, mental pabulum. 3. board, keep; la n. et le logement, board and lodging; avoir sa n. en argent, to be on board wages; *Mil:* n. chez l'habitant, billets with subsistence.

nous [nu], *pers.pron.* 1. (*a*) (*subject*) we; n. venons, we are coming; n. l'avons vu, we saw him; (*b*) (*object*) us; to us; il ne n. connaît pas, he does not know us; appelez-n., call us; lisez-le-n., read it to us; il n. en a parlé, he spoke to us about it; il n. en prêtera, he will lend us some; (*c*) (*reflexive*) n. n. chauffons, we are warming ourselves; n. n. sommes arrogé ce droit, we have arrogated that right to ourselves; *with many verbs is not rendered into English; see* S'EN ALLER, SE BATTRE, SE DÉPÊCHER, etc.; (*d*) (*reciprocal*) n. n. connaissons, we know each other. 2. (*stressed*) (*a*) (*subject*) we; n. deux, n. trois, we two, we three; n. et les domestiques, n. partons tout de suite, we and the servants will set off at once; c'est n. qui sommes à blâmer, it is we who are to blame; n. autres Anglais ne faisons pas comme vous, we English don't do as you do; ils sont plus riches que n., they are richer than we; n. l'avons fait n.-mêmes, we did it ourselves; (*b*) (*complement*) il resta chez n. tout un mois, he stayed with us, at our house, a whole month; un ami à n., a friend of ours; ce livre est à n., that book is ours, belongs to us; c'est à n. de jouer, it is our turn to play; c'est à n.-mêmes d'aviser, it is for us to take steps; entre n. soit dit, this is between ourselves; *F:* ce que c'est que de n.! such is life! n. deux, n. trois, n. tous, the two of us, the three of us, all of us; us two, us three, us all; combien d'argent avons-n. à n. deux (trois, quatre, tous)? how much money have we got between us? the two of us? etc. 3. (*plural of majesty, editorial 'we,' with concords in the singular*) we; n. avons décrété que . . ., we have decreed that . . .; n. sommes n.-même convaincu que . . ., we ourself are convinced that . . .. 4. *F:* (= VOUS) eh bien, petite, il paraît que n. n'avons pas été sage, well, my dear, I hear someone has been a naughty girl; et bien, ma petite fille, sommes-n. heureuse? well, my dear, are you, *F:* we, happy?

nous-même(s) [numɛm], *pers.pron. See* MÊME 1 (*c*) and NOUS 2, 3.

nouure [nuyːr], *s.f.* 1. *Hort:* setting (of fruit). 2. *Med:* rickets.

nouveau, -el, -elle[1], -eaux [nuvo, -ɛl], *a.* (*the form* nouvel *is used before m. sing. nouns beginning with a vowel or h 'mute'; also occ. before* et.) 1. new (invention, play, etc.); new-style (calendar, etc.); sujet toujours n., ever new topic; plaisir toujours n., pleasure that never stales; vêtu à la nouvelle mode, dressed in the latest fashion; habit n., coat of a new cut; modèle plus n., more up-to-date model; quelque chose de n., something new; il était n. qu'une femme se fît avocat, it was something new for a woman to be called to the bar; il n'y a rien de n., there is nothing new, no news; quoi de n.? what (is the) news? je suis n. dans ce métier, I am new to this trade; homme n. aux affaires, man new to, inexperienced in, business, etc.; *s.m.pl. Sch:* les nouveaux, the new boys; *Prov:* à nouvelles affaires, nouveaux conseils, sufficient unto the day is the evil thereof; rien n'est n. sous le soleil, there is nothing new under the sun; tout n. tout beau, everyone has a penny to spend at a new ale-house; *s.m.* j'ai appris du n., I have heard something new; I have some news; c'est du n.! that is news to me, to us; savez-vous du n.? have you any news? il y a du n. depuis hier, there are new developments since yesterday. 2. (*a*) new, recent, fresh; vin n., pommes de terre nouvelles, new wine, new potatoes; l'herbe nouvelle, the young grass; un homme n., an upstart, *novus homo*; (*b*) (*with adv. function* newly, recently; le nouvel arrivé, le n. venu, les nouveaux arrivés, les nouveaux venus, the new-comer(s); une nouvelle venue dans notre société, a newcomer to, in, our circle; les nouveaux convertis, les nouvelles converties, the new converts; je suis n. venu dans cette ville, I am new to this town; n. riche, upstart, nouveau riche; vin n.-tiré, new-drawn wine; des sentiers nouveaux, untrodden paths; *s.a.* MARIÉ 1. 3. another, a second, new, fresh, further, additional; un nouvel et éclatant exemple de sa libéralité, a fresh and conspicuous example of his open-handedness; un nouvel époux, another husband; commencer un n. chapitre, to begin a fresh chapter; nouvelle raison, further, additional, reason; n. silence, another pause; un nouvel Attila, a second Attila; jusqu'à nouvel ordre, till further order, until further notice; un nouvel acompte de cent francs, a further hundred francs on account; il met tous les jours un nouvel habit, he wears a different coat every day; (*cf.* habit nouveau in 1); la nouvelle génération, the rising generation; la nouvelle lune, the new moon; le nouvel an, the new year; *Sch:* nouveaux extraits, alternative extracts. 4. *adv.phr.* (*a*) de n., again; on se bat de n., they are fighting again; ses larmes coulaient de n., her tears had started afresh; (*b*) à n., (all over) again; étudier une question à n., to re-examine a question, to go into it again; *Com:* solde à n., balance brought forward; *F:* les "à nouveau," repeat orders. 5. *Pr.n.f. F:* la Nouvelle (= LA NOUVELLE-CALÉDONIE), the New Caledonia penal colony.

Nouveau-Brunswick [nuvobrœzvik], *Pr.n.m. Geog:* New Brunswick.

Nouveau-Mexique [nuvomeksik], *Pr.n.m. Geog:* New Mexico.

nouveau-né, -née [nuvone], *a. & s.* new-born (child); *pl. nouveau-nés, -nées.*

nouveauté [nuvote], *s.f.* 1. newness, novelty; le charme de la n., the charm of novelty; costume de haute n., costume in the latest style. 2. change, innovation; la n. répugne aux vieillards, old people hate change; c'est une n. que de vous voir sourire, it is something new, quite a change, to see you smile; ce fut une n. pour eux, it was a new experience for them. 3. new invention, new publication, etc.; se tenir au courant des nouveautés, to keep abreast of new ideas. 4. *pl. Com:* fancy articles, fancy goods, dry goods; marchand de nouveautés, linen-draper; magasin de nouveautés, draper's shop; (drapery and fancy goods) stores.

nouvelle[2] [nuvɛl], *s.f.* 1. (*a*) (piece of) news; bonne, mauvaise, n., good, bad, news; *Lit:* good, bad, tidings; une triste n., a sad piece of news, sad news; (en voilà la) première n., that's the first I've heard of it; recevoir une n., avoir n. de qch., to receive a piece of news, to have news of sth.; **débiter des nouvelles,** to spread news; **quelles nouvelles?** what is the news? **je vais aux nouvelles,** I am going in quest of information; *Journ:* **dernières nouvelles,** latest intelligence; **nouvelles judiciaires,** police intelligence; **nouvelles de l'intérieur,** home news; **nouvelles à la main,** (handwritten) broadsheet; *Journ:* **une grosse n.,** a scoop; *Fr.C:* **chef des nouvelles,** news editor, *U.S:* city editor; (*b*) *pl.* tidings, news (of, about, s.o.); **demander, (aller) prendre, des nouvelles de (la santé de) qn,** to inquire, ask, after s.o.('s health); **envoyer savoir des nouvelles de qn,** to send to ask after s.o.; **envoyez-moi de vos nouvelles,** let me hear from you; **j'ai (reçu) de ses nouvelles,** I have heard (i) from him, (ii) of him; **on n'eut plus jamais de ses nouvelles,** he was never heard of again; **il m'a demandé de ses nouvelles,** he asked me about him; *F:* **j'ai de vos nouvelles!** I have heard about your goings-on! **vous m'en direz des nouvelles,** you will be astonished at it, delighted with it, I'm sure you'll like it; **goûtez cela, vous m'en direz des nouvelles,** just you taste that! **vous aurez de mes nouvelles!** I'll give you something to think about! you shall hear from me! I'll make you sit up! *Prov:* **pas de nouvelles, bonnes nouvelles,** no news is good news; **les mauvaises nouvelles ont des ailes,** ill news flies apace. **2.** *Lit:* (long) short story.

Nouvelle-Amsterdam [nuvɛlamstɛrdam], *Pr.n.f. Geog:* New Amsterdam.

Nouvelle-Angleterre [nuvɛlɑ̃glətɛːr], *Pr.n.f. Geog:* New England.

Nouvelle-Bretagne [nuvɛlbrətaɲ], *Pr.n.f. Geog:* New Britain (in the East Indies).

Nouvelle-Calédonie [nuvɛlkaledɔni], *Pr.n.f. Geog:* New Caledonia; **en N.-C.,** in New Caledonia; *s.a.* NOUVEAU 5.

Nouvelle-Castille [nuvɛlkastiːj], *Pr.n.f. Geog:* New Castile.

Nouvelle-Delhi [nuvɛldɛli], *Pr.n.f. Geog:* New Delhi.

Nouvelle-Écosse [nuvɛlekɔs], *Pr.n.f. Geog:* Nova Scotia.

Nouvelle-Galles du Sud [nuvɛlgaldysyd], *Pr.n.f. Geog:* New South Wales; **dans la N.-G. du S.,** in New South Wales.

Nouvelle-Guinée [nuvɛlgine], *Pr.n.f. Geog:* New Guinea.

nouvellement [nuvɛlmɑ̃], *adv.* newly, lately, recently; **il était n. débarqué de New York,** he was fresh from New York.

Nouvelle-Orléans (la) [lanuvɛlɔrleɑ̃], *Pr.n.f. Geog:* New Orleans.

Nouvelles-Hébrides (les) [lenuvɛlzebrid], *Pr.n.f. pl. Geog:* the New Hebrides (Islands).

Nouvelle-Zélande [nuvɛlzelɑ̃ːd], *Pr.n.f. Geog:* New Zealand.

Nouvelle-Zemble [nuvɛlzɑ̃ːbl], *Pr.n.f. Geog:* Nova Zembla.

nouvellier [nuvɛlje], *s.m.* (*a*) *Lit.Hist:* writer of tales; (*b*) *A:* novelette writer, short-story writer.

nouvelliste [nuvɛlist], *s.m. & f.* **1.** *A:* news-monger, intelligencer. **2.** short-story writer. **3.** *Journ: A: F:* par writer, news writer; **n. à la main,** editor of, contributor to, the "wit and humour" column or the social gossip column.

nova [nɔva], *s.f. Astr:* nova; *pl. novæ.*

novaculite [nɔvakylit], *s.f. Geol:* novaculite.

novale [nɔval], *a.f. & s.f.* **1.** *Agr:* newly broken-up (land). **2.** *pl. A:* **(dîmes) novales,** tithes (on new land).

Novare [nɔvaːr], *Pr.n. Geog:* Novara.

novarois, -oise [nɔvarwa, -waːz], *a. & s. Geog:* (native, inhabitant) of Novara.

novateur, -trice [nɔvatœːr, -tris]. **1.** *a.* innovating (mind, etc.). **2.** *s.* innovator.

novation [nɔvasjɔ̃], *s.f. Jur:* **1.** novation, substitution (of new obligation for an old one); **n. de créance,** substitution (of debt). **2.** renewal (of lease, etc.). **3.** *Biol:* emergence.

novatoire [nɔvatwaːr], *a. Jur:* pertaining to, regarding, of the nature of, a novation.

novelette [nɔv(ə)lɛt], *s.f. Mus:* novelette.

novembre [nɔvɑ̃ːbr], *s.m.* November; **en n.,** in November; **au mois de n.,** in the month of November; **le premier, le sept, n.,** (on) the first, the seventh, of November, (on) November (the) first, (the) seventh, **le Onze N.,** Armistice Day.

nover [nɔve], *v.tr. Jur:* **1.** to substitute (debt). **2.** to renew (lease, etc.).

novice [nɔvis]. **1.** *s.m. & f.* novice (in convent); probationer (in profession); tiro, tyro; fresh hand (in trade); *Scouting:* tenderfoot; *Nau:* **n. au commerce,** apprentice to the merchant service; ordinary seaman; *F:* **ferveur de n.,** beginner's enthusiasm; *Prov:* **il n'est ferveur que de n.,** a new broom sweeps clean; **faire le n.,** to sham inexperience or ignorance. **2.** *a.* **être n. à, dans, qch.,** to be new to sth., unpractised in sth.; **il est encore n.,** he is still raw, still inexperienced; **encore n. à la guerre,** still new to war, still a tyro in war; **il n'est pas n.,** he is an old hand.

noviciat [nɔvisja], *s.m.* noviciate. **1.** (*a*) period of probation (of professing nun or monk); (*b*) apprenticeship (**à,** to); **faire son n.,** (i) to go through one's noviciate; (ii) to serve one's apprenticeship. **2.** building, quarters, allotted to the novices (in convent).

novocaïne [nɔvɔkain], *s.f. Pharm:* novocaine.

noyade [nwajad], *s.f.* **1.** drowning (fatality). **2.** *Fr.Hist:* (collective) execution by drowning; noyade (as carried out by Carrier in 1793).

noyage [nwajaːʒ], *s.m. Nau: etc:* flooding; **robinet, vanne, de n.,** flooding cock.

noyau, -aux [nwajo], *s.m.* **1.** stone (of fruit); kernel; **n. de cerise,** cherry-stone; **fruit à n.,** stone-fruit; **enlever le n. du fruit,** to stone the fruit; **eau, crème, de n.,** noyau (liqueur); *F:* **siège rembourré avec des noyaux de pêche,** hard seat. **2.** (*a*) *Ph: Biol:* nucleus (of atom, cell, comet, etc.); *Ph:* **n. atomique,** atomic nucleus; **n. naturellement radioactif,** naturally radioactive nucleus; **n. artificiellement radioactif,** artificially radioactive nucleus; **n. enfanté, engendré,** daughter nucleus; **n. original, n. père,** parent nucleus; **n. pair-pair, pair-impair,** even-even, even-odd, nucleus; **n. impair-impair, impair-pair,** odd-odd, odd-even, nucleus; *Mil:* **n. de bombe nucléaire,** (nuclear) bomb core; *Biol:* **n. de cristallisation,** nucleus of crystallization; (*b*) nucleus (of colony, etc.); *F:* **un petit n. de joueurs,** a small knot of players; *Navy:* **n. d'équipage,** skeleton crew; *Pol:* **n. communiste,** communist cell; *Mil:* **n. de résistance,** focus, nucleus, island, of resistance. **3.** *Tchn:* (*a*) *Const:* newel (of stairs); **escalier à n. plein,** winding stair; (*b*) stem, shank, (of bolt, screw); (*c*) plug, key (of cock); (*d*) hub (of wheel); (*e*) *El.E:* core (of armature); **pertes dans le n.,** core-losses; **n. aimanté,** magnet core; **n. magnétique,** magnetic core; **n. polaire,** pole core; **n. (en fer) feuilleté,** laminated core; (*f*) *Metall:* core (of mould); **grand n.,** nowel; **n. autosiccatif,** air-set core; **logement, portée, du n.,** core print; **coulage à n.,** core-casting; **couler à n.,** to cast upon a core; *s.a.* MOULAGE[2] 1; (*g*) *Civ.E:* **n. d'étanchéité,** watertight core; (*h*) **n. volcanique,** volcanic bomb.

noyautage [nwajotaːʒ], *s.m.* **1.** *Pol:* infiltration, setting up of (Communist) cells (**de,** in); **le n. des syndicats par les communistes,** the infiltration of the Communists into the trade-unions. **2.** *Metall:* coring (of mould).

noyauter [nwajote], *v.tr.* **1.** *Pol:* to set up (communist) cells in (trade-union, etc.); to establish groups of propagandists in (a society); to infiltrate. **2.** *Metall:* to core (mould); **machine à n.,** coring machine, core-making machine.

noyauterie [nwajotri], *s.f. Metall:* core-making.

noyauteur [nwajotœːr], *s.m. Metall:* (*pers.*) core maker.

noyauteuse [nwajotøːz], *s.f. Metall:* coring machine, core-making machine.

noyé [nwaje], *a.* **1.** (*a*) (i) drowned; (ii) drowning; *s.* **secours aux noyés,** first aid for the drowned; *Prov:* **un n. s'accroche à un brin de paille,** a drowning man will clutch at a straw; (*b*) *F:* (*of wine*) over-diluted; (*c*) *Games:* **boule noyée,** dead bowl. **2.** flooded (bunker, carburettor); choked (engine). **3.** (counter)sunk (screw); (nail) driven in flush; *Phot:* **monture noyée,** sunk mount (of lens); **vis à tête noyée,** countersunk screw; **n. dans le béton,** embedded in concrete; *El.E:* **plots noyés,** sunk studs. **4. roche noyée,** sunken rock. **5.** blurred (outline); swimming (eyes).

noyer[1] [nwaje], *s.m. Bot:* walnut (tree, wood); **n. (blanc) d'Amérique,** hickory, shell-bark; **n. cendré,** butter-nut.

noyer[2], *v.tr.* **(je noie, n. noyons; je noierai) 1.** to drown (s.o.); to swamp, inundate, deluge (the earth, etc.); **yeux noyés de larmes,** eyes brimming with tears; **champs noyés d'ombre,** fields bathed in shade; **leur faillite me noierait,** their failure would ruin me, *F:* would swamp me; *F:* **noyé de dettes,** sunk in debt; **noyé dans la foule,** lost in the crowd; **n. son chagrin dans le vin,** to drown one's sorrows in drink; **n. son vin, son whisky,** to put too much water into, to drown, one's wine or one's whisky; *s.a.* CHIEN 1. **2.** (*a*) to flood (bunker, carburettor, etc.); **n. la mèche de son briquet,** to flood one's lighter; (*b*) to bed (sth.) in cement; (*c*) to countersink (screw); to drive (nail) in flush; (*d*) *Nau:* **n. la terre,** to settle, lay, the land; (*of ship*) **coque noyée,** hull down; (*e*) *Paint:* to blend, mix (colours on canvas); (*f*) *Bowls:* to send (bowl) out of bounds. **3. n. le poisson,** (i) to play the fish; (ii) *F:* to tire out one's opponent; to discourage author, inventor, etc., by leaving his MS, his plans, etc., behind in the safe "by mistake"; to pigeon-hole.

se noyer, (*a*) **se n. (volontairement),** to drown oneself; **(par accident),** to be drowned; **il courait le risque de se n.,** he was in danger of drowning; **un homme qui se noie,** a drowning man; *Prov:* **un homme qui se noie s'attache à un brin de paille,** a drowning man will catch at a straw; *F:* **il est en train de se n.,** he is on the road to ruin, he is ruining his prospects; **il se noierait dans une goutte, un verre, d'eau,** *P:* **un crachat,** he comes a cropper at the least obstacle; he makes a mountain of every mole-hill; **se n. dans les détails,** to get bogged down in details, not to see the wood for the trees; (*b*) **se n. dans le sang,** to wallow in blood; **se n. dans le vin,** to steep oneself in drink; (*c*) **la nef se noie dans une demi-lumière,** the nave is bathed in a half-light.

noyeraie [nwajərɛ], *s.f.* walnut plantation.

noyon [nwajɔ̃], *s.m.* boundary-line (at bowls).

noyonnais, -aise [nwajɔnɛ, -ɛːz], *a. & s.* (native, inhabitant) of Noyon.

noyure [nwajyːr], *s.f. Tchn:* countersink, chamfered hole (for screw, etc.).

nu[1] [ny], *s.m. Gr.Alph:* nu.

nu[2]. **1.** *a.* (*a*) unclothed; naked (person); bare (shoulders, limbs, wire); *Art:* nude (figure); **être presque nu,** to have hardly anything on; *s.a.* CHEMISE 1; **mettez-vous torse nu,** strip to the waist; **elles se baignent toutes nues,** they bathe in the nude; *F:* **nu comme la main,** bare as the back of my hand; **mettre qn nu comme la main,** to strip s.o. to the buff; **nu comme un ver,** stark naked; NOTE: **nu** *before the noun that it qualifies is invariable and is joined to the noun by a hyphen;* **aller (la) tête nue, (les) pieds nus, (les) jambes nues, aller nu-tête, nu-pieds, nu-jambes,** to go bare-headed, barefooted, barelegged; **ceux qui sont nus,** the naked, the destitute; **visible à l'œil nu,** visible to the naked eye; **observer le ciel à l'œil nu,** to observe the heavens with the naked eye; **cheval nu,** barebacked horse; (*b*) uncovered, plain, undisguised; **sabre nu,** naked sword; **la vérité nue,** the plain, naked, truth; **exposer son âme toute nue,** to lay bare one's soul; (*c*) **vendre un cheval nu,** *A:* to sell a horse without saddle or bridle; **vendre des vins nus,** to make an extra charge for the casks, for the bottles; **châssis nu,** stripped chassis; *El:* **fil nu,** open wire, open-wire conductor; (*d*) bare (country, tree, room); *Tchn:* unequipped; *s.a.* PROPRIÉTAIRE 1, PROPRIÉTÉ 1. **2.** *s.m.* (*a*) *Art:* (the) nude; nudity; **des nus,** studies from the nude; **poser pour le nu,** to sit in the nude; (*b*) bare part (of wall, etc.). **3.** *adv.phr.* **à nu,** bare, naked; (*a*) **mettre qch. à nu,** to lay bare, expose, denude, uncover, strip, sth.; **mettre un terrain à nu,** to clear a piece of land; **mettre son cœur à nu,** to lay bare one's heart; **arbres mis à nu,** denuded trees; *s.a.* MISE 1; (*b*) **monter un cheval à nu,** to ride a horse bareback(ed).

nuage [nɥaːʒ], *s.m.* cloud; (*a*) **n. à grain, orageux,** rain cloud, thunder cloud; **n. en queue de vache, de chat,** cirrus, mare's tail; **n. en bandes,** stratus; **nuages pommelés,** mackerel sky; **n. en surfusion,** supercooled cloud; **sans nuages,** cloudless (sky); unclouded (life, future); unalloyed (happiness); **n. de poussière, de fumée,** cloud of dust, of smoke; **le ciel se couvrait de nuages,** the sky was clouding over; **ciel couvert de nuages,** overcast sky; **masses de nuages,** masses of cloud; *Mil: Navy:* **n. artificiel,** smoke-screen; (*of nuclear explosion*) **n. de base,** base surge; (*b*) haze, mist (on mirror, before the eyes); (*c*) gloom, shadow; **aucun n. ne vint, assombrir leur bonheur,** no cloud came to cast a gloom over their happiness; **il n'y a pas de bonheur sans nuages,** there is no such thing as perfect bliss; **un n. de tristesse assombrissait son front,** her face was clouded with sadness; **être, se perdre, dans les nuages,** to be in the clouds, day-dreaming; (*of orator, writer*) **se perdre dans les nuages,** to become obscure; (*d*) dash, tiny drop (of milk in a cup of tea).

nuagé [nɥaʒe], *a.* **1.** clouded (coat of fur, etc.). **2.** *Her:* nebuly.

nuageux, -euse [nɥaʒø, -øːz], *a.* (*a*) cloudy (weather); overcast (sky); clouded over; **état n. de l'horizon,** cloudiness, haziness, of the horizon; (*b*) hazy (thought, ideas).

nuançage [nɥɑ̃saːʒ], *s.m.* colouring, shading (of embroidery, etc.).

nuance [nɥɑ̃:s], *s.f.* (*a*) shade (of colour); hue; nuances variées, variegated hues; *Mus:* les nuances, the lights and shades (of expression); il joue sans nuances, he plays without any light and shade; (*b*) gradation, slight difference, shade (in meaning, in tone); une n. de regret, d'amertume, de mépris, a touch, a tinge, a suggestion, of regret, of bitterness, of contempt; journaux de toutes les nuances, newspapers of every hue, of every shade of opinion; il y a une n., there is a slight difference of meaning; je ne saisis pas la n., I don't quite see the difference; je ne vous le donne pas, je vous le prête, n.! I'm not giving it to you, I'm lending it, understand!

nuancé [nɥɑ̃se], *a.* made of various tints; shaded (feathers, embroidery); (design) showing light and shade; subtle, full of nuances; vers finement nuancés, verse full of delicate light and shade; voix nuancée d'un léger accent exotique, voice with slightly exotic inflexions; une fin de non-recevoir nuancée mais ferme, a moderately, but firmly, toned refusal.

nuancement [nɥɑ̃smɑ̃], *s.m.* shading, blending (of colours, tones).

nuancer [nɥɑ̃se], *v.tr.* (je nuançai(s); n. nuançons) 1. to blend, shade (colours) (de, with). 2. to vary (tone, etc); to express faint differences in (character, etc.); *Mus:* n. son jeu, to introduce light and shade into one's playing. 3. to moderate (refusal, etc.).

nuancier [nɥɑ̃sje], *s.m.* *Com:* sample card, chart (of colour range).

nubécule [nybekyl], *s.f.* *Med:* *Astr:* nubecula.

Nubie [nybi], *Pr.n.f.* *Geog:* Nubia.

nubien, -ienne [nybjɛ̃, -jɛn], *a. & s.* *Geog:* Nubian.

nubile [nybil], *a.* marriageable, nubile (age, girl); *Jur:* âge n., age of consent.

nubilité [nybilite], *s.f.* nubility; marriageable age.

nucal, nuchal, -aux [nykal, -o], *a.* *Anat:* nuchal.

nucelle [nysɛl], *s.f.* *Bot:* nucellus (of ovule).

nucifère [nysifɛ:r], *a.* *Bot:* nuciferous, nut-bearing.

nuciforme [nysifɔrm], *a.* *Bot:* *Anat:* nuciform.

nucivore [nysivɔ:r], *a.* nucivorous.

nucléaire [nykleɛ:r], *a.* nuclear; physique n., nuclear physics; rayonnement n., nuclear radiation; réaction n., nuclear reaction; fission n., nuclear fission; arme n., nuclear weapon; les puissances nucléaires, the Nuclear Powers.

nucléase [nyklea:z], *s.f.* *Ch:* nuclease.

nucléé [nyklee], *a.* *Biol:* *etc:* nucleate(d) (cell, etc.).

nucléide [nykleid], *s.m.* *Atom.Ph:* nuclide.

nucléine [nyklein], *s.f.* *Ch:* nuclein.

nucléique [nykleik], *a.* *Ch:* nucleic.

nucléiste [nykleist], *s.m.* nuclear scientist.

nucléobranche [nykleɔbrɑ̃:ʃ], *s.m.* *Moll:* nucleobranch; *pl.* Nucleobranchiata, Heteropoda.

nucléolaire [nykleɔlɛ:r], *a.* nucleolar.

nucléole [nykleɔl], *s.m.* *Biol:* nucleolus, nucleole.

nucléolé [nykleɔle], *a.* *Biol:* nucleolate(d).

nucléon [nykleɔ̃], *s.m.* *Atom.Ph:* nucleon.

nucléonique [nykleɔnik], *Atom.Ph:* 1. *a.* nucleonic, 2. *s.f.* nucleonics.

nucléophile [nykleɔfil], *a.* *Ch:* nucleophilic.

nucléophilie [nykleɔfili], *s.f.* *Ch:* nucleophilicity.

nucléoplasme [nykleɔplasm], *s.m.* *Biol.* nucleoplasm.

nucléoprotéide [nykleɔprɔteid], *s.f.* *Physiol:* nucleo-proteid.

nucléoside [nykleɔzid], *s.m.* *Bio-Ch:* nucleosid(e).

nucléothermique [nykleɔtɛrmik], *a.* *Atom.Ph:* nucleothermic.

nuclide [nyklid], *s.m.* *Atom.Ph:* nuclide.

nucule [nykyl], *s.f.* 1. *Bot:* nutlet. 2. *Moll:* nucula.

nudibranche [nydibrɑ̃:ʃ], *s.m.* *Moll:* 1. nudibranch; n. mauve, plumed aeolis. 2. *pl.* nudibranches, Nudibranchi(at)a.

nudisme [nydism], *s.m.* nudism.

nudiste [nydist], *s.m. & f.* nudist.

nudité [nydite], *s.f.* 1. (*a*) nudity, nakedness; (*b*) bareness (of rock, wall, etc.). 2. *Art:* (the) nude; peindre des nudités, to paint nude figures.

nue [ny], *s.f.* (*a*) *A. & Lit:* high cloud(s); l'éclair perce la nue, the lightning pierces the clouds; (*b*) *pl.* skies; *F:* porter, élever, qn, qch., (jusqu') aux nues, to laud, praise, s.o., sth., to the skies; *F:* to crack s.o., sth., up; se perdre dans les nues, to lose oneself in the clouds, in day-dreams; tomber des nues, (i) to arrive unexpectedly; (ii) to be thunderstruck; sauter aux nues, to leap, go wild, with joy, indignation, etc.

nuée [nɥe], *s.f.* (*a*) (large) cloud, thunder cloud, storm cloud; (*b*) n. de cendres (au-dessus d'un volcan), ash cloud; n. ardente, incandescent ash-cloud; (*c*) une n. d'insectes, de traits, a cloud of insects, of darts; une n. d'ennemis, a host of enemies; (*d*) cloud (in precious stone).

nuement [nymɑ̃], *adv.* = NÛMENT.

nue-propriété [nyprɔpriete], *s.f.* *Jur:* bare ownership, ownership without usufruct; *pl.* *nues-propriétés.*

nuer [nɥe], *v.tr.* *Tchn:* to match colours (in silk and wool).

nuire [nɥi:r], *v.ind.tr.* (*pr.p.* nuisant; *p.p.* nui; *pr.ind.* je nuis, il nuit, n. nuisons, ils nuisent; *pr. sub.* je nuise, n. nuisions; *p.d.* je nuisais; *p.h.* je nuisis; *fu.* je nuirai); n. à qn, à qch., to be hurtful, injurious, prejudicial, to s.o., to sth.; il cherche à vous n., he is trying to injure you (in business, etc.); cela ne nuira en rien, that will do no harm; cela nuira à sa réputation, it will injure, detract from, his reputation; fait qui aurait pu n. à son avancement, fact that might have prejudiced, proved an obstacle to, his promotion; cela vous nuira dans l'esprit du public, that will go against you with the public; n. aux intérêts de qn, to prejudice s.o.'s interests; ils se sont nui l'un à l'autre, they worked against each other's interests; they did each other harm; l'alcool nuit à la santé, alcohol is injurious to health; *F:* cela n'a pas nui à son succès, this was no slight contribution to his success; trop parler nuit, talking too much is harmful; *Jur:* dans l'intention de n., maliciously; *s.a.* ABONDANCE 1, CUIRE 2, DUIRE.

nuisances [nɥizɑ̃:s], *s.f.pl.* causes of harm; harmful effects, nuisances.

nuisibilité [nɥizibilite], *s.f.* harmfulness, injuriousness, noxiousness.

nuisible [nɥizibl̩], *a.* hurtful, harmful, noxious, detrimental, prejudicial (à, to); n. à la santé, detrimental to health; animaux, plantes, nuisibles, noxious, animals, plants; *s.m.pl.* les nuisibles, vermin.

nuisiblement [nɥizibləmɑ̃], *adv.* harmfully, injuriously.

nuit [nɥi], *s.f.* night; (*a*) la n., night time; la n. dernière, last night; cette n., (i) tonight; (ii) last night; la n. de lundi à mardi, du lundi au mardi, the night from Monday to Tuesday; je dormirai bien cette n., I shall sleep well tonight; j'ai beaucoup rêvé cette n., I dreamt a great deal last night; veiller jusqu'à une heure avancée de la n., to sit up far into the night; passer une bonne, une mauvaise, n., to have a good, bad, night('s rest); passer la n. à faire qch., to sit up all night, to spend the night, doing sth.; *F:* on a passé la n. (à faire la fête), we made a night of it; il ne passera pas la n., he will not live through the night; passer la n. chez des amis, to stay overnight with friends; (je vous souhaite une) bonne n., (I wish you) good night; toute la n., the whole night, all night long, the livelong night; j'ai pris le bateau de n., I took the night boat; (*of workman*) être de n., to be on night shift; vêtements de n., nightwear, night attire; *Com:* slumber wear; bonnet, filet, de n., slumber cap; oiseau de n., night-bird; *Paint:* effet de n., night effect, night piece; *Poet:* l'astre, la reine, des nuits, the queen of night, the moon; partir de n., to set off at night; voyager de n., la n., to travel by night, at night; n. et jour [nɥiteʒu:r], night and day; je n'ai pas dormi de la n., I did not close my eyes all night; I never slept a wink all night; faire de la n. le jour et du jour la n., to turn night into day and day into night; les Mille et une Nuits, the Arabian Nights; payer pour sa n., to pay for one's night's lodging; *s.a.* BLANC I 4, CONSEIL 1, SAC[1] 1; (*b*) darkness; la n. vient, tombe, il commence à faire n., il se fait n., night is falling; it is growing dark, getting dark; il fait déjà n., it is dark already; la n. était venue, night had come, had fallen, had closed in; à la n. tombante, at nightfall, at dusk; après la tombée de la n., à (la) n. close, à la n. faite, after dark; être surpris par la n., to be, to find oneself, overtaken by darkness; *Prov:* la n. tous les chats sont gris, when candles are away all cats are grey; la n. de l'ignorance, the darkness of ignorance; la n. se fit dans son esprit, darkness descended upon his mind; coutume dont l'origine se perd dans la n. des temps, custom the origin of which is lost in the mists of time; *s.a.* JOUR 1.

nuitamment [nɥitamɑ̃], *adv.* by night, in the night.

nuitée [nɥite], *s.f.* 1. whole night; longue n. passée parmi les bois, long night spent among the woods. 2. night's work; night-shift. 3. *A:* (cost of a) night's lodging.

nuiton, -onne [nɥitɔ̃, -ɔn], *a. & s.* *Geog:* (native, inhabitant) of Nuits-Saint-Georges.

nu-jambes [nyʒɑ̃:b], *adv.phr.* See NU[2] 1.

nul, nulle [nyl]. 1. (*with* ne *expressed or understood*) (*a*) *indef. a.* no, not one; n. espoir, no hope; il n'a nulle cause de se plaindre, he has no reason to complain; sans nulle vanité, without any conceit; *s.a.* PART[1] 3; (*b*) *indef.pron.* no one, nobody; n. ne le sait, no one knows; n. n'est prophète en son pays, no man is a prophet in his own country; n. que moi ne le sait, none but I knows of it; n. n'est mieux placé que nous pour . . ., nobody is better placed than we are to . . .. 2. (*a*) worthless (argument, effort); c'est un homme n., he is a man of no account, a mere cipher, a nonentity; esprit n., empty mind; élève n. en histoire, absolute dud at history; (*b*) *Jur:* n. et de n. effet, n. et sans effet, n. et non avenu, invalid, null and void; déclarer un décret n. et non avenu, to annul, to abate, a decree; considérer une lettre comme nulle et non avenue, to consider a letter as cancelled; acte qui rend une opération nulle, act that vitiates a transaction; bulletin (de vote) n., spoilt paper; *Sp:* course, manche, nulle, dead heat; "course nulle," "no race"; faire match n., to draw a game; partie nulle, drawn game, draw; balle nulle, no ball (at cricket); *Ling:* lettre nulle, unsounded letter; (*c*) non-existent; capitaux presque nuls, almost non-existent capital; (*d*) *Mec:* tension nulle, zero tension. 3. *s.f.* nulle, dummy letter (in cipher); null.

nullard, -arde [nyla:r, -ard], *a. & s.* *P:* useless (person); hopeless (person).

nullement [nylmɑ̃], *adv.* (*with* ne *expressed or understood*) not at all, by no means; n'être n. propre à qch., to be not at all suitable for sth.; nous ne sommes n. surpris, we are not in the least surprised; il n'est n. sot, he is by no means a fool; cela vous étonne?—n., does that surprise you?—by no means, in no wise; ce n'était n. sa place, he had no business at all to be there; il ne s'en porte n. mieux, he's not a whit better for it.

nullification [nyl(l)ifikasjɔ̃], *s.f.* nullification.

nullifier [nyl(l)ifje], *v.tr.* (*p.d. & pr.sub.* n. nullifiions, v. nullifiiez) to nullify, neutralize (effort, etc.).

nullipare [nyl(l)ipa:r], *a.* *Jur:* *etc:* nulliparous.

nullité [nyl(l)ite], *s.f.* 1. nullity, invalidity (of deed, marriage, etc.); frapper une clause de n., to render a clause void; cession atteinte de n., invalid assignment; sous peine de n., under pain of being declared void; *Jur:* action en n., action for avoidance of contract; demande en n., plea in abatement. 2. (*a*) nothingness; non-existence (of means); *F:* emptiness (of mind); n. des affaires, slackness, standstill, in trade; (*b*) incompetence; la n. de nos dirigeants, the incapacity of those at the head of affairs; sa n. en mathématiques, his inability to grasp the rudiments of mathematics. 3. nonentity; ce sera toujours une n., he will never be anybody.

nullivalant [nyl(l)ivalɑ̃], *a.* *Ch:* zero-valent.

nullivariant [nyl(l)ivarjɑ̃], *a.* *Ph:* *Ch:* invariant.

Numance [nymɑ̃:s], *Pr.n.f.* *A.Geog:* Numantia.

nûment [nymɑ̃], *adv.* (*a*) nakedly; (*b*) raconter n. les choses, to tell things as they are, frankly, without embellishments.

numéraire [nymerɛ:r]. 1. (*a*) *a.* (*of coins*) legal; valeur n., legal-tender value, numerary value; (*b*) *s.m.* metallic currency, specie, current coin; payer en n., to pay in cash; n. fictif, paper currency. 2. *s.m.* *Nau:* number-signal.

numéral, -aux [nymeral, -o], *a.* numeral; *s.* les numéraux cardinaux, the cardinal numerals.

numérateur [nymeratœ:r], *s.m.* *Mth:* numerator.

numératif, -ive [nymeratif, -i:v], *a.* *Gram:* (noun, adjective) of number.

numération [nymerasjɔ̃], *s.f.* 1. *Ar:* numeration; notation (of figures); n. décimale, decimal notation; n. binaire, binary notation. 2. count; n. globulaire, blood count.

numérique [nymerik], *a.* (*a*) numerical (value, ratio, superiority, etc.); (*b*) digital (information, etc.); analyse n., numerical analysis; ordre n. (normal), ascending numerical order; ordre n. inverse, descending numerical order; données numériques, numerical data; calculateur n., digital computer; traitement n. des données, digital processing of data.

numériquement [nymerikmɑ̃], *adv.* numerically.

numéro [nymero], *s.m.* number; (*a*) n. d'ordre, running number, serial number; donner un n. d'ordre à chaque dossier d'archives, to give a running number to each record file; *Th:* *Trans:* *Sp:* *etc:* n. du billet, du ticket, ticket number; tirer un bon, un mauvais, n., to draw a lucky, a wrong, number (at lottery, conscription, etc.); *Th:* *etc:* n. du vestiaire, cloakroom ticket; *Bank:* n. du chèque, cheque number; *Adm:* n. d'habitation n. du domicile, house number; j'habite, je demeure, au n. 10, I live at number 10; le pharmacien du n. 2, rue Lepic, the chemist at number 2, rue Lepic; **j'ai la chambre n. 20,** my room is number 20; *F:* **une maison à gros n.,** a brothel; *(b)* **n. de classification,** n. **distinctif,** designation number, specification number; **tenue n. un,** (i) *Mil:* full dress uniform; (ii) *F:* best clothes; *Mil:* **tenue n. deux,** walking-out dress; *F:* **mon parapluie n. deux,** my second-best umbrella; *Mil: Navy:* **n. matricule,** (i) official number (of man, of rating); (ii) (registered) number (of weapon); *Nau:* **n. (officiel) d'un bateau, d'un navire,** boat's, ship's, number; call letters, signal letters; *Com:* **marques et numéros des colis,** marks and numbers of cases; *Com: Ind:* **n. de lot,** lot number; *Ind: etc:* **n. de série, de fabrication,** serial number; *Tp:* **n. d'abonné,** subscriber's number; **n. d'appel,** telephone number; *Map: etc:* **n. d'une feuille (de carte),** sheet number; **n. (administratif) d'une route,** road number; *Journ:* number, issue (of periodical); **n. du jour, de la semaine, du mois; dernier n.,** current issue or number; **n. de Noël,** Christmas number, issue; **un ancien n., un n. déjà paru,** a back-issue, -number; **dans le n. de demain vous trouverez . . .,** in to-morrow's issue you will find . . .; **acheter un périodique au n.,** to buy a periodical a number at a time; "**vente au n.**", "single copies sold"; *(d)* number (of sewing-cotton, etc.); *Tex:* count (of yarn); *Com:* size (of stock sizes); *(e) Th: etc:* item, act; **le dernier n. du programme,** the last item, number, turn, on the programme; *F:* **il aime faire son petit n.,** he likes doing his little act; *(f) (of person)* **quel n.!** what a character! **c'est un drôle de n.!** he's a queer card, fish! **je connais le n.,** I know the sort of person he is, I have sized him up, *F:* I've got him taped.

numérotation [nymerɔtasjɔ̃], *s.m.,* **numérotation** [nymerɔtasjɔ̃], *s.f.* numbering (of houses, yarns, etc.); allocation of a (classification) number (to document, etc.); **n. d'un livre,** paging of a book.

numéroter [nymerɔte], *v.tr.* to number (street, etc.); *abs. Tp:* to dial (a number); **n. un livre,** to page, paginate, a book; **machine à n.,** paging machine; **voiture numérotée,** vehicle bearing a registered number; **plaque numérotée,** numbered identification plate; **n. des lettres,** to cross-reference letters; **dix caisses numérotées de 1 à 10,** ten cases numbered 1 to 10; *Mil:* **numérotez-vous (à partir de la droite)!** (from the right) number! *P:* **numérote tes os, que je te démolisse,** *(literally)* number off your bones, before I knock you to bits; *s.a.* ABATTIS 3.

numéroteur [nymerɔtœːr], *s.m.* numbering-machine, -stamp.

numide [nymid], *a. & s. A.Geog:* Numidian.

Numidie [nymidi], *Pr.n.f. A.Geog:* Numidia.

numismate [nymismat], *s.m.* numismatist.

numismatique [nymismatik]. **1.** *a.* numismatic. **2.** *s.f.* numismatics, numismatology.

numismatiste [nymismatist], *s.m.* = NUMISMATE.

nummulaire [nym(m)ylεːr], *s.f. Bot:* moneywort.

nummulite [nym(m)ylit], *s.f. Geol:* nummulite; **calcaire à nummulites,** nummulitic limestone.

nunatak [nynatak], *s.m. Geol:* nunatak.

Nunc dimittis [nɔ̃kdimitis], *s.m.inv. Ecc:* Nunc dimittis.

nuncupatif [nɔ̃kypatif], *a.m. Jur: A:* nuncupative (will); **faire un testament n.,** to nuncupate a will.

nuncupation [nɔ̃kypasjɔ̃], *s.f. Jur: A:* nuncupation, oral declaration (of will, deed, etc.).

nunnation [nyn(n)asjɔ̃], *Ling:* nunnation.

nuphar [nyfaːr], *s.m. Bot:* nuphar, yellow water-lily.

nu-pieds [nypje], *adv.phr. See* NU[2] 1.

nu-propriétaire [nyprɔprietεːr], *s.m. Jur:* bare owner; *pl.* nus-propriétaires.

nuptial, -iaux [nypsjal, -jo], *a.* nuptial, bridal; **marche nuptiale,** wedding-march, bridal march; **anneau n.,** wedding-ring; **la bénédiction nuptiale sera donnée à . . .,** the marriage will be celebrated at . . .

nuptialité [nypsjalite], *s.f.* marriage rate, nuptiality.

nuque [nyk], *s.f. (a)* nape of the neck; *Anat:* nucha; **saisir qn par la n.,** to catch hold of s.o. by the scruff of the neck; *(b)* poll (of horse).

Nuremberg [nyrε̃bεːr], *Pr.n. Geog:* Nuremberg; Nürnberg.

nurembergeois, -oise [nyrε̃bεrʒwa, -waːz], *a. & s. Geog:* Nuremberger.

nurse [nœrs], *s.f.* nanny, (children's) nurse.

nursery [nœrsəri], *s.f.* nursery.

nutant [nytɑ̃], *a. Bot:* nutant.

nutation [nytasjɔ̃], *s.f. Astr: Bot: Med:* nutation.

nu-tête [nytεːt], *adv.phr. See* NU[2] 1.

nutria [nytria], *s.m. Com:* nutria (fur).

nutricier, -ière [nytrisje, -jεːr], *a.* nourishing, nutritive.

nutriment [nytrimɑ̃], *s.m.* nutriment.

nutritif, -ive [nytritif, -iːv], *a.* nutritive, nourishing; **valeur nutritive,** food-value; **matière nutritive,** food material.

nutrition [nytrisjɔ̃], *s.f.* nutrition.

nutritionnel, -elle [nytrisjɔnεl], *a.* nutritional.

nutritionniste [nytrisjɔnist], *s.m. & f.* nutritionist, dietitian, dietician.

nutritivité [nytritivite], *s.f.* nutritiveness, nutriousness, food-value.

nyala [niala], *s.m. Z:* nyala.

Nyas(s)aland (le) [lənjasalɑ̃d], *Pr.n. Geog: A:* Nyasaland.

nyctaginacées [niktaʒinase], *s.f.pl. Bot:* Nyctaginaceae.

nyctalope [niktalɔp]. **1.** *a.* day-blind, hemeralopic. **2.** *s.m. & f.* person who sees best in the dark; hemeralope, hemeralops.

nyctalopie [niktalɔpi], *s.f. Med:* day-blindness, hemeralopia.

nyctalopique [niktalɔpik], *a. Med:* hemeralopic.

nyctéribides [nikteribid], *s.f.pl. Ent:* Nycteribiidae (family); the bat flies, bat parasites.

nycthéméral, -aux [niktemeral, -o], *a. Nat.Hist:* nyc(h)themeral (rhythm of life, etc.).

nycthémère [niktemεːr], *Nat.Hist:* **1.** *a.* nycterohemeral, nyctohemeral. **2.** *s.m.* nyc(h)themeron; *pl.* -ons, -a; full period of one night and one day.

nycticèbe [niktisεb], *s.m. Z:* Asiatic slow loris.

nyctipithèque [niktipitεk], *s.m. Z:* owl-monkey; night-ape; douroucouli.

nyctophonie [niktɔfɔni], *s.f. Psy:* nyctophonia.

nyctotempérature [niktɔtɑ̃peratyːr], *s.f. Bot:* nyctotemperature; temperature during the period of darkness.

nylgaut [nilgo], *s.m. Z:* nilgai.

nylon [nilɔ̃], *s.m. R.t.m:* nylon; **des nylons,** nylons, nylon stockings.

nymphal, -aux [nε̃fal, -o], *a.* nymphal.

nymphale [nε̃fal], *s.m. Ent:* nymphalid.

nymphalidés [nε̃falide], *s.m.pl. Ent:* Nymphalidae.

nymphe [nε̃ːf], *s.f.* **1.** *Myth:* nymph; *Cu:* **cuisses de n.,** frog's legs. **2.** *Ent:* nymph, pupa, chrysalis; **n. souterraine,** burrowing pupa. **3.** *pl. Anat:* nymphae; labia minora.

nymphéa [nε̃fea], *s.m. Bot:* nymphea, water nymph; common white water lily.

nymphéacées [nε̃fease], *s.f.pl. Bot:* nymphaeaceae.

nymphée [nε̃fe]. **1.** *s.m. or f. Gr.Ant:* nymphaeum; shrine (of a nymph); grotto. **2.** *s.f. Bot:* nymphea, water nymph; common white water lily.

nymphette [nε̃fεt], *s.f.* nymphet.

nympholepsie [nε̃fɔlεpsi], *s.f.* nympholepsy.

nympholepte [nε̃fɔlεpt]. **1.** *a.* nympholept; nympholeptic. **2.** *s.* nympholept.

nymphomane [nε̃fɔman], *s.f. Med:* nymphomaniac.

nymphomanie [nε̃fɔmani], *s.f. Med:* nymphomania.

nymphose [nε̃foːz], *s.f. Ent:* pupation.

nymphulines [nε̃fylin], *s.f.pl. Ent:* Nymphalinae.

nyonsais, -aise [njɔ̃zε, -εːz], *a. & s. Geog:* (native, inhabitant) of Nyons.

nyroca [niroka], *s.m.* **canard n.,** ferruginous duck.

nyssa [nis(s)a], *s.m. Bot:* nyssa, tupelo.

nystagme [nistagm], *s.m.,* **nystagmus** [nistagmys], *s.m. Med:* nystagmus.

O

O, o [o], *s.m.* (the letter) O, o; *Tp:* **O comme Oscar,**
O for Oliver.

ô [o], *int.* (*address or invocation*) O! oh! **ô mon fils!**
oh, my son! *Nau:* **ô! hisse!** yo-heave-ho! yoho!
Ecc: **les sept O de Noël,** the O's of Advent.

oaristys [ɔaristis], *s.f. Gr.Lit:* bucolic love-poem.

oasien, -ienne [ɔazjɛ̃, -jɛn]. **1.** *a.* oasis (vegetation,
etc.). **2.** *s.* **les oasiens du Sahara,** the oasis
dwellers of the Sahara.

oasis [ɔazis], *s.f. occ.m.* oasis; **une o. de calme au
centre d'une ville bruyante,** an oasis of calm in
the heart of a noisy town; **une o. de bonheur,** a
haven of happiness.

obbligato [obligato], *adv. Mus:* obbligato.

obcordé [ɔpkɔrde], **obcordiforme** [ɔpkɔrdifɔrm],
a. Bot: obcordate.

obdiplostémone [ɔpdiplɔstemɔn], *a. Bot:* obdiplo-
stemonous.

obédience [ɔbedjɑ̃:s], *s.f.* **1.** *Ecc:* (*R.C.Ch.*): (*a*)
dutiful submission to a superior; obedience; (*b*)
authorization (for monk, nun) to pass from one
convent to another; (*c*) *A:* **lettres d'o.,** ecclesiastical licence to teach (granted to members of
the teaching orders); (*d*) **musulman de stricte o.,**
a strict Moslem; (*e*) **pays d'o. communiste,**
countries of the Communist obedience. **2.**
Ecc.Hist: territories owning allegiance to the
Pope (during schism); obedience.

obédiencier [ɔbedjɑ̃sje], *s.m. Ecc:* obediencer,
obedientiary.

obédientiel, -elle [ɔbedjɑ̃tjɛl], *a. Ecc:* obediential.

obéir [ɔbeiːr], *v.ind.tr.* to obey; (*a*) **o. à qn,** to obey
s.o.; to be obedient to s.o.; **o. à qn au doigt et à
l'œil,** to be at s.o.'s beck and call; to obey s.o.
implicitly; *still used as v.tr. in* **faire o. la loi,**
to enforce obedience to the law; **se faire o. par
qn,** to compel, enforce, obedience from s.o.;
il sait se faire o., he commands obedience; he
can make himself obeyed; **il est obéi,** he is
obeyed; (*b*) **o. à qch.,** to yield, submit, to sth.;
to comply with sth.; **o. à un ordre,** to obey,
comply with, an order; **refuser d'o. à un ordre,**
to refuse to obey an order; **ses jambes refusaient
d'o.,** his legs refused to obey (him); **o. aux
moindres volontés de qn,** to be at the beck and
call of s.o.; **o. à la force,** to yield to force; **l'acier
obéit plus que le fer,** steel is more yielding, pliant,
than iron; *Av: Nau:* (*of ship, etc.*) **o. à la barre,**
to answer the helm; (*of aircraft*) **o. aux gouvernes,**
to respond to the controls.

obéissance [ɔbeisɑ̃:s], *s.f.* **1.** (*a*) obedience (à,
to); **il demandait une parfaite o. à ses volontés,**
he expected implicit obedience to his will; **payer
d'o.,** to obey; to knuckle under; **refuser o.,** to
refuse obedience; *Mil: etc:* to be guilty of
insubordination; **refus d'o.,** insubordination;
(*b*) dutifulness (to parents, teachers); submission
(to lawful authority); allegiance (to king); **être
sous l'o.,** to be under paternal
authority; **rendre o. à qn,** to obey s.o.; **rentrer
dans l'o.,** (i) to return to one's obedience; (ii) *F:*
to toe the line once more; **devoir o. à qn,** to owe
s.o. obedience, allegiance; **jurer o. au roi,** to
swear allegiance to the king; **se soumettre à l'o.
de qn,** to submit to s.o.'s authority. **2.** pliancy,
suppleness, elasticity (of copper, wood, etc.).

obéissant [ɔbeisɑ̃], *a.* **1.** obedient, dutiful (child,
person); docile (animal); submissive (people,
nation); **être o. envers, pour, vis-à-vis de, qn,**
to be obedient to s.o.; **votre très o. serviteur,**
your obedient servant; *Nau:* **navire o.,** ship that
answers the helm. **2.** (*of metals, wood, etc.*)
pliant, supple, elastic.

obèle [ɔbɛl], *s.m. Typ: Pal:* obelus, obelisk;
marquer un passage d'un o., to obelize a passage.

obélion [ɔbeljɔ̃], *s.m. Anat:* obelion.

obéliscal, -aux [ɔbeliskal, -o], *a.* obeliscal,
obeliscoid.

obélisque [ɔbelisk], *s.m.* obelisk; **l'o. de Cléo-
pâtre,** Cleopatra's Needle.

obérer [ɔbere], *v.tr.* (j'**obère,** n. **obérons;** j'**obérerai**)
to involve (s.o.) in debt; to encumber, burden,
(sth.) with debt; **homme fort obéré,** man who has
run deep in debt, who is sunk in debt; **finances
fort obérées,** heavily encumbered finances.

s'obérer, to run heavily into debt.

oberlandais, -aise [ɔbɛrlɑ̃dɛ, -ɛːz], *a. & s. Geog:*
(native, inhabitant) of the (Bernese) Oberland.

obèse [ɔbɛːz], *a. & s.m. & f.* obese, fat, corpulent
(person).

obésifuge [ɔbezify:ʒ], *a.* fat-reducing; **médicament
o.,** anti-fat remedy; slimming remedy; **régime
o.,** banting, slimming, diet.

obésité [ɔbezite], *s.f.* obesity, corpulence.

obi¹ [ɔbi], *s.m.* (*in Africa*) obeah man, doctor.

obi², *s.f. Japanese Cost:* obi.

obier [ɔbje], *s.m. Bot:* guelder rose, snowball tree.

obit [ɔbit], *s.m.* **1.** *Ecc:* (*a*) obit; anniversary mass
(for soul of departed); (*b*) money gift (to the
celebrant). **2.** serif (at top of letter).

obituaire [ɔbitɥɛ:r], *a. & s.m. Ecc:* (**registre**) **o.,**
obituary list; (i) register of deaths; (ii) obit book.

objectal, -aux [ɔbʒɛktal, -o], *a. Psy:* **choix o.,**
objective choice.

objecter [ɔbʒɛkte]. **1.** *v.tr.* to raise, interpose,
(sth.) as an objection; **je n'ai rien à o. à la proposition,** I have no objection to raise, nothing to
say, against the proposal; **on a objecté que . . .,**
the objection has been raised that . . .; **o. des
difficultés à, contre, qch.,** to plead difficulties
about sth.; **les raisons qu'il objecte,** the reasons
that he urges, alleges; **o. qch. à qn,** to bring
something up, to allege sth., against s.o.; **on lui
objecta sa jeunesse,** they took exception to his
youth; **on peut lui o. son âge,** his age is against
him; **on lui a objecté ses anciennes opinions,** his
former opinions were brought up against him;
o. la fatigue pour ne pas sortir, to plead tiredness
as an excuse for not going out. **2.** *abs. F:* **ils
objectent contre tout,** they bring up arguments
for or against everything.

objecteur [ɔbʒɛktœ:r], *s.m.* **o. de conscience,** conscientious objector.

objectif, -ive [ɔbʒɛktif, -iːv]. **1.** *a.* objective; **il est
très o.,** he is unbiased. **2.** *s.m.* (*a*) aim, object
(-ive), end; **atteindre son o.,** to attain one's object;
cette loi comporte un double o., this law has two
objects in view; (*b*) *Mil: etc:* objective; **o. principal, secondaire, intermédiaire, final,** primary,
secondary, intermediate, final, objective; **o.
lointain,** long-term objective; **attaque, neutralisation, prise, d'un o.,** attack, neutralization, capture, of an objective; **atteindre l'o.,** to reach the
objective; **dépasser, aller au-delà de, l'o.,** to
overreach the objective; (*c*) *Ball:* target; **o.
linéaire,** linear target; **o. ponctuel,** pinpoint target; **o. sur zone,** area target; **o. de circonstance,
o. fortuit, o. inopiné,** target of opportunity; **o.
fixe, o. immobile,** fixed, stationary, target; **o.
mobile, o. mouvant,** fleeting, moving, target;
o. terrestre, ground target; **o. aérien,** aerial
target, air target; **o. exactement repéré, localisé**
avec précision, pinpointed target; **choix de l'o.,**
des objectifs, target selection; **carte d'objectifs,**
target map; **dossier d'o.,** target folder; **étude des
objectifs,** target analysis; **recherche des objectifs,**
(i) search for targets; (ii) (*radar*) target acquisition; **zone des objectifs,** target area; **battre,
prendre à partie, un o.,** to engage a target; **o. à
battre,** target to be engaged; **attaque, prise à
partie, d'un o.,** engagement of a target; **changer
d'o.,** to shift target; **coiffer un o.,** to straddle a
target. **3.** *s.m.* (*a*) *Opt:* object glass, objective
(of microscope, etc.); **o. à immersion,** immersion
objective; (*b*) *Phot:* lens; **o. simple,** simple lens,
landscape lens; **o. composé,** compound lens; **o.
dédoublable,** doublet lens; **o. à portraits,** portrait
lens; **o. grand angulaire,** wide-angle lens; **o.
lumineux,** fast lens.

objection [ɔbʒɛksjɔ̃], *s.f.* objection; **faire, for-
muler, soulever, dresser, une o.,** to object (à,
contre, to); to make, raise, an objection; **ne plus
opposer d'o.,** to make no further objection;
répondre à une o., to meet an objection, to dispose of an objection; **o. de conscience,** conscientious objection.

objectivation [ɔbʒɛktivasjɔ̃], *s.f. Phil:* objectivation; objectification.

objectivement [ɔbʒɛktivmɑ̃], *adv.* objectively.

objectiver [ɔbʒɛktive], *v.tr. Phil:* to objectify.

objectivisme [ɔbʒɛktivism], *s.m. Phil:* objectivism.

objectiviste [ɔbʒɛktivist], *Phil:* **1.** *a.* objectivistic.
2. *s.m. & f.* objectivist.

objectivité [ɔbʒɛktivite], *s.f.* objectivity, objective-
ness.

objet [ɔbʒɛ], *s.m.* **1.** (*a*) object, thing (presented to
the senses); *Phil:* object; non-ego; **quel o.
affreux!** what a dreadful object! what a dreadful
sight! (*b*) *Gram:* object, complement; **o. direct,**
direct object. **2.** subject, (subject) matter; **l'o.
de nos méditations, de la conversation,** the subject
of our thoughts, of the conversation; *Jur:* **o.
d'un litige,** subject of an action; **faire l'o. d'un
entretien,** to form the subject of a conversation;
être l'o. de l'admiration générale, to be the subject of general admiration; **cela fera l'o. d'une
seconde conférence,** this will be dealt with in,
will be the subject of, a second lecture. **3.** (*a*)
object (of emotion); **o. de pitié,** object of pity,
pitiable object; **o. de raillerie, de risée,** butt,
laughing-stock; **ils étaient devenus les objets
d'une haine universelle,** they had become
objects of universal hatred; **dans l'o. aimé tout
est admirable,** everything concerned with the
object of one's love appears perfect; (*b*) object,
aim, purpose (of action); **il n'a pour o. que la
richesse,** wealth is his sole object; he has only
wealth in view; **l'optique a pour o. les lois de la
lumière,** optics is concerned with the laws of
light; **avec cet o. en vue,** with this end in view;
remplir son o., to attain one's end; **sans o.,** aimless, purposeless; **flâner sans o.,** to stroll aimlessly about; **cette demande est dès lors sans o.,**
this request is no longer applicable. **4.** (*a*)
article, thing; **o. de luxe,** luxury article; **o. d'art,**
objet d'art; **vendre toutes sortes d'objets,** to sell
all kinds of goods, things, articles; **objets trouvés,**
lost property; (*b*) *Jur:* **o. immobilier,** realty;
o. mobilier, personalty.

objurgation [ɔbʒyrgasjɔ̃], *s.f.* objurgation.

objurgatoire [ɔbʒyrgatwa:r], *a.* objurgatory
(words, etc.).

oblat [ɔbla], *s.m. Ecc:* oblate.

oblation [ɔblasjɔ̃], *s.f. Ecc:* oblation, offering.

obligataire [ɔbligatɛːr], *s.m. Fin:* **1.** (*a*) bond-holder, debenture holder; (*b*) holder of redeemable stock. **2.** obligee (whose bill has been backed, etc.).

obligatif, -ive [ɔbligatif, -iːv], *a.* **clause obligative,** guarantee clause.

obligation [ɔbligasjɔ̃], *s.f.* **1.** (*a*) (moral) obligation; duty; **je me sens dans l'o. de vous avertir que . . .,** I feel called upon, I feel compelled, to warn you that . . .; **remplir, s'acquitter de, ses obligations envers qn,** to fulfil one's obligations towards s.o.; to do one's duty by s.o.; **faire honneur, manquer, à ses obligations,** to meet, to fail to meet, one's obligations; **imposer à qn l'o. de faire qch.,** to make it binding upon s.o. to do sth.; **c'est une o. pour vous de le faire,** you are bound, it is your bounden duty, it is incumbent on you, to do so; **mettre qn dans l'o. de faire qch.,** to put s.o. under the obligation of doing sth.; **je me vois dans l'o. de . . .,** I find myself obliged to . . .; **cette clause entraîne pour vous l'o. de . . .,** this clause makes it incumbent on you to . . .; **se trouver dans l'o. de . . .,** to be under the necessity of . . .; *R.C.Ch:* **fête d'o.,** holiday of obligation; (*b*) **o. du service militaire,** liability to military service. **2.** *Jur:* (*a*) recognizance, bond; (*b*) **o. contractuelle,** privity in deed; **o. légale,** perfect, legal, obligation; **o. morale,** imperfect, moral, obligation (not enforceable at law); **o. alimentaire,** maintenance order; **contracter une o. irrévocable,** to enter into a binding agreement; *s.a.* S'ACQUITTER 1. **3.** *Com: Fin:* bond, debenture, redeemable stock; **obligations à la souche,** unissued debentures; **obligations à lots,** lottery bonds, premium bonds; **o. hypothécaire,** mortgage debenture; **o. de chemin de fer,** railway debenture; **o. au porteur,** bearer bond; **porteur d'obligations,** bondholder. **4.** obligation, favour; **avoir des obligations envers qn,** to be under an obligation to s.o.; to be beholden to s.o.; *F:* to owe s.o. a good turn; **créer une o. à qn,** to put s.o. under an obligation; **je vous ai de l'o. de m'avoir soutenu,** I am obliged to you for backing me up.

obligatoire [ɔbligatwaːr], *a.* obligatory; mandatory; compulsory (military service, etc.); binding (agreement, etc.); **décision o. pour tous,** decision binding on all parties; **l'uniforme est o.,** uniform must be worn; **il est o. de remplir le formulaire,** it is necessary to fill up the form; the form must be filled up; *s.a.* ARRÊT 1.

obligatoirement [ɔbligatwarmɑ̃], *adv.* compulsorily; **vous devez o. montrer votre passeport à la frontière,** it is necessary, you have, to show your passport at the frontier; *F:* **cela devait o. arriver!** it *had* to happen! it couldn't have been avoided!

obligé, -ée [ɔbliʒe]. **1.** *a.* (*a*) obliged, bound, compelled (**de faire qch.,** to do sth.); **invitation obligée,** duty invitation; (*b*) indispensable, necessary, usual (compliments, etc.); **tu es mon garçon d'honneur o.,** you will be my best man as a matter of course; (*c*) inevitable, sure to happen; *F:* **c'est o. qu'il rate son examen,** he's bound to fail his exam; (*d*) obliged, grateful; **être très o. à qn de qch.,** to be greatly obliged, very grateful, to s.o. for sth.; **je vous serai o. de vouloir bien fermer la porte,** I will be grateful if you will close the door; **bien o.!** many thanks! *Iron:* thank you for nothing! **2.** *s.* (*a*) person under obligation; *Jur:* obligee; **je suis votre o.,** you have put me under an obligation; (*b*) *Fin:* obligor (guaranteeing a bill).

obligeamment [ɔbliʒamɑ̃], *adv.* obligingly; courteously, kindly.

obligeance [ɔbliʒɑ̃ːs], *s.f.* obligingness; **ayez, veuillez avoir, l'o. de . . .,** would you be good enough to . . ., be so kind as to . . ., have the kindness to . . .; **homme d'une grande o.,** very obliging, helpful, man.

obligeant [ɔbliʒɑ̃], *a.* obliging, helpful; kind; civil; **c'est très o. de votre part,** it is very kind of you; **il m'a dit des choses très obligeantes,** he spoke very pleasantly to me; **il m'a dit des choses très obligeantes à votre égard,** he spoke very kindly of you.

obliger [ɔbliʒe], *v.tr.* (**j'obligeai(s); n. obligeons**) **1.** to oblige, constrain, bind, compel; **ma signature m'y oblige,** my signature binds me, holds me, to it; **votre devoir vous y oblige,** you are in duty bound to do it; **o. qn à,** *occ.* **de, faire qch.,** to compel, force, s.o. to do sth.; **la peur l'obligea à se taire,** fear made him silent; (*in the passive usu.* **de**) **être obligé de faire qch.,** to be obliged, bound, compelled, to do sth.; **rien ne m'oblige à les accompagner,** I am under no obligation to go with them; *Jur:* **o. qn de se tenir à la disposition de la justice,** to bind s.o. over to appear when called upon; *s.a.* NOBLESSE 1. **2. o. qn,** to oblige s.o., to do s.o. a favour; **o. qn de sa bourse,** to put one's purse at s.o.'s disposal; **vous m'obligeriez beaucoup en me prêtant vingt francs,** you would greatly oblige me by lending me twenty francs; **vous n'obligerez pas un ingrat,** you won't find me ungrateful; *A:* **obligez-moi de n'en rien dire,** oblige me by saying nothing about it; *Prov:* **qui oblige promptement oblige doublement,** he gives twice who gives quickly.

s'obliger: s'o. à faire qch., to bind oneself, to undertake, to engage oneself, to do sth.; to make a point of doing sth.; **s'o. par-devant notaire,** to sign a legal agreement; **s'o. pour qn,** to stand surety for s.o.

obliquangle [ɔblikɑ̃gl̩], *a.* oblique-angled.

oblique [ɔblik]. **1.** *a.* (*a*) *Geom: Gram: Mil: etc:* oblique (line, case, march, etc.); *s.a.* ACTION 5; (*b*) slanting (stitch); skew (arch); **regard o.,** side glance; **je jetai un coup d'œil o. sur son journal,** I had a squint at his paper; (*c*) *A:* indirect, crooked (means); underhand (behaviour); devious (ways); (*d*) **mariage o.,** marriage between persons of different generations. **2.** *s.m. Anat:* oblique muscle; **grand o. de l'œil,** superior oblique muscle; pathetic muscle. **3.** *s.f.* oblique line; **pluie qui tombe en o.,** slanting rain; *Mil:* **o. à droite,** right incline; *s.a.* STATIONNEMENT 1.

obliquement [ɔblikmɑ̃], *adv.* (*a*) obliquely, slantwise, aslant, diagonally; **couper le champ d'une planche o.,** to bevel (off), to cant, the edge of a board; (*b*) indirectly; (*c*) *A:* by underhand or unfair means.

obliquer [ɔblike], *v.i.* (*a*) to move in an oblique direction; to oblique; to edge (**sur, vers,** to); *Mil:* **o. à droite,** to incline to the right, to bear right; **obliquez à droite!** right incline! *Nau:* **o. sur tribord,** to edge to starboard; (*b*) to slant.

obliquité [ɔblikɥite], *s.f.* obliquity. **1.** obliqueness (of line, rays, etc.); skew. **2.** *A:* crookedness (of conduct).

oblitérateur, -trice [ɔbliteratœːr, -tris]. **1.** *a.* obliterating. **2.** *s.m.* cancel (for stamps, etc.).

oblitération [ɔbliterasjɔ̃], *s.f.* obliteration (of marks, writing, etc.); cancelling, cancellation (of stamps, etc.); **(cachet d')o.,** postmark; *Med:* **o. d'un conduit,** obliteration, obstruction, of a duct.

oblitérer [ɔblitere], *v.tr.* (**j'oblitère, n. oblitérons; j'oblitérerai**) **1.** to obliterate (marks, the past, etc.). **2.** to cancel, deface (stamp); **timbre oblitéré,** used stamp; *s.m.pl.* **les oblitérés d'une collection,** the used stamps in a collection.

oblong, -ongue [ɔblɔ̃, -ɔ̃ːg], *a.* oblong.

obnubilation [ɔbnybilasjɔ̃], *s.f. Med:* obnubilation; **o. matinale,** *F:* hangover.

obnubiler [ɔbnybile], *v.tr.* to obnubilate; (*a*) *A:* **ciel obnubilé,** overcast sky; (*b*) to cloud (mind, vision); (*c*) (*of idea, etc.*) to dominate (s.o.'s mind).

oboïste [ɔbɔist], *s.m. or f. Mus:* oboist, oboe player.

obole [ɔbɔl], *s.f.* (*a*) *A.Num:* (Greek) obolus, abol; (French) obole; (*b*) **je n'en donnerais pas une o.,** I wouldn't give a brass farthing, a stiver, for it; **donner son o.,** to make one's contribution; *B:* **l'o. de la veuve,** the widow's mite.

obombrer [ɔbɔ̃bre], *v.tr. Lit:* **1.** to cover (s.o.) with one's shadow. **2.** to cloud (the memory, etc.).

obreptice [ɔbrɛptis], *a.* obrepticious.

obrepticement [ɔbrɛptismɑ̃], *adv.* obrepticiously.

obreption [ɔbrɛpsjɔ̃], *s.f.* obreption; concealment of part of the truth.

obscène [ɔpsɛn], *a.* obscene (language, book); lewd (gesture); smutty (talk, song).

obscénité [ɔpsenite], *s.f.* **1.** obscenity; lewdness; *F:* smuttiness. **2. faire circuler des obscénités,** to circulate obscene books, pictures, etc.

obscur [ɔpskyːr], *a.* **1.** dark (night, room); gloomy (weather); sombre (tint); *F:* **salle obscure,** cinema; **il fait o.,** (i) it's dark; (ii) the sky is overcast. **2.** obscure; (*a*) difficult to understand; **sujets obscurs,** abstruse subjects; (*b*) indistinct, dim (horizon, etc.); **d'obscurs pressentiments,** dim forebodings; (*c*) unknown, lowly, humble (birth, parentage); **un écrivain o.,** an obscure, abstruse, recondite, writer; **un o. écrivain,** an unknown, obscure, writer. **3.** *Ph:* **chaleur obscure,** dark heat.

obscurantisme [ɔpskyrɑ̃tism], *s.m.* obscurantism.

obscurantiste [ɔpskyrɑ̃tist], *a. & s.m. & f.* obscurantist.

obscuration [ɔpskyrasjɔ̃], *s.f. Astr:* obscuration, occultation; *Cin:* **secteur d'o.,** obscuring blade (of shutter).

obscurcir [ɔpskyrsiːr], *v.tr.* to obscure; (*a*) to darken, cloud (the brightness of the sun, sky, etc.); (*b*) to dim (the sight, fame, mind); **yeux obscurcis par les larmes,** eyes dimmed with tears; (*c*) to obscure, fog, (situation, sense of passage).

s'obscurcir, to darken; to grow dark; to become grow, obscure or dim; (*of style, etc.*) to become obscure; **le ciel s'obscurcit,** the sky is clouding over; **son front s'obscurcit,** his brow darkened; **ma vue s'obscurcit,** my sight is growing dim; **sa raison s'obscurcit,** his reason is becoming clouded; **sa gloire s'est obscurcie,** his glory has dimmed.

obscurcissement [ɔpskyrsismɑ̃], *s.m.* (*a*) obscuration (of light, style, sense); darkening (of picture, of the sun, etc.); growing dim (of sight, of the mind); (*b*) blackout.

obscurcisseur [ɔpskyrsisœːr], *s.m.* dimmer.

obscuré [ɔpskyre], *a.* dark, darkened, dusky, shadowy (street, wings of moth, etc.).

obscurément [ɔpskyremɑ̃], *adv.* obscurely, dimly; **se rendre compte o. que . . .,** to be vaguely aware that . . ..

obscurité [ɔpskyrite], *s.f.* obscurity; (*a*) darkness (of night, of a cellar, etc.); (*b*) unintelligibility, obscureness (of speech, style, oracle, etc.); **tomber dans l'o.,** to lapse into obscureness; (*c*) dimness, uncertainty, vagueness (of the future, of the past); (*d*) obscurity (of birth, condition); **vivre dans l'o.,** to live in obscurity; **sortir de l'o.,** to become known; to spring, emerge, from obscurity; **tomber dans l'o.,** to sink into obscurity.

obsécration [ɔpsekrasjɔ̃], *s.f. Ecc:* obsecration; supplication.

obsédant [ɔpsedɑ̃], *a.* haunting (memory); obsessing (thought); **image obsédante,** obsessive image; *Psy:* **pensée obsédante,** compulsive thinking.

obsédé, -ée [ɔpsede], *s.* sufferer from an obsession; **o. sexuel,** sexual maniac.

obséder [ɔpsede], *v.tr.* (**j'obsède, n. obsédons; j'obséderai**) (*a*) to beset (prince, minister); (*b*) *O:* to importune, worry (s.o.); **obsédé par un fâcheux,** pestered by an intrusive fellow; (*c*) (*of devil, etc.*) to obsess (s.o.); (*d*) to obsess; **les pensées, souvenirs, qui m'obsèdent,** the thoughts, memories, that obsess me, that haunt me; **obsédé d'une, par une, idée,** obsessed by, with, an idea.

obséquent [ɔpsekɑ̃], *a. Geol:* **cours d'eau o.,** obsequent stream.

obsèques [ɔpsɛk], *s.f.pl.* obsequies; funeral (*esp.* state funeral, important funeral).

obséquieusement [ɔpsekjøzmɑ̃], *adv.* obsequiously.

obséquieux, -euse [ɔpsekjø, -øːz], *a.* obsequious.

obséquiosité [ɔpsekjozite], *s.f.* obsequiousness.

observable [ɔpsɛrvabl̩], *a.* observable.

observance [ɔpsɛrvɑ̃ːs], *s.f.* observance; (i) observing, keeping (of rule); (ii) rule observed; (iii) religious community; *Ecc:* **frères de l'étroite o.,** friars of the Strict Observance.

observantin [ɔpsɛrvɑ̃tɛ̃], *a. & s.m. Ecc: A:* (friar) Observant; Observant Friar; Franciscan of the Strict Observance.

observateur, -trice [ɔpsɛrvatœːr, -tris]. **1.** *s.* (*a*) observer (of events, of phenomena of nature, etc.; *Av: Mil:* of enemy's movements, etc.); spotter (of aircraft); *Mil: Navy:* **o. du but,** spotting officer; **o. des Nations Unies,** United Nations observer; (*b*) observer, keeper (of rules, laws). **2.** *a.* observant, observing.

observation [ɔpsɛrvasjɔ̃], *s.f.* **1.** observance, keeping (of laws, rules, feasts). **2.** observation; observing; (*a*) **o. des astres,** observation of heavenly bodies; **o. astronomique, météorologique,** astronomical, meteorological, observation; *Surv:* **observations sur le terrain,** observations in the field, field-work; **faire, prendre, une o.,** to take an observation; *Nau:* to take the sun; **être, se tenir, en o.,** to be on the lookout, on the watch; **tenir, mettre, qn, qch., en o.,** to keep, put, s.o., sth., under observation; to keep an eye on s.o., on sth.; **mettre un malade en o.,** to put a patient under observation; **esprit d'o.,** observant turn of mind; *Sp:* **le premier round a été un round d'o.,** they played a waiting game in the first round; (*b*) *Mil:* **armée d'o.,** army of observation; **poste d'o.,** observation post, station, observing post, station; observing point; look-out post; **o. aérienne,** aerial, air, observation; **o. terrestre,** ground, land, observation; **o. à courte distance, o. rapprochée,** close, near, observation; **o. à grande distance, o. lointaine,**

distant, far, observation; long-range observation; **o. à moyenne distance,** medium(-range) observation; **o. latérale,** observation from one, from the, flank; lateral observation; **o. bilatérale,** observation from both flanks, bilateral observation; **o. conjuguée,** combined observation, cross observation; **unité d'o.,** observing unit; *Av:* **avion d'o.,** observation aircraft; *s.a.* BALLON 1, TOUR[1]. **3.** (*a*) observation, remark; **faire une o.,** to make an observation, a remark; **si je puis me permettre une o.,** if I may be allowed to make an observation, to say sth.; **j'en fis l'o. à . . .,** I remarked on it to . . .; **point d'observations, s'il vous plaît!** no remarks, please! **il faisait toujours des observations à ses élèves,** he was always finding fault with his pupils; (*b*) **observations sur un auteur,** comments, notes, on an author; *Com: etc:* **pour observations,** for comments.

observatoire [ɔpsɛrvatwa:r], *s.m.* **1.** *Astr:* observatory. **2.** *Mil:* observation post.

observer [ɔpsɛrve], *v.tr.* to observe; (*a*) to keep (to), to comply with, to adhere to (rules, laws, etc.); **o. une stricte économie,** to practise strict economy; **ne pas o. la loi, le dimanche,** to break the law, the sabbath; **o. le silence,** to keep silence; to observe, preserve, silence; **o. les distances,** to keep one's distance, (i) *Mil: etc:* to keep, maintain, distance; (ii) to keep one's place; **o. les convenances,** to observe the conventions; **o. une attitude passive,** to maintain a passive attitude; **ne pas toujours o. ses devoirs,** to be lax in one's duties; **o. une promesse,** to keep a promise; **faire o. la loi, un décret,** to enforce obedience to the law, respect for a decree; (*b*) to watch (sth., s.o.); **on nous observe,** we are being watched; **observez votre langage,** keep a watch on your tongue; mind your language; **il observait tout autour de lui,** he observed, had his eye on, everything round him; **je l'observais faire,** I watched him doing it; (*c*) **o. les astres,** to observe, study, the stars; *Surv: etc:* **o. un angle,** to take, read, an angle; *Nau: etc:* **o. une étoile,** to sight a star; **o. le soleil,** to take the sun, to take a sight at the sun; **point observé,** position by observation; **navigation observée,** sailing by observation; (*d*) to note, notice; **faire o. qch. à qn,** to draw s.o.'s attention to sth.; to call sth. to s.o.'s notice; **je lui ai fait o. que . . .,** I pointed out to him that . . .; **comme le fait o. cet historien,** as this historian points out; **je vous prie d'o. que . . .,** may I ask you to note that . . .

s'observer, to be circumspect, careful, cautious, wary; to be on one's guard; to keep a watch on one's tongue, on one's manners.

obsession [ɔpsɛsjɔ̃], *s.f.* obsession ((i) by evil spirit; (ii) by idea or emotion); **o. de la violence,** obsession with violence.

obsession-impulsion [ɔpsɛsjɔ̃nɛ̃pylsjɔ̃], *s.f.* obsessive impulse; *pl. obsessions-impulsions.*

obsessionnel, -elle [ɔpsɛsjɔnɛl], *a.* obsessional.

obsidianite [ɔpsidjanit], *s.f. Miner:* obsidianite.

obsidienne [ɔpsidjɛn], *s.f.*, **obsidiane** [ɔpsidjan], *s.f. Miner:* obsidian; *F:* volcanic glass.

obsidional, -aux [ɔpsidjɔnal, -o], *a.* (*a*) obsidional (coin); *Rom.Ant:* **couronne obsidionale,** obsidional crown; (*b*) **fièvre obsidionale,** mass psychosis of the besieged.

obsolescence [ɔpsɔlɛs(s)ɑ̃:s], *s.f.* obsolescence.

obsolescent [ɔpsɔlɛs(s)ɑ̃], *a.* obsolescent.

obsolète [ɔpsɔlɛt], *a.* obsolete (word, etc.).

obsonine [ɔpsɔnin], *s.f. Med:* opsonin.

obsonique [ɔpsɔnik], *a.* opsonic.

obstacle [ɔpstakl], *s.m.* (*a*) obstacle (**à,** to); impediment, hindrance; **o. au progrès,** barrier to progress; **je ne veux pas être un o. à votre bonheur,** I do not want to stand in the way of your happiness; **le seul o. à leur réconciliation,** the only obstacle to their reconciliation; **avancer sans o.,** to advance unimpeded, without any obstacle; **dresser, susciter, des obstacles à qn,** to put obstacles in s.o.'s way, to hinder s.o.; **faire o. à qch., à qn,** to be a bar to sth.; to stand in the way of sth., of s.o.; **mettre o. à qch.,** to prevent, oppose, sth.; **je n'y vois pas d'o.,** I see no difficulty about it, no objection to it; **suivre qn à travers tous les obstacles,** to follow s.o. through thick and thin; (*b*) **course d'obstacles,** (i) *Turf:* steeplechase; (ii) *Sp:* hurdle race, obstacle race; **mettre un cheval sur les obstacles,** to put a horse over the jumps, over the fences; *Sp:* **parcours d'obstacles,** obstacle course; *Mil:* **o. artificiel, naturel,** artificial, natural, obstacle; **o. actif,** tactical obstacle; **o. passif,** protective obstacle; **établir, dresser, des obstacles,** to construct, set up, obstacles; *Av:* **balise d'o.,** obstruction marker; **feu d'o.,** obstruction, obstacle, light; **ligne de dégagement des obstacles,** obstacle, obstruction, clearance line; *Rail:* **o. sur la voie,** obstruction of the track; (*c*) *Jur:* **o. à la compensation,** bar to set-off; (*d*) *Dent:* **o. à l'occlusion,** occlusal interference.

obstétrical, -aux [ɔpstetrikal, -o], *a.* obstetric(al).

obstétrique [ɔpstetrik]. **1.** *a.* obstetric(al). **2.** *s.f.* obstetrics.

obstination [ɔpstinasjɔ̃], *s.f.* obstinacy, stubbornness, persistency; *F:* mulishness, pig-headedness; **o. à faire qch.,** doggedness, persistency, in doing sth.

obstiné, -ée [ɔpstine]. **1.** *a.* stubborn, self-willed, headstrong, obstinate, *F:* pig-headed (person); stubborn, dogged (resistance); persistent (cough, fever); **o. à se perdre,** bent on self-destruction; **o. dans ses principes,** unyielding in his principles. **2.** *s.* stubborn, obstinate, *F:* pig-headed, person.

obstinément [ɔpstinemɑ̃], *adv.* obstinately; stubbornly; mulishly, *F:* pig-headedly.

obstiner [ɔpstine], *v.tr. A:* **o. qn,** to make s.o. obstinate.

s'obstiner, to show obstinacy, stubbornness; **s'o. à qch., à faire qch.,** to persist in sth., in doing sth.; to be bent on sth., on doing sth.; **s'o. au silence,** to remain stubbornly, obstinately, silent; **il s'obstinait à la revoir,** he was set on, bent on, seeing her again; **s'o. dans une idée,** to persist in, cling to, an idea; **pluie qui s'obstine,** persistent rain.

obstruant [ɔpstryɑ̃]. **1.** *a.* obstructing, obstruent (matter, etc.). **2.** *s.m. Med:* obstruent.

obstructif, -ive [ɔpstryktif, -i:v], *a.* **1.** obstructive. **2.** *Med:* obstruent.

obstruction [ɔpstryksjɔ̃], *s.f.* (*a*) *Med:* obstruction; **o. intestinale,** stoppage of the bowels; (*b*) *Pol:* obstruction, *U.S:* filibustering; **faire de l'o.,** to filibuster; (*c*) blockage (of drains, etc.); choking; clogging; jamming (of bullet, etc.); (*d*) *Sp:* obstruction; **faire de l'o.,** to obstruct; (*e*) *Nau:* **o. littorale,** boom defence.

obstructionnisme [ɔpstryksjɔnism], *s.m. Pol:* obstruction(ism); *U.S:* filibustering.

obstructionniste [ɔpstryksjɔnist], *Pol:* **1.** *s.m.* obstructionist, *U.S:* filibusterer. **2.** *a.* obstructive, *U.S:* filibustering (tactics).

obstruer [ɔpstrye], *v.tr.* to obstruct, block (street, canal, the view); to choke (outlet); *Med:* to obstruct, to cause an obstruction in; **rue obstruée,** blocked street; **tuyau obstrué,** choked, blocked, pipe.

obtecté [ɔptɛkte], *a. Ent:* obtect, obtected (pupa).

obtempérer [ɔptɑ̃pere], *v.ind.tr.* (**j'obtempère, n. obtempérons; j'obtempérerai**) **o. à une sommation, aux magistrats,** to obey a summons, the magistrates; **o. à une requête,** to accede to, fall in with, a request; **o. à un ordre,** to comply with an order.

obtenir [ɔptəni:r], *v.tr.* (*conj. like* TENIR) to obtain, get (answer, permission, favour, result, satisfaction); to secure (promise, good value); to gain, procure (s.o.'s consent, etc.); to achieve (result); **comment avez-vous obtenu cet argent?** how did you come by, get, that money? **où cela s'obtient-il?** where can you get it? where can it be bought? **ça s'obtient facilement,** it's easy to get; **o. des renseignements,** to gain information; **o. qch. de qn,** to obtain, get, sth. from, of, s.o.; **un bon maître obtient de bons résultats,** a good teacher gets, achieves, good results; **j'ai obtenu de le voir,** I obtained, got, permission to see him; **il obtint d'être nommé président,** he managed to get himself elected president; **j'ai obtenu de lui qu'il vienne, qu'il viendrait, avec nous,** I have induced him to come with us; **j'obtins qu'il me prêtât cinq francs,** I got him, persuaded him, to lend me five francs; **ce privilège s'obtient très facilement,** this privilege is to be had for the asking.

obtenteur, -trice [ɔptɑ̃tœ:r, -tris], *s.* (*a*) *F:* one who obtains, gets; obtainer, getter; (*b*) *Hort: etc:* creator, grower (of a new variety).

obtention [ɔptɑ̃sjɔ̃], *s.f.* (*a*) obtaining (of favour, etc.); obtaining, attainment, acquisition (of diploma, etc.); **o. d'une température plus élevée,** reaching, obtaining, a higher temperature; (*b*) *Hort: etc:* creation, production (of a new variety).

obturant [ɔptyrɑ̃], *a.* that stops, closes up; **plaque obturante,** obturator; plate for closing an aperture.

obturateur, -trice [ɔptyratœ:r, -tris]. **1.** *a.* obturating, closing (cartridge, plate, etc.); *Anat:* **artère, veine, membrane, obturatrice,** obturator artery, vein, membrane; **muscle o.,** obturator muscle; *Mec.E: etc:* **anneau o.,** ring obturator; **aubage o.,** shutter vane; **volet o.,** shutter. **2.** *s.m.* (*a*) *Anat: Surg:* obturator, closing device (of cavity, aperture); (*b*) *Mec.E:* blank cap, blank flange, blind flange (for pipe, etc.); obturator, shutter; *I.C.E:* throttle; *Artil:* obturator, gas-check; **o. de joint,** gasket; **o. de vanne,** valve shutter; *Atom.Ph:* **o. à neutrons,** neutron shutter; (*c*) *Dent:* prosthetic speech-aid; **o. vélo-palatin,** obturator for cleft palate; (*d*) *Opt:* cap (of eyepiece); *Phot:* shutter (of camera); *Phot:* **o. à diaphragme iris,** iris-diaphragm shutter; **o. à guillotine,** drop shutter; **o. à rideau,** roller-blind shutter; **o. de plaque, o. focal,** focal-plane shutter; **o. central, o. au diaphragme,** diaphragm shutter; **o. programmé,** programmed shutter, program-type shutter; **o. rotatif,** rotary shutter; **armer l'o.,** to set the shutter; **o. toujours armé,** everset shutter; **déclancher l'o.,** to release the shutter; *Cin:* **o. à deux, trois, pales,** two-bladed, three-bladed, shutter.

obturation [ɔptyrasjɔ̃], *s.f.* (*a*) *Mec.E: Civ.E: etc:* obturation (of duct); closing (of cavity); blanking off (of pipe-line, tunnel); sealing (of vessel); **bride d'o.,** blank flange, blind flange; **plaque d'o.,** blanking plate; **composition isolante, enduit isolant, pour o.,** sealing compound; (*b*) *Dent:* filling, stopping (of tooth); **o. à la gutta-percha,** guttapercha stopping; **o. à l'amalgame,** amalgam filling; **o. métallique, plastique,** metal, plastic, filling; **o. temporaire,** temporary filling, stopping; **o. définitive,** permanent filling, stopping.

obturer [ɔptyre], *v.tr.* (*a*) *Mec.E: Civ.E: etc:* to stop, seal, obturate (pipe, aperture, etc.); to close (cavity); to blank off (pipeline, tunnel, etc.); **raccord en T obturé,** blanked-off T junction; (*b*) *Dent:* to fill, stop (a tooth).

obtus, -use [ɔpty, -y:z], *a.* **1.** blunt(ed) (point); rounded (leaf, etc.). **2.** dull, obtuse (person); **avoir l'esprit o.,** to be dull-witted, *F:* thick-headed, dim-witted. **3.** *Geom:* obtuse (angle).

obtusangle [ɔptyzɑ̃:gl], *a. Geom:* obtuse-angled (triangle).

obtusifolié [ɔptyzifɔlje], *a. Bot:* obtusifolious.

obus [ɔby], *s.m.* **1.** *Artil:* shell; **o. à coiffe, à ogive,** capped shell; **o. à ogive effilée,** long-shouldered shell; **o. à ogive pleine,** solid-headed shell; **o. à fausse ogive,** false-cap shell; **corps de l'o.,** body of the shell; **culot d'o.,** shell base; **o. à culot tronconique,** taper-based shell; **o. plein,** shot (shell); **o. réel, o. de combat,** service shell, live shell; **o. armé,** live shell; **o. chargé,** loaded shell; **o. explosif,** high-explosive shell; **o. à balles, à mitraille,** shrapnel (shell); **o. à balles à charge arrière,** base-burster shrapnel, rear-burster shrapnel; **o. à gaz, o. chimique, o. toxique,** gas shell, chemical shell; **o. de rupture,** armour-piercing shell; **o. de semi-rupture,** thick-walled shell; **o. éclairant,** illuminating shell, star shell, light shell; **o. fumigène,** smoke shell; **o. incendiaire,** incendiary shell; **o. traceur,** tracer shell; **o. d'exercice,** practice shell; **o. à blanc,** blank shell; **o. inerte,** blind-loaded shell; **faux o.,** dummy shell; **o. non explosé,** *F:* **o. qui a foiré,** blind shell, dud. **2.** *Aut:* conical valve plug (of pneumatic tyre).

obuser [ɔbyze], *v.tr. Artil:* to shell.

obus-fusée [ɔbyfyze], *s.m.* rocket-propelled shell; *pl. obus-fusées.*

obusier [ɔbyzje], *s.m. Artil:* howitzer; **o. de campagne,** field howitzer.

obusite [ɔbyzit], *s.f. Med: A:* shell-shock.

obvenir [ɔbvəni:r], *v.i.* (*conj. like* VENIR); *Jur:* to escheat, revert by escheat (**à,** to).

obvers [ɔbvɛ:r], *s.m.*, **obverse** [ɔbvɛrs], *s.m. Num:* observe (of coin, medal).

obversion [ɔbvɛrsjɔ̃], *s.f.* obversion.

obvie [ɔbvi], *a.* obvious.

obvier [ɔbvje], *v.ind.tr.* (*p.d. & pr.sub.* **n. obviions, v. obviiez**) **o. à qch.,** to obviate, prevent, sth.; **o. à un accident, à une maladie,** to take precautions against an accident, an illness; **pour o. à tout scandale,** to prevent any scandal.

oc [ɔk], *adv.* (*in Old Provençal*) yes; *Ling:* **la langue d'oc,** the dialect(s) of the south of France.

ocarina [ɔkarina], *s.m. Mus:* ocarina.

occase[1] [ɔkɑ:z], *a.f. Astr:* **amplitude o. d'un astre,** occiduous, western, amplitude of a star.

occase[2], *s.f. P:* (*a*) opportunity; **profiter de l'o.,** to make the most of the opportunity; (*b*) windfall; bargain; (*c*) **d'o.,** secondhand; **tuyaux d'o.,** stale news.

occasion [ɔkazjɔ̃, -kɑ-], *s.f.* 1. (*a*) opportunity, occasion, chance; **saisir une o.**, to take, seize, an opportunity; **prendre o. pour faire qch.**, **prendre l'o. de faire qch.**, to take the opportunity of doing sth.; **saisir, prendre, l'o. par les cheveux, aux cheveux**, to snatch at the opportunity; **vous n'avez qu'à saisir l'o.**, you have only to seize the opportunity; you have the ball at your feet; *Prov:* **l'o. est chauve**, opportunities are hard to seize; **l'o. fait le larron**, opportunity makes the thief; **je n'ai jamais eu l'o de le rencontrer**, I never had a chance, the opportunity, of meeting him; **avoir l'o. de faire qch.**, to have a chance to do sth., the opportunity of doing sth.; **si vous avez l'o. de . . .**, if you have occasion to . . .; **si l'o. se rencontre, si vous en trouvez l'o.**, if the opportunity comes your way; **attendre l'o.**, to bide one's time; **perdre, manquer, laisser échapper, l'o. de faire qch.**, to throw away, miss, the opportunity of doing sth.; **il ne faut pas laisser passer l'o.**, we must not miss the opportunity; **tu as vraiment manqué l'o.**, you've really missed the boat! **perdre une belle o. de faire qch.**, to throw away an excellent opportunity of doing sth.; **profiter de l'o.**, to take advantage of the opportunity; **suivant l'o.**, as occasion arises; **à l'o.**, (i) when the opportunity presents itself; (ii) if necessary; **à la première o.**, at the first opportunity; (*b*) *Com:* bargain; **soldes et occasions exceptionnels**, outstanding sales bargains; **c'est une véritable o.**, it's a real bargain; **montrer une o. à un client**, to show a customer a bargain. 2. (*a*) occasion, juncture; **à plusieurs occasions**, on several occasions; **en de rares occasions**, on rare occasions; *F:* once in a blue moon; **en toute o.**, on all occasions; **en toute autre o.**, at any other time; **toutes les occasions lui sont bonnes pour s'amuser**, he can find amusement, enjoy himself, in, under, any circumstances; **pour l'o.**, for the occasion; in this particular case; **à l'o. de son mariage**, on the occasion of his marriage; **je l'ai vu à l'o. du mariage de sa sœur**, I saw him at his sister's wedding; **par o.**, (i) by chance; (ii) now and then, occasionally; **en pareille o.**, (i) in similar circumstances; (ii) on such an occasion; **en cette o.**, at this juncture; **dans les grandes occasions**, on great occasions, on occasions of state; **il y a des occasions où . . .**, there are times when . . .; **leçons qui sont l'o. de plaisanteries**, lessons that give rise to jokes; (*b*) **d'o.**, (i) occasional; (ii) *A:* cheap, at a bargain price; (iii) secondhand; **héroïsme d'o.**, chance heroism; **vertu d'o.**, assumed virtue, virtue put on for the occasion; *Pej:* **musicien d'o.**, (indifferent) amateur musician; **acheter qch. d'o.**, to buy sth. secondhand; **voiture d'o.**, secondhand, used, car; **faire le neuf et l'o.**, to sell new and secondhand goods; **courir les occasions**, to look for bargains. 3. motive, reason, cause, occasion; **o. d'une dispute**, cause of a dispute; **c'est elle qui fut l'o. de la dispute**, it was about her that the quarrel arose; **différend à l'o. de . . .**, dispute about . . .; **donner o. à la médisance**, to give rise to scandal; **à l'o. de qn**, for the sake of, because of, s.o.; **dîner à votre o.**, dinner in your honour.

occasionnalisme [ɔkazjɔnalism], *s.m. Phil:* occasionalism.

occasionnaliste [ɔkazjɔnalist], *Phil:* (*a*) *a.* occasionalistic; (*b*) *s.m. & f.* occasionalist.

occasionnel, -elle [ɔkazjɔnɛl], *a.* occasional, acting as a cause; *Phil:* **cause occasionnelle**, occasional cause; **cause occasionnelle d'une révolte**, incident, opportunity, that led to a rising, a revolt; **rencontre occasionnelle**, chance meeting.

occasionnellement [ɔkazjɔnɛlmɑ̃], *adv.* occasionally; accidentally.

occasionner [ɔkazjɔne, -kɑ-], *v.tr.* (*rarely used except for unpleasant consequences*) to occasion, cause (dispute, etc.), to give rise to, to bring about (sth.); **retrait occasionné par le froid**, contraction due to cold; **la malpropreté occasionne des maladies**, dirt breeds disease; **le mauvais temps a occasionné de nombreuses grippes**, the bad weather has brought on many attacks of 'flu; **o. un retard**, to cause delay.

occident [ɔksidɑ̃], *s.m.* west; occident; *Hist:* **l'Empire d'O.**, the Western Empire; *Pol:* **l'O.**, the West.

occidental, -ale, -aux [ɔksidɑ̃tal, -o]. 1. *a.* west, western; **côte occidentale**, west coast; **l'Europe occidentale**, Western Europe; *Pol:* **les puissances occidentales**, the western powers, the West; *Hist: A:* **les Indes occidentales**, the West Indies; **Compagnie des Indes occidentales**, West India Company. 2. *s.* Westerner.

occidentalisation [ɔksidɑ̃talizasjɔ̃], *s.f.* westernization.

occidentaliser [ɔksidɑ̃talize], *v.tr.* to westernize, occidentalize.

occidentalisme [ɔksidɑ̃talism], *s.m.* occidentalism.

occipital, -aux [ɔksipital, -o], *Anat:* 1. *a.* occipital (lobe, artery, etc.). 2. *s.m.* occipital (bone).

occipito-atloïdien, -ienne [ɔksipitɔatlɔidjɛ̃, -jɛn], *a. Anat:* occipito-atlantal, occipito-atloid; *pl. occipito-atloïdiens, -iennes.*

occipito-bregmatique [ɔksipitɔbrɛgmatik], *a. Anat:* occipito-bregmatic; *pl. occipito-bregmatiques.*

occipito-frontal, -aux [ɔksipitɔfrɔ̃tal, -o], *a. Anat:* occipito-frontal.

occipito-mentonnier, -ière [ɔksipitɔmɑ̃tɔnje, -jɛːr], *a. Anat:* occipito-mental; *pl. occipito-mentonniers, -ières.*

occiput [ɔksipyt], *s.m. Anat:* occiput; the back of the head; **recevoir un coup sur l'o.**, to be hit on the back of the head.

occire [ɔksiːr], *v.tr.* (*a*) *A:* to kill, to slay; *used only in the inf., in the p.p.* **occis**, *and in the p.h. in the standing phr.*; **ceux que tu occis se portent bien**, those whom thou didst slay are whole; **quand il eut occis les paiens**, when he had slaughtered all the heathen; (*b*) *F: Hum:* **se faire o.**, to get killed, bumped off.

occiseur, -euse [ɔksizœːr, -øːz], *s. A:* slayer.

occitan [ɔksitɑ̃], *Ling:* 1. *a.* **langues occitanes, littérature occitane**, dialects, literature of the *langue d'Oc.* 2. *s.m. langue d'Oc, esp.* old Provençal.

occlure [ɔklyːr], *v.tr.* (*conj. like* CONCLURE, but *with p.p.* **occlus**); *Med: Surg: Ch:* to occlude; **paupières occluses**, occluded eyelids; *Lit:* **si la nuit occlut notre œil, c'est afin que nous écoutions plus**, if darkness veils our sight it is so that we may listen the more.

occlusif, -ive [ɔklysif, -iːv], *a.* occlusive, tending to occlude; *Ling:* **(consonne) occlusive**, occlusive (consonant).

occlusion [ɔklyzjɔ̃], *s.f.* 1. *Ch:* occlusion (of gases); *Meteor:* occlusion. 2. *Surg:* (*a*) occlusion (of the eyelids, etc.); (*b*) **o. intestinale**, obstruction, stoppage, of the bowels; atresia. 3. *Dent:* bite, occlusion; **o. acquise, o. habituelle**, acquired, habitual, occlusion; convenience occlusion; bite of convenience; **o. croisée, o. inversée**, crossbite; **o. équilibrée**, balanced bite, occlusion. 4. *Mch:* cut-off (of steam); *I.C.E: etc:* **o. complète d'une soupape**, full closure of a valve.

occlusionner [ɔklyzjɔne], *v.tr. Med: A:* to occlude.

occultation [ɔkyltasjɔ̃], *s.f. Astr:* occultation; **feu à occultations**, occulting, intermittent, light (of lighthouse, etc.); **o. des lumières**, blackout, screening, of light.

occulte [ɔkylt], *a.* occult (cause, science); secret (accounts); hidden (cause).

occultement [ɔkyltəmɑ̃], *adv.* occultly; secretly.

occulter [ɔkylte], *v.tr. Astr:* to occult; to hide, cut off (heavenly body) from view; *Rail: etc:* **o. un signal**, to occult a signal.

occulteur [ɔkyltœːr], *s.m.* occulter.

occultisme [ɔkyltism], *s.m.* occultism.

occultiste [ɔkyltist], *a. & s.m. & f.* occultist.

occupant, -ante [ɔkypɑ̃, -ɑ̃ːt]. 1. (*a*) *a.* occupying, in possession (of property, etc.); **autorité militaire occupante**, military occupation authority; *Jur:* **avoué o.**, solicitor in charge of a case; (*b*) *s.* occupier; occupant; *Mil:* member of the occupying, occupation, forces; *Jur:* **premier o.**, occupant; **possession à titre de premier o.**, occupancy. 2. *a. F:* that keeps one occupied; **enfant très o.**, child who gives a lot of trouble, who requires a lot of looking after.

occupation [ɔkypasjɔ̃], *s.f.* occupation. 1. occupancy, occupation, possession (of house, etc.); occupation (of conquered country, etc.); *Fr. Hist:* (1940-44) **l'O.**, the Occupation; **armée d'o.**, army of occupation. 2. (*a*) business, work, employment; **avoir de l'o.**, to be busy; **ne pas avoir d'o.**, (i) **être sans o.**, to be unemployed, out of a job; (ii) to have nothing to do; **donner de l'o. à qn**, to give s.o. (i) employment, (ii) sth. to do; **cela me donne de l'o.**, (i) it gives me something to do; (ii) I have my work cut out, my hands full; **sa toilette est l'unique o. de sa matinée**, her toilet occupies her whole morning; **voilà toute son o.**, that's all she cares about; **c'est toujours une o.!** it's something to do! (*b*) pursuit, profession; **occupations sédentaires**, sedentary pursuits.

occupationnel, -elle [ɔkypasjɔnɛl], *a. Med:* **thérapeutique occupationnelle**, occupational therapy.

occupé [ɔkype], *a.* 1. busy; engaged; **o. aux, des, préparatifs du voyage**, busy preparing, getting ready, for the journey; **o. à écrire un roman**, busy writing a novel; engaged in writing a novel; **c'est un homme fort o.**, he's a very busy man; **je suis o.**, (i) I'm busy; (ii) I'm engaged, not free; **elle n'est occupée que de sa petite personne**, she's entirely taken up with herself, with her own private affairs. 2. (*a*) **cette place est occupée**, this seat is engaged, taken; *Tp:* **ligne occupée**, line engaged, *U.S:* busy; (*b*) *Mil:* **territoire o.**, occupied territory.

occuper [ɔkype], *v.tr.* to occupy. 1. (*a*) to inhabit, reside in (house, etc.); (*b*) *Mil:* to hold, take possession of (town, fort, heights); (*c*) to fill, take up (time, space, attention, one's thoughts); **la lecture du rapport occupe la moitié de la séance**, the reading of the report takes up half the sitting; **faire qch. pour o. le temps**, to do sth. to fill in the time; (*d*) **o. un poste important**, to occupy, fill, an important post; **o. une chaire d'anglais**, to have a chair in English; **o. un rang élevé**, to hold a high rank; (*e*) *abs. Jur:* (*of solicitor or judge*) to be in charge of the case. 2. to give occupation to (s.o., the mind); **o. vingt ouvriers**, to employ twenty workmen; **o. qn**, to give s.o. something to do, something to think of; **le cas qui nous occupe**, the case in point, the case before us; **o. les enfants à des choses utiles**, to keep the children usefully occupied.

s'occuper. 1. to keep oneself busy; to employ oneself; **il aime à s'o.**, he likes being busy; **s'o. à qch.**, to be busy with sth.; **s'o. à faire qch.**, to be engaged in, busy, doing sth.; **s'o. à la lecture**, to spend one's time reading; **s'o. à écrire**, to be engaged in writing; **je bâtis un petit pavillon pour m'o.**, I am building a summerhouse for something to do. 2. **s'o. de qch.**, (i) to go in for, be interested in (music, photography, etc.); (ii) to apply one's thoughts to, to attend to, sth.; to be busy with sth.; **je vais m'o. de l'affaire**, I shall go into the matter; **il s'occupe un peu d'art**, he dabbles in art; **s'o. de deux choses à la fois**, to attend to two things at the same time; **il s'occupe de trop de choses**, he has too many irons in the fire; **nous allons maintenant nous o. de . . .**, we will now turn our attention to . . .; **il s'occupe de tout**, he attends to, sees to, everything; **ne vous occupez pas de vos bagages, on les enverra chercher**, don't bother about your luggage, it will be sent for; **je m'en occuperai**, I shall see to it, see about it; **qui s'occupe de ce qu'il dit?** who minds, who cares about, what he says? **occupe-toi de ce qui te regarde!** *P:* **de tes oignons!** mind your own business! *P:* **t'occupe pas!** don't you worry! never mind! **s'o. de qn**, to attend to s.o., to look after s.o.; *Com:* **est-ce qu'on s'occupe de vous?** are you being attended to, being served? **je m'occupe de vous trouver qch.**, I'm doing my best, trying hard, to find you sth.; **s'o. de grandes commandes**, to handle large orders; **la maison s'occupe d'une grande variété de marchandises**, the firm handles a great variety of goods; **je m'occupe surtout de . . .**, my special line is . . .; **il s'occupe d'importation**, he's in the import business.

occupeur [ɔkypœːr], *s.m.* occupant, tenant.

occurrence [ɔkyrɑ̃ːs], *s.f.* 1. occurrence, event; emergency, juncture, occasion; **en l'o.**, in, under, the circumstances, as it is, as it was; in this case; at this juncture; **d'o.**, sometimes. 2. *Ecc:* occurrence (of two festivals).

occurrent [ɔkyrɑ̃], *a.* occurring, occurrent (event, case).

océan [ɔseɑ̃]. 1. (*a*) *s.m.* ocean; **d'un o. à l'autre**, from coast to coast; *abs.* **l'O.**, the Atlantic; **un o. de blés**, a sea of corn; (*b*) *a. Lit: A:* **la mer océane**, the ocean sea; the Atlantic. 2. *Pr.n.m. Gr.Myth:* **Océan**, Oceanus.

océanide [ɔseanid], *s.f. Gr.Myth:* oceanid; ocean nymph.

Océanie (l') [lɔseani], *Pr.n.f. Geog:* Oceania; the South Sea Islands.

océanien, -ienne [ɔseanjɛ̃, -jɛn]. 1. *a.* oceanian, oceanic. 2. *s.* Oceanian; South Sea Islander.

océanique [ɔseanik], *a.* oceanic; **courants océaniques**, ocean currents; **climat o.**, oceanic climate, maritime climate.

océanite [ɔseanit], *s.m. Orn:* **pétrel o.**, Wilson's petrel.

océanodrome [ɔseanɔdrom], *s.m. Orn:* **o. de Leach**, Leach's fork-tailed petrel.

océanographe [ɔseanɔgraf], *s.m. & f.* oceanographer.

océanographie [ɔseanɔgrafi], *s.f.* oceanography.

océanographique [ɔseanɔgrafik], *a.* oceanographic(al).

océanologie [ɔseanɔlɔʒi], *s.f.* oceanology.

ocellaire [ɔsɛlɛːr], *a. Nat.Hist:* ocellar.

ocellation [ɔsɛlasjɔ̃], *s.f. Nat.Hist:* ocellation.

ocelle [ɔsɛl], *s.m.* 1. *Ent:* ocellus, simple eye. 2. *Nat.Hist:* ocellus (of peacock, etc.).

ocellé [ɔsɛlle], *a.* 1. *Nat.Hist:* ocellate; **dindon o.,** ocellated turkey. 2. ocellated (**de,** with).

ocelliforme [ɔsɛllifɔrm], *a.* ocelliform.

ocelot [ɔslo], *s.m. Z:* ocelot.

ochlocratie [ɔklɔkrasi], *s.f. Lit:* ochlocracy, mob rule.

ochna [ɔkna], *s.m. Bot:* ochna.

ochnacées [ɔknase], *s.f.pl. Bot:* Ochnaceae.

Ochosias [ɔkɔzjas], *Pr.n.m. B.Hist:* Ahaziah.

ochotone [ɔkɔtɔn], *s.m. Z:* pika; (*genus*) Ochotona.

ochotonidés [ɔkɔtɔnide], *s.m.pl. Z:* Ochotonidae.

ochracé [ɔkrase], *a. Nat.Hist:* ochraceous, ochreous.

ochrolite [ɔkrɔlit], *s.f. Miner:* ochrolite.

ochronose [ɔkrɔnoːz], *s.f. Med:* ochronosis.

ochrosporé [ɔkrɔspɔre], *a. Fung:* ochrosporous.

ocrage [ɔkraːʒ], *s.m.* ochring; *Phot:* **o. des plaques,** backing of plates.

ocre [ɔkr̥]. 1. *s.f.* ochre; **o. jaune, rouge,** yellow, red, ochre. 2. *a.inv.* ochre.

ocréa [ɔkrea], *s.f. Bot:* ocrea.

ocrer [ɔkre], *v.tr.* to ochre.

ocreux, -euse [ɔkrø, -øːz], *a.* (*a*) ochr(e)ous (clay); (*b*) ochre(-coloured); **le jaune o. qui indique une maladie de foie,** the muddy yellow (colour) indicative of a liver complaint.

oct(a)- [ɔkt(a)], **octo-** [ɔktɔ], *pref.* oct(a)-, octo-.

octac(h)orde [ɔktakɔrd], *a. & s.m. Mus:* octachord.

octaèdre [ɔktaɛdr̥]. 1. *a.* octahedral. 2. *s.m. Geom:* octahedron.

octaédrique [ɔktaedrik], *a.* octahedral.

octaédrite [ɔktaedrit], *s.f. Miner:* octahedrite.

octal [ɔktal], *a. Elcs:* (*computers*) **chiffre o.,** octal digit; **notation octale,** octal notation; **système de numération o.,** octal number system; **en o.,** octally.

octandre [ɔktɑ̃dr̥], *a. Bot:* octandrous.

octane [ɔktan]. 1. *a.f. Med: A:* octan (fever). 2. *s.m. Ch:* octane; **indice d'o.,** octane number; **degré d'o.,** octane rating; **essence à haut indice d'o.,** high-octane fuel, petrol; **carburant d'aviation à degré d'o. élevé,** high-octane aviation fuel.

octant [ɔktɑ̃], *s.m.* 1. *Astr: Astrol:* octant (position or aspect of heavenly body). 2. *Astr: Nau:* octant; quadrant. 3. **(constellation de) l'O.,** Octans.

octante [ɔktɑ̃ːt], *num.a. & s.m.inv. A: & Sw.Fr: Fr.C:* eighty.

octantième [ɔktɑ̃tjɛm], *num.a. & s.m.inv. A: & Sw.Fr: Fr.C:* eightieth.

octastyle [ɔktastil], *a. Arch:* octastyle.

octateuque [ɔktatøk], *s.m. B:* Octateuch.

octavaire [ɔktavɛːr], *s.m. Ecc:* octavarium.

octave[1] [ɔktaːv], *s.f. Ecc: Mus: Pros: etc:* octave.

Octave[2], *Pr.n.m. Rom.Hist:* Octavius.

Octavie [ɔktavi], *Pr.n.f. Rom.Hist:* Octavia.

octavien[1], **-ienne** [ɔktavjɛ̃, -jɛn], *a.* Octavian (library, etc.).

Octavien[2], *Pr.n.m. Rom.Hist:* Octavian(us).

octavier [ɔktavje], *v.i. Mus:* to octave.

octavin [ɔktavɛ̃], *s.m. Mus:* octave flute; piccolo.

octavo [ɔktavo]. 1. *adv.* eighthly. 2. *s.m. Publ:* octavo.

octavon, -onne [ɔktavɔ̃, -ɔn], *s.* octoroon.

octène [ɔktɛn], *s.m. Ch:* octene.

octet [ɔktɛt], *s.m.* 1. *Ch:* octet. 2. *Elcs:* (*computers*) octet, eight-bit byte.

octidi [ɔktidi], *s.m. Fr.Hist:* (*Republican Calendar*) eighth day of a decade.

octillion [ɔktiljɔ̃], *s.m.* (*a*) (*since* 1948) octillion (10^{48}); (*b*) (*before* 1948) a thousand quadrillions (10^{27}), *U.S:* octillion.

octo-. *See* OCT(A).

octobasse [ɔktɔbas], *s.m. Mus:* octobass.

octobre [ɔktɔbr̥], *s.m.* October; **en o.,** in October; **au mois d'o.,** in the month of October; **le premier, le sept., o.,** on October (the) first, (the) seventh; on the first, the seventh, of October.

octobriste [ɔktɔbrist], *s.m. Russian Hist:* Octobrist.

octocoralliaires [ɔktɔkɔraljɛːr], *s.m.pl. Coel:* Octocorallia, Alcyonaria.

octode [ɔktɔd], *s.f. Elcs:* octode.

octodon [ɔktɔdɔ̃], **octodonte** [ɔjtɔdɔ̃ːt], *s.m. Z:* octodon, pencil-tailed rat.

octodontidés [ɔktɔdɔ̃tide], *s.m.pl. Z:* Octodontidae.

octoèque [ɔktɔɛk], *s.m. Ecc:* octoechos, octaechos.

octogénaire [ɔktɔʒenɛːr], *a. & s.m. & f.* octogenarian.

octogonal, -aux [ɔktɔgɔnal, -o], *a.* octagonal, eight-angled, eight-sided.

octogone [ɔktɔgɔn], *Geom:* 1. *a.* octagonal. 2. *s.m.* octagon.

octogyne [ɔktɔʒin], *a. Bot:* octogynous.

octonaire [ɔktɔnɛːr], *s.m. A.Pros:* octonarian.

octopétale [ɔktɔpetal], *a. Bot:* octopetalous.

octoploïde [ɔktɔplɔid], *a. & s.m. Biol:* octoploid.

octopode [ɔktɔpɔd], *a. & s.m. Moll:* octopod; *s.m.pl.* **octopodes,** Octopoda.

octopodidés [ɔktɔpɔdide], *s.m.pl. Moll:* Octopodidae.

octopolaire [ɔktɔpɔlɛːr], *a. El.E:* eight-pole, octopolar (stator, etc.).

octostyle [ɔktɔstil], *a. Arch:* octastyle.

octosyllabe [ɔktɔsil(l)ab], **octosyllabique** [ɔktɔsil(l)abik], *a.* octosyllabic (word, verse).

octovalent [ɔktɔvalɑ̃], *a. Ch:* octovalent, octavalent.

octroi [ɔktrwa], *s.m.* 1. concession, grant(ing) (of a favour or privilege); **o. de crédits,** credit grant. 2. *O:* (*a*) town dues, city toll (on goods which are to be consumed within the town); octroi; *A:* **o. de mer,** dock dues (in Algiers and the colonies); (*b*) tollhouse.

octroiement [ɔktrwamɑ̃], *s.m.* granting, conceding.

octroyer [ɔktrwaje], *v.tr.* (**j'octroie, n. octroyons; j'octroierai**) to grant, concede, allow (**à,** to); **o. une charte à un pays,** to grant a country a charter; **o. un titre de noblesse à qn,** to confer a patent of nobility, a title, on s.o.; **il a bien employé le temps qu'on lui octroie,** he made good use of the time allocated to him; **s'o. des plaisirs,** to indulge in pleasures.

octuor [ɔktyoːr], *s.m. Mus:* octet, octette.

octuple [ɔktypl̥], *a. & s.m.* octuple, eightfold; **seize est l'o. de deux,** sixteen is eight times (as much as) two.

octupler [ɔktyple], *v.tr. & i.* to increase eightfold.

octyle [ɔktil], *s.m. Ch:* octyle.

octylène [ɔktilɛn], *s.m. Ch:* octylene.

octyne [ɔktin], *s.m. Ch:* octyne, octine.

oculaire [ɔkylɛːr]. 1. *a.* (*a*) ocular (demonstration, etc.); **loupe o.,** eye glass; **témoin o.,** eyewitness; (*b*) **hygiène o.,** hygiene of the eye. 2. *s.m.* (*a*) *Opt:* eyepiece, ocular; **o. micrométrique,** micrometer eyepiece; **o. à réticule, à fils,** cross-hair eyepiece; (*b*) *Cin:* viewfinder (of camera).

oculairement [ɔkylɛrmɑ̃], *adv.* ocularly; **démontrer o. que . . .,** to give a visible demonstration of the fact that. . . .

ocularist [ɔkylarist], *s.m.* ocularist.

oculé [ɔkyle], *a. Nat.Hist:* oculate, ocellate.

Oculi [ɔkyli], *s.m. Ecc:* Oculi Sunday.

oculifère [ɔkylifɛːr], *a. Nat.Hist:* oculiferous.

oculiforme [ɔkylifɔrm], *a. Biol:* oculiform, eye-shaped.

oculinidés [ɔkylinide], *s.m.pl. Coel:* Oculinidae.

oculiste [ɔkylist], *s.m.* oculist.

oculo-cardiaque [ɔkylɔkardjak], *a. Med:* oculocardiac (reflex); *pl. oculo-cardiaques.*

oculo-palpébral, -aux [ɔkylɔpalpebral, -o], *a. Anat:* oculopalpebral.

oculo-réaction [ɔkylɔreaksjɔ̃], *s.f.* oculoreaction, ophthalmoreaction; *pl. oculo-réactions.*

oculus [ɔkylys], *s.m. Arch:* oculus; bull's eye (window).

ocyphaps [ɔsifaps], *s.m. Orn:* crested bronzewing; (*genus*) Ocyphaps.

ocypode [ɔsipɔd], *s.m. Crust:* ocypode.

ocypodidés [ɔsipɔdide], *s.m.pl. Crust:* Ocypodidae.

ocytocine [ɔsitɔsin], *s.f. Physiol:* oxytocin.

ocytocique [ɔsitɔsik], *a. Obst:* oxytocic.

odalisque [ɔdalisk], *s.f.* odalisque, odalisk.

ode [ɔd], *s.f. Lit:* ode.

odelette [ɔdlɛt], *s.f.* short ode.

Odéon [ɔdeɔ̃], *s.m.* (*a*) *Gr.Ant:* odeum; (*b*) **(le Théâtre de) l'O.,** the Odeon theatre (in Paris).

odeur [ɔdœːr], *s.f.* 1. odour, smell; scent (of cigar, etc.); **sachet à o. de lavande,** lavender-scented sachet; **je sentais une o. de brûlé,** I could smell burning; **fleurs aux douces odeurs,** sweet-smelling flowers; **sans o.,** scentless; **bonne o.,** pleasant smell; fragrance; **mauvaise o.,** bad smell; reek, stench; **forte o. de varech,** tang of seaweed; **enlèvement des odeurs malsaines,** deodorizing; *F:* **ne pas être en o. de sainteté auprès de qn,** to be in s.o.'s bad books; *A:* **en mauvaise o. (auprès de qn),** in bad repute (with s.o.). 2. *usu. pl. Toil:* scent, perfume; **flacon d'odeurs,** bottle of scent.

odieusement [ɔdjøzmɑ̃], *adv.* odiously, hatefully.

odieux, -euse [ɔdjø, -øːz]. 1. *a.* odious; hateful (person, vice); abominable (crime); **être o. à qn,** to be hateful to s.o.; **il m'est o.,** I hate him; I find him odious; **il s'est rendu o.,** he made himself unbearable. 2. *s.m.* odiousness, hatefulness (of an action); **il supporta tout l'o. de la transaction,** he incurred all the odium of the transaction.

Odile [ɔdil], *Pr.n.f.* Odilia.

Odin [ɔdɛ̃], *Pr.n.m. Myth:* Woden, Odin.

Odoacre [ɔdɔakr̥], *Pr.n.m. Hist:* Odoacer.

odobénidés [ɔdɔbenide], *s.m.pl. Z:* Odobenidae.

odographe [ɔdɔgraf], *s.m.* hodograph, odograph.

odomètre [ɔdɔmɛtr̥], *s.m.* hodometer, odometer; pedometer.

odométrie [ɔdɔmetri], *s.f.* odometry.

Odon [ɔdɔ̃], *Pr.n.m.* Odo.

odonates [ɔdɔnat], *s.m.pl. Ent:* Odonata, Libellulidae, dragonflies.

odonatoptères [ɔdɔnatɔptɛːr], *s.m.pl. Ent:* Odonatoptera.

odontalgie [ɔdɔ̃talʒi], *s.f. Med:* odontalgia, toothache.

odontalgique [ɔdɔ̃talʒik], *a. & s.m. Med: Pharm:* odontalgic.

odontaspis [ɔdɔ̃taspis], *s.m. Ich:* odontaspis, sand shark.

odontoblaste [ɔdɔ̃tɔblast], *s.m. Anat:* odontoblast.

odontocètes [ɔdɔ̃tɔsɛt], *s.m.pl. Z:* (the) Odontoceti.

odontogénèse [ɔdɔ̃tɔʒenɛːz], *s.f.* odontogenesis.

odontoglosse [ɔdɔ̃tɔglɔs], **odontoglossum** [ɔdɔ̃tɔglɔsɔm], *s.m. Bot:* odontoglossum.

odontoïde [ɔdɔ̃tɔid]. 1. *a. Anat:* odontoid (process). 2. *s.f. Tchn:* profile (of (involute) gear teeth).

odontoïdien, -ienne [ɔdɔ̃tɔidjɛ̃, -jɛn], *a. Anat:* odontoid (ligament).

odontolit(h)e [ɔdɔ̃tɔlit], *s.f.* 1. *Miner:* odontolite. 2. (dental) tartar, odontolite.

odontologie [ɔdɔ̃tɔlɔʒi], *s.f. Med:* odontology.

odontologique [ɔdɔ̃tɔlɔʒik], *a. Med:* odontological.

odontologiste [ɔdɔ̃tɔlɔʒist], *s.m. & f. Med:* odontologist.

odontome [ɔdɔ̃tom], *s.m. Med:* odontoma, odontome; **o. complexe,** complex, composite, compound, odontoma.

odontophore [ɔdɔ̃tɔfɔːr], *s.m.* 1. *Moll:* (*a*) odontophore; (*b*) radula. 2. *Orn:* odontophorus.

odontorragie [ɔdɔ̃tɔraʒi], *s.f. Dent:* odontorrhagia.

odorant [ɔdɔrɑ̃], *a.* (*a*) sweet-smelling, fragrant, odoriferous (flower, etc.); (*b*) that smells, stinks; stinking.

odorat [ɔdɔra], *s.m.* (sense of) smell; **avoir l'o. fin, un o. exquis,** (i) to have a keen sense of smell, a good nose; (ii) to be perspicacious, shrewd; **mon o. était affecté par une odeur de poisson,** I was conscious of a smell of fish.

odorer [ɔdɔre]. 1. *v.tr.* (*a*) *A:* to smell; **et Dieu a odoré le sacrifice,** and God smelled the sacrifice; (*b*) (*of dog, etc.*) to scent (quarry, etc.); *abs.* **tous les animaux n'odorent pas,** not all animals have a sense of smell. 2. *v.i.* to smell (of sth.); to be fragrant; *with cogn. acc.* **o. la vanille,** to smell of vanilla; **ton haleine odorait le vin et la bouffarde,** your breath smelt of wine and tobacco.

odoriférant [ɔdɔriferɑ̃], **odorifique** [ɔdɔrifik], *a.* odoriferous, sweet-smelling, sweet-scented, fragrant.

odorimètre [ɔdɔrimɛtr̥], *s.m.* odorometer.

odorisant [ɔdɔrizɑ̃], *s.m. Ind:* strong-smelling additive (added to gas to aid detection of leaks).

odynère [ɔdinɛːr], *s.m. Ent:* odynerus.

Odyssée (l') [lɔdise], *s.f.* (*a*) *Gr.Lit:* the Odyssey; (*b*) odyssey, wanderings; **son voyage fut une véritable o.,** his journey was a real odyssey; **une o. de malheurs,** a tale of woes.

oécie [ɔesi], *s.f. Biol:* ooecium.

œcanthe [ekɑ̃ːt], *s.m. Ent:* oecanthus, tree cricket.

œcologie [ekɔlɔʒi], *s.f.* (o)ecology.

œcologique [ekɔlɔʒik], *a.* (o)ecological.

œcuménicité [ekymenisite], *s.f.* (o)ecumenicity.

œcuménique [ekymenik], *a. Ecc:* (o)ecumenical (council, etc.).

œcuménisme [ekymenism], *s.m.* (o)ecumenism.

œdémateux, -euse [edematø, -øːz], *a. Med:* oedematic, oedematose, oedematous.

œdème [edɛm], *s.m. Med:* oedema; **o. blanc douloureux,** white leg, milk leg; **o. généralisé,** anasarca.

œdicnème [ediknɛm], *s.m. Orn:* **o. (criard),** stone curlew, *F:* thick knee.

Œdipe [edip], *Pr.n.m. Gr.Lit:* Oedipus; **Œ. Roi,** Oedipus Rex, Oedipus Tyrannus; **Œ. à Colone,** Oedipus Coloneus; **complexe d'Œ.,** Oedipus complex; **tout l'art de nos Œdipes a échoué devant cette énigme,** all the art of our readers of riddles, of our disentanglers of mysteries, failed to solve the enigma.

œdipien, -ienne [edipjɛ̃, -jɛn], *a.* Œdipean; Œdipus (complex).

œil, *pl.* **yeux** [œːj, jø], *s.m.* **1.** eye; **o. de verre, o. artificiel,** glass, artificial, eye; **il a les yeux bleus,** he has blue eyes, his eyes are blue; **avoir de bons, de mauvais, yeux,** to have good, bad, (eye)sight; *P:* **avoir des yeux qui se croisent les bras, avoir un o. qui dit merde à l'autre,** to be cross-eyed; *P:* **mon o.!** my foot! **visible à l'o. nu,** visible to the naked eye; **regarder qch. d'un o. sec,** to look on dry-eyed; **pleurer d'un o. et rire de l'autre,** to laugh and cry at the same time; **on ne leur laissa que les yeux pour pleurer,** they were left only their eyes to weep with; **fermer, ouvrir, les yeux,** to close, open, one's eyes; **c'est moi qui lui ai fermé les yeux,** I was with him at the end; **je n'ai pas fermé l'o. de la nuit,** I didn't sleep a wink all night, I didn't have a wink of sleep all night; **faire qch. les yeux fermés,** to do sth. with one's eyes shut; **ouvrir de grands yeux,** to open one's eyes wide; to stare; **ouvrir les yeux à qn,** to open s.o.'s eyes; to enlighten s.o.; **cela me fit ouvrir les yeux,** it was an eye-opener for me; **il avait les yeux hors de la tête,** his eyes were starting from his head; **faire les petits yeux,** to screw up one's eyes; **regarder qn entre (les) deux yeux,** to look s.o. full in the face; to look s.o. squarely in the eye; **je ne pourrai jamais plus le regarder droit dans les yeux,** I shall never be able to look him in the face again; **les yeux dans les yeux,** gazing into each other's eyes; *P:* **t'as donc pas les yeux en face des trous?** (i) can't you get it? (ii) are you asleep? aren't you with us? *F:* **entre quatre(-z-)yeux, entre quat'z yeux,** in private, between you and me and the gatepost; **o. pour o., dent pour dent,** an eye for an eye, a tooth for a tooth; **il n'a d'yeux que pour elle,** he has eyes for no-one but her; **épouser une femme pour ses beaux yeux,** to marry a woman for her pretty face, for her (good) looks; to marry a woman for love; **ce qu'il en fait n'est pas pour vos beaux yeux,** he's not acting in an entirely disinterested manner; **ce n'est pas pour ses beaux yeux,** it's not entirely for his sake; **il ne travaille pour les beaux yeux de personne,** he doesn't do anything for love; **chose qui saute aux yeux,** sth. obvious, sth. that leaps to the eye; **cela saute aux yeux,** it's obvious, as plain as a pikestaff; you can see it with half an eye; **payer, demander, coûter, les yeux de la tête,** to pay, ask, cost, an exorbitant price, a (small) fortune, the earth; **avoir du travail par-dessus les yeux,** to be up to one's eyes in work; *F:* **taper de l'o.,** to be sleepy, drowsy; *F:* **je m'en bats l'o.,** I don't care a hoot, a damn; *F:* **battre l'o., tourner de l'o.,** (i) to faint; (ii) to die; *adv.phr.* **à l'o.,** (i) by the eye; (ii) *F:* free, buckshee; **mesurer qch. à l'o.,** to measure sth. by eye; *F:* **entrer à l'o.,** to get in free, gratis; *Th:* **la salle est pleine mais la moitié des places sont à l'o.,** the house is full, but half of it is paper; **repas à l'o.,** free meal; *P: O:* **avoir l'o.,** to have (sth. on) credit, tick. **2.** sight, look, eye; **cela charme les yeux,** it delights the eye; **dès que j'eus jeté les yeux sur lui . . .,** as soon as I had set eyes on him . . .; **attacher les yeux sur qn,** to fix one's eyes on s.o.; **chercher qn des yeux,** to look about for s.o.; **suivre qn des yeux,** to watch s.o.; *F:* **est-ce que vous avez vos yeux dans votre poche?** where are your eyes? **il n'a pas les yeux dans sa poche,** he is very observant; he keeps his eyes skinned; **il a les yeux plus grands que le ventre, que la panse,** his eyes are bigger than his belly; he's biting off more than he can chew; *F:* **regarder qn d'un o. noir,** to give s.o. a black look; **coupable aux yeux de la loi,** guilty in the eyes of the law; **aux yeux de Dieu, du monde,** in the sight of God, of the world; **avoir qch. sous les yeux,** to have sth. before one's eyes; **il l'a fait sous mes yeux,** he did it under my very eyes, in front of me; **mettre qch. sous les yeux de qn,** to bring sth. to s.o.'s notice, to draw s.o.'s attention to sth.; *Ten: etc:* **avoir la balle dans l'o.,** to have one's eye in; **cela manque d'o.,** it doesn't look well; there's no style about it; *Com:* **donner plus d'o. à un article,** to give an article a better appearance; *Prov:* **loin des yeux, loin du cœur,** out of sight, out of mind. **3.** attention, observation, notice; **avoir l'o.,** to be observant, sharp-eyed; **avoir l'o. sur qn, avoir qn à l'o.,** to keep an eye on s.o.; **voulez-vous avoir l'o. sur les enfants?** would you keep an eye on the children? **avoir l'o. à tout,** to see to everything; **ayez l'o. à ce que cela se fasse,** see that it's done; **j'y aurai l'o.,** I shall keep a lookout, keep my eyes open, *F:* skinned; **avoir l'o. ouvert, les yeux ouverts,** to have one's eyes about one; **ouvrir l'o.,** *F:* **l'o. et le bon,** to be on the watch, the lookout; to keep one's eyes skinned; **cela me fit ouvrir l'o.,** that put me on the alert; *A:* **avoir l'o. américain,** to be wide awake, on the alert; **on ouvrait l'o. de peur des brigands,** we were keeping our eyes open for robbers; *Nau:* **ouvrez l'o. devant!** look out forward; *F:* **risquer un o.,** to peep out; **fermer les yeux sur qch.,** to connive at sth.; to turn a blind eye; **fermer les yeux sur les défauts de qn,** to turn a blind eye to s.o.'s faults; **j'accepte les yeux fermés ce que vous m'en dites,** I'll take your word for it; **signer les yeux fermés,** to sign blind, *F:* on the dotted line; **pourquoi fermer les yeux à la vérité?** why shut your eyes to the truth? why blink the facts? **à vue d'o.,** (i) visibly; (ii) at first sight; **coup d'o.,** (i) view; (ii) glance; **reculer pour juger du coup d'o.,** to stand back to see what sth. looks like; **d'un coup d'o., j'avais jugé la situation,** I had taken in the situation at a glance; **du, au, premier coup d'o.,** at first sight, at the outset; **jeter un coup d'o. sur qch.,** to run one's eye, cast an eye, over sth.; **jeter un coup d'o. le long de la rue,** to look along, up, down, the street; **jeter un coup d'o. sur le journal,** to have a look at, to flick through, the paper; **sans jeter un coup d'o. par la vitre,** without even glancing through the window; **lancer un coup d'o. à qn,** to glance at s.o., to take a glance in s.o.'s direction; **avoir du coup d'o.,** (i) to be sure-sighted; (ii) to have good judgement; **voir, regarder, qn, qch., d'un bon o., d'un mauvais o.,** to look favourably, approvingly, on s.o., sth.; to look unfavourably, disapprovingly, on s.o., sth.; **voir du même o. que qn,** to see eye to eye with s.o.; *F:* **faire de l'o. à qn,** to give s.o. the glad eye; *F:* **faire les yeux doux à qn,** to make (sheep's) eyes at s.o.; **regarder qn du coin de l'o.,** to look at s.o. out of the corner of one's eye; **j'envisage le problème d'un autre o.,** I see the problem with a different eye, from another point of view; **regarder qn d'un o. en biais, d'un o. malveillant,** to look askance at s.o.; to give s.o. a dirty look; *F:* **taper dans l'o. de, à, qn,** to take someone's fancy; **faire les gros yeux à qn,** to look sternly, severely, reprovingly, at s.o.; **être très sur l'o.,** to be very strict, to have an eye to everything. **4.** (*a*) (*pl.* **œils**) eye (of needle, crane, hammer, bridle bit, anchor(-shank), volute, etc.); hole (of hinge); eye, eye-splice (on rope, cable); **piton à o.,** eye bolt; **o. de roue,** nave hole of wheel; *Artil:* **o. d'obus,** fuse hole; (*b*) **les yeux du pain, du gruyère,** the holes in bread, in gruyère (cheese); (*c*) **yeux du bouillon,** specks of fat on soup; **yeux d'une plante,** eyes, buds, of a plant; (*d*) **o. d'une plume,** spatule of a feather; (*e*) *Elcs: T.V:* **o. électrique,** electric eye; **o. magique, o. magnétique, o. cathodique,** magic eye, cathode eye, electron-ray tube. **5.** *Nau:* **l'o. du vent,** the eye of the wind, the wind's eye. **6.** (*in the sing. only*) (*a*) lustre, gloss, sheen (of materials, precious stones, etc.); (*b*) **ce vin a un o. louche,** this wine is not clear. **7.** *Typ:* face (of letter); **petit o.,** small face; **lettre d'un autre o.,** wrong fount.

œil-de-bœuf [œjdəbœf], *s.m.* **1.** (*a*) *Arch:* bull's eye, *œil-de-bœuf,* oculus, small circular window; (*b*) (round) wall clock; (*c*) *Hist:* the antechamber of the Great Hall, in the palace of Versailles; **gentilhomme de l'O.-de-b.,** gentleman in waiting. **2.** *Bot:* white oxeye, oxeye daisy, moonflower; *pl. œils-de-bœuf.*

œil-de-chat [œjdəʃa], *s.m.* **1.** *Lap:* cat's eye, tiger eye. **2.** *Bot:* nicker nut, bonduc seed; *pl. œils-de-chat.*

œil-de-Dieu [œjdədjø], *s.m. Bot:* pasque flower; *pl. œils-de-Dieu.*

œil-de-faisan [œjdəfəzɑ̃, -fe-], *s.m. Bot:* pheasant's eye (narcissus); *pl. œils-de-faisan.*

œil-de-paon [œjdəpɑ̃], *s.m. Miner:* pavonazzo; *pl. œils-de-paon.*

œil-de-perdrix [œjdəpɛrdri]. **1.** *s.m.* (*a*) (soft) corn (between toes); (*b*) small knot (in wood); *pl. œils-de-perdrix.* **2.** *a.inv.* (*of wine*) light claret-coloured.

œil-de-pie [œjdəpi], *s.m. Nau:* eyelet (in sail); *pl. œils-de-pie.*

œil-de-serpent [œjdəsɛrpɑ̃], *s.m. Miner:* toadstone; *pl. œils-de-serpent.*

œil-de-tigre [œjdətigr̥], *s.m. Lap:* cat's eye, tiger eye; *pl. œils-de-tigre.*

œil-du-monde [œjdymɔ̃ːd], *s.m. Miner:* hydrophane; *pl. œils-du-monde.*

œillade [œjad], *s.f.* glance; **lancer une o. à qn,** to glance meaningly at s.o.; **lancer des œillades à qn,** to make eyes at s.o.

œillard [œjaːr], *s.m. Mill:* millstone eye.

œillé [œje], *a.* of the nature of an eye; *Miner:* agate œillée, eye agate.

œillère [œjɛːr]. **1.** *a.f.* of the eye; (dent) **o.,** eye tooth, canine (tooth). **2.** *s.f.* (*a*) blinker, eye flap (of horse's harness); *U.S:* blind; **avoir des œillères,** to be narrow-minded, to have narrow views; to go through life in blinkers; **mettre les mains en œillères,** to shade one's eyes with one's hands; (*b*) *Med:* eye bath; (*c*) *A.Arm:* œillère (of helmet).

œillet [œjɛ], *s.m.* **1.** (*a*) *A:* little eye; (*b*) eyelet, eyelet-hole (of boots, sail, etc.); eye (of eye-bolt); (*c*) reinforcement (for perforations of sheet of paper); (*d*) *Salt Ind:* evaporating pan. **2.** *Bot:* pink; **o. des fleuristes,** clove pink, carnation; **o. jaspé, tiqueté,** picotee; **o. maritime,** sea-pink; **o. de(s) poète(s),** sweet-william; **o. des prés,** ragged robin; **o. de Pâques,** poet's narcissus, pheasant's eye; **o. d'Inde,** French marigold.

œilleteuse [œjətøːz], *s.f.* eyeletting machine.

œilletiste [œjətist], *s.m. Hort:* carnation grower.

œilleton [œjtɔ̃], *s.m.* **1.** *Hort:* (*a*) eye (bud); (*b*) sucker (of pineapple, etc.); offset, layer. **2.** (*a*) eyepiece shade (of telescope); (*b*) peephole (of rifle sight); *Phot:* eyepiece (of viewfinder); *Sm.a:* **o. de visée,** aiming aperture; (*c*) spy glass (in door); (*d*) *Mch:* **o. de bielle maîtresse,** wristpin hole, eye.

œilletonnage [œjtɔnaːʒ], *s.m. Hort:* layering.

œilletonner [œjtɔne], *v.tr. Hort:* (*a*) to layer (plant); (*b*) to disbud, remove buds from (plants, trees).

œillette [œjɛt], *s.f.* oil poppy, opium poppy; **huile d'o.,** poppy(-seed) oil.

œkoumène [ekumɛn], *s.m.* ecumene.

œnanthal [enɑ̃tal], *s.m. Ch:* oenanthal.

œnanthe [enɑ̃ːt], *s.m. Bot:* oenanthe, water dropwort.

œnanthique [enɑ̃tik], *a. Ch:* oenanthic (acid, ester).

œnanthylate [enɑ̃tilat], *s.m. Ch:* oenanthylate.

œnanthylique [enɑ̃tilik], *a. Ch:* oenanthylic.

œnilisme [enilism], **œnolisme** [enɔlism], *s.m.* alcoholism (caused by an excess of wine).

œnochoé [ənɔkɔe], *s.f. Gr.Ant:* œnochoë, wine pitcher.

œnocyte [enɔsit], *s.m. Ent:* oenocyte.

œnologie [enɔlɔʒi], *s.f.* oenology.

œnologique [enɔlɔʒik], *a.* oenological; **produits œnologiques,** chemicals (etc.) for improving or preserving wines; **station o.,** wine-testing laboratory.

œnologiste [enɔlɔʒist], *s.m. & f.,* **œnologue** [enɔlɔg], *s.m. & f.* oenologist.

œnomel [enɔmɛl], *s.m. Pharm:* honey-wine.

œnomètre [enɔmɛtr̥], *s.m.* oenometer.

œnométrie [enɔmetri], *s.f.* measurement of alcoholic content of wines; alcoholometry (of wines).

œnométrique [enɔmetrik], *a.* concerning the measurement of the alcoholic content of wine.

œnophile [enɔfil]. **1.** *a.* wine-loving. **2.** *s.m. & f.* wine lover; oenophilist.

œnothéracées [enɔterase], *s.f.pl. Bot:* Onagraceae, Oenotheraceae.

œnothère [enɔtɛːr], *s.m. Bot:* oenothera, evening primrose.

œrsted [ɛrstɛd], *s.m. El.Meas:* oersted.

œschynite [eʃinit], *s.f. Miner:* eschynite.

œsophage [ezɔfaːʒ], *s.m. Anat:* oesophagus, gullet.

œsophagectomie [ezɔfaʒɛktɔmi], *s.f. Surg:* oesophagectomy.

œsophagien, -ienne [ezɔfaʒjɛ̃, -jɛn], *a.* oesophageal (membrane, tube, probe).

œsophagisme [ezɔfaʒism], *s.m. Med:* oesophagism, spasm of the oesophagus.

œsophagite [ezɔfaʒit], *s.f. Med:* oesophagitis.

œsophago-gastrostomie [ezɔfagɔgastrɔstɔmi], *s.f. Surg:* œsophago-gastrostomy.

œsophagomalacie [ezɔfagɔmalasi], *s.f. Med:* œsophagomalacia.

œsophagoplastie [ezɔfagɔplasti], *s.f. Surg:* oesophagoplasty.

œsophagoscope [ezɔfagɔskɔp], *s.m. Med:* oesophagoscope.

œsophagoscopie [ezɔfagɔskɔpi], *s.f. Med:* oesophagoscopy.

œsophagostomie [ezɔfagɔstɔmi], *s.f. Surg:* oesophagostomy.

œsophagotomie [ezɔfagɔtɔmi], *s.f. Surg:* oesophagotomy.

œstradiol [estradjɔl], *s.m. Bio-Ch:* oestradiol.

œstral, -aux [estral, -o], *a. Physiol:* **cycle o.,** oestrous, sexual, cycle.

œstre [ɛstr̥], *s.m.* **1.** *Ent: Vet:* oestrus, gadfly, bot(t) fly; warble; **larve d'o.,** bot(t). **2.** oestrus, sexual impulse, sexual frenzy; (musical, poetical) afflatus.

œstridés [estride], *s.m.pl. Ent:* Oestridae.
œstriol [estriɔl], *s.m. Bio-Ch:* (o)estriol.
œstrogène [estrɔʒɛn], *a. & s.m. Physiol:* (o)estrogen.
œstrogénique [estrɔʒenik], *a. Physiol:* (o)estrogenic.
œstromanie [estrɔmani], *s.f.* oestromania.
œstrone [estrɔn], *s.f. Bio-Ch:* oestrone.
œstrus [estrys], *s.m. Physiol:* oestrus, estrus; *Vet: F:* heat.
œtite [etit], *s.f. Miner:* aetites, eagle stone; nodular limonite.
œuf [œf], *pl.* **œufs** [ø], *s.m.* **1.** (*a*) egg; *Biol:* ovum; **o. de poule,** hen's egg; **o. non fécondé, o. blanc, o. de couleuvre,** wind egg; **o. frais,** new laid egg; **o. du jour,** farm fresh egg; **o. en poudre,** dried, dehydrated, egg; *Cu:* **o. à la coque,** boiled egg; **o. mollet, o. à la mouillette,** soft-boiled egg; **o. dur,** hard-boiled egg; **œufs brouillés,** scrambled eggs; **o. sur le plat,** fried egg; **faire cuire un o. au plat,** to fry an egg; *P:* **elle a des œufs sur le plat,** she's flat-chested, as flat as a board; **passer à l'o.,** to coat with egg, *U.S:* to egg; **o. de Pâques, o. rouge,** Easter egg; **en o.,** egg-shaped; *P:* **va te faire cuire un o.,** go and boil your head; *Prov:* **il ne faut pas mettre tous ses œufs dans le même panier,** you shouldn't put all your eggs in one basket; *Prov:* **qui vole un o. vole un bœuf,** he that will steal a pin will steal a pound; *F:* **marcher sur des œufs,** to skate, tread, on thin ice; **il tondrait un o.,** he would skin a flint; **faire d'un o. un bœuf,** to make a mountain out of a molehill; **donner un o. pour avoir un bœuf,** to throw out a sprat to catch a mackerel; **tuer la poule aux œufs d'or,** to kill the goose that lays the golden egg(s); *F:* **écraser, tuer, détruire étouffer, qch. dans l'o.** to nip sth. in the bud; *P:* **espèce d'o.!** silly fool! (*b*) *pl.* eggs (of insect); spawn (of fish, etc.); *Pisc:* ova (for reproduction); (hard) roe (of fish); **un o. de hareng, de saumon,** a roe-corn from a herring, from a salmon; **œufs de homard,** berry. **2. o. en faïence,** nest-egg; **o. à repriser,** darning egg, darning mushroom; **o. à thé,** tea infuser.
œuf-de-vanneau [œfdəvano], *s.m. Bot: F:* fritillary; *pl. œufs-de-vanneau.*
œufrier [œfri(j)e], *s.m.* **1. o. en fil de fer,** wire egg holder (for boiling eggs). **2. o. (en faïence),** (china) egg stand (for the table).
œuvé [œve], *a.* hard-roed (fish); berried (lobster).
œuvre [œ:vr], *s.f.* **1.** (*a*) work; working; *O:* **il ne fait jamais o. de ses dix doigts,** he never does a hand's turn; **faire o. d'ami,** to behave, act, like a friend; **faire o. utile,** to do useful work; **à l'o.,** at work; **mettre qn à l'o.,** to set s.o. to work; **se mettre à l'o.,** to get down to work; **il est à l'o.,** he's started on it, is working on it; he's got down to work; *F:* **tu crois que c'est facile? bien, on te verra à l'o.,** you think it's easy? I'd like to see you try! **poursuivre l'o. commencée par X,** to carry on the work begun by X; **mettre (qch.) en o.,** (i) to use, make use of (sth.); to bring (sth.) into play, into use; (ii) to put (a piece of work) in hand; **mettre un traité en o.,** to implement a treaty; **mettre tout, tous les moyens, en o. pour faire qch.,** to use every possible means to get sth. done; to leave no stone unturned in order to do sth.; **mettre en o. toute son énergie, toute son industrie, pour faire qch.,** to devote all one's energy, all one's resources, to doing sth.; **mettre en o. un nouveau procédé de fabrication,** to bring a new manufacturing process into operation; **mettre de la pierre, du cuivre, en o.,** to work up stone, copper (into shape); **mettre des diamants en o.,** to set diamonds; **bois d'o.,** (constructional) timber (as opposed to firewood); **mise en o.,** (i) use; (ii) implementation, implementing, carrying into effect; (iii) working up; setting; *Ecc:* **o. de chair,** (carnal) knowledge; **elle eut un fils des œuvres de X,** she had a son by X; **il est fils de ses œuvres,** he's a self-made man; **renoncer à Satan, à ses pompes et à ses œuvres,** to renounce the Devil and all his works; *A:* **exécuteur des hautes œuvres,** executioner, hangman; (*b*) **bonnes œuvres,** (i) charity; gifts, donations, to charity; (ii) charitable organization; **faire de bonnes œuvres,** to do charitable work, social work; **quête au profit d'une o.,** collection in aid of a charity; **salle d'œuvres (de la paroisse),** parish hall. **2.** (finished) work, production; **les œuvres de la nature,** the works of nature; **œuvres d'un écrivain, d'un peintre,** works of a writer, of a painter; *Prov:* **à l'o. on connaît l'artisan,** a good carpenter is known by his chips. **3.** *Ecc:* fabric fund; *s.a.* BANC 1. **4.** (*a*) *Nau:* **œuvres vives,** quick works, vitals; **œuvres mortes,** dead works, upper works, topsides; **réparations dans les œuvres mortes,** repairs above the water line; (*b*) *Metalw:* **grosses œuvres,** heavy castings, forgings. **5.** *s.m.* (*a*) **gros o. (d'un bâtiment),** fabric (of a building); *Civ.E: Const:* **être à pied d'o.,** to be on site; **mourir à pied d'o.,** to die in harness; **amener du matériel à pied d'o.,** (i) *Civ.E:* to bring equipment on site; (ii) *Mil:* to bring equipment to the zone of operations; **mise à pied d'o.,** (i) *Civ.E: etc:* bringing on site; (ii) *Mil:* build-up (in the zone of operations); (*b*) *Lit: etc:* oeuvre; **l'o. de Molière, de Mozart,** the works of Molière, of Mozart (as a whole); **l'o. récent de X,** X's recent work; **lorsque nous considérons son o.,** when we consider his achievement; (*c*) **le Grand O.,** the philosopher's stone; (*d*) *adj.phr.* **dans o.,** inside (measurements, etc.); **escalier dans o.,** inside stair.
œuvrer [œvre]. **1.** *v.tr. A:* = OUVRER. **2.** *v.i.* to work (together); to strive, work (for peace, etc.).
offensant [ɔfɑ̃sɑ̃], *a.* **1.** offensive, insulting, abusive (remark, etc.). **2.** offending (person).
offense [ɔfɑ̃:s], *s.f.* **1.** offence; **faire une o. à qn,** to offend s.o.; **o. faite à Dieu,** offence against God. **2.** *Theol:* transgression, sin, trespass; **pardonne-nous nos offenses,** forgive us our trespasses; pardon our offences. **3.** *Jur:* **o. à la Cour,** contempt of Court.
offensé, -ée [ɔfɑ̃se], *s.* offended party, injured party.
offenser [ɔfɑ̃se], *v.tr.* **1. o. qn,** to offend s.o., to give offence to s.o., to hurt s.o.'s feelings; **soit dit sans vouloir vous o.,** with all due respect to you; **si je vous ai offensé par parole ou par action,** if I have offended you by word or deed. **2. o. qch.,** (*a*) to be detrimental to, to injure (eyesight, lungs, etc.); (*b*) to offend, to be offensive to, to shock (feelings, modesty, etc.); **son aigre qui offense l'oreille,** harsh sound that offends the ear; **o. la grammaire,** to offend against grammar; **o. les regards,** to be an eyesore. **3.** *Theol:* **o. Dieu,** to offend God; to sin, trespass, transgress, against God.
s'offenser, to take offence, to take umbrage (**de,** at); to be offended; **il s'offense d'un rien,** he takes offence at, takes exception to, the least thing; **il s'offense de ce que je ne vais pas le voir,** he is offended because I don't go and see him.
offenseur [ɔfɑ̃sœ:r], *s.m.* offender.
offensif, -ive [ɔfɑ̃sif, -i:v]. **1.** *a.* offensive (war, weapon); **armes offensives et défensives,** weapons of offence and defence; *s.a.* RETOUR 2. **2.** *s.f.* **offensive;** *Mil:* (the) offensive; **prendre, reprendre, l'offensive,** to assume, resume, the offensive **mener une offensive,** to carry out an offensive; **offensive de paix,** peace offensive; **mener une offensive diplomatique,** to attack in the field of diplomacy; **offensive de l'hiver,** cold spell; period of intense cold.
offensivement [ɔfɑ̃sivmɑ̃], *adv.* offensively; by attacking.
offerte [ɔfɛrt], *s.f. Ecc. A:* offertory.
offertoire [ɔfɛrtwa:r], *s.m. Ecc:* (*R.C.Ch.*) **1.** offertory. **2.** *Mus:* offertory, organ voluntary (played during the offertory).
office [ɔfis]. **1.** *s.m.* (*a*) office, functions, duty; **remplir l'o. de chancelier,** to fill the office of chancellor; **exercer l'o. de secrétaire,** to discharge the office, duties, of secretary; **faire o. de secrétaire,** to act as secretary; **fusible qui fait l'o., de commutateur,** fuse that serves, acts, as a switch; **la pilule a rempli son o.,** the pill did its job; **c'est mon o. de le faire,** it is my duty, my job, to do it; *adv.phr.* **d'o.** (i) officially; **agir d'o.,** to act in virtue, of one's office, ex officio; **avocat, expert, nommé d'o.,** barrister, expert, appointed by the court; *Adm:* **être mis à la retraite d'o.,** to be compulsorily retired; (ii) as a matter of course, of routine; automatically; **faire qch. d'o.,** to do sth. spontaneously, of one's own accord, as a matter of routine; *Publ:* **exemplaire d'o.,** (i) copy (of book) sent for publicity; (ii) copy sent on sale or return; **il a gagné d'o.,** it was a walkover for him; (*b*) service, turn; **accepter les bons offices de qn,** to accept the good offices of s.o.; (*c*) *Ecc:* Divine Service; office (for the day, etc.); **l'o. des morts,** the burial service; the Office for the Dead; **o. en plein air,** (i) open-air service; (ii) *Mil:* drumhead service; **livre d'o.,** prayer book; **aller à l'o.,** to go to church (*esp.* to Protestant service); **manquer l'o.,** to miss church; **fermer boutique pendant l'heure des offices,** to close during church time; (*d*) bureau, office; **o. de publicité,** advertising agency; *Adm:* **o. national de la propriété industrielle** = Patent Office; **o. de la main-d'œuvre,** employment exchange; **l'O. du Blé** = the National Wheat Board; *Ecc.Hist:* **le saint O.,** the Holy Office (of the Inquisition); (*e*) domestic staff, household. **2.** *s.f.* (*a*) (butler's) pantry; *Av:* galley; *Nau:* **o. du maître d'hôtel,** pantry; *Navy:* **matelot d'o.,** wardroom servant; (*b*) servant's hall; **dîner à l'o.,** to eat with the servants.
Offices [ɔfis], *Art:* **le Palais des O.,** the Uffizi Gallery (in Florence).
official, -aux [ɔfisjal, -o], *s.m. Ecc:* official principal, official.
officialisation [ɔfisjalizasjɔ̃], *s.f.* officialization, making (sth.) official.
officialiser [ɔfisjalize], *v.tr.* to make (sth.) official, to officialize (sth.).
officialité [ɔfisjalite], *s.f.* officiality.
officiant [ɔfisjɑ̃], *a. & s.m. Ecc:* officiating (priest); *s.* officiant.
officiel, -ielle [ɔfisjɛl]. **1.** *a.* official (statement, journal, source); formal (call, etc.); **à titre o.,** officially, formally; **se réunir à titre non o.,** to meet informally; **rendre qch o.,** to make sth. public; to make sth. official; **congé o.,** national holiday; **le Journal O.,** *s.m.* **l'Officiel** = the (official) Gazette; *Mil: Navy:* **être à l'O.,** to be gazetted. **2.** *s.* official; **les voitures des officiels,** the official cars; **les Officiels,** the official party.
officiellement [ɔfisjɛlmɑ̃], *adv.* officially.
officier[1] [ɔfisje], *v.i.* (*p.d. & pr.sub.* **n. officiions, v. officiiez**) (*a*) *Ecc:* to officiate; *R.C.Ch:* to celebrate mass; (*b*) **o. à table,** to officiate at table; *F:* **bien o. à table,** to eat and drink a lot.
officier[2], *s.m.* officer. **1. o. de l'état civil** = registrar (of births, marriages and deaths); **o. de justice,** law officer; *A:* **o. de paix,** police officer, official; **officiers ministériels,** a category of members of the legal profession, including greffiers, notaires, huissiers, avoués, commissaires-priseurs; **les officiers de l'église,** the church officers, officials. **2.** (*a*) *Mil:* (commissioned) officer; **o. de l'armée de terre,** army officer; **o. de l'armée active,** *F:* **o. d'active,** regular officer; **o. de réserve,** reserve officer; **o. subalterne,** junior officer, subordinate officer, *U.S:* company officer, company grade; **les officiers subalternes,** the subalterns and captains, *U.S:* company officers; **o. supérieur,** field officer, *U.S:* senior officer; **o. général,** general officer; **o. général commandant la 1ère armée,** general officer commanding 1st army; **o. breveté d'état-major, o. breveté de l'École de Guerre,** "passed Staff College" officer, P.S.C. officer, *U.S:* staff officer; **o. adjoint,** assistant (officer), adjutant, *U.S:* executive (officer); **o. de (corps de) troupe,** regimental officer; (*b*) *Navy:* **o. de marine,** naval officer; **o. de pont,** executive officer, deck officer; **o. de tir,** gunnery officer; **o. mécanicien,** engineer officer; **o. général,** flag officer; **o. de débarquement,** beach master; **o. marinier,** petty officer; *Fr.Navy:* **o. des équipages (de la flotte),** officer responsible for discipline aboard and controlling the personnel attending to a ship's helm, binnacle and signals; **o. de port,** harbour master. **3. O. de la Légion d'honneur,** Officer of the Legion of Honour; **O. d'Académie,** holder of the *palmes académiques,* an honour conferred for service in the educational field. **4.** (*with f.* **officière**) **o., officière, de l'Armée du Salut,** Salvation Army Officer.
officieusement [ɔfisjøzmɑ̃], *adv.* **1.** officiously. **2.** unofficially, semi-officially.
officieux, -euse [ɔfisjø, -ø:z]. **1.** *a.* (*a*) officious (**envers,** towards); over-obliging; **lettre d'allure officieuse,** letter that smacks of officiousness; (*b*) unofficial, semi-official; *Adm.* officious (information, etc.); **commission officieuse,** informal commission; *Journ:* **note d'origine officieuse,** inspired paragraph; **à titre o.,** unofficially; (*c*) kindly-meant (advice, etc.); *Theol:* **mensonge o.,** white lie. **2.** *s.* busybody.
officinal, -aux [ɔfisinal, -o], *a. Pharm:* officinal (preparation, plant); medicinal (plant).
officine [ɔfisin], *s.f.* **1.** (*a*) *Pharm:* dispensary; (*b*) (technical and legal term for) chemist's shop. **2.** den (of shady business); *Pej:* thieves' kitchen; **une o. d'intrigue,** a centre, a hotbed, of intrigue.
officiosité [ɔfisiozite], *s.f.* officiousness.
offrande [ɔfrɑ̃:d], *s.f. esp. Ecc:* offering (of gifts, of good wishes); *Ecc:* offertory (after kissing the pax); **l'o. est à dévotion,** everybody will be expected to contribute according to his means, to contribute as God has prospered him; **o. expiatoire,** sin offering, trespass offering; **déposer son o. dans le tronc,** to place one's offering in the alms box; *F:* **à chaque saint son o.,** all the people concerned will have to be squared.

offrant [ɔfrɑ̃], *s.m.* **le plus o. (et dernier enchérisseur),** the highest bidder.

offre [ɔfr̥], *s.f.* (*A: occ. s.m.*) (*a*) offer, proposal; tender (for contract); (*at auction sale*) bid; *Jur:* **o. réelle,** tender (and payment in court); **faire o. de qch.,** to offer sth.; **faire des offres de service à qn,** to offer to help s.o.; *Com:* to solicit orders; *Fin:* **o. publique d'achat,** takeover bid; (*b*) *Pol.Ec:* **l'o. et la demande,** supply and demand.

offrir [ɔfriːr], *v.tr.* (*pr.p.* **offrant;** *p.p.* **offert** [ɔfɛːr]; *pr.ind.* **j'offre, n. offrons;** *pr.sub.* **j'offre, n. offrions;** *imp.* **offre, offrons, offrez;** *p.d.* **j'offrais;** *p.h.* **j'offris;** *fu.* **j'offrirai)** to offer; (*a*) to give; to offer up (sacrifice); **je lui ai offert des fleurs,** I gave her some flowers; **ses collègues lui ont offert une pendule quand il a pris sa retraite,** his colleagues presented him with a clock when he retired; **c'est pour o.,** it's for a present; **o. un déjeuner à qn,** to invite s.o. to lunch(eon) (at a restaurant); to give, *F:* stand, s.o. lunch; **o. un déjeuner en l'honneur de qn,** to give a luncheon in s.o.'s honour, to give s.o. a luncheon; *F:* **il m'a offert à dîner,** he offered me dinner; **il s'offre un bon cigare,** he treats himself to a good cigar; **ne pas pouvoir s'o. qch.,** to be unable to afford sth.; **je voudrais pouvoir m'o. des vacances,** I wish I could afford a holiday; *F:* **s'o la tête de qn,** to make fun of s.o.; to take a rise out of s.o.; (*b*) **o. ses services,** to offer one's services; **on lui a offert une place de mécanicien,** he was offered a job as a mechanic; **o. le bras à une dame,** to offer one's arm to a lady; **o. la main à qn,** to hold out one's hand to s.o.; **o. son nom à une femme,** to propose (marriage) to a woman; *Mil:* **o. le combat,** to open fire (on the enemy); **s'o. comme guide,** to propose, offer, oneself as a guide; **o. de faire qch.,** to offer to do sth.; (*c*) **o. à qn l'occasion de faire qch.,** to give, offer, s.o. the opportunity of doing sth.; **je vous offre le choix,** I give, am giving, you the choice; **situation qui offre bien des avantages,** situation that offers many advantages; **le moindre petit plaisir qui s'offre à ma portée,** the least little pleasure that comes my way; (*d*) *Com:* **o. dix francs (de qch.),** (i) to offer, (ii) to bid, ten francs (for sth.); **combien m'en offrez-vous?** what will you give, offer, me for it? **le représentant lui offrait quelques nouveautés,** the traveller was showing, offering, him a few new lines; (*e*) **la campagne offre une vue splendide,** the countryside presents a magnificent view; **o. un abri,** to give shelter, cover; **ce légume offre une nourriture saine,** this vegetable provides wholesome food; **elle offre l'image d'une gaieté irrésistible,** she presents a picture of irresistible gaiety; **l'histoire en offre plusieurs exemples,** history affords several examples of it.

s'offrir. 1. (*of pers.*) to offer oneself; **s'o. au danger,** to court danger; **s'o. à faire qch.,** *A:* **s'o. de faire qch.,** to offer, volunteer, to do sth.; **s'o. à porter les bagages,** to offer to carry the luggage. **2.** (*of thg*) **quand l'occasion s'offrira,** when the opportunity occurs; **l'occasion s'offre trop belle pour ne pas la saisir,** the opportunity is too good to be missed; **le spectacle qui s'offrit à mes yeux, à ma vue,** the sight that met, greeted, my eyes; **deux moyens s'offrent à nous,** two courses are open to us.

offset [ɔfsɛt], *s.m. Typ:* offset; **machine (à imprimer) o.,** offset printing machine; **machine o. plate,** flat-bed offset machine; **rotative o.,** offset rotary machine; **impression o.,** offset printing; **o. en creux,** deep-etched offset, offset deep, intaglio offset.

offsetiste [ɔfsɛtist], *s.m.* lithographic printer.

offuscation [ɔfyskasjɔ̃], *s.f. A:* obfuscation; obscuration.

offusquer [ɔfyske], *v.tr.* **1.** *A:* (*a*) to obscure (the view, the sun); to obfuscate, befog, cloud (the mind, judgment); **le brouillard offusquait le paysage,** the haze blurred the landscape; (*b*) to dazzle (the eyes). **2.** to offend, shock (s.o.); **rien n'y offusque l'œil,** there is nothing in it to offend the eye; it has nothing to offend the eye.

s'offusquer. 1. *A:* (*of the sight, of the sun*) to become clouded, obscured. **2. s'o. de qch.,** to take offence at sth.; **il s'offusque d'un rien,** he is easily shocked.

oflag [ɔflag], *s.m. Mil.Hist:* oflag.

og(h)am [ɔgam], *s.m. Pal:* og(h)am; ogham alphabet.

ogival, -aux [ɔʒival, -o], *a.* ogival; (*incorrectly*) gothic (style, arch).

ogive [ɔʒiːv], *s.f.* **1.** *Arch:* (diagonal) rib (under a groin); **voûte d'ogives,** ribbed vault; **croisée d'ogives,** intersecting ribs (of a vault); (*incorrectly*) **arc en o.,** pointed arch. **2.** *Ball: etc:* conical point, head (of shell); warhead (of missile, torpedo); nose cone (of rocket); **fausse o.,** cap; **obus à o.,** capped shell; **o. classique,** conventional warhead; **o. atomique, nucléaire,** atomic, nuclear, warhead; **arme à ogives multiples,** multiple-warhead weapon.

ognette [ɔɲɛt], *s.f.* (stonecutter's, sculptor's) chisel.

ognon [ɔɲɔ̃], *s.m.* = OIGNON.

ognonet [ɔɲɔnɛ], *s.m.* small onion; onion set.

ogotone [ɔgɔtɔn], *s.m. Z:* pika.

ogre, ogresse [ɔgr̥, ɔgrɛs], *s.* (*a*) ogre, ogress; **manger comme un o.,** to eat like a horse, a pig; (*b*) *Hist:* **l'o. de Corse,** Napoleon; (*c*) *F:* glutton; (*d*) *s.f. P:* **ogresse,** landlady of a disreputable pub, dive.

Ogygie [ɔʒiʒi], *Pr.n.f. Gr.Ant:* Ogygia.

ogygien, -ienne [ɔʒiʒjɛ̃, -jɛn], *a. & s. Gr.Myth:* Ogygian, Ogygean.

oh [o], *int.* oh! O! **oh! hisse!** yo-heave-ho!

ohé [o(e)], *int.* (*a*) hi! hullo! (*b*) *Nau:* **o. du navire!** ship ahoy! **o. de la hune!** aloft there! up top!

ohm [oːm], *s.m. El.Meas:* ohm.

ohmique [omik], *a. El.E:* ohmic (resistance); **chute o.,** ohmic drop.

ohmmètre [ommɛtr̥], *s.m. El:* ohmmeter.

oïdie [ɔidi], *s.f. Fung:* oidium.

oïdiomycose [ɔidjɔmikoːz], *s.f. Med:* oidiomycosis.

oïdium [ɔidjɔm], *s.m.* oidium, vine mildew, powdery mildew; **faux o.,** brown rot.

oie [wa], *s.f.* (*a*) goose; **o. barrée,** bar-headed goose; **o. cendrée,** greylag (goose); **o. bernache, o. marine, o. à joues blanches,** barnacle goose; **o. d'Égypte,** Egyptian goose; **o. des neiges,** snow goose; **o. des moissons,** bean goose; **o. des moissons de Russie,** Sushkin's goose; **o. rieuse, o. à front blanc,** white-fronted goose; **o. à bec court,** pink-footed goose; **o. naine,** lesser white-fronted goose; **conte de ma mère l'O.,** fairy tale; **bête comme une o.,** as silly as a goose; *F:* **ne faites pas l'o.,** don't be silly, don't be an idiot; *F:* **une o. blanche,** an innocent young girl; **marcher au pas de l'o.,** to goose step; (*b*) **jeu de l'o.,** (i) *A:* the game of goose; (ii) any game of the snakes and ladders type.

oie-de-mer [wadəmɛːr], *s.f. Z:* dolphin, *F:* sea goose; *pl. oies-de-mer.*

oignon [ɔɲɔ̃], *s.m.* **1.** (*a*) onion; **petits oignons,** (i) spring onions; (ii) pickling onions; **aux petits oignons,** (i) *Cu:* stewed, etc., with spring onions; (ii) *F:* first-rate; *F:* **soigner qn aux petits oignons,** to treat s.o. (i) with great care; (ii) *Iron:* harshly; **chapelet, corde, d'oignons,** string of onions; **se mettre en rang d'oignons,** to form up in a row; *F:* **pensionnat qui défile en rang d'oignons,** school crocodile; **regretter les oignons d'Égypte,** to sigh for the fleshpots of Egypt; *F:* **être vêtu comme un o.,** to wear layers and layers of clothes; *P:* **occupe-toi, mêle-toi, de tes oignons,** mind your own business; *P:* **ce n'est pas tes oignons,** it's none of your business; *s.a.* PELURE; (*b*) *Bot:* bulb. **2.** (*a*) hard corn (*usu.* under sole of foot); (*b*) bunion. **3.** *A: F:* watch, turnip.

oignonade [ɔɲɔnad], *s.f. Cu:* onion stew.

oignonet [ɔɲɔnɛ], *s.m.* small onion; onion set.

oignonière [ɔɲɔnjɛːr], *s.f.* onion bed.

oïl [ɔil], *adv.* (*in old Fr.*) yes; *Ling:* **la langue d'o.,** the dialect(s) of northern France.

Oïlée [ɔile], *Pr.n.m. Gr.Lit:* Oileus.

oille [ɔːj], *s.f. Cu:* olio, olla podrida.

oindre [wɛ̃ːdr̥], *v.tr.* (*conj. like* CRAINDRE) **1.** *O:* to oil, to rub with oil; **s'o. d'huile,** to rub one's body with oil; *Prov:* **oignez vilain, il vous poindra, poignez vilain il vous oindra,** "Tender-handed stroke a nettle, And it stings you for your pains; Grasp it like a man of mettle, And it soft as silk remains." **2.** to anoint (king, etc.).

oing [wɛ̃], *s.m. A:* grease, lard; **vieux o.,** cart grease.

oint, ointe [wɛ̃, wɛ̃ːt], *a. & s.* anointed; **l'O. du Seigneur,** the Lord's Anointed.

oiseau, -eaux [wazo], *s.m.* **1.** (*a*) bird; **oiseaux domestiques, de basse-cour,** poultry; **o. de proie,** bird of prey; **oiseaux de volière, d'appartement,** cage birds; **o. de passage,** bird of passage; **être comme l'o. sur la branche,** to be here today and gone tomorrow; **perspective à vue d'o.,** bird's eye view; *Prov:* **c'est la plume qui fait l'o.,** fine feathers make fine birds; *F:* **l'o. n'y est plus, s'est envolé, les oiseaux sont dénichés,** the bird's flown; there's nobody there; **o. de mauvais augure,** bird of ill omen; **à vol d'o.,** as the crow flies; *adv.phr. F:* **aux oiseaux,** splendidly, beautifully (decorated, etc.); (*b*) *F:* (*of pers.*) **drôle d'o.,** queer type, odd sort of chap; **vilain o.,** bad lot, shady customer; **c'est l'o. rare, le bel o. bleu,** he's a *rara avis*; you don't often find people like him; **mon petit o.,** my pet; **o. des îles,** (i) creole; (ii) namby-pamby; (*c*) *Orn: F:* **o. à berceau,** bowerbird; **o. à berceau satiné,** satin bowerbird; **o. bleu, o. de Notre-Dame,** kingfisher; **o. boucher,** butcher bird; **o. du bon Dieu,** wren; **o. des Canaries,** canary; **o. de la croix,** bullfinch; **o. glorieux, o. des Indes,** pelican; **o. de Médée,** peacock; **o. de la Pentecôte,** golden oriole; **o. de paradis,** bird of paradise; (*d*) *Astr:* **O. de Paradis,** Apus, Bird of Paradise. **2.** *Const:* (bricklayer's) hod.

oiseau-chameau [wazoʃamo], *s.m. Orn: F:* ostrich; *pl. oiseaux-chameaux.*

oiseau-chat [wazoʃa], *s.m. Orn: F:* cat bird; *pl. oiseaux-chats.*

oiseau-cloche [wazoklɔʃ], *s.m. Orn:* (S. American) bellbird; *pl. oiseaux-cloches.*

oiseau-lyre [wazoliːr], *s.m. Orn:* lyre bird; *pl. oiseaux-lyres.*

oiseau-moqueur [wazomɔkœːr], *s.m. Orn:* mocking bird *pl. oiseaux-moqueurs.*

oiseau-mouche [wazomuʃ], *s.m. Orn:* humming bird; **o.-m. énicure,** slender shear-tail humming bird; **o.-m. porte-épée,** sword-bill humming bird; *pl. oiseaux-mouches.*

oiseau-rhinocéros [wazorinɔserɔs], *s.m. Orn:* rhinoceros hornbill; *pl. oiseaux-rhinocéros.*

oiseau-serpent [wazosɛrpɑ̃], *s.m. Orn:* anhinga, snake bird; *pl. oiseaux-serpents.*

oiseau-souris [wazosuri], *s.m. Orn:* coly, mouse-bird; *pl. oiseaux-souris.*

oiseau-tempête [wazotɑ̃pɛt], *s.m. Orn:* storm(y) petrel; *pl. oiseaux-tempête.*

oiseau-trompette [wazotrɔ̃pɛt], *s.m. Orn:* agami, trumpeter; *pl. oiseaux-trompettes.*

oiseler [wazle], *v.* **(il oiselle, n. oiselons; il oisellera) 1.** *v.i.* to go bird-catching. **2.** *v.tr. Ven:* (*a*) to train (hawk); (*b*) to fly (hawk).

oiselet [wazlɛ], *s.m. Lit:* small bird.

oiseleur [wazlœːr]. **1.** *s.m.* fowler, bird catcher. **2.** *a.m.* **vents oiseleurs,** Etesian winds.

oiselier [wazəlje], *s.m.* bird seller, bird fancier.

oiselle [wazɛl], *s.f.* (*a*) hen bird; **elle eut un petit sursaut d'o. effarée,** she gave a start like a frightened bird, sparrow; (*b*) *F:* innocent young girl.

oisellerie [wazɛlri], *s.f.* **1.** bird catching; bird breeding; bird selling. **2.** (*a*) bird shop; (*b*) aviary.

oiseusement [wazøzmɑ̃], *adv.* idly; unnecessarily.

oiseux, -euse [wazø, -øːz], *a.* **1.** *A:* idle, lazy, indolent. **2.** unnecessary; that adds nothing (to the matter); *F:* that doesn't cut any ice; **dispute oiseuse,** useless, pointless, quarrel; **explication oiseuse,** (i) unnecessary explanation; (ii) explanation that doesn't cut any ice; **il n'est peut-être pas o. de faire remarquer que . . .,** it is perhaps worthwhile pointing out that . . .; **épithète oiseuse,** otiose epithet.

oisif, -ive [wazif, -iːv]. **1.** *a.* idle; (*a*) unoccupied; **talent o.,** unapplied, dormant, talent; **capital o.,** uninvested, idle, capital; (*b*) lazy; **mener une vie oisive,** to lead an idle life. **2.** *s.* (*a*) person who has plenty of leisure time; person of independent means; (*b*) idler.

oisillon [wazijɔ̃], *s.m.* fledgling; young bird; small bird.

oisivement [wazivmɑ̃], *adv.* idly; in a lazy manner.

oisiveté [wazivte], *s.f.* idleness; (*a*) leisure; **dans mes heures d'o.,** in my leisure time; (*b*) laziness; **vivre dans l'o.,** to lead a life of idleness; **l'o. est (la) mère de tous les vices,** idleness is the root of all evil; Satan finds some mischief still for idle hands to do.

oison [wazɔ̃], *s.m.* **1.** *Orn:* gosling; *F:* **se laisser plumer comme un o.,** to let oneself be robbed, fleeced. **2.** *F:* (*with f.* **oisonne**) credulous person, mug, dope.

oisonnerie [wazɔnri], *s.f. F: O:* stupidity, simplicity.

okapi [ɔkapi], *s.m. Z:* okapi.

okénite [ɔkenit], *s.f. Miner:* okenite.

okonite [ɔkɔnit], *s.f. El.E: A:* okonite (insulating material).

okoumé [ɔkume], *s.m. Com:* **bois d'o.,** gaboon.

okra [ɔkra], *s.m. Bot:* okra.

olacacées [ɔlakase], *s.f.pl. Bot:* Olacaceae.

Oldenbourg [ɔldɛ̃buːr], *Pr.n.m. Geog:* Oldenburg.

oldenbourgeois, -oise [ɔldɛ̃burʒwa, -waːz], *a. & s. Geog:* Oldenburger.

oldhamite [ɔldamit], *s.f. Miner:* oldhamite.

oléacé [ɔlease], *Bot:* **1.** *a.* oleaceous. **2.** *s.f.pl.* **oléacées,** Oleaceae, the olive family.

oléagineux, -euse [ɔleaʒinø, -øːz], *a.* **1.** oleaginous, oily. **2.** oleaginous, oil-yielding; **graines oléagineuses,** *s.m.pl.* **oléagineux,** oilseeds, expeller seeds.

oléandre [ɔleɑ̃:dr̥], *s.m. Bot: A:* oleander.
oléandrine [ɔleɑ̃drin], *s.f. Ch:* oleandrin.
oléastre [ɔleastr̥], *s.m. Bot:* oleaster.
oléate [ɔleat], *s.m. Ch:* oleate.
olécrâne [ɔlekrɑ:n], *s.m. Anat:* olecranon.
olécrânien, -ienne [ɔlekrɑnjɛ̃, -jɛn], *a. Anat:* olecranal, olecranian.
oléfiant [ɔlefjɑ̃], **oléifiant** [ɔleifjɑ̃], *a. Ch:* oil-producing, oil-forming; *A:* **gaz oléfiant,** olefiant gas.
oléfines [ɔlefin], *s.f.pl. Ch:* olefin(e)s.
oléicole [ɔleikɔl], *a.* (*a*) olive-growing (land); (*b*) vegetable oil (industry).
oléiculteur [ɔleikyltœ:r], *s.m.* **1.** olive grower. **2.** olive-oil manufacturer.
oléiculture [ɔleikylty:r], *s.f.* oleiculture; (*a*) cultivation of the olive; (*b*) the olive-oil industry.
oléifère [ɔleifɛ:r], *a.* oil-producing, oleiferous.
oléiforme [ɔleifɔrm], *a.* oily; having the consistency of oil.
oléine [ɔlein], *s.f. Ch:* olein.
oléique [ɔleik], *a. Ch:* oleic (acid).
olénidés [ɔlenide], *s.m.pl. Paleont:* Olenidae.
olenus [ɔlenys], *s.m. Paleont:* Olenus, olenid.
oléo- [ɔleɔ], *pref.* oleo-.
oléobromie [ɔleɔbrɔmi], *s.f. Phot:* oleobrom process.
oléocalcaire [ɔleɔkalkɛ:r], *a.* oleocalcareous.
oléoduc [ɔleɔdyk], *s.m.* pipeline.
oléographie [ɔleɔgrafi], *s.f.* **1.** oleography, chromo-lithography. **2.** oleograph.
olé olé [ɔleɔle], *a. F:* **elle est un peu o. o.,** she's fast.
oléomargarine [ɔleɔmargarin], *s.f.* oleomargarine.
oléomètre [ɔleɔmɛtr̥], *s.m. Ind:* oleometer.
oléonaphte [ɔleɔnaft], *s.m. Ind:* heavy oil (distilled from tar).
oléophosphorique [ɔleɔfɔsfɔrik], *a.* oleophosphoric.
oléopneumatique [ɔleɔpnømatik], *a.* **amortisseur o.,** oil and air shock absorber.
oléoréfractomètre [ɔleɔrefraktɔmɛtr̥], *s.m.* oleorefractometer.
oléorésine [ɔleɔrezin], *s.f. Ch:* oleoresin.
oléorésineux-euse [ɔleɔrezinø, -ø:z], *a.* oleoresinous.
oléosaccharure [ɔleɔsakary:r], *s.m. Pharm:* oleosaccharum.
oléothorax [ɔleɔtɔraks], *s.m. Med:* oleothorax.
oléracé [ɔlerase], *a. Bot:* oleraceous.
oléum [ɔleɔm], *s.m. Ch:* oleum.
olfactif, -ive [ɔlfaktif, -i:v], *a.* olfactory, olfactive (nerve, cell).
olfaction [ɔlfaksjɔ̃], *s.f. Physiol:* olfaction; (i) (sense of) smell; (ii) smelling.
olfactométrie [ɔlfaktɔmetri], *s.f.* olfactometry.
oliban [ɔlibɑ̃], *s.m.* olibanum, frankincense.
olibrius [ɔlibriys], *s.m.* (*a*) *A:* (*from character in mystery plays*) braggart, swaggerer; **faire l'o.,** to brag; (*b*) *F: Pej:* eccentric.
olifant [ɔlifɑ̃], *s.m. Medieval Lit:* oliphant; ivory (hunting-)horn; **l'o. de Roland,** Roland's horn.
oligarchie [ɔligarʃi], *s.f.* oligarchy.
oligarchique [ɔligarʃik], *a.* oligarchic(al).
oligarque [ɔligark], *s.m.* oligarch.
oligiste [ɔliʒist], *a. & s.m. Miner:* (**fer**) **o.,** oligist (iron); haematite: **o. concrétionné,** kidney ore.
olig(o)- [ɔlig(ɔ)], *pref.* olig(o)-.
oligocarpe [ɔligɔkarp], *a. Bot:* oligocarpous.
oligocène [ɔligɔsɛn], *a. & s.m. Geol:* Oligocene.
oligochètes [ɔligɔkɛt], *s.m.pl. Ann:* Oligochaeta.
oligoclase [ɔligɔkla:z], *s.f. Miner:* oligoclase.
oligodendroglie [ɔligɔdɑ̃drɔgli], *s.f. Biol:* oligodendroglia.
oligodipsie [ɔligɔdipsi], *s.f. Physiol:* oligodipsia.
oligodynamique [ɔligɔdinamik], *a.* oligodynamic.
oligo-élément [ɔligɔelemɑ̃], *s.m. Biol:* trace element; *pl. oligo-éléments.*
oligohémie [ɔligɔemi], *s.f. Med:* oligohaemia.
oligoménorrhée [ɔligɔmenɔre], *s.f. Physiol:* oligomenorrhea.
oligomyodés [ɔligɔmjɔde], *s.m.pl. Orn:* Oligomyodae.
oligonite [ɔligɔnit], *s.f. Miner:* olignite.
oligophage [ɔligɔfa:ʒ], *a. Z:* oligophagous.
oligophrène [ɔligɔfrɛn], *a. & s.m. & f. Med:* oligophrenic.
oligophrénie [ɔligɔfreni], *s.f. Med:* oligophrenia.
oligophylle [ɔligɔfil], *a.* oligophyllous.
oligopole [ɔligɔpɔl], *s.m. Pol.Ec:* oligopoly.
oligosialie [ɔligɔsjali], *s.f. Med:* oligosialia.
oligosidère [ɔligɔsidɛ:r], *a. Miner:* oligosideric.
oligotriches [ɔligɔtriʃ], *s.m.pl. Prot:* Oligotricha.
oligotrophe [ɔligɔtrɔf], *a.* oligotrophic.
oligurie [ɔligyri], *s.f. Med:* oliguria.
olinder [ɔlɛ̃de], *v.i. A: Lit:* to draw one's sword.
olinet [ɔlinɛ], *s.m. Bot:* lycium, boxthorn.
olingo [ɔlɛ̃go], *s.m. Z:* pale-faced kinkajou.
olivacé [ɔlivase], *a.* olivaceous, olive-green.
olivaie [ɔlivɛ], *s.f.* olive plantation, olive grove.
olivaire [ɔlivɛ:r], *a. Anat: etc:* olivary, olive-shaped.
olivaison [ɔlivɛzɔ̃], *s.f.* **1.** olive harvest, olive crop. **2.** olive season.
olivâtre [ɔlivɑ:tr̥], *a.* inclined to olive in colour; sallow (complexion).
olive [ɔli:v], *s.f.* **1.** (*a*) olive; **huile d'o.,** olive oil; (*b*) *a.inv. & s.m.* olive-green. **2.** *Anat:* olivary body (of the medulla); **o. bulbaire,** olivary nucleus, inferior olivary body; **o. protubérentielle,** superior olivary nucleus; **o. cérébelleuse,** dentatus, corpus dentatum. **3.** (*a*) olive(-shaped button); frog (of frogged coat); toggle (of duffle coat); (*b*) (olive-shaped) knob, handle; (*c*) *Arch:* olive moulding; (*d*) *Fish:* lead weight (on line). **4.** *Moll:* olive shell; (*genus*) Oliva.
olivénite [ɔlivenit], *s.f. Miner:* olivenite.
oliver [ɔlive], *v.i. & v.tr.* to gather olives; **o. un champ,** to harvest the olives of a plantation.
oliveraie [ɔlivrɛ], *s.f.* olive plantation, olive grove.
oliverie [ɔlivri], *s.f.* (olive-)oil mill.
olivétain [ɔlivetɛ̃], *s.m. Ecc.Hist:* Olivetan (Benedictine).
olivète [ɔlivɛt], *s.f. Bot:* oil poppy, opium poppy.
olivette [ɔlivɛt], *s.f.* **1.** olive plantation, grove; **o. expérimentale,** trial ground (for olives). **2.** *pl.* dance to celebrate the gathering-in of the olive crop. **3.** olive-shaped grape. **4.** oval (shaped) tomato, plum tomato. **5.** imitation pearl, olivette, olivet.
oliveur, -euse [ɔlivœ:r, -ø:z], *s.* olive picker.
olividés [ɔlivide], *s.m.pl. Moll:* Olividae, the olive shells.
Olivie [ɔlivi], *Pr.n.f.* Olivia.
olivier[1] [ɔlivje], *s.m.* **1.** *Bot:* olive-(tree); *B.Hist:* **le Mont, le Jardin, des Oliviers,** the Mount of Olives; **se présenter un rameau d'o. à la main, l'o. à la main,** to come to sue for peace; to hold out the olive branch. **2.** olive-(wood).
Olivier[2], *Pr.n.m.* Oliver.
oliviforme [ɔlivifɔrm], *a.* olive-shaped, oliviform.
olivine [ɔlivin], *s.f. Miner:* olivine.
olivinite [ɔlivinit], *s.f. Miner:* olivinite.
ollaire [ɔllɛ:r], *a.f. Miner: used in* **pierre o.,** potstone; steatite.
olla-podrida [ɔjapɔdrida], *s.f.* olla podrida, olla, olio; (*a*) *Cu:* (mixed) stew; (*b*) medley, mixture.
olmèque [ɔlmɛk], *a. & s. Ethn:* Olmec.
oloffée [ɔlɔfe], *s.f. Nau:* luffing.
oloffer [ɔlɔfe], *v.i. Nau:* to luff.
olographe [ɔlɔgraf], *a. Jur:* holograph(ic), handwritten (will).
olographie [ɔlɔgrafi], *s.f.* **1.** holograph; holographic, handwritten, document. **2.** holography.
olographier [ɔlɔgrafje], *v.tr.* (*p.d. & pr.sub.* **n. olographiions, v. olographiiez**) to write (will, etc.) in holograph, in one's own handwriting.
olonnais, -aise [ɔlɔnɛ, -ɛ:z], *a. & s. Geog:* (native, inhabitant) of les Sables-d'Olonne.
oloronais, -aise [ɔlɔrɔnɛ, -ɛ:z], *a. & s. Geog:* (native, inhabitant) of Oloron-Sainte-Marie.
Olympe[1] [ɔlɛ̃:p], *Pr.n.m. Geog: Gr.Myth:* (Mount) Olympus; **les dieux de l'O.,** the Olympian gods.
Olympe[2], *Pr.n.f.* Olympia.
olympiade [ɔlɛ̃pjad], *s.f.* olympiad.
Olympie [ɔlɛ̃pi], *Pr.n.f. Geog:* Olympia.
olympien, -ienne [ɔlɛ̃pjɛ̃, -jɛn], *a. & s.* Olympian; **sa tête olympienne,** his godlike head; **les Olympiens,** the Olympians.
olympique [ɔlɛ̃pik], *a.* olympic; **les jeux olympiques,** the Olympic games; **stade o.,** olympic stadium; **champion o.,** olympic champion.
Olynthe [ɔlɛ̃:t], *Pr.n. A.Geog:* Olynthus.
olynthien, -ienne [ɔlɛ̃tjɛ̃, -jɛn]. **1.** *a. & s. A.Geog:* Olynthian. **2.** *s.f.pl.* **les Olynthiennes,** the Olynthiacs (of Demosthenes).
ombelle [ɔ̃bɛl], *s.f. Bot:* umbel; **en o.,** umbellate.
ombellé [ɔ̃bɛle], *a. Bot:* umbellate(d) (flower).
ombelliféracées [ɔ̃bɛliferase], *s.f.pl. Bot:* Umbelliferae.
ombellifère [ɔ̃bɛlifɛ:r], *Bot:* **1.** *a.* umbelliferous. **2.** *s.f.pl.* **ombellifères,** Umbelliferae, umbellifers.
ombelliférone [ɔ̃bɛliferɔn], *s.f. Ch:* umbelliferone.
ombelliforme [ɔ̃bɛlifɔrm], *a. Bot:* umbelliform, umbellar.
ombellique [ɔ̃bɛlik], *a. Ch:* umbellic (acid).
ombellula [ɔ̃bɛlyla], *s.f.,* **ombellule**[1] [ɔ̃bɛlyl], *s.f. Coel:* umbellula.
ombellule[2], *s.f. Bot:* umbellule, umbellet.
ombellulidés [ɔ̃bɛlylide], *s.m.pl. Coel:* Umbellulidae.
ombilic [ɔ̃bilik], *s.m.* umbilicus. **1.** *Anat:* navel. **2.** *Bot:* hilum. **3.** *Tchn:* navel-shaped depression. **4.** *Geom:* umbilic(us); umbilical point.
ombilical, -aux [ɔ̃bilikal, -o], *a.* (*a*) *Anat: Bot: etc:* umbilical; **cordon o.,** umbilical cord, navel string; **hernie ombilicale,** umbilical hernia; (*b*) *Ball:* **tour ombilicale,** umbilical tower (on rocket launching site); **cordon o.,** umbilical tether (of space suit).
ombilication [ɔ̃bilikasjɔ̃], *s.f.* umbilication.
ombiliqué [ɔ̃bilike], *a.* umbilicate(d); navel-shaped.
omble [ɔ̃:bl̥], *s.m. Ich:* **o. (chevalier),** char.
ombon [ɔ̃bɔ̃], *s.m. A.Arm:* umbo (of shield); boss.
omboné [ɔ̃bɔne], *a. Fung:* umbonate(d).
ombrage [ɔ̃bra:ʒ], *s.m.* **1.** shade (of trees); **se promener sous les ombrages,** to walk under the shady trees. **2.** umbrage; **prendre o., de qch.,** (i) (*of horse*) to shy at sth.; (ii) (*of pers.*) to take offence, umbrage, at sth.; **donner o., faire o., porter o., à qn,** to offend s.o.
ombragé [ɔ̃braʒe], *a.* **1.** shaded, shady (path, spot). **2.** *Her:* umbrated.
ombrager [ɔ̃braʒe], *v.tr.* (**il ombrageait**) (*a*) to shade; to protect (sth.) against the sun; **chemin ombragé de peupliers,** road shaded by poplars; (*b*) *Lit:* to overshadow.
s'ombrager **1. s'o. de qch.,** to shelter from, protect oneself against (the sun, heat, etc.). **2. s'o. d'un parasol,** to hold up one's sunshade, to take cover under a sunshade.
ombrageusement [ɔ̃braʒøzmɑ̃], *adv.* **1.** (*of horse*) skittishly. **2.** distrustfully.
ombrageux, -euse [ɔ̃braʒø, -ø:z], *a.* **1.** shy, skittish (horse, etc.). **2.** (*a*) (*of pers.*) easily offended; touchy, quick to take offence; (*b*) **l'opinion publique est ombrageuse à l'endroit de . . .,** public opinion is suspicious, sensitive, very touchy, with regard to . . .; **voir qch. d'un œil o.,** to look askance at something.
ombre[1] [ɔ̃:br̥], *s.f.* **1.** shadow; *Astr:* umbra; **projeter une o.,** to cast a shadow; **suivre qn comme son o.,** to follow, stick to, s.o. like his shadow; **ils sont comme l'o. et le corps,** they're inseparable; **il a peur de son o.,** he's scared of his own shadow; **o. chinoise,** silhouette; **ombres chinoises,** shadow theatre; *Opt: Geom:* **o. portée,** cast shadow. **2.** shade; **se reposer à l'o. d'un arbre,** to rest in the shade of a tree; **40° à l'o.,** 40°(C) in the shade; **plaine sans o.,** shadeless plain, plain exposed to the sun; *P:* **mettre qn à l'o.,** (i) to put s.o. in prison; (ii) to kill s.o.; **une o. de contrariété sur son visage,** a shadow of annoyance on his face; **jeter une o. sur la fête,** to cast a gloom over the festivities; **vivre dans l'o.,** to live in retirement; **se trouver dans l'o.,** to be suffering eclipse. **3.** darkness; **les ombres de la nuit,** the shades of night; **à l'o. de la nuit,** under the cover of darkness. **4.** (*a*) ghost, shade, shadowy figure; **l'o. d'Achille,** the shade of Achilles; *Lit:* **le royaume des ombres,** the land of the shades; **n'être plus que l'o. de soi-même,** to be merely the shadow of one's former self; to be worn to a shadow; (*b*) **vous n'avez pas l'o. d'une chance,** you haven't the ghost of a chance, the slightest chance; **il n'y a pas une o. de vérité dans ce récit,** there is not a particle of truth in this story; **pas une o. de surprise,** not a hint of surprise; **il n'a pas l'o. de bon sens,** he hasn't a grain, an atom, of common sense; **lâcher la proie pour l'o.,** to drop the substance for the shadow; **courir après une o.,** to catch at shadows; (*c*) *A:* simulacrum, pretence; **sous (l')o. de . . ., que . . .,** under the pretext, the cloak of . . ., under the pretext that . . .; (*d*) *Rom.Ant:* umbra (brought by guest). **5.** *Art:* **l'o. et la lumière,** light and shade; **mettre des ombres à un dessin,** to shade a drawing; **il y a une o. au tableau,** there's a fly in the ointment.
ombre[2], *s.f.* **terre d'ombre,** umber.
ombre[3], *s.m. Ich:* (*a*) **o. de rivière,** grayling; (*b*) **o. (chevalier),** char.
ombre[4], *s.m. Cards: A:* ombre.
ombré [ɔ̃bre], *a.* **1.** shaded (drawing); **chat argenté o.,** shaded-silver cat. **2.** striped (leopard skin, etc.).
ombrée [ɔ̃bre], *s.f. Geog:* (*in Alps*) ubac.
ombrelle [ɔ̃brɛl], *s.f.* **1.** sunshade, parasol. **2.** (*a*) *Moll:* umbrella shell; (*b*) *Coel:* umbrella (of jellyfish). **3.** *Av:* **o. de protection aérienne,** aerial umbrella.
ombrer [ɔ̃bre], *v.tr.* to shade (conservatory, drawing); to darken (eyelids, etc.); *Hort:* **paillasson à o.,** shading mat.
ombrette [ɔ̃brɛt], *s.f. Orn:* umbrette, hammer-headed stork, hammerkop.

ombreux, -euse [ɔ̃brø, -øːz], *a. Lit:* shady (walk, grove, etc.).
Ombrie [ɔ̃bri], *Pr.n.f. Geog:* Umbria.
ombrien, -ienne [ɔ̃brjɛ̃, -jɛn], *a. & s. Geog:* Umbrian.
ombrine [ɔ̃brin], *s.f. Ich:* umbrine, umbra.
ombromètre [ɔ̃brɔmɛtr̥], *s.m.* rain gauge, ombrometer.
ombrophile [ɔ̃brɔfil], *Bot:* **1.** *a.* ombrophilous (plant); **la forêt o.,** the tropical rain forest. **2.** *s.m.* ombrophile.
oméga [ɔmega], *s.m. Gr.Alph:* omega.
omelette [ɔmlɛt], *s.f.* (*a*) *Cu:* omelet(te); **o. aux fines herbes,** savoury omelette (*esp.* with chives); **o. aux confitures,** jam omelette; **on ne saurait faire une o., on ne fait pas d'o., sans casser des œufs,** you can't make an omelette without breaking eggs; (*b*) *F:* broken mess.
omental, -aux [ɔmɑ̃tal, -o], *a. Anat:* omental.
omentopexie [ɔmɑ̃tɔpɛksi], *s.f. Surg:* omentopexy.
omettre [ɔmɛtr̥], *v.tr.* (*conj. like* METTRE) to omit, miss out, pass over; to leave out (passage from letter, etc.); **o. de,** *A:* **à, faire qch.,** to fail, omit, neglect, to do sth.
omicron [ɔmikrɔn], *s.m. Gr.Alph:* omicron.
omis [ɔmi], (*a*) *a.* omitted; (*b*) *s.m. Mil:* passed over recruit.
omission [ɔmisjɔ̃], *s.f.* omission; *Typ: etc:* **signe d'o.,** caret; *Theol:* **péchés par action ou par o.,** sins of commission or omission; **péché, faute, d'o.,** sin of omission.
ommatidie [ɔmatidi], *s.f. Z:* ommatidium.
Ommeyades [ɔm(m)ejad], *Pr.n.m.pl.*, **Ommiades** [ɔm(m)jad], *Pr.n.m.pl. Hist:* the Ommiad dynasty, the Ommiads.
omni- [ɔmni], *pref.* omni-.
omnibus [ɔmnibys]. **1.** *s.m. A.Veh:* (horse) (omni)bus. **2.** *a.inv.* **train o.,** slow, stopping, train; *U.S:* accommodation train; **règles o.,** blanket rules; *El:* **barre o.,** busbar, slave.
omnicolore [ɔmnikɔlɔːr], *a.* of all colours, of many colours.
omnidirectionnel, -elle [ɔmnidirɛksjɔnɛl], *a.* omnidirectional.
omniforme [ɔmnifɔrm], *a.* omniform.
omnipotence [ɔmnipɔtɑ̃ːs], *s.f.* omnipotence.
omnipotent [ɔmnipɔtɑ̃], *a.* omnipotent, all-powerful.
omnipraticien, -ienne [ɔmnipratisjɛ̃, -jɛn], *s. Med:* general practitioner.
omniprésence [ɔmniprezɑ̃ːs], *s.f.* omnipresence.
omniprésent [ɔmniprezɑ̃], *a.* omnipresent.
omnirange [ɔmnirɑ̃ːʒ], *s.m. Nav: W.Tel:* omnirange, omnidirectional range.
omniscience [ɔmnisjɑ̃ːs], *s.f.* omniscience.
omniscient [ɔmnisjɑ̃], *a.* omniscient.
omnium [ɔmnjɔm], *s.m.* **1.** *Pol.Ec:* combine; **o. des pétroles,** oil combine. **2.** *Sp:* (*a*) open race; *Turf:* open handicap; *Golf:* open championship, *F:* the Open; (*b*) mixed race.
omnivore [ɔmnivɔːr]. **1.** *a.* omnivorous. **2.** *s.m. Z:* omnivore.
omo-hyoïdien [ɔmɔjɔidjɛ̃], *a. & s.m. Anat:* omohyoid; *pl. omo-hyoïdiens.*
omoïde [ɔmɔid], *s.m. Orn:* omoideum.
omophage [ɔmɔfaːʒ]. **1.** *a.* omophagous, omophagic. **2.** *s.m. & f.* omophagist.
omophagie [ɔmɔfaʒi], *s.f. Anthr:* omophagy, omophagia.
omoplate [ɔmɔplat], *s.f.* shoulder blade, scapula.
omphacite [ɔ̃fasit], *s.f. Miner:* omphacite.
Omphale [ɔ̃fal], *Pr.n.f. Gr.Myth:* Omphale.
omphalectomie [ɔ̃falɛktɔmi], *s.f. Surg:* omphalectomy.
omphalocèle [ɔ̃falɔsɛl], *s.f. Surg:* omphalocele, umbilical hernia.
omphalomésentérique [ɔ̃falɔmezɑ̃terik], *a. Anat:* omphalomesenteric.
omphalophlébite [ɔ̃falɔflebit], *s.f. Obst:* omphalophlebitis.
omphalorr(h)agie [ɔ̃falɔraʒi], *s.f. Obst:* omphalorrhagia.
omphalos [ɔ̃falɔs], *s.m. Gr.Ant:* omphalos; boss (of shield).
omphalosite [ɔ̃falɔzit], *s.f. Ter:* omphalosite.
omphalotomie [ɔ̃falɔtɔmi], *s.f. Obst:* omphalotomy.
omphalotripsie [ɔ̃falɔtripsi], *s.f. Obst:* omphalotripsy.
omphazite [ɔ̃fazit], *s.f. Miner:* omphacite.
on [ɔ̃], *indef. pron., always subject of verb; occ. becomes* **l'on,** *esp. after vowel sound to avoid hiatus.* **1.** (*indeterminate; the corresponding pronoun & poss. adj. of the complement are usu.* **soi(-même)** *and* **son**) one, people; we, they, etc.; (*a*) (*mankind in general*) **on ne sait jamais,** one, you, never can tell; **on ne saurait penser à tout,** one can't think of everything; **on ne saurait arrêter la langue des femmes,** there is no stopping women's tongues; **on n'en sait rien,** nobody knows anything about it; **avec de l'argent on est maître du monde,** with money a man commands the world; **on n'aime pas à être traité comme ça,** people don't like to be treated like that; *F:* **il faut bien qu'on mange,** a man, a girl, *must* eat; **partout où l'on trouve de ces fossiles,** wherever these fossils are to be found; **on ne connaît jamais son bonheur,** one never knows one's own happiness, how happy one is; **quand on demande à une jeune fille d'être sa, votre, femme,** when a man asks a girl to be his wife; when you ask a girl to be your wife; (*b*) **on était au sept mars,** it was the seventh of March; (*c*) (*people, opinion*) **on dit que . . .,** one says, men say, it is said, that . . .; **c'est lui, dit-on, qui . . .,** it is he, they say, it is said, who . . .; (*d*) (*unspecified pers. or people*) **on frappe à la porte,** someone's, somebody's, knocking; there's a knock at the door; **on a enfoncé la porte,** the door was burst open; **on a apporté le dessert,** the dessert was served, brought in; **on était fatigué de la guerre,** they, people, were tired of the war; **on demande une bonne cuisinière,** wanted, a good cook. **2.** (*specific pers. or group of people; in the complement a f. or pl. adj. may be used for greater precision; the f. or pl. p.p., considered by purists as F: is nevertheless used by some authors*) (*a*) **on parlait très peu au déjeuner,** there was very little talking over lunch; **on doit se coucher dans un grand dortoir,** we have to sleep in a large dormitory; **on ne s'était jamais séparés,** they had never been separated; **on n'est pas toujours jeune et belle,** a woman can't, women can't, be young and beautiful for ever; **on devient patiente quand on est maman,** one learns patience when one is a mother; **on voudrait que chacun soit heureux comme nous,** we should like everyone to be as happy as we are; **nous autres artistes, on ne fait pas toujours ce qu'on veut,** we artists cannot always do as we wish; **on attend le courrier,** we're waiting for the post; **on n'est pas méchant; c'est la vie qui l'est et qui nous force à l'être malgré soi,** we're not bad in ourselves; it's life that's hard and makes us so in spite of ourselves; (*in book*) **on montrera plus tard que . . .,** we shall show later that . . .; it will be shown later that . . .; (*b*) *F:* **alors, on y va?** well, shall we make a start? shall we move? **où va-t-on?** where are we going? **danse-t-on?** shall we dance? **quelqu'un!—on y va!** anyone there?—coming! (*2nd pers.*) **alors, on s'en va comme ça?** are you really going off like that? (*to child*) **on ne dit plus bonjour?** aren't you going to say "Good morning"? (*c*) *P:* **nous, on . . .,** we; **nous, on n'est pas des duchesses!** we're no duchesses! **puis nous, on s'est sauvés,** then (as for us) we got out, got going; **nous, on est tous égaux,** we're all equal.
onagracées [ɔnagrase], **onagrariacées** [ɔnagrarjase], *s.f.pl. Bot:* Onagraceae.
onagraire [ɔnagrɛːr], **onagre**[1] [ɔnagr̥], *s.f. Bot:* œnothera, evening primrose.
onagre[2], *s.m.* **1.** *Z:* onager, wild ass. **2.** *A.Arms:* (siege) onager.
onanisme [ɔnanism], *s.m.* onanism; masturbation.
onaniste [ɔnanist]. **1.** *a.* onanistic (practices, etc.). **2.** *s.m.* onanist.
once[1] [ɔ̃ːs], *s.f. Meas:* ounce; **perles à l'o.,** small pearls sold by weight; **il n'a pas une o. de sens commun,** he hasn't an ounce, a particle, of common sense.
once[2], *s.f. Z:* ounce, snow leopard, mountain panther.
onchidie [ɔ̃kidi], *s.f. Moll:* onchidium.
onchocercose [ɔ̃kɔsɛrkoːz], *s.f. Med:* onchocerciasis, onchocercosis, *F:* craw-craw.
oncial, -iaux [ɔ̃sjal, -jo], *a.* uncial (letter, MS.).
oncirostre [ɔ̃sirɔstr̥], *a. Orn:* with a hooked beak, hook-billed.
oncle [ɔ̃ːkl̥], *s.m.* uncle; **o. paternel, maternel,** uncle on the father's, the mother's, side; **o. à la mode de Bretagne,** (i) first cousin once removed; (ii) very distant relation; **o. de comédie,** o. **d'Amérique,** rich uncle (of fiction).
oncocerose [ɔ̃kɔseroːz], *s.f. Med:* onchocerosis.
oncosphère [ɔ̃kɔsfɛːr], *s.f.* oncosphere, embryonic tapeworm.
oncotique [ɔ̃kɔtik], *a. Biol:* **pression o.,** oncotic pressure.
oncques [ɔ̃ːk], *adv. A:* (*a*) ever; (*b*) (*with* **ne** *expressed or understood*) never.
onction [ɔ̃ksjɔ̃], *s.f.* **1.** *A:* oiling (of athlete, of machine, part, etc.). **2.** unction; (*a*) anointing; *Ecc:* **la sainte o., l'extrême-o.,** the last Sacrament, extreme unction; (*b*) unctuousness; **prêcher avec o.,** to preach with impressive eloquence, with unction, unctuously. **3.** *Theol:* unction.
onctueusement [ɔ̃ktɥøzmɑ̃], *adv.* unctuously, with unction.
onctueux, -euse [ɔ̃ktɥø, -øːz], *a.* **1.** (*a*) unctuous (to the touch); (*b*) greasy, oily (surface); saponaceous; oleaginous; (*c*) *Cu:* unctuous (to the taste); (*d*) *Art:* **blancs o.,** mellow whites. **2.** (*a*) unctuous (sermon, etc.); (*b*) *Pej:* oily (manner).
onctuosité [ɔ̃ktɥozite], *s.f.* (*a*) unctuousness; (*b*) *Pej:* oiliness (of manner, speech); (*c*) lubricating quality (of oil, etc.).
ondain [ɔ̃dɛ̃], *s.m. Agr:* swath.
ondatra [ɔ̃datra], *s.m. Z:* ondatra, muskrat.
onde [ɔ̃ːd], *s.f.* **1.** *Lit:* (i) billow; (ii) *Poet:* water, tide; sea, main; **sur la terre et sur l'o.,** on land and water; **sur les bords d'une o. limpide,** on the banks of a limpid stream; **l'o. amère,** the briny ocean; **l'O. noire,** the Styx; **les ondes de la foule,** the surging of the crowd. **2.** (*a*) wavy line; **cheveux en ondes,** waved hair; (*b*) corrugation; (*c*) *pl.* watering (on silk). **3.** (*a*) *Ph: etc:* **o. calorifique, o. lumineuse,** heat wave, light wave; **o. sonore,** sound wave; **o. ultra-sonore,** ultrasonic wave; *Ph: Av:* **o. de choc,** shock wave; *Atom.Ph:* base surge; *Nau:* **o. de marée,** tide wave, tidal wave; *Geol:* **o. séismique,** seismic wave; *Exp: Artil:* **o. explosive,** blast wave, detonation wave, explosive wave; *Artil:* **o. de bouche,** muzzle-blast wave; **o. à front raide,** steep-front wave; **o. plane,** plane wave; **o. sinusoïdale,** sine wave; **o. sinusoïdale plane,** plane sine wave; **o. stationnaire,** standing, stationary, wave; **ondes décalées,** waves out of phase; **o. enveloppe,** wave front; **o. progressive,** travelling wave; **o. réfléchie,** reflection wave; **amplitude, élongation, de l'o.,** wave amplitude; **forme d'o.,** wave form, shape; **longueur d'o.,** wavelength; *F:* **être sur la même longueur d'ondes,** to be on the same wavelength; **parcours de l'o.,** wave path, propagation path; **queue de l'o.,** wave tail; **gamme d'ondes,** wave band; **train d'ondes,** wave train; (*b*) *Elcs: W.Tel:* **ondes courtes,** short waves; **ondes ultra-courtes,** ultra-short waves; **ondes moyennes, petites ondes,** medium waves; **ondes longues, grandes ondes,** long waves; **o. millimétrique,** extremely-high-frequency wave; **o. centimétrique,** microwave, super-high-frequency wave; **o. décimétrique,** decimetric wave, ultra-high-frequency wave; **o. métrique,** metric wave, very-high-frequency wave; **o. décamétrique, o. haute fréquence,** decametric wave, high-frequency wave; **o. hectométrique, o. moyenne fréquence,** hectometric wave, medium-frequency wave; **o. kilométrique, o. basse fréquence,** kilometric wave; audio-frequency, low-frequency, wave; **o. myriamétrique,** myriametric wave, very-low-frequency wave; **collecteur d'ondes,** wave-collector; **détecteur d'ondes,** wave detector; **générateur d'ondes,** wave generator; **guide d'ondes,** wave guide; **o. radio-électrique,** radio wave; **o. hertzienne,** Hertzian wave; **o. ionosphérique,** sky wave, ionospheric wave; **o. de sol, de surface,** ground wave; **ondes amorties,** damped waves; **ondes entretenues,** continuous, sustained, undamped, waves; **o. d'émission, de transmission, de travail,** transmitting wave; **ondes dirigées,** directed waves, radio beam; **émission, transmission, à ondes dirigées,** beam emission, beam transmission; **transmettre un message par ondes dirigées,** to beam a message; **o. porteuse,** carrier wave; **o. réfléchie, o. d'écho,** echo (wave); *Mil:* **o. réfléchie par l'objectif,** target echo (of fire-control or range-finding radar); (*c*) **les ondes,** the radio; **mettre en ondes une pièce, etc.,** to put, produce, a play, etc., on the air, on the radio; **metteur en ondes,** producer, staging co-ordinator; **mise en ondes,** production, staging co-ordination; **par ordre d'entrée en ondes,** in order of speaking; *Mil: etc:* **la guerre des ondes,** electronic counter-measures.
ondé [ɔ̃de], *a.* **1.** waved, undulating, wavy (surface); waved (hair, etc.); watered (silk); grained (wood). **2.** *Her:* undé(e).
ondée [ɔ̃de], *s.f.* heavy shower; **il pleut par ondées,** it's showery (weather); **temps à ondées,** showery weather; *A:* **o. de coupes (de bâton),** shower, volley, of blows; *Lit:* **une brusque o. de tristesse,** a sudden pang of sadness.
ondemètre [ɔ̃dmɛtr̥], *s.m. El:* wavemeter; ondometer; *W.Tel:* **o. d'absorption,** wave trap.

onder [ɔ̃de], *v.i. & tr. A: & Lit:* to mark with wavy lines; to move, flow, in waves; **façade ondée par le temps,** façade weathered into a wave surface; **ses cheveux ne frisaient pas, ils ondaient,** her (his) hair was wavy rather than curly.
ondin, -ine [ɔ̃dɛ̃, -in], *s. Myth:* water sprite; *m.* nix; *f.* undine, nixie; (*of graceful swimmer*) **c'est une véritable ondine,** she's a real sea nymph, water sprite.
on-dit [ɔ̃di], *s.m.inv.* rumour, hearsay; **ce ne sont que des on-dit,** it's all idle talk.
ondographe [ɔ̃dɔgraf], *s.m. El: A:* ondograph.
ondoiement [ɔ̃dwamɑ̃], *s.m.* **1.** (*a*) undulation, wavy motion (of water, field of corn); (*b*) inconstancy, changeableness. **2.** *Ecc:* private baptism (in emergency).
ondoscope [ɔ̃dɔskɔp], *s.m. El:* ondoscope.
ondoyant [ɔ̃dwajɑ̃], *a.* **1.** undulating, wavy, billowy (motion, ground); swaying (crowd); **draperies ondoyantes,** flowing draperies; **blé o.,** waving corn. **2.** changeable, ever-changing, fluctuating (disposition, nature).
ondoyer [ɔ̃dwaje], *v.i.* **(j'ondoie, n. ondoyons; j'ondoierai) 1.** to undulate, wave, ripple; to float on the breeze; (*of clouds, flames, etc.*) to billow; **ses cheveux ondoyaient sur ses épaules,** her hair fell in waves over her shoulders; **un panache ondoie sur le casque,** a plume is waving over the helmet. **2.** *v.tr. Ecc:* to baptize privately (in emergency).
ondulant [ɔ̃dylɑ̃], *a.* **1.** undulating (landscape); waving (corn); flowing (mane, drapery). **2.** *Med:* **fièvre ondulante,** rock fever, undulant fever; **pouls o.,** erratic pulse.
ondulateur [ɔ̃dylatœːr], *s.m. Telecom:* undulator.
ondulation [ɔ̃dylasjɔ̃], *s.f.* **1.** (*a*) undulation (of water, etc.); wave motion; *Ph:* **la théorie des ondulations,** the undulatory theory; *El:* **o. de courant,** current ripple; (*b*) rise (and fall), undulation (in the ground); **les ondulations du terrain,** the rolling nature of the ground; **région à ondulations,** rolling country. **2.** *Hairdr:* wave (in hair); **se faire des ondulations,** to wave one's hair; **se faire faire des ondulations,** to have one's hair waved.
ondulatoire [ɔ̃dylatwaːr], *a. Ph:* undulatory; **mouvement o.,** wave motion.
ondulé [ɔ̃dyle], *a.* **1.** (*a*) undulating, rolling (ground); wavy, waved (hair); corrugated (iron, cardboard, paper); ripple (plate); **route ondulée,** switchback road; **toit en tôle ondulée,** corrugated-iron roof; (*b*) **bois à fibres ondulées,** wavy-grained, curly, wood. **2.** *s.m. Tex:* **o. de laine,** ripple cloth.
onduler [ɔ̃dyle]. **1.** *v.i.* to undulate, ripple; *P:* (*of pers.*) **o. de la toiture,** to have a screw loose. **2.** *v.tr.* to wave (the hair); to corrugate (iron, cardboard); **se faire o.,** to have one's hair waved.
onduleur [ɔ̃dylœːr], *s.m. El:* thyratron inverter.
onduleusement [ɔ̃dyløzmɑ̃], *adv.* sinuously.
onduleux, -euse [ɔ̃dylø, -øːz], *a.* undulating, wavy, sinuous; **ligne onduleuse,** wavy line; **plaine onduleuse,** undulating plain; **elle marche avec un léger mouvement o.,** she walks with a slight swaying motion.
onéreusement [ɔnerøzmɑ̃], *adv.* onerously.
onéreux, -euse [ɔnerø, -øːz], *a.* onerous; burdensome (tax, etc.); heavy (expenditure); **à titre o.,** subject to certain liabilities; subject to payment; *Jur:* for valuable consideration; **charge onéreuse pour le budget,** heavy charge on the budget.
onérosité [ɔnerozite], *s.f.* onerousness.
Onésime [ɔnezim], *Pr.n.m. Ecc.Hist:* Onesimus.
one-step [wɔnstɛp], *s. Danc:* one-step.
ongle [ɔ̃ːgl̩], *s.m.* **1.** (finger) nail; claw (of animal); talon (of bird of prey); **ongles des pieds, des orteils,** toenails; **o. incarné,** ingrowing nail; *F:* **il a les ongles en deuil,** his (finger) nails are dirty, his nails are in mourning; **coup d'o.,** scratch; **se faire les ongles,** to do, to cut, one's nails; to give oneself a manicure; **se faire faire les ongles,** to have a manicure; **rogner les ongles à un animal,** *F:* **à qn,** to cut an animal's, *F:* s.o.'s, claws; **se ronger les ongles,** (i) to bite one's nails; (ii) to be restless, impatient; **avoir les ongles crochus,** to be mean, avaricious; rapacious; **donner sur les ongles à qn,** to rap s.o. over the knuckles; **attaquer qn du bec et des ongles,** to go for s.o. tooth and nail; **payer rubis sur l'o.,** to pay to the last farthing; *O:* **faire rubis sur l'o.,** to drain one's glass to the last drop; **connaître, savoir, qch. sur le bout des ongles,** *A:* **savoir qch. sur l'o.,** to know sth. perfectly; **il est français jusqu'an bout des ongles,** he's French to the finger tips; **soldat jusqu'au bout des ongles,** every inch a soldier; *Prov:* **à l'o. on connaît le lion,** by his mark you shall know him. **2.** *Med:* onyx (in the eye).
onglé [ɔ̃gle], *a.* (*a*) armed with claws, with talons; (*b*) *Her:* unguled, hoofed.
onglée [ɔgle], *s.f.* tingling, aching (of numbed finger ends); **j'ai l'o.,** my fingers are numb, are tingling, with cold.
onglet [ɔ̃glɛ], *s.m.* **1.** (embroideress's) thimble. **2. o. de lame,** nail-hole, thumb-nail groove (in blade of penknife); fullering (of sword blade). **3.** *Bookb:* (*a*) guard, stub; butt (of single leaf); (*b*) binding strip (for map, etc.); (*c*) single-leaf cancel; cancel page; (*d*) tab (of thumb index or register); **dictionnaire à onglets,** thumb-indexed dictionary. **4.** (*a*) *Bot:* unguis, claw (of petal, etc.); (*b*) *Med:* pterygium; (*c*) *Z:* nictitating membrane. **5.** *Carp:* mitre; **boîte à o.,** mitre box; **tailler à o.,** to mitre; **assemblage à o.,** mitre joint. **6.** *Geom:* ungula (of sphere). **7.** *Engr:* = ONGLETTE.
onglette [ɔ̃glɛt], *s.f. Tls.* (*Engr.*): scorper, graver.
onglier [ɔ̃glije], *s.m.* **1.** manicure set. **2.** *pl.* nail scissors.
onguent [ɔ̃gɑ̃], *s.m. Pharm:* ointment, unguent, salve, liniment; **o. pour les yeux,** eyesalve; *A:* **o. souverain,** basilicon; *Prov:* **dans les petits pots les bons onguents,** good things are often wrapped in small parcels; little and good.
onguicule [ɔ̃gikyl], *s.m.* small nail, claw.
onguiculé [ɔ̃gikyle]. **1.** *a. Nat.Hist:* unguiculate(d). **2.** *s.m.pl. Z:* **unguiculés,** Unguiculata.
onguiforme [ɔ̃giform], *a. Nat.Hist:* unguiform, unciform, claw-shaped.
ongulé [ɔ̃gyle]. **1.** *a.* (*a*) *Anat:* nail-shaped; (*b*) *Z:* hoofed, ungulate (animal). **2.** *s.m.pl. Z:* **ongulés,** Ungulata, ungulates.
onguligrade [ɔ̃gyligrad], *a. & s.m. Z:* unguligrade.
onirique [ɔnirik], *a.* oneiric; **fantaisies oniriques,** dream phantasies; **symbole o.,** dream symbol.
onirisme [ɔnirism], *s.m. Psy:* (state of) hallucination.
onirocrite [ɔnirɔkrit], *s.m.* oneirocritic.
onirocritie [ɔnirɔkrisi], *s.f.* oneirocritics, oneirocriticism.
oniro-critique [ɔnirɔkritik]. **1.** *a.* oneirocritical. **2.** (*a*) *s.m.* oneirocritic; (*b*) *s.f.* oneirocritics, oneirocriticism; *pl. oniro-critiques.*
onirologie [ɔnirɔlɔʒi], *s.f.* oneirology.
onirologue [ɔnirɔlɔg], *s.m.* oneirologist.
oniromancie [ɔnirɔmɑ̃si], *s.f.* oneiromancy.
oniromancien, -ienne [ɔnirɔmɑ̃sjɛ̃, -jɛn], *s.* oneiromancer.
onirothérapie [ɔnirɔterapi], *s.f. Med:* oneirotherapy.
oniscidés [ɔniside], *s.m.pl. Crust:* Oniscidae.
onisciforme [ɔnisifɔrm], *a. Z:* onisciform.
onocentaure [ɔnɔsɑ̃tɔːr], *s.m. Myth:* onocentaur.
onoclée [ɔnɔkle], *s.f. Bot:* onoclea.
onomancie [ɔnɔmɑ̃si], *s.f.* onomancy.
onomastique [ɔnɔmastik], *a.* onomastic.
onomatomanie [ɔnɔmatɔmani], *s.f. Psy:* onomatomania.
onomatopée [ɔnɔmatɔpe], *s.f. Ling:* onomatopoeia.
onomatopéique [ɔnɔmatɔpeik], *a. Ling:* onomatopoeic(al), onomatopoetic.
onques [ɔ̃ːk], *adv. A:* = ONCQUES.
ontique [ɔ̃tik], *a. Phil:* ontal.
onto- [ɔ̃tɔ], *pref.* onto-.
ontogénèse [ɔ̃tɔʒenɛːz], *s.f.* ontogenesis, ontogeny.
ontogénétique [ɔ̃tɔʒenetik], *a.* ontogenetic, ontogenic.
ontogénie [ɔ̃tɔʒeni], *s.f. Biol:* ontogeny, ontogenesis.
ontogénique [ɔ̃tɔʒenik], *a.* ontogenetic, ontogenic.
ontologie [ɔ̃tɔlɔʒi], *s.f. Phil:* ontology.
ontologique [ɔ̃tɔlɔʒik], *a. Phil:* ontological.
ontologiquement [ɔ̃tɔlɔʒikmɑ̃], *adv. Phil:* ontologically.
ontologiser [ɔ̃tɔlɔʒise], *v.i. & tr.* to ontologize.
ontologisme [ɔ̃tɔlɔʒism], *s.m. Phil:* ontologism.
ontologiste [ɔ̃tɔlɔʒist], *s.m. Phil:* ontologist.
onusien, -ienne [ɔnyzjɛ̃, -jɛn], *a. F:* **expert o.,** UNO expert, specialist; *Pej:* **officine onusienne,** UNO propaganda centre.
onychophagie [ɔnikɔfaʒi], *s.f. Med:* nail biting.
onychite [ɔnikit], *a. Miner:* onyx-bearing.
onychomycose [ɔnikɔmikoːz], *s.f. Med:* onychomycosis.
onychophores [ɔnikɔfɔːr], *s.m.pl. Ent:* Onychophora.
onychoptôse [ɔnikɔptoːz], *s.f. Med:* onychoptosis.
onychose [ɔnikoːz], *s.f. Med:* onychosis.
onyx [ɔniks], *s.m. Miner:* onyx; **marbre o.,** onyx marble.
onyxis [ɔniksis], *s.m. Med:* onyxis, ingrowing (of nail).
onzain [ɔ̃zɛ̃], *s.m. Pros:* stanza of eleven lines.
onze [ɔ̃ːz], *num.a.inv. & s.m.inv.* (NOTES: (i) *the* e *of* **le, de,** *is not, as a rule, elided before* **onze** *and its derivatives:* **le onze** [ləɔ̃ːz] **avril;** *but* **entre onze** [ɑ̃trɔ̃ːz] **heures et midi,** *and occ.* **le train d'onze heures;** (ii) *except in* **il est onze heures** [ilɛ(t)ɔ̃zœːr] *there is no liaison between* **onze** *and a preceding word;* **vers les onze heures** [vɛrleɔ̃zœːr]), (*a*) eleven; **o. chevaux,** eleven horses; **nous n'étions que o.** [kəɔ̃ːz], **nous n'étions qu'o.,** there were only eleven of us; **il n'est qu'o. heures,** it is only eleven o'clock; **le o. avril,** the eleventh of April; **Louis Onze,** Louis the Eleventh; **au chapitre o.,** in chapter eleven; **deux o.,** two elevens; *P:* **prendre le train o.,** to go on Shanks's mare, pony; to go on foot; (*b*) *Fb: Cr:* **le o.,** the eleven; *Fb:* **le o. de France,** the French eleven, team.
onzième [ɔ̃zjɛm]. **1.** *num.a. & s.* (*for treatment in the word-group see* **onze** *above*) eleventh; **le o. jour,** the eleventh day. **2.** *s.m.* eleventh (part); **quatre onzièmes** [katrɔ̃zjɛm], four elevenths. **3.** *s.f. Mus:* eleventh.
onzièmement [ɔ̃zjɛmmɑ̃], *adv.* eleventhly, in the eleventh place.
o(o)- [ɔ(ɔ)], *pref.* o(o)-.
oocyste [ɔɔsist], *s.m. Biol:* oocyst.
oogénèse [ɔɔʒenɛːz], *s.f. Biol:* oogenesis, ovogenesis.
oogone [ɔɔgɔn], *s.f. Bot:* oogonium.
oolithe [ɔɔlit], *s.m., occ.f. Geol:* oolite; **o. ferrugineux,** roestone.
oolithique [ɔɔlitik], *a.* oolitic.
oologie [ɔɔlɔʒi], *s.f. Orn:* oology.
oologique [ɔɔlɔʒik], *a.* oologic(al).
oomycètes [ɔɔmisɛt], *s.m.pl. Fung:* Oomycetes.
oophore [ɔɔfɔːr], *s.m. Bot:* oophore.
ooplasme [ɔɔplasm], *s.m.* ooplasm.
ooscopie [ɔɔskɔpi], *s.f.* ooscopy.
oosphère [ɔɔsfɛːr], *s.f. Bot:* oosphere.
oospore [ɔɔspɔːr], *Bot:* **1.** *a.* oosporous, oosporic. **2.** *s.f.* oospore.
oostégite [ɔɔsteʒit], *s.f. Crust:* oostegite.
oothèque [ɔɔtɛk], *s.f. Ent: Moll:* ootheca.
ootide [ɔɔtid], *s.f. Biol:* ootid.
opacifier [ɔpasifje], *v.tr.* to make (sth.) opaque, to opacify (sth.).
s'opacifier, to become opaque, to opacify.
opacimètre [ɔpasimɛtr̥], *s.m.* opacimeter, densitometer.
opacimétrie [ɔpasimetri], *s.f. Opt:* opacimetry.
opacité [ɔpasite], *s.f.* **1.** opacity (of body); cloudiness (of liquid). **2.** darkness, denseness (of wood, of the intellect).
opah [ɔpa], *s.m. Ich:* opah, sunfish, moonfish.
opale [ɔpal]. **1.** *s.f.* opal; **o. incrustante,** siliceous sinter; **o. perlière,** pearl sinter; **o. xyloïde,** wood opal; **la côte d'O.,** the Pas-de-Calais coast. **2.** *a.inv.* opalescent; **verre o.,** opal glass; *El:* **ampoule o.,** pearl, inside-frosted, bulb.
opalescence [ɔpalɛs(s)ɑ̃ːs], *s.f.* opalescence.
opalescent [ɔpalɛs(s)ɑ̃], *a.* opalescent.
opalin, -ine [ɔpalɛ̃, -in]. **1.** *a.* opaline (hue, reflection). **2.** *s.f.* **opaline,** opaline. **3.** *s.f. Prot:* **opaline,** opalinid; *pl.* **opalines,** Opalinidae.
opalisation [ɔpalizasjɔ̃], *s.f.* opalizing; manufacture of opal glass.
opalisé [ɔpalize], *a.* **1.** opalized (stone, etc.). **2.** opalescent (haze, etc.).
opaliser [ɔpalize], *v.tr.* to opalize, to give an opalescent appearance to (sth.).
opaque [ɔpak], *a.* opaque.
ope [ɔp], *s.f. Const:* (*a*) aperture, opening (in a wall); (*b*) wall box, beam box.
open [ɔpɛn], *a. Golf:* open (championship).
opéra [ɔpera], *s.m.* **1.** opera; **grand o.,** grand opera; **o. bouffe,** opera bouffe, comic opera. **2.** opera house. **3.** *Games:* **faire o.,** to win the jackpot.
opérable [ɔperabl̩], *a. Surg:* operable (patient, tumour, etc.).
opéra-comique [ɔperakɔmik], *s.m.* opera comique, opera with spoken dialogue; *pl. opéras-comiques.*
opérande [ɔperɑ̃ːd], *s.m.* (*computers*) operand.
opérant [ɔperɑ̃], *a.* **1.** operative; **rendre un décret o.,** to put a decree into operation, to make a decree operative. **2.** *Theol:* operating (grace).
opérateur, -trice [ɔperatœːr, -tris], *s.* operator. **1.** (*a*) (machine) operator; *Typ:* machine setter; *Cin:* camera man; **o. des sons,** mixer; **o. de radio,** radio operator; (*b*) *St.Exch:* **o. à la hausse,** operator for a rise; bull; **o. à la baisse,** operator for a fall; bear; (*c*) operating surgeon. **2.** *s.m. Mec.E:* working piece or pieces (of a machine).

opératif, -ive [ɔperatif, -iːv], *a.* operative, active.

opération [ɔperasjɔ̃], *s.f.* **1.** operation, working (of God, nature); process; **opérations de l'esprit,** processes of the mind. **2.** (*a*) **opérations militaires,** military operations; **o. combinée,** combined operation; **o. mathématique,** mathematical operation; **champ, théâtre, d'opérations,** field, theatre, of operations; *Av:* **centre d'opérations,** operational centre; (*b*) (*computers*) **code o.,** operation code; **registre d'o.,** operation register; **o. unaire,** unary operation; (*c*) *F:* **o. baisse de prix,** price-slashing campaign; (*d*) **o. chirurgicale,** surgical operation; **subir une o.,** to undergo an operation; **faire l'o. de l'appendicite,** to perform an operation for appendicitis; to operate for appendicitis; **salle d'o.,** operating room; (in hospital) operating theatre; **o. à chaud,** emergency operation (for appendicitis, etc.); **o. à froid,** interval operation. **3.** (commercial) transaction; deal; speculation; **o. (réglée) au comptant,** cash transaction; *St.Exch:* spot deal; **opérations de Bourse,** Stock Exchange business or transactions; **o. à la hausse,** bull transaction; **o. à la baisse,** bear transaction; **o. blanche,** break-even transaction; *F:* **vous n'avez pas fait là une belle o.!** well, that wasn't a very good deal, a very good spec! **4.** *Typ:* **opérations,** table work.

opérationnel, -elle [ɔperasjɔnɛl], *a. Mil: Ind: etc:* operational; **recherche opérationnelle,** operational research, *U.S:* management science; **ambiance opérationnelle,** operational environment; **besoins opérationnels,** operational requirements; **coûts opérationnels,** operational costs; *Mth:* **calcul o.,** operational calculus.

opératoire [ɔperatwaːr], *a.* **1.** (mode, etc.) of operation; (*computers*) **instruction o.,** operational instruction. **2.** *Surg:* operative (mode of procedure, etc.); **médecine o.,** surgery.

operculaire [ɔpɛrkylɛːr]. **1.** *a. Biol:* opercular. **2.** *s.m. Ich:* opercle, opercular(e).

opercule [ɔpɛrkyl], *s.m.* cover, lid, cap; *Nat.Hist:* operculum; lid (of capsule, etc.); gill cover (of fish); *Nau:* **o. de hublot,** deadlight; *Navy:* **o. d'acier,** steel hatch-cover; *Tchn:* **o. de soupape,** valve plug.

operculé [ɔpɛrkyle]. **1.** *a. Nat.Hist:* operculate(d). **2.** *s.m.pl. Moll:* **operculés,** Operculata.

operculiforme [ɔpɛrkylifɔrm], *a.* operculiform.

opéré, -ée [ɔpere], *s.* patient (who has been operated upon).

opérer [ɔpere], *v.tr.* (**j'opère, n. opérons; j'opérerai**) to operate. **1.** to bring about, to work, to effect; **la foi opère des miracles,** faith works miracles; **o. le salut de qn,** to bring about the salvation of s.o.; **o. une grande réforme,** to carry out a great reform; *Mil:* **o. une retraite,** to effect a retreat; **o. un sondage,** (i) *Tchn:* to sink a bore-hole; (ii) *Pol.Ec: etc:* to take a sample test; to take an opinion poll. **2.** (*a*) to carry out, perform (multiplication, *Ch:* synthesis, etc.); (*b*) *Surg:* **o. un malade, un appendice, un abcès,** to operate on, perform an operation on, a patient, an appendix, an abscess; **être opéré pour (une hernie, etc.),** to be operated upon for (rupture, etc.); **être opéré de la pierre,** to be operated on for stone; **se faire o.,** to undergo, have, an operation; **o. qn à chaud,** to operate on s.o. in the acute stage; **o. qn à froid,** to operate on s.o. between attacks. **3.** (*a*) *abs.* (*of remedy*) to work, act; **son éloquence opéra sur la foule;** his eloquence swayed the crowd; (*b*) (*of rule, tendency, etc.*) to apply, obtain.

s'opérer, to be brought about, to take place; **le miracle s'est opéré tout seul,** the miracle came about of itself; **un changement complet s'était opéré dans sa vie,** a complete change had been brought about in his life; **une révolution s'opéra dans son esprit,** his attitude, opinions, feelings, underwent a complete change.

opérette [ɔperɛt], *s.f. Mus:* operetta; musical comedy; light opera.

Ophélie[1] [ɔfeli], *Pr.n.f.* Ophelia.

ophélie[2], *s.f. Ann:* ophelia.

ophiase [ɔfjaːz], *s.f.* (*a*) *Med:* alopecia, areata; (*b*) round bald patch (on crown of head).

ophicalcite [ɔfikalsit], *s.f. Miner:* ophicalcite.

ophicléide [ɔfikleiːd], *s.m. Mus: A:* **1.** ophicleide. **2.** ophicleidist.

ophidien, -ienne [ɔfidjɛ̃, -jɛn]. **1.** *a.* ophidian, snake-like. **2.** *s.m. Rept:* ophidian, *pl.* ophidians, Ophidia.

ophiocéphalidés [ɔfjɔsefalide], *s.m.pl. Ich:* Ophi(o)cephalidae.

ophioglosse [ɔfjɔglɔs], *s.m. Bot:* ophioglossum; **o. vulgaire,** adder's tongue.

ophiographie [ɔfjɔgrafi], *s.f.* ophiography.

ophiolâtrie [ɔfjɔlɑtri], *s.f.* ophiolatry.

ophiologie [ɔfjɔlɔʒi], *s.f.* ophiology.

ophiologiste [ɔfjɔlɔʒist], *s.m.* ophiologist.

ophiomorphique [ɔfjɔmɔrfik], *a.* ophiomorphic.

ophioplutéus [ɔfjɔplyteys], *s.m. Echin:* ophiopluteus.

ophisaure [ɔfisɔːr], *s.m. Rept:* glass snake; (*genus*) Ophi(o)saurus.

ophite[1] [ɔfit], *s.m. Miner:* ophite.

ophite[2], *s.m. Rel.H:* Ophite.

ophitique [ɔfitik], *a. Miner:* ophitic.

ophiure [ɔfjyːr], *s.f. Echin:* ophiuran, sand star, brittle star; *pl.* **ophiures,** Ophiurae.

ophiurides [ɔfjyrid], *s.m.pl. Echin:* Ophiuroidea, Ophiurae.

ophrys [ɔfris], *s.f. Bot:* ophrys; **o. abeille,** bee orchis, arachnites apiera; **o. araignée.** spider orchis; **o. mouche,** fly orchis.

ophtalmalgie [ɔftalmalʒi], *s.f. Med:* ophthalmalgia.

ophtalmie [ɔftalmi], *s.f. Med: etc:* ophthalmia; **o. des neiges,** snow blindness; *Vet:* **o. périodique,** pink-eye; moon blindness.

ophtalmique [ɔftalmik]. **1.** *a. Anat: Med:* opthalmic (nerve, salve, etc.). **2.** *s.m.* ophthalmic remedy.

ophtalmoblennorrhée [ɔftalmɔblenɔre], *s.f. Med:* ophthalmo-blennorrhea.

ophtalmocèle [ɔftalmɔsɛl], *s.f.* ophthalmocele.

ophtalmodynamomètre [ɔftalmɔdinamɔmɛtr], *s.m. Med:* ophthalmodynamometer.

ophtalmodynie [ɔftalmɔdini], *s.f. Med:* ophthalmodynia.

ophtalmographie [ɔftalmɔgrafi], *s.f.* ophthalmography.

ophtalmologie [ɔftalmɔlɔʒi], *s.f.* ophthalmology.

ophtalmologique [ɔftalmɔlɔʒik], *a.* ophthalmologic(al).

ophtalmologiste [ɔftalmɔlɔʒist], *s.m.* & *f.*, **ophtalmologue** [ɔftalmɔlɔg], *s.m.* & *f.* ophthalmologist, oculist.

ophtalmomalacie [ɔftalmɔmalasi], *s.f. Med:* opthalmomalacia.

ophtalmomètre [ɔftalmɔmɛtr], *s.m. Med:* ophthalmometer.

ophtalmométrie [ɔftalmɔmetri], *s.f. Med:* ophthalmometry.

ophtalmoplastie [ɔftalmɔplasti], *s.f. Surg:* ophthalmoplasty.

ophtalmoplégie [ɔftalmɔpleʒi], *s.f. Med:* ophthalmoplegia.

ophtalmoptose [ɔftalmɔptoːz], *s.f. Med:* ophthalmoptosin, ophthalmoptosis.

ophtalmo(-)réaction [ɔftalmɔreaksjɔ̃], *s.f.* ophthalmoreaction.

ophtalmorragie [ɔftalmɔraʒi], *s.f. Med:* ophthalmorrhagia.

ophtalmosaurus [ɔftalmɔsɔrys], *s.m. Paleont:* ophthalmosaurus.

ophtalmoscope [ɔftalmɔskɔp], *s.m. Med:* ophthalmoscope.

ophtalmoscopie [ɔftalmɔskɔpi], *s.f. Med:* ophthalmoscopy.

ophtalmoscopique [ɔftalmɔskɔpik], *a. Med:* ophthalmoscopic.

ophtalmostat [ɔftalmɔstat], *s.m.* ophthalmostat.

ophtalmotomie [ɔftalmɔtɔmi], *s.f. Surg:* ophthalmotomy.

opiacé [ɔpjase]. **1.** *a.* containing opium; opiated. **2.** *s.m.* opiate.

opiacer [ɔpjase], *v.tr.* (**j'opiaçai(s); n. opiaçons**) to opiate; to mix with opium.

opianique [ɔpjanik], *a. Ch:* opianic.

opiat [ɔpja], *s.m. A:* **1.** *Pharm:* (*a*) opiate, narcotic; (*b*) electuary. **2.** toothpaste.

opilation [ɔpilasjɔ̃], *s.f. Med:* oppilation, obstruction.

opiler [ɔpile], *v.tr. Med:* to oppilate, obstruct.

opiliacées [ɔpiljase], *s.f.pl. Bot:* Opiliaceae.

opilions [ɔpiljɔ̃], *s.m.pl. Arach:* harvest spiders.

opimes [ɔpim], *a.f.pl. used in* **dépouilles o.,** (i) *Rom.Ant:* spolia opima; (ii) rich profit.

opinant [ɔpinɑ̃], *s.m. A:* speaker, voter (in debate, etc.); **le premier o.,** the first speaker (on the subject of debate).

opiner [ɔpine], *v.i. O:* to opine; to be of opinion (que, that); **o. pour, contre, une proposition, en faveur d'une proposition,** to express an opinion, to vote, for, against, in favour of, a proposition; **o. de la tête,** to nod approval, to nod assent; **on opina pour une opération,** they were of opinion, they decided, that an operation was necessary; **o. à faire qch.,** to decide to do sth.; **o. pour que, à ce que, qch. se fasse,** to decide in favour of sth. being done; *s.a.* BONNET 1.

opiniâtre [ɔpinjɑːtr], *a.* obstinate; (*a*) self-opinionated; (*b*) self-willed, headstrong (child); stubborn (mule, mind, person); **idées opiniâtres,** hidebound notions; **o. à faire qch.,** set on doing sth.; (*c*) persistent, unyielding (cough, fight); **résistance o.,** stout, dogged, resistance; **haine o.,** unyielding, relentless, hatred.

opiniâtrement [ɔpinjɑtrəmɑ̃], *adv.* obstinately, stubbornly; stoutly; doggedly.

opiniâtrer (s') [sɔpinjɑtre], *v.pr. A:* to remain stubborn, obstinate; **s'o. dans une opinion,** to cling to an opinion, to be wedded to an opinion; **s'o. à faire qch.,** to persist stubbornly in doing sth., to work doggedly at sth.

opiniâtreté [ɔpinjɑtrəte], *s.f.* (*a*) obstinacy, stubbornness; (*b*) perseverance, determination, resolution.

opinion [ɔpinjɔ̃], *s.f.* opinion (de, of; **sur,** about); view, judgment; **opinions toutes faites,** cut and dried opinions; **affaire, chose, d'o.,** matter of opinion; *A:* **mal d'o.,** imaginary illness; **l'o. (publique),** public opinion; **créer un mouvement d'o.,** to excite public opinion; **sondage d'o.,** opinion poll; **avoir une o. sur qch.,** to have an opinion about sth.; **émettre une o.,** to give, advance, express, put forward, an opinion; **partager l'opinion de qn,** to agree with s.o.; **amener qn à son o.,** to bring s.o. round, over, to one's way of thinking; **suivant, selon, l'o. de . . .,** in the opinion of . . .; **avoir bonne, mauvaise, o. de qn,** to have a good, bad, opinion of s.o.; **je n'ai pas moins bonne o. de lui parce que . . .,** I think no worse of him because . . .; **avoir une o. favorable de qn,** to hold a favourable opinion of s.o.; **avoir une haute o. de qn,** to think highly of s.o.; **se faire une o. de, sur, qn, de qch.,** to form an opinion about s.o., sth.; **donner bonne o. de sa capacité,** to make a good impression; *A:* **aller aux opinions,** to put the matter to the vote; *Prov:* **autant de têtes autant d'opinions,** as many opinions as there are heads.

opiomane [ɔpjɔman]. **1.** *a.* opium-eating, opium-smoking (person, habit). **2.** *s.m.* & *f.* opium eater, smoker; opium addict, opiomaniac.

opiomanie [ɔpjɔmani], *s.f. Med:* opiomania.

opiophage [ɔpjɔfaːʒ]. **1.** *a.* opium-eating. **2.** *s.* opium eater.

opiophagie [ɔpjɔfaʒi], *s.f.* opium eating.

opisthobranche [ɔpistɔbrɑ̃ːʃ], *Moll:* **1.** *a.* opisthobranchiate. **2.** *s.m.pl.* **opisthobranches,** Opisthobranchia(ta).

opisthocèle, opisthocœle [ɔpistɔsɛl], *Z:* (*a*) *a.* opisthocœlous; (*b*) *s.m.* opisthocœlian.

opisthodome [ɔpistɔdɔm], *s.m. Gr.Ant:* opisthodome, opisthodomos.

opisthoglyphe [ɔpistɔglif], *Biol:* **1.** *a.* opisthoglyphous, opisthoglyphic. **2.** *s.m.pl. Rept:* **opisthoglyphes,** Opisthoglypha.

opisthognathisme [ɔpistɔgnatism], *s.m. Anat:* opisthognathism.

opisthographe [ɔpistɔgraf], *a.* opisthographic(al).

opisthotique [ɔpistɔtik], *a. Anat:* opisthotic.

opisthotonos [ɔpistɔtɔnɔs], *s.m. Med:* opisthotonos.

opium [ɔpjɔm], *s.m.* (*a*) opium; **fumerie d'o.,** opium den; (*b*) **la religion est l'o. du peuple,** religion is an opiate for the people, the masses.

opodeldoch [ɔpɔdɛldɔk], *s.m. Pharm:* opodeldoc, soap liniment.

opodidyme [ɔpɔdidim], *s.m. Ter:* opodidymus.

oponce [ɔpɔ̃ːs], *s.m. Bot:* opuntia, prickly pear.

opontiacées [ɔpɔ̃tjase], *s.f.pl. Bot:* Opuntiaceae.

opopanax [ɔpɔpanaks], *s.m. Bot: Pharm: etc:* opopanax.

opossum [ɔpɔsɔm], *s.m. Z:* opossum.

opothérapie [ɔpɔterapi], *s.f. Med:* opotherapy; organotherapy.

opothérapique [ɔpɔterapik], *a. Med:* opotherapeutic, organotherapeutic.

oppidum [ɔpidɔm], *s.m. Archeol:* oppidum.

oppien[1], **-ienne** [ɔpjɛ̃, -jɛn], *a. Rom.Hist:* Oppian.

Oppien[2], *Pr.n.m. Gr.Lit:* Oppian.

opportun, -une [ɔpɔrtœ̃, -yn], *a.* (*a*) opportune, seasonable, timely, well-timed, convenient; **attendre l'heure opportune,** to wait for the right moment; **arriver en temps o.,** to arrive opportunely, at the right moment; (*b*) expedient, advisable; **vous prendrez les mesures opportunes,** you will take such measures as are called for; **il ne semble pas o. que** + *sub.*, it does not seem advisable that . . .; **il serait o. de . . .,** it would be advisable to . . ..

opportunément [ɔpɔrtynemɑ̃], *adv.* opportunely, at the right moment.

opportunisme [ɔpɔrtynism], *s.m.* opportunism; time-serving; **faire de l'o.,** to swim with the tide.

opportuniste [ɔpɔrtynist]. **1.** *a.* time-serving. **2.** *s.m.* & *f.* opportunist; time-server.

opportunité [ɔpɔrtynite], *s.f.* **1.** (*a*) opportuneness, timeliness; appositeness (of phrase, etc.); (*b*) expediency, advisableness, advisability (of project, etc.). **2.** favourable occasion; opportunity.

opposabilité [ɔpozabilite], *s.f.* opposability.

opposable [ɔpozabl̩], *a.* **1.** opposable (à, to). **2.** *Jur:* demurrable.

opposant, -ante [ɔpozɑ̃, -ɑ̃:t]. **1.** *a.* opposing, adverse (party, etc.). **2.** *s.m.* (*a*) opponent; **o. d'une mesure,** voter against a measure; *Jur:* **se rendre o. à un acte, à un mariage,** to oppose an action, a marriage; (*b*) *Anat:* opponens (muscle); **o. du pouce, du petit doigt,** opponens pollicis, opponens minimi digiti.

opposé [ɔpoze]. **1.** *a.* (*a*) opposed, opposing (armies, characters, etc.); opposite (side, shore); contrary (interests, advice); antagonistic (interests); facing (angles); **angles opposés par le sommet,** vertically opposite angles; *Bot:* **feuilles opposées,** (i) opposite leaves; (ii) bifarious leaves; **suivre une direction opposée,** to go the opposite way; **naviguer à bord o.,** to be on the opposite tack; **navires faisant des routes directement opposées,** ships meeting; **nous faisions des routes directement opposées,** we were meeting end on; **leurs opinions sont diamétralement opposées,** their views are poles apart; **tons opposés,** contrasting colours; (*b*) **être o. à une mesure, à ce que qch. se fasse,** to be opposed to a measure; to be against a measure; to be opposed to sth. being done; to be against sth. being done; to be averse to sth. **2.** *s.m.* (*a*) the contrary, reverse, opposite (of sth.); **à l'o.,** on the contrary; **à l'o. de . . .,** contrary to . . .; *F:* **cet enfant est tout l'o. de son frère,** this child is just the opposite of his brother; (*b*) **la gare est à l'o.,** the station is (on the) opposite (side).

opposément [ɔpozemɑ̃], *adv.* in complete opposition; from a completely different point of view.

opposer [ɔpoze], *v.tr.* **1.** to oppose; to set (sth.) over against (sth.); **o. une équipe à une autre,** to match one team against another; **o. une glace à une fenêtre,** to set a mirror opposite a window; **les forces qui s'opposent,** the forces opposed to each other; **je n'ai rien à o. à ce raisonnement,** I have nothing to urge against, no objection to, this argument; **o. une vigoureuse résistance,** to put up, offer, a vigorous resistance; **o. une autorité à une autre,** to set one authority against another; *Jur:* **o. une exception,** to demur, to raise an objection in law; **o. son veto,** to exercise one's veto. **2.** to compare, to contrast (à, with); **o. le vice à la vertu,** to contrast vice with virtue.

s'opposer. s'o. à qch., to oppose sth.; to be opposed to sth.; **s'o. résolument à qch.,** to set one's face against sth.; **s'o. à un projet, à un mariage,** to set oneself, one's face, against, to stand in the way of, a scheme, a marriage; **il n'y a pas de loi qui s'y oppose,** there is no law against it; **rien ne s'oppose à votre succès,** nothing stands between you and success; **je m'y suis opposé de toutes mes forces,** I opposed it, resisted it, tooth and nail; **ma conscience s'oppose à faire cela,** it goes against my conscience to do that; **je ne m'oppose pas à ce qu'il le fasse,** I have no objection to his doing so; **il s'y oppose absolument,** he won't hear of it.

opposite [ɔpozit], *s.m.* (*a*) *A: or Lit:* opposite, contrary; **il est tout l'o. de son frère,** he is the exact opposite of his brother; **il pense tout l'o. de ce qu'il dit,** he thinks quite the reverse of what he says; (*b*) **à l'o.,** facing, in front of; **maison à l'o. de l'église,** house opposite to, facing, the church.

oppositif, -ive [ɔpozitif, -i:v], *a.* oppositive.

opposition [ɔpozisjɔ̃], *s.f.* **1.** (*a*) opposition; **faire une o. résolue à qch.,** to offer determined opposition to sth.; **mettre o. à qch.,** to oppose sth.; **agir en o. avec un droit,** to act in contravention of a right; **agir en o. avec la manière de voir de qn,** to act contrary to s.o.'s views; **se mettre en o. avec qn,** to come into conflict with s.o.; *Pol:* **le parti de l'o.,** the opposition; *Com:* **frapper d'o.,** to stop payment of (cheque, etc.); **voter une loi sans o.,** to vote a law *nem con*; (*b*) *Jur:* (i) distraint, execution; **o. sur titre,** attachment against securities; (ii) **mettre, former, o. à qch.,** to oppose, to lodge an objection to, to ask for an injunction against, sth.; **faire o. à une décision,** to appeal against a decision; **jugement susceptible d'o.,** judgment liable to stay of execution; (iii) caveat; **mettre o. à un mariage,** to put in, enter, a caveat to a marriage; to forbid the banns. **2.** contrast, antithesis; **par o. à qch.,** as opposed to sth.; **couleurs en o.,** contrasting colours. **3.** *Astr:* opposition (of planets); **o. supérieure, inférieure,** superior, inferior, opposition; **en o.,** in opposition.

oppositionnel, -elle [ɔpozisjɔnɛl], *Pol:* **1.** *a.* opposition (party). **2.** *s.* member of the opposition.

oppressant [ɔprɛsɑ̃, -pre], *a.* (*a*) oppressive; (*b*) overwhelming; depressing.

oppressé [ɔprɛse, -pre-], *a.* oppressed; **avoir la poitrine oppressée,** to feel as if one had a weight on one's chest, to feel a tightness across the chest; **malade o.,** patient who has difficulty in breathing.

oppresser [ɔprɛse, -pre-], *v.tr.* to oppress; (*a*) to weigh down; to lie heavy on (the chest, conscience, etc.); to impede (respiration); **oppressé par un asthme,** oppressed by asthma; (*b*) to deject, depress; **souvenirs qui oppressent,** depressing memories; **sa tristesse l'oppressait,** he was weighed down with sorrow.

oppresseur [ɔprɛsœ:r, -pre-]. **1.** *s.m.* oppressor. **2.** *a.m.* oppressive, tyrannical.

oppressif, -ive [ɔprɛsif, -i:v; -pre-], *a.* oppressive (government, etc.).

oppression [ɔprɛsjɔ̃, -pre-], *s.f.* oppression. **1. o. de la poitrine,** weight on, tightness of, the chest; difficulty in breathing; breathlessness. **2. o. d'un peuple,** oppression, crushing, of a nation.

oppressivement [ɔprɛsivmɑ̃-, -pre-], *adv.* oppressively, crushingly, tyranically.

opprimant [ɔprimɑ̃]. **1.** *a.* oppressing, oppressive; **une religion ni opprimée ni opprimante,** a religion neither oppressed nor oppressive. **2.** *s. See* OPPRIMÉ.

opprimé [ɔprime], *a.* oppressed, crushed, downtrodden (nation, etc.); *s.* **les opprimants et les opprimés,** the oppressors and the oppressed.

opprimer [ɔprime], *v.tr.* (*a*) to oppress, crush (down) (a people, the weak, etc.); (*b*) *A:* to kill, suppress.

opprobre [ɔprɔbr̥], *s.m.* disgrace, shame, opprobrium, infamy; **vivre dans l'o.,** to live in infamy; **couvert d'o.,** loaded, covered, with shame; **il est l'o. du genre humain,** he is a disgrace to mankind.

opsonine [ɔpsɔnin], *s.f. Med:* opsonin.

opsonique [ɔpsɔnik], *a. Med:* opsonic (index, etc.).

optant, -ante [ɔptɑ̃, -ɑ̃:t], *a. & s.* (person) exercising an option, optant; *Fin:* taker of an option; **les optants hongrois,** the people who elected to become Hungarian subjects.

optatif, -ive [ɔptatif, -i:v]. **1.** *a.* optative (formula, mood). **2.** *s.m. Gram:* optative (mood).

opter [ɔpte], *v.i.* to opt; **o. entre deux choses,** to choose, decide, to make one's option, between two things; **o. pour qch.,** to decide in favour of sth., to opt for sth., to choose sth.

opticien, -ienne [ɔptisjɛ̃, -jɛn], *s.* optician.

optimal, -aux [ɔptimal, -o], *a.* optimal.

optimaliser [ɔptimalize], *v.tr.* to perfect; to make as good as possible.

optimisation [ɔptimizasjɔ̃], *s.f.* optim(al)ization.

optimiser [ɔptimize], *v.tr.* (*computers*) to optim(al)ize; **programmation optimisée,** optimum programming.

optimisme [ɔptimism], *s.m.* optimism; sanguineness (à l'égard de, with regard to); **être porté à l'o.,** to be an optimist; to be of a sanguine, an optimistic, disposition, nature.

optimiste [ɔptimist]. **1.** *a.* optimistic (person); sanguine (disposition). **2.** *s.m. & f.* optimist.

optimum [ɔptimɔm], *a.inv. & s.m.inv. Biol:* optimum (conditions of life); *Pol.Ec:* **o. de population,** optimum population density; *pl. optimums, occ. optima.*

option [ɔpsjɔ̃], *s.f.* option, choice (**de, entre,** between); *St.Exch: etc:* **souscrire des valeurs à o.,** to buy an option on stock; **o. d'achat, pour acheter,** call; **o. de vente,** put; **jour d'o.,** option day; **levée d'o.,** exercise, taking up, of option; **demander une o. pour un sujet de film,** to ask for an option on the film rights (of a book, etc.); **prendre une o. sur tous les ouvrages à paraître d'un auteur,** to take an option on all the future works of an author; *Sch:* **matières à o.,** optional subjects.

optionnaire [ɔpsjɔnɛ:r], *s.m. Fin:* giver of an option.

optique [ɔptik]. **1.** *a.* optic (nerve); optic, visual (angle); optical (illusion); **télégraphie o.,** visual signalling; **axe o., banc o., centre o.,** optical axis, bench, centre; **diagramme o.,** optical pattern; **filtre o.,** optical filter; **portée o.,** optical range; **verre o.,** optical glass; **renversement o. de l'image,** optical reversal of image; (*of computer*) **analyse o., lecture o.,** optical scanning; **analyseur o.,** optical scanner, image dissector; **lecteur o.,** optical reader. **2.** *s.f.* (*a*) optics; **instruments d'o.,** *coll.* **optique,** optical instruments; **o. à façon,** practical optics, *U.S:* custom optics; **o. de haute précision,** high precision optics; **o. géométrique,** geometrical optics; **o. électronique, neutronique,** electron, neutron, optics; *Tg:* **transmettre par o.,** to communicate by visual signals; (*b*) **o. du théâtre,** stage perspective; (*c*) *A:* raree show; (*d*) optical system (of projector, etc.); (*e*) outlook; point of view.

optiquement [ɔptikmɑ̃], *adv.* optically.

opto-électronique [ɔptoelɛktrɔnik], *s.f.* opto-electronics.

optomètre [ɔptɔmɛtr̥], *s.m.* optometer.

optométrie [ɔptɔmetri], *s.f.* optometry.

optométrique [ɔptɔmetrik], *a.* optometrical.

optométriste [ɔptɔmetrist], *s.m. & f.* optometrist.

optophone [ɔptɔfɔn], *s.m.* optophone.

opulemment [ɔpylamɑ̃], *adv.* opulently.

opulence [ɔpylɑ̃:s], *s.f.* opulence, affluence; **vivre dans l'o.,** to live in affluence; **nager dans l'o.,** to be rolling in wealth; *F:* **l'o. de ses charmes,** her opulent figure.

opulent [ɔpylɑ̃], *a.* opulent, rich, monied, wealthy (person); affluent (circumstances); abundant (harvest, etc.); *F:* opulent, buxom (figure).

opuntia [ɔpɔ̃sja], *s.m. Bot:* opuntia.

opuntiales [ɔpɔ̃sjal], *s.f.pl. Bot:* Opuntiales.

opuntiées [ɔpɔ̃sje], *s.f.pl. Bot:* Opuntiaceae.

opus [ɔpys], *s.m.* **1.** *Arch:* **o. incertum,** opus incertum; **allée pavée en o. incertum,** path in crazy paving. **2.** *Mus:* opus.

opuscule [ɔpyskyl], *s.m.* opuscule; short (scientific, literary) treatise; pamphlet, tract; booklet.

or[1] [ɔ:r], *s.m.* **1.** gold; **or alluvionnaire,** placer gold; **or vierge,** native gold; **chercheur d'or,** gold digger; *Hist:* **la ruée vers l'or,** the gold rush; **or rouge,** red gold; **or vert,** electrum; **or blanc,** white gold; **or mat,** mat gold; **or moulu,** ormulu; **or mussif,** mosaic gold, dissulphide of tin; *F:* **or noir,** oil; **or brut,** gold in nuggets; **or en barres,** ingot gold; bullion; **c'est de l'or en barres,** (i) it's as safe as the Bank of England; (ii) he's as straight as a die; **or en poudre,** powdered gold; **poudre d'or,** gold dust; **vaisselle d'or, or orfévré,** gold plate; **montre d'or, en or,** gold watch; **en or massif,** gold (as opposed to gold-plated); *F:* **c'est en or,** it's easy to deal with; it's a piece of cake; *F:* **j'ai une femme en or,** I've a wonderful wife; my wife's worth her weight in gold; **or en feuille(s),** gold foil; **feuille d'or,** gold leaf; **or de coquille,** shell gold; **bracelet en plaqué (d')or,** rolled-gold bracelet; **acheter, vendre, payer, à prix d'or,** to buy, sell, at an exorbitant price; to pay a fortune (for sth.); **marché, affaire, d'or,** excellent bargain, business; **il vaut son pesant d'or,** he's worth his weight in gold; **cela vaut de l'or,** it's worth its weight in gold; **tout ce qui brille n'est pas or,** all that glitters is not gold; *Hist:* **le camp du Drap d'or,** the Field of the Cloth of Gold; **l'âge d'or,** *Lit:* **le siècle d'or,** the golden age; **tuer la poule aux œufs d'or,** to kill the goose that laid the golden eggs; **cœur d'or,** heart of gold; **parler d'or,** to speak words of wisdom; **je ne m'en départirais pas ni pour or ni pour argent,** I wouldn't part with it for love or money; **adorer le veau d'or,** to worship the golden calf; **manger dans l'or,** to eat off gold plate; **livre d'or,** (i) (official) visitors' book; (ii) roll of honour; *F:* **pont d'or,** offer of high salary (as inducement); *Geog: A:* **la Côte de l'Or,** the Gold Coast. **2. or (monnayé),** gold (specie); **payer qn en or,** to pay s.o. in gold; **nager dans l'or, rouler sur l'or, marcher sur l'or, être (tout) cousu d'or,** to be rolling in money. **3. or (de) couleur,** gold size. **4.** gold (colour); *Her:* or; **vieil or,** old gold; **chevelure d'or,** golden hair; **filet or,** gold (gilt) fillet; **avec titre en lettres d'or,** with a gilt-lettered title.

or[2], *conj.* now; **or, pour revenir à ce que nous disions,** now to come back to what we were saying; **or çà,** now then; **or . . ., donc . . .,** now . . ., therefore . . .; **or donc,** well then; **avant de le lire, je pensais que le livre était bon; or, il ne l'était pas,** before reading it, I thought the book was good; well, it wasn't.

oracle [ɔrɑkl̥], *s.m.* oracle; **style d'o.,** oracular style; **en (style d') o.,** oracularly; **rendre un o.,** to pronounce an oracle; **parler d'un ton d'o.,** to speak with assurance, sententiously, peremptorily; **parler comme un o.,** to talk like an oracle.

oraculaire [ɔrakylɛ:r], *a.* oracular.

orage [ɔraːʒ], *s.m.* (*a*) (thunder)storm; **pluie d'o.,** (i) thundery rain, thunderstorm; (ii) violent downpour; **orages locaux,** local thunder(storms); **le temps est à l'o.,** the weather's thundery; there's thunder in the air; **il va faire de l'o.,** there's a storm brewing; **l'o. s'est dissipé, est passé,** the storm has blown over; (*b*) **o. magnétique,** magnetic storm; **o. volcanique,** storm accompanying a volcanic eruption; (*c*) **o. politique,** political storm; **regard qui est à l'o.,** ominous look; **tout l'o. tombera sur vous,** you'll have to bear the brunt of the storm.

orageusement [ɔraʒøzmɑ̃], *adv.* stormily.

orageux, -euse [ɔraʒø, -øːz], (*a*) thundery (weather, sky, etc.); (*b*) stormy (season, sea, etc.); (*c*) agitated, stormy (life); stormy, heated (discussion, meeting).

oraison [ɔrɛzɔ̃], *s.f.* **1.** *A:* (*a*) oration, speech; *still so used in* **o. funèbre,** funeral oration; (*b*) *Gram:* **les parties de l'o.,** the parts of speech; **o. indirecte,** indirect speech. **2.** prayer; **faire ses oraisons,** to say one's prayers; **l'o. dominicale,** the Lord's Prayer.

oral, -aux [ɔral, -o]. **1.** *a.* (*a*) oral (tradition, teaching, examination); verbal (deposition); (*b*) *Anat:* oral (cavity). **2.** *s.m.* oral examination; viva voce examination; *F:* **rater l'o.,** to fail, to be ploughed in the oral, in the viva.

oralement [ɔralmɑ̃], *adv.* orally; by word of mouth.

oralité [ɔralite], *s.f.* orality.

oranais, -aise [ɔranɛ, -ɛːz], *a. & s. Geog:* (native, inhabitant) of Oran.

orange[1] [ɔrɑ̃ːʒ], *s.f.* **1.** (*a*) orange; **o. amère,** bitter orange, Seville orange; **o. douce,** (sweet) orange; **o. sanguine,** blood orange; **o. navel,** navel orange; **écorce d'orange,** orange-peel; (*b*) *A:* = ORANGER[1]. **2.** *s.m.* orange (colour); *a.inv.* orange(-coloured). **3.** *Hort:* (*a*) **o. musquée, o. rouge, o. d'hiver,** varieties of pear; (*b*) *P:* **o. à cochons, o. de Limousin,** potato.

Orange[2], *Pr.n. Geog:* **1.** Orange (in S. of Fr.); *Hist:* **le Prince d'O.,** the Prince of Orange. **2. le fleuve O.,** the Orange River; **l'État libre d'Orange,** the (Province of the) Orange Free State.

orangé [ɔrɑ̃ʒe], *a. & s.m.* orange (colour); orange-coloured.

orangeade [ɔrɑ̃ʒad], *s.f.* orangeade.

orangeat [ɔrɑ̃ʒa], *s.m.* candied orange peel.

orangeois, -oise [ɔrɑ̃ʒwa, -waːz], *a. & s. Geog:* (native, inhabitant) of Orange (in S. of Fr.).

oranger[1] [ɔrɑ̃ʒe], *s.m. Bot:* orange tree; **couronne de fleurs d'o.,** wreath of orange blossom; **eau de fleur(s) d'o.,** orange-flower water.

oranger[2], **-ère** [ɔrɑ̃ʒe, -ɛːr], *s. O:* orange seller.

oranger[3], *v.tr.* (**j'orangeai(s); nous orangeons**) to dye, colour, (sth.) orange.

orangeraie [ɔrɑ̃ʒrɛ], *s.f.* orange grove.

orangerie [ɔrɑ̃ʒri], *s.f.* orangery, greenhouse for oranges.

orangette [ɔrɑ̃ʒɛt], *s.f.* (unripe Seville) orange (for preserving).

orangisme [ɔrɑ̃ʒism], *s.m. Hist: Pol:* Orangism.

orangiste[1] [ɔrɑ̃ʒist], *Hist: Pol:* **1.** *s.m.* Orangeman (in Ireland). **2.** *a.* **parti o.,** Orange, Orangist, party (in the Netherlands).

orangiste[2], *s.m. Hort:* orange grower.

orangite [ɔrɑ̃ʒit], *s.f. Miner:* thorite.

orang-outan(g) [ɔrɑ̃utɑ̃], *s.m. Z:* orang-outang, orang-utan; *pl. orangs-outan(g)s.*

orant, -ante [ɔrɑ̃, -ɑ̃ːt], *Sculp: etc:* (*a*) *a.* praying (figure, on tomb); (*b*) *s.* praying figure, orant.

orateur [ɔratœːr], *s.m.* (*with occ. f.* **oratrice** [ɔratris], *but a woman is more usu. referred to as* **l'orateur**). **1.** orator, speaker; *occ. f.* oratress; **être né o.,** to be a born speaker; to be naturally eloquent; **o. de carrefour,** soap-box orator, stump orator, *U.S:* stump speaker. **2. l'o. de la compagnie,** the spokesman, -woman, of the party; *Pol:* (*in Eng., Canada*) **Monsieur l'O.,** Mr Speaker.

oratoire[1] [ɔratwaːr], *a.* oratorical (talent, etc.); **morceau o.,** oration; **l'art o.,** (the art of) oratory; public speaking; **débit o.,** oratorical delivery; **lutte o.,** battle of words.

oratoire[2], *s.m.* oratory. **1.** chapel for private worship. **2.** *Ecc:* (the religious society of the) Oratory; **les pères de l'O.,** the Oratorian fathers, the Oratorians.

oratoirement [ɔratwarmɑ̃], *adv.* oratorically.

oratorien [ɔratɔrjɛ̃], *a. & s.m. Ecc:* Oratorian (father).

oratorio [ɔratɔrjo], *s.m. Mus:* oratorio.

orbe[1] [ɔrb], *s.m.* orb. **1.** circle within the orbit (of planet). **2.** globe; sphere; heavenly body; **le sceptre et l'o.,** the sceptre and the orb; *Lit:* **l'o. rouge du soleil,** the red orb of the sun. **3.** *Ich:* **o. épineux,** globe fish, puffer(fish).

orbe[2], *a.* **1. mur o.,** blind wall. **2.** *Surg:* **coup o.,** bruise, contusion.

orbicole [ɔrbikɔl], *a.* **plante o.,** plant found in all regions of the world, with a world-wide distribution.

orbiculaire [ɔrbikylɛːr]. **1.** *a.* orbicular (bone, ligament); spherical, circular (movement); *Bot:* round-flowered. **2.** *s.m.* orbicular muscle; sphincter; **o. des paupières,** winking muscle.

orbitage [ɔrbitaːʒ], *s.m.* orbiting (of satellite, spacecraft).

orbitaire [ɔrbitɛːr], *a.* (*a*) *Anat:* orbital (nerve, etc.); **les arcades orbitaires,** the orbital arches **fosses orbitaires,** orbital cavities; (*b*) *Orn:* **plumes orbitaires,** orbital feathers.

orbital, -aux [ɔrbital, -o], *a. Astr: etc:* orbital; (motion) in an orbit; **vitesse orbitale,** orbital velocity; **moment o.,** orbital moment.

orbitale [ɔrbital], *s.f. Atom.Ph:* **o. atomique,** atomic orbital; **o. moléculaire,** molecular orbital.

orbite [ɔrbit], *s.f.* **1.** (*a*) orbit (of planet, spacecraft); **o. circulaire, elliptique, polaire,** circular, elliptical, polar, orbit; **o. d'approche, de rattrapage,** catch-up orbit (in orbital rendezvous); **o. d'attente,** parking orbit; **o. de transfert,** transfer orbit; **o. synchrone,** synchronous orbit; **en o., sur o.,** orbiting; in orbit; **sur o. terrestre, lunaire,** earth, moon, orbiting; **effectuer une dizaine de révolutions sur o. lunaire,** to orbit the moon ten times; **mettre, placer, (un satellite, etc.) en o.,** to put (a satellite, etc.) in orbit; **mettre un homme en o.,** to put a man into orbit; **se mettre en o.,** to enter, go into, orbit; **lancer (un satellite, etc.) sur o.,** to launch, boost, (a satellite, etc.) into orbit; **injecter (un satellite, etc.) en o.,** to inject (a satellite, etc.) into orbit; **modifier l'o. d'un véhicule spatial,** to change the orbit of a spacecraft; (*b*) *Ph:* orbit (of electron); (*c*) orbit, sphere of influence; *Pol:* **la Hongrie est attirée dans l'o. de la Russie,** Hungary is drawn into the Russian orbit. **2.** *Anat:* socket, orbit (of the eye); **les yeux lui sortaient des orbites,** his eyes were starting from their sockets.

orbitélaire [ɔrbitelɛːr], *a. Arach:* orbitelous; geometric (spider).

orbitèle [ɔrbitɛl], *s.m. Arach:* orbitelarian, orbitele, geometric spider; *pl.* **orbitèles,** Orbitelariae.

orbiter [ɔrbite], *v.i.* (*of satellite, etc.*) to orbit.

orbitoline [ɔrbitɔlin], *s.f. Paleont:* orbitolina.

orbitolite [ɔrbitɔlit], *s.f. Paleont:* orbitolite.

orbitostat [ɔrbitɔsta], *s.m. Anthr:* orbitostat.

Orcades (les) [lezɔrkad], *Pr.n.f.pl. Geog:* the Orkneys, the Orkney Islands; **les O. du Sud,** (i) the South Orkneys (S. hemisphere); (ii) the Southern Orkneys (Scot.).

orcanette, -ète [ɔrkanɛt], *s.f. Bot:* alkanet, dyer's bugloss.

orcéine [ɔrsein], *s.f. Ch:* orcein.

orchésographie [ɔrkezɔgrafi], *s.f. Danc: Mus:* orchesography; choreography.

orchestique [ɔrkɛstik], *a.* orchestic.

orchestral, -aux [ɔrkɛstral, -o], *a.* orchestral.

orchestrateur [ɔrkɛstratœːr], *s.m. Mus:* orchestrater, orchestrator.

orchestration [ɔrkɛstrasjɔ̃], *s.f. Mus:* orchestration, scoring.

orchestre [ɔrkɛstr̥], *s.m.* **1.** *Gr. & Rom.Ant: Th:* orchestra; **fauteuil d'o.,** orchestra stall. **2.** *Mus:* orchestra; (full) band (including strings); **représentation à grand o.,** performance with a full orchestra, with a full band; **o. d'archets,** string orchestra; **chef d'o.,** (i) conductor of the orchestra; (ii) bandmaster. **3.** *A:* orchestration.

orchestrer [ɔrkɛstre], *v.tr.* **1.** *Mus:* to orchestrate, to score (opera, etc.). **2.** *F:* to organize; **publicité bien orchestrée,** well-organized publicity.

orchidacées [ɔrkidase], *s.f.pl. Bot:* Orchidaceae.

orchidée [ɔrkide], *s.f.* **1.** *Hort:* orchid. **2.** *pl. Bot:* Orchid(ac)eae, orchids.

orchidopexie [ɔrkidɔpɛksi], *s.f. Surg:* orchidopexy.

orchidothérapie [ɔrkidɔterapi], *s.f. Med:* orchidotherapy.

orchidotomie [ɔrkidɔtɔmi], *s.f. Surg:* orchidotomy.

orchis [ɔrkis], *s.m. Bot:* orchis, wild orchid; **o. militaire,** military orchid, soldier orchid; **o. à deux feuilles,** butterfly orchid; **o. pourpre,** purple orchid; **o. taché,** spotted orchid.

orchite [ɔrkit], *s.f. Med:* orchitis.

Orchomène [ɔrkɔmɛn], *Pr.n. A.Geog:* Orchomenus.

orcine [ɔrsin], *s.f.*, **orcinol** [ɔrsinɔl], *s.m. Ch:* orcin, orcinol.

ord [ɔːr], *a. A: & Lit:* filthy.

ordalie [ɔrdali], *s.f. A:* ordeal; **o. de l'eau, du feu,** ordeal by water, by fire; **trancher une cause par o.,** to decide a case by ordeal.

ordinaire [ɔrdinɛːr]. **1.** *a.* (*a*) ordinary, usual, normal, habitual; **le cours o. des choses,** the ordinary course of things; **cela ne se fait pas en temps o.,** it isn't done in ordinary times, ordinarily, under ordinary circumstances; **sa façon o. de procéder,** his usual way of going about things; **dépasser les bornes ordinaires,** to go beyond the normal limits; **vêtements ordinaires,** everyday clothes; **vin o.,** table wine, beverage wine; **sa maladresse o.,** his habitual, usual, clumsiness; **sa réponse o. était que . . .,** his usual reply was that . . .; **il est o. de . . .,** it is usual, normal, to . . .; **peu o.,** unusual, uncommon, out of the ordinary; *F:* **ça alors, c'est pas o.!** well, that's odd if you like! *F:* **eh bien, celle-là n'est pas o.!** well, that's a good one! *Mth:* **fractions ordinaires,** vulgar fractions; *Mus:* **sons ordinaires,** open sounds (of instruments); *Fin:* **actions ordinaires,** ordinary shares; (*b*) **en vente chez votre fournisseur o.,** on sale at your normal supplier's, at the shop you normally deal with; **médecin o. du roi,** physician in ordinary to the king, to His Majesty; *Dipl: A:* **ambassadeur o.,** ambassador ordinary, resident ambassador; *Ecc:* **évêque o.,** diocesan bishop; (*c*) (= *not above the average*) **de taille o.,** ordinary-sized, average-sized; (*of pers.*) of average height; **au-dessus de la taille o.,** above average size; above average height; **ce ne sont pas des génies mais des hommes ordinaires,** they are not geniuses but men of average ability; **une existence tout o.,** a humdrum existence; **livre qui paraît o. au premier aspect,** book which appears commonplace at first sight; **il n'a rien d'o.,** there's nothing commonplace about him; *Pej:* **ce vin est très o.,** this is very indifferent wine; **des gens très ordinaires, tout à fait ordinaires,** (i) unpolished, uneducated, people; (ii) people in very humble circumstances. **2.** *s.m.* (*a*) custom, usual practice; **l'o. de mon existence,** my daily routine; **demain j'irai au bureau comme à mon o.,** tomorrow I shall go to the office as usual; *O:* **contre mon o., j'étais sorti,** contrary to my usual habit, I had gone out; (*b*) usual state of things; normal standard; **événement qui sort de l'o.,** unusual event; **une intelligence qui sort de l'o.,** an intelligence above the average; a brilliant brain; **cela sort de l'o.,** that's unusual; **menu supérieur à l'o.,** menu above the average; **avoir horreur de l'o.,** to have a horror of banality, of a humdrum existence; (*c*) everyday meal; daily bill of fare; *Mil:* (company) mess; *Husb:* daily feed; **auberge où l'o. est excellent,** inn where the fare, the food, the standard of the meals, is excellent; *Mil:* **caporal d'o.,** mess corporal; **fonds d'o.,** mess fund; **la troupe doit manger à l'o.,** privates must mess together; (*d*) *R.C.Ch:* **l'o. de la messe,** the ordinary of the mass; (*e*) *Ecc:* **l'o.,** the diocesan bishop; (*f*) *Post: A:* (the) regular mail service; (*g*) *Jur:* **régler une affaire à l'o.,** to refer a case from the criminal to the civil courts; (*h*) *adv.phr.* **d'o., à l'o.,** *A:* **selon l'o.,** usually, habitually, as a rule; **comme à l'o., comme d'o.,** as usual; **un hiver plus rude que d'o.,** an unusually hard winter.

ordinairement [ɔrdinɛrmɑ̃], *adv.* as a rule, ordinarily, usually.

ordinal, -aux [ɔrdinal, -o]. **1.** *a.* ordinal (adjective, etc.). **2.** *s.m. Ecc:* (*Anglican Ch.*) ordinal.

ordinand [ɔrdinɑ̃], *s.m. Ecc:* candidate for ordination; ordinand.

ordinant [ɔrdinɑ̃], *s.m. Ecc:* ordainer, ordinant.

ordinateur [ɔrdinatœːr], *s.m.* computer, data processing machine, *U.S:* data processer; **o. analogique,** analog computer; **o. arithmétique, o. numérique,** digital computer; **o. électronique,** electronic computer; **o. universel,** general-purpose computer; **o. spécialisé,** special-purpose computer; **o. scientifique,** scientific computer; **o. comptable,** accounting computer; **o. de bureau,** (i) desk-top computer; (ii) desk-size(d) computer; **l'ère des ordinateurs,** the computer age; **application sur o.,** computer application; **géré par o.,** computer-backed, computer-based; **commandé par o.,** computer-directed; **fourni par o.,** computer-fed; **établi par o.,** computer-produced, computer-prepared; **bande pour o.,** computer tape.

ordination [ɔrdinasjɔ̃], *s.f.* **1.** *Ecc:* ordination. **2.** *Tchn:* data processing.

ordiner [ɔrdine], *v.tr.* (*of computer*) to process (data).

ordinogramme [ɔrdinɔgram], *s.m.* flowchart, flow diagram, process chart (of computer).

ordonnance [ɔrdɔnɑ̃:s], *s.f.* **1.** order, (general) arrangement (of building, etc.); disposition, grouping (of picture, etc.). **2.** (*a*) statute, enactment, ordinance, order; **o. d'amnistie,** amnesty ordinance; **o. de police,** police regulation; **rendre une o.,** to issue an order; (*b*) *Jur:* judgment delivered by president of court, sitting alone; judge's order, decision, or ruling; (*c*) *Adm:* **o. de paiement,** order, warrant, for payment. **3.** *Mil:* **habit d'o.,** uniform, regimentals; **bottes d'o.,** ammunition boots, issue boots; **revolver d'o.,** regulation revolver, service revolver; **officier d'o.,** aide-de-camp; *Nau:* flag-lieutenant. **4.** *Mil:* (*a*) orderly; (*b*) *occ. m.* officer's servant. **5.** *Med:* prescription; **donner une o. à qn,** to prescribe, write out a prescription, for s.o.; *Pharm:* **préparer, exécuter, une o.,** to dispense, make up, *U.S:* to fill, a prescription; **délivré seulement sur o.,** available only on a doctor's prescription; **rayon d'ordonnances médicales,** dispensing department (in store, etc.).

ordonnancement [ɔrdɔnɑ̃smɑ̃], *s.m.* (*a*) *Ind: etc:* scheduling, sequencing (of production); timing (of decisions); putting in order; **o. de la production des pièces de rechange,** scheduling, sequencing, of spares; (*b*) *Adm:* order to pay.

ordonnancer [ɔrdɔnɑ̃se], *v.tr.* (**j'ordonnançai(s); n. ordonnançons**) **1.** to put in order; *Adm:* to pass (account) for payment; to sanction (expenditure); to initial (account). **2.** to schedule, to draw up a schedule for (a project, etc.).

ordonnancier [ɔrdɔnɑ̃sje], *s.m. Pharm:* register of prescriptions, prescription book.

ordonnateur, -trice [ɔrdɔnatœ:r, -tris]. **1.** *s.* (*a*) director, arranger; master of ceremonies, person in charge of the arrangements (for festival, party, etc.); **o. des pompes funèbres,** funeral director; **l'o. de la fête,** the organizer of the festivities; (*b*) person authorized to pass accounts. **2.** *a.* directing, managing.

ordonné, -ée [ɔrdɔne]. **1.** *a.* (*a*) orderly, well-ordered (life, arrangement, mind); **connaissances bien ordonnées,** well-digested knowledge; (*of computer*) **traitement non o.,** random processing; (*b*) (person) of regular habits; tidy (person); (*c*) *Ecc:* **prêtre o.,** ordained priest. **2.** *s.f. Mth:* **ordonnée,** ordinate; **axe des ordonnées,** Y-axis.

ordonnément [ɔrdɔnemɑ̃], *adv.* in an orderly fashion; tidily.

ordonner [ɔrdɔne], *v.tr.* **1.** (*a*) **o. qch.,** to arrange sth.; to set sth. to rights; **o. une maison,** to regulate a household; **le puzzle s'ordonne,** the pieces of the jigsaw puzzle are falling into place; everything is becoming clear; (*b*) *Mth:* to arrange (terms) in ascending or descending order; (*c*) *v.i.* **o. du sort de qn,** to dispose of the fate of s.o. **2.** to order, command, direct; (*a*) **o. à qn de faire qch.,** to order s.o. to do sth.; **o. à qn de monter, de descendre,** to order s.o. upstairs, downstairs; **on nous ordonna d'entrer, de sortir,** we were ordered in, out; **o. à qn de se taire,** to tell s.o. to be quiet; **il ordonna d'intercepter les avions,** he gave orders for the aircraft to be intercepted; **je vais o. qn'on le fasse,** I shall give orders to have it done; **o. une grève,** to call a strike; (*b*) **o. une punition à qn,** to order s.o. to be punished; **o. une enquête,** to order an enquiry; *Med:* **o. un remède à qn,** to prescribe a remedy for s.o.; (*c*) *Adm:* to enact, ordain (**que** + *ind.*, that); **la cour ordonna que M. le président serait interdit de ses fonctions,** the court ordained that the President should be suspended from his duties. **3.** *Ecc:* **o. un prêtre,** to ordain a priest; **o. qn prêtre,** to ordain s.o. priest; to confer holy orders on s.o.

ordovicien [ɔrdɔvisjɛ̃], *a.* & *s.m. Geol:* Ordovician.

ordre [ɔrdr̥], *s.m.* order. **1.** (*a*) methodical arrangement; **o. alphabétique, chronologique,** alphabetical, chronological, order; **ranger des mots par o. alphabétique,** to arrange words in alphabetical order; **certificats délivrés par o. de date,** certificates issued consecutively, in date order; (*computers*) **o. d'interclassement,** collating, collation, sequence; **numéro d'o.,** serial number; **avec o.,** methodically; **sans o.,** untidy; untidily, without method; unmethodical, unmethodically; *F:* higgledy-piggledy; **manque d'o.,** lack of order, of method; untidiness; **en bon o.,** (i) in (an) orderly fashion; (ii) in good order; **en o. parfait,** in apple-pie order; all shipshape; **en o. de bataille,** (i) in battle array; (ii) (*of troops on parade*) in order of precedence; **homme d'o.,** orderly, methodical, man; **il a de l'o.,** he is methodical, systematic, tidy; **il a l'esprit de l'o.,** he's a stickler for method; **mettre qch. en o., (re)mettre de l'o. dans qch.,** to set sth. in order, to rights; to tidy up (room); **mettre o. à ses affaires, mettre ses affaires en o.,** to put one's affairs in order, to settle one's affairs; to set one's house in order; **mettez un peu d'o. dans la chambre,** tidy up the room a bit; **mettre (bon) o. à un abus,** to put an end to, put a stop to, an abuse; **mise en o.,** ordering, arrangement (de, of); *Mil:* **o. serré,** close order; **o. ouvert, dispersé,** extended order; *Navy:* **o. de marche,** order of sailing; *I.C.E:* **o. d'allumage,** firing order; *Tchn: etc:* **être en o. de marche,** to be in working order; (*b*) *Jur:* **o. de succession,** canons of inheritance; **o. utile,** ranking (of creditor). **2.** orderliness, discipline; **assurer l'o.,** to preserve order; **maintenir l'o. dans une ville,** to maintain order, discipline, in a town, to police a town; **maintien de l'o.,** policing; **le service d'o.,** the (body of) officials responsible for order; **rappeler qn à l'o.,** to call s.o. to order; **à l'o.!** order! chair! **amis de l'o.,** law-abiding people; *Jur:* **o. public,** law and order; **délit contre l'o. public,** breach of the peace; **troubler l'o. (public),** to disturb the peace. **3. o. du jour,** (i) agenda, list of agenda (of meeting), business before the meeting; (ii) *Mil:* general orders, order of the day; **questions à l'o. du jour,** (i) items of the agenda, (ii) questions of the day; **question toujours à l'o. du jour,** evergreen topic; **la guerre froide est à l'o. du jour,** the cold war is very much in the news, is the fashion of the day; **l'o. du jour étant épuisé,** this being all the business; **passer à l'o. du jour,** to proceed with the business of the day (*i.e.* to set aside a motion); **passer à l'o. du jour sur une objection,** to overrule, brush aside, ignore, an objection; *Mil:* **venir à l'o.,** to come for general orders; *Mil:* **cité à l'o. (du jour)** = mentioned in despatches. **4.** (*a*) order (of architecture, plants, animals, etc.); class, division, category; **les trois ordres (de l'État),** the three orders, classes (of the State); **appartenir à un o., faire partie d'un o.,** to belong to an order, a category; **de premier o.,** first-class, first-rate (firm, workman, actor, performance, etc.); **dîner de premier o.,** first-rate dinner; **hôtel de troisième o.,** third-rate hotel; **un original de premier o.,** an oddity of the first water; **tireur de premier o.,** crack shot; **valeurs de premier o.,** gilt-edged stock; *Fin:* **obligation de premier o.,** prime bond; **renseignement d'o. général,** general information; **renseignements d'o. privé,** enquiries of a private nature; **de l'o. de . . .,** in, of, the order of . . .; in the region of . . .; **l'augmentation du chiffre d'affaires pourra bien être de l'o. de dix à douze mille francs,** the increase in business may well run to ten or twelve thousand francs; **une distance de l'o. de trois kilomètres,** a distance of about, some, three kilometres, three kilometres or so; **canal avec un tirant d'eau de l'o. de quatre mètres,** canal allowing for a draught of four metres or thereabouts; **dans cet o. d'idées,** in connection with this; (*b*) **o. religieux,** monastic order; **o. de chevalerie,** order of knighthood; *Jur:* **o. des avocats** = the Bar; **conseil de l'o. (des avocats)** = Bar Council; (*c*) *pl. Ecc:* holy orders; **recevoir, entrer dans les ordres,** to be ordained, to take holy orders; (*d*) *A.Theol:* order (of angels); **l'o. des séraphins,** the order of seraphim; (*e*) decoration (of an order); **l'O. de la Jarretière,** the Order of the Garter; **porter tous ses ordres,** to wear all one's decorations. **5.** (*a*) command, fiat; warrant; **o. par écrit,** written order; **o. d'exécution,** death warrant; **o. d'écrou, de levée d'écrou,** order to confine, to release, prisoner; **donner o. à qn de faire qch.,** to order s.o. to do sth.; **j'ai o. de rester ici,** I have orders to remain here; **je reçus l'o. de revenir,** I was ordered back; **je reçus l'o. de partir pour l'étranger,** I was ordered abroad; I was directed to proceed abroad; **donner des ordres à qn,** (i) to give s.o. orders; (ii) to order s.o. about; **par o., sur l'o., de qn,** by order of s.o.; **cela s'est fait sur les ordres de . . .,** it was done by the order of . . ., by command of . . .; **n'obéir qu'aux ordres de X,** to take orders only from X; **se mettre aux ordres de qn,** to put oneself at s.o.'s disposal; **s'enrôler sous les ordres de X,** to enlist under the command of X; **être aux ordres d'un client,** to wait upon a customer; **être aux ordres de qn,** to be at s.o.'s beck and call; **jusqu'à nouvel o.,** until further orders; until further notice; for the time being; **à moins d'o., sauf o., contraire,** in the absence of orders to the contrary; unless otherwise directed; *Mil: etc:* **o. d'appel (sous les drapeaux),** call-up papers; **o. de comparaître,** summons to attend; **ordres permanents,** standing orders; **confirmer un o. verbal par écrit,** to confirm a verbal order in writing; **o. de service courant,** routine order; **o. préparatoire,** warning order; **o. d'attaque,** (i) order to attack; (ii) order for an, the, attack; **o. d'opération,** operation order; **o. administratif et logistique,** administrative order; **o. particulier,** fragmentary order; **en vertu de l'o. d'opération No 7,** under operation order No 7; **en exécution des ordres reçus,** in compliance, in accordance, with order received; **ébaucher un o.,** to frame an order, to draft a tentative order; **rédiger un o.,** to draft an order; **la rédaction des ordres,** the drafting of orders; **donner, lancer, publier, un o.,** to issue an order; **diffuser un o.,** to disseminate an order; **la diffusion des ordres,** the dissemination of orders; **transmettre, faire passer, un o.,** to transmit, pass on, an order; **la transmission des ordres,** the transmission, passing-on, of orders; **annuler, révoquer, un o.,** to cancel an order; **rapporter un o.,** to rescind an order; **l'infanterie reçut l'o. d'attaquer,** the infantry was ordered to attack; *Navy:* **ordres cachetés,** sealed orders; *Nau:* **avoir reçu l'o. d'appareiller,** to be under sailing orders; (*b*) *Com:* **payez à l'o. de . . .,** pay to the order of . . .; **billet à o.,** promissory note; bill of exchange payable to order; **faire un billet à l'o. de qn,** to make a bill payable to s.o.; **d'o. et pour compte,** by order and for account; **compte d'o.,** suspense account (on balance sheet); (*c*) (*computers*) **ordres initiaux,** initial instructions, orders; **o. de contrôle des travaux,** job control statement; **o. de début des travaux,** job statement.

ordure [ɔrdy:r], *s.f.* **1.** (*a*) dirt, filth, muck; (*b*) excrement, dung, ordure; (*c*) filthiness, lewdness; **dire des ordures,** to use filthy language; to talk smut. **2.** *pl.* sweepings, refuse, rubbish; **ordures ménagères,** garbage, household refuse; **boîte, panier, bac, à ordures, aux ordures,** refuse bin, dustbin, *U.S:* trash can, garbage can; *P.N:* **défense de déposer des ordures,** shoot no rubbish; **ordures de ville,** town refuse; **service d'enlèvement des ordures,** refuse disposal departments. **incinérateur d'ordures,** refuse destructor, dust destructor; **tas d'ordures,** (i) muck heap; (ii) heap of street sweepings. **3.** *P:* **o.!** you rat! you skunk!

ordurier, -ière [ɔrdyrje, -jɛ:r]. **1.** *a.* obscene, filthy (book, song); filthy, foul (language); **écrivain o.,** obscene writer; **injures ordurières,** scurrilous abuse. **2.** *s.* scurrilous writer or talker; retailer of filth, of obscenities. **3.** *s.m.* *A:* dustbin; dustpan.

ore. *See* ORES.

oréade [ɔread], *s.f. Myth:* oread; grotto or mountain nymph.

orée [ɔre], *s.f. A:* & *Lit:* edge, verge, border, skirt (of a wood, etc.); (*still used in*) **à l'o. de la forêt,** on the edge of the forest; **elle apparut à l'o. du bois,** she emerged from the wood.

Orégon [ɔregɔ̃], *Pr.n.m. Geog:* Oregon.

oreillard [ɔrɛja:r]. **1.** *a.* lop-eared (horse, etc.). **2.** *s.m. Z:* long-eared bat. **3.** *s.m. F:* (*a*) hare; (*b*) donkey.

oreille [ɔrɛ:j], *s.f.* ear. **1. avoir mal à l'o., aux oreilles, avoir des douleurs d'o.,** to have earache; **aux oreilles courtes,** short-eared; **à longues oreilles,** long-eared; **couper les oreilles à un chien,** to crop a dog's ears; **mettre, porter, son chapeau sur l'o.,** to cock, wear, one's hat on one side, tilted (over one ear); **baisser l'o., avoir l'o. basse,** to be crestfallen, to look confused; **il partit l'o. basse,** he went off with his tail between his legs; (*of horse*) **secouer les oreilles, l'o.,** to toss its head; *F:* **secouer les oreilles à qn,** to give s.o. a flea in his ear; (*of horse*) **coucher les oreilles,** to set, lay, its ears back; to show signs of temper; **tirer les oreilles à un gamin,** to pull, tweak, a boy's ears; *F:* **il s'est (bien) fait tirer l'o.,** he needed, took, a lot of coaxing; **il ne s'est pas fait tirer l'o.,** he didn't have to be asked twice; **il ne se fit pas tirer l'o. pour . . .,** he showed no reluctance to . . .; **il se fait tirer l'o. pour payer,** it's hard to get money out of him; **montrer le bout de l'o.,** to show the cloven hoof; **autant lui pend à l'o.,** the same thing may very well happen to him any day; **être endette jusqu'aux oreilles, par-dessus les oreilles,** to be up to the ears, head over ears, in debt; *F:* **frotter, savonner, échauffer, les oreilles à qn,** to warm s.o.'s ears; **il lui frotta si bien les oreilles que . . .,** he gave him such a cuffing that . . .; **ils se sont pris par les oreilles,** they had a set-to; **il a toujours l'o. déchirée,** he's always in the wars;

Mil: fendre l'o. à un cheval, to clip a horse's ear (as a cast mark); *F:* fendre l'o. à qn, to retire (officer, official, etc.); *F:* il commence à m'échauffer les oreilles, he's beginning to get under my skin; enseigner à qn que les enfants ne se font pas par l'o., to tell s.o. the facts of life; *s.a.* DORMIR 1, LOUP[1] 1, PUCE 1. 2. (*a*) n'écouter que d'une o., to listen with half an ear; il m'est venu à l'o. que . . ., it has come to my ears that . . .; dire, souffler, qch. à l'o. de qn, to whisper sth. in s.o.'s ear; glissez-lui à l'o. ce petit avis, you might drop him this hint; dresser, tendre, l'o., ouvrir de grandes oreilles, to prick up one's ears; tendre l'o. au moindre bruit, to strain one's ears to catch the least sound; être tout oreilles, to be all ears, all attention; prêter l'oreille à qn, to lend an ear to s.o.; prêter une o. attentive à qn, à qch., to listen attentively to s.o., to sth.; avoir l'o. de qn, to have the ear of s.o.; fermer l'o. aux plaintes, à la vérité, to be deaf to complaints; to close one's ears to the truth; faire la sourde o., to pretend not to hear; to turn a deaf ear; il n'entend pas de cette o.-là, he is deaf in that ear, on that side; il ne l'entend pas de cette o.-là, he won't agree to that; he won't hear of it; *F:* casser les oreilles à qn, (i) to make a deafening noise; (ii) to drive s.o. crazy (with questions, etc.); si cela parvient aux oreilles du principal . . . ., if it should come to the ears of the headmaster . . .; ça lui entre par une o. et sort par l'autre, it goes in at one ear and out at the other; les oreilles doivent lui tinter, his ears must be tingling, burning; rebattre les oreilles à qn de qch., to din sth. in s.o.'s ears; (*b*) avoir l'o. fine, to have sharp ears, to be quick of hearing; être dur d'o., avoir l'o. dure, to be hard of hearing; avoir l'o. juste, avoir de l'o., to have a good ear, to have an ear for music; n'avoir pas d'o., n'avoir pas l'o. musicale, to have no ear for music; *Mus:* avoir l'o. absolue, to have absolute, perfect, pitch. 3. *Tchn:* ear (of porringer, of bale of goods); handle (of vase); lug, lobe, attachment, flange (of piece of machinery, etc.); palm (of anchor); horn (of cleat); mould board (of plough); wing (of thumb-screw); écrou à oreilles, wing nut, butterfly nut; *Furn:* bergère à oreilles, wing chair; casquette à oreilles, cap with ear flaps; faire une o. à une page, to dog-ear a page. 4. (*a*) *Bot: F:* o. d'homme, asarabacca; o. d'ours, bear's ear, auricula; o. de lièvre, (i) hare's ear; (ii) corn cockle; o. de souris, (i) mouse-ear chickweed, (ii) mouse-ear (scorpion grass), forget-me-not, (iii) mouse-ear (hawkweed); (*b*) *Moll:* o. de mer, ear shell, sea ear, haliotis, abalone; o. de Venus, white ear. 5. *Nau:* (*a*) o. de lièvre, leg-of-mutton sail; (*b*) o. d'âne, kevel.

oreiller [ɔreje; -rɛ-], *s.m.* 1. (*a*) pillow; prendre conseil de son o., to sleep on it; (*b*) o. pour dentelle aux fuseaux, lace cushion, pillow. 2. *Ich:* o. de mer, sea pincushion, sea barrow, mermaid's purse (skate's egg).

oreillère [ɔrɛjɛːr], *s.f. Ent:* earwig.

oreillette [ɔrɛjɛt], *s.f.* 1. (*a*) *Anat:* auricle (of the heart); (*b*) fauteuil à oreillettes, wing chair; casquette à oreillettes, cap with ear flaps; (*c*) ear (of a shell). 2. *Bot:* asarabacca.

oreillon [ɔrɛjɔ̃], *s.m.* 1. (*a*) *A.Arm:* ear-piece, cheek-piece (of helmet); (*b*) ear flap (of cap, sou'wester); (*c*) *Z:* earlet, tragus (of bat); (*d*) *Com:* oreillons d'abricots, (canned) apricots in halves. 2. *s.m.pl. Med:* oreillons, mumps.

orémus [oremys], *s.m.* (liturgical) prayer; dire, réciter des o., to recite prayers.

Orenbourg [orɛ̃buːr], *Pr.n.m. Geog:* Orenburg.

Orénoque (l') [lorenɔk], *Pr.n.m. Geog:* the Orinoco (river).

oreodon [oreɔdɔ̃], *s.m. Paleont:* oreodon.

oreodoxa [oreɔdɔksa], *s.m. Bot:* Oreodoxa.

oréophase [oreɔfaːz], *s.m. Orn:* oreophasis.

oréopithèque [oreɔpitɛk], **oreopithecus** [oreɔpitekys], *s.m. Paleont:* oreopithecus.

oréotrague [oreɔtraːg], *s.m. Z:* klipspringer.

ore(s) [ɔːr], *adv. A:* now; *still used in* d'o. et déjà, now and henceforth, here and now, *F:* right now.

Oreste [ɔrɛst], *Pr.n.m. Gr.Lit:* Orestes.

Orestie (l') [lɔrɛsti], *s.f. Gr.Lit:* the Oresteia.

orfèvre [ɔrfɛːvr], *s.m.* goldsmith, gold and silver smith; être o. en la matière, to be an expert in the matter; *Lit:* (*from Molière's L'Amour Médecin*) vous êtes o., Monsieur Josse! = nothing like leather! Quai des Orfèvres, police headquarters in Paris, = criminal investigation department.

orfévré [ɔrfevre], *a.* worked, wrought (by the goldsmith).

orfèvrerie [ɔrfɛvrəri], *s.f.* 1. (*a*) goldsmith's trade, craft, work; (*b*) goldsmith's shop. 2. (*a*) (gold, silver) plate; (*b*) jewellery.

orfraie [ɔrfrɛ], *s.f.* (*a*) *Orn:* sea eagle, erne; (*b*) pousser des cris d'o., to shriek at the top of one's voice.

orfroi [ɔrfrwa], *s.m. A: Ecc.Cost:* orphrey, orfray.

organdi [ɔrgɑ̃di], *s.m. Tex:* organdi(e); book muslin; *Bookb:* mull.

organe [ɔrgan], *s.m.* organ. 1. (*a*) les organes de la vue, de l'ouïe, the organs of sight, of hearing; (*b*) *Mec.E: etc:* part, component, element; unit; mechanism, device; les organes d'une machine, the parts, components, of a machine; o. accessoire, o. annexe, accessory; o. de commande, o. moteur, driving member; power unit; organes de commande, organes moteurs, driving gear; o. entraîné, driven member; o. de transmission, transmission member; organes de transmission, transmission gear; organes de manœuvre, working gear, operating gear; *Elcs:* o. d'entrée, de sortie, input, output, unit (of computer, etc.). 2. (*a*) voice; o. sonore, ringing voice; o. mâle et sonore, strong, manly, voice; (*b*) mouthpiece, spokesman, medium; journal qui est l'o. d'un parti, newspaper which is the organ of a party; certains organes, a certain section of the press; l'o. officiel, the official record; o. de publicité, advertising medium; (*c*) agent, means, medium; instrument (of a government, etc.); les juges sont les organes de la justice, judges are the organs, agents, of the law; judges administer the law; par un nouvel o., by another means, through another agency; je mettrai en œuvre les organes dont je dispose, I shall put in motion the machinery at my disposal; *Adm:* o. distributeur, distributing agency; o. livrancier, delivery agency; o. payeur, paying agency; *Mil: etc:* les organes de liaison, the liaison agencies.

organeau, -eaux [ɔrgano], *s.m. Nau:* (*a*) mooring ring; (*b*) anchor ring.

organicien, -ienne [ɔrganisjɛ̃, -jɛn], *s. Med:* organicist; *Ch:* organic chemist.

organicisme [ɔrganisism], *s.m. Med: Phil:* organicism.

organier [ɔrganje], *s.m. Mus:* organ builder.

organigramme [ɔrganigram], *s.m.* (*a*) administrative chart (of organization, etc.); operating chart; organization chart; plan; master sheet (of convoy, etc.); (*b*) (data) flow chart, (data) flow diagram, process chart (of computer programme).

organigraphe [ɔrganigraf], *s.m.* (flow chart) template (of computer).

organique [ɔrganik], *a.* organic (disease, chemistry, law).

organiquement [ɔrganikmɑ̃], *adv.* organically.

organisable [ɔrganizabl], *a.* organizable.

organisateur, -trice [ɔrganizatœːr, -tris]. 1. *a.* organizing. 2. *s.* organizer; promoter (of boxing match, etc.).

organisateur-conseil [ɔrganizatœrkɔ̃sɛːj], *s.m.* time and motion consultant; *pl. organisateurs-conseils.*

organisation [ɔrganizasjɔ̃], *s.f.* 1. organizing, organization; planning; (*a*) comité d'o., organizing committee; qualités d'o., organizing ability; défaut d'o., inadequacy of planning, of organization; (*b*) o. du travail, organization of work; job engineering; o. industrielle, industrial engineering; o. de la production, production engineering; ingénieur en o., management consultant; *Mil:* o. du terrain, field works, field defence; (*c*) (*computers*) o. des données, data organization; o. scientifique du travail (O.S.T.), organization and methods (O. & M.). 2. organization; (*a*) structure (of human body, of vegetable, of army, etc.); constitution (of the mind, etc.); (*b*) (organized) body (of workers, etc.); (*c*) (business, etc.) organization; *F:* set-up; O. des Nations Unies, United Nations Organization; o. de voyage, travel organization; une o. pour recueillir les nouvelles, an organization, a set-up, for collecting news; (*d*) l'o. militaire de l'O.T.A.N., the N.A.T.O. military build-up.

organisé [ɔrganize], *a.* 1. organic (body, life, etc.); êtres organisés, organic beings; la loi de croissance organisée, the law of organic growth. 2. organized, constituted; fête mal organisée, badly organized entertainment; voyage o., conducted tour; *F:* c'est du vol o., it's planned robbery; c'est une tête bien organisée, he, she, is level-headed; non o., unorganized. 3. société organisée, religion organisée, organized society, religion.

organiser [ɔrganize], *v.tr.* to organize. 1. to form; to furnish (a body) with organs. 2. to arrange; to put into working order (army, etc.); to get up, arrange (entertainment, contest, etc.); o. une réception pour qn, to organize, *F:* lay on, a reception for s.o.; o. un commerce, to set up a business; o. un voyage, to plan a journey; o. une révolte, to organize, plan, a revolt; o. son temps, to organize, plan, one's time.

s'organiser, to get down to work; to get settled; to settle down; il sait s'o., he knows how to organize himself.

organisme [ɔrganism], *s.m.* 1. organism, structure (of human body, etc.); *Med: Anat:* (the) system; mauvais pour l'o., bad for the system; un o. de fer, an iron constitution. 2. o. d'État, state agency, state authority; o. international du travail, international labour organization; un o. comme l'O.N.U., a body such as U.N.O.; *Nau:* o. de classification, regulatory body.

organiste [ɔrganist], *s.m. & f. Mus:* organist.

organite [ɔrganit], *s.m. Biol:* organoid; organelle.

organogel [ɔrganɔʒɛl], *s.m. Ch:* organogel.

organogène [ɔrganɔʒɛn], *a. Geol:* organogenic.

organogénèse [ɔrganɔʒenɛːz], *s.f.* organogenesis, organogeny.

organogénique [ɔrganɔʒenik], *a. Biol:* organogenetic.

organographie [ɔrganɔgrafin], *s.m.* organography.

organoleptique [ɔrganɔlɛptik], *a.* organoleptic.

organologie [ɔrganɔlɔʒi], *s.f. Biol:* organology.

organométallique [ɔrganɔmetalik], *a. Ch:* organometallic.

organopathie [ɔrganɔpati], *s.f. Med:* organopathy.

organosol [ɔrganɔsɔl], *s.m. Ch:* organosol.

organothérapie [ɔrganɔterapi], *s.f. Med:* organotherapy.

organsin [ɔrgɑ̃sɛ̃], *s.m.* thrown silk, organzine.

organsinage [ɔrgɑ̃sinaːʒ], *s.m. Tex:* throwing (of silk).

organsiner [ɔrgɑ̃sine], *v.tr. Tex:* to throw (silk); to twist twice, to organzine.

organsineur [ɔrgɑ̃sinœːr], *s.m. Tex:* throwster (of silk threads).

organum [ɔrganɔm], *s.m. A.Mus:* organum.

orgasme [ɔrgasm], *s.m. Physiol:* orgasm.

orgastique [ɔrgastik], *a. Physiol:* orgastic.

orge [ɔrʒ], *s.* barley. 1. *s.f.* (*a*) o. sans barbe, bald barley; o. à deux, à quatre, rangs, two-rowed, four-rowed, barley; o. trifirique, hooded barley; grain d'o., barley corn; *Tex:* toile (à) grain d'o., huckaback linen; meule d'o., barley mow; sucre d'o., barley sugar; tisane, eau, d'o., barley water; crème d'o., barley gruel; farine d'o., barley meal; *F:* faire ses orges, to make one's pile; (*b*) *Bot:* o. des rats, des murs, wall barley, way bent. 2. *s.m.* o. mondé, (i) hulled barley; (ii) barley water; o. perlé, pearl barley.

orgeat [ɔrʒa], *s.m.* orgeat (syrup); *F:* c'est une carafe d'o., he's a flabby, characterless, individual.

orgelet [ɔrʒəlɛ], *s.m.* stye (on the eye).

orgerie [ɔrʒəri], *s.f. Dial:* (*Normandy*) field of barley.

orgiaque [ɔrʒjak], *a.* orgiastic, orgiac (frenzy, feast).

orgiasme [ɔrʒjasm], *s.m. Gr.Ant:* (Bacchanalian) orgy.

orgiastique [ɔrʒjastik], *a. Gr.Ant:* Bacchanalian (orgy, etc.).

orgie [ɔrʒi], *s.f.* 1. *pl. Gr.Ant:* (Bacchanalian) orgies. 2. (*a*) orgy; drunken feasting; feast; (*b*) profusion, riot (of gay flowers, etc.); une o. de couleurs, a riot of colour.

orgue [ɔrg], *s.m.* 1. (*also Ecc: s.f.pl.* orgues) *Mus:* (*a*) organ; un bel o., de belles orgues, a fine organ; *but:* les meilleurs orgues sont fabriqués par . . ., the best organs are manufactured by . . .; grand o., (i) grand organ (in organ loft, as opposed to the o. du chœur); (ii) great (organ) (as opposed to positif, récit, *q.v.*); (iii) full organ (as a direction to player); o. du chœur, de la maîtrise, o. d'accompagnement, choir organ (located in choir); clavier du grand o., great manual; o. à plein jeu, o. plein, full organ; grandes orgues, grand organ; tenir l'o., les orgues, to be, preside, at the organ; Mlle X chantera au grand o., Miss X will sing (from the organ loft) accompanied by the grand organ; (*b*) o. de salon, American organ, harmonium. 2. o. de Barbarie, barrel organ, street organ; joueur d'o., organ grinder; (*c*) o. de cinéma, theatre organ. 3. *Coel:* o. de mer, organ-pipe coral, tubipore. 4. *Geol:* o. basaltique, columnar basalt; orgues de basalte, basalt columns. 5. *Nau: F:* tuyau d'o., scupper pipe.

orgueil [ɔrgœ:j], *s.m.* **1.** pride, arrogance, *F:* bumptiousness; **l'o. de la naissance,** pride of birth; **l'o. la dévore,** she is eaten up with pride; **crever d'o.,** to be bursting with pride; **ils déclarent avec o. que . . .,** they boast that . . .; **l'o. de la flotte,** the pride of the fleet; **mettre son o. à faire qch.,** to take a pride in doing sth.; **chatouiller l'o. de qn,** to tickle s.o.'s vanity. **2.** fulcrum (of lever).

orgueilleusement [ɔrgœjøzmɑ̃], *adv.* proudly; arrogantly.

orgueilleux, -euse [ɔrgœjø, -ø:z], *a.* proud, arrogant, *F:* bumptious; **une beauté orgueilleuse,** a proud, haughty, beauty; **être o. de sa maison, de ses richesses,** to be house-proud, purse-proud; *s.* **les orgueilleux,** the proud, the arrogant.

orgyie [ɔrʒii], *s.f. Ent:* tussock moth; vapourer moth.

oribate [ɔribat], *s.m. Arach:* wood mite.

oribatidés [ɔribatide], *s.m.pl. Arach:* Oribatidae.

oribi [ɔribi], *s.m. Z:* oribi.

orichalque [ɔrikalk], *s.m.* orichalc(h), orichalcum.

oriel [ɔrjɛl], *s.m. Arch:* oriel window.

orient [ɔrjɑ̃], *s.m.* **1.** (*a*) orient, east (of the sky, of the earth); *Lit:* **génie à son o.,** rising, budding, genius; (*b*) **le proche, le moyen, l'extrême, O.,** the Near, the Middle, the Far, East; **en O.,** in the East; **peuples d'O.,** Eastern, Oriental, nations; **cigarette d'O.,** Turkish cigarette; **tapis d'O.,** oriental carpet; *Ecc:* **l'Église d'O.,** the Eastern Church; *Hist:* **l'Empire d'O.,** the Byzantine Empire; (*c*) (*Freemasonry*) **le Grand O. (de France),** the Grand Lodge of France. **2.** water, orient (of pearl); **perle d'un bel o.,** orient pearl.

orientable [ɔrjɑ̃tabl̩], *a.* steerable; adjustable; rotatable; swivelling; free to turn, to swivel; revolving; directional; **raccord o.,** swivel connection, swivelling union, banjo connection; **tuyère o.,** directional nozzle; *Av:* **roulette de nez o.,** steerable nose wheel.

oriental, -ale, -aux [ɔrjɑ̃tal, -o]. **1.** *a.* (*a*) eastern, oriental; *Hist:* **les Indes orientales,** the East Indies; (*b*) **perle orientale,** (pearl of) orient; orient pearl; **rubis, saphir, o.,** orient ruby, sapphire. **2.** *s.* **les Orientaux,** Orientals, the peoples of the East.

orientaliser [ɔrjɑ̃talize], *v.tr.* to orientalize.

orientalisme [ɔrjɑ̃talism], *s.m.* orientalism.

orientaliste [ɔrjɑ̃talist], *s.m. & f.* orientalist.

orientation [ɔrjɑ̃tasjɔ̃], *s.f.* **1.** (*a*) orientation; **table d'o.,** orientation, panoramic, table; **perdre le sens de l'o.,** to lose one's sense of direction, one's bearings; *F:* **avoir la bosse de l'o.,** to have the bump of locality; **les événements leur ont permis de prendre une o. plus précise,** events enabled them to orientate themselves more precisely; **o. d'une maison, d'une église,** orientation, orientating, of a house, of a church; (*b*) *Sch:* **o. professionnelle,** vocational guidance; **o. scolaire (et professionnelle),** selection and guidance (for a particular type of education); **conseiller, -ère, d'o. scolaire et professionnelle,** vocational advisor; **conseil d'o.,** advisory council; (*c*) *Tchn:* steering; swivelling; rotating; steering (of crane, etc.); **roue d'o.,** directing wheel (of windmill); *Navy:* **o. d'un canon,** training of a gun; *Nau:* **o. des voiles,** trimming of the sails; *Av:* **o. de la roulette avant,** steering of the nose wheel; **à o. libre,** free-moving; adjustable; rotatable; (*d*) orientation (of computer). **2.** orientation, direction, aspect; **o. d'une maison,** orientation, aspect, of a house; **l'o. de la politique,** the trend of politics; *Nau:* **o. des voiles,** set, trim, of the sails.

orienté [ɔrjɑ̃te], *a.* (*a*) oriented, orientated; **salon o. au sud,** drawing room with a southerly aspect, facing south; (*b*) (*computers*) oriented; **graphe o., non o.,** oriented, non-oriented, graph; *Mth:* **vecteur o., non-o.,** directed, undirected, vector; (*c*) **ouvrage o. politiquement,** work, book, with a political bias; (*d*) *Nau:* (*of sail*) **bien o.,** in sailing trim; *W.Tel: etc:* **antenne orientée,** directional aerial.

orientement [ɔrjɑ̃tmɑ̃], *s.m.* **1.** (*a*) orienting, orientating (of building); (*b*) orientation; *Nau:* trimming (of sails). **2. prendre un o.,** to take a bearing.

orienter [ɔrjɑ̃te], *v.tr.* **1.** (*a*) to orient (building); (*b*) to slew, swing (crane, derrick, etc.); to train (gun); to point, direct (telescope); *Nau:* **o. des voiles,** to trim sails; **o. au plus près,** to brace sharp up; (*c*) to direct, guide; **o. ses efforts vers un but,** to direct one's efforts to(wards) an end; **o. un élève vers les belles-lettres,** to interest a pupil in literature; **o. une revue vers le goût féminin,** to slant a magazine for women readers; **o. la conversation vers d'autres sujets,** to turn the conversation into other channels. **2.** *Surv:* (*a*) to take the bearings of (spot); (*b*) to set (map) by the compass; (*c*) to draw the North-South line on (sketch map).

s'orienter. 1. to take, find, one's bearings; to get an idea of the lie of the land. **2.** (*a*) **il s'oriente vers la carrière diplomatique,** he is preparing to enter the diplomatic service; (*b*) **la politique de Cuba s'oriente vers le communisme,** Cuban politics are moving towards Communism.

orienteur, -euse [ɔrjɑ̃tœ:r, -ø:z]. **1.** *s. Sch:* **o. professionnel, orienteuse professionnelle,** careers master, mistress; vocational adviser, *U.S:* vocational guidance counselor. **2.** *s.m. Mil: etc:* pathfinder. **3.** *s.m. Surv:* (*instrument*) orientator.

orientite [ɔrjɑ̃tit], *s.f. Miner:* orientite.

orière [ɔrjɛ:r], *s.f.* hedge (bordering a field).

orifice [ɔrifis], *s.m.* aperture, hole, opening, orifice, mouth; *Mch:* **orifices d'admission, à l'introduction,** intake ports, steam ports; **o. d'échappement,** exhaust port; *I.C.E:* **o. de soupape,** valve port; **o. de visite,** inspection hole; *Hyd.E:* **o. noyé,** submerged orifice; **o. d'évacuation, de sortie,** outlet; *Metall:* **o. de coulée,** running gate; taphole (of blast furnace); *Anat:* **o. postérieur des fosses nasales,** choana, posterior naris.

oriflamme [ɔriflɑ:m, -am], *s.f.* (*a*) *Hist:* oriflamme (of the French kings); (*b*) streamer, banderole, decorative banner.

oriforme [ɔrifɔrm], *a.* mouth-shaped (aperture).

origan [ɔrigɑ̃], *s.m. Bot:* origanum; marjoram.

Origène [ɔriʒɛn], *Pr.n.m. Ecc.Hist:* Origen.

originaire [ɔriʒinɛ:r], *a.* **1.** originating (**de,** from, in); native (**de,** of); **il est o. de la Russie, du Havre,** he comes, hails, from Russia, from Le Havre; **habitant o. de . . .,** native inhabitant of . . .. **2.** (*a*) original (member); dating from the very beginning (of club, company, etc.); foundation (member); (*b*) *Jur:* original (writ, jurisdiction, etc.); originating (summons, etc.).

originairement [ɔriʒinɛrmɑ̃], *adv.* originally, at the beginning.

original, -ale, -aux [ɔriʒinal, -o], *a. & s.* **1.** original (text, manuscript); *Typewr:* top copy; **o. d'un tableau, d'une facture,** original of a picture, of an invoice; **copier qch. sur l'o.,** to copy sth. from the original; **en o.,** in the original; *A:* **savoir qch. d'o.,** to know sth. at first hand; **lire un auteur dans l'o.,** *A:* **d'o.,** to read an author in the original text or language; *Hist:* **recueil de textes originaux,** source-book; *Jur:* **(document) o.,** script; *Cin:* **copie originale (du film),** master print. **2.** (*a*) original (style, idea); inventive (genius); novel, fresh (idea); (*b*) odd, queer, eccentric (person, ways, etc.); **c'est un o.,** he's an eccentric, a character; *A:* **c'est un o. sans copie,** he's unique, there's nobody like him.

originalement [ɔriʒinalmɑ̃], *adv.* (*a*) in the original fashion; (*b*) in a novel, an original, manner; (*c*) oddly, eccentrically.

originaliser [ɔriʒinalize], *v.tr.* to give an original touch to (sth.).

originalité [ɔriʒinalite], *s.f.* (*a*) originality; (*b*) eccentricity, oddity; (*c*) **les grandes écoles constituent une des originalités de l'enseignement français,** the *grandes écoles* are one of the original features of the French educational system.

origine [ɔriʒin], *s.f.* origin. **1.** (*a*) beginning; **dès l'o.,** from the very beginning, from the outset; **à l'o., dans l'o.,** originally, in the beginning; **remonter à l'o. d'un événement,** to trace an event to its origin; (*b*) *Mth: Surv:* **(point) o.,** zero point; (*of vector*) head; **o. du temps,** zero on the time coordinate (of graph); (*c*) *Mil:* **o. d'étapes,** advanced base of supply. **2.** (*a*) extraction, birth (of person, family, nation); **être d'o. illustre,** to be of noble descent, of noble birth; **la colonie devait son o. à . . ., tirait son o. de . . .,** the colony owed its birth to . . .; (*b*) nationality; **il est d'o. anglaise, il est Anglais d'o.,** he is of English extraction, an Englishman by birth; (*c*) *Breed:* **livre d'origines,** stud book. **3.** (*a*) source, derivation (of thing); **o. d'un mot, d'une coutume,** derivation of a word, origin of a custom; **mots de même o.,** cognate words; **tirer son o. de . . .,** to originate with, from . . .; **la grève a pour o. les revendications de . . .,** the strike originated in the demands of . . .; *Post:* **bureau d'o.,** (postal) office of dispatch; *Cust:* **certificat d'o.,** certificate of origin; *Com:* **marchandises d'o.,** goods the source of which is guaranteed; **champagne d'o.,** vintage champagne; *Aut:* **pneus d'o.,** original tyres; *Ind:* **pièce d'o.,** original, factory-installed, component; *Com:* **emballage d'o.,** original packing; (*b*) *Arch: Mth: etc:* **point d'o.,** point of origin (of curve, etc.).

originel, -elle [ɔriʒinɛl], *a.* primordial, original; *used chiefly in the following phrases:* **péché o.,** original sin; **grâce originelle,** original grace; **tache originelle,** inherited taint; *but also* **valeur originelle d'un mot,** primary force of a word; *Geol:* **form originelle,** original form.

originellement [ɔriʒinɛlmɑ̃], *adv.* originally; **contrat vicié o.,** contract vitiated at its source, from the beginning; *Theol:* **l'homme est o. pécheur,** man is born in sin.

orignac [ɔriɲak], *s.m.*, **orignal, -aux** [ɔriɲal, -o], *s.m. Z:* American moose.

orillon [ɔrijɔ̃], *s.m.* **1.** (*a*) ear, lug, handle (of porringer, etc.); (*b*) *Fort: A:* orill(i)on (of bastion). **2.** (*a*) projection (in masonry); (*b*) mould board (of plough).

orin [ɔrɛ̃], *s.m. Nau:* buoy rope; **bouée d'o.,** anchor buoy.

oringuer [ɔrɛ̃ge], *v.tr. Nau:* to lift with a buoy rope.

oriol(l)e [ɔrjɔl], *s.m. Orn:* oriole.

oriolidés [ɔrjɔlide], *s.m.pl. Orn:* Oriolidae.

Orion [ɔrjɔ̃], *Pr.n.m. Gr.Myth: Astr:* Orion.

oripeau [ɔripo], *s.m.* **1.** tinsel, foil; Dutch gold. **2.** *pl.* **oripeaux;** (*a*) tawdry finery, cheap finery; (*b*) rags, old clothes (with traces of former finery).

orle [ɔrl], *s.m.* **1.** *Arch: Her:* orle; *Her:* **en o.,** in orle, orlewise. **2.** lip (of crater).

orlé [ɔrle], *a. Her:* orlée.

orléanais, -aise [ɔrleanɛ, -ɛ:z]. **1.** *a. & s. Geog:* (native, inhabitant] of Orleans. **2.** *Pr.n.m. Hist:* **l'O.,** the Orléanais.

orléanisme [ɔrleanism], *s.m. Hist:* Orleanism.

orléaniste [ɔrleanist], *Hist:* **1.** *s.m. & f.* Orleanist, supporter of the Orleans branch of the French monarchy. **2.** *a.* Orleanist (party); Orleanistic (opinions, leanings).

Orléans [ɔrleɑ̃]. **1.** *Pr.n. Geog:* Orleans; **la Nouvelle O.,** New Orleans. **2.** *s.f. Tex:* Orleans cloth.

ormaie [ɔrmɛ], *s.f.* elm grove.

orme [ɔrm], *s.m. Bot:* elm (tree, wood); **o. à larges feuilles,** broad-leaved elm; **o. blanc, o. de(s) montagne(s),** wych elm, witch elm, Scotch elm; **o. de cèdre,** red elm; **o. champêtre, à petites feuilles,** common elm, English elm; **o. subéreux, o. liège,** Dutch elm, cork elm; **maladie des ormes,** elm disease; *F:* **attendez-moi sous l'o.,** you can wait (for me) till the cows come home, till doomsday.

ormeau[1], **-eaux** [ɔrmo], *s.m. Bot:* (young) elm.

ormeau[2], **-eaux, ormet** [ɔrmɛ], **ormier** [ɔrmje], *s.m. Moll:* ormer, ear shell, sea ear, haliotis, abalone.

ormille [ɔrmi:j], *s.f.* **1.** (*a*) elm sapling; (*b*) small-leaved elm. **2.** (hedge)row, plantation, of young elms.

ormoie [ɔrmwa], *s.f.* elm grove.

ornateur, -trice [ɔrnatœ:r, -tris]. **1.** *a.* decorating (workman, etc.). **2.** *s.* decorator.

orne[1] [ɔrn], *s.m. Bot:* manna ash, flowering ash.

orne[2], *s.m. Vit:* furrow, (shallow) trench, between the vines.

orné [ɔrne], *a.* ornate (letter); illuminated initial (letter); ornate, florid (style).

ornemaniste [ɔrnəmanist], *s.m. Art: Arch:* ornamenter, ornament(al)ist.

ornement [ɔrnəmɑ̃], *s.m.* ornament; embellishment; *Mil:* ornament, badge (of helmet); *Mus:* **notes d'o.,** grace notes; **ajouter des ornements à qch.,** to ornament sth., **sans o.,** plain, unadorned; **surchargé d'ornements,** ornate; **ornements du style,** embellishments of style; *Ecc:* **ornements sacerdotaux,** vestments; **dessin d'o.,** decorative drawing; design; **la pudeur est le plus bel o. de la femme,** modesty is a woman's greatest ornament.

ornemental, -aux [ɔrnəmɑ̃tal, -o], *a.* ornamental, decorative.

ornementation [ɔrnəmɑ̃tasjɔ̃], *s.f.* ornamentation; decoration.

ornementer [ɔrnəmɑ̃te], *v.tr.* to ornament, to decorate.

ornéodides [ɔrneɔdid], *s.m.pl. Ent:* Orneodidae, the feather-winged moths.

ornéode [ɔrneɔd], *s.m. Ent:* feather-winged moth.

orner [ɔrne], *v.tr.* to ornament, embellish, decorate; **o. une fenêtre de fleurs,** to deck a window with flowers; **o. une robe de piqûres,** to trim a dress with stitching; **poignée ornée de rubis,** handle set with rubies; **robe ornée de galon d'or,** dress set off with gold braid; **salle ornée de drapeaux,** hall hung with flags; **hommes qui ont orné leur siècle,** men who have been the glory of their age.

ornière [ɔrnjɛːr], *s.f.* **1.** rut; **sortir de l'o.,** to get out of the rut; **sortir qn de l'o.,** to lift s.o. out of the rut. **2** groove (of tram rail, etc.); **rail à o.,** grooved rail; *A:* **chemin à ornières,** tram road.
ornithine [ɔrnitin], *s.f. Ch:* ornithin(e).
ornithodelphes [ɔrnitɔdɛlf], *s.m.pl. Z:* Ornithodelphia.
ornithogale [ɔrnitɔgal], *s.m. Bot:* ornithogalum; **o. à ombelle,** star-of-Bethlehem.
ornithogame [ɔrnitɔgam], *a. Bot:* (*of plants*) pollinated by birds, ornithophilous.
ornithogamie [ɔrnitɔgami], *s.f. Bot:* ornithophily.
ornithoïde [ɔrnitɔid], *a.* ornithoid.
ornithologie [ɔrnitɔlɔʒi], *s.f.* ornithology.
ornithologique [ɔrnitɔlɔʒik], *a.* ornithological.
ornithologiste [ɔrnitɔlɔʒist], **ornithologue** [ɔrnitɔlɔg], *s.m. & f.* ornithologist.
ornithomancie [ɔrnitɔmɑ̃si], *s.f.* ornithomancy.
ornithophile [ɔrnitɔfil], *a.* ornithophilous.
ornithopodes [ɔrnitɔpɔd], *s.m.pl. Paleont:* Ornithopoda; Ornithischia.
ornithoptère [ɔrnitɔptɛːr], *s.m.* (*a*) *A.Av:* ornithopter; (*b*) *pl. Ent:* **ornithoptères,** Ornithoptera.
ornithor(h)ynque [ɔrnitɔrɛ̃ːk], *s.m. Z:* ornithorhynchus, duck-billed platypus, duck bill, water mole.
ornithurés [ɔrnityre], *s.m.pl. Paleont:* Ornithurae.
ornithurique [ɔrnityrik], *a. Ch:* ornithuric.
orobanche [ɔrɔbɑ̃ːʃ], *s.f. Bot:* broomrape, chokeweed; **o. de Virginie,** beechdrops.
orobanchées [ɔrɔbɑ̃ke], *s.f.pl. Bot:* Orobanchaceae.
orobe [ɔrɔb], *s.m. or f.*, **orobus** [ɔrɔbys], *s.m. Bot:* orobus, bitter vetch.
orogénèse [ɔrɔʒenɛːz], *s.f. Geol:* orogenesis.
orogénie [ɔrɔʒeni], *s.f. Geol:* orogeny.
orogénique [ɔrɔʒenik], *a. Geol:* orogenic, orogenetic.
orographe [ɔrɔgraf], *s.m.* orologist.
orographie [ɔrɔgrafi], *s.f.* orography.
orographique [ɔrɔgrafik], *a.* orographic(al).
orologie [ɔrɔlɔʒi], *s.f.* orology.
orologique [ɔrɔlɔʒik], *a.* orological.
oromètre [ɔrɔmɛtr̥], *s.m.* orometer, mountain barometer.
orométrie [ɔrɔmetri], *s.f.* orometry.
orométrique [ɔrɔmetrik], *a.* orometric.
oronge [ɔrɔ̃ːʒ], *s.f. Fung:* royal agaric, Caesar's mushroom; **fausse o.,** fly agaric.
Oronte [ɔrɔ̃ːt], *Pr.n.m. Geog:* the (river) Orontes.
orophile [ɔrɔfil], *a. Bot:* **forêt o.,** mountain forest.
orophyte [ɔrɔfit], *a. Bot:* (*of plant*) adapted to mountain environment.
Orose [ɔroːz], *Pr.n.m. Hist:* Orosius.
orpaillage [ɔrpɑjaːʒ], *s.m.* gold washing.
orpailleur [ɔrpɑjœːr], *s.m.* gold washer.
Orphée [ɔrfe], *Pr.n.m. Gr.Myth:* Orpheus; **la lyre d'O.,** the Orphean lyre; *Th:* **O. aux Enfers,** Orpheus in the Underworld.
orphelin, -ine [ɔrfəlɛ̃, -in], *s.* orphan; *a.* orphan(ed); **o. de père,** fatherless (boy); **o. de mère,** motherless (boy); **o. en bas âge, il fut élevé par son oncle,** orphaned at an early age, he was brought up by his uncle.
orphelinage [ɔrfəlinaːʒ], *s.m.* **1.** orphanhood. **2.** *Ap:* (state of) being without a queen.
orphelinat [ɔrfəlina], *s.m.* orphanage; children's home.
orphéon [ɔrfeɔ̃], *s.m.* (*a*) choral society (*usu.* for men); male-voice choir; (*b*) musical society; (*c*) *F:* band.
orphéonique [ɔrfeɔnik], *a.* choral (society).
orphéoniste [ɔrfeɔnist], *s.m.* member of a choral society.
orphie [ɔrfi], *s.f. Ich:* garfish, green bone, sea pike, snipe fish.
orphique [ɔrfik], *a. Gr.Ant:* Orphean; Orphic (sect, literature); **les Orphiques,** (i) *s.m.pl.* the Orphic poems, (ii) *s.f.pl.* the Orphic festivities.
orphisme[1] [ɔrfism], *s.m. Gr.Ant:* Orphism, the religion of the Orphic mysteries.
orphisme[2], *s.m. Art:* Orphism.
orpiment [ɔrpimɑ̃], *s.m. Miner:* orpiment; yellow arsenic.
orpin [ɔrpɛ̃], *s.m.* **1.** *Miner:* orpiment; yellow arsenic. **2.** *Bot:* stonecrop; **o. âcre,** common stonecrop, wall pepper; **o. reprise, grand o.,** liveforever, live-long, orpin(e).
orque [ɔrk], *s.f. Z:* orc, grampus.
Orsay [ɔrsɛ], *F:* **le Quai d'O.,** the French Foreign Office (situated on the Quai d'Orsay).
orseille [ɔrsɛːj], *s.f. Bot: Dy:* archil, orchil; dyer's moss; **o. de terre,** cudbear.
orsellique [ɔrsɛl(l)ik], *a. Ch:* orsellic, orsellinic (acid).
ort [ɔːr], *A:* **1.** *a.inv.* gross (weight). **2.** *adv.* (weighed) gross.
orteil [ɔrtɛːj], *s.m.* toe; **gros o.,** big toe; **ongle d'o.,** toenail.
orthézien, -ienne [ɔrtezjɛ̃, -jɛn], *a. & s.* (native, inhabitant) of Orthez.
orthicon(oscope) [ɔrtikɔn(ɔskɔp)], *s.m. T.V:* orthicon.
orthite [ɔrtit], *s.f. Min:* orthite.
ortho [ɔrto], *a.inv.* ortho; **gneiss o.,** orthogneiss.
ortho- [ɔrtɔ], *pref.* ortho-.
orthobasique [ɔrtɔbazik], *a.* orthobasic.
orthocarbonique [ɔrtɔkarbɔnik], *a. Ch:* orthocarbonic (acid).
orthocentre [ɔrtɔsɑ̃ːtr̥], *s.m. Geom:* orthocentre (of triangle).
orthocentrique [ɔrtɔsɑ̃trik], *a. Mth:* orthocentric.
orthoceras [ɔrtɔseras], **orthocère** [ɔrtɔsɛːr], *s.m. Paleont:* orthoceras.
orthochlorite [ɔrtɔklɔrit], *s.f. Miner:* orthochlorite.
orthochromatique [ɔrtɔkrɔmatik], *a. Phot:* orthochromatic; **plaque o. à écran adhérent,** non-filter plate, N.F. plate.
orthochromatisation [ɔrtɔkrɔmatizasjɔ̃], *s.f. Phot:* orthochromatization.
orthochromatiser [ɔrtɔkrɔmatize], *v.tr. Phot:* to orthochromatize.
orthochromatisme [ɔrtɔkrɔmatism], *s.m.* orthochromatism.
orthoclase [ɔrtɔklɑːz], *s.f. Miner:* orthoclase.
orthodiagramme [ɔrtɔdjagram], *s.m.* orthodiagram.
orthodiagraphie [ɔrtɔdjagrafi], *s.f.* orthodiagraphy.
orthodontie [ɔrtɔdɔ̃ti], *s.f. Dent:* orthodontia.
orthodoxe [ɔrtɔdɔks]. **1.** *a.* (*a*) orthodox (church, doctrine); (*b*) sound (opinion, principle); conventional, correct (manner, etc.); **opinions peu orthodoxes,** unorthodox opinions. **2.** *s.* **les orthodoxes,** the orthodox.
orthodoxie [ɔrtɔdɔksi], *s.f.* (*a*) *Ecc:* orthodoxy; conformity; (*b*) soundness, orthodoxy (of opinions); correctness.
orthodromie [ɔrtɔdrɔmi], *s.f. Nau:* orthodromy, great-circle sailing.
orthodromique [ɔrtɔdrɔmik], *a.* **navigation o.,** great-circle sailing, orthodromic sailing.
orthoédrique [ɔrtɔedrik], *a.* orthometric (crystal).
orthoépie [ɔrtɔepi], *s.f. Ling:* orthoepy.
orthoépique [ɔrtɔepik], *a.* orthoepic.
orthogénèse [ɔrtɔʒenɛːz], *s.f. Biol:* orthogenesis.
orthognathe [ɔrtɔgnat], *a. Anthr:* orthognathous.
orthognathisme [ɔrtɔgnatism], *s.m.* orthognathism.
orthogneiss [ɔrtɔgnɛs], *s.m. Geol:* orthogneiss.
orthogonal, -aux [ɔrtɔgɔnal, -o], *a. Geom:* orthogonal; *Town P:* **plan o.,** grid layout, chequer-board layout.
orthogonalement [ɔrtɔgɔnalmɑ̃], *adv.* orthogonally, at right angles.
orthogonalité [ɔrtɔgɔnalite], *s.f.* orthogonality.
orthographe [ɔrtɔgraf], *s.f.* orthography, spelling; **faute d'o.,** spelling mistake; **o. d'usage,** literal spelling; **o. d'accord,** grammatical spelling.
orthographie [ɔrtɔgrafi], *s.f. Arch:* orthography; elevation plan (of building); normal profile, section (of fortification); *Geom:* orthogonal projection, orthographic projection.
orthographier [ɔrtɔgrafje], *v.tr.* (*p.d. & pr.sub.* **n. orthographiions, v. orthographiiez)** to spell (word) correctly; **mal o.,** to spell (word) incorrectly.
orthographique [ɔrtɔgrafik], *a.* **1.** *Gram:* orthographical; **réforme o.,** spelling reform; **concours o.,** spelling bee. **2.** *Geom:* orthographic (projection, etc.).
orthohydrogène [ɔrtɔidrɔʒɛn], *s.m.* orthohydrogen.
orthol [ɔrtɔl], *s.m. Phot:* ortol.
orthométrique [ɔrtɔmetrik], *a.* orthometric.
orthopédie [ɔrtɔpedi], *s.f.* orthop(a)edy, orthop(a)edics.
orthopédique [ɔrtɔpedik], *a.* orthop(a)edic.
orthopédiste [ɔrtɔpedist], *s.m. & f.* orthop(a)edist.
orthophonie [ɔrtɔfɔni], *s.f.* (*a*) *Ling:* orthoepy; (*b*) *Med:* speech therapy.
orthophonique [ɔrtɔfɔnik], *a.* **traitement o.,** speech therapy.
orthophoniste [ɔrtɔfɔnist], *s.m. & f.* speech therapist.
orthophorie [ɔrtɔfɔri], *s.f. Opt:* orthophoria.
orthophosphate [ɔrtɔfɔsfat], *s.m. Ch:* orthophosphate.
orthophosphorique [ɔrtɔfɔsfɔrik], *a. Ch:* orthophosphoric.
orthophyre [ɔrtɔfiːr], *s.m. Geol:* orthophyre.
orthopositonium [ɔrtɔpɔzitɔnjɔm], *s.m.*, **orthopositronium** [ɔrtɔpɔzitrɔnjɔm], *s.m. Atom.Ph:* orthopositronium.
orthoptère [ɔrtɔptɛːr]. **1.** *Ent:* (*a*) *a.* orthopterous, orthopteran, orthopteral; (*b*) *s.m.* orthopteron; orthopteran, orthopter; *pl.* **orthoptères,** Orthoptera. **2.** *s.m. A.Av:* orthopter.
orthoptéroïdes [ɔrtɔpterɔiːd], *s.m.pl. Ent:* Orthopteroidea.
orthoptie [ɔrtɔpti], *s.f. Med:* orthoptics.
orthoptique [ɔrtɔptik], *a. Mth: Med:* orthoptic.
orthor(h)aphes [ɔrtɔraf], *s.m.pl. Orn:* Orthorrhapha.
orthorhombique [ɔrtɔrɔ̃bik], *a. Cryst:* orthorhombic; trimetric.
orthoscopique [ɔrtɔskɔpik], *a. Phot:* orthoscopic (lens).
orthose [ɔrtoːz], *s.m. Miner:* orthoclase.
orthosélection [ɔrtɔselɛksjɔ̃], *s.f. Biol:* orthoselection.
orthosilicate [ɔrtɔsilikat], *s.m. Miner:* orthosilicate.
orthosilicique [ɔrtɔsilisik], *a. Ch:* orthosilicic.
orthostate [ɔrtɔstat], *s.m. Arch:* orthostat.
orthostatique [ɔrtɔstatik], *a. Med:* **albuminurie o.,** orthostatic, postural, albuminuria.
orthostatisme [ɔrtɔstatism], *s.m.* **1.** *Anat:* (*a*) (action of) standing upright; (*b*) upright posture. **2.** *Med:* postural complaints, diseases.
orthosympathique [ɔrtɔsɛ̃patik], *a. & s.m. Anat:* sympathetic (nerve).
orthotonos [ɔrtɔtɔnɔs], *s.m. Med:* orthotonus.
orthotrope [ɔrtɔtrɔp], *a.* **1.** *Bot:* orthotropous. **2.** *Const:* orthotropic.
orthoxylène [ɔrtɔksilɛn], *s.m. Ch:* orthoxylene.
ortie [ɔrti], *s.f.* **1.** *Bot:* nettle; **o. brûlante,** stinging nettle; **o. blanche, rouge,** white, red, dead nettle; **o. jaune,** yellow archangel; **o. grièche,** perennial nettle; *s.a.* FROC. **2.** *Coel:* **o. de mer,** sea anemone. **3.** *Vet:* (draining) rowel; seton.
ortié [ɔrtje], *a.* **fièvre ortiée,** nettlerash, urticaria.
ortier [ɔrtje], *v.tr.* (*p.d. & pr.sub.* **n. ortiions, v. ortiiez)** **1.** *Med:* to urticate (limb, etc.). **2.** (*of wine*) to sting (the palate).
ortive [ɔrtiːv], *a.f. Astr:* **amplitude o.,** ortive amplitude.
ortol [ɔrtɔl], *s.m. Phot:* ortol.
ortolan [ɔrtɔlɑ̃], *s.m. Orn:* ortolan bunting; *F:* **il ne mange pas des ortolans tous les jours,** he doesn't eat caviar every day.
ortstein [ɔrtʃtain], *s.m. Geol:* ortstein.
orvale [ɔrval], *s.f. Bot:* clary.
orvet [ɔrvɛ], *s.m. Rept:* slow-worm, blind-worm; **o. fragile,** common slow-worm.
orviétan [ɔrvjetɑ̃], *s.m.* (*a*) *A:* nostrum, quack medicine; (*b*) **marchand d'o.,** quack (doctor); charlatan.
oryctérope [ɔrikterɔp], *s.m. Z:* **o. (du Cap),** aardvark.
orysse [ɔris], *s.m. Ent:* oryssid; (*genus*) Oryssus.
oryx [ɔriks], *s.m. Z:* oryx; **o. algazelle,** scimitar-horned oryx; **o. gazelle,** gemsbok.
oryzomys [ɔrizɔmis], *s.m. Z:* rice rat; (*genus*) Oryzomys.
oryzopsis [ɔrizɔpsis], *s.m. Bot:* oryzopsis; mountain rice.
os[1] [ɔs; *pl.* o], *s.m.* bone; (*a*) **à, aux, gros os,** big-boned, bony; **qui a les os solides,** strong-boned; **sans os,** boneless; **n'avoir que la peau et les os, n'être qu'un paquet d'os** [do], to be nothing but skin and bone; **on lui voit les os,** he's nothing but a bag of bones; **voir qn en chair et en os,** to see s.o. in flesh and blood; **gelé jusqu'à la moelle des os, jusqu'au fond des os,** frozen to the marrow, to the bone; **mouillé, trempé, jusqu'aux os,** soaked to the skin, wet through; **casser, rompre, les os à qn,** (i) *A:* to break s.o. on the wheel; (ii) to beat s.o. black and blue; **il ne fera pas de vieux os,** he won't make old bones; he won't live long; he's not long for this world; **il y laissera ses os,** he'll die there; *P:* **l'avoir dans l'os,** to be diddled, taken in, had; (*b*) **os à moelle,** marrow bone; **ronger un os,** to pick, gnaw, a bone; *F:* **c'est un os bien dur à ronger,** it's a hard nut to crack; **il n'y a pas de viande sans os** [o], every rose has its thorn; *Ind:* **poudre, cendre, terre, d'os,** bone ash, bone earth; (*c*) **os de seiche,** cuttle bone; (*d*) *Farr:* **os coronaire,** small pastern; *Ven:* **os de cerf,** dew claws, false hoofs, of stag; (*e*) *F:* snag, hitch; **tomber sur un os,** to run up against a difficulty, a snag.
os[2], *s.m.*, **ôs** [ɔs], *s.m. Geol:* os; esker.
osan(n)e [ɔzan], *s.m. Ch:* glucosan(e).
osazone [ɔzazɔn], *s.f. Ch:* osazone.
oscabrion [ɔskabrjɔ̃], *s.m. Moll:* chiton.
Oscar [ɔskaːr], (*a*) *Pr.n.m.* Oscar; (*b*) *s.m. Cin: etc:* Oscar.
oscillaire [ɔsilɛːr], *s.f.*, **oscillaria** [ɔsilarja], *s.m. Algae:* oscillatoria, blue-green algae.

oscillant [ɔsil(l)ɑ̃], *a.* **1.** oscillating, (pendulum, machine, *El:* discharge); rocking (shaft); jigging (sieve, etc.); *Cin:* **miroir o. (pour enregistrement de la piste sonore),** mirror oscillator; *W.Tel:* **circuit o.,** oscillatory circuit. **2.** *Fin:* fluctuating (market). **3.** *Bot:* versatile (anther).

oscillateur, -trice [ɔsil(l)atœːr, -tris]. **1.** *a.* oscillating; *W.Tel:* **bobine oscillatrice, bobinage o.,** oscillating coil; **lampe oscillatrice,** oscillating valve; oscillator. **2.** *s.m. W.Tel: Elcs:* oscillator; oscillating coil; oscillation generator; vibrator; **o. maître, o. pilote,** master oscillator; **o. d'appoint,** booster oscillator; **o. à arc,** arc converter; **o. à lampe, à tube électronique,** valve oscillator, vacuum-tube oscillator; **o. à auto-oscillation, o. auto-entretenu,** oscillating transmitter; **o. à réaction,** feedback oscillator; *Atom.Ph:* **o. de pile,** reactor oscillator; **o. paramétrique,** parametric oscillator (of computer); **o. à blocage de phase,** phase-locked oscillator. **3.** *s.f. W.Tel: etc:* **oscillatrice,** oscillator.

oscillation [ɔsil(l)asjɔ̃], *s.f.* oscillation; (*a*) swing (of pendulum); **o. complète,** double oscillation (of pendulum); *W.Tel: etc:* **oscillations amorties, entretenues,** damped, sustained, oscillations; **oscillations en dents de scie,** saw-tooth wave; (*b*) rocking (of boat); *Av:* **o. de lacet,** snaking; **o. irrégulière,** buffeting; (*c*) *Mec.E:* vibration; *I.C.E:* **o. de vitesse,** hunting flutter; (*d*) fluctuation (of values, etc.); **oscillations de l'opinion publique,** variations in public opinion; **les oscillations du marché,** the fluctuations of the market; **oscillations climatiques,** (major) climatic changes.

oscillatoire [ɔsil(l)atwaːr], *a. Ph:* oscillatory (movement, circuit).

osciller [ɔsil(l)e], *v.i.* to oscillate; to sway. **1.** (*of pendulum*) to swing; (*of speedometer needle*) to flicker; (*of boat*) to rock; **faire o. un pendule,** to swing a pendulum; *W.Tel:* **faire o. une lampe,** to make a valve oscillate. **2.** (*a*) (*of pers.*) **o. entre deux opinions,** to waver between two opinions; (*b*) *Fin:* (*of markets, values*) to fluctuate.

oscillogramme [ɔsil(l)ɔgram], *s.m. El:* oscillogram.

oscillographe [ɔsil(l)ɔgraf], *s.m. Ph: El: Elcs:* oscillograph; **o. cathodique,** cathode-ray tube, oscillograph, oscilloscope.

oscillographique [ɔsil(l)ɔgrafik], *a.* oscillograph (curve, diagram, etc.); *Cin:* **équipage o.,** oscillograph recording apparatus.

oscillomètre [ɔsil(l)ɔmɛtr̥], *s.m. Med: Nau: etc:* oscillometer.

oscillométrie [ɔsil(l)ɔmetri], *s.f. Med:* oscillometry.

oscilloscope [ɔsil(l)ɔskɔp], *s.m.* oscilloscope; **o. à rayons cathodiques,** cathode-ray oscilloscope.

oscine [ɔsin], *s.f. Ent:* frit fly.

oscines [ɔsin], *s.m.pl. Orn:* Oscines.

osculaire [ɔskylɛːr], *a. Anat:* oscular (muscle).

osculateur, -trice [ɔskylatœːr, -tris], *a. Geom:* osculatory, osculating (curve); (*of curve*) **être osculatrice à une ligne,** to osculate with a line.

osculation [ɔskylasjɔ̃], *s.f. Geom:* osculation (of curves).

oscule [ɔskyl], *s.m. Z:* osculum (of sponge, etc.).

ose [oːz], *s.m. Ch:* (*esp. in comb.fm.*) ose; **les oses,** the monosaccharoses.

osé [oze], *a.* bold, daring(person, book, proposal); risqué (joke); **être trop o.,** to venture too far; *s.m.* **l'osé de ses doctrines,** the audaciousness, boldness, of his doctrines.

oseille [ozɛːj], *s.f.* (*a*) *Bot:* (common) sorrel; **o. aquatique,** water dock; **o. épinard,** spinach dock, herb patience; **o. des bois,** wood sorrel, cuckoo bread; **petite o., o. de brebis,** sheep sorrel; *P:* **la faire à l'o. à qn,** to put a fast one over on s.o.; to make a sucker of s.o.; (*b*) *Ch: F:* **sel d'o.,** salts of sorrel; (*c*) *P:* money, dough, lolly.

oser [oze], *v.tr.* **o. (faire) qch.,** to dare, venture, (to do) sth.; **je n'ose pas le faire;** I dare not do it; I am afraid to do it; **nul n'osait le proposer,** no one dared to propose it; **vous n'oseriez (pas)!** you would not dare! **j'ose croire que . . .,** I venture to think that . . .; **si j'ose (le) dire, si j'ose m'exprimer ainsi,** if I may venture to say so; if I may (make so bold as to) say so; if you don't mind my saying so; if you will forgive me for saying so; **s'il ose y aller seul,** if he is not afraid to go alone; **il n'ose pas me parler,** he is afraid to speak to me; **les bruits qu'il a osé répandre,** the rumours which he had the audacity to spread.

oseraie [ozrɛ], *s.f.* osier bed; osiery.

oseur, -euse [ozœːr, -øːz], *a. & s.* daring, bold (person).

oside [ozid], *s.m. Ch:* glycoside; (*esp. in comb.fm*) oside.

osier [ozje], *s.m.* **1.** *Bot:* osier, water willow; **o. blanc, vert,** velvet osier; **o. rouge,** red osier; **o. brun,** almond willow; **o. jaune,** golden willow; **o. à trois étamines,** almond-leaved willow. **2.** (*a*) **brin d'o.,** withy, withe; (*b*) wicker(work); *A:* **voiture en o.,** basket carriage; **panier d'o.,** wicker basket.

osiéricole [ozjerikɔl], *a.* **région o.,** osier-producing region.

osiériculteur [ozjerikyltœːr], *s.m.* osier grower.

osiériculture [ozjerikyltyːr], *s.f.* osier cultivation.

osiériste [ozjerist], *s.m.* (*a*) osier grower; (*b*) osier seller.

osiriaque [ozirjak], *a. Arch:* Osiride (pillar).

osirien, -ienne [ozirjɛ̃, -jɛn], *a. A.Egyptian Civ:* Osirian.

Osler [ozlɛːr], *Pr.n. Med:* **maladie d'O.,** Osler's disease.

Osmanli [ɔsmɑ̃li], *s.m. Hist:* Osmanli; Ottoman; *a.* **L'empire o.,** the Ottoman empire.

osmiate [ɔzmjat], *s.m. Ch:* osmiate, osmate.

osmie [ɔzmi], *s.f. Ent:* osmia.

osmieux, -euse [ɔzmjø, -øːz], *a. Ch:* osmious.

osmique [ɔsmik], *a. Ch:* osmic.

osmiridium [ɔzmiridjɔm], *s.m. Miner:* osmiridium.

osmium [ɔsmjɔm], *s.m. Ch:* osmium.

osmiure [ɔzmjyːr], *s.m. Ch:* **o. d'iridium,** iridium osmium alloy.

osmiuré [ɔzmjyre], *a. Miner:* osmium-bearing.

osmomètre [ɔsmɔmɛtr̥], *s.m.* osmograph, osmometer.

osmométrie [ɔzmɔmetri], *s.f.* osmometry.

osmométrique [ɔzmɔmetrik], *a.* osmometric.

osmondacées [ɔzmɔ̃dase], *s.f.pl. Bot:* Osmundaceae.

osmonde [ɔsmɔ̃ːd], *s.f. Bot:* osmund; **o. royale,** royal fern, water fern, flowering fern.

osmondite [ɔzmɔ̃dit], *s.f. Metall:* osmondite.

osmophore [ɔzmɔfɔːr], *s.m. Ch:* osmophore.

osmorégulateur [ɔzmɔregylatœːr], *s.m. Ph:* osmoregulator.

osmose [ɔsmoːz], *s.f. Ph: Biol:* osmosis; **o. électrique,** electro-endosmosis.

osmotactisme [ɔzmɔtaktism], *s.m. Biol:* osmotaxis.

osmotique [ɔsmɔtik], *a. Ph:* osmotic (pressure).

osone [ɔzɔn], *s.f. Ch:* osone.

osphrésiophilie [ɔsfrezjɔfili], *s.f. Psy:* osphresiophilia.

osphroménidés [ɔsfrɔmenide], *s.m.pl. Ich:* Osphromenidae.

osque [ɔsk], *a. & s. A.Geog: Ling:* Oscan.

Ossa [ɔssa], *Pr.n.m. A.Geog:* Ossa; *s.a.* PÉLION.

ossature [ɔsatyːr], *s.f.* **1.** *Anat:* frame, skeleton (of man or animal); **homme d'une o. puissante,** man of powerful frame, of powerful build. **2.** frame(work), carcass, skeleton, ossature (of building, etc.); **o. d'un pont,** main girders of a bridge; **l'o. terrestre,** the ossature of the earth; **l'o. de la langue française,** the structure, essentials, of the French language; **l'o. sociale,** the social structure.

ossaturé [ɔsatyre], *a.* stiffened with a framework (**de,** of); ribbed (**de,** with).

osse [ɔs], *s.m.* **1.** *Ethn:* Osset. **2.** *Ling:* Ossetic, Ossete.

osséine [ɔsein], *s.f. Ch:* ossein, ostein(e).

osselet [ɔslɛ], *s.m.* **1.** knuckle bone (of sheep); **jouer aux osselets,** to play at knuckle-bones, at dibs. **2.** *Anat:* ossicle; **les osselets de l'oreille,** the ossicles of the ear; the otic bones. **3.** *Vet:* osselet (on fetlock, etc.).

ossements [ɔsmɑ̃], *s.m.pl.* bones, remains (of dead men, animals); **retrouver les o. d'un explorateur,** to find the bones of an explorer.

osseret [ɔsrɛ], *s.m.* (butcher's) cleaver.

osserie [ɔsri], *s.f.* **1.** bone working. **2.** bone works.

ossète [ɔsɛt], *s.m.* **1.** *Ethn:* Osset. **2.** *Ling:* Ossetic, Ossete.

osseux, -euse [ɔsø, -øːz], *a.* bony; osseous (tissue); **système o.,** bone structure; **greffe osseuse,** bone graft; **figure, main, osseuse,** bony face, hand.

ossianique [ɔsjanik], **ossianesque** [ɔsjanɛsk], *a. Lit.Hist:* Ossianic (literature, etc.); Ossianesque (style).

ossianisme [ɔsjanism], *s.m. Lit.Hist:* Ossianism.

ossianiste [ɔsjanist], *s. Lit.Hist:* Ossianist.

ossicule [ɔsikyl], *s.m. Z:* ossicle.

ossification [ɔsifikasjɔ̃], *s.f. Med:* ossification.

ossifier [ɔsifje], *v.tr.* to ossify.

s'ossifier (*of tissue*) to ossify, to become ossified; to harden.

ossifluent [ɔsiflyɑ̃], *a. Med:* ossifluent (abscess).

ossifrage [ɔsifraːʒ], *s.m. Orn:* giant fulmar.

ossu [ɔsy], *a.* big-boned, raw-boned, bony.

ossuaire [ɔsɥɛːr], *s.m.* (*a*) heap of bones; (*b*) ossuary, charnel-house.

ostariophysaires [ɔstarjɔfizɛːr], *s.m.pl. Ich:* Ostariophysi.

ostéalgie [ɔstealʒi], *s.f. Med:* ostealgia.

ostéichthyens [ɔsteiktjɛ̃], *s.m.pl. Ich:* Osteichthyes.

ostéine [ɔstein], *s.f. Ch:* ostein(e), ossein.

ostéite [ɔsteit], *s.f. Med:* osteitis.

ostendais, -aise [ɔstɑ̃dɛ, -ɛːz], *a. & s. Geog:* (native, inhabitant) of Ostend.

Ostende [ɔstɑ̃ːd], *Pr.n. Geog:* Ostend.

ostensible [ɔstɑ̃sibl̥], *a.* (*a*) *A:* fit to be seen; that may be shown; (*b*) open, patent, to all; above-board; visible, apparent; **ils travaillaient d'une manière o. à renverser le gouvernement,** they were working openly to overthrow the government.

ostensiblement [ɔstɑ̃sibləmɑ̃], *adv.* openly, publicly; obviously; **o. poli,** markedly polite.

ostensif, -ive [ɔstɑ̃sif, -iːv], *a.* (*a*) *A:* intended to be shown, to be made public; (*b*) *Dipl:* **pièces ostensives,** open documents.

ostension [ɔstɑ̃sjɔ̃], *s.f. Ecc:* exposition (of the host, relics).

ostensoir [ɔstɑ̃swaːr], *s.m. Ecc:* monstrance, ostensory.

ostentateur, -trice [ɔstɑ̃tatœːr, -tris], *a. Lit:* ostentatious.

ostentation [ɔstɑ̃tasjɔ̃], *s.f.* ostentation, show; display; **avoir l'o. en horreur,** to have a horror of ostentation; **faire o. de sa misère,** to parade, make a parade of, one's poverty; **il fait o. de générosité,** he makes a show of generosity; **avec o.,** ostentatiously; **sans o.,** unostentatiously; **agir par o.,** to do sth. for the sake of ostentation, *F:* in order to show off.

ostentatoire [ɔstɑ̃tatwaːr], *a.* ostentatious.

ostentatoirement [ɔstɑ̃tatwarmɑ̃], *adv.* ostentatiously.

ostéo-arthrite [ɔsteɔartrit], *s.f. Med:* osteo-arthritis; ostearthritis.

ostéo-arthropathie [ɔsteɔartrɔpati], *s.f. Med:* osteoarthropathy.

ostéoblaste [ɔsteɔblast], *s.m. Biol:* osteoblast.

ostéochondrite [ɔsteɔkɔ̃drit], *s.f. Med:* osteochondritis.

ostéochondromatose [ɔsteɔkɔ̃drɔmatoːz], *s.f. Med:* osteochondromatosis.

ostéoclasie [ɔsteɔklazi], *s.f. Surg:* osteoclasis.

ostéoclaste [ɔsteɔklast], *s.m. Anat:* osteoclast.

ostéodentine [ɔsteɔdɑ̃tin], *s.f. Anat:* osteodentine.

ostéogène [ɔsteɔʒɛn], *a.* osteogenetic; bone-forming (cell).

ostéogénique [ɔsteɔʒenik], *a.* osteogenic.

ostéogénèse [ɔsteɔʒenɛːz], *s.f.*, **ostéogénie** [ɔsteɔʒeni], *s.f. Biol:* osteogeny, osteogenesis.

ostéoglossides [ɔsteɔglɔsid], **ostéoglossidés** [ɔsteɔglɔside], *s.m.pl. Ich:* Osteoglossidae; osteoglossids.

ostéographie [ɔsteɔgrafi], *s.f.* osteography.

ostéoïde [ɔsteɔid], *a.* osteoid.

ostéolépidés [ɔsteɔlepide], *s.m.pl. Paleont:* Osteolepidae.

ostéolite [ɔsteɔlit], *s.f. Miner:* osteolite.

ostéolithe [ɔsteɔlit], *s.m.* petrified bone.

ostéologie [ɔsteɔlɔʒi], *s.f.* osteology.

ostéologique [ɔsteɔlɔʒik], *a.* osteologic(al).

ostéologue [ɔsteɔlɔg], *s.m. & f.* osteologist.

ostéolyse [ɔsteɔliːz], *s.f. Med:* osteolysis.

ostéomalacie [ɔsteɔmalasi], *s.f. Med:* osteomalacia.

ostéome [ɔsteoːm], *s.m. Med:* osteoma.

ostéomyélite [ɔsteɔmjelit], *s.f. Med:* osteomyelitis.

ostéonécrose [ɔsteɔnekroːz], *s.f. Med:* osteonecrosis.

ostéopathie [ɔsteɔpati], *s.f.* osteopathy.

ostéopériostite [ɔsteɔperjɔstit], *s.f. Med:* osteoperiostitis.

ostéopétrose [ɔsteɔpetroːz], *s.f. Med:* osteopetrosis.

ostéophone [ɔsteɔfɔn], *s.m.* osteophone.

ostéophyte [ɔsteɔfit], *s.m. Med:* osteophyte.

ostéoplaste [ɔsteɔplast], *s.m. Anat:* osteoplast.

ostéoplastie [ɔsteɔplasti], *s.f. Surg:* osteoplasty.

ostéoporose [ɔsteɔpɔroːz], *s.f. Med:* osteoporosis.

ostéosarcome [ɔsteɔsarkoːm], *s.m. Med:* osteosarcoma.

ostéosclérose [ɔsteɔskleroːz], *s.f. Med:* osteosclerosis.

ostéosynthèse [ɔsteɔsɛ̃tɛːz], *s.f. Surg:* osteosynthesis.

ostéotome [ɔsteɔtɔm], *s.m. Surg:* (*instrument*) osteotome.

ostéotomie [ɔsteɔtɔmi], *s.f. Surg:* osteotomy.

Ostie [ɔsti], *Pr.n. Geog:* Ostia.

ostiole [ɔstjɔl], *s.m. Biol:* ostiole.

ostracé [ɔstrase], *a.* ostraceous.

ostraciser [ɔstrasize], *v.tr.* to ostracize.

ostracisme [ɔstrasism], *s.m.* ostracism; **frapper qn d'o.,** to ostracize s.o.

ostracodermes [ɔstrakɔdɛrm], *s.m.pl. Paleont:* Ostracodermi, ostracoderms.

ostracodes [ɔstrakɔd], *s.m.pl. Crust:* Ostracoda.

ostréicole [ɔstreikɔl], *a.* pertaining to oyster culture; **l'industrie o.,** the oyster industry.

ostréiculteur [ɔstreikyltœ:r], *s.m.* oyster farmer, oyster culturist.

ostréiculture [ɔstreikylty:r], *s.f.* ostreiculture, oyster farming.

ostréidés [ɔstreide], *s.m.pl. Moll:* Ostreidae.

ostréiforme [ɔstreifɔrm], *a. Z:* ostreiform.

ostrogot(h), -ot(h)e [ɔstrɔgo, -ɔt]. **1.** *a. Hist:* Ostrogothic. **2.** *s.* (*a*) *Hist:* Ostrogoth, Eastern Goth; (*b*) *F:* boor, barbarian; vandal; **quel o.!** what a savage! **un drôle d'o.,** an odd customer.

otacariose [ɔtakarjo:z], *s.f. Vet:* otacariasis.

otage [ɔta:ʒ], *s.m.* (*a*) hostage (**de,** for); **prendre une ville, qn, pour o.,** to take a town, s.o., as hostage; (*b*) guarantee, surety.

otalgie [ɔtalʒi], *s.f. Med:* otalgia, earache.

otalgique [ɔtalʒik], *a. Med:* otalgic.

otarie [ɔtari], *s.f. Z:* otary; otaria; eared seal; sea lion; sea bear; fur seal; *pl.* **otaries,** Otariidae.

ôté [ote], *p.p. used as prep., usu.inv.* barring, except; **ouvrage excellent ô. deux ou trois chapitres,** an excellent book, apart from, except for, two or three chapters.

ôter [ote], *v.tr.* to remove, take away; (*a*) **ô. des abus,** to suppress, do away with, abuses; **ô. le couvert,** to clear away, clear the table; **ô. des taches,** to remove stains; **ô. son pardessus, ses gants,** to take off one's overcoat, one's gloves; *A:* **ô. son chapeau à qn,** to raise one's hat to s.o.; *Mus:* **ô. la tirasse,** to shut off the pedal coupler (of organ); *Prov:* **en avril, n'ôtez pas un fil** = ne'er cast a clout till May be out; (*b*) **ô. qch. à qn,** to take sth. away from s.o.; to deprive s.o. of sth.; **l'amour ôte la raison aux hommes,** love deprives men of their reason; **ô. la vie à qn,** to kill s.o.; **ô. les illusions à qn,** to disillusion s.o.; **cela n'ôte rien à sa valeur,** that detracts nothing from its value; (*c*) **ô. qch. de qch.,** to take sth. away from sth.; **ôtez trois de cinq,** take away, deduct, three from five; **trois ôté de cinq égale deux,** three from five leaves two; **il me l'a ôté des mains,** he snatched it out of my hands; **ô. à qn le pain de la bouche,** to take the bread out of s.o.'s mouth; **on ne m'ôtera pas l'idée que . . .,** I can't get rid of the idea, get it out of my head, that . . .; nobody will rid me of the idea that . . .; **cela me l'a ôté tout à fait de l'esprit,** that drove, put, it entirely out of my head; (*d*) *A:* **ô. qn de (qch.),** to relieve s.o. of (anxiety, etc.); **cela nous ôte de doute,** that relieves us of doubt.

s'ôter, to remove oneself, to move away; *F:* **ôte-toi de là!** get out of the way! get out (of here)! *F:* **ôte-toi de devant mes yeux!** get out of my sight! *F:* **ôte-toi de là que je m'y mette!** that's my place if you don't mind! get out of there and give me some room!

Othon [ɔtɔ̃], *Pr.n.m. Hist:* Otho, Otto.

otididés [ɔtidide], *s.m.pl. Orn:* Otididae, the bustards.

otiorhynque [ɔtjɔrɛ̃:k], *s.m. Ent:* otiorhynchid.

otique [ɔtik], *a. Anat:* otic; **nerf o.,** otic nerve.

otite [ɔtit], *s.f. Med:* otitis; **o. moyenne,** otitis media; tympanitis.

otocyon [ɔtɔsjɔ̃], *s.m. Z:* otocyon; long-eared fox.

otocyste [ɔtɔsist], *s.m. Z:* otocyst.

otolit(h)e[1] [ɔtɔlit], *s.f. Anat: Z:* otolite, otolith.

otolithe[2] [ɔtɔlit], *s.m. Ich:* otholithus.

otologie [ɔtɔlɔʒi], *s.f.* otology.

otologiste [ɔtɔlɔʒist], *s.m. Med:* otologist, aurist, ear specialist.

otopiésis [ɔtɔpjezis], *s.f. Med:* otopiesis.

otoplastie [ɔtɔplasti], *s.f. Surg:* otoplasty.

oto-rhino-laryngologie [ɔtɔrinɔlarɛ̃gɔlɔʒi], *s.f. Med:* otorhinolaryngology.

oto-rhino-laryngologiste [ɔtɔrinɔlarɛ̃gɔlɔʒist], *s.m. or f.* ear, nose and throat specialist, otorhinolaryngologist; *pl. oto-rhino-laryngologistes.*

otorragie [ɔtɔraʒi], *s.f. Med:* otorrhagia, haemorrhage of the ear.

otorrhée [ɔtɔre], *s.f. Med:* otorrhoea.

otosclérose [ɔtɔsklero:z], *s.f. Med:* otosclerosis.

otoscope [ɔtɔskɔp], *s.m. Med:* otoscope, auriscope, ear speculum.

otoscopie [ɔtɔskɔpi], *s.f. Med:* otoscopy.

otospongiose [ɔtɔspɔ̃ʒjo:z], *s.f. Med:* otospongiosis.

Otrante [ɔtrɑ̃:t], *Pr.n. Geog:* Otranto.

ottoman, -ane [ɔtɔmɑ̃, -an]. **1.** *a. & s. Hist:* Ottoman. **2.** *s.f. Furn:* **ottomane,** divan, ottoman. **3.** *s.m. Tex:* grogram.

ou [u], *conj.* **1.** or; (*a*) (*two names for same thg*) **le baobab ou arbre à pain,** the baobab or monkey bread; **le patronyme ou nom de famille,** the family name or surname; (*b*) **voulez-vous du bœuf ou du jambon?** would you like beef or ham? **il lui est parfaitement égal d'être ici ou là,** he doesn't mind in the least whether he is here or there; **il vient trois ou quatre fois par jour,** he comes three or four times a day; **sept ou huit hommes,** seven or eight men; **l'un ou l'autre,** one or the other; **tôt ou tard,** sooner or later; **de gauche à droite ou inversement,** from left to right or vice versa; (*c*) (*with verb*) **entrez ou sortez,** either come in or go out; (*d*) (*with article*) **indiquez le ou les domaines . . .,** state the field or fields . . .; **l'examen du ou des systèmes,** the examination of the system or systems; (*e*) (*v. usu. in pl.*) **vous ou moi, nous lui en parlerons,** (either) you or I will speak to him about it; **vous ou lui, vous lui en parlerez,** (either) you or he will speak to him about it; **lui ou son frère va, vont, vous aider,** he or his brother will help you; (*f*) (*subjects mutually exclusive; concord always in the sing.*) **on ne savait pas encore si à Marie Tudor succéderait Marie Stuart ou Élizabeth,** it was not yet known whether Mary Tudor would be succeeded by Mary Stuart or Elizabeth; **l'une ou l'autre devait forcément monter sur le trône,** one or the other was bound to ascend the throne. **2.** (*second* **ou** *often strengthened with* **bien**) **ils exigeaient des paysans ou du blé ou (bien) de l'argent,** they demanded either wheat or money from the peasants. **3. ou bien,** or else; **il payera, ou bien il ira en prison,** he must pay, or else he will go to prison. **4.** *Elcs:* (*computers*) **circuit, mélangeur, OU,** OR circuit, OR gate; **élément OU,** OR element.

où [u], *adv.* **1.** *interr.* (*a*) (*direct speech*) where? **où habite-t-il?** where does he live? **où allez-vous?** where are you going? **où en êtes-vous?** how far have you got with it? where do you stand (in the matter)? **d'où venez-vous?** where do you come from? where have you been? **d'où êtes-vous?** where are you from? **d'où vient que . . .?** how does it happen, come about, that . . .? **d'où tenez-vous cela?** where did you learn that? how did you know? **par où?** (by) which way? **par où est-il passé?** which way did he go? **jusqu'où les a-t-il suivis?** how far did he follow them? (*b*) (*indirect speech*) **dis-moi où tu vas,** tell me where you are going; **je ne sais où aller,** I don't know where to go; **je vois où il veut venir,** I can see what he's getting at; (*c*) **n'importe où,** anywhere; **mettez-le n'importe où,** put it down anywhere; **il est allé je ne sais où,** I don't know where he's gone; *Pej:* **il est allé Dieu sait où,** he's gone to the devil for all I know (or care). **2.** *rel.* (*a*) where; **j'irai où vous voudrez,** I'll go where(ever) you wish; **l'endroit où sa voiture a quitté la route,** the place where his car went off the road; **partout où il va,** wherever he goes; **là où,** (there) where; **vous trouverez ma pipe là où je l'ai laissée,** you will find my pipe where I left it; **la source d'où découlent ces maux,** the source of these evils; **d'où on conclut que . . .,** from which it may be concluded that . . .; **la rue par où il a couru,** the street through, along, which he ran; **la maison d'où je sors,** the house I have just come out of; (*b*) when; **dans le temps où il était jeune,** in the days when he was young; **au moment où il arrivait le cheval mourut,** just as he arrived the horse died; (*c*) = **dans lequel, auquel, etc.) la maison où il demeure,** the house in which he lives, the house he lives in; **le terrible état où il est,** the dreadful state he is in; **au prix où se vend le sucre,** at the price sugar is fetching; **le rang où je suis parvenu,** the rank which I have attained; **le siècle où nous vivons,** the age we live in; *A:* **l'Amphitryon où je dîne,** mine host with whom I dine. **3.** (*concessive*) **où que vous soyez,** wherever you may be; **d'où que découlent ces maux,** whatever the source of these evils may be.

ouabaïne [wabain], *s.f. Ch:* ouabain.

ouache[1] [waʃ], *s.f. Nau:* = HOUACHE.

ouache[2], *s.f. Fr.C:* bear's den.

ouadi. *See* OUED.

ouaille [wa:j], *s.f.* **1.** *B.Lit. & Dial:* sheep. **2. le pasteur et ses ouailles,** the minister and his flock; **être parmi les ouailles d'un curé,** to sit under a priest.

ouais [wɛ], *int.* (*a*) *A:* (*of surprise*) what! my word! (*b*) *F: Iron:* **je vous l'apporterai demain, sans faute!—o.!** I'll bring it tomorrow without fail!—oh yeah!

ouakari [wakari], *s.m. Z:* uakari (monkey).

ouanderou [wɑ̃dru], *s.m. Z:* wanderoo (monkey).

ouaouaron [wɑwarɔ̃], *s.m. Fr.C:* bullfrog.

ouate[1] [wat], *s.f.* (*usu.* **la ouate,** *occ.* **l'ouate**) **1.** (*a*) wadding; **couverture doublée d'o.,** (wadded) quilt; (*b*) cotton wool; **o. hydrophile,** (absorbent) cotton wool; **vivre dans de la o.,** to have a comfortable life; to coddle oneself. **2. o. minérale,** slag wool. **3.** *Bot:* **herbe à o.,** silkweed, swallow wort.

ouate[2], *int. P:* rubbish! not a bit of it.

ouaté [wate], *a.* **1.** wadded, padded; **robe de chambre ouatée,** quilted dressing gown; **étoffe ouatée,** quilting; **couverture ouatée,** (wadded) quilt. **2.** woolly, fleecy (cloud, snow); soft (footstep); **profils ouatés,** woolly outlines.

ouater [wate], *v.tr.* **1.** to wad; to pad; to line with wadding; to quilt; **o. un manteau,** to line, quilt, a cloak (with wadding); *F:* **o. qn,** to (molly)coddle s.o. **2.** (*a*) **o. ses pas,** to tread softly, to deaden one's footsteps; **la neige ouate les abords du poste,** the snow muffles the sound of anything approaching the post; (*b*) **une brume épaisse ouate la vallée,** the valley is blurred by a thick mist.

ouateux, -euse [watø, -ø:z], *a.* (cotton-)woolly, fleecy, soft as cotton wool.

ouatier [watje], *s.m.* **1.** *Bot:* silkweed. **2.** *Tex:* quilting machine.

ouatinage [watina:ʒ], *s.m. Tex:* (*process*) quilting.

ouatine [watin], *s.f. Tex:* (*fabric*) quilting.

ouatiner [watine], *v.tr. Tex:* to quilt, to line (garment) with quilting.

ouatte [wat], *int. P:* rubbish! not a bit of it!

Oubangui [ubɑ̃gi], *Pr.n.m. Geog:* Ubangi (district, river); *Hist:* **les Territoires du Haut-O., l'O.-Chari,** the Ubangi-Chari.

oubanguien, -ienne [ubɑ̃gjɛ̃, -jɛn], *a. & s.m. Geog: Ling:* Ubangi.

oubli [ubli], *s.m.* **1.** (*a*) forgetting; **l'o. de ses devoirs,** the neglect of one's duties; **l'o. d'une offense,** the forgetting, forgiving, of an offence; **par o.,** inadvertently; by, through, an oversight; (*b*) forgetfulness; **l'o. de soi-même,** forgetfulness of self; (*c*) oblivion; **tomber dans l'o.,** to sink, fall, into oblivion, to be forgotten; **poème voué à l'o.,** poem doomed to oblivion, deservedly forgotten; **sauver qn, qch., de l'o.,** to rescue s.o., sth., from, oblivion. **2.** omission, oversight; **réparer un o.,** to rectify an omission.

oubliable [ubliabl̩], *a.* forgettable.

oubliance [ubliɑ̃:s], *s.f. A:* forgetfulness.

oublie [ubli], *s.f. A:* (*a*) *Ecc:* wafer; (*b*) *Com:* wafer (rolled into a cone, for ice cream, etc.).

oublier [ublije], *v.tr.* (*p.d. & pr.sub.* **n. oubliions, v. oubliiez**) to forget; (*a*) **j'ai oublié son nom,** I have forgotten his name; his name has slipped my memory; **o. le passé,** to forget the past; to let bygones be bygones; **faire o. son passé,** to live down one's past; **n'oubliez pas que . . .,** don't forget, bear in mind, that . . .; **o. de faire qch.,** to forget to do sth.; **un récit qu'il oubliait avoir déjà fait,** a story which he forgot he had told already; **on ne nous le laissera pas o.,** we shall never hear the last of it; **il mourut oublié de tous,** he died forgotten by all; (*b*) to overlook, neglect; **o. l'heure,** to forget, overlook, the time (of an engagement, etc.); **cela me fit complètement o. mon rendez-vous,** it sent my appointment clean out of my head, out of my mind; **o. les heures,** to lose count of time; **o. son devoir,** to neglect one's duty; **o. un mot,** to leave out a word; **o. ses intérêts,** to pay no attention to, be careless of, one's own interests; **o. son mouchoir,** to leave one's handkerchief behind; **un mouchoir s'oublie facilement,** it's easy to forget a handkerchief; **on n'oublia rien pour le faire avouer,** they left no stone unturned to make him confess; **ne m'oubliez pas dans vos prières,** remember me in your prayers.

s'oublier. 1. il ne s'oublie pas, he can look after himself, his own interests; he knows how to look after number one. **2.** to forget one's manners, to forget oneself; **il s'oublia jusqu'à la frapper,** he so far forgot himself that he struck her; **le chien s'est oublié sur le tapis,** the dog's made a mess on the carpet; **elles s'oublièrent à causer pendant la messe,** they forgot themselves and talked during mass. **3. s'o. à rêver,** to go off into a daydream; **elles s'oublièrent à causer,** while talking they lost all count of time.

oubliette [ubljɛt], *s.f. usu. pl.* oubliette, secret dungeon; *F:* **mettre, jeter, qch. aux oubliettes,** (i) to consign sth. to oblivion; (ii) to shelve sth. indefinitely.

oublieur, -euse[1] [ublijœːr, -øːz], *s.* forgetful person.

oublieux, -euse[2] [ublijø, -øːz], *a.* forgetful (de, of); **o. de ma présence,** oblivious of my presence; **o. de son devoir,** neglectful of his duty.

oued [wɛd], *s.m. Geog:* wadi; *pl. oueds, ouadi* [wadi].

Ouen [uɑ̃], *Pr.n.m.* Owen.

Ouessant [wesɑ̃], *Pr.n.m. Geog:* Ushant.

ouessantin, -ine [wɛsɑ̃tɛ̃, -in], *a. & s. Geog:* (native, inhabitant) of Ushant.

ouest [west]. **1.** *s.m. no pl.* west; **résider dans l'O.,** to live in the West (of a country); **les provinces de l'O.,** the western provinces; **un vent d'o.,** a westerly wind; **le vent (d')o.,** the west wind; **à l'o. de qch.,** (to the) west, (to the) westward, of sth.; **à l'o., dans l'o.,** in the west; **le vent est à l'o.,** the wind is west, there is a west wind; **borné à l'o. par . . .,** bounded on the west by . . .; **maison exposée à l'o.,** house facing west; **vers l'o.,** westward(s); *Nau:* **marche, route, vers l'o.;** *a.* **chemin o.,** westing; (*of the sun*) **passer à l'o.,** to west(er). **2.** *a.inv.* **côté o.,** western, west, side; **les régions o. de la France,** the westerly, western, parts of France.

ouest-allemand, -ande [wɛstalmɑ̃, -ɑ̃ːd], *a. & s.* West German; *pl. ouest-allemand(e)s.*

ouestir [wɛstiːr], *v.i.* (*of wind*) to veer to the west.

ouest-nord-ouest [wɛstnɔrwɛst], *a.inv.* west-north-west.

ouest-sud-ouest [wɛstsydwɛst], *a.inv.* west-south-west.

ouf [uf], *int.* **1.** (*sigh of relief*) ah! ha! what a relief! **2.** (*indicating oppression*) **o., on étouffe ici!** phew! it's stifling here! *F:* **avant de pouvoir dire o.!** before we could say Jack Robinson; *F:* **il n'a pas dit o.!** he didn't say a word.

Oufa [ufa], *Pr.n.m. Geog:* Ufa.

Ouganda [ugɑ̃da], *Pr.n. Geog:* Uganda.

Ougres [ugr], *s.m.pl. Ethn:* Ugrians.

ougrien, -enne [ugriɛ̃, -ɛn]. **1.** *a. & s. Ethn:* Ugrian. **2.** *s.m. Ling:* Ugric.

oui [wi], yes. **1.** *adv.* (*a*) **vient-il?—o.,** is he coming?—yes; **avez-vous faim?—o.,** are you hungry?—yes (, I am); **viendrez-vous?—o.,** will you come? yes (, I will); **pouvez-vous venir?—o.,** can you come?—yes (, I can); **l'aimez-vous?—o.,** do you love him?—yes (, I do); **il a dit o.,** he said yes; **je crois que o.,** *F:* **qu'o.,** I think so; **il m'assure que o.,** he assures me that it is so, that it's right; **faire signe que o., faire o. de la tête,** to nod one's head in agreement; **mais o., bien sûr que o.,** but of course, naturally; **o., o., allez toujours,** yes, get on with it; **je suis heureux, o., très heureux,** I'm happy, very happy indeed; **êtes vous satisfait?—o. et non,** are you satisfied?—well, yes, up to a point; *Nau:* **o., commandant!** aye, aye, sir; **eh, o.!** really! (*b*) (*interrogatively*) **ah, o.?** really, *F:* **tu viens, o.?** you're coming, aren't you? aren't you ever coming? *F:* **est-ce lui, o. ou non?** come on, out with it, is it him or not? *P:* (*not used in polite conversation*) **c'est-il o. ou merde?** is it bloody well yes or no? **2.** *s.m.inv.* **ce "o." m'a étonné,** that "yes" astonished me; (*in voting*) **deux cents o. et trois cents non,** two hundred ayes and three hundred noes; **se quereller pour un o., pour un non,** to quarrel about nothing, over a mere trifle; *F:* **prononcer le grand o.,** to get married, to take the plunge; **le grand o.,** the great "I will."

ouiche [wiʃ], *int. P:* (*denotes incredulity*) **croyez-vous qu'elle le fera?—ah o.!** do you think she'll do it?—don't you believe it! nothing of the kind! the hell she will!

oui-da, *A:* **oui-dà** [wida], *adv.* yes, of course; naturally!

ouï-dire [widiːr], *s.m.inv.* hearsay; **je ne le sais que par o.-d.,** I know it only by, from, hearsay; *Jur:* **simples o.-d.,** hearsay evidence.

ouïe [wi], *s.f.* **1.** (*a*) (sense of) hearing; audition; **avoir l'o. fine,** to have a keen, sharp, ear; to have excellent hearing; **avoir l'o. défectueuse,** to be hard of hearing; **à portée de l'o.,** within earshot, hearing distance; **à perte d'o.,** as far as the sound can reach; **être tout o.,** to be all ears, all attention; (*b*) *A:* **à l'o. de ces paroles . . .,** on hearing these words. . .. **2.** (*a*) *pl.* sound holes (of violin, etc.); (*b*) ear (of ventilator, etc.); inlet. **3.** *pl.* gills (of fish); *F:* **avoir les ouïes pâles,** to be, look, white about the gills.

oui-ja [wiʒa], *s.m. Psychics:* ouija.

ouillage [ujaːʒ], *s.m. Winem:* **1.** ullaging. **2.** ullage.

ouille [uːj], *int.* (*indicating pain*) ouch!

ouiller [uje], *v.tr.* to ullage (cask).

ouillère, ouillière [ujɛːr], *s.f. Vit:* space between rows of vines (used for other crops).

ouillette [ujɛt], *s.f. Winem:* uller.

ouïr [wiːr, uiːr], *v.tr.* (*used in the inf.; in p.p.* **ouï** *and compound tenses; in* **oyant, oyez;** *and occ. in p.h.* **j'ouïs.** *fu.* **j'ouïrai)** *A:* (= ENTENDRE) to hear; *still used for archaic effect; often Hum:* **ouïtes-vous jamais rien de pareil?** did you ever hear the like? (*modern use*) **nous avons ouï dire à notre père que . . .,** we have heard our father say that . . .; *Ecc:* **le dimanche la messe ouïras,** thou shalt hear mass on Sundays; *Jur:* **o. les témoins,** to hear the witnesses; *Adm: Jur: A:* **oyez! oyez! oyez!**

ouistiti [wistiti], *s.m. Z:* wistiti, marmoset.

oukase [ukɑːz], *s.m.* ukase.

ouléma [ulema], *s.m. Moham.Rel:* ulema.

oulice [ulis], *s.f. Carp:* **assemblage à o.,** forked mortice and tenon joint.

oullière [uljɛːr], *s.f. Vit:* = OUILLÈRE.

oulmière [ulmjɛːr], *s.f.* elm grove.

oumiak [umjak], *s.m. Nau:* umiak.

Oupanichads [upaniʃad], *s.f.pl. A.Lit:* the Upanishads.

Our [uːr], *Pr.n. A.Geog:* Ur.

ouragan [uragɑ̃], *s.m.* hurricane; **entrer en o. dans une pièce,** to burst into a room; **o. politique,** political storm.

Oural (l') [lural], *Pr.n. Geog:* (*a*) the Ural (river); (*b*) **l'O., les Montagnes de l'O.,** the Urals, the Ural Mountains.

ouralien, -ienne [uraljɛ̃, -jɛn], *a. Geog:* Uralian.

ouralite [uralit], *s.f. Miner:* uralite.

oural(it)isation [ural(it)izasjɔ̃], *s.f. Miner:* uralitization.

ouralo-altaïque [uraloaltaik], *a. Ethn: Ling:* Ural(o)-Altaic; *pl. ouralo-altaïques.*

ouraque [urak], *s.m. Anat:* urachus.

ourdir [urdiːr], *v.tr.* **1.** (*a*) *Tex:* to warp (linen, cloth); *Prov:* **à toile ourdie Dieu envoie le fil,** God helps those who help themselves; (*b*) to plait (straw); (*c*) *Ropem:* to warp (rope). **2.** to hatch (plot); to weave (intrigue).

ourdissage [urdisaːʒ], *s.m. Tex:* warping.

ourdisseur, -euse [urdisœːr, -øːz], *s.* **1.** *Tex:* warper. **2.** plotter; hatcher (of plot).

ourdissoir [urdiswaːr], *s.m. Tex:* (weaver's) warp beam; beaming frame, warping frame.

ourdissure [urdisyːr], *s.f.* = OURDISSAGE.

ourdou [urdu], *s.m. Ling:* Urdu.

ourébi [urebi], *s.m. Z:* oribi.

ourler [urle], *v.tr.* **1.** *Needlew:* to hem; **o. à jour,** to hemstitch. **2.** *Metalw:* to lap-joint (edges of metal sheets).

s'ourler, (*of waves*) to comb; to show white horses.

ourles [url], *s.m.pl. Med:* mumps.

ourlet [urlɛ], *s.m.* **1.** hem; **o. simple,** plain hem; **o. piqué,** stitched hem; **o. à jour,** hemstitched hem; **faux o.,** false hem; **point d'o.,** hemming; hemstitch; **hauteur de l'o.,** hemline. **2.** edge (of crater); helix, rim (of ear). **3.** *Metalw:* lap-joint, hem (at edge of metal sheets).

ourleur [urlœːr], *s.m.* **1.** (*attachment of sewing machine*) hemmer, binder. **2.** *Metalw:* (*tool for sheet metal*) hemmer.

ourlien, -ienne [urljɛ̃, -jɛn], *a. Med:* **fièvre ourlienne,** mumps.

ours, -e [urs], *s.* **1.** (*a*) *Z:* bear, *f.* she bear; **o. blanc,** polar bear; **o. brun,** brown bear; **o. grizzlé,** grizzly bear; **o. des cocotiers,** Malayan bear, sun bear; **o. à lunettes,** spectacled bear; **o. jongleur, o. lippu,** jungle bear, sloth bear, honey bear; *Paleont:* **o. des cavernes,** cave bear; **chasse à l'o.,** bear hunt(ing); **combats d'o.,** bear baiting; *Toys:* **o. Martin, o. en peluche,** Teddy bear; *F:* **o. mal léché,** (i) unlicked cub; (ii) boorish person; **quel o.!** what a boor! **votre o. de frère,** that surly brother of yours; *a.* **il est un peu o.,** he's a bit gruff, a bit of a boor; *Prov:* **il ne faut pas vendre la peau de l'o. avant de l'avoir tué,** don't count your chickens before they are hatched; (*b*) *Z:* **o. marin,** sea bear, fur seal; (*c*) *F:* (i) manuscript that has gone the rounds, that has been rejected many times; (ii) *Th:* play difficult to place; (iii) white elephant; (*d*) *Mil: P:* glasshouse; (*e*) *pl. P:* (*of woman*) **avoir ses o.,** to have the curse. **2.** *s.f. Astr:* **la Grande Ourse,** the Great Bear, the Big Dipper, Ursa Major, Charles' Wain, the Plough; **la Petite Ourse,** the Little Bear, the Little Dipper, Ursa Minor. **3.** *Bot:* **raisin d'o., cerise d'o.,** bearberry. **4.** *Geog:* **Grand Lac de l'O.,** Great Bear Lake.

ourserie [ursəri], *s.f. F:* bearishness, gruffness, surliness; boorishness.

oursin [ursɛ̃], *s.m.* **1.** *Echin:* sea urchin, sea hedgehog; **o. violet,** edible sea urchin. **2.** *Com:* bearskin; *Mil: A:* **bonnet d'o.,** bearskin.

ourson [ursɔ̃], *s.m.* **1.** bear's cub. **2.** black American bear. **3.** *A.Mil.Cost:* bearskin.

ousseau, -eaux [uso], *s.m. Nau:* well (of ship).

ous'que [uskə], *adv. P:* = **où est-ce que,** where; **ous'qu'il est?** where is he? **c'est là o. je suis né,** that's where I was born.

oust(e) [ust], *int. P:* **allez o.!** (i) now then, look sharp! get a move on! (ii) out you get! scram! **et o.! il lui flanque une beigne,** so he ups and catches him a clout.

outarde [utard], *s.f. Orn:* bustard; **o. barbue,** great bustard; **o. houbara,** houbara bustard; **o. canepetière,** little bustard.

outardeau, -eaux [utardo], *s.m.* young bustard.

outil [uti], *s.m.* (*a*) tool; implement; **o. à main,** hand tool; **o. à moteur,** power tool; **o. diamanté,** diamond tool; **o. de tour,** lathe tool; **o. coupant, o. de coupe, o. tranchant,** cutting tool, edge tool; **o. à deux tranchants,** two-edged, double-edged, tool; **o. à dégrossir,** roughing tool; **o. à dresser,** truing, facing, tool; **o. à planer,** planishing tool, planisher; **o. de terrassement,** earth-working tool; *Min: etc:* **o. de forage, de sondage,** boring, drilling, tool; *Metalw:* **o. à suivre,** gang die; **outils de jardinage,** garden tools; **boîte, coffre, à outils,** tool box, chest; **sac(oche) à outils,** toolbag; **trousse à outils,** tool kit; **planche à outils,** tool board; **petit magasin à outils,** *F:* **cagibi à outils,** tool crib; **l'homme n'était plus qu'un o. au service du dictateur,** man had become no more than a tool in the hands of the dictator; *Prov:* **à méchant ouvrier point de bons outils, les mauvais ouvriers ont toujours de mauvais outils,** a bad workman finds fault with, blames, his tools; (*b*) *P:* (*of pers.*) **un drôle d'o.,** a clumsy clot.

outillage [utijaːʒ], *s.m.* **1.** making, providing, of tools; tooling; **o. à main,** hand tooling; **petit o.,** millwright work. **2.** set of tools (of workman); gear, plant, equipment, machinery (of factory); *Aut: etc:* tool outfit, kit; **o. pour mécaniciens,** (set of) engineer's tools; *Av:* **o. de bord,** flight tool kit; **petit o.,** small tools; *Pol.Ec:* **o. national,** national capital equipment; *Ind: etc:* **installation, mise en place, de l'o.,** tooling-up.

outillé [utije], *a.* (*of workman*) supplied, equipped, with tools; (*of factory*) equipped with plant; **être bien o. en livres,** to have a good library.

outiller [utije], *v.tr.* to equip, fit out, supply, (workman) with tools, (factory) with plant.

s'outiller, to equip oneself, fit oneself out, with tools, plant; **s'o. en livres, de livres,** to provide oneself with books.

outillerie [utijri], *s.f.* (*a*) tool making; (*b*) tool selling.

outilleur [utijœːr], *s.m.* tool maker.

outrage [utraːʒ], *s.m.* outrage. **1.** flagrant insult (to morals; religion, good taste, etc.); **faire o. aux convenances,** to offend against propriety; **outrages à la morale, à la justice,** outrages against morals, upon justice; *Jur:* **o. (à l'égard de l'autorité publique),** (i) (*à agents*) insulting behaviour; (ii) (*à magistrat*) contempt of court; **o. aux bonnes mœurs, à la pudeur,** public act of indecency; indecent exposure; **faire (subir un) o. à qn,** to commit an outrage against, on, s.o.; **faire subir à une femme le(s) dernier(s), outrage(s),** to violate a woman. **2.** *A:* injury; *Lit:* **l'o. des ans,** the ravages of time.

outrageant [utraʒɑ̃], *a.* insulting, offensive (offer, refusal); scurrilous (accusation); **livre o. pour les bonnes mœurs,** book that offends one's moral sense; **plaisanteries outrageantes,** offensive, outrageous, jokes.

outrager [utraʒe], *v.tr.* (**j'outrageai(s); n. outrageons)** **1.** to insult; to attack scurrilously; **o. la vérité, le bon sens,** to fly in the face of truth, of common sense; **o. qn de soupçons odieux,** to insult s.o. with unpleasant suspicions. **2.** to outrage, violate (woman); to outrage (nature, the law); to desecrate (holy place); to abuse (hospitality).

outrageusement [utraʒøzmɑ̃], *adv.* insultingly, scurrilously; **il a été o. chassé,** he was kicked out in a most scandalous fashion.

outrageux, -euse [utraʒø, -øːz], *a.* insulting, scurrilous.

outrance [utrɑ̃ːs], *s.f.* excess; **les outrances d'un poète,** the audacities, extravagances, of a poet; *used esp. in the adv.phr.* **à o.,** to the utmost, to the bitter end; **guerre à o.,** war to the death; **attaque à o.,** all-out attack; **se battre à o.,** to fight desperately, to the death; **applaudir à o.,** to cheer to the echo; **industrialisme à o.,** out and out industrialism; **adulateur à (toute) o.,** out and out flatterer.

outrancier, -ière [utrɑ̃sje, -jɛːr]. **1.** *a.* carrying things to extremes, extremist; **nationalisme o.,** extreme nationalism. **2.** *s.* extremist; *F:* out-and-outer.

outre[1] [utr̥], *s.f.* **1.** goatskin bottle, leather bottle; water skin; **o. en cuir,** black-jack. **2.** *Moll:* **o. de mer,** ascidium; sea squirt.

outre[2]. **1.** *prep.* (*a*) (*used only in a few set phrases*) beyond; **o. mesure,** beyond measure, inordinately, unduly, over-; **travailler, se fatiguer, o. mesure,** to overwork, to overtire oneself, to overdo it; **se plaindre o. mesure,** to complain overmuch; **élaborer un argument o. mesure,** to over-labour, over-elaborate, an argument; **il serait o. nature de . . .,** it would be more than nature could bear, stand, to . . .; **poursuivre l'ennemi o. Somme,** to pursue the enemy beyond the Somme; (*b*) in addition to; **o. cette somme il me redoit . . .,** in addition to that sum he still owes me . . .; **o. cela . . .,** in addition to that . . ., besides . . ., moreover . . ., furthermore . . .; (*c*) *pref.* ultra; **outremarin,** ultramarine. **2.** *adv.* (*a*) further, beyond; **passer o., aller o.,** to go on, proceed further; **passer o. à un jugement, à une objection,** to disregard, to take no notice of, to overrule, a judgment, an objection; **passer o. à la loi,** to defy the law; to override the law; **passer o. à une interdiction,** to ignore a prohibition; **sa fermeté passa o. à toute opposition,** his firmness bore down all opposition; *A:* **j'irai plus o.,** I shall go further; (*b*) **en o.,** besides, moreover, further(more); also; again, over and above; **j'ai, en outre, deux neveux,** I have, besides, two nephews; (*c*) *A:* **transpercer qn d'o. en o.,** to run s.o. through (and through); (*d*) *prep.phr.* **en o. de,** in addition to, besides; **en o. de sa paye il reçoit . . .,** over and above his pay he gets . . .; (*d*) *conj.phr.* **o. que** + *ind.*, apart from the fact that . . ., not to mention the fact that . . .; besides, in addition to . . . (plus gerund).

outré [utre], *a.* (*a*) exaggerated, extravagant, overdone (praise, behaviour); far-fetched (thought); overstated; **d'une précision outrée,** hyper-accurate; **d'une activité outrée,** hyper-active; (*b*) carried away by indignation; **o. de colère,** beside oneself with anger; **o. d'avoir manqué son coup,** disgusted, furious, at having failed; (*c*) exhausted, tired out; (*of horse*) overridden, foundered.

outre-Atlantique [utratlɑ̃tik], *adv.phr.* on the other side of, across, the Atlantic.

outrecuidance [utrəkɥidɑ̃ːs], *s.f.* (*a*) *Lit:* presumptuousness, overweening conceit; (*b*) effrontery, impertinence.

outrecuidant [utrəkɥidɑ̃], *a.* (*a*) overweening, presumptuous, self-assertive; (*b*) impertinent (remark, etc.).

outre-Manche [utrəmɑ̃ːʃ], *adv.phr.* on the other side of, across, the Channel; in England; **nos voisins d'o.-M.,** our neighbours across the Channel.

outremer [utrəmɛːr], *s.m.* **1.** lapis lazuli. **2.** **(bleu d')o.,** ultramarine (blue).

outre-mer, *adv.phr.* overseas, beyond the sea(s); **commerce d'o.-m.,** oversea(s) trade; *Pol:* **départements d'o.-m.,** overseas departments (Martinique, Guadeloupe); **territoires d'o.,** overseas territories (New Caledonia, French Polynesia, etc.); **Ministre de la France d'Outre-mer,** Minister for Overseas Territories; **nos collègues d'o.-m.,** our colleagues from abroad.

outre-monts [utrəmɔ̃], *adv.phr.* beyond the mountains; **d'o.-m.,** tra(ns)montane.

outrepassé [utrəpɑse], *a. Arch:* **arc o.,** horsehoe arch.

outrepasser [utrəpɑse]. **1.** *v.tr.* to go beyond (a limit, one's rights); to act in excess of (one's right); to exceed (given orders); **o. ses pouvoirs,** to exceed one's commission; **o. les bornes de la vérité,** to go beyond the limits of truth; **son imagination outrepasse les faits,** his imagination outruns the facts. **2.** *v.i. Ven:* (*of hounds*) to overrun the scent, to check.

outrer [utre], *v.tr.* **1.** to carry (sth.) to excess, beyond reason; **o. les choses,** to exaggerate things; **o. un rôle,** to overdo a part; **o. l'éloge de qn,** to carry the praise of s.o. too far; to overpraise s.o.; **o. la mode,** to go beyond the fashion, to be ultra-fashionable; **o. le genre Zola,** to out-Zola Zola. **2.** to tire out, exhaust; **o. un cheval,** to overstrain, overwork, override, founder, a horse. **3.** to provoke (s.o.) beyond measure; **o. qn de colère,** to infuriate s.o.

s'outrer. *A:* **s'o. à travailler,** to overdo it; to overstrain oneself with working.

outre-Rhin [utrərɛ̃], *adv.phr.* beyond the Rhine; **d'o.-R.,** transrhenane.

outre-sarine [utrəsarin], *a. Sw.Fr:* German-speaking; *pl. outre-sarines.*

outre-tombe (d') [dutrətɔ̃ːb], *adv.phr.* from beyond the grave; posthumous.

outrigger [autrigœːr], *s.m. Row:* outrigger (boat).

outsider [utsidɛːr], *s.m.* outsider.

ouvala [uvala], *s.m. Geog:* uvala.

ouvarovite [uvarəvit], *s.f. Miner:* uvarovite.

ouvert [uvɛːr]. **1.** *a.* open; (*a*) **porte grande ouverte,** wide-open door; **tout grand o.,** wide open; **la bouche ouverte toute grande, il nous regardait,** he gazed at us open-mouthed; **gouffre o. à nos pieds,** abyss yawning at our feet; **plaie ouverte,** gaping wound; *Surg:* **à cœur o.,** open-heart (surgery); **accueillir qn à bras ouverts,** to welcome s.o. with open arms; *F:* **avoir la main ouverte,** to be open-handed; **faire qch. les yeux ouverts,** to do sth. with one's eyes open; **fleur ouverte,** flower in bloom; **intelligence ouverte,** ready understanding; **voyelle ouverte,** open vowel; *Fb:* **jeu o.,** open game; *s.a.* LIVRE[2]; (*b*) **ville ouverte,** open, unfortified, town; **maison ouverte à tous les vents,** house open, exposed, to all winds; **bateau o.,** open boat; **port o.,** (i) open, unprotected, harbour; (ii) port free from harbour dues, free port; **rade ouverte,** open roadstead; (*c*) **les bureaux sont ouverts de 10 heures à 5 heures,** the offices are open from 10 to 5; **o. la nuit,** open all night; **la collection est ouverte au public,** the collection is open to the public, is on view; **la Baltique est de nouveau ouverte à la navigation,** the Baltic is once more open to navigation; **compte o.,** open account, open credit; *s.a.* TABLE 1; (*d*) **caractère o.,** frank, open, nature; **avoir l'esprit o.,** to be open-minded; **parler à cœur o.,** to speak freely; **guerre ouverte,** open warfare; (*e*) **le gaz est o.,** the gas is on. **2.** *s.m. Nau:* fetch (of bay); **à l'o. de la baie,** off the entrance to the bay.

ouvertement [uvɛrtəmɑ̃], *adv.* openly, frankly; overtly; avowedly, undisguisedly; **il est socialiste o.,** he makes no secret of his socialism.

ouverture [uvɛrtyːr], *s.f.* **1.** (*a*) opening (of door, book, session, etc.); **l'o. de la chasse,** the first day of the shooting, the hunting, season; **o. d'un testament,** reading of a will; **o. d'hostilités,** outbreak of hostilities; **o. d'un compte, d'un crédit,** opening (up) of an account, of a credit; **conférence d'o.,** opening lecture; *Jur:* **il y a o. à cassation,** the way is open for an appeal; (*b*) **faire des ouvertures à qn,** to make overtures to s.o.; **je profiterai de la première o.,** I shall take the first opportunity; **ouvertures de paix,** overtures of peace; (*c*) *Mus:* overture (of opera, etc.); **l'o. du "Barbier de Séville,"** the overture to the "Barber of Seville"; (*d*) open state (of place of business, etc.); **heures d'o.,** business hours (of shop); visiting hours (of museum, etc.). **2.** (*a*) opening, aperture (in wall, etc.); mouth (of grotto); gap, break (in hedge); **les ouvertures (d'une maison),** the doors and windows; **pratiquer une o. dans la porte,** to cut a hole in the door; **flacon à large o.,** wide-mouthed flask; **ouvertures d'une machine,** (steam) ports of an engine; *Nau:* **o. de la chauffe,** stoke hole; **o. de tonnage,** tonnage opening; (*b*) width, span (of arch, etc.); spread (of compass legs); angular distance (between compass bearings); clearance, dimension (of spanner); gap (of rotor); *El.E:* **o. d'induit,** armature gap; (*c*) *Phot:* aperture; **o. relative,** aperture ratio, relative aperture; **o. utile,** working aperture, effective aperture. **3. o. de cœur,** frankness, open-heartedness; **o. d'esprit,** open-mindedness. **4.** *Av:* (parachute) opening; **o. retardée,** delayed opening.

ouvrabilité [uvrabilite], *s.f. Tchn:* workability.

ouvrable [uvrabl̥], *a.* **1.** workable, tractable (material). **2. jour o.,** working day; **heures ouvrables,** business hours, working hours.

ouvrage [uvraːʒ], *s.m.* work. **1.** (*a*) (*something to do*) **être sans o.,** to be unemployed; **il n'a pas d'o.,** he is out of work, out of a job; **se mettre à l'o.,** to set to work; **mettre qn à l'o.,** to set s.o. to work; **avoir du cœur à l'o.,** to work with a will; *Typ:* **o. de ville,** jobbing work; (*b*) workmanship; **l'o. l'emporte sur la matière,** workmanship is more important than the material; **plafond d'un o. achevé,** ceiling of finished workmanship. **2.** piece of work, product; **ouvrages d'un écrivain,** works of a writer; **o. en prose,** prose work; *Const:* **les gros ouvrages,** the rough work; **les menus ouvrages,** the smaller work; *Civ.E:* **ouvrages d'art,** (*generic term for*) bridges viaducts, tunnels, etc.; constructive works; *Fort:* **o. avancé,** outwork; **o. de brique,** brickwork; **ouvrages publics,** public works; **o. livré clef en main,** turnkey job; **ouvrages de dames,** needlework, fancywork, embroidery; **elle a toujours son ouvrage à la main,** she's never without her needlework; **table, corbeille, boîte, à o.,** work table, work basket, workbox; **ce chapitre de malheurs est votre o.,** this chapter of accidents is your doing; you've brought about this chapter of accidents; *s.f. F:* **c'est de la belle o.,** that's a nice bit of work.

ouvragé [uvraʒe], *a.* (*a*) worked; finished (product); (*b*) decorated; embroidered (cloth, etc.); (*c*) elaborate.

ouvrager [uvraʒe], *v.tr.* **(j'ouvrageai(s); n. ouvrageons)** *Tchn:* to work (metal, jewellery); to figure (velvets, brocades).

ouvraison [uvrɛzɔ̃], *s.f. Tchn:* (process of) working. **2.** material worked.

ouvrant [uvrɑ̃]. **1.** *a.* (*a*) opening (panel, etc.); *Aut:* sliding (roof); (*b*) *A:* **entrer dans une ville à portes ouvrantes,** to enter a town (i) when the gates open; (ii) without resistance; **à jour o.,** at break of day; **à audience ouvrante,** at the opening of the session. **2.** *s.m.* leaf (of door, shutter, etc.).

ouvré [uvre], *a.* (*a*) worked (timber); wrought (iron); finished (product, article); (*b*) decorated; embroidered (tablecloth, etc.); **linge o.,** diaper; diapered linen; **tissu o. à fleurs,** flowered material.

ouvreau [uvro], *s.m. Glassm:* tap-hole.

ouvre-boîte(s) [uvrəbwat], *s.m.* can opener, tin opener; *pl. ouvre-boîtes.*

ouvre-bouche [uvrəbuʃ], *s.m. Surg:* gag; *pl. ouvre-bouches.*

ouvre-bouteille(s) [uvrəbutɛːj], *s.m.* bottle opener; *pl. ouvre-bouteilles.*

ouvre-caisse(s) [uvrəkɛs], *s.m.* (packing-)case opener; *pl. ouvre-caisses.*

ouvrée [uvre], *s.f. A: & Dial:* (*an old measure of land*) = acre.

ouvre-gants [uvrəgɑ̃], *s.m.inv.* glove stretcher.

ouvre-huître(s) [uvrɥitr̥], *s.m.* oyster knife; *pl. ouvre-huîtres.*

ouvre-jante [uvrəʒɑ̃ːt], *s.m. Aut: etc:* rim opener, rim expander; *pl. ouvre-jantes.*

ouvre-lettres [uvrəlɛtr̥], *s.m.inv.* letter opener.

ouvrer [uvre], *v.tr.* (*a*) to work (up) (wood, copper, etc.); **facile à o.,** tractable, easily workable (material); (*b*) **o. du linge, du drap,** to diaper linen, cloth; (*c*) *abs. A:* **ne pas o. le dimanche,** not to work on Sundays.

ouvreur, -euse [uvrœːr, -øːz], *s.* **1.** (*a*) opener, person who opens; (*b*) *s.f.* **ouvreuse,** (i) *Th:* theatre attendant; (ii) *Cin:* usherette. **2.** *Cards:* player who opens the bidding; *Ski:* skier who goes down just before the race starts. **3.** *s.m. Paperm:* dipper, vatman. **4.** *s.f. Tex:* **ouvreuse,** cotton opener (machine).

ouvrier, -ère [uvrije, -ɛːr]. **1.** *s.* (*a*) worker; workman; working man; operative; **o. en bois, sur métaux,** woodworker, metal worker; **o. agricole,** agricultural worker, farm hand; **o. aux pièces,** piece worker; **o. à la journée,** day labourer; **o. d'usine,** factory worker; **o. spécialisé,** semi-skilled worker; **o. qualifié, professionnel,** skilled worker; **ouvriers syndiqués,** union men; organized labour; *Min:* **o. du fond,** miner, underground worker; **o. au jour,** surface worker; *Rail:* **o. de la voie,** platelayer, tracklayer, trackman; **o. de port,** docker; **conflits entre ouvriers et patrons,** labour disputes; *Prov:* **à l'œuvre on connaît l'o.,** a workman is known by his work; (*b*) *s.f.* **ouvrière,** (i) (female) factory worker; (ii) seamstress, dressmaker; *F:* **une ouvrière maison,** a visiting dressmaker; **première ouvrière,** forewoman; (*c*) *A: & Lit:* artisan, artist (in one's particular job); **le grand o., l'éternel o.,** God, the great Architect of the universe; **il est, a été, l'o. de sa fortune,** he is a self-made man. **2.** *a.* (*a*) **la classe ouvrière, les classes ouvrières,** the working class(es); **législation ouvrière,** labour legislation; **agitation ouvrière,** industrial unrest; labour unrest; **conflits ouvriers,** industrial disputes; labour disputes; **contrôle o.,** workers' control; **syndicat o.,** trade union; **association ouvrière,** workers' association; *O:* **train o.,** workmen's train; **logements ouvriers** = council flats; **quartier o.,** working-class district; **elle ne savait rien de l'enfance ouvrière,** she knew nothing of the background of a working-class child; (*b*) **abeille ouvrière,** worker bee; **fourmi ouvrière,** worker ant; (*c*) *A:* **jour o.,** working day; *s.a.* CHEVILLE 1.

ouvriérisme [uvrjerism], *s.m. Pol.Ec:* control by the workers; trade unionism.

ouvriériste [uvrjerist], *a. Pol.Ec:* workers' (movement, control, etc.).

ouvrir [uvriːr], *v.* (*pr.p.* **ouvrant**; *p.p.* **ouvert**; *pr.ind.* **j'ouvre, il ouvre, n. ouvrons**; *pr.sub.* **j'ouvre, n. ouvrions**, *imp.* **ouvre, ouvrons, ouvrez**; *p.d.* **j'ouvrais**; *p.h.* **j'ouvris**; *fu.* **j'ouvrirai**) **1.** *v.tr.* to open; (*a*) **o. une porte,** to open, unfasten, unlock, a door; **o. une malle,** to open, unlock, a trunk; **o. brusquement la fenêtre,** to fling open the window; **o. les portes toutes grandes à qn,** to open the doors wide for s.o.; to fling the doors wide open for s.o.; **o. sa maison à qn,** to throw open one's house to s.o.; to welcome s.o. to one's house; **o. une région au commerce,** to open up a district to trade; **o. la porte aux abus,** to open the door, the way, to abuses; **o. un robinet, le gaz,** to turn on a tap, the gas; *F:* **o. le poste,** to switch on (radio, television, etc.); **il n'a pas ouvert la bouche,** he didn't open his mouth; *El:* **o. le circuit,** to break, switch off, the current; **o. un verrou,** to draw a bolt; **o. les rideaux,** to draw back the curtains; **o. le lit,** to turn down the bedclothes; *Nau:* **o. les voiles,** to unfold the sails; *abs.* **nous ouvrons tous les jours à huit heures,** we open every day at eight; **o. à qn,** to answer the door to s.o.; to let s.o. in; **je me suis fait o.,** I got myself let in, I got them to let me in; **o. l'oreille,** to listen carefully; **o. les yeux de qn,** to open s.o.'s eyes, to disillusion s.o.; (*b*) **o. son cœur à qn,** to unburden oneself to s.o.; **cela ouvre l'appetit,** it sharpens the appetite; (*c*) to cut through, open up, perforate (wall, canal, mine); to cut (sth.) open; to lay (sth.) open; **o. qch. avec un couteau,** to cut sth. open; **o. qch. avec les dents,** to bite sth. open; **o. un pâté,** to cut into a pâté; *Mil:* **o. des tranchées,** to open, to break, trenches; **s'o. un chemin à travers la foule,** to cut, push, one's way through the crowd; **o. un chemin à travers la brousse,** to clear a way through the bush; *Surg:* **o. un abcès,** to open, to lance, an abscess; **o. une plaie,** to open up a wound; **une profonde entaille ouvrait le front,** the forehead was gashed with a deep cut; (*d*) to begin; to set going; **o. un débat,** to open, start, a debate; **o. le bal,** to open the ball; **o. les séances du Parlement,** to open Parliament; **o. une liste,** to head a list; **o. une parenthèse,** (i) to open a parenthesis; (ii) to embark on a digression; **o. des négociations,** to set negotiations on foot; **o. une école, une boutique,** to start a school, a shop; **o. boutique,** to set up shop; **o. la marche,** to lead the way; *Mil:* **o. le feu,** to open fire; *Fin:* **o. un emprunt,** to open a loan; **o. un crédit (en banque) à un voyageur,** to open a credit (with a bank) for a traveller; *Com:* **o. un compte chez qn,** to open (up) an account with s.o.; **o. une succession,** to apply for probate; (*e*) *Nau:* **o. deux amers,** to open two sea marks; **o. une baie,** to open a bay. **2.** *v.i.* to open; (*a*) **la scène ouvre par un chœur,** the scene opens with a chorus; (*b*) **le salon ouvrait sur le jardin,** the drawing-room opened on (to) the garden; (*c*) **les boutiques n'ouvrent pas les jours de fête,** the shops do not open on holidays; **le Parlement ouvre le cinq,** Parliament opens on the fifth.

s'ouvrir, to open; (*a*) **les boutiques s'ouvrent,** the shops are opening; (*of door, etc.*) **s'o. tout d'un coup,** to burst open; **la porte s'ouvrit en coup de vent,** the door flew open; **la foule s'ouvrit devant lui,** the crowd made way for him; **un gouffre s'ouvrait sous mes pieds,** a chasm opened out, yawned, under my feet; **le bal s'ouvrit par une valse,** the ball opened, began, started, with a waltz; (*b*) (*of pers.*) to become expansive, to open out; to unburden oneself; **s'o. à qn,** to talk freely, to unburden oneself, to s.o.; **s'o. de ses intentions, de ses scrupules, à qn,** to confide one's intentions, one's scruples, to s.o.

ouvroir [uvrwaːr], *s.m.* (*a*) workroom (in convent, etc.); (*b*) (ladies') work party, *U.S:* sewing bee; Dorcas Society.

ouwarowite [uvarɔvit], *s.f. Miner:* uvarovite.

ouzbek [uzbɛk]. **1.** *a. & s. Geog:* Uzbek. **2.** *s.m. Ling:* Uzbek.

Ouzbékistan [uzbekistan], *Pr.n. Geog:* **(République socialiste soviétique d')** Uzbekistan, Uzbek Soviet Socialist Republic.

ovaire [ɔvɛːr], *s.m. Anat: Bot:* ovary.

ovalaire [ɔvalɛːr], *a. Anat:* oval (foramen).

ovalbumine [ɔvalbymin], *s.f. Bio-Ch:* ovalbumin.

ovale [ɔval]. **1.** *a.* oval; egg-shaped, oviform; *Anat:* **fosse o.,** fossa ovalis; *Sp: F:* **ballon o.,** (i) rugger ball, *Journ:* oval; (ii) rugger. **2.** *s.m.* oval; **en o.,** oval(ly); *Mth:* **ovales de Descartes,** Cartesian ovals.

ovaler [ɔvale], *v.tr. Tex:* to throw (silk).

ovalisation [ɔvalizasjɔ̃], *s.f. Mec.E:* ovalization, wearing out of round (of cylinders, etc.).

ovaliser [ɔvalize], *v.tr.* to make oval; *Mec.E:* to ovalize; to wear out of round; **cylindre ovalisé,** ovalized cylinder.

s'ovaliser, to become ovalized; (*of piston*) to wear oval.

ovaliste [ɔvalist], *s.m. Tex:* (silk) thrower, throwster.

ovariectomie [ɔvarjɛktɔmi], *s.f. Surg:* ovariectomy.

ovarien, -ienne [ɔvarjɛ̃, -jɛn], *a. Anat: Bot:* ovarian.

ovariole [ɔvarjɔl], *s.f. Biol:* ovariole.

ovariotomie [ɔvarjɔtɔmi], *s.f. Surg:* ovariotomy.

ovarite [ɔvarit], *s.f. Med:* ovaritis.

ovate [ɔvat], *s.m. Rel.H:* ovate.

ovation [ɔvasjɔ̃], *s.f.* ovation; **faire une o. à qn,** to give s.o. an ovation; **être l'objet d'une o.,** to receive an ovation.

ovationner [ɔvasjɔne], *v.tr.* to acclaim (s.o.); to give (s.o.) an ovation.

ove [ɔːv], *s.m.* **1.** *Arch:* ovolo, ovum. **2.** egg-shaped section (of culvert).

ové [ɔve], *a.* egg-shaped, ovate (fruit, etc.).

ovi[1]**- ovo-** [ɔvi, ɔvɔ], *comb.fm. Nat.Hist:* ovi-, ovo-.

ovi[2]**-**, *comb.fm. Z:* ovi-.

ovibovine [ɔvibɔvine], *a. Z:* ovibovine.

ovibos [ɔvibɔs], *s.m. Z:* ovibos, musk ox.

ovicapsule [ɔvikapsyl], *s.f. Nat.Hist:* ovicapsule.

ovicelle [ɔvisɛl], *s.f. Z:* ovicell.

ovicule [ɔvikyl], *s.m. Arch:* small ovolo.

Ovide [ɔvid], *Pr.n.m. Lt.Lit:* Ovid.

ovidés [ɔvide], *s.m.pl. Z:* Ovidae.

oviducte [ɔvidykt], *s.m. Anat:* oviduct.

ovifère [ɔvifɛːr], **ovigère** [ɔviʒɛːr], *a. Z:* oviferous, ovigerous.

oviforme [ɔvifɔrm], *a.* oviform, egg-shaped.

ovigène [ɔviʒɛn], *a. Nat.Hist:* ovigenous.

ovin [ɔvɛ̃], *Husb:* **1.** *a.* **race ovine,** ovine race. **2.** *s.m.pl.* **ovins,** sheep.

ovinés [ɔvine], *s.m.pl. Z:* Ovinae.

ovipare [ɔvipaːr], *a. Z:* oviparous.

oviparisme [ɔviparism], *s.m.,* **oviparité** [ɔviparite], *s.f. Z:* oviparity.

ovipositeur [ɔvipozitœːr], *s.m. Ent:* ovipositor.

oviposition [ɔvipozisjɔ̃], *s.f.* oviposition.

ovisac [ɔvisak], *s.m. Nat.Hist:* ovisac.

oviscapte [ɔviskapt], *s.m. Ent:* oviscapt.

ovo-. *See* OVI[1]-.

ovocentre [ɔvɔsɑ̃ːtr̥], *s.m. Biol:* ovocentre.

ovocyte [ɔvɔsit], *s.m. Biol: Ent:* ovocyte; oöcyte.

ovogénèse [ɔvɔʒenɛːz], **ovogénie** [ɔvɔʒeni], *s.f.* ovogenesis, oogenesis.

ovoïdal, -aux [ɔvɔidal, -o], *a.* ovoidal.

ovoïde [ɔvɔid], *a.* ovoid, egg-shaped; *El.E:* **maillon o.,** egg insulator.

ovologie [ɔvɔlɔʒi], *s.f.* ovology.

ovomucoïde [ɔvɔmykɔid], *s.m. Bio-Ch:* ovomucoid.

ovoscope [ɔvɔskɔp], *s.m.* candler (for eggs).

ovotestis [ɔvɔtestis], *s.m. Biol:* ovotestis.

ovovivipare [ɔvɔvivipaːr], *a.* ovoviviparous.

ovoviviparité [ɔvɔviviparite], *s.f. Biol:* ovoviviparity.

ovulaire [ɔvylɛːr], *a.* ovular.

ovulation [ɔvylasjɔ̃], *s.f. Biol: Physiol:* ovulation.

ovule [ɔvyl], *s.m. Biol:* (*a*) ovule; (*b*) ovum.

owyhéeite [ɔvieeit], *s.f. Miner:* owyheeite.

oxacide [ɔksasid], *s.m. Ch:* oxyacid, hydroxy-acid.

oxalacétique [ɔksalasetik], *a. Ch:* oxalacetic.

oxalate [ɔksalat], *s.m. Ch:* oxalate; **o. de fer,** oxalate of iron, ferrous oxalate.

oxalémie [ɔksalemi], *s.f. Med:* oxal(a)emia.

oxalid(ac)ées [ɔksalid(as)e], *s.f.pl. Bot:* Oxalidaceae.

oxalide [ɔksalid], *s.f. Bot:* oxalis, wood sorrel.

oxalique [ɔksalik], *a. Ch:* oxalic (acid).

oxalis [ɔksalis], *s.m. Bot:* oxalis, wood sorrel.

oxalurie [ɔksalyri], *s.f. Med:* oxaluria.

oxalurique [ɔksalyrik], *a. Ch:* oxaluric.

oxalyle [ɔksalil], *s.m. Ch:* oxalyl.

oxalylurée [ɔksalilyre], *s.f. Ch:* oxalylurea, parabanic acid.

oxamide [ɔksamid], *s.m. Ch:* oxamide.

oxamique [ɔksamik], *a. Ch:* oxamic.

oxammite [ɔksamit], *s.f. Miner:* oxammite.

oxanilide [ɔksanilid], *s.m. Ch:* oxanilid(e).

oxanilique [ɔksanilik], *a. Ch:* oxanilic.

oxazine [ɔksazin], *s.f. Ch:* oxazin(e).

oxazole [ɔksazɔl], *s.m. Ch:* oxazole.

oxétone [ɔksetɔn], *s.f. Ch:* oxetone.

oxford [ɔksfɔrd], *s.m. Tex:* oxford skirting.

oxfordien, -ienne [ɔksfɔrdjɛ̃, -jɛn], **oxonien, -ienne** [ɔksɔnjɛ̃, -jɛn], *a. & s.* **1.** *a. & s. Geog:* Oxonian. **2.** *a. & s.m. Geol:* Oxfordian.

oxhydrique [ɔksidrik], *a. Ch:* oxyhydrogen, oxyhydric (blow pipe, etc.); *A.Th:* **lumière o.,** limelight.

oximation [ɔksimasjɔ̃], *s.f. Ch:* oximation.

oxime [ɔksim], *s.f. Ch:* oxim(e).

ox(y)- [ɔks(i)], *comb.fm.* ox(y)-.

oxyacétylénique [ɔksiasetilenik], *a.* oxyacetylene (blowpipe, gas, welding).

oxyacide [ɔksiasid], *s.m.* oxyacid.

oxyæna [ɔksiena], *s.m. Paleont:* Oxyaena.

oxycarboné [ɔksikarbɔne], *a.* containing carbon monoxide.

oxycarbonisme [ɔksikarbɔnism], *s.m. Med:* carbon-monoxide poisoning.

oxycellulose [ɔksisɛlyloːz], *s.f. Ch:* oxycellulose.

oxycéphale [ɔksisefal], *a.* oxycephalous.

oxychlorure [ɔksiklɔryːr], *s.m. Ch:* oxychloride.

oxycoupage [ɔksikupaːʒ], *s.m. Metalw:* oxygen cutting; oxyacetylene cutting out.

oxycouper [ɔksikupe], *v.tr. Metalw:* to flame cut.

oxycoupeur [ɔksikupœːr], *a. Metalw:* **chalumeau o.,** oxyacetylene cutting torch.

oxycrat [ɔksikrat], *s.m.* oxycrate.

oxydabilité [ɔksidabilite], *s.f.* oxidizability.

oxydable [ɔksidabl̥], *a.* (*a*) *Ch:* oxidizable, oxidable; (*b*) liable to rust.

oxydactyle [ɔksidaktil], *a. Z:* oxydactyl.

oxydant [ɔksidɑ̃]. **1.** *a.* oxidizing. **2.** *s.m.* oxidizer, oxidizing agent, oxidant.

oxydase [ɔksidaːz], *s.f. Bio-Ch:* oxidase.

oxydation [ɔksidasjɔ̃], *s.f. Ch:* oxidizing, oxidation; (*in engine, etc.*) corrosion; (*of boiler, etc.*) **épaisseur d'o.,** embedded scale; **forte o.,** heavy scale; *Metalw:* **o. anodique,** anodizing treatment.

oxyde [ɔksid], *s.m. Ch:* oxide; **o. de carbone, de plomb,** carbon monoxide, lead monoxide; **o. de cuivre,** cupric oxide, scale of copper; **o. de magnésium,** magnesium oxide; **o. de molybdène,** molybdenum oxide; **o. rouge de fer,** colcothar; **o. d'aluminium,** alumina; **o. de phénol,** diphenyl oxide, phenyl ether, diphenyl ether.

oxyder [ɔkside], *v.tr. Ch:* to oxidize.

s'oxyder, (i) to become oxidized; (ii) to rust; to become corroded.

oxydoréduction [ɔksidɔredyksjɔ̃], *s.f. Ch:* oxidoreduction.

oxygénable [ɔksiʒenabl̥], *a. Ch:* oxygenizable.

oxygénateur [ɔksiʒenatœːr], *s.m.* oxygenator.

oxygénation [ɔksiʒenasjɔ̃], *s.f. Ch:* oxygenation, oxidation.

oxygène [ɔksiʒɛn], *s.m. Ch:* oxygen; **o. liquide,** liquid oxygen, loxygen.

oxygéné, -ée [ɔksiʒene]. **1.** *a. Ch:* oxygenated; **eau oxygénée,** peroxide of hydrogen; *Hairdr:* **cheveux oxygénés,** peroxided hair. **2.** *Hairdr:* *s.f.* **une oxygénée,** *F:* a bleach.

oxygéner [ɔksiʒene], *v.tr.* (**il oxygène; il oxygénera**) to oxygenate, oxidize, oxygenize; *Hairdr:* to wash in peroxide, to bleach (hair).

s'oxygéner, *F:* to get, give oneself, a breath of fresh air.

oxygénothérapie [ɔksiʒenɔterapi], *s.f. Med:* oxygen treatment.

oxygnathe [ɔksignat], *a.* oxygnathous.

oxyhémoglobine [ɔksiemɔglɔbin], *s.f. Physiol:* oxyhaemoglobine.

oxyhydryle [ɔksiidril], *s.m. Ch:* hydroxyl.

oxylithe [ɔksilit], *s.f.* oxylith (for respiratory apparatus).

oxylophe [ɔksilɔf], *s.m. Orn:* **o. geai,** great spotted cuckoo.

oxymel [ɔksimɛl], *s.m.,* **oxymellite** [ɔksimɛlit], *s.m. Med:* oxymel.

oxymoron [ɔksimɔrɔ̃], *s.m. Rh:* oxymoron.

oxyrhinque, oxyrhynque[1] [ɔksirɛ̃ːk], *s.m. Ent:* oxyrhynchus.

oxyrhynque[2] [ɔksirɛ̃k], *s.m. Crust:* oxyr(r)hynchid; *pl.* Oxyr(r)hyncha.

oxysel [ɔksisɛl], *s.m. Ch:* oxysalt.

oxysulfure [ɔksisylfyːr], *s.m. Ch:* oxysulphide.

oxyton [ɔksitɔ̃], *a. Gram:* oxytone (word).

oxytonisme [ɔksitɔnism], *s.m. Ling:* oxytonesis.

oxyure [ɔksiyːr], *s.f. Ann:* oxyuris; **o. vermiculaire,** pin worm.

oxyurose [ɔksiyroːz], *s.f. Med:* oxyuriasis.

oyant [ɔjɑ̃], *A:* **1.** *a.* hearing, listening; (*cf.* OUÏR.) **2.** *s.m. Jur:* auditor.

oyat [ɔja], *s.m. Bot: F:* sea bent, sea reed; marram grass.

oyez [ɔje]. *See* OUÏR.

oyonnaxien, -ienne [ɔjɔnaksjɛ̃, -jɛn], *a. & s. Geog:* (native, inhabitant) of Oyonnax.

ozalid [ozalid], *s.m. R.t.m:* Ozalid.

ozène [ozɛn], *s.m. Med:* (= PUNAISIE) ozaena, ozena.

ozobrome [ɔzɔbrɔːm], *a. Phot:* **procédé o.,** ozobrome process.

ozobromie [ɔzɔbrɔmi], *s.f. Phot:* ozobromie.

ozokérite [ɔzɔkerit], *s. f.*, *occ.* **ozocérite** [ɔzɔserit], *s. f. Miner:* ozocerite, ozokerite.

ozonateur [ɔzɔnatœːr], *s.m.* ozonizer; ozone generator.

ozonation [ɔzɔnasjɔ̃], *s. f.* ozonization.

ozone [ɔzɔn, -oːn], *s.m. Ch:* ozone.

ozonide [ɔzɔnid], *s.m. Ch:* ozonide.

ozonisation [ɔzɔnizasjɔ̃], *s. f.* ozonization.

ozoniser [ɔzɔnize], *occ.* **ozoner** [ɔzɔne], *v.tr.* to ozonize.

ozoniseur [ɔzɔnizœːr], *s.m.*, *occ.* **ozoneur** [ɔzɔnœːr], *s.m.* ozonizer, ozone apparatus.

ozonium [ɔzɔnjɔm], *s.m. Fung:* ozonium.

ozonomètre [ɔzɔnɔmɛtr̩], *s.m. Ph:* ozonometer.

ozonométrie [ɔzɔnɔmetri], *s. f.* ozonometry.

ozonométrique [ɔzɔnɔmetrik], *a.* ozonometric.

ozonoscope [ɔzɔnɔskɔp], *s.m. Ch:* ozonoscope

ozonoscopique [ɔzɔnɔskɔpik], *a. Ch:* ozonoscopic.

ozonosphère [ɔzɔnɔsfɛːr], *s. f. Meteor:* ozonosphere.

ozotype [ɔzɔtip], *s.m. Phot:* ozotype.

P

P, p [pe], *s.m.* (the letter) P, p; *Tp:* **P comme Pierre,** P for Peter.

paca [paka], *s.m. Z:* paca.

pacage [paka:ʒ], *s.m.* **1.** pasture(land), pasturage. **2.** pasturing, grazing; *Jur:* **droit(s) de p.,** grazing rights, common of pasture, of pasturage; *Scot:* pasturage.

pacager [pakaʒe], *v.tr.* (**je pacageai(s); n. pacageons**) to pasture, graze (beasts, field); **faire p. du seigle,** to put animals to pasture on rye.

pacane [pakan], *s.f. Bot:* pecan nut.

pacanier [pakanje], *s.m. Bot:* pecan (tree).

pacemaker [peismeikɛːr], *s.m. Sp: Med:* pacemaker.

pacfung [pakfɔ̃], *s.m.* (Chinese) nickel-silver, paktong, pakfong.

pacha [paʃa], *s.m.* (*a*) pasha; (*b*) *F:* **mener une vie de p., faire le p.,** to lead an easy life; to sit back and take it easy; (*c*) *Navy: F:* **le p.,** the old man.

pachalik [paʃalik], *s.m. Hist:* pashalik.

pachnolite [paknolit], *s.f. Miner:* pachnolite.

pachomètre [pakɔmɛtr], *s.m. Meas:* pachymeter.

pachyblépharose [paʃiblefaroːz, paki-], *s.f. Med:* pachyblepharon.

pachyderme [paʃidɛrm, *occ.* paki-], *Z:* **1.** *a.* pachydermatous, thick-skinned. **2.** *s.m.* pachyderm; **les pachydermes,** the Pachydermata.

pachydermie [paʃidɛrmi, *occ.* paki-], *s.f. Med:* elephantiasis, pachydermia.

pachydermique [paʃidɛrmik, paki-], *a. F:* **1.** pachydermatous, thick-skinned. **2.** huge, mammoth.

pachylose [paʃiloːz, paki-], *s.f. Med:* pachylosis.

pachyméningite [paʃimenɛ̃ʒit, paki-], *s.f. Med:* pachymeningitis.

pachypleurite [paʃiplœrit, paki-], *s.f. Med:* pachypleuritis.

pachyrhizus [paʃirizys, paki-], *s.m. Bot:* pachyrhizus.

pachysalpingite [paʃisalpɛ̃ʒit, paki-], *s.f. Med:* pachysalpingitis.

pachytène [paʃitɛn, paki-], *a. Biol:* **stade p.,** pachytene stage.

pachyure [paʃiyːr, paki-], *s.f. Z:* **p. étrusque,** Etruscan shrew(-mouse).

pachyvaginite [paʃivaʒinit, paki-], *s.f. Med:* pachyvaginitis.

pacifiant [pasifjɑ̃], *a.* pacifying, calming.

pacificateur, -trice [pasifikatœːr, -tris], **1.** *a.* pacifying; peacemaking; pacificatory. **2.** *s.* pacifier; peacemaker.

pacification [pasifikasjɔ̃], *s.f.* pacification, pacifying; *Fr.Hist:* **Édits de p.,** pacificatory edicts (of the kings of France, during the Wars of Religion).

pacifier [pasifje], *v.tr.* (*p.d. & pr.sub.* n. **pacifiions, v. pacifiiez**) to pacify (country); to appease, to calm (crowd, the mind, etc.). **se pacifier,** to calm down.

pacifique [pasifik], *a.* (*a*) pacific, conciliatory, peaceable (person, etc.); **règlement p.,** peaceable settlement; *s. B:* **bienheureux les pacifiques,** blessed are the peacemakers; (*b*) peaceful, quiet (reign, etc.); **coexistence p.,** peaceful coexistence; (*c*) **l'océan P.,** the Pacific Ocean; (*d*) *Jur:* **possesseur p.,** uncontested owner.

pacifiquement [pasifikmɑ̃], *adv.* peaceably, quietly, calmly.

pacifisme [pasifism], *s.m. Pol:* pacifism.

pacifiste [pasifist], *a. & s.m. & f. Pol:* pacifist.

pack [pak], *s.m.* **1.** (ice-)pack (of the polar seas). **2.** *Rugby Fb:* pack.

packfond, packfong, packfung [pakfɔ̃], *s.m.* (Chinese) nickel-silver, packtong, packfong.

pacotille [pakɔtiːj], *s.f.* (*a*) *A:* (*goods taken on board by seamen or passengers for private sale*) mariner's venture, portage; private cargo; (*b*) **marchandises de p.,** shoddy goods; **meubles, maison, de p.,** gimcrack furniture, jerry-built house; **bijoux de p.,** paste jewellery; *Pej:* **un héroïsme de p.,** bogus heroism; (*c*) *A:* stock, quantity, job lot (of various goods).

pacotilleur, -euse [pakɔtijœːr, -øːz], *s. A:* **1.** merchant adventurer. **2.** dealer in shoddy goods.

pacquage [paka:ʒ], *s.m.* sorting and packing (of fish) in barrels.

pacquer [pake], *v.tr.* to sort and pack (fish) in barrels.

pacqueur, -eresse [pakœːr, -ɔrɛs], *s.* packer (of salt fish in barrels).

pacte [pakt], *s.m.* compact, pact, agreement; *Hist:* **le p. de la Société des Nations,** the Covenant of the League of Nations; **p. à quatre,** four-power pact; **faire un p. avec qn,** to enter into an agreement, to make a bargain, with s.o.; **p. de famille,** family settlement; *Fr.Hist:* the Family Compact (1761); *Jur:* **p. de quota litis,** champerty; **p. de préférence,** preference clause; *Com:* **p. social,** articles of association.

pactiser [paktize], *v.i.* **p. avec l'ennemi,** to make, enter into, a compact, to come to terms, to treat, with the enemy; **p. avec sa conscience,** to compound, to compromise, with one's conscience; **p. avec un crime,** to compound a felony.

Pactole (le) [ləpaktɔl]. **1.** *Pr.n.m. A.Geog:* the (river) Pactolus. **2.** *s.m.* **cette propriété est pour lui le, un, p.,** that estate of his is a regular gold mine.

padan [padɑ̃], *a. Geog:* of the (river) Po; **la plaine padane,** the plain of the Po.

paddock [padɔk], *s.m.* (*a*) paddock; (*b*) *P:* bed, *P:* pit.

paddocker (se) [səpadɔke], *v.pr. P:* to go to bed, to hit the hay, to pad down.

paddy [padi], *s.m. Com:* paddy (rice).

padine [padin], *s.f. Algae:* peacock's tail.

padischah, padisha [padiʃa], *s.m.* padishah.

padou(e) [padu], *s.m. Tex:* ferret; ribbon (half silk, half cotton).

padouan, -ane [padwɑ̃, -an], *a. & s. Geog:* Paduan.

Padoue [padu], *Pr.n.f. Geog:* Padua.

padouk [paduk], *s.m. Com:* padouk, padauk.

padre [padre], *s.m. Fr.C: Mil:* padre.

pæan [peɑ̃], *s.m.* paean.

pædogénèse [pedoʒenɛːz], *s.f. Biol:* p(a)edogenesis.

paf [paf]. **1.** *int.* slap! bang! **ses talons faisaient p. p. sur les dalles,** his heels went thump, thump, clump, clump, on the flags. **2.** *a.inv. P:* **être p.,** to be tipsy, tight, screwed.

pagaie [pagɛ], *s.f.* paddle (for canoe); **p. simple, p. à une pale(tte),** single paddle; **p. double, p. à double pale(tte),** double paddle.

pagaïe [paga:j], *s.f.*, **pagaille** [paga:j], *s.f.*, **pagale** [pagal], *s.f. A:* **pagaye** [paga:j], *s.f. F:* (*a*) *esp. Nau:* disorder, hurry; clutter (of objects); **faire de la p. (en manœuvrant),** to be all at sixes and sevens; **en p.,** in disorder; at random; **amener les vergues en p.,** to lower the yards by the run;

faire qch. en p., to bungle sth.; **tout ramasser en p.,** to bundle everything up; **tout était en p.,** everything was higgledy-piggledy; the things were all cluttered up, all in a clutter, in a mess; **convoi qui avance en p.,** convoy steaming all anyhow; **quelle p.!** what a mess! what a shambles! (*b*) **il y en a p.,** there's lots, any amount, of it; **avoir de l'argent en p.,** to be rolling in money.

pagailleur, -euse [pagajœːr, -øːz], **pagailleux, -euse** [pagajø, -øːz], *s. F:* muddler.

paganiser [paganize], *v.tr. & i.* to paganize, heathenize.

paganisme [paganism], *s.m.* paganism.

pagayer [pageje], *v.* (**je pagaie, je pagaye,** n. **pagayons; je pagaierai, je pagayerai**) **1.** *v.i.* (*a*) to paddle; (*b*) (*of paddleboat*) to bruise water. **2.** *v.tr.* **p. une périssoire,** to paddle a canoe.

pagayeur, -euse [pagɛjœːr, -øːz], *s.* paddler (of canoe).

page¹ [pa:ʒ], *s.f.* page (of book, etc.); **vous le trouverez (à la) p. 20,** you'll find it on page 20; *Journ:* **suite en p. 5, en dernière p.,** continued on page 5, on back page; **p. blanche,** blank page; *Typ:* **mettre en pages,** to make up; **metteur en pages,** clicker, maker-up; **mise en pages,** making up and imposing; page-setting; **belle p.,** right-hand page; **fausse p.,** left-hand page; **pages de départ,** prelims; **pages de garde,** end papers; **la plus belle p. de sa vie,** the finest chapter of his life; *F:* **être à la p.,** (i) to be up to date, with it; (ii) to be in the know; *F:* **se mettre à la p.,** to keep up with the times; *F:* **ne pas être à la p.,** to be behind the times; *F:* to be square; **tourner la p.,** (i) to let bygones be bygones; (ii) to turn over a new leaf; (iii) to draw a veil over sth.

page², *s.m.* **1.** page(-boy); **être sorti de p., être hors de p.,** (i) *A:* to have served one's time as a page, to be out of pagehood; (ii) to be no longer a boy; (iii) to be one's own master; *A:* **tour de p.,** schoolboy('s) trick. **2.** *A.Cost:* **p. de robe,** page, (dress-)clip. **3.** *Ven:* young (wild) boar (accompanying an old one).

page³, *s.m. P:* bed, *P:* pit, sack.

pageau, -eaux [paʒo], *s.m. Ich: F:* sea bream.

pagée [paʒe], *s.f. Fr.C:* fence section.

pagel [paʒɛl], *s.m.*, **pagelle** [paʒɛl], *s.f. Ich:* sea bream.

pageot [paʒo], *s.m. P:* bed, *P:* pit, sack.

pageoter (se) [səpaʒɔte], **pager (se)** [səpaʒe], *v.pr. P:* to go to bed, to hit the hay, to pad down.

pagination [paʒinasjɔ̃], *s.f.* paging, pagination; **faute de p.,** mistake in pagination.

paginer [paʒine], *v.tr.* to page, paginate (book, ledger, etc.).

pagne [paɲ], *s.m.* loincloth, pagne.

pagnon [paɲɔ̃], *s.m.* black broadcloth (as originally manufactured at Sedan by Pagnon).

pagnot [paɲo], *s.m. P:* bed, *P:* pit, sack.

pagnoter (se) [səpaɲote], *v.pr. P:* to go to bed; to get into bed; to hit the hay.

pagode [pagɔd]. **1.** *s.f.* (*a*) pagoda ((i) temple; (ii) coin); (*b*) (*nodding toy*) mandarin. **2.** *a.f.* **manches pagodes,** pagoda sleeves.

pagodite [pagɔdit], *s.f. Miner:* pagodite.

pagodon [pagɔdɔ̃], *s.m.* (small) Buddhist, Confucian, pagoda.

pagoscope [pagɔskɔp], *s.m. Ph:* pagoscope.

pagre [pagr], *s.m. Ich:* pagrus, porgy.

pagure [pagyːr], *s.m. Crust:* hermit crab, pagurian.

paidologie [pɛdɔlɔʒi], *s.f.* p(a)edology.

paidologique [pɛdɔlɔʒik], *a.* p(a)edologic(al).

paidologue [pɛdɔlɔg], *s.m. & f.* p(a)edologist.

paie [pɛ], *s.f.* **1.** (*a*) pay; wages; **livre de p.,** wage book; **feuille, bulletin, de p.,** pay (advice) slip; *Mil:* **haute p.,** special rate of pay (to re-enlisted men); (*b*) *Mil:* **les hautes paies,** the re-enlisted men (on a special rate of pay). **2.** payment; **jour de p.,** pay day; **faire, distribuer, la p.,** to pay out the wages. **3.** *F:* **c'est une mauvaise p.,** he's a bad, a slow, payer.

paiement [pɛmɑ̃], *s.m.* payment; discharge (of debt); **gros p.,** heavy disbursement; **paiements effectués par la caisse,** cash payments; **p. d'un compte,** settlement of an account; **p. d'avance,** payment in advance; prepayment; **p. contre livraison,** cash on delivery, C.O.D.; **p. à termes, par acomptes,** payment by instalments; **paiements échelonnés,** instalments; **p. comptant,** cash payment; **présenter un chèque au p.,** to present a cheque for payment; **défaut de p.,** non payment; **suspendre les paiements,** to stop payment; **jour de p.,** pay day; **conditions de p.,** terms of payment.

païen, -ienne [pajɛ̃, -jɛn], *a. & s.* pagan, heathen; **les dieux des païens,** the gods of the heathen; **le monde p.,** heathendom.

paierie [pɛri], *s.f. Adm:* paymaster's office; **p. générale,** (French government) pay office.

paillage [pɑjaːʒ], *s.m.* **1.** *Hort:* mulching. **2.** straw-bottoming (of chair).

paillard, -arde [pajaːr, -ard]. **1.** *a.* (*a*) *O:* (*of pers.*) lewd; dissolute; (*b*) **regard p.,** leer; **histoire paillarde,** risqué story; **chanson paillarde,** ribald, bawdy, song; **il eut un rire gras comme s'il découvrait aux paroles de son ami un sens p.,** he gave a fat chuckle as if he'd seen a dirty meaning in his friend's words. **2.** *s.* (*a*) *A:* tramp; ne'er-do-well; (*b*) *A:* lout, boor; (*c*) rake; **vieux p.,** dirty old man, old rake; (*d*) *s.f.* **paillarde,** loose-living woman.

paillarder [pajarde], *v.i.* (*a*) to live a dissolute life; (*b*) *A:* to idle away one's time; to live a life of ease.

se paillarder, *F:* (*a*) to have a high old time, a ball; (*b*) to have a good laugh.

paillardise [pajardiːz], *s.f.* **1.** profligacy; debauchery. **2. débiter des paillardises,** to make crude jokes; to tell risqué stories.

paillasse [pajas, pɑ-]. **1.** *s.f.* (*a*) straw mattress, paillasse, paliasse, pallet; (*b*) *Cu:* flank (of beef); (*c*) *P:* belly; **crever, trouer, la p. à qn,** to knife s.o. in the guts; (*d*) *Ch: etc:* (laboratory) bench; *Dom.Ec:* draining board (and support); (*e*) *P:* low prostitute, tart, bag. **2.** *s.m.* (*a*) *A:* clown, buffoon; *Th:* **Paillasse,** Pagliacci; (*b*) *Pol: F: A:* weathercock.

paillasserie [pajasri, pɑ-], *s.f. A:* clownery.

paillasson [pajasɔ̃, pɑ-], *s.m.* **1.** (*a*) (door)mat; *F:* **mettre la clef sous le p.,** to clear out, to flit; (*b*) *F:* servile person, *F:* doormat; (*c*) *Hort:* (straw) matting, mat; (*d*) *F:* old tennis racket. **2.** *P:* (*a*) **mener une vie de p.,** to lead a dissolute life; (*b*) low prostitute, tart, bag.

paillassonnage [pajasɔnaːʒ, pɑ-], *s.m. Hort:* covering (of seedlings, etc.) with (straw) matting; matting.

paillassonner [pajasɔne, pɑ-], *v.tr. Hort:* to cover, protect (seedlings, espaliers, etc.) with matting; to mat.

paille [pɑːj], *s.f.* **1.** (*a*) straw; **botte de p.,** truss of straw; **p. de litière,** loose straw; **p. de riz, d'Italie,** rice straw; **chapeau de p.,** straw hat; **chapeau de p. d'Italie,** Leghorn hat; **chaise de p.,** straw-bottomed chair; **homme de p.,** man of straw, dummy; **feu de p.,** flash in the pan; **être, coucher, sur la p.,** to be in extreme poverty, *F:* to be down and out; **mourir sur la p.,** to die in poverty; **réduire, mettre, qn sur la p.,** to ruin s.o.; **être comme un poisson sur la p.,** to be like a fish out of water; *Winem:* **vin de p.,** straw wine; dessert wine; *A:* **il a mis de la p. dans ses souliers,** he's feathered his (own) nest; *A:* **être à la p. jusqu'au ventre,** to be wallowing in luxury; *B:* **voir la p. dans l'œil du prochain,** to see the mote in one's brother's eye; *F:* **hacher de la p.,** to speak with a harsh (*esp.* guttural) accent; (*b*) **une p.,** a straw; **boire qch. avec une p.,** to drink sth. through a straw; **une p. indique d'où vient le vent,** a straw shows which way the wind blows; **rompre la p.,** to quarrel (with s.o.); **tirer à la courte paille,** to draw lots; *F:* **avoir, tenir, une p.,** to be drunk, tight; *F:* **voilà une p. que je ne t'ai pas vu,** it's ages since I last saw you; *F: Iron:* **il demande dix millions; une p.!** he's asking ten million(s); a mere trifle! (*c*) *a.inv.* straw-coloured; (*d*) *Cu:* **pailles au parmesan,** cheese straws. **2. menue p., p. d'avoine,** chaff. **3. p. de fer,** (i) iron shavings (for scrubbing floors); steel wool; (ii) *Metall:* hammer scale(s). **4.** *Nau:* **p. de bitte,** battledore, bitt pin. **5.** flaw (in gem, glass, etc.); flaw, blister, cleft (in metal); **la traduction présente quelques pailles,** the translation contains a certain number of imperfections.

paillé[1] [pɑje], *s.m. Husb:* stable litter (of straw and dung).

paillé[2], *a.* **1.** flawy (metal, gem, etc.); scaly (metal). **2.** straw-coloured (animal, mane, etc.). **3. vin p.,** straw wine; dessert wine.

paillebart [pɑjbaːr], *s.m. Const:* cob.

paille-de-mer [pɑjdəmɛːr], *s.f. Bot: F:* Posidonia; *pl. pailles-de-mer.*

paillée [pɑje], *s.f. Agr:* heap of sheaves (spread out on the threshing floor).

paille-en-cul [pɑjɑ̃ky], *s.m.*, **paille-en-queue** [pɑjɑ̃kø], *s.m. Orn:* tropic bird; *pl. pailles-en-cul, pailles-en-queue.*

paillement [pɑjmɑ̃], *s.m. Hort:* mulching.

pailler[1] [pɑje]. **1.** *s.m.* (*a*) farmyard, straw yard; **poularde, chapon, de p.,** barn-door fowl; (*b*) straw stack; (*c*) dunghill; *F:* **être sur son p.,** to be on one's own dunghill. **2.** *a.* (*f.* **paillère**) (*of fowl*) bred in the straw yard; **poularde paillère,** barn-door fowl.

pailler[2], *v.tr.* **1.** *Hort:* to cover, protect, (trees, plants, etc.) with straw; to mulch. **2.** to straw (a chair); *esp. in. p.p.* **chaise paillée,** rush-bottomed, straw-bottomed, chair.

paillet[1] [pɑjɛ], *s.m. Nau:* mat, fender; **p. d'abordage, p. makarov,** collision mat; **p. de défense,** mat fender; **p. de portage,** chafing mat.

paillet[2], *a.m. & s.m.* (vin) **p.,** pale red wine.

pailletage [pɑjətaːʒ], *s.m. Cost: etc:* spangling.

pailleté [pɑjte], *a.* spangled (de, with); pailletted.

pailleter [pɑjte], *v.tr.* (**je paillette, n. pailletons; je pailletterai**) to spangle.

pailleteur [pɑjtœːr], *s.m.* gold washer.

paillette [pɑjɛt], *s.f.* **1.** spangle, paillette; **p. d'esprit,** flash, spark, of wit. **2.** (*a*) grain of gold dust (in stream); (*b*) flake (of mica, etc.); **savon en paillettes,** soap flakes; (*c*) *Cu:* **paillettes au fromage,** cheese straws. **3.** (*a*) *Metall:* (forge) scale; (*b*) (*in goldsmith's work*) **p. de soudure,** grain of solder. **4.** flaw (in gem). **5.** *Bot:* palea, pale.

pailleur, -euse[1] [pɑjœːr, -øːz], *s.* **1.** straw merchant. **2.** *A:* chair mender.

pailleux, -euse[2] [pɑjø, -øːz], *a.* **1.** strawy (manure). **2.** flawy (iron, glass).

paillis [pɑji], *s.m. Hort:* mulch.

paillon [pɑjɔ̃], *s.m.* **1.** (large) spangle. **2.** (jeweller's) foil; **p. de soudure,** grain of solder. **3.** wisp of straw (in various technical processes). **4.** (*a*) **p. de bouteille,** straw case (for bottle); (*b*) **p. de boulanger,** baker's flat basket. **5.** *Watchm: Nau: etc:* link (of fusee chain, of cable chain). **6.** *P:* **faire des paillons à (son mari, sa femme),** to be unfaithful to, to deceive (one's husband, one's wife).

paillot [pɑjo], *s.m. O:* palliasse, straw mattress (for child's bed).

paillote [pɑjɔt], *s.f.* (*a*) straw hut; (*b*) (*in India*) matting (made of rice straw).

paimblotin, -ine [pɛ̃blɔtɛ̃, -in], *a. & s. Geog:* (native, inhabitant) of Paimbœuf.

paîment [pɛmɑ̃], *s.m. A:* = PAIEMENT.

paimpolais, -aise [pɛ̃pɔlɛ, -ɛːz], *a. & s. Geog:* (native, inhabitant) of Paimpol.

pain [pɛ̃], *s.m.* **1.** (*a*) bread; **p. de froment,** wheaten bread; **p. de seigle,** rye bread; **p. de sarrasin, p. noir,** buckwheat bread, black rye bread; **p. bis, p. de son,** brown bread; **p. complet,** wholemeal bread; **p. blanc,** white bread; **p. frais, p. rassis,** fresh bread, stale bread; *Mil:* **p. de guerre,** *A:* **p. de munition,** ration bread; **p. grillé,** toast; **p. perdu,** French toast; **p. de chien,** dog biscuit; **p. d'épice,** gingerbread; **p. de Gênes,** Genoa cake; **mettre qn au p. et à l'eau,** to put s.o. on bread and water; *Jewish Rel:* **p. azyme,** unleavened bread; *Ecc:* **p. eucharistique,** host; **p. d'autel, p. à chanter,** (unconsecrated) wafer; **donne-nous aujourd'hui notre p. de ce jour,** give us this day our daily bread; **p. du ciel,** manna; *B:* **p. de tribulation,** bread of tribulation; **bon comme le p., comme du bon p.,** good-hearted, good-natured; **acheter qch. pour une bouchée de p.,** to buy sth. for a mere song, for next to nothing; **il ne vaut pas le p. qu'il mange,** he isn't worth his salt; **manger son p. blanc le premier,** (i) to begin with the cake; (ii) to make a good, a flying, start; **manger son p. dans sa poche,** to be selfish, to keep one's good things to oneself; (*of cat*) **faire son p.,** to knead, to make bread; **recevoir plus de coups que de p.,** to get more kicks than ha'pence; *Prov:* **p. dérobé réveille l'appétit,** stolen kisses are more sweet; **savoir de quel côté son p. est beurré,** to know on which side one's bread is buttered; **avoir du p. sur la planche,** to have plenty of work on hand, on one's plate; *F:* **avoir son p. cuit,** to be nicely settled, in a good position; *s.a.* BÉNIT, LONG 1; (*b*) **gagner son p.,** to earn one's living; **ôter à qn le p. de la bouche,** to take the bread out of s.o.'s mouth; **mettre le p. à la main de qn,** to assure s.o. a livelihood, a job; **nul p. sans peine,** there is no reward without effort; it needs hard work to achieve success; **je ne mange pas de ce p.-là,** I'd rather starve; (*c*) *Bot: F:* **p. de pourceau,** sowbread; **p. de coucou,** cuckoo bread, wood sorrel; **p. de grenouille,** water plantain; **fruit à p.,** breadfruit; **arbre à p.,** breadfruit tree; **p. d'oiseau,** dithering grass; **p. de singe,** monkey bread. **2.** (*a*) loaf; **p. rond, p. boulot,** round loaf; **p. de quatre livres,** quarten loaf; **p. de ménage,** large (home-made) loaf; **p. moulé,** tin loaf; **p. de mie,** sandwich loaf; **p. de campagne, p. paysan,** farmhouse loaf; **petit p.,** (bread) roll; *Com:* **ça se vend, s'enlève, comme des petits pains,** it's selling like hot cakes; **acheter qch. pour une bouchée de p.,** to buy sth. for next to nothing, for a song; (*b*) **p. de savon,** cake of soap; **p. de beurre,** (i) pat, (ii) packet, of butter; *Husb:* **p. de noix, p. d'olives,** walnut cake, olive cake; *Husb:* **p. salé,** salt lick; *Art:* **p. (de peinture),** cake (of water colour); **p. de sucre,** sugar loaf; **sucre en pains,** loaf sugar; *Geog:* **(montagne en) p. de sucre,** sugar loaf (mountain); *Geol:* **p. fossile,** limepan. **3.** *A:* **p. à cacheter,** (sealing) wafer; **il n'a pas inventé les pains à cacheter,** he'll never set the Thames on fire. **4.** *P:* blow, punch; **flanque-lui un p.,** sock him one, give him a plug in the earhole.

pair [pɛːr]. **1.** *a.* even (number); *s.* **le p. et l'impair,** odd and even; *P.N:* **stationnement jours pairs,** parking on even dates (only); **(chez l'homme) les poumons sont des organes pairs,** man has two lungs; *s.* (*at roulette*) **jouer (sur) p.,** to play the even numbers; *Rail:* **voie paire,** up line. **2.** *s.m.* (*a*) equal; *A:* **c'est un homme sans p.,** he is without equal; *Lit:* **vivre avec qn, traiter qn, de p. en compagnon,** to treat s.o. as an equal; **vivre avec ses pairs,** to live with one's equals; **être jugé par ses pairs,** to be tried by one's peers; **sans p.,** unequalled; peerless; **hors (de) p.,** unrivalled, beyond compare; **succès hors p.,** unmatched success; **artiste hors (de) p.,** incomparable artist; **dans son domaine il est hors (de) p.,** in his own field he is unrivalled; (*b*) *adv.phr.* **de p. (avec),** (i) on a par, on an equal footing (with); (ii) at the same time (as), together (with); **marcher de p. avec qn,** (i) to keep pace with s.o.; (ii) to emulate s.o.; **ces industries ont marché de p.,** these industries have developed at the same pace, *pari passu*; **marcher de p. avec son époque,** to keep abreast of the times; **il va de p. avec les grands philosophes,** he ranks with the great philosophers; **le chômage va de p. avec les crises économiques,** unemployment and economic crises go hand in hand; (*c*) peer (of the realm); **les douze pairs de Charlemagne,** Charlemagne's twelve peers; **p. à vie,** life peer; (*in Eng.*) **Chambre des Pairs,** House of Lords; (*d*) (*of birds*) mate. **3.** *s.m.* (state of) equality, par; (*a*) *Fin:* **p. du change,** par of exchange; **le change est au p.,** the exchange is at par; **au-dessous, au-dessus, du p.,** below par, above par; **valeur au p., valeur du p.,** par value; (*b*) *adv.phr.* **au p.,** (i) *A:* level; (ii) au pair; **étudiante au p.,** au pair student, *F:* au pair (girl); **elle est chez eux au p.,** she's staying with them au pair; *A:* **être au p. de son travail,** to be up to date with one's work.

pairage [pɛraːʒ], *s.m. T.V:* pairing.

paire [pɛːr], *s.f.* pair; brace (of game birds, pistols); **p. de tourterelles,** pair of turtle doves; **p. de faisans,** brace of pheasants; **p. de bœufs,** yoke of oxen; **p. de chaussures, de gants,** pair of shoes, of gloves; **ça, c'est une autre p. de manches,** that's another story; **p. de lunettes, de ciseaux,** pair of spectacles, of scissors; *Elcs:* **p. d'ions,** ion pair; **p. d'impulsions,** pulse pair; **cable à paires,** paired cable; *El: Tp:* (*cable with two conductors*) **p. blindée,** shielded pair; **p. coaxiale,** coaxial pair; **p. torsadée,** twisted pair; **une p. d'amis inséparables,** a couple of inseparable friends; **ces tableaux font la p.,** these pictures make a pair, go together; *F:* **les deux font la p.,** the two of them are a pretty pair, are tarred with the same brush; *P:* **se faire la p.,** to clear out, to hook it.

pairement [pɛrmɑ̃], *adv. Mth:* **nombre p. pair,** multiple of four.
pairer (se) [səpɛre], *v.pr. (Eng. Parliament)* to pair (**avec,** with).
pairesse [pɛrɛs], *s.f.* peeress.
pairie [pɛri], *s.f.* peerage; **conférer une p. à qn,** to confer a peerage on s.o.
pairle [pɛrl], *s.m. Her:* pall; **en p.,** pallwise.
paisible [pezibl̥; pɛ-], *a.* (*a*) peaceful, peaceable, quiet (person); (*b*) peaceful, untroubled, quiet; **retraite p.,** quiet, calm, retreat; **silence p.,** undisturbed silence; (*c*) *Jur:* **possesseur p.,** uncontested owner.
paisiblement [pezibləmɑ̃; pɛ-], *adv.* peaceably, peacefully, quietly.
paissance [pɛsɑ̃:s], *s.f. Husb:* pasturing; **troupeaux en p. sur la montagne,** herds at pasture on the mountain-side.
paisseau, -eaux [pɛso], *s.m. Vit:* vine prop.
paisselage [pɛsla:ʒ], *s.m. Vit:* putting in of vine props.
paisseler [pɛsle], *v.tr.* (**je paisselle, n. paisselons; je paissellerai**) *Vit:* to prop up (vines).
paisselure [pɛsly:r], *s.f. coll. Vit:* hemp used to attach vines to props.
paisson [pɛsɔ̃], *s.m. Husb:* forest pasture; *Jur:* pannage.
paître [pɛ:tr̥], *v.* (*pr.p.* **paissant;** *pr.ind.* **je pais, il paît, n. paissons;** *pr.sub.* **je paisse, n. paissions;** *imp.* **pais, paissons, paissez;** *p.d.* **je paissais;** *fu.* **je paîtrai;** *no p.h.; the p.p.* **pu** *is used only in the phr. shown under* 2) **1.** *v.tr.* (*a*) *A: & Lit:* to take, drive, (cattle) to pasture; to feed, graze (cattle); (*b*) (*of animals*) to feed on (leaves, mast, etc.); to crop (grass); (*c*) *Ven:* **p. le faucon,** to feed the falcon; (*d*) **p. la meule,** to feed olives into the crushing mill. **2.** *v.i.* (*of animals*) to feed; to graze, browse; to pasture; **faucon qui a pu,** hawk that has fed; *F:* **je l'ai envoyé p.,** I sent him packing; I sent him about his business; I told him to go and jump in the lake; *O:* **allez p.!** get out!
se paître de qch., *A:* (*of animal*) to feed, to raven, on sth.; **les vautours se paissaient de la chair des morts,** the vultures battened on the corpses.
paix [pɛ], *s.f.* **1.** peace; (*a*) **faire la p.,** to make peace; **faisons la p.,** let us bury the hatchet; **faire la p. avec qn,** to make one's peace with s.o.; **proposer la p.,** to make overtures for peace, to hold out the olive branch; **demander la p.,** to sue for peace; **le pays est en p. avec . . .,** the country is at peace with . . .; **rester en p. avec un pays,** to remain at peace with a country; **en temps de p.,** in time(s) of peace; **p. à tout prix,** peace at any price; **p. plâtrée,** patched-up peace; *Hist:* **la p. de Dieu,** the truce of God; **p. romaine,** *pax romana*; (*b*) **observer, troubler, la p.,** to keep, to break, the peace; **la p. règne dans la ville,** the town is peaceful; **homme de p.,** man of peace; (*c*) **la p. des bois,** the peace, calm, of the woods; **la p. du tombeau,** the peace, quiet, of the grave; **p. à ses cendres!** peace to his ashes! peace to his memory! **vivre en p.,** to live in peace and quietness; **ma conscience est en p.,** my conscience is at peace; **dormir en p.,** to sleep peacefully; **laissez-moi en p.,** leave me in peace; **ne donner ni p. ni trêve à qn,** to give s.o. no peace; **il ne m'a laissé la p. que lorsque . . .,** he gave me no peace until . . .; *P:* **fiche-moi la p.!** don't bother me! shut up! **la p.!** hush! be quiet! **2.** *Ecc:* pax.
Pakistan [pakistɑ̃], *Pr.n.m. Geog:* Pakistan.
pakistanais, -aise [pakistanɛ, -ɛ:z], *a. & s.* Pakistani.
pal [pal], *s.m.* **1.** (*a*) pale, stake; *A:* **le supplice du p.,** impalement; (*b*) *Vit: etc:* planter, dibber; *Agr:* **p. injecteur,** injecting tube. **2.** *Her:* pale.
palabre [palabr̥], *s.f. occ. m. usu. pl.* palaver; (interminable) discussion; **après de longues palabres,** after an interminable discussion.
palabrer [palabre], *v.i.* to palaver; to make interminable speeches; to carry on interminable discussions.
palace [palas], *s.m.* de luxe hotel.
palade [palad], *s.f. Row:* stroke, pull (at the oar).
paladin [paladɛ̃], *s.m. Hist:* (*a*) paladin, knight (of Charlemagne's court); (*b*) knight-errant; chivalrous person.
palafitte [palafit], *s.m. Prehist:* lake dwelling.
palais¹ [palɛ], *s.m.* **1.** palace (of king, etc.); **le P. Bourbon,** the *Assemblée nationale*; **p. épiscopal,** bishop's palace. **2. p. de Justice,** law courts; **gens du p.,** lawyers, legal fraternity; **jour de palais,** court-day; **terme de p.,** legal term, forensic term; *Journ:* **courrier du p.,** police intelligence; law report.
palais², *s.m.* palate. **1.** (*a*) *Anat:* roof of the mouth; hard palate; **voile du p.,** soft palate; **la voûte du p.,** the palatine vault; **p. fendu,** cleft palate; (*b*) (sense of) taste; **avoir le p. fin,** to have a delicate palate. **2.** *Bot:* palate (of corolla of snapdragon, etc.).
palaïte [palait], *s.f. Miner:* palaite.
Palamède [palamɛd], *Pr.n.m. Gr.Myth:* Palamedes.
palan [palɑ̃], *s.m.* hoist, hoisting gear; *Mec.E: Nau:* pulley block, (purchase) tackle, whip; **p. simple,** single whip tackle; **p. à deux poulies simples,** double purchase gun tackle; **p. à deux poulies doubles, p. double,** twofold tackle, purchase; **p. à deux poulies triples,** threefold purchase; **p. à croc,** luff (tackle); **p. à vis,** worm block; **p. de garde,** guy tackle; **petit p., p. de, du, dimanche,** handy billy, jigger tackle, watch tackle, burton; **p. différentiel,** differential pulley block, planetary hoist; **p. à chaînes,** chain hoist; **p. d'apiquage,** lift tackle, purchase; **p. d'embarcation,** boat tackle; **p. de charge, d'étai,** garnet, stay tackle; **p. du gouvernail,** rudder tackle, relieving tackle; *Nau:* **livraison sous p.,** delivery under ship's tackle; **franco sous p.,** free alongside ship, free overboard, free overside, *U.S:* ex ship.
palanche [palɑ̃:ʃ], *s.f.* yoke, shoulder-piece (for carrying buckets, etc.).
palançon [palɑ̃sɔ̃], *s.m. Const:* lath, stake (in loam work).
palancre [palɑ̃kr̥], **palangre** [palɑ̃gr̥], *s.f. Fish:* trawl line, bottom line, *U.S:* trawl.
palancrer [palɑ̃kre], **palangrer** [palɑ̃gre], *v.i.* to fish with a trawl line.
palancrier [palɑ̃krje], **palangrier** [palɑ̃grje], *s.m. Nau:* small trawler.
palanguer [palɑ̃ge], *v.tr.* = PALANQUER².
palanque [palɑ̃:k], *s.f. Fort:* timber stockade, palank.
palanquée [palɑ̃ke], *s.f.* (*a*) sling load; draft, lift; (*b*) *Fish:* catch (of a fishing boat); (*c*) *P:* lashings, tons (of sth.).
palanquer¹ [palɑ̃ke], *v.tr. A.Fort:* to stockade.
palanquer², *v.tr. Nau:* to bowse, bouse (chain, etc.); to haul tight.
palanquin¹ [palɑ̃kɛ̃], *s.m.* palanquin.
palanquin², *s.m. Nau:* reef tackle.
Palaos (les) [lepalaos], *Pr.n.f.pl. Geog:* the Palau Islands.
palastre [palastr̥], *s.m.* (*a*) lock plate, back plate (of lock); (*b*) box (of lock); **serrure à p.,** case lock, box lock, rim lock.
palatal, -ale, -aux [palatal, -o], *a.* **1.** *Ling:* palatal; *s.f.* **palatale,** palatal; front consonant; **voyelle palatale,** front vowel. **2.** *Anat:* palatal, palatine (bones, etc.).
palatalisation [palatalizasjɔ̃], *s.f. Ling:* palatalization.
palatalisé [palatalize], *a. Ling:* palatalized.
palataliser [palatalize], *v.tr. Ling:* to palatalize.
palatial, -aux [palasjal, -o], *a.* **1.** *A:* **phrase palatiale,** legal phrase. **2.** (*rare*) palatial (building, etc.).
palatin¹, -ine [palatɛ̃, -in]. **1.** *a. & s. Hist:* palatine; **Comte p.,** Count Palatine; **la Princesse Palatine,** Princess Palatine. **2.** *a.* **Le Mont P.,** the Palatine Hill (at Rome). **3.** *s.f. A.Cost:* **palatine,** palatine, fur tippet.
palatin², **-ine,** *Anat:* (*a*) *a.* palatal, palatine; **os p.,** palatine bone; (*b*) *s.m.* palatine (bone).
Palatinat (le) [ləpalatina], *Pr.n.m. Hist:* the Palatinate.
palatite [palatit], *s.f. Med:* palatitis.
palato-dental, -aux [palatodɑ̃tal, -o], *a. Ling:* palatodental.
palato-glosse [palatoglɔs], *s.m. Anat:* palatoglossus; *pl. palato-glosses.*
palatogramme [palatogram], *s.m.* palatogram.
palato-pharyngien, -ienne [palatofarɛ̃ʒjɛ̃, -jɛn]. **1.** *a. Anat: Ling:* palato-pharyngeal. **2.** *s.m. Anat:* palato-pharyngeal muscle; *pl. palato-pharyngiens, -iennes.*
palatopharyngite [palatofarɛ̃ʒit], *s.f. Med:* palatopharyngitis.
palatoplastie [palatoplasti], *s.f. Surg:* palatoplasty.
palatorrhaphie [palatorafi], *s.f. Surg:* palatorrhaphy.
palâtre [palɑ:tr̥], *s.m.* = PALASTRE.
pale¹ [pal], *s.f.* **1.** stake, pale, paling (used for fences, etc.). **2.** (*a*) blade (of oar, paddle); wash (of oar); float, paddle board (of paddle wheel); (*b*) *Av: Nau:* blade (of propeller); (*in helicopter*) **p. de rotor,** rotor blade; **p. de l'aube,** aerofoil form of the blade; **angle de p.,** blade angle; **angle de calage de p.,** blade tilt; **courbure de la p.,** blade curvature; **dos de p.,** blade back; **face de p.,** blade face; **emplanture de la p.,** blade root; **pied, racine, de p.,** blade shank; **extrémité de p.,** blade tip; **garniture de p.,** blade packing; **manchon de p.,** blade cuff; **profil (de section) de p.,** blade section; **p. réglable,** adjustable blade; **à deux, à trois, à quatre, pales,** two-, three-, four-bladed; (*c*) *Mec.E:* vane (of fan, turbine, etc.); **p. mobile, orientable,** feathering blade (of turbine); (*d*) *Cin:* blade (of shutter); **obturateur à pales échancrées,** notched-blade shutter. **3.** sluice (gate); hatch (of mill); shut-off (of reservoir).
pale², *s.f. Ecc:* pall(a), chalice cover.
Pale³ (la), *s.f. Hist:* the English Pale.
pâle [pɑ:l], *a.* pale; *Lit: Med:* pallid; **à face p.,** pale-faced; **p. comme un linge, comme un mort, comme la mort,** as white as a sheet, as death; deadly pale; **être p. de colère,** to be white, livid, with rage; **teint p.,** pallid, ashen, bloodless, complexion; *s.a.* COULEUR 1, VISAGE; *Mil: P:* **se faire porter p.,** (i) to report sick; (ii) to sham sick; **bleu p.,** pale blue; **une p. clarté,** a pale, faint, light; **ses yeux pâles,** his lack-lustre eyes; **un sourire p.,** a wan, bleak, smile; *Lit:* **style p.,** colourless style.
palé [pale], *a. Her:* paly.
paléacé [palease], *a. Bot:* paleaceous.
paléage [palea:ʒ], *s.m. Nau:* shovelling (of grain, salt, etc.).
pale-ale [pɛlɛl], *s.m. Brew:* pale ale.
paléarctique [palearktik], *a.* palearctic.
palée [pale], *s.f.* **1.** *Civ.E:* row of piles; sheet piling. **2.** *Nau:* interval between strokes of blade.
palefrenier [palfrənje], *s.m.* groom, stableman, stable boy, ostler.
palefrenière [palfrənjɛ:r], *s.f.* horse girl, (girl) groom.
palefroi [palfrwa], *s.m. A:* palfrey.
pâlement [pɑlmɑ̃], *adv.* palely, wanly, dimly, pallidly.
Palémon [palemɔ̃]. **1.** *Pr.n.m. Myth:* Palaemon. **2.** *s.m. Crust: A:* palaemon.
pal(éo)- [pal(eo)], *comb.fm.* pal((a)eo)-.
paléoarchéologie [paleoarkeoloʒi], *s.f.* pal(a)eoarch(a)eology.
paléobiologie [paleobjoloʒi], *s.f.* pal(a)eobiology.
paléobiologique [paleobjoloʒik], *a.* pal(a)eobiological.
paléobiologiste [paleobjoloʒist], *s.m. & f.* pal(a)eobiologist.
paléobotanique [paleobotanik], *s.f.* pal(a)eobotany.
paléobotaniste [paleobotanist], *s.m.* pal(a)eobotanist.
paléocène [paleosɛn], *a. & s.m. Geol:* Pal(a)eocene.
paléochrétien, -ienne [paleokretjɛ̃, -jɛn], *a. Ant:* Pal(a)eo-Christian.
paléoclimat [paleoklima], *s.m.* pal(a)eoclimate.
paléoclimatologie [paleoklimatoloʒi], *s.f.* pal(a)eoclimatology.
paléocrystique [paleokristik], *a. Geol:* pal(a)eocrystic.
paléodictyoptères [paleodiktjoptɛ:r], *s.m.pl. Paleont:* Pal(a)eodictyoptera.
paléoécologie [paleoekoloʒi], *s.f.* pal(a)eoecology.
paléoethnologie [paleoɛtnoloʒi], *s.f.* pal(a)eoethnology, palethnology.
paléogène [paleoʒɛn], *a. & s.m. Geol: O:* Pal(a)eogene.
paléogéographie [paleoʒeografi], *s.f.* pal(a)eogeography.
paléogéographique [paleoʒeografik], *a.* pal(a)eographic.
paléographe [paleograf], *s.m. & f.* pal(a)eographer.
paléographie [paleografi], *s.f.* pal(a)eography.
paléographique [paleografik], *a.* pal(a)eographic.
paléographiquement [paleografikmɑ̃], *adv.* pal(a)eographically.
paléohistologie [paleohistoloʒi], *s.f.* pal(a)eohistology.
paléolithique [paleolitik], *a. & s.m.* Pal(a)eolithic (age).
paléologue [paleolog], *s.m. & f.* **1.** pal(a)eologist. **2.** *Hist:* **Michel P.,** Michael Palaeologus.
paléomagnétisme [paleomaɲetism], *s.m. Geol:* pal(a)eomagnetism.
paléométabole [paleometabol], *a. Biol:* pal(a)eometabolous.
paléontologie [paleɔ̃toloʒi], *s.f.* pal(a)eontology.
paléontologique [paleɔ̃toloʒik], *a.* **1.** pal(a)eontological. **2.** antiquated, prehistoric.
paléontologiste [paleɔ̃toloʒist], **paléontologue** [paleɔ̃tolog], *s.m. & f.* pal(a)eontologist.
paléopathologie [paleopatoloʒi], *s.f.* pal(a)eopathology.

paléophytologie [paleɔfitɔlɔʒi], *s.f. Bot:* pal(a)eophytology.
paléoplaine [paleɔplɛn], *s.f. Geol:* pal(a)eoplain.
paléopsychologie [paleɔpsikɔlɔʒi], *s.f. Psy:* pal(a)eo-psychology.
paléoptère [paleɔptɛːr], *Ent:* **1.** *a.* pal(a)eopteran (wings). **2.** *s.m.pl.* **paléoptères,** Pal(a)eoptera.
paléosol [paleɔsɔl], *s.m. Geol:* fossil soil.
paléothérium [paleɔterjɔm], *s.m. Paleont:* pal(a)eothere, pal(a)eotherium.
paléotropical, -aux [paleɔtrɔpikal, -o], *a. Geog:* pal(a)eotropical.
paléovolcanique [paleɔvɔlkanik], *a. Geol:* pal(a)eovolcanic.
paléozoïque [paleɔzɔik], *a. & s.m. Geol:* Pal(a)eozoic.
paléozoologie [paleɔzɔɔlɔʒi], *s.f.* pal(a)eozoology.
paléozoologique [paleɔzɔɔlɔʒik], *a.* pal(a)eozoological.
paléozoologiste [paleɔzɔɔlɔʒist], *s.m. & f.* pal(a)eozoologist.
Palerme [palɛrm], *Pr.n. Geog:* Palermo.
palermitain, -aine [palɛrmitɛ̃, -ɛn], *a. & s. Geog:* Palermitan.
paleron [palrɔ̃], *s.m.* shoulder blade, blade bone (of horse, ox, etc.); *Cu:* **p. de bœuf,** chuck.
Palestine [palɛstin]. **1.** *Pr.n.f. Geog:* Palestine. **2.** *s.f. Typ: A:* twenty-two point type.
palestinien, -ienne [palɛstinjɛ̃, -jɛn], *a. & s. Geog:* Palestinian.
palestre [palɛstr̥], *s.f. Gr.Ant:* pal(a)estra.
palestrique [palɛstrik], *a.* palaestral, palestral.
palet [palɛ], *s.m. Games:* **1.** quoit; **jouer au p., aux palets,** to play at quoits. **2.** metal disc (used for playing various games); (*for ice hockey*) puck.
paletot [palto], *s.m.* (*a*) (*usu.* rather short) overcoat; paletot; **p. de fourrure,** fur coat; *P:* **tomber, bondir, sauter, sur le p. à qn,** to attack s.o., to pitch into s.o.; (*b*) *P:* **p. de sapin, dernier p.,** coffin, wooden overcoat.
palette[1] [palɛt], *s.f.* **1.** (wooden) battledore. **2.** (*a*) blade (of oar); paddle, float board (of paddle wheel); dasher (of churn); plate (of trap); **roue à palettes,** blade wheel; **roue à palettes planes,** undershot water wheel; (*b*) vane, blade (of speed-damping apparatus, of rotary pump, etc.); *I.C.E:* **compresseur à p.,** vane supercharger; (*c*) plate (of electro-magnet); (*d*) pallet (of fork-lift truck, etc.); **marchandises sur palettes,** palletized goods; (*e*) *Rail:* semaphore arm; (*f*) *Cu:* shoulder (of mutton, pork); (*g*) *F:* shoulder blade; (*h*) *F:* kneecap. **3.** (painter's) palette; (printer's) slice; (gilder's) tip, pallet; (smith's) shovel; **p. à pansement,** (surgeon's) palette, flat splint; **p. à beurre,** Scotch hand, butter-pat; *Art:* **faire, charger, sa p.,** to set the palette.
palette[2], *s.f. A:* (barber-surgeon's) basin (for bleeding).
palettisation [palɛtizasjɔ̃], *s.f. Com:* palletization.
palettiser [palɛtize], *v.tr. Com:* to palletize.
palétuvier [paletyvje], *s.m. Bot:* mangrove.
pâleur [pɑlœːr], *s.f.* pallor, pallidness, paleness; wanness; **la p. de la mort,** the pallor of death; **d'une p. mortelle, effroyable,** as pale as death, ghastly pale, deadly pale.
pali [pali], *a. & s.m. Ling:* pali.
pâli [pɑli], *a.* wan, blanched (face, etc.).
palicare [palikaːr], *s.m. Gr.Hist:* palikar.
pâlichon, -onne [pɑliʃɔ̃, -ɔn], *a. F:* palish, somewhat, rather, pale.
palier [palje], *s.m.* **1.** (*a*) *Arch:* landing (of stairs), stairhead; **p. de repos,** half landing, halfpace; **nous sommes voisins de p.,** we live on the same floor; (*b*) stage, degree; **taxes imposées par paliers,** graduated taxation; **les différents paliers de la société,** the different social strata. **2.** (*a*) *Aut: Rail: etc:* level run, level stretch; **vitesse en p.,** speed on the level, on the flat; (*b*) *Av:* horizontal flight; **voler en p., attaquer le p.,** to fly level; (*c*) *Mth: etc:* plateau (of a graph); **le taux des naissances a atteint un p. ces dernières années,** the birthrate has levelled off in recent years; (*d*) **p. de came,** top of a cam. **3.** *Mch: Mec.E:* bearing; **p. d'arbre, p.-support,** (i) shaft bearing, spring bearing; (ii) (*pour élément lourd*) plummer block, pillow block; **p. de bielle,** connecting-rod bearing; **p. d'essieu,** axle bearing; **p. principal,** main bearing; **p. à billes,** ball bearing; **p. à rouleaux,** roller bearing; **p. à douille,** sleeve bearing; **p. à collet,** collar bearing, journal (bearing); **p. à potence, p. de suspension,** (bracket) hanger; **p. à cannelures,** collar bearing; **p. à rotule,** swivel bearing; **p. à blochets articulés, p. Mitchell,** pivoted-shoe bearing; **p. à segments pivotants,** tilting-pad bearing, slipper bearing; **p. fluide,** gas bearing; **p. glissant,** water bearing; **p. graisseur (automatique),** self-oiling, self-lubricating, bearing; **p. lisse,** plain bearing, (plain) journal bearing; **p. anti-frottement, p. (garni d') antifriction,** antifriction bearing; **p. régulé,** babbitted bearing, anti-friction bearing, white metal bearing; **chapeau, couvercle, de p.,** bearing cap, bearing keep; **corps de p.,** bearing standard; **support, chevalet, de p.,** (bearing) pedestal.
palière [paljɛːr], *a.f.* **porte p.,** landing door, door opening on to the landing; **marche p.,** *s.f.* **palière,** top step.
palification [palifikasjɔ̃], *s.f. Const: Civ.E:* piling (of ground for foundations, etc.).
palifier [palifje], *v.tr.* (*pr.sub. & p.d.* **n. palifiions, v. palifiiez**) *Const: Civ.E:* to pile (ground for foundations, etc.).
palikare [palikaːr], *s.m. Gr.Hist:* palikar.
palimpseste [palɛ̃psɛst], *a. & s.m.* palimpsest.
palindrome [palɛ̃droːm, -ɔm]. **1.** *s.m. Lit:* palindrome. **2.** *a.* palindromic (verse).
palingénèse [palɛ̃ʒenɛːz], *s.f. Geol:* palingenesis.
palingénésie [palɛ̃ʒenezi], *s.f.* palingenesis; regeneration.
palingénésique [palɛ̃ʒenezik], *a.* palingenetic.
palingénie [palɛ̃ʒeni], *s.f. Biol:* palingeny.
palinodie [palinɔdi], *s.f.* **1.** *Lit:* palinode. **2.** recantation, retraction; palinode; *O:* **chanter la p.,** to recant, retract.
palinodique [palinɔdik], *a.* palinodic.
palinodiste [palinɔdist], *s.m. & f.* palinodist.
Palinure [palinyːr]. **1.** *Pr.n.m. Rom.Lit:* Palinurus; **le cap P.,** Cape Palinuro. **2.** *s.m. Crust:* palinurid, spiny lobster, sea crayfish.
palinuridés [palinyride], *s.m.pl. Crust:* Palinuridae.
pâlir [pɑliːr]. **1.** *v.i.* to become pale, grow pale; (*of pers.*) to blanch; (*of light, star, etc.*) to grow dim, to pale; (*of colour*) to fade; **p. d'horreur, de terreur,** to turn pale, to blench, with horror, fright; **ses joues ont pâli,** his cheeks have lost their colour; **il avait pâli sur ses livres,** he had grown pale poring over his books; **son étoile pâlit,** his fame is on the decline, his star is on the wane; **faire p. les mérites de qn,** to outshine s.o., *F:* to put s.o. in the shade; **mes aventures pâlissent auprès des vôtres,** my adventures pale, sink into insignificance, beside yours. **2.** *v.tr.* to make (s.o., sth.) pale; to bleach (colours).
palis [pali], *s.m.* paling. **1.** (*a*) fence, picket fence; (*b*) enclosure (within picket fence). **2.** pale, stake, picket.
palissade [palisad], *s.f.* (*a*) palisade, fence, paling; picket fence; **entourer un champ d'une p.,** to fence a field; (*b*) *Fort:* stockade; (*c*) *Agr:* hedgerow; (*d*) (street) hoarding.
palissadement [palisadmɑ̃], *s.m.* palisading, fencing.
palissader [palisade], *v.tr.* (*a*) to palisade; to fence in, rail in; to enclose; (*b*) *Fort:* to stockade; (*c*) *Agr:* to make a hedgerow round (field, etc.).
palissadique [palisadik], *a. Bot:* palisade (tissue).
palissage [palisaːʒ], *s.m. Hort:* nailing up, training (of trailing plants, wall trees, etc.).
palissandre [palisɑ̃ːdr̥], *s.m. Bot:* Brazilian rosewood; purple wood; **faux p.,** jacaranda wood.
pâlissant [pɑlisɑ̃], *a.* (face) turning pale; fading, waning (light); fading, paling (colour).
palissé [palise], *a.* **1.** *Her:* palissé. **2.** *Hort:* (*of tree*) espalier-trained.
pâlissement [pɑlismɑ̃], *s.m.* **1.** paling, growing pale. **2.** pallidness.
palisser [palise], *v.tr. Hort:* to nail up, to train (trailing plants, wall trees, etc.); to arrange (trees) in espalier formation, to espalier.
palissois, -oise [paliswa, -waːz], *a. & s. Geog:* (native, inhabitant) of Lapalisse.
palisson [palisɔ̃], *s.m. Leath:* stake.
palissonner [palisɔne], *v.tr. Leath:* to stake.
palissonneur [palisɔnœːr], *s.m. Leath:* staker.
palladien, -ienne [pal(l)adjɛ̃, -jɛn], *a. Arch:* Palladian.
palladique [pal(l)adik], *a. Ch:* palladic.
palladium[1] [pal(l)adjɔm], *s.m. Cl.Myth:* palladium; *Lit:* **les lois sont le p. de la liberté,** the laws are the palladium, the safeguards, of liberty.
palladium[2], *s.m. Ch:* palladium.
pallasite [palazit], *s.f. Geol:* pallasite.
palléal, -aux [paleal, -o], *a. Moll:* **cavité palléale,** mantle cavity, palleal chamber.
palliateur, -trice [pal(l)jatœːr, -tris]. **1.** *a.* palliatory. **2.** *s.* palliator.
palliatif, -ive [pal(l)jatif, -iːv], *a. & s.m.* palliative.
palliation [pal(l)jasjɔ̃], *s.f.* palliation (of offence, disease, pain, etc.).
pallidum [palidɔm], *s.m. Anat:* globus pallidus.
pallier [pal(l)je], (*p.d. & pr.sub.* **n. palliions, v. palliiez**) **1.** *v.tr.* to palliate (offence, pain, disease). **2.** *v.ind.tr.* **p. aux conséquences d'une faute,** to mitigate the consequences of an error.
pallikare [palikar], *s.m. Gr.Hist:* palikar.
pallium [pal(l)jɔm], *s.m.* **1.** *Gr.Ant:* pallium. **2.** *Ecc:* (archbishop's) pall; pallium; *Her:* pall. **3.** *Anat: Z:* pallium.
palma-christi [palmakristi], *s.m.inv. Bot:* palma Christi, castor-oil plant.
palmaire [palmɛːr], *a. & s.m. Anat:* palmar (muscle).
palmarès [palmarɛs], *s.m. Sch: etc:* prize list; honours list; *T.V: etc:* **p. de la chanson** = top of the pops.
palmarium [palmarjɔm], *s.m. Hort:* palm house.
palmatifide [palmatifid], *a. Bot:* palmatifid.
palmatilobé [palmatilɔbe], *a. Bot:* palmatilobate, palmatilobed.
palmatinervé [palmatinɛrve], *a. Bot:* palminerved, palmately nerved, veined.
palmatipartite [palmatipartit], *a. Bot:* palmatipartite.
palmatiséqué [palmatiseke], *a. Bot:* palmatisect.
palmature [palmatyːr], *s.f.* (*a*) *Z:* palmation; (*b*) *Med:* palmature.
palme[1] [palm], *s.f.* **1.** *A:* (= PALMIER) palm (tree); **huile, beurre, sucre, vin, de p.,** palm oil, butter, sugar, wine. **2.** palm (branch); **remporter la p.,** to bear the palm; to win the victory; **décerner, céder, la p. à qn,** to assign, yield, the palm to s.o.; **p. du martyre,** martyr's crown, crown of martyrdom; **recevoir les palmes (académiques),** to be decorated by the Ministry of Education; (*of decoration*) **avec p.** = with bar. **3.** flipper, fin (of a frogman).
palme[2], *s.m. A.Meas:* hand, hand's-breadth, *A:* palm.
palmé [palme], *a.* **1.** *Bot:* palmate (leaf). **2.** *Orn:* web-footed; **pied p.,** webbed foot; **les oies ont les pieds palmés,** geese are web-footed; *P:* **les avoir palmées,** to be workshy.
palmer[1] [palme], *v.tr. Tchn:* **p. des aiguilles,** to flatten the heads of needles.
palmer[2] [palmɛːr], *s.m. Tchn:* micrometer calliper(s), wire gauge.
palmer[3], *v.i.* to swim wearing flippers, fins.
palmeraie [palmərɛ], *s.f.* palm grove, palm plantation.
palmette [palmɛt], *s.f.* **1.** *Bot:* dwarf fan-palm; palmetto. **2.** (*a*) *Hort:* fan-shaped espalier; (*b*) *Arch:* palm leaf (moulding); palmette.
palmier [palmje], *s.m.* palm tree; **p.-éventail,** fan palm; **p. nain,** dwarf fan-palm; palmetto; **p. nain sétifère,** bristly palmetto; **p. à huile,** oil palm; **p. à cire,** wax palm; **p. à sucre,** sugar palm; **p. royal,** royal palm; **p. pinot,** (Amazonian) cabbage palm; **p. bâche,** moriche palm, ita palm; **huile, beurre, de p.,** palm oil, palm butter; *Cu:* **cœurs de p.,** hearts of palm.
palmiérite [palmjerit], *s.f. Miner:* palmierite.
palmifide [palmifid], *a. Bot:* palmatifid.
palmiforme [palmifɔrm], *a. Bot:* palmiform.
palmilobé [palmilɔbe], *a. Bot:* palmilobate.
palmiparti, -ite [palmiparti, -it], *a. Bot:* palmatipartite.
palmipède [palmipɛd], *a. & s. Orn:* palmiped; web-footed (bird).
palmique [palmik], *a. Ch:* palmic (acid).
palmiséqué [palmiseke], *a. Bot:* palmatisect.
palmiste [palmist], *a. & s.m.* **1.** *Bot:* **(chou) p.,** (i) cabbage palm, cabbage tree, palmetto; (ii) palm cabbage. **2.** *Z:* **rat p.,** palm squirrel; *Ent:* **ver p.,** palm grub, worm, borer; **calandre p.,** palm weevil.
palmitate [palmitat], *s.m. Ch:* palmitate.
palmite [palmit], *s.m.* palm marrow.
palmitine [palmitin], *s.f. Ch:* palmitin.
palmitique [palmitik], *a. Ch:* palmitic (acid).
palmitone [palmitɔn], *s.f. Ch:* palmitone.
palmure [palmyːr], *s.f. Orn: Amph:* palmation.
Palmyre [palmiːr], *Pr.n.f. A.Geog:* Palmyra.
palmyréen, -enne [palmireɛ̃, -ɛn], **palmyrien, -ienne** [palmirjɛ̃, -jɛn], *a. & s. A.Geog:* Palmyrene.
palois, -oise [palwa, -waːz], *a. & s. Geog:* (native, inhabitant) of Pau.
palombe[1] [palɔ̃ːb], *s.f.* ring dove, wood pigeon.
palombe[2], *s.f.,* **palonne** [palɔn], *s.f. Ropem:* ground rope.
palombière [palɔ̃bjɛːr], **palomière** [palɔmjɛːr], **palonnière** [palɔnjɛːr], *s.f.* (*a*) net used for catching ring doves at migration time; (*b*) tree-top hide for ring-dove shooting.
palon [palɔ̃], *s.m. Ind:* (wooden) spatule.
palonneau [palɔno], *s.m. Veh:* swingle bar, whipple tree.

palonnier [palɔnje], *s.m.* (*a*) *Veh:* swingle bar, whipple tree; (*b*) *Av:* **p. (du gouvernail) de direction,** rudder bar, swing bar; (*c*) *Mec.E:* compensation bar, rocking lever; lifting beam (of travelling crane, etc.); *Aut:* **p. du frein,** compensator.

palot [palo], *s.m.* **1.** wooden spade (for digging worms). **2.** *pl. Fish:* stakes (along water's edge for fixing lines).

pâlot, -otte [pɑlo, -ɔt], *a.* palish, rather pale, wan; sickly-looking (child); peaky (look).

palotage [palɔta:ʒ], *s.m.* digging (with a *palot*).

paloter [palɔte], *v.tr.* to dig (with a *palot*).

palourde [palurd], *s.f. Moll:* clam; carpet shell; *F:* pullet shell.

palpabilité [palpabilite], *s.f.* palpability. **1.** tangibility, palpableness. **2.** obviousness.

palpable [palpabl̩], *a.* palpable. **1.** tangible. **2.** obvious, easily perceived, plain (truth, etc.); palpable (absurdity, error, imposture).

palpablement [palpabləmɑ̃], *adv.* palpably.

palpation [palpasjɔ̃], *s.f. Med:* palpation.

palpe [palp], *s.f. occ. m. Nat.Hist:* palpus, palp, feeler (of insect, of crustacean); barbel (of fish).

palpébral, -aux [palpebral, -o], *a. Anat:* palpebral.

palper [palpe]. **1.** *v.tr.* to feel; to examine (sth.) by feeling; *Med:* to palpate; **les aveugles reconnaissent les objets en les palpant,** the blind recognize objects by feeling them, by touch; **p. un article,** to finger an article; *F:* **p. (de l'argent),** to receive money, one's pay; to pocket money; *P:* **tu peux te p.!** nothing doing! don't you wish you could get it! *Nau:* **p. l'eau,** to hold up a boat (with the oar). **2.** *s.m. Med:* palpation.

palpeur, -euse [palpœ:r, -ø:z]. **1.** *a. Nat.Hist:* with long feelers. **2.** *s.m.* (*a*) *Mec.E: etc:* feeler (gauge); follower, testing spike; (*b*) (ultrasonic) probe; (*c*) *Dom.Ec:* **p. à signal lumineux,** rheostatic heat switch; (*d*) (*of computer*) pecker.

palpicorne [palpikɔrn], *a. Ent:* palpicorn.

palpigère [palpiʒɛ:r], *a. Ent:* palpigerous.

palpitant [palpitɑ̃]. **1.** *a.* palpitating, throbbing, quivering, fluttering; **elle restait là le cœur p.,** she stood there with her heart (all) in a flutter; **roman p. d'intérêt,** thrilling, exciting, novel; *O:* **ville palpitante d'activité commerciale,** city throbbing with business activity; **voilà qui est p.!** isn't that thrilling! **2.** *s.m. P:* heart, ticker.

palpitation [palpitasjɔ̃], *s.f.* palpitation; (*a*) quiver(ing) (of limb); flutter(ing) (of eyelid, of pulse); (*b*) violent beat(ing), throb(bing) (of the heart); **être sujet à des palpitations,** to be subject to palpitations.

palpiter [palpite], *v.i.* to palpitate; (*a*) (*of pulse, eyelid*) to flutter; (*of limb*) to quiver; (*b*) (*of heart*) to beat violently, to throb; (*of bosom*) to rise and fall, to heave; (*c*) to thrill (with pleasure, fear, hope); **mon cœur palpitait d'espoir,** my heart was throbbing, quivering, with hope; (*d*) **flammes qui palpitent,** quivering flames.

palplanche [palplɑ̃:ʃ], *s.f. Hyd.E: Min:* pile plank; sheeting pile; **rideau de palplanches,** sheet-pile wall; *Min:* **chasser par palplanches,** to forepole.

palsambleu [palsɑ̃blø], *int. A:* (*attenuated form of* **par le sang de Dieu**) 'Od's blood! 'sblood!

palsangué [palsɑ̃ge], **palsanguienne** [palsɑ̃gjɛn], *int. Dial: A:* (*esp. as used by peasants in older Fr. comedy*) 'sblood!

paltoquet [paltɔkɛ], *s.m. F:* (*a*) *O:* lout; (*b*) nonentity; (*c*) louse.

paluche [palyʃ], *s.f. P:* hand, mitt.

palud [paly], **palude** [palyd], *s.m. occ. f.* marsh.

paludarium [palydarjɔm], *s.m.* vivarium for amphibians.

paludéen, -enne [palydeɛ̃, -ɛn], *a.* (*a*) paludal; paludic; paludine; pertaining to marshes; **plante paludéenne,** marsh plant; (*b*) *Med:* malarial; **fièvre paludéenne,** malaria.

paludien, -ienne [palydjɛ̃, -jɛn], **paludier**[1], **-ière** [palydje, -jɛ:r], *a. & s. Geog:* (native, inhabitant) of the île de Batz.

paludier[2], **-ière,** *s.* worker in a salt marsh.

paludique [palydik], *a.* = PALUDÉEN.

paludisme [palydism], *s.m. Med:* paludism, malaria.

palus [palys], *s.m.* **1.** *A:* marsh. **2.** *Dial:* (*S.W. Fr.*) (*a*) alluvial plain (in valley); (*b*) wine from such areas.

palustre [palystr̩], *a.* palustral, palustrian, palustrine; paludous (plant, etc.); swampy, marshy (ground).

palynologie [palinɔlɔʒi], *s.f.* palynology.

pamban-manché [pɑ̃bɑ̃mɑ̃ʃe], *s.m. Nau:* pambanmanche; *pl. pambans-manchés.*

pâmé, -ée [pɑme]. **1.** *a.* (*a*) *A:* in a swoon; (*b*) *Her:* (*of dolphin*) pâmé; (*c*) *F:* **faire des yeux de carpe pâmée,** to show the whites of one's eyes. **2.** *s.f. Bot:* **pamée,** myrobalan.

Paméla [pamela], *Pr.n.f.* Pamela.

pamelier [pamlje], *s.m. Bot:* ferula, giant fennel.

pamelle [pamɛl], *s.f. Agr:* two-rowed barley.

pâmer [pɑme]. **1.** *v.i. & pr.* (*a*) *A:* to swoon, to faint (away); (*b*) **(se) p. de rire,** to be convulsed, to split one's sides, with laughter; **nous avons ri à nous p.,** we almost died with laughter, *F:* we laughed fit to burst; **se p. d'admiration,** to be in raptures (sur, over); **se p. de joie,** to be overjoyed, delighted; to be in raptures. **2.** *v.pr.* (*of steel*) to lose its temper (through overheating).

pâmoison [pɑmwazɔ̃], *s.f. A:* swoon, fainting fit; **tomber en p.,** to swoon; to faint away; to fall into a swoon.

pampa [pɑ̃pa], *s.f.* pampa (of S. America); *Bot:* **herbe des pampas,** pampas grass.

pampe [pɑ̃:p], *s.f. Agr:* blade, leaf (of corn).

Pampelune [pɑ̃plyn], *Pr.n. Geog:* Pamplona.

pampéro [pɑ̃pero], *s.m.* **1.** *Ethn:* pampean, pampero; Indian of the Pampas. **2.** (*also* **pamper** [pɑ̃pɛ:r]) pampero (wind).

pamphile [pɑ̃fil], *s.m.* **1.** *Cards:* mistigri(s). **2.** *A:* self-important man. **3.** *Ent:* skipper.

pamphlet [pɑ̃flɛ], *s.m.* (*usu.* scurrilous) pamphlet; lampoon.

pamphlétaire [pɑ̃fletɛ:r], *s.m. & f.* pamphleteer, lampooner.

Pamphylie [pɑ̃fili], *Pr.n.f. Geog:* Pamphylia.

pampiniforme [pɑ̃pinifɔrm], *a. Anat:* pampiniform.

pamplemousse [pɑ̃pləmus], *s.m.* (*a*) *Bot:* shaddock; (*b*) grapefruit.

pamplemoussier [pɑ̃pləmusje], *s.m.* grapefruit (tree).

pampre [pɑ̃:pr̩], *s.m.* **1.** vine branch, vine shoot (with leaves). **2.** *Arch: Art:* pampre.

pampsychisme [pɑ̃psiʃism], *s.m.* panpsychism.

pan[1] [pɑ̃], *s.m.* **1.** skirt, flap, flap end (of garment); tail (of shirt, coat); free end (of tie); **saisir qn par le p. de son habit,** to catch hold of s.o. by the coat tails. **2.** section, piece, surface; *Arch:* gore (of dome); **p. de voûte,** severy; **p. de mur,** bare wall, piece of wall; **p. d'un mur,** section, framing, of a wall; **p. de bois,** timber framing, wooden partition; **maison à pans de bois,** half-timbered house; **p. de comble,** side, panel, of a roof; **p. de ciel,** bit, patch, of sky; *Veh:* **p. latéral (de carrosserie),** flat. **3.** face, side (of angular building, etc.); **tour à huit pans,** eight-sided, octagonal, tower; **écrou (à) six pans,** hexagonal nut; **alésoir à six pans,** six-square broach; **entre pans,** across flats; **pans d'un prisme,** sides, faces, of a prism; **p. coupé,** cant-(wall); **à pans coupés,** with the corners cut off. **4.** *Ven:* game net.

Pan[2], *Pr.n.m. Myth:* Pan.

pan[3], *int.* **1.** bang! bif(f)! (*children playing*) **p.! p.! tu es mort!** bang! bang! you're dead! **2.** **entendre un p. p. à la porte,** to hear a rat-tat at the door; *F:* **faire p. p.,** to smack (a child).

pan-, *comb.fm.* pan-.

panabase [panaba:z], *s.f. Miner:* grey copper ore, tetrahedrite, fahlerz.

panace [panas], *s.m. Bot:* panax, ginseng.

panacée [panase], *s.f.* panacea; nostrum; cure-all.

panachage [panaʃa:ʒ], *s.m.* mixing (of colours, etc.); *Pol:* voting on the same "ticket" for candidates belonging to different parties; splitting (up) of one's vote.

panache [panaʃ], *s.m.* **1.** (*a*) plume, tuft (of waving feathers); **casque orné d'un p.,** plumed helmet; *F:* **avoir son p.,** to be slightly elevated, a bit tight; **p. de fumée,** (i) wreath of smoke (from chimney); (ii) trail of smoke (from moving locomotive); (*b*) *F:* **faire p.,** (*of rider*) to be pitched over the horse's head, to take a header; (*of cyclist*) to be pitched over the handlebars; (*of horse*) to turn a somersault; (*of car*) to overturn; **faire un p. complet,** to turn right over, to turn turtle; (*c*) *F:* **il a du p.,** he has an air about him; **y mettre du p.,** to carry it off with an air, with a flourish; **il aime le p.,** he likes to cut a dash. **2.** *Arch:* panache (of pendentive). **3.** *Hort:* stripe, variegation (of colours on flowers or leaves).

panaché [panaʃe], *a.* **1.** plumed (helmet, bird); feathered (tulip). **2.** parti-coloured, variegated, gaudy (bird, flower); **pré p. de marguerites,** meadow pied with daisies; **foule panachée,** motley crowd; **société panachée,** mixed society; *Cu:* **salade panachée,** mixed salad; **glace panachée,** mixed ice; **bière panachée,** *s.m.* **panaché,** shandy.

panacher [panaʃe], *v.tr.* **1.** to plume (helmet). **2.** (*a*) *Hort:* to variegate (with different colours); to impart colours to (flowers, etc.); (*b*) *Cards:* to arrange (cards) in alternate colours; (*c*) *Pol:* **p. un bulletin de vote,** to vote on the same "ticket" for candidates belonging to different parties; to split (up) one's vote. **3.** *v.i. & pr.* (*of flowers, etc.*) to become variegated.

panachure [panaʃy:r], *s.f.* streak, stripe of colour; variegation (on flowers, fruit, feathers); feathering (of tulip).

panade [panad], *s.f.* **1.** *Cu:* bread, milk and cheese soup; panada; *F:* **être dans la p.,** (i) to be in the soup, in a fix; (ii) to be down and out, on one's uppers. **2.** *a. & s.f. P:* spineless (individual); wet.

panader (se) [səpanade], *v.pr. A:* (*of peacock*) to strut.

panafricain [panafrikɛ̃], *a.* Pan-African.

panafricanisme [panafrikanism], *s.m.* Pan-Africanism.

panage [pana:ʒ], *s.m. Jur: Husb:* pannage.

panaire [panɛ:r], *a.* panary; pertaining to the making of bread.

panais[1] [panɛ], *s.m.* parsnip; *P:* **des p.!** not (bloody) likely!

panais[2], *s.m. P:* shirt tail.

Panama [panama]. **1.** *Pr.n.m. Geog:* Panama; **bois de p.,** quillai(a) bark, soap bark. **2.** *s.m. Com:* (*a*) panama hat; (*b*) straw hat.

Paname [panam], *Pr.n.m. P:* Paris.

panaméen, -éenne [panameɛ̃, -eɛn], **panamien, -ienne** [panamjɛ̃, -jɛn], *a. & s. Geog:* Panamanian.

panaméricain [panamerikɛ̃], *a.* Pan-American.

panaméricanisme [panamerikanism], *s.m.* Pan-Americanism.

panaméricaniste [panamerikanist], *a. & s.m. & f.* Pan-American.

panarabe [panarab], *a.* Pan-Arab.

panarabisme [panarabism], *s.m. Pol:* Pan-Arab movement Pan-Arabism.

panard [pana:r]. **1.** *a.* (*of horse*) with out-turned feet; knock-kneed; cow-hocked; **jument panarde,** cow-hocked mare. **2.** *s.m. P:* foot, hoof; *pl. P:* dogs, plates; **avoir les panards enflés,** to have swollen feet; **en avoir plein les panards,** to be fed up.

panaris [panari], *s.m.* (*a*) *Med:* whitlow; felon; (*b*) *Vet:* **p. interdigité,** foot rot.

panasiatisme [panazjatism], *s.m.* Pan-Asianism.

panatella [panatɛlla], *s.m.* panatella (cigar).

panathénaïque [panatenaik], *a. Gr.Ant:* Panathenaic, Panathenaean.

panathénées [panatene], *s.f.pl. Gr.Ant:* Panathenaea.

panathénien, -ienne [panatenjɛ̃, -jɛn], *a. Gr.Ant:* Panathenaean, Panathenaic.

panax [panaks], *s.m. Bot:* panax, ginseng.

panca [pɑ̃ka], *s.m.* punkah; **tireur de p.,** punkah boy, punkah wallah.

pancalier [pɑ̃kalje], *s.m. Hort:* savoy cabbage.

pancalisme [pɑ̃kalism], *s.m. Phil:* aestheticism.

pancardite [pɑ̃kardit], *s.f. Med:* pancarditis.

pancarte [pɑ̃kart], *s.f.* **1.** placard, bill; label (mounted on card); (show)card. **2.** *A:* jacket (for documents, etc.).

panchromatique [pɑ̃krɔmatik], *a. Phot:* panchromatic.

pancosmisme [pɑ̃kɔsmism], *s.m. Phil:* pancosmism.

pancrace[1] [pɑ̃kras], *s.m.* **1.** *Gr.Ant:* pancratium. **2.** *F: A:* **un docteur P.,** a champion arguer.

Pancrace[2], *Pr.n.m.* (Saint) Pancras.

pancratiaste [pɑ̃kratjast], *s.m. Gr.Ant:* pancrati(a)st.

pancratique [pɑ̃kratik], *a. Opt:* pancratic.

pancréas [pɑ̃kreɑs], *s.m. Anat:* pancreas.

pancréatectomie [pɑ̃kreatɛktɔmi], *s.f. Surg:* pancreatectomy.

pancréatico-duodénal, -aux [pɑ̃kreatikɔdɥɔdenal, -o], *a. Anat:* pancreaticoduodenal.

pancréatine [pɑ̃kreatin], *s.f. Ch:* pancreatin.

pancréatique [pakreatik], *a.* pancreatic (juice, etc.).

pancréatite [pɑ̃kreatit], *s.f. Med:* pancreatitis, inflammation of the pancreas.

pancréatotomie [pɑ̃kreatɔtɔmi], *s.f. Surg:* pancrea(to)tomy.

panda [pɑ̃da], *s.m. Z:* panda; **petit p.,** (small Himalayan) panda; **p. géant, grand p.,** giant panda.

pandactyle [pɑ̃daktil], *a. Z:* (*of hoofed mammal*) five-toed.

pandanacées [pɑ̃danase], *s.f.pl. Bot:* Pandanaceae.

pandanus [pɑ̃danys], *s.m. Bot:* pandanus; screw pine.

pandectes [pɑ̃dɛkt], *s.f.pl. Rom.Law:* pandects.

pandémie [pɑ̃demi], *s.f. Med:* pandemic (disease); pandemia.

pandémique [pɑ̃demik], *a. Med:* pandemic.

pandémonium [pɑ̃demɔnjɔm], *s.m.* pandemonium; (*a*) abode of demons; (*b*) *A. & Lit:* den of vice; (*c*) noisy, tumultuous, place.

pandermite [pɑ̃dɛrmit], *s.f. Miner:* pandermite.

pandiculation [pɑ̃dikylasjɔ̃], *s.f.* pandiculation.

pandit [pɑ̃di], *s.m.* (*Indian title*) pundit, pandit.

Pandore[1] [pɑ̃dɔːr]. **1.** *Pr.n.f. Gr.Myth:* Pandora; **le coffret, la boîte, de P.,** Pandora's box. **2.** *s.f. Moll:* pandora.

pandore[2], *s.m. F: A:* (*from hero of song by Nadaud*) policeman.

pandore[3], *s.f. A.Mus:* pandore.

pandoridés [pɑ̃dɔride], *s.m.pl. Moll:* Pandoridae.

pandour [pɑ̃duːr], *s.m.* (*a*) *Hist:* pandour, pandoor; (*b*) *F: A:* rapacious soldier, freebooter, brute.

pané[1] [pane], *a. Cu:* **1.** (*of meat, fish, etc.*) covered with, fried in, breadcrumbs. **2.** *A:* **eau panée,** toast and water; toast water.

pané[2], *a. P:* (stony) broke; down and out.

panégyrique [paneʒirik]. **1.** *s.m.* panegyric; **faire le p. de qn,** to panegyrize s.o. **2.** *a.* panegyric(al).

panégyriser [paneʒirize], *v.tr.* to panegyrize, to eulogize.

panégyriste [paneʒirist], *s.m.* panegyrist; eulogist.

panéiconographie [paneikɔnɔgrafi], *s.f.* paniconography.

panenthéisme [panɑ̃teism], *s.m. Theol:* panentheism.

paner [pane], *v.tr. Cu:* to bread(crumb); to cover (meat, fish, etc.) with breadcrumbs; to fry (chop, etc.) in breadcrumbs.

panerée [panre], *s.f.* basketful.

panet [panɛ], *s.m. P:* shirt tail.

paneterie [pantri], *s.f.* **1.** *A:* (*a*) pantler's office (in king's household, etc.); (*b*) the servants of the *paneterie.* **2.** (*a*) bread pantry; (*b*) bread store (in barracks, schools, etc.).

panetier [pantje], *s.m.* **1.** *Hist:* pantler. **2.** *Nau: A:* baker.

panetière [pantjɛːr], *s.f.* **1.** *A:* (shepherd's) scrip. **2.** (*a*) (i) (Breton, etc.) wooden bread box; (ii) bread bin; (*b*) (*for use on table*) bread basket. **3.** *Ent: F:* cockroach.

paneton [pantɔ̃], *s.m.* (baker's) bread basket.

pangène [pɑ̃ʒɛn], *s.m. Biol:* pangene.

pangénèse [pɑ̃ʒenɛːz], *s.f. Biol:* pangenesis.

pangermanique [pɑ̃ʒɛrmanik], *a.* Pan-German.

pangermanisme [pɑ̃ʒɛrmanism], *s.m.* Pan-Germanism.

pangermaniste [pɑ̃ʒɛrmanist], *a. & s.m. & f.* Pan-Germanist.

pangolin [pɑ̃gɔlɛ̃], *s.m. Z:* pangolin, scaly anteater; **p. pentadactyle,** Chinese pangolin; **p. à écailles tricuspides,** three-cusped pangolin.

panhellénien, -ienne [panɛl(l)enjɛ̃, -jɛn], **panhellénique** [panɛl(l)enik], *a.* Pan-Hellenic.

panhellénisme [panɛl(l)enism], *s.m.* Pan-Hellenism.

panic [panic], *s.m. Bot:* panic grass; **p. d'Italie,** Italian millet.

panicaut [paniko], *s.m. Bot:* eryngium; **p. maritime,** sea holly; **p. des Alpes,** Alpine sea holly.

paniconographie [panikɔnɔgrafi], *s.f.* paniconography.

paniconographique [panikɔnɔgrafik], *a.* paniconographic.

panicule [panikyl], *s.f. Bot:* panicle.

paniculé [panikyle], *a. Bot:* panicled, paniculate.

panier [panje], *s.m.* **1.** (*a*) basket; **p. à anse,** hand basket; **gros p.,** hamper; **p. à gibier,** game basket, hamper; **p. à papier,** wastepaper basket; **jeter qch. au p.,** to throw sth. into the wastepaper basket; to throw sth. away; **p. à ouvrage,** work basket; **p. à linge,** linen basket; **p. à friture,** basket for deep frying; **p. ramasse-couverts,** knife basket; **p. à provisions,** (i) shopping basket; (ii) luncheon basket, picnic basket; **p. à salade,** (i) salad shaker; (ii) *F:* prison van, Black Maria; **p. à bouteilles,** bottle carrier; **p. à chiens,** dog basket (for transporting animal); **p. à herbes,** grassbox (of lawn mower); **paniers (d'une bête de somme),** panniers (of pack animal); **mettre tous ses œufs dans le même p.,** to put all one's eggs in one basket; *F:* **on peut les mettre dans le même p.,** they're all tarred with the same brush; **être dans le même p.,** to be in the same boat; *F:* **c'est un p. percé,** he's a spendthrift; money burns a hole in his pocket; *s.a.* ANSE 1; (*b*) basketful; **p. de fruits, de fleurs,** basket(ful) of fruit, of flowers; **p. de Noël,** Christmas hamper; **le dessus du p.,** (i) the top layer (of goods in a basket); (ii) *F:* the pick of the basket, the best of the bunch; *F:* **le fond du p.,** the dregs; the scrapings of the barrel; *F:* **c'est un p. de crabes,** (i) they're a quarrelsome lot, they're all at each other's throats; (ii) it's a rat race; *F:* **videz le p.!** (come) out with it! (*c*) *Fish:* (i) lobster pot; (ii) **faire un p.,** to make a good catch; (*d*) *F:* family budget; (*e*) *Sp:* (*basketball*) basket; **faire un p.,** (i) to cage; (ii) *Fb: F:* to score a goal, to net (the ball). **2.** (*a*) *A: Veh:* (wicker) governess cart; pony carriage; *Aut:* wickerwork body; **p. roulant,** (child's) go-cart; (*b*) beehive. **3.** *Arch:* pannier, corbel. **4.** (*a*) *A.Cost:* pannier; hoop petticoat, hoop; **robe à paniers,** crinoline; (*b*) *P:* (woman's) buttocks.

panière [panjɛːr], *s.f.* (*a*) two-handled basket; (*b*) basketful.

panier-repas [panjerəpɑ], *s.m.* luncheon basket; *pl. paniers-repas.*

panifiable [panifjabl], *a.* **farine p.,** flour for bread; "strong" wheat flour; **céréales panifiables,** bread stuffs; bread crops, cereals, grains.

panification [panifikasjɔ̃], *s.f.* panification.

panifier [panifje], *v.tr.* (*p.d. & pr.sub.* **n. panifiions, v. panifiiez**) to turn, convert, (flour) into bread.

paniquard [panikaːr], *F:* (*a*) *a.* scaremongering, alarmist; (*b*) *s.m.* scaremonger, panic monger, alarmist.

panique [panik]. **1.** *a.* panic (terror). **2.** *s.f.* panic, scare; **pris de p.,** panic-stricken; **pris de p. ils s'enfuirent,** they fled in a panic; **sujet à la p.,** easily scared, *F:* panicky; **mesures dictées par la p.,** panic measures; **semeur de p.,** panic monger, scaremonger.

paniquer [panike], *F:* **1.** *v.tr.* to panic (s.o.); **il était paniqué par l'approche des examens,** he was thrown into a panic by the approach of the examinations. **2.** *v.i.* to (get into a) panic; to get panicky.

panis [panis], *s.m. Bot:* panic grass.

panislamique [panislamik], *a.* Pan-Islamic.

panislamisme [panislamism], *s.m.* Pan-Islamism.

panisque [panisk], *s.m. Myth:* panisc, panisk.

panka [pɑ̃ka], *s.m.* panka, punkah.

panlexique [pɑ̃lɛksik], *s.m.* universal lexicon.

panlogisme [pɑ̃lɔʒism], *s.m. Phil:* panlogism.

panmastite [pɑ̃mastit], *s.f. Med:* generalized mastitis.

panméristique [pɑ̃meristik], *a. Biol:* panmeristic.

panmixie [pɑ̃miksi], *s.f. Biol:* panmixia.

panne[1] [pan], *s.f.* **1.** (*a*) *Tex:* panne, plush; (*b*) *Her:* **pannes,** furs. **2.** (hog's) fat; lard.

panne[2], *s.f.* **1.** (*a*) *Nau:* **en p.,** hove to; **en p. sèche,** hove to under bare poles; **(se) mettre en p., prendre la p.,** to heave to, to bring to; **mettre un navire en p.,** to bring a ship to; **rouler p. sur p.,** to roll gunwale to; *F:* **faire p.,** rester en p., to be brought up all standing; (*b*) *F: A:* **être, tomber, dans la p.,** to be reduced to poverty, to come on hard times; (*c*) *Th: F:* (i) small part, insignificant part, bit part; (ii) (*also occ. s.m.*) actor, actress, fit only for small parts, bit parts. **2.** (mechanical) breakdown; (electrical) failure, *U.S:* outage; **en p.,** out of order; (*of electricity*) off; **p. intermittente,** intermittent breakdown; sporadic fault; **p. du métro,** hold-up, breakdown, on the underground; **p. de courant, d'électricité,** power failure; power cut; blackout; **p. de secteur,** mains failure; *W.Tel: T.V:* **p. d'émission,** technical fault, hitch; **p. de machine, de moteur,** engine trouble, engine failure; *I.C.E:* **p. d'allumage,** ignition trouble; **le moteur a eu une p.,** the engine broke down, refused to start, to go; **tomber en p. d'essence, en p. sèche,** to run out of petrol; (*of speaker*) **être en p. sèche,** to dry up; (*to motorist*) **vous êtes en p.?** have you broken down? *F:* won't she go? *F:* (*of pers.*) **être en p.,** to be stuck, to have come to a standstill; **rester, tomber, en p.,** to break down; **rester en p. devant une difficulté,** to stick at a difficulty; *F:* **laisser qn en p.,** to leave s.o. in the lurch; to let s.o. down; **elle est en p. de domestique,** she can't get any (domestic) help.

panne[3], *s.f.* **1.** *Const:* (*a*) purlin (of roof); **p. faîtière,** ridge purlin; **p. sablière,** eaves purlin; (*b*) pantile. **2. pannes de barrage, de port,** (harbour) boom.

panne[4], *s.f. Tchn:* **1. p. de marteau,** pane, peen, of a hammer; **p. fendue,** claw (of hammer); **p. bombée,** ball pane; **p. de marteau mécanique,** hammer block. **2.** flange (of H girder).

panne[5], *s.f.* **p. de nuages,** bank of clouds.

panne[6], *s.f.* (*in Flanders*) humid depression (in dunes).

panné [pane], *a. P:* (stony-)broke, on the rocks; penniless; down and out.

panneau, -eaux [pano], *s.m.* **1.** snare, net (for game); **tendre un p. à qn,** to set a trap for s.o.; **tomber, donner, dans le p.,** to fall into the trap. **2.** panel; **p. de lambris,** wainscot panel; **p. de porte,** door panel; **porte à panneaux,** panelled door; **à panneaux de chêne,** oak-panelled; **diviser un mur en panneaux,** to panel a wall; *Const:* **p. de revêtement,** wallboard; **panneaux vitrés,** glass panels, glass panelling; **p. chauffant,** heating panel; wall heater; *Aer:* **p. de déchirure,** ripping panel (of balloon). **3.** *Nau: etc:* (*a*) **entrée, ouverture, de p.,** hatchway, hatch opening; **p. d'accès,** access hatch, panel; **p. de visite,** inspection hatch, panel; **p. d'arrimage,** trimming hatch; **p. d'aération,** ventilation hatch; **p. de charge(ment), de déchargement,** cargo hatch; **p. de tonnage,** tonnage hatchway; **p. de descente,** hatchway, booby hatch; **p. de mer,** close hatch; **p. de vaigrage,** ceiling hatch; **p. à plat pont,** flush-deck hatch; *Av: Nau: etc:* **p. d'échappée,** escape hatch, panel; **p. ignifuge,** fire wall; **p. d'écoutille, p. de cale,** hatch cover; **p. à glissière,** sliding hatch; **p. à claire-voie, p. grillagé,** grated hatch; **barre, tringle, de p.,** batten; **condamner les panneaux,** to batten down the hatches, to cover and secure the hatches; **fermer le p.,** to close down the hatch; **nous avons des marchandises dans trois panneaux,** we have cargo in three holds; (*b*) *Navy:* **p. de dragage,** (minesweeping) kite. **4.** board; signboard; panel; (*a*) **p. d'affichage,** notice board, *U.S:* bill board; **p. à affiches, p. d'affichage, p. de publicité,** advertisement panel, hoarding; *Aut:* **p. indicateur,** road sign; **p. de signalisation (routière),** direction sign; traffic sign; *Av: etc:* **p. de signalisation,** signalling panel, panel signal; **signalisation par panneaux,** panel signalling; **p. de signalisation sol-air,** ground-air (liaison) panel, ground strip signal, displaying strip; **p. d'identification,** identification panel, distinguishing panel; **p. de jalonnement,** marking panel; (*b*) *El: Elcs:* **p. de commande,** control panel; **p. de contrôle,** test board; **p. de commutation,** switchboard, switch panel; **p. de distribution,** distribution switchboard; **p. de fusibles,** fuse panel; **p. de raccordement,** patch panel (of computer). **5.** (*a*) *A:* piece (of material); *F:* **crever dans ses panneaux,** to be suffocated; (*b*) *Dressm:* panel (of skirt, etc.). **6.** *Hort:* glass frame (for seeds, plants).

panneau-réclame [panoreklam], *s.m.* (advertisement) hoarding; *pl. panneaux-réclame.*

panneautage [panotaːʒ], *s.m.* **1.** netting of game (by poachers, etc.). **2.** panelling. **3.** *Av:* placing of ground strip signals.

panneauter [panote], *v.tr.* **1.** (*a*) to net, snare (game); (*b*) *abs.* to poach. **2.** *Hort:* to put (seedlings, etc.) under glass. **3.** to panel.

panneauteur [panotœːr], *s.m.* poacher.

pannequet [pankɛ], *s.m.* pancake.

panner [pane], *v.tr. Metalw:* to hammer (out) (copper, etc.).

panneresse [panrɛs], *s.f. Const:* stretcher (brick or stone).

panneton [pantɔ̃], *s.m.* **1.** web, bit (of key). **2. p. de fenêtre, d'espagnolette,** window catch.

pannicule [panikyl], *s.m. Anat:* panniculus; **p. adipeux,** panniculus adiposus.

Pannonie [panɔni], *Pr.n.f. A.Geog:* Pannonia.

pannonien, -ienne [panɔnjɛ̃, -jɛn], *a. & s. Geog:* Pannonian; **bassin p.,** middle Danubian, Pannonian, Hungarian, basin.

pannoter [panɔte], *v.tr.* = PANNEAUTER.

pano [pano], *s.m. Ling:* Panoan.

panonceau, -eaux [panɔ̃so], *s.m.* **1.** *A:* escutcheon. **2.** (*a*) escutcheon sign (over office of *avoué, notaire, huissier, etc.*); (*b*) sign (indicating bus stop, etc.).

panoplie [panɔpli], *s.f.* **1.** (*a*) panoply; full suit of plate armour; (*b*) set (of tools, kitchen utensils, etc.); *Toys:* **p. de soldat, de pompier,** soldier's, fireman's, outfit (for child); *F:* **p. de médailles,** full set of medals, *F:* gongs. **2.** weapons grouped ornamentally; (wall) trophy; panoply.

panoptique [panɔptik], *Arch:* **1.** *a.* panoptic(al). **2.** *s.m.* panopticon.

panorama [panɔrama], *s.m.* (*a*) *Art: etc:* panorama; (*b*) panorama, view; **un magnifique p. se déroulait devant nous,** a magnificent view, panorama, landscape, stretched out in front of us; (*c*) **p. de la littérature contemporaine,** comprehensive survey of contemporary literature.

panoramique [panɔramik]. **1.** *a.* panoramic; **vue p.,** panorama; *Rail:* **voiture p.,** observation coach, *U.S:* scenic car; *Aut:* **lunette p.,** wrapround rear window; **restaurant p.,** panoramic restaurant; *Surv:* **croquis p.,** panoram(ic) sketch, drawing; landscape sketch, drawing; *Phot:*

photo p., panoram(ic) photograph; (*radar*) indicateur p., plan-position indicator display; image p., plan-position indicator picture. 2. *s.m. Cin: T.V:* panning; p. horizontal, vertical, horizontal, vertical, panning.

panoramiquer [panɔramike], *v.i. Cin: T.V:* to pan.

panorpe [panɔrp], *s.f. Ent:* scorpion fly.

panorthodoxe [panɔrtɔdɔks], *a.* panorthodox.

panpsychisme [pɑ̃psyʃism], *s.m. Phil:* panpsychism.

pansage [pɑ̃saːʒ], *s.m.* grooming (of horse, etc.).

panse [pɑ̃ːs], *s.f.* 1. (*a*) *F:* belly; grosse p., paunch, pot belly; il a eu les yeux plus grands que la p., his eyes were bigger than his belly; *P:* se faire crever la p., to get knifed in the guts, to get killed; *P:* s'en faire crever la p., to blow one's guts out; (*b*) paunch, first stomach, rumen (of ruminant). 2. belly, bulge (of bottle, retort, vase, etc.); sound-bow (of bell); p. d'un a, d'un d., body, oval, of an a, of a d; *F: O:* il n'a pas fait une p. d'a, he hasn't done a stroke (of work), he's done damn all.

pansement [pɑ̃smɑ̃], *s.m. Med:* 1. (action of) dressing (a wound); faire un p., to dress a wound; to apply a dressing. 2. dressing; pack; (*used loosely for*) bandage; p. ouatiné, lint; p. compressif, compression bandage; p.-tampon, packing, pledget; p. chirurgical, surgical pack, dressing; p. post-opératoire, post-operative dressing; p. sec, humide, dry, wet, dressing; p. de fortune, improvised dressing; *Mil:* p. individuel, paquet individuel de p., first-aid dressing, kit; trousse de p., surgical dressing case; après l'application d'un premier p., after a first dressing has been applied; *F:* il faut mettre un p., you ought to put something over it, to put on a bandage.

panser [pɑ̃se], *v.tr.* 1. p. un cheval, to groom, rub down, a horse. 2. p. une blessure, to dress a wound; p. un blessé, to bandage a wounded man. 3. *A:* to feed (dogs, fowls).

panseur, -euse [pɑ̃sœːr, -øːz], *s.* (surgical) dresser.

pansinusite [pɑ̃sinyzit], *s.f. Med:* pansinusitis.

panslave [pɑ̃slaːv], *a.* Pan-Slav(ic).

panslavisme [pɑ̃slavism], *s.m.* Pan-Slavism.

panslaviste [pɑ̃slavist]. 1. *a.* Pan-Slav. 2. *s.m. & f.* Pan-Slavist.

pansophie [pɑ̃sɔfi], *s.f.* pansophy, universal science.

panspermie [pɑ̃spɛrmi], *s.f.*, **panspermisme** [pɑ̃spɛrmism], *s.m. Biol:* panspermy, panspermia.

panspermique [pɑ̃spɛrmik], *a. Biol:* panspermic.

pansu, -e [pɑ̃sy], *F:* 1. *a.* big-bellied, pot-bellied (person, bottle, etc.); tubby (person). 2. *s.* pot-bellied person, pot-belly.

pantagruélesque [pɑ̃tagryelɛsk], *a.* Pantagruelian.

pantagruélique [pɑ̃tagryelik], *a.* Pantagruelic, Gargantuan (meal, etc.).

pantagruélisme [pɑ̃tagryelism], *s.m.* Pantagruelism; Rabelaisian philosophy of life.

pantagruéliste [pɑ̃tagryelist], *s.m. & f.* Pantagruelist.

pantaine [pɑ̃tɛn], *s.f. Ven:* draw net.

pantaléon [pɑ̃taleɔ̃], *s.m. A.Mus:* pantaleon.

Pantalon [pɑ̃talɔ̃]. 1. (*a*) *Pr.n.m. Th:* Pantaloon; enlever une jeune fille à la barbe de P., to run off with a girl under an old man's very nose; (*b*) *s.m. A:* (i) pantaloon; buffoon; (ii) old dotard; (iii) hypocrite; (*c*) *s.m. Danc:* (*first figure of quadrille*) pantalon. 2. *s.m. Cost:* (*a*) (pair of) trousers, slacks; p. (de dame), slacks; pantalons fuseaux, drainpipe trousers; tissus pour pantalons, trouserings; (*b*) *A:* (*from red trousers worn by French soldiers*) p. rouge = redcoat; (*c*) *A:* (woman's) knickers. 3. *s.m. Aer:* p. d'eau, emergency water-ballast bag.

pantalonnade [pɑ̃talɔnad], *s.f.* (*a*) *Th.Hist:* burlesque scene, farce; pantaloonery; buffoonery; (*b*) piece of hypocrisy.

pantalonné [pɑ̃talɔne], *a.* wearing trousers.

pantalonnier, -ière [pɑ̃talɔnje, -jɛːr], *s. Ind:* trouser hand.

pante [pɑ̃ːt], *s.m. P:* (*a*) sucker, mug, easy mark; (*b*) un drôle de p., an odd type.

pantelant [pɑ̃tlɑ̃], *a.* (*a*) panting, gasping, heaving; (*b*) corps encore pantelants, bodies still quivering, still twitching.

panteler [pɑ̃tle], *v.i.* (je pantelle, n. pantelons; je pantellerai) to pant; to gasp.

pantellement [pɑ̃tɛlmɑ̃], *s.m.* panting.

pantène, pantenne [pɑ̃tɛn], *s.f.* 1. *Ven:* draw net; *Fish:* hoop net. 2. wicker tray (for drying fruit or moving silkworms). 3. en pantenne: (*a*) (*of ships, convoy*) in disorder; (*b*) vergues en pantenne, yards apeak (as sign of mourning).

pantequière [pɑ̃t(ə)kjɛːr], *s.f. Nau:* swifting tackle.

panthéisme [pɑ̃teism], *s.m.* pantheism.

panthéiste [pɑ̃teist]. 1. *a.* pantheist, pantheistic(al). 2. *s.m. & f.* pantheist.

panthéistique [pɑ̃teistik], *a.* pantheist, pantheistic(al).

panthéon [pɑ̃teɔ̃], *s.m.* pantheon; le P., the Pantheon (in Paris, in the crypt of which lie the famous dead of France); son nom restera au p. de l'histoire, his name will be famous in history.

panthère [pɑ̃tɛːr], *s.f.* 1. *Z:* panther; grande p. des fourreurs, jaguar; p. longibande, clouded leopard; p. des neiges, ounce, snow leopard. 2. (*a*) *A:* quick-tempered woman; (*b*) *P:* ma p., the wife, the missus.

panthérin [pɑ̃terɛ̃], *a.* pantherine.

pantière [pɑ̃tjɛːr], *s.f. Ven:* 1. draw net. 2. plain net game bag.

pantin [pɑ̃tɛ̃], *s.m. Toys:* jumping-jack; *F:* (*of man*) nonentity, mere puppet, stooge; p. politique, political jumping-jack, trimmer; mener une vie de p., to run wild.

pantinois, -oise [pɑ̃tinwa, -waːz], *a. & s. Geog:* (native, inhabitant) of Pantin.

pant(o)- [pɑ̃tɔ], *comb.fm.* pant(o)-.

Pantocrator [pɑ̃tɔkratɔːr], *a. & s.m.* (*a*) *Ecc.Art:* (Christ) P., (Christ) Pantocrator; (*b*) *Myth:* Zeus p., Zeus pantocrator, Zeus the all-ruler.

pantodon [pɑ̃tɔdɔ̃], *s.m. Ich:* chisel jaw: (*genus*) Pantodon.

pantographe [pɑ̃tɔgraf], *s.m.* 1. *Draw:* pantograph. 2. (any) lazy-tongs device; *esp.* pantograph (of electric train).

pantographique [pɑ̃tɔgrafik], *a.* pantographic(al).

pantographiquement [pɑ̃tɔgrafikmɑ̃], *adv.* pantographically.

pantoire [pɑ̃twaːr], *s.f. Nau:* (= *short rope with eye*) pendant.

pantois [pɑ̃twa], *a.* (*rare in f.*) 1. *A:* panting. 2. amazed, non-plussed, flabbergasted; en être tout p., to stand aghast.

pantomètre [pɑ̃tɔmɛtr̥], *s.m. Geom:* pantometer.

pantométrique [pɑ̃tɔmetrik], *a.* pantometric.

pantomime[1] [pɑ̃tɔmim], *s.m. Th: A:* pantomime (actor); mime; mimic.

pantomime[2], *s.f.* (*a*) *Th: etc:* mime; pantomime; (*b*) (= *significant gesticulation or play of features*); (panto)mime.

pantomimer [pɑ̃tɔmime], *v.tr. A:* to express, represent, (sth.) by pantomime; to mime (a play).

pantomimique [pɑ̃tɔmimik], *a. A:* pantomimic.

pantophobie [pɑ̃tɔfɔbi], *s.f. Psy:* pantophobia.

pantopodes [pɑ̃tɔpɔd], *s.m.pl. Arach:* Pantopoda, Pycnogonida.

pantoscope [pɑ̃tɔskɔp], *s.m. Phot: etc:* pantoscope.

pantothénique [pɑ̃tɔtenik], *a. Bio-Ch:* pantothenic (acid).

pantouflard [pɑ̃tuflaːr], *s.m. F:* stay-at-home, home-bird.

pantoufle [pɑ̃tufl̥], *s.f.* 1. (*a*) slipper; en pantoufles, (i) in one's slippers; (ii) at one's ease; rêver à la famille et à ses pantoufles, to dream of one's family and home life; ne pas quitter ses pantoufles, passer sa vie dans ses pantoufles, to live a stay-at-home life; *Lit:* cordonnier, mêlez-vous de votre p.! let the cobbler stick to his last; (*b*) *F:* quelle p.! what an idiot! raisonner comme une p., to talk nonsense, to talk through one's hat; jouer comme une p., to play very badly; et cætera p., and so on and so forth; (*c*) *F:* (i) civilian job; (ii) sum of money which may be demanded from any graduate of a *grande école* who does not remain in the service of the state; (*d*) *Farr:* (fer à) p., panton. 2. *A:* (slipper) bedpan.

pantoufler [pɑ̃tufle], *v.i. F:* 1. (*a*) to reason absurdly; (*b*) to engage in homely, friendly, conversation. 2. (*a*) to take it easy, to put one's feet up; (*b*) to be a stay-at-home; to lead a quiet, regular life; (*c*) (*of officer*) to take a civilian job; (*of civil servant*) to go into non-governmental employment.

pantouflerie [pɑ̃tufləri], *s.f.* 1. (*a*) slipper making, manufacture; (*b*) the slipper trade. 2. *A: F:* (*a*) absurd reasoning; (*b*) intimate chat.

pantouflier, -ère [pɑ̃tuflije, -ɛːr], *s.* (*a*) slipper manufacturer; slipper hand; (*b*) dealer in slippers.

pantoum [pɑ̃tum], *s.m.*, **pantoun** [pɑ̃tun], *s.m. Lit:* pantoum.

Pantruchard, -arde [pɑ̃tryʃaːr, -ard], *s. P: A:* Parisian.

Pantruche [pɑ̃tryʃ], *Pr.n.m. P: A:* Paris.

panty [pɑ̃ti], *s.m. Cost: F:* pantie girdle.

panure [panyːr], *s.f. Cu:* breadcrumbs; p. à l'anglaise, double p., egg and breadcrumb coating.

Panurge [panyrʒ]. 1. *Pr.n.m. Fr.Lit:* Panurge; ce sont les moutons de P., they follow one another like sheep. 2. *s.m. Harn:* runner, looped strap (for bearing rein). 3. *s.m. Ent:* digger bee, mining bee.

panzer [pɑ̃zɛːr], *s.m. Mil:* panzer.

paon [pɑ̃], *s.m.* 1. (*a*) *Orn:* peacock; pousser des cris de p., to screech like a peacock; se parer des plumes du p., to strut in borrowed plumes; fier comme un p., as proud as a peacock; *a.inv.* bleu p., peacock-blue; (*b*) pigeon p., fantail. 2. *Ent:* peacock butterfly; p. de nuit, wild silk moth, emperor moth. 3. p. de mer, (i) *Ich:* peacock fish; (ii) *Orn:* ruff. 4. *Astr:* le P., Pavo, the Peacock.

paonne [pan], *s.f. Orn:* peahen.

paonneau, -eaux [pano], *s.m.* peachick.

paonner [pane], *v.i.* to strut, *A:* to peacock; to preen oneself.

papa [papa], *s.m.* (*a*) (*form of address used by children*) papa; dad(dy); pa; (*used by adults*) father; (*to child*) embrasse (ton) p., give daddy a kiss; (*of children*) jouer au p. et à la maman, to play mummies and daddies; (*b*) *F:* un bon (gros) p., a nice, comfortable old gentleman; P. Martin, old Father Martin; (*c*) *F:* faire qch. à la p., to do sth. in a leisurely fashion; to do sth. simply; aller à la p., to dodder along; to potter along; (*d*) *F: Pej:* de p., old-fashioned; behind the times; antiquated; *s.a.* FILS 1, GÂTEAU 1.

papable [papabl̥], *a. F:* who is a likely candidate for the papacy.

papadie [papadi], *s.f. Gk. Orthodox Ch:* pope's wife.

papaïne [papain], *s.f. Pharm:* papain.

papal, -aux [papal, -o], *a.* papal.

papalin [papalɛ̃]. 1. *a. Pej:* popish, papistical. 2. *s.m. A:* (*a*) papal guard; (*b*) *Pej:* papal partisan.

papas [papas], *s.m. Gk. Orthodox Ch:* pope.

papauté [papote], *s.f.* papacy; les revendications de la p., the papal claims.

papaver [papavɛːr], *s.m. Bot:* papaver.

papavéracé [papaverase], *Bot:* 1. *a.* papaver(ace)ous. 2. *s.f.pl.* papavéracées, Papaveraceae, the poppies.

papavérine [papaverin], *s.f. Pharm:* papaverin(e).

papaye [papaːj, papɛ], *s.f. Bot:* papaw.

papayer [papaje, -eje], *s.m. Bot:* papaw (tree).

pape [pap], *s.m.* 1. *Ecc:* pope; le p. Pie X, Pope Pius X; *s.a.* FOU 2. 2. *Orn:* painted finch.

papegai [papgɛ], *s.m.* (*a*) *Orn: A:* popinjay; (*b*) (*archery*) popinjay.

papelard[1], **-arde** [paplaːr, -ard]. 1. *s. A:* sanctimonious person. 2. *a.* sanctimonious, canting (voice, etc.); il a un air p., he looks as if butter wouldn't melt in his mouth; he looks as sleek as a cat.

papelard[2], *s.m. F:* (piece of) paper; letter; handbill, notice; *pl.* identity papers; business papers; newspapers.

papelarder [paplarde], *v.i. A:* to cant.

papelardise [paplardiːz], *s.f. A:* sanctimoniousness, cant.

papelonné [paplɔne], *a. Her:* papelonné.

paperasse [papras], *s.f. Pej:* (*usu. pl. with coll. value*) de vieilles paperasses, old papers; old records; les paperasses administratives, official papers, records; (*coll. sing.*) c'est de la p.! it's just a lot of (old) papers!

paperasser [paprase], *v.i. Pej:* 1. to go through old papers, through old records. 2. to be for ever scribbling.

paperasserie [paprasri], *s.f. Pej:* 1. (accumulation of) old papers. 2. la p. (administrative), red tape.

paperassier, -ière [paprasje, -jɛːr], *Pej:* 1. *a.* (*a*) given to scribbling, to taking notes; (*b*) cluttered up with red tape. 2. *s.* (*a*) inveterate (i) scribbler, (ii) amasser of (old) papers; (*b*) red-tape merchant.

papesse [papɛs], *s.f. used in* la p. Jeanne, Pope Joan.

papeterie [pap(ə)tri], *s.f.* 1. (*a*) paper manufacturing; (*b*) paper mill, factory; (*c*) paper trade. 2. (*a*) stationery trade; (*b*) stationer's (shop); (*c*) stationery; (*d*) *O:* writing case.

papetier, -ière [paptje, -jɛːr]. 1. *s.* (*a*) paper manufacturer; (*b*) stationer. 2. *a.* (*a*) industrie papetière, paper industry; ouvrier p., paper maker; (*b*) *Ent:* mouche papetière, paper wasp.

papetier-libraire [paptjelibrɛːr], *s.m.* bookseller and stationer; *pl. papetiers-libraires.*

papeton [paptɔ̃], *s.m.* maize cob, corn cob.

paphien, -ienne [pafjɛ̃, -jɛn], *a. & s. A.Geog:* Paphian, of Paphos.

Paphlagonie [paflagɔni], *Pr.n.f. A.Geog:* Paphlagonia.

paphlagonien, -ienne [paflagɔnjɛ̃, -jɛn], *a. & s. A.Geog:* Paphlagonian.

papier [papje], *s.m.* **1.** (*a*) paper; **pâte à p.,** pulp; **p. à la main, p. cuve,** hand-made paper; **p. mécanique,** machine-made paper; **p. (en) continu,** (i) paper in rolls; (ii) continuous fanfold paper; **p. vergé,** laid paper; **p. d'alfa,** alfa, esparto, paper; **p. chiffon,** rag paper; **p. de Chine, p. de riz,** rice paper; **p. bulle,** manila paper; **p. vélin,** vellum paper; **p. du Japon,** Japanese vellum; **p. bible, p. pelure,** India paper; **p. bouffant,** featherweight paper; **p. buvard,** blotting paper; **p. carbone,** carbon paper; **p. collé,** sized paper; **p. paraffiné,** waxed paper; **p. couché,** art paper, (surface-)coated paper, baryta paper; **p. crêpe,** crepe paper; **p. cristal,** glassine, translucent, paper; **p. émeri,** emery paper; **p. abrasif, p. de verre,** glass paper, sandpaper; **frotter qch. au p. de verre,** to sandpaper sth.; **p. goudronné, p. bitumé,** tar paper, bituminized paper, bitumen felt, roofing felt; **p. gommé,** gummed paper; **p. gris,** brown paper; **p. kraft,** kraft; **p. filtre,** filter paper; **p. laboratoire,** (chemical) filter paper; **p. joseph,** (type of) filter paper; **p. à réactif,** test paper; **p. journal,** newsprint; **je vais l'envelopper dans du p. journal,** I'll wrap it up in newspaper; **p. (de) soie,** tissue paper; **p. sulfurisé,** butter paper, imitation parchment; **p. beurre, p. jambon, p. parcheminé,** greaseproof paper; **p. brillant,** glossy, glazed, paper; **p. demi-brillant,** semi-matt paper; **p. mat, non-satiné,** matt, unglazed, dull-finish, paper; **p. à cigarettes,** cigarette paper; *Phot:* **p. sensible,** sensitized paper; **p. au bromure (d'argent),** bromide paper; **p. pour effets doux,** soft paper; **p. autovireur,** self-toning paper; **p. charbon,** carbon paper, carbon tissue; autotype tissue; **p. calque, p. à calquer,** tracing paper; **p. toile,** tracing linen; **p. à écrire,** writing paper, notepaper; **p. à lettres,** notepaper, letter paper; **p. à en-tête,** headed, printed, notepaper; **p. (à lettres) toile,** cambric paper; **p. deuil,** black-edged paper; **p. pour machine à écrire,** *F:* **p. machine,** typing paper; **p. à dessin,** drawing paper; **p. écolier,** exercise paper; **p. brouillon,** rough paper, scribbling paper; **p. réglé,** ruled, lined, paper; **p. blanc, vierge,** blank paper; **p. quadrillé, p. à carreaux,** squared paper; **p. à musique,** manuscript paper; **p. d'emballage,** packing paper, wrapping paper; *Toil:* **p. à démaquiller, p. démaquillant,** cleansing tissue, face tissue; **p. hygiénique, p. toilette,** *P:* **p. torchette, p. cul,** toilet paper, lavatory paper, *F:* loo paper, *P:* bumf; **rouleau de p. hygiénique,** toilet roll; **p. peint, p. à tapisser, p. tenture,** wallpaper; **p. lavable,** washable wallpaper; **p. tue-mouches, p. attrape-mouches,** flypaper; (*b*) **un p.,** a sheet, bit, of paper; **p. volant,** loose sheet; **mettre qch. sur p.,** to put sth. down on paper; **notez plutôt cela dans votre carnet que sur un p.,** put it down in your notebook rather than on a scrap of paper; **(le jeu des) petits papiers,** (the game of) consequences; (*c*) **sur le p.,** on paper, in theory; **projet qui est beau sur le p.,** plan that is fine in theory, that looks good on paper; **sur le p. tout est résolu,** on paper, in principle, everything is decided; *Turf:* **jouer le p.,** to bet on form, on paper; (*d*) **p. mâché,** papier mâché; **avoir une mine de p. mâché,** to look washed-out; **jambes en p. mâché,** flabby legs. **2.** (*a*) paper, document; **papiers domestiques,** private papers, family papers; *Jur:* **papiers d'une affaire,** documents relating to a case; *Post:* **papiers d'affaires,** printed paper rate; **vieux papiers,** old papers, waste paper; *F:* **être dans les petits papiers de qn,** to be in s.o.'s good books; *F:* **rayez cela de vos papiers,** you shouldn't count on it; (*b*) *Jur:* **p. timbré,** stamped paper (for official and legal documents); **p. libre,** unstamped, plain, paper; (*c*) *Fin:* bill(s); **p. à longue échéance, à courte échéance, p. long, court,** long-dated, short-dated, bill, paper; **p. brûlant,** bills about to mature; **p. fait,** backed bills; **p. sur l'étranger,** foreign bill(s); (*d*) *pl. Adm:* **papiers (d'identité),** (identity) papers; **avoir ses papiers en règle,** to have one's papers in order; **faire viser ses papiers,** to have one's papers visa'd; **papiers du bord, de navire,** ship's papers; (*e*) *Journ: F:* article; (*f*) *F:* **lire un p.,** to read a paper (to a meeting of a society, etc.). **3. p. d'aluminium, d'étain, d'argent,** aluminium foil, lead foil, tinfoil. **4.** *Bot:* **arbre à p.,** paper mulberry.

papier-monnaie [papjemɔnɛ], *s.m.* paper money, paper currency; *pl. papiers-monnaie.*

papier-pierre [papjepjɛːr], *s.m.* papier mâché; *pl. papiers-pierre.*

papilionacé [papiljɔnase], *Bot:* **1.** *a.* papilionaceous; **orchis p.,** butterfly orchid. **2.** *s.f.pl.* **papilionacées,** Papilionaceae.

papilionidés [papiljɔnide], *s.m.pl. Ent:* Papilionidae.

papillaire [papil(l)ɛːr], *a. Anat: etc:* papillary; *Bot:* papillate (gland, etc.).

papille [papil, -piːj], *s.f. Anat: Bot:* papilla; **p. optique,** intraocular end of the optic nerve; blind spot; **p. gustative, du goût,** taste bud; **p. linguale,** lingual papilla; **p. caliciforme,** circumvalate papilla.

papillé [papil(l)e], *a. Bot: etc:* papillate, papillose.

papillectomie [papil(l)ɛktɔmi], *s.f. Surg:* papillectomy.

papilleux, -euse [papil(l)ø, papijø, -øːz], *a. Anat: etc:* papillose.

papillifère [papil(l)ifɛːr]. **1.** *a. Anat: Bot:* papilliferous. **2.** *s.m.pl. Moll:* **papillifères,** Papillifera.

papilliforme [papil(l)ifɔrm], *a.* papilliform.

papillite [papil(l)it, papijit], *s.f. Med:* papillitis.

papillomateux, -euse [papil(l)ɔmatø, papijɔmatø, -øːz], *a. Med:* papillomatous.

papillomatose [papil(l)omatoːz, papijomatoːz], *s.f. Med:* papillomatosis.

papillome [papil(l)oːm, papijoːm], *s.m. Med:* papilloma.

papillon [papijɔ̃], *s.m.* **1.** (*a*) *Ent:* butterfly; **p. feuille,** leaf butterfly; **p. de nuit,** moth; **p. comète (de Madagascar),** silver silk moth, tailed comet moth; **courir après des papillons,** to amuse oneself with trifles; **c'est un p.,** she's completely empty-headed, just a butterfly; **papillons noirs,** gloomy, melancholy, ideas; *F:* **minute p.!** just a moment; hold on a minute! *Cost:* **nœud p.,** bow tie; *Swim:* **(nage, brasse) p.,** butterfly stroke; (*b*) *Ich:* **p. de mer,** gunnel, butter fish; (*c*) *Z:* **épagneul p.,** papillon. **2.** (*a*) inset (in book); erratum slip; (*b*) leaflet, *esp.* publisher's blurb; (*c*) handbill, small poster; (*d*) inset map (in corner of large map); (*e*) rider (to document); (*f*) label; (*g*) *Aut: etc:* ticket; **on m'a collé un p. (sur le pare-brise),** I've been given a ticket (for parking in the wrong place, etc.). **3.** *Nau:* skysail, skyscraper, star gazer, moonraker. **4.** *Tchn:* (*a*) butterfly valve, throttle; throttle valve; *Aut:* disc-type throttle; **levier du p.,** throttle lever; **axe du p.,** throttle-valve spindle; *Mch:* **p. de la détente,** expansion damper; (*b*) thumb screw, butterfly nut, wing nut; (*c*) **(bec) p.,** bat's wing gas burner.

papillonnage [papijɔnaːʒ], *s.m.* **1.** fluttering; flitting (from place to place, person to person). **2.** *Ser:* emergence (of moth from cocoon). **3.** *Civ.E:* circular dredging.

papillonnant [papijɔnɑ̃], *a.* fluttering; flitting.

papillonnement [papijɔnmɑ̃], *s.m.* fluttering; flitting (from place to place, person to person).

papillonner [papijɔne], *v.i.* to flit about, to flutter about (from person to person); to pass rapidly (from one subject to another); (*of object in motion*) to twinkle; *T.V:* to flicker.

papillotage [papijɔtaːʒ], *s.m.* **1.** (*a*) **p. des yeux,** (i) blinking, (ii) dazzlement, of the eyes; **p. du style,** garishness of style; (*b*) *Cin: T.V:* flicker(ing); (*c*) *Typ:* mackling, slurring. **2.** *A:* (*a*) curling (of hair); (*b*) *A:* hair in curl papers.

papillotant [papijɔtɑ̃], *a.* flickering (light, etc.); twinkling (star).

papillote [papijɔt], *s.f.* **1.** *A:* curl paper; **être en papillotes, avoir la tête en papillotes,** to have one's hair in curl papers; **fer à papillotes,** curling-tongs. **2.** twist of paper; frill (round knuckle of ham, etc.); **(bonbons en) papillotes,** wrapped sweets; **p. à pétard,** Christmas cracker; **les yeux en p.,** with one's eyes screwed up; *F:* **tu peux en faire des papillotes,** it's no good, you can throw it away. **3.** *Cu:* buttered paper (for cooking chops, etc.); **côtelettes en papillotes,** chops grilled in buttered paper.

papillotement [papijɔtmɑ̃], *s.m.* **1.** dazzle. **2.** *Cin: etc:* flickering; *T.V:* flicker.

papilloter [papijɔte]. **1.** *v.i.* (*a*) (*of eyes*) to blink; (*of light*) to blink, twinkle; *Cin: etc:* to flicker; (*b*) to dazzle, glitter; **style qui papillote,** garish style; (*c*) *Typ:* to mackle, slur. **2.** *v.tr.* (*a*) *A:* to curl (hair); to put (hair) into curl papers, into curling pins; (*b*) *Cu:* to grill (chop, etc.) in buttered paper.

papin [papɛ̃], *s.m. Ent: F:* croton bug, German cockroach.

papion [papjɔ̃], *s.m. Z:* baboon; (*genus*) Papio.

papisme [papism], *s.m.* **1.** papism. **2.** *Pej:* popery, papistry.

papiste [papist]. **1.** *s.m. & f.* papist; (*a*) adherent of the papacy; (*b*) *Pej:* Roman Catholic. **2.** *a. Pej:* papistic(al); popish.

papistique [papistik], *a.* papistic(al).

papolâtre [papɔlɑtr], *Pej:* **1.** *a.* papolatrous. **2.** *s.m. & f.* papolater.

papolâtrie [papɔlɑtri], *s.f. Pej:* papolatry.

papotage [papɔtaːʒ], *s.m. F:* (*a*) chattering; gossiping; (*b*) chatter; gossip.

papoter [papɔte], *v.i. F:* to gossip; to chatter; to babble on.

papou, -oue [papu], *a. & s. Geog:* Papuan; *pl. papous, -oues.*

Papouasie [papwazi], *Pr.n.f. Geog:* (*a*) *A:* New Guinea; (*b*) Papua.

papouille [papuːj], *s.f. P:* tickle; squeeze; cuddle; *Pej:* **faire des papouilles,** to paw (s.o.).

papouiller [papuje], *v.tr. P:* to paw (s.o.).

pappe [pap], *s.m. Bot:* pappus.

pappeux, -euse [pap(p)ø, -øːz], *a. Bot:* pappose, downy.

pappifère [pap(p)ifɛːr], *a. Bot:* pappiferous.

paprika [paprika], *s.m. Bot: Cu:* paprika.

papule [papyl], *s.f.* **1.** *Med:* papula, papule; *F:* pimple; weal (of urticaria). **2.** *Bot:* papula, papule.

papuleux, -euse [papylø, -øːz], *a.* papulous, papulose; *F:* pimply.

papyracé [papirase], *a. Nat.Hist:* papyraceous, papery.

papyrologie [papirɔlɔʒi] *s.f.* papyrology.

papyrologique [papirɔlɔʒik], *a.* papyrological.

papyrologue [papirɔlɔg], *s.m. & f.* papyrologist.

papyrus [papirys], *s.m.* papyrus.

pâque [pɑːk]. **1.** *s.f.* (*a*) (Jewish) Passover; **manger la p.,** to eat the Passover, the paschal lamb; (*b*) *A:* **la grande P.,** Easter. **2.** (*a*) *s.f.pl.* **Pâques,** Easter; **joyeuses Pâques,** happy Easter; **faire ses Pâques,** to perform one's Easter duties, to take the sacrament at Easter; **Pâques fleuries,** Palm Sunday; *A:* **Pâques closes,** Quasimodo, Low Sunday; (*b*) *s.m.* (*contraction of* **jour de Pâques,** *used without article*) **Pâques,** Easter; **à Pâques prochain,** next Easter; **la semaine de Pâques,** Easter week; **le lundi de Pâques,** Easter Monday; **œufs de Pâques,** Easter eggs; *Geog:* **île de Pâques,** Easter Island; *Bot: F:* **fleur, herbe, de Pâques,** pasque flower; *F:* **remettre qch. à Pâques ou à la Trinité,** to put sth. off indefinitely; *F:* **faire Pâques avant les Rameaux,** to consummate a marriage before the ceremony.

paquebot [pakbo], *s.m. Nau:* (*a*) *A:* (steam-) packet; (*b*) (passenger and mail) steamer; **p. mixte,** passenger and cargo boat; (*c*) **p. (transatlantique),** (transatlantic) liner.

paquebot-poste [pakbopɔst], *s.m.* mail boat, mail steamer; *pl. paquebots-poste.*

paquer [pake], *v.tr.* to barrel (salt fish).

pâquerette [pɑkrɛt], *s.f. Bot:* daisy.

paquet [pakɛ], *s.m.* **1.** (*a*) parcel, packet; package; bundle; **p. de gens,** group of people; **p. de linge,** bundle of linen; **p. de lettres, de papiers,** packet, bundle, of letters, of papers; **faire un p.,** to make up, tie up, a parcel; to tie up a bundle; **expédier un p. par la poste,** to post a parcel; **p. de cigarettes, de lessive,** packet of cigarettes, of washing powder; **p. de bananes,** hand of bananas; **faire son p., ses paquets,** (i) to pack one's bags, to get ready to leave; (ii) to prepare for death; *F:* **prier la bonne de faire ses paquets,** to give the maid the sack; *F:* **donner son p. à qn,** (i) to give s.o. the sack; (ii) to give s.o. a piece of one's mind; **faire des paquets sur, contre, qn,** to speak ill of s.o.; **il a eu son p.,** I told him what I thought of him; **recevoir son p.,** to receive a reprimand; *F:* **porter son p.,** to be humpbacked; *Fin:* **p. d'actions,** parcel of shares; **ventes par petits paquets,** trickling sales, trickle of sales; **par petits paquets,** in driblets; *F:* **vous avez touché un joli p.,** you've made a nice bit; *F:* **il a perdu un p.,** he's dropped a packet; *F:* **risquer le p.,** (i) to risk it; to stick one's neck out; (ii) to go the whole hog; *F:* **mettre le p.,** to go all out; to pull out all the stops; **p. de neige,** heap of snow; snowdrift; **des paquets d'eau qui tombaient,** sheets of rain coming down; *Nau:* **p. de mer,** heavy sea, green sea; **embarquer un p. de mer,** to ship a (green) sea; *F:* **il a reçu le p. sur la tête,** he got the lot on his head; (*of pers.*) **quel p.!** (i) what a lump! (ii) *A:* what a clumsy lout! **c'est un p. de nerfs,** he's a bundle of nerves; **c'est un p. d'os,** he's all skin and bone; *A:* **avoir un p. sur la conscience,** to have a load on one's conscience; **avoir son p.,**

(i) to meet with disappointment; (ii) to be (thoroughly) drunk; to have a skinful, as much as one can carry; (b) *Rugby Fb:* pack; (c) *Typ:* **p. de composition,** parcel of type; take; (d) *A:* newly-born child; *P:* **elle va bientôt déposer son p.,** her baby's due any minute now, she'll drop it any time now. 2. *A:* (a) letters, mail; (b) mail boat, packet. 3. *Metall:* faggot.

paquetage [pakta:ʒ], *s.m.* 1. (a) parcelling; making up into packages; *Typ:* parcelling of type; (b) *Metall:* faggotting. 2. *Mil: etc:* (soldier's) pack; **faire son p.,** to stack one's kit.

paqueter [pakte], *v.tr.* (je paquette, n. paquetons; je paquetterai) 1. (a) to do (sth.) up into a parcel, into parcels; to parcel (sth.) up; (b) *Ind:* to bale; **presse à p.,** baling press. 2. *Metall:* to faggot. 3. *A:* (a) to put (s.o.) in bonds; to imprison (s.o.); (b) to incite (public) opinion against (s.o.).

paqueteur, -euse [paktœ:r, -ø:z], *s. Com: Ind:* packer.

paquetier [paktje], *s.m. Typ:* piece hand.

paqueur, -eresse [pakœ:r, -ərɛs], *s.* packer (of salt fish in barrels).

pâquis [paki], *s.m.* pasture.

par [par], *prep.* 1. (a) (*in relations of place*) **on y arrive p. un escalier,** the place is reached by a flight of stairs; **sa haute noblesse p. sa mère,** his high lineage on his mother's side; **jeter qch., regarder, p. la fenêtre,** to throw something, to look, out of the window; **il entra p. la fenêtre,** he came in at, through, the window; **p. mer et p. terre,** by land and sea; **p. monts et p. vaux,** over hill and dale; **il court p. les rues,** he runs about the streets; **p. tout le pays,** throughout, all over, the country; **se promener p. tout Paris,** to walk all over Paris; **p. latitude 10° nord,** in latitude 10° North; **passer p. Calais,** to travel by, via, Calais; **venez p. ici, allez p. là,** come this way, go that way; **c'est p. ici,** this is the way, it's this way; **p. où a-t-il passé?** which way did he go? how did he escape? *Geom:* **mener une tangente p. un point extérieur,** to draw a tangent through an exterior point; (b) (*in relations of time*) **p. un jour d'hiver,** on a winter's day; **c'était p. une belle journée de printemps,** it was on a fine day in spring; **mettez votre pardessus, p. le froid qu'il fait,** put on your overcoat in this cold weather; **ne sortez pas p. cette pluie, p. cette chaleur,** don't go out in this rain, in this heat; **p. temps de brume,** in foggy weather; **p. le passé,** in the past; **je l'ai averti p. trois fois,** I warned him three times. 2. (a) (*showing the agent*) (i) (*with a passive verb*) **il a été puni p. son père,** he was punished by his father; **action exercée p. une assemblée,** corporate action implemented by an assembly; **accablé p. l'inquiétude,** overcome by, with, anxiety; (ii) (*with an active verb*) **faire qch. p. soi-même,** to do sth. unaided; to do sth. on one's own initiative; **j'ai appris par les Martin que vous étiez malade,** I heard through, from, the Martins that you were ill; **faire faire qch. par qn,** to have sth. done by s.o.; *Breed:* **Gladiateur p. Monarch et Gladia,** Gladiator by Monarch out of Gladia; (b) (*showing the means, instrument*) **il fut salué p. des acclamations,** he was hailed with cheers; **réussir p. l'intrigue,** to succeed through intrigue; **il ne voit que p. tes yeux, il n'entend que p. tes oreilles,** he sees only through your eyes, he hears only through your ears; **attacher qch. p. une chaîne,** to fasten sth. by means of, with, a chain; **conduire qn p. la main,** to lead s.o. by the hand; **prendre qn p. le bras,** to take s.o. by the arm; **envoyer qch. p. la poste,** to send sth. by post, through the post; **je suis venu p. le train, p. le car,** I came by train, by bus; **je le jure p. le Styx,** I swear it by the Styx; **dame remarquable p. sa beauté,** lady remarkable for her beauty; **admirable p. la qualité,** admirable in quality; **bon p. nature,** kind by nature; **l'enfant qu'elle était p. nature sinon p. son âge,** the child she was by nature though not in years; **équation vraie p. elle-même,** equation true in itself; **appeler qn p. son nom,** to call s.o. by his name; (c) (*emphatic*) **vous êtes p. trop aimable,** you are far too kind; **il s'en assura p. lui-même,** he made sure of it on his own account; **j'ai connu cette existence p. moi-même,** I have personal knowledge of this kind of life; **examiner, juger, qch. p. soi-même,** to examine, judge, sth. (for) oneself. 3. (*showing cause, motive*) **faire qch. p. négligence, p. habitude, p. passe-temps,** to do sth. through carelessness, out of habit, by way of diversion; **j'ai fait cela p. amitié, p. respect, pour vous,** I did it out of friendship, out of respect, for you; **p.**

pitié! for pity's sake! **faire qch. p. pitié,** to do sth. out of pity; **je l'ai fait p. jeu,** I did it as a joke, for fun; **p. hasard,** by chance; **p. bonheur,** by good fortune; **il l'a épousée p. amour,** he married her for love. 4. (*distributive*) **p. ordre alphabétique,** in alphabetical order; **entrer deux p. deux,** to come in two by two, by twos, in twos; **je surveille sa conduite jour p. jour,** I watch his conduct day by day; **aller p. deux et trois, p. groupes de deux ou trois,** to go in twos and threes; **trois fois p. jour,** three times a day; **une fois p. dix années,** once in ten years; **mille francs p. an,** a thousand francs a year, per annum; **gagner tant p. semaine,** to earn so much per week, so much a week; **on les a p. douzaines, p. vingtaines,** they can be got, had, by dozens, by the score; *Post:* **au-dessus, p. 50 grammes . . .,** for each additional 50 grammes . . .; **attendre p. petits groupes,** to wait in small groups; **un guide p. groupe de six,** one guide per group of six, for each group of six; **couper qch. p. morceaux,** to cut sth. into pieces, to cut sth. up. 5. **p. + inf.** (a) (*after verbs of beginning and ending*) **commencer, débuter, finir, achever, terminer, p. faire qch.,** to begin, end, by doing sth.; (b) (*very occ. with other verbs*) **il se fatigue p. trop écrire,** he tires himself with writing too much; *Lit:* **l'amour ne cesse de se sauver p. aimer encore mieux ce qu'il aime,** love is for ever effecting its own salvation by loving still better the object of its love. 6. *adv.phr.* **p.-ci p.-là,** (i) hither and thither; (ii) now and then, at odd times; **c'est Charles p.-ci, Charles p.-là,** it's Charles here and Charles there. 7. *prep.phr.* **de p.** (a) **de p. le monde,** (i) somewhere in the world; (ii) throughout the world; (b) (= *A:* **de part**) **de p. le Roi,** by order of the King, in the name of the King; **promue à l'aristocratie de p. les millions de son père,** promoted to the aristocracy on the strength of her father's millions; **de p. la façon dont il s'y prend, on voit bien que . . .,** from his way of setting about it, one can see that . . .; **Dieu, de p. sa nature même, ne peut se tromper,** God, by His very nature, cannot err; **de p. les stipulations du traité,** by the stipulations of the treaty.

par(a)- [par(a)], *pref.* par(a)-.

Para¹ [para]. 1. *Pr.n.m. Geog:* Para. 2. *s.m.* Para rubber.

para², *s.m. Num:* para.

para³, *s.m. F: Mil:* paratrooper.

para-axial, -aux [paraaksjal, -o], *a. Opt:* paraaxial.

parabanique [parabanik], *a. Ch:* parabanic.

parabase [paraba:z], *s.f. Gr.Th:* parabasis.

parabellum [parabɛl(l)ɔm], *s.m. Sm.a:* automatic pistol.

parabenzène [parabɛ̃zɛn], *s.m. Ch:* parabenzene.

parabiose [parabjo:z], *s.f. Biol:* parabiosis.

parablaste [parablast], *s.m. Biol:* parablast.

parabole [parabɔl], *s.f.* 1. parable; **parler en, par, paraboles,** to speak in parables; **les Paraboles de Salomon,** the Book of Proverbs. 2. *Geom:* parabola.

parabolicité [parabɔlisite], *s.f.* parabolicness; **p. d'un miroir,** parabolic form of a mirror.

parabolique [parabɔlik], *a.* parabolic(al); (a) **enseignement p.,** teaching by parables; (b) *Geom:* **ligne p.,** parabolic line; **radiateur p.,** parabolic reflector; **miroir p.,** parabolic mirror; (*of spacecraft*) **vitesse p.,** parabolic velocity, escape velocity.

paraboliquement [parabɔlikmɑ̃], *adv. Lit: Geom:* parabolically.

paraboliser [parabɔlize], *v.tr. Opt:* to parabolize (mirror, etc.).

paraboloïdal, -aux [parabɔlɔidal, -o], *a. Mth:* paraboloidal.

paraboloïde [parabɔlɔid]. 1. *s.m. Geom:* paraboloid. 2. *a. Elcs:* **antenne p.,** dish aerial, antenna.

paraboulie [parabuli], *s.f. Psy:* parabulia.

parabuée [parabɥe], *s.f. O:* demister, anticondensation compound.

paracaséine [parakazein], *s.f. Bio-Ch:* paracasein.

Paracelse [parasɛls], *Pr.n.m.* Paracelsus.

paracentèse [parasɑ̃tɛ:z], *s.f. Surg:* paracentesis.

paracentral, -aux [parasɑ̃tral, -o], *a. Anat:* paracentral (lobe, etc.).

paracentrique [parasɑ̃trik], *a. Mth: Mec:* paracentric (curve, motion).

paracéphale [parasefal], *s.m. Ter:* paracephalus.

parachevable [paraʃvabl], *a.* perfectible.

parachèvement [paraʃɛvmɑ̃], *s.m.* finishing, completion; perfecting.

parachever [paraʃve], *v.tr.* (*conj. like* ACHEVER) to complete; to carry (sth.) through (to the end); to finish (sth.) off; to perfect; *Ind:* **p. la teinture,** to give the last dye.

parachor [parakɔ:r], *s.m. Ch:* parachor.

parachronisme [parakrɔnism], *s.m.* parachronism.

parachutage [paraʃyta:ʒ], *s.m.* parachute landing (of men, supplies); parachuting, dropping (by parachute), parachute drop, *U.S:* paradrop; baling out.

parachute [paraʃyt], *s.m.* 1. *Aer:* parachute; **p. dorsal,** back(-pack) parachute; **p. de poitrine,** chest-pack parachute; **p. ventral,** lap-pack parachute; **p. siège,** seat-pack parachute; **p. d'extraction,** pilot parachute; **ceinture, harnais, de p., parachute harness; corde d'ouverture de p.,** (parachute) rip cord; **p. (à ouverture) automatique,** self-opening parachute; **sangle d'ouverture automatique du p.,** (parachute) static line; **sac de p.,** parachute pack; **saut en p.,** parachute jump; **saut en p. avec ouverture retardée,** delayed jump; **sauter en p.,** to jump, to make a parachute jump, to bale out; **descente en p.,** parachute descent; **descendre en p.,** to parachute down; *Av:* **p. de freinage, p. de queue,** parachute brake, brake (para)chute, tail (para)chute. 2. **p. de mine,** safety device, safety clutch, safety brake (of pitshaft cage). 3. shock protector (of watch). 4. *A:* baby walker, go cart.

parachuter [paraʃyte], *v.tr. & i.* (a) to parachute, to drop by parachute, *U.S:* to paradrop; **il fut parachuté en France durant l'occupation,** he was dropped (by parachute) in France during the occupation; (b) *v.tr. F:* to pitchfork (s.o. into a job).

parachutisme [paraʃytism], *s.m.* parachuting.

parachutiste [paraʃytist]. 1. *s.m. & f.* parachutist. 2. *s.m.* paratrooper; *pl.* parachutistes, paratroops. 3. *a.* parachute; **détachements parachutistes,** parachute detachments; **troupes parachutistes,** parachute troops, paratroops; **sport p.,** parachuting.

paraclase [parakla:z], *s.f. Geol:* fault.

Paraclet (le) [ləparaklɛ], *s.m. Theol:* the Paraclete, the Holy Ghost, the Comforter.

paraclose [paraklo:z], *s.f. Nau:* panneaux de p., limber boards, limber plates.

paracousie [parakuzi], *s.f. Med:* paracusia.

paracrésol [parakrezɔl], *s.m. Ch:* paracresol.

paracyanogène [parasjanɔʒɛn], *s.m. Ch:* paracyanogen.

paracyste [parasist], *s.m.* paracyst.

parade¹ [parad], *s.f.* 1. *Equit:* stopping, checking, pulling up (of horse). 2. *Mil:* parade (for guard, etc.); guard mounting; **faire la p.,** to parade; **marcher au pas de p.,** (i) to march on parade, (ii) to march as if on parade; *P: A:* **défiler la p.,** to die; *Navy:* **faire parade,** to dress ship. 3. (a) (i) parade, show, ostentation; *Orn:* display; (ii) pomp and circumstance; **faire p. de ses bijoux,** to display, show off, one's jewels; **faire p. d'érudition,** to make a show, a parade, of learning; **il aime à faire p. de ses connaissances,** he is fond of airing, parading, his knowledge; **patriotisme de p.,** showy patriotism, all-on-the-surface patriotism; **habits de p.,** full-dress clothes; **lit de p.,** bed for lying in state; (*of body*) **être exposé sur un lit de p.,** to lie in state; (b) **p. de saltimbanques,** outside show, knockabout turn, given by travelling show, etc. (before performance inside the booth).

parade², *s.f.* 1. *Fenc:* parade, parry; *Box:* parry; **être prompt à la p.,** (i) to be quick at parrying; (ii) to be sharp at repartee; **il n'est pas heureux à la p.,** he is not good at repartee. 2. **la p. aux mines magnétiques fut trouvée en peu de semaines,** the answer to magnetic mines was found within a few weeks.

parader [parade], *v.i.* 1. (a) *Mil:* to parade; to go on parade; **faire p. des troupes,** to parade troops; (b) **faire p. un cheval,** to put a horse through its paces. 2. to make a display; *F:* to show off; *Orn:* to display; *F:* **p. sur les boulevards,** to strut about, show off, on the boulevards, to parade about the boulevards.

paradesmose [paradɛsmo:z], *s.f. Biol:* paradesmose.

paradeur, -euse [paradœ:r, -ø:z], *s.* ostentatious person, *F:* show-off.

paradiaphonie [paradjafɔni], *s.f. Tg:* conversation originating from crossed lines.

paradichlorobenzène [paradiklɔrɔbɛ̃zɛn], *s.m. Ch:* paradichlorobenzene.

paradigmatique [paradigmatik], *a. Ling:* paradigmatic.

paradigme [paradigm], *s.m. Ling:* paradigm.

paradis [paradi], *s.m.* paradise. **1. le P. terrestre,** the earthly paradise, the garden of Eden. **2. aller en p.,** to go to heaven, go to paradise; **c'est le p. sur terre,** it is heaven on earth, an earthly paradise; **le chemin du p.,** the narrow way; *F:* **faire son p. en, de, ce monde,** to lead a life of pleasure; *F:* **il ne l'emportera pas en p.** I'll be even with him yet; he won't get away with it; he'll have to pay for it; *O:* **sur ma part du p., je dis vrai,** as I hope to be saved, I am telling the truth; *Th: F: O:* **le p.,** the gallery, the gods; *Orn:* **oiseau de p.,** bird of paradise. **3.** *Hort:* paradise (apple).

paradiséidés [paradizeide], *s.m.pl. Orn:* Paradisaeidae, the birds of paradise.

paradisiaque [paradizjak], *a.* paradisiac(al), paradisaic(al), paradisial; **vallée d'une beauté p.,** valley of paradisiac beauty; **les joies paradisiaques,** the joys of paradise.

paradisier [paradizje], *s.m.* **1.** *Orn:* bird of paradise; **p. papou,** great bird of paradise; **p. de l'Empereur Guillaume,** Emperor William's bird of paradise; **p. de Rodolphe,** Prince Rudolph's bird of paradise; **p. magnifique,** magnificent bird of paradise. **2.** *Ich:* paradise fish.

paradiste [paradist], *s.m.* clown, mountebank (performing outside his booth).

parados [parado], *s.m. Fort:* parados.

paradoxal, -aux [paradɔksal, -o], *a.* paradoxical; **il serait p. qu'il votât avec la Gauche,** it would be paradoxical on his part to vote with the Left; *Med:* **pouls p.,** pulsus paradoxus.

paradoxalement [paradɔksalmɑ̃], *adv.* paradoxically.

paradoxe [paradɔks], *s.m.* paradox.

paradoxides [paradɔksidɛs], *s.m. Paleont:* Paradoxides.

paradoxologie [paradɔksɔlɔʒi], *s.f.* paradoxology.

paradoxure [paradɔksyːr], *s.m. Z:* paradoxure, palm cat, palm civet.

parafe [paraf], *s.m.* (*a*) paraph; flourish (following signature); (*b*) initials (of one's name); **mettre son p. au bas d'un acte,** to initial a document.

parafer [parafe], *v.tr.* to sign one's initials on, to put one's initials to, to initial (document); **p. une rectification,** to initial an alteration.

paraffènes [parafɛn], *s.m.pl. Ch:* (the) paraffin series.

paraffinage [parafinaːʒ], *s.m.* paraffining, oiling with paraffin.

paraffine [parafin], *s.f. Ch:* paraffin; *Com:* paraffin (wax); **p. amorphe,** petrolatum; **p. huileuse,** slack wax; **huile de p.,** liquid paraffin.

paraffiner [parafine], *v.tr.* to paraffin; to wax.

paraffineux, -euse [parafinø, -øːz], *a.* **distillat p.,** paraffin distillate.

paraffinique [parafinik], *a. Ch:* paraffinic; **carbures paraffiniques,** paraffin hydrocarbons.

parafiscal [parafiskal], *a. Adm:* **taxe parafiscale,** exceptional tax; special levy.

parafiscalité [parafiskalite], *s.f. Adm:* special levies.

paraformaldéhyde [parafɔrmaldeid], *s.m.,* **paraforme** [parafɔrm], *s.m. Ch:* paraform, paraformaldehyde.

parafoudre [parafudr̥], *s.m. El:* (*a*) lightning arrester, lightning protector (for electrical apparatus); **p. à cornes,** horn-type lightning arrester; *s.a.* SOUFFLAGE; (*b*) safety gap, spark arrester (of magneto, etc.).

parafouille [parafuːj], *s.f. Hyd.E:* cut-off (wall, etc.).

parage[1] [paraːʒ], *s.m. A:* birth, descent, parage; **personne de haut p.,** person of quality, of high degree, of high lineage.

parage[2], *s.m.* (*a*) paring, trimming (of iron, etc.); (*b*) *Tex:* dressing, sizing (of cloth); (*c*) *Vit:* dressing of the ground (before the winter); (*d*) trimming (of joints of meat).

parage[3], *s.m. usu. pl.* (*a*) *Nau:* sea area; stretch of ocean; **les parages du cap Horn,** the waters off Cape Horn; **parages des pilotes,** waters in which vessels require a pilot; (*b*) *always pl.* **dans les parages de . . .,** in the vicinity of, near . . .; **que faites-vous dans ces parages?** what are you are doing (around) here? in these parts?

paragénèse [paraʒenɛːz], *s.f. Biol: Geol:* paragenesis.

paragénésie [paraʒenezi], *s.f. Biol:* paragenesis.

paraglace [paraglas], *s.m. Nau:* ice fender.

paraglosse [paraglɔs], *s.m. Ent:* paraglossa.

paragneiss [paragnɛs], *s.m. Geol:* paragneiss.

paragnosie [paragnozi], *s.f. Med:* paragnosia.

paragoge [paragɔːʒ], *s.f. Gram:* paragoge.

paragogique [paragɔʒik], *a. Gram:* paragogic (letter, syllable).

paragonite [paragɔnit], *s.f. Miner:* paragonite.

paragramme [paragram], *s.m.* paragram.

paragraphe [paragraf], *s.m.* **1.** paragraph; *Jur: etc:* sub-clause (of contract, etc.); **diviser un chapitre en paragraphes,** to divide a chapter into paragraphs. **2.** section mark, paragraph.

paragraphie [paragrafi], *s.f. Med:* paragraphia.

paragrêle [paragrɛl], *a.inv. & s.m.* **(canon) p.,** gun discharged against hail clouds; **fusée p.,** cloud-dispersing charge.

Paraguay [paragwɛ], *Pr.n.m. Geog:* Paraguay (river or republic).

paraguayen, paraguéen, -enne [parag(w)ɛjɛ̃, -ɛn], *a. & s. Geog:* Paraguayan.

parahydrogène [paraidrɔʒɛn], *s.m. Ch:* parahydrogen.

paraison [parɛzɔ̃], *s.f. Glassm:* parison; ball (of molten glass); **moule p.,** parison mould.

paraître [parɛtr̥], *v.i.* (*pr.p.* **paraissant;** *p.p.* **paru;** *pr.ind.* **je parais, il paraît, n. paraissons;** *p.d.* **je paraissais;** *p.h.* **je parus;** *fu.* **je paraîtrai**) to appear. **1.** (*a*) to make one's appearance; (*of land, ship*) to heave in sight, to come up; (*of star, moon, etc.*) to appear, come out; (*of actor*) to appear, come on; **le jour commençait à p.,** the day was dawning; **un sourire parut sur ses lèvres,** a smile came to his lips; **ces bohémiens paraissent et disparaissent,** these gipsies come and go; **une croix parut à Jeanne dans l'air,** a cross appeared to Joan in the air; **p. chez qn,** to put in an appearance, *F:* to turn up, at s.o.'s house; **je ne veux pas p. dans l'affaire,** I don't want to appear in the business; *impers.* **il a paru des hommes qui . . .,** men have appeared who . . .; (*b*) (*of book, etc.*) to be published, to come out; (*of periodical*) to appear, to come out; **faire p. un livre,** to publish, bring out, a book; **le livre a paru hier,** the book came out yesterday; **le livre est déjà paru,** the book is already published, is already out, is in print; **sur le point de p.,** just ready; **vient de p.,** just out, just published; **un nouveau quotidien paraîtra au mois de mars,** a new daily will appear in March. **2.** (*a*) to be visible, apparent; **cette tache paraît à peine,** the stain is hardly visible; the stain hardly shows; **laisser p. ses sentiments,** to show, betray, one's feelings; **il a plus de connaissances qu'il n'en laisse paraître,** he has more knowledge than he cares to show; *A:* **cela paraît comme le nez au visage,** it's as plain as the nose on your face, as plain as a pikestaff; **faire p. qch.,** to show, display, sth.; to bring sth. to light; **il a fait p. peu d'intelligence dans ce travail,** he displayed, showed, little intelligence, gave little evidence of intelligence, in this work; (*b*) **chercher à p.,** to show off; to make a display; (*c*) *impers.* **il y paraît,** that is easy to see; that is quite apparent; **il a trop bu et il y paraît à sa démarche,** he has drunk too much and it is evident from his walk; **je suis très mal.—il n'y paraît pas,** I am very ill.—you don't look it, one would not have thought it; **elle va mieux, dans trois jours il n'y paraîtra plus,** she's better, in three days there'll be no trace of it; **sans qu'il y paraisse,** without its being apparent, although one would not think so. **3.** to seem, to look; (*a*) **il paraît triste,** he looks sad; **elle paraissait avoir vingt ans,** she seemed, appeared, to be about twenty; **elle a quarante ans, mais elle ne les paraît pas,** she is forty, but she doesn't look it; **elle paraît son âge,** she looks her age; **au téléphone, ce soir, il paraissait furieux,** on the phone this evening he sounded furious; **l'endroit lui parut familier,** the place seemed familiar to him; **il me paraît filer un mauvais coton,** he looks to me as if he were in a bad way; (*b*) *impers.* **il paraît qu'elle fait des vers,** it seems she writes poetry; **il ne paraît pas qu'il ait jamais visité Londres,** it does not appear that he ever visited London; **il me paraît que . . .,** it seems to me, it strikes me, that . . .; **à ce qu'il paraît,** (i) apparently; (ii) apparently (so), it would seem so; **à ce qu'il me paraît,** as far as I can judge; **il paraît que oui,** so it appears; **il paraît que non,** it appears not, it seems not; (*c*) **être et p.,** *s.m.* **l'être et le p., sont deux,** being and seeming, reality and appearance, are two different things.

parakératose [parakeratoːz], *s.f. Med:* parakeratosis.

parakinésie [parakinezi], *s.f. Med:* parakinesia, parakinesis.

paralalie [paralali], *s.f. Med:* paralalia.

paralaurionite [paralɔrjɔnit], *s.f. Miner:* paralaurionite.

paraldéhyde [paraldeid], *s.m. Ch:* paraldehyde.

paralexie [paralɛksi], *s.f. Med:* paralexia.

Paralipomènes (les) [leparalipɔmɛn], *s.m.pl. B.Lit:* the Paralipomena, (the Books of) Chronicles.

paralipse [paralips], *s.f. Rh:* paral(e)ipsis.

parallactique [paral(l)aktik], *a. Astr:* parallactic (angle, etc.).

parallaxe [paral(l)aks], *s.f. Astr: Opt: etc:* parallax; **sans p.,** parallax-free; **correction de p.,** correction for parallax; *Artil:* apex angle, displacement angle; **p. diurne,** diurnal parallax, geocentric parallax; **p. horizontale,** horizontal parallax; *T.V:* **p. de temps,** time parallax.

parallèle [paral(l)ɛl]. **1.** *a.* (*a*) **lignes parallèles,** parallel lines; *Gym:* **barres parallèles,** parallel bars; *Mch.-Tls:* **tour p.,** parallel lathe; **être p. à . . .,** to run parallel to, with . . .; **rue qui est p. à la rivière,** street that runs parallel to, with, the river; (*b*) similar; **mener une action p.,** to act with the same end in view; to carry out a parallel, a similar, action; to follow a similar course; (*c*) unofficial; **police p.,** unofficial police; *Fin: Pol.Ec:* **taux de change, marché, p.,** unofficial, illegal, rate of exchange, market. **2.** *s.f.* (*a*) *Mth:* parallel line, parallel; **tirer une p. au bord de la feuille,** to draw a parallel, a line parallel, to the edge of the sheet; (*b*) *Fort:* parallel (trench); **p. de départ,** trench, parallel, from which the assault, the attack, is made; (*c*) *El:* **en p.,** parallel, shunt; **alimentation en p.,** shunt feed; **couplage, montage, en p.,** parallel connection; **batteries en p.,** batteries in parallel; **résistance en p.,** shunt resistance. **3.** *s.m.* (*a*) *Geog:* parallel (of latitude); **situé sur le p. de . . .,** on the parallel of . . .; at latitude . . .; (*b*) comparison, parallel; **mettre qn en p. avec qn,** to compare s.o. with s.o.; **établir un p. entre . . . et . . .,** to draw a parallel between . . . and . . .; **Bible avec parallèles,** reference Bible; (*c*) **en p.,** at the same time, concurrently. **4.** *s.m. A:* parallel ruler, parallel rule.

parallèlement [paral(l)ɛlmɑ̃], *adv.* in a parallel direction (à, to, with); concurrently; **murs construits p.,** walls built parallel; **l'industrie suit p. la marche de la science,** the progress of science and industry follow a parallel course.

parallélépipède [paral(l)elepipɛd], *s.m. Geom:* parallelepiped.

parallélépipédique [paral(l)elepipedik], *a.* parallelepipedal, parallelepipedic.

parallélinervé [paral(l)elinɛrve], *a. Bot:* parallelinervate, parallelinerved.

parallélisation [paral(l)elizasjɔ̃], *s.f.* parallelization.

paralléliser [paral(l)elize], *v.tr.* (*a*) *Geom:* to make (lines) parallel; (*b*) to parallel, compare.

parallélisme [paral(l)elism], *s.m.* **1.** parallelism **(entre qch. et qch., de qch. à qch.,** between sth. and sth.); *Aut: Av:* **p. des roues,** wheel alignment; **vérifier le p. des roues,** to check the (wheel) alignment. **2.** *Phil:* parallelism.

paralléliste [paral(l)elist], *Phil:* **1.** *a.* parallelistic. **2.** *s.m. & f.* parallelist.

parallélogrammatique [paral(l)elɔgramatik], *a. Geom:* parallelogrammatic.

parallélogramme [paral(l)elɔgram], *s.m. Geom:* parallelogram; *Mec:* **p. des forces, des vitesses,** parallelogram of forces, of velocities; **p. articulé,** parallel motion.

paralogie [paralɔʒi], *s.f. Gram:* paralogy.

paralogisme [paralɔʒism], *s.m. Log:* paralogism, fallacious argument, fallacy.

paralume [paralym], *s.m. Ill:* diffuser.

paraluminite [paralyminit], *s.f. Miner:* paraluminite.

paralysant [paralizɑ̃], **paralysateur, -trice** [paralizatœːr, -tris], *a. Med: etc:* paralysing; **agent p.,** paralyser.

paralyser [paralize], *v.tr.* to paralyse; (*a*) *Med:* to affect with paralysis; **paralysé des deux jambes,** paralysed in both legs; (*b*) to paralyse, incapacitate; **lois qui paralysent l'industrie,** laws that cripple industry; **paralysé par l'effroi,** paralysed, helpless, with fear; **paralysé par la grève, par le brouillard,** strike-bound, fog-bound; (*c*) *Physiol: Med:* to inhibit (secretions, etc.).

paralysie [paralizi], *s.f.* (*a*) *Med:* paralysis; **p. agitante,** paralysis agitans, Parkinson's disease; **p. bilatérale,** diplegia, bilateral paralysis; **p. alterne,** hemiplegia; **p. (générale) progressive,** creeping paralysis; **p. générale,** (general) paresis, general paralysis; **p. pseudo-bulbaire,** pseudobulbar paralysis; *A:* **p. infantile,** infantile paralysis; **il tomba, frappé de p.,** he fell (to the ground), seized by a paralytic stroke; (*b*) **la p. des transports,** paralysis of the transport system; **esprit qui subit une espèce de p. momentanée,** mind momentarily paralysed.

paralytique [paralitik], *a. & s. Med:* paralytic.
paramagnétique [paramaɲetik], *a. Ph:* paramagnetic.
paramagnétisme [paramaɲetism], *s.m. Ph:* paramagnetism.
paramastite [paramastit], *s.f. Med:* paramastitis.
Par(r)amatta [paramata]. 1. *Pr.n. Geog:* Parramatta. 2. *s.m. Tex:* Paramatta tweed.
paramécie [paramesi], *s.f. Prot:* paramecium; slipper animalcule.
paramédical, -aux [paramedikal, -o], *a.* **services paramédicaux,** ancillary medical services.
paramélaconite [paramelakɔnit], *s.f. Miner:* paramelaconite.
paramères [paramɛːr], *s.f.pl. Ent:* parameres.
paramètre[1] [paramɛtr̥], *s.m. Mth:* parameter; *Av:* **p. de similitude,** advance diameter ratio (of propeller).
paramètre[2], *s.m. Anat:* parametrium.
paramétrique [parametrik], *a. Mth:* parametric, parametral.
paramétrite [parametrit], *s.f. Med:* parametritis.
paramidophénol [paramidɔfenɔl], **paraminophénol** [paraminɔfenɔl], *s.m. Ch:* paraminophenol.
paramilitaire [paramilitɛːr], *a.* paramilitary; **formations paramilitaires,** semi-military organizations (outside the regular army).
paramimie [paramimi], *s.f. Med:* paramimia.
paramnésie [paramnezi], *s.f. Med:* paramnesia.
paramorphique [paramɔrfik], *a. Miner:* paramorphic, paramorphous.
paramorphisme [paramɔrfism], *s.m.,* **paramorphose** [paramɔrfoːz], *s.f. Miner:* paramorphism, paramorphosis.
paramoustique [paramustik], *s.m. A:* anti-mosquito essence.
paramyotonie [paramjɔtɔni], *s.f. Med:* paramyotonia, paramyotone.
paraneige [paranɛːʒ], *s.m.* snow shield (over Alpine hut, railway).
parangon [parɑ̃gɔ̃], *s.m.* 1. *A:* comparison; **mettre deux choses en p.,** to compare two things. 2. paragon; (*a*) *A: & Lit:* pattern, model, type (of beauty, chivalry, etc.); **p. de vertu,** paragon of virtue; (*b*) diamond, precious stone without blemish. 3. *Typ:* **gros p.,** double pica; **petit p.,** two-line long primer.
parangonnage [parɑ̃gɔnaːʒ], *s.m. Typ:* justification (of different types).
parangonner [parɑ̃gɔne], *v.tr. Typ:* to justify (type, lines).
paranoïa [paranɔja], *s.f. Med:* paranoia.
paranoïaque [paranɔjak], *a. & s. Med:* paranoiac.
paranoïde [paranɔid], *a. Med:* paranoid.
paranthélie [parɑ̃teli], *s.f.* paranthelion.
paranthrope [parɑ̃trɔp], *s.m. Paleont:* paranthropus.
paranucléus [paranykleys], *s.m. Biol:* paranucleus.
parapet [parapɛ], *s.m.* parapet (of trench, bridge, etc.); *Fort:* breastwork; *A.Mil:* **franchir le p. (de la tranchée),** *F:* to go over the top.
paraphasie [parafazi], *s.f. Med:* paraphasia.
paraphasique [parafazik], *a. Med:* paraphasic.
paraphe [paraf], *s.m.* (*a*) paraph; flourish (following signature); (*b*) initials (of one's name).
parapher [parafe], *v.tr.* to sign one's initials on, to initial.
paraphernal, -aux [parafɛrnal, -o], *a. & s.m. Jur:* **(biens) paraphernaux,** wife's property (other than her dowry).
parapheur [parafœːr], *s.m.* file for letters awaiting signature.
paraphimosis [parafimozis], *s.m. Med:* paraphimosis.
paraphone [parafɔn], *a.* paraphonic.
paraphonie [parafɔni], *s.f. A.Gr.Mus: & Med:* paraphonia.
paraphrase [parafrɑːz], *s.f.* paraphrase; **sans tant de paraphrases,** without so much circumlocution; without so much beating about the bush.
paraphraser [parafrɑze], *v.tr.* (*a*) to paraphrase; (*b*) to expand, amplify, add to (story, speech).
paraphraseur, -euse [parafrɑzœːr, -øːz], *s.* paraphraser; verbose, *F:* long-winded, person.
paraphraste [parafrast], *s.m.* paraphrast.
paraphrastique [parafrastik], *a.* paraphrastic.
paraphrénie [parafreni], *s.f. Psy:* paraphrenia.
paraphyse [parafiːz], *s.f. Fung:* paraphysis.
paraplasme [paraplasm], *s.m. Biol:* paraplasm.
paraplégie [parapleʒi], *s.f. Med:* paraplegia; **p. spasmodique,** spastic paraplegia.
paraplégique [parapleʒik], *Med:* 1. *a.* paraplegic. 2. *s.m. & f.* paraplegic; **p. (spasmodique),** spastic.

parapluie [paraplɥi], *s.m.* 1. umbrella; **manche de p.,** umbrella stick; **carcasse, monture, de p.,** umbrella frame; **ouvrir son p.,** (i) to put up one's umbrella; (ii) *F:* to dodge one's responsibilities; *F:* **il a l'air d'avoir avalé un p.,** he looks as if he'd swallowed a poker. 2. *A:* **p. de chauffeur,** driver's waterproof coat. 3. *Tchn:* (*a*) *Metall:* splash board; (*b*) hood, rain cap (of chimney). 4. *Mil: Av:* **p. aérien,** aerial umbrella.
parapode [parapɔd], *s.m. Ann:* parapodium.
parapodie [parapɔdi], *s.f. Moll:* parapodium.
parapraxie [parapraksi], *s.f. Med:* parapraxia.
parapsychique [parapsiʃik], *a.* parapsychological.
parapsychisme [parapsiʃism], *s.m.,* **parapsychologie** [parapsikɔlɔʒi], *s.f.* parapsychology.
parasange [parasɑ̃ːʒ], *s.f. Meas:* parasang (of ancient Persia).
parascève [parasɛːv], *s.f.* (*a*) *Jew.Rel:* parasceve; (*b*) *R.C.Ch:* parasceve, Good Friday.
parascolaire [paraskɔlɛːr], *a.* extra-curricular.
parasélène [paraselɛn], *s.f. Meteor:* paraselene; mock moon.
parasexualité [parasɛksɥalite], *s.f.* parasexuality.
parasitage [parazitaːʒ], *s.m. El: W.Tel:* interference.
parasitaire [parazitɛːr], *a.* 1. *Med:* parasitic (disease). 2. *W.Tel:* **effet p.,** interference.
parasite [parazit]. 1. *s.m.* (*a*) *Biol:* parasite; **p. accidentel, permanent,** accidental, permanent, parasite; (*b*) parasite, hanger-on, sponger; **faire le, vivre en, p.,** to sponge; (*c*) *Elcs:* noise; *pl.* **parasites,** (i) *W.Tel: T.V:* interference; strays; (ii) (*radar*) clutter, *F:* grass; **parasites atmosphériques,** (i) *W.Tel:* atmospherics, statics; (ii) *T.V:* snow; **parasites dûs aux précipitations (atmosphériques),** precipitation statics; **sans parasites atmosphériques,** static(s)-free; **p. industriel,** man-made noise; (*radar*) **parasites dûs à la réflexion sur le sol, sur la mer,** ground clutter, return; sea clutter, return; **élimination des parasites,** (i) *W.Tel:* static(s) elimination, noise suppression; (ii) (*radar*) clutter elimination; **dispositif anti-parasites,** (i) *W.Tel:* interference, noise, eliminator, suppressor; (ii) (*radar*) anti-clutter device; **filtre anti-parasites,** (i) *W.Tel:* interference filter; (ii) (*radar*) anti-clutter device. 2. *a.* (*a*) *Biol:* parasitic (insect, plant, etc.); (*b*) extraneous; redundant (word, etc.); (*c*) *Elcs: Ph:* spurious (frequency, modulation, oscillation); parasitic (oscillation); **bruit p.,** parasitic, spurious, noise; (*radar*) **écho(s) parasite(s),** clutter; **écho(s) parasite(s) fixe(s),** permanent clutter; **écho(s) parasite(s) dû(s) à la pluie,** rain clutter; *Ph: etc:* **lumière, radiation, p.,** stray light, stray radiation; *El:* **courant p.,** stray current.
parasiter [parazite], *v.tr.* to parasitize; *Elcs: W.Tel:* to interfere.
parasiticide [parazitisid], *a. & s.* parasiticide; **onguent p.,** itch ointment; *Husb:* **bain p.,** sheep dip.
parasitique [parazitik], *a.* parasitical (habits, etc.).
parasitisme [parazitism], *s.m.* 1. parasitism, sponging (on others). 2. (*a*) *Biol:* parasitism; antagonistic symbiosis; (*b*) *Med:* parasitism (diseased state due to parasites).
parasitologie [parazitɔlɔʒi], *s.f.* parasitology.
parasitologiste [parazitɔlɔʒist], *s.m. & f.* parasitologist.
parasitose [parazitoːz], *s.f. Med:* parasitosis.
parasol [parasɔl], *s.m.* 1. (*a*) parasol, sunshade; beach umbrella; *Bot:* **fleur en p.,** umbellate flower; **magnolier (en) p.,** umbrella tree; **pin p.,** parasol pine, umbrella pine; (*b*) *Fung:* parasol mushroom. 2. (*a*) *Aut:* visor (over windscreen); (*b*) *Av:* parasol.
parasoleil [parasɔlɛːj], *s.m.* (*a*) sunshade (of telescope); (*b*) *Phot:* lens shade, lens hood.
parasolerie [parasɔlri], *s.f.* 1. umbrella trade. 2. umbrella factory.
parasolier [parasɔlje], *s.m. Bot: F:* umbrella tree.
parastatal [parastatal], *a.* (*in Belg.*) semi-public (institution, etc.).
parasurtension [parasyrtɑ̃sjɔ̃], *s.m. Rail:* surge absorber.
parasymbiose [parasɛ̃bjoːz], *s.f. Biol:* parasymbiosis.
parasympathique [parasɛ̃patik]. *Physiol:* 1. *a.* parasympathetic. 2. *s.m.* parasympathetic (nerve).
parasympathomimétique [parasɛ̃patɔmimetik], *a. Med:* parasympathomimetic.
parasynapsis [parasinapsis], *s.f. Biol:* parasynapsis.
parasynthétique [parasɛ̃tetik], *a. Ling:* parasynthetic.

parasyphilitique [parasifilitik], *a. Med:* parasyphilitic (affection).
paratactique [parataktik], *a. Gram:* paratactic (construction).
parataxe [parataks], *s.f. Gram:* parataxis.
parathormone [paratɔrmɔn], *s.f. Bio-Ch:* parathormone.
parathyroïde [paratirɔid], *Anat:* 1. *a.* parathyroid. 2. *s.f.* parathyroid (gland).
parathyroïdectomie [paratirɔidɛktɔmi], *s.f. Surg:* parathyroidectomy.
parathyroïdien, -ienne [paratirɔidjɛ̃, -jɛn], *a.* parathyroid(al).
paratonnerre [paratɔnɛːr], *s.m.* 1. lightning conductor, lightning rod. 2. *F:* (*pers.*) screen, decoy (*esp.* to divert the suspicions of a jealous husband).
parâtre [parɑtr̥], *s.m. O: Pej:* (*a*) stepfather; (*b*) unnatural father.
paratuberculeux, -euse [paratybɛrkylø, -øːz], *a.* paratuberculous.
paratuberculose [paratybɛrkyloːz], *s.f. Vet:* paratuberculosis, Johne's disease.
paratyphoïde [paratifɔid], *a. & s.f. Med:* paratyphoid (fever).
paravalanche [paravalɑ̃ːʃ], *s.m.* avalanche barrier.
paravane [paravan], *s.m. Navy:* paravane; **mettre à l'eau les paravanes,** to get out the paravanes.
paravent[1] [paravɑ̃], *s.m.* 1. (*a*) (draught) screen; folding screen; **papier à pliage p.,** fanfold paper; **comédie de p.,** play requiring virtually no scenery; (*b*) *F:* **Chinois de p.,** strange-looking person; figure of fun. 2. (*pers.*) screen; decoy.
paravent[2], *prep. A:* before; *conj.phr.* **p. que,** before; **p. qu'il soit peu,** ere long.
paraverse [paravɛrs], *s.m. Cost: A:* light-weight waterproof.
paravivipare [paravivipaːr], *a. Z:* paraviviparous.
paraxial, -aux [paraksjal, -o], *a.* paraxial.
paraxylène [paraksilɛn], *s.m. Ch:* paraxylene.
parbleu [parblø], *int.* (*attenuated form of* PARDIEU) good Lord, yes!
parc [park], *s.m.* 1. park; **p. national,** national park; nature reserve. 2. enclosure (for special purposes); **p. à voitures, p. de stationnement,** car park, *U.S:* parking lot; **p. pour chevaux,** paddock; **p. à bestiaux,** cattle pen; **p. à moutons,** sheep fold; **p. à huîtres,** oyster bed, park, oysterage; **p. à poisson,** fish pond (on trawler); **p. pour enfants,** play pen, nursery pen; *A:* **p. de combat de coqs,** cockpit; **mettre deux coqs en p.,** to pit two cocks; *Mil:* **p. d'artillerie,** artillery park; **p. à munitions,** ammunition depot; **p. à charbon,** coal depot; **p. aux combustibles,** fuel depot; **p. à mazout,** oil depot; *Petroleum Ind:* **p. à réservoirs, de stockage,** tank farm; *Rail:* **p. de wagons,** rolling-stock depot; *Nau: A:* **p. à boulets,** shot locker; **p. d'attractions,** fun fair. 3. fleet (of buses, cars, etc.); *Rail:* **p. ferroviaire,** rolling stock; **p. d'ordinateurs,** computer population, (total) number of computers in service; **le p. automobile français augmente de jour en jour,** the number of cars on the French roads is increasing daily; **le p. aérien français,** the French civil and military air forces. 4. **p. d'un navire,** waist of a ship.
parcage [parkaːʒ], *s.m.* 1. (*a*) parking (of cars); enclosing, penning (of cattle); folding (of sheep); laying down (of oysters); (*b*) car park, *U.S:* parking lot; (*c*) yardage (attached to factory, etc.). 2. manuring of ground by folding.
parcellaire [parsɛl(l)ɛːr], *a.* (*a*) divided into small portions, into parcels (of land); **cadastre p.,** *s.m.* **parcellaire,** detailed survey (of a commune); (*b*) **travail p.,** work divided into sections; **connaissance p. (d'un sujet),** compartmental knowledge (of a subject).
parcelle [parsɛl], *s.f.* (*a*) small fragment; particle (of gold, etc.); lot, plot, patch, parcel (of land); *For:* compartment (of forest); **thé sans une p. de sucre,** tea without a scrap of sugar; **il n'a pas la moindre p. de jugement,** he hasn't a particle, a scrap, of common sense; (*b*) **payer par parcelles,** to pay by small instalments.
parcellement [parsɛlmɑ̃], *s.m.* dividing (of land) into lots; parcelling (of land).
parceller [parsɛle], *v.tr.* to divide into small portions; to portion out (inheritance, etc.); **champ parcellé,** field divided into lots.
parce que [pars(ə)kə], (*a*) *conj.phr.* because; **je le dis parce que c'est vrai,** I say so because it is true; (*b*) *s.m.inv.* **des pourquoi et des parce que,** whys and wherefores.
parchemin [parʃəmɛ̃]. 1. *s.m.* (*a*) parchment; *Bookb: usu.* vellum; **p. en cosse,** rough vellum; *Bookb:* **p. de peau de mouton,** for(r)el; **visage de p.,** wizened, shrivelled, parchment-like, face;

manuscrit sur p., parchment manuscript; *F:* **allonger, étendre, le p.**, to pile up legal expenses; *Med:* **bruit de p.**, dry-leather creaking; (*b*) *pl.* title deeds, titles of nobility; diplomas; **être fier de ses parchemins**, to be proud of one's antecedents. **2. papier p.**, vegetable parchment, parchment paper. **3.** parchment (of coffee bean, etc.).

parcheminé [parʃəmine], *a.* (*a*) parchment-like, dried (skin, etc.); **sa joue parcheminée**, her shrivelled, wizened, cheek; (*b*) **papier p.**, parchment paper.

parcheminer [parʃəmine], *v.tr.* to give a parchment finish to (paper).

se parcheminer, to shrivel up; (*of the skin*) to become shrivelled; to take on an appearance of parchment.

parcheminerie [parʃəminri], *s.f.* **1.** (*a*) parchment making; (*b*) parchment trade. **2.** parchment factory.

parchemineux, -euse [parʃəminø, -øːz], *a.* parchment-like.

parcheminier, -ière [parʃəminje, -jɛːr], *s.* (*a*) parchment manufacturer; (*b*) dealer in parchment.

par-ci par-là [parsiparla], *adv.phr.* (*a*) here and there; hither and thither; *F:* all over the place; (*b*) now and then; at odd times.

parcimonie [parsimɔni], *s.f.* parsimony, excessive economy, meanness; **avec p.**, parsimoniously.

parcimonieusement [parsimɔnjøzmɑ̃], *adv.* parsimoniously, charily; in a mean way; **distribuer qch. p.**, to dole sth. out; **il va falloir vivre p.**, we shall have to live very carefully, consider every penny.

parcimonieux, -euse [parsimɔnjø, -øːz], *a.* parsimonious, mean, niggardly; **p. de louanges**, chary, sparing, of praise.

parclose [parkloːz], *s.f.* **1.** *Arch:* (wood) panel. **2.** *Veh:* *Furn:* seat framing. **3.** *pl.* *Nau:* limber boards, limber plates.

parcomètre [parkɔmɛtr̥], *s.m.* parking meter.

parcoriser [parkɔrize], *v.tr.* *Bookb:* to gather (the folded sections prior to binding).

parcourir [parkuriːr], *v.tr.* (*conj. like* COURIR) **1.** to travel through, go over (a stretch of country); **p. toutes les rues de la ville**, to wander through every street of the town; **p. une distance de plusieurs kilomètres**, to cover a distance of several kilometres; **nous avons parcouru pas mal de terrain**, we've covered, got over, a good deal of ground; **p. la campagne**, to scour the countryside; **on parcourt des kilomètres sans voir autre choses que des arbres**, you go for miles without seeing anything but trees; **un frisson me parcourut**, a shiver went through me; **p. les mers**, to sail the seas; **distance parcourue**, distance travelled, covered; (day's) run. **2.** to examine (cursorily); **p. qch. des yeux, du regard**, to glance at, over, sth.; **p. un livre**, to glance, skim, through a book; **p. une liste**, to look down a list; **parcourons ces pièces ensemble**, let's go over, run through, these documents together; **son regard parcourut l'horizon**, his eyes swept the horizon; *Nau:* **p. les coutures d'un navire**, to overhaul, run over, the seams of a ship.

parcours [parkuːr], *s.m.* **1.** (*a*) distance covered; **p. d'une conduite**, length, run, of a pipe line; **p. journalier d'un autobus**, daily mileage of a bus; **p. de 10 kilomètres**, run of 10 kilometres; **le car fait le p. entre la ville et la côte**, the coach runs between the town and the coast; **payer son p.**, to pay one's fare (for the journey); *Av:* **p. à l'atterrissage, au décollage**, landing, take-off, run; **p. au sol**, taxying distance; *Nau:* **p. d'une manœuvre**, lead of a rope; *Navy:* **régler le p. d'une torpille**, to set the range of a torpedo; (*b*) route (of procession, bus, train, etc.); course (of river, etc.); path (of crank, etc.); *Rail:* **avoir libre p. sur un réseau**, to have running rights over a system; (*c*) *Sp:* circuit, course; *Golf:* course, links; *Golf:* **à travers le p.**, through the green; **carte du p.**, (i) score card; (ii) map of the circuit; plan of the course; **connaître le p.**, (i) to know the course; (ii) *F:* *O:* to know the ropes; to know one's way about. **2.** *Jur:* (**droit de) p.**, commonage, right of pasture; *Scot:* pasturage. **3.** run, trip; **p. de garantie**, trial trip (of locomotive, etc.). **4. p. d'un poulailler**, (chicken) run.

pard [paːr], *s.m.* *Z:* serval, African wildcat.

pardalote [pardalɔt], *s.m.* *Orn:* pardalote, diamond bird, diamond sparrow.

par-deçà [pardəsa], *prep.* & *adv.* on this side (of).

par-dedans [pardədɑ̃], *prep., adv.* & *s.m.* within; *A:* **en mon p.-d. j'étais content**, I was inwardly pleased.

par-delà [pardəla], *adv.* & *prep.* beyond.

par-dehors [pardəɔːr], *adv.* & *prep.* outside; **la maison est belle par-dedans et p.-d.**, the house is beautiful inside and out.

par-derrière [pardɛrjɛːr], *prep.* & *adv.* behind; **médire qn p.-d.**, to run s.o. down behind his back.

par-dessous [pardəsu], *prep.* & *adv.* under, beneath, underneath; **passer p.-d. la porte**, to creep under the door; **j'ai passé p.-d.**, I crept under; **porter un gilet p.-d. son veston**, to wear a waistcoat under one's jacket.

par-dessus [pardəsy], *prep.* & *adv.* over (the top of); **sauter p.-d. la table**, to leap over the table; **jeter qch. p.-d. bord**, to throw sth. overboard; **p.-d. le marché**, into the bargain; **p.-d. tout**, above all; **un mouchoir autour de la tête, et son chapeau p.-d.**, a handkerchief round his head, with his hat on top; **j'ai sauté p.-d.**, I jumped over; *F:* **avoir p.-d. la tête de qch.**, to be unable to bear sth. any longer; to have had enough of sth.; **j'en ai p.-d. la tête**, I'm fed up, I can't stand it (any longer).

pardessus [pardəsy], *s.m.* **1.** overcoat. **2.** *Fr.C:* *F:* overshoe.

par-devant [pardəvɑ̃], *prep.* **1.** in front of; **passer p.-d. la maison**, to pass in front of the house. **2.** *Jur:* in front of, before; **acte signé p.-d. (le) notaire**, deed signed before, in the presence of, a lawyer.

par-devers [pardəvɛːr], *prep.* **1.** in the hands of; **retenir des papiers p.-d. soi**, to have papers in one's own custody, keeping. **2. p.-d. le juge**, before the judge.

pardi [pardi], *int.* *F:* (*a*) good Lord! good heavens! (*b*) of course! naturally!

pardienne [pardjɛn], **pardine** [pardin], **pardieu** [pardjø], *int.* *F:* *A:* & *Dial:* = PARDI.

pardon [pardɔ̃], *s.m.* pardon; (*a*) forgiveness (of an offence); **p. des injures**, forgiveness of injuries; **je vous demande p.**, I beg your pardon (de, for); **p.! mille pardons! mille fois p.!** I beg your pardon! excuse me! I'm (very) sorry! **p. de vous avoir retenu**, I'm sorry to have kept you; (*expressing contradiction*) **p. c'était hier que . . .**, I'm sorry, it was yesterday that . . .; (*in conversation*) **p.?** I beg your pardon? I didn't quite catch that; what did you say? *Jur:* **p. d'une offense conjugale**, condonation; (*b*) *Jur:* remission of a sentence; **il a reçu son p.**, he has been pardoned; (*c*) *Ecc:* (*in Brittany*) (local processional) pilgrimage; (*d*) *pl.* *Ecc:* papal indulgences; (*e*) *Jewish Rel:* **fête du Grand P.**, Day of Atonement, Yom Kippur; (*f*) *P:* **le père était déjà costaud, mais alors le fils, p.!** the father was beefy enough, but as for the son, good Lord!

pardonnable [pardɔnabl̥], *a.* (*a*) pardonable, forgivable, excusable (sin); (*b*) **vous êtes p. d'avoir oublié**, it is quite excusable that you should have forgotten.

pardonner [pardɔne], *v.tr.* to pardon, forgive; (*a*) **p. une faute**, to pardon a fault; **pardonnez la liberté que je prends**, excuse the liberty I am taking; **faute qui ne peut se p.**, offence that cannot be pardoned, that cannot be overlooked; *abs.* **maladie qui ne pardonne pas**, fatal disease; (*b*) **p. à qn**, *occ.* **p. qn**, to pardon s.o.; **Dieu me pardonne!** God forgive me! **la mort ne pardonne (à) personne**, death spares no one; **pardonnez-moi**, excuse me; **vous êtes tout pardonné**, it's all right, I quite understand; (*c*) **p. ses offenses à qn**, to forgive s.o. his offences; **p. à qn d'avoir fait qch.**, to pardon, forgive, s.o. for having done sth.; **pardonnez(-moi) si je vous contredis**, excuse my contradicting you; **je ne pardonne pas qu'il m'ait trompé**, I cannot forgive his having deceived me.

pardonneur, -euse [pardɔnœːr, -øːz], *s.* pardoner, forgiver.

paré [pare], *a.* **1.** *Nau:* **(qu'on soit) p.!** (make) ready! **p. à virer!** ready about! **p. à mouiller!** stand by the anchor! let her go! (*on steamer*) **p. à manœuvrer!** stand by below! **on est p.!** aye, aye, sir! all clear! **les machines sont parées à fonctionner**, the engines are in working order; steam is up; **l'ancre est parée**, the anchor is ready; **embarcation parée au dehors**, boat swung out. **2.** decorated, ornamented (**de**, with); (*of pers.*) dressed (up) (**de**, in); *Lit:* adorned (**de**, with); **salle parée pour une fête**, room decorated for a party; hall decorated for a fête; **femme trop parée**, overdressed woman; **elle était parée de tous ses atours, parée comme une châsse**, she was decked out in all her finery, all her jewels; **bal p.**, full dress ball. **3. morceau de viande p.**, dressed joint; **pièce parée**, (piece of) shoulder of beef.

paréatis [pareatis], *s.m.* *Jur:* *A:* proceedings to enforce a foreign judgement or an arbitrator's award.

pare-balles [parbal]. **1.** *s.m.inv.* (*a*) *Mil:* bullet shield; (*b*) marker's shelter (at shooting range, at butts). **2.** *a.inv.* bullet-proof (waistcoat); **verre p.-b.**, bullet-proof glass.

pare-battage [parbataːʒ], *s.m.* *Nau:* fender; *pl.* *pare-battages.*

pare-boue [parbu], *s.m.inv.* dashboard (of carriage); mudguard (of car, bicycle).

pare-brise [parbriːz], *s.m.inv.* *Aut:* *Av:* *etc:* windscreen, *U.S:* windshield.

pare-choc(s) [parʃɔk], *s.m.inv.* *Aut:* bumper; **p.-c. contre p.-c.**, bumper to bumper; **support de p.-c.**, bumper bracket.

pare-clous [parklu], *s.m.inv.* *Aut:* *Cy:* outer cover lining (of tyre).

pare-éclats [parekla], *s.m.inv.* *Mil:* **1.** splinter-proof shield (on trench parapet, field gun, etc.); *a.* *Navy:* **tôles p.-é.**, splinter plates; **pont p.-é.**, splinter-deck. **2. p.-é. de tranchée**, traverse.

pare-étincelles [paretɛ̃sɛl], *s.m.inv.* (*a*) fire guard; (*b*) *Rail:* *etc:* spark arrester, spark catcher (of engine, etc.); (*c*) *El:* arcing contact.

pare-feu [parfø], *s.m.inv.* fire break, fire belt, fire lane (in forest); **cloison p.-f.**, (i) fire wall, fire bulkhead, fire seal; (ii) fire guard; **plancher p.-f.**, fire floor.

pare-flamme [parflɑːm], *s.m.* *Ind:* flame guard; flame arrester, flame trap; *pl.* *pare-flammes.*

pare-fumée [parfyme]. **1.** *s.m.inv.* *Rail:* smoke shield (in roof of station). **2.** *a.inv.* **casque p.-f.**, smoke helmet.

parégorique [paregɔrik], *a.* & *s.m.* *Pharm:* paregoric.

pare-gouttes [pargut], *s.m.inv.* *Mec.E:* *etc:* splash guard, oil guard.

pareil, -eille [parɛːj]. **1.** *a.* (*a*) like, alike, similar; **ils sont pareils**, they are alike; **un tissu p. à celui-ci**, material like this, to match this; **en voici un tout p.**, here is one exactly like it; **p. à l'échantillon**, similar to sample, up to sample; **toutes choses pareilles**, all things being equal; (*b*) (*of time*) same, identical; **l'an dernier à p. jour**, this day last year; (*c*) such; like that; **en p. cas**, in a case like this, in such cases; **je n'ai rien fait de p.**, I did nothing of the kind, no such thing; **comment a-t-il pu faire une chose pareille!** how could he do such a thing! **avez-vous jamais entendu chose pareille!** did you ever hear of such a thing! **2.** *s.* (*a*) **mes pareils**, my equals, my peers; **à la façon de ses pareilles**, after the manner of her kind, as people of her sort do; **lui et ses pareils**, he and people like him; he and his like; (*b*) equal, fellow, match; **elle n'a pas sa pareille au monde**, she hasn't her equal on earth, there's no one like her; **de longtemps on ne verra pas son p.**, it will be long before we see his like, anyone like him, again; **il n'a pas son p. pour le travail**, there's no-one to equal him for work; **vous n'avez pas le p.?** you haven't its pair, the fellow to it? **sans p.**, peerless, matchless; unequalled; **méchanceté sans pareille**, unparalleled wickedness. **3.** *s.f.* **la pareille**, the like; **je n'ai jamais vu, entendu, la pareille**, I never saw, heard, anything like it; **rendre la pareille à qn**, to retaliate, to give s.o. tit for tat, to pay s.o. out, to pay s.o. back in his own coin; **si on me frappe je rends la pareille**, if any one hits me I hit back; *F:* **souhaiter la pareille à qn**, to reciprocate s.o.'s good wishes, to wish s.o. the same; **4.** *adv.phr.* *A:* **à la pareille**, (i) in the same way; (ii) in return. **5.** *s.m.* *P:* **c'est du p. au même**, it's just the same. **6.** *adv.* *P:* **(et) moi p.!** (and) so do I! me too!

pareillement [parɛjmɑ̃], *adv.* **1.** in a similar manner, *Lit:* in like manner. **2.** also; likewise; *F:* (*in answer to good wishes or to a toast*) the same to you! **et moi p.**, and so do I, so am I, so shall I, etc.; me too!

pare-insectes [parɛ̃sɛkt], *s.m.inv.* *Aut:* insect deflector.

pare-jambes [parʒɑ̃ːb], *s.m.inv.* *Motor Cy:* leg shields.

parélectronomie [parelɛktrɔnɔmi], *s.f.* *Physiol:* parelectronomy.

parélie [pareli], *s.f.* *Astr:* parhelion.

parelle [parɛl], *s.f.* *Bot:* **1.** yellow dock. **2.** parella (lichen).

pare-lumière [parlymjɛːr], *s.m.inv.* (*a*) *Aut:* anti-dazzle shield; (*b*) *T.V:* gobo.

parement [parmɑ̃], *s.m.* **1.** (*a*) adorning; (*b*) *Tchn:* dressing (of stone, etc.). **2.** (*a*) ornament; decoration, ornamentation (of façade, etc.); (*b*) cuff (of sleeve); (cuff or collar) facing; *pl.* facings (of coat, uniform); (*c*) **p. d'autel**, (altar) frontal;

(*d*) *Cu:* caul (wrapped round leg of mutton, etc.). **3.** *Const:* face, facing (of wall, etc.); (dressed) face (of stone, etc.); **p. en pierre de taille,** ashlaring; **brique de p.,** facing brick. **4.** kerb stone. **5. p. de fagot,** outside sticks, big sticks, of a faggot.

parementer [parmɑ̃te], *v.tr. Const:* to face (wall, etc.).

parementure [parmɑ̃ty:r], *s.f. Tail:* front and collar facings (of coat, etc.).

pare-mines [parmin], *s.m.inv. Navy:* paravane.

parémiologie [paremjɔlɔʒi], *s.f.* paroemiology.

parenchymal, -aux [parɑ̃ʃimal, -o], *a. Anat: Bot:* parenchymal.

parenchymateux, -euse [parɑ̃ʃimatø, -ø:z], *a. Anat: Bot:* parenchymatous.

parenchyme [parɑ̃ʃim], *s.m. Anat: Bot:* parenchyma.

pare-neige [parnɛ:ʒ], *s.m.inv.* snow break; snow fence; *Rail:* snow shed.

parent, -ente [parɑ̃, -ɑ̃:t]. **1.** *s.m.pl.* (*a*) parents; father and mother; **sans parents,** without parents, orphaned; **il a des parents jeunes,** his parents are young; *F:* **venez ce soir, les parents seront absents,** come this evening, the parents, the old people, will be out; *Sch:* **association des parents d'élèves** = parent-teacher association; **parents spirituels,** godparents; (*b*) *Lit:* forefathers, forbears; **nos premiers parents,** our first parents (Adam and Eve). **2.** *s.* (*a*) (blood) relation, relative; **son plus proche p.,** his next of kin; **être p. avec qn,** to be related to s.o.; **ils sont proches parents,** they are close, near, relations; **la tyrannie et le despotisme sont proches parents,** tyranny and despotism are closely connected, are near relations; **se prétendre p. de qn,** to claim relationship to s.o.; **le chat est p. du tigre,** the tiger is a member of the cat family; **l'art mycénien est p. de l'art crétois,** Mycenaean art has affinities with Cretan art; **c'est une de mes parentes,** she's a relation, a relative, of mine; **il est p. du ministre par son père,** he's a relation of the minister on his father's side; **p. par alliance,** relation by marriage; **nous sommes parents par alliance,** we are connected by marriage; **c'est là que reposent tous ses parents,** all his family are buried there; (*b*) **traiter qn en p. pauvre,** to treat s.o. like a poor relation; **le ministre se plaignait que son département fût traité en p. pauvre,** the minister complained that his department was treated like a poor relation, was a Cinderella; (*c*) *s.m. Atom. Ph:* parent. **3.** *a.* **langues parentes,** languages of the same group, of the same linguistic family; **intelligences parentes,** minds that think alike.

parentage [parɑ̃ta:ʒ], *s.m. A:* **1.** parentage, birth, lineage. **2.** *coll.* kindred, family, relations, connections.

parentaille [parɑ̃tɑ:j], *s.f. F: Pej:* **toute la p.,** the whole crew of relations; the whole blessed family.

parenté [parɑ̃te], *s.f.* **1.** (*a*) relationship; *Jur:* **p. naturelle,** consanguinity; **p. légale,** relationship by adoption; **p. civile,** affinity; **p. directe, en ligne directe,** lineal consanguinity; **p. collatérale,** collateral consanguinity; **p. du côté maternel,** relationship on the mother's side; **p. spirituelle,** relationship between godparents and godchild(ren); **ils ont le même nom, mais il n'y a entre eux aucune p.,** they have the same name but they are not in any degree related; **ils sont l'un et l'autre mes cousins issus de germain, donc au même degré de p. avec moi,** they are both my second cousins, and therefore of the same degree of relationship to me; **p. par alliance,** relationship, connection, by marriage; **ce mariage a créé des liens de p. entre les deux familles,** the two families are connected by this marriage; (*b*) relationship, affinity (between two languages, etc.); **une littérature qui a une p. évidente avec le romantisme,** literature that has a clear connection, relationship, with romanticism; **p. des goûts,** affinity of tastes. **2.** *coll.* family; relations; connections.

parentèle [parɑ̃tɛl], *s.f. A:* parentela; family, relations.

parentéral, -aux [parɑ̃teral, -o], *a. Med:* parenteral (administration of drugs).

parenthèse [parɑ̃tɛ:z], *s.f.* **1.** (*a*) *Gram:* parenthesis; (*b*) parenthesis, digression; **parenthèses qui font oublier le gros de l'histoire,** digressions which make one forget the main outlines of the story; **(soit dit) par p.,** incidentally, by the way. **2.** *Typ:* bracket; **ouvrir, fermer, la p.,** to open, close, the brackets; **mettre un mot entre parenthèses,** to put a word in brackets; **(soit dit) entre parenthèses,** incidentally, by the way; *F:* **avoir les jambes en parenthèses,** to be bow-legged.

paréo [pareo], *s.m. Cost:* pareo, grass skirt.

pare-oreilles [parɔrɛ:j], *s.m.inv. Sp:* ear shields.

pare-pierres [parpjɛ:r], *s.m.inv. Aut: A:* stone guard (for radiator, lamp).

pare-poussière [parpusjɛ:r], *s.m.inv.* **1.** *Cost:* (*a*) dust coat; (*b*) *A:* (lady's) motor-veil. **2.** *Tchn:* dust guard; dust cap (of valve, etc.).

parer¹ [pare], *v.tr.* **1.** to prepare; to dress, trim (meat, leather, timber, castings); to pare (horse's hoof, edges of leather); to tidy (garden path); *Nau:* to clear (cable, anchor, etc.). **2.** (*a*) **p. la mariée,** to dress the bride; **p. un enfant,** to dress a child in his best clothes; (*b*) to decorate, to embellish; to arrange (room, etc.) with care, with taste; **p. un autel,** to deck out an altar; **p. son style,** to embellish one's style; *Lit:* **l'espérance pare l'avenir de mille beautés,** hope paints the future in glowing colours; **p. ses marchandises,** to display one's goods to the best advantage.

se parer, to adorn oneself; to dress oneself up; to deck oneself out; **se p. de sa plus belle robe,** to deck oneself out in one's finest dress; **les noms les plus illustres dont se pare l'histoire,** the most famous names in history; *Pej:* **se p. d'un faux titre,** to parade a false title; **il se pare du nom de philosophe,** he calls himself a philosopher.

parer². **1.** *v.tr.* to avoid, ward off; (*a*) *Nau:* **p. un abordage,** to avoid, fend off, a collision; **p. un cap,** to clear, double, a headland; to give a headland a wide berth; **p. un grain,** to steer clear of a squall; (*b*) *Box: Fenc:* to parry, ward off (blow, thrust); (*c*) **p. qn contre, de, qch.,** to guard s.o. against (blow, misfortune). **2.** *v.ind.tr.* **p. à qch.,** to provide, guard, against sth.; to avert (accident); to obviate (difficulty); **on ne peut pas p. à tout,** one cannot guard against everything; accidents will happen; **p. aux besoins immédiats,** to provide for, meet, immediate needs; **p. au plus pressé,** to attend to the most urgent things first; **le plus grand danger auquel il reste à p.,** the greatest danger that remains to be countered; **la houille blanche pare au manque de charbon,** hydroelectric power compensates for the shortage of coal; **p. à l'imprévu,** to provide against accidents; **p. à l'échauffement d'un coussinet,** to guard against the heating of a bearing; *Fb:* (*of goalkeeper*) **p. à l'attaque,** to make a save; *Nau:* **p. à un grain,** to prepare to meet a squall; to reduce sail for a squall.

parer³, *Equit:* **1.** *v.tr.* to hold in, pull up (horse). **2.** *v.i.* **cheval qui pare bien,** horse that comes to a clean stop.

pare-radiateur [parradjatœ:r], *s.m. Aut:* stone guard; *pl. pare-radiateurs.*

parère [parɛ:r], *s.m. Jur:* expert opinion, advice (on commercial questions).

parésie [parezi], *s.f. Med:* paresis.

pare-soleil [parsɔlɛ:j], *s.m.inv.* **1.** sunshade (of telescope). **2.** *Aut: etc:* sun visor. **3.** *Cin:* ear.

pare-son [parsɔ̃], *s.m.inv. T.V:* gobo.

paresse [parɛs], *s.f.* (*a*) laziness, idleness; **par pure p.,** out of sheer laziness; **se laisser aller à la p.,** to drift into idleness; **prendre des habitudes de p.,** to acquire idle habits; **je goûtais une heure de p.,** I was enjoying an hour's laze; (*b*) **p. d'esprit,** sluggishness of mind; **p. du foie, de l'intestin,** sluggishness of the liver, of the bowels.

paresser [parese, -ɛse], *v.i.* to idle away one's time; to idle; to laze; **p. dans un fauteuil,** to laze in an armchair.

paresseusement [paresøzmɑ̃], *adv.* **1.** idly, lazily. **2.** *A:* (*a*) slowly; (*b*) sluggishly.

paresseux, -euse [paresø, -ø:z]. **1.** *a.* (*a*) lazy; idle; indolent; **p. comme une couleuvre, comme un lézard, comme un loir,** bone idle, bone lazy; **attitude paresseuse,** lazy attitude; **prendre la solution paresseuse,** to take the line of least resistance; **il est p. à, pour, se lever,** he's lazy about getting up, *F:* you can't get him out of bed (in the morning); (*b*) sluggish (liver, bowels, mind); slow-acting (spring, balance); **intelligence paresseuse,** slow, dull, intellect; (*c*) *Hort:* late (-ripening). **2.** *s.* lazy person, *F:* lazybones; **c'est un petit p.,** he's a lazy little beggar. **3.** *s.m. Z:* sloth.

paresthésie [parɛstezi], *s.f. Med:* paraesthesia.

parétique [paretik], *a. & s.m. & f. Med:* paretic.

pare-torpilles [partɔrpi:j], *s.m. & a.inv.* **(filet) p.-t.,** torpedo net; *N.Arch:* **caisson p.-t.,** bulge, blister.

pareur, -euse [parœ:r, -ø:z]. **1.** *s. Ind:* finisher, trimmer. **2.** *s.f. Tex:* **pareuse,** sizing machine (for cloth, thread, etc.).

pare-vent [parvɑ̃], *s.m.inv.* wind shield, screen (to protect camper's stove, etc.).

pare-vol [parvɔl], *a.inv.* anti-theft (lock, etc.).

parfaire [parfɛ:r], *v.tr.* (*conj. like* FAIRE; *used chiefly in inf. and p.p.*) to finish off, perfect, complete, round off (one's work, etc.); **après avoir parfait son éducation,** after finishing his education; **p. une somme,** to make up a sum (to the full amount).

parfaiseur [parfəzœ:r], *s.m. Tex:* comb manufacturer.

parfait [parfɛ]. **1.** *a.* perfect; (*a*) **Dieu seul est p.,** God alone is perfect; (*b*) perfect, incomparable; faultless; flawless; **le bonheur p. n'est pas sur la terre,** perfect happiness is not of this world; **beauté parfaite,** perfect, incomparable, beauty; **p. amour,** (i) perfect love; (ii) *Cu:* parfait amour; **sonnet p.,** flawless sonnet; **en ordre p.,** in perfect order; **crime p.,** perfect crime; **il est loin d'être p.,** he's no saint; **notre bonne est parfaite,** our maid's a treasure; **vous avez été p.,** you were wonderful, splendid; **(voilà qui est) p.!** (that's) splendid! fine! grand! wonderful! (*c*) perfect, complete; thorough; **exemple p.,** perfect example; **un p. gentilhomme,** a gentleman born and bred; **un p. honnête homme,** a thorough, perfect, gentleman; **un p. orateur,** a finished speaker; *F:* **un p. imbécile,** a complete fool, an out-and-out idiot; **en p. accord,** in full agreement; *Mus:* **accord p.,** perfect chord; **cadence parfaite,** perfect cadence; *Com:* **p. paiement,** payment in full; **jusqu'à p. paiement,** until fully paid; *Mth:* **nombre p.,** perfect number; **ensemble p.,** perfect group; *Ch:* **gaz p.,** perfect, ideal, gas; *Hyd:* **liquides parfaits,** perfect fluids; *Bot:* **fleur parfaite,** perfect flower; *Ent:* **insecte p.,** imago, perfect insect; *Carp:* **bois p.,** heart wood; *Lap:* **p. contentement,** matching set of diamonds. **2.** *s.m.* (*a*) perfection; **chercher le p. en toutes choses,** to look for perfection in everything; (*b*) *Gram:* perfect (tense); **verbe au p.,** verb in the perfect (tense); (*c*) *Cu:* ice (cream) (of one flavour); **p. au café,** coffee parfait; (*d*) *Rel.H:* **les parfaits,** the Perfecti.

parfaitement [parfɛtmɑ̃], *adv.* **1.** (*a*) perfectly; to perfection; **il a joué cette sonate p.,** he played this sonata to perfection; **cela m'ira p.,** that will do beautifully; (*of a hotel, etc.*) **on y est p.,** one is thoroughly comfortable, they do you perfectly, there; (*b*) completely, thoroughly; **je le sais p.,** I know it quite well, full well; **je l'admets p.,** I quite admit it; **je comprends p.,** I quite understand; **être p. maître d'un jeu,** to be perfect master of a game; **un éditeur p. imbécile,** a perfect fool of a publisher; **p. incorrect,** utterly false. **2.** (*emphatic answer*) that's so; quite so, certainly, exactly; **vous dites que vous l'avez vu?—p.,** you say you saw it?—certainly (I did).

parfilage [parfila:ʒ], *s.m. A:* **1.** unravelling, unpicking (of woven fabrics, of gold and silver lace); drizzling (a fashionable pastime in the 18th century). **2.** unravelled (gold or silver) thread.

parfiler [parfile], *v.tr.* to unravel, unpick (fabrics, gold or silver lace); *abs.* to pick threads; *A:* to drizzle; *Lit:* **on n'a jamais parfilé des riens avec plus de soin et de prétention,** never was the spinning of airy nothings taken more seriously.

parfilure [parfily:r], *s.f. A:* unravelled (gold or silver) thread.

parfois [parfwa], *adv.* sometimes, at times, occasionally, now and then; every now and then; **il arrive p. que . . .,** it happens now and again that . . .; it sometimes happens that . . ..

parfondre [parfɔ̃:dr], *v.tr.* to fuse (colours in enamel, etc.).

parfournir [parfurni:r], *v.tr. Com:* to make up (a quantity of goods ordered).

parfum [parfœ̃], *s.m.* **1.** perfume, fragrance, sweet smell, scent (of flower); bouquet (of wine); **fleurs au doux p.,** sweet-smelling flowers; *Lit:* **écrits qui ont un p. d'antiquité,** writings with a fragrance of antiquity; **le p. des louanges,** the sweet incense of praise. **2.** *Toil:* scent, perfume. **3.** flavour (of ice cream). **4.** *P:* **être au p.,** to be in the know, to be wise to sth.

parfumer [parfyme], *v.tr.* **1.** (*a*) to scent; **p. son mouchoir,** to scent one's handkerchief; **elle se parfume trop,** she uses too much scent; **elle se parfume à la violette,** she uses violet scent; **le jasmin parfume l'air du soir,** jasmine scents the evening air; **l'air parfumé du soir,** the balmy evening air; (*b*) *Cu:* to flavour **(avec, à,** with). **2.** *A:* to disinfect (with vinegar, fumes of sulphur, etc.).

parfumerie [parfymri], *s.f.* (*a*) perfumery; perfume and cosmetics (i) manufacture, (ii) trade; (*b*) (*shop or department in store*) parfumerie, perfumery; perfume and cosmetics department, counter; (*c*) (*product sold*) perfumery, perfume and cosmetics; **p. pour hommes,** toiletries for men.

parfumeur, -euse [parfymœːr, -øːz], *s.* perfumer.

pargasite [pargazit], *s.f. Miner:* pargasite.

pargué [parge], **parguienne** [pargjɛn], *int. A:* heavens!

parhélie [pareli], *s.m.* parhelion, mock sun (in solar halo), sun dog.

parhélique [parelik], *a.* parheliacal, parhelic.

pari [pari], *s.m.* **1.** bet, wager; **faire, offrir, un p.,** to make a bet; to lay a bet, a wager; **tenir, soutenir, un p.,** to take (up) a bet; **faire un p. inégal,** to lay (the) odds; **accepter, soutenir, un p. inégal,** to take (the) odds; **p. avec enjeu égal,** even bet; **p. avec report,** accumulator, *U.S:* if bet. **2.** betting; **je n'approuve pas les paris,** I disapprove of betting; **p. mutuel** = totalizator system, *F:* the tote.

paria [parja], *s.m.* (*a*) (*in India*) pariah, outcaste; (*b*) pariah, outcast.

pariade [parjad], *s.f.* (*of birds*) **1.** pairing. **2.** pairing season. **3.** pair.

parian [parjɑ̃], *s.m. Cer:* Parian biscuit, Parian.

paridés [paride], *s.m.pl. Orn:* Paridae, the tits.

paridigi(ti)dé [paridiʒi(ti)de], *Z:* (*a*) *a.* artiodactylous, even-toed; (*b*) *s.m.pl.* **paridigitidés,** Artiodactyla.

parien, -ienne [parjɛ̃, -jɛn], *a. & s. Geog:* Parian, of Paros.

parier [parje], *v.tr.* (*p.d. & pr.sub.* **n. pariions, v. pariiez**) to bet, to wager; **p. (à) cent contre un,** to bet, lay, a hundred to one; **p. le double contre le simple,** to bet two to one; **p. à égalité,** to lay even odds, evens; **p. sur, pour, un cheval,** to back a horse; **p. sur Destrier placé,** to back Destrier for a place; **p. avec qn,** to bet with s.o.; **p. gros,** to bet heavily; **p. de faire qch.,** to bet that one will do sth.; **p. (à) qui sautera le plus haut,** to bet who will jump the highest; **il y a gros, beaucoup, tout, à p. que . . ., il y a cent contre un à p. que . . .,** it's virtually certain, *F:* a dead cert, that . . .; the odds are a hundred to one that . . .; **je parie, je parierais, que . . .,** I'd bet that . . .; I'm almost certain that . . .; **j'aurais parié que cette pièce aurait obtenu quelque succès,** the odds were that the play would be successful; **vous avez soif, je parie,** I don't mind betting you're thirsty.

pariétaire [parjetɛːr], *s.f. Bot:* (wall) pellitory.

pariétal, -aux [parjetal, -o], *Anat: Bot: etc:* **1.** *a.* parietal; *Prehist:* **art p.,** cave painting. **2.** *s.m.* parietal (bone). **3.** *s.f.pl. Bot:* **pariétales,** Parietales.

parieur, -euse [parjœːr, -øːz], *s.* **1.** better, punter; *Sp: esp. Turf:* backer. **2.** betting man, woman; **c'est un p. enragé,** he's an inveterate gambler.

parigot, -ote [parigo, -ɔt], *s. P:* Parisian.

paripenné [paripɛnne], *a. Bot:* (*of leaves*) paripinnate.

Paris [pari], *Pr.n.m. Geog:* Paris; *A:* **premier P.,** leading article (in a Paris newspaper); **articles de P.,** fancy goods; **Monsieur de P.,** the public executioner; *Prov:* **P. ne s'est pas fait en un jour,** Rome was not built in a day.

Pâris [pɑris], *Pr.n.m. Gr.Lit:* Paris.

parisette [parizɛt], *s.f. Bot:* **p. à quatre feuilles,** herb Paris, (herb) true love.

parisianiser [parizjanize], *v.tr.* to Parisianize; to give a Parisian touch to (sth., s.o.).

parisianisme [parizjanism], *s.m.* **1.** Parisianism. **2.** Parisian idiom, way of speaking.

parisien, -ienne [parizjɛ̃, -jɛn]. **1.** (*a*) *a. & s.* Parisian, *f.* Parisienne; **esprit p.,** Parisian outlook; **pain p.** = French bread; **attache parisienne,** paper clip; (*b*) *Geog:* **le Bassin p.,** the Paris Basin; **l'agglomération parisienne,** Greater Paris. **2.** *Nau:* **vergue parisienne,** monkey spar. **3.** *s.f.* **parisienne,** (*a*) (workman's) overalls; (*b*) *Typ:* pearl (type).

parisis [parizis], *a.inv. Num.Hist:* minted at Paris.

parisyllabe [parisil(l)ab], **parisyllabique** [parisil(l)abik], *a.* parisyllabic.

paritaire [paritɛːr], *a.* (meeting) at which both sides are equally represented; **réunion p.,** round-table conference; *Ind: etc:* **gestion p.,** workers' participation in the management.

paritarisme [paritarism], *s.m. Pol.Ec:* (doctrine of) workers' participation in the management.

parité [parite], *s.f.* **1.** parity; equality (of rank, condition, value); **il n'y a pas de p. entre ces deux cas,** the two cases are not comparable; **établir une p. entre deux cas,** to show that the two cases are comparable; *Fin:* **p. de change,** equivalence of exchange; **change à (la) p.,** exchange at par; *Com:* **vendre des marchandises à Manchester p. Londres,** to sell goods in Manchester carriage paid to London or for an equivalent distance in any direction. **2.** *Mth:* evenness (of numbers, as opposed to oddness). **3.** *Atom.Ph:* parity.

parjure[1] [parʒyːr], *s.m.* perjury, *in the restricted senses of* (i) false swearing (as a moral offence); false oath; (ii) violation of one's oath; *cp.* **faux témoignage** *under* FAUX[1] I. 1.

parjure[2]. **1.** *a.* perjured, forsworn. **2.** *s.m. & f.* perjurer (who has violated his oath).

parjurer (se) [səparʒyre], *v.pr.* to forswear oneself, to perjure oneself; to be guilty of, commit, perjury (before God); *occ. v.tr. A:* **il a parjuré ses vœux,** he has broken his vows.

parka [parka], *s.f. Cost:* parka.

parkérisation [parkerizasjɔ̃], *s.f. Metalw:* parkerizing.

parkériser [parkerize], *v.tr. Metalw:* to parkerize (ferrous metals).

parking [parkiŋ], *s.m. F:* car park, parking place, *U.S:* parking lot.

Parkinson [parkinsɔn], *Pr.n. Med:* **maladie de P.,** Parkinson's disease.

parkinsonia [parkinsɔnja], *s.m. Bot:* parkinsonia; Jerusalem thorn.

parkinsonien, -ienne [parkinsɔnjɛ̃, -jɛn], *a. & s. Med:* (patient) suffering from Parkinson's disease; **tremblement p.,** parkinsonian tremor.

parkinsonisme [parkinsɔnism], *s.m. Med:* parkinsonism.

parlage [parlaːʒ], *s.m. F: O:* **1.** idle talk. **2.** talk, chat. **3.** glib speech (of canvasser, etc.).

parlant [parlɑ̃], *a.* (*a*) speaking; talking (creature, voice); **portrait p.,** speaking likeness, life-like portrait; **geste p.,** eloquent, meaningful, gesture; **des exemples parlants,** vivid examples; **voix parlante, voix chantante,** speaking voice, singing voice; *Tp:* **l'horloge parlante,** the speaking clock, *F:* Tim; (*b*) *F:* talkative, garrulous; **peu p.,** reticent, silent; (*c*) *Her:* **armes parlantes,** canting, allusive, arms.

parlé [parle]. **1.** *a.* spoken (language, word). **2.** *s.m.* patter (in song); spoken part (in opera).

parlement [parləmɑ̃], *s.m.* parliament; (*a*) *Fr. Hist:* high judicial court (in Paris and in each province); (*b*) (*modern times*) legislative assembly; (*in England*) **membre du p.,** member of parliament, M.P.; **au p.,** in parliament.

parlementage [parləmɑ̃taːʒ], *s.m.* parleying, parley.

parlementaire[1] [parləmɑ̃tɛːr]. **1.** *a. Pol:* parliamentary (government, etc.); **expression peu p.,** unparliamentary expression. **2.** *s.m.* (*a*) *Hist: Pol:* parliamentarian; (*b*) member of Parliament, *U.S:* congressman.

parlementaire[2], *O:* **1.** *s.m.* (*a*) *Mil:* bearer of a flag of truce; (*b*) *Navy:* **(vaisseau) p.,** cartel (ship). **2.** *a.* **drapeau p.,** *Navy:* **pavillon p.,** flag of truce, white flag.

parlementairement [parləmɑ̃tɛrmɑ̃], *adv.* parliamentarily; **s'exprimer peu p.,** to use unparliamentary language.

parlementarisme [parləmɑ̃tarism], *s.m.* parliamentary government; parliamentarism, parliamentarianism.

parlementer [parləmɑ̃te], *v.i.* (*a*) to parley, to hold a parley **(avec,** with); **nous parlementions depuis une heure,** we had been discussing matters for an hour; (*b*) to negotiate; (*c*) *F:* to talk, to argue, at length **(avec,** with).

parler [parle]. I. *v.i.* to speak, talk. **1.** (*a*) **p. haut,** to talk loudly; **p. bas,** to speak in a low voice; **p. tout haut,** to talk aloud; **p. entre ses dents,** to mumble; **parlez plus haut, plus fort!** speak up! **il parlait toujours très vite,** he always spoke very quickly; **p. du nez,** to speak through the nose, with a (nasal) twang; **p. à l'oreille de qn,** to whisper to s.o.; *Tp:* **on vous parle!,** I have a call for you; **s'enrouer à force de p.,** to talk oneself hoarse; **p. par gestes, du regard,** to talk by signs, by looks; **faire p. les animaux,** to put words into animals' mouths (in fables); *Pol:* **quand il parle à la Chambre,** when he addresses the House; **n'ayant pas l'habitude de p. en public,** being unaccustomed to speaking in public; **celui qui a parlé le premier, le dernier,** the first, last, speaker; *B:* **ainsi parle le Seigneur,** thus saith the Lord; **et Dieu parla ainsi,** and God spake on this wise; **il est bon de p. et meilleur de se taire,** speech is silver(n), silence is golden; (*b*) **parlez-vous sérieusement?** are you serious? do you really mean it? **laissez-le p.,** let him have his say; **je ne veux pas p. tout le temps,** I don't want to do all the talking; **p. pour p.,** to talk for talking's sake; **parlons peu et, mais, parlons bien,** let us be brief but to the point; **p. pour ne rien dire,** (i) to talk for the sake of talking; (ii) to make small talk; (iii) to talk through one's hat, to talk drivel; **elle ne sait pas p. pour ne rien dire,** she has no small talk; **il parle pour ne rien dire,** he's a windbag, a gasbag; **pour p. franc,** to put it bluntly, to speak candidly; **généralement parlant,** generally speaking; **savoir ce que p. veut dire,** to be able to take a hint; **faire p. qn,** to loosen s.o.'s tongue; **je ne peux pas le faire p.,** I cannot get a word out of him; **malgré sa timidité j'arrivai à le faire p.,** though he was shy I managed to draw him out; **on parlait très peu au déjeuner,** there was very little talking over breakfast; **façon de p.,** (i) way of speaking; (ii) manner of speech; **c'est une manière de p.,** it's a manner of speaking; **voilà ce qui s'appelle p.!** now you're talking! *P:* **tu parles!** (i) now you're talking! (ii) you're telling me! you bet! not half! *P: Iron:* **bonne cuisinière, tu parles! elle n'est pas fichue de faire cuire un œuf!** good cook be damned! my foot! she can't even boil an egg! *Iron:* **c'est bien à vous de p.!** you're a fine one to talk! *you* can talk! **cela parle tout seul,** *A:* **de soi,** it speaks for itself; **ces chiffres parlent d'eux-mêmes,** these figures speak for themselves; **si vous désirez qch. vous n'avez qu'à parler,** if you want anything you have only to speak; (*c*) **p. à qn,** to talk to s.o.; **se p. à soi-même,** *F:* **p. à son bonnet,** to talk to oneself; **il dit cela comme se parlant à lui-même,** he said it as if speaking to himself; **ne pas p.,** to keep one's own counsel; **n'en parlez à personne,** don't tell anyone about it, *F:* keep it dark; **elle a trouvé à qui p.,** (i) she has found s.o. to talk to; (ii) she has met, come up against, her match; **à qui croyez-vous p.?** who do you think you are talking to? **nous ne nous parlons pas à présent,** we are not on speaking terms at present; **ils se parlent quand ils se rencontrent,** they speak when they meet; *Nau:* **p. à un navire,** to speak a ship; (*d*) **p. de qn, de qch.,** to mention, to refer to, speak of, s.o., sth.; **il m'a parlé de ses projets,** he told me of his plans; **en avez-vous parlé aux autres?** have you said anything to the others about it? **il n'en parle jamais,** he never speaks of it, refers to it; **est-ce de moi que vous parlez?** do you mean me? **je sais qu'on parlait de moi,** I know they were discussing me; **si on parle de moi,** if any reference is made to me; **nous en parlerons après déjeuner,** we can talk it over after lunch; **n'en parlons plus,** let us drop the subject, let us say no more about it; **on a beaucoup parlé de cet incident,** much has been made of this incident; **cela ne vaut pas la peine d'en p.,** it isn't worth mentioning, talking about; **on parle de lui ériger une statue,** there is some talk of putting up a statue to him; **le renouveau du théâtre, dont on parle tant,** the much talked-of revival of the drama; **mal p. de qn,** to run s.o. down; **entendre p. de qn, de qch.,** to hear of, about, s.o., sth.; **j'entends beaucoup p. de lui,** I hear a good deal about him; **mon père ne veut pas en entendre p.,** father won't hear of it; **il ne veut plus entendre p. d'elle,** he doesn't want to hear her name mentioned again, to hear any more about her; **c'est la première fois que j'en entends p.,** this is the first I have heard of it; **je n'en ai jamais entendu p.,** I've never heard of it, about it; **faire p. de soi,** (i) to get talked about; (ii) to get a bad name; **on ne parle que de cela,** everyone's talking of it, it's common gossip; **p. de choses et d'autres,** to talk of one thing and another; **sans p. de cela, de lui,** to say nothing of that, of him; not to mention that, him; let alone that, him; *P:* **tu parles d'une occasion!** that was a chance in a lifetime! **tu parles d'une chance!** talk about luck! *Sch:* **p. sur l'histoire,** to lecture on history; (*e*) **p. pour, contre, qn,** to speak for, against, s.o.; (*f*) **son visage parle,** he has an expressive face; (*g*) (*of piano, organ, etc.*) **note qui ne parle pas,** note that is not sounding. **2.** *with cogn.acc.* (*a*) **p. français,** (i) to talk, speak, French; (ii) to speak plainly, intelligibly; **l'anglais se parle partout,** English is spoken everywhere; (*b*) **p. affaires, p. boutique,** to talk business, to talk shop; **p. musique, golf,** to talk about music; to talk golf; **p. raison,** to talk common sense, sensibly.

II. **parler,** *s.m.* (*a*) (way of) speaking; speech, language; **p. populaire,** uneducated speech; **p. provincial,** provincial speech, accent; **p. normand,** Norman dialect; **p. irlandais,** Irish brogue; *A:* **Philis au doux p.,** gentle-spoken Phyllis; (*b*) **avoir son franc p.,** to speak one's mind.

parleur, -euse [parlœːr, -øːz]. **1.** *s.* talker, speaker; **c'est un grand p.,** he never stops talking; **c'est un beau p.,** he's a facile speaker, a glib talker. **2.** *s.m. Tg:* sounder.

parloir [parlwaːr], *s.m.* **1.** (*a*) *A:* council room; (*b*) parlour, visiting room (of school, convent, etc.), locutory (of convent). **2.** *A:* council, assembly.

parlot(t)e [parlɔt], *s.f.* **1.** *A:* (*a*) (legal) debate; moot; (*b*) (legal) debating society. **2.** *F:* (*a*) *A:* **p. en plein air,** open-air discussion, debate; (*b*) talk, gossip; **la discussion a dégénéré en p.,** the debate degenerated into empty chatter.

parloter [parlɔte], *v.i. F:* to chatter, to talk about nothing in particular.

parlure [parlyːr], *s.f.* parlance.

Parme [parm], *Pr.n.f. Geog:* Parma.

parmélie [parmeli], *s.f. Moss:* parmelia.

Parménion [parmenjɔ̃], *Pr.n.m. Gr.Hist:* Parmenio.

Parmentier [parmɑ̃tje]. **1.** *Pr.n. Cu:* **potage, crème, P.,** (thick) potato soup; **hachis P.,** shepherd's pie; cottage pie. **2.** *s.f. A:* **parmentière** [parmɑ̃tjɛːr], potato (from A. Parmentier (1737-1813) who popularized the potato in France).

parmentiera [parmɑ̃tjɛra], *s.f. Bot:* candle tree (of Panama).

parmesan, -ane [parməzɑ̃, -an]. **1.** *a. & s. Geog:* Parmesan. **2.** *s.m.* Parmesan (cheese).

parmi [parmi]. **1.** *prep.* (*in modern Fr. used only before plural or coll. noun*) among, amongst; in the midst of; *Lit:* amid(st); **jouer p. les buissons,** to play among the bushes; **maisons disséminées p. les arbres,** houses scattered among the trees; **rôdant p. la foule,** wandering among the crowd; **nous souhaitons vous voir bientôt p. nous,** we hope you'll come and see us soon, that you'll soon be with us; **plusieurs, parmi lesquels X,** many, including X; **p. le silence de la nuit,** in the silence of the night; **un homme brave p. les braves,** a man of outstanding bravery; **un caractère fréquent p. les animaux,** a frequent characteristic among animals. **2.** *adv. A:* **il y en a des bons p.,** there are good ones among them.

Parnasse (le) [ləparnas], *Pr.n.m.* **1.** (*a*) *A.Geog:* Parnassus; **les filles du P.,** the Parnassian Maids; (*b*) *Fr.Lit.Hist:* the Parnassian School (of poetry, from 1860); (*c*) *s.m. Sch: A:* gradus (ad Parnassum). **2.** *Bot:* **gazon du P.,** grass of Parnassus.

parnassie [parnasi], *s.f. Bot:* **p. (des marais),** grass of Parnassus.

parnassien, -ienne [parnasjɛ̃, -jɛn]. **1.** *a.* Parnassian. **2.** *s.m.* (*a*) member of the Parnassian School (of French poetry); (*b*) *Ent:* parnassius (butterfly).

parnassin [parnasɛ̃], *s.m. Jewish Rel:* parnas(s).

parnelliste [parnɛlist], *s.m. Hist:* Parnellite.

parochial, -aux [parɔkjal, -o], *a.* parochial.

parodie [parɔdi], *s.f.* (*a*) parody; (*b*) skit (**de,** on); *Lit:* travesty (de, of).

parodier [parɔdje], *v.tr.* (*p.d. & pr.sub.* **n. parodiions, v. parodiiez**) to parody, to travesty, to burlesque; to take (s.o.) off.

parodique [parɔdik], *a. Lit:* parodic(al).

parodiste [parɔdist], *s.m. & f.* parodist.

parodonte [parɔdɔ̃ːt], *s.m. Anat:* periodontal tissue, periodontium.

parodontite [parɔdɔ̃tit], *s.f. Dent:* parodontitis, periodontitis.

parodontose [parɔdɔ̃toːz], *s.f. Dent:* periodontosis.

paroi [parwa], *s.f.* **1.** (*a*) *Const:* (partition) wall (between rooms); (*b*) wall (of rock, tent, furnace, cylinder); casing, wall, shell (of boiler); wall, crust (of horse's hoof); (rock) face; **la p. ouest de l'Aiguille du Dru,** the west face of the Aiguille du Dru; *Biol:* **p. d'une cellule,** cell wall; **chaudière à double p.,** double-shell boiler; *Const:* **ascenseur à p. lisse,** lift with doorless cabin; *N.Arch:* **p. longitudinale, latérale (de rouf),** (deck) house side; *Th:* **p. (d'une scène),** flat. **2.** inner side, surface (of vase, etc.); **p. de zinc d'une caisse,** zinc lining of a case; **p. d'un tunnel,** lining of a tunnel; **p. de l'estomac,** coat, lining, of the stomach. **3.** *For:* **arbre de p.,** border tree.

paroir [parwaːr], *s.m. Tls:* **1.** *Leath: Bookb:* parer, paring knife, scraper. **2.** *Metalw:* flatter; set hammer.

paroisse [parwas], *s.f.* **1.** parish; **la p. Saint-Jean,** the parish of Saint John's; **il n'est pas de la p.,** he's not from here; he's a foreigner; *F:* **porter des chaussettes de deux paroisses,** to be wearing odd socks. **2.** parish church. **3.** *coll.* parishioners, parish.

paroissial, -aux [parwasjal, -o], *a.* parochial, of the parish; **l'église paroissiale,** the parish church; **salle paroissiale,** parish, church, hall.

paroissien, -ienne [parwasjɛ̃, -jɛn]. **1.** *a.* parochial; **registre p.,** parish register. **2.** *s.* parishioner; *F:* **c'est un drôle de p.,** he's a queer customer, a queer stick; *s.a.* CURÉ. **3.** *s.m.* prayer book.

parole [parɔl], *s.f.* **1.** (spoken) word; remark; **il n'a prononcé aucune p.,** he didn't say a word; **perdre le temps en paroles,** to waste time talking; **vous perdez vos paroles,** it's not a bit of use your talking; you're wasting your breath; **la musique est de Schubert et les paroles de Heine,** the music is by Schubert and the words from Heine; **romance sans paroles,** song without words; **la p. de Dieu,** the word of God, the Scriptures; **cette p. le piqua,** this remark went home; **belles paroles,** fair words, *Iron:* fine words; **ni l'argent ni les belles paroles ne peuvent l'acheter,** it's not to be had for love or money; **avoir des paroles avec qn,** to have words with s.o. **2.** promise, word; *Mil:* parole; **donner sa p.,** to give one's word; **tenir (sa) p.,** to keep one's promise, one's word; to be as good as one's word; to abide by one's agreement; **il tint p.,** he was as good as his word; **manque de p.,** failure to keep one's word; breach of faith; **manquer à sa p.,** to break one's word; *Mil:* to break one's parole; **rendre sa p. à qn,** to release s.o. from his promise; **reprendre sa p.,** to retract one's promise; **il est (homme) de p., il a sa p., il n'a qu'une p.,** he's a man of his word; his word is as good as his bond; **(je vous en donne) ma p.! p. d'honneur!** (upon my) word of honour! **j'ai sa p.,** I have his word (on, for, it); **croire qn sur p.,** to take s.o.'s word; **je le crois sur votre p.,** I take your word for it; **prisonnier sur p.,** prisoner on parole. **3.** (*a*) speech, speaking; delivery; **avoir la p. nette,** to speak clearly; **avoir la p. embarrassée,** (i) to have an impediment in one's speech; (ii) to slur one's speech (on account of drink, etc.); **avoir la p. facile,** (i) to be an easy, fluent, speaker; (ii) to have the gift of the gab; to talk nineteen to the dozen; **ne pas avoir la p. facile,** to be slow of speech; **perdre la p.,** to lose the power, the faculty, of speech; **si les animaux avaient l'usage de la p.,** if animals could (only) speak; **retrouver la p.,** to find one's tongue again; (*of dying man*) **il a encore sa p.,** he can still speak; (*b*) (*action of speaking*) **la p. a été donnée à l'homme pour déguiser sa pensée,** speech was given to man to conceal his thoughts; **adresser la p. à qn,** to speak to s.o., to address s.o.; **couper la p. à qn,** to cut s.o. short, to interrupt s.o.; **l'émotion lui coupa la p.,** emotion left him speechless; **porter la p. (pour ses collègues),** to act as spokesman (for one's colleagues); **prendre la p.,** (to begin) to speak; to take the floor; **il a pris la p. à cette réunion,** he spoke at that meeting; **demander la p.,** to request leave to speak; *Pol:* to rise to a point of order; (*in parliament*) **obtenir la p.** = to catch the Speaker's eye; **donner la p. à qn,** to call on s.o. to speak; to call upon s.o. to address the meeting; **la p. est à M. X.,** Mr X will now speak; *Cards:* **passer p.,** to pass; **p.!** pass! no bid! **4.** eloquence, oratory; **la puissance de la p.,** the power of eloquence; **avoir le don de la p.,** to be a good speaker.

paroli [parɔli], *s.m.* (*at faro, etc.*) paroli, double stake; **faire p.,** to double; **il fit un faux p.,** he doubled his stakes and lost.

parolier [parɔlje], *s.m.* (*a*) *Th:* librettist, *esp.* writer of lyrics; (*b*) song writer.

paronomase [parɔnɔmɑːz], *s.f. Rh:* paronomasia.

paronychia [parɔnikja], *s.m.*, **paronyque** [parɔnik], *s.f. Bot:* paronychia, whitlow wort.

paronyme [parɔnim], *s.m.* paronym.

paronymie [parɔnimi], *s.f.* paronymy.

paronymique [parɔnimik], *a.* paronymous.

paroptique [parɔptik], *a.* paroptic, extra-retinal; **vision p.,** eyeless vision.

Paros [parɔs], *Pr.n. Geog:* (the island of) Paros; **marbre de P.,** Parian marble.

parosmie [parɔsmi], *s.f. Med:* parosmia.

parotide [parɔtid], *a. & s.f.* parotid (gland).

parotidectomie [parɔtidɛktɔmi], *s.f. Surg:* parotidectomy.

parotidien, -ienne [parɔtidjɛ̃, -jɛn], *a. Anat:* parotid, parotidean.

parotidite [parɔtidit], *s.f.* (*a*) *Med:* parotitis; **p. ourlienne,** mumps; (*b*) *Vet:* vives.

parotie [parɔti], *s.f. Orn:* parotia.

parotique [parɔtik], *a. Anat:* parotic (region, etc.).

parousie [paruzi], *s.f. Theol:* Parousia.

paroxysmal, -aux [parɔksismal, -o], **paroxysmique** [parɔksismik], *a.* paroxysmal; paroxysmic.

paroxysme [parɔksism], *s.m.* (*a*) *Med:* culminating point, crisis (of illness, fit); (*b*) paroxysm (of rage, laughter, etc.); **être au p. de la colère,** to be in a towering rage; **atteindre son p.,** to reach its highest point; **pousser qch. à son p.,** to carry sth. to extremes.

paroxystique [parɔksistik], *a.* paroxysmal, paroxystic.

paroxyton [parɔksitɔ̃], *a. & s.m. Gram:* paroxytone.

paroxytonique [parɔksitɔnik], *a. Gram:* paroxytonic, paroxytone.

parpaillot, -ote [parpajo, -ɔt], *s. Pej: A:* (*a*) Calvinist; (*b*) heretic; unbeliever.

parpaing [parpɛ̃], *s.m. Const:* parpen; bonder, bondstone; breeze block; through stone; **mur de p.,** parpen wall; **p. d'échiffre,** string wall (of stair).

parquage [parkaːʒ], *s.m.* = PARCAGE.

Parque [park], *Pr.n.f. Myth:* *usu. pl.* **les Parques,** the Parcae, the Fates.

parquement [parkəmɑ̃], *s.m.* penning (of cattle); folding (of sheep); parking (of cars, etc.).

parquer [parke], *v.tr.* **1.** (*a*) to pen (cattle); to fold (sheep); to confine (people); to put (horse) in paddock; to park (artillery, cars, etc.); to lay down a bed of (oysters); **moules parquées,** cultivated mussels; *F:* **maison où on se sent parqués comme des moutons,** house in which one feels cooped up, penned up; (*b*) *v.i.* (*of artillery, etc.*) to park; **les moutons parquent,** the sheep are in the fold. **2. p. une terre,** to manure a piece of ground (by enclosing cattle on it).

parquet [parkɛ], *s.m.* **1.** *A:* small enclosure; small fold, pen; (hen) run. **2.** (*a*) *Jur:* (i) well of the court; (ii) public prosecutor's room; **(membres du) p.,** public prosecutor and his deputies; **aller au p.,** to be appointed to the public prosecutor's department; **déposer une plainte au p.,** to lodge a complaint in court; (*b*) *St.Exch:* **le P.** = the Ring, the official market. **3.** (*a*) *Const:* (parquet) floor, flooring; **p. chauffant,** heated flooring; **p. de chêne,** oak parquet; **p. à l'anglaise,** parquet floor with pugging; **p. à bâtons rompus, à fougère, à points de Hongrie,** herring-bone flooring; **p. (en) mosaïque,** wood mosaic floor; **p. ciré,** waxed floor, polished floor; **lame de p.,** floor plank; (*b*) (wooden) backing (of wall mirror, of painting); *Phot:* **p. réversible,** reversing back; **p. d'adaptation,** adapter; (*c*) *Nau:* **p. de chargement,** dunnage; **p. de chauffe,** stokehold platform; **p. de la machine,** engine-room platform.

parquetage [parkətaːʒ], *s.m.* **1.** (*a*) making, laying, of floors; (*b*) flooring, floor. **2.** parquetry.

parqueter [parkəte], *v.tr.* **(je parquette, n. parquetons; je parquetterai)** (*a*) to floor; to lay a floor in (room, etc.); (*b*) to parquet; **p. en mosaïque,** to inlay (floor).

parqueterie [parkətri, -kɛ-], *s.f.* making, laying, of floors; **p. en mosaïque,** (i) inlaying; (ii) inlaid floor.

parqueteur [parkətœːr], *a.m. & s.m.* **(ouvrier) p.,** floor maker; floor layer; parquet maker; parquet layer.

parqueur, -euse [parkœːr, -øːz], *s.* oyster culturist.

parquier [parkje], *s.m.* (*a*) shepherd, goatherd, etc.; (*b*) oyster culturist.

parr [paːr], *s.m. Ich:* par(r), fingerling, brandling.

parrain [parɛ̃, pɑ-], *s.m.* (*a*) godfather, sponsor; *F:* uncle; **être p.,** to stand godfather (de, to); (*b*) proposer (of new member for club, learned society, etc.); sponsor.

parrainage [parɛnaːʒ], *s.m.* (*a*) sponsorship; (*b*) adoption (of one town by another).

parrainer [parɛne], *v.tr.* to sponsor; to act as godfather to.

parricide¹ [parisid]. **1.** *s.m. & f.* parricide. **2.** *a.* parricidal.

parricide², *s.m.* murder of ancestor in direct line; (crime of) parricide; *A: occ.* regicide.

parridés [paride], *s.m.pl. Orn:* Parridae.

parse [pars], *a. & s. Rel:* Parsee.

parsec [parsɛk], *s.m. Astr.Meas:* parsec.

parsemé [parsəme], *a.* **plumage p. de taches noires,** feathers dotted with black spots; **ciel p. d'étoiles,** sky studded, spangled, with stars; star-spangled sky; **champ p. de pâquerettes,** field sprinkled, dotted, with daisies; **le paysage est parsemé de fermes,** the countryside is dotted with farms; **barbe parsemée de gris,** greying beard.

parsemer [parsəme], *v.tr.* (*conj. like* SEMER) to strew, sprinkle (**de,** with); **p. un chemin de fleurs,** to strew a path with flowers; **des roses parsemaient le chemin,** the path was strewn with roses.

parsi, -ie [parsi], *a. & s. Rel:* Parsee.

parsisme [parsism], *s.m. Rel:* Parseeism.

part[1] [pa:r], *s.f.* **1.** share, part, portion; (*a*) **diviser un gâteau en plusieurs parts,** to divide a cake into portions, to share out a cake; **avoir la meilleure p.,** to have the best of the bargain; **la p. du lion,** the lion's share; **faire la p. (des bénéficiaires),** to allot the shares (to the beneficiaries); **vous lui faites la p. trop belle,** you favour him unduly; you let him off too easily; **il voulut contribuer pour sa p. à la conversation,** he made an effort to contribute his share to the conversation; **faire la p. du feu,** (i) to clear the ground (to prevent a fire spreading); (ii) *F:* to cut one's losses; **avoir une p. dans les bénéfices,** *F:* **une p. du gâteau,** to have a share, an interest, in the profits, *F:* a slice of the cake; to share in the profits; **mettre qn de p. (dans une affaire),** to give s.o. a share in the profits; **mettre qn de p. à demi,** to go half-shares with s.o.; to do a deal with s.o. on a fifty-fifty basis; *Fin:* **parts d'association,** partnership shares; **parts de fondateur,** founder's shares; **associé à p. entière,** full partner; **Français à p. entière,** person with full French citizenship; **avoir sa p. d'éloges,** to come in for a share, one's share, of praise; **avoir sa bonne p. d'éloges,** to come in for one's full share of praise; **une petite p. de vérité,** a modicum of truth; **ils viennent pour une bonne p. des environs de Lille,** they come very largely from the Lille area; (*b*) **pour ma p.,** as for me, as far as I am concerned; for my part; (speaking) for myself; **pour ma p. je n'attendrai pas,** I for one shall not wait; **j'en ai abattu six pour ma p.,** personally I shot down six; my share of the bag was six; (*c*) **prendre qch. en bonne p., en mauvaise p.,** to take sth. in good part, in bad part; **ne le prenez pas en mauvaise p.,** don't take it the wrong way; **employer un mot en bonne p.,** to use a word in a good sense; **expression qui peut se prendre en mauvaise p.,** expression that can be taken in a bad sense. **2.** share, participation; **avoir p. à qch.,** to have a hand, a share, in sth.; *F:* **avoir p. au gâteau,** to have a finger in the pie; **je n'ai pas eu de p. dans l'affaire,** I had no hand in, nothing to do with, the business; **prendre p. à qch.,** to take part in sth.; to join in sth.; to be a party to sth.; to share in sth.; **prendre p. à une cérémonie,** to assist at a ceremony; to take part in a ceremony; **prendre p. à la conversation, aux rires,** to join in the conversation, in the laughter; **ceux qui ont pris p. aux hostilités,** those who took part in the hostilities; **prendre p. à la joie de qn,** to share in s.o.'s joy; **prendre p. à une querelle,** to take part in, become a party to, a quarrel; **je n'y ai pris aucune p.,** I took no part in it; I had nothing to do with it; **faire p. de qch. à qn,** to inform s.o. of sth.; to tell s.o. about sth.; **faites-moi p. de vos soucis,** tell me (about) your troubles; **qui va lui faire p. de cette nouvelle?** who will break the news to him? who will tell him about this? **billet, lettre, de faire p.,** card, notice (announcing a wedding, a death, etc.); **faire la p. de qch.,** to take sth. into consideration; **il faut faire la p. de la jeunesse,** we should make allowances for youth; **faire la p. des choses, des circonstances,** to take circumstances into account; to be understanding; **faire la p. du diable,** to make allowances for human nature; **faire bonne p. à qch.,** to stress sth. **3.** (*a*) (*place where*) *adv.phrs.* **savoir, tenir, qch. de bonne p.,** to have it from a reliable source, on good authority; **nulle p.,** nowhere; **autre p.,** elsewhere, somewhere else; **nulle p. ailleurs,** nowhere else; **courir de p. et d'autre,** to run here and there; **faire des concessions de p. et d'autre,** to make concessions on both sides; **de toute(s) part(s),** on all sides, on all hands; **ils viennent de toutes parts,** they come from all parts, quarters; **de p. en p.,** through and through, right through; **d'une p.,** on the one hand; **d'autre p.,** on the other hand; in another connection; then again; (*b*) *prep.phr.* **je viens de la p. de . . .,** I represent . . .; I've come on behalf of . . .; **il est venu me voir de la part du maire,** he came to see me on behalf of the mayor; **une dépêche de la p. du colonel,** a despatch from the colonel; *Tp:* **c'est de la p. de qui?** who's speaking, *U.S:* calling? *adv.phr.* **dites-lui de ma p. que . . .,** tell him from me that . . .; **ce serait bien aimable de votre p.,** it would be very kind of you; **c'est une insolence de sa p.,** it's a piece of insolence on his part, it's (very) insolent of him; **pas d'insolences de votre p.!** none of your impudence! **cela étonne de sa p.,** that's astounding, coming from him. **4.** *adv.phr.* **à part,** apart, separately; **dîner à p.,** to dine apart, by oneself; **j'avais ma table à p.,** I had my table apart, my own table; **prendre qn à p.,** to take, draw, s.o. aside; **mettre de l'argent à p.,** to put money by, aside; to save money; **patriotisme à p., je ne voudrais pas . . .,** leaving patriotism aside, out of consideration, I should not like to . . .; **plaisanterie à p.,** joking apart; **emballage à p.,** packing extra; **c'est une femme à p.,** she's an exceptional woman; she's in a class of her own; **un genre à p.,** a class apart, by itself; **leur conversation avait une qualité à p.,** their conversation had a quality all its own; **et à p. lui?** who besides him? **à p. moi,** in my own heart; **je me disais à p. moi que . . .,** I was saying to myself that . . ., *Th:* **mots prononcés à p.,** words spoken aside; **à p. quelques exceptions,** with a few exceptions; **à p. quelques pages,** except for a few pages, with the exception of a few pages; **à p. cela tout va bien,** apart from that, barring that, putting that aside, all is well; *F:* **à p. que . . .,** apart from the fact that . . ., except that . . ..

part[2], *s.m.* **1.** (*of animal*) dropping (of young). **2.** *Jur:* new-born child.

partage [parta:ʒ], *s.m.* **1.** division; (*a*) (*into shares*) sharing, allotment, distribution, apportionment (of spoils, goods, etc.); *Jur:* partition (of real property); **p. de labeur,** division of labour; **faire le p. de qch.,** to divide, share out, sth.; *Cards:* **p. des atouts,** distribution of trumps; *Ch:* **coefficient de p.,** coefficient of distribution, of partition; (*b*) (*into sections, groups*) **p. d'un pays,** partition of a country; **il y a p. d'opinions,** opinions are divided; *Geog:* **ligne de p. des eaux,** watershed, *U.S:* divide; *Hyd.E:* **point, bief, de p.,** summit level (of canal). **2.** share, portion, lot; **avoir qch. en p.,** to have, receive, (a house, etc.) as one's share; **tomber, échoir, en p. à qn,** to fall to s.o.'s share, to s.o.'s lot; **la souffrance est le p. du genre humain,** suffering is the lot, portion, of mankind.

partagé [partaʒe], *a.* **1.** divided; *Bot:* parted (leaf). **2.** shared; **amour p.,** mutual affection; reciprocated love; **amour non p.,** unrequited love; *Golf:* **trou p.,** halved hole.

partageable [partaʒabl̩], *a.* dividable, divisible; shareable.

partageant [partaʒɑ̃], *s.m. Jur:* sharer; party interested (in a division).

partager [partaʒe], *v.tr.* (**je partageai(s); n. partageons**) **1.** (*a*) to divide (into shares); to parcel out; to apportion (property, etc.); to share (out) (loot, etc.); **la fortune devait être partagée également entre les deux filles,** the fortune was to be divided equally between the two daughters; **p. sa journée entre plusieurs occupations,** to divide one's day between a number of tasks, occupations; (*b*) to divide (into groups, sections, portions); **fleuve qui partage le pays en deux,** river that divides, cuts, the country into two; **question qui partage les savants,** question on which scientists are divided; *Pol:* **cette question a partagé la Chambre,** (i) this question divided the House; (ii) the House divided on this question; **les avis sont partagés,** opinions are divided; **partagé entre la haine et la pitié,** divided between hatred and pity; **p. le différend,** to split the difference; to compromise; *Navy:* **p. les homme en plats,** to divide the men into messes. **2.** to share; *abs.* **il faut lui apprendre à p.,** he should be taught to share; **p. qch. avec qn,** to share sth. with s.o.; **p. les bénéfices avec son associé,** to share the profits with one's partner; **ils se partagent les bénéfices par la moitié,** they go halves in the profits; *Fin: etc:* **p. proportionnellement,** to divide pro rata, *U.S:* to prorate; **p. le même sort,** to share the same fate; **p. la joie, l'avis, de qn,** to share s.o.'s joy, s.o.'s opinion; **p. les idées de qn,** to hold similar views to s.o.; to agree with s.o.'s views; **p. le repas de qn,** to share s.o.'s meal, to share a meal with s.o. **3. la nature l'a mal partagé,** he is poorly endowed by nature; **être bien partagé,** to be well provided for; **c'est vous le mieux partagé,** you have the best of it.

partageur, -euse[1] [partaʒœ:r, -ø:z], *a.* willing to share; generous; **ce garçon n'est pas p.,** this boy doesn't like sharing, is mean.

partageux, -euse[2] [partaʒø, -ø:z], *s. A:* partisan of the equal distribution of wealth, of property; socialist; communist.

partance [partɑ̃:s], *s.f. Nau:* departure; *so used esp. in* **navire en p.,** ship about to sail, just sailing, outward bound; **pavillon de p.,** Blue Peter; *Journ:* **navires en p.,** sailings; **en p. pour Bordeaux,** bound for Bordeaux; **avion en p. pour Toulouse,** aircraft taking off for Toulouse; *Rail: etc:* **prendre le premier train en p.,** to take the first train out, to leave.

partant[1] [partɑ̃], *adv. Lit:* consequently, therefore; **cela contribue à sa prospérité et p. à son bonheur,** it contributes to his prosperity and hence, so, to his happiness.

partant[2]. **1.** *a.* departing. **2.** *s.m.* (*a*) **les partants,** the departing guests, travellers, etc.; (*at hotel, etc.*) **les arrivants et les partants,** the arrivals and departures; (*b*) *Turf: etc:* starter; *F:* **je suis p.,** you can count me in; **il n'est pas p.,** he's a non-starter.

partenaire [partənɛ:r], *s.m. & f.* **1.** (*at sports, games, dancing*) partner; *Box:* sparring partner. **2.** opponent.

parterre [partɛ:r], *s.m.* **1.** (*a*) *A:* ground, earth; **faire un p.,** to fall down; (*b*) *F:* floor; **laver le p.,** to wash the floor. **2.** (*a*) flower bed; **p. de gazon,** lawn, grass plot; (*b*) *For:* felling. **3.** *Th:* (*a*) (the) pit; (the) area (of concert hall); *F:* **prendre un billet de p.,** to fall flat, to come a cropper; (*b*) (the) audience (in the pit).

parthe [part], *a. & s. A.Geog: A.Ethn:* Parthian; **lancer, décocher, la flèche du P.,** to fire a Parthian shaft, a Parthian shot.

parthenais, -aise [partənɛ, -ɛ:z], **parthenaisien, -ienne** [partənɛzjɛ̃, -jɛn], *a. & s. Geog:* (native, inhabitant) of Parthenay.

parthénocarpie [partenɔkarpi], *s.f. Bot:* parthenocarpy.

parthénocarpique [partenɔkarpik], *a. Bot:* parthenocarpic.

parthénogénèse [partenɔʒenɛ:z], *s.f. Biol:* parthenogenesis; virgin birth; **p. thélytoque,** thelytokous parthenogenesis; **p. arrhénotoque,** arrhenotokous parthenogenesis.

parthénogénétique [partenɔʒenetik], *a. Biol:* parthenogenetic.

Parthénon (le) [ləpartenɔ̃], *s.m. Gr.Ant:* the Parthenon.

parthénospore [partenɔspɔ:r], *s.f. Bot:* parthenospore.

parthique [partik], *a. A.Geog:* Parthian.

parti[1] [parti], *s.m.* **1.** party; (*a*) **le p. travailliste,** the labour party; **le p. conservateur,** the Conservative party; **le p. communiste,** *abs.* **le parti,** the Communist party, the Party; **guerre de partis,** party welfare; **esprit de p.,** party spirit; **homme de p.,** party man; **prendre p. pour, contre, qn,** to side with, against s.o.; **prendre, épouser, le p. de qn,** to take s.o.'s side, s.o.'s part; to take up the cudgels for s.o.; **il faut toujours prendre le p. de la maison,** you should never let the firm down; **être, se ranger, du p. de qn,** to side with s.o.; **abandonner son p.,** to desert one's party; *F:* to rat; (*b*) **un p. de Cosaques,** a party, band, troop, of Cossacks; (*c*) *A:* **le p. des armes, de la robe,** the profession of arms, the men of law. **2.** (*marriageable person*) **refuser un p.,** to refuse an offer of marriage; **c'est un bon p.,** he, she, is a good match, *F:* a good catch; he is very eligible; **petite ville où il n'y a pas de partis,** small town with no eligible men; **hésiter entre deux partis,** to be uncertain which of two people to marry. **3.** decision, choice, course; **hésiter entre deux partis,** to hesitate between two courses (of action); **prendre (un) p.,** to come to a decision, to make up one's mind, to declare oneself; **mon p. est pris,** my mind is made up; **en prendre son p.,** to resign oneself to the inevitable, to one's fate; to make the best of a bad job; to make the best of it; **prendre le p. de faire qch.,** to decide, resolve, to do sth.; **il ne savait quel p. prendre,** he did not know what course to take; **c'est un p. que je prends toujours,** I always adopt, take, this course; **il n'y a qu'un p. à prendre,** there's only one course open; **p. pris,** (i) set purpose; (ii) rank obstinacy (of opinion); bias; prejudice; **c'est un parti pris chez lui de . . .,** it is a fixed prejudice of his to . . .; **de p. pris,** (i) deliberately, of set purpose; (ii) out of sheer obstinacy; **critique sans p. pris de louange,** unbias(s)ed praise; *Prov:* **à p. pris point de conseil,** it is no use talking to a man whose mind is made up. **4.** advantage, profit; **tirer p. de qch.,** to make use of sth.; to utilize sth.; to turn sth. to account; to take advantage of (mistake, etc.); **tirer le meilleur p. de qch.,** to turn sth. to the best account; **il faut tirer le meilleur p. de cette affaire,** we must make all we can, make a good thing, out of this business; **tirer le meilleur p.**

possible de . . ., to make the best possible use of. . .. 5. (*a*) *A:* wages; (*b*) *F:* **faire un mauvais p. à qn**, (i) to ill-treat s.o., to handle s.o. roughly; to knock s.o. about; (ii) to kill s.o.; to do s.o. in.

parti², *a.* 1. *Her:* party per pale; *Sp: etc:* **une casaque (de jockey) partie de blanc et de vert**, a (jockey's) jacket half white, half green. 2. *Bot:* (*f. occ.* **partite**) partite, parted (leaf).

partiaire [parsjɛːr], *a. Jur:* **colon p.**, farmer who shares the produce of his farm with the landlord.

partial, -aux [parsjal, -o], *a.* partial (judge); bias(s)ed, unfair (critic); one-sided; **p. envers qn**, prejudiced, bias(s)ed, in favour of s.o.

partialement [parsjalmɑ̃], *adv.* partially, with partiality.

partialiste [parsjalist], *s.m. & f.* partialist.

partialité [parsjalite], *s.f.* 1. partiality (**envers**, for, to); bias, unfairness, one-sidedness; **critique pleine de p.**, bias(s)ed criticism. 2. *A:* faction, division.

participant, -ante [partisipɑ̃, -ɑ̃ːt]. 1. *a.* participating. 2. *s.* participant; participator (**de**, in); delegate, member (of a conference); competitor; contributor (to a fund, etc.).

participatif, -ive [partisipatif, -iːv], *a.* participative.

participation [partisipasjɔ̃], *s.f.* 1. participation; *Ecc:* **p. aux sacrements**, partaking of the sacraments; **cela s'est fait sans ma p.**, it was done without my taking any part in it; I had no hand in it, no share in it, nothing to do with it; *Pol:* **forte, faible, p. électorale**, heavy poll; small poll. 2. *Com:* share, interest (**à**, in); **p. aux bénéfices**, profit sharing; **compte en p.**, joint account; **opération en p.**, deal on joint account; *Publ:* **édition faite en p.**, edition published at the joint expense of publisher and author; *Jur:* **p. aux acquêts**, marriage settlement by which husband and wife share jointly acquisitions made after the marriage.

participe [partisip], *s.m. Gram:* participle; **p. présent, passé**, present, past, participle; **proposition p.**, participial phrase.

participer [partisipe], *v.i.* 1. **p. à qch.**: (*a*) to participate, have a share, an interest, in (profits, etc.); **il a participé à mes peines comme à mes plaisirs**, he shared my troubles as well as my pleasures; (*b*) to have a hand in, be a party to (plot, etc.); to share in, take (a) part in (work to be done, etc.); **voulez-vous p. à l'affaire?** would you like to be included in this, have a share in this, take part in this? 2. **p. de qch.**, to partake of, participate in, have some of the characteristics of, sth.

participial, -aux [partisipjal, -o], *a. Gram:* participial (phrase, etc.).

particulaire [partikylɛːr], *a. Ph:* particulate (matter).

particularisation [partikylarizasjɔ̃], *s.f.* particularization, particularizing.

particulariser [partikylarize], *v.tr.* 1. to particularize (a case, etc.). 2. to specify (details); to give particulars, details, of (sth.).

se particulariser, to distinguish oneself from others (**par**, through); *Pej:* to make oneself conspicuous.

particularisme [partikylarism], *s.m. Pol: Theol: etc:* particularism.

particulariste [partikylarist]. 1. *a.* particularistic. 2. *s.* particularist.

particularité [partikylarite], *s.f.* 1. detail; circumstance; **mémoire qui retient jusqu'aux moindres particularités d'un incident**, memory that retains the smallest details of an incident; **vous allez bientôt découvrir pourquoi j'insiste sur cette p.**, you will soon discover why I insist on this detail, this particular point. 2. (*a*) **la p. de ce cas ne permet pas d'en tirer des conclusions générales**, the special nature of this case prevents one from drawing general conclusions from it; (*b*) peculiarity; characteristic; **particularités d'une langue**, characteristics of a language; **les particularités de la grammaire**, grammatical anomalies; **cette p. remarquable de . . . +** *inf.*, this remarkable characteristic of . . . + *ger.*; **privilégiés qui croient à une p. d'essence de leur personne**, privileged people who believe themselves to be in a special category; **découvrir dans une œuvre une p. qui l'oppose à toutes les autres**, to discover in a work a particular characteristic that distinguishes it from any other.

particule [partikyl], *s.f.* 1. (*a*) particle, *F:* atom; **une p. de sable**, a grain of sand; *Miner:* **p. cristalline**, crystallite; (*b*) *Atom.Ph:* particle; **p. alpha, p. bêta**, alpha, beta, particle; **p. mésique**, meson; **p. émise**, emitted, ejected, particle; **p. élémentaire**, elementary particle; **p. fondamentale**, fundamental particle; **p. originale, p. primitive**, initial particle; **p. libre**, free, unbound, particle; **p. relativiste**, relativistic particle; **p. bombardante, p. projectile, p. incidente**, bombarding, incident, particle; **p. bombardée, p. cible**, bombarded, struck, particle; target particle; **p. chargée**, charged particle; **p. non chargée, p. neutre**, uncharged, neutral, particle. 2. *Gram:* particle; **avoir une p. à son nom**, to belong to the nobility, *F:* to have a handle to one's name.

particulé, -ée [partikyle], *a. & s. F:* (person) with a handle to his, her, name.

particulier, -ière [partikylje, -jɛːr]. 1. *a.* (*a*) particular, special; **mission particulière**, special mission; (*on passport*) **signes particuliers**, special peculiarities; **je n'ai rien de p. à vous dire**, I've nothing special, particular, to tell you; (*b*) peculiar, characteristic; **attitude qui lui est particulière**, an attitude that is characteristic of him, a characteristic attitude of his; **sa démarche bien particulière**, *Lit:* **une façon de marcher à lui particulière**, his own particular way of walking; **le condor est p. aux Andes**, the condor is peculiar to the Andes, is found only in the Andes; **on leur garantit l'usage de leurs coutumes et de leur religion particulières**, it was guaranteed that they should keep their own customs and religion; (*c*) unusual, uncommon; exceptional; peculiar; **faire un travail avec un soin p.**, to carry out a piece of work with exceptional, particular, care; **avoir des dispositions particulières pour les sciences**, to have an exceptional gift for science; **voilà qui est p.!** well, that's odd! that's peculiar! **roman d'un genre très p.**, novel of a particular type, with perverse tendencies; **mœurs particulières**, homosexuality; **amitié particulière**, unnatural friendship; (*d*) private (room, life, etc.); personal (account); **secrétaire p., particulière**, private secretary; **entrée particulière**, separate, private, entry; **salle de bain(s) particulière**, private bathroom; **leçons particulières**, private lessons, tuition; **j'ai des raisons particulières pour le désirer**, I have my own (private) reasons, reasons of my own, for wishing it; **à titre p.**, in a private capacity. 2. *s.* private person, private individual; **agir en tant que p., en (qualité de) simple p.**, to act in one's individual capacity, merely as a private individual; *Pej:* **il y a un p., une particulière, en bas, qui désirerait vous parler**, there's a person downstairs who would like to speak to you; **quel drôle de p.!** what a queer stick! **que nous veut ce p.?** what does that type want? 3. *s.m.* (*a*) **aller du p. au général**, to go from the particular, the specific, to the general; (*b*) **il est très aimable dans le p.**, he is very pleasant in his own home; **connaître qn dans le p.**, to know s.o. in private life; (*c*) *adv.phr.* **en p.**, (i) in particular; **notez en p. que . . .**, note particularly that . . .; (ii) **recevoir qn en p.**, to receive s.o. privately; **prendre qn en p.**, to draw s.o. aside; **les membres de cette communauté ne possèdent pas de biens en p.**, the members of this community have no personal property; (*d*) *A:* **en mon p.**, in my own mind; on my own account; **c'est ce que j'appelle en mon p. . . .**, it is what in my own mind I call . . .. 4. *s.f. A: F:* **particulière**, mistress.

particulièrement [partikyljɛrmɑ̃], *adv.* (*a*) particularly, (e)specially; **il aime tous les arts et p. la peinture**, he is fond of all the arts and especially painting; (*b*) particularly, outstandingly; **j'attire tout p. votre attention sur ce point**, I would like to draw your particular attention to this point; **avoir l'esprit de famille p. développé**, to have a particularly well-developed family spirit; **p. sensible à qch.**, exceptionally sensitive to sth.; **p. doué**, exceptionally, outstandingly, gifted; (*c*) in detail; **raconter qch. plus p.**, to tell sth. in greater detail, at greater length; (*d*) intimately; **je ne le connais pas p.**, I don't know him very well.

partie [parti], *s.f.* 1. part (of a whole); (*a*) **le tout est plus grand que sa p.**, the whole is greater than its part; **la plus grande p. des habitants**, the greater part of the inhabitants; **la plus grande p. du chemin**, the best part of the way; **pendant la plus grande p. du jour**, for the greater part of the day; **perdre la majeure p. de ses biens**, to lose the greater part of one's possessions; **une bonne p. des habitants**, a good many of the inhabitants; **une p. du papier est abîmée**, part, some, of the paper is damaged; **une bonne p. du papier est abîmée**, a good deal of the paper is damaged; much of the paper is damaged; **ses poèmes sont en grande p. incompréhensibles**, his poems are for the most part incomprehensible; **une p. de mon argent**, part of my money; **les parties du corps**, the parts of the body; **les parties génitales**, *F:* **les parties (honteuses)**, the genitals, *F:* private parts; **p. avant d'un navire**, forepart of a ship; *Gram:* **parties du discours**, parts of speech; **en p.**, partly, in part, in a measure; **en p. chaud, en p. froid**, partly hot, partly cold; **en totalité ou en p.**, wholly or partly; **les indications manquent en tout ou en p.**, indications are wholly or partly lacking; **en grande p.**, largely, to a great extent, in a great measure; **couper qch. en deux parties**, to cut sth. into two (parts); **contribuer pour p. aux frais de production**, to contribute in part to the expenses of production; **faire p. de qch.**, to be, form, part of sth.; **je ne fais plus p. de ce cercle**, I don't belong to this club any longer; **faire p. de la famille**, to be one of the family; **faire p. du bureau**, to be on the committee; **cela ne fait pas p. de mes fonctions**, that does not come within my duties; **c'est une p. essentielle, une p. intégrante, de mes fonctions**, it is part and parcel of my duties; **il fait p. de l'ambassade**, he is attached to the embassy; **faire p. des meubles**, to be part of the furnishings; (*of ship*) **faire p. d'une escadre**, to be attached to a squadron; (*b*) *Com:* (i) parcel, lot (of goods); **vendre qch. par parties**, to sell sth. in lots; **disposer d'une p. des marchandises**, to break bulk; (ii) **tenue des livres en p. simple, en p. double**, single entry, double entry bookkeeping; (iii) line, particular branch (of a business, profession); **dans quelle p. êtes vous?** what is your line (of business)? **ce n'est pas (de) ma partie**, that's not (in) my line; **les meilleurs acheteurs de la p.**, the best buyers in the trade; **je vois que vous êtes de la p.**, I see that you are in that line; I see you know all about it; (*c*) *Mus:* (*of the voice, of instrument*) part; **chant à trois parties**, three-part song; **chanter en parties**, to sing in parts; **chant en parties**, part singing; **parties d'orchestre**, orchestral parts; (*d*) (*of computer*) **p. d'adresse (d'une instruction)**, address part; **p. de bloc**, blockette; **p. type opération**, operation part, function part; **p. en virgule fixe**, fixed-point part. 2. (*a*) party; **p. de plaisir**, trip; picnic; outing; **la vie n'est pas une p. de plaisir**, life is no picnic; **organiser une p. de chasse**, to arrange, get up, a shoot, a shooting party, a day's hunting; **voulez-vous être de la p.?** will you join us? **j'étais de la p.**, I was one of the party; **dîner en p. fine**, (i) to dine in intimate tête-à-tête; (ii) to dine as a gay (mixed) party; (*b*) game, match, contest; *Ten:* match; **p. de cricket**, cricket match; *Golf:* **p. de trois**, three ball; **p. double**, foursome; **faire une p. de cartes, d'échecs**, to have, to play, a game of cards, of chess; **fin de p.**, end game; **milieu de p.**, middle game; **début de p.**, opening game; **il n'a plus personne pour faire sa p.**, he has nobody now to take a hand with him; **p. nulle**, draw, drawn game; (*in racing*) dead heat; **gagner la p.**, to win the game, the match; **la p. se trouve égale**, it is a close, even, match; *F:* **vous avez la p. belle**, you have the ball at your feet, now's your chance! **se mettre de la p.**, to give a hand, to join in; (*c*) duel; struggle; **p. inégale**, uneven struggle; **p. diplomatique**, diplomatic duel. 3. *Jur:* party (to dispute, etc.); (*a*) **p. en cause**, party to the case; **la p. lésée**, the injured party; **se rendre p. dans un procès**, to become party to an action; **être juge et p.**, to be judge in one's own case; **entendre les avocats des deux parties**, to hear counsel on both sides; **avoir affaire à forte p.**, to have a powerful opponent, *F:* a tough customer, to deal with; *Prov:* **qui n'entend qu'une p. n'entend rien**, there are two sides to every question; (*b*) *A:* **ma p.**, my opponent, the other side; **prise à p.**, suing of a magistrate for denial of justice; **prendre qn à p. (de qch., d'avoir fait qch.)**, to take s.o. to task, to call s.o. to account (for sth., for doing sth.); **je l'ai pris à p. ce matin**, I went for him about it this morning; (*c*) (*of barrister, etc.*) **ma p.**, my client; (*d*) **p. civile**, plaintiff claiming damages (in criminal case); **se constituer (en) p. civile**, to institute a civil action (in a criminal case); **se porter p. civile**, to bring a civil action against s.o. (concurrently with the criminal action); to sue s.o. for civil injury; (*e*) **les parties belligérantes**, the belligerent parties; **les hautes parties contractantes**, the high contracting parties.

partiel, -elle [parsjɛl], *a.* partial, incomplete; **paiement p.**, part payment; **éclipse partielle**, partial eclipse; **travailler à temps p.**, to have a part-time job, to work part time; *Pol:* **élection partielle**, by-election; *Mth:* **équation aux dérivées partielles**, partial differential equation.

partiellement [parsjɛlmɑ̃], *adv.* partially, partly, in part; **payer p.,** to pay (i) in part; (ii) *A:* by instalments.

partir [parti:r], *v.* (*pr.p.* **partant;** *p.p.* **parti;** *pr.ind.* **je pars, il part, n. partons, ils partent;** *pr.sub.* **je parte;** *p.d.* **je partais;** *p.h.* **je partis;** *fu.* **je partirai**) **1.** *v.tr. A:* to divide, part. **2.** *v.i.* (*the aux. is* **être,** *occ. P:* **avoir**) (*a*) to depart, leave; to start, to set out; to set off, go off; to go away; (*of ship*) to sail; (*of pers.*) to walk off, away; (*of horseman*) to ride off; (*of motorist*) to drive off; (*of aircraft*) to take off; *Ven:* (*of game*) to rise; **p. faire un tour d'inspection,** to go off, set off, on a round of inspection; **p. pour aller voir qn,** to set out, go off, to see s.o.; **je pars d'ici,** I'm going away, I'm leaving here; **je pars de la maison à huit heures,** I leave home at eight o'clock; **il est temps que je parte,** it's time I went, I left, I was off; **p. de Rome,** to leave, go away from, Rome; **p. pour, à, Paris, pour le, au, Canada, pour la, en, France, pour la, à la, campagne,** to set out, leave, for Paris, Canada, France, the country; **Mallarmé a dû p. pour un grand poème musical,** Mallarmé must have been aiming at, have set out to write, a great musical poem; **p. vers Paris,** to set out in the direction of Paris; **p. en voyage, en vacances,** to set out, go off, on a journey, on holiday; **p. chez qn,** to set out for s.o.'s house; **nous partons demain,** we're leaving, starting, tomorrow; **les domestiques n'étaient pas partis,** the servants had remained behind; **j'ai été content de le voir p.,** I was glad to see the back of him; **le train, le bateau, l'avion, part à dix heures,** the train leaves, the boat sails, the aircraft takes off, at ten (o'clock); **le train partait à dix heures,** the train was due to leave at ten (o'clock); **partez!** (i) get out! go! get off (with you)! (ii) *Sp:* go! **p. de ce monde,** to die, to depart this life; *F:* **elle allait p.,** she was going, dying; **p. à toute vitesse,** to set off at full speed; to hurry off; **p. au galop,** to set off at a gallop, to gallop away; **p. en avant,** to go on ahead; **p. comme une flèche, comme un trait,** to be off like a shot; to dart off; **nous voilà partis,** we're off; the train's (etc.) moving; **nous voilà (bien) mal partis,** (i) this isn't a very good, is rather a bad, start; (ii) the future doesn't look too bright, too good (for us); *F:* **la voilà partie!** she's off (on her favourite subject)! **les mots étaient à peine partis que . . .,** the words were hardly out of my, his, etc., mouth when . . .; **son nouveau livre est bien parti,** his new book has made a good start; **nous sommes partis pour une période de prospérité,** we are in for a period of prosperity; **p. de zéro,** to start from scratch; *Cards:* **p. d'une couleur,** to lead in a suit; *Aut:* **le moteur est parti du premier coup,** the engine started (at the) first go; **le fusil est tombé et est parti,** the gun fell and went off; **ces allumettes partent mal,** these matches strike badly, are bad strikers; *F:* **être parti,** to be tipsy, tight; **à moitié parti,** half-seas over; **p. à rire, p. d'un éclat de rire,** to burst out laughing; (*b*) to go, to give (way), to break; (*of button, etc.*) to come off; (*of cable*) to part, to give way; **la peinture commence à p.,** the paint's beginning to peel, to come off, to wear off; (*c*) to emanate, spring, proceed (**de,** from); **langage qui part du cœur,** words from the heart; **il est parti de rien,** he started from nothing; **partant du principe que . . .,** starting from the principle that . . .; **la Meuse part des Vosges,** the Meuse has its source in the Vosges; **une branche qui partait du tronc,** a branch growing out of the (tree) trunk; (*d*) *prep.phr.* **à p. de:** (i) **à p. d'aujourd'hui,** from today (onwards); **à p. du 15,** on and after the 15th; **comptant à p. d'hier,** reckoning from yesterday; **je serai libre à p. de trois heures,** I shall be free from three o'clock onwards, (any time) after three o'clock; **à p. de ce moment,** from that time onwards; **à p. de la route, il courut,** as soon as he got to the road, from the road onwards, he ran; (ii) **bâtir qch. à p. de rien,** to build sth. out of nothing; *Com:* **robes à p. de 50 francs,** dresses from 50 francs (upwards); (iii) **à p. de ces données, expliquez . . .,** given these facts, from these data, explain . . .; **il faut étudier les problèmes de la circulation à p. du nombre des véhicules,** any study of traffic problems must be based on the number of vehicles on the roads. **3. faire p.:** (*a*) to send off, dispatch (troops, etc.); **faire p. qn,** (i) to send s.o. away; to turn s.o. out; (ii) to turn s.o. away; (*b*) to remove, get out (stain, etc.); (*c*) to fire, discharge, let off (gun); to let off, set off (fireworks); to fire (rocket); to touch off (mine); to set (engine) going, to start (engine); (*d*) *Ven:* to start, put up (partridge, etc.); to flush (covey); (*e*) to start (some physical process); *Cu:* to bring (food) to the boil; (*f*) *Const:* **faire p. la pierre,** to split the stone.

partisan, -ane [partizɑ̃, -an]. **1.** *s.* partisan, follower; advocate, upholder, supporter (of custom, etc.); *Pol:* backer; **être p. d'une méthode,** to approve of a method, to believe in a method; **je suis p. de la réforme,** I am (all) for reform; **p. de la manière forte,** believer in the strong hand; *Pol:* **un p. convaincu des vieux partis traditionnels,** a true blue. **2.** *s.m. Mil:* guer(r)illa (soldier), partisan; **guerre de partisans,** guer(r)illa warfare. **3.** *a.* **querelles partisanes,** party, sectarian, quarrels; **esprit p.,** bias(s)ed mind.

partisanerie [partizanri], *s.f.* partisan spirit.

partita [partita], *s.f. Mus:* partita.

partiteur [partitœ:r], *s.m.* irrigation sluice.

partitif, -ive [partitif, -i:v], *a. & s.m. Gram:* partitive (noun, article).

partition [partisjɔ̃], *s.f.* **1.** *Pol:* partition, division. **2.** *Her:* quarter, partition (of shield). **3.** *Mus:* score; **écrire une p. sur "Othello,"** to set "Othello" to music; **p. d'orchestre,** full score; **p. piano et chant,** pianoforte and vocal score; **p. réduite,** compressed score, short score; piano score.

partouse, partouze [partu:z], *s.f. P:* orgy.

partout [partu], *adv.* (*a*) everywhere, on all sides, in every direction; **en tout et p.,** at all times and in all places; **chercher qch. p.,** to hunt for sth. high and low, everywhere; **faire savoir une nouvelle p.,** to broadcast a piece of news; **p. où,** wherever; **p. ailleurs,** anywhere else; **un peu p.,** all over the place; **un peu p. en France,** almost anywhere in France; **(nouvelles) de p.,** (news) from all quarters, from everywhere; **suivre qn p.,** to follow s.o. everywhere, *F:* all over the place; **souffrir de p.,** to feel pain, to be sore, all over; (*b*) all, all together; (*dominoes*) **trois, cinq, p.,** all three, all five; *Ten:* **quatre jeux p.,** four all; **set p.,** set all; *Nau:* (*to boat crew*) **sciez p.!** back together! (*to engine room*) **stoppez p.,** stop all engines.

partschine [partʃin], *s.f. Miner:* partschinite.

parturiente [partyrjɑ̃:t], *s.f.* parturient; woman in childbirth.

parturition [partyrisjɔ̃], *s.f.* parturition, childbirth; (*of animals*) dropping (of young); **en p.,** parturient.

parulidés [parylide], *s.m.pl. Orn:* Parulidae, American warblers.

parulie [paryli], *s.f. Med:* parulia, gumboil.

parure [pary:r], *s.f.* **1.** (action of) ornamenting, adorning; *Lit:* **la beauté sans p.,** beauty unadorned. **2.** (*a*) dress, finery; (*b*) ornament, head-dress; (*c*) set (of jewellery, of collar and cuffs, of lingerie, etc.); **p. de diamants,** set of diamonds; **p. de manchettes,** cuff links; (*d*) **les fleurs sont la p. d'un jardin,** flowers are the beauty of a garden. **3.** *Tchn:* parings (of leather, etc.); trimmings (of meat).

parurerie [paryrəri], *s.f.* costume jewellery and accessories trade.

parurier, -ière [paryrje, -jɛ:r], *s.* (i) manufacturer of, (ii) dealer in, costume jewellery and accessories.

parution [parysjɔ̃], *s.f. Publ:* appearance, publication, issue (of book); **dès p.,** as soon as published; from the date of publication.

parvenir [parvənir], *v.i.* (*conj. like* VENIR. *The aux. is* **être**) **1.** (*a*) to arrive; **p. à un endroit,** to arrive at, to reach, a place; to find one's way to a place; **votre lettre m'est parvenue,** your letter has reached me; I received your letter; **votre demande doit nous p. avant le 4,** your application must be in by the 4th; **ce fait parvint à ma connaissance,** this fact came to my knowledge; **un aboiement lointain lui parvint,** his ears caught a sound of distant barking; **faire p. qch. à qn,** to send, to forward, sth. to s.o.; **comment vous le faire p.?** how am I to get it to you? **enfin les sauveteurs sont parvenus jusqu'à lui,** at last the rescuers got to him; (*b*) **écrits anciens qui sont parvenus jusqu'à nous,** ancient writings which have survived to our times, which have been handed down to us. **2.** (*a*) to attain, reach (a great age, one's ends); to succeed; **p. au haut d'une montagne,** to reach the summit of a mountain; **p. à la dignité de maréchal,** to attain the dignity of field marshal; **p. à faire qch.,** to manage to do sth.; **il parvint à s'échapper,** he succeeded in escaping, he made good his escape; **p. à ses fins,** to achieve one's purpose; **sans y p.,** without success; **je parvins à ce qu'il fût placé dans mon bataillon,** I managed to have him posted to my battalion; (*b*) *abs.* to succeed in life; **le moyen de p.,** how to succeed; the way to get on; how to make one's way.

parvenu, -ue [parvəny], *s.* parvenu, self-made person; upstart; **les parvenus,** the newly rich; **toilettes trop riches qui sentent la parvenue,** over-elaborate clothes that smack of the newly rich.

parvifolié [parvifɔlje], *a. Bot:* parvifolious.

parvis [parvi], *s.m.* (*a*) parvis, square (in front of a church); (*b*) *B:* court (of Solomon's Temple); *Poet:* **les célestes p.,** the courts of heaven.

parvoline [parvɔlin], *s.f. Ch:* parvolin(e).

pas[1] [pɑ], *s.m.* **1.** step, stride, pace; footstep; (*a*) **mesurer une distance au p.,** to pace off a distance; **étalonner le p.,** to scale pace; **étalonnage du p.,** scaling, scale, of pace; **à chaque p.,** at every step; **p. à p.,** step by step, little by little; **allonger le p.,** to lengthen step, to step out; to put one's best foot forward; **raccourcir le p.,** to shorten step; **diriger, porter, ses p. vers un endroit,** to proceed, to make one's way, towards a place; **aller, marcher, à p. comptés,** to walk with measured tread; **aller, avancer, marcher, à grands p. (sur la route),** to stride along (the road); **il s'avança à grands pas,** he strode up (to us, to them, etc.); he came striding forward; **l'hiver arrive à grands pas,** winter is approaching rapidly; **s'éloigner à grands p.,** to stride away; to stalk off; **aller, marcher, à petits p.,** (i) (*of child, etc.*) to toddle (along); (ii) to walk with mincing steps; to mince along; **avancer, monter, descendre, entrer, sortir, à petits p.,** to toddle along, up, down, in, out; **faire un p.,** to take a step; **faire un p. en avant, en arrière,** to step forward, back; **cette expérience constitue un grand p. en avant,** this experiment constitutes an important step forward; *Mil: etc:* **"numéros impairs, un p. en avant!"** "odd numbers, one pace forward!" **p. de côté,** side step; **faire un p. de côté,** to take a step sideways; to step aside; **faire les cent p.,** to pace up and down; **faux p.,** (i) slip, stumble; (ii) (social) blunder, faux pas; **faire un faux p.,** (i) to stumble; (ii) to blunder, to make a faux pas; **le premier p.,** (i) the first step; (ii) *F:* the thin end of the wedge; **faire le premier p.,** to make the first move; **il n'y a que le premier p. qui coûte,** only the beginning is difficult; **faire un p. dans la bonne direction, dans la bonne voie,** to take a step in the right direction; **il a fait un grand p.,** he has made good progress, great strides; **c'est déjà un grand p. de fait,** that's already a great step forward; **faire des p. pour qn,** to go to some trouble for s.o.; **vous y perdrez vos p.,** you will get nothing for your pains; **j'y vais de ce p.,** I am going this instant, at once; **entendre des p., un bruit de p.,** to hear footsteps; **entendre un bruit de p. précipités,** to hear hurrying footsteps; **j'entends son p. léger,** I hear her light footstep; **entendre le p. rythmé des troupes en marche,** to hear the rhythmic tramp of troops marching; **j'entendis le p. d'un cheval,** I heard a horse's tread; **reconnaître le p. de qn,** to recognize s.o.'s step; **je l'ai reconnu à son p.,** I knew him by his step; **il demeure à deux pas d'ici, à deux p. de la maison,** he lives a few steps away, within a stone's throw from here, within a few steps of the house; **je n'ai que deux p. à faire d'ici chez moi,** it is only a step to my house; **il était à deux p. de nous,** he was within a couple of paces of us; **on n'y voit pas à trois p.,** you can't see three steps ahead; (*b*) pace; **au p.,** (i) at a walking pace; (ii) *P.N: Aut:* dead slow; **aller au p.,** to go at a walking pace, *Equit:* to ride at foot pace; **mettre son cheval au p.,** to walk one's horse; **marcher au p.,** (i) to walk, move at a walk; (ii) *Mil: etc:* to march in step, in time; **marche au p.,** march in step; **se mettre au p.,** to take step, to fall into step; *F:* **mettre qn au p.,** to reduce s.o. to obedience, to bring s.o. to heel; **être au p., marcher au p.,** to be in step, to keep step; **conserver, garder, le p.,** to keep in step; **marquer le p.,** (i) to mark time; (ii) *F:* to be behindhand, to be delayed; **changer le p.,** to change step; **perdre le p.,** to fall out of step; **n'être pas au p.,** to be out of step; **rompre le p.,** to break step; **hâter, presser, le p.,** to quicken (one's) pace; **ralentir le p.,** to slacken (one's) pace; **aller, marcher, du même p. que qn,** to keep pace with s.o.; **p. ordinaire,** marching step, ordinary step, pace; *O:* **p. accéléré, p. redoublé,** quick time, quick step; *Fr.Mil.Mus:* **p. redoublé,** military march; **p. cadencé,** quick march, quick time; **marcher au p. cadencé,** to march at attention, in quick time; **marche au p. cadencé,** march at attention, quick march; **prendre le, se**

mettre au, p. cadencé, (i) to break into quick march, into quick time; (ii) to fall into step; **p. de parade,** parade march, slow march; **p. de route,** route step, route order, march at ease; **marcher au p. de route,** to march at ease, at route step; **marche au p. de route,** march at ease, at route step; **p. de route, marche!** march at ease!; **prendre le, se mettre au, p. de route,** to break step; *Fr.Mil:* **p. sans cadence,** march at ease (executed in silence); **p. de gymnastique,** double time, double march; **prendre le p. de gymnastique,** to break into the double; **p. de charge,** charging pace; **avancer au p. de gymnastique, au p. de charge, au p. de course,** to advance at the double; **p. de l'oie,** goosestep; *Danc:* **p. de valse,** waltz step; **p. seul,** pas seul; (*c*) precedence; **avoir, prendre, le p. sur qn,** (i) to have, take, precedence of s.o.; (ii) to have a (considerable) lead over, to take the lead from, s.o.; (iii) to put s.o. into the background; **avoir l'honneur du p. sur qn,** to take precedence of s.o.; **disputer le p. à qn,** to contend for precedence with s.o.; **céder, donner, le p. à qn,** (i) to give s.o. precedence; (ii) to allow s.o. to pass, to overtake; **pour le chauffage central le charbon cède le p. au mazout,** solid fuel central heating is giving way to oil-fired central heating, oil-fired central heating is replacing solid fuel; (*d*) (*of computer*) **p. d'entraînement,** feed pitch; **p. longitudinal,** row pitch; **p. du programme,** programme stop. **2.** footprint, footmarks, tracks; **marcher sur les p. de qn,** (i) to follow in s.o.'s footprints, in s.o.'s tracks; (ii) to follow in s.o.'s footsteps; **s'attacher aux p. de qn,** to dog s.o., s.o.'s footsteps; **leur dévouement les entraîna sur ses p.,** their devotion carried them on behind him; *Prov:* **cela ne se trouve pas sous, dans, le p. d'un cheval,** (a thing like) that is not found every day; it doesn't grow on every hedge, it's not easily come by. **3.** (*a*) step (of stair); **p. de souris,** winder; (*b*) threshold (of door); **le p. de la porte,** the doorstep; **il est sur le p. de sa porte,** he's standing in his doorway; *Com:* **p. de porte,** goodwill; key money; **céder le pas de (la) porte,** to give up the goodwill (of a business). **4.** passage; (mountain) pass; strait; **le P. des Thermopyles,** the Pass of Thermopylae; **le P. de Calais,** the Straits of Dover; **mauvais p.,** tight corner, awkward situation; **tirer qn d'un mauvais p.,** to get s.o. out of a hole, out of a fix; **sauter le p.,** (i) to take a decided step, to take the plunge, to cross the Rubicon; (ii) (*of condemned criminal*) to die. **5.** *A:* **p. d'armes,** passage of arms. **6.** *Tchn:* (*a*) pitch, thread (of screw); **p. de vis mâle, femelle,** male, female, thread; **p. bâtard,** odd pitch; **p. exact,** even pitch; **p. fin, gros,** fine, coarse, thread; **p. normalisé,** unified thread; **p. du Congrès,** Congress pitch; **p. (système) international,** international standard thread; **p. national,** national thread; **p. américain,** American national thread, American (standard) thread; **p. anglais,** British standard thread; **p. (système) français,** French standard thread; **p. à droite, à gauche,** right-handed, left-handed, thread; **vis à p. à droite, à p. à gauche,** right-handed, left-handed, screw; **p. d'enroulement,** winding pitch, pitch of grooving; **p. des spires,** pitch of turns; (*b*) *Nau: Av:* pitch (of propeller); **grand p.,** high pitch, coarse pitch; **petit p.,** low pitch, fine pitch; **p. géométrique,** geometric pitch; **p. géométrique relatif,** pitch diameter ratio; **p. effectif,** effective pitch; **p. effectif relatif,** effective pitch ratio; **p. efficace,** experimental mean pitch; **commande de p.,** pitch control; **changement de p.,** pitch change; **vitesse de changement de p.,** rate of pitch change; **dispositif d'inversion du p.,** pitch reversing mechanism; **écart entre les p. (de l'hélice),** pitch range; **p. cyclique,** cyclic pitch (of helicopter); **p. collectif,** collective pitch; **p. angulaire de pale (d'hélice),** blade sweep; (*c*) *Mec.E:* **p. de denture,** pitch of gear; **p. diamétral,** diametral pitch; **p. de chaîne,** chain pitch; **p. de la chenille,** pitch of track (of tank, etc.); (*d*) *Artil: Sm.a:* **p. des rayures,** twist of the rifling; **p. constant, progressif,** uniform twist, increasing twist (of rifling); (*e*) *Cin:* **p. de l'image,** frame gauge; **p. de la perforation,** perforation gauge; **p. normal,** standard gauge; (*f*) *Tex:* shed.

pas², *neg.adv.* **1.** (*a*) (*used alone, or strengthening* **ne** *if the verb is expressed*) not; no; **je ne sais p.,** I don't know; **il n'a p. de pain,** he has no bread; **je ne l'ai p. encore vu,** I have not seen him yet; **p. toujours,** not always; **p. du tout,** not at all, by no means; *F:* not a bit of it; **pourquoi p.?** why not? **p. moi,** not I; **nous marchons peu ou p.,** we walk little or not at all; **qu'il vienne ou p. cela m'est égal,** it's all one to me whether he comes or not; I don't care whether he comes or not; *F:* **p. vrai?** really? **tu rentreras de bonne heure, p.?** you'll be home early, won't you? (*b*) *P:* (**ne** *omitted*) **ayez p. peur,** don't be afraid; **connais p.!** I don't know him, her! (*c*) (*strengthening* **non**) **affaibli mais non p. découragé,** weakened but not discouraged; **non p., s'il vous plaît!** not so, (if you) please! **non p. qu'il soit beau,** not that he is handsome; (*d*) (*qualifying an adj.*) **une ville p. belle,** not a beautiful town; **des lilas p. fleuris,** lilac not yet in bloom; **un individu p. trop mal tourné,** a quite good-looking man. **2. p. un:** (*a*) **p. un(e) ne répondit,** not one replied; **p. un mot ne fut dit,** not a word was spoken; **qui le croira?—p. un,** who will believe it?—no one, not a soul; (*b*) *F:* **fier, adroit, comme p. un, p. deux,** prouder, cleverer, than anyone; **il connaît Paris mieux que p. un,** he knows Paris better than anyone; **elle chante comme p. une,** she can sing with the best; **il sait l'anglais comme p. un,** he knows English if any man does; **il est menteur comme p. un,** he's a terrible liar.

pasan [pazɑ̃], *s.m. Z:* pasan, gemsbok.

pasang [pazɑ̃], *s.m. Z:* pasang, bezoar goat.

pascal¹, -aux [paskal, -o], *a.* paschal (lamb); Easter (communion, etc.); *R.C.Ch:* **faire son devoir p.,** to perform one's Easter duties; **les vacances pascales,** the Easter vacation, holiday(s).

Pascal.² 1. *Pr.n. Ph:* **principe de P.,** Pascal's law, principle. **2.** *s.m. Ph.Meas:* pascal; *pl. pascals.*

pascalien, -ienne [paskaljɛ̃, -jɛn], *a.* relating to Pascal.

pascoïte [paskɔit], *s.f. Miner:* pascoite.

pas-d'âne [pɑdɑːn], *s.m.inv.* **1.** (*a*) *A.Arms:* pas-d'âne, finger guard (of hilt); (*b*) *Harn: A:* port (of bit); (*c*) *Vet:* gag (for horse, dog, etc.). **2.** *Bot:* coltsfoot, hogweed.

pas-de-géant [pɑdʒeɑ̃], *s.m.inv. Gym:* giant stride.

paseng [pasɛ̃], *s.m. Z:* pasang, paseng, bezoar goat.

Pasiphaé [pazifae], *Pr.n.f. Gr.Myth:* Pasiphae.

paso doble [pasodɔbl̩], *s.m. Danc:* paso doble.

Pasquin [paskɛ̃]. **1.** *Pr.n.m.* Pasquino (the mutilated statue at Rome, to which lampoons were affixed). **2.** *s.m. A:* (*a*) lampooner; (*b*) *Th:* man-servant (in old comedy); (*c*) = PASQUINADE.

pasquinade [paskinad], *s.f. A:* pasquinade, lampoon, squib.

pasquiner [paskine], **pasquiniser** [paskinize], *v.tr. A:* to pasquinade; to lampoon.

passable [pɑsabl̩], *a.* **1.** passable, tolerable, fairly good; **écriture p.,** fairly good (hand)writing; (*in exam. etc.*) **obtenir une note p.,** to get a fairly good mark; *Sch:* (*in degree exam.*) **mention p.** = second class, division II; **c'est très p.,** it's not too bad. **2. une différence p.,** an appreciable difference.

passablement [pɑsabləmɑ̃], *adv.* passably, tolerably, fairly; **vin p. bon,** quite good, fairly good, wine; **dessiner p.,** to draw tolerably well; **il travaille p.,** he is working quite well; **il travaille très p.,** he is doing moderately well.

passacaille [pasakɑːj], *s.f.* **1.** *Mus: Danc: A:* passacaglia. **2.** *Cards:* **faire la p.,** to finesse a low trump (in ruffing).

passade [pɑsad], *s.f.* **1.** *F: Dial:* short stay; **je n'ai fait qu'une p. à Lyon,** I merely passed through Lyon, made a flying visit to Lyon. **2.** passing fancy, short liaison. **3.** (*a*) *Equit:* passade; (*b*) *Fenc:* pass, thrust. **4.** *Swim: O:* leapfrog(ging).

passage¹ [pɑsaːʒ], *s.m.* passage. **1.** (i) crossing (of sth.); (ii) passing over, through, across; going past (a place); (*a*) **p. des Alpes, d'un fleuve,** crossing of the Alps, of a river; **la rivière est de p. facile,** the river is easy to cross; *Hist:* **le p. du Rhin,** the crossing of the Rhine; *Nau:* **p. de la ligne,** crossing the line; **p. d'un train,** passing of a train; *Com:* **p. d'un représentant,** visit, call, of a traveller, a representative; **j'attends le p. du facteur,** I am waiting for the postman to pass; **chacun sourit sur son p.,** every one smiles as he, she, passes, as he, she, goes by; **guetter le p. de qn,** to waylay s.o., to lie in wait for s.o.; **il y a toujours du p. ici,** (i) there's always a lot of traffic here; (ii) there are always people coming and going, always crowds, here; **il bouleversa tout sur son p.,** he left chaos in his track, in his trail, in his train; **livrer p. à qn,** to allow s.o. to pass; **céder le p. à qn,** (i) to let s.o. pass first; (ii) to allow s.o. to overtake, to pass; *P.N:* **p. interdit (au public),** no entry; no thoroughfare; **le p. des harengs,** the passage of the herrings; **p. de Vénus (sur le disque du soleil),** transit of Venus; **oiseau de p.,** bird of passage; **plaisirs de p.,** transient pleasures; **droit de p.,** right of way; **payer un droit de p.,** to pay toll; **être de p. dans une ville,** to be making only a short stay in, to be only passing through, a town; **voyageur de p. à Paris,** traveller passing through Paris; *Mil:* **compagnie de p.,** forward replacement group, *U.S:* replacement company; *Com:* **nous n'avons que la clientèle de p.,** *F:* **que le p.,** we have only the chance customer, (*at hotel*) the chance guest; *Mus:* **note de p.,** passing note; **notes de p.,** grace notes; **j'ai noté au p. que . . .,** I noted in passing that . . .; *El:* **p. du courant,** flow of current; (*b*) *Nau:* passage; **payer son p.,** to pay for one's passage; **gagner son p.,** to work one's passage; **bateau de p.,** (i) ferry boat; (ii) *Navy: etc:* shore boat; **pouvez-vous me donner un p. dans votre embarcation?** can you give me a passage in your boat? **droits de p.,** ferry dues; (*c*) **p. du jour à la nuit, de la crainte à l'espoir,** transition, change, from day to night, from fear to hope; **avec le p. du temps,** as the days passed, as time went by; **le p. du gaz à l'électricité,** the changeover from gas to electricity; **le p. de la libre entreprise au collectivisme,** the changeover from free enterprise to collectivism; **le p. d'une économie du temps de guerre à une économie du temps de paix,** the conversion from a war economy to a peace economy; *Mil:* **le p. dans la réserve,** transfer to the reserve; **le p. d'une formation à une autre,** the passage from one formation to another; (*d*) *Metall:* pass (through rolling mill); (*e*) *F:* **p. à tabac,** third degree; (*f*) *W.Tel: T.V:* **ce morceau a eu beaucoup de passages,** this piece has been broadcast, televised, many times; (*g*) *Meteor:* **p. nuageux, pluvieux,** cloudy, rainy, interval; **ne vous en faites pas, ce n'est qu'un mauvais p.,** don't worry, it's just a bad patch; *Psy:* **un p. à vide,** a blank. **2.** (*a*) way, way through, thoroughfare; alley; roadway; gateway; *Nau:* channel; **profondeur d'eau dans le p.,** depth of water in the fairway; **le p. Nord-Ouest,** the North-West passage; **p. dans les montagnes,** mountain pass; **p. voûté,** archway; **se frayer, se faire, un p.,** to force, elbow, one's way through; **barrer le p. à qn,** to stand in s.o.'s way; to block s.o.'s way; (*b*) arcade (with shops on either side); (*c*) *Rail:* **p. à niveau,** level crossing; *U.S:* grade crossing; **p. en dessus, p. supérieur,** *Civ.E:* flyover, overpass; *Rail:* overbridge, bridge over; *U.S:* above grade crossing; **p. en dessous, p. inférieur,** *Civ.E:* **p. souterrain,** *Civ.E:* underground crossing, subway, underpass; *Rail:* underbridge, bridge under; *U.S:* below grade crossing; *Adm:* **p. pour piétons,** *F:* **p. clouté,** pedestrian crossing; *U.S:* crosswalk; (*d*) outlet (of pipe); waterway (of tap); **ménager un p. pour la fumée,** to provide an outlet for the smoke; (*e*) ferry; (*f*) crossing; *Mount:* pitch; **p. en artificiel,** artificial pitch. **3.** *Av:* pass; **l'avion effectua deux passages à basse altitude au-dessus des lignes ennemies,** the aircraft made two low passes over the enemy lines. **4.** (*a*) (short) part, portion; passage (of book, etc.); piece (of music, etc.); **un p. obscur de Virgile,** an obscure passage in Virgil; (*b*) *Mus:* cadenza. **5.** *Mil: etc:* **p. des consignes,** handing over, transmission, of (special) orders.

passage², *s.m. Equit:* passage.

passager¹, -ère [pɑsaʒe, -ɛːr]. **1.** *a.* (*a*) **oiseau p.,** migratory bird, bird of passage; (*b*) fleeting, short-lived, transitory (beauty, etc.); momentary (pain, etc.); (*c*) *F:* **rue passagère,** busy thoroughfare. **2.** *s.* (*a*) passer-by, passing traveller; (*b*) passenger (by sea or air); *Nau:* **p. d'entrepont,** steerage passenger; **p. clandestin,** stowaway.

passager², *v.tr. & i. Equit:* to passage.

passagèrement [pɑsaʒɛrmɑ̃], *adv.* momentarily, for a short time.

passageur [pɑsaʒœːr], *s.m.* ferryman.

passalidés [pasalide], *s.m.pl. Ent:* Passalidae.

passant, -ante [pɑsɑ̃, -ɑ̃ːt]. **1.** *a.* (*a*) (*of road, etc.*) (i) open to the public; (ii) busy; congested; (*b*) *Her:* passant. **2.** *s.* passer-by. **3.** *s.m.* (*a*) *Tls:* (woodcutter's) cross-cut saw; (*b*) *Harn:* keeper, guide; **p. coulant,** sliding keeper; **p. fixe,** fixed loop; **p. de courroie,** strap loop; (*c*) *Sm.a.* frog (for scabbard).

passation [pɑsasjɔ̃], *s.f.* drawing up, signing (of agreement); making (of contract); entering into (contract, lease, bargain); *Com:* placing (of order); *Fin:* passing (of dividend); *Jur:* filing (of return at registration office); *Book-k:* passing, making (of entries); entering (of items); **p. des pouvoirs,** transfer of power; *Com:* **15% à la p. de la commande,** 15% with order, when placing the order.

passavant [pɑsavɑ̃], *s.m.* **1.** *Nau:* (*a*) (fore-and-aft) gangway, catwalk; (*b*) waist (of ship). **2.** *Adm:* permit; *Cust:* transire.

passe [pɑːs], *s.f.* **1.** (*a*) passing, passage (of birds, etc.); **une longue p. de froid,** a long spell of cold; (*b*) *A:* permit, pass; **p. de chemin de fer,** (free) railway pass; (*still used in*) **mot de p.,** password; (*c*) **p. magnétique,** mesmeric pass; (*d*) *Fb: etc:* pass; **p. en avant,** forward pass; **p. en arrière,** back pass; *Ten:* **p. de jeu,** rally; (*e*) *Metalw:* cut (on lathe); **profondeur de p.,** depth of cut; **p. d'ébauche, de finition,** roughing, finishing, cut; (*welding*) **p. chaude,** hot pass; **p. étroite,** string bead; **p. sur l'envers,** back pass; (*f*) *F:* (prostitute's) "short time"; **maison, hôtel, de p.,** (prostitute's) house of call, assignation hotel; (*g*) (*at roulette*) any number above 18. **2.** (*a*) *Fenc:* pass, thrust; (*b*) **p. d'armes,** passage of arms, passage at arms. **3.** *Nau:* pass, fairway, harbour channel, navigable channel; gat (through shallows); **p. étroite,** narrows. **4.** (*a*) *Games: A:* port (at billiards); ring (at pall-mall) (through which the ball must pass); *hence* (*b*) *F:* **vous êtes en bonne p.,** it's all plain sailing, you're in a strong position; **être en (bonne) p. de . . .,** to be in a fair way to . . .; **il est en p. de faire fortune,** he looks as though he will make a fortune; **race en p. de disparaître,** race threatened with extinction; **être dans une mauvaise p., traverser une p. difficile,** to be in a tight corner; **on a franchi la mauvaise p.,** the worst is over; *Iron:* **être dans une jolie p.,** to be in a fine predicament. **5.** (*a*) *Typ:* overplus; **main de p., simple p.,** over-quire, overplus, extra sheets (of printing paper); paper overs; **double p.,** double overs; *Publ:* **exemplaires de p.,** surplus copies (of book); over copies; **tirer à 1000 exemplaires et la p., et la double p.,** to print 1050, 1100, copies; (*b*) *Com:* (i) odd money; (ii) **p. de caisse,** allowance to cashier for errors. **6.** (front) brim (of hat).

passé [pɑse]. **1.** *a.* (*a*) past, gone by; **événement p.,** past event; **la semaine passée,** last week; **il est quatre heures passées,** it is, has, gone four; it is after four; **il a quarante ans passés,** he is over forty, on the wrong side of forty; (*b*) over; **l'orage est p.,** the storm is over; (*c*) faded (colour, material); **beauté passée,** faded beauty. **2.** *s.m.* **le p.:** (*a*) the past; former times; **comme par le p.,** as in the past; **faire comme par le p.,** to go on as before; **fouiller dans le p. de qn,** to rake up s.o.'s past; **oublions le p.,** let bygones be bygones; **vivre dans le p.,** to live in the past; *Jur:* **p. chargé,** bad record; (*b*) *Gram:* past (tense); **verbe au p.,** verb in the past (tense); **p. antérieur,** pluperfect; **p. défini, simple,** preterite, past historic; **p. composé,** perfect (tense); (*c*) *Needlew:* **broderie au p.,** satin stitch embroidery. **3.** *prep.* beyond; **il est p. quatre heures,** it is, has, gone four; **p. les tranchées, pas un abri,** beyond the trenches there is no shelter; **p. cette date,** after this date; (NOTE. *Sometimes with the concord:* **passées les tranchées, passée cette date**).

passe-bande [pɑsbɑ̃ːd], *s.m. W.Tel:* band pass; *attrib.* **filtre p.-b.,** band-pass filter; *pl. passe-bandes.*

passe-bas, passe-basse [pɑsbɑ, pɑsbɑːs], *a. W.Tel:* **filtre passe-bas,** low-pass filter; *pl. passe-bas(ses).*

passe-bouillon [pɑsbujɔ̃], *s.m.inv. Cu:* soup strainer.

passe-boules [pɑsbul], *s.m.inv.* (*at fair*) (type of) Aunt Sally.

passe-carreau [pɑskaro], *s.m.* (tailor's) sleeve board; *pl. passe-carreaux.*

passe-cheval [pɑsʃ(ə)val], *s.m.* horse ferry; *pl. passe-chevaux.*

passe-corde [pɑskɔrd], *s.m. Tls:* (saddler's) drawing awl; *pl. passe-cordes.*

passe-cordon [pɑskɔrdɔ̃], *s.m.* bodkin; *pl. passe-cordons.*

passe-coude [pɑskud], *s.m.* elbow glove, long glove; *pl. passe-coudes.*

passe-crassane [pɑskrasan], *s.f.* (variety of) winter pear; *pl. passe-crassanes.*

passe-debout [pɑsdəbu], *s.m.inv. A: Cust:* transire (granted for 24 hours, and exempting from town-dues).

passe-déversoir [pɑsdevɛrswaːr], *s.m. Hyd.E:* spillback, spill channel, spillway; *pl. passe-déversoirs.*

passe-droit [pɑsdrwa], *s.m.* injustice; illegitimate favour; unfair promotion; **faire un p.-d. à qn,** to do an injustice to s.o. (by promoting a junior over his head); **le fils du patron a bénéficié d'un p.-d.,** the boss's son was promoted over the heads of others; *pl. passe-droits.*

passée [pɑse], *s.f.* **1.** *Ven:* (*a*) flight (of game birds); **chasse à la p.,** flighting; (*b*) net (for catching woodcock); (*c*) track (of game animal); **les passées d'un cerf,** the slot of a deer. **2.** (*a*) *Fish:* cast; (*b*) *Row: Swim:* stroke. **3.** *Geol: Min:* seam.

passefilage [pɑsfilaːʒ], *s.m.* darning.

passefiler [pɑsfile], *v.tr.* to darn.

passe-fils [pɑsfil], *s.m.inv. Nau: etc:* cord eye; grommet.

passefilure [pɑsfilyːr], *s.f.* darn.

passe-fleur [pɑsflœːr], *s.f. Bot:* **1.** pulsatilla, pasque flower. **2.** rose campion; *pl. passe-fleurs.*

passe-garde [pɑsgard], *s.f.inv. A.Arm:* passe-garde.

passège [pɑsɛːʒ], *s.m. Equit:* passage.

passéger [pɑseʒe], *v.tr. & i.* (**je passège, n. passégeons; je passégeai(s); je passégerai**) *Equit:* (*of rider*) to passage (horse); (*of horse*) to passage.

passe-haut [pɑso], *a.inv. W.Tel:* **filtre p.-h.,** high-pass filter.

passéisme [pɑseism], *s.m. Lit: Pej:* addiction to the past.

passéiste [pɑseist], *Lit: Pej:* (*a*) *a.* addicted to the past; (*b*) *s.m. & f.* person addicted to the past.

passe-lacet [pɑslasɛ], *s.m.* bodkin; *F:* **être raide comme un p.-l.,** to be (stony) broke; *pl. passe-lacets.*

passe-lait [pɑslɛ], *s.m.inv.* milk strainer.

passement [pɑsmɑ̃], *s.m.* (gold, silk) lace (for clothes); braid, braiding (for furniture).

passementer [pɑsmɑ̃te], *v.tr.* to trim (garment, etc.) with passementerie; to braid (edge of chair, etc.).

passementerie [pɑsmɑ̃tri], *s.f.* **1.** making or selling of passementerie. **2.** passementerie; trimmings.

passementier, -ière [pɑsmɑ̃tje, -jɛːr], *s.* maker of or dealer in passementerie.

passemèse [pɑsmɛːz], *s.f. Danc:* passamezzo, passemeasure.

passe-montagne [pɑsmɔ̃taɲ], *s.m.* balaclava helmet; *pl. passe-montagnes.*

passe-parole [pɑsparɔl], *s.m.inv. Mil:* order passed by word of mouth from the head to the rear of a column.

passe-partout [pɑspartu], *s.m.inv.* **1.** (*a*) master key, pass key; (*b*) **l'argent est un bon p.-p.,** money is a passport to everything, an open sesame; a golden key opens every door; **film p.-p.,** film of universal appeal; **formule p.-p.,** general purpose formula; **mot p.-p.,** general purpose word; (*c*) *W.Tel:* **filter p.-p.,** all-pass filter **2.** *Tls:* (*a*) cross-cut saw; (*b*) two-man saw. **3.** *Phot: etc:* (*a*) slip(-in) mount; **album p.-p.,** slip-in album; (*b*) passe-partout (frame); **p.-p. anglais (pour aquarelles),** white open mount, cut mount; (*c*) *Typ:* passe-partout plate, block.

passe-passe [pɑspɑs], *s.m. no pl.* legerdemain, sleight of hand, juggling; *esp.* **tour de p.-p.,** (i) conjuring trick; (ii) clever take-in, trick; **faire des tours de p.-p.,** to do conjuring tricks; **ce n'est pas un jeu de p.-p.,** there's no hocus-pocus about it.

passe-pied [pɑspje], *s.m.inv.* passepied (old Breton dance).

passe-pierre [pɑspjɛːr], *s.m. Bot:* **1.** samphire, sea fennel. **2.** (white, meadow) saxifrage; *pl. passe-pierres.*

passe-plats [pɑspla], *s.m.inv.* service hatch.

passepoil [pɑspwal], *s.m.* braid, piping (for garments).

passepoiler [pɑspwale], *v.tr.* to braid, to pipe (garment); **poche passepoilée,** welted pocket.

passeport [pɑspɔːr], *s.m.* (*a*) *Adm:* passport; *F:* **il porte son p. sur lui,** he carries his own recommendation with him; (*b*) *Nau:* sea pass, sea letter.

passe-purée [pɑspyre], *s.m.inv. Cu:* potato masher.

passer [pɑse]. I. *v.i.* **1.** (*the aux. is* **avoir** *or* **être**) to pass; to go (on, by, along); to proceed; (*a*) **p. d'un endroit à un autre,** to pass from one place to another; **p. sur un pont,** to cross (over) a bridge; **il est passé, a passé, devant la boutique,** he went by, passed (by), the shop; **p. par-dessus, par-dessous, qch.,** to get over, under, sth.; **l'auto lui a passé sur les jambes,** the car ran over his legs; **la bouteille a passé de main en main,** the bottle was passed round; **faire p. la bouteille, les gâteaux,** to hand round, pass round, send round, the bottle, the cakes; **par où est-il, a-t-il, passé?** which way did he go? **un cycliste qui passait par là,** a passing cyclist; **la prochaine fois que vous passerez par là,** when you are next that way; when you next pass that way; **le train passa à toute allure,** the train flew by; **les charrettes passent avec bruit,** the carts rumble by, clatter by; **une embarcation passa,** a boat passed (by); **le voilà qui passe!** there he goes! **je ne peux pas p.,** I can't get by; **je regardais p. la procession,** I was watching the procession; *Hist:* **ils ne passeront pas!** they shall not pass! **on ne passe pas,** no thoroughfare; *P.N:* **défense de p. sous peine d'amende,** trespassers will be prosecuted; **se ranger pour laisser p. qn,** to stand aside to make room for s.o.; **laissez passer,** admit bearer; **il parvint à s'évader et passa en Hollande,** he managed to escape and crossed into Holland; **p. à l'ennemi,** to go over to the enemy; to defect; **passons à la salle à manger,** let us go into the dining-room; **passons recevoir les invités,** let us go through and receive the guests; **après dîner on passa à la salle de billard,** after dinner we adjourned to the billiard room; *Sch:* **p. dans la classe supérieure,** to be moved up; **p. sur une difficulté, sur une faute,** to pass over a difficulty, over a mistake; **passons!** well, let it go at that! *adv.phr.* **en passant,** by the way; **une fois en passant,** once in a while, *F:* once in a blue moon; **remarque en passant,** passing, casual, remark; **dire, suggérer, qch. en passant,** to mention sth. casually, to throw out a casual suggestion; **(ceci) soit dit en passant,** by the way, incidentally; (*b*) **passons à autre chose,** (i) let us pass on to other matters; (ii) let us change the subject; **je passe maintenant à une autre question,** I shall now go on, proceed, turn, to another matter; **p. d'un système à un autre,** to change from one system to another; *Aut:* **p. en seconde, en deuxième (vitesse),** to go into, change into, second gear; (*c*) **p. à la postérité,** to go down to posterity, to survive; **il ne faut pas que ce domaine passe à d'autres,** this estate must not pass out of our hands; **glose qui a passé dans le texte,** gloss that has slipped into the text; *Equit:* **p. au trot, au galop,** to break into a trot, into a gallop; *Mil: etc:* **p. à l'offensive,** to switch over to the offensive; (*d*) **la route passe tout près du village,** the road runs quite close to the village; **notre chemin passe par les bois,** our way lies through the woods; **des frissons me passèrent par tout le corps,** I shuddered from head to foot; **il dit tout ce qui lui passe par la tête,** he says anything, the first thing, that comes into his head; **cela m'est passé de l'esprit,** it has quite slipped my memory; **mon dîner ne passe pas, n'a pas passé,** my dinner won't, wouldn't, go down; my dinner doesn't, didn't, agree with me; **il y a qch. qui ne passe pas,** something has upset my stomach; (*e*) to go through; **passez par la fenêtre,** go, get, through the window; **faire p. un tuyau à travers le mur,** to run a pipe through the wall; **par le crâne fracassé la cervelle passait,** through the shattered skull the brain protruded; **son pantalon était déchiré et la chemise passait,** his trousers were torn and his shirt hanging out; **il faut que le café passe très lentement,** coffee must percolate, filter, very slowly; *Fr.C:* **p. tout droit,** to oversleep; (*f*) *with cogn. acc.* **p. son chemin,** to go one's way; **passez votre chemin!** (i) move along! (ii) get out! (*g*) *W.Tel:* to be on; **cette chanson n'a pas encore passé à la radio,** this song has not been on the air yet; *Cin:* **ce film a passé la semaine dernière,** this film was on, was shown, last week; (*h*) **notre chiffre d'affaires a passé de deux millions à trois millions en cinq ans,** our turnover has increased, risen, from two million to three million in five years. **2.** (*aux.* **être**) **p. chez qn,** to call on s.o.; **il faut que je passe chez les Martin,** I must call on the Martins; **je passerai chez vous ce soir,** I'll come round this evening; **entrer en passant,** to drop in; **en passant, je suis entré dire bonjour,** I just looked in on my way by; **je ne fais que p. pour demander de vos nouvelles,** I only called, just dropped in, to see how you were; (*of commercial traveller*) **p. chez un client,** to call on, visit, *Com:* wait on, a customer; **est-ce que le facteur, le laitier, est passé?** has the post(man), the milkman, been? **3.** (*aux.* **avoir**) (*a*) to undergo, pass through; **p. par de rudes épreuves,** to experience some heavy trials; **j'ai passé par là,** I have been through it; **il a dû en p. par là, il a dû y p.,** he had to put up with it; **tout le monde y passe,** it happens to us all; *F:* **p. par toutes les couleurs de l'arc-en-ciel,** to turn all the colours of the rainbow; (*b*) **il la fait p. par où il veut,** he makes her do anything he wants; *F:* **il faut p. par là ou par la porte,** you must either do it or get out. **4.** (*aux. usu.* **avoir**) to pass away; (*a*) to disappear, to cease; **la douleur a passé,** the pain has passed off, has gone; **sa colère a vite passé,** his anger soon passed, cooled; **p. de mode,** to pass out of fashion; le vert est passé de mode, green is out of fashion; la nouveauté passera avec le temps, the novelty will wear off in time; s'il est espiègle, cela passera avec l'âge, if he is mischievous he will grow out of it; couleurs qui passent, colours that fade; il faut laisser p. l'orage, we must let the storm blow over; faire p. qch., to get rid of, do away with, sth.; prenez ce verre pour le faire p., drink this to wash it down; cela a fait p. mon mal de tête, it has cured my headache; j'espère que sa colère lui passera, I hope his anger will pass; laisser p. sa dernière chance, to miss one's last chance; (b) (of time) to elapse, to go by; des années ont passé depuis, years have passed, elapsed, since then; les années qui passent, the fleeting years; l'été a passé sans qu'on s'en aperçoive, summer has gone without our noticing it; les mois passent, the months are slipping by; à mesure que les années passent, as the years go by; comme le temps passe (vite)! how time flies! faire p. le temps, to pass the time. 5. (= TRÉPASSER) (aux. avoir or être) to die; il est, il a, passé dans mes bras, he died, passed away, in my arms; F: il a bien failli y p., he nearly kicked the bucket. 6. (a) (aux. avoir or être) to become; A: p. femme, to grow into a woman; la voilà passée femme, she is a woman now; p. capitaine, to be promoted captain, to a captaincy; p. commandant, to obtain one's majority; Sp: p. professionnel, to turn professional; ce mot de Molière est passé en proverbe, this saying of Molière's has become a proverb; (b) (aux. avoir) to be considered, to pass for; elle passe pour (être) très belle, she is considered, thought, (to be) very beautiful; she passes for a great beauty; p. pour riche, to be accounted rich; p. pour avoir fait qch., to be credited with having done sth.; p. pour exact, (i) (of pers.) to have a name for punctuality; (ii) (of fact) to be supposed to be correct; ceci passe pour vrai, this is believed, held, to be true; la maison passait pour être hantée, the house was believed to be haunted; se faire p. pour . . ., to pass oneself off as, for, . . .; se faire p. pour Français, to pose as a Frenchman; impers. il passe pour certain que . . ., it is commonly assumed as a fact that . . .. 7. (aux. avoir) to be accepted, to pass muster; la loi a passé, the bill has been carried, has gone through; cela peut passer, it will pass muster; monnaie qui ne passe plus, coinage that is no longer current; laisser p. une erreur, to overlook a mistake; qu'il revienne demain, passe encore, if he returns tomorrow, I have nothing to say against it, well and good; cela ne passe pas, that won't do; F: cette histoire-là ne passe pas, that story won't wash; enfin, passe pour lui! well, that's all right as far as he is concerned. 8. (aux. avoir) Jur: (of lawsuit) p. en jugement, to come up for judgment; l'affaire passera en janvier, demain, the case will be heard in January, comes on tomorrow; (of soldier) p. devant le conseil de guerre, to come up before a court martial.

II. passer, v.tr. 1. to pass, traverse, cross, go over (bridge, river, sea); to go through, pass through (a doorway, a gate); to cross (a threshold); p. la rivière à la nage, to swim (across) the river; p. la frontière, to go over, to cross, the frontier; arrêtez! vous avez passé la maison, stop! you've gone past the house. 2. (a) to convey, carry, across; to ferry (goods, passengers) over; voulez-vous me p.? will you ferry me across? p. des marchandises en fraude, to smuggle in goods; (b) p. qch. à qn, to hand sth. to s.o.; voulez-vous me p. l'eau, s'il vous plaît, please pass me the water; veux-tu p. les liqueurs? would you serve the liqueurs? p. une nouvelle, to hand on news; p. un avertissement à qn, to pass on a warning to s.o.; p. un droit à qn, to transfer a right to s.o.; Com: p. une commande, to place an order (de qch. à qn, for sth. with s.o.); Fb: p. le ballon, to pass the ball; p. le ballon en arrière, to pass back; Tp: passez-moi M. X, give me, put me through to, Mr X; p. sa colère sur qn, to vent one's wrath on s.o.; (c) p. qch. sur qch., to pass, move, sth. over sth.; p. une éponge sur le tableau, to wipe the blackboard; passons l'éponge là-dessus, let's say no more about it; se p. la main dans les cheveux, to run one's fingers through one's hair; elle passa sa main dans mon bras, she took my arm; p. sa tête par la fenêtre, to put one's head out of, in at, the window; p. la tête dehors, to stick, put, one's head out; je lui passai mon sabre à travers son corps, I ran my sword through his body, I ran him through with my sword; F: p. une jambe à qn, to trip s.o. up; p. une serviette sous son menton, to tuck a napkin under one's chin; je lui passai mes bras autour du cou, I hugged her round the neck; je lui passai mon bras autour de la taille, I slipped my arm round her waist; p. une chemise, une robe, to slip on a shirt, a dress; elle passa ses bas, she pulled on her stockings; il passa le poignard dans sa ceinture, he stuck the dagger in his belt; il passa la main sur sa bouche, he drew his hand across his mouth; p. la camisole de force à qn, to put a strait waistcoat on s.o., to put s.o. into a strait waistcoat; p. le fil dans le trou de l'aiguille, to pass the thread through the eye of the needle; Nau: p. une manœuvre, to reeve a rope; Bookb: p. (les nerfs) en carton, to lace in the bands; P: qu'est-ce que je vais lui p! I shan't half tell him off! (d) (to put sth. through a process) p. un couteau, un sabre, à la meule, to grind, sharpen, a knife, a sword; p. un couteau à la pierre, to hone a knife; p. (qch.) au tour, to turn (sth.) on a lathe; Metalw: p. par le laminoir, to cold roll; p. une table au brou de noix, to stain a table with walnut stain; p. du linge au bleu, to blue linen; p. de la viande au hachoir, to mince meat, to put meat through the mincer; p. un dessin à l'encre, to ink in a drawing; (of computer) p. en revue, to browse; p. des troupes en revue, to inspect, review, troops; p. un déserteur par les armes, to shoot a deserter; (e) Cin: to show (film); (of computer) to run (programme); on va p. des films ce soir, we're going to show some films this evening; salle qui passe Hamlet, cinema showing Hamlet; p. un disque, une bande, to put on, play, a record, a tape. 3. to pass, spend (time, one's life); p. son temps, le temps, à faire qch., to spend one's time (in) doing sth.; à quoi passez-vous le temps quand il n'est pas là? what do you do with yourself when he is away? pour p. le temps, in order to while away the time; p. les heures à dormir, to sleep the hours away; p. la nuit à causer, to talk the night away; ils passent la nuit en discussions, they spend the night in discussion; A: F: se la p. douce, to have an easy time, to take it easy. 4. to pass, go beyond, exceed, surpass; il a passé la soixantaine, he is in his sixties; A: elle passait alors cinquante ans, she was then over fifty, on the wrong side of fifty; cela passe ma capacité, that is beyond my powers; cela passe la mesure, les bornes, la plaisanterie, that's going too far; it's too much of a good thing; it's beyond a joke; A: son courage passe ses forces, his courage exceeds, is too much for, his strength; A: F: cela me passe, it passes my comprehension; it is above, beyond, my comprehension; F: that (quite) beats me! le vieux ne passera pas l'hiver, the old man won't outlive, last through, the winter; Prov: contentement passe richesse, contentment is better than wealth. 5. to pass over; (a) to excuse (fault, etc.); passez-le-moi cette fois, overlook it this time; on ne lui passe rien, nothing is overlooked; si vous me passez l'expression, if you will excuse the expression; on me passera de citer mon dernier livre, I trust I shall be forgiven if I quote my latest book; je vous passe cela, I grant you that; p. une fantaisie à qn, to indulge, humour, s.o.'s fancy; se p. une fantaisie, to gratify indulge, a whim; passez-moi ce caprice, forgive this whim of mine; (b) to omit, leave out; j'ai passé tout un chapitre, I skipped a whole chapter; p. qch. sous silence, to pass over sth. in silence, to make no mention of sth.; j'en passe et des meilleurs, there are many more even better than I could mention; (c) Cards: etc: p. son tour, abs. passer, to pass; passe! pass! no bid! 6. (a) Jur: p. un accord, to conclude an agreement; p. un contrat, to enter into, sign, a contract; acte passé devant (un) notaire, document drawn up before a lawyer; Book-k: p. écriture d'un article, to post an entry; p. écriture conforme, to reciprocate an entry; faire p. qch. aux écritures, to put sth. on the books; p. un article au journal, to post an entry in the journal; p. une somme au débit, to debit (an account) with a sum; (b) Pol: p. un projet de loi, une loi, to pass a bill, a law; (c) p. un examen, to sit for an examination. 7. to strain (liquid); to sift (flour, corn); p. le bouillon, to strain the soup; p. le café, to percolate the coffee.

se passer. 1. to happen; to take place; cela s'est passé il y a dix ans, it happened, took place, ten years ago; que se passe-t-il? qu'est-ce qui se passe? what's going on? what's happening? F: what's up? est-ce que la cérémonie s'est bien passée? did the ceremony go off all right? l'action de mon histoire se passe en France, the scene of my story is laid in France; leur lune de miel se passa à Naples, their honeymoon was spent in Naples; Th: le second acte se passe dans la rue, the second act is set in the street. 2. (a) to pass away, to cease; (of fashion) not to last; (of time) to elapse, go by, to be spent; mon mal de tête se passe, my headache is passing off; il faut que jeunesse se passe, youth will have its fling, its way; l'orage s'est passé, the storm has blown over; cela ne se passera pas ainsi, I shall not let it rest at that; (b) (of flowers, colours, beauty) to fade, decay, wither, fall off; (of wine, etc.) to deteriorate, to go off. 3. se p. de qn, de qch., to do without, to dispense with, s.o., sth.; je m'en passerai, I'll do without it; I shall manage without it; quand j'ai beaucoup à faire je me passe de déjeuner, when I am very busy I go without lunch; il ne peut se p. d'en parler, he just has to talk about it; je ne peux pas m'en p., I can't do without it; je ne peux pas me p. de lui, I can't spare him; I can't do without him; ces faits se passent de commentaires, these facts need no comment.

passerage [pasra:ʒ], s.f. Bot: pepperwort; p. cultivée, garden cress.

passereau, -eaux [pasro], s.m. Orn: 1. A: sparrow. 2. pl. passereaux, passeres, perchers, passerines, passeriformes.

passerelle [pasrɛl], s.f. 1. footbridge. 2. (a) Nau: p. (de commandement), bridge; p. de navigation, navigation bridge; compass bridge, compass platform; p. de manœuvre, p. arrière, docking, warping, bridge; p. volante, flying bridge, fore-and-aft bridge, catwalk; Navy: p. de majorité, de l'amiral, admiral's bridge; p. de débarquement, d'embarquement, gangway, gangplank, gangboard, brow; (b) Av: p. de débarquement, d'embarquement, (passenger) steps, passenger bridge; p. (de débarquement, d'embarquement) automotrice, automouvante, automotive passenger steps. 3. p. de grue, crane platform; p. de visite, catwalk.

passeresse [pasrɛs], s.f. Nau: small rope, line; esp. reeving line, heaving line, reef line.

passériformes [paseriform], s.m.pl. Orn: Passeriformes.

passerine [pasrin], s.f. 1. Orn: passerina, (N. American) bunting; p. bleue, indigo bird, bunting. 2. Bot: sparrow wort.

passerinette [pasrinɛt], s.f. Orn: (fauvette) p., subalpine, spectacled, warbler.

passe-rose [pasro:z], s.f. Bot: hollyhock, rose mallow; pl. passe-rose(s).

passe-ruban [pasrybɑ̃], s.m. ribbon threader; pl. passe-rubans.

passe-sauce [passo:s], s.m.inv. sauce strainer.

passe-temps [pastɑ̃], s.m.inv. pastime, diversion; hobby.

passe-thé [paste], s.m.inv. tea strainer.

passette [pasɛt], s.f. 1. small strainer. 2. Tex: heddle hook.

passeur, -euse [pasœ:r, -ø:z], s. 1. (a) ferryman, ferrywoman; (b) Pol: p. (de frontière), frontier runner; escape agent. 2. Tex: p. de chaînes, warp drawer; drawer-in; reacher-in.

passe-velours [pasvəlu:r], s.m.inv. Bot: cockscomb.

passe-volant [pasvɔlɑ̃], s.m. A: (a) Mil: Nau: dummy soldier or sailor, false muster; Mil: faggot; (b) dummy gun; (c) F: interloper, intruder, uninvited guest, gatecrasher; pl. passe-volants.

passe-vue(s) [pasvy], s.m. Phot: (a) (châssis) p.-v., slide carrier; (b) passe-vues, (slide) viewer.

passibilité [pasibilite], s.f. liability (de, to, for).

passible [pasibl], a. 1. passible, capable of feeling. 2. Jur: liable (de, to, for); p. d'une amende, liable to a fine; (of pers.) p. de l'impôt, liable for tax; p. du droit du timbre, subject to stamp duty.

passière [pasjɛ:r], s.f. Orn: hen sparrow.

passif, -ive [pasif, -i:v]. 1. a. (a) passive (obedience, resistance, etc.); Gram: voix passive, passive voice; (b) Com: dettes passives, debts due by us, by the firm; liabilities; Pol.Ec: commerce p., import trade. 2. s.m. (a) Gram: passive (voice); (b) Com: liabilities, debt; p. exigible, current liabilities; p. éventuel, contingent liabilities.

passifloracées [pasiflɔrase], s.f.pl., **passiflorées** [pasiflɔre], s.f.pl. Bot: Passifloraceae.

passiflore [pasiflɔ:r], s.f. Bot: passiflora, passion flower.

passim [pasim], Lt. adv. passim.

passing-shot [pasiŋʃɔt], s.m. Ten: passing shot.

passion [pasjɔ̃], s.f. 1. (a) la P., the Passion (of Christ); semaine de la P., Passion Week; souffrir mort et p., to suffer cruelly; Bot: fleur de la p., passion flower; (b) passion sermon; (c) Med:

p. iliaque, iliac passion. **2.** passion (intense emotion, violent love); **p. pour la musique,** passion for music; **se prendre d'une belle p. pour qn,** to fall violently in love with s.o.; **éprouver une grande p. pour qn, aimer qn à la p.,** to be passionately in love with s.o.; **la p. de la vérité,** a passion for truth; **avoir la p. de faire qch.,** to be passionately fond of doing sth.; **il a la p. des tableaux,** *F:* he is mad about pictures; **parler avec p., sans p.,** to speak passionately, dispassionately.

passionnaire [pɑsjɔnɛːr]. **1.** *s.m. Ecc:* passional, passionary. **2.** *s.f. Bot:* passion flower.

passionnant [pɑsjɔnɑ̃], *a.* exciting, enthralling, entrancing, thrilling (story, etc.); all-absorbing (sport); **œuvre passionnante à entreprendre,** fascinating piece of work to undertake, passionately interesting piece of work.

passionné [pɑsjɔne], *a.* passionate, impassioned, ardent; **p. de, pour, qn, qch.,** passionately fond of s.o., sth.; **p. contre qch.,** deeply prejudiced against sth.; **p. d'entreprendre ce voyage,** passionately keen, eager, to undertake this journey; **allocution passionnée,** impassioned speech; *s.* **un p. de musique,** a music enthusiast; **les passionnés du cinéma,** film fans.

passionnel, -elle [pɑsjɔnɛl], *a.* pertaining to the passions; **abandon p.,** indulgence of the passions; **crime p.,** love tragedy, crime due to jealousy, crime passionnel.

passionnément [pɑsjɔnemɑ̃], *adv.* passionately; **aimer qn, qch., p.,** to love s.o. passionately, to be passionately fond of s.o., sth.; **désirer p. qch.,** to have a passionate desire for sth.; to yearn, long, for sth.

passionner [pɑsjɔne], *v.tr.* (*a*) to impassion; to excite (s.o.) with passion; to interest passionately, to intrigue; **p. la foule,** to rouse, excite, the mob; **le sport le passionne,** he is passionately fond of, keen on, sport; **l'enthousiasme passionne son style,** enthusiasm lends passion to his style; **être passionné par la beauté de qn,** to be fired by s.o.'s beauty; **livre qui passionne,** passionately interesting, fascinating, book; (*b*) *A. & F:* to be passionately fond of, eager for (power, money, etc.).

se passionner, (*a*) **se p. de, pour, qch.,** to become passionately fond of, enthusiastic about, sth., to conceive a passion for sth.; (*b*) to fly into a passion, a rage; **ne vous passionnez pas,** don't lose your temper; **vous vous passionnez trop,** you get too worked up.

passionnette [pɑsjɔnɛt], *s.f. Lit:* passing fancy (**pour,** for).

passionniste [pɑsjɔnist], *s.m. Ecc:* Passionist (father).

passis [pasi], *a.m.pl.* (*of silkworms*) attacked by gattine.

passivation [pasivasjɔ̃], *s.f. Metalw: Paint:* passivation.

passivé [pasive], *a. Ch:* **fer p.,** passive iron.

passivement [pasivmɑ̃], *adv.* passively.

passiver [pasive], *v.tr. Ch: etc:* to passivate.

passivité [pasivite], *s.f.* passivity (of mind, of metals, etc.).

passoire [pɑswaːr], *s.f. Cu:* strainer; **p. à légumes,** colander; **p. à sucre,** sugar sifter; *Ind:* **presse à p.,** straining press; *Fb: etc: F:* (*of goalkeeper*) **c'est une p.,** he lets them all through.

passure [pɑsyːr], *s.f. Bookb:* **p. en carton,** lacing-in; **p. en colle,** pasting.

pastel [pastɛl], *s.m.* **1.** *Bot:* woad. **2.** *Art:* (*a*) pastel; **tableau au p.,** picture in pastel; **bleu p.,** pastel blue; (*b*) pastel drawing.

pasteller [pastɛle], *v.tr. & i.* to draw (portrait, etc.) in pastel, to pastel.

pastelliste [pastɛlist], *s.m. & f.* pastellist.

pastenague [pastənag], *s.f. Ich:* whip-tailed sting ray.

pastèque [pastɛk], *s.f.* water melon.

pasteur [pastœːr], *s.m.* **1.** shepherd; **peuple p.,** pastoral people; *Ecc:* **le bon P.,** the Good Shepherd. **2.** *Ecc:* pastor, *esp.* (Protestant) minister.

pasteurellose [pastœrɛloːz], *s.f. Vet: Med:* pasteurellosis; **p. des poules, des volailles,** chicken cholera.

pasteurien, -ienne [pastœrjɛ̃, -jɛn], *a.* Pasteurian (process, etc.); of Pasteur.

pasteurisateur [pastœrizatœːr], *s.m.* pasteurizer.

pasteurisation [pastœrizasjɔ̃], *s.f.* pasteurization.

pasteuriser [pastœrize], *v.tr.* to pasteurize (milk, etc.).

pastiche [pastiʃ], *s.m.* pastiche.

pasticher [pastiʃe], *v.tr.* to pastiche, do a pastiche of.

pasticheur, -euse [pastiʃœːr, -øːz], *s.* pasticheur.

pastillage [pastijaːʒ], *s.m.* **1.** *Cu:* (non-edible) decorative sugarwork. **2.** *Tchn:* pelletizing. **3.** *Cer:* baked clay figure.

pastille [pastiːj], *s.f.* **1.** pastille; lozenge; *Pharm:* **p. contre la toux, p. de pâte pectorale,** cough lozenge; **p. de menthe,** peppermint (tablet); **pastilles de chocolat,** chocolate drops. **2.** pastille, (aromatic) pellet (for fumigation). **3.** *Ind:* pellet (in plastic). **4.** (*a*) rubber patch (for inner tube of tyre); (*b*) reinforcement (for hole in papers for filing). **5.** (*a*) *Sm.a:* cartridge cap; (*b*) *Tp: etc:* **p. micro(phonique),** capsule (of transmitter); microphone inset; **p. d'écouteur,** earphone inset; (*c*) *Aut:* **pastilles en liège (du plateau d'embrayage),** cork inserts (of clutch plate).

pastiller [pastije], *v.tr. Tchn:* to pelletize; **machine à p.,** pelletizer.

pastilleur, -euse [pastijœːr, -øːz], *s. Ind:* (*a*) (*pers.*) pelletizer; (*b*) (*apparatus*) pelletizer.

pastis [pastis], *s.m.* (*a*) aniseed aperitif; (*b*) *F:* **quel p.!** what a muddle! what a mess! **un drôle de p.,** an unholy mess.

pastophore [pastɔfɔːr], *s.m.* (*a*) *Egyptian Ant:* pastophor(us); (*b*) *A:* priest.

pastoral, -aux [pastɔral, -o]. **1.** *a.* pastoral (life, poetry, *Ecc:* letter); **anneau p.,** episcopal ring. **2.** *s.f.* **pastorale,** (*a*) *Lit:* pastoral (play, poem); (*b*) *Ecc:* (bishop's) pastoral (letter).

pastoralement [pastɔralmɑ̃], *adv.* pastorally.

pastoraliste [pastɔralist], *s.m. & f. Lit:* pastoralist.

pastorat [pastɔra], *s.m.* pastorate.

pastorien, -ienne [pastɔrjɛ̃, -jɛn], *a.* Pasteurian (process, etc.); of Pasteur.

pastoureau, -eaux, -elle [pasturo, -ɛl]. **1.** *s. A: & Poet:* shepherd lad, lass. **2.** *s.f.* **pastourelle,** (*a*) *Lit:* pastoral (poem); (*b*) *Danc:* fourth figure of the quadrille; pastourelle.

pastruga [pastryga], *s.f. Ich:* pastruga (sturgeon).

pat [pat], *s.m.inv. Chess:* stalemate; *a.inv.* **faire p. son adversaire,** to stalemate, to give stalemate to, one's opponent; **le roi est p.,** the king is stalemated.

patache [pataʃ], *s.f.* **1.** *Nau:* (*a*) *A:* water-police vessel; (*b*) **p. de la douane,** custom-house tender, revenue cutter. **2.** (*a*) *A:* stage-cart; (*b*) *F:* ramshackle conveyance, rattletrap.

patachon [pataʃɔ̃], *s.m.* **1.** *A:* pilot of a *patache.* **2.** (*a*) *A:* stage-cart driver; (*b*) *P:* **mener une vie de p.,** to lead a rollicking life, a wild life.

patafioler [patafjɔle], *v.tr. P:* *used only in* **que le bon Dieu, que le diable, te, le, patafiole!** go to hell! to hell with him!

patagium [pataʒjɔm], *s.m.* **1.** *Rom.Cost:* patagium, gold edging. **2.** (*a*) *Z:* patagium, wing membrane (of bat, etc.); (*b*) *Ent:* patagium.

patagon, -onne [patagɔ̃, -ɔn]. **1.** *a. & s. Geog:* Patagonian. **2.** *s.m. Orn:* giant colibri, humming bird.

Patagonie [patagɔni], *Pr.n.f. Geog:* Patagonia.

patan, -ane [patɑ̃, -an], *a. & s. Ethn:* Pathan.

patapouf [patapuf]. **1.** *int.* flop! **faire p.,** to fall flop. **2.** *s.m. F:* **gros p.,** fat lump of a man, of a child.

pataquès [patakɛs], *s.m. F:* (*a*) faulty liaison; inversion of letters, of sounds (in speech); (*b*) gross blunder, boob (betraying illiteracy; *e.g.,* **je ne sais pas-t-à-qu'est-ce,** for **je ne sais pas à qui c'est).**

pataras [patara], *s.m. Nau:* preventer shroud.

patarasse [pataras], *s.f. Nau:* reaming iron.

patarasser [patarase], *v.tr. Nau:* to ream (seam).

patard [pataːr], *s.m. A:* small coin; **je n'en donnerais pas un p.,** I wouldn't give a (brass) farthing for it; **cela ne vaut pas un p.,** it isn't worth a doit.

patata [patata]. *See* PATATI.

patate [patat], *s.f.* **1.** *Bot:* batata; sweet potato; Spanish potato. **2.** (*a*) *F:* potato, spud; (*b*) *P:* idiot, clot; (*c*) *F:* **en avoir gros, lourd, sur la p.,** to have plenty to be sad about.

patati [patati], *F:* **et p. et patata,** and so on and so forth.

patatras [patatra], (*a*) *int. F:* crash! **et p., le voilà par terre!** and down he went with a wallop! (*b*) *s.m.* heavy fall.

pataud, -aude [pato, -oːd]. **1.** *s.* (*a*) puppy with big paws; (*b*) *F:* chubby child. **2.** *a. & s. F:* heavy, clumsy (person).

Pataugas [patogɑ], *s.m.inv. R.t.m:* rubber-soled canvas shoe.

pataugeage [patoʒaːʒ], *s.m.* (*a*) floundering, squelching, in the mud; (*b*) floundering (in a speech, etc.).

patauger [patoʒe], *v.i.* (**je pataugeai(s); n. pataugeons**) (*a*) to splash and flounder, to squelch, in the mud; (*b*) *F:* to become embarrassed, to get in a muddle, to flounder (in speech, in oral exam.); **p. parmi les adverbes et les adjectifs,** to be all at sea among, over, adverbs and adjectives; (*c*) to paddle, to wade (in sea, etc.).

patageur, -euse [patoʒœːr, -øːz], *s.* flounderer.

patchouli [patʃuli], *s.m. Bot: etc:* patchouli; **essence de p.,** patchouli oil.

pâte [pɑːt], *s.f.* **1.** (*a*) *Cu:* paste; pastry; **p. à pain,** dough; **p. brisée,** short pastry; **p. à choux,** chou pastry; **p. feuilletée,** flaky, puff, pastry; **p. lisse, p. à frire,** batter; **pâtes (d'Italie), pâtes alimentaires,** pasta, noodles; **mettre la viande en p.,** to cook a joint in pastry; **vous êtes d'une p. à vivre jusqu'à cent ans,** you're built to live to be a hundred; **être de la p. dont on fait les héros,** to be of the stuff that heroes are made of; **c'est une bonne p. (d'homme),** he's a good sort; **une p. molle,** an easily influenced, spineless, person; **mettre la main à la p.,** (i) to help with the cooking; to lend a hand; (ii) to get down to it; (*b*) *Cu:* **p. bleue,** blue cheese; **p. fraîche,** (fresh) cream cheese; **p. de coings,** quince cheese; **p. de fruits,** pâte de fruits, fruit jellies; **p. d'amandes,** (i) *A.Toil:* almond cream; (ii) *Cu:* almond paste; (*c*) *Cer:* paste, pâte; **p. dure,** pâte dure, hard paste; **p. tendre,** pâte tendre, soft paste; **p. doublée, p. sur p.,** pâte-sur-pâte; (*d*) *Paperm:* **p. à papier,** pulp; **p. de bois,** wood pulp; **p. de chiffons,** rag pulp; **p. dure, solide,** strong pulp; **p. de carton,** papier mâché; (*e*) *Mec.E:* **p. abrasive,** abrasive compound, grinding paste; **p. à joints,** sealing compound; gasket seal; **p. à souder,** soldering flux, paste; **p. isolante,** insulating compound; **p. à roder,** lapping compound; *Typ:* **p. à rouleaux,** roller composition; (*f*) **p. de chaux,** (plasterer's) putty; **p. dentifrice,** toothpaste; **p. pour chaussures,** shoe polish; **p. à polycopier,** hectograph jelly; **p. à modeler,** modelling clay; *Art:* **peindre dans la p., peindre en pleine p.,** to lay on the paint; to paint with a full brush; (*g*) *Geol:* magma. **2.** *Typ:* (printer's) pie; **mettre, laisser tomber, un paquet de composition en p.,** to pie a take; to make pie (of set matter). **3.** mash (for cramming poultry); **être, vivre, comme un coq en p.,** to live like a fighting cock.

pâté [pɑte], *s.m.* **1.** *Cu:* (*a*) **p. en croûte,** meat (etc.) pie; **petit p.,** patty, pasty; **croûte de p.,** pie crust; **p. du pauvre homme,** shepherd's pie, cottage pie; *F:* **quel gros p. que ce petit!** what a tubby little boy! (*b*) pâté; **p. en terrine,** pâté; potted meat; **p. de foie,** liver pâté; **p. maison,** pâté maison, special pâté (of the restaurant or household); (*c*) (*of children*) **faire des pâtés,** to make (i) sand castles, (ii) mud pies. **2.** (*a*) block (of houses); clump (of trees); (*b*) **p. de roches,** cluster of rocks; *Nau:* reef. **3.** *F:* blot, blob (of ink); **faire un p.,** to make a blot. **4.** *Typ:* (printer's) pie.

pâtée [pɑte], *s.f.* **1.** (*a*) mash (for poultry, pigs); dogs' food, cats' food; (*b*) *F:* thick, stodgy soup; (*c*) *F:* food (in general), *F:* grub; (*d*) *Ap:* **p. royale,** gelée royale, royal jelly. **2.** *P:* thrashing, good hiding.

pâtelette [pɑt(ə)lɛt], *s.f. Mil:* outer flap of pack.

patelin[1], **-ine** [patlɛ̃, -in], (*a*) *a.* smooth-tongued, smooth-spoken, mealy-mouthed; glib, *F:* smarmy (from the 15th cent. farce *Maistre Pierre Pathelin*); **voix pateline,** wheedling voice; **excuses patelines,** smarmy excuses; (*b*) *s. O:* smooth-tongue, wheedler.

patelin[2], *s.m. F:* (*a*) native village, place of birth; (*b*) village, small place; **ce n'est qu'un petit p.,** it's only a small place; **quel sale p.!** what a dump! what a hole!

patelin[3], *s.m. Tchn:* (small) assay crucible.

patelinage [patlinaːʒ], *s.m.,* **patelinerie** [patlin(ə)ri], *s.f. A:* smooth words and fair promises; mealy-mouthed flattery; humbug; soft sawder.

pateliner [patline], *A:* **1.** *v.i.* to speak, act, in an ingratiating manner, to be mealy-mouthed, *F:* to lay it on thick. **2.** *v.tr.* (*a*) **p. qn,** to make up to s.o.; to butter s.o. up; (*b*) **p. une affaire,** to carry sth. through with smooth words and fair promises.

patelineur, -euse [patlinœːr, -øːz], *s. A:* mealy-mouthed flatterer; wheedler.

patellaire [patɛlɛːr], *a. Physiol:* **réflexe p.,** patellar reflex, knee jerk.

patelle [patɛl], *s.f.* **1.** *Rom.Ant:* patella. **2.** *Moll:* patella, limpet. **3.** *Bot:* patella (of lichen).

patellé [patɛl(l)e], *a. Nat.Hist:* patellate.

patellidés [patɛl(l)ide], *s.m.pl. Moll:* Patellidae, patellidans.

patelliforme [patɛl(l)ifɔrm], *a.* patelliform, patellate, patelline, patelloid.

patène [patɛn], *s.f. Ecc:* paten.

patenôtre [patnoːtr̥], *s.f.* **1.** (*a*) *A:* paternoster, Lord's prayer; (*b*) *F:* prayer; (*c*) *F: A:* chaplet (consisting entirely of paternosters); *hence:* **dire ses patenôtres,** (i) to tell one's beads; (ii) to say one's prayers; *F: A:* **diseur, mangeur, de patenôtres,** hypocrite. **2.** *Arch:* paternoster; bead moulding. **3.** (*a*) *Hyd.E:* paternoster pump; noria; (*b*) *Min:* paternoster; bucket elevator.

patenôtrier [patnotrje], *s.m. Bot:* bead tree.

patent [patɑ̃], *a.* (*a*) patent, open to all; **lettres patentes,** letters patent; (*b*) obvious, evident, patent (fact, truth); **il est p. que . . .,** it is clear that . . .; *Jur:* **preuve patente,** proof positive.

patentable [patɑ̃tabl̥], *a.* (trade, etc.) subject to a licence, requiring a licence.

patentage [patɑ̃taːʒ], *s.m. Metall:* patenting.

patente [patɑ̃ːt], *s.f.* **1.** (*a*) licence (to exercise a trade or profession); **se faire inscrire à la p.,** to take out a licence; *Jur:* **p. retirée,** deprivation of the right to continue in a trade, profession; (*b*) tax (paid by merchants and professional men); **payer p.,** to be duly licensed. **2.** *Nau:* **p. (de santé),** bill of health; **p. nette,** clean bill of health; **p. brute, suspecte,** foul, touched, bill of health. **3.** *A:* (*a*) letters patent; (*b*) *Ind:* patent.

patenté, -ée [patɑ̃te]. **1.** *a.* (*a*) licensed; established, recognized (bookseller, etc.); *Jur:* **témoin p.,** witness of well-established position; **pilote p.,** licensed pilot; (*b*) *F:* **imbécile p.,** out-and-out fool. **2.** *s. Adm:* licensee, licensed dealer. **3.** *a. Dy:* patent (blue, etc.).

patenter [patɑ̃te], *v.tr.* to license.

pater [pateːr], *s.m.inv. Ecc:* (*a*) the Lord's prayer; **dire cinq p.,** to say five paternosters; *F:* **savoir qch. comme son p.,** to know a subject inside out; (*b*) great bead of a rosary; paternoster (bead).

pâter [pɑte], *v.i. Hort:* (*of fruit*) to become, get, woolly.

patère [pateːr], *s.f.* **1.** *Rom.Ant: Arch:* patera. **2.** (*a*) hat peg, coat peg; (*b*) curtain hook (for looping up the curtain).

paternalisme [paternalism], *s.m.* paternalism.

paternaliste [paternalist], *a.* paternalist.

paterne [patern], *a.* benevolent, smooth (tone), soft-spoken.

paternel, -elle [paternɛl], *a.* paternal; (*a*) **l'autorité paternelle,** paternal authority; **du côté p.,** on the father's side; **la maison paternelle** (the family) home; *s.m. P:* **le p.,** the old man, the governor; (*b*) fatherly, kindly (tone, advice); fatherly (care); **se montrer p. pour qn,** to treat s.o. in a fatherly way, in a paternal manner.

paternellement [paternɛlmɑ̃], *adv.* paternally, like a father.

paternité [paternite], *s.f.* paternity, fatherhood; *Jur:* **recherche de la p.,** affiliation; **recherche de p.,** action (by bastard) for affiliation; **attribuer la p. d'un enfant,** *F:* **d'un livre, à qn,** to father a child, *F:* a book, on s.o.; **revendiquer la p. d'un livre,** to claim the authorship of a book; **désavouer la p. d'un livre,** to repudiate the authorship of a book.

paternoïte [paternɔit], *s.f. Miner:* paternoite.

pater-noster [paternɔsteːr], *s.m.inv. Fish:* paternoster (line).

pâteux, -euse [pɑtø, -øːz], *a.* (*a*) pasty, clammy; **pain p.,** doughy bread; **poire pâteuse,** woolly pear; **chemin p.,** greasy, sticky, road; **langue pâteuse,** coated tongue; **bouche pâteuse,** dry mouth; (*b*) thick, dull; **vin p.,** wine of thick consistency; **encre pâteuse,** muddy ink; **voix pâteuse,** thick voice; **style, tableau, p.,** woolly style, painting; (*c*) (*of gem*) cloudy, milky.

pathan [patɑ̃], *a.* & *s.* Pathan.

pathétique [patetik], *Lit:* **1.** *a.* (*a*) pathetic, touching, moving (story, situation, tone); (*b*) *Anat:* **muscle p. (de l'œil),** pathetic muscle, superior oblique muscle. **2.** *s.m.* pathos, the pathetic.

pathétiquement [patetikmɑ̃], *adv.* pathetically.

pathétisme [patetism], *s.m.* the pathetic.

patho- [patɔ], *comb.fm.* patho-.

pathogène [patɔʒɛn], *a. Med:* pathogenic.

pathogénie [patɔʒeni], *s.f.,* **pathogénèse** [patɔʒɛnɛːz], *s.f.,* **pathogénésie** [patɔʒenezi], *s.f. Med:* pathogenesis.

pathogénétique [patɔʒenetik], *a. Med:* pathogenetic.

pathogénique [patɔʒenik], *a. Med:* pathogen(et)ic.

pathognomonie [patɔgnɔmɔni], *s.f. Med:* pathognomy.

pathognomonique [patɔgnɔmɔnik], *a. Med:* pathognomonic.

pathologie [patɔlɔʒi], *s.f.* pathology; **p. végétale,** plant pathology, phytopathology.

pathologique [patɔlɔʒik], *a.* pathological.

pathologiquement [patɔlɔʒikmɑ̃], *a.* pathologically.

pathologiste [patɔlɔʒist], *s.m.* & *f.* pathologist.

pathomanie [patɔmani], *s.f.* pathomania.

pathomimie [patɔmimi], *s.f. Psy:* pathomimesis.

pathophobie [patɔfɔbi], *s.f. Psy:* pathophobia.

pathopoétique [patɔpɔetik], *a.* pathopoietic.

pathos [patɔs, -oːs], *s.m.* affected pathos; bathos.

patibulaire [patibylɛːr]. **1.** *a.* relating to the gallows; **fourches patibulaires,** gibbet; **avoir une mine p.,** to wear a hangdog look; to look like a gallows bird. **2.** *s.m. A:* (*a*) gallows; (*b*) gibbet.

patiemment [pasjamɑ̃], *adv.* patiently.

patience[1] [pasjɑ̃ːs], *s.f.* **1.** patience, long-suffering; (*a*) **avoir de la p., prendre p.,** to have patience, to be patient; **prendre qch. en p.,** to bear sth. patiently; **montrer de la p. envers qn,** to be patient with s.o.; **attendre avec p.,** to wait patiently; **mettre la p. de qn à l'épreuve, à rude épreuve,** to try, to tax, s.o.'s patience; **ma p. est à bout, je suis à bout de p.,** my patience is exhausted, is at an end; **il a mis ma p. à bout,** I am out of all patience with him; **(prenez) p.! ayez de la p.!** (have) patience! **perdre p.,** to lose patience; **faire perdre p. à qn,** to exhaust s.o.'s patience; **s'armer, se munir, de p.,** to possess one's soul in patience; **jeu de p.,** puzzle, *esp.* jigsaw puzzle; **carte de p.,** jigsaw map, dissected map; (*b*) *Cards: A:* patience. **2.** *Ecc:* misericord (of choir stall). **3.** *Her:* salamander in flames. **4.** *Mil:* button stick.

patience[2], *s.f. Bot:* patience (dock); spinach dock; **grande p., p. officinale,** herb patience; **p. rouge,** bloodwort, bloody dock.

patient, -ente [pasjɑ̃, -ɑ̃ːt]. **1.** *a.* patient; (*a*) enduring; **être p. pour supporter la douleur physique,** to be capable of bearing pain patiently; (*b*) forbearing, long-suffering. **2.** *s.* (*a*) *A:* condemned man (about to be executed); (*b*) *A:* (*person undergoing torture*) sufferer; (*c*) patient (in surgical case).

patienter [pasjɑ̃te], *v.i.* to exercise patience; **patientez encore un peu,** possess your soul in patience for a little while longer; have a little more patience.

patin [patɛ̃], *s.m.* **1.** *A.Cost:* patten. **2.** (*a*) skate; **patins à roulettes,** roller skates; (*b*) runner (of sledge, etc.); skid (of aircraft); *Av:* **p. d'atterrissage,** landing skid; **p. de queue,** tail skid; (*c*) felt sole (for polishing floors); (*d*) *Aut:* **p. transbordeur,** motor trolley; (*e*) *P:* **chercher des patins (à qn),** to pick a quarrel (with s.o.); **prendre les patins (de qn),** to take up cudgels (on s.o.'s behalf). **3.** (*a*) slipper, (drag) shoe, skid (pan) (of wheel); (ball) housing; (*b*) shoe (of brake, etc.); brake block; *Mch:* **p. de glissière,** guide block; **p. de butée,** thrust pad; *El.E:* **p. isolant,** insulating pad; *Cin:* **p. presseur, de pression (de la fenêtre de vues),** pressure pad. **4.** (*a*) base, foot, flange (of rails); **largeur du p.,** width of rail base; (*b*) *Veh:* **p. de chenille,** track link, shoe; **chaîne sans fin à patins,** caterpillar chain; pedrail chain; (*c*) *Tls:* toe (of G cramp). **5.** (*a*) *Const:* patten, sole piece (of foundation); sill, sleeper (of staircase); (*b*) *N.Arch:* timber head. **6.** *P:* tongue; **rouler un p.,** to give s.o. a French kiss.

patinage[1] [patinaːʒ], *s.m.* **1.** skating; **p. à (la) voile,** skate sailing; **piste de p. artificielle,** ice, skating, rink. **2.** (*of wheel*) skidding; slipping; **p. de la courroie,** belt slip; **p. sur place (des roues),** spinning (of wheels).

patinage[2], *s.m. A: F:* pawing (of s.o.); monkeying about (with s.o.).

patine [patin], *s.f.* patina.

patiné [patine], *a.* (*a*) patinated (bronze); (*b*) *Furn:* fumed, weathered (oak); **vieille église patinée par le temps,** old church mellowed by time.

patiner[1] [patine], *v.i.* **1.** to skate; **p. sur des roulettes,** to roller skate. **2.** (*of wheel*) to skid, slip; (*of belt, clutch*) to slip; *Aut:* (*of wheels*) **p. sur place,** to spin.

patiner[2], *v.tr. A: F:* to paw (s.o.).

patiner[3], *v.tr.* to give a patina to, to patinate (bronze, etc.).

patinette [patinɛt], *s.f.* (child's) scooter; *A:* **p. automobile,** motor scooter.

patineur[1], **-euse** [patinœːr, -øːz], *s.* skater.

patineur[2], *s.m. A: F:* man who paws women.

patinoire [patinwaːr], *s.f.* skating rink, ice rink.

patio [patjo], *s.m. Arch:* patio.

pâtir [pɑtiːr], *v.i.* **1.** (*a*) *A:* to suffer; **il n'y a que les justes qui pâtissent ici-bas,** only the just suffer in this world; *O:* **pâtir pour qn,** to suffer on account of s.o.; **les bons pâtissent pour les méchants,** the good suffer for the wicked; (*b*) *A:* & *Lit:* to live in poverty; to suffer privation; *Com:* **les affaires pâtissent,** business is stagnating; (*c*) **p. de qch.,** to suffer on account of sth.; **p. de restrictions,** to suffer from restrictions. **2.** (*a*) to be in a state of contemplation, of inaction; (*b*) *s.m.* **le p.,** (i) contemplation; (ii) inaction.

pâtira(s) [pɑtira], *s.m. F:* scapegoat; butt.

pâtis [pɑti], *s.m.* grazing ground, pasture.

pâtissage [pɑtisaːʒ], *s.m. Cu:* (*a*) pastry making; (*b*) working up (of pastry, dough).

pâtisser [pɑtise], *Cu:* **1.** *v.i.* to make pastries; **elle pâtisse bien,** she's a good pastry cook, an excellent cake maker. **2.** *v.tr.* to work up (pastry, dough).

pâtisserie [pɑtisri], *s.f.* **1.** pastry; small cake; *coll.* pastries; *Com:* confectionery; **elle fait de la bonne p.,** she's a good pastrycook, she makes excellent pastries, cakes; **manger des pâtisseries,** to eat pastries; *Pej:* **c'est de la vraie p.!** it's just wedding-cake architecture! **2.** pastry making; **s'y connaître en p.,** to be an experienced pastrycook. **3.** (*a*) pastrycook's, confectioner's, business; (*b*) bakehouse (where pastries are made); (*c*) cake shop; confectioner's; teashop, tearoom.

pâtissier, -ière [pɑtisje, -jɛːr]. **1.** *s.* pastrycook; confectioner. **2.** *s.* (*owner of shop*) confectioner; tearoom proprietor. **3.** *a.* **crème pâtissière,** crème pâtissière.

pâtisson [pɑtisɔ̃], *s.m. Hort:* squash (melon).

patoche [patɔʃ], *s.f. P:* **1.** hand, paw. **2.** *O: Sch:* stroke, cut (with the cane).

patois [patwa]. **1.** *s.m.* (*a*) patois, provincial dialect; (*b*) jargon; (school, etc.) slang. **2.** *a.* patois, (word, etc.).

patoisant, -ante [patwazɑ̃, -ɑ̃ːt]. **1.** *a.* dialectal (language). **2.** *s.* person who speaks patois.

patoiser [patwaze], *v.i.* to speak in patois, to use provincialisms.

patoiserie [patwazri], *s.f. F:* imitation of patois, of provincial accent (on the stage, etc.).

pâton [pɑtɔ̃], *s.m.* **1.** *Husb:* ball of soft food (for cramming poultry); **p. de graisse,** plump little bird. **2.** *Paperm:* lump (in paper); *Cer:* lump of clay (added to turned piece to form handle, etc.).

patouillard [patujaːr], *s.m. Nau: F:* (old) tub.

patouille [patuːj], *s.f.* **1.** *F: Nau:* rope ladder. **2.** *F:* mud; *F:* goo; slush. **3.** *F:* water. **4.** *P:* squeeze; cuddle.

patouiller [patuje], *F:* **1.** *v.i.* to splash, flounder (in the mud). **2.** *v.tr.* to paw (s.o., sth.).

patouillet [patujɛ], *s.m. Min:* washing cylinder; washer (for ore); *Cer:* pug mill.

patouilleur [patujœːr], *s.m. Cer:* pugger, pug miller.

patouilleux, -euse [patujø, -øːz], *a. F:* (*a*) muddy, slushy; (*b*) choppy (sea).

patraque [patrak], *F:* **1.** *s.f. A:* (*a*) worn-out machine; (*b*) chronic invalid; old crock; (*c*) watch, ticker. **2.** *a.* (*of pers.*) out of sorts, seedy; under the weather.

pâtre [pɑːtr̥], *s.m. Lit:* herdsman; shepherd.

patriarcal, -aux [patriarkal, -o], *a.* patriarchal.

patriarcalement [patriarkalmɑ̃], *adv.* like a patriarch; patriarchally.

patriarcat [patriarka], *s.m.* **1.** *Ecc:* patriarchate. **2.** *Anthr:* patriarchy.

patriarche [patriarʃ], *s.m. B.Lit: Ecc: etc:* patriarch; **mener une vie de p.,** to live like a patriarch (surrounded by one's family).

patriarchie [patriarʃi], *s.f.* patriarchy.

patrice[1] [patris], *s.m. Rom.Hist:* (title of) patrician.

Patrice[2], *Pr.n.m.* Patrick.

patricial, -aux [patrisjal, -o], *a. Rom.Hist:* patrician; **dignité patriciale,** patrician rank.

patriciat [patrisja], *s.m. Rom.Hist:* patriciate. **1.** the order of the patricians. **2.** dignity of patrician.

patricien, -ienne [patrisjɛ̃, -jɛn], *a.* & *s. Rom.Hist: etc:* patrician; **manières patriciennes,** aristocratic bearing, outlook.

patriclan [patriklɑ̃], *s.m. Ethn:* patriclan, patrilineal clan.

patrie [patri], *s.f.* native land, country; fatherland, motherland; **mère p.,** mother country; **la p. des beaux-arts,** the home of the (fine) arts; **la p. de Rousseau est Genève,** Rousseau's birthplace is Geneva; Rousseau was born in Geneva; **mourir pour la p.,** to die for one's country.

patrilinéaire [patrilineɛːr], *a.* patrilineal, patrilinear.

patrimoine [patrimwan], *s.m.* patrimony, inheritance; heritage; estate; **le p. commun d'une nation,** the common inheritance of a nation; *Jur:* **séparation des patrimoines,** law under which the creditors of the deceased have prior claim on the estate; *Biol:* **p. héréditaire,** genotype.

patrimonial, -aux [patrimɔnjal, -o], *a.* patrimonial (estate, inheritance).
patrimonialement [patrimɔnjalmɑ̃], *adv.* patrimonially, by right of succession.
patrimonialiser [patrimɔnjalize], *v.tr. Jur:* to make patrimonial.
patrinite [patrinit], *s.f. Miner:* aikinite, needle ore.
patriofelis [patriɔfelis], *s.m. Paleont:* Patriofelis.
patriotard [patriɔtaːr], *s.m. F: Pej:* blatant patriot; flag-wagger; jingoist.
patriote [patriɔt]. **1.** *a.* patriotic (person). **2.** *s.* patriot; **il est mauvais p.,** he is unpatriotic, a bad patriot.
patriotique [patriɔtik], *a.* patriotic (song, speech, feelings, etc.).
patriotiquement [patriɔtikmɑ̃], *adv.* patriotically, like a patriot.
patriotisme [patriɔtism], *s.m.* patriotism; *Pej: A:* **p. de clocher,** parochialism.
patristique [patristik], *Theol:* **1.** *a.* patristic. **2.** *s.f.* patristics.
Patrocle [patrɔkl], *Pr.n.m. Gr.Lit:* Patroclus.
patrocline [patrɔklin], *a. Biol:* patroclinous, patroclinic.
patrologie [patrɔlɔʒi], *s.f. Rel.H:* patrology.
patron, -onne [patrɔ̃, -ɔn]. **1.** *s.* (*a*) patron, patroness; protector, protectress; **p. d'un bénéfice,** patron of a living; holder of the advowson; (*b*) patron saint (of person, church, etc.). **2.** (*a*) master, mistress (of house); employer (of labour); chief, head, owner (of firm, of business); proprietor, proprietress (of hotel); *F:* **adressez-vous au p., à la patronne,** you must speak to the boss; *Sch:* **p. de thèse de doctorat,** professor, tutor, supervising postgraduate student (preparing doctorate thesis); *Med:* **médecins assistants groupés autour de leur p.,** housemen, medical students, grouped around their specialist, *F:* chief; (*b*) *Nau:* skipper, master (of small vessel); shipmaster; coxswain (of boat crew); **p. de baleinière,** headsman. **3.** *s.m.* (*a*) pattern (for dress, embroidery); model; *Com:* stock size; **(taille) demi-p., p., grand p.** = small men's, men's, outsize (size); **très grand, extra grand, p.,** extra outsize; (*b*) template, templet; **p. ajouré,** stencil (plate); **colorié au p.,** coloured by stencil; **coloriage au p.,** stencil painting.
patronage [patrɔnaːʒ], *s.m.* **1.** (*a*) patronage; **apporter son p. à une œuvre,** to confer one's patronage upon an undertaking; *Com:* **nous vous prions de nous honorer de votre p.,** we hope you will honour us with your custom; (*b*) *Ecc:* advowson. **2.** (*a*) (church) club (for young people); guild; (*b*) headquarters of church guild.
patronal, -aux [patrɔnal, -o], *a.* **1.** of, pertaining to, the patron saint; **les saints patronaux,** the patron saints; **fête patronale,** parish feast, patronal festival. **2.** *Ind:* of, pertaining to, employers; **organisation patronale,** organization of employers; **syndicat p.,** employers' association.
patronat [patrɔna], *s.m.* **1.** *Rom.Ant: etc:* patronate, protection. **2.** *Ind:* (body of) employers; **le p. et le salariat,** employers and employed.
patronite [patrɔnit], *s.f. Miner:* patronite.
patron-jaquet [patrɔ̃ʒakɛ], *s.m.*, **patron-minet** [patrɔ̃minɛ], *s.m. A: used in phr.* **dès p.-j., dès p.-m.,** at early dawn, at peep of day.
patronner[1] [patrɔne], *v.tr.* (*a*) to cut out (shirt, etc.) on a pattern; (*b*) to stencil.
patronner[2], *v.tr.* to patronize, protect, support (person, hospital, charity ball, etc.); to sponsor (s.o.).
patronnesse [patrɔnɛs], *a. & s.f.* (*usu. Hum.*) **(dame) p.,** patroness (of a charity, fête, etc.).
patronnet [patrɔnɛ], *s.m.* pastrycook's boy.
patronnier, -ière [patrɔnje, -jɛːr], *s. Ind: Tex:* pattern maker.
patronyme [patrɔnim], *s.m.* patronym, patronymic, surname.
patronymique [patrɔnimik], *a.* patronymic; **nom p.,** (i) *Cl.Ant:* patronymic; (ii) surname.
patrouille [patruːj], *s.f. Mil: etc:* patrol; **p. aérienne,** air patrol; **p. à grande distance, à grand rayon d'action,** long-range patrol; **p. de découverte,** (i) *Mil:* scouting, exploration, patrol; (ii) *Av:* search patrol; **p. de reconnaissance,** (i) *Mil:* reconnaissance patrol, reconnoitring party; (ii) *Av:* reconnaissance air patrol; **p. de contact,** contact patrol; **p. de combat,** (i) *Mil:* combat patrol; (ii) *Av:* combat air patrol; **p. de harcèlement,** harassing patrol, nuisance patrol; **p. de liaison,** liaison patrol; **p. de sûreté,** protective patrol, security patrol; **formation de p.,** patrol formation; **p. de la circulation (routière),** traffic patrol; **en p.,** on patrol; **partir en, effectuer une, p.,** (i) *Mil: Av: Navy:* to patrol, to carry out a patrol; (ii) *Av:* to fly (in) a patrol; **envoyer une p.,** (i) *Mil:* to send out a patrol; (ii) *Av:* to send a patrol into the air; **envoyer qn, un groupe de combat, un avion, en p.,** to send s.o., a squad, an aircraft, on a patrol mission, on patrol duty.
patrouiller [patruje]. **1.** *v.tr.* to patrol; *Mil: Navy:* **p. sur la ligne,** to patrol the line. **2.** *v.tr. P:* to paw (s.o., sth.).
patrouilleur [patrujœːr]. **1.** *s.m.* (*a*) *Mil:* member of a patrol; scout; (*b*) *Av:* patrol aircraft, air scout; *Aer: A:* blimp; (*c*) *Navy:* patrol boat, ship, vessel; guard boat, scout. **2.** *a. Av:* **avion, bombardier, p.,** patrol aircraft, bomber; *Navy:* **bâtiment p.,** patrol boat, ship, vessel; *Nau:* **bâtiment p. des glaces,** ice-patrol vessel.
patte [pat], *s.f.* **1.** paw (of lion, cat, dog, monkey); foot (of bird); leg (of insect); *F:* (*of pers.*) (i) hand, paw, mitt; (ii) foot, hoof; *Ent:* **p. membraneuse, fausse p.,** pro-leg; *Crust:* **p. natatoire,** swimmeret; **p. de mouche,** fly's leg; *F:* **pattes de mouche,** cramped, badly-formed, handwriting; *F:* **pattes de lapin, de lièvre,** short side whiskers, sideboards; side-burns; *Th:* **p. de lapin (pour maquillage),** hare's foot; **pattes d'araignée,** (i) spider's legs; (ii) *F:* long, thin fingers; (iii) *F:* spidery handwriting; (iv) *Mec.E:* oil grooves, oil ways, grease channel (of bearing); *Cu: Fr.C:* **pattes de cochon,** pig's trotters; **marcher à quatre pattes,** to go on all fours, on one's hands and knees; **animaux à quatre pattes,** four-footed animals; **pattes de devant,** forelegs, forefeet; **pattes de derrière,** hind legs, feet; *F: A:* **mettre une affaire sur pattes,** to set a business on its feet; *F:* **aller à pattes,** to walk, to hoof it; **faire p. de velours,** (i) (*of cat*) to draw in its claws; (ii) to show the velvet glove; **coup de p.,** scratch, claw; pat; **donner un coup de p. à qn,** (i) to scratch, claw, s.o.; (ii) *F:* to have a dig at s.o.; **c'est un coup de p. à votre adresse,** that's a dig at you; **être sous la p. de qn,** to be under s.o.'s authority; **tenir qn sous sa p.,** to have s.o. at one's mercy, under one's thumb; **tomber sous la p. de qn,** to fall into s.o.'s clutches; **se tirer des pattes de qn,** to escape from s.o.'s clutches; **se faire faire les pattes,** to get caught; **en avoir plein les pattes,** (i) to be tired out (after a long walk); (ii) to be fed up; **(à) bas les pattes!** (i) (*to dog*) down, sir! (ii) *F:* hands off! (iii) *F:* no fighting here! *adv.phr.* (*of dog, etc.*) **à toutes pattes,** at full speed; *F:* **graisser la p. à qn,** to tip s.o., to oil s.o.'s palm; *F:* **il n'a jamais cassé trois pattes à un canard,** he'll never set the Thames on fire; *F:* **pantalon à pattes d'éléphant,** bell-bottomed trousers. **2.** (*a*) *Bot:* root (of anemone, etc.); (*b*) *occ.* foot (of wine glass). **3.** music pen. **4.** flap (of pocket, of envelope), tongue (of pocket-book). **5.** holdfast, clamp, clip, fastening; **pattes de soutien,** supporting legs; **p. d'attache,** (i) binding iron; (ii) *I.C.E: etc:* engine-bearer arm; lug; (iii) *Rail:* tongue attachment (of points); *Mec.E:* **p. d'attache, de fixation,** (anchor-) clip, fastening lug, fixing lug; **p. de sustentation, de suspension,** bracket; *Cy:* **p. de tension,** chain adjuster; *Nau:* **p. d'une ancre,** fluke, palm, of an anchor; **p. d'un grappin,** claw of a grapnel. **6.** *Dressm: etc:* tab, strap (on garment); **pattes d'épaule,** shoulder straps; **p. de bretelle,** (leather, cord) brace end; *Tail:* **pardessus à fermeture sous p.,** overcoat with fly front, fly-fronted overcoat; **poche sans p.,** cross-jetted pocket. **7.** *Dial:* rag, duster. **8.** *Nau:* (*a*) **p. d'élingue, p. à barriques,** (pair of) barrel hooks; can hook; **pattes d'embarcation,** boat slings; (*b*) cringle (of sail, reef, etc.); **p. de bouline,** grommet, cringle (for bowline bridle).
patté [pate], *a. Her:* paty.
patte-d'araignée [patdarɛɲe], *s.f. Bot:* love in a mist; *s.a.* PATTE 1; *pl. pattes-d'araignée.*
patte-de-griffon [patdəgrifɔ̃], *s.f. Bot:* stinking hellebore; *pl. pattes-de-griffon.*
patte-de-lièvre [patdəljɛːvr], *s.f. Bot:* hare's-foot trefoil; rabbit-foot clover; *pl pattes-de-lièvre.*
patte-de-loup [patdəlu], *s.f. Bot:* gipsywort, water horehound; *pl. pattes-de-loup.*
patte-d'oie [patdwa], *s.f.* **1.** cross-roads; fork; Y-junction; *Aer:* goose foot, eta patch. **2.** crow's foot (wrinkle about the eyes). **3.** *Bot:* chenopodium, goose foot. **4.** *Hyd.E:* dolphin (of bridge). **5.** *Nau:* **p.-d'o. de corps-mort,** mooring bridle. **6.** *W.Tel:* crow's foot (of aerial); *pl. pattes-d'oie.*
patte-fiche [patfiʃ], *s.f.* holdfast; *pl. pattes-fiches.*
patte-mâchoire [patmɑʃwaːr], *s.f. Arach: Crust:* maxilliped(e); *pl. pattes-mâchoires.*
pattemouille [patmuːj], *s.f. Dom.Ec:* damping cloth.
patte-nageoire [patnaʒwaːr], *s.f. Z:* flipper; *pl. pattes-nageoires.*
patte-pelu(e) [pat(ə)pəly], *s.m. & f. O: F:* sneak, pussyfoot; *pl. pattes-pelu(e)s.*
patter [pate]. **1.** *v.tr. Mus:* to draw staves on (paper). **2.** *v.i.* (*of hare, etc.*) to scratch up earth (with its paws).
pattinson(n)age [patɛ̃sɔnaːʒ], *s.m. Metall:* pattinsonization; Pattinson's desilverizing process (for lead).
pattu [paty], *a.* **1.** *F:* large-pawed, broad-pawed, rough-footed (dog, etc.); sturdy-legged (pers.). **2.** feather-legged (hen, pigeon).
patudo [patydo], *s.m. Ich:* blackfin tunny, obese tunny, big-eye tuna.
pâturable [pɑtyrabl̩], *a.* pasturable (plain, etc.); suitable for pasture, for grazing.
pâturage [pɑtyraːʒ], *s.m.* **1.** grazing; *Jur:* (*a*) **bail de p.,** lease of grazing rights; (*b*) **droit de p.,** right of common; common of pasturage. **2.** (*a*) pasture, grazing ground; sheep walk, run; **p. en forêt,** forest pasture; (*b*) *pl.* pasture land.
pâturant [pɑtyrɑ̃], *a.* grazing (animal).
pâture [pɑtyːr], *s.f.* **1.** food, feed, fodder (of animals); **leurs cadavres servirent de p. aux oiseaux de proie,** their bodies became food for, were devoured by, birds of prey; **livre qui donne de la p. à l'esprit, qui est une p. intellectuelle,** book that provides food for the mind. **2.** (*a*) pasture; *Jur:* **vaine p.,** (right of) common; **mettre les chevaux en p.,** to turn the horses out to grass; (*b*) pasture, grazing ground.
pâturer [pɑtyre]. **1.** *v.i.* (*of cattle, etc.*) to graze, to feed. **2.** *v.tr.* (*of cattle, etc.*) to graze (on) (meadow).
pâturin [pɑtyrɛ̃], *s.m. Bot:* meadow grass, *U.S:* spear grass; **p. des prés,** (i) smooth-stalked meadow grass; (ii) *U.S:* blue grass; **p. commun,** rough meadow grass; **p. des bois,** wood poa.
paturon [patyrɔ̃], *s.m.* **1.** pastern (of horse). **2.** *Bot: F:* (kind of) pumpkin.
pauciflore [posiflɔːr], *a. Bot:* pauciflorous.
paucité [posite], *s.f. A:* paucity.
Paul [pɔl], *Pr.n.m.* Paul; *s.a.* PIERRE[2].
Paula [pola], **Paule** [poːl], *Pr.n.f.* Paula.
Paul-Émile [pɔlemil], *Pr.n.m. Rom.Hist:* Aemilius Paulus.
paulette [polɛt], *s.f. A:* tax paid every nine years by magistrates and other holders of hereditary offices (first farmed by Paulet under Henri IV).
paulicien [polisjɛ̃], *s.m. Rel.H:* Paulician.
Paulin [polɛ̃], *Pr.n.m. Rel.H:* Paulinus.
Pauline [polin], *Pr.n.f.* Paulina, Pauline.
paulinien, -ienne [polinjɛ̃, -jɛn], *Ecc.Hist:* (*a*) *a.* Pauline (doctrine, writings); (*b*) *s.* Paulinian.
paulinisme [polinism], *s.m. Rel.H:* Paulinism.
pauliste[1] [polist], *s.m. & a. R.C.Ch:* Paulist.
pauliste[2], *a. & s.m. & f. Geog:* (native, inhabitant) of São Paulo.
paulo-post-futur [polopɔstfytyːr], *s.m. Gr.Gram:* paulo-post future.
paulownia [polɔnja], *s.m. Bot:* paulownia.
paume [poːm], *s.f.* **1.** (*a*) palm (of hand); (*b*) hand (as a measure of horses). **2.** *Games:* **(jeu de) p.,** (i) tennis (N.B. not lawn tennis); (ii) tennis court; **courte p.,** court tennis, close tennis; **longue p.,** open-air tennis (the forerunner of lawn-tennis); *Fr.Hist:* **Le Serment du Jeu de P.,** the Tennis-Court Oath (1789). **3.** *Carp:* halved joint.
paumé, -ée[1] [pome], *P:* **1.** *a.* broke; down and out. **2.** *s.* (*pers.*) derelict, wreck; down-and-out.
paumée[2] [pome], *s.f. Meas: Equit:* hand.
paumelle[1] [pomɛl], *s.f.* **1.** *Nau: etc:* (sailmaker's) palm; hand leather. **2.** *Leath:* graining board. **3.** (*a*) plate (of door hinge); (*b*) door hinge, lift-off hinge; **p. double,** H-hinge.
paumelle[2], *s.f. Agr:* two-rowed barley.
paumer [pome], *v.tr. P:* **1.** *O:* to smack, slap (s.o.'s face, etc.). **2.** to nab, cop (thief); **p. qn marron,** to catch s.o. red-handed; **se faire p.,** to get nabbed, copped. **3.** to pinch, swipe. **4.** to lose.
se paumer, *P:* **1.** to get lost. **2.** to go to the dogs, to become a down-and-out.
paumet [pomɛ], *s.m. Nau: etc:* (sailmaker's) palm; hand leather.
paumier, -ière [pomje, -jɛːr], *s. Hist:* palmer.
paumoyer [pomwaje], *v.tr.* **(je paumoie, n. paumoyons; je paumoierai) 1.** to measure the height of (flax, hemp, etc.) in hand's breadths. **2.** *Nau:* to underrun (rope).
se paumoyer, *Nau:* to climb hand over hand.
paumure [pomyːr], *s.f. Ven:* palm (of deer's antlers).

Paunie [poni], *s.m. & f. Ethn:* Pawnee.

paupérisation [poperizasjɔ̃], *s.f.* impoverishment, impoverishing; reducing to poverty, to destitution.

paupériser [poperize], *v.tr.* to reduce to poverty, to destitution.

paupérisme [poperism], *s.m.* pauperism; destitution; **réduire une nation au p.**, to reduce a nation to destitution, to extreme poverty.

paupière [popjɛːr], *s.f.* (*a*) eyelid; **ouvrir la p.**, to wake up; **fermer la paupière**, (i) to go to sleep; (ii) to close one's eyes in death; **fermer la p. à qn**, to close s.o.'s eyes (as a last duty); (*b*) *Z:* **p. interne**, nictitating membrane.

paupiette [popjɛt], *s.f. Cu:* (meat) olive.

paurométabole [porɔmetabɔl], *a. & s. Ent:* paurometabolous (insect).

pauropodes [porɔpɔd], *s.m.pl. Myr:* Pauropoda, pauropods.

pause [poːz], *s.f.* **1.** pause; *Fb: etc:* half time; *Ind: etc:* meal break; **la p. du café, la p.-café**, the coffee break, (=) the tea break; **faire une p.**, to pause, to make a pause, a stop. **2.** *Mus:* (i) rest, pause; (ii) semibreve rest; (iii) bar's rest; *F:* **compter des pauses**, to mark time; to be kept waiting for nothing. **3.** *Mil:* period (of drill), lesson, training session.

pauser [poze], *v.i.* **1.** *Mus:* to pause. **2.** *Mus: A:* to dwell (on a note). **3.** *F: Dial:* to kick one's heels.

Pausilippe [pozilip], *Pr.n.m. Geog:* Posilippo.

paussidés [poside], *s.m.pl. Ent:* Paussidae, paussids.

pauvre [poːvr̥]. **1.** *a.* (NOTE: *if this a. is placed before the s. it usu. indicates a nuance of pity, scorn or condescension*) (*a*) **p.**, *A:* **p. d'argent**, poor; *F:* hard up; **un homme p.**, a poor man; **p. comme un rat d'église, comme Job**, as poor as a church mouse, as Job; **il est devenu p.**, he has become poor, has lost his money; **p. de talent et de ressources**, lacking in talent and resources; *F:* **p. d'esprit**, dull-witted; **vie p. en événements**, uneventful life; **minerai p. en métal**, ore with a low metal content; **mélange p.**, (i) *Aut:* weak mixture; (ii) *Av:* lean mixture; (*b*) poor, unfortunate; **un p. aveugle**, a poor blind man; **le p. homme!** poor chap! **p. de moi!** poor me! (*c*) (*used when speaking of person who is dead*) **mon p. père disait toujours . . .**, my poor father always used to say . . .; (*d*) shabby (dress, furniture, etc.); lame, paltry (excuse); **de pauvres vers**, poor verse; **un p. dîner**, a wretched, meagre, dinner; not much of a dinner; **deux pauvres mille francs**, a paltry two thousand francs; **au bout de trente ans de travail il avait amassé cinq ou six pauvres mille francs**, at the end of thirty years' work he had saved a miserable five or six thousand francs; **assis auprès d'un p. feu**, seated by a small, dull, fire; **p. sujet**, barren subject; *F:* (*pers.*) **c'est un p. type**, he's not much, he's a wet; **p. idiot!** silly fool! **2.** *s.m. & f.* poor man, poor woman; *Adm: A:* pauper; **les pauvres et les riches**, the poor and the rich; **la bière est le champagne des pauvres**, beer is the poor man's champagne; *B:* **bienheureux les pauvres en esprit**, blessed are the poor in spirit; *F:* **les pauvres d'esprit**, the feeble-minded, the dull-witted; those of limited intelligence; *Adm: A:* **taxe des pauvres**, poor rate; *Th: A:* **droit des pauvres**, entertainment tax.

pauvrement [povrəmɑ̃], *adv.* poorly, wretchedly; **vivre p.**, to live on a small income; **p. vêtu**, poorly, shabbily, dressed; **pièce p. meublée**, poorly furnished room; **peindre p.**, to paint indifferently; **élevé p.**, brought up in poverty, in poor circumstances.

pauvresse [povrɛs], *s.f.* (*a*) poor woman; *Adm:* pauper; (*b*) beggar-woman; **une petite p.**, a little beggar-girl.

pauvret, -ette [povrɛ, -ɛt], (*a*) *a. A: Lit:* poor; (*b*) *s. F: O:* **le p., la pauvrette**, the poor little thing.

pauvreté [povrəte], *s.f.* **1.** (*a*) poverty; *Ecc:* **vœu de p.**, vow of poverty; *Prov:* **p. n'est pas vice**, poverty is no vice, no sin, no disgrace, no crime; **p. du sol**, poverty, lack of fertility, of the soil; **p. en céréales**, lack of cereal crops (in a region); (*b*) poorness (of language); baldness (of style, etc.); **p. d'idées**, (i) lack, dearth, of ideas; (ii) poorness, poverty, of ideas. **2. n'écrire que des pauvretés**, to write nothing but commonplaces; to write poor stuff.

pauxi [poksi], *s.m. Orn:* pauxi.

pavage [pavaːʒ], *s.m.* **1.** (action of) paving; **pierre de p.**, paving stone; **carreau de p.**, paving flag. **2.** pavement. **3.** *Ph.Geog:* pavement.

pavane [pavan], *s.f. Danc: Mus:* pavan(e).

pavaner (se) [səpavane], *v.pr.* to strut about; to make a display of oneself.

pavé [pave], *s.m.* **1.** (*a*) paving stone, paving block; **p. d'échantillon**, standard paving stone; stone set; **p. refendu**, paving stone of half-size; *Lit:* **c'est le p. de l'ours**, (allusion to La Fontaine's fable) (i) save me from my friends! (ii) it's like breaking a butterfly on the wheel; *F:* **un p. dans la mare**, a (nice) bit of scandal; (*b*) **p. de pain d'épice**, slab of gingerbread; (*c*) *F: Publ:* large tome; *Journ:* **p. publicitaire**, prominent advertisement, advertisement that hits you in the eye. **2.** (*a*) pavement, paving; **p. en briques, en béton**, brick pavement, concrete pavement; **p. en verre**, glass pavement; (*b*) paved road, carriage road, highway; *Aut: F:* **brûler le p.**, to race along, to eat up the miles; (*c*) *A:* paved sides of (unpaved) throughfare, footway; **prendre le haut du p.**, (i) to walk on the inside, on the wall side, of the pavement; (ii) *F:* to lord it; **céder le haut du p. à qn**, (i) to let s.o. walk on the inside; (ii) to give way to s.o.; *F:* **ici, c'est M. X qui tient le haut du p.**, it is Mr X who is the big man here; it is Mr X who bosses the show; (*d*) the street, the streets; **battre le p.**, (i) to loaf about the streets, about town; (ii) to tramp the streets in search of work; **être sur le p.**, (i) to be homeless, on the streets; (ii) to be out of work; **mettre une famille sur le p.**, to turn a family into the street; **mettre qn sur le p.**, to turn s.o. out of his job. **3. p. d'organigramme**, box (of flow chart of computer).

pavement [pavmɑ̃], *s.m.* **1.** *A:* (action of) paving. **2.** (ornate) pavement; **p. en mosaïque**, mosaic floor(ing).

paver [pave], *v.tr.* to pave (street, courtyard, etc.) **rue pavée en bois**, wood-paved street; *Prov:* **l'enfer est pavé de bonnes intentions**, the road to hell is paved with good intentions; *F:* **la ville en est pavée, les rues en sont pavées**, it's as common as dirt, you can find it, them, everywhere; *F:* **avoir le gosier pavé**, to have a cast-iron throat.

paveton [pavətɔ̃], *s.m. P:* paving stone.

paveur [pavœːr], *s.m.* paver, paviour.

Pavie [pavi]. **1.** *Pr.n.f. Geog:* Pavia. **2.** *s.f. Hort:* clingstone (peach).

pavillon [pavijɔ̃], *s.m.* **1.** (*a*) *A:* tent; *Her:* pavilion, tent; (*b*) *Ecc:* veil of ciborium; (*c*) detached house; **p. de banlieue**, suburban house; **pavillons jumelés**, semi-detached houses; **p. du garde, p. d'entrée (d'une propriété)**, (gate) lodge; **p. de jardin**, summerhouse; **p. de chasse**, shooting lodge, box; **p. de golf**, golf pavilion, club house; **le P.**, the Pump Room; (*d*) (*isolated building in hospital, university, etc.*) block; (*e*) (*structure projecting or rising above a main building*) **comble en p.**, pavilion roof; (*e*) *Aut:* roof head, dome, body ceiling; *Furn:* canopy (over bed, etc.); (*e*) *Mus:* **p. chinois**, pavillon chinois. **2.** (*a*) horn (of hooter, loudspeaker, siren); bell (of brass instrument); mouth (of funnel); *Bot:* vexillum, standard, banner (of pea flower); *Tp:* **p. d'écouteur**, earpiece; *Mec:* (*on test bed*) **p. d'entrée**, (air) intake duct; (*b*) *Anat:* **p. de l'oreille**, pavilion, auricle, external ear. **3.** *Nau:* flag, colours; *Navy:* **le p. de l'amiral**, the admiral's flag; **p. de beaupré**, jack; **p. de compagnie, d'armateur**, house flag; *A:* **p. couplé**, waft; **p. de départ, p. de partance**, Blue Peter; **p. noir, de pirate**, Jolly Roger; black flag; **p. de poupe**, ensign; **p. de quarantaine**, yellow flag; **p. de détresse**, flag of distress; **p. (de) pilote**, pilot flag; **p. de complaisance**, flag of convenience; **hisser, arborer, son p.**, to hoist one's colours; **montrer son p.**, to show, display, one's colours; **battre un p.**, to fly a flag; **saluer du p.**, to dip the flag; **sous le p. anglais**, (ship) flying the British flag; (cargoes) in British bottoms; *Jur:* (*in war*) **loi du p.**, immunity of ship carrying neutral flag from search by warship of any other nation; **le p. couvre la marchandise**, the flag covers the cargo; **amener son p.**, *A:* **baisser (le) p.**, (i) *Navy:* to strike one's flag, to surrender; (ii) to admit defeat; **mettre p. bas devant qn**, to yield, give in, to s.o.; **clouer son p.**, to nail one's colours to the mast.

pavillonnaire [pavijɔnɛːr], *a. Town P: Pej:* suburban, subtopian (development).

pavillonnerie [pavijɔnri], *s.f. Nau:* **1.** flag loft. **2.** *coll.* flags.

pavimenteux, -euse [pavimɑ̃tø, -øːz], *a.* **1.** (*of stone*) suitable for paving. **2.** *Anat:* **épithélium p.**, pavement epithelium.

pavlovien, -ienne [pavlɔvjɛ̃, -jɛn], *a. Physiol:* Pavlovian.

pavlovisme [pavlɔvism], *s.m. Physiol:* Pavlovian theories (as a whole).

pavois [pavwa], *s.m.* **1.** *A.Arm:* (body-)shield; pavis(e); **élever qn sur le p.**, (i) *Hist:* to raise (newly elected king) on the shield, (ii) to extol s.o. to the skies. **2.** *Nau:* (*a*) bulwark; **p. de poulaine**, headboard; (*b*) *coll.* flags (for dressing ship); dressing; **mettre, hisser, le grand p.**, to dress over all, full; **metre, hisser, le petit p.**, to dress with masthead flags; **sous le grand p.**, dressed full; **sous le petit p.**, dressed with masthead flags.

pavoisement [pavwazmɑ̃], *s.m.* (*a*) *Nau:* dressing ship; (*b*) decking, decorating (of house, etc.) with flags.

pavoiser [pavwaze]. **1.** *v.tr.* (*a*) *Nau:* to dress (ship); *abs.* to dress ship; (*b*) to deck, decorate (house, etc.) with flags; to put out bunting, flags; **rues pavoisées**, streets gay with bunting. **2.** *v.i.* (*a*) *F:* to rejoice, to put out the flags; **il n'y a pas de quoi p.**, it's nothing to make a song and dance about; **aujourd'hui il pavoise, mais demain ce sera une autre histoire!** he may put out the flags today, but tomorrow it will be another story! (*b*) *P:* (i) *Box:* to bleed (from the nose), to have one's claret tapped; (ii) (*of woman*) to have the curse.

pavonazzo [pavɔnadzo], *s.m.* pavonazzo (marble).

pavot [pavo], *s.m. Bot:* poppy; **p. rouge, des moissons**, corn poppy, field poppy; **p. somnifère**, opium poppy; **p. de Tournefort**, oriental poppy; **p. cornu**, horn(ed) poppy, sea(side) poppy; **p. d'Islande**, Iceland poppy; **tête de p.**, poppy head; **graine(s) de p.**, poppy seed; **huile de p.**, poppy seed oil.

Pawnee [poni], *s.m. & f. Ethn:* Pawnee.

paxille [paksiːj], *s.m. Fung:* paxillus.

payable [pɛjabl̥], *a.* payable; *Com:* **p. à la livraison**, payable on delivery; **p. à vue, à l'ordre**, payable at sight, to order; **effet p. au premier mai**, bill due on 1st May; **devenir p.**, to fall due.

payant, -ante [pɛjɑ̃, -ɑ̃ːt]. **1.** *a.* (*a*) paying; **spectateur p.**, spectator who pays (for admission); **élèves payants**, paying pupils; (*b*) charged for; **spectacle p.**, show with charge for admission; **toutes les places sont payantes**, no free seats; **entrée payante**, no free admission, pay at the gate; (*c*) (*agency, etc.*) charging a fee; **école payante**, fee-paying school; **pont p.**, toll bridge; **lieux payants**, public conveniences; (*d*) **travail p., affaire payante**, work, business, that pays, profitable work, business; *F:* **ce n'est pas p.**, it's not worth the trouble. **2.** *s.* payer; *F: Pej:* **les cochons de payants**, the mugs (who pay full price).

paye [pɛːj], *s.f.* = PAIE.

payement [pɛjmɑ̃], *s.m.* = PAIEMENT.

payer [peje, pɛ-], *v.tr.* (**je paye, je paie, n. payons; je payerai, je paierai**) to pay; (*a*) **p. qn**, to pay s.o.; **se faire p.**, to collect one's money; **combien vous a-t-il fait p.?** how much did he charge you? **faire p. les riches**, to soak the rich; **p. qn sur la recette**, to pay s.o. out of the takings; **on paye les pompiers sur la caisse de la ville**, the firemen are paid out of the town funds; **p. qn de ses services**, to pay s.o. for his services; **trop payé, trop peu payé**, overpaid, underpaid; **on me payerait que je ne le ferais pas**, I would not do it even if I were paid; *F:* **p. qn de la même monnaie**, to pay s.o. back in his own coin; *P:* (*when offering large note in payment*) **voilà monsieur, payez-vous**, here you are, take it out of that; **il me paie d'ingratitude**, he repays me with ingratitude; **p. qn de paroles, de mots**, to put s.o. off with fine words; **je ne me paie pas de mots, de phrases**, mere words are no good; I'm not to be taken in with fine words; **p. de sa personne**, (i) to risk one's own skin; (ii) to take a personal share in the work, to do one's bit; to bear the brunt (of the work, of the fight); **p. d'audace**, (i) to take the risk; (ii) to face the music; (iii) *also* **p. d'effronterie**, to brazen it out; to put a bold face on it; *s.a.* MINE[2] 1; *abs.* **il paie mal**, he is a bad payer; **cette maison paie mal**, this firm pays badly, doesn't give very good wages; (*b*) **p. qch.**, to pay, discharge, settle (debt, fine, bill, etc.); **p. la note, les dépenses**, to pay, to foot, the bill; **p. rubis sur l'ongle**, to pay on the nail, on the dot; **pension payée sur un revenu**, pension charged on an income; *Com:* **p. un effet**, to honour a bill; **refuser de p. une traite**, to dishonour a bill; **congés payés**, holidays with pay; (*c*) **p. qch.**, to pay for sth.; **p. qch. à qn**, to pay s.o. for sth.; **je le lui ai payé cent francs**, I paid him a hundred francs for it; **p. son passage par son travail**, to work one's passage; **p. un dîner à qn**, to stand s.o. a dinner; **p. une tournée**, to stand a round (of drinks); *abs.* **c'est moi qui paye**, I'll stand this; it's my round; **je me suis payé une**

glace, I treated myself to an ice; **se p. la figure, la tête de qn,** to make fun of s.o.; to take a rise out of s.o.; *F:* **se p. la peau de qn,** to take it out of s.o.; **s'en p.,** to have a good time; **s'en p. une tranche,** to have a good laugh; **p. d'avance,** to pay in advance; to prepay (carriage, etc.); **la viande a été payée,** the meat has been paid for; **port payé,** carriage paid; post paid; *Tg:* **réponse payée,** answer prepaid; (*c*) **j'ai payé son silence dix mille francs,** I paid him ten thousand francs to hold his tongue; **c'est bien payé,** that's a stiff price; **il a payé sa témérité de sa vie,** he paid for his rashness with his life; **cela ne se paie pas,** it's invaluable, money can't buy it; **faire p. ses méfaits à qn,** to bring s.o. to account; **vous me le paierez!** you'll pay for this! I'll make you sorry (for this)! **je le lui ferai p.,** I'll make him pay for that; **j'ai payé pour cela; je suis payé pour le savoir,** I've learnt it to my cost; **un avantage chèrement payé,** a dearly bought advantage; **je l'ai payé cher,** I paid dearly for it (e.g. for my rashness, etc.); **p. pour les coupables,** to pay for the misdeeds of others; (*d*) *v.i. F:* **commerce qui paie,** profitable business, business that pays.

payeur, -euse [pɛjœːr, -øːz]. **1.** *s.* payer; **c'est un bon p.,** he is a good payer, a prompt payer. **2.** *s.m. Adm: etc:* disbursements officer; payments officer; paying cashier; *Mil: Navy:* paymaster; *Bank:* teller.

payol [pɛjɔl], *s.m. Nau:* ceiling.

pays[1] [pe(j)i], *s.m.* country; (*a*) land; **le beau p. de France,** the fair land of France; **p. de provenance,** country of origin; **visiter des p. étrangers,** to visit foreign countries, lands; **les p. chauds,** the tropics; **battre du p.,** (i) to roam about; (ii) *F:* to wander from one's subject; **il a vu du p.,** he has seen the world, travelled far, travelled (about) a great deal; **faire voir du p. à qn,** to lead s.o. a pretty dance (in pursuit); *F:* **le p. des songes,** dreamland; (*b*) region, district, locality; **vous n'êtes donc pas de ce p.?** so you don't belong to these parts? **p. perdu,** out-of-the-way place; *F:* **être en p. de connaissance,** to be among friends, to feel at home; **c'est la coutume du p.,** it is the custom of the country; **denrées du p.,** home (-grown) produce; **vin de p., du p.,** local wine; (*c*) **p. de montagne(s),** hill country; **p. maritime,** maritime country; **p. sans côtes marines,** land-locked country; *pl.* **p. bas,** lowlands; **p. côtiers,** coastal regions; (*d*) native land, home, birth-place; **mal du p.,** homesickness; nostalgia; **avoir le mal du p.,** to be homesick; **écrire au p.,** to write home; **dans mon p.,** where I come from; **le p. des tigres,** the home of the tiger; *F:* **il est bien de son p.!** well, he *is* green!

pays[2], **payse** [pe(j)i, pe(j)iːz], *s. F:* fellow-country-man, -woman; **nous sommes p.,** we are from the same parts, the same place, the same village; **c'est une payse,** she's from our village.

paysage [peizaːʒ], *s.m.* **1.** landscape; scenery. **2.** *Art:* landscape (painting); **peintre de paysages,** landscape painter; **faire du p.,** to paint landscapes; *F:* **cela fait bien dans le p.,** it looks well in the picture; it looks, sounds, well.

paysager [peizaʒe], *a.m. used in* **jardin p.,** landscape garden; **dessinateur de jardins paysagers,** landscape gardener.

paysagiste [peizaʒist]. **1.** *s.m.* landscape painter. **2.** *a.* (*a*) landscape (painter); (*b*) **(jardinier) p.,** landscape gardener.

paysan, -anne [peizɑ̃, -an], *s. & a.* **1.** *s.* (*a*) countryman, -woman; (*b*) **p. (propriétaire),** farmer; **p. (salarié),** farm labourer; (*c*) *Hist:* **les paysans,** the peasants, the peasantry; (*d*) *Pej:* peasant, clod. **2.** *a.* country, rustic.

paysanesque [peizanɛsk], *a. F:* rustic (gaiety, etc.).

paysannat [peizana], *s.m.* (*a*) country people; (*b*) farmers; farming community (of a country, region).

paysannerie [peizanri], *s.f.* **1.** (*a*) country ways, habits, etc.; (*b*) = PAYSANNAT. **2.** *Lit: A:* story, play, depicting peasant life.

Pays-Bas (les) [lepeibɑ], *Pr.n.m. Geog:* the Netherlands.

pé [pe], *s.m.* (the letter) p.

péage [peaːʒ], *s.m.* **1.** toll, charge (for bridges, canals, on motorways, etc.); **pont à p.,** toll bridge; **acquitter le p.,** to pay the toll; **autoroute à p.,** toll motorway; *P.N: Aut:* **p. à 200 m.,** toll at 200 metres. **2.** toll house.

péageois, -oise [peaʒwa, -waːz], *a. & s. Geog:* (native, inhabitant) of (i) Bourg-de-Péage, (ii) Péage-de-Roussillon.

péager, -ère [peaʒe, -ɛːr], *s.* toll collector.

péan [peɑ̃], *s.m. Gr.Ant:* paean; song of triumph, of thanksgiving.

peau, -eaux [po], *s.f.* **1.** (*a*) skin; **vêtement à même la p., sur la p.,** garment next to the skin; **maladie de p.,** skin disease; **beauté à fleur de p.,** skin-deep beauty; **prendre qn par la p. du cou,** to take s.o. by the scruff of the neck; *F:* **il a des peaux sous le menton,** he's got dewlaps; **faire p. neuve,** (i) (*of snake*) to cast its slough, its skin; (ii) (*of pers.*) to turn over a new leaf; **il n'a que la p. et les os, les os lui percent la p.,** he's nothing but skin and bone; **crever dans sa p.,** to be bursting (i) with health, (ii) with anger, (iii) out of one's clothes; **ne pas tenir dans sa p.,** to be bursting with pride, with joy, with high spirits; **il mourra dans la p. d'un imbécile,** he'll be a fool until his dying day; **il mourra dans sa p., il ne changera jamais de p.,** he'll never alter; he's incorrigible; *F:* **femmes en p.,** women with low-cut dresses; **la p. lui démange,** (i) his skin's itching; (ii) *F:* he's itching for trouble; **je ne voudrais pas être dans sa p.,** I wouldn't like to be in his shoes; **risquer sa p.,** to risk one's life; **sauver sa p.,** to save one's bacon; **vendre cher sa p.,** to sell one's skin, one's life, dearly; **craindre pour sa p.,** to fear for one's skin; **je ne donne pas cher pour sa p.,** I wouldn't give much for his chances; **il travaille au dictionnaire depuis vingt ans et il finira par y laisser sa p.,** he's been working on the dictionary for twenty years and he'll die in harness; **il est parti pour une expédition en Afrique et il y a laissé sa p.,** he went on an expedition to Africa and left his bones there; *F: A:* **avoir la p. courte,** to be lazy; *F:* **avoir qn dans sa p.,** to be crazy about s.o.; *F:* **il l'a dans la p.,** he's mad on her; *F:* **se sentir mal dans sa p.,** to feel uncomfortable; *Th:* **entrer dans la p. d'un personnage,** to identify oneself with a character; to get right inside a part; *P:* **trouer la p. à qn,** to kill s.o., to bump s.o. off; *P:* **j'aurai ta p.!** I'll get you! *P:* **il ne sait pas quoi faire de sa p.,** he doesn't know where to put himself; *P:* **travailler pour la p.,** to work for nothing; to have one's trouble for nothing; *P:* **la p.! p. de balle (et balai de crin)!** nothing doing! no fear! (*b*) *P: O:* old hag; old tart, old bag; *P:* (*of girl*) **p. (de chien),** tart. **2.** (*a*) hide, pelt, fell, fur (of animals); **peaux vertes,** raw hides, raw skins, pelts; **p. de lapin,** (i) rabbit skin; (ii) *P:* (*woman*) tart; *F: A:* **bas en p. de lapin,** stockings worn inside out; *F:* **communiste, etc. en p. de lapin,** would-be communist, etc.; (*b*) prepared hide, leather; **p. de cheval,** horse hide; **p. de mouton,** sheepskin; **p. de chevreau,** kid; **p. de daim,** buckskin; **p. de veau,** calfskin, box calf; **p. de requin,** shagreen; **p. de taupe,** moleskin (fur); **p. sciée,** split hide; *F:* **p. d'âne,** diploma; *P:* **c'est une vraie p. de vache,** he's a stinker; (*c*) **p. de tambour,** (i) drum parchment; (ii) drumhead; (*d*) *Tex:* **p. d'ange,** angel skin; **3.** (*a*) peel, skin (of fruit); **p. d'orange,** orange skin; (*b*) **p. à saucisses,** sausage skin. **4.** (*a*) coating, film, skin (of boiled milk, etc.); (*b*) *Metall:* **p. de crapaud,** scabbing.

peau-bleu [poblø], *s.m. Ich:* common sand shark; *pl. peaux-bleus.*

peaucier [posje], *a. & s.m. Anat:* **(muscle) p.,** platysma.

peaufiner [pofine], *v.tr.* (*a*) to polish (sth.) with a chamois leather; (*b*) *F:* to finick, niggle, over (a piece of work).

Peau-Rouge [poruːʒ], *s.m. & f. & a.* Red Indian, Redskin; *pl. Peaux-Rouges.*

peausserie [posri], *s.f.* **1.** (*a*) skin dressing; (*b*) skin-dressing trade. **2.** *coll.* skins.

peaussier [posje], *s.m.* (*a*) skinner, skin dresser; (*b*) fellmonger; (*c*) *F:* dermatologist; (*d*) *a. & s.m.* **(muscle) p.,** platysma.

pébrine [pebrin], *s.f. Ser:* pebrine.

pébriner (se) [səpebrine], *v.pr. Ser:* to contract pebrine.

pec [pɛk], *a.m.* **hareng p.,** freshly salted herring.

pécaïre [pekaiːr], *int. Dial:* (*S. of Fr.*) oh dear! heavens!

pecan [pekɑ̃], *a. & s.m. Bot:* **(noix) p.,** pecan.

pécari [pekari], *s.m. Z:* peccary; Mexican hog.

peccabilité [pɛkabilite], *s.f. Theol:* peccability.

peccable [pɛkabl], *a.* peccable, liable to sin.

peccadille [pɛkadiːj], *s.f.* peccadillo; slip.

peccamineux, -euse [pɛkaminø, -øːz], *a.* sinful.

peccant [pɛkɑ̃], *a. A.Med:* peccant (humour).

peccavi [pɛkavi], *int.* peccavi.

pecco [pɛko], *s.m.* pekoe (tea).

pêchable [pɛʃabl], *a.* **rivières pêchables,** fishing, fishable, streams.

pêchant [pɛʃɑ̃], *a. Fish:* **ligne pêchante,** good fishing line; **leurre p.,** good bait.

pechblende [pɛʃblɛ̃ːd], *s.f. Miner:* pitchblende, uraninite.

pêche[1] [pɛːʃ], *s.f.* (*a*) peach; (*b*) *P:* blow, biff; **flanque-lui une p.,** swipe him one!

pêche[2], *s.f.* **1.** fishing; **p. à la truite,** trout fishing; **p. à la sardine, à la morue,** sardine fishing, cod fishing; **p. à la ligne,** angling; **p. à la mouche,** fly fishing; **p. à la cuiller,** trolling, spinning; **p. à la main,** tickling, *Scot:* guddling; **grande p.,** deep-sea fishing; **la p. des perles,** pearl fishing; **la p. du corail,** coral fishery; **aller à la p.,** to go fishing; **p. à pied,** fishing for crabs, shellfish, etc. on the seashore when the tide is out; **articles de p.,** fishing tackle, implements; **port de p.,** fishing port. **2.** catch; **faire une heureuse p.,** to get a good haul; *B:* **la p. miraculeuse,** the miraculous draught of fishes. **3.** fishery; **grande p.,** high-sea fishery, great fishery; **petite p., p. côtière,** coastal fishery, inshore fishery; **p. au chalut,** trawling; **p. à la baleine,** whaling; **p. à la crevette,** shrimping.

péché [peʃe], *s.m.* sin; trespass, transgression; **les péchés mortels, capitaux,** the deadly sins; *F:* **laid comme les sept péchés capitaux,** as ugly as sin; *A:* **dire les sept péchés mortels de qn,** to blacken s.o.'s character; to say dreadful things about s.o.; **unis dans le p.,** living in sin; **mourir dans le p.,** to die in sin; **mourir dans son p.,** to die unrepentant; *F:* **pour mes péchés, je fus nommé à . . .,** for my sins, I was appointed to . . .; **son p. mignon,** his besetting sin, fault; *Prov:* **p. avoué est à demi pardonné,** a fault confessed is half redressed; **p. caché est à demi pardonné,** where there is no scandal it is easy to forgive; **à tout p. miséricorde,** there is mercy for everything; **péchés de jeunesse,** indiscretions of youth; **rechercher les vieux péchés de qn,** to rake up s.o.'s past.

pécher [peʃe], *v.i.* **(je pèche, n. péchons; je pécherai)** to sin; to trespass; **p. contre le ciel,** to sin against heaven; **p. par ignorance,** to err through ignorance; **p. contre la politesse,** to offend against the laws of courtesy; **construction qui pèche contre les règles de la langue,** construction contrary to the rules of the language; **il pèche par trop de timidité,** his fault, failing, is his excessive shyness; **il ne pèche pas par la modestie,** he does not err on the side of modesty; **p. par excès, par défaut,** to exceed, fall short of, what is required; **le raisonnement pèche,** the argument is at fault.

pêcher[1] [peʃe], *s.m.* peach tree; **(couleur) fleur de p.,** peach colour.

pêcher[2], *v.tr.* **1.** (*a*) to fish for (eels, trout, etc.); **p. à la ligne,** to angle (with rod and line); **p. à la mouche,** to fish with a fly; **p. à la cuiller,** to troll, to spin (for trout, etc.); **p. des truites à la main,** to tickle, *Scot:* guddle, trout; **p. un étang,** to drag a pond (for fish); **p. un câble,** to sweep for a cable; **p. des perles, du corail,** to dive for pearls, for coral; **p. la baleine,** to hunt whales; **toujours pêche qui en prend un,** every little helps; **p. des compliments,** to fish for compliments; **p. en eau trouble,** to fish in troubled waters; (*b*) **p. au plat,** to dig one's fork or spoon into the dish; (*c*) *Games:* (*at dominoes*) to draw (from the reserve). **2. p. une truite,** to catch a trout; **p. un cadavre,** to fish up a dead body; *F:* **où avez-vous pêché cela?** where did you pick that up? where did you get hold of that?

péchère [peʃɛːr], *int. Dial:* (*S. of Fr.*) oh dear (me)!

pêcherie [pɛʃri], *s.f.* fishery, fishing ground.

pêchette [pɛʃɛt], *s.f. Fish:* dipping net.

pécheur, pécheresse [peʃœːr, peʃrɛs]. **1.** *s.* sinner, offender, transgressor; **vieux p.,** hardened old sinner. **2.** *a.* sinning; *B:* **la femme pécheresse,** the woman who was a sinner.

pêcheur, -euse [pɛʃœːr, -øːz]. **1.** *s.* fisher, fisherman, -woman; **p. à la ligne,** angler; **p. au chalut,** trawler; **p. de baleines,** whaler; **p. de phoques,** sealer; **p. de perles,** pearl diver; **p. d'éponges,** sponge diver; **p. de corail,** coral diver; **nœud de p.,** fisherman's bend; *Ecc:* **l'anneau du p.,** the Fisherman's ring, the Pope's seal; *a.* **bateau p.,** fishing smack. **2.** *s.m.* fishing smack, boat.

péchopal [peʃɔpal], *s.m. Miner:* pitch opal.

pechstein [pɛʃtajn], *s.m. Miner:* pitchstone.

péchurane [peʃyran], *s.m.* pitchblende, uraninite.

peckhamite [pɛkamit], *s.f. Miner:* peckhamite.

pécoptéris [pekɔpteris], *s.m. Paleont:* pecopteris.

pécore [pekɔːr], *s.f.* (*a*) *A:* creature, animal; (*b*) *A:* stupid person; (*c*) *F:* silly, stuck-up, girl, woman.

pecque [pɛk], *s.f. A:* ignorant and pert young woman.

pectase [pɛktɑːz], *s.f. Ch:* pectase.

pectate [pɛktat], *s.m. Ch:* pectate.

pecten [pɛktɛn], *s.m. Moll:* pecten, scallop.

pectine [pɛktin], *s.f. Ch:* (*a*) pectin(e); (*b*) vegetable jelly.

pectiné [pɛktine], *a. Nat.Hist:* pectinate(d), pectinal; comb-shaped; pectenoid; **structure pectinée,** pectination.

pectinéal-aux [pɛktineal, -o], *a. Anat:* pectineal.

pectinibranche [pɛktinibrɑ̃:ʃ], *a. Moll:* pectinibranch(ian), pectinibranchiate.

pectinidés [pɛktinide], *s.m.pl. Moll:* Pectinidae, pectinids.

pectique [pɛktik], *a. Ch:* pectic (acid).

pectisable [pɛktizabl̥], *a. Ch:* pectizable.

pectisation [pɛktizasjɔ̃], *s.f. Ch:* pectization.

pectiser [pɛktize], *v.tr. Ch:* to pectize.

pectolite [pɛktɔlit], *s.f. Miner:* pectolite.

pectoral, -aux [pɛktɔral, -o]. **1.** *a.* pectoral (muscle, fin, medicine); **sirop p.,** pectoral syrup, expectorant; **pastille de pâte pectorale,** cough lozenge. **2.** *s.m.* pectoral, breast plate (of Jewish high priest).

pectoriloquie [pɛktɔrilɔki], *s.f. Med:* pectoriloquy.

pectose [pɛkto:z], *s.m. Bio-Ch:* pectose.

péculat [pekyla], *s.m.* peculation, embezzlement.

péculateur [pekylatœ:r], *s.m.* peculator; embezzler.

pécule [pekyl], *s.m.* (*a*) *Rom.Ant:* peculium; (*b*) savings; store (of money); nest egg; **perdre son p.,** to lose all one's savings; (*c*) earnings of convict (handed to him on discharge); (*d*) *Mil: Navy:* gratuity (on discharge).

pécune [pekyn], *s.f. A:* money; fortune.

pécuniaire [pekynjɛ:r], *a.* pecuniary; **améliorer sa situation p.,** to improve one's financial position; **être dans un embarras p.,** to be short of money; **intérêt p.,** (i) money interest; (ii) insurable interest; **peine p.,** fine.

pécuniairement [pekynjɛrmɑ̃], *adv.* pecuniarily.

pécunieux, -euse [pekynjø, -ø:z], *a. A:* wealthy.

pédagogie [pedagɔʒi], *s.f.* pedagogy, pedagogics.

pédagogique [pedagɔʒik], *a.* pedagogic(al), educational; **méthodes pédagogiques,** teaching methods.

pédagogiquement [pedagɔʒikmɑ̃], *adv.* pedagogically.

pédagogisme [pedagɔʒism], *s.m. Pej:* pedagogism, pedantry.

pédagogue [pedagɔg], *s.m. & f.* (*a*) pedagogue; educationalist; (*b*) *Pej:* pedagogue, pedant.

pédale [pedal], *s.f.* **1.** pedal (of cycle, machine, piano, etc.); (*a*) *Mec.E:* pedal, treadle (of lathe, grindstone, etc.); **tour, machine à coudre, à p.,** foot, pedal, treadle, lathe; treadle sewing machine; *Aut: Mch: etc:* **p. d'accélérateur,** accelerator pedal; **p. de commande,** control pedal; **commande par p.,** pedal control; **p. de débrayage, d'embrayage,** clutch pedal; **p. de changement de vitesse,** gear (-change) pedal; **p. de frein,** brake pedal; **frein à p.,** foot brake; *Cy:* **p. à scies,** rat-trap pedal; *Av:* **p. de direction, de palonnier,** rudder pedal; **attelage, tringlage, de p.,** pedal linkage; **tringle de traction, de p.,** pedal pull-rod; **axe (d'articulation) de p.,** pedal fulcrum; **course de la p.,** pedal stroke; **course morte de la p.,** pedal clearance; **ressort de rappel de p.,** pedal return spring; **agir sur la p.,** to depress the pedal; **lâcher la p.,** to release the pedal; (*b*) *Mus:* (i) (*of piano*) **petite p.,** soft pedal; **grande p.,** loud pedal, damper pedal; (ii) (*of organ*) **clavier de pédales,** pedal board, clavier; pedalier; **p. expressive,** swell pedal; **p. de combinaison,** composition pedal; (*c*) *El:* **p. de parquet,** floor contact; *Tp:* **p. d'appareil téléphonique,** press(el) switch, push-to-talk button; (*d*) *F:* **perdre les pédales,** to get all balled up. **2.** *Mus:* pedal (note). **3.** *P:* (*a*) homo(sexual), queer; (*b*) **être de la p.,** to be a homo, a queer, one of them.

pédalé [pedale], *a. Bot:* pedate (leaf).

pédaler [pedale], *v.i.* **1.** to pedal; (*a*) to work a treadle; (*b*) to cycle. **2.** *P:* (*a*) to go at top speed, to rush along; (*b*) to run away, beat it.

pédaleur, -euse [pedalœ:r, -ø:z], *s.* pedalist, pedal(l)er; cyclist.

pédalfer [pedalfɛ:r], *s.m. Geol:* pedalfer.

pédaliacées [pedaljase], *s.f.pl. Bot:* Pedaliaceae.

pédalier [pedalje], *s.m.* **1.** crank gear (of cycle, etc.); **axe p.,** crank axle. **2.** pedal board (of organ); pedalier.

pédaline [pedalin], *s.f. Hatm:* pedaline.

pédalo [pedalo], *s.m.* pedal craft, water bicycle.

pédant, -ante [pedɑ̃, -ɑ̃:t]. **1.** *s.* pedant. **2.** *a.* pedantic.

pédanterie [pedɑ̃tri], *s.f.* pedantry.

pédantesque [pedɑ̃tɛsk], *a.* pedantic.

pédantesquement [pedɑ̃tɛskəmɑ̃], *adv.* pedantically.

pédantiser [pedɑ̃tize], *v.i.* to pedantize, to play the pedant.

pédantisme [pedɑ̃tism], *s.m.* pedantism.

pédantocratie [pedɑ̃tɔkrasi], *s.f.* pedantocratic government.

pédard [peda:r], *s.m. A: P:* (*a*) cyclist who obstructs the traffic; (*b*) road-hog (cyclist); scorcher.

pédates [pedat], *s.m.pl. Z:* Pedata.

pédé [pede], *s.m. P:* homo, queer, pansy, sod.

pédéraste [pederast], *s.m.* p(a)ederast, sodomite, homosexual.

pédérastie [pederasti], *s.f.* p(a)ederasty, sodomy.

pédérastique [pederastik], *a.* p(a)ederastic, homosexual.

pédèse [pedɛ:z], *s.f. Ph:* pedesis.

pédesouille [pedzu:j], *s.m. P:* clumsy lout, oaf.

pédestre [pedɛstr̥], *a.* pedestrian; (journey) on foot.

pédestrement [pedɛstrəmɑ̃], *adv.* on foot.

pédestrianisme [pedɛstrianism], *s.m. A:* pedestrianism.

pédestrien, -ienne [pedɛstri(j)ɛ̃, -jɛn], *s. Sp: A:* pedestrian, competitor in a walking or running match.

pédète [pedɛt], *s.f. Z:* jumping hare (of Southern Africa), springhaas.

pédétidés [pedetide], *s.m.pl. Z:* Pedetidae.

pédiatre [pedjatr̥], *s.m. Med:* pediatrician, pediatrist.

pédiatrie [pedjatri], *s.f. Med:* pediatry, pediatrics.

pédicellaire [pedisɛl(l)ɛ:r], *s.m. Echin:* pedicellaria.

pédicelle [pedisɛl], *s.m. Nat.Hist:* pedicel, pedicle.

pédicellé [pedisɛl(l)e], *a. Bot:* pedicellate, pediculate.

pédicelline [pedisɛl(l)in], *s.f. Z:* pedicellina.

pédicellinidés [pedisɛl(l)inide], *s.m.pl. Z:* Pedicellinidae.

pédiculaire [pedikylɛ:r]. **1.** *a.* pedicular, pediculous, lousy; *Med:* **maladie p.,** phthiriasis, pediculosis. **2.** *s.f. Bot:* lousewort, wood-betony; **p. des bois,** red rattle.

pédiculates [pedikylat], *s.m.pl. Ich:* Pediculati.

pédicule [pedikyl], *s.m. Biol:* pedicle.

pédiculé [pedikyle]. **1.** *a.* pediculate, pedicellate. **2.** *s.m.pl. Ich:* **pédiculés,** Pediculati.

pédiculidés [pedikylide], *s.m.pl. Ent:* Pediculidae.

pédiculose [pedikylo:z], *s.f. Med:* pediculosis.

pédicure [pediky:r], *s.m. & f.* chiropodist.

pédicurer [pedikyre], *v.tr.* to pedicure.

pédicurie [pedikyri], *s.f.* chiropody.

pédieux, -euse [pedjø, -ø:z], *a. Anat:* pedal; **les muscles p.,** the muscles of the foot.

pedigree [pedigre], *s.m. Breed:* pedigree.

pédiluve [pedily:v], *s.m. Med:* foot bath.

pédimane [pediman], *a. Z:* pedimanous.

pédiment [pedimɑ̃], *s.m. Geol:* (rock) pediment.

pédimentation [pedimɑ̃tasjɔ̃], *s.f. Geol:* pedimentation.

pédipalpe [pedipalp], *Arach:* **1.** *a.* pedipalpous. **2.** *s.m.* (*a*) (*appendage*) pedipalp(us); (*b*) pedipalp(id), whip scorpion, scorpion spider; *pl.* **pédipalpes,** Pedipalpida.

pédiplaine [pediplɛn], *s.f. Geol:* pediplain, pediplane.

pédiplanation [pediplanasjɔ̃], *s.f. Geol:* pediplanation.

pédobaptisme [pedɔbatism], *s.m. Rel:* p(a)edobaptism.

pédocal [pedɔkal], *s.m. Geol:* pedocal.

pédogénèse[1] [pedɔʒenɛ:z], *s.f. Geol:* pedogenesis.

pédogénèse[2], *s.f. Biol:* p(a)edogenesis.

pédogénétique [pedɔʒenetik], *a. Geol:* pedogenic.

pédologie[1] [pedɔlɔʒi], *s.f. Geol:* pedology.

pédologie[2], *s.f. Med:* p(a)edology.

pédologique[1] [pedɔlɔʒik], *a. Geol:* pedologic(al); **équilibre p.,** soil equilibrium.

pédologique[2], *a. Med:* p(a)edological.

pédologue[1] [pedɔlɔg], *s.m. & f. Geol:* pedologist.

pédologue[2], *s.m. & f. Med:* p(a)edologist.

pédomètre [pedɔmɛtr̥], *s.m.* pedometer.

pédomorphose [pedɔmɔrfo:z], *s.f. Biol:* neotenia.

pédonculaire [pedɔ̃kylɛ:r], *a. Bot:* peduncular.

pédoncule [pedɔ̃kyl], *s.m. Nat.Hist.* peduncle; *Bot:* stem, stalk.

pédonculé [pedɔ̃kyle], *a. Nat.Hist:* pedunculate; stalked.

pédophilie [pedɔfili], *s.f. Psy:* p(a)edophilia.

pedzouille [pɛdzu:j], *s.m. P:* (clumsy) lout, oaf.

peeliste [pilist], *s.m. & f.*, **peelite** [pilit], *s.m. & f. Eng.Hist:* Peelite.

Pégamoïd [pegamɔid], *s.m. R.t.m:* Pegamoid.

péganite [peganit], *s.f. Miner:* peganite.

Pégase [pega:z], *Pr.n.m.* **1.** *Gr.Myth: Astr:* Pegasus. **2.** *Ich:* pegasus (fish).

pegmatite [pɛgmatit], *s.f. Miner:* pegmatite.

pegmatoïde [pɛgmatɔid], *a. Miner:* pegmatoid.

pégomancie [pegɔmɑ̃si], *s.f.* pegomancy.

pégot [pego], *s.m. Orn: F:* alpine accentor.

pègre [pɛgr̥]. **1.** *s.f.* thieves (as a class); the underworld; *A:* **la haute p.,** the mobsmen, the swell mob; **basse p.,** petty thieves. **2.** *s.m. A: P:* thief; **p. de la haute,** swell-mobsman.

pehl(e)vi [pɛlvi], *s.m. Ling:* pahlavi.

peignage [pɛɲa:ʒ], *s.m. Tex:* combing, carding (of wool, etc.); **p. du chanvre,** hackling.

peigne [pɛɲ], *s.m.* **1.** (*a*) comb; **p. de coiffure,** hair comb; **p. fin, p. à l'indienne,** (fine) tooth-comb; **passer (un document) au p. fin,** to go through (a document) with a (fine) toothcomb; *Hairdr:* **coup de p.,** comb-out; **se donner un coup de p.,** to run a comb through one's hair; *A: F:* **donner un coup de p. à qn,** to give s.o. a thrashing; *F:* **être sale comme un p.,** to be (completely) filthy; (*b*) *Bot:* **p. (-) de (-) Vénus,** scandix, shepherd's needle. **2.** (*a*) *Tex:* (i) card (for wool); gill, hackle (for hemp); (ii) **p. d'abattage,** doffing knife, doffer, comb (of carding machine); (iii) **p. de métier à tisser,** reed; (*b*) **p. à décor,** (house painter's) graining comb; (*c*) *Metalw:* **p. à fileter,** screw-chasing tool; comb, chaser; die box, die head; (*d*) *Coop:* **p. à jable,** croze iron; (*e*) toothed plate (of safety razor, etc.); (*f*) comb (of escalator); (*g*) *P:* (burglar's) crowbar, jemmy. **3.** (*a*) *Moll: F:* pecten; comb(shell); scallop; (*b*) *Arach:* pecten, comb (of scorpion); (*c*) *Orn:* pecten, comb (of bird's eye).

peigné [pɛɲe], *a.* **1.** combed; **bien p.,** well-groomed (person); trim (garden); carefully smoothed out (style); **mal p.,** unkempt, bedraggled, slatternly, (student, appearance); **chevelure mal peignée,** tousled head of hair; *s.* **une mal peignée,** a slattern. **2.** *Tex:* (*a*) worsted (yarn); **tissus de laine peignée,** worsted fabrics, worsteds; (*b*) *s.m.* worsted (yarn).

peigne-à-loup [pɛɲalu], *s.m. Bot:* (fuller's) teasel; *pl. peignes-à-loup.*

peigne-cul [pɛɲky], *s.m.*, **peigne-derche** [pɛɲdɛrʃ], *s.m. P:* (*pers.*) (*a*) nonentity; creep; (*b*) rotter, skunk; *pl. peigne-culs; peigne-derches.*

peignée [pɛɲe], *s.f.* **1.** *Tex:* cardful (of wool, flax, hemp). **2.** *F:* thrashing, good hiding.

peigner [pɛɲe], *v.tr.* **1.** (*a*) to comb (out) (the hair, etc.); **p. un enfant,** to comb a child's hair; **p. son style,** to smooth (out) one's style; *F:* **p. la girafe,** to waste one's time; **c'est comme p. la girafe,** it's like painting the Forth Bridge; *Prov:* **on ne peut pas p. un diable qui n'a pas de cheveux,** you can't take the breeks off a Highlander; (*b*) *F: A:* to thrash (s.o.). **2.** (*a*) *Tex:* to card, comb (wool); to hackle (hemp); (*b*) *Metalw:* to chase (screw thread, etc.).

se peigner. **1.** to comb, brush, do, one's hair. **2.** *F: O:* (*esp. of women*) to fight; to have a set-to, a scrap.

peignerie [pɛɲri], *s.f. Tex:* combing works.

peigneur, -euse [pɛɲœ:r, -ø:z], *Tex:* **1.** *s.* (*a*) wool comber; (*b*) **p. à la machine,** combing-machine tenter. **2.** *s.f.* **peigneuse:** (*a*) wool-combing machine; (*b*) hackling machine; (*c*) **peigneuse enleveuse,** doffing cylinder; porcupine.

peigne-zizi [pɛɲzizi], *s.m. P:* (*pers.*) nonentity; creep; *pl. peigne-zizis.*

peignier, -ière [pɛɲje, -jɛ:r], *s. Toil:* comb maker.

peignoir [pɛɲwa:r], *s.m.* (*a*) *Hairdr:* cape, overall (to protect customer's clothes); (*b*) (lady's, boxer's) dressing gown; house coat; **p. de bain,** bath robe.

peignons [pɛɲɔ̃], *s.m.pl. Tex:* cardings.

peignures [pɛɲy:r], *s.f.pl. Toil:* combings.

peiller, -ière [pɛje, -jɛ:r], *s.*, **peillier, -ière** [pɛlje, -jɛ:r], *s.* **peillereau** [pɛjro], *s.m.* rag collector; rag merchant; ragman.

peilles [pɛ:j], *s.f.pl. Paperm:* rags.

peinard [pɛna:r]. **1.** *s.* (*a*) *A:* toiler; (**père**) **p.,** toil-worn old man; (*b*) *A:* **vieux p.,** old rake; (*c*) *P:* easy-going man; **faire qch. en (père) p.,** to do sth. in a leisurely fashion; to take it easy. **2.** *a. P:* (*a*) **rester peinard(e),** to take things easy; **tiens-toi peinard(e),** keep quiet; take it easy; **père p.,** easy-going man; (*b*) **être p.,** to be well off.

peinardement [pɛnardəmɑ̃], *adv. P:* quietly, slyly.

peindre [pɛ̃:dr̥], *v.tr.* (*pr.p.* **peignant;** *p.p.* **peint;** *pr.ind.* **je peins, il peint, n. peignons, ils peignent;** *p.d.* **je peignais;** *p.h.* **je peignis;** *fu.* **je peindrai**) **1.** to paint; **p. qch. en vert,** to paint sth. green; **p. (une surface) au pistolet,** to spray the paint on (a surface); **p. qch. à la chaux,** to whitewash sth.; **p. une carte,** to colour a map; (*of woman*) **se p.,** to make up. **2.** to paint, portray, depict, represent (in colours); **p. un coucher de soleil,** to paint a sunset; **p. à l'huile, à l'aquarelle,** to paint in oils, in water colours; **elle est à p.,** she's worthy of an artist's brush; she is a perfect picture; **il était à p.!** he looked too funny for words! **se faire p.,** to have one's portrait painted;

p. les caractères, to portray character; **p. tout en beau**, to paint everything in rosy colours; **p. tout en laid**, to disparage everything; **la terreur peinte sur son visage**, the terror depicted on his face; **la cruauté était peinte sur son visage**, cruelty was stamped on his face; **l'innocence se peint sur son front**, innocence is written on his brow; *Lit:* **déjà la mort se peint sur son visage**, already his face is taking on the hue of death; **sa douleur ne saurait se p.**, his grief is indescribable; **cette action le peint bien, achève de le peindre**, that action is typical of him.

peine [pɛn], *s.f.* **1.** punishment, penalty; **p. corporelle, capitale**, corporal, capital, punishment; **la p. de mort**, the death penalty; **sous p. de mort, de la vie**, on pain, under penalty, of death; *A.Jur:* **condamné à la p. forte et dure**, condemned to be pressed to death, to the peine forte et dure; **p. contractuelle**, penalty for non-performance (of contract); **porter la p. de qch.**, to suffer for sth., to be punished for sth.; **pendant la durée de sa p.**, while he was undergoing his sentence; *Lit:* **porter la p. de la célébrité**, to pay the penalty of fame; **âmes en p.**, souls in Purgatory; **errer comme une âme en p.**, to wander about like a lost soul. **2.** (*a*) pain, sorrow, affliction; **peines de cœur**, sorrows that go to the heart; **faire de la p. à qn**, to grieve, distress, s.o.; **je m'en suis séparé avec beaucoup de p.**, I was very sorry to part with it; **nous apprenons avec p. que . . .**, we are sorry, grieved, to hear that . . .; **cela fait p. à voir**, it is painful to see; **être, se mettre, en p. de qn**, to be troubled, uneasy, anxious, about s.o.; to worry about s.o.; (*b*) **être, tomber, dans la p.**, to be in trouble, in distress; to fall on evil days; **je ne peux pas le laisser dans la p.**, I cannot leave him in distress. **3.** pains, trouble, labour; **prendre, se donner, de la p. pour faire qch.**, to take trouble, take pains, to do sth.; **ne pas ménager sa p. pour . . .**, to spare no trouble (in order) to . . .; **se donner beaucoup de p.**, to take great pains; **donnez-vous, prenez, la p. de vous asseoir**, please take a seat; **ne prenez pas la p. d'y répondre**, don't trouble to answer it; **je prends beaucoup de peine(s) pour . . .**, I am at great pains to . . .; **en vous donnant un peu de p. vous y arriverez**, with a little trouble, with a little effort, you will manage it; **vous perdez votre p.**, you are wasting your time; **c'est p. perdue**, it is a waste of effort, of time; **qu'est-ce que je vais vous donner pour votre p.?** what shall I give you for your trouble, for the trouble you have taken? **en être pour sa p.**, to have all one's trouble for nothing; **cela vaut la p. d'essayer**, it's worth trying; **cela n'en vaut pas la p.**, it's not worth the trouble; **ce n'est pas la p. de changer de robe**, you needn't bother to change your dress; **ce n'est pas la p. que nous revenions**, it's not worth while our coming back; *Iron:* **c'était bien la p. de venir!** we might just as well have stayed at home! **je perds ma p. à raisonner avec vous**, it's no use, it's a waste of breath, arguing with you; **cela ne m'a donné, ne m'a coûté, aucune p.**, I didn't have any, it was no, trouble at all; **homme de p.**, odd-job man; **mourir à la p.**, to die (i) of overwork, (ii) in harness, (iii) without reaching one's goal, achieving one's purpose; **toute p. mérite salaire**, a labourer is worthy of his hire. **4.** difficulty; **j'ai eu de la p. à en trouver**, I had some difficulty in finding any; **j'ai eu toutes les peines du monde à le trouver**, I had the utmost difficulty in finding it; **j'ai p. à croire que** + *sub.*, it is difficult for me to believe that . . ., I find it hard to believe that . . .; **vous aurez (de la) p. à le croire**, you will hardly believe it; **avoir p. à retenir ses larmes**, to be on the brink of tears; **j'ai, j'ai eu, p. à ne pas pleurer**, I could weep, could have wept; **ne jamais être en p. de trouver une excuse**, never to be at a loss for an excuse; **avec p., à grand-p.**, with (great) difficulty; **nous joignons à grand-p. les deux bouts**, it takes us all our time to make both ends meet; **je n'ai pas eu grand-p. à le faire**, it wasn't much trouble; **fortune acquise à grand-p.**, hard-earned fortune; **sans p.**, (i) easily; (ii) willingly; **vous concevez sans p. ma déception**, you can easily imagine my disappointment. **5.** *adv.phr.* **à p.**, hardly, barely, scarcely; (*a*) **c'est à p. si je le connais**, I hardly know him; **hostilité à p. déguisée**, thinly disguised hostility; **il demeure à cent pas à p.**, he lives barely a hundred yards away; (*b*) **à p. Jean eut-il le sceptre en main (qu')il changea de politique**, no sooner had John come to power than he changed his policy; **à p. étions-nous sortis qu'il se mit à pleuvoir**, hardly had we gone out when it began to rain.

peiné [pene], *a.* pained, grieved, upset, concerned (de, at).

peiner [pene]. **1.** *v.tr.* (*a*) to pain, grieve, upset, distress (s.o.); **vous l'avez peinée**, you have hurt her feelings; *impers.* **il me peine beaucoup de . . .**, it distresses me very much to . . .; (*b*) to fatigue, tire; **métier qui peine beaucoup**, strenuous profession. **2.** *v.i.* (*a*) to toil, labour, drudge; *F:* to sweat (à, at); **p. comme un cheval**, to work like a slave; **il est toujours à p.**, he is always hard at it; **le garçon peinait sur son travail**, the boy was sweating over his work; *Aut:* **le moteur peine**, the engine is labouring; *Const: etc:* **poutre qui peine beaucoup**, beam carrying a heavy load; (*b*) **p. à faire qch.**, to be loth, reluctant, to do sth.

peint [pɛ̃], *a.* (*a*) **papier p.**, wallpaper; **vitraux peints**, stained-glass windows; (*b*) *Lit:* **papillons peints d'azur et d'or**, butterflies tinted with blue and gold.

peintre [pɛ̃:tr̥], *s.m.* painter. **1.** (*f. occ.* **peintresse**) **(artiste) p.**, artist; **une femme p.**, a woman artist; **elle était un p. amusant**, she was an amusing painter; **il fut un p. fidèle des mœurs de son époque**, he was a faithful portrayer of the manners of his time; **p. de portraits**, portrait painter, portraitist; **p. en miniature**, miniature painter; **p. sur ivoire, sur porcelaine**, ivory painter, china painter; **p. de blason**, heraldic painter; **p. de l'air, de la marine**, official airforce, navy, painter. **2. p. en bâtiment(s), p. décorateur**, (house) painter; **p. au pochoir**, stenciller; **p. en lettres**, signwriter; *Th:* **p. de décors**, scene painter; *Med:* **colique des peintres**, painters' colic, lead colic.

peintre-graveur [pɛ̃tr(ə)gravœ:r], *s.m.* artist engraver, painter engraver; *pl. peintres-graveurs.*

peintre-vitrier [pɛ̃tr(ə)vitrije], *s.m.* (house) painter and glazier; *pl. peintres-vitriers.*

peinturage [pɛ̃tyra:ʒ], *s.m. F:* daubing, painting daubs.

peinture [pɛ̃ty:r], *s.f.* **1.** (action, art of) painting; (*a*) **étudier la p.**, to study painting; **faire de la p.**, to paint; **p. à l'huile**, oil painting, painting in oils; **p. à l'aquarelle**, water-colour (painting), painting in water colours; **p. de mœurs**, portrayal of manners, of customs; (*b*) **p. en bâtiments**, (house) painting; **p. au pistolet**, spray painting. **2.** picture, painting; *F:* **je ne peux pas le voir en p.**, I can't bear the sight of him; **p. des mœurs de l'époque**, picture, description, of the morals of the period. **3.** paint, colour; **couche de p.**, coat of paint; *P.N:* **prenez garde, attention, à la p.!** wet paint, mind the paint! **p. à la colle, en détrempe**, size paint, distemper; **p. lumineuse**, luminous paint; **p. (à) émulsion**, emulsion paint; **p. (à l')aluminium**, aluminium paint; **p. au minium**, red-lead paint; **p. métallique**, metallic paint; **p. cellulosique**, cellulose paint; **p. (-)émail, p. émaillée**, enamel (paint); **p. émaillée au four**, stove enamelling; **p. d'apprêt, p. de fond**, priming (paint), primer; *Mil: etc:* **p. bigarrée, p. en zébrures**, disruptive paint (for camouflage); **p. anticorrosive**, anti-corrosive paint; **p. antirouille**, anti-rust paint; *Nau: etc:* **p. anti-parasites**, anti-fouling paint; **p. résistant aux acides**, acid-resisting paint; **p. ignifuge**, fireproof paint.

peinturer [pɛ̃tyre], *v.tr.* (*a*) *O:* to cover (wall, etc.) with a coat of paint; to paint; (*b*) *abs. F:* to paint daubs, to daub.

peinturlurer [pɛ̃tyrlyre], *v.tr. F:* to paint (building, etc.) in all the colours of the rainbow; to daub (with colour).

péjoratif, -ive [peʒɔratif, -i:v], *a. & s.m.* pejorative; disparaging, depreciatory (sense, etc.).

péjoration [peʒɔrasjɔ̃], *s.f. Ling:* pejoration.

péjorativement [peʒɔrativmɑ̃], *adv.* pejoratively.

pékan [pekɑ̃], *s.m. Z:* pekan, fisher (cat).

Pékin [pekɛ̃]. **1.** *Pr.n.m. Geog:* Pekin(g); *Husb:* **canard P.**, Pekin(g) (duck). **2.** *s.m.* (*a*) *Tex:* Pekin (fabric); (*b*) *Mil: F: O:* civilian; **être en p.**, to be in mufti, in civvies.

pékiné [pekine], *a.* candy-striped (cloth, etc.).

pékinois, -oise [pekinwa, -wa:z], (*a*) *a. & s. Geog:* Pekin(g)ese; (*b*) *a. & s.m.* (*dog*) **(épagneul) p.**, pekin(g)ese, *F:* peke.

péko(ë) [peko(e)], *s.m.* pekoe (tea).

pelade [pəlad], *s.f.* **1.** *Tchn:* pelt wool, skinwool. **2.** *Med:* alopecia.

peladique [pəladik], *a.* peladic.

pelage [pəla:ʒ], *s.m.* **1.** (*a*) *Leath:* removing the hair (from), unhairing (of skins); (*b*) *Agr:* removing of top layer of soil (to destroy vegetation); (*c*) peeling (of fruit). **2.** coat, wool, fur (of animal); pelage; **le tigre a un p. rayé**, the tiger has a striped coat.

Pélage [pela:ʒ], *Pr.n.m. Rel.H:* Pelagius.

pélagianisme [pelaʒjanism], *s.m. Rel.H:* Pelagianism.

Pélagie [pelaʒi], *Pr.n.f.* Pelagia.

pélagien[1], **-ienne** [pelaʒjɛ̃, -jɛn], *a. Oc: A:* pelagian.

pélagien[2], **-ienne** *a. & s. Rel.H:* Pelagian, (follower) of Pelagius.

pélagique [pelaʒik], *a. Oc:* pelagic, pelagian (fauna, etc.); **région p.**, pelagic zone; **dépôt p.**, pelagic deposit.

pélagodrome [pelagɔdro:m], *s.m. Orn:* **p. marin**, frigate petrel.

pelagothuria [pelagɔtyrja], *s.f. Z:* pelagothuria.

pelain [pəlɛ̃], *s.m. Leath:* lime pit.

pelainage [pəlɛna:ʒ], *s.m. Leath:* liming.

pelainer [pəlɛne], *v.tr. Tan:* to lime (the skins).

pélamide[1] [pelamid], *s.f. Rept:* sea snake.

pélamide[2], **pélamyde**, *s.f. Ich:* pelamid, pelamyd.

pelard [pəla:r], *a. For:* **bois p.**, barked wood.

pélargonique [pelargɔnik], *a. Ch:* pelargonic.

pélargonium [pelargɔnjɔm], *s.m. Bot:* pelargonium; (i) stork's bill; (ii) *Hort: F:* geranium.

Pélasges [pela:ʒ], *s.m.pl. Gr.Hist:* Pelasgians, Pelasgi.

pélasgien, -ienne [pelazʒjɛ̃, -jɛn], **pélasgique** [pelazʒik], *a.* Pelasgic.

pélastre [pelastr̥], *s.m. Tchn:* blade, scoop (of shovel).

pelé[1] [p(ə)le], *a.* bald; **peau pelée**, bare, hairless, skin, hide; **campagne pelée**, bare, naked, countryside; *s. F:* **un vieux p.**, an old baldpate; **il n'y avait que trois pelés et un tondu, que trois teigneux et un p.**, there was only a handful of nobodies, of odds and sods.

pelé[2], *a.* peeled (fruit, etc.).

pélécanidés [pelekanide], *s.m.pl. Orn:* Pelecanidae, the pelicans.

Pélécaniformes [pelekanifɔrm], *s.m.pl. Orn:* Pelecaniformes.

pélécanoïde [pelekanɔid], *s.m. Orn:* diving petrel; (*genus*) Pelecanoides.

pélécanoïdidés [pelekanɔidide], *s.m.pl. Orn:* Pelecanoididae.

pélécypodes [pelesipɔd], *s.m.pl. Moll:* Pelecypoda, pelecypods.

Pélée[1] [pele], *Pr.n.m. Gr.Myth:* Peleus.

pélée[2], *s.f. Z:* reebok; (*genus*) Pelea.

Pélée[3], *Pr.n. Geol:* **cheveux de P.**, Pele's hair.

péléen, -enne [peleɛ̃, -ɛn], *a. Geol:* Pelean (eruption).

pèle-fruits [pɛlfrɥi], *s.m.inv.* fruit knife.

pêle-mêle [pɛlmɛl]. **1.** *adv.* pell-mell; **mettre tout p.-m.**, to jumble everything up; **ils vivent p.-m. avec leurs bêtes**, they live all together with their animals; **dans cette maison tout est p.-m.**, in this house everything is in disorder, is higgledy-piggledy; **des faits trop nombreux présentés p.-m.**, too many facts presented without any idea of order, of arrangement. **2.** *s.m.inv.* (*a*) jumble; muddle; medley; untidy accumulation; **un p.-m. sans nom de vieux bidons, de chaussures, d'objets hétéroclites**, an indescribable heap, jumble, of old cans, shoes and objects of all descriptions; **l'effroyable p.-m. politique**, the terrifying political muddle; (*b*) frame for holding several photographs.

pèle-osier [pɛlozje], *s.m.inv. Tchn:* osier stripper.

peler[1] [p(ə)le], *v.tr.* (**je pèle, n. pelons; je pèlerai**) to unhair, depilate (skin, hide); to scald (carcase); *F:* **p. qn**, to strip s.o. (of all his property, etc.).

se peler, (*of animal*) to lose its hair; (*of skin*) to grow bare.

peler[2]. **1.** *v.tr.* to peel, skin (vegetables, fruit); to peel off (the bark of a tree); **p. une orange à vif**, to remove the skin and pith from an orange; **p. la terre**, to strip the turf off the ground; **p. les allées**, to clear, rake, the (garden) paths. **2.** *v.i. & pr.* (*of skin, etc.*) to peel; (*of snake*) to slough.

pèlerin, -ine [pɛlrɛ̃, -in]. **1.** (*a*) *s.m. A:* traveller; (*b*) *s.* (*the f.* **pèlerine** *is rarely used*) pilgrim; *Eng.Hist:* **les (pères) Pèlerins**, the Pilgrim Fathers; *Prov:* **rouge au soir, blanc au matin, c'est la journée du p.**, evening red and morning grey sets the traveller on his way; (*c*) *F:* (i) queer customer; (ii) bloke, type. **2.** *s.m.* (*a*) *Ich:* basking shark; (*b*) *Orn:* peregrine falcon; (*c*) *Ent:* migratory grasshopper. **3.** *s.f.* **pèlerine**; (*a*) cape, cloak; (*b*) hooded cape; (*c*) *Moll:* scallop, comb (shell), pecten.

pèlerinage [pɛlrina:ʒ], *s.m.* **1.** pilgrimage; **aller en p., faire un p.**, to go on a pilgrimage. **2.** place of pilgrimage.

pelham [pɛlam], *s.m. Harn:* pelham.

péliade [peljad], *s.f. Rept:* **(vipère) p.**, adder.

pélican [pelikɑ̃], *s.m.* **1.** *Orn:* pelican; **p. blanc,** white pelican; **p. frisé,** Dalmatian pelican; *Her:* **p. avec sa piété,** pelican in her piety. **2.** (*a*) *Tls:* (bench) holdfast; (*b*) *Dent: Dist: A:* pelican.

péliom [peljɔm], *s.m. Miner:* peliom.

Pélion [peljɔ̃], *Pr.n.m. Geog:* (Mount) Pelion; *Lit:* **entasser P. sur Ossa,** to pile Pelion on Ossa; to leave no stone unturned.

pelisse [pəlis], *s.f.* **1.** fur-lined coat. **2.** *A.Mil. Cost:* hussar's pelisse.

pélite [pelit], *s.f. Miner:* pelite.

pélitique [pelitik], *a. Geol:* pelitic.

pellagre [pɛl(l)agr], *s.f. Med:* pellagra.

pellagreux, -euse [pɛl(l)agrø, -øːz]. **1.** *a. Med:* pellagrous. **2.** *s.* pellagrin.

pelle [pɛl], *s.f.* **1.** shovel, scoop; (*a*) **p. à charbon, à feu,** coal scoop, shovel; **p. à tarte,** tart slice; **p. à fromage,** cheese scoop; **p. à main, à poussière, à ordures,** dustpan; **p. à four,** (baker's) oven peel; **ramasser qch. à la p.,** to shovel sth. up; **enlever qch. à la p.,** to shovel sth. away; **remuer, ramasser, l'argent à la p.,** to be rolling in money; *F:* **ramasser une pelle,** to have a spill (off a cycle); to take a toss (off a horse); to come a cropper; (*b*) *Civ.E: etc:* **p. automatique, mécanique,** (i) grab, power shovel; (ii) shovel dredger; **p. à vapeur,** steam shovel; navvy. **2.** (child's) spade (at seaside). **3.** blade (of oar).

pelle-à-cheval [pɛlaʃəval], *s.f. Agr:* soil leveller; *pl. pelles-à-cheval.*

pelle-bêche [pɛlbɛʃ], *s.f. Mil:* entrenching tool, shovel, spade; *pl. pelles-bêches.*

pellée [pɛle], *s.f.* shovelful.

pelle-pioche [pɛlpjɔʃ], *s.f.* pick and shovel; *pl. pelles-pioches.*

peller [pɛle], *v.tr.* to shovel, to turn with a shovel.

pelleron [pɛlrɔ̃], *s.m.* (baker's) peel.

pellet [pɛlɛ], *s.m. Pharm:* pellet.

pelletage [pɛltaːʒ], *s.m.* shovelling.

pelletée [pɛlte], *s.f.* shovelful, spadeful.

pelleter [pɛlte], *v.tr.* (**je pellette** [pɛlt], **n. pelletons; je pelletterai** [pɛltre]) to shovel, to turn with a shovel.

pelleterie [pɛltri], *s.f.* **1.** *coll.* fur skins, peltry. **2.** (*a*) fur making; (*b*) fur trade, furriery.

pelleteur [pɛltœːr], *s.m.* **1.** (*pers.*) shoveller. **2.** (mechanical) excavator.

pelleteuse [pɛltøːz], *s.f. Civ.E:* (mechanical) excavator; **p. chargeuse,** front-end loader.

pelletier, -ière [pɛltje, -jɛːr]. **1.** *s.* furrier. **2.** *s.f. Ent:* **pelletière,** casemaking clothes moth.

pelletiérine [pɛltjerin], *s.f. Pharm:* pelletierin(e).

pelletisation [pɛlətizasjɔ̃], *s.f. Metall:* pelletization.

pelleverser [pɛlvɛrse], *v.tr. Agr:* to loosen, break up (soil in furrows of ploughed field).

pelliculage [pɛl(l)ikylaːʒ], *s.m.* **1.** *Phot:* stripping (of plate or film). **2.** *Bookb:* lamination (of jacket).

pelliculaire [pɛl(l)ikylɛːr], *a.* pellicular (metal, etc.); *El:* **effet p.,** skin effect, Kelvin effect; *Phot:* **négatif p.,** film negative; **papier négatif p.,** stripping film.

pellicule [pel(l)ikyl], *s.f.* **1.** (*a*) pellicle; thin skin; skin (on jelly, boiled milk, etc.); **p. de glace, d'huile, sur un étang,** film of ice, of oil, on a pond; *Tchn:* **p. lubrifiante,** oil film; (*b*) grape skin; skin (of coffee, cocoa, bean); cuticle (of rice, etc.); (*c*) (i) *Phot:* film; **p. en bobine,** roll film; (ii) *Cin:* stock; **p. inversible,** reversible stock; **p. vierge,** non-exposed stock. **2.** *pl.* (*a*) **pellicules (du cuir chevelu),** scurf, dandruff; (*b*) **pellicules du vin de Porto,** beeswing.

pelliculé [pɛl(l)ikyle], *a. Bookb:* (*of jacket*) laminated.

pelliculer [pɛl(l)ikyle], *v.tr. Phot:* to strip (plate).

pelliculeux, -euse [pɛl(l)ikylø, -øːz], *a.* scurfy (scalp).

pellin [pɛlɛ̃], *s.m.* (timber of) roble, evergreen beech.

pellon [pɛlɔ̃], *s.m. Tchn:* founder's shovel (for moulding sand).

pellucide [pɛl(l)ysid], *a.* (*a*) *Lit:* pellucid, limpid; (*b*) *Biol:* pellucid, transparent.

pelmatozoaires [pɛlmatozɔɛːr], *s.m.pl. Echin:* Pelmatozoa; pelmatozoans.

pélobate [pelɔbat], *s.m. Amph:* pelobatid (toad), spadefoot toad; **p. brun,** European spadefoot.

pélobatidés [pelɔbatide], *s.m.pl. Amph:* Pelobatidae.

pélodyte [pelɔdit], *s.m. Amph:* pelodytid, parsley frog.

pélomédusidés [pelɔmedyzide], *s.m.pl. Rept:* Pelomedusidae.

pélopée [pelɔpe], *s.m. Ent:* pelopaeus, mud dauber.

pélophage [pelɔfaːʒ], *a. Z:* limivorous, mud-eating.

Pélopon(n)èse (le) [ləpelɔpɔnɛːz], *Pr.n.m. Geog:* (the) Peloponnesus, (the) Peloponnese; *A.Hist:* **la guerre du P.,** the Peloponnesian War.

pélopon(n)ésien, -ienne [pelɔpɔnezjɛ̃, -jɛn], *a. & s.* Peloponnesian.

pélorie [pelɔri], *s.f. Bot:* peloria.

pélorié [pelɔrje], *a. Bot:* peloriate, peloric.

pélorisme [pelɔrism], *s.m. Bot:* pelorism.

pelotage [p(ə)lɔtaːʒ], *s.m.* **1.** winding (of skeins of wool, string) into balls. **2.** (*in billiards, tennis, etc.*) knocking the balls about. **3.** *P:* cuddling, necking.

pelotari [p(ə)lɔtari], *s.m.* pelota player.

pelote [p(ə)lɔt], *s.f.* **1.** ball, clew (of wool, string); card (of cotton, thread, etc.); wad (of cotton wool, etc.); pellet (of clay, etc.); **mettre de la laine en p.,** to ball wool; to wind wool into a ball; **p. à épingles, à aiguilles,** pincushion; **p. de neige,** snowball; **p. de beurre,** pat of butter; *F:* **faire sa (petite) p.,** to make one's pile; to feather one's nest; **avoir les nerfs en p.,** to be irritable, nervy, *F:* a bit jumpy. **2.** blaze, star (on horse's forehead). **3.** *Z:* **p. digitale,** pad (on the foot of certain animals); *Ent:* **p. adhésive,** pad. **4.** *Games:* **p. basque,** pelota. **5.** *Mil: P:* **la pelote,** the defaulters' squad; **faire la p.,** to do punishment drill.

peloter [p(ə)lɔte]. **1.** *v.tr.* (*a*) to wind (wool, string, etc.) into a ball; (*b*) *A: F:* to handle (s.o.) roughly; to maul (s.o.) about; (*c*) *P:* to paw, maul (a woman); to flatter (s.o.); to suck up to (s.o.). **2.** *v.i.* (*in billiards, tennis, etc.*) to knock the balls about; *A:* **p. en attendant partie,** to put in time (before coming to business, while awaiting events).

peloteur, -euse [p(ə)lɔtœːr, -øːz]. **1.** *s.* (*a*) *Tex:* (*pers.*) ball winder; (*b*) *F:* (i) flatterer; (ii) cuddler. **2.** *s.f.* **peloteuse,** balling machine.

peloton [p(ə)lɔtɔ̃], *s.m.* **1.** ball, clew (of wool, string, etc.). **2.** group (of people); cluster (of bees, caterpillars); *Rac:* **le p.,** the main body (of runners); the bunch; **emmener le p.,** to lead the field. **3.** *Mil:* (*a*) troop (of cavalry), platoon (of tanks, armoured cars, etc.); *A:* half-company (of infantry); *Artil:* **p. de pièce,** gun detachment, gun crew, gun squad; (*b*) class, party; **p. d'élèves sous-officiers, d'élèves caporaux,** N.C.O.'s class; **p. d'instruction,** training unit, training platoon (for soldiers); **p. de discipline, p. de punition, p. des punis,** punishment squad; **p. d'exécution,** firing party, firing squad.

pelotonner [p(ə)lɔtɔne], *v.tr.* to ball; to wind (wool, string, etc.) into a ball.

se pelotonner. 1. to curl up (into a ball, as a hedgehog); to coil, roll, oneself up; to huddle up; **pelotonné dans les couvertures,** snugly rolled up in the blankets; **se p. entre les bras de qn,** to snuggle into s.o.'s arms. **2.** (*a*) to gather into groups; (*b*) to huddle, crowd, cluster, together; (*of badly trained troops*) to bunch; (*c*) (*of bees*) to cluster.

pelotonneur, -euse [p(ə)lɔtɔnœːr, -øːz], *Tex:* **1.** *s.* (*pers.*) ball winder. **2.** *s.f.* **pelotonneuse,** balling machine.

pelousard, -arde [p(ə)luzaːr, -ard], *s. F:* racegoer.

pelouse[1] [p(ə)luːz], *s.f.* lawn; plot (of grass); **on dansera sur la p.,** there will be dancing on the green; *Golf:* **p. d'arrivée,** (putting) green; *Turf:* **la P.,** the public enclosures, the ground within the track; the green.

pelouse[2], *s.f.*, **pelouze** [p(ə)luːz], *s.f. Ann:* nereid.

peloux [pəlu], *s.m. Geog:* (*material transported*) rainwash.

pelta[1] [pɛlta], *s.m. Nau:* (*a*) (*on Newfoundlander*) unskilled hand; (*b*) *Pej:* landlubberly sailor.

pelta[2], *s.f.*, **pelte** [pɛlt], *s.f. Gr.Ant:* pelta.

peltandra [pɛltɑ̃dra], *s.m. Bot:* peltandra.

peltaste [pɛltast], *s.m. A.Gr.Mil:* peltast.

pelté [pɛlte], *a. Bot:* peltate.

Peltier [pɛltje], *Pr.n. El:* **effet P.,** Peltier effect.

peltigera [pɛltiʒera], *s.m. Moss:* peltigera.

Pelton [pɛltɔn], *Pr.n. Tchn:* **roue, turbine, P.,** Pelton wheel.

pelu [p(ə)ly], *a.* hairy; *Z:* **tatou p.,** hairy armadillo.

peluche [p(ə)lyʃ], *s.f.* (*a*) *Tex:* plush; **p. à brides,** loop plush; **p. bouclée,** bouclé plush; *A:* **p. long-poil,** long-pile shag; **ours en p.,** teddy bear; (*b*) (piece of) fluff.

peluché [p(ə)lyʃe], *a.* **1.** *Tex:* shaggy, nappy (material). **2.** *Bot:* hairy (flower, leaf).

pelucher [p(ə)lyʃe], *v.i.* (*of worn material*) to become fluffy, nappy; to shed fluff.

pelucheux, -euse [p(ə)lyʃø, -øːz], *a.* **1.** shaggy. **2.** fluffy (thread, material, paper, etc.); downy (fruit, plant); **non p.,** fluffless (blotting-paper, etc.).

peludo [pelydo], *s.m. Z:* peludo, hairy armadillo.

pelure [p(ə)lyːr], *s.f.* (*a*) peel, skin (of apple, onion, etc.); paring, peel (of vegetables); rind (of cheese); shell (of cocoa bean); **p. d'oignon,** dark rosé wine; *Com:* **papier p. (pour copies de lettres),** copying paper; **papier p. (d'oignon),** onion-skin paper; (*b*) *F:* outer garments; outdoor clothes; **enlever sa p.,** to peel; (*c*) *Rec:* master matrix.

pelvetia [pelvesja], *s.f. Algae:* pelvetia, channelled wrack, holy wrack.

pelvien, -ienne [pɛlvjɛ̃, -jɛn], *a.* (*a*) *Anat:* pelvic; **ceinture pelvienne,** pelvic girdle; **cavité pelvienne,** pelvic cavity; **membres pelviens,** pelvic limbs; (*b*) *s.f.pl. Ich:* **pelviennes,** pelvic fins.

pelvimètre [pɛlvimɛtr], *s.m.* pelvimeter.

pelvimétrie [pɛlvimetri], *s.f.* pelvimetry.

pelvipéritonite [pɛlviperitɔnit], *s.f. Med:* pelviperitonitis.

pelvis [pɛlvis], *s.m. Anat:* false pelvis.

pelvitomie [pɛlvitɔmi], *s.f. Obst:* pelviotomy.

pélycosauriens [pelikɔsɔrjɛ̃], *s.m.pl. Paleont:* Pelycosauria, pelycosaurs, pelycosaurians.

pemmican [pɛm(m)ikɑ̃], *s.m.* pemmican.

pemphigoïde [pɛ̃figɔid], *a. Med:* pemphigoid.

pemphigus [pɛ̃figys], *s.m.* **1.** *Med:* pemphigus. **2.** *Ent:* pemphigus, gall insect.

pemphredon [pɛ̃fredɔ̃], *s.m. Ent:* pemphredon.

penaille [pənɑːj], *s.f. A:* rags, tatters.

penaillon [pənɑjɔ̃], *s.m. A:* **1.** rag. **2.** *P:* monk.

pénal, -aux [penal, -o], *a.* penal (code); **clause pénale,** penalty clause (in contract).

pénalement [penalmɑ̃], *adv.* penally; from a penal point of view.

pénalisation [penalizasjɔ̃], *s.f. Sp:* penalization, penalizing.

pénaliser [penalize], *v.tr. Sp: Games:* to penalize; **p. un concurrent de dix points,** to penalize a competitor ten points.

pénalité [penalite], *s.f.* **1.** penal system. **2.** *Jur: Sp: etc:* penalty; *Fb:* **point, coup de pied, de p.,** penalty spot, kick.

penalty [penalti], *s.m. Fb:* penalty; *pl. penaltys.*

pénard [penaːr], *s.m.* = PEINARD.

pénates [penat], *s.m.pl.* (*a*) *Rom.Ant:* penates, household gods; (*b*) **regagner ses p.,** to return home; **établir ses p.,** to set up house.

penaud [pəno], *a.* crestfallen, shamefaced; **rester p.,** to look foolish, sheepish; **d'un air p.,** sheepishly, shamefacedly.

pencatite [pɑ̃katit], *s.f. Miner:* pencatite.

penchant [pɑ̃ʃɑ̃]. **1.** *a.* (*a*) sloping, inclined, leaning (wall, tower); (*of horse*) **encolure penchante,** lop neck; (*b*) *A:* tottering (empire); declining (power); (heavenly body) on its downward course. **2.** *s.m.* (*a*) slope; **sur le p. de la colline,** on the hillside; **être sur le p. de sa ruine,** to be on the brink, verge, of ruin; to be on the downward path; **sur le p. de l'âge,** in one's declining years; (*b*) **p. à, pour, vers, qch.,** inclination to, propensity for, tendency to, sth.; leaning towards sth.; **p. à faire qch.,** inclination to do sth.; **grand p. pour le mensonge,** great propensity for lying; **un p. à la boisson,** a fondness, partiality, for drink; **encourager un p. pour les livres, pour la lecture,** to encourage a taste for reading; **avoir un p. au mysticisme,** to have a bent towards mysticism; to incline to mysticism; **il avait un malheureux p. pour les cartes,** card playing was his curse; **suivre, se laisser aller à, ses penchants,** to follow one's inclinations, one's natural tastes; **redresser un mauvais p.,** to overcome a bad tendency; (*c*) **avoir un penchant pour qn,** to be rather fond of s.o., partial to s.o.; to have a leaning towards s.o.; **le p. qui m'attire vers elle,** my penchant for her; her attraction for me.

penché [pɑ̃ʃe], *a.* **1.** leaning; **la tour penchée de Pise,** the leaning tower of Pisa; *F:* **prendre des airs penchés,** to stand, recline, like a drooping lily. **2.** stooping; **p. sur le berceau,** bending over the cradle; **il marche p.,** he walks with a stoop.

penchement [pɑ̃ʃmɑ̃], *s.m.* **1.** leaning (of wall, etc.). **2.** stoop, bend; **p. de tête,** (i) bending of the head; (ii) nod.

pencher [pɑ̃ʃe], *v.* to incline, bend, lean. **1.** *v.tr.* **p. la tête (sur qch.),** to bend one's head (over sth.); **p. une cruche,** to tilt a jug; **p. la tête en avant,** to bend, lean, forward; **p. les épaules,** to stoop; **p. l'avion,** to bank. **2.** *v.i.* (*a*) to lean (over); **mur qui penche,** leaning wall; **le navire penche sur le côté,** the ship is listing, has a list, is heeling over; **faire p. la balance,** to weigh down the scale, to turn the scale; **la balance penche de leur côté,** the scales are tipping in their favour; **l'arbre penche sous le poids des fruits,** the tree is bent down by the weight of the fruit; **terrain qui penche,** sloping ground; **il penche vers**

la ruine, he is on the brink of ruin; (*b*) **p. vers le, pour le,** *A:* **au, socialisme,** to tend towards, have a leaning for, socialism; **p. vers, pour,** *A:* **à, l'indulgence,** to incline, lean, towards indulgence; **p. pour,** *A:* **à, faire qch.,** to be inclined to do sth.; **p. pour cette solution,** to prefer this solution.

se pencher. 1. to incline, bend, stoop, lean; **se p. en avant,** to bend forward; **se p. (en, au) dehors,** to lean out; **se p. à, par, la fenêtre,** to lean out of the window. **2. se p. sur,** (i) to be interested in; to study; (ii) to feel for; **se p. sur les souffrances du peuple,** to feel for the underdog.

pendable [pɑ̃dabl̩], *a.* (*a*) *A:* that deserves hanging; **cas p.,** hanging matter; *F:* **le cas n'est pas p.,** it's nothing serious, nothing to make a fuss about; (*b*) outrageous, abominable (trick, etc.).

pendage [pɑ̃daːʒ], *s.m. Geol: Min:* dip (of seam); **angle de p.,** angle of dip; **fort, faible, p.,** high angle, low angle, dip; **p. périclinal,** centroclinal dip.

pendagemètre [pɑ̃daʒmɛtr̥], *s.m. Geol:* dip meter.

pendaison [pɑ̃dɛzɔ̃], *s.f.* (*a*) (action of) hanging; **exécution par p.,** death by hanging; (*b*) **p. de la crémaillère,** housewarming (party).

pendant [pɑ̃dɑ̃]. **I.** *a.* **1.** hanging, pendent; *Arch:* **clef pendante,** hanging keystone; pendant; **moustache pendante,** drooping moustache; **joues pendantes,** flabby, baggy, cheeks; **oreilles pendantes,** flap ears, lop ears; **lapin, chien, aux oreilles pendantes,** lop-eared rabbit, flap-eared dog, dog with pendulous ears; *Jur:* **fruits pendants par (les) racines,** growing crops, uncut crops, standing crops. **2.** pending, undecided, outstanding (lawsuit, question, etc.); **la question reste pendante,** the question remains in suspense, in abeyance.

II. **pendant,** *s.m.* **1.** pendant; **p. (d'oreille),** (i) drop ear-ring; (ii) bob cherry; *Mil:* **p. de ceinturon,** sword-belt sling, frog. **2.** counterpart, match, fellow, pendant (of picture, ornament, etc.); **ces deux tableaux (se) font pendant,** these two pictures make a pair.

III. **pendant. 1.** *prep.* during; **p. l'été,** during the summer; in summer; **p. les week-ends,** at weekends; **restez là p. quelques minutes,** stay there for a few minutes; **p. le voyage,** in the course of the journey; **p. sa convalescence,** during his convalescence; **route bordée d'arbres p. un kilomètre,** road bordered, lined, with trees for a kilometre. **2.** *conj.phr.* **p. que,** while; whilst; **vous pourrez sortir p. que je serai là,** you'll be able to go out while I'm there; **amusons-nous p. que nous sommes jeunes,** let us have a good time while we are young; **p. que j'y pense,** while I think of it; **p. que vous y êtes,** while you're about it. **3.** *adv.* **avant la guerre et p.,** before and during the war; **vous lisez le journal après le déjeuner; moi je le lis p.,** you read the paper after breakfast; I read it while I am having mine.

pendard, -arde [pɑ̃daːr, -ard], *s. F:* gallows-bird; rogue; rotter; good-for-nothing.

pendeloque [pɑ̃dlɔk], *s.f.* (*a*) *Lap:* pendeloque; drop ear-ring; tear drop; (*b*) pendeloque, pendant, drop, crystal (of chandelier); (*c*) *F: O:* (torn) shred (of cloth hanging from garment).

pendentif [pɑ̃dɑ̃tif], *s.m.* **1.** *Arch:* pendentive; **en p.,** hanging. **2.** pendant (worn round the neck).

penderie [pɑ̃dri], *s.f.* **1.** *Tan:* drying house (for skins). **2.** wardrobe, hanging cupboard. **3.** *A:* hanging (of person).

pendiller [pɑ̃dije], *v.i.* to dangle, to hang loose.

pendillon [pɑ̃dijɔ̃], *s.m.* **1.** *Clockm:* pendulum rod. **2.** pendant; drop (of crystal chandelier).

Pendjab (le) [ləpɛ̃dʒab], *Pr.n.m. Geog:* the Punjab.

pendjabi [pɛ̃dʒabi], *s.m. Ling:* Punjabi.

pendoir [pɑ̃dwaːr], *s.m.* hook (for hanging bacon, etc.).

pendouiller [pɑ̃duje], *v.i. P:* to hang loosely, slackly, untidily; to dangle.

pendre [pɑ̃ːdr̥]. **1.** *v.tr.* (*a*) to hang (sth.) up; **p. du linge pour le faire sécher,** to hang the washing out to dry; **p. qch. au mur,** to hang sth. on the wall; **p. une lampe au plafond,** to hang a lamp from the ceiling; **p. la crémaillère,** to give a house-warming party; *F:* **il est toujours pendu à mes jambes,** he follows me about like a dog; *F:* **être toujours pendu au cou de qn,** to be always in s.o.'s arms; *F:* **elle est toujours pendue au téléphone,** she's never off the line; (*b*) to hang (on the gallows); *Prov:* **le bruit pend l'homme,** give a dog a bad name and hang him; **il fut pendu haut et court,** he was well and truly hanged; **dire pis que p. de qn,** to malign s.o., to run s.o. down; **il ne vaut pas la corde pour le p.,** he isn't worth the rope to hang him with; *F:* **qu'il aille se faire p.,** let him go and jump in the lake, go to hell; **je veux être pendu si . . .,** I'll be hanged if . . .; **il se pendit par désespoir,** he hanged himself out of despair. **2.** *v.i.* (*a*) to hang; **fruits qui pendent à un arbre,** fruit hanging on a tree; **cheveux qui pendent sur son dos,** hair hanging down one's back; **les voiles pendaient le long des mâts,** the sails were flapping idly against the masts; **un foulard pendait du panier,** a scarf was hanging out of the basket; (*b*) **jupe qui pend par derrière,** skirt hanging down, dipping, at the back; (*c*) **cela lui pend sur la tête,** it's threatening him, hanging over his head; *F:* **ça lui pend au nez,** he's got it coming to him.

se pendre à qch., to hang on, cling, to sth.; **se p. au cou de qn,** to hang round s.o.'s neck; to hug s.o.; **se p. à la sonnette,** to pull the bell violently; **se p. à un arbre,** to hang oneself from a tree.

pendu [pɑ̃dy]. **1.** *a.* hanged; hung, hanging; **lampe pendue au plafond,** lamp hanging from the ceiling; **aussitôt pris aussitôt p.,** no sooner said than done; **avoir la langue bien pendue,** to be a great talker; not to be able to stop talking. **2.** *s.* person who has been hanged or who has hanged himself; **sec comme un p.,** as thin as a lath, a rake; *s.a.* CORDE 1. **3.** *Bot: F:* **l'homme p.,** man orchid.

pendulaire [pɑ̃dylɛːr], *a.* swinging, pendulous, pendular (motion); **effet p.,** pendulum effect; **avoir un mouvement p.,** to pendulate; *Trans:* **migration p.,** commuting.

pendule [pɑ̃dyl]. **1.** *s.m.* (*a*) *Ph: Mec.E:* pendulum; **p. balistique,** ballistic pendulum; **p. compensé, p. compensateur,** compensated pendulum; **p. libre,** free pendulum; **p. asservi,** slave pendulum; **p. de torsion,** torsion pendulum; **p. physique,** compound, physical, pendulum; *Mch:* **p. à boules,** pendulum governor, ball governor; (*b*) balancer (of torpedo); (*c*) *Mount:* **faire un p.,** to do a pendulum traverse. **2.** *s.f.* clock; **p. mère,** master clock; **p. asservie,** slave clock; **p. à gaine,** grandfather clock; **p. murale,** hanging clock, wall clock; **p. à coucou,** cuckoo clock; **p. électrique,** electric clock; *Ind:* **p. de pointage,** time clock; *Pej:* **sujet de p.,** objet d'art.

penduler [pɑ̃dyle]. **1.** *v.i. Mount:* to do a pendulum traverse. **2.** *v.tr. Ind:* to time (work, operation) approximately.

pendulette [pɑ̃dylɛt], *s.f.* small clock, carriage clock, travelling clock.

penduleur [pɑ̃dylœːr], *s.m. Ind:* timekeeper.

penduline [pɑ̃dylin], *s.f. Orn:* **(rémiz) p.,** penduline tit(mouse).

pendulisant [pɑ̃dylizɑ̃], *s.m.* dowser who uses a pendulum.

pêne [pɛn], *s.m.* bolt (of lock); latch; **p. biseauté,** bevelled bolt; **p. coulant, à ressort,** spring bolt; **serrure à p. dormant,** dead lock.

péneau [peno], *s.m. Nau:* **ancre en p.,** anchor a-cockbill; **faire p.,** to clear for anchoring.

Pénée (le) [ləpene], *Pr.n.m. Geog:* the (river) Peneus.

pénée [pene], *s.m. Crust:* peneus.

pénéidés [peneide], *s.m.pl. Crust:* Peneidae.

Pénélope [penelɔp]. **1.** *Pr.n.f.* Penelope; **le travail de P.,** Penelope's web; **c'est la toile de P.,** it's never-ending. **2.** *s.f. Orn:* penelope, guan.

pénéplaine [peneplɛn], *s.f. Geol:* peneplain, peneplane.

pénéplanation [peneplanasjɔ̃], *s.f. Geol:* peneplanation.

pénéplaner [peneplane], *v.tr. Geol:* to peneplain, peneplane; to erode to a peneplain.

pénétrabilité [penetrabilite], *s.f.* penetrability; *Petroleum Ind:* **p. (d'une graisse) après malaxage,** worked penetrability.

pénétrable [penetrabl̩], *a.* penetrable.

pénétrance [penetrɑ̃ːs], *s.f. Biol:* penetrance.

pénétrant [penetrɑ̃]. **1.** *a.* penetrating; sharp (object); piercing (wind, cold); pervasive, obtrusive, strong, (smell); subtle (poison, scent); searching, keen (glance); acute, discerning (person); *Ph:* **rayonnement p.,** penetrating radiation; **esprit p., intelligence pénétrante,** keen, sharp, shrewd, mind; mind of deep insight; *Surg:* **plaie pénétrante,** perforating wound. **2.** *s.f. Mil:* **pénétrante,** axial route, road.

pénétration [penetrasjɔ̃], *s.f.* **1.** (*a*) penetration (of chemical, bullet); (*b*) penetration, insight; acuteness (of mind); acumen, shrewdness; **il juge les hommes avec p.,** he is a keen judge of men; (*c*) *Pol.Ec:* **p. des marchés étrangers,** penetration of foreign markets. **2.** impregnation (of wood). **3.** *Petroleum Ind:* penetration; **p. à l'aiguille des cires de pétrole,** needle penetration of petroleum waxes; **p. après malaxage, sans malaxage,** worked, unworked, penetration. **4. p. médicale,** availability of medical attention.

pénétré [penetre], *a.* penetrated, impressed, imbued **(de,** with); **homme p. de son importance,** man filled with, full of, his own importance; **p. d'idées fausses,** filled with false ideas; **p. de pitié, d'horreur,** filled with pity, with horror; **être p. d'une vérité,** to be firmly convinced of a truth; **d'un ton p.,** in a voice full of conviction; **d'un air p.,** with an earnest air.

pénétrer [penetre], *v.* **(je pénètre, n. pénétrons; je pénétrerai)** to penetrate. **1.** *v.i.* to enter, make one's way; **p. dans la forêt,** to penetrate into the forest; **il pénétra jusqu'au cabinet du roi,** he forced his way to the king's cabinet; **la baïonnette pénétra jusqu'au poumon,** the bayonet penetrated to the lung; **p. très avant dans le cœur humain,** to probe deeply into the human heart; **un cambrioleur a pénétré dans la maison,** a burglar broke into the house; **l'eau avait pénétré partout,** the water had got in everywhere; **il faut donner à la teinture le temps de p.,** the dye must be allowed to sink in, to soak in; **p. dans une couche pétrolifère,** to drill in. **2.** *v.tr.* (*a*) **l'eau pénètre les corps poreux,** water penetrates, impregnates, porous bodies; **la balle pénétra l'os,** the bullet penetrated, pierced, the bone; **il a pénétré le passé,** he has seen clearly into the past; **essayer de p. l'avenir,** to try to see into the future; **p. un secret,** to fathom a secret; **il sait p. les caractères,** he has an insight into character; **p. la pensée, les intentions, de qn,** to see through s.o.; **p. les raisons d'une ligne de conduite,** to get to the bottom of a policy; (*b*) **être pénétré d'un sentiment, d'une idée,** to be imbued with a feeling, an idea; **votre lettre m'a pénétré de douleur,** your letter has deeply distressed me, has filled me with grief.

se pénétrer. 1. (*of substances*) to combine, to interpenetrate. **2.** (*a*) (*of wood, etc.*) to become impregnated **(de,** with); to imbibe (dye, etc.); **se p. de chaleur,** to get thoroughly warm; **la terre se pénètre de la chaleur du soleil,** the earth absorbs the heat of the sun; (*b*) **se p. d'une idée,** to let an idea sink in; to absorb an idea.

pénétromètre [penetrɔmɛtr̥], *s.m. Tchn:* penetrometer.

penfieldite [penfildit], *s.f. Miner:* penfieldite.

pénibilité [penibilite], *s.f.* laboriousness, painfulness.

pénible [penibl̩], *a.* **1.** laborious, arduous, hard (task, etc.); laboured, heavy (breathing, style); **chemin p.,** rough, difficult, road; **vie p.,** hard, difficult, life. **2.** painful, distressing (spectacle, necessity, news, etc.); **l'idée m'est trop p.,** I can't bear the idea of it; **c'est un sujet p. qu'il faut éviter,** that is a painful subject which we must avoid; **p. à voir,** painful to see; **il m'était p. d'être soupçonné, qu'on me soupçonnât,** it was painful to me to be suspected. **3.** *F:* (*of pers.*) difficult; **avoir un caractère p.,** to have a difficult character; **ce qu'elle est p.!** she's impossible! **ce que tu es p.!** what a nuisance you are!

péniblement [penibləmɑ̃], *adv.* laboriously, arduously, painfully; with difficulty; **avancer, aller, marcher, p.; suivre p. son chemin,** to labour along, to toil along, to plod along, to trudge along; **respirer p.,** to breathe heavily, with difficulty; **le moteur fonctionne p.,** the engine is labouring; *F:* **il a trouvé p. 1.000 électeurs,** he had a job to scrape together 1,000 voters.

péniche [peniʃ], *s.f. Nau:* **1.** *A:* pinnace, shallop. **2.** canal boat, barge; coal barge; lighter; **p. aménagée en habitation,** houseboat; *Mil:* **p. de débarquement,** landing craft, barge. **3.** *P: A:* boot.

pénicillé [penisil(l)e], *a. Anat: Z:* penicillate.

pénicilliforme [penisil(l)ifɔrm], *a.* penicilliform.

pénicillinase [penisil(l)inaːz], *s.f. Bac:* penicillinase.

pénicilline [penisil(l)in], *s.f.* penicillin.

pénicillino-résistant [penisiljɔrezistɑ̃], *a.* penicillin-resistant; *pl. pénicillino-résistant(e)s.*

pénicillium [penisil(l)jɔm], *s.m. Fung:* penicillium (mould).

pénien, -ienne [penjɛ̃, -jɛn], *a. Anat:* penial, penile.

pénil [penil], *s.m. Anat:* mons pubis.

péninsulaire [penɛ̃sylɛːr], *a. & s.m. & f.* peninsular; (native, inhabitant) of a peninsula.

péninsule [penɛ̃syl], *s.f.* peninsula; **P. Ibérique,** Iberian Peninsula.

pénis [penis], *s.m. Anat:* penis.

pénitence [penitɑ̃ːs], *s.f.* **1.** penitence, repentance; **psaumes de la p.,** penitential psalms; *s.a.* DOS 1. **2.** (*a*) penance; **sacrement de p.,** sacrament of penance; **faire p.,** to do penance **(de,** for); **faire**

qch. pour p., to do sth. (i) as a penance, (ii) as a punishment; *F:* **mettre un enfant en p.,** to punish a child, *esp.* to put a child in the corner; **il est en p.,** he is in disgrace; *F:* **c'est une rude p. que d'aller chez eux,** it's really torture going to see them; *F:* **dînez chez nous, si vous ne craignez pas de faire p.,** come and have dinner with us if you think it won't be too much of a penance; (*b*) *Games:* forfeit.

pénitencerie [penitɑ̃sri], *s.f. R.C.Ch:* **1.** penitentiary (office) (in Rome). **2.** penitentiaryship.

pénitencier [penitɑ̃sje], *s.m.* **1.** *Ecc.* (*R.C.Ch*): penitentiary (priest, granting special dispensations); **Grand P.,** Grand Penitentiary. **2.** (*a*) penitentiary, reformatory prison; **p. agricole,** agricultural settlement for youths guilty of minor offences; (*b*) convict station; *a. A:* **navire p.,** hulks.

pénitent, -ente [penitɑ̃, -ɑ̃:t]. **1.** *a.* penitent, repentant, contrite; **vie pénitente,** life of penitence, of repentance. **2.** *s.* (*a*) (*person doing penance*), penitent; (*b*) *Ecc:* Penitent. **3.** *s.m. Geol:* pinnacle (of rock or snow).

pénitentiaire [penitɑ̃sjɛ:r], *a.* penitentiary (system); **maison p.,** penitentiary.

pénitential, -iaux [penitɑ̃sjal, -jo], **pénitentiel, -ielle** [penitɑ̃sjɛl]. **1.** *a.* penitential; **psaumes pénitentiaux,** penitential psalms; **œuvres pénitentielles,** works of penance. **2.** *s.m.* **pénitentiel,** penitential (book).

pennage [pɛn(n)a:ʒ], *s.m. Ven:* plumage (of bird of prey).

pennatifide [pɛn(n)atifid], *a. Bot:* pennatifid.

pennatilobé [pɛn(n)atilɔbe], *a. Bot:* pennatilobate.

pennatiséqué [pɛn(n)atiseke], *a. Bot:* pennatisect(ed).

pennatulaire [pɛn(n)atylɛ:r], *s.m. Coel:* pennatularian.

pennatule [pɛn(n)atyl], *s.f. Coel:* sea pen; (*genus*) Pennatula.

pennatulidés [pɛna(n)tylide], *s.m.pl. Coel:* Pennatulidae.

penne [pɛn], *s.f.* **1.** (*a*) quill(-feather), long wing feather, tail feather; pinna; (*b*) feather (of arrow). **2.** (*a*) *Nau:* peak (of lateen yard); **faire la p.,** to peak the yard; (*b*) *Tex:* warp end; (*c*) *Nau:* mop; **p. à brai,** pitch mop.

penné [pɛn(n)e], *a. Nat.Hist:* pennate, pinnate(d).

penniforme [pɛn(n)ifɔrm], *a.* penniform.

pennine [pɛn(n)in], *s.f. Miner:* penninite, pennine.

pennon [pɛn(n)ɔ̃], *s.m.* **1.** pennon. **2.** feather (of arrow).

Pennsylvanie [pɑ̃silvani, pɛ̃-], *Pr.n.f. Geog:* Pennsylvania.

pennsylvanien, -ienne [pɑ̃silvanjɛ̃, pɛ̃-, -jɛn], *a. & s. Geog:* Pennsylvanian.

pénologie [penɔlɔʒi], *s.f.* penology.

pénombre [penɔ̃:bŗ], *s.f.* (*a*) penumbra; (*b*) half light, semi-darkness, shadowy light, semi-obscurity; **rester dans la p.,** to remain inconspicuous, in the background.

penon [pənɔ̃], *s.m. Nau:* dog vane.

pensable [pɑ̃sabl], *a.* thinkable; conceivable.

pensant [pɑ̃sɑ̃], *a.* thinking (man, woman); **bien p.,** orthodox, right-thinking, right-minded (in religion or politics); **mal p.,** (i) unorthodox, heretical; (ii) uncharitable, ill-disposed.

pense-bête [pɑ̃sbɛt], *s.m. F:* memory jogger, memory tickler; *pl. pense-bêtes.*

pensée¹ [pɑ̃se], *s.f. Bot:* pansy.

pensée², *s.f.* **1.** thought; **grandes pensées,** lofty thoughts; *Lit:* **les Pensées de Marc-Aurèle,** the Meditations of Marcus Aurelius; **pensées détachées,** stray thoughts; **se laisser aller au fil de ses pensées,** to follow the thread of one's thoughts; **absorbé, perdu, dans ses pensées,** lost in thought; **arrêter sa p. sur un fait,** to fix one's thoughts on a fact; to dwell on a fact; **se représenter clairement qch. par la p.,** to have a clear conception, a clear idea, of sth.; **il me vint dans la p. que . . .,** the thought occurred to me, I had a notion, that . . .; **entrer dans la p. de qn,** to understand what is in s.o.'s mind; **désastre toujours présent à ma p.,** disaster always in my thoughts; **je l'ai fait dans la p., avec la p., que . . .,** I did it with the idea that . . .; **dire sa p.,** to speak one's mind; **a-t-il dit réellement sa p.?** does he really mean what he said? is that really his opinion? **dans sa p. il n'y avait aucun danger,** in his opinion there was no danger; **saisir la p. de qn,** to grasp s.o.'s meaning; **libre p.,** free thought, free thinking; **à la seule p. d'y aller elle . . .,** at the mere thought of going there she . . .; **rappelez-moi à la p. de votre mère,** remember me to your mother; *F:* **il n'est pas tourmenté par ses pensées,** his thoughts don't give him much to worry about; he's not very bright. **2.** intention; **quelle est votre p.?** what have you got in (your) mind? **j'avais la p. de pousser jusqu'à Paris,** I had some idea, some thought, of going as far as Paris; **changer de p.,** to change one's mind; **saisir la p. de qn,** to grasp s.o.'s intention.

penser [pɑ̃se]. I. *v.* to think. **1.** *v.ind.tr.* (*a*) **p. à qn, à qch.,** to think of, to let one's thoughts dwell on, s.o., sth.; **la personne à qui je pense,** the person whom I have in mind; **il pense à elle,** he is thinking of her; **il ne pense plus qu'à elle,** he is quite taken up with her; **à quoi pensez-vous?** (i) what are you thinking of? about? a penny for your thoughts; (ii) how could you (think of such a thing)! **p. tout haut,** to think aloud; **on ne saurait p. à tout,** one can never think of everything; **quand je pense à ce qui aurait pu arriver!** when I think of what might have happened! **je l'ai fait sans y p.,** I did it without thinking; (**y**) **pensez-vous!** what an idea! don't you believe it! *F:* **est-ce qu'il a donné un bon pourboire?—pensez-vous! (tu penses!)** did he give a good tip?—you're joking? no fear! what, him? **vous n'y pensez pas!** you don't mean it! **n'y pensez plus,** put it out of your mind, forget all about it; **je n'y ai plus pensé,** I forgot all about it; **ah, j'y pense!** by the way! **la vieillesse arrive sans qu'on y pense,** old age comes on without our having given it a thought; **rien que d'y p., mon sang bout,** the mere thought (of it) makes my blood boil; **p. à faire qch.,** (i) to think of doing sth.; (ii) to remember to do sth.; **je n'ai pas pensé à vous avertir,** (i) I never thought of warning you; (ii) I forgot to warn you; (*b*) **faire p. qn à qch.,** to remind s.o. of sth.; **il me fait p. à mon frère,** he reminds me, puts me in mind, of my brother; **faites-moi p. à lui écrire,** remind me to write to him. **2.** *v.i.* **manière de p.,** attitude of mind; **il pense par lui-même,** he thinks for himself; **je pense comme vous,** I agree with you, I am of your way of thinking; **à ce que je pense,** to my mind, to my way of thinking; **voilà ma façon de penser,** that is my way of thinking; **révélations qui donnent à p.,** revelations that give food for thought; **ne disant mot, il n'en pensait pas moins,** though he said nothing he thought all the more; **comme bien vous pensez, j'ai refusé,** I declined, as you may suppose; **pensez donc!** just fancy! **3.** *v.i. with cogn.acc.* (*a*) **p. vacances,** to think about holidays; **p. philosophie,** to think in philosophical terms; (*b*) **il faut p. européen,** we must think European. **4.** *v.tr.* (*a*) **p. qch.,** (i) to think, believe, sth.; (ii) to imagine, picture, sth.; **il dit tout ce qu'il pense,** he says all that he thinks; **je le pensais bien,** I thought as much, I thought so; **à ce que je pense,** to my mind, in my opinion; **je pense que c'est vrai,** I believe it is true; **je pensais que le livre avait déjà paru,** I was under the impression that the book was already out; **je pense que oui, que non,** I think so, I think not; **pensez si j'étais furieux,** you can imagine how angry I was; **je ne savais plus que p.,** I no longer knew what to think; I was quite nonplussed; (*b*) **je le pense fou,** I think he's mad, insane; (*c*) **p. qch. de qn, de qch.,** to think sth. of s.o., of sth.; **que pensez-vous de lui?** what do you think of him? what is your opinion of him; **j'en pense le plus grand bien,** I have a very high opinion of him, her, it; **p. du mal de qn,** to have a poor opinion of s.o.; *Iron:* **eh bien, qu'est-ce que vous pensez maintenant de ses théories?** well, what price his theories now? **je lui ai dit carrément ce que j'en pensais, ce que je pensais, ma façon de p.,** I told him straight what I thought; I gave him a piece of my mind; (*d*) **p. faire qch.:** (i) to expect to do sth.; **je pense le voir demain,** I have hopes of seeing him tomorrow; **il pensait pouvoir réussir,** he believed he could succeed; (ii) (= FAILLIR) **il a pensé se noyer,** he was nearly drowned, he had a narrow escape from drowning; **j'ai pensé mourir de rire,** I nearly died with laughter; **les médecins ont pensé me tuer,** *Lit:* **m'ont pensé tuer,** the doctors nearly killed me; (*e*) **p. qch.,** to think sth. out; **j'ai déjà pensé le problème,** I have already examined the problem; **les plans ont été mal pensés,** the plans were badly conceived; **c'est lui qui a pensé ce procédé,** it is he who invented this process.

II. **penser**, *s.m. A:* thought; **le p. abstrus des philosophes allemands,** the abstruse thinking of the German philosophers.

penseur, -euse [pɑ̃sœ:r, -ø:z], *s.* thinker; **libre p.,** freethinker; *a. A:* **l'homme p.,** the thinking man; **regard p.,** contemplative, thoughtful, reflective, eyes, look.

pensif, -ive [pɑ̃sif, -i:v], *a.* thoughtful, pensive (person); pensive, abstracted (air).

pension [pɑ̃sjɔ̃], *s.f.* **1.** pension, allowance; **p. sur l'État,** government pension; **p. de retraite,** (retirement) pension; *Mil: Navy:* retired pay; **p. viagère,** life annuity; **p. alimentaire,** allowance for board; *Jur:* alimony; **il fait à sa sœur une p. de 20.000 fr.,** he allows his sister 20,000 fr. a year. **2.** (*a*) (*payment for board* (*and lodging*)) **être en p., prendre p., chez qn,** to board with s.o.; **p. entière,** full board; **chambre et p.** board and residence; **cheval en p.,** horse at livery (stable); *O:* **titres en p.,** pawned stock; (*b*) **p. de famille, p. bourgeoise,** residential hotel, pension (pronounced as in French); boarding house. **3.** (*a*) boarding-school fees; (*b*) (private) boarding school; **mettre un enfant en p., dans une p.,** to send a child to a boarding school.

pensionnaire [pɑ̃sjɔnɛ:r], *s.m. & f.* **1.** (*a*) pensioner; **p. de l'État,** State pensioner; (*b*) *Hist:* **le Grand P. (de Hollande),** the Grand Pensionary. **2.** boarder (i) in boarding house, (ii) in boarding school; guest, resident (in hotel); paying guest (in private house); inmate (of mental hospital, etc.); (in-)patient (in hospital); **prendre, avoir, des pensionnaires,** to take, have, boarders, paying guests; **elle a l'air d'une petite p.,** she looks like a schoolgirl; **rougir comme une p.,** to blush like a schoolgirl. **3.** *Th:* actor under contract to a company.

pensionnat [pɑ̃sjɔna], *s.m.* **1.** (*a*) boarding school; (*b*) boarding establishment (attached to school). **2.** (school) boarders.

pensionné, -ée [pɑ̃sjɔne]. **1.** *a.* pensioned (soldier, employee). **2.** *s.* pensioner.

pensionner [pɑ̃sjɔne], *v.tr.* to pension; to grant a pension to (s.o.).

pensivement [pɑ̃sivmɑ̃], *adv.* pensively, thoughtfully; abstractedly.

penstémon [pɛ̃stemɔ̃], *s.m. Bot:* pentstemon, *esp.* beard tongue.

pensum [pɛ̃sɔm], *s.m.* (*a*) *Sch:* imposition; lines; extra work (given as punishment); (*b*) unpleasant task.

pent(a)- [pɛ̃t(a)], *pref.* pent(a)-.

pentaalcool [pɛ̃taalkɔl], *s.m. Ch:* pentite, pentitol.

pentabromure [pɛ̃tabrɔmy:r], *s.m. Ch:* pentabromide.

pentachlorure [pɛ̃taklɔry:r], *s.m. Ch:* pentachloride.

pentacle [pɛ̃takl̥], *s.m.* pentacle.

pentacorde [pɛ̃takɔrd], *s.m. Mus: A:* pentachord.

pentacrine [pɛ̃takrin], *s.m. Paleont: Echin:* pentacrinus; pentacrinite.

pentacrinidés [pɛ̃takrinide], *s.m.pl. Paleont: Echin:* Pentacrinidae.

pentadactyle [pɛ̃tadaktil], *a. Nat.Hist:* pentadactyl.

pentade [pɛ̃tad], *s.f.* pentad.

pentadécagone [pɛ̃tadekagɔn], *s.m. Geom:* pentadecagon.

pentaèdre [pɛ̃taɛdŗ], *Geom:* **1.** *a.* pentahedral. **2.** *s.m.* pentahedron.

pentaérythrite [pɛ̃taeritrit], *s.f.*, **pentaérythritol** [pɛ̃taeritritɔl], *s.m. Ch:* pentaerythritol.

pentagonal, -aux [pɛ̃tagɔnal, -o], *a. Geom:* pentagonal.

pentagone [pɛ̃tagɔn]. **1.** *Geom:* (*a*) *a.* pentagonal; (*b*) *s.m.* pentagon. **2.** *Pr.n.m. U.S: Mil:* **le P.,** the Pentagon.

pentagramme [pɛ̃tagram], *s.m.* pentagram.

pentagyne [pɛ̃taʒin], *a. Bot:* pentagynous.

pentagynie [pɛ̃taʒini], *s.f. Bot:* pentagynia.

pentalcool [pɛ̃talkɔl], *s.m. Ch:* pentite, pentitol.

pentalpha [pɛ̃talfa], *s.m.* pentalpha, five-pointed star.

pentamère [pɛ̃tamɛ:r]. **1.** *a. Nat.Hist:* pentamerous. **2.** *s.m. Paleont:* pentamerus; pentamerid.

pentaméridés [pɛ̃tameride], *s.m.pl. Paleont:* Pentameridae.

pentamètre [pɛ̃tamɛtŗ], *a. & s.m. Pros:* pentameter.

pentaméthylène [pɛ̃tametilɛn], *s.m. Ch:* pentamethylene.

pentaméthylènediamine [pɛ̃tametilɛndjamin], *s.f. Ch:* pentamethylenediamine.

pentamoteur, -trice [pɛ̃tamɔtœ:r, -tris], *a. A:* five-engined.

pentandre [pɛ̃tɑ̃:dr], *a. Bot:* pentandrous.

pentandrie [pɛ̃tɑ̃dri], *s.f. Bot:* pentandria.

pentane [pɛ̃tan], *s.m. Ch:* pentane.

pentanoïque [pɛ̃tanɔik], *s.m. Ch:* pentanoic acid.

pentanol [pɛ̃tanɔl], *s.m. Ch:* pentanol.

pentanone [pɛ̃tanɔn], *s.f. Ch:* pentanone.

pentapétale [pɛ̃tapetal], *a. Bot:* pentapetalous.

pentaploïde [pɛ̃taplɔid], *s.m. Biol:* pentaploid.

pentapodie [pɛ̃tapɔdi], *s.f. Pros:* pentapody.

pentapole [pɛ̃tapɔl], *s.f. A.Hist:* pentapolis.

pentarchie [pɛ̃tarʃi], *s.f.* pentarchy.

pentarchique [pɛ̃tarʃik], *a.* pentarchical.

pentarque [pɛ̃tark], *s.m.* pentarch.

pentastomides [pɛ̃tastɔmid], *s.m.pl. Ent:* Pentastomida, Linguatulida.

pentastyle [pɛ̃tastil], *Arch:* **1.** *a.* pentastyle. **2.** *s.m.* pentastylos.

pentasulfure [pɛ̃tasylfy:r], *s.m. Ch:* pentasulphide; *Miner:* **p. d'antimoine,** red sulphide of antimony.

pentasyllabe [pɛ̃tasil(l)ab]. **1.** *a.* pentasyllabic. **2.** *s.m.* pentasyllable.

Pentateuque (le) [ləpɛ̃tatø:k], *s.m. B:* the Pentateuch.

pentathionate [pɛ̃tatjɔnat], *s.m. Ch:* pentathionate.

pentathionique [pɛ̃tatjɔnik], *a. Ch:* pentathionic.

pentathle [pɛ̃tatl̥], *s.m.*, **pentathlon** [pɛ̃tatlɔ̃], *s.m. Sp:* (*Olympic Games, etc.*) pentathlon.

pentatome [pɛ̃tatɔm], *s.f. Ent:* pentatomid.

pentatomidés [pɛ̃tatɔmide], *s.f.pl. Ent:* Pentatomidae.

pentatomique [pɛ̃tatɔmik], *a. Ch:* pentatomic.

pentatonique [pɛ̃tatɔnik], *a. Mus:* pentatonic (scale).

pentavalence [pɛ̃tavalɑ̃:s], *s.f. Ch:* pentavalence, quinquivalence.

pentavalent [pɛ̃tavalɑ̃], *a. Ch:* pentavalent, quinquivalent.

pente [pɑ̃:t], *s.f.* **1.** (*a*) slope; incline; gradient, *U.S:* grade; **p. ascendante,** uphill slope, slope up, *U.S:* upslope; rising gradient, *U.S:* upgrade; **p. descendante,** downhill slope, slope down, *U.S:* downslope; falling gradient, *U.S:* downgrade; **forte p., p. raide, p. rapide,** steep slope; steep gradient, grade; steep hill; **p. douce, p. faible,** gentle slope; low gradient, grade; **à faible, à forte, p.,** gently, steeply, sloping; with a low, steep, gradient; **colline à vingt-cinq pour cent de p.,** hill with a gradient of one in four; *P.N: Aut:* **p. 10%,** hill 1 in 10. *Rail:* **poteau indicateur de p.,** gradient post; **p. graduelle,** gradual slope; **p. à pic,** vertical slope; **en p.,** sloping; shelving; **rue en p.,** steep street; **rivage, côte, en p.,** sloping bank; shelving shore; *Oc:* **p. continentale,** continental slope; **p. d'une rivière,** fall of a river; **rupture de p.,** change of slope, of gradient; *Geol:* **p. limite,** angle of rest; *P:* **avoir la dalle en p., avoir une p. dans le gosier,** to have a perpetual thirst; *F:* **être sur la p. du mal,** to be on the downward path, to be going downhill; *F:* **être sur une, sur la, mauvaise p.,** (i) to be in a bad way; (ii) to be past hope, beyond recovery; (*b*) *Civ.E:* **p. transversale (d'une route),** camber (of a road); *N.Arch:* **pont en p.,** cambered deck; *Const:* **p. d'un toit,** pitch of a roof; *Mch.-Tls:* **pente (d'affûtage),** rake angle (of tool); *Mth:* **p. d'une courbe,** slope of a curve; *Surv: etc:* **angle de p.,** angle of slope; **échelle des pentes,** scale of slopes; **correction de p.,** correction for slope; **ligne de changement de p.,** fall line; **ligne de plus grande p.,** principal line; (*c*) *Av:* slope (of flight path); **p. de montée, de descente,** slope at take-off, at landing; **pentes de montée ou de descente très accentuées,** steep slopes at take-off or landing, steep flight-path slopes; **indicateur de p.,** inclinometer; *Aut:* gradient meter; (*d*) *Lit:* bent, inclination, propensity; **avoir une p. naturelle à, pour, vers, qch.,** to have a natural bent for sth.; **suivre sa p.,** to follow one's bent, one's inclinations. **2.** *Elcs: W.Tel:* slope, transconductance, mu (of valve). **3.** valance, hangings (of bed, canopy, curtain).

pentécostaire [pɑ̃tekɔstɛ:r], *a. Ecc:* Pentecostal.

Pentecôte [pɑ̃tko:t], *s.f.* Pentecost; Whitsun, Whitsuntide; **dimanche de la P.,** Whit Sunday; *Ecc:* **deuxième, etc., dimanche après la P.,** second, etc., Sunday after Pentecost.

pentédécagone [pɛ̃tedekagɔn], *s.m. Geom:* pentadecagon.

Pentélique (le) [ləpɑ̃telik], *Geog:* **1.** *Pr.n.m.* Mount Pentelicus. **2.** *a.* **marbre p.,** Pentelican marble.

pentène [pɛ̃tɛn], *s.m. Ch:* pentene.

Penthée [pɑ̃te], *Pr.n.m. Gr.Myth:* Pentheus.

Penthésilée [pɑ̃tezile], *Pr.n.f. Gr.Lit:* Penthesilea.

penthiofène, penthiophène [pɛ̃tjɔfɛn], *s.m. Ch:* penthiophene.

penthode [pɛ̃tɔd], *s.f. Elcs:* pentode, five-electrode tube, three-grid tube.

penthore [pɛ̃tɔ:r], *s.m. Bot:* penthorum; ditch stonecrop.

pentière [pɑ̃tjɛ:r], *s.f.* slope (of a mountain).

pentite [pɛ̃tit], *s.f.*, **pentitol** [pɛ̃titɔl], *s.m. Ch:* pentite, pentitol.

pentlandite [pɛ̃tlɑ̃dit], *s.f. Miner:* pentlandite.

pentode [pɛ̃tɔd], *s.f. Elcs:* pentode, five-electrode tube, three-grid tube.

pentolite [pɛ̃tɔlit], *s.f. Exp:* pentolite.

pentomique [pɛ̃tɔmik], *a. U.S: Mil:* pentomic.

pentosanne [pɛ̃tɔzan], *s.m. Ch:* pentosan.

pentose [pɛ̃to:z], *s.m. Ch:* pentose.

pentoside [pɛ̃tɔzid], *s.m. Ch:* pentosid(e).

pentosurie [pɛ̃tɔzyri], *s.f. Med:* pentosuria.

pentothal [pɛ̃tɔtal], *s.m. Pharm: R.t.m:* Pentothal.

pentremites [pɛ̃tremites], *s.m. Paleont: Echin:* Pentremites; pentremitid.

pentryl [pɛ̃tril], *s.m. Exp:* pentryl.

pentstémon [pɛ̃tstemɔ̃], *s.m. Bot:* pentstemon.

pentu [pɑ̃ty], *a. Dial:* sloping.

penture [pɑ̃ty:r], *s.f.* strap hinge (of door, etc.); **p. et gond,** hook and hinge; *pl. Nau:* **pentures du gouvernail,** rudder bands, braces, chalders; **pentures des sabords,** port hinges.

pénultième [penyltjɛm], *a. & s.f.* penultimate; **la syllabe p.,** *s.* **la pénultième,** the penult, the penultimate (syllable), the last syllable but one.

pénurie [penyri], *s.f.* (*a*) scarcity, dearth, shortage (of money, goods, staff, etc.); lack (of words); *Pol.Ec:* **p. de dollars,** dollar gap; (*b*) poverty.

péon [peɔ̃], *s.m.* (*in S. & Central America*) peon.

pépé [pepe], *s.m. F:* grand-dad, grandpa.

pépée [pepe], *s.f.* (*a*) (*child's language*) dolly; (*b*) *P:* girl, bird, popsy, doll.

pépère [pepɛ:r], *F:* **1.** *s.m.* (*a*) easy-going old buffer; **c'est un gros p.,** (i) he's a big, placid fellow; (ii) (*of child*) he's a quiet, chubby little chap; (*b*) grand-dad, grandpa. **2.** *a.* (*a*) **une somme p.,** a nice fat sum (of money); **un gueuleton p.,** a really good blowout; (*b*) **un petit coin p.,** a nice quiet, snug, little spot; **une petite situation p.,** a cushy little job; (*c*) (*of pers.*) easy-going. **3.** *adv. Aut:* **rouler p.,** to bumble along.

péperin [peprɛ̃], *s.m.*, **peperino** [peperino], *s.m. Geol:* peperino.

pépette, pépète [pepɛt], *s.f. P:* **de la p., des pépettes,** money, brass, lolly.

pépie [pepi], *s.f.* pip (disease of the tongue of fowls); *hence F:* **avoir la p.,** to have a perpetual thirst; **elle n'a pas la p.,** she never stops talking.

pépiement [pepimɑ̃], *s.m.* cheep(ing), chirp(ing), peep(ing) (of birds).

pépier [pepje], *v.i.* (*of birds*) to cheep, chirp, peep.

pépin[1] [pepɛ̃], *s.m.* **1.** pip (of apple, grape, etc.); *P: O:* **avoir un p. pour qn,** to be in love with, to be gone on, s.o.; to be crazy about s.o.; *P:* **avoir avalé un p.,** to be pregnant. **2.** *F:* hitch; **avoir un p.,** to be in trouble, in difficulties.

pépin[2], *s.m. F:* (*a*) umbrella, gamp, brolly; (*b*) parachute, 'chute.

Pépin[3], *Pr.n.m. Hist:* Pepin.

pépinière [pepinjɛ:r], *s.f.* **1.** *Hort:* seed bed; nursery (of young trees). **2.** *F:* nursery (of young actors, young communists, etc.); *Pej:* breeding-ground (of anarchists).

pépiniériste [pepinjerist], *s.m. & f.* nurseryman, nursery gardener.

pépite [pepit], *s.f.* nugget (of gold); *F:* **il n'a plus une p.,** he hasn't a (brass) farthing left.

péplide [peplid], *s.f. Bot:* peplis; **p. pourpière,** water purslane.

péplum [peplɔm], *s.m. Gr.Ant:* peplos, peplum.

pépon [pepɔ̃], *s.m.*, **péponide** [pepɔnid], *s.f. Bot:* pepo.

pepsinase [pɛpsina:z], *s.f.*, **pepsine** [pɛpsin], *s.f. Bio-Ch:* pepsin.

pepsique [pɛpsik], *a. Physiol:* peptic.

pepsis [pɛpsis], *s.m. Ent:* pepsis; tarantula hawk (wasp).

peptidase [pɛptida:z], *s.f. Bio-Ch:* peptidase.

peptide [pɛptid], *s.m. Ch: Physiol:* peptide.

peptique [pɛptik], *a.* peptic; *Med:* **ulcère p.,** peptic ulcer.

peptisable [pɛptizabl̥], *a. Ch:* peptizable.

peptisation [pɛptizasjɔ̃], *s.f. Ch:* peptization.

peptogène [pɛptɔʒɛn]. **1.** *a.* peptogenic. **2.** *s.m.* peptogen.

peptonate [pɛptɔnat], *s.m. Bio-Ch:* peptonate.

peptone [pɛptɔn], *s.f. Physiol: Ch:* peptone.

peptonisable [pɛptɔnizabl̥], *a. Ch:* peptonizable.

peptonisation [pɛptɔnizasjɔ̃], *s.f.* peptonization.

peptoniser [pɛptɔnize], *v.tr.* to peptonize.

peptonurie [pɛptɔnyri], *s.f. Med:* peptonuria.

péquenot [pekno], *s.m. P:* clodhopper, country bumpkin; clot.

péquin [pekɛ̃], *s.m. Mil: F: O:* civilian.

per- [pɛr], *pref.* per-.

peracarides [pɛrakarid], *s.f.pl. Crust:* Peracarida.

peracétique [pɛrasetik], *a. Ch:* peracetic.

peracide [pɛrasid], *s.m. Ch:* peracid.

pérambulation [perɑ̃bylasjɔ̃], *s.f.* **1.** (*rare*) perambulation. **2.** *Surv:* measuring, surveying (of piece of land).

péramèle [peramɛl], *s.m. Z:* bandicoot; (*genus*) Perameles.

péramélidés [peramelide], *s.m.pl. Z:* Peramelidae.

perazotate [pɛrazɔtat], *s.m. Ch:* pernitrate.

perazotique [pɛrazɔtik], *a. Ch:* pernitric (acid).

perborate [pɛrbɔrat], *s.m. Ch:* perborate.

perbromure [pɛrbrɔmy:r], *s.m. Ch:* perbromide.

perbunan [pɛrbynɑ̃], *s.m. Ch: R.t.m:* Perbunan.

perc [pɛrk], *s.m. Metall:* tapping iron.

perçage [pɛrsa:ʒ], *s.m.* (*a*) piercing, boring, drilling, punching; **outils de p.,** drills, boring tools; (*b*) broaching, tapping (of cask).

percale [pɛrkal], *s.f. Tex:* percale; cotton cambric.

percaline [pɛrkalin], *s.f. Tex:* percaline; *Dressm: etc:* glazed lining; calico; *Bookb:* cloth.

perçant [pɛrsɑ̃], *a.* piercing, penetrating (eyes, shriek); keen, sharp (wits); shrill (voice); **coup de sifflet p.,** sharp, shrill, whistle; **vent p.,** keen, piercing, wind; **à la vue perçante,** keen-sighted; keen-eyed; **regarder qn d'un œil p.,** to look s.o. through and through.

percarbonate [pɛrkarbɔnat], *s.m. Ch:* percarbonate.

perce [pɛrs], *s.f.* **1.** *Tls:* borer, drill, punch. **2.** **perces d'une flûte, etc.,** holes of a flute, etc. **3.** **barrique en p.,** broached cask; **mettre un fût, le vin, en p.,** to broach a cask, the wine; **mise en p.,** broaching, tapping.

percé [pɛrse]. **1.** *a.* (*a*) pierced, bored (hole, etc.); **chaise percée,** (night) commode; **p. de vers,** wormeaten (fruit, wood); **cœur p. de douleur,** grief-stricken heart; *F:* **c'est un panier p.,** he's a spendthrift; (*b*) (*of garments, etc.*) in holes; **habit p.,** coat out at elbows; **pantalon p.,** trousers with a hole in the seat; **mur p. à jour par la canonnade,** wall pierced with shell holes; **complot p. à jour,** plot brought to light; (*c*) *Her:* pierced, perforate. **2.** *s.m. Mil:* breakthrough.

perce-bois [pɛrs(ə)bwa], *Ent:* **1.** *a.* wood-boring. **2.** *s.m.inv.* wood borer; (*in ships*) teredo; **abeille p.-b.,** carpenter bee.

perce-boîte(s) [pɛrs(ə)bwat], *s.m.* tin piercer; *pl. perce-boîtes.*

perce-bouchon [pɛrs(ə)buʃɔ̃], *s.m.* cork borer; *pl. perce-bouchons.*

perce-courroie(s) [pɛrs(ə)kurwa], *s.m.inv. Mec.E: Aut:* belt punch.

percée [pɛrse], *s.f.* opening (action or aperture). **1.** (*a*) cutting (in a forest); break (in hedge, etc.); glade; vista; **faire une p. dans un bois,** to make an opening in, cut a passage through, a wood; **la ville a plusieurs percées qui mènent à la rivière,** the town has several openings on to the river; **faire une p. entre deux quartiers,** to open up a thoroughfare between two districts; (*b*) (window or door) opening (in wall). **2.** (*a*) *Mil:* breakthrough; *Fb:* run through; *Meteor:* **p. des nuages,** break(through) in the clouds; **faire une p.,** to break through; **nous avons fait une p. assez avant dans la Provence,** we pushed, penetrated, a good way into Provence; (*b*) *Av:* letdown; (*c*) **p. (technologique),** breakthrough. **3.** *Metall:* **p. (de coulée),** (i) tapping (of blast furnace), (ii) tap hole; **faire la p.,** to tap. **4.** *Ph.Geog:* (river) gap; transverse valley.

perce-feuille [pɛrs(ə)fœ:j], *s.f. Bot:* hare's ear; *pl. perce-feuilles.*

percement [pɛrs(ə)mɑ̃], *s.m.* **1.** perforation; piercing (of heart, ear, etc.); boring (of hole, passage); opening (of street); cutting (of canal); tunnelling (of mountain); sinking (of well); *Min:* **p. de galeries,** driving of levels, of galleries. **2.** opening (in forest, etc.).

perce-muraille [pɛrs(ə)myrɑ:j], *s.f. Bot:* wall pellitory; *pl. perce-murailles.*

perce-neige [pɛrs(ə)nɛ:ʒ], *s.m. or f.inv. Bot:* snowdrop.

percentage [pɛrsɑ̃ta:ʒ], *s.m. Adm:* percentage.

percentile [pɛrsɑ̃til], *s.m.* (per)centile.

perce-oreille [pɛrsɔrɛ:j], *s.m. Ent:* earwig; *pl. perce-oreilles.*

perce-pierre [pɛrs(ə)pjɛ:r], *s.f. Bot:* **1.** samphire, sea fennel. **2.** (white, meadow) saxifrage; *pl. perce-pierres.*

percepta [pɛrsɛpta], *s.m.pl. Psy:* percepta, percepts, sense-data.

percepteur, -trice [pɛrsɛptœ:r, -tris]. **1.** *a.* perceiving, discerning; **organes percepteurs,** organs of perception. **2.** *s.m. Adm:* collector of taxes.

perceptibilité [pɛrsɛptibilite], *s.f.* **1.** perceptibility (through the senses); audibility (of sound). **2.** **p. d'un impôt,** possibility of collecting a tax.

perceptible [pɛrsɛptibḷ], *a.* **1.** perceptible (à, by, to); discernible; **p. à l'oreille,** audible. **2.** collectable, collectible (tax).

perceptiblement [pɛrsɛptibləmɑ̃], *adv.* perceptibly; audibly.

perceptif, -ive [pɛrsɛptif, -iːv], *a.* perceptive; perceptional; *Phil:* perceptual; **les facultés perceptives,** the apprehensive faculties.

perception [pɛrsɛpsjɔ̃], *s.f.* **1.** perception (through the senses). **2.** *Adm:* (*a*) collection, receipt (of taxes, duties, rent); levying (of taxes); **maximum de p.,** highest scale of taxation; maximum charge; **minimum de p.,** (i) *Post:* minimum rate, (ii) minimum fare, charge; **(bureau de) p.,** tax-collector's office, revenue office; (*b*) collectorship.

percer [pɛrse], *v.* **(je perçai(s); n. perçons) 1.** *v.tr.* (*a*) to pierce, to go through, pass through (sth.); **p. l'air de ses cris,** to pierce the air with one's cries; **vous me percez les oreilles,** you're deafening me; **p. un abcès,** to lance an abscess; **p. qn d'un coup d'épée,** to run s.o. through; to run a sword through s.o.; **p. qn d'un coup de couteau,** to stab s.o.; **p. qn d'un coup de baïonnette,** to bayonet s.o.; **p. qn de part en part,** to run s.o. through (and through); **le soleil perce les nuages,** the sun is breaking through the clouds; **la pluie a percé mon pardessus,** the rain has gone, soaked, through my overcoat; **le remords lui perçait le cœur,** remorse pierced his heart; **p. le cœur à qn,** to cut s.o. to the heart; **p. l'avenir,** to foresee the future; **p. un secret,** to penetrate a secret; **p. la foule,** to make one's way, to break, through a crowd; (*b*) to perforate; to make a hole, an opening, in (sth.); to sink (well); **p. un mur,** to make a hole in a wall; **p. un tonneau,** to broach, tap, a cask; **p. un coffre-fort,** to crack a safe; **p. une porte dans un mur,** to make, open, a door in a wall; *Metall:* **p. le haut fourneau,** to tap the furnace; **p. un fer à cheval,** to punch the holes in a horseshoe; **p. les lobes des oreilles,** to pierce the lobes of the ears; (*c*) **p. un trou,** to drill, bore, a hole; **p. un tunnel dans une montagne,** to drive a tunnel through a mountain; **machine à p.,** drilling machine. **2.** *v.i.* to pierce; to come, break, through; **ses dents percent,** he is cutting his teeth; **l'abcès a percé,** the abscess has burst; **la vérité perce tôt ou tard,** truth will out (sooner or later); **auteur qui commence à p.,** author who is beginning to make his way, to attract attention, to come to the front, to make a name; **discours où perçait la jalousie,** speech in which jealousy was apparent, could be detected; speech that savoured of jealousy.

percerette [pɛrs(ə)rɛt], *f.* (*a*) gimlet; (*b*) awl; (*c*) cork borer.

percésoces [pɛrsezɔs], *s.m.pl. Ich:* Percesoces, percesocids.

percette [pɛrsɛt], *s.f. Tls:* (*a*) gimlet; (*b*) awl; (*c*) cork borer.

perceur, -euse [pɛrsœːr, -øːz]. **1.** *s.* borer; driller (of rivet holes, etc.); drilling-machine operator; puncher (of sheet metal, etc.). **2.** *s.f.* **perceuse,** boring, drilling, machine; **perceuse à main,** hand drill; **perceuse électrique,** electric drill; **perceuse de roches,** rock drill; **perceuse multibroche,** multiple-spindle drill(ing machine); **p. monobroche,** single-spindle drill(ing machine); **p. radiale,** radial drill(ing machine); **p. à percussion,** impact drill(ing machine). **3.** *s.m.* **p. de coffres-forts,** safe breaker.

percevable [pɛrsəvabḷ], *a.* **1.** perceivable. **2.** leviable (tax); *Tp:* **faire une communication p. à l'arrivée,** to reverse the charge.

Perceval [pɛrsəval], *Pr.n.m.* Percival.

percevoir [pɛrsəvwaːr], *v.tr.* (*pr.p.* **percevant;** *p.p.* **perçu;** *pr.ind.* **je perçois, n. percevons, ils perçoivent;** *pr.sub.* **je perçoive, n. percevions, ils perçoivent;** *p.d.* **je percevais;** *p.h.* **je perçus;** *fu.* **je percevrai) 1.** to perceive, discern (with the senses, the intellect); **p. un bruit,** to hear, catch, a sound; **il perçut leur anxiété,** he noticed their anxiety. **2.** to collect, gather (taxes, rents, etc.); to levy (taxes); **taxe perçue,** postage paid; **cotisations à p.,** contributions still due; **p. un droit,** to charge a fee.

perchage [pɛrʃaːʒ], *s.m. Orn: etc:* perching.

perchal [pɛrʃal], *s.m. Z:* nesokia, bandicoot.

perche[1] [pɛrʃ], *s.f.* **1.** (*a*) (thin) pole; **perches à houblon,** hop poles; *Sp:* **saut à la p.,** pole vaulting; **p. de saut,** vaulting pole; **sauteur à la p.,** pole vaulter; *F:* **grande p.,** tall, lanky person, *F:* maypole, hop pole, bean pole; **p. de bachot,** punt pole, setting pole; **conduire un bateau à la p.,** to pole, punt, a boat; **tendre la p. à qn,** to give s.o. a helping hand, a broad hint; **p. d'échafaudage,** scaffolding pole; *El:* **p. de prise de courant,** trolley arm (of trolleybus, etc.); *Rail:* **p. à accrocher,** coupling pole; (*b*) *Agr:* beam (of plough). **2.** *A.Meas:* rod, pole, perch.

perche[2], *s.f. Ich:* perch; **p. goujonnière,** ruff; **p. noire,** small-mouthed black bass; **p. soleil,** sunfish; **p. de mer,** sea bass.

Perche[3] **(le),** *Pr.n.m. Geog:* the Perche (region).

perché [pɛrʃe]. **1.** *a.* perched, perched up; **poules perchées,** roosting hens; **château p. sur une colline,** castle perched on a hill. **2.** *s.m.* **tirer des faisans au p.,** to shoot pheasants sitting.

perchée [pɛrʃe], *s.f. Orn:* roost, group of birds at roost.

percher [pɛrʃe]. **1.** *v.i.* (*of birds*) to perch, roost; *F:* **il perche au quatrième,** he lives up on the fourth floor; **où perchez-vous?** where do you hang out? *F:* **où ça perche, ce trou-là?** where on earth is the place? **2.** *v.tr. F:* **p. un vase sur une armoire,** to perch a vase on top of a wardrobe.

se percher. (*of bird*) **se p. sur une branche,** to alight, perch, on a branch; *F:* **il est allé se p. à Montmartre,** he has gone to live at the top of Montmartre; *F:* **tâchez de vous p. de manière à dominer la foule,** try and find a spot from which you can see over the heads of the crowd.

percheron, -onne [pɛrʃərɔ̃, -ɔn], *a. & s. Geog:* (native, inhabitant) of Perche; **cheval p.,** *s.m.* **percheron,** percheron (draught horse).

perche-truite [pɛrʃtrɥit], *s.f. Ich:* large-mouthed black bass; green bass; *pl. perches-truites.*

percheur, -euse [pɛrʃœːr, -øːz]. **1.** *a.* perching, roosting (bird, fowl); **l'alouette n'est pas percheuse,** the lark is not a perching bird; **oiseau p.,** percher. **2.** *s.m.pl. Orn:* **percheurs,** perchers.

perchis [pɛrʃi], *s.m. For:* pole plantation.

perchiste [pɛrʃist], *s.m. & f.* (*a*) acrobat (who uses a perch pole); (*b*) pole vaulter.

perchlorate [pɛrklɔrat], *s.m. Ch:* perchlorate.

perchloré [pɛrklɔre], *a. Ch:* perchlorinated.

perchlorique [pɛrklɔrik], *a. Ch:* perchloric.

perchlorure [pɛrklɔryːr], *s.m. Ch:* perchloride; **p. de fer,** ferric chloride.

perchman [pɛrʃman], *s.m. Cin: T.V:* boom operator; *pl. perchmen.*

perchoir [pɛrʃwaːr], *s.m.* (bird's) perch, roost.

perchromique [pɛrkrɔmik], *a. Ch:* perchromic.

percidés [pɛrside], *s.m.pl. Ich:* Percidae, percids, perches.

perclus [pɛrkly] (*f.* **percluse** [pɛrklyːz], *F:* **perclue**), *a.* (*a*) stiff-jointed, anchylosed (person); **jambe percluse,** stiff leg; **il est p. de sa jambe gauche,** he has lost the use of his left leg; **p. de rhumatismes,** crippled with rheumatism; *A:* **il a le cerveau p.,** his brain is anchylosed; (*b*) stupefied; paralysed (with fright, etc.).

percnoptère [pɛrknɔptɛːr], *s.m. Orn:* **p. d'Égypte,** Egyptian vulture.

perco(t) [pɛrko], *s.m. F:* **1.** percolator. **2.** *Mil: O:* man who makes the coffee for his comrades. **3.** *A:* flying rumour, baseless report.

perçoir [pɛrswaːr], *s.m. Tls:* (*a*) punch; drill, borer, broach; **p. à couronne,** square bit; **p. à rochet,** ratchet brace; **p. en spirale,** screw auger; (*b*) awl, gimlet; (*c*) *Metall:* tapping iron; (*d*) *Archeol:* perforator.

percolateur [pɛrkɔlatœːr], *s.m.* (coffee) percolator.

percolation [pɛrkɔlasjɔ̃], *s.f. Petroleum Ind:* percolation.

percomorphes [pɛrkɔmɔrf], *s.m.pl. Ich:* Percomorphi, percomorphs.

percussion [pɛrkysjɔ̃], *s.f.* (*a*) percussion; impact; *Exp:* **amorce à p.,** percussion primer; **amorce à p. centrale,** centre-fire primer; *Sm.a:* **fusil à p.,** percussion gun; **p. centrale,** centre fire; **p. périphérique,** rim fire; (*b*) *Med:* sounding (by percussion); percussion; (*c*) **presse à p.,** stamping press; *Bookb:* nipping press; (*d*) *Mus:* **instruments à p.,** percussion instruments.

percussionniste [pɛrkysjɔnist], *s.m. & f. Mus:* percussion player.

percutané [pɛrkytane], *a. Med:* percutaneous.

percutant [pɛrkytɑ̃], *a.* (*a*) percussive; *Artil:* **fusée percutante,** percussion fuse; **obus p.,** *s.m.* **percutant,** percussion-fuse shell; **tir p.,** percussion fire; **pointe percutante,** firing pin (of gun); (*b*) trenchant, forceful, incisive; **argument p.,** argument that strikes home; **discours p.,** forceful speech; **style p.,** trenchant, incisive, style.

percuter [pɛrkyte]. **1.** *v.tr.* (*a*) to strike (sth.) sharply; *Sm.a:* **p. l'amorce,** to strike the primer; **l'avion percuta une colline,** the plane crashed into a hillside; (*b*) *Med:* to sound (chest) by percussion; to percuss. **2.** *v.i.* **l'avion percuta au sol,** the plane crashed to the ground; **la voiture percuta contre un arbre,** the car crashed into a tree.

percuteur [pɛrkytœːr], *s.m.* (*a*) striker, hammer (of gun, of fuse); needle (of rifle); firing pin (of machine gun); striker (of torpedo); plunger (of fuse); (*b*) *Med:* plexor.

percuti-réaction [pɛrkytireaksjɔ̃], *s.f. Med:* percutaneous reaction; *pl. percuti-réactions.*

percylite [pɛrsilit], *s.f. Miner:* percylite.

perdable [pɛrdabḷ], *a.* losable; **la partie n'est plus p.,** the game cannot be lost now.

perdant, -ante [pɛrdɑ̃, -ɑ̃ːt]. **1.** *a.* losing; **billet p.,** blank (ticket, at lottery); **partir p.,** to have no hope of winning. **2.** *s.* loser. **3.** *s.m.* **p. de la marée,** ebb of the tide.

perdeur, -euse [pɛrdœːr, -øːz], *s. used esp. in* **perdeur, -euse, de temps,** time-waster.

perd-fluide [pɛrflyid], *s.m.inv. El:* earth (circuit) (of lightning rod, etc.).

perdisulfurique [pɛrdisylfyrik], *a. Ch:* peroxydisulphic (acid).

perditance [pɛrditɑ̃ːs], *s.f. El:* leakage conductance, leakance.

perdition [pɛrdisjɔ̃], *s.f.* **1.** *Ecc:* perdition; **le chemin de la p.,** the road that leads to destruction. **2.** *Nau:* **navire en p.,** ship (i) in distress; (ii) breaking up; (iii) sinking; (iv) driven ashore. **3. lieu de p.,** den of vice.

perdre [pɛrdṛ], *v.tr.* **1.** to ruin, destroy; **le jeu le perdra,** gambling will be the ruin of him; **vous vous perdrez par cette démarche,** such a step will be your undoing; **cette faillite nous perd,** this failure means, spells, ruin for us; *A. & Lit:* **p. qn d'honneur,** to ruin s.o.'s honour, to disgrace, dishonour, s.o.; **p. qn de réputation,** to ruin s.o.'s reputation. **2.** to lose; (*a*) **p. son père, sa vie,** to lose one's father, one's life; **p. une bataille, un procès,** to lose a battle, a lawsuit; **p. la partie,** (i) to lose the game; (ii) to go to the wall; **cette faute lui fit p. la partie,** this mistake lost him the match, the game; **p. la raison,** *F:* **le nord, la boussole,** to lose one's reason, become insane; **p. le fil,** to lose the thread (of the conversation); **p. haleine,** to get out of breath; *P:* **p. le goût du pain,** to die; **p. une habitude avec le temps, en vieillissant,** to outgrow, grow out of, lose, a habit; **faire p. une habitude à qn,** to break s.o. of a habit; **p. sa bourse,** to lose one's purse; **cela se perd facilement,** it is easily lost; **vous ne perdrez rien pour attendre,** you will lose nothing by waiting; **il ne perdra rien pour attendre,** my revenge will keep; I'll be even with him yet; **n'avoir rien à p.,** to have nothing to lose; **je l'ai payé cher, mais je consentirais à p. quelque chose dessus,** it cost me a lot, but I wouldn't mind dropping a bit on it; **p. son chemin,** to lose one's way; **le guide l'a perdu,** the guide led him astray; **perdre son temps,** to waste (one's) time; to fritter the time away; **p. du temps,** to lose time; **faire qch. sans p. de temps,** to do sth. without losing any time; to lose no time in doing sth.; **il ne perd pas de temps,** he doesn't waste any time; he doesn't let the grass grow under his feet; **il n'y a pas de temps, un instant, à p.,** there is no time to lose, to be lost; **p. du terrain,** to lose ground; (*of swimmer, etc.*) **p. pied, terre, fond,** to get out of one's depth; **p. qn, qch., de vue,** to lose sight of s.o., sth.; **ne perdez pas de vue que . . .,** bear in mind that . . .; **p. une occasion,** to miss (i) an opportunity, (ii) a bargain; *Ven:* (*of stag*) **p. son bois,** to lose its horns; (*b*) **p. cent hommes prisonniers,** to lose a hundred men taken prisoner. **3.** *abs.* (*a*) **vous n'y perdrez pas,** you won't lose, won't be out of pocket, by it; **savoir, ne pas savoir, p.,** to be a good, bad, loser; (*b*) **la marée perd,** the tide is ebbing; (*c*) **fût qui perd,** cask that is leaking; leaking cask; (*d*) **le grain perd en vieillissant,** grain loses in value, deteriorates, with age; **p. dans l'estime de qn,** to fall in s.o.'s estimation; (*e*) *Nau:* to fall, to drop, astern; *Sp: etc:* **p. (sur ses concurrents),** to fall behind, to drop behind.

se perdre. 1. to be lost; (*a*) **le navire se perdit corps et biens,** the ship was lost with all hands; (*b*) **se p. dans la foule,** to vanish, disappear, lose oneself, in the crowd; **sa voix se perdit parmi les rires,** his voice was lost in the laughter; **le son alla se p. au loin,** the sound died away in the distance; **usage qui se perd,** custom that is disappearing, falling into disuse; **être perdu dans ses pensées,** to be wrapt, lost, in thought; **se p. dans les sables,** to peter out; (*c*) (*of mechanical power, etc.*) to be wasted, to run to waste; (*of liquid*) to leak away, to escape. **2.** to lose one's way; **il s'est perdu dans le bois,** he got lost in the wood; *F:* **ma tête s'y perd, je m'y perds,** I can't make head or tail of it, I'm all at sea; **se p. en conjectures,** to be lost in conjecture.

perdreau, -eaux [pɛrdro], *s.m.* young partridge, partridge poult; *Cu:* partridge.
perdrigon [pɛrdrigɔ̃], *s.m. Hort:* perdrigon (plum).
perdrix [pɛrdri], *s.f.* partridge; **p. grise,** common, grey, partridge; *U.S:* Hungarian partridge; **p. rouge,** red-legged partridge; **p. bartavelle,** Greek partridge; **p. gambra, p. de Barbarie,** Barbary partridge; **p. blanche, p. de neige,** ptarmigan; **p. de mer,** pratincole; **compagnie de p.,** covey of partridges.
perdu [pɛrdy], *a.* **1.** ruined; **nous sommes perdus,** we are ruined, *F:* done for; **p. de dettes,** up to the eyes, neck, in debt; **ma robe est perdue,** my dress is ruined; **p. de rhumatisme(s),** martyr to rheumatism, crippled with rheumatism; **femme perdue,** fallen woman; **âme perdue,** lost soul; *s.* **crier comme un p.,** to shout like a madman. **2.** lost; **peine perdue,** wasted, lost, labour; **ce furent des efforts perdus,** all my efforts went for nothing; **à mes moments perdus, à mes heures perdues,** in my spare time; in my idle moments; **sentinelle perdue,** advanced sentry; **petit trou p.,** little out-of-the-way place; **il habite un trou p.,** he lives at the back of beyond; **p. dans ses pensées,** lost, wrapt, in thought; **j'ai la tête perdue,** I'm utterly bewildered, completely at a loss; **ne lui en dites pas davantage, ce sont paroles perdues,** don't say any more to him about it, you're wasting your breath; **c'est peine perdue,** it's a waste of time, of effort; *Com:* **emballage p.,** non-returnable packing; *Typ:* **illustrations à marges perdues, à fond p.,** bled-off illustrations; *Fin:* **argent placé à fonds p.,** money invested in an annuity; *Mec:* **mouvement p.,** idle motion. **3. reprise perdue,** invisible darn; **cheville à tête perdue,** pin with a sunk head; *Const:* **pierre perdue,** sunk stone, stone embedded in mortar or cement. **4.** *adv.phr.* **à corps p.,** without restraint, recklessly; **se jeter à corps p. dans la mêlée,** to hurl oneself into the fray; **tirer à coup p.,** to fire at random.
père [pɛːr], *s.m.* **1.** (*a*) father, *Breed:* sire; **de p. en fils,** from father to son, from generation to generation; **ils étaient médecins de p. en fils,** for generations there had been a doctor in the family; **ils dirigent l'entreprise de p. en fils depuis un siècle,** they have been directors of the firm, father and son, for a hundred years; *Prov:* **tel p. tel fils,** like father like son; **M. Martin p.,** Mr Martin senior; **p. de famille,** family man; *Jur:* **bon p. de famille,** prudent administrator (of family wealth); **valeurs de p. de famille,** gilt-edged securities; *Aut:* **conduire en p. de famille,** to bumble along; *Th:* **p. noble,** heavy father; **nos pères,** our forefathers, our ancestors; *F: O:* **petit p.,** daddy; **le p. Jean,** old John; (*b*) **p. nourricier,** foster father. **2.** *Ecc:* father; (*a*) **les Pères de l'Église,** the Fathers (of the Church); **le Saint-Père,** the Holy Father, the Pope; **p. spirituel,** (i) *Ecc:* father confessor; (ii) spiritual father; mentor; **les pères capucins,** the Capuchin fathers; **un p. carme,** a Carmelite father; **le (Révérend) P. X,** Father X; (*b*) **notre P. qui êtes aux cieux,** our Father which, who, art in heaven. **3.** *Theol:* **le Père, le Fils et le Saint-Esprit,** the Father, the Son, and the Holy Ghost. **4.** *Rom. Ant:* **les pères conscrits,** the Conscript Fathers.
Pérée [pere], *Pr.n.f. A.Geog:* Peraea.
pérégrin [peregrɛ̃], *s.m. Rom.Ant:* peregrine, alien.
pérégrinateur, -trice [peregrinatœːr, -tris], *s.* (*rare*) peregrinator.
pérégrination [peregrinasjɔ̃], *s.f.* peregrination.
pérégriner [peregrine], *v.i. A:* (*a*) to peregrinate; (*b*) to amble along.
pérégrinité [peregrinite], *s.f. A.Jur:* peregrinity.
Père-Lachaise (le) [ləpɛrlaʃɛːz], *Pr.n.m.* famous Paris cemetery.
péremption [perɑ̃psjɔ̃], *s.f. Jur:* time limitation (in a suit); **p. d'instance,** extinction of an action (no step having been taken within the statutory time); **dévolu par p.,** lapsed.
péremptoire [perɑ̃ptwaːr], *a.* **1.** (*a*) peremptory (tone); (*b*) **argument p.,** unanswerable, decisive, argument. **2.** *Jur:* **délai p.,** strict time limit; **exception p.,** peremptory exception.
péremptoirement [perɑ̃ptwarmɑ̃], *adv.* peremptorily.
pérennant [perɛn(n)ɑ̃], *a. Bot:* perennating (rhizome, etc.).
pérenne [perɛn], *a.* perennial; **source p.,** permanent spring.
pérennibranche [perɛn(n)ibrɑ̃ːʃ], *Rept:* **1.** *a.* perennibranch, perennibranchiate. **2.** *s.m.pl.* **pérennibranches,** Perennibranchiata, perennibranchiates, perennibranches.
pérenniser [perɛn(n)ize], *v.tr.* to prolong, to perennialize, to perpetuate.
pérennité [perɛn(n)ite], *s.f.* perenniality, everlastingness, perpetuity.
péréquation [perekwasjɔ̃], *s.f. Adm:* equalization (of taxes, salaries); *Rail:* **p. des prix,** standardizing of freight charges, of tariffs; **faire la p. des salaires,** to equalize wages.
perfectibilité [pɛrfɛktibilite], *s.f.* perfectibility.
perfectible [pɛrfɛktibl̩], *a.* perfectible, improvable.
perfectif, -ive [pɛrfɛktif, -iːv], *a. & s.m. Gram:* perfective.
perfection [pɛrfɛksjɔ̃], *s.f.* (*a*) perfection; **toucher à la p.,** to attain perfection; **à la p.,** *A:* **en p., dans la p., avec une rare p.,** to perfection, perfectly; with rare perfection; **avoir toutes les perfections,** to be perfect, faultless; **la p. même,** perfection itself; (*b*) *F:* **notre femme de ménage, c'est une p.,** our daily help's a treasure.
perfectionnement [pɛrfɛksjɔnmɑ̃], *s.m.* **1.** perfecting (of machine, method); improving; further training; **p. en cours d'emploi,** in-service training; **brevet de p.,** patent relating to improvements; *Sch:* **cours de p.,** refresher course. **2.** improvement; **apporter des perfectionnements à qch.,** to improve sth.
perfectionner [pɛrfɛksjɔne], *v.tr.* **1.** to perfect; to bring (sth.) to perfection. **2.** to improve (machine, method, one's style).
se perfectionner dans, en, qch., to improve one's knowledge of (language, sciences, etc.); **se p. en allemand,** to improve one's German.
perfectionneur, -euse [pɛrfɛksjɔnœːr, -øːz], *s. Ind:* perfecter, improver.
perfectionnisme [pɛrfɛksjɔnism], *s.m.* perfectionism.
perfectionniste [pɛrfɛksjɔnist], *a. & s.m. & f. Rel:* perfectionist.
perfeuillé [pɛrfœje], *a. Bot:* perfoliate.
perfide [pɛrfid]. **1.** *a.* treacherous (**envers,** to); perfidious; falsehearted (friend, etc.); false (promises, etc.); **vin p.,** treacherous wine. **2.** *s.* traitor, deceiver.
perfidement [pɛrfidmɑ̃], *adv.* perfidiously, treacherously, falsely.
perfidie [pɛrfidi], *s.f. Lit:* (*a*) treachery, perfidy, perfidiousness; false-heartedness; **avoir la p. de faire qch.,** to have the treachery to do sth.; (*b*) treacherous act, act of treachery, of perfidy; **faire une p. à qn,** to commit an act of treachery against s.o.; to play s.o. false.
perfo [pɛrfo], *s.f. F:* **1.** card punch. **2.** key-punch operator, *F:* punch girl.
perfolié [pɛrfɔlje], *a. Bot: Ent:* perfoliate.
perforage [pɛrfɔraːʒ], *s.m.* boring, drilling, perforation.
perforant [pɛrfɔrɑ̃], *a.* perforating, perforative; **balle perforante,** penetrating bullet; **obus p.,** armour-piercing shell; *Anat:* **muscle p.,** perforating muscle; **ulcère p.,** perforative ulcer; **insecte p.,** borer.
perforateur, -trice [pɛrfɔratœːr, -tris]. **1.** *a.* perforative, perforating; **pince perforatrice,** ticket punch. **2.** (*a*) *s.m.* perforator; drill; punch; **p. à papier,** paper punch; **p. à air comprimé,** percussion tool; **p. à charge creuse,** jet gun perforator; (*b*) *s.m. or f. Tg:* (tape) perforator; **p. de bande,** tape perforator; punch; **p. d'arrivée,** receiving perforator, punch; (*c*) *s.m. or f. Elcs:* (*for computers, etc.*) perforator; card punch; (key) punch; **p. (à alimentation) automatique,** automatic feed punch; **p. de bande,** tape punch; **p. de cartes,** card punch (unit); **p. à clavier,** keyboard perforator; **p. duplicateur de cartes,** duplicating card punch; **p. imprimeur de clavier,** printing keyboard perforator; **p. récapitulateur,** summary punch. **3.** *s.f.* **perforatrice:** (*a*) *Civ.E:* rock drill, driller, borer; drilling machine; **perforatrice à colonne,** column drill; **perforatrice d'avancement,** drifter drill; (*b*) *Cin:* perforating machine; (*c*) (*pers.*) puncher, key-punch operator, punch girl.
perforatif, -ive [pɛrfɔratif, -iːv], *a.* perforative; *s.m. Surg:* perforator (for bones); **trépan p.,** cephalotome.
perforation [pɛrfɔrasjɔ̃], *s.f.* **1.** (*a*) perforation, perforating; boring; drilling; **p. mécanique,** machine drilling; **appareil de p.,** borer; driller; (*b*) puncturing (of tyre, etc.); (*c*) *Elcs:* (*computers*) punching, perforation; **p. complète,** chad type perforation; **p. partielle,** chadless perforation; **p. hors-texte,** overpunching; **p. intercalée,** interstage punching; **p. multiple,** multiple punching; **p. normale,** normal stage punching; **perforations en grille,** lace punching; **atelier de p.,** punching room, section. **2.** (*a*) hole, puncture (in tyre, etc.); (*b*) *Cin:* perforation; (*c*) *Elcs:* (*computers*) perforation, punch, (code) hole; **p. d'entraînement,** feed hole, sprocket hole; **p. hors-texte,** overpunch; zone punch; (*d*) *Med:* perforation.
perforé [pɛrfɔre]. **1.** *a.* (*a*) *Anat:* **espaces perforés,** perforated spaces (of brain); (*b*) **carte perforée,** (i) punch card, tab(ulating) card; (ii) punched card; **machine à cartes perforées,** punched card machine; **bande perforée,** (i) music roll (of piano player); (ii) punched tape (of computer). **2.** *s.m.pl. Coel:* **perforés,** Perforata.
perforer [pɛrfɔre], *v.tr.* **1.** (*a*) to perforate; to bore (through), to drill (material); to punch (leather, etc.); (*b*) *Elcs:* (*computers*) (i) (*of machine*) to perforate (tape, etc.); to punch hole in (card); (ii) (*of pers.*) to key punch; **p. en série,** to gang punch. **2.** to puncture (tyre, etc.).
perforeur, -euse [pɛrfɔrœːr, -øːz]. **1.** *s.* card punch operator, puncher; *f.* card punch girl. **2.** *s.f.* **perforeuse,** perforator; card punch, key punch.
performance [pɛrfɔrmɑ̃ːs], *s.f.* **1.** (*a*) *Sp:* performance (in a race, etc.); (*b*) achievement, good performance; **accomplir une p.,** to perform well; to show up well; **c'est une p.!** that's quite sth.! **2.** *pl. Aut: Av:* **performances,** performance data; *Elcs:* (*computers*) **analyse des performances,** performance evaluation; **tableau comparatif des performances,** performance analysis.
perfusion [pɛrfyzjɔ̃], *s.f. Physiol:* perfusion.
Pergame [pɛrgam], *Pr.n.m. A.Geog:* Pergamum, Pergamos.
Pergaménien, -ienne [pɛrgamenjɛ̃, -jɛn], *a. & s. A: Geog:* Pergamenian, Pergamene.
pergamine [pɛrgamin], *s.f.* **papier p.,** artificial parchment.
pergélisol [pɛrʒelisɔl], *s.m. Geol:* permafrost, pergelisol.
pergola [pɛrgɔla], *s.f.,* **pergole** [pɛrgɔl], *s.f.* pergola.
Pergolèse [pɛrgɔlɛːz], *Pr.n.m. Mus.Hist:* Pergolesi, Pergolese.
péri[1] [peri], *s.m. & f.* (oriental) peri; genius; fairy.
péri[2], *a. Her:* (baton) couped.
péri- [peri], *pref.* peri-.
périadénite [periadenit], *s.f. Med:* periadenitis.
périanal, -aux [perianal, -o], *a. Anat:* perianal.
Périandre [perjɑ̃ːdr̥], *Pr.n.m. Gr.Hist:* Periander.
périanthe [perjɑ̃ːt], *s.m. Bot:* perianth.
périapte [perjapt], *s.m.* periapt, amulet.
périartérite [periarterit], *s.f. Med:* periarteritis.
périarthrite [periartrit], *s.f. Med:* periarthritis; **p. scapulo-humérale,** frozen shoulder.
périarticulaire [periartikylɛːr], *a. Anat:* periarticular.
périblaste [periblast], *s.m. Biol:* periblast.
périblastula [periblastyla], *s.f. Biol:* periblastula.
périblème [periblɛm], *s.m. Bot:* periblem.
péribole [peribɔl], *s.m. Arch:* peribolus, peribolos.
péricarde [perikard], *s.m. Anat:* pericardium.
péricardectomie [perikardɛktɔmi], *s.f. Surg:* pericardectomy.
péricardiotomie [perikardjɔtɔmi], *s.f. Surg:* pericardiotomy.
péricardique [perikardik], *a. Anat:* pericardial.
péricardite [perikardit], *s.f. Med:* pericarditis.
péricarpe [perikarp], *s.m. Bot:* pericarp.
péricarpial, -aux [perikarpjal, -o], **péricarpique** [perikarpik], *a. Bot:* pericarpial, pericarpic.
périchondre [perikɔ̃ːdr̥], *s.m. Anat:* perichondrium.
périchondrite [perikɔ̃drit], *s.f. Med:* perichondritis.
périclase [periklɑːz], *s.m. Miner:* periclase, periclasite.
Périclès [periklɛs], *Pr.n.m. Gr.Hist:* Pericles.
périclinal, -aux [periklinal, -o], *a. Geol:* periclinal.
péricline [periklin], *s.f. Miner:* pericline.
périclitant [periklitɑ̃], *a.* unsound. shaky (business, undertaking).
péricliter [periklite], *v.i.* (*of business, undertaking*) to be in danger, in jeopardy; **ses affaires périclitent,** his business is in a bad way; **faire p. une entreprise,** to jeopardize, endanger, an undertaking.
péricolite [perikɔlit], *s.f. Med:* pericolitis.
péricope [perikɔp], *s.f. Ecc:* pericope.
péricopides [perikɔpid], *s.m.pl. Ent:* Pericopidae.
péricrâne [perikrɑːn], *s.m. Anat:* pericranium.
péricrocote [perikrɔkɔt], *s.m. Orn:* pericrocotus, minivet.
péricycle [perisikl̩], *s.m. Bot:* pericycle.
péricystite [perisistit], *s.f. Med:* pericystitis.
périderme [peridɛrm], *s.m. Bot: Z:* periderm.
péridermique [peridɛrmik], *a. Nat.Hist:* peridermal, peridermic.

péridesme [peridɛsm], *s.m. Bot:* peridesm.

péridesmique [pɛridesmik], *a. Bot:* peridesmic.

péridinidés [peridinide], *s.m.pl. Biol:* Peridiniidae, peridinians.

péridiniens [peridinjɛ̃], *s.m.pl. Biol:* Peridinieae, peridinians.

péridinium [peridinjɔm], *s.m. Biol:* peridinium, peridinid.

péridium [peridjɔm], *s.m. Bot:* peridium.

péridot [perido], *s.m. Miner:* peridot, chrysolite, olivine.

péridotite [peridɔtit], *s.f. Miner:* peridotite.

périfolliculite [perifɔl(l)ikylit], *s.f. Med:* perifolliculitis.

périgée [periʒe], *s.m. Astr:* perigee; **la lune est à son p.;** *adj. O:* **la lune est périgée,** the moon is in perigee.

périglaciaire [periglasjɛːr], *a. Geog:* periglacial.

Périgord [perigɔːr], *Pr.n.m. Geog:* Perigord.

périgordien, -ienne [perigɔrdjɛ̃, -jɛn], *a. & s.m. Prehist:* Perigordian.

périgourdin, -ine [perigurdɛ̃, -in], *a. & s.* (native, inhabitant) of Périgord.

périgyne [periʒin], *a. Bot:* perigynous.

périhélie [perieli], *Astr:* **1.** *s.m.* perihelion. **2.** *a.* **planète p.,** planet in perihelion.

périhépatite [periepatit], *s.f. Med:* perihepatitis.

périjove [periʒɔːv], *s.m. Astr:* perijove.

péril [peril], *s.m.* peril, danger; risk, hazard; *Lit:* **se jeter dans le p.,** to rush into peril; to hazard one's life; **au p. de sa vie,** at the risk of one's life, in peril of one's life; **en p.,** in danger, in peril; **mettre qch. en p.,** to imperil, jeopardize, sth.; **territoire en p. d'invasion,** territory in danger of invasion; *Ins:* **p. de mer,** risk and peril of the seas; sea risk; **à ses risques et périls,** at one's own risk.

périlleusement [perijøzmɑ̃], *adv.* perilously.

périlleux, -euse [perijø, -øːz], *a.* perilous, hazardous, dangerous; **saut p.,** somersault.

périlogie [perilɔʒi], *s.f. Elcs:* (*computers*) software.

périlymphe [perilɛ̃ːf], *s.f. Anat:* perilymph.

périmé [perime], *a.* **1.** *Jur:* barred by limitation. **2.** out-of-date (coupon, etc.); expired (bill); (ticket) no longer valid; lapsed (money order, ticket, etc.); **méthode périmée,** out-of-date, old-fashioned method; method now superseded.

périmer [perime], *v.i. Jur:* to lapse, to become out of date; **laisser p. un droit,** to allow a right to lapse; to forfeit a right.

périmétral, -aux [perimetral, -o], *a.* peripheral, perimetric.

périmètre [perimɛtr̥], *s.m.* (*a*) *Geom:* perimeter, periphery; *Anthr:* **p. thoracique,** chest measurement; (*b*) area, sphere (of influence, of protection, etc.); *Adm:* **p. d'agglomération** = borough area, urban district (in which public services provided by the town are available); **p. de captage,** catchment area (of a well, within which pollution is forbidden); (*c*) *Opt:* (*instrument*) perimeter.

périmétrie [perimetri], *s.f. Opt:* perimetry.

périmétrique [perimetrik], *a.* perimetric, peripheral.

périmétrite [perimetrit], *s.f. Med:* perimetritis.

périmorphose [perimɔrfoːz], *s.f. Cryst:* perimorphism.

périmysium [perimizjɔm], *s.m. Anat:* perimysium.

périnatal, -als [perinatal], *a. Med:* perinatal.

périnéal, -aux [perineal, -o], *a. Anat: Surg:* perineal (hernia, etc.).

périnée [perine], *s.m. Anat:* perineum.

périnéoplastie [perineɔplasti], *s.f. Surg:* perineoplasty.

périnéorraphie [perineɔrafi], *s.f. Obst:* perineorrhaphy.

périnéotomie [perineɔtɔmi], *s.f. Surg:* perineotomy.

périnéphrétique [perinefretik], *a. Anat:* perinephric, perirenal.

périnéphrite [perinefrit], *s.f. Med:* perinephritis.

périnèvre [perinɛːvr̥], *s.m. Anat:* perineurium.

périnévrite [perinevrit], *s.f. Med:* perineuritis.

periodate [pɛrjɔdat], *s.m. Ch:* periodate.

période [perjɔd]. **1.** *s.f.* (*a*) period (of recurring phenomenon, *e.g.* of planet's revolution); *Geol:* period, cycle; *Nau:* **p. de roulis,** period of (ship's) rolling motion; *Ph:* **p. d'une onde,** period of a wave; **nombre de périodes par seconde,** frequency (of sound wave, of oscillation); *Mth:* **p. d'une fraction décimale,** repetend of a (recurring) decimal; **p. d'un seul chiffre,** single repetend; (*b*) **p. biologique,** biological half life; *Atom.Ph:* **p. radioactive,** half(-)life (period); (*c*) *Elcs:* (*computers*) **p. de balayage,** scan period; **p. d'extinction,** decay time; **p. de régénération,** regeneration period; **p. de taxation,** charging period; (*d*) *Med:* period (between recurring phases of an illness); (*e*) *Physiol:* monthly period, menstruation. **2.** *s.f.* period of time; age, era; **première p. de l'existence,** early stages of life; **longue p. de pluie, de beau temps,** long spell of rain, of fine weather; **je suis dans une p. de guignon,** I am having a run of bad luck; *Mil:* **p. de repos,** spell of rest in billets. **3.** *s.f.* (*a*) *Gram: Rh:* period, complete sentence; (*b*) *Mus:* phrase. **4.** *s.m.* (*a*) *Lit:* **le plus haut p. (de la gloire, de l'éloquence, etc.),** the highest point, pitch, degree, the height, acme (of glory, of eloquence, etc.); **le plus haut p. de son influence,** the zenith of his influence; (*b*) *A:* **le dernier p. (de la vie, etc.),** the last stage (of life, etc.).

périodemètre [perjɔdmɛtr̥], *s.m. Atom.Ph:* period meter.

périodicité [perjɔdisite], *s.f.* periodicity (of comet, etc.); (recurrence) frequency, interval; frequency of issue (of a publication); *Elcs:* (*computers*) **p. moyenne des révisions,** mean time between overhauls.

periodique [pɛrjɔdik], *a. Ch:* per-iodic.

périodique [perjɔdik]. **1.** *a.* (*a*) periodical, recurrent, recurring (at regular intervals); intermittent; cyclic; **fraction p.,** recurring, repeating, decimal; **fonction p.,** cyclic function; **erreur p.,** cyclic error; **fièvre p.,** recurrent fever; **feuille p.,** periodical publication; (*b*) *Astr: Lit: Mus:* periodic. **2.** *s.m.* periodical (publication).

périodiquement [perjɔdikmɑ̃], *adv.* periodically; at regular intervals.

périodonte [perjɔdɔ̃ːt], *s.m. Anat:* periodontium, periodontal tissue.

périodontite [perjɔdɔ̃tit], *s.f. Dent:* periodontitis.

periodure [pɛrjɔdyːr], *s.m. Ch:* periodide.

périœciens [perjesjɛ̃], *s.m.pl. Geog:* perioeci.

périœsophagien, -ienne [perjezɔfaʒjɛ̃, -jɛn], *a. Anat:* peri(o)esophageal.

périœsophagite [perjezɔfaʒit], *s.f. Med:* peri(o)esophagitis.

périopht(h)alme [perjɔftalm], *s.m. Ich:* mud skipper; (*genus*) Periophthalmus.

périople [perjɔpl̥], *s.m. Vet:* periople.

périoplique [perjɔplik], *a. Vet:* perioplic.

périoste [perjɔst], *s.m. Anat:* periosteum.

périostique [perjɔstik], **périosté** [perjɔste], **périostéal, -aux** [perjɔsteal, -o], *a. Anat:* periosteal.

périostite [perjɔstit], *s.f. Med:* periostitis.

periostose [perjɔstoːz], *s.f. Med:* periostosis.

périovulaire [perjɔvylɛːr], *a. Anat:* periovular.

péripate [peripat], *s.m. Ent:* peripatus.

péripatéticien, -ienne [peripatetisjɛ̃, -jɛn], *a. & s.,* **péripatétique** [peripatetik], *a.* (*a*) *A.Phil:* peripatetic; (*b*) *s.f. F:* **péripatéticienne,** prostitute, street walker.

péripatétisme [peripatetism], *s.m.* peripateticism.

péripétie [peripesi], *s.f.* **1.** (*a*) *Lit:* peripet(e)ia, peripety; (*b*) sudden change of fortune or situation (in novel, in life). **2.** *pl.* vicissitudes, ups and downs (of life); **après bien des péripéties,** after many mishaps, many adventures.

périphérie [periferi], *s.f.* **1.** (*a*) *Geom:* periphery; circumference; (*b*) **p. d'un colis,** girth of a parcel. **2.** outskirts (of town); **les quartiers de la p.,** the outlying districts.

périphérique [periferik]. **1.** *a.* peripheral, peripheric; **rues, quartiers, périphériques,** outlying streets, districts; **boulevard p.,** ring road; *Elcs:* (*computers*) **équipement, appareil, p.,** peripheral equipment, device. **2.** *s.m. Elcs:* (*computers*) peripheral; **tampon de p.,** peripheral buffer; **p. à mémoire tampon,** buffered peripheral; **transfert entre périphériques,** peripheral transfer.

périphlébite [periflebit], *s.f. Med:* periphlebitis.

périphrase [perifrɑːz], *s.f. Gram:* periphrasis, periphrase, circumlocution; **en, par, p.,** periphrastically.

périphraser [perifrɑze], *v.i.* to be loquacious, long-winded, prolix.

périphrastique [perifrastik], *a. Gram:* periphrastic (tense, etc.).

périplasme [periplasm], *s.m. Ent:* periplasm.

périple [peripl̥], *s.m.* (*a*) *A.Geog: Lit:* periplus; (*b*) (long) tour.

péripneumonie [peripnømɔni], *s.f. Vet:* contagious bovine pleuropneumonia.

péripneustique [peripnøstik], *a. Ent:* peripneustic.

périprocte [periprɔkt], *s.m. Echin:* periproct.

périprostatique [periprɔstatik], *a. Anat:* periprostatic.

périprostatite [periprɔstatit], *s.f. Med:* periprostatitis.

périptère [periptɛːr], *Arch:* **1.** *a.* peripteral. **2.** *s.m.* peripteros, periptery.

périr [periːr], *v.i.* (*the aux. is* **avoir**, *A: also* **être**) **1.** to perish, to die (unnaturally); to be destroyed; (*of ship*) to be wrecked, lost; **p. dans un incendie,** to die, perish, in a fire; **p. gelé,** to be frozen to death; **p. de sa propre main,** to die by one's own hand; **il périt un bon nombre de personnes,** many lives were lost; **faire p. qn,** to kill s.o.; to put s.o. to death; **faire p. qn sous le bâton,** to beat, cudgel, s.o. to death; **je péris de froid,** I'm perishing (with cold); *F:* I'm freezing t_ ..eath; **p. d'ennui,** to be bored to death; **empires qui ont péri,** empires that have decayed, fallen into ruin; **son nom ne périra pas,** his name will live (on); **p. victime de son devoir,** to fall a victim to duty; **p. victime d'un accident,** to die as a result of an accident. **2.** *Jur:* to lapse.

périrectite [perirɛktit], *s.f. Med:* perirectitis.

périsarc, périsarque [perizark], *s.m. Z:* perisarc.

périsciens [peris(s)jɛ̃], *s.m.pl. Geog:* periscii.

périscolaire [periskɔlɛːr], *a.* extra-curricular (activities).

périscope [periskɔp], *s.m. Mil: Navy: etc:* periscope.

périscopique [periskɔpik], *a.* periscopic (lens, view); (*of submarine*) **en plongée p.,** at periscope depth.

périsigmoïdite [perisigmɔidit], *s.f. Med:* perisigmoiditis.

périspermatique [perispɛrmatik], *a. Bot:* perispermal, perispermic.

périsperme [perispɛrm], *s.m. Bot:* perisperm.

périsplénite [perisplenit], *s.f. Med:* perisplenitis.

périspomène [perispɔmɛn], *a. & s.m. Gr.Gram:* perispomenon, perispome.

périsporiacées [perispɔrjase], *s.f.pl. Fung:* Perisporiaceae.

périsprit [perispri], *s.m. Psychics:* astral body.

périssable [perisabl̥], *a.* perishable.

périssodactyle [perisɔdaktil], *Z:* **1.** *a.* perissodactyl(lous), perissodactylate. **2.** *s.m.* perissodactyl; *pl.* **périssodactyles,** Perissodactyla.

périssoire [periswaːr], *s.f.* (single-seater river) canoe; **faire de la p.,** to go (in for) canoeing; to canoe.

périssologie [perisɔlɔʒi], *s.f. Ling:* pleonasm.

péristaltique [peristaltik], *a. Physiol:* peristaltic, vermicular (motion).

péristaltisme [peristaltism], *s.m. Physiol:* peristalsis.

péristère [peristɛːr], *s.m. Ecc:* (eucharistic) dove.

péristérite [peristerit], *s.f. Miner:* peristerite.

péristole [peristɔl], *s.f. Physiol:* peristaltic motion (of the intestines); peristole.

péristomal, -aux [peristɔmal, -o], *a. Nat.Hist:* peristom(i)al.

péristome [peristoːm], *s.m. Nat.Hist:* peristome, peristomium.

péristyle [peristil], *Arch:* **1.** *a.* peristylar (columniation, etc.). **2.** *s.m.* peristyle.

périsystole [perisistɔl], *s.f. Physiol:* perisystole.

péritectique [peritɛktik], *a.* peritectic.

périthèce [peritɛs], *s.m. Fung:* perithecium.

périthoracique [peritɔrasik], *a. Anat:* perithoracic.

péritoine [peritwan], *s.m. Anat:* peritoneum.

péritomie [peritɔmi], *s.f.* peritomy, circumcision.

péritonéal, -aux [peritɔneal, -o], *a. Anat:* peritoneal.

péritonéoscopie [peritɔneɔskɔpi], *s.f. Med:* peritoneoscopy.

péritonite [peritɔnit], *s.f. Med:* peritonitis.

péritrachéen, -éenne [peritrakeɛ̃, -eɛn], *a. Ent:* peritracheal.

péritriches [peritriʃ], *s.m.pl. Prot:* Peritricha, peritrichans.

péritrophique [peritrɔfik], *a. Ent:* peritrophic (membrane).

pérityphlite [peritiflit], *s.f. Med:* perityphlitis.

périurétérite [periyreterit], *s.f. Med:* periureteritis.

périutérin [periyterɛ̃], *a. Anat:* periuterine.

périvasculaire [perivaskylɛːr], *a. Anat:* perivascular.

périviscéral, -aux [periviseral, -o], *a. Anat:* perivisceral.

périviscérite [periviserit], *s.f. Med:* perivisceritis.

perlaire [pɛrlɛːr], *a.* nacr(e)ous, pearly.

perlasse [pɛrlas], *s.f.* pearl ash, crude carbonate of potash.

perle [pɛrl], *s.f.* **1.** (*a*) pearl; **p. fine,** real pearl; **p. de culture,** cultured pearl; **fil de perles,** string of pearls; **nacre de p.,** mother-of-pearl; **c'est une p. à sa couronne,** it's a feather in his cap; **jeter des perles devant les pourceaux,** to cast pearls before swine; **ma nouvelle bonne est une p.,** my new maid is a treasure; **c'est la p. des bonnes,** she's a treasure (of a maid); **c'est la p. des maris,** he is a jewel, a gem, of a husband; blanc de p., poudre de p., pearl white, pearl powder; *a.inv.* gants gris p., pearl-grey gloves; (*b*) *Sch:* gem, howler; *F:* c'est une p., it's a peach; (*c*) *P:* lâcher une p., to fart; (*d*) *Bot: F:* herbe aux perles, gromwell. 2. (*a*) bead (of glass, metal, etc.); (*b*) perles de rosée, beads of dew; *Poet:* les perles de l'aurore, the morning dew. 3. *Pharm:* pearl (capsule). 4. *Typ:* pearl, diamond; five-point type. 5. *Ent:* water fly.

perlé [pɛrle], *a.* 1. (*a*) resembling pearls; pearly (teeth, etc.); *El:* accumulateur p., milky accumulator; riz p., husked rice; orge p., pearl barley; (*b*) set with pearls, pearled; (*c*) beaded; (*d*) rires perlés, ripples of laughter, rippling laughter. 2. (*of needlework, musical execution, etc.*) tastefully, exquisitely, done; finished; *O: F:* c'est p., it's perfect. 3. corded (cotton); laine perlée, crochet wool.

perlèche [pɛrlɛʃ], *s.f. Med:* angular stomatitis.

perler [pɛrle]. 1. *v.tr.* (*a*) to pearl; (i) to set (sth.) with pearls; (ii) to make (sth.) like pearls; (*b*) to pearl (barley); to husk (rice); (*c*) to twice boil (sugar); (*d*) to execute (piece of embroidery, of music) to perfection; *A:* p. ses phrases, to round off one's sentences; *Mus:* p. une roulade, to sing a run with every note clear cut. 2. *v.i.* (*a*) (*of tears, sweat, etc.*) to form in beads; la sueur perlait sur son front, beads of perspiration stood out on his forehead; (*b*) (*of sugar*) to bead.

perleur, -euse [pɛrlœːr, -øːz], *a. & s.f.* moulin p., *s.f.* perleuse, rice husker, huller.

perlides [pɛrlid], *s.m.pl. Ent:* Perlidae, stone flies.

perlier, -ière [pɛrlje, -jɛːr], *a.* containing, producing, pearls; pearl-bearing; huître perlière, pearl oyster; bateau p., pearler; mulette perlière, pearl mussel.

perlimpinpin [pɛrlɛ̃pɛ̃pɛ̃], *s.m.* 1. poudre de p., quack powder, wonder-working powder; *F:* tout ça, c'est de la poudre de p., that's all my eye, that's all bunkum. 2. *F:* un p. (de qch.), a dash, a soupçon, (of sth.).

perlite [pɛrlit], *s.f.* 1. *Miner:* perlite. 2. *Metall:* pearlite.

perlitique [pɛrlitik], *a. Geol:* perlitic.

perloïdes [pɛrlɔid], *s.m.pl. Ent:* Plecoptera, stone flies.

perloir [pɛrlwaːr], *s.m. Metalw:* perloir.

perlon [pɛrlɔ̃], *s.m. Ich:* seven gills.

perlot [pɛrlo], *s.m. P:* tobacco, baccy.

perlure [pɛrlyːr], *s.f. Ven:* pearl (of antler).

permagel [pɛrmaʒɛl], *s.m. Geol:* permafrost, pergelisol.

Permalloy [pɛrmalɔi], *s.m. Metall: R.t.m:* Permalloy.

permanence [pɛrmanɑ̃ːs], *s.f.* 1. permanence; p. d'une race, continued existence of a race; assemblée en p., permanent assembly; l'assemblée se déclara en p., the assembly declared that it would sit until the conclusion of the business; être attaché en p. à une maison, to be permanently attached to a firm. 2. building, room, etc., always open to the public; p. électorale, (parliamentary candidate's) committee rooms; p. de police, police station open night and day; p. nocturne, all-night service; la p. comprend trois employés, la p. est assurée par trois employés, a skeleton staff of three people is always on duty; être de p., to be on duty, on call. 3. *Sch:* heure de p., prep. period.

permanencier, -ière [pɛrmanɑ̃sje, -jɛːr], *s.* duty officer, engineer, etc.

permanent [pɛrmanɑ̃]. 1. *a.* permanent (court, etc.); standing (order, committee); abiding (peace); l'armée permanente, the standing, regular, army; d'une façon permanente, permanently; *Cin:* spectacle p., *s.m.* permanent, continuous performance; *Ph:* aimant p., permanent magnet; *Dressm:* pli p., permanent pleat. 2. *s.m.* permanent representative, agent, etc. 3. *s.f. Hairdr:* permanente, permanent wave, *F:* perm; permanente chez soi, home perm.

permanenter [pɛrmanɑ̃te], *v.tr. F: Hairdr:* to perm.

permanganate [pɛrmɑ̃ganat], *s.m. Ch:* permanganate; p. de potassium, potassium permanganate, permanganate of potash.

permanganique [pɛrmɑ̃ganik], *a. Ch:* permanganic.

perme [pɛrm], *s.f.* (= PERMISSION) *Mil: P:* 1. leave. 2. pass.

perméabilimètre [pɛrmeabilimɛtr̥], *s.m.* permeameter.

perméabilité [pɛrmeabilite], *s.f.* permeability, perviousness; *Ph:* p. à faible aimantation, permeability under low magnetizing.

perméable [pɛrmeabl̥], *a.* 1. permeable, pervious (à, to); *Cin:* écran p. au son, sound-porous screen. 2. (*a*) sensitive, susceptible (à, to); (*b*) influenceable.

perméamètre [pɛrmeamɛtr̥], *s.m. Ph: Geol:* permeameter.

perméance [pɛrmeɑ̃ːs], *s.f. Magn:* permeance, permeation.

perméation [pɛrmeasjɔ̃], *s.f. Med:* permeation.

permettre [pɛrmɛtr̥], *v.tr.* (*conj. like* METTRE) to permit, allow; ici la chasse n'est pas permise, shooting is not allowed, not permitted, here; p. qch. à qn, to allow s.o. sth.; on ne me permet pas le vin, I am not allowed wine; p. à qn de faire qch., to allow s.o. to do sth.; to let s.o. do sth.; to give s.o. leave to do sth.; *Lit:* permettez-moi de vous présenter mon frère, let me introduce my brother; mon honneur ne me permettrait pas de . . ., it would not be consistent with my honour to . . .; cet héritage lui permit de prendre sa retraite, this legacy enabled him, made it possible for him, to retire; mes moyens ne me le permettent pas, I cannot afford it; les climats froids ne permettent pas la culture de la vigne, the vine cannot be grown in cold climates; qu'il me soit permis de . . ., I beg to . . .; may I . . .? est-il permis d'entrer? may I come in? s'il est permis de s'exprimer ainsi, if I, we, may say so; permis à vous de ne pas me croire, you are at liberty, are free, to believe me or not; permis à vous de rire! it's all right for you to laugh! il se croit tout permis, he thinks he can do anything he likes; he thinks he's above the law; il n'est pas permis à tout le monde de . . ., not everyone can, is able to . . .; not everyone is capable of . . .; permettez-moi de vous dire, que je vous dise . . ., may I be allowed to say that . . .; excuse me, but . . .; permettez! excuse me! not so fast! vous permettez? may I? si Dieu le permet, God willing; si le temps le permet, weather permitting; dès que les circonstances le permettront, as soon as circumstances allow; cela ne permet pas de doute, there's no doubt about it; se p. un cigare, un verre de vin, to indulge in, to allow oneself, a cigar, a glass of wine; il se permet bien des choses, he takes a good many liberties; he takes a good, great, deal upon himself.

se permettre, se p. de faire qch., to take the liberty of doing sth.; to venture to do sth.; je me permets d'attirer votre attention sur . . ., I venture to draw, take the liberty of drawing, your attention to . . .; je me permettrai de vous faire observer que . . ., allow me to observe that . . .; je me permettrai de venir vous voir demain, I will take the liberty of calling on you tomorrow; puis-je me p. de vous offrir une cigarette? may I offer you a cigarette?

permien, -ienne [pɛrmjɛ̃, -jɛn], *a. & s.m. Geol:* Permian.

permis [pɛrmi]. 1. *a.* allowed, permitted; lawful; legitimate; allowable, permissible. 2. *s.m. Adm:* permit; licence; p. de chasse, shooting licence; game licence; p. de port d'arme, gun licence; p. de séjour (pour des étrangers) = certificate of registration; p. d'inhumer, permission to dispose of a body; p. de construire, de bâtir, building licence; *Aut:* p. (de conduire), driving licence; p. transports en commun, licence to drive a public service vehicle; p. poids lourds, heavy goods vehicle licence; p. de circulation, (i) car licence; (ii) *Rail:* free pass; passer son p. de conduire, to take one's driving test; *Min:* p. de recherche, prospecting licence; p. d'exploitation, mining permit, concession; *Cust:* p. de chargement, de déchargement, loading permit; discharging permit; p. d'entrée, clearance inwards; p. de sortie, clearance outwards.

permissif, -ive [pɛrmisif, -iːv], *a.* (*a*) *Rail:* bloc p., permissive blocking; (*b*) permissive (attitude, etc.).

permission [pɛrmisjɔ̃], *s.f.* (*a*) permission, leave; demander, donner, la p. de faire qch., to ask, give, permission to do sth.; accorder à qn la p. de . . ., to grant s.o. leave to . . .; agir sans la p. de ses supérieurs, to act without the permission, authority, of one's superiors; il n'a pas même demandé la p., he didn't even ask permission; p. pleine et entière de circuler, full permission to come and go; avec la gracieuse p. de . . ., by courtesy of . . .; avec votre p., if I may say so; I'm sorry, excuse me, but . . .; avec votre p. je dirai que c'est un franc crétin, if you'll excuse the expression, he's a bloody fool; *Jur:* p. de construire, building permission; p. de voirie, permission to occupy the public highway; (*b*) *Mil: etc:* leave (of absence); (*less than 24 hours*) pass; p. supplémentaire, special leave; p. exceptionnelle, emergency leave, pass; p. de convalescence, sick leave; p. pour affaires de famille, compassionate leave; p. permanente, permanent pass; *Navy:* p. de terre, d'aller à terre, liberty ticket; en p., (i) on leave; (ii) on pass; demander une p., to apply for leave; feuille, titre, de p., (i) *Mil:* pass for leave; (ii) *Navy:* liberty ticket; toutes les permissions sont suspendues, all leave is stopped, is cancelled; il s'est marié pendant sa p., he got married while on leave.

permissionnaire [pɛrmisjɔnɛːr], *s.m.* 1. person possessing a permit; licence holder. 2. *Mil: etc:* man on pass, on leave; *Navy:* liberty man; liste des permissionnaires, liberty list; cahier des permissionnaires, leave book; rappel des permissionnaires, recall of military personnel on leave; *a.* officier p., officer on leave.

permissivité [pɛrmisivite], *s.f.* permissiveness.

permittivité [pɛrmitivite], *s.f. El:* permittivity, dielectric constant.

permo-carbonifère [pɛrmɔkarbɔnifɛːr], *a. & s.m. Geol:* Permocarboniferous; *pl. permo-carbonifères.*

permonosulfurique [pɛrmɔnɔsylfyrik], *a. Ch:* permonosulphuric.

permutabilité [pɛrmytabilite], *s.f.* permutability, interchangeability.

permutable [pɛrmytabl̥], *a.* permutable, interchangeable.

permutant, -ante [pɛrmytɑ̃, -ɑ̃ːt], *s.* exchanger, one who exchanges (posts, etc.) with s.o.; fonctionnaire cherchant un p., civil servant seeking an exchange.

permutation [pɛrmytasjɔ̃], *s.f.* 1. exchange of posts; *Mil:* transfer; prendre un nouveau poste par p., to exchange into a new post; p. pour convenance personnelle, voluntary transfer, transfer at one's own request. 2. *Mth: etc:* permutation; transposition (of figures, letters); *Mth:* permutations de n objets r à r, permutations of n things r at a time (nPr). 3. *Ling:* metathesis.

permutatrice [pɛrmytatris], *s.f. El:* rectifying commutator; rectifier (of alternating current).

permuter [pɛrmyte], *v.tr.* 1. (*a*) *O:* to exchange (post) (avec qn, with s.o.); *abs.* to exchange posts (with colleague); (*b*) *El:* to change over (by switching). 2. *Mth: etc:* to permute.

Pernambouc [pɛrnɑ̃buk], (*a*) *Pr.n. Geog:* Pernambuco; (*b*) *s.m. Bot:* Pernambuco wood.

pernette [pɛrnɛt], *s.f. Sw.Fr:* ladybird.

pernettya [pɛrnetija], *s.m. Bot:* pernettya.

pernicieusement [pɛrnisjøzmɑ̃], *adv.* perniciously.

pernicieux, -ieuse [pɛrnisjø, -jøːz], *a.* pernicious, injurious, harmful; les effets p. de . . ., the ill effects of . . .; influence pernicieuse, pernicious influence; anémie pernicieuse, pernicious anaemia.

perniciosité [pɛrnisjozite], *s.f. Med:* pernicious nature (of disease).

pernion [pɛrnjɔ̃], *s.m. Med:* pernio, chilblain.

pernitrique [pɛrnitrik], *a. Ch:* pernitric.

peroba [pɛrɔba], *s.m.* p. jaune, ipé peroba; p. rose, peroba rosa.

pérodictique [perɔdiktik], *s.m. Z:* potto, sloth (monkey).

pérognathe [perɔgnat], *s.m. Z:* pocket mouse, (*genus*) Perognathus.

péromysque [perɔmisk], *s.m. Z:* white-footed mouse; (*genus*) Peromyscus.

péroné [perɔne], *s.m. Anat:* fibula.

péronéo-tibial, -aux [perɔneɔtibjal, -o], *a. Anat:* peroneotibial.

péronier, -ière [perɔnje, -jɛːr], *Anat:* 1. *a.* peroneal (artery, etc.). 2. *s.m.* peroneus.

péronisme [perɔnism], *s.m. Pol:* Peronism.

péronnais, -aise [perɔnɛ, -ɛːz], *a. & s. Geog:* (native, inhabitant) of Péronne.

péronnelle [perɔnɛl], *s.f. F:* silly half-wit (of a girl).

péronospora [perɔnɔspɔra], *s.m. Fung:* peronospora.

péronosporacées [perɔnɔspɔrase], *s.f.pl. Fung:* Peronosporaceae.

péronosporales [perɔnɔspɔral], *s.f.pl. Fung:* Peronosporales.

péronosporées [perɔnɔspɔre], *s.f.pl. Fung:* Peronosporaceae.

péroraison [perɔrɛzɔ̃], *s.f.* peroration.

pérorer [perɔre], *v.i.* to hold forth; to speechify spout, orate.

péroreur, -euse [perɔrœːr, -øːz], *s.* speechifier, *F:* spouter.

per os [pɛrɔs], *adv.phr. Med:* administration p. os, peroral administration, administration per os.

pérose [peroːz], *s.f. Vet:* perosis.

pérote [perɔt], *a. & s. Geog:* (native, inhabitant) of Pera (quarter of Istanbul).

Pérou (le) [ləperu], *Pr.n.m. Geog:* Peru; *F:* **gagner le P.**, to make a big fortune; **ce n'est pas le P.**, it's no great catch, it is not highly paid; *Pharm:* **écorce du P.**, Peruvian bark; **baume du P.**, balsam of Peru.

Pérouse [peru:z], *Pr.n.f. Geog:* Perugia; **lac de P.**, lake Trasimene.

perowskite, perovskite [perɔvskit], *s.f. Miner:* perovskite.

peroxyacide [perɔksiasid], *s.m. Ch:* peroxy acid.

peroxydase [perɔksida:z], *s.f. Bio-Ch:* peroxidase.

peroxydation [perɔksidasjɔ̃], *s.f. Ch:* peroxidation.

peroxyde [perɔksid], *s.m. Ch:* peroxide; **p. de manganèse**, manganese peroxide.

peroxyder [perɔkside], *v.tr. Ch:* to peroxidize.

peroxysel [perɔksisel], *s.m. Ch:* peroxy salt.

perpendiculaire [perpɑ̃dikylɛ:r]. **1.** *a.* (*a*) *Geom: etc:* perpendicular (**à, sur,** to); plumb, upright; (*b*) *Arch:* (*in England XIVth-XVth c.*) perpendicular (style); (*c*) **l'écriture des Chinois est p.**, the Chinese write vertically. **2.** *s.f.* (*a*) **abaisser une p.**, to drop, draw, a perpendicular (**à, sur,** to); *Nau:* **sur la p. du vent**, with the wind abeam; *N.Arch:* **longueur entre perpendiculaires**, length between perpendiculars; (*b*) *Surv:* offset.

perpendiculairement [perpɑ̃dikylɛrmɑ̃], *adv.* perpendicularly; sheer.

perpendicularité [perpɑ̃dikylarite], *s.f.* perpendicularity.

perpète, perpette (à) [aperpɛt], *adv.phr. P:* for ever; for life; **condamné à p.**, sentenced for life, given a lifer; **jusqu'à p.**, till the cows come home.

perpétration [perpetrasjɔ̃], *s.f.* perpetration.

perpétrer [perpetre], *v.tr.* (**je perpètre, n. perpétrons; je perpétrerai**) to perpetrate (crime, etc.).

perpétuation [perpetɥasjɔ̃], *s.f.* perpetuation (of the species, etc.).

Perpétue [perpety], *Pr.n.f. Rel.H:* Perpetua.

perpétuel, -elle [perpetɥɛl], *a.* (*a*) perpetual; everlasting; **calendrier p.**, perpetual calendar; **secrétaire p. de l'Académie française**, perpetual secretary to the French Academy; **rente perpétuelle, constituée en p.**, rent in perpetuity; perpetuity; perpetual annuity; **le mouvement p.**, perpetual motion; (*b*) constant, endless (strife, chatter); never-ending; **commentaire p.**, running commentary; **perpétuelles récriminations**, constant recriminations; **de perpétuelles difficultés d'argent**, never-ending, constant, financial difficulties; **sa réussite est un miracle p.**, his success remains a perpetual miracle.

perpétuellement [perpetɥɛlmɑ̃], *adv.* (*a*) perpetually, everlastingly; **l'âme vivante, p. changeante**, the living soul, for ever changing; **tous les animaux sont p. en guerre**, all animals are perpetually in a state of war; (*b*) constantly; **opinions qui oscillent p.**, constantly changing opinions; **assemblée p. délibérante**, permanent assembly; **la maison est p. en réparations**, the house is constantly, always, under repair; **il arrive p. en retard**, he's always late; he's never on time.

perpétuer [perpetɥe], *v.tr.* to perpetuate; **p. l'espèce**, to perpetuate the species; **il désirait un fils pour p. son nom**, he wanted a son to carry on his name; **p. le souvenir de qn**, to keep s.o.'s memory alive; **p. une tradition ancienne**, to keep up an ancient tradition; **p. un abus**, to perpetuate an abuse.

se perpétuer, to remain, survive; to become established; **espèces qui se perpétuent**, species that survive; **usage qui se perpétue**, custom that has become established; **se p. dans son œuvre**, to live on in one's work; **se p. dans une charge**, to remain indefinitely in an office.

perpétuité [perpetɥite], *s.f.* perpetuity; endlessness; **à p.**, in perpetuity, for ever; **travaux forcés à p.**, penal servitude for life; *Adm:* **concession à p.**, grant (of a grave) in perpetuity.

perpignan [perpiɲɑ̃], *s.m.* **1.** *Bot:* nettle tree. **2.** (nettle tree) stock, handle (of whip).

perpignanais, -aise [perpiɲanɛ, -ɛ:z], *a. & s. Geog:* (native, inhabitant) of Perpignan.

perplexe [perplɛks], *a.* **1.** perplexed, puzzled; embarrassed (as to choice). **2.** *A:* perplexing (situation).

perplexité [perplɛksite], *s.f.* perplexity; **saisi de p.**, perplexed.

perquisiteur, -trice [perkizitœ:r, -tris]. **1.** *s.m. Jur:* searcher (in virtue of search warrant). **2.** *a.* searching (look, etc.).

perquisition [perkizisjɔ̃], *s.f. Jur:* thorough search or inquiry; **p. domiciliaire**, searching of a house; house search; **mandat de p.**, search warrant; **faire une p. chez qn**, to search s.o.'s premises.

perquisitionner [perkizisjɔne], *v.i. Jur:* to make, conduct, a search (of premises, etc.); **p. dans une maison, au domicile de qn**, to search a house.

perquisitionneur [perkizisjɔnœ:r], *s.m. Jur:* searcher (in virtue of search warrant).

perrayeur [perajœ:r], *s.m.* (slate) quarryman, slateman.

perré [pere], *s.m. Civ.E:* stone pitching, facing (of road, embankment); dry wall.

Perrette [perɛt], *Pr.n.f.* Perrette; **boîte à P.**, (i) *A:* money-box, money laid by; (ii) secret funds (of an association).

perreyer [perɛje], *v.tr. Civ.E:* to pitch (road, embankment) (with pebbles).

perrhénate [perenat], *s.m. Ch:* perrhenate.

perrhénique [perenik], *a. Ch:* perrhenic.

perrier [perje], *s.m.* quarryman (in slate quarry).

perrière [perjɛ:r], *s.f.* **1.** (*a*) stone quarry; (*b*) (*in Anjou*) slate quarry. **2.** *A.Arms:* mangonel, perrier.

perron [perɔ̃], *s.m.* **1.** *Arch:* (flight of) steps (leading to building); perron; *U.S:* stoop. **2.** *Rail:* **p. de chargement**, loading platform.

perroquet [perɔkɛ], *s.m.* **1.** (*a*) *Orn:* parrot; **p. jacko**, (West African) grey parrot; **p. à gros bec**, great-billed parakeet; **p. de la Nouvelle-Zélande**, (i) kaka; (ii) kea; **p. de mer**, puffin; **bâton, échelle, de p.**, (i) parrot's perch; (ii) *F:* tall, narrow house; (*b*) *F:* (*pers.*) parrot; (*c*) *Ich:* **p. de mer**, parrot fish, scarus; **p. (des coraux)**, pudding wife; (*d*) *F:* (i) absinthe; (ii) pastis with mint; *P: A:* **étrangler un p.**, to swill down a glass of absinthe.

perruche [peryʃ, pe-], *s.f.* **1.** *Orn:* (*a*) parakeet, small (long-tailed) parrot; (*b*) hen parrot; (*c*) **p. inséparable**, lovebird; **p. ondulée**, budgerigar; (*d*) *F:* garrulous woman. **2.** *Nau:* mizzen topgallant sail.

perruque [peryk, pe-], *s.f.* (*a*) wig; **p. de théâtre**, theatrical wig; *A:* **p. à marteaux**, bob wig; **p. à nœuds**, tie wig; **p. à bourse**, bag wig; **tête à p.**, barber's block; *F: O:* **tête à p., vieille p.**, old fogey, old fossil; (*b*) *Bot:* **arbre à (la) p., aux perruques**, wig sumac, Venetian sumac; young fustic; smoke tree; (*c*) *Fish:* tangled line; *F:* bird's nest; (*d*) *P:* **faire de la p.**, to do sth. on the side.

perruquer [peryke, pe-], *v.tr. Fish:* to tangle, *F:* make a bird's nest in (the line).

perruquerie [perykri, pe-], *s.f. F: A:* **1.** (old) fog(e)ydom, fogyism. **2.** (*a*) old-fashioned idea or usage; (*b*) *pl.* relics of the past.

perruquier, -ière [perykje, -jɛ:r, pe-], *s.* (*a*) wig maker; (*b*) *A:* hairdresser, barber; *f.* barber's wife.

pers [pɛ:r], *a.* sea-green, grey, or purplish-blue (according to contexts); **Minerve aux yeux p.**, grey-eyed Minerva.

persan, -ane [persɑ̃, -an]. **1.** *a. & s. Geog:* Persian. **2.** *s.m. Ling:* Persian. **3.** *a. Z:* **chat p.**, Persian cat; **(cheval) p.**, Persian arab, Persian horse; **lévrier p.**, saluki.

Perse¹ [pers]. **1.** *Pr.n.f. Geog:* Persia; **tapis de P.**, Persian rug, carpet; *Bot:* **graine de P.**, common buckthorn seed. **2.** *a. & s. A.Geog:* (native, inhabitant) of ancient Persia; Persian. **3.** *s.m. Ling: A:* Persian. **4.** *s.f. Tex:* chintz.

Perse², *Pr.n.m. Lt.Lit:* Persius.

persécutant [persekytɑ̃], *a.* persecuting.

persécuté, -ée [persekyte]. **1.** *a. & s.* persecuted (person). **2.** *s.* sufferer from persecution mania.

persécuter [persekyte], *v.tr.* (*a*) to persecute; (*b*) to importune, harass, pester; **être persécuté par ses créanciers**, to be dunned by one's creditors.

persécuteur, -trice [persekytœ:r, -tris]. **1.** *s.* persecutor. **2.** *a.* (*a*) persecuting; (*b*) harassing, pestering, troublesome.

persécution [persekysjɔ̃], *s.f.* (*a*) persecution; **essuyer de cruelles persécutions**, to be cruelly persecuted, to suffer cruel persecution; *Med:* **manie, folie, délire, de la p.**, persecution mania; (*b*) *occ.* importunity.

Persée [perse], *Pr.n.m. Gr.Myth: Astr:* Perseus.

perséides [perseid], *s.f.pl. Astr:* Perseids.

perséite [perseit], *s.f.*, **perséitol** [perseitɔl], *s.m. Ch:* perseitol, perseite.

persel [persɛl], *s.m.* persalt; peroxy salt.

Perséphone [persefɔn], *Pr.n.f. Gr.Myth:* Persephone.

Persépolis [persepolis], *Pr.n.f. A.Geog:* Persepolis.

perséulose [perseylo:z], *s.m. Ch:* perseulose.

persévérance [perseverɑ̃:s], *s.f.* perseverance (**à faire qch.**, in doing sth.); **avec p.**, perseveringly.

persévérant [perseverɑ̃], *a.* persevering.

persévération [perseverasjɔ̃], *s.f. Med:* perseveration.

persévérer [persevere], *v.i.* (**je persévère, n. persévérons; je persévérerai**) **1.** to persevere (**dans,** in); **p. dans le mal**, to continue in sin; **p. dans le bien, à bien faire, à faire le bien**, to persevere in one's efforts to lead a good life, to do good; **il n'a guère persévéré**, he didn't show much perseverance; **il faut p.**, you must persevere. **2.** *A:* (*of thgs*) to continue, persist; **la fièvre persévère**, the fever persists.

persicaire [persikɛ:r], *s.f. Bot:* persicaria, lady's thumb; **p. âcre**, water pepper, smart weed.

persicot [persiko], *s.m.* liqueur flavoured with peach kernels, etc.; persico, persicot.

persiennage [persjena:ʒ], *s.m. Const:* shuttering.

persienne [persjɛn], *s.f.* (slatted) shutter.

persiflage [persifla:ʒ], *s.m.* (ill-natured) banter; persiflage.

persifler [persifle], *v.tr.* to ridicule (s.o.); to make fun (ill-naturedly) of (s.o.).

persifleur, -euse [persiflœ:r, -ø:z]. **1.** *s.* (ill-natured) banterer; persifleur. **2.** *a.* derisive, superciliously ironical (tone, etc.).

persil [persi], *s.m.* **1.** *Bot:* parsley; **p. des fous, faux p.**, fool's parsley; **p. noir**, horse parsley; **p. sauvage**, anthriscus. **2.** *P: O:* **aller au p., faire son p.**, (i) (*of prostitute*) to walk the streets; (ii) (*of man*) to go whoring; (iii) to parade around (to attract attention).

persillade [persijad], *s.f. Cu:* (*a*) beef salad (seasoned with chopped parsley, etc.); (*b*) sauce seasoned with parsley.

persillé [persije], *a.* **1.** spotted (with green); **fromage à pâte persillée**, blue cheese. **2.** (*of meat*) marbled; **jambon p.**, jellied ham into which chopped parsley has been introduced.

persiller [persije], *v.tr. Cu:* to sprinkle with parsley.

persimmon [persimɔ̃], *s.m. Bot:* persimmon (tree).

persique [persik], *a.* (ancient) Persian; *Geog:* **le Golfe P.**, the Persian Gulf; *Arch:* **statue p.**, caryatid.

persistance [persistɑ̃:s], *s.f.* **1.** persistence, persistency (**à faire qch.**, in doing sth.); **avec p.**, persistently, doggedly; **la p. de ces vertus**, the enduring quality of these virtues. **2.** (*a*) persistence, continuance (of fever, etc.); **p. optique, p. des impressions lumineuses**, persistence of vision; (*b*) *Elcs:* **p. d'écran**, afterglow; **écran à p.**, persistence screen.

persistant [persistɑ̃], *a.* **1.** persistent (efforts, etc.). **2.** lasting, enduring (perfume, etc.); *Bot:* (*of leaves*) persistent, indeciduous; **pluie persistante**, steady downpour.

persister [persiste], *v.i.* to persist. **1. p. dans sa résolution de faire qch.**, to persist in, to adhere to, one's determination to do sth.; **il faut p.**, you must persist, keep up your effort; **p. à faire qch.**, to persist in doing sth.; **il y persiste**, he persists in it; he sticks to it; he adheres to it. **2. la fièvre persiste**, the fever continues, pursues, its course; **la beauté persiste mais évolue**, beauty remains but changes.

personée [persɔne], *a.f. Bot:* personate (corolla).

personnage [persɔna:ʒ], *s.m.* personage; (*a*) person of rank, of distinction; **devenir un p.**, to rise to eminence; **les personnages remarquables de l'histoire**, the prominent characters, the prominent figures, in history; **être un p.**, to be somebody, *F:* to be a big shot; **se prendre pour un p.**, to think no small beer of oneself; (*b*) *Pej:* person, individual; **c'est un sot p.**, he's a fool (of a fellow); **c'est un triste p.**, he's a poor specimen; **c'est un vil p., un vilain p.**, he's a swine; (*c*) (public) image (of politician, etc.); (*d*) *Lit:* character (in play, in novel); **les personnages**, the dramatis personae; **c'est un vrai p. de roman**, he might have stepped out of a novel; (*e*) **p. principal d'un tableau**, central figure in a painting.

personnalisation [persɔnalizasjɔ̃], *s.f.* personalization, personification.

personnaliser [persɔnalize], *v.tr.* (*a*) to personify, personalize (vice, virtue, etc.); (*b*) to give a personal touch to; *Com:* to personalize.

personnalisme [persɔnalism], *s.m. Phil:* personalism.

personnaliste [persɔnalist], *s.m. & f. Phil:* personalist.

personnalité [persɔnalite], *s.f.* personality. **1.** (*a*) individuality, individual characteristics; **il a de la p.**, he has (real) personality, individuality; *Jur:* (*of corporation, etc.*) **acquérir la p. civile, juridique, morale**, to become an artificial, fictitious, person; to acquire legal status; (*b*) *A:* egotism. **2.** person, personage, personality; **toutes les personnalités de la ville**, all the people of consequence, *F:* all the notables, of the town; **c'est une p.**, he's an important man, *F:* he's somebody. **3.** *pl.* **faire des personnalités à qn**, to make personal, offensive, remarks to s.o.

personne [pɛrsɔn]. **1.** *s.f.* person; (*a*) (*individual*) **la p. dont je parlais,** the person of whom I was speaking; **les quelques personnes présentes,** the few people present; **une assemblée de trois cents personnes,** an assembly of three hundred people; **une tierce p.,** a third party; **passer par une tierce p., par p. interposée,** to negotiate, to go through, a third party, a third person; **ce n'était pas une p. à demeurer en repos,** he, she, was not somebody who could remain idle; **cela coûte 3 francs par p.,** it costs 3 francs per head; **une p. âgée,** an elderly person; **jeune p.,** young woman, girl; *Pej:* young person; **une vieille p. très respectable,** a very respectable old woman; **les grandes personnes,** adults, grown-ups; **être bonne p.,** to be a good sort; **l'efficacité de la méthode dépend de la p. qui l'applique,** the efficiency of the method depends on the person who applies it; *Jur:* **personnes physiques ou morales,** individual and legal entities; **erreur sur la p.,** mistaken identity; **p. future,** child yet to be born; **personnes à la charge,** dependents; (*of writer, etc.*) **la p. et l'œuvre,** the man and his work; *Theol:* **un (seul) Dieu en trois personnes,** one God in three Persons; (*b*) (*one's own self*) **soigner sa p.,** to like one's comfort; to coddle oneself; **être satisfait, faire grand cas, de sa (petite) p.,** to be self-satisfied, to think no small beer of oneself; *A:* **je parle à ma p.,** I'm talking to myself; **en p.,** in person, personally; **je l'ai vu en p.,** I saw him personally, in the flesh; **le roi vint en p.,** the king came in person; **il est la bonté en p.,** he is kindness itself, kindness personified; **il est l'avarice en p.,** he is avarice personified; **il faudra vous présenter en p.,** you will have to apply, appear, in person; *Iron: or Hum:* **personne ne pensait à ma pauvre petite p.,** nobody thought of poor little me; (*c*) (*the human body*) **elle est bien (faite) de sa p.,** she's very attractive, good-looking; **exposer sa p.,** to expose oneself to danger; to risk death; **payer de sa p.,** (i) to spare no effort; (ii) to give no thought to the possibility of danger; *Jur:* **répondre de la p. de qn,** to stand surety for s.o.; *O:* **s'assurer de la p. de qn,** to arrest s.o.; (*d*) *Gram:* **écrire à la troisième p.,** to write in the third person; **en français la deuxième p. du pluriel peut faire fonction de singulier,** in French the second person plural may function as a singular. **2.** *pron.indef.m.inv.* (*a*) (*with vaguely implied negation*) anyone, anybody; **y a-t-il p. qui ose le dire?** is there anyone who dares to say so? **il s'y connaît comme p.,** nobody is more expert at it than he is; **il le sait aussi bien, mieux, que p.,** nobody knows it better than he does; **il sait mieux que p. que . . .,** nobody is more aware than he is that . . .; **il travaille plus fort que p.,** he works harder than anyone; nobody works harder than he does; **je ne dois rien à p.,** I don't owe anything to anyone; I don't owe anyone a penny; (*b*) (*with ne expressed or understood*) no one, nobody; **p. n'est venu,** nobody has come; **qui est là?—p.,** who's there?—nobody; **que p. ne sorte,** nobody is to leave; **j'épouserai ma cousine ou p.,** I shall marry my cousin or nobody; **il n'y a p. de blessé,** nobody has been injured; there were no casualties; **il n'y a p. de plus heureux que moi,** nobody is happier than I am; **p. (d')autre n'était à bord,** there was no one else on board; **p. de vous, d'entre vous, n'a rien remarqué?** did no one among you notice anything? **dans cette maison p. ne se connaissait,** in this house no one knew any one else; (*with fem. concord by attraction*) **p. de ces demoiselles n'est sortie,** none of the young ladies has, have, gone out; (*c*) (*the negation is implied in some other part or word of the sentence*) **il est inutile que vous dérangiez p.,** you needn't disturb anybody; **sans nommer p.,** without naming anybody, without mentioning any names, naming no names.

personnel, -elle [pɛrsɔnɛl]. **1.** *a.* (*a*) personal (letter, business, interest, *Gram:* pronoun, mood); **question personnelle,** personal issue; **craindre pour sa sûreté personnelle,** to go about in bodily fear; **strictement p., invitation personnelle,** not transferable (ticket, pass); **objets personnels,** personal belongings; **fortune personnelle,** private means; *Jur:* **action personnelle,** personal action at law; (*b*) **maîtrise personnelle,** self mastery, self control; **intérêt p.,** self-interest; (*c*) *F:* selfish; **joueur trop p. pour être un bon équipier,** too selfish a player to be a good member of the team. **2.** *s.m.* (*a*) personnel, staff (of institution, school, business firm); hands (of factory, farm, etc.); (hotel) servants, staff; employees; **service du p.,** personnel department; **chef du p.,** personnel manager; **direction du p.,** staff management; **p. de direction,** management; **p. d'encadrement,** supervisory personnel; **p. de maîtrise,** foremen; **p. non cadre,** non-supervisory personnel; **p. ouvrier,** workmen, hands; **p. technique,** engineering staff; **p. d'exécution,** line; **p. d'administration,** administrative personnel, staff; **p. de bureau,** clerical staff, office staff, secretarial staff; **p. sédentaire,** indoor staff, personnel; **p. du service actif, des services extérieurs; p. de chantier,** outdoor personnel, staff; **p. de service,** staff on duty; **p. réduit,** reduced staff, skeleton staff; **faire partie du p. de . . .,** to be on the staff of . . .; **manquer de p., ne pas avoir tout son p.,** to be understaffed, inadequately staffed, short-handed; (*b*) *Mil: etc:* personnel, manpower; *Navy:* complement; **direction du, des, personnel(s) militaire(s); section du p.** = Department of the Adjutant General; **service du p.,** personnel services; **officier chargé du p.,** personnel officer; **p. officier,** commissioned personnel; **p. non officier,** other ranks, *U.S:* enlisted personnel; **tout le p.,** all ranks; **p. médical, p. sanitaire,** medical personnel, medical establishment; **p. des transmissions,** signal personnel; **p. du génie, du renseignement,** engineer, intelligence, personnel; **P. Féminin de l'Armée de Terre (P.F.A.T.)** = Women's Royal Army Corps (W.R.A.C.); *Av:* **p. de l'aviation,** aviation personnel; **p. de l'Armée de l'Air** = Air Force personnel; **p. navigant,** flying personnel, aircrew; **p. non navigant, p. au sol,** *F:* **p. rampant,** ground personnel, staff; ground crew; **P. Féminin de l'Armée de l'Air (P.F.A.A.)** = Women's Royal Air Force (W.R.A.F.); *Navy:* **p. des machines,** engine-room complement; **p. non officier,** lower-deck ratings; *F:* the lower deck; *Navy: Nau:* **p. navigant,** sea-going personnel, ship's personnel; **p. sédentaire,** shore personnel, staff; **P. Féminin de l'Armée de Mer (P.F.A.M.)** = Women's Royal Naval Service (W.R.N.S.).

personnellement [pɛrsɔnɛlmɑ̃], *adv.* personally, in person; as far as I am, he is, etc., concerned; **lectures à faire par les élèves p.,** reading to be done by the pupils in their own time.

personnificateur, -trice [pɛrsɔnifikatœ:r, -tris], *s.* personifier.

personnification [pɛrsɔnifikasjɔ̃], *s.f.* **1.** (*a*) personification (of inanimate nature, etc.); (*b*) impersonation. **2.** *Jur:* **p. civile,** status of body corporate.

personnifié [pɛrsɔnifje], *a.* **la vertu personnifiée,** virtue personified; **l'honnêteté personnifiée,** the personification of honesty.

personnifier [pɛrsɔnifje], *v.tr.* (*p.d. & pr.sub.* **n. personnifiions, v. personnifiiez**) (*a*) to personify (inanimate object, virtue, vice, etc.); (*b*) to impersonate; **elle personnifie en soi toute la bonté humaine,** she is the personification of all human kindness; **il me semblait p. le citoyen transatlantique,** he seemed to me to typify the transatlantic citizen.

perspectif, -ive [pɛrspɛktif, -i:v]. **1.** *a.* perspective (plan); **échelle perspective,** scenographic(al) scale. **2.** *s.f.* **perspective:** (*a*) *Art: etc:* (linear) perspective; **perspective aérienne,** aerial perspective; **perspective cavalière,** isometric projection; **perspective à vol d'oiseau,** bird's-eye perspective, bird's-eye view (of country, etc.); **dessin en perspective,** drawing in perspective; (*b*) outlook, view, prospect; **triste perspective que celle-là,** it is a dreary outlook; **la perspective n'est pas des plus rassurantes,** the prospect, outlook, is none too promising; **avoir qch. en perspective,** to have sth. in view, in prospect; **aucune perspective d'accord,** no prospect of agreement; **j'envisage avec plaisir la perspective des vacances, la perspective de le revoir,** I am looking forward to the holidays, to seeing him again; **pour la voir sous sa vraie p.,** to see her in her proper perspective; **la p. de peines graves,** the prospect of severe penalties; **perspectives d'avenir d'une entreprise,** future prospects of an undertaking; **je n'ai d'autre perspective que le travail,** I see nothing before me, ahead of me, but work; **perspective démographique, perspective de population,** population forecast; (*c*) **dans la perspective de . . .,** from the point of view of . . .; (*d*) vista; **une longue perspective de hêtres,** a long vista of beech trees.

perspectivisme [pɛrspɛktivism], *s.m. Phil:* perspectivism.

perspectiviste [pɛrspɛktivist], *s.m.* (*a*) painter of urban scenes; (*b*) artist drawing the maximum effect from perspective.

perspicace [pɛrspikas], *a.* perspicacious, shrewd.

perspicacité [pɛrspikasite], *s.f.* perspicacity, insight, acumen, shrewdness; **avec p.,** shrewdly.

perspicuité [pɛrspikɥite], *s.f. A:* perspicuity, perspicuousness.

perspiration [pɛrspirasjɔ̃], *s.f.* transpiration.

persuadé [pɛrsɥade], *a.* persuaded, convinced, sure (**de,** of; **que,** that); **c'est le portefeuille que j'étais p. avoir laissé dans le tiroir,** it is the wallet (which) I was sure I had left in the drawer.

persuader [pɛrsɥade], *v.tr. & pr.* (NOTE: *for the v.pr. the concord of the p.p. in the compound tenses should depend on whether the reflexive pronoun is a direct or indirect object; but in modern French usage the p.p. is almost always invariable*) **1.** (*a*) *Lit:* **p. qch. à qn,** to persuade s.o. of sth., to make s.o. believe sth.; **toutes les sottises qu'un parleur insinuant pourrait p. au peuple,** all the stupidities that an insinuating speaker could persuade people to believe; (*b*) **je ne saurais me le p.,** I cannot bring myself to believe it; **il s'était persuadé être dans son droit,** he had persuaded himself that he was right; **j'ai eu peine à lui p. que vous fussiez un excellent officier,** I had difficulty in persuading him that you were an excellent officer; **ils se sont persuadé que . . .,** they are convinced that . . .. **2. p. qn,** to persuade, convince, s.o.; **p. qn de qch., de faire qch.,** to persuade, convince, s.o. of sth.; to persuade s.o. to do sth.; **j'ai fini par les p.,** in the end I convinced them, persuaded them, talked them round, got round them; **il s'en est persuadé,** he is convinced of it; **nous sommes persuadés que . . .,** we are convinced, confident, that . . .; **je les ai persuadés de partir,** I persuaded them to go. **3. p. à qn de faire qch.,** to persuade, induce, s.o. to do sth.; **il s'est laissé p. d'aller en Grèce,** he let himself be persuaded to go to Greece; **aucun argument ne pouvait lui p. de le faire,** no argument could induce, persuade, him to do it.

persuasible [pɛrsɥazibl̩], *a.* persuadable, persuasible.

persuasif, -ive [pɛrsɥazif, -i:v], *a.* persuasive (manner); convincing (language); **d'un ton p.,** persuasively.

persuasion [pɛrsɥazjɔ̃], *s.f.* **1.** persuasion; **à force de p. je le fis renoncer à ce projet,** I managed to talk him out of this plan. **2.** conviction, belief; **ébranler la p. de qn,** to shake s.o.'s belief; **nous avons l'intime p. que . . .,** we are firmly persuaded that . . ..

persuasivement [pɛrsɥazivmɑ̃], *adv.* persuasively.

persulfate [pɛrsylfat], *s.m. Ch:* persulphate; **p. d'ammoniaque,** ammonium persulphate.

persulfure [pɛrsylfy:r], *s.m. Ch:* persulphide.

persulfurique [pɛrsylfyrik], *a. Ch:* persulphuric (acid).

perte [pɛrt], *s.f.* **1.** ruin, destruction; **il court à sa p.,** he is heading for disaster, is on the high road to ruin; *Nau:* **p. corps et biens,** loss of vessel with all hands; total loss; *Ins:* **p. présumée,** presumptive loss; **p. censée totale,** constructive total loss. **2.** loss (of money, relative, lawsuit, battle, sight, reason, etc.); **profits et pertes,** profit and loss; **passer une p. par profits et pertes,** to write off a loss; **subir de grandes pertes,** to sustain, suffer, heavy losses, *Mil:* heavy casualties; *Mil:* **combler les pertes,** to make good (the) losses; **remplacement des pertes,** replacement of casualties; **grosses pertes en vie humaine,** heavy loss of life; **vendre qch. à p.,** to sell sth. at a loss; **se retirer (d'une affaire) à p.,** to withdraw with a loss; **être en p.,** to be out of pocket; **je suis en p. de 500 francs,** I'm 500 francs to the bad, out of pocket, down; **p. sèche,** dead loss; **à p. de vue,** as far as the eye can see; **p. de temps,** waste of time; **parler en pure p.,** to talk to no purpose, to waste one's breath; **dépense en pure p.,** wasteful expenditure; *Geog:* **p. d'un fleuve, d'une rivière,** water sink, disappearance underground of a river; **p. de connaissance,** loss of consciousness; fainting. **3.** (*a*) loss, leakage; **p. de chaleur,** loss of heat; *Aer:* **p. de force ascensionnelle, de poussée,** loss of lift; *Mec.E: etc:* **p. de charge, de pression,** pressure drop, drop in pressure; *El:* **p. de charge,** drop in voltage, loss of pressure; **p. de courant, d'intensité,** leakage of current; **p. à la terre,** earth leakage; **perte(s) dans le fer,** iron, core, losses; (*b*) *Med:* (i) issue, discharge; (ii) flooding, uterine h(a)emorrhage; **pertes blanches,** leucorrhoea.

perthite [pɛrtit], *s.f. Miner:* perthite.

pertinacité [pɛrtinasite], *s.f. Lit:* pertinacity, pertinaciousness.

pertinemment [pɛrtinamɑ̃], *adv.* 1. pertinently, appositely, relevantly. 2. **j'en parle p.,** I speak with knowledge; **je sais p. qu'ils sont à Londres,** to my certain knowledge they are in London; **savoir qch. p.,** to know sth. for a fact.

pertinence [pɛrtinɑ̃:s], *s.f.* pertinence, pertinency, appositeness, relevance; **avec p.,** competently.

pertinent [pɛrtinɑ̃], *a.* pertinent, apposite, relevant (à, to); **faits pertinents,** relevant facts; **non p.,** irrelevant.

pertuis [pɛrtɥi], *s.m.* 1. *A:* hole, opening. 2. sluice; *Metall:* tap-hole. 3. *Geog:* (*a*) narrows (of a river); (*b*) strait(s), (narrow) channel; (*c*) (*in the Jura*) pass.

pertuisane [pɛrtɥizan], *s.f. A.Arms:* partisan, halberd.

pertuisanier [pɛrtɥizanje], *s.m. A.Mil:* halberdier.

pertuisien, -ienne [pɛrtɥizjɛ̃, -jɛn], *a. & s. Geog:* (native, inhabitant) of Pertuis.

perturbateur, -trice [pɛrtyrbatœ:r, -tris]. 1. *a.* disturbing, upsetting; **force perturbatrice,** perturbational force. 2. *s.* disturber, upsetter; **p. de la paix, du repos public,** disturber of the peace; brawler.

perturbation [pɛrtyrbasjɔ̃], *s.f.* (*a*) perturbation, agitation of mind; (*b*) *Astr:* perturbation (of elliptic motion, etc.); (*c*) disturbance; **p. magnétique,** magnetic disturbance; **perturbations atmosphériques,** atmospheric disturbances; *W.Tel: etc: F:* atmospherics; *Meteor:* **(courant de) p.,** depression; cyclone; *Ind: etc:* **p. dans le service,** breakdown; technical hitch; (*d*) *Med: etc:* disorder.

perturber [pɛrtyrbe], *v.tr.* to disturb (the peace); **p. le repos public,** to cause a disturbance.

pérugin, -ine [peryʒɛ̃, -in]. 1. *a. & s. Geog:* (native, inhabitant) of Perugia; Perugian. 2. *Pr.n.m. Hist. of Art:* **le P.,** Perugino.

pérule [peryl], *s.f. Bot:* perula.

péruvien, -ienne [peryvjɛ̃, -jɛn], *a. & s. Geog:* Peruvian.

pervéance [pɛrveɑ̃:s], *s.f. Elcs:* perveance.

pervenche [pɛrvɑ̃:ʃ], *s.f.* (*a*) *Bot:* periwinkle; **bleu** (*inv.*) **p.,** periwinkle blue; (*b*) **des yeux de p..** forget-me-not eyes.

pervers, -erse [pɛrvɛ:r, -ɛrs]. 1. *a.* perverse, depraved; immoral; **goûts p.,** vicious, depraved, tastes; **machination perverse,** diabolical plot; **conseils p.,** evil advice. 2. *s.* (*a*) depraved, immoral, person; (*b*) **p. sexuel,** sexual pervert.

perversement [pɛrvɛrsəmɑ̃], *adv.* perversely.

perversion [pɛrvɛrsjɔ̃], *s.f.* (*a*) perversion (of taste, morals); (*b*) warping (of the mind); (*c*) **p. sexuelle,** sexual perversion.

perversité [pɛrvɛrsite], *s.f.* perversity, perverseness.

perverti, -ie [pɛrvɛrti], *a. & s.* perverted, depraved, corrupted (person).

pervertir [pɛrvɛrti:r], *v.tr.* to pervert (person, taste, meaning); to deprave; to corrupt.

se pervertir, to become perverted, depraved; to grow vicious.

pervertissement [pɛrvɛrtismɑ̃], *s.m.* perverting.

pervertisseur, -euse [pɛrvɛrtisœ:r, -ø:z]. 1. *a.* perverting. 2. *s.* perverter.

pervibrateur [pɛrvibratœ:r], *s.m. Civ.E:* vibrator, concrete-vibrating machine.

pervibration [pɛrvibrasjɔ̃], *s.f. Civ.E:* vibration (of concrete).

pervibrer [pɛrvibre], *v.tr. Civ.E:* to vibrate (concrete).

pervibreur [pɛrvibrœ:r], *s.m. Civ.E:* vibrator, concrete-vibrating machine.

pérylène [perilɛn], *s.m. Ch:* perylene.

pesade [pəzad], *s.f. Equit:* pesade, rearing (of horse).

pesage [pəza:ʒ], *s.m.* 1. weighing; **appareil, bascule, de p.,** weighing machine; **bureau de p.,** weigh-house; **droits de p.,** weighing dues; *Civ.E:* **p. automatique par charges dosées,** batching process. 2. *Turf:* (*a*) weighing in; (*b*) weighing-in room; (*c*) paddock; the enclosure.

pesamment [pəzamɑ̃], *adv.* heavily; (*of movement, etc.*) inelegantly, clumsily; **parler p.,** to speak ponderously.

pesant [pəzɑ̃]. 1. *a.* (*a*) heavy, weighty, unwieldy (body, burden, etc.); ponderous, inelegant, clumsy, dull (style, writer); sluggish (mind); **avoir la tête pesante,** to feel heavy-headed; **cheval p. à la main,** horse heavy in, on, hand; **marcher à pas pesants,** to walk heavily; to lumber along; **entrer, sortir, à pas pesants,** to lumber in, out; *adv.* **deux livres p.,** two pounds in weight; (*b*) *Ph:* ponderable (gas, etc.). 2. *s.m.* **cela vaut son p. d'or,** it is worth its weight in gold; *F:* (*of story, etc.*) **valoir son p. de moutarde,** to be very funny.

pesanteur [pəzɑ̃tœ:r], *s.f.* 1. weight; *Ph:* gravity; **p. spécifique,** specific gravity. 2. (*a*) heaviness; **p. de tête,** heaviness in the head; **j'ai une p. d'estomac,** there is something lying heavy on my stomach; (*b*) inelegance, unwieldiness (of movement, walk); (*c*) dullness, sluggishness (of mind).

pèse [pɛ:z], *s.m. P:* money, cash, lolly; **être au p.,** to be well off, rolling (in it).

pèse-acide [pɛzasid], *s.m.* acid hydrometer, acidimeter; *pl. pèse-acides.*

pèse-alcool [pɛzalkɔl], *s.m.* alcoholometer; *pl. pèse-alcools.*

pèse-bébé [pɛzbebe], *s.m.* baby scales; *pl. pèse-bébés.*

pesée [pəze], *s.f.* 1. (*a*) weighing; *Box:* weigh-in; *Turf:* (i) (*before race*) weighing in; (ii) (*after race*) weighing out; **faire la p. de qch.,** to weigh sth.; (*b*) amount weighed at one time; **faire bonne p.,** to give generous weight; (*c*) (= *piece of bread added to make up the weight of a loaf*) make-weight. 2. force, leverage, effort; **exercer une p. (avec un levier),** to prize; **exercer des pesées sur une porte,** to try to force a door; **forcer un couvercle d'une seule p.,** to force a lid with a single wrench.

pèse-esprit [pɛzɛspri], *s.m.* spirit hydrometer, alcoholometer; *pl. pèse-esprit(s).*

pèse-lait [pɛzlɛ], *s.m.inv.* lactometer, milk gauge.

pèse-lettre(s) [pɛzlɛtr̥], *s.m.* letter balance, letter scales; *pl. pèse-lettres.*

pèse-liqueur [pɛzlikœ:r], *s.m.* alcoholometer; *pl. pèse-liqueurs.*

pèsement [pɛzmɑ̃], *s.m. Medieval Art:* **p. des âmes,** weighing of the souls.

pèse-moût [pɛzmu], *s.m.inv. Brew:* saccharometer.

pèse-personne [pɛzpɛrsɔn], *s.m.* bathroom scales; *pl. pèse-personnes.*

peser [pəze], *v.* (**je pèse, n. pesons; je pèserai**) 1. *v.tr.* to weigh; **p. un paquet,** to weigh a parcel; **p. les quantités requises,** to weigh (out) the required amounts; **machine à p.,** weighing machine; **p. ses paroles,** to weigh one's words; **pesez vos paroles,** think before you speak; **réponse bien pesée,** carefully thought out, careful, answer; **p. un avis,** to ponder a piece of advice; *Sp:* **se p., se faire, p.,** to weigh in. 2. *v.i.* (*a*) to weigh; to have weight; to be heavy; **il ne pèse pas lourd,** (i) he doesn't weigh much; (ii) *F:* he doesn't count for much, he's of no importance; **paquet qui pèse deux kilos,** parcel weighing two kilos; **combien le paquet a-t-il pesé?** how much did the parcel weigh? *F:* **ça pèse son petit poids,** (i) it's quite a good weight; (ii) *P:* it's bloody heavy; **viande qui pèse sur l'estomac,** meat that lies heavy on the stomach; **mes péchés pèsent sur mon âme,** my sins lie heavy on my soul; **cet impôt pèse lourdement sur les commerçants,** this tax presses heavily on tradesmen; **un silence pesait sur l'assemblée,** a heavy silence hung, brooded, over the meeting; **le sommeil pesait sur eux,** they were weighed down with sleep; **le temps lui pèse,** time hangs heavily on his hands; **une lourde responsabilité pèse sur lui,** he is weighed down by a heavy responsibility; **sa famille lui pèse sur les bras,** his family is a burden to him; **sa responsabilité lui pèse,** he feels the weight of his responsibility; (*b*) to bear, to press hard (on sth.); **p. sur un levier,** to bear on a lever; *Nau:* **p. sur une manœuvre,** to heave, haul, on a rope; to bouse a rope; **p. sur un mot,** to lay stress on a word.

pèse-sel [pɛzsɛl], *s.m.* salinometer; *pl. pèse-sel(s).*

pèse-sirop [pɛzsiro], *s.m.* syrup hydrometer; *pl. pèse-sirop(s).*

peseta [pezeta], *s.f.* (*a*) *Num:* peseta; (*b*) *pl. P:* pesetas, money, dough, lolly.

pésètes, pésettes [pezɛt], *s.f.pl. P:* money, dough, lolly.

pesette[1] [pəzɛt], *s.f.* assay scales.

pesette[2], *s.f. Bot: F:* vetch.

peseur, -euse [pəzœ:r, -ø:z]. 1. *s.* weigher; weighman, scalesman. 2. *a.* **trémie peseuse,** weighing hopper.

pèse-urine [pɛzyrin], *s.m.* urinometer; *pl. pèse-urine(s).*

péseux, -euse [pezø, -ø:z], *a. P:* rich, rolling in it.

pèse-vin [pɛzvɛ̃], *s.m.inv.* oenometer.

peso [pezo], *s.m. Num:* peso.

peson [pəzɔ̃], *s.m.* balance; *esp.* **p. à ressort,** spring balance; **p. à contrepoids,** lever balance, steelyard.

pesquié [pɛskje], *s.m. Dial:* (*S. of Fr.*) fish pond.

pessaire [pɛs(s)ɛ:r], *s.m. Med:* pessary.

pesse[1] [pɛs], *s.f.,* **pessereau** [pɛsro], *s.m. Bot:* horse tail, equisetum.

pesse[2], *s.f. Bot:* picea, spruce.

pesseau [pɛso], *s.m.* vine prop.

pesseler [pɛs(ɛ)le], *v.tr.* (**je pesselle, n. pesselons**) to prop (vines).

pessimisme [pesimism, pɛ-], *s.m.* pessimism.

pessimiste [pesimist, pɛ-]. 1. *a.* pessimistic. 2. *s.m. & f.* pessimist.

peste [pɛst], *s.f.* (*a*) plague, pestilence, *A:* pest; **p. bovine,** cattle plague; rinderpest; **p. noire,** bubonic plague, *Hist:* the Black Death; *F:* **fuir qn comme la p.,** to avoid s.o. like the plague, like poison; *A:* **p.!** bless my soul! man alive! *A. & Lit:* **p. soit du vieux fou!** a plague on, deuce take, the old fool! (*b*) *F:* **c'est une p. que cet enfant!** what a plague, what a pest, that child is! **petite p.,** little devil, little pest.

pester [pɛste], *v.i.* **p. contre qn, qch.,** to storm, curse, rave, at s.o., sth.; **p. contre le mauvais temps,** to curse the (bad) weather; *abs.* **il pestait,** he was grumbling, cursing.

pesteux, -euse [pɛstø, -ø:z], *a. Med:* pertaining to the plague; **bacille p.,** plague bacillus; **rat p.,** plague-carrying rat.

pesticide [pɛstisid]. 1. *a.* pesticidal. 2. *s.m.* pesticide.

pestifère [pɛstifɛ:r], *a.* pestiferous, pestilential (air).

pestiféré, -ée [pɛstifere], *a. & s.* plague-stricken (person); *F:* **fuir qn comme un p.,** to avoid s.o. like the plague.

pestilence [pɛstilɑ̃:s], *s.f.* (*a*) *A:* pestilence; (*b*) stench, stink.

pestilencieux, pestilentieux, -euse [pɛstilɑ̃sjø, -ø:z], *a. A:* pestilential.

pestilent [pɛstilɑ̃], *a.* pestilent.

pestilentiel, -elle [pɛstilɑ̃sjɛl], *a.* (*a*) pestilential; (*b*) stinking, foetid; **odeur pestilentielle,** stench.

pet [pɛ], *s.m.* 1. (*a*) *P:* breaking of wind; fart; **faire un p.,** to break wind, to (let a) fart; *F:* **ça ne vaut pas un p. (de lapin),** it isn't worth a tinker's curse, isn't worth a cuss; *F:* **il n'a pas un p. de bon sens,** he hasn't an atom of sense; (*b*) *P:* **il va y avoir du p.,** (i) look out for squalls; (ii) there's going to be a nice bit of scandal; **faire du p.,** to kick up a row; **porter le p.,** (i) to lay a charge (against s.o.); (ii) to blab, squeal; **p.! p.!** look out! **faire le p.,** to be on the watch, on the look out; (*c*) [pɛt] *P:* **je lui ai flanqué un p.,** I socked him one; **ta voiture a pris un p.,** your car's taken a bash.

pétainiste [petenist], *a. & s.m. & f. Hist:* follower of Pétain, Pétainist.

pétalaire [petalɛ:r], *a. Bot:* petaline.

pétale [petal], *s.m. Bot:* petal.

pétalé [petale], *a. Bot:* petalled, petalous.

pétaliforme [petalifɔrm], *a. Bot:* petaliform.

pétalin, -ine [petalɛ̃, -in], *a. Bot:* petaline.

pétalisme [petalism], *s.m. Gr.Hist:* petalism.

pétalite [petalit], *s.f. Miner:* petalite.

pétalodé [petalɔde], *a. Bot:* petalodic.

pétalodie [petalɔdi], *s.f. Bot:* petalody.

pétalodontidés [petalɔdɔ̃tide], *s.m.pl. Paleont:* Petalodontidae; petalodonts.

pétaloïde [petalɔid], *a. Bot:* petaloid.

petalostemon [petalɔstemɔ̃], **petalostemum** [petalɔstemɔm], *s.m. Bot:* prairie clover; (*genus*) Petalostemon.

pétanielle [petanjɛl], *s.f. Agr:* (variety of) poulard wheat.

pétanque [petɑ̃:k], *s.f.* game of bowls (in S. of Fr.).

pétanqueur [petɑ̃kœ:r], *s.m. pétanque* player.

pétant, -ante [petɑ̃, -ɑ̃:t], *a. P:* **à neuf heures pétantes,** on the stroke of nine.

pétarade [petarad], *s.f.* (*a*) (*of horse*) (succession of) farts; (*b*) crackling, loud discharge (of fireworks); promiscuous firing (of arms); (*c*) *Aut:* backfiring.

pétarader [petarade], *v.i.* (*a*) (*of horse*) to let off a succession of farts; (*b*) (*of fireworks*) to crackle; to emit a succession of bangs; (*c*) *I.C.E:* (*of engine*) to backfire.

pétard [peta:r], *s.m.* 1. (*a*) *Mil: A:* petard; (*b*) *Min:* shot, blast; **faire partir un p.,** to fire a blast; to touch off a shot; (*c*) *Rail:* detonator, fog signal; **faire éclater un p.,** to detonate a fog signal; (*d*) (*firework*) cracker, banger; **grand p.,** thunder flash; (*e*) *P:* gun, gat. 2. *F:* (*a*) noise, row; **faire du p.,** to kick up a row; (*b*) **être en p.,** to be in a flaming temper. 3. *P:* backside, bum; **se manier le p.,** to get a move on, to shift one's fanny.

pétardage [petarda:ʒ], *s.m.,* **pétardement** [petardəmɑ̃], *s.m. Min: Civ.E:* fragmentation (of rock) by blasting.

pétarder [petarde]. 1. *v.tr.* to blow up (wall, gate) with a petard; to blast (rock). 2. *v.i.* (*a*) *I.C.E:* to backfire; (*b*) *F:* to kick up a row.

pétardier [petardje], *s.m.* (*a*) *Mil: A:* petard firer; (*b*) *P:* rowdy.

pétase [petɑːz], *s.m. A.Gr.Cost:* petasus.

pétasite [petazit], *s.m. Bot:* butterbur, sweet-scented coltsfoot.

pétasse [petas], *s.f. P:* **1.** prostitute, tart. **2.** fear, funk; **avoir la p.,** to be in a (blue) funk.

Pétaud [peto], *Pr.n.m. used only in* **la cour du roi P.,** a house misruled, where everyone is master.

pétaudière [petodjɛːr], *s.f.* disorderly meeting; regular bear garden.

pétauriste [petɔrist], *s.m. Z:* petaurist, flying phalanger; taguan.

pet-d'âne [pɛdɑːn], *s.m. Bot:* cotton thistle; *pl. pets-d'âne.*

pet-de-nonne [pɛd(ə)nɔn], *s.m. Cu:* (type of) fritter; *pl. pets-de-nonne.*

pétéchiale [peteʃjal], *a. Vet:* **fièvre p.,** anasarca.

pétéchies [peteʃi], *s.f.pl. Med:* petechiae.

pet-en-l'air [petɑ̃lɛːr], *s.m.inv. Cost: F:* (*man's*) short indoor jacket; *P:* bum freezer.

péter [pete], *v.i.* (**je pète, n. pétons; je péterai**) **1.** *P:* (*a*) to break wind, to fart; **envoyer p. qn,** to send s.o. packing, to hell, about his business; **p. plus haut que le cul, plus haut que son derrière,** (i) to show off, swank; to be above oneself; (ii) to try to bite off more than one can chew; **p. dans la soie,** (i) to dress luxuriously; (ii) to show off, swank; (iii) to be rich, rolling in it; (*b*) *v.tr. F:* **p. du feu, des flammes,** to be bursting with energy, with vitality; to be a live wire; *P:* **p. la faim, la p.,** to be ravenously hungry, to be ready to eat a horse. **2.** (*of burning wood, etc.*) to crack, crackle; (*of cork, etc.*) to pop; (*of fire-arm, balloon, etc.*) to burst; *F:* (*of chair, etc.*) to break, to give way; *F:* (*of string, etc.*) to snap; *F:* **p. de santé,** to be bursting with health; **tous les boutons étaient prêts à p.,** all the buttons were about to burst off; *F:* **la tête me pète,** my head feels as if it's going to burst; *P:* **manger à s'en faire p. la sous-ventrière,** to eat till one is about to burst; *F:* **il faut que ça pète ou que ça dise pourquoi,** it's got to succeed, come off, whatever happens; *F:* **si vous hésitez plus long-temps, l'affaire va vous p. dans la main,** if you hesitate any longer, the business is going to fizzle out.

pète(-)sec [pɛtsɛk], *s.m.inv. F:* martinet.

péteur, -euse[1] [petœːr, -øːz], *s. P: A:* (*a*) farter; (*b*) ill-mannered lout; oaf; (*c*) coward.

péteuse[2] [petøːz], *s.f. Ich: F:* bitterling.

péteux, -euse[3] [petø, -øːz], *P: s.* coward, funk; *a.* in a funk.

péthidine [petidin], *s.f. Pharm:* pethidine.

pétillant [petijɑ̃], *a.* crackling (fire); semi-sparkling (wine); sparkling (eyes, wit); sprightly (wit); **margarine non pétillante,** non-spitting, non-splashing, margarine.

pétillement [petijmɑ̃], *s.m.* crackling (of burning wood); sparkling, fizzing, bubbling (of champagne); sparkling (of the eyes); **p. de la jeunesse,** sparkle of youth.

pétiller [petije], *v.i.* (*of burning wood*) to crackle; (*of drink*) to sparkle, fizz, bubble; (*of eyes*) to sparkle; **p. de joie,** to bubble over with joy; **livre qui pétille d'esprit,** book sparkling, scintillating, with wit.

pétiolaire [pesjɔlɛːr], *a. Bot:* petiolar.

pétiole [pesjɔl], *s.m. Bot:* petiole, leaf stalk, foot-stalk.

pétiolé [pesjɔle]. **1.** *a. Bot: Ent:* petiolate(d). **2.** *s.m.pl. Ent:* **pétiolés,** Petiolata.

pétiolule [pesjɔlyl], *s.m. Bot:* petiolule.

pétiolulé [pesjɔlyle], *a. Bot:* petiolulate.

petiot, -ote [pətjo, -ɔt], *a. & s. F:* tiny (child); **un p.,** a little 'un; **ma petiote,** my little girl; **viens ici, p.,** come here, little chap, little 'un, young 'un.

petit, -ite [pəti, -it], *a. & s.* **1.** *a.* (*a*) small; little; **un p. homme,** a little man; **c'est un homme p.,** he's small, short; **une petite maison,** a small house; **une toute petite maison,** a tiny little house; **p. bruit,** slight sound; **petite brise,** light breeze; **p. bois,** chopped wood; sticks; **faire une petite visite,** to pay a short visit, a short call; **à une petite distance de la gare,** at a short distance from the station; **mes chaussures sont trop petites,** my shoes are too small (for me); **ce cheval est p. pour sa race,** this horse is small for its breed; **en p.,** on a small scale, in miniature; **ce musée était le Louvre en p.,** the museum was a miniature Louvre; **p. à p.,** little by little, bit by bit; gradually; inch by inch; **à petites étapes,** by easy stages; **se faire tout p.,** (i) to make oneself as small, as inconspicuous, as possible; (ii) to cower (**devant,** before, in front of); **en me faisant tout p. je me suis frayé un chemin à travers la foule,** by making myself as small as possible, I managed to slip through the crowd; **j'avais une petite auto,** I had a toy car; **le monde est p.,** it's a small world; *F:* **le p. endroit, le p. coin,** the lavatory, the loo; (*b*) (*indicating appreciation or disapproval*) **une petite lettre de ma nièce,** a nice little letter from my niece; *F:* **un p. coup de rouge,** a nice drop of red wine; **p. misérable!** little wretch! **mais ma petite Louise . . .,** but my dear Louise . . .; **eh bien, et cette petite santé?** well, how are you? **elle s'inquiète toujours de sa petite santé,** she's always worrying about her precious health; (*c*) lesser, minor; **les petits talents,** the lesser talents; **les petits prophètes,** the minor prophets; **p. jury,** petty jury; *Sch:* **les petites classes,** the lower forms; **la petite industrie,** small-scale industry; **la petite chirurgie,** minor surgery; **petite guerre,** sham fight; *Com:* **petite caisse,** petty cash; *Iron:* (*of Napoleon III*) **Napoléon le p.,** Napoleon the Less; *Astr:* **la petite Ourse,** the Lesser, Little, Bear; *Bot:* **petite éclaire,** lesser celandine; **petite douve,** lesser spearwort; **p. cyprès,** ground cypress; **petite ciguë,** fool's parsley; **p. prêcheur,** Jack in the pulpit; **p. houx,** butcher's broom, knee holly; *Comest:* **petits fours,** petits fours; **petits pois,** (garden) peas; **p. salé** = streaky bacon; (*d*) *s.m.* **l'infiniment p.,** the infinitesimally small, the infinitesimal. **2.** *a.* (*a*) small, insignificant, unimportant, petty; minor; **p. commerçant,** small shopkeeper; **les petits propriétaires,** the small landowners; **la petite propriété,** small-holdings; **petites routes,** minor roads; **un partisan de la petite Angleterre,** a little Englander; **ce n'est pas une petite affaire,** that's no small matter; **par suite d'un p. accident,** owing to a slight, minor, accident, a slight mishap; **j'ai un p. rhume,** I've a slight cold, a bit of a cold; **un p. vin du pays,** a light local wine; **les petites gens,** *s.* **les petits,** people in humble circumstances; **les grands et les petits,** great and small; (*in U.S.*) **p. blanc,** poor white; **p. prince,** petty prince; *Ecc:* **les petites sœurs des pauvres,** the Little Sisters of the Poor; (*b*) feeble, poor, delicate; **il a une petite santé,** he's never really well; there's always something the matter with him. **3.** *a.* mean, petty, paltry; ungenerous; **c'est un p. esprit,** he's a got a small mind; he's very petty, niggling; **petites âmes,** (i) mean-spirited people; (ii) small-minded people. **4.** (*a*) *a.* **p. enfant,** little child; **petite fille,** little girl; **un p. bonhomme de six ans,** a little boy of six; **un p. Anglais,** an English boy; **les petits Anglais,** English children; **les petits Martin sont arrivés,** the Martin children have arrived; **j'ai vu les trois petites Thomas,** I saw the three little Thomas girls, Mrs Thomas' three little daughters; **livres pour les tout petits,** books for (very) young children, for the very young; **p. chien,** puppy; **p. chat,** kitten; **p. renard,** fox cub; (*b*) *s.* little boy; little girl; **le petit, la petite,** the baby; **pauvre petit(e),** poor little thing; *Sch:* **les petits,** the juniors; (*to child*) **viens ici, petit(e),** come here (my) dear; *F:* (*term of affection*) (*to woman*) **bonjour, mon p.,** good morning, my dear; *P:* **sortir avec une petite,** to go out with a girl, a bit of skirt; (*c*) *s.m.* young (of animal); **les petits d'un chien, d'un chat, d'un lion, d'un loup,** a dog's puppies, pups; a cat's kittens; a lion's whelps; a wolf's cubs; **p. du phoque,** seal calf, seal pup; **p., p., p.!** (*call to poultry to come and feed*) come along, come along! chuck! chuck! **faire des petits,** to have young; (*of bitch*) to pup, to whelp; (*of lion, etc.*) to whelp; (*of sow*) to farrow; (*of cat*) to kitten; (*of wolf*) to cub; *F:* (*of money*) to increase, multiply; to bear interest.

Petit(-)Belt (le) [ləpətibɛlt], *Pr.n.m. Geog:* the Little Belt (of the Baltic).

petit-beurre [pətibœːr], *s.m. Comest: R.t.m:* Petit beurre; *pl. petits-beurre.*

petit-bois [pətibwɑ], *s.m. Const:* window bar; *pl. petits-bois.*

petit-bourgeois, petite-bourgeoise [pətiburʒwa, pətitburʒwaːz]. **1.** *a.* (*a*) lower-middle class; (*b*) *Pej:* narrow-minded. **2.** *s.* (*a*) member of the lower-middle class; (*b*) narrow-minded person; *pl. petit(e)s-bourgeois(e)s.*

petit-cheval [pətiʃval], *s.m.* (*a*) *Mch:* donkey engine; (*b*) (**jeu de**) **petits-chevaux,** petits chevaux; *pl. petits-chevaux.*

petit-cousin, petite-cousine [pətikuzɛ̃, pətitkuzin] *s.* second cousin; *pl. petit(e)s-cousin(e)s.*

petite-fille [p(ə)titfiːj], *s.f.* grand-daughter; *pl. petites-filles.*

petite-maîtresse [pətitmɛtrɛs], *s.f. A:* belle; *pl. petites-maîtresses.*

petitement [p(ə)titmɑ̃], *adv.* (*a*) to a limited extent, in small quantities; (*b*) poorly, meanly, pettily; **se venger p.,** to take a mean revenge; **elle est logée p.,** she lives in poky lodgings; **vivre p.,** to live meagrely; to skimp.

petite-nièce [p(ə)titnjɛs], *s.f.* great-niece; *pl. petites-nièces.*

petite-oie [p(ə)titwa], *s.f. A:* (*a*) *Cu:* giblets; (*b*) (dress) accessories; *pl. petites-oies.*

petites-maisons [p(ə)titmɛzɔ̃], *s.f.pl. A:* lunatic asylum, madhouse.

petitesse [pətitɛs], *s.f.* **1.** (*a*) smallness, littleness, diminutiveness (of any object); slenderness (of figure); **p. d'une chambre,** smallness, pokiness, of a room; (*b*) meanness, pettiness, shabbiness; paltriness; **p. d'un don,** paltriness of a gift; **p. d'esprit,** narrow-mindedness. **2. faire des petitesses,** to do mean, shabby, actions; **quelle p.!** what a mean trick!

petit-fer [pətifɛːr], *s.m. Const:* (metallic) window bar; *pl. petits-fers.*

petit-fils [p(ə)tifis], *s.m.* grandson; *pl. petits-fils.*

petit-gris [p(ə)tigri], *s.m.* **1.** *Z:* miniver. **2.** squirrel (fur); calabar. **3.** *Comest:* edible brown snail; *pl. petits-gris.*

pétition [petisjɔ̃], *s.f.* (*a*) petition, memorial; **faire droit à une p.,** to grant a petition; **présenter une p. à qn,** to petition s.o.; **p. émanant de qn,** petition from s.o.; *Jur:* **obtenir (un pardon, etc.) par p.,** to sue out (a pardon, etc.); (*b*) *Log:* **p. de principe,** petitio principii; **faire une p. de principe,** to beg the question.

pétitionnaire [petisjɔnɛːr], *s.m. & f.* petitioner.

pétitionnement [petisjɔnmɑ̃], *s.m.* petitioning.

pétitionner [petisjɔne], *v.i.* to petition.

petit-lait [p(ə)tilɛ], *s.m.* whey; *F:* **ça se boit comme du p.-l.,** it slips down easily; **boire du p.-l.,** to take it in easily, to lap it up; *pl. petits-laits.*

petit-lion [pətiljɔ̃], *s.m. Z:* lion-monkey; *pl. petits-lions.*

petit-maître [pətimɛtr̥], *s.m. A:* fop, coxcomb; *pl. petits-maîtres.*

petit-nègre [pətinɛgr̥], *s.m. Ling: F:* pidgin, petit nègre.

petit-neveu [p(ə)tinvø], *s.m.* **1.** great nephew. **2.** *pl.* **nos petits-neveux,** our descendants.

pétitoire [petitwaːr], *a. Jur:* **action p.,** *s.m.* **pétitoire,** claim of ownership, of real estate; *Scot:* petitory suit.

petit-père [pətipɛːr], *s.m.* **1.** *Ecc: A:* Augustinian hermit. **2.** (*used in translations from the Russian*) little father; *pl. petits-pères.*

petit-poivre [pətipwavr̥], *s.m. Bot:* agnus castus, chaste tree; Abraham's balm; *pl. petits-poivres.*

petit-russe [pətirys], *a. & s. Hist:* Little Russian; *pl. petits-russes.*

petits-enfants [p(ə)tizɑ̃fɑ̃], *s.m.pl.* grandchildren.

petiveria [pɛtivɛrja], *s.m. Bot:* petiveria, guinea-hen weed.

pétochard [petɔʃaːr], *s.m. P:* coward, funk.

pétoche [petɔʃ], *s.f. P:* fear, funk; **avoir la p.,** to be in a funk.

pétoire [petwaːr], *s.f.* **1.** (child's) pop gun. **2.** *F:* poor sort of gun, gat.

peton [pətɔ̃], *s.m. F:* (*in nursery speech*) tiny foot, tootsy-wootsy; *pl.* tootsies.

pétoncle [petɔ̃ːkl̥], *s.m. Moll:* scallop.

pétoulet [petulɛ], *s.m. P:* buttocks, backside; **avoir le p. à zéro,** to be in a blue funk.

Pétrarque [petrark], *Pr.n.m.* Petrarch.

pétré [petre], *a. Geog:* stony; *used esp. in* **l'Arabie Pétrée,** Arabia Petraea.

pétrel [petrɛl], *s.m. Orn:* petrel; **p. océanite, p. de Wilson,** Wilson's petrel; **p. diablotin,** black-capped petrel; **p. damier,** Cape pigeon; pintado petrel; **p. cul-blanc,** Leach's petrel; **p. des neiges,** snow petrel; **p. de Bulwer,** Bulwer's petrel; **p. de Kermadec,** Kermadec petrel; **p. de Castro,** Madeiran petrel; **p. à lunettes,** white-chinned petrel; **p. à ailes blanches,** white-winged, collared, petrel; **p. tempête,** storm petrel; **p. glacial,** fulmar; **p. géant,** giant fulmar.

pétreux, -euse [petrø, -øːz], *a.* stone-like; *esp. Anat:* **os p.,** petrosal, petrous, bone; **sinus p.,** otic bone; petrous sinus.

pétri [petri], *a.* kneaded, moulded (**de,** out of); **un homme p. d'amour-propre,** a man eaten up with self-conceit; **p. d'ignorance,** steeped in ignorance; *A:* **il est p. d'honneur,** he is the soul of honour.

pétricole [petrikɔl], *s.f. Moll:* petricola.

pétricolidés [petrikɔlide], *s.m.pl. Moll:* Petricolidae.

pétrifiant [petrifjɑ̃], *a.* petrifying, petrifactive.

pétrification [petrifikasjɔ̃], *s.f.* petrification, petrifaction.

pétrifier [petrifje], *v.tr.* (*p.d. & pr.sub.* n. **pétri-fiions,** v. **pétrifiiez**) 1. to petrify; **bois pétrifié,** petrified, fossilized, wood; **pétrifié de peur, d'admiration,** petrified, paralysed, with fear; motionless in admiration; **nouvelle qui pétrifie,** petrifying news. 2. to encrust with lime.
se pétrifier. 1. to turn into stone; to petrify; **son sourire se pétrifia,** his smile became fixed. 2. to become encrusted with lime.
pétrin [petrɛ̃], *s.m.* kneading trough; **p. mécanique,** mechanical kneader, kneading machine (for bread making, for clay, etc.); *F:* **se mettre dans le p.,** to get into trouble, into a mess, into a fix; *F:* **être dans le p., dans un beau p.,** to be in a hole, in a tight corner, in a mess, in the soup, in the cart; **un beau p.!** here's a fine mess!
pétrinal [petrinal], *s.m. A.Arms:* petronel.
pétrir [petri:r], *v.tr.* (*a*) to knead (dough, bread); to knead, pug, shape, mould (clay); **vase pétri d'argile,** vase moulded in clay; (*b*) **p. l'esprit de qn,** to mould, shape, a person's character; (*c*) *Med:* **p. un muscle,** to knead a muscle.
pétrissage [petrisa:ʒ], *s.m.* (*a*) kneading (of dough, bread); kneading, pugging, shaping, moulding (of clay); (*b*) moulding, shaping (of character); (*c*) *Med:* petrissage.
pétrisseur, -euse [petrisœ:r, -ø:z]. 1. *s.* kneader; dough mixer. 2. *s.f.* **pétrisseuse,** kneading machine.
pétrochimie [petroʃimi], *s.f.* (*a*) petrochemistry; (*b*) petrochemical industry.
pétrochimique [petroʃimik], *a.* petrochemical; **l'industrie p.,** the petrochemical industry; petro-chemicals.
pétrochimiste [petroʃimist], *s.m. & f.* petro-chemist; petrochemical engineer.
pétrocorien, -ienne [petrokɔrjɛ̃, -jɛn], *a. & s. Geog:* (native, inhabitant) of Périgueux.
pétrodrome [petrodro:m], *s.m. Z:* forest elephant shrew.
pétrogale [petrogal], *s.m. Z:* rock wallaby; (*genus*) Petrogale.
pétrogénèse [petroʒenɛ:z], *s.f. Geol:* petrogenesis.
pétroglyphe [petroglif], *s.f.* petroglyph.
pétrographe [petrograf], *s.m. & f.* petrographer.
pétrographie [petrografi], *s.f. Geol:* petro-graphy.
pétrographique [petrografik], *a.* petrographic(al).
pétrolage [petrola:ʒ], *s.m.* 1. kindling with paraffin. 2. petrolage, oiling (of mosquito breeding grounds).
pétrolatum [petrolatɔm], *s.m. Pharm:* petrolatum.
pétrole [petrɔl], *s.m.* petroleum, (mineral) oil; **p. brut,** (crude) petroleum, crude oil, crude; **p. brut à base paraffinique,** paraffin-base crude; **p. brut doux,** sweet crude; **p. raffiné, rectifié,** refined, rectified, petroleum, oil; **p. lampant,** paraffin (oil), lamp oil, *U.S:* kerosene; **gisement, nappe, de p.,** oil deposit, oil pool; **puits de p.,** oil well; **canalisation de p.,** oil line; **droits d'extrac-tion de, du, p.,** oil rights, royalties; **trouver du p.,** to strike oil; **production de p.,** oil production; **raffinage du p.,** petroleum, oil, refining; **raffi-nerie de p.,** petrol, oil, refinery; **distillation du p.,** distillation of petroleum, oil distillation; **résidus de la distillation du p. brut,** crude bottoms; **coke de p.,** petroleum coke; **éther de p.,** petro-leum ether; **gelée de p.,** petroleum jelly; **lampe à p.,** paraffin lamp, *U.S:* kerosene lamp; **moteur à p.,** (heavy-)oil engine, petroleum engine; **navire qui chauffe au p.,** oil-fired ship; *Mil:* **p. enflammé,** liquid fire; *St.Exch:* **les pétroles, les valeurs de p.,** oils, oil shares.
pétroléochimie [petroleoʃimi], *s.f.* petrochem-istry; petrochemical industry.
pétroléochimique [petroleoʃimik], *a.* petro-chemical.
pétroler [petrole], *v.tr.* 1. to kindle, to set fire to, (sth.) with paraffin oil. 2. to oil (pools, etc.) against mosquitoes.
pétrolette [petrolet], *s.f.* (*a*) *F: O:* baby car; (*b*) *F:* moped.
pétroleuse [petrolø:z], *s.f. Hist:* (1871) incendiary, pétroleuse.
pétrolier, -ière [petrolje, -jɛr]. 1. *a.* **l'industrie pétrolière,** the petroleum, (mineral-)oil, industry; **port p.,** oil port; **flotte pétrolière,** tanker fleet; **expert p.,** oilman; *St.Exch:* **valeurs pétrolières,** oil shares. 2. *a. & s.m.* (navire) p.**,** tanker; **p. de haute mer,** sea-going tanker; **p. côtier,** coastal tanker; **p. géant,** giant tanker, supertanker, mammoth tanker. 3. *s.m.* oilman; petroleum engineer. 4. *s.f.pl. St.Exch:* **pétrolières,** oils, oil shares.
pétrolifère [petrolifɛ:r], *a.* petroliferous, oil-bearing; **champ, gisement, p.,** oilfield; **gîtes pétrolifères,** oil-bearing sediments; **sable p.,** oil

sand; **lentille de sable p.,** oil lens; **séries pétroli-fères,** oil-bearing series; **zone p.,** oil zone.
pétrolochimie [petroloʃimi], *s.f.* petrochemistry; petrochemical industry.
pétrolochimique [petroloʃimik], *a.* petrochemical.
pétrologie [petroloʒi], *s.f.* petrology.
pétromyidés [petromiide], *s.m.pl. Z:* Petromyidae.
pétromys [petromis], *s.m. Z:* rock rat.
pétromyzonidés [petromizonide], *s.m.pl. Ich:* Petromyzonidae; lampreys.
Pétrone [petron], *Pr.n.m. Lt.Lit:* Petronius.
Pétronille [petroni:j], *Pr.n.f.* Petronilla.
pétrosilex [petrosileks], *s.m. Miner:* petrosilex, felsite.
pétrosiliceux, -euse [petrosilisø, -ø:z], *a. Geol:* (micro-)felsitic.
pétrousquin [petruskɛ̃], *s.m. P:* 1. backside, rump, bum; **tomber sur son p.,** to sit down with a bump, *U.S:* to do a pratfall. 2. (*a*) civilian, civvy; (*b*) fellow, type, chap; (*c*) (*with f.* **pétrous-quine**) person from the back of beyond, *U.S:* from the backwoods, the sticks.
pétulance [petylɑ̃:s], *s.f.* liveliness, irrepressible-ness (of spirits); friskiness (of horse); **parler avec p.,** to speak impetuously.
pétulant [petylɑ̃], *a.* lively, irrepressible, full of spirits; frisky (horse).
pétun [petɛ̃], *s.m. A:* tobacco.
pétuner [petyne], *v.i. A:* to smoke, to indulge in tobacco.
pétunia [petynja], *s.m. Bot:* petunia.
pétunsé [petɛ̃se], *s.m.,* **pétunzé** [petɛ̃ze], *s.m. Miner: Cer:* petuntse, china stone.
petzite [petzit], *s.f. Miner:* petzite.
peu [pø]. 1. *adv.* (*a*) little; **p. ou point,** little or none; **manger p.** (**ou point**)**,** to eat little (or noth-ing); **nous marchons p. ou point,** we walk very little or not at all; **ils ne reçoivent que p.** ou point **de traitement,** they receive only a very small salary, if any (at all); **ni p. ni point,** none at all; **p. de viande,** not much meat, very little meat; **si p. qu'il pleuve, pour p. qu'il pleuve,** je resterai à la maison, however little it rains, even if it only rains a little, I shall stay at home; **ce n'est pas p. dire,** that's saying a good deal; **quelque p.,** to a slight extent; **je suis quelque p. surpris,** I am somewhat surprised; **être quelque p. connaisseur, médecin,** to be something of a connoisseur, of a doctor; **il est quelque p. jaloux,** he is a bit jealous; **tant soit p.,** somewhat; **je suis tant soit p. confus,** I am somewhat embarrassed; *s.a.* TANT 1; **c'est p. (que) de parler,** talking is not enough; (*indef. pron. neut.* **p. de chose,** (very) little, not much; **j'ai p. de chose de neuf à vous dire,** I have little new to tell you; **c'est bien p. de chose que cet obstacle-là,** that obstacle is of very little significance, impor-tance; **pour si p. de chose,** for so small a matter; **j'y ai été pour p. de chose,** I had (very) little to do with it; (*b*) few; **p. de gens,** few people; **p. de jours après,** not long after; **p. d'heures après,** not many hours later; **en p. de mots,** in a few words; **p. d'entre eux avaient voyagé,** few of them had travelled; **combien p. de ces explorateurs ont survécu!** how few of these explorers have survived! (*c*) not very; un-; **p. utile,** not very useful; **p. intelligent,** unintelligent, not over-intelligent; **peu seyant,** not very becoming, rather unbecoming; **opinion p. sou-tenable,** untenable opinion; **p. honnête,** dis-honest; **p. profond,** shallow; **p. abondant,** scarce; **les gens p. énergiques,** unenergetic people. 2. *s.m.* (*a*) little, bit; **j'ai fait le p. que j'ai pu,** I did what little I could; **le p. qu'il y a est à votre disposition,** you are welcome to the little there is; **donnez-m'en si p. que rien,** give me the least little bit, the least little drop; **j'ai perdu le p. d'argent que je possédais,** I have lost what little money I had; **le p. d'instruction qu'il a,** (i) his inadequate, scanty, education; (ii) what little education he has had; **son p. d'éducation lui a nui,** his lack of education has been against him; **son p. d'éducation lui a été précieux,** what little education he received has been invaluable to him; **nous avons vendu le p. de biens qui nous restaient,** we sold what little property we had left; **le p. de conversation qui avait lieu pendant le repas,** c'était leur hôte qui en faisait les frais, such conversation as went on during the meal came from their host; **mon p. de mémoire,** my lack of memory, my poor memory; **il a p. fait pour nous,** he has done (very) little for us; *A:* **homme de p.,** man of humble birth; **il a un p. moins, un p. plus, de quarante ans,** he's a little under, a little over, forty; **un p. de vin,** a little wine; **un tout petit p.,** a tiny bit, drop; **un tout petit p. de vin,** just a drop of wine; **encore un p.,**

a little more, a few more; **encore un p. de vin?** a little more wine? **il sait un p. d'anglais,** he knows a little English, has a smattering of English; **vous êtes allé un p. loin!** you went rather far, a bit far! **je suis un p. en retard,** I'm a bit late; *F:* **c'est un p. bien!** that's really good! *F:* **ça, c'est un p. fort!** that's a bit too much of a good thing, a bit much! **elle est un p. musicienne,** she's quite musical; she knows a bit about music; **il a un p. l'air étranger,** he has a slightly foreign appearance; **pour un p. on eût crié,** we very nearly shouted; **pour un p. je l'aurais jeté dehors,** for two pins I would have thrown him out; **écoutez un p.,** just listen; *F:* **viens un p.!** come here! **pressez-vous un p.,** hurry up, buck up, a bit; *F:* **excusez du p.!** is that all? *P:* **très p. pour moi!** not for me! I'm not having any! *P:* **un p., mon neveu!** you bet! rather! **p. à p.,** gradually; by degrees; little by little; **fort p.,** very little; **vivre p., to** live on next to nothing; (*b*) (*of time*) **restez encore un p.,** stay a bit, a little (while), longer; **p. après,** shortly after-(wards); **sous p., dans p., avant p., d'ici p.,** soon, before long; in the near future; **depuis p.,** lately; recently; **il avait appris depuis p. que . . .,** he had recently learnt that . . .; **j'ai manqué le train de p.,** I just missed the train; **il y a p., a little while ago, not (very) long ago; recently.
peucédan [pøsedɑ̃], *s.m. Bot:* peucedanum.
peuchère [pøʃɛ:r], *int. Dial:* (*S. of Fr.*) good gracious! heavens!
peuh [pø], *int.* pooh!
peuhl, peul [pøl], *a. & s.m. Ethn: Ling:* Peu(h)l, Fulah.
peulven [pølvɛn], *s.m.* (*in Brittany*) peulven, menhir.
peuplade [pœplad], *s.f.* small tribe, clan (of primitive peoples).
peuple [pœpl], *s.m.* 1. (*a*) people, nation; **le p. français,** the French people; **les peuples euro-péens,** the peoples, nations, of Europe; **peuples primitifs,** primitive peoples; **le p. élu,** the chosen race; (*b*) *A:* population (of a town, etc.). 2. (*a*) people (considered as a political entity); **le roi et son p.,** the king and his subjects; **le gouverne-ment du p.,** **par le p. et pour le p.,** government of the people, by the people and for the people; (*b*) **le p.,** the people, the masses; the proletariat; **les gens du p.; le petit, le menu, p.,** the lower, the working, classes; *Pej:* **le bas p.,** the riff-raff; **sortir du p.,** to be of humble origins; to have a working-class background; **mettre qch. à la portée du p.,** to bring sth. within the reach of the masses; **écrire pour le p.,** to write for the popular market; **gagner la faveur du p.,** to win the favour of the public; **qch. qui plaît au p.,** sth. with a popular appeal; **se pencher sur les souffrances du p.,** to feel for the underdog; (*c*) *a.inv. Pej:* common, vulgar; **ça fait p.,** that's vulgar, common; **expressions p.,** common, uneducated, expressions; **elle avait un je ne sais quoi de p.,** there was something low, vulgar, about her. 3. *A:* (*a*) crowd; **un p. de . . .,** a large number of . . .; a flock of . . .; (*b*) public, audience.
peuplé [pœple], *a.* inhabited; **pays très p.,** densely populated country.
peuplement [pœpləmɑ̃], *s.m.* 1. settlement, populating (of a region); stocking (of fish pond, game preserve, etc.); **régions à faible p.,** sparsely populated areas. 2. *For:* plantation; stand (of timber-trees); crop; **p. mélangé,** mixed stand; **consistance du p.,** crop density; *Bot:* **p. végétal,** vegetation (of an area).
peupler [pœple]. 1. *v.tr.* to people, populate (country); to stock (poultry yard, fish pond); **p. un parc de gibier,** to stock a park with game; **hêtres qui peuplent la crête,** beeches that clothe the crest; **rues peuplées de gens,** streets thronged, crowded, with people; **ville peuplée de souvenirs,** town full of memories. 2. *v.i.* to multiply, to breed.
se peupler, to become (densely) populated; **l'espace s'est peuplé peu à peu,** the empty space has gradually filled (up) with people.
peupleraie [pœplərɛ], *s.f. For:* poplar plantation.
peuplier [pœplije], *s.m.* poplar; **p. blanc, de Hollande,** white poplar, abele; **p. noir,** black poplar; **p. gris, grisard, grisaille,** grey poplar; **p. d'Italie,** Lombardy poplar; **p. suisse,** black Italian poplar; **p. baumier,** balsam poplar; **p. du Canada,** black cottonwood; **p. tremble,** aspen; **bois de p.,** cottonwood.
peur [pœ:r], *s.f.* 1. fear, fright; dread; **nous avions une grande p. du patron,** we stood in great fear, in awe, of the boss; **avoir p.,** to be, feel, frightened; **avoir p. du chien,** to be frightened, afraid, of the dog; **avoir p. de**

l'obscurité, to be afraid of the dark; **j'avais p. pour lui,** I was frightened on his account; I was afraid for him; **j'avais p. de vous gêner,** I was afraid I might be in your way, might disturb you; **n'ayez pas p.!** don't be afraid! **j'en ai bien p.,** I'm afraid so; **c'est trop tard, j'en ai p.,** it's too late, I'm afraid; **je mourais de p.,** I was dying of fright; **j'ai p. qu'il (ne) soit en retard,** (i) I'm worried in case he should be late; (ii) I'm afraid he may be late; **j'ai grand-p. qu'il n'oublie,** I'm very much afraid he may forget; **elle avait p. de chanceler, et qu'il s'en aperçût,** she was afraid of staggering, and of his noticing it; **j'avais si p. que tu ne viennes pas,** I was so afraid you might not come, you would not come; **(chien) qui a p. du coup de fusil,** gun-shy (dog); *F:* **vous n'avez pas p.!** you *have* got a nerve! *Iron:* **comme il est obéissant cet enfant, ça fait p.!** it's amazing how obedient that child is! **prendre p.,** to take fright; **être saisi par la p.,** to be terror-stricken; **la p. lui fit abandonner la tentative,** he was scared out of the attempt; *F:* **avoir la p. au ventre, avoir une p. bleue,** to have one's heart in one's boots, *F:* to be in a blue funk, to be scared to death; **avoir une p. bleue de qn,** to go in terror of s.o.; to be terrified of s.o.; **j'ai eu une p. bleue, cela m'a donné une belle p.,** I got an awful fright, it gave me an awful fright, *F:* it put me in a blue funk; **en être quitte pour la p.,** to get off with a fright; **il a eu plus de p. que de mal,** he is, was, more frightened than hurt; **faire p. à qn,** to frighten s.o.; to give s.o. a fright; **vous m'avez fait si p.!** you gave me such a fright! **cet homme-là me fait p.,** I'm terrified of that man; **être laid à faire p.,** to be frightfully ugly; **se faire p.,** to take fright, get frightened; **sans p.,** fearless, fearlessly. **2.** (*a*) *prep.phr.* **de p. de,** for fear of (sth.); **de p. de nous égarer,** for fear of losing our way; (*b*) *conj.phr.* **de p. que . . . (ne)** + *subj.* for fear that; **de p. que nous (n')oublions,** for fear we should forget, in case we forget; **prenez mon bras de p. que vous ne tombiez,** take my arm in case you fall, so that you don't fall.

peureusement [pœrøzmɑ̃], *adv.* timorously, timidly, nervously.

peureux, -euse [pœrø, -øːz]. **1.** *a.* timorous (person, glance); easily frightened; nervous; timid (nature); shy, skittish (horse); **être p. en affaires,** to be timid in business, to refuse to take risks in business; **p. comme un lièvre,** as timid as a hare. **2.** *s.* timid, nervous, person; **petit p.!** you little coward!

peut-être [pøtɛtr̥], *adv.* (*a*) perhaps, maybe, possibly; **p.-ê. (bien) que oui, p.-ê. (bien) que non,** perhaps so, perhaps not; **il est p.-ê. rentré chez lui,** he may have gone home; **p.-ê. s'est-il fait mal, il s'est p.-ê. fait mal, p.-ê. qu'il s'est fait mal,** perhaps he's hurt; he may be hurt; **p.-ê. bien qu'il viendra,** he will very likely, possibly, come; **j'ai p.-ê. vu trois personnes,** I saw perhaps three people; (*b*) *Iron:* **j'en sais quelque chose, p.-ê.!** I suppose you'll credit me with knowing something about it! **nous n'étions pas, p.-ê., fatigués,** oh no, *we* weren't tired! **vous n'attendez p.-ê. pas que je vous accompagne?** you don't expect me to go with you, I presume? I suppose? (*c*) *s.m.inv.* **il n'y a pas de p.-ê.,** there's no maybe, no perhaps, about it.

peyotl [pɛjɔtl̥], *s.m. Bot:* peyote.

pèze [pɛːz], *s.m. P:* money, dough, lolly; **un vieux tout à fait au p.,** a stinkingly rich old man.

pézize [peziːz], *s.f. Fung:* peziza.

pfennig [pfenig], *s.m. Num:* pfennig.

pff [pf], **pfft** [pfit], **pffut** [pfyːt], *int.* pooh!

phacélite [faselit], *s.f. Miner:* phacelite, kaliophilite.

phacochère [fakɔʃɛːr], *s.m. Z:* warthog.

phacolite [fakɔlit], *s.f. Miner:* phacolite.

phacomètre [fakɔmɛtr̥], *s.m. Opt:* phacometer.

Phaéton [faetɔ̃]. **1.** *Pr.n.m. Gr.Myth:* Phaethon. **2.** *s.m. A.Veh:* phaeton. **3.** *s.m.* coachman, driver. **4.** *s.m. Orn:* tropic bird.

phage [faːʒ], *s.m.* phage, bacteriophage.

phagédène [faʒedɛn], *s.f. Med:* (*a*) rodent ulcer; (*b*) *A:* boulimia.

phagédénique [faʒedenik], *a. Med:* phagedenic.

phagédénisme [faʒedenism], *s.m.* phaged(a)ena.

phagocytaire [fagɔsitɛːr], *a. Biol:* phagocytic.

phagocyte [fagɔsit], *s.m. Biol:* phagocyte.

phagocytose [fagɔsitoːz], *s.f. Biol:* phagocytosis.

phalacrocoracidés [falakrɔkɔraside], *s.m.pl. Orn:* Phalacrocoracidae, the cormorants.

phalange [falɑ̃ːʒ], *s.f.* **1.** (*a*) *Gr.Ant: Mil:* phalanx; (*b*) *Spanish Pol:* **la P.,** the Falange, Falangist party; (*c*) *Lit:* host, army; **les célestes phalanges,** the heavenly hosts. **2.** (*a*) *Anat:* phalanx, phalange, finger or toe bone; **p. unguéale,** ungual phalanx; (*b*) *P:* **phalanges,** hands, mitts, fists. **3.** *Bot:* phalanx.

phalanger [falɑ̃ʒe], *s.m. Z:* phalanger.

phalangéridés [falɑ̃ʒeride], *s.m.pl. Z:* Phalangeridae.

phalangette [falɑ̃ʒɛt], *s.f.* (*a*) *Anat:* phalangette, ungual phalanx, top joint (of finger, toe); (*b*) *Farr:* coffin bone.

phalangien, -ienne [falɑ̃ʒjɛ̃, -jɛn], *a. Anat:* phalangeal.

phalangine [falɑ̃ʒin], *s.f. Anat:* second joint, middle joint (of finger, toe).

phalangiste [falɑ̃ʒist]. **1.** *s.m. A.Gr.Mil:* phalangite. **2.** *s.m. & f. Pol:* Falangist; *a.* **parti p.,** Falangist party.

phalanstère [falɑ̃stɛːr], *s.m. Hist. of Pol.Ec:* phalanstery.

phalanstérien, -ienne [falɑ̃sterjɛ̃, -jɛn], *a.* phalansterian; Fourierist.

phalaris [falaris], *s.m. Bot:* canary grass, ribbon grass, lady's garters.

phalarope [falarɔp], *s.m. Orn:* phalarope; **p. à bec large, p. platyrhynque,** grey, *U.S:* red, phalarope; **p. à bec étroit, p. hyperbolé,** red-necked, *U.S:* northern, phalarope.

phalène [falɛn], *s.f.* (*occ. s.m. in poetry*) *Ent:* phalaena, moth; **p. mouchetée,** currant moth; **p. d'hiver,** winter moth.

phalère[1] [falɛːr], *s.f. Ent:* phalera (moth); **p. bucéphale,** buff-tip.

phalère[2], *s.f. Gr. & Rom.Ant:* phalera.

Phalère[3], *Pr.n.m. A.Geog:* Phalerum.

phalline [fal(l)in], *s.f. Bio-Ch:* phallin.

phallique [fal(l)ik], *a.* phallic; **emblème p.,** phallic symbol.

phallisme [fal(l)ism], *s.m. Rel.H:* phall(ic)ism.

phalloïde [fal(l)ɔid], *a. Nat.Hist:* phalloid; *Fung:* **amanite p.,** amanita phalloides, death cap.

phallus [fal(l)ys], *s.m.* phallus; *Fung:* **p. impudique,** stinkhorn.

phallusie [fal(l)yzi], *s.f. Z:* phallusia.

phanariote [fanarjɔt], *a. & s. Hist:* Phanariot.

phanère [fanɛːr], *s.m. Biol:* superficial body growth (*e.g.* hair, nails, teeth, feathers).

phanérocristallin [fanerɔkristalɛ̃], *a. Miner:* phanerocrystalline.

phanérogame [fanerɔgam], *Bot:* **1.** *a.* phanerogamic, phanerogamous. **2.** *s.f.* phanerogam; **les phanérogames,** the Phanerogamia.

phanérogamie [fanerɔgami], *s.f. Bot:* phanerogamy.

phanérophyte [fanerɔfit], *s.f. Bot:* phanerophyte.

phanotron [fanɔtrɔ̃], *s.m. Elcs:* phanotron, phanatron.

phantasme [fɑ̃tasm], *s.m.* phantasm; optical illusion.

phantastron [fɑ̃tastrɔ̃], *s.m. Elcs:* phantastron.

pharamineux, -euse [faraminø, -øːz], *a. F:* fantastic, colossal; **un rhume p.,** a whale of a cold.

pharaon [faraɔ̃], *s.m.* **1.** *Hist:* Pharaoh; **les tombeaux des pharaons,** the tombs of the Pharaohs. **2.** *Cards:* faro.

pharaonien, -ienne [faraɔnjɛ̃, -jɛn], **pharaonique** [faraɔnik], *a.* Pharaonic.

phare[1] [faːr], *s.m.* **1.** *Nau:* lighthouse; **p. marin,** marine light; **p. à éclats,** flashing light; **p. à occultations, à éclipses,** occulting light; **p. intermittent, p. isophase,** intermittent light; **p. (à feu) fixe,** fixed light; **p. fixe à éclats,** fixed and flashing light; **p. (à feu) tournant,** revolving light; **p. flottant,** lightship; **gardien de p.,** lighthouse keeper. **2.** *Av:* beacon; **p. aéronautique,** air (navigation) light; **p. d'aéroport,** airport beacon; **p. d'atterrissage,** landing light; **p. de balisage, de jalonnement (de route), p. de ligne, de navigation,** airway beacon; **p. de repérage,** landmark beacon; **jalonner une route aérienne (avec des phares),** to beacon a route; **p. code,** code beacon (conveying special information); **p. à éclats, à éclipses,** blinker (beacon); **p. tournant,** rotating beacon; **p. hertzien,** radio beacon. **3.** *Aut: etc:* headlight; **p. encastré,** built-in headlight; **baisser les phares, mettre les phares en code,** to dip the headlights; **p. code,** dipped headlight; **p. anti-brouillard,** foglight, foglamp; **p. de recul,** reversing light; **p. orientable, p. auxiliaire, p. de repérage,** spotlight; *Av:* **p. aéronautique,** (air) navigation light; **p. de roulement,** taxi light; *Ill:* **p. d'éclairage,** floodlight; *Mil:* **p. cuirassé,** armoured searchlight.

phare[2], *s.m. Nau:* sails and yards (of a mast); **p. de grand mât,** mainsails.

Pharès [farɛs]. *See* MANÉ.

pharillon [farijɔ̃], *s.m. Fish:* flare; **pêche au p.,** flare fishing.

pharisaïque [farizaik], *a.* Pharisaic(al); hypocritical.

pharisaïquement [farizaikmɑ̃], *adv.* Pharisaically; hypocritically.

pharisaïsme [farizaism], *s.m.* Pharisaism, Phariseeism; hypocrisy.

pharisien, -ienne [farizjɛ̃, -jɛn], *s.* (*a*) *Rel.H:* Pharisee; (*b*) Pharisee, formalist; hypocrite.

pharmaceutique [farmasøtik]. **1.** *a.* pharmaceutic(al). **2.** *s.f.* pharmaceutics.

pharmacie [farmasi], *s.f.* **1.** pharmacy; dispensing. **2.** (*a*) pharmacy; chemist's shop; (*b*) dispensary. **3.** (*a*) pharmaceuticals; medicines; (*b*) **(armoire à) p.,** medicine chest, cabinet; **p. portative,** first-aid kit.

pharmacien, -ienne [farmasjɛ̃, -jɛn], *s.* pharmacist, dispensing chemist; dispenser.

pharmacodynamie [farmakɔdinami], *s.f. Med:* pharmacodynamics.

pharmacodynamique [farmakɔdinamik], *a.* pharmacodynamic.

pharmacognosie [farmakɔgnozi], *s.f.* pharmacognosy.

pharmacolit(h)e [farmakɔlit], *s.f. Miner:* pharmacolite.

pharmacologie [farmakɔlɔʒi], *s.f.* pharmacology.

pharmacologique [farmakɔlɔʒik], *a.* pharmacological.

pharmacologiste [farmakɔlɔʒist], *s.m. & f.,* **pharmacologue** [farmakɔlɔg], *s.m. & f.* pharmacologist.

pharmacomanie [farmakɔmani], *s.f. Psy:* pharmacomania.

pharmacopée [farmakɔpe], *s.f.* pharmacopoeia.

Pharnace [farnas], *Pr.n.m. A.Hist:* Pharnaces.

Pharsale [farsal], *Pr.n. A.Geog:* **1.** Pharsalus. **2.** **2.** *Pr.n.f.* Pharsalia (district of Thessaly); *Rom. Hist:* **la bataille de P.,** the battle of Pharsalia; *Lt.Lit:* **la P.,** (Lucan's) Pharsalia.

pharyngal, -aux [farɛ̃gal, -o], *a. Ling:* pharyng(e)al.

pharyngé [farɛ̃ʒe], *a. Anat:* pharyng(e)al.

pharyngectomie [farɛ̃ʒɛktɔmi], *s.f. Surg:* pharyngectomy.

pharyngien, -ienne [farɛ̃ʒjɛ̃, -jɛn], *a. Anat:* pharyngeal.

pharyngite [farɛ̃ʒit], *s.f. Med:* pharyngitis; **p. subaiguë,** subacute pharyngitis, relaxed throat.

pharyngobranche [farɛ̃gɔbrɑ̃ːʃ], *Ich:* **1.** *a.* pharyngobranchial. **2.** *s.m.* pharyngobranch.

pharyngoglosse [farɛ̃gɔglɔs], *a. Anat:* pharyngoglossal.

pharyngognates [farɛ̃gɔgnat], *s.m.pl. Ich:* Pharyngognathi.

pharyngo-laryngé [farɛ̃gɔlarɛ̃ʒe], *a. Med:* **syndrome p.-l.,** pharyngitis; *pl. pharyngo-laryngé(e)s.*

pharyngo-laryngite [farɛ̃gɔlarɛ̃ʒit], *s.f. Med:* pharyngolaryngitis.

pharyngoscope [farɛ̃gɔskɔp], *s.m. Med:* pharyngoscope.

pharyngoscopie [farɛ̃gɔskɔpi], *s.f. Med:* pharyngoscopy.

pharyngotomie [farɛ̃gɔtɔmi], *s.f. Med:* pharyngotomy.

pharynx [farɛ̃ːks], *s.m. Anat:* pharynx.

phasco(lo)gale [faskɔ(lɔ)gal], *s.m. Z:* phascogale; brush-tailed marsupial rat.

phascolome [faskɔlɔm], *s.m. Z:* wombat.

phascolosome [faskɔlɔzoːm], *s.m. Ann:* phascolosoma.

phase [fɑːz], *s.f.* **1.** *Astr:* phase, phasis (of moon, etc.). **2.** (*a*) phase, stage, period; **les phases d'une maladie,** the stages, phases, of an illness; *Ind:* **phases de fabrication,** processing stages; **la première, la dernière, p. de la modernisation de l'équipement,** the initial, the final, stage of the modernization of equipment; (*of computer*) **p. de compilation,** compiling phase; **p. d'exécution,** run phase; (*b*) *El:* **en p.,** in phase, in step; **mettre en p.,** to phase, to bring into step, to synchronize; **mise en p.,** phasing, bringing into step, synchronization; **relais de mise en p.,** phasing relay; **angle de p.,** phase angle; **avance, retard, de p.,** phase lead, lag; **être en avance, en retard, de p.,** to lead, to lag, in phase; **angle d'avance de p.,** angle of lead in phase; **changement, déplacement, de p.,** phase shift; **changeur de p.,** phase shifter; **convertisseur de p.,** phase converter; **décalage de p.,** difference of phase, phase displacement; **décalé en p.,** differing in phase; **équilibrage de p.,** phase compensation; **inversion de p.,** phase reversal, phase inversion; **inverseur de p.,** phase inverter; **régulateur de p.,** phase advancer; **rapport de p.,** phase relationship; (*c*) *Atom.Ph:* phase, zone; **p. alpha, bêta, gamma,** alpha, beta, gamma, phase; **p. initiale,**

initial, starting, phase; **p. gazeuse, liquide,** vapour, liquid, zone; **diagramme de p.,** phase diagram; (*d*) *Metall:* **changement de p.,** phase transformation.
phasé [fɑze], *a. El:* phased; **à enroulement p.,** phase-wound (rotor).
phaséline [fazelin], *s.f. Bio-Ch:* phaselin.
phasemètre [fɑzmɛtr̥], *s.m. El:* phasemeter; **p. enregistreur,** phase recorder.
phaséole [fazeɔl], *s.f. Bot:* haricot bean.
phaséoline [fazeɔlin], *s.f. Bio-Ch:* phaseolin.
phaséolunatine [fazeɔlynatin], *s.f. Ch:* phaseolunatin.
phasianelle [fazjanɛl], *s.f. Moll:* pheasant shell; (*genus*) Phasianella.
phasianidés [fazjanide], *s.m.pl. Orn:* Phasianidae.
phasitron [fɑzitrɔ̃], *s.m. Elcs:* phasitron.
phasme [fasm], *s.m. Ent:* phasma; stick insect, walking stick.
phasmidé [fasmide], *s.m. Ent:* (*a*) phasmid; spectre insect; (*b*) *pl.* **phasmidés,** Phasmidae.
phasmoptères [fazmɔptɛːr], *s.m.pl. Ent:* Phasmoptera.
phasotron [fɑzɔtrɔ̃], *s.m. Atom.Ph:* synchrocyclotron.
phéacien, -ienne [feasjɛ̃, -jɛn], *a. & s. Myth:* Phaeacian.
Phébé [febe], *Pr.n.f.* Phoebe.
phébéen, -éenne [febeɛ̃, -eɛn], *a.* Phoebean.
Phébus [febys]. **1.** *Pr.n.m. Myth:* Phoebus, Apollo. **2.** *s.m. A:* (*a*) **parler p., donner dans le p.,** to talk bombast; to indulge in fine talk; to speechify; (*b*) (*pers.*) glib talker; grandiloquent talker.
Phédon [fedɔ̃], *Pr.n.m. Gr.Lit:* Phaedon.
Phèdre[1] [fɛdr̥], *Pr.n.m. Cl.Lit:* Phaedrus.
Phèdre[2], *Pr.n.f. Myth:* Phaedra.
phégoptère [fegɔptɛːr], *a.* growing under beeches.
phellandrène [fɛl(l)ɑ̃drɛn], *s.m. Ch:* phellandrene.
phelloderme [fɛl(l)ɔdɛrm], *s.m. Bot:* phelloderm.
phellogène [fɛl(l)ɔʒɛn], *Bot:* **1.** *a.* phellogen(et)ic (layer). **2.** *s.m.* phellogen.
phénacétine [fenasetin], *s.f. Pharm:* phenacetin.
phénacéturique [fenasetyrik], *a. Ch:* phenaceturic.
phénacite [fenasit], *s.f. Miner:* phenakite, phenacite.
phénacyle [fenasil], *s.m. Ch:* phenacyl.
phénakisti(s)cope [fenakisti(s)kɔp], *s.m. A:* phenakistoscope, thaumatrope, zoetrope.
phénanthrène [fenɑ̃trɛn], *s.m. Ch:* phenanthrene.
phénanthridine [fenɑ̃tridin], *s.f. Ch:* phenanthridine.
phénanthridone [fenɑ̃tridɔn], *s.f. Ch:* phenanthridone.
phénanthrol [fenɑ̃trɔl], *s.m. Ch:* phenanthrol.
phénanthroline [fenɑ̃trɔlin], *s.f. Ch:* phenanthroline.
phénate [fenat], *s.m. Ch:* phenolate.
phénazine [fenazin], *s.f. Ch:* phenazine.
phénazone [fenazɔn], *s.f. Ch:* phenazone.
phénétidine [fenetidin], *s.f. Ch:* phenetidine.
phénétole [fenetɔl], *s.m. Ch:* phenetol(e).
phengite [fɛ̃ʒit], *s.f. Miner:* phengite.
Phénicie [fenisi], *Pr.n.f. A.Geog:* Phoenicia.
phénicien, -ienne [fenisjɛ̃, -jɛn]. **1.** *a. & s. A.Geog:* Phoenician. **2.** *s.m. Ling:* Phoenician.
phénicine [fenisin], *s.f. Dy: A:* phenicin(e); indigo purple.
phénylbutazone [fenilbytazɔn], *s.f.* phenylbutazone.
phénique [fenik], *a. Ch:* **acide p.,** carbolic acid, phenic acid, phenol.
phéniqué [fenike], *a. Pharm:* carbolic; **eau phéniquée,** carbolic lotion, weak phenol solution; **gaze phéniquée,** carbolated gauze.
phéniquer [fenike], *v.tr. Pharm: etc:* to carbolize.
phénix [feniks], *s.m.* **1.** (*a*) *Myth:* phoenix; (*b*) phoenix, paragon, rara avis; *Pej:* **ce n'est pas un p.,** he's no genius. **2.** *Husb:* Yokohama cock, phoenix fowl. **3.** *Ent:* chaerocampa celerio.
phén(o)- [fen(ɔ)], *pref.* phen(o)-.
phénobarbital [fenɔbarbital], *s.m. Pharm:* phenobarbital.
phénocristal [fenɔkristal], *s.m. Geol:* phenocryst.
phénogénétique [fenɔʒenetik], *a. Biol:* phenogenetic.
phénol [fenɔl], *s.m.* (*a*) *Ch:* phenol, phenyl alcohol; (*b*) *Com:* carbolic acid.
phénolate [fenɔlat], *s.m. Ch:* phenolate, phenoxide.
phénolique [fenɔlik], *a. Ch:* phenolic.
phénologie [fenɔlɔʒi], *s.f. Biol: Meteor:* phenology.
phénolphtaléine [fenɔlftalein], *s.f. Ch:* phenol(-) phthalein.
phénolsulfonique [fenɔlsylfɔnik], *a. Ch:* phenolsulphonic.
phénoménal, -aux [fenɔmenal, -o], *a.* phenomenal; prodigious, amazing; **une bêtise phénoménale,** a phenomenal, an outstanding, piece of stupidity.
phénoménalement [fenɔmenalmɑ̃], *adv.* phenomenally, amazingly.
phénoménalisme [fenɔmenalism], *s.m. Phil:* phenomenalism.
phénomène [fenɔmɛn], *s.m.* (*a*) phenomenon; **les phénomènes de la nature,** the phenomena of nature; **p. électrique,** electrical phenomenon; **p. économique,** economic phenomenon; *F:* **c'est un p. de vous voir ici,** it's a wonder seeing you here; (*b*) (*pers.*) (i) phenomenon, marvel; (ii) *F:* freak, outlandish character; **jeune p.,** infant prodigy; *F:* (*of one's children*) **mes trois phénomènes,** my three bright specimens; *F:* **un p. vivant,** a living wonder; (*c*) freak (of nature); (*in fairs*) **montreur de phénomènes,** freak showman; (*d*) *Ph:* event.
phénoménisme [fenɔmenism], *s.m. Phil:* phenomenalism.
phénoméniste [fenɔmenist], *s.m. & f. Phil:* phenomen(al)ist.
phénoménologie [fenɔmenɔlɔʒi], *s.f. Phil:* phenomenology.
phénoménologique [fenɔmenɔlɔʒik], *a. Phil:* phenomenologic(al).
phénoménologue [fenɔmenɔlɔg], *s.m. & f. Phil:* phenomenologist.
phénoplaste [fenɔplast], *s.m. Ch:* phenoplast, phenolic resin.
phénosafranine [fenɔsafranin], *s.f. Ch:* phenosafranin(e).
phénotype [fenɔtip], *s.m. Biol:* phenotype.
phénotypique [fenɔtipik], *a.* phenotypical.
phénoxazine [fenɔksazin], *s.f. Ch:* phenoxazine.
phénylacétaldéhyde [fenilasetaldeid], *s.m. Ch:* phenylacetaldehyde.
phénylacétamide [fenilasetamid], *s.m. Ch:* phenylacetamide.
phénylacétique [fenilasetik], *a. Ch:* phenylacetic.
phénylalanine [fenilalanin], *s.f. Ch:* phenylalanine.
phénylamine [fenilamin], *s.f. Ch:* (*a*) phenylamine; (*b*) aniline.
phenylbenzène [fenilbɛ̃zɛn], *s.m. Ch:* phenylbenzene, diphenyl.
phényle [fenil], *s.m. Ch:* phenyl.
phénylé [fenile], *a. Ch:* phenylated; (*in compounds*) phenyl.
phénylène [fenilɛn], *s.m. Ch:* phenylene.
phényléthylène [feniletilɛn], *s.m. Ch:* phenylethylene.
phénylhydrazine [fenilidrazin], *s.f. Ch:* phenylhydrazine.
phénylique [fenilik], *a. Ch:* phenylic.
phéochromocytome [feɔkromositɔm], *s.m. Med:* phacochromocytoma.
phéon [feɔ̃], *s.m. Her:* pheon.
phéophycées [feɔfise], *s.f.pl. Algae:* Phaeophyceae, Laminariaceae.
phérécratéen [ferekrateɛ̃], **phérécratien** [ferekrasjɛ̃], *a.m. & s.m. Pros:* pherecratean, pherecratic (verse).
phérormone [ferɔrmɔn], *s.f. Ap:* queen substance.
phi [fi], *s.m. Gr.Alph:* phi.
phiale [fjal], *s.f. Gr.Ant:* phiale.
Philadelphie [filadɛlfi], *Pr.n.f. Geog:* Philadelphia.
philadelphien, -ienne [filadɛlfjɛ̃, -jɛn], *a. & s. Geog:* Philadelphian.
philanthe [filɑ̃ːt], *s.m. Ent:* philanthus; digger wasp.
philanthrope [filɑ̃trɔp], *s.m. & f.* philanthropist.
philanthropie [filɑ̃trɔpi], *s.f.* philanthropy; **avec p.,** philanthropically.
philanthropique [filɑ̃trɔpik], *a.* philanthropic(al).
philanthropiquement [filɑ̃trɔpikmɑ̃], *adv.* philanthropically.
philanthropisme [filɑ̃trɔpism], *s.m.* philanthropism.
philatélie [filateli], *s.f.,* **philatélisme** [filatelism], *s.m.* philately, stamp collecting.
philatélique [filatelik], *a.* philatelic.
philatéliste [filatelist]. **1.** *s.m. & f.* philatelist, stamp collector. **2.** *a.* philatelic.
Philémon [filemɔ̃], *Pr.n.m. Myth: Gr.Lit:* Philemon; **ils sont comme P. et Baucis,** they're just like Darby and Joan.
philépitte [filepit], *s.f. Orn:* philepitta.
philépittidés [filepitide], *s.m.pl. Orn:* Philepittidae.
philharmonique [filarmɔnik], *a.* philharmonic (society, etc.).
philhellène [filɛlɛn]. **1.** *s.m.* Philhellene. **2.** *a.* philhellenic.
philhellénisme [filɛlenism], *s.m.* philhellenism.
Philippe [filip], *Pr.n.m.* Philip; *Hist:* **P. le Bel,** Philip the Fair (of France); **P. le Beau,** Philip the Handsome (of Spain); **P. le Hardi,** (i) Philip the Rash (of France); (ii) Philip the Bold (of Burgundy); **P.-Auguste,** Philip Augustus (of France).
Philippes [filip], *Pr.n. A.Geog:* Philippi.
philippien, -ienne [filipjɛ̃, -jɛn], *a. & s. A.Geog:* Philippian.
philippin, -ine [filipɛ̃, -in], *a. & s. Geog:* Filipino.
Philippine [filipin]. **1.** *Pr.n.f.* Philippa. **2.** *s.f.* (*double almond*) Philippina, philopoena, philippine.
Philippines (les) [lefilipin], *Pr.n.f.pl. Geog:* the Philippines.
philippique [filipik], *s.f.* philippic (oration).
philippsite [filipsit], *s.f. Miner:* bornite.
Philis [filis], *Pr.n.f.* Phyllis.
philistin, -ine [filistɛ̃, -in], *a. & s.* (*a*) *A.Geog: B.Lit:* Philistine; (*b*) (*unenlightened person*) philistine.
philistinisme [filistinism], *s.m.* philistinism; lack of taste.
phillipsite [filipsit], *s.f. Miner:* phillipsite.
phil(o)- [fil(ɔ)], *pref.* phil(o)-.
philo [filo], *s.f. Sch: F:* philosophy class (= upper VIth form).
Philocrate [filɔkrat], *Pr.n.m. Gr.Hist:* Philocrates.
Philoctète [filɔktɛt], *Pr.n.m. Gr.Lit:* Philoctetes.
philologie [filɔlɔʒi], *s.f.* philology.
philologique [filɔlɔʒik], *a.* philological.
philologiquement [filɔlɔʒikmɑ̃], *adv.* philologically.
philologue [filɔlɔg], *s.m. & f.* philologist.
Philomèle [filɔmɛl], *Pr.n.f.* (*a*) *Myth:* Philomela; (*a*) *Poet:* philomel, the nightingale; *Orn:* **rossignol p.,** nightingale.
Philon [filɔ̃], *Pr.n.m. Hist:* Philo; **P. le Juif,** Philo Judaeus.
philoptère [filɔptɛːr], *s.m. Ent:* philopterid.
philoptéridés [filɔpteride], *s.m.pl. Ent:* Philopteridae.
philosophailler [filɔzɔfɑje], *v.i. Pej:* to philosophize.
philosophale [filɔzɔfal], *a.f. A:* **la pierre p.,** the philosophers' stone.
philosophard [filɔzɔfaːr], *a. Pej:* philosophizing.
philosophe [filɔzɔf]. **1.** *s.m. & f.* philosopher; **supporter un malheur en p.,** to bear a misfortune philosophically. **2.** *a.* philosophical.
philosopher [filɔzɔfe], *v.i.* to philosophize.
philosophie [filɔzɔfi], *s.f.* **1.** philosophy; **p. de la nature,** natural philosophy; **prendre les choses avec p.,** to take things philosophically; *Sch:* **classe de p.,** philosophy class (= upper VIth, arts). **2.** *Typ:* long primer; ten-point type.
philosophique [filɔzɔfik], *a.* philosophical; philosophic.
philosophiquement [filɔzɔfikmɑ̃], *adv.* philosophically.
philosophisme [filɔzɔfism], *s.m.* philosophism.
Philostrate [filɔstrat], *Pr.n.m. Gr.Lit:* Philostratus.
philotechnique [filɔtɛknik], *a.* philotechnic (association, etc.); fond of, devoted to, the (industrial) arts.
philtre [filtr̥], *s.m.* (love) philtre.
phimosis [fimozis], *s.m. Med:* phimosis.
Phinée(s)[1] [fine], *Pr.n.m. B:* Phine(h)as.
Phinée[2], *Pr.n.m. Gr.Myth:* Phineus.
phlébectasie [flebɛktazi], *s.f. Med:* phlebectasia.
phlébectomie [flebɛktɔmi], *s.f. Surg:* phlebectomy.
phlébite [flebit], *s.f. Med:* phlebitis.
phlébographie [flebɔgrafi], *s.f. Med:* phlebography.
phlébographique [flebɔgrafik], *a.* phlebographical.
phlébologie [flebɔlɔʒi], *s.f. Anat:* phlebology.
phléborragie [flebɔraʒi], *s.f. Med:* phleborrhagia.
phlébosclérose [flebɔskleroːz], *s.f. Med:* phlebosclerosis.
phlébotome [flebɔtɔm], *s.m.* **1.** *Surg:* lancet. **2.** *Ent:* blood sucking sand fly, phlebotomus; *pl.* **phlébotomes,** Phlebotomi.
phlébotomie [flebɔtɔmi], *s.f. Med:* phlebotomy.
phlegmasie [flɛgmazi], *s.f. Med:* phlegmasia.
phlegmon [flɛgmɔ̃], *s.m. Med:* phlegmon.
phlegmoneux, -euse [flɛgmɔnø, -øːz], *a.* phlegmonic, phlegmonous.
phléole [fleɔl], *s.f. Bot:* phleum, *F:* cat's tail grass; **p. des prés,** timothy grass, meadow cat's tail grass.
phlobaphène [flɔbafɛn], *s.m. Ch:* phlobaphene.

phloème [flɔɛm], *s.m. Bot:* phloem.

phlogistique [flɔʒistik], *A.Ch:* 1. *a.* phlogistic. 2. *s.m.* phlogiston.

phlogopite [flɔgɔpit], *s.f. Miner:* phlogopite; rhombic mica.

phlorétine [flɔretin], *s.f. Ch:* phloretin.

phlorétique [flɔretik], *a. Ch:* phloretic.

phlori(d)zine [flɔrizin], *s.f. Ch:* phlor(h)izin.

phloroglucine [flɔrɔglysin], *s.f.*, **phloroglucinol** [flɔrɔglysinɔl], *s.m. Ch:* phloroglucin(ol).

phlox [flɔks], *s.m. Bot:* phlox; **p. subulé,** moss pink, phlox pink.

phlyctène [fliktɛn], *s.f. Med:* phlyct(a)ena, vesicle, pimple, (water) blister, bleb.

phlycténoïde [fliktenɔid], *a. Med:* phlyctenoid.

phlycténule [fliktenyl], *s.f. Med:* phlyctenule, phlyctenula.

phobie [fɔbi], *s.f. Med:* phobia; morbid fear; **la p. de la guerre,** aversion from, to, war; **avoir une p. du téléphone,** to have a horror of the telephone.

phobique [fɔbik], *a. Med:* 1. relating to a phobia, phobic. 2. (*pers.*) subject to a phobia, to a morbid fear.

Phocée [fɔse], *Pr.n.f. A.Geog:* Phocaea.

phocéen, -enne [fɔseɛ̃, -ɛn], *a. & s. A.Geog:* Phocaean; **la cité phocéenne,** Marseille(s).

phocène [fɔsɛn], *s.f. Z:* (= MARSOUIN) porpoise.

Phocide [fɔsid], *Pr.n.f. Geog:* Phocis.

phocidés [fɔside], *s.m.pl. Z:* Phocidae.

phocidien, -ienne [fɔsidjɛ̃, -jɛn], *a. & s. Geog:* Phocian.

phocomèle [fɔkɔmɛl], *Ter:* 1. *a.* phocomelic, phocomelous. 2. *s.m.* phocomelus.

phocomélie [fɔkɔmeli], *s.f. Ter:* phocomelia.

phœnicite [fenisit], *s.f. Miner:* phoenicite.

phœnicochroïte [fenikɔkrɔit], *s.f. Miner:* phoenicochroite, phenicochroite, phoenicite.

phœnicoptéridés [fenikɔpteride], *s.m.pl. Orn:* Phoenicopteridae, the flamingoes.

phœnix [feniks], *s.m. Bot:* phoenix.

pholade [fɔlad], *s.f. Moll:* pholas, piddock, stone-borer.

pholadidés [fɔladide], *s.m.pl. Moll:* Pholadidae.

pholcodine [fɔlkɔdin], *s.f.* pholcodine.

pholidote [fɔlidɔt], *Z:* 1. *a.* scaly. 2. *s.m.pl.* **pholidotes,** Pholidota, the pangolins.

pholiote [fɔljɔt], *s.f. Fung:* pholiota.

phonation [fɔnasjɔ̃], *s.f. Physiol: Ling:* phonation.

phonatoire [fɔnatwaːr], *a.* phonatory.

phonautographe [fɔnotɔgraf], *s.m. Ac:* phonautograph.

phone [fɔn], *s.m. Ac.Meas:* phon.

phonématique [fɔnematik], *Ling:* 1. *a.* phonematic. 2. *s.f.* phonematics.

phonème [fɔnɛm], *s.m. Ling:* phoneme, phone.

phonemètre [fɔnmɛtr̥], *s.m. Ac:* phonmeter.

phonémique [fɔnemik], *a. Ling:* phonemic.

phonendoscope [fɔnɑ̃dɔskɔp], *s.m. Med:* phonendoscope.

phonéticien, -ienne [fɔnetisjɛ̃, -jɛn], *s.* phonetist, phonetician.

phonétique [fɔnetik]. 1. *a.* phonetic. 2. *s.f.* phonetics.

phonétiquement [fɔnetikmɑ̃], *adv.* phonetically.

phonétisme [fɔnetism], *s.m.* phonetism.

phonétiste [fɔnetist], *s.m. & f.* phonetician.

phoniatre [fɔnjatr̥], *s.m. & f. Med:* phoniatric specialist.

phoniatrie [fɔnjatri], *s.f. Med:* phoniatry, phoniatrics.

phonie [fɔni], *F:* (= RADIOPHONIE, TÉLÉPHONIE); *Mil:* **parler en p.,** to radio, phone, a message.

phonique [fɔnik]. 1. *a.* phonic; acoustic; **signal p.,** sound signal; *Tp:* **appel p.,** audible call (apparatus); buzzer; **isolation p.,** sound proofing. 2. *s.f.* phonics.

phonocamptique [fɔnɔkɑ̃ptik], *a. Ac:* that reflects sound.

phonocapteur [fɔnɔkaptœːr], *s.m. Cin: etc:* sound reproducer, sound reproducing unit.

phonocardiogramme [fɔnɔkardjɔgram], *s.m. Med:* phonocardiogram.

phonocardiographie [fɔnɔkardjɔgrafi], *s.f. Med:* phonocardiography.

phonogénie [fɔnɔʒeni], *s.f. Cin: W.Tel:* good transmitting quality (of the voice); **épreuve de p.,** microphone test.

phonogénique [fɔnɔʒenik], *a.* **voix p.,** good broadcasting voice; *Cin:* voice suitable for sound recording.

phonogramme [fɔnɔgram], *s.m. Cin: etc:* sound record.

phonographe [fɔnɔgraf], *s.m.* (*a*) *A:* phonograph; (*b*) gramophone, *U.S:* phonograph.

phonographie [fɔnɔgrafi], *s.f.* 1. phonography; (*a*) phonetic spelling; (*b*) automatic recording of sounds. 2. gramophone recording.

phonographique [fɔnɔgrafik], *a.* phonographic.

phonolit(h)e [fɔnɔlit], *s.f. Miner:* phonolite.

phonolit(h)ique [fɔnɔlitik], *a. Miner:* phonolitic.

phonologie [fɔnɔlɔʒi], *s.f. Ling:* phonology.

phonologique [fɔnɔlɔʒik], *a.* phonologic(al).

phonologue [fɔnɔlɔg], *s.m. & f. Ling:* phonologist.

phonomètre [fɔnɔmɛtr̥], *s.m. Ph:* phonometer.

phonométrie [fɔnɔmetri], *s.f. Ph:* phonometry.

phonométrique [fɔnɔmetrik], *a. Ph:* phonometric.

phonomimie [fɔnɔmimi], *s.f.* lip reading.

phonomimique [fɔnɔmimik], *a.* lip-reading (exercises, etc.).

phonon [fɔnɔ̃], *s.m. Ph:* phonon.

phonoscope [fɔnɔskɔp], *s.m. Ph:* phonoscope.

phono-télémétrique [fɔnɔtelemetrik], *a. Navy:* **signaux phono-télémétriques,** sound-ranging signals.

phonothèque [fɔnɔtɛk], *s.f.* record library.

phono-visuel [fɔnɔvizɥɛl], *a. Cin:* **enregistrement p.-v.,** sound and picture recording; *pl. phono-visuel(le)s.*

phoque [fɔk], *s.m.* (*a*) *Z:* seal; **p. à capuchon,** hooded seal; **p. macrorhine, p. à trompe,** sea elephant, elephant seal; **p. barbu,** bearded seal; **p. marbré,** mottled seal; **chasse aux phoques,** sealing; **pêcherie de phoques,** seal fishery; **chasseur de phoques,** sealer; **souffler comme un p.,** to blow like a grampus; (*b*) *Com:* sealskin; **manteau de p.,** sealskin coat; *Ski:* **peaux de p.,** skins.

phoquier, -ière [fɔkje, -jɛːr]. 1. *a.* concerning seals, sealing (industry, etc.); **flotte phoquière,** sealing fleet. 2. *s.m. Nau:* sealer, seal-hunting boat.

phorésie [fɔrezi], *s.f. Biol:* phoresy.

phorides [fɔrid], *s.m.pl. Ent:* Phoridae.

phormium [fɔrmjɔm], *s.m. Bot:* phormium; New Zealand flax.

phorone [fɔrɔn], *s.f. Ch:* phorone.

phosgène [fɔsʒɛn], *s.m. Ch:* phosgene (gas); carbonyl chloride.

phosgénite [fɔsʒenit], *s.f. Miner:* phosgenite, horn lead.

phospham [fɔsfam], *s.m. Ch:* phospham.

phosphatage [fɔsfataːʒ], *s.m. Agr:* (*a*) phosphating, fertilizing with phosphates; (*b*) *Winem:* treating (of grapes) with phosphates.

phosphatase [fɔsfataːz], *s.f. Bio-Ch:* phosphatase.

phosphate [fɔsfat], *s.m. Ch:* phosphate; **p. de chaux,** phosphate of lime, calcium phosphate.

phosphaté [fɔsfate], *a. Ch:* phosphatic, phosphated.

phosphater [fɔsfate], *v.tr.* 1. *Metalw:* to phosphate. 2. *Agr:* to treat with phosphates, to phosphate.

phosphaterie [fɔsfatri], *s.f.* phosphate mine.

phosphatide [fɔsfatid], *s.m. Bio-Ch:* phosphatide.

phosphatier [fɔsfatje], *s.m.* 1. phosphate miner, miner of phosphate rock. 2. **(navire) p.,** phosphate-carrying vessel.

phosphatique [fɔsfatik], *a. Ch:* phosphatic (acid).

phosphaturie [fɔsfatyri], *s.f. Med:* phosphaturia.

phosphaturique [fɔsfatyrik], *a. Med:* phosphaturic.

phosphène [fɔsfɛn], *s.m.* 1. *Physiol:* phosphene. 2. *Ent:* firefly.

phosphényle [fɔsfenil], *s.m. Ch:* phosphenyl.

phosphine [fɔsfin], *s.f. Ch:* phosphine.

phosphite [fɔsfit], *s.m. Ch:* phosphite.

phosphoaminolipide [fɔsfɔaminɔlipid], *s.m. Bio-Ch:* phosphoaminolipid(e).

phospholipide [fɔsfɔlipid], *s.m. Bio-Ch:* phospholipid(e), phosphatide.

phosphomolybdique [fɔsfɔmɔlibdik], *a. Ch:* phosphomolybdic.

phosphonium [fɔsfɔnjɔm], *s.m. Ch:* phosphonium.

phosphore [fɔsfɔːr], *s.m. Ch:* phosphorus; **p. rouge, amorphe,** red, amorphous, phosphorus; **p. blanc,** yellow phosphorus.

phosphoré [fɔsfɔre], *a.* 1. phosphorated, containing phosphorus; **allumettes phosphorées,** phosphorus matches. 2. *Ch:* **hydrogène p.,** phosphuretted hydrogen.

phosphorer [fɔsfɔre]. 1. *v.tr.* to phosphorate. 2. *v.i. F:* to exert the grey matter.

phosphorescence [fɔsfɔrɛs(s)ɑ̃ːs], *s.f.* phosphorescence; **luire par p., entrer en p.,** to phosphoresce.

phosphorescent [fɔsfɔrɛs(s)ɑ̃], *a.* phosphorescent.

phosphoreux [fɔsfɔrø], *a.m.* (*the f.* **-euse** *is rare*) *Ch:* phosphorous (compound, acid); **bronze p.,** phosphor bronze.

phosphorique [fɔsfɔrik], *a. Ch:* phosphoric (acid).

phosphorisation [fɔsfɔrizasjɔ̃], *s.f.* phosphorization.

phosphoriser [fɔsfɔrize], *v.tr. Ch:* to phosphorize.

phosphorisme [fɔsfɔrism], *s.m. Med:* phosphorism.

phosphorite [fɔsfɔrit], *s.f. Miner:* phosphorite.

phosphoritique [fɔsfɔritik], *a.* phosphoritic.

phosphorogène [fɔsfɔrɔʒɛn]. 1. *a.* phosphorogenic. 2. *s.m.* phosphorogen(e).

phosphorographie [fɔsfɔrɔgrafi], *s.f.* phosphorography.

phosphorographique [fɔsfɔrɔgrafik], *a.* phosphorographic.

phosphoroscope [fɔsfɔrɔskɔp], *s.m.* phosphoroscope.

phosphoryle [fɔsfɔril], *s.m. Ch:* phosphoryl.

phosphotungstate [fɔsfɔtœ̃gstat], *s.m. Ch:* phosphotungstate.

phosphure [fɔsfyːr], *s.m. Ch:* phosphide.

phosphuré [fɔsfyre], *a. Ch:* phosphuretted.

phosphydrique [fɔsfidrik], *a. Ch:* **acide p.,** phosphine.

phot [fɔt], *s.m. Phot:* phot (= 10,000 luces).

Photin [fɔtɛ̃], *Pr.n.m. Ecc.Hist:* Photinus.

photisme [fɔtism], *s.m. Biol:* photism.

photo- [fɔtɔ], *pref.* photo-.

photo [fɔto], *s.f.* (*a*) *F:* photograph, photo; **prendre une p.,** to take a photograph; **p. surprise,** informal shot; (*b*) **faire de la p.,** to take photographs, to go in for photography.

photobactérie [fɔtɔbakteri], *s.f.* photobacterium.

photobiologie [fɔtɔbjɔlɔʒi], *s.f.* photobiology.

photocalque [fɔtɔkalk], *s.m. Ind:* phototype (from tracing); blueprint, brown print.

photocartographe [fɔtɔkartɔgraf], *s.m.* photographic plotter.

photocatalyse [fɔtɔkataliːz], *s.f. Ch:* photocatalysis.

photocathode [fɔtɔkatɔd], *s.f. Elcs:* photocathode, photoelectric cathode.

photocellule [fɔtɔsɛlyl], *s.f.* photoelectric cell, photocell.

photocéramique [fɔtɔseramik]. 1. *a.* photoceramic (process). 2. *s.f.* photoceramics.

photochimie [fɔtɔʃimi], *s.f.* photochemistry.

photochimique [fɔtɔʃimik], *a.* photochemical.

photochromie [fɔtɔkrɔmi], *s.f.* 1. photochromy, colour photography. 2. photochrome.

photochromique [fɔtɔkrɔmik], *a.* photochromic, photochromatic.

photo-cisaille [fɔtɔsizaːj], *s.f.* (photographer's) proof cutter; trimming board; *pl. photo-cisailles.*

photocléistogame [fɔtɔkleistɔgam], *a. Bot:* photocleistogamous.

photocollographie [fɔtɔkɔlɔgrafi], *s.f.* photocollography.

photocollotypie [fɔtɔkɔlɔtipi], *s.f. Phot.Engr:* **p. à la gélatine bichromatée,** chromocollotypy.

photocomposer [fɔtɔkɔ̃poze], *v.tr. Typ:* to filmset.

photocomposeuse [fɔtɔkɔ̃pozøːz], *s.f. Typ:* film setter.

photocomposition [fɔtɔkɔ̃pozisjɔ̃], *s.f. Typ:* photocomposition, film setting.

photoconducteur, -trice [fɔtɔkɔ̃dyktœːr, -tris]. *Elcs:* 1. *a.* photoconductive, photo-conducting. 2. *s.m.* photoconductor. 3. *s.f.* **photoconductrice,** photoconductive cell.

photoconductibilité [fɔtɔkɔ̃dyktibilite], **photoconductivité** [fɔtɔkɔ̃dyktivite], *s.f. Elcs:* photoconductivity.

photoconduction [fɔtɔkɔ̃dyksjɔ̃], *s.f. Elcs:* photoconduction, photoconductive effect.

photocopie [fɔtɔkɔpi], *s.f.* photocopy.

photocopier [fɔtɔkɔpje], *v.tr.* (*conj. like* COPIER) to photocopy; to photostat.

photocopieur [fɔtɔkɔpjœːr], *s.m.* photocopier.

photocopiste [fɔtɔkɔpist], *s.m. & f.* photostat operator.

photocourant [fɔtɔkurɑ̃], *s.m. Elcs:* photocurrent.

photodermatose [fɔtɔdɛrmatoːz], *s.f. Vet: Med:* photodermatosis.

photodésintégration [fɔtɔdezɛ̃tegrasjɔ̃], *s.f. Atom. Ph:* photodisintegration.

photodiode [fɔtɔdjɔd], *s.f. Elcs:* photodiode, photoconductive diode.

photodissociation [fɔtɔdis(s)ɔsjasjɔ̃], *s.f. Ch:* photodissociation.

photodynamique [fɔtɔdinamik], *a.* photodynamic.

photo(-)élasticimètre [fɔtɔelastisimɛtr̥], *s.m.* device for measuring photoelasticity; *pl. photo(-)élasticimètres.*

photo(-)élasticimétrie [fɔtɔelastisimetri], *s.f.* measurement of photoelasticity.

photo(-)élasticité [fɔtɔelastisite], *s.f.* photoelasticity.

photo(-)électricité [fɔtɔelɛktrisite], *s.f.* photoelectricity; photoelectric current.

photo(-)électrique [fɔtɔelɛktrik], *a.* photoelectric (cell, effect); *pl. photo(-)électriques.*

photo(-)électron [fɔtoelɛktrɔ̃], *s.m. Atom.Ph:* photoelectron; *pl. photo(-)électrons.*

photo(-)émetteur, -trice [fɔtoemɛtœːr, -tris], *a.* photo-emittent; *pl. photo(-)émetteurs, -trices.*

photo(-)émissif, -ive [fɔtoemisif, -iːv], *a.* photo-emissive; **cellule photo(-)émissive,** photoemissive cell, phototube; *pl. photo(-)émissifs, -ives.*

photo(-)émission [fɔtoemisjɔ̃], *s.f. Elcs:* photo-emission, photoemissive effect, photoelectric emission.

photo-finish [fɔtofiniʃ], *s.f.inv. Sp:* (*a*) photo finish; (*b*) photo-finish camera.

photofission [fɔtofisjɔ̃], *s.f. Atom.Ph:* photo-fission.

photogène [fɔtɔʒɛn], *a. Ph:* photogenic, photo-genetic.

photogénèse [fɔtɔʒenɛːz], *s.f.* photogenesis.

photogénie [fɔtɔʒeni], *s.f.* **1.** production of light. **2.** photogenic qualities.

photogénique [fɔtɔʒenik], *a.* **1.** actinic. **2.** *Phot:* photogenic, that photographs well.

photogéologie [fɔtɔʒeɔlɔʒi], *s.f.* photogeology.

photoglyptie [fɔtɔglipti], *s.f. Phot:* woodbury type, photoglyphy.

photoglyptique [fɔtɔgliptik], *a.* photoglyptic.

photogramme [fɔtɔgram], *s.m. Cin:* frame.

photogrammètre [fɔtɔgram(m)ɛtr], *s.m.* photo-grammetrist.

photogrammétrie [fɔtɔgram(m)etri], *s.f.* photo-grammetry; photographic surveying.

photogrammétrique [fɔtɔgram(m)etrik], *a.* photo-grammetric.

photographe [fɔtɔgraf], *s.m. & f.* photographer; **p. amateur, professionnel,** amateur, professional, photographer; **reporter p., p. de presse,** press photographer; **porter des photos à développer chez un p.,** to take some photographs to the photographer's to be developed.

photographie [fɔtɔgrafi], *s.f.* **1.** photography; **p. aérienne,** aerial photography; **p. en couleurs,** colour photography; **faire de la p.,** to go in for photography; to take photographs. **2.** (*a*) photograph; (photographic) print; **p. aérienne,** aerial photograph; **p. oblique,** oblique photo-graph; **p. panoramique,** panoram photograph; **prendre une p. de qn,** to take s.o.'s photograph; **il s'est fait faire sa p.,** he's had his photograph taken: **satellite qui transmet des photographies de la terre,** satellite that transmits, returns, photographs of the earth; (*b*) *Cin:* still.

photographier [fɔtɔgrafje], *v.tr.* (*p.d. & pr.sub.* **n. photographiions, v. photographiiez**) to photo-graph; to take a photograph of (sth.); **se faire p.,** to have one's photograph taken, to be photo-graphed.

photographique [fɔtɔgrafik], *a.* photographic (reproduction, description, etc.); **appareil p.,** camera; *Surv:* **levé p.,** photographic survey(ing); *Av:* **reconnaissance p.,** photo-reconnaissance.

photographiquement [fɔtɔgrafikmɑ̃], *adv.* photo-graphically.

photograveur [fɔtɔgravœːr], *s.m.* photoengraver, process engraver, photogravurist; block maker.

photogravure [fɔtɔgravyːr], *s.f.* photoengraving; photogravure (process or print); *Elcs:* photo-engraving, photoetching; **p. sur zinc,** (i) zinco-graphy; (ii) zincograph; **p. en couleurs,** colour photoengraving; **chambre noire pour p.,** process-type camera.

photo-ionisation [fɔtɔjɔnizasjɔ̃], *s.f. Elcs:* photo-ionization.

photokinésie [fɔtɔkinezi], *s.f. Biol:* photokinesis, photocinesis.

photolithographe [fɔtɔlitɔgraf], *s.m.* photo-lithographer.

photolithographie [fɔtɔlitɔgrafi], *s.f.* **1.** photo-lithography. **2.** photolithograph.

photolithographier [fɔtɔlitɔgrafje], *v.tr.* (*p.d. & pr.sub.* **n. photolithographiions, v. photolitho-graphiiez**) to photolithograph; to reproduce by photolithography.

photolithographique [fɔtɔlitɔgrafik], *a.* photo-lithographic; **gravure p.,** photolithography.

photologie [fɔtɔlɔʒi], *s.f.* photology.

photoluminescence [fɔtɔlyminɛs(s)ɑ̃ːs], *s.f.* photo-luminescence.

photoluminescent [fɔtɔlyminɛs(s)ɑ̃], *a.* photo-luminescent.

photolyse [fɔtɔliːz], *s.f. Biol: Bot:* photolysis.

photomacrographie [fɔtɔmakrɔgrafi], *s.f.* (*a*) photomacrography, macrophotography; (*b*) photomacrograph, macrophotograph.

photomagnétique [fɔtɔmaɲetik], *a.* photomag-netic.

photomécanique [fɔtɔmekanik], *a.* photomech-anical (process, etc.).

photométallographie [fɔtɔmetal(l)ɔgrafi], *s.f.* photolithography from a metal plate.

photomètre [fɔtɔmɛtr], *s.m.* photometer; **p. à éclats,** flicker photometer; **p. à tache d'huile,** grease-spot photometer; *Phot:* **p. de pose,** actino-meter; **p. de tirage,** print meter.

photométrie [fɔtɔmetri], *s.f.* photometry; **p. spectrale,** spectrophotometry.

photométrique [fɔtɔmetrik], *a.* photometric(al).

photomicrographie [fɔtɔmikrɔgrafi], *s.f.* **1.** photomicrography. **2.** photomicrograph.

photomicrographique [fɔtɔmikrɔgrafik], *a.* photo-micrographic.

photomitrailleuse [fɔtɔmitrajøːz], *s.f. Mil.Av:* camera gun.

photomontage [fɔtɔmɔ̃taːʒ], *s.m.* photomontage.

photomorphose [fɔtɔmɔrfoːz], *s.f. Biol:* photo-morphosis.

photomultiplicateur, -trice [fɔtɔmyltiplikatœːr, -tris], *Elcs:* **1.** *a.* photomultiplier. **2.** *s.m.* photomultiplier (tube).

photon [fɔtɔ̃], *s.m. Opt.Meas:* photon.

photonastie [fɔtɔnasti], *s.f. Bot:* photonasty; floral reaction to light.

photonastique [fɔtɔnastik], *a. Bot:* photonastic (flower).

photonégatif, -ive [fɔtɔnegatif, -iːv], *a. Biol:* photonegative, exhibiting negative phototro-pism.

photoneutron [fɔtɔnøtrɔ̃], *s.m. Atom.Ph:* photo-neutron.

photonique [fɔtɔnik], *a. Ph:* photonic.

photonucléaire [fɔtɔnykleɛːr], *a.* photonuclear.

photopériode [fɔtɔperjɔd], *s.f. Biol:* photoperiod.

photopériodisme [fɔtɔperjɔdism], *s.m. Bot:* photo-periodism.

photophile [fɔtɔfil], *a. Biol:* photophile, photo-philic.

photophobie [fɔtɔfɔbi], *s.f. Med:* photophobia.

photophone [fɔtɔfɔn], *s.m. Hist. of Tp:* photo-phone, radiophone.

photophonique [fɔtɔfɔnik], *a. Cin:* **bande p.,** sound track (of film).

photophore [fɔtɔfɔːr], *s.m.* **1.** *Med: etc:* photo-phore; endoscope. **2.** *Nau:* light buoy. **3.** (miner's) cap lamp.

photophorèse [fɔtɔfɔrɛːz], *s.f. Ph:* photophoresis.

photopile [fɔtɔpil], *s.f. Elcs:* photovoltaic cell.

photopique [fɔtɔpik], *a. Opt:* photopic; *Med:* **bain p.,** light bath.

photoplan [fɔtɔplɑ̃], *s.m.* photomap.

photopolymérisation [fɔtɔpɔlimerizasjɔ̃], *s.f. Ch:* photopolymerization, photochemical poly-merization.

photopositif, -ive [fɔtɔpɔzitif, -iːv], *a. Biol:* photo-positive, exhibiting positive phototropism.

photopoudre [fɔtɔpudr], *s.f. Phot:* flashlight powder.

photoprojecteur [fɔtɔprɔʒɛktœːr], *s.m.* slide projector.

photoproton [fɔtɔprɔtɔ̃], *s.m. Atom.Ph:* photo-proton.

photopsie [fɔtɔpsi], *s.f. Med:* photopsia, photopsy.

photoréaction [fɔtɔreaksjɔ̃], *s.f. Ch:* photo-reaction.

photorésistance [fɔtɔrezistɑ̃ːs], *s.f.* photoresis-tance.

photorésistant, -ante [fɔtɔrezistɑ̃, -ɑ̃ːt], *a.* photo-resistive; **cellule photorésistante,** photoconduc-tive cell.

photorésistivité [fɔtɔrezistivite], *s.f.* photo-resistivity; photoresistance; photoconductivity.

photo-robot [fɔtɔrɔbo], *s.m. Jur:* identikit (pic-ture); *pl. photos-robots.*

photoroman [fɔtɔrɔmɑ̃], *s.m.* story told in photo-graphs.

photosensibilisation [fɔtɔsɑ̃sibilizasjɔ̃], *s.f.* pho-tosensitization.

photosensibilité [fɔtɔsɑ̃sibilite], *s.f.* photosensi-tivity.

photosensible [fɔtɔsɑ̃sibl], *a.* photosensitive.

photosphère [fɔtɔsfɛːr], *s.f. Astr:* photosphere.

photostat [fɔtɔsta], *s.m.* photostat.

photostop [fɔtɔstɔp], *s.m.* street photography.

photostoppeur, -euse [fɔtɔstɔpœːr, -øːz], *s.* street photographer.

photosynthèse [fɔtɔsɛ̃tɛːz], *s.f.* photosynthesis.

photosynthétique [fɔtɔsɛ̃tetik], *a.* photosynthetic.

phototactisme [fɔtɔtaktism], *s.m. Biol:* photo-tactism.

phototaxie [fɔtɔtaksi], *s.f. Biol:* phototaxis, phototaxy.

phototélégraphe [fɔtɔtelegraf], *s.m. Tg:* photo-telegraph.

phototélégraphie [fɔtɔtelegrafi], *s.f. Tg:* photo-telegraphy.

photothécaire [fɔtɔtekɛːr], *s.m. & f.* librarian of photographic library.

photothéodolite [fɔtɔteɔdɔlit], *s.m. Surv:* photo-theodolite.

photothèque [fɔtɔtɛk], *s.f.* photographic library.

photothérapie [fɔtɔterapi], *s.f.* phototherapy.

photothérapique [fɔtɔterapik], *a. Med:* photo-therapeutic; **bain p.,** light bath.

phototopographie [fɔtɔtɔpɔgrafi], *s.f.* phototo-pography, photographic survey(ing); **p. aérienne,** aerial surveying.

phototransistor [fɔtɔtrɑ̃zistɔːr], *s.m.,* **phototran-sistron** [fɔtɔtrɑ̃zistrɔ̃], *s.m.* phototransistor.

phototropisme [fɔtɔtrɔpism], *s.m. Bot:* photo-tropism.

phototype [fɔtɔtip], *s.m. Phot.Engr:* **1.** phototype; **p. positif,** direct positive; **p. négatif,** direct negative. **2.** collotype (print).

phototypie [fɔtɔtipi], *s.f.* collotype (process).

phototypographie [fɔtɔtipɔgrafi], *s.f.* phototypo-graphy; halftone reproduction; block process.

phototypographique [fɔtɔtipɔgrafik], *a.* photo-typographic, half-tone (process, etc.).

phototypogravure [fɔtɔtipɔgravyːr], *s.f.* photo-typogravure, heliography.

photovoltaïque [fɔtɔvɔltaik], *a.* photovoltaic; **cellule p.,** photovoltaic, photochemical, photo-electrolytic, cell.

photozincographie [fɔtɔzɛ̃kɔgrafi], *s.f.* photo-zincography.

phragmite [fragmit], *s.m.* **1.** *Bot:* reed. **2.** *Orn:* **p. (des joncs),** sedge warbler; **p. aquatique,** aquatic warbler.

phrase [frɑːz], *s.f.* **1.** sentence; **p. bien construite,** well-constructed sentence; **p. toute faite,** cliché, stock phrase, stereotyped form of words; **faire des phrases, faire de grandes phrases,** to speak in flowery, pretentious, language, in a grandilo-quent style; **sans phrases,** (i) straight out, with-out mincing matters; (ii) just like that, without more ado; *Gram:* **membre de p.,** phrase. **2.** *Mus:* phrase. **3.** *Fenc:* **p. d'armes,** phrase.

phrasé [frɑze], *s.m. Mus:* phrasing.

phraséologie [frazeɔlɔʒi], *s.f.* (*a*) phraseology; (*b*) *Sch:* phrase book (for learning vocabulary).

phraséologique [frazeɔlɔʒik], *a.* phraseological.

phraser [frɑze]. **1.** *v.i.* (*a*) to phrase; **p. bien,** to phrase well, to use well-chosen expressions; (*b*) to speak in a grandiloquent style. **2.** *v.tr.* (*a*) to phrase, to express in phrases; (*b*) *Mus:* to phrase.

phraseur, -euse [frɑzœːr, -øːz], *s. Pej:* phrase-monger, speechifier.

phratrie [fratri], *s.f. Gr.Ant: etc:* phratry.

phréatique [freatik], *a. Geol:* phreatic; **nappe p.,** ground water, phreatic water.

phréatophyte [freatɔfit], *s.f. Bot:* phreatophyte.

phrénicectomie [frenisɛktɔmi], *s.f. Surg:* phrenic-ectomy.

phrénicotomie [frenikɔtɔmi], *s.f. Surg:* phrenico-tomy.

phrénique [frenik], *a. Anat:* phrenic (nerve, artery).

phrénite [frenit], *s.f. Med:* inflammation of the diaphragm.

phrénitis [frenitis], *s.m. Med:* **1.** inflammation of the diaphragm. **2.** phrenitis, delirium.

phrénocardie [frenɔkardi], *s.f. Med:* phreno-cardia.

phrénologie [frenɔlɔʒi], *s.f.* phrenology.

phrénologique [frenɔlɔʒik], *a.* phrenological.

phrénologiste [frenɔlɔʒist], *s.m.* phrenologist.

phronime [frɔnim], *s.f. Crust:* phronima.

phrygane [frigan], *s.f. Ent:* phryganea, *esp.* caddis fly, may fly, caperer; **larve de p.,** caddis worm; *Fish:* caddis bait.

Phrygie [friʒi], *Pr.n.f. A.Geog:* Phrygia.

phrygien, -ienne [friʒjɛ̃, -jɛn], *a. & s. A.Geog:* Phrygian; *Hist:* **bonnet p.,** Phrygian cap (as emblem of liberty); liberty cap.

phrynosome [frinozoːm], *s.m. Rept:* phrynosoma.

phtaléine [ftalein], *s.f. Ch:* phthalein.

phtalide [ftalid], *s.m. Ch:* phthalide.

phtalimide [ftalimid], *s.m. Ch:* phthalimide.

phtaline [ftalin], *s.f. Ch:* phthalin.

phtalique [ftalik], *a. Ch:* phthalic, alizaric (acid).

phtalocyanine [ftalɔsjanin], *s.f. Ch:* phthalo-cyanine; **p. du platine,** platinum phthalocyanine.

phtanite [ftanit], *s.f. Miner:* phthanite.

phtinobranches [ftinɔbrɑ̃ːʃ], *s.m.pl. Ich:* Lopho-branchii, Syngnathidae.

phtiriase [ftirjɑːz], **phtiriasis** [ftirjasis], *s.f. Med:* phthiriasis.

phtisie [ftizi], *s.f. Med: A:* phthisis; (pulmonary) consumption; **p. galopante,** galloping con-sumption.

phtisiogénèse [ftizjɔʒenɛːz], *s.f. Med:* phthisio-genesis.

phtisiogénique [ftizjɔʒenik], *a. Med:* phthisiogenic.

phtisiologie [ftizjɔlɔʒi], *s.f. Med:* phthisiology, study of tuberculosis.

phtisiologue [ftizjɔlɔg], *s.m. & f. Med:* phthisiologist, tuberculosis specialist.

phtisiothérapie [ftizjɔterapi], *s.f. Med:* phthisiotherapy.

phtisique [ftizik], *Med:* **1.** *a.* phthisical, consumptive. **2.** *s.* consumptive.

phycologie [fikɔlɔʒi], *s.f.* phycology.

phycologiste [fikɔlɔʒist], **phycologue** [fikɔlɔg], *s.m. & f.* phycologist.

phycomycètes [fikɔmisɛt], *s.m.pl. Fung:* Phycomyceteae, phycomecetes.

phyl-. *See* PHYL(O)-.

phylactère [filaktɛːr], *s.m.* **1.** phylactery. **2.** *Medieval Art:* scroll.

phylactolémates [filaktɔlemat], *s.m.pl. Z:* Phylactolaemata.

phylarchie [filarʃi], *s.f. Gr.Hist:* phylarchy.

phylarque [filark], *s.m. Gr.Hist:* phylarch.

phyle [fil], *s.m. O: Biol:* phylum.

phylétique [filetik], *a.* phyletic; phylogenetic.

phyllie [fili], *s.f. Ent:* leaf insect, walking leaf.

phyllite [fil(l)it], *s.f. Miner:* phyllite; mica slate.

phyllo- [fil(l)ɔ], *pref.* phyllo-.

phyllocactus [fil(l)ɔkaktys], *s.m.* phyllocactus.

phylloclade [fil(l)ɔklad], *s.m. Bot:* phylloclade.

phyllode [fil(l)ɔd], *s.f. Bot:* phyllode.

phyllodromie [fil(l)ɔdrɔmi], *s.f. Ent: F:* Croton bug, German cockroach.

phyllogène [fil(l)ɔʒɛn], *a. Bot:* phyllogenetic, phyllogenous.

phylloïde [fil(l)ɔid], *a.* phylloid, leaflike.

phyllophage [fil(l)ɔfaːʒ]. **1.** *a.* phyllophagous. **2.** *s.m. Ent:* phyllophaga, *U.S:* June bug.

phyllopode [fil(l)ɔpɔd], *Crust:* **1.** *a.* phyllopodous. **2.** *s.m.* phyllopod.

phylloptéryx [fil(l)ɔpteriks], *s.m. Ich:* phyllopteryx.

phyllorhine [fil(l)ɔrin], *s.m. Z:* phyllorhine (bat).

phyllosome [fil(l)ɔzoːm], *s.m. Crust:* phyllosoma.

phyllostachys [fil(l)ɔstakis], *s.m. Bot:* phyllostachys.

phyllostomidés [fil(l)ɔstɔmide], *s.m.pl. Z:* Phyllostom(at)idae.

phyllotaxie [fil(l)ɔtaksi], *s.f. Bot:* phyllotaxis.

phylloxéra, phylloxera [filɔksera], *s.m. Ent:* phylloxera; **p. du chêne,** oak pest.

phylloxéré [filɔksere], *a.* phylloxerized (vine).

phylloxérien, -ienne [filɔkserjɛ̃, -jɛn], *a.* **phylloxérique** [filɔkserik], *a. Vit:* phylloxerna.

phyl(o)- [fil(ɔ)], *pref.* phyl(o).

phylogénèse [filɔʒenɛːz], *s.f.,* **phylogénie** [filɔʒeni], *s.f. Biol:* phylogenesis, phylogeny.

phylogénétique [filɔʒenetik], **phylogénique** [filɔʒenik], *a. Biol:* phylogenetic, phylogenic.

phylogéniste [filɔʒenist], *s.m. & f.* phylogenist.

phylum [filɔm], *s.m. Biol:* phylum.

phymatidés [fimatide], *s.m.pl. Ent:* Phymatidae.

physalie [fizali], *s.f. Coel:* physalia, *F:* Portuguese man-of-war.

physalis [fizalis], *s.m. Bot:* ground cherry, winter cherry; (*genus*) Physalis.

physalite [fizalit], *s.f. Miner:* physalite.

physalospore [fizalɔspɔːr], *s.m. Fung:* physalospora.

physe [fiːz], *s.f. Moll:* physa.

physicalisme [fizikalism], *s.m.* physicalism.

physicien, -ienne [fizisjɛ̃, -jɛn], *s.* **1.** physicist. **2.** natural philosopher.

physicisme [fizisism], *s.m.* physicism.

physico-chimie [fizikɔʃimi], *s.f. no pl.* physicochemistry.

physico-chimique [fizikɔʃimik], *a.* physicochemical; *pl. physico-chimiques.*

physico-chimiste [fizikɔʃimist], *s.m. & f.* physicochemist; *pl. physico-chimistes.*

physico-mathématique [fizikɔmatematik], *a.* physicomathematical; *pl. physico-mathématiques.*

physico-mécanique [fizikɔmekanik], *a.* physicomechanical; *pl. physico-mécaniques.*

physico-théologique [fizikɔteɔlɔʒik], *a.* physicotheological; *pl. physico-théologiques.*

physio- [fizjɔ], *pref.* physio-.

physiocrate [fizjɔkrat], *s.m. Pol.Ec:* physiocrat.

physiocratie [fizjɔkrasi], *s.f. Pol.Ec:* physiocracy.

physiocratique [fizjɔkratik], *a.* physiocratic.

physiogénèse [fizjɔʒenɛːz], *s.f.* physiogenesis.

physiogénie [fizjɔʒeni], *s.f.* physiogeny.

physiognomonie [fizjɔgnɔmɔni], *s.f.* physiognomy, study of facial features.

physiognomonique [fizjɔgnɔmɔnik], *a.* physiognomonic(al), physiognomic(al).

physiognomoniste [fizjɔgnɔmɔnist], *s.m. & f.* physiognomist; one who studies physiognomy.

physiographe [fizjɔgraf], *s.m.* physiographer.

physiographie [fizjɔgrafi], *s.f.* physiography, physical geography.

physiographique [fizjɔgrafik], *a.* physiographical.

physiologie [fizjɔlɔʒi], *s.f.* physiology; **p. végétale,** plant physiology.

physiologique [fizjɔlɔʒik], *a.* physiological; *Bio-Ch:* **solution p.,** normal saline solution; physiological salt solution.

physiologiquement [fizjɔlɔʒikmɑ̃], *adv.* physiologically.

physiologiste [fizjɔlɔʒist], *s.m. & f.,* **physiologue** [fizjɔlɔg], *s.m. & f.* physiologist.

physionomie [fizjɔnɔmi], *s.f.* physiognomy; cast of features; face, countenance; (*of thg*) appearance, aspect, specific character; **p. repoussante,** repulsive countenance; **à mauvaise p.,** ill-favoured, ugly, *U.S:* homely; **il manque de p.,** his face lacks character; **jeu de p.,** play of features; **la paisible p. des rues,** the peaceful aspect, peaceful appearance, of the streets; **région qui a une p. particulière,** region with a character of its own; **p. littéraire,** literary profile, literary character; **esquisse d'une p. littéraire,** thumbnail sketch of a literary personality, character sketch.

physionomique [fizjɔnɔmik], *a.* physiognomical.

physionomiste [fizjɔnɔmist], *s.m.* physiognomist; judge of character from the face; good judge of faces; *F:* **je ne suis pas p.,** I've no memory for faces.

physiopathologie [fizjɔpatɔlɔʒi], *s.f. Med:* physiopathology.

physiothérapeute [fizjɔterapøt], *s.m. & f.* physiotherapeutist, physiotherapist.

physiothérapie [fizjɔterapi], *s.f. Med:* physiotherapy.

physiothérapique [fizjɔterapik], *a.* physiotherapeutic.

physiothérapiste [fizjɔterapist], *s.m. & f.* physiotherapist.

physique [fizik]. **1.** *a.* physical; (*a*) **douleur p.,** bodily pain; **culture p.,** physical culture; **force p.,** physical force, strength; **il n'y a pas d'empêchement p. à cela,** there is no physical impossibility in that; **certitude p.,** physical certainty; (*b*) **chimie p.,** physical chemistry. **2.** *s.f.* (*a*) (i) physics; (ii) natural philosophy; **p fondamentale, générale, pure,** fundamental physics; **p. expérimentale,** experimental physics; **p. nucléaire,** nuclear physics; **p. du globe,** geophysics; (*b*) *Sch:* text book on physics; **appareil de p.,** (piece of) physical apparatus. **3.** *s.m.* physique (of person); (i) external appearance; (ii) constitution; **il a un beau p.,** he has a fine physique; he is a fine figure of a man; **il a le p. de l'emploi,** he looks the part; **comment est-il au p.?** what is he like to look at? what does he look like? **d'un p. agréable,** attractive, pleasant to look at.

physiquement [fizikmɑ̃], *adv.* physically, materially; **p. il est mieux que son frère,** he is better looking than his brother; **p. impossible,** physically impossible.

physocliste [fizɔklist], *Ich:* **1.** *a.* physoclistic. **2.** *s.m.* physoclist; *pl.* **physoclistes,** Physoclisti.

physogastrie [fizɔgastri], *s.f. Z:* physogastry.

physostegia [fizɔsteʒja], *s.m. Bot:* physostegia, false dragon's head.

physostigma [fizɔstigma], *s.m. Bot:* physostigma, Calabar bean.

physostigmine [fizɔstigmin], *s.f. Ch:* physostigmine.

physostome [fizɔstɔm], *Ich:* **1.** *a.* physostomatous. **2.** *s.m.* physostome; *pl.* **physostomes,** Physostomi.

phytéléphas [fitelefas], *s.m. Bot:* phytelephas.

phytine [fitin], *s.f. Ch:* phytin.

phyto- [fitɔ], *comb.fm.* phyto-.

phytobézoard [fitɔbezɔaːr], *s.f. Physiol:* phytobezoar.

phytobiologie [fitɔbjɔlɔʒi], *s.f.* phytobiology.

phytobiologique [fitɔbjɔlɔʒik], *a.* phytobiological.

phytocénose [fitɔsenoːz], *s.f. Bot:* phytocoenosis.

phytochimie [fitɔʃimi], *s.f.* phytochemistry.

phytoécologie [fitɔekɔlɔʒi], *s.f.* phytoecology, plant ecology.

phytoécologique [fitɔekɔlɔʒik], *a.* phytoecological.

phytogène [fitɔʒɛn], *a. Geol:* phytogenic.

phytogénèse [fitɔʒenɛːz], **phytogénésie** [fitɔʒenezi], *s.f. Biol:* phytogenesis.

phytogénétique [fitɔʒenetik], *a. Biol:* phytogenetic(al).

phytogéographe [fitɔʒeɔgraf], *s.m. & f.* phytogeographer.

phytogéographie [fitɔʒeɔgrafi], *s.f.* phytogeography.

phytogéographique [fitɔʒeɔgrafik], *a.* phytogeographic(al); **carte p.,** plant-distribution map.

phytographie [fitɔgrafi], *s.f.* phytography, descriptive botany.

phytohormone [fitɔɔrmɔn], *s.f. Bio-Ch:* phytohormone.

phytoïde [fitɔid], *a.* phytoid.

phytol [fitɔl], *s.m. Bio-Ch:* phytol.

phytolacca [fitɔlaka], *s.m. Bot:* phytolacca.

phytolaccacées [fitɔlakase], *s.f.pl. Bot:* Phytolaccaceae.

phytolaque [fitɔlak], *s.m. Bot:* redweed, poke weed.

phytologie [fitɔlɔʒi], *s.f.* phytology.

phytomètre [fitɔmɛtr], *s.f. Ent:* plusia.

phytomonadines [fitɔmɔnadin], *s.f.pl. Prot:* Phytomonadina.

phytoparasite [fitɔparazit], *s.m.* phytoparasite.

phytopathologie [fitɔpatɔlɔʒi], *s.f. Bot:* phytopathology, plant pathology.

phytopathologique [fitɔpatɔlɔʒik], *a.* phytopathological.

phytopathologiste [fitɔpatɔlɔʒist], *s.m. & f.* phytopathologist, plant pathologist.

phytophage [fitɔfaːʒ]. **1.** *a.* phytophagous; plant-eating. **2.** *s.m.pl. Ent:* **phytophages,** Phytophaga.

phytopharmaceutique [fitɔfarmasøtik], *a.* phytopharmacological.

phytopharmacie [fitɔfarmasi], *s.f.* phytopharmacology.

phytoplancton [fitɔplɑ̃ktɔ̃], *s.m. Bot:* phytoplankton.

phytophthora [fitɔftɔra], *s.m. Fung:* phytophthora.

phytopte [fitɔpt], *s.m. Arach:* phytoptid, blister mite.

phytosociologie [fitɔsɔsjɔlɔʒi], *s. Bot:* phytosociology.

phytostérol [fitɔsterɔl], *s.m. Ch:* phytosterol.

phytotechnie [fitɔtɛkni], *s.f.* phytotechny.

phytothérapie [fitɔterapi], *s.f.* phytotherapy.

phytotomidés [fitɔtɔmide], *s.m.pl. Orn:* Phytotomidae.

phytotomie [fitɔtɔmi], *s.f.* phytotomy.

phytotron [fitɔtrɔ̃], *s.m.* plant laboratory.

phytozoaire [fitɔzɔɛːr], *s.m.* phytozoon; zoophyte.

pi [pi], *s.m.* **1.** *Gr.Alph:* pi; *Mth:* π. **2.** *Atom.Ph:* pion, pi-meson.

pia [pja], *s.m. Bot:* pia.

piaculaire [pjakylɛːr], *a. Lit:* piacular, expiatory.

piaf [pjaf], *s.m. P:* sparrow.

piaffe [pjaf], *s.f. F: A:* ostentation, show; **faire de la p.,** to swagger; to cut a dash.

piaffé [pjafe], *s.m. Equit:* (*a*) piaffe, piaffer; (*b*) pawing the ground.

piaffement [pjafmɑ̃], *s.m. Equit:* pawing (the ground).

piaffer [pjafe], *v.i.* **1.** *A:* to swagger; to show off. **2.** (*of horse*) (*a*) to paw the ground; (*b*) to prance; (*c*) *F:* **p. d'impatience,** to fidget.

piaffeur, -euse [pjafœːr, -øːz]. **1.** *a. & s.* pawing; prancing, high-stepping, mettlesome (horse); high-stepper. **2.** *P: A:* (*of pers.*) (*a*) *s.* swaggerer; (*b*) *s.f.* **piaffeuse,** high-stepper.

piaillard, -arde [pjɑjaːr, -ard], *a. & s.* cheeping (bird); *F:* squalling, squawking (child).

piaillement [pjɑjmɑ̃], *s.m.* cheeping (of bird); *F:* squalling, squawking (of child).

piailler [pjɑje], *v.i.* (*of small birds*) to cheep; *F:* (*of children, etc.*) to squall, squeal; to squawk; **la louve et ses quatre petits qui piaillaient,** the wolf and her four squeaking cubs.

piaillerie [pjɑjri], *s.f.* (continuous) cheeping (of birds); *F:* squeaking, squalling, squawking, squealing (of children, etc.).

piailleur, -euse [pjɑjœːr, -øːz], *s.* (*of bird*) cheeper; *F:* (*of pers.*) squaller, squealer, squawker.

pian [pjɑ̃], *s.m. Med:* framboesia, yaws, pian.

piane-piane [pjanpjan], *adv. F:* very slowly, very softly, very gently.

pianino [pjanino], *s.m. Mus:* pianino.

pianissimo [pjanisimo]. **1.** *adv. & s.m. Mus:* pianissimo. **2.** *adv. F:* gently, softly.

pianiste [pjanist], *s.m. & f.* pianist.

pianistique [pjanistik], *a. Mus:* pianistic; **une œuvre p.,** a work for (the) piano.

piano[1] [pjano], *s.m.* piano; **p. à queue,** grand piano; **p. (à queue) de concert, de salon,** concert, drawing-room, grand; **p. demi-queue,** boudoir grand; **p. quart de queue,** small, miniature, grand; **p. droit,** upright piano; **p. mécanique,** piano player, player piano; *F:* **p. du pauvre, p. à bretelles,** accordion; **jouer du p.,** to play the piano; **sonate pour p. et violon,** sonata for piano and violin.

piano[2], *adv. & s.m. Mus:* piano, softly.

Pianola [pjanɔla], *s.m. R.t.m:* Pianola.
piano-piano [pjanopjano], *adv. F:* very slowly, very softly, very gently.
pianotage [pjanɔta:ʒ], *s.m. F:* strumming (on piano).
pianoter [pjanɔte], *v.i. F:* to strum (on piano); **ses doigts pianotent sur la nappe,** his fingers are drumming, tapping out a tune, on the tablecloth.
pianoteur, -euse [pjanɔtœ:r, -ø:z], *s. F:* strummer.
piariste [pjarist], *s.m. Ecc:* Piarist.
piassava [pjasava], *s.m. Bot: Com:* piassaba, piassava; **balai en p.,** piassaba brush, broom.
piastre [pjastr̥], *s.f. Num:* piastre; *Fr.C:* dollar.
piat [pja], *s.m. Orn: F:* young magpie.
piauhau [pjoo], *s.m. Orn: F:* chatterer, cotinga; *pl. piauhaus.*
piaulard, -arde [pjola:r, -ard], *a. & s. F:* peeping, cheeping (chicken); whimpering, whining (child); whiner.
piaule [pjo:l], *s.f. P:* digs.
piaulement [pjolmɑ̃], *s.m.* peeping, cheep(ing) (of chicks); *F:* whimpering, whining (of children).
piauler [pjole], *v.i.* (*of chicks*) to peep, cheep; *F:* (*of children*) to whine, whimper.
piaulis [pjoli], *s.m. F:* cheeping, squeaking, shrill crying (of birds, children).
piballe [pibal], *s.f. Ich:* glass eel, elver.
pible [pibl̥], *s.m.* (*a*) *A:* poplar; (*b*) *Nau:* **mât à p.,** pole mast.
pibou [pibu], *s.m. Dial: F:* poplar (tree).
pibroch [pibrɔk], *s.m. Mus:* **1.** pibroch. **2.** bagpipe.
pic[1] [pik], *s.m.* **1.** pick, pickaxe; **p. de tailleur de pierre,** stone-dressing pick; **p. pneumatique,** pneumatic pick, drill; **p. à main,** miner's pick; **p. à tranche,** mattock. **2.** *Cards:* pique (at piquet). **3.** (mountain) peak; *adv.phr.* **à p.,** perpendicular(ly), sheer, abrupt; **sentier à p.,** precipitous path; **côte à p.,** bluff, sheer, coast; **promontoire à p., cap à p.,** bold headland; bluff; **rocher qui s'élève à p. au-dessus de la mer,** rock rising sheer, abruptly, from the sea; (*of ship, etc.*) **couler à p.,** to sink straight to the bottom; to sink like a stone; **tomber à p.,** (i) to be, to fall, sheer; (ii) *F:* to happen at the right moment, in the nick of time; *F:* **il est arrivé à p.,** he turned up in the nick of time, just at the right moment. **4.** *Nau:* (*a*) peak (of sail, of gaff); **drisse à p.,** peak halyard; (*b*) **l'ancre est à p.,** the anchor is apeak, is up and down; **virer à p.,** to heave short.
pic[2], *s.m. Orn:* woodpecker; **p. épeiche,** great spotted woodpecker, pied woodpecker; **p. épeichette,** lesser spotted woodpecker, barred woodpecker; **p. noir,** black woodpecker; **p. vert,** green woodpecker; **p. cendré,** grey-headed woodpecker; **p. mar,** middle-spotted woodpecker; **p. brun d'Asie,** Asiatic rufous woodpecker; **p. tridactyle,** three-toed woodpecker; **p. syriaque,** Syrian woodpecker; **p. à dos blanc, p. leuconote,** white-backed woodpecker; **p. à bec d'ivoire,** (North American) ivory-billed woodpecker; **p. maçon,** nuthatch.
pica[1] [pika], *s.m. Typ:* pica.
pica[2], *s.m. Med: Vet:* pica.
picador [pikadɔ:r], *s.m.* picador.
picage [pika:ʒ], *s.m.* **1.** *Lacem:* pricking (of design). **2.** *Vet:* feather picking.
picaillons [pikajɔ̃], *s.m.pl. P:* (*a*) small coins; coppers; (*b*) money; **avoir des p.,** to have money, to be rich, rolling in it.
picard, -arde [pika:r, -ard], *a. & s. Geog:* (native, inhabitant) of Picardy.
Picardie [pikardi], *Pr.n.f. Geog:* Picardy.
picarel [pikarɛl], *s.m. Ich:* picarel.
picaresque [pikarɛsk], *a.* picaresque (novel).
piccolo [pikɔlo], *s.m.* **1.** *Mus:* piccolo; **joueur de p.,** piccoloist, piccolo player. **2.** light wine (of the locality).
pice [pis], *s.f. Num: A:* pice.
pichenette [piʃnɛt], *s.f.* flip, flick, fillip (of the finger); **d'une p. il chassa une mouche sur sa manche,** he flicked a fly off his sleeve.
pichet [piʃɛ], *s.m.* (small) jug; pitcher (for wine or cider).
picholette [piʃɔlɛt], *s.f. Sw.Fr:* wine carafe (of 3 decilitres).
picholine [pikɔlin], *s.f. Cu:* pickled olive.
picidés [piside], *s.m.pl. Orn:* Picidae, the woodpeckers.
piciformes [pisifɔrm], *s.m.pl. Orn:* Piciformes.
pickeringite [pik(ə)rɛ̃ʒit], *s.f. Miner:* pickeringite.
picklage [pikla:ʒ], *s.m. Leath:* pickling (of hides).
pickpocket [pikpɔkɛ(t)], *s.m.* pickpocket.
pick-up [pikœp], *s.m.* **1.** *Rec:* pick-up; record player. **2.** *Veh:* pick-up; *pl. pick-ups.*
picofarad [pikɔfarad], *s.m. El.Meas:* picofarad.
picoïde [pikɔid], *s.m. Orn:* three-toed woodpecker.
picoler [pikɔle], *v.i. P:* to be fond of the bottle, to tipple.
picoleur [pikɔlœ:r], *s.m. P:* tippler, boozer.
picolet [pikɔlɛ], *s.m.* staple (of lock).
picoline [pikɔlin], *s.f. Ch:* picoline.
picorée [pikɔre], *s.f.* (*a*) *A:* pilfering (of fruit, etc.); (*b*) (*of birds*) **aller à la p.,** to go in search of food.
picorer [pikɔre]. **1.** *v.i.* (*a*) (*of bird, etc.*) to forage; to pick, scratch, about, for food; to peck; to feed; (*b*) *A:* to appropriate, snap up, unconsidered trifles; to pilfer. **2.** *v.tr. A:* to pilfer (fruit, etc.).
picoreur [pikɔrœ:r], *s.m. A:* pilferer.
picoseconde [pikɔsəgɔ̃:d], *s.f. Meas:* picosecond.
picot [piko], *s.m.* **1.** (*a*) splinter (of wood); (*b*) barb, point (of barbed wire); (*c*) **entraînement à picots,** sprocket drive. **2.** pick hammer. **3.** wedge (as used in timbering of mine shaft). **4.** *Needlew: Lacem:* picot. **5.** (*a*) *Dial:* (*Normandy*) turkey; (*b*) *P:* fool, idiot.
picotage [pikɔta:ʒ], *s.m.* **1.** *Min:* wedging (of timbers of shaft). **2.** pricking, tingling, smarting.
picotant [pikɔtɑ̃], *a.* tingling, stinging.
picote [pikɔt], *s.f. Vet:* cowpox; *F:* smallpox.
picotement [pikɔtmɑ̃], *s.m.* pricking, tingling, smarting (sensation).
picoter [pikɔte], *v.tr.* **1.** (*a*) to prick tiny holes in (sth.); **visage picoté de petite vérole,** pockmarked face, face pitted with smallpox; (*b*) (*of bird*) to peck, peck at (fruit, etc.); (*c*) to produce a tingling sensation in (sth.); **la fumée me picotait les yeux,** the smoke made my eyes sting, smart; *O: F:* **ne picote pas ta sœur,** don't tease your sister; *Equit:* **p. son cheval,** to prick one's horse lightly (with the spur); to give one's horse a touch of the spurs. **2.** (*a*) *Min:* to wedge (timbering of shaft); (*b*) *Needlew: etc:* to picot, to put picots on (piece of lace, etc.). **3.** *v.i.* to smart, tingle; **j'ai les yeux qui me picotent,** my eyes are smarting.
picoterie [pikɔtri], *s.f. A: F:* teasing; pinpricks.
picoteur, -euse [pikɔtœ:r, -ø:z]. **1.** *s. F: A:* teaser, tease. **2.** *s.f. Needlew: etc:* worker who makes picots; picot-stitch hand.
picotin [pikɔtɛ̃], *s.m.* **1.** *A.Meas:* peck. **2.** *Husb:* peck of oats, feed of oats.
picotite [pikɔtit], *s.f. Miner:* chromic spinel; picotite.
picoture [pikɔty:r], *s.f.* spot, mark (caused by pricking or pecking); pinhole (in leather, etc.); **fruit couvert de picotures,** fruit that has been pecked.
picramique [pikramik], *a. Ch:* picramic (acid).
picrate [pikrat], *s.m.* **1.** *Ch:* picrate. **2.** *P:* poor quality wine, plonk.
picraté [pikrate], *a. Ch:* picrated.
picride [pikrid], *s.f. Bot:* ox tongue.
picrique [pikrik], *a. Ch:* picric (acid).
picris [pikris], *s.m. Bot:* picris.
picrol [pikrɔl], *s.m. Ch:* picrol.
picrolite [pikrɔlit], *s.f. Miner:* picrolite.
picroméride [pikrɔmerid], **picromérite** [pikrɔmerit], *s.f. Miner:* picromerite.
picrotoxine [pikrɔtɔksin], *s.f. Med:* picrotoxin.
picryle [pikril], *s.m. Ch:* picryl.
Pictes [pikt], *s.m.pl. Ethn: Hist:* Picts.
pictique [piktik], *a. Ethn:* Pictish.
pictogramme [piktɔgram], *s.m.* pictogram, pictograph.
pictographe [piktɔgraf], *s.m.* pictograph.
pictographie [piktɔgrafi], *s.f.* pictography, picture writing.
pictographique [piktɔgrafik], *a.* pictographic.
picton [piktɔ̃], *s.m. P:* (red) wine.
pictural, -aux [piktyral, -o], *a.* pictorial; worthy of an artist's brush.
picturalement [piktyralmɑ̃], *adv.* pictorially; as in a picture.
picul [pikyl], *s.m. A.Meas:* picul.
pic(-)vert [pikvɛ:r], *s.m. Orn:* green woodpecker; *pl. pics(-)verts.*
pidgin [pidʒin], *s.m. Ling:* pidgin.
pie [pi]. **1.** *s.f.* (*a*) *Orn:* magpie; **p. bleue,** Spanish blue magpie; **p. bleue à calotte noire,** azure-winged magpie; **voleur comme une p.,** as thievish as a magpie; *F:* **jaser, bavarder, comme une p.,** to chatter like a magpie; *F:* **elle est bavarde comme une p. (borgne),** she's a regular chatterbox, a confirmed gossip; *s.a.* NID; (*b*) *F:* chatterbox; (*c*) *Orn:* **p. agace, p. de buisson,** shrike; **p. de mer,** oyster catcher; (*d*) *Comest:* **fromage à la p.,** green cheese; (*i.e.* containing herbs). **2.** (*a*) *s.m. or f.* piebald horse, mare; (*b*) *a.inv.* **cheval p., jument p.,** (i) piebald, (ii) skewbald, horse, mare; **vache p.,** black and white cow; **vache p. rouge, rouge p.,** red and white cow; **pigeon p.,** black and white pigeon; **voiture p. (de la police)** = Panda car.
pie[2], *a.f. A:* pious, charitable; *still used in* **œuvre(s) pie(s),** charitable deed(s), good deed(s), work(s).
Pie[3], *Pr.n.m.* Pius.
pié [pje], *s.m. Poet:* = PIED.
piéça [pjesa], *adv. A:* long since.
pièce [pjɛs], *s.f.* **1.** piece (as a whole); (*a*) **p. de bétail, de gibier,** head of cattle, of game; **p. anatomique,** anatomical specimen; **p. de musée,** museum piece; **les plus belles pièces de sa collection,** the finest specimens, pieces, in his collection; *A:* **p. de mariage,** commemorative medal given by bridegroom to bride during marriage ceremony; **p. de blé,** wheatfield; **p. d'avoine,** field of oats; **p. d'eau,** sheet of water, piece of water; ornamental lake; **p. de rhum,** puncheon of rum; **p. de vin,** barrel, cask, of wine; **vin en p.,** wine in the cask, in the wood; *Nau:* **p. à eau,** water cask; **p. de monnaie,** coin; **p. de dix francs,** *F:* **grosse p.,** ten-franc piece; **petites pièces,** small change; **donner la p. à qn,** to give s.o. a tip; to tip s.o.; **p. d'étoffe,** roll of material; **p. de toile,** bolt of canvas, of sailcloth; *Pyr:* **p. d'artifice,** firework; *Cu: Pyr: etc:* **p. montée,** set piece; **p. de résistance,** pièce de résistance; **coûter tant la p.,** to cost so much each, apiece; **ils coûtent dix francs p.,** they cost ten francs each, apiece; **vendre son mobilier p. à p., p. par p.,** to sell one's furniture piece by piece; **ils se vendent à la p.,** they are sold singly, separately; **marchandises à la p.,** piece goods; **travailler à la p., aux pièces,** to do piece work; **être aux pièces,** to be on piece work; *F:* **on n'est pas aux pièces,** we're not in a hurry; **être payé à la p., aux pièces,** to be paid piece rates; (*b*) *Artil:* gun; **p. d'artillerie,** piece of ordnance; **grosse p.,** heavy gun; **p. de petit calibre, p. légère,** light gun; **p. de campagne,** field gun; *Fort: Navy: etc:* **p. de tourelle,** turret gun; **pièces jumelées,** twin guns, guns in pairs; **p. directrice,** directing gun, piece; **chef de p.,** number one, squad leader, *U.S:* chief of (piece) section; **armer une p.,** to man a gun; **p. parée, prête, à faire feu,** gun at the ready; *Hist:* **p. à culasse,** breech-loader; **p. de trois,** three-pounder; *Navy:* **p. de marine, p. de bord,** naval gun; *A:* **p. de batterie,** broadside gun; **p. de chasse,** fore(most) gun, bow-chaser; **p. de retraite,** aft(er) gun, stern-chaser; **p. axiale, p. tirant des deux bords,** axial gun, gun firing all round; (*c*) *Tchn:* **p. moulée,** moulding; (plaster, etc.) cast; *Metall:* **p. coulée, moulée, fondue, venue de fonderie,** casting; **grosses pièces,** heavy castings; **p. coulée, moulée, fondue, en coquille,** chilled casting; **p. coulée, moulée, (en coquille) sous pression,** die casting; **p. coulée, fondue, au sable,** sand casting; **p. creuse,** hollow casting; **p. emboutie, estampée,** pressing, stamping; **p. forgée, venue de forge,** forging; **p. matricée,** drop forging; **p. profilée,** shaped piece; **p. brute de fonderie,** rough casting; (*d*) **p. (de théâtre),** play; **p. en trois actes,** three-act play; **monter une p.,** to put on a play; to cast a play; **tirer une p. d'un roman,** to dramatize a novel; *F: A:* **jouer une p. à qn, faire p. à qn,** to play a trick or a joke on s.o.; *F:* to pull s.o.'s leg; (*e*) *Jur: Adm: etc:* document; **pièces d'un procès,** documents in a case; **p. justificative,** document in proof; relevant paper; **p. à conviction,** exhibit (in criminal case); **nous avons remis ces pièces à notre avoué,** we have handed these papers to our solicitors; **juger, décider, sur pièces,** to decide on documentary evidence; **p. annexe, p. jointe,** enclosure; **p. à l'appui,** document, voucher, in support; supporting document; **pièces à l'appui d'une demande,** documents in support of a request; **présenter une demande avec pièces à l'appui,** to hand in, submit, a request with documents in support; **p. de caisse,** cash voucher; *Adm: etc:* **p. secrète,** secret document; *Nau:* **pièces de bord,** ship's papers; *F:* **c'est la meilleure p. de son dossier,** it is his strongest card; (*f*) *adj. & adv.phr.* **tout d'une p.,** all of a piece; **marcher tout d'une p.,** to walk stiffly, ungracefully; **homme tout d'une p.,** (i) blunt man; (ii) narrow-minded man; **faire sa nuit tout d'une p.,** to sleep right through the night (without waking up); **s'asseoir tout d'une p.,** to flop down; **tomber tout d'une p.,** to fall headlong. **2.** piece (as part of a whole); (*a*) **p. de bœuf,** joint of beef; **pièces d'une armure,** pieces of armour; **être armé de toutes pièces,** to be fully armed, armed at all points; **créer une**

armée de toutes pièces, to create an army out of nothing; **histoire inventée de toutes pièces,** made-up story; **affaire montée de toutes pièces,** trumped-up business, job; *A:* **habiller qn de toutes pièces,** (i) to give s.o. a drubbing; (ii) to say everything that is bad about s.o.; (*b*) *Mec.E:* part (of machine, of clock, etc.); **pièces constituantes d'un mécanisme,** component parts, components, details, of a mechanism; **pièces d'automobile, d'avion,** motor-car, aircraft, parts; *Civ.E: Const:* **pièces d'une charpente,** members of a frame; **pièces mobiles,** moving parts; **pièces fixes, statiques,** fixed, static, parts; **p. rapportée;** *also* **p. collée,** (i) patch; insert; (ii) *F:* outsider, odd man out; **pièces de rechange, pièces détachées,** replacement parts, spare parts, spares, duplicate parts, duplicates, single components; (*c*) patch; **mettre, poser, une p. à un vêtement,** to patch a garment; (*d*) room (of house); **un appartement de trois pièces, un trois pièces,** a three-roomed flat; (*e*) *Games:* (chess) piece; (draughts) man; **faire p. à qn,** to checkmate s.o.; (*f*) *Her:* piece, ordinary, charge; **p. honorable,** honourable ordinary; **burelé de dix pièces,** barruly of ten pieces. **3.** fragment, bit; **fait de pièces et de morceaux,** made of bits and pieces, of odds and ends; **vêtements en pièces,** tattered, ragged, garments; **mettre qch. en pièces,** to break sth. to bits, into fragments; to break sth. to pieces; to pull sth. to pieces; to tear (garment, etc.) to pieces; **briser qch. en pièces,** to shatter sth.; *F:* **mettre qn en pièces,** to slander s.o.; to pull s.o. to pieces; **tailler l'ennemi en pièces,** to cut the enemy to pieces; *F:* **apres l'accident on l'a ramassé en pièces détachées,** after the accident he was picked up in little bits; *adv.phr.* **p. à p.,** bit by bit, piece by piece.

piécette [pjesɛt], *s.f.* **1.** (*a*) small coin; (*b*) *Num: A:* peseta. **2.** short play, playlet, curtain raiser.

pied [pje], *s.m.* **1.** (*a*) foot (of man, of hoofed animal); **pieds de devant, de derrière, d'un cheval,** forefeet, hind feet, of a horse; **p. bot,** club foot; **avoir les pieds plats,** to be flat-footed; *F:* **avoir les pieds nickelés,** (i) to sit tight, to refuse to budge; (ii) to be lazy; **un poney au p. sûr,** a sure-footed pony; **des enfants aux pieds agiles,** quick-footed children; *Lit:* **Achille aux pieds légers,** swift-footed Achilles; **elle a le p. petit, un petit p.,** she has small feet; *F:* **être bête comme ses pieds,** to be unbelievably stupid, so stupid it isn't true; **il n'avait pas de souliers aux pieds,** he had no shoes to his feet; *F:* (*of footwear*) **il n'y a pas de p.,** both feet are the same; *F:* **il y a du p. (dans la chaussette),** (i) there's plenty of time; (ii) we'll manage all right; **la neige durcie craquait sous les pieds,** the hard snow was crunching under our feet; **se jeter aux pieds de qn,** to throw oneself at s.o.'s feet; (*to dog*) **au p.!** heel! **partir du bon p.,** to make a good start, to put one's best foot foremost; **être sur le bon p.,** to be in a good, sound, position; **avoir bon p. bon œil,** to be hale and hearty; **aller de bon p. avec une affaire,** to make good progress, get on swimmingly, with a business; **avoir toujours le p. en l'air,** to be always on the go; **p. gauche,** left foot; **partir du p. gauche,** to make a bad start; **être sur le p. gauche,** to be in an awkward predicament, in a fix; **se lever du p. gauche,** to get out of bed on the wrong side; **il ne peut pas mettre un p. devant l'autre,** (he's so weak) he can hardly crawl, hardly put one foot in front of the other; **il retombe toujours sur ses pieds,** he always falls on his feet; *F:* **avoir les pieds chauds,** to be in clover; *F:* **tenir les pieds chauds à qn,** to keep s.o. on the go; *St.Exch: F:* **pieds humides,** outside brokers; **de la tête aux pieds, de p. en cap** [dəpjetɑ̃kap], from head to foot, from top to toe; **armé de p. en cap,** armed from head to foot, to the teeth, *Lit:* cap-à-pie; **trempé de la tête aux pieds,** soaked from head to foot; **lutter des pieds et des mains,** to fight tooth and nail; **faire des pieds et des mains pour . . .,** to do one's utmost, to move heaven and earth, (in order) to . . .; *F:* **faire du p. à qn,** (i) to give s.o. a kick (as a warning); (ii) to play footy-footy, footsie, with s.o.; *F:* **ça lui fera les pieds!** that'll serve him right! *P:* **il me casse les pieds,** he's a frightful bore; **mettre p. à terre** [pjetatɛːr], to get out (of car, etc.); to dismount (from horse); to step ashore, to land (from boat); **mettre p. sur une île,** to set foot on an island, to land on an island; **jamais je ne remettrai les pieds chez lui,** I'll never set foot in his house again; **je n'ai pas mis les pieds au congrès,** I didn't go near the congress; **je n'ai pas mis le p. dehors de toute la journée,** I haven't set foot outside all day; *F:* **mettre les pieds dans le plat,** to put one's foot in it, to drop a brick; *F:* **ne pas savoir sur quel p. danser,** not to know which way to turn; **marcher sur les pieds de qn,** to tread on s.o.'s toes; *F:* **lever le p.,** to abscond, to bolt; **faire qch. au p. levé,** to do sth. straight off, at a moment's notice; **composer une épigramme au p. levé,** to throw off an epigram; **prendre qn au p. levé,** to catch s.o. unawares, unprepared, *F:* on the hop; **frapper du p.,** to stamp (one's foot); **pousser qch. du p.,** to kick sth.; **repousser qch. du p.,** to push, kick, sth. aside (with one's foot); to spurn sth.; (*b*) **coup de p.,** kick; **donner, envoyer, un coup de p. à qn,** to kick s.o.; **il y a des coups de pied** (*P:* **au cul**) **qui se perdent,** there's no hope for some people; some people are past praying for; **chasser qn à coups de p.,** to kick s.o. out; **recevoir des coups de p.,** to get kicked; **enfoncer une porte à coups de p.,** to kick a door in; *F:* **il ne se donne pas des coups de p.,** he's always pleased with himself; he thinks he can do no wrong; he's always blowing his own trumpet; *F:* **c'est le coup de p. de l'âne,** that's the unkindest cut of all; *Fb:* **coup de p. tombé,** drop kick; **coup de p. de coin,** corner (kick); **coup de p. de but,** goal kick; **coup de p. croisé,** cross kick; (*c*) **à p.,** on foot, walking; **voyageur à p.,** walker; pedestrian; **aller à pied,** to walk, *F:* to foot it; **il faudra faire le trajet à p.,** we shall have to walk it, go on foot; **retourner à p.,** to return on foot, to walk back; **faire deux kilomètres à p.,** to walk two kilometres; **vous en avez pour vingt minutes à p.,** it will take you twenty minutes to walk (it), twenty minutes on foot; **course à p.,** foot race; **mettre qn à p.,** to dismiss, sack, s.o.; **mettre un jockey à p.,** to suspend a jockey; **être mis à p.,** to be dismissed, sacked; **mise à p.,** (i) dismissal (of employee); (ii) withdrawal of (jockey's) licence; (*d*) **sur p.,** standing; on one's feet; **il est sur p. de bonne heure,** he's up (and about) early; **récolte sur p.,** standing crop; **bétail sur p.,** livestock on the hoof; **mettre une armée sur p.,** to raise an army; to equip an army; **mettre un comité sur p.,** to set up a committee; **remettre une affaire sur p.,** to get a business going, on its feet, again; **il n'y a qu'un médecin qui vous remettra sur p.,** only a doctor will get you on your feet again, will pull you round; **il est de nouveau sur p.,** he's up and about, getting about, again; (*e*) **être en p.,** to hold an appointment; to be on the active list; **portrait en p.,** full-length portrait; (*f*) *Cu:* **p. de veau,** calf's foot; **p. de cochon, p. de mouton,** pig's, sheep's, trotter; *F:* **jouer un p. de cochon à qn,** to play a dirty trick on s.o.; to let s.o. down; (*g*) *P:* fool, idiot; **quel p.!** what a clot! what a nit! **jouer comme un p.,** to play badly, to be an atrocious player; **il conduit comme un p.,** he's a shocking driver; (*h*) *Bootm:* **p. de fonte,** last. **2.** (*a*) footing; foothold; **avoir le p. marin,** to be a good sailor; **perdre p.,** (i) to lose one's foothold; (ii) to get out of one's depth; **une vague lui fit perdre p.,** a wave carried him off his feet, out of his depth; **avoir p.,** (i) to feel the ground (firm) under one's feet; (ii) (*of swimmer*) to be within one's depth; **ne pas avoir p.,** to be out of one's depth; **le p. me manqua,** I lost my footing, I slipped; **tenir p.,** to hold one's ground; to stand fast; **tenir p. à qn,** to stand up to s.o.; **prendre p.,** (i) to get a foothold, a footing; (ii) to take root; **l'ennemi prit p. dans le village,** the enemy gained a foothold in the village; **coutume qui prend p.,** custom that is gaining ground; **armée sur le p. de guerre, de paix,** army on a war footing, on a peace footing; **être sur le même p. que qn,** to be on an equal footing with s.o.; to be on terms of equality with s.o.; **être, se mettre, sur un bon p. avec qn,** to be, to get, on good terms with s.o.; **établir une maison sur un grand p.,** to set up (i) house, (ii) a business, on a large scale; **vivre sur un grand p.,** to live on a grand scale; **sur un p. tout nouveau,** on quite new lines; **sur quel p. vit-il?** in what sort of style does he live? **payer qn sur le p. de . . .,** to pay s.o. at the rate of . . ., on the scale of . . .; **je ne puis pas continuer à ce p.-là,** I can't go on at that rate, on that scale; (*b*) footprint, track (of animal); *Typ: O:* **p. de mouche,** paragraph mark. **3.** (*a*) foot (of stocking, tree); foot, base (of column, wall); foot (of mountain); *Her:* **p. de l'écu,** base of the shield; **le village est situé p. de la montagne,** the village lies at the foot of the mountain; **p. d'un escalier, d'un lit,** foot of a staircase, of a bed; *Geom:* **p. d'une perpendiculaire,** foot of a perpendicular; **p. d'une courbe,** toe of a curve; *Surv: etc:* **p. de la verticale,** ground plumb point; (*of wall*) **avoir du p.,** to have batter; **donner plus de p. à une échelle,** to give more slope to a ladder; *Civ.E: etc:* **à p. d'œuvre,** on site; **coût des matériaux à p. d'œuvre,** cost of materials (delivered) on site; **se mettre à p. d'œuvre,** to get down to work; **reprendre un travail à p. d'œuvre,** to start again from the beginning; (*b*) leg (of chair, table, etc.); stem, foot (of glass); **table à trois pieds,** three-legged table; **p. de lampe, de lampadaire,** lampstand; **lampe sur p.,** standard lamp; **p. de flèche (de grue, etc.),** jib foot (of crane, etc.); **p. de poteau (télégraphique, etc.),** pole butt; **p. de tube électronique,** (vacuum) valve stem; (*c*) stalk (of plant); stock (of vine); **p. de céleri, d'asperges, de salade,** head of celery, of asparagus, of lettuce; **cent pieds d'arbres,** a hundred standing trees; *Hort:* **p. mère,** stool; (*d*) stand, rest (for telescope, etc.); *Phot:* foot; **p. d'atelier,** studio stand; **p. à trois branches,** tripod; **p. à branches coulissantes,** sliding tripod; **pieds d'un tour,** standards of a lathe; *Laund:* **p. à manches, p. à repasser,** sleeve board; (*e*) *Nau:* step, heel (of mast); (*f*) *Bookb:* tail (of book); (*g*) *Dressm:* **p. du col,** sham of the collar. **4.** (*a*) *Meas:* foot; **p. carré,** square foot; **p. cube,** cubic foot; **donnez-lui un p., il en prendra quatre,** give him an inch and he'll take an ell; **c'est un Napoléon au petit p.,** he's a miniature Napoleon, Napoleon on a small scale, a tinpot Napoleon; **p. à p.** [pjeapje], foot by foot, step by step; **reculer p. à p.,** to fall back step by step; **disputer le terrain p. à p.,** to dispute the ground inch by inch; to dispute every inch of the ground; (*b*) foot rule; *Fr.C:* **p. de roi,** folding rule(r); **p. à coulisse,** (i) calliper square; (ii) (shoemaker's) size stick. **5.** *Pros:* (metrical) foot; **vers de dix pieds,** ten-foot verse, line.

pied-à-terre [pjetatɛːr], *s.m.inv.* pied-à-terre; small flat (in a town).

pied-bleu [pjeblø], *s.m. Fung:* wood blewit; *pl. pieds-bleus.*

pied-bot [pjebo], *s.m.* club-footed person; *pl. pieds-bots.*

pied-d'alouette [pjedalwɛt], *s.m. Bot:* larkspur; delphinium; *pl. pieds-d'alouette.*

pied-de-banc [pjedbɑ̃], *s.m. Mil: P:* non-commissioned officer, N.C.O.; *esp.* sergeant; *pl. pieds-de-banc.*

pied-de-biche [pjedbiʃ], *s.m.* **1.** bell pull. **2.** (*a*) (dentist's) molar forceps; (*b*) nail extractor, nail claw; (*c*) crow bar, spike bar; (*d*) presser foot (of sewing machine). **3.** cabriole leg (of chair, table, etc.); *pl. pieds-de-biche.*

pied-de-chat [pjedʃa], *s.m. Bot: F:* chasteweed, cat's foot; *pl. pieds-de-chat.*

pied-de-cheval [pjedʃəval], *s.m. F:* large oyster; *pl. pieds-de-cheval.*

pied-de-chèvre [pjedʃɛːvr], *s.m.* **1.** *Bot:* pimpinella, burnet saxifrage. **2.** ground-sill, footing (of heavy sheers); *pl. pieds-de-chèvre.*

pied-de-corbeau [pjedkɔrbo], *s.m. Bot: F:* crowfoot; *pl. pieds-de-corbeau.*

pied-de-griffon [pjedgrifɔ̃], *s.m. Bot: F:* stinking hellebore, bear's foot; *pl. pieds-de-griffon.*

pied-de-lion [pjedljɔ̃], *s.m. Bot: F:* lion's foot; *pl. pieds-de-lion.*

pied-de-loup [pjedlu], *s.m. Bot:* **1.** club moss. **2.** gipsy wort; *pl. pieds-de-loup.*

pied-de-pigeon [pjedpiʒɔ̃], *s.m. Bot: F:* dove's foot; *pl. pieds-de-pigeon.*

pied-de-poule [pjedpul]. **1.** *a. & s.m. Tex:* broken check, houndstooth (material). **2.** *s.m. Bot: F:* (*a*) woolly andropogon; (*b*) dog's tooth grass; *pl. pieds-de-poule.*

pied-de-veau [pjedvo], *s.m. Bot:* lords and ladies, cuckoo pint, wake robin; *pl. pieds-de-veau.*

pied-d'oiseau [pjedwazo], *s.m. Bot: F:* bird foot, bird's foot; *pl. pieds-d'oiseau.*

pied-droit [pjedrwɑ], *s.m.* **1.** *Civ.E:* pier (of arch, of bridge). **2.** *Arch:* (*a*) engaged pier, *A:* pied-droit; (*b*) jamb, pier (of window, etc.); *pl. pieds-droits.*

piédestal, -aux [pjedɛstal, -o], *s.m.* pedestal; **mettre qn sur un p.,** to put s.o. on a pedestal; to hero-worship s.o.

pied-livre [pjeliːvr], *s.m. Mec.Meas:* foot-pound; *pl. pieds-livres.*

pied-noir [pjenwaːr]. **1.** *s.m. Bot:* (*disease*) black root (rot). **2.** *s.m. & f. F:* Algerian-born Frenchman, Frenchwoman; **pieds-noirs rapatriés (en France),** repatriated Algerians. **3.** *Nau: O:* stoker; *pl. pieds-noirs.*

piédouche [pjeduʃ], *s.m.* small pedestal (for busts, cups, etc.); piedouche.

pied-plat [pjepla], *s.m.* despicable person, *F:* rotter; *pl. pieds-plats.*
piédroit [pjedrwa], *s.m.* = PIED-DROIT.
pied-tonne [pjetɔn], *s.m. Mec.Meas:* foot-ton; *pl. pieds-tonnes.*
piège [pjɛ:ʒ], *s.m.* trap, snare; **p. à mâchoire,** jaw trap, gin trap; **p. à loups,** mantrap; **p. en forme de fosse,** pitfall; *Geol:* **p. à pétrole, p. pétrolifère, p. stratigraphique,** oil trap; *Elcs:* **p. à ions,** ion trap; **armer, dresser, tendre, un p.,** to set a trap (à, for); **amorcer un p.,** to bait a trap; **dresser un p. à qn,** to set a trap for s.o.; **prendre un animal au p.,** to trap an animal; **chasse au p. et au filet,** trapping and netting; **attirer l'ennemi dans un p.,** to ambush the enemy; **être entraîné dans un p.,** to be lured into a trap; **donner, tomber, dans le p., se prendre au p.,** to walk, fall, into the trap; **se laisser prendre au p.,** to be caught in the trap; **être pris à son propre p.,** to be caught in one's own trap, to be hoist with one's own petard; **dictée pleine de pièges,** dictation full of traps, of pitfalls.
piégeage [pjeʒa:ʒ], *s.m.* trapping (of animals).
piège-attrape [pjɛʒatrap], *s.m.* booby trap; *pl. pièges-attrape.*
piéger [pjeʒe], *v.tr.* (**je piège, n. piégeons; je piégeai(s); je piégerai**) 1. to trap (animal). 2. *Mil:* (*a*) **p. une mine,** to make a mine into a booby trap; (*b*) **p. une route,** to booby-trap a road.
piégeur [pjeʒœ:r], *s.m.* trapper.
pie-grièche [pigriɛʃ], *s.f.* 1. *Orn:* shrike; **p.-g. écorcheur,** butcher bird, red-backed shrike; **p.-g. rousse,** woodchat shrike; **p.-g. grise,** great grey shrike; **p.-g. à poitrine rose,** lesser grey shrike; **p.-g. isabelle,** isabelline shrike; **p.-g. masquée,** masked shrike. 2. *F:* (*woman*) shrew; *pl. pies-grièches.*
pie-mère [pimɛ:r], *s.f. Anat:* pia mater; *pl. pies-mères.*
pie-mérien, -ienne [pimerjɛ̃, -jɛn], *a. Anat:* of the pia mater.
Piémont [pjemɔ̃]. 1. *Pr.n.m. Geog:* Piedmont. 2. *s.m. Geol:* **(plaine de) p.,** piedmont (plain), *U.S:* benchland; **glacier de p.,** piedmont glacier.
piémontais, -aise [pjemɔ̃tɛ, -ɛ:z], *a. & s. Geog:* Piedmontese.
piémontite [pjemɔ̃tit], *s.f. Miner:* piedmontite.
piéride [pjerid], *s.f.* 1. *Myth:* **les Piérides,** the Pierides; the nine Muses. 2. *Ent:* pierid; **p. du chou,** cabbage white butterfly; **p. gazée,** black-veined white butterfly.
piéridés [pjeride], *s.m.pl. Ent:* Pieridae.
Piérie [pjeri], *Pr.n.f. A.Geog:* Pieria; the birth-place of the Muses.
piérien, -ienne [pjerjɛ̃, -jɛn], *a. Myth: A.Geog:* Pierian.
pierrage [pjɛra:ʒ], *s.m. Metalw:* honing.
pierraille [pjɛrɑ:j], *s.f.* broken stones, rubble, gravel; ballast; road metal.
pierre¹ [pjɛ:r], *s.f.* stone; (*a*) *Miner:* **p. d'aimant,** lodestone; **p. à chaux, p. calcaire,** limestone; **p. à plâtre,** plaster stone, gypsum; **p. à filtrer,** filtering stone; **p. abrasive,** grindstone; **p. d'aigle,** eagle-stone; aetites; **p. d'alun,** alum stone, alumite, alunite; **p. de croix,** cross stone, staurolite; **p. d'émeri,** emery stone; **p. de grès,** grit stone; **p. météorique,** meteoric stone; **p. de meule, p. meulière,** grindstone grit, buhrstone, burrstone; **p. de touche,** touchstone; **p. ponce,** pumice (stone); **p. de savon,** soapstone; **p. de soleil,** sunstone; (*b*) **une p.,** a stone; **tas de pierres,** heap of stones; **pierres de gué,** stepping stones; *Geol:* **p. branlante,** rocking stone; *Ecc. Arch:* **p. d'autel,** altar stone; **p. d'achoppement,** stumbling block; *Prov:* **p. qui roule n'amasse pas mousse,** a rolling stone gathers no moss; **avoir un cœur de p.,** to have a heart of stone; **assaillir qn à coups de pierres,** to pelt s.o. with stones; **jeter la p. à qn,** to cast a stone at s.o.; to accuse s.o.; *F:* **c'est une p. dans votre jardin,** that's a dig at you; **faire d'une p. deux coups,** to kill two birds with one stone; **jour à marquer d'une p. blanche,** red-letter day; *F:* **malheureux comme les pierres,** (i) bitterly unhappy; (ii) (stony) broke; (*c*) *Prehist:* **âge de la p.,** stone age; **âge de la p. taillée,** palaeolithic age; **âge de la p. polie,** neolithic age; **outils en p.,** flint implements; **p. levée,** menhir, standing stone; (*d*) *Const:* **p. à bâtir,** building stone; **p. de taille,** ashlar, freestone; **p. taillée,** cut stone, hewn stone, dressed stone; **p. non taillée, p. brute,** uncut stone, unhewn stone, undressed stone; rough stone; **taille de la p.,** stone cutting; **tailleur de p.,** stone cutter, stone dresser; **p. angulaire,** corner stone; **p. d'arête,** quoin stone; **p. d'attente, d'arrachement,** toothing stone, tooth; **poser la première p.,** to lay the foundation stone; **assise de pierre(s),** course of stone(s); **mur de p.,** stone wall; **mur en pierres sèches,** drystone wall; **ouvrage en p.,** stone work; **démolir un édifice p. à p.,** to demolish a building stone by stone; **il ne reste pas p. sur p. de l'ancienne Carthage,** there is no stone of ancient Carthage left standing; (*e*) **p. (de bijouterie),** gem, jewel; **p. précieuse, p. gemme,** precious stone; gem; **p. fine,** semi-precious stone; **p. (précieuse) brute,** rough (stone), stone in the rough; **p. (précieuse) taillée,** cut stone, cut gem; **pierres de couleur,** coloured stones; **p. d'azur,** azure stone, lazulite, lapis lazuli; **p. d'évêque,** bishop's stone, amethyst; **p. de jade, p. néphritique,** jade stone, nephritic stone; **p. de lune,** moonstone; **p. de soleil,** sunstone, aventurine; **p. d'imitation, p. factice, p. fausse,** imitation stone, paste; *Astrol:* **p. bénéfique,** *F:* **p. de bonheur,** birthstone; (*f*) *Tchn:* **p. à affûter, à aiguiser, à morfiler, à repasser,** whetstone, grindstone, sharpening stone; **p. à huile,** oilstone, hone, honing stone; **passer un outil à la p. à huile,** to hone a tool; **p. à briquet,** (lighter) flint; **p. à fusil,** gun flint; **fusil à p.,** flint gun, flint lock; (*g*) **p. lithographique,** lithographic stone; **p. à encrer,** ink slab; **gravure sur p.,** stone engraving; **mettre un dessin sur la p.,** to put a drawing on the stone; (*h*) *Med:* stone, calculus; (*i*) grit (in pear).
Pierre², *Pr.n.m.* Peter; **découvrir saint P. pour couvrir saint Paul,** to rob Peter to pay Paul; **P. et Paul; P., Paul et Jacques,** Tom, Dick and Harry.
pierré(e) [pjɛre], *s.f. Const:* drystone drain.
pierrefittois, -oise [pjɛrfitwa, -wa:z], *a. & s. Geog:* (native, inhabitant) of Pierrefitte-sur-Seine.
pierrer [pjɛre], *v.tr.* to hone.
pierreries [pjɛr(ə)ri], *s.f.pl.* precious stones, jewels, gems.
pierrette¹ [pjɛrɛt], *s.f.* small stone, pebble.
pierrette², *s.f.* 1. *Th:* Pierrette. 2. *Orn: F:* hen sparrow.
pierreux, -euse [pjɛrø, -ø:z]. 1. *a.* (*a*) stony (ground, road, etc.); gravelly (bed of river); gritty (pear); *Anat:* petrous; (*b*) *Med:* (i) calculous (formation); (ii) (patient) suffering from calculus. 2. *s. Med:* person suffering from calculus. 3. *s.f. P: A:* **pierreuse,** street walker.
pierrier [pjɛrje], *s.m.* 1. *Agr:* stone drain. 2. *Artil: A:* swivel gun; *A:* perrier. 3. *Geol:* scree slope.
Pierrot [pjɛro]. 1. *Pr.n.m. F:* Peterkin, little Peter. 2. *s.m.* (*a*) *Th:* Pierrot; clown; (*b*) *Orn: F:* sparrow; (*c*) *F:* bumpkin; idiot, fool; **c'est un drôle de p.,** he's a queer fish; (*d*) *P:* **étrangler un p.,** to knock back a glass of white wine; (*e*) *F:* double blank (in game of dominoes).
pierrures [pjɛry:r], *s.f.pl. Ven:* pearls (of base of deer's antlers).
piéta, pietà [pjeta], *s.f. Ecc.Art:* pietà.
piétage [pjeta:ʒ], *s.m.* 1. *Nau:* draught marks. 2. **p. femelle, mâle,** locating hole, stud.
piétaille [pjetɑ:j], *s.f. Mil: A: P:* foot-sloggers, infantrymen, P.B.I.
piété [pjete], *s.f.* (*a*) piety; **homme d'une grande p.,** man of great piety, extremely pious man; **œuvres de p.,** charitable works; good works; *Com:* **articles de p.,** devotional objects; (*b*) **p. filiale,** filial piety, devotion.
piètement [pjɛtmɑ̃], *s.m. Furn:* support; legs (and crossbars); *Tchn:* (i) seating, seat; (ii) mounting, mount.
piéter [pjete], *v.* (**je piète, n. piétons; je piéterai**) 1. *v.i.* (*a*) (*at bowls, etc.*) to toe the line; to stand fair; (*b*) *Ven:* (*of pheasant, etc.*) to run (instead of flying). 2. *v.tr.* (*a*) *A:* **p. qn contre qch.,** to incite s.o. to resist against sth.; (*b*) **p. le gazon,** to cut the grass close to the roots; (*c*) *Nau:* to mark the draught in feet on (ship).
se piéter, *A:* to dig one's heels into the ground; to stand firm; to show stubbornness.
piétin [pjetɛ̃], *s.m.* (*a*) *Vet:* foot rot; (*b*) (*in cereals*) root rot.
piétinement [pjetinmɑ̃], *s.m.* stamping, trampling (with the feet); *Hort:* treading (of light soil); **p. sur place,** marking time.
piétiner [pjetine]. 1. *v.tr.* to trample, stamp, on (sth.); to trample (sth.) down; to tread (sth.) under foot; *Hort:* to tread (light soil); *Ind:* **p. l'argile,** to tread the clay. 2. *v.i.* **p. d'impatience,** to stamp (one's feet) with impatience, impatiently; **p. sur place,** to mark time; **on piétine, on n'avance pas,** we are (merely) marking time; **l'instruction piétine,** the judge's investigation is making no headway; **p. de rage,** to dance with rage; **p. sur le feu pour l'éteindre,** to stamp out the fire; *v.i. & tr.* **p. (sur) le cadavre de qn,** to speak ill of the dead.
piétisme [pjetism], *s.m. Rel.H:* Pietism.
piétiste [pjetist], *a. & s.m. & f. Rel.H:* Pietist.
piéton, -onne [pjetɔ̃, -ɔn], *s.* (*a*) pedestrian; **sentier pour piétons,** *a.* **sentier p.,** footpath; **col p.,** mountain pass traversed by footpath; **passage pour piétons,** pedestrian crossing; *P.N: Rail:* **passage interdit aux piétons** = passengers are requested to cross the line by the bridge, the underground passage; (*b*) *A:* country postman.
piètre [pjɛtr], *a.* wretched, poor; lame, paltry (excuse); **un p. musicien,** a poor musician; **c'est un bien p. docteur,** he's a pretty miserable doctor; **faire p. figure,** to cut a poor figure; **p. consolation,** cold comfort; **maison de p. apparence,** shabby(-looking) house.
piètrement [pjɛtrəmɑ̃], *adv.* wretchedly, poorly; **vêtu p.,** shabbily, poorly, dressed.
pieu¹, -ieux [pjø], *s.m.* 1. stake, post; **on avait enclos le terrain de pieux,** the ground had been staked off; *F:* (*pers.*) **raide comme un p.,** as stiff as a post; *Nau:* **p. d'amarrage,** mooring-post; bollard. 2. *Civ.E: etc:* pile; **p. creux,** tubular pile; **enfoncer, battre, un pieu,** to drive (in) a pile.
pieu², *s.m. P:* bed; *P:* kip; **se mettre au p.,** to go to bed; to get into bed; *P:* to doss down, to hit the hay, to kip down.
pieusement [pjøzmɑ̃], *adv.* (*a*) piously, reverently; (*b*) dutifully.
pieuter (se) [səpjøte], *v.pr. P:* to go to bed; *P:* to doss down, to hit the hay, to kip down.
pieuvre [pjœ:vr], *s.f.* (*a*) *Moll:* octopus; (*b*) *F:* (*of pers.*) parasite, limpet, leech; (*c*) *Aut:* elastic or spring tie for roof rack.
pieux, -euse [pjø, -ø:z], *a.* (*a*) pious; **legs p.,** charity bequest; (*b*) dutiful, (respectfully) devoted.
pièze [pjɛ:z], *s.f. Ph.Meas:* pieze.
piézoclase [pjezɔklɑ:z], *s.f. Geol:* compression joint, compression fracture.
piézocristallisation [pjezɔkristalizasjɔ̃], *s.f. Miner:* piezocrystallization.
piézo-électricité [pjezɔelɛktrisite], *s.f.* piezo-electricity.
piézo-électrique [pjezɔelɛktrik], *a.* piezo-electric; **pilotage p.-é.,** crystal control, crystal drive; **à pilotage p.-é.,** crystal-controlled, crystal-driven; *pl. piézo-électriques.*
piézographe [pjezɔgraf], *s.m.* piezograph.
piézomètre [pjezɔmɛtr], *s.m. Ph:* piezometer.
piézométrie [pjezɔmetri], *s.f. Ph:* piezometry.
piézométrique [pjezɔmetrik], *a. Ph:* piezometric(al).
pif¹ [pif], *int.* **p., paf!** (*denoting a sequence or exchange of sharp blows, of revolver shots, etc.*) bang, bang! crack, crack! smack, smack!
pif², *s.m. P:* 1. large nose; bottle-nose; *P:* conk. 2. **faire qch. au p.,** to do sth. by guess(work).
piffard [pifa:r], *s.m. P:* person with a long, big, nose, with a conk.
piffer [pife], *v.tr. P:* **j'peux pas le p.,** I can't stand (the sight of) him, I can't stomach him.
piffomètre [pifɔmɛtr], *s.m. P:* **au p.,** (i) by guess-work, *U.S: F:* gues(s)timate; (ii) by chance; **aller au p.,** to play it by ear.
piffre,¹ -esse [pifr, -ɛs], *s. P: A:* greedy-guts, fatty.
piffre², *s.m.* (large) hammer (used by gold beater).
piffrer (se) [səpifre], *v.pr. A: P:* to guzzle, to gorge.
pigamon [pigamɔ̃], *s.m. Bot:* meadow rue.
pige [pi:ʒ], *s.f.* 1. (*a*) (arbitrary) measure; *Sp:* (*bowls*) distance between bowl and marker; (*b*) measuring rod; *Aut:* **p. de niveau d'huile,** dip-stick. 2. *Typ:* take; amount of copy to be set up in a given time; **travail à la p.,** piece work; *Journ:* **être payé à la p.,** to be paid by the line. 3. *P:* year (of age, of prison sentence); **à, pour, soixante piges il n'est pas mal,** he's not bad for sixty. 4. *P:* **faire la p. à qn,** to go one better than s.o.; to leave s.o. standing.
pigeon, -onne [piʒɔ̃, -ɔn], *s.* 1. *Orn:* pigeon, *f.* hen pigeon; **p. mâle, femelle,** cock pigeon, hen pigeon; **p. domestique, p. de volière,** domestic pigeon; **p. migrateur,** passenger pigeon; **p. voyageur,** carrier pigeon, homing pigeon; **p. (à) grosse gorge,** pouter; **p. biset, p. de roche,** rock dove, rock pigeon; **p. colombin, p. bleu,** stock dove; **p. ramier,** ring dove, wood pigeon; **p. à capuchon,** jacobin; **p. romain,** runt; **p. à cravate, p. cravaté,** turbit; **p. paon,** fantail; **p. brésilien,** helmet pigeon; **p. bouvreuil,** archangel; **p. tambour,** tambourine pigeon; **p. du Cap,** Cape pigeon, pintado petrel; **p. d'argile,** clay pigeon (for shooting); *Danc:* **aile de p.,** pigeon wing;

Games: **p. vole,** children's game with forfeits; *F:* **loger comme, avec, les pigeons,** to live in an attic. **2.** *F: (pers.)* sucker; **plumer un p.,** to fleece a mug, a sucker; *(at gaming)* to pluck a pigeon. **3.** *s.m. Const:* (*a*) builder's plaster; (*b*) hard lump, nodule (in lime). **4.** *Nau:* **aile de p.,** skysail, skyscraper.

pigeonite [piʒɔnit], *s.f. Miner:* pigeonite.

pigeonnage [piʒɔnaːʒ], *s.m. Const:* plaster work; stucco.

pigeonnant [piʒɔnɑ̃], *a. Cost:* **soutien-gorge p.,** uplift brassière.

pigeonneau, -eaux [piʒɔno], *s.m.* **1.** young pigeon; squab. **2.** *F: (pers.)* sucker.

pigeonner [piʒɔne], *v.tr. F:* to swindle, to cheat; to dupe; *(at cards)* to fleece; **je me suis laissé, fait, p.,** I've been had.

pigeonnier, -ière [piʒɔnje, -jɛːr]. **1.** *a.* relating to the breeding or keeping of pigeons; **l'industrie pigeonnière,** pigeon breeding. **2.** *s.m.* pigeon house, dovecot(e), pigeonry, columbarium. **3.** *s.m. F:* garret, attic. **4.** *s.m. F: Th:* the gods.

piger [piʒe], *v.tr.* **(je pigeai(s); n. pigeons) 1.** *F: & Dial:* to measure. **2.** *P:* (*a*) to look at (sth.); **pige-moi ça!** take a look at that! just look at that! (*b*) **p. un rhume,** to catch a cold; *O:* **se faire p.,** to get nabbed, collared; (*c*) to understand; **il n'y a rien pigé,** he didn't catch on; **piges-tu la combine?** d'you see their, my, little game? d'you get what they're, we're, up to? *abs.* **tu piges?** get it? **je pige,** the penny's dropped; **je ne pige rien aux maths,** I haven't a clue about maths.

pigiste [piʒist], *a. & s.m. & f. Journ:* (journalist) paid at space rates.

pigment [pigmɑ̃], *s.m.* pigment.

pigmentaire [pigmɑ̃tɛːr], *a.* pigmentary; **maladie p.,** macular skin affection; **cellule p.,** pigment cell, colour cell.

pigmentation [pigmɑ̃tasjɔ̃], *s.f.* pigmentation.

pigmenté [pigmɑ̃te], *a.* pigmented.

pigmenter [pigmɑ̃te], *v.tr.* to pigment.

pigmenteux, -euse [pigmɑ̃tø, -øːz], *a.* pigmentary, pigmentous.

pigmentophage [pigmɑ̃tɔfaːʒ], *s.m. Anat:* pigmentophage.

pignade [piɲad], *s.f. (esp. in the Landes)* plantation of maritime pines.

pigne [piɲ], *s.f. Bot:* pine cone, fir cone.

pignet [piɲɛ], *s.m. Bot:* spruce.

pignocher[1] [piɲɔʃe]. *F:* **1.** (*a*) *v.tr.* to pick at (one's food); (*b*) *v.i.* to pick at one's food. **2.** *v.tr. & i. Art:* to paint with little niggling strokes.

pignocher[2] **(se),** *v.pr. P:* to have a set-to; to come to blows.

pignocheur, -euse [piɲɔʃœːr, -øːz], *s. F:* **1.** small eater, person who picks at his food. **2.** *Art:* niggler.

pignon[1] [piɲɔ̃], *s.m. Const:* gable (end); **maison à p.,** gabled house; **p. à redans,** (crow-)stepped gable; **avoir p. sur rue,** (i) to own a house (of one's own); (ii) to own property; to be a person of substance; (iii) *(of shopkeeper)* to have well-situated premises; **bordure de p.,** bargeboard.

pignon[2], *s.m. Mec.E:* pinion; gear; **p. droit,** spur pinion, spur gearing; **p. de chaîne,** sprocket wheel, chain sprocket (of motor cycle, etc.); **arbre porte-p.,** gear shaft; **p. de crémaillère,** rack pinion; **grand p.,** front chain wheel (of bicycle; *Aut:* **p. de boîte de vitesses,** gear pinion; **p. du centre du différentiel,** axle-drive bevel gear; **p. à deux vitesses, p. multiple,** cluster gear; **p. d'angle, p. conique,** bevel gear, pinion; mitre gear; **p. d'attaque, de commande, d'entraînement,** driving gear, pinion; drive gear, pinion; **p. de distribution,** timing gear, pinion; valve gear pinion; **p. fou, p. intermédiaire,** idle(r) gear; **p. planétaire,** spider pinion; **p. satellite,** planet gear, pinion, wheel; **p. tendeur,** jockey wheel; **p. principal d'engrenage planétaire,** sun gear; **p. et couronne d'entraînement,** crown wheel and pinion.

pignon[3], *s.m. Bot:* pignon, pine seed, pine kernel; (pin) **p.,** parasol pine; **p. d'Inde,** pignon, physic nut, Barbados nut.

pignonnerie [piɲɔn(ə)ri], *s.f. Mec.E:* gear train, assembly train.

pignoratif, -ive [pignɔratif, -iːv], *a. Jur:* pignorative; **contrat p.,** contract of sale with option of redemption.

pignoration [pignɔrasjɔ̃], *s.f. Jur:* pignoration; pledging; pawning.

pignouf [piɲuf], *s.m. P:* **1.** boor, lout. **2.** *O:* miser, skinflint.

pika [pika], *s.m. Z:* pika, rock rabbit.

piklage [piklaːʒ], *s.m. Leath:* pickling.

pila [pila], *s.f. Moll:* apple snail, apple shell.

pilaf [pilaf], *s.m. Cu:* pilaf, pilao, pilaw, pulao.

pilage [pilaːʒ], *s.m.* pounding, crushing, grinding (in mortar, mill, etc.).

pilaire [pilɛːr], *a. Anat:* pilar, pilary; relating to the hair.

pilastre [pilastr̥], *s.m. Arch:* pilaster; **pilastres de porte,** gateway piers; **p. (de rampe) d'escalier,** newel (at bottom of handrail).

Pilate[1] [pilat], *Pr.n.m. Hist:* **Ponce P.,** Pontius Pilate; *Lit:* **être renvoyé de Caïphe à P.,** to be driven from pillar to post.

Pilate[2], *Pr.n.m. Geog:* (Mount) Pilatus.

pilau, pilaw [pilo], *s.m.* = PILAF.

pilchard [pilʃaːr], *s.m. Ich:* pilchard.

pile[1] [pil], *s.f.* **1.** pile; heap (of coins, books); stack (of wood); **mettre en p.,** to heap, to stack, to pile up. **2.** pier (of bridge); mole; **p. culée,** abutment pier. **3.** (*a*) *El:* battery; cell; **p. sèche,** dry cell; **p. à liquide, p. humide,** wet cell; **p. de polarisation,** bias cell, battery; **p. solaire,** solar cell; **p. galvanique,** column battery; **p. non amorcée,** inert cell; **p. usée,** weak cell; *Tp:* **p. de ligne,** line battery; **p. de rechange,** spare battery (for torch, etc.); (*b*) *Atom.Ph:* **p. atomique,** atomic pile, nuclear reactor; **p. couveuse,** breeder reactor. **4.** *Fish:* snood, snell.

pile[2], *s.f.* (*a*) *Tchn:* beating trough, beating engine, stamping trough (for sugar, paper, etc.); bed (of powder mill); (*b*) *A:* **mettre qn à la p. et au verjus,** to ill-treat s.o.; *F:* **flanquer, donner, une p. à qn,** to give s.o. a thrashing; *F:* **recevoir une p.,** to have a crushing defeat.

pile[3]. **1.** *s.f.* reverse (of coin); **p. ou face,** heads or tails; **jouons à p. ou face à qui commencera,** let's toss to see who begins. **2.** *adv.* (*a*) *A:* **tomber p. sur le dos,** to fall flat on one's back; (*b*) *F:* **s'arrêter p.,** to stop short; to come to a dead stop; to stop dead; **vous tombez p.,** you've come just at the right moment; **ça tombe p.,** that comes just at the right moment, in the nick of time; that's just what was wanted now; **à six heures p.,** on the dot of six.

pile[4], *s.f. Her:* pile.

pilée [pile], *s.f. Paperm:* troughful.

piler [pile], *v.tr.* (*a*) to pound; to crush, bruise, grind, bray (in mortar, mill, etc.); to powder, pestle (drug); to grind (almonds); to stamp, beat (skins); **p. menu,** to grind small; **poivre pilé,** ground pepper; *F:* **p. du poivre,** (i) to bump up and down in the saddle; (ii) to talk scandal; (iii) to make no headway (in undertaking, etc.); *Cy: F:* **p. une montée,** to toil up a hill; (*b*) *F:* to thrash (s.o.); **être à p.,** to be objectionable, to deserve a good thrashing; **en p.,** to have a bad time of it; **notre équipe s'est fait p.,** our team was badly beaten, got a good thrashing; (*c*) *v.i. F:* to brake abruptly; to jam on the brakes.

pilet [pilɛ], *s.m. Orn:* **(canard) p.,** pintail (duck).

pileum [pileɔm], *s.m. Orn:* pileum, cap.

pileur, -euse[1] [pilœːr, -øːz], *s. (pers.)* pounder, beater, grinder; (ore) crusher; stamp man.

pileus [pileys], *s.m. Fung:* pileus.

pileux, -euse[2] [pilø, -øːz], *a.* pilose, pilous, hairy; **système p.,** hair; **bulbe p.,** hair root.

pilier [pilje], *s.m.* (*a*) pillar, column; post; shaft (of column); strut (of aircraft); (*b*) *Min:* **p. de remblai,** cog, chock; *Geol:* **p. (d'érosion),** chimney rock; (*c*) *Dent:* abutment; *Anat:* **piliers du voile du palais,** folds of the palatoglossus muscle, pillars of the fauces; (*d*) *Astr:* **p. solaire,** sun pillar; (*e*) *Rugby Fb:* prop forward; (*f*) support, mainstay; **commerce qui est devenu un p. du pays,** trade that has become a mainstay of the country; *(of pers.)* **un p. d'église,** a pillar, staunch supporter, of the church; *Pol:* **un p. du parti,** a pillar, mainstay, of the party; *F: Pej:* **p. de café, de bar, de bistrot,** frequenter of pubs; bar lounger; **c'est un vrai p. de bar,** he's always propping up the bar; **p. d'antichambre,** hanger-on (of minister, etc.); (*g*) *P:* **piliers,** fat, solid, sturdy, legs; **être ferme sur ses piliers,** to be steady on one's pins.

pilifère [pilifɛːr], *a. Bot:* piliferous.

piliforme [pilifɔrm], *a. Nat.Hist:* piliform.

pillage [pijaːʒ], *s.m.* (*a*) pillage, looting, plunder(ing) (by soldiers, etc.); **mettre une ville au p.,** to sack a town; **se livrer au p.,** to loot; (*b*) (i) pilfering, filching; (ii) waste(fulness); **maison qui est tout au p.,** house where wastefulness, pilfering, is rampant; (*c*) plagiarism.

pillard, -arde [pijaːr, -ard]. **1.** *a.* (*a*) pillaging; given to, fond of, plundering; (*b*) thieving, pilfering; (*c*) *(of dog)* given to worrying; (*d*) predatory. **2.** *s.* (*a*) pillager, looter, plunderer; (*b*) pilferer.

piller [pije], *v.tr.* **1.** (*a*) to pillage, plunder, loot, sack, ransack (town, etc.); **p. le dictionnaire à la recherche d'adjectifs,** to ransack the dictionary for adjectives; (*b*) to rob (s.o.); (*c*) **p. un auteur,** to plagiarize, steal from, an author. **2.** *(of dog)* to seize, attack, worry; **pille! pille!** at him! go for him! tear him!

pilleri [pijri], *s.m. Orn: F:* house sparrow.

pillerie [pijri], *s.f. O:* extortion; theft; profiteering.

pilleur, -euse [pijœːr, -øːz]. **1.** *a.* given to plunder; **domestique p.,** pilfering servant. **2.** *s.* pillager, plunderer; *Nau:* **p. d'épaves,** wrecker.

pilloter [pijɔte], *v.tr. A: (of bees)* to despoil, plunder (flowers).

pilocarpe [pilɔkarp], *s.m.,* **pilocarpus** [pilɔkarpys], *s.m. Bot:* pilocarpus.

pilocarpine [pilɔkarpin], *s.f. Ch:* pilocarpine.

pilomoteur [pilɔmɔtœːr], *a.m. Anat:* pilomotor; **muscle p.,** erector pili, pilomotor muscle.

pilon [pilɔ̃], *s.m.* **1.** pounder, pounding device; (*a*) *Pharm: etc:* pestle; (*b*) rammer, earth rammer, punner; **p. à air comprimé,** pneumatic rammer; (*c*) (ore-crushing) stamp; *Min:* **p. à chute libre,** gravitation stamp; (*d*) **p. mécanique, à vapeur,** power hammer, steam hammer; **mettre un livre au p.,** to pulp a book; (*e*) *Tex:* **moulin à pilons,** beetling machine. **2.** (*a*) drumstick (of fowl); (*b*) wooden leg; **homme à p.,** man with a wooden leg.

pilonnage [pilɔnaːʒ], *s.m.* **1.** pounding, ramming, punning, stamping, tamping; *Mil:* pounding (of position) with shells; heavy bombing; **p. des radiations,** radiation bombardment. **2.** *Aut: A:* knocking (of engine).

pilonner [pilɔne]. **1.** *v.tr.* to pound (drugs, etc.); to pulp (paper, etc.); to ram, beat, pun (earth, concrete, etc.); to stamp (ore); to pug (clay); to full (cloth); *Mil:* to flatten, pound (with shells, bombs). **2.** *v.i.* (*a*) *F:* to work hard, to slog; (*b*) *Aut: A: (of engine)* to knock.

pilorhize [pilɔriːz], *s.f. Bot:* pileorhiza, root cap.

pilori[1] [pilɔri], *s.m.* pillory; **clouer, mettre, qn au p.,** to pillory s.o.; to hold s.o. up to public indignation.

pilori[2], *s.m. Z:* **p. de Cuba,** pilori, hutia conga.

pilorier [pilɔrje], *v.tr. (p.d. & pr.sub.* **n. piloriions, v. piloriiez)** to pillory (s.o.); to put (s.o.) in the pillory.

pilo-sébacé [pilɔsebase], *a. Physiol:* pilosebaceous; *pl. pilo-sébacé(e)s.*

piloselle [pilɔzɛl], *s.f. Bot:* mouse-ear (hawkweed).

pilosisme [pilɔzism], *s.m. Anat:* pilosis; *Bot:* pilosism.

pilosité [pilozite], *s.f.* (*a*) *Nat.Hist:* pilosity; (*b*) hairiness.

pilot [pilo], *s.m.* **1.** *Civ.E:* pile; **p. de support,** foundation pile; **p. de pont,** bridge pile; **p. à vis,** screw pile; **soutenir un édifice au moyen de pilots,** to pile a structure. **2.** heap of salt (in salt pans).

pilotage[1] [pilɔtaːʒ], *s.m. Const:* **1.** pile driving. **2.** pile work.

pilotage[2], *s.m.* **1.** *Nau:* pilotage, piloting; **p. d'entrée, de sortie,** inward, outward, pilotage; **p. libre, obligatoire,** free, compulsory, pilotage; **bureau de p.,** pilot office; **zone de p.,** pilot(age) waters; **(droits, frais, de) p.,** pilotage (dues); (*b*) steering; **p. automatique,** automatic steering. **2.** *Av:* pilotage, piloting, flying; **poste de p.,** cockpit; **p. automatique,** automatic flying, flight; **appareil gyroscopique de p.,** gyropilot; **p. aux instruments,** instrument flying, flight; **p. à vue,** visual flying; **p. sans visibilité,** blind flying; **école de p.,** flying school. **3.** *Aut:* driving (of racing car). **4.** *Rail:* hand signalling. **5.** *El: Elcs:* control, drive; **p. par diapason,** tuning-fork oscillator drive; **p. par quartz, p. piézo-électrique,** crystal control, crystal drive; **à p. par quartz, à p. piézo-électrique,** crystal-controlled, crystal-driven. **6.** *Atom.Ph:* fine control, fine regulating.

pilote [pilɔt], *s.m.* **1.** (*a*) *Nau:* (i) helmsman, steersman; **p. automatique,** automatic steerer; (ii) pilot; *A:* **p. côtier, p. lamaneur,** coast(ing) pilot, inshore pilot, hobbling pilot, hobbler; *A:* **p. hauturier,** deep-sea pilot; **p. de mer,** sea pilot; **p. de port,** harbour pilot, dock pilot; **p. fluvial,** river pilot; **p. breveté,** licensed pilot; **brevet de p.,** pilot's licence; (*b*) *Av:* pilot; **avion sans p.,** pilotless aircraft; **p. d'acrobatie,** acrobatic pilot, acrobat; **p. d'essais,** test pilot; **p. convoyeur, de convoyage,** ferry pilot; **p. de ligne,** airline pilot; **p. commandant de bord,** pilot in command; **premier p.,** first, senior, pilot; **second p.,** second pilot; **élève p.,** pilot trainee; **p. breveté,** licensed pilot; *Mil.Av:* certified pilot; **p. automatique,** automatic pilot, *F:* George; *Mil.Av:* **officier p.,** pilot officer; **sous-officier p.,** non-commissioned pilot, sergeant pilot; (*c*) driver, pilot, (of racing car, etc.); **ne parlez pas au p.,** don't speak to the man at the wheel; (*d*)

il fut l'un des pilotes du fauvisme, he was one of the leaders of fauvism; (*e*) *attrib.* **bateau p.,** pilot boat, cutter; **usine, installation, p.,** pilot factory, pilot plant; *Elcs:* **fréquence p.,** pilot frequency, control, frequency; *Meteor:* **ballon p.,** pilot balloon; *Rail:* **locomotive, train, p.,** pilot engine; pilot train; *Tex:* **drap p.,** pilot cloth. **2.** *Elcs:* master oscillator, driving oscillator; **p. à quartz, p. piézo-électrique,** crystal-driven, crystal-controlled, oscillator. **3.** *Atom.Ph:* (fine) control system; **p. automatique,** automatic-control assembly. **4.** *Ich:* pilot fish. **5.** *Metalw:* nose (of reamer).

piloter[1] [pilɔte], *v.tr. Civ.E:* to drive piles into (sand, etc.).

piloter[2], *v.tr.* **1.** (*a*) *Nau:* (i) to steer (ship); (ii) to pilot (ship); **p. à l'entrée, à la sortie,** to pilot in, out; (*b*) *Av:* to pilot, fly (aircraft); **p. aux instruments,** to fly by instruments, by dead reckoning; **p. sans visibilité,** to fly blind; **p. à vue,** to do, practise, contact flying, visual flying; (*c*) to drive, pilot (racing car, etc.); (*d*) *F:* **p. qn dans Londres,** to guide, show, s.o. round London. **2.** *Rail:* to hand-signal (train).

pilotin [pilɔtɛ̃], *s.m. Nau:* apprentice (in Merchant Service).

pilotis [pilɔti], *s.m. Civ.E:* piling; **bâti sur p.,** built on piles; **p. de support,** pile foundation; **p. d'acier,** steel piling; **machine à arracher les p.,** pile extractor; **affermir le sol avec des p.,** to pile the ground; to drive piles into the ground.

pilou [pilu], *s.m. Tex:* flannelette, cotton flannel, Canton flannel.

pilpoul [pilpul], *s.m. Jewish Rel:* pilpul.

pilsen [pilsɛn], *s.f. Brew:* = lager.

pilulaire [pilylɛːr]. **1.** *a. Pharm:* pilular. **2.** *s.f. Bot:* pillwort. **3.** *s.m. Vet:* balling gun.

pilule [pilyl], *s.f. Pharm:* pill; **"la p.",** "the pill"; **la p. et la limitation des naissances,** the pill and birth control; **p. mercurielle,** blue pill; *F:* **prendre la p.,** (i) to meet with a rebuff, to be thwarted; to come to grief; to be defeated; (ii) to be on "the pill"; **avaler la p.,** (i) to swallow the pill, to submit to the humiliation; (ii) to swallow sth. hook, line and sinker.

pilulier [pilylje], *s.m.* (*a*) pill box; (*b*) pill machine.

pilum [pilɔm], *s.m. Rom.Ant:* pilum, javelin.

pimarique [pimarik], *a. Ch:* pimaric (acid).

pimbêche [pɛ̃bɛʃ], *a. & s.f.* affected, *F:* stuck-up (girl, woman).

pimélique [pimelik], *a. Ch:* pimelic (acid).

pimélite [pimelit], *s.f. Miner:* pimelite.

piment [pimɑ̃], *s.m.* **1.** (*a*) *Bot:* pimento, capsicum; Jamaica pepper, allspice; bayberry; **p. royal,** bog myrtle, Dutch myrtle; *Cu:* **p. rouge,** (i) red pepper; (ii) chilli; pimento; **p. (en poudre),** (i) red pepper; paprika; (ii) Cayenne pepper; **p. doux,** sweet pepper; (*b*) **le p. de l'aventure,** the spice of adventure; **donner du p. à une histoire,** to add piquancy to a story. **2.** *Bot:* **faux p.,** winter cherry, Jerusalem cherry. **3.** *A:* piment, spiced honey-sweetened wine.

pimentade [pimɑ̃tad], *s.f. Cu: O:* pimento sauce.

pimenté [pimɑ̃te], *a. Cu:* highly-spiced.

pimenter [pimɑ̃te], *v.tr. Cu:* to season (sth.) with pimento, with red pepper; **p. son récit,** to give piquancy, spice, to one's story.

pimpant [pɛ̃pɑ̃], *a.* smart, spruce, spick and span (dress, person); **femme pimpante,** chic and attractive woman; **une pimpante petite ville,** a gay and spruce little town.

pimple [pɛ̃pl̩], *s.m. Ich:* ichneumon fly; (*genus*) Pimpla.

pimprenelle [pɛ̃prənɛl], *s.f. Bot:* burnet, bloodwort; **p. aquatique,** brookweed, water pimpernel.

pin [pɛ̃], *s.m.* pine (tree); **p. maritime, p. de Bordeaux,** pinaster, maritime pine, sea pine, star pine, cluster pine; **p. d'Écosse,** Scotch pine, Scotch fir; **p. sylvestre, suisse, p. de Genève, de Russie, à mâtures,** Norway pine; **p. d'Alep, de Jérusalem,** Aleppo pine; **p. pignon, p. (en) parasol,** parasol pine, stone pine, umbrella pine; **p. à trochets,** pitch pine; **p. à longues feuilles, à balais,** long-leaved pine, broom pine; **p. cembro,** Siberian pine; Cembra or yellow pine; **p. de montagne,** silver pine, white pine; **p. de Virginie,** scrub pine; **pomme de p.,** pine cone; fir cone.

pinacle [pinakl̩], *s.m.* pinnacle; *esp.* ridge ornament (of roof); **porter qn au p., mettre qn sur le p.,** to extol s.o.; to praise s.o. to the skies; **être au, sur le, p.,** to be at the top of the tree, at the summit of power, of fame.

pinaciolite [pinasjɔlit], *s.f. Miner:* pinakiolite.

pinacoïde [pinakɔid], *Cryst:* **1.** *a.* pinacoidal. **2.** *s.m.* pinacoid.

pinacol [pinakɔl], *s.m. Ch:* pinacol.

pinacolique [pinakɔlik], *a. Ch:* pinacolic.

pinacone [pinakɔn], *s.f. Ch: A:* pinacone.

pinacothèque [pinakɔtɛk], *s.f.* picture gallery, art gallery; **la p. de Munich,** the Munich Pinakothek.

pinaillage [pinɑjaːʒ], *P:* quibbling.

pinailler [pinɑje], *v.i. P:* to quibble, split hairs; to be finicky.

pinailleur, -euse [pinɑjœːr, -øːz], *s. P:* quibbler, hair-splitter.

pinard [pinaːr], *s.m. P:* wine, plonk.

pinardier [pinardje], *s.m. Nau: F:* wine tanker.

pinasse[1] [pinas], *s.f. Nau:* pinnace, shallop.

pinasse[2], *s.f. Bot:* Norway pine.

pinastre [pinastr̥], *s.m. Bot:* pinaster, maritime pine.

pinatypie [pinatipi], *s.f. Phot:* pinatype, three-colour process.

pinçage [pɛ̃saːʒ], *s.m. Hort:* (*a*) pinching off, nipping off (of buds); (*b*) topping.

pince [pɛ̃ːs], *s.f.* **1.** (*a*) grip, hold (of tool, hand, etc.); **avoir bonne p.,** to have a strong grip; (*b*) *P:* **gare la p.!** mind you don't get nabbed, pinched! **2.** (*a*) *Tls:* pincers; pliers; nippers; *Metalw:* tongs; *Surg:* forceps; **petites pinces,** tweezers; *Toil:* **p. à épiler,** tweezers; **pince(s) coupante(s),** cutting pliers, (cutting) nippers, wire cutters; **p. à long bec,** long-nose pliers; **p. à bec effilé,** needle-nose pliers; **p. à bec de canard,** duckbill pliers; **p. (à) bec-de-corbin,** bent-nose pliers; **pinces plates,** flat-nose pliers; **pinces rondes, p. à bec rond,** round-nose pliers; **pinces multiprises,** adjustable pliers; **pinces universelles,** combination pliers; **p. à gaz, p. de plombier,** gas pliers; **p. à plomber,** sealing tongs; **p. à river,** riveting pliers, tongs; **p. à river à bouterolle fixe, à bouterolle interchangeable,** riveting pliers, fixed-die, removable-die, pliers; **p. à sertir,** crimping pliers; **p. à souder,** soldering pliers, tongs; **p. à emporte-pièce,** punch; **p. à emporte-pièce pour courroie,** belt punch; **p. à emporte-pièce à revolver,** revolver-head punch; *Metall: Metalw:* **pinces à creuset,** crucible tongs; **pinces à four,** furnace tongs; **pinces à lingot,** ingot tongs; **pinces de forgeron,** anvil tongs, smith's tongs; *El.E:* **p. à dénuder,** stripping pliers; **pinces à fusibles,** fuse tongs; **pinces isolantes,** insulated pliers; *Surg: etc:* **p. anatomique, p. à tissus,** tissue forceps; **p. à dissection,** dissecting forceps; **p. à pansement,** dressing forceps, pliers; **p. à instruments,** steriliser forceps; **p. chirurgicale,** surgical forceps, pliers; **p. hémostatique,** hemostatic forceps; **p. pour suture,** suture forceps; *Dom.Ec: etc:* **p. à sucre,** sugar tongs; **p. à escargots,** snail tongs; *Toil:* **p. à ongles,** nail clippers; *Fish:* **p. à dégorger,** gag; (*b*) clip; *Typ:* gripper; **p. à cravate,** tie clip; **p. à pantalon, p. de cycliste,** trouser clip, bicycle clip; **p. (à cheveux),** (i) (hair) grip; (ii) clip (for setting hair); **p. à papier,** paper clip; **p. à linge,** clothes peg, *U.S:* clothes pin; **p. à ressort,** spring clip; clamp; *Ch: etc:* **p. de Mohr, p. d'arrêt,** (Mohr) pinchcock, rubber-tube clip; *Ch:* **p. pour tube à essais,** test-tube holder; **p. à serviette,** (dentist's) towel clip; *Surg:* **p. à artère, p. artérielle, p. hémostatique,** artery clip; **fixer avec des pinces, avec une p.,** to clamp on; *Typ:* **p. à ressort,** spring gripper; **came de pinces,** tumbler; **taquet de p.,** gripper guide; **prise de p.,** gripper bite; **repère de p.,** gripper mark; **ligne de pinces,** gripper line; **marge, blanc, de pinces,** gripper margin, gripper allowance; *El.E:* **p. de raccordement,** connecting clamp, connector; **raccord à p.,** clamp connection; **p. porte-électrode,** electrode holder; **p. pour fil terminal,** terminal clamp; **p. pour essais,** test clip; **p. crocodile,** alligator clip (for cable, wire, etc.); **p. de serrage, p. américaine,** (holding) collet (for tool); **p. élastique,** spring collet; (*c*) **p. (à levier, à soulever),** crowbar, lifting bar; pinch bar; tommy bar; **p. (à) pied-de-biche,** claw (bar), spike lever; **p. (pied-de-biche) à clous,** nail claw; *Min:* **p. de mineur,** gad; *Rail:* **p. à rails,** track lifter; **talon d'une p.,** heel of a crow-bar. **3.** *Arach:* **p. des bibliothèques,** book scorpion, chelifer. **4.** (*a*) claw, nipper (of crab, etc.); *P:* hand, paw, fist; *P:* **serre-moi la p.!** give us your paw! (*b*) incisor, front tooth, nipper (of herbivorous animal); (*c*) toe, point (of horse's hoof or shoe); *P:* (*of pers.*) **aller à pinces,** to hoof it. **5.** *Dressm:* dart; pleat.

pincé [pɛ̃se]. **1.** *a.* affected, supercilious; prim (person, style, etc.); glum (face); **sourire p.,** tight-lipped smile; wry smile; **répondre d'un ton p.,** to answer stiffly, starchily. **2.** *s.m. Mus:* (*a*) pizzicato; (*b*) **p. étouffé,** acciaccatura.

pinceau, -eaux [pɛ̃so], *s.m.* **1.** (*a*) (artist's) paint brush; **coup de p.,** stroke of the brush; **avoir le p. hardi, délicat,** to have a bold, delicate, touch; (*b*) **p. à colle,** paste brush; (*c*) *F: A:* broom, (sweeping) brush; (*d*) *P:* leg; foot; **affûter des pinceaux,** to walk, to hoof it; **s'embrouiller les pinceaux,** to get tied (up) in knots. **2.** *Opt:* **p. de lumière,** pencil of light; *Ph:* **p. sonore,** sound beam; *Elcs:* **p. électronique,** electron beam; **p. radar,** radar strobe.

pinceauter [pɛ̃sote], *v.tr. Ind:* to touch up (colour of wallpaper design, etc., with brush).

pince-cul [pɛ̃sky], *s.m.*, **pince-fesses** [pɛ̃sfɛs], *s.m. inv. P:* rowdy party, dance, *U.S:* shindig; *pl. pince-cul(s).*

pincée [pɛ̃se], *s.f.* (*a*) pinch (of salt, snuff, etc.); (*b*) *F:* **une bonne p. (de billets),** a good wad of notes.

pince-feuilles [pɛ̃sfœːj], *s.m.inv. A:* paper clip, paper clamp.

pince-guiches [pɛ̃sgiʃ], *s.m.inv.* hair grip.

pincelier [pɛ̃səlje], *s.m. Paint:* dipper, dip cup.

pince-maille [pɛ̃smɑːj], *s.m. F: A:* niggard, skin-flint, old screw; pinchpenny; *pl. pince-maille(s).*

pincement [pɛ̃smɑ̃], *s.m.* **1.** (*a*) pinching, nipping; (*b*) pang, twinge (of regret, etc.); **il a eu un p. au cœur,** his heart missed a beat. **2.** *Mus:* plucking (of strings of guitar, etc.). **3.** *Hort:* pinching off, nipping off (of buds). **4.** *Aut:* toe-in (of front wheels).

pince-monseigneur [pɛ̃smɔ̃sɛɲœːr], *s.f.* (burglar's) jemmy; *pl. pinces-monseigneur.*

pince-nappe [pɛ̃snap], *s.m.* tablecloth clamp; *pl. pince-nappes.*

pince-nez [pɛ̃sne], *s.m.inv.* pince-nez.

pince-notes [pɛ̃snɔt], *s.m.inv.* spring clip (for papers).

pince-oreille [pɛ̃sɔrɛːj], *s.m. F:* earwig; *pl. pince-oreilles.*

pince-pantalon [pɛ̃spɑ̃talɔ̃], *s.m.* bicycle clip, trouser clip; *pl. pince-pantalons.*

pincer [pɛ̃se], *v.tr.* (**je pinçai(s), n. pinçons**) **1.** to pinch, nip; (*a*) **se p. le doigt dans la porte,** to nip, catch, squeeze, one's finger in the door; **son grand-père lui pinça la joue,** her grandfather pinched her cheek; **p. les lèvres,** to purse one's lips; **p. les lèvres pour ne pas rire,** to pinch, bite, one's lips to stop laughing; **se p. le nez pour ne pas sentir une odeur,** to pinch, hold, one's nose to avoid a bad smell; *P:* **on lui pincerait le nez qu'il en sortirait encore du lait,** he's wet behind the ears; **vêtement qui pince la taille,** tight-waisted garment; *A:* **p. qn sans rire,** to have a sly dig at s.o.; *F:* **ça pince dur ce matin!** it's pretty nippy, there's a nip in the air, this morning; (*b*) *Hort:* (i) to nip off (buds); (ii) to top (plant); (*c*) *Aut:* **faire p. les roues avant,** to toe in the front wheels; (*d*) *Mus:* to pluck (strings of harp, etc.); *abs.* **p. de la harpe,** to play, touch, the harp; **p. de la guitare,** to pluck, play, the guitar; (*e*) *Dressm:* to put darts in (a garment). **2.** to grip, hold fast; **p. qch. dans des tenailles,** to grip sth. with pincers; *Nau:* **p. le vent,** to hug the wind; *F:* **p. un voleur, un rhume,** to catch a thief, a cold; **se faire p.,** to get pinched, caught, nabbed, copped; **il s'est fait p. en sautant de la fenêtre,** the police collared him as he jumped out of the window; *F:* **en p. pour qn, qch.,** to be keen on, crazy about, s.o., sth.; to have a soft spot for s.o.

pince-sans-rire [pɛ̃ssɑ̃riːr], *s.m.inv.* man of dry (and ironical) humour; *a.* **répondre d'un air de p.-s.-r.,** to answer drily, with dry sarcasm.

pincette [pɛ̃sɛt], *s.f.* **1.** *O:* light pinch, nip; *was thus used in* **embrasser qn à (la) p., en p.,** to pinch s.o.'s cheeks while giving him (or her) a kiss. **2.** (*a*) tweezers; **pincettes anatomiques,** tissue forceps; (*b*) *pl.* (fire) tongs; pair of tongs; *F:* **il n'est pas à prendre avec des pincettes,** (i) I wouldn't touch him with a barge pole, with a pair of tongs; (ii) he's unapproachable, like a bear with a sore head; (*c*) *P:* legs, pins; **tricoter des pincettes,** (i) to dance; (ii) to run like mad; **se tirer des pincettes,** to make off, to scram; **affûter ses pincettes,** to run, skedaddle; to get moving.

pinchard [pɛ̃ʃaːr], *a.* iron grey, dark grey (horse).

pinchart [pɛ̃ʃaːr], *s.m.* (artist's) three-legged folding stool.

pinchbeck [pinʃbɛk], *s.m. Metall:* pinchbeck.

pinchina(t) [pɛ̃ʃina], *s.m. Tex: A:* coarse woollen material (from Toulon).

pinçon [pɛ̃sɔ̃], *s.m.* **1.** pinch mark (on the skin); blood blister; **mon bras était couvert de pinçons,** my arm was black and blue. **2.** *Farr:* toe-clip (of horse-shoe).

pinçure [pɛ̃syːr], *s.f.* **1.** pinching, pinch. **2.** *Tex:* crease, wrinkle (made in material during fulling).

Pindare [pɛ̃daːr], *Pr.n.m. Gr.Lit:* Pindar.

pindaresque [pɛ̃darɛsk], **pindarique** [pɛ̃darik], *a.* Pindaric (ode).
Pinde (le) [ləpɛ̃:d], *Pr.n.m. A.Geog:* Pindus; *Lit:* **les filles du P.**, the Muses.
pinéal, -aux [pineal, -o], *a. Anat:* pineal; **glande pinéale**, pineal gland, pineal body.
pinéalome [pinealo:m], *s.m. Med:* pinealoma.
pineau, -eaux [pino], *s.m.* (*a*) type of grape; (*b*) (kind of) apéritif (made of wine and brandy).
pinède [pinɛd], *s.f.* (*in S. of Fr.*) pine forest.
pinène [pinɛn], *s.m. Ch:* pinene.
pineraie [pinrɛ], *s.f.* pine plantation, pinewood.
pinet [pinɛ], *s.m. Fung:* saffron milk cap, milky agaric.
pingo [pɛ̃go], *s.m. Geol:* pingo, hydrolaccolith.
pingouin [pɛ̃gwɛ̃], *s.m. Orn:* (*a*) auk; **grand p.**, great auk; **petit p., p. torda**, razorbill, razor-billed auk; (*b*) **p. royal**, king penguin; **p. impérial**, Emperor (penguin).
pingouinière [pɛ̃gwinjɛ:r], *s.f.* auk rookery.
ping-pong [piŋpɔ̃:g], *s.m. no pl. R.t.m:* ping pong (*R.t.m.*), table tennis.
pingre [pɛ̃:gr], *F:* **1.** *a.* miserly, mean, stingy; **il est p. comme tout**, he's an awful miser, he's as mean as can be. **2.** *s.m.* & *f.* miser, skinflint, *U.S:* tight wad.
pingrerie [pɛ̃grəri], *s.f. F:* stinginess, niggardliness, meanness.
pinguécula [pɛ̃gɥekyla], **pinguicula**[1] [pɛ̃gɥikyla], *s.f. Med:* pinguecula, pinguicula.
pinguicula[2], **pinguicule** [pɛ̃gɥikyl], *s.f. Bot:* pinguicula.
pinguite [pɛ̃gɥit], *s.f. Miner:* pinguite.
pinicole [pinikɔl], *a. Z:* pinicolous.
pinière [pinjɛ:r], *s.f.* pine plantation, pinewood.
pinifère [pinifɛ:r], *a.* piniferous.
pinique [pinik], *a. Ch:* pinic.
pinite [pinit], *s.f.* **1.** *Miner:* pinite. **2.** *Ch:* pinite, pinitol.
pinnatifide [pin(n)atifid], *a. Bot:* pinnatifid.
pinnatilobé [pin(n)atilɔbe], *a. Bot:* pinnatolobed, pinnatilobate, pinnately lobed.
pinnatipède [pin(n)atipɛd], *a.* & *s.m. Orn:* pinnatiped.
pinnatiséqué [pin(n)atiseke], *a. Bot:* pinnatisect.
pinne [pin], *s.f. Moll:* pinna.
pinné [pin(n)e], *a. Nat.Hist:* pinnate(d), pennate.
pinnidés [pin(n)ide], *s.m.pl. Moll:* Pinnidae.
pinnipède [pin(n)ipɛd], *a.* & *s.m. Z:* pinniped; *pl.* **pinnipèdes**, Pinnipedia.
pinnoïte [pin(n)ɔit], *s.f. Miner:* pinnoite.
pinnothère [pin(n)ɔtɛ:r], *s.m. Crust:* pinnotherid.
pinnule [pinnyl], *s.f.* **1.** *Bot: Z:* pinnule. **2.** sight vane, sight (of alidade, sextant, etc.); **p. à fils**, cross-hair sight; **p. à œilleton**, aperture sight.
pinocytose [pinɔsito:z], *s.f.* pinocytosis.
pinonique [pinɔnik], *a. Ch:* pinonic.
pinot [pino], *s.m.* Pinot grape (grown *esp.* in Burgundy).
pinque [pɛ̃:k], *s.f. Nau:* narrow-sterned sailing ship (of the Mediterranean); pink, pinkie.
pinsbeck [pinsbɛk], *s.m. Metall:* pinchbeck.
pinson, -onne [pɛ̃sɔ̃, -ɔn], *s. Orn:* finch; **p. des arbres**, chaffinch; **p. du Nord, des Ardennes**, brambling; **p. des neiges**, snow finch; **être gai comme un p.**, to be as gay as a lark.
pinta [pɛ̃ta], *s.m. Med:* pinta.
pintade [pɛ̃tad], *s.f.* (*a*) *Orn:* guinea fowl; **p. mâle**, guinea cock; **p. femelle**, guinea hen; (*b*) *F: Bot:* fritillary; (*c*) *F:* pretentious, stuck-up, woman.
pintadeau, -eaux [pɛ̃tado], *s.m. Orn:* young guinea fowl; guinea poult.
pintadine [pɛ̃tadin], *s.f.* pearl oyster.
pintadoïte [pɛ̃tadɔit], *s.f. Miner:* pintadoite.
pintadon [pɛ̃tadɔ̃], *s.m. Cu:* guinea fowl.
pinte [pɛ̃:t], *s.f.* (*a*) *Meas:* (i) *A:* (*in Fr.*) pint (*about* 0·9 litres); (ii) (*Eng: U.S:*) pint; *F:* & *Dial:* **une p. de lait**, half a litre of milk; (iii) *Fr.C:* quart; (*b*) *O: F:* **s'offrir, se payer, se faire une p. de bon sang**, to laugh loud and long; to enjoy a joke to the full; to have a good time; **faire une p. de mauvais sang**, to fret and fume; to get all hot and bothered.
pinter [pɛ̃te], *v.i.* & *tr. P:* (*a*) to swill (beer, wine); to booze; (*b*) **se p.**, to get tight, sozzled.
pin-up [pinœp], *s.f.inv. P:* pin-up girl; *a.* **croyez-vous qu'elle est p.-u.!** what a smasher!
piochage [pjɔʃa:ʒ], *s.m.* **1.** digging; breaking (of ground) with a pick. **2.** *F:* hard work, swotting; slogging; **le p. qui précède les examens**, swotting for exams.
pioche [pjɔʃ], *s.f.* **1.** (*a*) pickaxe, pick, mattock; **donner les premiers coups de p.**, to break ground; (*b*) **p. à bourrer**, tamping pick. **2.** *F:* (hard) work, slog; grind; **vingt heures de p.**, twenty hours hard at it. **3.** stock (at dominoes).
pioche-hache [pjɔʃaʃ], mattock; *pl.* *pioches-haches.*
piochement [pjɔʃmɑ̃], *s.m.* digging, breaking of ground (with a pick).
piocher [pjɔʃe]. **1.** *v.tr.* (*a*) to dig (with a pick); to pick; (*b*) *F:* to grind, swot, at (sth.); **p. son allemand**, to swot up, mug up, one's German. **2.** *v.i.* (*a*) to dig; to delve (**dans**, into); *F:* **p. dans une assiette de gâteaux**, to help oneself from a plate of cakes; *P:* **pioche (dans le plat)!** dig in! (*b*) (*at dominoes*) to draw from the stock; (*c*) to slog, to sweat; **il faut tout le temps p.**, it's a constant grind.
piocheur, -euse [pjɔʃœ:r, -ø:z]. **1.** *s.m. Civ.E:* *etc:* pickman, digger, navvy. **2.** *s.m.* & *f. Sch:* *F:* hard worker; swot, swotter; slogger. **3.** *s.f.* *Civ.E:* **piocheuse**, digger, mechanical excavator, navvy; **piocheuse-défonceuse**, excavator.
piochon [pjɔʃɔ̃], *s.m. Tls:* (*a*) mortise axe; (*b*) weeding hoe.
piolet [pjɔlɛ], *s.m.* piolet, (mountaineer's) ice axe.
pion[1] [pjɔ̃], *s.m.* **1.** (*a*) *A:* foot-soldier; (*b*) *Sch:* *F:* (i) = junior master (in charge of preparation); (ii) *Pej:* (assistant) master; **il a un petit air p.**, he looks like a (poor) schoolmaster; (*c*) *F:* narrow-minded pedant. **2.** (*a*) *Chess:* pawn; **p. passé**, passed pawn; (*b*) *Draughts:* piece, man; **prendre un p.**, to take a man; *s.a.* DAMER 1.
pion[2], *s.m. Atom.Ph:* pion, pi-meson.
pioncer [pjɔ̃se], *v.i.* (**je pionçai(s); n. pionçons**) *P:* to sleep, to kip down, to doss down; **p. ferme**, to be fast asleep.
pionceur, -euse [pjɔ̃sœ:r, -ø:z], *s. P:* sleeper, snoozer.
pionne [pjɔn], *s.f. Sch: F:* = assistant mistress (in charge of preparation).
pionner [pjɔne], *v.i.* (*a*) to take pawns (at chess); (*b*) to exchange men (at draughts).
pionnier [pjɔnje], *s.m.* **1.** *Mil: etc:* pioneer; **faire œuvre de p.**, to pioneer, to blaze a trail, to break new ground. **2.** *Pol:* (*in Communist countries*) = (boy) scout. **3.** *Tchn:* portable workbench.
piotter [pjɔte], *v.i. Orn:* (*of nestlings*) to cheep.
pioupiou [pjupju], *s.m. P: A:* (foot-)soldier = Tommy (Atkins); *pl.* *pioupious.*
pipa [pipa], *s.m. Amph:* pipa, Surinam toad.
pipe[1] [pip], *s.f.* pipe. **1.** pipe, tube (for liquid, gas); **p. d'alimentation**, feed (pipe); *W.Tel:* **p. d'entrée**, lead-in tube, leading-in insulator; *I.C.E:* **p. de refoulement**, exhaust elbow connection; *Av:* **p. à réaction**, ejector (pipe). **2.** pipe, large cask (for wine, spirits, etc.). **3.** (*a*) (tobacco) pipe; **p. de, en, bruyère**, briar pipe; **p. en terre**, clay pipe; **p. hollandaise**, churchwarden (pipe); **je fume la p.**, I smoke a pipe (habitually); I'm a pipe smoker; **si on fumait une p.?** how about a pipe? *F:* **mettez ça dans votre p.!** put that in your pipe and smoke it; **terre de p.**, pipe clay; **passer qch. à la terre de p.**, to pipe-clay sth.; *P:* **casser sa p.**, to die, to kick the bucket; *F:* **nom d'une p.!** heavens above! *P:* **tête de p.**, ridiculous or grotesque person; figure of fun; *P:* **huit francs par tête de p.**, eight francs a head; *P:* **se fendre la p.**, to split one's sides laughing, to laugh one's head off; (*b*) **une p. de tabac**, a pipe(ful) of tobacco; (*c*) *P:* cigarette. **4.** *Bot:* **p. de tabac**, Dutchman's pipe.
pipe[2], *s.f. P:* (*back formation from* PIPER 2 (*a*)) **prendre la p., remporter une p.**, to get badly caught out; to lose on a deal; to come to grief, come a cropper (on the Stock Exchange).
pipé [pipe], *a.* loaded (dice); marked (cards).
pipeau, -eaux [pipo], *s.m.* **1.** *Mus:* (reed) pipe; shepherd's pipe; **p. de chasse**, bird call. **2.** *pl.* limed twigs (to snare birds); snare.
pipécoline [pipekɔlin], *s.f. Ch:* pipecolin(e).
pipée [pipe], *s.f.* (*a*) bird snaring, bird catching (with bird calls and limed twigs); *Prov:* **on ne prend pas les vieux merles à la p.**, you can't catch an old bird with chaff; (*b*) *A:* deceit.
pipelet, -ette [piplɛ, -ɛt], *s. F:* (*a*) concierge, porter (of block of flats, etc.), *U.S:* janitor; (*b*) gossip.
pipe-line [piplin], *s.m.* pipeline; *pl.* *pipe-lines.*
piper [pipe]. **1.** *v.i.* (*a*) *A:* (*of small birds*) to peep, cheep; (*b*) *F:* **ne pas p.**, not to say a word; to keep silent. **2.** *v.tr.* (*a*) to lure (birds by means of bird calls); *F:* **p. qn**, to dupe, decoy, trick, s.o.; **se faire p.**, to get caught; (*b*) **p. les dés**, to load, cog, dice; **p. une carte**, to mark a card.
pipéracé [piperase], *Bot:* **1.** *a.* piperaceous. **2.** *s.f.pl.* **pipéracées**, Piperaceae.
piperade [pipərad], *s.f. Cu:* (*in Basque country*) omelette filled with sweet peppers and tomatoes.
pipérales [piperal], *s.f.pl. Bot:* Piperales.
pipérazine [piperazin], *s.f. Ch:* piperazine.
pipérideïne [piperidein], *s.f. Ch:* piperidein(e).
pipéridine [piperidin], *s.f. Ch:* piperidin(e).
pipérin [piperɛ̃], *s.m.*, **pipérine** [piperin], *s.f. Ch:* piperin(e).
pipérique [piperik], *a. Ch:* piperic (acid).
pipéronal [piperɔnal], *s.m. Ch:* piperonal.
pipérylène [piperilɛn], *s.m. Ch:* piperylene.
pipette [pipɛt], *s.f.* (*a*) *Ch: etc:* pipette; **p. jaugée**, graduated pipette; **p. pèse-acide**, hydrometer syringe; (*b*) **p. d'échantillonnage**, thief tube; **p. tâte-vin**, plunging siphon, liquor thief.
pipetter [pipɛte], *v.tr.* to pipette, to draw off (with a pipette).
pipeur, -euse [pipœ:r, -ø:z]. **1.** *s.* (*a*) bird lurer; (*b*) *F: A:* (*at cards, etc.*) cheat, sharper; **p. de dés**, dice-loader, dice-cogger. **2.** *a. A:* deceitful, cheating, beguiling (hope, dream).
pipi[1] [pipi], *s.m. F:* (*a*) **faire p.**, to piddle, to pee; (*child's language*) to wee-wee; **aller faire p.**, to spend a penny, to pay a call, to pay a visit, to see a man about a dog, to have a look at the plumbing, to shed a tear for Nelson, to do sth. no one else can do for you; **c'est comme si je faisais p. dans un violon**, it's like water off a duck's back; (*b*) urine; (*child's language*) wee-wee; **il y a du p. de chien sur le tapis**, the dog's made a puddle on the carpet; *P:* **du p. de chat**, poor quality wine, cat's piss.
pipi[2], *s.m. Orn:* pipit; *s.a.* PIPIT.
pipidés [pipide], *s.m.pl. Amph:* Pipidae.
pipier, -ière [pipje, -jɛ:r]. **1.** *a.* **industrie pipière**, (tobacco) pipe industry. **2.** *s.m.* pipe maker, manufacturer.
pipistrelle [pipistrɛl], *s.f. Z:* (small) bat; pipistrelle.
pipit [pipit], *s.m. Orn:* pipit; **p. rousseline**, tawny pipit; **p. des prés, p. farlouse**, meadow pipit, meadow titlark; **p. de Richard**, Richard's pipit; **p. maritime, p. obscur**, rock pipit; **p. des arbres, p. des buissons**, tree pipit; **p. spioncelle**, water, alpine, pipit; **p. indien**, Indian tree pipit; **p. de la Petchora**, Petchora pipit; **p. à gorge rousse**, red-throated pipit; **p. des rivages**, Scandinavian rock pipit.
Pipo [pipo]. **1.** *Pr.n.f. P:* = **l'École polytechnique.** **2.** *s.m. P:* student at the *École polytechnique.*
pipridés [pipride], *s.m.pl. Orn:* Pipridae.
piquage [pika:ʒ], *s.m.* **1.** (machine) stitching. **2.** *Av:* nose dive. **3.** (*a*) cutting, dressing (of building stone); (*b*) chipping, scaling (of boiler). **4.** pitting (of metal). **5.** digging (of peat, etc.). **6.** tapping (of cask); **faire un p. de fût**, *F:* to suck the monkey; to broach the Admiral.
piquant [pikɑ̃]. **1.** *a.* (*a*) pricking; pointed; keen; prickly, thorny (plant); stinging (nettle); **les feuilles du houx sont piquantes**, holly leaves are prickly; **l'eau était froide, les cailloux piquants**, the water was cold and the pebbles sharp and pointed; (*b*) **tissu rêche et p.**, harsh, prickly material; **barbe piquante**, bristly, prickly, beard; **un vent vif et p.**, a sharp, biting wind; **goût p.**, piquant flavour; *Cu:* **sauce piquante**, piquant sauce; **vin p.**, tart wine; *F:* **eau piquante**, aerated, fizzy, water; **l'odeur piquante de l'ammoniaque**, the bitter, pungent, smell of ammonia; (*c*) mordant; **style p.**, pungent style; **paroles piquantes**, words with a sting (in them); **remarques piquantes**, sharp, biting, cutting, remarks; (*d*) **beauté piquante**, piquant, striking, stimulating, beauty; **remarques intéressantes et piquantes**, interesting and stimulating remarks; **il est p. de retrouver . . .**, it is intriguing, stimulating, to find . . . . **2.** *s.m.* (*a*) prickle, thorn (of plant); quill, spine (of porcupine); spike (of barbed wire, etc.); **les piquants d'un hérisson**, the bristles of a hedgehog; (*b*) piquancy; pungency (of style); **donner du p. à qch.**, to give a touch of piquancy to sth.; **le changement donne du p. à la vie**, variety is the spice of life.
pique[1] [pik]. **1.** *s.f.* (*a*) *A.Arms:* pike; **bois de p.**, pikestaff; **fer de p.**, pike head; (*b*) *A:* pike's length; *F:* **être à cent piques au-dessus de qn**, to be miles above, immensely superior to, s.o.; **il est à cent piques au-dessous de son frère**, he isn't a patch on, can't hold a candle to, his brother. **2.** *s.f.* (*a*) (pointed) tip (of alpenstock, etc.); (*b*) peg, standard (of 'cello); (*c*) *Mus:* dash, dot (indicating staccato). **3.** *s.m. Cards:* spade(s); **jouer (du) p.**, to play a spade; to play spades.
pique[2], *s.f.* **1.** *O:* pique, ill-feeling; **par p.**, out of spite; **il y a de la p. entre eux**, they have had a tiff. **2.** taunt, spiteful remark, *F:* dig; **jeter, lancer des piques à qn**, to get at s.o.
piqué, -ée [pike], *a.* **1.** (*a*) quilted (coverlet, garment); padded (door); **p. à la machine**, machine-quilted; machine-stitched; (*b*) *s.m.* quilting; piqué. **2.** *Cu:* larded (meat). **3.** (*a*) wormeaten (wood, book); (damp-, dust-, mould-)spotted

(mirror, etc.); foxed (page, engraving); pitted (metal); **p. des mouches,** fly-spotted; **ciel p. d'étoiles,** sky studded with stars, star-spangled sky; **vêtement p. des vers,** motheaten garment; *P:* **ne pas être p. des vers, des hannetons,** to be first-rate; (*b*) *a. & s. F:* crack-brained (person); loony; **c'est une vieille piquée,** the old girl's a bit weak in the top storey. **4.** sour, tart (wine); (wine) that has turned acid. **5. d'un ton p.,** in a ruffled tone. **6.** *Mus:* **notes piquées,** staccato notes. **7.** *s.m. Phot:* clearness of detail. **8.** (*a*) *Av:* **descente piquée,** *s.m.* **piqué,** vertical dive, nose dive; **descendre en p.,** to nose dive; **attaquer en p.,** to dive bomb; **bombardement en p.,** dive bombing; **attaque en p.,** dive-bombing attack; (*b*) *Golf:* **approche piquée,** short approach; *Bill:* **coup p.,** chop shot.

pique-assiette [pikasjɛt], *s.m. & f.inv. F:* sponger; parasite, *U.S:* freeloader.

pique-bœuf [pikbœf], *s.m.* **1.** (*a*) ox-team driver, goadsman; (*b*) goad. **2.** *Orn:* beefeater, ox-pecker; *pl. pique-bœufs* [pikbœf].

pique-bois [pikbwɑ], *s.m.inv. Fr.C: Orn:* woodpecker.

pique-feu [pikfø], *s.m.inv.* poker; fire rake.

pique-fleurs [pikflœːr], *s.m.inv.* (glass) flower holder; (wire) pin holder.

pique-nique [piknik], *s.m.* picnic; **faire un p.-n.,** to go for a picnic; to picnic; *pl. pique-niques.*

pique-niquer [piknike], *v.i.* to (have a) picnic.

pique-niqueur, -euse [piknikœːr, -øːz], *s.* picnicker; *pl. pique-niqueurs, -euses.*

pique-notes [piknɔt], *s.m.inv.* spike file, bill file.

piquer [pike], *v.tr.* **1.** (*a*) to prick, sting; (*of flea*) to bite; **p. qn avec qch.,** to prick s.o. with (pin, thorn, etc.); **être piqué par une guêpe, par les orties,** to be stung by a wasp, by the nettles; *F:* **quelle mouche vous pique?** what's biting you? **p. un cheval de l'éperon,** to prick, spur, a horse; **p. des deux,** (i) to spur on one's horse, to gallop off; (ii) to hurry up; **p. les bœufs,** to goad the oxen; **p. un animal d'un bâton,** to prod an animal with a stick; **p. qn d'honneur,** to put s.o. on his mettle; **la moutarde pique la langue,** mustard stings one's tongue; **moutarde qui pique,** hot mustard; **vent qui pique,** keen, biting, wind; **ça pique,** it pricks, stings, smarts; it hurts; *F:* (*to unshaven man*) you're all bristly; (*b*) *Med:* to give (s.o.) an injection; **p. qn à la morphine,** to inject s.o. with (a dose of) morphia; *F:* **p. un chien,** to put a dog down, to put a dog to sleep; (*c*) to pique, offend (s.o.); **p. qn au vif,** to cut s.o. to the quick, to touch s.o. on the raw; **p. la jalousie de qn,** to arouse, awaken, s.o.'s jealousy; **p. la curiosité de qn,** to arouse, excite, s.o.'s curiosity. **2.** (*a*) **p. une surface,** to eat into, to pit, a surface; (*of worms*) to eat into (wood); (*b*) to spot, to mark; **miroir piqué par l'humidité,** damp-spotted, mildewed, mirror; **livre piqué par l'humidité,** mildewy book; **mains piquées de tâches de rousseur,** freckled hands; (*c*) **p. une pierre, un moellon,** to dress a stone; **p. une chaudière,** to scale, chip, a boiler; **p. de la tourbe,** to dig peat; *P:* **se p. le nez,** to tipple; to hit the bottle. **3.** *Nau:* **p. l'heure,** to strike the hour; to strike (so many) bells. **4.** (*a*) to prick, puncture (sth.); to backstitch; to quilt (counterpane, etc.); to pink (silk); *Bookb:* to stab (folded sheet); **p. du cuir,** to stitch leather; **p. à la machine,** to machine (stitch); **p. un dessin sur un tissu,** to prick a design on a piece of material; *Cu:* **p. de la viande,** to lard meat; *A:* **p. son chapeau,** to pin on one's hat; *abs.* **p. dans une assiette,** to help oneself from a plate (*esp.* with fork, cocktail stick, etc.); *F:* **p. dans l'assiette de qn,** (i) to steal from s.o.'s plate; (ii) to sponge on s.o.; *Fish:* **p. un poisson,** to strike a fish; *v.i.* **le poisson pique,** the fish is nibbling (at the bait); (*b*) to mark off (name on list); *Sch: F:* **p. une bonne note,** to get a high mark; to come out well (in an exam); (*c*) *Mus:* **p. une note,** to play a note staccato; (*d*) *F:* to pinch, swipe (**qch. à qn,** sth. from s.o.); **je ne l'ai pas volé, je l'ai piqué sur un chantier,** I didn't steal it, I "found" it lying around. **5.** to stick, insert (sth. into sth.); **p. une rose dans sa ceinture,** to tuck, stick, a rose in one's belt. **6.** (*a*) **p. une tête,** to take a header, to dive; (*b*) *v.i.* **p. de l'avant,** (i) *Nau:* to go down by the bows; (ii) *Av:* to nosedive; *Av:* **p. de haut sur un ennemi,** to dive down on an enemy; **descente trop piquée,** too steep a dive; **p. de l'aile,** to drop a wing; **p. à pleins gaz,** to power dive; *Nau:* **p. sur une île,** to head for an island; **il piqua droit sur B.,** he headed straight for B.; **p. dans le vent,** to drive head into the wind. **7.** *F:* **p. un soleil, un fard,** to blush; **p. un petit somme,** to have forty winks; **p. une attaque d'hystérie,** to have a fit of hysteria, to throw a fit; **p. une crise de larmes,** to burst into a flood of tears, *F:* to turn on the taps.

se piquer. 1. (*a*) to prick, sting, oneself; (*b*) (i) to give oneself an injection; (ii) to take drugs; **il se pique,** he's a drug addict, a needle fiend. **2.** to take offence, to get irritated; **elle se pique pour un rien,** she takes offence at the slightest thing; she's very touchy. **3. se p. de qch., de faire qch.,** to pride oneself on sth., on doing sth.; **se p. de littérature,** to pride oneself on one's literary taste, one's knowledge of literature; **se p. de ponctualité,** to pride oneself on being punctual. **4. se p. au jeu,** to get excited, to warm up, over a game; to be stimulated by opposition; **je m'étais piqué au jeu,** I was on my mettle. **5. se p. pour qn,** to take a fancy to s.o. **6.** to become spotted (with rust, dust, mould, etc.); (*of metals*) to pit; (*of wood*) to become wormeaten; (*of clothes, etc.*) to become motheaten. **7.** (*of wine*) to turn acid, sour.

piquet[1] [pikɛ], *s.m.* **1.** (*a*) peg, stake, post; **p. d'attache,** tethering stake, post; **mettre, attacher, les chevaux au p.,** to tether the horses; **p. de tente,** tent peg; **planter, lever, le p.,** to pitch, to strike, camp; *Artil.* **p. de mire,** ranging stake; *Nau:* **p. de retenue,** anchor stake; *Fb:* **p. de coin,** corner flag; (*at croquet*) **toucher le p. final,** to peg out; **droit comme un p.,** as straight as a ramrod; **raide comme un p.,** as stiff as a post, as a poker; *F:* **qu'est-ce que tu fais là planté comme un p.?** what are you doing standing there like a stuffed dummy? (*b*) *Hatm: etc:* **p. de fleurs,** cluster of flowers. **2.** (*a*) *Mil: etc:* picket; **p. en armes,** inlying picket; **p. d'incendie,** fire picket; **piquets de grève,** strike pickets; **être de p.,** to be on picket; *Sch:* **être au p.** = to stand in the corner; (*b*) *Elcs:* **p. radar,** radar picket; *Navy:* **destroyeur, escorteur, p. radar,** radar-picket destroyer, escort.

piquet[2], *s.m. Cards:* piquet; **faire un p.,** to play a hand at piquet; **un (jeu de) p.,** a pack of cards for piquet, a piquet pack; **p. normand,** piquet normand, three-handed piquet; **p. voleur,** piquet voleur, four-handed piquet; **p. Rubicon,** Rubicon piquet.

piquetage [piktaːʒ], *s.m.* **1.** pegging, staking (of camp); *Civ.E: Surv:* marking out (of road, railway track, etc.); *Min:* **p. d'un terrain,** pegging out of a claim. **2.** picketing (by strikers, etc.). **3.** *Lacem:* pricking (of the card).

piqueter [pikte], *v.tr.* (**je piquette, n. piquetons; je piquetterai**) **1.** to peg out, stake out (claim, camp); *Civ.E: Surv:* to mark out, stake out (road, ground, etc.). **2.** to picket (approaches to works, etc.). **3.** to spot, dot; **piqueté de noir,** dotted with black; *Lacem:* **p. le carton,** to prick the card; **aiguille à p.,** pricker.

piqueton [piktɔ̃], *s.m.* (*a*) *Wine-m:* second wine; (*b*) *P:* (red) wine; **boire un coup de p.,** to knock back some wine.

piquette [pikɛt], *s.f.* **1.** (*a*) *marc* diluted with water; (*b*) poor quality wine; tart, acid, vinegary, wine; *F:* **ça n'était pas de la p.,** that was no small matter. **2.** *P:* **prendre une p.,** (i) to get a good thrashing; (ii) to be overwhelmingly defeated.

piqueur, -euse [pikœːr, -øːz], *s.* **1.** *s.m.* (*a*) *Ven:* whipper-in; huntsman; **les piqueurs,** the whips; (*b*) *Equit:* groom; (*c*) *Equit:* outrider. **2.** *s. Ind:* (*a*) (leather) stitcher; **piqueuse en ganterie de peau,** glove stitcher; **piqueur, piqueuse, de, en, bottines,** shoe stitcher, upper stitcher; (*b*) *esp. f.* sewer; **piqueuse à la machine,** stitcher; (*c*) *Lacem:* pricker. **3.** *s.m. Min: etc:* hewer, pickman; **p. de granit,** (i) granite feller; (ii) granite dresser; *Mch:* **p. de chaudières,** scurfer. **4.** *s.m.* (*a*) overseer (of workmen); (*b*) *Rail:* foreman platelayer. **5.** *s.* **p. de vin,** wine taster.

piqueux [pikø], *s.m. Ven:* (chief) whipper-in.

piquier [pikje], *s.m. Mil.Hist:* pike-bearer, pikeman.

piquoir [pikwaːr], *s.m. Art:* (draughtsman's) needle; pricker.

piquouse [pikuːz], *s.f. P:* shot (of a drug), fix.

piqûrage [pikyraːʒ], *s.m. Tex:* repair of defects (in cloth).

piqûre [pikyːr], *s.f.* **1.** (*a*) prick, sting, bite (of insect); **p. d'épingle,** pin prick; **p. de puce,** flea-bite; (*b*) subcutaneous injection, (hypodermic) injection; **p. de morphine,** (subcutaneous) injection of morphia, *F:* shot of morphia; **faire une p. à qn,** to give s.o. an injection. **2.** puncture, small hole; pit (in metal, etc.); (*a*) **p. de vers,** wormhole (in wood, book); moth-hole (in garment); **p. d'aiguille,** pinhole (in leather, etc.); (*b*) (back)stitching (of material, leather); quilting; **piqûres sellier,** saddle stitching; **fixé par une p.,** stitched down, fixed by a row of stitching; **point de p.,** lockstitch (of sewing machine). **3.** (*a*) *Bookb:* **p. métallique,** stabbing; (*b*) *Publ:* (stabbed) pamphlet. **4.** spot, speck (of rust, dust, mould); foxing (of paper); pitting (in metal); **p. de mouches,** fly-speck; *Phot:* **p. due aux poussières,** pinhole (on negative).

piqûreuse [pikyrøːz], *s.f. Tex:* repair hand.

piranha [piraɲa], *s.m. Ich:* piranha, piraña, caribe.

pirate [pirat], *s.m.* (*a*) pirate; *Av:* **p. aérien,** hijacker, skyjacker; (*b*) plagiarist, pirate; **pirates financiers,** financial buccaneers; (*c*) *a. W.Tel:* **émetteur p.,** pirate station.

pirater [pirate], *v.* (*a*) *v.i.* to practise piracy, to lead the life a pirate; (*b*) *v.tr.* to pirate, plagiarize.

piraterie [piratri], *s.f.* **1.** (*a*) piracy; *Av:* **p. aérienne,** hijacking, skyjacking; (*b*) plagiarism, piracy. **2.** act of piracy.

piratinère [piratinɛːr], *s.m. Bot:* piratinera; **p. de Guyane,** snake-wood.

piratique [piratik], *a.* piratical.

piraya [piraja], *s.m. Ich:* piranha, piraña, caribe.

pire [piːr]. **1.** *comp.a.* worse; (*a*) **une catastrophe p. que la guerre,** a catastrophe worse than war; **le père ne vaut pas grand-chose mais le fils est p.,** the father is a pretty poor specimen but the son is worse; **cent fois p.,** a hundred times worse; **cela est bien p.,** that's much worse; **tomber d'un mal dans un p.,** to jump out of the frying pan into the fire; **le remède est p. que le mal,** the cure is worse than the complaint; the remedy is worse than the disease; *Prov:* **il n'est p. eau que l'eau qui dort,** still waters run deep; (*b*) (*with neuter or indef.pron.*) **qch. de p.,** sth. worse; **rien n'est p. que . . .,** nothing is worse than . . .; **ce qui est p.,** what is worse. **2.** *sup.* **le p., la p., les pires,** the worst; (*a*) *a.* **les pires inventions de l'humanité,** the worst inventions of mankind; **un voyou de la p. espèce,** the worst kind of scoundrel; **le p. des malheurs,** the worst of all misfortunes; **nos pires erreurs,** our worst mistakes; (*b*) *s.* (*though some grammarians advocate the use of* **pis** *for the noun, the modern tendency is to use* **pire**) **le p. de l'histoire, c'est que . . .,** the worst of the story is that . . .; **le p. de tout,** the worst of all; **le meilleur et le p.,** the best and the worst; **pour le meilleur et pour le p.,** for better, for worse; **s'attendre au p.,** to expect the worst; **les pessimistes ont la crainte constante du p.,** pessimists always expect the worst.

Pirée (le) [ləpire], *Pr.n.m. Geog:* Piraeus; *Lit:* **prendre le P. pour un homme,** to make a ridiculous mistake; not to know that Queen Anne is dead.

piriforme [pirifɔrm], *a.* pear-shaped, pyriform.

Pirithoüs [piritɔys], *Pr.n.m. Gr.Myth:* Pirithous.

pirogue [pirɔg], *s.f.* **1.** pirogue; (dugout) canoe. **2.** canoe.

piroguier [pirɔgje], *s.m.* paddler (in a pirogue).

pirola [pirɔla], *s.m.,* **pirole** [pirɔl], *s.f. Bot:* pyrola.

pirolacées [pirɔlase], *s.f.pl. Bot:* Pyrolaceae, Pirolaceae.

pirouette [pirwɛt], *s.f.* **1.** whirligig (toy). **2.** *Danc: Equit:* pirouette; **faire la p.,** (i) to pirouette, to perform a pirouette; (ii) to reverse one's opinions, one's policy; *F:* **répondre par des pirouettes,** to reply (to sth. serious) with a joke.

pirouettement [pirwɛtmɑ̃], *s.m.* pirouetting; series of pirouettes.

pirouetter [pirwɛte], *v.i.* to pirouette.

pirssonite [pirsɔnit], *s.f. Miner:* pirssonite.

pis[1] [pi], *s.m.* udder, dug (of cow, etc.).

pis[2], *adv., a. & s.m.* **1.** *comp.* worse; (*a*) *adv.* **p. que tout cela,** worse than all that; **il y a p.,** there is, are, worse; **cela ne vaut ni mieux ni p.,** it comes to about the same thing; **je ne fais ni mieux ni p. que tant d'autres,** I do neither better nor worse than so many others; *A:* **mettre qn à faire p., à p. faire,** to challenge s.o. to do his worst; *A:* **c'est à qui p. fera,** they are each trying to behave worse than the other; **de p. en p.,** worse and worse; **aller de mal en p.,** to go from bad to worse; **tant p.!** it can't be helped! never mind! **cent fois p.,** a hundred times worse; **il a fait bien p.,** he did much worse; (*b*) (*with adj. function*) (i) **cela serait encore p.,** that would be worse still; **ce qui est p.,** what is worse; **et qui p. est . . .,** and what is worse . . .; **D. était p. qu'un mauvais poète,** D. was something worse than a bad poet; **rien de p.,** nothing worse; (ii) **le malade est p. que jamais,** the patient is worse; (*c*) *s.neut.* **pour ne pas dire p.,** to say no more; **il a fait tout cela et p.,** he did all that and something even worse; **on eût pu craindre p.,** something worse might have been feared; **je m'attendais à p.,** I expected something worse; **il a changé,**

mais en p., he has changed, but for the worse. 2. *sup.* le p., the worst; (*a*) (*with adj. function*) ce qu'il y a de p., (i) what is worst; (ii) the worst there is; (*b*) *s.neut.* c'est le p., this is the worst; le p. c'est qu'il ne reconnait pas son erreur, the worst of it is that he does not admit his mistake; faire de son p., to do one's worst; faites du p. que vous pourrez, do your worst; il a choisi le p., he chose the worst course; mettre les choses au p., to suppose, assume, the worst; en mettant les choses au p., if the worst comes to the worst; at the very worst; prendre les choses au p., pousser tout au p., to put the worst face on things; au p., vous le perdrez, at worst, you will lose it.

pisaille [piza:j], *s.f.* field pea, grey pea.

pis(-)aller [pizale], *s.m.inv.* last resort, resource; makeshift.

pisan, -ane [pizɑ̃, -an], *a. & s. Geog:* (native, inhabitant) of Pisa; Pisan.

piscatoire [piskatwa:r], *a.* piscatory, piscatorial.

piscénois, -oise [pisenwa, -wa:z], *a. & s.* (native, inhabitant) of Pézenas.

piscicole [pisikɔl]. 1. *a.* piscicultural; établissement p., fish farm, fish-breeding establishment, centre. 2. *s.f. Ann:* piscicola.

pisciculteur [pisikyltœ:r], *s.m.* pisciculturist, fish breeder.

pisciculture [pisikylty:r], *s.f.* pisciculture; fish breeding.

pisciforme [pisifɔrm], *a.* fish-shaped, pisciform; *Anat:* os p., pisciform bone.

piscine [pisin], *s.f.* 1. (*a*) fish pond; (*b*) swimming pool; p. olympique, regulation-length swimming pool; p. de plein air, open-air swimming pool; p. couverte, indoor swimming pool. 2. *Ecc:* piscina. 3. *Atom.Ph:* (réacteur à) p., swimming-pool-type reactor.

piscivore [pisivɔ:r], *a.* piscivorous.

pise[1] [pi:z], *s.f. Crust:* spider crab.

Pise[2], *Pr.n.f. Geog:* Pisa.

pisé [pize], *s.m. Const:* pisé, rammed earth; construction en p., cobwork; mur en p., mud wall, cob wall.

piser [pize]. 1. *v.tr. Const:* to ram (earth). 2. *v.i. Ven:* mettre un chevreuil à p., to start a deer.

Pisidie [pisidi], *Pr.n.f. A.Geog:* Pisidia.

pisiforme [piziform], *a.* pea-shaped; pisiform (bone, etc.).

Pisistrate [pizistrat], *Pr.n.m. Gr.Hist:* Pisistratus.

pisoir [pizwa:r], *s.m. Const:* rammer.

pisolit(h)e [pizɔlit], *s.f. Geol:* pisolite, peastone.

pisolit(h)ique [pizɔlitik], *a. Geol:* pisolitic; calcaire p., pisolite.

pison [pizɔ̃], *s.m. Const:* rammer (for making pisé).

pissaladière [pisaladjɛ:r], *s.f. Cu: Dial:* p. niçoise, (open) onion and tomato tart, garnished with anchovies or sardines and olives.

pissasphalte [pisasfalt], *s.m. Miner:* pissasphalt, maltha.

pissat [pisa], *s.m.* urine (of horse, donkey, etc.).

pisse [pis], *s.f. P:* (*not used in polite company*) piss, pee, urine.

pissée [pise], *s.f. P:* (*not used in polite company*) (*a*) une bonne p., a good piss; (*b*) downpour (of rain).

pisse-froid [pisfrwa], *s.m.inv. P:* (*of person*) cold fish.

pissement [pismɑ̃], *s.m.* (*a*) *P:* (*not used in polite company*) pissing; (*b*) *F:* p. de sang, passing blood with the urine.

pissenlit [pisɑ̃li], *s.m. Bot:* dandelion; *P:* manger les pissenlits par la racine, to be dead, to be pushing up the daisies.

pisser [pise], *v.i.* (*a*) *P:* (*not used in polite company*) to piss, to pee, to shed a tear for Nelson, to have a look at the plumbing, to see a man about a dog; avoir envie de p., to want to piss, to pee, to spend a penny; c'est comme si je pissais dans un violon, it's like water off a duck's back; laisse p.! let it ride! *s.a.* MÉRINOS; (*b*) *P:* tonneau qui pisse, leaky barrel; (*c*) *F:* (*with cogn.acc.*) p. du sang, (i) to pass blood with the urine; (ii) to bleed like a stuck pig; (*d*) *Journ: P:* p. de la copie, to churn it out; (*e*) *impers. P:* (*of rain*) ça pisse dur, it's coming down in buckets.

pissette [pisɛt], *s.f. Ch:* washing bottle, wash bottle.

pisseur, -euse[1] [pisœ:r, -ø:z], *s. P:* (*a*) (*not used in polite company*) c'est un p., he's always going off to piss; (*b*) *Journ:* p. de copie, writer who churns it out; (*c*) *s.f.* pisseuse, (i) baby girl; (ii) woman, bird; skirt; tart.

pisseux, -euse[2] [pisø, -ø:z], *a. F:* (*a*) of, resembling, urine; smelling of urine; (*b*) stained with urine; (*c*) filthy; (*d*) (*of colour*) faded, washed-out, yellow(ed); jaune p., dingy yellow.

pisse-vinaigre [pisvinɛgr], *s.m.inv. P:* (*a*) *A:* miser; (*b*) grumbler, grouser.

pissoir [piswa:r], *s.m. F:* urinal.

pissoter [pisɔte], *v.i. P:* to be always pissing, peeing.

pissotière [pisɔtjɛ:r], *s.f. F:* 1. *A:* small dribbling fountain. 2. (public) urinal.

pistache [pistaʃ]. 1. *s.f. Bot:* pistachio (nut); *P: O:* avoir sa p., to be drunk. 2. *a.inv.* pistachio (green).

pistachier [pistaʃje], *s.m.* 1. *Bot:* pistachio tree. 2. *Ind:* pistachio nut drier.

pistage [pista:ʒ], *s.m.* (*a*) *Sp: etc:* tracking; (*b*) *F:* spying on (s.o.); keeping track of (s.o.); (*of police*) shadowing; tailing (suspect); (*c*) *O:* touting (for customers, etc.).

pistard, -arde [pista:r, -ard], *s.* 1. *Cy:* track racer. 2. skier (on run).

pistation [pistasjɔ̃], *s.f. Pharm:* powdering, pestling (of ingredients).

piste [pist], *s.f.* 1. *Ven:* track, trail, scent; suivre la p., to follow (i) the track, (ii) the footprints; le chien suivait la p. d'un lièvre, the hound was following the track, scent, of a hare, was tracking a hare; p. tracée par une voiture dans la neige, tracks of a car in the snow; être sur la p. de qn, de qch., (i) to be on the track of s.o., sth.; (ii) to be in search of s.o., sth.; faire fausse p., suivre une fausse p., to be on the wrong track; perdre la p. de qn, to lose track of s.o. 2. *Sp: etc:* (*a*) racecourse; la grande p., the three-kilometre course, the full course; (*b*) running track; racetrack, racing track; p. cendrée, cinder track; p. d'obstacles, obstacle track; p. individuelle, lane (of straight track); courses de p., track racing; tour de p., lap; *F:* être en p., to be in the running; vous êtes toujours en p.? you're still in? you haven't been knocked out yet? (*c*) *Aut: etc:* p. de vitesse, racing track; p. d'autodrome, speedway; *Cy:* machine de p., racer, racing machine; p. d'essai, test track; essai sur p., track test; (*d*) p. de cirque, ring; directeur de p., ringmaster; p. de patinage, skating rink; p. de ski, ski piste, run; p. de luge, de toboggan, luge, toboggan, run; p. de danse, dance floor; (*e*) *Av:* runway; p. d'envol, take-off strip; p. principale, main runway; p. de secours, emergency runway; p. en dur, paved runway, tarmac; p. bétonnée, concrete runway; terrain à deux pistes, double-strip runway; terrain à pistes multiples, multi-strip runway; balisage de p., runway markings; feux de p., runway lights; p. d'atterrissage, landing strip; p. de roulement, de dégagement, taxi way; p. en terre, mud strip; (*e*) p. muletière, mule track, pack trail; p. pour cavaliers, p. cavalière, bridle path; p. impraticable pour les voitures, path, track, unsuitable for motor vehicles; p. pour piétons, footpath; *Civ.E:* p. en rondins, corduroy road, track; *Adm:* route à double p., dual carriageway; p. cyclable, cycle track p. de ravitaillement, drive-in (for refuelling). 3. *Rec:* track (of tape recorder); *Cin:* p. sonore, soundtrack; (*of computer*) p. d'alimentation, feed track; p. de base de temps, p. de référence, clock track; p. d'éjection, ejection track; p. d'insertion, insertion track.

pister[1] [piste], *v.tr.* (*a*) p. un lièvre, to track a hare; *abs.* le chien piste très bien, the dog tracks very well; p. qn, to shadow s.o.; p. un cambrioleur, to be on the track of a thief; attention, on nous piste! look out, there's someone on our track! faire p. qn, to have s.o. watched; (*b*) *O:* p. des clients, (i) to keep track of customers; (ii) to tout for customers.

pister[2], *v.tr. Pharm:* to powder, pestle (ingredients).

pisteur [pistœ:r], *s.m.* (*a*) tracker; *esp.* police spy; (*b*) *O:* (hotel) tout; (*c*) *Ind:* progress chaser.

pistil [pistil], *s.m. Bot:* pistil.

pistillaire [pistil(l)ɛ:r], *a. Bot:* pistillar, pistillary.

pistillé [pistil(l)e], *a. Bot:* pistillate.

pistillifère [pistil(l)ifɛ:r], *a. Bot:* pistilliferous.

Pistoie [pistwa], *Pr.n.f. Geog:* Pistoia.

pistolage [pistɔla:ʒ], *s.m. Tchn:* spraying plastic (on a mould).

pistole [pistɔl], *s.f.* 1. *A.Num:* pistole. 2. *A:* être à la p., to be treated as a first-class misdemeanant (in prison, with permission to purchase one's own comforts).

pistoler [pistɔle], *v.tr. F: Tchn:* to spray (paint).

pistolet [pistɔlɛ], *s.m.* 1. (*a*) pistol; *F:* gun; *A:* p. d'arçon, horse pistol; *O:* pistolets de combat, duelling pistols; p. automatique, automatic pistol; *Mil:* haut p.! raise pistol! remettre, rengainer, le p., to return pistol; p. à air comprimé, air pistol; *Sp:* p. de starter, starting pistol; *Toys:* p. à bouchon, pop gun; p. à amorces, cap pistol; mettre à qn le p. sous la gorge, to hold a pistol to s.o.'s head; *F:* c'est un drôle de p., he's a queer customer, an odd type; (*b*) *Artil: etc:* p. de tir, firing pistol; p. de signalisation, p. signaleur, signalling pistol; p. lance-fusées, flare pistol, pyrotechnic pistol; (*c*) p. de manœuvre, jet gun (for astronauts to move in space); (*d*) *Tchn:* p. à peinture, p. vaporisateur, paint gun, spray gun; peinture au p., spray painting, spraying; peindre au p., to paint with a spray gun, to spray; p. graisseur, lubricating gun, grease gun; p. de distribution d'essence, petrol pump delivery nozzle; *Const:* p. de scellement, (i) cartridge gun; (ii) cartridge-assisted fixing tool; sealing gun; (*e*) p. d'abattage, humane killer (for slaughtering animals). 2. *Min:* borer, drill, chisel; p. à tête carrée, cross-mouthed chisel; p. pneumatique, pneumatic (hand) drill. 3. *Nau:* (*a*) p. d'embarcation, davit; (*b*) p. d'amure, bumpkin. 4. (*a*) *Cu:* (milk) roll; (*b*) *Com:* half bottle of champagne. 5. *Draw:* French curve. 6. *F:* bed urinal, *F:* bottle.

pistolet-mitrailleur [pistɔlɛmitrajœ:r], *s.m.* machine pistol, automatic pistol; *pl. pistolets-mitrailleurs.*

pistomésite [pistɔmezit], *s.f. Miner:* pistomesite.

piston[1] [pistɔ̃], *s.m.* 1. (*a*) *Mec.E:* piston (of machine, pump, jack, etc.); p. à air, à eau, air, water, piston; p. flottant, libre, floating, free, piston; p. à fourreau, trunk piston; *Mch:* p. (de machine) à vapeur, steam piston; p. compensateur, p. d'équilibre, balance, balancing, piston; p. tiroir, piston valve; p. de soupape, valve piston; machine, moteur, à piston(s), piston engine; *Artil:* p. de frein (de tir), buffer piston, recoil piston; p. de cylindre à gaz, gas-cylinder piston; axe de p., piston pin; embout d'axe de p., piston-pin chamfer, plug; corps de p., piston body, barrel; garnitures de p., piston packings; garnir un p., to pack a piston; jupe de p., piston skirt; p. à jupe pleine, full-skirt-type piston; tête de p., piston head, crown; tige de p., piston rod; course du p., piston stroke, travel; deux courses du p., up-and-down stroke; *I.C.E:* claquement du p., piston slap; *Aut:* p. d'amortisseur, shock-absorber piston, dashpot piston; (*b*) *Hyd.E:* piston plongeur, plein, plunger (of force pump, etc.); ram (of hydraulic press); p. à clapet, valve piston, bucket (of pump), sucker (of suction pump); clapet à p. plongeur, plunger valve; ascenseur à p. plongeur, plunger lift, *U.S:* plunger elevator; (*c*) *El.E:* plunger (of accumulator, wave guide, etc.); p. de court-circuit, short-circuit plunger; p. de verrouillage, locking plunger; commutateur à p., plunger switch; (*d*) *F:* avoir du p., to have friends at court, to be well backed; il est arrivé à coups de p., he succeeded through backstairs influence; he was pushed up; faire obtenir une place à qn à force de p., to boost s.o. into a job. 2. *Mus:* (*a*) valve (of saxhorn, etc.); (*b*) cornet à pistons, *F:* piston, (i) cornet; (ii) cornet (player). 3. spring stud (releasing camera front, etc.).

piston[2], *s.m. A: Mil: P:* (= CAPISTON) captain.

piston[3], *s.m. Sch: F:* candidate for, student of, the *École Centrale.*

pistonnage [pistɔna:ʒ], *s.m.* 1. *F:* backstairs influence, string pulling, wire pulling. 2. *Petroleum Min:* swabbing.

pistonner [pistɔne], *v.tr.* 1. *F:* to use one's influence to help (s.o.); to pull strings, wires, for (s.o.); to push (s.o.); il s'est fait p., he got s.o. to pull strings for him. 2. *Petroleum Min:* to swab (out) (a well).

pistonneur, -euse [pistɔnœ:r, -ø:z], *s. F:* friend at court.

pistou [pistu], *s.m. Cu:* soupe de, au, p., vegetable soup flavoured with basil.

pitaine [pitɛn], *s.m. P:* (= CAPITAINE) captain, cap.

pitance [pitɑ̃:s], *s.f.* 1. *A:* (*in convent, etc.*) allowance (of food). 2. se faire une maigre p., to eke out a living; être réduit à une maigre p., to be reduced to a mere pittance; to be on short commons.

pitangue [pitɑ̃:g], *s.m. Orn:* tyrant, American flycatcher; (*genus*) Pitangus.

pitchoun, pitchounette [pitʃun, pitʃunɛt], *a. & s. Dial:* (*Provence*) little (one).

pitchpin [pitʃpɛ̃], *s.m. Bot:* pitchpine, (long-leaf) yellow pine, stiff-leaved pine.

pite [pit]. 1. *s.f. Bot:* (*a*) American aloe; (*b*) silk grass. 2. *s.m. Tex:* pita, pita flax, *Com:* coir.

piteusement [pitøzmɑ̃], *adv.* piteously; miserably; il a échoué p. à son examen, he failed miserably in his examination.

piteux, -euse [pitø, -ø:z], *a.* piteous, woeful, pitiable, miserable; **avoir l'air bien p., faire piteuse mine,** to look crestfallen; **faire (une assez) piteuse figure,** to cut a (pretty) poor, miserable, figure; **faire piteuse chère,** to make a poor meal; **p. élève,** poor pupil; **p. résultat,** poor, miserable, result; **être dans un p. état,** to be in a poor way.

pithécanthrope [pitekɑ̃trɔp], *s.m. Anthr:* pithecanthropus, pithecanthrope.

pithécanthropien, -ienne [pitekɑ̃trɔpjɛ̃, -jɛn], *a. Anthr:* pithecanthropic.

pithécisme [pitesism], *s.m.* pithecism.

pithécoïde [pitekɔid], *a.* pithecoid.

pithiatique [pitjatik], *a. Med:* pithiatic.

pithiatisme [pitjatism], *s.m. Med:* pithiatism.

pithivérien, -ienne [pitiverjɛ̃, -jɛn], *a. & s. Geog:* (native, inhabitant) of Pithiviers.

Pithiviers [pitivje], (*a*) *Pr.n.* Pithiviers; (*b*) *s.m. Cu:* **(gâteau de) p.,** almond tart.

pitié [pitje], *s.f.* pity, compassion; **avoir p. de qn,** to pity, have pity on, s.o.; **prendre p. de qn, prendre qn en p.,** to take pity on s.o.; **sans p.,** pitiless(ly), merciless(ly), ruthless(ly); **par p.,** for pity's sake; **out of pity; regarder qn d'un œil de p.,** to look compassionately at s.o.; **faire p.,** to arouse pity, compassion; **il me faisait p.,** I felt sorry for him; **cela faisait p. à voir,** it was pitiable to see (it); **il fait p., c'est p. de le voir,** it is pitiful to see him; **c'est p. qu'il soit resté seul,** it is sad that he should have been left alone; **c'est à faire p.!** it's lamentable! it's pitiful! **il chante à faire p.,** he is a shocking, terribly bad, singer; **quelle p.!** (i) what a pity! (ii) what a sad sight! **c'est grande p. (que . . .),** it's a terrible pity (that . . .); *F:* **vraiment, quand je vous vois agir ainsi vous me faites p.,** I'm really sorry for you, my heart bleeds for you, when I see you behaving in this way.

piton [pitɔ̃], *s.m.* **1.** *Tchn:* (metal) eye, eye bolt; *Mount:* piton, peg; **p. de levage,** lifting eye; **p. de cervelle,** rudder eye; **p. à vis,** screw eye; screw ring; **p. à boucle,** ring bolt. **2.** (*a*) peak (of mountain); (*b*) *P:* (large) nose, *P:* conk.

pitonnage [pitɔna:ʒ], *s.m. Mount:* planting of pitons, pegs.

pitonner [pitɔne], *v.i. Mount:* to plant pitons, pegs.

pitoyable [pitwajabl], *a.* **1.** *A:* compassionate (**à, envers,** to). **2.** (*a*) pitiable, pitiful, piteous, lamentable (tale, condition, etc.); **il a une santé p.,** he has very poor health; (*b*) paltry, despicable, wretched (excuse, etc.); **écrire d'une manière p.,** to write in a painfully poor style.

pitoyablement [pitwajabləmɑ̃], *adv.* pitifully; **il chante p.,** he's a terribly bad singer; it's (really) painful to hear him sing.

pitpit [pitpit], *s.m. Orn:* pipit; *s.a.* PIPIT.

pitre [pitr], *s.m.* **1.** (circus) clown; (conjuror's) stooge. **2.** *F:* clown, buffoon; **faire le p.,** to clown, play the buffoon, to act the fool.

pitrerie [pitrəri], *s.f. F:* piece of clowning; foolery, buffoonery.

pittidés [pit(t)ide], *s.m.pl. Orn:* Pittidae.

pittizite [pit(t)izit], *s.f. Miner:* pitticite, pittizite.

pittoresque [pitɔrɛsk]. **1.** *a.* (*a*) picturesque; graphic (description, style); (*b*) *A:* pictorial (magazine). **2.** *s.m.* picturesqueness; vividness (of style, etc.).

pittoresquement [pitɔrɛskmɑ̃], *adv.* picturesquely; in a picturesque manner, style.

pittosporacées [pitɔspɔrase], *s.f.pl. Bot:* Pittosporaceae.

pittosporum [pitɔspɔrɔm], *s.m. Bot:* pittosporum; pittospore.

pituitaire [pitɥitɛ:r], *a. Anat:* pituitary (gland, membrane).

pituite [pitɥit], *s.f. Med:* (*a*) phlegm; (*b*) catarrh.

pituiteux, -euse [pitɥitø, -ø:z], *a. O: Med:* pituitous, subject to catarrh.

pityle [pitil], *s.m. Orn:* pitylus.

pityriasique [pitirjazik], *a. Med:* pityriasic.

pityriasis [pitirjazis], *s.m. Med:* pityriasis.

pivalique [pivalik], *a. Ch:* pivalic.

pive [pi:v], *s.m. P:* wine, plonk.

pivert [pivɛ:r], *s.m. Orn:* green woodpecker.

pivette [pivɛt], *s.f.* green glass of inferior quality.

pivoine [pivwan]. **1.** *s.f. Bot:* peony; **rougir comme une p.,** to blush scarlet. **2.** *s.m. or f. Orn: F:* bullfinch. **3.** *a.inv.* peony-red.

pivois [pivwa], *s.m. P:* wine, plonk.

pivot [pivo], *s.m.* **1.** pivot; (*a*) *Mec.E:* pin, pintle, axis; spindle (of potter's wheel, of tripod mounting, etc.); swivel (of gun, etc.); stud (of spring, etc.); *Mec:* fulcrum (of lever); *Rail:* bolster (of flat wagon); **p. à rotule,** ball pivot, journal; **p. central,** centre pin, pivot (of turntable, crane, etc.); *Machine-Tls:* **p. d'entraînement,** catch pin (of lathe); *Nau: Av: etc:* **p. de compas, de boussole,** centre pin of a compass; *Veh:* **p. de fusée (d'essieu),** king pin, bolt; **à p., monté sur p.,** pivoted, swivelling; *Civ.E:* **grue à p.,** revolving crane; *Artil:* **canon à p.,** swivel gun; *El.E:* **p. de porte-balai,** brush pillar; (*b*) *Dent:* pivot, post; **p. radiculaire,** root post; **dent à p.,** pivot tooth, crown; (*c*) *Mil:* **p. d'un mouvement d'ensemble,** pivot (man) of a movement; **p. de manœuvre,** pivot of manoeuvre; **p. fixe, mobile,** fixed, moving, pivot; (*d*) central figure (of drama, etc.); king pin, key man (of industry, etc.); **l'agriculture et l'industrie sont les pivots de la richesse d'une nation,** agriculture and industry are the central factors on which the wealth of a nation depends; (*e*) *pl. F:* legs, pins; **mal assuré sur ses pivots,** rather unsteady on his pins. **2.** *Bot:* tap root. **3.** *Ven:* pedicule (of deer). **4.** *Games:* (*basket ball*) pivot.

pivotal, -aux [pivɔtal, -o], *a.* pivotal.

pivotant [pivɔtɑ̃], *a.* **1.** pivoting; (*a*) swivelling (base, etc.); slewing (crane, etc.); (*b*) *Mil:* wheeling (wing, movement). **2.** *Bot:* tap-rooted (tree, plant); **racine pivotante,** tap root.

pivotement [pivɔtmɑ̃], *s.* **1.** pivoting, turning, swivelling. **2.** slewing (of crane jib, etc.).

pivoter [pivɔte], *v.i.* **1.** (*a*) to pivot; to swivel, revolve; to turn, hinge (**sur,** upon); **faire p. qch.,** to turn, swivel, sth. round; **faire p. un fauteuil tournant,** to swing round a swivel chair; (*of pers.*) **p. sur ses talons,** to swing round on one's heels; (*b*) *Aut:* to slew round; (*c*) *Mil: etc:* (*of troops*) to wheel; to change direction; **faire p. un escadron,** to wheel a squadron; **faire p. une flotte,** to pivot a fleet; (*d*) *F:* **faire p. qn,** to boss s.o. about. **2.** *Bot:* (*of plant*) to form a tap root.

piz [pi], *s.m. Geog:* (*in Switz.*) peak.

pizza [pidza], *s.f. Cu:* pizza.

pizzicato [pidzikato], *s.m. Mus:* pizzicato.

placage [plaka:ʒ], *s.m.* **1.** (*a*) veneering (of wood); **bois de p.,** veneer; **feuille, feuillet, de p.,** leaf of veneer; (*b*) *Lit: Mus: F:* patchwork (composition). **2.** plating (of metal); **p. au chrome,** chromium plating; **feuilles de p.,** metal sheets (for plating). **3.** flashing (of glass). **4.** *Geol:* superficial deposit. **5.** *Rugby Fb:* tackle.

plaçage [plasa:ʒ], *s.m.* placing (of guests at dinner, etc.); allotment of sites (of booths at fair, etc.).

placagiste [plakaʒist], *s.m.* veneer manufacturer.

placard [plaka:r], *s.m.* **1.** wall cupboard, wall press; **p. aux provisions,** larder. **2.** (*a*) poster, bill, placard; **p. officiel,** public notice; *Journ:* **p. (de réclame),** advertisement (in newspaper); (*b*) *A:* lampoon; (*c*) (diplomatic) document (on parchment). **3.** *Typ:* **épreuve en p.,** slip proof, galley proof. **4.** (*a*) *Nau:* patch (on sail); *Aer:* **p. pour le raccordement du cordage,** rigging patch; (*b*) *A: Nau:* **p. de dalot,** scupper-leather; (*c*) panel (of door); **porte à p.,** panelled door.

placardage [plakarda:ʒ], *s.m.* billposting; posting up (of advertisement).

placarde [plakard], *s.f. P:* (*a*) public square; (*b*) (*of street hawker*) **une bonne p.,** a good pitch; (*c*) good job; (*d*) hide-out, hiding place.

placarder [plakarde], *v.tr.* **1.** *Const:* to build a wall cupboard. **2.** (*a*) **p. une affiche,** to stick a bill on a wall; to post up a bill; (*b*) **p. un mur,** to stick bills on a wall, to placard a wall with posters; (*c*) *A:* to lampoon (s.o.). **3.** *Typ:* to pull (matter) in slips. **4.** *Nau:* to patch (sail).

placardeur [plakardœ:r], *s.m.* bill sticker, billposter.

place [plas], *s.f.* place. **1.** (*a*) position; *Sch:* (*in competition*) **avoir une bonne p.,** to be well placed; **changer sa chaise de p.,** to shift one's chair; **mettre qch. en place,** to put sth. in its place, in position; to set, fit, mount, sth.; **tout remettre en p.,** to tidy things away, to tidy up; **mise en p.,** putting into place, into position; setting, fitting, mounting; **mise en p. d'un tuyau,** fitting of a pipe; **mise en p. du moteur,** positioning of the engine; *Mil:* **mise en p. des forces de couverture,** positioning and deployment of the covering forces; **zone de mise en p.,** forming-up position, *U.S:* assembly area; **tout est à sa p.,** everything's in its place; everything's shipshape; **remettez vos livres à leur p.,** put your books away; **ce livre a sa p. dans votre bibliothèque,** you ought to have this book in your library; **ils y sont à leur p.,** they are not out of place there; **ces documents ont été examinés en bonne p.,** these documents were high on the list for discussion; **remettre qn à sa p.,** to put s.o. in his place; to sit on, snub, s.o.; **à vos places!** take your places, your seats; *Mil:* posts! **voulez-vous prendre ma p.?** would you like to change places with me? **il ne peut pas rester en p.,** he can't keep still; he's a fidget; **il ne tient pas en p. aujourd'hui,** he is very fidgety today; **son nom a pris p. dans l'histoire,** his name has taken its place, found a place, in history; *s.a.* LIEU[1] 1; (*b*) stead; **je viens à la p. de mon père, au lieu et p. de mon père,** I've come instead of my father, in my father's place; **à votre p. je . . .,** in your place, if I were you, I . . .; **j'ai signé à sa p.,** I signed in his stead; (*c*) **faire p. à qch.,** to give place to sth.; **la joie fit p. à la crainte,** joy gave place to fear; (*d*) room; **occuper beaucoup de p.,** to take up a great deal of room; **nous n'avons pas de p. pour mettre un piano,** we have no room for a piano; **faire p. à qn,** to make room, make way, for s.o.; **(faites) p.!** make room! make way! stand aside! **faites-moi un peu de p.,** give me a little room, make room for me; **p. aux dames!** ladies first! **céder, laisser, la p. à qn, à un navire,** to give way to s.o., to a ship; **il y a p. pour une juridiction spéciale,** there is room for a special tribunal; **sincérité qui ne laisse p. à aucun doute,** sincerity that leaves no room for doubt; **l'amour tient grande p. dans ce roman,** love looms large in this novel; *Nau:* **p. pour éviter,** swinging room; *s.a.* NET 1. **2.** (*a*) seat; *Th: etc:* **prendre p.,** to take one's seat; **restez à votre p.,** keep your seat; **louer deux places au théâtre,** to book two seats at the theatre; **il n'y avait pas une p.,** there wasn't a seat to be found, to be had; **petites places,** cheap seats; **p. d'honneur,** place, seat, of honour (at dinner party, etc.); **p. avant, arrière,** front seat, back seat (in car); **voiture à deux, à quatre, places,** two-seater, four-seater; *Aut:* **une deux places,** a two-seater; **il y a deux places de libres,** there are two seats vacant; **nombre de places d'une voiture, d'une salle,** seating capacity of a car, of a hall; **prix des places,** (i) fares; (ii) prices of admission; (*on bus, etc.*) **"les places, s'il vous plaît!"** "fares, please!" **payer p. entière,** to pay (i) full fare; (ii) full price; (*b*) situation, office, post; **quitter, perdre, sa p.,** to leave, to lose, one's job; **une personne en p.,** a person in high office; (*of servant*) **être en p.,** to be in a situation, in service; **être sans p.,** to be out of work, out of a job; *F:* **les places sont chères,** it's hard to get a job. **3.** locality, spot; (*a*) **p. publique,** public square, market-place; **p. d'armes,** drill ground, parade ground; *O:* **voiture de p.,** cab; *Turf:* **être laissé sur p.,** to be left standing; **sur p.,** on the spot; on site; **faire du sur p.,** to mark time; **il lut la lettre sur p.,** he read the letter then and there; **personnel engagé sur p.,** staff engaged locally; **rester sur p.,** (i) to be left on the field (dead or wounded); (ii) to stay put; **quitter la p.,** to give up the attempt; **par places,** here and there; (*b*) **p. marchande,** market centre; **droits de p.,** stall rent, stallage; **achats sur p.,** local purchases; **prix sur p.,** loco-price; **avoir du crédit sur la p.,** to be a sound man; **faire la p.,** to canvass for orders; *Com:* **prix sur la p.,** market price; *Com: Bank:* **les affaires de la p.,** local business; (*c*) *Mil:* **p. forte, p. de guerre,** fortress, fortified town; fortified place; *s.a.* ARTILLERIE 1; (*d*) *Nau:* **p. à quai,** berthing; (*e*) **p. à charbon,** charcoal kiln (in forest).

placé [plase], *a. & s.m.* **1.** *Turf:* placed (horse); **chevaux non placés,** unplaced horses, (horses that) also ran; *s.a.* JOUER II 1. **2.** *Equit:* **cheval bien p.,** horse that stands well.

placebo [plasebo], *s.m. Med:* placebo.

placement [plasmɑ̃], *s.m.* **1.** (*a*) placing (of piece of furniture, of servant, of apprentice); investing (of money); **bureau, office, de placement(s),** (i) employment bureau, office, agency, (servants') registry office; (ii) labour exchange; (*b*) *Com:* sale, disposal; **trouver un p. rapide, sûr, pour un article,** to find a quick, a ready, sale for an article. **2.** investment; **faire des placements,** to invest money, to make investments; **p. avantageux,** good investment; *F:* **p. de père de famille, de tout repos,** gilt-edged investment.

placenta [plasɛ̃ta], *s.m. Bot: Obst:* placenta.

placentaire [plasɛ̃tɛ:r]. **1.** *a. Anat: Obst: Bot:* placental (vessels, murmur, etc.); placentary; *Obst:* **gâteau p.,** placenta. **2.** *s.m.pl. Z:* **placentaires,** Placentalia, Eutheria.

placentation [plasɛ̃tasjɔ̃], *s.f. Bot:* placentation.

placentin, -ine [plasɑ̃tɛ̃, -in], *a. & s.* (native, inhabitant) of Piacenza.

placentographie [plasɛ̃tɔgrafi], *s.f. Obst:* placentography.

placer[1] [plase], *v.tr.* (je plaçai(s); n. plaçons) to place. 1. (*a*) to put, set (in a certain place), to find a place, places, for (spectators, guests, etc.); *Th: etc:* **p. qn,** to show s.o. to his seat; **p. une table près de la fenêtre,** to put, set, place, a table near the window; **vous êtes mieux placé que moi pour en juger,** you're better placed than I am to judge; **vous êtes bien placé pour le savoir,** you're in a position to, you ought to, know; **être particulièrement bien placé pour faire qch.,** to be in a unique position for doing sth.; *F:* **vous êtes plutôt mal placé pour parler de la sorte,** you're a fine one to talk like that; *F:* **ne pas pouvoir en placer une,** not to be able to get a word in edgeways; **p. qn sur le trône,** to set s.o. on the throne; **p. un soldat en sentinelle,** to post a (soldier on) sentry (duty); **maison bien placée,** well-situated house; **confiance mal placée,** misplaced confidence; *F:* **il a le cœur bien placé,** his heart is in the right place; *F:* **elle a des rondeurs bien placées,** she comes out in the right places; *Mil:* **p. des tranchées,** to site trenches; *s.a.* MOT 1; (*b*) to place (s.o.); to find a post, a job, for (s.o.); **p. des ouvriers,** to find employment for workmen; **gens bien placés,** people of good position; **fille difficile à p.,** daughter who is difficult to marry, settle; (*c*) to invest, put out (money); **p. (de l'argent) en rente,** to invest in stock. 2. (*a*) to sell, dispose of (goods); **valeurs difficiles à p.,** bills difficult to negotiate; **p. son stock,** to clear out one's stock; **marchandises qui se placent facilement,** goods that sell readily; **p. des billets de loterie,** to dispose of lottery tickets; (*b*) **bien p.** ses aumônes, to give to deserving charities; **p. son affection sur qn,** to make s.o. the object of one's affection.

se placer. 1. to take one's seat, one's place (at dinner party, etc.); to take up one's position, one's stand; **à côté de la règle se place l'exception,** there is an exception to every rule; **dites-moi où me p.,** tell me where to sit. 2. to obtain, find, a situation, a post; **chercher à se p. chez qn,** to try to find a job, employment, with s.o.; **se p. comme domestique,** to go into service.

placer[2] [plasɛːr], *s.m. Min:* 1. placer. 2. gold mining.

placet[1] [plasɛ], *s.m. A:* footstool.

placet[2], *s.m. A:* petition, address; *Jur:* (plaintiff's) claim.

placeur, -euse [plasœːr, -øːz], *s.* 1. manager of an employment agency. 2. *Com: Fin:* placer, seller. 3. (*a*) steward (at public meetings); (*b*) *Th:* **les placeuses,** the seat attendants, box openers; (*c*) *Av:* (*to guide aircraft to parking bay*) marshaller; (*d*) *Typ:* layout man.

placide[1] [plasid], *a.* placid, good-tempered, calm; unruffled (temper).

Placide[2]. *Pr.n.m. Ecc.Hist:* Placidus.

placidement [plasidmɑ̃], *adv.* placidly, calmly.

placidité [plasidite], *s.f.* placidity, good temper, serenity, calmness.

placier, -ière [plasje, -jɛːr]. 1. *s.m. Adm:* clerk in charge of the letting (of market pitches). 2. *s.m. Com:* commercial traveller, agent, canvasser; door-to-door salesman, *U.S:* drummer. 3. *s.* clerk (at Labour Exchange). 4. *s. Cin: Th:* usher, usherette.

placoderme [plakɔdɛrm], *s.m. Paleont:* placoderm; *pl.* **placodermes,** Placodermi.

placodonte [plakɔdɔ̃ːt], *s.m. Paleont:* placodont; *pl.* **placodontes,** Placodontia.

placoïde [plakɔid], *a. Nat.Hist:* placoid.

Placoplâtre [plakɔplɑtr], *s.m. Const: R.t.m:* plasterboard.

placothèque [plakɔtɛk], *s.f.* filing cabinet for address plates.

plafond [plafɔ̃], *s.m.* 1. (*a*) ceiling; **p. de plâtre,** plaster ceiling; **p. à nervures,** ribbed ceiling; **p. lambrissé,** panelled ceiling; **p. vitré,** glazed roof; **chambre haute, basse, de p.,** high-, low-ceilinged room; *F:* être bas de **p.,** to be stupid, dim, thick; **tableau exposé au p.,** skied picture; *s.a.* ARAIGNÉE 1; (*b*) *Mch:* **p. de chaudière, de la boîte à feu,** boiler crown, fire-box crown; *Nau:* **p. de ballast,** tank top; **p. de tunnel (d'arbre),** top of (shaft) tunnel; (*c*) *Meteor:* **plafond (nuageux),** ceiling (of clouds); **hauteur du p.,** ceiling height; **p. nul,** ceiling unlimited; **p. zéro,** ceiling zero; *Av:* **indicateur de hauteur du p.,** ceiling-height indicator; (*d*) *Cu:* **p. (de four),** baking sheet. 2. (*maximum attainable or permissible*) (*a*) **prix p.,** maximum price; ceiling (price); **fixer un p. à un budget,** to fix a ceiling to a budget; **il a atteint son p.,** he's hit his ceiling; **crever le p.,** to exceed the limit; *Aut:* **voiture avec un p. de . . .,** car with a maximum speed of . . .; (*b*) *Av:* ceiling, flying height (of aircraft); **p. de croisière,** cruising ceiling; **p. opérationnel,** operational ceiling; **p. pratique, p. d'utilisation,** economy ceiling, service ceiling; **p. théorique, p. absolu,** absolute ceiling; **p. maximum,** maximum flying height; **vitesse de p.,** holding-off speed; (*c*) *Cards:* (i) "above the line" (on bridge scorer); (ii) (form of) contract bridge; plafond. 3. *Hyd.E:* bottom, depth of bottom (of canal, reservoir, etc.); *Nau:* floor (of hold). 4. *Min:* roof (of a level).

plafonnage [plafɔnaːʒ], *s.m. Const:* ceiling work.

plafonné [plafɔne], *a.* **salaire p.,** wage ceiling (above which no percentage deduction is made for social insurance contributions).

plafonnement [plafɔnmɑ̃], *s.m.* **la production automobile est en plein p.,** car production has reached its ceiling.

plafonner [plafɔne]. 1. *v.tr.* to ceil (room). 2. *v.i. Av:* to fly at the ceiling, at the limit of height; *Aut:* to go at maximum speed; to go flat out; *Pol.Ec:* **les prix plafonnent à . . .,** prices have reached the ceiling of . . .; **la production plafonne,** output has reached its ceiling; *F:* **il plafonne,** he's hit the ceiling, he's reached his maximum.

plafonneur [plafɔnœːr], *s.m.* plasterer of ceilings.

plafonnier [plafɔnje], *s.m.* ceiling light, (electric) ceiling fitting; *Aut:* roof light.

plage [plaːʒ], *s.f.* 1. (*a*) beach; **jouer sur la p.,** to play on the beach; *Poet:* **une p. lointaine,** a distant shore; *Geol:* **p. soulevée,** raised beach; *Mil:* **débarquement sur p.,** beach landing; **détachement de p.,** beach party; **commandant de p.,** beach commander; **officier régulateur de p.,** beach master; **obstacles de p.,** beach obstructions; (*b*) seaside resort. 2. *Navy:* free-board deck (of battleship); **p. avant,** forecastle; **p. arrière,** (i) *Navy:* quarter deck; (ii) *Aut:* window shelf. 3. (*a*) area; *Opt:* **p. lumineuse,** light area, high light; **p. sombre, p. d'ombre,** dark area; *Phot:* **plages à teinter,** area, expanses, (of the negative) to be tinted; (*b*) range; *Mec.E:* **p. de fonctionnement, d'utilisation,** operating range, usable range (of machine, apparatus, etc.); **p. de puissance,** range of power; **p. de mesure,** measuring range; *Elcs:* **p. de fréquences,** frequency range; *W.Tel:* **p. d'écoute (d'un appareil),** tuning range; *Com:* **p. de prix,** price range; (*c*) band (of gramophone record); gap (in a recorded magnetic tape). 4. **les quatre plages du ciel,** the four cardinal points.

plagal, -aux [plagal, -o], *a. Mus:* plagal (mode, cadence).

plagiaire [plaʒjɛːr], *a. & s.m.* plagiarist (de, from); plagiarizing; **prédicateur p. de Bossuet,** preacher who plagiarizes Bossuet.

plagiat [plaʒja], *s.m.* plagiarism, plagiary; **faire un p. à un auteur,** *F:* to lift a passage from an author.

plagier [plaʒje], *v.tr.* (*p.d. & pr.sub.* **n. plagiions, v. plagiiez**) to plagiarize; *F:* to crib from (an author).

plagiocéphale [plaʒjɔsefal], *a. Anthr:* plagiocephalic, plagiocephalous.

plagiocéphalie [plaʒjɔsefali], *s.f. Anthr:* plagiocephaly.

plagioclase [plaʒjɔklɑːz], *s.f. Miner:* plagioclase, triclinic feldspar.

plagionite [plaʒjɔnit], *s.f. Miner:* plagionite.

plagiostome [plaʒjɔstɔm], *s.m. Ich:* plagiostome.

plaid[1] [plɛ], *s.m. Jur: A:* (*a*) sitting (of court); (*b*) plea, pleading.

plaid[2] [plɛd], *s.m. Tex:* 1. *Cost:* plaid. 2. travelling rug.

plaidable [plɛdabl̩], *a. Jur:* pleadable.

plaidailler [plɛdɑje], *v.i.* to go to law continually over trifling causes; to litigate.

plaidailleur [plɛdɑjœːr]. 1. *a.m.* litigious. 2. *s.m.* constant litigant.

plaidant [plɛdɑ̃], *a. Jur:* pleading (counsel); **les parties plaidantes,** the litigants.

plaider [plɛde], *v.tr.* to plead (a cause); to argue (in a court of law); to allege (sth.) in plea; **p. pour qn,** to plead in favour of s.o.; **plaidez pour moi,** plead, intercede, for me (**auprès de,** with); **il plaide bien,** he is a good advocate; **il aime à p.,** he is fond of going to law, of litigation; **la cause s'est plaidée hier,** the case was heard, came on, yesterday; **p. la jeunesse de l'accusé,** to plead the prisoner's youth; **son défenseur va p. la folie,** his counsel will plead insanity, will put forward a plea of insanity; **p. le faux pour savoir le vrai,** to make a false allegation in order to get at the truth; **p. coupable, non coupable,** to plead guilty, not guilty; **s'arranger vaut mieux que p.,** to come to an arrangement is better than going to law; *abs.* **il faudra p.,** they, we, I, etc., will have to go to court.

plaideur, -euse [plɛdœːr, -øːz], *s.* 1. litigant, suitor. 2. litigious person.

plaidoirie [plɛdwari], *s.f.* 1. pleading. 2. counsel's speech.

plaidoyer [plɛdwaje], *s.m. Jur:* address to the Court (*usu.* by counsel, *esp.* for the defence); speech for the defence; **on lui interdit tout p.,** he was not allowed to plead his cause, to say a word in self-defence; **mon p. démontre que . . .,** my argument shows that . . ..

plaie [plɛ], *s.f.* 1. (*a*) wound, sore; **p. profonde,** deep(-seated) wound; **p. béante, ouverte,** open wound; **p. contuse, p. par instrument contondant,** contused wound; **p. pénétrante,** perforating wound; **p. incise, p. par instrument tranchant,** incised wound; **p. de lit,** bed sore; **p. par arme à feu,** gunshot wound; **p. par déchirure,** lacerated wound; **p. des parties molles,** flesh wound; **mendiant qui montre ses plaies,** beggar who shows his sores; **rouvrir d'anciennes plaies,** to open old sores; **retourner le couteau dans la p.,** to turn the knife in the wound; **ne rêver que plaies et bosses,** to be bent on quarrelling; to be always ready for a row; (*b*) **p. sociale,** social evil; **mettre le doigt sur la p.,** to put one's finger on the source of the trouble. 2. (*a*) affliction, evil; **les dix plaies d'Égypte,** the ten plagues of Egypt; (*b*) *F:* (*of pers.*) pest, menace; **quelle p.!** what a pest!

plaignant, -ante [plɛɲɑ̃, -ɑ̃ːt], *a. & s. Jur:* plaintiff; prosecutor, *f.* prosecutrix; **partie plaignante,** plaintiff, complainant.

plaignard, -arde [plɛɲaːr, -ard], *F: A:* 1. *a.* complaining, whining, querulous. 2. *s.* complainer, whiner.

plain[1] [plɛ̃], *a. A:* level, flat, even; **velours p.,** plain velvet; **plaine campagne,** level country.

plain[2], *s.m. Leath:* lime pit.

plainage [plɛnaːʒ], *s.m. Leath:* liming.

plain-chant [plɛ̃ʃɑ̃], *s.m. Mus:* plainsong, plain chant; *pl. plains-chants.*

plaindre [plɛ̃ːdr̥], *v.tr.* (*pr.p.* **plaignant;** *p.p.* **plaint;** *pr.ind.* **je plains, il plaint, n. plaignons, ils plaignent;** *pr.sub.* **je plaigne;** *p.d.* **je plaignais;** *p.h.* **je plaignis;** *fu.* **je plaindrai**) 1. to pity; **je le plains,** I am sorry for him; **il est fort à p.,** he is greatly to be pitied; **plus à p. qu'à blâmer,** more sinned against than sinning; **il n'est pas en humeur d'être plaint,** he is in no mood to be pitied. 2. *A. & Dial:* to grudge; **p. qch. à qn,** to grudge s.o. sth.; **on n'a pas plaint l'argent,** there was no stint of money; **il ne (se) plaint pas sa peine,** he spares himself no trouble.

se plaindre, to complain. 1. to make complaint; to moan, groan. 2. **souffrir sans se p.,** to suffer without complaining, without murmuring; **se p. de qn, de qch.,** to complain of, about, to find fault with, s.o., sth.; **il n'y a pas de quoi vous p., vous n'avez pas à vous p.,** you have nothing to complain of, you needn't grumble; **les gens qui ont à se p.,** people with a grievance; **se p. que +** *ind. or sub.*; **il se plaignait qu'on ne le payait pas exactement,** he complained that he was not paid punctually; **on se plaint que vous vous conduisiez mal, de ce que vous vous êtes mal conduit,** people complain that you behave, behaved, badly.

plaine [plɛn], *s.f.* 1. plain; flat open country; **p. d'exercices,** drill ground; *Geol:* **p. d'inondation,** flood plain; *Geog:* **haute p.,** meseta. 2. *Fr.Hist:* **la P.,** the Plain the moderates (in the National Convention).

plainer [plɛne], *v.tr. Leath:* to lime.

plain-pied [plɛ̃pje], *s.m.* 1. suite of rooms on one floor; **occuper un p.-p.,** to live in a flat. 2. *adv. phr.* **de p.-p.,** on one floor, on a level; **maison de p.-p.,** single-storey house; bungalow; **salon de p.-p. avec le jardin,** drawing-room on a level with the garden; **de p.-p. avec,** (i) flush with; (ii) on an equal footing with; **sauter de p.-p. dans le roman,** to plunge straight into the novel; *s.a.* PONT[1] 2.

plainte [plɛ̃ːt], *s.f.* 1. moan, groan; **pousser des plaintes,** to moan, to wail, to lament, to groan. 2. (*a*) complaint; **motif de p.,** cause for complaint; (*b*) *Jur:* indictment, complaint; **porter p., donner p., déposer une p., contre qn,** to lodge a complaint against s.o. (**auprès de,** with); to bring an action against s.o.; to sue s.o.; **porter p. en justice,** to institute an action at law; **retirer sa p.,** to withdraw one's charge; **p. en diffamation,** action for libel.

plaintif, -ive [plɛ̃tif, -iːv], *a.* (*a*) plaintive, doleful (tone); (*b*) querulous (person, tone).

plaintivement [plɛ̃tivmɑ̃], *adv.* (*a*) plaintively, dolefully; (*b*) querulously.

plaire [plɛːr], *v.ind.tr.* (*pr.p.* **plaisant**; *p.p.* **plu**; *pr.ind.* **je plais, il plaît, n. plaisons, ils plaisent**; *pr.sub.* **je plaise**; *p.d.* **je plaisais**; *p.h.* **je plus, n. plûmes**; *fu.* **je plairai**) **p. à qn,** to please s.o., to be agreeable to s.o.; **cet homme me plaît,** I like this man; **vous lui plaisez beaucoup,** he is greatly taken with you; **cette vie ne me plaît guère,** I don't like this life very much; **elle a chanté trois chansons qui ont plu,** she sang three songs that went down well; **chercher à p. à qn,** to set out to please s.o., to curry favour with s.o.; **on ne peut p. à tout le monde,** one cannot please everybody; **elle cherche à lui p.,** (i) she tries to please him; (ii) she is setting her cap at him; **elle ne lui plaît pas,** he is not attracted to her, he doesn't care for her; **je le ferai si cela me plaît,** I shall do it if I please, if I choose, if I want to; **cela vous plaît à dire,** you are pleased to say so; (i) you're saying that as a joke, for fun; you're joking; (ii) that's all very well! *impers.* **s'il vous plaît,** (if you) please; **il ne me plaît pas de faire cela,** I do not choose, like, to do that; **vous plairait-il de nous accompagner?** would you like to come with us? **vous plairait-il de vous asseoir?** would you like to sit down? please take a seat; **il me plaît qu'il le fasse,** (i) I would like him to do it; (ii) I'm very pleased that he's doing it; **plaît-il?** I beg your pardon? I didn't catch that; what did you say? **comme il vous plaira,** as you like (it); **faites comme il vous plaira,** please yourself; do as you please; **quand il vous plaira,** when you please; whenever you like; **plaise à Dieu qu'il vienne!** God grant that he may come! *Jur:* **plaise au tribunal adopter mes conclusions,** that is my case, my Lord; **à Dieu ne plaise (que . . .),** God forbid (that . . .); **à Dieu ne plaise que je me permette de critiquer . . .,** far be it from me to dare to criticize . . .; **plût au ciel, plût à Dieu, que . . .!** I wish to heaven, to God, that . . .!

se plaire, to take pleasure; to be pleased, be happy; to thrive; **je me plais beaucoup à Paris,** I enjoy, I love, being in Paris; **vous plaisez-vous au collège?** do you like it, are you happy, at school? **il ne se plaît pas dans son nouvel entourage,** he is unhappy in his new surroundings; **ils se sont plu à me tourmenter,** they took pleasure in teasing me; **la vigne se plaît sur les coteaux,** the vine thrives, does well, on hillsides; the vine likes hillsides.

plaisamment [plɛzamɑ̃], *adv.* (*a*) pleasantly; (*b*) funnily, amusingly; (*c*) ludicrously, ridiculously.

plaisance[1] [plɛzɑ̃ːs], *s.f.* (*a*) *A:* pleasure; (*b*) **bateau de p.,** yacht, pleasure boat; **lieu de p.,** pleasure ground; **maison de p.,** house, place, in the country; **port de p.,** marina; **navigation de p., la p.,** yachting; **pêche de p.,** amateur fishing, fishing for sport.

Plaisance[2], *Pr.n.f. Geog:* Piacenza.

plaisancier [plɛzɑ̃sje], *s.m.* **1.** yacht; pleasure boat. **2.** (*a*) yachtsman; yacht owner; member of crew (of pleasure boat); (*b*) amateur fisherman, game fisherman.

plaisant [plɛzɑ̃]. **1.** *See* PLAIRE. **2.** *a.* (*a*) pleasant, agreeable; **un homme p.,** a pleasant man; **p. au regard,** pleasing to the eye; (*b*) funny, amusing, droll; **ton moitié p., moitié colère,** half joking, half angry tone; **un homme p.,** an amusing man; *s.m.* **le (plus) p. de l'affaire c'est que . . .,** the funniest thing about it is that . . ., the cream of the joke is that . . .; (*c*) (*always before the noun*) ridiculous, absurd, ludicrous (person, answer); **un p. homme!** an absurd man! **plaisante excuse!** what a ridiculous excuse! **3.** *s.m. A:* wag, joker; **des mauvais plaisants,** practical jokers; **faire le p.,** to act the fool.

plaisanter [plɛzɑ̃te]. **1.** *v.i.* to joke, jest; to speak in jest; **je ne plaisante pas,** I am serious, in earnest; I'm not joking; **dire qch. en plaisantant,** *F:* **dire qch. histoire de p.,** to say sth. jokingly, in jest, for a joke, for fun; **p. sur qch.,** to joke about sth.; **vous plaisantez!** you're joking! you don't mean it! **il aime à p.,** he must have his little joke; **on ne doit pas p. avec ces sentiments-là,** such feelings are not to be trifled with; **c'est un homme avec qui on ne plaisante pas,** he is not a man to be trifled with; **est-ce que j'ai l'air de p.?** do I look as if I'm joking? **il ne plaisante pas là-dessus,** (i) he takes such matters seriously; (ii) he won't stand any nonsense about it. **2.** *v.tr.* **p. qn (sur, pour, qch.),** to tease s.o. (about sth.); to poke fun at s.o.; **on la plaisantait de ce qu'il venait si souvent,** they teased her about his coming so often.

plaisanterie [plɛzɑ̃tri], *s.f.* joke, jest; joking, jesting; **p. acérée,** gibe; **dire des plaisanteries,** to crack jokes; **faire, jouer, des plaisanteries à qn,** to play pranks, tricks, (practical) jokes, on s.o.; **une mauvaise p.,** (i) a silly joke; (ii) a spiteful trick; **vous poussez trop loin la p.,** you are carrying the joke too far; **tourner une chose en p.,** to laugh a thing off; **cela passe la p.,** that's beyond a joke; **entendre la p.,** to know how to take a joke; **il n'entend pas la p.,** it doesn't do to joke with him; he can't take a joke; **p. à part,** joking apart; **par p.,** for fun, for a joke; **faire, dire, qch. par p.,** to do, say, sth. in fun, in jest, by way of a joke.

plaisantin [plɛzɑ̃tɛ̃], *s.m.* practical, malicious, joker.

plaisir [plɛziːr, -e-], *s.m.* pleasure. **1.** delight; **c'est pour moi un grand p. d'être présent,** it is a great pleasure to me, I am delighted, to be present; **c'est un réel p. d'apprendre que . . .,** it is very gratifying, a real pleasure, to learn that . . .; **j'apprends avec p. que vous êtes de mon avis,** I am glad to hear you agree with me; **c'était p. de l'entendre,** it was a pleasure to hear him; **faire p. à qn,** to please s.o.; **cela m'a fait p. de le revoir,** it gave me great pleasure to see him again; **cela me fait grand p. de vous voir,** I'm very pleased to see you; **cela me fait p. qu'il vienne,** I am very glad, very pleased, that he is coming; **cela me ferait le plus grand p.!** I should like that of all things; it would give me the greatest pleasure; **cela m'a fait grand p.,** it afforded me great pleasure; **cela me fait (infiniment de) p. de vous voir si gai,** it's a (real) pleasure to see you so cheerful; **cela fait p. à voir,** it is pleasant to see, to look at; **une chose qui fait p. à voir,** a thing that is a joy to see; **voulez-vous me faire p.?** will you do me a favour? **faire à qn le p. de . . .,** to do s.o. the favour of . . .; **voulez-vous me faire le p. de vous taire!** will you *please* be quiet, shut up! **ils vous prient de leur faire le p. de dîner avec eux,** they request the pleasure of your company to dinner; **je me ferai un p. de vous accompagner,** it will be a pleasure, I shall esteem it a pleasure, I shall be delighted, to go with you; **j'ai le p. de vous apprendre que . . .,** I have pleasure in informing you, I'm pleased to be able to tell you, that . . .; **j'aurai le p. de vous voir,** I shall have the pleasure of seeing you; **au p. de vous revoir,** good-bye; I hope we shall meet again; *P:* **au p.!** nice seeing you! **prendre (du) p. à qch.,** to take pleasure in sth.; to enjoy sth.; **je prends grand p. à la musique,** I derive great pleasure from music; I delight in music; I am very fond of music; **j'ai pris p. à la musique,** I enjoyed the music; **je prends p., j'ai p., à vous faire savoir que . . .,** I have pleasure in informing you that . . .; **avoir p. à faire qch.,** to take pleasure in doing sth.; **il y a p. à l'écouter,** it is a pleasure to listen to him; **gâter le p. de qch.,** to mar the enjoyment of sth.; *F:* to take the gilt off the gingerbread; **à votre bon p.,** (i) at your convenience; (ii) at your discretion; as and when you want; **faire qch. à son bon p.,** to do sth. when one chooses, in one's own sweet time; **avec p.!** with pleasure! (I shall be) delighted! **à p.,** (i) wantonly, without cause; (ii) ad lib; **répandre comme à p. des nouvelles fausses,** to spread false news wantonly; **potin inventé à p.,** gleefully invented (piece of) scandal; **se tourmenter à p.,** to worry for the sake of worrying; **vous en aurez à p.,** you shall have as much as you want; **c'est par p. que vous faites cela?** are you doing that because you like it? for the fun of the thing? **parler pour le p. de parler,** to talk for the sake of it; *Psy:* **principe de p.,** pleasure principle. **2.** (*a*) amusement, enjoyment; **plaisirs mondains,** social pleasures; **(argent pour) menus plaisirs,** pocket money; *A:* **intendant des menus plaisirs (du roi),** Master of the Revels; **jouer (aux cartes, etc.) pour le p., pour son p.,** to play (cards, etc.) for love; **train de p.,** excursion train; **partie de p.,** pleasure trip, pleasure party; picnic, outing; **ville de p.,** pleasure resort; (*b*) **le p., les plaisirs,** dissipation; **plaisirs sensuels,** sensual indulgence; **vie de plaisirs,** gay life; **lieu de p.,** place of amusement; night haunt. **3.** *Cu:* cornet(-shaped wafer).

plamer [plame], *v.tr. Leath:* to lime.

plan[1] [plɑ̃]. **1.** *a.* even, level, flat (ground, surface); plane (surface); *Geom:* **angle p.,** plane angle; **triangle p.,** plane triangle; **courbe plane,** plane curve; *Mth:* **coordonnées planes,** planar coordinates; *Ph:* **écoulement p.,** plane flow; **onde plane,** plane wave; **optiquement p.,** optically flat; *W.Tel:* **antenne à réflecteur p.,** plane-reflector antenna. **2.** *s.m.* plane; (*a*) *Geom: etc:* **p. axial,** axial plane; **p. horizontal,** horizontal plane; **p. horizontal de référence,** horizontal reference-plane; **p. vertical,** vertical plane; **p. incliné,** (i) inclined plane; (ii) *Min:* chute, shoot (for sending down coal, ore, etc.); **p. médian,** mid plane; **p. sécant,** cutting plane; **p. tangent,** tangent plane; *Draw:* **p. de projection,** plane of projection; **p. géométrique,** geometric plane, ground plane; *Draw: Surv:* **p. de défilement,** plane of defilade; *Surv:* **p. de référence,** datum plane, level; *Astr:* **p. de l'écliptique, de l'équateur céleste,** plane of the ecliptic, of the celestial equator; *Ball:* **p. de tir,** plane of fire, of departure; *Mec:* **p. de rotation,** plane of spin; *Opt:* **p. focal,** focal plane; **p. focal arrière,** back focal plane; **p. d'incidence,** plane of incidence; **p. de réflexion, de réfraction,** plane of reflection, of refraction; **p. de sortie,** aperture plane (of lens); **p. image,** image plane; **p. optique,** optical flat; **p. d'épreuve,** proof plane (for electroscopic test); **p. d'eau,** (i) (broad) stretch, sheet, of water; reach (of a river); (ii) *Hyd.E:* water level (of canal, etc.); **p. automoteur,** (i) *Min:* jinny; (ii) *Rail:* inclined track, (self-acting) incline; *Tls:* **p. d'un rabot,** sole of a plane; *Nau:* **p. d'arrimage premier,** ground tier; *Miner:* **p. d'un cristal,** face, plane, of a crystal; **p. de clivage,** cleavage plane; **p. de glissement,** slip plane; **p. d'hémitropie,** twinning plane; **p. de symétrie,** plane of symmetry; *Geol:* **p. de cassure, de fracture,** fracture plane; **p. de charriage, de poussée,** thrust plane; **p. de faille,** fault plane; **p. de séparation,** joint plane; **p. de stratification,** bedding plane; *Magn:* **p. de polarisation,** plane of polarisation; *Metall:* **p. de joint,** flash line; *Anat:* **p. orbital,** orbital plane; **p. sagittal,** sagittal plane; *Dent:* **p. occlusal, p. d'occlusion,** occlusal plane; (*b*) **premier p.,** (i) *Art: etc:* foreground; (ii) *Th:* downstage; (iii) *Cin:* close shot; *Cin:* **gros p.,** close-up; **p. moyen,** medium shot; **p. général,** long shot; **p. américain, p. italien,** close medium shot; *Art: etc:* **second p.,** middle ground; **cette question occupe le premier p.,** this question is very much to the fore; **passer au second p.,** (i) (*of project, etc.*) to be put aside, to be pushed into the background; (ii) (*of pers.*) to take a back seat; **reléguer qn au second p.,** to relegate s.o. to a subordinate position; to push s.o. out of the limelight; **un artiste de premier p.,** an artist of the first rank; a first-rate artist; **un artiste de second p.,** a second-rank artist; an artist not quite of the first rank; **sur le p. national,** on a nation-wide basis, scale; **sur le, au, p. politique,** (i) in the political field, sphere; (ii) from the political point of view; (*c*) *Av:* plane, surface, wing; **p. (à profil d'aile),** aerofoil, airfoil; **p. à courbure variable,** variable-camber plane; **p. fixe horizontal,** (horizontal) stabiliser, tail plane; **p. fixe vertical,** vertical stabiliser; **p. mobile,** movable surface, control surface; **p. déflecteur,** deflector surface, baffle flap; **p. intercepteur,** spoiler; **p. sustentateur,** lifting surface; **p. de dérive,** tail fin; **p. inférieur, supérieur,** lower wing or plane, upper wing or plane (of biplane); (*d*) *Dom.Ec:* **p. de travail,** working surface (of kitchen unit); worktop; **p. de cuisson,** boiling-ring unit, *F:* top (of cooker).

plan[2], *s.m.* **1.** (*a*) plan, drawing; draught, draft, plan (of building, machine, structure, etc.); blueprint; diagram; **p. à vol d'oiseau, p. cavalier,** bird's-eye view; **p. géométral,** ground plan; **p. de coupe,** section (drawing); **p. transversal,** cross section; **p. d'ensemble,** general plan, general assembly; *N.Arch:* general arrangement drawing; **p. sommaire,** sketch plan; **tracer un p.,** to draw a plan; *Mch: etc:* **p. de montage,** assembly drawing, erection plan; *Arch: Const:* **plans et devis,** draughts and estimates; *N.Arch:* **p. des formes,** lines plan; **p. des couples, p. latitudinal,** body plan; **p. longitudinal,** sheer plan, sheer drawing, sheer draft; **p. des capacités,** capacity plan; **p. d'exécution,** "as fitted" drawing; *El.E:* **p. de câblage,** wiring diagram; (*b*) *Surv:* map; plan; **p. cadastral,** cadastral map, survey; **p. de ville, p. urbain, p. des rues,** town plan; street plan; **p. sommaire du terrain,** sketch map; *Mil:* **p. directeur,** battle map; **levé d'un p.,** plotting, surveying; **lever le p. d'une région,** to plot, survey, an area; to map out an area. **2.** plan, scheme, project, design; **p. réalisable, irréalisable,** workable, unworkable, plan; **p. bien conçu,** well conceived plan; **p. très étudié,** well thought-out plan; **ébaucher un p.,** to rough out a plan; **élaborer un p.,** to work out a plan; **établir, arrêter, le p. d'un roman,** to work out the plan of a novel; to plan, frame, a novel; **sans p. arrêté,** without any, following no, preconceived plan; **modifier un p. pré-établi,** to alter, modify, a pre-arranged plan; **mettre un p.**

en application, exécuter un p., to implement, carry out, a plan; **bouleverser, faire échouer, les plans de qn,** to upset s.o.'s plans, *F:* put a spoke in s.o.'s wheel; **vos propositions ne cadrent pas avec nos plans,** your proposals do not fit in with our plans; *Adm: etc:* **p. d'aménagement,** development plan; **p. d'exploitation rationnelle,** scientific control unit; **p. de servitudes,** zoning plan; **p. économique,** economic plan; **p. de travail,** work project; scheme of work; **p. d'échantillonnage,** sampling project; *Sch:* **p. d'éducation,** scheme of education; **p. d'études,** plan, programme, of studies; curriculum; **p. détaillé de composition,** skeleton essay; *Mil:* **p. d'attaque, de campagne, d'opérations,** plan of attack, of campaign, of operations; **p. de mobilisation,** mobilisation plan; **p. de(s) feux,** fire plan, fire scheme; **p. d'emploi de l'artillerie,** artillery plan; **p. d'engagement des réserves,** plan of engagement of reserves; *Av:* **p. de vol,** flight plan; **éléments du p. de vol,** flight-plan data; *Av: Nau:* **p. d'arrimage,** stowage plan; **p. de chargement,** cargo plan; *Trans:* **p. d'enlèvement,** loading plan, plan of transport; *Med:* **p. de traitement,** treatment plan; *Fin:* **p. d'amortissement,** redemption table.

plan³, *s.m.* (= PLANT); **laisser qn en p.,** to leave s.o. in the lurch; to leave s.o. stranded; **laisser qch. en p.,** to leave off in the middle of sth.; **rester en p.,** to be stranded, to be abandoned in mid-stream.

plan⁴, *s.m. V:* metal tube containing precious objects hidden in the anus.

planage [plana:ʒ], *s.m.* smoothing, planing (of wood); planishing, planing (of metal); **machine de p.,** planing machine.

planaire [planɛ:r]. **1.** *a.* planar; **graphe p.,** planar graph; **vecteur p.,** plane vector. **2.** *s.f. Ann:* turbellarian; planarian; *F:* flatworm; (*genus*) Planaria; *pl.* **planaires,** Turbellaria.

planar [plana:r], *s.m. Elcs:* (*a*) double diffusion; (*b*) planar method.

planarité [planarite], *s.f. Mth:* planarity.

planchage [plɑ̃ʃa:ʒ], *s.m. O:* boarding; structure made of boards.

planche [plɑ̃:ʃ], *s.f.* **1.** (*a*) *Const: etc:* board; plank; (flooring) batten; **p. bouvetée,** match-board; **p. d'échafaud(age),** scaffold board; **revêtement en planches,** sheeting; **p. de ciel, de plafond,** head board, roof plank; **p. de parquet,** floor(ing) board; **p. mobile,** loose board, plank; **planches de recouvrement,** weatherboarding; **p. à clin,** feather-edged board, *U.S:* clapboard; *Carp:* **p. à dresser,** shooting board; *Metalw:* **p. à trousser,** loam board, strickle board; **p. à dessin,** drawing board; **p. de salut,** plank (clutched by drowning man); **c'est ma (dernière, seule) p. de salut,** it's my sheet anchor, my last hope; **p. pourrie,** assistance which is in itself dangerous accepted as a last resort; *A:* **faire la p. à qn, aux autres,** to smooth the way for s.o., for (the) others; *Swim:* **faire la p.,** to float, swim, on one's back; (*b*) *Dom.Ec:* **p. à (couper le) pain,** bread board; **p. à couteaux,** knife board; **p. à découper,** cutting board; **p. à hacher,** chopping board; **p. à laver,** washboard; **p. à pâtisserie,** pastry board; **p. à fromage,** cheese board; **p. à repasser,** ironing board; **p. porte-bouteilles,** bottle rack; *F:* **p. à pain, p. à repasser,** woman as flat as a board; (*c*) *Aut:* **p. de bord, p. tablier,** instrument board, dashboard, fascia board; (*d*) *Nau:* **p. de débarquement, d'embarquement, p. pour embarquer,** gang plank; brow; **p. à roulis,** side board (of bunk), bunk board; **p. de bordure,** boundary plank; **planches de fardage,** dunnage planks; *N.Arch:* **p. d'ouverture,** cross spall; *Com: Nau:* **jour de p.,** lay day; *Nau: A:* **passer à la p.,** to walk the plank; (*at the seaside*) **"les planches",** the broad walk (on the sand); (*e*) *Th:* **monter sur les planches,** to go on the stage; **être sur les planches,** to be on the stage, *F:* to tread the boards; **brûler les planches,** to act with fire; (*f*) *Med: A:* back-board; (*g*) *Sch: A:* blackboard; (*h*) *Sp: F:* ski; (*i*) shelf (of cupboard, etc.); **p. réservée aux livres,** bookshelf; *Mil:* **p. à paquetage,** equipment shelf; *F:* **avoir du pain sur la p.,** (i) *A:* to have money put by, to have a nest-egg; (ii) to have plenty of work to do, to have enough on one's plate; (*j*) (metal) plate, sheet; *Metall:* **p. de cuivre,** copper sheet; *Sm.a:* **p. d'élévateur,** magazine follower; **p. de hausse,** sight leaf; (*k*) *Min:* block of slate. **2.** (*a*) *Art: Engr:* (i) (metal) plate, (wood)cut, block (for printing, etching, engraving, etc.); (ii) (printed) plate, (wood)cut, engraving; **dictionnaire avec planches en couleurs,** dictionary with colour plates; *Engr:* **p. de trait,** key plate (in key transfer); (*b*) *Typ:* (i) plate (of type); block (of illustration); *Fin:* **faire fonctionner la p. à billets,** to issue paper money in excessive quantities; (ii) (stereotyped) plate, stereotype; (*c*) *Phot:* **coup de p.,** (i) plate marking; (ii) plate mark (on print). **3.** (*a*) *Agr:* land (*i.e.* space between water furrows); **labour en planches,** ploughing in lands; (*b*) (rectangular) flower bed; **p. d'oignons,** strip, bed, of onions; **p. de fraisiers,** strawberry bed.

planchéiage [plɑ̃ʃeja:ʒ], *s.m.* (*a*) boarding, planking (of partition, of deck); (*b*) flooring (of room, etc.).

planchéier [plɑ̃ʃeje], *v.tr.* (*p.d. & pr.sub.* **n. planchéiions, v. planchéiiez**) (*a*) to board (partition, etc.); to board over, plank over (deck, etc.); to batten (floor); (*b*) to floor (room, etc.).

plancher¹ [plɑ̃ʃe], *v.i. F: Sch:* (*a*) to be called up to demonstrate something on the blackboard; (*b*) to take an (oral) exam.

plancher², *s.m.* **1.** (*a*) (boarded) floor; **p. en ciment,** cement floor; *F:* **débarrassez-moi le p.!** get out! clear out! beat it! scram! **le p. des vaches,** terra firma; *Adm:* **prix p.,** bottom price; (*b*) planking (of deck); floor-plates (of engine-room); flooring (of trench); *Aut: Av:* floor board; **p. oblique,** toe-board; *Mil: etc:* **p. non glissant,** duck-board; *Rail:* **p. roulant,** travelling platform; **élément de p.,** floor panel (of aircraft, ship, bridge, etc.); (*c*) roadway, road covering (of bridge); (*d*) *Hyd.E:* bottom (of lock); (*e*) tread (of stirrup); (*f*) *Anat:* floor (of cavity); **p. de la bouche,** floor of the mouth; **p. des fosses nasales,** nasal floor. **2.** *A:* ceiling.

planchette [plɑ̃ʃɛt], *s.f.* **1.** small plank or board; *Phot:* **p. d'objectif,** lens panel; *Artil:* **p. de chargement,** loading-tray (of gun). **2.** (*a*) *Surv:* plane table; surveyor's table; **mettre la p. en station,** to set up the plane table; **cheminement à la p.,** plane-table traverse; **opérateur à la p.,** plane tabler; **travail à la p.,** plane tabling; (*b*) map board; (*c*) *Artil:* (i) fighting map; (ii) range-card. **3.** *Typ:* **p. de galée à coulisse,** slice of a slice galley. **4.** *Psychics:* planchette. **5.** *Wr:* **p. japonaise,** monkey climb.

planchon [plɑ̃ʃɔ̃], *s.m.* **p. d'embarquement,** gang-plank.

plançon [plɑ̃sɔ̃], *s.m.* **1.** *Hort:* (*a*) sapling; (*b*) set, slip (for planting). **2.** plank timber.

plan-concave [plɑ̃kɔ̃ka:v], *a. Opt:* plano-concave (lens); *pl. plan-concaves.*

plan-convexe [plɑ̃kɔ̃vɛks], *a. Opt:* plano-convex (lens); *pl. plan-convexes.*

plancton [plɑ̃ktɔ̃], *s.m. Biol:* plankton; **essaim de p.,** natural phytoplankton community.

planctonique [plɑ̃ktɔnik], *a. Biol:* planktonic, relating to plankton.

planctonologie [plɑ̃ktɔnɔlɔʒi], *s.f.* plankt(on)ology.

planctonologiste [plɑ̃ktɔnɔlɔʒist], *s.m. & f.* plankt(on)ologist.

planctonophage [plɑ̃ktɔnɔfa:ʒ], *Biol:* **1.** *a.* planktivorous (fish, etc.). **2.** *s.m.* plankton feeder.

plan-cylindrique [plɑ̃silɛ̃drik], *a. Opt:* plano-cylindrical; *pl. plan-cylindriques.*

plane¹ [plan], *s.m. Bot:* plane tree; **faux p.,** sycamore, false plane, great maple.

plane², *s.f. Tls:* (*a*) drawing knife; **p. droite,** straight drawing knife; **p. creuse,** hollowing knife; (*b*) turning chisel, planisher, finishing tool.

plané¹ [plane], *s.m.* rolled gold, gold casing.

plané², *a. & s.m. Av:* gliding; **angle de p.,** gliding angle; **vol. p.,** (i) glide; gliding flight; volplane; (ii) (*of birds*) soaring flight; **descendre en vol p.,** to volplane down; *F:* **faire un vol p.,** to fall (heavily); to pitch down (head first).

planéité [planeite], *s.f.* inherent flatness (of plane surface).

planement [planmɑ̃], *s.m.* **1.** hovering (of bird); floating (of balloon). **2.** *Av:* gliding; **angle de p.,** gliding angle.

planer¹ [plane], *v.tr.* **1.** to smooth, make even; to plane or shave (wood). **2.** (*a*) to planish (metals); (*b*) to roll (gold).

planer², *v.i.* **1.** (*a*) (*of bird*) to soar; to hover; (*of balloon*) to float; *F:* **il plane dans les airs,** his ambition soars high; *abs. F:* **il plane,** he's in the clouds; (*b*) *Av:* to glide; to volplane. **2.** (*a*) (*of mist, etc.*) to hover; **une brume légère planait sur la forêt,** a slight mist hung over the forest; **un silence glacé plane sur la campagne,** a chill silence broods over the countryside; **un grand danger plane au-dessus de vous,** a great danger hangs over you; (*b*) to look down (from the air, from on high); **p. sur les siècles passés,** to survey, contemplate, bygone ages.

planétaire [planetɛ:r]. **1.** *a.* (*a*) *Astr:* planetary (system, etc.); (*b*) *Mec.E:* **engrenage p.,** (sun-and-)planet gear; *s.m.* **p. du différentiel,** differential bevel wheel; (*c*) world-wide; global. **2.** *s.m.* planetarium, orrery.

planétarium [planetarjɔm], *s.m. Astr:* planetarium.

planète [planɛt], *s.f. Astr:* planet; **grande p.,** major planet; **les planètes intérieures,** the inner planets (Mercury and Venus); **les planètes extérieures,** the outer planets; **il est né sous une heureuse p.,** he was born under a lucky star.

planétisation [planetizasjɔ̃], *s.f.* globalization.

planétoïde [planetɔid], *s.m. Astr:* planetoid.

planeur¹ [planœ:r], *s.m.* planisher (of metals).

planeur², *s.m. Av:* **1.** glider; sailplane. **2.** aeroplane (considered apart from engine).

planeuse [planø:z], *s.f. Tls:* planing machine; planishing machine.

planèze [planɛ:z], *s.f. Geol:* planeze.

plani- [plani], *pref.* plani-.

planidium [planidjɔm], *s.m. Ent:* planidium.

planificateur, -trice [planifikatœ:r, -tris]. **1.** *a.* planning; **autorité planificatrice,** planning authority. **2.** *s.m. & f.* planner; *Pej:* systematizer (gone mad).

planification [planifikasjɔ̃], *s.f. Pol.Ec: Elcs:* (*computers*) planning; **p. des naissances,** family planning.

planifié [planifje], *a. Pol.Ec:* planned.

planifier [planifje], *v.i.* (*p.d. & pr.sub.* **n. planifiions, v. planifiiez**) *Pol.Ec: etc:* to plan.

planiforme [planifɔrm], *a.* planiform.

planigraphe [planigraf], *s.m.* planigraph.

planimétrage [planimetra:ʒ], *s.m. Surv:* plotting.

planimètre [planimɛtr], *s.m. Geom:* planimeter; surface integrator; **p. polaire,** polar planimeter.

planimétrie [planimetri], *s.f.* planimetry.

planimétrique [planimetrik], *a.* planimetric(al).

planipennes [planipɛn], *s.m.pl. Ent:* Planipennia.

planirostre [planirɔstr], *a.* planirostral.

planisme [planism], *s.m. Pol.Ec:* planning.

planiste [planist]. **1.** *a. Pol.Ec:* **la folie p.,** planning mania. **2.** *s.m.* planner.

planisphère [planisfɛ:r], *s.m. Astr: Geog:* planisphere.

planking [plaŋkiŋ], *s.m. Sp: A:* surf-riding.

plankton [plɑ̃ktɔ̃], *s.m. Biol:* plankton.

planning [planiŋ], *s.m.* (*a*) *Ind:* planning; *Civ.E:* **p. à chemin critique,** critical path planning, scheduling; **p. du chantier,** job planning; *Elcs:* (*computers*) **p. de production,** product planning; (*b*) *Ind:* work schedule; (*of production*) **se poursuivre suivant le p.,** to be on schedule; (*c*) **p. familial,** family planning.

planomanie [planɔmani], *s.f. Psy:* planomania.

planomètre [planɔmɛtr], *s.m. Mec.E:* planometer, surface plate.

planorbe [planɔrb], *s.f. Moll:* planorbid.

planorbidés [planɔrbide], *s.m.pl. Moll:* Planorbidae.

planque [plɑ̃:k], *s.f. P:* (*a*) hiding place, hide-out; (*b*) safe job; (*c*) cushy job.

planqué [plɑ̃ke], *s.m. P:* (*a*) *Mil: etc:* shirker; (*b*) person who has got himself a soft job.

planquer [plɑ̃ke], *v.tr. P:* (*a*) to hide (sth.), to stash (sth.); (*b*) to put (money) by; (*c*) to put, to stick, to shove, to dump (sth. somewhere); (*d*) to plant (stolen goods).

se planquer. *P:* (*a*) to take cover, shelter; to go to ground; (*b*) to lie flat; (*c*) to park (oneself) (somewhere); (*d*) to get a cushy job.

plant [plɑ̃], *s.m. Hort:* **1.** (*a*) (nursery) plantation (of trees, bushes); (*b*) **p. de choux,** cabbage patch. **2.** (*a*) sapling, set, slip; **jeunes plants,** seedlings; (*b*) vine plant.

plantage [plɑ̃ta:ʒ], *s.m.* **1.** planting (of trees, plants). **2.** (*a*) patch of ground under cultivation; (*b*) (sugar, coffee, tobacco,) plantation.

plantain [plɑ̃tɛ̃], *s.m.*, **plantago** [plɑ̃tago], *s.m. Bot:* plantain; (*genus*) Plantago; **grand p.,** greater plantain; **p. d'eau,** water plaintain; **p. lancéolé,** ribgrass, ribwort.

plantaire [plɑ̃tɛ:r], *a. Anat:* plantar; **voûte p.,** plantar arch.

plantanier [plɑ̃tanje], *s.m. Bot:* plantain (of banana type).

plantard [plɑ̃ta:r], *s.m. Hort:* (*a*) sapling; (*b*) set, slip (for planting).

plantation [plɑ̃tasjɔ̃], *s.f.* **1.** (*a*) planting (of trees, seeds); (*b*) erection (of telegraph poles, etc.); *Th:* **p. de décor,** erection of scenery. **2.** (sugar, tobacco, tea,) plantation; **p. d'oranges,** orange grove; **p. de fraisiers,** strawberry field.

plante¹ [plɑ̃:t], *s.f.* sole (of the foot).

plante[2], *s.f.* plant; **p. potagère,** herb or vegetable; **p. marine,** seaweed; **p. à fleurs,** flowering plant; **plantes vertes, à feuilles persistantes,** evergreens; **p. d'appartement,** (indoor) pot plant, house plant; **p. de serre,** hothouse plant; **le Jardin des Plantes,** the Botanical Gardens (of Paris); *P:* **une belle p.,** a fine specimen (of humanity).

planté [plɑ̃te], *a.* **1.** planted; **colline plantée d'arbres,** hill planted with trees; **un champ p. en betterave,** a field put to beet. **2.** situated, placed; **maison bien plantée,** pleasantly situated house; **oreilles bien plantées,** well-set ears; **un enfant bien p.,** a sturdy, healthy, child; *F:* **ne la laissez pas plantée là,** don't leave her standing there.

planter [plɑ̃te], *v.tr.* **1.** to plant, set (seeds, flowers); **p. une avenue,** to lay out an avenue; **p. du céleri dans une rigole,** to trench celery. **2.** to fix, set (up); **p. un pieu dans le sol,** to drive, stick, a stake in the ground; to set a stake; **borne plantée entre deux champs,** boundary-stone set between two fields; **p. une échelle contre le mur,** to plant, fix, set, a ladder against the wall; **p. un drapeau,** (i) to set up, raise, a flag; (ii) *F:* to leave without paying one's bill; **p. sa tente,** to pitch one's tent; *F:* **p. son chapeau sur la tête,** to stick one's hat on one's head; **p. un baiser sur la joue de qn,** to plant a kiss on s.o.'s cheek; *F:* **p. là qn,** to leave s.o. in the lurch, to desert s.o.; **elle l'a planté là,** she (has) jilted him; **je ne vous planterai pas là,** I won't let you down.

se planter, to stand, take one's stand (firmly); **se p. sur ses jambes,** to take a firm stand; **se p. devant qn,** to plant oneself, to stand squarely, in front of s.o.

planteur [plɑ̃tœːr], *s.m.* **1.** (*a*) planter, grower (of vegetables, etc.); **p. de pommes de terre,** potato grower; **p. de tabac,** tobacco farmer, grower; **p. de thé,** tea planter; *F:* **p. de choux,** man who has retired and who devotes himself to his garden; (*b*) planter, settler (in new colony). **2. p. mécanique** = PLANTEUSE.

planteuse [plɑ̃tøːz], *s.f. Agr:* potato planting machine.

plantier [plɑ̃tje], *s.m.* (*in S.W. France*) young vine shoot.

plantigrade [plɑ̃tigrad], *a. & s.m. Z:* plantigrade.

plantoir [plɑ̃twaːr], *s.m. Hort:* dibble, dibber; **semer, repiquer, au p.,** to dibble.

planton [plɑ̃tɔ̃], *s.m.* (*a*) *Mil:* orderly; **être de p.,** to be on orderly duty; *F:* **faire le p.,** to kick, cool, one's heels; (*b*) runner; commissionaire.

plantule [plɑ̃tyl], *s.f. Bot:* plantlet.

plantureusement [plɑ̃tyrøzmɑ̃], *adv.* copiously, abundantly.

plantureux, -euse [plɑ̃tyrø, -øːz], *a.* **1.** copious, abundant; **repas p.,** lavish meal; *F:* **appas p.,** buxom charms (of woman). **2.** rich, fertile (countryside); luxuriant (vegetation).

planula [planyla], *s.f.*, **planule** [planyl], *s.f. Coel:* planula.

planure[1] [planyːr], *s.f.* (wood) shaving(s).

planure[2], *s.f. Dial:* **1.** plain, flat countryside. **2.** *Min:* (*in Belg.*) horizontal layer (in coal seam).

plaquage [plakaːʒ], *s.m.* **1.** *Rugby Fb:* tackle. **2.** *P:* chucking, forsaking (*esp.* of lover); **alors c'est un p. en règle?** so he, she, has definitely chucked you? so you definitely chucked him, her?

plaque [plak], *s.f.* **1.** (*a*) plate, sheet (of metal); slab (of marble, chocolate, etc.); patch (of snow, vegetation, etc.); **p. de blindage, d'acier,** armour plate; **p. de cuirasse,** plate of armour; **p. de cuivre,** copper plate; **p. de fer,** iron plate; **p. de, en, fonte,** cast-iron plate; **p. de, en, tôle,** sheet iron; **p. de plomb,** lead plate (for accumulator, etc.); **p. de zinc,** zinc plate; **p. de verre,** glass plate; *Join:* **p. de contre-plaqué,** (sheet of) veneer; *Carp:* **p. rapportée,** flitch; **poutre à plaques rapportées,** flitch beam; (*b*) *Dom.Ec:* **p. de cheminée,** fireback; **p. de propreté,** (i) finger plate (of door); (ii) enamel tray (of cooker); **p. chauffante,** hotplate; **p. de four,** baking sheet; (*c*) *Artil:* **p. de crosse,** trail plate (of gun); **p. de base,** base plate (of mortar); *Sm.a:* **p. de couche,** butt plate (of rifle); (*d*) *Civ.E: Mec.E:* **p. d'assise, de fondation,** (i) *Const: etc:* base plate, bottom plate, foundation plate; (ii) *Mch:* bed plate, base plate; **p. de fermeture,** cover plate; **p. d'obturation, p. obturatrice,** blanking plate; **p. de regard, de trou de visite, de trou d'homme, p. d'égout,** manhole cover; **p. de protection,** protective plate; **p. de revêtement,** lining plate; **p. de renfort,** backing plate, stiffening plate; **p. (de) support,** support plate; *Mec.E:* **p. de fixation,** clamping plate; **p. de jonction,** gusset plate; **p. de liaison,** plate fitting; **p. de montage,** base board, assembly plate; **p. de raccord, p. adaptatrice,** adapter plate; **p. entretoise,** spacer, spacing, plate; *Rail:* **p. de garde,** hornplate (of locomotive); axle guard (of coach); *Mch:* **p. tubulaire,** flue sheet, tube sheet (of boiler); *Metall:* **p. modèle,** match, pattern, plate (of foundry mould); *Ind:* **p. d'autel,** bridge plate (of furnace); *N.Arch:* **p. de parquet de chauffe,** stokehold plate; (*e*) *Rail:* **p. d'assise de rail,** bearing plate, sole plate; **p. (d'assise) d'aiguille,** bed plate for points; **p. de serrage (de rail),** rail clip; **p. d'enraillement,** re-railing plate; **p. tournante, p. de manœuvre,** turntable, *Min:* switch plate (of tram road); **p. tournante sur galets,** turntable on rollers; **batterie de plaques tournantes,** series of (wagon) turntables; **faire tourner une p. tournante, une p. de manœuvre,** to turn a turntable, *Min:* a switch plate; (*f*) **p. tournante,** pivot; **c'est la p. tournante du projet,** the plan hinges on it; **Bruxelles est la p. tournante du Marché Commun,** Brussels is the hub of the Common Market; (*g*) *El: Elcs:* plate; anode; **p. d'accumulateur,** accumulator plate; **p. de pile,** battery plate; **p. négative, positive,** negative, positive, plate; **p. à grille, à grillage,** grid plate; **p. empâtée, tartinée,** pasted plate; **p. de (mise à la) terre,** ground plate, earth plate; *W.Tel:* **accord de p.,** anode tuning; **circuit, courant, de p.,** plate circuit, plate current; **conductance de p.,** plate conductance; **détection p.,** anode detection, anode rectification; **écran de p.,** anode screen; **impédance de p.,** plate impedance; **résistance de p.,** plate resistance; **tension de p.,** plate voltage, anode voltage; *Elcs:* (*computers*) **p. à circuit imprimé,** printed circuit card; **p. d'identification,** badge; **p. à trous,** aperture plate; (*h*) *Engr: Typ:* **p. de trait,** key plate; **p. d'offset en creux,** offset deep plate, deep-etched plate; **p. machine,** machine plate, press plate; **châssis porte-p.,** plate-holding frame; (*i*) *Phot:* **p. photographique,** photographic plate; **p. anti-halo,** anti-halo, anti-halation, plate; **p. autochrome,** autochrome plate; **p. contraste,** contrast plate; **p. rapide,** rapid plate; **p. sensible,** sensitive plate; **p. sensibilisée,** sensitized plate; **châssis porte-plaque,** plate holder; **p. stéréoscopique,** stereo slide; (*j*) *Opt:* **p. porte-objet,** slide(r) (of microscope); (*k*) *Dent:* **p. de prothèse,** denture base, plate; **p. de contention,** retention plate. **2.** (*a*) (ornamental) plaque (of metal, porcelain, pewter, etc.); **p. commémorative,** commemorative, *esp.* votive, tablet; **p. funéraire, mortuaire, en cuivre,** church brass; (*b*) **p. de porte,** door plate; name plate; **p. de cuivre (d'avocat, de médecin, etc.),** brass plate; **avant trente ans il avait sa p. de cuivre dans Harley Street,** before he was thirty he had his name up in Harley Street; **p. indicatrice de rue,** name plate (of street); (*c*) *Ind:* **p. signalétique,** rating plate (of engine, etc.); **p. de constructeur,** manufacturer's name plate (on machine, apparatus, etc.); (*d*) *Adm: etc:* **p. d'identité, d'identification,** identification plate, number plate; (soldier's) identity disc; **p. de garde champêtre,** rural policeman's badge; *A:* **p. de cocher,** cabman's badge; **p. d'un ordre,** star of an order; **p. d'immatriculation,** licence plate, *Aut: etc:* number plate; *Aut:* **p. de police, p. de contrôle, p. matricule, p. minéralogique, p. réglementaire,** number plate; **p. de police, de contrôle, etc., maquillée,** false number plate. **3.** *Hort:* **p. de gazon,** sod. **4.** (*a*) *Med:* plaque; **p. bactérienne, microbienne,** bacterial plaque; **p. muqueuse,** mucous plaque; **p. psoriasique,** psoriatic plaque; *Physiol:* **p. sanguine,** red blood disc; (*b*) *Anat:* **plaques de Peyer,** Peyer's patches, glands; (*c*) *Orn:* **plaques incubatrices,** brooding patches.

plaqué [plake], *a. & s.m.* **1. (métal) p.,** plated metal, plated goods; electroplate; *F:* **c'est du p.,** it's false, cheap. **2. (bois) p.,** veneered wood.

plaque-adresse [plakadrɛs], *s.f.* address plate; *pl. plaques-adresses.*

plaque-chicane [plakʃikan], *s.f.* baffle plate; *pl. plaques-chicanes.*

plaquemine [plakmin], *s.f. Bot:* persimmon.

plaqueminier [plakminje], *s.m. Bot:* **1. p. ébénier,** ebony. **2. p. de Virginie,** persimmon (tree).

plaque-modèle [plakmɔdɛl], *s.f. Metall:* die; *pl. plaques-modèles.*

plaquer [plake], *v.tr.* **1.** (*a*) to veneer (wood); to plate (metal); to flash (glass); to lay on (plaster); to lay down (turf); **presse à p.,** veneering press; **plaqué de sang, de boue,** caked with blood, with mud; **maison plaquée de dartres,** house showing patches of decay; *F: O:* **p. un soufflet à qn,** to smack s.o.'s face; **p. qch. au nez de qn,** to cast sth. in s.o.'s teeth; **se p. les cheveux sur le front,** to plaster one's hair down on one's forehead; *v.i.* **cheveux qui plaquent sur le front,** hair that lies flat on the brow; **le vent lui plaquait son manteau sur les jambes,** the wind blew his coat against his legs; **il avait les épaules plaquées au mur,** he stood with his shoulders to the wall; **p. son chapeau sur ses oreilles,** to pull, cram, one's hat down over one's ears; (*b*) *Rugby Fb:* to tackle, bring down (opponent); (*c*) *Mus:* **p. un accord,** to strike (and hold) a chord. **2.** (*a*) *F:* to abandon, desert, *F:* ditch, chuck (s.o.); to leave (s.o.) in the lurch; **pourquoi l'avez-vous plaqué?** why did you jilt him, throw him over? (*b*) *v.i. F:* **j'ai plaqué tout de suite,** I gave up at once.

se plaquer. 1. se p. contre le sol, contre un mur, to lie flat on the ground, to flatten oneself against a wall; *F:* **se p. par terre,** to fall at full length. **2.** *Av:* to pancake.

plaque-semelle [plaksəmɛl], *s.f. Civ.E: Mec.E: etc:* foundation plate; *pl. plaques-semelles.*

plaquette [plakɛt], *s.f.* **1.** plaquette, small plate (of metal, wood, etc.); thin slab (of stone, etc.); stock (plate) (of revolver); *Mch:* metal disc (of washer); *Aut:* **p. (d'un frein à disque),** pad; **p. à cosses,** tag board; *El.E:* terminal strip; (*computers*) **p. à circuit imprimé,** printed circuit card; **p. embrochable, p. interchangeable,** plug-in unit. **2.** thin booklet (bound in thin boards); brochure. **3. plaquettes sanguines,** blood platelets, hematoblasts.

plaqueur [plakœːr], *s.m.* **1.** (*a*) plater (of metal); (*b*) veneerer. **2.** *Rugby Fb:* tackler.

plasma [plasma], *s.m.* **1.** *Biol: Miner:* plasma; **p. sanguin,** blood plasma. **2.** *Ph:* (*ionized gas*) plasma; **p. primordial,** ylem; **p. électronique,** electron plasma; **propulsion par p.,** plasma propulsion; **fusée, moteur, à p.,** plasma rocket, plasma engine.

plasmagène [plasmaʒɛn], *a.Ph:* plasma-producing.

plasmaphérèse [plasmafereːz], *s.f. Med: Physiol:* plasmaphaeresis, plasmapheresis, plasmaphoresis.

plasmatique [plasmatik], *a.* plasmatic, plasmic.

plasmifier [plasmifje], *v.tr.* (*p.d. & pr.sub.* **n. plasmifiions, v. plasmifiiez**) *Ph:* to transform (a gas) into plasma.

plasmine [plasmin], *s.f. Bio-Ch:* plasmin.

plasmique [plasmik], *a.* plasmic.

plasmocyte [plasmɔsit], *s.m. Biol:* plasmocyte.

plasmod(i)e [plasmɔd(i)], *s.f. Biol:* plasmodium.

plasmodium [plasmɔdjɔm], *s.m. Biol:* plasmodium.

plasmogamie [plasmɔgami], *s.f. Bot:* plasmogamy.

plasmologie [plasmɔlɔʒi], *s.f.* plasmology.

plasmolyse [plasmɔliːz], *s.f. Biol:* plasmolysis.

plasmopara [plasmɔpara], *s.m. Fung:* plasmopara.

plaste [plast], *s.m. Bot:* plastid.

plasterboard [plastərbɔrd], *s.m. Const:* plasterboard.

plastic [plastik], *s.m.* explosive gelatin, jelly, plastic.

plasticage [plastikaːʒ], *s.m.* plastic bomb attack, incident.

plasticien [plastisjɛ̃], *s.m.* **1.** *Tchn:* plastics technician. **2.** plastic surgeon.

plasticité [plastisite], *s.f.* plasticity.

plastide [plastid], *s.m. Biol:* plastid.

plastie [plasti], *s.f.* plastic surgery.

plastifiant [plastifjɑ̃], (*a*) *a.* plastifying (agent); (*b*) *s.m.* plasticizer.

plastification [plastifikasjɔ̃], *s.f.* plastification, plasticization; *Bookb: etc:* lamination.

plastifier [plastifje], *v.tr.* (*p.d. & pr.sub.* **n plastifiions, v. plastifiiez**) to plasticize; *Bookb:* to laminate; **jaquette plastifiée,** laminated jacket; **machine à p.,** laminator.

plastigel [plastiʒɛl], *s.m.* plastigel.

plastiquage [plastikaːʒ], *s.m.* plastic bomb attack, incident.

plastique [plastik]. **1.** *a.* plastic; **aux formes plastiques,** with a fine figure; *Adm:* **alignement p.,** building line; *Ind: Com:* **matière p.,** plastic; **bois p.,** plastic wood; **caractère p.,** malleable nature. **2.** *s.f.* (*a*) plastic art, art of modelling; (*b*) figure, physique (of an actress or dancer); **danseuse d'une belle p.,** dancer with a beautifully modelled figure. **3.** *s.m. Ind:* plastic; **p. expansé, p. mousse,** expanded, foam, plastic; **plastiques acryliques, vinyliques,** acrylic, vinyl, plastics; **p. stratifié,** laminate plastic.

plastiquement [plastikmɑ̃], *adv.* plastically; **p. très belle,** sculpturally beautiful.

plastiquer [plastike], *v.tr.* to attack, damage, destroy (sth.) with plastic explosive.

plastiqueur, -euse [plastikœːr, -øːz], *s.* person responsible for a plastic bomb explosion.

plastisol [plastizɔl], *s.m.* plastisol.

plastomère [plastɔmɛːr], *s.m. Ch:* plastomer.

plastomètre [plastɔmɛːtr̥], *s.m. Tchn:* plastometer.

plastotype [plastɔtip], *s.f. Typ:* plastotype.

plastron [plastrɔ̃], *s.m.* **1.** breastplate (of cuirass). **2.** *Mec.E:* drill plate. **3.** (*a*) (fencer's) plastron, pad, fencing jacket; *Games:* (*baseball*) body shield; (*b*) *F:* butt, target (of jokes); **je suis las de vous servir de p.,** I am tired of being your butt; (*c*) *Z:* plastron (of tortoise, of echinoderm). **4.** *Cost:* **p. de chemise,** (man's) shirt front; **faux p., p. mobile,** false shirt front; dicky, dickey; **chemise à p.,** starched shirt, *F:* boiled shirt. **5.** *Mil:* (*in manœuvres*) exercise target, skeleton enemy.

plastronner [plastrɔne]. **1.** *v.tr.* to put a plastron on (s.o.). **2.** *v.i.* (*a*) to practise hits on the plastron (worn by the fencing-master); (*b*) *F:* to throw out one's chest, to pose, strut, attitudinize.

plastronneur, -euse [plastrɔnœːr, -øːz], *s. F:* person who puts on airs, who poses; swaggerer; affected person, poseur.

plat [pla]. **1.** *a.* (*a*) flat, level; **le pays p.,** the lowlands; **soulier p.,** low-heeled, flat, shoe; **avoir la poitrine plate, les pieds plats,** to be flat-chested, flat-footed; **teinte plate,** flat tint; **cheveux plats,** straight hair; **mer plate,** smooth sea; **calme p.,** dead calm; *F:* **bourse plate,** empty purse; **vis à tête plate,** screw with countersunk head; **vaisselle plate,** (solid) gold plate or silver plate; *Cu:* **plates côtes,** top ribs (of beef); *s.a.* COUTURE 2, RIME; (*b*) flat, dull, insipid, tame; platitudinous (answer); **traduction plate,** flat, dull, bald, translation; **style p.,** platitudinous, commonplace, style; **vin p.,** dull, flat, wine; *I.C.E:* **moteur p.,** unresponsive engine; **c'est un p. personnage,** he's a worm, a contemptible fellow; *A:* **c'est un pied p.,** he is a man of no consequence; **faire de plates excuses,** to make (i) a contemptible, shabby, apology, (ii) paltry excuses; *s.m.* **faire du p. à qn,** (i) to flatter s.o., to pay compliments to s.o., *F:* to toady (to) s.o.; (ii) *P:* to make advances to s.o.; *s.a.* VALET 2; (*c*) *adj. & adv.phr.* **à p.,** flat; **pierres à p.,** stones laid flat; **couché à p. sur le sol,** lying flat on the ground; **avirons à p.!** feather (your oars)! **tomber à p. (ventre),** to fall flat on one's face; **se mettre à p. ventre devant qn,** to grovel before s.o.; **la pièce est tombée à p.,** the play fell flat, was a complete failure; **pneu à p.,** flat tyre; tyre that is down; **accus à p.,** flat battery; *F:* **être à p.,** (i) to be exhausted, all in; (ii) *Aut: etc:* to have a flat tyre; **j'étais complètement à p.,** I was completely run down; **cette maladie l'a mis à p.,** this illness has taken it out of him; *Av:* **descendre à p.,** to pancake (to the ground); *Bookb:* **feuilles à p.,** flat sheets; *Carp:* **assemblage à p.,** butt-joint. **2.** *s.m.* (*a*) flat (part) (of hand, of sword, etc.); blade (of oar, of the tongue); face (of hammer); *Bookb:* **plats,** boards, sides; **p. supérieur,** front side, front board; **p. inférieur,** off side, off board; **plats toile, plats papier,** cloth boards, paper boards; *Cu:* **p. de côtes,** top ribs (of beef); *Glassm:* **p. de verre,** square, pane, of glass; piece of glass plate; *Metall:* **p. (de fer),** flat (iron) bar; *Sp:* **le p.,** flat racing; **course de p.,** flat race; (*b*) *Cu:* dish (container or contents); **p. à rôtir, à four,** baking dish; *F:* **mettre les petits plats dans les grands,** to make a great spread; to spare no expense; **mettre les pieds dans le p.,** to put one's foot in it; *A:* **il nous a donné, servi, un p. de son métier,** he played us one of his tricks; *F:* **en faire tout un p. (à qn),** to make a great fuss, a great song and dance, about sth. (to s.o.); to pile on the agony; *Navy:* **faire p. avec . . .,** to mess with . . .; **camarade de p.,** messmate; (*c*) *Cu:* course (at dinner, etc.); **trois plats et un dessert,** three courses and a sweet; **p. de résistance,** main course, main dish; plat de résistance; **petits plats,** delicacies; **faire de bons petits plats,** to prepare, cook, delicacies with loving care; **p. cuisiné,** ready-cooked dish (bought at delicatessen shop); *s.a.* JOUR 3; (*d*) pan, scale (of balance, etc.); **p. de quête,** collection plate; *A:* **p. à barbe,** shaving dish, barber's basin; (*e*) *Swim:* **faire un p.,** to do a belly flop.

Plata [plata], *Pr.n.f. Geog:* **le Rio de la P.,** the (River) Plate.

plataléidés [plataleide], *s.m.pl. Orn:* Plataleidae, the spoonbills.

platanaie [platanɛ], *s.f. Bot:* plantation of plane trees.

platane [platan], *s.m. Bot:* plane tree, platan; **faux p.,** sycamore (maple); *Aut:* **s'écraser contre un p.,** to hit a tree.

plataniste [platanist], *s.m. Z:* river dolphin.

plat-bord [plabɔːr], *s.m. Nau:* **1.** gunwale, gunnel; **hauteur au-dessus du p.-b.,** height above the hull. **2.** low freeboard deck (of monitor); *pl. plats-bords.*

plate [plat], *s.f.* **1.** *Nau:* (*a*) punt; (*b*) flat-bottomed fishing boat. **2.** *A.Arm:* piece of plate armour; **batteur de p.,** maker of plate armour.

plateau, -eaux [plato], *s.m.* **1.** (*a*) tray; **p. à thé,** tea tray; **p. d'argent,** silver salver; **p. à fromage,** cheese board; **p. de fromage,** dish of assorted cheeses, cheese platter, board; (*b*) **p. d'une balance,** pan, scale, of a balance; *Ethn:* **négresse à plateaux,** plate-wearing, labret-wearing, negress; (*c*) shelf (of oven, etc.); **p. à savon,** soap dish; **p. d'une table,** top of a table, table top; **p. d'amiante,** asbestos (stove) mat; *Surg:* **p. pour instruments,** instrument tray; **p. pour stérilisation,** sterilising tray; *Nau:* **p. à roulis,** swinging tray, *F:* fiddle. **2.** *Geog:* (*a*) plateau, tableland; **p. marécageux,** high moor; **p. continental,** continental shelf; (*b*) *Nau:* sand beach, shallow; (*c*) *Med:* dead level (of a disease). **3.** platform; (*a*) *Artil:* **p. chargeur,** loading platform; (*b*) *Th:* floor (of the stage); *Cin:* set; **p. tournant,** revolving stage; **répétition sur le p.,** rehearsal on the set; *Cin:* **secrétaire de p.,** script girl; (*c*) *Const:* board, plank; **p. d'échafaudage,** scaffold board; (*d*) *Aut: etc:* **(camion) p.,** flat truck; **p. de manutention,** dolly. **4.** *Tchn:* (*a*) face plate, chuck (plate), table (of lathe, etc.); **p. à centrage automatique,** auto-centring chuck; **p. à couronne,** gear-driven face plate; **p. à hauteur variable,** rising table; **p. circulaire automatique,** self-acting circular table; **p. diviseur, p. indicateur,** index plate, dial; **p. indicateur des avances,** feed-index plate; **p. porte-chariot à aléser, à fraiser, à planer,** boring, milling, facing, head; **p. porte-pièce,** work plate, work table; **p. toc, p. porte-mandrin,** catch plate, dog plate; dog chuck; **p. mobile (d'une presse à vis),** follower (of a screw press); *Typ:* **p. flottant,** floating platen; (*b*) *Mch: Mec.E:* plate, disc, flange; *Mch:* **accouplement à plateaux,** flange, plate, coupling; **p. d'accouplement,** coupling flange, plate; **p. d'arbre de butée,** thrust-shaft flange; **p. de cylindre,** cylinder cover; **p. avant, arrière, de cylindre,** front, back, cylinder cover; **p. de friction,** friction disc; **p. d'excentrique,** eccentric disc, sheave; **p. oscillant,** wrist plate (of rocking valves); *Aut: etc:* **embrayage à plateaux,** plate, disc, clutch; **p. d'embrayage,** clutch plate, disc; **p. de pression d'embrayage,** clutch pressure plate; *Cy:* **p. de pédalier,** front chain wheel; *Nau:* **p. d'aile d'hélice,** propeller-blade flange; (*c*) *Ch:* **p. de colonne de distillation,** plate of distilling column; **p. de colonne de fractionnement,** tray of fractioning column; *Atom.Ph:* **p. en chicane,** baffle plate; **p. à cloche,** bubble cap; **p. à barbotage, à coupelles,** bubble plate; (*d*) *Rail:* **p. de butoir,** buffer plate; **p. de tampon,** buffer disc; (*e*) *El:* **p. d'annonciateur,** annunciator disc (of bell); (*f*) *Mus:* key (of Boehm flute, etc.); (*g*) *Nau:* **p. d'ancre,** anchor buoy.

plateau-étau [platoeto], *s.m. Mch.Tls:* vice plate; *pl. plateaux-étaux.*

plateau-manivelle [platomanivɛl], *s.m. Mec.E:* disc crank; *pl. plateaux-manivelles.*

plate-bande [platbɑ̃ːd], *s.f.* **1.** *Hort:* (*a*) grass border; border; (*b*) flower bed; *F:* **ne marchez pas dans mes plates-bandes,** mind your own business. **2.** *Arch:* plat band; (i) flat arch; (ii) flat moulding; lintel course; *pl. plates-bandes.*

platée[1] [plate], *s.f. Arch:* (solid) foundation (of concrete).

platée[2], *s.f. F:* dishful (of food, etc.).

Platée, *Pr.n.f. A.Geog:* Plataea.

platéen, -enne [plateɛ̃, -ɛn], *a. & s. A.Geog:* Plataean.

plate-forme [platfɔrm], *s.f.* **1.** (*a*) platform (of bus, etc.); flat roof (of house); footplate (of locomotive); apron (of lock, of dock entrance). *Artil: etc:* **p.-f. de tir,** gun platform; **p.-f. de mitrailleuse,** machine-gun platform; **p.-f. tournante,** gun turntable; **p.-f. de chargement, de déchargement,** loading, unloading, platform; *Nau:* **p.-f. de cale,** platform deck; *Navy:* **p.-f. d'envol,** flying(-off) platform (for aircraft); **p.-f. d'atterrissage, d'apontage,** landing platform; **p.-f. de lancement,** (i) *Av:* launching platform (for aircraft); (ii) *Ball:* launch(ing) pad (for rocket); **p.-f. (marine) de forage (pétrolier),** oil rig, (oil-)drilling rig, platform; *Const: etc:* **p.-f. suspendue,** hanging stage; **p.-f. volante,** flying stage; *Civ.E: Min:* **p.-f. de déversement,** tipping stage; *Nau:* **p.-f. flottante,** floating stage; *Rail:* **p.-f. roulante,** flat truck, open truck; **p.-f. de transport auto,** car carrier; *Min:* **p.-f. de roulage, de roulement,** trolley; *Ball:* **p.-f. chenillée (pour le transport des fusées),** crawler; (*b*) *Civ.E:* **p.-f. des terrassements,** formation level, road bed; *Geol:* **p.-f. rocheuse,** level stretch of rock; **p.-f. d'abrasion,** rock bench. **2.** *Pol:* platform; *pl. plates-formes.*

platelage [platlaːʒ], *s.m.* **1.** *N.Arch:* plating (upon which armour is bolted). **2.** *Civ.E:* floor(ing) (of bridge); planking.

plate-longe [platlɔ̃ːʒ], *s.f. Harn:* (*a*) kicking strap; (*b*) leading rein; *pl. plates-longes.*

platement [platmɑ̃], *adv.* flatly. **1.** (*a*) dully, prosaically, baldly; (*b*) contemptibly, meanly. **2.** *A:* plainly, without beating about the bush.

plateresque [plat(ə)rɛsk], *a. Arch:* plateresque.

platerie [platri], *s.f.* earthenware or china dishes; flatware.

plateure [platyːr, -œːr], *s.f. Min:* horizontal fold (in coal seam); flat seam, vein.

plat-fond [plafɔ̃], *s.m. Nau:* well (of boat); *pl. plats-fonds.*

plathelminthes [platɛlmɛ̃ːt], *s.m.pl. Ann:* platyhelminthes, platelminthes.

platière [platjɛːr], *s.f.* (*a*) water-splash (across road); (*b*) stretch of level ground (at foot of hill).

platin [platɛ̃], *s.m. Nau:* flat (showing at low tide); shoal, shallow.

platinage [platinaːʒ], *s.m.* plating (of copper, etc.) with platinum; platinization.

platinate [platinat], *s.m. Ch:* platinate.

platine[1] [platin], *s.f.* plate (of lock, watch, etc.); lock (of firearm), gun-lock plate; platen (of printing press, of typewriter); follower (of press); stage (of microscope); turntable (of record player); **p. à chariot,** mechanical stage; **les platines d'un canif,** the shell of a penknife; *Sm.a:* **p. à double détente,** hair-trigger lock; *P: A:* **avoir une fameuse p.,** to have the gift of the gab.

platine[2], *s.m. Ch:* platinum; **p. iridié,** platino-iridium; **mousse, éponge, de p.,** platinum sponge; **fil de p.,** platinum wire; **p. laminé,** platinum foil; **noir de p.,** platinum black.

platiné [platine], *a.* **1.** (*a*) platinum-plated, platinized; *Metall: Miner:* **iridium p.,** platino-iridium; (*b*) **cheveux platinés,** platinum-blond hair; **une blonde platinée,** a platinum blonde. **2.** platinum-tipped (screw); *El.E:* **grain p.,** platinum point (of make-and-break); *Aut: F:* **vis platinées,** points.

platiner [platine], *v.tr.* to platinize, to plate with platinum.

platineux, -euse [platinø, -øːz], *a.* platinous.

platinifère [platinifɛːr], *a.* platiniferous.

platinique [platinik], *a. Ch:* platinic.

platiniridium [platiniridjɔm], *s.m. Metall: Miner:* platinoiridium, platiniridium.

platinite [platinit]. **1.** *s.m. Metall:* nickel-steel alloy. **2.** *s.f. Miner:* platinite.

platinocyanure [platinɔsjanyːr], *s.m. Ch:* platinocyanide; **p. de barium,** barium platinocyanide.

platinoïde [platinɔid], *a.* platinoid.

platinotypie [platinɔtipi], *s.f. Phot:* platinotype.

platitude [platityd], *s.f.* **1.** flatness, dullness (of character, style, etc.); vapidity (of style). **2.** (*a*) commonplace remark, platitude; **dire, débiter, des platitudes,** to platitudinize; (*b*) servile action; **faire des platitudes à qn,** to truckle to s.o.; to fawn and cringe to s.o.

platocyanure [platɔsjanyːr], *s.m. Ch:* platinocyanide.

Platon [platɔ̃], *Pr.n.m.* Plato.

platonicien, -ienne [platɔnisjɛ̃, -jɛn]. **1.** *a.* Platonic (school, philosopher). **2.** *s.* Platonist.

platonique [platɔnik], *a.* **1.** Platonic (love, etc.). **2.** useless; futile; **tentative p.,** futile attempt; **protestation p.,** ineffective protest.

platoniquement [platɔnikmɑ̃], *adv.* Platonically.

platonisme [platɔnism], *s.m.* Platonism.

plâtrage [plɑtraːʒ], *s.m.* plastering (of wall, field, wine); *Const:* plaster work; *F:* **c'est du p., tout ça,** that's all lath and plaster, all rubbishy stuff.

plâtras [plɑtrɑ], *s.m.* debris of plaster work, broken bricks and mortar; rubble.

plâtre [plɑːtr̥], *s.m.* **1.** (*a*) plaster; **p. fin, p. de moulage,** plaster of Paris; **p. aluné,** marble cement; **pierre à p.,** gypsum; **p. cru,** unburnt gypsum; **p. cuit,** burnt gypsum, plaster of Paris; **p. au sas,** sifted plaster; **enduire qch. de p.,** to plaster sth. over; (*b*) *pl.* plaster work (on house, etc.); pargeting; **essuyer les plâtres,** (i) to occupy a house before the plaster is dry; (ii) to be the first occupant of a house; *F:* (*of new product, etc.*) **on ne l'a pas acheté car on veut laisser les autres essuyer les plâtres,** we haven't bought it as we want to let other people try it out first; (*c*) (face-)paint (*esp.* of clown). **2.** plaster cast; *Med:* **p. de marche,** walking cast.

plâtre-ciment [plɑtrəsimɑ̃], *s.m.* plaster-cement; *pl. plâtres-ciments.*

plâtrée [plɑtre], *s.f. Arch:* (solid) foundation (of concrete).

plâtrer [plɑtre], *v.tr.* **1.** (*a*) to plaster (wall, ceiling); to plaster up (hole, crack); *F:* **se p. (le visage),** to plaster one's face with make-up; (*b*) *F:* to plaster up, hide (fault, defect); to smooth over, patch up (a quarrel); (*c*) *Med:* **appareil plâtré,** cast; **p. une jambe,** to put a leg in plaster. **2.** (*a*) to plaster, to gypsum (field); to dress (the soil) with sulphate of lime; (*b*) to plaster (wine), to clear (wine) with gypsum.

plâtrerie [plɑtrəri], *s.f.* plaster works; **travaux de p.,** plaster work, plastering.

plâtreux, -euse [plɑtrø, -øːz], *a.* plastery; gypseous; chalky (water, soil).

plâtrier [plɑtrije], *s.m.* **1.** plasterer. **2.** calciner of gypsum.

plâtrière [plɑtrijɛːr], *s.f.* **1.** gypsum quarry, chalk pit. **2.** plaster kiln, gypsum kiln.

plâtroir [plɑtrwaːr], *s.m.* plastering-trowel.

plat-ventre [plavɑ̃ːtr̥], *s.m.inv. Swim: F:* belly-flop.

platy- [plati], *comb.fm.* platy-; **platybasique,** platybasic; (skull) wide at the base; **platydactyle,** platydactylous.

platybasique [platibazik], *a.* platybasic; (skull) wide at the base.

platycéphale [platisefal], *a.* platycephalic, platycephalous.

platycerium [platiserjɔm], *s.m. Bot:* platycerium.

platycnémie [platiknemi], *s.f. Anthr:* platycnemia.

platycnémique [platiknemik], *a.* platycnemic.

platydactyle [platidaktil], *a.* platydactylous.

platymètre [platimɛtr̥], *s.m. El:* platymeter.

platypétale [platipetal], *a. Bot:* platypetalous.

platyr(r)hinien, -ienne [platirinjɛ̃, -jɛn], *Z:* **1.** *a.* platyr(r)hine. **2.** *s.m.pl.* **platyr(r)hiniens,** Platyr(r)hina.

platystémon [platistemɔ̃], *s.m. Bot:* Californian poppy.

plausibilité [plozibilite], *s.f.* plausibility (of statement).

plausible [plozibl̥], *a.* plausible (statement); **cela rend p. la théorie,** that makes the theory plausible.

plausiblement [plozibləmɑ̃], *adv.* plausibly.

Plaute [ploːt], *Pr.n.m. Lt.Lit:* Plautus.

play-back [plɛbak], *s.m. Rec: etc:* playback.

plèbe [plɛb], *s.f.* (the) plebs; (the) lower orders, (the) common people.

plébéianisme [plebejanism], *s.m.* plebeianism.

plébéien, -ienne [plebejɛ̃, -jɛn], *a. & s.* plebeian.

plébiscitaire [plebisitɛːr], *a.* plebiscitary.

plébiscite [plebisit], *s.m.* plebiscite.

plébisciter [plebisite], *v.tr.* (*a*) to vote for (s.o., sth.) by plebiscite; (*b*) *F:* **p. qn,** to measure somebody's popularity.

plécoptères [plekɔptɛːr], *s.m.pl. Ent:* Plecoptera.

plectognathe [plɛktɔgnat], *Ich:* **1.** *a.* plectognath(ous). **2.** *s.m.* plectognath; **les plectognathes,** the Plectognathi.

plectre [plɛktr̥], *s.m. Mus:* plectrum.

pléiade [plejad], *s.f. Astr: Lit:* pleiad; *Myth:* **les Pléiades,** the Atlantides, Pleiades.

plein[1] [plɛ̃]. **1.** *a.* full; (*a*) filled, replete (**de,** with); **p. de vie,** full of life; **bouteille pleine,** full bottle; **pleine bouteille,** bottleful (**de,** of); **p. verre,** bumper; **pleine charrette, pleine auto,** cartful, carful; **joues pleines,** full, plump, cheeks; **p. comme un œuf,** full as an egg, chock-full; *F:* **être p.,** to be drunk; *F:* to have a skinful; **salle pleine à craquer,** hall, room, full to bursting point; **sac p. à craquer, tout p., de pommes de terre,** sack bulging, bursting, with potatoes; **avoir le ventre p.,** to have eaten one's fill, to be full; **ne parle pas la bouche pleine,** don't speak with your mouth full; **j'ai le cœur p.,** my heart is full; **cave pleine de vin,** cellar full of wine; *Nau:* **p. chargement,** full cargo; **navire p. d'eau,** waterlogged ship; **mourir p. de jours,** to die old, full of years; **entreprise pleine de dangers,** enterprise fraught with dangers; **p. de gaieté,** overflowing with high spirits; **il a les doigts pleins d'encre,** he has inky fingers; **bois p. de gibier,** wood teeming with game; (*b*) (*of animals*) full; big (with young); pregnant; **chienne, chatte, jument, brebis, vache, chèvre, pleine,** bitch in pup, cat with kittens, mare in foal, ewe with lamb, cow with calf, goat in kid; (*c*) complete, entire, whole; **pleine lune,** full moon; **p. sud,** due south; **pleine mer,** (i) high tide; (ii) the high sea(s); **végétaux de pleine terre,** open-air plants; **arriver à pleine maturité,** to come to full maturity; **reliure pleine peau,** full leather binding; **p. pouvoir,** full power; *Jur:* power of attorney; **p. consentement,** full consent; **de p. gré,** of one's own free will; *Bill:* **prendre la bille pleine, demi-pleine,** to strike the ball full, half full; *s.a.* FOUET 2; (*d*) solid (tyre, axle, etc.); **trait p., ligne pleine,** continuous line; *El.E:* **fil p.,** solid wire; **table en acajou p.,** solid mahogany table; **brique pleine,** solid brick; **écrou p.,** blind nut; (*e*) **en plein** + *sb:* **en p. visage,** full, right, in the face; **la boulette l'atteignit en p. œil,** *F:* the pellet hit him slap in the eye; **en p. hiver,** in the depth, the middle, of winter; **en p. air,** in the open, alfresco; *s.m.* **un p. air,** an open-air portrait; **en p. jour,** (i) in broad daylight; (ii) publicly; **en pleine rue,** in the open street, openly; **s'arrêter en p. milieu de la place,** to stop right in the middle of the square; **en pleine nuit,** in the (very) middle of the night, at dead of night; **en pleine saison,** in the height of the season; **en pleine moisson,** right in the middle of the harvest; **semer en pleine terre,** to sow in the open ground, out-of-doors, in the open; **en pleine mer,** out at sea, in the open sea, on the high sea(s); **en pleine ville,** right in the town; **nager en pleine eau,** to swim in deep water; **en pleins champs,** in the open fields; **la maison est située en pleine campagne,** the house stands in the open; **en p. tribunal,** in open court; **en p. travail,** in the midst of the, his, work; **être en p. travail,** to be (i) hard at work, (ii) (*of factory etc.*) in full production; **en pleine activité,** in full swing; (*f*) **à p.** + *sb.* **respirer à pleine poitrine, à pleins poumons,** to breath deep; **boire à p. verre,** to drink deep; to drink (sth.) down; **crier à pleine gorge, à pleine poitrine,** to shout at the top of one's voice, lustily; **apporter des fleurs à pleins bras,** to bring flowers in armfuls; **mordre dans qch. à pleine bouche,** to take a big bite out of sth.; **à pleines voiles,** with all sails set, under full sail; *s.a.* MAIN 1; (*g*) *adv.* **il avait des larmes p. les yeux,** his eyes were full of tears; **il a des livres p. ses poches,** he has his pockets stuffed with books; **avoir de l'argent p. les poches,** to be flush with money); **apporter des fleurs p. les bras,** to bring flowers in armfuls; **nous avions du vent p. la voile,** the wind filled our sail; *F:* **en avoir p. les jambes, les pattes, les bottes,** to be fagged out; **en avoir p. la vue de qn,** to be impressed by s.o.; **en mettre p. la vue à qn,** to impress s.o.; *P:* **tout p.,** very, very much, very many; **elle est mignonne tout p.,** she's awfully sweet; she's a peach, a darling; **tout p. de gens,** any amount of people, lots of people; **si vous voulez être tout p. gentil . . .,** if you want to be very nice . . .; *Nau:* **porter p.,** to keep her full; **près et p.,** full and by; by and large. **2.** *s.m.* (*a*) plenum, fully occupied space; **pleins et vides d'un bâtiment,** solid and hollow parts of a building; **mettre dans le p.,** to hit the bull's eye; *Mch:* **faire le p. des chaudières,** etc., to fill the boilers, etc.; to fill up; **eau pour faire le p.,** make-up water; *Aut: Av:* **faire le p. d'essence, d'eau,** to fill up with petrol, with water; **faites le p., s'il vous plaît,** fill up the tank, please, *F:* fill her up; *Nau:* **faire le p. des vivres,** to complete with provisions; **faire le p. avec du charbon,** to complete the freight, fill up, with coal; *Nau:* (*of ship*) **avoir son p.,** to be fully laden; **avoir le grand p. des soutes,** to be full up with coal or oil; (*b*) full (extent, height, etc.); **la lune est dans son p.,** the moon is at the full; **être dans le p. de sa beauté,** to be at the height, in the full bloom, of one's beauty; **le p. (de la mer),** high tide; **au p. (de la mer),** (i) at high tide; (ii) (*of ship*) aground, high and dry, neaped; (*of the tide*) **battre son p.,** to be at the full; **la saison bat son p., c'est le p. de la saison,** the season is at its height, is in full swing; *adv.phr.* **travailler à p.,** to work full out; (*c*) **en p. dans le centre,** full, right, in the middle; **se trouver en p. dans le faisceau des projecteurs,** to find oneself full in the beams of the searchlights; (*d*) downstroke (in writing); *Typ:* thick stroke.

plein[2], *a. Her:* **écu p.,** shield of a single tincture; **armes pleines,** arms without any difference.

pleinairisme [plɛnɛrism], *s.m.* cult of the open air; open-air spirit.

pleinairiste [plɛnɛrist], *s.m. & f. F:* fresh-air fiend.

pleinement [plɛnmɑ̃], *adv.* fully, entirely, quite, to the full.

plein-emploi [plɛnɑ̃plwa], *s.m.inv. Pol.Ec:* full employment.

plein-temps [plɛ̃tɑ̃], *a.inv.* full-time; **médecin p.-t.,** full-time doctor (in a hospital).

plein-vent [plɛ̃vɑ̃], *s.m.* **1.** *Hort:* hardy fruit tree. **2.** isolated tree; *pl. pleins-vents.*

pléistocène [pleistɔsɛn], *a. & s.m. Geol:* pleistocene.

plénier, -ière [plenje, -jɛːr], *a. A:* full, complete; absolute; (*still used in*) **cour, indulgence, plénière,** plenary court, indulgence.

plénièrement [plenjɛrmɑ̃], *adv.* plenarily.

plénipotentiaire [plenipɔtɑ̃sjɛːr], *a. & s.m.* (*a*) plenipotentiary; (*b*) *s.m.* authorized agent (with full powers to act).

plénitude [plenityd], *s.f.* plenitude, fullness (of time, faculties, power, etc.); completeness (of victory, success, etc.); **p. d'estomac,** repletion; *B:* **c'est de la p. du cœur que la bouche parle,** out of the abundance of the heart the mouth speaketh.

pléochroïque [pleɔkrɔik], *a. Cryst:* pleochroic.

pléochroïsme [pleɔkrɔism], *s.m. Cryst:* pleochroism.

pléomorphe [pleɔmɔrf], *a. Biol: Ch:* pleomorphic.

pléomorphisme [pleɔmɔrfism], *s.m. Biol: Ch:* pleomorphism.

pléonasme [pleɔnasm], *s.m.* pleonasm; **par p.,** pleonastically; (*of word*) **faire p. avec . . .,** to be pleonastic when used with . . ..

pléonaste [pleɔnast], *s.m. Miner:* pleonast, iron spinel.

pléonastique [pleɔnastik], *a.* pleonastic.

plérome [pleroːm], *s.m.* **1.** *A.Phil:* pleroma. **2.** *Bot:* plerome.

plésiosaure [plezjɔsɔːr], *s.m.* (*a*) *Paleont:* Plesiosaurus; (*b*) *F:* old fossil.

plessimètre [plɛsimɛtr̥], *s.m. Med:* pleximeter.

plessite [plɛsit], *s.f. Miner:* plessite.

plet [plɛ], *s.m. Nau:* fake, (single) turn (of coil of rope).

pléthodontidés [pletɔdɔ̃tide], *s.m.pl. Amph:* Plethodontidae.

pléthore [pletɔːr], *s.f.* (*a*) *Med:* plethora; (*b*) superabundance, plethora.

pléthorique [pletɔrik], *a.* (*a*) *Med:* full-blooded, plethoric; (*b*) superabundant; **année p.,** year of superabundance of crops; *Sch:* **classe p.,** overcrowded class.

pleur [plœːr], *s.m.* **1.** *Lit: Poet: usu. pl.* tear; **verser des pleurs,** to shed tears; **fondre en pleurs,** to dissolve into tears; **cessez vos pleurs,** dry your tears; **être tout en pleurs,** to be bathed in tears, to be all tears; **elle n'eut pas un p.,** she did not shed a single tear. **2.** bleeding (of vine, etc.).

pleuracanthe [plœrakɑ̃ːt], *s.m. Paleont:* Pleuracanthus.

pleurage [plœraːʒ], *s.m. Ac:* wow.

pleural, -aux [plœral, -o], *a. Anat:* pleural.

pleurant, -ante [plœrɑ̃, -ɑ̃ːt]. **1.** *a.* weeping, given to tears. **2.** *s. Art:* weeper, mourner.

pleurard, -arde [plœraːr, -ard]. **1.** *a.* whimpering, fractious (child); whining, tearful (voice); tearful, weepy (eyes); **voix pleurarde (d'un homme gris),** maudlin voice (of a drunken man). **2.** *s.* whimperer; *F:* blubberer, cry-baby.

pleure-misère [plœrmizɛːr], *s.m. & f.inv.* person who is always pleading poverty.

pleure-pain [plœrpɛ̃], *s.m.inv. A:* = PLEURE-MISÈRE.

pleurer [plœre]. **1.** *v.tr.* (*a*) to weep, mourn, for (s.o., sth.); to bewail; **p. (la mort de) qn,** to mourn (the death of) s.o.; **p. sa jeunesse perdue,** to mourn for one's lost youth; **p. ses péchés,** to mourn over one's sins; to bewail one's sins; **mourir sans être pleuré,** to die unmourned, unwept; **on ne l'a pleuré que d'un œil,** few tears were shed for him; (*b*) **p. toutes les larmes de ses yeux, de son corps,** to cry one's eyes out; **p. des larmes de sang,** to weep tears of blood; **p. misère,** to plead poverty. **2.** *v.i.* (*a*) to weep, to shed tears, to cry (**sur,** over; **pour,** for); **p. sur le sort de l'héroïne,** to weep over the heroine; **p. de joie,** to weep for joy; **p. de dépit,** to weep from vexation; **p. à chaudes larmes,** to cry bitterly, copiously; **elle pleurait à chaudes larmes,** she was in a passion of tears, she was sobbing her heart out; **se perdre les yeux, se brûler les yeux, à force de p.,** to cry one's eyes out; **p. bruyamment,** *F:* **p. comme un veau,** to blubber; (*of woman*) **p. comme une Madeleine,** to weep one's eyes out; **s'endormir en pleurant,** to cry oneself to sleep; **p. tout son content,** to have a good cry; to cry one's fill; **faire p. qn,** to make s.o. cry, to wring tears from s.o.; **une chanson triste à faire p.,** a song to bring tears to your eyes; **c'est à faire p.,** it's enough to make you cry; **c'est à faire p. de rire,** it's enough to make you weep with laughing; **c'est bête à p.,** it's lamentably stupid; *F:* **je veux ça ou je pleure,** give it (to) me or I'll scream; (*b*) (*of the eyes*) to water, to run; **roche, robinet, qui pleure,** dripping rock, dripping tap; (*c*) *Hort:* (*of vines, trees*) to bleed; (*d*) (*of river*) to start (and drip).

pleurerie [plœr(ə)ri], *s.f. F:* snivelling, whining.

pleurésie [plœrezi], *s.f. Med:* pleurisy; **p. sèche, p. avec épanchement,** dry, wet, pleurisy; **fausse p.** = PLEURODYNIE.

pleurétique [plœretik], *Med:* **1.** *a.* pleuritic (pain). **2.** *s.m. & f.* pleurisy patient.

pleureur, -euse[1] [plœrœːr, -øːz]. **1.** *s.* (*a*) one who weeps; whimperer; (*b*) mute; hired mourner; (*c*) *s.f.pl. Cost: A:* **pleureuses**, weepers. **2.** *a.* weeping, whimpering, tearful, lacrymose; *F:* **drame p.**, sloppy play; sobstuff; **roche pleureuse**, weeping rock; **saule p.**, weeping willow; *Z:* **(singe) p.**, weeper.

pleureux, -euse[2] [plœrø, -øːz], *a.* tearful; on the brink of tears.

pleurite [plœrit], *s.f. Med:* dry pleurisy.

pleurnichage [plœrniʃaːʒ], *s.m. Pej:* = PLEURNICHERIE.

pleurnichard, -arde [plœrniʃaːr, -ard], *s. F:* crybaby; sniveller.

pleurnichement [plœrniʃmɑ̃], *s.m. Pej:* = PLEURNICHERIE.

pleurnicher [plœrniʃe], *v.i.* to whimper, whine, snivel, grizzle.

pleurnicherie [plœrniʃri], *s.f. Pej:* whimpering, whining, snivelling, grizzling; **des pleurnicheries sans fin**, constant whining.

pleurnicheur, -euse [plœrniʃœːr, -øːz]. **1.** *s.* whiner, sniveller, whimperer, grizzler; crybaby. **2.** *a.* whimpering, snivelling, peevish, fractious (child, voice, etc.).

pleurocarpe [plœrɔkarp], *a. Bot:* pleurocarpous.

pleurodynie [plœrɔdini], *s.f. Med:* pleurodynia; neuralgia of the chest-wall.

pleuronecte [plœrɔnɛkt], *s.m. Ich:* pleuronect; *pl.* **pleuronectes**, Pleuronectidae.

pleuronectidés [plœrɔnɛktide], *s.m.pl. Ich:* Pleuronectidae.

pleuropéricardite [plœrɔperikardit], *s.f. Med:* pleuropericarditis.

pleuropneumonie [plœrɔpnømɔni], *s.f. Med:* pleuro-pneumonia.

pleuropneumonique [plœrɔpnømɔnik], *a. Med:* pleuro-pneumonic.

pleurotrèmes [plœrɔtrɛm], *s.m.pl. Ich:* Pleurotremata.

pleurote [plœrɔt], *s.m. Fung:* pleurotus.

pleurotomie [plœrɔtɔmi], *s.f. Surg:* pleurotomy.

pleutre [pløtr̥], *s.m. F: O:* (*a*) cad; contemptible fellow; (*b*) coward.

pleutrerie [pløtrəri], *s.f. O:* (*a*) caddish trick; piece of ill-breeding; (*b*) cowardice.

pleuvasser [plœvase], **pleuviner** [plœvine], *v. impers. F:* to drizzle.

pleuvoir [plœvwaːr], *v.* (*pr.p.* **pleuvant**; *p.p.* **plu**; *pr.ind.* **il pleut, ils pleuvent**; *p.d.* **il pleuvait**; *p.h.* **il plut**; *fu.* **il pleuvra**) to rain. **1.** *v.impers.* **il pleut à verse, à seaux, à torrents,** *F:* **des cordes,** *P:* **comme vache qui pisse,** *Lit:* **il pleut des hallebardes,** it's raining hard, fast; the rain's pouring down; it's pouring (with rain), it's raining in buckets, it's raining cats and dogs; **il pleut à petites gouttes,** it's drizzling; **que faites-vous les jours où il pleut?** what do you do on wet, rainy, days? **il pleuvait des coups,** blows fell thick and fast; **comme s'il en pleuvait,** in great quantities, in thousands. **2.** *occ. pers. F:* **faire p. des coups, des baisers, sur qn,** to rain, shower, blows, kisses, on s.o.; **l'argent pleut chez lui,** money is always coming in to him; **les invitations lui pleuvent de tous les côtés,** invitations are pouring in on him, are raining on him, from all sides.

pleuvoter [plœvɔte], *v.i. F:* to drizzle.

plèvre [plɛːvr̥], *s.f. Anat:* pleura.

plexiforme [plɛksifɔrm], *a.* plexiform.

Plexiglas [plɛksiglas], *s.m. R.t.m:* Plexiglass.

plexus [plɛksys], *s.m. Anat:* plexus; **p. solaire,** solar plexus; **p. cardiaque,** cardiac plexus; **p. hypogastrique,** plexus hypogastricus; **p. mésentérique,** mesenteric plexus; **p. cœliaque,** plexus coeliacus.

pleyon [plɛjɔ̃], *s.m.* **1.** *Arb:* shoot trained back. **2.** withe, osier tie.

pli[1] [pli], *s.m.* **1.** (*a*) pleat; fold; *Dressm:* **p. creux, rentré, double p.,** box pleat, inverted pleat; **p. inverti,** inverted pleat; **petit p.,** tuck; **jupe à plis d'accordéon,** accordion-pleated skirt; **plis couchés, plats,** flat pleats; **faire des plis à une robe,** to pleat a dress; **les plis d'un rideau,** the folds of a curtain; **faire un p. à une page,** to turn down a page; *Nau:* **p. d'un cordage,** coil, fake, of a rope; *Hairdr:* **mise en plis,** set; **faire une mise en plis à qn,** to set s.o.'s hair; (*b*) wrinkle, pucker (of cloth, of the forehead); curl (of the lip); *Geol:* fold; **p. de terrain,** undulation of the ground; *Geol:* **p. anticlinal, synclinal,** upfold, downfold; (*of garment*) **faire des plis,** to pucker, wrinkle; **robe qui ne fait pas un p.,** dress that fits like a glove, without a wrinkle; *F:* **tout cela ne fait pas un p.,** (i) that's fine, perfect; (ii) it's all plain sailing; *s.a.* REPLI; (*c*) crease; **faire un p. à qch.,** to crease sth.; **pantalon bien marqué d'un p.,** well-creased trousers; **faux p.,** (unintentional) crease; **tissu qui a pris des faux plis, des mauvais plis,** (badly) creased material; (*d*) (i) habit, custom; (ii) turn; **prendre le p.,** to get into the habit of; *F:* **les enfants prennent aisément de mauvais plis,** children easily acquire bad habits; **donner un bon p. à une affaire,** to give a favourable turn to a business. **2.** bend (of the arm, leg); **p. du jarret,** hollow of the knee. **3.** (*a*) cover, envelope (of letter); **sous p. séparé,** under separate cover; **nous vous envoyons sous ce p. . . .,** we send you herewith . . ., please find enclosed . . .; **sous p. secret,** in an envelope marked "secret"; (*b*) letter, note, message; *Navy:* **p. cacheté,** sealed orders; *Nau: etc:* **plis consulaires,** consular packages. **4.** *Cards:* **faire un p.,** to take a trick.

pli[2], *s.m. Tch:* ply (of laminated wood, tyre).

pliable [plijabl̥], *a.* foldable; pliable, flexible (wood, character); **canot p.,** folding boat; **esprit p.,** (i) mind easily swayed; (ii) docile mind.

pliage [pliaːʒ], *s.m.* folding, creasing (of linen, paper, etc.); bending (of metal, etc.); **p. accordéon, p. paravent,** fan folding; **papier en continu à p. paravent,** continuous fanfold paper.

pliant [plijɑ̃]. **1.** *a.* that bends or folds; (*a*) pliant, flexible; (*of character, etc.*) docile, tractable, accommodating; (*b*) folding (chair, bed, table, eye-glasses); collapsible (spring, opera glass); *Aut:* **capote pliante,** collapsible hood; **cartonnages pliants,** folding cardboard boxes; *Phot: etc:* **pied p.,** folding tripod. **2.** *s.m.* folding chair or stool; camp stool.

plicatif, -ive [plikatif, -iːv], *a. Bot:* plicate(d).

plicatile [plikatil], *a. Nat.Hist:* plicatile.

plie [pli], *s.f. Ich:* plaice.

plié [plije], *s.m. Danc:* plié.

pliement [plimɑ̃], *s.m.* folding; creasing.

plier [plije], *v.* (*p.d. & pr.sub.* **n. pliions, v. pliiez**) **1.** *v.tr.* (*a*) to fold, fold up (linen, fan, letter, etc.); to strike (tent); *Nau:* to furl (sail); *Bookb: etc:* **machine à p.,** folding machine; *s.a.* BAGAGE 1; (*b*) (= PLOYER) to bend (bough, cane, metal, etc.); **p. les reins,** to stoop; **p. le genou,** to bend the knee; **vieillard presque plié en deux,** old man nearly bent double; *Ind:* **machine à p.,** bending machine, bending press; (*c*) **p. la tête,** to bow the head; to submit; **p. qn à la discipline,** to bring s.o. under discipline; **p. un cheval,** to break a horse; *F:* **être plié au métier,** to be broken in; **p. qn à faire qch.,** to train s.o. to do sth.; (*d*) to adapt; **les Parisiennes savent p. la mode à leur avantage,** Parisian women know how to adapt fashion to suit themselves. **2.** *v.i.* (*a*) to bend; **roseau qui plie mais ne rompt pas,** reed that bends but does not break; **mieux vaut p. que rompre,** better bend than break; **poutre qui plie sous le poids,** beam that bends, gives, sags, under the weight; (*b*) to submit, yield; (*of troops in battle*) to give way; **p. sous les ordres de qn,** to bow, submit, to s.o.'s orders; **tout plie devant lui,** he carries all before him; (*c*) *Danc:* to bend the knees.

se plier, (*a*) to bend; (*b*) **se p. aux circonstances, à la discipline,** to yield, bow, submit, to circumstances; to conform to discipline; **se p. aux lois,** to obey the law; **se p. à l'étude,** to bend one's mind to study; (*c*) (*of parapet, etc.*) **se p. au terrain,** to adapt itself to the ground.

plieur, -euse [plijœːr, -øːz], *s.* **1.** folder (of cloth, paper, etc., *esp.* of newspapers). **2.** *s.f.* **plieuse,** folding machine; bending machine.

pli-faille [plifaːj], *s.m. Geol:* thrust fault; *pl. plis-failles.*

Pline [plin], *Pr.n.m. Lt.Lit:* Pliny; **P. l'Ancien, le Jeune,** Pliny the Elder, the Younger.

plinien, -ienne [plinjɛ̃, -jɛn], *a. Geol:* Plinian; **éruption plinienne,** Plinian eruption.

plinthe [plɛ̃ːt], *s.f.* **1.** *Arch:* plinth (of column). **2.** (*a*) skirting board, washboard (of room); plinth; (*b*) plinth (course) (of rubble wall).

pliocène [pliɔsɛn], *a. & s.m. Geol:* Pliocene.

pliodynatron [pliɔdinatrɔ̃], *s.m. Ph:* pliodynatron.

plioir [pliwaːr], *s.m.* **1.** *Bookb:* folder, bone blade (for folding paper); paper knife. **2.** winder (for fishing line).

plion [pliɔ̃], *s.m.* **1.** *Arb:* shoot trained back. **2.** withe, osier tie.

pliopithèque [pliɔpitɛk], *s.m. Paleont:* Pliopithecus.

plique [plik], *s.f. Med:* **p. polonaise,** plica (polonica); Polish plait.

plissage [plisaːʒ], *s.m.* pleating, kilting (of material, etc.); crinkling (of paper).

plissé [plise]. **1.** *a.* (*a*) pleated (dress, (shirt-)front); kilted (skirt); (*b*) **les lèvres plissées,** with puckered lips; **front p.,** wrinkled brow; (*c*) *Geol:* **chaîne plissée,** (range of) folded mountains. **2.** *s.m.* pleat(ing), pleats; tucks; kilting.

plissement [plismɑ̃], *s.m.* **1.** pleating (of material); corrugation (of sheet metal). **2.** crumpling (of material); puckering (of the skin); crinkling (of paper); *Geol:* fold.

plisser [plise]. **1.** *v.tr.* (*a*) to pleat, fold, kilt (skirt, etc.); (*b*) to crease, crumple; to crinkle (paper); to corrugate (metal, paper); **un sourire plissait sa figure, ses lèvres,** a smile wrinkled his face, puckered his lips; **p. les yeux,** to screw up one's eyes. **2.** *v.i. & pr.* (*a*) to have folds, creases, pleats; (*b*) to crease, crumple, pucker; **rideau qui (se) plisse parfaitement,** curtain that falls in perfect folds; **linge qui plisse mal,** linen that shows creases.

plisseur, -euse [plisœːr, -øːz]. **1.** *s.* pleater, folder. **2.** *s.f.* **plisseuse,** pleating machine.

plissure [plisyːr], *s.f.* **1.** (art of) pleating, kilting. **2.** pleats.

pliure [pliyːr], *s.f. Bookb:* **1.** folding (of printed sheets into sections). **2.** folding room, folding department.

ploc[1] [plɔk], *s.m.* **1.** hair (from cow, dog, etc.). **2.** waste wool. **3.** *Nau:* sheathing-felt, caulking-felt.

ploc[2], *int.* (*a*) splat! (*b*) splosh! plop!

plocéidés [plɔseide], *s.m.pl. Orn:* Ploceidae, the sparrows, the weavers.

ploërmelais, -aise [plɔɛrməlɛ, -ɛːz], *a. & s. Geog:* (native, inhabitant) of Ploërmel.

ploiement [plwamɑ̃], *s.m.* folding, bending (of material, paper, etc.); *Mil: A:* ployment; reducing of front from line to column; closing.

plomb [plɔ̃], *s.m.* **1.** lead; (*a*) *Miner: Ind:* **p. jaune,** wulfenite; **p. rouge,** crocoite; **p. carbonaté,** cerusite; **p. dur, aigre,** hard lead; **p. antimonié,** antimonial lead; **p. d'œuvre,** crude lead; **p. tétraéthyle,** tetraethyl lead (additive); **p. laminé, en feuilles,** sheet lead; **p. filé,** lead wire; **tuyau de p.,** lead pipe; **papier de p.,** lead-foil; **blanc de p.,** white lead; *s.a.* MINE[1] 2; *F:* **sommeil de p.,** heavy sleep; **ciel de p.,** leaden, grey, sky; **soleil de p.,** oppressively hot sun; **teint couleur de p.,** leaden complexion; **n'avoir pas de p. dans la tête,** to be harum-scarum; to lack ballast; *s.a.* COLIQUE 2, CUL 1; *Typ:* **lire sur le p.,** to read in the metal; **distribuer le p.,** to distribute the type; (*b*) *Arch:* **plombs,** lead work, leads (of window); **mise en p.,** leading. **2.** *Ven:* shot; **petit, menu, p.,** small shot, bird shot; **gros p.,** buck-shot, swan-shot; *s.a.* AILE 1. **3.** *pl.* (*a*) *A:* (housemaid's) sink; (*b*) lead roof; **les plombs,** the leads; *Hist:* **les Plombs,** the Piombi (at Venice); (*c*) = MITTE 1. **4.** (*a*) lead (weight); **p. de ligne de pêche,** sinker; *Nau:* **p. de sonde,** sounding lead, plummet; **jeter, lancer, le p. de sonde,** to heave the lead; *F:* **mets qui est un p. sur l'estomac,** dish that lies heavy on the stomach; **avoir un p. sur la langue,** to keep a secret; (*b*) **fil à p.,** plumb line; **p. d'un fil à p.,** (plumb-)bob; plummet; **à p.,** upright, vertically, sheer; perpendicular; **tomber à p. sur qch.,** to fall plumb on to sth.; **le soleil donne à p. sur nous,** the sun is beating straight down on our heads. **5.** *Com: Cust:* **p. (de garantie),** lead stamp, seal. **6.** *El:* **p. (fusible, de sûreté),** fuse, cut-out; **faire sauter les plombs,** to blow the fuses; **un p. a fondu,** a fuse has blown.

plombage [plɔ̃baːʒ], *s.m.* **1.** (*a*) leading, plumbing; *Cer:* lead glazing; (*b*) **p. des dents,** stopping, filling, of teeth; **perdre un p.,** to lose a filling. **2.** *Cust:* sealing (of packages). **3.** *Agr:* rolling, stamping down (of ground).

plombaginacées [plɔ̃baʒinase], *s.f.pl. Bot:* Plumbaginaceae.

plombagine [plɔ̃baʒin], *s.f. Miner:* black lead, graphite, plumbago.

plombate [plɔ̃bat], *s.m. Ch:* plumbate.

plombe [plɔ̃ːb], *s.f. P:* hour (struck); **voilà quatre plombes,** it's striking four; **ça fait une p. que je t'attends,** I've been waiting a whole solid hour for you.

plombé [plɔ̃be], *a.* **1.** (*a*) leaded; **vitres plombées,** leaded windows; **toit p.,** lead(-covered) roof; **ligne de pêche plombée,** shotted fishing line; *Cust: etc:* **caisse plombée,** sealed crate; **canne plombée,** loaded stick; (*b*) **j'ai la tête plombée,** my head feels like lead. **2.** leaden-hued; leaden, murky (sky); livid (complexion).

plombée [plɔ̃be], *s.f.* **1.** *Fish:* sinker, shot. **2.** *Const:* plumbing (of a wall, etc.).

plomber [plɔ̃be], *v.tr.* **1.** to lead; (*a*) to cover, sheathe, (sth.) with lead; (*b*) to weight (sth.) with lead; (*c*) *Cer:* to glaze (earthenware). **2.** to give a leaden, livid, hue to (complexion, sky). **3.** **p. une dent,** to stop, fill, a tooth. **4.** *Const:* **p. un mur,** to plumb a wall. **5.** *Cust:* to seal; to affix leads to (goods). **6.** *Agr:* to roll (the ground); to stamp down the ground round (newly planted tree, etc.). 7. *P:* (*a*) to shoot s.o.; (*b*) to infect (s.o.) with syphilis, to give (s.o.) the pox. 8. *v.i. P:* (*a*) (*of the hour*) to strike; (*b*) **p. du goulot**, to have a bad breath.

se plomber, (*of sky, complexion*) to take on a leaden hue.

plomberie [plɔ̃bri], *s.f.* 1. lead work; plumbing. 2. (*a*) lead works; (*b*) lead industry; (*c*) plumber's shop.

plombeur [plɔ̃bœːr], *s.m.* 1. *Cust:* affixer of seals (to bales, etc.) 2. *Agr:* (heavily weighted) roller.

plombeux [plɔ̃bø], *a.* plumbous; plumbeous.

plombier, -ière [plɔ̃bje, -jɛːr]. 1. *a.* connected with lead or lead working. 2. *s.m.* (*a*) worker in lead; (*b*) plumber.

plombières [plɔ̃bjɛːr], *s.f. Cu:* ice cream (with preserved fruits) (*from the name of the town*).

plombifère [plɔ̃bifɛːr], *a.* plumbiferous, lead-bearing; *Cer:* **glaçure p.**, lead glaze.

plombique [plɔ̃bik], *a.* plumbic.

plombite [plɔ̃bit], *s.m. Ch:* plumbite; *Petroleum Ind:* **solution du p.**, doctor solution.

plombure [plɔ̃byːr], *s.f.* leads, cames (of stained-glass window).

plonge [plɔ̃ːʒ], *s.f.* 1. washing up (in restaurant); **faire la p.**, to wash up. 2. bowl (of sink); **évier à deux plonges**, two-bowl sink, double sink (unit).

plongé [plɔ̃ʒe], *a. Bot:* submerged (plant).

plongeant [plɔ̃ʒɑ̃], *a.* 1. plunging; **tir p.**, plunging fire; **vue plongeante**, view from above, bird's eye view. 2. *Dressm:* falling freely, in straight lines; **décolleté p.**, plunging neckline.

plongée [plɔ̃ʒe], *s.f.* 1. (*a*) plunge, dive; **p. sous-marine autonome**, skin diving, free diving, scuba diving; (*b*) (*of submarine*) submergence, submersion; **effectuer sa p., se mettre en p.**, to dive, to submerge; **vitesse en p.**, speed submerged; **barres de p.**, hydroplanes; **p. raide**, crash dive. 2. dip, slope, incline (of ground); *Geol:* sudden dip (in ocean bed). 3. (*a*) *Arch:* declivity, slope (of roof); (*b*) *Mil:* superior slope (of parapet). 4. *Cin: T.V:* high angle shot; bird's eye view.

plongement [plɔ̃ʒmɑ̃], *s.m.* 1. plunging (of sth. into liquid); bobbing under (of angler's float); immersion (in study, etc.). 2. dip, dipping (of ground). 3. pitching (of ship).

plongeoir [plɔ̃ʒwaːr], *s.m.* (*a*) diving board, diving stage; (*b*) diving tower.

plongeon [plɔ̃ʒɔ̃], *s.m.* 1. *Orn:* diver; **p. arctique, lumme, à gorge noire**, black-throated diver, *U.S:* black-throated, Pacific, loon; **p. imbrin, glacial**, great northern diver, *U.S:* common loon; **p. catmarin, p. à gorge rousse**, red-throated diver, *U.S:* red-throated loon; **p. à bec blanc**, white-billed diver, *U.S:* yellow-billed loon. 2. *Swim:* plunge, dive; **p. à la hussarde**, pike dive; **p. de haut vol**, high dive; **p. en canard**, surface dive, duck dive; **faire le p.**, (i) to dive; (ii) to duck (one's head); (iii) *F:* to make up one's mind, to take the plunge; (iv) *F:* to give a low bow, to bow deeply.

plonger [plɔ̃ʒe], *v.* (**je plongeai(s); n. plongeons**) 1. *v.i.* to plunge; (*a*) to dive, to take a header; **appareil à p.**, diving apparatus; **l'œil plonge dans l'abîme**, one looks down sheer into the abyss; *F:* **p. dans sa poche pour y prendre de la monnaie**, to dive into one's pocket for change (*b*) to become immersed; (*of submarine*) to submerge; **p. raide**, to crash-dive; (*of angler's float*) to bob under; (*c*) **les murs plongent dans le fossé**, the walls plunge steeply into the moat; (*d*) *Nau:* (*of ship*) **p. dans le creux de la lame**, to s(c)end; **p. du nez**, to pitch; to bury her nose in the sea; (*e*) (*of coal-seam, etc.*) to dip; **la route plonge brusquement**, the road dips suddenly. 2. *v.tr.* to plunge, immerse (s.o., sth., in liquid); to quench (steel, etc.); to dip (candles); **p. qn dans la douleur, dans la misère**, to plunge s.o. into grief, into poverty; **p. la main dans sa poche**, to thrust one's hand, *F:* to dive, into one's pocket; **p. le regard dans l'abîme**, to peer into the depths; **p. un poignard dans le cœur de qn**, to drive, plunge, thrust, a dagger into s.o.'s heart; **p. qn dans un cachot**, to thrust s.o. into a dungeon.

se plonger, (*a*) to immerse oneself (**dans**, in); (*b*) **se p. dans l'étude, dans le plaisir**, to give oneself up completely to study, to pleasure; **se p. dans le sang**, to wallow in blood; **plongé dans ses pensées**, immersed, lost, in thought; **plongé dans la méditation**, deep in meditation; **plongé dans le sommeil**, deep in sleep, fast asleep; **nous étions plongés dans nos préparatifs, dans nos livres**, we were immersed in our preparations, in our books; **il était plongé dans la lecture du journal**, he was deep in his newspaper; **plongé dans le vice**, steeped in vice.

plongeur, -euse [plɔ̃ʒœːr, -øːz]. 1. *a.* (*a*) diving (bird, etc.); (*b*) **piston p.**, plunger piston; **clapet, pompe, à piston p.**, plunger valve, pump. 2. *s.m.* (*a*) diver; **p. de haut vol**, high diver; **agents plongeurs**, riverside police; (*b*) (professional) diver; **cloche à plongeurs**, diving-bell; (*c*) **p. sous-marin autonome**, skin diver. 3. *s.m.* (*a*) *Paperm: etc:* dipper, vatman; (*b*) washer-up, bottle washer (in restaurant). 4. *s.m. Orn:* diver, diving bird. 5. *s.m.* (*a*) plunger (of pump or press); **p. de tête de bielle**, connecting-rod dipper; **p. de transfert**, transfer plunger; (*b*) plunger (of explosive mine); (*c*) *Typewr:* **p. d'interligne**, line-feed sprocket; (*d*) *Elcs:* transverse plate (of wave guide).

ploque [plɔk], *s.f.* = PLOC[1].

ploquer [plɔke], *v.tr. Nau: A:* **p. le bordage d'un navire**, to felt, caulk, the planks of a ship.

se ploquer, (*of woollen mattress*) to become lumpy.

plosive [ploziːv], *s.f. Ling:* plosive (consonant); stopped consonant; stop.

plot [plo], *s.m.* 1. (*a*) *For:* log sawn up in planks; (*b*) *Hatm:* form; (*c*) *Aut:* **mettre une voiture sur plots**, to lay up a car. 2. (*a*) *El:* (contact) stud; **p. mobile**, plug; **p. noyé**, sunk stud; **p. de distribution**, distribution, distributor, segment; **culot à p. central**, single-contact base (of electric bulb); **lampe à un p.**, single-contact bulb; **culot à deux plots**, double-contact base; *Aut:* **p. de démarrage**, foot-starter stud; *A:* **système à plots**, surface-contact system (of tram); (*b*) *I.C.E:* **distributeur (d'allumage) à huit plots**, eight-point distributor; (*c*) *Mec.E:* **p. d'arrêt**, stop pin; (*d*) (*computers*) hub, socket. 3. (*a*) *Adm: Aut:* cat's eye (marking road); (*b*) *Av:* **p. lumineux d'atterrissage**, flush marker light; (*c*) *Sp:* **p. de départ**, starting point.

Plotin [plɔtɛ̃], *Pr.n.m.* Plotinus.

plou [plu], *s.m. Dial:* (*in place names of Brittany*) village; tribe.

plouc(k) [pluk], *s.m. P:* idiot, nit.

plouf [pluf], *int.* & *s.m.* (*onomat.*) plop! splosh!

ploutocrate [plutɔkrat], *s.m.* plutocrat.

ploutocratie [plutɔkrasi], *s.f.* plutocracy.

ploutocratique [plutɔkratik], *a.* plutocratic.

ployable [plwajabl], *a.* pliable, flexible.

ployage [plwajaːʒ], *s.m.* 1. bending (of branch, metal, etc.); *Mec.E:* **essai de p.**, bending test. 2. bend.

ployer [plwaje], *v.* (**je ploie, n. ployons; je ploierai**) 1. *v.tr.* (*a*) to bend (branch, tree, metal, the knee); (*b*) *A: Mil:* to ploy (troops). 2. *v.i.* to bow (under yoke, burden); **p. devant l'ennemi**, to give way before the enemy; (*cf.* PLIER) **mes genoux ployèrent sous moi**, my knees gave way under me; **le poids des fleurs fait p. la tige**, the weight of the flowers bends down the stem.

pluche[1] [plyʃ], *s.f. A:* = PELUCHE.

pluche[2], *s.f. F: Mil:* peeling, paring (of potatoes); **les pluches**, cook-house fatigue.

pluie [plɥi], *s.f.* rain; (*a*) **p. violente, battante, diluvienne, torrentielle**, pouring rain, pelting rain, downpour; **p. d'orage**, thunder rain, shower; **p. fine**, drizzle; **p. pénétrante**, soaking rain; **goutte de p.**, raindrop; **nuages chargés de p.**, rain-laden clouds; **le temps est à la p.**, it looks like rain; **le temps se met à la p.**, it is turning wet; **temps de p.**, rainy, wet, weather; **p. persistante**, settled rain; **la saison des pluies**, the rainy season; (*in tropics*) the rains; **les pluies ont commencé**, the rainy season has set in; *Meteor:* **quantité de p. annuelle**, annual rainfall, annual precipitation; **hauteur moyenne des chutes de pluie**, average rainfall; **par un jour de p.**, on a wet day; on a rainy day; **jour sans p.**, rainless day; **ne sortez pas sous la p.**, don't go out in the wet; **être sous la p.**, to be in the rain; **"craint la p."**, "to be kept dry"; **parler de la p. et du beau temps**, to talk about the weather, of nothing in particular, of one thing and another; *F:* **il n'était pas tombé de la dernière p.**, there were no flies on him; *Prov:* **après la p. le beau temps**, every cloud has a silver lining; *s.a.* ABATTRE 5; *F:* **faire la p. et le beau temps**, to be the boss; to rule the roost; **il fait la p. et le beau temps chez lui**, when father says turn we all turn; **c'est lui qui fait la p. et le beau temps ici**, he's the big noise around here; (*b*) *Cin:* (*streaks appearing on screen during the showing of a damaged film*) rain; (*c*) **p. d'or**, (i) shower of gold; (ii) *Pyr:* golden rain; **douche en p.**, shower (bath); *B:* **il tomba du ciel une p. de feu**, it rained fire from heaven; **p. de balles**, hail of bullets; **p. de sable**, sandstorm.

plum [plym], *s.m. P:* bed, pit.

plumage [plymaːʒ], *s.m.* plumage, feathers (of bird); **oiseaux à beau p.**, birds of plumage; **p. d'été, d'hiver**, summer, winter, plumage.

plumail, -aux [plymaːj, -o], *s.m.* 1. feather duster, feather brush. 2. *A:* = PLUMET 1 (*a*).

plumaison [plymɛzɔ̃], *s.f.* (*a*) plucking (of fowl); (*b*) *F:* fleecing (of pers.).

plumard [plymaːr], *s.m.* 1. feather duster, feather brush. 2. *P:* bed.

plumarder (se) [s(ə)plymarde], *v.pr. P:* to go to bed, to get into bed, to kip down, to hit the hay.

plumasseau, -eaux [plymaso], *s.m.* 1. feather duster, feather brush. 2. *Vet: Surg:* pledget.

plumasserie [plymasri], *s.f.* feather trade.

plumassier, -ière [plymasje, -jɛːr], *s.* feather dresser, feather dealer, plumassier.

plumbaginacées [plœ̃baʒinase], *s.f.pl. Bot:* Plumbaginaceae.

plumboferrite [plœ̃bɔfɛrit], *s.f. Miner:* plumboferrite.

plumbojarosite [plœ̃bɔʒarɔzit], *s.f. Miner:* plumbojarosite.

plum-cake [plœmkɛk], *s.m.* plum cake; *pl. plum-cakes.*

plume[1] [plym], *s.f.* 1. (*a*) feather; **p. de paon**, peacock's feather; **oiseau sans plumes**, callow, unfledged, bird; **gibier à plumes**, game birds; **porter une p. à son chapeau**, to wear a feather in one's hat; *A:* **arracher, tirer, une p. de l'aile à qn**, to cheat s.o.; to pluck s.o.; *F:* **il y a laissé, il a perdu, des plumes**, he was the loser by it; he didn't get off scot free; *F:* **craindre pour ses plumes, avoir chaud aux plumes**, to go in fear of one's life; *F:* **ils allaient me voler dans les plumes**, they were going to attack me, pounce on me, grab me; *A:* **jeter la p. au vent**, to take a decision by spinning a coin; to toss up; *Lit:* **passer une, la, p. par le bec à qn**, to frustrate s.o.'s hopes; to thwart s.o.; **léger comme une p.**, as light as a feather; *Prov:* **la belle p. fait le bel oiseau, c'est la p. qui fait l'oiseau**, fine feathers make fine birds; *s.a.* PAON; (*b*) **lit (oreiller, etc.) de plumes, de plume**, feather bed (pillow, etc.); **se mettre, s'ensevelir, dans la p.**, to get, snuggle, into bed; (*c*) *Fish:* quill. 2. (*a*) **p. (d'oie)**, quill (pen); (*b*) (pen) nib; **stylo à p. ou stylo à bille?** fountain pen or ball point? **p. à dessin**, drawing pen; **dessin à la p.**, pen (-and-ink) drawing; **p. tubulaire (pour dessin)**, barrel pen, crow quill; *Tchn:* **enregistreur à p.**, pen recorder; **trait de p.**, stroke of the pen; **guerre de p.**, paper war; **prendre la p. (en main), mettre la main à la p.**, to put pen to paper; **avoir la p. facile**, to be a ready, an easy, writer; **sous la p. de**, under the signature of; **écrire au courant de la p.**, to write as the spirit takes one; **mots restés au bout de la p.**, words that have been left out; **vivre de sa p.**, to make one's living by writing, to live by one's pen, to be a professional writer. 3. (*a*) *Coel:* **p. marine, p. de mer**, sea pen; (*b*) *Moll:* pen (of squid).

plume[2], *s.m. P:* bed, pit.

plumeau, -eaux [plymo], *s.m.* 1. feather duster, whisk; *F:* **un vieux p.**, an old stick-in-the-mud; a back number. 2. *Fish:* large fly. 3. eiderdown (quilt). 4. *Bot:* water violet.

plume-de-paon [plymdəpɑ̃], *s.f. Algae: F:* sea lettuce; *pl. plumes-de-paon.*

plumée[1] [plyme], *s.f. A:* penful, dip (of ink).

plumée[2], *s.f. Stonew:* draft.

plumée[3], *s.f.* (*a*) plucking (of poultry); (*b*) *F:* fleecing (of s.o.); (*c*) *P:* thrashing.

plumer [plyme]. 1. *v.tr.* to pluck (poultry); *F:* to fleece (s.o.); *Dom.Ec:* to scrape (asparagus); *s.a.* PIGEON 2. 2. *v.i. Row:* to feather.

se plumer, *P:* to go to bed, *P:* to kip down.

plumet [plymɛ], *s.m.* 1. (*a*) plume (of helmet, etc.); *P:* **avoir son p.**, to be drunk, tight; (*b*) ostrich feather (as head ornament). 2. *Nau:* **p. de pilote**, dog-vane.

plumeté [plymte], *Her:* (*of field*) plumetty.

plumetis [plymti], *s.m. Needlew:* 1. (raised) satin-stitch. 2. dotted Swiss (muslin).

plumeur, -euse[1] [plymœːr, -øːz], *s.* (poultry) plucker.

plumeux, -euse[2] [plymø, -øːz], *a.* feathery, plumose.

plumier [plymje], *s.m.* (*a*) pen-tray; (*b*) pen-box, pencil-box or -case.

plumiste [plymist], *s.m.* artist in feathers.

plumitif [plymitif], *s.m.* 1. *Jur:* minute-book (of clerk of court). 2. *F: A:* quill-driver, pen-pusher.

plumosite [plymɔzit], *s.f. Miner:* plumosite, fibrous jamesonite.

plum-pudding [plœmpudiŋ], *s.m.* plum pudding, Christmas pudding; *pl. plum-puddings.*

plumulaire [plymylɛːr], *s.f. Coel:* Plumularia.

plumularidés [plymylaride], *s.m.pl. Coel:* Plumulariidae.

plumule [plymyl], *s.f. Nat.Hist:* plumule.

plupart (la) [laplypaːr], *s.f.* the most, the greatest part, the greater part, number; (*with pl. concord*) **la p. des hommes croient . . .**, most men, the majority of men, believe . . .; **la p. des citoyens,** the main body, the bulk, the majority, of the citizens; **la p. furent d'avis que . . .**, the majority considered that . . .; **la p. d'entre eux,** most of them; (*with sing. concord*) **la p. du monde ignore ses intérêts,** most people do not know where their interest lies; **la p. du temps,** (i) most of the time; (ii) in most cases, generally; **pour la p.,** for the most part, mostly.

plural, -aux [plyral, -o], *a.* plural (vote, etc.).

pluraliser [plyralize], *v.tr.* to pluralize; to put into the plural.

pluralisme [plyralism], *s.m. Phil: etc:* pluralism.

pluraliste [plyralist], *a. & s. Phil: etc:* pluralist.

pluralité [plyralite], *s.f.* (*a*) plurality, multiplicity; **p. des bénéfices,** plurality of benefices, pluralism; (*b*) majority; **élu à la p. des voix,** elected by a majority; (*c*) *Gram:* **signe de la p.,** sign of the plural.

pluri- [plyri], *pref.* pluri-.

pluriatomique [plyriatɔmik], *a.* polyatomic.

pluricellulaire [plyriselylɛːr], *a. Biol:* pluricellular.

pluridenté [plyridɑ̃te], *a.* pluridentate.

pluridisciplinaire [plyridisiplinɛːr], *a.* multidisciplinary; **recherche p.,** multi-field research.

pluriel, -elle [plyrjɛl], *a. & s.m. Gram:* plural; **au p.,** in the plural.

pluriflore [plyriflɔːr], *a. Bot:* multiflorous, many-flowered.

plurilatéral, -aux [plyrilateral, -o], *a. Pol: etc:* **accord p.,** multilateral agreement.

pluriloculaire [plyrilɔkylɛːr], *a. Bot:* plurilocular, multilocular.

plurispécifique [plyrispesifik], *a. Nat.Hist:* of mixed species; of several, many, species.

plurivalence [plyrivalɑ̃ːs], *s.f. Ch:* plurivalence, polyvalence.

plurivalent [plyrivalɑ̃], *a.* plurivalent.

plus [ply] (*often pronounced* [plys] *when at the end of the word group; the liaison of s should be made in front of a vowel;* **plus on est de fous, plus on rit** [plyzɔ̃nɛdfuplyzɔ̃ri]) **1.** *adv.* (*a*) more; **ils sont beaucoup p. nombreux,** they are far more numerous; **il est p. grand que moi,** he is taller than I; **je ne suis pas p. grand que lui,** I am no taller than he (is); **elle est p. attentive que vous,** she is more attentive than you; **elle écoute p. attentivement,** she listens more attentively; **une fenêtre p. haute que large,** a window higher than it is wide, higher than its width; **elle était p. femme que sa sœur,** she was more of a woman than her sister; **il a p. de patience que moi,** he has more patience than I; **il me faut une maison deux fois p. grande que celle-ci,** I want a house twice as large as this; **je gagne p. que vous,** I earn more than you; **il n'en est pas p. avancé (pour cela),** he is none the wiser (for it); **p. qu'à moitié** (*often* [plyskamwatje]), *A:* **p. d'à moitié** [plydamwatje], more than half (done, etc.); **p. d'une fois,** more than once; **pendant p. d'une heure,** for over an hour; **p. d'un auteur y a fait allusion,** more than one writer has alluded to it; **bâtiment qui ne marche pas à p. de quinze nœuds,** ship that does not exceed fifteen knots; **la maladie pas p. que les obstacles, non p. que les obstacles, ne put le vaincre,** neither disease nor difficulties could vanquish him; **p. de dix hommes,** more than, over, ten men; **il a p. de vingt ans,** he is over twenty; **p. loin,** farther on; **p. tôt,** sooner; **pour ne pas dire p.** (*often* [plys]), to say the least; **p. . . . (et) p. . . .,** the more . . ., the more . . .; **p. je lis de livres, p. j'apprends,** the more books I read the more I learn; **p. on est de fous p. on rit,** the more the merrier; **p. je lis, moins je retiens,** the more I read the less I remember; *Prov:* **p. on se presse, moins on arrive; p. on se dépêche moins on réussit,** more haste less speed; **qui p. qui moins,** some (do it, have, etc.) more, some less; *P:* **tant p. ses arguments sont mauvais, tant p. il y croit,** the worse his arguments are the more he believes in them; *P:* **tant p. (qu')il boit, tant p. il a soif,** the more he drinks the thirstier he gets; **et qui p. est,** and what is more, moreover; **25° à l'ombre et qui p. est, en septembre, 25°** in the shade, and what's more in September, and in September, too; **p. célèbre est le roman qu'il s'agit de porter à l'écran, p. l'adaptation s'en avère difficile,** the more famous the novel to be filmed, the greater the difficulties of adaptation; **j'en ai trois fois p. qu'il ne m'en faut,** I have three times as much as I want; **il ne m'aide pas; bien p., il m'empêche de travailler,** he's no help to me; what's more, he stops me from working; **il y en a tant et p.,** there is any amount of it; **il n'en fait que p. de mal,** he does (all) the more harm; *s.a.* AUTANT 4; (*b*) (**le**) **p.,** most; **la p. longue rue, la rue la p. longue, de la ville,** the longest street in the town; **la p. belle dame,** the most beautiful lady; **c'est vous qui avez fait le p. de fautes,** you have made (the) most mistakes; **c'est à trente ans qu'elle a été le p. belle,** she was at her best at thirty; *s.a.* LE[1] 2 (*b*); **une ascension des p. hasardeuses,** a most perilous ascent; **ce que je désire le p.,** what I most desire; **mon p. ancien ami,** my oldest friend; **c'est tout ce qu'il y a de p. simple,** nothing is simpler; nothing could be simpler; **c'est on ne peut p. embêtant,** it is most annoying; (*c*) **ne . . . p.** (*with negative expressed or understood*), no more, no longer, not again; **je ne veux p. de cela,** I want no more of that; I don't want any more of that; **je ne la verrai p.,** I shall never see her again; **il ne voit p. personne,** he has ceased to see anybody; **il n'est p.,** he is no more; he is dead; he has passed away; **cela n'existe p.,** that is a thing of the past; **on n'en trouve p. (maintenant)** it is not, they are not, to be found today; **je ne suis p. d'âge à danser,** I'm past dancing; **il n'est p. temps de fuir,** it is too late to flee; **je n'ai p. d'argent,** I have no money left; **je n'ai p. soif, merci,** I've had enough, thank you; *F:* **boire jusqu'à p. soif,** to drink one's fill; **deux femmes p. très jeunes,** two women no longer very young; **sans p. attendre,** without waiting any longer; **p. de doute,** there is no more doubt about it; **p. d'espoir,** good-bye to hope; **p. de potage, merci,** no more soup, thank you; **p. rien,** nothing more; **y allez-vous quelquefois?—p. maintenant,** do you go there?—not any more, not now; **p. que dix minutes!** only ten minutes left! *s.a.* QUE[3] 9; (*d*) *adv.phr.* **non p.,** (not) either; **je n'en ai pas non p.,** I have not any either; **je n'avais pas non p. oublié le vin,** I had not forgotten the wine either; nor had I forgotten the wine; **ni moi non p.,** neither do I, neither did I, neither shall I, neither can I, etc.; **il n'en a pas, ni moi non p.,** he hasn't any, nor have I, neither have I; **jamais non p. je n'avais songé à . . .,** nor had I ever thought of . . .; **il ne semble pas non p. que . . .,** nor does it seem that . . .; **ils étaient sortis sans non p. y penser,** they had gone out without thinking of it either; **vous n'en avez guère non p.,** you haven't much either; **non p. que son frère elle ne vous ressemble,** she is no more like you than her brother is; (*e*) [plys] plus, also, besides, in addition; **sept p. neuf p. un** [sɛtplysnœfplysœ̃], seven plus nine plus one; **deux étages p. un grenier,** two floors plus an attic; **il fait p. 20 (degrés),** it's 20°; **cent francs d'amende, p. les frais,** a hundred francs fine and costs; *Golf:* **p. quatre** [plyskatr̥], plus four; (*f*) *adv.phr.* **de p.,** more; **que puis-je dire de p.?** what more, what else, can I say? **une journée de p.,** one day more; **il a trois ans de p. que moi,** he is three years my senior; **de p. . . .,** moreover . . ., by the same token . . .; **rien de p., merci,** nothing more, nothing else, thank you; **de p. en p.,** more and more; **on craignait de p. en p. que . . .,** there was a growing fear that . . .; **de p. en p. disposé à . . .,** increasingly disposed to . . .; **de p. en p. froid,** colder and colder; **en p.,** in addition; (i) into the bargain; (ii) extra; **son père nous acheta une maison, et un mobilier de salon en p.,** her father bought us a house, and a drawing-room suite besides, into the bargain; **le vin est en p.,** wine is extra; *F:* **il y en a trois en p. de lui,** there are three others besides him; **en p. de ce qu'il me doit,** over and above what he owes me; **p. ou moins** [plyzumwɛ̃], more or less; **ni p. ni moins,** neither more or less; **ce n'est ni p. ni moins qu'un scandale,** it's an absolute scandal. **2.** *s.m.* (*a*) more; **qui peut le p. peut le moins,** he who can do more can do less; **sans p.,** (just that and) nothing more; **je vous donnerai dix francs sans p.,** I will give you not a penny more than ten francs; **sans p. il les mit à la porte,** without more ado he turned them out; (*b*) most; **faites le p. que vous pourrez,** do the most you can; **au p., tout au p.,** at (the very) most, at the utmost, at the best; **dans une semaine au p.,** within a week (at most); **c'est tout au p. s'il est midi,** it is twelve o'clock at the latest, at the outside; **c'est tout au p. s'il put rentrer,** it was all he could do to get home; **c'est tout au p. si nous pourrons arriver demain,** at best we cannot arrive before tomorrow; (*c*) *Mth:* plus (sign); (*d*) *Golf:* **le p.** [ləplys], the odd.

plusie [plyzi], *s.f. Ent:* gamma moth, plusia.

plusieurs [plyzjœːr], *a. & pron. pl.* several; **p. personnes l'ont remarqué,** a number of persons noticed it; **de p. manières,** in more ways than one; **j'en ai p.,** I have several, I have quite a number; **perceuse à p. broches,** multiple-spindle drilling machine; **un ou p.,** one or more; *Prov:* **à p. la besogne va vite, à p. mains l'ouvrage avance,** many hands make light work.

plus-payé [plypeje], *s.m.* over-payment; *pl. plus-payés.*

plus-pétition [plyspetisjɔ̃], *s.f. Jur:* plus petitio, pluris petitio, demand for more than is due; *pl. plus-pétitions.*

plus-que-parfait [plyskəparfɛ], *s.m. Gram:* pluperfect (tense); *pl. plus-que-parfaits.*

plus-value [plyvaly], *s.f.* **1.** (*a*) *Pol.Ec: etc:* increase in value, increment value, appreciation, unearned increment (of land, etc.); surplus, excess yield (of tax, etc.); **les recettes présentent une p.-v. de . . .,** the receipts show an increase of . . .; *Fin:* **actions qui ont enregistré une p.-v.,** shares that show (an) appreciation; (*b*) *Fin:* appreciated surplus, betterment, appreciation (of shares); **impôt sur les plus-values,** betterment tax. **2.** extra payment (in addition to sum as per contract); *pl. plus-values.*

Plutarque [plytark], *Pr.n.m. Gr.Lit:* Plutarch.

plutéus [plyteys], *s.m. Echin:* pluteus (of sea urchin).

Pluton [plytɔ̃], *Pr.n.m. Myth:* Pluto.

plutonien, -ienne [plytɔnjɛ̃, -jɛn], **plutonique** [plytɔnik], *a.* (*a*) *Myth:* Plutonian, Plutonic; (*b*) *Geol:* plutonian, plutonic.

plutonigène [plytɔniʒɛn], *a. Atom.Ph:* **réacteur p.,** plutonium reactor.

plutonisme [plytɔnism], *s.m. Geol:* plutonism.

plutoniste [plytɔnist], *s.m.* plutonist.

plutonium [plytɔnjɔm], *s.m. Ch:* plutonium.

plutôt [plyto], *adv.* (*a*) rather, sooner; **p. la mort que l'esclavage,** sooner death than slavery; **p. mourir!** I would rather die! **p. souffrir que mentir,** it is better to suffer than to lie; I had rather suffer than tell a lie; **il récite p. qu'il ne chante,** he recites rather than sings; **demande p. à ta mère,** (you'd) better ask your mother; **vous me tuerez p. que j'y consente,** you can kill me before I consent; **ne pleurez pas, riez p.,** don't cry, laugh instead; **j'ai tort, dites-vous; écoutez p.,** you say I'm wrong, but listen; **pouvez-vous venir à six heures?—p. la demie,** can you come at six?—make it half-past; (*b*) rather, on the whole; **les prix sont p. soutenus,** prices are steady on the whole; **il faisait p. froid (que chaud),** the weather was cold if anything; **les pommes sont p. petites cette année,** apples run rather small, somewhat small, this year; apples are on the small side this year; **discours p. long,** speech on the long side.

pluvial[1], -iaux [plyvjal, -jo]. **1.** *a.* pluvial; (*a*) of rain; **eau pluviale,** rain-water; (*b*) rainy (season, etc.). **2.** *s.m. Geog:* pluvial.

pluvial[2], -iaux, *s.m. Ecc:* cope, *A:* pluvial.

pluvian [plyvjɑ̃], *s.m. Orn:* crocodile-bird.

pluvier [plyvje], *s.m. Orn:* plover; **p. doré,** golden plover; **p. à collier,** ringed plover, sand-lark; **p. doré américain,** American golden plover; **p. doré asiatique,** Asiatic golden plover; **p. asiatique,** Caspian plover; **p. sociable,** sociable plover; **p. à queue blanche,** white-tailed plover; **p. guignard,** dotterel; **p. argenté, varié,** grey plover, *U.S:* black-bellied plover.

pluvieux, -ieuse [plyvjø, -jøːz], *a.* rainy (season); wet (weather); pluvious.

pluviner [plyvine], *v.i. F:* to drizzle.

pluviographe [plyvjɔgraf], *s.m. Meteor:* recording rain-gauge; self-registering rain-gauge.

pluviomètre [plyvjɔmɛtr̥], *s.m. Meteor:* rain-gauge, pluviometer, udometer.

pluviométrie [plyvjɔmetri], *s.f.* pluviometry.

pluviométrique [plyvjɔmetrik], *a.* pluviometric, udometric; **hauteur p.,** rainfall.

pluviométrographe [plyvjɔmetrɔgraf], *s.m.* = PLUVIOGRAPHE.

pluvioscope [plyvjɔskɔp], *s.m.* pluvioscope.

pluviôse [plyvjoːz], *s.m. Fr.Hist:* fifth month of the Fr. Republican calendar (Jan.-Feb.).

pluviosité [plyvjozite], *s.f. Meteor:* rainfall, precipitation (of a region).

pnéodynamique [pneɔdinamik], *s.f. Physiol:* pneodynamics.

pnéomètre [pneɔmɛtr̥], *s.m. Med: etc:* pneometer, spirometer.

pneu [pnø], *s.m.* **1.** (pneumatic) tyre, *U.S:* tire; **p. agraire, agricole,** agricultural, land, tyre; **p. avion,** aircraft tyre; **p. (à) basse, (à) haute, pression,** low, high, pressure tyre; **p. neige,** snow tyre; **p. antidérapant,** non-skid tyre; **p. camionnette,** light giant tyre, *U.S:* light truck tire; **p. ballon,** balloon tyre; **p. à carcasse**

métallique, metallic-cord tyre; **p. à carcasse textile,** textile-cord tyre; **p. à carcasse radiale,** radial-ply tyre; **p. à carcasse croisée,** cross-ply tyre; **p. course,** racing tyre; **p. cru,** green, uncured, tyre; **p. cuirassé,** armoured tyre; **p. à flanc blanc,** white-wall tyre; **p. forestier,** forestry tyre; **p. génie civil,** earth-mover tyre; **pneus jumelés,** twin, dual(-mounted), tyres; **p. lisse,** smooth(-tread) tyre; **p. moto,** motor-cycle tyre; **p. poids lourd,** giant tyre, *U.S:* truck tire; **p. de rechange, de secours,** spare tyre; **p. rechapé,** retreaded tyre; retread; **p. sans chambre, tubeless,** tubeless tyre; **p. à talons,** beaded(-edge), clincher, tyre; **p. tourisme,** car tyre, *U.S:* auto tire; **p. vélo,** (bi)cycle tyre; **p. à clous,** studded tyre; **p. à cordes, p. câblé,** corded tyre; *A:* **p. à tringles,** wired tyre, straight-side tyre; **vieillissement du p., des pneus,** tyre creep. **2.** = PNEUMATIQUE 2 (*b*); *pl. pneus.*

pneuma [pnøma], *s.m. Gr.Phil:* pneuma.

pneumarthrose [pnømartro:z], *s.f. Med:* pneumarthrosis.

pneumaticité [pnømatisite], *s.f. Orn:* pneumaticity.

pneumaticohydraulique [pnømatikɔidrɔlik], *a.* pneumaticohydraulic.

pneumatique [pnømatik]. **1.** *a.* pneumatic; air-; **machine p.,** air-pump; **machine p. à deux corps,** double-barrelled air-pump; **outil p.,** compressed-air tool, pneumatic tool; **canot p.,** rubber dinghy; **matelas p.,** air bed, mattress. **2.** *s.m.* (*a*) pneumatic tyre; (*b*) (*in Paris*) express letter (transmitted by pneumatic tube). **3.** *s.f.* pneumatics.

pneumatocèle [pnømatɔsɛl], *s.m. Med:* pneumatocele.

pneumatologie [pnømatɔlɔʒi], *s.f.* pneumatology.

pneumatolyse [pnømatɔli:z], *s.f. Geol:* pneumatolysis.

pneumatolytique [pnømatɔlitik], *a. Geol:* pneumatolytic.

pneumatomètre [pnømatɔmɛtr̥], *s.m. Physiol:* pneumatometer, spirometer.

pneumatométrie [pnømatɔmetri], *s.f.* pneumatometry.

pneumatophore [pnømatɔfɔ:r]. **1.** *a.* pneumatophorous. **2.** *s.m.* (*a*) *Bot:* pneumatophore; (*b*) *Z:* pneumatophore, pneumatocyst.

pneumatose [pnømato:z], *s.f. Med:* pneumatosis.

pneumaturie [pnømatyri], *s.f. Med:* pneumaturia.

pneumectomie [pnømɛktɔmi], *s.f. Med:* (*a*) pneumectomy; (*b*) pneumonectomy.

pneumo [pnømo], *s.m. Med: F:* artificial pneumothorax.

pneumobacille [pnømɔbasil], *s.m. Bac:* pneumobacillus.

pneumocèle [pnømɔsɛl], *s.f. Med:* pneum(at)ocele.

pneumococcémie [pnømɔkɔksemi], *s.f.* pneumococcemia.

pneumococcie [pnømɔkɔksi], *s.f. Med:* pneumococcia.

pneumoconiose [pnømɔkɔnjo:z], *s.f. Med:* pneumoconiosis.

pneumocoque [pnømɔkɔk], *s.m. Bac:* pneumococcus.

pneumogastrique [pnømɔgastrik], *a. & s.m. Anat:* pneumogastric (nerve).

pneumographe [pnømɔgraf], *s.m.* pneumograph, pneumatograph, stethograph.

pneumographie [pnømɔgrafi], *s.f. Med:* pneumography.

pneumolithe [pnømɔlit], *s.m. Med:* pneumolith, pneumonolith.

pneumologie [pnømɔlɔʒi], *s.f. Med:* pneumology.

pneumologue [pnømɔlɔg], *s.m. & f. Med:* lung specialist.

pneumonectomie [pnømɔnɛktɔmi], *s.f. Med:* (*a*) pneumectomy; (*b*) pneumonectomy.

pneumonie [pnømɔni], *s.f. Med:* pneumonia, congestion of the lungs; **p. caséeuse,** interstitial pneumonia; **p. lobaire, franche, fibrineuse,** acute, croupous, lobar, pneumonia; **p. lobulaire,** catarrhal, lobular, pneumonia; broncho-pneumonia; **p. d'un seul poumon,** single pneumonia; **p. double,** double pneumonia.

pneumonique [pnømɔnik], (*a*) *a. Med:* pneumon(it)ic; (*b*) *s.* patient suffering from pneumonia.

pneumonite [pnømɔnit], *s.f. Med:* pneumonitis.

pneumopathie [pnømɔpati], *s.f. Med:* pneumonopathy.

pneumopéricarde [pnømɔperikard], *s.m. Med:* pneumopericardium.

pneumopéritoine [pnømɔperitwan], *s.m. Med:* pneumoperitonitis.

pneumopleurésie [pnømɔplørezi], *s.f. Med:* pleuro-pneumonia.

pneumorragie [pnømɔraʒi], *s.f. Med:* h(a)emorrhage of the lungs, pneumor(r)hagia.

pneumoséreuse [pnømɔserø:z], *s.f. Med:* pneumoserosa.

pneumothérapie [pnømɔterapi], *s.f. Med:* pneumotherapy.

pneumothorax [pnømɔtɔraks], *s.m. Med:* pneumothorax; **p. artificiel,** artificial pneumothorax.

pneumotomie [pnømɔtɔmi], *s.f. Surg:* pneumotomy.

pneumotoxine [pnømɔtɔksin], *s.f. Bac:* pneumotoxin.

pneumotyphoïde [pnømɔtifɔid], *s.f. Med:* pneumotyphoid.

Pô (le) [lɔpo], *Pr.n.m. Geog:* the (river) Po.

poacées [pɔase], *s.f.pl. Bot:* Poaceae.

pochade [pɔʃad], *s.f.* (*a*) rapid sketch, rough sketch; (*b*) essay, report, etc., hastily dashed off.

pochage [pɔʃa:ʒ], *s.m. Cu:* poaching (of egg, etc.).

pochard, -arde [pɔʃa:r, -ard], *s. P:* drunkard, boozer.

pocharder [pɔʃarde], *v.tr. P:* to make (s.o.) drunk, tight.

se pocharder, *P:* to get drunk, tight, stoned; to booze.

pocharderie [pɔʃardəri], *s.f. P:* boozing, drinking.

pochardise [pɔʃardi:z], *s.f. P:* drunkenness; habitual drinking, *P:* boozing, lifting the elbow.

poche[1] [pɔʃ], *s.f.* **1.** pocket; **p. de poitrine,** breast pocket; **p. de côté,** side pocket; **p. à portefeuille, p. intérieure,** inside breast pocket; **p. de pantalon, de culotte,** trouser pocket; **p. (à) revolver,** hip pocket; **p. plaquée, rapportée,** patch pocket; **p. carnier,** poacher pocket; *F:* **faire les poches à qn,** to go through s.o.'s pockets; **couteau de p.,** pocket knife; **carnet de p.,** pocket book; **livre de p.,** paperback; *Phot:* **appareil de p.,** pocket camera; **argent de p.,** pocket money; **avoir la p. vide,** to have empty pockets, to be penniless; **avoir toujours la main à la p.,** to be always paying out; **mettre la main à la p.,** to pay up; to shell out; **payer qn de sa p.,** to pay s.o. from one's own pocket; **j'y suis de ma p.,** I'm out of pocket by it; **j'y ai été de ma p.,** I had to stump up; **j'ai cent francs en p.,** I have a hundred francs on me; **mettre qch. dans sa p.,** to put sth. in one's pocket, to pocket sth.; *F:* **s'en mettre plein les poches,** to make a fortune; **chapeau qui se met dans la p.,** hat that rolls up for the pocket; *F:* **vous le mettriez dans votre p.,** he's no match for you, you could put him in your pocket; **mettez ça dans votre p. (et votre mouchoir dessus),** put that in your pipe and smoke it; **connaître qch. comme (le fond de) sa p.,** to know sth. intimately, through and through, inside out; **je connais le voisinage comme ma p.,** I know every inch of the neighbourhood, I know the neighbourhood like the back of my hand; **il n'a pas la, sa, langue dans sa p.,** he's a great talker, he has plenty to say for himself; **mettre son orgueil dans sa p.,** to pocket, swallow, one's pride; **mettre sa langue dans sa p.,** to hold one's tongue; **ne pas avoir les yeux dans sa p.,** not to go about with one's eyes shut; **c'est dans la p.,** it's in the bag; **tenir une affaire dans sa p., avoir une affaire en p.,** to have a matter well in hand; **des poches pleines de bonbons,** pocketfuls of sweets. **2.** (*a*) bag, pouch, sack; paper bag; case; crop (of bird); *Cu:* **p. à douille,** forcing bag; piping bag; **p. d'avoine,** sack of oats; **p. à cartes,** map case; *F:* **acheter chat en p.,** to buy a pig in a poke; **p. d'air,** (i) *Av:* air pocket; (ii) *Hyd.E:* airlock; *Aer:* **p. à air,** air pocket (of observation balloon); *Mch:* **p. à huile,** oil pan; (*b*) *Biol: Med:* sac; **p. du fiel,** gall-bladder; *Obst:* **p. des eaux,** bag of waters; *Moll:* **p. du noir,** ink sac, bag; *Arb:* **p. de résine,** resin gall. **3.** *Ven:* purse net, bag net. **4.** (*a*) pucker (in garment); **pantalon qui fait des poches aux genoux,** trousers that are baggy at the knees; (*b*) **poches sous les yeux,** bags, pouches, under the eyes; (*c*) loop (of written b, g, h, etc.). **5.** *Geol:* (*a*) pothole; (*b*) wash-out; (*c*) **p. d'eau,** water pocket; **p. de minerai,** nest of ore; **p. à cristaux,** druse, geode; *Petroleum Ind:* **p. de gaz,** natural gas pocket.

poche[2], *s.f. Cu: etc:* ladle; *Metall:* **p. à couler, p. de fonderie,** casting ladle; **p. à laitier,** slag ladle.

poche[3], *s.m. Publ: F:* paperback.

pochée [pɔʃe], *s.f.* pocketful.

pocher[1] [pɔʃe]. **1.** *v.tr.* (*a*) *Cu:* to poach (eggs); *F:* **p. l'œil à qn,** to black, bung up, s.o.'s eye; **œil poché,** black eye; *P:* **la ferme, ou je te poche un œil!** shut up, or I'll give you a sock in the eye! (*b*) (*in writing*) **lettres pochées,** blobbed letters, blind letters. **2.** (*a*) *v.tr.* to make (trousers) baggy at the knees; (*b*) *v.i.* (*of clothes*) to pucker; to get baggy.

pocher[2], *v.tr.* **1.** to dash off (sketch, essay, etc.). **2.** to stencil (design, etc.).

pochet [pɔʃɛ], *s.m.* (horse's) nose-bag.

pocheteau, -eaux [pɔʃ(ə)to], *s.m. Ich: F:* skate.

pochetée [pɔʃte], *s.f.* **1.** pocketful; *P:* **il en a une p.!** he's an awful fool! *Hence* **2.** *P:* duffer, stupid.

pocheter [pɔʃte], *v.tr.* (**je pochette, n. pochetons; je pochetterai** [*F:* pɔʃtre]) *A:* to keep (sth.) in one's pocket for some time.

pochette [pɔʃɛt], *s.f.* **1.** (*a*) small pocket; pouch; handbag, *esp.* clutch bag; (*b*) **p. de compas,** pocket case of mathematical instruments; (*c*) *Phot:* **p. de papier,** packet of paper; (*d*) envelope with metal fastener; (*e*) *Com:* **p. de papeterie,** compendium; **p. d'allumettes,** book of matches; (*f*) *Rec:* sleeve (of record). **2.** *Ven:* purse-net. **3.** *A:* pocket violin; *A:* kit. **4.** fancy handkerchief.

pochette-surprise [pɔʃɛtsyrpri:z], *s.f.* surprise packet; *pl. pochettes-surprises.*

pocheur [pɔʃœ:r], *s.m. Metall:* ladler; ladle-man.

pocheuse [pɔʃø:z], *s.f. Dom.Ec:* egg poacher.

pochoir [pɔʃwa:r], *s.m.* stencil(-plate); **peindre, passer, qch. au p.,** to stencil sth.; **peinture au p.,** stencilling; **peintre au p.,** stenciller.

pochon[1] [pɔʃɔ̃], *s.m. Ind:* ladle; shovel.

pochon[2], *s.m.* **1.** (*a*) stencil brush; (*b*) blob (in loop of letter); blind letter. **2.** *P:* (*a*) black eye; (*b*) blow, *F:* sock, in the eye.

pochouse [pɔʃu:z], *s.f. Cu:* fresh-water fish dish.

podagre [pɔdagr̥]. **1.** *s.f.* podagra, gout (in the feet). **2.** *a. & s.* podagrous, gouty (person).

podalique [pɔdalik], *a. Obst:* **version p.,** podalic version.

podarge [pɔdarʒ], *s.m. Orn:* frogmouth.

podargidés [pɔdarʒide], *s.m.pl. Orn:* Podargidae, the frogmouths.

podestat [pɔdɛsta], *s.m. Italian Adm. & Hist:* Podesta.

podicipiformes [pɔdisipifɔrm], *s.m.pl. Orn:* Podicipiformes.

podicipitidés [pɔdisipitide], *s.m.pl. Orn:* Podicipidae, the grebes.

podium [pɔdjɔm], *s.m. Rom.Ant: etc:* podium; *Sp.* (winner's) rostrum; *Pol:* speaker's platform.

podobranche [pɔdɔbrɑ̃:ʃ], *a. Crust:* podobranchial, podobranchiate.

podobranchie [pɔdɔbrɑ̃ʃi], *s.f. Crust:* podobranch; podobranchia.

podocarpe [pɔdɔkarp], *s.m. Bot:* yellow-wood.

podolite [pɔdɔlit], *s.f. Miner:* podolite.

podologie [pɔdɔlɔʒi], *s.f. Med:* podology.

podomètre [pɔdɔmɛtr̥], *s.m.* **1.** pedometer. **2.** *Farr:* horse-shoe gauge.

podophthalme [pɔdɔftalm], *a. Z:* podophthalmate, stalk-eyed.

podophylle [pɔdɔfil], *s.m. Bot:* podophyllum.

podophyllin [pɔdɔfilɛ̃], *s.m.*, **podophylline** [pɔdɔfilin], *s.f. Ch:* podophyllin.

podostémacées [pɔdɔstemase], *s.f.pl. Bot:* Podostemaceae.

podot, -ote [pɔdo, -ɔt], *a. & s. Geog:* (native, inhabitant) of Le Puy.

podsol, podzol [pɔdsɔl, pɔdzɔl], *s.m. Geol:* podzol, podsol.

podsolique, podzolique [pɔdsɔlik, pɔdzɔlik], *a. Geol:* podzolic, podsolic.

podsolisation, podzolisation [pɔdsɔlizasjɔ̃, pɔdzɔlizasjɔ̃], *s.f. Geol:* podzolization, podsolization.

podsoliser, podzoliser [pɔdsɔlize, pɔdzɔlize], *v.tr.* to podzolize, podsolize.

pœcile [pesil], *s.m. Gr.Ant:* poecile, painted portico.

pœcilogale [pesilɔgal], *s.m. Z:* white-naped weasel, striped weasel.

pœcilotherme [pesilɔtɛrm], *Z:* **1.** *a.* cold-blooded (animal, reptile, etc.); poikilothermic, poikilothermal, poikilothermous. **2.** *s.m.* **pœcilotherme,** cold-blooded animal.

poêle[1] [pwal, pwa:l], *s.f.* **1.** frying pan; **p. à confitures,** preserving pan; *F:* **sauter de la p. dans le feu, dans la braise,** to jump out of the frying pan into the fire; **tenir la queue de la p.,** to be in charge; *F:* to run the show. **2.** panful.

poêle[2], *s.m.* **1.** (*a*) *A:* (marriage-)canopy; (*b*) *Ecc:* canopy (held over the Sacrament in procession). **2.** (funeral) pall; **porteurs des cordons du p.,** pall bearers; **les cordons du p. étaient tenus par . . .,** the pall bearers were . . ..

poêle[3], *s.m.* **1.** stove; **p. à feu continu,** slow-burning stove, slow-combustion stove; **p. à gaz,** gas stove; **p. de cuisine,** cooking-range; kitchen stove; cooker; **p. flamand,** cooking range (on high feet). **2.** *Dial:* (*in N. of Fr.*) (heated) living-room.

poêlée [pwale], *s.f.* panful.

poêler [pwale], *v.tr.* to cook in a frying pan (with carrots and bacon).

poêlerie [pwalri], *s.f.* (*a*) stove manufacture, trade; (*b*) *coll.* stoves and boilers.

poêlette [pwalɛt], *s.f.* small frying-pan.

poêlier [pwalje], *s.m.* (*a*) dealer in stoves and kitchen ranges; (*b*) stove setter.

poêlon [pwalɔ̃], *s.m.* small (earthenware or metal) saucepan; casserole.

poème [pɔɛm], *s.m.* poem; *F:* **c'est un p.,** it's priceless.

poésie [pɔezi], *s.f.* **1.** poetry. **2.** poem; piece of poetry.

poétaillon [pɔetɑjɔ̃], *s.m.* poetaster.

poétastre [pɔetastr̥], *s.m.* poetaster.

poète [pɔɛt]. **1.** *s.m.* poet; **Madame X est un p. distingué,** Mrs X is a distinguished poet(ess); *A:* **p. de cour,** courtier-poet; **méchant p.,** poetaster, rhymester. **2.** *a.* **femme p.,** woman poet; poetess.

poétereau, eaux [pɔetro], *s.m.* poetaster.

poétesse [pɔetɛs], *s.f.* poetess.

poético- [pɔetikɔ-], *pref. Lit:* poetico-.

poétique [pɔetik]. **1.** *a.* (*a*) poetic (inspiration, talent, muse, licence); **l'art p.,** the art of poetry; (*b*) poetical (works, passage, expression, genius). **2.** *s.f.* poetics.

poétiquement [pɔetikmɑ̃], *adv.* poetically.

poétisation [pɔetizasjɔ̃], *s.f.* poet(ic)izing.

poétiser [pɔetize]. **1.** *v.i.* to write poetry, to poetize. **2.** *v.tr.* to poet(ic)ize; to treat (sth.) poetically.

poétraillon [pɔetrɑjɔ̃], *s.m.* poetaster.

pogne [pɔɲ], *s.f.* **1.** *Cu:* kind of *brioche* made in Romans (Drôme). **2.** *P:* hand; **être à la p. de qn,** to be under s.o.'s thumb.

pognon [pɔɲɔ̃], *s.m. P:* money, lolly, dough.

pognophores [pɔɲɔfɔːr], *s.m.pl. Z:* Pognophora.

pogonia [pɔgɔnja], **pogonie** [pɔgɔni], *s.f. Bot:* pogonia.

pogrom [pɔgrɔm], *s.m.* pogrom.

pogromiste [pɔgrɔmist], *s.m.* pogromist.

poids [pwɑ], *s.m.* weight. **1.** (*a*) heaviness; **fléchir sous le p. de qch.,** to give way under the weight of sth.; **appuyer de tout son p. sur qch.,** to lean on sth. with the whole of one's weight; **perdre du p.,** to lose weight; **reprendre du p.,** to put on weight again; **vendre au p.,** to sell by weight; **vendre qch. au p. de l'or,** to sell sth. for its weight in gold; **le p. n'y est pas,** this is short weight; **faire bon p.,** to give good weight; **ajouter qch. pour faire le p.,** to throw sth. in as a makeweight; **monnaie de p.,** coin of standard weight; *Ch:* **p. atomique,** atomic weight; **p. moléculaire,** molecular weight; **p. spécifique,** *Ph:* specific weight; *Ch:* specific gravity; **liquide de p. spécifique élevé,** high-gravity liquid; *Box:* **p. coq,** bantam-weight; **p. lourd,** heavy-weight; **p. moyen,** middle weight; **p. mouche,** fly-weight; *Box: Wr: Turf:* **p. à volonté,** catch-weight; *s.a.* PLUME 1; (*b*) importance; **donner du p. à qch.,** to give weight to sth.; **son opinion a du p.,** his opinion carries weight; **chiffres qui ajoutent du p. à sa thèse,** figures that add weight to his argument; **gens de p.,** people of weight, of consequence, *F:* **il ne fait pas le p.,** he's not up to scratch. **2.** (*a*) weight (of balance); **p. de dix kilogrammes,** ten-kilogram weight; **p. mobile, p. curseur,** sliding weight (of steelyard, etc.); **poids et mesures,** weights and measures; **faux p.,** false weights; **vendre à faux p.,** to give short weight; **avoir, faire, deux p. et deux mesures,** to have one law for the rich and another for the poor, one law for one's friends and another for one's foes; *Jew.Hist:* **le Poids du sanctuaire,** the shekel of the sanctuary; *F:* **peser qch. au p. du sanctuaire,** to examine sth. thoroughly; (*b*) **les p. d'une horloge,** the weights of a clock; (*c*) *Sp:* shot, weight; **lancer le p.,** to put the shot; **p. et haltères,** (i) heavy weights and dumb-bells; (ii) *Gym:* weight lifting; (*d*) *Adm:* **les Poids et Mesures,** (i) the Weights and Measures Department; (ii) the office of the inspector of weights and measures; **p. public,** public weighing office, weigh-bridge. **3.** load, burden; *Av:* **p. en ordre de vol,** laden weight; **p. au décollage,** take-off weight; **p. à l'atterrissage,** landing weight; **p. utile,** live weight; useful load; *Av:* payload; **p. mort,** (i) dead weight; (ii) *Const:* dead load; **jeter tout ce qui fait p.,** to throw away all dead weight; **p. brut,** gross weight; *Veh:* **p. en charge,** laden weight; *Aut:* **p. lourd,** heavy lorry; *N.Arch:* **p. (d'un navire),** displacement; *Nau:* **p. au lancement,** launching weight; **p. de charge,** load (of valve, etc.); *Mec.E:* **p. du cheval,** weight per horse-power; **le p. des impôts,** the burden of taxation; **écrasé sous le p. des ans,** crushed by the weight of years; **porter le p. du jour et de la chaleur,** to bear the burden and heat of the day; **le p. de la bataille,** the brunt of the battle; **soutenir le p. de la colère de qn,** to bear the brunt of s.o.'s displeasure; **que je n'aie plus ce p. sur la conscience!** if only I could rid myself of that load on my conscience!

poignamment [pwaɲamɑ̃], *adv.* poignantly.

poignant [pwaɲɑ̃], *a.* poignant (thought, regret); heart-gripping, painfully sharp (emotion); **spectacle p.,** (i) agonizing, (ii) thrilling, sight; **chagrin p.,** heartbreak.

poignard [pwaɲaːr], *s.m.* (*a*) dagger, poniard; **coup de p.,** stab; **donner un coup de p. à qn, percer qn d'un coup de p.,** to stab s.o.; **la nouvelle lui fut un coup de p.,** the news cut him to the heart; (*b*) (highlander's or midshipman's) dirk.

poignarder [pwaɲarde], *v.tr.* (*a*) to stab (s.o.); *Lit:* to poniard (s.o.); (*b*) to cut (s.o.) to the heart.

poigne [pwaɲ], *s.f. F:* (hand-)grip, grasp; **c'est un homme à p., de p.,** he is a strong, energetic, man; **montrer de la p.,** to show energy, to be equal to the situation; **il manque de p.,** he lacks grip.

poignée [pwaɲe], *s.f.* **1.** (*a*) handful; **jeter de l'argent à p.,** to scatter money lavishly, abundantly; **à poignées,** in handfuls; by the handful; **p. d'hommes,** handful, small number, of men; **p. de foin,** wisp of hay; (*b*) **p. de main,** handshake, handgrip; **donner une p. de main à qn,** to shake hands with s.o.; **quitter qn sur une p. de main,** to leave s.o. after shaking hands, with a handshake. **2.** (*a*) handle (of door, cycle); handle, grasp (of oar); hilt (of sword); haft, handhold (of tool); horn (of a plane); **p. de chasse d'eau,** cistern pull; *Av: etc:* **p. de verrouillage,** locking handle; **bêche à p. en étrier, à p. en croix,** stirrup-handled spade, crutch-handled spade; *Aut: etc:* **p. à condamnation,** handle with locking device, with safety catch; **p. de tirage (d'une portière),** pull-to handle; (*b*) *Sm.a: etc:* grip (of pistol); small (of rifle-butt); **p. de culasse mobile,** bolt handle; **fusil à p.-pistolet,** pistol-grip rifle; **pistolet avec p.-magasin,** stock-and-magazine pistol; *Artil:* **p. de culasse,** breech-block handle. **3.** hank (of thread, etc.).

poignet [pwaɲɛ], *s.m.* **1.** wrist; **faire qch. à la force du p.,** to do sth. by sheer strength of arm; *F:* **gagner de l'argent à la force du p.,** to make money by sheer hard work. **2.** (*a*) wristband (of shirt); (*b*) cuff (of coat, dress); (*c*) **poignets de manches,** cuff-protectors.

poïkilotherme [pɔikilɔtɛrm], *Z:* **1.** *a.* cold-blooded (animal, reptile, etc.); poikilothermic, poikilothermal, poikilothermous. **2.** *s.m.* poicilotherm, poikilotherm, cold-blooded animal.

poil [pwal], *s.m.* **1.** (*a*) (*of animal*) hair, fur; **p. de chameau,** camel's hair; **p. de chèvre,** goat's hair; **p. de chèvre d'Angora,** mohair; **à p. long,** long-haired, shaggy; **caresser un chat dans le sens du p.,** to stroke a cat the way of the fur, with the fur; **cheval à p.,** bare-backed horse; **monter à p.,** to ride bareback(ed); **faire le p. à un cheval,** to clip a horse; *P:* **faire le p. à qn, avoir du p. de qn,** (i) to fleece s.o.; (ii) to be too sharp for s.o., to get the better of s.o.; (iii) to tell s.o. off; **tomber sur le p. à qn,** to go for s.o.; *Ven:* **chien dressé au p. et à la plume,** dog trained to both fur and feather; *s.a.* BÊTE 1, RAS[1] 1; (*b*) coat (of animals); **cheval d'un beau p.,** sleek horse; **cheval de p. noir,** black horse; **chien au p. rude,** wire-haired dog; **chien à p. dur,** rough-coated dog; **fox à p. dur,** wire-haired fox terrier; (*c*) nap (of cloth); pile (of velvet); **drap à long p.,** shaggy cloth; **velours à trois poils,** three-pile velvet; **velours en p. soie naturelle,** velvet with a real silk pile; **journaux de toute nuance et de tout p.,** newspapers of every shade and hue; *s.a.* BRAVE 1; (*d*) **poils d'une brosse,** bristles of a brush. **2.** (*of men*) hair (on the body); *F:* **il a du p.,** (i) he's got guts; (ii) he's got plenty of energy, of go; **p. de Judas,** red hair; **sans p. au menton,** beardless; **poils follets,** down; *P:* **à p.,** naked; **se mettre à p.,** to strip to the skin, to the buff; *F:* **avoir un p. (dans la main),** to be workshy; *F:* to have a bone in one's leg. **3.** *F:* mood, temper; **être de bon, de mauvais, p.,** to be in a good, bad, mood. **4.** (*a*) **réglage fait au quart de p.,** adjustment, tuning, done to a hair's breadth; fine tuning, etc.; (*b*) *F:* **au (petit quart de) p.,** super; dead accurate; spot on; **à un p. près,** as near as dammit; **un p. plus vite,** a fraction faster; *int.* **au p.!** wonderful! super! **5.** (*of plants*) down, pubescence.

poilant [pwalɑ̃], *a. P:* screamingly funny.

poiler (se) [səpwale], *v.pr. P:* to split one's sides with laughter.

poileux, -euse [pwalø, -øːz], *a.* hairy.

poilu [pwaly]. **1.** *a.* (*a*) hairy, shaggy; (*b*) nappy, shaggy (material); (*c*) *Nat.Hist:* pilose. **2.** *s.m.* *F:* French soldier (1914-1918).

poinçon[1] [pwɛ̃sɔ̃], *s.m.* **1.** (*a*) (engraver's) point; chasing-chisel; (*b*) awl, bradawl; *Needlw:* stilleto; (sailmaker's) stabber; *Dom.Ec:* **p. à glace,** ice pick; *Nau:* **p. à épisseur,** marline spike. **2.** (*a*) (perforating) punch; *Rail: etc:* (pair of) cancels; (*computers*) punch knife; **(coup de) p. sur un billet,** punch hole in a ticket; **p. à river,** riveting punch; (*b*) die, stamp; **p. à chiffrer,** number punch, figure stamp; (*c*) stamped mark; **p. de contrôle, de garantie,** hall-mark, inspection stamp; *Sm.a:* **p. d'essai,** proof-mark. **3.** *Rec:* negative record, stamper; **p. de réserve,** master negative. **4.** *Const:* (*a*) king post, crown post; (*b*) **p. d'échafaudage,** scaffolding pole; (*c*) **p. d'une grue,** post of a crane; (*d*) *Av:* support strut.

poinçon[2], *s.m.* large cask; puncheon.

poinçonnage [pwɛ̃sɔnaːʒ], *s.m.* **1.** pricking, boring. **2.** (*a*) punching; (*b*) stamping, marking; hall-marking.

poinçonner [pwɛ̃sɔne], *v.tr.* **1.** (*a*) to prick, bore; (*b*) to punch. **2.** (*a*) to punch, clip (ticket, etc.); (*b*) to stamp, hall-mark (metal objects).

poinçonneur [pwɛ̃sɔnœːr], *s.m.* (*a*) *Ind:* puncher; **p. de tôle,** sheet-iron puncher; (*b*) *Trans:* ticket collector.

poinçonneuse [pwɛ̃sɔnøːz], *s.f.* **1.** stamping, punching, machine; punch; ticket punch; (*computers*) card punch; **p. récapitulatrice,** summary punch. **2.** *Trans:* (*pers.*) ticket collector.

poindre [pwɛ̃ːdr̥], *v.* (*pr.p.* **poignant;** *p.p.* **point;** *pr.ind.* **il point, ils poignent;** *pr.sub.* **il poigne;** *p.d.* **il poignait;** *p.h.* **il poignit;** *fu.* **il poindra;** *used esp. in infin., pr.ind., and fu.*) **1.** *v.tr.* (*a*) *A:* to sting; *s.a.* OINDRE 1; (*b*) (*apparently a back-formation from* POIGNANT) **une irritation sourde lui poignait le cœur,** he was in the grip of a vague irritation. **2.** *v.i.* (*of daylight*) to dawn, break; (*of plants, etc.*) to come up, sprout, come out, appear; **l'aube va p.,** daybreak is at hand; (*of ship*) **p. à l'horizon,** to heave in sight; *F:* **je sens p. un rhume,** I feel a cold coming on; **je vis p. un sourire sur ses lèvres,** I saw a smile dawning, hovering, on her, his, lips; I saw the beginning of a smile on his, her, lips.

poing [pwɛ̃], *s.m.* fist; *A:* hand; **poings nus,** naked fists, bare knuckles; **pieds et poings liés,** bound hand and foot; **sabre, revolver, au p.,** sword, revolver, in hand; **serrer les poings,** to clench one's fists; **menacer qn du p., montrer le p. à qn,** to shake one's fist at s.o.; **dormir à poings fermés,** to sleep soundly, like a top, like a log; **coup de p.,** blow with the fist; punch; **donner un coup de p. à qn,** to punch s.o., give s.o. a punch; **se battre à coups de p., faire le coup de p.,** to fight with one's fists, to use one's fists; to resort to fisticuffs; **il tomba sur eux à coups de p.,** he went for them with his fists; **se mordre, se ronger, les poings,** to gnaw one's fingers (with impatience); *s.a.* FRAPPER 1, HANCHE 1.

point[1] [pwɛ̃], *s.m.* **1.** hole (in strap). **2.** (*a*) *Needlew:* stitch; **p. glissé, coulé,** (running) stitch; **p. droit, p. devant,** running stitch; **p. arrière,** back stitch; **p. de piqûre,** (i) back stitch; (ii) (*on machine*) lock stitch; **p. de chausson, p. russe, p. d'épine,** herring bone stitch; **p. d'arêtes,** feather stitch; **p. de reprise,** darning stitch; **p. noué,** knot stitch; **p. de navette,** lock stitch (on machine); **p. redoublé,** double lock stitch; **p. de chaînette,** chain stitch; **p. roulé,** whipping; **p. turc,** pin stitch; **p. d'armes, tortillé,** French knot; **p. croisé,** cross stitch; **petit p.,** petit point; **gros p.,** gros point; **p. de Holbein, p. droit,** (*in tapestry*) Holbein stitch, Italian stitch; **p. de languette, de feston,** blanket stitch, buttonhole stitch; **p. perdu,** blind stitch, slip stitch; **coudre qch. à points perdus,** to blind-stitch sth.; **faire un p. à un vêtement,** to put a few stitches in a garment, to sew up, run up, a tear in a garment; *Prov:* **un p. (fait) à temps en épargne cent,** a stitch in time saves nine; *Knitting:* **p. de riz,** moss stitch; **p. de riz double,** double moss stitch; **p. mousse,** plain knitting, garter stitch; (*b*) (needle-)point lace; **p. d'Alençon,** Alençon point; **p. de Bruxelles,** Brussels lace; **p. de Milan,** punto di Milano; (*c*) (*acute pain*) stitch; **avoir un p. au dos,** to have a stabbing pain in one's back; **p. de côté,** stitch in one's side. **3.** point (in time); **le p. du jour,** daybreak; **au p. du jour,** at daybreak, at the first streak of dawn; **être sur le p. de faire qch.,** to be on the point of doing sth.; **sur le p. de mourir,** at, on, the point of death, about to die; **être sur le p. de partir,** to be about to start, on the eve of starting, on the point of starting; **être sur le p.**

de s'évanouir, to be on the verge of fainting; **on était tous sur le p. de se battre,** we were all within an inch of a fight; **arriver à p. nommé, juste à p.,** to arrive in the nick of time; **le livre parut à p. nommé,** the book appeared just at the right moment; **tomber, venir, à p.,** to come at the right moment; *Prov:* **tout vient à p. à qui sait attendre,** everything comes to him who waits. **4.** point (in space); (*a*) **p. de départ,** starting point, point of departure; **p. d'arrivée,** point of arrival, place of arrival; *Ball:* point of impact; **p. de chute,** (place of) fall; *Golf:* **guetter le p. de chute de la balle,** to watch, mark, where the ball pitches; *Ph:* **p. d'application,** point of application (of a force); **p. bas, p. haut, d'une onde,** trough, crest, of a wave; *Ball: etc:* **p. à battre,** point to be aimed at, to be fired at; **p. de mire,** sighting point; **p. de visée, p. visé,** *Artil: Sm.a:* point aimed at, aiming point; (*atom bombs*) desired ground zero; **p. origine de tir, p. d'où l'on tire,** firing point; **p. de repère (de tir),** aiming, ranging mark; **p. d'impact,** point of impact; **p. moyen d'impact, d'un groupement,** mean point, centre, of impact; centre of dispersion; *Artil:* **p. futur,** predicted point; (*atom bombs*) **p. zéro,** ground zero; *Mil: etc:* **p. de direction,** point of direction (for troops, etc., to march on); **p. de dispersion,** dispersal point (of column, convoy, etc.); **p. de ralliement,** rallying point; **p. initial,** initial point (of a march); *Av:* **p. de survol, p. en route,** way point; *Trans:* **p. de chargement, de déchargement,** loading, unloading, place, point; **p. d'embarquement,** (i) *Nau: etc:* embarking point; (ii) *Av:* enplaning place, point; (iii) *Rail:* entraining place, point; (iv) *Road Trans:* enbussing place, point, *U.S:* entrucking place, point; **p. de débarquement,** (i) *Nau: etc:* disembarking, landing, place; (ii) *Av:* deplaning, landing, place, point; (iii) *Rail:* detraining place, point; (iv) *Road Trans:* debussing place, point; *U.S:* detrucking place, point; *Av:* **p. de largage,** drop point; (bomb) release-point; *Mth:* **p. conjugué,** conjugate point; **p. de rebroussement,** cusp (of curve); **p. d'intersection de deux droites,** point of intersection of two straight lines; **le cercle coupe le triangle en deux points, aux points, A et B,** the circle intersects the triangle at (the two) points A and B; **p. de croisement, d'intersection, de deux rues,** point of intersection of two streets; *Mth: Surv:* **p. origine,** zero point; **p. coté,** spot height; **p. (coté) sur la carte,** landmark (on a map); **p. caractéristique, p. remarquable, p. saillant, du terrain,** conspicuous point, outstanding point, of the ground; feature of the ground; landmark; **p. de référence,** reference point, reference object, datum (point); **p. de station,** station; **p. géodésique,** geodetic point; **p. trigonométrique,** trig(onometrical) point; **carnet de points,** trig-point booklet; **calculer, relever, un p.,** to plot a point; **p. relevé,** plotted point; **p. intersecté,** intersected point, intersection point; **p. cardinal,** cardinal point; **p. quadrantal,** quadrantal point, inter-cardinal point; **p. d'orientation,** orienting, orientation, point; **orientation sur un p.,** setting by object; **p. de repère,** reference mark; landmark; bench mark; *Av:* **p. de repère (sur un itinéraire),** position mark (on a route); **p. du terrain à la verticale,** plumb point; *Av: Nau:* **p. à terre,** landmark; **faire le p.,** to take bearings, to find position on a map, to prick the chart; *Av: Nau:* to determine one's position, to work out a position; *Nau:* to take the ship's bearing, to determine the ship's position; *F:* to take, shoot, the sun; **faire le p. (d'une question),** to take stock of (a question); **calcul du p.,** determination of the position, position finding; **p. estimé,** dead reckoning (position); **p. observé,** fix, position, by observation; **p. par radio, par T.S.F.,** radio fix; *Nau:* **p. en vue de terre,** fix, position, by land bearings; **p. transporté,** running fix; **carte à grand p., à petit p.,** large-scale, small-scale, chart; **p. d'eau,** (i) water hole (in desert); (ii) tap (in camp site); **p. d'eau intermittent,** non-perennial water point; **de divers points,** from different places, quarters; **p. d'observation,** observation point; **p. de vue,** (i) (*panorama*) viewpoint, view; (ii) point of view, viewpoint, standpoint; **à tous (les) points de vue,** in all respects, in every respect; **au, du, p. de vue international,** from an international point of view, angle; *F:* **du p. de vue caractère,** as far as his character is concerned; **considérer qch. sous son véritable p. de vue,** to see sth. in its true aspect; **p. sensible,** critical, sensitive, vital, point; **défense des points sensibles,** defence of vital, of critical, points; **points vitaux, points d'importance, stratégique ou tactique,** key points; *Pol:* **p. chaud,** (i) marginal seat; (ii) (*theatre of war, etc.*) hot spot; *Tchn:* **p. critique,** critical point; **p. fixé,** fixed point; *Av:* **essai au p. fixe,** static test; **faire le p. fixe,** to run the engines (in order to check them); **p. de fixation,** attach(ment) point; **p. d'amarrage, d'ancrage,** tie point, anchor point (of girder, etc.); **p. d'appui,** (i) *Mec:* fulcrum (of lever), purchase, bearing surface; (ii) *Const:* (point of) support; (iii) rest (for hand, foot, etc.); (iv) *Mil:* strong point, defended locality; **p. d'appui de la flotte,** naval base, outlying station; **p. d'articulation,** joint; **p. de contact,** contact point, point of contact; pitch point (of gear); **p. de décollement,** separation point; **p. d'équilibre,** point of equilibrium, null point; **p. de suspension,** suspension point (of pendulum, hanging stage, etc.); *Elcs:* **p. de transition,** transition point (of wave guide); *Atom.Ph:* **p. du réseau,** lattice point (of reactor); **p. de transition,** transition point; **p. limite de retour, p. de non-retour,** point of no return; **p. mort,** (i) *Aut:* neutral gear; (ii) *Book-k:* break-even point; (*of computer*) **p. d'arrêt, p. d'interruption,** break point; **p. de connexion,** branch point; **p. de contrôle,** check point; **p. machine,** index point; **p. de référence,** bench mark; **p. de réglage,** set point; **p. de reprise,** check point; re-run point, re-start point; **p. de retour,** re-entry point; *Nau:* **p. lumineux,** lighting point; *Mec.E:* **p. de graissage,** lubricating point; *Com:* **p. de vente,** stockist; (*b*) **au p.,** (i) *Opt:* in focus; (ii) *I.C.E:* in tune; **pas au p.,** out of focus; **parfaitement au p.,** (thoroughly) tried and tested; **plan parfaitement au p.,** well thought-out plan; **technique au p.,** perfected technique; *F:* **c'est au p.,** it's just, exactly, right; **mettre au p.,** to focus (lens, image); to bring (image) into focus; to perfect (design, etc.); to tune (engine); to position (machine tool); to adjust (sth.); to finish off, to touch up (sth.); to vet (sth.); **mettre une question au p.,** to narrow a question down to its essentials; to restate a question; **mettre une affaire au p.,** to make a matter quite clear; **cette question n'a pas été mise au p.,** this question (i) is not yet ready for discussion, (ii) has not been clarified, cleared up; **le cahier des charges a été mis au p. en fonction de vos observations,** the specifications have been brought into line with your observations, have been revised in accordance with your observations; **quand le cahier des charges aura été mis au p.,** when the specifications are definitely completed; **on a mis au p. une commande électronique simple,** a simple electronic control has been developed, devised; **il faut mettre au p. des règles d'exploitation,** operating procedures should be established; **les détails du contrat seront mis au p. d'ici la fin de l'année,** the details of the contract will be finalized before the end of the year; **mettre au p. l'organisation d'un banquet,** to make final arrangements for a banquet; **nous avons mis au p. la description du système,** we have made final adjustments to the description of the system; **il mettait son rapport au p.,** he was putting the final, finishing, touches to his report; **le projet est désormais mis au p.,** the scheme has now been put into its final form; **mettre au p. une technique,** to perfect a technique; **cette question reste à mettre au p.,** this question remains to be settled; **les détails n'ont pas été mis au p.,** the details have not been worked out; **mettre au p. le réglage d'une came,** to time a cam; (*computers*) **ces programmes seront bientôt mis au p.,** these programmes will soon be checked out, soon be debugged; *Journ:* **mettre un article au p.,** to sub-edit an article, *F:* to lick an article into shape; **travail de mise au p.,** sub-editorial work, sub-editing; **mise au p.,** focusing (of lens); perfecting (of technique, etc.); tuning (of engine); adjusting; *Opt:* **mettre l'objectif hors de mise au p.,** to put the lens out of focus; **mise au p. hélicoïdale,** focusing (lens) mount; **anneau de mise au p.,** focusing ring; **dépoli de mise au p.,** focusing glass, screen; **loupe de mise au p.,** focusing glass; **échelle de mise au p.,** focusing scale; **vis de mise au p.,** focusing screw; **voile de mise au p.,** focusing cloth; *Ind:* **ingénieur des mises au p.,** development engineer; **recherche et mise au p.,** research and development; **mise au p. d'une question,** restatement of a question; **permettez-moi la mise au p. suivante,** may I be allowed to make the following correction, amendment; (*c*) *Anat:* punctum; **p. d'ossification,** ossification point; **p. rétinien correspondant,** corresponding retinal point; **p. craniométrique,** craniometric point; (*d*) *Nau:* **p. de voile,** clew, corner, of a sail; **p. de vent,** weather clew; **p. sous le vent,** lee clew; **p. de drisse,** gaff-sail peak; **renfort de p.,** clew patch; *s.a.* AMURE, ÉCOUTE[2]; (*e*) *Her:* point. **5.** (*a*) point, dot, tick; punctuation mark; **mettre les points sur les i.,** (i) to dot one's i's; (ii) *F:* to make one's meaning perfectly plain, not to mince words (with s.o.); **faute d'un p., Martin perdit son âne,** for want of a nail the shoe was lost; **p. (final),** full stop, *U.S:* period; **un p., c'est tout,** (i) (*Sch: at end of dictation*) full stop, that's all; (ii) *F:* and that's that; **deux points,** colon; **p. d'interrogation,** question mark; **p. d'exclamation,** exclamation mark; *Tg:* **points et traits,** dots and dashes (of Morse alphabet); *Hebrew Gram:* **p.-voyelle,** vowel point; **hébreu sans points-voyelles,** unpointed Hebrew; **faire un p. en face d'un nom,** to put a tick to a name; to tick off a name; (*b*) *Mus:* **p. (d'augmentation),** dot; **p. d'orgue, d'arrêt,** pause, fermata; **points détachés,** staccato dots; (*c*) *Games:* point, score; **faire trente points,** to score thirty (points); **jouer cinq francs le p.,** to play for five-franc points; **marquer les points,** to keep the score; *Bill:* **je vous fais cent points,** I'll play you a hundred up; **p. volé,** fluke; *Box:* **gagner aux points,** to win on points; **battu aux points,** beaten on points; **rendre des points à qn,** to give s.o. points, to be more than a match for s.o.; **il vous rend des points à tous les deux,** he can give both of you points; *Sp: F:* **donner des points à (certains coureurs),** to back-mark; *Ten:* **il fait le p.,** he plays a winning shot; **il ne fait pas le p.,** he doesn't put the ball away; **marquer des points,** to score; (*d*) *Sch:* mark; **mauvais p.,** bad mark; **bon p.,** good mark, good point; (*e*) *Typ:* point; **caractères de huit points,** eight-point type; (*f*) speck, spot, dot; **le navire n'est qu'un p. à l'horizon,** the ship is a mere speck on the horizon; **p. noir,** (i) *Meteor:* small black cloud announcing a storm; (ii) *F:* a cloud on the horizon; (iii) *Aut:* black spot; *Med:* **points noirs,** blackheads, comedones; (*g*) *Fin:* (i) **hausse, baisse, d'un p.,** rise, fall, of one point; (ii) **silver-p.,** silver point; **silver-p. d'entrée,** silver import point; **silver-p. de sortie,** silver export point; **gold-p. d'entrée,** gold import point; **gold-p. de sortie,** gold export point. **6.** (*a*) point, stage, degree; extent; **p. d'ébullition,** boiling point; **p. de combustion,** burning point; **p. d'éclair,** flash point; **p. de fusion, de congélation,** melting point, freezing point; *Ch:* **p. de nuage,** cloud point; *Elcs:* **p. de Curie,** Curie point; **p. isoélectrique,** isoelectric point; *Metall:* **p. chaud,** hot spot; (*Aerodynamics*) **p. de décollement,** separation point; **jusqu'à un certain p.,** to a certain extent, in some measure, in some degree, up to a certain point; **au p. où en sont les choses,** as matters stand; **à ce p. que, à tel p. que, au p. que . . .,** to such a pitch, so much so, that . . .; **il est riche au p. d'ignorer sa fortune,** he is so rich that he doesn't know what he is worth; **vous n'êtes pas malade à ce p.-là,** you are not as ill as all that; **au dernier p.,** to, in, the last degree; (*b*) case, state, condition; **en bon p.,** in good condition; in good fettle; **le commerce est en mauvais p.,** trade is in a bad way; *F:* **être mal en p.,** to be in a bad way; **être plus mal en p.,** to be worse off; (*c*) **à p.,** in the right condition; ready; *Cu:* done to a turn, (*of steak*) medium; **remettre une machine à p.,** to overhaul, to tune up, a machine. **7.** point, particular; **discuter un p. d'histoire,** to discuss a point, a question of history; *Jur:* **p. de fait,** issue; **p. de droit,** point of law; **le p. capital,** the main point; **le grand p. c'est de . . .,** the great thing is to . . .; **c'est là le p.,** that's the point; **j'attire votre attention sur ce p.,** I would draw your attention to this point; **p. d'honneur,** point of honour; **mettre son p. d'honneur à ne pas céder,** to make it a point of honour not to yield; **sur ce p.,** on that score; **sur ce p. nous sommes d'accord,** on that point we are agreed; **équiper qn en tout p.,** to equip s.o. fully; to fit s.o. out (with uniform, etc.); **avoir raison en tous points,** to be right in every particular; **admirable en tous points,** admirable in every way; **de tous points,** in all respects, in every particular; **exécuter un ordre de p. en p.,** [dəpwɛ̃tɑ̃pwɛ̃], to execute an order exactly, to the letter, in every particular; *s.a.* CHATOUILLEUX. **8.** *War Adm:* **points textiles,** *F:* **des points,** clothing coupons.

point[2], *adv. A: Dial: Lit:* = PAS[2] (*often with an affectation of archaism*); *A: F:* **p. d'affaires,** nothing doing; *remains the standard form in the phr.* **peu ou p.,** little or not at all; **je n'en ai p.,** I've none at all; *hardly ever used in the* *comparative, or before* **si, beaucoup, tant, assez** *and similar advs.; often used in preference to* **pas** *if standing alone*; **le connaissez-vous?—p.!** do you know him?—not at all.

pointage [pwɛ̃taːʒ], *s.m.* (*a*) checking, ticking off, pricking (of items, account, names in list, etc.); scrutiny (of votes, of electoral roll, etc.); *Nau:* pricking (of chart); *Elcs:* (*radar, etc.*) plotting; **p. de déchargement,** tally of discharging; (*b*) timekeeping (at factory); timing (of race); scoring, marking (of game); *Ind:* **pendule de p.,** time clock, attendance clock; **carte de p.,** time card; (*c*) aiming, laying (of gun, rifle, etc.); pointing (of telescope, etc.); *Artil: etc:* **appareil de p.,** (collimating) sight; **p. au niveau,** quadrant aiming, laying; **p. direct, indirect,** direct, indirect, laying; **p. en direction, p. latéral,** aiming, laying, in direction; training; **mécanisme de p. en direction,** traversing gear, mechanism; **secteur denté de p. en direction,** traversing arc; **volant de p. en direction,** traversing handwheel; **p. en hauteur, p. vertical,** aiming, laying, for elevation; **mécanisme de p. en hauteur,** elevating gear, mechanism; **secteur denté, crémaillère de p. en hauteur,** elevating arc; **manivelle, volant, de p. en hauteur,** elevating handle, handwheel; **correction de p.,** correction of aim; *Sm.a:* **chevalet de p.,** aiming stand or rest, aiming tripod; *Navy:* **circulaire de p.,** training rack (for torpedoes); (*d*) marking (of playing cards); (*e*) *Metalw:* (i) tack, temporary welding; (ii) indentation.

pointal, -aux [pwɛ̃tal, -o], *s.m.* stay, strut, prop.

pointe [pwɛ̃ːt], *s.f.* **1.** (*a*) point (of pin, knife, sword, etc.); tip, head (of arrow, lance); nose (of bullet); toe (of shoe); top (of tree, spire); **p. d'aiguille,** (i) needle point; (ii) *Rail:* point of a switch blade; *s.a.* PERCUTANT; **p. d'une épigramme,** point, sting, of an epigram; **coup de p.,** thrust; *A:* **se frayer un chemin du tranchant et de la p.,** to make one's way cutting and thrusting; **gagner qch. à la p. de l'épée,** to win sth. after a great struggle; **p. d'asperge,** asparagus tip, point; **p. de tour,** lathe centre; **hauteur des pointes,** height of centres (of a lathe); **en p.,** tapering; **aller en p.,** to taper, to end in a point; **tailler en p.,** to point (stick, pencil, etc.); **toit en p.,** sharp, pointed, roof; **porter la barbe en p.,** to wear a pointed beard, a peaked beard; *Nau:* **brasser en p.,** to brace up, to trim (sails) sharp; *Av:* **p. avant (du fuselage),** nose cone; **p. de lance,** spear head; *Fenc:* **coup de p.,** lunge; *Fish:* **anneau de p.,** end ring; *Mec.E:* **(mesure) entre pointes,** between centres; *El.E:* **pouvoir des pointes,** power of points; *Anat:* **p. de la langue,** tip of the tongue, apex linguae; **marcher, se tenir, sur la p. des pieds,** to walk, stand, on tip-toe; **entrer, sortir, sur la p. des pieds,** to tiptoe in, out; **retomber sur la p. des pieds,** to come down on (the points of) one's toes; *Danc:* **pointes,** point work; **faire des pointes,** to dance on points; (*in organ pedal playing*) **"pointe,"** "toe"; *F:* **s'asseoir sur la p. des fesses,** to sit on the edge of a chair; (*of submarine*) **rendre de la p.,** to incline at a steep angle; *Mus:* **p. de l'archet,** point of the bow (of violin, etc.); *Mil:* **pointes antichar,** tank teeth, dragon's teeth; (*b*) peak (*Mth:* of curve, *Med:* of fever); *El:* **p. d'une charge,** peak of a load; **couvrir la p. de charge,** to cope with the peak consumption; **charge de p.,** peak load; **p. de courant,** current surge; *Mch: etc:* **puissance de p.,** peak power; **heures, période, de p.,** (i) peak hours, peak period, rush hours; (ii) *T.V: W.Tel:* peak viewing, listening, period; **enregistreur de p.,** peak recorder, maximum-demand recorder; **indicateur de p.,** peak indicator; maximum-demand meter, indicator; **pointes et paliers,** peaks and plateaus; *Ind:* **machine, dynamo, de p.,** stand-by engine, dynamo, etc.; (*c*) *Mil:* point (of advanced guard); **chevaux de p.,** leaders (of gun team, etc.); **faire une p.,** to push a small force far in advance of main army; **pousser sa p.,** to push forward; **pousser une p. sur . . .,** to launch a spearhead against . . .; *F:* **pousser une p. jusqu'à la digue, jusque chez un ami,** to go as far as to the jetty, to drift round to a friend's house; **ayant du temps de reste, nous avons poussé une p. jusqu'à Venise,** having some time to spare we made a detour as far as Venice; *Navy:* **tir en p.,** firing ahead; **être à la p. de, être à la p. du progrès en,** to set the pace in; **cette entreprise est à la p. de l'automation,** this firm sets the pace in automation; **cette entreprise est en p.,** this firm is in the forefront; **ce savant est à la p. de la recherche,** this scientist is in the forefront of research; **industrie de p.,** advance technology industry; (*d*) *Row:* **aviron de p.,** oar (as opposed to scull); **canot armé en p.,** single-banked boat; **avirons en p.,** single-banked oars; **ramer, nager, en p.,** to row (as opposed to sculling); **nage en p.,** rowing; **huit de p.,** eight(-oared boat); (*e*) **p. du jour,** day-break; **p. de douleur,** twinge of pain; **sentir une petite p. au cœur,** to feel a pang; **parler avec une p. d'accent étranger,** to speak with a hint of a foreign accent; **p. d'ironie,** hint, touch, of irony; **p. d'ail, de vanille,** touch of garlic, soupçon, dash, of vanilla; *F:* **avoir une p. de vin,** to have had a drop too much; *O:* **il a sa p.,** he's had a little drop; *Sp:* **p. de vitesse,** spurt, sprint; **p. finale,** final spurt; **vitesse de p.,** highest speed; (*f*) (i) *A:* witty phrase; conceit; **pointes et bons mots,** quips and cranks; (ii) punch line (of joke); (iii) dig; dirty crack. **2.** *Geog:* **p. (de terre),** foreland, head(land); cape; spit, tongue (of land); *Nau:* **gouverner de p. en p.,** to steer along the coast. **3.** *Tls:* (*a*) (stonemason's) point; (*b*) *Carp:* **p. carrée,** bradawl; (*c*) **p. à tracer, de traçage,** scriber; (*d*) **p. sèche,** (etcher's) point; etching needle; point (of pair of compasses); **p. pour taille douce,** engraving needle; (*e*) *Typ:* bodkin; (*f*) *Metall:* **p. de mouleur,** moulding pin. **4. p. de Paris,** wire nail; **p. sans tête,** brad; **p. à ardoise,** slate peg; *Arch:* **p. de diamant,** nail-head (ornamentation); **(chaussures à) pointes,** spiked shoes; *F:* spikes. **5.** *Med:* **pointes de feu,** ignipuncture. **6.** (*a*) (triangular) napkin, diaper (for infant); (*b*) fichu; (*c*) *Nau:* gore (of sail); **p. de canot,** canvas.

pointé [pwɛ̃te], *a. Mth:* (*of plane*) on which a fixed point of origin has been selected for the vectors.

pointeau, -eaux [pwɛ̃to], *s.m.* **1.** *Mec.E:* centre-punch; **coup, trou, de p.,** centre mark, punch mark; **amorcer au p.,** to centre dot. **2.** (*a*) *I.C.E:* needle, float spindle (of carburettor); **siège du p.,** needle-valve seating; **agir sur le p.,** to tickle the carburettor; **p. d'huile,** pin lubrication valve; (*b*) **p. de soupape (de pneu),** valve needle; (*c*) *Typewr:* **p. d'interligne,** line-space gauge. **3.** (*pers.*) checker.

pointement [pwɛ̃tmɑ̃], *s.m.* **1.** *O:* = POINTAGE. **2.** (*a*) sprouting (of plant); (*b*) *Geol:* outcrop (of seam).

pointer¹ [pwɛ̃te], *v.tr.* **1.** (*a*) to check, tick off, prick off (items, names on list); to tally (goods); to scrutinize (electoral roll, votes, etc.); *Nau:* to prick (the chart); *Typ:* to register (the sheets); **p. un emplacement sur la carte,** to plot a site on the map; (*b*) *Mus:* (i) to dot (a note); **note pointée,** dotted note; (ii) to perform (passage) in a staccato manner; (*c*) *Ind:* **p. (à l'arrivée, à la sortie),** to clock in, to clock out, off. **2.** to point, level, train (telescope, etc.); to train, aim, lay (gun); to train (searchlight) (**sur,** on); *Artil: etc:* **p. une pièce sur un but,** to bring a gun to bear on a mark; **p. en direction,** to aim in direction, to lay for line, to traverse; **p. la pièce en direction,** to aim the gun in azimuth; **p. en hauteur,** to lay for elevation; **p. la pièce en hauteur,** to lay the gun for range; *Navy:* **p. par le travers,** to train on the beam. **3.** *Needlew:* to tack (seam, etc.). **4.** *Sp:* (*bowls*) to aim.

se pointer, *P:* to turn up, to show up; **ne fais pas ça, si le patron se pointait!** don't do that! supposing the boss showed up! **on ne peut se p. à n'importe quelle heure chez les gens,** you can't turn up at someone's house at any old time.

pointer². **1.** *v.tr.* (*a*) to thrust, prick, stab, deliver point (with sword, etc.); **p. son adversaire,** to thrust at one's opponent; (*b*) to point (needles); to sharpen (pencil); **p. un bœuf,** to slaughter a bullock (for meat); (*c*) (*of horse, etc.*) **p. les oreilles,** to prick up its ears. **2.** *v.i.* to appear; (*of plant*) to sprout, to spring up, to come up; (*of wind*) to rise; (*of bird*) to soar; (*of horse*) to rear; (*of steeple*) to jut upwards; **le clocher pointe sur le ciel,** the steeple stands up against the sky; **partout les clochers pointent,** steeples rise on all sides. **3. machine à p.,** jig-boring machine.

pointer³ [pwɛ̃tœːr], *s.m. Z:* pointer.

pointerie [pwɛ̃tri], *s.f.* wire-nail works, trade.

pointerolle [pwɛ̃trɔl], *s.f. Tls: Coal Min:* (*a*) dresser, small pick; (*b*) point of miner's drilling tool.

pointe-sèche [pwɛ̃tsɛʃ], *s.f.* **1.** dry-point etching. **2.** (pair of) dividers; *pl. pointes-sèches.*

pointeur¹ [pwɛ̃tœːr], *s.m.* **1.** checker; tallyman, timekeeper; (billiard) marker, scorer. **2.** *Artil:* gun layer. **3.** *Typ:* pointer, layer-on. **4.** *Elcs:* pointer, sensor (of satellite, spacecraft, etc.); **p. solaire,** sun pointer, sensor; **p. stellaire,** star pointer, sensor; **les pointeurs terrestres accrochent, se braquent sur, la terre,** the earth sensors lock on to the earth.

pointeur², -euse [pwɛ̃tœːr, -øːz], *s.* **1.** one who points; pointer; sharpener (of tools, etc.). **2.** *Tchn:* jig-borer operator.

pointier [pwɛ̃tje], *s.m.* nail maker.

pointil [pwɛ̃til], *s.m. Glassm:* pontil, punty, ponty.

pointillage¹ [pwɛ̃tijaːʒ], *s.m.* (*a*) *Art: etc:* dotting, stippling; *Psy:* **test de p.,** dotting test; (*b*) *Med:* massage using one or more fingers.

pointillage², *s.m. A:* cavilling.

pointille [pwɛ̃tiːj], *s.f. A:* punctilio, trifle.

pointillé [pwɛ̃tije]. **1.** *a.* dotted (line); stippled (engraving); spotted (pattern); *Tex:* pin-head (cloth); **ligne pointillée, trait p.,** dotted line. **2.** *s.m.* (*a*) dotted line; **détacher suivant le p.,** tear along the dotted line; (*b*) stippling; stippled engraving; **dessin au p.,** stippled design.

pointillement [pwɛ̃tijmɑ̃], *s.m. Med:* massage using one or more fingers.

pointiller¹ [pwɛ̃tije], *v.tr.* **1.** to dot; **roue à p.,** dotting wheel. **2.** *Engr:* to stipple. **3.** *Glassm:* to polish with a pontil.

pointiller², *A:* **1.** *v.i.* (*a*) to cavil, bicker (over trifles); (*b*) to split hairs. **2.** *v.tr.* to plague, bait (s.o.); to annoy (s.o.) with pinpricks; to nag (s.o.).

pointillerie [pwɛ̃tijri], *s.f. A:* **1.** captiousness. **2.** hair splitting.

pointilleur [pwɛ̃tijœːr], *s.m.* device for drawing dotted lines.

pointilleusement [pwɛ̃tijøzmɑ̃], *adv.* **1.** carpingly, captiously. **2.** touchily.

pointilleux, -euse [pwɛ̃tijø, -øːz], *a.* **1.** captious (person); carping (critic); touchy (person). **2.** (*a*) particular (**sur,** about); fastidious (as to); **p. dans le choix de ses relations,** particular in the choice of his acquaintances; (*b*) finical, finicky (person).

pointillisme [pwɛ̃tijism], *s.m. Art:* pointillism(e).

pointilliste [pwɛ̃tijist], *Art:* (*a*) *s.m. & f.* pointillist(e); (*b*) *a.* pointillist(ic).

pointis [pwɛ̃ti], *s.m.* pointed end of island in a river.

pointomètre [pwɛ̃tɔmɛtr], *s.m. Sculp:* pointing machine.

pointu [pwɛ̃ty]. **1.** *a.* (*a*) sharp-pointed (knife, etc.); **menton p.,** pointed chin; **oreilles pointues,** pointed ears; (*of dog, A: of pers.*) prick ears; **aux oreilles pointues,** prick-eared; **chapeau p.,** sugar-loaf hat; **plume pointue,** fine nib; (*b*) **caractère p.,** touchy disposition; **voix pointue,** shrill voice; *F:* (*in S. of Fr.*) **parler p.,** to talk with a Parisian accent; *s.a.* RIRE I. 1; (*c*) *Nau:* (*of wind*) scant, shy; (*d*) *I.C.E: F:* **moteur p.,** hotted up, souped up, engine. **2.** *s.m.* (*a*) small Mediterranean fishing boat; (*b*) *Fb: F:* toe punt.

pointure [pwɛ̃tyːr], *s.f.* **1.** size (in boots, gloves, collars, etc.); **j'ai six de p.,** I take sixes (in gloves, etc.); *F:* **tu ne fais pas la p.,** you're not up to it. **2.** *Typ:* (*a*) point spur; (*b*) point; (*c*) point holes (for registration).

point-virgule [pwɛ̃virgyl], *s.m.* semicolon; *pl. points-virgules.*

poire [pwaːr], *s.f.* **1.** *Hort:* pear; *F:* **entre la p. et le fromage,** over the walnuts and wine; **garder une p. pour la soif,** to put by something for a rainy day; **couper la p. en deux,** to compromise, to split the difference; **la p. est mûre,** the moment is ripe. **2.** (*a*) (pear-shaped) bulb (of camera shutter, etc.); pear switch (of electric light); pear push (of bell); **p. (d'une balance romaine),** weight, bob (of a steelyard); **p. à poudre,** powder flask; *Tchn:* **p. de pulvérisateur,** spray bulb; *Med:* **p. à injection,** douche; (*b*) *Cu:* part of silverside, cross cut; (*c*) pear-shaped diamond; pear-shaped ear pendant. **3.** *P:* (*a*) head, nut; (*b*) mug, sucker, easy mark; **il a une bonne p.,** (i) he looks a decent sort; (ii) he looks a bit of a mug; **c'est une bonne p.,** he's a sucker; **est-ce que tu me prends pour une p.?** what sort of a sucker do you take me for? *A:* **l'impôt des poires,** income tax, the mugs' tax; (*c*) *A:* **faire sa p.,** to fancy oneself; to put on airs.

poiré [pware] *s.m.* perry.

poireau, -eaux [pwaro], *s.m.* **1.** (*a*) *Bot:* leek; *F:* **le P.,** = *le Mérite agricole*; (*b*) *P:* simpleton, clot; **faire le p.,** to be kept waiting; to kick one's heels; to cool one's heels; **rester planté comme un p.,** to be rooted to the ground. **2.** *Med: F:* wart; *Vet:* papilloma; *Med: F:* **p. de la suie,** soot cancer.

poireauter [pwarɔte], *v.i. P:* to be kept waiting; to kick one's heels; to cool one's heels.

poirée [pware], *s.f. Bot:* white beet.

poirer [pware], *v.tr. P:* to catch, nab (s.o.).

se poirer, *P:* to have a good time.

poirette [pwarɛt], *s.f. Bot:* small pear.

poirier [pwarje], *s.m.* (*a*) pear tree; *Gym:* **faire le p.**, to do a head stand; (*b*) pear-tree wood, timber.

poiroter [pwarɔte], *v.i.* = POIREAUTER.

pois [pwɑ], *s.m.* **1.** *Bot:* pea; **p. à gratter**, common cowitch, stinging cowitch; **p. à rames**, climbing peas; **p. bedeau**, rosary pea tree; **p. café**, bird's foot trefoil; **p. carrés**, marrowfats; **p. chiche**, chickpea; **p. chinois**, soya bean; **p. cochon**, wayaka plant; **p. Congo**, Congo pea; **p. de pigeon, des champs**, field pea, gray pea; **p. de senteur**, sweet pea; **p. gourmand, mange-tout**, edible podded pea, sugar pea; **p. nains**, dwarf peas; **p. sabre**, red bean; **p. vivace, de Chine**, everlasting pea; *F:* **la fleur des pois**, the pick of the bunch; *s.a.* FÈVE 1. **2.** *Cu:* **des petits p., des p. verts**, green peas; **p. cassés**, split peas; **farine de p. cassés**, pease flour; **purée de p.**, (i) thick pea soup; (ii) pease pudding, *Scot:* pease-brose; (iii) *F:* pea-souper (fog). **3.** *Med:* **p. à cautère**, issue pea. **4.** *Pyr:* **p. fulminant**, toy torpedo. **5.** *Tex: Needlew:* **cravate bleue à p. blancs**, blue tie with white spots; blue polka dot tie; **tissu, tulle, à p.**, spotted material, net; **p. de broderie**, embroidered spot.

poise [pwa:z], *s.m. Ph.Meas:* poise.

poiseuille [pwazœ:j], *s.m. Ph.Meas:* 1/10 poise.

poison [pwazɔ̃], *s.m.* **1.** (*A. & Dial. s.f.*) poison; *F:* **ce vin est un vrai p.**, this wine is poisonous stuff; *P:* **c'est une vraie p.**, she's a pest, a poisonous creature; **cet enfant est un petit p.**, that child's a little horror; **quel p. ce travail!** how boring this work is! what a bind! *Bot:* *F:* **arbre p.**, poison ivy. **2.** *A:* **accusation de p.**, charge of poisoning; **le p. de la calomnie**, poisonous slander. **3.** *Ch:* (catalyst) poison; *Atom.Ph:* **p. de fission**, fission poison.

poissant [pwasɑ̃], *a. F:* (*a*) sticky; (*of pers.*) **il est p.**, I can't shake him off; (*b*) unlucky.

poissard, -arde [pwasa:r, -ard]. **1.** *a.* vulgar, low (manners, song); Billingsgate (language). **2.** *s.f.* **poissarde**; (*a*) fishwife; (*b*) *F:* vulgar, foul-mouthed, woman; **langage de poissarde**, Billingsgate.

poisse[1] [pwas], *s.f. F:* **1.** bad luck; tough luck; **jour de p.**, bad day (at races, etc.); **c'est la p.!** my luck's out! just my luck! **quelle p.!** what a bind! **2.** *O:* poverty; **être dans la p.**, to be hard up.

poisse[2], *s.m. P:* **1.** thief. **2.** pimp. **3.** layabout; good-for-nothing.

poisser [pwase], *v.tr.* **1.** to pitch; to coat (sth.) with cobbler's wax; **fil poissé**, waxed thread. **2.** (*a*) to make (hands, etc.) sticky (with jam, gum, etc.); (*b*) *abs.* (*of substance*) to be sticky. **3.** *P:* (*a*) to steal, pinch (sth.); (*b*) to catch, nab (s.o.); (*c*) to plague (s.o.).

poisseur, -euse[1] [pwasœ:r, -ø:z], *s.* **1.** *P: O:* thief, cheat. **2.** *s.m. Harn:* pitch pot attached to sewing machine.

poisseux, -euse[2] [pwasø, -ø:z]. **1.** *a.* (*a*) coated with pitch; (*b*) sticky; slimy.

poisson [pwasɔ̃], *s.m.* **1.** fish; **p. ange**, angel fish, bat fish, damsel fish; **p. à poumons**, lung fish; **p. archer, cracheur**, archer fish; **p. à trompe**, tube-snouted mormyrid; **p. aux quatre-yeux**, *F:* **quatre-z-yeux**, four-eyed fish; **p. aveugle des Rocheuses**, Rocky Mountains' blindfish; **p. boule**, puffer; **p. chat**, catfish; **p. chat cuirassé**, armoured catfish; **p. chirurgien**, surgeon fish; **p. coffre**, boxfish, trunkfish; **p. combattant**, fighting fish; **p. criard**, Chinese crying fish; **p. d'eau douce**, fresh-water fish; **p. de mer**, salt-water fish; **p. dollar**, lookdown fish; **p. électrique africain**, electric catfish; **p. épieu**, marlin; **p. feuille**, leaf fish; **p. globe**, sunfish; **p. grenouille**, frogfish, angler; **p. hache**, hatchet fish; **p. juif tacheté**, spotted jewfish; **p. loup**, wolf fish; **p. lune**, sunfish, moonfish; **p. noir de l'Alaska**, Alaskan blackfish; **p. panthère**, panther fish; **p. papillon**, butterfly fish; **p. perroquet**, pudding-wife; **p. pilote**, pilot fish; **p. plat** flat fish; **p. porc-épic**, porcupine fish; **p. rasoir**, shrimp fish; **p. rouge**, goldfish; **p. scie**, sawfish; **p. scorpion** scorpion fish; **p. suceur**, sucking fish, sucker; **p. télescope**, telescope fish; **p. trompette**, trumpet fish, long-snouted catfish; **p. volant**, flying fish; **manger du p.**, to eat fish; *F:* **donner à manger aux poissons**, to be seasick, to feed the fishes; **p. d'avril**, first of April hoax; **p. d'avril!** April fool! **être comme le, un, p. dans l'eau**, to be in one's element; **être comme un p. hors de l'eau**, to be like a fish out of water; *F:* **gros p.**, big business man; **les gros poissons mangent les petits**, (i) might is right; (ii) the small trader (etc.) is swallowed up by big business; **donner un petit p. pour en avoir un gros**, to throw out a sprat to catch a mackerel; *F:* **il ne faut pas apprendre aux poissons à nager**, don't teach your grandmother to suck eggs; *F:* **il avalerait la mer et les poissons**, he's got a perpetual thirst; he drinks like a fish; *P:* **attraper, engueuler, qn comme du p. pourri**, to give s.o. a good slanging; **noyer le p.**, to confuse the issue; *F:* **faire des yeux de p. frit**, to stare (vacantly) into space; *Astr:* **les Poissons**, Pisces, the Fishes; *s.a.* APPÂT 1, CHAIR 2, QUEUE[1] 1. **2.** *P:* pimp. **3.** (*a*) *Ent:* **p. d'argent**, silver fish; (*b*) *Rept:* **p. de sable**, medicinal skink.

poisson-lune [pwasɔ̃lyn], *s.m. Ich:* sunfish, moonfish; *F:* **elle a une figure de p.-l.**, she's moon-faced, she's got a face like a full moon; *pl. poissons-lunes.*

poissonnaille [pwasɔnɑ:j], *s.f.* (small) fry.

poissonnerie [pwasɔnri], *s.f.* fish market; fish shop.

poissonneux, -euse [pwasɔnø, -ø:z], *a.* (*of lake, river*) full of fish, abounding with fish.

poissonnier, -ière [pwasɔnje, -jɛ:r]. **1.** *s.* fish-monger, fishwife. **2.** *s.f.* **poissonnière**, fish kettle. **3.** *s.m.* fish chef.

poitevin, -ine [pwatvɛ̃, -in], *a. & s. Geog:* (native, inhabitant) of (i) Poitou, (ii) Poitiers.

Poitou [pwatu], *Pr.n.m. Geog:* Poitou.

poitrail [pwatra:j], *s.m.* **1.** (*a*) *Const:* breast-summer; (*b*) *Tls:* breast piece (of a breast drill). **2.** (*a*) breast (of horse); (*b*) *Harn:* breast strap, breastplate.

poitrinaire [pwatrinɛ:r], *a. & s. A:* consumptive.

poitrine [pwatrin], *s.f.* **1.** chest; **rhume de p.**, cold on the chest; *A:* **s'en aller de la p.**, to be in the last stages of consumption, to be dying of consumption; *A:* **être attaqué de la p.**, to be in a decline; **chanter, crier, à pleine p.**, to sing, shout, at the top of one's voice; **respirer à pleine, p.**, to breathe deep; *Mus:* **voix de p.**, chest voice; **ut de p.**, high C from the chest. **2.** (*a*) chest; **se croiser les bras sur la p.**, to fold one's arms across one's chest; **tour de p.** (i) (*of man, child*) chest measurement; (ii) (*of woman*) bust measurement; **avoir la p. plate**, to be flat-chested; **avoir la p. haute, basse**, to be high-breasted, low-breasted; **dans l'eau jusqu'à la p.**, breast-deep, breast-high, in water; (*b*) *Cu:* breast (of veal); brisket (of beef).

poitriner [pwatrine], *v.i.* (*a*) *F:* to stick out one's chest; (*b*) *P:* to posture, swagger.

poitrinière [pwatrinjɛ:r], *s.f.* **1.** *Harn:* breast strap. **2.** (weaver's) breast beam.

poivrade [pwavrad], *s.f.* (*a*) vinaigrette, poivrade (sauce) (for calf's head, etc.); (*b*) **manger des artichauts à la p.**, to eat artichokes (raw) with pepper and salt; (*c*) *P:* boozing.

poivre [pwavr], *s.m.* **1.** (*a*) pepper; **p. blanc, noir**, white, black, pepper; **p. long**, long pepper; **p. de Cayenne, p. d'Amérique**, Cayenne pepper, red pepper; **grain de p.**, peppercorn; **p. moulu**, ground pepper; *Com:* **p. grabeau**, ground pepper of inferior quality; *F: A:* **moudre du p.**, to trudge wearily along (on sore feet); **livre qui manque de p.**, book that lacks spice, that lacks pep; *s.a.* PILER; *a.inv.* **p. et sel**, pepper-and-salt (colour); **cheveux p. et sel**, grizzly, iron-grey, hair; (*b*) **p. indien d'Éthiopie, de Guinée**, malaguetta pepper, grains of paradise; **p. à queue**, cubeb(a); cubeb pepper; **p. de la Jamaïque**, sweet pepper, pimento; (*c*) *P:* brandy. **2.** *Bot:* **p. d'eau**, water pepper; **p. des murailles**, biting yellow stonecrop; **p. de Brabant**, sweet gale, bog myrtle; **p. sauvage, petit p., p. des moines**, agnus castus, chaste tree, Abraham's balm.

poivré [pwavre], *a.* peppery (food); pungent (smell); *F:* **paroles poivrées**, caustic speech; **récit p.**, spicy tale; **prix p.**, stiff, exorbitant, price.

poivrer [pwavre], *v.tr.* **1.** to pepper; to season (salad, etc.) with pepper; *F:* **p. ses paroles, ses écrits**, to pepper, spice, one's words, one's writings (with licentiousness, etc.); **p. l'addition, une note (d'hôtel), etc.**, to stick it on. **2.** *P:* to infect (s.o.) with venereal disease; *P:* to give (s.o.) a dose.

se poivrer, *P:* to get drunk.

poivrier [pwavrije], *s.m.* **1.** *Bot:* pepper plant. **2.** pepper pot. **3.** *P:* drunkard; **vol au p.**, robbing of drunken men, *U.S:* lush rolling.

poivrière [pwavrijɛ:r], *s.f.* **1.** pepper plantation. **2.** (*a*) pepper pot; (*b*) *Arch:* (small overhanging) watch turret, *F:* pepper-pot (turret).

poivron [pwavrɔ̃], *s.m.* pimento, sweet pepper.

poivrot [pwavro], *s. P:* drunkard, boozer.

poix [pwɑ, -a], *s.f.* (*a*) (pine)pitch; *esp.* cobbler's wax; **p. sèche**, resin; **noir comme p.**, pitch-dark; (*b*) **p. liquide**, tar; **p. de Judée**, asphalt; **enduire de p.**, to pitch; to wax (thread, etc.); **avoir de la p. aux mains**, to have sticky fingers (where money is concerned).

poix-résine [pwɑrezin], *s.f.* resin.

poker [pɔkɛ:r], *s.m.* (*a*) *Cards:* poker; **p. dice**, *P:* **p. d'as**, poker dice; *F:* **coup de p.**, (piece of) bluff; (*b*) *Tchn:* poker.

Polack [pɔlak], *s.m. P: Pej:* Pole, Polack.

polacre[1] [pɔlakr̥], *s.f.* **1.** *A.Nau:* (*three-masted Mediterranean vessel*) polacca. **2.** *Nau:* main jib of a lateen.

polacre[2], *s.m.* = POLAQUE[1].

polaire [pɔlɛ:r]. **1.** *a. Geog: Astr: El: Mth:* polar; *Astr:* **l'étoile p.**, *s.f.* **la p.**, the pole star, the lodestar, Polaris; **distance p.**, polar distance; **hauteur p.**, polar altitude; *Geog:* **cercle p.**, polar circle; **lièvre p.**, polar, Arctic, hare; **nuit p.**, polar night; **froid p.**, intense, Arctic, cold; *El: Magn:* **champ p.**, polar field; **molécule p.**, polar molecule; **pièce p., masse p.**, pole piece; **cornes polaires**, pole tips; **épanouissement p.**, pole shoe; **noyau p.**, pole core; *Mth:* **expression p.**, polar notation; **coordonnées polaires**, polar co-ordinates; **vecteur p.**, polar vector; **courbe p.**, polar curve; **triangle p.**, polar triangle; *Biol:* **globule p.**, polar body, globule. **2.** *s.f.* (*a*) *Mth:* polar; (*b*) *Av:* polar curve (of wing).

polaque[1] [pɔlak], *s.m. Hist:* Polack; Polish cavalryman (in the French army during 17th century).

polaque[2], *s.f. A.Nau:* polacca.

polar[1], **-are** [pɔlar], *s. Sch: F:* swot.

polar[2], *s.m. Publ: F:* detective story, whodunit.

polarimètre [pɔlarimɛtr̥], *s.m. Ph:* polarimeter.

polarimétrie [pɔlarimetri], *s.f. Ph:* polarimetry.

polarimétrique [pɔlarimetrik], *a. Ph:* polarimetric.

polarisabilité [pɔlarizabilite], *s.f. Ph:* polarizability.

polarisable [pɔlarizabl̥], *a. Ph:* polarizable.

polarisant [pɔlarizɑ̃], *a.* polarizing (apparatus, microscope).

polarisateur, -trice [pɔlarizatœ:r, -tris], *Ph:* **1.** *a.* polarizing (prism, current). **2.** *s.m.* polarizer.

polarisation [pɔlarizasjɔ̃], *s.f.* **1.** *Ph:* polarization, polarizing (of light; *El:* of electrodes); *Opt:* **plan de p.**, plane of polarization; **p. dans un plan**, plane polarization; **p. rotatoire**, rotary polarization; **p. irrégulière**, erratic polarization; **p. circulaire**, circular polarization; *El:* **courant de p.**, polarizing current. **2.** *Elcs: W.Tel:* **p. positive, négative**, positive, negative, bias; **p. automatique**, automatic bias; (*radar*) self bias; **p. de cathode**, cathode bias; **p. de coupure**, cut-off bias, grid bias; **p. de grille**, grid bias; **p. négative de grille**, negative grid voltage; **p. nulle**, zero bias; **pile de p.**, grid battery, bias cell; **pile de p. de grille**, C battery, control-grid battery; **résistance de p. de grille**, bias resistor, grid resistance; **résistance de p. automatique**, grid-leak resistor; **tension de p.**, bias voltage; **tension de p. de grille**, grid polarization voltage.

polariscope [pɔlariskɔp], *s.m. Opt:* polariscope.

polarisé [pɔlarize], *a. Ph:* polarized; *F:* **il est p. par les mathématiques**, he's obsessed with, by, maths; he's mad on maths; he's fanatical about maths.

polariser [pɔlarize], *v.tr. Ph:* to polarize; **p. l'intérêt sur un aspect particulier d'un problème**, to centre interest on a particular aspect of a problem.

se polariser, *v.pr.* to be polarized.

polariseur [pɔlarizœ:r], *s.m. Opt:* polarizer.

polarité [pɔlarite], *s.f.* (*a*) *Ph: El:* polarity; **p. normale**, straight polarity; **p. inverse**, reverse polarity; **inversion de la p.**, reversal of polarity; **inverseur de p.**, see-saw amplifier; **indicateur de p.**, polarity indicator; **indication de p.**, terminal marking; *W.Tel:* **p. négative, positive, du signal image**, negative, positive, picture phase, polarity; (*b*) *Biol:* **p. de l'œuf**, polarity of the ovum; (*c*) **c'est un sujet à polarités multiples**, this subject has many aspects.

polarogramme [pɔlarɔgram], *s.m. Ch:* polarogram.

polarographe [pɔlarɔgraf], *s.m. Ch: R.t.m:* Polarograph.

polarographie [pɔlarɔgrafi], *s.f. Ch:* polarography.

polarographique [pɔlarɔgrafik], *a. Ch:* polarographic.

polaroïd [pɔlarɔid], *s.m. Opt: R.t.m:* polaroid.

polastre [pɔlastr̥], *s.m. Plumb:* soldering pan.

polatouche [pɔlatuʃ], *s.m. Z:* flying squirrel, flying phalanger, polatouche.

polder [pɔldɛ:r], *s.m. Geog:* polder.

poldérisation [pɔlderizasjɔ̃], *s.f. Geog:* empoldering.

pôle [po:l], *s.m.* pole; (*a*) *Geog:* **p. nord, sud,** north, south, pole; **p. magnétique,** magnetic pole; **p. géographique,** true pole; **p. terrestre,** terrestrial pole; *Astr:* **p. céleste,** celestial pole; *Geom:* **p. d'un cercle,** pole of a circle; (*b*) *Magn:* **p. d'un aimant,** pole of a magnet; **p. nord,** north(-seeking) pole, red pole; **p. sud,** south(-seeking) pole, blue pole; **p. conséquent,** consequent pole; **p. saillant,** salient pole; **pôles de même nom,** like poles; **pôles de nom contraire,** opposite poles; *F:* **p. d'attraction,** magnet, centre of attraction; (*c*) *El:* **p. positif,** positive pole, terminal; anode; **p. négatif,** negative pole, terminal; cathode; **p. de commutation,** commutation pole, interpole; **distance entre pôles,** pole pitch; **écartement des pôles,** pole spacing; (*d*) *Cryst:* **p. analogue,** analogous pole; **p. antilogue,** antilogous pole; (*e*) *Anat:* **p. frontal,** polus frontalis; **p. occipital,** polus occipitalis.

polémarque [polemark], *s.m. Gr.Ant:* polemarch.

polémique [polemik]. **1.** *a.* polemic(al). **2.** *s.f.* (*a*) polemic, controversial discussion, controversy; (*b*) *Theol:* polemics.

polémiquer [polemike], *v.i.* to polemize.

polémiser [polemize], *v.i.* to polemize.

polémiste [polemist], *s.m.* controversialist, polemist.

polémoine [polemwan], *s.f. A: Bot:* polemonium.

polémoniacées [polemonjase], *s.f.pl. Bot:* Polemoniaceae.

polémonie [polemoni], *s.f. Bot:* polemonium; **p. bleue,** Greek valerian, Jacob's ladder.

polémonium [polemonjom], *s.m. Bot:* polemonium.

poli [poli]. **1.** *a.* (*a*) polished (marble, etc.); buffed (metal); burnished, bright (steel, etc.); glossy, sleek (coat of animal); **p. comme la glace,** as smooth as ice; *Ind:* **parties polies,** bright parts (of machinery, etc.); **bright works;** (*b*) polished, elegant (style, writer); polite, courteous (person, manners); **les Japonais sont un peuple p.,** the Japanese are a polite race; **être très p. avec qn,** to be very polite, very courteous, to s.o.; **toute la famille s'est montrée très polie envers moi,** the whole family were very courteous to me; **peuple p.,** cultured, polite, people; **refus p.,** polite refusal; **enfant p.,** polite, well-mannered, child; (*to child*) **sois p.!** mind your manners! **il a été tout juste p. avec moi,** he was just about polite to me; he just missed being rude; **se montrer peu p.,** to be rude, discourteous. **2.** *s.m.* polish, gloss; **p. brillant,** high polish; **bois qui prend un beau p.,** wood that takes a high polish.

polianite [poljanit], *s.f. Miner:* polianite.

polianthe [poljã:t], *s.m. Bot:* tuberose; (*genus*) Polianthes.

police¹ [polis], *s.f.* **1.** *A:* government, administration; organization. **2.** maintenance of law and order; policing; **exercer, faire, la p.,** to maintain law and order; **p. des réunions,** maintenance of order (by the police) at (public) meetings; **quand plusieurs centaines de personnes délibèrent ensemble, il leur faut une sorte de p. intérieure,** when several hundred people meet for discussions, they need their own (private) system of maintaining order; **p. du roulage, de la circulation,** traffic regulations; **numéro, plaque, de p. d'un véhicule,** registration number of a vehicle; **contrevenir aux règlements de p.,** to contravene police regulations; (*at hotel*) **feuille, fiche, de p.,** (police) registration form; *Mil:* **salle de p.,** guard room; **poste de p.,** guard house; **piquet de p.,** police picket. **3. la p.,** the police (force); **force de p. des Nations Unies,** police force of the United Nations; **p. municipale, rurale,** municipal, country, police (force); **p. de la circulation, de la route,** traffic police; **p. militaire,** military police; **p. judiciaire (P.J.)** = Criminal Investigation Department (C.I.D.); **p. mondaine, p. des mœurs** = vice squad; **appeler p. secours** = to dial 999 (for the police); **être de, dans, la p.,** to be a member of the police force, to be in the police; **agent de p.,** police constable, policeman; **inspecteur de p.** = police inspector; **commissaire de p.** = police inspector (in the C.I.D.); **commissariat de p.,** police station; **le préfet de p.,** the chief commissioner of the Paris police; **la préfecture de p.,** the headquarters of the Paris police; **dénoncer qn à la p.,** to denounce s.o. to the police; **remettre qn entre les mains de la p.,** to give s.o. in charge; **la p. est à vos trousses,** the police are after you.

police², *s.f.* **1.** (*a*) (insurance) policy; **p. ouverte, non évaluée,** open policy; **p. d'assurance (sur la) vie, (contre l')incendie,** life insurance, fire insurance, policy; **p. à temps, à terme,** time policy;

p. à forfait, policy for a specific amount; **p. évaluée, non évaluée,** valued, non-valued, policy; **p. flottante,** floating policy, floater; **p. type, standard policy;** *M.Ins:* **p. à navire dénommé,** named (ship) policy; **p. d'abonnement, p. flottante, p. ouverte,** floating policy, open policy, open cover; **p. sur corps,** hull, ship, policy; **p. sur facultés,** cargo policy; **prendre une p.,** to take out a policy; (*b*) *Com:* **p. de chargement,** bill of lading; (*c*) *El:* **p. mixte (force et lumière),** all-in agreement. **2.** *Typ:* scale of assortment, bill of type, bill of a fount.

policer [polise], *v.tr.* (je poliçai(s); n. poliçons) to bring (country) under orderly government; to organize (country); *A. & Lit:* to civilize.

polichinelle [polifinel], *s.m.* **1.** Punch, Punchinello; **théâtre de p.,** Punch and Judy show; **secret de p.,** open secret; **voix de p.,** shrill, quavering voice. **2.** *F:* (*a*) ugly, misshapen, person; figure of fun; (*b*) **faire le p.,** to act the buffoon; (*c*) **mener une vie de p.,** to go the pace, to lead a rackety life; (*d*) (*pers.*) weathercock. **3.** *P:* (*not used in polite company*) **avoir un p. dans le tiroir,** to be pregnant, *P:* to have a bun in the oven.

polichineller [polifinele], *v.i. F:* to play the clown, to act the buffoon.

policier, -ière [polisje, -jɛ:r]. **1.** *a.* **enquête policière,** police enquiry; **chien p.,** police dog; **état sous un régime p.,** police state; **roman p.,** detective novel, story. **2.** *s.m.* (*a*) police officer; (*b*) detective; (*c*) *F:* detective novel, story.

policlinique [poliklinik], *s.f. Med:* policlinic.

poliment [polimã], *adv.* politely, courteously.

polio [poljo], *s.f. Med: F:* polio.

polioencéphalite [poljoãsefalit], *s.f. Med:* polioencephalitis.

poliomyélite [poljomjelit], *s.f. Med:* poliomyelitis.

poliomyélitique [poljomjelitik], *a. & s.m. & f. Med:* poliomyelitic, *F:* polio (case).

polir [poli:r], *v.tr.* **1.** to polish (steel, marble, wood); to burnish, buff (metal, etc.); to smooth, make glossy (animal's coat); **chaises polies par l'usage,** chairs shiny with use; **pâte à p. les métaux,** metal polish; **machine à p.,** buffing machine; **se p. les ongles,** to polish one's nails. **2.** to polish (one's mind, style, manners, etc.).

polissable [polisabl], *a.* polishable.

polissage [polisa:ʒ], *s.m.* polishing, burnishing, smoothing, buffing; **p. au feutre,** bobbing; **p. électrolytique,** electrolytic polishing, electro-polishing.

polissement [polismã], *s.m.* **1.** *A: except in Tex:* polishing. **2.** *A:* civilizing.

polisseur, -euse [polisœ:r, -ø:z]. **1.** *s.* polisher; **p. d'aiguilles,** needle polisher; **p. d'armes blanches,** sword furbisher; **p. de pierres précieuses,** gem cutter. **2.** *s.f.* **polisseuse,** polishing machine; grinding machine; buffing machine.

polissoir [poliswa:r], *s.m. Tls:* polisher, burnisher; polishing tool, polishing machine; buff stick; buff(ing) wheel; *Toil:* nail polisher.

polissoire [poliswa:r], *s.f.* **1.** polishing brush (for shoes, etc.). **2.** meule p., (cutler's) polishing stone; polishing wheel. **3.** *Ind:* polishing shop.

polisson, -onne [polisõ, -on]. **1.** *s.* (*a*) street urchin; (*b*) scamp, little wretch; **mon p. de neveu,** my scamp of a nephew; (*c*) *A:* (i) depraved, licentious, person; (ii) man affecting mischievous, childish, behaviour. **2.** *a.* (*a*) **enfant p.,** mischievous child; (*b*) **propos polissons,** smutty talk; **regard p.,** leer; **conte p.,** dirty story.

polissonner [polisone], *v.i.* **1.** *A:* to be licentious, bawdy. **2.** (*of child*) (*a*) to be mischievous, naughty; (*b*) to roam the streets.

polissonnerie [polisonri], *s.f.* **1.** (child's) act of mischief; mischievousness. **2.** (*a*) questionable behaviour; (*b*) questionable remark; smutty joke.

polissure [polisy:r], *s.f.* **1.** polishing. **2.** polish (of metals, etc.).

poliste [polist], *s.f. Ent:* polistes.

politesse [polites], *s.f.* (*a*) politeness; good manners; courtesy; **la p. la plus élémentaire exige que . . .,** it is only common politeness to . . .; **je lui apprendrai la p.!** I'll show him how to behave! **brûler la p. à qn,** (i) to leave s.o. abruptly, without saying goodbye; to give s.o. the slip; (ii) to fail to keep an appointment with s.o.; (iii) to steal a march on s.o.; (*b*) **faire des politesses à qn,** (i) to greet, (ii) to treat, s.o. courteously, politely; **faire échange de politesses,** to exchange compliments; **formules de p.,** (i) polite, conventional, phrases (used in conversation); (ii) conventional beginning and ending (of a letter); **se confondre en politesses,** to fall over oneself to be polite.

politicaille [politika:j], *s.f.* **politicaillerie** [politikɑj(ə)ri], *s.f. F: Pej:* wire pulling, political manœuvring, *U.S:* playing politics; peanut politics.

politicailler [politikaje], *v.i. F: Pej:* to indulge in wire pulling, in political manœuvring.

politicailleur [politikajœ:r], *s.m.,* **politicard** [politika:r], *s.m. F. Pej:* wire puller, political manœuvrer.

politicien, -ienne [politisjɛ̃, -jɛn], *s. usu. Pej:* politician.

politico-économique [politikoekonɔmik], *a.* politico-economic; *pl. politico-économiques.*

politicologie [politikolɔʒi], *s.f.* political economy.

politicologue [politikolɔg], *s.m. & f. Pol:Ec:* political economist, *U.S:* political scientist.

politicomanie [politikomani], *s.f.* politicomania.

politique [politik]. **1.** *a.* (*a*) political (party, rights, institutions); (**homme) p.,** politician; **le corps p.,** the body politic; **sciences politiques,** political science; **économie p.,** economics; (*b*) politic, prudent, shrewd (person, behaviour); diplomatic (answer, conduct). **2.** *s.f.* (*a*) policy; **p. intérieure, extérieure,** home policy, foreign policy; **considérer comme de bonne p. de . . .,** to consider it (good) policy to . . .; **p. de la porte ouverte,** open-door policy; (*b*) polity; **système de p. positive,** a system of positive polity; (*c*) politics; **étudier la p.,** to study politics; **p. de clocher,** parish-pump politics; **se jeter, se lancer, dans la p.,** to go into politics. **3.** *s.m.* (*a*) *Hist:* politique; (*b*) political prisoner.

politiquement [politikmã], *adv.* (*a*) politically; **être p. d'accord avec qn,** to share s.o.'s political ideas; **penser p.,** to think from a political point of view; (*b*) politically, diplomatically.

politiquer [politike], *v.i. A: F:* **1.** to dabble in politics. **2.** to talk politics.

politiqueur, -euse [politikœ:r, -ø:z], *s. A: F:* armchair politician; dabbler in politics.

politisation [politizasjõ], *s.f.* politization; **la p. des syndicats ouvriers,** the political orientation of the trade unions.

politiser [politize], *v.tr.* to politicize, to give a political aspect to sth.; **p. des élections syndicales,** to give (trade) union elections a political basis; to bring politics into union elections.

politologie [politolɔʒi], *s.f.* political economy.

poljé [poljɛ], *s.m. Geog:* polje.

polka [polka], *s.f.* **1.** *Danc: Mus:* polka. **2.** (quarryman's) hammer.

pollakiurie [pol(l)akiryi], *s.f. Med:* pollakiuria.

pollen [pol(l)ɛn], *s.m. Bot:* pollen; *Ap:* bee bread; **taux du p.,** pollen count.

pollénographie [pol(l)enografi], *s.f.* palynology.

polletais, -aise [polte, -ɛ:z], *a. & s. Geog:* (native, inhabitant) of Le Pollet (near Dieppe); *s.m. Nau:* **grand p.,** Dieppe herring boat.

pollex [polɛks], *s.m. Anat: Orn:* pollex.

pollicial, -aux [pol(l)isjal, -o], *a. Anat: Orn:* pollicial.

pollicitation [pol(l)isitasjõ], *s.f. Jur:* pollicitation, tentative offer.

pollination [pol(l)inasjõ], *s.f. A: Bot:* pollination.

pollinide [pol(l)inid], *s.m.,* **pollinie** [pol(l)ini], *s.f. Bot:* pollinium.

pollinifère [pol(l)inifɛ:r], *a.* polliniferous.

pollinique [pol(l)inik], *a. Bot:* pollinic; **sac p.,** pollen sac; **tube p.,** pollen tube.

pollinisateur, -trice [pol(l)inizatœ:r, -tris], (*a*) *a.* pollinating; (*b*) *s.m.* pollinator.

pollinisation [pol(l)inizasjõ], *s.f. Bot:* pollination; **p. directe,** self pollination; **p. croisée, indirecte,** cross pollination.

polliniser [pol(l)inize], *v.tr. Bot:* to pollinate.

polliniseur [pol(l)inizœ:r], *a.* **oiseaux polliniseurs,** (flower-)pollinating birds.

pollinose [pol(l)ino:z], *s.f.,* **pollinosis** [pol(l)inozis], *s.m. Med:* pollinosis, hay fever.

Pollion [pol(l)jõ], *Pr.n.m. Rom.Hist:* Pollio.

polluant [pol(l)qã], *s.m.* pollutant, agent of pollution; **des polluants atmosphériques,** pollution in the atmosphere, atmospheric pollution.

pollucite [pol(l)ysit], *s.f. Miner:* pollucite.

polluer [pol(l)qe], *v.tr.* (*a*) *A: & Lit:* to pollute, defile; to profane (holy place); (*b*) to pollute (atmosphere, etc.).

pollution [pol(l)ysjõ], *s.f.* (*a*) *A: & Lit:* pollution, defilement; profanation (of holy place); (*b*) *Med:* pollution; (*c*) **p. atmosphérique, p. de l'air,** atmospheric pollution, pollution of the atmosphere; **p. des cours d'eau,** river pollution; **agent de p.,** pollutant.

Pollux [pol(l)yks], *Pr.n.m. Gr.Myth: Astr:* Pollux.

polo [polo], *s.m.* **1.** *Sp:* polo. **2.** *Cost:* (*a*) *O:* polo-necked jersey; (*b*) sweat shirt; (*c*) *A:* (woman's) round knitted cap.

polochon [pɔlɔʃɔ̃], *s.m. P:* bolster; **combat bataille, à coups de p., de polochons,** pillow fight; **partie de p.,** nap, snooze.
Pologne [pɔlɔɲ], *Pr.n.f. Geog:* Poland.
polois, -oise [pɔlwa, -wa:z], *a. & s. Geog:* (native, inhabitant) of Saint-Pol.
poloïste [pɔlɔist], *s.m. Sp:* polo player.
polonais, -aise [pɔlɔnɛ, -ɛ:z]. **1.** *Geog:* (*a*) *a.* Polish; (*b*) *Const:* **appareil p.,** double Flemish bond; (*c*) *s.* Pole; **soûl comme un P.,** as drunk as a lord. **2.** *s.m. Ling:* Polish. **3.** *s.m. Fung:* (*a*) saffron milk cap; (*b*) boletus edulis. **4.** *s.f. Cost: Danc: Mus:* **polonaise,** polonaise. **5.** *s.f. Cu:* **polonaise,** meringue-covered pastry containing kirsch and preserved fruit.
polonisant, -ante [pɔlɔnizɑ̃, -ɑ̃:t], *s.* Polish scholar.
polonium [pɔlɔnjɔm], *s.m. Ch:* polonium.
poltron, -onne [pɔltrɔ̃, -ɔn]. **1.** *a.* easily frightened, timid, cowardly, *F:* funky. **2.** *s.* coward, *F:* funk; *F:* **c'est un p. révolté,** the worm has turned.
poltronnerie [pɔltrɔnri], *s.f.* **1.** cowardice; timidity. **2.** cowardly action; **céder n'est pas toujours une p.,** to yield is not always an act of cowardice.
poly- [pɔli], *pref.* poly-.
polyacide [pɔliasid], *a. & s.m. Ch:* polyacid.
polyacrylate [pɔliakrilat], *s.m. Ch:* polyacrylate.
polyacrylique [pɔliakrilik], *a. Ch:* polyacrylic.
polyadelphe [pɔliadɛlf], *a. Bot:* polyadelphous.
polyadénite [pɔliadenit], *s.f. Med:* polyadenia.
polyadénome [pɔliadenɔm], *s.m. Med:* polyadenoma.
polyadique [pɔliadik], *a.* polyadic.
polyalcool [pɔlialkɔl], *s.m. Ch:* polyalcohol.
polyamide [pɔliamid], *s.m. Ch:* polyamide.
polyandre [pɔliɑ̃:dr, -jɑ̃-], *a. Anthr: Bot:* polyandrous.
polyandrie [pɔliɑ̃dri, -jɑ̃-], *s.f.* **1.** *Anthr:* polyandry. **2.** *Bot:* polyandria.
polyandrique [pɔliɑ̃drik, -jɑ̃-], *a.* polyandric.
polyanthe [pɔliɑ̃:t, -jɑ̃-], *a. Bot:* polyanthous.
polyarchie [pɔliarʃi], *s.f.* polyarchy.
polyarthrite [pɔliartrit], *s.f. Med:* polyarthritis; **p. chronique évolutive,** rheumatoid arthritis.
polyarticulaire [pɔliartikylɛ:r], *a. Med:* polyarticular.
polyatomique [pɔliatɔmik], *a. Ch:* polyatomic.
polybasique [pɔlibɑzik], *a. Ch:* polybasic.
polybasite [pɔlibɑzit], *s.f. Miner:* polybasite.
Polybe [pɔlib], *Pr.n.m. Gr.Lit:* Polybius.
polybranches [pɔlibrɑ̃:ʃ], *s.m.pl. Moll:* Polybranchia, Polybranchiata.
Polycarpe[1] [pɔlikarp], *Pr.n.m.* (Saint) Polycarp.
polycarpe[2], *s.m. Bot:* polycarpon.
polycarpellé [pɔlikarpɛl(l)e], *a. Bot:* polycarpellary.
polycarpique [pɔlikarpik], **polycarpien, -ienne** [pɔlikarpjɛ̃, -jɛn], *a. Bot:* polycarpic, polycarpous.
polycellulaire [pɔlisɛlylɛ:r], *a. Biol:* polycellular.
polycentrique [pɔlisɑ̃trik], *a.* polycentric.
polycéphale [pɔlisefal], *a. Ter:* polycephalous.
polychètes [pɔlikɛt], *s.m.pl. Ann:* Polychaeta.
polychroïque [pɔlikrɔik], *a. Cryst:* polychroic, pleochroic.
polychroïsme [pɔlikrɔism], *s.m. Cryst:* polychroism, pleochroism.
polychromatophilie [pɔlikromatɔfili], *s.f. Med:* polychromatophilia.
polychrome [pɔlikro:m], *a.* polychrome, polychrom(at)ic.
polychromie [pɔlikromi], *s.f.* polychromy.
polychromisme [pɔlikromism], *s.m.* polychromism.
polyclades [pɔliklad], *s.m.pl. Z:* Polycladida.
polyclinique [pɔliklinik], *s.f. Med:* polyclinic.
polycondensat [pɔlikɔ̃dɑ̃sa], *s.m. Ch:* condensation polymer.
polycondensation [pɔlikɔ̃dɑ̃sasjɔ̃], *s.f. Ch:* condensation, polymerization; polycondensation.
polycopie [pɔlikɔpi], *s.f.* **1.** manifolding, stencilling, duplicating, process. **2.** (duplicated) copy.
polycopier [pɔlikɔpje], *v.tr.* (*conj. like* COPIER) to duplicate, to manifold; *O:* to (hecto)graph, to jellygraph; to stencil, to cyclostyle; *Sch:* **cours polycopié,** duplicated lecture notes.
polycorde [pɔlikɔrd], *s.m. A.Mus:* polychord.
polycotylédone [pɔlikɔtiledɔn], *a. Bot:* polycotyledonous.
polycrase [pɔlikra:z], *s.f. Miner:* polycrase.
Polycrate [pɔlikrat], *Pr.n.m. Gr.Hist:* Polycrates.
polyculture [pɔlikylty:r], *s.f.* polyculture, mixed farming.
polycyclique [pɔlisiklik], *a. Ch: Ph:* polycyclic; *Elcs:* multi-frequency.

polycylindrique [pɔlisilɛ̃drik], *a. I.C.E:* multicylinder (engine).
polycythémie [pɔlisitemi], *s.f. Med:* polycyth(a)emia.
polydactyle [pɔlidaktil], *Z:* (*a*) *a.* polydactyl(ous); (*b*) *s.m. & f.* polydactyl.
polydactylie [pɔlidaktili], *s.f.,* **polydactylisme** [pɔlidaktilism], *s.m.* polydactyly, polydactylism.
polydipsie [pɔlidipsi], *s.f. Med:* polydipsia.
polydymite [pɔlidimit], *s.f. Miner:* polydymite.
polyèdre [pɔliɛdr, -jɛ-], *Geom:* **1.** *a.* polyhedral. **2.** *s.m.* polyhedron; solid angle.
polyédrique [pɔliedrik, -je-], *a. Geom:* polyhedral, polyhedric.
polyembryonie [pɔliɑ̃brijɔni, -jɑ̃-], *s.f. Biol:* polyembryony.
polyergue [pɔliɛrg, -jɛ-], *s.m. Ent:* polyergus.
polyester [pɔliɛstɛ:r, -jɛ-], *s.m. Ch:* polyester.
polyestérification [pɔliesterifikasjɔ̃, -jɛ-], *s.f.* polyesterification.
polyéthylène [pɔlietilɛn, -je-], *s.m. Ch:* polyethylene, polythene.
polygala [pɔligala], *s.m.,* **polygale** [pɔligal], *s.m.* **1.** *Bot:* milkwort; (*genus*) Polygala. **2.** *Bot: Pharm:* **p. de Virginie,** Senega root, snakeroot.
polygalacées [pɔligalase], **polygalées** [pɔligale], *s.f.pl. Bot:* Polygalaceae.
polygame [pɔligam]. **1.** *a.* polygamous (person, animal, plant). **2.** *s.m. & f.* polygamist.
polygamie [pɔligami], *s.f.* **1.** *Anthr: Bot:* polygamy. **2.** *A: Bot:* polygamia.
polygamique [pɔligamik], *a.* polygamous.
polygénétique [pɔliʒenetik], *a. Ch:* polygenetic.
polygénie [pɔliʒeni], *s.f. Biol:* polygeny.
polygénique [pɔliʒenik], *a.* (*a*) *Anthr:* polygenic; (*b*) *Geol:* polygenetic.
polygénisme [pɔliʒenism], *s.m. Anthr:* polygenism.
polygéniste [pɔliʒenist], *s.m. & f. Anthr:* polygenist.
polyglobulie [pɔliglɔbyli], *s.f. Med:* polyglobulia.
polyglotte [pɔliglɔt]. **1.** *a. & s.m. & f.* polyglot. **2.** *s.f.* polyglot Bible.
polyglottisme [pɔliglɔtism], *s.m.* polyglottism.
polygonacées [pɔligɔnase], *s.f.pl. Bot:* Polygonaceae.
polygonal, -aux [pɔligɔnal, -o], *a. Mth: etc:* polygonal; *Const:* **appareil p.,** polygonal rubble; *Geol:* **sol p.,** polygon soil; patterned ground.
polygonation [pɔligɔnasjɔ̃], *s.f.* polygonation.
polygone [pɔligɔn]. **1.** *a.* polygonal. **2.** *s.m.* (*a*) *Geom:* polygon; *Mec:* **p. des forces,** polygon of forces; *El:* **montage en p.,** polygon connection; (*b*) *Mil: Artil:* experimental range, proving ground, shooting range; **p. d'essais,** test site (of atomic bomb, etc.).
polygraphe [pɔligraf], *s.m.* **1.** *Typ:* polygraph. **2.** (*a*) versatile writer; (*b*) *Pej:* voluminous writer.
polygraphie [pɔligrafi], *s.f. Typ:* polygraphy.
polygraphique [pɔligrafik], *a.* **les industries polygraphiques,** printing and kindred trades.
polygynie [pɔliʒini], *s.f.* polygyny.
polyhalite [pɔlialit], *s.f. Miner:* polyhalite.
polyhybride [pɔliibrid], *s.m. Biol:* polyhybrid.
polyhybridisme [pɔliibridism], *s.m. Biol:* polyhybridism.
polyisoprène [pɔliizɔprɛn], *s.m. Ch:* polyisoprene.
polylobe [pɔlilɔb], **polylobé** [pɔlilɔbe], *a. Arch:* multifoil.
polymastie [pɔlimasti], *s.f. Anat:* polymastia, polymasty.
polymastigines [pɔlimastiʒin], *s.f.pl. Prot:* Polymastiga, Polymastigida.
polymastodon [pɔlimastɔdɔ̃], *s.m. Paleont:* polymastodon.
polymèle [pɔlimɛl], *a. & s.m. Ter:* polymelian.
polymélie [pɔlimeli], *s.f. Ter:* polymelia, polymely.
polymère [pɔlimɛ:r]. **1.** *a. Ch:* polymeric; *Biol:* polymerous. **2.** *s.m. Ch:* polymer; **p. acryloïde,** acryloid polymer; **p. éthylénique,** ethylene polymer.
polymérie [pɔlimeri], *s.f. Ch:* polymerism; polymeria; *Biol:* polymery.
polymérisation [pɔlimerizasjɔ̃], *s.f. Ch:* polymerization; curing, processing (of resin); **p. conjointe,** conjunct polymerization; **p. thermique,** thermal polymerization; **inhibiteur de p.,** short stopper; *Dent:* **p. d'une prothèse,** curing, processing, of a denture.
polymériser [pɔlimerize], *v.tr. Ch:* to polymerize; to cure, process (resin); *Dent:* **p. une prothèse,** to cure, process, a denture.
polyméthylène [pɔlimetilɛn], *s.m. Ch:* polymethylene.
polymètre [pɔlimɛtr], *s.m. Elcs:* (*computers*) all-purpose meter.

polymignite [pɔlimiɲit], *s.f. Miner:* polymignyte, polymignite.
polymnia [pɔlimnja], *s.m. Bot:* polymnia.
Polymnie [pɔlimni]. **1.** *Pr.n.f. Myth:* (the Muse) Polyhymnia. **2.** *s.f. Ann:* polymnia.
polymorphe [pɔlimɔrf], *a. Biol: Ch:* polymorphous, polymorphic, pleomorphic; *Elcs:* (*of computer*) **système p.,** polymorphic system.
polymorphique [pɔlimɔrfik], *a.* polymorphic.
polymorphie [pɔlimɔrfi], *s.f.,* **polymorphisme** [pɔlimɔrfism], *s.m. Biol: Ch:* polymorphism.
polymyosite [pɔlimjɔzit], *s.f. Med:* polymyositis.
Polynésie [pɔlinezi], *Pr.n.f. Geog:* Polynesia.
polynésien, -ienne [pɔlinezjɛ̃, -jɛn], *a. & s. Geog:* Polynesian.
polynévrite [pɔlinevrit], *s.f. Med:* polyneuritis.
Polynice [pɔlinis], *Pr.n.m. Gr.Lit:* Polynices.
polynoé [pɔlinɔe], *s.f. Ann:* polynoid, scale worm; (*genus*) Polynoe.
polynôme [pɔlino:m], *s.m. Alg:* polynomial.
polynucléaire [pɔlinykleɛ:r], *a. Biol:* polynuclear; **leucocyte p.,** polynuclear leucocyte.
polynucléé [pɔlinyklee], *a. Biol:* polynucleate.
polynucléose [pɔlinykleo:z], *s.f. Med:* polynucleosis.
polyol [pɔljɔl], *s.m. Ch:* polyalcohol.
polyonychie [pɔljɔniki], *s.f. Med:* polyonychia.
polyopie [pɔljɔpi], *s.f. Opt:* polyopia.
polyopsie [pɔljɔpsi], *s.f. Opt:* polyopsia, polyopsy.
polyose [pɔljo:z], *s.m. Ch:* polyose.
polyoxyméthylène [pɔliɔksimetilɛn, -jɔ-], *s.m. Ch:* polyoxymethylene.
polype [pɔlip], *s.m.* **1.** *Coel:* polyp. **2.** *Med:* polypus, polyp.
polypeptide [pɔlipɛptid], *s.m. Ch:* polypeptide.
polypeptidique [pɔlipɛptidik], *a.* polypeptide (chain, etc.).
polypétale [pɔlipetal], *a. Bot:* polypetalous.
polypeux, -euse [pɔlipø, -ø:z], *a. Med:* polypous.
polyphage [pɔlifa:ʒ]. **1.** *a. Med: Z:* polyphagous. **2.** *s.m.pl. Ent:* **polyphages,** Polyphaga.
polyphagie [pɔlifaʒi], *s.f. Biol: Med:* polyphagia.
polyphasé [pɔlifɑze], *a. El: Elcs:* polyphase, multiphase (current, system).
Polyphème [pɔlifɛm], *Pr.n.m. Myth:* Polyphemus.
polyphénol [pɔlifenɔl], *s.m. Ch:* polyphenol.
polyphone [pɔlifɔn], *a.* polyphonic.
polyphonie [pɔlifɔni], *s.f.* polyphony.
polyphonique [pɔlifɔnik], *a.* polyphonic.
polyphylétisme [pɔlifiletism], *s.m. Biol:* polyphyly.
polyphyodonte [pɔlifjɔdɔ̃:t], *a. & s.m. Z:* polyphyodont.
polypide [pɔlipid], *s.m. Prot:* polypide.
polypier [pɔlipje], *s.m. Coel:* polypary.
polyplacophores [pɔliplakɔfɔ:r], *s.m.pl. Moll:* Polyplacophora.
polyploïde [pɔliplɔid], *a. & s.m. & f. Biol:* polyploid.
polyploïdie [pɔliplɔidi], *s.m. Biol:* polyploidy.
polypnée [pɔlipne], *s.f. Med:* polypnoea.
polypode [pɔlipɔd]. **1.** *a. & s.m. Z:* polypod; *s.m.pl.* **polypodes,** Polypoda. **2.** *s.m. Bot:* polypod(y); polypodium; **p. vulgaire, du chêne,** wall fern; **p. phégoptère,** beech fern.
polypodiacées [pɔlipɔdjase], *s.f.pl. Bot:* Polypodiaceae.
polypodie [pɔlipɔdi], *s.f. Ter:* polypodia.
polypoïde [pɔlipɔid], *a. Z: Med:* polypoid.
polypore [pɔlipɔ:r], *s.m. Fung:* polyporus.
polypose [pɔlipo:z], *s.f. Med:* polyposis.
polypotome [pɔlipɔtɔm], *s.m. Surg:* polypotome.
polyprène [pɔliprɛn], *s.m. Ch:* polyprene.
polypropylène [pɔliprɔpilɛn], *s.m. Ch:* polypropylene.
polyprotodontes [pɔliprɔtɔdɔ̃:t], *s.m.pl. Z:* Polyprotodontia.
polyptère [pɔliptɛ:r], *s.m. Ich:* bichir; lungfish; (*genus*) Polypterus.
polyptyque [pɔliptik], *s.m. Art:* polyptych.
polysaccharide [pɔlisakarid], *s.m. Ch:* polysaccharide.
polyscope [pɔliskɔp], *s.m. Opt:* polyscope.
polysémie [pɔlisemi], *s.f. Ling:* polysemia.
polysémique [pɔlisemik], *a. Ling:* polysemous.
polysépale [pɔlisepal], *a. Bot:* polysepalous.
polysérite [pɔliserit], *s.f. Med:* polyserositis.
polysoc [pɔlisɔk], *s.m. Agr:* multiple plough, gang plough.
polyspermie [pɔlispɛrmi], *s.f. Biol:* polyspermia, polyspermy.
polystélie [pɔlisteli], *s.f. Bot:* polystely.
polystélique [pɔlistelik], *a. Bot:* polystelic.
polystic [pɔlistik], **polystichum** [pɔlistikɔm], *s.m. Bot:* Polystichum.
polystyle [pɔlistil], *a. Arch:* Polystyle (hall, temple).

polystyrène [polistirɛn], **polystyrolène** [polystirɔlɛn], *s.m. Ch:* polystyrene.
polysulfure [polisylfy:r], *s.m. Ch:* polysulphide.
polysyllabe [polisil(l)ab]. 1. *a.* polysyllabic (word). 2. *s.m.* polysyllable.
polysyllabique [polisil(l)abik], *a.* polysyllabic.
polysyllabisme [polisil(l)abism], *s.m.* polysyllabism.
polysyllogisme [polisil(l)ɔʒism], *s.m.* polysyllogism.
polysyllogistique [polisil(l)ɔʒistik], *a.* polysyllogistic.
polysyndète [polisɛ̃dɛt], *s.f. Rh:* polysyndeton.
polysynthèse [polisɛ̃tɛːz], *s.f. Ling:* polysynthesis.
polysynthétique [polisɛ̃tetik], *a. Ling:* polysynthetic.
polytechnicien, -ienne [politɛknisjɛ̃, -jɛn], *s.* (i) student at, (ii) graduate of, the *École polytechnique.*
polytechnique [politɛknik], *a.* polytechnic; *s.a.* ÉCOLE.
polyterpène [politɛrpɛn], *s.m. Ch:* polyterpene.
polythéisme [politeism], *s.m.* polytheism.
polythéiste [politeist], *a. & s.m. & f.* polytheist.
polythéistique [politeistik], *a.* polytheistic.
polythélie [politeli], *s.f. Anat:* polythelia.
polythène [politɛn], *s.m.* polythene, polyethylene.
polytraumatisé, -ée [politromatize], *a. & s.* (patient) having multiple injuries.
polytric [politrik], *s.m. Moss:* polytrichum.
polytypique [politipik], *a.* polytypic.
polyuréthanne [poliyretan], *s.m.* polyurethan(e).
polyurie [poliyri], *s.f. Med:* polyuria, polyuresis.
polyurique [poliyrik], *a. Med:* polyuric.
polyvalence [polivalɑ̃ːs], *s.f. Ch:* polyvalence, multivalency; *Tchn:* versatility (of equipment, plant, etc.).
polyvalent [polivalɑ̃]. 1. *a.* polyvalent, multivalent; multiple-purpose (building, etc.); *Mil:* multi-mission (aircraft, weapon, etc.); **outil p.,** versatile tool; *Elcs:* (*of computer*) **calculateur p.,** general purpose computer; **notation polyvalente,** polyvalent notation; **programme p.,** generalized routine. 2. *s.m.* (*a*) *Adm:* special tax inspector; (*b*) *Sch:* teacher who specializes in several subjects.
polyvinyle [polivinil], *s.m.* polyvinyl; **acétate de p.,** polyvinyl acetate; **chlorure de p.,** polyvinyl chloride.
polyvinylique [polivinilik], *a.* polyvinyl; **acétal p.,** polyvinyl acetal; **alcool p.,** polyvinyl alcohol.
polyvoltin [polivɔltɛ̃], *a.* (*esp. of silkworms*) polyvoltine.
Polyxène [poliksɛn], *Pr.n.f. Gr.Lit:* Polyxena.
pomacé [pɔmase], *a.* pomaceous.
pomaderris [pɔmadɛris], *s.m. Bot:* pomaderris.
pomaison [pɔmezɔ̃], *s.f. Hort:* cabbaging season, season when cabbages come to a head.
pombé [pɔ̃be], *s.m.* pombe, millet beer.
pomelo [pomelo], *s.m. Bot:* pomelo; grapefruit.
Poméranie [pɔmerani], *Geog:* Pomerania; *Z:* **loulou de P.,** Pomeranian (dog), *F:* pom.
poméranien, -ienne [pɔmeranjɛ̃, -jɛn], *a. & s. Geog:* Pomeranian.
pomiculteur [pɔmikyltœːr], *s.m.* orchardist, fruit grower.
pomifère [pɔmifɛːr], *a. Bot:* pomiferous.
pommade [pɔmad], *s.f.* (*a*) pomade, pomatum (for the hair, etc.); (*b*) ointment (for skin troubles); *cp.* **pour les lèvres,** lip salve; (*c*) *F:* flattery; soft soap; **passer de la p. (dans les cheveux) à qn,** to flatter s.o.; to butter s.o. up.
pommader [pɔmade], *v.tr.* to pomade (one's hair, etc.).
pommadin [pɔmadɛ̃], *s.m. O: P:* (*a*) dandy; (*b*) hairdresser's assistant.
pomme [pɔm], *s.f.* 1. (*a*) apple; **p. à couteau,** eating apple, dessert apple; **p. à cidre,** cider apple; **p. sauvage,** crab apple; **compote de pommes,** (i) stewed apples, apple purée; (ii) apple sauce; **p. de discorde,** apple of discord; **chaque jour une p. conserve son homme** = an apple a day keeps the doctor away; *F:* (*of child*) **il est haut comme trois pommes,** he's only a little nipper, he's about as big as three penn'orth of coppers, he'd come knee-high to a grasshopper; *Anat: F:* **p. d'Adam,** Adam's apple; (*b*) **p. de terre,** potato; *Cu:* **pommes (de terre) frites,** chipped potatoes, chips, French fried potatoes; *F:* French fries; **pommes (de terre) à l'anglaise,** boiled potatoes; **pommes paille,** potato straws; **pommes chips,** potato crisps; **pommes (de terre) sautées,** sauté potatoes; **purée de pommes de terre,** mashed potatoes, potato puree; **bifteck aux pommes,** steak and chips; *F:* **tomber dans les pommes,** to pass out, to faint; (*c*) *F:* **p. épineuse,** thorn apple; **p. de merveille,** balsam apple; **p. de savon,** China berry; *A:* **p. d'amour,** tomato; *A:*

love apple; (*d*) **p. de chêne,** oak apple; **p. de pin,** pine cone; (*e*) *P:* **aux pommes,** first-rate. 2. *Bot:* pome; heart (of lettuce, cabbage). 3. (*a*) knob (of bedstead, walking stick, etc.); head (of cabbage, lettuce, etc.); rose (of watering can, etc.); (*b*) *Nau:* (i) truck (of mast); **p. de girouette,** acorn; **p. de racage,** parrel truck; (ii) diamond (knot) (in foot rope, etc.); (*c*) *P:* (i) head, nut; (ii) face, mug; **sucer la p. à qn,** to kiss s.o., to give s.o. a smacker; (iii) **ma p., ta p., sa p.,** etc., me, myself; you, yourself; him, her, himself, herself, etc.; (*d*) *F:* idiot; **pauvre p.!** you poor sucker!
pommé [pɔme], *a.* 1. *a.* (*a*) (*of cabbage, lettuce, etc.*) round (like an apple); rounded; **chou p.,** white-heart cabbage; **laitue pommée,** cabbage lettuce; **choux bien pommés,** fine heads of cabbage; *hence* (*b*) *F:* complete, utter, absolute, downright (fool, blunder, etc.); **repas p.,** first-rate dinner, slap-up dinner; **maladresse pommée,** downright, out-and-out, blunder; **en voilà des pommés!** they're enormous! they're whoppers! (*c*) *F:* lost, all at sea. 2. *s.m. Cu:* apple turnover.
pommeau, -eaux [pɔmo], *s.m.* pommel (of sword, saddle); butt (of fishing rod); **canne à p.,** knobbed stick.
pomme-cannelle [pɔmkanɛl], *s.f. Bot:* sweetsop; *pl.* **pommes-cannelles.**
pommelé [pɔmle], *a.* dappled, mottled; **jument gris p.,** dapple-grey mare; **ciel p.,** mackerel sky.
pommeler (se) [səpɔmle], *v.pr.* (**il se pommelle;** *il se pommellera*) 1. (*of sky*) to become dappled with small clouds. 2. (*of horse's coat*) to become dappled, mottled (with darker patches).
pomme-liane [pɔmljan], *s.f. Bot:* water lemon; *pl.* **pommes-lianes.**
pommelle [pɔmɛl], *s.f.* pierced cover, (lead) grating, strainer (over drain pipe, etc.).
pommer [pɔme], *v.i. & pr.* (*of cabbage, lettuce, etc.*) to form a head, heart; to heart, to head, to loaf; (*of lettuce*) to cabbage.
pommeraie [pɔmrɛ], *s.f.* apple orchard.
pommeté [pɔmte], *a. Her:* bourdonnée.
pommetier [pɔmtje], *s.m. Fr.C:* crab(-apple) tree.
pommette [pɔmɛt], *s.f.* 1. knob; ball ornament. 2. cheek bone; **pommettes saillantes,** prominent cheek bones; **petite vieille aux pommettes rouges,** little apple-cheeked old woman. 3. *Fr.C:* crab apple. 4. (*instrument*) fruit picker.
pommier [pɔmje], *s.m.* 1. (*a*) apple tree; **p. sauvage,** crab(-apple) tree; (*b*) **p. d'amour,** Jerusalem cherry tree. 2. *Cu:* apple roaster.
pomologie [pɔmɔlɔʒi], *s.f.* pomology.
pomologique [pɔmɔlɔʒik], *a.* pomological.
pomologiste [pɔmɔlɔʒist], *s.m. & f.,* **pomologue** [pɔmɔlɔg], *s.m. & f. Hort:* pomologist.
Pomone [pɔmɔn], *Pr.n.f. Myth:* Pomona.
pompadour [pɔ̃paduːr], *a.inv. & s.m.* Pompadour (style, design).
pompage [pɔ̃paːʒ], *s.m.* 1. pumping (up, out) (of water, etc.); **p. par commande excentrique,** back-crank pumping; **p. magnétique,** magnetic pumping; **p. pour faire, pour obtenir, le vide,** vacuum generation; **câble de p.,** pumping line; **chevalet de p.,** pumping jack; **station de p.,** pump(ing) station. 2. *Elcs:* exhaust(ion), evacuation (of vacuum valve). 3. (*a*) *El:* hunting; (*b*) (*maser*) pumping.
pompe¹ [pɔ̃p], *s.f.* pomp, ceremony, display; *Lit:* **renoncer aux pompes du siècle,** to renounce the pomps and vanities of this wicked world; **p. funéraire, funèbre,** obsequies, funeral; **pompes funèbres,** undertaking; **entrepreneur de pompes funèbres,** undertaker, funeral furnisher, *U.S:* mortician; **employé des pompes funèbres,** undertaker's assistant, mute.
pompe², *s.f.* 1. pump; (*a*) *Ph: Mec.E:* **p. aspirante,** suction pump, lift pump; **p. (re)foulante,** force pump; **p. aspirante et foulante,** lift-and-force pump; **p. à induction,** induction pump; **p. à jet,** jet pump; **p. alternative, p. à mouvement alternatif,** reciprocating pump; **p. à mouvement continu,** continuous-action pump; **p. à double effet,** double-acting pump; **p. à simple effet,** single-acting pump; **p. rotative,** rotary pump; **p. centrifuge,** centrifugal pump; **p. centrifuge à diffuseur,** turbo-pump; **p. principale,** main pump; **p. secondaire,** auxiliary pump; **p. auxiliaire,** booster pump; **p. à bras, à main,** hand pump; **p. à pied,** foot pump; **p. à moteur,** motor pump; **p. à vapeur,** steam(-driven) pump; **p. (à commande) électrique,** electric pump; **p. éolienne, à vent,** wind pump; **axe de p.,** pump spindle; **corps, cylindre, de p.,** pump body, barrel, cylinder; **p. à un, à trois, corps,** one-throw, three-throw, pump; **étage de p.,** pump stage; **p. à un étage, à deux étages,** one-

stage, two-stage, pump; **p. à plusieurs étages, p. multicellulaire,** multi-stage pump; **garniture, presse-étoupe, de p.,** pump pack, gland; **p. sans garniture, sans presse-étoupe,** packless, glandless, pump; **raccord, tuyauterie, de p.,** pump connection; **régulateur de p.,** pump governor; **bâtiment, chambre, compartiment, des pompes,** pump house, room, compartment; **p. à ailette, à palette,** vane pump; **p. à clapet,** (flap-)valve, pump; **p. sans clapet,** valveless pump; **p. à diaphragme, à membrane,** diaphragm pump; **p. à engrenage,** gear pump; **p. à piston, p. à (piston) plongeur,** piston, plunger, pump; **p. à piston creux, à piston plein,** hollow-piston, solid-piston, pump; **p. à hélice,** propeller pump; **p. à turbine,** turbine pump, impeller pump; **p. à vis,** screw pump; **p. à étrier,** stirrup pump; *F:* **coup de p.,** breakdown; *F:* **avoir le coup de p.,** to be fagged out, exhausted, *U.S:* pooped; *F:* **le coup de p. de onze heures,** that sinking feeling; *F:* **à toutes pompes,** as quickly as possible, at top speed; *Gym: F:* **faire des pompes,** to do pushups, press-ups; (*b*) **p. à air, p. pneumatique,** air pump, pneumatic pump; **p. à mercure,** mercurial air pump; **p. à vide,** vacuum pump; **p. à vide élevé,** high-vacuum pump; **p. de diffusion,** diffusion pump; **p. de compression,** compression pump, compressor; **p. de sur(com)pression,** booster pump; *Aut: Av:* **p. à pneu(matique)s,** (tyre) inflator; **p. à pneu(matique)s automatique,** mechanical (tyre) inflator; **p. à bicyclette,** bicycle pump; *Nau: Civ.E:* **p. de scaphandre,** diver's pump; (*c*) *Hyd:* **p. à eau, p. hydraulique,** water pump, hydraulic pump; **la p. du village,** the village pump; **eau de p.,** pump water; *F:* **Château la Pompe,** Adam's ale; **p. d'arrosage,** irrigating pump; **p. de jardin,** garden syringe; **p. à, d', incendie,** fire pump, fire engine; **les pompes,** fire-brigade equipment (generally); **p. à amorçage automatique,** self-priming pump; **p. d'amorçage,** priming, primer, pump; **p. à débit constant,** constant-flow pump; **p. à débit variable,** variable-delivery pump, adjustable-discharge pump; variable-flow pump; *Nau:* **p. de service,** water-service pump; **p. sanitaire,** sanitary pump; *Mch: Ind: Civ.E:* **p. d'alimentation, p. alimentaire,** feed pump, donkey pump; **p. d'alimentation électrique, à moteur, à vapeur,** electric motor, steam, feed pump; **p. d'alimentation en eau,** water feed pump; **p. d'alimentation de chaudière,** boiler feed pump; **p. d'épuisement, d'extraction,** discharge pump, brine pump, pumping engine; *Av:* scavenge(r) pump; **épuiser l'eau à la p.,** to pump out the water; *Nau:* **p. de cale,** bilge pump; **p. de(s) ballast(s),** ballast pump; **p. de chargement,** cargo pump; **p. d'assèchement,** stripping pump (of tanker); **p. à chapelet, à godets, à auges,** chain pump, chain of buckets, noria, paternoster; (*d*) *Mch: I.C.E:* **p. de circulation (d'eau, de combustible, d'huile),** (water, fuel, oil) circulation or circulating pump; **p. des circuits de réfrigérant,** coolant pump; **p. à graisse, p. de graissage,** grease gun, lubricating pump; **p. à huile,** oil pump; *I.C.E:* **p. à essence,** (i) petrol pump; (ii) petrol station; **p. (de station-service) à débit visible,** sight-feed petrol pump; **p. à carburant, à combustible,** fuel pump; **p. d'alimentation en combustible,** fuel-feed pump; **p. de suralimentation, de gavage (en combustible),** (fuel) booster pump; **p. d'injection (de carburant)** (fuel) injection pump (of diesel engine); **p. d'injection directe,** direct-injection pump; *Aut:* **p. de reprise,** accelerating pump; *Av:* **p. à main, p. à plateau oscillant,** wobble pump; **p. à effet venturi,** pump working with a venturi effect; (*e*) **p. à bière,** beer pull, beer engine; **bière à la p.,** beer on draught; (*f*) *Med:* pump, ejector; **p. à salive,** saliva pump, ejector; **p. à sein,** breast pump, reliever; **p. stomacale,** stomach pump; (*g*) *Atom.Ph:* **p. ionique,** ionic pump. 2. *Mus:* (*a*) slide (of trombone); (*b*) **p. d'accord,** tuning slide (of wind instrument). 3. **serrure à p.,** Bramah lock. 4. *Meteor:* **p. de mer,** waterspout. 5. *Tail:* **travail à la p.,** jobbing. 6. *P:* **pompes,** shoes, beetle-crushers.
Pompée [pɔ̃pe], *Pr.n.m. A.Hist:* Pompey.
Pompéi [pɔ̃pei], *Pr.n.f. Geog:* Pompeii.
pompéien, -ienne [pɔ̃pejɛ̃, -jɛn], *a. & s.* Pompeian.
pomper [pɔ̃pe]. 1. *v.tr.* (*a*) to pump (water, air); to suck up, suck in (liquid); *F:* to pump, draw information out of (s.o.); *F:* **p. ferme,** to pump away; **p. en circuit fermé,** to pump through the loop; *F:* **tu me pompes l'air,** you're exhausting me, wearing me out; (*b*) *Elcs:* to exhaust, evacuate (vacuum valve). 2. *v.i.* (*a*) to pump; (*b*) (*of engine, governor, etc.*) to hunt; (*c*) *Sch:*

F: (i) to swot; (ii) to copy from s.o.; (*d*) *P:* to tipple, booze; (*e*) **être pompé,** to be worn out, fagged out, exhausted; (*f*) (*referring to sun after rain*) **ça pompe,** it's drying well.

pomperie [pɔ̃pri], *s.f. Petroleum Ind:* pumping station.

pompette [pɔ̃pɛt], *a. F:* tight, tipsy.

pompeusement [pɔ̃pøzmɑ̃], *adv.* pompously.

pompeux, -euse [pɔ̃pø, -øːz], *a.* pompous.

pompier [pɔ̃pje], *s.m.* **1.** (*a*) maker of pumps; (*b*) pumpman. **2.** (*a*) fireman; **ligne de p.,** lifeline; (*b*) *Art: Lit: F:* conventionalist; formulist; uninspired writer, artist; *a.* conventional, uninspired, traditional (style, art). **3.** *A: F:* drinker, boozer. **4.** (*f.* **pompière**) *Tail: Dressm:* jobbing tailor; alteration hand.

pompiérisme [pɔ̃pjerism], *s.m. F: Art: Lit:* conventionalism; formulism.

pompile [pɔ̃pil], *s.m. Ent:* pompilid, hunting wasp.

pompilidés [pɔ̃pilide], *s.m.pl. Ent:* Pompilidae.

pompiste [pɔ̃pist]. **1.** *s.m. & f. Aut:* (petrol) pump assistant, attendant. **2.** *s.m. Nau:* pumpman.

pompon [pɔ̃pɔ̃], *s.m.* **1.** pompom, ornamental tuft; **en France le p. de laine rouge orne toujours le béret des marins,** in France sailors still wear caps with a red pompom; *F:* **à lui le p.,** he's easily first; he's streets ahead (of the others); *F:* **ça, c'est le p.!** that's the limit! *F:* **avoir son p.,** to be tight, tipsy. **2.** *Toil: O:* powder puff.

pomponner [pɔ̃pɔne], *v.tr.* to ornament; to dress elegantly, with care.

ponant [pɔnɑ̃], *s.m. A.Geog:* **1.** (*in the Mediterranean*) West (as opposed to Levant). **2.** (the) Atlantic Ocean.

ponantais [pɔnɑ̃tɛ], *a. A.Geog:* **1.** western. **2.** Atlantic; **côte ponantaise,** Atlantic coast.

ponçage [pɔ̃saːʒ], *s.m.* **1.** pumicing; sandpapering; rubbing down (of paint). **2.** *Draw:* pouncing (of pattern upon material).

ponce [pɔ̃ːs], *s.f.* **1.** (**pierre**) **p.,** pumice (stone). **2.** *Draw:* (*a*) pounce; (*b*) pouncing bag. **3.** (thick black) stencil ink.

ponceau[1], **-eaux** [pɔ̃so], *s.m. Civ.E: Rail:* culvert.

ponceau[2], **-eaux,** *s.m.* **1.** *Bot:* (corn) poppy. **2.** *s.m. & a.inv.* ponceau, poppy-red, flaming red (ribbon, silk).

poncelet [pɔ̃slɛ], *s.m. Ph.Meas:* poncelet.

Ponce Pilate [pɔ̃spilat], *Pr.n.m. B.Hist:* Pontius Pilate.

poncer [pɔ̃se], *v.tr.* (**je ponçai(s); n. ponçons**) **1.** to pumice; to sandpaper; to polish (metal, etc.) with pumice stone, etc.; to rub down (paint); **machine à p.,** sandpapering machine. **2.** *Leath:* (*a*) to stone (a skin); **pierre à p.,** stockstone; (*b*) to fluff, frizz (a skin). **3.** *Draw:* to pounce; **tampon à p.,** pouncing pad.

poncette [pɔ̃sɛt], *s.f. Needlew: etc:* pounce.

ponceur [pɔ̃sœːr], *s.m. Tchn:* (*pers.*) sandpaperer; sander.

ponceux, -euse[1] [pɔ̃sø, -øːz], *a.* pumiceous (rock, etc.).

ponceuse[2], *s.f.* sandpapering machine; sander, grinder; **p. à bande(s),** belt grinder; **p. à plat,** surface-belt sander.

poncho [pɔ̃tʃo], *s.m. Cost:* poncho.

poncif [pɔ̃sif]. **1.** *s.m. A:* (*a*) pouncing pattern; (*b*) pounced drawing. **2.** *a. & s.m. Art: Lit: F:* (*a*) conventional (piece of work), (work) lacking originality; stereotyped (plot, scheme, effect, colouring); (*b*) *s.m.* conventionalism. **3.** *s.m.* = PONCIS.

poncis [pɔ̃si], *s.m. Metall:* dust bag (for moulds); facing dust.

ponction [pɔ̃ksjɔ̃], *s.f.* (*a*) *Surg:* puncture; tapping (of lung, etc.); pricking (of blister); (*b*) **impôt qui fait une p. importante sur la fortune des épargnants,** tax that makes a large hole in people's savings.

ponction-biopsie [pɔ̃ksjɔ̃bjɔpsi], *s.f.* aspiration-biopsy.

ponctionner [pɔ̃ksjɔne], *v.tr. Surg:* to puncture; to tap (lung, dropsical patient, etc.); to prick (blister).

ponctualité [pɔ̃ktɥalite], *s.f.* punctuality.

ponctuation [pɔ̃ktɥasjɔ̃], *s.f. Gram: etc:* punctuation, pointing.

ponctué [pɔ̃ktɥe], *a.* **1.** punctuated (manuscript, etc.). **2.** dotted (line); spotted (leaf, wing, etc.).

ponctuel, -elle [pɔ̃ktɥɛl], *a.* **1.** punctual (**dans, en,** in); **p. en tout,** punctual in everything; **p. à remplir ses devoirs,** punctual in the execution of his duties. **2. source ponctuelle de chaleur,** pinpoint flame; **lampe ponctuelle,** lamp giving a pinhole beam of light; **source de lumière ponctuelle,** pinpoint source of light; *Mil:* **objectif p.,** pinpoint target.

ponctuellement [pɔ̃ktɥɛlmɑ̃], *adv.* punctually.

ponctuer [pɔ̃ktɥe], *v.tr.* to punctuate, point (sentence, etc.); to mark, emphasize, accentuate (one's words in speaking).

ponctulé [pɔ̃ktyle], *a. Ent: etc:* punctulate(d), punctuate; punctiform.

pondaison [pɔ̃dɛzɔ̃], *s.f.* **1.** laying (of eggs). **2.** egg-laying time.

pondérabilité [pɔ̃derabilite], *s.f.* ponderability, ponderableness.

pondérable [pɔ̃derabl̥], *a.* ponderable, weighable.

pondéral, -aux [pɔ̃deral, -o], *a.* ponderal.

pondérateur, -trice [pɔ̃deratœːr, -tris], *a.* balancing; preserving the balance, the equilibrium; **éléments pondérateurs du marché,** stabilizing factors of the market.

pondération [pɔ̃derasjɔ̃], *s.f.* balance, ponderation; (*a*) equipoise, equilibrium; (*b*) *Art: Lit:* proper balance (of parts); **conserver quelque p.,** to retain a sense of measure; (*c*) level-headedness; coolness; poise (of a person); (*d*) *Pol.Ec:* weighting (of index).

pondéré [pɔ̃dere], *a.* (*a*) well-balanced (mind); cool, level-headed, poised (person); **avoir des vues pondérées sur une question,** to take a balanced view of a question; (*b*) *Pol.Ec:* **indice p.,** weighted index; **moyenne pondérée,** weighted average; **moyenne non pondérée,** unweighted average.

pondérer [pɔ̃dere], *v.tr.* (**je pondère, n. pondérons; je pondérerai**) (*a*) to balance (powers, etc.); *Art:* **p. les masses dans une composition,** to achieve a balanced composition; (*b*) *Pol.Ec:* **p. un indice,** to weight an index.

pondéreux, -euse [pɔ̃derø, -øːz], *a.* weighty; bulky; *s.m.* **la flotte des pondéreux,** ships carrying heavy cargo.

pondeur, -euse [pɔ̃dœːr, -øːz]. **1.** *a.* (egg-)laying (bird, moth, etc.); **poule pondeuse,** laying hen. **2.** *s.f.* **pondeuse,** (i) laying bird, layer; (ii) *F:* woman who has a lot of children; **toutes les poules ne sont pas bonnes pondeuses,** not all hens are good layers. **3.** *s.m. F:* **p. de prose,** prolific author. **4.** *s.f. Bot: F:* **pondeuse,** egg plant, white aubergine.

Pondichéry [pɔ̃diʃeri], *Pr.n.m. Geog:* Pondicherry.

pondoir [pɔ̃dwaːr], *s.m.* **1.** laying place (for hens); nest box. **2.** *Ent:* ovipositor.

pondre [pɔ̃ːdr̥], *v.tr.* (*a*) (*of birds, etc.*) to lay (eggs); **œuf frais pondu,** new laid egg; (*b*) *F:* (*of writer, speaker*) to bring forth, produce, give birth to (poem, speech, etc.).

poney [pɔnɛ], *s.m.* pony.

pongé(e) [pɔ̃ʒe], *s.m. Tex:* pongee.

pongidés [pɔ̃ʒide], *s.m.pl. Z:* Pongidae.

pongiste [pɔ̃ʒist], *s.m.* table-tennis player.

pongitif, -ive [pɔ̃ʒitif], *a.* stabbing (pain).

ponogènes [pɔnɔʒɛn], *s.m.pl. Physiol:* fatigue products, fatigue stuff.

ponor [pɔnɔːr], *s.m. Geog:* swallowhole, ponor.

ponot, -ote [pɔno, -ɔt], *a. & s. Geog:* (native, inhabitant) of Le Puy.

pont[1] [pɔ̃], *s.m.* **1.** (*a*) bridge; **p. en brèche humide,** wet-gap bridge; **p. en brèche sèche,** dry-gap bridge; **p. aqueduc,** aqueduct (bridge); **p. viaduc,** viaduct (bridge); **p. pour piétons,** footbridge; **p.-route,** road bridge; **p. de chemin de fer,** railway bridge; **p. à une voie, à deux voies,** single-lane, two-lane, bridge; **p. biais,** skew bridge, oblique bridge; **p. droit,** straight bridge; **p. permanent,** permanent bridge; **p. provisoire,** temporary bridge; **p. volant,** flying bridge; *Rail:* loading board or gangway; **p. de circonstance, p. de fortune, p. improvisé,** emergency bridge, makeshift bridge; *Adm:* **les Ponts et Chaussées,** the department of civil engineering, the Highways Department; **p. en maçonnerie,** masonry bridge; **p. en béton (armé),** (reinforced-)concrete bridge; **p. en pierre,** stone bridge; **p. voûté, p. en arc, p. à arches,** arched bridge; **p. à voûte, à arche, surbaissée,** bridge with diminished arch; **p. en bois,** wooden bridge, timber bridge; **p. de, sur, chevalets; p. de, sur, tréteaux,** trestle bridge; **p. sur contre-fiches,** strut-framed bridge; **p. de, sur, pilot(i)s,** pile bridge; **p. métallique,** metal bridge, girder bridge, iron bridge, steel bridge; **p. métallique démontable,** movable metal bridge; **p. à poutres, à longerons,** girder bridge; **p. à poutres en caisson, p. tubulaire,** box (girder) bridge; **p. à poutre en arc,** steel-arch bridge; **p. à poutres armées, p. sur poutres en treillis,** truss bridge; **p. en treillis,** lattice bridge; **p. bow-string,** bow-string bridge; **p. suspendu,** suspension bridge; **p. suspendu à armatures,** hanging truss bridge; **p. cantilever, p. à consoles, p. en encorbellement,** cantilever bridge; **p. à bascule, p. basculant, p. levant, p.-levis,** bascule bridge, counterpoise bridge, lift bridge, drawbridge; **p. tournant, p. pivotant,** turning bridge, turn bridge, swing bridge, swivel bridge; **p. à tablier inférieur,** bottom-road bridge, through bridge; **p. à tablier intermédiaire,** through bridge; **p. à tablier supérieur,** deck bridge; *Mil:* **p. en ciseaux,** scissors bridge; **char poseur de p.,** bridge-laying tank; **p. flottant, p. de bateaux,** floating bridge, pontoon bridge, boat bridge; *Mil:* **p. d'équipage,** pontoon bridge; **p. de radeaux,** raft bridge; **p. par portières,** bridge by rafts; **p. de tonneaux,** barrel, cask, bridge; **p. d'outres,** inflated-skin bridge; **jeter, lancer, un p. sur un cours d'eau,** to lay, throw, a bridge, across a river; to bridge a river; **démonter, replier, un p.,** to dismantle, break up, a bridge; **faire sauter un p.,** to blow up, blast, a bridge; *Mil:* **tête de p.,** bridgehead; *Av:* **p. aérien,** airlift; *F:* **faire le p.,** to take the intervening working day(s) off; to make a long weekend of it; *F:* **jour de p.,** working day intervening between a Sunday and a public holiday, and also taken as a holiday; **faire le p. à qn,** to help s.o. by acting as an intermediary; *F:* **faire un p. d'or à qn,** to make s.o. a lucrative offer to entice him to change his job; **on lui a fait un p. d'or,** they made it worth his while; **couper, brûler, les ponts avec qn, son passé,** to cut oneself off from s.o., from one's past; **vivre sous les ponts,** to be a tramp; **p. aux ânes,** *pons asinorum*; **c'est le p. aux ânes,** anyone but a fool can do that; (*b*) *Meas:* **p. à bascule,** weighbridge; (*c*) *Metall:* **p. de chauffe,** fire bridge, flame bridge, furnace bridge; (*d*) *Ind: Trans: etc:* platform, ramp, stage, bridge; **p. de chargement,** loading bridge, handling platform; **p. de décharge, p. à chariots culbuteurs,** tipping stage; *Aut:* **p. élévateur de garage,** garage repair ramp, lifting ramp, platform; *Const: Paint:* **p. volant,** hanging stage; *Rail:* **p. roulant,** slide bridge, portable ramp; (*e*) *Ind:* crane; **p. roulant,** (i) overhead crane, travelling crane; (ii) *Rail:* traverser, traverse table, *U.S:* transfer table; **p. roulant à benne (prenante), à crochet,** (overhead) travelling crane with grab, with hook; **p. roulant gerbeur,** (overhead) travelling stacking crane; **p. roulant d'atelier,** shop traveller; *Metall:* **p. (roulant) de coulée,** pouring, ladle, crane; (*f*) *El.E:* bridge; **couplage, montage, en p.,** bridge connection: **(couplé, monté) en p.,** bridge-connected; **p. de raccordement,** connection bridge, bridge connector; **p. de capacitance, de capacité,** capacitance bridge; **p. d'éclatement,** spark gap; **p. d'induction,** inductance bridge; **p. de mesure,** measuring bridge; **p. de mesure à fil,** slidewire measuring bridge; **p. de résistance,** resistor bridge; **p. de Wheatstone,** Wheatstone's bridge; **p. polaire,** bridge piece (of accumulator); (*g*) *Anat:* **p. de Varole, de Varoli,** pons Varolii; (*h*) *Dent:* bridge; (*i*) *Wr:* bridge. **2.** *N.Arch: Nau:* deck (of ship); **p. avant,** foredeck; **p. arrière,** after deck; **p. principal,** main deck; **p. supérieur, p. des gaillards,** upper deck; **p. inférieur,** lower deck; **navire à un p.,** single-decker, single-deck, ship; **navire à deux, à trois, ponts,** two-, three-decker; **homme, matelot, de p.,** deck hand, *Navy:* upper-deck rating; **monter sur le p.,** to go, come, on deck; **être sur le p.,** to be on deck; **tout le monde sur le p.!** *Nau:* all hands on deck! *Navy:* clear lower deck! *Nau:* **commander tout le monde sur le p.,** to pipe up all hands; **passage, voyage, sur le p.,** deck passage; **passager de p., muni d'un billet de p.,** deck passenger; *Com:* **sur p.,** free on board, f.o.b; **p. ras, p. plat, p. de plain-pied,** flush deck; **p. à coffre,** well deck; *Navy:* **p. oblique,** angled deck (of aircraft-carrier); **faux p.,** orlop deck; **p. (de) dunette,** poop deck; **p. du gaillard,** forecastle deck; **p. de passerelle, p. (du) château,** bridge deck; **p. des superstructures,** superstructure deck; **p. découvert, p. exposé,** weather deck; **p. de cloisonnement,** bulkhead deck; **p. de résistance,** strength deck; **p. de tonnage,** tonnage deck; **p. des embarcations,** boat deck; **p. des emménagements, p. des premières,** saloon deck; **p. promenade,** promenade deck, sun deck, hurricane deck (on liner); **p. de manœuvre,** hurricane deck; *Navy:* **p. d'envol,** flight deck (of aircraft-carrier, etc.). **3.** *Mec.E:* live axle; *Rail:* **alimentation sur deux ponts à 600 volts,** power transmission through two live axles at 600 volts; *Aut:* **p. arrière,** rear axle (and drive); final drive; **p. arrière flottant,** floating rear axle. **4.** *Cost: A:* flap (of trousers). **5.** *Cards:* bridge (i.e. bend in card inserted by sharper in the pack); **couper dans le p.,** (i) to cut the pack at the bridge; (ii) *F:* to walk into the trap, to walk into it, to swallow it whole.

Pont[2] **(le),** *Pr.n.m. A.Geog:* **1.** the (Kingdom of) Pontus. **2. le P.-Euxin,** the Euxine, the Black Sea.

pont-abri [pɔ̃abri], *s.m. N.Arch:* shelter deck, awning deck; *pl. ponts-abris.*

pontage [pɔ̃taːʒ], *s.m.* **1.** bridge building; bridging; **matériel de p.,** bridging equipment; **p. par portières,** bridging by rafts; *Mil: etc:* **manœuvre de p., école de p.,** bridge drill, pontoon drill. **2.** *Nau:* decking.

pont-aqueduc [pɔ̃ak(ə)dyk], *s.m.* aqueduct bridge; *pl. ponts-aqueducs.*

pont-barrage [pɔ̃baraːʒ], *s.m.* dam, barrage, carrying a road; *pl. ponts-barrages.*

ponte[1] [pɔ̃ːt], *s.f.* (*a*) laying (of eggs); **lieu de p. (des mouches, etc.),** breeding place; (*b*) **vendre la p. de ses poules,** to sell the eggs laid by one's own hens.

ponte[2], *s.m. Gaming:* punter, punt.

ponte[3], *s.m. F:* pundit; big shot.

ponté [pɔ̃te], *a.* decked (boat); **non p.,** open, undecked (boat).

pontépiscopien, -ienne [pɔ̃tepiskɔpjɛ̃, -jɛn], *a. & s. Geog:* (native, inhabitant) of Pont-l'Évêque.

ponter[1] [pɔ̃te], *v.tr.* **1.** to lay the decks of (vessel). **2.** (*a*) to bridge (river, etc., *esp.* with pontoon bridge); (*b*) to incorporate (boat) into a pontoon bridge. **3.** *abs. Wr:* to make a bridge.

ponter[2], *v.i. Gaming:* to punt; **p. cher,** to punt high.

pontet [pɔ̃tɛ], *s.m.* **1.** *Sm.a:* (*a*) trigger guard; (*b*) scabbard catch (of bayonet, etc.). **2.** *Harn:* saddle bow.

pont-grue [pɔ̃gry], *s.m. Ind:* bridge-crane, overhead travelling crane; *pl. ponts-grues.*

pontien [pɔ̃tjɛ̃], *a. & s.m. Geol:* Pontian.

pontier [pɔ̃tje], *s.m.* (*a*) keeper of swing bridge; (*b*) operator of travelling crane.

pontife [pɔ̃tif], *s.m.* (*a*) pontiff; **le souverain P., le P. romain,** the sovereign pontiff, the Pope; (*b*) *F:* **les pontifes (des lettres, etc.),** the pundits (of literature, etc.).

pontifiant [pɔ̃tifjɑ̃], *a. F:* pontificating, that lays down the law.

pontifical, -aux [pɔ̃tifikal, -o]. **1.** *a.* pontifical, papal. **2.** *s.m.* pontifical.

pontificalement [pɔ̃tifikalmɑ̃], *adv.* pontifically.

pontificat [pɔ̃tifika], *s.m.* pontificate.

pontifier [pɔ̃tifje], *v.i.* (*p.d. & pr.sub.* **n. pontifiions v. pontifiiez**) (*a*) to pontificate, to officiate as a pontiff; (*b*) *F:* to act, speak, pompously; to pontificate; to lay down the law.

pontil [pɔ̃til], *s.m. Glassm:* pontil, punty, ponty.

Pontin [pɔ̃tɛ̃], *a.* **les marais Pontins,** the Pontine Marshes.

pontique [pɔ̃tik], *a. A.Geog:* Pontic.

pontissalien, -ienne [pɔ̃tisaljɛ̃, -jɛn], *a. & s. Geog:* (native, inhabitant) of Pontarlier.

pontivien, -ienne [pɔ̃tivjɛ̃, -jɛn], *a. & s. Geog:* (native, inhabitant) of Pontivy.

pont-l'Abbiste [pɔ̃labist], *a. & s. Geog:* (native, inhabitant) of Pont-l'Abbé; *pl. pont-l'Abbistes.*

pont-l'évêque [pɔ̃levɛk], *s.m.inv.* Pont-l'Évêque cheese.

pont l'Évêquois, -oise [pɔ̃levɛkwa, -waːz], *a. & s.* (native, inhabitant) of Pont-l'Évêque; *pl. pont-l'Évêquois, -oises.*

pont-levis [pɔ̃l(ə)vi], *s.m.* **1.** drawbridge (of castle, etc.); lift bridge (of canal); **p.-l. à fléau, à balancier,** lever drawbridge. **2.** *Ind:* swinging platform; *pl. ponts-levis.*

Pont-Neuf [pɔ̃nœf]. **1.** *Pr.n.m.* famous old bridge in Paris; **être solide, se porter, comme le P.-N.,** to be as strong as a horse, as fit as a fiddle; **vieux comme le P.-N.,** as old as the hills. **2.** *s.m. A:* popular song, ballad. **3.** *attrib. Cu:* **pommes p.-n.,** chipped potatoes, chips.

pontocaspien, -ienne [pɔ̃tɔkaspjɛ̃, -jɛn], *a.* Pontocaspian.

pontois, -oise[1] [pɔ̃twa, -waːz], *a. & s. Geog:* (native, inhabitant) (i) of Pons [pɔ̃ːs], (ii) of Pont-sur-Yonne, (iii) of Pont-en-Royans.

Pontoise[2] [pɔ̃twaːz], *Pr.n. Geog:* Pontoise (near Paris); *F:* **vous revenez de P.,** you've been wool-gathering! **il a l'air de revenir de P.,** he looks half-dazed.

pontoisien, -ienne [pɔ̃twazjɛ̃, -jɛn], *a. & s. Geog:* (native, inhabitant) of Pontoise.

ponton [pɔ̃tɔ̃], *s.m.* **1.** *A:* hulk; prison ship. **2.** *Mil:* (*a*) pontoon; (*b*) section of pontoon bridge; **train de pontons,** bridge train. **3.** (*a*) *Nau:* hulk, pontoon; **p. de relevage,** lifting pontoon, camel; **p. à mâture,** sheer hulk; (*b*) **p. d'incendie,** fire float; (*c*) *Petroleum Min:* **p. de forage,** drilling barge. **4.** (floating, pontoon) landing stage.

pontonage [pɔ̃tɔnaːʒ], *s.m.* (*a*) bridge toll; (*b*) ferry dues.

ponton-allège [pɔ̃tɔ̃alɛːʒ], *s.m. Nau:* hulk, lighter; *pl. pontons-allèges.*

ponton-bigue [pɔ̃tɔ̃big], *s.m. Nau:* sheer hulk; *pl. pontons-bigues.*

ponton-grue [pɔ̃tɔ̃gry], *s.m.* floating crane, pontoon crane; **p.-g. à portique,** floating gantry; *pl. pontons-grues.*

ponton-mâture [pɔ̃tɔ̃mɑtyːr], *s.m. Nau:* sheer hulk; *pl. pontons-mâture.*

pontonnier [pɔ̃tɔnje], *s.m.* **1.** *Mil:* pontoneer, pontonier (who builds pontoon bridges); **le corps des pontonniers,** the bridge train. **2.** (bridge, ferry) toll collector. **3.** landing stage attendant. **4.** (*a*) keeper of swing bridge; (*b*) operator of travelling crane.

pontorsonnais, -aise [pɔ̃tɔrsɔnɛ, -ɛːz], *a. & s. Geog:* (native, inhabitant) of Pontorson.

pont-portique [pɔ̃pɔrtik], *s.m.* transporter bridge; *pl. ponts-portiques.*

pont-promenade [pɔ̃prɔmnad], *s.m. Nau:* promenade deck; sun deck; **p.-p. abrité,** shelter deck; hurricane deck; *pl. ponts-promenades.*

pontuseau, -eaux [pɔ̃tyzo], *s.m. Paperm:* chain line.

pont-viaduc [pɔ̃vjadyk], *s.m.* viaduct bridge; *pl. ponts-viaducs.*

pool [pul], *s.m.* **1.** *Pol.Ec: etc:* pool; common stock, fund; combine; syndicate. **2. p. dactylographique,** typing pool.

pop[1] [pɔp], *a. F:* **musique p.,** pop music.

pop'art [pɔpaːr], *s.m. F:* **pop**[2] [pɔp], *s.m.* pop art.

pope [pɔp], *s.m. Ecc:* pope (of the Greek church).

popeline [pɔplin], *s.f. Tex:* poplin; **p. fil à fil,** end-on-end poplin.

poplité [pɔplite], *a. Anat:* popliteal (muscle, nerve, artery).

popote [pɔpɔt]. *F:* **1.** *s.f.* (*a*) (child's word for) soup; (*b*) **faire la p.,** to do the cooking; (*c*) kitchen; *Mil: etc:* canteen; *Mil:* **p. des officiers,** officer's mess; **faire p. ensemble,** to mess together; (*d*) messmate. **2.** *a.inv.* homely, stay-at-home, quiet (person); **mari p.,** husband swamped with household chores; **elle est terriblement p.,** she's never out of the kitchen, always busy about the house.

popotier [pɔpɔtje], *s.m. F:* canteen manager; mess officer.

popotin [pɔpɔtɛ̃], *s.m. P:* buttocks, backside, rump; **tortiller du p.,** to wiggle one's hips; **se manier le p.,** to hurry, to get a move on; **se trémousser, se remuer, le p.,** to dance, to shake a leg.

Poppée [pɔp(p)e], *Pr.n.f. Rom.Hist:* Poppaea.

populace [pɔpylas], *s.f. Pej:* populace, rabble, riff-raff.

populacier, -ière [pɔpylasje, -jɛːr], *a.* of the rabble; common, vulgar.

populage [pɔpylaːʒ], *s.m. Bot:* marsh marigold.

populaire [pɔpylɛːr]. **1.** *a.* popular; (*a*) *Pol: etc:* of the people; **démocratie p., république p.,** people's democracy, republic; **insurrection p.,** uprising of the people; **manifestation p.,** mass demonstration; (*b*) **tradition p.,** folk tradition; **chanson p.,** (i) folk song; (ii) popular song, song of the day; **expression p.,** (i) expression used by uneducated people; (ii) slang expression; (iii) popular expression; **il n'a pas de succès comme orateur p.,** as a speaker he does not appeal to the masses; **les classes populaires,** the working classes; **un quartier p.,** a working-class district; (*c*) *Th: etc:* **places populaires,** *s.f.* **populaires,** cheap seats; (*d*) popular; **roi, général, p.,** popular king, general; **se rendre p.,** to make oneself popular; **mesure p.,** popular measure, measure that receives popular approval. **2.** *s.m. A:* **le p.,** the (common) people.

populairement [pɔpylɛrmɑ̃], *adv.* (*a*) popularly; (*b*) **s'exprimer p.,** (i) to talk in an uneducated manner; (ii) to talk slang.

popularisation [pɔpylarizasjɔ̃], *s.f.* popularization.

populariser [pɔpylarize], *v.tr.* (*a*) to popularize (an idea, a science); (*b*) **sa gaieté le popularise,** his cheerfulness makes him popular.

popularité [pɔpylarite], *s.f.* popularity.

population [pɔpylasjɔ̃], *s.f.* (*a*) population; **les populations rurales,** the country people, the rural population; **la p. civile,** *Mil:* **les populations,** civilians; **la p. active,** the working population; **recensement de la p.,** population census; (*b*) flora and fauna (of a region).

populeux, -euse [pɔpylø, -øːz], *a.* **1.** populous; densely populated. **2.** *Pej:* **quartier p.,** low, common, working-class, district.

populine [pɔpylin], *s.f. Ch:* populin.

populisme [pɔpylism], *s.m. Hist: Lit:* populism.

populiste [pɔpylist], *a. & s.m. & f. Hist: Lit:* populist.

populo [pɔpylo], *s.m. F:* (*a*) the (common) people; *Pej:* the rabble; (*b*) crowd; people; **c'est plein de p.!** what a crowd; **il y avait des flics et un peu de p. désœuvré,** there were some cops and a few people with nothing to do standing around.

poquet [pɔkɛ], *s.m. Agr:* seed hole; **le semis en p. est utilisé surtout pour les grosses graines,** sowing in seed holes is done mainly for large seeds.

poracé [pɔrase], *a. Med:* porraceous, leek-green.

poranie [pɔrani], *s.f. Echin:* cushion(-)star.

porc [pɔːr], *s.m.* **1.** (*occ.* [pɔrk] *in sing.*) pig, *U.S:* hog; **p. sauvage,** wild boar; **p. destiné à l'engraissement,** porker; **p. châtré,** hog; **gardeur de porcs,** swineherd; **peau de p.,** pigskin; *F: O:* **être comme un p. à l'auge,** to be in clover; *F:* (*of pers.*) **c'est un p.,** (i) he's a dirty pig; (ii) he's a glutton. **2.** *Cu:* pork; **rôti de p.,** roast (of) pork; **côte de p.,** spare-rib; **côtelette de p.,** pork chop.

porcelaine [pɔrsəlɛn], *s.f.* **1.** cowrie, porcelain shell. **2.** *Cer:* porcelain; china; **p. dure,** hard-paste porcelain; **p. tendre,** soft-paste, artificial, porcelain; **p. tendre anglaise, p. phosphatique,** bone china; **p. sanitaire,** sanitary ware; **être comme un éléphant dans un magasin de p.,** to be like a bull in a china shop. **3.** *a.inv.* (*a*) (*of horse*) blue-grey; (*b*) **chien p.,** porcelain harrier.

porcelainier, -ière [pɔrsəlɛnje, -jɛːr]. **1.** *a.* of, pertaining to, porcelain; **industrie porcelainière,** porcelain, china, industry. **2.** *s.m.* porcelain manufacturer.

porcelanique [pɔrsəlanik], *a.* porcellaneous, porcellanic (shell).

porcelanite [pɔrsəlanit], *s.f. Miner:* porcelain jasper; porcel(l)anite.

porcelet [pɔrsəlɛ], *s.m.* **1.** young pig; piglet. **2.** *Ent:* woodlouse.

porcellane [pɔrsɛlan], *s.f. Crust:* hairy porcelain crab; (*genus*) Porcellana.

porcelle [pɔrsɛl], *s.f. Bot:* cat's ear.

porc-épic [pɔrkepik], *s.m.* **1.** (*a*) *Z:* porcupine; (*b*) *F:* (*pers.*) prickly customer. **2.** *Ich:* **p.-é. de mer,** porcupine fish; *pl. porcs-épics* [pɔrkepik].

porchaison [pɔrʃɛzɔ̃], *s.f. Ven:* boar(-hunting) season.

porche [pɔrʃ], *s.m.* porch.

porcher[1], **-ère** [pɔrʃe, -ɛːr], *s.* (*a*) swineherd; (*b*) *F:* dirty, uncouth, person.

porcher[2], *s.m. Bot:* bendy tree.

porcherie [pɔrʃəri], *s.f.* (*a*) pigsty; piggery; (*b*) *F:* (*dirty or untidy place*) pigsty.

porcin [pɔrsɛ̃]. **1.** *a.* (*a*) porcine; **élevage p., industrie porcine,** pig breeding; **peste porcine,** hog cholera, swine fever; **viande porcine,** pork; (*b*) **yeux porcins,** piggy eyes; **sourire p.,** hog-like grin. **2.** *s.m.pl.* **porcins,** swine; pigs; *U.S:* hogs.

pore [pɔːr], *s.m.* pore (of skin, plant, stone); **il sue l'orgueil par tous les pores,** he oozes conceit at every pore.

porencéphalie [pɔrɑ̃sefali], *s.f. Med:* porencephalia.

poreux, -euse [pɔrø, -øːz], *a.* (*a*) porous; (*b*) *Cer:* porous, unglazed (ware).

poricide [pɔrisid], *a. Bot:* poricidal.

poriforme [pɔrifɔrm], *a.* poriform.

porion [pɔrjɔ̃], *s.m. Min:* (*in N. of Fr.*) overman; foreman; **p. de surface,** banksman.

porisme [pɔrism], *s.m. A.Geom:* porism.

poristique [pɔristik], *a. A.Mth:* porismatic, poristic.

porite [pɔrit], *s.m. Coel:* porite.

porno [pɔrno], *a. F:* pornographic, obscene; off-colour (joke, etc.).

pornocratie [pɔrnɔkrasi], *s.f. Hist:* pornocracy.

pornographe [pɔrnɔgraf], *s.m.* **1.** *A:* author of a work on prostitution. **2.** pornographer.

pornographie [pɔrnɔgrafi], *s.f.* (*a*) pornography; (*b*) obscenity.

pornographique [pɔrnɔgrafik], *a.* pornographic.

porocéphalidés [pɔrɔsefalide], *s.m.pl. Z:* Porocephalidae.

porogamie [pɔrɔgami], *s.f. Bot:* porogamy.

porokératose [pɔrɔkeratoːz], *s.f. Med:* porokeratosis.

poroscopie [pɔrɔskɔpi], *s.f.* poroscopy.

porose [pɔroːz], *s.f. Med:* porosis.

porosimètre [pɔrozimɛtr], *s.m.* porosimeter.

porosité [pɔrozite], *s.f.* porosity, porousness.

porphine [pɔrfin], *s.f. Ch:* porphin.

porphyre[1] [pɔrfiːr], *s.m.* **1.** *Miner:* porphyry; **p. rouge,** red porphyry; **p. kératique,** hornstone porphyry. **2.** *Pharm:* slab (of porphyry) (for triturating drugs); porphyry muller.

Porphyre[2], *Pr.n.m. Gr.Phil:* Porphyrius.

porphyrie [pɔrfiri], *s.f. Med:* porphyria; *F:* royal purple disease.

porphyrien [pɔrfirjɛ̃], *a. Gr.Phil:* Porphyrian.

porphyrine [pɔrfirin], *s.f. Ch:* porphyrin.

porphyrinurie [pɔrfirinyri], *s.f. Med:* porphyrinuria.

porphyrion [pɔrfirjɔ̃], *s.m. Orn:* porphyrio; **p. bleu,** purple gallinule.

porphyrique [pɔrfirik], *a. Miner:* porphyritic.

porphyriser [pɔrfirize], *v.tr. Pharm:* to grind, triturate (on slab).

porphyrite [pɔrfirit], *s.f. Miner:* porphyrite.

porphyritique [pɔrfiritik], *a.* porphyritic.

porphyroblaste [pɔrfirɔblast], *s.m. Miner:* porphyroblast.

porphyrogénète [pɔrfirɔʒenɛt], *a. Hist:* porphyrogenitus; born in the purple.

porphyroïde [pɔrfirɔid], *a. Geol:* pseudoporphyritic.

porpite [pɔrpit], *s.f. Coel:* porpitoid.

porque [pɔrk], *s.f. N.Arch:* web frame (to strengthen ship).

porquer [pɔrke], *v.tr.* to strengthen (ship) with a *porque*.

porracé [pɔrase], *a. A: esp. Med:* porraceous, leek-green.

porreau, -eaux [pɔro], *s.m. A. & Dial:* leek.

porrection [pɔrrɛksjɔ̃], *s.f. Ecc:* porrection.

porrette [pɔrɛt], *s.f.* young leek plant.

port[1] [pɔːr], *s.m.* **1.** harbour, port; *Lit:* haven; **p. naturel,** natural harbour; **p. abrité,** sheltered harbour; **p. exposé,** open harbour; unsafe harbour; **p. à barre,** bar harbour, bar port; **p. à, de, marée,** tidal harbour; **p. de toute marée, p. en eau profonde,** deep-water harbour; **capitaine de p.,** harbour master; **droits de p.,** harbour dues; port charges; **p. artificiel,** artificial port; **p. préfabriqué,** prefabricated port; **p. de quarantaine,** quarantine harbour; **entrer dans le p.,** to enter harbour; **entrer au p.,** to come into port; **au p.,** in port; **quitter le p.,** to leave port, to clear the harbour; **arriver à bon p.,** to come safe into port; **amener, conduire, qch. à bon p.,** (i) to deliver sth. safely; (ii) to arrive at a satisfactory solution; *F:* **le p. des navires perdus,** Davy Jones' locker. **2.** (*a*) (*town*) port; **p. de mer, p. maritime,** seaport; **p. fluvial,** river port; **p. de commerce, p. marchand,** commercial port; **p. de guerre, p. militaire,** naval port, naval base; **p. de pêche,** fishing port; **p. pétrolier,** oil port; **p. de constructions navales,** shipbuilding port; *Nau: Navy:* **les ports de la métropole,** the home ports; **p. d'armement,** port of registry, *U.S:* port of documentation; **p. d'attache,** home port, port of commissioning; **p. d'escale, p. de relâche, p. intermédiaire,** port of call; **p. de relâche (forcée), p. de refuge, p. de salut,** port of necessity, port, harbour, of refuge; **p. de départ,** port of departure, of sailing; **p. de destination,** port of destination; **p. d'arrivée,** port of arrival; **p. d'embarquement,** port of embarkation; **p. de débarquement,** port of disembarkation, *U.S:* debarkation, port of landing; *Cust:* **p. d'entrée,** port of entry; **p. de charge(ment),** port of loading, of shipment; **p. de décharge(ment),** port of discharge, of delivery; **p. de transbordement,** port of transhipment; **p. de transit,** port of transit; *Com:* **p. autonome,** autonomous port; **p. franc,** free port; **p. ouvert,** open port; (*b*) *Av:* **p. aérien,** airport.

port[2], *s.m.* **1.** (*a*) (act of) carrying; *Adm:* **permis de p. d'armes,** permit for carrying firearms; **p. d'armes,** shooting licence, gun licence; **p. d'arme prohibée,** carrying a weapon without a licence; *Mil:* **se mettre au p. d'armes,** to shoulder arms; (*b*) wearing (of uniform, etc.); manner of carrying (sword, etc.); **p. illégal de décoration,** unlawful wearing of decoration; **le p. de la barbe est de rigueur,** the wearing of beards is compulsory. **2.** cost of transport; porterage, carriage (of luggage, goods); postage (of parcel, letter); charge for delivery (of telegram); *Com:* **ports de lettres, frais de p.,** postage, postal charges; **p. payé, perçu; franc de p.,** carriage paid, post paid; **en p. dû,** carriage forward. **3.** bearing, gait, carriage (of person); *Bot:* habit (of plant); **un p. de reine,** a queenly carriage, the bearing of a queen. **4.** *Nau:* (*a*) burden, tonnage (of ship); (*b*) **p. en lourd,** dead weight. **5.** *Mus:* **p. de voix,** glide, portamento, *F:* scoop.

port[3], *s.m. Dial:* mountain pass (in the Pyrenees).

portabilité [pɔrtabilite], *s.f.* portability, portableness.

portable [pɔrtabl̥], *a.* **1.** portable (burden). **2.** wearable, presentable (garment, etc.). **3. dette p.,** debt payable at the address of payee.

portage [pɔrtaːʒ], *s.m.* **1.** (*a*) porterage, conveyance, transport (of goods); **frais de p.,** porterage; (*b*) portage; (i) conveying of a boat across land between navigable waters; **faire le p. d'un canot,** to porter a boat; (ii) stretch of water where such conveyance is necessary; (iii) ground over which the boat is carried. **2.** *Nau:* nip (of rope).

portager [pɔrtaʒe], *v.i. Fr.C:* to portage.

portail [pɔrtaːj], *s.m.* principal door, portal (of church, etc.).

portal [pɔrtal], *a. Anat:* portal.

portance [pɔrtɑ̃ːs], *s.f. Av:* lift (per unit area); **p. nulle,** zero lift; **angle de p. nulle,** no-lift angle; **composante de p.,** lift component; **coefficient de p.,** lift coefficient; **pente de coefficient de p.,** lift-coefficient slope.

portant [pɔrtɑ̃]. **1.** *a.* (*a*) bearing, carrying (part of machine, etc.); **force portante (d'un aimant),** portative force (of a magnet); **à bout portant,** point blank; *Av:* **surface portante,** aerofoil; *Nau:* **vent p.,** fair wind; (*b*) **être bien p.,** to be in good health; **être mal portant,** to be in poor health, to be unwell. **2.** *s.m.* (*a*) *Tchn:* bearer, upright; supporter, stay, strut; *Th:* **p. (de décor),** framework of a flat; (*b*) (lifting) handle (of trunk, etc.); (*c*) armature, keeper (of magnet); (*d*) **p. d'une roue,** tread of a wheel; (*e*) lengthening strap (of a shoulder belt).

portatif, -ive [pɔrtatif, -iːv], *a.* portable; easily carried; **machine à écrire portative,** portable (typewriter); **poste de télévision p., poste de radio p.,** portable television, radio; **outil p.,** portable tool; **armes portatives,** small arms; *A.Mus:* **orgue p.,** portative organ; *Com:* **glaces portatives,** ices to take away, for home consumption.

porte [pɔrt], *s.f.* **1.** (*a*) gateway, doorway, entrance; **portes d'une ville,** gates of a town; *A:* **arriver à porte(s) ouvrante(s), fermante(s),** to arrive at the opening, at the closing, of the gates; **le métro dessert les portes de Paris,** the metro, underground, lines run to the (old) gates of Paris; *Pol.Ec:* **politique de la porte ouverte,** the open-door policy; **p. cochère, charretière,** carriage entrance, gateway, **les portes de l'enfer,** the gates of hell; **être aux portes de la mort, aux portes du tombeau,** to be at death's door; **la géometrie est la porte des sciences mathématiques,** geometry is the gateway to mathematics; *Myth:* **la p. d'ivoire,** the ivory gate; *Hist:* **la P. ottomane, la sublime P.,** the (Sublime) Porte, the Turkish government; (*b*) *Ind:* **p. de visite,** inspection door, manhole door, cover; **p. de foyer, de chargement,** fire door; *Min: etc:* **p. d'aérage,** air gate, trap (door); (*c*) *Hyd.E:* **p. à flot,** tide gate; **p. d'écluse,** dock gate; lock gate; sluice gate; **p. à trappe,** drop gate; (*d*) *Nau:* **p. d'un barrage,** gate in a boom; (*e*) *Av:* hatch; (*f*) *Ski:* gate, pair of flags; (*g*) (*computers*) gate. **2.** door (of house); **p. d'entrée,** entrance door, front door, street door; **p. de derrière, de service,** back door; tradesmen's entrance; **p. à deux battants,** double door; **p. de dégagement, petite p.,** back door, side door; *F:* **entrer dans une profession par la petite p.,** to get into a profession by the back door, *Navy:* through the hawse hole; **p. dérobée, fausse p.,** jib door; **p. feinte, fausse p.,** blind door; **p. battante,** swing door; **p. tournante,** revolving door; **p. vitrée,** glass door; **p. roulante, p. glissante, p. coulissante,** sliding door; **p. coulante,** portcullis; **p. à claire-voie,** gate (with lattice bars, slats, etc.); **portes d'une armoire, d'une voiture,** doors of a wardrobe, of a car; **aller ouvrir la p.,** to answer the door; **gagner, prendre, la p.,** to make for the door; to make off; **montrer, faire prendre, la p. à qn,** to throw s.o. out; **faire la p.,** (i) (*at monastery*) to keep the door; (ii) to tout at the shop door; *F:* **je lui ai parlé entre deux portes,** I spoke to him for a brief moment; **agir à p. close, à portes ouvertes,** to act secretly, openly; **trouver p. close,** (i) to find nobody at home; (ii) to be denied the door; to have the door shut in one's face; **mettre, jeter,** *F:* **flanquer, qn à la p.,** (i) to kick s.o. out (of doors); (ii) to throw s.o. out; (iii) to give s.o. the sack; **refuser, fermer, sa p. à qn,** to refuse s.o. admission; to close one's door to s.o.; **je ne puis pas leur fermer la p.,** I can't turn them away, refuse to let them in; **la société lui a fermé ses portes,** he is shut out, excluded, from society; **se ménager une p. de sortie,** to arrange a way out, a means of escape; **vous avez frappé à la bonne p.,** you've come to the right person; **frapper, heurter, à toutes les portes,** to try every door, every means (to obtain sth.); *F:* **habiter, demeurer, à la p. de qn,** to live next door to s.o.; **habiter p. à p., être voisins de p. à p.,** to be next-door neighbours; *s.m. Com:* **p.(-)à(-)p.,** door-to-door (i) transport, (ii) canvassing, selling; **faire du p.(-)à(-)p.,** to go from door to door (selling, canvassing, etc.); **mendier de p. en p.,** to beg from door to door; **demander la p.,** to call for the concierge to open the door; **défendre sa p.,** (i) to be "not at home"; (ii) *Sch:* to sport one's oak; *Lit:* **il faut qu'une p. soit ouverte ou fermée,** there can be no middle course; **écouter aux portes,** to eavesdrop; **impôt sur les portes et fenêtres** = window tax. **3.** eye (of hook and eye). **4.** *usu. pl. Geog:* gorge; defile, pass; **les Portes de Fer,** the Iron Gates. **5.** *a. & s.f. Anat:* (**veine**) **p.,** portal (vein).

porté [pɔrte]. **1.** *a.* (*a*) inclined, disposed; **être p. à l'indulgence,** to be inclined to be indulgent; **être p. à la colère,** to be quick-tempered; **p. à faire qch.,** inclined to do sth., given to doing sth.; **être p. à oublier,** to be apt to forget; **p. sur qn, qch.,** fond of s.o., of sth.; **être p. sur la bouche,** to be fond of one's food; (*b*) *Art:* **ombre portée,** projected shadow; (*c*) **il est mieux p. de . . .,** it is more fashionable to . . .; **le bleu est très bien p. cette année,** blue is very fashionable this year; *F:* **c'est tout p.,** it's on the spot, ready to hand. **2.** *s.m.* (*of garment*) wear; appearance.

porte-adresse [pɔrtadrɛs], *s.m.inv.* luggage-label holder.

porte-aéronefs [pɔrtaerɔnɛf], *s.m.inv. Navy:* aircraft carrier.

porte(-)à(-)faux [pɔrtafo], *s.m.inv.* (*a*) *Civ.E: Mec.E:* overhang, cantilever; **en p. à f.,** cantilever, overhanging, overhung; back-balanced (crankshaft, etc.); **palier en p. à f.,** outboard bearing; **poutre en p. à f.,** cantilever beam, girder; **être en p. à f. par rapport à . . .,** to overhang . . .; (*b*) instability; **situation en p. à f.,** uncertain, unstable, position; **jugement en p. à f.,** ill-founded judgement.

porte-affiches [pɔrtafiʃ], *s.m.inv.* advertisement board; notice board.

porte-aiguille [pɔrteɡɥiːj], *s.m. Surg:* needle holder; *pl. porte-aiguille(s).*

porte-aiguilles [pɔrteɡɥiːj], *s.m.inv.* needle case.

porte-aiguillon [pɔrteɡɥijɔ̃], *a.inv. Ent:* aculeate; having a sting.

porte-alésoir [pɔrtalezwaːr], *s.m. Tchn:* tool holder (of machine tool); brace chuck; side rest (of lathe); *pl. porte- alésoir(s).*

porte-allumettes [pɔrtalymɛt], *s.m.inv.* match holder.

porte-amarre [pɔrtamaːr], *s.m.inv. Nau:* line-throwing apparatus; **canon p.-a.,** line-throwing gun; **fusée, flèche, p.-a.,** line-throwing rocket.

porte-amorce [pɔrtamɔrs], *s.m.inv. Artil: etc:* fuse cup; cap chamber (of fuse); primer holder.

porte-ampoule [pɔrtɑ̃pul], *s.m.inv. El:* lamp holder, bulb holder.

porte-assiette [pɔrtasjɛt], *s.m.* table mat; *pl. porte-assiettes.*

porte-auge [pɔrtoːʒ], *s.m.inv.* hodman, mason's labourer.

porte-avions [pɔrtavjɔ̃], *s.m.inv. Navy:* aircraft carrier; **p.-a. d'attaque, d'escorte,** assault carrier, escort carrier.

porte-bagages [pɔrt(ə)bagaːʒ], *s.m.inv.* **1.** (*a*) luggage rack, luggage stand; (*b*) *Aut: etc:* (luggage) carrier; luggage grid. **2.** luggage strap. **3.** *Rail:* trolley.

porte-baguette [pɔrt(ə)bagɛt], *s.m. Sm.a:* cleaning-rod sleeve; *pl. porte-baguette(s).*

porte-baguettes [pɔrt(ə)bagɛt], *s.m.inv.* stick holder (on drum).

porte-baïonnette [pɔrt(ə)bajɔnɛt], *s.m.* bayonet frog; *pl. porte-baïonnette(s).*

porte-balais [pɔrt(ə)balɛ], *s.m.inv. El:* brush holder (of dynamo, etc.); **ensemble p.-b.,** brush assembly (of computer).

porteballe [pɔrt(ə)bal], *s.m. A:* packman, pedlar.

porte-balles [pɔrt(ə)bal], *s.m.inv. Ten:* ball net.

porte-bannière [pɔrt(ə)banjɛːr], *s.m.* banner bearer; *pl. porte-bannière(s).*

porte-bât [pɔrt(ə)bɑ], *s.m.inv.* pack animal.

porte-bébé(s) [pɔrt(ə)bebe], *s.m.inv.* **1.** baby carrier (on bicycle). **2.** carry cot.

porte-bijoux [pɔrt(ə)biʒu], *s.m.inv.* jewel stand; jewel box.

porte-billets [pɔrt(ə)bijɛ], *s.m.inv.* notecase, *U.S:* billfold.

porte-bobines [pɔrt(ə)bɔbin], *s.m.inv.* **1.** reel stand, holder. **2.** *Tex:* creel (of frame).

porte-bois [pɔrt(ə)bwa], *s.m.inv.* (*a*) caddis worm; (*b*) caddis bait.

porte-bombes [pɔrt(ə)bɔ̃ːb], *s.m.inv. Mil.Av:* (*a*) bomb rack (in aircraft); (*b*) bomb carrier.

porte-bonheur [pɔrt(ə)bɔnœːr], *s.m.inv.* **1.** charm, amulet, mascot; **petit cochon p.-b.,** lucky pig; **conserver qch. comme p.-b.,** to keep sth. for luck. **2.** bangle.

porte-bougie [pɔrt(ə)buʒi], *s.m.* candlestick; *pl. porte-bougies.*

porte-bouquet [pɔrt(ə)bukɛ], *s.m.* flower holder; flower vase; *pl. porte-bouquets.*

porte-bouteille [pɔrt(ə)butɛːj], *s.m.* bottle stand; coaster; *pl. porte-bouteilles.*

porte-bouteilles [pɔrt(ə)butɛːj], *s.m.inv.* (*a*) bottle rack; (wine) bin; (*b*) bottle carrier.

porte-brancards [pɔrt(ə)brɑ̃kaːr], *s.m.pl. Harn:* tugs.

porte-bras [pɔrt(ə)bra, -brɑ], *s.m.inv.* arm rest, arm strap (in car, etc.).

porte-brosses [pɔrt(ə)brɔs], *s.m.inv.* **p.-b. (à dents),** toothbrush holder.

porte-cadenas [pɔrt(ə)kadnɑ], *s.m.inv.* padlock fitting (for trunk, etc.).

porte-cannes [pɔrt(ə)kan], *s.m.inv.* stick rack.

porte-caractères [pɔrt(ə)karaktɛːr], *s.m.inv.* print member (of computer).

porte-carafe [pɔrt(ə)karaf], *s.m.* **1.** decanter stand; coaster. **2.** milk-bottle carrier; *pl. porte-carafes.*

porte-carte [pɔrt(ə)kart], *s.m.* map case, map holder; *pl. porte-cartes.*

porte-cartes [pɔrt(ə)kart], *s.m.inv.* (*a*) (visiting-) card case; (*b*) card tray.

porte-cartons [pɔrt(ə)kartɔ̃], *s.m.inv.* portfolio stand.

porte-chaîne [pɔrt(ə)ʃɛn], *s.m.inv. Surv:* chainman; fore-chainman.

porte-chaise [pɔrt(ə)ʃɛːz], *s.m. A:* (sedan) chairman; *pl. porte-chaises.*

porte-chapeau [pɔrt(ə)ʃapo], *s.m.* **1.** hat peg; *pl. porte-chapeaux.* **2.** *inv. Bot:* Christ's thorn.

porte-chapeaux [pɔrt(ə)ʃapo], *s.m.inv.* hat stand; hat rack.

porte-charbon(s) [pɔrt(ə)ʃarbɔ̃], *s.m.inv. El:* carbon holder (of arc lamp, of magneto).

porte-chars [pɔrt(ə)ʃaːr], *s.m.inv. Mil:* tank transporter.

porte-chaussures [pɔrt(ə)ʃosyːr], *s.m.inv.* shoe rack.

porte-cible [pɔrt(ə)sibl̩], *s.m.* target-stand; *pl. porte-cibles.*

porte-cigare [pɔrt(ə)sigaːr], *s.m.inv.* cigar-holder.

porte-cigares [pɔrt(ə)sigaːr], *s.m.inv.* cigar case.

porte-cigarette [pɔrt(ə)sigarɛt], *s.m.inv.* cigarette holder.

porte-cigarettes [pɔrt(ə)sigarɛt], *s.m.inv.* cigarette case.

porte-clés, porte-clefs [pɔrt(ə)kle], *s.m.inv.* **1.** turnkey, prison warder. **2.** (*a*) **étui** *m* **p.-c.,** bell key-ring; (*b*) (*in hotel*) key board.

porte-containers [pɔrt(ə)kɔ̃tɛnɛːr], *s.m.inv. Nau:* container ship.

porte-copie [pɔrt(ə)kɔpi], *s.m. Typewr:* copy holder; *pl. porte-copie(s).*

porte-coupures [pɔrt(ə)kupyːr], *s.m.inv.* notecase, *U.S:* billfold.

porte-coussinet [pɔrt(ə)kusinɛ], *s.m. Tchn:* die head; *pl. porte-coussinets.*

porte-couteau [pɔrt(ə)kuto], *s.m.* knife rest; *pl. porte-couteau(x).*

porte-crayon [pɔrt(ə)krɛjɔ̃], *s.m.* (*a*) pencil-case; (*b*) **p.-c. de compas,** pencil point; (*c*) *Art:* port-crayon; *pl. porte-crayon(s).*

porte-croisée [pɔrt(ə)krwaze], *s.f.* French windows; *pl. portes-croisées.*

porte-croix [pɔrt(ə)krwa], *s.m.inv. Ecc:* cross bearer, crucifer.

porte-crosse [pɔrt(ə)krɔs], *s.m.* **1.** *Ecc:* crosier bearer. **2.** *Mil: A:* rifle-bucket; *pl. porte-crosse(s).*

porte-culasse [pɔrt(ə)kylas], *s.m. Artil: Sm.a:* breech ring.

porte-cylindres [pɔrt(ə)silɛ̃ːdr̥], *s.m.inv. Tex:* roller beam.

porte-disques [pɔrt(ə)disk], *a. & s.m.inv.* (*a*) **(chevalet) p.-d.,** record rack; (*b*) **mallette p.-d.,** record case.

porte-documents [pɔrt(ə)dɔkymɑ̃], *s.m.inv.* document case; briefcase.

porte-drapeau [pɔrt(ə)drapo], *s.m. Mil:* officer carrying the regimental colour; colour bearer; *pl. porte-drapeau(x).*

porte-drapeaux [pɔrt(ə)drapo], *s.m.inv.* flag holder (for decorations).

portée [pɔrte], *s.f.* **1.** (*a*) period of gestation (of animal); (*b*) *Const:* bearing (of beam); span (of roof, bridge); distance between (telegraph, etc.) poles, span (of the poles); **poutre de vingt mètres de p.,** girder with a twenty-metre span; (*c*) *Nau:* burden, tonnage (of ship); **p. en lourd, en poids,** deadweight (capacity); **p. en volume,** measurement capacity; **p. utile,** cargo(-carrying) capacity. **2.** (*a*) litter, brood (of animals); farrow (of pigs); **une p. de chiots,** a litter of puppies; **animaux de la même p.,** litter mates; (*b*) *Mec.E:* bearing surfaces; race (of ball bearing); **p. à cannelure,** thrust bearing; **portées d'un arbre,** (main) journals; **p. de fusée (d'essieu), p. lisse,** journal bearing; *Nau:* **p. de l'arbre de couche,** propeller-shaft bearing, main(-shaft) bearing; (*c*) projection (of part of building beyond wall); projecting ledge; *Mec.E: etc:* boss (on shaft, etc.); throat (of punching machine); (*d*) *Metall:* (core) print (of pattern); **p. du noyau,** core print; (*e*) *Hyd.E:* discharge, flow (of water from river, pipe, etc.); (*f*) *Mus:* stave; **au-dessus de la p.,** in alt; (*g*) *Surv:* chain (length). **3.** (*a*) reach (of arm, etc.); reach, radius (of crane jib, lever, etc.); range (of gun, broadcasting station, etc.); scope (of treaty, etc.); compass (of voice, etc.); **à p. (de tir, etc.),** within range; **à bonne p.,** at an effective range; **à p. de jet,** within throwing distance, within throwing range; **à p. d'arc, de trait,** within bow shot; **à p. de fusil,** *Mil:* within rifle range, *Sp:* within gunshot; **se tenir à p. de fusil,** to keep within rifle range; **à p. de canon,** within gun range, *O:* within cannon shot; *Navy:* **à p. de lancement (de torpille),** within torpedo range; **hors de p. (de tir, etc.),** out of range; **se tenir hors de p. des canons ennemis,** to keep out of range of enemy guns; **(à) courte p., (à) petite p.,** (at) short range; **(à) grande p., (à) longue p.,** (at) long range; **(à) moyenne p.,** (at) mean range; **la plus grande p.,** the maximum range; **canon, pièce, à longue p.,** long-range gun; **tir à grande, à longue, p.,** long-range fire; **se battre à grande, à longue, p.,** to fight at long range; **p. efficace,** effective range; **variation de p. due à l'échauffement du tube,** warming-up effect; **dépasser en p. l'artillerie adverse,** to outrange enemy, hostile, artillery; **à p. de (la) voix,** within call; **à p. d'oreille,** within hearing, within earshot; **hors de p. de la voix humaine,** out of range of the human voice; **cette partition est hors de p. de ma voix,** this score is beyond the compass of my voice; **p. optique, p. visuelle,** visual range; **à p. des signaux,** within signalling distance; *W.Tel:* **p. radio,** radio range; **poste émetteur, station émettrice, à grande p.,** high-power station; *Atom.Ph:* **p. réelle, p. vraie,** practical range, true range; **p. massique,** mass range; **p. résiduelle,** residual range; *Elcs:* (*of computer*) **p. dynamique,** dynamic range; **p. d'une grue, d'un mât de charge,** radius, reach, of a crane (jib), of a cargo-boom; **à ma p.,** within my reach; **à p. (de . . .),** within reach (of . . .); **hors de ma p.,** (i) beyond my reach; (ii) beyond the compass of my voice; (iii) beyond my understanding; (iv) beyond my means; **hors de p. (de . . .),** out of reach (of . . .); **à p. de la main,** (i) within (hand)reach; (ii) within striking distance; **cela passe la p. de mon esprit,** it is beyond my comprehension, beyond me; **la science à la p. du public,** science for the general public, for the non-specialist; science for all; **il ne sait pas se mettre à la p. de son auditoire,** he cannot adapt himself to his audience; **il faut rester à la p. de son auditoire,** one should avoid speaking over the heads of one's audience; **livre à la p. de tout le monde,** (i) book available, accessible, to everybody; (ii) book that anyone can understand; (*b*) **la p. d'une affirmation,** the full significance of a statement; **il ne se rendait pas compte de la p. de ces paroles,** he did not realize the full implication of these words; **affirmation d'une grande p.,** statement of far-reaching effect; weighty statement; **conséquences d'une p. incalculable,** far-reaching consequences. **4.** *Meteor:* angle of the wind; *Nau: Av:* **p. à babord, à tribord,** angle of the wind to port, to starboard.

porte-écuelle [pɔrtekɥɛl], *s.m.inv. Ich:* lepadogaster, (Cornish) sucker, sucking fish.

porte-électrodes [pɔrtelɛktrɔd], *s.m.inv.* electrode holder.

porte-empreinte [pɔrtɑ̃prɛ̃ːt], *s.m. Dent:* impression tray; *pl. porte-empreintes.*

porte-en-dehors [pɔrtɑ̃dəɔːr], *s.m.inv. Row:* outrigger.

porte-enseigne [pɔrtɑ̃sɛɲ], *s.m.inv. Mil: A:* colour bearer.

porte-épée [pɔrtepe], *s.m.inv.* sword knot, frog.

porte-éperon [pɔrteprɔ̃], *s.m.* spur strap; *pl. porte-éperon(s).*

porte-épingles [pɔrtepɛ̃ːgl], *s.m.inv.* pin tray.

porte-éponge(s) [pɔrtepɔ̃ːʒ], *s.m.inv.* sponge dish; sponge holder, basket.

porte-étendard [pɔrtetɑ̃daːr], *s.m.inv.* **1.** standard bearer (in cavalry). **2.** stirrup socket, bucket, shoe (for staff of standard).

porte-étiquette [pɔrtetikɛt], *s.m.inv.* label holder.

porte-étriers [pɔrtetrije], *s.m.inv. Equit:* stirrup strap.

porte-fainéant [pɔrt(ə)fɛneɑ̃], *s.m.inv. A:* carter's seat (attached to shaft of heavy dray).

portefaix [pɔrtəfɛ], *s.m.* **1.** *A:* porter; *esp.* (i) street-porter; (ii) dock hand, stevedore. **2.** caddis worm.

porte-fanion [pɔrt(ə)fanjɔ̃], *s.m.inv. Mil:* orderly bearing headquarters flag.

porte-fenêtre [pɔrt(ə)fənɛtr̥], *s.f.* French window; *pl. portes-fenêtres.*

portefeuille [pɔrt(ə)fœːj], *s.m.* (*a*) portfolio (for drawings, papers, etc.); *A:* **p. d'un écrivain,** unpublished works, manuscripts, of a writer; (*b*) *A:* school bag, satchel; (*c*) *Pol:* **recevoir le p. de . . .,** to be made Minister of . . .; **ministre sans p.,** minister without portfolio; **ambitionner un p.,** to aim at office; **accepter un p.,** to accept office; (*d*) wallet, notecase, *U.S:* billfold; **avoir un p. bien garni,** to be rich; *F:* **ferme ton p., c'est moi qui paye,** you're showing your medals; (*e*) *Fin:* **effets en p., p. effets,** bills in hand, holdings; **p. (titres),** investments, securities; **société de gestion de p.,** unit trust; **avoir toute sa fortune en p.,** to have all one's fortune in stocks and shares; (*f*) **p. d'assurances,** portfolio (of insurance broker), insurance book; (*g*) **jupe p.,** wrap-over skirt; *F:* **lit en p.,** apple-pie bed.

porte-ficelle [pɔrt(ə)fisɛl], *s.m.inv.* twine holder.

porte-filière [pɔrt(ə)filjɛːr], *s.m. Tls:* screw stock; die stock; *pl. porte-filières.*

porte-film [pɔrt(ə)film], *s.m. Phot:* film holder (in camera); *Cin:* rack; *pl. porte-film(s).*

porte-flambeau [pɔrt(ə)flɑ̃bo], *s.m.inv.* (*a*) torch bearer; (*b*) *A:* **(valet) p.-f.,** linkman, link-boy, link.

porte-fleurs [pɔrt(ə)flœːr], *s.m.inv.* flower holder.

porte-foret [pɔrt(ə)fɔrɛ], *s.m. Tls:* (*a*) drill holder; drill stock; bit holder; (*b*) drill chuck; **arbre p.-f.,** drilling spindle; *pl. porte-forets.*

porte-fort [pɔrt(ə)fɔːr], *s.m.inv. Jur:* **1.** guarantee. **2.** guarantor.

porte-fouet [pɔrt(ə)fwɛ], *s.m.inv.* **1.** *A: Veh:* whip socket; whip bucket. **2.** *Metalw:* milling spindle.

porte-fraise [pɔrt(ə)frɛːz], *s.m. Metalw:* milling spindle; *pl. porte-fraises.*

porte-fusain [pɔrt(ə)fyzɛ̃], *s.m.inv. Art:* port-crayon; crayon holder.

porte-fusée [pɔrt(ə)fyze], *s.m. Aut:* (*a*) kingpin support; (*b*) steering stub axle, *U.S:* steering knuckle; *pl. porte-fusées.*

porte-fusible [pɔrt(ə)fyzibl̩], *s.m. El:* fuse holder; *pl. porte-fusibles.*

porte-fusil [pɔrt(ə)fyzi], *s.m.* gun rack; *pl. porte-fusils.*

porte-fût(s) [pɔrt(ə)fy], *s.m.inv.* barrel stand; gantry.

porte-giberne [pɔrt(ə)ʒibɛrn], *s.m.inv. Mil: A:* cartridge-box belt.

porte-gibier [pɔrt(ə)ʒibje], *s.m.inv.* game carrier.

porte-glaive [pɔrt(ə)glɛːv], *s.m.* **1.** *Hist:* **(chevalier) p.-g.,** sword bearer. **2.** *Ich:* sword tail; *pl. porte-glaives.*

porte-glissière [pɔrt(ə)glisjɛːr], *s.m.inv. Mec.E:* slide-bar bracket.

porte-graine [pɔrt(ə)grɛn], *s.m. & a.m. inv: For:* **(arbre) p.-g.,** seed-bearer (tree).

porte-greffe(s) [pɔrt(ə)grɛf], *s.m.inv. Hort:* stock; understock.

porte-guidon [pɔrt(ə)gidɔ̃], *s.m.inv. Mil:* guidon (bearer).

porte-habit(s) [pɔrtabi], *s.m.inv.* **1.** suitcase (with fitted hangers). **2.** clothes rack; hall stand. **3.** coathanger.

porte-haubans [pɔrt(ə)obɑ̃], *s.m.inv. Nau:* chain-wale, chain board channel; *pl.* the chains.

porte-hélice [pɔrtelis], *s.m.inv. N.Arch:* tail-shaft bracket; **arbre p.-h.,** tail-end shaft, screw shaft, propeller shaft; **support d'arbre p.-h.,** stern bracket of the propeller shaft.

porte-hélicoptères [pɔrtelikɔptɛːr], *s.m.inv. Nau:* helicopter carrier.

porte-isolateur [pɔrtizɔlatœːr], *s.m. Tg:* pin (of insulator); *pl. porte-isolateurs.*

porte-jarretelles [pɔrt(ə)ʒartɛl], *s.m.inv.* suspender belt, *U.S:* garter belt.

porte-journaux [pɔrtʒurno], *s.m.inv.* newspaper rack.

porte-jupe [pɔrt(ə)ʒyp], *s.m.* skirt hanger; *pl. porte-jupe(s).*

portelais, -aise [pɔrtəlɛ, -ɛːz], *a. & s. Geog:* (native, inhabitant) of Le Portel.

porte-lame [pɔrt(ə)lam], *s.m. Tchn:* blade holder; cutter bar (of drill); *pl. porte-lame(s).*

porte-lance [pɔrt(ə)lɑ̃ːs], *s.m. A.Mil:* (*a*) lancer; (*b*) lance bucket; lance holder; *pl. porte-lance(s).*

porte-lanterne [pɔrt(ə)lɑ̃tɛrn], *s.m.* lamp bracket; *pl. porte-lanterne(s).*
porte-lettres [pɔrt(ə)lɛtr̥], *s.m.inv.* letter case.
porte-liqueurs [pɔrt(ə)likœːr], *s.m.inv.* (*a*) liqueur stand; (*b*) liqueur tray.
porte-livres [pɔrt(ə)livr̥], *s.m.inv.* book rest.
porte-lof [pɔrt(ə)lɔf], *s.m. Nau: A:* portlast, portoise; *pl. porte-lofs.*
portelone [pɔrt(ə)lɔn], *s.m. Nau:* cargo door, cargo port.
porte-loupe [pɔrt(ə)lup], *s.m.inv.* lens-holder; magnifying-glass stand.
porte-lunette [pɔrt(ə)lynɛt], *s.m.* die head; *pl. porte-lunettes.*
porte-lyre [pɔrt(ə)liːr], *s.m.inv. Orn:* lyre bird.
porte-malheur [pɔrt(ə)malœːr], *s.m.inv.* **1.** bringer of bad luck, Jonah; bird of ill omen. **2.** *Ent: F:* blaps, darkling beetle, churchyard beetle.
porte-manchon [pɔrt(ə)mɑ̃ʃɔ̃], *s.m.inv.* mantle holder, fork (of gas burner).
portemanteau, -eaux [pɔrt(ə)mɑ̃to], *s.m.* **1.** *A:* portmanteau. **2.** coat (-and-hat) rack, stand; *F:* **épaules en p.,** sloping shoulders. **3.** *Nau:* davit(s). **4.** *s.f. Hist:* train bearer (to the queen).
porte-masse [pɔrt(ə)mas], *s.m.inv.* mace bearer.
porte-matrice [pɔrt(ə)matris], *s.m.* (*a*) *Metalw:* die holder (of punching machine, etc.); (*b*) *Dent:* matrix retainer; *pl. porte-matrices.*
portement [pɔrtəmɑ̃], *s.m. B.Hist:* **le p. de croix,** (Christ's) bearing of the Cross.
porte-menu [pɔrt(ə)məny], *s.m.* menu holder; *pl. porte-menu(s).*
porte(-)mine [pɔrt(ə)min], *s.m.* propelling pencil; *pl. porte-mine(s), portemines.*
porte-mire [pɔrt(ə)miːr], *s.m.* (*a*) *Artil: etc:* sight arm; (*b*) *Surv:* staff holder, rod(s)man; *pl. porte-mires.*
porte-molette [pɔrt(ə)mɔlɛt], *s.m.* milling tool; knurling tool; *pl. porte-molettes.*
porte-monnaie [pɔrt(ə)mɔnɛ], *s.m.inv.* purse.
porte-montre(s) [pɔrt(ə)mɔ̃ːtr̥], *s.m.inv.* (*a*) watch stand; (*b*) show case (for watches).
porte-mors [pɔrt(ə)mɔːr], *s.m.inv.* cheek piece (of bridle); **anneau p.-m.,** bit ring.
porte-mousqueton [pɔrt(ə)muskətɔ̃], *s.m.inv.* **1.** carbine swivel (on bandolier). **2.** snap hook (on watch chain, etc.).
porte-munitions [pɔrt(ə)mynisjɔ̃], *a.inv. Mil:* **véhicule p.-m.,** ammunition carrier.
porte-musc [pɔrt(ə)mysk], *s.m.inv. Z:* (**chevrotain**) **p.-m.,** musk deer.
porte-musique [pɔrt(ə)myzik], *s.m.inv.* music case; music folio
porte-objectif [pɔrtɔbʒɛktif], *s.m.* **1.** *Phot:* lens holder, lens mount. **2.** nose piece (of microscope); *pl. porte-objectifs.*
porte-objet [pɔrtɔbʒɛ], *s.m.* (i) (object) slide; (ii) stage (of microscope); *pl. porte-objet(s).*
porte-or [pɔrtɔːr], *s.m.inv. A:* gold purse; = sovereign case.
porte-outil(s) [pɔrtuti], *s.m.inv.* tool holder (of machine tool); brace chuck; slide rest (of lathe); **p.-o. revolver,** revolving tool holder, turret.
porte-papier [pɔrt(ə)papje], *s.m.inv.* **1. p.-p. (hygiénique),** toilet-paper, toilet-roll, fixture, fitting, holder. **2.** *Phot:* (**panneau**) **p.-p.,** enlarging easel. **3.** *Typewr:* **rouleau p.-p.,** platen, cylinder, impression roller.
porte-paquet(s) [pɔrt(ə)pakɛ], *s.m.inv.* luggage rack.
porte-parapluies [pɔrt(ə)paraplɥi], *s.m.inv.* umbrella stand.
porte-parole [pɔrt(ə)parɔl], *s.m.inv.* (*a*) spokesman, mouthpiece (of deputation, etc.); (*b*) **ce journal est le p.-p. de l'opposition,** this paper is the mouthpiece of the opposition, is the organ of the opposition.
porte-pelle [pɔrt(ə)pɛl], *s.m.inv.* fire-iron stand.
porte-phare [pɔrt(ə)faːr], *s.m.inv. A: Aut:* headlamp bracket.
porte-pieds [pɔrt(ə)pje], *s.m.inv. Med:* foot rest.
porte-pincettes [pɔrt(ə)pɛ̃sɛt], *s.m.inv.* fire-iron stand.
porte-pipes [pɔrt(ə)pip], *s.m.inv.* pipe rack.
porte-plaque [pɔrt(ə)plak], *s.m.* **1.** *Phot:* plate carrier; steel sheath. **2.** *Aut:* number-plate bracket; *pl. porte-plaques.*
porte-plat [pɔrt(ə)pla], *s.m.* (dish) stand; *pl. porte-plat(s).*
porte-plume [pɔrt(ə)plym], *s.m.inv.* penholder; *O:* **p.-p. (à) réservoir,** fountain-pen; **p.-p. réservoir à remplissage automatique,** self-filling pen.
porte-pneu [pɔrt(ə)pnø], *s.m.inv. Aut:* tyre carrier, tyre holder.
porte-poussière [pɔrt(ə)pusjɛːr], *s.m.inv. Fr.C:* dustpan.
porte-queue [pɔrt(ə)kø], *s.m.inv.* **1.** train bearer. **2.** *Ent:* swallowtail.
porte-queues [pɔrtəkø], *s.m.inv. Bill:* cue rack.
porter[1] [pɔrte]. **1.** *v.tr.* (*a*) to carry; to bear, support (burden, etc.); **elle portait un panier,** she was carrying a basket; **p. qn en triomphe,** to carry s.o. shoulder high; **p. le fardeau de la responsabilité,** to bear the weight of the responsibility; **p. la peine de ses méfaits,** to suffer the penalty for one's misdeeds; **la lettre porte la date du 2 juin,** the letter is dated June 2nd; **livre portant le titre de . . .,** book bearing the title of . . ., book entitled . . .; **travail qui porte la marque des interruptions,** work bearing the mark of interruptions; **barque qui porte bien sa toile,** boat that carries her canvas well; *F:* **il porte bien son vin,** he carries his drink well, he knows how to carry his drink; *Nau:* **p. un feu,** to show a light; *abs.* **croyez-vous que la glace porte,** do you think that the ice will bear? **l'eau salée porte mieux que l'eau douce,** salt water is more buoyant than fresh (water); **ces abus portent en eux leur propre châtiment,** these abuses carry their own punishment; *F:* **il ne le portera pas loin!** I'll be even with him yet! I'll make him pay for it! *O:* **l'un portant l'autre,** taking one thing with another; on an average; **elle porte quarante ans,** she looks forty; **elle porte bien son âge,** (i) she looks her age; (ii) she wears well; **elle ne porte pas son âge,** she doesn't look her age; **il porte plus, moins, que son âge,** he looks older, younger, than he is; *F:* **p. beau,** to have a fine presence; **p. qn dans son cœur,** to have a great affection for s.o.; *abs. Tail:* **de quel côté portez-vous, Monsieur?** which way do you dress, Sir? *abs. O:* **elle porte depuis trois mois,** she has been pregnant for three months; **les juments portent onze mois,** the gestation period of a mare is eleven months; (*b*) to produce; **animaux qui portent plus de deux petits,** animals that bear more than two young; **le plus grand scélérat que la terre ait porté,** the greatest rogue that has ever been born; **p. des fruits,** to bear fruit; **terres qui portent du blé,** wheat-producing lands; **argent qui porte intérêt,** money that bears, brings in, interest; **cela vous portera bonheur,** that will bring you luck; *Prov:* **la nuit porte conseil,** seek counsel from your pillow; sleep on it; (*c*) **le chameau porte deux bosses,** the camel has two humps; **p. des cornes,** (i) (*of animal*) to have horns; (ii) *F:* (*of husband*) to be a cuckold; **p. des lunettes,** to wear spectacles; **p. du noir,** to wear black; **p. une bague,** to wear a ring; **il portait un chapeau neuf,** he was wearing a new hat; **p. la soutane, les armes,** to be a priest, a military man; **le bleu se porte beaucoup cette année,** blue is very much worn, is very fashionable, this year; **c'est mal porté,** one can't (possibly) wear that; **c'est très bien porté,** my dear, it's just right; **le nom qu'on porte,** the name one bears; **je ne porte jamais beaucoup d'argent sur moi,** I never carry, have, much money on me; **p. des cicatrices,** to bear scars; **p. la tête haute,** to carry one's head high; *F:* **le p. haut,** to think no small beer of oneself; *Mil:* **portez armes!** shoulder arms! **p. le sabre,** to port swords; *Her:* **p. d'argent à la croix de gueules,** to bear argent, a cross gules; *Nau:* (*of ship*) **p. tout dessus,** to have all sails set; (*d*) to carry, convey, take (sth. somewhere); **p. qch. dans la maison, p. qch. dehors,** to carry sth. in, out; **p. une lettre à la poste,** to take a letter to the post; **c'est moi qui leur ai porté la nouvelle,** it was I who brought, conveyed, the news to them; **p. le lait, les journaux, à domicile,** to deliver milk, newspapers, at the door; **il porta le verre à ses lèvres,** he raised the glass to his lips; **p. qn en terre,** to bury s.o.; to carry s.o. to his grave; **courant, marée, qui porte au sud,** current, tide, that sets to the south; **p. la mort partout,** to carry death everywhere; (*e*) **p. un coup à qn, p. la main sur qn,** to strike s.o., to aim, strike, a blow at s.o.; **cela nous a porté un grand coup,** that was a severe blow to us; *abs.* **fusil qui porte à mille mètres,** rifle that carries, has a range of, a thousand metres; **il porta la main à son revolver,** his hand went to his revolver; **il porta la main à sa casquette,** he touched his cap; **p. ses regards sur qn,** to look at s.o.; **p. qn aux nues,** to praise s.o. to the skies; *Lit:* **les pavés sur lesquels il avait tant de fois porté ses pas,** the pavements on which he had so often walked; **p. son attention sur qch.,** to give sth. one's attention; **je porterai votre proposition à la connaissance du conseil d'administration,** I shall bring your suggestion to the notice of the board; **p. un différend devant un tribunal,** to bring a dispute before a court; **p. une accusation contre qn,** to lodge a complaint against s.o.; to bring, lay, a charge against s.o.; **p. qch. à la connaissance de qn,** to bring sth. to s.o.'s knowledge; **p. qch. à la perfection,** to bring sth. to perfection; (*f*) to inscribe, enter; **p. une position sur une carte,** to mark, show, a position on a map, a chart; *Mth:* **p. un point en abscisse, en ordonnée,** to plot the abscissa, the ordinate, of a point; **p. qch. en compte à qn,** to charge sth. to s.o.'s account; **les frais lui seront portés en compte,** the expenses will be charged to his account; **portez cela sur, à, mon compte,** put that down to me, to my account; **portez-le sur la note,** put it, charge it, on the bill; **p. une somme au crédit de qn,** to place a sum (of money) to s.o.'s credit; *Nau:* **p. un homme au rôle de l'équipage,** to enter a seaman on the ship's books; *Mil: etc:* **p. qn déserteur,** to declare s.o. a deserter; **p. qn disparu,** to report s.o. missing; **p. qn manquant à l'appel,** to report s.o. absent from roll call; **se faire p. malade,** to report sick; (*g*) to induce, incline, prompt; **p. qn à qch.,** to incite s.o. to sth.; **tout me porte à croire que . . .,** everything leads, inclines, me to believe that . . .; **propagande qui pourrait p. la foule à se soulever,** propaganda that might lead to rebellion; **sa bonté le porta à écouter notre prière,** his kind nature prompted him, induced him, to listen to our request; (*h*) to raise, carry; **p. la température à 100°,** to raise the temperature to 100°; **p. la production au maximum,** to raise production to a maximum; **les historiens portent le nombre à douze cents,** historians put the number as high as twelve hundred; **si vous pouviez p. la somme à mille francs,** if you could raise, increase, the sum to a thousand francs; (*i*) to show, manifest, entertain (interest, affection, respect, for s.o., sth.); **par la tendresse que je vous porte,** by the love I bear you; (*j*) to declare, state; **le texte du traité porte ces mots . . .,** the text of the treaty bears these words, declares, says . . .; **avec une clause conditionnelle portant que . . .,** with a proviso to the effect that . . .; **le rapport ne porte rien de tout cela,** nothing of the kind is mentioned in the report; **la loi porte que . . .,** the law provides that . . .; *Mil: etc:* **la décision porte que . . .,** it is stated in orders that . . .; **p. témoignage,** to bear witness. **2.** *v.i.* (*a*) to rest, bear; **tout le poids porte sur cette poutre,** all the weight bears on this beam; **la discussion porte toujours sur le même sujet,** the discussion always turns on the same subject; **la philosophie porte sur tous les aspects de la vie,** philosophy is concerned, has to do, with all aspects of life; **l'invention porte sur . . .,** the invention relates to . . .; **résolution portant sur une question,** resolution bearing on, dealing with, a matter; **faire p. son attention sur qch.,** to bring one's mind to bear on sth.; **sur quoi porte sa plainte?** what is the ground of his complaint? what is he complaining of? **la perte a porté sur nous,** we incurred the loss; we had to stand the loss; (*b*) to hit (a target, a mark); **aucun des coups, des coups de feu, ne porta,** none of the blows, of the shots, took effect; **le coup, l'insulte, a porté,** the shot, the insult, went home; **chaque coup, chaque mot, porte,** every shot, every word, tells; **coup qui porte, qui a porté,** home thrust; **style qui porte,** telling style; **son discours a porté sur ses auditeurs,** his speech made an impact on his audience; **je me rendis compte à leurs visages que son plaidoyer avait porté,** I saw by their faces that he had made his point; **vin qui porte à la tête,** wine that goes to the head; **sa voix porte bien,** his voice carries well; **ce bruit me porte sur les nerfs,** the noise gets on my nerves; **sa tête a porté sur le trottoir,** his head hit, struck, knocked against, the pavement; (*c*) *Nau:* (*of sail*) to fill, draw; **les voiles portent bien,** the sails are full; **portez plein!** keep her full! (*d*) *Nau:* **laisser p.,** to bear away; **laisser p. sur un navire,** to bear down upon, to run down, a ship; **p. à terre,** to stand in for the land; **p. à route,** to keep the course, to stand upon the course.
se porter. 1. to go, proceed (to a place); **se p. au secours de qn,** to go to s.o.'s help; *Navy:* **se p. en tête de la flotte,** to take up a position ahead; **la foule se porta vers les hauteurs,** the crowd made for the heights; **le sang se porta à sa tête,** the blood went to his head; **se p. aux dernières extrémités,** to go to extremes; **se p. à des voies de fait,** to commit acts of violence; to commit an assault; **son regard se portait vers son frère,** he looked towards his brother, his eyes turned towards his brother; *Mil:* **se p. en avant,** to advance; **la conversation s'est portée sur**

l'Extrême-Orient, the conversation turned to the Far East. **2.** (*of health*) to be; **se bien p., se p. à merveille, se p. comme un charme,** to be in good health; to be in, to enjoy, the best of health; to be as fit as a fiddle; **il n'est rien de tel que de se bien p.,** there is nothing like good health; **comment vous portez-vous?** how are you? **je ne m'en porte pas plus mal,** I am none the worse for it. **3. se p. candidat, caution,** to offer oneself, to come forward, to stand, as candidate, as surety.

porter[2], *s.m. used in the phr.* **au p.,** in the wearing, while being worn; **ce chandail ne se déforme pas au p.,** this sweater doesn't lose its shape through wear; **la montre se remonte elle-même au p.,** the watch winds itself up while being worn, is self-winding when worn.

porter[3] [pɔrtɛːr], *s.m. Brew:* porter.

porte-rame [pɔrt(ə)ram], *s.m.inv. Nau:* rowlock.

porte-raviers [pɔrt(ə)ravje], *s.m.inv.* hors-d'œuvres dish.

portereau, -eaux [pɔrt(ə)ro], *s.m.* **1.** *Artil:* carrying bar. **2.** (*in river*) (*a*) stake; (*b*) staked off basin.

porte-respect [pɔrt(ə)rɛspɛ], *s.m.inv.* **1.** *O:* person of imposing appearance. **2.** *A:* weapon (carried for self-defence); life-preserver.

porte-ressort [pɔrt(ə)rəsɔːr], *s.m.* spring carrier; *pl. porte-ressorts.*

porte-revues [pɔrt(ə)rəvy], *s.m.inv.* newspaper, magazine, rack.

porterie [pɔrtəri], *s.f.* gatehouse (of convent).

porte-robe [pɔrt(ə)rɔb], *s.m.* dress hanger; *pl. porte-robes.*

porte-rôties [pɔrt(ə)roti], *s.m.inv.* toast rack.

porte-roue [pɔrt(ə)ru], *s.m.inv. Aut:* **p.-r. (de rechange),** wheel carrier; spare-wheel axle, clip.

porte-sabot [pɔrt(ə)sabo], *s.m.* brake-shoe holder; *pl. porte-sabots.*

porte-sabre [pɔrt(ə)sɑbr̥], *s.m.inv. A: Mil:* (*a*) sword frog; (*b*) sword clip (on bicycle).

porte-savon [pɔrt(ə)savɔ̃], *s.m.inv.* soap dish.

porte-scie [pɔrt(ə)si], *s.m.inv.* saw frame.

porte-segment [pɔrt(ə)sɛgmɑ̃], *s.m. I.C.E:* piston-ring carrier.

porte-serviette(s) [pɔrt(ə)sɛrvjɛt], *s.m.inv.* (*a*) towel rail; towel horse; **rouleau p.-s.,** roller (for roller towel); (*b*) napkin case; (*c*) *Dent:* napkin holder.

porte-tapisserie [pɔrt(ə)tapis(ə)ri], *s.m.inv.* curtain rail, curtain rod (on door).

porte-taraud [pɔrt(ə)taro], *s.m. Tls:* tap holder; *pl. porte-tarauds.*

porte-timbre [pɔrt(ə)tɛ̃ːbr̥], *s.m.inv.* bell holder, bell support.

porte-tartines [pɔrt(ə)tartin], *s.m.inv.*, **porte-toasts** [pɔrt(ə)tost], *s.m.inv.* toast rack.

porte-tolet [pɔrt(ə)tɔlɛ], *s.m.inv. Nau:* (rowlock) poppet.

porte-torpille(s) [pɔrt(ə)tɔrpiːj], *Navy:* (*a*) *s.m.inv.* torpedo spar, torpedo boom; (*b*) *a.inv.* **canot p.-t.,** torpedo boat.

porte-trait [pɔrt(ə)trɛ], *s.m. Harn:* trace tug; *pl. porte-trait(s).*

porteur, -euse [pɔrtœːr, -øːz]. **1.** *s.* (*a*) bearer, carrier (of message, etc.); **p. de télégrammes,** telegraph boy, messenger; **p. de nouvelles,** bearer, bringer, of news; **j'arrivais p. d'heureuses nouvelles,** I arrived bringing good news; **p. d'une lettre,** bearer of a letter; **prière de donner la réponse au p.,** please hand the reply to bearer; **il entra p. d'un énorme paquet,** he came in carrying a huge parcel; *Mil: etc:* **p. d'ordres,** messenger; (*b*) (railway, etc.) porter; **p. de la halle,** market porter; *A:* **p. de chaise,** chairman; **chaise à porteurs,** sedan chair; **p. d'eau,** (i) water carrier; (ii) *Cy.Rac:* rider who acts as squire to his leader; (*c*) *Med:* **p. de germes,** (germ) carrier; (*d*) *Fin:* **p. d'un chèque,** bearer, endorsee, payee, of a cheque; **p. de titres,** holder of stock, stockholder; **p. d'actions,** shareholder, stockholder; **p. d'un effet,** bearer, holder, payee, of a bill of exchange or draft; **payable au p.,** payable to bearer; **effets au p.,** bearer stock(s); **p. d'obligations,** bondholder; **titre au p.,** bearer bond, negotiable instrument. **2.** *s.m.* (*a*) *Nau:* (dredger's) mud barge; hopper (barge); (*b*) *Aut:* **gros p.,** large (petrol) tanker; (*c*) *Av:* **(avion) gros, moyen, p.,** large, medium, transport aircraft. **3.** *s.f.* **porteuse:** (*a*) *Min:* (*Central Fr.*) longitudinal beam, girder; (*b*) *Elcs:* **carrier; déplacement de la p.,** carrier shift. **4.** *a.* (*a*) **cheval p.,** near horse (of team); **animal p.,** pack animal; **essieu p.,** bearing axle; *Rail:* **roues porteuses,** carrying wheels (of locomotive); *a. & s.m.* **(câble) p.,** suspension cable; (*b*) *El: Elcs:* **courant p.,** carrier current; **équipement de courant p.,** carrier equipment; **fréquence porteuse,** carrier frequency; **onde porteuse,** carrier wave; **transmission à suppression d'onde porteuse,** suppressed carrier transmission.

porte-veine [pɔrt(ə)vɛn], *s.m.inv. F:* lucky charm, mascot.

porte-vent [pɔrt(ə)vɑ̃], *s.m.inv.* **1.** air duct; wind chest (of organ); mouth tube (of bagpipe). **2.** *Metall:* blast pipe, main; **coude p.-v.,** goose neck. **3.** *Aer: A:* trousers (of kite balloon).

porte-verge [pɔrt(ə)vɛrʒ], *s.m.inv. Ecc: etc:* verger, beadle.

porte-vêtements [pɔrt(ə)vɛtmɑ̃], *s.m.inv.* coat hanger, clothes hanger.

porte-voix [pɔrt(ə)vwa], *s.m.inv.* speaking tube, speaking pipe; loudhailer; megaphone.

Port-Fouad [pɔrfwad], *Pr.n.m. Geog:* Port Fuad.

portier, -ière[1] [pɔrtje, -jɛːr], *s.* (*a*) *Lit:* gatekeeper; **Saint Pierre, p. du paradis,** St Peter who guards the gates of Paradise; (*b*) *Ecc:* porter, *f.* port(e)ress (of convent); **sœur portière,** sister portress; (*c*) caretaker, *U.S:* janitor (of block of flats); (*d*) (hotel, etc.) commissionaire; (*e*) *Fb: etc:* goalkeeper.

portier-consigne [pɔrtjekɔ̃siɲ], *s.m. Mil:* gatekeeper (of fortress); warden (of arsenal); *pl. portiers-consigne.*

portière[2] [pɔrtjɛːr], *a.f. Husb:* (cow, ewe, etc.) of an age to bear.

portière[3], *s.f.* **1.** door (of carriage, car, railway carriage). **2.** door curtain.

portière[4], *s.f.* **1.** raft, cut (of pontoon bridge). **2. portières de dames (d'un canot),** (rowlock) poppets.

portillon [pɔrtijɔ̃], *s.m.* **1.** wicket(-gate); kissing-gate; *Rail:* (foot passengers') side gate (at level crossing); **p. d'accès,** ticket barrier; **p. automatique,** automatic gate; *F:* **ses mots se bousculent au p.,** he can't get his words out. **2.** *Dial:* small pass (in the Pyrenees).

portion [pɔrsjɔ̃], *s.f.* portion; share; part; **p. de viande,** portion, helping, of meat; **p. de gâteau,** slice of cake; **par portions égales,** in equal shares; **par petites portions,** in batches; in consignments; in driblets; **p. de maison à louer,** part of a house to let; *Jur:* **p. virile,** lawful share (of succession); *Elcs:* (*computers*) **p. horizontale (d'une carte),** curtate; **p. des rangées inférieures, supérieures,** lower, upper, curtate; *s.a.* CONGRU.

portionnaire [pɔrsjɔnɛːr], *s.m. & f. Jur:* sharer (in an estate); portioner.

portionner [pɔrsjɔne], *v.tr.* **1.** to portion out; to divide (food, etc.) into shares, portions. **2.** to apportion (prize money, etc.).

portique [pɔrtik], *s.m.* **1.** (*a*) portico, porch; *Gr.Phil:* **le P.,** the Porch, the Stoic body; (*b*) *Fb:* **p. du but,** goal mouth; (*c*) *Rail:* gantry. **2.** *Gym:* cross beam (for attaching gymnastic apparatus); (gymnasium) gallows. **3.** *Mec.E:* **p. roulant, grue à p.,** travelling-gantry crane. **4.** *Av:* **p. pour essais de vol statique,** captive-flight gantry, rig.

portland [pɔrtlɑ̃(ːd)], *s.m.* Portland cement.

portlandien [pɔrtlɑ̃djɛ̃], *s.m. Geol:* Portlandian oolite.

Porto [pɔrto]. **1.** *Pr.n.m. Geog:* Oporto. **2.** *s.m.* (*also* **vin de P.**), port; **vieux p.,** old port; **p. rouge,** ruby port; **p. blanc,** white port.

portor [pɔrtɔːr], *s.m. Geol:* portor (marble).

portoricain, -aine [pɔrtɔrikɛ̃, -ɛn], *a. & s. Geog:* Porto Rican, Puerto Rican.

Porto Rico [pɔrtoriko], *Pr.n.m. Geog:* Porto Rico, Puerto Rico.

portraire [pɔrtrɛːr], *v.tr. Used only in inf. A: & Lit:* **1.** to draw, paint, the portrait of (s.o.). **2.** (*of author*) to portray.

portrait [pɔrtrɛ], *s.m.* **1.** (*a*) portrait; **p. en pied, en buste,** full-length, half-length, portrait; **p. très ressemblant,** speaking likeness; **faire le p. de qn,** to make, paint, draw, a portrait of s.o.; **c'est le p. vivant de son père,** he is the living image of his father; **p. de qn, de qch., en prose, en vers,** description of s.o., sth., in prose, in verse; portrait in words; **p. littéraire,** character sketch; (*b*) *P:* face; *P:* **il s'est abîmé le p.,** he's messed his face up; **je vais lui abîmer le p.,** I'm going to spoil his beauty for him; **se payer le p. de qn,** to make fun of s.o. **2. l'art du p.,** the art of portraiture; portrait painting.

portrait-charge [pɔrtrɛʃarʒ], *s.m. Lit:* unkind character sketch; *pl. portraits-charges.*

portrait-interview [pɔrtrɛɛ̃tɛrvju], *s.m. Journ:* close-up; *pl. portraits-interviews.*

portraitiste [pɔrtrɛtist], *s.m.* portrait painter.

portraiture [pɔrtrɛtyːr], *s.f. A: & Lit:* **1.** portrait. **2.** portrayal; portraiture.

portraiturer [pɔrtrɛtyre], *v.tr.* (*rare*) to portray.

Port-Saïd [pɔrsaid], *Pr.n.m. Geog:* Port Said.

port-salut [pɔrsaly], *s.m.inv.* Port-Salut (cheese).

portuaire [pɔrtɥɛːr], *a.* **installations portuaires,** harbour installations; **équipement p.,** harbour, port, equipment.

portugais, -aise [pɔrtygɛ, -ɛːz]. **1.** *a. & s.* Portuguese. **2.** *s.m. Ling:* Portuguese. **3.** *s.f.* **portugaise:** (*a*) Portuguese oyster; (*b*) head lashing (of sheers); (*c*) *s.f.pl. P:* **portugaises,** ears, lugs, lugholes; **avoir les portugaises ensablées,** (i) to be deaf; (ii) not to take it in; **je vais t'embouteiller les portugaises,** I'll split your ears for you.

Portugal [pɔrtygal], *Pr.n.m. Geog:* Portugal; **aller au P.,** to go to Portugal; *Toil: O:* **eau de P.,** *s.m.* **portugal,** angel water.

portulaca [pɔrtylaka], *s.m. Bot:* portulaca; *F:* purslane.

portulacacées [pɔrtylakase], *s.f.pl. Bot:* Portulacaceae.

portulan [pɔrtylɑ̃], *s.m. Nau: A:* portolano, portulan.

portune [pɔrtyn], *s.m. Crust:* portunian; (*genus*) Portunus.

portunidés [pɔrtynide], *s.m.pl. Crust:* Portunidae.

port-vendrais, -aise [pɔrvɑ̃drɛ, -ɛːz], *a. & s. Geog:* (native, inhabitant) of Port Vendres.

porzane [pɔrzan], *s.f. Orn:* crake; **p. poussin,** little crake; **p. marouette,** spotted crake.

posage [pozaːʒ], *s.m.* (*used mainly in plumbing and building*) placing, laying (down) (of pipes, cables, rails); fixing, fitting; setting (of boilers); laying (of bricks).

pose [poːz], *s.f.* **1.** (*a*) fitting, fixing; installation (of equipment, machinery); laying (of pipes, carpet; *Rail:* track); *Rail:* **p. volante,** laying of a temporary track; **p. définitive,** laying of the permanent way; **train de p.,** track-laying train; **p. de câbles sous-marins,** submarine-cable laying; *N.Arch:* **p. de la quille,** keel laying; *Const:* **p. de la première pierre,** laying of the foundation stone; (*b*) *Mil:* posting, stationing (of sentry); (*c*) *Games:* (*dominoes*) pose; **à vous la p.,** you play first, it's your start. **2.** (*a*) pose, posture; (*b*) *Art:* pose; **elle ne sait pas garder la p.,** she can't hold the pose, she's a poor sitter; **faire des heures de p.,** to sit (as a model); (*c*) posing, affectation; **sans p.,** unaffected(ly); *F:* **le faire à la p.,** to swank, to show off; (*d*) *Golf:* **p. d'une balle,** lie of a ball. **3.** *Phot:* (*a*) exposure; **temps de p.,** exposure time; **p. instantanée,** instantaneous exposure; **manque de p.,** under exposure; **salon de p.,** (photographer's) studio; (*b*) time exposure.

posé [poze], *a.* **1.** (*a*) sitting (bird); **tirer sur un faisan p.,** to shoot a sitting pheasant; (*b*) *Her:* **lion p.,** lion statant, lion posé; **p. en pal,** palewise; **p. en fasce,** fesswise. **2.** staid, serious, calm, grave, sedate (person); steady (person, bearing, etc.); **écrire à main posée,** to write slowly, carefully; **écriture posée,** calligraphic hand; **voix posée,** even, steady, voice; **avancer à pas posés,** to move slowly, steadily, forward. **3.** *s.m.* **il est plus facile de tirer au p.,** it's easier to shoot a sitting bird. **4.** *s.f. Nau:* **posée,** beaching strand, graving beach.

pose-cigare(s) [pozsigaːr], *s.m.inv.* cigar rest.

posément [pozemɑ̃], *adv.* staidly, sedately, soberly, calmly; steadily, without hurry, deliberately.

posemètre [pozmɛtr̥], *s.m. Phot:* exposure meter.

pose-mines [pozmin], *a.inv. Navy:* **navire p.-m.,** minelayer.

pose-plumes [pozplym], *s.m.inv.* pen rack, pen tray.

poser [poze]. **1.** *v.i.* (*a*) to rest, lie (on sth.); **poutre qui pose sur un mur,** beam that rests on a wall; (*b*) to pose (as artist's model); to sit (for an artist, for one's portrait); **p. pour le buste,** *v.tr.* **p. le buste,** to sit for the bust; **qui a posé cette statue?** who sat for this statue? *F:* **faire p. qn,** to keep s.o. waiting; *F:* **je ne pose pas à l'ange,** I don't pretend to be an angel; (*c*) to pose, to take up an attitude; to show off; **p. pour la galerie,** to play to the gallery; **tu croyais que je posais?** did you think I was being affected, showing off? **2.** *v.tr.* (*a*) to put, place, lay down (sth. somewhere); **p. un livre sur la table,** to put a book (down) on the table; **il l'a posé avec violence sur la table,** he banged it down on the table; **p. son chapeau,** to put down one's hat; **p. les armes,** to lay down one's arms; **p. un avion,** to land an aircraft; (*at chess, etc.*) **p. une pièce,** to move a piece; **p. (le premier domino),** to pose; **p. un soldat en sentinelle,** to post a soldier as sentry; **p. sa candidature,** to stand as a candidate (**à,** for); **p. une question à qn,** to ask s.o. a question; **ces questions se posent d'elles-mêmes,** these questions crop up of their own accord, automatically; **p. la question de confiance,** to table a motion of confidence; **p. un problème à qn,** to set s.o. a problem; **ce barrage a posé de grands problèmes aux ingénieurs,** this dam presented the engineers with serious problems; **un nouveau problème se pose,** we are faced with a new problem; **p. une règle de conduite,** to lay down a rule of conduct; *Jur:* **je pose en fait que** + *ind.*, I submit that . . .; (*b*) to put up, fix (up) (curtain, etc.); to hang (bell); to lay (bricks, carpet, foundation stone, rivets, rails, pipes, mines); to set (stones, rivets, boiler); to fit (a watch glass, etc.); *N.Arch:* **p. la quille,** to lay the keel; **p. une vitre,** to put in a pane of glass; *F:* **p. l'électricité,** to put in electricity; *abs. Const:* **p. à cru,** to build without foundations; (*c*) **le moindre succès pose un auteur,** the slightest success establishes an author's reputation; (*d*) to suppose, admit, grant; **posons le cas que cela soit, le cas posé que cela soit,** supposing, admitting, that that is the case; **cela p., il s'ensuit que . . .,** assuming this to be true, it follows that . . .; *Ar:* **je pose deux et je retiens un,** put down two, carry one; (*e*) *Art:* **p. un modèle,** to pose a model; (*f*) *Mus:* **bien p. la voix,** to pitch (one's voice) correctly.

se poser. 1. (*of bird*) to settle, alight (**sur,** on); *Av:* (*of pilot, aircraft*) to land. **2.** (*a*) **se p. dans le monde,** to establish a position in society; **homme bien posé,** man of good standing; (*b*) *P:* **se p. là,** to be first rate; **il se pose un peu là,** (i) he's a hefty chap; (ii) he's just right for the job. **3. se p. en réformateur,** to set up as, to pose as, a reformer; **se p. en savant,** to claim to be, pretend to be, a scholar.

poseur, -euse [pozœːr, -øːz], *s.* **1.** *Tchn:* layer (of pipes, cables, etc.); *Rail:* **p. de rails, de voie,** platelayer; **p. (de pierres de taille),** setter; *Navy:* **p. de mines,** minelayer. **2.** *a. & s.* (person) who poses; **il est p.,** he's always (i) striking attitudes, (ii) swanking, putting on side; **elle est un peu poseuse,** she's rather affected.

posidonie [pɔzidɔni], *s.f. Algae:* posidonia.

positif, -ive [pozitif, -iːv]. **1.** *a.* (*a*) positive, actual real (fact, etc.); **c'est p.,** it's a positive fact; *Gram:* **degré p.,** positive degree (of comparison); (*b*) *Mth: El: etc:* positive (number, pole, etc.); *Phot:* **papier p.,** printing-out paper; (*c*) practical, unsentimental, matter-of-fact (person); **philosophie positive,** positive philosophy; **esprit p.,** (i) practical mind; (ii) precise mind. **2.** *s.m.* (*a*) *Phil:* reality; what is certain, actual, real; (*b*) *Mus:* choir organ (of full organ); (*c*) *Phot:* positive; print.

position [pozisjɔ̃], *s.f.* position. **1.** (*a*) situation, site (of house, town, etc.); position (of ship at sea, of aircraft, of spacecraft, etc.); *Astr:* position, place (of star); *Nau: Av:* **p. (obtenue) par relèvement,** fix, position by bearing; **donner, indiquer, sa p.,** to give, indicate, one's position; **message de p.,** position report; **renseignements sur la p.,** position data; **repère de p.,** position mark, sign; **feux de p.,** (i) *Nau:* riding lights; (ii) *Aut:* parking lights; *Aut:* **stationner en deuxième p.,** to double park; *Astr:* **p. apparente, moyenne, d'une étoile,** apparent, mean, place of a star; **astronomie de p.,** field, position, astronomy; *Ball:* **p. estimée,** dead-reckoning position; **p. extrapolée, p. future,** predicted position; *Golf:* **la p. de la balle,** the lie of the ball; *Mth:* **appliquer la règle de fausse p.,** to proceed by trial and error; (*b*) *Mus:* position, shift (of hand on violin, of slide in trombone); **deuxième p.,** second position, half shift (on violin); (*c*) *Mil:* (tactical) position; **p. clé,** key position; **p. dominante,** commanding position; **p. masquée,** position behind cover; **p. en bretelle,** switch (position); **occuper, s'établir sur, une p.,** to take up a position; **prendre p. sur la cote 304,** to take up position on hill 304; **guerre de p.,** position warfare; **p. organizée,** organized position; **p. défensive, p. de défense,** defensive position; **p. de couverture,** covering position; **p. de résistance,** main defensive position, *U.S:* battle position; **p. de soutien,** supporting position; **p. de repli, de recueil,** position to fall back on; *U.S:* reserve battle position; **p. de recueil des éléments de couverture,** position for the covering force to fall back on; **p. de rechange,** alternate position; **p. factice, p. simulée,** dummy position; *Artil: etc:* **p. de batterie,** battery position, field emplacement; (*of tank*) **p. à défilement de coque, à défilement de tourelle,** hull-down, turret-down, position; **aménager, organiser, une p.,** to organize a position; **prendre d'assaut les positions ennemies,** to storm the enemy positions; **s'emparer d'une p.,** to capture a position; **prendre pied dans les positions ennemies,** to gain a foothold in the enemy positions; (*d*) **prendre p. (sur une question),** to take, adopt, a definite position on a matter; (*e*) *Tp:* **p. d'opératrice,** operator's position, switchboard position; **p. urbaine,** local position; **p. de communications interurbaines, régionales,** trunk, toll, position; **p. internationale,** international position, *U.S:* foreign service position; **p. desservie, non desservie,** staffed, unstaffed, position, *U.S:* occupied, unoccupied, position. **2.** (*a*) posture, attitude (of the body, arm, head, etc.); *Golf:* stance; **fausse p., p. étriquée,** cramped position; *Anat:* **p. de repos,** rest position (of hand, mandible, etc.); *Obst:* **p. anormale,** malposition; (*in handwriting*) **p. correcte des doigts,** correct grip; *Danc:* **les cinq positions des jambes,** the five positions of the feet; *Med:* **p. genu-pectorale,** knee-chest position; *Mil: etc:* **p. du tireur (au fusil, etc.),** firing position of the (individual) soldier, of the marksman; **p. couchée, p. à plat ventre,** lying, prone, position; **p. à genoux,** kneeling position; **p. debout,** standing position; (*b*) *Av:* attitude (of aircraft); **p. de vol,** attitude of flight; **p. d'atterrissage,** landing attitude; **contrôleur de p.,** attitude controller; **gyroscope (contrôleur) de p.,** attitude gyro(scope); (*c*) *Mec.E:* position (of part of mechanism); **p. de repos, p. "coupé,"** *El: Mch:* "off" position; *Mch.Tls:* running idle; **p. de fonctionnement, p. de travail, p. "marche," p. "contact,"** "on" position; **mettre le levier en p. de fonctionnement, en p. "marche,"** to put, set, the lever in the operating position; **p. au point mort,** dead-centre position; **p. centrale,** central, centric, position; **p. excentrique, p. excentrée,** eccentric position; *Av:* **p. des volets, de l'atterrisseur,** flap, landing-gear, position. **3.** (*a*) condition, circumstances; (social) status; **p. enviable, peu enviable,** enviable, unenviable, situation; **p. gênante,** embarrassing situation; **il est dans une meilleure p. au point où il en est,** he is better off where he is; **nous allons faire l'inventaire pour nous rendre compte de notre p.,** we are going to take stock to see how we stand; **voici ma p.,** this is how I am situated, how I stand; **être en p. de faire qch.,** to be in a position to do sth.; (*b*) *Fin: St.Exch:* position, account; **la solvabilité d'un tiré dépend de la p. de son compte en banque,** the solvency of a drawee depends on the position of his bank account; *St.Exch:* **p. acheteur, p. vendeur,** bull, bear, position, account; **p. de place,** market (position). **4.** (*a*) post, situation, job; (*b*) **société cherche cadre p. II,** firm requires executive (grade II). **5.** stating, formulation (of problem, etc.); **la p. du problème, de la question, sous tous ses aspects,** the stating of the problem in full; **p. du problème, de la question,** aspect(s) of the problem.

positionnement [pozisjɔnmɑ̃], *s.m. Tchn:* positioning; (*of computer*) **bras de p.,** positioning arm.

positionner [pozisjɔne], *v.tr.* **1.** *Tchn:* to position. **2.** *Bank:* to calculate the balance of (an account).

positionneur [pozisjɔnœːr], *s.m. Tchn:* positioner.

positionneuse [pozisjɔnøːz], *s.f. Bank:* calculating machine (used for working out the balance of an account).

positionniste [pozisjɔnist], *s.m. & f.* bank clerk (who works out the balances of accounts).

positivement [pozitivmɑ̃], *adv.* positively. **1. répondre p.,** to answer positively; to answer yes or no; **je ne le sais pas p.,** I don't know it for certain, for an actual fact. **2.** *El:* **électrisé p.,** positively electrified.

positivisme [pozitivism], *s.m.* **1.** (*a*) *Phil:* positivism; (*b*) materialism. **2.** *Biol: etc:* positive nature (of reaction, etc.).

positiviste [pozitivist], *a. & s.m. & f., Phil:* positivist.

positivité [pozitivite], *s.f. El: Phil:* positivity.

positon [pozitɔ̃], *s.m. Atom.Ph:* positon, positron.

positonium [pozitɔnjɔm], *s.m. Atom.Ph:* positronium.

positron [pozitrɔ̃], *s.m. Atom.Ph:* positron, positon.

positronium [pozitrɔnjɔm], *s.m. Atom.Ph:* positronium.

Posnanie [pɔsnani, pɔz-], *Pr.n.f. Hist:* the province of Posen; Posnania; *Geog:* (province of) Poznan.

posnanien, -ienne [pɔsnanjɛ̃, pɔz-, -jɛn], *a. & s. Geog:* (native, inhabitant) of Poznan (town or province).

posologie [pozɔlɔʒi], *s.f. Med: etc:* posology; dos(i)ology; dosage (of drug).

posologique [pozɔlɔʒik], *a.* posological.

possédant, -ante [pɔsedɑ̃, -ɑ̃ːt], *a. & s.* **les possédants, les classes possédantes,** the propertied classes; the well-to-do; *F:* the "haves."

possédé, -ée [pɔsede]. **1.** *a.* possessed (**de,** by, of); infatuated, dominated (by passion, idea, etc.); **être p. du démon,** to be possessed of the devil. **2.** *s.* person possessed; madman, maniac; **se démener comme un p.,** to carry on like a madman.

posséder [pɔsede], *v.tr.* (**je possède, n. possédons; je posséderai**) **1.** to be in possession of (sth.); (*a*) to possess, own; to enjoy the possession of (sth.); to have (wealth, property, etc.); **la bibliothèque de la ville possède trois de ses manuscrits,** the town library has three of his manuscripts; **posséder un titre,** to hold a title; **p. le secret de qn,** to be in possession of s.o.'s secret; **on possède déjà des données sur . . .,** we are already in possession of data on, about . . .; **p. qn pendant quelques jours,** to have s.o. (staying with one) for a few days; **p. un million,** to be worth a million; (*b*) to have a thorough knowledge of, be master of (subject, etc.); **p. (à fond) une langue,** to have a thorough knowledge of a language, to be proficient in a language; (*c*) *Lit:* to curb, control; **tâchez de p. votre langue,** try to curb your tongue; **p. son âme en paix,** to possess one's soul in peace; (*d*) (*of passion, ideas*) to dominate; **le désespoir le possède,** he is filled with despair; **quel démon le possède?** what devil possesses him? **tous étaient possédés de la même illusion,** they all laboured under the same delusion. **2.** (*a*) **p. le cœur d'une femme,** to win a woman's heart; **p. une femme,** to have sexual intercourse with a woman; (*b*) *F:* to fool (s.o.); **je me suis fait p.,** I've been had.

se posséder, to control oneself, one's temper; **elle ne se possédait plus,** she was no longer able to control herself; **il ne se possédait plus de joie,** he was beside himself with joy.

possesseur [pɔsɛsœːr], *s.m.* possessor, owner; occupier; **comment êtes-vous devenu p. de cette montre?** how did you get, come by, this watch?

possessif, -ive [pɔsɛsif, -iːv], *a. & s.m.* (*a*) *Gram:* possessive (adjective, pronoun); (*b*) *F:* **une mère possessive,** a possessive mother.

possession [pɔsɛsjɔ̃], *s.f.* **1.** possession; **s'assurer la p. de qch.,** to take steps to obtain sth., to acquire sth.; **il ne faut pas que ce papier tombe en sa p.,** he mustn't see, get hold of, this paper; **être en p. de qch.,** to be in possession of sth., *Jur:* to be possessed of sth., to own sth.; **en pleine p. de ses facultés,** in full possession of one's faculties; *Com:* **nous sommes en p. de votre lettre du 4 mars,** we are in receipt of, have received, your letter of 4th March; **être en p. de l'estime publique,** to be held in public esteem; *Jur:* **les terres dont je suis en p.,** the estates of which I am possessed; **avoir qch. en sa p.,** to have sth. in one's possession; **entrer en p. d'un héritage,** to enter into possession of an inheritance; **entrée en p. d'un patrimoine,** accession to an estate; **prendre p. de qch.,** to take possession of sth.; to take over (authority, the customs, etc.); to assume (power, authority); **prise de p.,** taking possession, taking over; **reprendre p. de qch.,** to resume possession of sth.; **mettre qn en p. de qch.,** to put s.o. in possession of sth.; **mettre qn en p. d'un emploi,** to invest s.o. with an office; **nous désirons être mis en p. de preuves (de ce) que . . .,** we wish to be furnished with proof that . . .; **remettre qn en p. de sa fortune,** to restore his fortune to s.o.; **rentrer en p. de qch.,** to regain possession of sth.; to recover sth.; **rester en p. de qch.,** to remain in possession of sth.; to retain possession of sth.; *Prov:* **p. vaut titre,** possession is nine points of the law; *Jur:* possession is title (in respect of movables); *Jur:* **p. de fait,** actual possession. **2.** property, estate; *pl.* possessions. **3.** possession (by evil spirit). **4. p. de soi-même,** self-control.

possessionnel, -elle [pɔsɛsjɔnɛl], *a. Jur:* possessional.

possessoire [pɔsɛswaːr], *Jur:* **1.** *a.* possessory; **intenter une action p.,** to undertake an action for possession (of land). **2.** *s.m.* possessory right (in real estate).

posset [pɔsɛ], *s.m. A.Cu:* posset.

possibiliste [pɔsibilist], *a. & s. Hist:* possibilist.

possibilité [pɔsibilite], *s.f.* (*a*) possibility; **la p. d'une guerre,** the possibility of a war; **envisager toutes les possibilités,** to envisage, consider, all possibilities; **avoir des doutes sur la p. d'un accord,** to doubt the possibility of an agreement; **possibilités d'avancement,** possibilities, scope, for advancement; **appareil aux nombreuses**

possibilités, versatile machine; **voir la p. de faire qch.,** to consider it possible to do sth.; to see one's way to doing sth.; (*b*) possibility, feasibility; **croyez-vous à la p. du projet,** do you consider that the plan is feasible? **si j'en ai la p.,** if there is any possibility, if it is feasible; **si j'ai la p. de vous joindre,** if it is possible for me, if I can manage, to meet you, get in touch with you; (*c*) (*at youth hostel, etc.*) **p. de faire la cuisine,** cooking facilities; (*d*) *pl.* **il ne connaît pas ses possibilités,** he doesn't know his own capacity, his own capabilities; **chacun doit payer selon ses possibilités,** each should pay according to his means; **l'accumulation des victimes surpassa de beaucoup les possibilités que pouvait offrir notre cimetière,** the number of victims greatly exceeded the capacity of our cemetery; (*e*) *For:* amount (of timber) a forest is capable of producing permanently; *Min:* **possibilités pétrolières d'une région,** oil prospects of a region.

possible [pɔsibl̩]. **1.** *a.* possible; (*a*) **croire une chose p.,** to believe a thing to be possible, feasible; **tout est p. à celui qui veut,** where there's a will there's a way; **cela ne m'est pas p.,** it isn't possible for me; I find it impossible; it's beyond my power, my means; **il lui est p. de venir,** it's possible for him to come; it isn't impossible, out of the question, for him to come; **juger p. de faire qch.,** to see one's way to doing sth.; to consider it possible to do sth.; **projet qu'il n'est pas p. d'exécuter,** plan that is impossible to carry out, put into execution; **cela n'est pas p. à faire,** it can't be done; **c'est p.!** *F:* **p.!** possibly! it's (quite) possible! very likely! **est-ce p.? ce n'est pas p.!** *F:* **pas p.!** it's not possible! impossible! you don't mean it! **est-il p. de faire des fautes pareilles!** how can people make such mistakes! **si p.,** if possible; **si c'est p.,** if possible (= if imaginable); *F:* **si c'est p.!** (i) good heavens! you don't mean it! (ii) aren't you ashamed of yourself? (*b*) **il est p. que** + *subj.*, it is possible that . . .; **il est bien p. que . . .,** it is quite likely, quite on the cards, that . . .; **est-il p. que . . .?** is it possible that . . .? can it be true that . . .? **il est p. qu'il fasse froid cette nuit,** it may be cold tonight; **il est tout juste p. qu'il réussisse,** it is just possible that he will succeed; *occ. with ind.* (*to indicate certitude, or conditional of hypothesis*) **il est p. qu'il en sait plus long qu'il n'en veut dire,** it is possible that he knows more than he cares to say; **est-il p. que vous serez toujours aussi bête?** will you really always be so stupid? (*c*) (*with idea of superlative, maximum or minimum*) **aussitôt que p.,** as soon as possible; **le plus tôt p.,** as early, as soon, as possible; **le moins souvent p.,** as infrequently as possible; **il écrit des lettres le moins souvent p.,** he writes letters as little as possible; he tries to avoid writing letters; **il a fait toutes les sottises possibles,** he did every stupid thing he possibly could; he couldn't have done anything more stupid if he had tried; **tous les détails possibles,** every possible detail; **le meilleur style p.,** the best possible style, the best style possible; **dans la plus large mesure p.,** as far as possible; *Corr: Com:* **le plus tôt qu'il vous sera p.,** at your earliest convenience; NOTE. **possible** *usu. remains invariable when placed after a plural noun preceded by* **le plus de, le moins de,** *or when adverbial;* **le plus, le moins, de détails possible,** as many, as few, details as possible; **courir le moins de risques possible,** to run as few risks as possible; **le moins de fautes p.,** as few mistakes as possible; **ordres exécutés le mieux p.,** orders carried out as well as possible; (*d*) **M. X., président p.,** Mr X, a suitable, possible, acceptable, president; **M. X., p. président,** Mr X, the possible (future) president; **elle le considérait comme un mari p.,** she considered him as an acceptable husband; *F:* **ces gens-là ne sont pas possibles,** these people are really impossible. **2.** *s.m.* what is possible; **dans la mesure du p.,** as far as possible; **faire tout son p. pour . . .,** to do all one can, to do one's utmost, one's level best, to make every endeavour, to try one's hardest, to . . .; **scrupuleux au p.,** scrupulous to a degree; extremely scrupulous; **il s'est montré aimable au p.,** he was as pleasant as could be; he could not have been nicer; **il a été sage au p.,** he has been as good as gold.

possiblement [pɔsibləmɑ̃], *adv.* possibly.

post- [pɔst], *pref.* post-.

postabdomen [pɔstabdɔmɛn], *s.m. Z:* postabdomen.

post-abortum [pɔstabɔrtɔm], *s.m.inv. Obst:* post-abortal period.

post(-)accélération [pɔstakselerasjɔ̃], *s.f. Elcs:* post-deflexion acceleration.

postage [pɔsta:ʒ], *s.m.* posting (of letters, etc.).

postal, -aux [pɔstal, -o], *a.* postal (service, etc.); **service p. aérien,** airmail service; **caisse d'épargne postale** = national savings bank; **carte postale,** postcard.

postbiblique [pɔstbiblik], *a.* post-Biblical.

postcombustion [pɔstkɔ̃bystjɔ̃], *s.f.* after-burning (of rocket, turbojet); **appareil, dispositif, de p.,** afterburner; **commande de p.,** reheat actuation; **dispositif de régulation de p.,** reheat fuel control system.

postcommunion [pɔstkɔmynjɔ̃], *s.f. Ecc:* post-communion.

post(-)cure [pɔstky:r], *s.f.* (*of T.B. cases*). **1.** readjustment. **2.** readjustment centre.

postdate [pɔstdat], *s.f.* post-date.

postdater [pɔstdate], *v.tr.* to post-date, to date forward (cheque, etc.).

postdental, -ale, -aux [pɔstdɑ̃tal, -o], *a.* & *s.f. Ling:* postdental (consonant).

postdiluvien, -ienne [pɔstdilyvjɛ̃, -jɛn], *a.* **1.** postdiluvial. **2.** *Hist:* postdiluvian; since the Flood.

poste[1] [pɔst], *s.f.* **1.** *A:* (*a*) post, relay (of horses;) **chevaux de p.,** post-horses; **maître de p.,** post-master; **aller, voyager, en p.,** to travel post; **aller un train de p., courir la p.,** to go post-haste; **ne courez pas la p.!** take your time! (*b*) stage (between relays). **2.** (*a*) post; **les Postes et Télécommunications,** the postal services; = the Post Office; **par p. aérienne,** by airmail; **p. aux armées,** forces mail; **sac de p.,** mailbag; **envoyer une lettre, un paquet, par la p.,** to send a letter, a parcel, by post; **mettre une lettre à la p.,** to post a letter; **je vais vous l'envoyer par la p.,** I'll post it to you, send it to you by post; **Directeur des Postes** = regional postmaster; (*b*) **(bureau de) p.,** post office; **Grande P.,** (i) = General Post Office, G.P.O.; (ii) head, general, post office (in a town); **receveur, -euse, des postes,** postmaster, postmistress; *Fr.C:* **maître de p.,** postmaster; **employé(e) des postes,** post-office clerk; counter hand; **la p. ouvre à 9 heures,** the post office opens at 9 o'clock.

poste[2], *s.m.* **1.** (*a*) post, station (of soldier, sailor, worker, etc.); **(être) en p. à . . .,** (to be) stationed at . . .; **être à son p.,** to be at one's post; **quitter, abandonner, son p.,** to leave, abandon, one's post; **ne pas être à son p.,** to be absent, away, from one's post; *Mil:* **abandon de p. en présence de l'ennemi,** desertion of post before the enemy; *Mil: Navy:* **à vos postes!** take post! to your post! stand by! **désigner leurs postes aux hommes,** to station the men; *Ind:* **p. de travail,** operation station (in factory); *Mil: Navy:* **p. de combat,** action station, battle station; *Av:* **p. du mitrailleur,** gunner's station; *Nau: Navy:* **postes d'abandon,** boat stations; **à vos postes d'abandon!** everyone to his boat! **postes de mouillage,** anchor stations; **être fidèle au p.,** to stick to one's post; **être solide au p.,** to be still going strong; (*b*) *Mil:* **petit p.,** picket; **p. avancé,** advanced, outlying, post; **p. détaché, p. isolé,** detached post; **p. d'écoute,** listening post, station; **p. de guet, de surveillance, d'observation,** lookout post, observation post; **p. d'observation aérienne,** air observation post; **p. de recueil (des traînards, etc.),** (straggler, etc.) collecting post; **p. de relais de brancardiers,** stretcher relay post; *Trans: etc:* **p. de contrôle,** control post, checking station, check point; (*c*) *Min:* **p. au charbon, p. à l'extraction,** working shift; **p. d'entretien,** repairing shift; **p. de jour, de nuit,** day, night, shift. **2** (*a*) **p. d'incendie,** (i) fire station; (ii) (fire) hydrant; **p. de police,** (i) police post, station; (ii) *Mil:* guard room; **conduire qn au p.,** to escort s.o. to the police station, *F:* to run s.o. in; **p. frontière,** frontier post; **p. d'essence,** petrol pump; filling station; **p. de la Croix-Rouge,** Red Cross station; **p. de secours,** (i) rescue station; (ii) *Med:* first aid post, dressing station; (iii) *Mil:* field dressing station, regimental aid post; *Mil:* **p. de garde,** guard house, guard room; **chef de p.,** guard commander; (*b*) *Rail:* **p. d'aiguillage,** switch tower; **p. de signaux,** signal tower; **p. sémaphorique,** block-section post, block station; (*c*) *Mil:* **p. de commandement,** headquarters (H.Q.), *U.S:* command post (C.P.), *Navy:* control room; **p. central (de conduite, de direction) de tir,** fire-direction centre; **p. de conduite, de direction, de tir,** fire-control station; *Navy:* fire-control room; *Navy:* **p. de direction de tir (avant),** fore control; **p. de direction de tir arrière,** after control; *Mil:* **p. de transmissions,** signal station; **p. optique,** visual (signal) station; *Av:* **p. de pilotage,** cockpit, flight deck, pilot's compartment; (*d*) *El:* **p. abaisseur de tension,** transformer station; **p. de couplage,** switching station; (*e*) *Elcs: W.Tel:* **p. de radio (télégraphie),** radio, wireless, station; **p. de radio à ondes dirigées,** beam station; **p. de radioalignement,** radio-range station, **p. radiophonique,** radio-telephone station; **p. d'interception radio,** radio intercept station; **p. privé,** private station; **p. émetteur,** sending, broadcasting, station; **p. récepteur,** receiving station; *Av:* **p. du radio,** radio operator's station, compartment; *Nau:* **p. de T.S.F., de radio,** radio, wireless, room; wireless house; (*computers*) **p. de consultation, d'interrogation,** inquiry station; **p. de lecture,** brush, reading, sensing, station; **p. de perforation,** punching station; (*f*) *Tp:* **p. téléphonique,** telephone station; **p. (téléphonique) public,** (public) call office, box; **p. privé, p. d'abonné,** subscriber's telephone; **p. (intérieur, supplémentaire).** extension; **poste 35,** extension 35; **entrée de p. (d'un abonné),** telephone lead-in; **p. groupé,** shared line, party-line, telephone; **ligne à postes groupés,** shared, party, line; **p. central téléphonique,** (telephone) exchange; **p. central automatique, manuel,** automatic, manual, exchange. **3.** set; (*a*) *W.Tel: etc:* **p. radio, p. de T.S.F.,** radio, wireless, set; **p. de télévision,** television set; **p. (radio) portatif,** portable radio; **p. à galène,** crystal set; **p. à lampes,** valve set; **p. à piles,** battery set; **p. à transistor,** transistor set; **p. à modulation de fréquence,** frequency modulation receiver, set; **p. émetteur,** transmitter, transmitting set; **p. récepteur,** receiver, receiving set; **p. émetteur-récepteur,** transmitter-receiver set, transceiver; *F:* **allumer, éteindre, le p.,** to switch on, switch off, the radio, television; *Elcs:* (*computers*) **p. appelant,** calling set; **p. d'utilisateur,** user's set; (*b*) *Tp:* **p. mural,** wall telephone; **p. mobile,** desk telephone (set); **p. d'opératrice,** operator's telephone set; (*c*) *Mil: Navy:* **p. de conduite de tir,** director, predictor; (*c*) *Tls:* **p. de soudure,** welding set; **p. de soudure autogène,** welder generator. **4.** (*a*) **à p. fixe,** permanently located, fixed; *Nau:* **mettre les ancres à p.,** to stow the anchors; (*b*) *Nau:* berth (of ship); **p. à quai, p. d'amarrage,** mooring berth; **p. de mouillage,** anchoring berth; **p. d'évitage,** clear berth, swinging berth; **p. de chargement, de déchargement,** loading, discharging, berth; **donner un p. à un navire,** to berth a ship; (*of ship*) **être, ne pas être, à son p.,** to be in, out of, station. **5.** *Nau: Navy:* accommodation, quarters; **p. d'équipage,** crew's accommodation, crew's quarters, crew space; (*in merchant service*) forecastle; **p. des matelots,** seamen's, sailors', quarters; *Navy:* **p. des aspirants,** gun room, *U.S:* junior officers' quarters; **p. des maîtres,** warrant officers' wardroom. **6.** post, appointment, job. **7.** *Book-k:* (*a*) entry (in books); (*b*) heading.

poste[3], *s.f. usu. pl. Arch:* Vitruvian scroll.

posté [pɔste], *a. Ind:* **travail p.,** shift working; **travailleurs postés,** shift workers.

post-éducation [pɔstedykasjɔ̃], *s.f.* further education.

poste-fond [pɔstəfɔ̃], *s.m.inv. Min:* face working; **rendement par p.-f.,** output per face working.

postembryonnaire [pɔstɑ̃brjɔnɛ:r], *a.* postembryonic, postembryonal.

poster[1] [pɔste], *v.tr.* to post, set (sentry, etc.); to station (men); to post (the guns at a shoot).

se poster, to take up a position; to take one's stand.

poster[2], *v.tr.* to post, mail (letter, etc.).

postérieur [pɔsterjœ:r]. **1.** *a.* posterior; (*a*) (*of time*) subsequent (**à,** to); later; **événement p. de dix ans à son décès,** event that occurred ten years after his death; (*b*) (*of place*) hinder, hind, back; **partie postérieure de la tête,** back part of the head; (*c*) *Ling:* back (vowel). **2.** *s.m. F:* posterior, buttocks, bottom, stern, backside, behind.

postérieurement [pɔsterjœrmɑ̃], *adv.* subsequently (**à,** to); at a later date.

posteriori (à) [apɔsterjɔri], *Lt.adv.phr.* a posteriori.

postériorité [pɔsterjɔrite], *s.f.* posteriority (of date).

postérité [pɔsterite], *s.f.* posterity; (*a*) descendants; *Jur:* **laisser p.,** to leave issue; **mourir sans (laisser de) p.,** to die without issue; (*b*) **la p.,** succeeding generations, generations yet unborn.

postface [pɔstfas], *s.f.* postscript, postface (to book).

postformation [pɔstfɔrmasjɔ̃], *s.f. Biol:* post-formation.

postglaciaire [pɔstglasjɛːr], *a. Geol:* postglacial.
posthite [pɔstit], *s.f. Med:* posthitis.
posthomérique [pɔstɔmerik], *a. Gr.Lit:* post-Homeric.
posthume [pɔstym], *a.* posthumous (child, work, etc.); **gloire, renommée, p.,** posthumous fame.
posthumement [pɔstymmɑ̃], *adv.* posthumously.
posthypophysaire [pɔstipɔfizɛːr], *a. Anat:* post-hypophyseal.
posthypophyse [pɔstipɔfiːz], *s.f. Anat:* posthypophysis.
postiche [pɔstiʃ], *a.* **1.** *A:* (*a*) superadded; (*b*) out of place. **2.** (*a*) false (hair, etc.); **cils postiches,** artificial eyelashes; **mèche p.,** hair-piece; *A:* **dent p.,** false tooth; (*b*) *s.m.* (i) wig; (ii) piece of false hair, hair piece. **3.** *s.f. O: P:* (street hawker's) sales talk.
posticheur [pɔstiʃœːr], *s.m.* **1.** (*a*) wig and postiche maker; (*b*) seller of wigs and postiches. **2.** *O: P:* street hawker.
postier, -ière [pɔstje, -jɛːr]. **1.** *s.* post-office employee. **2.** *s.m. A:* post-horse.
postillon [pɔstijɔ̃], *s.m.* **1.** *A.Trans:* postilion. **2.** (*a*) message (sent up the line when flying a kite); **cerfs-volants en postillon,** string of kites on the same cable; (*b*) **envoyer des postillons,** to spit, sputter, splutter, in speaking. **3.** *Hyd.E: etc:* ball valve.
postillonner [pɔstijɔne], *v.i.* to spit, splutter, sputter (in speaking).
postillonneux, -euse [pɔstijɔnø, -øːz], (*a*) *a.* spluttering; (*b*) *s.* splutterer, person who splutters, spits.
post-impressionnisme [pɔstɛ̃prɛsjɔnism], *s.m. Art:* post-impressionism.
post-impressionniste [pɔstɛ̃prɛsjɔnist], *a. & s.m. & f. Art:* post-impressionist.
postliminium [pɔstliminjɔm], *s.m. Rom.Jur:* postliminy.
postlude [pɔstlyd], *s.m. Mus:* postlude.
postmarqueuse [pɔstmarkøːz], *s.f. Elcs:* (*computers*) post printer.
postméridien, -ienne [pɔstmeridjɛ̃, -jɛn], *a.* post-meridian.
postnatal, -als [pɔstnatal], *a.* postnatal; **soins postnatals,** postnatal care.
postopératoire [pɔstɔperatwaːr], *a. Med:* post-operative (care, etc.).
postoral, -aux [pɔstɔral, -o], *a. Anat:* postoral.
postpalatal, -aux [pɔstpalatal, -o], *a. Anat: Ling:* postpalatal.
post-partum [pɔstpartɔm], *s.m.inv. Obst:* post-partum.
postpliocène [pɔstpliɔsɛn], *a. & s.m. Geol:* Post-Pliocene.
postposer [pɔstpoze], *v.tr.* (*a*) *A:* **p. qch. à qch.,** to value sth. less than sth.; (*b*) *Gram:* to place after.
postposition [pɔstpozisjɔ̃], *s.f.* postposition; **verbe à p.,** phrasal verb, compound verb.
post-prandial, -aux [pɔstprɑ̃djal, -o], *a.* post-prandial.
postscolaire [pɔstskɔlɛːr], *a.* continuation (classes, etc.); **enseignement p.,** further education.
post-scriptum [pɔstskriptɔm], *s.m.inv.* postscript, P.S.; **en p.-s.,** by way of postscript.
postsynchronisation [pɔstsɛ̃krɔnizasjɔ̃], *s.f. Cin:* postsynchronization; *F:* dubbing.
postsynchroniser [pɔstsɛ̃krɔnize], *v.tr. Cin:* to postsynchronize; *F:* to dub.
postulant, -ante [pɔstylɑ̃, -ɑ̃ːt], *s.* (*a*) candidate, applicant (for post); (*b*) *Ecc:* postulant.
postulat [pɔstyla], *s.m. Geom: Phil:* postulate, assumption; **admettre qch. en p.,** to postulate sth.; to assume sth.
postulateur [pɔstylatœːr], *s.m. Ecc:* postulator (in canonization trial).
postulation [pɔstylasjɔ̃], *s.f.* **1.** *Ecc: etc:* postulation. **2.** *Jur:* **p. devant un tribunal,** representation before a tribunal.
postulatum [pɔstylatɔm], *s.m.* = POSTULAT.
postuler [pɔstyle]. **1.** *v.tr.* (*a*) to solicit, ask for, apply for (situation, etc.); (*b*) *Ecc:* **p. un tel pour évêque,** to postulate so and so for a bishop. **2.** *v.tr. Phil: etc:* to postulate. **3.** *v.i.* (*of lawyer*) to conduct a suit; to act on behalf of a client.
post-universitaire [pɔstyniversitɛːr], *a.* post-graduate; *pl. post-universitaires.*
postural, -aux [pɔstyral, -o], *a.* postural.
posture [pɔstyːr], *s.f.* **1.** posture, attitude (of the body, etc.); *Med:* **réflexes de p.,** postural reflexes. **2.** position, footing (in society, in business matters, etc.); **être en p. de faire qch.,** to be in a position, in a situation, to do sth.; **être en bonne, en mauvaise, p. pour . . .,** to be well placed, badly placed, in a good, bad, position, to . . .; *F:* **surprendre qn en mauvaise p.,** to catch s.o. bending; **comment vous êtes-vous placé dans une telle p.?** how did you get into such a fix?
postvélaire [pɔstvelɛːr], *Ling:* (*a*) *a.* post-velar; (*b*) *s.f.* post-velar phoneme.
postverbal, -aux [pɔstvɛrbal, -o], *a. Ling:* post-verbal.
pot [po], *s.m.* (*before* **à, au, aux,** *in compounds occ.* [pɔt]) **1.** (*a*) pot, jug, can, jar; **p. de terre,** earthenware pot; **p. d'étain,** pewter tankard; **p. de confiture,** pot of jam; **pot de chambre,** chamber (pot); *F:* (*for child*) **petit p.,** potty; **p. de fleurs,** pot of flowers; plant in a pot; **pot(s) à fleurs** [poaflœːr], flower pot(s); **p. à grains** [poagrɛ̃], seed bed, hot bed; **pot(s) à colle** [poakɔl], glue pot(s); *F:* **p. de colle,** bore, sticker, pain in the neck; **pot(s) à bière** [poabjɛːr], beer mug(s); **pot(s) à eau** [pɔtao, poao], water jug(s); **p. à lait** [poalɛ], **p. au lait** [pɔtolɛ], milk jug, milk can; **p. à moineau,** pigeon hole; **mettre en p.,** to pot (plant, meat, etc.); **mise en p.,** potting; **p. au noir,** container for wax, polish, etc.; *Nau:* **le p. au noir** [pɔtonwaːr, poonwaːr], (i) the pitch pot; (ii) the doldrums; the cloud-ring; *F:* **c'est le p. au noir,** (i) it's a wretched business; (ii) it's a hopeless tangle, muddle; *Games:* **jouer au p.,** to play bits, moshie (with marbles); *P:* **allons prendre un p.,** let's go and have a drink; **être invité à un p.,** to be invited for drinks; *P:* **avoir du p., avoir un coup de p.,** to be lucky; **manque de p.,** hard luck; *F:* **payer les pots cassés,** to carry the can; to be left holding the baby; **dîner à la fortune du p.,** to take pot luck; **courir à la fortune du p.,** to go somewhere on the off-chance; *O:* **faire p. à part,** to keep oneself to oneself; *F:* **c'est le p. de terre contre le p. de fer,** he's met more than his match; **en trois coups de cuiller à p.,** in a twinkling; **il est bête, sourd, comme un p.,** he's a prize idiot, as deaf as a post; **il a une voix de p. fêlé,** he has a cracked voice; **p. fêlé dure longtemps,** creaking gates hang long; *P:* **en avoir plein le p. (de),** to be fed up (with); **pêcher pour le p.,** to fish for the pot; **la politique de la poule au p.,** policy ensuring that everyone has a reasonable standard of living; **c'est dans les vieux pots qu'on fait la bonne soupe,** there's many a good tune played on an old fiddle; *s.a.* ANSE 1, ROSE[1] 1, TABAC 2, TOURNER 2; (*b*) *Ch: Ind:* pot, crucible; **p. à injection,** injection chamber; *Metall:* **p. de cémentation,** case-hardening box; **p. à recuire, de recuit,** annealing pot; *Tex:* **p. de filature,** spinning can; *Glassm:* **p. à cueillir,** melting pot; *Gasm:* **p. d'évacuation,** seal pot. **2.** (*a*) *Hyd.E:* **p. de presse,** hydraulic ram; (*b*) **p. d'échappement,** (i) *Mch:* exhaust tank, exhaust pit, exhaust chamber; (ii) *I.C.E:* silencer, muffler; (*c*) **p. de cheminée,** chimney pot; (*d*) **p. à feu** [poafø], (i) *Pyr:* stinkball, fireball; (ii) *Pyr:* flare; (iii) *Arch:* flame ornament. **3.** *Paperm:* **papier au p.,** pot(t) paper. **4.** *P:* buttocks, backside; **se manier le p.,** to hurry, to get a move on.
potabilité [pɔtabilite], *s.f.* fitness for drinking, potability, potableness.
potable [pɔtabl], *a.* **1.** drinkable, fit to drink; **eau p.,** drinking water; *A:* **or p.,** potable gold. **2.** *F:* fair; good enough; **travail p.,** tolerably good work.
potache [pɔtaʃ], *s.m. Sch: F:* schoolboy (attending *collège* or *lycée*).
potage [pɔtaːʒ], *s.m.* (*a*) soup; **p. déshydraté,** dehydrated, powdered, soup; (*b*) *A:* stew; (*c*) *A: & Lit:* **pour tout p.,** altogether, all in all, all told.
potager, -ère [pɔtaʒe, -ɛːr]. **1.** *a.* of, for, the pot; for cooking; **herbes potagères,** pot herbs; **plante potagère,** vegetable; **jardin p.,** kitchen garden; **2.** *s.m.* (*a*) kitchen garden; (*b*) *A:* kitchen stove; cooker; (*c*) *O:* (workman's) dinner can, pail.
potalia [pɔtalja], *s.m.,* **potalie** [pɔtali], *s.f. Bot:* potalia.
potamique [pɔtamik], *a.* potamic, of streams and rivers.
potamobiologie [pɔtamɔbjɔlɔʒi], *s.f.* biology of streams and rivers.
potamochère [pɔtamɔʃɛːr], *s.m. Z:* potamochoerus; (African) river hog.
potamogale [pɔtamɔgal], *s.m. Z:* otter shrew.
potamogalidés [pɔtamɔgalide], *s.m.pl. Z:* Potamogalidae.
potamogeton [pɔtamɔʒetɔ̃], *s.m. Bot:* potamogeton.
potamogétonacées [pɔtamɔʒetɔnase], *s.f.pl. Bot:* Potamogetonaceae.
potamologie [pɔtamɔlɔʒi], *s.f. Geog:* potamology.
potamoplancton [pɔtamɔplɑ̃ktɔ̃], *s.m. Biol:* potamoplankton.
potamot [pɔtamo], *s.m. Bot:* pondweed; water spike.
potamotoque [pɔtamɔtɔk], *a. Ich:* potamodromous, anadromous.
potard [pɔtaːr], *s.m. P:* chemist; pharmacy student.
potasse [pɔtas], *s.f.* (*a*) *Ch:* potash; **mine de p.,** potash mine; **chlorate de p.,** potassium chlorate; **p. sulfatée,** sulphate of potash; **solution, lessive, de p. caustique,** potassium lye; (*b*) *Com:* (impure) potassium carbonate; **p. d'Amérique,** pearl ash.
potassé [pɔtase], *a.* containing potash; combined with potassium.
potasser [pɔtase], *v.tr. & i. Sch: F:* to swot at (sth.); to mug up (subject); **p. un examen,** to swot up for an examination.
potasseur [pɔtasœːr], *s.m. Sch: F:* swot.
potassier, -ière [pɔtasje, -jɛːr], *a.* potash (industry, production, etc.).
potassique [pɔtasik], *a. Ch:* (of, containing) potassium; potassic (salt).
potassisme [pɔtasism], *s.m.* potassium poisoning.
potassium [pɔtasjɔm], *s.m. Ch:* potassium; **bichromate de p.,** potassium bichromate.
pot-au-feu [pɔtofø], *s.m.inv.* **1.** soup pot, stock pot. **2.** beef broth. **3.** boiled beef with vegetables; *F:* **faire aller le p.-au-f.,** to keep the house going; to keep the pot boiling. **4.** (*a*) *a.inv. & s.f. F:* stay-at-home, sit-by-the-fire (woman); (*b*) *a.inv.* plain, homely, commonplace (matter or person).
potazote [pɔtazɔt], *s.m.* potash and nitrogenous fertilizer.
pot-bouille [pobuːj], *s.f. P: A:* **1.** ordinary fare, menu. **2. elles font p.-b. ensemble,** they keep house, live, together; *pl. pots-bouilles.*
pot-de-vin [podvɛ̃], *s.m. F:* **1.** gratuity, tip. **2.** (*a*) illicit commission, bribe; (*b*) hush money; *pl. pots-de-vin.*
pote[1] [pɔt], *a.f. A: F:* (*of the hand*) big, swollen; clumsy.
pote[2], *s.f. Min:* socket for pit prop; post hole.
pote[3], *s.m. & f. P:* friend, pal.
poteau, -eaux [pɔto], *s.m.* **1.** post, pole, stake; *Min:* pit prop; *Rugby Fb:* goalpost; **p. d'huisserie,** doorpost, window post, jamb; **p. de réverbère,** lamp-post; *Surv:* **p. de borne,** boundary pole; **p. indicateur,** signpost; **p. télégraphique,** telegraph pole; **p. (de ligne) électrique,** post, pole, carrying electric cables; **poteaux couplés,** H-type pole; **p. en A,** A-pole; **p. en béton,** concrete pole; **poteaux de treuil,** windlass standards; **p. de refend,** head post; *Const:* **p. cornier,** corner post, corner stud; *Sp:* **p. de départ,** starting post; *Turf:* (*of horse*) **rester au p.,** to be left at the post; **se présenter au p.,** to come under starter's orders; **p. d'arrivée,** winning post; **être coiffé au p., se faire battre, coiffer, sur le p.,** to be beaten at the post; *Rugby Fb:* **tirer entre les poteaux,** to put the ball between the posts; **marquer entre les poteaux,** to score under the posts; *Nau:* **p. d'amarrage,** bollard; *F:* **dormir comme un petit p.,** to sleep like a log; **p. d'exécution,** *F:* **le p.,** execution post (for s.o. about to be shot); **mettre qn au p.,** to put s.o. against the wall; *F:* **X au p.!** down with X! **2.** *P: O:* chum, pal.
poteau-frontière [pɔtofrɔ̃tjɛːr], *s.m.* frontier post; *pl. poteaux-frontière.*
poteau-tourillon [pɔtoturijɔ̃], *s.m. Hyd.E:* heel post (of lockgate); *pl. poteaux-tourillons.*
potée [pɔte], *s.f.* **1.** (*a*) *O:* potful, jugful (of water, etc.); mugful (of beer); (*b*) *Cu:* stew (*esp.* cabbage and carrots boiled slowly with ham, pork, etc.); (*c*) *F: O:* swarm (of children, etc.); **j'en ai une p.,** I have quite a lot. **2.** *Tchn:* (*a*) red-ochre solution; (*b*) **p. (d'étain),** putty powder; **p. d'émeri,** emery powder, flour of emery; **p. de fer,** rust-putty; **p. de montagne,** rotten stone; (*c*) *Metall:* luting loam; (*d*) *Tan:* **mettre les peaux en p.,** to lay away (hides); **mise en p.,** laying away.
potelé [pɔtle], (*a*) *a.* plump and dimpled (arm, etc.); chubby (cheek, child); (*b*) *s.m.* plumpness.
poteler [pɔtle], *v.tr.* (**je potelle, n. potelons; je potellerai**) *Min:* to set (pit prop) in its socket.
potelet [pɔtlɛ], *s.m.* small post, strut, prop; stanchion; rail post, banister.
potelle [pɔtɛl], *s.f. Min:* pit-prop socket; post hole.

potence [pɔtɑ̃:s], *s.f.* **1.** *A:* crutch. **2.** gallows, gibbet; **mettre, attacher, qn à la p.,** to hang s.o. on the gallows; **échapper à la p.,** to cheat the gallows; **il sent la p.,** he'll end his days on the gallows; **gibier de p.,** gallows bird. **3.** (*a*) *Const: Mch: etc:* support, arm, cross piece, bracket; jib (of crane); *Cy:* stem (of handlebar); **en p.,** T-shaped; *Mil:* **formation en p.,** formation with one flank thrown back at right angles; **table en p.,** cross-table; (*b*) (hoisting) derrick; *Artil:* loading davit; (*c*) fork (of gas mantle); (*d*) standard, sliding rule (for measuring men, animals); (*e*) *Nau:* spider; **p. de drôme,** gallows bitt; **p. à flexibles,** hose boom; **p. de transbordement,** cargo-loading crane, whipping crane; *Fish:* **p. de chalut,** trawl gallows; *Min:* **p. de puits,** well gallows.

potencé [pɔtɑse], *a. Her:* potent; **croix potencée,** potent cross.

potentat [pɔtɑ̃ta], *s.m.* potentate; **p. de la banque,** banking magnate.

pot-en-tête [pɔtɑ̃tɛt], *s.m. A: Mil:* (*type of helmet*) pot; *pl. pots-en-tête.*

potentialisation [pɔtɑ̃sjalizasjɔ̃], *s.f. Pharm:* potentiation.

potentialiser [pɔtɑ̃sjalize], *v.tr. Pharm:* to potentiate.

potentialité [pɔtɑ̃sjalite], *s.f.* potentiality.

potentiel, -elle [pɔtɑ̃sjɛl]. **1.** *a.* potential; **les ressources potentielles de l'Afrique,** the potential resources of Africa. **2.** *s.m.* (*a*) potentialities; **le p. militaire d'un pays,** the military potentialities of a country; (*b*) *Mch: etc:* **p. (d'utilisation),** useful life; lifetime (of engine, etc.); **moteur arrivé en fin de p.,** time-expired engine; **p. recommandé entre révisions: 900 heures,** recommended overhaul interval: 900 hours; (*c*) *El:* potential; **différence de potentiel,** potential difference; **p. redox,** oxido-reduction potential; *W.Tel:* **p. de grille,** grid potential; (*d*) *Petroleum Ind:* **p. maximal d'un puits,** open flow potential; **p. nominal,** rated potential; (*e*) *Gram:* potential (mood); (*f*) **p. humain,** human potential; **p. de travail,** working potential; (*g*) *Med:* **p. évoqué,** evoked potential; **p. de membrane,** membrane potential.

potentiellement [pɔtɑ̃sjɛlmɑ̃], *adv.* potentially.

potentiel-vecteur [pɔtɑ̃sjɛlvɛktœ:r], *s.m. Mth:* vector potential; *pl. potentiels-vecteurs.*

potentille [pɔtɑ̃ti:j], *s.f. Bot:* potentilla, cinquefoil; **p. ansérine,** silverweed, goose grass.

potentiomètre [pɔtɑ̃sjɔmɛtr̥], *s.m. Elcs:* potentiometer, *F:* pot; *Cin:* fader (of sound); **p. automatique X-Y,** electronic X-Y recorder.

potentiométrie [pɔtɑ̃sjɔmetri], *s.f. Elcs:* potentiometry.

potentiométrique [pɔtɑ̃sjɔmetrik], *a. Elcs:* potentiometric.

poter [pɔte], *v.tr. Golf:* (*a*) to put(t) (ball); (*b*) *abs.* to hole out.

poterie [pɔtri], *s.f.* **1.** (*a*) pottery (works); (*b*) potter's workshop, studio; (*c*) potter's art. **2.** pottery; **p. de terre, commune,** earthenware; **p. de grès,** stoneware; **p. de Delft,** Delft (ware). **3.** *O:* (*a*) **p. d'étain,** pewter (ware); (*b*) **p. en fonte,** cast-iron ware.

potérium [pɔterjɔm], *s.m. Bot:* burnet.

poterne [pɔtɛrn], *s.f.* **1.** *Fort:* postern. **2.** *A:* rear entrance (to castle, etc.); postern(-gate). **3.** vaulted passage under a platform.

potestas [pɔtɛstas], *s.f. Rom.Jur:* potestas; *pl. potestates.*

potestatif, -ive [pɔtɛstatif, -i:v], *a. Jur:* potestative; **condition p.,** potestative condition.

potet [pɔtɛ], *s.m. Agr: Hort:* seed hole.

poteur [pɔtœ:r], *s.m. Golf:* putter (club or pers.).

poteyage [pɔtɛja:ʒ], *s.m. Tchn:* (*a*) refractory wash, crucible wash; (*b*) (applying a) refractory dressing.

poteyer [pɔtɛje], *v.tr. Tchn:* to dress, to wash.

pothos [pɔtɔs], *s.m. Bot:* pothos.

potia(t) [pɔtja], *s.m. Min:* pit-prop socket; post hole.

potiche [pɔtiʃ], *s.f.* **1.** (large) vase (*esp.* of Chinese or Japanese porcelain). **2.** (*pers.*) figurehead.

potichomanie [pɔtiʃɔmani], *s.f.* potichomania.

Potidée [pɔtide], *Pr.n.f. A.Geog:* Potidaea.

potier [pɔtje], *s.m.* **1.** potter; **terre de p.,** potter's clay. **2. p. d'étain,** pewterer. **3.** *Ent:* potter bee.

potin[1] [pɔtɛ̃], *s.m.* **1.** (*a*) pinchbeck (metal); (*b*) pewter; white metal; **p. jaune,** brass; **p. gris,** grey pewter; **p. à assiettes,** plate pewter. **2.** *Tchn:* iron boiler (of distilling apparatus).

potin[2], *s.m., F:* **1.** (*a*) piece of gossip; (*b*) *pl.* gossip, tittle-tattle. **2.** clatter, row, rumpus; **faire du p.,** to make a fuss; to kick up a row.

potinage [pɔtina:ʒ], *s.m. F:* (*a*) tittle-tattle, gossip, scandal; (*b*) piece of gossip.

potiner [pɔtine], *v.i. F:* to tittle-tattle, gossip.

potinier, -ière [pɔtinje, -jɛ:r], *F:* **1.** *a.* gossipy. **2.** *s.* gossip(er), scandalmonger. **3.** *s.f. O:* **potinière,** gossip-place, gossiping-corner, gossip-shop. **4.** *s.f. Tchn:* **potinière,** iron boiler (of distilling apparatus).

potion [posjɔ̃], *s.f. Med:* potion, draught, drink.

potiron [pɔtirɔ̃], *s.m.* pumpkin.

potologie [pɔtɔlɔʒi], *s.f.* treatise on drinks.

potologique [pɔtɔlɔʒik], *a.* relating to the study of drinks.

potomane [pɔtɔman], *Med:* (*a*) *a.* dipsomaniacal; (*b*) *s.m. & f.* dipsomaniac.

potomanie [pɔtɔmani], *s.f. Med:* potomania, dipsomania.

potomètre [pɔtɔmɛtr̥], *s.m. Bot:* potometer.

poto-poto [pɔtopɔto], *s.m.inv. Geog:* mud of a mangrove swamp.

potorou [pɔtɔru], *s.m. Z:* potoroo, rat kangaroo.

pot-pourri [popuri], *s.m.* (*a*) *Cu: A:* hotchpotch; (*b*) *Mus: etc:* pot pourri, medley; (*c*) (*perfumery*) pot pourri; *pl. pots-pourris.*

potron-ja(c)quet [pɔtrɔ̃ʒakɛ], *s.m.,* **potron-minet** [pɔtrɔ̃minɛ], *s.m. used only in the phrase F:* **dès p.-j., dès p.-m.,** at early dawn, at break of day.

Pott [pɔt], *Pr.n.m. Med:* **mal de P.,** Pott's disease.

pottique [pɔtik], *Med:* (*a*) *a.* relating to Pott's disease; **gibbosité p.,** gibbus; (*b*) *s.m. & f.* person suffering from Pott's disease.

potto [pɔto], *s.m. Z:* potto, agwantibo.

pou, poux [pu], *s.m.* **1.** (*a*) louse, *pl.* lice; **p. du pubis,** crab (louse); **être mangé de poux,** to be eaten up with lice; **œuf de p.,** nit; *F:* **laid comme un p.,** as ugly as sin; *P:* **chercher des poux (dans la tête) (à qn),** to be over-critical (of s.o.); to be always picking on (s.o.); (*b*) **p. de mouton,** sheep tick; **p. d'oiseau,** bird mite; **p. de bois,** psocus, book louse, death-watch beetle; (*c*) *Bot: F:* **herbe aux poux,** lousewort; *Hort:* **le p. de San José,** San Jose scale. **2.** *Crust:* **p. de mer,** sea louse. **3.** *A: Av: F:* **p. du ciel,** flying flea.

pouacre [pwakr̥], *a. & s.m. & f. A: F:* **1.** dirty, filthy, unwashed (person). **2.** mean, stingy (person).

pouacrerie [pwakrəri], *s.f. A: F:* **1.** dirt, filth. **2.** meanness, stinginess.

pouah [pwa], *int.* faugh! ugh!

poubelle [pubɛl], *s.f.* (regulation pattern) dustbin, refuse bin, *U.S:* trash can; **p. à pédale,** pedal bin; *F:* **c'est la p. de la maison,** he's a regular dustbin; **faire les poubelles,** to rout about in the dustbins; **jeter qch. à la p.,** (i) to put sth. in the dustbin, to throw sth. away; (ii) *F:* to reject, to treat (offer, suggestion, etc.) as rubbish.

pouce [pu:s], *s.m.* **1.** (*a*) thumb; *F:* **donner un coup de p. à qn, qch.,** (i) to give s.o., sth., a push; to shove sth. on; to influence s.o.; (ii) to deflect the course of (justice, etc.); (iii) *A: P:* to strangle, throttle (s.o.); **donner le coup de p. à qch.,** to give the finishing touches to sth.; **fait au p.,** faultless, flawless; *F:* **morceau sur le p.,** snack; **manger sur le p.,** to have a (quick) snack (standing); **lire un livre du p.,** to skim the pages of a book; **se tourner les pouces,** to twiddle one's thumbs; **serrer les pouces à qn,** (i) *A:* to apply the thumb-screw to s.o. (as a mode of torture); (ii) *F:* to put the screws on s.o.; to bully s.o. (into a confession); to clamp down on s.o.; **sucer son p.,** (i) to suck one's thumb; (ii) to indulge in childish pleasures; **mettre les pouces,** to give in, to knuckle under; *Fr.C:* **faire du p., voyager sur le p.,** to hitch-hike; *F:* **et le p.,** and something besides, and a bit over; *F:* **s'en mordre les pouces,** to regret it; **s'asseoir sur le p.,** to have nowhere to sit; *Sch: P:* **p.!,** pax! **p. cassé!,** end the pax! *s.a.* LÉCHER 1; (*b*) *occ:* big toe. **2.** *Meas:* inch; *Prov:* **si on lui en donne un p. il en prendra long comme le bras,** give him an inch and he'll take an ell; **ne pas lâcher un p. de terrain,** (i) not to yield ground; (ii) not to yield an inch; **ne pas perdre un p. de sa taille,** to draw oneself up to one's full height.

pouce-pied [puspje], *s.m. Crust:* (type of) goose barnacle; *pl. pouces-pieds.*

Poucet [pusɛ], *Pr.n.m.* **le Petit P.,** Hop-o'-my-thumb, Tom Thumb (*from Perrault's tale*).

poucettes [pusɛt], *s.f.pl.* **1.** *A:* thumb-cuffs, -fetters. **2.** thumbscrew (instrument of torture); **mettre les p. à qn,** to put on, tighten, the screw.

Pouchkine [puʃkin], *Pr.n.m.* Pushkin.

poucier [pusje], *s.m.* **1.** thumbstall. **2.** thumb piece (of door latch).

poud [pud], *s.m. Meas:* pood, pud (Russian measure = 16,38 kg).

pou(t)-de-soie, poult-de-soie [putswa], *s.m. Tex:* poult-de-soie; grained taffeta; *pl. poux-de-soie; poul(l)ts-de-soie.*

poudet [pudɛ], *s.m.* **poudette** [pudɛt], *s.f.* pruning knife (used for vines and fruit trees in S. of Fr.).

pouding [pudiŋ, -ɛ̃:g], *s.m.* (steamed) pudding.

poudingue [pudɛ̃:g], *s.m. Miner:* conglomerate, pudding stone.

poudrage [pudra:ʒ], *s.m.* powdering; dusting on (of powder, etc.).

poudre [pudr̥], *s.f.* **1.** *A:* dust; *F:* **jeter de la p. aux yeux de qn,** to throw dust in s.o.'s eyes; to blind s.o. to the facts; to show off; **c'est de la p. aux yeux,** it's only window dressing, it's all bluff, it's all eyewash, it's all my eye. **2.** powder; (*a*) **p. d'or,** gold dust; **p. à lever,** *Fr.C:* **p. à pâte,** baking powder; *Com.Cu:* **p. pour gâteau,** cake mix; **p. abrasive,** grinding powder; **p. dentifrice,** tooth powder; **réduire qch. en p.,** (i) to reduce sth. to powder; to powder, pulverize, sth.; (ii) to smash sth. to smithereens; *F:* **réduire un argument en p.,** to demolish an argument; **savon en p.,** soap powder; **café en p.,** instant coffee; **sucre en p.,** (i) caster sugar; (ii) *Fr.C:* icing sugar; **p. de tabac,** snuff; **p. de bois (piqué des vers),** bore dust; **p. de corne,** horn meal; **p. à blanchir, de blanchiment,** bleaching powder; *Metall:* **p. à cémenter,** cementation powder; **p. brune,** cocoa powder; *Pharm:* **p. purgative,** laxative powder; **p. vermifuge,** worm powder; (*b*) (face) powder; **p. de riz,** toilet powder, face powder. **3.** (*generic term for*) explosives (*including gunpowder, cordite, dynamite, etc.*); **p. de chasse,** sporting powder; **p. à canon,** gunpowder; *Ven:* **p. de plomb,** dust shot, small shot; **p. sans fumée,** smokeless powder; **p. vive,** fast-burning powder; **p. lente,** slow-burning powder; *A:* **tirer à poudre,** to fire blank cartridge; **p. de mine,** blasting powder; *Phot:* **p. éclairante, p. éclair,** flash powder; *F:* **être (vif) comme la p.,** to be very excitable, touchy, to be fiery-tempered; **la nouvelle se répandit comme une traînée de p.,** the news spread like wildfire; **il n'a pas inventé la p.,** he won't set the Thames on fire; **faire parler la p.,** to start a war; *Hist:* **la Conspiration des poudres,** the Gunpowder Plot; *s.a.* BARIL, FEU[1] 1, MOINEAU.

poudré [pudre], *s.m.* process consisting of dusting powdered glass through a screen over hot ironware for enamelling.

poudrederizé [pudrədrize], **poudrerizé** [pudrərize], *a. O: F:* plastered with face-powder.

poudrement [pudrəmɑ̃], *s.m. O:* powdering.

poudrer [pudre]. **1.** *v.tr.* to powder; to sprinkle with powder; to dust on (flour, etc.); **se p.,** to powder (one's face, etc.). **2.** *v.i.* (*a*) *Ven:* (*of hunted hare, etc.*) to raise a dust; (*b*) *Tex:* (*of material*) to give off dust when shaken. **3.** *v.i. Fr.C:* **il poudre,** the snow is drifting.

poudrerie [pudrəri], *s.f.* **1.** (gun)powder factory, powder mill. **2.** *Fr.C:* blizzard; drifting, driving, snow.

poudrette [pudrɛt], *s.f.* fine powder; (*a*) dried and powdered night-soil (for manure); poudrette; (*b*) (*of bird*) **faire la p.,** to take a dust bath.

poudreux, -euse[1] [pudrø, -ø:z]. **1.** *a.* (*a*) dusty (clothes, road, books); *A:* **pied p.,** vagabond; (*b*) powdery; **neige poudreuse,** powdered, powdery, snow. **2.** *s.f.* **poudreuse,** powdered snow.

poudreuse[2], *s.f.* **1.** (*a*) *Cu:* sugar sprinkler; sugar castor; (*b*) *Agr:* (*for insecticides*) duster. **2.** *Furn: O:* dressing-table.

poudrier [pudrije], *s.m.* **1.** *A:* = POUDRIÈRE 1 (*a*). **2.** *Toil:* powder box; powder case; compact. **3.** *O:* gunpowder maker, seller; worker in a (gun)-powder factory.

poudrière [pudrijɛ:r], *s.f.* **1.** *A:* (*a*) sand-box; pounce-box; (*b*) powder-flask, powder-horn. **2.** powder magazine. **3.** = POUDRERIE.

poudrin [pudrɛ̃], *s.m.* **1.** spindrift, spray. **2.** frozen snow; fine hail.

poudroiement [pudrwamɑ̃], *s.m.* dusty condition; clouds of dust (raised on road, etc.); dust haze.

poudroyant [pudrwajɑ̃], *a.* dusty (road).

poudroyer [pudrwaje], *v.* (**il poudroie; il poudroiera**) **1.** *v.tr.* to cover (sth.) lightly with dust. **2.** *v.i.* to form clouds of dust; **la route poudroie,** the road is smothered in dust, the dust whirls up from the road.

pouf [puf]. **1.** *int.* (*a*) (*of person or thing falling*) plop! flop! plump! wallop! (*b*) (*denoting relief, oppressive heat, etc.*) phew! **2.** *s.m.* (*a*) puff, inflated advertisement; (*b*) *P:* **faire un p.,** (i) to go off without paying one's bill; (ii) to go bankrupt; (*c*) *Furn:* pouf; humpty; (*d*) *Cost: A:* bustle.

pouffant [pufɑ̃], *a. F:* excruciatingly funny, side-splitting; **dans ce rôle il est p.**, in that part he's a perfect scream.
pouffement [pufmɑ̃], *s.m. F:* **1.** guffawing. **2.** *pl.* guffaws.
pouffer [pufe], *v.i.* **p. (de rire),** to burst out laughing, to guffaw; **il pouffait de rire,** he was bubbling over with laughter; **p. dans son mouchoir,** to stifle one's laughter.
pouffiasse [pufjas], *s.f. P:* slattern, slut.
pouh [pu], *int.* pooh!
pouillard [pujaːr], *s.m. Orn:* poult ((i) young pheasant; (ii) young partridge).
Pouille[1] [puːj], *Pr.n.f. Geog:* Apulia.
pouille[2], *s.f. P:* poverty; squalor.
pouillé [puje], *s.m. Ecc.Hist:* terrier (of abbey, diocese, etc.).
pouiller[1] [puje], *v.tr.* (*a*) *A:* to search for lice on (s.o.); (*b*) *A: F:* to go through (a text) with a fine tooth comb.
se pouiller, *F:* to scratch oneself (as if searching for lice).
pouiller[2], *v.tr. A:* to abuse, slang, revile (s.o.)
pouillerie [pujri], *s.f.* **1.** *F:* (*a*) abject poverty; (*b*) squalid miserliness. **2.** (*a*) *F:* filthy place, lousy hole; (*b*) *A:* (*in hospital, etc.*) stripping room (for removing patient's rags).
pouilles [puj], *s.f.pl. used only in A:* **dire, chanter, p. à qn,** to make offensive remarks to s.o., to jeer at s.o., to revile s.o.
pouilleux, -euse [pujø, -øːz]. **1.** *a.* (*a*) lousy, verminous; (*b*) **bois p.,** cankered timber. **2.** *a.* wretched; abjectly poor; **quartier p.,** slum; *Geog:* **la Champagne pouilleuse,** Dry Champagne. **3.** (*a*) *Engr:* (*of block*) badly cut, irregular, broken. **4.** *s.* (*a*) tramp; (*b*) *Orn:* (pheasant, partridge) poult.
pouillot [pujo], *s.m. Orn:* warbler; **p. siffleur,** wood warbler; **grand p., p. véloce,** chiff-chaff; **p. boréal,** arctic, Eversmann's, warbler; **p. brun,** dusky warbler; **p. verdâtre, brillant,** greenish warbler; **p. de Pallas,** Pallas's warbler; **p. de Schwarz,** Radde's bush warbler; **p. de Bonelli,** Bonelli's warbler; **p. fitis, chantre,** willow warbler, willow wren; **p. à grands sourcils,** yellow-browed warbler.
pouillous(s)e [pujus], *s.f. Nau:* main staysail.
poulaille [pulɑːj], *s.f.* (*a*) poultry, fowls; (*b*) *P:* the cops.
poulailler[1] [pulɑje], *s.m.* (*a*) hen house, hen roost; (*b*) poultry cart; (*c*) poor, poky little house; (*d*) *Th: F:* (top) gallery; the gods.
poulailler[2], **-ère** [pulɑje, -ɛːr], *s.* poulterer.
poulaillerie [pulɑjri], *s.f.* poultry market.
poulain [pulɛ̃], *s.m.* **1.** (*a*) colt, foal; (*b*) *Box: etc:* trainee; **p. d'un tel,** trained by so and so; (*c*) young protégé; *Sch:* favourite pupil. **2.** *Furs:* pony skin. **3.** *Tchn:* (*a*) skid (for unloading barrels, etc.); (*b*) *N.Arch:* dog-shore.
poulaine [pulɛn], *s.f.* **1.** *Cost: A:* (*a*) Polish leather; (*b*) poulaine; **souliers à la p.,** cracowes, crakows; **à courte p.,** with short pointed toes. **2.** *Nau:* (*a*) (ship's) head; **lisse de p.,** headrail; **pavois de p.,** head board; (*b*) *pl.* latrines (for crew), *F:* the heads; *P:* **gabier de poulaines,** lubber.
poulard [pulaːr], *a. & s.m. Agr:* **(blé) p.,** cone wheat, poulard wheat.
poularde [pulard], *s.f. Cu:* poulard; fattened pullet.
poulbot [pulbo], *s.m.* street urchin (of Paris, as drawn by Francisque Poulbot).
poule [pul], *s.f.* **1.** (*a*) hen; *Cu:* fowl; **p. au pot,** boiled chicken; **p. (à faire à la casserole, au pot),** boiling fowl, boiler; **être empêtré comme une p. qui n'a qu'un poussin,** to be as flustered as an (old) hen with (only) one chick; **ma (petite) p.!** my dear, my pet! **la p. aux œufs d'or,** the goose that laid the golden egg; **lait de p.,** (non-alcoholic) egg flip, egg nog; *F:* **quand les poules auront des dents,** when pigs (begin to) fly; *F:* **c'est la p. qui chante qui a fait l'œuf,** if the cap fits, wear it; *F:* **il habite au delà des poules,** he lives at the back of beyond; *F:* **il avait l'habitude de plumer la p.,** he was in the habit of fleecing people; *s.a.* CHAIR 3, LAIT 1, MOUILLÉ, 1; (*b*) **p. d'eau,** moorhen, *U.S:* Florida gallinule; **p. faisane,** hen pheasant; **p. de Guinée, de pharaon,** guinea fowl, hen; **p. d'Inde,** turkey-hen; **p. des sables,** pratincole; **p. des bois,** hazel hen; **p. de neige,** grouse; **petite p. de bruyère,** grey hen; **p. des steppes,** Pallas's sand grouse; **p. sultane,** purple gallinule; (*c*) *Ich:* **p. de mer,** John Dory; (*d*) *P:* (fast young) woman; bird; tart; **p. de luxe,** high-class tart; call girl. **2.** (*a*) (*at games*) pool; (*b*) (*at races*) sweepstake; (*c*) *Fenc: etc:* pool; **p. à l'épée,** fencing pool, tournament; **p. au pistolet,** pistol-shooting match. **3.** *Danc:* third figure of the quadrille; la poule. **4.** *a. Metalw:* **acier p.,** blister steel. **5.** *P:* **la p.,** the police.
poulet [pulɛ], *s.m.* **1.** (*a*) chicken, chick; **p. d'Inde,** young turkey; **p. fermier,** free-range chicken; (*b*) *Cu:* chicken; **p. de chair,** broiler; (*c*) **mon p.,** (i) (*to child*) pet; (ii) (*to man*) sweetheart; (*d*) **c'est du p.!** it's child's play! *P:* it's a cinch! (*e*) *P:* policeman, cop. **2.** *P:* riding horse; nag. **3.** (witty, playful, amorous) letter.
pouletier [pultje], *s.m.* poulterer.
poulette [pulɛt], *s.f.* **1.** young hen, pullet; **p. d'eau,** moorhen. **2.** *F:* girl, lass. **3.** *Cu:* **sauce à la p.,** poulette (sauce). **4.** *Tchn:* eel.
pouliage [pulјaːʒ], *s.m. Nau:* blocks, tackle.
pouliche [puliʃ], *s.f.* filly.
poulichon [puliʃɔ̃], *s.m.* baby colt.
poulie [puli], *s.f.* **1.** pulley ((i) sheave, (ii) block); **p. simple, double,** single block, double block; **p. fixe,** fixed pulley, standing block; **p. à cône,** cone pulley; *s.a.* GRADIN 2; **p. à gorge,** grooved pulley; **p. à empreintes pour chaînons,** chain pulley; **p. coupée,** snatch block; **p. à violon,** fiddle block; *Nau: etc:* **p. vierge,** sister block; **p. à fouet,** tail block; **p. de retour,** leading block; **p. à croc,** hook block; **p. métallique,** steel block; **p. de charge,** cargo block; **p. de renvoi,** guide pulley; **p. mobile,** running block; **p. à réas multiples,** purchase block; *Nau:* **p. de pied de mât,** nine pin block; **p. à câble,** rope wheel; **p. à émerillon,** swivel block; **p. d'assemblage,** made block. **2.** (belt) pulley; driving wheel; **p. folle,** loose pulley; **d'entraînement,** drive, driving, pulley; **p. étagée,** stepped pulley; **p. de tension,** tension pulley, idler (pulley); **p. en deux pièces,** split pulley.
poulie-volant [pulivɔlɑ̃], *s.f. Mch:* driving fly-wheel; *pl. poulies-volants.*
poulier [pulje], *s.m. Oc:* shingle bank, sand bank.
poulieur [puljœːr], *s.m.* pulley maker, wooden-block maker.
poulin [pulɛ̃], *s.m. N.Arch:* dog-shore.
poulinement [pulinmɑ̃], *s.m.* foaling (of mare).
pouliner [puline], *v.i.* (*of mare*) to foal.
poulinière [pulinjɛːr], *a. & s.f.* **(jument) p.,** brood mare; **bonne p.,** good breeder.
pouliot[1] [puljo], *s.m. Bot:* pennyroyal.
pouliot[2], *s.m.* windlass (on dray, etc.).
pouliste [pulist], *s. Fenc:* contestant (in a pool).
poulot, -otte [pulo, -ɔt], *s. F:* (*in addressing children*) (my) pet, darling.
poulotter [pulɔte], *v.tr. F:* to coddle, to pamper.
poulpe [pulp], *s.m. Moll:* octopus.
pouls [pu], *s.m. Physiol:* pulse; *Med:* **p. fréquent,** quick, rapid, pulse; **p. faible,** weak, low, pulse; **p. intermittent,** irregular pulse; **p. paradoxal,** pulsus paradoxus; **p. artériel,** arterial pulse; **p. veineux,** venous pulse; **tâter le p. à qn,** (i) to feel s.o.'s pulse; (ii) to sound s.o. as to his intentions; **prendre le p. à qn,** to take s.o.'s pulse; **chercher, trouver le p. à, de qn,** to feel s.o.'s pulse; **voyons votre p.,** let me feel your pulse; **se tâter le p.,** to reflect; to think things over.
poult-de-soie [putswa], *s.m. Tex:* poult-de-soie; *pl. poults-de-soie.*
poumon [pumɔ̃], *s.m.* (*a*) *Anat:* lung; **p. d'acier,** iron lung; **respirer à pleins poumons,** to draw a deep breath; **crier à pleins poumons,** to shout at the top of one's voice; **avoir les poumons faibles,** to be weak-lunged; **cracher ses poumons,** to cough phlegm; to cough one's lungs up; **s'user les poumons,** to wear one's lungs out (with shouting); (*b*) *Bot: F:* **herbe aux poumons,** lungwort.
Pounah [puna], *Pr.n.m. Geog:* Poona.
pounding [paundiŋ], *s.m. Nau:* pounding.
poupard [pupaːr]. **1.** *s.m.* (*a*) baby in long clothes; chubby baby; (*b*) baby doll (without arms and legs); (*c*) *Crust:* edible crab. **2.** *a.* chubby (as a baby); **physionomie pouparde,** baby face.
poupart [pupaːr], *s.m. Crust:* edible crab.
poupe [pup], *s.f.* **1.** *Nau:* stern, poop; **feu de p.,** stern light; **avoir le vent en p.,** (i) to have the wind aft, to sail before the wind; (ii) *F:* to be in luck, in favour; to be favoured by fortune; **se trouver en p. d'un autre navire,** to be astern of another ship; **naviguer beaupré sur p.,** to be in the wake of another ship. **2.** *Astr:* Puppis, Poop, Stern.
poupée [pupe], *s.f.* **1.** (*a*) doll; **p. de son,** stuffed doll; **p. de chiffon,** rag doll; **p. articulée,** jointed doll; **elle a un visage de p.,** she has a doll's face, a face like a doll; **maison de p.,** doll's house; **jouer à la p.,** to play with dolls; (*b*) *F: A:* (*of girl*) doll. **2.** (*a*) puppet; (*b*) (tailor's) dummy; (milliner's) block; (*c*) (engraver's) dabber. **3.** *F:* finger bandage; bandaged finger, dolly. **4. p. de tour,** headstock, poppet (head), of a lathe; **p. mobile,** tailstock, sliding poppet; **p. porte-pièce,** work head (of lathe); **p. de cabestan,** capstan head. **5.** *Nau:* **p. d'amarrage,** bollard; belaying pin; **p. de guindeau,** windlass end; **p. de treuil,** warping end. **6.** *Geol:* **p. du lœss,** loess doll.
poupelin [puplɛ̃], *s.m.* (*a*) *F:* babe, suckling; (*b*) *Cu:* cake dipped in melted butter.
poupelinier [puplinje], *s.m. Cu:* cake mould for a *poupelin.*
poupin, -ine [pupɛ̃, -in], *a.* rosy(-cheeked); **visage p.,** baby face; **faire le p.,** to smirk.
poupiner [pupine], *v.tr. O:* to dress up (child, etc.) like a doll; to doll (s.o.) up.
poupon, -onne [pupɔ̃, -ɔn], *s.* baby.
pouponnage [pupɔnaːʒ], *s.m. Pej:* coddling, fussing over (child).
pouponner [pupɔne], (*a*) *v.tr.* to mother; to coddle; (*b*) *v.i. F:* to be pregnant.
pouponnière [pupɔnjɛːr], *s.f.* (*a*) babies' room (in day nursery); (*b*) day nursery; (*c*) (baby) walker.
poupoule [pupul], *s.f. A: F:* darling.
pour [puːr]. **I.** *prep.* for. **1.** (*a*) instead of; **allez-y p. moi,** go for me, instead of me; **il me prend p. un autre,** he takes me for someone else; **mot p. mot,** word for word; **il y a six ans jour p. jour,** six years ago to the day; **recevoir de l'or p. des billets,** to receive gold in exchange for notes; **agir p. qn,** to act on s.o.'s behalf; (*b*) (*introducing a predicative complement*) **il me veut p. femme,** he wants me for, as, his wife; **je l'ai eu p. maître,** I had him, for, as a master; **tenir qn p. fou,** to regard s.o. as a madman; **passer p. dangereux,** to be considered dangerous; **laisser qn p. mort,** to leave s.o. for dead; **il n'a p. arme qu'un bâton,** his only weapon is a stick; **il faut prendre le progrès p. but,** we must make progress our aim; *F:* **c'est p. de bon, p. de vrai,** I mean it, I'm serious; (*c*) (*direction*) **je pars p. la France,** I am starting for France; **le train p. Paris,** the Paris train; (*d*) (i) (*time, esp. futurity*) **je vais en Suisse p. quinze jours,** I am going to Switzerland for a fortnight; **p. toujours,** for ever; **s'engager p. trois ans,** to enlist for three years; **je n'ai rien p. le moment,** I have nothing for the time being; **il sera ici p. quatre heures,** he will be here by four o'clock; (ii) (*to the amount of*) **j'en ai p. huit jours,** it will take me a week; **trois coups p. un franc,** three shots a franc; **donnez-moi p. deux francs de chocolat,** give me two francs' worth of chocolate; **j'en ai p. mon argent,** I have got my money's worth; **en être p. son argent,** to be out of pocket; **il en est p. sa peine,** all his efforts were for nothing, were wasted; **p. toute réponse il secoua la tête,** his only reply was to shake his head; **être p. beaucoup, p. peu, dans une affaire,** to count for much, for little, in a business; *s.a.* MOINS 1; (*e*) (*purpose*) **je suis ici p. affaires,** I am here on business; **vêtements p. hommes,** clothes for men; **tissus p. robes,** dress materials; **remède p. la fièvre,** remedy against fever; **devoir p. le lendemain,** task for the next day; **j'épargne p. quand je serai vieux,** I am saving for my old age; **p. la cause de l'humanité,** in the cause of humanity; **c'est p. cela qu'il est venu,** that is why he came; **je viens p. le compteur,** I've come about the (gas, etc.) meter; *conj.phr. A:* **p. ce que** = PARCE QUE; *s.a.* QUOI[1] 1; (*f*) because of, for the sake of; **écrire p. soi,** to write for one's own satisfaction; **p. l'amour de Dieu,** for heaven's sake; **c'est p. vous que j'ai tant travaillé,** it is for your sake that I worked so hard; **faites-le p. moi,** do it for my sake; **je l'aime p. lui-même,** I love him for his own sake; **être estimé p. ses vertus,** to be esteemed for one's virtues; **j'avais peur p. lui,** I was nervous on his account; **mourir p. sa patrie,** to die for one's country; **prendre qch. p. sa santé,** to take sth. for (the good of) one's health; **l'art p. l'art,** art for art's sake; **épouser qn p. son argent,** to marry s.o. for his (her) money; **p. la forme,** for form's sake; **beaucoup de bruit p. rien,** a lot of fuss; *Lit:* much ado, about nothing; (*g*) in favour of; **parler p. qn,** to speak in favour of s.o.; **la loi est p. vous,** the law is on your side; **je suis p. le libre échange,** I am (all) for free trade; *adv. F:* **moi, je suis p.,** (as far as I am concerned) I am in favour of it; **le vote est p.,** the voting is for it, *Pol:* the ayes have it; **parler p. et contre,** to speak for and against; **je n'ai rien à dire p. ou contre,** I have nothing to say one way or the other; (*h*) **comme p. . . .,** as in the case of . . .; **p. mon compte,** for my part, as far as I am concerned; **il est grand, intelligent, p. son âge,** he is tall, clever, for his age; **p. ce qui est de . . .,** as concerns . . ., as regards . . ., with regard to . . .; **p. ce qui est**

de cela, as far as that is concerned, as far as that goes; **p. (ce qui est de) moi,** as for me, for my part; **p. moi c'est une crise de foie,** in my opinion it's a liver attack; **p. moi, je veux bien,** personally, I am willing; **p. ce qu'il fait il peut aussi bien aller jouer,** for all he is doing he may as well go and play; **p. cela,** for all that; *F:* **p. de la chance, c'est de la chance,** you're, we're, etc., in luck and no mistake; **p. un été chaud, c'est un été chaud,** this is a hot summer, right enough; (*i*) for lack of; **p. un moine l'abbaye ne chôme pas,** nobody can be considered indispensable; (*j*) per; **dix p. cent,** ten per cent; **acheter du trois p. cent,** to buy three per cents; (*k*) **contribuer p. une part égale à la dépense,** to contribute equal shares to the expenses; (*l*) **être bon p. les animaux,** (i) to be good with animals; (ii) to be kind to animals. **2. pour** + *inf.*, (*a*) (in order) to; **il faut manger p. vivre,** one must eat to live; **p. ainsi dire,** so to speak; **il s'en va p. ne jamais revenir,** he is going away and will never come back; he is going away for good; **il est rentré chez lui p. trouver que sa femme était sortie,** he got home, only to find that his wife had gone out; **diviser p. régner,** divide and rule; (*b*) (*after* **assez, trop**) **être trop faible p. marcher,** to be too weak to walk; **assez âgé pour aller à l'école,** old enough to go to school; (*c*) considering; **il est bien ignorant p. avoir étudié si longtemps,** he is very ignorant considering how long he has studied; (*d*) although; **p. être petit, il n'en est pas moins brave,** though small, he is none the less brave; **p. avoir échappé aux pirates, je n'étais pas encore en sûreté,** although I had escaped from the pirates, I was not yet safe; **p. aimer mon mari, je ne hais pas mes frères,** much as I love my husband, I do not necessarily hate my brothers; **nous ne perdrons rien p. attendre,** we shall lose nothing by waiting; (*e*) because of; **être puni p. avoir désobéi,** to be punished for having disobeyed; **p. avoir bâclé un sonnet il se croit poète,** because he dashed off a sonnet he thinks himself a poet; **je le sais pour l'avoir vu, p. l'avoir éprouvé,** I know it from having seen it; I know it by experience; **je le reconnais p. l'avoir vu au cercle,** I recognize him from having seen him at the club; **je m'intéresse à lui p. avoir lu son livre,** I'm interested in him because I've read read his book; **il est mort p. avoir trop bu, trop travaillé,** he died of drink, of overwork; *Sch:* **on l'avait privé de sortie p. avoir coupé l'électricité,** he had been gated for cutting off the electricity; (*f*) of a nature to; **cela n'est pas p. me surprendre,** that does not come as a surprise to me; **cette amitié n'était pas p. lui plaire,** this friendship was not to his liking; **ces questions n'étaient pas p. m'embarrasser,** these questions did not embarrass me in the slightest; **votre sévérité n'est pas p. les encourager,** your severity is not calculated to encourage them; **il n'y a que les Parisiens p. avoir de ces reparties,** there's nobody like a Parisian for giving you a pat answer; **il n'y a que les Anglais p. ne jamais se laisser démonter,** there's nobody like the English for never getting flummoxed; **il y aura des gens p. me traiter d'imbécile,** there will be people who will call me a fool; (*g*) *F:* about to; **être pour partir,** to be about to start, on the point of departure; (*h*) **mourir p. mourir, mieux vaut être noyé que pendu,** death for death, if die we must, it is better to drown than to be hanged; *P:* **p. causer, on cause,** we talk, and no mistake. **3.** (*a*) **p. que** + *sub.* in order that; **je vous dis cela p. que vous soyez sur vos gardes,** I am telling you this in order to put you on your guard; **il est bien tard p. qu'elle sorte seule,** it is very late for her to go out alone; **il est trop tard p. qu'elle sorte,** it is too late for her to go out; **mettez-le là, p. qu'on ne l'oublie pas,** put it there so that it won't be forgotten; (*b*) (*concessive*) **pour** (+ *adj.* or *sb.*) **que** + *sub.*, however; although; **p. court qu'il soit, le livre est très intéressant,** short as it is, the book is very interesting; *Lit:* **p. grands que soient les rois ils sont ce que nous sommes,** great though kings are they are but as we are; **cette situation, p. terrible qu'elle soit,** this situation, terrible though it may be; **p. médecin qu'on soit, on n'en est pas moins homme,** one is none the less a man for being a doctor; **l'art, p. variable qu'il soit, doit rester l'art,** art, vary as it will, must still remain art; (*elliptically*) **Pierre, p. agile de corps, était lent d'esprit,** Peter, although physically quick, was mentally slow; (*c*) **p. peu que** + *sub.*, if only, if ever; **p. peu que vous hésitiez vous êtes fichu,** if you hesitate for a moment, if you hesitate at all, it's all up with you; **p. peu que nous ayons un rayon de soleil tous les oiseaux se mettent à chanter,** at the first ray of sunshine all the birds begin to sing.

II. **pour,** *s.m.* **peser le p. et le contre,** to weigh the pros and cons; **entendre le p. et le contre,** to hear both sides; **il y a du p. et du contre,** there is something to be said on both sides.

Pourâna [purana], *s.m. Lit:* Purana.

pourboire [purbwa:r], *s.m.* tip, gratuity; **donner un p. au porteur,** to tip the porter.

pourceau, -eaux [purso], *s.m.* **1.** (*a*) hog, pig, swine; *pl. usu.* swine; *Prov:* **jeter des perles aux pourceaux,** to cast pearls before swine; **se conduire comme un p.,** to behave like a swine; (*b*) *F: Pej:* (*pers.*) swine. **2.** (*a*) **p. de mer,** porpoise; (*b*) *Z:* **p. ferré,** hedgehog; (*c*) *Ent:* **petit p.,** hawkmoth.

pour-cent [pursɑ̃], *s.m.inv.* percentage, rate per cent; **à quel p.-c. s'est fait l'emprunt?** at what rate per cent was the loan floated?

pourcentage [pursɑ̃ta:ʒ], *s.m.* (*a*) percentage ((i) of moisture, etc.; (ii) of commission)); amount per cent; rate (of interest); (*b*) *Civ.E:* **rampe à fort p.,** steep gradient.

pourchas [purʃa], *s.m.* pursuit, chase; research.

pourchasser [purʃase], *v.tr.* to pursue, to follow hot on the track of (game, etc.); **p. un débiteur,** to dun, harry, a debtor; **p. un criminel,** to hunt, pursue, a criminal; **pourchassé par un souvenir,** haunted by a memory; *St.Exch:* **p. le découvert,** to raid the shorts, the bears; *F:* **p. la poussière,** to be for ever dusting.

pourchasseur, -euse [purʃasœ:r, -ø:z], *s.m.* eager pursuer; **p. de dots,** dowry hunter.

pour(-)compte [purkɔ̃:t], *s.m.* undertaking to sell goods on behalf of a third party.

pourfendeur, -euse [purfɑ̃dœ:r, -ø:z], *s. A:* **p. de géants,** swashbuckler, swaggerer, bully.

pourfendre [purfɑ̃:dr̥], *v.tr.* (*a*) *A:* to cleave in twain; (*b*) to attack, to strike at (prejudices, abuses, etc.).

pourget, pourjet [purʒɛ], *s.m. Ap:* insulating mixture (for beehives).

pourim [purim], *s.m.* (Jewish feast of) Purim.

pourlèche [purlɛʃ], *s.f. Med:* angular stomatitis.

pourlèchement [purlɛʃmɑ̃], *s.m.* licking (of one's chops).

pourlécher [purleʃe], *v.tr.* (**je pourlèche, n. pourléchons; je pourlécherai**) **1.** *A:* to lick (sth.) over; *still used in* **se p. les babines, s'en p.,** to lick one's chops. **2.** *O:* to polish up, finish with care (verses, sketch, etc.).

pourparler [purparle], *s.m. usu. pl.* (*a*) *Mil:* parley; (*b*) diplomatic conversation; pourparlers; **entrer en pourparlers, entamer des pourparlers,** to begin negotiations, to enter on, enter into, negotiations (**avec,** with); **être en pourparler(s) avec qn,** to be in negotiation with s.o.

pourpenser [purpɑ̃se], *v.tr. A:* to ponder over.

pourpier [purpje], *s.m. Bot:* purslane; **p. de mer,** sea purslane, purslane orach; **p. des marais, p. sauvage,** water purslane.

pourpière [purpjɛ:r], *s.f. Bot:* water purslane.

pourpoint [purpwɛ̃], *s.m. A.Cost:* pourpoint, doublet; *F: A:* **rembourrer son p.,** to stuff oneself (with food).

pourpointier [purpwɛ̃tje], *s.m. A.Cost:* pourpoint maker, seller.

pourpre [purpr̥]. **1.** *s.f.* (*a*) purple (dye) (of the ancients); (*b*) purple robe; (i) royal or imperial dignity; **né dans la p.,** born in the purple; (ii) **la p. romaine,** the cardinalate purple. **2.** (*a*) *s.m.* crimson; rich red (colour); **le p. lui monta au visage,** he turned crimson, he flushed up; *Physiol:* **p. rétinien,** red pigment, visual purple; *Poet: occ. f.* **les dernières pourpres du couchant,** the last glow of sunset; (*b*) *a.* **manteau p.,** crimson cloak; **il devint p.,** he turned purple (with rage, etc.). **3.** *s.m. Her:* purpure. **4.** *s.m. Med: A:* purpura, *F:* purples. **5.** *s.m. Moll:* dog whelk, purple.

pourpré [purpre], *a.* purple, crimson; *Med:* **fièvre pourprée des montagnes Rocheuses,** Rocky Mountains spotted fever, rickettsiosis.

pourprer (se) [səpurpre], *v.pr.* to become, to turn, purple.

pourprier [purprije], *s.m. Moll:* purpura; purple (fish).

pourprin [purprɛ̃], *s.m. Hort:* purple colour.

pourpris [purpri], *s.m. A:* enclosure; abode, home; *Poet:* **le(s) céleste(s) p.,** the heavenly abodes.

pourquoi [purkwa]. **1.** *adv. & conj.* why? **p. faire?** what for? **p. cela?** why so? **p. êtes-vous venu?** what have you come for? **p. Jean s'en va-t-il?** why is John going away? **mais p. donc?** what on earth for? **voilà p.,** that's (the reason) why; **p. pas? p. non?** why not? **je ne sais pas p. il a dit ça,** I don't know what he said that for, why he said that; **je ne vois pas p. vous lui écririez,** I can't see the point of your writing to him; *F:* **vous le ferez ou vous me direz p.,** you shall do it or I'll know the reason why; *F:* **demandez-moi p.,** I can't tell why, *F:* ask me another! **c'est p. . . .,** therefore . . .; for that reason . . .; **voici p. cela a eu lieu,** that's why it happened. **2.** *s.m.inv.* **je ne sais pas le p.,** I don't know the reason why, the why and the wherefore; **les p. et les comment,** the whys and the wherefores; **dites-moi le p. et le comment de la chose,** tell me the why and the how of it.

pourri [puri]. **1.** *a.* rotten (fruit, wood); rotted (wood); putrid (flesh); damp, dank (air, weather); **un œuf p.,** an addle(d) egg; **viande pourrie,** bad, rotten, meat; **été p.,** wet summer; *Mount:* **neige, glace, pourrie,** hazardous, crumbly, snow; thin, dangerous, ice; **rocher p.,** disintegrated, mouldered, rock; *F:* **planche pourrie,** broken reed; **membre p.,** black sheep (of society, etc.); **il est p. de vices,** he is full of vices, rotten to the core; **homme p. de préjugés,** man steeped in prejudice; **p. d'orgueil,** eaten up with self-conceit; **il est p.,** (i) he is eaten up with disease (*esp.* venereal); (ii) he is corrupt; **enfant p.,** spoilt child; **des gens pourris,** degenerate people; **société pourrie,** corrupt society; **gouvernement p.,** corrupt government; **il est p. par la racine,** he's a nasty piece of work; he's rotten to the core; *int. P:* **p.!** you swine! you stinker! **2.** *s.m.* (*a*) rotten, decayed, part; **le p. d'une pomme,** the rotten part of an apple; (*b*) **sentir le p.,** to smell of decay, of rot.

pourridié [puridje], *s.m. Hort:* root rot.

pourrir [puri:r]. **1.** *v.i.* (*a*) to rot, decay, putrefy; to become rotten; to go bad; (*of hay, etc.*) to rot; (*of egg*) to addle; **p. en prison,** to rot in prison; **faire p.,** to rot (wood, etc.); (*b*) (*of abscess, etc.*) to mature, to come to a head. **2.** *v.tr.* to rot; **l'eau avait pourri le bois,** the water had rotted the wood.

se pourrir, (*a*) (*of fruit, etc.*) to go bad; (*of egg*) to addle; (*b*) to deteriorate; **laisser p. la situation,** to allow the situation to deteriorate.

pourrissable [purisabl̥], *a.* liable to rot, to decay.

pourrissage [purisa:ʒ], *s.m.* **1.** *Paperm:* rotting. **2.** *Cer:* souring.

pourrissant [purisɑ̃], *a.* rotting, decaying, putrefying.

pourrissement [purismɑ̃], *s.m.* (*a*) rot(ting), decay; (*b*) deterioration; degradation; **p. d'une situation,** deterioration of a situation.

pourrissoir [puriswa:r], *s.m.* **1.** muck heap. **2.** *Paperm:* steeping vats.

pourriture [purity:r], *s.f.* **1.** (*a*) rotting, rot, decay; **p. du bois,** wood rot; dote; **p. sèche (du bois),** dry rot; **p. de l'aubier,** sap-wood rot; **p. du cœur,** heart rot (in wood); *Med: A:* **p. d'hôpital,** hospital gangrene; **en p.,** putrescent, rotting; **tomber en p.,** to rot, decay, putrefy; to rot away; **son grabat était une p.,** his miserable bed was no better than rotten straw, was foul beyond expression, was only fit to burn; (*b*) *Vet:* core, (liver) rot (of sheep); *Ap:* **p. du couvain,** foul brood; *Wine-m:* **p. noble,** Botrytis cenerea. **2.** rottenness (of wood, of society); degeneracy. **3.** *F:* **p.!** you swine!

poursuite [pursɥit], *s.f.* **1.** (*a*) pursuit; chase (of enemy ship); tracking (of criminal); **être à la p. de qch.,** to be in pursuit of sth.; **se mettre, s'élancer, à la p. de qn,** to set off, set out, in pursuit of s.o.; to chase after s.o.; **envoyer qn à la p. de qn,** to send s.o. after s.o.; **c'est une p. vaine,** it's a wild goose chase; **la p. des richesses,** the pursuit of wealth; *Cy:* **champion de p.,** pursuit champion; *Com:* **p. du client,** follow-up system; **p. d'un travail, d'une action, etc.,** carrying out of a piece of work, action, etc. *Psy:* **tâche de p.,** pursuit test; (*b*) *Elcs:* tracking (of aircraft, missile, satellite, etc.); **dispositif de p. optique,** tracking servo-optical system; **radar de p.,** tracking radar; **station de p.,** tracking station; **réseau de p.,** tracking network. **2.** *usu. pl. Jur:* lawsuit, action; prosecution; suing (of a debtor); **poursuites publiques,** public prosecution; **faire, diriger, engager, entamer, initier, intenter, commencer, exercer, des poursuites (judiciaires) contre qn,** to take, institute, proceedings, to take (legal) action, against s.o.; **avant de déclencher des poursuites judiciaires,** before calling for a prosecution; **p. en expropriation,** action in expropriation; **vous vous exposez à des poursuites de la part du Conseil,** you are laying yourself open to prosecution by the Council. **3.** *Games:* spanners.

poursuiteur [pursɥitœːr], *s.m. Cy: F:* pursuit cyclist.

poursuivable [pursɥivabl], *a.* **1.** pursuable. **2.** *Jur:* actionable.

poursuivant, -ante [pursɥivɑ̃, -ɑ̃ːt]. **1.** *a. Jur:* prosecuting (party). **2.** *s.* (*a*) *A:* applicant (for post); suitor (for woman); (*b*) *Jur:* plaintiff, prosecutor; (*c*) *Her:* **p. d'armes,** poursuivant (at arms); (*d*) pursuer; *esp.* tagger, 'it' (in game of tag).

poursuivre [pursɥiːvr], *v.tr.* (*conj. like* SUIVRE) **1.** (*a*) to pursue; to go after, make after (s.o., an animal); to chase (enemy ship, *F:* s.o.); **p. l'ennemi,** to pursue, harry, the enemy; **p. une femme,** to press one's attentions on a woman; *A:* **p. une femme en mariage,** to woo a woman; **ce songe me poursuit,** that dream haunts me; **poursuivi par la guigne,** dogged by bad luck; (*b*) *A:* **p. un emploi,** to seek a post. **2.** *Jur:* **p. qn (en justice),** to prosecute s.o.; to sue (debtor); to proceed against s.o.; **il n'y a pas lieu à p.,** the case need not be proceeded with; there is no case; **p. la contrefaçon,** to take action for infringement of patent. **3.** to pursue, continue, proceed with, go on with (story, one's studies, etc.); **p. un travail,** to carry on a piece of work; **il faut p. la chose,** we must go through with it; **p. sa pointe,** to pursue one's course (to the end), *F:* to stick to it; **p. sa carrière,** to continue, follow, one's career; **p. un avantage,** to follow up an advantage; to press an advantage; **les préparatifs se poursuivent,** preparations are continuing, going forward; **p. un but,** to work towards an end; **p. une politique,** to pursue a policy; *abs.* **poursuivez,** go on, continue (your story).

pourtant [purtɑ̃], *adv.* nevertheless, however, still, (and) yet; **il est intelligent, et p. il a commis une grosse erreur,** he is intelligent and yet he has made a bad blunder; **vous n'allez p. pas nous quitter?** you're surely not going to leave us? **mais si, p., je l'ai vu!** oh yes, I really *have* seen it!

pourthiea, pourthiœa [purtjea], *s.m. Bot:* photinia.

pourtour [purtuːr], *s.m.* **1.** (*a*) periphery, circumference, compass (of building, space); **les murs de la ville ont 3000 mètres de p.,** the town walls are 3000 metres round; **p. d'une cathédrale,** precincts of a cathedral; **mur de p.,** enclosure wall (of prison, town, etc.); (*b*) mount (of photograph, etc.). **2.** *Th:* promenade, gangway (round stalls and boxes).

pourtournant [purturnɑ̃], *a.* surrounding (wall, etc.).

pourtraire [purtrɛːr], *v.tr.* (*conj. like* TRAIRE) *A. & Hum:* to portray.

pourvoi [purvwa], *s.m. Jur:* (*a*) appeal (*esp.* to the *Cour de cassation*); (*b*) **p. en grâce,** petition for mercy; **p. en révision,** appeal for review.

pourvoir [purvwaːr], *v.* (*pr.p.* **pourvoyant;** *p.p.* **pourvu;** *pr.ind.* **je pourvois, il pourvoit, n. pourvoyons, ils pourvoient;** *pr.sub.* **je pourvoie;** *p.d.* **je pourvoyais;** *p.h.* **je pourvus;** *fu.* **je pourvoirai**) to provide. **1.** *v.ind.tr.* **p. aux besoins de qn,** to provide for, see to, attend to, the wants of s.o.; **p. à une éventualité,** to provide for, to take steps to meet, a contingency; **il sera pourvu à votre protection,** your protection will be provided for; **p. aux frais d'un voyage,** to defray the cost of a journey; **p. à un emploi,** to fill a post; **on n'y a pas pourvu,** no provision has been made for it; **siège à p.,** seat to be filled; **j'avais pourvu à ce que rien ne manquât,** I had seen to it that nothing should be lacking. **2.** *v.tr.* (*a*) **p. qn de qch.,** to supply, provide, furnish, equip, s.o. with sth.; **se p. d'argent,** to provide oneself with money; **p. qn d'une charge,** to invest s.o. with, appoint s.o. to, an office; **les pays les mieux pourvus en richesses minières,** the countries most richly endowed with mineral wealth; *abs. A:* **p. sa fille,** to provide one's daughter with a husband, to settle one's daughter; (*b*) to equip, fit (**de,** with); **les bicyclettes sont pourvues de garde-boue,** bicycles are fitted, provided, with mudguards.

se pourvoir. *Jur:* (*a*) **se p. en cassation,** to lodge an appeal with the Supreme Court; **se p. en appel,** to lodge an appeal; (*b*) **se p. en grâce,** to petition for mercy.

pourvoirie [purvwari], *s.f. Hist:* store; **droit de p.,** right of purveyance.

pourvoyeur, -euse [purvwajœːr, -øːz], *s.* **1.** purveyor, provider; contractor; caterer; *Artil:* ammunition-server, supply number. **2.** procurer, procuress.

pourvu [purvy], *s.m. Ecc.Hist:* incumbent of a living.

pourvu que [purvykə], *conj.phr.* provided (that) so long as; **faites tout ce que vous voudrez p. que vous me laissiez tranquille,** do what you please, so long as, if only, you leave me alone; **p. qu'il ne fasse pas de gaffes!** I only hope he won't make any blunders! **p. que nous ne manquions pas d'essence!** if only we aren't short of petrol! **p. qu'il vienne!** I do hope he'll come!

poushtou [puʃtu], *s.m. Ling:* Pashto, Pushtu.

poussa(h) [pusa], *s.m.* (*a*) (toy) tumbler, tumble-over; (*b*) *F:* potbellied individual.

poussage [pusaːʒ], *s.m. Rail: Nau:* pushing.

poussard [pusaːr], *s.m. Const:* trave.

poussardage [pusardaːʒ], *s.m. Const:* (action of) putting up traves.

poussarder [pusarde], *v.tr. Const:* to put up traves between (props).

pousse [pus], *s.f.* **1.** growth (of leaves, hair, feathers); **p. des dents,** cutting of teeth. **2.** young shoot, sprout; *Bot:* **première p.,** first shoot; **p. terminale,** leading shoot. **3.** *Vet:* broken wind (in horses); heaves. **4.** ropiness (of wine). **5.** *Cu:* rising.

poussé [puse]. **1.** *a.* elaborate (ornamentation, etc.); deep, searching, thorough (study); **travail trop p.,** work with too much finicky detail; **il aboutit à un scepticisme assez p.,** he carries scepticism to some lengths, pretty far; **faire des études très poussées,** to pursue one's studies to a very advanced level; *Phot:* **cliché trop p.,** over-developed negative; *I.C.E:* **moteur p.,** high-efficiency engine, *F:* hotted-up engine. **2.** *s.m. Mus:* (*violin, etc.*) up-bow.

pousse-au-crime [pusokrim], *s.m.inv. P:* strong wine or fiery spirits; = mother's ruin.

pousse-avant [pusavɑ̃], *s.m.inv. Tls:* (wood-engraver's) dog-leg chisel.

pousse-broche [pusbrɔʃ], *s.m.inv. Tchn:* pin punch.

pousse-café [puskafe], *s.m.inv. F:* (glass of) liqueur (after coffee); chaser; pousse-café.

pousse-cailloux [puskaju], *s.m.inv. P: A:* infantry man, foot-slogger.

pousse-cul [pusky], *s.m.inv. F: A:* bumbailiff.

poussée [puse], *s.f.* **1.** *Mec:* (*a*) thrust; **p. latérale d'une voûte, du terrain,** lateral thrust of an arch, of the ground; **p. des terres,** thrust of the ground; **p. au vide,** bulging; *Civ.E:* thrust passing outside material; **p. d'une hélice,** thrust of a propeller; **p. nominale,** rated thrust; **p. axiale,** end thrust; **p. en avant,** propulsive force, propulsion; **inverseur de p.,** thrust reverser; *Av:* (*of engine*) **développer une p. de 20.000 kilos au décollage,** to develop, produce, a 20,000 kilo thrust at take-off; (*b*) pressure; *esp.* **p. du vent,** wind pressure; **centre de p.,** aerodynamic centre, centre of pressure; *Ph:* **axe de p.,** aerodynamic axis; (*c*) buoyancy (of liquid); **p. verticale de l'eau,** buoyancy of water; **force de p.,** upward thrust; **centre de p.,** centre of buoyancy, of immersion; (*d*) lift (of balloon, of aeroplane). **2.** (*a*) **la p. de la foule,** the pushing, pressure, of the crowd; **la p. des affaires,** the pressure of business; (*b*) *Com: Fin:* **forte p. en hausse,** strong upward tendency (of the market); **p. inflationniste,** inflationary tendency. **3.** push, shove; **donner une p. à qn,** (i) to give s.o. a push; (ii) *F:* to give s.o. a leg up; **écarter qch. d'une p.,** to push, shove, sth. aside; **ouvrir une porte d'une violente p.,** to burst a door open. **4.** (*a*) sprouting, growth; **nouvelle p. de cheveux,** new growth of hair; **p. de boutons,** outbreak of pimples; **p. dentaire,** teething; (*b*) **p. de la sève, p. radiculaire,** rising of the sap; *Med:* **p. de fièvre,** sudden rise of temperature; (*c*) **p. vitale,** vital impetus; (*d*) upsurge; (*e*) *Pol.Ec:* the bulge.

pousse-fiche(s) [pusfiʃ], *s.m.inv. Tchn:* pin-punch.

pousse-pied [puspje], *s.m.inv. Nau:* small light craft.

pousse-pointe(s) [puspwɛ̃ːt], *s.m.inv.* nail punch.

pousse-pousse [puspus], *s.m.inv.* **1.** jinricksha, rickshaw, pedicab. **2.** rickshaw-man.

pousser [puse]. **1.** *v.tr.* (*a*) to push, shove, thrust; **ne poussez pas!** don't push! don't shove! **p. qn du coude, du pied, du genou,** to nudge s.o.; **p. une embarcation au large,** to shove off a boat; **les vents poussent le navire,** the winds drive the ship forward; **l'hélice pousse le navire,** the propeller thrusts the ship forward; (*of wind*) **p. un navire à la côte,** to blow a ship ashore; **p. le verrou,** to shoot the bolt; **p. la porte,** (i) to push the door to; (ii) to push the door open; **p. qn au pouvoir,** (i) to raise s.o. to power; (ii) to thrust s.o. into power; *O:* **p. un tunnel,** to drive a tunnel (**à travers,** through); *Min:* **p. les galeries,** to push on the levels; **p. un troupeau,** to drive a herd of cattle, a flock of sheep; *Sp:* **p. le ballon,** to dribble the ball; *P:* **pousse ton char!** shift your carcass! *Aut:* **p. le moteur,** to strain the engine; *Join:* **p. des moulures,** to do moulding by hand; *Const:* **p. à la main,** to fashion (stone, plaster) by hand; *Bookb:* **p. (un titre, des filets),** to gold tool; *Nau:* **p. la barre,** to move the tiller from one side or the other; **p. le point d'une voile d'embarcation,** to set the sail (to port or to starboard); (*boating*) **p. du fond,** to punt; *Mus:* (*violin, etc.*) **poussez,** up bow; *Av:* **l'avion pousse dans la main,** the plane thrusts against the hand-control; the plane tends to rise; (*b*) to drive, impel, urge, actuate; **p. qn à faire qch.,** to push s.o. into doing sth.; (*of circumstances, etc.*) **p. au crime,** to be an incentive to crime; **p. la main à qn,** to force s.o.'s hand; **il se sentit poussé à prendre la parole,** he felt an impulse to speak; he felt prompted to speak; **poussé par la pitié,** prompted by pity; **poussé par la nécessité,** under the pressure of necessity; **poussé par des motifs secrets,** impelled, actuated, by secret motives; (*c*) to push on, urge forward (piece of work); to pursue deeply, to extend (studies); to elaborate (ornamentation, etc.); *F:* to exaggerate; *abs. Fenc:* to thrust; **p. une attaque à fond,** to push, thrust, drive, an attack home; **p. une promenade jusqu'à la ville,** to walk on as far as the town; *O:* **p. sa pointe,** to persevere; **p. trop loin une plaisanterie,** to carry a joke too far; **p. la guerre jusqu'au bout,** to carry the war to its conclusion; **licence poussée jusqu'au cynisme,** licence carried to the point of cynicism; **p. la vente de qch.,** to push the sale of sth.; **p. un article aux enchères,** to run up the bidding for sth.; **p. un cheval,** (i) to urge on a horse; (ii) to try a horse's mettle, to extend a horse; **p. un malade,** to keep a patient going as long as possible; **p. un élève,** to push on a pupil; **elle désirait vivement p. sa fille,** she was anxious for her daughter to get on; *P:* **faut pas p.!** that's a bit much! *Mch:* **p. les feux,** to raise steam, to stoke up; *Nau:* **p. l'allure à vingt nœuds,** to increase speed to twenty knots; **p. une botte à qn,** (i) *Fenc:* to lunge at s.o.; (ii) *F:* to attack s.o.; to have a dig at s.o.; *Husb:* **p. une femelle au lait,** to prolong lactation; **p. d'avoine un cheval,** to overfeed a horse with oats; *s.a.* BOUT 1; (*d*) (*of trees, etc.*) to put out, shoot (out), grow (leaves, roots); (*e*) to utter (cry); to heave (sigh); **p. un hourra,** to give a cheer; **en poussant un cri,** with a cry; (*f*) *F:* **je leur ai poussé un petit laïus,** I said a few words to them, I made a little speech; *F:* **en p. une,** to give a song; (*g*) **p. un mouton,** to skin a sheep. **2.** *v.i.* (*a*) to push, to put on pressure; **p. à la roue,** to put one's shoulder to the wheel; *F:* **avoue que tu as poussé à la roue!** admit that you've helped a bit! (*b*) to push on, push forward, make one's way (to a place); **p. tout doucement jusque chez qn,** to stroll, drift, round to s.o.'s house; *Nau:* (*of boat*) **p. au large,** to put off, push off, shove off; **p. à l'effet,** to strive after effect; **p. au noir,** (i) (*of painting, etc.*) to darken; (ii) to see the gloomy side of things; (*c*) to extend; **l'entr'acte pousse parfois à la demi-heure,** the interval sometimes runs to as much as half an hour; (*d*) (*of plants, etc.*) to grow, shoot, burgeon; (*of hair, nails*) to grow; (*of tree*) **p. en hauteur,** to spindle; **laisser p. sa barbe,** to grow a beard; (*of plant*) **commencer à p.,** to sprout; **le soleil fait p. les plantes,** the sun is bringing on the plants; **les dents commencent à lui p.,** he is beginning to cut his teeth; **tous ces enfants poussent,** all these children are growing up, are shooting up; *Lit:* **dès que les blés seront poussés,** as soon as the corn has sprung up; **le dindon pousse le rouge,** the turkey's caruncle becomes red; (*e*) *Vet:* (*of horse*) to break wind; (*f*) *Const:* **p. en dehors,** to bulge.

se pousser. **1.** to push oneself forward; to make one's way (in society, etc.); to shove, elbow, one's way to the front; **elle sait se p. dans le monde,** she's very pushing. **2.** to move up (to give s.o. else room); *P:* **pousse-toi,** shove up.

pousse-toc [pustɔk], *s.m. Mec.E:* driving-plate pin, driver (of lathe); *pl. pousse-tocs.*

poussette [pusɛt], *s.f.* **1.** (game of) push-pin. **2.** (*a*) *F:* (child's) pushchair; (*b*) *Dom.Ec:* shopping trolley. **3.** *Cy:* pushing (from behind).

pousseur, -euse [pusœːr, -øːz], *s.* **1.** (*a*) pusher, shover; (*b*) *s.f. Tls:* **pousseuse,** pusher; *Rail:* wagon pinch bar; *Nau:* push boat. **2.** *Lit:* heaver (of sighs); utterer (of fine phrases).

pousseux [pusø], *s.m. Fish:* prawn net, shrimp net, shove net.

pousse-wagon [pusvagɔ̃], *s.m.inv. Rail:* light engine (running on or beside the track, for pushing one or more coaches for short distances).

poussier [pusje], *s.m.* (*a*) *Min:* coal dust, screenings; **p. d'anthracite,** culm; **p. de minerai,** ore slime; **p. de mottes,** peat litter, tan litter; (*b*) *Const:* stone dust; (*c*) *Pyr:* gunpowder dust; (*d*) *Metalw:* **p. de moulage,** facing sand.

poussière [pusjɛːr], *s.f.* **1.** (*a*) dust; **enlever la p. des meubles,** to dust the furniture; **enlever la p. de qch. avec une brosse,** to brush the dust off sth.; *s.a.* SECOUER 2; **nuage de p.,** cloud of dust; **p. cosmique** cosmic dust; **faire de la p.,** (i) to raise the dust; (ii) *P:* to strut about, to show off; *impers.* **il fait tant de p.,** there are such clouds of dust; **s'en aller en p.,** to crumble into dust; **mettre, réduire, qch. en p.,** (i) to reduce sth. to dust; (ii) to smash sth. to atoms; **réduit en p.,** (i) reduced to dust; (ii) mouldering; **charbon en p.,** coal dust; *F:* **tirer qn de la p.,** to raise s.o. from the dust, from the dunghill; **mordre la p.,** to bite the dust; *Min:* **coup de p.,** coal-dust explosion; *Nav:* **p. navale,** small vessels, small fry; (*b*) speck, grain, of dust; *F:* **cela m'a coûté dix mille francs et des poussières,** this cost me ten thousand francs plus (a little bit). **2. p. d'eau,** (fine) spray; *Nau:* spindrift. **3. p. d'or,** gold dust; *Ind:* **p. de foret,** bore dust, borings. **4. p. fécondante, p. des fleurs,** pollen. **5. une p. d'étoiles,** a cloud of stars.

poussiéreux, -euse [pusjerø, -øːz], *a.* **1.** dust-like, dust-coloured. **2.** dusty, covered with dust.

poussif, -ive [pusif, -iːv], *a.* (*a*) broken-winded, wind-broken (horse); heavy [hiːvi] (horse); (*b*) wheezy, short-winded (person); puffing (engine).

poussin [pusɛ̃], *s.m.* **1.** (*a*) chick; (*b*) *Cu:* spring chicken; (*c*) *F:* young child; *F:* **mon p.,** pet. **2.** *Mil.Av: F:* (first year) officer cadet.

poussinesque [pusinɛsk], *a. Art:* of Poussin; in the style of Poussin.

poussinet [pusinɛ], *s.m. F:* (*child*) **mon p.,** my (little) pet.

poussinière [pusinjɛːr], *s.f.* **1.** (*a*) chicken coop; (*b*) (chicken) incubator. **2.** *Astr: A:* **la P.,** the Pleiades.

poussivement [pusivmɑ̃], *adv.* breathlessly.

poussoir [puswaːr], *s.m.* **1.** (*a*) push (button) (of electric bell, repeater watch, etc.); bolt spring (of bayonet); thumb piece, button (of machine-gun firing mechanism); *Mec.E:* push rod; *I.C.E:* **p. de soupape,** push rod of a valve; valve lifter; *Mec.E:* **p. à ressort,** trigger; (*b*) *Elcs:* (*computers*) key; **p. de chargement (de programme),** load key. **2.** *Tls:* driver, punch.

poutargue [putarg], *s.f. Dial: Cu:* salted and pressed tunny or mullet roe.

poutassou [putasu], *s.m. Ich:* small Mediterranean cod.

pout-de-soie [putswa], *s.m. Tex:* poult-de-soie; *pl. pouts-de-soie.*

pouteria [puterja], *s.m. Bot:* pouteria.

poutine [putin], *s.f. Pisc:* small fry.

poutrage [putraːʒ], *s.m.*, **poutraison** [putrɛzɔ̃], *s.f.* framework of beams; joist framing.

poutre [putr̥], *s.f. Const:* **1. p. en bois,** wooden beam; **grosse p.,** balk; **p. de faîte,** ridge piece, roof tree; **p. de plancher,** ceiling joist; summer (beam); summertree; **p. posée,** beam with ends loose; **p. encastrée,** beam with fixed ends; **maison aux poutres apparentes,** half-timbered house. **2.** girder; **p. à âme pleine,** plate girder; **p. armée,** trussed girder; **p. composée,** built up girder; **p. contre-fichée,** lattice girder; **poutres jumelées, p.-caisson, p. creuse,** box girder; **p. en console, en encorbellement,** cantilever girder, overhung girder; **p. à, en, porte-à-faux,** cantilever beam; **p. de démontage,** lifting beam; **p. roulante,** small travelling crane, small gantry; *Nau:* **p. du navire,** hull girder; *Av:* **p. de liaison, de réunion, de queue,** tail boom, tail girder.

poutrelle [putrɛl], *s.f.* (*a*) small beam, girder; balk, joist; *Av:* spar (of wing); *Const:* **p. à griffe,** claw balk; **p. articulée,** jointed balk; (*b*) flitch (of timber); (*c*) road bearer (of pontoon bridge); (*d*) *Artil: etc:* skid.

pouture [putyːr], *s.f. Husb:* stall fattening (of animals for butchery).

poutzer [putze], *v.tr. Sw.Fr:* to clean.

pouvoir [puvwaːr]. **I.** *v.tr.* (*pr.p.* **pouvant;** *p.p.* **pu;** *pr.ind.* **je puis** or **je peux** (always **puis-je** [pɥiːʒ]), **tu peux, il peut, n. pouvons, ils peuvent;** *pr.sub.* **je puisse, n. puissions;** *p.d.* **je pouvais;** *p.h.* **je pus;** *fu.* **je pourrai** [pure]) **1.** to be able; "can"; **je ne peux (pas) le faire,** I can't do it; I am unable to do it; **nous ne pouvons absolument pas le faire,** we cannot possibly do it; **cela ne peut (pas) se faire,** it cannot be done; **comment a-t-il pu dire cela?** how could he say that? **il aurait pu le faire s'il avait voulu,** he could have done it if he had wanted to; **lâchez le chien pour qu'il puisse courir un peu,** let the dog loose so that he can have a run; **on aurait pu entendre voler les mouches,** you could have heard a pin drop; **vous n'auriez pas pu l'empêcher,** you could not have prevented it; **faire tout ce qu'on peut,** to do one's (level) best, the best one can, the best in one's power (**pour,** to); **j'ai fait toutes les démarches que j'ai pu,** I took every step that I possibly could; **j'espère p. vous aider,** I think I can help you, I hope to be able to help you; **j'ai pu le revoir,** I managed, was able, contrived, to see him again; **je n'y puis rien,** I cannot help it; **on n'y peut rien,** (i) it can't be helped; (ii) there is nothing that can be done; **ils n'y peuvent rien,** they are powerless in the matter; **je ne peux rien au fait accompli,** I cannot undo what has been done; **ne p. qu'y faire,** to be unable to resist; to be unable to help it; **il a été on ne peut plus grossier,** he was as rude as could be; he was most rude; **j'en suis on ne peut plus content,** I'm so pleased about it; **elle est on ne peut plus contente,** she is as pleased as can be, *F:* as pleased as Punch; **il travaille on ne peut mieux,** he couldn't work better; **il est on ne peut plus loyal,** he is absolutely faithful; **les effets de ces courants intenses sont on ne peut plus remarquables,** the effects of these high-voltage currents are most remarkable; **n'en plus p.,** to be tired out, exhausted; to be at the end of one's tether; **il n'en peut plus (de fatigue),** he is quite exhausted, he is worn out, tired out, *F:* dog tired, dead beat, tired; **les chevaux n'en peuvent plus,** the horses are exhausted; **ils n'en peuvent plus de demeurer là,** they cannot face living there any longer; **je n'en peux plus de soif,** I'm dying of thirst; *s.a.* MAIS 1; **sauve qui peut,** every man for himself; **dépenser le moins d'argent qui se puisse,** to spend the least money possible; **on ne peut pas ne pas l'admirer,** one cannot help admiring him; **je la rassurai comme je pus,** I reassured her as well as I could; **je viendrai aussitôt que je pourrai,** I will come as soon as I can; *v.pr.* **si cela se peut, si faire se peut,** if it can be done, if possible; **aussi souvent que faire se peut,** so often as I, we, you, possibly can; as often as possible; **cela ne se peut pas,** (i) that cannot be; (ii) it cannot be done; **M. X? qu'est-ce qu'il peut bien me vouloir?** Mr X? whatever can he want? **où pouvait-il bien être à cette heure?** wherever could he be at this time? **la loi ne peut rien contre lui,** the law can't touch him. **2.** "may"; (*a*) to be allowed; **vous pouvez partir,** you may go; **puis-je entrer?** may I, shall I, come in? **quand pourrai-je emménager?** when can I move in? *F:* **si l'on peut dire, si je puis dire,** if I may say so; (*b*) (*optative*) **puissé-je arriver à temps!** I hope to heaven I arrive in time! **puissiez-vous dire vrai!** may what you say be true! I hope what you say is true! **puisse-t-il défendre nos lois!** may he defend our laws! **3.** to be possible, probable; **cela peut (bien) être,** *v.pr.* **cela se peut (bien),** it may be; it is quite possible; maybe! possibly! **avec de la chance je peux réussir,** with luck I may succeed; **il a pu se tromper, il a pu le faire sans le vouloir,** he may have made a mistake, he may have done it unintentionally; **la porte a pu se fermer toute seule, la porte peut s'être fermée toute seule,** the door may have closed of its own accord; **nous pourrions le trouver si nous nous dépêchions,** we might find him if we hurried; **la chose aurait pu arriver plus tôt,** it might have happened sooner; **il peut, pourrait, avoir dix ans,** he may be ten years old; **il pouvait avoir dix ans,** he may, might, have been ten; **advienne que pourra,** come what may; **tout de même vous auriez (bien) pu faire moins de bruit,** all the same you could have made less noise; **s'il se peut,** if (it is) possible; **il fait encore plus froid, s'il se peut,** it's even colder, if that's possible; **il aurait pu être son père,** he was old enough to be her father; **il peut se faire, il peut arriver, que** + *sub.*, *v.pr.* **il se peut que** + *sub.*, it may be, may happen, that . . .; **il a pu se faire que . . .,** *Lit:* **il s'est pu faire que . . .,** it may have happened that . . .; **il se pourrait fort bien que . . .,** it is quite possible, quite on the cards, that . . .; **il se pourrait bien qu'il réussisse,** he will succeed as likely as not; he's quite likely to succeed; **il pourrait bien se faire que . . .,** it is not at all unlikely that . . .; **il se peut qu'il ne soit pas coupable,** he may not be guilty; **il se peut qu'il vienne,** he may come.

II. pouvoir, *s.m.* **1.** (*a*) power, force, means; **il n'est au p. de personne de vous aider,** nobody can help you; **il n'est pas en mon p. de . . .,** it is not within my power to . . .; **être en p. de faire qch.,** to be able, in a position, to do sth.; **je vous aiderai de tout mon p.,** I will do all I possibly can to help you, I will help you to the utmost of my power, of my capacity, I will help you all I can; **cela passe mon p.,** that is beyond my power, my capacity; **en dehors de mon p.,** beyond my power; (*b*) *Ch: Ph: etc:* power; **p. absorbant,** absorptivity, absorptive power; **p. antidétonant,** antiknock value (of a fuel); **p. agglutinant,** bonding strength, caking capacity; **p. éclairant,** illuminating power; **p. calorifique (d'un combustible),** calorific value; **p. radiant,** radiating capacity; **p. freinant,** braking power; **p. inducteur spécifique,** dialectric constant, permittivity; **p. grossissant,** magnifying power; *Opt:* **p. rotatoire,** rotatory power; *Pol.Ec:* **p. d'achat,** purchasing power. **2.** influence; power; **avoir un p. absolu sur qn,** to have complete power over s.o.; **acquérir un grand p. sur qn,** to gain a firm hold over s.o.; **tomber au p. de l'ennemi,** to fall into enemy hands, into the hands of the enemy; **être au p. de qn,** to be in s.o.'s power; **il est en mon pouvoir,** he is my power; **les Pays-Bas étaient tombés au p. de l'Espagne,** the Netherlands had come under Spanish rule. **3.** authority; (*a*) **p. paternel,** paternal authority; (*b*) competence, power; **demander des pouvoirs pour conclure la paix,** to ask for powers to conclude peace; **en dehors de mes pouvoirs,** not within my competence; not within my sphere; **il est en dehors de mes pouvoirs de . . .,** it does not rest with me to . . .; **agir en dehors de ses pouvoirs,** to act *ultra vires*; (*c*) **p. politique,** political power; **ambitionner le p.,** to aim at power; **prendre le p.,** (i) to assume power; (ii) to come into office, to take office; **prise du p.,** assumption of power; **arriver, venir, au p.,** to come into power, into office; **détenir le p.,** to be in power; **le parti au p.,** the party in power; **abus de p.,** abuse, misuse, of power; **p. noir,** black power; **quand les Libéraux sont au p.,** when the Liberals are in power; **les pouvoirs publics,** the administration, the authorities; **p. exécutif,** executive power, the executive; **p. législatif,** legislative power; **p. judiciaire,** judicial power, the judiciary; (*d*) *Rel:* **p. spirituel,** spiritual power; **p. temporel,** temporal power. **4.** *Jur:* power of attorney; procuration; letters of procuratory; **p. discrétionaire,** discretionary powers; **munir qn d'un p.,** to furnish s.o. with full powers; **avoir, recevoir, plein(s) pouvoir(s) pour agir,** to have full powers, to be (fully) empowered, authorized, to act; **exercer un p.,** to exercise powers of attorney; **conférer, donner, pleins pouvoirs à qn pour . . .,** to empower s.o. to . . .; **pouvoir(s) régulier(s),** credentials; **montrer ses pouvoirs,** to show one's credentials; **se présenter sans pouvoirs réguliers,** to come without full credentials; *Com:* **p. pour assemblée générale,** proxy for general meeting; **p. impératif,** special proxy; *s.a.* FONDÉ 2. **5.** *A:* heavy stick, cudgel (carried by *incroyable*).

pouzolzia [puzɔlzja], *s.m. Bot:* pouzolzia.

pouzzolane [puzɔlan], *s.f.* pozzolana; **p. en pierre,** trass.

Pouzzoles [puzɔl, -dzɔl], *Pr.n. Geog:* Pozzuoli.

powellite [powɛlit], *s.f. Miner:* powellite.

poyaudin, -ine [pwajodɛ̃, -in], *a. & s. Geog:* (native, inhabitant) of la Puisaye.

poyou [pwaju], *s.m. Z:* poyou.

pradéen, -enne [pradeɛ̃, -ɛn], *a. & s. Geog:* (native, inhabitant) of Prades.

pradelle [pradɛl], *s.* meadow.

præmunire [premynire], *Eng.Hist:* **statut de p.,** writ of præmunire.

praesidium [prezidjɔm], *s.m. Pol:* (*in U.S.S.R.*) Praesidium.

pragmatagnosie [pragmatagnozi], *s.f. Med:* pragmatagnosia.

pragmaticisme [pragmatisism], *s.m. Phil:* pragmaticism.

pragmatique [pragmatik]. **1.** *a.* pragmatic (sanction, philosophy). **2.** *s.f. Hist:* Pragmatic Sanction.

pragmatiquement [pragmatikmɑ̃], *adv.* pragmatically.

pragmatisme [pragmatism], *s.m.* **1.** *Phil:* pragmatism. **2.** *Elcs:* (*computers*) pragmatics.

pragmatiste [pragmatist], *s.m. & f. Phil:* pragmatist.

pragois, -oise [pragwa, -waːz], *a. & s. Geog:* (native, inhabitant) of Prague.

Praguerie [pragri], *s.f. Fr.Hist:* (revolt of the) Praguerie (1439-1443).
prahau, praho [prao], *s.m. Nau:* proa.
praire [prɛːr], *s.f. Moll:* venus (clam); *Dial:* **fausse p.,** cockle.
prairial, -aux [prɛrjal, -o]. **1.** *a. Bot:* **plante prairiale,** meadow plant. **2.** *s.m. Fr.Hist:* ninth month of Fr. Republican Calendar (May-June).
prairie [prɛri], *s.f.* **1.** (*a*) meadow; **p. irrigable,** water meadow; **p. temporaire,** ley; (*b*) grassland, *U.S:* prairie. **2.** *Geog:* **la Prairie,** the Prairies.
praiss [prɛs], *s.m. Cust:* praiss.
prâkrit [prɑkri], *s.m. Ling:* Prakrit.
pralin [pralɛ̃], *s.m.* **1.** *Hort:* dressing (applied to root of rose bush, etc. when planting). **2.** *Cu:* praline mixture.
pralinage [pralinaːʒ], *s.m.* **1.** *Hort:* dressing (of root at time of planting). **2.** *Cu:* manufacture of praline.
praline [pralin], *s.f.* **1.** (*a*) *Cu:* praline; (*b*) *P:* **ça paraît un peu (cucul) la p.,** it seems (i) a bit out-of-date, old hat; (ii) rather silly. **2.** *P:* blow, bash, whack.
praliné [praline], *Cu:* **1.** *a.* containing ground praline; **chocolat p.,** praline chocolate. **2.** *s.m.* cake containing almonds and praline.
praliner [praline], *v.tr.* **1.** *Hort:* to dress (roots of rose bush, etc. at time of planting). **2.** *Cu:* to brown (almonds, etc.) in sugar; to crisp (almonds, etc.).
pralineur, -euse [pralinœːr, -øːz], *s. Cu:* praline maker, manufacturer.
pram [pram], *s.m.,* **prame** [pram], *s.f. A.Nau:* pram, praam; Dutch barge.
prandial, -aux [prɑ̃djal, -o], *a.* prandial.
prangos [prɑ̃gɔs], *s.m. Bot:* prangos.
prao [prao], *s.m. Nau:* proa.
prase [prɑːz], *s.m. Miner:* prase; *Lap:* pebble; **p. de topaze,** false topaz.
praséodyme [prazeodim], *s.m. Ch:* praseodymium.
praséolite [prazeolit], *s.f. Miner:* praseolite.
prasin [prazɛ̃], *a. Lit:* prasine, prasinous; *Rom. Ant:* green (faction).
prasium [prazjɔm], *s.m. Bot:* hedge nettle.
prasopale [prazɔpal], *s.f. Miner:* prasopal.
pratelle [pratɛl], *s.f. Bot:* red pratelle.
praticabilité [pratikabilite], *s.f.* practicability, practicableness (of project, road, etc.); feasibility, feasibleness; *Tchn:* **étude de p.,** feasibility study.
praticable [pratikabl]. **1.** *a.* practicable; (*a*) feasible (plan, idea, etc.); (*b*) passable, negotiable (road, ford, etc.); (*c*) *Th:* practicable (door, window); (*d*) *A:* sociable; (person) easy to get on with. **2.** *s.m.* (*a*) *Th:* practicable door, window, balcony, etc.; (*b*) *Cin:* movable platform for camera or projectors.
praticien, -ienne [pratisjɛ̃, -jɛn]. **1.** *a.* practising; **(médecin) p.,** practitioner. **2.** *s.m.* (*a*) (legal, medical) practitioner; (*b*) practical man, expert; craftsman (as opposed to layman); (*c*) *Art:* sculptor's assistant, rougher-out, pointer.
praticulteur [pratikyltœːr], *s.m.* grassland specialist.
praticulture [pratikyltyːr], *s.m.* cultivation of meadows.
pratincole [pratɛ̃kɔl], *a. Orn:* living in meadows; **glaréole p.,** pratincole.
pratiquant [pratikɑ̃], *a.* practising (religious observances); *a. & s.* **(catholique) p.,** practising Catholic.
pratique¹ [pratik], *a.* **1.** practical, useful (method, article, etc.); handy (gadget, etc.); convenient (time, bus, etc.); **avoir l'esprit p.,** to have a practical turn of mind; **avoir beaucoup de sens p.,** to have a great deal of practical common sense; to be very businesslike; **proposition d'ordre p.,** practical proposition; **connaissance p. d'un procédé,** practical knowledge of a process; **connaissance p. d'un sujet,** working knowledge of a subject; *Sch:* **travaux pratiques,** practical (work); *Ph:* **unité p.,** practical unit; *Nau:* **pilote p.,** hobbling pilot, hobbler. **2.** *A:* experienced (person). **3.** *s.m. Nau:* **p. (d'une côte),** pilot, sailor, well acquainted with a coast.
pratique², *s.f.* **1.** practice; application (of theory); **mettre qch. en p.,** to put sth. into practice; to apply (system, etc.); *O:* **réduire qch. en p.,** to make sth. practicable; **inutilisable dans la p.,** of no practical value; **c'est de p. courante,** it is quite commonly done; it is the usual practice; it is quite usual; **en p.,** in practice. **2.** (*a*) practice, method, experience; **il a une grande p. des hommes,** he has a wide experience of men; **p. du théâtre,** practice of the theatre, theatrical experience; **la p. d'un sport,** the practice of a sport; **s'entretenir dans la p. d'un sport,** to keep up a sport; **on se perfectionne par la p.,** practice makes perfect; **perdre la p., de qch.,** to lose the knack of sth.; to get out of practice; **avoir une longue p. de qch.,** to have a long personal experience of sth.; **êtes-vous dans la p. des affaires?** are you a practical business man? **effectuer des calculs par p.,** to calculate by rule of thumb; *Art:* **peindre de p.,** to paint from memory, without a model; (*b*) *Jur:* practice (of the law); **terme de p.,** legal term; **en termes de p.,** in legal parlance; (*c*) *A:* **p. des témoins,** tampering with the witnesses; bribing of the witnesses; (*d*) *pl.* dealings; **avoir des pratiques avec l'ennemi,** to have dealings with the enemy; (*e*) associating, association **(de,** with); **il avait vécu dans la p. des employés de ministères,** he had associated with civil servants. **3.** practice, usage; **pratiques religieuses,** religious practices, religious observances; **pratiques clandestines,** underhand practices or dealings. **4.** *A:* (*a*) practice (of lawyer or doctor); (*b*) custom, business (of tradesman); (*of customer*) **donner sa p. à qn,** to give s.o. one's custom. **5.** *A:* (*a*) (lawyer's) client; (doctor's) patient; (*b*) (tradesman's) customer. **6.** *Jur:* **libre p.,** free exercise (of one's religion, etc.); *Nau:* **avoir libre p.,** to be out of quarantine; to have pratique; **donner libre p. à un navire,** to admit a ship to pratique. **7.** (puppet showman's) squeaker. **8.** *Const:* **pierre de p.,** rough-hewn stone.
pratiquement [pratikmɑ̃], *adv.* **1.** practically, in a practical manner. **2.** (*a*) in actual fact; (*b*) in practice; (*c*) practically, virtually; **p. impossible,** virtually, well-nigh, impossible.
pratiquer [pratike], *v.tr.* **1.** to practise (rules, one's religion, virtues, etc.); to put into practice; to employ, to use; **il pratique le football,** he plays football; **elle pratique la natation,** she's a (keen) swimmer; **p. une méthode,** to employ a method; **voilà comment cela se pratique ici,** this is the custom here, this is how it is usually done here; **p. les conseils de qn,** to put s.o.'s advice into practice; **passage alpin déjà connu et pratiqué,** Alpine pass already known and used; **p. la chirurgie,** to practise surgery; *Surg:* **p. une intervention sur qn,** to operate on s.o.; *abs.* **il ne pratique pas,** he doesn't practise (his religion); **médecin qui pratique dans cette ville,** doctor who practises in this town; **il ne pratique plus,** he is no longer in practice; *Com:* **les cours pratiqués, les cours qu'on a pratiqués,** the prices (at which bargains were) made; the ruling prices; **cours pratiqués au comptant,** business done for cash; **les prix qui se pratiquent à Paris,** the prices ruling in Paris. **2.** *Const: etc:* **p. un escalier dans l'épaisseur d'un mur,** to cut a stair in, to fit a stair into, the thickness of a wall; **p. une ouverture, un trou, dans un mur,** to make an opening, a hole, in a wall; *Min:* **p. une galerie,** to drive a gallery; **p. un sentier,** to make, to open out, a path; **p. des sondages,** to put down bore holes; *Const:* **p. la pierre,** to hew stone. **3.** (*a*) to frequent; to associate with (s.o.); *A:* **p. les femmes,** to frequent women; **j'ai pratiqué le monde,** I have lived in the world; **je ne pratique pas le grand monde,** I do not move in society; *O:* **p. un livre,** to use, to study, a book;' (*b*) *A:* **p. les témoins,** to tamper with the witnesses; to bribe the witnesses.
praw [prao], *s.m. Nau:* proa.
praxéen, -éenne [prakseɛ̃, -eɛn], *a. & s. Rel.H:* Praxean.
praxéologie [prakseolɔʒi], *s.f.* praxeology, praxiology.
praxinoscope [praksinɔskɔp], *s.m.* praxinoscope.
praxique [praksik], *a. Anat:* motor (area, etc.).
praxis [praksis], *s.f. Phil:* praxis.
Praxitèle [praksitɛl], *Pr.n.m. Gr.Ant:* Praxiteles.
pré [pre], *s.m.* meadow; **prés salés,** saltings, salt meadows; *A:* **aller sur le p.,** to fight a duel.
pré- [pre], *pref.* prae-, pre-; fore-; ante-.
préaccentuation [preaksɑ̃tɥasjɔ̃], *s.f. Elcs:* pre-emphasis.
préachat [preaʃa], *s.m.* **1.** buying (of article) before it is up for sale to the general public. **2.** prepayment.
préadamisme [preadamism], *s.m. Hist:* preadamitism.
préadamite [preadamit]. **1.** *a.* preadamic. **2.** *s.* preadamite.
préadaptation [preadaptasjɔ̃], *s.f. Biol:* preadaptation.
préalable [prealabl]. **1.** *a.* (*a*) previous (**à,** to); **formalités préalables au débat,** formalities that precede the debate; **réclamer, poser, demander, la question p.,** to call for, to move, the previous question; *Tp: etc:* **appareil à payement p.,** prepayment coin box; penny-in-the-slot machine; (*b*) preliminary (agreement, arrangement, etc.); **bombardement sans déclaration p.,** bombardment without warning; **à titre de mesure p.,** as a preliminary; (*c*) (*computers*) **faire un tri p.,** to screen. **2.** *s.m.* prerequisite, condition; preliminary; **au p.,** to begin with, first of all, as a preliminary, beforehand.
préalablement [prealabləmɑ̃], *adv.* (*a*) previously; (*b*) as a preliminary, beforehand, before anything else.
préallumage [prealymaːʒ], *s.m. I.C.E: etc:* pre-ignition; *Rockets:* preliminary rocket stage.
Préalpes (les) [leprealp], *Pr.n.f.pl. Geog:* the Alpine foreland.
préalpin [prealpɛ̃], *a. Geog:* of the Alpine foreland.
préambule [preɑ̃byl], *s.m.* preamble (**de,** to); *Mus:* prelude.
préamplificateur [preɑ̃plifikatœːr], *F:* **préampli,** *s.m. Elcs: Cin:* first-stage (sound) amplifier; preamplifier, *F:* preamp.
pré-anesthésie [preanɛstezi], *s.f. Med:* pre-anaesthesia.
préassemblage [preasɑ̃blaːʒ], *s.m. Const:* sub-assembly.
préau, -aux [preo], *s.m.* (*a*) (court)yard (of building, *esp.* prison yard); open space (of cloister); (*b*) *Sch:* covered (part of) playground; (*c*) courtyard (for patients in hospital).
préavertissement [preavɛrtismɑ̃], *s.m. Rail:* distant signal.
préavis [preavi], *s.m.* previous, advance, notice; **sans p.,** without notice, warning; **exiger un p. de trois mois,** to require three months' notice; **p. de grève,** strike warning.
préaviser [preavize], *v.tr.* to give previous notice to (s.o.); to warn (s.o.) beforehand.
prébaccalauréat [prebakalɔrea], *s.m. Sch:* examination taken two years before the *baccalauréat.*
prébende [prebɑ̃ːd], *s.f.* **1.** *Ecc:* prebend. **2.** (*a*) sinecure, *F:* cushy job; (*b*) *F:* bribery.
prébendé [prebɑ̃de], **prébendier, -ière** [prebɑ̃dje, -jɛːr], *Ecc:* **1.** *a.* prebendal (canonry, etc.). **2.** *s.m.* prebendary.
pré-bois [prebwɑ], *s.m.* grazing forest; *pl. prés-bois.*
précâblé [prekɑble], *a.* prewired.
précaire [prekɛːr]. **1.** *a.* (*a*) precarious (tenure, authority, life, etc.); (*b*) delicate (health); precarious (state of health); (*c*) **commerce p.,** trade between belligerent nations carried out under a neutral flag. **2.** *s.m. Jur:* precarium; (*a*) precarious tenure; **jouir d'un bien par p.,** to enjoy the precarious use of an estate; (*b*) precarious holding.
précairement [prekɛrmɑ̃], *adv.* precariously.
précambrien, -ienne [prekɑ̃brjɛ̃, -jɛn], *a. & s.m. Geol:* Precambrian.
pré-capitalisme [prekapitalism], *s.m. Pol.Ec:* pre-capitalist movement, economy.
précapitaliste [prekapitalist], *a. Pol.Ec:* pre-capitalist(ic).
précarence [prekarɑ̃ːs], *s.f.* vitamin, etc., deficiency (in diet).
précarité [prekarite], *s.f.* precariousness.
précatif, -ive [prekatif, -iːv], *a.* precative, precatory; *Jur:* **legs p.,** precatory trust.
précaton [prekatɔ̃], *s.m. Tchn:* drawplate (for gold wire).
précaution [prekosjɔ̃], *s.f.* **1.** precaution; **prendre des précautions,** to take precautions (**pour,** for); *F:* **prendre ses précautions,** to go to the loo; **mesures de p.,** precautionary measures; **à titre de p., par mesure de p.,** as a precaution; **apporter des précautions à faire qch.,** to observe care in doing sth.; **précautions oratoires,** introductory remarks (to gain the goodwill of the listener, reader). **2.** caution, wariness; care; **avec p.,** cautiously; carefully.
précautionné [prekosjɔne], *a.* cautious, wary; careful.
précautionner [prekosjɔne], *v.tr. O:* to warn, caution (**contre,** against).
se précautionner contre qch., to take precautions, to provide, to guard, against sth.
précautionneusement [prekosjɔnøzmɑ̃], *adv.* cautiously, warily; carefully.
précautionneux, -euse [prekosjɔnø, -øːz], *a.* cautious, wary; careful.
précédemment [presedamɑ̃], *adv.* previously, already, before, earlier; **articles p. énumérés,**

articles enumerated above; **quelque chose que j'ai dit p.**, something I said earlier on.

précédence [presedɑ̃:s], *s.f.* precedence (**de**, of); priority (**de**, over).

précédent [presedɑ̃]. **1.** *a.* preceding, previous, former; **à la page précédente**, on the preceding page; **cette page et la précédente**, this page and the one before; **le jour p.**, the day before, the previous day. **2.** *s.m.* precedent; **créer un p.**, to create, set, a precedent; **cela ne constituera aucun p. pour les décisions à prendre**, this will not prejudice future decisions, will not constitute a precedent; **fait sans p.**, unprecedented occurrence; *Jur:* **les précédents** = case-law; *s.a.* CAUSE 2.

précéder [presede], *v.tr.* (*conj. like* CÉDER) **1.** to precede; to go before (s.o., sth.); to take place before (sth.); **faire p. de**, to prefix with; **la musique précède les troupes**, the band marches in front of the troops; **précédé de, par, deux laquais**, preceded by two footmen; **l'empire qui a précédé la république**, the empire which preceded the republic; **l'antichambre qui précède le salon**, the antechamber leading to the drawing-room; *abs.* **la page qui précède**, the preceding page, the page before; **ce qui précède**, the foregoing. **2. p. qn (en dignité)**, to have precedence of s.o.

préceinte [presɛ̃:t], *s.f. N.Arch:* bend, wale.

précellence [presɛlɑ̃:s], *s.f.* pre-eminence.

précelles [presɛl], *s.f.pl. Dent:* forceps (for stoppings, etc.).

précepte [presɛpt], *s.m.* precept.

précepteur, -trice [presɛptœ:r, -tris], *s.* (*a*) (family) tutor, (private) teacher; *Lit:* preceptor, *f.* preceptress; (*b*) **il a consenti à être mon p. en politique**, he agreed to be my political mentor, guide.

préceptoral, -aux [presɛptɔral, -o], *a.* tutorial.

préceptorat [presɛptɔra], *s.m.* tutorship.

précession [presɛsjɔ̃], *s.f. Astr: etc:* precession.

préchambre [preʃɑ̃bɽ], *s.f.* pre-combustion chamber (of Diesel engine), antechamber.

préchantre [preʃɑ̃tɽ], *s.m. Ecc:* precentor.

préchargement [preʃarʒmɑ̃], *s.m. Exp:* preloading.

préchauffage [preʃofa:ʒ], *s.m.* pre-heating.

préchauffer [preʃofe], *v.tr.* to pre-heat.

préchauffeur [preʃofœ:r], *s.m.* pre-heater.

préchaulage [preʃola:ʒ], *s.m. Sug.-R:* addition of lime (to the syrup).

prêche [prɛ:ʃ], *s.m. Protestant Ch:* **1.** (*a*) sermon; (*b*) *F:* sermon, lecture; telling off. **2.** *A:* assembly (of worshippers). **3.** *A:* place of worship, meeting-house.

prêche-malheur [prɛʃmalœ:r], *s.m. & f.inv. A: & Lit:* prophet(ess) of woe; *f.* Cassandra.

prêcher [prɛʃe], *v.tr.* **1.** (*a*) to preach (the Gospel, etc.) (**à**, to); **p. l'avent**, to preach the Advent sermons; **p. malheur**, to preach desolation and despair; **p. l'économie**, to preach economy; *abs.* **il prêche mal**, he is a poor preacher; *F:* **il est toujours à p.**, he is for ever sermonizing, preachifying; **p. d'exemple**, to practise what one preaches; **il prêche d'exemple**, his example is as good as a sermon; (*b*) **p. à qn de faire qch.**, to exhort, urge, s.o. to do sth.. **2.** *F:* to preach to (s.o.), to lecture (s.o.); to tell (s.o.) off; **on le prêchait sans cesse là-dessus**, he was eternally being lectured on the subject; *F:* **p. un converti**, to preach to the converted.

prêcheresse [prɛʃərɛs], *a. & s.f. Ecc:* Dominican (nun).

prêcherie [prɛʃri], *s.f. O: F:* sermonizing, preachifying.

prêcheur, -euse [prɛʃœ:r, -ø:z]. **1.** *a.* (*a*) *Ecc:* Dominican (friar); (*b*) *F:* sermonizing (person). **2.** *s. F:* sermonizer, preacher.

prêchi-prêcha [preʃipreʃa], *F:* **1.** *int.* stop preaching! don't go on about it! dry up! **2.** *s.m.inv.* sermonizing. **3.** *s.m.inv.* **c'est un p.-p.**, he, she, is for ever giving us lectures, going on at us.

préchrétien, -ienne [prekretjɛ̃, -jɛn], *a.* pre-Christian.

précieusement [presjøzmɑ̃], *adv.* **1.** very carefully; **garder qch. p.**, to treasure up sth.. **2.** *Lit:* with preciosity, preciously, affectedly.

précieux, -euse [presjø, -ø:z]. **1.** *a.* (*a*) precious; **les métaux précieux**, the precious metals; **pierres précieuses**, precious stones; gems; **ce privilège lui a été p.**, this privilege was precious to him; **bijou qui m'est p. pour ses souvenirs**, jewel precious to me on account of the memories that it recalls; **cela m'est aussi p. que la vie même**, it is the very breath of life to me; *Rel:* **le P. sang**, the Precious Blood; (*b*) valuable (advice, help, time, person); (**à**, to); (*c*) affected, euphuistic, mannered (style, language); (*d*) *Art:* **touche précieuse**, delicate finish. **2.** *s.m. Lit:* preciosity. **3.** *s.f. Fr.Lit.Hist:* **précieuse**, précieuse.

préciosité [presjozite], *s.f.* (*a*) *Lit:* preciosity; (*b*) affectation, affectedness.

précipice [presipis]. *s.m.* (*a*) chasm, abyss; (*b*) **tirer qn d'un p.**, to rescue s.o. from ruin.

précipitabilité [presipitabilite], *s.f.* precipitability.

précipitable [presipitabl̥], *a. Ch:* precipitable.

précipitamment [presipitamɑ̃], *adv.* precipitately, headlong, in a hurry; **descendre p. l'escalier**, to rush downstairs; **entrer, sortir, monter, descendre, p.**, to rush or hurry in, out, up, down; **sortir p. de la chambre**, to dash out of the room; **revenir p.**, to hurry, rush, back; **agir trop p.**, to be too precipitate; to be in too much of a hurry.

précipitant [presipitɑ̃], *s.m. Ch:* precipitant; precipitating agent.

précipitateur [presipitatœ:r], *s.m. Ch:* precipitator.

précipitation [presipitasjɔ̃], *s.f.* **1.** (*a*) precipitation, violent hurry, great haste; **sortir avec p.**, to rush, dash, out; **se lever avec p.**, to get up hastily; (*b*) excessive haste; **sans p.**, deliberately, without undue haste; **il ne faut pas confondre vitesse et p.**, speed is not synonymous with haste; haste is one thing and speed another; **travail fait avec p.**, hasty, scamped, work; (*c*) **la p. d'un départ imprévu**, the rush, scurry, of an unexpected departure. **2.** (*a*) *Ch: Ph:* precipitation; (*b*) *Meteor:* precipitation; (*c*) *Atom.Ph:* **p. radioactive primaire**, close-in fall-out.

précipité [presipite]. **1.** *a.* (*a*) precipitate; hasty (person, decision); hurried, headlong (flight, etc.); abrupt (departure); racing (pulse); **s'avancer à pas précipités**, to rush along, forward; **un bruit de pas précipités**, quick footsteps; **la course précipitée du temps**, the headlong course of time; (*b*) *Ch:* precipitated (chalk, etc.). **2.** *s.m. Ch: etc:* precipitate; **p. électrolytique**, electrolytic precipitate; **p. galvanique**, electrodeposit.

précipiter [presipite], *v.tr.* **1.** (*a*) to throw down, hurl down, dash down (sth.); **p. qch. par la fenêtre**, to hurl, throw, sth. out of the window; **p. qn dans le désespoir**, to plunge s.o. into despair; **p. un peuple dans la guerre**, to precipitate a nation into war; (*b*) *Ch:* to precipitate (a substance); *v.i.* (*of substance*) to precipitate; to form a precipitate. **2.** to hurry, hasten; to rush; to accelerate; to precipitate (events); **p. ses pas**, to hasten one's steps; **p. son départ**, to put forward, to precipitate, one's departure; **il ne faut rien p.**, we must not be in too much of a hurry over anything; we must not rush things.

se précipiter. **1.** (*a*) to dash, to rush headlong, to make a rush (**sur**, at, upon); **se p. pour faire qch.**, to rush to do sth.; **se p. dans les bras l'un de l'autre**, to rush into one another's arms; **se p. sur l'ennemi**, to swoop down on the enemy; **les événements se précipitent**, events are moving fast; (*b*) *Ch:* to precipitate, to be precipitated. **2.** to be hasty; **il ne faut pas vous p.**, you must not be too hasty.

précipitine [presipitin], *s.f. Bio-Ch:* precipitin.

précipito-diagnostic [presipitɔdjagnɔstik], *s.m. Bio-Ch:* precipitin test.

précipitueux, -euse [presipitɥø, -ø:z], *a.* precipitous, sheer (slope).

préciput [presipy], *s.m. Jur:* **1.** portion of an estate or inheritance that devolves upon one of the co-heirs over and above his equal share with the others. **2. p. conventionnel**, benefit stipulated in the marriage settlement in favour of the surviving spouse. **3.** *A:* supplementary salary granted to certain civil servants.

précis [presi]. **1.** *a.* precise, exact, accurate, definite (time, explanation, etc.); unambiguous (term, etc.); **exiger d'une façon précise que . . .**, to call definitely for . . .; **à deux heures précises**, at two o'clock precisely; at two o'clock sharp; **à deux heures trois quarts, heure précise**, at a quarter to three precisely; **je suis parti sans raison précise**, I left for no definite reason; **répondre à des besoins p.**, to answer definite needs; **on lui avait ordonné en termes p. de . . .**, he had been ordered in precise terms to . . .; *Artil:* **tir p.**, accurate fire. **2.** *s.m.* abstract, summary, précis (of document, etc.); epitome; *Sch:* **p. d'histoire de France**, short history of France; précis of French history.

précisément [presizemɑ̃], *adv.* **1.** (*a*) precisely, exactly; **s'exprimer p.**, to express oneself in exact terms; (*b*) **c'est p. l'homme que je cherche**, he is just the man I am looking for; **c'était vous?—p.!** it was you?—exactly! **2.** as it happens, as it happened; **j'ai lu p. dans le journal que . . .**, as a matter of fact, I read in the paper that . . ..

préciser [presize], *v.tr.* (*a*) to specify; to state (sth.) precisely; **il faut p. vos affirmations**, you must be more explicit in your statements; *Jur:* **p. la portée d'un article**, to define (more) accurately the meaning of a clause; **p. des règles de procédure**, to specify rules of procedure; **p. les détails**, to go into more, greater, further, detail; **je tiens à p. que . . .**, I wish to make it clear that . . .; **il a bien précisé que . . .**, he clearly indicated that . . .; he specifically stated that . . .; **veuillez nous p. . . .**, please let us know; **p. la date de . . .**, to give the exact date of . . ., to say for certain when . . .; **à une date qui n'a pas encore été précisée**, at a date still unspecified; at a date to be announced later; **sans rien p.**, (i) without going into details; (ii) without pinning oneself down to anything; (*b*) *abs.* to be precise, explicit; to make a definite statement; **précisions**, let us have, give, the exact details; let us be quite clear (about it).

se préciser, (*of ideas*) to become clear, explicit; (*of a danger, etc.*) to take shape.

précision [presizjɔ̃], *s.f.* **1.** precision, preciseness, exactness, accuracy; **s'exprimer avec p.**, to speak precisely, unambiguously; **répondre avec p.**, to answer precisely, accurately; **p. de tir**, accuracy of fire; **tir de p.**, precision fire; **avec une p. toute mathématique**, with mathematical precision; *Tchn:* **travail de p.**, precision work; **instruments de p.**, precision instruments. **2. donner, apporter, des précisions sur qch.**, to give precise details, exact information, about sth.; **demander des précisions sur qch.**, to ask for fuller information, for full particulars, about sth.

précisionniste [presizjɔnist], *a. & s.m.* **(mécanicien) p.**, precision engineer.

précité [presite], *a.* previously cited, aforesaid, above(-mentioned); **la résolution précitée**, the above resolution.

préclassique [preklasik], *a.* preclassical.

précoce [prekɔs], *a.* precocious (talent, child, etc.); early, forward (season, fruit); **enfant p. pour son âge**, child who is advanced for his age; precocious child; **mariage p.**, early marriage; **sénilité p.**, premature senility.

précocement [prekɔsmɑ̃], *adv.* precociously; early.

précocité [prekɔsite], *s.f.* precocity; precociousness; earliness, forwardness (of season); *Breed:* precocity.

précolique [prekɔlik], *a. Med:* antecolic.

précolombien, -ienne [prekɔlɔ̃bjɛ̃, -jɛn], *a.* pre-Columbian.

précombustion [prekɔ̃bystjɔ̃], *s.f.* precombustion; **moteur Diesel à chambre de p.**, Diesel engine with ante-chamber; precombustion engine.

précompte [prekɔ̃:t], *s.m. Fin:* (*a*) advance deduction (from an account); (*b*) deduction at source (of income tax, etc. from wages).

précompter [prekɔ̃te], *v.tr. Fin:* to deduct beforehand, to begin by deducting; to deduct (income tax, etc.) at source; **p. la Sécurité Sociale sur le salaire de qn**, to deduct National Insurance from s.o.'s pay; **p. les mensualités pour achats à crédit sur le salaire de qn**, to deduct hire purchase payments from s.o.'s pay.

préconcassage [prekɔ̃kasa:ʒ], *s.m. Stonew:* breaking-down.

préconcept [prekɔ̃sɛpt], *s.m.* preconcept.

préconceptif, -ive [prekɔ̃sɛptif, -i:v], *a. Phil:* preconceptual.

préconception [prekɔ̃sɛpsjɔ̃], *s.f.* preconception, prenotion; prejudice.

préconcevoir [prekɔ̃səvwa:r], *v.tr.* (*conj. like* CONCEVOIR) to preconceive.

préconçu [prekɔ̃sy], *a.* preconceived; **idée, opinion, préconçue**, preconception; preconceived idea, opinion.

préconditionné [prekɔ̃disjɔne], *a. Com:* packaged.

préconis(at)eur [prekɔniz(at)œ:r], *s.m.* preconizer.

préconisation [prekɔnizasjɔ̃], *s.f.* (*a*) *R.C.Ch:* preconizing, preconization; (*b*) strong recommendation.

préconiser [prekɔnize], *v.tr.* **1.** *Ecc:* to preconize (bishop); to approve the appointment of (bishop). **2.** to (re)commend (s.o., sth.); to advocate (course of action).

préconnaissance [prekɔnɛsɑ̃:s], *s.f. O:* foreknowledge, precognition.

préconnaître [prekɔnɛtɽ], *v.tr.* (*conj. like* CONNAÎTRE) *O:* to have an intuition of (sth.).

préconscient [prekɔ̃sjɑ̃], *a. & s.m. Psy:* preconscious; **de manière préconsciente,** preconsciously.
préconsonantique [prekɔ̃sɔnɑ̃tik], *a. Ling:* preconsonantal.
préconstruction [prekɔ̃stryksjɔ̃], *s.f.* prefabrication, preconstruction.
précontraindre [prekɔ̃trɛ̃:dr̥], *v.tr.* (*conj. like* CONTRAINDRE) *Const:* to prestress.
précontraint [prekɔ̃trɛ̃], *a.* prestressed; **béton p.,** prestressed concrete; *s.m.* **pont en p.,** prestressed concrete bridge.
précontrainte [prekɔ̃trɛ̃:t], *s.f.* prestress; **appliquer le procédé de la p.,** to prestress.
précordial, -aux [prekɔrdjal, -o], *a. Anat: Med:* precordial.
précordialgie [prekɔrdjalʒi], *s.f. Med:* precordialgia.
précraquage [prekraka:ʒ], *s.m. Petroleum Ind:* primary cracking.
précuire [prekɥi:r], *v.tr.* (*conj. like* CUIRE) to precook; to cook in advance; **aliments précuits,** ready-cooked food.
précultural, -aux [prekyltyral, -o], *a. Agr:* **travaux préculturaux,** preliminary preparation (of land for cultivation).
précurseur [prekyrsœ:r]. **1.** *s.m.* precursor, forerunner; *Lit:* harbinger (of spring, etc.). **2.** *a.m.* precursory; **indices, signes, précurseurs,** premonitory signs; antecedent signs; *Mil:* **détachement p.,** advance detachment.
prédateur, -trice [predatœ:r, -tris]. **1.** *a.* predatory; **oiseau p.,** bird of prey. **2.** *s.m.* bird, beast, of prey; predator.
prédavitique [predavitik], *a.* pre-Davidic.
prédécéder [predesede], *v.i.* (*conj. like* DÉCÉDER) to predecease, to die first.
prédécès [predesɛ], *s.m.* predecease.
prédécesseur [predesesœ:r], *s.m.* predecessor; **nos prédécesseurs,** (i) our ancestors; (ii) our predecessors.
prédéfini [predefini], *a. Elcs:* (*computers*) **paramètre p.,** preset parameter; **processus p.,** predefined process.
prédelle [predɛl], *s.f. Ecc.Art:* predella.
prédénommé [predenɔme], *a.* aforesaid, aforementioned.
prédésinentiel, -ielle [predezinɑ̃sjɛl], *a. Ling:* preterminal.
prédestinateur [predɛstinatœ:r], *s.m.* predestinator.
prédestinatianisme [predɛstinasjanism], *s.m.* predestinationism; predestinarianism.
prédestinatien, -ienne [predɛstinasjɛ̃, -jɛn], *a. & s.* predestinationist; predestinarian.
prédestination [predɛstinasjɔ̃], *s.f.* predestination.
prédestiné [predɛstine]. **1.** *a.* predestined; foredoomed, fated (à, to). **2.** *s. Theol:* predestinate.
prédestiner [predɛstine], *v.tr.* to predestinate, predestine (à, to).
prédéterminant [predetɛrminɑ̃], *a. Theol:* predetermining.
prédétermination [predetɛrminasjɔ̃], *s.f.* predetermination.
prédéterminé [predetɛrmine], *a.* predetermined; **calculateur à séquence prédéterminée,** consecutive sequence computer; **paramètre p.,** preset parameter.
prédéterminer [predetɛrmine], *v.tr.* to predetermine.
prédéterminisme [predetɛrminism], *s.m. Phil:* predeterminism.
prédial, -aux [predjal, -o], *a. Jur:* predial, praedial (servitude, etc.); landed (property); real (estate).
prédiastolique [predjastɔlik], *a. Physiol:* prediastolic.
prédicable [predikabl̥], *a. Log:* predicable.
prédicament [predikamɑ̃], *s.m. Phil:* predicament, category.
prédicant [predikɑ̃], *s.m. Ecc:* predicant.
prédicat [predika], *s.m. Gram: Log:* predicate; *Log:* sentential, prepositional, function.
prédicateur, -trice [predikatœ:r, -tris], *s.* preacher; *Med:* **main de p.,** preacher's hand.
prédicatif, -ive [predikatif, -i:v], *a. Gram:* predicative.
prédication [predikasjɔ̃], *s.f.* **1.** preaching; *Hist:* **la p. de la Croix,** the preaching of the Cross. **2.** sermon. **3.** *Log:* predication.
prédictif, -ive [prediktif, -i:v], *a.* predictive.
prédiction [prediksjɔ̃], *s.f.* prediction. **1.** predicting, foretelling. **2.** forecast; *Psy:* **p. d'un test,** predictive efficiency of a test.
prédigéré [prediʒere], *a.* predigested.
prédigestion [prediʒɛstjɔ̃], *s.f. Physiol:* predigestion.
prédilection [predilɛksjɔ̃], *s.f.* predilection; **avoir une p. pour qn,** to have a partiality for s.o.; **montrer une p. pour qch.,** to show a marked preference for sth.; **auteur de p.,** favourite author; **par p.,** for preference.
prédire [predi:r], *v.tr.* (*conj. like* DIRE *except pr.ind. second pers. pl. & imp.,* **v. prédisez**) to predict, prophesy, foretell, forecast; **p. une éclipse,** to predict an eclipse; **p. quel sera l'avenir de . . .,** to foretell the future of . . ..
prédiseur, -euse [predizœ:r, -ø:z], *s.* predictor.
prédisposant [predispozɑ̃], *a.* predisposing.
prédisposé [predispoze], *a.* predisposed (à, to; **en faveur de,** in favour of); prejudiced (**contre,** against); prone (à, to); **p. aux accidents,** accident-prone; **p. au rhume,** subject to colds; **p. au doute,** having a tendency to, inclined to, doubt.
prédisposer [predispoze], *v.tr.* to predispose. **1.** **cette vie l'avait prédisposé à la goutte,** this life had predisposed him to gout. **2.** **p. qn en faveur de qn,** to predispose s.o. in s.o.'s favour; **p. qn contre qn,** to prejudice, bias, s.o. against s.o.
prédisposition [predispozisjɔ̃], *s.f.* **1.** predisposition (à, to); **p. à l'arthrite,** predisposition to arthritis; arthritic diathesis; **p. au vice,** propensity to vice; **avoir des prédispositions pour la vie monastique,** to be predisposed to monastic life; **p. aux accidents,** proneness to accidents. **2.** predisposition (**en faveur de,** in favour of); prejudice, bias (**contre,** against).
prédistillation [predistilasjɔ̃], *s.f. Ch:* predistillation; **colonne de p.,** predistillation column.
prednisolone [prɛdnizɔlɔn], *s.f. Pharm:* prednisolone.
prednisone [prɛdnizɔn], *s.f. Pharm:* prednisone.
prédominance [predɔminɑ̃:s], *s.f.* predominance, prevalence.
prédominant [predɔminɑ̃], *a.* predominant, predominating, prevailing, prevalent; *Astrol:* **astre p.,** dominant star.
prédominer [predɔmine]. **1.** *v.i.* to predominate, prevail, to have the upper hand (**sur,** over); to be uppermost; to be in the ascendant. **2.** *v.tr.* **l'intérêt prédomine tout,** (self-)interest always comes first.
prédomme [predɔm], *s.m. Bot:* annual clary, common sage.
prédorsal, -aux [predɔrsal, -o], *a. Anat:* predorsal.
prédynastique [predinastik], *a.* predynastic.
pré-électoral, -aux [preelɛktɔral, -o], *a.* preelection (promises, etc.).
préemballer [preɑ̃bale], *v.tr. Com:* to package (goods).
préembryon [preɑ̃briɔ̃], *s.m. Bot:* pro-embryo.
préembryonnaire [preɑ̃briɔnɛ:r], *a. Bot:* proembryonal, pro-embryonic.
prééminence [preeminɑ̃:s], *s.f.* pre-eminence (**sur,** over).
prééminent [preeminɑ̃], *a.* pre-eminent.
préempter [preɑ̃pte], *v.tr.* to pre-empt; to obtain (sth.) by pre-emption.
préemptif, -ive [preɑ̃ptif, -i:v], *a.* pre-emptive.
préemption [preɑ̃psjɔ̃], *s.f.* pre-emption; **droit de p.,** right of pre-emption.
préétabli [preetabli], *a.* pre-established; *Phil:* **harmonie préétablie,** pre-established harmony.
préétablir [preetabli:r], *v.tr.* to pre-establish.
préexcellence [preeksɛlɑ̃:s], *s.f.* pre-eminence; incomparable superiority.
préexilien, -ienne [preegziljɛ̃, -jɛn], *a.*, **préexilique** [preegzilik], *a. B.Hist:* pre-exile, preexilian, pre-exilic.
préexistant [preegzistɑ̃], *a.* pre-existent, preexisting.
préexistence [preegzistɑ̃:s], *s.f.* pre-existence.
préexistentiel, -ielle [preegzistɑ̃sjɛl], *a.* preexistent.
préexister [preegziste], *v.i.* to pre-exist; **la cause préexiste à l'effet,** the cause is pre-existent to the effect.
préfabrication [prefabrikasjɔ̃], *s.f. Const:* prefabrication; unit construction.
préfabriqué [prefabrike]. **1.** *a.* prefabricated. **2.** *s.m.* (*a*) **le p.,** prefabricated units; (*b*) *F:* (*house*) prefab.
préfabriquer [prefabrike], *v.tr.* to prefabricate.
préface [prefas], *s.f.* **1.** preface, foreword (à, **de,** to); **quelques mots à titre de p.,** a few words of preface, a few prefatory words; **l'incompréhension est la p. de la dispute,** lack of understanding leads to quarrels. **2.** *Ecc:* preface.
préfacer [prefase], *v.tr.* **p. l'ouvrage de qn,** to write a preface to, for, s.o.'s work.
préfacier [prefasje], *s.m.* prefacist, prefacer.
préfanage [prefana:ʒ], *s.m. Agr:* drying fodder for silage.
préfectoral, -aux [prefɛktɔral, -o], *a.* prefector(i)al; of the prefect; *Fr.Adm:* **le corps p.,** the senior staff of the *préfecture.*
préfecture [prefɛkty:r], *s.f.* **1.** *Rom.Ant:* (*a*) prefectship; (*b*) prefecture. **2.** *Fr.Adm:* prefecture; (*a*) chief town of a *département* = county town; (*b*) prefect's residence and offices; (*c*) prefect's term of office; (*d*) appointment as prefect, office of prefect. **3.** **la P. de police,** the headquarters of the (Paris) police. **4.** **p. maritime,** (i) area under command of a port-admiral; (ii) naval superintendent's office, port-admiral's office. **5.** *R.C.Ch:* **p. apostolique,** prefecture apostolic.
préférable [preferabl̥], *a.* preferable (à, to); more advisable; **il serait p. de le revoir,** it would be better to see him again; **il serait p. que l'on constituât un fonds de garantie,** it would be preferable to establish a guarantee fund.
préférablement [preferabləmɑ̃], *adv.* preferably (à, to); in preference (à, to).
préféré, -ée [prefere], *a. & s.* favourite; **lectures préférées des enfants,** children's favourite reading.
préférence [preferɑ̃:s], *s.f.* **1.** preference; **de p.,** preferably; **de p. à . . .,** in preference to . . .; **donner, accorder, la p. à qn,** to give s.o. preference (**sur,** over); **choisir qn de, par, p. à tout autre,** to choose s.o. in preference to any other, rather than any other; *Jur:* **p. d'un créancier,** priority of a creditor; **droits de p.,** priority rights; *Fin:* **actions de p.,** preference shares, preferred shares; *Pol.Ec:* **p. pour la liquidité,** liquidity preference; **p. impériale,** imperial preference. **2.** *pl.* marks of preference; distinctions, favouritism.
préférentiel, -elle [preferɑ̃sjɛl], *a.* preferential (treatment, tariff); **vote p.,** preferential voting, system.
préférer [prefere], *v.tr.* (**je préfère, n. préférons; je préférerai**) to prefer (à, to); to like better; **je préfère le cidre au vin,** I prefer cider to wine, I would rather have cider than wine; **p. l'honneur à l'argent,** to put honour before riches; **à vivre sans honneur il préfère mourir,** he would rather die than live in disgrace; **je préférerais que vous veniez,** I would rather you came; **il préféra mourir plutôt que de se rendre,** *F:* **il préféra mourir que de se rendre,** he preferred death to surrender; **je préfère la viande bien cuite,** I prefer meat well done; **je vous préfère triste,** I would rather have you sad.
préfet [prefɛ], *s.m.* **1.** (*a*) *Rom.Ant:* prefect; **le p. des Gaules,** the prefect of Gaul; (*b*) *Fr.Adm:* prefect, administrator of a French *département*; (*c*) *Fr.C: Adm:* reeve; = chairman of urban council. **2.** **le p. de police,** the prefect, chief commissioner, of the Paris police. **3.** *Navy:* **p. maritime,** port-admiral; commander-in-chief of the port. **4.** *Sch:* (*a*) **p. (des études),** master responsible for discipline (*in certain boarding schools*); vice-principal; (*b*) *Belg:* headmaster (of boys' grammar school). **5.** *Ecc:* **p. apostolique,** prefect apostolic.
préfète [prefɛt], *s.f.* (*a*) *F:* the prefect's wife; (*b*) *Sch: Belg:* headmistress (of girls' grammar school).
préfeuille [prefœ:j], *s.f. Bot:* prophyll(um), bracteole; palea.
préfiguration [prefigyrasjɔ̃], *s.f.* prefiguration; foreshadowing.
préfigurer [prefigyre], *v.tr.* to prefigure; to foreshadow.
préfinancement [prefinɑ̃smɑ̃], *s.m. Fin:* prefinancing.
préfix [prefiks], *a.* predetermined (day, place); *Jur:* **douaire p.,** stipulated jointure.
préfixal, -aux [prefiksal, -o], *a. Ling:* prefixal.
préfixation [prefiksasjɔ̃], *s.f. Ling:* prefixation, prefixing.
préfixe [prefiks]. **1.** *s.m.* (*a*) *Gram:* prefix; (*b*) code letter. **2.** *a.* prefixed (particle).
préfixé [prefikse], *a.* (*computers*) **notation préfixée,** prefix notation, parentheses-free notation; Polish notation, Lukasiewicz notation.
préfixer [prefikse], *v.tr.* **1.** to fix, settle (date, etc.) beforehand. **2.** to prefix; **p. une particule au verbe,** to prefix a particle to the verb.
préfleuraison [preflœrɛzɔ̃], **préfloraison** [preflɔrɛzɔ̃], *s.f. Bot:* aestivation, prefloration.
préfoliaison [prefɔljɛzɔ̃], **préfoliation** [prefɔljasjɔ̃] *s.f. Bot:* vernation, prefoliation.
préformage [prefɔrma:ʒ], *s.m. Tchn:* preforming.

préformant [prefɔrmɑ̃], *a. Ling:* preformant, preformative.
préformation [prefɔrmasjɔ̃], *s.f.* preformation.
préformationnisme [prefɔrmasjɔnism], *s.m. Biol:* preformationism.
préforme [prefɔrm], *s.f. Tchn:* preform.
préformé [prefɔrme], *a.m. Cost:* **soutien-gorge p.,** preformed brassière.
préformer [prefɔrme], *v.tr. Tchn:* to preform.
préformisme [prefɔrmism], *s.m.* preformism.
préfractionnateur [prefraksjɔnatœːr], *s.m. Petroleum Ind:* prefractionator.
prégaton [pregatɔ̃], *s.m. Tchn:* drawplate (for gold wire).
pré-gazon [pregazɔ̃], *s.m. Agr:* artificial pasture; *pl. prés-gazons.*
prégénérique [preʒenerik], *s.m. Cin:* pre-credits sequence.
prégénital, -aux [preʒenital, -o], *a. Psy:* pregenital.
préglaciaire [preglasjɛːr], *a. & s.m. Geol:* preglacial (period).
prégnance [pregnɑ̃ːs], *s.f. Psy:* pregnancy, vitality, significance.
prégnant [pregnɑ̃], *a.* **1.** (*of animal*) pregnant; with young. **2.** *Gram:* **construction prégnante,** pregnant construction. **3.** *Psy:* pregnant, vital, significant.
prégnation [pregnasjɔ̃], *s.f. Physiol: O:* pregnancy.
prégustation [pregystasjɔ̃], *s.f.* (*a*) tasting (of food before serving); (*b*) *R.C.Ch:* tasting (of bread and wine before communion).
préhellénique [preɛllenik], *a.* pre-Hellenic.
préhenseur [preɑ̃sœːr]. **1.** *a.m.* prehensile, prehensory (organ). **2.** *s.m.pl. Orn:* **préhenseurs,** Psittaciformes.
préhensible [preɑ̃sibl̩], *a.* prehensible.
préhensile [preɑ̃sil], *a.* prehensile (tail, etc.).
préhension [preɑ̃sjɔ̃], *s.f.* (*a*) gripping; **appareil de p.,** gripping device; *Com:* **(pot) avec nervures de p.,** (jar) with handy grip; (*b*) *A.Jur:* seizure; **droit de p.,** right of the State to appropriate trees at a fixed price for shipbuilding.
préhistoire [preistwaːr], *s.f.* prehistory.
préhistorien, -ienne [preistɔrjɛ̃, -jɛn], *s.m.* prehistorian.
préhistorique [preistɔrik], *a.* prehistoric; **station p.,** (prehistoric) type station, type site; **site p.,** prehistoric site; *F:* **c'est vraiment p.!** it must have come out of the Ark!
préhnite [prenit], *s.f. Miner:* prehnite.
préhnitique [prenitik], *a. Ch:* prehnitic.
préhominien [preɔminjɛ̃], *s.m. Paleont:* prehominid; *pl.* **préhominiens,** Prehominidae.
préhumain [preymɛ̃], *a.* prehuman.
préimprimé [preɛ̃prime], *a.* preprinted.
préindustriel, -ielle [preɛ̃dystr(i)jɛl], *a.* preindustrial.
préislamique [preislamik], *a. Hist:* pre-Islamic.
préjudice [preʒydis], *s.m.* prejudice, detriment; (moral) injury; wrong, damage; *Jur:* tort; **porter, faire, p. à qn,** to inflict injury, loss, on s.o.; (*of action*) to be prejudicial to s.o.'s interests; **au p. de qn,** to the prejudice, detriment, of s.o.; **à mon p.,** to my detriment; **sans p. de . . .,** without prejudice to . . .; **sans p. de mes droits,** without prejudice to my rights, without prejudicing my rights; **accepter un principe sans p. des mesures déjà prises,** to accept a principle without prejudice to the measures already taken; *Psy:* **délire de p.,** (type of) persecution delusion.
préjudiciable [preʒydisjabl̩], *a.* prejudicial, injurious, detrimental (**à,** to); *Jur:* tortious; **démarche p.,** harmful step.
préjudiciaux [preʒydisjo], *a. & s.m.pl. Jur:* **(frais) p.,** security for costs (before appeal).
préjudiciel, -elle [preʒydisjɛl], *a. Jur:* interlocutory (question, etc.); pre-judicial (action).
préjudicier [preʒydisje], *v.i.* (*pr.sub. & p.d.* **n. préjudiciions v. préjudiciiez**) to be detrimental, prejudicial (**à,** to); to harm, injure (cause, etc.).
préjugé [preʒyʒe], *s.m.* **1.** *Jur:* precedent (in law). **2.** presumption; **les préjugés sont contre lui,** appearances are against him; **c'est un p. en sa faveur,** that is a presumption in his favour. **3.** prejudice, preconception; *pl.* antiquated ideas; **avoir un p. sur qch.,** to have a preconceived idea about sth.; **avoir un p. pour, vers, qch.,** to have a prejudice in favour of sth.; **nourrir des préjugés à l'égard de qch.,** to entertain prejudices about sth.; **gens à préjugés,** prejudiced people; **gens sans préjugés,** unprejudiced people; **préjugés de vieille fille,** old maid's prejudices; **p. favorable,** preconceived favourable opinion; prejudice in favour of (s.o., sth.).
préjuger [preʒyʒe], *v.tr.* (*conj. like* JUGER) **1.** to prejudge; **sans p. la solution de la question,** without prejudice to, without prejudicing, the solution of the question; **autant qu'on peut p.,** as far as one can judge beforehand. **2.** *v.ind.tr.* **p. de qch.,** to make too hasty a judgement about sth.; **p. de ses forces,** to overestimate one's strength.
prélart [prelaːr], *s.m. Nau: etc:* tarpaulin.
prélasser (se) [səprelase], *v.pr.* (*a*) *A:* to look important; to strut about; (*b*) to lounge, loll, take one's ease (in an armchair, etc.); **le chat se prélassait au soleil,** the cat was basking in the sunshine.
prélat [prela], *s.m.* prelate.
prélature [prelatyːr], *s.f.* prelature, prelacy.
prélavage [prelavaːʒ], *s.m.* preliminary wash; rinse through.
prélaver [prelave], *v.tr.* to give a preliminary wash to; **les casseroles doivent être prélavées avant d'être mises dans une machine à laver la vaisselle,** saucepans should be prewashed, rinsed, before being put in a washing-up machine.
prêle, prèle [prɛl], *s.f. Bot:* horsetail, scouring rush, shave grass.
prélecture [prelɛktyːr], *s.f.* preliminary proof reading (carried out by printer); (*of computer*) **tête de p.,** pre-read head.
prélegs [prelɛ, -ɛg], *s.m. Jur:* preference legacy.
préléguer [prelege], *v.tr.* (*conj. like* LÉGUER) *Jur:* to bequeath (sth.) as a preference legacy.
préler [prele], *v.tr.* (**je prèle, n. prélons; je prèlerai**) to rub, polish (fine woodwork), with a scouring rush; **p. une anche de basson,** to rub down, fine down, a bassoon reed.
prélèvement [prelɛvmɑ̃], *s.m.* **1.** deduction in advance; setting apart of a certain portion, share, of a whole; **p. d'échantillons,** sampling; **faire un p. de lait,** to take away a certain quantity of milk (as a sample); *Med:* **p. de sang,** taking of blood (for a test); **faire un p. dans la gorge de qn,** to take a swab of s.o.'s throat; **p. sur le prix des billets,** tax on (the price of) tickets; entertainment tax; **p. sur le capital, sur la fortune,** capital levy, tax on capital; *For:* **p. global,** depletion. **2.** (*a*) sample; *Med:* swab; (*b*) amount, quantity, sum, deducted; *Bank:* = standing order (for payment of electricity, etc. account).
prélever [prelve], *v.tr.* (*conj. like* LEVER) to deduct, set apart, (portion or share from whole) in advance; **p. la dîme,** to levy tithes; **p. dix pour cent sur une somme,** to make an advance deduction of ten per cent from a sum of money; **p. une commission de deux pour cent sur une opération,** to charge a commission of two per cent on a transaction; **dividende prélevé sur le capital,** dividend paid out of capital; **une fois la crème prélevée . . .,** when the cream has been skimmed off . . .; **p. un échantillon,** to take, cut off, a sample; *Med:* **p. une goutte de sang,** to take a drop of blood (for a test).
préliminaire [prelimineːr]. **1.** *a.* preliminary; **vue p.,** preview. **2.** *s.m.pl.* **les préliminaires de (la) paix,** the preliminaries to peace, the peace preliminaries; **préliminaires d'un traité,** preamble of a treaty.
préliminairement [preliminɛrmɑ̃], *adv.* preliminarily, by way of preliminary.
prélittéraire [preliterɛːr], *a.* preliterate.
prélogique [prelɔʒik], *a.* prelogic(al).
prélude [prelyd], *s.m. Mus:* prelude; **les éclairs sont le p. de l'orage,** lightning is the prelude to the storm; **les préludes à une conférence,** the preliminaries to a conference.
préluder [prelyde], *v.i.* **1.** *Mus:* to prelude, to play a prelude. **2. p. à qch.,** to be a, serve as, prelude to sth.; **il préludait à son grand ouvrage par de petits essais,** a series of minor works led up to his masterpiece.
prem [prɛm], *a. & s.m. & f. F: Sch:* first, top; **c'est elle la p.,** she's come out top.
prématuration [prematyrasjɔ̃], *s.f. Med:* premature birth.
prématuré, -ée [prematyre], (*a*) *a. & s.* premature (baby); (*b*) *a.* premature, untimely; **mort prématurée,** untimely death; *I.C.E:* **allumage p.,** pre-ignition.
prématurément [prematyremɑ̃], *adv.* prematurely, before the proper time; abortively; **mourir p.,** to die before one's time.
prématurité [prematyrite], *s.f.* prematureness, prematurity.
prémédication [premedikasjɔ̃], *s.f. Med:* preoperative treatment.
préméditation [premeditasjɔ̃], *s.f.* premeditation; **avec p.,** wilfully, deliberately; *Jur:* with malice aforethought, with malice prepense.
préméditer [premedite], *v.tr.* to premeditate; **de dessein prémédité,** of set purpose; designedly; **insulte préméditée,** deliberate insult, studied insult; **elle n'avait pas prémédité de lui demander de rester,** she hadn't planned, intended, to ask him to stay.
prémélange [premelɑ̃ːʒ], *s.m.* pre-mixing (of gas and air, etc.).
préménopause [premenɔpoːz], *s.f.* premenopause.
prémenstruel, -elle [premɑ̃stryɛl], *a.* premenstrual.
prémentionné [premɑ̃sjɔne], *a.* aforementioned.
prémices [premis], *s.f.pl. A: & Lit:* **1.** first fruits; **p. du bétail,** firstlings of cattle. **2.** early beginnings; **les p. de la jeunesse,** the first blush of youth.
premier, -ière [prəmje, -jɛːr], *a. & s.* first. **1.** (*a*) (*in time*) **le p. jour du mois,** the first day of the month; **le p. janvier,** the first of January; **le p. de l'an,** New Year's day; **dans les premiers jours de mai,** in the early part of May; **les premiers mois de l'année,** the early, first, months of the year; **les premières heures après minuit,** the small hours; **les douze premiers Césars,** the first twelve Caesars; **les trois premières années,** the first three years; **il reçut sa première éducation à . . .,** he received his early education at . . .; **dans les premiers temps,** at first; **en p. (lieu),** in the first place, firstly, in the first instance, first and foremost; **la question d'argent vient toujours en p.,** money is always the first consideration; **dès le p. jour,** from the first day; from the beginning; from the outset; **du, au, p. coup,** at the first attempt; **deviner qch. du, au, p. coup,** to guess sth. straight away, at the first go; **arriver le p.,** to arrive first; **nous sommes arrivés tout les premiers,** we were the (very) first to arrive; **il est arrivé dans les tout premiers,** he was among the first to arrive; **arriver beau p., bon p.,** to come in an easy first, to win in a canter; *Prov:* **les premiers vont devant; p. arrivé, p. servi; p. venu, p. moulu;** first come first served; **Priestley le p. a fait cette expérience,** Priestley was the first to carry out this experiment; **être le p. à faire qch.,** to be first to do sth.; **vous êtes le p. qui me fassiez (or qui me fasse) cette objection,** you are the first to make this objection; **je suis tout le p. à reconnaître que . . .,** I am the very first to acknowledge that . . .; **elle rompit le silence la première,** she was the first to break the silence; **les premiers venus,** the first comers; the first to arrive; **le p. venu vous dira cela,** anybody will tell you that; **ce n'est pas le p. venu,** he isn't just anybody; **je passerai chez vous au p. jour,** I'll drop in, call, at the first opportunity; (*at hairdresser's*) **au p. de ces messieurs,** next gentleman, please; *F:* **il n'a pas le p. sou,** he hasn't a penny (to bless himself with); **armes prêtes à servir au p. signal,** weapons ready for use at a moment's notice; **p. discours,** maiden speech; *Nau:* **p. voyage,** maiden voyage (of a ship); *Engr:* **p. état,** first state; *Fin:* **p. cours,** opening price; **frais de p. établissement,** initial outlay, expenses; *Aut:* **première (vitesse),** first, bottom, (gear); **monter une côte en première,** to climb a hill in first; **la première guerre mondiale,** the first world war; (*b*) **couleur première d'une robe,** original colour of a dress; **sens p. d'un mot,** original meaning of a word; **cause première d'un malheur,** prime, primary, cause of a misfortune; **vérité première,** basic truth; **cette bonne impression première se confirma,** the initial good impression was confirmed; **sa pauvreté première,** the poverty of his early days; *Meteor:* **p. arc,** primary rainbow; *Ind:* **matières premières,** raw materials. **2** (*in place*) **première (rue) à gauche,** first (street) on the left; **tomber la tête la première,** to fall head first, headlong; **p. étage,** first floor, *U.S:* second story; **demeurer au p.,** to live on the first floor; *Journ:* **p. (article),** leading article; **p. plan,** foreground; **la première voiture près de la locomotive,** the carriage next to the engine; *Th:* **les premières (loges),** the first-tier boxes; **être aux premières loges,** to have a front seat; to be well placed (for seeing sth.); *Mount:* **p. de cordée,** leader, first, on the rope. **3.** (*in rank*) **au p. rang,** in the first rank; **le tout premier,** the foremost; **au tout p. rang,** in the foremost rank; *Sp: etc:* **prendre la première place,** to take the lead; **le p. chirurgien de Paris,** the leading surgeon in Paris; **p. ministre,** Prime Minister, Premier; **p. mineur,** mine foreman; **p. commis,** principal clerk; **p. clerc,** (lawyer's) head clerk; *Navy:* **p. maître,** chief petty officer; **capitaine en p.,** senior captain; *Sch:* **maître en p.,** senior master; **p. choix,**

best quality, finest quality; **travail de première urgence,** work of immediate urgency; **événement de (toute) première importance,** event of the first, highest, importance; event of vital importance; *Jur:* **p. intéressé,** preferential creditor; *Rail: etc:* **billet de première (classe),** first-class ticket; **voyager en première,** to travel first (class); *Mth:* **nombres premiers,** prime numbers; **nombres premiers entre eux,** incommensurable numbers; *Th:* **p. rôle,** leading part, lead; **jouer les premiers rôles,** to play the leads; **jeune p.,** juvenile lead; **jeune première,** leading lady; *Sch:* **(classe de) première** = sixth form; **(classe de) première supérieure,** class preparing for entrance to the *École normale supérieure*; **il est le p. de sa classe,** he's the top of his form; *P:* **de première,** first-rate; **c'est une menteuse de première,** she's an out-and-out liar; **un gueuleton de première,** a first-class blowout. **4.** *s.f.* **première:** (*a*) head saleswoman; *Dressm: etc:* forewoman; (*b*) *Mount:* first ascent; *Th: etc:* first performance, first night, première; *Cin: U.S:* first run; **première mondiale,** world première; (*c*) *Typ:* first proof; (*d*) *Com:* **première de change,** first of exchange; (*e*) *Bootm:* inner sole, insole.

premièrement [prəmjɛrmɑ̃], *adv.* first, firstly, in the first place.

premier-né, première-née [prəmjene, prəmjɛrne], *a. & s.* first-born; *pl. premiers-nés, premières-nées.*

premier-Paris [prəmjepari], *s.m. A:* leading article, leader (in Paris newspapers); *pl. premiers-Paris.*

prémilitaire [premilitɛːr], *a.* premilitary.

prémisse [premis], *s.f. Log:* premise, premiss.

prémolaire [premɔlɛːr], *s.f. Anat:* premolar (tooth); bicuspid.

prémoniteur, -trice [premɔnitœːr, -tris], *a.* premonitory.

prémonition [premɔnisjɔ̃], *s.f.* premonition.

prémonitoire [premɔnitwaːr], *a.* premonitory (sign).

prémontage [premɔ̃taːʒ], *s.m. Tchn:* prefabrication.

prémonter [premɔ̃te], *v.tr. Tchn:* to prefabricate (units).

prémontré, -ée [premɔ̃tre], *a. & s. Ecc.Hist:* Premonstrant, Premonstratensian.

prémoulé [premule], *a. Metalw:* precast (machinery parts).

prémourant [premurɑ̃], *s.m. Jur:* predeceaser.

prémunir [premyniːr], *v.tr.* **p. qn contre qch.,** (i) to caution, forewarn, guard, s.o., to put s.o. on his guard, against sth.; (ii) to secure s.o. against sth.

se prémunir contre qch., to provide against sth.; to take precautions against sth.; to be prepared for sth.; to be on one's guard against sth.

prenable [prənabl], *a.* **1.** that can be taken; seizable; pregnable (town or fort). **2.** *A:* corruptible; **il n'est pas p.,** he cannot be bribed.

prenant, -ante [prənɑ̃, -ɑ̃ːt]. **1.** *a.* (*a*) *Fin:* **partie prenante,** (i) payee; (ii) recipient, receiver; (*b*) **queue prenante,** prehensile tail; **doigts prenants,** clutching fingers; (*c*) sticky; **glu prenante,** sticky bird lime; (*d*) engaging; **sa voix est aussi prenante que jamais,** her voice is as fascinating as ever; (*e*) **c'est trop p.,** it takes up too much time. **2.** *s.* (*a*) taker (of bet); (*b*) bidder.

prénatal [prenatal], *a.* (*the masc. pl. is* **prénatals** *or* **prénataux**) prenatal, ante-natal (period, etc.).

prendre [prɑ̃ːdr], *v.* (*pr.p.* **prenant;** *p.p.* **pris;** *pr.ind.* **je prends, tu prends, il prend, n. prenons, v. prenez, ils prennent;** *pr.sub.* **je prenne, n. prenions, ils prennent;** *imp.* **prends, prenons, prenez;** *p.d.* **je prenais, n. prenions;** *p.h.* **je pris, n. prîmes;** *fu.* **je prendrai**) to take. **I.** *v.tr.* **1.** (*a*) to take (up), take hold of (sth.); **p. les armes,** to take up arms; **p. un cheval par la bride,** to take hold of a horse by the bridle; **p. brusquement qch.,** to snatch (up) sth., to seize hold of sth.; **p. qn par les cheveux,** to take hold of, to grasp, to seize, s.o. by the hair; **je suis allé p. mon pardessus,** I went to get my overcoat; **p. qch. avec des pincettes,** to pick up sth. with a pair of tongs; *F:* **il n'est pas à p. avec des pincettes,** I wouldn't touch him with a barge pole; **je sais comment le p.,** I know how (i) to handle him, (ii) to get round him; **p. qch. à un tas,** to take sth. from a heap; **p. qch. dans un tiroir,** to take sth. from, out of, a drawer; **p. qch. sur la table,** to take sth. from, off, the table; **p. un livre sur un rayon,** to take a book down from a shelf; **p. un enfant sur ses genoux,** to take a child on one's lap; **p. qch. sous une chaise,** to take sth. from under a chair; **je l'ai prise dans mes bras,** I took her in my arms; **il a pris le livre sous son manteau,** he put the book under, inside, his coat; **vêtement qui prend (bien) la taille,** close-fitting garment; **exemple pris dans la Bible, chez Fénelon,** example taken from the Bible, from Fénelon; **p. qn dans un coin,** to take s.o. into a corner; **je n'y prends ni je n'y mets,** I am neither understating nor overstating the case; I am not exaggerating in either direction; **où avez-vous pris cela?** (i) where did you get that? where did you take that from? (ii) where did you get that idea? (*b*) **p. qch. à sa charge, en charge,** to take charge of, take care of, sth.; (*computers*) **p. en charge une instruction de programme,** to staticize a programme; **p. des pensionnaires,** to take boarders, lodgers; **p. qch. sur soi,** to take responsibility for sth.; **p. sur soi de faire qch.,** to take it upon oneself to do sth., to do sth. off one's own bat; **il prit sur lui de ne pas se plaindre,** he vowed, undertook, not to complain; **elle prit sur elle de sourire,** she forced herself to smile; **p. sur soi (pour . . .),** to get a grip on oneself, to keep a firm hold on oneself (in order to . . .); **p. la direction d'une affaire,** to take over the management of a business; **p. qn, qch., au sérieux,** to take s.o., sth., seriously; **vous avez mal pris mes paroles** you have misunderstood me, misunderstood what I said; **il a très mal pris la chose,** he took it very badly; he didn't take it too well; **prendre qch. à cœur,** to take sth. to heart; (*c*) **p. qch. à qn,** to take sth. from s.o.; *Lit:* **la mort lui a pris son fils,** death has robbed him, deprived him, of his son; **cela me prend tout mon temps,** it takes (up) all my time; **cela prend du temps,** it takes time, it requires time; **combien de temps cela vous a-t-il pris?** how long did it take you? **cela m'a pris deux heures,** it took me two hours; **mon temps est entièrement pris,** I haven't a free minute; **il y a à p. chez les uns et les autres,** there is something to be gleaned from various, different, sources; **c'est autant de pris sur l'ennemi,** that's so much to the good; **j'ai dû p. sur mes économies,** I had to draw on my savings; (*d*) **prenez ce que je vous offre,** take what I'm offering you; **dites-moi ce que vous prenez pour cela,** tell me what you charge for that; *F:* **ce tailleur prend cher,** he's an expensive tailor; **c'est à p. ou à laisser,** take it or leave it; **j'en prends et j'en laisse,** (i) I'm taking that with a pinch of salt; (ii) I'm doing just as much as I feel inclined to; **p. les choses comme elles sont,** to take things as they are, as one finds them; **à tout p.,** on the whole, taking it all in all, taking it by and large, all things considered; **à bien p. les choses,** properly considered; rightly speaking; **prenons qu'il en soit ainsi,** supposing this is the case; assuming this is so; *F:* **en p. à son aise,** to take it easy; to slack; **il en prend trop à son aise,** he's really too casual; **il est inutile de le p. de haut,** there's no need to be scornful, disdainful, to be so superior about it; **prenez-le sur un autre ton,** I don't like the way you're taking it; there's no need to take it in that (superior) way. **2.** to take, seize, catch, capture; (*a*) **p. une ville d'assaut,** to take a town by assault; **p. qn à la gorge,** to seize s.o. by the throat; **odeur qui prend à la gorge,** smell that catches the throat, that catches one in the throat; **p. un poisson, un voleur,** to catch a fish, a thief; *Prov:* **tel est pris qui croyait p.,** it's a case of the biter bit; (*of sail, etc.*) **p. le vent,** to catch the wind; **se faire p.,** to get caught; **je ne veux pas risquer de me faire p.,** I don't want to risk detection; **se laisser p.,** to let oneself be caught; **il s'y laissa p.,** he fell into the trap; **se laisser p. aux flatteries,** to succumb to flattery; **se laisser p. aux belles paroles,** to let oneself be taken in by glib talk, by fine words; **p. qn à voler,** to catch s.o. stealing; **être pris à faire qch.,** to be caught doing sth.; **p. qn sur le fait,** to catch s.o. in the act; **parfois je me prends à sourire,** sometimes I catch myself smiling; **je vous y prends!** I've caught you (at it)! **que je vous y prenne!** let me catch you at it! **on ne m'y prendra pas!** I know better; **on ne m'y prendra plus,** I shan't be caught, taken in, again; **être pris par le brouillard,** to be caught in the fog; **la pluie nous a pris en route,** we were caught in the rain; **il se prit le pied contre une racine et tomba,** he caught his foot, his toe, on a root, and fell; **la peur le prit, il fut pris de frayeur,** he was seized with fright; **il fut pris d'un rire convulsif,** he was seized with uncontrollable laughter; **elle fut prise d'une crise de larmes,** she burst into tears; (*b*) (*can take direct or indirect object; always indirect with impers. const.*) **le vin lui, le, prit à la tête,** the wine went to his head; **une odeur âcre lui, le, prit au nez,** a pungent smell caught his nostrils; **l'envie lui prend de partir,** he is seized with a desire to go away; **si jamais l'envie vous en prenait,** if ever you should feel so inclined; **il lui prit un accès de rire, un étourdissement,** he was seized with a fit of laughter, with dizziness; **il lui prend des lubies impossibles,** he is subject to extraordinary whims; **qu'est-ce qui lui prend?** what's come over him? what's up with him (now)? **bien lui en prit,** it was lucky for him that he did; **bien vous en a pris d'aller le voir,** it was a good thing you called on him. **3.** (*a*) **j'irai, je passerai, vous p. demain matin à votre hôtel,** I shall call for you at your hotel tomorrow morning; **je viendrai p. les bagages,** I shall come for the luggage; (*of taxi*) **p. un client,** to pick up a fare; (*to driver*) **déposez-moi où vous m'avez pris,** put me down where you picked me up; (*of train*) **p. des voyageurs,** to take up, pick up, passengers; (*of boat*) **p. des marchandises,** to take in cargo; *Nau:* **p. de l'eau douce,** to fill up with fresh water; *Com:* **pris à l'usine,** ex works; (*b*) **p. des billets,** to buy, take, book, tickets; **p. un billet direct pour Londres,** to book (straight) through to London; (*in hotel*) **p. une chambre,** to book, take, a room; **p. un jour de congé,** to take a day off; **il n'a pas pris de vacances l'année dernière,** he didn't take, have, a holiday last year; **p. des renseignements,** to make inquiries; **p. des précautions,** to take precautions; **Denise prenait sa leçon de piano,** Denise was having her music lesson; **p. des notes,** to take notes; (*to secretary*) **voulez-vous p. une lettre?** will you take (down) a letter? **p. un rendez-vous,** to make an appointment; **je peux vous p. mardi à dix heures,** I can take you, give you an appointment, on Tuesday at ten o'clock; (*c*) **p. un associé,** to take a partner; **p. un ouvrier,** to engage, take on, a worker; **on ne prend plus personne à l'usine,** no more hands, workers, are required at the factory; no extra labour required; (*of man*) **p. femme,** to get married; *F:* **p. une femme,** to take a woman; **consentez-vous à prendre Monsieur X comme époux,** will you take this man to be your lawful wedded husband? **p. qn comme secrétaire,** to engage s.o. as one's secretary; **p. qn comme exemple,** to take s.o. as an example; (*d*) **p. une personne, une chose, pour une autre,** to mistake, take, one person, one thing, for another; **on le prit pour un général,** he was taken for a general; **p. qn pour qn d'autre,** to mistake s.o. for s.o. else; **il se prend pour un grand homme,** he thinks himself a great man; **on vous a fait p. du quartz pour des diamants,** they've palmed off quartz on you as diamonds; **il se faisait p. pour un colonel,** he passed himself off as a colonel; (*e*) to take, eat, have (food); **p. un remède,** to take (some) medicine; *A:* **p. médecine,** to take a purge; **p. un bain,** to have a bath; **chaussures qui prennent l'eau,** shoes that let in water; (*to guest*) **qu'est-ce que vous pren(dr)ez?** what will you have? what can I offer you? *F:* **p. un verre,** to have a drink; *F:* **qu'est-ce que tu vas p.!** you're for it! *F:* **qu'est-ce que j'ai pris!** I really caught it (that time)! *P:* **je sors d'en p.!** I've had some, thank you! I'm not having any! (*f*) **p. des habitudes,** to acquire habits; **p. froid,** to catch cold; **p. feu,** to catch fire; **p. goût à qch.,** to acquire a taste for sth.; **p. racine,** to take root; **p. congé de qn,** to leave s.o.; to say goodbye to s.o.; (*g*) to take on, assume; **p. un air de fête,** to take on a festive appearance; **les arbres prennent une couleur d'automne,** the trees are taking on autumn tints; **p. un ton sévère,** to put on a severe manner; to speak in a severe tone; **il a essayé de p. un ton dégagé,** he tried to put on an airy manner; **p. un air innocent,** to put on an innocent air; **p. l'accent du midi,** to acquire a southern accent; **p. du poids,** to put on weight; (*of animal*) **p. chair,** to put on flesh; **nom qui prend un "s" au pluriel,** noun that takes an "s" in the plural; (*h*) **p. de l'âge,** to be getting on in years; *Turf:* **cheval prenant quatre ans,** horse rising four (years); (*i*) *Med:* **p. du sang,** to draw off blood. **4. p. le train, le bateau, l'avion,** to take the train, the boat, the plane; to go by boat, by plane, by air; **prenez une chaise,** take a chair; sit down; **p. le chemin de, pour, Paris,** to take the road to Paris; **p. à travers champs,** to strike across the fields; *Aut:* **p. un virage,** to take a corner; to round a corner; *abs.* **p. à gauche,** bear (to the) left, take the turning on the left, fork left; *Nau:* **p. le large,** to take to the open sea; **le cheval prit le trot, le gallop,** the horse broke into a trot, into a gallop; **parchemin qui ne prend pas l'encre,** parchment that will not take the ink; *F: Tp: abs.* **on vous demande au téléphone; prenez dans le salon,** you're wanted on the telephone; take the call in the drawing-room.

II. **prendre,** *v.i.* 1. (*a*) (*of mortar*) to set; (*of jelly, etc.*) to set, to congeal, to coagulate; (*of mayonnaise*) to take; (*of milk*) to curdle; **le ciment, la gelée, n'a pas pris,** the cement, jelly, has not set; (*b*) to freeze; **la rivière a pris, est prise,** the river has, is, frozen over; (*c*) (*of pump, etc.*) to get choked, fouled up; (*of engine, etc.*) to seize, to jam; (*d*) *Cu:* to catch (in the pan); **le lait, le bœuf, a pris,** the milk, the beef, has caught. 2. **arbres qui n'ont pas pris,** trees that did not take root, did not strike; **le feu a pris,** the fire has taken, has caught; **allumettes qui prennent mal, qui ne prennent pas,** matches that won't strike; **le vaccin a pris,** the vaccine has taken (effect); **cette mode a pris, prendra,** this fashion has caught on, will catch on; **la pièce a pris,** the play has caught on, is a hit; *F:* **ce truc-là prend toujours,** that trick is always successful; **cela ne prend pas!** that won't do! it's no go! it won't wash! **ça ne prend pas avec moi,** you can't put that over on me. 3. **rue qui prend au numéro 21 de la grand-rue,** street that turns off at No. 21 in the high street.

se prendre. 1. (*a*) to catch, to be caught; **son manteau se prit dans la porte, à un clou,** her coat (got) caught in the door, on a nail; (*b*) (*of jelly, milk, etc.*) to congeal; to coagulate; to curdle; (*c*) **se p. d'amitié pour qn,** to take a liking to, for s.o., form a friendship with s.o.; **ils se sont pris d'amitié,** they have struck up a friendship. 2. **se p. à pleurer, à rire,** to begin to weep, to laugh; **se p. à songer à . . .,** to start thinking about . . .. 3. **s'en p. à qn,** to attack, blame, s.o.; to cast, lay, the blame on s.o.; to lay the blame at s.o.'s door; *F:* to go for s.o.; **s'en p. inopinément à qn,** to round on s.o.; **ne t'en prends qu'à toi-même,** you have only yourself to blame, you have nobody to thank but yourself. 4. **s'y p.: il sait comment s'y p.,** he knows how to go about it, how to set about it, how to manage it; **je sais comment m'y p. avec lui,** I know how to deal with him; **comment vous y prenez-vous pour ne jamais vous salir?** how do you manage never to get dirty? **vous vous y prenez mal,** you're going the wrong way to work; you're setting about it the wrong way; **s'y p. maladroitement,** to bungle; **il s'y est pris maladroitement,** he made a bungle, a mess, of it; **il s'y prend bien,** he sets, goes, about it in the right way; he does extremely well; **il ne s'y est pas mal pris,** he has managed it pretty, quite, well; **s'y p. à deux fois,** to make two attempts (before succeeding); **pourquoi s'y p. à deux fois?** why have two goes at it? **j'ai dû m'y p. à trois fois,** I was obliged to have three shots at it.

III. **prendre,** *s.m. A:* (*used in the phr.*) **en venir au fait et au p.,** to come to the point.

prénégociation [prenegɔsjasjɔ̃], *s.f.* (*usu. in pl.*) *Pol:* preliminary negotiation.

Préneste [prenɛst], *Pr.n. A.Geog:* Praeneste.

preneur, -euse [prənœːr, -øːz]. 1. *s.* (*a*) taker; **p. d'absinthe,** absinthe drinker; **p. de tabac,** snuff taker; (*b*) captor; **p. de rats,** ratcatcher; *Adm:* rodent exterminator; *W.Tel:* **p. de son,** sound engineer; (*c*) *Com: Fin:* bargainer; buyer, purchaser; payee (of cheque); **p. d'une lettre de change,** purchaser, taker, of a bill; **avoir (trouvé) p. pour qch.,** to have found a purchaser for sth.; **je suis p.,** I'll take it; **si ce n'est pas trop cher je suis p.,** if it isn't too expensive I'm interested; *F:* **une fille qui n'a pas trouvé p.,** a girl who's been left on the shelf; (*d*) *Jur:* lessee, leaseholder; (*e*) *Turf:* **les preneurs,** the takers of odds. 2. *a.* (*a*) buying, purchasing; (*b*) *Min: etc:* **benne preneuse,** clam-shell bucket.

prénom [prenɔ̃], *s.m.* (*a*) Christian name; first name, *U.S:* given name; **j'ai le p. de Charles,** my Christian name is Charles; (*b*) *Rom.Ant:* praenomen.

prénommé [prenɔme], *a.* (*a*) called, named; (*b*) *Jur:* above-named, fore-mentioned.

prénommer [prenɔme], *v.tr.* to give (a child) a (Christian) name; **il se prénomme Jean,** his Christian, given, name is John.

prénotion [prenɔsjɔ̃], *s.f.* prenotion.

prénuptial, -aux [prenypsjal, -o], *a.* antenuptial, prenuptial; *Med:* **examen p.,** premarital examination.

préoccupant [preɔkypɑ̃]. 1. *a.* (*a*) preoccupying (idea, etc.); (*b*) worrying. 2. *s.m.* previous occupant (of house, etc.).

préoccupation [preɔkypasjɔ̃], *s.f.* 1. *A:* prejudice, prepossession; **exempt de p.,** free from bias. 2. preoccupation, abstractedness; absence of mind; **être dans la p.,** to be preoccupied. 3. preoccupation (de, with); (*a*) **sa p. d'élégance,** her concern for elegance; **ma seule p. a été d'assurer . . .,** my only care, concern, has been to ensure . . .; **être, devenir, la p. de qn,** to engross s.o.'s attention, s.o.'s thoughts; (*b*) anxiety; **s'élever au-dessus des préoccupations matérielles,** to rise above material cares, above material considerations. 4. preoccupation, preoccupancy; occupation (of house, etc.) at an earlier date.

préoccupé [preɔkype], *a.* 1. preoccupied, taken up (de, with); **il est p. de perfectionner la machine,** his mind is set on, he is taken up with, perfecting the machine. 2. **être p.,** to be preoccupied, absentminded; **répondre d'un ton p.,** to answer (i) absentmindedly, (ii) in a worried tone of voice.

préoccuper [preɔkype], *v.tr.* 1. *A:* to prejudice, bias (s.o., s.o.'s mind); to prepossess. 2. to preoccupy, engross (s.o., s.o.'s mind); **son devoir le préoccupe toujours,** he is always preoccupied with his duty; **le problème qui nous préoccupe,** the problem which is exercising our minds; **elle a quelque chose qui la préoccupe,** she has something on her mind, is preoccupied; **sa santé me préoccupe,** I am anxious about his health.

se préoccuper de qch., de faire qch., to give one's attention, to attend, see, to sth.; to be engaged in doing sth.; **je me préoccupe peu que les élections se fassent cette année ou plus tard,** it doesn't matter to me whether the elections are held this year or later; **on se préoccupe de la disparition de X,** we are, people are, worried about the disappearance of X; **il ne se préoccupe pas (de savoir) si je suis vivant ou mort,** he doesn't care whether I am dead or alive.

préolympique [preɔlɛ̃pik], *a. Sp:* **entraînement p.,** Olympic training, training for the Olympic games.

préopératoire [preɔperatwaːr], *a.* preoperative.

préoperculaire [preɔpɛrkylɛːr], *s.m. Ich:* preopercular.

préopercule [preɔpɛrkyl], *s.m. Ich:* preopercle, preoperculum.

préopinant, -ante [preɔpinɑ̃, -ɑ̃ːt], *s.* previous speaker; *Pol:* **l'honorable p.,** the honourable gentleman who has just spoken.

préopiner [preɔpine], *v.i.* to speak, to vote, first.

préoral, -aux [preɔral, -o], *a. Z:* preoral.

préordination [preɔrdinasjɔ̃], *s.f.* preordination.

préordonné [preɔrdɔne], *a.* preordained; predetermined.

préordonner [preɔrdɔne], *v.tr.* to preordain; to predetermine.

prépalatal, -ale, -aux [prepalatal, -o], *a.* & *s.f. Ling:* antepalatal, prepalatal (consonant).

préparateur, -trice [preparatœːr, -tris], *s.* 1. preparer, mixer, maker (of a substance, drug, etc.); dresser (of lithographic stone, etc.); **p. en pharmacie,** assistant to a dispensing chemist. 2. *Sch:* assistant (in laboratory, etc.); demonstrator. 3. *O: Sch:* tutor; coach. 4. **les préparateurs d'une révolution,** those who brought about, paved the way for, a revolution.

préparatifs [preparatif], *s.m.pl.* preparations; **p. de guerre, de départ,** preparations for war, for departure; **faire ses p. de départ,** to prepare for departure; **faire les p. d'un repas,** to make preparations for a meal; **p. pour la réception de qn, pour recevoir qn,** preparations for the reception of s.o., for receiving s.o.; *in sg.* **sans aucun préparatif,** without any preparation.

préparation [preparasjɔ̃], *s.f.* 1. (*a*) preparation, preparing; **p. à la guerre,** preparing for war; **p. mécanique du charbon,** coal dressing; *Mus:* **p. d'une dissonance,** preparation of a discord; **parler sans p.,** to speak extempore; **annoncer une nouvelle sans p.,** to blurt out a piece of news; **les échantillons sont en p.,** the samples are in preparation, are being prepared; (*b*) *Ind:* dressing (of a raw material, of wool, etc.); (*c*) *Sch:* (*work done as preliminary to passage to be translated in class, etc.*) preparation; **classe de p. aux grandes écoles,** form preparing pupils for entrance examination to one of the *grandes écoles.* 2. (*a*) *Pharm: etc:* preparation; **p. anatomique,** anatomical preparation, specimen; **p. de démonstration,** demonstration object; (*b*) *Com: Cu:* **p. pour gâteau,** cake mix.

préparationnaire [preparasjɔnɛːr], *s.m.* & *f. Sch:* student preparing for the entrance examination to one of the *grandes écoles.*

préparatoire [preparatwaːr], *a.* preparatory; **démarches préparatoires,** initiatory, preparatory, preliminary, steps; *Sch:* **cours p.** = infants' class; **classe p.,** form preparing pupils for the entrance examination to one of the *grandes écoles*; *For:* **coupe p.,** advance cutting; (*computers*) **analyse p.,** preanalysis.

préparer [prepare], *v.tr.* 1. (*a*) to prepare; to make ready, get ready (meal, speech, lesson, etc.); to take the preliminary steps for (the establishment of sth., etc.); **p. un traité,** to arrange a treaty; **p. un devis,** to get out an estimate; *Mus:* **p. une dissonance,** to prepare a discord; **p. du thé, du punch,** to brew tea, punch; **elle avait préparé un bon déjeuner pour les enfants,** she had prepared a good lunch, got a good lunch ready, for the children; **p. un lit pour qn,** to make up a bed for s.o.; **les vêtements étaient préparés sur le lit,** the clothes were laid out, put out, on the bed; (*b*) *Ind:* to dress (raw material, wool, cotton, etc.); **machine à p. le coton,** cotton-dressing machine. 2. **p. qn à qch.,** (i) to prepare, (ii) to fit, train, s.o. for sth.; **p. un élève à un examen,** to prepare, coach, a pupil for an examination; **préparé aux fonctions publiques,** trained for public office; **p. qn à une nouvelle,** to prepare s.o. for a piece of news. 3. **p. un examen,** to prepare for an examination; to read for an examination.

se préparer. 1. **de grands événements se préparent,** great events are about to take place; **un orage se prépare,** a storm is brewing; *impers.* **il se prépare quelque chose,** there's something in the wind, in the air; there's something afoot. 2. **se p. à un examen, à répondre,** to prepare for an examination; to get ready to reply; **se p. à, pour, un voyage,** to get ready for a journey; to make preparations for a journey; **se p. à partir,** to get ready to leave; *Mil: Navy:* **se p. au combat, à combattre,** to prepare for action; **se p. à faire qch.,** to prepare, take steps, to do sth.

préperceptif, -ive [prepɛrsɛptif, -iːv], *a. Psy:* preperceptive.

préperforé [preperfɔre], *a.* prepunched (card).

prépondérance [prepɔ̃derɑ̃ːs], *s.f.* preponderence (sur, over).

prépondérant [prepɔ̃derɑ̃], *a.* preponderant, preponderating; **voix prépondérante,** casting vote; **jouer un rôle p.,** to play a leading part.

préposé, -ée [prepoze], *s.* 1. *Adm:* official (*esp.* in a minor capacity); traffic warden; **p. (des postes),** postman; **p. des douanes,** customs officer; *Rail:* **p. à la distribution des billets,** booking clerk; *Jur:* **p. à la caisse de dépôts et de consignation,** official receiver; *F: Hum: O:* **p. au cordon,** porter (of block of flats). 2. *Jur:* **commettant et p.,** principal and agent; **préposés,** agents and servants.

préposer [prepoze], *v.tr.* **p. qn à une fonction,** to appoint s.o. to an office; to put s.o. in charge of a job; **p. qn comme, pour, chef de service,** to appoint s.o. (as) departmental head; **je vous prépose à la confection du dessert,** you can be in charge of preparing the dessert.

prépositif, -ive [prepozitif, -iːv], *a. Gram:* 1. prepositive (word, particle, etc.). 2. **locution prépositive,** prepositional phrase.

préposition [prepozisjɔ̃], *s.f. Gram:* preposition.

prépositionnel, -elle [prepozisjɔnɛl], *a. Gram:* prepositional.

prépositivement [prepozitivmɑ̃], *adv. Gram:* prepositionally; (employed) as a preposition.

prépotence [prepɔtɑ̃ːs], *s.f.* 1. prepotence, prepotency; dominance. 2. *Biol:* prepotency.

prépubertaire [prepybɛrtɛːr], *a. Physiol:* prepubertal, prepuberal, prepubescent.

prépuberté [prepybɛrte], *s.f. Physiol:* prepuberty.

prépuce [prepys], *s.m. Anat:* prepuce, foreskin.

préputial, -aux [prepysjal, -o], *a. Anat:* preputial.

préraphaélisme [prerafaelism], *s.m. Art: etc:* Pre-Raphaelism.

préraphaélite [prerafaelit], *a.* & *s.m. Art: etc:* Pre-Raphaelite.

prérasage [prerazaːʒ], *s.m.* **lotion de p.,** before-shave, pre-shave, lotion.

préreconnaissance [prerəkɔnɛsɑ̃ːs], *s.f.* preliminary exploration (for oil, etc.).

préréfrigération [prerefriʒerasjɔ̃], *s.f. Ind:* precooling.

préréfrigérer [prerefriʒere], *v.tr. Ind:* to pre-cool.

préréglage [prereglaːʒ], *s.m. El: Elcs:* presetting.

préréglé [preregle], *a. El: Elcs:* preset.

prérégler [preregle], *v.tr. El: Elcs:* (*conj. like* RÉGLER) to preset.

prérogative [prerɔgatiːv], *s.f.* 1. prerogative; **la p. royale,** the royal prerogative. 2. **p. parlementaire,** parliamentary privilege.

préromain [prerɔmɛ̃], *a. Hist:* pre-Roman.

préroman [prerɔmɑ̃], *a. Arch: etc:* pre-romanesque.

préromantique [prerɔmɑ̃tik], *a. Lit: etc:* pre-romantic.

préromantisme [prerɔmɑ̃tism], *s.m. Lit: etc:* pre-romanticism; the pre-romantic period.

près [prɛ]. **1.** *adv.* near; **il habite tout p.,** he lives close by, quite near, near at hand, close at hand; **plus p.,** nearer; *Artil:* (*in range finding*) **plus p. 300!** down 300 (metres)! **2.** *adv.phr.* (*a*) **à . . . p:** **à cela p. nous sommes d'accord,** except on that point, with that one exception, we are agreed, are in agreement; **à ce détail p.,** except for this detail; **à cela p. que, à cette différence p. que,** except that; **à peu d'exceptions p.,** with (a) few exceptions; **ce théodolite nous donne les mesures à cinq centimètres p.,** this theodolite is accurate to within five centimetres; **il devinerait votre poids à un milligramme p.,** he would guess your weight to the nearest milligramme; **j'ai été payé à un sou p.,** I was paid to the last halfpenny; **je ne suis pas à un sacrifice p.,** I am ready to make a sacrifice; **nous n'en sommes pas à un ou deux jours p.,** a day or two more or less doesn't matter; **je ne suis pas à cela p.,** I haven't come to that yet; *F:* **je l'ai raté à deux minutes p.,** I missed him by two minutes; (*b*) **à peu de chose(s) p.;** **un chef-d'œuvre à peu de chose p.,** little short of a masterpiece; **il y en a mille à peu de choses p.,** there are a thousand of them, as near as makes no difference; (*c*) **à peu p.,** nearly, about, approximately; **le travail est à peu p. achevé,** the work is almost, about, completed; **à peu p. satisfait,** fairly satisfied; **à peu p. cent personnes,** about a hundred people; *Lit:* **il lui tint à peu p. ce langage,** he spoke to him more or less in the following terms; he spoke to him something like this; **à peu p. la même chose,** very much, pretty much, the same (thing); **il va à peu p. de même,** he is much about the same; **à peu p. exact,** about right; **il était à peu p. certain que . . .,** it was fairly, tolerably, certain that . . ., it was all but certain that . . .; (*d*) **à beaucoup p.: le mieux équipé à beaucoup p.,** by far the best equipped; **ce n'est pas à beaucoup p. la somme qu'il me faut,** that's nothing like, nowhere near, the sum I require; **il n'est pas à beaucoup p. aussi grand que vous,** he is not as tall as you by a long way, *F:* by a long chalk; he is not nearly so tall as you; (*e*) **au plus p.,** to the nearest point; *Nau:* **courir au plus p.,** to sail on a wind, close to the wind, on a bowline; **courir au plus p. serré,** to sail close-hauled; (*f*) **de p.,** close, near, from close to; **il a vu la mort de p.,** he has looked death in the face; **tirer de p.,** to fire at close range; **rasé de p.,** close-shaved; **examiner, surveiller, qch. de p.,** to examine, watch, sth. closely; **à y regarder de p.,** on close inspection; **suivre qn, qch., de p.,** to follow hard, close, on s.o., sth.; **examiner, regarder, qch. de plus p.,** to get a nearer view of sth., to look closer; **en y regardant de plus p., on s'aperçut que . . .,** on closer examination it was discovered that . . .; **il n'y regarde pas de si p.,** he is not so particular as all that; **quand je l'ai vu de p.,** when I saw him at close quarters. **3.** (*a*) *prep. phr.* **p. de qn, de qch.,** *Adm: Jur:* **p. qn, p. qch.,** near, close, to, s.o., sth.; **asseyez-vous p. de moi,** sit by me; **p. de l'endroit où j'étais assis,** near to where I was sitting; **p. de là,** nearby; **assis tout p. du feu,** sitting close to the fire; **situé p. (de) l'église,** situated near the church; **nous habitons p. de chez eux,** we live near (to) them; **ambassadeur p. le gouvernement français,** ambassador to the French government; **ma marraine m'écrivit de venir p. d'elle,** my godmother wrote to ask me to make a home with her; *Nau:* **naviguer p. de terre,** to sail along the land, to keep close inshore; **courir p. du vent,** to sail close to the wind; **il est p. de midi,** it is nearly, close on, twelve; **je me sentais p. de pleurer,** I could have wept; **être p. d'éclater en sanglots,** to be on the brink of tears; **elle a tout p. de vingt ans,** she is very nearly twenty; **il y a p. de dix ans,** nearly ten years ago; close on, not far short of, ten years ago; **p. de partir,** on the point of starting, about to start; **j'ai été p. de les attraper,** I nearly caught them; **nous ne sommes pas p. de le revoir,** it will be a long time before we see him again; we shan't see him again soon; **il est p. de sa fin,** he is nearing his end; **il n'est pas p. de recommencer,** he won't do it again in a hurry; **est-il p. d'avoir fini?** is he anywhere near finished? *A:* (= AUPRÈS DE) **p. de son frère il paraît beau,** alongside of his brother, compared with his brother, he looks handsome; (*b*) *adv.phr.* **être (très) p. de ses sous,** to be mean, tight-fisted; **être très p. de ses intérêts, suivre ses intérêts de très p.,** to keep a close watch on one's interests.

présage [preza:ʒ], *s.m.* presage, portent, foreboding; **mauvais p.,** bad omen; **oiseau de sinistre p.,** bird of ill omen.

présager [prezaʒe], *v.tr.* (**je présageai(s); n. présageons**) to presage. **1.** to (fore)bode, portend, betoken; **ils croient que les éclipses présagent le malheur,** they believe that eclipses portend evil; **l'horizon rouge le soir présage le vent,** a red sky in the evening is a sign of windy weather; **j'entendis un craquement qui ne présageait rien de bon,** I heard an ominous crack. **2.** to predict, to augur; **de tout cela je ne présage rien de bon,** I cannot think that any good will come out of that.

présalaire [presalɛ:r], *s.m.* = student's grant.

pré-salé [presale], *s.m.* (*a*) salt meadow; (*b*) salt-meadow sheep; (*c*) salt-meadow lamb, mutton; *pl. prés-salés.*

présanctifié [presɑ̃ktifje], *a. Ecc:* presanctified; **la Messe des présanctifiés,** the Mass of the Presanctified.

Presbourg [prɛzbu:r], *Pr.n. Geog:* Pressburg, Bratislava.

presbyacousie [prɛzbjakuzi], *s.f. Med:* presby(a)cusis.

presbyophrénie [prɛzbjɔfreni], *s.f. Med:* presbyophrenia.

presbyte [prɛzbit], (*a*) *a.* presbyopic, presbytic, long-sighted (person), (*b*) *s.m. & f.* presbyte, presbyope.

presbytéral, -aux [prɛzbiteral, -o], *a.* priestly, of a priest; **maison presbytérale,** presbytery.

presbytérat [prɛzbitera], *s.m. Ecc:* presbyterate, priesthood.

presbytère [prɛzbitɛ:r], *s.m. Ecc:* **1.** (*priest's residence*) presbytery. **2.** (*ecclesiastical assembly*) diocesan presbytery.

presbytérianisme [prɛzbiterjanism], *s.m. Ecc. Hist:* Presbyterianism.

presbytér(i)at [prɛzbiter(j)a], *s.m. Rel.H: Presbyterian Ch:* eldership.

presbytérien, -ienne [prɛzbiterjɛ̃, -jen], *a. & s.* Presbyterian.

presbytie [prɛzbisi], *s.f.*, **presbytisme** [prɛzbitism], *s.m.* presbyopia, presbytia, long-sightedness; **p. augmentante,** increasing presbyopia.

presbytique [prɛzbitik], *a.* presbyopic, presbytic.

prescience [presjɑ̃:s, prɛss-], *s.f.* prescience, foreknowledge (**de,** of).

prescient [presjɑ̃, prɛss-], *a.* prescient (**de,** of).

préscientifique [presjɑ̃tifik], *a.* prescientific.

prescripteur [prɛskriptœ:r], *s.m.* (*a*) *attrib.* **médecin p.,** prescribing doctor; (*b*) *Pol.Ec:* (*pers. or group*) dictator (of consumer choice).

prescriptibilité [prɛskriptibilite], *s.f. Jur:* prescriptibility.

prescriptible [prɛskriptibl], *a. Jur:* prescriptible.

prescription [prɛskripsjɔ̃], *s.f.* **1.** *Jur:* prescription; *Jur:* **p. extinctive,** extinctive prescription, negative prescription, time limitation; **p. acquisitive,** acquisitive prescription, positive prescription; **invoquer la p.,** to raise a defence under the statute of limitations; **il y a p.,** the time limit has passed. **2.** (*a*) *Med:* (i) direction(s) (for treatment); (ii) (*more usu.* ORDONNANCE) prescription; (*b*) regulation(s) (issued by technical institute, in works, etc.); **contraire aux prescriptions,** contrary to regulations; **prescriptions légales,** official instructions, official regulations; **prescriptions relatives à la sûreté,** safety regulations; (*c*) *pl. Ind:* specifications.

prescrire [prɛskri:r], *v.tr.* (*conj. like* ÉCRIRE) **1.** to prescribe, ordain, lay down (time, law, conduct, etc.); to stipulate for (quality, etc.); to prescribe (remedy) (**à,** to); **dans le délai prescrit,** within the prescribed, required, time; **à la date prescrite,** on the date fixed; **dans les limites prescrites,** within due limits; **charge prescrite,** specified load; **qualité prescrite,** stipulated quality. **2.** *Jur:* to prescribe; to render invalid by prescription; to bar by the statute of limitations; **chèque prescrit,** out-of-date cheque; **arrérages prescrits,** statute-barred interest.

se prescrire, *Jur:* to become void by prescription; to be statute-barred, to be barred by limitation; **ces dettes se prescrivent par cinq ans,** these debts are barred after five years have elapsed.

préséance [preseɑ̃:s], *s.f.* precedence (**sur,** of); priority (**sur,** to); **avoir la p. sur qn,** to take precedence of s.o.

préséchage [preseʃa:ʒ], *s.m. Ind:* preliminary drying.

présélecteur [preselɛktœ:r], *s.m. Tchn:* preselector.

présélection [preselɛksjɔ̃], *s.f.* **1.** *Tchn:* preselection. **2.** *Mil:* preliminary aptitude tests (for men called up for military service).

présélectionner [preselɛksjɔne], *v.tr. Tchn:* to preselect.

présence [prezɑ̃:s], *s.f.* **1.** (*a*) *A:* bearing; **homme de noble p.,** man of noble presence; (*b*) **avoir de la p.,** to have a forceful personality; **cet acteur manque de p.,** this actor has no personality, *F:* can't put it across. **2.** presence, attendance; **sa p. nous ranime,** his presence cheers us up; **le maire nous honorera de sa p.,** the mayor will honour us with his presence; **il ignore votre p.,** he doesn't know that you are here; **faire acte de p.,** to put in an appearance, *F:* to show up; *Sch:* **régularité de p.,** regular attendance; **registre de p.,** attendance register; *Ind:* **feuille de p.,** time sheet; **l'appel nominal constate deux cents présences,** the roll call establishes that two hundred were present; **en p.,** face to face, facing one another, in view of one another; **mettre les deux parties en p.,** to bring the two parties face to face; to bring the parties together; **en p. de la mort,** in the presence of death; in face of death, faced with death; **en p. de ces faits,** in view of these facts, faced with these facts, with these facts before one; **en p. de cette situation,** confronted with this situation; **louer qn en sa p.,** to praise s.o. to his face; **cela s'est fait en ma p.,** it was done in my presence; **cela s'est dit en ma p.,** it was said in my hearing; **il l'a dit en ma p.,** he said it in front of me, in my presence, while I was there; **je ne parlerai qu'en p. de mon avocat** = I refuse to say anything except in the presence of my lawyer; *Theol:* **p. réelle,** real presence; (*b*) **p. d'esprit,** presence of mind; **conserver sa p. d'esprit,** to keep one's presence of mind; to keep (all) one's wits about one.

présénile [presenil], *a. Psy:* presenile.

présensibilisé [presɑ̃sibilize], *a. Phot: etc:* presensitized.

présent[1] [prezɑ̃], *a.* present; (*a*) **les personnes présentes,** those present; **toute autre personne présente,** any other person present; **les présents exceptés,** present company excepted; **être p. à un spectacle,** to be present at a performance; (*in minutes of meeting*) **étaient présents . . .,** were present . . .; **les Africains sont de plus en plus présents à l'O.N.U.,** the Africans are more and more in evidence in the United Nations; **cela m'est toujours p. à l'esprit,** it is always present in my mind; I always keep it in mind; **il n'est pas p. à ce que je dis,** he is not attending to what I say; *Mil: etc:* **p.!** (here) sir!, present! yes (sir)! **p. au corps,** doing regimental duty; **la présente convention,** this convention; **la présente (lettre),** the present letter, this letter; *Jur:* **par la présente,** hereby, by these presents; **le conseil déclare par la présente que . . .,** the council hereby resolve that . . .; **savoir faisons par ces présentes que . . .,** know all men by these presents that . . .; *A:* **à tous ceux qui ces présentes verront, salut,** to all to whom these presents may come, greeting; **le temps p.,** *s.m.* **le présent,** the present (time); **pour le p.,** for the present, for the time being; **à présent,** (just) now; **jusqu'à p.,** up to the present; until now, as yet; **dès à p.,** (i) (even) now; (ii) from now on, henceforth; **quant à p.,** as for now; **à p. que . . .,** now that . . .; *Gram:* **verbe au p.,** verb in the present (tense); **le p. du subjonctif,** the present subjunctive; (*b*) **esprit p.,** alert mind, quick mind; ready wit.

présent[2], *s.m.* present, gift; *A:* **p. de noces,** wedding present; **faire un p. à qn,** to make s.o. a present; **faire p. de qch. à qn, donner qch. en p. à qn,** to make a present of sth.; to s.o.; to give sth. to s.o. for a present; to present s.o. with sth.

présentable [prezɑ̃tabl], *a. F:* presentable (person, clothing, etc.); **je ne suis pas p.,** I am not fit to be seen; I am hardly fit for company.

présentateur, -trice [prezɑ̃tatœ:r, -tris]. **1.** *s.* (*a*) presenter (of a bill, etc.); introducer, presenter (of a person); (*b*) *Ecc:* patron, presenter (of a living); (*c*) master of ceremonies, M.C.; *W.Tel: T.V:* announcer; **p. (de disques),** disc jockey. **2.** *a.* presenting.

présentation [prezɑ̃tasjɔ̃], *s.f.* **1.** (*a*) presentation (of bill, play, etc.); *Bank:* **p. à l'encaissement d'un chèque,** presentation of a cheque for clearance; *Com:* **payable à p.,** payable on demand, on presentation, at sight; (*b*) appearance, presentation, arrangement, layout; **livre de bonne p.,** well-produced book; **p. originale des tableaux dans un musée,** original presentation of the paintings in a gallery; **je n'aime pas la p. des marchandises chez mon épicier,** I don't like the way my grocer arranges, displays, his stock; *F:* (*of pers.*) **avoir une bonne p.,** to have a good appearance; to show oneself to advantage; **il n'a aucune p.,** he's nothing much to look at; he doesn't know how to make the best of himself; (c) presentation (of a theory, etc.); (d) *Obst:* presentation. 2. (a) (formal) introduction (**à qn**, to s.o.); presentation (at court); **lettre de p.**, letter of introduction; **faire les présentations**, to make the introductions; to introduce people; *Ecc:* **la P. de la Vierge**, (Feast of) the Presentation (of the Blessed Virgin Mary); **la P. de l'Enfant Jésus (au Temple)**, the Presentation of the Infant Jesus at the Temple; *Mil:* **p. du drapeau**, trooping the colour; (b) *Com:* **p. de collections**, fashion show, parade; **p. d'un nouveau roman**, launching of a new novel; (c) *Cin:* trailer, *U.S:* preview. 3. *Av:* approach; **p. trop courte**, undershoot; **p. trop longue**, overshoot; **faire une deuxième p.**, to come round again. 4. *Elcs:* display (of information on radar screen); **système de p. des données**, data display system.

présentement [prezɑ̃tmɑ̃], *adv. Dial: & A:* at present, now; **je viens de lui écrire p.**, I have just written to him this minute; **à louer p.**, to let with immediate possession

présenter [prezɑ̃te], *v.tr.* 1. to present, offer; (a) **p. qch. à qn**, to present s.o. with sth.; to present sth. to s.o.; **p. son bras à une dame**, to offer a lady one's arm; **p. sa main à qn**, to hold out one's hand to s.o.; **p. une excuse à qn**, to offer an apology to s.o.; **p. l'olivier**, to hold out the olive branch; **p. ses hommages à qn**, to pay one's respects to s.o.; **p. ses compliments à qn**, to present one's compliments to s.o.; **p. ses pièces d'identité**, to submit proofs of identity; **p. son passeport**, to produce, show, one's passport; *Com:* **p. une traite à l'acceptation**, to present a bill for acceptance; *Sch:* **p. le français (à un examen)**, to present, take, French (at an examination); *F:* **p. un examen**, to sit for an exam; (*of mannequin*) **p. une robe**, to model a dress; *Mil:* **p. les armes**, to present arms; **armes au présentez-armes** [prezɑ̃tearm], arms at the present [pri'zent]; **présentez armes!** present arms! *Nau:* **p. un mât**, to point up a mast; (b) **il me présenta tous les faits**, he put, laid before me, all the facts of the case; he stated all the facts; **p. des conclusions**, to bring up, submit, conclusions (at a meeting); **p. un argument**, to bring forward an argument; **présentez-lui la chose gentiment**, put it to him nicely; **p. une motion à l'assemblée**, to put a motion to the meeting; *Pol:* **p. un projet de loi**, to bring in, to introduce, a bill; to table a bill; **son travail est bien présenté**, his work is well set out; **affaire qui présente des difficultés**, matter that presents difficulties; **compte qui présente un solde créditeur de 50.000 francs**, account that shows a credit balance of 50,000 francs; **présenter des traits communs**, to exhibit, offer, similar features; **p. l'aspect de qch.**, to look like, be like, sth. 2. **p. qn à qn**, to present, introduce, s.o. to s.o.; **p. qn pour une décoration**, to put s.o. forward for a decoration; **p. qn comme candidat**, to present s.o., to put s.o. up, as a candidate; *Mil:* **p. une troupe** = to receive the reviewing officer. 3. *v.i.* **il présente bien**, he is a man of good appearances; **jeune homme présentant bien**, young man of good appearance.

se présenter. 1. to present itself; to arise, occur; **une occasion se présente (de faire qch.)**, an opportunity presents itself, offers, occurs (for doing sth.); **lorsqu'une difficulté se présente**, when a difficulty arises; **un beau spectacle se présenta à mes yeux**, a fine sight met my eyes; **un nouveau paysage se présenta à notre vue**, a new landscape opened up in front of us; **si le cas se présente**, if the case arises, occurs; **si une autre occasion se présente**, if another opportunity arises; **la question des loyers se présente de nouveau**, the rent question has come to the fore again; **attendre que quelque chose se présente**, to wait for something to turn up; **la chose se présente bien**, the matter looks promising; **l'affaire se présente sous un jour nouveau**, the matter appears in a new light. 2. to present oneself; *Mil: etc:* to report oneself; **se p. à, pour, un examen**, to present oneself for, go in for, go up for, an examination; **se p. chez qn**, to call on s.o.; **s'il se présente des malades**, if any patients turn up; **se p. à qn**, (i) to introduce oneself to s.o.; (ii) to appear before, report oneself to, s.o.; *Jur:* **se p. contre qn**, to appear against s.o.; **se p. au danger**, to expose oneself to danger; **se p. aux élections**, to stand (as a candidate) at the elections; **se p. comme candidat**, to offer oneself, to come forward, as a candidate; **il se présente bien**, he knows how to make a good impression on (being introduced to) people. 3. (a) *Obst:* to present; **l'enfant se présente mal**, the child presents badly; (b) *Av:* **se p. trop court sur la piste**, to undershoot; **se p. trop long**, to overshoot.

présenteur, -euse [prezɑ̃tœːr, -øːz], *s.* presenter; presentor.

présentoir [prezɑ̃twaːr], *s.m.* (a) (wooden) stand for vase, figure; (b) *Com:* display unit.

présérie [preseri], *s.f. Ind:* (a) pre-production; **avion de p.**, pre-production aircraft; (b) test series, pilot series; prototype series.

préservateur, -trice [prezɛrvatœːr, -tris], *a.* preserving, preservative (**de**, from); **la vaccine est préservatrice de la variole**, vaccine is a preventive against smallpox.

préservatif, -ive [prezɛrvatif, -iːv]. 1. *a. & s.m.* preservative; preventive (**contre**, of); protective; *Nau: etc:* **enduit p. (de carène, etc.)**, antifouling composition. 2. *s.m. Hyg:* **préservatif**, (contraceptive) sheath.

préservation [prezɛrvasjɔ̃], *s.f.* preservation, protection, safeguarding (of crops, etc.).

préserver [prezɛrve], *v.tr.* to preserve, to protect (**de**, from); **p. qn d'un danger**, to protect s.o. from a danger; **le ciel m'en préserve!** heaven forbid! **à préserver de l'humidité**, to be kept dry.

présidant [prezidɑ̃], *a.* presiding, in the chair.

préside [prezid], *s.m.* (*in Spanish-speaking countries*) fortified post; presidio; **désordre dans les présides marocains**, disorder in the Moroccan presidios.

présidence [prezidɑ̃ːs], *s.f.* 1. (a) presidency; **la p. de la République**, the Presidency of the Republic; (b) chairmanship; **être appelé à exercer la p. de . . ., être nommé à la p. de . . .**, to be appointed chairman of . . .; **p. de monsieur X**, Mr X in the chair; (c) board (of a company); **la Banque fait partie de la p. de la société**, the Bank has a representative, is represented, on the Board of the company. 2. president's house. 3. *Hist:* (Bombay, Madras) Presidency.

président, -ente [prezidɑ̃, -ɑ̃ːt], *s.* 1. (a) president (of legal tribunal, etc.); presiding judge; (b) **le P. de la Republique**, the President of the Republic; **la Présidente**, the President's wife. 2. (a) chairman (of a meeting, committee, etc.); **être élu p.**, to be voted into the chair; **Monsieur le p., Madame la présidente, permettez-moi de . . .**, Mr Chairman, Madam Chairman, allow me to . . .; (b) *Pol.Hist:* **le p. du Conseil** = the Prime Minister; NOTE: **M. le Président** *is used as a form of address to all past Présidents du Conseil*; (c) **p. du jury**, (i) *Jur:* foreman of the jury; (ii) *Sch:* chief examiner; (iii) (*for a competition*) chairman of the judging committee; (d) *Ind: Com:* **p. directeur général**, chairman and managing director.

présidentiel, -elle [prezidɑ̃sjɛl]. 1. *a.* presidential; **prendre possession du fauteuil p.**, (i) to assume the presidency (of a state); (ii) (*at a meeting*) to take the chair. 2. *s.f. pl.* **les présidentielles**, the presidential elections.

présider [prezide], *v.tr. & i.* (a) **p. un conseil**, to preside over a council; to be chairman of a council; **le conseil municipal est présidé par le maire**, the municipal council is presided over by the mayor; (b) to preside, to be in the chair, to take the chair; **p. (à) une réunion**, to preside at, over, a meeting; *abs.* **qui présidera ce soir?** who will be in the chair tonight? who will preside tonight? (c) **la justice doit p. à la politique**, justice should be the principal factor in determining policy; **p. aux destinées de . . .**, to preside over the destinies of . . .; **p. aux préparatifs du dîner**, to direct the preparations for dinner; **p. à l'ouverture du courrier**, to superintend the opening of the letters.

présidial, -aux [presidjal, -o], *a. & s.m. Fr.Hist:* presidial.

présidium [prezidjɔm], *s.m. Pol:* presidium, praesidium.

présignalisation [presiɲalizasjɔ̃], *s.f. Aut: Adm:* presignalling; **panneau de p.**, advance sign.

présignification [presiɲifikasjɔ̃], *s.f.* presignification.

presle [prɛːl], *s.f. Bot:* horsetail.

présomptif, -ive [prezɔ̃ptif, -iːv], *a.* presumptive; **héritier p.**, heir presumptive, *esp.* heir apparent.

présomption [prezɔ̃psjɔ̃], *s.f.* 1. presumption, presumptive evidence; *Ins:* **il y a p. de perte**, the ship is a presumptive loss; *Jur:* **p. de fait**, presumption of fact; **preuve par p.**, circumstantial evidence, presumptive evidence. 2. presumption, presumptuousness; **rabattre la p. de qn**, to make s.o. sing small, to put s.o. in his place.

présomptivement [prezɔ̃ptivmɑ̃], *adv.* presumptively.

présomptueusement [prezɔ̃ptɥøzmɑ̃], *adv.* presumptuously.

présomptueux, -euse [prezɔ̃ptɥø, -øːz], *a.* presumptuous, presuming; *F:* brash; *s.* **un jeune p.**, a presumptuous young man.

présphygmique [presfigmik], *a. Physiol:* presphygmic.

presque [prɛsk], *adv.* (*the final* **e** *is not usu. elided except in* **presqu'île**, *though modern usage is flexible*) 1. (a) almost, nearly; **ouvrage p. achevé**, work almost completed, all but completed; **c'est p. impossible**, it's almost, next to, impossible; **je les ai p. tous**, I have nearly all of them; **il est p. temps**, it's about time; **c'est p. de la folie**, it's only a little short of madness; **je l'admirais p.**, I almost admired him; (b) **il a donné un p. démenti à sa sœur**, he practically contradicted his sister; **j'en ai la p. certitude**, I am almost certain of it; **malgré la p. absence de femmes**, although there were hardly any women present; **la p. totalité des électeurs**, nearly the whole of the electors. 2. (*with negative*) scarcely, hardly; **p. jamais**, hardly ever, scarcely ever, almost never; **p. rien**, scarcely anything, next to nothing; **p. personne, personne ou p.**, hardly anyone, next to nobody; **elle n'a p. pas de voix**, she has no voice to speak of; she has hardly any voice; **ils étaient là p. sans exception**, they attended almost without exception.

presqu'île [prɛskil], *s.f. Geog:* peninsula (*usu.* with narrow isthmus); **la p. de Malacca**, the Malay Peninsula.

pressage [prɛsaːʒ], *s.m.* (a) *Dom.Ec: etc:* pressing; **p. à la vapeur**, steam pressing; (b) **p. des disques**, pressing, moulding, of (gramophone) records; (c) *Glassm:* pressing.

pressant [prɛsɑ̃], *a.* pressing, urgent (**need, request, danger, etc.**); **ouvrage écrit dans des circonstances pressantes**, work written under pressure; **en termes pressants**, in pressing terms, emphatically; **cas p.**, urgent case; emergency.

presse [prɛs], *s.f.* 1. press, pressing-machine; squeezer; (a) **p. hydraulique**, hydraulic press; **p. à emballer, à balles**, baler; **p. à forger**, forging press; **p. à cingler**, crocodile squeezer; **p. hydraulique à estamper**, drop-forging press; *Navy:* **p. de pointage en hauteur**, hydraulic elevating ram (of turret); **p. mécanique**, power press; **p. à main, à serrer**, clamp, hand screw; **p. à vis**, screw press; **p. à balancier**, fly press; **travailler du métal à la p.**, to stamp metal; **pièces découpées à la p.**, stamped-out pieces; **p. à frapper**, coining press; **p. à copier**, letter press, copying press; *Carp:* **p. à main**, screw-clamp; holdfast; **p. à raquette**, (tennis) racket press; (b) **p. à imprimer, d'imprimerie**, printing press; **p. à bras**, hand press; **p. à platine**, platen press; **p. rotative**, rotary press; **p. à double impression**, perfecting press; **p. à épreuves**, proof press; **p. lithographique**, lithographic press; **livre sous p.**, book in the press; **prêt à mettre sous p.**, ready for press; **nous mettons sous p.**, we are going to press; (c) *Bookb: etc:* **p. à rogner**, guillotine; plough. 2. press; newspapers; **la p. technique**, the technical press; **attaché de p.**, press attaché; **photographe de p.**, press photographer; **campagne de p.**, press campaign; **la liberté de la p.**, the liberty of the press; **avoir bonne, mauvaise, p.**, (i) to have a good, bad, press; (ii) to be in, out of, favour; to be in good, bad, odour; *Publ:* **service de p.**, publicity (department); **exemplaire de service de p.**, press copy, review copy. 3. (a) pressure, congestion (in a crowd, in traffic); press, crowd, throng; **la p. était à mourir**, we were nearly crushed to death; **fendre la p.**, to force one's way through the crowd; **il n'y a pas p. à ses allocutions, à l'écouter**, people don't exactly flock to hear him (speak); *A:* **la p. y est**, everyone is flocking to it; **se tirer de la p.**, to cut adrift from the rest (of the gang, etc.); (b) *A:* (i) impressment (of men to the navy); (ii) press-gang. 4. (a) haste, urgency; **il n'y a pas de p.**, there's no hurry; (b) **p. des affaires**, pressure of business; **moments de p.**, busy periods.

pressé [prese], *a.* 1. (a) compressed; *Tchn:* pressed; **citron p.**, (i) squeezed lemon; (ii) fresh lemon juice; **tas de papier bien p.**, pile of tightly compressed paper; *Metalw:* **p. à froid**, cold-pressed; **pièce pressée**, pressing; (b) *s.m. Glassm:* pressing; (c) crowded, close together; **pressés les uns contre les autres**, crowded together; **foule pressée**, tightly packed crowd; **en rangs pressés**, in serried ranks; (d) **coups pressés**, blows that follow in quick succession; **frapper qn à coups pressés**, to rain blows on s.o. 2. (a) **p. par la faim**, torn by the pangs of hunger; **p. d'argent**, pressed for money; (b) in a hurry; **je**

suis très p., I'm in a great hurry; I'm very pressed for time; **p. de partir,** in a hurry to go, to leave; **p. d'arriver,** in a hurry, impatient, to arrive; **avoir un air p.,** to look as though one is in a hurry; **il n'est pas p. de le vendre,** he's in no hurry to sell it; (*c*) urgent, pressing (work, etc.); **ce n'est pas p.,** it's not urgent, there's no hurry; *s.m.* **aller, courir, au plus p.,** to attend to the most urgent thing(s) first; **aussitôt qu'il eut touché son argent, il n'eut rien de plus p. que de le dépenser,** as soon as he had received his money he could hardly wait to spend it.

presse-artère [prɛsartɛːr], *s.m.inv. Surg:* artery forceps.

presse-bouton [prɛsbutɔ̃], *a.inv.* push-button; **la guerre p.-b.,** push-button war; push-button warfare.

presse-cartes [prɛskart], *s.m.inv.* (*computers*) card weight.

presse-citron [prɛssitrɔ̃], *s.m.inv.* lemon squeezer.

pressée [prese], *s.f.* **1.** pressing (of cider apples, etc.). **2.** cider-pressful (of apples, etc.). **3.** amount (of juice, etc.) expressed; pressings.

presse-étoffe [prɛsetɔf], *s.m.inv.* presser foot (of sewing machine).

presse-étoupe(s) [prɛsetup], *s.m.inv. Mch:* stuffing box, packing box (and gland); **garniture de p.-é.,** packing.

presse-fruits [prɛsfrɥi], *s.m.inv.* fruit squeezer; juice extractor.

presse-garniture [prɛsgarnityːr], *s.m.inv.* = PRESSE-ÉTOUPE(S).

presse-livres [prɛslivr̥], *s.m.inv.* book ends.

presselle [prɛsɛl], *s.f.* tweezers, spring nippers.

pressentiment [prɛsɑ̃timɑ̃, prɛ-], *s.m.* presentiment, forewarning; foreboding; misgiving; **j'ai comme un p. que . . .,** I have a feeling that . . .; **des pressentiments de goutte,** vague, ill-defined, twinges of gout.

pressentir [prɛsɑ̃tiːr, prɛ-], *v.tr.* (*conj. like* SENTIR) **1.** to have a presentiment of (sth.), to have a feeling that sth. is going to happen; **p. le danger,** to have a presentiment of danger; **faire, laisser, p. qch.,** to foreshadow, portend, sth.; **faire p. qch. à qn,** to give s.o. an inkling of sth.; **événement qui se fait p.,** event that casts its shadow before it; **on a laissé p. de nouvelles démarches,** a hint was given that new steps would be taken. **2. p. la pensée de qn,** to endeavour to ascertain s.o.'s thoughts; **p. qn (sur qch.),** (i) to sound s.o. (on sth.); (ii) to approach s.o. (about sth.).

presse-pantalon [prɛspɑ̃talɔ̃], *s.m.* trouser press, trouser stretcher; *pl. presse-pantalon(s).*

presse-papier(s) [prɛspapje], *s.m.inv.* **1.** paper weight. **2.** *Typewr:* paper clamps, fingers.

presse-purée [prɛspyre], *s.m.inv.* potato masher; vegetable press.

presser [prese], *v.tr.* **1.** to press, to squeeze (lemon, sponge, etc.); to press, mould (gramophone record); *Metalw:* **p. à froid,** to cold press; **p. du raisin, des pommes,** to press grapes, apples; **p. un vêtement,** to steam-press a garment; **p. qn entre, dans, ses bras, p. qn contre son cœur,** to clasp s.o. in one's arms; **p. les rangs,** to close up the ranks; *A:* **p. son style,** to compress one's style; **il m'entraînait en me pressant le bras,** he dragged me off clutching me by the arm; **p. un bouton,** to press, push, put one's finger on, a button, a switch. **2.** (*a*) **la faim le pressait,** he was overcome with hunger, he was overwhelmed by (severe) pangs of hunger; **pressé par ses créanciers,** hard pressed, dunned, by his creditors; **p. l'ennemi,** to press hard upon the enemy; **ville pressée de toutes parts,** town beset on all sides; **p. qn de questions,** to ply s.o. with questions, to question s.o. closely; **on le pressa de questions sur ce point,** he was pressed upon this point; (*b*) **p. qn de faire qch.,** to press, urge, s.o. to do sth.; **je savais qu'il me presserait enfin d'exécuter mon projet,** I knew that he would finally bring pressure to bear on me to make me carry out my plan. **3.** to hurry (s.o.) on; to accelerate, speed up (work, movement); **p. le pas,** to quicken one's pace, to walk more quickly; **p. la mesure,** (i) *Mus:* to quicken, accelerate, the tempo; (ii) to press the pace; to increase the speed; **p. un cheval,** to push on a horse; **il est inutile d'essayer de p. les ouvriers,** it's useless to try to make the workmen hurry (up); **rien ne me presse plus maintenant,** there's nothing urgent (to be done) now; **qu'est-ce qui vous presse?** why are you in such a hurry? what's your hurry? *abs.* **le temps presse,** time presses; **l'affaire presse,** the matter is urgent; **il n'y a rien qui presse; rien ne presse;** *F:* **ça ne presse pas,** there's no hurry.

se presser. 1. to press, crowd; **la foule se pressait autour de lui,** the mob pressed, crowded, round him; **ici les souvenirs se pressent dans ma mémoire,** here memories crowd in on me. **2.** to hurry, make haste; **se p. de faire qch.,** to make haste to do sth.; **pressez-vous!** hurry up! **répondre sans se p.,** to answer deliberately, leisurely; **ne vous pressez pas,** don't hurry; take your time; **se p. de monter, de descendre, de partir, de revenir,** to hurry up, down, away, back. **3.** to snuggle; **elle se pressa contre lui,** she snuggled (up) against him.

presse-raquette [prɛsrakɛt], *s.m.* racket press; *pl. presse-raquettes.*

pressé-soufflé [presesufle], *s.m. no pl. Glassm:* mould blowing.

presseur, -euse [prɛsœːr, -øːz], *s.* **1.** *Ind:* presser (of materials, etc.); pressman (of oil, wine, etc.); **p. à la presse hydraulique,** pressing-machine minder. **2.** *s.m.* presser bar, presser foot (of sewing machine).

presse-viande [prɛsvjɑ̃ːd], *s.m.inv.* juice extractor (for meat).

pressier [prɛsje], *s.m. Typ:* pressman.

pressing [prɛsiŋ], *s.m. Com:* (*a*) steam pressing; (*b*) *F:* (i) dry cleaner's; (ii) dry cleaning.

pressiographe [prɛsjɔgraf], *s.m. Tchn:* pressure recorder.

pressiomètre [prɛsjɔmɛtr̥], *s.m. Mec:* pressure gauge.

pression [prɛsjɔ̃], *s.f.* **1.** pressure; (*a*) **p. atmosphérique,** atmospheric pressure; *Meteor:* **haute, basse, p.,** high, low, pressure; *Med:* **p. artérielle,** arterial blood pressure; **p. veineuse,** venous blood pressure; **p. différentielle,** pulse pressure; *Bot:* **p. osmotique,** osmotic pressure; **p. en colonne d'eau,** hydraulic head; **p. de bas en haut,** upthrust (of fluid); **bière (à la) p.,** beer on draught; (*in café*) **un demi p.** = a half of draught (beer); *Ind:* **p. effective, de service,** working pressure; **commandé, mû, par simple p. du doigt,** with finger-tip control; *Aut: etc:* **contrôleur de p.,** pressure gauge (for tyres); *Mch:* **machine à haute, basse, p.,** high-pressure, low-pressure, engine; **faire monter la p., mettre (la chaudière) sous p.,** to get up steam; **sous toute p.,** at full pressure; **clapet d'excès de p.,** relief valve; **alimenté sous p.,** pressure-fed; *Mec:* **p. inverse,** back pressure; **graissage sous p.,** pressure greasing; (*aerodynamics*) **p. génératrice,** kinetic pressure; *Av:* **effet de p. extérieure,** ram(ming) effect; **cabine sous p.,** pressurized cabin (of aircraft, spacecraft); (*b*) *El:* tension; **sous p.,** under tension; (*c*) **vis de p.,** binding screw; (*d*) **exercer une p. sur qn,** to bring pressure to bear on s.o.; **faire p. sur qn,** (i) to influence s.o.; (ii) to threaten s.o., to intimidate s.o.; **groupe de p.,** pressure group; **p. démographique,** population pressure; *F:* (*of pers.*) **être sous p.,** to be pent up; **agir sous la p. des circonstances,** to act under the pressure of circumstances. **2. un bouton (à) p., un, une, p.,** a press stud, snap fastener, *F:* popper.

pressirostre [prɛs(s)irɔstr̥], *s.m. Orn:* plover snipe.

pressoir [prɛswaːr], *s.m.* (*a*) wine press; **p. à cidre,** cider press; **p. à huile,** (i) oil press; (ii) expeller; (*b*) press house, press room.

pressostat [prɛsɔsta], *s.m. Ind:* pressure controller.

Presspahn [prɛspɑn], *s.m. El.E:* Presspahn (*R.t.m.*).

pressurage [prɛsyraːʒ, pre-], *s.m.* **1.** (*a*) pressing (of grapes for wine); (*b*) extortion. **2.** (*a*) wine from the second pressing; pressurage; (*b*) fee paid for use of the press; pressurage.

pressurer [prɛsyre, pre-], *v.tr.* **1.** (*a*) to press (grapes for wine); (*b*) to press out (the juice). **2.** to squeeze, grind down, overtax, extort money from (s.o.); **impôts qui pressurent le peuple,** taxes that bear heavily on the people; *F:* **se p. le cerveau,** to rack one's brains.

pressureur, -euse [prɛsyrœːr, pre-, -øːz], *s.* **1.** *Winem: etc:* pressman, press-house hand. **2.** exploiter.

pressurisation [prɛsyrizasjɔ̃, pre-], *s.f.* pressurization.

pressuriser [prɛsyrize, pre-], *v.tr.* to pressurize; *Av: etc:* **cabine pressurisée,** pressurized cabin.

prestance [prɛstɑ̃ːs], *s.f.* fine presence, imposing appearance; **avoir une belle p.,** to have a fine presence.

prestant [prɛstɑ̃], *s.m. Mus:* diapason (stop) (of organ).

prestataire [prɛstatɛːr], *s.m.* **1.** *Hist:* person liable to statute labour. **2.** *Mil:* soldier (i) claiming, (ii) drawing, allowances; *Adm:* person receiving benefits, allowances.

prestation [prɛstasjɔ̃], *s.f.* **1.** prestation (of dues, tolls); furnishing, provision, lending, loan(ing) (of money); performance (of statute labour). **2.** *Jur:* **p. de serment,** taking of an oath, taking the oath; *Hist:* **p. de foi et hommage,** oath of fealty and act of homage. **3.** (*a*) *Mil:* **prestations (en nature, en deniers),** allowances (in kind, in money); *Adm:* **p. en nature,** service charge (paid by tenant to landlord); (*b*) war indemnity. **4.** *Ins:* benefit; *Adm:* allowance; benefit; **verser les prestations,** to pay out benefits; **prestations familiales** = family allowances, maternity benefits and rent allowance; **prestations sociales,** national insurance benefits. **5.** *Sp:* *F:* **fournir une belle p.,** to play well.

preste [prɛst], *a.* quick, sharp, nimble (in movement, action, speech, etc.); alert; prompt; *A:* **p!.** quick! sharp's the word! **être p. à la réplique,** to be smart at repartee; **avoir la main p.,** to be skilful with one's hands; to have a light touch; **maman avait la main p.,** mother was always quick to give me a slap.

prestement [prɛstəmɑ̃], *adv.* quickly; promptly.

prestesse [prɛstɛs], *s.f.* quickness (and agility); alertness.

prestidigitateur, -trice [prɛstidiʒitatœːr, -tris], *s.* conjurer; illusionist.

prestidigitation [prɛstidiʒitasjɔ̃], *s.f.* conjuring, legerdemain, sleight of hand; **tour de p.,** conjuring trick.

prestige [prɛstiːʒ], *s.m.* **1.** *A:* marvel; **qui tient du prestige,** marvellous (dexterity, etc.). **2.** *Lit:* glamour (of a name, of glory, etc.); **le p. de son éloquence,** the magic of his eloquence. **3.** prestige, high reputation; **médiocre et sans p.,** mediocre and undistinguished; **publicité de p.,** prestige advertising.

prestigieux, -euse [prɛstiʒjø, -øːz], *a.* (*a*) marvellous, wonderful, amazing; (*b*) **un nom p.,** a great name; (*c*) **la plus prestigieuse des écoles,** the school with the greatest prestige.

prestissimo [prɛstisimo], *adv.* & *s.m. Mus:* prestissimo.

presto [prɛsto], *adv.* & *s.m. Mus:* presto.

prestolet [prɛstɔlɛ], *s.m. F:* priestling.

pré-stop [prestɔp], *s.m. Aut:* "Halt sign ahead" sign; *pl. pré-stops.*

présuccession [presyksɛsjɔ̃], *s.f. Jur:* anticipated succession (to one's estate).

présumable [prezymabl̥], *a.* presumable (**de la part de qn,** of s.o.).

présumé [prezyme], *a.* supposed, presumed; **ses intentions présumées,** his supposed, hypothetical, intentions; **son fils p.,** his putative son; **innocent ou p. tel,** innocent or presumedly innocent.

présumer [prezyme], *v.tr.* to presume. **1. p. qn innocent, que qn est innocent,** to presume, assume, s.o. (to be) innocent; to presume that s.o. is innocent; **p. le bien de son prochain,** to presume, suppose, good of one's neighbour; **le coupable présumé, le présumé coupable,** the supposed culprit; **le voleur, l'assassin, présumé,** the alleged thief, murderer; **nouvelle que l'on présume être vraie,** news that is supposed, presumed, assumed, to be true; **il est à p., on présume, qu'il est mort,** the presumption is that he is dead; **sa conduite laisse p. la folie, donne lieu de p. la folie,** his conduct points to madness, suggests that he is mad. **2.** (*a*) **p. de faire qch.,** to presume to do sth.; **aussitôt qu'on présume en jouir,** whenever one thinks one will enjoy it; (*b*) **trop p. de soi,** to presume too much, to be too presuming, to show presumption; **trop p. de son savoir,** to presume too much on one's knowledge; **trop p. de ses forces,** to over-estimate, over-rate, one's strength.

présupposé [presypoze], (*a*) *a.* presupposed; (*b*) *s.m.* presupposition.

présupposer [presypoze], *v.tr.* to presuppose; to take (sth.) for granted; to imply; **cette profession présuppose de longues études,** this profession implies, calls for, long years of study.

présupposition [presypozisjɔ̃], *s.f.* presupposition.

présure [prezyːr], *s.f.* rennet; **p. microbienne,** cultured rennet.

présurer [prezyre], *v.tr.* **p. du lait,** to set, coagulate, curdle, milk (with rennet).

présystole [presistɔl], *s.f. Physiol:* presystole.

présystolique [presistɔlik], *a. Physiol:* presystolic.

prêt[1] [prɛ], *a.* **1.** ready; prepared; **le dîner est-il p.?** is dinner ready? **p. à l'emploi, p. à servir,** ready for use; **p. pour la guerre,** prepared for war; *Scouting:* **toujours p.,** be prepared; *Sp:* **à vos marques! prêts? partez!** on your marks! set! go! **il faut être p. dans un quart d'heure,** we, you, must be ready in a quarter of an hour;

tenez-vous p. pour onze heures, be ready for eleven, to leave at eleven; **être p. à tout,** (i) to be ready, game, for anything; (ii) to be prepared to do anything (to achieve one's purpose); **p. à,** *A:* **p. de, faire qch.,** ready, prepared, to do sth.; **p. à faire n'importe quoi,** ready to do anything; **p. à partir,** ready to start, leave, go; **être p. à commencer,** to be all set to begin; **vêtements prêts à porter,** *s.m.* **le p. à porter,** ready-made clothes. 2. *Lit:* **p. à,** *A:* **p. de,** + *inf.*, on the point of (doing sth.); **p. à mourir,** at the point of death.

prêt², *s.m.* 1. loan (of money, of a book, etc.); (*of book in library*) **exclu du p.,** not to be taken away; **cent francs de p.,** a loan of a hundred francs; **p. à terme,** loan at notice; **p. à court terme,** short loan; **p. à long terme,** long-term loan; **p. à découvert,** loan on overdraft; **p. à la petite semaine,** loan by the week, with payment of weekly interest; **p. d'honneur,** loan on trust; **caisse de prêts,** loan bank; **p. sur gage,** loan against security; **p. hypothécaire,** mortgage loan; **p. garanti,** secured loan; **p. sur titres,** advance on securities; **p. à intérêt,** loan at interest; **p. à usage,** commodatum; **prêts au jour le jour,** money at call, call money; **intérêt de p., sur p.,** interest on loan; **à titre de p.,** as a loan, on loan. 2. (*a*) *Mil:* official sum allocated for the subsistence and equipment of a soldier; **p. franc,** subsistence allowance; (*b*) advance (on pay, wages).

prêtable [prɛtabl̥], *a.* lendable, loanable.

prêtaillage [pretajaːʒ], *s.m. Const:* dressing (of building stone).

prêtailler [pretaje], *v.tr. Const:* to dress (building stone).

pretantaine [prətɑ̃tɛn], **prétantaine** [pretɑ̃tɛn], *s.f. used in the phr.* **courir la p.,** to be always gadding about, having a gay time.

prêt-à-porter [prɛtapɔrte], *s.m. coll.* ready-made clothing.

prêt-bail [prɛbaj], *s.m. no pl. Pol.Ec:* lease-lend, lend-lease; **loi de p.-b.,** lend-lease act; **p.-b. réciproque,** reverse lease-lend.

prêté [prete]. 1. *a.* lent, loaned. 2. *s.m.* **c'est un p. rendu, un p. pour un rendu,** it's tit for tat, he's (etc.) been paid back in his (etc.) own coin.

prétendant, -ante [pretɑ̃dɑ̃, -ɑ̃ːt], *s.* 1. **p. (à qch.),** applicant, candidate (for a situation, etc.); claimant (of an inheritance, etc.); pretender (to a throne). 2. *s.m.* suitor.

prétendre [pretɑ̃ːdr̥], *v.tr.* 1. to claim (sth.) as a right; to require (sth.); (*a*) *A: & Lit:* **p. un cinquième,** to lay claim to a fifth (share); **p. part à qch.,** to claim a share in sth.; **p. qn en mariage,** to seek s.o. in marriage; **que prétendez-vous de moi?** what do you require of me? (*b*) **je prétends être obéi,** I expect to be obeyed; **prétendez-vous me faire la loi?** do you think you have the right to dictate to me, to lay down the law to me? **p. avoir le droit de faire qch.,** to claim the right to do sth. 2. *A:* to mean, intend; **il prétendait partir le lendemain,** he intended, meant, to start the next day. 3. to maintain, assert; to claim; **je prétends que ce n'est pas vrai,** I maintain that it is not true; **on prétend que . . .,** people say that . . ., claim that . . .; it is said that . . .; **à ce qu'on prétend,** as it is said, asserted; as people claim; **à ce qu'il prétend,** according to him; **je ne prétends pas tout savoir,** I don't claim to know everything; **je ne prétends pas qu'il l'ait fait,** I don't say that he did it; **un meuble qu'on prétend d'époque,** a piece of furniture claimed, stated, to be a genuine antique; **ils prétendent être de nos amis,** they claim to be friends of ours; **je ne prétends pas qu'il le fera,** I don't guarantee that he will do it; **on le prétend fou,** they say he is mad; **il prétend être le fils d'un inventeur célèbre,** he claims to be the son of a famous inventor; **il se prétend de nos parents,** he claims to be a relation of ours. 4. *v.ind.tr.* **p. à qch.,** to lay claim to sth.; **p. à l'esprit,** to lay claim to wit; to consider oneself witty; **p. aux honneurs,** to aspire to honours; *Lit:* **p. à la main de qn,** to aspire to marry s.o.

prétendu¹, -ue [pretɑ̃dy]. 1. *a.* alleged; would-be; bogus; **p. crime, voleur,** alleged crime, thief; **un p. baron,** a self-styled, bogus, baron; **un p. rendez-vous d'affaires,** a bogus business meeting; **un rendez-vous p. d'affaires,** a so-called business meeting; **prétendus progrès,** so-called progress; **un p. bel esprit,** a would-be wit; **p. expert,** (i) self-styled, (ii) so-called, expert. 2. *A: & Dial:* (*a*) *s.* **mon p., ma prétendue,** my fiancé, fiancée, my future husband, wife; **les prétendus,** the engaged couple; (*b*) **mon p. gendre,** my prospective, future, son-in-law; my son-in-law to be.

prétendu², *a. Civ.E:* prestressed (concrete).

prétendument [pretɑ̃dymɑ̃], *adv.* (*a*) allegedly; (*b*) wrongly supposed.

prête-nom [prɛtnɔ̃], *s.m. usu. Pej:* person who lends his name (to enterprise, contract, etc.); figurehead, dummy, man of straw; *pl. prête-noms.*

pretentaine [prətɑ̃tɛn], **prétentaine** [pretɑ̃tɛn], *s.f.* = PRETANTAINE.

prétentiard, -arde [pretɑ̃sjaːr, -ard], *F:* 1. *a.* pretentious. 2. *s.* pretentious person.

prétentieusement [pretɑ̃sjøzmɑ̃], *adv.* pretentiously.

prétentieux, -euse [pretɑ̃sjø, -øːz]. 1. *a.* pretentious (person, manner, house, style). 2. *s.* pretentious person; **c'est un p.,** he's (very) pretentious; he considers himself a superior being.

prétention [pretɑ̃sjɔ̃], *s.f.* (*a*) pretension, claim (à, to); **renoncer à ses prétentions,** to renounce one's claims; **exposé détaillé des prétentions du demandeur,** detailed statement of claim; **avoir des prétentions à la sagesse,** to have some claim to wisdom; **elle n'affiche aucune p. à la beauté,** she makes no pretension to beauty; **elle a des prétentions justifiées à la beauté,** she can justifiably claim to be beautiful; **je n'ai pas la p. de remporter le prix,** I don't for a moment suppose I shall get the prize; **je n'ai pas la p. de vous être supérieur,** I don't pretend, claim, to be better than you are; (*b*) **homme à prétentions,** pretentious man; **homme sans prétention(s),** unassuming, unpretentious, man; **maison sans prétention(s),** unpretentious house; **écrire avec p.,** to write in a pretentious style; **avoir des prétentions artistiques,** to have artistic pretensions, *F:* to be arty; (*c*) (*in advertisement for a job*) **envoyer curriculum vitae et prétentions,** send curriculum vitae and state salary required.

prêter [prete], *v.tr.* 1. (*a*) to lend, *U.S:* to loan; **p. qch. à qn,** to lend sth. to s.o.; **il m'a prêté sa maison pour les vacances,** he lent me his house for the holidays; **p. de l'argent à un ami,** to lend a friend some money; **p. sur gage(s),** to lend against security; **p. à la petite semaine,** to make a short-term loan at a high rate of interest; *s.m.* **ami au p., ennemi au rendre,** good at borrowing but bad at giving back; (*b*) **p. son appui, son concours, à qn,** to give s.o. one's support, to back s.o. (up); **p. la main à qn,** to lend s.o. a hand, to help s.o.; **p. l'oreille,** to listen; to pay attention (to what s.o. is saying); **p. attention,** to pay attention; **p. serment,** to take an oath, to be sworn, to swear; **p. le flanc à l'ennemi,** to expose one's flank to the enemy; **p. son nom,** to allow one's name to be used; (*c*) **chose qui prête un prétexte à . . .,** sth. that serves as pretext for . . . . 2. to attribute; **prêter aux autres ses propres défauts,** to attribute one's own failings to others; **p. à qn tous les torts,** to lay the blame on s.o. else; **l'esprit qu'on lui prête,** the wit attributed to him; **on me prête des discours dont je suis innocent,** I am credited with speeches of which I am innocent; *A:* **on lui prête d'avoir opéré des miracles,** he is credited with having wrought miracles. 3. *abs.* (*a*) (*of gloves, cloth, etc.*) to stretch, to give; (*b*) **c'est un sujet qui prête,** the subject is full of possibilities. 4. *v.ind.tr.* **p. à qch.,** to give rise to sth.; **privilège qui prête aux abus,** privilege that lends itself to abuses, that gives rise to abuses, that opens the door to abuses; **son accent prêtait à rire,** his accent invited, gave rise to, laughter.

se prêter. 1. to lend oneself, to be a party (à, to); **il se prête tant qu'il peut,** he shows himself as tractable, as accommodating, as possible; **se p. à un accommodement,** to consent to, fall in with, an arrangement; **se p. à une fraude,** to countenance a fraud. 2. **se p. au plaisir,** to give oneself up to pleasure, to indulge in pleasure. 3. **se p. à qch.,** to lend itself to sth.; to be adapted, suited, to sth.; **sujet qui se prête à des développements variés,** subject that lends itself to a varied treatment; **cette terre ne se prête pas à la culture des céréales,** this land is not suitable for the cultivation of cereals; **si le temps s'y prête,** weather permitting.

préter- [pretɛr], *pref.* preter-.

prétérit [preterit], *s.m. Gram:* preterite (tense); **au p.,** in the preterite.

prétérition [preterisjɔ̃], *s.f.* 1. *Rh:* preterition, pretermission. 2. *Jur:* preterition (of heir by testator).

prétermission [pretɛrmisjɔ̃], *s.f. Rh:* pretermission, preterition.

préternaturel, -elle [pretɛrnatyrɛl], *a.* preternatural.

prétest [pretɛst], **prétesting** [pretɛstiŋ], *s.m. Com: etc:* pretest, pretesting.

prétester [pretɛste], *v.tr.* to pretest.

préteur [pretœːr], *s.m. Rom.Hist:* praetor.

prêteur, -euse [prɛtœːr, -øːz]. 1. *s.* lender (*esp.* of money); *Jur:* bailor; **p. sur gages,** (i) *Jur:* pledgee; (ii) pawnbroker. 2. *a.* ready, willing, to lend; **je ne suis pas p.,** I am not one to lend; I don't believe in lending.

prétexte¹ [pretɛkst], *s.m.* pretext, excuse, plea; **ce n'était qu'un p.,** it was only a pretext, a blind; **pour lui, tout était p. à discussions,** he treated everything as a pretext, an excuse, for argument; **le premier p. venu,** the first excuse to hand, the first excuse that comes into one's mind; **prendre, tirer, p. de qch. pour faire qch.,** to make a pretext of sth. for doing sth.; **prendre p. que . . .,** to pretend that . . .; **il n'y avait aucun p. à cela, à faire cela,** there was no excuse for that, for doing that; **sous p. de . . .,** on the pretext, on a plea, of . . .; **sous p. de me consulter,** on, under, the pretext, of consulting me; **il sortit sous p. de mettre une lettre à la poste,** he went out ostensibly to post a letter, on the pretext of posting a letter; **sous p. d'économie,** on the plea of economy; **sous aucun p.,** on no account, not on any account, under no circumstances; **saisir le p.,** to make the most of the opportunity.

prétexte², *a. & s.f. Rom.Ant:* (toga) praetexta.

prétexter [pretɛkste], *v.tr.* to give, allege, as a pretext, to pretext, to plead; **p. la fatigue,** to plead fatigue; **p. qch. pour faire qch.,** to make sth. an excuse for doing sth.

prêt-location [prɛlɔkasjɔ̃], *s.m. no pl. Pol.Ec:* lease-lend.

prétoire [pretwaːr], *s.m. Rom.Ant:* praetorium; *B:* judgment hall; *Jur:* (floor of the) court.

prétonique [pretɔnik], *a. Ling:* pretonic (accent).

prétorial, -aux [pretɔrjal, -o], *a. Rom.Ant:* praetorial.

prétorien, -ienne [pretɔrjɛ̃, -jɛn], *a. & s.m. Rom. Ant:* Praetorian.

prêtraille [prɛtrɑːj], *s.f. Pej: O:* the priests, the clergy.

prêtraillon [prɛtrɑjɔ̃], *s.m. Pej:* priestling.

prétraitement [pretrɛtmɑ̃], *s.m. Tchn:* pretreatment.

prêtre [prɛtr̥], *s.m.* 1. priest; **grand p.,** high priest; *Prov:* **il faut que le p. vive de l'autel,** the labourer is worthy of his hire. 2. *Ich: F:* atherine.

Prêtre-Jean [prɛtrəʒɑ̃], *Pr.n.m. Myth:* Prester John.

prêtre-ouvrier [prɛtruvrije], *s.m.* worker priest; *pl. prêtres-ouvriers.*

prêtresse [prɛtrɛs], *s.f.* priestess.

prêtrise [prɛtriːz, pre-], *s.f.* priesthood; **recevoir la prêtrise,** to take (holy) orders.

prêtrophobe [prɛtrɔfɔb], *a. & s.m. & f.* anti-clerical.

prétrot [pretro], *s.m. Orn: F:* redstart.

prétuberculeux, -euse [pretybɛrkylø, -øːz], *Med:* 1. *a.* pretubercular, pretuberculous. 2. *s.* pretuberculous patient.

préture [pretyːr], *s.f. Rom.Hist:* praetorship.

preuve [prœːv], *s.f.* 1. proof, evidence; (*a*) **donner les preuves de son amitié,** to give proofs, signs, tokens, of one's friendship; **p. évidente de culpabilité,** clear proof of guilt; **et la p. c'est que . . .,** and in proof of this . . .; **comme p. à l'appui . . .,** to support my case . . .; **en p.,** as a proof; **faire la p. de qch.,** to prove sth.; **faire la p. d'une multiplication,** to prove a multiplication; **faire la p. par neuf,** to cast out the nines; **faire p. d'intelligence et de courage,** to give proof of, evidence of, to show, display, intelligence and courage; **faire ses preuves,** to prove oneself; to show one's mettle; **cette méthode a fait ses preuves,** this method has stood the test of time, of experience; **fournir la p. contraire,** to produce proof to the contrary; **comme p., il nous a fait observer que . . .,** by way of proof, he mentioned that . . .; **s'il faut une p. à ces affirmations,** if proof is needed for these statements; **à p.,** witness; **le directeur est incapable, à p. le déficit de la maison,** the manager is incompetent, witness the firm's deficit; **à p. que . . .,** witness the fact that . . .; (*b*) *Jur:* **le soin, l'obligation, de faire la p. incombe à . . .,** the onus of proof, the burden of proof, lies with . . .; **commencement de (la) p.,** *prima facie* evidence; **p. directe,** direct evidence; **p. indirecte,** circumstantial evidence; **p. patente,** proof positive; **p. littérale,** documentary, evidence, evidence in writing; **preuves testimoniales,** (witnesses') evidence; **preuves intrinsèques, naturelles,** internal evidence; **preuves extrinsèques, artificielles,** external evidence. 2. test(ing) of the alcoholic strength (of wine, etc.).

preux [prø], *A: & Lit:* 1. *a.m.* gallant, valiant, stout, doughty; **p. chevalier,** gallant knight. 2. *s.m.* valiant knight; champion.

prévaloir [prevalwa:r], *v.i.* (*conj. like* VALOIR, *except in the pr.sub.* **je prévale, n. prévalions**) to prevail; to get the advantage; to have the upper hand; **p. sur, contre, qch., qn,** to prevail over, against, sth., s.o.; **faire p. son droit,** to make good one's, right; **faire p. son opinion,** to win acceptance for one's opinion; **qui prévaut encore,** which still obtains.

se prévaloir de qch. (*a*) to avail, oneself of sth.; to take advantage of sth.; **se p. d'un droit,** to exercise a right; (*b*) to presume on (one's birth, wealth).

prévaricateur, -trice [prevarikatœ:r, -tris], *Lit:* 1. *a.* unjust, dishonest (judge, etc.). 2. *s.* unjust judge; betrayer of his trust.

prévarication [prevarikasjɔ̃], *s.f. Lit:* abuse of trust, breach of trust; maladministration of justice.

prévariquer [prevarike], *v.i. Lit:* (*of judge, etc.*) to depart from justice; to betray one's trust.

prévélaire [prevele:r], *a. Ling:* prevelar.

prévenance [prev(ə)nɑ̃:s, pre-], *s.f.* 1. attention, kindness, consideration; **manquer de p.,** to be inconsiderate. 2. **avoir des prévenances pour qn,** to be attentive to s.o.; **combler qn de prévenances,** to shower attentions on s.o.

prévenant [prɛv(ə)nɑ̃, pre-], *a.* 1. kind, attentive, considerate, obliging (**envers,** to); **vous êtes toujours si p.,** you are always so thoughtful. 2. pleasing, prepossessing (manner, appearance). 3. *Theol:* prevenient (grace).

prévenir [prɛv(ə)ni:r, pre-], *v.tr.* (*conj. like* VENIR *but with aux.* AVOIR) 1. (*a*) to forestall, anticipate (s.o., s.o.'s desires, etc.); **p. un concurrent,** to forestall a competitor; *Ecc:* **que ta grâce nous prévienne et nous accompagne toujours,** that thy grace may always prevent and follow us; (*b*) **p. une maladie, un danger,** to prevent, ward off, stave off, an illness, a danger; **p. un malheur, un accident,** to avert an accident; *Prov:* **mieux vaut p. que guérir,** prevention is better than cure. 2. to predispose, to bias; **p. qn en faveur de qn,** to predispose s.o. in favour of s.o.; **p. qn contre qn,** to prejudice s.o. against s.o., to set s.o. against s.o.; *abs.* **son visage prévient en sa faveur,** he has a prepossessing face. 3. (*a*) to inform, apprise, forewarn; **p. qn de qch.,** to inform, advise, s.o. of sth., to give s.o. notice of sth.; **p. l'autorité,** to give notice to the authorities; **je vais le p. que vous êtes ici,** I will let him know that you are here; **on m'avait prévenu que la police était à mes trousses,** I had been warned that the police were after me; **vous auriez dû m'en p.,** you ought to have let me know; you ought to have told me of it beforehand; you ought to have warned me; **partir sans p. (personne),** to go off, leave, without warning (anybody); (*b*) *abs. Aut:* (i) to (give a) signal; (ii) to sound one's horn.

préventif, -ive [prevɑ̃tif, -i:v], *a.* 1. preventive (medicine, etc.); **défense préventive contre la maladie,** prevention of disease; **à titre p.,** as a preventive; **mesure imposée à titre p.,** preventive measure; **exercer un effet p.,** to act as a deterrent; *Cards:* **ouverture préventive,** pre-emptive bid; shut-out bid; *Adm:* **régime p.,** censorship of the press; *Mil:* **guerre préventive,** preventive war. 2. *Jur:* **détention préventive,** detention on suspicion, detention awaiting trial.

prévention [prevɑ̃sjɔ̃], *s.f.* 1. predisposition (**en faveur de,** in favour of); prejudice, bias (**contre,** against); **avoir de la p. contre qn,** to be prejudiced against s.o.; **observateur sans p.,** unprejudiced, unbias(s)ed, observer. 2. *Jur:* imprisonment on suspicion; **être en état de p.,** to be in custody, committed for trial, in confinement under remand; **mise en p.,** committal for trial; indictment (for minor offence); charge; **faire trois mois de p.,** to be kept three months in prison awaiting trial. 3. **p. contre la maladie,** prevention of disease; *Adm:* **la p. routière,** road safety (i) measures, (ii) squad; **p. contre la pollution,** pollution control.

préventionnaire [prevɑ̃sjɔnɛ:r], *s.m. & f. Jur:* person remanded in custody.

préventivement [prevɑ̃tivmɑ̃], *adv.* (*a*) *Jur:* **arrêter qn p.,** to arrest s.o. on suspicion; **détenu p.,** committed for trial; (*b*) *Med:* as a preventive.

préventorium [prevɑ̃tɔrjɔm], *s.m.* observation sanatorium, preventorium; *pl. préventoriums*; *occ. préventoria.*

prévenu, -ue [prɛv(ə)ny, pre-]. 1. *a.* prejudiced, predisposed, bias(s)ed (**contre,** against; **en faveur de,** in favour of); **non prévenu,** unprejudiced, unbias(s)ed. 2. *Jur:* (*a*) *a.* **p. de vol,** accused of, charged with, theft; (*b*) *s.* **le p., la prévenue,** the prisoner, the accused (of a DÉLIT); **p. administratif,** detainee (considered as a potential danger to a visiting statesman, etc.).

préverbe [preverb], *s.m. Gram:* verbal prefix.

pré-verger [prevɛrʒe], *s.m.* meadow planted with fruit trees; *pl. prés-vergers.*

prévertébral, -aux [prevɛrtebral, -o], *a. Anat:* prevertebral.

prévisibilité [previzibilite], *s.f.* foreseeability.

prévisible [previsibl], *a.* foreseeable; that can be, could have been, foreseen.

prévision [previzjɔ̃], *s.f.* (*a*) anticipation, expectation; **en p. de qch.,** in the expectation, in anticipation, of sth.; **selon toute p.,** in all likelihood; **contre toute p.,** contrary to all expectations; **si mes prévisions sont exactes,** if my expectations are fulfilled; **au-delà des prévisions,** beyond all expectation, in excess of what was foreseen; **dépasser les prévisions,** to surpass anticipation, to exceed all expectation; **prévisions dépassées par les événements,** forecast overtaken by events; (*b*) *Meteor:* **p. (météorologique),** (weather) forecast; **p. journalière,** daily forecast; **p. à longue échéance,** long-range forecast; **p. sur période prolongée,** extended forecast; **p. sur période courte,** short-range forecast; **p. en altitude,** upper-air forecast; **p. en surface,** surface forecast; **Bureau des Prévisions Météorologiques,** Weather Forecast Bureau; (*c*) *Fin:* provision, reserve; **p. pour créances douteuses,** reserve for bad, doubtful, debts; **p. pour moins-value,** provision for depreciation; **prévisions pour fluctuations du change,** allowance, provision, for exchange fluctuations; **prévisions budgétaires,** budget estimates.

prévisionnel, -elle [previzjɔnɛl], *a.* estimated.

prévisionniste [previzjɔnist], *s.m. Pol.Ec:* forecaster.

prévocalique [prevɔkalik], *a. Ling:* prevocalic.

prévoir [prevwa:r], *v.tr.* (*conj. like* VOIR *except in fu. and condit.*, **je prévoirai, je prévoirais**) 1. to foresee, forecast, anticipate (events, etc.); *abs.* to foretell the future; **on prévoyait que . . .,** it was foreseen, anticipated, that . . .; **il était facile de p. que les pourparlers ne mèneraient à rien,** it was easy to see that the talks would break down, would come to nothing; **p. toutes les réponses,** to foresee, anticipate, all the answers; *abs.* **gouverner c'est p.,** to govern is to see ahead; **tout laisse prévoir . . .,** all signs point to . . .; **rien ne fait p. un changement de temps,** there appears to be no prospect of a change in the weather; *A:* **p. de pouvoir faire qch.,** to foresee the possibility of doing sth. 2. to take measures beforehand; to provide for (sth.); **dépenses prévues au budget,** expenses provided for in the budget; **dépenses à p.,** expenses involved; expenses to allow for; **chiffre prévu pour les dépenses,** estimate of expenditure; **la loi n'a pas prévu un cas semblable,** the law makes no provision for a case of this kind; **article qui prévoit un cas,** clause under which a case is dealt with; **ceci a été prévu dans le projet,** this has been catered for, provided for, in the plan; **l'installation de cet ordinateur est prévue pour l'année prochaine,** this computer is scheduled, is due, for installation next year; **la réunion est prévue pour demain,** the meeting is arranged for, will be held, tomorrow; **le gouvernement a prévu la construction de 100.000 maisons,** the government has provided for, planned for, the construction of 100,000 houses; **le début de la construction est prévu pour bientôt,** the construction work is planned, scheduled, *U.S:* slated, to start soon; **le personnel prévu dans le contrat,** the personnel laid down in the agreement; **on ne peut pas tout p.,** one cannot provide for, arrange for, everything; **p. des rectifications,** to allow for readjustments; **l'heure prévue pour le départ,** the (i) advertised, (ii) planned, time of departure; **il prévoit une visite au Brésil,** he is planning to visit Brazil; *abs.* **p. pour le pire,** to plan for the worst, with the worst in mind; **comme prévu,** as was planned, foreseen; *F:* **nous arriverons demain comme prévu,** we shall arrive tomorrow as planned.

prévôt [prevo], *s.m.* 1. (*a*) *Jur:* provost (judge of a *cour prévôtale*); (*b*) *Mil:* assistant provost marshal; **grand p.,** provost marshal; (*c*) **p. (militaire),** officer in military police; (*d*) *Fenc:* **p. de salle,** assistant fencing master. 2. *Hist: Ecc: A:* provost; *A:* **Grand P. de France, de l'Hôtel,** grand Provost of France, of the Household.

prévôtal, -aux [prevotal, -o], *a.* provostal, relating to provost duty; *Jur: Hist:* (*esp. in 1815*) **cour prévôtale,** provostal court (temporary criminal court without appeal); summary court; *Mil:* **service p.,** provost duty.

prévôtalement [prevotalmɑ̃], *adv. Jur:* in accordance with the justice of the provostal court; summarily, without right of appeal.

prévôté [prevote], *s.f.* 1. *Hist:* (*a*) provostship; (*b*) district under a provost; provostry. 2. *Mil:* (*a*) provost marshal's establishment; military police establishment; (*b*) military police service.

prévoyance [prevwajɑ̃:s], *s.f.* foresight, forethought, precaution; **mesure de p.,** measure of precaution; *Adm: A:* **p. sociale,** national insurance; **p. collective,** collective welfare measures; **fonds de p.,** (i) *Com: Ind:* contingency fund; reserve fund; (ii) *Adm: etc:* (staff) provident fund, scheme; **société de p.,** provident society; **il a toujours vécu avec p.,** he has always lived providently; **sans p.,** improvident(ly).

prévoyant [prevwajɑ̃], *a.* provident; foreseeing; far-sighted (administration, etc.).

prévu [prevy], (*a*) *a.* planned, envisaged; **dans les conditions prévues,** under the conditions foreseen; *Trans:* **vitesse prévue,** designed speed; **charge prévue,** rated load; specified load; *Mil:* **contre-attaque prévue,** counter attack with reserves; (*b*) *s.m.* **le p. et l'imprévu,** the foreseen and the unforeseen, the expected and the unexpected; *s.a.* PRÉVOIR.

priant [priɑ̃], (*a*) *a.* praying, kneeling in prayer; (*b*) *s.m.* kneeling statue (in prayer).

Priape[1] [priap], *Pr.n.m. Cl.Myth:* Priapus.

priape[2], *s.m. Anat:* priapus.

priapéen, -éenne [priapeɛ̃, -eɛn], *a. Cl.Myth:* Priapean.

priapique [priapik], *a.* priapic; phallic; **emblème p.,** phallic symbol.

priapisme [priapism], *s.m. Med:* priapism.

priapuliens [priapyljɛ̃], *s.m.pl. Ann:* Priapul(o)ida.

pricéite [priseit], *s.f. Miner:* priceite.

prié, -ée [prije], *A:* 1. *a.* (*a*) invited (guest); (*b*) **dîner p.,** formal dinner, set dinner. 2. *s.* (invited) guest.

prie-Dieu [pridjø]. 1. *s.m.inv.* (*a*) prie-dieu, praying desk, prayer stool; (*b*) *A:* (hour of) prayer. 2. *s.f.inv. Ent: F:* praying mantis.

prier [prije], *v.tr.* (*p.d. & pr.sub.* **n. priions, v. priiez**) 1. to pray; (*a*) **p. Dieu, la Vierge,** to pray to God, to the Virgin (Mary); *F:* **je prie Dieu, le ciel, de ne pas avoir à rester longtemps ici,** I'm praying I won't have to stay here too long; (*b*) *v.i.* **p. pour qn,** to pray, intercede, for s.o.; **p. pour la paix,** to pray for peace. 2. (*a*) to beg, beseech, entreat; **il l'a prié, en termes pressants, de . . .,** he begged him, with some insistence, to . . .; **elle accepta l'invitation après s'être fait un peu p.,** she accepted the invitation after a little persuasion; **ne vous faites pas tant p.,** don't take so much asking, so much persuading; **consentir sans se faire p.,** to consent readily, willingly; not to have to be asked twice; (*b*) to ask, request; **p. qn de faire qch.,** to ask s.o. to do sth.; **priez-le d'attendre,** please ask him to wait; **puis-je vous p. de vouloir bien fermer la porte?** would you be kind enough, might I ask you, to close the door? **p. qn d'entrer,** to ask s.o. in; **p. qn de sortir,** (i) to ask s.o. to leave; (ii) to ask s.o. to come out; **dites-moi, je vous prie,** would you please tell me; **passez-moi le sel, je vous prie,** (would you) please pass me the salt; **restez, je vous en prie,** do stay, please; **je vous en prie,** (i) (*affirmative answer*) please do, of course! (ii) (*when thanked for sth.*) but it was a pleasure; I'm so glad that I could help; please! *F:* that's all right! *U.S: F:* you're welcome! (*emphatic after interrog.*) **croyez-vous, je vous prie, que je puisse . . .?** I ask you, do you believe that I could . . .? *F:* **je vous prie de croire que . . .,** you can take it from me that . . .; **ne recommencez pas, je vous prie!** now don't do it again, (if you) please! *Corr:* **je vous prie de bien vouloir recevoir l'assurance de mes sentiments les meilleurs,** yours sincerely; *Ind: etc:* **le personnel est prié d'arriver à 9 heures précises,** the staff are requested to arrive punctually at nine o'clock. 3. (*a*) *A: & Lit:* to invite; **p. qn à dîner,** to invite s.o. to dinner; **être prié chez qn,** to be invited to s.o.'s house; (*b*) (*formal invitation*) **Monsieur et Madame X prient Monsieur et Madame Y de leur faire l'honneur d'assister à . . .,** Mr and Mrs X request the pleasure of Mr and Mrs Y's company at . . ..

prière [prijɛːr], *s.f.* **1.** prayer; **faire, dire, ses prières,** to say one's prayers; **faire la p.,** to offer prayer; to pray (in common); to put up a prayer; **après la p.,** after prayers; **se mettre en prières,** to kneel down and pray; **être en prières,** to be at prayers; **seigneur, écoutez ma p.,** O Lord, hear my prayer; **la p. en commun se faisait à neuf heures,** family prayers were at nine o'clock; **p. avant le repas, après le repas,** grace before meat, after meat. **2.** request, entreaty; **rester sourd aux prières de qn,** to remain deaf to s.o.'s entreaties; **être accessible aux prières,** to be open to requests; **faire une p. à qn,** to make a request of s.o.; **faire qch. à la prière de qn,** to do sth. at s.o.'s request; **p. de ne pas fumer,** please do not smoke, you are requested not to smoke; **p. de fermer la porte,** please close the door; *Com:* **p. de nous couvrir par chèque,** kindly remit by cheque.

prieur, -eure [prijœːr], *s. Ecc:* prior, prioress.

prieural, -aux [prijœral, -o], *a. Ecc:* prioral.

prieuré [prijœre], *s.m.* **1.** priory. **2.** priorship.

prima donna [prima dɔn(n)a], *s.f.inv.* prima donna.

primage[1] [primaːʒ], *s.m. Mch:* primage, priming.

primage[2], *s.m. Nau:* primage; *A:* hat money.

primaire [primɛːr], *a.* (*a*) primary; **enseignement p., école p.,** primary education, school; *El:* **courant p.,** primary current, inducing current; **enroulement p.,** *s.m.* **primaire,** primary winding; *Astr:* **planète p.,** primary planet; *Geol:* **roches primaires,** primary rocks; **ère p.,** *s.m.* **primaire,** primary (era); *Pol.Ec:* **secteur p.,** primary industries (agriculture and extractive industries); *Psy:* **test des aptitudes mentales primaires,** test of primary mental abilities; *Jur:* **un(e) délinquant(e) p.,** *s.* **un(e) p.,** a first offender; (*b*) *Pej:* of limited outlook; *s.* **c'est un p.,** he's a man of limited outlook, with a primary school outlook.

primarisme [primarism], *s.m. usu. Pej:* limited outlook; narrow dogmatism.

primarité [primarite], *s.f.* primariness.

primat [prima], *s.m.* **1.** *Ecc:* primate. **2.** paramountcy, preeminence, primacy (of function, etc.).

primata [primata], *s.m. Fin:* **p. de change,** first of exchange; **p. d'un chèque,** original cheque.

primate [primat], *s.m. Z:* primate.

primatial, -aux [primasjal, -o], *a. Ecc:* primatial, primatical.

primatie [primasi], *s.f. Ecc:* primateship, primacy.

primauté [primote], *s.f.* **1.** *Ecc:* primacy. **2.** (*a*) priority; *Lit:* **gagner qn de p.,** to forestall s.o.; (*b*) lead (at cards, etc.).

primavera [primavera], *s.m. Bot: Com:* primavera, white mahogany (tree and timber).

prime[1] [prim]. **1.** *a.* (*a*) *A:* first; *still used in the phrases* **de p. abord,** to begin with; at first; **de p. face,** at first sight; *Lit:* **de p. saut,** (i) on the first impulse; (ii) at the first attempt, at once; **dans ma p. jeunesse,** in my earliest youth; **je vous parle de mes primes années,** I am talking of my earliest years; (*b*) *Mth:* **n p. (n′),** n prime (n′). **2.** *s.f.* (*a*) *Ecc:* Prime; **chanter p.,** to sing the Prime; (*b*) *Fenc:* prime; (*c*) *Agr:* **orge de p.,** winter barley; (*d*) *Com:* prime wool.

prime[2], *s.f.* **1.** (*a*) *Fin: Ins:* premium; **faire p.,** to be at a premium; **p. de remboursement,** premium on redemption; (*of stocks*) **être à p., se vendre à p.,** to be, sell, at a premium; (*b*) *St. Exch:* **marché à p.,** (i) option (bargain); put, call; (ii) option market; **doubles primes,** double option, put and call; **p. pour lever, p. acheteur,** call (option); buyer's option; **p. pour livrer, p. vendeur,** (put) option; seller's option; **lever la p.,** to take up the option; **abandonner la p.,** to relinquish the forfeit, the option money; **acheter à p.,** to give for the call; **faire des opérations à p.,** to deal in options; **réponse des primes,** option day; **p. comportant le droit de livrer,** put option; **achat d'encore autant à p.,** call of more; **achat du double à p.,** call of twice more; **acheter la p. à livrer,** to give for the call; **acheter la p. à recevoir,** to give for the put; **vendeur de primes,** taker of option money; **acheteur de primes,** giver of option money. **2.** (*a*) *Com: Adm: etc:* subsidy; grant; **p. de réexportation,** drawback; **p. d'achat,** rebate, allowance; **p. à la construction,** building subsidy (given to people building houses for personal occupation); *Ind:* **p. spéciale d'équipement,** (State) development subsidy (paid to firms setting up new factories, etc., in development areas); **p. d'insalubrité,** grant towards improving insanitary conditions; (*b*) bonus; *Ind:* **p. de salissure,** dirt money; **p. de transport,** transport allowance; **p. de déménagement,** removal allowance; **p. de vie chère,** cost-of-living bonus; **p. (payée) aux employés,** bonus paid to employees; *Pol.Ec:* **p. à l'exportation,** export bonus; *Ind: etc:* **p. de rendement,** output bonus; *Agr:* **p. pour l'arrachage des vignes excédentaires,** compensation, bonus, for the uprooting of surplus vines; *Mil:* **p. de démobilisation,** demobilization gratuity; **p. d'engagement, de rengagement,** bounty on voluntary enlistment, on re-engagement; **p. fixe, p. journalière,** daily subsistence allowance; **p. de capture,** reward offered for the apprehension of a deserter; (*c*) *Com:* gift (on presentation of so many coupons); free gift.

prime[3], *s.f. Lap:* (rock-crystal) pebble; **p. de topaze,** false topaz.

primefleur [primflœːr], *s.f. A: Lit:* first bloom; **en sa p. de nouveauté,** in the first blush of its newness.

primer[1] [prime], *v.tr.* **1.** to excel, surpass; to take precedence of, take the lead of (s.o., sth.); **p. tout,** to take the first place; to come first; **considération qui prime toutes les autres,** consideration of the first importance; *O:* **être primé par qn,** to rank after s.o.; *abs.* **p. par, en, qch.,** to excel, take the lead, in sth.; *Jur:* **p. qn en hypothèque,** to have priority over s.o. (in claim on mortgaged property). **2.** *Agr:* to dig, harrow, dress, (ground) for the first time (in the season). **3.** *v.i. Astr:* (*of tide*) to prime.

primer[2], *v.tr.* **1.** to award a prize to (cattle at show, etc.); **taureau primé,** prize bull; **roman primé,** prize-winning novel. **2.** to give, award, a bonus to (s.o., sth.); **industrie primée,** subsidized industry.

primer[3], *v.i. Mch:* (*of boiler*) to prime.

primerose [primroːz], *s.f. Bot:* hollyhock.

primesaut [primso], *s.m. Lit:* first impulse

primesautier, -ière [primsotje, -jɛːr], *a* impulsive, spontaneous; ready, quick; **avoir l'esprit p.,** (i) to be impulsive; (ii) to be quick-witted.

primeur [primœːr], *s.f.* **1.** newness, freshness; **lire un livre dans sa p.,** to read a book on first publication; **avoir la p. d'une nouvelle,** to be the first to hear a piece of news; *Journ:* **p. d'une grosse nouvelle,** scoop; **vins bons dans la p.,** wines that are palatable when young. **2.** (*a*) early season; (*b*) *Hort: etc:* early product; **cultiver des primeurs,** to grow early, young, vegetables (and, or, fruit).

primeuriste [primœrist], *s.m. & f.* early fruit and vegetable grower.

primevère [primvɛːr], *s.f. Bot:* primula; **p. à grandes fleurs,** primrose, oxlip; **p. commune,** cowslip; **p. des jardins,** polyanthus; **p. farineuse,** bird's eye primrose; **p. officinale,** mountain primrose.

primidi [primidi], *s.m. Hist:* first day of the decade (in the French Republican calendar).

primine [primin], *s.f. Bot:* primine (of ovule).

primipare [primipaːr]. **1.** *a.* primiparous (woman, animal). **2.** *s.f.* primipara.

primitif, -ive [primitif, -iːv], *a.* **1.** (*a*) primitive, primeval, original, earliest; *Ling:* **mot p.,** primitive, radical, word; *Gram:* **temps primitifs,** primary tenses; *Opt:* **couleurs primitives,** primary colours, (i) the seven colours of the spectrum; (ii) red, green, and blue; *Geol:* **roches primitives,** primitive rocks; *Mec.E:* **(cercle) p.,** pitch circle, pitch line, primitive circle (of gearing); *s.m. Hist. of Art:* **les primitifs,** the primitives; the early masters; (*b*) first, original; **la question primitive,** the original question; *Fin:* **souscripteur p.,** original subscriber. **2. méthodes primitives,** primitive, crude, methods; **mœurs primitives,** primitive customs or manners. **3.** *s.f. Mth:* **primitive,** primitive.

primitivement [primitivmɑ̃], *adv.* primitively; (*a*) originally; (*b*) primevally.

primitivisme [primitivism], *s.m.* primitivism.

primitivité [primitivite], *s.f.* primitiveness (of manners, etc.).

primo [primo], *adv.* firstly, in the first place.

primogéniture [primɔʒenityːr], *s.f. Jur:* primogeniture; **droit de p.,** right of primogeniture; **succession par p.,** (succession by) primogeniture.

primo-infection [primɔɛ̃fɛksjɔ̃], *s.f. Med:* primary infection; *pl. primo-infections.*

primordial, -aux [primɔrdjal, -o]. **1.** *a.* (*a*) primordial; *Biol:* **cellule primordiale,** primordial cell; **fins primordiales d'une société,** original aims of an association; **nécessité primordiale,** prime necessity; (*b*) of prime importance; **appareil où la légèreté est primordiale,** machine in which lightness is of primary importance; (*c*) primeval. **2.** *s.m. Jur:* original document.

primordialement [primɔrdjalmɑ̃], *adv.* (*a*) primordially; primarily; (*b*) primevally.

primovaccination [primɔvaksinasjɔ̃], *s.f.* primary vaccination.

primulacées [primylase], *s.f.pl. Bot:* Primulaceae.

primuline [primylin], *s.f. Ch:* primuline.

Primus [primys], *Pr.n.m. R.t.m:* Primus stove.

prince [prɛ̃ːs], *s.m.* prince; **p. royal, impérial,** crown prince; **p. du sang,** prince of the blood; *Hist:* **le P. Noir,** the Black Prince; **les Princes de l'Église,** the Princes of the Church; **le p. des poètes,** the very prince of poets; **le p. des ténèbres, de ce monde,** the prince of darkness, of this world; **jeux de p.,** the sport of kings; **il est bon p.** he's a decent chap, a good fellow; he is open handed; **traiter qn en p.,** to treat s.o. like a prince, royally, in princely fashion. *Jur:* **le fait du p.,** restraint of princes.

prince(-)de(-)galles [prɛ̃sdəgal], *a. & s.m.inv. Tex:* broken check (material), Prince of Wales (check).

princeps [prɛ̃sɛps], *a.inv. used only in the phr.* **édition(s) p.,** first edition(s), editio princeps (of classical author).

princesse [prɛ̃sɛs], *s.f.* **1.** princess; **p. royale,** princess royal; **p. impériale,** crown princess; *F:* **prendre des airs de p.,** to be affected; *F:* **aux frais de la p.,** at government, the firm's, expense, *F:* on the house. **2.** *attrib.* **amande p.,** soft-shelled almond; **robe p.,** princess(e) (style) dress; **dentelle p.,** appliqué lace.

princier, -ière [prɛ̃sje, -jɛːr], *a.* princely; **de naissance princière,** of princely birth; **habitation princière,** palatial house; **honoraires princiers,** princely fees.

princièrement [prɛ̃sjɛrmɑ̃], *adv.* like a prince, in princely fashion; **il est p. payé,** he gets a princely salary; **il nous a reçus p.,** he entertained us magnificently, royally.

principal, -aux [prɛ̃sipal, -o]. **1.** *a.* principal, chief, leading (person, thing); **associé p.,** senior partner; **agent p.,** head agent; **mobile p. d'une action,** prime motive of an action; *Av:* **nervure principale,** main rib (of wing); **but p.,** main object, chief object; **produit p. d'une région,** main, staple, product of a region; **un des principaux actionnaires,** a major shareholder; *Gram:* **proposition principale,** main clause, head clause; *Jur:* **p. locataire,** head lessee; **auteur p. d'un crime,** principal of a crime in the first degree; *Mus:* **violon p.,** principal violin, leading violin; *Geom:* **axe p. d'une courbe,** principal axis of a curve; *El:* **câble p.,** main cable; **chaudière principale,** main boiler (of ship, etc.); **p. clerc,** lawyer's) head clerk. **2.** *s.m.* (*a*) principal, chief; headmaster, head (of college, school); chief partner, senior partner (of a business); (lawyer's) head clerk; **les principaux d'une ville,** the principal, leading, citizens of a town; (*b*) principal thing, chief thing, great thing, main point; **le p. est de réussir,** the great thing is to succeed; **le p. est que personne n'en sache rien,** the main thing is that no one shall know anything about it; **le p. est qu'il est déjà sur les lieux,** the great thing is that he is already on the spot; (*c*) *Com: Jur:* principal, capital sum.

principalat [prɛ̃sipala], *s.m. Sch:* principalship, headmastership.

principalement [prɛ̃sipalmɑ̃], *adv.* principally, chiefly, mainly.

principat [prɛ̃sipa], *s.m. Rom.Hist:* principate.

principauté [prɛ̃sipote], *s.f.* **1.** (*a*) principality; **la p. de Galles,** the principality of Wales; (*b*) principality, princedom. **2.** *pl. Theol:* **les Principautés,** the Principalities (the fifth order of angels).

principe [prɛ̃sip], *s.m.* **1.** principle; primary cause; beginning, source; **aboutir à un accord de p.,** to reach an agreement in principle; **par cet acte le gouvernement est frappé dans son p.,** this action strikes at the root of all government; **p. mère,** fundamental principle; **le p. de la vie,** the principle of life; **p. de nos actions,** mainspring of our actions; *adv.phr.* **dans le p.,** in the beginning; **dès le p.,** from the outset. **2.** principle, fundamental, truth; **les principes de la géométrie,** the principles of geometry; **le p. d'Archimède,** Archimedes' principle; **poser qch. en p.,** to lay down sth. as a principle; *Mil:* **principes d'emploi des armes,** weapon-employment philosophy. **3.** *Ch:* element, constituent, ingredient (of a substance); **p. gras, amer, actif,** fatty, bitter, active, principle or constituent. **4.** (*rule of conduct*) principle; **par p.,** on principle; **en p.,** (i) as a rule; (ii) provisionally; (iii) d.v. (*deo volente*); (iv) there should be; (v) theoretically, in theory; **avoir pour p. de . . .,** to make it a matter of principle to . . .; **relâchement des principes,** relaxing of principles, of moral standards; **sans principes,** unprincipled; **rester fidèle à ses principes,** to stick to one's principles.

principicule [prɛ̃sipikyl], *s.m.* princeling, princelet, petty prince.

printanier, -ière [prɛ̃tanje, -jɛːr], *a.* spring (season, flowers, etc.); **étoffes printanières,** spring materials, spring suitings; **potage p.,** soup made with spring vegetables; vegetable soup; **température printanière,** spring-like temperature; *F:* **vous êtes bien printanière avec cette robe,** you look very spring-like in that dress.

printanisation [prɛ̃tanizasjɔ̃], *s.f. Agr:* vernalization.

printemps [prɛ̃tɑ̃], *s.m.* (*a*) spring, springtime; **au p.,** in (the) spring; **une belle soirée de p.,** a lovely spring evening; **dans les premiers jours du p.,** in early spring; **on sent dans l'air les effluves du p.,** you can smell spring in the air; *Fr.C: F:* **avoir la fièvre du p.,** to have spring fever; *Prov:* **une hirondelle ne fait pas le p.,** one swallow doesn't make a summer; (*b*) *Lit:* **le p. de la vie,** the springtime, heyday, of life; **elle mourut dans le p. de sa vie,** she died in the springtime of life; *A: & Poet:* **jeune fille de dix-huit p.,** maiden of eighteen summers.

printing [printiŋ], *s.m. F:* teleprinter.

priodonte [priodɔ̃ːt], *s.m. Z:* giant armadillo.

prion [priɔ̃], *s.m. Orn:* prion.

prioniens [priənjɛ̃], *s.m.pl. Ent:* Prioninae.

prionops [priənɔps], *s.m. Orn:* prionops.

priorat [priəra], *s.m.* priorate, priorship.

prioritaire [priəritɛːr], (*a*) *s.* priority holder; **être p.,** to have priority; (*b*) *a.* priority; **droits prioritaires,** priority rights; *Fin:* **achat p.,** preemptive purchase; **action p.,** preference share; **route p.,** major road; *Aut:* **le véhicule venant de la droite est p.,** the vehicle coming from the right has priority.

priorité [priərite], *s.f.* priority; *Jur:* priority of claim; **p. absolue, relative,** preemptive, non-preemptive, priority; **droits de p.,** priority rights; **réclamer la p.,** to claim the right to speak first; *Com:* **actions de p.,** preference shares, preferred stock; **avoir la p. sur,** to take precedence over; to override; *esp. Trans:* **carte de p.,** queue ticket; *F:* **laissez passer les priorités!** ticket holders first! *Aut:* **p. (de passage),** right of way; *P.N:* **p. à droite** = give way (*i.e.* to vehicles coming from the right).

pris [pri], *a.* **1.** (*a*) occupied, taken; **cette place est-elle prise?** is this seat taken? **tout est p.,** everything is taken, booked; **avoir les mains prises,** to have one's hands full; **il avait sa journée prise,** his whole day was busy, full; (*b*) (*of pers.*) engaged; occupied; busy; **je suis très p. ce matin,** I'm very busy this morning; **impossible ce soir, je suis p.,** I can't this evening, I'm busy, I've got another engagement. **2.** (*a*) **p. de peur,** panic stricken; **p. de remords,** smitten with remorse; **p. de colère,** in a rage, a passion; **p. de vin, de boisson,** drunk, under the influence of drink, *F:* the worse for wear, fuddled; (*b*) **avoir le nez p.,** to have one's nose blocked (up) (with a cold); **avoir la gorge prise,** to have a sore throat. **3. bien p.,** well-proportioned; shapely; **elle est de taille bien prise,** she has a good figure. **4.** (*of jelly, etc.*) set; (*of river, etc.*) frozen over.

prisable [prizabl], *a. Lit:* worthy of esteem; estimable.

Priscien [prisjɛ̃], *Pr.n.m. Rom.Hist:* Priscian(us).

Priscille [prisil], *Pr.n.f.* Priscilla.

Priscillien [pris(s)iljɛ̃], *Pr.n.m. Rel.H:* Priscillian.

prise [priːz], *s.f.* **1.** hold, grasp, grip; (*a*) **trouver p. à qch.,** to get a grip, a hold, of sth.; to get, secure, a purchase on sth.; **avoir p. sur qn,** to have a hold on, over, s.o.; *Nau:* **l'ancre est en p.,** the anchor bites, is holding; **lâcher p., quitter p.,** (i) to lose one's hold, to let go; (ii) *F:* to give in; **donner p. à la calomnie,** to lay oneself open to calumny; **donner p. aux reproches** to lay oneself open to reproaches; **nul n'a prise sur lui,** no one has any hold over him; *abs.* **trouver p.,** to take hold; **je n'avais pas de p. (pour me hisser, etc.),** I had no purchase, no hold (with which to pull myself up, etc.); *Wr:* **simple p. de tête à terre,** half Nelson; **double p. de tête à terre,** Nelson; **toutes prises autorisées,** (with) no holds barred; (*b*) **être aux prises,** to be at close quarters; **être aux prises avec qn,** to be at grips with s.o.; **en venir aux prises,** to come to grips; to come to close quarters; to grapple with one another; **mettre qn aux prises avec qn,** to pit s.o. against s.o.; **mettre les gens aux prises,** to set people by the ears; **mettre aux prises des intérêts,** to bring interests into conflict; **aux prises avec l'adversité,** fighting against adversity; **les difficultés avec lesquelles je suis aux prises,** the difficulties with which I have to contend, to deal; **il est aux prises avec la justice,** he is up against the law; **avoir une p. avec qn,** to have a passage at arms with s.o.; (*c*) *Mec.E:* engagement, mesh(ing), pitch(ing); **en p.,** in gear, engaged; **mettre en p.,** to engage; **se mettre en p.,** to engage; **mise en p.,** engaging; **être en p. avec un pignon,** to mesh, be in mesh, with a spur wheel; **pignons constamment en p., de p. constante,** constant-mesh gear; **mécanisme de p. directe,** direct-drive mechanism; **en p. directe sur le moteur,** coupled direct to the motor; *Aut:* **en p. (directe),** in top (gear); **être en p. (directe) avec son temps,** to be in touch with contemporary reality, *F:* to be with it; **hors de p.,** out of gear; (*d*) *Mus:* entry (of fugue subject). **2.** solidification, congealing, setting; **ciment à p. lente, rapide,** slow-setting, quick-setting, cement; (*of cement*) **faire p.,** to set; **p. à l'air,** air hardening. **3.** taking (up); (*a*) *Mil: etc:* **p. de poste,** taking up of one's position; **p. d'armes,** parade under arms; (*b*) capture; **p. d'une ville, d'un voleur,** taking, capture, of a town, of a thief; **p. en mer,** capture at sea; *Jur:* **p. de corps,** arrest; **la p. de la Bastille,** the fall of the Bastille; **le code qui régit le droit de p. entre belligérants,** the Law of Warlike Capture; *Chess:* **pièce en p.,** piece, pawn, en prise; (*c*) collecting; **p. de colis à domicile,** collection of parcels; (*d*) **p. de vues,** *Phot:* taking of photographs; *Cin: T.V:* shooting; *Cin:* **p. de vue,** shot; take; **p. de vues à la lampe éclair, au flash, au magnésium,** flashlight photography; *Cin: T.V:* **p. de vue à distance,** long shot; **p. de vue rapprochée,** close shot; **p. de vues à l'extérieur,** outside shooting; **p. de vue en mouvement,** travelling shot; *T.V:* **p. de vues directe, en direct,** live broadcast; *Cin: T.V:* **p. de son,** sound take, sound recording; **appareil de p. de son,** sound recorder; (*e*) *Nau:* prize; **être de bonne p.,** to be (a) lawful prize, *F:* to be fair game; **part de p.,** prize money; **cour des prises,** prize court; **équipage de p.,** prize crew; (*f*) *St. Exch:* **p. de bénéfices,** profit taking. **4.** (*thing taken*) (*a*) **p. de poisson,** catch of fish; (*b*) **p. de quinine,** dose of quinine; **p. de tabac,** pinch of snuff; **il m'offrit une p.,** he offered me a pinch of snuff; **je n'en donnerais pas une p. de tabac,** I wouldn't give a pinch of snuff, a thank you, for it; **p. de minerai,** sample of ore; **p. d'essai,** sample for analysis, assay sample; test portion; *Med:* **faire une p. de sang,** to take a blood specimen, sample. **5.** (*d*) *Mch: Mec.E: etc:* **p. d'air,** (i) ventilation aperture; (ii) *I.C.E:* air intake, inlet; (iii) *Aer:* air scoop, bleed; **p. de gaz latérale,** downcomer, downtake (in blast furnace); **p. de vapeur,** (i) intake, input, of steam; (ii) steamcock, steam valve, throttle valve, injection cock; **p. de vidange,** drain connector; **p. de remplissage,** filler connector; *Mec.E: Aut:* **point de p. de force,** power take-off, P.T.O.; **p. de pression,** pressure bleed; **p. d'eau,** (i) intake of water; (ii) cock, valve, tap; fire-hydrant plug; hydrant; (iii) water catchment; (iv) canal regulator; (v) offtake (of canal from river, etc.); (vi) water crane; **faire une p. à une rivière,** to tap a river; (*b*) *El:* **p. de courant,** (i) collecting, intake, of current; (ii) current collector (of trolley); (iii) connector, plug-and-socket, point; **p. (de courant) femelle,** socket (connector); **p. (de courant) mâle,** plug (connector); **p. (de courant) murale,** (wall) plug (socket); point; **p. de courant force,** power plug, point; **p. multiple,** multi-terminal connector, connection block, multiple point; **p. de dérivation, p. intermédiaire,** tapping point; **p. de bobine,** coil tap; **p. de terre,** ground, earth, connection; ground, earth, plate; **faire une p. sur un câble, sur un enroulement,** to tap a cable, a coil.

prisée [prize], *s.f. Jur:* **p. (et estimation),** valuation (of goods); appraisement, appraisal (before auction).

priser¹ [prize], *v.tr.* to snuff (sth.) up (through the nose); *abs.* to take snuff; **poudre à p., tabac à p.,** snuff.

priser², *v.tr.* (*a*) *Lit:* to appraise, value (goods); (*b*) to set a (high) value on sth.; to prize, value, treasure (sth.); to think highly of (s.o.).

priseur¹, -euse [prizœːr, -øːz], *s.* snuff taker.

priseur², *s.m.* **(commissaire-) p.,** (official) valuer, appraiser (of goods).

prismatique [prismatik], *a.* prismatic; **couleurs prismatiques,** prismatic colours; *Exp:* **poudre p.,** prismatic powder.

prismatisation [prismatizasjɔ̃], *s.f.* prismatization.

prismatiser [prismatize], *v.tr.* to prismatize.

prismatoïde [prismatɔid], *s.m. Geom:* prismatoid.

prisme [prism], *s.m.* prism; *Geom:* **p. droit,** right prism; **p. oblique,** oblique, slanting, prism; *Opt:* **p. à dispersion,** dispersing prism; **p. redressant les images, p. redresseur,** erecting prism; **p. réflecteur,** reflecting prism; **p. à réflexion totale,** total-reflexion prism; **jumelle(s) à prismes,** prism(atic) binoculars; *Dent:* **prismes (de l'émail),** enamel prisms, rods.

prismé [prisme], *a.* prismatic.

prismoïde [prismɔid], *s.m. Geom:* prismoid.

prisographe [prizəgraf], *s.m. Civ.E: Const:* prisometer.

prison [prizɔ̃], *s.f.* **1.** (*a*) prison, gaol, jail; *Mil: Navy:* cell(s); *F:* glasshouse; **aller en p.,** to go to prison, to jail; **être mis en p.,** to be put in prison; **réintégrer un homme en p.,** to recommit a man (to prison); **s'échapper, s'évader, de p.,** to break prison; **il a été en p.,** he has been in prison, *F:* he has done time; *A:* **p. pour dettes,** debtors' prison; *F:* **aimable, gracieux, comme une porte de p.,** grumpy, disagreeable; as forbidding as a prison gate; **triste comme une porte de p.,** as cheerful as a prison; (*b*) *Lit:* **le corps est la p. de l'âme,** the body is the prison of the soul; **dans la p. des soucis et des tâches médiocres,** imprisoned, confined, by cares and humdrum tasks. **2.** imprisonment; **faire de la p., garder la p.,** *F:* **tirer de la p.,** to be in prison; to serve a sentence of imprisonment, *F:* to do time, to do a stretch; **cinq ans de p.,** five years' imprisonment, five years' confinement; **condamné à la p. perpétuelle,** sentenced to imprisonment for life; *Mil:* **donner à un homme trois jours de p.,** to give a man three days' cells.

prison-école [prizɔ̃ekɔl], *s.f. Jur:* = Borstal institution; approved school; *pl. prisons-écoles.*

prisonnier, -ière [prizənje, -jɛːr]. **1.** *s.* prisoner; **p. de guerre,** prisoner of war; **camp de prisonniers (de guerre),** prison camp; prisoner-of-war camp; **p. d'État,** prisoner of state; **p. de droit commun,** prisoner under common law; **faire qn p.,** to take s.o. prisoner; **les prisonniers qu'on avait faits sur les Espagnols,** the prisoners taken from the Spanish; **Murat mit Klenau en déroute et lui fit dix mille prisonniers,** Murat routed Klenau and took ten thousand of his men prisoner; **se constituer p.,** to give oneself up; **il fut emmené p.,** he was taken away in custody; he was marched off under guard. **2.** *s.m.* (*a*) *Mec.E:* stud (pin, bolt), set bolt, standing bolt, set pin; **p. à clavette,** cotter stud bolt; **p. borgne,** blind stud bolt; (*b*) *Tchn:* (*plastics industry*) insert. **3.** *a.* (*a*) imprisoned, in prison; captive; (*b*) *Mec.E:* fixed, set.

privadois, -oise [privadwa, -waːz], *a. & s. Geog:* (native, inhabitant) of Privas.

privatif, -ive [privatif, -iːv]. **1.** *Gram:* (*a*) *a.* privative; (*b*) *s.m.* privative prefix. **2.** *a.* **peine privative de liberté,** sentence depriving the convicted person of his liberty; prison sentence. **3.** *a. Jur:* **droit p.,** exclusive right; (*of flat, etc.*) **avec jardin p.,** with exclusive use of garden.

privation [privasjɔ̃], *s.f.* **1.** deprivation, loss; **p. de commandement,** deprivation of command; **p. de la vue,** loss of sight; **p. de sortie,** (i) *Mil:* stoppage of pass (as punishment); (ii) *Sch:* gating; *Jur:* **p. de droits civils, civiques,** loss of civil rights. **2.** privation, hardship; **vivre dans la p., vivre de privations,** to live in privation, in poverty; **les privations de la guerre,** the hardships of war; **s'imposer des privations,** (i) to deprive oneself; (ii) to fast.

privautés [privote], *s.f.pl.* (undue) familiarity; **prendre des p., avec qn,** to take liberties, to be over-familiar, *F:* to go a bit too far, with s.o.

privé [prive]. **1.** *a.* (*a*) private (individual, life, enterprise, etc.); *P.N:* **propriété privée,** private property; **la charité privée,** private charity; **séance privée,** private sitting; **intérêts privés,** private interests, by(e) interests; **considérations d'ordre p.,** by(e) considerations; **se réunir en séance privée,** to sit in private; *Jur:* **agir en son (propre et) p. nom,** to act in one's own name; **renseignements privés,** private information, *F:* inside information; (*b*) *Hist:* **le Conseil p.,** the Privy Council; (*c*) *A:* tame (animal, etc.). **2.** *s.m.* (*a*) private (life); **le p.,** private (as opposed to nationalized) industry; **parler à qn en p.,** to speak to s.o. in private; **il se présente sous un jour tout différent dans le p.,** he appears in a completely different light in private life; **il était fonctionnaire avant de prendre un emploi dans le p.,** he was a civil servant before taking up a job in a private firm; **match joué dans le p.,** match played in private, privately; (*b*) *A:* privy, water closet.

privément [privemɑ̃], *adv. A:* privately, as a private individual; secretly.

priver [prive], *v.tr.* to deprive; **p. qn de qch.,** to deprive s.o. of sth.; to debar s.o. from sth.; (*to child*) **tu seras privé de dessert,** you'll have to go without your pudding; **être privé de travail,** to be thrown out of work; **je ne vous en prive pas?** can you spare it? I'm not depriving you? **être privé de toutes les jouissances de la vie,** to be cut off from all the enjoyments of life; **privé de tout espoir,** bereft of all hope; **l'indignation l'avait privé de la parole,** indignation had deprived, bereft, him of speech; *Mil:* **terrain, angle, p. de feux,** dead ground, dead angle.

se priver de qch., to do, to go, without sth.; to deprive oneself of sth.; to deny oneself sth.; **se p. de viande,** (i) to abstain from meat; (ii) to stint oneself of meat; **se p. pour ses enfants,** to deny oneself for one's children.

privilège [privilɛːʒ], *s.m.* **1.** privilege; (*a*) **les privilèges de la noblesse,** the privileges of the nobility; **c'est là un p. de la vieillesse,** that is a privilege, a prerogative, of old age; **la raison est le p. de l'homme,** the gift of reason is the privilege of man alone; **jouir du p. de faire qch., avoir le p. de faire qch.,** to be privileged to do sth., to enjoy the privilege of doing sth.; **violer les privilèges de qn,** to invade s.o.'s privileges; *Iron:* **il a le p. de me déplaire,** I have a particular dislike for him; (*b*) licence, grant; **p. d'une banque,** bank charter; **accorder un p. à qn,** to license s.o. **2.** *Com: Jur:* preferential right, preference; **p. de créancier,** creditor's preferential claim; **p. d'hypothèque,** mortgage charge; **p. général,** general lien; **avoir un p. sur qch.,** to have a lien, a charge, on sth.

privilégié, -ée [privileʒje]. **1.** *a.* (*a*) privileged; **les classes privilégiées,** the privileged classes; (*b*) licensed; **banque privilégiée,** chartered bank; (*c*) **créancier p.,** preferential creditor; **action privilégiée,** preference share; **créance privilégiée,** preferential debt, preferred debt, privileged debt; (*c*) *Fish:* **poissons privilégiés,** fishes protected by law. **2.** *s.* privileged person; **quelques privilégiés l'ont vu,** a privileged few have seen it; **la classe des privilégiés,** the privileged class.

privilégier [privileʒje], *v.tr.* (*pr.sub. & p.d.* **n. privilégiions, v. privilégiiez**) to privilege; to license; to grant a charter to (bank, etc.).

prix [pri], *s.m.* **1.** (*a*) value, worth, cost; **connaître le p. d'un ami,** to know a friend's worth, the value of a friend; **il semble ignorer le p. du temps,** he doesn't seem to know the value of time; **à tout p.,** at all costs; **faire qch. à p. d'argent,** to do sth. for money; **se vendre à p. d'or,** (i) to sell oneself for gold; (ii) (*of foods*) to fetch huge prices; **à aucun p.,** not on any terms, not at any price; **au p. de,** (i) at the price of; (ii) in comparison with; **faire qch. au p. de dépenses énormes,** to do sth. at enormous cost; **fortune amassée au p. de tant de haines,** fortune piled up at the cost of so much hatred; **c'est peu de chose au p. de ce que j'espérais,** it is little compared with what I had hoped for; **p. pour p.,** on a fair comparison; **attacher beaucoup de p., un grand p., à qch.,** to set a high value on sth.; to set great store by sth.; **tenir qch. en haut p.,** to prize sth. highly; (*b*) price; **bas, haut, p.,** low, high, price; **p. le plus bas, dernier p.,** lowest price; *F:* rock-bottom price; **acheter qch. à bas p., à juste p.,** to buy sth. at a low price, at a fair price; **p. d'achat,** purchase price, cost; **p. de vente,** (i) selling price; (ii) consideration for sale; **p. au comptant,** cash price; **p. courant,** current price, market price; **p. fort, p. (de) catalogue,** full price, list price, catalogue price; (*of book*) published price; **p. à forfait, p. forfaitaire,** agreed price, contract price, fixed price; **p. de nomenclature,** list price; **p. imposé,** administered price, agreed fair price; **p. net,** net price, trade price; **p. faible,** (i) low price; (ii) discount price; **p. initial,** prime cost; **à, au, p. coûtant; au p. de revient,** at cost price; **établir le p. de revient d'un travail,** to cost a job; **p. de gros, en gros,** wholesale price; *St.Exch:* **p. du report,** contango rate, continuation rate; *Fin:* **p. du change,** (exchange) premium; *Pol.Ec:* **p. plancher,** floor price; **p. plafond,** ceiling price; **blocage des p.,** price freezing, price pegging; **indice des p.,** price index; **faire le p. à qn,** to quote a price to s.o.; **vous pouvez l'acheter si vous y mettez le p.,** you can buy it at a price; **je vous ferai un p. (d'ami),** I'll let you have it cheap, I'll give you special terms; **avoir un p., des p.,** to get special terms; *F:* **si tu n'es pas content c'est le même p.,** it comes to the same thing whether you like it or not; **une voiture dans mes p.,** a car within my means; **c'est plutôt dans mes p.,** that's more in my line; *St.Exch:* **actions cotées au p. de . . .,** shares quoted at the rate of . . .; **(magasin à) p. unique,** one-price store; (*in restaurant*) **(repas à) p. fixe,** table d'hôte (meal), set meal; **articles de p.,** expensive, costly, articles; **coûter un p. fou,** to cost the earth; **c'est hors de p.,** the price is prohibitive; **fourrures hors de p.,** furs at extravagant prices, at ransom prices; **ce vieux piano a bien son p.,** this old piano is surely worth something; **n'avoir pas de p.,** (i) to be priceless, beyond price; (ii) to be worthless; **je vous le céderai pour un p. raisonnable,** I'll let you have it at a fair price; **mettre à p. la tête de qn,** to put a price on s.o.'s head; **mise à p. d'un domaine,** upset price of an estate; (*at auction*) **mise à p.,** (i) reserve price; (ii) opening bid; **mettre un tableau à p. 20.000 francs,** to start the bidding for a picture at 20,000 francs; *F:* **c'est plutôt dans les grands p.,** it's a bit steep! (*c*) charge; **p. d'un trajet, du voyage,** fare; **je n'ai pas le p. de mon voyage,** I haven't my fare, the price of my ticket; *Nau:* **p. de la traversée,** passage money; *Th: etc:* **le p. des fauteuils est de 20 francs,** a seat in the stalls is 20 francs; *Ind:* **p. pour matériel,** quotation for plant. **2.** reward, prize; (*a*) **remporter le p.,** to win, carry off the prize; **le p. Nobel,** the Nobel Prize; **un p. Nobel,** a Nobel prize-winner; *Rac:* **Grand P.,** Grand Prix; **remporter le p. d'histoire,** to carry off, to take, to win, the history prize; **distribution des p.,** prize giving; *Sch:* speech day; **livre de p.,** prize book; **pour p. des peines,** as a reward, recompense, for his trouble; (*b*) *Sp:* challenge cup race, prize race; *Turf:* **p. à réclamer,** selling plate.

prix-courant [prikurɑ̃], *s.m. Com:* price list; catalogue; *pl. prix-courants.*

prix-étalon [prietalɔ̃], *s.m. Com:* standard costs; *pl. prix-étalons.*

prix-fixe [prifiks], *s.m. F:* (*a*) *A:* fixed-price store; (*b*) restaurant with a fixed-price meal; *pl. prix-fixes.*

pro- [prɔ], *pref.* pro-.

pro [pro], *s.m.inv. Sp: F:* pro.

proaction [prɔaksjɔ̃], *s.f. Psy:* proaction.

proamnios [prɔamnjɔs], *s.m. Biol:* proamnion.

probabiliorisme [prɔbabiljɔrism], *s.m. Theol:* probabiliorism.

probabilioriste [prɔbabiljɔrist], *s.m. & f. Theol:* probabiliorist.

probabilisme [prɔbabilism], *s.m. Theol: Phil:* probabilism.

probabiliste [prɔbabilist], *s.m. & f. Theol: Phil:* probabilist.

probabilité [prɔbabilite], *s.f.* probability, likelihood; *Mth:* **calcul des probabilités,** theory of probability; **fonction de p.,** probability function; **selon toute(s) probabilité(s),** in all likelihood, most probably; *Ins:* **probabilités de la vie,** expectation of life.

probable [prɔbabl̩], *a.* probable, likely; **il est p. qu'elle viendra,** she is likely to come, she will probably come; **peu p.,** hardly probable, improbable, unlikely; **éventualité peu p.,** remote prospect; **il est peu p., n'est pas p., qu'elle vienne,** she is not likely to come, it is not likely that she will come; **c'est peu p.,** I should hardly think so; **c'est très peu p.,** it is most unlikely; **c'est plus que p.,** it is more than likely.

probablement [prɔbabləmɑ̃], *adv.* probably, in all likelihood; **il pleuvra p.,** it is likely to rain, it will probably rain.

probant [prɔbɑ̃]. **1.** *a.* probative, convincing, conclusive, cogent (proof, evidence, reason, etc.); **peu p.,** unconvincing; *Jur:* **document en forme probante,** document in an authentic form; **force probante d'un reçu non timbré,** probatory force of an unstamped receipt. **2.** *s.m. Biol:* type specimen.

probation [prɔbasjɔ̃], *s.f.* (*a*) *Ecc:* probation, probationary period; (*b*) *Jur:* probation; **agent de p.,** probation officer.

probatoire [prɔbatwaːr], *a.* probatory; probative; *Sch:* **examen p.,** grading examination (to determine level reached by the pupil).

probe [prɔb], *a. Lit:* honest, upright; **homme p.,** man of integrity.

probité [prɔbite], *s.f.* probity, uprightness, integrity, honesty; **être d'une p. à toute épreuve,** to be of proven integrity; **c'est la p. même,** he is the soul of honesty, the soul of honour.

problématique [prɔblematik]. **1.** *a.* problematic(al) (question, opinion, result, etc.); questionable (mode of life); **seconde édition encore p.,** still problematic(al) second edition. **2.** *s.f. Phil:* problematics.

problématiquement [prɔblematikmɑ̃], *adv.* problematically.

problématisation [prɔblematizasjɔ̃], *s.f. Phil:* problematization.

problème [prɔblɛm], *s.m.* problem; **p. de mathématiques,** mathematical problem; **p. d'arithmétique,** sum; **le p. de l'origine de l'homme,** the problem of the origin of man; **problèmes politiques,** political problems; **ce sont de faux problèmes dès le départ,** these are basically false problems; (*computers*) **p. d'évaluation comparative, p. de référence,** benchmark problem; **p. de file d'attente,** queueing problem; **p. test,** check problem; **cela pose des problèmes,** *int.* **p.!** that's a difficulty, a problem; *F:* **il n'y a pas de p.,** (i) that's easy, simple; (ii) naturally! of course! **pas de problèmes!** certainly! **votre ami est un vrai p. pour moi,** your friend's a real problem, a real puzzle, to me; **pendant les vacances ce garçon était un constant p.,** during the holidays the boy was a constant problem, *F:* a continual headache.

problo(que) [prɔblo, prɔblɔk], *s.m. & f. F:* landlord, *f.* landlady (of rented flat, etc.); **le p. réclame son loyer,** the landlord's asking for the rent; **les probloques sont deux vieilles filles,** the owners are a couple of spinsters.

proboscide [prɔbɔsid], *s.f. Ent:* proboscis; *A: Lit:* trunk (of elephant).

proboscidien, -ienne [prɔbɔsidjɛ̃, -jɛn], *a. & s.m. Z:* proboscidian; *s.m.pl.* **proboscidiens,** Proboscidea.

procaïne [prɔkain], *s.f. Ch:* procaine.

procambial, -aux [prɔkɑ̃bjal, -o], *a. Bot:* procambial.

procambium [prɔkɑ̃bjɔm], *s.m. Bot:* procambium.

procédé [prɔsede], *s.m.* **1.** (*a*) proceeding, dealing, conduct; **je ne sais pas quel p. employer,** I do not know what line of action to take; **procédés honnêtes,** (i) courteous behaviour; (ii) square dealing; **homme à procédés,** man of gentlemanly behaviour; **échange de bons procédés,** exchange (i) of courtesies, of civilities, (ii) of friendly services; **user d'un bon p. envers qn,** to act handsomely by, towards, s.o.; **vous avez les bons procédés de votre côté,** yours has been the right way of setting about it; **c'est un échange de bons procédés,** one good turn deserves another; (*b*) *pl. A:* duel preliminaries. **2.** *Ind: etc:* process, way; method (of working); **p. de travail,** operating process; **p. de fabrication,** manufacturing process; **p. chimique,** chemical process; *Mil:* **procédés de combat,** tactical methods; *Pej:* **cela sent le p.,** it seems artificial. **3.** tip (of a billiard cue).

procéder [prɔsede], *v.* (*conj. like* CÉDER) **1.** *v.i.* (*a*) *Theol:* to proceed (**de,** from); **le Saint-Esprit procède du Père et du Fils,** the Holy Ghost proceeds from the Father and the Son; (*b*) to originate (**de, in**); **sa maladie procède de l'intempérie du climat,** his illness arises from, has its origin in, the bad climate; (*c*) to proceed; to act; **p. avec méthode,** to act, proceed, methodically; **p. par élimination,** to proceed by elimination; **façon de p.,** method, procedure; **en procédant ainsi,** by so doing; by acting in this way; **pour démonter le filtre p. de la façon suivante,** (to) remove the filter (proceed) as follows; **le programme procédera de la façon suivante,** the (computer) programme will take the following action; *Jur:* **p. contre qn,** to proceed, take proceedings, against s.o. **2.** *v.ind.tr.* (*a*) **p. à une enquête,** to institute, initiate, an enquiry; **procédons au choix d'un nom,** let us go on to the choice of a name; (*b*) **faire p. à une étude géologique,** to undertake a piece of geological research; **p. au lavage à grande eau de la cour,** to get down to a thorough washing down of the courtyard.

procédural, -aux [prɔsedyral, -o], *a.* procedural.

procédure [prɔsedyːr], *s.f.* **1.** *Jur: etc:* procedure; **règles, mode, de p.,** (rules, order of) procedure; **terme de p.,** law, legal, term; **p. militaire en campagne,** regulations for field courts martial. **2.** *Jur:* proceedings; **p. de faillite,** bankruptcy proceedings. **3.** (*computers*) procedure.

procédurier, -ière [prɔsedyrje, -jɛːr]. **1.** *a.* (*a*) (*of pers.*) litigious; pettifogging (lawyer, etc.); quibbling; who complicates proceedings, *F:* uses too much red tape; **les Normands sont très procéduriers,** the Normans are always going to law; (*b*) **formalités procédurières,** lengthy formalities, *F:* formalities bound up in red tape. **2.** *s.* litigious person; pettifogger; quibbler.

procéleusmatique [prɔseløsmatik], *a. A.Pros:* proceleusmatic.

procellaire [prɔsɛlɛːr], *s.f. Orn:* procellarian, procellarid.

procellariidés [prɔsɛllariide], *s.m.pl. Orn:* Procellariidae, the petrels.
procellariiformes [prɔsɛllariifɔrm], *s.m.pl. Orn:* Procellariiformes.
procéphalique [prɔsefalik], *a. Z:* procephalic.
procès [prɔsɛ], *s.m.* **1.** proceedings at law; action at law; cause, case; **p. civil,** lawsuit, suit; **p. criminel,** (criminal) trial; **engager un p.,** to engage in a lawsuit; **faire, intenter, un p. à qn,** (i) to bring, enter, an action against s.o.; to institute proceedings against s.o.; to sue s.o.; to go to law with s.o.; to bring s.o. to law; (ii) to prosecute s.o.; **être en p. avec qn,** to be at law with s.o.; **intenter un p. en divorce à qn,** to institute divorce proceedings against s.o.; **gagner son p.,** to win one's case; **perdre un p.,** to fail in, lose, a suit, case; **abandonner un p.,** to withdraw an action; **les journaux sont remplis de p. en divorce,** the papers are full of divorce cases; *A:* **faire le p. à qn,** to prosecute s.o.; **faire un p. à qn pour qch.,** to accuse s.o. of sth., to take s.o. to task for sth.; **faire le p. de qn, qch.,** to criticize s.o., sth.; **sans autre forme de p.,** without (any) further ceremony; **on lui a retiré son emploi sans autre forme de p.,** he was dismissed, sacked, out of hand, without any further ceremony; **on l'a chassé sans autre forme de p.,** he was turned out neck and crop. **2.** *Anat:* process; **p. ciliaires,** ciliary processes.
processif, -ive [prɔsɛsif, -iːv], *a.* **1.** litigious, fond of litigation. **2. formes processives,** forms of legal procedure. **3.** *Pol.Ec:* **p. ou récessif,** progressive or recessive.
procession [prɔsɛsjɔ̃], *s.f.* **1.** procession; **aller en p.,** to go, walk, in procession; **une longue p. de touristes,** a long trail, procession, string, of tourists. **2.** *Theol:* **la P. du Saint-Esprit,** the Procession of the Holy Ghost.
processionnaire [prɔsɛsjɔnɛːr], *a. & s.f. Ent:* **(chenille) p.,** processionary (caterpillar).
processionnal, -aux [prɔsɛsjɔnal, -o], *s.m. Ecc:* processional, book of processional hymns.
processionnel, -elle [prɔsɛsjɔnɛl], *a.* processional (hymn, march).
processionnellement [prɔsɛsjɔnɛlmɑ̃], *adv.* in procession, processionally.
processionner [prɔsɛsjɔne], *v.i.* to go, walk, in (a) procession.
processuel, -elle [prɔsɛsɥɛl], *a.* processual.
processus [prɔsesys, -sɛ-], *s.m.* **1.** *Anat:* process. **2.** (*a*) progress, course, process; **le p. de l'évolution,** the evolutionary process; (*b*) method, process; **le p. est toujours le même,** the method of operation, the process, is always the same; (*c*) *Elcs:* (*computers*) process; **p. itératif,** iterative process; **p. récurrent,** recursive process.
procès-verbal [prɔsɛvɛrbal], *s.m.* **1.** (official) report; proceedings, minute(s) (of meeting); record (of evidence, etc.); **dresser p.-v.,** to draw up a report, to report; **tenir le p.-v. des réunions,** to keep the minutes of the meetings; **le p.-v. de la dernière séance fut approuvé,** the minutes of the last meeting were approved; **registre des procès-verbaux,** minute-book; *Nau:* **p.-v. de visite,** certificate of survey; **p.-v. des avaries,** protest. **2.** policeman's report (against s.o.); **dresser le p.-v. d'un délit; dresser un p.-v. contre, à, qn,** to make an official entry of, take down the particulars of, a minor offence; *F:* to take s.o.'s name and address; *F:* **j'ai attrapé un p.-v.,** I've been had up; *F:* **on m'a collé un p.-v. (sur mon pare-brise),** I've got a ticket; *pl. procès-verbaux.*
prochain [prɔʃɛ̃]. **1.** *a.* (*a*) nearest; **le village p.,** the nearest village; **allez à la prochaine pharmacie,** go to the nearest chemist's; **cause prochaine,** proximate cause, immediate cause; (*b*) next; **dimanche p.,** next Sunday, on Sunday next; **la semaine prochaine,** next week; **dans les prochains jours,** in the next few days; **pour les trois prochains jours,** for the next three days; **le trois du mois p.,** on the third of next month; *Com:* **fin p.,** at the end of next month; **le p. numéro,** the next number (of periodical); **la prochaine session,** the next, forthcoming, session; **j'en ferai autant pour vous à la prochaine occasion,** I shall do as much for you at the first opportunity; **arrêtons-nous au p. hôtel que nous apercevrons,** let us stop at the next hotel that we see; **la chambre prochaine,** the next room; (*c*) near at hand; (i) **une auberge prochaine,** a neighbouring inn; (ii) **son p. départ, son départ p.,** his approaching, impending, departure; **l'orage p.,** the coming, impending, storm; **la paix est prochaine,** peace is (near) at hand; **on me prévint de l'arrivée prochaine de la police,** I was warned of the early, impending, arrival of the police; **dans un avenir p.,** in the near future, before long. **2.** *s.m.* neighbour, fellow creature, fellow being; **aime ton p. comme toi-même,** love thy neighbour as thyself; **nos prochains,** our fellow creatures, our fellow beings.
prochainement [prɔʃɛnmɑ̃], *adv.* shortly, soon; at an early date.
proche [prɔʃ]. **1.** *adv.* near; **il demeure ici p.,** he lives close to here; **tout p.,** close at hand; **de p. en p.,** step by step, by degrees; **l'incendie s'étend de p. en p.,** the fire spreads by degrees; **p. de mourir,** near death, approaching death; **nous étions proche(s) de la ruine,** we were on the verge of ruin; **être p. de ses intérêts,** to keep a close watch on one's interests. **2.** *a.* near, neighbouring; **la ville la plus p.,** the nearest town; **mon plus p. voisin,** my nearest neighbour; **le printemps tout p.,** the approaching spring; **l'heure est p.,** the hour is at hand; **ses proches (parents),** his near relations; **ils sont proches parents,** they are closely related.
Proche-Orient (le) [ləprɔʃɔrjɑ̃], *Pr.n.m. Geog:* The Middle East.
proche-oriental, -aux [prɔʃɔrjɑ̃tal, -o], *a. Geog:* Middle-Eastern.
prochile [prɔkil], *s.m. Z:* sloth bear.
prochinois, -oise [prɔʃinwa, -waːz], *a. & s. Pol:* pro-Chinese, *esp.* Maoist.
prochlorite [prɔklɔrit], *s.f. Miner:* prochlorite, ripidolite.
prochordés [prɔkɔrde], *s.m.pl. Nat.Hist:* Prochorda, Prochordata, Protochordata.
prochromosome [prɔkromozoːm], *s.m. Biol:* prochromosome.
prochronisme [prɔkrɔnism], *s.m.* prochronism; ante-dating (of historical event).
procidence [prɔsidɑ̃ːs], *s.f. Med:* prolapse, prolapsus (of womb, etc.).
proclamateur, -trice [prɔklamatœːr, -tris]. **1.** *a.* proclaiming. **2.** *s.* proclaimer.
proclamation [prɔklamasjɔ̃], *s.f.* proclamation; **faire une p.,** to issue a proclamation.
proclamer [prɔklame], *v.tr.* to proclaim, declare, publish; **p. un édit,** to publish, promulgate, an edict; **il fut proclamé avoir le mieux fait,** he was declared to have done the best; **p. le résultat du scrutin,** to declare the poll; **on proclama que . . .,** it was given out that . . .; **p. qn roi,** to proclaim s.o. king; **il n'appartient pas à un particulier mais au juge de p. l'innocence d'un condamné,** it is not for an individual but for the judge to proclaim the innocence of a condemned man; **il proclamait la nécessité d'en finir,** he made a great point about the necessity of finishing with it.
proclise [prɔkliːz], *s.f. Ling:* proclisis.
proclitique [prɔklitik], *a. & s.m. Ling:* proclitic.
proclive [prɔkliːv], *a. Anat:* proclivous.
proclivité [prɔklivite], *s.f.* slope, incline, inclination (of the ground); *Anat:* proclivousness.
Procné [prɔkne], *Pr.n.f. Gr.Myth:* Procne.
procnia [prɔknia], *s.m. Orn:* bell bird.
procœlique [prɔkelik], *a. Z:* procoelous.
procombant [prɔkɔ̃bɑ̃], *a. Bot:* procumbent.
proconsul [prɔkɔ̃syl], *s.m. Hist:* proconsul.
proconsulaire [prɔkɔ̃sylɛːr], *a.* proconsular.
proconsulat [prɔkɔ̃syla], *s.m.* proconsulate, proconsulship.
Procope [prɔkɔp], *Pr.n.m. Gr.Lit:* Procopius.
procoracoïde [prɔkɔrakɔid], *s.m. Anat:* procoracoid.
procordés [prɔkɔrde], *s.m.pl. Z:* Protochordata, Protochordates.
procrastination [prɔkrastinasjɔ̃], *s.f.* procrastination.
procréateur, -trice [prɔkreatœːr, -tris]. **1.** *a.* procreative. **2.** *s.* procreator.
procréation [prɔkreasjɔ̃], *s.f.* procreation, begetting.
procréer [prɔkree], *v.tr.* to procreate, to beget.
Procruste [prɔkryst], *Pr.n.m. Gr.Lit:* Procrustes.
proctalgie [prɔktalʒi], *s.f. Med:* proctalgia.
proctite [prɔktit], *s.f. Med:* proctitis.
proctocèle [prɔktosɛl], *s.f. Med:* proctocele.
proctologie [prɔktɔlɔʒi], *s.f. Med:* proctology.
proctologue [prɔktɔlɔg], *s.m. & f. Med:* proctologist.
proctoptôse [prɔktɔptoːz], *s.m. Med:* proctoptosis.
proctotrupe [prɔktɔtryp], *s.m.,* **proctotrype** [prɔktɔtrip], *s.m. Ent:* proctotrupid, proctotripid.
proctotrupides [prɔktɔtrypid], *s.m.pl.,* **proctotrypidés** [prɔktɔtripide], *s.m.pl. Ent:* Proctotrupidae, Proctotrypidae, Syrphidae.
procurable [prɔkyrabl̩], *a.* procurable, obtainable.
procuratèle [prɔkyratɛl], *s.f. Rom.Hist:* procuratorship.
procurateur [prɔkyratœːr], *s.m. Hist:* procurator; **le p. de Judée,** the Procurator of Judea.
procuratie [prɔkyrasi], *s.f. Italian Hist:* procuratorship.
procuration [prɔkyrasjɔ̃], *s.f. Com: Fin: Jur:* procuration, proxy, power of attorney, letters of procuratory; **p. générale,** full power of attorney; **par p.,** per procurationem, per pro; **signature par p.,** procuration signature; **agir par p.,** to act by procuration, by proxy; **voter par p.,** to vote by proxy; **donner (la) p. à qn, revêtir qn de p.,** (i) to confer powers of attorney on s.o.; (ii) to appoint s.o. as one's proxy.
procuratoire [prɔkyratwaːr], *a.* procurationary.
procuratrice. *See* PROCUREUR.
procure [prɔkyːr], *s.f. Ecc:* (*a*) procuracy; (*b*) procurator's offices.
procurer [prɔkyre], *v.tr.* **p. qch. à qn,** to procure, obtain, get, sth. for s.o.; **c'est moi qui lui ai procuré cet emploi,** it was I who found this job for him, who got him this job; **se p. de l'argent,** to raise, obtain, find, money; **se p. une clientèle,** to work up a connection; **où peut-on se p. ce livre?** where can one get this book? **où vous êtes-vous procuré cela?** where did you get that? **impossible à se p.,** unobtainable.
procureur, procuratrice [prɔkyrœːr, prɔkyratris], *s.* **1.** *Jur:* procurator, proxy. **2.** *s.m. Jur:* (*a*) *A:* attorney (at law); (*b*) **p. de la République** = public prosecutor, *U.S:* district attorney; **p. général** = Attorney General. **3.** *Ecc:* bursar (of a religious order).
procureuse [prɔkyrøːz], *s.f.* **1.** *Jur: A:* attorney's wife. **2.** procuress.
procursif, -ive [prɔkyrsif, -iːv], *a. Med:* **épilepsie procursive,** procursive epilepsy.
Procuste [prɔkyst], *Pr.n.m. Gr.Myth:* Procrustes; **un lit de P.,** a Procrustean bed; **le lit de P.,** the bed of Procrustes.
Procyon [prɔsjɔ̃], *Pr.n.m. Astr:* Procyon.
procyonidés [prɔsjɔnide], *s.m.pl. Z:* Procyonidae.
prodiastase [prɔdjastɑːz], *s.f. Ch:* proenzyme, zymogen.
prodigalement [prɔdigalmɑ̃], *adv.* prodigally; lavishly.
prodigalité [prɔdigalite], *s.f.* **1.** prodigality, lavishness; **la p. de la nature,** the prodigality, bountifulness, of nature. **2.** wastefulness, prodigality; **ses prodigalités l'ont ruiné,** his extravagance has ruined him.
prodige [prɔdiːʒ], *s.m.* prodigy, wonder; **c'est un p.,** (i) he is a prodigy; (ii) it is something prodigious; **faire des prodiges,** to do, work, wonders; to perform miracles; **tenir du p.,** appear extraordinary, inexplicable; **un p. de cruauté,** a monster of cruelty; *a.* **enfant p.,** infant prodigy.
prodigieusement [prɔdiʒjøzmɑ̃], *adv.* prodigiously; **il était p. vieilli,** he had aged terribly; **p. intelligent,** prodigiously clever.
prodigieux, -euse [prɔdiʒjø, -øːz], *a.* (*a*) *Lit:* prodigious, miraculous; (*b*) prodigious, extraordinary, amazing; **ce p. génie,** this prodigious, extraordinary, genius; **une foule prodigieuse,** a stupendous crowd; *s.m.* **le p.,** the prodigious, the extraordinary.
prodigue [prɔdig]. **1.** *a.* (*a*) prodigal, lavish, unsparing (de, of); **p. d'excuses,** profuse in apologies; **être p. de son argent,** to spend lavishly; to be free with one's money; (*b*) prodigal, wasteful, spendthrift, thriftless; *B:* **l'enfant p.,** the Prodigal Son. **2.** *s.* prodigal, spendthrift, squanderer.
prodiguer [prɔdige], *v.tr.* **1.** to be prodigal, lavish, of (sth.); to lavish (sth.); **p. qch. à qn,** to lavish sth. on s.o.; **p. sa santé, ses forces,** to be unsparing of one's health, of one's strength; **il ne prodigue pas les éloges,** he is sparing, chary, of praise. **2.** to waste, squander, throw away (sth.).
se prodiguer. 1. to lay oneself out to please. **2. se p. en éloges,** to be lavish of praise. **3. le médecin se prodigue pour ses malades,** the doctor does not spare himself to help his patients.
pro domo [prodɔmo], *a. & adv.phr.* **plaidoyer p.d.,** plea in one's own cause, speech in one's own defence; **plaider p.d.,** to plead in person.
prodrome [prɔdroːm], *s.m.* prodrome (de, to); (i) *Med:* premonitory symptom (of disease); (ii) preamble (to a treatise, to a science).
prodromique [prɔdrɔmik], *a. Med:* prodromal, prodromic.
producer [prɔdjusœːr], *s.m. Cin: etc:* producer.
producteur, -trice [prɔdyktœːr, -tris]. **1.** *a.* productive (de, of); producing; **régions productrices d'un pays,** productive regions of a country; **capital p. d'intérêt,** interest-bearing capital; *Ind:* **appareil p.,** generating apparatus; generator (of gases). **2.** (*a*) *s.* producer; (*b*) *s.m. Cin:* backer.

productibilité [prɔdyktibilite], *s.f.* productibility.

productible [prɔdyktibl̩], *a.* producible.

productif, -ive [prɔdyktif, -iːv], *a.* (*a*) productive; fertile (soil, etc.); *Pol.Ec:* **personnel p., main-d'œuvre productive,** productive labour; (*b*) **actions productives d'un dividende de . . .,** shares yielding a dividend of . . ..

production [prɔdyksjɔ̃], *s.f.* **1.** *Jur: etc:* production; exhibiting; **p. des pièces,** exhibition of documents; **p. d'un témoin,** production, bringing forward, of a witness; **p. d'une carte d'identité,** production of an identity card. **2.** (*a*) producing, production; generation (of electricity, steam, etc.); raising (of steam); **étude de la p. du son,** study of the production of sound; *Mus: etc:* **p. de la voix,** voice production; *Atom.Ph:* **p. de neutrons par fission,** fission production of neutrons; (*b*) *Pol.Ec: Ind: etc:* production; **moyens de p.,** (i) means of production; (ii) capital equipment; **biens de p.,** (i) producer goods; (ii) capital equipment; **capacité de p.,** output capacity, production capacity; **augmenter la p.,** to increase production, output; **ralentir la p.,** to slow down production; to reduce (the) output; **taux de p.,** rate of production; **coûts, frais, de p.,** production costs; **les prix restent stables à la p.,** production prices, costs of manufacture, are stable; *Ind:* **p. à la chaîne,** line-flow production; **p. en masse, en série,** mass production; **p. continue,** continuous production; **p. sur commande,** production to order; **ordonnancement de la p.,** sequencing; **p. agricole,** agricultural production, output; **productions de plein champ,** field crops; **productions maraîchères,** market-garden produce; **p. littéraire,** literary output; **productions du génie,** works of genius; *Pol.Ec:* **p. nationale,** national product; (*c*) *Cin: T.V: etc:* producer; **directeur de p.,** producer; **Monsieur X a assuré la p. de ce film,** Mr X has sponsored this film; **p. à grand spectacle,** spectacular production, film; (*d*) *Med:* **p. accidentale, p. tissulaire,** growth; excrescence.

productivité [prodyktivite], *s.f.* productivity, productiveness; productive capacity; yield-capacity (of a forest, etc.).

produire [prɔdɥiːr], *v.tr.* (*pr.p.* **produisant;** *p.p.* **produit;** *pr.ind.* **je produis, il produit, n. produisons, ils produisent;** *p.d.* **je produisais;** *p.h.* **je produisis;** *fu.* **je produirai**) **1.** to produce, bring forward, adduce (evidence, claim, reason, etc.); **p. un témoin,** to produce, bring forward, a witness; *A:* **c'est moi qui l'ai produite dans le monde,** it was I who introduced her into society, who brought her out; **p. un film, une artiste,** to produce a film, an artiste; *abs. Jur:* **p. à une liquidation, faillite,** to prove claims in bankruptcy and liquidation. **2.** to produce, yield; to bring forth, bear (offspring, etc.); **arbre qui produit beaucoup (de fruits),** tree that bears a great deal of fruit; **argent qui produit de l'intérêt,** money that yields interest; **p. de la chaleur,** to generate heat; **p. de la vapeur,** to generate, raise, produce, steam; **p. des ondes,** to set up waves; **p. cent voitures par jour,** to produce, turn out, a hundred cars a day; **le monopole des tabacs produit des millions à l'État,** the tobacco monopoly brings in millions to the State; *abs.* **p. beaucoup,** (i) to produce a great deal of work; (ii) (*of land, etc.*) to yield well, to produce large crops; **le rôle du poète est de p.,** the role of the poet is to create, is creative. **3.** to produce, bring about (result, effect); to bring on (disease); **son apparition produisit un grand émoi,** his appearance caused, gave rise to, great excitement; **p. une impression favorable,** to produce, create, a favourable impression; **p. des protestations,** to provoke protest.

se produire. 1. se p. (dans le monde), to come forward; to make one's way (in society). **2.** (*a*) to occur, happen, arise; to take place; to come into being; **les changements qui se sont produits depuis cinquante ans,** the changes that have come about in the last fifty years; **si vous saviez le changement qui s'est produit en lui!** if you knew the change that has come over him! **il pourrait se p. des incidents,** there might be trouble; (*b*) *Th: etc:* to appear.

produit [prɔdɥi], *s.m.* **1.** (*a*) product; produce; **produits agricoles, maraîchers,** agricultural, market-gardening, produce; **p. industriel,** industrial product; **produits de base,** (i) basic, (ii) staple, commodities or products; **produits de consommation,** consumer goods; **produits de marque,** branded goods; **produits manufacturés,** manufactured goods, products; manufactures; **produits finis, semi-finis,** finished, semi-finished, products; **produits dérivés,** derivatives; by-products; **produits de rejet,** waste products; **les produits et les sous-produits de la distillation du pétrole,** the products and by-products of oil distillation; *Petroleum Ind:* **p. d'addition,** additive, *F:* dope; *Metalw:* **p. de départ,** test piece; *Metall:* **p. de germination,** nucleating agent; **produits chimiques,** chemicals; **produits pharmaceutiques,** pharmaceuticals; **produits de beauté,** beauty preparations; cosmetics; **produits de nettoyage,** cleaning materials; **p. d'étanchéité,** sealing compound; **produits diététiques, de régime,** health foods; *Pol.Ec:* **p. national brut,** gross national product; (*b*) proceeds; yield; **p. d'une vente,** proceeds of a sale; **p. net,** net earnings; net proceeds; **p. casuel,** casual profit; *Com:* **le p. de la journée,** the day's takings, receipts; **le p. de dix années de travail,** the product, result, of ten years' work; *Pol.Ec:* **produits immatériels,** services (rendered). **2.** *Mth:* product (of multiplication).

proembryon [prɔɑ̃briɔ̃], *s.m.* proembryo.

proème [prɔɛm], *s.m.* proem, preamble, prelude (de, to).

proéminence [prɔeminɑ̃ːs], *s.f.* prominence. **1.** prominency. **2.** protuberance, projection.

proéminent [prɔeminɑ̃], *a.* prominent, projecting, protuberant; jutting out.

proenzyme [prɔɑ̃zim], *s.f. Bio-Ch:* proenzyme, zymogen.

prof [prɔf], *s.m. & f. F: Sch:* (= PROFESSEUR) **le, la, p. de maths,** the maths master, mistress; **p. de fac(ulté),** (i) prof; (ii) don; lecturer.

profanateur, -trice [prɔfanatœːr, -tris], *s.* profaner; desecrator.

profanation [prɔfanasjɔ̃], *s.f.* profanation; desecration.

profane [prɔfan]. **1.** *a.* profane; (*a*) secular (history, music, etc.); (*b*) unhallowed, ungodly; (*c*) impious, sacrilegious. **2.** *s.* (*a*) uninitiated person, layman, *F:* outsider (in art, science, law, etc.); (*b*) *Ecc:* person outside the fold; (*c*) *A:* irreverent, ungodly, person.

profaner [prɔfane], *v.tr.* **1.** to profane; to desecrate (church, etc.); to violate (a grave). **2.** to misuse, degrade (one's genius, talent, etc.).

proférer [prɔfere], *v.tr.* (**je profère, n. proférons; je proférerai**) to utter (a word, an insult, an oath); **sans p. une (seule) parole,** without a word; **p. une accusation contre qn,** to bring an accusation against s.o.

proferment [prɔfɛrmɑ̃], *s.m. Bio-Ch:* proferment, proenzyme, zymogen.

profès, -esse [prɔfɛ, -ɛs], *a. & s. Ecc:* professed (monk, nun, house).

professer [prɔfese], *v.tr.* **1.** to profess (religion, doctrine, opinion); **p. une grande estime pour qn,** to profess great esteem, a high regard, for s.o.; **p. des opinions,** to hold views. **2.** to teach; to be a professor of, a lecturer in (French, etc.); to exercise (a calling); **il professe la physique au lycée,** he teaches physics at the *lycée*; *abs.* **il professe à la Sorbonne,** he is a professor at the Sorbonne.

professeur [prɔfɛsœːr], *s.m.* **1.** (school)master, mistress; (naval, etc.) instructor; **p. (de faculté),** (i) professor; (ii) = senior lecturer; reader; **elle est p. d'anglais,** (i) she teaches English; (ii) she is professor of, a lecturer in, English; **p. principal,** form master; **p. de première** = sixth form master; **p. titulaire,** master, mistress, who has the *agrégation* or who is of sufficiently long standing; **p. de dessin,** drawing master, mistress; **p. de chant,** singing master, mistress; **p. de natation,** swimming instructor; **Monsieur le Professeur X,** Professor X. **2.** professor (of a faith); **p. d'athéisme,** avowed atheist.

profession [prɔfɛsjɔ̃], *s.f.* **1.** profession (of a religion, doctrine, etc.); **p. de foi,** profession of faith; *Ecc:* **faire p. (dans un ordre),** to make one's profession, to profess oneself (in an order); **faire p. de qch.,** to profess sth.; **il fait p. d'athéisme, de socialisme,** he professes himself an atheist, a socialist. **2.** (*a*) profession, occupation, calling, business, trade; **sans p.,** (i) having no trade or profession; *Adm:* not gainfully employed; (ii) (*married woman filling in form*) married woman; housewife; **p. libérale,** (liberal) profession; **médecin de (sa) p.,** doctor by profession; **menuisier de p.,** carpenter by trade; **ballerine de p.,** professional ballet dancer; **les membres des professions libérales,** the professional classes; **il fait p. de remettre les clôtures en état,** his trade, his job, is to repair fences; (*b*) **(les membres de) la p.,** the profession; **usages de la p.,** professional practices.

professionnalisme [prɔfɛsjɔnalism], *s.m. Sp:* professionalism.

professionnel, -elle [prɔfɛsjɔnɛl]. **1.** *a.* (*a*) professional; vocational; **orientation professionnelle,** vocational guidance; **aptitudes, connaissances, professionnelles,** professional qualifications; **école professionnelle** = technical school; **enseignement p., formation professionnelle,** vocational training; **maladies professionnelles,** occupational diseases; **sélection professionnelle,** personnel selection; **journal, organe, p.,** trade journal, paper; **dans les milieux professionnels,** in the profession, the trade; (*b*) by profession, professional; **écrivain p.,** writer by profession; *Sp:* **joueur p.,** professional (player); **le football p.,** professional football. **2.** *s.* (*a*) *esp. Sp:* professional; (*b*) **c'est un p. de la haine,** he makes a profession of hatred; **c'est un p. du retard,** he's inevitably late; he always arrives late; (*c*) *s.f. F:* **professionnelle,** prostitute, tart.

professionnellement [prɔfɛsjɔnɛlmɑ̃], *adv.* professionally.

professoral, -aux [prɔfɛsɔral, -o], *a.* professorial; **le corps p.,** the body of teachers, the teaching profession; *Pej:* **ton p.,** pedantic tone.

professorat [prɔfɛsɔra], *s.m.* **1.** professorship; lectureship; teaching post. **2.** *coll.* the body of teachers, the teaching profession; **choisir le p.,** to choose teaching as one's profession, to decide to be a schoolmaster, etc.

profil [prɔfil], *s.m.* **1.** (*a*) profile, side-face; **voir, dessiner, qn de p.,** to see, draw, s.o. in profile, side-face; (*b*) *Journ:* profile. **2.** *Const: Mec.E: etc:* profile, contour, outline, section, shape; **projeter qch. en p.,** to project sth. in profile; **p. en long,** longitudinal section; *Geog:* **p. longitudinal,** longitudinal profile (of valley); **p. en travers,** cross section; **p. d'un rail,** section of a rail; **p. de marches,** nosing of steps; **p. de l'horizon,** skyline; **le p. terrestre,** the contour of the earth; **carte des profils de route,** contour (road) map; *Mil:* **ouvrage à fort p., à faible p.,** massive, slight, work; *Const:* **p. intérieur,** inner shape; *Av:* **traînée de p.,** profile drag; *Surv:* **p. des parties vues et cachées,** visibility diagram. **3.** (*a*) graph, curve, profile; **construire le p. de,** to chart; (*b*) (*in statistics*) **p. saisonnier,** seasonal adjustment. **4.** (*a*) **p. médical,** medical history; (*b*) (*in advertisement*) **société chimique recherche personne ayant le p. suivant,** a chemical firm is looking for a man with the following qualifications and experience. **5.** *Elcs:* (*computers*) pattern; **p. binaire,** bit pattern.

profilage [prɔfilaːʒ], *s.m.* (*a*) profiling; (*b*) *Metalw:* shaping; (*c*) streamlining (of car body, etc.).

profilé [prɔfile]. **1.** *a.* (*a*) streamlined; *Aut:* **arrière p.,** fastback; *Av:* **capot de moteur p.,** low-drag engine cowling; (*b*) *Const: Metalw:* extruded, sectional, structural; **pièce profilée,** shaped piece; **poutre profilée,** structural beam; **fers profilés,** sectional irons; *Aut:* **châssis en fer p.,** rolled-section chassis; *Tls:* **fraise profilée,** profile cutter. **2.** *s.m. Const: Metalw:* (extruded, structural) shape, section; rolled bar, section; extrusion; **gros p.,** heavy section; **p. léger,** light section; **profilés en acier,** steel sections, shapes; sectional steel; **p. à, en, T,** T section, T iron, T bar; **p. en U,** channel bar; **profilés pour construction,** constructional steelwork.

profilée [prɔfile], *s.f.* side view (of object); **toute une p. d'arcs et de ponts,** a long range of arches and bridges.

profilement [prɔfilmɑ̃], *s.m. Fort:* ground plan.

profiler [prɔfile], *v.tr.* **1.** to profile; to draw (sth.) in section; to draw out a profile of (sth.). **2.** to cut, to machine, (sth.) to a special shape; to shape (a piece); **p. une pièce sur modèle,** to cut a piece to pattern; **machine à p.,** profiling machine, shaping machine.

se profiler, to stand out in profile, to be outlined, to be silhouetted (**à, sur, contre,** on, against); **collines qui se profilent à l'horizon, contre le ciel bleu,** hills that are outlined, that stand out, on the horizon, against the blue sky; **une solution commence à se p.,** we are beginning to see the way to a solution.

profilographe [prɔfilɔgraf], *s.m. Civ.E:* profilograph.

profilomètre [prɔfilɔmɛtr̥], *s.m. Mec.E: etc:* profilometer, profilograph, contour follower.

profit [prɔfi], *s.m.* profit, benefit; **petits profits d'un domestique,** servant's perquisites; **profits et pertes,** profit and loss; **se tromper à son p.,** to make a mistake to one's own advantage; **faire (son) p. de qch.,** to profit by sth.; **faites-en votre p.,** (i) profit by that; (ii) take that to heart;

vendre à p., to sell at a profit; **mettre qch. à p.**, to turn sth. to account; **tirer p. de qch.**, (i) to reap, derive, benefit or advantage from sth.; (ii) to make use of sth., to utilize sth.; **tirer tout le p. possible de qch.**, to turn sth. to the best account; **il y a un grand p. à le faire**, it is highly profitable to do it; **travail sans p.**, unprofitable, profitless, work; **j'en eus peu de p.**, I gained little advantage from it; *Prov:* **le p. de l'un est le dommage de l'autre**, my gain is your loss; **p. maritime**, bottomry interest; *prep.phr.* **au p. de qn**, on behalf of, for the benefit of, s.o.; **représentation au p. des pauvres**, performance in aid of, for the benefit of, the poor; **souscrire un chèque au profit de qn**, to write out a cheque in favour of s.o.; **les socialistes perdront au p. des communistes**, votes will swing from the Socialists to the Communists; *Jur:* **p. du défaut**, benefit of non-appearance of the other party.

profitable [prɔfitabl̩], *a.* profitable; advantageous (**à, pour**, to); **affaire p.**, paying business.

profitablement [prɔfitabləmɑ̃], *adv.* profitably.

profitant [prɔfitɑ̃], *a. F:* **1.** (*a*) thriving (child); (*b*) economical (material, food, etc.). **2.** profit-seeking (person).

profiter [prɔfite], *v.i.* **1.** (*a*) **p. de qch.**, to take advantage of sth.; to turn sth. to account; to derive benefit from sth.; **p. d'un conseil**, to benefit from advice; **p. de l'occasion**, to seize the opportunity; **les habitants de Grenoble profitent de la montagne**, the inhabitants of Grenoble are fortunate in having the mountains (near them); **il profita de ce que tout le monde dormait encore pour s'esquiver**, he took advantage of the fact that everyone was still asleep to slip away; (*b*) **p. sur une vente**, to make a profit on a sale; **il profite beaucoup à faire cela**, he benefits very much by doing that. **2. p. à qn**, to profit s.o.; to be profitable to s.o.; to benefit s.o.; to turn out to s.o.'s advantage; **rien ne lui a profité**, nothing has been of any profit, benefit, to him; **à quoi (cela) profitera-t-il d'y aller?** what advantage will you have in going? how will going there help you? **thésauriseurs dont l'argent ne profite à personne**, hoarders whose money is of no use to anybody, whose money benefits no one; **faire p. son argent**, to lay out one's money to advantage; *impers.* **il nous profite plus de vendre**, it is more advantageous, more profitable, for us to sell it. **3.** *F:* (*of child, plant, etc.*) to thrive, grow; **p. en sagesse**, to grow in wisdom; **les enfants profitent à vue d'œil**, the children are filling out visibly. **4.** *F:* **étoffe qui profite**, material that wears well, profitable material.

profiterole [prɔfit(ə)rɔl], *s.f. Cu:* profiterole.

profiteur, -euse [prɔfitœːr, -øːz], *s.* **1.** *Pej:* profiteer; **profiteurs de guerre**, war profiteers. **2.** *Pol.Ec:* profit taker.

profond [prɔfɔ̃]. **1.** *a.* (*a*) deep (well, lake, cave, wound, etc.); **puits p. de six mètres**, well six metres deep; **révérence profonde**, low, profound, deep, bow; **voix profonde**, deep voice; **ici le lac devient plus p.**, here the lake deepens, gets deeper; **peu p.**, shallow; (*b*) deep-seated; **raisons profondes d'un événement**, underlying causes of an event; **cause profonde de . . .**, underlying cause of . . .; *Anat:* **vaisseau p.**, profunda; (*c*) profound (wisdom, scholarship, etc.); deep (thinker); deep, sound (sleep); **il y a une profonde différence**, the difference goes deep, there is a profound difference; **écouter qn avec un intérêt p.**, to listen to s.o. with profound, absorbed, interest; **le silence devint plus p.**, the silence deepened; **p. soupir**, deep(-drawn) sigh; heavy sigh; **aversion profonde**, deep-rooted aversion; **p. désespoir**, deep, blank, despair; **p. dégoût**, deep disgust; thorough distaste; **p. scélérat**, downright, utter, scoundrel; *Psy:* **arriéré p.**, mental defective. **2.** *adv.* **creuser p.**, to dig deep; **enterrer qch. plus p.**, to bury sth. deeper; **retentir p.**, to give a hollow sound. **3.** *s.m.* depth; **au plus p. de mon cœur**, in the depths of my heart, in my heart of hearts; **au plus p. de la nuit**, at dead of night, in the dead of night; **au plus p. des bois**, in the inmost recesses of the woods. **4.** *s.f. P:* **profonde**, pocket.

profondément [prɔfɔ̃demɑ̃], *adv.* profoundly, deeply; **réfléchir p.**, to think deeply, intently; to think hard; **haïr qn p.**, to hate s.o. intensely; **p. vexé**, extremely annoyed; **p. endormi**, sound asleep; **saluer p.**, **s'incliner p.**, to make a deep bow; **p. versé dans qch.**, deeply versed in sth.

profondeur [prɔfɔ̃dœːr], *s.f.* **1.** depth (of well, river, cave, etc.); **les profondeurs d'un bois**, the depths of a wood; **avoir dix mètres de p.**, to be ten metres deep, ten metres in depth; **en p.**, **dans le sens de la p.**, in depth; *Av:* **p. de l'aile**, chord; **p. du col-de-cygne**, throat depth; *Opt:* **p. de foyer**, depth of focus; *Geol:* **roche de p.**, plutonic rock; **le peu de p. du lac**, the shallowness, lack of depth, of the lake. **2.** profoundness, depth; **la p. de son savoir**, the profoundness, profundity, depth, of his knowledge; **p. des sentiments**, depth of feelings.

pro forma [prɔfɔrma], *a.phr.inv. Com:* **facture p.f.**, pro forma invoice.

profus [prɔfy], *a.* profuse; abundant; lavish (praise).

profusément [prɔfyzemɑ̃], *adv.* profusely; lavishly; in abundance.

profusion [prɔfyzjɔ̃], *s.f.* (*a*) profusion, profuseness; abundance; **avoir tout à p.**, to have everything in profusion; **répandu à profusion**, scattered broadcast; (*b*) lavishness; **donner avec p.**, to give lavishly, without stint; **dépenser de l'argent à p.**, to spend lavishly.

progamique [prɔgamik], *a. Biol:* progamous.

progéniture [prɔʒenityːr], *s.f.* progeny, progeniture, offspring (of animals, *Hum:* of persons).

progéria [prɔʒerja], **progérie** [prɔʒeri], *s.f. Med:* progeria.

progestatif, -ive [prɔʒɛstatif, -iːv]. **1.** *a. Anat:* **corps p.**, corpus luteum, yellow body. **2.** *s.m. Physiol:* progestogen.

progestérone [prɔʒɛsterɔn], *s.f. Physiol:* progesterone.

proglottis [prɔglɔtis], *s.m. Ann:* proglottis, proglottid.

prognathe [prɔgnat], *a. Anthr:* prognathous, prognathic; underhung, undershot (jaw); *a. & s.* (person) with an underhung, undershot, jaw.

prognathie [prɔgnati], *s.f.*, **prognathisme** [prɔgnatism], *s.m.* prognathism, prognathy; **p. inférieur(e)**, **p. mandibulaire**, mandibular protrusion, protraction of the mandible, underhung jaw; **p. supérieur(e)**, maxillary protrusion, protrusion of the maxilla; **p. bimaxillaire**, double protrusion.

Progné [prɔgne]. **1.** *Pr.n.f. Gr.Myth:* Procne. **2.** *s.m. Orn:* **(rossignol) p.**, sprosser, thrush nightingale.

prognostic [prɔgnɔstik], *s.m. A:* = PRONOSTIC.

prognostique [prɔgnɔstik], *a. Med:* prognostic (sign, etc.).

programmabilité [prɔgramabilite], *s.f.* programmability.

programmable [prɔgramabl̩], *a.* programmable.

programmateur, -trice [prɔgramatœːr, -tris]. **1.** *s.* (*pers.*) (*a*) *Elcs:* (*computers*) programmer; scheduler; (*b*) *T.V: etc:* programmer. **2.** *s.m.* (*device*) programmer (of computer); automatic control (of washing machine, etc.).

programmation [prɔgramasjɔ̃], *s.f.* (*a*) programming, planning; **p. à longue échéance**, long-range planning; (*b*) *Elcs:* (*computers*) programming; **aides à p.**, software; **p. linéaire**, linear programming, linear optimization; **p. à accès sélectif**, random access programming.

programmatique [prɔgramatik], *s.f.* programmatics.

programme [prɔgram], *s.m.* (*a*) (concert, cinema, etc.) program(me); **p. de télévision**, television programme, telecast; (*at theatre, etc.*) **acheter un p.**, to buy a programme; (*b*) *Sch:* **p. (d'études)**, curriculum; syllabus; **les auteurs au, du p.**, the set books; **ce n'est pas au p.**, it's not in the syllabus; *Mil:* **p. d'instruction**, training programme, syllabus; (*c*) *Pol:* programme (of political party); (party) platform; (*d*) *Ind: etc:* programme; schedule; **p. à longue échéance**, long-range plan, forward plan; **p. de fabrication**, **de production**, production programme, schedule; **p. d'entretien courant**, servicing schedule; **p. de renouvellement (du matériel, etc.)**, (equipment, etc.) replacement schedule; **p. de recherche nucléaire**, nuclear research programme; *Fin:* **p. d'investissements**, investment programme; (*e*) *Elcs:* (*computers*) program(me), routine; **p. codé**, coded programme; **p. d'analyse**, trace programme, routine; **p. en boucle**, **p. fermé**, closed routine; **p. enregistré**, stored programme; **p. heuristique**, heuristic programme; **bibliothèque de programmes**, programme library, routine library.

programmé [prɔgrame], *a.* **enseignement p.**, programmed teaching; (*of computer work*) **arrêt p.**, coded stop, programme stop; **contrôle p.**, programmed check, routine check.

programmer [prɔgrame], *v.tr.* to program(me).

programmerie [prɔgramri], *s.f. Elcs:* (*computers*) software.

programmeur, -euse [prɔgramœːr, -øːz], *s.* (*pers.*) programmer.

progrès [prɔgrɛ], *s.m.* (*a*) (*usu. pl.*) progress; **il marquait sur la carte les p. de l'armée**, he marked on the map the progress, advances, of the army; **ils regardaient avec horreur les p. de l'incendie**, with horror they watched the fire gaining hold, spreading; **les p. d'une épidémie**, the progress, spreading, of an epidemic; **les p. de l'inondation**, the rising, spreading, of the flood; **les p. de la maladie**, the progress, development, of an illness; (*b*) progress, advancement, improvement; development; **un p. sensible**, appreciable progress; **il a fait des p. en anglais**, he has made progress, has improved, has come on (well), in English; **ce trimestre votre fils n'a fait aucun p.**, your son has made no progress this term; **la science a réalisé de sérieux p.**, science has made considerable progress, has advanced considerably; **suivre les p. d'une science**, to keep abreast of a science; **suivre les p. d'une affaire**, to keep track of a matter; **cette époque de p.**, this age of progress; **tous ces prétendus p.**, all this so-called progress, these so-called improvements; **croire au p.**, to believe in progress; **on n'arrête pas le p.**, progress cannot be checked; *F:* **il y a du p.**, things are improving; **être ami du p.**, to be progressive; *Pol:* **parti du p.**, progressive party.

progresser [prɔgrese, -ɛse], *v.i.* (*a*) to progress, advance; to make (head)way; to gain ground; (*b*) to improve; (*c*) (*computers*) **faire p.**, to increment.

progressif, -ive [prɔgresif, -iːv; -ɛsif], *a.* (*a*) progressive, forward (movement, etc.); *Pol: O:* **parti p.**, progressive party; (*b*) **impôt p.**, **à taux p.**, progressive, graduated, tax; **surtaxe progressive**, graduated surtax; (*c*) gradual (growth, development); **l'amélioration progressive du rendement**, the gradual improvement in productivity; *Sch:* **son cours n'est pas p.**, his course is not graded according to difficulty; *Med:* **paralysie progressive**, creeping paralysis; *Sm.a:* **pas p.**, gaining twist (of rifling).

progression [prɔgrɛsjɔ̃], *s.f.* **1.** (*a*) progress(ion); moving forward; advancement; **recettes en p.**, receipts on the increase; (*b*) **il n'y a pas de p.**, there is no grading, graduation. **2.** *Mth:* **p. arithmétique**, **par différence**, arithmetical progression; **p. géométrique**, **par quotient**, geometrical progression; **p. harmonique**, harmonic progression.

progressionnel, -elle [prɔgrɛsjɔnɛl], *a.* progressional.

progressisme [prɔgresism, -ɛsism], *s.m.* **1.** belief in progress, progressionism. **2.** *Pol:* advanced socialist doctrine.

progressiste [prɔgresist, -ɛsist], *Pol:* **1.** *s.m. & f.* (*a*) progressist, progressionist; (*b*) advanced socialist. **2.** *a.* (*a*) progressive (party); (*b*) left-wing; (*c*) forward-looking.

progressivement [prɔgresivmɑ̃, -ɛsi-], *adv.* progressively, gradually; step by step.

progressivité [prɔgresivite, -ɛsivite], *s.f.* progressiveness; *Fin:* progressive increase (in taxation).

prohiber [prɔibe], *v.tr.* to prohibit, forbid; **p. à qn de faire qch.**, to prohibit s.o. from doing sth., to forbid s.o. to do sth.; **mariage entre degrés prohibés**, marriage within the prohibited degrees; **p. le tabac à qn**, to forbid s.o. tobacco; **marchandises prohibées**, prohibited goods; **temps prohibé**, close season (for hunting, fishing, etc.); close time.

prohibitif, -ive [prɔibitif, -iːv], *a.* **1.** prohibitory (law, etc.). **2.** prohibitive (price, duty). **3.** *Ecc:* inhibitive (decree).

prohibition [prɔibisjɔ̃], *s.f.* prohibition, *U.S: Hist:* **loi de p.**, prohibition law.

prohibitionnisme [prɔibisjɔnism], *s.m. Pol.Ec: etc:* prohibition(ism).

prohibitionniste [prɔibisjɔnist], *a. & s.m. Pol.Ec: etc:* prohibitionist.

prohibitoire [prɔibitwaːr], *a. Jur:* prohibitory.

proie [prwɑ, -a], *s.f.* (*a*) prey; *Ven:* quarry; **oiseau de p.**, (i) bird of prey; (ii) cruel, rapacious, person; **bête de p.**, beast of prey; predatory animal, predator; (*b*) *A:* prize, spoil, booty (in war); (*c*) **être**, **devenir**, **la p. de qn, de qch.**, to be, become, the prey, victim, of s.o., sth.; **les renards font leur p. des poules et des agneaux**, foxes prey on hens and lambs; **la ville fut la p. des flammes**, the town was consumed, destroyed, by fire; **être en p. aux remords**, to be a prey to remorse; **être en p. au doute**, to be tormented by doubt, possessed with doubt; **être en p. à une violente émotion**, to be prey to a violent emotion; **être en p. à la douleur**, to be grief-stricken; **tomber en p. à . . .**, to fall a prey to . . ..

projecteur [prɔʒɛktœːr], *s.m.* 1. (*a*) *Tchn:* projector, discharger; p. de fumée, smoke discharger; p. lance-fusée, pyrotechnic projector, rocket projector; (*b*) *Sp:* ball trap (for pigeon shooting); p. à main, pistol ball trap. 2. *Cin: etc:* projector; p. cinématographique, p. de cinéma, cinema projector; p. de diapositives, transparency, slide, projector; p. stéréoscopique, stereo projector. 3. (*a*) p. de signalisation, signal(ling) lamp, morse lamp, blinker; p. optique de télécommunications, light-beam transmitter; *Av:* p. (de signalisation) de bord, signal searchlight (of aircraft); (*b*) projector, floodlight (of monument, shop window, etc.); illuminer (un bâtiment, etc.) par projecteurs, to floodlight (a building, etc.); donner un coup de p. sur qch., to flash a searchlight on sth.; p. orientable, spotlight; *Th:* diriger les projecteurs sur un acteur, to direct, turn, the spotlights on an actor; *Av:* p. d'atterrissage, landing-area floodlight; p. de piste, runway floodlight; *Mil:* batterie, unité, de projecteurs, searchlight battery, unit; (*c*) *Cin: Phot:* p. à main, pistol light; p. d'appoint, fill(-in) light; p. de fond, back light; p. intensif, spotlight, cone light; (*d*) *Aut:* headlight; p. auxiliaire orientable, spotlight.

projecteur-pulvérisateur [prɔʒɛktœrpylverizatœːr], *s.m.* spray-painting apparatus; *pl. projecteurs-pulvérisateurs.*

projectif, -ive [prɔʒɛktif, -iːv], *a.* 1. projective (co-ordinates, etc.). 2. impulsive (force). 3. *Psy:* tests projectifs, projective tests.

projectile [prɔʒɛktil], *a. & s.m.* projectile; missile; *Artil:* p. creux, d'éclatement, shell; p. plein, p. perce-cuirasse, solid projectile, armour-piercing shot; p. terre-à-avion, ground-to-air missile; p. avion-à-terre, air-to-ground missile, air-to-surface missile.

projection [prɔʒɛksjɔ̃], *s.f.* 1. (*a*) projection; throwing forward, up, out (of heavy body, liquid, etc.); (*welding*) flash, splatter; splashing; *Mch: etc:* p. d'eau, priming; *Ind:* p. de sable, sand blasting; *Geol:* projections volcaniques, (volcanic) ejecta; (*b*) *Cin: etc:* projection; appareil de p., projector; cabine de p., projection room, booth; p. par transparence, rear projection; conférence avec projections, lecture (illustrated) with slides, with film strips; (*c*) beam (of light); p. électrique, searchlight beam. 2. (*a*) *Mth: Arch: etc:* projection, plan; p. horizontale, ground plan; *N.Arch:* p. transversale, body plan (of ship); p. longitudinale, sheer drawing; p. horizontale, half-breadth plan; (*b*) *Mapm:* projection; p. centrale, p. gnomonique, gnomonic projection; p. conique, polyconique, conical, polyconical, projection; p. conforme, orthomorphique, conformal, orthomorphic, projection; p. (conique) conforme de Lambert, Lambert conformal (conical) projection; p. conique sécante, secant conical projection; p. cylindrique, cylindrical projection; p. cylindrique conforme de Lambert, Lambert conformal cylindrical projection; p. équivalente, equal-area projection; p. polyédrique, polyhedric projection; p. de Mercator, Mercator's projection; p. homalographique, homalographic projection; p. orthographique, orthographic projection; p. perspective, perspective projection; p. stéréographique, stereographic projection; p. zénithale, zenithal projection; p. zénithale équidistante, zenithal, azimuthal, equidistant projection.

projectionniste [prɔʒɛksjɔnist], *s.m. & f. Cin:* projectionist.

projecture [prɔʒɛktyːr], *s.f.* 1. *Arch:* projection, projecture, ledge. 2. *Bot:* rib.

projet [prɔʒɛ], *s.m.* (*a*) plan, project; scheme; faire, former, un p., to make, draw up, devise, a plan; to concoct a scheme; projets à longue échéance, long-range planning, forward planning; réaliser un p., to carry out a plan; envisager un p. de faire qch., former le p. de faire qch., to plan to do sth.; p. irréalisable, impracticable plan; avoir des projets sur qch., to have designs on sth.; to have one's eye on sth.; p. qui a échoué, plan that failed; quels sont vos projets pour cet été? what are your plans for this summer? what do you plan to do this summer? (*b*) plan (of building, etc.); blueprint; rough sketch, preliminary design; draft (of novel, document, etc.); préparer un p., to prepare plans; p. d'ordre du jour, draft agenda; p. de contrat, draft agreement, draft contract; p. de loi, (draft) bill; établir un p. de loi, to draft a bill; bâtiment en p., proposed, projected, building; bâtiment à l'état de p., building still only in the planning stage.

projeter [prɔʒ(ə)te], *v.tr.* (je projette, n. projetons; je projetterai) 1. (*a*) to project, cast (shadow); to project (beam of light, etc.); to throw back (reflection); les arbres projetaient leurs ombres sur les prés au soleil couchant, the trees cast their shadows across the fields at sunset; la lampe projetait la silhouette des deux hommes sur le mur, the light of the lamp projected the silhouettes of the two men on the wall; (*b*) p. un film, to screen a film, to show a film (on the screen); p. ses photos, to show one's slides, one's transparencies; (*c*) l'explosion les projeta dans la haie, the explosion flung, hurled, them into the hedge; volcan qui projette des cendres, volcano that ejects ash. 2. to plan; p. un voyage, to plan, consider, contemplate, a journey; je projette de partir demain, I'm thinking of starting, leaving, tomorrow; I'm planning to start tomorrow; ils projettent de nouveaux travaux, they are planning new work; *abs.* on a beau p., it's no use planning.

se projeter, to project, stand out; (*of cliff*) to jut out; le navire se projetait sur l'horizon, the ship stood out on the horizon; à midi les ombres se projettent au nord, at noon shadows are cast to the north; une ombre se projeta sur le mur, a shadow fell on the wall, was cast on the wall.

projeteur, -euse [prɔʒtœːr, -øːz], *s.* designer, planner.

prolabé [prɔlabe], *a. Med:* prolapsed.

prolactine [prɔlaktin], *s.f. Biol:* prolactin (hormone).

prolamine [prɔlamin], *s.f. Bio-Ch:* prolamin.

prolan [prɔlɑ̃], *s.m. Physiol:* prolan.

prolapsus [prɔlapsys], *s.m. Med:* prolapsus, prolapse.

prolégomènes [prɔlegɔmɛn], *s.m.pl. Lit: etc:* prolegomena.

prolepse [prɔlɛps], *s.f. Rh: Gram:* prolepsis, anticipation.

proleptique [prɔlɛptik], *a. Gram: Med:* proleptic.

prolétaire [prɔletɛːr], *a. & s.m. & f.* proletarian.

prolétariat [prɔletarja], *s.m.* proletariat.

prolétarien, -ienne [prɔletarjɛ̃, -jɛn], *a.* proletarian.

prolétarisation [prɔletarizasjɔ̃], *s.f.* proletarianization.

prolétariser [prɔletarize], *v.tr.* to proletarianize; bourgeois qui se prolétarisent, middle class people who become members of the proletariat.

prolifératif, -ive [prɔliferatif, -iːv], *a. Biol: Med:* proliferative.

prolifération [prɔliferasjɔ̃], *s.f.* (*a*) *Nat.Hist:* proliferation; (*b*) traité de non p. des armes nucléaires, nuclear non-proliferation treaty.

prolifère [prɔlifɛːr], *a. Nat.Hist:* proliferous; *Med:* kyste p., proliferous cyst.

proliférer [prɔlifere], *v.tr. & i.* (il prolifère; il proliférera) *Nat.Hist:* to proliferate.

prolification [prɔlifikasjɔ̃], *s.f. Nat.Hist:* prolification.

prolifique [prɔlifik], *a.* prolific.

proligération [prɔliʒerasjɔ̃], *s.f. Biol:* proliferation.

proligère [prɔliʒɛːr], *a. Biol:* proligerous; *Med:* kyste p., proliferous cyst.

proline [prɔlin], *s.f. Ch:* prolin(e).

prolixe [prɔliks], *a.* prolix, diffuse; verbose, long-winded.

prolixement [prɔliksəmɑ̃], *adv.* diffusely; verbosely; at great length.

prolixité [prɔliksite], *s.f.* prolixity; verbosity.

prolo [prɔlo], *s.m. P:* proletarian.

prologue [prɔlɔg], *s.m.* prologue (de, to).

prolongateur [prɔlɔ̃gatœːr], *El:* (*a*) *a. & s.m.* (cordon, fil,) p., (flexible lead) extension; (*b*) *s.m.* connector.

prolongation [prɔlɔ̃gasjɔ̃], *s.f.* prolongation (in time); protraction, lengthening; p. d'un séjour, lengthening, extension, of a stay; p. de congé, d'un billet, extension of leave, of a (railway) ticket; *Sch:* p. de la scolarité, raising of the school-leaving age; p. d'une lettre de change, renewal of a bill; *Mus:* p. d'une note, holding of a note; *Fb: etc:* jouer les prolongations, to play extra time; après deux prolongations, after two periods of extra time.

prolonge [prɔlɔ̃ːʒ], *s.f.* 1. (*a*) *A.Artil:* prolonge, trail-rope; (*b*) lashing rope. 2. (*a*) *A.Mil:* ammunition wag(g)on, forage wag(g)on; (*b*) p. d'artillerie, gun carriage (at military funeral).

prolongé [prɔlɔ̃ʒe], *a.* 1. (*a*) long(-continued); of long, prolonged, duration; absence prolongée, prolonged absence; applaudissements prolongés, long, prolonged, applause; match très p., long drawn-out match; soupir p., long-drawn sigh; (*b*) (*of street, line, etc.*) extended, lengthened; (*c*) *F:* jeune fille prolongée, girl who is taking a long time to get married. 2. prolate (ellipsoid).

prolongement [prɔlɔ̃ʒmɑ̃], *s.m.* (*a*) prolongation (in space); continuation; lengthening, extension (of wall, street, railway, etc.); sur le p. de . . ., in prolongation of . . .; *Bot:* prolongements médullaires, medullary rays; (*b*) prolonging, prolongation (in time); les prolongements d'une affaire, the developments, consequences, arising from a piece of business.

prolonger [prɔlɔ̃ʒe], *v.tr.* (je prolongeai(s); n. prolongeons) 1. to prolong (in time); to protract, extend; to draw out, spin out (discourse, etc.); *Med:* p. qn, to keep s.o. alive; p. un armistice, to extend (the time of) an armistice; il prolongea ses adieux, he spun out his farewells; visite très prolongée, protracted call; *Rail:* p. un billet, to extend a ticket; *Mil:* p. de trois jours la permission d'un homme, to extend a man's leave by three days; *Com:* p. une lettre de change, to renew a bill; *Mus:* p. une note, to hold a note. 2. to prolong (in space); to lengthen, extend (wall, street, line of battle, etc.); *Mth:* p. une droite, to produce a line. 3. *Nau:* p. un promontoire, une côte, to coast a headland, to coast along a shore.

se prolonger, to be prolonged; to continue, extend; la guerre se prolongea jusqu'à l'année suivante, the war went on, was carried on, until the following year.

promenade [prɔmnad], *s.f.* 1. (*a*) walking; la p. est le meilleur des exercices, walking is the best form of exercise; (*b*) walk; drive; outing, excursion; trip; faire une p. (à pied), to go for a walk; faire une p. à la campagne, (i) to go for a walk in the country; (ii) to go for a drive, a ride, in the country; (iii) to go for an outing into the country; faire une p. pour détendre sa colère, to walk off one's anger; faire une p. à cheval, to go for a ride, to go riding; faire une p. à bicyclette, to go for a bicycle ride; faire une p. en voiture, to go for a drive, to go out in the car; p. en bateau, row; sail; boat trip; faire faire une p. à qn, to take s.o. (i) for a walk, (ii) for a drive; p. militaire, route march; p. des chevaux, exercising and watering of the horses; ce n'est qu'une p., it's only a short walk; it's not far; aujourd'hui c'est une p. d'aller de Paris à New York, today Paris–New York is only a short trip; faire un bout de p., to go for a short walk, a short stroll; cela nous fera un but de p., that will be somewhere (interesting) to go. 2. (*place for walking*) promenade; (public) walk; parade; avenue; p. plantée d'arbres, avenue lined with trees; les Champs-Élysées sont une belle p., the Champs-Élysées is a beautiful avenue.

promener [prɔmne], *v.tr.* (je promène, n. promenons; je promènerai) 1. (*a*) to take (s.o.) for a walk, a drive, etc.; (*b*) to take, lead, (s.o.) about; cela vous promènera un peu, that will get, take, you out a bit; p. des amis à travers Paris, to show friends round Paris; p. un chien, to exercise a dog, to take a dog for a walk; il promène ses tristes pensées partout, he carries his gloomy thoughts with him everywhere; *Lit:* p. partout le carnage, to carry death and destruction everywhere. 2. p. sa main sur qch., to pass, run, one's hand over sth.; il promenait ses doigts sur toutes les cordes, he ran his fingers over all the strings; p. ses yeux, son regard, sur qch., to run one's eye over sth.; to let one's eyes wander over sth.; p. sa pensée, son esprit, sur qch., to cast one's thoughts, one's mind, over sth.

se promener, (*a*) to walk; to go for a walk, a drive, a ride; se p. dans les rues, to walk, stroll, about the streets; se p. dans sa chambre, to pace up and down (in) one's room; (*to child*) viens te p. avec papa, come for a walk with daddy then; mener p. les enfants, to take the children for a walk; laisser p. les chiens, to let the dogs run (about); to let the dogs off the lead; (*b*) *F:* envoyer qn (se) p., envoyer p. qn, to send s.o. about his business, to send s.o. packing; va te p.! get out! scram! envoyer tout p., to give everything up, to chuck everything; (*c*) *F:* voilà encore ton livre qui se promène, there's your book lying about again! il laisse p. ses affaires partout, he leaves his things all over the place.

promenette [prɔmnɛt], *s.f.* go-cart, *U.S:* baby walker.

promeneur, -euse [prɔmnœːr, -øːz], *s.* **1.** walker; pedestrian; **il y avait quelques promeneurs attardés,** there were a few people still strolling about. **2.** *(a) A:* (tourist) guide; *(b)* **promeneuse d'enfants,** mother's help (who takes children for a walk).

promenoir [prɔm(ə)nwaːr], *s.m.* promenade; (covered) walk; lounge (of concert hall, etc.); lobby (of law courts, etc.); promenade deck (of liner).

promesse [prɔmɛs], *s.f.* **1.** *(a)* promise, assurance; **p. de mariage,** promise of marriage; **faire une p.,** to make a promise; **tenir sa p.,** to keep one's promise; **manquer à sa p., violer sa p.,** to break one's promise; **violation de p. de mariage,** breach of promise; **se rendre sous p. de la vie,** to surrender on the promise that one's life will be spared; *B:* **les enfants de la p.,** the children of the promise; *(b)* **un beau ciel plein de promesses de chaleur,** a beautiful sky full of the promise of heat; **entreprise pleine de promesses,** promising undertaking; **non que le livre ne contienne des promesses,** not that the book is without signs of promise. **2.** *Com: etc:* undertaking to pay, promissory note, note of hand.

Prométhée [prɔmete], *Pr.n.m. Gr.Myth:* Prometheus; *Lit:* **P. enchaîné, délivré,** Prometheus Bound, Unbound.

prométhéen, -enne [prɔmeteɛ̃, -ɛn], *a.* Promethean.

prométhéum [prɔmeteɔm], **prométhium** [prɔmetjɔm], *s.m. Ch:* promethium.

prometteur, -euse [prɔmɛtœːr, -øːz], *a. & s.* **1.** (person) quick to promise, ready to make promises. **2.** promising, attractive (invitation); full of promise.

promettre [prɔmɛtr̥], *v.tr.* (*conj. like* METTRE) to promise. **1.** *(a)* **p. qch. à qn,** to promise s.o. sth.; **p. à qn sa fille en mariage,** to promise s.o. one's daughter in marriage; **p. à qn de faire qch.,** to promise s.o. to do sth.; **se p. de travailler,** to resolve, make up one's mind, to work; **il m'a promis qu'il le ferait,** he promised me that he would do it; **il a fait mieux qu'il n'avait promis,** he was better than his word; **je vous attendrai, je vous le promets,** I'll wait for you, I promise; *F:* **je vous promets qu'on s'est amusé(s),** I'll say we had a good time; *Prov:* **p. et tenir sont deux,** saying and doing are different things; it is one thing to promise and another to perform; promises are made to be broken; *(b)* **se p. qch.,** to promise oneself sth.; to set one's hopes, one's mind, on sth.; **je me promets (de boire) une bière,** I'm looking forward to (having) a beer; **je m'en promets,** I'm looking forward to having, expecting to have, a good time. **2.** *(a)* **le temps promet de la chaleur,** it promises to be hot; it looks as though it will be (a) hot (day); **le temps promet de s'améliorer,** the weather promises, bids fair, to improve; **le jeune homme promet un bel avenir,** the young man shows promise of, appears to be destined for, a fine future; **il promet d'éclipser tous ses rivaux,** he bids fair to eclipse all his rivals; *(b) abs.* **les vignes promettent,** the vines look promising, are full of promise; **enfant qui promet,** promising child; **c'est un plan qui promet,** the plan has possibilities; *F:* **ça promet!** (i) that looks promising! (ii) *Iron:* that looks bad! the outlook's a bit grim! ***that's*** **a fine outlook! il répond de façon insolente et il n'a que six ans; ça promet!** he answers insolently and he's only six; that's a good start!

promis, -ise [prɔmi, -iːz]. **1.** *a.* *(a)* promised; **la Terre promise,** the Promised Land; *Prov:* **chose promise, chose due,** a promise is a promise; *(b)* **p. à,** destined for; **jeune homme p. à un brillant avenir,** young man destined for, with every promise of, a brilliant future. **2.** *A: & Dial:* *(a)* *a.* engaged (to be married); *(b)* *s.* fiancé(e).

promiscuité [prɔmiskɥite], *s.f.* promiscuity, promiscuousness; **en p.,** promiscuously.

promission [prɔmisjɔ̃], *s.f. B:* **la Terre de P.,** the Promised Land.

promissoire [prɔmiswaːr], *a. Jur:* promissory.

promo [prɔmo], *s.f. Sch: F:* year (of students), *U.S:* class.

promontoire [prɔmɔ̃twaːr], *s.m. Geog: Anat:* promontory; *Geog:* headland, head, cape.

promoteur, -trice [prɔmɔtœːr, -tris], *s.* *(a)* promoter, originator (**de,** of); *(b) Sp: etc:* promoter, organizer; *Com:* **p. de ventes,** sales promoter; *(c)* **p. (de construction), p.(-constructeur),** property developer; *(d) s.m. Ch:* (catalytic) accelerator.

promotion [prɔmosjɔ̃], *s.f.* **1.** *(a)* promotion; *Lit:* preferment; **p. à l'ancienneté, au choix,** promotion by seniority, by selection; *(b)* list of promotions, of appointments; list of nominations (to an order, etc.); **p. rouge, p. violette,** list of nominations to the Legion of Honour, to the *palmes académiques*; *(c) abs.* rise in the standard of living; **p. ouvrière, sociale,** rise in the social scale. **2.** *coll.* persons promoted, decorated; = Honours List; *Sch:* (*of students*) year, *U.S:* class; *Navy:* term (of cadets); **le premier de sa p.,** the first in his year; **il est de ma p.,** he was in my year; **les promotions à la voirie,** people after whom streets have been named. **3.** *Com:* **p. des ventes,** sales promotion.

promotionnel, -elle [prɔmosjɔnɛl], *a. Com:* **vente promotionnelle** = special offer, bargain offer.

promouvable [prɔmuvabl̥], *a.* (*of employee*) promotable.

promouvoir [prɔmuvwaːr], *v.tr.def.* (*conj. like* MOUVOIR, *but used esp. in inf., in p.p.* **promu** *and compound tenses, and occ. in p.h.* **il promut, ils promurent**) *(a)* to promote; **être promu lieutenant, au grade de lieutenant,** to be promoted to lieutenant; **être promu à l'épiscopat,** to be raised to the episcopate, to be made a bishop; *(b)* to encourage, to further, to favour the development of; **p. la recherche scientifique,** to encourage scientific research.

prompt [prɔ̃], *a.* prompt, quick, ready; hasty; **prompte** [prɔ̃ːt] **réponse,** prompt reply, ready answer; **esprit p.,** quick mind; ready wit; **être d'humeur prompte,** to be hasty-tempered; **il est p. à la colère, à se fâcher,** he loses his temper, flares up, easily; **p. à agir,** quick to act; **p. à la riposte,** prompt, quick, in repartee; **prompte vengeance, justice,** speedy revenge, justice; **prompte guérison,** quick, speedy, cure; **avoir la main prompte,** to be always ready with a slap; to be always ready to strike (a blow); *Lit:* **l'esprit est p. et la chair infirme,** the spirit is willing but the flesh is weak; *A:* **sa joie fut prompte,** his joy was of short duration; *Adm: A:* **droit de prompte expédition,** *s.f. F:* **prompte,** fee paid to Government department for attending to a business more expeditiously than if it were dealt with in the ordinary course; priority fee.

prompt-bourgeon [prɔ̃burʒɔ̃], *s.m. Bot:* secondary shoot, bud; accessory shoot, bud; *pl. prompts-bourgeons.*

promptement [prɔ̃t(ə)mɑ̃], *adv.* promptly, quickly.

promptitude [prɔ̃tityd], *s.f.* **1.** promptitude, promptness; quickness, alertness (of movement, of mind, etc.); **avec toute la p. possible,** as quickly as possible, with all possible dispatch; **obéir avec p.,** to be prompt, quick, to obey. **2.** hastiness; **p. à croire le mal,** readiness to believe evil.

prompto [prɔ̃to], *adv. P:* pronto.

promptuaire [prɔ̃ptɥɛːr], *s.m. Ecc: A:* promptuary.

promu, -ue [prɔmy], *a. & s.* (person) who has been promoted, has received a decoration, etc.; *Sch:* **les nouveaux promus** = this year's graduates (of a *grande école*); **les promotions à la voirie favorisent autant l'intérêt des promoteurs que la mémoire des promus,** naming streets after people serves the interest of the promoters as much as it perpetuates the memory of those so honoured.

promulgateur, -trice [prɔmylgatœːr, -tris]. **1.** *a.* promulgating. **2.** *s.* promulgator.

promulgation [prɔmylgasjɔ̃], *s.f.* promulgation, publication, proclamation (of a law, etc.).

promulguer [prɔmylge], *v.tr.* to promulgate (law); to publish, to issue (decree).

promycélium [prɔmiseljɔm], *s.m. Bot:* promycelium.

pronaos [prɔnaɔs], *s.m. Gr.Ant:* pronaos.

pronateur [prɔnatœːr], *a. & s.m.* (**muscle**) **p.,** pronator.

pronation [prɔnasjɔ̃], *s.f.* prone position, pronation; **en p.,** prone (hand, position, etc.).

prône [proːn], *s.m.* **1.** *Ecc:* sermon, homily; **faire le p.,** to preach (the sermon) and give out the announcements for the week; **recommander qn au p.,** (i) to ask the prayers of the congregation for s.o.; (ii) *F: A:* to report s.o. (to his superiors). **2.** *F: A:* lecture, rebuke, wigging.

pronéphros [prɔnefrɔs], *s.m. Biol: Anat:* pronephros.

prôner [prone], *v.tr.* **1.** *A:* *(a) Ecc:* to preach to (congregation); *(b)* to rebuke (s.o.). **2.** *(a)* to praise, extol (s.o. to praise,); boost (sth.); *(b)* to recommend (strongly); **p. la modération,** to preach moderation.

prôneur, -euse [pronœːr, -øːz], *s.* **1.** *A:* *(a) Ecc:* preacher; *(b) F:* sermonizer. **2.** *(a) A:* extoller; *(b) usu. Pej:* booster; **p. d'un certain régime (alimentaire),** food faddist; **p. du régime végétarien,** rabid vegetarian.

pronom [prɔnɔ̃], *s.m. Gram:* pronoun.

pronominal, -aux [prɔnɔminal, -o], *a. Gram:* pronominal (adjective, verb).

pronominalement [prɔnɔminalmɑ̃], *adv.* pronominally.

prononçable [prɔnɔ̃sabl̥], *a.* pronounceable.

prononcé [prɔnɔ̃se]. **1.** *a.* pronounced, decided, (well-)marked (character, taste, feature, etc.); **nez p.,** prominent nose; **courbe prononcée,** sharp curve; **parler l'anglais avec un accent étranger très p.,** to speak English with a strong, marked, foreign accent; **peu p.,** faint. **2.** *s.m. Jur:* decision; terms (of decision); **p. du jugement,** verdict.

prononcement [prɔnɔ̃smɑ̃], *s.m.* pronouncement.

prononcer [prɔnɔ̃se], *v.tr.* (**je prononçai(s); n. prononçons**) to pronounce. **1.** *(a)* **sans p. un mot,** without uttering one word; without saying a word; **il prononça quelques mots entre ses dents,** he muttered a few words; **j'entendis p. mon nom,** I heard my name (mentioned); **son nom est toujours prononcé avec respect,** he is always mentioned with respect; **il ne faut jamais p. son nom,** you must never mention him, his name; *(b)* **p. un discours,** to deliver, make, a speech; *Jur:* **p. une sentence,** to pass, deliver, a sentence; to pronounce sentence; *abs.* **p. en faveur de qn, contre qn,** to decide, declare, in favour of s.o., against s.o.; **p. sur l'état d'un malade,** to pronounce on the condition of a patient; **p. sur une question,** to adjudge, adjudicate, a question, to adjudicate upon a question. **2.** to articulate; **mot difficile à p.,** word hard to pronounce; **mal p. un mot,** to mispronounce a word; **cette lettre ne se prononce pas,** this letter is not pronounced.

se prononcer, to declare, pronounce, express, one's opinion, one's decision; to make a decision; **se p. contre un projet,** to decide against a plan; **se p. sur une question,** to come to a conclusion, to a decision, about a matter; **le médecin ne s'est pas encore prononcé,** the doctor has not yet given his verdict.

prononciation [prɔnɔ̃sjasjɔ̃], *s.f.* **1.** delivery (of speech); bringing in (of verdict, etc.); passing (of sentence). **2.** pronunciation (of syllable, language, etc.); **défaut de p.,** defect in pronunciation; faulty articulation; **faute de p.,** mispronunciation, mistake in pronunciation; **dictionnaire de p.,** pronouncing dictionary.

pronostic [prɔnɔstik], *s.m.* **1.** forecast; **p. des courses,** racing forecast; **un heureux p.,** a happy omen; *Turf:* **les pronostics d'un tuyauteur,** a tipster's selections; **concours de pronostics de football,** football pool. **2.** *Med:* prognosis.

pronostication [prɔnɔstikasjɔ̃], *s.f.* prognostication, forecast(ing).

pronostique [prɔnɔstik], *a. Med:* prognostic (sign, etc.).

pronostiquer [prɔnɔstike], *v.tr.* **1.** to forecast. **2.** *Med:* to prognose; **p. au plus grave,** to give a very serious prognosis; to anticipate, expect, the worst.

pronostiqueur, -euse [prɔnɔstikœːr, -øːz], *s.* prognosticator, forecaster.

pronotum [prɔnɔtɔm], *s.m. Ent:* pronotum.

pronucléus [prɔnykleys], *s.m. Biol:* pronucleus.

pronunciam(i)ento [prɔnɔ̃sjam(j)ɛnto], *s.m.* pronunciamento, manifesto.

propadiène [prɔpadjɛn], *s.f. Ch:* propadiene.

propagande [prɔpagɑ̃ːd], *s.f.* *(a) Ecc:* **Congrégation de la P.,** Congregation, College of (the) Propaganda; *(b)* propaganda; publicity; **p. de guerre,** warmongering; *Com:* **faire de la p.,** to advertise, publicize.

propagandisme [prɔpagɑ̃dism], *s.m.* propagandism.

propagandiste [prɔpagɑ̃dist], *s.m. & f.* propagandist.

propagateur, -trice [prɔpagatœːr, -tris]. **1.** *a.* propagating, propagative. **2.** *s.* propagator, spreader (of news, disease, etc.); **p. de fausses nouvelles,** spreader of false news.

propagation [prɔpagasjɔ̃], *s.f.* **1.** spread(ing), propagation, propagating (of knowledge, disease, news, etc.). **2.** *(a)* **p. d'une maladie vers l'ouest,** westward spread of a disease; *Ph:* **p. des ondes,** wave propagation; *(b)* **p. d'une espèce,** propagation of a species.

propager [prɔpaʒe], *v.tr.* (**je propageai(s); n. propageons**) to propagate; to spread (abroad); to disseminate (news); **p. une méthode,** to popularize a method; **p. le son,** to propagate sound.

se propager. 1. (*a*) (*of disease, news, fire, etc.*) to spread; (*b*) (*of sound, light, etc.*) to be propagated; **la lumière se propage en ligne droite,** light is propagated in a straight line. 2. (*of creatures*) to propagate, reproduce.
propagule [prɔpagyl], *s.f. Moss:* propagulum, propagule.
propane [prɔpan], *s.m. Ch:* propane.
propanier [prɔpanje], *s.m. Nau:* propane carrier.
propanol [prɔpanɔl], *s.m. Ch:* propanol.
propanone [prɔpanɔn], *s.f. Ch:* propanone.
propargyle [prɔparʒil], *s.m. Ch:* propargyl.
proparoxyton [prɔparɔksitɔ̃], *s.m. Ling:* proparoxytone.
propédeute [prɔpedøt], *s.m. & f. Sch: A:* first year student (taking preliminary course for arts or science degree).
propédeutique [prɔpedøtik]. 1. *a.* propaedeutic(al). 2. *s.f.* propaedeutics; *Sch: A:* **(l'année de) p.,** an intermediate year of study at the start of a degree course in arts or science.
propène [prɔpɛn], *s.m. Ch:* propene, propylene.
propénoïque [prɔpenɔik], *s.m. Ch:* propenoic.
propension [prɔpɑ̃sjɔ̃], *s.f.* 1. propensity, tendency, inclination (**à,** to). 2. *Ph: A:* attraction.
propényle [prɔpenil], *s.m. Ch:* propenyl.
propénylique [prɔpenilik], *a. Ch:* propenylic.
Properce [prɔpɛrs], *Pr.n.m. Rom.Lit:* Propertius.
properdine [prɔpɛrdin], *s.f. Physiol:* properdin.
propergol [prɔpɛrgɔl], *s.m.* (rocket) propellant.
propérispomène [prɔperispɔmɛn], *s.m. Gr.Gram:* properispomenon.
prophage [prɔfaːʒ], *s.m. Bac:* prophage.
propharmacien, -ienne [prɔfarmasjɛ̃, -jɛn], *s. Med:* (country) practitioner with permit to dispense his, her, own medicines.
prophase [prɔfaːz], *s.f. Biol:* prophase.
prophète, prophétesse [prɔfɛːt, prɔfetɛs], *s.* prophet; seer; *f.* prophetess; prophesier; **p. de malheur,** prophet of evil; **parler en p.,** to speak like a prophet; to prophesy; **il s'est montré bon p.,** he proved a true prophet; *B:* **les grands, les petits, prophètes,** the major, minor, prophets; *Moham.Rel:* **le P.,** the Prophet; **nul n'est p. en, dans, son pays,** no man is a prophet in his own country.
prophétie [prɔfesi], *s.f.* prophecy. 1. prophesying; **le don de p.,** the gift of prophecy. 2. prophetic saying; **la p. s'est accomplie,** the prophecy was fulfilled.
prophétique [prɔfetik], *a.* prophetic(al).
prophétiquement [prɔfetikmɑ̃], *adv.* prophetically.
prophétiser [prɔfetize], *v.tr.* to prophesy; **ces paroles prophétisaient sa grandeur future,** these words were prophetic of his future greatness; *abs.* **il commença par p.,** he began by prophesying; **elle avait prophétisé vrai,** she had shown herself a true prophet.
prophétisme [prɔfetism], *s.m.* (*a*) **p. (biblique),** prophetism; (*b*) (political, etc.) prophecy.
prophylactique [prɔfilaktik], *Med:* 1. *a. & s.m.* prophylactic. 2. *s.f.* prophylaxis.
prophylaxie [prɔfilaksi], *s.f.* prophylaxis; prevention of disease.
propice [prɔpis], *a.* (*of deity, wind, person, moment, etc.*) propitious (**à,** to s.o.; to, for, sth.); auspicious; favourable (**à,** to); **être né sous une étoile p.,** to have been born under a lucky star; **lieu retiré p. à la méditation,** secluded spot that lends itself to meditation; **rendre propices les dieux,** to propitiate the gods; **peu p.,** (i) unpropitious; (ii) inauspicious (moment, etc.); **si la fortune nous est p.,** if all goes well with us.
propiolique [prɔpjɔlik], *a. Ch:* propiolic.
propionate [prɔpjɔnat], *s.m. Ch:* propionate.
propione [prɔpjɔn], *s.f. Ch:* propione.
propionique [prɔpjɔnik], *a. Ch:* propionic (acid).
propionyle [prɔpjɔnil], *s.m. Ch:* propionyl.
propithèque [prɔpitɛk], *s.m. Z:* sifaka lemur; (*genus*) Propithecus.
propitiateur, -trice [prɔpisjatœːr, -tris], *s.* propitiator.
propitiation [prɔpisjasjɔ̃], *s.f.* propitiation; *Jew. Rel:* **sacrifice de p.,** peace offering.
propitiatoire [prɔpisjatwaːr]. 1. *a.* propitiatory (rite, sacrifice); **don p.,** propitiatory gift, sop to Cerberus. 2. *s.m. B.Hist:* propitiatory; mercy seat.
propitier [prɔpisje], *v.tr.* (*pr.sub. & p.d.* **n. propitiions, v. propitiiez**) *A:* to propitiate.
propodite [prɔpɔdit], *s.m. Crust:* propodite.
propolis [prɔpɔlis], *s.f.* propolis, bee glue.
propolisation [prɔpɔlizasjɔ̃], *s.f. Ap:* propolization.
Propontide [prɔpɔ̃tid], *Pr.n.f. A.Geog:* Propontis (now Sea of Marmora).
proportion [prɔpɔrsjɔ̃], *s.f.* 1. proportion; ratio; percentage; **les proportions du corps,** the proportions of the body; **varier en p. directe, en p. inverse,** to vary in direct ratio, in inverse ratio; **p. harmonique, géométrique,** harmonic ratio; geometrical ratio; geometric proportion; *Ar:* **règle de p.,** rule of three; *Ch:* **loi des proportions multiples,** law of multiple proportions; *Fin:* **p. de la monnaie d'or par rapport à la circulation,** gold ratio; **p. du cuivre à l'étain dans l'alliage,** proportion of copper to tin in the alloy; **p. d'alcool dans un vin,** percentage of alcohol in a wine, alcohol content of a wine; **à p., en p. (de),** in proportion (to); **estimer qn à p. de ses efforts,** to value, judge, s.o. by what he does, by the work he does; **en p. de ses forces,** in proportion to his strength; **à p. que** + *ind.*, as; **hors de toute p. avec,** out of all proportion to; **défaut de p.,** disproportion, lack of proportion (**entre,** between); **toute(s) proportion(s) gardée(s),** all things considered, taking everything into consideration, making all due allowance; **alliage contenant du nickel dans des proportions restreintes,** alloy containing a small, a limited, percentage of nickel. 2. *pl.* size; **salle de vastes proportions,** vast hall, hall of imposing dimensions; capacious room, room of ample proportions; **son usine a pris des proportions considérables,** his factory has grown to a considerable size; **grève qui prend des proportions considérables,** strike that is assuming serious proportions; **cela sort des proportions ordinaires,** this is extraordinary, on an extraordinarily large scale, beyond the normal run of things; **dans de plus vastes proportions,** on a greater, wider, scale; **si les commandes diminuent dans de sérieuses proportions,** if orders should decrease, drop (off), to any extent.
proportionnaliste [prɔpɔrsjɔnalist], *s.m. & f. Pol:* proportionalist.
proportionnalité [prɔpɔrsjɔnalite], *s.f.* proportionality; **la p. entre x et y,** the proportion which *x* bears to *y*; *Fin:* **p. de l'impôt,** fixed rate system of taxation.
proportionné [prɔpɔrsjɔne], *a.* 1. (*a*) proportioned; **bien p.,** well-proportioned (body, etc.); (*b*) fully-fashioned (stockings, etc.). 2 proportionate, suited (**à,** to); **lectures proportionnées à l'âge d'un enfant,** reading suitable to the age of a child.
proportionnel, -elle [prɔpɔrsjɔnɛl]. 1. *a.* proportional (**à,** to); **inversement p.,** inversely proportional, in inverse ratio (**à,** to); *Cust:* **droit p.,** ad valorem duty; *Fin:* **impôt p.,** tax at a fixed rate, percentage. 2. *s.f. Mth:* **moyenne proportionnelle entre a et b,** mean proportional between a and b.
proportionnellement [prɔpɔrsjɔnɛlmɑ̃], *adv.* proportionally, proportionately, in proportion (**à,** to); pro rata.
proportionnément [prɔpɔrsjɔnemɑ̃], *adv.* in due proportion, in due ratio, proportionally (**à,** to).
proportionner [prɔpɔrsjɔne], *v.tr.* **p. qch. à qch.,** to proportion, adjust, adapt, sth. to sth.; to regulate sth. in proportion to sth.; **p. les peines aux délits,** to make the punishment fit the crime.
propos [prɔpo], *s.m.* 1. *Lit:* purpose, resolution; intention; **suivons notre p.,** let us proceed with our resolution; **avoir le ferme p. de faire qch.,** to have the firm intention of doing sth.; **agir de p. délibéré,** to act deliberately, with set purpose. 2. subject, matter; **à ce p., à p.,** talking of this, in connection with this, while we're on the subject, by the way; **à p., avez-vous lu ce livre,** by the way, while I think of it, à propos, that reminds me, have you read this book? **à tout p.,** at every turn; at any time, at any moment; **à tout p. et sans p.,** in season and out of season; **une irritation qui se manifestait à tout p.,** an irritation which kept cropping up all the time; **dire qch. à p.,** to say sth. to the point; to say sth. appropriate; **mot jeté à p.,** timely word; **observation à p.,** well-timed observation; apt observation; **remarque faite à p.,** apt, relevant, remark; **faire qch. à p.,** to do sth. at the right moment; **tu viens à p.,** you've come at the right moment, in the nick of time; **juger à p. de . . .,** to consider it advisable, a good thing, to . . .; **vous ferez ce que vous jugerez à p.,** you will use your own discretion, act as you think fit; **savoir se taire à p.,** to know when to remain silent, when to say nothing; **mal à p.,** at the wrong time, at the wrong moment; **plaisanter à p. et hors de p.,** to jest in and out of season; *adj.phr.* **hors de p.,** (i) ill-timed; (ii) irrelevant; out of place; **il serait hors de p. de . . .,** it would be out of place to . . .; it wouldn't be suitable, wouldn't do, to . . .; *prep.phr.* **à p. de,** in connection with, on the subject of, apropos of, à propos of (sth.); **à p. de rien,** for nothing at all, for no reason whatever, *F:* for no earthly reason; **se quereller à p. de rien,** to quarrel about nothing; **à p. d'un rien,** for a mere trifle; **à p. de tout et de rien,** without any obvious motive; **à p. de quoi? à quel p.?** in what connection? about what? what about? à propos of what? 3. remark; *pl.* talk, gossip; **p. offensant,** offensive remark; **p. méchants,** malicious gossip; **p. flatteurs,** flattering remarks; **des p. de table,** table talk; mealtime conversation; **changer de p.,** to change the subject; **tenir des p. (moqueurs) sur qn,** to make (scathing) remarks about s.o.; **se moquer des p. d'autrui,** not to care, not to worry, about other people's gossip; *A:* **entrer en p. avec qn,** to enter into conversation with s.o.
proposant [prɔpozɑ̃], *s.m.* 1. (protestant) student in divinity; proposant. 2. *Ins:* proposer.
proposer [prɔpoze], *v.tr.* to propose (plan); to propound (theory, idea); **p. un amendement,** to move an amendment; **p. une définition pour un mot,** to suggest a definition for a word; **p. un problème à résoudre,** to put forward a problem to be solved; **p. qn, qch., comme modèle,** to hold s.o., sth., up as a model; **je te l'ai proposé maintes fois,** I've suggested it to you time and time again; **p. de l'argent à qn,** to offer s.o. money; **il m'a proposé des tapis,** he tried to sell me some carpets; **p. qn pour son successeur,** to propose, recommend, s.o. as one's successor; **être proposé pour un emploi,** to be suggested, proposed, recommended, for a job; **p. un candidat,** to propose, put forward, a candidate; **p. que l'on fasse qch.,** to suggest that sth. should be done; **je lui ai proposé de le faire,** I proposed, suggested, that he should do it; *abs.* **l'homme propose et Dieu dispose,** man proposes but God disposes.
se proposer. 1. **se p. pour qch.,** to propose oneself, offer one's services, for sth.; **se p. comme secrétaire,** to offer to act as secretary; **se p. pour un emploi,** to apply for a job. 2. **se p. qch.,** to have sth. in view; to be considering sth.; **se p. de faire qch.,** to propose to do sth.; **je me propose de rester huit jours à Paris,** I propose, mean, intend, to stay in Paris for a week; **que vous proposez-vous de faire?** (i) what are your plans? what do you intend to do? (ii) what are you going to do about it?
proposeur, -euse [prɔpozœːr, -øːz], *s.* proposer (of scheme, idea, etc.); mover (of amendment).
proposition [prɔpozisjɔ̃], *s.f.* 1. proposal, proposition; **faire une p.,** to make a proposal; (*in an assembly*) to put, propose, a motion; **mettre une p. aux voix,** to put a motion to the vote; **propositions relatives à la formation de . . .,** proposals for the formation of . . .; **propositions de paix,** peace proposals; **p. de mariage,** proposal of marriage; *Rel.H:* **pain de p.,** shew bread. 2. (*a*) *Log: Mth: etc:* proposition; (*b*) *Gram:* clause; **p. principale,** principal clause, main clause; (*c*) *Mus:* subject (of fugue).
propositionnel, -elle [prɔpozisjɔnɛl], *a. Log:* propositional.
propre [prɔpr]. 1. *a.* (*a*) proper; **la Grèce p.,** Greece proper; **mouvement p. d'un astre,** real movement of a star; **oscillation p.,** natural oscillation; **signification p. d'un mot,** proper meaning of a word; **faire qch. en p. personne,** to do sth. in person; to go personally, *Jur:* in propria persona; **ce n'est pas, au sens p. . . .,** it is not in the proper sense . . .; **faire qch. de son p. mouvement,** to do sth., of one's own accord; **il me dit en propres terms que . . .,** he told me in so many words that . . .; **ceci est la p. maison où il logeait,** this is the very house in which he stayed; **ce sont là ses propres paroles,** these are his very words; (*b*) peculiar (**à,** to); **ces amphibes sont propres aux mers articques,** these amphibians belong to the arctic seas; **symptôme p. à une maladie,** symptom peculiar to a disease; **une façon de marcher à lui p.,** his own particular, characteristic, way of walking; **vice p.,** inherent vice; (*c*) *Ph:* **vibration p.,** natural beat; *Ac:* **résonance p.,** natural resonance; (*d*) own; **chacun a une façon p. de faire les choses,** everyone has his own way of doing things; **ses idées lui sont propres,** his ideas are his own; **avec ce charme qui lui est p.,** with that charm which is his alone; **voir avec ses propres yeux,** to see with one's own eyes; **je n'ai pas de ressources qui me soient propres,** I have no resources of my own; **dans votre p. maison,** in your own house; **je le lui ai remis en**

main p., I delivered it to him personally, into his own hands; à remettre en main p., to be delivered to the addressee in person; (e) appropriate, proper, fit(ting); le mot p., the appropriate, proper, word; p. à qch., (*of persons and things*) adapted, fitted, suited, to sth.; p. à faire qch., (i) (*of pers.*) fit(ted) to do sth.; (ii) (*of thgs*) adapted, calculated, to do sth.; exercice p. à aiguiser l'intelligence, exercise calculated to sharpen the wits; p. à tout, fit for anything; p. à rien, good for nothing; *Prov:* qui est p. à tout n'est p. à rien, a Jack of all trades is master of none; (f) neat, clean (clothing, person); linge p. clean linen; chambre p. et nette, clean and tidy room; p. comme un sou neuf, as clean as a new pin; *F:* nous voilà propres! we're in a nice, fine, mess! ça, c'est du p.! well, that's a nice mess! that's disgusting! *s.m. Sch:* recopier au p., to make a fair copy; (g) le chat est très p., the cat is a very clean animal; mon bébé était p. à treize mois, my baby was dry at thirteen months; (h) *Atom.Ph:* clear. 2. *s.m.* (a) property, attribute, nature, characteristic; le p. de cette nation, the characteristic of this nation; le p. des poissons est de nager, the nature of fish is to swim; c'est le p. des caractères inférieurs de faire étalage d'autorité, it is characteristic of inferior natures to make a show of authority; (b) proper or literal sense (of a word); employer un mot au p., to use a word in its literal sense; (c) avoir qch. en p., to possess sth. in one's own right; (d) *Jur:* p. d'une femme mariée (*also* biens propres), separate property of a married woman; (e) *Ecc:* special service; *esp.* p. des saints, Proper of Saints.

propre(-)à(-)rien [prɔprarjɛ̃], *s.m.* good-for-nothing, dead loss; c'est un p.-à-r., he's a good-for-nothing, a ne'er-do-well, *F:* a dead loss; *pl. propres(-)à(-)rien.*

proprement [prɔprəmɑ̃], *adv.* 1. (a) properly; in fact; *F:* well and truly; c'est à ces pensées que convient p. le nom d'idées, it is to thoughts of this type that the word ideas is properly applied; cet état est p. un état de guerre, this constitutes strictly speaking, accurately speaking, a state of war; c'est là p. l'affaire du gérant, this is really, strictly speaking, a matter for the manager; Sparte était p. un camp, Sparta was in effect a camp; l'effet est p. stupéfiant, the effect is perfectly, absolutely, simply, literally, nothing short of, stupefying; *F:* il s'est fait avoir p., he was properly, well and truly, had; (b) à p. parler, properly speaking, strictly speaking; to be quite accurate; il n'y a pas, à p. parler, de recrutement de main-d'œuvre, there is strictly speaking no recruiting of labour; (c) p. dit, properly so called; actual; pierres précieuses p. dites, precious stones proper; l'histoire p. dite, history properly speaking; nous fabriquons la machine p. dite, mais nous achetons certains accessoires, we manufacture the machine itself, the actual machine, but we buy some accessories. 2. (a) chambre p. rangée, neatly arranged room; neat and tidy room; cet enfant ne sait pas manger p., this child doesn't know how to eat cleanly; animal qui mange p. dans votre main, animal that eats delicately out of your hand; (b) well; efficiently; with dignity; mourir p., to meet one's end with dignity, with courage; il chante assez p., he sings tolerably well.

propret, -ette [prɔprɛ, -ɛt], *a. F:* neat, tidy.

propreté [prɔprəte], *s.f.* cleanliness; cleanness, neatness, tidiness; être d'une extrême p., to be exceedingly clean, very tidy; *Navy:* postes de p., cleaning stations.

propréteur [prɔpretœːr], *s.m. Rom.Hist:* propraetor.

propréture [prɔpretyːr], *s.f. Rom.Hist:* propraetorship.

propriétaire [prɔprietɛːr], *s.m. & f.* 1. proprietor, proprietress; owner, holder; se rendre p. de qch., to acquire sth.; p. unique, sole owner; qui est le p. de ce livre? who owns this book? whose book is this? p. foncier, (i) ground landlord; (ii) landed proprietor; landowner; être p., (i) to be a landed proprietor, a man of property, a landowner; (ii) to have a house of one's own; le p. de cette terre, the holder, owner, of this piece of land; *Jur:* p. indivis, joint owner; nu p., bare owner. 2. landlord, landlady.

propriétaire-occupant [prɔprietɛrɔkypɑ̃], *s.m.* owner-occupier; *pl. propriétaires-occupants.*

propriété [prɔpriete], *s.f.* 1. (a) proprietorship, ownership; property; p. privée, publique, private, public, property; nue p., bare ownership, ownership without usufruct; pleine p. (foncière), freehold; p. libre, property held in fee simple; freehold; p. collective, collective ownership, commons; p. individuelle, individual ownership, severalty; p. indivise, joint ownership, coparcenary; titres de p., title deeds; conserver la p. de ses biens, to retain the property in one's estate; p. littéraire, intellectuelle, literary property; copyright; p. dramatique, dramatic rights; p. industrielle, patent rights; (b) property, estate; holding; p. foncière, landed property, landed estate; propriétés immobilières, real property, real estate, realty; p. mobilière, personal estate. 2. property, characteristic, peculiar quality (of matter, of a metal, plant, etc.); les propriétés de la matière, the properties of matter. 3. propriety, correctness (of terms, language, etc.).

proprio [prɔpri(j)o], *s.m. P:* landlord; le p. les a mis à la porte, the landlord threw them out.

propriocepteur [prɔprijɔsɛptœːr], *s.m. Physiol:* proprioceptor.

proprioceptif, -ive [prɔprijɔsɛptif, -iːv], *a.* proprioceptive.

propulser [prɔpylse], *v.tr.* 1. *Av: Nau: etc:* to propel. 2. *Metall:* métal propulsé en barres, extruded metal.

propulseur [prɔpylsœːr]. 1. *a. Av: Nau: etc:* propellent, propulsive, impelling, impulsive. 2. *s.m.* propeller; p. à hélice, screw propeller. 3. *s.m.* propulsion device, system; p. nucléaire pour fusées, nuclear rocket propulsion system; avion à p. atomique, nuclear aircraft.

propulsif, -ive [prɔpylsif, -iːv], *a. Av: Nau: etc:* propulsive, propelling (power, wheel, screw, etc.).

propulsion [prɔpylsjɔ̃], *s.f.* propulsion, propelling; impulsion, impelling; drive, driving; mouvement de p., propulsive motion; drive; la p. du sang par le cœur, the propulsion of the blood by the heart; mode de p., means of propulsion; p. mécanique, mechanical propulsion, power; véhicule à p. mécanique, mechanically propelled vehicle; moteur de p., propulsion engine; p. par fusée(s), par réaction, jet propulsion; réacteur de p., propulsion jet; à p. atomique, atomic-powered; p. nucléaire, nuclear propulsion; navire, sous-marin, à p. nucléaire, nuclear-powered ship, submarine; fusée à p. nucléaire, nuclear-propelled rocket; p. (d'un homme) par fusée individuelle, personal rocket propulsion; p. électrique, electric drive, propulsion; véhicule à p. électrique, electrically propelled, powered, vehicle; p. diesel-électrique, diesel-electric drive, propulsion; p. turbo-électrique, turbo-electric drive, propulsion; *Elcs:* p. ionique, thermo-ionique, ionic, thermoionic, drive or propulsion; p. par plasma, plasma drive; p. par photons, photon drive.

propylamine [prɔpilamin], *s.f. Ch:* propylamine.

propyle [prɔpil], *s.m. Ch:* propyl.

propylée [prɔpile], *s.m. Gr.Ant:* propylaeum; les Propylées, the Propylaea.

propylène [prɔpilɛn], *s.m. Ch:* propylene, propene.

propylique [prɔpilik], *a. Ch:* propylic; alcool p., propyl alcohol, propanol.

propylite [prɔpilit], *s.f. Miner:* propylite.

propylitisation [prɔpilitizasjɔ̃], *s.f. Geol:* propylitization.

propyne [prɔpin], *s.m. Ch:* propyne, propine.

propynoïque [prɔpinɔik], *s.m. Ch:* propynoic, propinoic.

proquesteur [prɔkɥɛstœːr], *s.m. Rom.Ant:* proquaestor.

prorata [prɔrata], *s.m.inv.* proportional part, proportion, share; paiement au p., payment pro rata; au p. de qch., in proportion to sth., proportionately to sth.

prorogatif, -ive [prɔrɔgatif, -iːv], *a.* proroguing, prorogating.

prorogation [prɔrɔgasjɔ̃], *s.f.* 1. *Pol:* prorogation (of parliament). 2. *esp. Jur:* extension of time; le président demanda au Sénat une p., the president asked the Senate to extend his period of office; p. d'enquête, leave to protract an enquiry.

proroger [prɔrɔʒe], *v.tr.* (je prorogeai(s); n. prorogeons) 1. to prorogue, adjourn (parliament). 2. *Com: Jur:* to extend (time limit); to grant leave that (enquiry) be continued, protracted; *Jur:* p. une caution, un engagement, to enlarge bail, a recognisance.

prosaïque [prozaik, prɔ-], *a.* prosaic; commonplace; unimaginative; matter-of-fact.

prosaïquement [prozaikmɑ̃, prɔ-], *adv.* prosaically; in a matter-of-fact manner.

prosaïsme [prozaism, prɔ-], *s.m.* (a) prosaism, prosaic style; le p. de la vie, the prosaicness, dullness, flatness, tediousness, of life; (b) matter-of-factness.

prosateur, -trice [prozatœːr, -tris, prɔ-], *s.* prose writer, prosaist; morceaux choisis des prosateurs, selected prose writings.

proscenium [prɔs(s)enjɔm], *s.m. Gr. & Rom.Ant: Th:* proscenium.

proscripteur [prɔskriptœːr], *s.m.* proscriber, banisher.

proscription [prɔskripsjɔ̃], *s.f.* 1. (a) proscription; banishment, outlawry; (b) p. d'un usage, prohibiting, doing away with a practice. 2. *Jur:* p. de biens, selling of property left behind by an absconding debtor.

proscrire [prɔskriːr], *v.tr.* (*conj. like* ÉCRIRE) (a) to proscribe, outlaw, banish (a person); p. qn d'une société, to proscribe, ostracize, s.o. from a society; (b) p. un usage, to do away with, to condemn, a practice; p. l'usage d'un mot, to forbid the use of a word.

proscrit, -ite [prɔskri, -it]. 1. *a.* proscribed (person, thing); cet usage est p., this practice is taboo. 2. *s.* proscript, outlaw, refugee.

prose [proːz], *s.f.* 1. prose; écrire en p., to write in prose; *F:* j'ai reçu de sa p., I have had a letter from him; une vie où la p. ne manquait pas, a life for the most part prosaic. 2. *Ecc:* prose, sequence.

prosécrétine [prɔsekretin], *s.f. Physiol:* prosecretin.

prosecteur [prɔsɛktœːr], *s.m. Sch:* prosector; demonstrator (in anatomy).

prosectorat [prɔsɛktɔra], *s.m. Sch:* prosectorship, post of demonstrator (in anatomy).

prosélyte [prɔzelit], *s.* proselyte; *Hebrew Hist:* p. de justice, proselyte of righteousness, of the covenant; p. de la porte, proselyte of the gate.

prosélytique [prɔzelitik], *a.* proselytical, proselytizing.

prosélytisme [prɔzelitism], *s.m.* proselytism.

prosenchyme [prɔzɑ̃ʃim], *s.m. Bot:* prosenchyma.

proserpinaca [prɔzɛrpinaka], *s.m. Bot:* proserpinaca.

Proserpine [prɔzɛrpin], *Pr.n.f. Myth:* Proserpine, Proserpina, Persephone.

prosimiens [prɔsimjɛ̃], *s.m.pl. Z:* Prosimii, Lemuroidea, prosimians.

prosiphon [prɔsifɔ̃], *s.m. Moll:* prosiphon.

prosobranches [prɔzɔbrɑ̃ːʃ], *s.m.pl. Moll:* Prosobranchia, Prosobranchiata, Streptoneura.

prosodiaque [prɔzɔdjak], *a.* prosodiac(al), prosodic.

prosodie [prɔzɔdi], *s.f.* prosody; p. musicale, adaptation of words to music, of music to words.

prosodier [prɔzɔdje], *v.* (*p.d. & pr.sub.* n. prosodiions, v. prosodiiez) (a) *v.tr.* to mark the prosody, the rhythm, of; (b) *v.i. Mus:* to combine words and music.

prosodique [prɔzɔdik], *a.* prosodic(al).

prosodiste [prɔzɔdist], *s.m.* prosodist.

prosoma [prɔzɔma], *s.m. Z:* prosoma.

prosopis [prɔzɔpis], *s.m. Bot:* mesquite; (*genus*) Prosopis.

prosopite [prɔzɔpit], *s.f. Miner:* prosopite.

prosopopée [prɔzɔpɔpe], *s.f.* 1. *Rh:* prosopopoeia, personification. 2. *F: A:* ranting speech; tirade.

prospecté, -ée [prɔspɛkte], *s. Com:* customer, prospect, prospective buyer.

prospecter [prɔspɛkte], *v.tr.* 1. *Min: etc:* to prospect. 2. *Com:* to investigate, examine (potential market, etc.); p. la clientèle, to canvass for customers.

prospecteur, -trice [prɔspɛktœːr, -tris]. 1. *s. esp. Min:* prospector. 2. *s. Com: etc:* canvasser. 3. *s.m. Civ.E: Min:* prospecting machine, drill.

prospectif, -ive [prɔspɛktif, -iːv]. 1. *a.* prospective. 2. *s.f. Phil: etc:* la prospective, research into the future evolution of humanity; futurology, forecasting the future.

prospection [prɔspɛksjɔ̃], *s.f.* 1. *Phil:* looking forward. 2. *Min:* prospecting; *Civ.E:* prospection; p. pétrolière, oil prospecting; p. d'après les fragments rencontrés, shoading; p. biologique, biological prospecting. 3. canvassing.

prospectus [prɔspɛktys], *s.m.* 1. prospectus. 2. handbill, leaflet; distribuer des p., to give out handbills; p. publicitaire, brochure.

prospère [prɔspɛːr], *a.* 1. favourable (à, to). 2. prosperous, thriving, flourishing (person, business).

prospèrement [prɔspɛrmɑ̃], *adv.* prosperously.

prospérer [prɔspere], *v.i.* (je prospère, n. prospérons; je prospérerai) to prosper, thrive; to do well.

prospérité [prɔsperite], *s.f.* prosperity, prosperousness; air de p., prosperous appearance; *Com:* vague de p., boom.

prostate [prɔstat], *s.f. Anat:* prostate gland; prostate; *F:* **un vieux affligé d'une p.,** an old man with prostate trouble.

prostatectomie [prɔstatɛktɔmi], *s.f. Surg:* prostatectomy.

prostatique [prɔstatik], *a. Anat:* prostatic.

prostatite [prɔstatit], *s.f. Med:* prostatitis.

prostatorrhée [prɔstatɔre], *s.f. Med:* prostatorrh(o)ea.

prosternation [prɔstɛrnasjɔ̃], *s.f.* (*a*) prostrating oneself, falling prostrate (in adoration, attitude of respect); (*b*) grovelling, kowtowing.

prosternement [prɔstɛrn(ə)mɑ̃], *s.m.* (*a*) prostrate attitude; (*b*) *Lit:* humiliation.

prosterné [prɔstɛrne], *a.* prostrate; *B:* **les rois des nations, devant toi prosternés,** the kings of the nations, falling down before Thee.

prosterner [prɔstɛrne], *v.tr.* (*a*) *A: & Lit:* **le vent prosterne les arbres,** the wind is laying the trees flat, is bending the trees to the ground; (*b*) **il prosterna sa tête devant l'empereur,** he bowed his head to the ground before the emperor.

se prosterner, (*a*) to prostrate oneself (**devant,** before); to bow down (**devant,** to, before); (*b*) to grovel (**devant,** before); to kowtow (**devant,** to).

prosternum [prɔstɛrnɔm], *s.m. Ent:* prosternum.

prosthèse [prɔstɛːz], *s.f. Gram:* pro(s)thesis.

prosthétique [prɔstetik], *a.* pro(s)thetic.

prostigmine [prɔstigmin], *s.f. Pharm: R.t.m:* Prostigmin.

prostituée [prɔstitɥe], *s.f.* prostitute; harlot; *B:* (**Babylone**) **la grande p.,** (Babylon) the great whore.

prostituer [prɔstitɥe], *v.tr.* to prostitute (person, talent, etc.).

se prostituer, to prostitute oneself.

prostituteur [prɔstitytœːr], *s.m. A:* prostitutor.

prostitution [prɔstitysjɔ̃], *s.f.* prostitution; **la p. de la justice, de la presse,** the prostitution of justice, of the press; **maison de p.,** brothel, house of ill repute.

prostration [prɔstrasjɔ̃], *s.f.* (*a*) *Rel:* prostration; (*b*) *Med:* prostration, (nervous) exhaustion.

prostré [prɔstre], *a.* prostrate(d); (physically or mentally) exhausted.

prostyle [prɔstil], *s.m. Arch:* prostyle; *a.* **temple p.,** prostyle temple.

prosyllogisme [prɔsilɔʒism], *s.m.* prosyllogism.

protactinium [prɔtaktinjɔm], *s.m. Ch:* prot(o)-actinium.

protagon [prɔtagɔ̃], *s.m. Bio-Ch:* protagon.

protagoniste [prɔtagɔnist], *s.m.* (*a*) *A.Gr.Th:* protagonist; (*b*) protagonist, leading spirit (in an undertaking).

protal [prɔtal], *s.m. Sch: F:* head (of *lycée*).

protamine [prɔtamin], *s.f. Bio-Ch:* protamin(e).

protandre [prɔtɑ̃ːdr̥], *a. Bot:* protandrous.

protandrie [prɔtɑ̃dri], *s.f. Bot:* protandry.

protandrique [prɔtɑ̃drik], *a. Z:* protandric, protandrous.

protane [prɔtan], *s.m.* (*rare*) *Ch:* methane.

protarse [prɔtars], *s.m. Ent: Arach:* protarsus.

protase [prɔtɑːz], *s.f. A.Th: Ling:* protasis.

protatique [prɔtatik], *a. A.Th:* protatic; introductory.

prote [prɔt], *s.m. Typ:* foreman, overseer; **p. à la composition,** head of the composing room, case overseer; **p. aux machines,** machine-room manager; **p. à tablier,** working foreman.

protéacées [prɔtease], *s.f.pl. Bot:* Proteaceae.

protéase [prɔteɑːz], *s.f. Bio-Ch:* protease.

protecteur, -trice [prɔtɛktœːr, -tris]. **1.** *s.* (*a*) protector, protectress; (*b*) patron, patroness (of letters, art, etc.); **se donner des airs de p.,** to put on a patronizing manner. **2.** *s.m. Mec.E: etc:* protector, shield; guard (for machine tool, etc.); **p. de scie,** saw guard; *Mch:* **p. de niveau d'eau,** water-level guard, protector. **3.** *a.* (*a*) protecting (god, care, etc.); **société protectrice des animaux,** Society for the Prevention of Cruelty to Animals; (*b*) patronizing (tone, manner, etc.); **prendre un air p. avec qn,** to patronize s.o.; **un petit signe de tête p.,** a patronizing nod; (*c*) *Tchn:* protective (device, apparatus, etc.); **appareil p.,** safety guard; (*d*) *Pol.Ec:* protective (duty, tariff, etc.).

protectif, -ive [prɔtɛktif, -iːv], *a. Lit:* protective; **erreur protective,** protective illusion.

protection [prɔtɛksjɔ̃], *s.f.* **1.** (*a*) protection (contre, from, against); *Mil:* cover; **p. civile,** civil defence; **p. diplomatique,** diplomatic protection; **p. antirouille, p. contre la rouille,** protection against rust, rust proofing, rust prevention; **p. contre les rats,** ratproofing; **p. contre le feu, contre les incendies,** fire protection; *For:* fire conservancy; **forêt de p.,** protected forest; **œuvre de p. de l'enfance,** child-welfare association; **sous la p. de la police,** under police protection; **dispositif de p.,** safety device, protective device; *Mil:* protective disposition, set-up; security set-up; **p. thermique,** heat shield; **couche, enduit, de p.,** protective coating; **écran de p.,** protective screen; *Elcs: W.Tel:* **p. contre les émissions parasites,** protection against spurious emissions, spurious-frequency rejection; (*of computer*) **p. de mémoire,** memory, storage, protection; *Bot:* **tissus de p.,** protective layer; (*b*) *Pol.Ec:* protection; **système de p.,** protective system; **système de la p.,** protectionism; (*c*) (*pers.*) protector; **le Seigneur est notre p.,** the Lord is our protection. **2.** (*a*) patronage; influence; **être sous la p. de qn,** to be s.o.'s protégé; **prendre qn sous sa p.,** to take s.o. under one's wing; **solliciter la p. de qn,** to ask for s.o.'s help, s.o.'s support; to ask s.o. to use his influence on one's behalf; **avoir de la p.,** to have influential friends, friends at court; *Pej:* **par p.,** through influence; through friends at court; **regarder qn d'un air de p.,** to look at s.o. patronizingly, in a superior manner; (*b*) (*pers.*) **avoir de hautes protections,** to have influential friends, friends at court.

protectionnisme [prɔtɛksjɔnism], *s.m. Pol.Ec:* protection(ism).

protectionniste [prɔtɛksjɔnist], *s. & a. Pol.Ec:* protectionist.

protectorat [prɔtɛktɔra], *s.m.* protectorate.

Protée [prɔte]. **1.** *Pr.n.m. Myth:* Proteus. **2.** *s.m. Amph:* olm; (*genus*) Proteus. **3.** *s.f. Bot:* protea.

protéen, -enne [prɔteɛ̃, -ɛn], *a.* protean.

protégé, -ée [prɔteʒe]. **1.** *a.* protected; *P.N: Aut:* **passage p.,** priority of passage (over vehicles entering from minor road ahead). **2.** *s.* (*a*) favourite; protégé; *f.* protégée; (*b*) dependant; (*c*) **un p. britannique,** a British-protected person.

protège-aile [prɔtɛʒɛl], *s.m. Av:* wing skid; *pl. protège-ailes.*

protège-bas [prɔtɛʒbɑ], *s.m.inv. Cost:* socklet (worn to protect stocking from rough shoes).

protège-cahier [prɔtɛʒkaje], *s.m.* exercise-book cover; *pl. protège-cahiers.*

protège-cheville [prɔtɛʒʃəviːj], *s.m.inv. Fb:* ankle pad.

protège-courroie [prɔtɛʒkurwɑ], *s.f. Mch:* belt housing; *pl. protège-courroies.*

protège-dents [prɔtɛʒdɑ̃], *s.m.inv. Box:* gum shield.

protège-jambes [prɔtɛʒʒɑ̃ːb], *s.m.inv. Motor Cy:* leg shield.

protège-livre [prɔtɛʒlivr̥], *s.m.* reading jacket, paper cover (for book); *pl. protège-livres.*

protège-main [prɔtɛʒmɛ̃], *s.m.inv. Ind:* hand shield, hand guard.

protège-mine [prɔtɛʒmin], *s.m.inv.* pencil protector, pencil cap.

protège-nez [prɔtɛʒne], *s.m.inv. Mount:* **lunettes comportant un p.-n.,** glasses fitted with a nose shield.

protège-oreilles [prɔtɛʒɔrɛːj], *s.m.inv.* ear protector; *Rugby Fb:* scrum cap.

protège-parapluie [prɔtɛʒparaplɥi], *s.m.* umbrella cover; *pl. protège-parapluies.*

protège-pointe(s) [prɔtɛʒpwɛ̃ːt], *s.m.inv.* point protector; pencil cap.

protège-poumons [prɔtɛʒpumɔ̃], *s.m.inv.* lung protector.

protéger [prɔteʒe], *v.tr.* (**je protège, n. protégeons; je protégeai(s); je protégerai**) **1.** (*a*) to protect, to shelter, shield, guard (**contre,** against, from); **se p. de qch.,** to protect oneself from sth.; to guard against sth.; **p. qch. par un brevet,** to patent sth.; **protégé de, par, qn,** protected by s.o.; **forts qui protègent une ville,** forts that protect a town; (*b*) *Pol.Ec:* to protect (industry, etc.). **2.** (*a*) to patronize; to be a patron of (the arts, etc.); (*b*) to give (s.o.) one's support; to use one's influence on behalf of (s.o.); **il est très protégé au ministère,** he has influential friends at the ministry; **il sait qu'il est protégé par le ministre,** he knows that he has the minister behind him; (*c*) **p. une femme,** to keep a mistress.

protège-radiateur [prɔtɛʒradjatœːr], *s.m.* radiator grille; *pl. protège-radiateurs.*

protège-tibia [prɔtɛʒtibja], *s.m. Sp:* shin guard, shin pad; *pl. protège-tibias.*

protège-tympan [prɔtɛʒtɛ̃pɑ̃], *s.m.inv.* ear plug.

protéide [prɔteid], *s.f. Bio-Ch: O:* proteid.

protéidés [prɔteide], *s.m.pl. Amph:* Proteidae, the olms.

protéiforme [prɔteifɔrm], *a.* infinitely variable; protean.

protéinate [prɔteinat], *s.m. Pharm:* **p. d'argent,** silver proteinate.

protéine [prɔtein], *s.f. Ch:* protein.

protéinothérapie [prɔteinɔterapi], *s.f. Med:* protein therapy.

protéinurie [prɔteinyri], *s.f. Med:* proteinuria.

protéique[1] [prɔteik], *a.* protean.

protéique[2], *a. Ch:* protein(ic) (substance); **assise p.,** aleurone layer.

protèle [prɔtɛl], *s.m. Z:* aardwolf; (*genus*) Proteles.

protélytroptères [prɔtelitrɔptɛːr], *s.m.pl. Ent. Paleont:* Protelytroptera.

protéoflavine [prɔteɔflavin], *s.f. Ch: Biol:* flavoprotein, *F:* yellow enzyme.

protéolyse [prɔteɔliːz], *s.f. Bio-Ch:* proteolysis.

protéolytique [prɔteɔlitik], *a. Bio-Ch:* proteolytic.

protéose [prɔteoːz], *s.f. Bio-Ch:* proteose.

Protéphémères [prɔtefemɛːr], *s.m.pl. Ent: Paleont:* Protephemeroptera.

protérandrie [prɔterɑ̃dri], *s.f. Bot:* protandry, proterandry.

protérandrique [prɔterɑ̃drik], *a. Bot:* protandric.

protéroglyphe [prɔterɔglif], *Rept:* **1.** *a.* proteroglyphic. **2.** *s.m.* proteroglyph; *pl.* **protéroglyphes,** Proteroglypha.

protérogyne [prɔterɔʒin], *a. Bot:* protogynous, proterogynous.

protérogynie [prɔterɔʒini], *s.f. Biol:* proterogyny.

Protésilas [prɔtezilɑːs], *Pr.n.m. Gr.Myth:* Protesilaus.

protestable [prɔtɛstabl̥], *a. Com: Jur:* (bill) which may be protested.

protestant, -ante [prɔtɛstɑ̃, -ɑ̃ːt], *a. & s.* Protestant.

protestantisme [prɔtɛstɑ̃tism], *s.m.* Protestantism.

protestataire [prɔtɛstatɛːr]. **1.** *a.* (letter, etc.) of protest. **2.** *s.m. & f.* protester, objector.

protestation [prɔtɛstasjɔ̃], *s.f.* **1.** declaration, affirmation; **faire une p., des protestations, de son innocence,** to protest, declare, one's innocence. **2.** protest; **faire une p. contre qch.** to make a protest against sth.; **élever des protestations énergiques,** to raise a strong protest; **réunion de p.,** protest meeting, indignation meeting; **laisser passer sans p. une affirmation,** to allow a statement to pass unchallenged.

protester [prɔtɛste]. **1.** *v.tr.* (*a*) to protest; solemnly to declare; **je vous proteste que je l'ai fait,** I assure you that I did it; **il proteste n'avoir rien fait de pareil,** he protests, vows, swears, that he did no such thing; (*b*) *Com:* **p. un billet, une traite,** to protest a bill. **2.** *v.i.* (*a*) **p. de son innocence,** to protest one's innocence; (*b*) **p. contre qch.,** to protest, make a protest, against sth.; **p. contre une affirmation,** to challenge a statement; **p. mollement,** to make a mild protest; **sa vie entière proteste contre ces allégations,** his whole life gives the lie to these allegations; **tout le monde proteste,** everybody is up in arms about it; *Jur:* **p. de violence,** to act under protest.

protêt [prɔtɛ], *s.m. Com: Jur:* protest; **signifier un p.,** to give notice of a protest; **dresser un p.,** to make a protest; **dresser p. d'un effet,** to protest a bill; **p. faute de payement,** non-payment and protest; **p. faute d'acceptation,** protest for non-acceptance.

proteus [prɔteys], *s.m. Bac:* proteus.

prothalame [prɔtalam], *s.m. Lit:* prothalamion.

prothalle [prɔtal], *s.m.*, **prothallium** [prɔtaljɔm], *s.m. Bot:* prothallium, prothallus.

prothèse [prɔtɛːz], *s.f.* **1.** *Ling:* pro(s)thesis. **2.** (*a*) *Surg:* prosthesis, prosthetics; (*b*) (**appareil de**) **p.,** prosthesis; artificial limb, etc.; **p. dentaire,** dental prosthesis; false, artificial, teeth; denture, plate; **p. auditive,** hearing aid. **3.** *Ecc:* (*Gr. Orthodox Ch.*) prothesis (of the eucharistic elements).

prothésiste [prɔtezist], *s.m. & f.* prosthesist; artificial-limb maker, repairer; **p.-dentaire,** dental technician, mechanic.

prothétique [prɔtetik], *a.* (*a*) *Ling:* pro(s)thetic; (*b*) *Surg:* prosthetic; **appareil p.,** artificial limb, etc.; *Dent:* **traitement p.,** prosthetic dentistry.

prothoracique [prɔtɔrasik], *a. Ent:* prothoracic.

prothorax [prɔtɔraks], *s.m. Ent:* prothorax.

prothrombine [prɔtrɔ̃bin], *s.f. Physiol:* prothrombin.

protide [prɔtid], *s.m.* protid(e).

protiste [prɔtist], *s.m. Biol:* protist, unicellular organism; *pl.* **protistes,** Protista.

protistologie [prɔtistɔlɔʒi], *s.f.* protistology.

protium[1] [prɔsjɔm], *s.m. Bot:* protium.

protium[2], *s.m. Ch:* protium.

prot(o)- [prɔt(ɔ)], *pref.* prot(o)-.

proto [prɔto], *s.m. Sch: F:* head (of *lycée*).

protoascomycètes [prɔtɔaskɔmisɛt], *s.m.pl. Fung:* Protoascomycetes.

proto-attique [prɔtɔatik], *a. Cer:* proto-Attic (vase); *pl. proto-attiques.*

protobasidomycètes [prɔtɔbazidɔmisɛt], *s.m.pl. Fung:* Protobasidomycetes.

protoblaste [prɔtɔblast], *s.m. Biol:* protoblast.

protoblattoptères [prɔtɔblatɔptɛ:r], *s.m.pl. Ent: Paleont:* Protoblattoptera.

protocanonique [prɔtɔkanɔnik], *a. B:* protocanonical.

protocératops [prɔtɔseratɔps], *s.m. Rept: Paleont:* protoceratops.

protochordés [prɔtɔkɔrde], *s.m.pl. Nat.Hist:* Prochorda, Pro(to)chordata.

protococcus [prɔtɔkɔkys], *s.m.*, **protocoque** [prɔtɔkɔk], *s.m. Bot:* protococcus.

protocolaire [prɔtɔkɔlɛ:r], *a.* protocolar; formal; **clauses protocolaires d'accord,** formal provisions of agreement.

protocolairement [prɔtɔkɔlɛrmɑ̃], *adv.* according to protocol; by protocol.

protocole [prɔtɔkɔl], *s.m.* **1.** protocol, ceremonial etiquette; **chef du P.** = Marshal of the Diplomatic Corps. **2.** protocol, draft (treaty). **3.** *Typ:* list of proofreader's signs, symbols.

protocordés [prɔtɔkɔrde], *s.m.pl. Nat.Hist:* Prochorda, Pro(to)chordata.

protocorinthien, -ienne [prɔtɔkɔrɛ̃tjɛ̃, -jɛn], *a.* proto-Corinthian.

protodonates [prɔtɔdɔnat], *s.m.pl. Ent: Paleont:* Protodonata.

protodorique [prɔtɔdɔrik], *a. Arch:* proto-Doric.

protogermanique [prɔtɔʒɛrmanik], *a. & s.m. Ling:* proto-Germanic.

protogine [prɔtɔʒin], *s.m. Geol:* protogine.

protogyne [prɔtɔʒin], *a. Bot:* protogynous.

protogynie [prɔtɔʒini], *s.f. Bot:* protogyny.

protohémiptères [prɔtɔemiptɛ:r], *s.m.pl. Ent: Paleont:* Protohemiptera.

protohippus [prɔtɔipys], *s.m. Paleont:* protohippus.

protohistoire [prɔtɔistwa:r], *s.f.* protohistory.

protohistorien, -ienne [prɔtɔistɔrjɛ̃, -jɛn], *s.* protohistorian.

protohistorique [prɔtɔistɔrik], *a.* protohistoric.

protolyse [prɔtɔli:z], *s.f. Ch:* protolysis.

protolytique [prɔtɔlitik], *a. Ch:* **réaction p.,** ion exchange.

protomartyr [prɔtɔmarti:r], *s.m.* protomartyr.

protomycénien, -ienne [prɔtɔmisenjɛ̃, -jɛn], *a.* proto-Mycenean.

proton [prɔtɔ̃], *s.m. Atom.Ph:* proton.

protonéma [prɔtɔnema], *s.m. Moss:* protonema.

protonique[1] [prɔtɔnik], *a. Gram: Ling:* protonic, pretonic.

protonique[2], *a. Atom.Ph:* protonic.

protonotaire [prɔtɔnɔtɛ:r], *s.m. Ecc:* protonotary.

protopathie [prɔtɔpati], *s.f.* protopathy.

protophosphure [prɔtɔfɔsfy:r], *s.m. Ch:* protophosphide.

protophyte [prɔtɔfit], *s.m. Bot:* protophyte; *pl.* **protophytes,** Protophyta.

protoplasma [prɔtɔplasma], *s.m.*, **protoplasme** [prɔtɔplasm], *s.m. Biol:* protoplasm.

protoplasmique [prɔtɔplasmik], *a. Biol:* protoplasmic.

protoplaste [prɔtɔplast], *s.m. Biol:* protoplast.

protoptère [prɔtɔptɛ:r], *s.m. Ich:* protopterus, African lung fish.

protorthoptères [prɔtɔrtɔptɛ:r], *s.m.pl. Ent: Paleont:* Protorthoptera.

protospore [prɔtɔspɔ:r], *s.f. Biol:* protospore.

protothériens [prɔtɔterjɛ̃], *s.m.pl. Z:* Prototheria.

prototype [prɔtɔtip], *s.m.* prototype.

prototypique [prɔtɔtipik], *a.* prototypal, prototypic(al).

protoures [prɔtu:r], *s.m.pl. Ent:* Protura.

protoxyde [prɔtɔksid], *s.m. Ch:* protoxide.

protozoaire [prɔtɔzɔɛ:r]. **1.** *s.m. Z:* protozoan; **les protozoaires,** the Protozoa. **2.** *a.* protozoal, protozoan, protozoic.

protozoologie [prɔtɔzɔɔlɔʒi], *s.f.* protozoology.

protracteur, -trice [prɔtraktœ:r, -tris], *Anat:* **1.** *a.* protractor (muscle). **2.** *s.m.* protractor (muscle).

protractile [prɔtraktil], *a.* protractile.

protraction [prɔtraksjɔ̃], *s.f.* protraction, drawing out.

protrus [prɔtry], *a.* protrusive (jaw, etc.).

protrusion [prɔtryzjɔ̃], *s.f.* protrusion.

protubérance [prɔtyberɑ̃:s], *s.f.* protuberance. **1.** *Astr:* **p. solaire,** solar prominence; *Anat:* **protubérances du crâne,** protuberances, *F:* bumps, of the cranium; **p. (cérébrale),** *pons varolii.* **2.** knob (on stick, etc.); **couvert de protubérances,** knobbly.

protubérant [prɔtyberɑ̃], *a.* protuberant.

protubérantiel, -ielle [prɔtyberɑ̃sjɛl], *a. Astr:* protuberantial.

protuteur, -trice [prɔtytœ:r, -tris], *s. Jur:* acting guardian.

protypographique [prɔtipɔgrafik], *a.* **bibliothèque p.,** manuscript library; manuscript room (of library).

prou [pru], *adv. A:* much; many; *still used in the phrases:* **peu ou p.,** more or less; not much; not many; **ni peu ni p.,** not at all; none at all.

proue [pru], *s.f.* prow, stem, bows (of ship).

prouesse [pruɛs], *s.f.* **1.** *Lit:* prowess, valour. **2.** (*a*) *Lit:* feat of valour; (*b*) feat; **se lever avant l'aube en guise de p.,** to get up before dawn, as if one were performing a feat; *Iron:* **voilà une belle p.!** well, that's a fine feat!

proustien, -ienne [prustjɛ̃, -jɛn], *a. Lit:* Proustian.

proustite [prustit], *s.f. Miner:* proustite.

prout [prut], *s.m. P:* fart.

prouter [prute], *v.i. P:* to fart.

prouvable [pruvabl], *a.* provable.

prouver [pruve], *v.tr.* **1.** to prove (fact, the truth of sth.); **p. le bien-fondé d'une réclamation,** to substantiate a claim; to make good one's claim; **p. une accusation contre qn,** to bring a charge home to s.o.; **cela n'est pas encore prouvé,** that remains to be proved; **p. clair comme le jour que . . .,** to make it as clear as daylight that . . . *Prov:* **qui veut trop p. ne prouve rien,** he spoils his case who tries to prove too much. **2. p. sa capacité,** to give proof, show proof, of (one's) capacity; **il aimait à p. sa force,** he liked to show off his strength; **l'événement prouve qu'il avait raison,** the event shows him to have been right.

provenance [prɔvnɑ̃:s], *s.f.* **1.** source, origin; provenance; **de p. anglaise,** of English origin; **pays de p.,** country of origin; **train en p. de Bordeaux,** train from Bordeaux. **2.** *pl. Cust:* **les provenances,** imports.

provençal, -ale, -aux [prɔvɑ̃sal, -o]. **1.** *a. & s. Geog:* Provençal; of Provence. **2.** *s.m. Ling:* Provençal.

provençalisant, -ante [prɔvɑ̃salizɑ̃, -ɑ̃:t], *s.* student of Provençal (language, literature, etc.).

provençalisme [prɔvɑ̃salism], *s.m. Ling:* Provençal expression.

Provence [prɔvɑ̃:s], *Pr.n.f. Geog:* Provence.

provende [prɔvɑ̃:d], *s.f.* **1.** *A:* provisions, victuals; **aller à la p.,** to go foraging; to go marketing. **2.** *Husb:* provender, fodder.

provenir [prɔvni:r], *v.i.* (*conj. like* VENIR) to proceed, result, arise, come (**de,** from); to originate (**de,** in); **mot qui provient du latin,** word that comes from Latin; **d'où proviennent ces difficultés?** what do these difficulties arise from? *Jur:* **les enfants provenant, provenus, de ce mariage,** the children issuing from this marriage; **revenu provenant d'une propriété,** income issuing, arising, out of an estate; **tout l'argent qui en provient,** all the money which accrues from it; **un bruit qui provient du sous-sol,** a noise coming up from the basement.

provenu [prɔv(ə)ny], *s.m.* proceeds.

proverbe [prɔvɛrb], *s.m.* **1.** proverb; *B:* **le Livre des Proverbes,** the Book of Proverbs; **passer en p.,** to become a proverb; to become proverbial. **2.** *Th:* proverb.

proverbial, -aux [prɔvɛrbjal, -o], *a.* proverbial.

proverbialement [prɔvɛrbjalmɑ̃], *adv.* proverbially.

proverbialiser [prɔvɛrbjalize], *v.tr.* to proverbialize (sth.); to make (sth.) into a proverb.

providence [prɔvidɑ̃:s], *s.f.* providence; **aller contre la p.,** to fly in the face of providence; **être la p. de qn,** to be s.o.'s good angel; **c'est une p. que vous ne soyez pas encore parti,** it's providential that you haven't gone yet; **l'État P.,** the Welfare State.

providentialisme [prɔvidɑ̃sjalism], *s.m.* providentialism; belief in providence.

providentialiste [prɔvidɑ̃sjalist], *s.m. & f.* believer in providence.

providentialité [prɔvidɑ̃sjalite], *s.f.* providential character (of an event).

providentiel, -elle [prɔvidɑ̃sjɛl], *a.* (*a*) providential; **secours p.,** providential help; (*b*) **rencontre providentielle,** providential, fortunate, encounter; **un ami p.,** a friend in need.

providentiellement [prɔvidɑ̃sjɛlmɑ̃], *adv.* providentially.

provignage [prɔviɲa:ʒ], *s.m. Vit:* provining, layering (of vine).

provignement [prɔviɲ(ə)mɑ̃], *s.m.* (*a*) *Vit:* provining, layering (of vine); (*b*) *Ling:* enriching of vocabulary (with derivatives of existing words).

provigner [prɔviɲe], *v.tr. Vit:* to provine, layer (vine).

provin [prɔvɛ̃], *s.m. Vit:* layered branch, stock.

province [prɔvɛ̃:s], *s.f.* **1.** (*a*) *A:* country, state; (*b*) province; **la p. du Poitou, du Languedoc,** the province of Poitou, of Languedoc; **la p. de Bourgogne, de Normandie,** the province of Burgundy, of Normandy. **2.** (*in opposition to the capital*); (*a*) **la p.,** the provinces, the country; **vivre en p.,** to live in the provinces, in the country; **vie de p.,** provincial life, country life; **de p.,** small-town(ish); **cousin de p.,** country cousin; **il est bien de sa p.,** he's very provincial, very countrified; **manières de p.,** provincial, countrified, ways; **il arrive du fond de sa p.,** he's fresh from the provinces, he's just arrived from the depths of the country; **aller en p.** = to leave Town; (*b*) *a.inv. F:* **cela fait p.,** that's very provincial; **ils sont très p.,** they're very provincial, countrified.

Provinces Maritimes (les) [leprɔvɛ̃smaritim], *Pr.n.f.pl. Geog:* The Maritime Provinces (of Canada).

Provinces Unies (les) [leprɔvɛ̃syni], *Pr.n.f.pl. Hist:* the United Provinces (of the Netherlands).

provincial, -ale, -aux [prɔvɛ̃sjal, -o]. **1.** *a.* provincial, country; *Pej:* countrified (manners, etc.); small-town(ish); parochial. **2.** (*a*) *s.* provincial; man, woman, from the country; (*b*) *s.m. Ecc:* provincial.

provincialat [prɔvɛ̃sjala], *s.m. Ecc:* provincialate.

provincialement [prɔvɛ̃sjalmɑ̃], *adv.* provincially, in a provincial, countrified, manner.

provincialiser [prɔvɛ̃sjalize], *v.tr.* to provincialize.

provincialisme [prɔvɛ̃sjalism], *s.m.* provincialism; provincial, regional (i) word, expression, (ii) pronunciation.

provincialité [prɔvɛ̃sjalite], *s.f.* provinciality.

provinois, -oise [prɔvinwa, -wa:z], *a. & s. Geog:* (native, inhabitant) of Provins.

proviseur [prɔvizœ:r], *s.m. Sch:* headmaster (of a *lycée*).

provision [prɔvizjɔ̃], *s.f.* **1.** provision, store, stock, supply; **faire p. de charbon,** to lay in a stock of coal; **p. de cartouches, de blé,** supply of cartridges, of corn; **nos provisions sont épuisées,** our supplies, provisions, are exhausted; **provisions de bouche,** food; **provisions de guerre,** munitions; **faire ses provisions,** to go shopping; **sac, panier, à provisions,** shopping bag, basket; **une bonne p. de courage,** a good reserve of courage. **2.** *Jur:* **jugement par p.,** provisional judgment. **3.** (*a*) advance made to person receiving damages not yet definitely assessed; (*b*) *Com: Fin:* funds, cover, reserve, margin; *Jur:* sum paid into court; **verser une p., des provisions, verser une somme à titre de p.,** to pay a deposit; **p. d'une lettre de change,** consideration for a bill of exchange; **faire p. pour une lettre de change,** to provide for, protect, a bill; **insuffisance de p.,** insufficient funds (to meet cheque, etc.); **chèque sans p.,** dishonoured, *F:* dud, bouncing, cheque; (*c*) **p. pour créances douteuses,** bad-debts reserve; (*d*) retaining fee (given to lawyer); (*e*) commission (paid to agent). **4.** *Ecc:* conferring of a post or benefice (upon s.o.); **(lettres de) provisions,** letters confirming an appointment, *esp.* an appointment to a living.

provisionnel, -elle [prɔvizjɔnɛl], *a.* **1.** *A:* = PROVISOIRE. **2.** *Jur:* provisional (division of estate, etc.). **3.** *Fin:* **acompte p.,** payment (of income tax) made on provisional assessment.

provisionnellement [prɔvizjɔnɛlmɑ̃], *adv.* **1.** *A:* = PROVISOIREMENT. **2.** *Jur:* provisionally.

provisionner [prɔvizjɔne], *v.tr. Com:* to give consideration for (a bill); *Bank:* **p. un compte,** to pay money into an account.

provisoire [prɔvizwa:r]. **1.** *a.* provisional, provisory; acting, temporary; **nommé à titre p.,** appointed provisionally; **dividende p.,** interim dividend; **gérant p.,** acting manager; *Jur:* **sentence p.,** provisional judgment, judgment ad interim; **mise en liberté p.,** *F:* **la p.,** conditional discharge; **gouvernement p.,** provisional, interim, government; **habitation p.,** emergency dwelling; temporary accommodation. **2.** *s.m.* (*a*) what is provisional, temporary; **parfois le p. dure longtemps,** the provisional can sometimes last a long time; **s'installer dans le p.,** to treat sth. temporary as permanent; (*b*) provisional nature (of appointment, etc.).

provisoirement [prɔvizwarmɑ̃], *adv.* provisionally, temporarily, for the time being, in the meantime.

provisorat [prɔvizɔra], *s.m. Sch:* headmastership (of a *lycée*).

provitamine [prɔvitamin], *s.f. Bio-Ch:* provitamin.

provocant [prɔvɔkɑ̃], *a.* **1.** provoking, provocative, aggressive (language, tone, etc.). **2.** provocative, tantalizing, alluring (smile, glance, etc.); **elle lui lançait des œillades provocantes,** she was making eyes at him.

provocateur, -trice [prɔvɔkatœːr, -tris]. **1.** *a.* provocative; **agent p.,** agent provocateur. **2.** *s.* (*a*) aggressor; (*b*) instigator, provoker (of disturbance, etc.).

provocatif, -ive [prɔvɔkatif, -iːv], *a.* provocative.

provocation [prɔvɔkasjɔ̃], *s.f.* **1.** provocation; **il se fâche à la moindre p.,** he gets angry on the slightest provocation; **lancer des provocations à qn,** to hurl provoking remarks at s.o.; **p. en duel,** challenge to a duel; *Jur:* **plaider excuse de p.,** to plead provocation. **2.** instigation; **p. au crime,** incitement to crime. **3.** *O:* **p. au sommeil,** inducement to sleep.

provoqué, -ée [prɔvɔke], *s. Jur:* victim of unprovoked assault.

provoquer [prɔvɔke], *v.tr.* **1.** to provoke; (*a*) **p. qn en duel,** to challenge s.o. to a duel; to call s.o. out; **s'il n'avait pas été provoqué, il n'aurait pas frappé,** if he had not been provoked he would not have struck the blow; (*b*) (*of woman*) to make advances to (a man). **2.** to induce, instigate; **p. qn au crime, à commettre un crime,** to instigate s.o. to crime; to incite s.o. to commit a crime; **p. la révolte,** to instigate a revolt; **p. qn à boire,** to egg s.o. on to drink. **3.** (*a*) to bring about, achieve (desired result, reform, etc.); **p. un appel d'air,** to create a draught; **p. le sommeil,** *abs.* **p. au sommeil,** to induce sleep; *Med:* **p. la sueur,** to induce perspiration; (*b*) to cause, bring about (war, catastrophe, etc.); to give rise to (dissatisfaction, etc.); to call forth, stir up (passion, feeling, etc.); **p. une explosion,** to cause an explosion; **bactéries qui provoquent la fermentation,** bacteria that provoke fermentation, that give rise to fermentation; **sa colère provoqua un nouvel accès de fièvre,** his anger brought on a new bout of fever; **p. la curiosité de tous,** to arouse universal curiosity; **p. la gaieté,** to cause, provoke, cheerfulness; *F:* to add to the gaiety of nations; **p. un sourire,** to raise a smile; **p. des commentaires,** to give rise to comments; **p. une réponse généreuse,** to produce a generous response.

proxénète [prɔksenɛt], *s.m. & f.* procurer, procuress; pander.

proxénétisme [prɔksenetism], *s.m.* procuring; pimping.

proximal, -aux [prɔksimal, -o], *a. Z: Anat:* proximal.

proximité [prɔksimite], *s.f.* **1.** proximity, nearness, vicinity, adjacency; propinquity; **à p.,** near at hand, close by; **j'ai tous mes outils à p.,** I have all my tools at hand, to hand; **à p. de . . .,** close to . . .; **demeurer à p. de qch.,** to live in the immediate neighbourhood, in the vicinity, of sth.; **hôtel à p. de la gare,** hotel within easy reach of the station. **2. p. du sang,** near relationship.

proyer [prwaje], *s.m. Orn:* **(bruant) p.,** common bunting, corn bunting, bunting lark.

prozymase [prɔzimaːz], *s.f. Bio-Ch:* proenzyme, zymogen.

pruche [pryːʃ], *s.f. Fr.C: Bot:* hemlock.

prude [pryd]. **1.** *a.* prudish. **2.** *s.f.* prude.

prudemment [prydamɑ̃], *adv.* prudently, cautiously; carefully; with prudence.

prudence [prydɑ̃ːs]. **1.** *s.f.* prudence; carefulness; **agir avec p.,** to act prudently; **c'est une simple mesure de p.,** it is merely a question of prudence; **avoir la p. du serpent,** to have the wisdom of the serpent; *Prov:* **p. est mère de sûreté,** look before you leap; safety first! **2.** *Pr.n.f.* Prudence.

prudent [prydɑ̃], *a.* prudent, discreet (person, answer, conduct); conservative (estimate, etc.); **il serait p. d'enfermer ces papiers,** it would be advisable to lock up these papers; **il serait p. que vous restiez encore un peu,** it would be just as well for you to stay a little longer; **il faut être très p. en . . .,** the greatest care must be taken in . . .; **se montrer plus zélé que p.,** to show more zeal than discretion; *F:* to throw the baby out with the bath water.

pruderie [prydri], *s.f.* **1.** prudery, prudishness; **se détourner avec p.,** to turn away prudishly. **2. des pruderies de vieille fille,** old maid's pruderies.

prud'homie [prydɔmi], *s.f. A:* **1.** probity, integrity. **2.** wisdom.

prud'homme [prydɔm], *s.m.* **1.** *A:* man of experience and integrity. **2. conseil des prud'hommes,** conciliation board (of employers and workers, in industrial disputes).

Prudhomme (Joseph) [ʒozɛfprydɔm], *Pr.n.m. Fr.Lit:* character invented by Henri Monnier (1852), given to the utterance of sententious platitudes; he is the personification of the pompous and empty-headed bourgeois; **c'est un p.,** he's a pompous ass.

prudhommerie [prydɔmri], *s.f.* pomposity, sententiousness.

prudhommesque [prydɔmɛsk], *a.* pompous, sententious.

pruine [prɥin], *s.f.* bloom (on fruit).

pruiné [prɥine], **pruineux, -euse** [prɥinø, -øːz], *a. Bot:* pruinose; covered with bloom; velvety.

pruinosité [prɥinozite], *s.f. Bot: Ent:* pruinescence.

prulaurasine [prylɔrazin], *s.f. Ch:* prulaurasin.

prune [pryn], *s.f.* **1.** (*a*) *Bot:* plum; **p. de Damas,** damson; **eau de vie de prunes,** plum brandy; **un verre de p.,** a glass of plum brandy; **prunes à l'eau de vie,** brandy plums; *P:* **avoir sa p.,** to be drunk, tight; *F:* **aux prunes,** (i) next summer; (ii) last summer; (*b*) *P:* **pour des prunes,** for nothing; **je ne veux pas me déranger pour des prunes,** I'm not going to put myself out for nothing; **des prunes!** no fear! not (bloody) likely! **2. p. d'icaque, de coco, de coton, des anses,** coco plum. **3.** *P: A:* (*a*) (rifle) bullet; (*b*) blow; slap. **4.** *a.inv.* plum-coloured.

prune-abricot [prynabriko], *s.f. Hort:* (*U.S.*) plumcot; *pl. prunes-abricots.*

pruneau, -eaux [pryno], *s.m.* **1.** (*a*) prune; (*b*) *F: O:* **p. (délavé),** dark-skinned, swarthy, girl or woman. **2.** *P:* (*a*) bruise(mark); black eye; (*b*) (rifle)bullet; (*c*) quid of tobacco.

prunées [pryne], *s.f.pl. Bot:* Prunaceae, Amygdalaceae.

prunelaie [prynlɛ], *s.f.* plum orchard.

prunelée [prynle], *s.f.* plum jam.

prunelle [prynɛl], *s.f.* **1.** *Bot:* (*a*) sloe; **(liqueur de) p.,** sloe gin; (*b*) prunella, self-heal. **2.** pupil (of the eye); **chérir qn comme la p. de ses yeux, tenir à qch. comme à la p. de ses yeux,** to cherish s.o., sth., like the apple of one's eye; *F:* **jouer de la p.,** to make eyes (at s.o.). **3.** *Tex:* prunella.

prunellier [prynɛlje], *s.m.* blackthorn, sloe bush.

prunier [prynje], *s.m.* plum tree; **p. de Damas,** damson tree; **p. d'Amérique, d'Espagne,** hog plum; **p. trilobé, p. du Japon,** Japanese plum (tree); *F:* **secouer qn comme un p.,** (i) to give s.o. a good shaking; (ii) to tell s.o. off.

prurigineux, -euse [pryriʒinø, -øːz], *a. Med:* pruriginous, that makes one itch.

prurigo [pryrigo], *s.m. Med:* prurigo.

prurit [pryri(t)], *s.m. Med:* pruritus, itching.

Prusse [prys], *Pr.n.f. Geog: Hist:* Prussia; **la P. orientale,** East Prussia; **bleu de P.,** Prussian blue; *F:* **travailler pour le roi de P.,** to work for nothing, for love; *F:* **aller voir le roi de P.,** to have a look at the plumbing, to go to the loo.

prussianiser [prysjanize], *v.tr.* to Prussianize.

prussianisme [prysjanism], *s.m.* Prussianism.

prussiate [prysjat], *s.m. Ch:* prussiate, cyanide; **p. jaune,** potassium ferrocyanide; **p. rouge,** potassium ferricyanide.

prussien, -ienne [prysjɛ̃, -jɛn], *a. & s. Geog: Hist:* Prussian; **troupes dressées à la prussienne,** troops drilled in the Prussian fashion.

prussique [prysik], *a. Ch: A:* prussic (acid).

prytane [pritan], *s.m. Gr.Ant:* prytanis.

prytanée [pritane], *s.m.* **1.** *Gr.Ant:* prytaneum. **2. le P. militaire de la Flèche,** the Military School of la Flèche (for sons of officers).

psallette [psalɛt], *s.f.* choir school.

psalliote [psaljɔt], *s.f. or m. Fung:* agaric(us); **p. champêtre,** common, field, mushroom.

psalmique [psalmik], *a.* psalmic.

psalmiste [psalmist], *s.m.* psalmist.

psalmodie [psalmɔdi], *s.f.* **1.** (*a*) *Ecc:* intoning; (*b*) singsong, droning. **2.** (*a*) intoned psalm; (*b*) *O:* monotonous string of complaints.

psalmodier [psalmɔdje], *v.* (*pr.sub. & p.d.* **n. psalmodiions, v. psalmodiiez**) **1.** *v.i.* to intone, chant; to psalmodize. **2.** *v.tr.* to intone (office, etc.); **p. qch.,** to drone out sth.; to recite sth. monotonously, in a singsong voice.

psalmodique [psalmɔdik], *a.* psalmodic.

psaltérion [psalterjɔ̃], *s.m.* psaltery.

Psammétique, Psammétik [psametik], *Pr.n.m. A.Hist:* Psammetichus.

psammite [psammit], *s.m. Miner:* psammite.

psammitique [psammitik], *a.* psammitic; **roche p.,** sandstone.

psammome [psamom], *s.m. Med:* psammoma.

psammophile [psam(m)ɔfil], *a.* sand-loving (lizards, reptiles); psammophile (plants, etc.).

psammophyte [psam(m)ɔfit], *Bot:* **1.** *a.* psammophytic. **2.** *s.m.* psammophyte.

psaume [psoːm], *s.m.* psalm.

psautier [psotje], *s.m.* **1.** psalter, psalm book. **2.** *Z: A:* psalterium, omasum.

pschent [pskɛnt], *s.m. Egyptian Ant:* pschent.

psélaphidés [pselafide], *s.m.pl. Ent:* Pselaphidae.

pseudarthrose [psødartroːz], *s.f. Med:* pseudoarthrosis.

pseudesthésie [psødɛstezi], *s.f.* pseudaesthesia.

pseud(o)- [psød(ɔ)], *pref.* pseud(o)-.

pseudo [psødo], *s.m. F:* **c'est du p.,** it's pseudo, fake, phoney, bogus.

pseudo-adiabatique [psødɔadjabatik], *a. Meteor:* pseudoadiabatic; *pl. pseudo-adiabatiques.*

pseudo-archaïque [psødɔarkaik], *a.* pseudo(-) archaic; *pl. pseudo-archaïques.*

pseudobrookite [psødɔbrukit], *s.f. Miner:* pseudobrookite.

pseudo-bulbaire [psødɔbylbɛːr], *a. Med:* pseudobulbar; *pl. pseudo-bulbaires.*

pseudo-bulbe [psødɔbylb], *s.m. Bot:* pseudobulb; *pl. pseudo-bulbes.*

pseudocarpe [psødɔkarp], *s.m. Bot:* pseudocarp.

pseudo-catholique [psødɔkatɔlik], *a.* pseudo-catholic; *pl. pseudo-catholiques.*

pseudo-chrysalide [psødɔkrizalid], *s.f. Ent:* pseudochrysalis; *pl. pseudo-chrysalides.*

pseudo-code [psødɔkɔd], *s.m. Elcs:* (*computers*) pseudo code, interpretive code; *pl. pseudo-codes.*

pseudo-cumène [psødɔkymɛn], *s.m. Ch:* pseudocumene.

pseudo-démence [psødɔdemɑ̃ːs], *s.f. Med:* pseudodementia.

pseudogamie [psødɔgami], *s.f. Bot:* pseudogamy.

pseudo-gothique [psødɔgɔtik], *a.* pseudo-gothic; *pl. pseudo-gothiques.*

pseudogyne [psødɔʒin], *s.f. Ent:* pseudogyne.

pseudo-hallucination [psødɔalysinasjɔ̃], *s.f. Psy:* pseudohallucination; *pl. pseudo-hallucinations.*

pseudo-hermaphrodisme [psødɔɛrmafrɔdism], *s.m.* pseudohermaphroditism.

pseudo-instruction [psødɔɛ̃stryksjɔ̃], *s.f. Elcs:* (*computers*) pseudo-instruction; quasi instruction; *pl. pseudo-instructions.*

pseudo-lamellibranches [psødɔlamɛlibrɑ̃ːʃ], *s.m. pl. Moll:* Pseudolamellibranchia.

pseudo-membrane [psødɔmɑ̃bran], *s.f. Med:* pseudomembrane, false membrane; *pl. pseudo-membranes.*

pseudo-membraneux, -euse [psødɔmɑ̃branø, -øːz], *a.* pseudomembranous; *pl. pseudo-membraneux, -euses.*

pseudo-méningite [psødɔmenɛ̃ʒit], *s.f. no pl. Med:* meningism(us), pseudomeningitis.

pseudomère [psødɔmɛːr], *s.m. Ch:* pseudomer.

pseudomérie [psødɔmeri], *s.f. Ch:* pseudomerism.

pseudomérique [psødɔmerik], *a. Ch:* pseudomeric.

pseudomorphe [psødɔmɔrf], *Miner:* **1.** *a.* pseudomorphous, pseudomorphic. **2.** *s.m.* pseudomorph.

pseudomorphique [psødɔmɔrfik], *a. Miner:* pseudomorphic.

pseudomorphisme [psødɔmɔrfism], *s.m.,* **pseudomorphose** [psødɔmɔrfoːz], *s.f. Miner:* pseudomorphosis.

pseudonitrol [psødɔnitrɔl], *s.m. Ch:* pseudonitrol.

pseudonyme [psødɔnim]. **1.** (*a*) *a.* pseudonymous; (*b*) *s.m.* pseudonymous author, writer. **2.** *s.m.* pseudonym; assumed name; nom de plume; **sons le p. de . . .,** signing himself . . ..

pseudo-nymphe [psødɔnɛ̃ːf], *s.f. Ent:* pseudochrysalis, pseudo-nymph; *pl. pseudo-nymphes.*

pseudo-parasite [psødɔparazit], *s.m.* pseudoparasite; *pl. pseudo-parasites.*

pseudo-parasitisme [psødɔparazitism], *s.m.* pseudoparasitism.

pseudo-périodique [psødɔperjɔdik], *a. Mth: etc:* pseudoperiodic; *pl. pseudo-périodiques.*

pseudopode [psødɔpɔd], *s.m. Biol:* pseudopod(ium).

pseudo-rage [psødɔraːʒ], *s.m. Vet:* pseudorabies; bulbar paralysis.

pseudo-rhumatisme [psødɔrymatism], *s.m. Med:* pseudorheumatism; *pl. pseudo-rhumatismes.*

pseudo-rubis [psødɔrybi], *s.m.inv. Miner:* rose quartz, Bohemian ruby.

pseudo-saphir [psødɔsafiːr], *s.m. Miner:* blue quartz; *pl. pseudo-saphirs.*

pseudo-scorpion [psødɔskɔrpjɔ̃], *s.m. Arach:* pseudoscorpion; *pl.* **pseudo-scorpions,** Pseudoscorpionida.

pseudosmie [psødɔsmi], *s.f. Med:* pseudosmia.

pseudo-sphère [psødɔsfɛːr], *s.f. Geom:* pseudosphere; *pl. pseudo-sphères.*

pseudo-sphérique [psødɔsferik], *a.* pseudospherical; *pl. pseudo-sphériques.*
pseudo-spore [psødɔspɔːr], *s.f. Biol:* pseudospore; *pl. pseudo-spores.*
pseudosuichens [psødɔsykjɛ̃], *s.m.pl. Paleont:* Pseudosuchia, pseudosuchians.
pseudotsuga [psødɔtsyga], *s.m. Bot:* pseudotsuga; **p. de Douglas,** Douglas pine, Douglas spruce.
pseudo-tuberculose [psødɔtybɛrkyloːz], *s.f. Med: Vet:* pseudotuberculosis; *Vet:* caseous lymphadenitis; *pl. pseudo-tuberculoses.*
pseudo-tumeur [psødɔtymœːr], *s.f. Med:* false tumour; *pl. pseudo-tumeurs.*
pseudo-vecteur [psødɔvɛktœːr], *s.m. Mth:* pseudovector; *pl. pseudo-vecteurs.*
pseudo-vitesse [psødɔvitɛs], *s.f.* pseudovelocity.
psi [psi], *s.m. Gr.Alph:* psi; *Atom.Ph:* **fonction p.,** wave function.
psiloceras [psilɔseras], *s.m. Paleont:* psiloceras, psiloceran.
psilomélane [psilɔmelan], *s.f. Miner:* psilomelane.
psilose [psiloːz], *s.f. Ling:* psilosis.
psilotacées [psilɔtase], *s.f.pl. Bot:* Psilotaceae.
psilure [psilyːr], *s.m. Ent:* **p. moine,** nun (moth).
psitt [pst], *int. & s.m.* (*to attract attention*) psst!
psittacidés [psitaside], *s.m.pl. Orn:* Psittacidae.
psittaciformes [psitasifɔrm], *s.m.pl. Orn:* Psittaciformes.
psittaciné [psitasine], *a. & s.m. Orn:* psittacine; *s.m.pl.* **psittacinés,** Psittacinae.
psittacinite [psitasinit], *s.f. Miner:* psittacinite.
psittacisme [psitasism], *s.m.* psittacism; automatic, parrot-like, speech.
psittacose [psitakoːiz], *s.f. Med: Vet:* psittacosis.
psithyre [psitiːr], *s.m. Ent:* cuckoo bee.
psoas [psɔas], *s.m. Anat:* psoas, psoatic muscle; **p. iliaque,** psoas major, psoas magnus; **petit p.,** psoas minor, psoas parvus.
psocidés [psɔside], *s.m.pl. Ent:* Psocidae.
psoïtis [psɔitis], *s.m. Med:* psoitis, inflammation of the psoas.
psocoptères [psɔkɔptɛːr], *s.m.pl. Ent:* Psocoptera, booklice.
psocoptéroïdes [psɔkɔpterɔid], *s.m.pl. Ent:* Psocopteroidea.
psophomètre [psɔfɔmɛtr̥], *s.m. Tp: Tg:* psophometer.
psoque [psɔk], *s.m. Ent:* psocid.
psore [psɔːr], *s.f.,* **psora** [psɔra], *s.f. Med:* psora.
psoriasique [psɔrjazik], **psoriasistique** [psɔrjazistik], *a. Med:* psoriatic.
psoriasis [psɔrjazis], *s.m. Med:* psoriasis.
psorique [psɔrik], *a. Med:* psoric.
psoropte [psɔrɔpt], *s.m. Ent:* psoroptid.
psoroptique [psɔrɔptik], *a. Ent: Vet:* psoroptic.
pst(t) [pst], *int.* pstt!
psychagogie [psikagɔʒi], *s.f.* psychagogy.
psychagogique [psikagɔʒik], *a.* psychagogic.
psychalgie [psikalʒi], *s.f. Med:* psychalgia.
psychanalyse [psikanaliːz,] *s.f.* psychoanalysis; **p. (industrielle),** human engineering.
psychanalyser [psikanalize], *v.tr.* to psychoanalyse.
psychanalyste [psikanalist], *s.m. & f.* psychoanalyst; **romancier p.,** psychoanalytical novelist.
psychanalytique [psikanalitik], *a.* psychoanalytical.
psychasthénie [psikasteni], *s.f. Med:* psychasthenia.
psychasthénique [psikastenik], *a. Med:* psychasthenic.
Psyché [psiʃe]. **1.** *Pr.n.f. Gr.Myth:* Psyche. **2.** *s.f.* (*a*) *Ent:* psyche, psychid; (*b*) cheval glass, swing mirror.
psychédélique [psikedelik], *a. Psy:* psychedelic.
psychédélisme [psikedelism], *s.m. Psy:* psychedelism.
psychiatre [psikjatr̥], *s.m. & f.* psychiatrist.
psychiatrie [psikjatri], *s.f.* psychiatry.
psychiatrique [psikjatrik], *a.* psychiatric; **hôpital p.,** psychiatric, mental, hospital.
psychidés [psikide], *s.m.pl. Ent:* Psychidae.
psychique [psiʃik], *a.* psychic; *Cards:* **annonce p.,** psychic bid.
psychisme [psiʃism], *s.m.* psychism.
psychiste [psiʃist], *s.m.* psychist.
psych(o)- [psik(ɔ)], *pref.* psych(o)-.
psychobiologie [psikɔbjɔlɔʒi], *s.f.* psychobiology.
psychobiologique [psikɔbjɔlɔʒik], *a.* psychobiologic(al).
psychochirurgie [psikɔʃiryrʒi], *s.f.* psychosurgery.
psychocritique [psikɔkritik], *Lit:* **1.** *s.f.* psychological criticism. **2.** *s.m.* psychological critic.
psychodramatique [psikɔdramatik], *a.* psychodramatic.
psychodrame [psikɔdram], *s.m.* psychodrama.
psychogalvanique [psikɔgalvanik], *a.* **réflexe p.,** psychogalvanic reflex.
psychogène [psikɔʒɛn], *a.* psychogenic.
psychogénèse [psikɔʒenɛːz], *s.f.* psychogenesis.
psychogénétique [psikɔʒenetik], *a.* psychogenetic.
psychogénie [psikɔʒeni], *s.f. Med:* psychogenesis.
psychogénique [psikɔʒenik], *a. Med:* psychogenic (disorder).
psychogramme [psikɔgram], *s.m.* **1.** *Psychics:* psychogram, spirit writing. **2.** *Psy:* psychogram, profile.
psychographe [psikɔgraf], *s.m. Psychics:* psychographist.
psychographie [psikɔgrafi], *s.f.* **1.** *Psy:* psychography. **2.** *Psychics:* psychography, automatic writing.
psychoïde [psikɔid], *a.* psychoid.
psycholeptique [psikɔlɛptik], *a.* psycholeptic.
psycholinguistique [psikɔlɛ̃gɥistik], *s.f.* psycholinguistics.
psychologie [psikɔlɔʒi], *s.f.* psychology; **p. clinique,** clinic psychology; **p. génétique,** genetic psychology; **p. en profondeur, p. abyssale,** depth psychology; **p. individuelle,** individual psychology.
psychologique [psikɔlɔʒik], *a.* psychological; **le moment p.,** the psychological moment.
psychologiquement [psikɔlɔʒikmɑ̃], *adv.* psychologically.
psychologisme [psikɔlɔʒism], *s.m.* psychologism.
psychologiste [psikɔlɔʒist], *a.* psychologistic.
psychologue [psikɔlɔg]. **1.** *s.m. & f.* psychologist. **2.** *a.* psychological.
psychomachie [psikɔmaʃi], *s.f.* psychomachy.
psychomancie [psikɔmɑ̃si], *s.f.* psychomancy.
psychométricien, -ienne [psikɔmetrisjɛ̃, -jɛn], *s.* psychometrician.
psychométrie [psikɔmetri], *s.f.* psychometry.
psychométrique [psikɔmetrik], *a.* psychometric.
psychomoteur, -trice [psikɔmɔtœːr, -tris], *a.* psychomotor (centre, nerve fibre, etc.).
psychonévrose [psikɔnevroːz], *s.f.* psychoneurosis.
psychonévrotique [psikɔnevrɔtik], *a.* psychoneurotic.
psychopathe [psikɔpat]. **1.** *a.* psychopathic. **2.** *s.m. & f.* psychopath.
psychopathie [psikɔpati], *s.f.* psychopathy.
psychopathique [psikɔpatik], *a.* psychopathic (state, personality).
psychopathologie [psikɔpatɔlɔʒi], *s.f.* psychopathology.
psychopathologique [psikɔpatɔlɔʒik], *a.* psychopathological.
psychopédagogie [psikɔpedagɔʒi], *s.f.* the application of experimental psychology to education.
psychopharmacologie [psikɔfarmakɔlɔʒi], *s.f.* psychopharmacology.
psychopharmacologique [psikɔfarmakɔlɔʒik], *a.* psychopharmacologic(al).
psychopharmacologiste [psikɔfarmakɔlɔʒist], *s.m. & f.* psychopharmacologist.
psychophysicien, -ienne [psikɔfizisjɛ̃, -jɛn], *s.* psychophysicist.
psycho(-)physiologie [psikɔfizjɔlɔʒi], *s.f.* psychophysiology.
psycho(-)physiologiste [psikɔfizjɔlɔʒist], **psycho(-)physiologue** [psikɔfizjɔlɔg], *s.m. & f.* psychophysiologist.
psychophysique [psikɔfizik]. **1.** *a.* psychophysical. **2.** *s.f.* psychophysics.
psychose [psikoːz], *s.f.* **1.** *Med:* psychosis; **p. traumatique,** shellshock. **2.** obsession; **p. de guerre,** war scare.
psychosé, -ée [psikoze], *a. & s. Med:* psychotic.
psychosensoriel, -ielle [psikɔsɑ̃sɔrjɛl], *a.* psychosensorial.
psychosexuel, -elle [psikɔsɛksɥɛl], *a.* psychosexual.
psychosocial, -aux [psikɔsɔsjal, -o], *a.* psychosocial.
psychosociologie [psikɔsɔsjɔlɔʒi], *s.f.* social psychology.
psychosomatique [psikɔsɔmatik], *Med:* **1.** *a.* psychosomatic. **2.** *s.f.* psychosomatics.
psychotechnicien, -ienne [psikɔtɛknisjɛ̃, -jɛn], *s.* psychotechnician.
psychotechnie [psikɔtɛkni], *s.f.* psychotechnology, psychotechnics.
psychotechnique [psikɔtɛknik]. **1.** *a.* psychotechnic(al). **2.** *s.f.* psychotechnology, psychotechnics.
psychothérapeute [psikɔterapøːt], *s.m.* psychotherapist.
psychothérapeutique [psikɔterapøtik]. **1.** *a.* psychotherapeutic. **2.** *s.f.* psychotherapeutics.
psychothérapie [psikɔterapi], *s.f.* psychotherapy.
psychothérapique [psikɔterapik], *a.* psychotherapeutic; **centre p.,** psychotherapy centre; **intervention p.,** psychotherapeutic treatment.
psychotique [psikɔtik], *a. & s.m. & f. Med:* psychotic.
psychotonique [psikɔtɔnik], *Med:* **1.** *a.* mood-elevating. **2.** *s.m.* mood elevator.
psychotrine [psikɔtrin], *s.f. Ch:* psychotrine.
psychotrope [psikɔtrɔp], *a. & s.m.* psychotropic (substance).
psychromètre [psikrɔmɛtr̥], *s.m. Meteor:* psychrometer.
psychrométrie [psikrɔmetri], *s.f. Meteor:* psychrometry.
psychrophile [psikrɔfil], *a. Biol:* psychrophile, psychrophilous.
psylle¹ [psil], *s.m.* (Indian) snake charmer.
psylle², *s.f. Ent:* psylla, psyllid, jumping plant louse.
psyllidés [psilide], *s.m.pl. Ent:* Psyllidae.
psyllium [psiljɔm], *s.m. Pharm:* psyllium.
ptarmique [ptarmik], *s.f. Bot:* sneezewort.
pténoglosses [ptenɔglɔs], *s.m.pl. Moll:* Ptenoglossa.
ptéranodon [pteranɔdɔ̃], *s.m. Paleont:* pteranodon.
ptéréon [ptereɔ̃], *s.m. Anat:* pterion.
ptéridophytes [pteridɔfit], *s.f.pl. Bot:* Pteridophyta.
ptéridospermales [pteridɔspɛrmal], *s.f.pl.,* **ptéridospermées** [pteridɔspɛrme], *s.f.pl. Paleont:* Pteridospermaphyta.
ptérine [pterin], *s.f. Ent:* pterin(e), pteridine.
ptérion [pterjɔ̃], *s.m. Anat:* pterion.
ptéro- [pterɔ], *pref.* ptero-.
ptérobranches [pterɔbrɑ̃ːʃ], *s.m.pl. Z:* Pterobranchia.
ptérocarpe [pterɔkarp], *a. Bot:* pterocarpous.
ptérocère [pterɔsɛːr], *s.m. Moll:* scorpion shell.
ptéroclididés [pterɔklidide], *s.m.pl. Orn:* Pteroclididae, Pterocletidae.
ptérodactyle [pterɔdaktil]. **1.** *a.* pterodactylous, pterodactyloid. **2.** *s.m. Paleont:* pterodactyl, pterodactylian.
ptérodactylidés [pterɔdaktilide], *s.m.pl. Paleont:* Pterodactylidae.
ptéromale [pterɔmal], *s.m. Ent:* pteromalid.
pteromalides [pterɔmalid], *s.m.pl. Ent:* Pteromalidae.
ptérophore [pterɔfɔːr], *s.m. Ent:* pterophorid, plume moth.
ptérophoridés [pterɔfɔride], *s.m.pl.* Pterophoridae.
ptéropodes [pterɔpɔd], *s.m.pl. Moll:* Pteropoda, pteropods.
ptérosaurien [pterɔsɔrjɛ̃], *s.m. Paleont:* pterosaurian; *pl.* **ptérosauriens,** Pterosauria, Pterosauri.
ptérygion [pteriʒjɔ̃], *s.m. Med:* pterygium.
ptérygode [pterigɔd], *s.m. Ent:* pterygode, pterygodum.
ptérygoïde [pterigɔid], *s.f. Anat:* pterygoid; *a.* **apophyse p.,** pterygoid process.
ptérygoïdien, -ienne [pterigɔidjɛ̃, -jɛn], *a. & s.m. Anat:* pterygoid (muscle).
ptérygo-maxillaire [pterigɔmaksilɛːr], *a. Anat:* pterygomaxillary; *pl. ptérygo-maxillaires.*
ptérygo-palatin [pterigɔpalatɛ̃], *a. Anat:* pterygopalatine; *pl. ptérygo-palatins.*
ptérygopode [pterigɔpɔd], *s.m. Ich:* pterygopodium, clasper.
ptérygotes [pterigɔt], *s.m.pl. Ent:* Pterygota; **p. paléoptères,** Palaeodictyoptera.
pterygotus [pterigɔtys], *s.m. Paleont:* pterygotus.
ptérylie [pterili], *s.f. Orn:* pteryla, feather tract.
ptérylographie [pterilɔgrafi], *s.f. Orn:* pterylography.
ptérylose [pteriloːz], *s.f. Orn:* pterylosis, arrangement of feathers.
ptiline [ptilin], *s.f. Ent:* ptilinum.
ptilonorhynchidés [ptilɔnɔrɛ̃kide], *s.m.pl. Orn:* Ptilonorhynchidae.
ptilonorhynque [ptilɔnɔrɛ̃ːk], *s.m. Orn:* bowerbird.
ptiloris [ptilɔris], *s.m. Orn:* **p. à gorge d'acier,** rifle bird.
ptine [ptin], *s.m. Ent:* ptinid; (*genus*) Ptinus.
ptinidés [ptinide], *s.m.pl. Ent:* Ptinidae.
ptolémaïque [ptɔlemaik], *a.* Ptolemaic.
Ptolémée [ptɔleme], *Pr.n.m. A.Hist:* Ptolemy; **P. Évergète,** Ptolemy Euergetes; *Astr:* **système de P.,** Ptolemaic system.
ptoléméen, -éenne [ptɔlemeɛ̃, -eɛn], **ptoloméen, -éenne** [ptɔlɔmeɛ̃, -eɛn], *a. Astr:* Ptolemaic (system).
ptomaïne [ptɔmain], *s.f. Bio-Ch:* ptomaine.
ptose, ptôse [ptoːz], *s.f. Med:* (visceral) ptosis.
ptosis, ptôsis [ptozis], *s.f. Med:* ptosis (of eyelid).
ptyalagogue [ptjalagɔg], *a. Med:* ptyalagogic.

ptyaline [ptjalin], *s.f. Bio-Ch:* ptyalin.
ptyalisme [ptjalism], *s.m. Med:* ptyalism.
puant [pɥɑ̃], *a.* (*a*) stinking, foul-smelling, fetid; *Ven:* **bêtes puantes,** mustelids (that leave a strong scent); *Fr.C: F:* **bête puante,** skunk; *Ch: F:* **gaz p.,** hydrogen sulphide, sulphuretted hydrogen; **boule puante,** stink bomb; (*b*) (*of pers.*) (offensively) pretentious; eaten up with self-conceit; *F:* **type p.,** stinker.
puanteur [pɥɑ̃tœːr], *s.f.* stink, stench; foul smell.
pubère [pybɛːr], *a.* pubescent; who has arrived at the age of puberty.
pubertaire [pybɛrtɛːr], *a.* **âge p.,** age of puberty.
puberté [pybɛrte], *s.f.* puberty.
pubérulent [pyberylɑ̃], *a. Bot:* pubescent, covered with light down.
pubescence [pybɛsɑ̃ːs], *s.f. Nat.Hist:* pubescence, downiness.
pubescent [pybɛsɑ̃], *a. Bot:* pubescent, downy (plant, fruit).
pubien, -ienne [pybjɛ̃, -jɛn], *a. Anat:* pubic; **région pubienne,** pubes.
pubiotomie [pybjɔtɔmi], *s.f. Obst:* pubiotomy.
pubis [pybis], *s.m. Anat:* pubis, pubic bone.
publiable [pybliabl̩], *a.* publishable; **peu p.,** hardly publishable; scarcely fit for publication.
public, -ique [pyblik]. **1.** *a.* (*a*) public (life, meeting, monument, etc.); open (meeting); **tenir une séance publique,** to hold an open meeting, a public meeting; **la chose publique,** (i) public welfare, the public service; (ii) state, government, commonwealth; **service p.,** public utility (service); **autorité publique,** local, statutory, authority; **travailler pour le bien p.,** to work for the common good; **tous les citoyens dévoués au bien p.,** all public-spirited citizens; **questions d'intérêt p.,** public matters; **les hommes publics,** men in public life; **force publique,** (civil) police; **la dette publique,** the national debt; *Jur:* **marché p.,** market overt; *A:* **marchande publique,** woman keeping open shop, and entitled to enter into commitments without her husband's sanction; *Adm:* **le ministère p., la partie publique,** the public prosecutor; (*b*) **femme publique, fille publique,** prostitute; **maison publique,** brothel. **2.** *s.m.* **le p.,** the public, the people; **le grand p.,** the general public, *F:* the man in the street; *Publ:* **livres pour le grand p.,** general books; **placer des actions dans le p.,** to place shares with the public; **se faire entendre devant un nombreux p.,** to perform before a large audience; **un bon p.,** an easygoing, easily pleased, audience; **être bon p.,** to be easily persuaded, *F:* an easy mark; **le p. est prié de ne pas cueillir les fleurs,** the public are requested not to pick the flowers; **en p.,** in public, publicly.
publicain [pyblikɛ̃], *s.m.* (*a*) *Hist:* tax gatherer; *B:* publican; (*b*) *A:* extortioner, bloodsucker.
publication [pyblikasjɔ̃], *s.f.* **1.** publication; publishing; (*a*) **p. d'un ordre,** issue of an order; **p. de mariage,** publication of banns; **p. de vente aux enchères,** notice of sale by auction; (*b*) publication (of a book); **ouvrage en cours de p.,** work in course of publication. **2.** publication, published work; **p. périodique,** periodical.
publiciste [pyblisist], *s.m.* (*a*) *A:* publicist; writer on law or politics; (*b*) journalist; (*c*) *F:* publicist, publicity agent.
publicitaire [pyblisitɛːr]. **1.** *a.* pertaining to publicity, to advertising; **manifestation entreprise dans un but p.,** demonstration with a view to publicity, to advertisement; **dépenses publicitaires,** publicity, advertising, expenses; **agence p.,** advertising agency; **vente p.,** promotional sale. **2.** *s.m. & f.* publicity man; publicist; *F:* adman.
publicité [pyblisite], *s.f.* (*a*) publicity; **donner une regrettable p. à une affaire privée,** to give unfortunate publicity to a private matter; (*b*) publicity, advertising; build-up; **p. lumineuse,** neon signs; **p. radiophonique,** commercials; **faire de la p.,** to advertise; **p. collective,** group advertising; **p. directe,** direct advertising (to selected individuals); **p. tapageuse,** vulgar publicity; **p. d'amorçage,** advance publicity; *Jur:* **p. mensongère,** misleading representations; **agence, agent, de p.,** advertising agency, agent; **frais de p.,** advertising costs, expenses; *Com: Journ:* **chef de la p.,** advertising manager; head of the publicity department; **exemplaires de p.,** press copies; **faire appel à la grande p. pour lancer un article,** to conduct a wide publicity campaign, to advertise widely, in order to launch an article on the market.
publier [pyblije], *v.tr.* (*pr.sub. & p.d.* **n. publiions, v. publiiez**) **1.** to publish, make public; to make known; to proclaim; **p. un ordre,** to issue an order; **p. la nouvelle que . . .,** to release the news that . . .; **p. qch. sur, par-dessus, les toits,** to proclaim sth. from the housetops. **2.** to publish (book, newspaper, etc.); **ce journal est publié sur seize pages,** this paper runs to sixteen pages.
publiquement [pyblikmɑ̃], *adv.* publicly; in public; openly.
puccinia [pysinja], *s.m. Fung:* puccinia.
puce [pys]. **1.** *s.f.* (*a*) flea; **piqûre de p.,** fleabite; *F:* **marché aux puces, les puces,** flea market; **marchand de puces,** junk dealer; old-clothes man; *F:* **avoir la p. à l'oreille,** to be uneasy, suspicious; **mettre la p. à l'oreille à qn,** to rouse s.o.'s suspicions; **cela m'a mis la p. à l'oreille,** it made me suspicious, it made me smell a rat; *F:* **secouer les puces à qn,** (i) to give s.o. a good thrashing; (ii) to tell s.o. off; (*b*) **p. terrestre, p. de terre,** flea beetle; **p. pénétrante,** chigoe, jigger; **p. aquatique, p. d'eau,** water flea; (*c*) *Bot: F:* **arbre à la p.,** poison ivy, poison oak; **herbe aux puces,** flea bane; (*d*) *Crust:* **p. de mer,** sandhopper; (*e*) *Games:* **jeu de (la) p.,** tiddlywinks. **2.** *a.inv.* puce(-coloured).
puceau, -elle [pyso, -ɛl]. **1.** *a.* virgin. **2.** *s.m.* virgin. **3.** *s.f.* maid(en), virgin; *Hist:* **la Pucelle d'Orléans,** the Maid of Orleans.
pucelage [pyslaːʒ], *s.m.* **1.** maidenhead, virginity. **2.** *Bot:* **petit p.,** great periwinkle. **3.** *Conch:* cowrie.
puceron [pysrɔ̃], *s.m.* plant louse, greenfly, aphis; **p. du pêcher,** peach fly; **p. lanigère,** woolly aphis.
puceronnière [pysrɔnjɛːr], *s.f. Hort:* powder bellows.
pucerotte [pysrɔt], *s.f. Ent: F:* (*a*) greenfly; (*b*) vine flea beetle.
puche [pyʃ], *s.f.* shrimping net.
pucher [pyʃe], *v.tr.* to ladle out (pitch, syrup, etc.).
puchérite [pyʃerit], *s.f. Miner:* pucherite.
puchette [pyʃɛt], *s.f.* peat drag.
pucheux [pyʃø], *s.m. Sug.-R:* syrup ladle.
pucier [pysje], *s.m.* **1.** *Bot: F:* flea bane. **2.** *P:* bed, *P:* fleabag; **dix heures de p.,** ten hours' kip.
pucrasie [pykrazi], *s.f. Orn:* pukras (pheasant).
pudding [pudiŋ], *s.m. Cu:* (steamed) pudding.
puddlage [pydlaːʒ], *s.m. Metall:* puddling.
puddler [pydle], *v.tr. Metall:* to puddle.
puddleur [pydlœːr], *s.m. Metall:* **1.** puddler. **2.** **p. mécanique,** puddling machine.
pudeur [pydœːr], *s.f.* (*a*) modesty, *esp.* sexual modesty; sense of decency; **sans p.,** unblushing(ly), shameless(ly); **agir sans la moindre p.,** to act without any sense of shame; **être sans p.,** to have no feelings of shame; **avoir perdu toute p.,** to have lost all sense of shame; **rougir de p.,** to blush for shame; **je ne veux pas jouer les Pères de la p., mais . . .,** I don't want to appear a prude, but . . .; **commettre un outrage à la p.,** to offend people's sense of decency; *Jur:* **attentat à la p.,** indecent assault; **outrage public à la p.,** indecent exposure; (*b*) (sense of) discretion, reticence; **il a eu la p. de n'en pas parler,** he was discreet enough, was careful, not to talk about it; **une espèce de p. l'empêchait de le raconter,** a kind of reticence prevented him from talking about it.
pudibond, -onde [pydibɔ̃, -ɔ̃ːd], *a.* **1.** *A:* modest, chaste. **2.** easily shocked; prudish. **3.** *s.m. & f.* prude.
pudibonderie [pydibɔ̃dri], *s.f.* prudishness.
pudicité [pydisite], *s.f.* (*a*) chastity, modesty; (*b*) sense of decency.
pudique [pydik], *a.* modest; chaste.
pudiquement [pydikmɑ̃], *adv.* modestly, with natural delicacy.
pudu [pydy], *s.m. Z:* pudu.
puer [pɥe], *v.i.* to stink; (*a*) **fromage qui pue,** strong (-smelling), smelly, cheese; **ça pue ici,** there's a nasty smell here; it stinks here; **p. comme un rat mort, comme un bouc, comme une charogne, comme la peste,** to stink like a goat, to stink to high heaven; (*b*) *with cogn. acc.* **p. l'ail, le tabac,** to smell, stink, of garlic, of tobacco; **il puait le vin,** he was reeking of wine; **article qui pue la flatterie,** article oozing with flattery.
puériculteur, -trice [pɥerikyltœːr, -tris]. **1.** *s.* specialist in infant welfare. **2.** *s.f.* **puéricultrice,** nursery nurse.
puériculture [pɥerikyltyːr], *s.f.* rearing of children; child care; child, infant, welfare; **p. anténatale,** prenatal care; **suivre un cours de p.,** to take a course in infant welfare.
puéril [pɥeril], *a.* (*a*) puerile, of a child; **l'âge p.,** childhood; *Med:* **respiration puérile,** puerile breathing; (*b*) *Pej:* puerile, childish, infantile; **excuse puérile,** childish excuse; **tu es p. de le croire,** it's childish, infantile, of you to believe that.
puérilement [pɥerilmɑ̃], *adv.* childishly.
puérilisme [pɥerilism], *s.m. Med:* puerilism.
puérilité [pɥerilite], *s.f.* **1.** puerility, childishness, **2.** **s'attacher aux puérilités,** to be attached to childish things.
puerpéral, -aux [pɥɛrperal, -o], *a. Obst:* puerperal (complications, etc.); **fièvre puerpérale,** puerperal fever.
puerpéralité [pɥɛrperalite], *s.f. Obst:* puerperium.
Puerto Rico [pwɛrtoriko], *Pr.n.m. Geog:* Puerto Rico, Porto Rico.
puffin [pyfɛ̃], *s.m. Orn:* shearwater; **p. des Anglais,** Manx shearwater; **p. à bec grêle,** short-tailed shearwater, Tasmanian mutton bird; **p. fuligineux,** New Zealand mutton bird, sooty shearwater; **p. cendré,** Cory's shearwater; **p. majeur,** great shearwater; **petit p.,** little, *U.S:* allied, shearwater; **p. obscur,** Audubon's shearwater.
pugilat [pyʒila], *s.m.* (*a*) pugilism, boxing; (*b*) fight, *F:* set-to; **le jardin fut la scène d'un p.,** the garden was the scene of a fight, a brawl.
pugilisme [pyʒilism], *s.m.* pugilism, boxing.
pugiliste [pyʒilist], *s.m.* pugilist, boxer.
pugilistique [pyʒilistik], *a.* pugilistic.
pugnace [pygnas], *a.* pugnacious.
pugnacité [pygnasite], *s.f.* pugnacity, pugnaciousness.
puîné, -ée [pɥine], *a. & s.* younger (brother or sister).
puis [pɥi], *adv.* **1.** (*a*) then, afterwards, after that, next; **p. il s'est remis à lire,** then he went back to his reading; **p. il me donna tous les détails,** he went on to give me all the details; (*b*) (*in space*) **à gauche l'église, p. quelques vieilles maisons,** on the left the church, then a few old houses; (*c*) (*in enumeration; not translated in Eng.*) **tout homme a deux pays, le sien et p. la France,** every man has two countries, his own and France; **et p. c'est tout,** and that's all; and that's all there is to it; (*d*) **et p.,** and then, moreover, besides; **et p.? et p. quoi? et p. après?** (i) what then? what next? (ii) *F:* (and) so what? **2.** *Poet: Lit: A:* **puis** [pɥis] . . . **que** (= PUISQUE), since, seeing that; **puis donc** [pɥisdɔ̃ːk] **qu'il en est ainsi . . .,** since matters stand thus . . ..
puisage [pɥizaːʒ], *s.m.* drawing (up) (of water).
puisard [pɥizaːr], *s.m.* sunk draining trap; drain tank; draining well; cesspool, sink; *Min: Mch: etc:* sump, well; *Nau:* bilge well, drainage well, drain pot; *I.C.E:* **p. (d'alimentation) d'huile,** oil-feeding sump; **p. de retour d'huile,** crank-case sump; *Nau:* **p. de tunnel (d'arbre),** (shaft-) tunnel well.
puisatier [pɥizatje], *s.m.* **1.** (*a*) well maker, well sinker; (*b*) *Min:* shaft sinker. **2.** *Min:* sumpman.
puisement [pɥizmɑ̃], *s.m.* = PUISAGE.
puiser [pɥize], *v.tr.* (*a*) to draw (water) (**à, dans,** from); **p. de l'eau à la rivière, dans le tonneau,** to draw water from the river, from the barrel; *abs. F:* **p. dans le plat,** to help oneself, *F:* to dig in; *F:* **il n'y a qu'à y p.,** you have only to put out your hand; (*b*) **p. des consolations dans la religion,** to derive consolation from religion; **p. des forces en soi-même,** to draw strength from within oneself; **p. une idée chez un auteur,** to take, get, an idea from an author; *abs.* **p. à la source, aux sources,** to go to the source, to the fountain-head; to draw on the original authorities; **auteur qui puise partout,** author who draws his matter from many sources.
puisette [pɥizɛt], *s.f.* ladle, scoop.
puiseur, -euse [pɥizœːr, -øːz], *s.* **1.** drawer (of water, etc.). **2.** *Paperm:* vatman; dipper.
puisoir [pɥizwaːr], *s.m. Ind:* ladle, scoop.
puisque [pɥisk(ə)], *conj.* (**puisqu'** *before* **il(s), elle(s), on, en, un(e),** *and today frequently before any initial vowel*) (*a*) since, as, seeing that; **je le ferai, puisqu'il le faut,** I shall do it, since I must; **venez donc aussi, puisque vous êtes là,** come (along) too, seeing that you are here; (*b*) **p. je te dis que je l'ai vu!** but I tell you I saw it! *s.a.* PUIS 2.
puissamment [pɥisamɑ̃], *adv.* (*a*) **navire p. armé,** heavily armed ship; **position p. défendue par l'artillerie,** position strongly defended by the artillery; (*b*) powerfully; **homme p. charpenté,** powerfully built man; *Iron:* **c'est p. raisonné!** that's a fine, powerful, bit of reasoning! (*c*) **contribuer p. à qch.,** to make an important contribution to sth.; (*d*) exceedingly, extremely; **p. riche,** exceedingly rich.

puissance [pɥisɑ̃:s], *s.f.* **1.** (*a*) power, force, strength; *Phil:* potency; yield (of nuclear weapon); **la p. de la parole, de l'habitude,** the power of the word, the force of habit; **aucune p. humaine ne pourrait le sauver,** no human power could save him; **p. du vent,** strength of the wind; *Ball:* **p. de perforation,** perforating, penetrating, power (of projectile); *Mil:* **p. de, du, feu,** fire power; **p. défensive, offensive,** defensive, offensive, power; **p. offensive, défensive, d'une flotte,** fighting efficiency of a fleet; *Mec:* **p. vive,** kinetic energy; *Opt:* **p. lumineuse,** candle power (of lamp, searchlight, etc.); *Pol.Ec:* **p. d'achat,** purchasing power; *Tchn:* **p. ascensionnelle,** lifting power (of balloon, etc.); **grue d'une p. de levage de vingt tonnes,** crane with a lifting capacity of twenty tons; (*b*) *Mec.E: Mch:* power, output (of engine, motor, etc.); **moteur de grande p.,** heavy-duty engine; **à pleine, à toute, p.,** at full power; **p. de pointe,** peak power output; *Av:* **p. au décollage,** take-off power; **réacteur fonctionnant à pleine p.,** jet engine running, working, at full throttle; **maximum de p.,** maximum output; **excédent de p.,** margin of power; **p. à vide,** no-load power; **p. effective, p. réelle,** effective, actual, output, power; **p. nominale,** nominal output, rated power; **p. utile,** operating, useful, power; *Ind: etc:* **p. horaire,** output per hour; **p. en chevaux(-vapeur),** horse power; **p. effective en chevaux,** effective, actual, horse-power; **p. indiquée,** indicated horse-power; **p. nominale (en chevaux),** nominal horse-power, horse-power rating; **p. normale,** normal, service, horse-power; **p. sur l'arbre, p. au frein,** shaft horse-power, brake horse-power; **calcul de la p. des moteurs,** engine rating; *I.C.E:* **formule de p.,** rating formula; *Adm:* **p. fiscale d'une auto,** treasury rating of a car; (*c*) *El: Elcs:* (electric) power; dissipation, rated power (of resistance); **p. installée,** installed capacity; **p. électromécanique,** electrical horse power; **p. d'entrée, de sortie,** input, output, power; **p. fournie,** power output; **p. (maximum) disponible,** available power; **p. limite admissible,** operating limit, *U.S:* overload level; *W.Tel:* **p. reçue,** signal strength; **p. d'antenne,** aerial capacity; **p. reçue par l'antenne,** aerial input; **p. d'émission,** radiating power; **p. émise,** radiated power; **p. haute fréquence,** radio-frequency power; **poste émetteur à haute p.,** high-power radio transmitter; **lampe de p.,** power valve. **2.** (*a*) *Min:* **p. d'une couche (de houille, etc.),** thickness of a seam (of coal, etc.); (*b*) *Mth:* **p. d'un nombre,** power of a number; **élever un nombre à la nième p.,** to raise a number to the nth power; **dix p. quatre,** ten to the fourth. **3. avoir qn en sa p.,** to have s.o. in one's power; **réduire qn sous sa p.,** to get s.o. into one's power; *A:* **détenir qn en p.,** to hold s.o. under restraint, forcibly; **être en p. de mari,** to be under a husband's control, authority; *Jur:* **femme en p. de mari,** feme covert; **p. paternelle,** authority of father (or mother when father is dead) over child; **l'Espagne était alors à l'apogée de sa p.,** Spain was then at the height of her power. **4.** (*a*) *Pol:* **les Grandes Puissances,** the Great Powers; **les puissances européennes,** the European Powers; **p. mondiale,** world power; **les puissances établies,** the powers that be; (*b*) *Theol:* **les puissances,** the (angelic) powers; **les puissances célestes,** the powers above; **les puissances des ténèbres,** the powers of darkness. **5. en p.,** (*a*) in posse, potential(ly); **l'arbre est en p. dans la graine,** the tree in posse lies hidden in the seed; (*b*) in being; **flotte en p.,** fleet in being; (*c*) *Com:* **client en p.,** potential customer.

puissancique [pɥisɑ̃sik], *a. Mec.E:* **masse p.,** weight : power relation (lbs : HP).

puissant [pɥisɑ̃], *a.* (*a*) powerful; **homme p.,** powerful, influential, man; **armée puissante,** powerful army; *s.* **les puissants de ce monde,** the great of this world; (*b*) **remède p.,** potent, powerful, remedy; **argument p.,** weighty argument; **en p. relief,** in bold relief; **une des plus puissantes maisons du pays,** one of the leading firms in the country; (*c*) (*of pers., etc.*) strong; **muscles puissants,** powerful muscles; **conviction puissante,** strong conviction; **moteur p., freins puissants,** powerful engine, brakes; **voix puissante,** powerful voice; **vent p.,** strong wind; (*d*) *A:* fat, stout, (*e*) *Min:* **couche puissante,** thick seam.

puits [pɥi], *s.m.* **1.** (*a*) well; hole; **p. de sondage,** boring; **p. artésien,** artesian well; **p. abyssinien, p. instantané,** driven well, drive well, tube well, Abyssinian well; **p. à ciel ouvert,** open well; uncovered well; **p. à bras,** pump well; **p. à poulie,** draw well; **p. absorbant, p. perdu,** dead well, cesspool; *Geol:* **p. naturel,** swallowhole; **p. à diamants,** diamond pipe; **eau de p.,** well water; **p. de science,** learned person, fount of knowledge; **ce qu'on lui dit tombe dans un p.,** anything he is told goes no further; **cela est tombé dans le p.,** it has been entirely forgotten; *B:* **le p. de l'abîme,** the bottomless pit; (*b*) *Cu:* **p. d'amour,** jam puff; cream puff. **2.** (*a*) shaft, pit (of mine); **p. d'aérage,** air shaft, ventilation shaft; **p. d'appel, d'air,** downcast shaft; **p. d'extraction,** winding shaft; **p. aux échelles,** ladderway, ladder shaft; **p. intérieur,** blind shaft; (*b*) *Petroleum Min:* **p. de décantation,** clear well; **p. fou,** wild well; **p. improductif, sec,** duster; (*c*) *Const:* **p. d'attente, de soutien,** well foundation; **p. d'amarre,** anchor block (of suspension bridge); **p. d'aqueduc,** inspection, cleaning, hole; **p. de lumière,** light well; (*d*) *Ind:* **p. de montage,** erecting pit. **3.** *N.Arch:* well deck; **p. à chaînes, aux chaînes,** chain locker, chain well, cable locker; **p. de (la) dérive,** drop-keel housing; centre-board case, trunk, well; **p. de tonnage,** tonnage well. **4. p. pour mitrailleuse,** machine gun pit; *Ball:* **p. de lancement,** launching silo. **5.** *Elcs:* (*computers*) bin.

puits-fontaine [pɥifɔ̃tɛn], *s.m.* spout well; *pl. puits-fontaines.*

Pulchérie [pylkeri], *Pr.n.f. A.Hist:* Pulcheria.

pulicaire [pylikɛ:r], *s.f. Bot:* pulicaria, fleabane.

pulicidés [pyliside], *s.m.pl. Ent:* Pulicidae.

pull [pul], *s.m. Cost: F:* pullover.

pullman [pulman], *s.m. Rail:* Pullman car.

pullorose [pyl(l)ɔro:z], *s.f, Vet:* pullorum disease.

pull-over [pulɔvœ:r, pylɔvɛ:r], *s.m. Cost:* pullover, sweater.

pullulation [pylylasjɔ̃], *s.f.,* **pullulement** [pylylmɑ̃], *s.m.* (*a*) pullulation, rapid multiplication (of plants, animals, etc.); (*b*) *F:* swarming (of insects, children, etc.).

pulluler [pylyle], *v.i.* to pullulate; (*a*) to multiply rapidly; (*b*) to be found in profusion; to swarm.

pulmonaire [pylmɔnɛ:r]. **1.** *a.* (*a*) pulmonary, pulmonic; **artère p.,** pulmonary artery; **congestion p.,** congestion of the lungs; (*b*) *Mch:* **chaudière p.,** reheating boiler. **2.** *s.m. & f.* consumptive. **3.** *s.f. Bot:* pulmonaria, lungwort; **p. commune,** bottle of all sorts.

pulmoné [pylmɔne]. *Moll:* **1.** *a.* pulmonate, pulmobranchiate. **2.** *s.m.pl.* **pulmonés,** Pulmonata.

pulmonie [pylmɔni], *s.f. Med: A:* **1.** pneumonia. **2.** consumption.

pulmonique [pylmɔnik], *a. & s. Med:* pulmonic (person); suffering from lung disease.

pulpaire [pylpɛ:r], *a. Dent:* pulpar, pulpal.

pulpation [pylpasjɔ̃], *s.f. Pharm: etc:* pulping (of a substance).

pulpe [pylp], *s.f.* **1.** pulp; **p. de betterave,** beet pulp; **p. à papier,** paper pulp; **p. dentaire,** dental pulp; **réduire qch. en p.,** to reduce sth. to a pulp; to pulp sth. **2.** pad (of finger or toe).

pulpectomie [pylpɛktɔmi], *s.f. Dent:* pulpectomy.

pulper [pylpe], *v.tr. Pharm: etc:* to pulp; to reduce (sth.) to pulp.

pulpeux, -euse [pylpø, -ø:z], *a.* pulpy; pulpous.

pulpite [pylpit], *s.f. Med:* pulpitis.

pulpotomie [pylpɔtɔmi], *s.f. Dent:* pulpotomy.

pulque [pulke], *s.m. Dist:* pulque.

pulsant [pylsɑ̃], *a.* pulsating; *Astr:* **étoile pulsante,** pulsating star, Cepheid variable, Cepheid.

pulsar [pylsa:r], *s.m. Astr:* pulsar.

pulsateur, -trice [pylsatœ:r, -tris]. **1.** *a.* pulsating. **2.** *s.m. Husb:* pulsator.

pulsatif, -ive [pylsatif, -i:v], *a.* pulsatory; **douleur pulsative,** throbbing pain.

pulsatile [pylsatil], *a.* pulsatile (tumour, etc.).

pulsatille [pylsati:j], *s.f. Bot:* pulsatilla, pasque flower.

pulsation [pylsasjɔ̃], *s.f.* **1.** (*a*) pulsation, throbbing; beating (of the heart, etc.); (*b*) throb; (heart) beat. **2.** *Ph:* pulsation; *El:* pulsatance; *Mec.E:* (pressure) fluctuation.

pulsatoire [pylsatwa:r], *a.* pulsatory (movement, etc.); *El:* **courant p.,** pulsating current.

pulser [pylse]. **1.** *v.i.* to pulse; to pulsate; to beat; to throb. **2.** *v.tr.* to extract (air from a room, etc.); **chauffage par air pulsé,** warm-air heating.

pulsimètre [pylsimɛtr̥], *s.m. Med:* pulsimeter, sphygmometer.

pulsion [pylsjɔ̃], *s.f.* pulsion; propulsion; *Psy:* impulse; **p. de mort,** death wish, instinct.

pulsomètre [pylsɔmɛtr̥], *s.m. Ind:* pulsometer, pulsator; (steam-condensing) vacuum pump.

pulsoréacteur [pylsɔreaktœ:r], *s.m. Av:* aeropulse, aero-resonator, pulso-jet; reso-jet.

pultacé [pyltase], *a.* pultaceous, pulpy.

pultation [pyltasjɔ̃], *s.f.* pulping, reducing to pulp.

pulvérin [pylverɛ̃], *s.m.* **1.** *A:* (*a*) mealed gunpowder; (*b*) powder-flask. **2.** coal dust. **3.** (fine) spray (of water).

pulvérisable [pylverizabl̥], *a.* (*a*) pulverizable (substance); (*b*) (liquid) that can be sprayed.

pulvérisateur [pylverizatœ:r], *s.m.* (*a*) pulverizer (of hard substances); (*b*) spray(er); vaporizer; atomizer.

pulvérisation [pylverizasjɔ̃], *s.f.* (*a*) pulverization, pulverizing, crushing (of hard substances); (*b*) atomization, atomizing; spraying (of liquids).

pulvériser [pylverize], *v.tr.* (*a*) to pulverize; to grind, reduce, (substance) to powder; **charbon pulvérisé,** pulverized coal; *F:* **p. qn,** to pulverize s.o.; **la locomotive a pulvérisé le camion,** the engine smashed the lorry to smithereens; *Sp: F:* **p. un record,** to smash a record; (*b*) to spray, atomize (liquid); *I.C.E:* **p. l'essence,** to atomize the petrol.

pulvériseur [pylverizœ:r], *s.m. Agr:* disc harrow.

pulvérulance [pylverylɑ̃:s], *s.f. Ent:* pruinescence.

pulvérulence [pylverylɑ̃:s], *s.f.* pulverulence, powderiness; dustiness.

pulvérulent [pylverylɑ̃], *a.* **1.** pulverulent, powdery; dusty. **2.** *Ent:* pruinose. **3.** *s.m.* powder.

pulvinaire [pylvinɛ:r], *s.f. Ent:* pulvinaria, vine scale.

pulvinar [pylvina:r], *s.m. Rom.Ant: Anat:* pulvinar.

pulviné [pylvine], *a. Bot:* pulvinate(d).

pulvino [pylvino], *s.m. Civ.E:* substructure of an arch dam.

puma [pyma], *s.m. Z:* puma; cougar; American panther.

pumicite [pymisit], *s.f.,* **pumite** [pymit], *s.f. Miner:* pumice (stone).

pumiqueux, -euse [pymikø, -ø:z], *a.* pumiceous, pumicose.

pumpernickel [pumpɛrnikɛl], *s.m.* pumpernickel; Westphalian rye bread.

puna [pyna], *s.f.* **1.** *Geog:* puna (of the Andes). **2.** *Med: A:* mountain sickness.

punais, -aise[1] [pynɛ, -ɛ:z]. **1.** *a. A:* foul-smelling, foetid; *Dial:* **œuf p.,** rotten egg. **2.** *a. & s. Med:* (person) suffering from oz(a)ena.

punaise[2] [pynɛ:z], *s.f.* **1.** *Ent:* bug; **p. des lits,** bed bug, house bug; **p. des bois,** stinkbug; **p. rouge (des jardins),** firebug; **maison infestée de punaises,** bug-ridden house; *F:* **p. de sacristie,** bigoted churchwoman; *F:* **plat comme une p.,** servile, cringing; *int. F: Dial:* (*S. of Fr.*) **punaise(s)!** good heavens! **2.** drawing pin, *U.S:* thumb tack.

punaiser [pynɛze], *v.tr.* to fasten with drawing pins, *U.S:* to thumbtack.

punaisie [pynɛzi], *s.f. Med:* oz(a)ena.

punaisot, punaizot [pynɛzo], *s.m. Z: F:* skunk.

punch[1] [pɔ̃:ʃ], *s.m. Cu:* punch; **bol à p.,** punch-bowl.

punch[2] [pœnʃ], *s.m.* (*a*) *Box:* punch; (*b*) *F:* punch, dynamism; **manquer de p.,** to lack punch.

puncheur [pœnʃœ:r], *s.m.* boxer with plenty of punch.

punching-ball [pœnʃiŋbol], *s.m. Box:* punching ball, punch ball; *pl. punching-balls.*

punctiforme [pɔ̃ktifɔrm], *a.* punctiform (aperture, markings, etc.); **source de lumière p.,** pinhole source of light.

punctum cæcum [pɔ̃ktɔmsekɔm], *s.m. Anat:* blind spot (of the eye).

punicacées [pynikase], *s.f.pl. Bot:* Punicaceae.

punique [pynik], *a. Hist:* Punic; **les guerres puniques,** the Punic Wars; **foi p.,** Punic faith; treachery.

punir [pyni:r], *v.tr.* to punish (offender, offence); to avenge (offence, crime); **p. qn de mort, de prison,** to punish s.o. with death, with imprisonment; **p. qn d'un crime, pour un mensonge,** to punish s.o. for a crime, for a lie; **p. qn d'avoir fait qch., pour avoir fait qch.,** to punish s.o. for having done sth., for doing sth.; **être puni par où l'on a péché,** to reap what one has sown; **être puni de ses crimes,** to pay the penalty for one's crimes; *Mil:* **homme puni,** defaulter.

punissable [pynisabl̥], *a.* punishable.

punisseur, -euse [pynisœ:r, -ø:z]. **1.** *a.* punishing; **un dieu p. des méchants,** an avenging God. **2.** *s.* punisher.

punitif, -ive [pynitif, -i:v], *a.* punitive.

punition [pynisjɔ̃], *s.f.* **1.** punishing; punishment; **échapper à la p.,** to escape punishment, to go unpunished; **donner une p. à qn,** to inflict a punishment, a penalty, on s.o.; **proportionner la p. à l'offense,** to make the punishment fit the crime; **en p. de qch.,** as a punishment for sth.;

par, pour, p., for, by way of, punishment; as a punishment; *Mil:* **registre de punitions,** conduct book; *Nau:* **cahier, livre, de punitions,** defaulters' book, *F:* black book. **2.** *Games:* forfeit.
puntarelle [pɔ̃tarɛl], *s.f. Com:* coral chippings.
pupaison [pypɛzɔ̃], *s.f.*, **pupation** [pypasjɔ̃], *s.f. Ent:* pupation.
pupe [pup], *s.f. Ent:* **1.** pupa case. **2.** pupa, chrysalis.
pupillaire[1] [pypil(l)ɛ:r], *a. Jur:* pupil(l)ary, pertaining to a ward.
pupillaire[2], *a. Anat:* pupil(l)ary (membrane, etc.).
pupillarité [pypil(l)arite], *s.f. Jur:* (*a*) pupil(l)age; (*b*) pupil(l)arity; wardship.
pupille[1] [pypil]. **1.** *s.m. & f. Jur:* ward; **pupilles de la Nation,** war orphans; **pupilles de l'État,** orphans in state care. **2.** *s.f.* **enfant en p.,** child in pupil(l)age.
pupille[2], *s.f. Anat:* pupil (of the eye); *Opt:* **pupilles de contact,** micro-corneal contact lenses.
pupillométrie [pypil(l)ɔmetri], *s.f.* pupillometry.
pupilloscopie [pypil(l)ɔskɔpi], *s.f. Med:* pupilloscopy, skiascopy.
Pupin [pypɛ̃], *Pr.n.m. Tp:* **bobine P.,** loading coil, Pupin coil.
pupinisation [pypinizasjɔ̃], *s.f. Tp:* loading (of line) with inductances; pupinization.
pupiniser [pypinize], *v.tr. Tp:* to load, pupinize (long-distance line); **câble pupinisé,** coil-loaded cable.
pupipare [pypipa:r], *Ent:* **1.** *a.* pupiparous. **2.** *s.m.pl.* **pupipares,** Pupipara.
pupitrage [pypitra:ʒ], *s.m. Elcs:* (*computers*) console operator control.
pupitre [pypitr̥], *s.m.* **1.** desk; stand; **p. à musique, p. d'orchestre,** music stand; *Tp: etc:* **p. de distribution,** switch desk; *Elcs:* (*computers*) **p. (de commande),** control desk, console; **p. de poursuite (des missiles, avions, etc.),** (missile, aircraft, etc.) tracking console. **2.** (wine-bottle) rack. **3.** *Mus:* group (of instruments); **le p. des premiers violons, des clarinettes, etc.,** the first violins, the clarinets, etc.; **chef de p.,** leader (of a group).
pupitreur, -euse [pypitrœ:r, -ø:z], *s. Elcs:* (*computers*) console operator.
pur [py:r], *a.* pure. **1.** (*free from foreign elements*) **or p.,** pure gold; **vin p.,** neat, unmixed, unwatered, wine; **liquide p. de tout mélange,** liquid free from all admixture; **p. hasard,** pure chance, mere chance; **par p. accident j'appris que . . .,** by sheer accident, by the merest chance I heard that . . .; **la pure vérité,** the simple, plain, honest, unvarnished, truth; **ce bruit est une pure invention,** this rumour is a pure fabrication; **p. coquin,** downright rogue; **c'est p. et simple,** that's clear, uncompromising; *Fin:* **ordre (de payer) p. et simple,** unconditional order; **c'est de la paresse pure et simple,** it's pure and simple, pure unadulterated, laziness; **c'est de la folie pure, de la pure folie,** it is sheer folly, sheer madness; **par pure malice,** out of pure, sheer, malice; **en p. don,** as a free gift; **travailler en pure perte,** to work uselessly, to no purpose; **être en état de pure nature,** to be (i) in a state of nature, (ii) stark naked; **cheval p. sang,** thoroughbred horse. **2.** (*free from taint*) **air p.,** pure air; **ciel p.,** clear sky, cloudless sky; **femme pure,** chaste woman; **conscience pure,** clear conscience; **être p. de tout crime,** to be innocent of all crime; **style, goût, p.,** pure style, taste; **l'anglais p.,** pure English, English undefiled; **réputation pure,** untarnished reputation; **félicité pure,** unalloyed happiness; **gloire pure,** untarnished glory; *s. Pol: etc:* **un p.,** an uncompromising member of a party; an out-and-out socialist, etc.; a true blue.
purbeckien [pyrbɛkjɛ̃], *a. & s.m. Geol:* Purbeckian, upper Portlandian.
pureau, -eaux [pyro], *s.m. Const:* bare, gauge (of roofing slate, tile, etc.).
purée [pyre], *s.f.* (*a*) *Cu:* purée; **p. de pommes de terre,** *abs.* **purée,** potato purée, mashed potatoes; **p. de pois,** (i) pease pudding; (ii) (*fog*) peasouper; *F:* **p. de septembre,** wine; (*b*) *F:* **être dans la p.,** to be hard up, (stony) broke; (*c*) *int. P:* **p.!** (i) hell! (ii) you twerp! (*d*) *a. P:* poor, wretched.
purement [pyrmɑ̃], *adv.* (*a*) purely; **vivre p.,** to live a chaste life; (*b*) simply, merely; **p. et simplement,** (i) simply and solely; (ii) unreservedly; **résigner sa charge p. et simplement,** simply to resign.
pureté [pyrte], *s.f.* purity, pureness (of substance, liquid, air, morals, style, etc.); clearness (of the sky); **vœux de p.,** vows of chastity.
purgatif, -ive [pyrgatif, -i:v], *a. & s.m. Med:* purgative.
purgation [pyrgasjɔ̃], *s.f.* **1.** *Med:* (*a*) purging; (*b*) purgative, purge. **2.** *Theol:* purgation.
purgatoire [pyrgatwa:r], *s.m. Theol:* purgatory; **les âmes du p.,** the souls in purgatory; **faire son p. sur terre, en ce monde, de son vivant,** to live a life of purgatory, to go through purgatory (in one's lifetime).
purge [pyrʒ], *s.f.* **1.** (*a*) *Med:* purge; (*b*) *A:* disinfection (of goods, etc.); (*c*) *Tex:* cleaning (of yarn); removal of fluff; (*d*) *Pol:* purge. **2.** (*a*) *Mch:* blow-off, draining; **soupape de p.,** blow-off valve, drain valve; **robinet de p.,** blow-off cock, drain cock, relief cock, mud cock; **tuyau de p.,** (i) blow-off pipe; (ii) drain; (*b*) air valve (*esp.* of submarine); *Mec.E:* **vis de p.,** bleed screw. **3.** *Jur:* redemption, paying off (of mortgage).
purgeage [pyrʒa:ʒ], *s.m. Tex:* cleaning (of silk thread).
purgeoir [pyrʒwa:r], *s.m.* purifying tank, filtering tank (of canal water supply, etc.).
purger [pyrʒe], *v.tr.* (**je purgeai(s); n. purgeons**) to purge, clean, cleanse, clear; (*a*) **p. un malade,** to purge a patient; to give a patient a laxative; **p. les intestins,** to clear out the bowels; (*b*) **p. l'or,** to refine gold; **p. le fer par le cinglage,** to purify iron by shingling; **p. un pays de voleurs,** to rid a country of bandits; (*c*) **p. ses terres de dettes,** to clear, disencumber, rid, free, one's estate of debt; **p. sa conscience,** to clear one's conscience (*esp.* by confession); **se p. d'une accusation,** to clear oneself of an accusation; **se p. de ses vices,** to purge oneself of one's vices; **p. une hypothèque,** to redeem, pay off, a mortgage; *Nau:* **p. la quarantaine,** to clear one's quarantine; *Com:* **p. les dossiers,** to cancel and strip files; (*d*) *Tex:* to clean (silk thread) of its fluff; (*e*) *Mch:* to blow off, blow out, blow through, drain (a cylinder, etc.); *Mec.E:* to bleed; **p. la vapeur,** to blow off steam.
se purger, to take a purgative, a laxative.
purgerie [pyrʒəri], *s.f. Sug.-R:* purgery, sugar-drying house, curing house.
purgeur [pyrʒœ:r]. **1.** *a.* purging, cleansing; *Mch:* **robinet p.,** (i) drain cock, waste cock; (ii) air cock. **2.** *s.m.* (*a*) purger, cleanser, purifier; *Ind:* **p. de gaz,** gas purifier; (*b*) *Mch:* **p. de vapeur,** (i) blow-off gear, pet cock; (ii) (*also* **p. d'eau),** steam separator, steam trap; **p. d'air,** air cock; (*c*) *I.C.E:* *A:* compression tap.
purifiant [pyrifjɑ̃], *a.* purifying, cleansing.
purificateur, -trice [pyrifikatœ:r, -tris]. **1.** *a.* purifying, cleansing. **2.** *s.* purifier, cleanser.
purification [pyrifikasjɔ̃], *s.f.* purification. **1.** purifying (of metals, etc.); cleansing (of the blood, etc.); **installation pour la p. de l'air,** air-purifying plant. **2.** *Ecc:* (*a*) purification (of the chalice after communion); (*b*) **(fête de) la P.,** Feast of the Purification (of the Virgin Mary).
purificatoire [pyrifikatwa:r]. **1.** *a.* purificatory, purificative. **2.** *s.m. Ecc:* purificator, (celebrant's) communion cloth.
purifier [pyrifje], *v.tr.* (*pr.sub. & p.d.* **n. purifiions, v. purifiiez**) to purify, cleanse (air, water, morals, etc.); to sweeten (air, water); to refine (metal); **âme purifiée de toute souillure,** soul cleansed of all stains.
puriforme [pyrifɔrm], *a. Med:* puriform, pussy (expectoration, etc.).
purin [pyrɛ̃], *s.m, Agr:* liquid manure; **fosse à p.,** urinarium, liquid manure pit, sump.
purine [pyrin], *s.f. Ch:* purin(e).
purique [pyrik], *a. Ch:* **base p.,** purine base.
purisme [pyrism], *s.m.* purism (of language, style, etc.).
puriste [pyrist]. **1.** *s.m. & f.* (*a*) purist (in language, style, etc.); (*b*) *A:* puritan. **2.** *a.* (*s*) puristical; (*b*) *A:* puritanical.
puritain, -aine [pyritɛ̃, -ɛn]. **1.** *s.* puritan. **2.** *a.* puritan, puritanical.
puritainement [pyritɛnmɑ̃], *adv.* puritanically.
puritanisme [pyritanism], *s.m.* puritanism.
purot [pyro], *s.m.* liquid manure pit.
purotin [pyrɔtɛ̃], *s.m. P:* down-and-out; person who is always hard up, on the rocks.
purpura [pyrpyra], *s.m. Med:* purpura, purples.
purpuracé [pyrpyrase], *a.* **1.** purple, purpuraceous. **2.** *Med:* purpuric.
purpurigène [pyrpyriʒɛn], *a. Biol:* purpurogenous.
purpurin, -ine [pyrpyrɛ̃, -in]. **1.** *a.* (*a*) (near-) crimson; (*b*) purplish. **2.** *s.f.* **purpurine:** (*a*) *Ch:* purpurin; (*b*) *Dy:* madder purple; (*c*) purple bronze (varnish).
purpurique [pyrpyrik], *a. Ch: Med:* purpuric.
purpurite [pyrpyrit], *s.f. Miner:* purpurite.
purpuroxanthine [pyrpyrɔksɑ̃tin], *s.f. Ch:* purpuroxanthin.
pur-sang [pyrsɑ̃], *s.m.inv.* thoroughbred (horse).
purulence [pyrylɑ̃:s], *s.f. Med:* purulency.
purulent [pyrylɑ̃], *a. Med:* purulent; **foyer p.,** abscess.
pus [py], *s.m. Med:* pus, matter.
puseyisme [pyzeism], *s.m. Rel.H:* Puseyism.
puseyiste [pyzeist], *Rel.H:* **1.** *a.* Puseyistic. **2.** *s.m. & f.* Puseyite.
pusher [puʃɛ:r], *s.m. Civ.E:* pusher tractor.
push-pull [puʃpul], *a. & s.m.inv. Elcs:* push-pull (amplifier, circuit).
pusillanime [pyzil(l)anim], *a. Lit:* pusillanimous; faint (heart); faint hearted (person).
pusillanimité [pyzil(l)animite], *s.f. Lit:* pusillanimity; faint-heartedness; **avec p.,** pusillanimously; faint-heartedly.
pustule [pystyl], *s.f.* **1.** *Med:* pustule; *F:* pimple; **se couvrir de pustules,** to pustulate; **p. maligne,** malignant pustule; **pustules varioliques,** small-pox pustules. **2.** *Bot:* pustule, wart, blister. **3.** *Geol:* mound; **p. fumerolle,** fumarole mound.
pustulé [pystyle], *a. Bot:* pustulate(d), pustular.
pustuleux, -euse [pystylø, -ø:z], *a. Med:* pustulous, *F:* pimply.
putain [pytɛ̃], *s.f.* (*not used in polite conversation*) *P:* (*a*) prostitute, tart; (*b*) (*intensive use with s.*) **cette p. de guerre,** this bloody war; (*c*) *int.* hell! dammit!
putasser [pytase], *v.i. P:* (*not used in polite conversation*) (*a*) to go whoring; to chase the skirts; (*b*) to live as a prostitute, to be on the game.
putasserie [pytasri], *s.f. P:* (*not used in polite conversation*) (*a*) whoring; (*b*) living as a prostitute; (*c*) **quelle p.!** what a bloody mess!
putassier, -ière [pytasje, -jɛr], *P:* (*not used in polite conversation*) **1.** *a.* worthy of a prostitute, a tart; **langage p.,** obscene, bawdy, language. **2.** *s.m.* whoremonger, woman chaser.
putatif, -ive [pytatif, -i:v], *a.* putative, supposed, presumed, reputed; **père p.,** putative father; *Jur:* **mariage p.,** putative marriage.
putativement [pytativmɑ̃], *adv.* putatively, reputedly, by repute.
pute [pyt], *s.f. P:* (*not used in polite conversation*) prostitute, tart; **fils de p.,** son of a bitch.
putéal [pyteal], *s.m. Rom.Ant:* puteal, well curb.
putier [pytje], *s.m.*, **putiet** [pytjɛ], *s.m.* wild cherry, bird cherry (tree).
putinerie [pytinri], *s.f.*, **putinisme** [pytinism], *s.m. P:* (*not used in polite conversation*) (*a*) (habitual) prostitution; (*b*) low sensuality.
Putiphar [pytifa:r], *Pr.n.m. B.Hist:* Potiphar.
putois [pytwa], *s.m.* (*a*) polecat, fitchet; **p. (d'Amérique),** skunk; **p. de Virginie,** pekan; *F:* **crier comme un p.,** to squeal like a pig; to kick up a hell of a row; (*b*) (*fur*) fitchet; skunk.
putréfactif, -ive [pytrefaktif, -i:v], *a.* putrefactive.
putréfaction [pytrefaksjɔ̃], *s.f.* putrefaction, decomposition, decay; *Med:* sepsis; **matière en p.,** putrefying matter.
putréfiable [pytrefjabl̥], *a.* putrescible, putrefiable.
putréfier [pytrefje], *v.tr.* to putrefy, rot; to decompose (sth.).
se putréfier, to putrefy; to become putrid.
putrescence [pytrɛs(s)ɑ̃:s], *s.f.* putrescence, putrefaction; *Med:* sepsis.
putrescent [pytrɛs(s)ɑ̃], *a.* putrescent.
putrescibilité [pytrɛs(s)ibilite], *s.f.* putrescibility.
putrescible [pytrɛs(s)ibl̥], *a.* putrescible, liable to putrefy.
putrescine [pytrɛs(s)in], *s.f. Bio-Ch:* putrescine.
putride [pytrid], *a.* putrid, tainted (matter, water, etc.); **fermentation p.,** putrefactive fermentation; *A:* **fièvre p.,** putrid fever.
putridité [pytridite], *s.f.* putridity, putridness; **ce monsieur était une petite p.,** this man was positively noisome, *F:* a perfect stinker.
putsch [putʃ], *s.m. Pol:* putsch.
putt [pœt, pyt], *s.m. Golf:* putt.
putter[1] [pœtœ:r, py-], *s.m. Golf:* putter.
putter[2] [pœte, pyte], *v.tr. Golf:* to putt.
putting [pœtiŋ, pytɛ̃:ʒ], *s.m. Golf:* putting green.
putto [pyto], *s.m. Art:* putto; *pl. putti.*
puy [pɥi], *s.m.* **1.** *Geol:* puy. **2.** *A.Fr.Lit: etc:* literary, musical, society.
puzzle [pyzl̥], *s.m.* (jigsaw) puzzle.
pyarthrose [pjartro:z], *s.f. Med:* pyarthrosis.
pycnide [piknid], *s.f. Fung:* pycnidium.
pycnique [piknik], *a. Psy:* pyknic (type).
pycnite [piknit], *s.f. Miner:* pycnite.
pycnodontes [piknɔdɔ̃:t], *s.m.pl. Paleont:* Pycnodonti.
pycnogonide [piknɔgɔnid], *s.m. Arach:* pycnogonid; *pl.* **pycnogonides,** Pycnogonida.
pycnolepsie [piknɔlɛpsi], *s.f. Med:* pyknolepsy.

pycnomètre [piknɔmɛtr̥], *s.m. Ph:* pycnometer, picnometer.
pycnonote [piknɔnɔt], *s.m. Orn:* bulbul; (*genus*) Pycnonotus.
pycnonotidés [piknɔnɔtide], *s.m.pl. Orn:* Pycnonotidae.
pycnose [pikno:z], *s.f. Med:* pycnosis.
pycnospore [piknɔspɔ:r], *s.f. Fung:* pycnospore.
pycnosporé [piknɔspɔre], *a. Fung:* pycnosporic.
pycnostyle [piknɔstil], *a. & s.m. Arch:* pycnostyle.
pyélite [pjelit], *s.f. Med:* pyelitis.
pyélographie [pjelɔgrafi], *s.f. Med:* pyelography.
pyélo(-)néphrite [pjelɔnefrit], *s.f. Med:* pyelonephritis.
pyéloscopie [pjelɔskɔpi], *s.f. Med:* pyeloscopy.
pyélotomie [pjelɔtɔmi], *s.f. Surg:* pyelotomy.
pyémie [pjemi], *s.f. Biol: Med:* pyaemia.
pygargue [pigarg], *s.m. Orn:* sea eagle; **p. à tête blanche,** American bald eagle; **p. à queue blanche,** white-tailed, *U.S:* gray, sea eagle; **p. de Pallas,** Pallas's sea eagle.
pygmée [pigme], *a. & s.m. & f.* pygmy.
pygméen, -enne [pigmeɛ̃, -ɛn], *a.* pygm(a)ean, pygmy.
pygope [pigɔp], *s.m. Rept:* pygopus, (Australian) finfoot lizard.
pygopodes [pigɔpɔd], *s.m.pl. Orn:* Pygopodes.
pygopodidés [pigɔpɔdide], *s.m.pl. Rept:* Pygopodidae.
pyjama [piʒama], *s.m.* pyjamas, *U.S:* pajamas; **un p.,** a suit of pyjamas; **dormir en p.,** to sleep in pyjamas.
pyknolepsie [piknɔlɛpsi], *s.f. Med:* pyknolepsy.
Pylade [pilad], *Pr.n.m. Gr.Lit:* Pylades.
Pylée [pile], *Pr.n.f. A.Geog:* Pyle.
pyléphlébite [pileflebit], *s.f. Med:* pylephlebitis.
pyléthrombose [piletrɔ̃bo:z], *s.f. Med:* pylethrombosis.
pylône [pilo:n], *s.m.* **1.** *A.Arch:* pylon (of Egyptian temple). **2.** pylon; steel tower; **p. métallique** (i) (iron framework) tower (conveying electric power, on aerodrome, etc.); (ii) lattice mast (supporting telegraph wires, etc.); **grue à p.,** tower crane; *Rail:* **p. de signaux,** signal post; *W.Tel: etc:* **antenne p.,** tower antenna; **p. d'émission,** radiating tower; **p. relais de télévision,** television relay tower.
pylore [pilɔ:r], *s.m. Anat:* pylorus.
pylorectomie [pilɔrɛktɔmi], *s.f. Surg:* pylorectomy.
pylorique [pilɔrik], *a. Anat:* pyloric.
pylorisme [pilɔrism], *s.m. Med:* constriction of the pylorus.
pyloroplastie [pilɔrɔplasti], *s.f. Surg:* pyloroplasty.
pylorospasme [pilɔrɔspasm], *s.m. Med:* pylorospasm.
pyobacillose [pjɔbasilo:z], *s.f. Vet:* pyobacillosis.
pyocyanine [pjɔsjanin], *s.f. Bio-Ch:* pyocyanin.
pyocyanique [pjɔsjanik], *a.* **bacille p.,** bacillus pyocyaneus.
pyocyste [pjɔsist], *s.m. Med:* pyocyst.
pyocyte [pjɔsit], *s.m. Med:* pyocyte.
pyodermite [pjɔdɛrmit], *s.f. Med:* pyodermatitis.
pyogène [pjɔʒɛn], *a. Med:* pyogenic.
pyogénie [pjɔʒeni], **pyogénèse** [pjɔʒenɛ:z], *s.f. Med:* pyogenesis.
pyohémie [pjɔemi], *s.f. Med:* pyaemia.
pyohémique [pjɔemik], *a. Med:* pyaemic.
pyoïde [pjɔid], *a. Med:* pyoid.
pyoktanine [pjɔktanin], *s.f. Pharm:* pyoctanin.
pyolabrinthite [pjɔlabrɛ̃tit], *s.f. Med:* pyolabrinthitis.
pyonéphrose [pjɔnefro:z], *s.f. Med:* pyonephrosis.
pyophagie [pjɔfaʒi], *s.f. Med:* pyophagia.
pyophtalmie [pjɔftalmi], *s.f. Med:* pyophthalmia.
pyopneumothorax [pjɔpnømɔtɔraks], *s.m. Med:* pyopneumothorax.
pyorrhée [pjɔre], *s.f. Med:* pyorrhea; **p. alvéolo-dentaire,** pyorrhea alveolaris.
pyorrhéique [pjɔreik], *a. Med:* pyorrheal, pyorrheic.
pyothorax [pjɔtɔraks], *s.m. Med:* pyothorax; empyema.
pyracanthe [pirakɑ̃:t], *s.f. Bot:* pyracanth, *F:* Christ's, Egyptian, thorn; evergreen thorn.
pyrale [piral], *s.f. Ent:* pyralis, *F:* meal moth, bee moth; **p. des pommes,** codling moth.
pyralides [piralid], *s.f.pl.,* **pyralidés** [piralide], *s.m.pl. Ent:* Pyralidae.
pyralididés [piralidide], *s.m.pl. Ent:* Pyralididae.
Pyrame [piram], *Pr.n.m. A.Lit:* Pyramus.
pyramidal, -aux [piramidal, -o], *a.* pyramidal; *A:* **succès p.,** tremendous, colossal, success.
pyramidalement [piramidalmɑ̃], *adv.* pyramidally.
pyramide [piramid], *s.f.* pyramid; *Geol:* **p. d'érosion,** erosion column; **p. des fées, p. coiffée,** (capped) earth pillar; *Gym:* **faire une p.,** to make a human pyramid.
pyramidé [piramide], *a.* pyramidal.
pyramidellidés [piramidɛlide], *s.m.pl. Moll:* Pyramidellidae.
pyramider [piramide], *v.i.* to rise in a pyramid, to form a pyramid; to pyramid.
pyramidion [piramidjɔ̃], *s.m. Arch:* pyramidion (of obelisk, etc.).
pyran [pirɑ̃], *s.m.,* **pyranne** [piran], *s.m. Ch:* pyran.
pyranomètre [piranɔmɛtr̥], *s.m. Ph:* pyranometer.
pyrargyrite [pirarʒirit], *s.f. Miner:* pyrargyrite, argyrythrose, dark-red silver ore; aerosite.
pyrauste [pirost], *s.f. Ent:* pyrausta.
pyrazine [pirazin], *s.f. Ch:* pyrazine.
pyrazol(e) [pirazɔl], *s.m. Ch:* pyrazole.
pyrazoline [pirazɔlin], *s.f. Ch:* pyrazoline.
pyrazolone [pirazɔlɔn], *s.f. Ch:* pyrazolone.
pyrène [pirɛn], *s.m. Ch:* pyrene.
pyrénéen, -enne [pireneɛ̃, -ɛn], *a. Geog:* Pyrenean.
Pyrénées (les) [lepirene], *Pr.n.f.pl. Geog:* the Pyrenees.
pyrénéisme [pireneism], *s.m. Mount:* Pyrenean climbing, mountaineering.
pyrénéite [pireneit], *s.f. Miner:* Pyrenean black garnet.
pyrénine [pirenin], *s.f. Biol:* pyrenin.
pyrénoïde [pirenɔid], *a. Bot:* pyrenoid.
pyrénomycètes [pirenɔmisɛt], *s.m. Fung:* pyrenomycetes.
pyrèthre [pirɛtr̥], *s.m.* **1.** *Bot:* (*a*) feverfew, pyrethrum; (*b*) *F:* pellitory of Spain. **2. poudre de p.,** pyrethrum (powder), insect powder.
pyréthrine [piretrin], *s.f. Pharm:* pyrethrin.
pyrétique [piretik], *a. Med:* pyretic.
pyrétogène [piretɔʒɛn], *a.* pyretogenetic.
pyrétologie [piretɔlɔʒi], *s.f. Med:* pyretology.
pyrétothérapie [piretɔterapi], *s.f. Med:* pyretotherapy.
Pyrex [pirɛks], *s.m. Glassm: R.t.m:* Pyrex.
pyrexie [pirɛksi], *s.f. Med:* pyrexia, fever.
pyrexique [pirɛksik], *a. Med:* pyrexial, pyrexic, febrile.
pyrgéomètre [pirʒeɔmɛtr̥], *s.m. Ph:* pyrgeometer.
pyrhéliomètre [pireljɔmɛtr̥], *s.m. Ph:* pyrheliometer.
pyrhéliométrique [pireljɔmetrik], *a. Ph:* pyrheliometric.
pyridazine [piridazin], *s.f. Ch:* pyridazin(e).
pyridine [piridin], *s.f. Ch:* pyridin(e).
pyridique [piridik], *a. Ch:* pyridic.
pyridone [piridɔn], *s.f. Ch:* pyridone.
pyridoxine [piridɔksin], *s.f. Bio-Ch:* pyridoxin.
pyriforme [pirifɔrm], *a. Bot:* pyriform.
pyrimidine [pirimidin], *s.f. Ch:* pyrimidin(e).
pyrite [pirit], *s.f. Miner:* (iron) pyrites; **p. de cuivre, p. cuivreuse,** copper pyrites, chalcopyrite; **p. arsenicale,** arsenopyrites, mispickel; **p. blanche, crêtée,** marcasite; **p. capillaire,** millerite.
pyriteux, -euse [piritø, -ø:z], *a. Miner:* pyritic, pyritous (copper, etc.).
pyritifère [piritifɛ:r], *a. Miner:* pyritiferous (shale, etc.).
pyr(o)- [pir(ɔ)], *pref.* pyr(o)-.
pyroacétique [pirɔasetik], *a.* pyroacetic; **éther p.,** acetone.
pyroarséniate [pirɔarsenjat], *s.m.* pyroarsenate.
pyroborique [pirɔbɔrik], *a. Ch:* pyroboric.
pyrocatéchine [pirɔkateʃin], *s.f.,* **pyrocatéchol** [pirɔkateʃɔl], *s.m. Phot:* pyrocatechin, pyrocatech(in)ol.
pyrochlore [pirɔklɔ:r], *s.m. Minor:* pyrochlore.
pyroclastique [pirɔklastik], *a. Geol:* pyroclastic.
pyrocollodion [pirɔkɔlɔdjɔ̃], *s.m.* pyrocollodion.
pyroélectricité [pirɔelɛktrisite], *s.f.* pyroelectricity.
pyroélectrique [pirɔelɛktrik], *a.* pyrolectric.
pyroforique [pirɔfɔrik], *a. Ch:* pyrophoric.
pyrofuge [pirɔfy:ʒ], *a.* fire-extinguishing.
pyrogallate [pirɔgal(l)at], *s.m. Ch:* pyrogallate.
pyrogallique [pirɔgal(l)ik], *a. Ch:* pyrogallic.
pyrogallol [pirɔgal(l)ɔl], *s.m. Ch:* pyrogallol.
pyrogénation [pirɔʒenasjɔ̃], *s.f. Ch: Ph:* pyrogenation.
pyrogène [pirɔʒɛn], *a.* **1.** *Geol:* pyrogenic, pyrogenous. **2.** *Med:* pyrogenous, pyrogenic, fever-producing.
pyrogéné [pirɔʒene], *a. Ch:* **acide p.,** pyro acid; **huile pyrogénée,** empyreumatic oil.
pyrogénèse [pirɔʒenɛ:z], *s.f. Ph:* pyrogenesis.
pyrogénésique [pirɔʒenezik], **pyrogénétique** [pirɔʒenetik], *a.* pyrogenetic.
pyrognostique [pirɔgnɔstik], *a.* pyrognostic.
pyrograver [pirɔgrave], *v.tr.* to pyrograph.
pyrograveur, -euse [pirɔgravœ:r, -ø:z], *s.m. & f.* pyrographer.
pyrogravure [pirɔgravy:r], *s.f.* pyrogravure, poker work.
pyrolacées [pirɔlase], *s.f.pl. Bot:* Pyrolaceae.
pyrolâtre [pirɔlɑ:tr̥]. **1.** *a.* fire-worshipping. **2.** *s.* fire worshipper, pyrolater.
pyrolâtrie [pirɔlɑtri], *s.f.* fire worship, pyrolatry.
pyrole [pirɔl], *s.f. Bot:* pyrola, wintergreen.
pyroligneux, -euse [pirɔliɲø, -ø:z], *a. Ch:* pyroligneous (acid).
pyrolignite [pirɔliɲit], *s.f. Ch:* pyrolignite.
pyrolusite [pirɔlyzit], *s.f. Miner:* pyrolusite; polianite.
pyrolyse [pirɔli:z], *s.f. Ch:* pyrolysis.
pyromancie [pirɔmɑ̃si], *s.f.* pyromancy.
pyromane [pirɔman], *s.m. & f.* pyromaniac.
pyromanie [pirɔmani], *s.f.* pyromania.
pyroméconique [pirɔmekɔnik], *a.* pyromeconic (acid).
pyromellique [pirɔmɛlik], *a. Ch:* pyromellitic.
pyrométamorphisme [pirɔmetamɔrfism], *s.m. Geol:* pyrometamorphism.
pyromètre [pirɔmɛtr̥], *s.m. Ph: Metall:* pyrometer; **p. à cadran,** dial pyrometer; **p. à lunette,** optical pyrometer; **p. à radiation totale,** radiation pyrometer.
pyrométrie [pirɔmetri], *s.f.* pyrometry.
pyrométrique [pirɔmetrik], *a.* pyrometric(al).
pyromorphite [pirɔmɔrfit], *s.f. Miner:* pyromorphite.
pyromucique [pirɔmysik], *a.* pyromucic (acid).
pyrone [pirɔn], *s.f. Ch:* pyrone.
pyrope [pirɔp], *s.m. Miner:* pyrope.
pyrophage [pirɔfa:ʒ], *a.* fire-eating.
pyrophane [pirɔfan], *a.* pyrophanous.
pyrophanite [pirɔfanit], *s.f. Miner:* pyrophanite.
pyrophore [pirɔfɔ:r], *s.m. Ch: Ent:* pyrophorus.
pyrophorique [pirɔfɔrik], *a. Metall: etc:* pyrophoric; **alliage p.,** pyrophoric alloy.
pyrophosphate [pirɔfɔsfat], *s.m. Ch:* pyrophosphate.
pyrophosphoreux, -euse [pirɔfɔsfɔrø, -ø:z], *a. Ch:* pyrophosphorous.
pyrophosphorique [pirɔfɔsfɔrik], *a. Ch:* pyrophosphoric.
pyrophyllite [pirɔfil(l)it], *s.f. Miner:* pyrophyllite.
pyrophysalite [pirɔfizalit], *s.f. Miner:* pyrophysalite.
pyrophyte [pirɔfit], *s.m. Bot:* pyrophyte.
pyropneumatique [pirɔpnømatik], *a.* hot-air (engine, etc.).
pyroscaphe [pirɔskaf], *s.m. Nau.Hist:* steamship.
pyroscope [pirɔskɔp], *s.m. Ph: Metall:* pyroscope.
pyroscopie [pirɔscɔpi], *s.f.* pyroscopy.
pyrosis [pirozis], *s.m. Med:* pyrosis, *F:* heartburn.
pyrosmalite [pirɔsmalit], *s.f. Miner:* pyrosmalite.
pyrosome [pirozo:m], *s.m. Moll:* pyrosome; (*genus*) Pyrosoma.
pyrosphère [pirɔsfɛ:r], *s.f. Geol: A:* pyrosphere.
pyrostat [pirɔsta], *s.m.* pyrostat.
pyrostilpnite [pirɔstilpnit], *s.f. Miner:* pyrostilpnite, fireblende.
pyrosulfate [pirɔsylfat], *s.m. Ch:* pyrosulphate.
pyrosulfite [pirɔsylfit], *s.m. Ch:* pyrosulphite.
pyrosulfurique [pirɔsylfyrik] *a. Ch:* pyrosulphuric.
pyrosulfuryle [pirɔsylfyril], *s.m. Ch:* pyrosulphuryl.
pyrotartrique [pirɔtartrik], *a. Ch:* pyrotartaric.
pyrotechnicien, -ienne [pirɔtɛknisjɛ̃, -jɛn], *s.* pyrotechnist; explosives expert.
pyrotechnie [pirɔtɛkni], *s.f.* pyrotechnics, pyrotechny.
pyrotechnique [pirɔtɛknik]. **1.** *a.* pyrotechnic(al). **2.** *s.f.* pyrotechnics, pyrotechny.
pyrotherium [pirɔtɛrjɔm], *s.m. Paleont:* pyrotherium.
pyroxène [pirɔksɛn], *s.m. Miner:* pyroxene.
pyroxéneux, -euse [pirɔksenø, -ø:z], *a. Miner:* pyroxenic.
pyroxénite [pirɔksenit], *s.f. Miner:* pyroxenite.
pyroxyle [pirɔksil], *s.m.,* **pyroxyline** [pirɔksilin], *s.f. Ch:* pyroxyle, pyroxyline; *A:* gun-cotton.
pyroxylé [pirɔksile], *a. Exp:* pyroxiline (explosive).
pyroxylique [pirɔksilik], *a. Ch:* pyroligneous, *A:* pyroxylic.
pyrrhique [pir(r)ik]. **1.** *a.* Pyrrhic (verse, etc.). **2.** *s.m. Pros:* Pyrrhic (foot). **3.** *s.f.* Pyrrhic (dance).
pyrrhocore [pirɔkɔ:r], *s.m.,* **pyrrhocoris** [pirɔkɔris], *s.m. Ent:* pyrrhocorid.
pyrrhocoridés [pirɔkɔride], *s.m.pl. Ent:* Pyrrhocoridae.

Pyrrhon [pirrɔ̃], *Pr.n.m. Gr.Phil:* Pyrrho.

pyrrhonien, -ienne [pir(r)ɔnjɛ̃, -jɛn], *A.Gr.Phil:* 1. *a.* Pyrrhonic, Pyrrhonian. 2. *s.* Pyrrhonist.

pyrrhonisme [pir(r)ɔnism], *s.m. A.Gr.Phil:* Pyrrhonism.

pyrrhotine [pir(r)ɔtin], *s.f.*, **pyrrhotite** [pir(r)ɔtit], *s.f. Miner:* pyrrhotine, pyrrhotite, magnetic pyrites.

Pyrrhus [pir(r)ys], *Pr.n.m.* Pyrrhus; victoire à la P., Pyrrhic victory.

pyrrol(e) [pirɔl], *s.m. Ch:* pyrrol(e).

pyrrolidine [pirɔlidin], *s.f. Ch:* pyrrolidin(e).

pyrroline [pirɔlin], *s.f. Ch:* pyrrolin(e).

pyruvique [piryvik], *a. Ch:* pyruvic.

Pythagore [pitagɔːr], *Pr.n.m. Gr.Phil:* Pythagoras; **la table de P.**, the Pythagorean table; the multiplication table; **théorème de P.**, Pythagoras' theorem.

pythagoréen, -enne [pitagɔreɛ̃, -ɛn], *a.* Pythagorean.

pythagoricien, -ienne [pitagɔrisjɛ̃, -jɛn], *a. & s.* Pythagorean.

pythagorique [pitagɔrik], *a.* Pythagorean.

pythagorisme [pitagɔrism], *s.m.* Pythagoreanism, Pythagorism.

Pythéas [piteas], *Pr.n.m. Gr.Hist:* Pytheas.

pythiade [pitjad], *s.f. Gr.Ant:* pythiad.

pythie [piti]. 1. *s.f. Gr.Rel:* pythoness. 2. *Pr.n.f.* la P., Pythia.

pythien, -ienne [pitjɛ̃, -jɛn], *a.* 1. Pythian. 2. *pl.* jeux pythiens, Pythian games.

pythiques [pitik]. 1. *a.pl.* Pythian (games, etc.). 2. *s.f.pl.* les Pythiques, the Pythians, the Pythian Odes (of Pindar).

python [pitɔ̃], *s.m.* python; **p.(-)tigre**, rock python; **p. réticulé**, reticulate python.

pythonisse [pitɔnis], *s.f. Gr.Ant:* pythoness; *B:* la p. d'Endor, the Witch of Endor.

pyurie [piyri], *s.f. Med:* pyuria.

pyxide [piksid], *s.f. Arch: Z:* pyxis; *Bot:* pyxidium, pyxis.

Q

Q, q [ky], *s.m.* (the letter) Q, q; *Tp:* Q comme Quintal, Q for Queenie; *Nau:* **le pavillon Q,** the quarantine flag; *Med:* **fièvre Q.,** Q fever; *El: facteur Q.,** Quality factor; *Telecom:* **code Q.,** Q signal.

Q-mètre [kymɛtr], *s.m. El: Meas:* Q-meter.

quadragénaire [kwadraʒenɛːr], *a. & s.m. & f.* quadragenarian.

quadragésimal, -aux [kwadraʒezimal, -o], *a.* quadragesimal; lenten (fast, etc.).

Quadragésime [kwadraʒezim], *s.f. Ecc:* (le dimanche de) la Q., Quadragesima (Sunday).

quadrangle [kwadrɑ̃ːgl], *s.m. Geom:* quadrangle.

quadrangulaire [kwadrɑ̃gylɛːr], *a.* quadrangular, four-angled; four-cornered (building, etc.).

quadrangulairement [kwadrɑ̃gylɛrmɑ̃], *adv.* quadrangularly.

quadrangulé [kwadrɑ̃gyle], *a.* quadrangular.

quadrant [k(w)adrɑ̃], *s.m. Mth: Biol:* quadrant.

quadrantal, -aux [kwadrɑ̃tal, -o], *a. Mth:* quadrantal (sector).

quadrat¹ [kwadra], *a. Astrol:* **aspect q.,** *s.m.* **quadrat,** quartile aspect, quadrature (of two heavenly bodies).

quadrat² [k(w)adra], *s.m. Typ:* quadrat, quad.

quadrateur [kwadratœːr], *s.m. pers.* who tries to square the circle, who attempts the impossible.

quadratifère [kwadratifɛːr], *a. Miner:* with square facets.

quadratin [k(w)adratɛ̃], *s.m. Typ:* em quadrat, em quad.

quadratique [kwadratik], *a.* **1.** *Mth:* quadratic (form, etc.); **moyenne q.,** quadratic mean. **2.** *Cryst:* quadratic, tetragonal. **3.** *Ph:* **vitesse q. moyenne,** mean square velocity.

quadratrice [kwadratris], *s.f. Mth:* quadratrix.

quadrature [kwadratyːr], *s.f.* **1.** *Mth:* quadrature, squaring (*esp.* of the circle); *F:* **chercher la q. du cercle,** to try to square the circle; to attempt the impossible. **2.** *Astr: Ph:* quadrature; **marées de q.,** neap tides, neaps. **3.** train, dial work (of watch, clock).

quadrette [k(w)adrɛt], *s.f.* team of four bowls players.

quadri- [kwadri], *pref.* quadri-.

quadribasique [kwadribazik], *a. Ch:* quadribasic, tetrabasic.

quadricapsulaire [kwadrikapsylɛːr], *a.* quadricapsular.

quadricentenaire [kwadrisɑ̃tənɛːr], *s.m.* quadricentennial.

quadriceps [kwadrisɛps], *Anat:* **1.** *a.* quadricipital. **2.** *s.m.* quadriceps (femoris).

quadrichromie [kwadrikrɔmi], *s.f.* four-colour printing.

quadricolore [kwadrikɔlɔːr], *s.m. Orn:* pintailed nonpareil.

quadricuspidé [kwadrikyspide], *a.* quadricuspid, quadricuspidate.

quadricycle [kwadrisikl], *s.m. Veh:* quadricycle.

quadridenté [kwadridɑ̃te], *a. Bot:* quadridentate.

quadridigité [kwadridiʒite], *a. Z:* quadridigitate.

quadridimensionnel, -elle [kwadridimɑ̃sjɔnɛl], *a.* four-dimensional.

quadriel [kwadrjɛl], *s.m. Ling:* quadrual.

quadriennal, -aux [kwadrijɛnal, -o], *a.* quadrennial. **1.** lasting for four years. **2.** occurring every four years; *Agr:* **assolement q.,** four-year rotation; *s.a.* DÉCHÉANCE 2.

quadrifide [kwadrifid], *a.* quadrifid, four-cleft (calyx, leaf).

quadrifolié [kwadrifɔlje], *a. Bot:* quadrifoliate.

quadriforme [kwadriform], *a. Cryst:* quadriform.

quadrige [kwadriːʒ], *s.m. Rom.Ant:* quadriga.

quadrigémellaire [kwadriʒemɛlɛːr], *a.* **grossesse q.,** pregnancy resulting in the birth of quadruplets.

quadrijugué [kwadriʒyge], *a.* quadrijugate.

quadrijumeaux [kwadriʒymo]. **1.** *a.m.pl. Anat:* **tubercules q.,** the quadrigeminal bodies, the corpora quadrigemina (of the brain). **2.** *s.m.pl. Biol:* quadruplets.

quadrilatéral, -aux [kwadrilateral, -o], *a.* quadrilateral, four-sided.

quadrilatère [k(w)adrilatɛːr], *a. & s.m. Mth: Mil: etc:* quadrilateral; *Mth:* **q. complet,** complete quadrilateral; **q. gauche,** skew quadrilateral; **q. irrégulier,** irregular quadrilateral; *Aut:* **q. articulé,** Ackerman quadrilateral system.

quadrilitère [kwadrilitɛːr], *a. Ling:* quadriliteral.

quadrillage [kadriʒ], *s.m.* **1.** (*a*) cross-ruling, squaring (of paper, map); (*b*) *Mil: etc:* partitioning (of a zone in order to carry out search operations). **2.** (*a*) (pattern of) checks, squares; chequer work; (*b*) *Mapm:* grid, graticule; **q. international,** standard grid; **q. kilométrique,** kilometric grid; **q. perspectif,** perspective grid; **éléments numériques du q.,** grid data; **lettre du q.,** grid letter; **nord du q.,** grid north; **gisement par rapport au nord du q.,** grid bearing; (*c*) *Town P:* chequer-board layout; grid layout.

quadrille [kadriːj]. **1.** *s.m.* (*a*) quadrille (dance, air); set of quadrilles; **q. des lanciers,** (set of) lancers; (*b*) *Cards: A:* quadrille. **2.** (*a*) *s.m. or f.: A:* troop (of horsemen at a tournament, etc.); (*b*) *s.f.* (*bull-fighting*) quadrille, the matador and his assistants.

quadrillé [kadrije], *a.* squared, cross-ruled; checked; squared (cloth); **papier q.,** squared paper; (*computers*) coordinate paper; **carte quadrillée,** grid map; *Adm: Aut:* **zone quadrillée,** box junction; **bouton q.,** roughened thumb piece.

quadriller [kadrije], *v.tr.* (*a*) to rule in squares, to cross-rule (paper); (*b*) to comb (out) (a district for enemies, criminals, etc.).

quadrillion [k(w)adriljɔ̃, -ijɔ̃], *s.m.* = QUATRILLION.

quadrilobe [kwadrilɔb], *s.m. Arch:* quatrefoil.

quadrilobé [kwadrilɔbe], *a. Bot:* quadrilobate.

quadrimestre [kwadrimɛstr], *s.m. Book-k:* four-monthly (accounting) period.

quadrimoteur, -trice [k(w)adrimɔtœːr, -tris], *a. & s.m. Av:* four-engined (aircraft).

quadrinôme [kwadrinoːm], *a. Mth:* quadrinomial.

quadripale [kwadripal], *a.* four-bladed (propeller).

quadriparti [kwadriparti], **quadripartite** [kwadripartit], *a.* (*a*) *Bot:* quadripartite; (*b*) *Pol: etc:* quadripartite (treaty, etc.); **conférence quadripartite,** four-power conference.

quadripartition [kwadripartisjɔ̃], *s.f.* quadripartition.

quadripétale [kwadripetal], *a. Bot:* with four petals.

quadriplace [kwadriplas], (*a*) *a.* four-seater; (*b*) *s.m. Av:* four-seater plane.

quadriplane [kwadriplan], *s.m. Av:* quadruplane.

quadriplégie [kwadripleʒi], *s.f. Med:* quadriplegia, tetraplegia.

quadripolaire [kwadripɔlɛːr], *a.* quadripolar.

quadripôle [kwadripoːl], *s.m. El:* quadripole.

quadrique [kwadrik], *a. & s.f. Mth:* quadric.

quadriréacteur [kwadrireaktœːr], *a. & s.m. Av:* four-engined (jet aircraft).

quadrirème [kwadrirɛm], *s.f. A.Nau:* quadrireme.

quadrisyllabe [kwadrisil(l)ab], *s.m.* quadrisyllable.

quadrisyllabique [kwadrisil(l)abik], *a.* quadrisyllabic.

quadrivalence [kwadrivalɑ̃ːs], *s.f. Ch:* quadrivalence, tetravalence.

quadrivalent [kwadrivalɑ̃], *a. Ch:* quadrivalent, tetravalent.

quadrivalve [kwadrivalv], *a.* quadrivalve, quadrivalvular.

quadrivium [kwadrivjɔm], *s.m. Sch: A:* quadrivium.

quadrumane [k(w)adryman]. **1.** *a.* quadrumanous, four-handed (animal). **2.** *s.m.* quadrumane; *pl.* **quadrumanes,** Quadrumana.

quadrupède [k(w)adrypɛd]. **1.** *a.* quadruped(al), four-footed (animal). **2.** *s.m.* quadruped.

quadruplateur [kwadryplatœːr], *s.m. Rom.Hist:* quadruplator.

quadruple [k(w)adrypl], *a. & s.m.* quadruple, fourfold; **être payé au q.,** to be repaid fourfold; **payer le q. du prix,** to pay four times the price; **vingt est le q. de cinq,** twenty is four times (as much as) five; *Hist:* **la Q. Alliance,** the Quadruple Alliance; *Mus:* **q. croche,** hemidemisemiquaver.

quadruplé, -ée [k(w)adryple], *s.* quadruplet, *F:* quad.

quadruplement¹ [k(w)adrypləmɑ̃], *s.m.* quadrupling; *Rail:* **q. des voies (d'une ligne),** quadrupling of a line.

quadruplement², *adv.* quadruply, fourfold.

quadrupler [k(w)adryple], *v.tr. & i.* to quadruple; to increase (one's fortune, etc.) fourfold.

quadruplets, -plettes [k(w)adryplɛ, -plɛt], *s.pl. Biol:* quadruplets.

quadruplette [kwadryplɛt], *s.f. A.Cy:* four-seater bicycle, quadruplet.

quadruplex [kwadryplɛks], *s.m. Tg:* quadruplex (system).

quadruplication [kwadryplikasjɔ̃], *s.f.* quadruplication.

quadruplique [kwadryplik], *s.f. A.Jur:* (defendant's) rebutter; **exception opposée à la q.,** (plaintiff's) surrebutter.

quadrupôle [kwadrypoːl], *s.m. El:* quadrupole, quadripole.

quai [ke], *s.m.* (*a*) *Nau:* quay; wharf; pier; **à quai,** alongside the quay, berthed; **aborder, venir, à q.,** to come alongside, to berth; **amener un navire à q.,** to bring a ship alongside, to berth a ship; **q. à marée,** tidal wharf; **q. à charbon, à houille,** coal wharf; **q. des pétroliers,** oil wharf; **droits de q.,** quayage, wharfage; pier dues; **gardien, propriétaire, de q.,** wharfinger; *Com:* (*of goods*) **à prendre, livrable, à q.,** ex-quay, ex-wharf; *Nau:* **mise à q.,** dismissal (of member of crew); (*b*) embankment (along river); **les bouquinistes des quais,** the second-hand booksellers along the embankments (in Paris); *F:* **le Q. d'Orsay,** the French Foreign Office; (*c*) *Rail:* platform; *P.N:* **accès aux quais,** to the trains; **billet de q.,** platform ticket; **q. d'arrivée,** arrival platform, *Mil:* detraining platform; **q. de départ,** departure platform, *Mil:* entraining platform; **q. de transbordement,** trans-shipping platform; **q. entre voies,** island platform; **le train est à q.,** the train is in; **à, de, quel q. part le train?** which platform does the train leave from? **q. haut,** high platform (as in English station); (*d*) *Rail:*

etc: **q. de chargement, de déchargement,** loading. off-loading, platform; **q. en cul-de-sac,** bay, dock.

quaiage [keaːʒ], *s.m.* quayage, wharfage.

quaiche [kɛʃ], *s.f. Nau:* ketch.

quaker, -eresse [kwɛkœːr, -(ə)rɛs; kwa-], *s.* Quaker, Quakeress; Friend.

quakerisme [kwɛkrism, kwak(ə)rism], *s.m.* Quakerism.

qualifiable [kalifjabl̩], *a.* **1.** that may be characterized (de, as); **homicide q. de meurtre,** homicide that falls under the definition of murder; **conduite peu q.,** unwarrantable conduct. **2.** subject to qualification; qualifiable.

qualificateur [kalifikatœːr], *s.m. Ecc:* qualificator (attached to ecclesiastical tribunal).

qualificatif, -ive [kalifikatif, -iːv], *Gram:* **1.** *a.* qualifying, qualificative (adjective, etc.). **2.** *s.m.* qualificative, qualifier.

qualification [kalifikasjɔ̃], *s.f.* **1.** *(a)* **q. de qn de qch.,** calling s.o. sth.; **q. de faussaire,** calling s.o. a forger; *Pol.Ec:* **q. de région,** area rating; *Com:* **q. des emplois,** job evaluation; *(b) Gram:* qualifying (of noun, etc.); *(c) Fin:* qualifying (by acquisition of shares); *(d) Jur:* legal definition (of crime, etc.). **2.** designation, name, title; **q. de traître,** designation as a traitor; **attribuer à qn la q. de faussaire,** to call s.o. a forger; **s'attribuer la q. de colonel,** to call oneself a colonel. **3.** qualification; **q. professionnelle,** professional qualifications; *Sp:* **obtenir sa q.,** to qualify.

qualifié [kalifje]. **1.** *a.* *(a)* **q. pour faire qch.,** qualified to do sth.; **ouvrier q., non q.,** skilled, unskilled, worker; **personne qualifiée,** (i) qualified person; (ii) *A:* person of quality, of rank; (iii) *A:* person of importance, of standing; **le ministre q.,** the competent minister; **je suis certainement q. pour en parler,** I am surely entitled, qualified, to speak of, about, it; *(b) Jur:* **vol q.,** aggravated theft. **2.** *a. & s. Sp:* **(cheval, coureur) q.,** qualifier; **équipe qualifiée,** qualifying team.

qualifier [kalifje], *v.tr.* (*p.d. & pr.sub.* **n. qualifiions v. qualifiiez**) **1.** to style, call, term, qualify; **acte qualifié (de) crime,** action termed a crime; **piquette qualifiée de vin de marque,** poor quality wine offered, passed off, as vintage wine; **q. qn de son titre, de son grade,** to address, designate, s.o. by his correct title; **q. qn de charlatan, de menteur,** to call s.o. a quack, a liar; **q. une entreprise d'escroquerie,** to describe an undertaking as a swindle; **ouvrage qui a été qualifié immoral,** work that has been called immoral; **q. durement qn,** to call s.o. hard names; **conduite qu'on ne saurait q.,** unspeakable, most objectionable, conduct. **2.** *Gram:* to qualify; **l'adjectif sert à q. le substantif,** the adjective serves to qualify the noun. **3.** to qualify; **mes connaissances me qualifient à entreprendre cet ouvrage,** my knowledge qualifies me to undertake this work; *Sp:* **la seconde place aux championnats de France qualifie pour les Jeux Olympiques,** a second place in the French championships qualifies for the Olympic Games.

se qualifier. 1. se q. colonel, to call, style, oneself colonel. **2.** *(a)* **se q. pour une fonction,** to qualify for an office; *(b) Sp:* to qualify; **il s'est qualifié pour la finale,** he qualified for the finals.

qualitatif, -ive [kalitatif, -iːv], *a.* qualitative; *Ch:* **analyse qualitative,** qualitative analysis.

qualitativement [kalitativmɑ̃], *adv.* qualitatively.

qualité [kalite], *s.f.* **1.** quality; *(a) (degree of excellence)* **commerçant bien connu par la bonne, la mauvaise, q. de sa marchandise,** tradesman well known for the high, poor, quality of his goods; **de première q.,** high-grade, high-quality; first-rate; **blé de première q.,** prime wheat; **vin de (première) q.,** choice wine; **vin de q. inférieure,** wine of inferior quality; inferior wine; **minerai de q. inférieure,** low-grade ore; **qualités de thé,** leaf grades (of tea); **q. industrielle d'une roche,** commercial value of a rock; **q. industrielle,** industrial grade; **q. ordinaire,** regular grade; *Nau:* **qualités évolutives,** steering qualities; **qualités nautiques,** weatherly qualities; *Elcs:* **q. de transmission,** transmission performance; **indice de q.,** quality index; **facteur de q.,** Q (factor), quality factor; *Mus:* **q. de la note,** tone quality (of an instrument, etc.); *(b) (excellence)* **vin qui a de la q.,** wine that has quality; **personne qui a beaucoup de qualités,** person who has many good qualities, many good points. **2.** *(a)* quality, property (of sth.); **drogue qui a des qualités fébrifuges,** drug with antifebrile properties; *(b)* intrinsic nature (of sth.); *Jur:* **q. substantielle d'un crime,** essence of a crime. **3.** qualification, capacity; profession, occupation; **décliner ses titres et qualités,** to enumerate one's titles and qualifications; to give an account of oneself; to introduce oneself; *Adm:* **nom, prenom et q.,** surname, Christian name and occupation or description; **il nous révéla sa q. de prêtre,** he disclosed the fact that he was a priest; **agir en q. de tuteur,** to act in one's capacity as guardian; **en sa q. d'avocat,** (in his capacity) as a barrister; *Jur:* **ès qualités,** ex officio, in one's capacity (as); **avoir q. pour agir,** to be qualified, empowered, entitled, authorized, to act; to have authority to act; **avoir les qualités requises pour occuper un poste,** to have the necessary qualifications for a post; to be qualified for a post; **avoir q. de citoyen,** to rank as a citizen; **avoir q. d'électeur,** to be qualified to vote. **4.** *A:* title, rank (of noble, etc.); **gens de q.,** people of quality; gentlefolk. **5.** *Jur:* **qualités d'un jugement,** record of proceedings before judgement.

quand [kɑ̃], when. **1.** *conj.* *(a)* **je lui en parlerai q. je le verrai,** I'll mention it to him when I see him; **elle a dit qu'elle lui en parlerait q. elle le verrait,** she said she would mention it to him when she saw him; *F:* **q. je vous le disais!** didn't I tell you so! **q. vous aurez fini!** when you've finished! *(b)* **q. (même),** (i) even if, even though, although; **q. il me l'affirmerait je n'en croirais rien,** even if he assured me it was so I wouldn't believe it; **je n'en voudrais pas q. (bien) même on me le donnerait,** I wouldn't have it as a gift; (ii) **je le ferai q. même,** I'll do it all the same, nevertheless, in spite of everything; *(c) A: & Dial:* if; **ça ne m'étonnerait pas q. il pleuvrait,** I shouldn't wonder if it rained. **2.** *adv.* **q. viendra-t-il?** when will he come? **dites-moi q. il viendra,** tell me when he will come; **n'importe q.,** no matter when, at any time; **jusqu'à q. serez-vous à Paris?** till when, how long, will you be in Paris? **depuis q. êtes-vous à Paris?** how long have you been in Paris? since when have you been in Paris? **depuis q. les enfants fument-ils?** (i) how long have the children been smoking? (ii) since when do children smoke? **à q. le mariage?** when will the wedding be? **de q. est ce journal?** what is the date of this paper? **pour q. est la réunion,** when is the meeting? *F:* *(when pouring drink)* **dites-moi q.,** say when; *F:* **à q.?** until when? **3.** *(a) prep.phr. A: & Fr.C:* **q. et,** with; at the same time as; *Fr.C. & Dial:* **je suis arrivé q. (et) lui,** I arrived with him, at the same time as him; *(b) adv. & prep.phr. A:* **q. et q.,** at the same time (as).

quant [kɑ̃], *a.* *(a) A:* whenever; **quantes fois que . . .,** as often as . . .; *(b) Jur:* **toutes et quantes fois que . . .,** whenever . . ., every time that . . ..

quant à [kɑ̃ta], *adv.phr.* as for; **q. à moi,** as for me, for my part; as far as I am concerned; **q. à cela,** as for that, for that matter; as far as that goes; **q. à l'avenir,** as for the future; **q. au reste des habitants,** as for the rest of the inhabitants; as far as the rest of the inhabitants are concerned; **q. à le demander, je n'y aurais pas songé,** as for asking for it, I wouldn't have dreamt of it; **le rapport est exact q. à ce qu'il dit,** the report is accurate as far as it goes; **q. à savoir si cette politique a été suivie, c'est un point sur lequel les avis sont partagés,** whether that policy has been followed is a matter of controversy; **les doutes que j'ai éprouvés q. à son intelligence,** the doubts I entertained about his intelligence.

quanta [kwɑ̃ta], *s.m.pl.* *See* QUANTUM.

quant-à-moi [kɑ̃tamwa], *s.m.inv. Lit:* dignity, reserve.

quant-à-soi [kɑ̃taswa], *s.m.inv.* dignity, reserve; *used in the phrases:* **se mettre, se tenir, rester, sur son q.-à-s.; prendre, tenir, son q.-à-s.,** to stand on one's dignity, to be stand-offish.

quantième [katjɛm], *s.m.* day of the month; **quel q. (du mois), le q. du mois, sommes-nous?** *F: (incorrectly)* **quel est le q. (du mois)? quel q. avons-nous?** what day of the month, what date, is it? **montre à quantièmes,** calendar watch.

quantifiable [kɑ̃tifjabl̩], *a.* quantifiable.

quantificateur [kɑ̃tifikatœːr], *s.m. Log: Mth:* quantifier; **q. universel,** universal quantifier; **q. existentiel,** existential operator, quantifier.

quantification [kɑ̃tifikasjɔ̃], *s.f.* **1.** *Log:* quantification (of predicate). **2.** *Ph:* quantization; **distorsion de q.,** quantization distortion.

quantifier [kɑ̃tifje], *v.tr.* **1.** *Log:* to quantify (the predicate). **2.** *Ph:* to quantize.

quantique [kwɑ̃tik], *a. Ph: etc:* **théorie q.,** quantum theory; **nombre q.,** quantum number; **nombre q. de spin nucléaire,** nuclear spin quantum number; **mécanique q.,** quantum mechanics; **énergie q.,** quantum energy; **rendement q.,** quantum efficiency, quantum yield.

quantitatif, -ive [kɑ̃titatif, -iːv], *a.* **1.** quantitative; *Ch:* **analyse quantitative,** quantitative analysis. **2.** *Gram:* **adjectif q.,** adjective of quantity; **adverbe q.,** adverb of degree. **3.** *Pol.Ec:* **théorie quantitative,** quantity theory.

quantitativement [kɑ̃titativmɑ̃], *adv.* quantitatively.

quantitativiste [kɑ̃titativist], *s.m. Pol.Ec:* quantity theorist.

quantité [kɑ̃tite], *s.f.* **1.** *(a) Mth: Pros: etc:* quantity; **q. d'eau tombée,** rainfall; *Mth:* **q. à soustraire,** subtrahend; *Pros:* **faute de q.,** false quantity; *(b) El:* amperage; *(c) Ph:* **q. de lumière,** quantity of light; **q. de chaleur,** thermal content; *Mec:* **q. de mouvement,** momentum, impulse. **2.** quantity, abundance; **en q.,** in quantity, in bulk; **en q. considérable, en grande q.,** *F:* **en q. industrielle,** in large quantities; **par petites quantités,** in small quantities, amounts; **médicament à prendre en petite q.,** medicine to be taken in small doses, quantities; **donnez-m'en cette q.-là,** give me that much; **q. de gens,** a lot of people, a great number of people; **venez pour faire q.,** come along and help swell the numbers.

quantum, *pl.* **-a** [kwɑ̃tɔm, -a], *s.m.* **1.** *Ch: Mth: Ph:* quantum; **théorie des quanta,** quantum theory; **q. virtuel,** virtual quantum. **2.** amount, proportion, ratio; **fixer le q. des dommages-intérêts,** to fix the amount of damages, to assess the damages; **on vous assignera un q. sur les bénéfices,** a certain proportion of the profits will be assigned to you.

quapalier [kwapalje], *s.m. Bot: F:* sloanea.

quarantaine [karɑ̃tɛn], *s.f.* **1.** (about) forty, some forty; **une q. de jours,** about forty days; **une q. de mots,** forty words or so; **approcher de la q.,** to be getting on for forty; **avoir passé la q.,** to be over forty, in the forties; *Ecc:* **la sainte Q.,** Lent. **2.** quarantine; **faire (la) q.,** to be in quarantine; **mettre un navire, des passagers, en q.,** to quarantine a ship, passengers; **pavillon de q.,** quarantine flag; **lever la q.,** to admit a ship to pratique; **purger la q.,** to clear one's quarantine; *F:* **mettre qn en q.,** *A:* **à la q.,** to send s.o. to Coventry. **3.** *Bot: F:* annual stock.

quarantainier [karɑ̃tɛnje], *s.m. Nau:* ratline stuff.

quarante [karɑ̃ːt], *num.a.inv. & s.m.inv.* forty; **page q.,** page forty; **au chapitre q. de . . .,** in the fortieth chapter of . . .; **demeurer au numéro q.,** to live at number forty; **les Q.,** the Forty, the French Academy; *F:* **je m'en moque, je m'en fiche, comme de l'an q.,** I don't care a rap, a damn; I don't care two hoots; *Ten:* **q. à, q. partout,** deuce; *R.C.Ch:* **les (prières des) q. heures,** the forty hours (devotion); **la semaine de q. heures,** *F:* **les q. heures,** the forty-hour week; **les années q.,** the forties (1940-1949); *Med:* **dites quarante-quatre** = say ninety-nine.

quarante-huitard [karɑ̃tɥitaːr], *Pej: F:* **1.** *s.m. Fr.Hist:* revolutionary of 1848. **2.** *a.* **attitude quarante-huitarde,** revolutionary outlook; *pl. quarante-huitard(e)s.*

quarantenaire [karɑ̃tnɛːr]. **1.** *a.* *(a)* lasting, that has lasted, for forty years; of forty years; *(b) Nau:* (relating to) quarantine; *(c)* quarantinable. **2.** *s.m. Nau:* quarantine anchorage.

quarantenier [karɑ̃tənje], *s.m. Nau:* ratline stuff.

quarantième [karɑ̃tjɛm], *num.a. & s.m.* fortieth.

quarderonner [kardərɔne], *v.tr. Arch:* to round off an angle (with a quarter round).

quark [kwark], *s.m. Atom.Ph:* quark.

quarre [kaːr], *s.f.* cut (in pine trunk for tapping resin).

quart¹ [kaːr], *a.* *(a) A:* fourth; *s.m.* fourth person, fourth party; **un q. voleur survint,** a fourth robber arrived; **le q. denier,** interest at 25%; *(b)* **le tiers et le q.,** everybody; anybody; *F:* **il se fiche du q. comme du tiers,** he doesn't give a damn for anything, for anybody; *(c) A.Med:* **fièvre quarte,** quartan ague, fever; **fièvre double quarte,** double quartan.

quart², *s.m.* **1.** quarter, fourth part; *(a)* **donner un q. de tour à une vis,** to give a screw a quarter turn; *Com:* **remise du q.,** discount of 25%; **q. d'heure,** quarter of an hour; **dans un petit q. d'heure,** in (rather) less than a quarter of an hour; in ten minutes or so; **nous en voilà débarrassés pour le q. d'heure,** we're rid of him for the time being, for the moment; *F:* **passer un mauvais, sale, q. d'heure,** to have a trying moment, a bad time of it; **faire passer un mauvais q. d'heure à qn,** to give s.o. a bad time, a gruelling time; **le q. d'heure de Rabelais,** the hour of reckoning; **trois quarts,** three quarters; **portrait de trois quarts,** three-quarter face, semi-profile portrait; **la mer couvre les trois quarts du globe,** the sea covers three quarters of the globe; *F:* **les**

trois quarts du temps, most of the time, more than half the time; *F:* être aux trois quarts ivre, to be three parts drunk, to be three sheets in the wind, to be half-seas over; *F:* aux trois quarts mort, nearly, all but, dead; il est deux heures et q., deux heures un q., it's a quarter past two; il est deux heures moins le q., *occ.* moins un q., it's a quarter to two; à cinq heures trois quarts, at a quarter to six; l'horloge a sonné le q., les trois quarts, the quarter has struck, the three-quarters have struck; the clock has struck the quarter, the three-quarters; *Watchm:* pièce des quarts, quarter repeater; q. de cercle, (i) *Geom:* quadrant of a circle, quarter circle; (ii) dividers with arc; (iii) *Surv: etc:* quadrant; *Mil:* q. de conversion, wheel through 90°; *Mus:* q. de soupir, semi-quaver rest; *Typ:* q. de feuille, quarter page; *Sp:* q. de finale, quarter final; *s.a.* PIANO 1; (*b*) *Fort:* slope of 1 in 4; *Artil:* coup de q., shot arriving with ¼ slope of descent; (*c*) *Typ:* q. gras, four-to-pica rule. 2. *Nau:* q. (de vent), point of the compass (= 11° 15′); nord-est q. est, north-east by east; changer la route de deux quarts vers l'est, to alter (the) course two points to the east; venir de 16 quarts, to alter course 16 points. 3. (*a*) *Nau:* watch; q. en bas, watch below; q. en haut, watch on deck; q. par bordées, watch and watch; q. au mouillage, anchor watch; petit q., dog watch; être de q., to be on watch; prendre le q., to come on watch; faire le q., (i) to keep watch, (ii) *F:* (*of prostitute*) to walk her beat; (*of policeman*) battre son q., to be on one's beat; l'officier de q., the officer of the watch; homme de q., watch-keeper; faire bon q., to keep a good lookout; bon q.! all's well! (*b*) *Mil:* portion of a unit on duty, in readiness to move, etc.; officier de q., officer on duty (in a company's trench-system); (*c*) *Ind:* shift; (*d*) *P:* police station. 4. (*a*) *esp. Mil:* mug (holding a quarter of a litre); (*b*) small barrel. 5. un q. de beurre, a quarter of a kilo of butter, 250 grammes of butter.

quartage [kartaːʒ], *s.m. Min:* quartering.

quartager [kartaʒe], *v.tr. Agr:* to plough (field) a fourth time.

quartaine [kartɛn], *a.f. Med: A:* quartan (fever, ague).

quartan [kartɑ̃], *s.m.*, **quartan(n)ier** [kartanje], *s.m. Ven:* four-year-old boar.

quartation [kartasjɔ̃], *s.f. Metall:* quartation (of gold, silver).

quartaut [karto], *s.m.* quarter cask, octave cask.

quart-de-brie [kardəbri], *s.m. P:* large nose, conk; *pl. quarts-de-brie.*

quart-de-pouce [kardəpus], *s.m. Tex:* linen prover, thread counter; weaver's glass; *pl. quarts-de-pouce.*

quart-de-rond [kardərɔ̃], *s.m.* (*a*) *Arch: etc:* quarter round, quadrant, ovolo; (*b*) *Tls:* quarter-hollow moulding plane, quarter-round; *pl. quarts-de-rond.*

quarte [kart], *s.f.* 1. *Meas: A:* quart. 2. *Mus:* fourth. 3. *Fenc:* quart, quarte, carte; parer en q., to parry in carte. 4. *El: Elcs:* four-wire circuit; quad; q. torsadée, spiral four, spiral quad; q. D.M., multiple twin quad; câble à quartes, quad cable. 5. *Vet:* (seime) q., quarter crack.

quartefeuille [kart(ə)fœːj], *s.f. Her:* quatrefoil.

quartenier [kartənje], *s.m.* 1. *Hist:* official in charge of a municipal district. 2. *Ven:* four-year-old boar.

quarter [karte], *v.tr. Min:* to quarter.

quarteron[1], **-onne** [kart(ə)rɔ̃, -ɔn], *a. & s. Ethn:* quadroon.

quarteron[2], *s.m.* 1. *A.Meas:* quarter, fourth part (of a hundred, of a pound); demi-q., baker's dozen. 2. small group, handful (of people).

quartet [kartɛ], *s.m. Elcs:* (*computers*) four-bit byte.

quartette [kwartɛt], *s.m.* 1. *Mus:* quartet (of jazz, etc., musicians); short quartet. 2. *Biol:* quartet.

quartettiste [kwartɛtist], *s.m.* member of a jazz quartet.

quartidi [k(w)artidi], *s.m. Fr.Hist:* (*Republican Calendar*) fourth day of the decade.

quartier [kartje], *s.m.* 1. quarter, fourth part; (*a*) couper qch. en quatre quartiers, to cut sth. into four quarters; bois de q., firewood logs split into four; quartered logs; q. de la lune, de l'année, quarter of the moon, of the year; la lune est au premier q., au dernier q., the moon is in the first quarter, at three quarters, in its last quarter; *Nau:* marée de q., neap tide; *A:* toucher un q. de pension, to draw a quarter's pension; (*b*) *Cu:* q. d'agneau, de bœuf, quarter of lamb, of beef; cinquième q., offal; (*c*) *Her:* quartiers de l'écusson, quarters, quarterings, of the shield; (*d*) *Bill:* balk. 2. (*a*) part, portion; mettre qch. en quartiers, to tear sth. to pieces; son corps fut mis en quartiers, his body was quartered, was dismembered; *A:* je me mettrais en quatre quartiers pour lui, I would do anything for him, for his sake; q. de gâteau, portion of cake; q. d'orange, quarter, section, of orange, orange segment; q. de terre, plot of land; q. de pierre, block of (shaped) stone; q. de lard, gammon of bacon; q. de chevreuil, haunch of venison; q. d'un cheval, horse's quarters; (*b*) *Bootm:* quarter, galosh; (*c*) *Harn:* q. de selle, sweat flap; petits quartiers, skirts; (*d*) *Farr:* quarter (of hoof); (*e*) *Const:* q. d'un escalier, quarter pace of stairs; q. tournant, winding quarter. 3. (*a*) district, neighbourhood, ward (of town); les bas quartiers, (i) the slums; (ii) lower part of the town; q. des spectacles, theatreland; q. réservé, red-lamp district; q. des affaires, business district, *U.S:* downtown; q. résidentiel, bourgeois, residential district, *U.S:* uptown; je ne suis pas du q., I don't come from this area, district; (*in Belg.*) rentrer au q., to go back home; faire des visites de q., to pay calls near at hand; médecin de q., local practitioner; bureau de q., branch office (of bank, etc.); branch post office; cinéma de q., local cinema; (*b*) part, section (of building, establishment); (*c*) *Nau:* quarter; de quel q. vient le vent? from what quarter is the wind blowing? what quarter is the wind in? (*d*) *Mil:* quarters; rentrer au q., to return to quarters, to barracks; avoir q. libre, to be off duty; *A:* mettre l'alarme au q., to flutter the dovecotes; quartiers d'hiver, winter quarters; prendre ses quartiers d'hiver, to go into winter quarters; Q. général, headquarters; Grand Q. général, General Headquarters; *F: O:* chien de q., sergeant-major. 4. quarter, mercy; faire, donner, q. à qn, to grant, give, s.o. quarter; demander q., to ask for quarter; to cry quarter; point de q.! no quarter! il ne fait de q. à personne, he spares nobody, shows nobody any mercy. 5. *adv.phr.* (*a*) *A:* à q., apart; se tenir à q., to stand apart, to hold aloof; mettre qch. à q., to put, set, sth. aside; (*b*) sans q., without delay.

quartier-maître [kartjemɛtr̥], *s.m.* 1. *Mil: A:* quartermaster. 2. *Navy:* leading seaman; *pl. quartier(s)-maîtres.*

quartilage [kwartilaːʒ], *s.m.* (*statistics*) division into quartiles.

quartile [kwartil]. 1. *a. Astrol:* q. aspect, quartile aspect; quartile. 2. *s.m.* (*statistics*) quartile.

quartique [kwartik], *s.f. Mth:* quartic.

quarto [kwarto], *adv.* fourthly.

quartolet [kwartɔlɛ], *s.m. Mus:* quadruplet.

quartz [kwarts], *s.m.* (*a*) *Geol:* quartz, rock crystal; q. naturel, mother quartz; cristal de q., quartz crystal; q. enfumé, smoky quartz, cairngorm; q. aventuriné, flamboyant quartz; q. à or libre, free-milling quartz; moulin à q., quartz mill, quartz battery; (*b*) *Elcs:* crystal; q. piézo-électrique, q. pour oscillateur, piezo-crystal; piloté par q., crystal-controlled; oscillateur à, piloté par, q., crystal(-controlled) oscillator; horloge à q., quartz-crystal clock; (*computers*) ligne à retard à q., quartz delay line.

quartzeux, -euse [kwartsø, -øːz], *a.* quartzose, quartzous, quartzy (rock, etc.); sable q., quartz sand.

quartzifère [kwartsifɛːr], *a.* quartziferous; diorite q., quartz diorite.

quartzifié [kwartsifje], *a. Geol:* crystallized into quartz.

quartzine [kwartsin], *s.f. Miner:* quartzine.

quartzique [kwartsik], *a.* quartzic.

quartzite [kwartsit], *s.f.* quartzite, quartz rock.

quasar [kwazar, ka-], *s.m. Astr:* quasar.

quasi[1] [kazi], *s.m. Cu:* chump end (of loin of veal or beef).

quasi[2], *adv.* quasi, almost; q. aveugle, almost blind; all but blind; je n'ai q. rien senti, I felt scarcely anything; prédire q. d'instinct, comment . . ., to predict, so to speak instinctively, how . . .; une q.-amitié, a sort of friendship, a quasi-friendship; élu à la q.-unanimité, elected by a practically unanimous vote; j'en ai la q-certitude, I am all but certain of it; I am virtually certain of it.

quasi-besoin [kazibəzwɛ̃], *s.m. Psy:* quasi need; *pl. quasi-besoins.*

quasi-contrat [kazikɔ̃tra], *s.m. Jur:* quasi contract, implied contract, virtual contract; *pl. quasi-contrats.*

quasi-délit [kazideli], *s.m. Jur:* quasi delict, technical offence; *pl. quasi-délits.*

quasiment [kazimɑ̃], *adv. F:* almost, as it were, as one might say; to all intents and purposes; q. guéri, as good as cured; practically cured; il m'a q. mis à la porte, he practically turned me out.

Quasimodo [kazimɔdo], *s.f.* 1. *Ecc:* First Sunday after Easter, Quasimodo, Low Sunday; le lundi de (la) Q., Low Monday. 2. Quasimodo, the Hunchback of Notre-Dame (*a character in Victor Hugo's Notre-Dame de Paris*); laid comme Q., as ugly as sin.

quasi-possession [kazipɔsɛsjɔ̃], *s.f. Jur:* quasi easement, apparent easement, apparent servitude; *pl. quasi-possessions.*

quasi-usufruit [kaziyzyfrɥi], *s.m. Jur:* quasi usufruct, imperfect usufruct; *pl. quasi-usufruits.*

quassia [kwasja], *s.m.* 1. *Bot:* quassia (tree). 2. *Pharm: etc:* quassia; q. en copeaux, quassia chips.

quassier [kwasje], *s.m. Bot:* quassia (tree); (*a*) quassia amara; (*b*) q. de la Jamaïque, bitter wood, bitter ash (of the West Indies).

quassine [kwasin], *s.f.* quassin.

quater [kwatɛr], *Lt.adv.* (*a*) fourthly; in the fourth place; (*b*) (*in street numbers*) 12 q., 12 D.

quaternaire [kwatɛrnɛːr]. 1. *a. Ch: Geol: Mth: etc:* quaternary. 2. *s.m. Geol:* Quaternary (era). 3. *s.m. Pros:* tetrameter.

quaterne [kwatɛrn], *s.m.* (*a*) quatern, four winning numbers drawn in a lottery; (*b*) four numbers called on one horizontal line in lotto, bingo.

quaterné [kwatɛrne], *a. Bot:* quaternate (leaves).

quaternifolié [kwatɛrnifɔlje], *a. Bot:* with quaternate leaves.

quaternion [kwatɛrnjɔ̃], *s.m.* 1. quaternion, four-leaved manuscript. 2. *Mth:* quaternion.

quatorze [katɔrz], *num.a.inv. & s.m.inv.* 1. fourteen; page q., page fourteen; au chapitre q. de . . ., in the fourteenth chapter of . . .; *Hist:* Louis Q., Louis the Fourteenth; le q. juillet, the fourteenth of July, Bastille Day; *s.a.* MIDI[1] 1. 2. *Cards:* (*at piquet*) quatorze; (*at belote*) nine of trumps; *s.a.* QUINTE 2.

quatorzième [katɔrzjɛm]. 1. *num.a. & s.* fourteenth. 2. *s.m.* fourteenth (part).

quatorzièmement [katɔrzjɛmmɑ̃], *adv.* fourteenthly, in the fourteenth place.

quatrain [katrɛ̃], *s.m. Pros:* quatrain.

quatre [katr̥], *num.a.inv. & s.m.inv.* four; les q. saisons, the four seasons; *Hist:* Henri Q., Henry the Fourth; le q. août, the fourth of August; demeurer au numéro q., to live at number four; à q. pattes, on all fours; *A:* conduire à q., to drive four-in-hand; morceau à q. mains, (piano) duet; piece for four hands; les q. mois de septembre, the four months, September, October, November, December; pain de q. livres, quartern loaf; q. chiffres, large bills, bills running into four figures; *Th: F:* nous avons décroché les q. chiffres, the takings run into four figures; *Nau:* cordage en q., four-stranded rope; *P:* fil en q., strong brandy; *Mth: A:* les q. règles, the four fundamental processes, addition, subtraction, multiplication and division; (*computers*) à q. adresses, four-address; *Pol:* les Q. Grands, the Big Four; *Row:* un q., a four; un q. barré, a coxed four; un q. sans barreur, a coxless four; par q., in fours; se mettre par q., to form fours; *Mil:* colonne par q., column of fours; à droite par q., droite! form fours,—right! il est arrivé q. ou cinquième, he arrived fourth or fifth; *F:* un de ces q. jours, un de ces q. matins, one of these (fine) days, sometime soon; il demeure à q. pas (d'ici), he lives close by; pour les q. jours que j'ai à vivre, for all the days that are left to me; ménager ses q. sous, to be careful of one's small savings; une petite maison de q. sous, a little tuppeny-halfpenny house; maison exposée aux quatre vents, house exposed to the four winds; éparpillés aux q. coins du monde, scattered to the four corners of the earth; étendu les q. fers en l'air, sprawling on his back; clair comme deux et deux font q., as clear as daylight; monter l'escalier q. à q., to go upstairs four steps at a time, in a furious hurry; to rush upstairs; avoir la tête en q., to have a splitting headache; un vent à vous couper la figure en q., a cutting, icy, wind; se couper, se mettre, en q. pour faire qch., to do one's utmost to accomplish sth.; il se couperait, se mettrait, en q. pour vous, he would do anything, would go through fire and water, for you; il s'est mis en q. pour m'aider, he bent over backwards to help me; être tiré à q. épingles, to be immaculately turned out; il faut le tenir à q., it takes four men to hold him; je me tenais à q. pour ne pas rire, it all I was could do to stop myself from laughing; *s.a.* CHEMIN 1, CHEVEU 1, ÉPICE, JEUDI, MANGER I. 1, MARCHAND 1, ŒIL 1, PATTE 1, TEMPS 4, TRAVAILLER 2, VÉRITÉ 2, VOLONTÉ 2.

Quatre-Cantons [katr(ə)kɑ̃tɔ̃], *s.m.pl. Geog:* **le lac des Q.-C.,** the Lake of Lucerne.
quatre-cent-vingt [kat(rə)sɑ̃vɛ̃], *s.m.inv. Mil:* 420-millimetre gun.
quatre-de-chiffre [katrədəʃifr̥], *s.m.inv. Ven:* figure-four trap.
quatre-épices [katrepis], *s.f.inv. Bot:* fennel flower.
quatre-feuilles [katrəfœːj], *s.m.inv. Arch: Her:* quatrefoil.
quatre-fleurs [katrəflœːr], *s.f.pl.* **tisane des q.-f.,** infusion (of borage, mint, lime and verbena).
quatre-huit [katrɥit], *s.m.inv. Mus:* (*a*) four-eight time; (*b*) piece in four-eight time.
quatre-mâts [katrəmɑ], *s.m.inv.* four-masted ship; four master; **q.-m. barque,** four-masted barque; **q.-m. carré,** square-rigged four master; **q.-m. goélette,** four-masted schooner.
quatre-quarts [katrkaːr], *s.m.inv. Cu:* (type of) rich Madeira cake, *U.S:* = pound cake.
quatre-saisons [katrəsɛzɔ̃], *s.f.inv.* **1.** *Hort:* perpetual fruiting, flowering, variety, **fraisier des q.-s.,** perpetual-fruiting strawberry; **laitue des q.-s.,** all-the-year-round lettuce. **2. marchand(e) des q.-s.,** fruit and vegetable stallholder; barrow boy.
Quatre-Temps [katrətɑ̃], *s.m.pl. Ecc:* Ember days; **semaine des Q.-T.,** Ember week; **jeûner les Q.-T.,** to observe the Ember fast.
quatre-vingt [katrəvɛ̃]. *See* QUATRE-VINGTS.
quatre-vingt-dix [katrəvɛ̃dis], *num.a. & s.m.* ninety.
quatre-vingt-dixième [katrəvɛ̃dizjɛm], *num.a. & s.m.* ninetieth.
quatre-vingtième [katrəvɛ̃tjɛm], *num.a. & s.m.* eightieth.
quatre-vingt-neuf [katrəvɛ̃nœf], *s.m.* eighty-nine; *Fr.Hist:* first year of the French Revolution (1789).
quatre-vingts [katrəvɛ̃], *num.a. & s.m.; omits the final* s *when followed by another numeral adjective or when used as an ordinal*; eighty; **ils étaient quatre-vingts,** there were eighty of them; **page quatre-vingt,** page eighty; **quatre-vingt-un** [katrəvɛ̃œ̃], eighty-one; **quatre-vingt-onze** [katrəvɛ̃ɔ̃ːz], ninety-one; **quatre-vingt-onzième,** ninety-first.
Quatre-vingt-treize [katrəvɛ̃trɛːz], *s.m. Fr.Hist:* first year of the Terror (1793).
quatrième [katrijɛm]. **1.** *num.a. & s.* fourth; (*a*) **habiter au q. (étage),** to live on the fourth floor, *U.S:* the fifth floor; (*b*) *Med:* **q. maladie,** fourth disease; (*c*) *Mil:* **la q. arme,** the fourth arm; (*d*) *Ven:* **q. tête,** fourth head (of antlers); stag with its fourth head. **2.** *s.m.* fourth (drink, cake, etc.). **3.** *s.f.* (*a*) sequence of four (in card games); (*at piquet*) quart; **q. majeure,** quart major; (*b*) *Sch:* (i) **(classe de) q.,** approx. third form (of grammar school); (ii) the third-form classroom.
quatrièmement [katrijɛm(ə)mɑ̃], *adv.* fourthly; in the fourth place.
quatriennal [katrijɛn(n)al], *a.* = QUADRIENNAL.
quatrillion [k(w)atriljɔ̃], *s.m.* **1.** (*since* 1948) quadrillion (10^{24}); *U.S:* septillion. **2.** (*before* 1948) a thousand billion(s) (10^{15}); *U.S:* quadrillion.
quattrocentiste [kwatrotʃɛntist], *s.m. Art: Lit:* quattrocentist.
quattrocento [kwatrotʃɛnto], *s.m. Art: Lit:* quattrocento.
quatuor [kwatɥɔːr], *s.m. Mus:* quartet(te), quatuor; **q. à cordes,** string quartet.
quayage [kejaːʒ], *s.m.* quayage, wharfage.
que¹ [k(ə)], *rel.pron.m. & f., sg. & pl.* (*of pers.*) that, whom; (*of thg*) that, which; (*in the neut.*) which, what; (*in Engl. ellipsis of the relative is frequent.*) **1.** (*subject*) *A: still found in the phrs.* **advienne que pourra, advienne qu'advienne,** come what may; **faites ce que bon vous semble,** do as you think fit. **2. il mourut en brave soldat qu'il était,** he died like the gallant soldier he was; he died as became a gallant soldier; **pauvre malheureux que je suis!** poor wretch that I am! **menteur que tu es!** you liar! **de radical qu'il était, il devint socialiste,** from being a radical, he turned socialist; **couvert qu'il était de poussière il ne voulait pas entrer,** covered with dust as he was he didn't want to come in; **purs mensonges que tout cela!** that's all a pack of lies! **(c'est un) drôle de garçon que Pierre,** (he's) a queer fish, is Peter; **c'est une belle maison que la vôtre, que la sienne,** yours, his, is a fine house; **c'est chose dangereuse que de critiquer,** to criticize is a dangerous thing; **ce serait se tromper que de croire que . . .,** it would be a mistake to believe that . . .; *P:* **c'est moi que je vous ramène,** I'll see you home; **mais je suis là que je bavarde!** but I'm standing here talking! *P:* **c'est moi que je suis le chef!** I'm the boss! *Lit:* **du temps que les bêtes parlaient,** at the time when animals could speak. **3.** (*object*) (*a*) (*introducing a defining clause in the ind.*) **l'homme que vous voyez,** the man whom, that, you see; **montrez-moi les livres que vous avez achetés,** show me the books you have bought; **c'est un homme que personne ne respecte,** he is a man whom no one respects; *A:* **voici un homme que je crois qui pourra vous aider,** here is a man who I think can help you; *P:* **le garçon que je sors avec,** the boy I'm going out with; (*b*) (*introducing a defining clause in the sub.*) **c'est le seul de ses romans que je lise avec plaisir,** it is the only novel of his that I read with pleasure; **c'est le meilleur que nous ayons,** it is the very best we have; **il n'est venu personne que je sache,** no one has come that I know of; **c'est un des meilleurs dîners que j'aie faits,** it is one of the best dinners I have ever had; **une demi-heure de grammaire est le maximum qu'un enfant puisse supporter,** half an hour of grammar is as much as a child can stand; (*c*) (*introducing a continuative clause, usu. in the ind.*) **une petite maison des faubourgs, que personne ne connaissait,** a little suburban house that nobody knew; (*d*) (*in the construction* **c'est . . . que . . .**); **c'est vous que j'ai vu hier?** was it you I saw yesterday? **c'est la plus âgée que nous préférons,** we like the eldest best; (*e*) *P:* **quoi qu'il a dit?** what did he say? *s.a.* QUOI² 1. **4.** (*adv. use*) (*a*) **pendant (les) dix mois qu'il languit encore,** during the ten months that he continued to languish; **les années qu'il avait langui en prison,** the years during which he had languished in prison; **les jours qu'il fait chaud,** on (the) days when it is warm; **un jour que j'étais de service,** one day when I was on duty; **du temps que les automobiles n'existaient pas,** before cars existed; **ce n'est plus la peine, depuis le temps que nous attendons,** it isn't worth while now that we have waited so long; **depuis trois mois que j'habite Paris,** for the three months I have been living in Paris; **les trois ans que j'ai habité à Paris,** the three years (during which) I lived in Paris; **je regrette les cinquante francs que ce livre m'a coûté,** I wish I had the fifty francs this book cost me; **je le ferai coûte que coûte,** I shall do it cost what it may; **je l'achète, vaille que vaille,** I will buy it whether it's worth the money or not; *A:* (= **où**) **en l'état qu'elle est,** in the state in which she is; (*b*) *P:* **où que vous allez?** where are you going? **d'où que tu sors?** where have you sprung from? **combien que vous l'avez vendu?** what did you sell it for? **5. ce que.** *See* CE¹ 3.
que², *interr.pron.neut.* what? **1.** (*object*) (*a*) **que voulez-vous?** what do you want? **que voulez-vous que j'y fasse?** how can I help it? **que dit Jean?** what does John say? what is John saying? **qu'a répondu Pierre?** what did Peter reply? **qu'y a-t-il à voir dans cette ville?** what is there to be seen in this town? **que faire?** what can I, we, one, do? what's to be done? **que dire?** what could I say? what am I to say? **que penser?** what am I to think? what was I to think? **il ne savait que dire, que penser, que faire,** he didn't know what to say, what to think, what to do; **dites-moi que faire,** tell me what to do; **je n'ai que faire de vos souhaits,** I don't want your good wishes; *Lit:* **vous n'aviez que faire de parler,** you had no business to speak; (*b*) (= LEQUEL) **que prendrez-vous, du lait ou de la crème?** which will you take, milk or cream? **2.** (*a*) (*logical subject*) **qu'est-il arrivé? que s'est-il passé?** what has happened? **que lui est-il donc arrivé?** what ever has happened to him? (*b*) **qu'êtes-vous?** what are you? **qu'est-ce** [kɛːs]? what is it? **nous étions ruinés; que devenir?** we were ruined; what was to become of us? *s.a.* QU'EST-CE QUE, QU'EST-CE QUI. **3.** (*adv. use*) (*a*) (= POURQUOI) **que ne le disiez-vous?** why didn't you say so? (*b*) (*exclamatory*) (i) (= COMME) **qu'il est beau!** how handsome he is! **que c'est bien vrai!** how true! **que je n'aimerais pas ça!** how I should hate that! **que je voudrais vous expliquer les dangers que vous courez!** how I should like to explain to you the dangers you are running! *Lit:* **qu'avec plaisir je vous revois!** with what pleasure I behold you again! (ii) (= COMBIEN) **que de déceptions!** how many disappointments! **que de gens!** what a lot of people! (iii) (= A QUOI) *Lit:* **que vous profite cette dignité?** what use is this high position to you?
que³, *conj.* that; but (that); lest; (*in Engl. ellipsis of "that" is frequent*); **1.** (*introducing a subordinate clause or its equivalent*) **il me dit que c'était vrai,** he told me (that) it was true; **je vois qu'il me trompe,** I see (that) he is deceiving me; **je ne doute pas qu'il (ne) consente,** I have no doubt he will consent; **je désire qu'il vienne,** I want him to come; **la peur qu'on ne découvrît sa retraite,** his fear lest his retreat should be discovered; **il serait étrange qu'on le fît,** it would be strange if that were done; **qu'il soit toujours en retard, je ne me l'explique pas,** why he should always be late I just don't understand; **je pense que non,** I think not. **2.** (*a*) (*imperative or optative*) **qu'elle entre!** let her come in! **Dieu dit: que la lumière soit,** God said, Let there be light; **que Dieu lui pardonne! que Dieu lui fasse grâce!** may God forgive him! **que le bon Dieu vous bénisse!** God bless you! **que je vous y reprenne!** just let me catch you at it again! (*b*) (*hypothetical*) **que la machine vienne à s'arrêter et il y aura un accident,** let the machine stop and there will be an accident; (*c*) (i) **(soit) que . . . ou (soit) que; qu'il pleuve ou qu'il fasse du vent,** whether it rains or blows; (ii) **que . . . ou non; que tu le veuilles ou non,** whether you wish it or not. **3.** (*a*) *linking up two verbs in the conditional,* **ces questions, nous ne les poserions pas qu'elles se poseraient d'elles-mêmes,** if we did not ask these questions, they would crop up of themselves; **il l'affirmerait que je ne le croirais pas,** even if he said it was true, I would not believe it; (*b*) **que . . . ne,** *after negative clause;* **il ne se passe jamais une année qu'il ne nous écrive,** a year never goes by without his writing to us. **4.** *for* **que** *in compound conj. phrases,* **afin que, attendu que, avant que, bien que, depuis que, pourvu que, etc.,** *see under these words.* **5.** (*a*) *equivalent to* **afin que, alors que, avant que, depuis que, puisque, sans que, tant que, etc.; approchez qu'on vous entende,** come nearer so that we can hear you; **approchez que je vous parle,** come nearer and let me speak to you; **il ne s'était pas écoulé deux secondes que j'entendis un coup de feu,** two seconds had not elapsed when I heard a shot; **je ne le quitterai pas que l'affaire ne soit terminée,** I will not leave him till the matter is concluded; **il y a trois jours que je ne l'ai vu,** it is three days since I saw him, I haven't seen him for three days; **vous n'aviez donc pas entendu, que vous ne disiez rien?** you didn't hear then, since you said nothing? **ne partez pas que je ne vous aie parlé,** don't go before I have had a talk with you; *F:* **il y en avait, qu'on ne savait qu'en faire,** there was such a lot that we didn't know what to do with them; (*b*) *A: equivalent to* **tel que, etc.; je suis dans une colère que je ne me sens pas,** I am too angry for words. **6.** *to avoid repetition of conj.* **parce que vous êtes bon et que vous êtes juste,** because you are good and because you are just; **quand il entrera et qu'il vous trouvera ici,** when he comes in and finds you here; **quoiqu'il pleuve et qu'il fasse froid,** although it is rainy and cold; **comme il avait soif et que le vin était bon,** as he was thirsty and the wine was good; **si on vient et qu'on veuille me consulter,** if anyone comes and wants to consult me. **7. à ce que, de ce que,** *introducing a noun clause when the head verb takes a complement with* **à** *or* **de; je ne m'attendais pas à ce qu'on entrât,** I did not expect anyone to come in; **on s'alarmait de ce qu'il ne reparaissait pas,** alarm was felt at his failure to appear again; **de ce que je ne dis rien il ne faut pas conclure que je ne vois rien,** just because I say nothing it does not follow that I see nothing. **8.** (*in comparison*) (*a*) **aussi grand que moi,** as tall as I (am); **plus fort que son frère,** stronger than his brother; **moins fort que vous,** not so strong as you; **tout autre que moi,** anyone but me; **j'ai un autre parapluie que celui-là,** I have another umbrella besides that one; **il vaut mieux se taire que de mentir,** it is better to say nothing than to tell a lie; **vous écrivez plus correctement que vous (ne) parlez,** you write more correctly than you speak; **je ne suis pas si bête que de le faire,** I am not so stupid as to do it; **il habite la même maison que moi,** he lives in the same house as I do; (*b*) (*with haplology*) **je ne demande pas mieux que (= que que) cela soit,** I ask for nothing better than that it should be so; **si cet enfant est à elle, quoi de plus simple qu'elle le reprenne?** if the child is hers, what could be simpler than for her to take him back? **9.** (*a*) **ne . . . que,** only; **il n'est que blessé,** he is only wounded; **il n'a qu'une jambe,** he has only one leg; **on ne vit qu'à Paris,** it is only in Paris that one really lives; **on ne m'a donné que des conseils,** all I got was advice; **il ne fait qu'entrer et sortir,** he does nothing but go in and out; **il n'a fait qu'entrer**

et sortir, he just slipped, *F:* popped, in and out again; **je n'ai fait que le toucher,** I only touched it; **il n'y a que le colonel qui puisse donner des ordres,** only the colonel can give orders; **il n'y a que lui qui le sache,** he is the only one who knows about it; no one else but he knows about it; **il n'y a que la reliure d'abîmée,** only the binding is damaged; **je ne sais que vous capable de l'entreprendre,** I don't know any one but you that is fit to undertake it; **je ne le ferai que si on me le dit,** I won't do it unless I'm told to, I'll do it only if I'm told to; **il ne fait que de sortir,** he has only just gone out; **il ne viendra qu'après le dîner,** he will not come until after dinner; **ce ne fut qu'en 1880 qu'il commença,** he did not begin until 1880; **je n'ai pu le faire qu'à la hâte,** I could only do it in a hurry; **je n'en ai que trop,** I have all too many; **il n'est arrivé que trop vite,** he came all too soon; **il n'y a qu'à se soumettre,** there is nothing for it but to submit; **il n'y avait que lui à ne pas paraître ému,** he was the only person to appear unmoved; **il n'est que de faire preuve d'énergie,** we, you, need only show energy; *F:* **si je connais Teissier? mais je ne connais que lui!** do I know Teissier? why, there's no-one I know better! (*with ne under-stood*) **il me faudrait un million de francs—que cela!** I should require a million francs—is that all (= only that)? **c'est vrai, n'est-ce pas?—que trop vrai,** it's true, isn't it?—only too true; (*b*) **sans . . . que; j'étais sans ami que mon chien,** I had no friend but my dog; I had only my dog for a friend; (*c*) (*with haplology of* **ne**) **ne . . . pas que,** not only; **il n'y a pas que lui qui le sache,** he is not the only one who knows it; **il n'y avait pas que les esclaves qui fussent opprimés,** not only the slaves were oppressed; **l'homme ne vit pas que de pain,** man does not live by bread alone; **elle est très jolie—il n'y a pas que la beauté,** she is very pretty—beauty isn't everything; (*d*) **ne . . . plus, jamais, guère, que; il ne me reste plus que vingt francs,** I have only twenty francs left; **il n'y avait plus qu'à mourir,** there was nothing left but to die; there was nothing for it but to die; **plus que dix minutes!** only ten minutes left! **je ne bois jamais que de l'eau,** I never drink anything but water; **ce mot n'est guère usité qu'à Lyon,** the word is hardly used except in Lyons; (*e*) **ne . . . pas plus tôt . . . que, à peine . . . que; il n'eut pas plus tôt paru qu'on l'assaillit de questions,** no sooner had he appeared, did he appear, than questions were showered upon him; **à peine était-il rentré que le téléphone retentit,** he had scarcely come in when the telephone bell rang. **10.** (*in imitation of Latin*) *Lit:* **que si,** if; **que si vous savez la vérité, il est de votre devoir de la révéler,** if you know the truth, it is your duty to reveal it. **11.** (*a*) *F:* **ah! que non! que si! que oui!** ah! surely not! surely yes! **que non pas!** not at all! (*b*) *P:* **"Allez-vous-en," que je lui dis,** "get out!" says I to him; **"Pas du tout," qu'il dit,** "By no means," says he; **pourquoi que vous n'avez rien dit?** why didn't you say anything? **il va au cercle—qu'il dit!** he goes to the club—so he says! (*c*) (*intensive*) *F:* **ton chapeau est dans un état, que c'est une horreur!** your hat is in a terrible state! **on nous a régalé que rien n'y manquait,** we were given a slap-up feed.

qué [ke], *interr.pron. Dial. & P:* (= QUOI² 1 (*f*)) **qué qu'i'dit?** what does he say? **qué, c'est toi!** why, it's you!

Québec [kebɛk], *Pr.n.m. Geog:* Quebec; **le Q.,** Quebec Province.

québecois, -oise [kebɛkwa, -waːz], *a. & s. Geog:* Quebecer; (native, inhabitant) of Quebec.

québrachite [kebraʃit, -kit], *s.f. Ch:* quebrachitol.

quebracho [kebratʃo], *s.m.*, **quebraco** [kebrako], *s.m. Bot:* quebracho.

quèche [kɛʃ], *s.f. Nau:* ketch.

quechua [ketʃwa], *s.m. Ling:* Quechua.

quel, quelle [kɛl], *a. & pron.* what, which. **1.** (*correlative*) (*a*) **q. que soit le résultat, je le ferai,** whatever the result may be, I will do it; **quelle que soit mon affection pour vous, je ne peux pas faire l'impossible,** however great my affection for you, much as I love you, I cannot achieve the impossible; **quels que soient ces hommes . . .,** whoever these men may be . . .; **q. que soit l'endroit où,** wherever, no matter where; **quelle que soit la façon dont,** no matter how; in whatever way; (*b*) (*occ.* = **quelque . . . que**) **sous quelle forme que ce soit,** under whatever form; **à quelle époque que ce soit,** at whatever time; (*c*) **voilà en quels termes il me parla,** that is the way he spoke to me; **mettez-moi à n'importe quelle table,** put me at any table you like; (*d*) **tel q.** *See* TEL 2. **2.** (*interrogative*) (*a*) **quelle réponse a-t-il faite?** what reply did he make? **quelle heure est-il?** what is the time? what time is it? **dites-moi quelle heure il est,** tell me the time; **q. livre avez-vous pris?** what, which, whose, book did you take? **quelles mains ont fait cela?** by whose hands was it done? **avec q. argent?** with whose money? **de quelle couleur est votre chapeau?** what colour is your hat? **q. homme?** which man? **q. genre d'homme est-ce?** *A:* **q. homme est-ce?** what sort, manner, of man is he? **q. est cet arbre?** what sort of tree is this? **en q. lieu le trouver?** where shall we find it? *F:* **quelle mouche vous a piqué?** what's bitten you? **q. mal y a-t-il?** what's wrong with (doing) this? what harm is there in it? **en q. honneur?** why should I? **de q. droit?** what right has he, have you? **je ne sais q. auteur a dit . . .,** some author or other has said . . .; **on ne sait q. sera la vainqueur,** there is no knowing who will be the winner; **je sais quelle lettre vous attendez,** I know what letter you are expecting; **Dieu sait quelles choses il va s'imaginer!** God knows what he will imagine! (*b*) **quels sont ces messieurs?** who are these gentlemen? **quelle est la longueur, la largeur, de la pièce?** how long, wide, is the room? *A:* **voilà quelle je suis et quelle je veux être,** behold me as I am, and as I wish to be; (*c*) (*subject*) **de ces deux projets q. est le plus sûr?** of these two plans which is the safer? **3.** (*exclamatory*) **q. homme!** what a man! **quelle bonté!** how kind! **quelle ne fut pas sa surprise lorsque . . .!** you can imagine his surprise when . . .; *F:* **quelle horreur!** how shocking! *A. & Lit:* **quelle audace est la vôtre!** what audacity on your part!

quelconque [kɛlkɔ̃ːk], *a.* **1.** any (whatever); **décrire un cercle passant par trois points quelconques,** to describe a circle passing through any three points; **les proportions des éléments sont absolument quelconques,** the elements may be in any proportions; **entrer par l'une q. des portes,** to enter by one or other of the doors. **2.** **un q. général X,** some general X or other; **l'auto s'arrêta devant un q. pavillon japonais,** the car stopped in front of a vaguely Japanese pavilion; **répondre d'une façon q.,** to make some sort of reply; **causer de choses quelconques,** to chat on indifferent topics. **3.** *F:* (*a*) **c'est un homme très q.,** he is a very ordinary, commonplace, kind of man; **on ne peut pas lui donner un emploi q.,** we can't give him an ordinary job, *F:* any old job; **prenez un chapeau q.!** take any old hat! *F:* **son travail est q.,** his work isn't up to much; (*b*) *s.m. A:* **le q. des vêtements qu'il portait,** the want of any distinction in his dress.

quelea [kelea], *s.m. Orn:* quelea.

quellement [kɛlmɑ̃], *adv. A: used only in the phr.* **tellement q.,** after a fashion, tolerably well.

quelque [kɛlk(ə)]. **1.** *a.* (*a*) some, any; **il arrivera q. jour,** he will arrive some day; **adressez-vous à q. autre,** apply to someone else; **avez-vous q. ami qui puisse vous aider?** have you any friend who can help you? **n'avez-vous pas q. ami qui puisse vous aider?** haven't you some friend who can help you? (*b*) some, some little, a few; **pendant q. temps,** for some time, for a brief period; **il y a quelques jours,** a few days ago, some days ago; **il y a q. courage à faire cela,** it needs some (little) pluck to do that; **je ressentais q. inquiétude,** I felt some slight uneasiness; **leurs quelques minutes d'entretien,** their few minutes of conversation; **ses quelques cents francs de retraite de l'État,** his few hundred francs of State pension; **ces quelques mille francs qu'il m'a prêtés,** those few thousand francs he lent me; (cp. 2 (*a*)); **quelques centaines de mètres,** a few hundred metres; **cent et quelques mètres,** a hundred metres plus; **vingt francs et q.,** twenty francs odd; **nous étions quarante et quelques,** there were rather more than forty of us; **deux cents et q.,** two hundred and something; two hundred odd; (*c*) (*correlative to* **qui, que** + *sub.*) **quelque . . . qui, que,** whatever, whatsoever; **q. ambition qui l'agite,** whatever ambition moves him; **q. chose qu'il vous ait dite,** whatever (thing) he said to you (cp. QUELQUE CHOSE); **quelques fautes qu'il ait commises,** whatever faults he has committed; **sous q. prétexte que ce soit,** under any pretext whatever; **tout traité de q. nature qu'il soit,** every treaty of whatsoever character; **de q. côté que vous regardiez . . .,** look which way you will . . .. **2.** *adv.* (*a*) some, about; **q. dix ans,** some, about, ten years; **les quelque mille francs qu'il m'a prêtés,** the thousand francs or so, or thereabouts, that he lent me; (cp. 1 (*b*)); *see* PEU 1, QUELQUE PART; (*b*) (correlative to *que* + *sub.*); **quelque . . . que,** however; **q. grandes que soient ses fautes,** however great his faults may be; **q. amoureuse qu'elle fût,** however much in love she was; (*intensive*) *F:* **q. méchant qu'il fût, il ne voulut pas consentir à cette combinaison,** wicked as he was, he would not agree to this plan.

quelque chose [kɛlkəʃoːz], *indef.pron.m.inv.* something, anything; **q. c. me dit qu'il viendra,** something tells me he will come; **avez-vous q. c. à dire?** have you anything to say? **s'il a q. c. à dire, qu'il le dise,** if he has anything to say, anything to tell, let him say it, let him speak out; **vous a-t-il dit q. c.?** did he tell you anything? **je pense à q. c. qu'on m'a dit,** I am thinking of something I was told; (cp. QUELQUE 1 (*c*)); **voilà un tableau qui dit q. c.!** that's a picture that has some appeal, *F:* that's got something; **son nom me dit q. c.,** his name rings a bell; **q. c. de nouveau, d'autre, de ridicule,** something new, something else, something ridiculous; *F:* **il a q. c.,** there's something the matter with him; **il y a q. c.,** there's something up, something afoot, something the matter; **il y est pour q. c.,** he has (had) something to do with it, he has a hand in it; **il a q. c. à la gorge,** there's something wrong with his throat, something the matter with his throat; **cela m'a fait q. c.,** I felt it a good deal; **ça te ferait vraiment q. c. si je m'en allais?** would you really mind if I went away? **ça, c'est q. c.!** that's really something! **allons prendre q. c.,** let's have a drink; *Mil: etc: F:* **prendre q. c.,** to take, get, a bashing; **je vais prendre q. c.,** I shall catch it; *P:* **vous y travaillerez q. c. comme deux ans,** you'll be at it for about two years; *s.m. F:* **il lui manque un petit q. c.,** he's slightly lacking somewhere.

quelquefois [kɛlkəfwa], *adv.* (*a*) sometimes, now and then; (*b*) *F:* in case; **q. qu'il serait arrivé,** in case he'd arrived.

quelque part [kɛlkəpaːr], *adv.* **1.** somewhere; **je suis sûr qu'il se cache q. p.,** I am sure he is hiding somewhere; **cela doit bien venir de q. p.,** it must come from somewhere; *F:* **aller q. p.,** to disappear for a moment; to go to the loo; *F:* **donner à qn un coup de pied q. p.,** to give s.o. a kick in the pants; *P:* **les ordres du patron, moi je me les mets q. p.,** I don't give a bloody damn about the boss's orders. **2.** (*correlative to* **que** + *sub.*) **q. p. qu'il fouillât, rien de suspect,** wherever he rummaged, he found nothing suspicious.

quelqu'un, quelqu'une [kɛlkœ̃, kɛlkyn]; *pl.* **quelques-uns, -unes** [kɛlkəzœ̃, -yn], *indef. pron.* **1.** *m. & f.* (*A: in sg.*) one (or other); **vous le trouverez surement dans q. des autres magasins de la ville,** you are sure to find it in one of the other shops in the town; **le mot est inconnu dans cette province; il s'emploie peut-être dans quelqu'une des autres,** the word is unknown in this province; it is perhaps used in one of the others; **quelqu'une de ces dames va s'en occuper,** one of the ladies will see to it; **quelques-uns des magasins,** some of the shops; **nous sommes restés quelques-uns, restées quelques-unes, à parler,** a few of us remained to chat; **j'ai lu quelques-unes des lettres,** I have read a few of the letters; **cela arrivera q. de ces jours,** it will happen one of these days; **quelques-un(e)s d'entre nous,** a few of us. **2.** (*a*) *m.* someone, somebody; anyone, anybody; **q. me l'a dit,** someone told me so; **est-il venu q.?** has anybody come? **si q. vient,** if anybody comes; *Com:* **quelqu'un!** shop! *F:* **y a q.!** (the place, *esp.* the w.c., is) engaged! **il est venu une dame, q. d'assez âgé,** a lady called, someone elderly; **q. de plus,** some one extra; **q. de trop,** one too many; **adressez-vous à q. d'autre,** apply to someone else; **y a-t-il eu q. de blessé?** was anyone wounded, injured? **il me faut q. d'assez fort pour . . .,** I want someone strong enough to . . .; **elle lui rappelait q. de déjà vu,** she reminded him of someone she had seen before; *F:* **elle se croit déjà q.,** she thinks she is somebody already; **est-il q.?** is he anybody? **ils sont q. dans leur village,** they are somebodies in their own village; *P:* **c'est q., ça alors!** (i) that's something (extraordinary)! (ii) that's a damn nuisance! (*b*) **c'est q. ou quelqu'une?** is it a man or a woman, *F:* male or female?

quémander [kemɑ̃de]. **1.** *v.i.* to beg (from door to door). **2.** *v.tr.* **q. qch. à qn,** to beg for, solicit, sth. from s.o.

quémanderie [kemɑ̃dri], *s.f. O:* begging; solicitation; cadging (for sth.); sponging; **ce sont des quémanderies sans fin,** he is eternally asking for something, always pestering me for something.

quémandeur, -euse [kemɑ̃dœːr, -øːz], *s.* beggar; cadger; sponger; **je déteste les quémandeurs de places, d'emplois,** I hate people who are just on the lookout for a cushy, soft, job.

quenaupe [k(ə)no:p], *s.f. Mil: P: A:* pipe.
quench [kwenʃ], *s.m. Petroleum Ind:* quenching.
qu'en-dira-t-on (le) [ləkɑ̃diratɔ̃], *s.m.inv.* what people will say; gossip, tittle-tattle; **se moquer du, des, qu'en-dira-t-on,** not to care what people say.
quenelle [kənɛl], *s.f. Cu:* quenelle.
quenotte [kənɔt], *s.f. F:* (*in nursery language*) tooth, toothy-peg.
quenouille [kənu:j], *s.f.* **1.** distaff; **royaume qui tombe en q.,** kingdom that falls to the distaff (side). **2.** (*a*) bedpost (of four-poster bed); (*b*) *Arb:* quenouille-trained fruit tree; (*c*) *Metall:* stopper rod (of casting ladle); **tampon de q.,** stopper end. **3.** *Bot:* cat's tail, reed mace, bulrush; *Agr:* **quenouilles de maïs,** stem of maize.
quenouillée [kənuje], *s.f. Tex:* amount of wool on a distaff.
quenouillère [kənujɛ:r], *s.f. Metall:* stopper rod (of casting ladle).
quenouillette [kənujɛt], *s.f.* **1.** *A:* small distaff. **2.** *N.Arch:* stern timber. **3.** *Nau:* **q. de cap-de-mouton,** sheer pole; **q. de trélingage,** futtock staff. **4.** = QUENOUILLE 2 (*c*).
quenouillon [kənujɔ̃], *s.m. Nau:* hank or tow (for caulking).
quensélite [kɑ̃selit], *s.f. Miner:* quenselite.
quenstedtite [kɑ̃stetit], *s.f. Miner:* quenstedtite.
quérable [kerabl̩], *a.* (rent, allowance) that must be applied for or called for in person; *Ins:* **primes quérables,** premiums collected by the Company's servants.
quercétine [kɛrsetin], *s.f. Ch:* quercetin, quercitin.
quercinois, -oise [kɛrsinwa, -wa:z], *a. & s. Geog:* (native, inhabitant) of the Quercy region; *s.m. Ling:* Quercy dialect.
quercite [kɛrsit], **quercitol** [kɛrsitɔl], *s.m. Ch:* quercitol.
quercitrin [kɛrsitrɛ̃], *s.m.*, **quercitrine** [kɛrsitrin], *s.f. Ch:* quercitrin.
quercitron [kɛrsitrɔ̃], *s.m. Bot:* quercitron (oak); black oak, dyer's oak.
Quercy [kɛrsi], *Pr.n.m. Geog:* (the) Quercy (region).
querelle [kərɛl], *s.f.* **1.** quarrel, dispute; difference, altercation; *F:* row, wrangle; **faire (une) q. à qn,** to pick a quarrel with s.o.; **chercher q. à qn,** to try to pick a quarrel with s.o.; **se prendre de q. avec qn,** to begin to quarrel with s.o.; to fall foul of s.o.; **avoir une q. avec qn,** to have a quarrel, an altercation, a row, with s.o.; **prendre part à une q.,** to join in a quarrel, *Jur:* to become a party in a dispute; **être en q. avec qn,** to be at variance, at loggerheads, with s.o.; **q. d'Allemand, mauvaise q.,** trumped-up quarrel, forced quarrel; **querelles de famille,** family squabbles; **q. d'amoureux,** lovers' tiff; **q. d'ivrognes,** drunken brawl; **soulever des querelles de préséance,** to quarrel about precedence. **2.** feud; **familles en q. ouverte,** families in open feud; **épouser, embrasser, la q. de qn,** to take up s.o.'s quarrel, s.o.'s cause; **prendre q. pour qn,** to take up the cudgels for s.o.
quereller [kərɛle], *v.tr.* **q. qn,** to quarrel with s.o.; **femme qui querelle son mari,** wife who nags her husband; **aimer à q.,** to be fond of quarrelling, of wrangling, of bickering.
se quereller, to quarrel, wrangle; to have words, to fall out (**avec,** with); to have a tiff; **se q. sur des riens,** to quarrel over trifles; **faire q. les gens,** to set people at variance, at loggerheads.
querelleur, -euse [kərɛlœ:r, -ø:z]. **1.** *s.* quarreller, wrangler. **2.** *a.* quarrelsome (person); **une (femme) querelleuse,** a shrew, a nagger, a scold.
quérimonie [kerimɔni], *s.f. Ecc:* querimony.
quérir [keri:r], *v.tr. used only in the infinitive after the verbs* **aller, venir, envoyer; aller q. qn, qch.,** to go and fetch s.o., sth. (*esp.* the police); to go for s.o., sth.; **envoyer q. main forte,** to send for the police.
quernage [kɛrna:ʒ], *s.m. Min:* (*a*) slate splitting; (*b*) **plan de q.,** rift plane, cleavage plane.
querner [kɛrne], *v.tr. Min:* to split (slate).
querneur [kɛrnœ:r], *s.m. Min:* slate splitter.
quernon [kɛrnɔ̃], *s.m.* grain surface (of block of slate).
quernure [kɛrny:r], *s.f.* line of cleavage (of slate).
querre [kɛ:r], *v.tr. A:* = QUÉRIR.
quérulence [kerylɑ̃:s], *s.f. Psy:* paranoia quaerula.
quérulent [kerylɑ̃], *a. & s. Psy:* querulent.
qu'es-aco, -aquo [kɛzako], *adv.phr. Dial:* (*S. of Fr.*) what's this? what's the matter?
quésiteur [kezitœ:r], *s.m. A.Jur:* examining magistrate.
qu'est-ce que [kɛskə], *interr.pron.* what? (*a*) (*object*) **qu'est-ce que vous voulez?** what do you want? (*b*) **qu'est-ce que la grammaire?** what is grammar? *F:* **qu'est-ce que c'est que cet homme-là!** what on earth is that man! **qu'est-ce que c'est que ça?** what's that? **qu'est-ce que tout cela qu'un avertissement?** what's all that but a warning? (*c*) *P:* (= COMBIEN) **qu'est-ce que vous êtes de personnes ici?** how many are there of you here? **qu'est-ce qu'il fait beau!** how fine it is! **qu'est-ce qu'on rigole!** what a laugh! (*d*) *F:* (= POURQUOI) **qu'est-ce que tu avais besoin d'aller lui dire ça?** why did you have to go and say that to him?
qu'est-ce qui [kɛski], *interr.pron.* (*used as subject*) **1.** what? **qu'est-ce qui est arrivé?** what has happened? **2.** *F:* (= QUI EST-CE QUI) who? **qu'est-ce qui est là?** who's there? **3.** (*in indirect questions*) *F:* (*a*) (= **ce qui**) **je vous demande un peu qu'est-ce qui lui prend!** what's taken him, I ask you! (*b*)(= QUI) **je ne savais pas qu'est-ce qui était là,** I didn't know who was there.
questeau, -eaux [kɛsto], *s.m. A:* silver, jewellery, box.
questeur [kɥɛstœ:r], *s.m.* (*a*) *Rom.Hist:* quaestor; (*b*) *Fr.Adm:* (*any one of the treasurers of the parliamentary assemblies*) questor.
question [kɛstjɔ̃], *s.f.* **1.** (*a*) question, query; (*computers*) **q. codée,** coded question; **faire, poser, adresser, une q. à qn,** to put a question to s.o.; to ask s.o. a question; to ask a question of s.o.; **presser qn de questions,** to press, ply, s.o. with questions; *Sch:* **questions à choix multiples,** multiple-choice questions; **son adhésion ne fait pas q.,** there is no doubt, no question, of his adherence; his adherence is beyond question; **mettre qch. en q.,** to question sth.; to challenge (statement, s.o.'s honour); to cavil at sth.; **remettre une affaire en q.,** to take up a matter again; **remettre en q. une décision,** to revise a decision; **les journaux mettent en q. l'avenir de l'alliance,** the papers are questioning whether the alliance will hold; **tout remettre en q.,** *F:* to put everything back into the melting-pot; **voici un point qui fait q.,** this is a debatable point; **il n'y a pas de q.,** there is no doubt about it; (*b*) question, matter, point, issue; **poser une q.,** to state a question, an issue; **la q. est mal posée,** the question is badly stated; **je voudrais vous consulter sur une q. d'affaires,** I wish to consult you on a matter of business; **questions d'actualité,** topics of the day; **c'est une q. de bon sens!** that's just common sense! **ce n'est qu'une q. d'argent,** it is simply a question of money; **il ne saurait être q. de les inviter,** we couldn't think of inviting them; **l'affaire, la personne, en q.,** the matter, the person, in question; **c'est une simple q. de temps,** it is simply a matter of time; **la q. d'argent vient toujours en premier,** money is always the first consideration; **il est fort q. d'amour dans ses essais,** a great deal is said about love, there is much about love, in his essays; *F:* **la q. alcoolisme,** the problem of alcoholism; *F:* **q. boulot, je me débrouille,** as far as work goes, I get on all right; **ce n'est pas là la q.,** that is not the point; **c'est là la q.,** that is the question; **sortir de la q.,** to wander from the point, from the subject; **rappeler qn à la q.,** to ask s.o. to keep to the question; to call s.o. to order; **de quoi est-il q.?** what is the question (in hand)? what is the matter? what is it all about? **il n'a jamais été q. de cela,** that was never contemplated; there was never any question of that; **il ne saurait être q., il est hors de q., pour nous de . . .,** it is quite out of the question for us to . . .; **qu'il n'en soit plus q.,** let us say no more about it; let the subject be closed, be dropped; **après le premier chapitre il n'est plus q. de lui,** after the first chapter no further mention is made of him; **il est q. de savoir s'il viendra,** the question is whether he will come; **il est q. de lui élever une statue,** there is some talk of raising a statue to him; **il est q. qu'il revienne cette année,** there is some talk of his returning this year; **il n'est pas q. qu'il revienne si promptement,** there is no question of his returning so soon; (*c*) *Jur:* (point at) issue; **q. de fait, de droit,** issue of fact, of law; *Rom.Jur:* **questions perpétuelles,** quaestiones; *s.a.* CONFIANCE, ORDRE 3, PRÉALABLE, PRÉJUDICIEL, SECONDAIRE 2. **2.** *Hist:* question; judicial torture; the rack; **appliquer la q. à qn, mettre qn à la q.,** *A:* **appliquer qn à la q.,** to put, submit, s.o. to the question, to the rack; to torture s.o.; *A:* **être soumis à la q.,** to be put to the question, to be tortured; **q. ordinaire,** the common question; **q. extraordinaire,** the question extraordinary.
questionnaire [kɛstjɔnɛ:r], *s.m.* **1.** list, set, of questions; questionnaire. **2.** *A:* torturer, executioner.
questionner [kɛstjɔne], *v.tr.* **1.** to question (s.o.). to ask (s.o.) questions. **2.** *A:* to torture (s.o.).
questionneur, -euse [kɛstjɔnœ:r, -ø:z], *a. & s.* (person) fond of, given to, asking questions; inquisitive (person); **c'est un éternel q.!** he's always, for ever, asking questions!
questorien, -ienne [kɥɛstɔrjɛ̃, -jɛn]. **1.** *a.* quaestorial. **2.** *s.m.* former quaestor.
questure [kɥɛsty:r], *s.f.* **1.** quaestorship. **2.** *Fr. Adm:* fiscal department (of the parliamentary assemblies).
quête[1] [kɛt], *s.f.* **1.** (*a*) quest, search; **se mettre en q. de qch., aller à la q. de qch.,** to set out, go, in search of sth.; **gens en q. de plaisirs,** pleasure seekers; **je ne suis pas en q. de compliments,** I'm not out, *F:* fishing, for compliments; **un journaliste en q. de copie fut témoin de l'accident,** a journalist looking for copy witnessed the accident; (*b*) *Ven:* (i) (*of men*) beating (for the game); (ii) (*of dogs*) tracking, scenting; quartering. **2.** *Ecc: etc:* collection; **faire la q.,** to take up the collection, take round the plate; (*in an emergency*) to pass the hat round.
quête[2], *s.f. N.Arch:* rake (of the stern post).
quêter [kete], *v.tr.* (*a*) to collect (alms, etc.); *abs.* to take up the collection; (*b*) to seek (for) (approval, praise, etc.); **q. des compliments,** to fish, angle, for compliments; (*c*) (*of dogs*) to seek game; *abs.* to quarter.
quêteur, -euse [kɛtœ:r, -ø:z], *s.* **1.** alms collector; *Ecc:* taker of the collection. **2. q. de compliments,** person who fishes for compliments. **3.** *Ven:* dog on the scent of game; **chien bon q.,** good tracking dog.
quêteux [kɛtø], *s.m. Fr.C:* beggar.
quetsche [kwɛtʃ], *s.f.* (*a*) *Hort:* quetsch(e) (plum); (*b*) *Dist:* quetsch.
quetschier [kwɛtʃje], *s.m. Hort:* quetsch plum tree.
quetzal [kwɛtzal], *s.m.* **1.** *Orn:* quetzal. **2.** *Num:* quetzal; *pl. quetzales.*
queue[1] [kø], *s.f.* **1.** *Z:* tail; **couper la q. à un cheval, à un agneau,** to dock a horse, a horse's tail; to tail a lamb; **cheval à longue q.,** long-tailed horse; **cheval à q. écourtée,** bobtail (horse); **q. à l'anglaise,** (horse's) nicked tail; **q. de renard,** fox's brush; **pigeon à q. de paon,** fantail (pigeon); **q. de rat,** rat tail; *Hairdr:* **q. de cheval,** pony tail; **q. de poisson,** (i) fish tail; (ii) *Aut: F:* tail wobble, wobbling (on greasy road); *Aut:* **faire une q. de poisson (à qn),** to cut in (on s.o.); *F:* (*of play, novel, etc.*) **finir en q. de poisson,** to fizzle out; **sans q.,** tailless; **à la q. gît le venin,** the sting is in the tail; **il s'en retourna la q. entre les jambes,** he went off with his tail between his legs; *F:* **pas la q. d'un, d'une,** not the slightest appearance of one; not a blessed one; *Astr:* **q. de dragon,** dragon's tail; **q. de Lion,** Denebola; *s.a.* BOULON, BRIDER 1, DIABLE 1, NUAGE. **2.** (*a*) tail (of comet, of kite, of a letter); trail (of meteor); stem (of crotchet or quaver); handle (of a pan); stalk (of fruit, flower); shank (of button); pin (of brooch); tailpiece (of violin); label, tongue (of document); train (of comet, of dress); end (of a piece of material); pigtail, queue (of hair); *Const:* tail; fang, tang, shank (of tool, knife); lug (of electric accumulator); rod, stem (of valve); stick (of stick bomb); tail planes (of aircraft); rudder, tail (of windmill); **avion sans q.,** tailless aircraft; **bouton à q.,** shanked button; **habit à q.,** (swallow-)tail coat; **piano à q.,** grand piano; *Nau:* **à q. lourde,** heavy by the stern; tail-heavy; *Typ:* **lettre à q. inférieure,** descending letter; **tranche de q.,** edge tail; *F:* **ajouter des queues aux zéros,** (i) to write "9" instead of "o"; (ii) to cook the books; *Petroleum Ind:* **q. de chargement,** boom; (*b*) *Carp:* = QUEUE-D'ARONDE 1; *Const:* **en q. de paon,** fan-shaped. **3.** (*a*) (tail) end, fag end (of a procession, of a class, of a political party, of a book, of winter, of a piece of business, etc.); tailings (of ore, grain, etc.); **être en q., former la q., du cortège,** to tail the procession; **venir en q. (du cortège),** to bring up the rear; *Turf:* **arriver en q.,** to come in at the tail end; **être à la q. de la classe,** to be at the bottom of the class; *Wine-m:* **vin de q.,** inferior wine (from the last of the grapes); *Dist: etc:* **produits de q.,** tailings; **une histoire sans q. ni tête,** a jumbled, disconnected story; a story that one cannot make head or tail of; **prendre une affaire par la tête et par la q.,** to take a matter in hand; *Rail:* **voiture en q. de train, en q. du train,** carriage at the back, in the rear, of the train; **wagon de q.,** end carriage; **groupe de q.,** rear portion; *Fish:* **q. de filet,** cod end; *Petroleum Ind:* **queues de distillation,** tails, bottoms; (*b*) *Mil:* rear (of army); **bataillon de q.,** rear battalion; **attaquer une armée en q.,** to attack

an army in the rear; *Navy:* **colonne de q.,** rear column; (*c*) *Cards:* bonus for winning the rubber. **4.** (*a*) queue, file (of people); **q. du pain, du beurre,** bread queue; butter queue; **faire (la) q.,** to form a queue; to stand in a line, in a queue; to queue up, line up, form up; **prendre la q., se mettre à la q.,** to get into the queue; **à la q.!** get in the queue! **à la q. leu leu,** (i) in a single file; (ii) helter skelter; *O:* **avoir qn en q.,** to have s.o. at one's heels; (*b*) *Fish:* **q. de madrague,** wall composed of (tunny) nets. **5.** *Bill:* (*a*) cue; **la grande q.,** the long butt; (*b*) **fausse q.,** miscue; **faire fausse q.,** to miscue. **6.** *Metall:* **q. de lion,** tilting lever.

queue[2], *s.f.* hone, whetstone; **q. à huile,** oil stone.

queue-d'aronde [kødarɔ̃:d], *s.f.* **1.** *Carp:* dovetail, fantail; **assemblage à q.-d'a.,** dovetailing; **q.-d'a. recouverte,** lapped dovetail; **à q.-d'a.,** dovetailed. **2.** *Bot: F:* arrowhead; *pl. queues-d'aronde.*

queue-de-carpe [kødkarp], *s.f. Tls:* iron cramp; *pl. queues-de-carpe.*

queue-de-chat [kødʃa], *s.f.* **1.** cat-o'-nine-tails. **2.** mare's tail, colt's tail (cloud); cirrus; *pl. queues-de-chat.*

queue-de-cheval [kødʃəval], *s.f.* **1.** *Anat:* cauda equina. **2.** *Bot:* shave grass, horse tail, scouring rush. **3.** *Hairdr:* pony tail. **4.** *Turkish Hist:* tail; *pl. queues-de-cheval.*

queue-de-cochon [kødkɔʃɔ̃], *s.f.* **1.** *Tls:* auger bit, gimlet. **2.** *Tex:* pigtail; *pl. queues-de-cochon.*

queue-de-lion [kødljɔ̃], *s.f. Bot:* leonurus, motherwort; *pl. queues-de-lion.*

queue-de-loup [kødlu], *s.f. Bot:* field cow-wheat, melampyrum; *pl. queues-de-loup.*

queue-de-morue [kødmɔry], *s.f.* **1. (habit à) q.-de-m,** swallow-tail coat, *F:* tails; **mettre sa q.-de-m.,** to wear tails. **2.** (painter's) flat brush. **3.** plank shaped like a fish's tail; *pl. queues-de-morue.*

queue-de-mouton [kødmutɔ̃], *s.f. Arch:* wreath-like ornament; *pl. queues-de-mouton.*

queue-de-paon [kødpɑ̃], *s.f. Arch:* fan-shaped ornament; *pl. queues-de-paon.*

queue-de-pie [kødpi], *s.f.* = QUEUE-DE-MORUE 1; *pl. queues-de-pie.*

queue-de-porc [kødpɔr], *s.f. Bot:* hog's fennel, sow's fennel; *pl. queues-de-porc.*

queue-de-rat [kødra], *s.f.* **1.** (birch-bark) snuff-box (with leather tail on lid). **2.** *Tls:* (*a*) rat tail, rat-tailed file; (*b*) reamer. **3.** small wax taper. **4.** *Nau:* pointed-up rope end; **faire une q.-de-r. à un cordage,** to point a rope. **5.** *Vet:* rat tail (of horse); *pl. queues-de-rat.*

queue-de-renard [kødrəna:r], *s.f.* **1.** *Bot:* (*a*) field cow-wheat; (*b*) love-lies-bleeding; (*c*) fox-tail (grass). **2.** *Tls:* firmer chisel; *pl. queues-de-renard.*

queue-de-scorpion [kødskɔrpjɔ̃], *s.f. Bot:* caterpillar, scorpion's tail; *pl. queues-de-scorpion.*

queue-de-souris [kødsuri], *s.f. Bot:* creeping cereus, rat's tail cactus; *pl. queues-de-souris.*

queue-de-vache [kødvaʃ]. **1.** *s.f. Const:* skirts, skirt roof; *pl. queues-de-vache.* **2.** *a.inv. F:* **cheveux q.-de-v.,** mousy hair; **couleur q.-de-v.,** brownish colour.

queue-de-vinaigre [kødvinɛ:gr], *s.f. Orn: F:* African waxbill; astrild; *pl. queues-de-vinaigre.*

queue-fourchue [køfurʃy], *s.f. Ent:* puss-moth; *pl. queues-fourchues.*

queue-rouge [køru:ʒ], *s.f.* jester; *pl. queues-rouges.*

queursage [kœrsa:ʒ], *s.m. Leath:* slating.

queurse [kœrs], *s.f. Leath:* slater.

queussi-queumi [køsikømi], *adv. Dial:* likewise.

queutage [køta:ʒ], *s.m. Bill: etc:* pushing; push (stroke).

queuter [køte], *v.i.* (*a*) *Bill: etc:* to push the ball; to play a push stroke; **coup queuté,** push stroke; (*b*) *P:* to miss.

queux[1] [kø], *s.f. A:* hone, whetstone.

queux[2], *s.m. A:* cook; *used only in* MAÎTRE-QUEUX; *Hist:* **grand q. de France,** Superintendent of the King's kitchens.

qui[1] [ki], *rel.pron.m. & f. sg. & pl.* **1.** (*subject*) (*of pers. or higher animal*) who, that; (*of thg*) which that; (*a*) (*introducing a defining clause in the ind.*) **homme, femme, qui sait le français, man,** woman who knows French; **phrases qui ne sont pas françaises,** sentences that are not French; **il y a beaucoup de gens qui savent cela,** there are many people who know that; **un romancier qui, me dit-on, est encore lu,** a novelist who I am told is still read; **je prendrai le premier qui se présentera,** I shall take the first who presents himself; **Notre Père qui es aux cieux,** our Father, who, which, art in heaven; (*b*) (*introducing a defining clause in the sub.*) **il me faut un livre qui traite de ces questions,** I want a book dealing with these questions; **il a pu m'échapper quelque chose qui ressemblât à une promesse,** I may have let fall something that sounded like a promise; **il y a peu de gens qui sachent cela,** there are few people who know that; **vous êtes le seul qui sachiez votre leçon,** you are the only one who knows his lesson; **qu'a-t-il accompli qui n'ait pas péri avec lui?** what did he accomplish that did not perish with him? **il n'y a personne qui ne comprenne cela,** there is no one who does not understand that; (*c*) (*introducing a continuative clause, usu. in the ind.*) **ils se rendirent à son bureau, qui n'était pas loin,** they went round to his office, which was not far away; **dans ce match, qui était son premier, l'équipe a fait preuve de . . .,** in this their first match, the team showed . . .; **je le vois qui vient,** I see him coming; **je l'entends qui approche,** I hear him coming; **je viens de le rencontrer qui traversait le boulevard,** I have just met him as he was crossing the boulevard; **j'ai le cœur qui m'étouffe,** I feel like choking; I can hardly breathe; **Mirabeau aurait fait mieux, (lui) qui voulait sauver la monarchie,** Mirabeau would have been more successful, anxious as he was to save the monarchy; **c'est un homme charmant, et qui a du talent,** he is a charming man, and talented; **c'est une simple farce, et qui est médiocre,** it's a mere farce and a poor one at that; (*d*) (*in the construction* **c'est . . . qui . . .**) **c'est la plus âgée qui a répondu,** it was the eldest who answered; **c'est vous qui me l'avez dit,** you told me so; **ce n'est pas lui qui a répondu,** it was not he who answered. **2.** (*a*) (= **celui qui,** *esp. in proverbs*) **qui vivra verra,** he who lives will see; **tout vient à point à qui sait attendre,** all things come to him who waits; **sauve qui peut,** every man for himself; **qui sème l'injustice récoltera le chagrin,** he that sows iniquity shall reap sorrow; **le fasse qui voudra,** let him do it who likes; **vienne qui voudra,** let them all come; *P:* **. . . comme qui dirait . . .,** . . . so to speak . . .; (*b*) *neut.pron.* (= **ce qui**) **qui plus est,** what is more; **qui pis est,** what is worse; **son pouls battait à 120, au lieu de 66, qui était son état normal,** his pulse was beating at 120, instead of 66, which was its normal state; **voilà qui me plaît,** this is what I like; (*c*) (*very usual in dictionary definitions*) **monarchique: qui appartient à la monarchie,** monarchical: pertaining to monarchy; **invendable: qui ne peut se vendre,** unsaleable: that cannot be sold; **affairé: qui a beaucoup à faire,** busy: who has much to do; (*d*) **ce qui.** *See* CE[1] 3. **3.** (*after prep., with pers. occ. with thg, as antecedent*) whom, *occ.* which; (*in Engl. there may be ellipsis of the relative*) (*a*) **voilà l'homme à qui je pensais, de qui je parlais,** there is the man of whom I was thinking, speaking; there is the man (whom) I was thinking about, speaking about; **il cherche quelqu'un avec qui jouer,** he is looking for some one to play with; **il n'y a personne à qui s'adresser,** there is nobody to apply to; **il a trouvé à qui parler,** he's met his match; **l'officier aux ordres de qui j'ai obéi,** the officer whose orders I obeyed; **le champ sur qui tombait la nuit,** the field on which night was falling; **le journal à qui j'emprunte ces faits,** the paper from which I take these facts; (*b*) (*without antecedent*) **qui aurait prédit ces événements, on l'aurait traité de fou,** if anyone had foretold these events, we should have said he was mad; **adressez-vous à qui vous voudrez,** apply to whom you please, to whoever you like, to anyone you like; **allez chercher qui vous savez,** go and fetch you know who(m). **4.** (*occ. object* = **celui que**) **il est bien gardé, qui Dieu garde,** he is well cared for, who is in the care of God. **5.** (*indefinite use*) some; **on se dispersa, qui d'un côté, qui d'un autre,** we scattered, some going one way, some another. **6.** (*correlative to* **que** + *sub.*) (*a*) **qui que,** who(so)ever, whom(so)-ever; **qui que vous soyez, parlez,** who ever you are, speak; **soyez poli envers qui que vous rencontriez,** be polite to whoever, anyone, you meet; **qui que ce soit qui vous ait dit cela . . .,** whoever told you that . . .; **qui que ce soit qui sonne, ne laissez pas entrer,** whoever rings, no matter who rings, don't admit him; (*b*) **qui que ce soit,** anyone (whatever); **je défie qui que ce soit de . . .,** I challenge anyone to . . .; **je n'ai trouvé qui que ce soit,** I found no one whatever; **il ne parlait à qui que ce fût,** he spoke to no one whatever; **je ne dois un centime à qui que ce soit,** I don't owe any man anything (whatever).

qui[2], *interr.pron.m.sg.* **1.** who? whom? (*a*) **qui a dit cela?** who said that? **savez-vous qui a dit cela?** do you know who said that? **qui désirez-vous voir?** whom do you wish to see? **dites-moi qui vous désirez voir,** tell me whom you wish to see; **qui vient à la réunion?** who is coming, who are coming, to the meeting? **devinez qui est arrivé le premier,** guess who was here first; **de qui parlez-vous?** of whom are you speaking? **à qui est ce canif?** whose is this knife? who owns this knife? whose knife is this? **de qui êtes-vous fils?** whose son are you? **pour qui est ce livre?** who is that book for? **qui trouver de plus pauvre que lui?** whom could you find poorer than he (is)? **qui d'autre?** who(m) else? **elle épouse je ne sais plus qui,** she's marrying I forget who(m); **c'est à qui entrera le premier,** it's who shall come in first; each one tries to come in first; **c'était à qui l'aiderait,** they vied with each other in helping him; *F:* **il est là,—qui ça? qui donc?** he's there,—who? *P:* **qui (c'est) qui** = QUI EST-CE QUI; **qui c'est qui couche là?** who sleeps there? **qui qui t'a dit ça?** who told you that? (*b*) (= LEQUEL) **qui des deux a raison?** which of the two is right? **qui de vous me suivra?** who of you will follow me? **on ne sait à qui des deux s'adresser,** one does not know which of the two to apply to. **2.** (= QU'EST-CE QUI) **qui t'amène si matin?** what brings you so early? **qui vous presse?** what's your hurry? **je ne sais qui m'a retenu de le gifler,** I don't know what kept me from slapping his face; *s.a.* QUI EST-CE QUE, QUI EST-CE QUI.

quia (à) [akɥia], *adv.phr.* **être à q.,** to be nonplussed, in a quandary, floored, at a loss; **réduire, mettre, qn à q.,** to nonplus, floor, stump, s.o.

quiberonnais, -aise [kibərɔnɛ, -ɛ:z], *a. & s. Geog:* (native, inhabitant) of Quiberon.

quibinaire [kibinɛ:r], *a. Elcs:* (*computers*) **code q.,** quibinary code.

quibus [kɥibys], *s.m. P: A:* money, the needful, the wherewithal.

quiça [kɥisa], *s.f. Z:* quica.

qui c'est qui [kisɛki], **qui c'est que** [kisɛk(ə)], *Dial. & P:* = QUI EST-CE QUI, QUI EST-CE QUE.

quiche [kiʃ], *s.f. Cu:* **q. lorraine,** quiche lorraine, egg and bacon tart.

quiché [kiʃe], *s.m. Ling:* Quiche.

quichenotte [kiʃ(ə)nɔt], *s.f. Cost:* coiffe worn by women in Vendée.

Quichotte, Don [dɔ̃kiʃɔt], *Pr.n.m. Spanish Lit:* Don Quixote; **agir en D. Q.,** to act quixotically.

quichottisme [kiʃɔtism], *s.m.* **(don) q.,** quixotism, quixotry.

quichua [kiʃɥa], *s.m. Ling:* Quechua.

quick [kwik], *s.m. Ten: F:* porous cement tennis court.

quick-freezing [kwikfriziŋ], *s.m. R.t.m:* quick-freeze(r), deepfreeze (*R.t.m.*).

quiconque [kikɔ̃:k], *indef.pron.m.sg.* **1.** who(so)-ever; **q. désobéira sera puni,** whoever disobeys, anyone who disobeys, shall be punished; **je le protégerai contre q. l'attaquera,** I shall protect him against whoever attacks him. **2.** (= **qui que ce soit**) **il m'aidera mieux que q.,** he will help me better than anyone (else); **pas un mot de cela à q.,** not a word of that to anybody; **ce serait téméraire de la part de q.,** it would be rash on anyone's part; **elle était sûre de faire mieux que q. de ses amies,** she was sure she could do better than any of her friends; *A: F:* **tout un q. peut se payer ce luxe-là,** anyone can afford that luxury.

quidam, *A:* **quidane** [kɥidam, kidam, kidan], *s.* (*a*) *Jur:* person (name unknown); **lesdits quidams, lesdites quidanes,** the said persons; (*b*) *A:* **survint un q.,** someone, an individual, appeared.

quiddité [kɥid(d)ite], *s.f. Phil:* quiddity.

quiescence [kɥiɛs(s)ɑ̃:s], *s.f. Hebrew Gram: etc:* quiescence.

quiescent [kɥiɛs(s)ɑ̃], *a.* (*a*) *Hebrew Gram: etc:* quiescent (letter); (*b*) *Biol:* quiescent.

qui est-ce que [kiɛskə], *interr.pron.m.sg.* whom? **qui est-ce que vous désirez voir?** whom do you wish to see?

qui est-ce qui [kiɛski], *interr.pron.m.sg.* who? (*a*) **qui est-ce qui vous l'a dit?** who told you so? **qui est-ce qui va arriver le premier?** who will be the first to arrive? (*b*) (*in indirect questions*) *F:* **je ne sais pas qui est-ce qui vous a dit ça,** I don't know who told you that.

quiet, -ète [kjɛ, -ɛt], *a. A:* calm.

quiètement [kɥiɛtmɑ̃], *adv. A:* calmly.

quiétisme [kɥietism, kje-], *s.m. Rel.H:* quietism.

quiétiste [kɥietist, kje-]. **1.** *s.m. & f. Rel.H:* quietist. **2.** *a.* quietist(ic).

quiétude [kɥietyd, kje-], *s.f.* quietude; *Theol:* **oraison de q.,** prayer of quiet.

quignon [kiɲɔ̃], *s.m.* chunk, hunch, hunk; *esp.* **q. de pain,** hunk of bread.
quilboquet [kilbɔkɛ], *s.m.* mortise gauge.
quillage [kijaːʒ], *s.m. A:* keelage (dues).
quillaja [kijaʒa], *s.m. Bot:* quillai(a) (tree); **q. savonneux,** soap-bark tree.
quillard [kijaːr], *s.m.* **1.** Jurançon wine. **2.** *Mil: F:* soldier who is about to be, who has just been, demobbed.
quille[1] [kiːj], *s.f.* **1.** *(a)* ninepin, skittle(pin); *F:* **se tenir droit comme une q.,** to hold oneself as straight as a ramrod; **jeu de quilles,** (i) set of ninepins, of skittles; (ii) ninepins, etc., set up for play; (iii) skittle alley; *Bill:* **partie de quilles,** pin pool; **être reçu comme un chien dans un jeu de quilles,** to be treated as an intruder, to be given a cold welcome; to be made as welcome as a dog on a putting green; *F:* **être planté comme une q.,** to be rooted to the spot; *A:* **trousser, prendre, son sac et ses quilles,** to decamp bag and baggage; *(b) P:* leg, pin; **il ne tient pas sur ses quilles,** he's shaky on his pins; **jouer des quilles,** to run hard, skedaddle; **être sur ses quilles,** to be in good health, in good form; *(c) F:* **la q.,** (i) *Mil:* demob (of National Serviceman); (ii) *Sch:* holidays. **2.** *(a)* glove stretcher; *(b)* (stone) wedge; plug (used in quarrying); *(c)* (wheelwright's) auger; *(d)* screw-cutting tap; *(e)* stump (of a tree); *(f) Tail:* gusset.
quille[2], *s.f.* **1.** *N.Arch:* keel; **fausse q.,** false keel, outer keel, slab keel, shoe; **q. à bulbe, q. lestée,** bulb keel (of yacht); **q. de sécurité,** slide keel, drop keel (of yacht); **q. de roulis, q. latérale,** bilge keel; **q. d'échouage,** grounding keel, docking keel; **q. plate,** plate keel, flat keel; *(of seaplane)* **q. centrale,** keel; **q. d'angle,** chine (on seaplane keel); **poser la q. d'un navire,** to lay down a ship; *(of boat)* **la q. en l'air,** bottom up. **2.** *Av:* **q. de voilure,** wing bolster beam.
quillé [kije], *a. N.Arch:* keeled, provided with a keel.
quiller [kije]. **1.** *v.i. (a)* to throw for first play (at skittles); *(b)* to set up the skittles. **2.** *v.tr. F: A:* to throw skittles, etc., at (s.o.); to shy things at (s.o.).
quillette [kijɛt], *s.f.* willow cutting (for planting).
quilleur [kijœːr], *s.m. Games:* skittle-alley, bowling-alley, attendant (who gathers up the skittles).
quillier [ki(l)je], *s.m.* **1.** wheelwright's drill. **2.** *(a)* skittle alley; *(b)* set of skittles.
quillon [kijɔ̃], *s.m.* **1.** cross bar, cross guard (of sword, *A:* of sword-bayonet). **2.** *A:* piling pin (of upper band of the Lebel rifle).
quimperlois, -oise [kɛ̃pɛrlwa, -waːz], *a. & s. Geog:* (native, inhabitant) of Quimperlé.
quimpérois, -oise [kɛ̃perwa, -waːz], *a. & s. Geog:* (native, inhabitant) of Quimper.
quinaire [k(ɥ)inɛːr]. **1.** *a. Mth:* quinary (system, etc.); *Ent: Bot:* pentamerous. **2.** *s.m. Rom.Ant: Num:* quinarius.
quinaldine [kinaldin], *s.f. Ch:* quinaldine.
quinaldique [kinaldik], *a. Ch:* **acide q.,** quinaldic, quinaldinic, acid.
quinalizarine [kinalizarin], *s.f. Ch:* quinalizarin.
quina-quina [kinakina], *s.m. Bot:* balsam tree.
quinaud [kino], *a. A:* abashed, confused; **rester q.,** to look foolish, to hang one's head; to feel crushed.
quinauderie [kinaudri], *s.f. A:* nonsense; affected style.
quincaille [kɛ̃kɑːj], *s.f. A: (a)* (piece of) hardware; **(marchandise de) q.,** ironmongery; *(b) F:* copper coins, coppers.
quincaillerie [kɛ̃kɑjri], *s.f.* **1.** hardware, ironmongery. **2.** hardware (i) business, (ii) shop. **3.** *F:* cheap jewellery.
quincaillier [kɛ̃kɑje], *s.m.* hardware merchant; ironmonger.
quinconce [kɛ̃kɔ̃ːs], *s.m.* quincunx; arrangement in fives; staggered arrangement (of at least three rows); **arbres en q.,** trees planted in quincunx, in alternate rows; *Metalw:* **rivetage en q.,** staggered riveting, zigzag riveting, cross riveting.
quinconcial, -aux [kɛ̃kɔ̃sjal, -o], *a.* quincuncial.
quindécagone [kɥɛ̃dekagɔn], *s.m.* quindecagon.
quindécennal, -aux [kɥɛ̃desɛnal, -o], *a.* quindecennial.
quindécimvir [kɥɛ̃desimviːr], *s.m. Rom.Hist:* quindecemvir.
quindécimviral [kɥɛ̃desimviral], *a. Rom.Hist:* relating to the quindecemviri.
quindécimvirat [kɥɛ̃desimvira], *s.m. Rom.Hist:* quindecemvirate.
quine [kin], *s.m.* **1.** series of five winning numbers (in a lottery); quinto; *F: A:* **c'est un q. à la loterie,** it's a chance in ten thousand. **2.** two fives (in backgammon).
quiné [kine], *a. Bot:* quinate (leaflet).
quinhydrone [kinidrɔn], *s.f. Ch:* quinhydrone.
quinidine [kinidin], *s.f. Ch:* quinidine, chinidine.
quinine [kinin], *s.f. (a)* quinine; *(b) Pharm:* (sulphate of) quinine.
quininisme [kininism], *s.m.,* **quinisme** [kinism], *s.m. Med:* cinchonism, quininism.
quinique [kinik], *a. Ch:* quinic (acid).
quinite [kinit], *s.f. Ch:* quinitol.
quinizarine [kinizarin], *s.f. Ch:* quinizarin.
quinnat [kina], *s.m. Ich:* quinnat.
quinoa [kinɔa], *s.m. Bot:* quinoa.
quinoléine [kinɔlein], *s.f. Ind: Ch:* quinoline, chinoline.
quinoléique [kinɔleik], *a. Ch:* quinolinic (acid); of quinoline.
quinométhane [kinɔmetan], *s.m. Ch:* quinomethane.
quinone [kinɔn], *s.f. Ch:* quinone.
quinonique [kinɔnik], *a. Ch:* quinoid, quinonoid.
quinophtalone [kinɔftalɔn], *s.f. Ch:* quinaldine.
quino-quino [kinɔkinɔ], *s.m. Bot:* balsam tree.
quinoxalines [kinɔksalin], *s.f.pl. Ch:* quinoxalines.
quinquagénaire [k(ɥ)ɛ̃k(w)aʒenɛːr], *a. & s.m. & f.* quinguagenarian.
Quinquagésime [k(ɥ)ɛ̃kwaʒezim], *s.f. Ecc:* Quinquagesima (Sunday); Shrove Sunday.
quinquangulaire [k(ɥ)ɛ̃kwɑ̃gylɛːr], *a.* quinquangular.
quinquennal, -aux [k(ɥ)ɛ̃k(ɥ)ɛnal, -o], *a.* quinquennial; *Russian Hist:* **le Plan q.,** the Five-Year Plan; **jeux quinquennaux,** quinquennalia.
quinquennalité [k(ɥ)ɛ̃k(ɥ)ɛnalite], *s.f.* quinquennial.
quinquennat [k(ɥ)ɛ̃k(ɥ)ɛna], *s.m.* five-year period, quinquenniad.
quinquennium [k(ɥ)ɛ̃k(ɥ)ɛnjɔm], *s.m.* quinquennium.
quinquérème [k(ɥ)ɛ̃k(ɥ)erɛm], *s.f. A.Nau:* quinquereme, quinquireme.
quinquet [kɛ̃kɛ], *s.m. (a)* (Argand) lamp; *(b) pl. P:* eyes; **allumer ses quinquets,** to stare; *A:* **moucher les quinquets à qn,** to give s.o. one in the eye.
quinquévir [k(ɥ)ɛ̃k(ɥ)evir], *s.m. Rom.Hist:* quinquevir.
quinquina [kɛ̃kina], *s.m. (a) Pharm:* cinchona, quinquina (bark, tree); Peruvian bark; **q. rouge,** red bark; *(b)* aperitif wine flavoured with quinquina; **vin de q.,** tonic wine.
quinquinisme [kɛ̃kinism], *s.m. Med:* cinchonism.
quint [kɛ̃], *a. A:* **1.** fifth; *Hist:* **Charles-Q.,** Charles the Fifth (Holy Roman Emperor). **2.** *A.Med:* **fièvre quinte,** quintan fever. **3.** *A:* tax paid on a piece of jewellery.
quintain [kɛ̃tɛ̃], *s.m. Pros:* quintain.
quintaine [kɛ̃tɛn], *s.f. A.Mil:* quintain; **courir la q.,** to tilt at the quintain; **servir de q. à qn,** to be the object of s.o.'s attack.
quintal, -aux [kɛ̃tal, -o], *s.m. Meas:* **1.** *A:* quintal = *approx.* hundredweight. **2. q. (métrique)** = 100 kilogrammes.
quintan [kɛ̃tɑ̃], *s.m. A.Mil:* quintain.
quintane [kɛ̃tan], *a. Rom.Ant:* **voie q.,** road parallel with main road which was used as a market; *A.Med:* **fièvre q.,** quintan (fever).
quintaton [kɛ̃tatɔ̃], *s.m. Mus:* quintaton.
quintau [kɛ̃to], *s.m. Agr:* stook.
quinte [kɛ̃ːt], *s.f.* **1.** *Mus: (a)* fifth, quint; **fausse q., q. diminuée,** diminished fifth; **q. augmentée,** augmented fifth; **q. juste,** perfect fifth; *(b) A:* tenor violin, viola. **2.** *Cards: (at piquet, etc.)* quint (sequence of five of the same suit); **q. majeure,** quint major; *P: A:* **avoir q. et quatorze,** to suffer from syphilis. **3.** *Fenc:* quint(e); **parer en q.,** to parry in quinte. **4.** *(a)* **q. de toux,** fit of coughing; *(b) F:* caprice, crotchet; fit of bad temper.
Quinte-Curce [k(ɥ)ɛ̃tkyrs], *Pr.n.m. Lt.Lit:* Quintus Curtius.
quintefeuille [kɛ̃tfœːj], *(a) s.f. Her: Bot:* cinq(ue)foil; *(b) s.m. Arch:* cinquefoil.
quinter [kɛ̃te], *v.tr. A:* to hallmark (after the tax has been paid).
quinterol [kɛ̃t(ə)rɔl], *s.m. A: Nau:* fifth rower on each bank of a galley.
quinteron, -onne [kɛ̃t(ə)rɔ̃, -ɔn], *s. Ethn:* quintroon.
quintessence [kɛ̃tesɑ̃ːs], *s.f.* quintessence.
quintessencié [kɛ̃tesɑ̃sje], *a.* quintessential; **pensées quintessenciées,** sublimated thoughts.
quintessenciel, -elle [kɛ̃tesɑ̃sjɛl], *a.* quintessential.
quintessencier[1] [kɛ̃tesɑ̃sje], *v.tr.* to quintessence, to quintessentialize.
quintessencier[2], *s.m. Alch:* seeker after the philosopher's stone.
quintette [k(ɥ)ɛ̃tɛt], *s.m. Mus:* quintet(te).
quinteux, -euse [kɛ̃tø, -øːz], *a.* **1.** *Med:* **toux quinteuse,** fitful cough. **2.** *F:* capricious, crotchety (person); **cheval q.,** restive, jibbing, horse; jibber.
quintidi [k(ɥ)ɛ̃tidi], *s.m. Fr.Hist:* (Republican Calendar) Fifth day of the decade.
quintidodécaèdre [k(ɥ)ɛ̃tidɔdekaɛdr], *a.* composed of five dodecahedrons.
quintil [k(ɥ)ɛ̃til], *s.m. Pros:* quintain, using two rhymes.
Quintilien [kɥɛ̃tiljɛ̃], *Pr.n.m.* Quintilian.
quintilla [k(ɥ)ɛ̃tila], *s.m. Pros:* octosyllabic quintain.
quintillion [k(ɥ)ɛ̃tiljɔ̃], *s.m.* **1.** *(since* 1948) quintillion (10^{30}). **2.** *(before* 1948) trillion (10^{18}), *U.S:* quintillion.
quintinois, -oise [kɛ̃tinwa, -waːz], *a. & s.* (native) of Quintin.
quintioctaèdre [k(ɥ)ɛ̃tiɔktaɛdr], *a.* composed of five octahedrons.
quintivalent [k(ɥ)ɛ̃tivalɑ̃], *a. Ch:* quinquevalent, quinquivalent.
quinto [kɥɛ̃to], *Lt.adv. (abbr.* 5°) fifthly.
quintolet [kɛ̃tɔlɛ], *s.m. Mus:* quintole(t), quintuplet.
quinton [kɛ̃tɔ̃], *s.m. Mus:* quinton.
quintoyer [k(ɥ)ɛ̃twaje], *v.i. Mus: (of organ pipe, wind instrument)* to produce the harmonic octave-fifth faintly with the fundamental tone.
quintuple [k(ɥ)ɛ̃typl], *a. & s.m.* quintuple, fivefold; **être payé au q.,** to be repaid fivefold; **trente est (le) q. de six,** thirty is five times as much as six; *Mus:* **q. croche,** semihemidemisemiquaver.
quintuplé, -ée [k(ɥ)ɛ̃typle], *s.* quintuplet, *F:* quin.
quintupler [k(ɥ)ɛ̃typle], *v.tr. & i.* to quintuple; to increase fivefold; to multiply by five.
se quintupler, to increase fivefold.
quintuplet, -ette [k(ɥ)ɛ̃typlɛ, -ɛt], *s.* quintuplet, *F:* quin.
quinuclidine [k(ɥ)inyklidin], *s.f. Ch:* quinuclidine.
quinzain [kɛ̃zɛ̃], *a.inv. A.Ten:* **ils sont q.,** they are fifteen all.
quinzaine [kɛ̃zɛn], *s.f.* **1.** (about) fifteen, some fifteen; **une q. de francs,** fifteen francs or so. **2.** *(a)* fortnight; **dans la q.,** within a fortnight; **remettre une cause à q.,** to adjourn a case for a fortnight; *(b)* fortnight's pay, wages.
quinze [kɛ̃ːz], *num.a.inv. & s.m.inv.* **1.** fifteen; **q. joueurs,** fifteen players; *Fr.Hist:* **Louis Q.,** Louis the Fifteenth; **le q. mai,** (on) the fifteenth of May; **j'arriverai le q.,** I'll arrive on the fifteenth; **demeurer au (numéro) q.,** to live at number fifteen; **au chapitre q. de . . .,** in the fifteenth chapter of . . .; *Ten:* **q. à, q. partout,** fifteen all; *Rugby Fb:* **le q. de France,** the French fifteen. **2. q. jours,** a fortnight; **dans q. jours,** in a fortnight; **aujourd'hui en q.,** today fortnight; **demain en q.,** a fortnight from tomorrow, tomorrow fortnight; **tous les q. jours,** every fortnight, once a fortnight, fortnightly; every other week. **3.** *Fin:* **q. du mois,** mid month, mid (-month) account.
Quinze-Vingts [kɛ̃zvɛ̃]. **1.** *s.m.pl. Hist:* **les Q.-V.,** the Hospital for the blind (originally 300) in Paris. **2.** *s.m. A:* **un quinze-vingt(s),** (i) an inmate of this hospital; (ii) a blind person.
quinzième [kɛ̃zjɛm]. **1.** *num. a. & s.* fifteenth. **2.** *s.m.* fifteenth (part).
quinzièmement [kɛ̃zjɛmmɑ̃], *adv.* fifteenthly; in the fifteenth place.
quipo [kipɔ], **quipu** [kipy], *s.m. Archeol:* quipo, quipu.
quiproquo [kiprɔko], *s.m.* mistake (taking of one thing for another); misunderstanding; **il y a eu q.,** (i) we misunderstood each other; (ii) I took you, him, for someone else; I was taken for someone else.
quiqui [kiki], *s.m.* **1.** *P:* Adam's apple; **serrer le q. à qn,** to throttle, garrotte, s.o. **2.** *Dial:* chicken.
quirat [kira], *s.m. Jur:* joint ownership (in a ship).
quirataire [kiratɛːr], *s.m. Jur:* joint owner (of a ship).
Quirinal [kirinal], *a. & s.m.* **le mont Q.,** the Quirinal; **le palais du Q.,** the Quirinal.
quiritaire [kɥiritɛːr], *a. Rom.Jur:* quiritarian.
quirite [kɥirit], *s.m. Rom.Hist:* Roman citizen.
quisling [k(ɥ)isliŋ], *s.m. F:* quisling; traitor.
quittance [kitɑ̃ːs], *s.f. Com:* receipt, discharge, (ac)quittance; **q. de loyer,** rent receipt; **q. pour solde,** receipt in full; **q. double,** duplicate receipt; **q. libératoire, finale,** receipt in full (discharge); **donner q. à qn,** (i) to give s.o. a receipt in full; (ii) to forgive s.o.

quittancer [kitɑ̃se], *v.tr.* **(je quittançai(s))** *Com:* to receipt (bill).

quitte [kit], *a.* **1.** free, quit, rid (**de,** of); discharged (**de,** from); **être q. de dettes,** to be out of debt; **je suis q. envers vous,** I am no longer in your debt; **nous sommes quittes,** I am quits with you; **tenir qn q. de qch.,** to release s.o. from, let s.o. off, sth.; **je vous tiens q. du reste,** never mind the remainder; **en être q. pour, avec, qch.,** to get off, come off, be let off, with sth.; **il en a été q. pour la peur,** he got off, escaped, with a fright; **j'en suis q. pour une petite politesse,** it costs me a little civility; **ils en ont été quittes à bon marché, à bon compte,** they came off, got off, cheap(ly); **nous voilà q. à q.,** now we're quits, square; **jouer à q. ou (à) double, jouer q. ou double,** to play double or quits. **2.** *inv. in the following adv. uses;* **q. à,** even if it entails; **je le ferai, q. à être grondé,** I'll do it even if I'm scolded; I'll do it and chance the scolding; **elles avaient un salon, q. à coucher dans une mansarde,** they had a drawing-room, even though they had to sleep in an attic; **j'abandonne ce travail, q. à le reprendre plus tard,** I am giving up this work, but may perhaps resume it later; **j'irai jusqu'au bout, q. à en mourir,** I shall carry on to the end, live or die; **le gouvernement suspendit brusquement les opérations, q. à les reprendre quelques semaines plus tard,** the government suddenly suspended operations, only to resume them a few weeks later; **tu te marieras, q. à le regretter,** you'll get married and be sorry for it; **il accepta ses cadeaux, q. à être ingrat envers lui plus tard,** he accepted his gifts, though he did not scruple to be ungrateful to him later; **je le ferai, q. à ce qu'elle m'en blâme par la suite,** I'll do it even though she may blame me afterwards; (*occ. agreeing*) **ils refusent toutes concessions quittes à perdre leurs places,** they will not make any concessions, even if it means losing their jobs.

quitter [kite], *v.tr.* **1.** *A:* **q. qn d'une dette,** to discharge s.o. of a debt; to free, release, s.o. from a debt. **2.** (*a*) *A:* **q. qch. à qn,** to give up, resign, sth. to s.o.; **je vous quitte la place,** I leave you in possession; (*b*) **q. la partie,** to throw up one's cards; to throw up the sponge; to cry off. **3.** to leave, quit (place, person); to vacate (office); **q. la chambre,** (i) to leave the room; (ii) (*of invalid*) to leave one's room; (iii) (*at hotel*) to vacate one's room; **q. le lit,** to leave one's bed; **q. ses habits,** to take off one's clothes; **q. sa peau,** (i) (*of snake*) to cast its slough; (ii) (*of pers.*) to make a radical change (in one's habits); **après avoir passé le fleuve, la voiture quitta la grande route,** after crossing the river, the car turned off the main road; **q. le droit chemin,** to swerve from the straight path, from the path of duty; (*of train*) **q. les rails,** to jump the metals; **q. sa famille,** (i) to desert the home; (ii) (*of young pers.*) to leave the family home; *Nau:* **q. la jetée, le quai,** to cast off; **q. le service,** to leave, quit, the service; **q. le théâtre,** to give up the stage; **q. les affaires,** to retire from business; to give up business; **q. ses mauvaises habitudes,** to leave off, give up, one's bad habits; **q. la vie, ce monde,** to depart this life; **quel plaisir de tout q.!** how nice to get away from it all! *Sch:* **il quitte l'université cet été,** he's going down this summer; **ses yeux ne la quittaient pas; il ne l'a pas quittée des yeux, du regard,** he never took his eyes off her; **ne le quittez pas des yeux,** keep your eye on him; do not let him out of your sight; *F:* **il ne quitte pas sa femme d'une semelle,** he never lets his wife out of his sight; **son image ne me quitte pas,** I can't get him out of my mind, I can't forget him; **ils se sont quittés bons amis,** they parted good friends; *abs.* **je tâcherai de q. de bonne heure,** I I will try to leave early, to get away early; *Tp:* **ne quittez pas!** hold the line! hold on! hang on! don't ring off! don't hang up! *W.Tel:* **ne quittez pas l'écoute!** don't switch off!

quitus [k(ɥ)itys], *s.m. Com:* receipt in full; *Jur:* quietus, quittance, final discharge (from debt, liability, office, etc.); **donner à qn q. de sa gestion,** to give s.o. final discharge from his financial administration; **obtenir son q.,** to obtain one's quietus, one's quittance, one's final discharge; **obtenir q. des sommes dues au Trésor,** to obtain a quietus of the sum due to the Treasury.

qui-vive [kiviːv], *s.m.inv. Mil:* sentry's challenge; *F:* **être, se tenir, sur le q.-v.,** to be on the qui-vive, on the alert, on the look out; *s.a.* VIVRE 1.

qui-vous-savez [kivusave], (*in lieu of*) *Pr.n.m. & f.* You-Know-Who.

quoailler [k(w)ɔaje], *v.i.* (*of horse*) to swish its tail constantly.

quodlibet [k(w)ɔdlibɛ], *s.m. Mus:* quodlibet.

quoi[1] [kwa], *rel.pron.neut.* what. **1.** (*a*) *with* **ce** *as antecedent, expressed or understood;* **c'est ce à q. je m'attendais,** that is what I was expecting; **ce sur q. l'on discute,** what is being discussed; the matter under discussion; **ce à q. je m'oppose, ce contre q. je proteste, c'est . . .,** what I object to is . . .; **c'est en q. vous vous trompez,** that is where you are wrong; **ce pour q. il avait lutté,** what he had fought for; **après q.,** after which; **sur q.,** on which; **moyennant q.,** for which; *A. & Jur:* **q. faisant . . .,** doing which . . .; **q. disant . . .,** saying which . . .; (*b*) (= LEQUEL, LAQUELLE) **la mort, contre q. rien ne prévaut,** death, against which nothing can prevail; **il a bien autre chose à q. penser!** he has something else to think about! **un autre fait, à q. vous n'avez pas pris garde,** another fact, which you have left out of consideration. **2. de q.: il a de q. vivre,** he has enough to live on; **nous n'avons pas de q. payer,** we have not the means to pay; we haven't the wherewithal; **nous n'avions pas de q. nous payer à dîner,** we hadn't enough money to treat ourselves to dinner; *F:* **il a de q.,** he's well off, comfortably off; **il y a de q. vous faire enrager,** it's enough to drive you mad; **il y avait de q.!** with good reason! **il n'y a pas de q. être fier,** there's nothing to be proud of; **il n'y a pas de q. chanter victoire,** there's no occasion to crow; **il n'y a pas de q.,** no thanks, no apologies, are needed; don't mention it; **avez-vous de q. écrire?** have you anything to write with? **donnez-moi de q. écrire,** give me some writing materials; **et donnez-moi de q. m'asseoir,** and give me something to sit on; **il faut trouver de q. allumer le feu,** we must find something to light the fire with; **pour faire du feu, il faut avoir de q.,** to make a fire, you must have the wherewithal; *P:* (*as a threat*) **de q.?** what did you say? **3. sans q.: travaille, sans q. tu ne mangeras pas,** work, otherwise you won't eat. **4.** *F:* **comme q., montrer comme q. la chose est possible,** to show that the thing is possible; **voilà comme q. je me suis trouvé là,** that's how I happened to be there; **comme q. . . .,** it only goes to show that . . .; *P:* **une lettre, comme q. j'étais malade,** a letter saying I was ill; **il m'a dit comme q. il mourait de faim,** he told me he was starving. **5.** (*correlative to* **qui, que** + *sub.*) **q. qui, q. que;** (*a*) **q. qui survienne, restez calme,** whatever comes of it, keep calm; **q. que vous entendiez, ne dites rien,** whatever you hear, say nothing; **q. qu'il en soit . . .,** however that may be . . ., be that as it may . . ., at all events . . .; **q. qu'il dise . . .,** whatever he says . . .; **q. qu'en aient dit les journaux . . .,** in spite of the statements in the papers . . .; **q. qu'on fasse, il n'est jamais content,** no matter what you do, whatever you do, he's never satisfied; (*b*) **q. que ce soit,** (i) anything (whatever); (ii) whatever it may be; **puis-je vous être utile en q. que ce soit?** can I be of help to you in any way? **avez-vous dit q. que ce soit?** did you speak at all? did you say anything at all? **je n'ai besoin de q. que ce soit,** I am not in need of anything at all, of anything whatsoever; **q. que ce soit qui l'en empêche,** whatever may be preventing him.

quoi[2], *interr.pron.neut.* what? **1.** (*a*) (*subject*) **qui ou q. vous a donné cette idée?** who or what gave you the idea? **quoi d'autre pourrait m'amener chez toi?** what else could bring me to your house? **q. de plus beau que ces couchers de soleil?** what could be more beautiful than these sunsets? **q. de nouveau?** what news? **q. de plus simple?** what could be simpler, easier? **eh bien! q.?** well, what about it? (*b*) (*object*) **vous désirez q.?** what is it you want? **une meute? pour chasser q.?** a pack? to hunt what? **elle buvait un cocktail—un q.?** she was drinking a cocktail—a what? **les journaux ne savent (pas) q. inventer,** the papers don't know what to invent next; *s.a.* IMPORTER[2] 2, JE-NE-SAIS-QUOI; *Dial. & P:* **q. qu'il dit?** (= **qu'est-ce qu'il dit?**) what does he say? **q. que vous voulez?** what do you want? (*c*) (*after prepositions*) **de q. parlez-vous?** what are you talking about? **à q. pensez-vous?** what are you thinking of? **dites-moi en q. je puis vous être utile,** tell me how, in what respect, I can help you; **en q. cela vous regarde-t-il?** what business is it of yours? *Sch:* **en q. est-il bon?** what's he good at? **à q. bon (faire qch.)?** what's the use, the good (of doing sth.)? **en q. est-ce? c'est en q.?** what is it made of? **il s'élança avant de voir après quoi il sautait,** he made his bound before he saw what (it was) he was jumping at; (*d*) *F:* (*and ill-bred,* = PARDON?) what? **on te demande, mon enfant—q.?** you are wanted, my dear—what? **et vos cousines?—q., mes cousines?** and your cousins? —well, what about them! **2.** *int.* **q.! mais q.! q. donc!** what! what's that? **q., c'est vous!** what, is it you! *F:* **enfin, q.! c'est la vie!** well, well, such is life! **elle vous aime, q.!** in short, she loves you; **j'en ai assez, q.!** I'm simply fed up!

quoiqu' [kwak], *conj.* = QUOIQUE *before* **il(s), elle(s), on, en, un(e),** *and today frequently before any word beginning with a vowel.*

quoique [kwak(ə)]. **1.** *conj. usu.* + *sub.* (al)-though; (*a*) **quoiqu'il soit pauvre il est généreux,** although he is poor he is generous; **q. nous soyons parents et que nous habitions le même département, je ne l'ai jamais vu,** although we are related, and live in the same department, I have never seen him; (*b*) (*with ellipsis of verb*) **je suis heureux q. garçon,** I am happy though a bachelor; (*c*) *occ. with ind. F:* **nous recevons souvent des coups, q., vous savez, nous en donnons aussi,** we often receive blows, but then, of course, we hit back. **2.** *prep. P:* **q. ça il vous est fidèle,** in spite of that, nevertheless, he is faithful to you.

quolibet [kɔlibɛ], *s.m.* **1.** gibe; **poursuivre qn de quolibets,** to gibe, jeer, at s.o.; **quolibets à l'adresse de qn,** digs at s.o. **2.** *Mus:* quodlibet.

quorum [kɔrɔm], *s.m.* quorum.

quota [k(w)ɔta], *s.m.* quota; **sondage par q.,** quota sampling.

quote-part [kɔtpaːr], *s.f.* share, quota, portion; contribution *pro rata*; *pl. quotes-parts.*

quotidien, -ienne [kɔtidjɛ̃, -jɛn]. **1.** *a.* daily, everyday; of daily occurrence; **la vie quotidienne,** everyday life; **notre pain q.,** our daily bread; *Med: A:* **fièvre quotidienne,** quotidian fever. **2.** *s.m.* (*a*) **les quotidiens,** the daily papers, the dailies; (*b*) **le q.,** everyday life. **3.** *s.f. A: F:* **une quotidienne,** a daily (charwoman, etc.).

quotidiennement [kɔtidjɛnmɑ̃], *adv.* daily, every day.

quotidienneté [kɔtidjɛnte], *s.f.* everyday life, humdrum existence.

quotient [kɔsjɑ̃], *s.m.* **1.** *Mth:* quotient; *Physiol:* **q. respiratoire,** respiratory quotient. **2. q. électoral,** electoral quota; **q. de la capitalisation boursière par le dernier bénéfice annuel,** price-earnings ratio; **système du q. familial,** system of (income) tax relief in respect of dependents; *Psy:* **q. d'intelligence, intellectuel,** intelligence quotient, I.Q.

quotité [kɔtite], *s.f.* quota, share, amount, proportion; **la q. du dégrèvement fiscal,** the extent of taxation relief; *Jur:* **q. disponible,** share of estate in the free disposal of the testator, disposable portion of estate; **q. de cens,** property qualification; **impôt de q.,** coefficient tax.

quottement [kɔtmɑ̃], *s.m. Mec.E:* engaging, catching (of gearing).

quotter [kɔte], *v.i. Mec.E:* (*of gearing*) to engage, catch.

R

R, r [ɛːr], *s.m.* (the letter) R, r; *Ling:* **r. cacuminal,** point r, dental r; **r. vélaire,** uvular r; **rouler les r,** to roll one's r's; *Tp:* **R comme Raoul,** R for Robert; **ne mangez des huîtres que dans les mois en R,** eat oysters only in the months with an r in them.

ra [rɑ], *s.m.inv. Mus:* ruffle, ruff (on the drum).

rab [rab], *s.m. esp. Mil:* P: extra; bit, drop, more; **un petit r.?** won't you have a drop more? **faire du r.,** to do a bit of extra work; to work late (without extra pay).

rabâchage [rabɑʃaːʒ], *s.m.,* **rabâchement** [rabɑʃmɑ̃], *s.m.* (tedious) repetition; harping (on words, etc.).

rabâcher [rabɑʃe]. **1.** *v.i.* to be everlastingly repeating the same thing. **2.** *v.tr.* **ils rabâchent toujours la même chose,** they are always harping on the same string; *Sch:* **r. une leçon,** to go over a lesson until one knows it by heart.

rabâcherie [rabɑʃri], *s.f. usu. pl.* (tedious) repetition; harping; **le sujet se prêtait à mille rabâcheries,** the subject lent itself to endless repetition.

rabâcheur, -euse [rabɑʃœːr, -øːz], (a) *a.* repetitive (person); **il est très r.,** he's always repeating himself, always harping on the same thing; (b) *s.* person who is always repeating himself, herself.

rabais [rabɛ], *s.m.* **1.** *Com:* reduction (in price); allowance, rebate, discount, abatement; **r. en cas de payement comptant,** discount for cash; **faire un r. sur qch.,** to make a reduction, an allowance, on sth.; **au r.,** poor quality; cheap and nasty; **faire qch. au r.,** to do sth. on the cheap; **refuser un travail au r.,** to refuse an underpaid job; to refuse to work on the cheap; **vendre qch. au r.,** to sell sth. at a discount, at a reduced price; **vente au grand r.,** sale at greatly reduced prices. **2.** *Fin:* A: depreciation (of coinage). **3.** fall, abatement (of flood waters).

rabaissant [rabɛsɑ̃], *a.* disparaging, derogatory.

rabaissement [rabɛsmɑ̃], *s.m.* **1.** lowering ((i) of curtain, etc., (ii) of prices). **2.** (a) depreciation, disparagement, running down (of person, of performance); (b) humbling (of person).

rabaisser [rabese], *v.tr.* **1.** to lower (sth., one's voice); to reduce, lower (price); to depreciate (coinage); *F:* **r. son vol,** to do things on a smaller scale; **r. le caquet à qn,** to make s.o. sing small; to sit on s.o. **2.** (a) to depreciate, disparage, belittle (person, talent, etc.); **ne le rabaissez pas comme ça,** don't run him down like that; (b) to humble (s.o., s.o.'s pride). **3.** (a) to cut back (tree, plant, etc.); (b) *Bookb:* to cut, trim (the boards).

raban [rabɑ̃], *s.m. Nau:* (a) (small) rope; **rabans de ferlage,** furling lines, gaskets; **rabans de ris,** reef earings, gaskets; **r. d'empointure,** rope band, roband, head earing (of a sail); *O:* **être entre la vergue et le r.,** to be three sheets in the wind; to be drunk; (b) **r. de barre de cabestan,** swifter; (c) lashing (of hammock).

rabane [raban], *s.f.* raffia matting; *Hort:* **r. de raphia,** grass mat.

rabaner [rabane], **rabanter** [rabɑ̃te], *v.tr.* **1.** to fit rope bands into (sail). **2.** to pass a gasket round (sail).

rabat [raba], *s.m.* **1.** bands (of clerical costume); turned-down piece; flap (of handbag pocket, cardboard box, etc.). **2.** *O:* reduction (in price); rebate. **3.** *Ven:* beating (for game). **4.** *Metalw:* spring beam, rabbet (of drop hammer).

rabat-eau [rabao], **rabat-l'eau** [rabalo], *s.m.inv.* splash guard (of grindstone).

rabat-joie [raba3wa], *a. & s.inv.* **1.** *s.m. A:* damper, disappointment. **2.** (*of pers.*) c'est un, une, **r.-j.,** he, she, is a wet blanket, a killjoy, a spoil-sport; **elle est un peu r.-j.,** she's a bit of a wet blanket.

rabattable [rabatabl], *a.* that can be folded back; *Aut:* **coupé à capote r.,** drophead coupé; **siège r.,** reclining seat; *N.Arch:* **cheminée r.,** hinged funnel.

rabattage [rabataːʒ], *s.m.* **1.** *Com:* lowering (of prices). **2.** *Hort:* cutting back (of shoots). **3.** (a) *Ven:* beating (for game); (b) heading back (of game); heading off (of fugitives).

rabattant [rabatɑ̃], *s.m.* flap; folding leaf; **un tiroir secret caché sous le r.,** a secret drawer hidden under the drop front.

rabattement [rabatmɑ̃], *s.m.* **1.** folding back; (a) *Geom:* rabatment (of triangle, etc.); *Draw:* **r. américain,** third angle projection; (b) **charrette à r.,** tip-up cart; **paroi à r.,** hinged side, drop side (of railway wagon, etc.); *Nau:* **cheminée à r.,** hinged funnel. **2.** gradual wheeling movement (of an army). **3.** *Jur:* annulment of (provisional) verdict by default.

rabatteur, -euse [rabatœːr, -øːz], *s.* **1.** *Pej:* (a) (i) *Com:* tout; *esp.* hotel tout; (ii) procurer; (b) *s.f.* **rabatteuse,** procuress, decoy. **2.** *s.m. Ven:* beater. **3.** *s.m. Agr:* (*machine*) pick-up.

rabattre [rabatṛ], *v.tr.* (*conj. like* BATTRE) **1.** to fold (sth.) back; to bring (sth.) down (to a lower level); to shut down (lid); to lower, pull down (a blind, etc.); to turn down (one's collar, etc.); to tilt back (seat of a car); to tone down (colour); *Geom:* to rabatte, rotate (plane); *Needlew:* to turn down; to stitch down; **r. une couture,** (i) to fell a seam, (ii) to press down, flatten, a seam; *Metalw:* **r. un collet sur une tôle, r. le bord d'une tôle,** to flange a plate, to turn over the edges of a plate; **r. une inégalité,** to hammer down an irregularity; **r. un clou,** to burr a nail; **porte rabattue contre la paroi,** door folded back to the wall; **le vent rabat la fumée,** the wind is beating down the smoke; **cheval qui rabat les oreilles,** horse that lays its ears back. **2.** to reduce, lessen, diminish; (a) *Com:* **r. tant du prix,** to take, *F:* knock, so much off the price; to make a reduction of so much on the price; **combien voulez-vous en r.?** what reduction will you make on it? **je n'en rabattrai pas un sou,** I won't take a halfpenny less for it; **r. les centimes,** to knock off the centimes; **il faut r. la moitié de ce qu'il dit,** you must discount half of what he says; **tout compté et tout rabattu,** after making every allowance; *abs.* **r. du prix,** to reduce, lower, one's price; (b) **r. l'orgueil de qn,** to lower, take down, humble, s.o.'s pride; *abs.* **r. de sa fierté,** to lower, pocket, one's pride; **r. de ses prétentions, en r.,** to climb down, to draw in one's horns; **il ne veut rien r. de ses prétentions,** he won't budge from his position; *F:* **r. le caquet à qn,** to make s.o. sing small; (c) *Hort:* to cut back (tree, branch, etc.) **r. sévèrement,** to cut back close; (d) *Knitting:* **r. les mailles,** to cast off. **3.** (a) **r. le gibier,** (i) to beat up the game; (ii) to head back the game; **r. les flammes,** to beat back the flames; (b) to head off (game, fugitives). **4.** *v.i.* **il faut r. à (main) droite,** you must turn off, bear, to the right.

se rabattre. 1. **col qui se rabat sur les épaules,** collar that falls, turns back, on the shoulders; **table qui se rabat,** folding table. **2.** (a) **l'armée se rabattit sur la ville, vers le sud,** the army fell back upon the town, in a southerly direction; *Mil:* **se r. sur le flanc de l'ennemi,** to swing inwards, to roll up the enemy's flank; **se r. vers la base,** to drop back towards the base; (b) **se r. sur qch., à faire qch.,** to fall back upon a course of action, upon doing sth.; **ayant épuisé ce sujet, il se rabattit sur la politique,** having exhausted this subject, he fell back on politics; (c) *Aut:* to cut in (in front of car after overtaking it).

rabattu [rabaty], *a.* turned down; **col r.,** turn-down collar, low collar; **chapeau r.,** slouch hat; **couture rabattue,** run and fell seam.

rabattue [rabaty], *s.f. Nau: A:* drift rail.

rabbin [rabɛ̃], *s.m.* (*voc. case* rabbi) *Jewish Rel:* rabbi; **grand r.,** Chief Rabbi.

rabbinage [rabinaːʒ], *s.m. Pej:* rabbinics.

rabbinat [rabina], *s.m. Jewish Rel:* rabbinate.

rabbinique [rabinik], *a.* rabbinical; **études rabbiniques,** rabbinics.

rabbinisme [rabinism], *s.m.* rabbinism.

rabbiniste [rabinist], *s.m. & f.* rabbinist.

rabdomancie [rabdɔmɑ̃si], *s.f.* rhabdomancy.

rabdomancien, -ienne [rabdɔmɑ̃sjɛ̃, -jɛn], *s.* rhabdomancer, (water)diviner.

rabe [rab], *s.m. esp. Mil:* P: extra; bit, drop, more.

rabelaiserie [rablɛzri], *s.f.* **1.** Rabelaisianism; coarse, broad, humour. **2.** Rabelaisian joke; broad joke.

rabelaisien, -ienne [rablɛzjɛ̃, -jɛn], *a.* Rabelaisian, broad (humour, etc.).

rabes [rab], *s.f.pl.* **r. de morue,** salted cod roe.

rabiau [rabjo], *s.m. A:* = RABIOT.

rabiauter [rabjote], *v.i. A:* = RABIOTER.

rabiauteur [rabjotœːr], *s.m. A:* = RABIOTEUR.

rabibochage [rabibɔʃaːʒ], *s.m. F:* (a) tinkering up, patching up; (b) reconciliation, making it up; patching up (of quarrel).

rabibocher [rabibɔʃe], *v.tr. F:* **1.** (a) to tinker up, patch up (sth.); (b) to patch up (quarrel); to reconcile (two people); **ils se sont rabibochés,** they made it up. **2.** to put (gambler) on his legs again.

rabiot [rabjo], *s.m.* P: **1.** (a) second helping; *Mil:* surplus of food (after distribution of rations); buckshee; (b) illicit profits (on forage, on food supplies). **2.** (a) extra work; (b) *Mil:* extra period of service (owing to imprisonment).

rabiotage [rabjotaːʒ], *s.m. Mil:* P: scrounging.

rabioter [rabjote], *v.i.* P: **1.** (a) to appropriate, scrounge, surplus food, etc.; (b) *v.tr.* to wangle (sth.); *Mil:* **j'ai rabioté deux jours de perm,** I've scrounged two extra days' leave. **2.** to make illicit profits; to make a bit on the side.

rabioteur, -euse [rabjotœːr, -øːz], *s.* P: **1.** scrounger; wangler. **2.** person who makes a bit on the side.

rabique [rabik], *a. Med:* rabic (virus, animal).

râble¹ [rɑːbl], *s.m.* back (of hare, rabbit, etc.; *F:* of person); *Cu:* **r. de lièvre,** saddle of hare; *F:* **il m'a sauté sur le r.,** (i) he jumped on me; (ii) he cornered me.

râble², *s.m. Tls:* **1.** fire rake. **2.** *Metall:* rabble, strike; *Dy: Glassm:* stirrer.

râblé [rɑble], *a.* broad-backed, strong-backed (animal, person).

râblure [rɑblyːr], *s.f. N.Arch:* rabbet, groove.

rabobiner [rabɔbine], *v.tr. P:* to patch up, tinker up (sth.).

raboin [rabwɛ̃], *s.m. P:* **1.** *A:* the Devil. **2.** gipsy.

rabonnir [rabɔniːr]. **1.** *v.tr.* to improve, better (wine, etc.). **2.** *v.i.* (*of wine, etc.*) to improve.

rabot [rabo], *s.m.* **1.** *Join:* plane; **r. à moulures,** moulding plane; **r. cintré, à semelle cintrée,** compass plane; **r. rond,** round plane; **r. denté, à dents, à coller,** tooth(ing) plane; **r. à languette,** grooving plane, tongue-plane; **fer de r.,** plane iron; **fût de r.,** plane stock; **passer le r. sur une planche,** to run the plane over a plank; **passer le r. sur un ouvrage,** to polish up a piece of work. **2. r. d'ébouage,** road scraper; **r. en caoutchouc,** squeegee. **3.** *A:* **r. coupe-cors,** corn plane. **4.** *Min:* coal plough.

rabotage [rabɔtaːʒ], *s.m.*, **rabotement** [rabɔtmɑ̃], *s.m. Join:* planing; **atelier de r.,** planing mill, shop.

rabote [rabɔt], *s.f. Cu: Dial:* (baked) apple dumpling.

raboter [rabɔte], *v.tr.* **1.** (*a*) to plane (wood); (*b*) to file down (horse's hoof); **r. son style,** to polish one's style; **la houle rabote les rochers,** the swell of the sea wears away the rocks. **2.** *P: A:* **r. l'argent de qn,** to steal, pinch, s.o.'s money.

raboteur [rabɔtœːr], *s.m. Join:* (*pers.*) planer; **r. à la machine,** planing-machine tenter.

raboteuse[1] [rabɔtøːz], *s.f. Join:* planing machine, planer.

raboteux, -euse[2] [rabɔtø, -øːz], *a.* **1.** rough, uneven; **bois r.,** knotty wood; **pays r.,** rough, rugged, country; **chemin r.,** rough, bumpy, road. **2.** unpolished, rugged (style, etc.); rough (performance).

rabotin [rabɔtɛ̃], *s.m. Tls:* drag (for surfacing stone).

raboture [rabɔtyːr], *s.f.* shavings (from a plane).

rabougri [rabugri], *a.* stunted, dwarfed (plant, person, etc.); scraggy (vegetation).

rabougrir [rabugriːr]. **1.** *v.tr.* to stunt the growth of (sth.). **2.** *v.i. & pr.* to become stunted.

rabougrissement [rabugrismɑ̃], *s.m.* stuntedness; scragginess (of vegetation).

rabouiller [rabuje], *v.tr. & v.i. Dial:* to muddy (water, before fishing).

rabouillère [rabujɛːr], *s.f.* nursery burrow (of rabbit).

rabouilleur, -euse [rabujœːr, -øːz], *s. Dial:* angler in muddied waters.

rabouin [rabwɛ̃], *s.m. P:* **1.** *A:* the Devil. **2.** gipsy.

rabouter [rabute], *O:* **raboutir** [rabutiːr], *v.tr.* (*a*) to join, set, (lengths of wood, iron, etc.) end to end; to butt (lengths) together; to splice up; (*b*) *Needlew:* to join up (lengths of material).

raboutissage [rabutisaːʒ], *s.m.* joining (of objects) end to end; butting together; splicing (up).

rabrouer [rabrue], *v.tr.* to snub (s.o.); to treat (s.o.) brusquely, in an offhand manner; *F:* to give (s.o.) a good dressing down; to jump down (s.o.'s) throat; to sit on (s.o.).

rabroueur, -euse [rabruœːr, -øːz], *a. & s.* brusque, offhand, surly (person).

raca [raka], *int. B:* raca; *A: & Lit:* **crier r. à, sur, qn,** to hurl abuse at s.o.; to insult s.o.

racage [rakaːʒ], *s.m. Nau:* parrel, parral.

racahout [rakau], *s.m. Cu:* rac(c)ahout.

racaille [rakɑːj], *s.f.* rabble, riff-raff; scum, dregs (of the population).

racambeau, -eaux [rakɑ̃bo], *s.m. A: Nau:* boom iron.

racanette [rakanɛt], *s.f. Orn: Ven:* teal.

raccastillage [rakastijaːʒ], *s.m. Nau:* repairs to upper works.

raccastiller [rakastije], *v.tr.* to repair the upper works of (ship).

raccommodable [rakɔmɔdabl̩], *a.* mendable, repairable.

raccommodage [rakɔmɔdaːʒ], *s.m.* **1.** mending, repairing (of furniture, garments, etc.); darning (of stockings, etc.). **2.** mend, repair; darn.

raccommodement [rakɔmɔdmɑ̃], *s.m.* reconciliation; making up (of a quarrel).

raccommoder [rakɔmɔde], *v.tr.* **1.** (*a*) to mend, repair (dress, watch, etc.); to darn (stocking); to patch (garment); (*b*) *A:* to set (a matter) to rights; to make amends for (blunder, etc.); (*c*) *A:* **l'air de la mer vous raccommodera,** the sea air will restore you to health. **2.** to reconcile (two persons); to heal the breach between (two persons); **ils se sont raccommodés,** they made it up; they became friends again.

raccommodeur, -euse [rakɔmɔdœːr, -øːz], *s.* **1.** mender, repairer. **2.** *Coal Min:* (underground) maintenance man.

raccompagner [rakɔ̃paɲe], *v.tr.* to accompany back, to see back; **je vais vous r.,** I'll take you back, see you home.

raccord [rakɔːr], *s.m.* **1.** *Tp: etc:* linking up (of subscribers, etc.). **2.** (*a*) join(ing), juncture (in a building, a picture, etc.); **papier sans raccords,** (wall)paper with no pattern repeat; **faire des raccords (de peinture),** to touch up (the paintwork); **faire des raccords dans une tapisserie, un roman,** to join up tapestry, parts of a novel; *Toil: F:* **faire un r.,** to touch up one's face, one's makeup; *Cin:* **scène de r.,** flash; *Th:* **nous allons faire un r. pour la doublure qui joue ce soir,** we'll run through the cues for the understudy who is playing tonight; (*b*) *Elcs:* (*computers*) link; *Rec:* splice; **faire un r. à (une bande magnétique),** to splice (a tape). **3.** *Mec.E:* adapter, adaptor (of part of a machine or apparatus); connection, coupling, coupler (of adjacent parts); connector (of wires or tubes); joint, junction (of end pieces or pipes); nipple, union (of pipes); **bouchon de r.,** adapter plug; **r. universel,** universal adapter, coupling; *I.C.E:* **r. de tuyau, de tubulure, d'échappement,** exhaust-pipe, exhaust-stack, adapter; *El:* **r. mâle et femelle,** plug and socket connection; **r. de lampe,** lamp adapter, connector; **r. articulé,** articulated connection, coupling; **r. banjo, r. oscillant,** banjo connection; **r. flexible,** flexible connection coupling; **r. en col de cygne,** gooseneck coupling; **r. à brides,** flanged fitting; **r. orientable,** swivel connection; *Mec.E:* **r. de pompe,** pump connection; *Av:* **r. d'essais au sol,** ground-test coupling; *Rail:* **r. de rail,** rail joint; **r. de tuyaux,** pipe union, connection, coupling; **r. de tuyau flexible,** hose union, connection, coupling; hose nippling; **r. flexible de tuyauterie,** flexible hose connection; **tuyau, manchon, de r.,** connecting pipe, connection sleeve; **r. manchon,** joint union; **r. coudé,** elbow union; **r. en T,** T union; **raccord en Y,** breeches pipe; **r. d'arrivée d'huile,** oil-inlet union; **r. fileté,** union nut, screwed socket; **r. à vis,** union-nut joint; **r. mobile,** movable union; *I.C.E:* **r. de durite,** rubberhose coupling; **r. de cylindre,** cylinder nipple; **r. de filtre d'essence,** fuel-filter nipple; **r. de graissage,** grease nipple; *Phot:* **r. de déclenchement,** teat of pneumatic release.

raccordement [rakɔrdəmɑ̃], *s.m.* **1.** adjusting; levelling (of two floors or surfaces); bringing (parts) into line, making (parts) flush; *Rail: Civ.E:* easement, transition (of curves, of segments of railway or road by a curve); **rayon de r. (d'une courbe),** transition radius (of a curve); *Rail:* **r. des angles par des courbes,** adjustment of angles by curves; *Mapm:* **(ligne de) r. (d'une feuille),** sheet line. **2.** *Arch: etc:* joining; *Tp:* linking-up (of subscribers); **taxe de r.,** installation charge (for electricity, telephone, etc.). **3.** (*a*) *Civ.E: Mec.E:* connecting, connection, coupling; **pièces de r.,** making-up lengths (of piping, etc.); **collerette de r.,** mating flange; **embase de r.,** connector base; *Av:* **bretelle de r.,** connecting taxiway (in aerodrome); *Rail:* **courbe de r.,** junction curve; **ligne, voie, de r.,** (i) junction line, loop line; (ii) side line, private siding (leading to a factory, etc.); (*b*) *El: Elcs:* (i) connecting, connection; (ii) branch (circuit), by-pass; **r. telex,** telex connection; **boîte de r.,** connecting box (for cables, etc.); **borne de r.,** connecting terminal; **câble de r.,** connecting cable; **fiche de r.,** connection plug.

raccorder [rakɔrde], *v.tr. Arch: Mec.E: etc:* (*a*) to join (up), connect, unite, couple; to link up (**avec,** with); *El:* **r. transversalement,** to cross-connect; **r. à la masse, à la terre,** to earth, to ground; (*b*) to bring (parts) into line; to make (parts) flush; (*c*) *Elcs:* (*computers*) to branch, connect; to patch; *Rec:* to splice (a tape).

se raccorder, to fit together, to blend; to square together.

raccourci [rakursi]. **1.** *a.* shortened (skirt, etc.); short, squat (stature); abridged (plan, account); *Geom:* oblate (ellipsoid); curtate (cycloid); *Her:* couped; **à bras raccourcis,** with all ones' strength, with all one's force; **tomber à bras raccourcis sur qn,** to go for s.o. tooth and nail. **2.** *s.m.* (*a*) *O:* abridgment, abridged version; (*b*) **en r.,** (i) briefly, in brief; (ii) on a small scale, in miniature; **voici l'histoire en r.,** this, in brief, is the story; these are the outlines of the story; **raconter qch. en r.,** to tell sth. briefly, in a few words; **la famille est la société en r.,** the family is society in miniature; (*c*) *Art:* foreshortening; **bras en r.,** foreshortened arm; (*d*) short cut (to a place); **prendre (par) un r.,** to take a short cut.

raccourcir [rakursiːr]. **1.** *v.tr.* (*a*) to shorten; to make (string, skirt, etc.) shorter; to take up (sleeve, etc.); to reduce the length of (sth.); **r. ses pas,** to take shorter steps; **r. le pas,** to shorten step; *Artil:* **r. le tir,** to shorten, lessen, the range; **raccourcir son bras,** to draw up one's arm; **chat qui se raccourcit pour bondir,** cat that draws itself up, that crouches, to spring; **r. son chemin,** to take a short cut; *P:* **r. qn,** to guillotine s.o., to cut s.o.'s head off, to top s.o.; (*b*) to abridge, curtail; to cut down (trousers into shorts, etc.); to cut (speech, etc.) short; (*c*) *Art:* to foreshorten. **2.** *v.i. & pr.* to grow shorter; to shorten; **toile qui (se) raccourcit,** cloth that shrinks; **les jours (se) raccourcissent,** the days are growing shorter, are drawing in, closing in.

raccourcissement [rakursismɑ̃], *s.m.* shortening. **1.** (*a*) reducing (in length); (*b*) abridging, abridgment; (*c*) *Art:* foreshortening. **2.** (*a*) growing shorter; **le r. des jours en automne,** the drawing in of the days in autumn; (*b*) shrinking (of cloth, etc.).

raccours [rakuːr], *s.m. Tex:* shrinking.

raccoutrage [rakutraːʒ], *s.m.*, **raccoutrement** [rakutrəmɑ̃], *s.m. A:* mending (of knitted garment, etc.).

raccoutrer [rakutre], *v.tr. A:* to mend, repair (knitted garment, ladder in stocking, etc.); *Ind:* to make good (by hand, defective hosiery, etc.).

raccoutreur, -euse [rakutrœːr, -øːz], *s. A: Ind:* mender (of defective hosiery).

raccoutumer (se) [sərakytyme], *v.pr.* to reaccustom oneself, to get reaccustomed (**à,** to).

raccroc [rakro], *s.m.* **1.** (*a*) *Games: esp. Bill:* fluke, lucky stroke; **coup de r.,** fluky shot, stroke; **par r.,** by a fluke; (*b*) *A:* **visiteurs de r.,** chance visitors, visitors that drop in. **2.** *F:* **faire le r.,** (i) to tout; (ii) (*of prostitute*) to walk the streets.

raccrochage [rakrɔʃaːʒ], *s.m.* (*a*) *Jur:* accosting; (*b*) touting.

raccrocher [rakrɔʃe], *v.tr.* **1.** (*a*) to hook up, hang up, (sth.) again; *Tp:* **r. (l'appareil),** to put down the receiver; to ring off; to hang up; (*b*) *abs.* to give up; **ce boxeur devrait r.,** it's time this boxer gave up, retired. **2.** *F:* to recover (sth.); to lay hold of (sth.) again; to get hold of (s.o.) again. **3.** to stop (s.o., in the street, etc.); (*of prostitute*) to accost (passer-by). **4.** to get hold of, secure, (sth.) by a fluke. **5.** *abs. Bill: etc:* to make flukes, a fluke; to fluke.

se raccrocher. 1. se r. à qch., to clutch hold of sth.; to catch on to sth.; **se r. à une espérance,** to catch at, cling to, a hope; **se r. à tout,** to clutch at every chance, at every straw. **2.** *A:* **se r. à qn,** to attach oneself to s.o. again; to take up with s.o. again; to become friends with s.o. again; **se r. au service,** to take up, one's duties again; to resume one's duties. **3.** *Gaming: etc: F:* to recoup one's losses.

raccrocheur, -euse [rakrɔʃœːr, -øːz]. **1.** *a. F:* fetching; **un titre r.,** a fetching headline, a headline with appeal. **2.** *s.f.* **raccrocheuse,** street walker, tart.

race [ras], *s.f.* race. **1.** ancestry, descent; strain; **être de r. juive,** to be of Jewish race, of Jewish descent; **de r. noble,** of noble race, of noble blood; **immigrants de r. latine,** immigrants of Latin blood; *A:* **ne point laisser de r.,** to leave no descendants. **2.** stock, breed, blood; **la r. humaine,** the human race; **la r. blanche,** the white race; **la r. chevaline,** the horse species; **r. canine,** canine race; **améliorer, croiser, les races,** to improve, to cross, breeds; **chien, taureau, de r., qui a de la r.,** pure-bred dog, bull; pedigree dog, bull; **cheval de r.,** thoroughbred horse; **r. croisée,** crossbreed; **de r. croisée,** crossbred; *Prov:* **bon chien chasse de r.,** what's bred in the bone comes out in the flesh; (*of pers.*) **avoir de la r.,** to be distinguished, aristocratic; **style de r.,** distinguished style. **3. la r. des hommes de loi,** lawyers (considered collectively); *F:* **quelle (sale) r.!** what a brood! what a set!

racé [rase], *a.* (*of animal*) thoroughbred; true to race; true to stock; (*of pers.*) aristocratic; distinguished; **Basque r.,** pure Basque; *F: Aut: etc:* **profil r.,** pure profile.

racémate [rasemat], *s.m. Ch:* racemate.

racème [rasɛm], *s.m. Bot:* raceme.

racémeux, -euse [rasemø, -øːz], *a. Bot:* racemose.

racémique [rasemik], *a. Ch:* racemic (acid, compound).

racémisation [rasemizasjɔ̃], *s.f. Ch:* racemization.

racémiser [rasemize], *v.tr. Ch:* to racemize.

racer [rasɛːr], *s.m.* racer; (*a*) race horse; (*b*) racing yacht; (*c*) *A:* (light) racing car.

raceur, -euse [rasœːr, -øːz], *s. Breed:* pedigree sire, dam.

rachat [raʃa], *s.m.* (*a*) *Com: Fin: etc:* repurchase, buying back; buying in (of goods); *St.Exch:* **rachats,** covering purchases; **offre de r.,** take-over bid; *Jur:* **r. d'une servitude,** commutation of an easement, of a right of user; **pacte de r.,** covenant of redemption; **avec faculté de r.,** with option of repurchase, of redemption; **r. des captifs,** ransom of the prisoners; **r. de cargaison,** ransom of cargo; (*b*) *Ins:* surrender (of policy); redemption (of annuity, etc.); **valeur de r.,** surrender value; (*c*) *Mil: A:* buying out of the service; (*d*) *A:* **r. des bans (de mariage),** marriage licence; (*e*) *Theol:* atonement.

rache [raʃ], *s.f.* (*a*) dregs (of tar); (*b*) *Carp: esp. Nau:* mark (made on timber indicating work to be done).

rachée [raʃe], *s.f.* sprouting stump (of tree).

Rachel [raʃɛl], *Pr.n.f.* Rachel.

racher [raʃe], *v.tr. Carp:* to mark (timber, as indication of work to be done).

rachetable [raʃtabl̩], *a.* redeemable (stock); atonable (sin).

racheter [raʃte], *v.tr.* (*conj. like* ACHETER) **1.** (*a*) to repurchase; to buy (sth.) back; *Com:* to buy (sth.) in; **r. (en surenchérissant),** to take over; (*b*) to redeem (debt, pledge, etc.); **Jésus-Christ est mort pour r. les hommes,** Christ died to redeem mankind; *F:* **r. ses défauts par ses agréments,** to redeem, make up for, compensate for, one's shortcomings, by one's agreeable qualities; **r. ses péchés,** to atone for one's sins; **r. son honneur,** to retrieve one's honour; **r. son passé,** to atone for one's past; to make good; **r. cher son bonheur,** to pay dear for one's happiness; (*c*) *Ins:* to surrender (policy); to redeem (annuity); (*d*) to ransom (prisoner); (*e*) *A:* **r. un jeune homme (du service militaire),** to buy a young man out (of military service). **2.** to buy again; to make a further purchase of (sth.); **r. du même drap,** to buy some more of the same cloth.

se racheter. 1. to redeem oneself; (*of child*) to make up (for bad behaviour). **2.** *St.Exch:* to cover short sales, shorts.

racheteur, -euse [raʃtœːr, -øːz], *s.* buyer back; redeemer (of stock, etc.).

racheux, râcheux, -euse [raʃø, rɑʃø, -øːz], *a.* knotty (wood).

rachialgie [raʃjalʒi], *s.f. Med:* rachialgia.

rachianalgésie [raʃjanalʒezi], **rachianesthésie** [raʃjanɛstezi], *s.f. Med:* rachianalgesia, rachi-anaesthesia.

rachidien, -ienne [raʃidjɛ̃, -jɛn], *a. Anat:* rachidian (bulb, canal, etc.).

rachiglosses [raʃiglɔs], *s.m.pl. Moll:* Rachiglossa.

rachis [raʃis], *s.m. Anat: Bot:* rachis.

rachitigène [raʃitiʒɛn], *a. Med:* rachitogenic.

rachitique [raʃitik], *a. & s. Med:* rachitic; *F:* rickety.

rachitis [raʃitis], *s.m.*, **rachitisme** [raʃitism], *s.m.* **1.** *Med:* rachitis; *F:* rickets. **2.** *Bot:* rachitis, abortion (of the seed).

rachitome [raʃitɔm], *s.m. Surg:* rachitome.

racial, -aux [rasjal, -o], *a.* racial.

racinage [rasinaːʒ], *s.m.* **1.** *coll. A:* (edible) **roots. 2.** *Tex: A:* walnut dye. **3.** *Bookb:* tree-marbling (of cover).

racinal, -aux [rasinal, -o], *s.m. Const: etc:* (*a*) (foundation) beam, sleeper, bolster; main sill (of sluice); sole (of crane); (*b*) *pl.* grillage.

racine [rasin], *s.f.* **1.** (*a*) root (of plant, hair, nail, tumour, etc.); *Anat:* **r. de la langue,** radix linguae; *Bot:* **r. pivotante,** tap root; *Com:* **r. de gingembre,** ginger race; **r. d'une montagne,** foot of a mountain; **de vieilles racines de dents,** old stumps (of teeth); **jeter, pouser, des racines,** to throw out roots, to strike (root); **prendre r.,** to take root; *F:* **quand elle fait des visites, elle prend r. chez les gens,** when she calls, comes, there's no getting rid of her; **affection aux racines profondes,** deep-rooted affection; *Lit:* **ces vices jettent dans l'âme de profondes racines,** these vices become deeply rooted in the soul; **couper le mal dans sa r.,** to strike at the root of the evil; **atteindre le mal dans sa r.,** to go to the root of the evil; (*b*) *Mth:* **r. carrée, cubique,** square root, cube root; **r. quatrième,** fourth root; (*c*) *Ling:* **r. d'un mot,** root of a word; etymon. **2.** *Fish:* **r. (anglaise),** silkworm gut; silk gut.

raciné [rasine], *a.* **1.** *Bot:* having roots. **2.** *Bookb:* marbled; **veau r.,** marbled calf; tree calf.

racine-asperge [rasinaspɛrʒ], *s.f. Bot:* air root, breathing stem (of aquatic plant); *pl. racines-asperges.*

racineau, -eaux [rasino], *s.m.* prop, stake, support (for young plant).

racine-échasse [rasineʃas], *s.f. Bot:* stilt root; *pl. racines-échasses.*

racinement [rasinmɑ̃], *s.m.* taking root, rooting.

raciner [rasine]. **1.** *v.i. A:* to strike root, take root; to root. **2.** *v.tr.* (*a*) *Tex: A:* to dye with walnut; (*b*) *Bookb:* to marble (the covers).

racineur [rasinœːr], *s.m. Bookb:* marbler.

racinien, -ienne [rasinjɛ̃, -jɛn], *a. Lit:* Racinian.

racique [rasik], *a.* racial; *attrib.* race.

racisme [rasism], *s.m.* racialism, *esp. U.S:* racism.

raciste [rasist], *a. & s.m. & f.* racialist, *esp. U.S:* racist.

racket [rakɛt], *s.m. F:* racket.

racketter [rakɛtɛːr], **racketteur** [rakɛtœːr], *s.m. F:* racketeer.

raclage [rɑklaːʒ], *s.m.* **1.** (*a*) scraping; (*b*) raking (of the ground). **2.** *For:* thinning of the under-brush.

racle [rɑːkl̩], *s.f.* (*a*) *Tls:* scraper; (*b*) doctor (of calico-printing roller).

raclée [rɑkle], *s.f.* **1.** *F:* (*a*) hiding, licking, thrashing; **flanquer, administrer, une r. à qn,** to give s.o. a thrashing, a licking; **recevoir sa r. en homme,** to take one's licking, one's punishment, like a man; (*b*) defeat. **2.** surface hoeing.

raclement [rɑkləmɑ̃], *s.m.* scraping.

racler [rɑkle], *v.tr.* **1.** to scrape (skin, horn, carrot, etc.); **r. une allée,** to rake a drive; *F:* **r. les fonds de tiroir,** to scrape the barrel; **r. du, le, violon,** to scrape, saw, on the fiddle; **r. un air,** to scrape out a tune (on the fiddle); **vin qui racle le gosier,** wine that rasps the throat; **se r. la gorge,** to clear one's throat; **la police les a raclés,** the police made a clean sweep of them. **2.** *For:* to thin out (underbrush). **3.** *Carp:* to scrape, polish, smooth (surface).

raclerie [rɑkləri], *s.f.* **bois de r.,** carving wood.

raclette [rɑklɛt], *s.f. Tls:* (*a*) scraper; (*b*) *Phot: etc:* squeegee; (*c*) *Paperm: Typ: etc:* doctor; (*d*) *Hort:* hoe; (*e*) (baby's) pusher.

racleur, -euse [rɑklœːr, -øːz]. **1.** *s.* scraper; *F:* **r. de violon,** scraper on the fiddle. **2.** *s.m. I.C.E:* **(segment) r. d'huile,** scraper ring.

racloir [rɑklwaːr], *s.m. Tls:* (*a*) scraper, scraping-tool; (*b*) (cooper's) hoop-shave, spokeshave; (*c*) squeegee; (*d*) *Typ:* slice; (*e*) *Paperm: etc:* doctor; (*f*) shoescraper (outside front door).

racloire [rɑklwaːr], *s.f.* **1.** strickle, strike. **2.** *Tls:* spokeshave. **3.** tongue scraper.

raclons [rɑklɔ̃], *s.m.pl.* (pan) scrapings; (road) sweepings.

raclure [rɑklyːr], *s.f.* (*a*) scrapings (of wood, horn, brick, etc.); (*b*) rubbish.

racolage [rakɔlaːʒ], *s.m.* **1.** (*a*) *A:* recruiting (for the army or navy); (*b*) *A:* crimping; impressing (of men into the army or navy); (*c*) **r. de partisans,** enlisting of supporters. **2.** *Jur:* r. **(sur la voie publique),** soliciting, accosting (in a public place).

racoler [rakɔle], *v.tr.* **1.** (*a*) *A:* to recruit (men for the army or navy); (*b*) *A:* to crimp, impress (men into the army or navy); (*c*) *Pej:* **r. des partisans,** to enlist supporters; **r. des clients,** to tout for customers. **2.** *Jur:* **r. (sur la voie publique),** to solicit, accost (in a public place).

racoleur, -euse [rakɔlœːr, -øːz], *s.* **1.** (*a*) *A:* recruiting sergeant; (*b*) *A:* crimp; (*c*) *Pej:* tout; propagandist. **2.** *s.f.* **racoleuse,** prostitute, street walker.

racon [rakɔ̃], *s.m. Elcs:* radar beacon, racon.

racontable [rakɔ̃tabl̩], *a.* relatable, tellable; that can be told.

racontage [rakɔ̃taːʒ], *s.m. O:* story, piece of gossip, piece of tittle-tattle; **racontages,** tittle-tattle; chit-chat; idle talk.

racontar [rakɔ̃taːr], *s.m. F:* story, piece of gossip; **ce n'est que des racontars,** it's all talk; it's nothing but ill-natured gossip.

raconter [rakɔ̃te], *v.tr.* to tell, relate, narrate, recount (tale, fact, adventures); **r. de longues histoires,** to spin long yarns; **vous vous êtes laissé r. des histoires,** you have been listening to gossip; **l'histoire qu'on lui a racontée était fausse,** the story told to him was untrue; **il en a raconté de belles,** he told some fine, tall, stories; **il vous en raconte,** he's telling you a tall story; **il raconta ses aventures, ses souffrances,** he told of his adventures, of his sufferings; **je vous raconterai cela plus tard,** I shall tell you all about it later; **voilà ce qu'on raconte,** that is what people are saying; **on a raconté que . . .,** it has been rumoured, said, that . . .; **il raconta s'être vu face à face avec un revenant,** he told how he had come face to face with a ghost; **qu'est-ce qu'il raconte là?** what ever is he talking about? **il nous a raconté comment cela s'était passé,** he told us how it had happened; *abs.* **il raconte bien,** he knows how to tell a story; he tells a good story; **allez, racontez!** get on with it! out with it!

raconteur, -euse [rakɔ̃tœːr, -øːz]. **1.** *s.* (*a*) (story) teller, narrator; **les raconteurs du passé,** people who tell stories of the past; (*b*) (*public entertainer*) raconteur, raconteuse. **2.** *a.* **la vieillesse raconteuse,** (i) garrulous old age; (ii) garrulous old people.

racoon [rakun], *s.m. Z:* rac(c)oon.

racornir [rakɔrniːr], *v.tr.* to make (sth.) hard or tough (as horn); **se r. les mains,** to make one's hands horny; **le feu a racorni le cuir,** the fire has hardened, has shrivelled up, the leather; **visage racorni,** wizened face.

se racornir, (*a*) to grow horny, hard, tough; to harden; to shrivel up; (*b*) (*of pers.*) (i) to become wizened; (ii) to grow callous; (iii) to lose one's elasticity of mind.

racornissement [rakɔrnismɑ̃], *s.m.* (*a*) hardening; toughening; (*b*) shrivelling.

racquérir [rakeriːr], *v.tr.* (*conj. like* ACQUÉRIR) to recover; to acquire (sth.) again; to get (sth.) back.

racquitter [rakite], *v.tr.* to recoup, indemnify (s.o.).

rad [rad], *s.m. Atom.Ph: Meas:* rad.

radar [radaːr], *s.m.* radar; **r. à impulsions,** pulse radar; **r. à modulation de fréquence,** frequency-modulation radar; **r. à ondes entretenues,** continuous-wave radar; **r. diversité,** diversity radar; **r. Doppler,** Doppler radar; **r. acoustique,** sound radar; **r. primaire, secondaire,** primary, secondary, radar; **balayage r.,** radar scan; **r. à balayage latéral,** sideways-looking radar; **couverture r.,** radar cover(age); **écho r.,** radar echo; **écran r.,** radar screen, radarscope; **faisceau r.,** radar beam; **image r.,** radar picture; **opérateur r.,** radar operator, radarman; **poste r.,** radar set; **station r.,** radar station; *Mil:* **r. militaire tactique,** military tactical radar; **r. de localisation, de repérage,** locator radar; **r. de localisation des mortiers,** mortar-locating radar; *Mil: Av: Navy:* **r. d'exploration, de recherche,** search radar; **r. de surveillance, de veille,** surveillance radar, watch radar; **r. de veille aérienne,** air-surveillance radar; **r. d'acquisition, de désignation d'objectif, de détection,** acquisition radar; **r. de détection lointaine,** early-acquisition radar; **accrochage d'un objectif par le r.,** radar lock-on; **r. d'alerte,** warning radar; **r. d'alerte lointaine, éloignée,** early-warning radar; **r. de poursuite,** tracking radar; **r. panoramique,** plan position indicator (P.P.I.); **r. d'altimétrie, de sitométrie, de site,** height-finding radar; **r. de tir,** fire-control radar; **r. de bord,** *Av:* airborne radar, *Nau:* ship's radar; **r. anti-collision,** anti-collision radar; **r. de navigation,** navigational radar; **r. de radio-navigation, balise r.,** radar beacon; **navigation au r.,** radar navigation; *Av:* **r. d'aérodrome,** airport radar; **r. d'avion,** airborne radar; **r. d'approche,** approach radar; **r. d'atterrissage,** landing radar; **r. de contrôle de la navigation aérienne,** air-traffic control radar; **r. de navigation à très basse altitude,** terrain-following radar; **r. de détection, d'évitement, d'obstacles,** obstacle-avoidance radar; terrain-avoidance, terrain-warning, radar; *Ball:* **r. de guidage des missiles,** missile site radar; **r. d'autoguidage,** homing radar; **autoguidage par r.,** radar homing.

radariser [radarize], *v.tr.* to equip with radar.

radariste [radarist], *s.m. or f.* radar operator; radar engineer, mechanic.

rade [rad], *s.f.* **1.** (*a*) *Nau:* roadstead, roads; **en r.,** in the roads; **mettre un navire en r.,** to lay up a ship; **r. foraine, ouverte,** open roadstead; **r. fermée,** sheltered roadstead; **bonne r. du nord,** roads well sheltered from the north; (*b*) *F:* **laisser qn en r.,** to leave s.o. in the lurch; **rester en r.,** to be stuck; to be left out in the cold; **projet laissé en r.,** plan that has been shelved; **tomber en r.,** to break down. **2.** *P:* bar, pub.

radeau, -eaux [rado], *s.m.* raft. **1. r. de fortune,** emergency raft; **r. de barriques,** barrel raft; **r. de sauvetage,** life raft. **2.** raft, float (of logs carried down river).

radeleur [radlœːr], **radelier** [radəlje], *s.m.* **1.** raftman, raftsman. **2.** *Sw.Fr:* mooring man (for lake craft).

rader[1] [rade], *v.tr.* **1.** *A:* to strike (grain, salt, in the measure). **2.** *Const:* to split (block of stone).

rader[2]. **1.** *v.tr. Nau:* to bring (ship) into the roads **2.** *v.i. P:* (*of prostitute*) to solicit.

radeuse [radøːz], *s.f. P:* tart, street walker.

radiaire [radjɛːr]. **1.** *a. Nat.Hist:* radiate(d). **2.** *s.m. Z: A:* radiary; **les radiaires,** the Radiata.

radial¹, -ale, -aux [radjal, -o]. **1.** *a. Mth: etc:* radial; **pierres radiales d'un puits,** radial stones of a well; *Aut:* **pneumatique à carcasse radiale,** radial-ply tyre. **2.** *s.f.* **radiale,** radial road.

radial², -ale, -aux, *Anat:* (*a*) *a.* radial (muscle, nerve); (*b*) *s.m.* radial muscle, nerve; (*c*) *s.f.* **radiale,** radial vein, artery.

radialement [radjalmɑ̃], *adv.* radially.

radiamètre [radjamɛtr̥], *s.m. Atom.Ph:* radiation meter.

radian [radjɑ̃], *s.m. Mth:* radian (arc, angle).

radiance [radjɑ̃ːs], *s.f.* radiance.

radiant [radjɑ̃]. **1** *a. Astr: Bot: Ph: etc:* radiant; **chaleur radiante,** radiant heat; **pouvoir r.,** radiating capacity. **2.** *s.m. Astr:* radiant (point).

radiateur [radjatœːr], *s.m.* radiator; (*a*) **r. de chauffage central,** central-heating radiator; **r. à eau chaude,** hot-water radiator; **r. à circulation d'huile,** oil-filled radiator; **r. électrique,** electric fire; electric radiator; **r. parabolique,** (electric) bowl fire; **r. à convection,** convector heater; **r. soufflant,** fan heater; (*b*) *Aut: etc:* **r. à nid d'abeilles, r. alvéolaire,** honeycomb radiator, cellular radiator; **r. à ailettes, à nervures,** gilled, ribbed, radiator; **r. refroidi par ventilateur,** fan-cooled radiator; *Av:* **r. à lamelles,** secondary surface radiator; (*c*) *Ph:* **r. intégral,** black body.

radiatif, -ive [radjatif, -iːv], *a.* radiative.

radiation¹ [radjasjɔ̃], *s.f.* (*a*) erasure, striking out, crossing out; cancellation (of debt, etc.); *Jur:* **r. d'hypothèque,** entry of satisfaction of mortgage; (*b*) striking off the roll; dismissal from employment; disbarment (of barrister); striking off (of solicitor).

radiation², *s.f.* radiation; (*a*) *Ph: Elcs:* **r. cosmique,** cosmic radiation; **r. thermique,** thermal radiation; *Ch:* **r. ionisante, non ionisante,** ionizing, non-ionizing, radiation; *Elcs:* **r. (de) haute fréquence,** high-frequency radiation; **champ de r.,** radiation field; *W.Tel:* **zone de r.,** radiation zone; (*b*) *Atom.Ph:* **r. alpha, bêta, gamma,** alpha, beta, gamma, radiation; alpha-ray, beta-ray, gamma-ray, emission; **r. neutronique,** neutron radiation; **radiations instantanées, résiduelles, induites,** initial, residual, induced, radiation; **compteur, indicateur, de r.,** radiation counter, radiation survey meter; **détecteur de r.,** radiation detector, monitor; **mesure des radiations,** radiation measurement; **danger des radiations,** radiation hazard; **troubles dûs aux radiations,** radiation sickness.

radical, -ale, -aux [radikal, -o]. **1.** *a.* (*a*) *Mth. Bot: etc:* radical; *Mth:* **signe r.,** radical, root, sign; **axe, centre, r.,** radical axis, centre; (*b*) *Pol:* radical; (*c*) radical, complete; **changement r.,** complete, radical, change; **réformes radicales,** radical, sweeping, reforms. **2.** *s. Pol:* radical. **3.** *s.m.* (*a*) *Gram: Ling:* root, radical; (*b*) *Mth:* radical, root sign; (*c*) *Ch:* radical; group; **radicaux libres,** free radicals.

radicalaire [radikalɛːr], *a. Ch:* **réaction r.,** reaction giving rise to free radicals.

radicalement [radikalmɑ̃], *adv.* radically; **changer qch. r.,** to make a radical change in sth.; to change sth. radically; *Jur:* **r. nul,** null and void, absolutely void.

radicaliser [radikalize], *v.tr.* **r. l'opinion de qn,** to harden s.o.'s attitude; **se r.,** to become more extreme.

radicalisme [radikalism], *s.m. Pol:* radicalism.

radical-socialisme [radikalsɔsjalism], *s.m. Pol:* radical socialism.

radical-socialiste [radikalsɔsjalist], *s.m. & f. Pol:* radical socialist; *pl. radicaux-socialistes.*

radicant [radikɑ̃], *a. Bot:* radicant, radicating (stem, leaf).

radication [radikasjɔ̃], *s.f. Bot:* radication.

radicelle [radisɛl], *s.f. Bot:* radicel, rootlet.

radicicole [radisikɔl], *a. Nat.Hist:* radicicolous.

radicivore [radisivɔːr], *a. Ent: Z:* root-eating; rhizophagous, radicivorous.

radiculaire [radikylɛːr], *a.* (*a*) *Bot:* radicular; **poil r.,** root hair; (*b*) *Anat: Dent:* of the roots.

radicule [radikyl], *s.f. Bot:* radicle.

radiculite [radikylit], *s.f. Med:* radiculitis.

radié [radje], *a. Nat.Hist: etc:* radiate(d), rayed; *Bot:* **fleur radiée,** ray flower.

radier¹ [radje], *s.m.* **1.** *Civ.E:* frame, floor, bed; strengthening revetment (of masonry, concrete); sill (of lock gate); apron (of dock, basin, etc.); invert (of tunnel, sewer, etc.); (*in N.Africa*) concrete ford (across a wadi). **2. r. de fondation,** foundation raft; **immeuble fondé sur r.,** building on floating foundations.

radier², *v.tr.* (*p.d. & pr.sub.* **n. radiions, v. radiiez**) to erase; to strike (sth.) out; to strike (sth., s.o.) off, cross (sth., s.o.) off (a list, etc.); **r. le nom de qn,** to strike s.o.'s name off the rolls (of a society); **se faire r.,** to get one's registration cancelled, one's name removed, from the list; *Jur:* **r. une inscription hypothécaire par une mention sur le registre,** to enter a memorandum of satisfaction of mortgage on the register.

radier³, *v.i.* (*of pers.*) to beam.

radiesthésie [radjɛstezi], *s.f.* radiesthesia; dowsing; **faire de la r.,** to dowse.

radiesthésique [radjɛstezik], *a.* dowsing, water divining.

radiesthésiste [radjɛstezist], *s.m. & f.* radiesthesist; dowser; water-finder, water-diviner.

radieux, -euse [radjø, -øːz], *a.* radiant (sun, eyes, etc.); **ciel r.,** dazzling sky; **elle entra radieuse,** she came in beaming (with joy).

radifère [radifɛːr], *a. Miner:* radiferous, containing radium.

radin [radɛ̃], *a. & s.m. P:* mean, stingy (person).

radiner [radine], *v.i. P:* to come (back); to turn up; *Mil:* to arrive at the end of the day's march; to reach camp, billets; **alors? tu te radines!** so you're back.

radio- [radjɔ], *pref.* radio-.

radio [radjo], *F:* **1.** *s.m.* (*a*) radiogram, radio telegram; *attrib.* **message r.,** radio, wireless, message; (*b*) radio operator; (radio) telegraphist. **2.** *s.f.* (*a*) radio, wireless; **à la r.,** on the wireless; **il a parlé, passé, à la r. hier soir,** he broadcast, was on the air, on the radio, last night; **R. Moscou,** Radio Moscow; **r. pirate,** pirate station, pirate radio; (*b*) radiotelegraphy; (*c*) radiotelephony; (*d*) radio (set); (*e*) X-ray photograph; **passer à la r., passer une, la, r.,** to be X-rayed.

radio(-)actif, -ive [radjɔaktif, -iːv], *a.* radioactive; *Atom.Ph:* **période radioactive,** half-life (period); **déchets radioactifs,** radioactive waste; **constante radioactive,** radioactive constant, decay constant; **équilibre r.,** radioactive equilibrium; **série radioactive,** radioactive series.

radio(-)activité [radjɔaktivite], *s.f.* radioactivity; **r. artificielle, naturelle,** artificial, natural, radioactivity; **r. alpha, bêta, gamma,** alpha, beta, gamma, radioactivity; **r. instantanée, initiale,** initial (radio) activity; **r. résiduelle, rémanente,** residual (radio) activity; **r. induite,** induced (radio) activity.

radio(-)alignement [radjɔaliɲ(ə)mɑ̃], *s.m. Av:* radio-range airway; *Nau:* radio-beacon route; *Meteor:* **r. arrière,** back course; **émetteur de r.,** radio-range transmitter; **faisceau de r.,** radio-range beam; leg; **navigation par r.,** radio-range navigation; **voler par r.,** to fly airways.

radio(-)altimètre [radjɔaltimɛtr̥], *s.m. Av:* radio altimeter; radar altimeter.

radio(-)amateur [radjɔamatœːr], *s.m.* radio amateur, *F:* ham.

radio(-)astronome [radjɔastrɔnɔm], *s.m. & f.* radio astronomer.

radio(-)astronomie [radjɔastrɔnɔmi], *s.f.* radio astronomy.

radiobalisage [radjɔbalizaːʒ], *s.m.* (*a*) setting up of a radio-range system; (*b*) radio-beacon navigation; *Av:* airways navigation, flying airways.

radiobalise [radjɔbaliːz], *s.f.* radio beacon; marker beacon; **r. en éventail,** fan marker beacon.

radiobaliser [radjɔbalize], *v.tr.* (*a*) to equip (a route) with a radio-navigation system; (*b*) *Av: abs.* to fly airways.

radio(-)bélinogramme [radjɔbelinɔgram], *s.m.* radio photograph, photogram.

radio(-)bélinographie [radjɔbelinɔgrafi], *s.f.* radio photography.

radiobiologie [radjɔbjɔlɔʒi], *s.f.* radiobiology.

radioborne [radjɔbɔrn], *s.f. Av:* radio range beacon.

radiocarbone [radjɔkarbɔn], *s.m.* radiocarbon.

radiocarpien, -ienne [radjɔkarpjɛ̃, -jɛn], *a. Anat:* radio(-)carpal.

radiocentrique [radjɔsɑ̃trik], *a. Town P:* **plan r.,** concentric plan.

radiochimie [radjɔʃimi], *s.f.* radiochemistry; radiation chemistry.

radiochimique [radjɔʃimik], *a.* radiochemical.

radiocobalt [radjɔkɔbalt], *s.m.* radioactive cobalt, cobalt 60.

radiocolloïde [radjɔkɔlɔid], *s.m.* radiocolloid.

radiocommande [radjɔkɔmɑ̃ːd], *s.f.* radio control.

radiocommander [radjɔkɔmɑ̃de], *v.tr.* to radio-control.

radiocommunication [radjɔkɔmynikasjɔ̃], *s.f.* radiocommunication.

radiocompas [radjɔkɔ̃pɑ], *s.m. Av:* radio compass.

radioconducteur [radjɔkɔ̃dyktœːr], *s.m.* radio conductor; coherer.

radiocorps [radjɔkɔːr], *s.m.* radioactive body.

radiocristallographie [radjɔkristalɔgrafi], *s.f.* X-ray crystallography.

radio-cubital, -aux [radjɔkybital, -o], *a. Anat:* cubitoradial.

radiodermite [radjɔdɛrmit], *s.f. Med:* radiodermatitis; X-ray dermatitis.

radiodétecteur [radjɔdetɛktœːr,], *s.m.* radiodetector.

radiodétection [radjɔdetɛksjɔ̃], *s.f.* radiodetection.

radiodiagnostic [radjɔdjagnɔstik], *s.m. Med:* radiodiagnosis.

radiodiascopie [radjɔdjaskɔpi], *s.f.* radiodiascopy.

radiodiffuser [radjɔdifyze], *v.tr. W.Tel:* to broadcast; **r. en direct,** to broadcast live.

radiodiffusion [radjɔdifysjɔ̃], *s.f. W.Tel:* broadcasting; **r. en direct,** live broadcasting.

radiodramaturgie [radjɔdramatyrʒi], *s.f.* radio theatre.

radioélectricien, -ienne [radjɔelɛktrisjɛ̃, -jɛn], **radioélectronicien, -ienne** [radjɔelɛktrɔnisjɛ̃, -jɛn], *s.* radio (and television) specialist, technician, engineer; radioelectrician; electronics engineer.

radioélectricité [radjɔelɛktrisite], *s.f.* radioelectricity.

radioélectrique [radjɔelɛktrik], *a.* radioelectric; (*radar*) **axe r.,** scan axis.

radio(-)élément [radjɔelemɑ̃], *s.m. Atom.Ph:* radioelement.

radio-émission [radjɔemisjɔ̃], *s.f.* **1.** broadcasting. **2.** broadcast.

radio-étoile [radjɔetwal], *s.f. Astr:* radio star; *pl. radio-étoiles.*

radio-exposition [radjɔɛkspozisjɔ̃], *s.f.* exposure to radiation.

radiogène [radjɔʒɛn], *a.* X-ray emitting; **ampoule r.,** X-ray tube.

radiogénique [radjɔʒenik], *a.* **1.** (*produced by radioactive decay*) radiogenic. **2.** *F:* **il a une voix r.,** he has a good broadcasting voice.

radiogoniomètre [radjɔgɔnjɔmɛtr̥], *s.m.* radiogoniometer, direction finder; **r. de bord,** (i) *Av:* aircraft direction finder; (ii) *Nau:* ship's direction finder; **r. à cadre compensé,** compensated-loop direction finder; **r. à oscilloscope,** cathode-ray direction finder.

radiogoniométrie [radjɔgɔnjɔmetri], *s.f.* radiogoniometry; direction finding.

radiogoniométrique [radjɔgɔnjɔmetrik], *a.* radiogoniometric; direction-finding; **position donnée par relèvements radiogoniométriques,** position by directional findings; **cadre r.,** direction-finding loop.

radiogramme [radjɔgram], *s.m.* **1.** (*a*) radiograph, X-ray photograph; (*b*) skiagraph, radiogram. **2.** radiogram, radio telegram.

radiographe [radjɔgraf], *s.m. & f.* radiologist.

radiographie [radjɔgrafi], *s.f.* (*a*) radiography, X-ray photography; **r. collective,** mass radiography; **r. de contrôle,** follow-up radiography; **r. du crâne,** cephalography; (*b*) X-ray photograph, radiograph; **r. du crâne,** cephalogram.

radiographier [radjɔgrafje], (*p.d. & pr.sub.* **n. radiographiions, v. radiographiiez**) *v.tr.* to radiograph; to X-ray.

radiographique [radjɔgrafik], *a.* radiographic; **examen r.,** X-ray examination.

radioguidage [radjɔgidaːʒ], *s.m. Av: Nau:* radio control; radio direction; radio guidance; *Ball:* homing; *Av:* **r. d'aérodrome,** instrument landing system (ILS); **navigation par r.,** radio aid navigation.

radioguidé [radjɔgide], *a.* radio-controlled; guided (missile).

radioguider [radjɔgide], *v.tr.* to radio-control.

radiohuméral, -aux [radjɔymeral, -o], *a. Anat:* radiohumeral.

radio-interféromètre [radjɔɛ̃tɛrferɔmɛtr̥], *s.m.* radio interferometer; *pl. radio-interféromètres.*

radio-iode [radjɔjɔd], *s.m. Atom.Ph:* radio-iodine, radioactive iodine.

radioisotope [radjɔizɔtɔp], *s.m.* radioisotope, radioactive isotope.

radio(-)journal [radjɔʒurnal], *s.m. W.Tel:* (broadcast) news, news bulletin.

radiolabile [radjɔlabil], *a.* radiosensitive.

radiolaire [radjɔlɛːr], *a. & s.m. Prot:* radiolarian; *pl.* **radiolaires,** Radiolaria.

radiolarite [radjɔlarit], *s.f. Geol:* radiolarite; radiolarian ooze.

radiole [radjɔl], *s.f. Echin:* spine (of sea urchin).

radiolé [radjɔle], *a. Nat.Hist:* radiate(d), rayed.
radiolésion [radjɔlezjɔ̃], *s.f. Med:* X-ray lesion; lesion caused by a radioactive substance; radiation injury.
radiolite[1] [radjɔlit], *s.m. Moll:* radiolite.
radiolite[2], *s.f. Miner:* radiolite.
radiolocation [radjɔlɔkasjɔ̃], *s.f.*, **radio-localisation** [radjɔlɔkalizasjɔ̃], *s.f.* radiolocation.
radiologie [radjɔlɔʒi], *s.f.* radiology.
radiologique [radjɔlɔʒik], *a.* radiological; **examen r.**, X-ray examination; **guerre r.**, radiological warfare.
radiologiste [radjɔlɔʒist], **radiologue** [radjɔlɔg], *s.m. & f.* radiologist.
radioluminescence [radjɔlyminɛs(s)ɑ̃:s], *s.f.* radioluminescence.
radioluminescent [radjɔlyminɛs(s)ɑ̃], *a.* radioluminescent.
radio-maillage [radjɔmɑja:ʒ], *s.m. Av: etc:* **guidage par r.-m.**, grid guidance.
radio-mailles [radjɔmɑ:j], *s.f.pl. Av. etc:* **guidage par r.-m.**, grid guidance.
radiométallographie [radjɔmetalɔgrafi], *s.f.* radiometallography.
radiomètre [radjɔmɛtr̥], *s.m. Ph:* radiometer.
radiométrie [radjɔmetri], *s.f. Ph:* radiometry.
radiométrique [radjɔmetrik], *a.* radiometric; **magnitude r. d'une étoile**, radiometric magnitude of a star.
radiomicromètre [radjɔmikrɔmɛtr̥], *s.m.* radiomicrometer.
radiomusculaire [radjɔmyskylɛ:r], *a. Anat:* radiomuscular.
radionavigant [radjɔnavigɑ̃], *s.m. Nau: & A.Av:* radio officer, radio operator.
radionavigation [radjɔnavigasjɔ̃], *s.f.* radio navigation.
radionécrose [radjɔnekro:z], *s.f. Med:* radionecrosis; X-ray necrosis.
radionucléide [radjɔnykleid], *s.m.*, **radionuclide** [radjɔnyklid], *s.m.* radionuclide, radioactive nucl(e)ide.
radio-opacité [radjɔɔpasite], *s.f.* radiopacity.
radio-opaque [radjɔɔpak], *a.* radiopaque.
radiopathologie [radjɔpatɔlɔʒi], *s.f.* radiopathology.
radiophare [radjɔfa:r], *s.m. Nau: Av:* radio beacon; **r. directionnel, r. d'alignement fixe,** radio-range beacon; **r. tournant,** rotating (radio) beacon; **r. omnidirectionnel,** omnidirectional, omnirange, beacon; *Av:* **r. d'alignement de piste,** runway localizer; localizer beacon; **r. de jalonnement,** locator beacon; **r. de repérage,** airport marker beacon; **r. d'atterrissage,** landing beacon.
radiophone [radjɔfɔn], *s.m.* radiophone.
radiophonie [radjɔfɔni], *s.f.* radiophony; wireless telephony; broadcasting.
radiophonique [radjɔfɔnik], *a.* radiophonic; **pièce r.,** radio play.
radiophosphore [radjɔfɔsfɔ:r], *s.m. Atom.Ph:* radio-phosphorus.
radiophotographie [radjɔfɔtɔgrafi], *s.f.*, *F:* **radiophoto** [radjɔfɔto], *s.f.* X-ray photograph, radiophotograph.
radioprotection [radjɔprɔtɛksjɔ̃], *s.f.* protection against radiation.
radioralliement [radjɔralimɑ̃], *s.m.* homing (of missiles, etc.); **phare, balise, de r.,** radio homing beacon.
radiorécepteur [radjɔresɛptœ:r], *s.m.* radio (receiving set).
radiorepérage [radjɔrəpera:ʒ], *s.m.* radiolocation.
radioreportage [radjɔrəpɔrta:ʒ], *s.m. W.Tel:* broadcasting (of news, etc.); running commentary (of a match, etc.).
radioreporter [radjɔrəpɔrtɛ:r], *s.m. W.Tel:* commentator.
radioroman [radjɔrɔmɑ̃], *s.m. W.Tel:* radio serial.
radioroute [radjɔrut], *s.f. Av:* radio-beacon route; airway.
radioscopie [radjɔskɔpi], *s.f.* radioscopy; X-ray examination.
radioscopique [radjɔskɔpik], *a.* **examen r.,** X-ray examination; fluoroscopic observation.
radiosensibilité [radjɔsɑ̃sibilite], *s.f.* radiosensitivity.
radiosensible [radjɔsɑ̃sibl̥], *a.* radiosensitive, radiation-sensitive.
radiosignalisation [radjɔsiɲalizasjɔ̃], *s.f. Av: Nau:* radio direction sending; transmission of navigational aids.
radiosondage [radjɔsɔ̃da:ʒ], *s.m. Meteor:* radiosondage.
radiosonde [radjɔsɔ̃:d], *s.f.* **1.** *Meteor:* radiosonde. **2.** *Av:* radio altimeter.
radiosource [radjɔsurs], *s.f. Astr:* radio source.
radiostéréoscopie [radjɔstereɔskɔpi], *s.f.* radiostereoscopy.
radiostrontium [radjɔstrɔ̃tjɔm], *s.m. Atom.Ph:* radio strontium, strontium 90.
radiosusceptibilité [radjɔsysɛptibilite], *s.f.* radiosensitivity.
radio-taxi [radjɔtaksi], *s.m.* radio taxi; *pl. radiotaxis.*
radiotechnique [radjɔtɛknik], *s.f.* radiotechnology.
radiotélégramme [radjɔtelegram], *s.m.* radio telegram.
radiotélégraphie [radjɔtelegrafi], *s.f.* radio telegraphy, wireless telegraphy.
radiotélégraphier [radjɔtelegrafje], *v.tr.* (*conj. like* TÉLÉGRAPHIER) to radio (a telegram).
radiotélégraphique [radjɔtelegrafik], *a.* radiotelegraphic, wireless.
radiotélégraphiste [radjɔtelegrafist], *s.m. & f.* radiotelegraphist.
radiotéléphone [radjɔtelefɔn], *s.m.* radiotelephone, radiophone.
radiotéléphoner [radjɔtelefɔne], *v.tr. & i.* to radiotelephone.
radiotéléphonie [radjɔtelefɔni], *s.f.* radiotelephony, wireless telephony.
radiotéléphonique [radjɔtelefɔnik], *a.* radiotelephonic, wireless, *F:* radio (message, etc.).
radiotéléphoniste [radjɔtelefɔnist], *s.m. & f.* radiotelephonist.
radiotélescope [radjɔtelɛskɔp], *s.m.* radio telescope.
radiothéâtre [radjɔteɑtr̥], *s.m.* radio theatre.
radiotélévisé [radjɔtelevize], *a.* **ce discours sera r.,** this speech will be broadcast on both radio and television.
radiothérapeute [radjɔterapø:t], *s.m. & f.* radiotherapist; radiotherapeutist.
radiothérapie [radjɔterapi], *s.f.* radiotherapy; X-ray treatment; radiotherapeutics, radiation therapy.
radiothérapique [radjɔterapik], *a.* radiotherapic.
radiothorium [radjɔtɔrjɔm], *s.m. Ch:* radiothorium.
radis [radi], *s.m.* radish; **r. noir,** horseradish; **ne pas avoir un r.,** to be without a penny, *F:* to be (stony) broke; **je ne dépense pas un r. de plus,** I'm not spending a penny more; *A:* **piquer un r.,** to blush, to flush up.
radium [radjɔm], *s.m.* radium; *F:* **montre (au) r.,** watch with luminous hands, dial.
radiumbiologie [radjɔmbjɔlɔʒi], *s.f.* radiobiology.
radiumthérapeute [radjɔmterapø:t], *s.m.* radiumtherapist.
radiumthérapie [radjɔmterapi], *s.f.* radiumtherapy.
radius [radjys], *s.m. Anat:* radius.
radja(h) [radʒa], *s.m.* raja(h).
radoire [radwa:r], *s.f. A:* strickle, strike.
radome, radôme [rado:m], *s.m.* (*radar*) radome.
radon [radɔ̃], *s.m. Ch:* radon.
radotage [radɔta:ʒ], *s.m.* (*a*) disjointed, rambling, conversation; (*b*) **tomber dans le r.,** to fall into one's dotage.
radoter [radɔte], *v.i.* (*a*) to talk in a rambling, disjointed, incoherent, manner; **il commence à r.,** he's getting a bit gaga; (*b*) to keep on repeating oneself; (*c*) *v.tr. F:* **qu'est-ce qu'il radote?** what's he rambling on about?
radoterie [radɔtri], *s.f.* (*a*) disjointed, rambling, incoherent, conversation; (*b*) endless, senseless, repetition.
radoteur, -euse [radɔtœ:r, -ø:z]. **1.** *s.* dotard; person in his, her, dotage. **2.** *a.* **discours r., (i)** rambling, disjointed, incoherent, (ii) repetitive, speech; **il est un peu r.,** he's a bit gaga.
radoub [radu], *s.m.* **1.** *Nau:* repair, refitting, graving (of ship); **navire en r.,** ship under repair, in dry dock; **bassin, forme, de r.,** graving dock, dry dock; **cale de r.,** graving slip; **chantier de r.,** yard. **2.** *Pyr: A:* re-working (of powder).
radoubage [raduba:ʒ], *s.m. Nau:* repairing of the hull (of ship); docking.
radouber [radube], *v.tr.* **1.** *Nau:* (*a*) to repair the hull of (ship); to dock (ship in dry dock); *v.i.* (*of vessel*) to be under repair; (*b*) to mend, repair (net); *F:* to patch (sth.) up. **2.** *Pyr: A:* to re-work (damp) powder.
radoubeur [radubœ:r], *s.m.* (ship) repairer, refitter; graver.
radoucir [radusi:r], *v.tr.* to calm, soften; to calm, smooth (s.o.) down; to mollify (s.o.); **la pluie a radouci le temps,** the rain has brought milder weather; **le bonheur l'a radouci,** happiness has made him calmer, more gentle.
se radoucir. 1. (*of s.o.'s mood, etc.*) to grow calmer, to calm down; (*of pers.*) to recover one's temper. **2.** (*of the weather*) to grow milder.
radoucissement [radusismɑ̃], *s.m.* (*a*) softening (of character, voice, etc.); calming down (of temper, etc.); (*b*) getting milder, change for the better (of the weather).
radula [radyla], *s.f.*, **radule** [radyl], *s.f. Moll:* radula.
Raf [raf; ɛ:r a ɛf], *s.f. F:* the Royal Air Force, the R.A.F.
rafale [rafal], *s.f.* (*a*) squall; strong gust, blast (of wind); **le vent souffle par rafales,** the wind blows in squalls, the wind is gusty; **vent à rafales, qui souffle en rafales,** blustering wind; gusty wind; **temps à rafales,** squally weather; **r. de pluie,** cloudburst; (*b*) burst (of gunfire); **tir par rafales,** fire by bursts; **r. de cinq à six cartouches,** burst of five or six rounds.
rafalé [rafale], *a.* **1.** (*of ship*) struck by a squall; disabled by a squall or by squalls. **2.** *A: F:* (*of pers.*) cleaned out; down and out.
rafalement [rafalmɑ̃], *s.m. A: F:* impecuniosity, want, distress; dire straits.
rafaler [rafale], *v.tr. A: P:* to bring (s.o.) into low water, to the verge of ruin; to bring s.o. to ruin.
raffermir [rafɛrmi:r], *v.tr.* **1.** to harden (once more); to make (sth.) firm(er); **le soleil a raffermi les chemins,** the sun has hardened the roads. **2.** (*a*) to confirm, strengthen (s.o.'s authority, resolution); to fortify, reinforce restore (s.o.'s courage, spirit); to steady (prices, etc.); **r. le crédit d'une maison,** to re-establish a firm's credit; **r. qn dans un projet,** to confirm s.o. in a project; **prendre qch. pour se r. les nerfs,** to take sth. to steady one's nerves; **cela raffermirait ma position,** it would strengthen my position; (*b*) **r. un poteau,** to firm up a post.
se raffermir. 1. (*a*) (*of ground, muscle, etc.*) to harden; (*b*) **sa santé s'est raffermie,** his health has improved; he has recovered his health; **ses jambes se raffermissent,** his legs are growing stronger again. **2. son autorité, son crédit, se raffermit,** he is recovering his authority, his credit; **les prix se raffermissent,** prices are steadying, are hardening; **il se raffermit dans sa résolution,** he is more determined than ever.
raffermissement [rafɛrmismɑ̃], *s.m.* **1.** hardening (again); making firm(er) (of substance). **2.** (*a*) strengthening, confirmation (of authority, power, etc.); improvement, building up (of health); (*b*) hardening, steadying (of prices).
raffinade [rafinad], *s.f.* refined sugar.
raffinage [rafina:ʒ], *s.m. Ind:* (oil, sugar, etc.) refining.
raffiné [rafine], *a.* **1.** *Ind:* refined (sugar, etc.); *s.m. Petroleum Ind:* **du brut et du r.,** crude and refined (products). **2.** (*a*) subtle (mind, pleasure, etc.); delicate (taste, etc.); polished (manners, style, etc.); **analyse raffinée,** subtle analysis; **cuisine raffinée,** choice cuisine; (*b*) **peuple r.,** highly civilized nation; **gourmet r.,** fine gourmet; *s.m.* **un r.,** a man of taste, of discernment; *Pej:* **un petit r.,** a finicky little man.
raffinement [rafinmɑ̃], *s.m.* (over-)refinement; affectedness, affectation (of language, style, manners, tastes); subtlety (of thought, policy); refinement (of luxury, cruelty).
raffiner [rafine], *v.tr.* **1.** to refine (sugar, oil, etc.). **2.** (*a*) to polish (one's style, manners, etc.); (*b*) *abs.* **r. sur l'élégance, sur la propreté,** to carry elegance, cleanliness, to a point of fanaticism; **vous raffinez!** you're being too subtle!
raffinerie [rafinri], *s.f.* (oil, sugar) refinery.
raffineur, -euse [rafinœ:r, -ø:z], *s.* **1.** (oil, sugar) refiner; sugar boiler. **2.** *s.f. Paperm:* **raffineuse,** refining engine, refiner.
raffinose [rafino:z], *s.m. Ch:* raffinose.
rafflesia [raflɛzja], *s.m.*, **rafflésie** [raflezi], *s.f. Bot:* rafflesia.
rafflésiacées [raflezjase], *s.f.pl. Bot:* Rafflesiaceae.
raffolement [rafɔlmɑ̃], *s.m. F:* infatuation (**de,** for).
raffoler [rafɔle], *v.i. F:* **r. de qn, de qch.,** to be infatuated with, to dote on (s.o.); to adore, to be mad on (s.o., sth.).
raffut [rafy], *s.m. F:* noise, row, shindy; **faire du r.,** to kick up a row, a dust; **un r. du diable,** the devil's own row; a hell of a row.
raffûtage [rafyta:ʒ], *s.m.* (re)sharpening, (re)-setting (knife, tool, etc.).
raffûter [rafyte], *v.tr.* to (re)sharpen, (re)set (tool).
rafiau, rafiot [rafjo], *s.m. Nau:* (*a*) (Mediterranean) skiff; (*b*) *Pej:* **(vieux) r.,** old tub.
rafistolage [rafistɔla:ʒ], *s.m. F:* mending up, patching up.

rafistoler [rafistɔle], *v.tr. F:* to mend up, patch up (sth.); to get (sth.) going again.

rafistoleur, -euse [rafistɔlœːr, -øːz], *s. F:* patcher up; **c'est un r.,** he's always mending sth., patching sth. up.

rafle¹ [rɑːfl], *s.f.* **1.** stalk (of raisins, grapes). **2.** cob (of maize).

rafle², *s.f.* **1.** (*a*) *A:* looting, pillaging; (*b*) *F:* **r. d'étalage avec bris de devanture,** smash-and-grab raid; (*c*) *F:* round-up, raid, comb-out (by the police). **2.** *Dice:* pair-royal; **faire r.,** to make a clean sweep; to sweep the board.

rafler [rɑfle], *v.tr.* (*a*) to sweep off, carry off (contents of a house, etc.); (*b*) (*of police*) to round up (criminals); (*c*) *Gaming:* **r. le tout,** to sweep the board.

raflouage [rafluaːʒ], **raflouement** [raflumɑ̃], **raflouer** [raflue]. *See* RENFLOUAGE, RENFLOUEMENT, RENFLOUER.

rafraîchir [rafrɛʃiːr], *v.tr.* **1.** to cool, refresh (sth.); **la pluie a rafraîchi l'air,** the rain has cooled the air; **r. l'eau avec de la glace,** to cool the water with ice; to ice the water; **r. une pièce,** to air a room; **cela vous rafraîchira le sang,** it will cool your blood, freshen you up. **2.** (*a*) to freshen up, revive (colour, painting); to do up, renovate (picture, wall, etc.); to touch up (edged tool, etc.); to recut (groove); to revive, stir up (mortar); to recultivate (soil); to prune (tree roots); **r. les cheveux et la barbe à qn, la queue d'un cheval,** to trim, clip, s.o.'s hair and beard, a horse's tail; *Nau:* **r. un câble,** (i) to freshen (the nip of) a cable; (ii) to trim (the end of) a cable; *Mil:* **r. des troupes,** to rest troops; (*b*) **r. la mémoire à qn,** to refresh s.o.'s memory; **r. à qn la mémoire de qch.,** to revive s.o.'s memory of sth.; *F:* **je vais vous r. la mémoire!** I'll help you remember! **r. son anglais,** to brush up one's English. **3.** *v.i.* **mettre le vin à r. à la cave,** to put the wine to cool in the cellar.

se rafraîchir. **1.** (*of the weather*) to grow, turn, cooler. **2.** (*a*) to refresh oneself; (*b*) *F:* to have a drink, sth. to drink.

rafraîchissant [rafrɛʃisɑ̃]. **1.** *a.* refreshing; cooling; **petite pluie rafraîchissante,** light rain that cools, refreshes, the atmosphere; refreshing rain; **le jus de citron est une boisson rafraîchissante,** fresh lemon is a refreshing drink; **simplicité rafraîchissante,** refreshing simplicity. **2.** *a. & s.m. Med: A:* laxative; cooling (medicine).

rafraîchissement [rafrɛʃismɑ̃], *s.m.* **1.** (*a*) cooling (of temperature, liquid, etc.); *Mch:* **r. par ruissellement, à pluie,** shower cooling (of steam); **r. par pulvérisation,** spray cooling; (*b*) freshening up, restoring (of picture, etc.); reviving (of colour); (*c*) refreshing, refreshment (of one's memory, spirit); brushing up (of one's knowledge); *Sch: O:* **cours de r.,** refresher course. **2.** *usu. pl.* (*a*) refreshments (at a dance, etc.); cold drinks; **si on s'arrêtait prendre un r. (dans un café),** what about stopping for a cold drink? (*b*) *Mil: Nau: A:* fresh supplies, fresh provisions.

rafraîchisseur [rafrɛʃisœːr], *s.m.*, **rafraîchissoir** [rafrɛʃiswar], *s.m. O:* ice bucket, wine cooler.

ragage [ragaːʒ], *s.m.* chafing (of cable); **plaque, tôle, de r.,** chafing piece, plate.

ragaillardir [ragajardiːr], *v.tr.* (*a*) to revive (s.o.), to make (s.o.) feel better; **sa cure l'a ragaillardi,** his treatment has revived him, made him feel a new man; (*b*) to cheer (s.o.) up, *F:* to buck (s.o.) up; **ce vin m'a ragaillardi,** this wine has cheered me up.

rage [raːʒ], *s.f.* **1.** *Vet: Med:* rabies, hydrophobia. **2.** (*a*) rage, fury, frenzy; **écumer de r.,** to foam with rage; **une r. à tout casser,** a tearing, towering, rage; **il fait r.,** he's moving heaven and earth; **la tempête fait r.,** the storm is raging; **l'incendie faisait r.,** the fire was blazing furiously; *F:* **cela fait r.,** it is quite the rage, all the rage; (*b*) passion, mania (for sth.); **avoir la r. du jeu,** to have a passion for gambling; **r. d'écrire,** mania for writing; *O:* **aimer qn, qch., à la r.,** to love s.o. to distraction; to be mad about sth.; to have a mania for sth.; *F:* **c'est pas de l'amour, c'est de la r.,** that's not love, it's madness; (*c*) acute pain; **r. de dents,** raging toothache.

rageant [raʒɑ̃], *a. F:* infuriating.

rager [raʒe], *v.i.* **(je rageai(s); n. rageons)** *F:* to rage; to be in a rage; to fume; **il rageait qu'on ne fît aucune attention à lui,** it riled him, he was furious, that no one paid any attention to him; **elle rageait de le voir fêté et entouré,** it made her mad to see him surrounded with admirers; **ça me fait r. de voir ça!** it makes me wild, infuriated, to see it!

rageur, -euse [raʒœːr, -øːz], *a. & s.* (*a*) violent-tempered (person); (*b*) *a.* infuriated (tone, reply); **répondre d'un ton r.,** to answer in a temper.

rageusement [raʒøzmɑ̃], *adv.* furiously; in a violent temper.

raglan [raglɑ̃], *s.m. Tail:* raglan coat; *a.inv.* **manches r.,** raglan sleeves.

raglanite [raglanit], *s.f. Miner:* raglanite.

ragondin [ragɔ̃dɛ̃], *s.m. Z:* coypu; *Com:* nutria (fur).

ragot¹, -ote [rago, -ɔt]. **1.** *s.m. Ven:* boar in its third year. **2.** *a. & s.* (*a*) *A:* stumpy, dumpy, squat, stocky (person); (*b*) stocky, cobby (horse). **3.** *s.m. Veh:* shaft hook, breeching hook.

ragot², *s.m. F:* **1.** piece of (ill-natured) gossip, of tittle-tattle. **2.** *pl.* (ill-natured) gossip, tittle-tattle.

ragoter [ragɔte], *v.i. F:* to gossip.

ragotin [ragɔtɛ̃], *s.m. A: F:* mis-shapen dwarf (from a character in Scarron's *Roman comique*).

ragoût [ragu], *s.m.* **1.** (*a*) *Cu: A:* spice; (*b*) *O:* spice, savour, relish (of novelty, etc.). **2.** *Cu:* stew, ragout; **r. de mouton,** stewed mutton; **(faire) cuire qch. en r.,** to stew sth.

ragoûtant [ragutɑ̃], *a. usu. with neg. or Iron:* attractive, tempting, inviting, appetizing; **ce n'est pas très r.,** it's not very attractive, inviting; **peu r.,** unpleasant; disgusting; *Iron:* **c'est r. ce que vous faites là!** *that's* a nice job you're on!

ragoûter [ragute], *v.tr.* (*a*) *A:* to revive, restore, the appetite of (invalid, etc.); (*b*) *with neg.* **cela ne me ragoûte pas,** I don't like the idea of it.

ragrafer [ragrafe], *v.tr.* to hook, clasp, (dress, belt, etc.) again.

ragrandir [ragrɑ̃diːr], *v.tr.* to enlarge (again), to re-enlarge.

se ragrandir, to grow larger (again); to widen out, broaden out (again).

ragréage [ragreaːʒ], *s.m.* (*a*) *Nau:* refit(ting); (*b*) *Const:* **r. (d'une façade, etc.),** (i) finishing, polishing, (ii) cleaning (of a façade, etc.).

ragréer [ragree], *v.tr.* **1.** *Nau:* (*a*) to re-rig (a ship); **se r. d'une vergue,** to ship a new yard; (*b*) to refit (a ship). **2.** *Const:* (*a*) to finish, polish; to clean up, trim up (joint, etc.); (*b*) to restore (brickwork, etc.); to clean (building).

ragré(e)ment [ragremɑ̃], *s.m.* **1.** re-rigging (of ship). **2.** *Const:* (*a*) finishing, polishing (of surface); trimming up (of joint, etc.); (*b*) repairing (of wall, etc.); cleaning (of façade of building, etc.).

raguer [rage]. **1.** *v.tr.* to chafe, rub (a rope); *Nau:* **r. le fond,** to be in shoal water, to make foul water; (*of anchor*) to drag. **2.** *v.i.* (*of rope*) to chafe, rub.

ragusain, -aine [ragyzɛ̃, -ɛn], *a. & s.* (native, inhabitant) of Ragusa.

Raguse [ragyːz], *Pr.n.f. Geog:* Ragusa.

rahat-lokoum [raatlokum], **rahat-loukoum** [raatlukum], *s.m.* Turkish delight.

rai [rɛ], *s.m.* (*sing. occ.* **rais**) **1.** spoke (of wheel); rowel (of spur). **2.** *Lit:* **r. de lumière,** slant, slanting ray, of light.

raid [rɛd], *s.m.* **1.** *Mil:* raid; **r. (aérien),** air raid. **2.** *Sp: A:* long-distance rally, endurance test, flight.

raide [rɛd]. **1.** *a.* (*a*) stiff (limb, joints, corpse, attitude, drapery, etc.); tense (cord, etc.); tight, taut (rope); **corde r.,** tightrope; **mettre un câble au r.,** to take up the slack in a cable; **les amarres sont trop raides,** the moorings are too tight; **cheveux raides,** straight and wiry hair; **barbe r.,** wiry, bristly, beard; (*b*) **vol r.,** swift and straight flight; **coup r. comme une balle,** lightning blow, stinging blow; *F:* stinger; **réponse r.,** stinging rejoinder; (*c*) stiff, starchy (manner, etc.); inflexible, unbending, unyielding (character, temper, etc.); **assis r. sur sa chaise,** sitting bolt upright in, on, his chair; (se) **tenir r.,** to maintain an unbending attitude; **morale r. et sévère,** inflexible and austere code of morals; (*d*) steep (stair, slope); abrupt (hill, path); (*e*) *F:* **histoire r.,** (i) tall story; (ii) queer, odd, surprising story; **ça c'est un peu r.!** (i) that's a bit thick; (ii) that's too bad! **il en raconte de raides,** he tells some strange yarns, tales; **il en a vu de(s) raides,** he's had some queer experiences; (*f*) *P:* **être r. (comme un passe-lacet),** to be (stony) broke; (*g*) *P:* **boire du r.,** to drink raw, neat, spirits; (*h*) *Mil: P:* **se faire porter r.,** to report sick. **2.** *adv.* (*a*) **filer r.,** to speed, to go at a terrific rate; **côte qui grimpe r.,** stiff, steep, slope; **mener qn un peu r.,** to treat s.o. roughly, harshly; **mener une affaire r.,** to act promptly, with decision; **frapper r.,** to strike hard; **boire r.,** to drink hard; *Sp:* **frapper la balle r.,** to strike the ball hard; (*b*) **tuer qn r.,** to kill s.o. outright, on the spot; **tomber r. mort,** to drop dead.

rai-de-cœur [rɛdəkœːr], *s.m. Art:* leaf and dart (moulding); *pl. rais-de-cœur.*

raidement [rɛdmɑ̃], *adv.* stiffly; tensely.

raideur [rɛdœːr], *s.f.* **1.** stiffness (of limb, joints, movement, outline, etc.); tightness (of rope); tenseness (of cord, etc.); **r. cadavérique,** rigor mortis; **donner plus de r. à qch.,** to stiffen sth. **2.** stiffness, starchiness (of manner, style, etc.); inflexibility (of mind, character, etc.); severity; **apporter trop de r. dans les affaires,** to be too uncompromising in business; **répondre avec r.,** to answer (i) stiffly, (ii) in an overbearing manner. **3.** steepness, abruptness (of a slope, etc.). **4.** *A:* **lancer une pierre avec r.,** to throw a stone hard; **se défendre avec r.,** to fight every inch of the ground.

raidillon [rɛdijɔ̃], *s.m.* (short and steep) rise (in a road); abrupt path.

raidir [rɛdiːr], *v.tr.* **1.** (*a*) to stiffen (limb, etc.); to tighten, tauten (rope, etc.); to haul (rope) taut; (*b*) **r. qn,** to make s.o. obdurate, intractable; (*c*) **r. sa volonté, ses forces,** to stiffen one's will; to brace oneself. **2.** *v.i.* to stiffen; to grow stiff, taut.

se raidir. **1.** (*of limbs, joints, of the body, etc.*) to stiffen, to grow stiff; (*of cable, etc.*) to grow taut, to tauten; **leurs bras se raidissent sur les rames,** their arms stiffen to the oars. **2. se r. contre le malheur,** to steel, harden, brace, oneself against misfortune; **allons, raidissez-vous!** come on, pull yourself together! *A:* **se r. sous le faix,** to strain under the load.

raidissement [rɛdismɑ̃], *s.m.* stiffening; tautening; *Mec.E: etc:* **nervure de r.,** stiffening rib.

raidisseur [rɛdisœːr], *s.m. Tchn:* wire stretcher, tightener; *N.Arch: etc:* stiffener; *Av:* stringer; *a.* **hauban r.,** straining tie, stay.

raie¹ [rɛ], *s.f.* **1.** line, stroke; *O:* **faire une r. sur du papier,** to draw a line on paper. **2.** (*a*) streak, stripe (on animal); streak (in marble, etc.); stripe (on materials); **chaussettes à raies,** striped socks; (*b*) *Opt:* **raies du spectre, raies spectrales,** spectrum lines, spectral lines; **r. d'absorption, de dispersion,** absorption, dispersion, line; **r. de résonance,** resonance line, radiation. **3.** parting, *U.S:* part (in the hair); **porter la r. à droite, à gauche, au milieu,** to part one's hair on the right, on the left, in the middle. **4.** (*a*) *Agr:* (i) furrow; (ii) ridge (between furrows); (*b*) **la r. du dos,** the ridge of the back. **5.** *Ten:* **balle sur la r.,** ball on the line.

raie², *s.f. Ich:* ray, skate; **r. bouclée,** thornback; **r. grise,** bordered ray; **r. blanche,** flapper skate; **r. lisse,** smooth ray; **r. miroir,** spotted ray; **r. mêlée,** painted ray; **r. mosaïque,** undulate ray; **r. fleurie,** flowered ray; **r. manta,** manta ray, devilfish.

raifort [rɛfɔːr], *s.m.* horseradish.

rail [rɑːj], *s.m.* (*a*) rail; **r. à adhérence,** adhesion rail; **r. à crémaillère,** rack rail; **r. à gorge, r. à ornière, r. plat,** tram rail; **r. à patin, r. Vignoles,** flange rail, flat-footed rail, Vignoles rail; **r. méplat,** flat rail; **r. noyé,** sunken rail; **r. saillant,** raised rail, edge rail; *Rail:* **r. contre(-)aiguille,** stock rail (of cross over); **r. fixe,** main rail (of crossover); **r. mobile,** switch rail; point rail, tongue rail; **r. de roulement, r. de voie,** running rail; **r. d'évitement,** crossing rail, rail for turn-out; **r. conducteur, r. de contact,** conductor rail, contact rail, live rail (of electrified railways); **r. de prise de courant,** collector rail, third rail; **r. de retour,** fourth rail; **poser des rails,** to lay rails; (*of train*) **quitter les rails, sortir des rails,** to jump, leave, the rails, the metals; to derail; **remettre l'économie sur les rails,** to put the economy on its feet again; (*b*) railways; **travailleurs du r.,** railwaymen; **usagers du r.,** railway users; **coordination du r. et de la route, coordination r.-route,** co-ordination of rail and road transport.

railbond [rɛlbɔ̃d], *s.m. Rail:* rail bond.

railbondage [rɛlbɔ̃daːʒ], *s.m. Rail:* rail bonding.

railler [rɑje], *v.tr.* to laugh at, make fun of (s.o.); **on le raille de ce qu'il porte toujours un parapluie,** they laugh, poke fun, at him for always carrying an umbrella; *abs.* **je ne raille pas,** I'm not joking.

se railler de qn, de qch., *A:* to poke fun at, mock at, scoff at, s.o., sth.; **se r. d'une menace,** to make light of a threat.

raillerie [rɑjri], *s.f.* **1.** (*a*) joking; **il n'entend pas r.,** he can't take a joke; **il n'entend pas r. là-dessus,** he is very touchy on that point; *A:* **entendre la r.,** to be a great quiz; **r. à part, sans r.,** joking apart, seriously; **cela passe la r.,** that's going beyond a joke; (*b*) poking fun (at s.o., sth.); (unkind) teasing; **être soumis à la r.,** to be an object of scorn, a butt for unkind remarks. 2. (*a*) *O:* joke; (*b*) unkind, malicious, remark; **recueillir des railleries,** to be scoffed at.

railleur, -euse [rɑjœːr, -øːz]. 1. *a.* mocking, malicious (person, tone, etc.); **d'un air r.,** with a mocking air. 2. *s.* scoffer.

railleusement [rɑjøzmɑ̃], *adv.* mockingly, in a mocking, malicious, manner.

railure [rɛlyːr], *s.f.* groove (alongside the eye of a needle).

rain [rɛ̃], *s.m. Dial:* edge (of forest).

rainage [rɛnaːʒ], *s.m. Tchn:* grooving, fluting; slotting.

raineau, -eaux [rɛno], *s.m. Civ.E:* bind-beam, tie beam (on heads of piles).

rainer [rɛne], *v.tr. Tchn:* to groove, flute; to slot (nut, etc.); **fraiseuse à r.,** slot drilling machine.

raineter [rɛnte], *v.tr.* (**je rainette, n. rainetons**) *Carp: etc:* to trace saw lines on (timber).

rainette[1] [rɛnɛt], *s.f.* 1. **r. (verte),** tree frog; **r. à poche, à bourse,** marsupial frog; **r.(-)maki,** (South American) leaf frog. 2. *Hort:* rennet, pippin (apple); **r. grise,** russet.

rainette[2], *s.f.* 1. *Carp: etc:* tracing iron. 2. *Leath:* race knife.

raineuse [rɛnøːz], *s.f. Carp:* grooving machine.

rainurage [rɛnyraːʒ], *s.m.* slotting.

rainure [rɛnyːr], *s.f.* 1. (*a*) *Carp: Mec.E: etc:* groove, channel, furrow, rabbet; slot, groove (of cam, of armature, etc.); *Mch:* spline (of shaft); **r. en T,** T-slot; **r. d'aération,** vent groove; **r. de dégagement,** clearance groove; **r. de graissage,** oil groove; **r. de clavette,** keyway, key slot; *Mch:* **r. annulaire d'un piston,** piston-ring groove; **à rainure(s),** grooved, channelled, slotted, fluted (drill, etc.); **trou à deux rainures** two-spline hole; *El.E:* **induit à rainures,** slotted armature; (*b*) *Anat:* **rainures d'un os** grooves in a bone. 2. *Astr:* rille (on the moon).

rainure-guide [rɛnyrgid], *s.m. Mec.E:* guide groove, guide slot, guideway; *pl. rainures-guides.*

rainurer [rɛnyre], *v.tr. Carp: etc:* to cut a groove, slot, in, on (sth); to slot.

rainureuse [rɛnyrøːz], *s.f. Mec.E:* slotting machine, slotter.

raiponce [rɛpɔ̃ːs], *s.f. Bot:* rampion; *occ.* lamb's lettuce.

raire[1] [rɛːr], *v.i.* (*conj. like* TRAIRE, *but the only forms in common use are* **il rait, ils raient**) *Ven:* (*of stag*) to bell, to troat.

raire[2], *s.m.* belling, troating (of stag).

rais [rɛ], *s.m. See* RAI.

raisin [rɛzɛ̃], *s.m.* 1. (*a*) **le r., du r.,** grapes; **un r.,** a (variety of) grape; **grappe de r.,** (i) bunch of grapes, (ii) *Artil: A:* grape-shot; **(grain de) r.** grape; **raisins de cuve, de vigne,** wine grapes; **raisin(s) de table, de treille,** table grapes, dessert grapes; **raisins secs,** raisins; **vin de raisins secs,** raisin wine; **raisins de Corinthe,** (dried) currants; **raisins de Smyrne,** sultanas; *s.a.* FIGUE 1; (*b*) (*at restaurant, etc.*) **comme dessert je prendrai du r.,** for dessert, I'll have grapes. 2. *Bot:* **r. de loup,** black nightshade; **r. de renard,** herb Paris; true love; **r. de mer,** (i) ephedra, shrubby horsetail; (ii) *Algae:* bladder wrack; (iii) *Moll:* sea grapes, cuttle-fish eggs; **r. d'Amérique,** redweed; *s.a.* OURS. 3. *Paperm:* **grand r.** (*so called from its former watermark*) approx. = royal.

raisiné [rɛzine], *s.m.* 1. fruit preserved in grape juice; raisiné. 2. *P:* (spilt) blood; **faire du r.,** to have a nose bleed.

raison [rɛzɔ̃], *s.f.* 1. reason, motive, ground (**de,** for); **pour une r. ou une autre,** for one reason or another; **raisons d'affaires, de famille,** business reasons, family reasons; **demander la r. de qch.,** to ask the reason for sth.; **quelle r. a-t-il pu avoir pour . . .?** what reason, motive, could he have had for . . .? **ce n'est pas une r.,** that doesn't follow; **nos raisons d'espérer,** our reasons, grounds, for hope; **pour des raisons personnelles,** on personal grounds; **pour des raisons de convenance,** on grounds of expediency; **pour quelle r.?** for what reason? what for? **pas tant de raisons!** don't argue so much! **sans r.,** without reason, groundlessly, needlessly; **en, pour, r. de qch.,** by reason of, on account of, sth.; **absent pour r. de santé,** absent on account of, because of, ill health; **en r. de son âge,** by reason of his age, because of his age; **en r. d'un deuil récent,** owing to a recent bereavement; *Lit:* **pour r. à moi connue,** for reasons best known to myself; **à plus forte r. . . .,** with greater reason . . ., all the more . . .; **r. de plus,** all the more reason; **c'est une r. de plus pour le congédier,** that's another argument, all the more reason, for dismissing him; **r. d'être,** raison d'être; **r. d'être de qch.,** reason for the existence of sth., grounds, object, justification, of sth.; **le duel n'avait plus aucune r. d'être,** there was no further object in fighting the duel; **ce qu'il a dit n'avait absolument pas de r. d'être,** what he said was quite uncalled for; **la r. pour laquelle il est venu,** the reason why he came; **il y a une r. à ce que vous le fassiez,** there is a reason for your doing it; **il y a de bonnes raisons pour s'y mettre dès maintenant,** there is much to be said for beginning now. 2. reason (= *faculty of reasoning*); **il n'a plus sa r.,** his mind is unhinged, deranged; **il n'a pas toute sa r.,** he is not quite in his right mind; **ses malheurs ont troublé sa r.,** his misfortunes have affected his mind; **ramener qn à la r.,** to bring s.o. to his senses; **revenir à la r.,** to come to one's senses; **avoir toute sa r.,** to be in possession of one's reason; to be sane, in one's right mind; **vous perdez la r.!** have you taken leave of your senses? **avez-vous votre r.?** are you in your right senses? are you out of your mind? **manque de r.,** irrationality; **mettre qn à la r.,** to bring s.o. to his senses; **se mettre à la r.,** to come to one's senses, to see reason; **parler r.,** to talk sense; **entendre r.,** to listen to reason; **faire entendre r. à qn,** to make s.o. see reason; **rendre r. de qch.,** to give an explanation of sth., to explain sth., to account for sth. (*cf.* 4); **agir contre toute r.,** to act contrary to all reason; **faire qch. sans rime ni r.,** to do sth. without rhyme or reason; **la raison a ses heures,** there are times for reasonableness; **l'âge de r.,** years of discretion; **avoir l'âge de r.,** to have come to years of discretion; *A:* **être de r.,** imaginary being, creation of the mind; **mariage de r.,** marriage of convenience. 3. reason, justification; **avoir r.,** to be right; **avoir r. en qch.,** to be right about sth.; **avoir r. de faire qch.,** to be justified, right, in doing sth.; **donner r. à qn,** (i) to declare, admit, that s.o. is right; (ii) to declare s.o. to be in the right, to decide in s.o.'s favour; *F:* to back s.o. up; **l'événement lui donna r.,** he was justified in the event; **c'est r. qu'il vous soit reconnaissant,** it is only right that he should be grateful to you; **on lui a demandé r. de sa conduite,** he has been called upon to account for his conduct; **ce n'est pas r. d'agir ainsi,** there is no justification for such an action; **se faire une r.,** to accept the inevitable, to make the best of a bad job; **il se fait une r. de travailler le dimanche,** he has resigned himself to working on Sundays; **avec (juste) r.,** rightly; **boire plus que de r.,** to drink to excess, more than one ought, more than is good for one; **comme de r.,** as a matter of course, as one might expect; **à telle fin que de r.,** as occasion may require; to meet any emergency; *Jur:* **pour valoir ce que de r.,** to be used as may be thought proper. 4. satisfaction, reparation; **demander r. d'un affront,** to demand satisfaction for an insult; **faire r. à qn,** (i) to give s.o. satisfaction (by accepting his challenge to a duel); (ii) to answer s.o.'s toast; **se faire r. à soi-même,** to take the law into one's own hands; **rendre r. de qch.,** to give satisfaction for sth.; *cf.* 2; **tirer r. de qn,** to obtain satisfaction from s.o.; **avoir r. de qn, de qch.,** to overcome, get the better of, get the upper hand of, s.o., sth.; **avoir r. de toute opposition,** to break down all opposition; *A:* **avoir des raisons avec qn,** to have words with s.o.; **chercher des raisons à qn,** to try to pick a quarrel with s.o. 5. *Com:* **r. sociale,** name, style (of a firm); trade name. 6. *Mth:* **r. géométrique, arithmétique,** geometrical ratio, arithmetical ratio; **r. directe, inverse,** direct, inverse, ratio; **r. (de progression arithmétique),** common difference; **r. (de progression géométrique),** common ratio; **extrême r.,** ultimate ratio; **le poids est en r. directe du volume,** the weight is directly proportional to the volume; **on admire un homme en r. de ce qu'il vaut,** a man is admired in proportion to his worth; **l'illumination varie en r. inverse du carré de la distance,** the illumination varies inversely as the square of the distance; **travail payé à r. de dix francs l'heure,** work paid at the rate of ten francs an hour; **à r. de deux par minute,** at the rate of two per, a, minute; **à r. de huit mots par ligne,** (on the basis of) eight words to a line.

raisonnable [rɛzɔnabl̩], *a.* 1. reasonable, sensible; **être r.,** rational being; **soyez r.,** be sensible, reasonable; do listen to reason; **à son âge il devrait être plus r.,** he is old enough to know better; **interprétation r.,** reasonable interpretation; **il est r. de croire que . . .,** it is reasonable to believe that. . . . 2. (*a*) **prix r.,** reasonable, fair, price; (*b*) **revenu r.,** reasonable, adequate, income; **d'une grandeur r.,** reasonably large, *F:* decent-sized; **un r. paquet d'actions,** a fair-sized block of shares.

raisonnablement [rɛzɔnabləmɑ̃], *adv.* 1. reasonably, rationally; **gens qui pensent r.,** people who think in a reasonable manner; **tout ce qu'on pouvait r. demander,** all that one could reasonably ask for. 2. (*a*) reasonably, fairly (large, etc.); moderately, in moderation; **maison r. grande,** reasonably large, *F:* decent-sized, house; **manger r.,** to eat reasonably, in moderation; (*b*) *F:* fairly well, reasonably well; **il travaille r.,** he works fairly well.

raisonné [rɛzɔne], *a.* reasoned (analysis, argument, etc.); **exposé r. d'un procédé,** rationale of a process; **grammaire raisonnée de la langue française,** a rational, analytical, French grammar; *Com:* **catalogue r.,** descriptive catalogue.

raisonnement [rɛzɔnmɑ̃], *s.m.* (*a*) reasoning; **r. formel,** formal reasoning; **surpasser qn par la puissance du r.,** to surpass s.o. in power of reasoning; **homme de r. juste,** man who argues soundly; man of sense; (*b*) (line of) argument; **prouver par le r. qu'une crainte est mal fondée,** to reason a fear away; *F:* **faire des raisonnements à perte de vue,** to argue without end; **pas de raisonnements!** don't argue, don't answer back!

raisonner [rɛzɔne]. 1. *v.i.* (*a*) to reason (**sur,** about, upon); to argue (**sur,** about); **r. juste,** to argue soundly, correctly; **r. mal,** to argue illogically; *F:* (*play on the words* **raisonner** *&* **résonner**) **r. comme un tambour,** to talk nonsense, talk through one's hat; (*b*) *F:* to wrangle; to argle-bargle; **ne raisonnez pas tant,** don't be so argumentative; (*c*) *Nau: A:* **r. avec les autorités du port,** to show the ship's papers (on entering port); **faire r. un navire,** to hail a ship. 2. *v.tr.* (*a*) **r. ses actions,** to consider, study, one's actions; (*b*) **r. qn,** to reason with s.o., to try to bring s.o. to reason; **il faut vous r.,** you must try to be reasonable.

raisonneur, -euse [rɛzɔnœːr, -øːz]. 1. *a.* (*a*) reasoning, rational; (*b*) argumentative (person, spirit). 2. *s.* (*a*) reasoner, arguer; **un fort r.,** a powerful arguer, reasoner; *Th:* (*in the plays of Augier, Dumas fils, etc.*) the mentor; the guide, philosopher and friend; (*b*) *F:* arguer, argumentative person; **ne faites pas le r.,** don't argue; don't answer back.

raja(h) [raʒa], *s.m.* raja(h).

rajeton [raʒtɔ̃], *s.m. Ich:* young ray, skate.

rajeunir [raʒœniːr]. 1. *v.tr.* (*a*) to rejuvenate (s.o.); to restore (s.o.) to youth, to make (s.o.) young again; **ce chapeau la rajeunit de dix ans,** this hat makes her look ten years younger; **vous la rajeunissez de dix ans,** you are making her out to be ten years younger than she is! **ça me rajeunit,** it makes me feel much younger; **le voilà grand jeune homme; ça ne nous rajeunit pas!** he's a young man now; that doesn't make us feel any younger! **le comité a besoin d'être rajeuni,** the committee needs new blood; (*b*) to renovate, do up (clothes, furniture, etc.); to revive (a word, expression, etc.); (*c*) to prune (tree). 2. *v.i.* to grow young again; to be restored to youth; to get younger; **vous avez rajeuni,** you are looking years younger; **je le trouve rajeuni,** he seems, looks, younger to me.

se rajeunir. 1. to make oneself look younger. 2. to make oneself out younger than one is.

rajeunissant [raʒœnisɑ̃], *a.* (hat, etc.) that makes one look younger; youthful (style, etc.); **crème de beauté rajeunissante,** rejuvenating cream; **traitement r.,** rejuvenating treatment.

rajeunissement [raʒœnismɑ̃], *s.m.* 1. (*a*) making young again, rejuvenation (of s.o.); (*b*) renewal, renovation (of sth.); (*c*) pruning (of tree). 2. (*a*) growing young again, rejuvenescence; (*b*) **cure de r.,** rejuvenation; (*c*) *Geol:* rejuvenation.

rajeunisseur [raʒœnisœːr], *s.m.* rejuvenator; renovator (**de,** of).

rajidés [raʒide], *s.m.pl. Ich:* Rajidae.

rajout [raʒu], *s.m.* addition; extension (to a building, etc.); *Publ:* **faire des rajouts sur épreuves,** to make additions at proof stage.

rajouter [raʒute], *v.tr.* to add (sth.); to add more of (sth.); **r. du sel,** to add some salt, to put in some extra salt; *Rail:* **r. une voiture,** to put on another coach, an extra coach; *F:* **en r.,** to lay it on thick; **n'en rajoute pas!** don't exaggerate!

Rajpoute, Rajput [raʒput], *a. & s.* Rajput.

rajustement [raʒystəmɑ̃], *s.m.* readjustment, putting in order; **les syndicats réclament un r. des salaires,** the trade unions are demanding a readjustment of the wage structure, a wage increase.

rajuster [raʒyste], *v.tr.* (*a*) to readjust (sth.); to put (sth.) straight; **r. le tir,** to readjust, correct, one's aim; **r. sa cravate,** to put one's tie straight; **se r.,** to tidy oneself (up), to put one's clothes straight; (*b*) **r. les salaires,** to readjust the wage structure, to bring wages into line with the cost of living.

rajusteur, -euse [raʒystœːr, -øːz], *s.* repairer.

raki [raki], *s.m.* raki.

râlage [rɑlaːʒ], *s.m. F:* (*a*) (the fact of) being in a bad temper; (*b*) protest, grumbling.

râlant [rɑlɑ̃], *a.* **1.** (*a*) *Med:* **respiration râlante,** rhonch(i)al breathing; (*b*) **champ de bataille couvert de blessés râlants,** battlefield covered with wounded at their last gasp. **2.** *F:* enraging, maddening; **c'est vraiment r. d'avoir manqué cet avion,** it's really infuriating to have missed the plane.

râle[1] [rɑːl], *s.m. Orn:* rail; **r. de genêts,** corncrake; **r. d'eau,** water rail; **r. poussin,** little crake; **r. marouette,** spotted crake; **r. de Baillon,** Baillon's crake.

râle[2], *s.m.*, **râlement** [rɑlmɑ̃], *s.m.* **1.** rattle (in the throat); **le r. (de la mort),** the death rattle. **2.** *Med:* râle, rhonchus; **r. bulleux,** bubbling râle; **r. humide,** moist râle.

ralenti [ralɑ̃ti]. **1.** *a.* slow(er); **au trot r.,** at a slow trot. **2.** *s.m.* (*a*) slow motion; *Aut:* **prendre un virage au grand r.,** to take a corner dead slow; *Cin:* **film tourné au r.,** slow-motion picture; **scène au r.,** scene in slow motion; *Ind:* (*of works*) **marcher, tourner, au r.,** to slow down production; **travail au r.,** go-slow strike; (*b*) *I.C.E: Mch:* idle, idling, idle running, slow running; **au r.,** idle; **(à) l'extrême r.,** full idle; **(au) r. de vitesse maximum,** fast idle; **essai de r.,** idling test; **plage de r.,** idle range; **vitesse de r.,** idle speed; **moteur au r.,** idling engine, engine throttled down; **mettre le moteur au r.,** to idle, throttle down, the engine; *Av:* **r. de prise de terrain,** approach idling; (*of engine*) **prendre le r., se mettre au r.,** to slow down; **tourner au r.,** to idle, to run idle, to run slow; **ressort de r.,** idle spring; **soupape de commande de r.,** idling control valve; **vis de réglage de r.,** idling adjusting screw.

ralentir [ralɑ̃tiːr], *v.tr.* & *i.* to slacken, slow down (one's pace, movements, etc.); to decelerate; **r. l'allure,** to slacken the pace; **le train ralentissait (sa marche, son allure),** the train was slowing down; *P.N:* **ralentir!** slow! *Artil:* **r. le feu,** to slow down the fire; *Nau: etc:* **r. les feux,** to bank the fires; *Nau: etc:* **r. la marche,** to reduce speed; **r. ses efforts,** to reduce one's efforts; to ease up; **r. le pas,** to slacken one's pace, to slow down; **j'ai été obligé de r.,** I was obliged, forced, to slow down; (*of car driver*) **r. à chaque tournant,** to slow down at each bend.

se ralentir, (*of movements*) to slacken, slow down; (*of zeal, etc.*) to abate, relax, flag; (*of passion*) to abate; **l'offensive ennemie commence à se r.,** the enemy offensive is beginning to slacken.

ralentissement [ralɑ̃tismɑ̃], *s.m.* slackening, slowing up, slowing down (of a movement, etc.); deceleration; **r. de vitesse,** decrease of speed; *Av:* **r. à l'atterrissage,** landing deceleration; *Atom.Ph:* **r. des neutrons,** slowing down of neutrons; **densité de r. (des neutrons),** slowing-down density; **r. de zèle,** abatement, cooling, flagging, of zeal; **r. des affaires,** falling off, decline, of business; **périodes de r. dans les affaires,** slack times in business; **r. de la production,** slowing down of production; **r. d'un moteur à ressort,** lag of a spring motor.

ralentisseur [ralɑ̃tisœːr], *s.m.* **1.** *Mec.E: etc:* idler, retarder; (automatic) braking device; speed reducer. **2.** *Atom.Ph:* moderator; **r. de neutrons,** neutron moderator; **r. de particules,** particule moderator, spirotron; **r. organique,** organic moderator; **réacteur à r. organique,** organic-moderated reactor.

ralentisseur-refroidisseur [ralɑ̃tisœrrəfrwadisœːr], *s.m.* moderator coolant; *pl. ralentisseurs-refroidisseurs.*

râler [rɑle], *v.i.* **1.** (*a*) to rattle (in one's throat); to be at one's last gasp, in the throes of death; (*b*) to be in agony; to suffer terribly. **2.** (*of tiger, etc.*) to growl. **3.** *F:* (*a*) *A:* to haggle; (*b*) to be in a foul temper; to create; to be hopping mad; to bellyache, to gripe.

râleur, râleux, -euse [rɑlœːr, rɑlø, -øːz], *a.* & *s. P:* (*a*) *A:* haggling, stingy (person); *s.* haggler; (*b*) bad-tempered (person); *s.* grumbler, bellyacher; *a.* **il est terriblement r.,** he's always bellyaching, griping, about sth.

raligner [raliɲe], *s.m. Fish:* **pêche au r.,** seine, dragnet, trailnet, fishing.

ralingue [ralɛ̃ːg], *s.f.* **1.** (*a*) *Nau:* bolt rope (of sail); **r. de fond, de bordure,** foot rope; **r. de têtière,** head rope; **r. de chute,** leech rope; (*b*) *Nau:* awning rope; (*c*) *Fish:* **r. supérieure (de filet),** balk; (*d*) *Av:* **r. de suspension,** suspension band. **2.** **tenir les voiles en r.,** to keep the sails shivering, shaking.

ralinguer [ralɛ̃ge], *Nau:* **1.** *v.tr.* to rope (a sail). **2.** *v.i.* (*of the sails*) to shiver, to shake in the wind; **faire r. les voiles,** to shiver, shake, the sails.

raller[1] [rale], *v.i. Ven:* (*of stag*) to bell, to troat.

raller,[2] *v.i.* (*conj. like* ALLER) *F:* to go again; *used only in* **il va, vient, reva, revient,** he goes, comes back, goes again, comes back again.

rallidés [ralide], *s.m.pl. Orn:* Rallidae.

rallié, -iée [ralje], *s.* rallier, one who rallies (to a cause, etc.); *Fr.Hist:* **les ralliés,** Royalists and Imperialists who accepted the Republic.

ralliement, *A:* **rallîment** [ralimɑ̃], *s.m.* (*a*) rally(ing), assembly (of troops, ships, etc.); **mot de r.,** password; **point de r.,** rallying point, rendezvous position; (*b*) *Av:* homing (of aircraft); (*c*) (i) winning over (of adherents, etc.); (ii) going over (to a political party, etc.).

rallier [ralje], *v.tr.* (*p.d.* & *pr.sub.* **n. ralliions, v. ralliiez**) **1.** (*a*) to rally, assemble (troops, ships, etc.); (*b*) *Mil:* to rejoin; **les éclaireurs rallièrent leur unité,** the scouts rejoined, made their way back to, their unit; **r. le bord,** to rejoin one's ship; (*c*) *Nau:* **r. la terre,** to stand in for land, to haul in; **r. le vent,** to haul to the wind; (*d*) to join (a political party, etc.); (*e*) *abs.* to rally; to assemble. **2.** to rally, to win (s.o.) over, to bring (s.o.) round (to a party, opinion, etc.); **cette proposition rallia tous les suffrages,** this proposal met with general acceptance.

se rallier. 1. (*a*) (*of troops, ships, etc.*) to rally; (*b*) *Nau:* **se r. à terre,** to hug the shore. **2.** **se r. à un parti,** to rally to, to throw in one's lot with, join, a party; **se r. à une opinion,** to concur in an opinion, to come round to an opinion; to adopt a point of view.

ralliformes [ralifɔrm], *s.m.pl. Orn:* Gruiformes.

rallonge [ralɔ̃ːʒ], *s.f.* (*a*) extension piece (of lifting jack, etc.); eking piece, lengthening piece; *Min:* lengthening rod (of borer); *Mec.E:* **r. d'arbre,** extension shaft; **foret à r.,** extension drill; (*b*) extension leaf, extra leaf (of table); **table à rallonge(s),** extending table; *F:* **nom à r.,** double-barrelled name; (*c*) addition; **mettre une r. à une jupe,** to lengthen a skirt; (*d*) *F:* bribe; additional payment (over and above the official price); (*e*) *F:* **demander une, de la, r. (au patron),** to ask for a rise.

rallongement [ralɔ̃ʒmɑ̃], *s.m.* lengthening, extension; **r. d'une jupe,** lengthening, letting down, of a skirt.

rallonger [ralɔ̃ʒe], **(je rallongeai(s); n. rallongeons)** (*a*) *v.tr.* to lengthen; to make longer (a curtain, table, etc.); **r. une jupe,** (i) to let down a skirt; (ii) to lengthen a skirt (by adding a piece); (*b*) *v.i. F:* **les jours rallongent,** the days are drawing out.

se rallonger, to grow longer; *F:* **par ce chemin vous vous rallongez,** if you take that road, you're going a long way round.

rallongi(s) [ralɔ̃ʒi], *s.m. F:* supposed short cut that makes the journey longer.

rallumer [ralyme], (*a*) *v.tr.* to relight (lamp, fire); to rekindle (fire); to light (sth.) again; to revive (anger, hope, etc.); (*b*) *v.i. I.C.E:* to ignite automatically.

se rallumer, to rekindle; to light up again; to blaze up again; (*of anger, etc.*) to revive; (*of war*) to break out again.

rallye [rali], *s.m. Sp: Aut:* (*a*) race meeting; (*b*) (car) rally; (*c*) treasure hunt (in cars).

rallye(-paper) [rali(pepœːr)], *s.m. Sp:* paper chase; *pl. rallye-papers.*

ralstonite [ralstɔnit], *s.f. Miner:* ralstonite.

ramad(h)an [ramadɑ̃], *s.m. Moslem Rel:* Ramadan.

ramage [ramaːʒ], *s.m.* **1.** floral design; **ouvrages à ramages,** flowered work; **robe à grands ramages,** dress with a bold floral pattern. **2.** (*a*) song, warbling, twittering, chirping (of birds); (*b*) *F:* prattling (of children); prattle.

ramager [ramaʒe], *v.i.* **1.** to print floral designs (on material). **2.** (*of birds*) to sing, warble, twitter.

ramaigrir [ramɛgriːr]. **1.** *v.tr.* to make (person, animal) thin again. **2.** *v.i.* to become, grow, thin again.

ramaigrissement [ramɛgrismɑ̃], *s.m.* **1.** (*a*) (act of) growing thin; (*b*) (act of) making thin. **2.** thinness; emaciation.

ramaire [ramɛːr], *a. Bot:* ramal.

ramarder [ramarde], *v.tr.* to mend (fishing nets).

ramas [ramɑ], *s.m. F:* (*a*) heap, pile, collection, raggle-taggle assortment (of old clothes, books, etc.); (*b*) band, motley crew (of undesirable persons).

ramassage [ramɑsaːʒ], *s.m.* gathering, collecting, picking up; **r. à la main,** hand picking, picking by hand; **r. à la pelle,** shovelling up; **lait de grand r.,** milk collected over a wide area; *Rail:* **automotrice de r.,** railcar connecting country districts with mainline station; *Adm:* **service de r. des écoliers, r. scolaire,** school bus service.

ramasse [ramɑːs], *s.f.* **1.** (*in the Alps*) sledge; *Mount:* **filer, descendre, en r.,** to glissade. **2.** cleaning rod (for fowling piece).

ramassé [ramɑse], *a.* **1.** thick-set, stocky, squat (person); stocky, cobby (horse). **2.** compact (machine, style, etc.); *Art:* **composition, peinture, ramassée,** concentrated composition, painting.

ramasse-couverts [ramɑskuvɛːr], *s.m.inv.* plate basket, cutlery basket.

ramassement [ramɑsmɑ̃], *s.m.* gathering up.

ramasse-miettes [ramɑsmjɛt], *s.m.inv.* crumb tray, crumb scoop.

ramasse-plis [ramɑspli], *s.m.inv. Rail: Post:* mail-bag apparatus, postal express pouch.

ramasse-poussière [ramɑspusjɛːr], *s.m.inv.* dust-pan.

ramasser [ramɑse], *v.tr.* **1.** (*a*) to gather (sth.) together (in a mass); **village ramassé autour de son église,** village clustering round its church; **r. à la pelle,** to shovel up; **le tigre ramasse son corps avant de bondir,** the tiger crouches, gathers itself, before springing; **le hérisson ramasse son corps en boule,** the hedgehog rolls itself into a ball; **r. toutes ses forces,** to gather, muster, all one's strength; (*b*) *Nau:* **r. une voile,** to take in, truss up, a sail. **2.** to collect, gather (different things, persons); **r. les cartes, les dominos,** to gather up the cards, the dominoes; **ramasse ta musique!** gather up your music and stop playing! **r. ses affaires,** to collect one's belongings together; **r. de l'argent,** to collect money; to scrape money together; *F:* to make one's pile; **r. les débris de son armée,** to collect, to get together, the fragments of one's army; **r. des bribes de connaissances,** to pick up scraps of knowledge; *P:* **se faire r.,** (i) to be run in (by the police); (ii) to get told off, ticked off; *Aut: F:* **r. un procès-verbal,** to get a ticket. **3.** to pick up, take up; **r. vivement qch.,** to snatch sth. up; **r. son mouchoir,** to pick up one's handkerchief; *Fb:* **r. le ballon,** to gather the ball; **r. un ivrogne,** to help a drunken man up, to help him to his feet; *F:* **il est à r. à la petite cuiller,** he's in a terrible state, mess; *F:* **r. une bûche, une pelle,** to come a cropper; *F:* **r. un rhume,** to catch, pick up, a cold.

se ramasser. 1. to collect, gather (into a crowd); **toutes les espérances s'étaient ramassées autour de lui,** he had become the centre of every hope. **2.** (*a*) (*of animal*) to double up; to roll itself up; (*b*) (*of pers.*) to gather oneself (for an effort); (*of tiger, etc.*) to crouch (for a spring); **tigre ramassé avant de sauter,** tiger crouched ready to spring. **3.** (*a*) to pick oneself up (after a fall); (*b*) *P:* **se r. par terre,** to fall (down), to come a cropper.

ramassette [ramɑsɛt], *s.f.* **1.** pick-up attachment (for scythe). **2.** (*in Belg. and N.Fr.*) dustpan.

ramasseur, -euse [ramɑsœːr, -øːz]. **1.** *s.* collector, gatherer; **r. de lait,** collector of milk (from farms); **r. de mégots,** collector, picker-up, of cigarette ends, *U.S:* sniper; *Ten: etc:* **r. de balles,** ball boy. **2.** *s.m. Tchn:* pick-up (of pick-up baler, etc.). **3.** *a.* **pelle ramasseuse,** mechanical shovel, excavator.

ramasseuse-botteleuse [ramɑsøzbɔtløːz], *s.f.*, **ramasseuse-presse** [ramɑsøzprɛs], *s.f. Agr:* pick-up baler; *pl. ramasseuses-botteleuses, ramasseuses-presses.*

ramassis [ramɑsi], *s.m. F: Pej:* heap, pile (of thgs); bunch (of people).

ramazan [ramazɑ̃], *s.m. Moslem Rel:* Ramadan.

rambarde [rɑ̃bard], *s.f. Nau: etc:* (guard) rail; breast work; *esp.* poop rail or forecastle rail; rails and stanchions.

rambervelais, -aise [rɑ̃bɛrvəlɛ, -ɛːz], **rambuvetais, -aise** [rɑ̃byvtɛ, -ɛːz], *a.* & *s. Geog:* (native, inhabitant) of Rambervillers.

rambin [rɑ̃bɛ̃], *s.m. P:* **1.** **faire du r. à qn,** to flatter, make up to, s.o. **2.** excuse; **marcher au r.,** to try to make excuses, to wriggle out.

rambiner [rɑ̃bine], *P:* **1.** *v.tr.* (*a*) to reconcile; (*b*) to cheer, buck (s.o.) up. **2.** *v.i.* to make peace; **il vaut mieux r.,** it's better to come to an understanding, put things right, patch things up.

rambineur, -euse [rɑ̃binœːr, -øːz], *s. P:* **1.** patcher-up (of quarrels). **2.** flatterer.

rambolitain, -aine [rɑ̃bɔlitɛ̃, -ɛn], *a. & s. Geog:* (native, inhabitant) of Rambouillet.

ramdam(e) [ramdam], *s.m.* **1.** *Moslem Rel:* Ramadan. **2.** *P:* noise, row, din.

rame[1] [ram], *s.f.* **1.** (*a*) *Hort:* stick, prop (for peas, etc.); (*b*) *A:* branch (of tree); (*c*) *F:* **avoir la r.,** to be lazy, bone-idle; **ne pas en fiche une r.,** not to do a stroke (of work). **2.** *Tex:* tenter (of loom).

rame[2], *s.f.* oar, scull; **embarcation à huit rames,** eight-oared boat; **aller à la r.,** to row; **faire le tour de l'île à la r.,** to row round the island; **faire force de rames,** to row hard; **le bateau filait à toute(s) rame(s),** the boat was going at full speed; *A:* **mettre un homme à la r.,** to sentence a man to the galleys; *A:* **tirer, être, à la r.,** (i) to ply the oars; to pull at the oar; (ii) *F:* to work like a galley slave; **faire fausse r.,** to catch a crab; *Nau:* **lève rames!** oars!

rame[3], *s.f.* **1.** ream (of paper). **2.** (*a*) string, tow (of barges); (*b*) *Rail:* **r. (de wagons),** (i) rake, set, string (of carriages, of trucks); (ii) made-up train; **la r. directe pour Tours,** the through coach(es) for Tours; **collision entre deux rames du Métro,** collision between two underground trains.

ramé[1] [rame], *a. Hort:* (*of peas, etc.*) trained on sticks; propped, supported, by sticks; **petits pois ramés,** staked peas.

ramé[2], *a. Orn:* **vol r.,** slow-winged flight, flapping flight (of large birds).

ramé[3], *a. Artil: A:* **boulets ramés,** chain-shot, bar-shot.

ramé[4], *a. Ven: Her:* **cerf r.,** stag attired.

rameau, -eaux [ramo], *s.m.* **1.** (*a*) (small) branch, bough, twig (of tree); **le R. d'or,** the Golden Bough; *s.a.* OLIVIER[1] 1; (*b*) *Ecc:* (processional) palm; **le dimanche des Rameaux, les Rameaux,** Palm Sunday; (*c*) *pl.* antlers (of stag). **2.** branch, ramification (of family, civilization, language, etc.). **3.** (*a*) *Anat:* ramification (of artery, vein, etc.); (*b*) *Min:* vein; (*c*) *Geol:* outlying massif (of mountain range).

ramée [rame], *s.f.* **1.** green boughs, branches (forming an arbour); arbour. **2.** small wood, leafage (for burning or fodder).

ramenard, -arde [ramnaːr, -ard], *P:* **1.** *a.* self-important. **2.** *s.* swank; big mouth.

ramendable [ramɑ̃dabl̩], *a.* **1.** *Agr:* ready to be manured again. **2.** (*a*) *Fish:* mendable (net); (*b*) (*of gilt frame*) renewable, reparable.

ramendage [ramɑ̃daːʒ], *s.m.* **1.** *Agr:* re-manuring (of fields). **2.** (*a*) *Fish:* mending (of nets); (*b*) renewing, repairing (gilt frames).

ramender [ramɑ̃de], *v.tr.* **1.** *Agr:* to manure (field, etc.) again. **2.** to mend (fishing net); to renovate (gilt frame); to re-dye.

ramènement [ramɛnmɑ̃], *s.m. A:* withdrawing, drawing back (of hand, foot, etc.).

ramener[1] [ramne], *v.tr.* (*conj. like* MENER) **1.** to bring (s.o., sth.) back (again); (*a*) **r. qn chez lui en voiture,** to drive s.o. home; *Nau:* **r. qn à bord,** to bring s.o. off (from land); **r. qn à terre,** to bring s.o. off (from a vessel); **quand vous irez à la ville, vous ramènerez deux fûts de cidre,** when you go to town bring me back two barrels of cider; (*b*) **r. qn à la vraie foi, au devoir, à la question,** to recall s.o., bring s.o. back, to the true faith, to his duty, to the question; **r. un malade à la vie,** to bring a patient round; **elle s'est évanouie; nous allons la r. à elle,** she's fainted; we'll try to bring her round; **r. la conversation sur un sujet,** to lead the conversation back to a subject; to hark back to a subject; **r. ses pensées en arrière,** to cast one's thoughts back; **r. sa science,** to parade one's knowledge; *P:* **r. sa gueule, sa fraise, la r.,** to have a big mouth, to like to talk big; to like to lay down the law; (*c*) **r. tout à un seul principe,** to reduce everything to a single principle; **morale qui ramène tout au plaisir,** code of morals founded on pleasure; **il ramène tout à lui,** he thinks the whole world revolves around him; *Mth:* **r. une fraction à sa plus simple expression,** to reduce a fraction to its simplest terms; **r. le prix d'un article à . . .,** to bring down the price of an article to . . .; *Ph:* **volume ramené aux conditions normales de température et de pression,** volume corrected for temperature and pressure; *Aut: etc:* **r. le compteur à zéro,** to reset the speedometer to 0, to zero; **r. la semaine de 42 à 40 heures,** to cut, reduce, the working week from 42 to 40 hours; (*d*) **r. son chapeau sur ses yeux,** to pull down, draw down, one's hat over one's eyes; **r. le poing,** to draw back one's fist; **il ramena les couvertures jusqu'à son menton,** he pulled up the blankets up to his chin; **ramené en arrière par le vent,** pulled back by the wind; (*e*) *Equit:* **r. un cheval,** to rein in a horse; **r. son cheval au pas,** to rein in. **2. r. un autre à son opinion,** to bring s.o. over, round, to one's opinion (again); **r. les rebelles,** to win back the rebels. **3.** (*a*) **r. la paix,** to restore peace; **r. une vieille mode,** to revive an old fashion; (*b*) **ce fut lui qui ramena la partie,** he it was who restored the fortunes of the game, who pulled the game together again.

se ramener, (*a*) *F:* (*of pers.*) to come, arrive; *F:* to turn up, roll along; (*b*) **toutes ces suggestions se ramènent à une seule,** all these suggestions may be reduced to one; **voici à quoi se ramène son raisonnement,** this is what his argument amounts to, comes (down) to, *F:* boils down to.

ramener[2], *s.m. Equit:* position "in hand," flexed.

rameneur, -euse [ramnœːr, -øːz], *s.* **1.** bringer back, restorer; **r. de courage,** heartener; *a.* **des nouvelles rameneuses d'espoir,** heartening news. **2.** *P:* swank, bragger; line-shooter.

ramequin [ramkɛ̃], *s.m. Dom.Ec:* ramekin, ramequin.

ramer[1] [rame], *v.tr.* **1.** *Hort:* to stick, prop, stake (peas, beans, etc.); *F:* **il s'y entend comme à r. des choux,** he wouldn't know which was the business end of a chisel; he doesn't know which end of a cow you get the milk from. **2.** *Tex:* to tenter (cloth).

ramer[2], *v.i.* to row; to pull (at the oar); **r. en couple,** to scull; **r. jusqu'au rivage,** to pull ashore; **r. à rebours,** to back the oars; to back water; *P:* **bien r.,** to work like stink; **il a bien ramé pour faire sa fortune,** he worked hard to make his fortune.

ramer[3], *v.tr. Rail:* to distribute, sort out (railway wagons or trucks) into lifts.

ramer[4], *v.i.* (*of stag*) to grow its horns.

ramereau, -eaux [ram(ə)ro], *s.m.*, **ramerot** [ram(ə)ro], *s.m. Orn:* young wood pigeon.

ramescence [ramɛs(s)ɑ̃ːs], *s.f. Bot:* ramification, branching.

ramette[1] [ramɛt], *s.f. Typ:* job-chase.

ramette[2], *s.f. Paperm:* ream (of small notepaper).

rameur, -euse[1] [ramœːr, -øːz], *s.* rower; oarsman, oarswoman; **r. de couple,** sculler.

rameuter [ramøte], *v.tr.* **1.** *Ven:* to call in (the hounds). **2.** to stir up (the mob) again.

rameux, -euse[2] [ramø, -øːz], *a. Nat.Hist:* ramose, ramous; branching, branched, branchy.

rami [rami], *s.m. Cards:* rummy.

ramie [rami], *s.f.* **1.** *Bot:* ramie, ramee, china grass, grass cloth plant. **2. (toile de) r.,** grass cloth.

ramier [ramje], *a.m. & s.m.* **1.** *Orn:* **(pigeon) r.,** ring dove, wood pigeon. **2.** *F:* lazybones.

ramification [ramifikasjɔ̃], *s.f.* ramification; (*a*) branching; (*b*) branch; **les ramifications des artères, du réseau ferroviaire,** the ramifications of the arteries, of the railway network; **étendre de toutes parts ses ramifications,** to branch out in every direction.

ramifié [ramifje], *a.* ramified, branching; *Ch:* **à chaîne ramifiée,** branched; *Sch:* **programme r.,** branching programme.

ramifier [ramifje], *v.tr. & pr.* to ramify, branch out, divide.

ramiflore [ramiflɔːr], *a. Hort:* ramiflorous.

ramille [ramiːj], *s.f.*, **ramillon** [ramijɔ̃], *s.m.* **1.** branchlet, twig. **2.** *pl.* small wood (for lighting fires).

Raminagrobis [raminagrɔbis], *s.m. F:* puss (from the old cat in La Fontaine's fables).

ramingue [ramɛ̃ːg], *a. Equit:* stubborn (horse), (horse) disobedient to the spur.

ramoindrir [ramwɛ̃driːr], *v.tr.* to decrease, diminish, lessen.

ramolli, -ie [ramɔli], *F:* **1.** *a.* soft-witted, soft-headed. **2.** *s.* imbecile, dodderer.

ramollir [ramɔliːr], *v.tr.* **1.** to soften (wax, etc.). **2.** to enervate, weaken (s.o., s.o.'s courage).

se ramollir. 1. to soften; to grow soft; **son cœur s'est un peu ramolli,** his heart has softened a little. **2.** (*a*) **son cerveau se ramollit,** he has softening of the brain; (*b*) *F:* **il se ramollit,** he is getting soft(-witted), is going daft.

ramollissant [ramɔlisɑ̃], *a. & s.m. Med: A:* emollient.

ramollissement [ramɔlismɑ̃], *s.m.* softening; *Med:* **r. du cerveau,** softening of the brain.

ramollo(t) [ramɔlo], *a. & s.m. F:* **un vieux r.,** an old crock, a dodderer, a has-been; **il est un peu r.,** he's a bit gaga.

ramonage [ramɔnaːʒ], *s.m.* **1.** chimney sweeping; *Const:* **registre de r.,** soot door; *Petroleum Ind:* **r. des canalisations,** pigging; *Mch:* **r. des tubes de chaudière,** boiler-tube cleaning. **2.** *Mount:* chimney climbing.

ramoner [ramɔne]. **1.** *v.tr.* to sweep (chimney); to take out (flue); *Mch:* to clean (fire tubes); *F: A:* **r. qn de la belle façon,** to give s.o. a good telling off, a good dressing down. **2.** *v.i. Mount:* to climb a chimney.

ramoneur [ramɔnœːr], *s.m.* **1.** chimney sweeper; sweep; *A:* **petit r.,** chimney-boy, climbing-boy; **2.** *Petroleum Ind: etc:* go-devil (for cleaning pipe lines); soot blower.

ramoneuse [ramɔnøːz], *s.f.* (*a*) chimney-cleaning apparatus; (*b*) *Sm.a:* pull-through.

rampant [rɑ̃pɑ̃], *a.* **1.** (*a*) *Her:* **lion r.,** lion rampant; (*b*) *a. & s.m. Arch:* sloping (part); **voûte, arche, rampante,** rampant arch, vault; (*c*) *s.m. Metall:* uptake flue. **2.** (*a*) creeping (plant, animal); crawling (animal); **bête rampante,** *F:* creepy-crawly; (*d*) grovelling, cringing (person, character); low, mean (condition in life); pedestrian (style); (*c*) *Surg:* **bandage r.,** spiral bandage; (*d*) *Av: F:* **personnel r.,** *s.m.,* **les rampants,** the Kiwis, ground staff.

rampe [rɑ̃ːp], *s.f.* **1.** *A:* flight of stairs. **2.** (*a*) slope, incline, rise (of hill, etc.); **r. d'entrée d'un gué,** slope, bank, leading down to a ford; *Veh:* **démarrer en r.,** to start off up a slope; **vitesse en r.,** speed when (hill) climbing; *Const:* **r. des chevrons,** pitch of the roof rafters; (*b*) *Civ.E:* (rising) gradient, upgrade, *U.S:* grade; **r. brute,** uncompensated gradient; **r. nette,** gradient compensated for curves; **route de montagne avec des rampes de 20%,** mountain road with gradients of 20%, of 1 in 5; *Rail: etc:* **traction en r.,** upgrade traction; **voie (ferrée) à fortes rampes,** line with steep gradients; (*c*) ramp (in road); **r. d'accès d'un pont,** sloping approach, (approach) ramp, of a bridge; **rampes d'un échangeur,** ramps of a cloverleaf, of an interchange; *Fort:* **rampes d'un bastion,** ramps of a bastion; (*d*) ramp, gangway; **r. mobile,** portable ramp, movable gangway; **r. relevable,** retractable ramp; *Rail: etc:* **r. de chargement, d'embarquement,** loading ramp; **r. de déchargement, de débarquement,** unloading ramp; *Rail:* **r. d'enraillement, de remise (sur rail),** re-railing ramp, guide plate; *Nau:* **r. d'accostage,** landing ramp; *Av:* **r. (pneumatique) d'évacuation,** (inflated) escape slide; *Ball:* **r. de lancement (de missiles),** launching ramp, launcher, launching rail(s) (of missiles). **3.** *Mec.E:* inclined plane; **r. hélicoïdale,** (i) skews (of engagement dogs, etc.); (ii) *Opt:* focusing mount(ing); *Mch: etc:* **r. de graissage, r. à huile,** lubricating rack, oil distributor, oil manifold; *Aut:* **r. des culbuteurs,** valve rocker shaft; *I.C.E:* **r. d'allumage,** ignition harness; **r. de soufflage,** hot-air blower; **r. d'injection principale, auxiliaire,** main, pilot, fuel pipe (of turbo-jet). **4.** banisters, hand rail (of stair); *P:* **lâcher la r.,** to die; *F:* **tenir bon la r.,** to be still going strong. **5.** *Ill:* (*a*) **r. au néon,** neon strip light; *Cin:* **r. de projecteurs,** bank of projectors; (*b*) *Th:* footlights, float(s); **être sous les feux de la r.,** to be in the limelight, in the blaze of publicity; *F:* **la pièce n'a pas passé la r.,** the play failed to get across; *F:* **cette chanson-là ne passera pas la r.,** that song won't get over; (*c*) *Av:* **r. (lumineuse) d'atterrissage,** landing lights, contact lights. **6.** *A:* bank (of oars).

rampeau, -eaux [rɑ̃po], *s.m.* (*a*) *Games:* (*esp. dice*) deciding throw; (*b*) *F:* **faire r.,** to be all square.

rampement [rɑ̃pmɑ̃], *s.m.* creeping, crawling

ramper [rɑ̃pe], *v.i.* **1.** (*a*) *A:* to climb; (*b*) *Arch: Mec.E: etc:* to slope, to incline, to ramp. **2.** (*of animal or pers.*) to creep; to crawl; (*of plant*) to creep, trail; **gagner la porte en rampant,** to creep, crawl, to the door; **entrer, sortir, monter, en rampant,** to crawl in, out, up; **r. à quatre pattes dans le fossé,** to creep along the ditch on all fours; **r. devant les grands,** to truckle, cringe, to the great; to grovel before the great; to fawn upon the great; **style qui rampe,** uninspired, prosy, style; **r. dans la misère,** to live in abject poverty.

rampon(n)eau, -eaux [rɑ̃pɔno], *s.m.* **1.** (toy) tumbler, tumble-over, tumbling doll. **2.** type of small knife. **3.** *P:* blow, knock (received in a brawl, etc.).

Ramsès [ramsɛːs], *Pr.n.m. A.Hist:* Rameses, Ramses.

ramule [ramyl], *s.m.* branchlet.

ramure [ramyːr], *s.f.* **1.** branches, boughs, foliage. **2.** antlers (of stag); *Her: Ven:* attire (of a deer).

ramuscule [ramyskyl], *s.m.* little twig.

ranatre [ranatr̥], *s.f.*, **ranatra** [ranatra], *s.f. Ent:* ranatra.

rancard [rɑ̃kaːr], *s.m. P:* **1.** information, tip, gen. **2.** date, rendezvous.

rancarder [rɑ̃karde], *v.tr. P:* **1.** to tip (s.o.) off; **se r.,** to find out. **2.** to make a date with (s.o.).

rancart [rɑ̃kaːr], *s.m.* **1. mettre qch., qn, au r.,** to discard sth.; to retire (officer, official); to shelve (sth.); to side-track (s.o., sth.); **mise au r. d'un projet,** shelving of a plan; *F:* **elle est au r.,** she's on the shelf. **2.** *F:* date, rendezvous.

rance[1] [rɑ̃ːs], *a.* rancid, rank (butter, oil, etc); *F:* **une vieille fille un peu r.,** a faded old maid; *s.m.* **sentir le r.,** to smell rancid.

rance[2], *s.f.* **1.** *Coop:* wooden stand (for casks, etc.). **2.** *N.Arch:* wooden prop.

ranch [rɑ̃ːʃ], *s.m.* ranch; **exploiter un r.,** to ranch; **propriétaire d'un r.,** rancher, ranch man, cowman.

ranche [rɑ̃ːʃ], *s.f.* rung, round, peg (of a rack or peg ladder).

rancher [rɑ̃ʃe], *s.m.* **1.** peg ladder, rack ladder. **2.** jib (of crane).

ranchet [rɑ̃ʃɛ], *s.m.* stanchion, upright (of railway truck, etc.).

ranci [rɑ̃si], *a.* rancid.

rancidité [rɑ̃sidite], *s.f.* rancidity, rancidness.

rancir [rɑ̃siːr], *v.i.* to become, grow, rancid.

rancissement [rɑ̃sismɑ̃], *s.m.*, **rancissure** [rɑ̃sisyːr], *s.f.* growing, becoming, rancid; souring (of butter, etc.).

rancœur [rɑ̃kœːr], *s.f.* rancour; bitterness (of mind); resentment; **j'ai gardé de cette déception, une r.,** this disappointment still rankles (in my mind).

rançon [rɑ̃sɔ̃], *s.f.* ransom; **mettre qn à r.,** to hold s.o. to ransom; **payer la r. de qn,** to ransom s.o.; **la r. du progrès,** the price paid for progress; the penalty of progress

rançonnement [rɑ̃sɔnmɑ̃], *s.m.* (*a*) holding (of s.o., of town) to ransom; (*b*) *F:* extortion, fleecing.

rançonner [rɑ̃sɔne], *v.tr.* (*a*) to hold (s.o., town, ship) to ransom; to exact a ransom from (s.o.); to ransom (s.o.); (*b*) *F:* to fleece (customer, etc.).

rançonneur, -euse [rɑ̃sɔnœːr, -øːz]. **1.** *a.* extortionate (innkeeper, etc.). **2.** *s.* extortioner.

rancune [rɑ̃kyn], *s.f.* rancour, spite, malice, grudge; **satisfaire une r. personnelle,** to satisfy a private grudge; **sentiment de r.,** feeling of pique; **garder r. à qn, avoir de la r. contre qn,** to harbour resentment against s.o., to have a spite against s.o., to bear s.o. malice, ill will (**d'avoir fait qch.,** for having done sth.); **je ne lui garde pas de r.,** I bear him no malice; **par r.,** out of spite; **sans r.,** (i) without malice, without ill feeling; (ii) no hard feelings! no ill feelings! (iii) let bygones be bygones; **il y a de vieilles rancunes entre eux,** there is bad blood between them; **cela a excité bien des rancunes,** it caused much heartache.

rancuneux, -euse [rɑ̃kynø, -øːz], *a. A:* = RANCUNIER.

rancunier, -ière [rɑ̃kynje, -jɛːr], *a. & s.* grudge-bearing, vindictive, rancorous, spiteful (person, character).

rand [rɑ̃ːd]. **1.** *Pr.n.m. Geog:* **le R.,** the Rand. **2.** *s.m. Num:* (*S. Africa, etc.*) rand.

randanite [rɑ̃danit], *s.f.* randannite.

Randolphe [rɑ̃dɔlf], *Pr.n.m.* Randolph.

randonnée [rɑ̃dɔne], *s.f.* **1.** *Ven:* circuit (made by hunted game). **2.** *Aut: Cy: etc:* outing, run, trip, excursion; **être en r.,** (i) to be touring; (ii) to be out for a good long run; **faire une (longue) r.,** to make a long tour, to have a long run; **randonnées de week-end,** weekend excursions, trips, runs.

rang [rɑ̃], *s.m.* **1.** (*a*) row, line (of trees, seats, columns, etc.); *Typewr:* row; **une machine à quatre rangs de touches,** a four-bank machine; **remettre un livre à son r.,** to put a book back in its place; **r. de tricot,** row of knitting; **r. d'oignons,** row of onions; **r. de perles,** row, string, rope, of pearls; *Th:* **premier r. des fauteuils d'orchestre,** first row of the stalls; **cinq jours de r.,** five days in a row; (*b*) *Mil:* rank (= row in line abreast); **sur un r., sur deux rangs,** in single rank, in two ranks; **par rangs de trois, de quatre,** three, four, abreast; **se rassembler, se mettre, en rangs; former les rangs,** to fall into rank, into line; to form line, to fall in; **"formez vos rangs!"** "fall in!" **se rassembler, se former, en ligne sur un r., sur deux rangs, sur trois rangs,** to fall, form, in single rank, in two ranks, in three ranks; **rassembler, mettre, les hommes, la troupe, sur trois rangs,** to draw up men, troops, in three ranks, three deep; **"rassemblement en ligne sur trois rangs!"** "form three deep!" **serrer les rangs,** to close ranks, to close up; **"serrez les rangs!"** "close up!" **avancer en rangs serrés,** to advance in close order; **exercice de r. serré,** *F:* **le r. serré,** close-order drill; **rompre les rangs,** to break ranks, to break off, to be dismissed; to fall out (for a short break); **"rompez vos rangs!"** "dismiss!" **quitter les, sortir des, rangs,** to fall out (of line), to break rank; **permettre à un homme de quitter les, de sortir des, rangs,** to fall out a man; **rentrer, revenir, dans les rangs,** (i) to fall in again; (ii) to return to the ranks; **homme du r.,** private; **officier sorti du r.,** officer promoted from the ranks, ranker, *U.S:* mustang; **sortir du r.,** (i) (*of an officer*) to rise from the ranks; (ii) to get out of the ruck, to make one's name; *F:* **rentrer dans le r.,** (i) (*of pers.*) to give in, to knuckle under, to submit; (ii) (*of situation*) to be normal again; **tout est désormais rentré dans le r.,** everything is now normal again; (*c*) **se mettre sur les rangs,** (i) *A:* to enter the lists (at a tournament); (ii) to enter the lists, to come forward (as a candidate), to put in (for a job); **être sur les rangs,** to be a competitor; **j'appris qu'il y avait déjà quelqu'un sur les rangs,** I was told that there was already someone in the field; (*d*) *Fr.C:* farm service road, country road. **2.** (*a*) rank, place; station (in life); **avoir r. de colonel,** to hold the rank of colonel; **r. élevé,** high rank; **dame de haut r.,** lady of rank; **selon son r.,** according to one's rank; **il préféra ne pas sortir de son r.,** he preferred to keep to his own station in life; *A:* **vaisseau de premier r.,** first-rate man-of-war; *F:* **de premier r.,** first-class, first-rate; **arriver au premier r.,** to come to the front; **il est au premier r. de sa profession,** he is at the top of the tree in his profession; **tenir le premier r. parmi . . .,** to hold the foremost place among . . .; **venir au troisième r., en troisième r.,** to rank third; **passer au second r.,** to receive secondary consideration; **par r. d'âge, de taille,** according to age, height; **être mis sur le même r.,** to be placed on the same footing; **occuper un r. supérieur, inférieur, à qn,** to rank above, below, s.o.; **prendre r., avoir r., avant, après, qn,** to rank before, after s.o.; **avoir, prendre, même r. que . . .,** (i) (*of person, debt, mortgage, etc.*) to rank equally with . . .; (ii) (*of share, debenture*) to rank pari passu with . . .; **il a pris r. parmi les grands poètes,** he has taken his place among the great poets; **mettre qn au r. des plus grands écrivains,** to rank, reckon, count, s.o. among the greatest writers; **déchoir du r. que l'on a occupé,** to fall from one's high position; **prendre r. dans un parti,** to join a party; (*b*) (*in restaurant*) **chef de r.,** chef de rang; (*c*) **r. social,** social status; **il faut tenir notre r.,** we have got to keep up our position. **3.** *Mth: etc:* rank; **méthodes statistiques de rangs,** rank-order statistics. **4.** *Typ:* composing frame.

range[1] [rɑ̃ːʒ], *s.f. Civ.E:* row (of paving stones).

range[2] [rɑ̃dʒ], *s.m.* **1.** (*statistics*) range. **2.** *Telecom:* range.

rangé [rɑ̃ʒe], *a.* **1. bataille rangée,** pitched battle. **2.** tidy, orderly, well-ordered (room, desk, etc.). **3.** steady (person); **être r.,** to lead a well-ordered life; **homme r. dans ses habitudes,** man of regular habits; **fille rangée,** dutiful daughter.

rangée [rɑ̃ʒe], *s.f.* row, line (of persons, trees); **r. de perles,** row, rope, of pearls; **r. de sièges, de loges,** tier of seats, of boxes; **r. de chiffres,** array of figures; (*of computers*) **r. de contrôle,** check row; **binaire par r.,** row binary.

rangement [rɑ̃ʒmɑ̃], *s.m.* (*a*) tidying, putting in order; storage; (*computers*) storage, reading (into computer store); **la manie du r.,** mania for tidiness; **volume de r.,** storage space; **(meuble de) r.,** storage unit; **r. incorporé,** built-in cupboard; **r. de cuisine,** kitchen cabinet; (*in computer work*) **r. par interclassement,** sequencing by merging; **emplacement de r. (en mémoire),** bucket; (*b*) arrangement; **r. rationnel,** logical arrangement; **le r. des voitures à l'exposition était bien fait,** the arrangement of the cars in the exhibition was well done.

ranger [rɑ̃ʒe], *v.tr.* (**je rangeai(s); n. rangeons**) **1.** to arrange; to draw up, marshal (troops, etc.). **2.** (*a*) to put (sth.) away; to put (sth.) back in its place; to stow away, tidy away (objects); to stow (goods); (*of computers*) to rank; **r. par classe,** to classify; **r. en mémoire,** to store; **rangez vos livres,** put away your books; **r. le linge dans l'armoire,** to put away the linen in the cupboard; (*b*) **r. la foule,** to keep the crowd back, in its place; *Aut:* **r. une voiture,** to pull in to the side. **3.** (*a*) to arrange, tidy; to put, set (things) to rights, in order; **r. une chambre,** to tidy a room; (*b*) **le mariage l'a rangé,** marriage has steadied him down, has made him settle down; *F:* (*of criminal*) **être rangé (du côté) des voitures,** to reform. **4. r. qn parmi les grands écrivains,** to rank s.o. amongst the great writers; **on peut r. ces faits, ces faits se rangent, dans une autre catégorie,** these facts fall into another category. **5. r. une ville sous sa puissance,** to bring a town under one's power; **r. qn de son côté,** to win s.o. over to one's side; *A:* **r. qn à la raison,** to bring s.o. to reason. **6.** *Nau:* **r. la terre, la côte,** to range the land, to run along (the) shore, to hug the coast; **r. la terre,** to keep the land aboard. **7.** *Nau:* **le vent range le nord,** the wind is veering round to the north.

se ranger. **1.** (*a*) (*of troops, etc.*) to draw up, line up; (*b*) (*of car, etc.*) **se r. le long du trottoir,** to pull up at the kerb; *Nau:* **se r. à quai,** to berth. **2. se r. du côté de qn,** to take sides, to side, with s.o.; **se r. avec la majorité,** to come into line with the majority; **se r. à l'opinion de qn,** to fall in with, come over to, s.o.'s opinion; to agree with s.o.'s opinion; **se r. à l'avis de qn,** to come round to s.o.'s way of thinking; **si le public se range à cet avis,** if this view commends itself to the public. **3. se r. (de côté),** to get out of the way; to draw to one side; to stand aside; *Aut:* (*of car*) to pull over to one side; **se r. contre le mur,** to draw back against the wall; **on se rangea pour nous laisser passer,** they stood aside to make room for us; **on se rangea pour le laisser passer,** they made way for him to pass; **rangez-vous!** stand back! (get) out of the way! **4. Il s'est rangé,** (i) he has steadied down, settled down; (ii) he has got married. **5.** *Nau:* **le vent se range au nord,** the wind is veering round to the north.

rangette [rɑ̃ʒɛt], *s.f. Games:* taw; **jouer à la r.,** to have a game of taw, to play marbles.

rangeur, -euse [rɑ̃ʒœːr, -øːz], *s.* sorter, arranger; tidier.

Rangoon, Rangoun [rɑ̃gun], *Pr.n.m. Geog:* Rangoon.

rani [rani], *s.f.* ranee.

ranidés [ranide], *s.m.pl. Amph:* Ranidae, the true frogs.

raniforme [ranifɔrm], *a. Z:* frog-like, raniform.

ranimation [ranimasjɔ̃], *s.f.* resuscitation; reanimation.

ranimer [ranime], *v.tr.* to revive; to put new life into (s.o., sth.); (*a*) to restore (fainting person) to consciousness, to life; **on le ranima avec un verre d'eau-de-vie,** they brought, pulled, him round, brought him to, with a glass of spirits; **Jésus ranima Lazare,** Jesus raised Lazarus from the dead; (*b*) to revive (dying fire, drooping plant, faded colour); to stir up (the fire); **r. la colère, l'espoir, l'amour, de qn,** to reawaken, rekindle, s.o.'s anger, hope, love; **r. la conversation,** to put new life into the conversation; to liven up the conversation; (*c*) to cheer, *F:* buck, (s.o.) up again; **r. l'assemblée,** to put fresh life into the meeting; **ce discours ranima les troupes,** this speech heartened the troops, put fresh heart into the troops.

se ranimer, to revive; (*a*) to come to life again; (*of fire*) to burn up; **elle ne fut pas longtemps à se r.,** she soon came round; **les affaires se raniment,** business is looking up; (*b*) to cheer up.

ranin [ranɛ̃], *a.* frog-like, raniform; *Anat:* ranine (vein).

ranine [ranin], *s.f. Crust:* ranina.

ransomite [rɑ̃sɔmit], *s.f. Miner:* ransomite.

ranule [ranyl], *s.f. Med:* ranula, *F:* frog tongue.

ranz [rɑ̃(ːs)], *s.m.* **r. des vaches,** ranz-des-vaches (Swiss pastoral melody).

raonnais, -aise [rɑnɛ, raɔnɛ, -ɛːz], *a. & s. Geog:* (native, inhabitant) of Raon-l'Étape.

Raoul [raul], *Pr.n.m.* Ralph, Rollo, Rodolph, Rudolph.

raout [raut], *s.m. A:* (social) party; reception, at-home; rout.

rapace [rapas], *a.* **1.** rapacious, predacious (animal, bird); **bêtes rapaces,** predatory animals; *s.m.pl. Z:* **les rapaces,** *A:* the raptores; birds of prey. **2.** rapacious, grasping (person).

rapacité [rapasite], *s.f.* rapacity; rapaciousness; **avec r.,** rapaciously.

râpage [rɑpaːʒ], *s.m.* rasping; grating (of sugar, etc.); grinding (of wood, etc.).

rapakiwi [rapakivi], *s.m. Geol:* rapakivi.

rapapillotage [rapapijɔtaːʒ], *s.m. A: P:* reconciliation, making it up.

rapapilloter [rapapijɔte], *v.tr. A: P:* to reconcile (persons).

se rapapilloter, *A:* to make it up.

rapatelle [rapatɛl], *s.f.* haircloth.

rapatriage [rapatrija:ʒ], *s.m. A. & Dial: F:* reconciliation.

rapatriement [rapatrimɑ̃], *s.m.* **1.** repatriation (of soldiers, sailors, etc.). **2.** *Dial:* reconciliation.

rapatrié, -iée [rapatrije]. **1.** *a.* repatriated; **soldats rapatriés,** homecoming soldiers. **2.** *s.* repatriate.

rapatrier [rapatrije], *v.tr.* (*p.d. & pr.sub.* **n. rapatriions, v. rapatriiez**) **1.** to repatriate; to send (s.o.) home (from abroad). **2.** *Dial:* to reconcile.

se rapatrier, *A: & Dial:* to make it up.

râpe¹ [rɑ:p], *s.f.* **1.** rasp; (*a*) grater; **r. à muscade,** nutmeg grater; (*b*) rough file. **2.** *Med:* rasping murmur (of the heart).

râpe², *s.f.* = RAFLE¹.

râpé [rɑpe]. **1.** *a.* (*a*) grated (sugar, cheese, etc.) rasped; (*b*) worn out, threadbare (garment); *F:* **avoir l'air r.,** to look shabby. **2.** *s.m.* (*a*) rape wine; (*b*) *F:* odd remnants of wine (mixed and re-bottled); (*c*) grated cheese.

râper [rɑpe], *v.tr.* **1.** to rasp (wood); to grate (sugar, nutmeg, etc.); to grind (snuff, etc.). **2.** to wear (garment) threadbare.

râperie [rɑpri], *s.f. Sug.R:* crushing mill.

rapetassage [raptasa:ʒ], *s.m. F:* **1.** patching up; cobbling. **2.** patched-up work.

rapetasser [raptase], *v.tr. F:* to patch up, do up (garment); to cobble (shoe); to piece together (literary work).

rapetasseur [raptasœ:r], *s.m.* cobbler.

rapetissant [raptisɑ̃], *a.* **verre r.,** diminishing glass.

rapetissement [raptismɑ̃], *s.m.* shortening, reducing, diminishing, shrinking, dwarfing.

rapetisser [raptise]. **1.** *v.tr.* to make (sth.) smaller; to reduce; to shorten (garment); to shrink (material); **la distance rapetisse les objets,** distance makes objects look smaller; **sa maison rapetisse les autres,** his house dwarfs the others; **il lui fallait se r. pour monter dans la voiture,** he had to stoop in order to get into the car; **figure rapetissée,** shrunken face. **2.** *v.i. & pr.* to shorten; to become shorter, smaller; (*of materials*) to shrink.

râpette [rɑpɛt], *s.f. Bot: F:* madwort.

râpeur, -euse¹ [rɑpœ:r, -ø:z], *s. Tchn:* rasper (of wood, etc.); grinder (of snuff, etc.).

râpeux, -euse² [rɑpø, -ø:z], *a.* raspy (tongue); harsh (wine); grating (noise).

Raphaël [rafaɛl], *Pr.n.m.* Raphael.

raphaëlois, -oise [rafaɛlwa, -wa:z], *a. & s. Geog:* (native, inhabitant) of Saint-Raphaël.

raphanus [rafanys], *s.m. Bot:* raphanus.

raphé [rafe], *s.m. Anat: Bot:* raphe.

raphia [rafja], *s.m. Bot: Com:* raphia (grass), raffia.

raphide [rafid], *s.f. Bot:* raphide.

raphidés [rafide], *s.m.pl. Orn:* Raphidae, the dodos.

raphidie [rafidi], *s.f. Ent:* raphidiid; raphidian.

rapiat, -ate [rapja, -at]. *F:* **1.** *a.* stingy, avaricious (person). **2.** *s.* miser, skinflint.

rapide [rapid]. **1.** *a.* (*a*) rapid, swift, fast; **r. comme la pensée, une flèche, l'éclair,** as swift as thought, as an arrow, as lightning; **épidémie r. à se propager,** epidemic swift to spread; **faire des progrès rapides,** to make rapid progress; **j'en eus le souvenir r.,** a swift memory of it came back to me; **la r. conclusion des négociations,** the speedy conclusion of the negotiations; **fusil à tir r.,** quick-firing rifle; *Sp:* **piste r.,** fast track; **palan à action r.,** quick-acting hoist; **après un tour r. en Europe,** after a rapid, quick, tour of Europe; (*computers*) **imprimante r.,** high-speed printer; **lecteur r.,** high-speed reader; **mémoire à accès r.,** fast access store; quick-access store; **mémoire r.,** fast store; **mémoire très r.,** scratch-pad memory; **rebobinage r.,** high-speed rewind; **report r.,** high-speed carry, ripple-through carry; (*b*) steep, rapid (slope). **2.** *s.m.* (*a*) rapid (in river); (*b*) express (train).

rapidement [rapidmɑ̃], *adv.* (*a*) rapidly, swiftly; **le temps passe r.,** time flies; (*b*) steeply.

rapidité [rapidite], *s.f.* (*a*) rapidity, swiftness; *Sp:* fastness (of track); **avec la r. de l'éclair,** with lightning speed; (*computers*) **r. de modulation,** modulation rate; (*b*) steepness (of slope).

rapiéçage [rapjesa:ʒ], *s.m.* **1.** = RAPIÈCEMENT. **2.** patchwork.

rapiècement [rapjɛsmɑ̃], *s.m.* patching (of garment).

rapiécer [rapjese], *v.tr.* (**je rapiéce, n. rapiéçons; je rapiécerai**) to piece, patch (garment, etc.).

rapiécetage [rapjesta:ʒ], *s.m. A:* = RAPIÉÇAGE.

rapiéceter [rapjeste], *v.tr.* (**je rapiécette, n. rapiécetons; je rapiécetterai**) *A:* = RAPIÉCER.

rapière [rapjɛ:r], *s.f.* rapier; *A:* **traîneur de r.,** swashbuckler.

rapin [rapɛ̃], *s.m. F:* **1.** art student (*esp.* the junior in the studio). **2.** bad painter; dauber, daubster.

rapinade [rapinad], *s.f. F:* piece of bad painting; daub.

rapine [rapin], *s.f. Lit:* (*a*) rapine, pillage, depradation; **habitudes de r.,** predatory habits; (*b*) **vivre de r.,** to live by rapine; **enrichi par ses rapines,** grown rich by fleecing others.

rapiner [rapine], *v.tr. & i.* to pillage.

rapinerie [rapinri], *s.f.* plundering, pillaging.

rapineur, -euse [rapinœ:r, -ø:z], *s.* plunderer, pillager.

raplapla(t) [raplapla], *a.inv. F:* **1.** commonplace, trite. **2.** (*of pers.*) without energy, washed out.

rappareillement [raparɛjmɑ̃], *s.m.* matching; completing (of a set).

rappareiller [rapareje], *v.tr.* to match, complete (a set of china, etc.).

rappariement [raparimɑ̃], *s.m.* (action of) matching, completing (a pair).

rapparier [raparje], *v.tr.* (*p.d. & pr.sub.* **n. rappariions, v. rappariiez**) to match, complete (a pair); to pair (two things); to find the fellow of (glove, stocking).

rappel [rapɛl], *s.m.* **1.** (*a*) recall (of general, ambassador, etc.); **lettres de r.,** letters of recall; *Ven:* **r. des chiens,** calling off of the hounds; (*b*) *Com: etc:* calling in (of sum advanced, etc.); (*c*) **r. à l'ordre,** call(ing) to order; **r. à la question,** recall(ing) to the question; (*d*) *Mil:* **r. sous les drapeaux,** recall to the colours (of reservists); (*e*) *Th:* curtain call; (re)call (of actor). **2.** *Art:* **r. de lumière,** high lights (in design). **3.** (*a*) reminder; *Com:* **r. de compte, d'échéance,** reminder of account due, of due date; **lettre de r.,** (letter of) reminder; (*b*) **r. de traitement, de solde,** back pay. **4.** *Jur:* repeal, recall (of decree). **5.** *Mch: Mec.E: etc:* (*a*) readjustment; **vis de r.,** adjusting screw; **r. de l'usure,** taking up of the wear; (*b*) back motion; **piston de r.,** drawback piston; **ressort de r.,** return spring, drawback spring; pull-back spring (of brake, etc.); **bras de r.,** compensating arm; **dispositif de r. à la position neutre,** return-to-neutral mechanism; *Typewr:* **r. de chariot, r. arrière,** (i) return of carriage; (ii) backspace key, back spacer; **r. de chariot avec changement de ligne,** automatic line-spacer; (*c*) **fil de r.,** bracing wire, straining wire; **tige de r.,** stay rod; *Mch:* **barre de r.,** drag link. **6.** *Mil:* **battre le r.,** to call, beat, to arms; *F:* **battre le r. de ses amis,** to drum up one's friends. **7.** *Nau:* **r. de roulis, r. au vent,** weather roll, **fort coup de r.,** weather lurch. **8.** suspicion, touch, faint smell. **9.** *Mount:* doubled rope; roping down; **faire une descente en r.,** to come down on a doubled rope; to rope down. **10.** *Bac:* **dose de r.,** booster dose; **injection, piqûre, de r.,** booster injection.

rappelable [raplabl̩], *a.* **1.** recallable (reservist, etc.). **2.** repealable (decree, etc.).

rappeler [raple], *v.tr.* (*conj. like* APPELER) **1.** to call (s.o.) again, afresh; *Tp:* to ring, *U.S:* call, again, back. **2.** (*a*) to recall (s.o.); to call, summon, (s.o.) back; **r. un général, un ambassadeur, un exilé,** to recall a general, an ambassador, an exile; **r. un acteur,** to call for, recall, an actor; to give an actor a recall; **être rappelé trois fois,** to take three curtain calls; **r. qn au pouvoir,** to recall s.o. to office; **r. son chien,** to call off one's dog; **les affaires l'ont rappelé à Paris,** business called, summoned, him back to Paris; **on l'a rappelé de Paris,** he has been called away from Paris; (*b*) **r. qn à l'ordre,** to call s.o. to order; **r. qn à son devoir,** to recall s.o. to the paths of duty; **r. qn à la vie,** to restore s.o. to life; to resuscitate s.o.; to bring s.o. round; (*c*) **r. son courage,** to summon up one's courage (again). **3.** (*a*) to call back, recall, (sth.) to mind; **r. sa jeunesse,** to call one's youth back to memory; to recall one's youth; **r. d'anciens griefs,** to rake up old grievances; **rappelez-moi votre nom,** what was your name again? **r. qch. à qn,** to recall sth., to s.o., to remind s.o. of sth.; **vous me rappelez mon oncle,** you remind me of my uncle; you put me in mind of my uncle; **cela me rappelle mon enfance,** it brings back my childhood to me; **une figure qui rappelle la vôtre,** a face not unlike yours; **rappelez-moi à son bon souvenir,** remember me (kindly) to him; **elle me rappelle que nous y allons ce soir,** she has reminded me that we are going there tonight; **choses qu'il vaut autant ne pas r.,** things best forgotten; (*b*) *Adm. & Com. Corresp:* **dans votre réponse r. la référence D.H./L.M.,** reference: D.H./L.M.; **prière de r. ce numéro,** in reply please quote this number. **4. r. un décret,** to repeal, recall, a decree; **r. (par téléphone) un message,** to cancel a message (by phone). **5.** *Mec.E: etc:* to draw back (part, etc.); **soupape rappelée sur son siège par un ressort,** valve closed by a spring, spring-loaded valve; *Typewr:* **r. le chariot,** (i) to return the carriage; (ii) to backspace; (*b*) (*of guy rope*) to brace back; (*of tie rod*) to tie, stay. **6.** *Art:* **r. la lumière,** to distribute the high lights (in a painting). **7.** *Nau:* (*of ship*) (*a*) **r. au vent, au roulis,** to weather-roll; (*b*) **r. sur son ancre,** to swing to the anchor. **8.** *Bill:* **r. les billes,** to bring the balls together. **9.** *v.i. Mount:* to come down a doubled rope; to rope down. **10.** *v.i. Ven:* (*of pheasant*) to crow.

se rappeler qch., to recall, recollect, remember, sth.; to call sth. to mind; **rappelez-vous ce que vous m'avez dit,** remember what you told me; **je ne me le rappelle pas,** I do not remember it; **se r. (d')avoir promis qch.,** to remember having promised sth.; **je me rappelle que vous me l'avez dit,** I remember that you told me (so); **je ne me rappelle pas que vous me l'ayez dit,** I don't remember your telling me (so), that you told me; **rappelez-vous que ce n'est qu'une enfant,** bear in mind that she is only a child.

rappliquer [raplike]. **1.** *v.tr.* to re-apply (poultice, etc.). **2.** *v.i. P:* to come back; *P:* to hike back; **r. à la maison,** to make tracks for home; **il a rappliqué à minuit,** he rolled in at midnight.

rappointir [rapwɛ̃ti:r], *v.tr.* to sharpen the tip (of a bradawl, etc.).

rappointis [rapwɛ̃ti], *s.m. Const:* key.

rapport [rapɔ:r], *s.m.* I. **1.** yield, return, profit; **r. d'un capital, d'une terre,** yield of, return on, capital; yield of land; **capital en r.,** interest-bearing, productive, capital; **maison de r.,** block of flats (for letting); **d'un bon r.,** profitable; that brings in a fair, a good, return; that pays well; **arbre d'un bon r.,** good bearer; **actions d'un bon r.,** shares that bring in a good return; **commerce d'un bon r.,** trade that brings in a good profit; **emploi d'un bon r.,** profitable employment; **terre d'un bon r.,** land that makes, yields, a good return, that brings in a good income. **2.** (*a*) account, report, statement; **faux r.,** false report, misstatement; *F:* **faire des rapports,** to tell tales (out of school); **au r. de cet auteur . . .,** according to this author . . .; (*b*) *Adm: Jur:* (official) report; return (of expenses, etc.); survey; *Adm:* **r. collectif,** joint report; **r. périodique, r. d'avancement (des travaux),** progress report; **envoyer un r.,** to send in a report; **faire, rédiger, un r. sur qch.,** to make, draw up, a report on sth.; **r. rédigé par . . .,** report by . . .; **présenter, soumettre, un r. à qn sur qch.,** to render, furnish, present, a report to s.o. concerning, on, sth.; *Parl:* **faire un r. sur l'état de la question,** to report progress; *Com: Ind:* **r. de gestion,** annual report (of company); **r. des commissaires (aux comptes),** audit(ors') report; **r. financier,** treasurer's report; **r. moral,** chairman's, president's, report; **r. sur la situation générale de la société,** company's (background) report; *Jur:* **r. d'enquête,** report of enquiry, of investigation, of survey; **r. d'expert(ise),** expert's report, survey(or's) report, appraisement; *Nau: etc:* **r. d'avarie(s),** damage report; *Nau:* **r. de mer, r. du capitaine,** (ship's) protest, captain's (sworn) report; *Av:* **r. d'incident,** failure report; (*c*) *Mil:* daily parade for issue of orders; **"au rapport!" "read!" heure du r.,** orderly hour; **salle des rapports,** orderly room; **être porté au r. du commandant de compagnie,** to have to appear before, to report to, the company's commander (as a defaulter); (*d*) *Ven:* **faire son r.,** to report on the outcome of the beating. **3.** (*a*) **terres de r.,** made ground, artificial soil; *Metalw:* **(forgeage) faux r.,** die shift; (*b*) *Tchn:* **pièces de r.,** (i) parts secured to one another; built-up parts (of machinery, etc.); (ii) inlaid pieces, mosaic work; (iii) *Metall:* false cores, draw-backs; (*c*) *Tex:* repeat (of design); (*d*) *Jur:* **r. (d'une donation, d'un bien, etc.) à une succession,** restoration (of a bequest, a property, etc.) to a succession; bringing into hotchpot; (*e*) *pl. A:* (i) repeating (of food); (ii) flatulence; **j'ai des rapports,** (i) my food repeats; (ii) I suffer from wind.

II. **rapport. 1.** relation, connection (**avec,** with); **sans r. avec le sujet,** irrelevant (to the subject); without any bearing on the subject; **avoir r. à qch.,** to relate, refer, to sth.; **la question a un r. très étroit avec . . .,** the question bears closely upon . . ., the question is intimately connected with . . .; *F:* **je ne dirai rien, r. à ton père,** I'll say nothing because of your father; *adv.phr.* **en r. avec qch.,** in keeping with sth., in harmony with sth.; **rôle en r. avec votre dignité,** role in keeping with your dignity; **par r. à qch.,** (i) with regard to sth.; with respect to sth.; in relation to sth.; (ii) in comparison with, compared with, sth.; **sous le r. de qch.,** with regard to, with respect to, sth.; in respect of sth.; **sous ce r.,** in this respect; **sous le r. de l'intelligence,** in point of intelligence; **sous tous les rapports,** in all respects, in every respect, in every way, on every account; **examiner une question sous tous les rapports,** to examine a question in all its implications; **la maison est trop grande, et peu désirable sous d'autres rapports,** the house is too large, and undesirable in other respects. **2.** (*a*) *Mth: Mec.E: etc:* ratio, proportion; **r. arithmétique, géométrique,** arithmetical, geometrical, ratio; **r. de corrélation,** correlation ratio; **dans le r. de . . .,** in the ratio of . . .; **(dans le) r. de un à trois,** (in the) ratio of one to three; **le r. maître-élèves est de 1 pour 20,** the staff-student ratio is 1 to 20; *T.V:* **r. hauteur-largeur de l'image,** aspect ratio; *I.C.E:* **r. entre la longueur et le diamètre d'une chambre de combustion,** aspect ratio; *Ph: etc:* **r. d'amplitude (des mouvements ondulatoires, des mouvements saisonniers, etc.),** amplitude ratio (of wave motions, of seasonal variations, etc.); *Oc:* **r. des amplitudes (des marées),** ratio of tidal range; *Atom.Ph:* **r. atomique,** atomic ratio; **r. isotopique,** abundance ratio; **r. molaire,** molar ratio; *Av: etc:* **r. du poids mort au poids utile,** proportion, ratio, of the gross load to the net load; *Av:* **r. portance-traînée,** lift-drag ratio; *Mec:* **r. tension-déformation,** strength-strain ratio; (*b*) *Mec.E:* **r. de denture, r. des engrenages,** gear ratio; **r. de démultiplication, de réduction,** reduction(-gear) ratio; **r. pondéral,** mass ratio; **r. volumétrique,** swept volume (of cylinder); **r. de surmultiplication,** overdrive ratio; *I.C.E:* **r. de suralimentation** boost ratio; **indicateur de r. de pression,** ratiometer (of jet engine); *N.Arch:* **r. de compensation (d'un gouvernail compensé),** balance ratio (of balanced rudder); (*c*) *El:* **r. de transformation,** voltage ratio; *Elcs:* **r. signal-bruit, signal-image,** signal-to-noise, signal-to-image, ratio; **r. de déviation,** deviation ratio; **r. de discrimination (1 à 0),** one-to-zero ratio; **r. d'impulsions,** break-make ratio; **r. de sélection,** selection ratio. **3.** (*a*) relations (between persons); **mettre qn en r. avec qn,** to bring s.o. into contact, put s.o. in touch, with s.o.; **avoir des rapports avec qn,** (i) to have dealings, relations, with s.o.; (ii) to be in touch with s.o.; **j'ai eu des rapports avec eux,** I have come into contact with them; **avoir de bons rapports avec qn,** to be on good terms with s.o.; **bons rapports avec la France,** good understanding with France; **cesser tout r. avec qn,** to break off all relations with s.o.; **rapports de commerce,** business relations, dealings, connections; **entretenir des rapports amicaux avec qn,** to be on friendly terms with s.o.; **rapports patient-médecin, patrons-ouvriers,** patient-doctor, labour-management, relations; (*b*) **rapports sexuels,** sexual intercourse; **avoir des rapports avec une femme,** to have sexual intercourse with a woman; **r. interrompu,** coitus interruptus.

rapportable [rapɔrtabl], *a.* **1.** *Jur:* (sum, property) that must be restored to a succession. **2.** *Tchn:* **pièces rapportables,** pieces that fit together. **3.** referable, attributable (**à,** to).

rapportage [rapɔrtaːʒ], *s.m.* **1.** *Sch: etc:* taletelling, *F:* sneaking. **2.** piece of taletelling; underhand report.

rapporté [rapɔrte], *a.* **1. terre rapportée,** made ground. **2.** (*a*) built-up (machine); compound (girder); (*b*) added, separate (part); **étau à mâchoires rapportées,** vice with detachable jaws, with inserted jaws; **moteur à culasse rapportée,** engine with detachable head; *Mec.E:* **alluchons rapportés,** inserted teeth; *Carp:* **languette rapportée,** loose tongue, slip tongue; *Dressm:* **manche rapportée,** set-in sleeve; *Bootm:* **chaussure sans bout r.,** plain front shoe; **bout r.,** toe-cap; *Phot:* **épreuve avec fond r.,** combination print; (*c*) **pièces rapportées,** inlaid work, mosaic work.

rapporter [rapɔrte], *v.tr.* **1.** (*a*) to bring back (sth. of a size to be carried); *Ven:* (*of dog*) to retrieve (game); **rapportez-moi un kilo de sucre,** bring me back a kilo of sugar; **r. ce qu'on a emprunté,** to bring back, return, restore, what one has borrowed; **il a rapporté de Chine beaucoup d'objets d'art,** he brought home many curios from China; **chien qui rapporte bien,** good retriever; *Jur:* **r. une donation, etc., à une succession,** to restore a donation, etc., to a succession; (*b*) to get, win; **il a rapporté beaucoup de gloire de cette campagne,** he got, derived, much glory from this campaign; **il n'en a rapporté que de la honte,** all he got out of it was disgrace; (*c*) **r. des terres pour élever une terrasse,** to cart earth to build up a terrace; (*d*) *Tchn:* to add, join, put in, insert (pieces, in order to build up a machine or form a mosaic pattern). **2.** to bring in, bear, yield, produce; **placement qui rapporte cinq pour cent,** investment that brings in, bears, yields, five per cent; **arbres qui rapportent beaucoup,** trees that yield, produce, much fruit, that yield a good profit; **cela ne rapporte rien,** it doesn't pay; *abs.* **la publicité rapporte,** it pays to advertise; **affaire qui rapporte,** paying business. **3.** (*a*) to report, give an account of (sth.); **r. un fait,** to report, relate, a fact; **il rapporte l'avoir vu lui-même,** he reports that he saw it himself; **il est rapporté dans l'histoire que . . .,** it is on record that . . .; (*b*) *v.i.* **r. sur un projet,** to report, present a report, on a plan; (*c*) *Sch: F:* to tell tales; **il est toujours à r.,** he is always taletelling, talebearing, *F:* sneaking; **r. sur le compte de qn,** *F:* to tell on s.o.; *Pej:* **r. une histoire,** to repeat a story; **vous n'auriez pas dû le r.,** you should not have repeated it. **4.** to refer, ascribe; **r. qch. à une cause,** to attribute, ascribe, sth. to a cause; **r. un événement à une époque,** to assign, refer, an event to a period; *A:* **famille qui rapporte son origine à tel ancêtre,** family that ascribes its origin to, that traces its descent from, that claims descent from, such or such an ancestor; **r. tout à soi, à ses intérêts,** to have nothing but one's selfish interests in view; to view everything in terms of self. **5.** *Book-k:* **r. un article,** to post an item. **6.** *Jur: etc:* to rescind, revoke (decree, etc.); to re-open (case of bankruptcy); *Adm:* to withdraw, cancel, (order); **r. un ordre de grève,** to call off a strike. **7.** *Surv: etc:* **r. un angle,** to plot, set off, lay off, an angle. **8.** *v.i. Nau:* **les marées rapportent,** the tides are increasing.

se rapporter. 1. (*a*) to agree, tally (**avec,** with); **couleurs qui se rapportent bien,** colours that go well together; (*b*) to fit together; **le pignon ne se rapporte pas avec l'arbre,** the pinion does not fit the shaft. **2.** to refer, relate (**à,** to); to have reference (to); **passage qui se rapporte à un autre,** passage that relates, refers, has reference, to another; **le traité et les ratifications qui s'y rapportent,** the treaty and the appurtenant ratifications; **les documents qui se rapportent à l'affaire,** the relevant documents. **3. s'en r. à qn, au témoignage de qn,** to refer to, to rely on, to put one's faith in, s.o., s.o.'s evidence; **je m'en rapporte à vous,** (i) I take your word for it; (ii) I shall abide by your decision, I leave it to you.

rapporteur, -euse [rapɔrtœːr, -øːz], *s.* **1.** (*a*) talebearer, tell-tale, sneak; *a.* **écolier r.,** talebearing schoolboy; (*b*) *Ven:* **chien r.,** retriever; (*c*) *s.m.* tell-tale (of organ bellows). **2.** *s.m.* reporter, recorder; (*a*) *Pol:* **r. d'une commission,** chairman of a committee (who reports to the House); **r. d'une conférence,** rapporteur of a conference; (*b*) *Mil:* judge advocate (at court martial). **3.** *s.m. Mth: Surv: etc:* protractor; **r. à limbe complet,** circular protractor.

rapprendre [raprɑ̃ːdr], *v.tr.* (*conj. like* PRENDRE) **1.** to learn (sth.) (over) again. **2.** to teach (sth.) again (**à,** to).

rapprêter [raprete], *v.tr. Tex: etc:* to dress (material, etc.) again.

rapprochage [raprɔʃaːʒ], *s.m.* (action of) thinning (a hedge, etc.).

rapproché [raprɔʃe], *a.* near (in space or time) (**de,** to); **les forts rapprochés de la frontière,** the forts in proximity to the frontier; **maisons très rapprochées,** houses very close, near, to one another; **yeux rapprochés,** eyes set close together; close-set eyes; *Navy:* **combat r.,** close action; **séances très rapprochées,** meetings held at very short intervals, at near intervals; **espèces rapprochées,** closely related species.

rapprochement [raprɔʃmɑ̃], *s.m.* **1.** bringing together; (*a*) **r. des lèvres d'une plaie,** bringing, placing, together of the edges of a wound; (*b*) **r. de deux personnes,** bringing together, reconciling, of two persons; (*c*) comparison, parallel; **r. de faits, d'idées,** setting side by side, putting together, comparing, of facts, ideas, **établir un r. inattendu entre Cicéron et Démosthène,** to establish unlooked-for points of similarity in Cicero and Demosthenes. **2.** nearness, proximity, closeness (of two objects). **3.** coming together; (*a*) **plus grand r. vers l'intimité,** closer approach to intimacy; (*b*) reconciliation; rapprochement. **4.** *Navy:* rate of approach, closing rate (of opposing ships or fleets).

rapprocher¹ [raprɔʃe], *s.m. Ven:* following the scent (of an animal).

rapprocher², *v.tr.* **1.** to bring (sth.) near (again); to bring (s.o.) part of the way; **rapprochez la lampe que vous avez éloignée,** bring back the lamp you've moved away. **2.** (*a*) to bring (objects) nearer, closer, together; **r. les lèvres d'une plaie,** to draw together, join, unite, the lips of a wound; **r. qch. de qch.,** to bring, put, sth. nearer to sth.; **r. une chaise du feu,** to draw up a chair to the fire; **les avions ont rapproché les distances,** aircraft have made distances seem less; **une lunette rapproche les objets,** a field-glass makes objects look nearer, brings things near; (*b*) to bring together; to create a fellowship between (two persons); **un intérêt commun les rapproche,** a common interest brings, draws, them together; **un goût commun la rapprochait du jeune homme,** a taste in common, a common interest, drew her towards the young man; (*c*) to bring together again, to reconcile (two persons); **cette maladie de l'enfant les avait rapprochés,** the child's illness had drawn them together again. **3. r. des faits, des idées,** to put together, to put side by side, to compare, facts, ideas; **en rapprochant différents indices, j'arrivai à l'opinion que . . .,** putting two and two together, I formed the opinion that . . .. **4.** *Ven:* to follow the scent (of an animal).

se rapprocher. 1. (*a*) **se r. de qn, de qch.,** to draw near(er) to s.o., to sth.; (*b*) **se r. d'un navire,** to gain on a ship (*e.g.* in pursuit). **2. plan qui se rapproche d'un autre,** plan that bears a resemblance to another, that approximates to, is not unlike, another; **son costume se rapprochait d'un uniforme,** his clothes looked almost like a uniform; **se r. de la vérité,** to approximate to the truth; **cela se rapproche de la perfection,** it is an approach to perfection. **3. se r. de qn,** to become reconciled, to make it up, with s.o.; **la France et l'Espagne s'étaient rapprochées,** a rapprochement had taken place between France and Spain; France and Spain had drawn together.

rapprocheur [raprɔʃœːr], *s.m. Ven:* tufter.

rapproprier [raprɔprije], *v.tr.* (*conj. like* APPROPRIER). *F:* **1.** to clean (sth.) again; to refurbish. **2.** to put (sth.) in order again.

rapprovisionner [raprɔvizjɔne], *v.tr.* to reprovision (town after a siege, etc.); to restock (shop, etc.); *Com:* **se r.,** to restock.

rapsode [rapsɔd], *s.m.* = RHAPSODE.

rapsoder [rapsɔde], *v.tr.* = RHAPSODER.

rapsodie [rapsɔdi], *s.f.* = RHAPSODIE.

rapsodique [rapsɔdik], *a.* = RHAPSODIQUE.

rapsodiste [rapsɔdist], *s.m.* = RHAPSODIST.

rapt [rapt], *s.m. Jur:* abduction of a minor (by force, menace, or fraud); kidnapping; **r. par séduction,** abduction with consent.

raptores [raptɔres], *s.m. Orn: A:* Raptores; birds of prey.

raptus [raptys], *s.m. Psy:* raptus.

râpure [rɑpyːr], *s.f.* raspings; (*a*) gratings; (*b*) filings.

raquer [rake], *v.tr. P:* to fork out; to cough up.

raquette [rakɛt], *s.f.* **1.** *Games:* (i) racket, racquet; (ii) battledore; (iii) bat (for table tennis); **r. mousse,** sponge bat; *Ten:* **n'être pas en r.,** to be off one's game; **mettre la balle dans la r. de son adversaire,** to play on to one's opponent's racket; *Aut: F:* **coups de r.,** jolts, jars, backlash; bumping (off the springs). **2.** regulating lever (of watch). **3.** snowshoe. **4.** *Bot:* (*a*) (thick, fleshy) joint (of nopal, etc.); (*b*) *F:* prickly pear, Indian fig; nopal. **5.** *Cu:* foreshin. **6.** *Rail:* loop. **7.** rocket (carrying a warhead).

raquetteur [rakɛtœːr], *s.m. Fr.C:* snowshoer

raquet(t)ier [rakɛtje], *s.m.* racquet maker; battledore maker.

rara [rara], *s.m. Orn:* plant cutter.

rare [rɑːr], *a.* **1.** rare (book, insect, *Ch:* substance); **visites rares (et éloignées),** visits few and far between; **une des rares personnes qui . . .,** one of the few people who . . .; *s.* **je suis un, une, des rares à aimer, qui aiment, la pluie,** I am one of the few who like rain; **se faire r.,** to be seldom seen; **vous devenez r. comme les beaux jours,** you are quite a stranger; **il est r. qu'on le voie,** one seldom, rarely, sees him, it; one doesn't often see it, him; **la main-d'œuvre était r.,** there was a shortage of labour; *Com: F:* **l'argent est r.,** money is scarce, tight; **il n'était pas r. qu'il fit des plaisanteries,** he often made jokes; *F:* **ça n'aurait rien de r.,** that wouldn't be anything out of the ordinary; *F:* **ça serait bien r. que** + *sub.*, it's hardly likely that . . .; *Med:* **pouls r.,** slow, feeble, pulse. **2.** (*a*) rare, uncommon, extraordinary, exceptional (merit, beauty, talent, etc.); **r. courage,** rare courage, singular courage; (*b*) unusual (occurrence). **3.** thin, sparse, scanty (hair, grass, etc.). **4.** *Ph:* rare (atmosphere, etc.).

raréfaction [rarefaksjɔ̃], *s.f.* (*a*) rarefaction (of gas, air, etc.); (*b*) depletion (of supplies, etc.); growing scarcity (of labour, of money); **la r. du blé,** the decrease in the yield of wheat; the dwindling production of wheat; **la r. du bison,** the dying out of the bison; **la r. du charbon,** the gradual exhaustion of coal.

raréfiable [rarefjabl], *a. Ph:* rarefiable.

raréfiant [rarefjɑ̃], *a. Ph:* rarefying, rarefactive.

raréfier [rarefje], *v.tr.* (*p.d. & pr.sub.* **n. raréfiions, v. rarifiiez**) (*a*) *Ph:* to rarefy; (*b*) to deplete; to make (sth.) scarce.

se raréfier, (*a*) to become rarefied, to rarefy; to get thinner; (*b*) to become scarce; to grow rare, rarer; **les arrivages de charbon se sont raréfiés à cause de la grève,** coal deliveries have become rare, infrequent, because of the strike.

rarement [rarmɑ̃], *adv.* rarely, seldom, infrequently, not often; **on le voit r.,** one rarely, seldom, sees him; one doesn't often see him.

rareté [rarte], *s.f.* **1.** (*a*) rarity, tenuity (of gas, etc.); (*b*) scarceness, scarcity, dearth (of objects, money, etc.); **r. des pluies,** scarcity of rain; drought; **vos parents se plaignent de la r. de vos lettres,** your parents complain of the infrequency of your letters, that you don't write more often; (*c*) novelty, singularity, unusualness (of phenomenon); **je voudrais le voir pour la r. du fait,** I should like to see it as a curiosity. **2.** (*a*) rare object; **cabinet plein de raretés,** cabinet full of rare objects; (*b*) rare occurrence; **c'est une r. (que) de vous voir,** you have become quite a stranger.

rarissime [rarisim], *a.* exceedingly rare, extremely rare.

rarranger [rarɑ̃ʒe], *v.tr.* (*conj. like* ARRANGER) to re-arrange; to set (sth.) to rights again.

ras[1] [rɑ]. **1.** *a.* (*a*) close-cropped (hair, head); close-shaven (beard, chin); short-napped (velvet, etc.); **couper r. les cheveux,** to crop the hair short, close; **à poil r.,** (i) short-haired (dog); (ii) smooth, short-napped (cloth); (*b*) bare, blank; **en rase campagne,** in the open country; **table rase,** tabula rasa; **faire table rase de qch.,** to make a clean sweep of sth.; **sa mémoire est une table rase,** his memory is a complete blank; (*c*) **mesure rase,** full measure (but not heaped); stricken measure (of corn, etc.); **cuillerée rase,** level spoonful; **verser du vin, etc., à qn à r. bord,** to fill s.o.'s glass to the brim; to fill s.o.'s glass brimfull; *P:* **en avoir r. le bol, bord,** to be fed up to the back teeth; (*d*) *Nau:* **bateau r.,** flat-bottomed boat; **navire r. (sur l'eau),** low-built ship; **bâtiment r.,** dismasted vessel; **pont r.,** flush deck; (*e*) **écueil r.,** reef awash. **2.** *s.m.* (*a*) short-nap cloth; (*b*) *Nau:* **r. de carène,** floating stage; (repairing) raft, punt; (*c*) *Nau:* reef awash; spit. **3.** *prep.phr.* **à, au, r. de,** (on a) level with, flush with; **vaisseau chargé au r. de l'eau,** vessel laden to the water line; **voler au r. du sol,** to fly close to the ground; to skim (along) the ground; **pullover r. le cou,** crewneck sweater, straight-necked sweater.

ras[2], *s.m.* = RAZ.

ras[3], *s.m.* (*in Ethiopia*) ras.

rasade [rɑzad], *s.f.* brimfull glass (of wine, etc.); bumper; **se verser une r.,** to fill one's glass (to the brim).

rasage [rɑzaːʒ], *s.m.* **1.** shaving (of the beard); shave; **lotion après r.,** after-shave lotion. **2.** *Tex:* shearing (of stuffs). **3.** *Metalw:* shaving.

rasance [rɑzɑ̃ːs], *s.m. Ball:* grazing (of fire), flatness (of trajectory); **effet de r.,** grazing effect.

rasant [rɑzɑ̃], *a.* **1.** (*a*) *Ball:* **tir r.,** grazing fire; **trajectoire rasante,** flat trajectory; **fortification rasante,** rasant, low-built, fortification; **vol r.,** flight that skims the ground; (*b*) *Opt:* **angle r.,** grazing, glancing, angle; **incidence rasante,** grazing incidence (of X-rays, etc.); **éclairage r.,** grazing lighting; **lumière rasante,** oblique, (almost) horizontal, lowdown, light; **vue rasante,** view over an open, flat, country. **2.** *F:* boring (person); dull, boring (speech, etc.).

rasbora [rasbɔra], *s.m. Ich:* rasbora.

rascasse [raskas], *s.f. Ich:* scorpion fish; *F:* hog fish; **r. blanche,** stargazer.

rascettes [rasɛt], *s.f.pl. Anat:* rasceta; (*in palmistry*) rascettes, bracelets.

rasé [rɑze], *a.* **1.** shaven; **r. de près,** close-shaven; **visage entièrement r.,** clean-shaven face. **2.** *Nau:* **bâtiment r.,** dismasted ship, *A:* razee. **3.** (horse) that has lost mark of mouth.

rasement [rɑzmɑ̃], *s.m.* **1.** = RASAGE. **2.** razing (of fortress, etc.). **3.** (*of horse*) loss of mark of mouth.

rase-mottes [rɑzmɔt], *s.m.inv. Av:* **vol en r.-m.,** very low flying; skimming; *F:* hedge hopping; **faire du, voler en, r.-m.,** to skim the ground, *F:* to do hedge hopping, to hedge hop; **mitrailler en r.-m.,** to strafe; **bombarder en r.-m.,** to skip bomb; **bombardement en r.-m.,** skip bombing.

rase-pet [rɑzpɛ], *s.m.inv. P:* **(veston) r.-p.,** bum-freezer.

raser [rɑze], *v.tr.* **1.** (*a*) to shave (s.o.'s head, beard, etc.); to shear (cloth); **raser qn,** to shave s.o., to give s.o. a shave; **se faire r.,** to get shaved; to have, get, a shave; **se r. la moustache,** to shave off one's moustache; **les soldats sont tenus de se r.,** shaving is compulsory in the army; *Furs:* **peau rasée,** sheared skin; *F:* **demain on rase gratis,** that'll be the day! (*b*) *F:* to bore (s.o.); **ça me rase,** this puts years on me, this bores me stiff. **2.** (*a*) to raze (fortress, etc.); to raze (building) to the ground; to pull down (house); to level (house, etc.) with the ground; *Nau:* to cut down, *A:* to razee (ship); (*b*) to strike (grain) (in the measure); (*c*) to construct (road, etc.) level with the ground (without embankments, etc.); (*d*) (*of animal*) **r. les oreilles,** to put back its ears. **3.** (*a*) to graze, brush, skim (over), pass close to, (surface, etc.); **l'hirondelle rase le sol,** the swallow is skimming the ground; **la balle lui rasa l'épaule,** the bullet grazed his shoulder; (*b*) **r. la côte, le mur,** to hug the shore, the wall; **je vis quelqu'un qui rasait l'église,** I saw someone pass close by the church.

se raser. **1.** (*a*) to shave; (*b*) *F:* to be bored. **2.** *Ven:* (*of game*) to squat.

rasette [rɑzɛt], *s.f.* **1.** *Organ:* tuning wire (of reed pipe). **2.** *Agr:* skim coulter. **3.** *Tex:* velvet-shearing machine.

raseur, -euse [rɑzœːr, -øːz], *s.* (*pers.*) **1.** shaver; *Tex:* **r. de velours,** velvet shearer. **2.** *F:* bore.

rash [raʃ], *s.m. Med:* rash.

rasibus [rɑzibyːs], *adv. F:* **couper r.,** to cut quite close; **la balle me passa r. de l'oreille,** the bullet grazed my ear.

rasoir [rɑzwaːr], *s.m.* **1.** (*a*) razor; **r. à manche,** straight razor; **r. évidé,** hollow-ground razor; **r. de sûreté, r. mécanique, américain,** safety razor; **r. électrique,** electric razor, shaver; **repasser un r.,** (i) to hone, (ii) to strop, a razor; **pierre à r.,** hone; **cuir à r.,** strop; (*b*) *Tex:* knife (of shearing machine); (*c*) *Dom.Ec:* **r. à légumes,** vegetable peeler; (*d*) *F:* (*pers.*) bore; *a.* boring; **que c'est r.!** what a bore, a bind! **2.** *Ich:* razor fish.

rason [rɑzɔ̃], *s.m. Ich:* razor fish.

raspecon [raspəkɔ̃], *s.m. Ich:* stargazer.

raspite [raspit], *s.f. Miner:* raspite.

rassasiant [rasazjɑ̃], *a.* (*a*) satisfying (meal, etc.); (*b*) satiating, filling (food, etc.); cloying.

rassasié [rasazje], *a.* **1.** satisfied; *F:* full. **2.** surfeited, sated (**de,** with); **r. de plaisirs,** cloyed with pleasures.

rassasiement [rasazimɑ̃], *s.m.* **1.** satisfying (of hunger, etc.). **2.** (*a*) full meal; full satisfaction (of hunger, etc.); (*b*) satiety, surfeit.

rassasier [rasazje], *v.tr.* (*p.d. & pr.sub.* **n. rassasiions, v. rassasiiez**) **1.** to satisfy (hunger, passion); **r. qn, la faim de qn,** to satisfy s.o., s.o.'s hunger; **les fruits ne rassasient pas,** fruit does not fill a man; **r. son regard à contempler qch.,** to feast one's eyes on sth.; **r. sa curiosité,** to satisfy one's curiosity. **2.** to sate, satiate, surfeit, cloy (**de,** with); **r. qn de bonne chère, de fêtes, etc.,** to sate, satiate, surfeit, s.o. with good fare, with entertainments, etc.; **r. qn d'injures,** to heap insults on s.o.

se rassasier, to eat one's fill; **se r. d'un mets, de plaisirs, etc.,** to take one's fill of, to glut, gorge, oneself with, a dish, pleasures, etc.; **ici l'œil, la vue, se rassasie de belles choses,** here the eye feeds, feasts, on beautiful objects.

rassemblement [rasɑ̃bləmɑ̃], *s.m.* **1.** assembling, collecting, gathering (of documents, troops, etc.); *Mil:* fall in; parade; **(accusé de) retard au r.,** (charged with being) late on parade; **r. en colonne par quatre,** falling in in column of fours; **sonner le r.,** to sound the assembly; **rassemblement!** fall in! form up! (*computers*) **r. de données,** data acquisition, data collection, data gathering; **instruction de r.,** extract instruction. **2.** assemblage, crowd, gathering; *Pol:* rally; **lieu de r.,** rallying point; **provoquer un r.,** to draw a crowd; *Mil:* **r. de l'ennemi,** hostile concentration; *Ven:* **r. de la meute,** meet.

rassembler[1] [rasɑ̃ble], *v.tr.* **1.** to reassemble; to bring (persons, etc.) together again. **2.** to assemble, muster (troops, etc.); to collect, to gather together, get together (persons, things); **r. ses idées,** to collect one's thoughts; to get, put, one's thoughts together; **r. toutes les pièces d'un procès,** to bring together all the documents of a case; **r. toutes ses forces,** to muster, to gather up, summon up, all one's strength; *Equit:* **r. un cheval,** to gather a horse.

se rassembler. **1.** to re-assemble. **2.** to assemble, to come together, to get together, to flock together; *Mil:* to fall in, to form up, to muster; **ils se rassemblèrent autour de lui,** they gathered round him, they all came round him.

rassembler[2], *s.m. Equit:* gathering (of horse).

rasseoir [raswaːr], *v.tr.* (*conj. like* ASSEOIR) **1.** to reseat (s.o.); to seat (s.o.) again; **r. une statue sur sa base,** to replace, set up again, a statue on its base. **2.** to settle, compose (one's ideas, s.o.'s mind).

se rasseoir. **1.** to sit down again; to resume one's seat; **rasseyez-vous,** take your seats again; sit down again; **faire r. qn,** to make s.o. sit down again. **2.** *A:* to recover one's composure; to calm down. **3.** (*of liquid*) to settle; **attendre que le vin se rasseye, laisser r. le vin,** to let the wine settle.

rassérènement [raserɛnmɑ̃], *s.m.* **1.** clearing (up) (of the sky, etc.). **2.** (*a*) restoring the serenity (of the mind, etc.); (*b*) recovering of one's equanimity, one's peace of mind.

rasséréner [raserene], *v.tr.* (**je rassérène, n. rassérénons; je rassérénerai**) **1.** to clear (up) (the weather). **2.** to calm (s.o.); to restore (s.o.'s) equanimity, peace of mind.

se rasséréner. **1.** (*of the weather*) to clear (up). **2.** (*of pers.*) to recover one's serenity, one's equanimity, one's spirits, one's peace of mind; to brighten up; **son front se rasséréna,** his brow cleared.

rassir [rasiːr], *v.i. F:* to get stale; **je laisse r. mon pain,** I let my bread go stale.

rassis [rasi]. **1.** *a.* (*a*) settled, calm, staid, sedate, sober (disposition, mind); **personne de sens r.** person of sane, ripe, well-balanced, judgment; **faire qch. de sens r.,** to do sth. coolly, soberly, calmly, collectedly; **avoir l'esprit r.,** *F:* to have ballast; (*b*) **pain r.,** stale bread. **2.** *s.m. A:* (*of liquid*) **prendre son r.,** to settle.

rassortiment [rasɔrtimɑ̃], *s.m.* = RÉASSORTIMENT.

rassortir [rasɔrtiːr], *v.tr.* = RÉASSORTIR.

se rassortir, = SE RÉASSORTIR.

rassurant [rasyrɑ̃], *a.* reassuring, heartening (news, etc.); **bruits peu rassurants,** disquieting (i) noises, (ii) rumours.

rassurer [rasyre], *v.tr.* **1.** to reassure, cheer, hearten; **je suis assez peu rassuré,** I have my misgivings. **2.** to stay, strengthen (wall, arch of bridge).

se rassurer. **1.** to get over one's apprehensions; to feel reassured; **rassurez-vous (là-dessus),** make yourself easy, set your mind at ease, at rest (on that point). **2.** (*of the weather*) to become settled.

rasta [rasta], *s.m.*, **rastaquouère** [rastakwɛːr], *s.m. F: Pej:* flashy (foreign) adventurer.

Rastignac [rastiɲak], *s.m.* clever, smart and unscrupulous adventurer (character in the novels of Balzac).

rat [ra], *s.m.* **1.** (*a*) rat; **r. des champs,** fieldmouse; **r. surmulot,** brown rat, grey rat, Norway rat; **r. noir,** black rat; **r. d'égout,** sewer rat; *Lit:* **le r. de ville et le r. des champs,** the town mouse and the country mouse; **mort aux rats,** rat poison, *A:* ratsbane; **chasse aux rats,** rat catching; **preneur de rats,** rat-catcher; *F:* **avoir un r., des rats, dans la tête,** to have a bee in one's bonnet; to be capricious; **prendre un r.,** (i) (*of gun, etc.*) to miss fire, misfire; (ii) (*of plan, etc.*) to miscarry, misfire; **serrure qui a un r.,** lock that won't work; *P:* **être, vivre comme un, r.,** to be stingy, mean, miserly; **c'est un r.,** he's a miser; *F:* **être fait comme un r.,** to be caught out; *s.a.* CHAT 1, QUEUE-DE-RAT, S'ENNUYER; (*b*) **r. musqué,** musk rat, musquash; **r. à trompe africain,** African elephant shrew; **r. arboricole du Brésil,** Brazilian tree rat; **r. à mamelles multiples,** multimamillate rat; **r. hérissé,** spiny rat; **r. palmiste,** African ground squirrel; **r. de Gambie,** hamster rat of Gambia; **r. roussard,** striped mouse; **r. rayé,** striped rat, striped grass mouse; **r. des moissons,** (European) harvest mouse; **r. de rizière,** (American) rice rat; **r. des cotonniers,** (American) cotton rat; **r. géant (des Indes),** bandicoot; **r. d'eau,** water vole, *F:* water rat; **r. à bourse,** gopher; **r. d'Égypte, de Pharaon,** ichneumon, mongoose, Pharoah's rat; **r. d'Amérique,** guinea pig; (*c*) *Ich:* stargazer. **2. r. de cave,** (i) (*pers.*) *A:* exciseman; (ii) wax taper (sold coiled or folded); **r. d'église,** (i) devout attender at church services; (ii) minor church official; **pauvre comme un r. d'église,** as poor as a church mouse; *s.a.* GUEUX 4; **r. d'hôtel,** flashy hotel thief; **petit r. (d'Opéra),** young ballet girl (still attending dancing class); *F:* **mon petit r.,** darling.

rata [rata], *s.m.* (*a*) *Mil: P:* (= RATATOUILLE) stew, skilly; *F:* **nous avons eu un maigre r.,** we had a lousy meal; (*b*) *P:* **ne pas s'endormir sur le r.,** to be active, wide awake, on the spot.

ratafia [ratafja], *s.m.* ratafia (liqueur).

ratage [rata:ʒ], *s.m. F:* **1.** failure; misfire. **2.** *A:* rat colony (in ship, etc.).

ratanhia [ratanja], *s.m. Bot: Med:* rhatany.

rataplan [rataplɑ̃]. **1.** *s.m.* rat-tat, rub-a-dub (of a drum). **2.** *a. F:* ridiculous.

ratapoil [ratapwal], *a. F:* ridiculous.

ratatiné [ratatine], *a.* shrivelled, shrunken (apple, face, person, etc.); crinkled (parchment); **petite vieille ratatinée,** wizened little old woman.

ratatinement [ratatinmɑ̃], *s.m.* **1.** shrivelling up; crinkling (of parchment, etc.). **2.** wizened, shrunken, condition.

ratatiner [ratatine], *v.tr. & pr.* **1.** to shrivel (up); to shrink, to dry up; (*of parchment*) to crinkle up. **2.** *P:* (*a*) to destroy, smash; (*b*) to bump (s.o.) off; (*c*) to beat (s.o.) up.

ratatouille [ratatu:j], *s.f. Cu:* **1.** (*a*) ratatouille; **r. niçoise,** dish of fried aubergines, tomatoes, pimentos and onions; (*b*) *P:* stew. **2.** *P:* beating, pasting.

rate[1] [rat], *s.f. Anat:* spleen; *F:* **épanouir, dilater, désopiler, la r. de qn,** to make s.o. shake with laughter; **se dilater la r.,** to have a good laugh; **ne pas se fouler la r.,** to take things pretty easy; to be rather slack; *A:* **décharger sa r. (sur qn),** to vent one's spleen (on s.o.); *Bot: F:* **herbe à la r.,** hart's tongue fern.

rate[2], *s.f.* female of the rat; she rat.

raté[1] [rate], *a. A:* **1.** rat-eaten, rat-gnawed (fruit, etc.). **2.** *P:* pock-marked (face).

raté[2], **-ée.** **1.** *a.* miscarried, ineffectual; **coup r.,** (i) shot that has missed the mark; (ii) misfire; (iii) (*in golf*) fluffed shot; fluff; **affaire ratée,** business that has miscarried, that has come to nothing; *Av:* **atterrissage r.,** bad landing; **ce fut une vie ratée,** his life was a failure; nothing he tried came off. **2.** *s.* (*of pers.*) failure, *F:* wash-out. **3.** *s.m.* misfire (of gun, etc.; *I.C.E:* of engine); **le moteur avait des ratés,** the engine was misfiring.

râteau, -eaux [rɑto], *s.m.* **1.** *Tls:* (*a*) *Hort: etc:* rake; *Agr:* **r. mécanique, r. à cheval,** raker, sulky rake; **r. ameulonneur,** buck rake, hay stacker; **r. faneur,** tedder; **r. faneur-andaineur,** side-delivery rake and tedder; (*b*) *Typ:* scraper (of hand press); *Nau:* (i) blunt scraper; (ii) **r. de pont,** squeegee; (*c*) *Toil: F:* big-toothed comb; dressing comb; *P:* (bug) rake; *Equit: F:* curry comb; (*d*) (croupier's) rake. **2.** wards (of a lock). **3.** *Clockm:* recoiling click; regulator. **4. table en râteaux,** table with branches.

ratel [ratɛl], *s.m. Z:* ratel.

râtelage [rɑtla:ʒ], *s.m.* (action of) raking.

râtelée [rɑtle], *s.f.* rakeful (of hay, etc.).

râteler [rɑtle], *v.tr.* (**je râtelle, n. râtelons; je râtellerai**) **1.** *Agr:* to rake up (hay, etc.). **2.** = RATISSER.

râteleur, -euse [rɑtlœ:r, -ø:z], *s. Agr:* raker (*esp.* of hay).

râtelier [rɑtəlje], *s.m.* **1.** rack (in a stable); *F:* **quand il n'y a plus de foin dans le r.,** when we're broke; *F:* **manger au r. de qn,** to live at s.o.'s expense; *F:* **manger à deux râteliers,** (i) to have two strings to one's bow; to derive one's income from two sources; (ii) to have a foot in both camps; *F:* **manger à plusieurs, à tous les, râteliers,** to take one's profit where one finds it; to profit (without scruple) from any situation. **2.** (*a*) **r. d'armes, aux armes, à outils, à pipes, etc.,** arm rack, tool rack, pipe rack, etc.; *F:* **remettre ses armes au r.,** to leave the service; *Nau:* **r. d'amarrage; r. à, de, cabillots,** belaying-pin rack; pin rails; range of belaying-pins; **r. du grand-mât,** fife rail; **r. à seaux,** bucket rack; (*b*) *Bill:* cue rest. **3.** (*a*) *A:* (upper or lower) row of teeth; (*b*) *F:* set of false teeth; denture. **4.** *A:* **r. de perles,** gorget of pearls. **5.** *Tex:* creel (of spinning frame); **r. à bobines,** bobbin board.

râtelures [rɑtly:r], *s.f.pl.* rakings.

ratepennade [rat(ə)pɛnad], *s.f.* (*S. of Fr.*) *Z:* bat.

rater [rate]. **1.** *v.i.* (*a*) (*of gun*) to miss fire, misfire; to fail to go off; (*b*) (*of gun, motor engine*) to misfire; (*c*) (*of enterprise, etc.*) to fail; to miscarry, misfire. **2.** *v.tr.* (*a*) **r. son coup,** to miss one's shot, to miss the mark; (*in golf*) to fluff (a shot); *F:* (*children playing*) **raté!** yah, missed! **r. un lièvre,** to miss a hare; **coup qui rate le but,** bad shot; **il raterait un éléphant, une vache, dans un couloir,** he couldn't hit an elephant, a haystack, a barn-door; (*b*) *F:* **r. une affaire, un coup,** to mess up a piece of business, to fail in an attempt; **r. son train,** to miss one's train; **je l'ai raté de deux minutes, à deux minutes près,** I missed him by two minutes; **r. une place,** to fail to get a job; **r. son bac.,** to fail in one's *baccalauréat* exam.; **j'ai raté l'occasion,** I missed the opportunity, the chance.

rathite [ratit], *s.f. Min:* rathite.

ratiboiser [ratibwaze], *v.tr. P:* **1.** to filch, pinch (sth.); **r. qch. à qn,** to do s.o. out of sth.. **2.** to fleece (s.o.), to clean (s.o.) out. **3.** (*a*) to do for (s.o.); **le voilà ratiboisé,** he's done for; (*b*) to do (s.o.) in, to bump (s.o.) off. **4. je vais me faire r.,** I'm going to get my hair cropped, to be shorn.

ratichon [ratiʃɔ̃], *s.m. P: Pej:* priest.

ratichonne [ratiʃɔn], *s.f. P: Pej:* nun.

raticide [ratisid], (*a*) *a.* rat-killing, anti-rat; (*b*) *s.m.* rat poison, raticide.

ratier [ratje], *a. & s.m.* **(chien) r.,** ratter.

ratière [ratjɛ:r], *s.f.* **1.** rat trap. **2.** *Nau:* **(fanal de) r.,** stern light. **3.** *Tex:* dobby.

ratificateur, -trice [ratifikatœ:r, -tris], (*a*) *a.* ratifying; (*b*) *s.* ratifier.

ratificatif, -ive [ratifikatif, -i:v], *a.* ratifying (act, etc.).

ratification [ratifikasjɔ̃], *s.f.* ratification, confirmation, approval (of a decision, etc.).

ratifier [ratifje], *v.tr.* (*p.d. & pr.sub.* **n. ratifiions, v. ratifiiez**) to ratify (treaty, act, etc.); to confirm, approve (decision, etc.).

ratinage [ratina:ʒ], *s.m. Tex:* friezing.

ratine [ratin], *s.f. Tex:* frieze, ratteen, petersham.

ratiner [ratine], *v.tr. Tex:* to frieze, friz(z) (cloth).

ratineuse [ratinø:z], *s.f.* friezing machine.

ratiocinage [rasjɔsina:ʒ], *s.m. Pej:* hair splitting, quibbling, making of meaningless distinctions.

ratiocination [rasjɔsinasjɔ̃], *s.f.* ratiocination; *Pej:* over-subtle reasoning, hair splitting.

ratiociner [rasjɔsine], *v.i.* to ratiocinate; *Pej:* to split hairs.

ration [rasjɔ̃], *s.f.* ration(s), allowance; (horse's) feed; **r. réduite, diminuée,** short rations; **mettre qn à la r.,** to put s.o. on short commons, on short rations; **r. de combat,** iron rations; **r. de campagne, r. forte,** field ration; *Nau:* **rations d'embarcations,** boat rations; **rations imposées en temps de guerre,** wartime rations; *Mil: etc:* **cahier de rations,** victualling book; *Physiol:* **r. calorique,** caloric intake; **r. alimentaire,** food intake; *F: usu. Iron:* **recevoir sa r. de coups,** to get one's full ration of blows.

rationalisation [rasjɔnalizasjɔ̃], *s.f.* (*a*) *Pol.Ec:* rationalizing (of industry); rationalization; (*b*) *Psy:* rationalization.

rationalisé [rasjɔnalize], *a. Elcs:* rationalized (unit, formula).

rationaliser [rasjɔnalize], *v.tr.* to rationalize.

rationalisme [rasjɔnalism], *s.m. Phil:* rationalism.

rationaliste [rasjɔnalist], *a. & s.m. & f. Phil:* rationalist.

rationalité [rasjɔnalite], *s.f.* rationality.

rationnaire [rasjɔnɛ:r], *s.m. & f. War Adm:* ration-book holder.

rationnel, -elle [rasjɔnɛl], *a.* **1.** *a.* (*a*) rational (system; *Mth:* quantity; *Astr:* horizon); **mécanique rationnelle,** theoretic mechanics, pure mechanics; **organisation rationnelle de l'industrie,** rationalization of industry; (*b*) rational, reasonable, sensible. **2.** *s.m.* **le r.,** the rational (as opposed to the irrational).

rationnellement [rasjɔnɛlmɑ̃], *adv.* rationally; **utiliser r. qch.,** to use sth. reasonably, in a proper manner; **agir r.,** to act rationally, sensibly.

rationnement [rasjɔnmɑ̃], *s.m.* rationing.

rationner [rasjɔne], *v.tr.* to ration; (*a*) **r. une garnison, un convalescent,** to put a garrison, a convalescent, on (short) allowance, on rations; **être rationné,** to be on short allowance; (*b*) **r. le pain, etc.,** to ration bread, etc.; (*c*) **r. l'avoine à ses chevaux,** to stint one's horses of oats.

Ratisbonne [ratizbɔn, -is-], *Pr.n.f. Geog:* Ratisbon, Regensburg.

ratissage [ratisa:ʒ], *s.m.* **1.** (*a*) raking; (*b*) scraping (of vegetables, etc.). **2.** *Gaming:* raking in (of the stakes). **3.** *F:* combing, thorough search (of district, by police, etc.). **4.** *Const:* primer, priming coat (for fresh plaster).

ratisser [ratise], *v.tr.* **1.** (*a*) to rake; (*b*) to hoe; to scuffle (path, etc.); (*c*) to scrape (skins, vegetables, etc.). **2.** (*a*) (*at casino, etc.*) **r. les mises,** to rake in the stakes; *F:* **la police les a ratissés,** the police nabbed the lot; (*b*) *P:* **il est complètement ratissé,** he's (i) ruined, (ii) broke to the wide, absolutely cleaned out. **3.** *F:* (*a*) to search, comb (a district); **la police a ratissé tout le quartier,** the police searched, combed, the entire district; (*b*) *Rugby Fb:* **r. le ballon,** to rake up the ball (in a scrum).

ratissette [ratisɛt], *s.f. Tchn:* (*a*) (brickmaker's) scraper; (*b*) fire hook (for raking furnace fire).

ratissoir [ratiswa:r], *s.m.* **ratissoire** [ratiswa:r], *s.f. Tls:* (*a*) hoe, scuffle; (*b*) scraper.

ratissure [ratisy:r], *s.f.* (*a*) raking(s); (*b*) scraping(s).

ratite [ratit], *s.m. Orn:* ratite (bird); *pl.* **ratites,** Ratitae.

rat-kangourou [rakɑ̃guru], *s.m. Z:* kangaroo rat; *pl. rats-kangourous.*

raton[1] [ratɔ̃], *s.m.* **1.** little rat; *F:* (*to child*) **mon r.,** my (little) pet. **2.** *Z:* procyon; **r. laveur,** raccoon; **r. crabier,** crab-eating raccoon. **3.** *P: Pej:* Arab.

raton[2], *s.m. Cu:* cheese cake.

raton(n)ade [ratɔnad], *s.f. A: P:* (*esp. in Algeria*) punitive raid against the Arabs; Arab bashing.

ratoncule [ratɔ̃kyl], *s.f. Bot:* mousetail.

rattachage [rataʃa:ʒ], *s.m.* **1.** fastening, tying (up); *Tex:* piecing. **2.** linking up, connecting (of events, etc.).

rattachement [rataʃmɑ̃], *s.m.* **1.** (*a*) fastening, tying up; (*b*) *Pol:* re-attachment; **le r. de l'Alsace à la France,** the return of Alsace to France; (*c*) *Mil: etc:* attachment (of s.o. to a unit, etc.); **r. pour ordre,** attachment for the purpose of defining a status. **2.** *Surv: etc:* rabattement.

rattacher [rataʃe], *v.tr.* **1.** to fasten, tie (up), (sth.) again; to refasten, retie; **rattachez le chien,** tie up the dog (again); *Tex:* **r. les fils cassés,** to piece broken threads. **2.** (*a*) **les liens qui vous rattachent à la famille,** the ties that bind one to the family; **cette passion seule le rattachait à l'existence,** this passion was all that he had to live for; (*b*) **r. une question à une autre,** to link up, connect, one question with another; (*c*) **r. une province à un État,** to incorporate a province into a state; (*d*) *Mil: etc:* to attach (s.o. to a unit, etc.); **rattaché pour ordre,** attached for the purpose of defining a status.

se rattacher à qch. **1.** to be fastened to sth. **2.** to be connected with sth.; **cette question se rattache à une autre,** this question is linked up with another, depends on another; **les vertus qui se rattachent à la terre,** the virtues bound up in the soil; **en ce qui se rattache à . . .,** with regard to . . ..

rattacheur, -euse [rataʃœ:r, -ø:z], *s. Tex:* piecer.

rat-taupe [rato:p], *s.m. Z:* mole rat; *pl. rats-taupes.*

ratteindre [ratɛ̃:dr], *v.tr.* (*conj. like* ATTEINDRE) *O:* **1.** to retake, recapture; to catch (s.o.) again. **2.** to overtake (s.o.); to catch up with (s.o.).

ratteler [ratle], *v.tr.* (*conj. like* ATTELER) to harness again, to reharness.

rattrapable [ratrapabl], *a.* **erreur r.,** error that can be retrieved, corrected; **ces heures perdues qui ne sont pas rattrapables,** lost hours never to be recovered.

rattrapage [ratrapa:ʒ], *s.m.* **1.** *Mec.E:* compensation, correction (**de, du,** for); taking up (**de, du,** of); **r. du jeu,** taking up of play; **r. de l'usure,** taking up of, compensation for, wear; wear take-up. **2.** *Sch:* **cours de r.,** special course, extra tuition, for (i) late beginners, (ii) backward pupils. **3.** *Pol.Ec:* adjustment (of wages in relation to the cost of living, etc.). **4.** *Typ: Typewr:* catchword.

rattrape-jeu [ratrapʒø], *s.m.inv. Mec.E:* **(dispositif) r.-j.,** device for taking up play.

rattraper [ratrape], *v.tr.* **1.** to recapture; to catch (s.o., sth.) again; *F:* **on ne m'y rattrapera pas! bien fin qui m'y rattrapera!** you won't catch me doing that again! once bitten, twice shy! **je vous rattraperai!** I'll get my own back on you. **2.** to overtake; to catch (s.o.) up; to catch up on (s.o.); to come up with (s.o.); **r. l'arriéré de besogne, to clear up, catch up with,** arrears of work. **3. r. son argent, sa santé,** to recover one's money, one's wealth; **r. le temps perdu,** to make up for lost time; **r. du sommeil,** to catch up on lost sleep. **4.** *Mec.E:* **r. le jeu, l'usure,** to take up the play, the wear; to tighten up; **r. les différences de montage,** to accommodate the differences in assembling. **5.** to correct, retrieve (mistake, etc.); to take back (remark); *Cu:* **r. une mayonnaise,** to salvage a mayonnaise, to make a mayonnaise take again.

se rattraper. 1. **se r. à une branche, à un cordage,** to save oneself by catching hold of a branch, of a rope. 2. **se r. de ses pertes,** to make up, make good, one's losses; **on perd sur la nourriture, mais on se rattrape sur la boisson,** we lose on the food, but we make it up on the drink; **si vous lui donniez du temps, il pourrait se r.,** if you gave him time he would catch up again. 3. (*a*) to check oneself, hold oneself back (before making an unfortunate remark, etc.); (*b*) to redeem oneself; **se r. auprès de qn,** to get back into favour with s.o.

raturage [ratyraːʒ], *s.m.* 1. erasing, scratching out. 2. scraping (of parchment, etc.).

rature [ratyːr], *s.f.* 1. erasure (in manuscript, etc.); **faire une r.,** to scratch out, cross out, a word. 2. scraping(s) (of parchment, tin, etc.).

raturer [ratyre], *v.tr.* 1. to erase, scratch out, cross out (word); to put one's pen through (word). 2. to scrape (parchment, etc.).

raucité [rosite], *s.f.* raucousness; hoarseness.

rauque [roːk], *a.* hoarse, raucous, rough, harsh, raw (voice, etc.); **à mon âge on a la voix un peu r.,** at my age the voice becomes a little rough.

rauquement [rokmɑ̃], *s.m.* snarl (of tiger, etc.).

rauquer [roke], *v.i.* (of tiger, etc.) to snarl.

rauvite [rovit], *s.f. Miner:* rauvite.

ravage[1] [ravaːʒ], *s.m. usu. pl.* havoc, devastation, ravages; **le r. des passions, du typhus,** the ravages of passion, of typhus; **faire des ravages,** to work havoc; **l'orage fit de grands ravages dans les récoltes,** the storm wrought great havoc among the crops, played havoc with the crops, made havoc of the crops.

ravage[2], *s.m. Fr.C: Ven:* (moose, etc.) yard.

ravagé [ravaʒe], *a.* (*a*) devastated (countryside, etc.); (*b*) **visage r.,** (i) ravaged face, face on which life has left its mark; (ii) haggard, distraught, face; (iii) face distorted by passion, etc.; **visage r. de rides,** deeply lined face; **visage r. par la petite vérole,** face pitted with smallpox; (*c*) *F:* **il est complètement r.!** he's quite mad!

ravageant [ravaʒɑ̃], *a.* destructive, devastating.

ravagement [ravaʒmɑ̃], *s.m.* ravaging.

ravager [ravaʒe], *v.tr.* **(je ravageai(s); n. ravageons)** to ravage, devastate; to lay (country) waste; to make havoc of, play havoc with (sth.).

ravageur, -euse [ravaʒœːr, -øːz]. 1. *a.* ravaging, devastating (storm, etc.). 2. *s.* ravager; **les ravageurs des cultures,** birds, insects, etc., that destroy, ravage, the crops; the enemies of the crops.

raval [raval], *s.m. Min:* deepening (of pit, shaft).

ravalaison [ravalɛzɔ̃], *s.f.* downstream migration of fish.

ravalant [ravalɑ̃], *a.* debasing, degrading.

ravalé [ravale]. 1. *a.* **bas ravalés,** stockings about one's heels. 2. *a.* & *s.m.* **(saumon) r.,** kelt.

ravalement [ravalmɑ̃], *s.m.* 1. (*a*) *Const:* (i) resurfacing and repointing, scraping, re-dressing (of stonework); (ii) roughcasting, rough-coating, plastering; *F: Pej:* **elle fait son r.,** she's putting on her makeup, her face; (*b*) *Const: etc:* hollowing out (of recess); (*c*) cutting back, cutting low (of tree); trimming (of branches); (*d*) *O:* disparagement, depreciation (of s.o., of s.o.'s merit); loss of prestige; snubbing, slighting (of s.o.). 2. (*a*) *Const:* (coat of) rough-cast, plaster; (*b*) *Const: etc:* (hollowed out) recess; *N.Arch:* fall, break (of ship's deck); (*c*) (i) snub, slight; (ii) *O:* **imposer un r. à qn,** to lower s.o. in public estimation.

ravaler [ravale], *v.tr.* 1. to swallow (sth.) again, to swallow (sth.) down; **r. un sanglot,** to choke down a sob; **r. ses paroles,** (i) to resist the temptation to speak; to check oneself; (ii) to retract a statement; **je lui ferai r. ses paroles,** I'll make him eat his words. 2. (*a*) to degrade (s.o.); **r. sa femme au rôle de servante,** to treat one's wife like a servant; **r. l'homme au-dessous des animaux,** to relegate man to a level below that of dumb animals; **voilà jusqu'où la passion nous ravale,** (i) this is the level to which passion has reduced us; (ii) this is an example of what passion can lead to; (*b*) to disparage, depreciate, run down (s.o., s.o.'s merit); to take (s.o.) down; to snub, slight (s.o.). 3. *Hort:* to cut back, cut low (tree); to trim (branches). 4. *Const:* (*a*) to re-dress, to resurface and repoint (stonework); to scrape (wall); (*b*) to roughcast, rough-coat, plaster (wall, etc.); (*c*) to hollow out a recess in (wall, etc.). 5. *v.i.* (*a*) *Nau:* (*of the wind*) to back; (*b*) *Ven:* (*of old stag*) to go back.

se ravaler, to degrade, lower, debase, oneself; **vous ne vous ravaleriez pas jusque-là,** you would not stoop to that.

ravaleur [ravalœːr], *s.m. Const:* roughcaster, plasterer.

ravaudage [ravodaːʒ], *s.m.* 1. (*a*) mending, patching (of old clothes); darning (of stockings, etc.); (*b*) botching, bungling. 2. (*a*) mend (in garment); darn (in stocking); (*b*) *F:* piece of botched work; botch. 3. *F: A:* idle talk.

ravauder [ravode], *v.tr.* 1. (*a*) to mend, patch (old clothes, etc.); to darn (stockings, etc.); (*b*) to botch, bungle (work). 2. *F: A:* to abuse, upbraid, scold (s.o.). 3. *v.i. F: A:* (*a*) to engage in idle talk; (*b*) to potter about the house; (*c*) to rummage about.

ravaudeur, -euse [ravodœːr, -øːz], *s.* (*a*) mender (of garments); darner (of stockings, etc.); (*b*) *F:* botcher, bungler.

rave[1] [raːv], *s.f. Bot:* 1. rape, coleseed. 2. *Hort:* (i) radish; (ii) turnip; **céleri r.,** celeriac.

rave[2], *s.f. Tex:* floss (silk).

rave[3], *s.f. A.Min:* (miner's) lamp.

rave[4], *s.f.* **r. de poissons,** fish roe, *esp.* salted cod's roe (used as bait).

ravelin [ravlɛ̃], *s.m. A.Fort:* ravelin.

ravenala [ravənala], *s.m. Bot:* ravenala.

ravenelle [ravnɛl], *s.f. Bot:* 1. wallflower. 2. wild radish.

ravennate [ravɛn(n)at], *a.* & *s. Geog:* (native, inhabitant) of Ravenna.

Ravenne [ravɛn], *Pr.n.f. Geog:* Ravenna.

ravet [ravɛ], *s.m. Ent: F:* cockroach.

ravi [ravi], *a.* 1. entranced, enraptured; **être ravi en extase,** to be in an ecstatic trance. 2. delighted **(de,** with); overjoyed **(de,** at); **r. de joie,** overjoyed; **je suis r. de vous voir,** I am delighted to see you; **je suis r. que vous ayez réussi,** I am delighted that you have succeeded; **d'un air r.,** delightedly.

ravier [ravje], *s.m.* 1. radish dish; hors-d'œuvres dish. 2. *Agr:* turnip silo.

ravière [ravjɛːr], *s.f. Hort:* (*a*) radish bed; (*b*) turnip field.

ravigote [ravigɔt], *s.f. Cu:* ravigote sauce.

ravigoter [ravigɔte], *v.tr. F:* to cheer (s.o.) up, buck (s.o.) up; **un petit verre va le r.,** a drop of spirits will put new life into him.

ravilir [raviliːr], *v.tr.* to degrade, debase, vilify.

ravin [ravɛ̃], *s.m.* ravine, gully.

ravine [ravin], *s.f.* (*a*) *A:* (mountain) torrent; (*b*) gully.

ravinée [ravine], *s.f.* gully; ravine.

ravinement [ravinmɑ̃], *s.m.* gullying, hollowing out (of the ground by running water).

raviner [ravine], *v.tr.* (*of storm torrents*) to gully, hollow out, channel (the ground); to furrow, cut up (the roads, etc.).

ravineux, -euse [ravinø, -øːz], *a.* full of ravines; gullied (hillside); (road) washed away, cut up, by the rain.

ravir [raviːr], *v.tr.* 1. to ravish, carry off (s.o.); **r. qch. à qn,** to rob s.o. of sth.; to steal sth. from s.o.; **on lui avait ravi son enfant,** her child had been torn from her. 2. to delight (s.o.); **cela ne me ravissait pas,** I wasn't happy about it; **belle à r.,** ravishingly beautiful; **elle chante à r.,** she sings charmingly; she has a delightful voice; **cela lui va à r.,** she looks charming in it.

raviser (se) [səravize], *v.pr.* to change one's mind; to alter one's mind; to think better of it; to think again.

ravissant [ravisɑ̃], *a.* 1. *A:* ravening (wolf, etc.). 2. entrancing, bewitching; ravishing, delightful; lovely.

ravissement [ravismɑ̃], *s.m.* 1. carrying off, ravishing, ravishment; *Poet:* rape (of sth.). 2. rapture, ecstasy, delight; **être dans le r.,** to be in a transport of delight, in raptures.

ravisseur, -euse [ravisœːr, -øːz]. 1. *a.* predatory, *A:* ravening (wolf, etc.). 2. *s.m.* ravisher; (*a*) plunderer; (*b*) abductor (of a woman); (*c*) **r. (d'enfant),** kidnapper.

ravitaillement [ravitɑjmɑ̃], *s.m.* 1. *Mil: Navy: Av:* supply **(en,** of); revictualling, provisioning, refilling, replenishment **(en,** with); **r. (en carburant),** refuelling; (*a*) *Mil:* **r. automatique,** automatic supply; **r. journalier,** daily supply; **r. en armes,** supply of weapons; **r. en effets d'habillement,** clothing supply; **r. en explosifs,** supply of explosives; **r. en munitions,** ammunition supply, replenishment; **r. en vivres,** food supply; **distribuer, répartir, le r. en fonction des besoins,** to issue, distribute, supplies as required; **distribution du r.,** issue of supplies; **le r. s'effectuait, se faisait, à la nuit tombée,** rations went up after dark; **axe de r.,** main line of supply, *U.S:* main supply route; **axe de r. et d'évacuation,** axis of supply and evacuation; **base de r.,** supply base; **centre de r.,** supply point, refilling point, loading centre; **dépôt de r.,** (i) (supply) dump (of a division or lower unit); (ii) (supply) depot (of a corps or higher unit); **colonne, convoi, de r.,** supply column; **gare de r.,** railhead, refilling station; **officier chargé du r.,** supply officer; **écoulement du r.,** flow of supplies; (*b*) *Nau: Navy:* taking in of supplies, completing, victualling; **r. à la mer,** replenishment, refuelling, at sea; *Navy:* logistic support at sea, *U.S:* underway logistic support; **convoi de r.,** supply, logistic, convoy; (*c*) *Av:* **r. par air, par avion(s),** air supply; **r. en vol,** (in-)flight refuelling; **entonnoir de r. en vol,** drogue; **perche de r. en vol,** refuelling boom; **sonde de r. en vol,** refuelling probe; (*d*) *Ind: etc:* supplying with fuel, lubricants, etc.; **le r. des grandes villes est un des problèmes de nos jours,** maintaining supplies in large cities is one of the problems of today; *F:* **aller au r.,** to go shopping. 2. supplies (of food, fuel, etc.).

ravitailler [ravitɑje], *v.tr. Mil: Navy: Av: Ind: etc:* to supply, provision, revictual, refill, replenish **(en,** with); to feed (prisoners of war, etc.); **r. une place forte (en vivres, munitions, etc.),** to (re-)supply a stronghold (with provisions, ammunitions, etc.); **r. par air (des unités encerclées, etc.),** drop suppplies to (encircled units, etc.); **r. un bâtiment à la mer,** to replenish, revictual, refuel, a ship at sea; **r. un avion en vol,** to refuel an aircraft in flight; **r. une ville en viande, en carburant,** to supply a town with meat, with fuel.

se ravitailler, *Mil: Navy: Av: Ind: etc:* to take in (fresh) supplies, replenish, revictual **(en,** with); **se r. (en carburant),** to refuel; **se r. en eau,** to replenish with water; *Mil:* **se r. à un dépôt de base,** to be supplied from a base depot; *Navy:* **se r. à la mer,** to replenish, revictual, refuel, at sea; *Av:* **se r. en vol,** to refuel in flight; *F:* **on peut se r. facilement à la ville voisine,** it's easy to do one's shopping, to stock up, in the nearby town.

ravitailleur [ravitɑjœːr], *s.m.* 1. *Mil:* carrier (of ammunition, etc.). 2. *Navy:* supply ship, replenishment ship, *U.S:* logistic-support ship; **r. à la mer, r. de la flotte,** fleet supply ship, fleet replenishment ship; *U.S:* underway replenishment ship; **r. d'aviation,** seaplane tender; **r. de destroyers,** destroyer tender; **r. de sous-marins,** submarine tender, (submarine) parent ship; **r. en munitions,** ammunition ship; **r. de région,** regional supply ship.

ravivage [ravivaːʒ], *s.m.* reviving, brightening up (of colour, metal surface, etc.); cleaning, filing up (of metal surfaces); rechasing (of screw thread); trimming (of edges of wound).

ravivement [ravivmɑ̃], *s.m.* renewal, renewing (of pain, sorrow, etc.); revival, reviving, reliving (of memories, etc.); *Med:* refreshing (of edges of a wound).

raviver [ravive], *v.tr.* 1. to revive (fire, strength, hope, memory, pain); to poke (up), revive (the fire); to give a fillip to (ambition, memory); **son inquiétude s'est ravivée,** his anxiety made itself felt, came to life again; he began to feel anxious again; **la conflagration s'est ravivée,** the fire broke out again. 2. to brighten up, to touch up (colour, metal surface, etc.); to clean, file up (surfaces to be soldered); to rechase (screw-thread); **r. une plaie,** (i) to trim a wound; (ii) to re-open an old sore; to revive an old sorrow.

ravoir[1] [ravwaːr], *v.tr.* (*used only in the infinitive*) 1. (*a*) to have (sth.) (once) again; (*b*) to get (sth.) back again; to recover (sth.); **tâchez de r. cette lettre,** try to get that letter back. 2. *F:* (*in neg.*) to clean (up); to scrape off; **je n'arrive pas à r. cette casserole,** I can't get this pan properly clean.

se ravoir, *A:* to recover one's strength; to recruit (after illness, etc.).

ravoir[2], *s.m. Fish:* trap net (covered by the sea at high tide); net stretched across a stream.

ravoure [ravuːr], *s.m.* (*in Switz.* & *Fr.Alps*) band of red (in sky, at sunrise or sunset).

rayage [rɛjaːʒ], *s.m. O:* **rayement** [rɛmɑ̃], *s.m.* 1. (*a*) scratching, scoring (of plate, glass, etc.); (*b*) ruling (of paper, etc.); (*c*) striping, streaking (of fabric, etc.); (*d*) *Artil: etc:* rifling (of gun); grooving (of cylinder, etc.). 2. striking out (of word, etc.); striking off (of name from list).

rayé [reje], *a.* 1. striped, streaked **(de,** with); **pantalon r.,** striped trousers; **tablier r. rouge et bleu,** red and blue striped apron; **pelage r. de bandes sombres,** coat (of animal) streaked with black; **chat orange r.,** orange tabby cat. 2. lined, ruled (paper, etc.). 3. (*a*) rifled, grooved (gun); **âme rayée,** rifle(d) bore; **r. à gauche, à droite,** rifled to the left, to the right; (*b*) scratched (glass etc.); scored (cylinder, etc.).

rayer [reje], *v.tr.* **(je raie, je raye, n. rayons; je raierai, je rayerai) 1.** (*a*) to scratch (glass, plate, etc.); to score (cylinder, etc.); (*b*) to rule, line (paper, etc.); (*c*) to stripe, streak (fabric, etc.); (*d*) to rifle (gun); to groove (cylinder, etc.). **2.** to strike out, expunge, delete (word, line, conviction, etc.); to remove s.o.'s name (**de**, from); (*on form*) **r. les mentions inutiles,** delete where inapplicable; **on vous a rayé, on a rayé votre nom, de la liste,** you, your name, has been struck off the list; *Mil:* **r. qn des contrôles,** to strike s.o. off the strength; **r. qch. des contrôles,** to write sth. off charge; *Navy:* **r. un bâtiment de l'activité,** to take a ship off the active list; **r. la pension de qn,** to suppress, stop, s.o.'s pension; *Com:* **r. un article,** to cross out, cancel, an item; *F:* **rayez cela de vos papiers!** you needn't count on that any longer! *F:* **r. une ville de la carte,** to wipe a town off the map.

rayère [rɛjɛːr], *s.f.* **1.** *Arch:* dreamhole. **2.** *Hyd.E:* channel, head race (of overshot wheel); flume, leat.

ray-grass [rɛgrɑːs], *s.m.inv. Agr:* rye grass; **r.-g. anglais,** perennial rye grass, English meadow grass; **r.-g. de France,** false oat.

rayon[1] [rɛjɔ̃], *s.m.* **1.** (*a*) *Opt:* ray, beam, gleam (of light); **faisceau de rayons,** bundle of rays, *Elcs:* beam; **r. lumineux,** light ray, luminous ray; **un faible r. de lumière,** a faint gleam of light; **r. de lumière blanche,** ray of white light; **r. de lune,** moonbeam; **r. de soleil,** sunbeam; **les rayons du soleil, les rayons solaires,** the rays of the sun, the solar rays; *Meteor:* **le r. vert,** the green ray, the green flash; **émettre, envoyer, lancer, des rayons,** to beam; **diriger les rayons d'une lanterne sur qn, sur qch.,** to flash a lantern on to s.o., on to sth.; **r. d'espérance,** ray, gleam, of hope; (*of pers., thg*) **c'est un vrai r. de soleil,** he's, she's, it's, a real joy; it's a perfect, a sheer, delight; *P:* **en connaître un r.,** to know a lot; (*b*) *Physiol:* **r. visuel,** (i) visual ray, beam; (ii) line of sight; (*c*) *Ph:* **rayons convergents,** converging rays; **rayons émergents,** emergent rays; **r. incident,** incident ray; **r. marginal,** marginal ray; **r. oblique,** oblique, slant, ray; **l'obliquité des rayons du soleil dans le voisinage des pôles,** the obliquity of the sun's rays in the vicinity of the poles; **r. rasant,** skimming, tangent, ray; **r. réfléchi,** reflected ray; **rayons réfléchis par une surface polie,** rays reflected by a polished surface; **r. réfracté,** refracted ray; (*d*) *Rad.-A: Atom.Ph: etc:* **r. alpha, bêta, gamma,** alpha, beta, gamma, ray; **rayons actiniques, chimiques,** actinic, chemical, rays; **rayons cosmiques,** cosmic rays; **rayons infra-rouges,** infra-red rays; **rayons ultra-violets,** ultra-violet rays; **rayons X,** X-rays; **rayons X pénétrants,** deep X-rays; **rayons (X, etc.) doux, mous,** soft (X-, etc.) rays; **rayons (X, etc.) ultra-mous, rayons limites,** grenz rays; **rayons (X, etc.) durs,** hard (X-, etc.) rays; **rayons (X, etc.) moyens,** medium-hard (X-, etc.) rays; *Med:* **mal des rayons,** radiation sickness; (*in popular Lit:*) **rayons de la mort, rayons qui tuent,** death rays; (*e*) *Elcs:* **r. électronique,** electron beam, ray; electron trajectory; **rayons cathodiques,** cathode rays; **r. positif, r. canal,** positive ray, canal ray. **2.** (*a*) radius (of circle, *Mec.E:* of eccentric, gear wheel, etc.); **r. de courbure, de courbe,** radius of curvature, of curve; **r. équatorial,** equatorial radius; **r. polaire,** polar radius; *Mth:* **r. vecteur,** radius vector; *Mec.E:* **r. primitif,** pitch radius (of gearing); *Rail: etc:* **r. de raccordement,** transition radius (of transition curve); *Veh:* **r. de braquage,** steering radius; **r. de giration, de virage,** radius of gyration, of turn; **r. de rotation,** turning circle, radius; *Nau:* **r. d'évitage,** swinging radius; (*b*) range; **dans un r. de deux kilomètres, à deux kilomètres de r.,** within a radius of two kilometres; **r. d'action,** (i) *Veh:* cruising radius, steaming range (of ship); range, radius of action or operation (of aircraft, submarine, etc.); (ii) radius of action (of weapon); (iii) transmitting range (of radio station); **avion, sous-marin, à grand r. d'action,** long-range aircraft, submarine; *Mil:* **r. de destruction (d'une arme),** radius of destruction (of weapon); **r. d'efficacité d'une arme,** weapon radius (of action); *Com:* **r. d'action d'une campagne publicitaire,** coverage, range, of an advertising campaign; **r. de livraison,** delivery area; **cette entreprise a étendu son r. d'action,** this firm has extended the scope of its activities. **3.** (*a*) spoke (of wheel); **r. droit,** radial spoke; **r. tangent,** tangent spoke; (*b*) **étoile à cinq rayons,** five-point star; (*c*) *Bot:* **rayons médullaires,** medullary rays; (*d*) *Ich:* (*part of fin*) ray; spoke.

rayon[2], *s.m.* **1. r. de miel,** honeycomb; **miel en r.,** honey in the comb. **2.** (*a*) shelf (of cupboard, bookcase, etc.); *pl.* set of shelves; (*b*) *Com:* (*in shop*) (i) department; (ii) counter; **magasin à rayons multiples,** department store; **r. des soldes,** bargain counter; **chef de r.,** (i) head, (ii) buyer, of department; shopwalker; *F:* (*in self-service stores*) **le cinquième r.,** the non-food section; **c'est votre r.,** that's something that concerns you; that's in your line; **ce n'est pas mon r.,** that's nothing to do with me, that's not in my line; I don't know anything about that.

rayon[3], *s.m. Hort:* drill; (small) furrow (for planting seed); **r. d'oignons, de laitues,** row of onions, of lettuce.

rayonnage[1] [rɛjɔnaːʒ], *s.m. coll.* spokes (of wheel).

rayonnage[2], *s.m.* (*a*) shelving; (set of) shelves; (*b*) shelf space.

rayonnage[3], *s.m. Hort:* drilling, furrowing (of plot).

rayonnant [rɛjɔnɑ̃], *a.* **1.** (*a*) *Ph:* radiant (heat); radiating, radiative (power); (*b*) radiant, beaming (face); (face) wreathed in smiles; radiant (beauty); **r. de joie,** radiant, beaming, with joy; **r. de santé,** glowing with health; **joie rayonnante,** radiant joy. **2.** (*a*) *Nat.Hist:* radiating (umbel, etc.); (*b*) *Her: Gothic Arch:* rayonnant (crown, window tracery).

rayonne [rɛjɔn], *s.f. Tex:* rayon.

rayonnement [rɛjɔnmɑ̃], *s.m.* (*a*) *Ph:* radiation; **r. de faible, de grande, énergie,** low-level, high-level, radiation; **r. diffusé,** scattered radiation; **r. cosmique,** cosmic radiation; **r. parasite,** perturbing, spurious, radiation; stray radiation; **r. thermique,** thermal, caloric, radiation; heat radiation; **r. d'un corps noir,** black body radiation, Planckian radiation; *Atom.Ph:* **r. radioactif,** radioactive radiation; **r. alpha, bêta, gamma,** alpha, beta, gamma, radiation; **r. de freinage,** bremsstrahlung; **r. ionisant,** ionizing radiation; **r. neutronique,** neutron radiation; **r. instantané,** initial, prompt, radiation; **r. résiduel,** residual radiation; **r. pénétrant,** penetrating radiation; **protection contre le r.,** glow screen; (*b*) radiance, effulgence; **le r. du soleil, de la vérité,** the radiance of the sun, of truth; **dans le plein r. de sa beauté,** in the full radiance of her beauty; (*c*) influence; diffusion; **le r. de la culture française,** the influence of French civilization.

rayonner[1] [rɛjɔne], *v.i.* (*a*) *Ph:* to radiate; *W.Tel:* **r. dans l'antenne,** to howl; (*b*) to beam, shine; **il rayonnait de joie, la joie rayonnait sur son visage,** he was radiant, beaming, with joy; his face shone with joy; (*c*) **six avenues rayonnent autour de la place,** six avenues radiate from the square; **pendant huit jours nous avons rayonné autour d'Avignon,** we did a week's sightseeing based on Avignon, we made Avignon our centre for a week's sightseeing; (*d*) **la culture française rayonne sur le monde entier,** French civilization influences, is an influential force throughout, the (whole) world.

rayonner[2], *v.tr.* to fit with shelves; to shelve (room, shop, etc.).

rayonner[3], *v.tr. Hort:* to drill, furrow.

rayonnés [rɛjɔne], *s.m.pl. Z: A:* radiata.

rayonneur [rɛjɔnœːr], *s.m. Hort:* (*Tls:*) drill.

rayure [rɛjyːr], *s.f.* **1.** (*a*) stripe, streak; **à rayures,** striped; (*b*) scratch, score; (*c*) groove; *Sm.a:* rifling, groove of the rifling (of gun). **2.** (*a*) striking out, expunging (of conviction); striking off (of name); (*b*) erasure.

raz [rɑ], *s.m.* **r. (de courant),** strong current (in isthmus or estuary); race; **r. de marée,** (i) tidal wave; (ii) *Pol: etc:* landslide.

razon [rɑzɔ̃], *s.m. Ich:* razor fish.

razzia [razja], *s.f.* (*a*) incursion, raid, foray, razzia; (*b*) *A: F:* (police) raid; (*c*) *F:* **faire (une) r.,** to make a clean sweep (**sur,** of); **le public a fait (une) r. sur les nouveaux modèles,** the public snapped up all the new models.

razzier [razje], *v.tr.* (*p.d. & pr.sub.* **n. razziions, v. razziiez**) to raid; to make a raid, an incursion on (s.o., sth.).

r(e)- [r(ə)], **ré-** [re], *pref.* **1.** re-, again. **2.** re-, back. **3.** *intensive, but usu. with little force and not translated in Eng.; e.g.* **recourber,** to bend; **reluire,** to shine. NOTE. *It is impossible to list all words in* **(r(e)-** *and* **ré;** *as a guide to translation it should be noted that those having the sense of repetition can almost invariably be translated by the addition of the adverb* again, *and that many of them have a* **re-** *form in English, e.g.* **réadmettre,** to readmit, to admit again; **reclasser,** to reclassify, to classify again. *Those having the sense of return can usually be translated by the addition of* back, *though many have also a* **re-** *form; e.g.* **revenir,** to come back; **repousser,** to push back; to repulse; **retourner,** to return; to turn back.

ré [re], *s.m.inv. Mus:* **1.** (*a*) (the note) D; (*b*) the D string (of violin, etc.). **2.** re (in the Fixed Do system).

réa [rea], *s.m. Mec.E:* sheave; pulley wheel; **r. à rais,** spokesheave; **r. plein,** disc sheave; **r. à billes, à rouleaux, à roulements,** roller sheave.

réabonnement [reabɔnmɑ̃], *s.m.* renewal of subscription (**à,** to).

réabonner [reabɔne], *v.tr. & pr.* to renew (s.o.'s, one's) subscription (**à,** to).

réabsorber [reapsɔrbe], *v.tr.* to reabsorb.

réabsorption [reapsɔrpsjɔ̃], *s.f.* reabsorption, reabsorbing.

réaccoutumer [reakutyme], *v.tr.* to re-accustom (**à,** to).

réactance [reaktɑ̃ːs], *s.f. El:* reactance; **bobine de r.,** reaction coil, choking coil, choke; **r. acoustique,** acoustic reactance; **r. de capacité,** capacitative reactance; **r. d'électrode,** electrode reactance; **coefficient de r.,** reactive factor; **tube (de) r.,** reactance valve, tube.

réacteur, -trice [reaktœːr, -tris]. **1.** *s. Pol: A:* reactionary. **2.** (*a*) *s.m. Av: Mec.E:* jet engine, jet motor; reaction engine, reaction motor; **r. inversé,** retro rocket; **r. de propulsion,** propulsion-jet engine; **r. de sustentation,** lift-jet engine; **r. à simple corps,** single-shaft engine; **r. à double corps,** two-shaft, twin-spool, engine; **r. à triple corps,** three-shaft, triple-shaft, engine; **r. à simple flux,** (single-flow) turbo jet; **r. à double flux,** by-pass engine, fan engine, turbo fan; **r. à triple corps et à double flux,** triple-shaft fan engine; (*b*) jet aircraft. **3.** *s.m. Atom.Ph:* (atomic, nuclear) reactor; atomic, nuclear, pile; **r. (auto)générateur, r. sur(ré)générateur, r. producteur de matière fissile,** breeder (reactor); **r. générateur d'énergie, r. de puissance,** power reactor; **r. d'énergie nulle, r. à puissance zéro,** zero-power reactor; **r. à fission,** fission reactor; **r. à fusion (contrôlée, ménagée),** (controlled) fusion reactor; **r. expérimental, industriel,** experimental, industrial, reactor; **r. à combustible circulant,** circulating reactor; **r. à combustible fluidisé,** fluidized reactor; **r. à l'uranium naturel,** natural-uranium reactor; **r. à l'uranium enrichi,** enriched-uranium reactor; **r. au plutonium,** plutonium reactor; **les réacteurs rapides régénèrent le combustible,** fast reactors breed fuel; **r. à neutrons épithermiques, r. épithermique,** epithermal reactor; **r. à neutrons intermédiaires, r. intermédiaire,** intermediate reactor; **r. à neutrons rapides, r. rapide,** fast (neutron) reactor; **r. sur(ré)générateur à neutrons rapides,** fast breeder; **r. à neutrons thermiques, r. thermique,** thermal reactor; **r. à réseau,** lattice reactor; **r. modéré à l'eau, à modérateur en eau,** water-moderated reactor; **r. modéré au graphite, à modérateur en graphite,** graphite-moderated reactor; **r. refroidi au gaz, au sodium, r. à refroidissement au gaz, au sodium,** gas-cooled, sodium-cooled, reactor; **r. modéré et refroidi à l'eau lourde, légère,** heavy-water, light-water, moderated and cooled reactor; **r. modéré à l'eau lourde et refroidi à l'eau légère,** heavy-water moderated, light-water cooled reactor; **r. modéré et refroidi par fluide organique, r. à modérateur et à réfrigérant organiques,** organic moderated and cooled reactor; **r. propulseur de fusée,** rocket pile; *Nau: Navy:* **r. marin,** marine nuclear reactor; **r. propulseur de navire,** ship-propulsion reactor.

réactif, -ive [reaktif, -iːv]. **1.** *a.* (*a*) reactive; **non r.,** non-reactive; *Ch:* **papier r.,** reagent paper, test paper; *Mec:* **force réactive,** reactive force; *Physiol:* **les nerfs sensitifs des personnes âgées sont moins réactifs que ceux de sujets plus jeunes,** the sensory nerves of old people are less reactive than those of younger individuals; *Psy:* **inhibition réactive,** reactive inhibition; **l'impulsivité est essentiellement réactive,** impulsiveness is essentially reactive; (*b*) *El: Elcs:* reactive, *attrib:* feedback; **courant r.,** reactive current; **couplage r.,** feedback coupling; **charge réactive,** reactive load; **puissance réactive,** reactive power, reactive volt-ampere. **2.** *s.m.* (*a*) *Ch:* reagent; **r. à base de mercure,** mercury reagent, mercury composition; **r. d'attaque,** etching solution; **r. organique,** organic reagent; (*b*) *Physiol: Psy: etc:* reaction agent; **notre milieu est un r. puissant pour notre comportement,** we are highly reactive to our environment.

réactimètre [reaktimɛtr̥], *s.m. Atom.Ph:* reactivity meter.

réaction [reaksjɔ̃], *s.f.* reaction. 1. (*a*) *Ch: Atom. Ph:* **r. chimique,** chemical reaction; **r. endothermique, exothermique,** endothermic, exothermic, reaction; **r. réversible, équilibrée,** reversible reaction; **faire la r. des alcaloïdes,** to test for alkaloids; **r. de fission, de fusion,** fission, fusion, reaction; **r. en chaîne,** chain reaction; **r. (en chaîne) auto-entretenue,** self-maintaining, self-sustaining, (chain) reaction; **r. inverse,** back reaction; **r. nucléaire, thermonucléaire, photonucléaire,** nuclear, thermonuclear, photonuclear, reaction; **r. nucléaire en chaîne,** nuclear chain reaction; **r. nucléaire artificielle, induite, provoquée,** artificial, induced, nuclear reaction; **r. nucléaire spontanée,** spontaneous nuclear reaction; (*b*) *El.E: Elcs:* reaction, retroaction; feedback; **r. d'anode,** anode reaction; **r. d'induit,** armature reaction; **bobine de r.,** reaction coil, choking coil, choke; **r. capacitive,** capacitance feedback; **r. d'intensité,** current feedback; **r. de tension,** voltage feedback; **r. électromagnétique, électrostatique,** electromagnetic, electrostatic, feedback; *W.Tel:* **r. dans l'antenne,** howling; **r. positive,** regeneration; **r. acoustique,** acoustic regeneration; (*c*) **à réaction,** regenerative; **amplificateur, récepteur, à r.,** regenerative amplifier, receiver; **couplage à r.,** regenerative coupling; **montage à r.,** regenerative circuit; (*d*) *Mec:* reaction; *Ball:* kick (of rifle, etc.); **r. réciproque,** interaction; **r. d'appui,** reaction of support; **pouvoir de r.,** reactivity; *Aut:* **tube de r.,** torque tube; *Typ:* **presse à r.,** perfecting machine; *Mec.E:* **moteur à r.,** jet engine, reaction engine, reaction motor; **propulsion par r.,** jet propulsion, reaction propulsion; **avion, appareil, à r.,** jet (-propelled) aircraft, jet plane, *F:* jet; **turbine à r.,** reaction turbine; **aubage à r.,** reaction blades (of turbine); **étage de r.,** reaction stage (of turbine); **vitesse de r.,** reaction rate; *Hyd.E:* **roue à r.,** reaction wheel. 2. (*a*) *Physiol:* reaction, response (of organ, tissue, etc.); *Med:* test; **r. auditive, tactile, visuelle,** auditory, tactile, visual, reaction; **r. biologique,** biological response; **r. de défense,** defensive response; defence reaction; **r. motrice,** motor response; **r. cutanée,** (i) cutaneous, skin, reaction; (ii) skin test; **r. de dégénérescence,** degenerative reaction; **r. de sédimentation globulaire,** blood sedimentation test; **r. de Wassermann,** (i) Wassermann reaction; (ii) Wassermann test; **r. de l'organisme humain à l'infection microbienne,** reaction of the human organism to bacterial infection; (*b*) afterglow (after a bath); (*c*) *Psy: etc:* **psychologie de r.,** behaviourism; **temps de r.,** reaction time; **r. conditionnelle,** conditioned reflex, response; **r. circulaire,** circular reaction, reflex, response, behaviour; **sans r.,** non-reactive; **r. à une situation nouvelle,** reaction to a new situation; **avoir des réactions lentes,** to be slow to react; *F:* **il a protesté?—non, aucune r.,** did he protest? —no, there was no reaction; **cette voiture a de bonnes réactions,** this car responds well, is easy to handle; (*d*) *St.Exch:* **vive r. du sterling sur le marché des changes,** sharp reaction of the pound sterling on the (foreign) exchange market; **forte r. des pétroles en clôture,** strong reaction of oils, of oil shares, at the close; (*e*) *Pol:* **la r.,** (i) reactionary attitude; (ii) reactionaries; **partis de r.,** reactionary parties.

réactionnaire [reaksjɔnɛːr], *a. & s.m. & f. Pol:* reactionary.

réactionnel, -elle [reaksjɔnɛl], *a. Ch: El: etc:* reactive; *Psy:* **formation réactionnelle,** reaction formation.

réactivateur [reaktivatœːr], *s.m. Ch: Elcs: Med:* reactivator.

réactivation [reaktivasjɔ̃], *s.f.* reactivation (of catalyst, electron tube, etc.); **r. de la tuberculose par excès de fatigue,** reactivation of tuberculosis by excess of fatigue.

réactiver [reaktive], *v.tr.* 1. to restart; to revive; to regenerate; **r. le feu,** to revive, poke (up), the fire; *Med:* **r. la circulation,** to restore the circulation. 2. *Ch: Elcs: Med:* to reactivate (a catalyst, an absorbent, an electron tube, a serum, a microbial disease, etc.).

réactivité [reaktivite], *s.f.* (*a*) *Psy:* reactivity (to stimulation); (*b*) *Med:* reactivity (to immunization, etc.); **r. naturelle, acquise,** natural, acquired, reactivity; (*c*) *Ch: Atom.Ph:* reactivity (of substance, atomic pile, etc.); *Atom.Ph:* **r. négative,** negative reactivity; **r. résiduelle,** residual, shut-down, reactivity; **facteur de r.,** reactivity factor; **variation de r.,** reactivity drift.

réactogène [reaktɔʒɛn], *a. Med: etc:* (substance, etc.) that provokes a reaction.

réadaptation [readaptasjɔ̃], *s.f.* 1. rehabilitation (of refugees). 2. re-education. 3. *Med:* readjustment, rehabilitation.

réadapter [readapte], *v.tr.* 1. to rehabilitate. 2. to re-educate. 3. to readjust.

réadjudication [readʒydikasjɔ̃], *s.f.* readjudication; re-allocation.

réadjuger [readʒyʒe], *v.tr.* (*conj. like* JUGER) to readjudicate, re-allocate.

réadmettre [readmɛtr̥], *v.tr.* (*conj. like* METTRE) to readmit; to admit again.

réadmission [readmisjɔ̃], *s.f.* readmission; readmittance.

réadopter [readɔpte], *v.tr.* to readopt.

réadoption [readɔpsjɔ̃], *s.f.* readoption.

réadresser [readrɛse], *v.tr. F:* to re-address.

ready-made [rɛdimɛd], *s.m.inv. Art:* objet trouvé.

réaffecter [reafɛkte], *v.tr.* **r. qn à son premier emploi,** to re-instate s.o. in his former job; **r. une subvention à sa destination première,** to re-allocate funds to their original use.

réafficher [reafiʃe], *v.tr.* to stick up (a poster) again; to post (up) (a notice) again.

réaffirmation [reafirmasjɔ̃], *s.f.* reaffirmation.

réaffirmer [reafirme], *v.tr.* to reaffirm.

réaffûtable [reafytabl̥], *a.* that can easily be reground, regrindable.

réaffûtage [reafytaːʒ], *s.m.* regrinding (of blade, etc.).

réaffûter [reafyte], *v.tr.* to regrind.

réagine [reaʒin], *s.f. Med:* reagin.

réagir [reaʒiːr], *v.i.* 1. to react (**sur,** on; **contre,** against; **à,** towards); **r. contre ses passions,** to wrestle with one's passions; **r. réciproquement,** to interact. 2. to fight back.

réagissant [reaʒisɑ̃], *a.* reacting.

réaimanter [reɛmɑ̃te], *v.tr.* to remagnetize.

réajournement [reaʒurnəmɑ̃], *s.m.* readjournment.

réajourner [reaʒurne], *v.tr.* to readjourn.

réajustement [reaʒyst(ə)mɑ̃], *s.m.* readjustment; putting in order; setting right; settling (of quarrel); **r. des salaires,** readjustment of wages, of wage levels.

réajuster [reaʒyste], *v.tr.* to readjust (sth.); to put (sth.) straight, right; to repair (sth.); **r. sa cravate,** to put one's tie straight; **se r.,** to tidy oneself (up), to put one's clothes straight; **r. une querelle, deux personnes,** to settle a quarrel, to reconcile two people.

réal[1], **-aux** [real, -o], *a. A:* royal; *Hist:* **la galère réale,** *s.f.* **la réale,** the royal galley.

réal[2], **-aux,** *s.m. Num:* real.

réalésage [realezaːʒ], *s.m. Metalw:* reboring; *Aut: F:* rebore; *I.C.E:* **piston à cote de r.,** oversize piston.

réaléser [realeze], *v.tr.* (*conj. like* ALÉSER) *Metalw:* to rebore.

réalgar [realgaːr], *s.m. Miner:* realgar; red arsenic.

realia [realja], *s.f.pl. Phil:* realia, real things.

réalisable [realizabl̥], *a.* 1. realizable; feasible; **projet r.,** workable plan. 2. *Fin:* realizable, available; **actif r.,** current assets.

réalisateur, -trice [realizatœːr, -tris]. 1. (*a*) *a.* **esprit r.,** productive mind; mind that can plan things, work things out; (*b*) *s.* realizer, worker out (of a plan); author, creator (of work of art, etc.); *Tchn:* designer (of machine, etc.); builder, constructor (of building, equipment, etc.); (*c*) *Cin: T.V: etc:* producer. 2. *s. Fin:* seller (of shares).

réalisation [realizasjɔ̃], *s.f.* 1. (*a*) realization, carrying out, accomplishment (of plan, etc.); creation (of work of art, etc.); designing (of building, etc.); building, construction (of equipment, etc.); **les dernières réalisations de la technique moderne,** the latest developments in modern technology; **nous sommes très fiers de cette r.,** we are very proud of this achievement; (*b*) *Cin: T.V: etc:* production; (*c*) *Town P:* building scheme. 2. *Fin: Bank: etc:* realization; utilization, availment; concluding (of bargain, transaction, etc.); **r. d'actions,** selling out of shares; *Com:* **r. du stock,** clearance sale.

réaliser [realize], *v.tr.* to realize. 1. (*a*) to achieve (sth.); to carry out, work out (sth.); to create (a work of art, etc.); to build, construct (equipment, etc.); *Ind: etc:* **réalisé à la demande,** made, built, to order; custom-built, custom-made; **r. un plan,** to implement, carry out, carry through, a plan; **r. une ambition,** to achieve an ambition; **on sait le bel effort réalisé par X,** we know what X has accomplished, achieved; **pour r. la guérison, il vous faudra . . .,** to ensure a cure you will have to . . .; **ne pas r. entièrement la perfection,** to come, fall, (somewhat) short of perfection; (*b*) *Cin: T.V: etc:* to produce (a programme). 2. (*a*) to make, realize (a profit); *St.Exch:* **les cours réalisés au marché d'aujourd'hui,** today's prices; (*b*) *Fin: etc:* **r. des actions,** to sell out shares; **r. sa fortune,** to realize one's assets. 3. *F:* to realize; **ne pas r. les difficultés d'une entreprise,** not to realize the difficulties of an undertaking; **je réalise mon danger,** I realize my danger; *abs.* **tu as réalisé à temps,** you've realized, understood, in time.

se réaliser, (*of projects, of hopes, etc.*) to be realized; to be achieved; to materialize; (*of dream, etc.*) to come true.

réalisme [realism], *s.m. Art: Lit: Phil:* realism.

réaliste [realist]. 1. *a.* realistic; **homme d'État r.,** realistic, practical, statesman. 2. *a. & s.m. & f. Lit: Art: Phil:* realist; **chanteuse r.,** cabaret singer.

réalité [realite], *s.f.* 1. (*a*) reality; actuality, fact; **être près de, au-dessus de, au-dessous de, loin de, la r.,** to be near, over, under, wide of, the mark; **en r.,** in reality; really; in actual fact; **la r. dépasse quelque fois la fiction,** truth is sometimes stranger than fiction; **ce n'est pas ainsi dans la r.,** it's not like that in real life; **l'idéal et la r.,** the ideal and the real; **s'en tenir aux réalités,** to stick to realities, to facts; **les réalités de tous les jours,** the realities, facts, of everyday life; (*b*) *Psy:* **principe de r.,** reality principle. 2. *Theol:* real presence.

réaménagement [reamenaʒmɑ̃], *s.m.* refitting.

réaménager [reamenaʒe], *v.tr.* to refit.

réanimation [reanimasjɔ̃], *s.f.* resuscitation; reanimation.

réanimer [reanime], *v.tr.* to reanimate, revive.

réannexer [reanɛkse], *v.tr.* to reannex.

réannexion [reanɛksjɔ̃], *s.f.* reannexation.

réapparaître [reaparɛtr̥], *v.i.* (*conj. like* APPARAÎTRE; *the aux. is usu.* être) to reappear.

réapparition [reaparisjɔ̃], *s.f.* reappearance.

réapprendre [reaprɑ̃dr̥], *v.tr.* (*conj. like* APPRENDRE) to relearn; to learn (lesson, etc.) again.

réapprentissage [reaprɑ̃tisaːʒ], *s.m.* relearning; new apprenticeship; **cinq ans que je n'ai cohabité avec une femme! réapprentissage!** five years of living without a wife! everything to learn over again!

réapprovisionnement [reaprɔvizjɔnmɑ̃], *s.m.* replenishing of supplies; revictualling; reprovisioning; *Com:* restocking, reordering; *Sm.a:* refilling (of rifle magazine, etc.); **seuil de r.,** reorder point; **commande de r.,** replenishing order.

réapprovisionner [reaprɔvizjɔne], *v.tr. & pr.* to replenish (s.o.'s, one's) supplies (**en,** of); *Com:* to reorder; to restock (shop) (**en,** with); *Sm.a:* to refill (rifle magazine, etc.).

réargenter [rearʒɑ̃te], *v.tr.* to resilver, replate (forks and spoons, etc.).

réargenture [rearʒɑ̃tyːr], *s.f.* resilvering, replating.

réarmement [rearməmɑ̃], *s.m.* (*a*) *Mil: etc:* rearming, rearmament, *Nau:* refitting; recommissioning; *Tchn:* resetting (of a system); *Sm.a:* recocking (of rifle, etc.); *Pol:* **r. moral,** moral rearmament; (*b*) *El.E:* reset (of contactor, etc.); **r. automatique, r. à la main,** automatic, hand, reset.

réarmer [rearme], *v.tr.* 1. (*a*) *Mil:* to rearm; (*b*) *Sm.a: etc:* to recock (gun, etc.); to reset (a system). 2. *Nau:* to refit, recommission; to put (vessel) into commission again.

réarrangement [rearɑ̃ʒmɑ̃], *s.m.* rearrangement; *Ch:* (molecular) rearrangement.

réarranger [rearɑ̃ʒe], *v.tr.* (*conj. like* ARRANGER) to rearrange.

se réarranger, *Ch:* to isomerize.

réarrimage [rearimaːʒ], *s.m. Nau:* restowing.

réarrimer [rearime], *v.tr. Nau:* to restow (cargo).

réassemblage [reasɑ̃blaːʒ], *s.m.* re-assembly (of computer programme).

réassembler [reasɑ̃ble], *v.tr.* to re-assemble (computer programme).

réassignation [reasiɲasjɔ̃], *s.f. Jur:* new summons, fresh summons.

réassigner [reasiɲe], *v.tr. Jur:* to re-summon; to summon (witness, etc.) again.

réassortiment [reasɔrtimɑ̃], *s.m.* 1. (*a*) (re)-matching (of colours, etc.); (*b*) *Com:* restocking. 2. (*a*) **réassortiments difficiles à faire,** articles difficult to match; (*b*) *Com:* new stock.

réassortir [reasɔrtiːr], *v.tr.* (*conj. like* ASSORTIR) 1. to (re)match (ribbons, etc.). 2. *Com:* to restock (shop); **se r.,** to replenish one's stock.

réassortisseuse [reasɔrtisøːz], *s.f.* (*in supermarket, etc.*) shelf filler.

réassumer [reasyme], *v.tr.* to reassume.

réassurance [reasyrɑ̃ːs], *s.f.* reinsurance, reassurance (of a risk); **police de r.,** reinsurance policy; **effectuer une r.,** to lay off a risk.

réassurer [reasyre], *v.tr.* to reinsure, reassure (a risk).
réassureur [reasyrœːr], *s.m.* reinsurer.
réatteler [reatle], *v.tr.* (*conj. like* ATTELER) to put (the horses) to again.
réavertir [reavɛrtiːr], *v.tr.* to warn, caution, (s.o.) again; to give (s.o.) a fresh warning; to send (s.o.) a second notice.
rebaisser [rəbese]. **1.** *v.tr.* to lower (sth.) again. **2.** *v.i.* **les prix ont remonté puis rebaissé,** prices have gone up and then fallen again.
rebaptisation [rəbatizasjɔ̃], *s.f.* rebaptism.
rebaptiser [rəbatize], *v.tr.* to rebaptize, to re-christen; to rename; **la rue a été rebaptisée,** the street has been renamed.
rébarbatif, -ive [rebarbatif, -iːv], *a.* grim, forbidding, unprepossessing (face, aspect); surly (humour); **style r.,** unpleasing, dull, *F:* stodgy, style; **sujet r.,** unattractive, dull, subject.
rebarrer [rəbare], *v.tr. Mus:* to renew the base bar of (violin).
rebâtir [rəbɑtiːr], *v.tr.* to rebuild (house, church, etc.); to reconstruct (novel, etc.); *Const:* **r. par le pied,** to underpin.
rebattre [rəbatr], *v.tr.* (*conj. like* BATTRE) **1.** (*a*) to beat, hammer, (sth.) again; **r. un matelas,** to remake a mattress; (*b*) **r. les cartes,** to reshuffle the cards. **2.** *F:* **r. les oreilles à qn de qch.; r. toujours la même chose aux oreilles de qn,** to say the same thing over and over again; to din sth. into s.o.'s ears; **j'en ai les oreilles rebattues,** I hear (of) nothing else; I am sick (and tired) of hearing (about) it; **j'en suis rebattu,** I have heard it over and over again.
rebattu [rəbaty], *a.* (*a*) *A:* **sentier r., les vieux sentiers rebattus,** the beaten track; (*b*) hackneyed, trite (subject, story).
rebec [rəbɛk], *s.m. A.Mus:* rebec(k).
rébec(c)a [rebɛka], *s.f. or m. P:* **faire du r.,** (i) to grouse, to bellyache; (ii) to kick up a row, a shindy; **y a de la r.,** there's a hell of a rumpus, a row.
Rébecca [rebɛka], *Pr.n.f.* Rebecca.
rebé(c)quer (se) [sərəbeke], *v.pr.* (**je me rebè(c)que, n.n. rebé(c)quons; je me rebé(c)querai**) *F:* to answer back; to protest, to be up in arms (about sth.).
rebec(que)tant [rəbɛktɑ̃], *a. P:* encouraging, appetizing; (sth.) that bucks you up.
rebec(que)ter [rəbɛkte], *v.* (*conj. like* BECQUETER) *P:* **1.** *v.tr.* to buck (s.o.) up. **2.** *v.i. & pr.* to make it up; to put things right; to buck up.
rebe(c)queur, -euse [rəbekœːr, -øːz], *a. & s. F:* insolent, impertinent (person).
rebelle [rəbɛl]. **1.** *a.* (*a*) rebellious, intractable (person, spirit, etc.); stubborn, obstinate (fever, etc.); **r. à la loi, à toute discipline,** unamenable to law, to discipline; **matière r.,** unworkable material; **minerai r.,** refractory ore; **chevelure r.,** rebellious hair; *Med:* **fièvre, ulcère, r.,** obstinate fever, ulcer; **matière r. à la poésie,** subject ill-suited to be treated poetically; (*b*) *Jur:* contumacious. **2.** *s.m. & f.* rebel.
rebeller (se) [sərəbele], *v.pr.* (*a*) to rebel, to rise, to revolt (**contre,** against); (*b*) to protest.
rébellion [rebeljɔ̃], *s.f.* (*a*) rebellion, rising, revolt; **acte de r.,** rebellious act; **en état de r.,** insurgent; (*b*) *Jur:* contumacy; **faire r. à la justice,** to resist the authority of the Court; (*c*) *coll.* **négocier avec la r.,** to negotiate with the rebels.
rébellionnaire [rebeljɔnɛːr], *s.m. & f. Jur:* (*a*) rebel; (*b*) contumacious person.
rebiffe [rəbif], *s.f. F:* (*a*) revolt; **faire de la r.,** to kick over the traces; to get one's back up; to be up in arms (about sth.); (*b*) vengeance.
rebiffement [rəbifmɑ̃], *s.m. F:* indignant refusal to obey; bristling up; kicking (at an order).
rebiffer [rəbife], *F:* **1.** *v.tr.* **r. qn,** to snub s.o.; to set s.o. down. **2.** *v.i.* **r. (au truc),** to start all over again; to have another shot, another go.
se rebiffer, *F:* to bristle up, bridle up (in protest); to get one's back up; to kick (at sth.); to kick over the traces; **faire r. qn,** to get s.o.'s back up; **se r. contre qch.,** to kick against sth., to be up in arms against sth.
reblanchir [rəblɑ̃ʃiːr]. **1.** *v.tr.* (*a*) to whiten, whitewash (sth.) again; (*b*) to launder (garment) again. **2.** *v.i.* to grow white again.
reblochon [rəblɔʃɔ̃], *s.m.* reblochon (cheese).
rebobinage [rəbɔbinaːʒ], *s.m.* rewinding.
rebobiner [rəbɔbine], *v.tr.* to rewind.
reboire [rəbwaːr], *v.tr.* (*conj. like* BOIRE) to drink again; **jamais je ne reboirai de ce vin,** I shall never (i) touch that wine again, (ii) drink such wine again.
reboisement [rəbwazmɑ̃], *s.m.* **1.** afforestation; retimbering (of land). **2.** retimbering (of mine level).
reboiser [rəbwaze], *v.tr.* **1.** to afforest; to re-timber (land). **2.** to retimber (a mine level).
rebond [rəbɔ̃], *s.m.* (*a*) rebound, bounce (of ball, etc.); (*b*) **les rebonds d'un torrent,** the surging of a torrent; (*c*) rounded shape.
rebondi [rəbɔ̃di], *a.* rounded, chubby (cheeks); plump (body); **femme aux formes rebondies,** buxom woman; **petite femme rebondie,** plump little woman; **ventre r.,** corporation; **bourse rebondie,** well-filled purse.
rebondir [rəbɔ̃diːr], *v.i.* (*a*) to rebound; (*of ball*) to bounce; (*b*) (*of torrent, etc.*) to surge; (*c*) *F:* to start off again; **sa lettre a fait r. l'affaire,** his letter has brought the business back into the public eye.
rebondissant [rəbɔ̃disɑ̃], *a.* (*a*) rebounding, bouncy; (*b*) surging.
rebondissement [rəbɔ̃dismɑ̃], *s.m.* (*a*) rebound(ing); resilience; bounce; (*b*) surging; (*c*) (exciting) new development (in a case, story, etc.); **après le r. des affaires,** after business had taken a step forward; **l'histoire des épidémies comportant des rebondissements imprévus,** the history of epidemics and their unexpected recurrences.
rebord [rəbɔːr], *s.m.* **1.** edge, border, rim; hem (of garment); lip (of cup, etc.); helix (of the ear); **r. d'une fenêtre,** window sill, ledge; *Mec.E:* **r. saillant d'une came,** cam head. **2.** (*of sheet metal, pipes, etc.*) raised edge, flange; **à r.,** with raised edge, flanged.
reborder [rəbɔrde], *v.tr.* **1.** (*a*) to put a new edging or border to (sth.); to re-hem (garment); (*b*) to reflange (pipe, etc.). **2. r. qn dans son lit,** to tuck s.o. up (in bed) again.
rebot [rəbo], *s.m. Games:* pelota.
rebotter (se) [sərəbɔte], *v.pr.* to put on one's boots again.
rebouchage [rəbuʃaːʒ], *s.m.*, **rebouchement** [rəbuʃmɑ̃], *s.m.* **1.** stopping (up), blocking up, again; recorking (of bottle). **2.** *Carp: etc:* stopping (before painting); *Civ.E: etc:* back filling; *Petroleum Min:* plugging back (of a well).
reboucher [rəbuʃe], *v.tr.* **1.** (*a*) to stop, block, (sth.) up again; to recork (bottle), to put the cap back on (tube, bottle); (*b*) to fill up (trench, etc.). **2.** *Carp: etc:* to stop out (woodwork) (with putty, etc.); *Petroleum Min:* **r. un sondage,** to plug back a well.
rebouclage [rəbuklaːʒ], *s.m. Tex:* defect (in the weave, giving uneven tension).
rebouillir [rəbujiːr], *v.i.* (*conj. like* BOUILLIR) to boil (up) again; **faire r.,** to reboil (jam, etc.).
rebouiser [rəbwize], *v.tr.* **1.** *F: A:* to patch, cobble (old shoes); to do up (old hat, etc.). **2.** *P:* to kill, bump off, do in (s.o.).
rebours [rəbuːr]. **1.** *a. A:* cross-grained (wood, *F:* person); cantankerous (spirit, person); intractable (horse). **2.** *s.m.* wrong way (of the grain, of the nap); contrary, reverse; *adv.phr.* **à r., au r.,** against the grain, against the hair, the wrong way, backwards; **réciter l'alphabet à r.,** to say the alphabet backwards; **prendre tout à r.,** to take everything the wrong way, to misconstrue everything; **il faut interpréter les rêves à r.,** dreams go by contraries; **compliment à r.,** backhanded compliment; **prendre à r. une rue à sens unique,** to enter a one-way street at the wrong end; **caresser un chat à r.,** to stroke a cat the wrong way; **snobisme à r.,** inverted snobbery; *Tchn:* (*rocket launching*) **compte à r.,** countdown; *adj.phr.* **rampe à r.,** backward slope; **esprit à r.,** perverse, *F:* bloody-minded, outlook; *prep.phr.* **à, au, r. de . . .,** contrary to . . .; **des opinions à r. des nôtres,** opinions diametrically opposed to ours, that go dead against ours.
rebourser [rəburse], *v.tr. Tex:* to raise (the nap).
reboursoir [rəburswaːr], *s.m. Tex:* napping comb.
reboutement [rəbutmɑ̃], *s.m.* bone setting.
rebouter [rəbute], *v.tr.* **1.** *A:* to replace, put back in its place. **2.** (*of bone setter*) to set (broken limb, etc.); to reduce (dislocation).
rebouteur, -euse, rebouteux, -euse [rəbutœːr, rəbutø, -øːz], *s. F:* bonesetter.
reboutonner [rəbutɔne], *v.tr. & pr.* to rebutton; to button up (garment) again; **reboutonne-toi!** button up your clothes!
rebras [rəbra], *s.m.* **1.** cuff (of sleeve); gauntlet (of glove). **2.** flap (of book jacket).
rebrider [rəbride], *v.tr.* to bridle (horse) again.
rebroder [rəbrɔde], *v.tr.* to re-embroider.
rebrousse [rəbrus], *s.f. Tex:* napping comb.
rebroussement [rəbrusmɑ̃], *s.m.* **1.** graining, boarding (of leather); napping (of cloth). **2.** (*a*) turning back; *Mth:* retrogression (of curve); *Geol:* sharp change in direction (of fold); **point de r.,** point of reflection; cusp; **arête de r.,** cuspidal edge; (*b*) turning (of edge of tool); bending back, curling up (of point of nail under the hammer).
rebrousse-poil (à) [arəbruspwal], *adv.phr.* **brosser un chapeau à r.-p.,** to brush a hat against the nap, the wrong way; **caresser le chat à r.-p.,** to stroke the cat the wrong way, against the fur; *F:* **prendre qch. à r.-p.,** to take sth. in the wrong sense, the wrong way; *F:* **prendre qn à r.-p.,** to get on the wrong side of somebody; to rub s.o. up the wrong way.
rebrousser [rəbruse], *v.tr.* **1.** (*a*) to turn up, brush up (hair, nap); *F:* **r. qn,** to rub s.o. up the wrong way; (*b*) to grain, board (leather); to nap (cloth); *Tan:* to strike (skins). **2.** (*a*) **rebrousser chemin,** to retrace one's steps, to turn back; **faire r. chemin à qn,** to head s.o. off; to drive, chase, s.o. back; (*b*) *v.i.* (*of path, etc.*) to turn back; (*of curve*) to retrogress.
se rebrousser, (*of edge of tool*) to turn (up); (*of nail, point*) to bend back, to curl up; **bois qui fait r. la hache,** wood that turns the edge of the axe.
rebroussette [rəbrusɛt], *s.f. Tex:* napping comb.
rebrousseur [rəbrusœːr], *s.m. Tan:* striker.
rebroussoir [rəbruswaːr], *s.m. Tex:* napping comb.
rebuffade [rəbyfad], *s.f.* rebuff; snub; *F:* slap in the face.
rebuffer [rəbyfe], *v.tr.* to rebuff; to snub.
rébus [rebys], *s.m.* (*a*) picture puzzle; rebus; (*b*) *A:* enigma; **parler par r.,** to speak in riddles; (*c*) *F:* illegible writing.
rebut [rəby], *s.m.* **1.** *A:* repulse, rebuff; **essuyer un r.,** to meet with a rebuff, to suffer a snub, to be snubbed. **2.** (*a*) *O:* throwing away, rejection, scrapping; (*b*) (**article de**) **r.,** reject; rubbish; **papier de r.,** waste paper; **habits de r.,** cast-off clothing; *Ind:* **pièces de r., les rebuts,** rejects; throw-outs, wasters; **marchandises de r.,** rubbishy goods, trash; **mettre qch. au r.,** to throw sth. away; to discard (clothing); to scrap (ship, machinery); to reject (casting, etc.); to dispose of, throw away (rubbish); **mise au r.,** disposal; throwing away; *Post:* **bureau des rebuts,** dead-letter office; **case r.,** reject pocket (of punch(ed) card sorter); (*c*) *Pej:* (*of pers.*) waster; **le r. de la population,** the scum, dregs, of the population.
rebutant [rəbytɑ̃], *a.* **1.** tiresome, irksome; deadly dull, uphill, disheartening (work); tedious, tiresome (conversations); tiresome (person). **2. homme r.,** man with a brusque, overbearing manner; **homme à l'abord r.,** unapproachable man.
rebuter [rəbyte], *v.tr.* **1.** to rebuff, repulse; to be very short with (s.o.). **2.** to reject, discard, cast aside, throw aside (goods, etc.). **3.** (*a*) to dishearten, discourage; to take all the heart out of (s.o.); **ce travail les rebute,** they find the work deadly dull, discouraging; (*b*) **r. un cheval,** to make a horse sullen by overwork. **4.** to shock, disgust (s.o.); **sa vulgarité me rebute,** his vulgarity disgusts me; **sa physionomie me rebute,** I find him unprepossessing; *F:* I can't stand the sight of him.
se rebuter. 1. to become discouraged, disheartened; to lose heart; to give up the attempt; **se r. devant un obstacle, une dépense,** to balk at a difficulty, at an expense. **2.** to feel disgusted; to have a feeling of revulsion.
récabite [rekabit], *s.m.* Rechabite.
recacheter [rəkaʃte], *v.tr.* (*conj. like* CACHETER) to seal (letter) (up) again.
recalage[1] [rəkalaːʒ], *s.m. Mec.E:* retiming.
recalage[2], *s.m. Sch: F:* failure, being ploughed (at an exam.).
recalcifiant [rəkalsifjɑ̃], *s.m.* calcifying agent.
recalcification [rəkalsifikasjɔ̃], *s.f.* recalcification.
recalcifier [rəkalsifje], *v.tr.* to (re)calcify.
récalcitrance [rekalsitrɑ̃ːs], *s.f.* recalcitrance, refractoriness; rebellion (against authority); insubordination.
récalcitrant, -ante [rekalsitrɑ̃, -ɑ̃ːt]. **1.** *a.* recalcitrant, refractory, obstinate, rebellious (person, horse). **2.** *s.* recalcitrant; rebel.
récalcitrer [rekalsitre], *v.i.* to rebel (against authority); *F:* to kick (**contre,** against).
recalcul [rəkalkyl], *s.m.* recalculation, recomputation.
recalculer [rəkalkyle], *v.tr.* to calculate (sth.) again; to recompute; to make a fresh computation of (sth.); to work (sth.) out again.

recalé, -ée [rəkale], *a. & s. Sch: F:* failed (candidate); **les recalés,** the failures.

recaler[1] [rəkale], *v.tr.* **1.** to wedge up (sth.) again; to rechock (sth.). **2.** to reset, readjust (timing gear, etc.). **3.** *Carp:* to shoot, smooth (joint). **4.** *F: A:* to set (s.o.) up again, to put new life into (s.o.); to set (tradesman, etc.) on his feet again.

recaler[2], *v.tr. Sch: F:* to fail, plough (s.o. in an exam.); **être recalé,** to be ploughed, to fail.

récalescence [rekalɛs(s)ɑ̃:s], *s.f. Ph:* recalescence.

recaoutchoutage [rəkautʃuta:ʒ], *s.m.* re-rubbering (of material); retreading (of tyre).

recaoutchouter [rəkautʃute], *v.tr.* to re-rubber (material); to retread (tyre).

récapitulateur, -trice [rekapitylatœ:r, -tris]. **1.** *s.* recapitulator. **2.** *a.* (*of computer*) **perforateur r.,** summary punch.

récapitulatif, -ive [rekapitylatif, -i:v], *a.* recapitulatory, recapitulative; (*of computer*) **carte récapitulative,** summary (-punch) card; **tableau r.,** summary table; **perforatrice récapitulative,** summary punch.

récapitulation [rekapitylasjɔ̃], *s.f.* (*a*) recapitulation; summing up; (*b*) summary, résumé; **faire la r. des témoignages, etc.,** to recapitulate, sum up, the evidence, etc.

récapituler [rekapityle], *v.tr.* to recapitulate; to summarize, to sum up (proceedings); *Sch:* to go quickly through (the work) again, to revise.

recapturer [rəkaptyre], *v.tr.* to recapture.

recarburation [rəkarbyrasjɔ̃], *s.f. Ch: Metall:* recarburization, recarbonization, recementation.

recarburer [rəkarbyre], *v.tr. Ch: Metall:* to recarburize; to recarbonize (steel).

recarder [rəkarde], *v.tr.* to card (wool) over again; to tease out (mattress) again.

recarrelage [rəkarla:ʒ], *s.m.* re-paving; re-tiling.

recarreler [rəkarle], *v.tr.* (*conj. like* CARRELER) to re-pave, re-tile (floor).

recasement [rəkɑzmɑ̃], *s.m.* **1.** rehousing. **2.** resettlement.

recaser [rəkɑze], *v.tr. F:* (*a*) to find another job for (s.o.); (*b*) to rehouse, resettle (s.o.).

recasser [rəkɑse], *v.tr.* to break (sth.) again.

recéder [rəsede], *v.tr.* (*conj. like* CÉDER) **r. qch. à qn,** (i) to let s.o. have sth. back again; (ii) to resell sth. to s.o.; (iii) to sell sth. back to s.o.

recel [rəsɛl], *s.m.,* **recelé** [rəs(ə)le], *s.m.,* **recélé** [rəsele], *s.m.,* **recèlement** [rəsɛlmɑ̃], *s.m. Jur:* **1.** receiving and concealing (of stolen goods); *F:* fencing; *Scot:* resetting. **2.** concealment (of child, of part of estate of deceased person); harbouring (of criminal).

receler [rəsle], *v.tr.* (**je recèle, n. recelons; je recèlerai**); **recéler** [rəsele], *v.tr.* (**je recèle, n. recélons; je recélerai**) *Jur:* **1.** to receive, *Scot:* reset (stolen goods). **2.** (*a*) to conceal (child, part of estate of deceased person); to harbour (criminal); (*b*) **la terre recèle de grands trésors,** the earth conceals great treasures; great treasures lie hidden within the earth; **ville qui recèle beaucoup de curiosités,** town that has many places of interest.

receleur, -euse [rəs(ə)lœ:r, -ø:z], *s. Jur:* receiver (of stolen goods), *F:* fence, *Scot:* resetter.

récemment [resamɑ̃], *adv.* recently, lately, of late.

récence [resɑ̃:s], *s.f. Psy:* recency; **effet de r.,** law of recency.

recensement [rəsɑ̃smɑ̃], *s.m.* (*a*) *Adm:* census; return (of population, of horses, etc.); *Mil:* registration; **faire un r.,** to take a census; **r. des accidents,** recording of accidents; **agent chargé du r.,** recording official; **r. des événements de l'année,** review of the year; (*b*) *Com:* new inventory; checking off (of accounts); (*c*) counting (of votes); **faire le r. des voix,** to count the votes.

recenser [rəsɑ̃se], *v.tr.* (*a*) to take the census of (a town, etc.); to record; *Mil:* to register; (*b*) to check off (goods); (*c*) to count (votes).

recenseur, -euse [rəsɑ̃sœ:r, -ø:z], *s.* (*a*) census taker; enumerator; (*b*) compiler of inventory; (*c*) teller (of votes).

recension [rəsɑ̃sjɔ̃], *s.f.* recension (of text).

récent [resɑ̃], *a.* recent (event, etc.); **la mémoire en est encore récente,** it happened within recent memory; **j'en ai la mémoire récente,** my recollection of it is fresh, distinct; it is fresh in my mind.

recentrer [rəsɑ̃tre], *v.tr. Sp:* to centre, to cross (the ball).

recepage [rəsəpa:ʒ], **recépage** [rəsepa:ʒ], *s.m.* cutting back (of trees, plants, etc.).

recepée [rəsəpe], **recépée** [rəsepe], *s.f.* **1.** clearing (in forest). **2.** (tree) stump.

receper [rəsəpe], **recéper** [rəsepe], *v.tr.* (**je recèpe, n. recepons, n. recépons; je recéperai**) **1.** to cut back (tree, vine stock, leaving only the stump). **2.** to saw (piles) down to level; to raze (wall).

récépissé [resepise], *s.m.* (*a*) (acknowledgement of) receipt; *Bank: Fin:* **r. de dépôt,** deposit receipt; **r. de versement,** receipt for payment, deposit receipt; **r. de souscription (à des actions),** application receipt (for shares); *Com: Cust:* **r. à l'expéditeur, au destinataire,** receipt for the sender, for the consignee (of goods); **r. de douane,** custom-house receipt; **r. d'entrepôt,** warehouse receipt; **r. de transit,** transit bond; **r. warrant,** warrant; **r. postal,** postal receipt; **r. de dépôt d'un télégramme, d'une lettre chargée,** receipt for a telegram, for a registered letter; (*b*) acknowledgement (of complaint, etc.).

réceptacle [resɛptakl̩], *s.m.* **1.** *a.* receptacle; repository, (*b*) *F: A:* nest (of thieves, etc.). **2.** *Hyd.E: etc:* collector (of water, steam, etc.). **3.** *Bot:* (*a*) receptacle, torus; (*b*) *Algae: Fung:* receptacle.

récepteur, -trice [resɛptœ:r, -tris]. **1.** *a.* (*a*) receiving; *Tg: Tp:* **appareil r.,** receiving apparatus; *W.Tel: etc:* **poste r.,** receiving (i) station, (ii) set; **bobine réceptrice,** machine reel (of computer); *Mec.E:* **arbre r.,** driven shaft; (*b*) **milieu r.,** receptive medium, milieu. **2.** *s.m.* (*a*) *Bank:* receiver, recipient (of current account, etc.); (*b*) *Physiol:* receptor (of stimulus); (*c*) *Mec.E: Mch:* driven part (of machine); (*d*) *Hyd.E: etc:* receiver, collector (of overflow water, etc.); **r. de douche,** shower receptor; *Mec.E:* **r. d'huile,** oil saver, save-all; (*e*) *Tp:* **r. (téléphonique),** (telephone) receiver; **décrocher le r.,** to remove, lift, the receiver; **raccrocher le r.,** to replace, hang up, the receiver; *Tg:* **r. (télégraphique),** (telegraph) receiver; **r. Morse,** Morse receiver, tape machine; **r. bélinographique,** facsimile receiver; **r. imprimant, r. à encre,** inker; (*f*) *W.Tel: etc:* **r. radio,** radio set, wireless set; **r. de télévision,** television receiver, set; **r. portatif,** portable receiver; **r. de poche,** mini receiver, mini radio; **r. en diversité,** diversity receiver; **r. en oscillation, r. rayonnant un signal,** blooper; **r. haute fréquence,** radio-frequency receiver; **r. autodyne,** autodyne receiver; **r. hétérodyne,** heterodyne receiver, beat receiver; **r. super-hétérodyne,** superheterodyne receiver; **r. homodyne,** zero-beat receiver; **r. de secours, de sécurité,** emergency receiver; **r. radar,** radar receiver; responder (connected with an interrogator); **r. panoramique,** plan position indicator receiver, P.P.I. receiver; *T.V: etc:* **r. d'images,** picture receiver; (*g*) (*computers*) **r. de cartes,** card stacker (of punched card machine); **r. de données,** data receiver (of computer); **r. de fac-similé,** facsimile receiver; **r. perforateur,** reperforator; receiving perforator; **r. perforateur imprimeur,** printing, *U.S:* printer, perforator; **r. de télémesure,** telemetering receiver; (*h*) *Av:* **r. d'axe de descente,** glide-slope receiver; **r. de navigation,** navigation receiver; **r. de radiobalise,** marker-beacon receiver. **3.** *s.f. El.E:* **réceptrice,** dynamo energized by a generator; dynamo driven as a motor; motor-transmitter (of electric drive).

réceptif, -ive [resɛptif, -i:v], *a.* receptive.

réception [resɛpsjɔ̃], *s.f.* **1.** (*a*) receipt (of letter, order, etc.); **accuser r. de qch.,** to acknowledge receipt of sth.; **avis de r., accusé de r.,** advice of delivery; acknowledgement of receipt; (*b*) *Com:* receipt, reception, receiving, taking delivery (of goods); **à la, dès, r. de votre envoi,** on receipt of your parcel, of the goods forwarded; **dans les dix jours après r.,** within ten days of receipt; **payer à la r.,** to pay on receipt; (*c*) *Ind:* acceptance, taking over (of equipment, machines, etc., from manufacturer); **essais (officiels) de r.,** acceptance test; *Av:* **vol de r.,** acceptance flight; *Mil:* **tir de r.,** acceptance firing; (*d*) *Th:* acceptance (of new play for performance). **2.** (*a*) welcome; **faire une bonne r. à qn,** to welcome s.o. warmly, to give s.o. a good reception; (*b*) reception (of candidate by learned body, etc.); **discours de r. d'un nouvel académicien,** (i) address of welcome to new member of the *Académie*; (ii) answering speech of the new member; (*c*) (official, court) reception; party; **offrir une r. (à qn),** to entertain (s.o.); **salon, salle, de r.,** reception room; *Adm: etc:* **(indemnité pour) frais de r.,** entertainment allowance; *O:* **jour de r.,** at-home day; (*d*) (hotel) reception desk, office; *Com: etc:* enquiry office; **adressez-vous à la r.,** (i) ask at the reception desk; (ii) ask at the enquiry office. **3.** *Tp: Tg: W.Tel: Elcs:* receiving, reception; **appareil, poste, de r.,** receiving set; **intensité, niveau, de r.,** signal strength, reception level; **r. au casque,** headphone reception; *W.Tel:* **r. au son,** aural reception, Morse reception; **r. en haut-parleur,** loudspeaker reception; **r. sur cadre,** loop reception; *Tg:* **r. sur bande,** receiving by tape; *W.Tel: Elcs:* **r. à réaction, r. autodyne,** autodyne reception; **r. en diversité,** diversity reception; **r. multiple,** multiple reception; **r. en direct, r. directe,** direct reception; (*computers*) **r. en case,** pocketing; **case de r.,** stacker.

réceptionnaire [resɛpsjɔnɛ:r], *a. & s.m. & f.* **1.** *Com: Ind:* receiving (agent, clerk); (hotel) receptionist; *Ind:* **ingénieur r.,** acceptance-test engineer; *Av:* **pilote r.,** acceptance-test pilot. **2.** *s.m. Com:* receiver, consignee (of goods, shipment); receiver, last buyer (at produce exchange).

réceptionner [resɛpsjɔne], *v.tr. Com: Ind:* to check and sign for (goods on delivery); to take delivery of (parcel).

réceptionniste [resɛpsjɔnist], *s.m. & f.* receptionist.

réceptivité [resɛptivite], *s.f.* receptivity; *Med:* **en état de r.,** liable to infection.

recerclage [rəsɛrkla:ʒ], *s.m.* re-hooping (of cask).

recercler [rəsɛrkle], *v.tr.* to re-hoop (cask).

recès [rəsɛ], *s.m.* = RECEZ.

récessif, -ive [resesif, -i:v], *a. Biol: Pol.Ec:* recessive.

récession [resɛsjɔ̃], *s.f. Pol.Ec:* recession.

récessivité [resesivite], *s.f. Biol:* recessiveness.

recette [rəsɛt], *s.f.* **1.** receipts, returns; *Th: etc:* takings, *Sp:* gate money; **dépenses et recettes,** expenses and receipts; outgoings and incomings; **la r. est bonne,** (i) the money is coming in well; (ii) the takings are good; (*of play, film, etc.*) **faire r.,** to be a draw, an attraction, a success; **ce film ne fera pas r.,** this film won't have much success. **2.** (*a*) collection (of bills, by bank messenger, etc.); **faire la r. (des traites, etc.),** to collect moneys due; (*b*) receiving; receipt (of stores); *Ind: etc:* acceptance (from contract); taking over (of machine, etc.); checking and signing for (goods); **prendre qch. en r.,** to accept (delivery of) sth.; **essais de r.,** acceptance trials (of ship, etc.); *Artil:* **tir de r.,** acceptance firing test. **3.** *Adm:* (*a*) receivership, collectorship (of rates and taxes, etc.); (*b*) receiver's office, collector's office; **r. des douanes,** receiver's office for the customs. **4.** *Min:* landing, onsetting station; **r. du fond,** bottom landing; **r. du jour,** top landing; bank; **r. à eau,** lodgment. **5.** (*a*) *Cu:* recipe (for dish, etc.); (*b*) *Med: A:* prescription; (*c*) **recettes de métier,** trade dodges; tricks of the trade.

recevabilité [rəsəvabilite], *s.f. Jur:* admissibility (of an appeal, etc.).

recevable [rəsəvabl̩], *a.* **1.** *Jur:* (*a*) admissible (evidence, etc.); receivable, allowable; **excuse non r.,** inadmissible excuse; (*b*) *Com:* **marchandises bonnes et recevables,** goods in sound condition and fit for acceptance. **2.** *Adm:* **être r. à faire qch.,** to be entitled to do sth.; **être r. dans une demande,** to be entitled to proceed with a claim.

receveur, -euse [rəsəvœ:r, -ø:z], *s.* **1.** (*a*) receiver (of sth.); addressee (of telegram, etc.); (*b*) *Med:* (*blood transfusion*) **r. universel,** universal recipient. **2.** (*a*) *Adm:* **r. des Finances,** district collector (of taxes); **r. des contributions directes,** tax collector; **r. des contributions indirectes,** collector of excise; **r. des douanes,** collector of customs; **r., receveuse, des Postes (et Télécommunications),** postmaster, postmistress; **r. buraliste,** tobacconist; **r. de l'enregistrement** = receiver of registry fees and stamp duties; *St.Exch:* **r. de la prime,** taker of the rate; **r. des épaves,** wreck master; (*b*) (bus) conductor, conductress; (*c*) *s.f. Th:* **receveuse,** (seat) attendant, usherette; programme girl. **3.** *Min:* lander, banksman. **4.** *Sp:* (*at baseball*) catcher. **5.** *s.m. Clockm:* **r. mécanique,** fly.

recevoir [rəsəvwa:r], *v.tr.* (*pr.p.* **recevant;** *p.p.* **reçu;** *pr.ind.* **je reçois, il reçoit, n. recevons, ils reçoivent;** *pr.sub.* **je reçoive, n. recevions;** *p.d.* **je recevais;** *p.h.* **je reçus;** *fu.* **je recevrai**) **1.** (*a*) to receive, get (letter, present, etc.); **r. qch. de qn,** to receive sth. from s.o.; **je ne recevais pas encore d'appointements,** I wasn't getting a salary yet; **r. un prix,** to get, win, a prize; **r. un conseil,** to receive, be given, advice; *Ecc:* **r. la communion, l'absolution,** to receive communion, absolution; *Book-k:* **compte, intérêts, à r.,** account, interest, receivable; **nous avons bien reçu votre lettre,** we have received your letter safely; *Com:* we are in receipt of your letter; *Corr:* **recevez, Monsieur, l'assurance de mes sentiments distingués,** yours faithfully; (*b*) to receive (punishment, wound, etc.); to incur (blame); **r. des injures,** to receive, meet with, insults; to be insulted; **la lune reçoit sa lumière du soleil,** the moon gets, receives, its light from the sun. **2.** (*a*) to receive, welcome (s.o.); **r. qn à bras ouverts,** to welcome, receive, s.o. with open arms; **être mal reçu,** to meet with a poor reception; to be made feel unwelcome; (*b*) to entertain (friends, etc.); to receive (clients, etc.); **r. des amis à dîner,** to have friends to dinner; *abs.* **ils reçoivent très peu,** they do not do much entertaining; **elle sait r.,** she knows how to entertain, how to give a good party; **ils se reçoivent beaucoup,** they are always entertaining each other; *F:* they are always in and out of each other's houses; *O:* **elle reçoit le mardi,** Tuesday is her at-home day; **le médecin reçoit à 6 heures,** the doctor's surgery is at 6 o'clock; *Sp:* **équipe qui reçoit,** home side, team; (*b*) to receive, admit; *Sch:* **élèves reçus en première,** pupils admitted, promoted, to the top form; (*in letter to friends, etc.*) **pouvez-vous nous r.?** (i) can you put us up? (ii) can we come and see you? **elle reçoit des pensionnaires,** she takes boarders, lodgers, P.G.'s; (*c*) **être reçu à un examen,** to pass an exam(ination); **être reçu bachelier,** to take, get, one's degree; **être reçu premier,** to be, come out, first, top; **être reçu avocat,** to be called, admitted, to the bar; **être reçu médecin,** to qualify as a doctor; *Nau:* **être reçu capitaine,** to be promoted to captain, to get one's captain's certificate; (*e*) *A: & Lit:* **être reçu à faire qch.,** to be authorized, free, to do sth.; **je ne serais pas reçu à . . .,** I could not presume to . . .; **serait-on reçu de dire que . . .?** would it be permissible to say that . . .? (*f*) to receive, take; **mortaises pour r. des tenons,** mortises to take tenons; **creuset qui reçoit le minerai en fusion,** crucible that receives the molten metal; **fleuve qui reçoit des affluents,** river into which tributaries flow. **3.** *Lit:* to accept, admit (opinion, excuse, etc.); **ne r. jamais aucune chose pour vraie,** never to accept anything as true; **coutumes reçues,** accepted customs.

se recevoir, (*of horse, athlete, etc.*) to land (after jump); **sauteur qui se reçoit sur la jambe droite,** jumper who lands on the right foot.

recez [rəse], *s.m.* **1.** *Hist:* recess, ordinance (of the Imperial Diet, of the Diet of the Hanseatic League). **2.** *Dipl:* minutes (of convention).

réchabite [rekabit], *s.m.* Rechabite.

rechampi(s) [rəʃɑ̃pi], **réchampi(s)** [reʃɑ̃pi], *s.m. Paint:* border of contrasting colour.

rechampir [rəʃɑ̃piːr], **réchampir** [reʃɑ̃piːr], *v.tr. Paint:* to set off (one colour against another); to line (a contour).

rechampissage [rəʃɑ̃pisaːʒ], **réchampissage** [reʃɑ̃pisaːʒ], *s.m. Paint:* setting off (one colour against another); lining (a contour).

rechange[1] [rəʃɑ̃ːʒ], *s.m.* (*a*) replacement; **linge de r., vêtements de r.,** change of linen, of clothes; **r. de vêtements,** spare set of clothes; **matériel de r.,** duplicate, standby, equipment; **trousse de r.,** duplicate set (of tools, etc.); *Mec.E: Aut: etc:* **pièces de r.,** *abs.* **rechanges,** spare parts, spares; **mât de r.,** spare mast; *El:* **pile de r.,** spare battery, refill (for torch); **j'aurai soin de prendre des chaussures de r.,** I shall be careful to take a change of shoes, a spare pair of shoes; (*b*) **solution de r.,** alternative solution; **je n'ai pas envie de prendre le train, mais il n'y a pas de solution de r.,** I don't want to go by train, but there's no alternative, no other solution, nothing else I can do; **le gouvernement s'est assuré une majorité de r.,** the government made sure of a scratch majority.

rechange[2], *s.m. Com:* re-exchange (of a bill); redraft.

rechanger [rəʃɑ̃ʒe], *v.tr.* (*conj. like* CHANGER) to change, to exchange (sth.) again; *Aut:* **il va falloir r. la roue,** we shall have to change the wheel again.

rechanter [rəʃɑ̃te], *v.tr.* to sing again; to repeat.

rechapage [rəʃapaːʒ], *s.m. Aut:* retreading (of tyre).

rechaper [rəʃape], *v.tr.* to retread (tyre); **pneu rechapé,** retread.

réchappé, -ée [reʃape], *s.* survivor (of disaster, wreck, etc.); **r. de potence,** gallow's bird.

réchapper [reʃape]. **1.** *v.i.* (*the aux. is* **avoir** *or* **être**) to escape (de, from); **r. d'un péril, d'une maladie,** to escape from a peril; to recover from, get over, a dangerous illness; **il a réchappé du naufrage,** he was saved from, he survived, the wreck; **il était réchappé de la Grande Guerre,** he had come through the Great War; **il n'en réchappera pas,** it is all up with him. **2.** *v.tr. A:* to rescue, save (s.o.) (**de,** from).

recharge [rəʃarʒ], *s.f.* (*a*) refill (for ball-point pen, etc.); (*b*) recharging, recharge (of battery); **mettre l'accumulateur en r.,** to put the battery on charge.

rechargeable [rəʃarʒabl̩], *a.* (*a*) that takes a refill; (*b*) that can be recharged.

rechargement [rəʃarʒəmɑ̃], *s.m.* **1.** (*a*) recharging (of accumulator); (*b*) reloading (of vehicle); relading (of ship). **2.** *Civ.E:* remetalling (of road); reballasting, consolidation (of railway track).

recharger [rəʃarʒe], *v.tr.* (*conj. like* CHARGER) **1.** (*a*) to recharge (accumulator); (*b*) to reload (lorry, gun, etc.); to relade, reload (ship); to make up (the fire). **2.** to charge (the enemy) again. **3.** *Jur: A:* to recommit (prisoner, on a writ of detainer). **4.** *Civ.E:* to remetal (road); to reballast, consolidate (railway track); to thicken, strengthen (axle, tool, etc.).

rechargeur [rəʃarʒœːr], *s.m. El:* replenisher.

rechasser [rəʃase]. **1.** *v.tr.* to chase out, turn out, expel (s.o.) again. **2.** *v.i.* to go hunting (or shooting) again.

réchaud [reʃo], *s.m.* **1.** (*a*) boiling ring; **r. (avec four),** (small portable) stove; cooker; **r. à pétrole,** oil stove; **r. électrique,** electric boiling plate, ring; **r. à gaz (à un feu),** gas ring; **r. de camping,** camping stove; (*b*) **r. à souder,** soldering-iron heater; (*c*) hot plate; plate warmer; chafing dish. **2.** *Hort:* layer of fresh manure (on hot bed).

réchauffage [reʃofaːʒ], *s.m.* (*a*) reheating; warming up; *F:* dishing up, rehashing (of sth. old as new); (*b*) *Mec.E: Metall: etc:* reheating, reheat process; **dispositif de r.,** reheater; *Mch:* **chaudière à r.,** exhaust-heat boiler; *Metall:* **four de r.,** reheating furnace; *I.C.E:* **r. (préliminaire),** preheating (of mixture); *Elcs:* **filament de r.,** (cathode) heater, heating filament (of electron tube).

réchauffant [reʃofɑ̃], *a. & s.m. Med:* calefacient.

réchauffe [reʃoːf], *s.f. I.C.E:* reheat, afterburning (in jet engine); **injecteur de r.,** afterburner jet.

réchauffé [reʃofe]. **1.** *a.* (*a*) **plat r.,** warmed-up dish; (*b*) **une vieille querelle réchauffée,** an old quarrel that has been stirred up again; **plaisanterie réchauffée,** stale joke. **2.** *s.m.* (*a*) warmed-up dish; **plat qui sent le r.,** food that tastes as though it had been warmed up; (*b*) *Pej:* rehash; stale news, joke; **ça sent le r., c'est du r.,** we've heard that (one) before.

réchauffement [reʃofmɑ̃], *s.m.* **1.** reheating, warming up; **un lent r. de l'atmosphère,** a gradual warming (up) of the atmosphere; **le r. de la température pendant le mois d'avril,** the increase in temperature during April. **2.** *Hort:* layer of fresh manure (on hot bed).

réchauffer [reʃofe], *v.tr.* **1.** to reheat; to warm (sth.) again, to make (sth.) hot again; **(faire) r. le potage,** to warm up the soup; **voilà qui vous réchauffera,** this will warm you up; *Metall:* **four à r. les barres,** bar-heating furnace; *Paint: Dy:* **r. une couleur,** to warm up a colour; *Lit:* **r. un serpent dans son sein,** to nourish a viper in one's bosom; **r. une vieille histoire,** to revive an old story, to dish up an old story. **2. r. le courage, le zèle, de qn,** to rekindle, stir up, s.o.'s courage, zeal; **r. le cœur à qn.,** to comfort s.o., to put new heart into s.o.; **cela me réchauffe le cœur de l'entendre,** it does my heart good to hear him. **3.** *Hort:* **r. une couche,** to put fresh manure on a hot bed.

se réchauffer, to warm oneself (up); **je ne pouvais pas me r.,** I couldn't get warm.

réchauffeur [reʃofœːr], *s.m.* heating, warming, device; *Mec.E: Mch:* (re)heater; *Mch:* **r. à condensation,** condenser heater; **r. d'eau d'alimentation,** feed-water (re)heater; **r. de vapeur,** steam heater; **r. d'huile,** oil heater; **purge de r.,** heater drain; *I.C.E:* **r. d'admission,** pre-heater, intake heater; **r. d'air,** air (re)heater; **r. d'air d'admission,** air-intake heater; **boîte, enveloppe, de r.,** heater barrel; **serpentin r.,** heating coil; *Av:* **r. de cabine,** cabin heater; *Agr:* **r. au pétrole,** oil heater; *Rail:* **r. d'aiguilles,** de-icer (for points).

réchauffoir [reʃofwaːr], *s.m. Dom.Ec:* plate warmer (in stove, radiator).

rechauler [rəʃole], *v.tr.* (*a*) to renew whitewash on (wall); (*b*) to cover up (scandal, etc.).

rechaumage [rəʃomaːʒ], *s.m. Agr:* successive planting (of wheat in the same field).

rechaumer [rəʃome], *v.tr. Agr:* to plant (field with wheat) several years running.

rechaussement [rəʃosmɑ̃], *s.m. Hort:* banking up (foot of tree, etc.).

rechausser [rəʃose], *v.tr.* **1.** (*a*) to put (s.o.'s) shoes or boots on again (for him); (*b*) to fit (s.o.) with new boots; (*c*) **r. une voiture,** to fit a car with new tyres. **2.** (*a*) *Const:* to underpin (structure); (*b*) *Const:* to line the foot of (wall, etc.); (*c*) *Hort:* to bank up the foot of (tree, etc.).

se rechausser, to put one's shoes, one's shoes and stockings, on again.

rechausseuse [rəʃosøːz], *s.f. Hort:* ridge plough, ridger (for banking up the foot of trees).

rêche [rɛʃ], *a.* harsh, rough (surface, wine, humour); (*of pers.*) prickly, difficult (to get on with); **étoffe r.,** fabric rough to the touch.

rechemiser [rəʃ(ə)mize], *v.tr. Mec.E: I.C.E:* to reline (cylinder, boiler).

recherchable [rəʃɛrʃabl̩], *a. Jur:* **délit r.,** punishable offence.

recherche [rəʃɛrʃ], *s.f.* **1.** (*a*) search; pursuit; *Lit:* quest; **la r. de la vérité,** the search for, after, truth; **r. des plaisirs,** pleasure seeking; **r. d'un déserteur,** search for a deserter; *Jur:* **r. de paternité,** affiliation; *Com:* **r. de débouchés,** market research; marketing; *Navy:* **r. et attaque des sous-marins,** search for and attacking of submarines; **être à la r. de qn, de qch.,** to be in search of s.o., sth.; to be looking for, on the lookout for, s.o., sth.; **il est toujours à la r. de son intérêt,** he always has an eye to his own interest(s); **aller, partir, se mettre, à la r. de qn,** to set out, off, in search of s.o.; to go off, set out, to look for s.o.; **j'ai couru à la r. d'un médecin,** I ran for, to find, a doctor; (*in hotel*) **r. de personnes,** paging; **toxicomanes à la r. de leur drogue,** drug addicts in search of their drug; *Min:* **r. de filons,** prospecting; **r. pétrolifère,** oil prospecting; (*skiing*) **position de r. de vitesse,** streamlined position; (*b*) *Sch: etc:* research; **r. scientifique, médicale,** scientific, medical, research; **r. appliquée,** industrial research; **r. expérimentale,** experimental research; *Ind:* **r. et mise au point,** research and development; **centre, service, de r.,** research centre, department; **faire de la r.,** to be a research worker; **maître de r.,** research scientist, scientific research worker (at university); **faire des recherches sur qch.,** (i) to do research on sth.; (ii) to enquire into sth.; **en poursuivant mes recherches je découvris que . . .,** my research led me to discover that . . .; in the course of my research I found, discovered, that . . .; (*c*) *El: Elcs:* **r. de dérangements,** locating of faults; (*computers*) trouble shooting; (*in computer work*) **r. opérationnelle,** operations, operational, research; **r. par chaînage,** chaining research; **r. dichotomique,** dichotomizing, binary, search; **r. documentaire,** information retrieval; (*d*) searching; *Nau:* **droit de r.,** right of search (at sea). **2.** effort, affectation, studied refinement, studied elegance; **mis avec r.,** dressed with studied elegance, with meticulous care; **style sans r.,** straightforward, unaffected, style.

recherché [rəʃɛrʃe], *a.* **1. article (très) r.,** article in great request, in great demand; **article peu r.,** article in limited demand; **personne très recherchée,** person much sought after. **2.** (*a*) choice, elaborate, exquisite (jewels, dress, etc.); **toilette recherchée,** studied elegance of dress; **d'un travail r.,** of exquisite workmanship; **paroles recherchées et choisies,** studied, well-chosen, words; (*b*) *Pej:* strained, affected mannered, laboured (style, expression, etc.); *s.m.* **éviter le r.,** to steer clear, keep clear, of all affectation.

rechercher [rəʃɛrʃe], *v.tr.* (*a*) to search for, search into, inquire into (causes, etc.); *Tp: etc:* **r. un dérangement,** to try to locate a fault; **r. l'auteur d'un crime,** (i) to try to trace, identify, the author of a crime; (ii) to seek out, search for, make a search for, the author of a crime; **homme recherché par la police,** man wanted by the police; *Ch:* **r. un élément dans un composé,** to test for an element in a compound; **r. un nom dans un fichier,** to search through a file for a name; **recherchez le nom du représentant qui est passé la semaine dernière,** look up, find out, the name of the representative who called last week; (*in advertisement*) **société recherche représentants,** firm requires representatives; *Mth:* **r. la valeur de l'inconnue,** to (try to) find the value of the unknown quantity; **r. un mot dans le dictionnaire,** to look up a word in the dictionary; (*b*) **désirer une chose sans vraiment la r.,** to want sth. without going out of one's way to look for it; **je ne recherche pas la complication,** I'm not looking for complications; **r. une femme en mariage,** to seek a woman's hand in marriage; (*c*) **r. l'esprit,** to strive after wit; **il recherchait toujours la conversation d'hommes qui parlaient de leur profession,** he was always eager to talk with men who spoke of their own profession.

rechercheur [rəʃɛrʃœːr], *s.m. O:* researcher; research worker; seeker, inquirer.

rechignant [rəʃiɲɑ̃], *a.* tiresome, disheartening, *F:* off-putting (work, etc.).

rechigné [rəʃiɲe], *a.* sour-tempered, sour-faced, surly, (person); sour (humour, expression, etc.).

rechignement [rəʃiɲ(ə)mɑ̃], *s.m.* **1.** sourness, sullenness. **2. r. devant la besogne,** jibbing at work.

rechigner [rəʃiɲe], *v.i. F:* **1.** to jib; to look sour, sullen (when asked to do sth.); **faire qch. en rechignant, sans r.,** to do sth. with a bad grace, with a good grace; **r. à, devant, la besogne,** to jib, ba(u)lk, boggle, at (i) work, (ii) a job; **r. à faire qch.,** to jib at doing sth.; to boggle, at, about, doing sth. **2.** *Hort: (of plants)* to grow badly; to make a poor show; to be bad doers.

rechigneur, -euse [rəʃiɲœːr, -øːz], **rechigneux, -euse** [rəʃiɲø, -øːz], *s.* grumbler; surly, sour-tempered, person.

rechoir [rəʃwaːr], *v.i. (conj. like* CHOIR) *A: (a)* to fall again; *(b) Med:* to have a relapse.

rechoper [rəʃɔpe], *v.tr. P:* to catch (s.o.) again; to get another smack at (s.o.); **je le rechoperai au tournant,** I'll find a chance of getting even with him.

rechute [rəʃyt], *s.f.* **1.** *Med:* relapse, setback; **faire, avoir, une r.,** to have a relapse. **2. r. dans le péché, dans le vice,** relapse into sin, into vice; backsliding.

rechuter [rəʃyte], *v.i.* **1.** *Med:* to have a relapse, a setback. **2.** to backslide.

récidive [residiːv], *s.f.* **1.** repetition of an offence; backsliding; relapse (into crime). **2.** recurrence (of a disease).

récidiver [residive], *v.i.* **1.** to repeat an offence; to relapse into crime. **2.** *(of disease)* to recur; **la tumeur récidivera,** the tumour will recur, will grow again. **3.** *F:* to do sth. again.

récidiviste [residivist], *s.m. & f.* recidivist, habitual criminal; old, hardened, offender; *F:* old lag; **il est r. de la conduite en état d'ivresse,** he has been convicted before for drunken driving.

récidivité [residivite], *s.f.* **1.** recidivism. **2.** *(of disease)* liability, tendency, to recur.

récif [resif], *s.m.* reef; **r. en barrière,** barrier reef; **r. en bordure, frangeant,** fringing reef; **r. sous-marin,** submerged reef; **r. de fond,** bottom rock; **r. de corail, corallien,** coral reef.

récipé [resipe], *s.m. Med: A:* recipe, prescription.

récipiendaire [resipjɑ̃dɛːr], *s.m. & f.* member elect, new member (of learned body, etc.) *(thus termed esp. on the occasion of his reception).*

récipient [resipjɑ̃], *s.m. (a)* container, vessel, receptacle; (storage) bin; **r. cylindrique,** drum; **r. métallique,** metal container; **r. en tôle,** iron container; **r. à fond de cuivre,** copper-bottomed vessel; *(b) Tchn:* tank; receiver (of air pump, of retort; for gas, condensation water, etc.); *(computers)* bin; *Ind: etc:* **r. à déchets,** waste receiver; **r. à pression,** pressure vessel; **r. d'expansion,** expansion tank, vessel; **r. de mélange,** mixing tank; **r. de stockage,** storage container, bin; **r. de transfert,** transfer container; *Mch:* **r. d'eau chaude,** hot well; *Atom.Ph:* **r. de réacteur,** reactor tank, vessel; **r. compensateur, r. de compensation,** surge tank; *Ch:* **r. à pression,** pressure flask; **r. florentin,** florentine flask, receiver.

réciprocation [resiprɔkasjɔ̃], *s.f. A:* reciprocation.

réciprocité [resiprɔsite], *s.f.* reciprocity (of services, etc.).

réciproque [resiprɔk]. **1.** *a. (a)* reciprocal, mutual (benefits, love, duties, etc.); *(b) Gram: Mth: Log:* reciprocal (verb, pronoun, quantities, terms, etc.); convertible (terms); inverse (ratio); *Geom:* converse (propositions); *Mec:* reversible (motion); **action r.,** mutual interaction; *(c) (computers)* **exclusion r.,** exclusive OR operation, non-equivalence operation; **implication r.,** equivalence. **2.** *s.f. (a)* **rendre la r. à qn,** to pay s.o. back in his own coin; **je vous rendrai la r.,** I'll be even with you; *(b) Log: Geom:* converse; *Mth:* reciprocal.

réciproquement [resiprɔkmɑ̃], *adv.* reciprocally. **1.** mutually; **ils s'aident r.,** they help one another. **2.** conversely; vice-versa.

recirculation [rəsirkylasjɔ̃], *s.f. Ind: Atom.Ph:* recirculation; recycling.

recirculer [rəsirkyle], *v.i. Ind: Atom.Ph: (of fluid, water, etc.)* to recirculate.

récit [resi], *s.m.* **1.** narration, narrative; account; recital, relation (of events); **faire un r. exact de qch.,** to give an exact account of sth.; **il nous fit le r. de ses aventures,** he gave us an account of his adventures; he told us of his adventures. **2.** *Mus: (a)* solo (in a concerted piece); *(b)* swell box (of organ); swell organ; **jeux de r., clavier de r.,** solo organ, swell organ.

récital [resital], *s.m.* (music, organ) recital; **chanteur qui donne un r.,** singer who is giving a recital; **r. poétique,** recital of poetry; *pl. récitals.*

récitant, -ante [resitɑ̃, -ɑ̃ːt], *a. & s. Mus: (a)* solo (voice, instrument) (in concerted piece); *(b) (in oratorio)* narrator.

récitateur, -trice [resitatœːr, -tris], *s.* reciter.

récitatif [resitatif], *s.m. Mus:* recitative.

récitation [resitasjɔ̃], *s.f.* **1.** *(a)* recitation, reciting; *(b) Sch:* **apprendre une r.,** to learn a poem (or prose passage) by heart. **2.** *Mus: A:* singing of a recitative.

réciter [resite], *v.tr.* **1.** *(a)* to recite (poem, etc.); *(b) Sch: A:* **r. les leçons,** to say the lessons; **faire r. les leçons,** to hear the lessons; **faire r. la leçon aux enfants,** to hear the children their lesson. **2.** *A:* to repeat, relate, tell (story, etc.). **3.** *v.i. Mus: A:* to sing a recitative.

réclamant, -ante [reklamɑ̃, -ɑ̃ːt; -kla-], *s. (a)* complainer; *(b) Jur:* claimant.

réclamation [reklamasjɔ̃, -kla-], *s.f.* complaint; objection, protest; claim; *Navy:* request; *Navy:* **cahier de réclamations,** request book; **faire, déposer, une r.,** (i) to make a complaint; to complain; (ii) to make, put forward, a claim; (iii) to lodge a protest; (iv) *Sp:* to lodge, make, an objection; **(bureau, service, des) réclamations,** complaints office, department; **toutes réclamations devront être adressées à . . .,** all complaints to be addressed to . . .; **la mauvaise qualité de cet article a donné lieu à r.,** the poor quality of this product gave cause for complaint, gave rise to complaints; **prouver le bien-fondé d'une r.,** to substantiate a claim; **faire droit à une r.,** to entertain, allow, a claim; **ne pas faire droit à, rejeter, une r.,** to refuse, disallow, a claim; **r. d'indemnité,** claim for compensation; *Rail: Trans:* **r. pour perte, pour avarie, pour retard,** claim for loss, for damage, for delay (in transit); *Jur:* **r. en dommages-intérêts,** claim for damages; *Jur:* **action en r. d'état,** action of legitimate child to claim his status.

réclame [reklaːm, -klam], *s.f.* **1.** *(a)* advertising; **pas d'affaires sans r.. .,** it pays to advertise; **faire de la r.,** to advertise; **faire de la r. pour qn,** to boost s.o.; *Com:* **article (en) r.,** special offer; **vente r.,** bargain sale; *(b)* advertisement; **r. lumineuse,** illuminated sign; **r. à éclipse,** flashing sign; *(c)* **cela ne lui fait pas de r.,** that's no advertisement for him; it; that won't bring him, it, much success. **2.** *(a) A.Typ:* catchword; *(b) Th:* cue.

réclamer [reklame, -kla-]. **1.** *v.i.* to complain, to lodge a complaint; **r. contre qch.,** to protest against sth.; to object to sth.; *Jur:* **r. contre une décision,** to appeal against a decision; **r. auprès de qn,** to lodge a complaint with s.o. **2.** *v.tr. (a)* to lay claim to (sth.), to claim (sth.); **r. son droit** to claim one's right; **dividende non réclamé,** unclaimed dividend; *Turf:* **course à r.,** selling race; *(b)* to claim (sth.) back, to demand (sth.) back **(à,** from); **r. son argent,** to ask for one's money back; **r. de l'argent à qn,** to dun s.o.; *(c)* to crave, beg, for (sth.); **je réclame votre indulgence,** I beg your indulgence; **son âme réclamait une amitié solide,** his soul craved for a true friendship; *(d)* to call for (s.o., sth.); **r. qch., qn, à grands cris,** to call (out) for, to clamour for, sth., s.o.; **le parterre réclama l'auteur,** the pit called for the author; **le peuple réclamait le sang des tyrans,** the people demanded the blood of the tyrants; *(e)* **machine, blessure, qui réclame beaucoup de soins,** machine, wound, that requires much attention; **plante qui réclame des soins continuels,** plant that calls for, demands, requires, continual care; *(f) A:* **r. les saints,** to call upon the saints (for help).

se réclamer de qn, de qch., to appeal to s.o., sth.; to call s.o., sth., to witness; to quote s.o. as one's authority (for a statement); to claim kinship with s.o.; **vous pouvez vous r. de moi,** you may use my name (as a reference).

réclameur, -euse [reklamœːr, -øːz, -kla-], *s.* protester, objector, complainer.

reclamper [rəklɑ̃pe], *v.tr. Nau:* to fish (sprung mast).

reclassement [rəklasmɑ̃], *s.m.* **1.** *(a)* reclassifying; reclassification; regrouping, rearranging; rearrangement; relocation; resequencing; *(b)* regrading (of civil servants, etc.). **2.** *(a)* rehabilitation; *(b)* rehousing.

reclasser [rəklase], *v.tr.* **1.** *(a)* to reclassify; to regroup, rearrange, redistribute; to resequence; *(b)* to regrade (civil servant, etc.). **2.** to rehabilitate.

réclinaison [reklinezɔ̃], *s.f.* **1.** *(a)* angle of inclination from the vertical; *(b) (position of)* plane that inclines from the vertical. **2.** *Surg: A:* reclination (of cataract).

récliné [rekline], *a. Bot:* reclinate.

récliner [rekline]. **1.** *v.i.* to incline from the vertical. **2.** *v.tr.* to tilt (sth.) backwards.

reclouer [rəklue], *v.tr.* to nail (sth.) (up) again.

reclure [rəklyːr], *v.tr. (used only in the infinitive, the p.p.* **reclus,** *and the compound tenses)* to shut up, seclude, sequester, confine (s.o.).

se reclure, to shut oneself up, to seclude oneself.

reclus, -use [rəkly, -yːz]. **1.** *a.* secluded; cloistered; **mener une existence recluse,** to lead a cloistered life, the life of a recluse; **une mère de famille guère moins recluse dans sa maison qu'une religieuse dans son cloître,** a mother almost as confined to her home as a nun in her cloister. **2.** *s. (a) Ecc:* (i) hermit, recluse; *f.* anchoress; (ii) cloistered monk, nun; *(b)* recluse; **il ne sort plus, il vit en r.,** he no longer goes out, he lives the life of a recluse.

reclusion [rəklyzjɔ̃], **réclusion** [reklyzjɔ̃], *s.f.* **1.** reclusion, seclusion, retirement. **2.** *Jur:* **r. criminelle** = hard labour; **r. à perpétuité,** life sentence.

reclusionnaire [rəklyzjɔnɛːr], **réclusionnaire** [reklyzjɔnɛːr], *s.m. & f. Jur:* = person condemned to a sentence of hard labour; convict.

reco [rəko], *s.f. Mil: F:* recce.

récognitif, -ive [rekɔgnitif, -iːv], *a.* recognitory, recognitive; *Jur:* **acte r. et conformatif,** act of ratification and acknowledgement.

récognition [rekɔgnisjɔ̃], *s.f. Phil:* recognition, identification.

recoiffer [rəkwafe], *v.tr.* **1. r. qn,** to do, comb, s.o.'s hair again; **se r. avant de sortir,** to comb one's hair before going out. **2. se r.,** to put on one's hat again; **il salua Madame X et se recoiffa,** he greeted Mrs X and put on his hat again. **3. r. une bouteille,** to put the cap back on a bottle.

recoin [rəkwɛ̃], *s.m.* nook, recess; **coins et recoins,** nooks and corners.

récolement [rekɔlmɑ̃], *s.m. Jur: (a)* verification; checking (of inventory, etc.); *(b) A:* **r. des dépositions,** reading of the depositions (to witnesses).

récoler [rekɔle], *v.tr. Jur: (a)* to verify, check, re-examine (accounts, etc.); to check (inventory, etc.); *(b) A:* **r. les témoins,** to read over their depositions to witnesses.

recollage [rəkɔlaːʒ], *s.m.* gluing up (again), sticking together (again) (of broken object).

récollection [rekɔlɛksjɔ̃], *s.f. Theol:* recollection (in God).

recollement [rəkɔlmɑ̃], *s.m.* **1.** gluing together again; sticking up again. **2.** setting (of broken bone).

recoller [rəkɔle]. **1.** *v.tr. (a)* to paste, glue (sth.) together again; to repaste, restick; *(b) Sch: F:* to plough, fail (s.o.) again. **2.** *v.i. P:* **ça recolle maintenant,** they've made it up again, they are friends once more.

se recoller, *(of broken bone)* to knit; *(of wound)* to heal; *P:* **ils se sont recollés,** they are living together again.

récollet, -ette [rekɔlɛ, -ɛt], *s. Rel.H:* Recollect (friar or nun).

récoltable [rekɔltabl̩], *a.* ready for harvesting, for picking; **fruits récoltables en août,** fruit ready for picking in August.

récoltant, -ante [rekɔltɑ̃, -ɑ̃ːt], *a. & s.* **(propriétaire) r.,** farmer who harvests his own crops, who farms his own land.

récolte [rekɔlt], *s.f.* **1.** *(a)* harvesting (of grain); vintaging (of grapes); **faire une r.,** to produce a crop; **faire la r. du blé, des foins,** to harvest the wheat, the hay; *(b)* collecting, gathering (of documents, etc.). **2.** *(a)* harvest, crop(s); vintage; **r. sur pied,** standing crop; **rentrer la r.,** to get in, gather in, the harvest, the crops; **il nous faut attendre la nouvelle r.,** we must wait for the new crop, for this year's harvest; **r. améliorante,** crop that enriches the soil; **r. dérobée,** catch crop; *(b) Gold Min: etc:* winnings; *(c)* collection (of documents, objects, etc.).

récolter [rekɔlte], *v.tr.* **1.** to harvest (wheat, etc.); **r. le raisin,** to pick, harvest, the grapes; **ces fraises se récoltent en juin,** these strawberries are ready for picking in June; *Prov:* **qui sème le vent récolte la tempête,** he who sows the wind shall reap the whirlwind. **2.** to collect, gather (documents, anecdotes, etc.); **je n'en ai récolté que des coups et des injures,** all I got out of it was blows and insults; **le profit de l'effort ne se récolte pas au moment même,** hard work does not (always) give immediate results.

recommandable [rəkɔmɑ̃dabl̥], *a.* **1.** (*a*) (*of qualities, etc.*) to be commended, worthy of commendation; (*of pers.*) estimable, commendable; **peu r.,** undesirable; (*b*) (*of hotel, etc.*) to be recommended, recommendable; **hôtel peu r.,** not a good hotel; a poor hotel. **2.** advisable, recommendable; **il serait r. de . . .,** it would be well, advisable, to . . ..

recommandataire [rəkɔmɑ̃datɛːr], *s.m. Com:* (*on bill of exchange*) referee in case of need.

recommandatif, -ive [rəkɔmɑ̃datif, -iːv], *a.* recommendatory; **lettre recommandative,** letter of recommendation, of introduction.

recommandation [rəkɔmɑ̃dasjɔ̃], *s.f.* **1.** recommendation, recommending (of s.o., of hotel, etc.); **je viens sur la r. d'un de vos clients,** I have come on the recommendation of one of your customers; **(lettre de) r.,** (i) letter of recommendation, of introduction; (ii) testimonial; *A:* **avoir qn en grande r.,** to hold s.o. in high esteem. **2.** recommendation, injunction, advice; **suivre les recommandations de qn,** to follow s.o.'s instructions, s.o.'s advice. **3.** registration (of letter or parcel). **4.** *Jur: A:* (writ of) detainer.

recommandatoire [rəkɔmɑ̃datwaːr], *a.* recommendatory; (letter) of recommendation.

recommandé [rəkɔmɑ̃de], *a.* **1.** (*a*) recommended (hotel, product, etc.); *Tchn:* approved, preferred (product, etc.); **lubrifiant r.,** approved lubricant; **modèle de foret r.,** preferred-type drill; (*b*) *F:* **ce n'est pas très r.,** it's not a good thing (to do); I shouldn't do it if I were you. **2.** *Post:* registered; *s.m.* **envoi en r.,** *F:* **un r.,** registered letter, parcel; **les recommandés,** the registered mail.

recommander [rəkɔmɑ̃de], *v.tr.* **1.** (*a*) **r. qn à un employeur éventuel,** to recommend s.o. to a prospective employer; **r. un hôtel,** to recommend an hotel; **cet hôtel se recommande par sa cuisine,** this hotel is to be recommended for its cooking; (*b*) **r. son âme à Dieu,** to commend one's soul to God; (*c*) **r. qch. à l'attention de qn,** to call s.o.'s attention to sth.; (*d*) **une personne que sa fortune et son nom recommandent autant que son talent,** s.o. who merits consideration on account of his name and fortune as much as for his talent. **2. r. la prudence à qn,** to advise s.o. to be prudent, careful; **je vous recommande de . . .,** I strongly advise you to . . .; **je vous recommande la discrétion,** I must beg you to be discreet. **3.** to register (letter, parcel). **4.** *Jur: A:* to lodge a detainer against (s.o.).

se recommander. 1. se r. à qn, to beg s.o.'s help, s.o.'s protection; **se r. à Dieu,** to commend oneself to God. **2. se r. de qn,** to refer to s.o.; to give s.o. as a reference; **écrire en se recommandant de qn,** to write mentioning s.o.'s name; **il se recommande de lui-même,** he is, carries with him, his own recommendation. **3. se r. de qch.,** to be known, remarkable, to merit consideration, for sth.

recommencement [rəkɔmɑ̃smɑ̃], *s.m.* beginning again, restarting; **au moment du r. des hostilités,** when hostilities were renewed; **l'histoire est un perpétuel r.,** history is always repeating itself; history is a series of beginnings.

recommencer [rəkɔmɑ̃se], *v.* (**je recommençai(s); n. recommençons**) **1.** *v.tr.* to begin, start, (sth.) (over) again; **r. sa vie,** to start life afresh, to make a fresh start in life; **les autorités devront faire r. l'examen,** the authorities will have to set fresh examination papers; **r. à** (*occ.* **de**) **faire qch.,** to begin to do, to begin doing, sth. again; **c'est toujours à r.,** there's no end to it; **tout est à r.,** we shall have to start all over again. **2.** *v.i.* (*a*) to do it again; to begin again; to start afresh; **je vous pardonne, mais ne recommencez pas!** I forgive you, but don't do it again! **le voilà qui recommence!** he's doing it again! he's at it again! **r. de plus belle, sur nouveaux frais,** to begin again with fresh vigour; to begin again more vigorously, harder, worse, than ever; (*b*) (*of bad weather, etc.*) to begin again, to start again; (*of war, epidemic*) to break out again.

recomparaître [rəkɔ̃parɛtr̥], *v.i.* (*conj. like* COMPARAÎTRE) *Jur:* to appear again (before the court).

récompense [rekɔ̃pɑ̃ːs], *s.f.* **1.** (*a*) recompense, reward; **mille francs de r.,** a thousand francs reward; **en r., pour r., de vos services,** as a reward for your services; in return for your services; **ce revers de fortune fut la juste r. de ses crimes,** this reverse of fortune was a just retribution for his crimes; (*b*) (*at prize show, etc.*) **distribution des récompenses,** giving out of the awards, of the prizes; awarding of the prizes. **2.** *A:* compensation, amends.

récompenser [rekɔ̃pɑ̃se], *v.tr.* **1.** to reward, recompense (person, action); **r. les services de qn,** to give s.o. sth. in return for his services; **r. qn de qch.,** to reward s.o. for sth.; **l'honnêteté est toujours récompensée,** honesty always pays. **2.** *A:* to compensate, to make amends for (neglect, etc.).

recomplètement [rəkɔ̃plɛtmɑ̃], *s.m. Mil:* **dépôt de r.,** replacement depot.

recomposer [rəkɔ̃poze], *v.tr.* **1.** (*a*) *Ch:* to recompose, recombine (elements); (*b*) to re-knit, reunite (family). **2.** (*a*) *Typ:* to reset (matter); (*b*) *Lit:* to re-write.

recomposition [rəkɔ̃pozisjɔ̃], *s.f.* **1.** *Ch: etc:* recombining. **2.** *Typ:* resetting.

recomptage [rəkɔ̃taːʒ], *s.m.* recount.

recompter [rəkɔ̃te], *v.tr.* to recount, to count again.

réconciliable [rekɔ̃siljabl̥], *a.* reconcilable (persons, evidence).

réconciliateur, -trice [rekɔ̃siljatœːr, -tris], *s.* reconciler.

réconciliation [rekɔ̃siljasjɔ̃], *s.f.* (*a*) reconciliation; **amener une r. entre deux personnes,** to bring about a reconciliation, to heal the breach, between two people; *Jur:* **r. des époux,** condonation of matrimonial infidelity; (*b*) *R.C.Ch:* reconciliation; **r. d'une église profanée,** reconsecration of secularized church.

réconcilier [rekɔ̃silje], *v.tr.* (*pr.sub. & p.d.* **n. réconciliions, v. réconciliiez**) (*a*) to reconcile (persons, inconsistencies); to make it up between (persons); to bring (persons) together again; **les voilà réconciliés,** now they are friends again; **se r. avec Dieu,** to make one's peace with God; (*b*) *R.C.Ch:* to reconcile (heretic, etc.).

reconditionnement [rəkɔ̃disjɔnmɑ̃], *s.m.* reconditioning.

reconditionner [rəkɔ̃disjɔne], *v.tr. Com:* to recondition.

reconduction [rəkɔ̃dyksjɔ̃], **réconduction** [rekɔ̃dyksjɔ̃], *s.f.* (*a*) *Jur:* renewal (of lease); **tacite r.,** renewal by tacit agreement; (*b*) **r. d'une politique,** continuation of a policy.

reconduire [rəkɔ̃dɥiːr], *v.tr.* (*conj. like* CONDUIRE) (*a*) to see, escort, drive, (s.o.) home; to accompany, take, bring, (s.o.) back (to a place); **je l'ai reconduit chez lui,** I took him home; **je vais vous r. jusqu'à la gare,** I'll see you, drive you, to the station; **r. qn à la frontière,** to expel (an alien); **r. l'ennemi l'épée dans les reins,** to drive the enemy back helter-skelter; (*b*) to see, show, (s.o.) out; to accompany (s.o.) to the door; **Baptiste, reconduisez madame,** Baptiste, show Mrs X out; (*c*) *Jur:* to renew (lease, etc.); *Adm:* **r. des mesures temporaires de sécurité,** to extend short-term safety measures.

reconduite [rəkɔ̃dɥit], *s.f.* (*a*) seeing (of s.o.) home; accompanying, escorting, bringing, taking, (of s.o.) back (to a place); (*b*) showing out (of s.o.); showing (of s.o.) to the door.

réconfort [rekɔ̃fɔːr], *s.m.* (*a*) comfort, consolation; **quelques paroles de r.,** a few comforting words; a few words of comfort; (*b*) stimulant; *F:* **une petite goutte de r.,** a little drop of sth. to cheer you up.

réconfortant [rekɔ̃fɔrtɑ̃]. **1.** *a.* (*a*) strengthening, stimulating; tonic (medicine); **aliment sain et r.,** wholesome food; (*b*) comforting, cheering (words, letter, etc.). **2.** *s.m.* tonic, stimulant.

réconforter [rekɔ̃fɔrte], *v.tr.* **1.** to strengthen, fortify, refresh (s.o.); to act as a tonic to (s.o.); **il est l'heure de se r.,** it's time to take a little refreshment. **2.** to comfort; to cheer (s.o.) up.

reconnaissable [rəkɔnɛsabl̥], *a.* recognizable (**à,** by, from, through); **il n'est plus r.,** you wouldn't know him again; he has altered past recognition; **il est facilement r. à sa balafre,** he is easily recognized by his scar.

reconnaissance [rəkɔnɛsɑ̃ːs], *s.f.* **1.** recognition (of s.o., of sth.); **il m'adressa un sourire de r.,** he gave me a smile of recognition; *Mil: etc:* **signal de r.,** recognition signal. **2.** (*a*) acknowledgement (of promise, debt); recognition (of government); **r. d'une faute,** avowal, admission, of a lapse; (*b*) *Com:* note of hand; *Jur:* acknowledgement of indebtedness (in writing); *Com:* **donner une r. à qn,** to give s.o. an i.o.u.; **r. de mont-de-piété,** pawn ticket; (*c*) *Jur:* **r. d'un enfant naturel,** affiliation of an illegitimate child; (*d*) (*computers*) **r. de caractères, de formes,** character, pattern, recognition. **3.** *Mil: etc:* reconnaissance, reconnoitring; *F:* recce; *Mil:* **r. terrestre, r. du terrain,** ground reconnaissance; **r. d'une position,** reconnaissance of a position; **r. en force,** reconnaissance in force; **r. par le feu,** reconnaissance by fire; **détachement, élément, de r.,** reconnaissance or reconnoitring detachment, element, party; **véhicule de r.,** reconnaissance car; **r. stratégique, tactique,** strategical, tactical, reconnaissance; **r. rapprochée, à courte distance,** close reconnaissance; **r. à grande distance, r. lointaine, r. en profondeur,** distant, long-range, reconnaissance; **r. à vue, r. optique,** reconnaissance by sight, visual reconnaissance; **r. optique de nuit,** night visual reconnaissance; **r. électronique, r. radar,** electronic, radar, reconnaissance; **(être) en r.,** (to be) reconnoitring, on a reconnaissance; **effectuer, faire, une r.,** to make reconnaissance, to do reconnaissance work, to reconnoitre; **envoyer (qn, une unité) en r.,** to send (s.o., a unit) on a reconnaissance; *Av:* **appareil, aviation, de r.,** reconnaissance aircraft, aviation; *abs.* **la r.,** reconnaissance aviation; **r. aérienne,** air, aerial, reconnaissance; **patrouille de r.,** reconnaissance patrol; **sortie, vol, de r.,** reconnaissance sortie, flight; **r. photo(graphique),** photo(graphic) reconnaissance; **bande (mosaïque) de r. (photographique),** reconnaissance (photographic) strip; (*b*) *Civ.E: Mil: etc:* inspection, exploration, examination; *Min:* prospecting; **r. du terrain,** exploration, exploring, proving, of the ground; **r. des terrains en profondeur,** exploration of the subsoil; **r. sur le terrain,** going over the ground; **r. préalable des lieux, de l'emplacement,** preliminary exploration, inspection, of the place, of the site; *Min:* **r. d'un gisement,** proving of a deposit; **r. géophysique,** geophysical prospecting; *Mil:* **il sera procédé à une r. de la frontière,** the frontier will be inspected; (*c*) *Surv:* reconnaissance, surveying, charting; **levé de r.,** (i) exploratory survey; (ii) reconnaissance sketch, map; **r. du littoral,** charting of the coast. **4.** (*a*) gratitude, gratefulness; **témoigner de la r. à qn,** to show gratitude to s.o.; **pour témoigner ma, sa, r. de ce service,** in acknowledgement of my, his, gratitude for this service; **il m'adressa un sourire de r.,** he gave me a grateful smile; **avec r.,** gratefully; **je lui en avais beaucoup de r.,** I was most grateful to him for it; *F:* **il n'a même pas la r. du ventre,** he isn't even grateful for his board and lodging; (*b*) **r. de, pour, la bonté de Dieu,** thankfulness for the kindness of God; **avec r.,** thankfully.

reconnaissant [rəkɔnɛsɑ̃], *a.* (*a*) grateful (**envers,** to; **de,** for); **être r. à qn de qch.,** to be grateful to s.o. for sth.; **je vous suis r. de m'avoir prévenu,** I am grateful to you for having given me a warning; (*b*) thankful (**de,** for).

reconnaître [rəkɔnɛtr̥], *v.tr.* (*conj. like* CONNAÎTRE) **1.** (*a*) to recognize; to know (s.o., sth.) again; **se r.,** (i) to collect oneself, pull oneself together; (ii) to get one's bearings; **donnez-moi le temps de m'y r.,** give me time to take it in; **c'est à ne pas s'y r.,** it's all very confusing; **je ne m'y reconnais plus,** I'm all at sea; I've lost my bearings; *Nau:* **r. la terre,** to sight land, to make land; *Nau:* **r. un feu,** to make (out) a light; **r. un navire, un avion,** to identify a ship, an aircraft; **r. un corps à la morgue,** to identify a body in the mortuary; **r. qn à sa démarche, à sa voix,** to recognize, know, tell, s.o. by his walk, by his voice; **il fut reconnu de l'agent, des voyageurs,** he was recognized by the policeman, by the travellers; **se r. dans ses enfants,** to recognize oneself, see oneself, in one's children; **ils se reconnurent tout de suite frères d'armes,** they recognized each other at once as brothers in arms; **comment m'avez-vous reconnu comme Américain,** how did you know I was, spot me as, an American? **gaz qui se reconnaît à son odeur,** gas recognizable by its smell; **on reconnaît là la main de l'homme,** one can see the hand of man in it; **je vous reconnais bien là!** that's just like you! that's you all over! **je le reconnaîtrais à des kilomètres, entre mille,** I'd know him from miles away, anywhere; (*b*) to distinguish (one thing from another); **ils se ressemblent tant qu'on ne peut les r.,** they are so alike that one cannot tell them apart; **jumeaux impossibles à r.,** identical twins; (*c*) (*computers*) to identify. **2.** (*a*) to recognize, acknowledge (truth, right, government, etc.); to acknowledge, admit (mistake); *Bank:* to credit; **r. l'indépendance d'un pays,** to recognize the independence of a country; **r. qn pour maître, pour chef,** to acknowledge s.o. as one's master, as one's leader; **faire r. qn pour chef,** to proclaim s.o. leader; **c'est le chef reconnu de la rébellion,** he is the acknowledged leader of the rebellion; **r. qch. pour vrai,** to acknowledge sth. to be true, to admit the truth of sth.; **reconnu pour, comme, incorrect,** admittedly incorrect; **on lui reconnaît du génie,** he is an acknowledged genius; **il a raison, reconnaissons-le,** he's right, let us admit it; we must admit that he's right; **se r. coupable,** to acknowledge, admit, one's guilt; **il fut reconnu coupable,** he was found (to be) guilty; **un voleur reconnu comme tel,** an admitted thief; *Mil: etc:* **être reconnu apte,** to be passed fit; **r. à qn un droit,** to acknowledge s.o.'s right to sth.; **r. qu'on s'est trompé, r. de s'être trompé,** to admit, own, that one was mistaken, to admit to being mistaken; (*b*) *Jur:* **r. un enfant,** to acknowledge a child; **r. qn pour son héritier,** to name s.o. as one's heir, one's beneficiary; **r. sa signature,** to acknowledge one's signature. **3.** (*a*) *Mil:* to reconnoitre, make a reconnaissance of (a position, an area, etc.); to explore (the ground); **r. le contour apparent du dispositif ennemi,** to find out the outline of the enemy layout; (*b*) *Civ.E: Mil: etc:* to explore, inspect; *Min:* to prospect; to prove (the nature of the ground, a mineral deposit, etc.); **r. les lieux,** to examine, inspect, the place; *Min:* **r. l'emplacement d'un filon,** to locate a vein; *Rail:* **r. l'état des lignes,** to find out the state, the condition, of the lines; (*c*) *Surv:* **non reconnu,** unsurveyed. **4.** *Mil:* to challenge (patrol, etc.); **se faire r. par une sentinelle,** to give an account of oneself (to a sentry). **5. r. une faveur, etc.,** to be grateful for a favour, etc.; **je voudrais r. vos services,** I should like to make some return for, to do sth. in return for, your services.

reconquérir [rəkɔ̃keriːr], *v.tr.* (*conj. like* CONQUÉRIR) to regain, recover, reconquer (province); to regain (s.o.'s esteem); **r. une province sur l'ennemi,** to reconquer, to win back, a province from the enemy; **r. sa dignité, sa liberté,** to recover one's dignity, one's liberty.

reconquête [rəkɔ̃kɛt], *s.f.* reconquest.

reconsidération [rəkɔ̃siderasjɔ̃], *s.f.* reconsideration.

reconsidérer [rəkɔ̃sidere], *v.tr.* (*conj. like* CONSIDÉRER) to reconsider.

reconsolidation [rəkɔ̃sɔlidasjɔ̃], *s.f.* reconsolidation.

reconsolider [rəkɔ̃sɔlide], *v.tr.* to reconsolidate.

reconstituant [rəkɔ̃stitɥɑ̃], *a.* & *s.m. Med:* reconstituent, restorative, tonic.

reconstituer [rəkɔ̃stitɥe], *v.tr.* (*a*) to reconstitute; to reconstruct (a crime); to restore (badly damaged building, etc.); to recreate, reconstruct (destroyed computer file, etc.); to replenish (one's stock); (*b*) to restore (s.o.'s health).

reconstitution [rəkɔ̃stitysjɔ̃], *s.f.* reconstitution, reconstruction (of a government, company, etc.); restoration (of badly damaged building, etc.); re-creation, reconstruction (of computer file, etc.); **r. d'un crime,** reconstruction of a crime.

reconstruction [rəkɔ̃stryksjɔ̃], *s.f.* reconstruction, rebuilding; *Adm:* **r. des régions occupées,** rehabilitation of occupied territories.

reconstruire [rəkɔ̃strɥiːr], *v.tr.* (*conj. like* CONSTRUIRE) to reconstruct, rebuild.

reconter [rəkɔ̃te], *v.tr.* to relate, tell, (sth.) (over) again.

reconvention [rəkɔ̃vɑ̃sjɔ̃], *s.f. Jur:* counter claim; cross action.

reconventionnel, -elle [rəkɔ̃vɑ̃sjɔnɛl], *a. Jur:* **demande reconventionnelle,** counter claim.

reconventionnellement [rəkɔ̃vɑ̃sjɔnɛlmɑ̃], *adv. Jur:* as a cross action, as a counter claim.

reconversion [rəkɔ̃vɛrsjɔ̃], *s.f. Pol.Ec:* (*a*) reconversion; **r. d'une fabrique de chars en usine d'automobiles,** conversion of a tank factory for the manufacture of cars; **r. technique,** adaptation to new (economic) techniques; (*b*) redeployment (of workers).

reconvertir [rəkɔ̃vɛrtiːr], *v.tr. Pol.Ec:* (*a*) to reconvert; **r. l'industrie de guerre,** to turn over war factories to peacetime production; (*b*) **se r.,** to change one's type of employment, to reorientate one's activities; **elle peut se r. dans le journalisme,** she can turn over to journalism.

reconvoquer [rəkɔ̃vɔke], *v.tr.* **1.** to convoke again; to call (an assembly, etc.) together again; to re-summon (an assembly, etc.). **2.** *Adm:* to invite (s.o.) to another interview.

recopier [rəkɔpje], *v.tr.* (*conj. like* COPIER) (*a*) to recopy; to copy (sth.) (over) again; to take another copy of (sth.); (*b*) (*of author*) to revise (part of work already written); (*c*) (*computers*) to transcribe.

recoquillement [rəkɔkijmɑ̃], *s.m.* (*a*) curling up, cockling, shrivelling; (*b*) dog-earing (of pages).

recoquiller [rəkɔkije], *v.tr.* (*a*) to curl (sth.) up; to cockle, shrivel (sth.); (*b*) **pages recoquillées,** dog-eared pages.

se recoquiller, to curl up, cockle, shrivel.

record [rəkɔːr]. **1.** *s.m. Sp: etc:* record; **battre le r.,** to break, beat, the record; **détenir le r.,** to hold the record; **r. mondial, du monde, de distance,** world distance record; **pour la maladresse, il bat tous les records,** he beats all the records as far as clumsiness is concerned. **2.** *attrib.* (*a*) *Sp: etc:* **vitesse r.,** record speed; **dans, en, un temps r.,** in record time; **dans un, le, temps r. de . . .,** in a, the, record time of . . .; **attirer une affluence r.,** (i) (*of event*) to draw record crowds; (ii) (*of play, etc.*) to attract (a) record audience(s); (*b*) *Pol.Ec: etc:* record production; maximum, peak (output, etc.); **chiffre r.,** record figure; **chiffre r. d'accidents,** highest accident figure to date.

recorder[1] [rəkɔrde], *v.tr. A:* (*a*) *Th:* **r. un rôle,** to con a part; to go over a part; *Sch:* **r. sa leçon,** to go over one's lesson; (*b*) **r. les acteurs,** to run the actors through their parts; (*c*) *F:* **r. sa leçon à qn,** to put a person up to what he has to say.

se recorder, *A:* to run over, go through, one's part; *F:* **laissez-moi me r.,** give me time to think (and remember).

recorder[2], *v.tr.* **1.** to rope up (bale) again; to retie (packet). **2.** to measure (bundle of firewood). **3.** to twist (the strands of a rope) again. **4.** to restring (racket).

recordman [rəkɔr(d)man], *s.m.* record holder; *pl. recordmen.*

recordwoman [rəkɔr(d)woman], *s.f.* woman record holder; *pl. recordwomen.*

recorriger [rəkɔriʒe], *v.tr.* (*conj. like* CORRIGER) to correct (sth.) again; to revise.

recors [rəkɔːr], *s.m. Jur: A:* (*a*) process-server's assistant; *F:* bailiff's man; (*b*) **les r. de la justice,** the minions of the law.

recoucher [rəkuʃe]. **1.** *v.tr.* (*a*) to put (s.o.) to bed again; (*b*) to lay (person, object) down again. **2.** *v.i.* to put up again (at hotel); to sleep again (in same bed).

se recoucher, (*a*) to go to bed again; to go back to bed; to get back into bed; (*b*) **se r. par terre,** to lie down (on the ground) again.

recoudre [rəkudr̥], *v.tr.* (*conj. like* COUDRE) (*a*) to sew (a seam) again; to sew (garment) up again; to sew (button) on again; **r. une déchirure à gros points,** to run up a tear; (*b*) to link (memories, impressions).

recouler [rəkule], *v.tr. Mec.E:* to run up; **r. le métal aux coussinets,** to run up patent metal in the brasses.

recoupage [rəkupaːʒ], *s.m.* **1.** RECOUPEMENT. **2.** (re)blending (of wines).

recoupe [rəkup], *s.f.* **1.** (*a*) *Mill:* second flour; sharps, middlings; (*b*) chips (of stone); (*c*) chippings, cuttings (of metal, etc.); (*d*) scraps, fragments (from the table). **2.** *Agr:* (= REGAIN) aftermath, second crop. **3.** raw spirit diluted to standard strength. **4.** *Min:* cross drive; drift.

recoupé [rəkupe], *a.* (*a*) *Const:* stepped (foot of wall, embankment, etc.); battered (embankment); (*b*) *Her:* party per fess.

recoupement [rəkupmɑ̃], *s.m.* **1.** (*a*) stepping (of embankment, of foot of wall); (*b*) batter (of stepped wall). **2.** (*a*) *Surv:* resection; **méthode du r.,** resection method; (*b*) *Mil: Journ:* cross-checking (of information); **moyens de r.,** cross checks; **effectuer, faire, des recoupements,** to cross-check.

recouper [rəkupe], *v.tr.* **1.** (*a*) to cut (sth.) again; (*b*) to cut again (at cards); (*c*) *Const:* to step (wall, embankment, etc.). **2.** to (re)blend (wines, etc.). **3.** to confirm, support; to cross check; **les deux témoignages se recoupent,** the two statements support one another. **4.** to overlap; **deux champs d'action qui se recoupent,** two fields of action which overlap.

recoupette [rəkupɛt], *s.f. Mill:* third flour.

recouponnement [rəkupɔnmɑ̃], *s.m. Fin:* renewal of coupons.

recouponner [rəkupɔne], *v.tr. Fin:* to renew the coupons of (share certificate).

recourbé [rəkurbe], *a.* bent, curved; bent back; reflexed; **poignée recourbée,** crooked handle, crook handle; **races de bétail à cornes recourbées,** crumpled-horn breeds of cattle; *Orn:* **bec r.,** recurved bill.

recourbement [rəkurbəmɑ̃], *s.m.* bending.

recourber [rəkurbe], *v.tr.* **1.** to bend (sth.) again. **2.** to bend (down, back, round).

recourbure [rəkurbyːr], *s.f.* bend, curve; curvature; **la r. des cornes d'un chamois,** the curved shape of a chamois' horns.

recourir [rəkuriːr], *v.i.* (*conj. like* COURIR) **1.** (*a*) to run again; *v.tr.* **r. un cerf,** to hunt a stag for the second time; (*b*) **r. jusque chez soi,** to run back home (for sth.). **2.** (*a*) **r. à qn, à l'aide de qn,** to call in s.o. for help; to have recourse to s.o., to apply to s.o., to turn to s.o.; to resort to (moneylender); **r. à qch.,** to have recourse to sth.; to resort to (measures, stratagem, etc.); **r. à la justice,** to take legal proceedings; **r. à la violence,** to resort to violence; to have recourse to violence; **r. aux armes,** to appeal to arms; **r. aux services de qn,** to requisition s.o.'s services; to call on s.o.'s services; (*b*) *Jur:* **r. en grâce,** to petition for mercy.

recours [rəkuːr], *s.m.* (*a*) recourse, resort, resource; **r. à l'arbitrage,** appeal to arbitration; **en dernier r.,** as a last resort; **mon seul r. est la soumission complète,** complete submission is my sole resource; **Dieu est mon r.,** God is my refuge; **avoir r. à qn, à qch.,** to have recourse to s.o., to sth.; to call on s.o. for help; *Jur: Com:* **se réserver le r.,** to reserve the right of recourse; (*b*) *Jur:* **r. en cassation,** appeal; **r. en grâce,** appeal for mercy, petition for reprieve; **les condamnés ont été informés du rejet de leur r. en grâce,** the condemned men have been informed of the rejection of their appeal; **avoir un r. sur un chargement, etc.,** to have a lien upon a cargo, etc.; **n'avoir aucun r. contre qn,** (i) to have no claim whatever on s.o.; (ii) to have no remedy at law; **r. contre des tiers,** recourse against third parties; *Ins:* **s'assurer contre le r. des tiers,** to insure against a third party claim.

recousu [rəkuzy], *a.* re-sewn, sewn up again.

recouvrable [rəkuvrabl̥], *a.* recoverable (moneys, etc.); collectable (debt).

recouvrage [rəkuvraːʒ], *s.m.* re-covering (of umbrella, etc.).

recouvrement[1] [rəkuvrəmɑ̃], *s.m.* **1.** (*a*) recovery (of health, force, etc.); (*b*) recovery, collection (of debts, bill, etc.); **faire un r.,** to recover, collect, a debt; **r. par la poste,** payment for goods by cash on delivery; payment of taxes, etc., through collection by the postman. **2.** *pl.* outstanding debts; **recouvrements restant à faire en fin d'exercice,** (book) debts outstanding at the end of the financial year.

recouvrement[2], *s.m.* **1.** re-covering, covering again. **2.** (*a*) covering; **le r. des champs par les sables du désert,** the covering (over) of the fields by the sands of the desert; (*b*) cover, covering; **r. d'une montre à savonnette,** cover of a hunter; *Tchn:* **plaque, tôle, de r.,** covering plate; **r. en contre-plaqué, r. métallique,** plywood, metal, covering; (*c*) (over)lapping; lap (of slates, glazing, etc.); (over)lap (of photographs in mosaic, of map sheets); *Geol:* overlap (of strata); overthrust (of recumbent folds); **à r.,** lapped; lap-jointed; **en r.,** overlapping; **poser des planches à r.,** to lap boards; **planches à r.,** weatherboarding; *N.Arch:* **r. d'about,** butt lap, end lap; **r. des cans,** seam lap, landing; *Phot:* **r. latéral, longitudinal,** side lap, end lap; **r. total,** full-size overlap; *Geol:* **r. horizontal,** heave (of thrust fault); **lambeau de r.,** outlier; *Mch:* **r. du tiroir,** lap, cover, of the slide valve; **r. à l'admission, r. extérieur,** steam lap, outside lap; **r. à l'échappement, r. intérieur,** exhaust lap, inside lap; *Mec.E:* **assemblage, joint, à r.,** (over)lap joint; **rivetage à r.,** (over)lap riveting; **soudure à r.,** (over)lap weld(ing); (*computer*) **(segment de) r.,** overlay.

recouvrer [rəkuvre], *v.tr.* **1.** to recover, retrieve, get back (one's freedom, one's property); to regain (health, strength, freedom). **2.** to recover, collect, get in (debts, taxes, etc.); **créances à r.,** outstanding debts (due to us).

recouvrir [rəkuvriːr], *v.tr.* (*conj. like* COUVRIR) **1.** to cover (sth.) (over) again; to re-cover (umbrella, roof, etc.). **2.** (*a*) to cover (sth.) (over); to overlay (sth.); to cap (sth.) (de, with); **fauteuil recouvert de velours,** armchair covered in velvet, velvet-covered armchair; **la neige recouvre la plaine,** the snow covers the plain; **jardin recouvert de mauvaises herbes,** garden overgrown with weeds; **ces théories recouvrent un fait,** these theories have a factual basis; *Mec.E:* **r. un palier,** to line a bearing-block; (*b*) **r. ses défauts,** to cover up, hide, one's faults. **3.** to (over)lap; **ardoises qui se recouvrent,** overlapping slates.

se recouvrir, (*of the sky*) to cloud over, to become overcast (again).

recracher [rəkraʃe]. **1.** *v.tr.* to spit (sth.) out again. **2.** *v.i.* to spit again; *P:* **j'ai craché et recraché pour les dettes de monsieur,** I have had to stump up again and again to pay this young man's debts.

récréance [rekreɑ̃:s], *s.f.* **1.** *Jur:* provisional usufruct of estate, etc. under dispute at law. **2.** *Dipl:* **lettres de r.,** (ambassador's) letters of recall.

récréatif, -ive [rekreatif, -i:v], *a.* entertaining, amusing (occupation, etc.); recreative; **lecture(s) récréative(s),** light reading; **séance récréative,** entertainment.

recréation [rəkreasjɔ̃], *s.f.* re-creating, re-creation.

récréation [rekreasjɔ̃], *s.f.* **1.** recreation, amusement; relaxation; **la peinture n'est pour lui qu'une r.,** painting is only an amusement, a hobby, for him. **2.** *Sch:* recreation, break, playtime, *U.S:* recess; *Ecc:* (*in convent*) recreation; **cour de r.,** playground; **les enfants étaient en r.,** the children were at play.

recréer [rəkree], *v.tr.* to recreate; to create, establish (sth.) again; **il fut obligé de se recréer une clientèle,** he had to build up a new connection, a new clientele.

récréer [rekree], *v.tr. A: & Lit:* **1.** to enliven, refresh (the mind, etc.); to please (the eye). **2.** to divert, amuse, entertain.

se récréer, *A: & Lit:* to take some recreation, some diversion; to divert oneself; **faire qch. pour se r.,** to do sth. by way of recreation, as a recreation, for one's own amusement.

récrément [rekremɑ̃], *s.m. Med: etc:* recrement.

recrépiment [rəkrepimɑ̃], *s.m.* = RECRÉPISSAGE.

recrépir [rəkrepi:r], *v.tr.* (*a*) to roughcast again; to renew the roughcast; to replaster; to repoint (wall, etc.); (*b*) to patch up (s.o., sth.); *F: O:* **r. son visage,** to do up one's face.

recrépissage [rəkrepisa:ʒ], *s.m. Const:* coating again with rough-cast; replastering; repointing.

recreuser [rəkrøze], *v.tr.* to hollow (sth.) out again; to dig, go deeper into (ground, question, etc.).

récri [rekri], *s.m. Ven:* full cry (of hounds).

récrier (se) [sərekrije], *v.pr.* (*conj. like* CRIER) **1. se r. d'admiration (à la vue de qch.),** to exclaim, cry out, in admiration (at the sight of sth.). **2. se r. contre, sur, qch.,** to cry out, expostulate, protest, against sth.; **se r. sur les procédés de qn,** to take exception to s.o.'s actions, to what s.o. is doing; **il n'y a pas de quoi se r.,** there is nothing to make a fuss about. **3.** *Ven:* (*of hounds*) to be in full cry.

récriminateur, -trice [rekriminatœ:r, -tris], *a.* recriminative, querulous.

récrimination [rekriminasjɔ̃], *s.f.* recrimination.

récriminatoire [rekriminatwa:r], *a.* recriminatory.

récriminer [rekrimine], *v.i.* to recriminate; **r. contre qn,** to recriminate against s.o.; *abs.* **rien ne sert de r.,** recrimination serves no purpose, it's no use recriminating.

récrire [rekri:r], *v.tr.* (*conj. like* ÉCRIRE) **1.** to rewrite; to write (sth.) over again ((i) to make a fresh copy; (ii) to recast, put into new shape). **2.** *abs.* (*a*) to write (to s.o.) again; (*b*) to write an answer (to s.o.); to answer (s.o.'s letter).

recristallisation [rəkristalizasjɔ̃], *s.f.* recrystallization.

recristalliser [rəkristalize], *v.tr. & i.* to recrystallize.

recroiser [rəkrwɑze], *v.tr.* **1.** to recross; **r. qn,** to meet, pass s.o. again (in the street). **2.** to intersect again.

recroiseté [rəkrwɑzte], *a. Her:* **croix recroisetée,** cross crosslet.

recroître [rəkrwɑ:tr], *v.i.* (*conj. like* CROÎTRE) (*of plant*) to grow again, to spring up again; (*of river*) to rise again.

recroquevillé [rəkrɔkvije], *a.* (*a*) shrivelled, curled up, cockled (leaf, parchment, etc.); (*b*) (fingers) clenched, knotted (by rheumatism); (*c*) **r. dans un fauteuil,** curled up, huddled (up) in an armchair.

recroquevillement [rəkrɔkvijmɑ̃], *s.m.* curling up, huddling (up).

recroqueviller (se) [sərəkrɔkvije], *v.pr.* (*a*) (*of leather, parchment, etc.*) to shrivel (up) (with the heat); to curl up; to cockle; to crumple up; (*of flower*) to wilt; **se r. de peur,** to wilt with fear; (*b*) (*of fingers*) to curl in, to clench (with rheumatism); (*c*) (*of pers., animal*) to curl up, huddle (up).

récrouir [rekrui:r], *v.tr. Metalw:* to reheat.

recru[1] [rəkry], *a.* **r. (de fatigue),** tired out, worn out (by exertion); tired to death, dead tired.

recrû, recru[2] [rəkry], *s.m. For:* new growth (of copse-wood).

recrudescence [rəkrydes(s)ɑ̃:s], *s.f.* recrudescence; renewed outbreak, fresh outbreak (of fire, disease, disorder); **r. du froid,** new spell of cold weather.

recrudescent [rəkrydes(s)ɑ̃], *a.* recrudescent.

recrue [rəkry], *s.f. Mil:* **1.** *A:* (*a*) new levy (of men); (*b*) recruiting; **faire la r. de qn,** to recruit s.o. (to a party, etc.). **2.** recruit; new member, fresh adherent (of party, company, etc.); *Mil:* **jeune r.,** raw recruit; **le nouveau parti a fait de nombreuses recrues dans la bourgeoisie,** the new party made many recruits among the middle class, was largely recruited from the middle class.

recrutement [rəkrytmɑ̃], *s.m.* recruiting, recruitment (of soldiers, etc.); engaging (of a staff, etc.); *Pol: etc:* **campagne de r.,** membership drive.

recruter [rəkryte], *v.tr.* to recruit (regiment, party); to bring (regiment) up to strength; to recruit (men, supporters); to enlist, beat up (supporters); **parti qui se recrute surtout parmi le peuple,** party drawn largely from the workers; **les officiers de cavalerie se recrutaient pour une bonne part dans la vieille noblesse,** cavalry officers were largely recruited from among the old nobility.

recruteur [rəkrytœ:r]. **1.** *a.* **officier, sergent, r.,** recruiting officer, sergeant. **2.** *s.m.* recruiter.

recta [rɛkta], *F:* **1.** *adv.* **payer, arriver, r.,** to pay on the nail; to arrive punctually, on the dot; **ça me conduirait r. au ridicule,** that would lay me open to ridicule, make me look a fool, straight away. **2.** *a.inv.* punctual; **ils sont r. et font un gros travail,** they're punctual, they arrive on the dot, and get through a lot of work.

rectal, -aux [rɛktal, -o], *a. Anat:* rectal.

rectangle [rɛktɑ̃:gl], *Geom:* **1.** *a.* right-angled (triangle, etc.). **2.** *s.m.* rectangle; *Ten:* **r. de service,** service court; *T.V:* **r. blanc,** "for adults only" sign.

rectangulaire [rɛktɑ̃gylɛ:r], *a.* rectangular; *Mth:* right-angled (co-ordinates, etc.).

recteur, -trice [rɛktœ:r, -tris]. **1.** *s.m.* (*a*) *Sch:* = vice-chancellor (of university, who is also responsible for the schools of the region); (*b*) *Ecc:* (i) *A:* rector (of Jesuit college); (ii) (*in Brittany*) parish priest; (iii) priest who serves a church other than a parish church. **2.** *a.* (*a*) *A:* **esprit r.,** guiding spirit; (*b*) *Orn:* **penne rectrice,** *s.f.* **rectrice,** tail feather, rectrix.

rectifiable [rɛktifjabl], *a.* rectifiable.

rectifiant [rɛktifjɑ̃], *a. El:* **contact r.,** rectifying contact; *Mth:* **plan r.,** *s.m.* **rectifiant,** rectifying plane.

rectificateur, -trice [rɛktifikatœ:r, -tris]. **1.** *s.* rectifier. **2.** *s.m.* (*a*) *Dist: etc:* rectifier; (*b*) *El:* **r. de courants,** current rectifier; (*c*) *Typ:* **r. de marge,** side-guide mark; (*d*) *Ch:* stripper.

rectificatif, -ive [rɛktifikatif, -i:v]. **1.** *a.* rectifying; *Book-k:* **écriture rectificative,** correcting entry; *Com:* **facture rectificative,** amended invoice. **2.** *s.m.* (*a*) *Adm:* corrigendum (to circular, to pay roll, etc.); (*b*) *Ch: Ind:* corrective.

rectification [rɛktifikasjɔ̃], *s.f.* rectification. **1.** (*a*) amendment, correction (of document, text, etc.); rectification, correction (of calculation, mistake, etc.); adjustment, correction (of account, prices, etc.); (*b*) *Opt: etc:* adjustment (of instrument); correction (of the setting of instrument); **les rectifications du sextant,** the sextant adjustments; (*c*) *Civ.E: etc:* rectification (of boundaries, design, layout, etc.); **r. du tracé d'une route, du tracé d'une ligne de chemin de fer,** rectification, straightening, of the alignment of a road, of a railway; *Rail:* **r. du tracé d'une courbe,** rectification of the alignment of a curve; *Mth:* **r. d'une courbe,** rectification of a curve. **2.** *Mec.E:* (*a*) tru(e)ing, rectifying (of surface with emery wheel, etc.); (*b*) (precision) grinding; **r. à sec, avec arrosage,** dry, wet, grinding; **r. à l'enfilade,** straight-through grinding; **r. en plongée,** plunge-cut grinding; **r. par chariotage,** traverse grinding; **r. plane,** surface grinding. **3.** *Ch: Ind:* rectifying, redistilling (of alcohol, petroleum, etc.); *Petroleum Ind:* **tour de r.,** stripping tower. **4.** *El:* rectification (of current); **r. par grille,** grid rectification.

rectifier [rɛktifje], *v.tr.* (*p.d. & pr.sub.* **n. rectifiions, v. rectifiiez**) **1.** (*a*) to amend, correct (document, text, etc.); to rectify, correct (calculation, mistake, etc.); to put (mistake) right; to adjust, correct (account, prices); to amend (account); to reform, correct (habit); to tighten, straighten (tie); *Mil: etc:* **r. l'alignement,** to correct the dressing, to dress the ranks; *Artil: etc:* **r. le tir,** to correct the range; (*b*) *Opt: etc:* to adjust (instrument); to correct (setting of instrument); (*c*) *Civ.E: etc:* to rectify (boundary, design, layout, etc.); **r. le tracé d'une route, d'une ligne de chemin de fer,** to rectify, straighten, the alignment of a road, of a railway; *Rail:* **r. le tracé d'une courbe,** to rectify the alignment of a curve; *Mth:* **r. une courbe,** to rectify a curve. **2.** *Mec.E:* (*a*) to true, rectify (a surface with emery wheel); to straighten, form (with press); **meule à r.,** grinding wheel; **presse à r.,** straightening, forming, press; **rectifié au marteau,** shortpeened; (*b*) *Mec.E:* to grind (true); **r. à la cote,** to grind to size. **3.** *Ch:* to rectify, re-distil (alcohol, petroleum, etc.); **alcool rectifié,** rectified alcohol. **4.** *El:* to rectify (current). **5.** *P:* to kill (s.o.), to bump (s.o.) off.

rectifieur [rɛktifjœ:r], *s.m. Mec.E:* grinding-machine operator.

rectifieuse [rɛktifjø:z], *s.f. Mec.E:* grinder, grinding machine; **r. de soupapes,** valve cutter; **r. à table cylindrique,** cylindrical grinder.

rectiligne [rɛktiliɲ]. **1.** *a.* (*a*) rectilinear; *occ.* rectilineal; linear (movement); (*b*) **conduite r.,** unswerving, straightforward, conduct; **esprit r.,** mind that can see only straight ahead. **2.** *s.m. Phot:* **r. grand angulaire,** wide-angle rectilinear lens.

rectilinéaire [rɛktilineɛ:r], *a. Phot:* rapid rectilinear (lens).

rectite [rɛktit], *s.f. Med:* proctitis, rectitis.

rectitude [rɛktityd], *s.f.* **1.** straightness (of line). **2.** rectitude; (*a*) correctness, soundness, rightness, sanity (of judgment); (*b*) uprightness, righteousness, integrity, propriety (of conduct).

recto [rɛkto], *s.m.* recto, right-hand side (of page); first page (of single leaf); *Bookb:* front side, front board; **r. d'une carte postale illustrée,** view side of a picture postcard; **r. d'une traite,** face of a draft.

rectocèle [rɛktɔsɛl], *s.f. Med:* rectocele.

recto-colite [rɛktɔkɔlit], *s.f. Med:* procto-colitis, rectocolitis.

rectopexie [rɛktɔpɛksi], *s.f. Surg:* rectopexy.

rectoral, -aux [rɛktɔral, -o], *a.* rectorial.

rectorat [rɛktɔra], *s.m.* rectorship, rectorate; vice-chancellorship.

rectoscope [rɛktɔskɔp], *s.m. Med:* proctoscope, rectoscope.

rectoscopie [rɛktɔskɔpi], *s.f. Med:* proctoscopy, rectoscopy.

rectotomie [rɛktɔtɔmi], *s.f. Surg:* rectotomy.

recto-urétral, -aux [rɛktɔyretral, -o], *a. Anat:* recto-urethral.

recto-vaginal, -aux [rɛktɔvaʒinal, -o], *a. Anat:* rectovaginal.

recto-vésical, -aux [rɛktɔvezikal, -o], *a. Anat:* rectovesical.

rectum [rɛktɔm], *s.m. Anat:* rectum.

reçu [rəsy]. **1.** *a.* received, accepted, recognized, prevailing (opinion, custom, etc.). **2.** *s.m. Com:* (*a*) **r. de marchandises, d'argent, etc.,** receipt, voucher, for goods, money, etc.; **r. certifié,** accountable receipt; **r. à valoir,** receipt on account; (*b*) **au r. de votre lettre,** on receipt of your letter, on receiving your letter; **payer au r.,** to pay on delivery.

recueil [rəkœj], *s.m.* **1.** *A:* collecting, harbouring; *still so used occ. as in Mil:* **poste de r.,** medical-aid post (for men who have fallen out on the march); **position, base, de r.,** fall-back position. **2.** collection, compilation (of poems, laws, etc.); miscellany; **r. choisi, r. de morceaux choisis,** selection, anthology; **r. de prières,** book of prayers; **r. des lois,** compendium of laws; **r. de jurisprudence,** case book; **r. de locutions,** phrase book.

recueillement [rəkœjmɑ̃], *s.m.* (*a*) collectedness, self-communion, introversion, meditation, contemplation; *Theol:* (state of) recollection; (*b*) **r. d'esprit,** composure.

recueilli [rəkœji], *a.* **1.** collected, meditative, contemplative, introspective (person, frame of mind); *Theol:* recollected. **2.** (*of chapel, etc.*) favourable to meditation; silent, quiet.

recueillir [rəkœji:r], *v.tr.* (*conj. like* CUEILLIR) **1.** (*a*) to collect, gather (anecdotes, curios, fragments, etc.); to set down (s.o.'s words); **r. les miettes,** to gather up the crumbs; **r. l'eau de pluie,** to catch the rainwater; **r. des nouvelles,** to pick up news; **r. des renseignements,** to obtain, pick up, information; **r. le consentement de qn,** to obtain, get, s.o.'s consent; **contes recueillis dans la tradition orale,** stories handed on by word of mouth; **r. les ouvrages d'un auteur,** to make a collection of an author's works; (*b*) **r. ses forces,** to collect, gather, all one's strength; **r. les restes d'une armée,** to gather up what remains of an army; **r. ses idées,** to collect one's thoughts; (*of apparatus*) **r. les sons,** to pick up sounds. **2.** (*a*) to get in, gather (crops, etc.); to recover (by-products, etc.); **r. le fruit de ses travaux,** to reap the fruit of one's labours; (*b*) **r. un héritage,** to inherit; (*c*) **r. les suffrages,** to be elected, to win the election; **r. des louanges,** to win praise; **r. la**

couronne, to succeed to the crown. 3. r. un pèlerin, un malheureux, to take in, to shelter, to give hospitality to, a pilgrim, someone in need; r. un orphelin, to give an orphan a home; r. des naufragés, to pick up shipwrecked men.
se recueillir, to collect oneself, one's thoughts; to commune with oneself; to retire within oneself; to be plunged in meditation; to turn one's thoughts to God.
recuire [rəkɥi:r], *v.tr.* (*conj. like* CUIRE) 1. to cook, bake, (sth.) again; *Cer:* to rebake, rekiln. 2. *Tchn:* to reheat; to anneal, temper (steel); to anneal (glass); to reboil (syrup); to reburn (cement); **r. après trempe,** to draw, let down, the temper of (tool); **r. de l'acier par le flambage,** to blaze off steel.
recuisson [rəkɥisɔ̃], *s.f.* 1. recooking; rebaking. 2. reheating; tempering (of steel); annealing (of glass).
recuit, -ite [rəkɥi, -it]. 1. *a.* (*a*) cooked, baked, again; **poulet cuit et r.,** chicken cooked to a cinder; (*b*) annealed; **r. au blanc, au bleu,** bright-annealed, blue-annealed; **r. en pot, en vase clos,** box-annealed; **fil de fer r.,** annealed steel wire; **non r.,** unannealed. 2. *s.m.* **recuit,** *s.f.* **recuite,** reheating; *Tchn:* tempering, annealing (of steel); annealing (of glass); reboiling (of syrup); reburning (of lime); **r. adoucissant,** soft annealing; **r. blanc,** bright annealing; **r. bleu,** blue annealing; **r. complet,** full annealing; **r. différentiel,** differential annealing; **r. de libération des tensions,** stress-release annealing; **r. noir,** black annealing; **r. en vase clos,** box annealing, close annealing; **r. de surface,** skin annealing.
recul [rəkyl], *s.m.* 1. retirement, recession (of sea water, etc.); retreat (of glacier, etc.); backing (of horse, cart); setback (in business, in health, etc.); **(mouvement de) r.,** backward movement, retiring movement; **il eut un brusque mouvement de r.,** he shrank back, started back; **r. d'un levier de commande,** return of a control lever; *Bill:* **combiner un effet de r.,** to bring off a screwback; *Av:* **hauban, câble, de r.,** dragwire; *Aut:* **phare de r.,** reversing light; *Ling:* **r. de la langue,** retraction of the tongue; *Med:* **grâce aux antibiotiques la tuberculose est en net r.,** thanks to antibiotics tuberculosis is in marked recession, is becoming less and less frequent. 2. (*a*) *Ball:* recoil (of cannon); kick (of rifle); **canon sans r.,** recoilless gun; (*b*) *Nau:* slip (of propeller). 3. room to move back; *Ten:* **cinq mètres de r.,** five-yard runback (behind base line); *Art:* **statue qui manque de r.,** statue that cannot be viewed in proper perspective, from the right distance; **nous manquons de r. pour écrire l'histoire du 20e siècle,** we are too near the 20th century to be able to write its history; **avoir, prendre, du r.,** to have, adopt a detached attitude (to a situation). 4. *Meteor:* backing (of the wind).
reculade [rəkylad], *s.f.* (*a*) backward movement, falling back, retreat; backing (of carriage); (*b*) *F:* (*in debate, etc.*) retreat (from a position); climbing down; **une honteuse r.,** a miserable climb down.
reculage [rəkyla:ʒ], *s.m. Min:* shifting, transport (of coal, ore), from the face to the loading point.
reculé [rəkyle], *a.* distant, remote (time, place); **ancêtres reculés,** remote ancestors; **à une époque reculée,** at a remote period; **à une date reculée,** at an early date; **à une période reculée du moyen âge,** in the earlier (period of the) Middle Ages; **dans un avenir r.,** in a distant, remote, future.
reculée, *s.f.* 1. backing space, backing room. 2. (*in the Jura*) blind valley.
reculement [rəkylmɑ̃], *s.m.* 1. *A:* backing (of horse, carriage, etc.). 2. moving back (of sth., in space or time); extension (of boundaries); postponement (of an event). 3. breeching, breech band (of harness). 4. *Const: etc:* batter (of wall).
reculer¹ [rəkyle]. 1. *v.i.* to move back, step back, draw back, recede; to fall back, to retreat; (*of horse*) to back; (*of car*) to back; (*of gun*) to recoil; (*of rifle*) to kick; (*of glacier*) to retreat; **r. d'un pas,** to fall back, step back, a pace; (*of car, etc.*) **r. contre qch.,** to back into sth.; **faire r. qn,** to make s.o. fall back; **la police nous fit r. jusqu'au trottoir,** the police moved us back to the pavement; **faire r. un cheval,** to back a horse; **ses affaires ont reculé,** his business has fallen off, has had a setback; **on dit que la civilisation recule,** people say civilization is going back, is on the downgrade; **il n'y a plus moyen de r.,** there is no going back; **il ne recule jamais,** he never draws back; he never flinches; **r. devant qch.,** to draw back, shrink, from sth.; to recoil, flinch, before sth.; *F:* to back out of sth.; **r. devant la dépense,** to shrink from incurring the expense, *F:* to jib, boggle, at the expense; **ne r. devant rien,** to shrink from nothing; *F:* to stick at nothing; **r. à faire qch.,** to shrink from doing sth.; to hesitate to do sth.; *F:* to jib at doing sth.; **il ne recule à rien,** he is ready for anything; **r. pour mieux sauter,** (i) to step back in order to have a better take-off; (ii) to procrastinate; to put off the evil day. 2. *v.tr.* (*a*) to move (s.o., sth.) back; **r. les chaises,** pull back, push back, the chairs; **r. un cheval,** to rein back, to back, a horse; **r. les frontières,** to push forward, extend, the frontiers; **r. l'origine de l'homme à un passé très lointain,** to trace the origin of man (back) to a remote past; (*b*) **r. un paiement, un mariage,** to postpone, defer, put off, a payment, a marriage; **r. de faire qch.,** to put off doing sth.
se reculer, to draw back; to stand back; to step back, to move back; **reculez-vous de là,** stand back from there.
reculer², *s.m.* 1. *Equit:* backing (of horse). 2. *Tls:* (clockmaker's) file.
reculons (à) [ar(ə)kylɔ̃], *adv.phr.* **aller, marcher, à r.,** (i) to walk backwards; (ii) to lose ground; (*of business, etc.*) to be in recession; **sortir à r.,** to go out backwards; to back out.
récupérabilité [rekyperabilite], *s.f. Ind:* salvage value.
récupérable [rekyperabl], *a.* (*a*) recoverable; salvageable; **heures récupérables,** (i) time that can be made good; (ii) *Ind: etc:* time to be made good (at normal rates); **ferraille r.,** scrap metal; (*b*) *F:* (*of pers.*) **il est tout de même r.,** we'll make sth. of him yet.
récupérateur [rekyperatœ:r], *s.m. Ind: Mch: etc:* 1. regenerator, recuperator; hot-blast stove; *Metall:* **r. cylindrique,** Cowper stove. 2. *Artil:* recuperator; **r. à ressort, à huile,** spring recuperator, oil recuperator; *a.* **ressort r.,** recuperator spring. 3. *Mch: etc:* **r. d'huile,** oil extractor. 4. **r. de ferrailles,** salvage dealer, scrap metal merchant.
récupération [rekyperasjɔ̃], *s.f.* 1. (*a*) *Jur:* recuperation, recovery (of debt); (*b*) *Ind:* recovery (of waste products, etc.); salvage; **four à r.,** regenerative furnace; **chambre de r.,** regenerating chamber; *El.Rail:* **freinage par r.,** regenerative braking; (*c*) recovery (of spacecraft); (*d*) (*computers*) **r. de données,** information retrieval; (*e*) recoupment (of losses); (*f*) *F:* scrounging. 2. recuperation, recovery (from illness).
récupéré [rekypere]. 1. *a. Ind: etc:* reclaimed; salvaged (goods). 2. *s.m. Mil:* invalided man called up again for active service.
récupérer [rekypere], *v.tr.* (**je récupère, n. récupérons; je récupérerai**) 1. (*a*) to recover (debt, etc.); *F:* **j'ai récupéré le livre que je lui avais prêté,** I've got back the book I lent him; *F:* **je l'ai récupéré au bar,** I retrieved him from, fished him out of, the bar; (*b*) *F:* **r. ses forces,** *abs.* **récupérer,** to recuperate, to recover (one's strength). 2. (*a*) *Ind: etc:* to recover (waste products); to salvage; **r. de la ferraille,** to collect, recover, scrap (metal); (*b*) to give a new job to, find alternative employment for (s.o. unable to continue his present work); (*c*) *F:* to scrounge. 3. (*a*) to retrieve, recoup (a loss); (*b*) to make up (lost time, etc.); **la journée chômée sera récupérée,** the lost day will be made up. 4. *Fish:* to wind in (the line).
récurage [rekyra:ʒ], *s.m.* scouring, cleaning.
récurer [rekyre], *v.tr.* 1. to scour, clean (pots and pans). 2. **r. une vigne,** to give a vineyard a third ploughing.
récureur, -euse [rekyrœ:r, -ø:z]. 1. *s.* (*pers.*) scourer, dishwasher. 2. *s.m.* scourer, scouring agent.
récurrence [rekyrɑ̃:s], *s.f.* 1. turning back (of nerve, vein, etc.). 2. *Med:* recurrence (of fever). 3. (*computers*) recursion.
récurrent [rekyrɑ̃], *a.* 1. *Anat:* recurrent (nerve, vein). 2. recurrent, recurring; *Med:* **fièvre récurrente,** *s.f.* **récurrente,** recurrent fever; *Mth:* **série récurrente,** recurrent series. 3. (*in computer work*) **processus r.,** recursive process.
récusable [rekyzabl], *a. Jur:* challengeable, exceptionable, untrustworthy (witness); **témoignage r.,** impugnable evidence.
récusant, -ante [rekyzɑ̃, -ɑ̃:t], *s.* 1. *Jur:* challenger. 2. *Eng.Hist:* recusant.
récusation [rekyzasjɔ̃], *s.f.* 1. *Jur:* disclaiming competence; **r. de témoin, d'arbitre,** challenge of, exception to, objection to, a witness, an arbitrator; **r. de témoignage,** impugnment of evidence. 2. disclaimer.
récuser [rekyze], *v.tr.* (*a*) *Jur:* to challenge, take exception to, object to (witness, etc.); to impugn (evidence); (*b*) to reject.
se récuser, *Jur:* to decline to give an opinion; to declare oneself incompetent to judge; to disclaim competence.
recyclage [rəsikla:ʒ], *s.m.* 1. (*a*) *Sch:* reorientation (of course of study); (*b*) *Ind: etc:* retraining (of staff); readaptation (to new techniques, etc.); **la technologie moderne exige qu'un spécialiste soit soumis à un r. périodique,** in modern technology it is necessary for specialists to attend periodical refresher courses. 2. *Ind: etc:* reprocessing; *Petroleum Min:* rerun, recycling (of gas in oilfield); *Atom.Ph: etc:* recycling (of coolant, fissionable material, etc.).
recycler [rəsikle], *v.tr.* 1. (*a*) *Sch:* to reorientate (pupil's studies); (*b*) *Ind: etc:* to retrain (staff); to readapt (personnel) (to new techniques). 2. *Ind: etc:* to reprocess.
rédacteur, -trice [redaktœ:r, -tris], *s.* (*a*) writer, drafter (of deed, communiqué, etc.); writer (of article); *Adm: A:* = junior executive officer; **r. technique,** technical writer; (*b*) *Journ:* member of staff (of newspaper, etc.); *Publ:* sub-editor; *Publ: Journ:* **r. en chef, rédactrice en chef,** editor; **r. aux actualités, r. de la chronique du jour, r. au service des informations,** news editor; **r. sportif,** sports editor; **r. parlementaire,** parliamentary correspondent; **r. politique,** political correspondent; *T.V: W.Tel:* **r. du journal parlé,** newscaster.
rédaction [redaksjɔ̃], *s.f.* 1. (*a*) drafting, drawing up, wording, writing (of deed, parliamentary bill, etc.); building up (of map); (*b*) *Journ:* editing; editorship. 2. *Journ:* (*a*) *coll.* editorial staff; **faire partie de la r.,** to be on the staff (of a paper); (*b*) **(bureau de) r.,** (newspaper) office(s). 3. *Sch:* essay, composition.
rédactionnel, -elle [redaksjɔnɛl], *a.* editorial; **publicité rédactionnelle,** publicity article.
redan [rədɑ̃], *s.m.* 1. *Fort:* redan. 2. (*a*) step (in the coping of a wall built on sloping ground); step (in gable); **pignon à redans** (crow-, corbie-) stepped gable; (*b*) step (under hull of speedboat, of hydroplane); **hydroplane à redans multiples,** multi-stepped hydroplane; (*of hydroplane*) **courir sur le redan,** to plane along the water; (*c*) *Geol:* step fault.
reddingite [rɛdɛ̃ʒit], *s.f. Miner:* reddingite.
reddition [rɛdisjɔ̃, rɛddi-], *s.f.* 1. surrender (of town, of ship). 2. rendering (of account); *Jur:* **action en r. de compte,** action for an account. 3. *Rail:* **r. de voie,** liberating of track. 4. **r. de lumière,** shedding of light.
redécouverte [rədekuvɛrt], *s.f.* rediscovery.
redécouvrir [rədekuvri:r], *v.tr.* (*conj. like* COUVRIR) to rediscover.
redéfaire [rədefɛ:r], *v.tr.* (*conj. like* DÉFAIRE) to undo (sth.) again.
redélayage [rədelɛja:z], *s.m.* retempering.
redemander [rədmɑ̃de], *v.tr.* 1. to ask for (sth.) again; to ask for more of (sth.), for a second helping of (sth.). 2. to ask for (sth.) back (again).
rédempteur, -trice [redɑ̃ptœ:r, -tris]. 1. *a.* redeeming. 2. *s.* redeemer; **le R.,** (Christ) the Redeemer.
rédemption [redɑ̃psjɔ̃], *s.f.* (*a*) redemption, redeeming ((i) *Theol:* of man, (ii) *Jur:* of loan, etc.); **la r. des péchés,** the redemption of sins; (*b*) *A:* ransom(ing) (of prisoner).
rédemptoriste [redɑ̃ptɔrist], *s.m. Ecc:* Redemptorist (father).
redent [rədɑ̃], *s.m.* (*a*) *Arch:* cusp; (*b*) = REDAN 2.
redenté [rədɑ̃te], *a. Arch:* cuspate.
redéranger [rəderɑ̃ʒe], *v.tr.* (*conj. like* DÉRANGER) to put (thgs) out of order again; to upset (sth.) again; to disturb, inconvenience, (s.o.) again.
redescendre [rədesɑ̃dr, -dɛ-]. 1. *v.i.* (*a*) to come, go, down again; **le chemin redescend,** the path is going downhill again; **la mer redescend,** the tide is going out again; **le baromètre redescend,** the glass is falling again; (*b*) *Nau:* (*of the wind*) to back. 2. *v.tr.* (*a*) to take (picture, etc.) down again; to let (s.o.) down again (with a rope); to bring (s.o., sth.) down again; (*b*) **r. l'escalier,** to come down the stairs, downstairs, again; **r. le fleuve,** (i) to go down the river again; (ii) to go down the river.
redevable [rəd(ə)vabl]. 1. *a.* **être r. de qch. à qn,** to be indebted to s.o. for sth.; to owe (one's life, etc.) to s.o.; to be accountable to s.o. (for money held in trust, etc.); **vous ne m'êtes r. de rien,** I have no claim on you; **je vous suis r. de cent francs,** I still owe you a hundred francs. 2. *s.m. & f. A:* debtor.

redevance [rəd(ə)vɑ̃:s], *s.f.* (*a*) rent; **r. emphytéotique,** ground rent; *Tp: etc:* **r. annuelle,** yearly rental; (*b*) dues; (*c*) royalty; **redevances d'auteur,** author's royalties; **droit de possession moyennant r.,** right of property on royalty; **r. à payer à l'État,** government royalty; **r. pétrolière,** oil royalty; (*d*) (television, etc.) licence fee; (*e*) fee; **moyennant une légère r.,** for a small fee.

redevancier, -ière [rəd(ə)vɑ̃sje, -jɛ:r], *s.* (rent, etc.) payer; person liable for the payment of royalty, licence fee, etc.

redevenir [rədəvni:r], *v.i.* (*conj. like* DEVENIR) to become (sth., s.o.) again; **r. jeune,** to grow young again; **r. amoureux de qn,** to fall in love with s.o. again; **r. malade,** to fall ill again; **le temps redevient froid,** it is turning cold again.

redevoir [rəd(ə)vwa:r], *v.tr.* (*conj. like* DEVOIR) to owe a balance of (a sum on an account, etc.); **il me redoit dix francs,** he still owes me ten francs; **il m'est redû vingt francs,** there are twenty francs still owing to me; *Com:* **redoit M. Martin,** balance due (to us) from Mr Martin.

rédhibition [redibisjɔ̃], *s.f. Jur:* annulment of sale (owing to latent defect); redhibition.

rédhibitoire [redibitwa:r], *a.* (*a*) *Jur:* **vice r.,** redhibitory defect (in horse, etc.); latent defect that makes a sale void; (*b*) **la peur est une infirmité r. pour un homme d'action,** to suffer from fear is incompatible with being a man of action; **être étranger ici est r.,** being a foreigner here rules you out.

rédie [redi], *s.f. Vet:* redia.

rediffuser [rədifyze], *v.tr. W.Tel: T.V:* to repeat (a programme).

rediffusion [rədifyzjɔ̃], *s.f. W.Tel: T.V:* repeat broadcast, showing; second broadcast.

rédiger [rediʒe], *v.tr.* (**je rédigeai(s); n. rédigeons**) **1.** to draw up, to draft, to word, to write (out) (agreement, programme, invoice, letter, etc.); to write (article); **à l'heure où le présent article est rédigé,** at the time of writing; **r. la correspondance d'une maison,** to conduct the correspondence of a firm. **2.** *Journ:* to edit; to be the editor of (a paper, etc.); (*computers*) **r. un programme,** to program(me).

rédimer [redime], *v.tr. A: & Lit:* to redeem; to buy (s.o.) off; **se r. par le repentir,** to redeem oneself by repentance.

redingote [rədɛ̃gɔt], *s.f. Cost:* (*a*) frock coat; (*b*) (woman's) tailored, fitting, coat.

rédingtonite [redɛ̃ntɔnit], *s.f. Miner:* redingtonite.

rédintégration [redɛ̃tegrasjɔ̃], *s.f.* (*a*) *Psy:* redintegration; (*b*) *Cryst:* **r. des cristaux,** redintegration of crystals.

redire [rədi:r], *v.tr.* (*conj. like* DIRE) **1.** to tell, say, (sth.) again; to repeat (sth.); **on ne saurait trop r. que . . .,** it cannot be said, pointed out, too often that. . . . **2.** *abs.* **trouver à r. à qch.,** to take exception to sth.; to find fault with, carp at, *F:* pick holes in, sth.; **je ne vois rien à r. dans cet ouvrage,** I can see nothing to criticize in this work; **on trouve à r. à ce que vous sortiez si souvent,** people don't like, people criticize, your going out so often; **il n'y a rien à r. à cela,** there's nothing to be said against that.

rediseur, -euse [rədizœ:r, -ø:z], *s. A:* repeater, tell-tale, *F:* blab.

redissoudre [rədisu:dr], *v.tr.* (*conj. like* DISSOUDRE) to redissolve; to dissolve (sth.) again.

redistillation [rədistilasjɔ̃], *s.f.* redistillation, redistilling; **appareil de r.,** secondary still; *Petroleum Ind:* **unité de r.,** rerunning unit.

redistiller [rədistile], *v.tr.* to redistil; *Petroleum Ind:* to rerun.

redistribuer [rədistribɥe], *v.tr.* to redistribute; to re-allocate; *Cards:* to redeal.

redistribution [rədistribysjɔ̃], *s.f.* redistribution; re-allocation.

redit [rədi], *s.m. A:* **dits et redits,** gossip, tittle-tattle.

redite [rədit], *s.f.* (useless) repetition; **éviter les redites,** to avoid repeating oneself.

redondance [rədɔ̃dɑ̃:s], *s.f.* redundance, redundancy; (*computers*) **contrôle par r.,** redundancy check.

redondant [rədɔ̃dɑ̃], *a.* redundant (word, style); pleonastic (word); (*computers*) **code r.,** redundant code.

redonder [rədɔ̃de], *v.i.* (*a*) to be redundant; (*b*) to be in excess; **ouvrage qui redonde de citations,** work chock-full, over-full, of quotations, *F:* stiff with quotations.

redonnais, -aise [rədɔnɛ, -ɛ:z], *a. & s. Geog:* (native, inhabitant) of Redon.

redonne [rədɔn], *s.f. Cards:* redeal.

redonner [rədɔne]. **1.** *v.tr.* (*a*) to give (sth.) again; *Th:* **je vois qu'on redonne "Hamlet,"** I see "Hamlet" is being given again; I see "Hamlet" is coming on again, is on again; (*b*) to give more of (sth.); (*c*) to give (sth.) back; to restore, return; **voici qui vous redonnera des forces,** this will restore your strength, put new life into you; (*c*) *abs. Cards:* to redeal. **2.** *v.i.* (*a*) **r. dans un piège, dans des excès,** to fall into a trap, into excesses, again; (*b*) **le froid redonne,** the cold has set in again; **la pluie redonna de plus belle,** the rain began again, came on again, worse than ever; (*c*) **la cavalerie redonna avec un nouveau courage,** the cavalry charged again, returned to the charge, with new courage; (*d*) **la chute lui redonna dans la colonne vertébrale,** the fall jarred his spine; (*e*) **r. dans l'exagération,** to go on exaggerating.

redorer [rədɔre], *v.tr.* to regild.

redormir [rədɔrmi:r], *v.i.* (*conj. like* DORMIR) to sleep again.

redoublant, -ante [rədublɑ̃, -ɑ̃:t], *s. Sch:* pupil who is repeating a year, who has stayed down.

redoublé [rəduble], *a.* **rime redoublée,** double rime; **battre qn à coups redoublés,** to thrash s.o. soundly; *s.a.* PAS[1] 1; *Ling:* **parfait r.,** reduplicated perfect.

redoublement [rədubləmɑ̃], *s.m.* **1.** redoubling (of joy, zeal, etc.); **avec un r. de zèle, de colère,** with redoubled zeal, anger. **2.** *Ling:* reduplication. **3.** *Mus:* doubling (of note in chord).

redoubler [rəduble]. **1.** *v.tr.* (*a*) to redouble, increase (dose, s.o.'s fears, one's efforts, etc.); **r. le chagrin de qn,** to add to s.o.'s grief; **r. ses cris,** to redouble one's cries; to shout louder than ever; (*b*) *Sch:* **r. (une classe),** to stay down; (*c*) to reline (garment). **2.** *v.i.* (*a*) (*of efforts, cries, pain, ardour, etc.*) to redouble; **la pluie redoubla,** the rain came on worse than ever; (*b*) **r. de zèle,** to redouble one's zeal, to be more zealous than ever; **r. d'efforts,** to strive harder than ever, to redouble one's efforts; *A:* **r. de jambes,** to mend one's pace.

redoul [rədul], *s.m. Bot:* myrtle-leaved (tanner's) sumach.

redoutable [rədutabl], *a.* redoubtable, formidable; deadly (scourge); **homme r. à l'État,** man to be feared by the state, dangerous to the state; **ennemi r.,** formidable, dangerous, enemy; **concurrence r.,** dangerous competition; *P:* **c'est une r. emmerdeuse,** she's the bloodiest nuisance I ever met.

redoutablement [rədutabləmɑ̃], *adv. F:* extremely, terribly.

redoute [rədut], *s.f.* **1.** *Fort:* redoubt. **2.** (*a*) *A:* gala evening (at dance hall); (*b*) *A:* ridotto; (i) fancy-dress ball; (ii) casino.

redouté [rədute], *a.* dreaded, feared.

redouter [rədute], *v.tr.* **1.** to fear, dread (s.o., sth.); to be in awe of (s.o., sth.); **je le redoute,** I am afraid of him; **r. d'apprendre qch.,** to dread, to be in fear of, hearing sth.; **je redoute surtout de . . .,** the thing I fear most is to . . .; **r. que . . . + (ne) + sub.,** to be afraid that. . . . **2. plante qui redoute un sol humide,** plant that cannot stand a damp soil.

redoux [rədu], *s.m. Meteor:* rise in temperature; **neige de r.,** snow associated with the warming of the atmosphere, with milder weather.

redox [rədɔks], *Ch:* **1.** *a.* redox; **processus r.,** redox process; **potentiel r.,** redox potential. **2.** *s.m.* oxidation reduction, redox.

rèdre [rɛdr], *s.m. Fish:* herring net.

redressage [rədrɛsa:ʒ], *s.m.* **1.** = REDRESSEMENT. **2.** *Metalw:* straightening out. **3.** re-schooling (of horse). **4.** *Leath:* finishing.

redresse [rədrɛs], *s.f.* (*a*) *Nau:* **palans de r.,** righting tackle; (*b*) *P:* **c'est un type à la r.,** (i) he's wide awake, knows what he's up to; (ii) he's a tough guy; he knows how to get his own way.

redressé [rədrese], *a.* erect, upright; inclined at a high angle; *Geol:* **couches redressées,** tilted strata.

redressement [rədrɛsmɑ̃], *s.m.* **1.** (*a*) re-erecting (of fallen post, etc.); setting up again (of fallen object, etc.); (*b*) righting (of a boat); **canot à r.,** self-righting boat; (*c*) *Opt:* erecting (of inverted image); **oculaire à r.,** erecting eyepiece. **2.** (*a*) straightening (of path, piece of wood, etc.); tru(e)ing (of a surface); flattening-out (of curled paper, etc.); *Mil:* re-establishing (of one's line); *Hist:* **le r. de la Marne,** the recovery on the Marne; **r. économique,** economic recovery; **maison de r.** = Borstal (school); (*b*) *El: Elcs:* rectifying (of current); (voltage) rectification; **r. d'une seule alternance,** half-wave rectification; **r. de deux alternances, r. biphasé,** full-wave rectification; **valve de r.,** rectifier, rectifying valve; (*c*) rectification, redress(ing), righting, amendment (of wrong, mistake, etc.); *Book-k:* **écriture de r.,** correcting entry; (*d*) *Opt: Phot:* correction of distortion; (*e*) *Dent:* straightening, regulation (of teeth).

redresser [rədrese], *v.tr.* **1.** (*a*) to re-erect, (fallen statue, etc.); to set (sth.) upright again; (*b*) to right (boat, aeroplane); (*c*) *Av:* **r. l'avion (avant l'atterrissage),** to lift the nose of the plane (before landing); *abs.* to pull on the joystick; (*d*) *Opt:* to erect (inverted image). **2.** (*a*) to straighten (out) (path, bent wood, warped metal, affair, etc.); to true (surface); *Mil:* **r. la ligne, se r.,** to straighten out, re-establish, one's line; **r. une embarcation,** to trim a boat; *Nau:* **r. la barre,** to right the helm; (*b*) **r. la tête,** (i) to hold up one's head; to look up; (ii) (*with indignation*) to bridle up; (*c*) *El:* to rectify (current, voltage); **machine à courant redressé,** commutating machine; (*d*) to redress, to right (wrong, grievance); to rectify (mistake); to adjust (account); **r. l'enfance coupable,** to reclaim young delinquents; (*e*) *Opt: Phot:* to correct distortion in (image).

se redresser. **1.** (*a*) to stand up straight again; **se r. sur son séant,** to sit up again; (*b*) (*of boat*) to right; to get upright. **2.** (*a*) to draw oneself up, to hold one's head high; **il se redressa fièrement,** he drew himself up proudly; (*b*) to bridle up. **3.** to mend one's ways. **4.** *Av:* to flatten out (after a dive).

redresseur, -euse [rədrɛsœ:r, -ø:z]. **1.** *s.* (*a*) righter (of wrongs, etc.); **r. de torts,** knight errant; Don Quixote; (*b*) *Tchn:* straightener (of bent pieces of mechanism, etc.). **2.** *s.m.* (*a*) *El: Elcs:* rectifier (of current, voltage); **r. à une alternance, r. demi-onde,** half-wave rectifier; **r. à deux alternances, r. pleine-onde,** full-wave rectifier; **r. à commande magnétique,** magnetron rectifier; **r. à grilles commandées,** grid-controlled rectifier; **r. à lampe, à tube,** vacuum-tube rectifier, kenotron; **r. au sélénium, au silicium,** selenium, silicon, rectifier; **r. à vapeur de mercure,** mercury-vapour rectifier; **r. électrolytique,** electrolytic-cell rectifier; **r. mécanique,** mechanical rectifier; **r. sec, r. à semi-conducteurs,** dry rectifier; (*b*) turbine stator ring (of gas turbine engine). **3.** *a.* (*a*) **dispositif r.,** (i) *El:* rectifying device; (ii) *Opt:* erecting device; **valve redresseuse,** rectifying valve; **prisme r.,** erecting prism; *Phot:* **viseur r.,** reversal finder; (*b*) **mesures redresseuses,** corrective measures, measures calculated to restore the balance.

redû [rədy], *s.m.* balance due.

réducteur, -trice [redyktœ:r, -tris]. **1.** *a. Ch: Phot: Tchn:* reducing; *attrib.* reduction; *Ch:* **agent r.,** reducing agent; **gaz r.,** reducing gas; **flamme réductrice,** reducing flame; *Metall:* **creuset r.,** reducing crucible; *Mec.E:* **ensemble r.,** reduction gear assembly; **système r.,** gear-down mechanism; *Av:* **dispositif r. de bruit,** noise-reducing device, equipment. **2.** *s.m.* (*a*) *Ch: Phot:* reducer, reducing agent; **r. de Farmer,** Farmer's reducer; (*b*) *Mec.E:* (i) reducer; (ii) reduction gear, reduction unit; **r. de vitesse,** speed reducer; **r. à vis sans fin, à vis tangente,** worm gear (reduction); **r. à satellites,** epicyclic gear (reduction); **ce moteur est offert avec ou sans r.,** this engine is offered with geared or direct drive; *Mch:* **r. de course,** stroke reducer; **r. de pression,** reducing valve; *Av: etc:* **r. de bruit,** noise reducer; *Av:* **r. de trim,** trim gear; (*c*) *El:* **r. de tension,** potential reducer, attenuator; attenuating potentiometer; *Th:* **r. d'éclairage,** dimmer; (*d*) *Med:* (fracture) reducer, reducing apparatus; (*e*) *Anthr:* **(Indiens) réducteurs de têtes,** (Indian) head shrinkers.

réductibilité [redyktibilite], *s.f.* reducibility, reducibleness, reductibility.

réductible [redyktibl], *a.* reducible (amount, fraction, *Surg:* fracture).

réduction [redyksjɔ̃], *s.f.* **1.** (*a*) reduction (of amount, of taxation, etc.); restriction, cutting down (of expenditure); abatement; **r. homothétique,** scaling down; *Mth:* **r. d'une fraction à sa plus simple expression,** reduction of a fraction to its simplest expression; **r. à l'horizontale,** reduction to the horizontal; **échelle, compas, de r.,** reducing scale, compass; *Log:* **r. à l'absurde,** *reductio ad absurdum*; *Jur:* **r. de peine,** mitigation of penalty; **r. de dons et legs,** abatement of gifts and legacies; **action en r.,** action in abatement (by heirs); **r. à un grade inférieur,** *Mil:* reducing (of a man); *Navy:* disrating; *Fin:* **r. de capital,** writing down of capital; (*b*) *Surg:* **r. d'une fracture, etc.,** setting, reducing, of a fracture, etc.; **r. sanglante,** open reduction; (*c*) *Mec.E:* gearing down (of machinery); gear ratio; *El:* **r. de tension,** stepping down of voltage; (*d*) *Ch: Metall:* reduction; (*e*) conquest (of a province); capture by siege, reduction (of a town). **2.** (*a*) **réductions de salaires,** cuts in wages, wage cuts; **réductions sur les traitements,** salary cuts; **supprimer les réductions,** to restore the cuts; *Com:* **grandes réductions de prix,** great reductions (in price); **réductions sur la quantité,** discount, concessions, for quantities; *Bank:* **r. du taux de l'escompte,** lowering of the bank rate; (*b*) *Mus:* **r. pour piano, pour orgue,** short score (of opera, etc.); (*c*) reduced copy, reduction (of statue, picture, etc.); smaller edition; **bateau, maison, en r.,** scaled-down model of a ship, house.

réductionnel, -elle [redyksjɔnɛl], *a. Biol:* **mitose réductionnelle,** reduction division, meiosis.

réduire [redɥiːr], *v.tr.* (*pr.p.* **réduisant;** *p.p.* **réduit;** *pr.ind.* **je réduis, il réduit, n. réduisons;** *p.d.* **je réduisais;** *p.h.* **je réduisis;** *fu.* **je réduirai**) to reduce. **1.** (*a*) **r. la pression,** to reduce, relieve, the pressure; *Nau: etc:* **r. la vitesse,** to reduce speed; **r. le prix d'un article,** to reduce, lower, bring down, cut, the price of an article; *Bank:* **r. le taux de l'escompte,** to lower the bank rate; **r. ses dépenses,** to reduce, curtail, cut down, one's expenses; **r. les libertés publiques,** to curtail, restrict, public liberties; **l'amoindrissement des revenus a réduit la natalité,** the reduction of incomes has brought down the birth rate; **r. un ouvrage,** to abridge a work; **r. un dessin,** to reduce a design, to bring a design down to a smaller scale; **réduit de moitié, au quart,** reduced to half, a quarter of, the natural size; **r. une dissolution,** to boil down a solution; **r. un homme à un grade inférieur,** *Mil:* to reduce a man; *Navy:* to disrate a man; *Fin:* **r. le capital,** to write down the capital; *El:* **r. la tension,** to step down the voltage; (*b*) **r. du grain en farine, du bois en cendres,** to reduce grain to flour, wood to ashes; **réduit en poussière,** reduced to dust; **r. qch. en miettes,** to crumble sth. up; to pound sth. to atoms; **r. des francs en centimes,** to reduce francs to centimes; (*c*) *Ch: etc:* **r. un oxyde,** to reduce an oxide; *Cu:* **r. une sauce,** to reduce a sauce; (*d*) *Mth:* **r. deux fractions au même dénominateur,** to reduce, bring, two fractions to a common denominator; (*e*) *Mus:* **r. une partition,** to arrange a score for the piano. **2.** (*a*) **r. qn à la misère, au désespoir,** to reduce s.o. to poverty; to drive s.o. to despair; **r. qn à demander pardon,** to reduce, compel, s.o. to ask for pardon; **j'en suis réduit à . . ., à faire . . .,** I am reduced to . . ., to doing . . .; (*b*) **r. une ville, une province,** to reduce a town, to subjugate a province; **r. qn par la famine,** to starve s.o. into submission; **r. un cheval,** to break a horse. **3.** *Surg:* to reduce (fracture, dislocation, etc.). **4.** *Sw.Fr. F:* to tidy away.

se réduire. 1. se r. au strict nécessaire, to confine oneself to what is strictly necessary. **2. voilà où se réduit votre argument,** that is what your argument amounts to, comes to; **les frais se réduisent à peu de chose,** in fact the expenses come to very little; **toute la difficulté se réduit à savoir si . . .,** the whole difficulty comes down, *F:* boils down, to the question of whether . . .; **à quoi se réduit tout cela?** what is the upshot of it all? what does all that boil down to? **se r. en poussière,** to crumble into dust; **la sauce s'est réduite,** the sauce has boiled down, boiled away; **faire r. un sirop,** to boil down a syrup; **ces bruits se réduisent à rien,** these rumours boil down to nothing. **3.** *Sw.Fr:* to hide (oneself).

réduit[1] [redɥi], *a.* reduced; **prix r.,** reduced, cut, price; **billet à prix r.,** cheap ticket; **mécanisme r.,** reduced mechanism; **modèle r.,** scaled-down model; *Publ:* **édition réduite,** abridged edition; *Cin:* **film (de format) r.,** substandard film; *Ins:* **assurance à prime réduite,** low-premium insurance; **assurance à tarif r.,** low-rate insurance; **aller à vitesse réduite,** to go at a reduced speed; *Com:* **débouchés réduits,** restricted market.

réduit[2], *s.m.* **1.** (*a*) small, poor room or dwelling; closet; **un misérable r.,** a wretched hovel; **il dormait dans un r. sans fenêtres et sans porte,** he slept in a sort of alcove without windows or door; **ce réduit qualifié laboratoire,** a poor little room that went under the name of laboratory; (*b*) alcove (in library, etc.); nook; **r. servant de placard,** alcove used as a cupboard. **2.** (*a*) *Fort:* keep, redoubt; (*b*) *N.Arch:* (i) gun casement; (ii) armoured citadel (of battleship).

réduplicatif, -ive [redyplikatif, -iːv], *a.* **1.** *Bot:* reduplicate, reduplicative (aestivation). **2.** *Ling:* reduplicated (verb, etc.); reduplicating (particle).

réduplication [redyplikasjɔ̃], *s.f. Bot: Ling: etc:* reduplication.

rédupliqué [redyplike], *a. Bot:* reduplicate (leaf).

réduve [redyːv], *s.m. Ent:* reduvius, assassin bug.

réduviidés [redyviide], *s.m.pl. Ent:* Reduviidae.

réédification [reedifikasjɔ̃], *s.f.* rebuilding, re-erection.

réédifier [reedifje], *v.tr.* (*conj. like* ÉDIFIER) to rebuild; to re-erect (monument, etc.).

rééditer [reedite], *v.tr.* (*a*) to republish, re-issue (book, etc.); (*b*) to republish (libel); to rake up (old slander); *F:* **il a réédité la scène qu'il nous avait faite l'an dernier,** he gave us a new version of the scene he had made last year.

réédition [reedisjɔ̃], *s.f.* (*a*) re-issue (of book, etc.), republication; (*b*) *F:* **c'est une réédition du match France-Écosse de l'année dernière,** it's last year's France-Scotland match all over again; **la situation actuelle est une r. de celle d'il y a six mois,** the present situation is a repetition of what happened six months ago.

rééducatif, -ive [reedykatif, -iːv], *a.* **thérapie rééducative,** occupational therapy.

rééducation [reedykasjɔ̃], *s.f. Med:* re-education (of nerve-centres after paralysis, etc.); rehabilitation; **r. des mutilés,** rehabilitation of disabled men; **centre de r. (professionnelle)** rehabilitation centre.

rééduquer [reedyke], *v.tr. Med:* to re-educate (nerve-centres, etc.); to rehabilitate (the disabled).

réel, -elle [reɛl]. **1.** *a.* (*a*) real, actual; **c'est r.,** it's a fact; **personnage imaginaire ou personnage r.,** real or imaginary person; *Opt:* **image réelle,** true image; **un fait r. et incontestable,** a true and incontestable fact; *Ethn:* **parenté réelle,** blood relationship; *Mth:* **nombre r.,** real number; **calculateur à valeurs réelles,** absolute value computer; (*b*) **il était le chef r. de la maison sous le titre de secrétaire général,** he was the real head of the firm under the title of general secretary; **salaire nominal et salaire r.,** nominal wage rate and net earnings; *Com: etc:* **offre réelle,** cash offer, offer in cash; (*c*) (*before noun*) **éprouver un r. bien-être,** to have a real feeling of well-being; **prendre un r. plaisir à faire qch.,** to take real pleasure in doing sth.; (*d*) *Jur:* of real estate; **action réelle,** real action. **2.** *s.m.* **le réel,** the real, reality; **il faut rester dans le r.,** we must stick to realities.

réélection [reelɛksjɔ̃], *s.f.* re-election.

rééligibilité [reeliʒibilite], *s.f.* re-eligibility.

rééligible [reeliʒibl̩], *a.* re-eligible.

réélire [reeliːr], *v.tr.* (*conj. like* ÉLIRE) to re-elect.

réellement [reɛlmɑ̃], *adv.* (*a*) really; in reality; actually; in actual fact; **pensez-vous r. que . . .?** do you really think that . . .? **tous veulent être r. heureux,** everyone has a desire to be truly happy; **une seule action r. bonne,** one single really good action; (*b*) *Jur:* **saisir r.,** to seize, attach, real estate.

réembarquer [reɑ̃barke], *v.tr. & i.* to re-embark.

réembaucher [reɑ̃boʃe], *v.tr.* to re-engage, re-employ (labour).

réembobinage [reɑ̃bɔbinaːʒ], *s.m. Cin:* re-winding.

réembobiner [reɑ̃bɔbine], *v.tr. Cin:* to re-wind.

réembobineuse [reɑ̃bɔbinøːz], *s.f. Cin:* rewinder.

réémetteur [reemɛtœːr], *s.m. T.V: W.Tel:* relay transmitter.

réemploi [reɑ̃plwa], *s.m.* re-employment.

réemployer [reɑ̃plwaje], *v.tr.* = REMPLOYER.

réemption [reɑ̃psjɔ̃], *s.f. Jur:* (right of) redemption.

réencadrer [reɑ̃kadre], *v.tr.* to reframe (a picture).

réenclenchement [reɑ̃klɑ̃ʃmɑ̃], *s.m. Mec.E: etc:* reset; **r. automatique,** self reset; **r. à la main,** hand reset.

réenclencher [reɑ̃klɑ̃ʃe], *v.tr. Mec.E:* to re-engage (gear).

réendosser [reɑ̃dose], *v.tr.* to put on (one's coat, etc.) again.

réengagement [reɑ̃gaʒmɑ̃], *s.m. Mil:* re-enlisting, re-enlistment.

réengager (se) [sәreɑ̃gaʒe], *v.pr. Mil:* to re-enlist.

réenregistrement [reɑ̃rәʒistrәmɑ̃], *s.m.* re-recording.

réenregistrer [reɑ̃nrәʒistre], *v.tr.* to re-record; to store back (into computer store).

réenroulement [reɑ̃rulmɑ̃], *s.m.* rewinding.

réenrouler [reɑ̃rule], *v.tr.* to rewind.

réensemencement [reɑ̃s(ә)mɑ̃smɑ̃], *s.m. Agr:* re-sowing.

réensemencer [reɑ̃s(ә)mɑ̃se], *v.tr. Agr:* to resow (field, etc.).

réenvahir [reɑ̃vaiːr], *v.tr.* to re-invade, to invade again.

rééquilibre [reekilibr̥], *s.m.* restoration, recovery, of balance, of poise; **traitement qui favorise le r. mental,** treatment that tends to restore mental equilibrium.

rééquilibrer [reekilibre], *v.tr.* to restore the balance of (sth.); **r. le budget,** to rebalance the budget.

rééquipement [reekipmɑ̃], *s.m.* re-equipment.

rééquiper [reekipe], *v.tr.* to re-equip.

réer [ree], *v.i. Ven:* (*of stag*) to bell; to troat.

réescompte [reɛskɔ̃ːt], *s.m. Com:* rediscount, new discount.

réescompter [reɛskɔ̃te], *v.tr. Com:* to rediscount; to discount (bill) again.

réessayage [reɛsɛjaːʒ], *s.m. Tail: etc:* second fitting.

réessayer [reɛseje], *v.tr.* (*a*) *Tail:* to give a second fitting for (suit, etc.); (*b*) to try (sth.) again; *abs.* to have another try.

réestimation [reɛstimasjɔ̃], *s.f.* new estimation; reappraisal; revaluation.

réestimer [reɛstime], *v.tr.* to estimate, value, appraise (sth.) again, a second time; to re-appraise; to revalue (goods, etc.).

réétudier [reetydje], *v.tr.* to study (sth.) again.

réévaluation [reevalɥasjɔ̃], *s.f.* **1.** revaluation, new appraisement (of property, etc.); *Fin:* **r. du franc,** revaluation of the franc. **2.** reassessment, reappraisal.

réévaluer [reevalɥe], *v.tr.* to revalue; to appraise, estimate, again; *Fin:* **r. le franc,** to revalue the franc.

réexamen [reɛgzamɛ̃], *s.m.* re-examination.

réexaminer [reɛgzamine], *v.tr.* to re-examine.

réexpédier [reɛkspedje], *v.tr.* (*conj. like* EXPÉDIER) **1.** to send on, to (re)forward (sth.); to retransmit (telegram); to reship (goods). **2.** to send back (sth., *F:* s.o.).

réexpédition [reɛkspedisjɔ̃], *s.f.* **1.** sending on, (re-)forwarding; retransmission (of telegram); reshipment (of goods); redirection (of parcel). **2.** sending back, return (to sender).

réexportateur [reɛkspɔrtatœːr], *s.m.* re-exporter.

réexportation [reɛkspɔrtasjɔ̃], *s.f.* re-exportation.

réexporter [reɛkspɔrte], *v.tr.* to re-export.

réexposer [reɛkspoze], *v.tr.* to re-expose.

refaçon [rәfasɔ̃], *s.f.* remaking, refashioning.

refaçonner [rәfasɔne], *v.tr.* to remake, refashion.

réfaction [refaksjɔ̃], *s.f.* **1.** *Com:* allowance, reduction, rebate, drawback (on goods not up to sample, etc.); allowance (for loss in transport). **2.** repairs (to property, under repairing lease).

refaire [rәfɛːr], *v.tr.* (*conj. like* FAIRE) **1.** to remake; to do (piece of work, etc.) again; to make (journey, acquaintance) again; **r. une phrase,** to recast a sentence; **r. une pièce,** to rewrite a play; **r. sa malle,** to pack one's trunk again; *F:* (*in pub. etc. when ordering a new round of drinks*) **à r.,** same again, please; **c'est à r.,** it will have to be done (over) again; **si c'était à r.,** if I had to do it again; (*computers*) **r. une carte (perforée),** to repunch a card. **2.** (*a*) to do up (a dress, a house, etc.) again; to repair, mend; to recover (one's health, strength); **à une vieille maison il y a toujours à r.,** if you have an old house there are always repairs to be done; *F:* **elle se refait une beauté,** she's redoing her face, titivating herself; (*b*) *Equit:* to make (a horse). **3.** *F:* (*a*) to dupe, do, bilk, diddle (s.o.); to take (s.o.) in; **on vous a refait,** you've bought, been sold, a pup; **être refait,** to be had; **je suis refait de dix francs,** I have been done, tricked, out of ten francs; (*b*) **r. qch. à qn,** to rob s.o. of sth.; **on m'a refait mon porte-monnaie,** I've had my purse pinched. **4.** (*of stag*) **r. sa tête,** to grow a new set of antlers. **5.** *v.i. Cards:* to redeal.

se refaire. 1. (*a*) to recover one's health; to recuperate; to pick up again; **il s'est bien refait,** he has made a good recovery; (*b*) **à mon âge on ne peut pas se r.,** at my age a man can't change his ways. **2.** *Com: etc:* to retrieve one's losses; to recoup oneself; to re-establish one's affairs.

refaiseur, -euse [rәfәzœːr, -øːz], *s.* **1.** remaker. **2.** *P: A:* swindler.

refait [rәfɛ]. **1.** *a.* prepared, squared (timber); made (horse); twice-laid (rope). **2.** *s.m. Ven:* new horns (of stag). **3.** *s.m. Cards:* (*trente et quarante*) refait.

réfection [refɛksjɔ̃], *s.f.* **1.** (*a*) remaking; rebuilding (of bridge, etc.); repairing, restoration; doing up; **r. des rues,** street repairs; **route en r.,** road under repair, road up; (*b*) *Jur:* **r. d'un acte,** redrafting of an act (to make it valid). **2.** (*a*) *A:* restoration to health; (*b*) *Ecc:* (*in convent*) meal (eaten in common).

réfectionner [refɛksjɔne]. **1.** *v.tr. Tchn: F:* to repair, overhaul; to do up (a house, etc.). **2.** *v.i.* to take some refreshment.

réfectoire [refɛktwaːr], *s.m.* refectory, dining hall (in monasteries, schools, etc.).

réfectorier, -ière [refɛktɔrje, -jɛːr], *s. Ecc:* refectorian.

refend [rəfɑ̃], *s.m.* **1.** splitting, slitting, ripping; **bois de r.,** longitudinally cut wood, wood in planks. **2.** (*a*) *Const:* **pierre de r.,** corner stone; **mur de r.,** internal partition (wall), cross wall; **ligne de r.,** joint line on façade (of building); (*b*) poster site on wall at right angles to the road; (*c*) *Hort:* espalier wall.

refendage [rəfɑ̃daːʒ], *s.m. Leath:* splitting, slitting (of skins).

refendre [rəfɑ̃ːdr̥], *v.tr.* to split, cleave (slates); to slit (leather); to rip (timber); **bambou refendu,** split cane.

refendu [rəfɑ̃dy], *s.m.* split bamboo fishing rod.

refente [rəfɑ̃ːt], *s.f.* splitting, sawing, ripping.

référé [refere], *s.m. Jur:* summary procedure; **(ordonnance de) r.,** order delivered by judge sitting in chambers; provisional order, injunction; **juger en r.,** to try a case (sitting) in chambers.

référence [referɑ̃ːs], *s.f.* reference; referring; (*a*) **livre, ouvrage, de r.,** reference book, work of reference; **faire r. à un ouvrage,** to refer to a work, a book; **références au bas des pages,** footnotes; **indemnité fixée par r. au traitement,** compensation fixed with reference to, according to, salary; *Med: etc:* **groupe de r.,** reference group; *Tchn:* **calibre de r.,** reference gauge; **température de r.,** reference temperature; *El:* **circuit de r.,** reference circuit; *Tp:* **niveau téléphonique de r.,** reference telephone power; *Surv: etc:* **r. topographique,** map reference; **niveau de r.,** datum level, reference level; **plan de r.,** datum plane, plane of reference; *Astr:* **système de r. céleste,** celestial reference system; *Nau:* **position, point, de r.,** reference position; *Elcs:* (*computers*) **point de r.,** benchmark; **problème de r.,** benchmark problem; **article de r.,** reference record; **champ (magnétique) de r.,** reference field; (*b*) *Corr: etc:* reference (on letter, document); **r. à rappeler,** in replying please quote; (*c*) *Com:* sample book, book of patterns; (*d*) *pl.* **références,** (i) (employee's) reference, testimonial; (ii) *Com:* clientele, customers (of manufacturer, etc.).

référencer [referɑ̃se], *v.tr. Com: F:* (*a*) to put a reference on (a letter); (*b*) to classify (sample, pattern) in a sample book.

référendaire [referɑ̃dɛːr], *s.m.* **1.** *Jur:* chief clerk (of commerical court). **2.** *Fr.Hist:* **Grand R. (du Sénat impérial),** Great Referendary. **3.** *a.* pertaining to a referendum, referendary.

référendariat [referɑ̃darja], *s.m. Jur: Hist:* office, position, of chief clerk of commercial court, of referendary.

referendum, référendum [referɛ̃dɔm], *s.m.* referendum.

référentiel, -ielle [referɑ̃sjɛl]. **1.** *a.* referential. **2.** *s.m. Mth: etc:* reference frame, frame of reference, reference system.

référer [refere], *v.* (**je réfère, n. référons; je référerai**) **1.** *v.tr.* (*a*) to refer, ascribe (**qch. à qch.,** sth. to sth.); to refer, attribute (**qch. à qn,** sth. to s.o.); (*b*) *Jur:* **r. un serment (décisoire) à qn,** to tender back a decisive oath to s.o. **2.** *v.i. Jur:* **r. à qn d'une question,** to refer a matter to s.o.; **en r. à la cour,** to report to the court; to submit the case to the court.

se référer. 1. se r. à qch., to refer to sth.; **me référant à ma lettre du 20 ct,** with reference to my letter of the 20th inst. **2. se r. à qn,** to ask s.o.'s opinion; **s'en r. à qn, à l'avis de qn,** to refer, leave, the matter to s.o., to s.o.'s decision; **se r., s'en r., à qn d'une question,** to refer a matter to s.o.

refermer [rəfɛrme], *v.tr.* to reclose; to shut, close (door) again; to shut up (box) again; to close up (grave, etc.) again; **il referma la porte sur lui,** he closed the door after him.

se refermer, (*of door*) to close (again); (*of wound*) to close up, to heal; **le couvercle se referma avec un bruit sec,** the lid snapped to.

referrer [rəfere], *v.tr.* to reshoe (horse, etc.).

refeuillé [rəføje], *a. Carp:* **joint r.,** rabbet, rebate, *Scot:* check, joint.

refeuillement [rəføjmɑ̃], *s.m. Carp:* re-rabbeting.

refeuiller [rəføje], *v.tr. Carp:* to re-rabbet, make an additional rabbet.

reficher [rəfiʃe], *v.tr. Const:* to re-point (a wall).

refil [rəfil], *s.m. P:* **aller au r.,** to be sick, to throw up.

refiler [rəfile], *v.tr. P:* **r. qch. à qn,** (i) to fob off, palm off, sth. on s.o.; to foist, unload, sth. on s.o.; to work sth. off on s.o.; (ii) to give s.o. sth.; **se faire r. qch.,** to get palmed off with sth.

réfléchi [refleʃi], *a.* **1.** (*a*) reflected (light, etc.); (*b*) (*computers*) **code binaire r.,** reflected binary code, Gray code, cyclic code. **2.** reflective, thoughtful, serious-minded (person); deliberate, considered (action, opinion); premeditated (crime); **réponse (bien) réfléchie,** careful answer; **opinion peu réfléchie,** inconsiderate, hasty, opinion; **tout bien r.,** everything considered, after due consideration. **3.** (*a*) *Bot:* reflexed (petal, etc.); (*b*) *Gram:* reflexive verb, pronoun).

réfléchir [refleʃiːr]. **1.** *v.tr.* to reflect, to throw back (image, light, sound, at a certain angle); to bend back (light); to reverberate (sound). **2.** (*a*) *v.i.* **r. à, sur, qch.,** to reflect on sth., to ponder, consider, weigh, sth.; to turn sth. over in one's mind; **je vais r. à la réponse à faire,** I shall consider what answer we should give; **réfléchissez-y,** think it over; **réfléchissez avant d'agir,** think well before you act; **réfléchissez donc!** think again! think it over! **donner à r. à qn,** to give s.o. food for thought, cause for reflection; **cela lui a donné à r.,** that made him think twice; **après avoir beaucoup réfléchi,** after much thought; **parler sans r.,** to speak without thinking, hastily; **agir sans avoir suffisamment réfléchi,** to act without due reflection; **c'est tout réfléchi,** my mind is made up already; (*b*) *v.tr.* **il réfléchit que . . .,** he reflected that . . .; it occurred to him that . . ..

se réfléchir, (*of light, heat, sound, etc.*) to be reflected, to be thrown back; (*of sound*) to reverberate; **le caractère d'un temps se réfléchit dans les controverses de ce temps,** the characteristics of an age are reflected, revealed, in its controversies.

réfléchissant [refleʃisɑ̃], *a.* **1.** reflecting, reflective (surface, etc.). **2.** *A:* reflective, thoughtful (person); **peu r.,** thoughtless, rash.

réfléchissement [refleʃismɑ̃], *s.m.* reflection, reflecting (of light, heat, sound, etc.); reverberation (of sound).

réflectance [reflɛktɑ̃ːs], *s.f. Opt: etc:* reflectance, reflectivity.

réflecteur, -trice [reflɛktœːr, -tris]. **1.** *a.* reflecting (mirror, etc.); **écran r.,** reflecting panel; **pouvoir r.,** reflectance, reflectivity; **revêtement r.,** reflector coating; *Atom.Ph:* **substance réflectrice,** tamper material. **2.** *s.m.* (*a*) reflector (of lamp); *Phot: Cin:* reflecting panel, reflector (to reflect light on to the subject); **r. à miroir,** (i) mirror reflector; (ii) *Sm.a:* reflector; *El:* **r. à charbon passant,** hole reflector; *Aut: etc:* **r. à bascule,** tilting reflector; **r. plan, convexe, parabolique,** plane, convex, parabolic, reflector; **braquer les réflecteurs de l'histoire sur . . .,** to turn the searchlights of history on to . . .; (*b*) *Opt:* reflecting telescope, reflector; (*c*) *Ac:* (sound) reflector; **r. parabolique de son,** sound concentrator; (*d*) *Elcs: W.Tel:* **r. d'antenne,** aerial reflector; (*radar*) **r. métallique, r. triangulaire,** corner reflector; (*e*) *Atom.Ph:* (i) reflector (of reactor); (ii) tamper (material); **r. de neutrons,** neutron reflector; **r. électronique,** electron mirror; **réacteur avec r.,** reflected reactor; **réacteur sans r.,** bare, naked, reactor.

réflectif, -ive [reflɛktif, -iːv], *a.* reflective.

réflectivité [reflɛktivite], *s.f. Physiol:* **avoir une bonne r.,** to have good reflexes.

réflectomètre [reflɛktɔmɛtr̥], *s.m.* reflectometer.

réflectorisé [reflɛktɔrize], *a.* equipped with reflectors.

reflet [rəflɛ], *s.m.* (*a*) reflection; reflected light, image; *Art:* accidental light; **r. des eaux,** gleam on the waters; **les reflets de la lune sur le lac,** the reflection of the moon on the lake; **chevelure à, aux, reflets d'or,** hair with glints of gold; **r. des glaces,** ice blink; **reflets changeants,** ever-changing colours; **reflets irisés,** play of (iridescent) colours; **jeter des reflets variés,** to present a play of colours; **il n'est qu'un pâle r. de son père,** he's only a pale reflection of his father, *F:* he isn't a patch on his father; **l'écriture, r. de la personnalité,** handwriting as an indication of character; **la langue, qui est toujours le r. de l'esprit de chaque génération,** language, which always reflects the outlook of its generation; (*b*) *Petroleum Ind:* **r. d'une huile,** cast of an oil; **r. gras,** greasy lustre.

refléter [rəflete], *v.tr.* (**je reflète, n. reflétons; je refléterai**) to reflect (scattered light); to send back, throw back (light, colour); **le Louvre se reflète dans la Seine,** the Louvre is mirrored in the Seine; **mes paroles ne reflétaient nullement mes sentiments,** what I said in no way reflected, was no indication of, what I was feeling, thinking.

refleurir [rəflœriːr], *v.i.* **1.** to flower, blossom, again; to reflower, reblossom; **toute la nature est refleurie,** all nature is blossoming again; *occ. v.tr. Lit:* **ses petits-enfants refleurissaient son cœur,** his grandchildren made his heart young again. **2.** (*of art, literature*) to flourish again; to undergo a revival; **faire r. les arts,** to revive the arts. **3.** *v.tr.* **r. une tombe,** to put fresh flowers on a grave.

refleurissement [rəflœrismɑ̃], *s.m.* **1.** *Bot:* second flowering, blossoming; reflorescence. **2.** revival (of art, literature).

reflex [rəflɛks]. **1.** *a. & s.m. Phot:* **(appareil) r.,** reflex camera; **r. à un objectif, à deux objectifs,** single-lens, twin-lens, reflex camera. **2.** *a. Elcs:* reflex (circuit).

réflexe [reflɛks]. **1.** *a. Ph: Physiol:* reflex (light, action, etc.). **2.** *s.m.* (*a*) *Physiol:* reflex; **r. rotulien,** knee reflex, knee jerk; **r. achilléen,** Achilles' reflex; **r. plantaire,** plantar reflex; (*b*) reflex, reaction; **avoir du r., des réflexes,** to react quickly.

réflexibilité [reflɛksibilite], *s.f. Ph:* reflexibility.

réflexible [reflɛksibl̥], *a. Ph:* reflexible (ray).

réflexif, -ive [reflɛksif, -iːv], *a. Phil: etc:* reflexive; *Mth:* **relation réflexive,** reflexive relation.

réflexion [reflɛksjɔ̃], *s.f.* **1.** (*a*) *Ph:* reflection, reflexion (of image, light, sound, etc.); **r. spéculaire,** specular reflection; **r. sporadique,** sporadic reflection; **r. totale,** total reflection; **prisme à r. totale,** total-reflection prism; **angle de r.,** angle of reflection; **coefficient de r.,** reflection coefficient; reflectance; **facteur de r.,** reflection factor, reflectance; (*b*) *Atom.Ph:* reflection (of neutron beam, etc.); *Rad.A:* back-scattering, back-diffusion (of neutrons, X-rays, etc.); (*c*) *Elcs:* **électrode de r.,** reflection, reflecting, electrode; **gain, perte, par r.,** reflection gain, loss; (*Radar*) **intervalle de r. (d'une impulsion),** reflection interval (of a pulse). **2.** reflection, thought; **être plongé dans ses réflexions,** to be deep in thought; **agir sans r.,** to act rashly, inconsiderately, without thinking, without forethought, carelessly; **cela mérite r.,** it is worth thinking over; **cela exige de la r.,** it requires consideration; **cela demandait mûre r.,** it required careful thought; **(toute) r. faite, à la r.,** on thinking it over; everything considered; on (further) consideration, on reflection; on second thoughts; when you come to think of it; **à la r. vous changerez d'avis,** on reflection, when you think it over, you will change your mind; **il ne fit pas cette r. qu'elle pourrait être absente,** it didn't occur to him, he never considered the possibility, that she might not be there. **3.** remark; **une r. désobligeante,** an unpleasant remark.

réflexivité [reflɛksivite], *s.f.* reflexivity.

réflexogène [reflɛksɔʒɛn], *a. Physiol:* reflexogenic; reflexogenous; **zone r.,** trigger area.

réflexologie [reflɛksɔlɔʒi], *s.f. Psy:* reflexology.

réflexologique [reflɛksɔlɔʒik], *a.* reflexological.

réflexologiste [reflɛksɔlɔʒist], *s.m. & f. Med:* reflexologist.

refluement [rəflymɑ̃], *s.m.* refluence, flowing back; reflux.

refluer [rəflye], *v.i.* (*a*) to flow back; (*of the tide*) to ebb; **le sang lui reflua au visage,** the blood surged to, his, her, cheeks; **le sang lui reflua du visage,** the blood ebbed from his, her, face; (*b*) (*of invading horde, etc.*) to fall back, to surge back; (*c*) to sweep back; **l'eau reflua sur la berge,** the water washed up on to the bank; **une partie des fuyards reflua dans la Suisse,** some of the fugitives poured into Switzerland; **à la fin du match, la foule a reflué vers la ville,** after the match the crowd swept back towards the town.

reflux [rəfly], *s.m.* (*a*) reflux, flowing back; ebb(ing) (of tide); ebb tide; **le flux et le r.,** the ebb and flow; (*b*) surging back (of crowd, etc.).

refondre [rəfɔ̃ːdr̥], *v.tr.* **1.** to remelt; to recast (metal, a bell); to recoin, remint (money); to fuse (metal, etc.) again. **2.** *Nau:* **r. un navire,** to refit a ship entirely. **3. r. un poème,** to recast, remodel, a poem; *A:* **on ne peut pas se r.,** one cannot change one's nature.

refonte [rəfɔ̃ːt], *s.f.* **1.** recasting, remelting (of metals, etc.); recoinage (of money). **2.** refitting, refit (of ship). **3.** recasting (of treatise, play, etc.); remodelling, reorganization (of factory, etc.); (entire) re-shaping (of plans); reconstruction.

reforestation [rəfɔrɛstasjɔ̃], *s.f.* reafforestation.

reforger [rəfɔrʒe], *v.tr.* (*conj. like* FORGER) to reforge.

réformable [refɔrmabl̥], *a.* **1.** reformable (abuse, etc.). **2.** (*a*) (judgment) liable to be reversed on appeal); (*b*) *Mil:* (*man*) who may be discharged; (*horse*) that may be cast.

reformage [rəfɔrmaːʒ], *s.m. Petroleum Ind:* reforming; cracking.

réformateur, -trice [refɔrmatœːr, -tris]. **1.** *a.* reforming. **2.** *s.* reformer.

réformation [refɔrmasjɔ̃], *s.f.* reformation, reform; *Rel.H:* **la R.,** the Reformation.

réformatoire [refɔrmatwaːr], *a.* reformatory, reformative.

réforme [refɔrm], *s.f.* **1.** reformation, reform (of abuses, of the calendar, etc.); *A:* **école de r.,** reformatory (for young delinquents); **mettre la r. dans une administration,** to reform an administration; *Rel.H:* **la R.,** the Reformation. **2.** (*a*) *Mil: etc:* (i) discharge (for physical unfitness); invaliding out; rejection (of recruit for physical unfitness); **r. temporaire,** deferment (of military service); **congé de r.,** sick leave, temporary discharge; **traitement de r.,** reduced pay, half pay; **commission de r.,** special medical board; (ii) **r. (d'un officier) par mesure de discipline,** cashiering, dismissal from the service; (iii) **r. des chevaux,** casting of horses; **chevaux de r.,** cast horses; **mettre (qn, un cheval) à la r.,** (i) to discharge (man, officer) from the service, to put (officer) on half pay; (ii) to dismiss, cashier (officer); (iii) to cast (horse); (*b*) *Ind:* **r. du matériel,** scrapping of plant; **matériel en r.,** scrapped plant.

réformé, -ée [refɔrme]. **1.** *a.* (*a*) *Rel.H:* reformed (church, religion); (*b*) invalided (out of the army, etc.); (*c*) (officer) on half pay; (*d*) (officer) cashiered, dismissed from the service; (*e*) cast (horse); (*f*) scrapped (machinery); *F:* cast off (clothing). **2.** *s.* (*a*) *A:* protestant; member of one of the Reformed Churches; (*b*) *s.m. Mil: etc:* man invalided out of the service; **réformés de guerre avec invalidité,** disabled ex-servicemen; **r. temporaire,** (i) deferred recruit; (ii) soldier, etc. on temporary discharge.

reformer [rəfɔrme], *v.tr.* (*a*) to form again, to re-form (battalion, etc.); **r. les rangs,** to fall into line again; (*b*) to reblock (hat); (*c*) **des nuages se reforment,** clouds are forming again; *Pol:* **l'opposition se reformait,** the opposition was uniting for action, was gathering itself together again.

réformer [refɔrme], *v.tr.* **1.** (*a*) to reform (one's conduct, an abuse, the laws, etc.); (*b*) to retrench (expenditure). **2.** *Jur:* (*of a court of appeal*) **r. un jugement,** to reverse a decision. **3.** (*a*) *Mil: Navy:* (i) to discharge (soldier, etc.) as unfit; to retire (officer); to invalid (a man) out of the army; (*of recruit*) **réformé pour myopie,** rejected on account of short-sightedness; (ii) to dismiss (officer) from the service; to cashier; (iii) to cast (horse); (*b*) to condemn, scrap (equipment); *Ind:* **r. le matériel,** to scrap the plant.

reforming [rəfɔrmiŋ], *s.m.* reforming (of crude oil).

réformisme [refɔrmism], *s.m. Pol:* reformism.

réformiste [refɔrmist], *a.* & *s.m.* & *f. Pol: Rel.H:* reformist.

refouillement [rəfujmɑ̃], *s.m.* (*in sculpture*) deep carving (of stone).

refouiller [rəfuje], *v.tr.* (*of sculptor*) to carve deeply into (the stone, to bring out the relief).

refoulant [rəfulɑ̃], *a.* **1. pompe refoulante,** force pump. **2.** *Psy:* repressing, repressive, inhibiting.

refoulé, -ée [rəfule], *Psy:* **1.** *a.* repressed; inhibited. **2.** *s.* person suffering from repression, from inhibition.

refoulement [rəfulmɑ̃], *s.m.* **1.** (*a*) pressing back; driving back, forcing back (of the enemy, etc.); driving, forcing, in or out (of pin, bolt); stemming (of the tide, of invasion); backing (of train); upsetting, jumping up (of metal); tamping (of earth, etc.); compressing (of gas); (*b*) *Hyd.E:* (i) delivery, discharge, output (of pipe); (ii) lift (of pump); **soupape de r.,** delivery valve (of pump); **conduit de r.,** delivery pipe; (*c*) *Mch:* back flow, backward flow (of water, etc.); **tuyau de r.,** exhaust pipe; (*d*) *Psy:* (unconscious) repression, suppression (of desires); suppressed desire; inhibition. **2.** *Tex:* remilling (of cloth).

refouler [rəfule], *v.tr.* **1.** (*a*) to drive back, force back, press back; *Adm:* to expel, to turn back (an alien); to stem (attack); to compress (water, gas, etc.); to drive, force, in or out (bolt, pin, etc.); (*of ship*) to stem (the tide, the current); to back (train); to upset, jump up (metal); to tamp (earth, etc.); to deliver, discharge (water); **r. l'ennemi,** to drive back, press back, hurl back, the enemy; *Artil:* **r. un projectile à poste,** to ram home a projectile; *Metall:* **machine à r. le métal,** extruding machine; **être refoulé,** to be driven back or borne backwards; **r. ses sentiments,** to repress, suppress, contain, one's feelings; **r. ses larmes, ses sanglots,** to check, force back, keep back, one's tears; to gulp down one's sobs; *Psy:* **r. un instinct dans l'inconscient,** to drive back an instinct into the unconscious; to repress an instinct; (*b*) *v.i. Mec.E: etc:* (*of pin*) to go the wrong way; **le boulon refoule,** the bolt refuses; (*c*) *v.i.* **la mer, la marée, refoule,** the tide is ebbing, is on the ebb. **2.** *Tex:* to re-mill (cloth). **3.** *v.i. P:* to stink; to have foul breath.

refouleur [rəfulœːr], *s.m. Ind:* compressor; *Hyd.E:* force pump.

refouloir [rəfulwaːr], *s.m.* (*a*) *Min:* tamping tool; (*b*) *Artil:* rammer; (*c*) *Metalw:* jumper, jumping hammer.

réfractaire [refraktɛːr]. **1.** *a.* (*a*) refractory rebellious, insubordinate (person); **r. à la loi,** unwilling to accept the law; *Psy:* **période psychologique r.,** refractory period; *Fr.Hist:* **prêtre r.,** non-juring priest; (*b*) *Tchn:* refractory (ore); fireproof, fire (brick, clay, etc.); **tampon r.,** plug of fireclay; (*c*) **r. aux acides,** acid-proof; **le coton est r. à la teinture,** cotton does not take dyes well; **organisme r. au poison,** organism unaffected by poison, proof against poison. **2.** *s.* (*a*) refractory person; rebel; conscientious objector; defaulter; (*b*) *F:* bad character.

réfractant [refraktɑ̃], *a. Ph:* refracting, refractive (surface, etc.).

réfracté [refrakte], *a.* **1.** refracted (ray). **2.** *Med:* **dose réfractée,** repeated dose.

réfracter [refrakte], *v.tr. Ph:* to refract, bend (rays, etc.).

se réfracter, to be refracted, to suffer refraction.

réfractérité [refrakterite], *s.f.* refractoriness.

réfracteur [refraktœːr]. **1.** *a.m.* refracting. **2.** *s.m.* refractor, refracting telescope.

réfractif, -ive [refraktif, -iːv], *a. Ph:* refractive.

réfraction [refraksjɔ̃], *s.f.* refraction, bending (of rays, neutron beam, etc.); **double r.,** double refraction, birefringence; **à double r.,** birefracting, birefractive, birefringent; **r. atmosphérique,** atmospheric refraction; **indice de r.,** index of refraction, refractive index; *Opt:* **dispositif optique à r.,** refracting, refractive, optical system; *Cin:* **film à r.,** three-D(imensional) film.

réfractionniste [refraksjɔnist], *s.m.* & *f. Opt:* optometrist.

réfractivité [refraktivite], *s.f.* refractivity.

réfractomètre [refraktɔmɛtr̥], *s.m. Ph:* refractometer; **r. à parallaxe,** parallax refractometer; **r. à immersion,** immersion refractometer, dipping refractometer.

réfractométrie [refraktɔmetri], *s.f.* refractometry.

refrain [rəfrɛ̃], *s.m.* **1.** (*a*) refrain, burden (of a song); **chanter de vieux refrains,** to sing old songs, old ditties; (*b*) **c'est son r. continuel, avec lui c'est toujours le même r.,** he's always harping on the same string; **c'est le r. (de la ballade),** it's the same old story. **2. r. en chœur,** chorus.

réfrangibilité [refrɑ̃ʒibilite], *s.f. Ph:* refrangibility.

réfrangible [refrɑ̃ʒibl̥], *a. Ph:* refrangible.

refrappage [rəfrapaːʒ], *s.m.,* **refrappement** [rəfrapmɑ̃], *s.m.* recoining, recoinage.

refrapper [rəfrape], *v.tr.* **1.** to strike (s.o., sth.) again; to knock again (at the door). **2.** to recoin (gold or silver).

refrènement [rəfrɛnmɑ̃], *s.m. Lit:* curbing (of instincts, etc.).

refréner [rəfrene], *v.tr.* (**je refrène, n. refrénons; je refrénerai**) to curb, bridle, restrain (one's passions, etc.); to control (a passion).

réfrigérant [refriʒerɑ̃]. **1.** *a.* (*a*) refrigerating, cooling (action, apparatus); freezing (mixture); (*b*) refrigerant (medicine). **2.** *s.m.* (*a*) refrigerator, condenser (of still); cooler, refrigerator (of freezing apparatus); *Ind:* **r. à cheminée,** cooling tower; **r. à ruissellement,** surface cooler; **r. soufflé,** forced-draught cooler; (*b*) *Med:* refrigerant.

réfrigérateur, -trice [refriʒeratœːr, -tris]. **1.** *a.* refrigerating (apparatus, etc.); **appareil r.,** refrigerator. **2.** *s.m.* refrigerator; *F:* frig, fridge; cooler; **r. à absorption,** absorption refrigerator; **r. à compression,** compression refrigerator.

réfrigératif, -ive [refriʒeratif, -iːv], *a.* & *s.m. Med: A:* refrigerant, refrigerative.

réfrigération [refriʒerasjɔ̃], *s.f.* refrigeration; chilling (of meat, etc.); *Ind:* **tour de r.,** cooling tower.

réfrigérer [refriʒere], *v.tr.* (**je réfrigère, n. réfrigérons; je réfrigérerai**) to refrigerate; **viande réfrigérée,** chilled meat; *Trans:* **camion réfrigéré,** refrigerated van; *Rail:* **wagon réfrigéré,** refrigerated wagon; *U.S:* refrigerator car.

réfringence [refrɛ̃ʒɑ̃ːs], *s.f. Ph:* refringency; refractivity.

réfringent [refrɛ̃ʒɑ̃], *a. Ph:* refringent, refractive, refracting.

refrognement [rəfrɔɲmɑ̃], *s.m. A:* = RENFROGNEMENT.

refrogner [rəfrɔɲe], *v.tr. A:* = RENFROGNER.

refroidi [rəfrwadi], *s.m. P:* corpse, stiff.

refroidir [rəfrwadiːr]. **1.** *v.tr.* (*a*) to cool, chill (air, water, temperature, etc.); **laisser r. le lait, le potage,** to let milk, soup, cool off; (*b*) *Mec.E: Ind:* to cool (engine, fluid, etc.); *Metall:* to quench (hot metal in oil or cold water); *Art:* to cool, decrease (a colour); **r. par l'air,** to air-cool; **refroidi par (l')air,** air-cooled; **r. par l'eau,** to water-cool; **refroidi par (l')eau,** water-cooled; **refroidi par ventilateur,** fan-cooled; *Ph: Ind:* (*of gas*) **refroidi par détente, par dilatation,** cooled by expansion; (*c*) to cool, chill (friendship, passion, zeal, etc.); to damp (sympathy); to cool (off), dash (s.o.'s enthusiasm); (*d*) *P:* to kill (s.o.), to do (s.o.) in, *U.S:* to make cold meat of (s.o.); *U.S:* to cool (s.o.). **2.** *v.i.* & *pr.* (*a*) to grow cold; to cool down, to cool off; **laisser r. son thé,** to let one's tea get cold; **le temps a refroidi, s'est refroidi,** it has grown colder; **l'enthousiasme se refroidit,** enthusiasm is cooling off; (*b*) *Med:* **se r.,** to catch a chill.

refroidissement [rəfrwadismɑ̃], *s.m.* **1.** (*a*) cooling (of air, water, temperature, etc.); **r. du temps,** fall in temperature; (*b*) *Mec.E: Ind:* cooling (of engine, fluid, etc.); *Metall:* quenching (of hot metal in oil or cold water); slacking (of blast furnace); **r. naturel,** self-cooling; **r. accéléré, forcé,** forced cooling; **r. canalisé,** ducted cooling; **r. préalable,** pre-cooling; **r. par air, par eau,** air cooling, water cooling; **départ de l'eau de r.,** cooling-water outlet; **r. par fluide, par liquide,** fluid cooling, liquid cooling; **r. forcé par fluide, par liquide,** forced-fluid, forced-liquid, cooling; **fluide, liquide, de r.,** cooling fluid, liquid; coolant; **r. par diffusion,** effusion cooling; **r. par évaporation,** evaporative cooling; *Metall:* **r. brusque,** quenching; **agent de r.,** cooling agent, coolant; **dispositif, système, de r.,** cooling system; **ailette de r.,** cooling fin, flange, vane; **bac, cuve, de r.,** cooling tank, pond; **chemise, manchon, de r.,** cooling jacket; *Atom. Ph:* **système, installation, de r. du combustible,** fuel-cooling system, installation; **boucle de r.,** coolant loop; (*c*) *Art:* cooling, decreasing (of colour). **2.** *Med:* **attraper un r.,** to catch a chill. **3. r. (de l'amitié),** cooling off (of friendship).

refroidisseur [rəfrwadisœːr]. **1.** *a.* cooling; **agent r.,** cooling agent, coolant; **système r.,** cooling system (of reactor, etc.). **2.** *s.m.* (*a*) *Mec.E: Ind:* cooler, refrigerator unit; (*in spacecraft, etc.*) heat-sink; **r. à l'huile,** oil-cooler; **r. à tuyauterie double, tubulaire, r. à double enveloppe,** double-pipe chiller; *El:* **r. de transformateur,** transformer cooler; (*b*) *Atom.Ph:* cooler, coolant; **r. primaire, secondaire,** primary, secondary, cooler or coolant; **r. intermédiaire,** intercooler, intercoolant.

refuge [rəfyːʒ], *s.m.* refuge; (*a*) **Dieu est mon r.,** God is my refuge; **(lieu de) r.,** place of refuge; **chercher r.,** to seek refuge; (*b*) *Adm: A:* **maison de r.,** almshouse; (*c*) *Mount:* (Alpine) refuge; (climbers') hut; *Mil:* **r. de blessés,** collecting station; (*d*) **r. d'oiseaux,** bird sanctuary; (*e*) (*on road*) (i) layby, parking place; (ii) street refuge, traffic island; (*f*) *A:* pretext, evasion.

réfugié, -ée [refyʒje], *s.* refugee.

réfugier (se) [sərefyʒje], *v.pr.* to take refuge; to find shelter; to shelter; **se r. chez qn,** to take refuge with s.o.; **les voleurs se réfugièrent dans les montagnes,** the robbers took to the mountains; **se r. dans les mensonges,** to take refuge in lying, to have recourse to lies; to fall back on lies.

refuir [rəfɥiːr], *v.i. Ven:* to double back.

refuite [rəfɥit], *s.f.* **1.** *A:* excuse, pretext; delay (to gain time). **2.** *Ven:* double, doubling back.

refus [rəfy], *s.m.* **1.** (*a*) refusal; denial; **essuyer un r.,** to meet with a refusal; **r. de faire qch.,** refusal to do sth.; **sur son r. de se rendre,** on his refusal, refusing, to surrender; **r. d'obéissance à un ordre,** refusal to obey, non-compliance with, an order; **r. d'obéissance,** (i) insubordination; (ii) *Jur:* contempt of court; **le r. d'entendre M. X a été une grosse faute,** the denial of a hearing to Mr X was a serious blunder; *F:* **ce n'est pas de r.,** I can't say no to that; I accept gladly; **je n'admettrai pas de r.,** I won't take no for answer; *O:* **accepter qch. au r. d'un autre,** to accept sth. which has been refused by s.o. else; **ce n'est pas à son r.,** he has not had the refusal of it;

Tchn: **battre, enfoncer, (un pieu, etc.) (jusqu') à r. (de mouton),** to drive in (a pile, etc.) as far as possible; to drive (a pile) to refusal; to drive (a pile) home; **visser, serrer, un boulon à r.,** to screw a bolt home, tight; (*b*) *Equit:* refusal. **2.** (*a*) thing refused; *Agr:* (*in pasture*) plant left, not eaten (by grazing animals); *O:* **il ne veut pas du r. d'un autre,** he doesn't want s.o. else's leavings; (*b*) *Min:* **r. de crible,** oversize; **r. de broyage,** tailings.

refusable [rəfyzabl̩], *a.* refusable; **une telle offre n'est pas r.,** one cannot refuse an offer like this, such an offer.

refusant, -ante [rəfyzɑ̃, -ɑ̃:t]. **1.** *a.* refusing. **2.** *s.* refuser.

refusé, -ée [rəfyze]. **1.** *a.* refused, rejected; *Mil:* **aile refusée,** refused wing; *Post:* **lettre refusée,** blind letter. **2.** *s.* (*a*) artist, etc., whose work has been rejected; *Art:* **salon des refusés,** exhibition of rejected work; (*b*) *Sch:* candidate who has failed (an examination).

refuser [rəfyze], *v.tr.* **1.** (*a*) to refuse, decline (sth.); to turn down (offer); *abs:* **r. tout net,** to give a flat refusal, to refuse point blank; **r. de faire qch.,** to refuse to do sth.; **r. de payer une traite,** to dishonour a bill; **elle refusa qu'on la reconduisît,** she refused to be seen home; **r. qch. d'un geste,** to wave sth. away; **r. mille francs d'un tableau,** to refuse a thousand francs for a picture; **r. qch. à qn,** to refuse, deny, s.o. sth.; **se r. qch.,** to deny, grudge, oneself sth.; *F:* **il ne se refuse rien,** he doesn't stint himself; **il ne lui avait rien refusé,** he had refused her nothing; **r. toute qualité à qn,** to refuse to see any good in s.o.; **r. tout talent à qn,** to deny that s.o. has any talent; to refuse to admit that s.o. has any talent; **r. la porte à qn,** to close one's door to s.o.; to deny s.o. admittance; *Mil:* **r. l'aile,** to refuse a wing; (*b*) (*of horse*) **r. (l'obstacle),** to refuse, to ba(u)lk; *Mil:* **r. le combat,** to decline battle; (*c*) (*of ship*) **r. de virer,** not to obey the helm; to miss stays; (*d*) *Civ.E:* **le pieu refuse le mouton,** the pile will go no deeper, has reached hard bottom, has been driven to refusal. **2.** (*a*) **r. un homme (pour le service militaire),** to reject a man (for military service), to turn a man down; *Sch:* **r. un candidat,** to refuse, fail, a candidate (at an examination); **être refusé,** to fail; (*b*) *Th: etc:* **r. du monde,** to turn people away. **3.** *v.i.* (*a*) *Nau:* (*of the wind*) to draw forward, to veer forward, to haul, to scant; (*b*) **ne r. à aucune besogne,** to shrink from no work, from no task.

se refuser à qch., to object to, to set one's face against, to resist, sth.; **les circonstances s'y refusent,** circumstances will not allow it; **se r. à l'évidence,** to shut one's eyes to the evidence; **sol qui se refuse aux arbres fruitiers,** soil on which fruit trees will not grow; **se r. à faire qch.,** to refuse, decline, to do sth.; **la plume se refuse à décrire ces atrocités,** the pen recoils from describing these atrocities; **il ne se refusait pas à reconnaître que . . .,** he didn't mind admitting that . . ..

refuseur, -euse [rəfyzœ:r, -ø:z], *s.* refuser.

réfutable [refytabl̩], *a.* refutable, confutable.

réfutateur, -trice [refytatœ:r, -tris], *s.* refuter, confuter.

réfutatif, -ive [refytatif, -i:v], *a.* refutative.

réfutation [refytasjɔ̃], *s.f.* refutation, rebuttal, rebutment, disproof (de, of).

réfuter [refyte], *v.tr.* to refute, confute (s.o.'s theory); to disprove (theory, statement).

reg [rɛg], *s.m. Geog:* reg, gravel desert (in Sahara).

regâchage [rəgɑʃa:ʒ], *s.m.* retempering.

regagner [rəgaɲe], *v.tr.* **1.** (*a*) to regain, recover, win back (s.o.'s confidence, affection, etc.); **r. qn,** to win s.o. back; (*b*) to recover, win back, get back (money, position, in battle, etc.); **r. le temps perdu,** to make up for lost time; **on regagne le prix d'un article de bonne qualité,** buying a good article is an economy in the long run. **2.** to get back to (a place); to reach (a place) again; to regain (the shore, one's ship, etc.); **r. son foyer,** to return to one's home; *Nau:* **r. le large,** to head out to sea again, to make for the open sea again.

regaillardir [rəgajardi:r], *v.tr.* = RAGAILLARDIR.

regain [rəgɛ̃], *s.m.* **1.** *Agr:* (i) aftermath, aftergrowth, aftercrop, second growth; (ii) fog. **2.** renewal (of youth, beauty, success, etc.); **r. d'activité,** renewal, revival, of activity; **r. de vente,** revival of sales, fresh fillip to sales; **r. de vie,** new lease of life; **un r. d'intérêt,** a fresh interest (in sth.).

régal [regal], *s.m.* (*a*) (sumptuous) feast, banquet; (*b*) exquisite dish; **pour nous le gibier est un r.,** for us game is a treat; **c'est un vrai r. de l'écouter,** it is a treat, a pleasure, to listen to him; *pl. régals.*

régalade [regalad], *s.f. F:* **1.** (*a*) regaling, treating (of s.o.); (*b*) treat; **boire à la r.,** to drink without touching the lips with the glass or bottle. **2.** *A:* & *Dial:* blazing fire of small wood.

régalage [regala:ʒ], *s.m. Civ.E:* levelling (of ground, etc.).

régalant [regalɑ̃], *a. F: O:* diverting, amusing; *esp. in the phr.* **cela n'est pas r.,** that's no joke.

régale[1] [regal], *s.f. Fr.Hist:* regale (= royal prerogative), *esp.* prerogative of enjoying the revenues of vacant sees and abbacies.

régale[2], *a.f. Ch:* **eau r.,** aqua regia.

régale[3], *s.f. Organ:* vox humana.

régalec [regalɛk], *s.m. Ich:* oarfish.

régalement [regalmɑ̃], *s.m. Civ.E:* levelling (of ground, etc.).

régaler[1] [regale], *v.tr.* to level; to spread (earth, etc.) evenly.

régaler[2], *v.tr. F:* to entertain, feast (one's friends, etc.); **r. qn de qch.,** to regale, entertain, s.o. with sth.; to treat s.o. to sth.; *abs.* **c'est moi qui régale,** I'm standing treat.

se régaler, *F:* to feast (**de,** on); to treat oneself (**de,** to); **on s'est bien régalé,** we had a good meal, we did ourselves well.

régalien, -ienne [regaljɛ̃, -jɛn], *a. Hist:* pertaining to the royal prerogative; regalian; **droits régaliens,** regalia, regalities.

regard [rəga:r], *s.m.* **1.** (*a*) look, glance, gaze; **r. de côté, en coulisse,** sidelong glance; **r. terne, vitreux,** glassy stare; **r. dur, torve,** stony stare; **yeux sans r.,** dull, lack-lustre, eyes; **jeter un r. à qn,** to glance at s.o.; to give s.o. a look; to catch s.o.'s eye; **jeter un r. sur qch.,** to cast a glance at, over, sth.; to glance at, over, sth.; **il suffit d'y porter vos regards,** to look at it is enough; **chercher qn du r.,** to look round for s.o.; **interroger qn du r., lancer à qn un r. interrogateur,** to give s.o. a questioning look; to look at s.o. inquiringly; **lancer un r. furieux à qn,** to glare at s.o.; **ses regards exprimaient son indignation,** his expression showed his indignation; **abaisser sur qn un r. favorable,** to look favourably on s.o.; **détourner le r.,** to look away, to avert one's eyes (de, from); **porter ses regards du côté de . . .,** to look, cast one's eyes, in the direction of . . .; *Mil: etc:* **conserver le r. droit devant soi,** to keep one's eyes to the front; **promener ses regards sur qch.,** (i) to let one's eyes roam over sth.; (ii) to eye, scan, sth.; **couler un r. sur qn,** to cast a glance at s.o.; **arrêter son r. sur qn,** to let one's eye dwell upon s.o.; **ne pas arrêter ses regards sur qn,** to look past s.o.; to ignore s.o.; **appuyer son r. sur qn,** to stare at s.o.; **r. appuyé,** stare; **exposé aux regards,** exposed to view; **caché aux regards,** out of sight; hidden from view, from observation; **à l'abri des regards,** screened from observation; **attirer le(s) regard(s),** to draw the eye, to attract attention, to be conspicuous; **échapper aux regards,** to escape notice, to escape observation; *adv. & prep.phrs.* **en r. de qch.,** (i) opposite, facing, sth.; (ii) taking sth. into account; **le symbole N est placé en r. de chaque nouvelle règle,** the symbol N is placed against each new rule; **texte avec illustration en r.,** text with illustration on the opposite page; **au r. de qch.,** in comparison with sth., compared with sth.; (*b*) *Astrol: A:* (= ASPECT) aspect (of the heavens). **2.** (*a*) **r. (d'accès, de visite),** manhole (of sewer, water main, etc.); inspection hole; *Av:* **r. de visite,** inspection port, window; (*b*) **(trou de) r.,** peephole, sight hole (of oven, etc.); draught hole (of furnace); observation aperture, slit (in scientific apparatus, etc.; (*c*) *Mch:* **r. de lavage,** wash-out hole; **r. de nettoyage,** cleaning hole, eye. **3.** *Geol:* upthrow side (of fault); inlier. **4.** control; *Jur:* **droit de r.,** right of inspection. **5.** attention; **l'assemblée a arrêté son r. sur la question,** the assembly has turned its attention to the question.

regardant, -ante [rəgardɑ̃, -ɑ̃:t]. **1.** *a.* (*a*) close (-fisted), stingy, mean (person); (*b*) particular (**pour,** about); **ménagère très regardante,** careful housewife; (*c*) *Her:* regardant. **2.** *s. A:* onlooker, spectator.

regarder [rəgarde], *v.tr.* **1.** (*a*) to regard, consider (s.o., sth.); **je regarde comme un honneur de vous servir,** I count it an honour to serve you; **r. qch. comme un crime, comme illicite,** to regard, look on, sth. as a crime, as unlawful; **se r. comme un héros,** to consider oneself, think oneself, a hero; (*b*) **ne r. que ses intérêts,** to consider only one's own interests; **vous ne regardez pas que . . .,** you don't consider that . . .; (*c*) *v.ind.tr.* **r. à qch.,** to pay attention to sth.; to be particular about sth.; **il ne regarde pas à la dépense, il n'y regarde pas,** he doesn't mind the expense; **sans r. à la dépense,** regardless of expense; **je ne regarde pas à vingt francs, je n'y regarde pas pour vingt francs,** I am not particular, worried, about twenty francs more or less; *abs.* **quand elle achète, elle n'y regarde pas,** when she's buying something she doesn't worry about the price; **y bien r., y r. à deux fois, pour faire qch., avant de faire qch.,** to consider sth. carefully; to think twice about doing sth., before doing sth.; **je n'y regarde pas de si près,** I don't look at things as closely as that; I'm not as particular, fussy, as (all) that; **je n'y regarde pas à un jour ou deux,** it doesn't matter to me within a day or two; **à y r. de près,** on close inspection, looking at it closely; **à y bien r.,** on thinking it over; (*d*) (*of thgs*) to concern (s.o.); **cela me regarde,** that's my business, my look out; **cela ne vous regarde pas,** that's no concern, no business, of yours; that's none of your business; **en ce qui me regarde,** as far as I am concerned; **en ce qui regarde nos projets,** as far as our plans are concerned; (*e*) *A:* to regard (persons); to attach importance to (thgs); **ne regarde point les personnes, dit le Seigneur,** thou shalt not regard persons, saith the Lord; **je ne regarde rien quand il faut servir un ami,** nothing matters, nothing can deter me, when I have a friend to serve. **2.** (*a*) to look at (sth., s.o.); **r. qn dans les yeux,** to look s.o. in the eyes; **r. qn fixement,** to stare at s.o.; **r. qn du coin de l'œil,** to look at s.o. out of the corner of one's eye; **r. qn de travers, avec méfiance,** to look askance at s.o.; to look at s.o. suspiciously; **r. qn en face,** (i) to look s.o. in the face; (ii) to stand up to s.o.; **ils se regardaient en chiens de faïence,** they were staring, glaring, at each other; **se faire r.,** to attract attention; to make oneself conspicuous; **r. qn faire qch.,** to watch s.o. doing sth.; **je regardais s'allumer les étoiles,** I watched the stars coming out; **si vous m'aidiez, au lieu de me r. faire,** supposing you helped me instead of looking on; **r. tomber la pluie,** to watch the rain (falling); *F:* **regardez-moi cet idiot!** look at that idiot! what an idiot! *F:* **non, mais tu ne m'as pas regardé!** what d'you take me for? you needn't think you can count on me! (*b*) *abs.* **r. à la fenêtre,** to look in at the window; **r. par la fenêtre,** to look out of the window; **r. dans ses papiers,** to look among one's papers; **r. dans un télescope,** to look through a telescope; **r. à la loupe, au microscope,** to look through a magnifying glass, a microscope; **r. à sa montre,** to look at one's watch, at the time; **r. en arrière,** to look back; **puis-je r.?** may I look? **r. par le trou de la serrure,** to look, peep, through the keyhole; **je regarde s'il est là,** I'm looking to see if he's there. **3.** to look on to, to face (sth.); **la maison regarde le midi,** the house faces south; **nos deux maisons se regardent,** our houses are opposite each other; *abs.* **fenêtre qui regarde sur le jardin,** window that looks on to, faces, the garden; **l'aiguille aimantée regarde toujours le nord,** the magnetic needle always points north.

regardeur, -euse [rəgardœ:r, -ø:z], *s. A:* watcher, onlooker.

regarnir [rəgarni:r], *v.tr.* to regarnish; to refill (one's pocket, one's purse); to re-stock (larder, etc.); to re-cover (furniture); to retrim (dress, etc.); *Mch: Mec.E:* to repack (stuffing-box); to refill, reline (bearing).

regarni(s) [rəgarni], *s.m. For:* (*a*) replanting (empty spaces with trees); (*b*) saplings grown as replacements (for dead trees in a new plantation).

regarnissage [rəgarnisa:ʒ], *s.m. For:* after-culture.

régate [regat], *s.f.* **1.** regatta; **r. à voiles,** sailing regatta; yacht races; **r. à rames, à l'aviron,** (rowing) regatta; boat races. **2.** *Cost:* (*a*) (narrow) sailor-knot tie; (*b*) (*hat*) boater.

régater [regate], *v.i. Y:* to race, to take part in a regatta.

régatier [regatje], *s.m. Y:* competitor in a (sailing) race, in a regatta.

regayer [rəgɛje], *v.tr. Tex:* to hatchel, hackle (hemp).

regayoir [rəgɛjwa:r], *s.m. Tex:* hatchel, hackle.

regayure [rəgɛjy:r], *s.f. Tex:* residue (of hackled hemp).

regazéification [rəgɑzeifikasjɔ̃], *s.f.* **r. de gaz naturel liquéfié,** gasification of liquid (natural) gas.

regazéifier [rəgɑzeifje], *v.tr.* (*conj. like* GAZÉIFIER) to gasify (liquid gas).

regazonner [rəgɑzɔne], *v.tr.* to returf.

regel [rəʒɛl], *s.m.* (*a*) renewed frost; (*b*) *Ph:* regelation.

regélation [rəʒelasjɔ̃], *s.f.* regelation.

regeler [rəʒle], *v.tr. & i.* **(il regèle; il regèlera)** to freeze (sth.) again; *impers.* **voilà qu'il regèle,** it's freezing again.

régence [reʒɑ̃:s], *s.f.* **1.** (*a*) regency; *Fr.Hist:* **la R.,** the Regency (of Philip of Orleans (1715–1723)); (*b*) *Sch: A:* mastership (in a *collège*). **2.** fob-chain. **3.** *a.inv.* **des mœurs R.,** (i) *A:* profligacy (reminiscent of the *Régence* period); (ii) elegant manners; *Arch: Furn:* **style R.,** Régence style.

régénérateur, -trice [reʒeneratœ:r, -tris]. **1.** *a.* regenerating, regenerative; *Ecc:* **eau régénératrice,** baptismal water; *Atom.Ph:* **pile régénératrice,** breeder reactor. **2.** *s. Lit:* (*pers.*) regenerator. **3.** *s.m.* (*a*) *Ind: etc:* regenerator; regenerating plant; regenerating furnace; **r. d'huile de turbine,** turbine oil conditioner; *Elcs:* **r. de composante continue,** direct current restorer; **r. d'impulsions,** pulse regenerator; (*b*) *Agr:* **r. de prairie,** prairie breaker; scarifier.

régénératif, -ive [reʒeneratif, -i:v], *a.* regenerating, regenerative.

régénération [reʒenerasjɔ̃], *s.f.* **1.** regeneration. **2.** reclamation (of land). **3.** *Ind:* recuperation; reconditioning; *Atom.Ph:* breeding; regeneration (of fuel in reactor); *Elcs:* (*computers*) **r. de signaux,** signal regeneration, reshaping; **faisceau de r.,** holding beam; **période de r.,** regeneration period; **mémoire à r.,** regenerative store.

régénérer [reʒenere], *v.tr.* **(je régénère, n. régénérons; je régénérerai) 1.** to regenerate. **2.** to reactivate (catalyst).

régénérescence [reʒeneresɑ̃:s], *s.f. Med: etc:* rejuvenation.

régent, -ente [reʒɑ̃, -ɑ̃:t], *s.* **1.** regent. **2.** *Fin: A:* director (of the Bank of France). **3.** *Sch:* (*a*) *A:* form-master (in a *collège*); (*b*) (*in Belg.*) (secondary) schoolmaster. **4. le R.,** the Regent diamond. **5.** *a.* **reine régente, prince r.,** Queen Regent, Prince Regent.

régenter [reʒɑ̃te]. **1.** *v.i. Sch: A:* to teach; to be a form-master. **2.** *v.tr.* (*a*) *Sch: A:* to teach (a form); (*b*) to domineer over, dictate to (s.o.); **il veut tout r.,** he wants to run everything, *F:* to boss the whole show.

reggien, -ienne [rɛdʒjɛ̃, -jɛn], *a. & s. Geog:* (native, inhabitant) of Reggio.

régicide[1] [reʒisid]. **1.** *s.m. & f.* (*pers.*) regicide. **2.** *a.* regicidal.

régicide[2], *s.m.* (*crime*) regicide.

régie [reʒi], *s.f.* **1.** *Jur: etc:* (*a*) administration, stewardship (of property, etc.); management, control; **en r.,** (i) in the hands of trustees; (ii) under state supervision; **succession en r.** = succession in the hands of the Public Trustee; **théâtre en r.,** state-managed theatre; **mise sous r. d'une industrie,** bringing of an industry under state control; **r. du dépôt légal,** copyright department; (*b*) public corporation; state-owned company; (*c*) *Mil:* **(compte de) r. d'avances,** imprest account. **2.** (*a*) **r. des impôts indirects,** excise (administration); (*b*) Customs and Excise; **employé de la r.,** exciseman. **3.** *T.V: Cin:* central control room; **salle de r.,** control room; **chef de r.,** director.

Régille [reʒil], *Pr.n. A.Geog:* **le lac R.,** Lake Regillus.

regimbement [rəʒɛ̃b(ə)mɑ̃], *s.m.* refractoriness; rebellion, rebelling, *F:* kicking **(contre,** against).

regimber [rəʒɛ̃be], *v.i.* (*of horse, F: of pers.*) to kick **(contre,** at, against); to jib, to ba(u)lk **(contre,** at); *F:* **il est toujours à (se) r.,** he's always rebelling at, revolting against, jibbing at, sth.

regimbeur, -euse [rəʒɛ̃bœ:r, -ø:z], *a. & s. F:* refractory (person, mule); recalcitrant; rebel.

régime [reʒim], *s.m.* **1.** (*a*) *A:* government; rule; (*b*) form of government or of administration; regime; **r. des hôpitaux,** hospital regulations; hospital rules; **le r. du travail,** the organization of labour; *Jur:* **r. de la communauté (de biens),** husband's and wife's joint estate; **r. de la communauté réduite aux acquêts,** community of acquisitions made during married life; **r. de la séparation de biens,** marriage settlement under which husband and wife administer their separate properties; *A:* **mariée sous le r. dotal,** married under the dotal system; *Fr.Hist:* **l'ancien r.,** the old regime (before 1789); **changement de r.,** change of regime; **r. parlementaire,** parliamentary regime; parliamentary system; **le r. actuel,** the present regime; the present order of things; **établir un nouveau r.,** to set up a new regime; **r. spécial,** special treatment (of prisoners). **2.** (*a*) *Mec.E: Mch:* **r. (nominal),** rating (of engine, motor, generator, etc.); **r. (de fonctionnement, de marche),** operating conditions, working conditions, operation, running (of engine, motor); speed (of engine, etc.); rate (of combustion, acceleration, etc.); **r. de marche normal,** normal working, operating, conditions; **r. constant, permanent,** steady operation or running, constant load (of machine); steady state (of generator or electric system); **(marche) en r. constant,** in steady operation, at constant load; **r. continu,** continuous rating, operating; **r. fort, rapide, accéléré,** high rate; **r. faible, lent,** low rate; **r. maximum,** maximum rate; **charge de r.,** rated load; **pression de r.,** normal or working pressure; **puissance de r.,** normal power; **r. de puissance,** power range; **vitesse de r.,** rated or working speed; *Av: Nau: etc:* **r. de croisière,** cruising speed; *Aut:* **r. de ville,** town conditions; **en r. de ville ma voiture fait neuf litres (aux cent kilomètres)** = in town my car does thirty miles to the gallon; *F:* **le moteur a changé de r.,** the engine has changed its note; *Mec.E: Aut:* **gardez ce r.,** keep to this speed; *Atom.Ph:* **r. de démarrage du réacteur,** rise of reactor; (*b*) *El.E:* **r. de charge (d'un accumulateur),** charging rate; **charge de r.,** normal charge; **r. de décharge (d'un accumulateur),** time rate; **décharge à faible r.,** low-rate discharge; **courant, tension, de r.,** normal current, voltage; **variations de r.,** load variations; (*c*) mode of operation (of electric or telephone system, of commercial or industrial concern, etc.); (*c*) *Geog:* flow, regime (of river, etc.); **cours d'eau à r. uniforme,** stream with a constant, uniform, rate of flow; **r. climatérique,** climatic conditions, climate; **r. thermique,** temperature regime, pattern; **r. des précipitations,** rainfall regime, pattern. **3.** *Med:* diet; **r. lacté,** milk diet; **être au r.,** to be on a diet; **se mettre au r.,** to diet; *Sp:* **r. d'entraînement,** training; **à ce r. il ne tiendra pas longtemps,** he won't last long with the sort of life he's leading. **4.** *Gram:* object; **cas r.,** objective case; **r. direct, indirect,** direct, indirect, object. **5.** bunch, cluster (of bananas, dates); stem (of bananas).

régiment [reʒimɑ̃], *s.m.* (*a*) regiment; **r. actif,** regiment of the regular army; **r. de réserve,** regiment of the reserve; *Eng:* **r. territorial,** regiment of the territorial army; *Fr:* **r. de marche,** temporary regiment (made up of elements from different units); **r. du type normal,** normal-type regiment; **r. de montagne,** mountain regiment; **r. motorisé,** motorized regiment; *Fr:* **r. d'artillerie, du génie,** artillery, engineer, regiment; **r. parachutiste,** parachute regiment; **r. de chasseurs parachutistes,** parachute rifle regiment; **r. aérotransporté, r. aéromobile,** air-transported, airmobile, regiment; (*b*) (= *Army*) **aller au r.,** to join the army; **ça ne se faisait pas comme ça au r.,** that wasn't the way in the army; **quand j'étais au r.,** when I was in the army; when I was doing my military service; (*c*) **entouré d'un r. d'admirateurs,** surrounded by a host, a swarm, of admirers.

régimentaire [reʒimɑ̃tɛ:r], *a.* regimental; **dépôt r.,** regimental depot; **école r.,** regimental educational school; **train r.,** field train, regimental supply train.

reginglard [rəʒɛ̃gla:r], *s.m. F:* little local wine (with a slightly sharp taste).

reginglette [rəʒɛ̃glɛt], *s.f. A:* snare (for small birds).

région [reʒjɔ̃], *s.f.* region; territory; area; *Mil:* **r. militaire,** military district, = (northern, southern, etc.) command; **les régions polaires,** the polar regions; **r. du coton, du maïs,** cotton-growing, maize-growing, area; cotton belt, corn belt; **r. minière,** mining district; **r. à population dense,** densely populated area; **passer ses vacances dans la r. de Royan,** to spend one's holiday in the Royan area; **dans nos régions,** in our region, in the area where we live; *Anat:* **la r. lombaire,** the lumbar region; *Magn:* **r. attractive,** field of attraction.

régional, -ale, -aux [reʒjɔnal, -o]. **1.** *a.* regional, local; **comité r.,** local committee; **concours r.,** (regional) (agricultural) show; **expressions régionales,** regional expressions; **restaurant qui se spécialise en cuisine régionale,** restaurant specializing in regional dishes. **2.** *s.f.* **régionale,** provincial branch (of an association).

régionalisation [reʒjɔnalizasjɔ̃], *s.f.* regionalization.

regionaliser [reʒjɔnalize], *v.tr.* to regionalize.

régionalisme [reʒjɔnalism], *s.m.* regionalism.

régionaliste [reʒjɔnalist]. **1.** (*a*) *a.* regional; **roman r.,** regional novel; (*b*) *s.m. & f.* regionalist; regional novelist, etc. **2.** *a. Pol: etc:* regionalistic.

régir [reʒi:r], *v.tr.* (*a*) to govern, rule; to manage (estate); to direct (undertaking); **les lois qui nous régissent,** the laws that govern us; (*b*) *Gram:* to govern (case, noun).

régisseur [reʒisœ:r], *s.m.* manager; agent, steward, *Scot:* factor (of estate); (farm) bailiff; *Th:* stage manager; *Cin:* assistant director; *Mil:* **r. d'avances,** imprest holder.

registration [rəʒistrasjɔ̃], *s.f. Mus:* registration.

registre [rəʒistr̥], *s.m.* **1.** register, record; *Com:* account book; **r. des délibérations, des procès-verbaux,** minute book (of committee, etc.); **r. à souche(s),** counterfoil book, stub book; **rapporter un article sur un r.,** to post, enter, an item in a register; **tenir r. des événements,** to note events in one's books, to take note of events; *Adm:* **les registres de l'état civil,** the registers of births, marriages, and deaths; **tenue du r.,** registration; **r. du commerce,** Commercial, Trade, Register; *Breed:* **r. des chevaux,** stud book; *Mec.E:* **r. d'une machine,** log book of a machine; **noter des résultats sur le r.,** to log results. **2.** *Mus:* register; (i) compass, (ii) tone quality (of the voice, of an instrument). **3.** *Typ:* register (of page with page). **4.** (*a*) **r. d'aérage,** ventilation flap; **r. de cheminée,** register, damper (of furnace or chimney); **r. à guillotine,** sliding damper; (*b*) *Mch:* **r. de prise de vapeur,** regulator lever, throttle (valve) (of steam engine); **manœuvre de r.,** throttling; (*c*) (stop) register, draw stop, stop knob (of organ). **5.** *Elcs:* (*computers*) register; **r. d'index,** index register, modifier register, B-box; **r. d'instruction,** instruction register, location counter, programme address counter.

registrer [rəʒistre], *v.tr. Mus:* to registrate.

réglable [reglabl̥], *a.* adjustable; variable (at will).

réglage [regla:ʒ], *s.m.* **1.** ruling (of paper). **2.** (*a*) regulating, adjusting, adjustment, setting (of apparatus, watch, etc.); rating (of chronometer); **r. approximatif, r. au jugé,** rough adjustment; **r. de précision,** fine adjustment; **r. automatique,** automatic control; automatic adjustment; self adjustment; **à r. automatique,** self-adjusting; self-regulating; self-timing; **r. à la main,** hand adjustment; manual control; (*b*) *Artil:* **r. du tir,** adjustment of fire, ranging, spotting; **tir de r.,** adjustment fire, registering fire; **coup de r.,** ranging, sighting, shot; (*c*) *Atom.Ph:* regulating (of reactor); (*d*) *Elcs: W.Tel:* adjustment; control; tuning; **réglages,** dial readings; **r. d'intensité, de puissance (du son),** volume control; **r. de la luminosité,** brightness control (of electron tube); **changer de r.,** to switch over, tune in, to another station; (*computer*) **point de r.,** set point.

règle [rɛgl̥], *s.f.* **1.** (*a*) *Carp: Mec.E: etc:* rule, ruler; **r. à araser,** strickle board; straight edge; **r. à dessin, à dessiner,** drawing rule; *occ.* T-square; **r. à parallèles,** parallel ruler; **r. divisée,** scale; **r. à calcul,** slide rule; (*b*) *Surv:* measuring rod; **r. à éclimètre, r. de visée,** sight rule, sight vane; (*c*) *Mec.E:* guide bar, motion bar. **2.** rule (of conduct, art, grammar, arithmetic, etc.); **les règles du duel,** the code of honour, the duelling code; *Ecc:* **r. d'un ordre,** rule of an order; **la r. de Saint-Benoît,** the Rule of Saint Benedict; *Nau:* **règles de la route de mer, règles de route,** the rule of the road (at sea); *Av:* **règles de vol à vue,** visual flight rules; *Com: Ind:* **règles d'exploitation,** operating rules; **r. majoritaire,** majority rule; **règles d'un jeu,** rules of a game; **les règles du jeu,** the rules of the game; **l'arbitre veille à ce que tout se passe dans les règles,** the umpire sees fair play; **fixer des règles pour une procédure,** to regulate a procedure; *Com:* **pour la bonne r. . . .,** for order's sake . . .; **se faire une r. de se coucher de bonne heure,** to make it a rule to go to bed early; to make a practice, a point, of going to bed early; **mettre qch. en r.,** to put sth. in order; **je vais tout mettre en r.,** I am going to put everything to rights; **se mettre en r. avec les autorités,** to put oneself right with the authorities; **tout est en r.,** everything is in order, correct; **votre passeport est-il en r.?** is your passport in order? **oui, je suis en r.,** yes, all my papers are in order; **reçu en r.,** formal receipt; *A:* **affaire en r.,** duel in proper form, according to rule; *F:* **bataille en r.,** regular set-to, stand-up fight; **en r. générale,** as a general rule; **agir dans les règles,** to act according to rule; **jouer selon les règles,** to play according to rule; to play the game; **il est de r. de lui rendre visite, qu'on lui rende visite,** we make it a rule to go and see him; **comme c'est la r., comme de r.,** as is the rule; **r. d'or,** golden rule; *Mth:* **les quatre règles,** the four fundamental processes; *Ar:* **r. de trois,** rule of three; **r. conjointe,** chain rule. **3. prendre qn, qch., pour r.,** to take s.o., sth., as a guide, as an example. **4.** *Physiol: F:* **avoir ses règles,** to have one's period, the curse.

réglé [regle], *a.* **1.** ruled (paper, etc.); **papier non r.,** plain paper. **2.** (*a*) regular, well-ordered; fixed; steady; **vie réglée,** well-ordered life; **à des heures réglées,** at set, stated, hours; *Equit:* **allure réglée,** steady gait; *Const:* **assises réglées,** courses of uniform height; **il est r. comme une horloge,** he's as regular as a clock; *F:* **c'est r. comme du papier à musique,** it's inevitable, it's bound to happen; (*b*) **l'affaire est réglée,** the business is settled; **carburateur mal r.,** badly regulated carburettor; (*c*) *Physiol:* **fillette déjà réglée,** girl who is already having her (menstrual) periods; **femme bien, mal, réglée,** woman whose periods are regular, irregular.

règlement [rɛgləmɑ̃], *s.m.* **1.** settlement, adjustment (of difficulty, of account, etc.); *Com:* payment; **r. judiciaire,** rule of Court; **r. à l'amiable,** amicable settlement; *Com:* **mode, lieu, de r.,** method, place, of payment; **faire un r. par chèque,** to pay by cheque; **en r. de,** in settlement of; **pour r. de tout compte,** in full settlement; **faire un r. de compte(s) (avec qn),** to take the law into one's own hands; *St.Exch:* **jour du r.,** account day, settling day. **2.** (*a*) regulation(s); statutes (of university, etc.); **les règlements de la douane,** the customs regulations; **règlements internes,** internal regulations (of company, etc.); **r. intérieur d'une assemblée,** rules of procedure of an assembly; standing orders; **règlements de police,** by(e)-laws; (*b*) *Mil:* regulations, manual; **les règlements militaires,** army regulations; **r. provisoire,** provisional regulations; **r. d'instruction,** training manual; **r. d'éducation physique,** manual of physical training; **r. du service en campagne,** field service regulations. **3.** *O:* rule; **se faire un r. de vie,** to adopt a rule of life.

réglementaire [rɛgləmɑ̃tɛːr], *a.* regular, statutory, prescribed; *Mil:* **tenue r.,** regulation uniform, uniform of service pattern; *Nau:* **les feux réglementaires,** the regulation lights; **ce n'est pas r.,** it's not according to regulations, not in order; it's against the rules.

réglementairement [rɛgləmɑ̃tɛrmɑ̃], *adv.* in the regular, prescribed, manner; according to the rules.

réglementarisme [rɛgləmɑ̃tarism], *s.m.* regimentation; excessive regulation.

réglementariste [rɛgləmɑ̃tarist], *a.* **pays r.,** regulationist country.

réglementateur, -trice [rɛgləmɑ̃tatœːr, -tris]. **1.** *a.* (*a*) fond of regulations; obsessed by regulations; (*b*) given to making rules and regulations. **2.** *s.* (*a*) lover, partisan, of rules and regulations; (*b*) maker, compiler, of rules and regulations.

réglementation [rɛgləmɑ̃tasjɔ̃], *s.f.* **1.** making of rules (and regulations). **2.** regulating, regulation; bringing under regulation; **r. du trafic des changes,** exchange control; **r. des prix,** price control. **3.** *coll.* regulations; rules; **se documenter sur la r. du travail,** to gather information on labour regulations, regulations concerning the employment of labour.

réglementer [rɛgləmɑ̃te], *v.tr.* to regulate; to make rules for (sth.); to bring (sth.) under regulation; **r. le droit de grève,** to control the right to strike; **industries réglementées,** regimented industries.

régler [regle], *v.tr.* (**je règle, n. réglons; je réglerai**) **1.** to rule (paper, etc.). **2.** (*a*) to regulate, order (one's life, conduct, expenditure, etc.); **r. sa journée,** to plan one's day; **r. ses dépenses sur son revenu,** to cut one's coat according to one's cloth; **r. sa vie d'après un but à atteindre,** to plan one's life with a certain aim in view; *Sp:* **r. l'allure,** to set the pace; *Hyd.E:* **r. une rivière,** to control the flow of a river; *Mil:* **r. le tir,** to range; (*b*) to regulate, adjust, set (mechanism); to adjust (compass); to rate (chronometer); **r. une montre,** (i) to regulate a watch; (ii) to set a watch right; **r. sa montre sur le signal horaire,** to set, time, one's watch by the time signal; **la pendule est bien réglée,** the clock keeps good time; *I.C.E:* **r. l'allumage, les soupapes,** to time the ignition, the valves; **r. le moteur,** to tune the engine; *Navy:* **r. une torpille,** to set a torpedo; *W.Tel:* **r. une fréquence sur une autre,** to adjust, synchronize, one frequency with another; (*c*) *Nau:* **r. les quarts,** to set the watches. **3.** (*a*) to settle (question, quarrel, piece of business); **r. ses affaires,** to put one's business in order; **l'affaire s'est réglée à l'amiable,** the business was settled on a friendly basis; (*b*) *Com:* to settle (an account); **r. une note,** to pay a bill; **r. une succession,** to settle an estate; *Book-k:* **r. les livres,** to balance, make up, the books; **r. son compte, ses comptes, avec qn,** (i) to settle one's account(s), one's bill(s), with s.o.; (ii) to settle accounts with s.o., to have one's own back on s.o.; **r. de vieux comptes,** to pay off old scores; **r. son compte à qn,** to kill s.o.; **r. le boucher, le boulanger,** to pay the butcher, the baker; *abs.* **c'est moi qui règle,** this is on me; **r. par chèque,** to pay by cheque.

réglet [reglɛ], *s.m.* (*a*) *Arch:* reglet; (*b*) carpenter's rule; (*c*) *Typ: A:* (= FILET) (brass) rule; reglet.

réglette [reglɛt], *s.f.* **1.** small rule, scale. **2.** slide(r) (of a slide rule). **3.** strip (of metal); guide strip (of machine tool, etc.); *Typ:* reglet; *Tp:* **r. d'annonciateurs,** drop-mounting; **r. de jacks,** jack-strip; **r. de raccordement,** terminal strip; *Artil:* **r. de repérage,** direction bar, rule.

réglette-bloc [reglɛtblɔk], *s.f.* fluorescent lamp fitting; *pl. réglettes-blocs.*

réglette-jauge [reglɛtʒoːʒ], *s.f. Aut:* dipstick (for sump); *pl. réglettes-jauges.*

régleur, -euse [reglœːr, -øːz], *s.* **1.** (*pers.*) regulator, adjuster (of mechanism); ruler (of paper, etc.). **2.** *s.m.* expansion valve (of refrigerator). **3.** *s.f.* **régleuse,** ruling machine (for paper).

réglisse [reglis]. **1.** *s.f. Bot:* liquorice. **2.** *s.m. or f. Comest:* **(bâton de) r.,** stick of liquorice; *Pharm:* **pâte de r.,** (extract of) liquorice.

réglo [reglo], *P:* (*a*) *a.inv.* (*of papers*) in order; **c'est un type r.,** he's on the level; (*b*) *adv.* **il s'est conduit r. avec moi,** he's acted straight with me.

réglure [reglyːr], *s.f.* ruling (of or on paper); **r. serrée,** close ruling.

régnant [reɲɑ̃], *a.* reigning (sovereign, opinion, beauty); ruling (family); prevailing (wind, opinion); prevalent (disease); **prince r.,** prince regnant.

règne [rɛɲ], *s.m.* **1.** (vegetable, animal, mineral) kingdom. **2.** reign (of a king, of truth, reason, etc.); **sous le r. de Louis XIV,** in the reign of Louis XIV; **période entre deux règnes,** interregnum; **nous sommes sous le r. des banquiers,** we are in the hands of the bankers.

régner [reɲe], *v.i.* (**je règne, n. régnons; je régnerai**) **1.** (*of monarch*) to reign, rule; (*of conditions, opinion, disease*) to prevail, to be prevalent; to obtain; **r. en maître,** to reign supreme; **l'art de r.,** the art of ruling; kingship; **r. sur l'opinion,** to dominate opinion; **le calme règne,** calm prevails; **la mode qui règne actuellement,** the prevailing fashion; **le mauvais temps régnant à cette époque,** the bad weather prevailing at that time; **le silence règne dans le camp,** silence reigns in the camp; *Lit:* **elle règne dans mon cœur,** she reigns in my heart. **2.** *A:* to extend; **une galerie règne le long du bâtiment,** a gallery runs, extends, along the building.

regommage [rəgɔmaːʒ], *s.m. A:* retreading (of tyre).

regommer [rəgɔme], *v.tr. A:* to retread (tyre).

regonflement [rəgɔ̃fləmɑ̃], *s.m.* **1.** reinflation, refilling (of balloon); blowing up (again) (of tyres, etc.). **2.** swelling, surging up (of flood waters).

regonfler [rəgɔ̃fle]. **1.** *v.tr.* (*a*) to reinflate, refill (balloon, etc.); to blow up, pump up (tyre); (*b*) *F:* to cheer (s.o.) up; to put new life into (s.o., sth.); **il est regonflé à bloc,** he's on top of the world again. **2.** *v.i.* (*of water*) to swell, rise; to surge.

regorgeant [rəgɔrʒɑ̃], *a.* overflowing, abounding (**de,** with); *F:* cram full (**de,** of).

regorgement [rəgɔrʒəmɑ̃], *s.m.* **1.** overflow(ing); superabundance. **2.** flowing back (up a drain, etc.). **3.** *Med:* **miction par r.,** involuntary micturition (caused by excessive retention of urine).

regorger [rəgɔrʒe], *v.* (**je regorgeai(s); n. regorgeons**) **1.** *v.i.* (*a*) (*of river, recipient, etc.*) to overflow, run over; (*of jug, etc.*) to brim over; (*b*) to abound (**de,** in); **le marché regorge de cet article,** the market is glutted with this article; **les trains regorgent de gens,** the trains are packed with people; **les rues regorgeaient de monde,** the streets were crowded, teeming, swarming, with people; **magasins qui regorgent de marchandises,** shops chock-full of goods; **sa maison regorge de livres,** his house is cram full of books; **sacs regorgeant de blé,** sacks bursting with corn; **il regorge de santé,** he is bursting with health; (*c*) (*of water*) to flow back (up a drain, etc.). **2.** *v.tr.* **r. sa nourriture,** to bring up, regurgitate, one's food; *F:* **faire r. à qn ce qu'il a volé,** to make s.o. disgorge, cough up, what he has stolen.

régosol [regɔsɔl], *s.m. Geol:* regosol.

regoûter [rəgute], *v.tr. & i.* **1.** to have another snack. **2.** (*a*) **r. (à, de) qch.,** to have another taste of sth., to taste sth. again; (*b*) **je commence à r. la vie,** I am beginning to enjoy life again.

regradation [rəgradasjɔ̃], *s.f. Biol:* regeneration.

regrader [rəgrade], *v.tr. Biol:* to regenerate.

regrat [rəgra], *s.m. A:* huckstering; buying and reselling of food, etc., at second hand; *Hist:* regrating.

regrattage [rəgrataːʒ], *s.m.* scraping, regrating (of a wall).

regratter [rəgrate]. **1.** *v.tr. Const:* to scrape, rub down, regrate (a wall). **2.** *v.i. A:* to huckster; to deal in food, etc., at second hand for small profits; *Hist:* to regrate.

regratterie [rəgratri], *s.f. A:* **1.** huckstery, huckstering. **2.** huckster's wares; broken food bought for resale.

regrattier, -ière [rəgratje, -jɛːr], *s. A:* huckster; hucksterer, hucksteress; dealer in food, etc., at second hand; *Hist:* regrater.

regréer [rəgree], *v.tr. Nau:* to re-rig (a ship).

regreffage [rəgrɛfaːʒ], *s.m. Hort:* regrafting.

regreffer [rəgrefe], *v.tr. Hort:* to regraft, to insert a second graft.

régresser [regrese], *v.i.* to regress; to diminish (in quantity, intensity).

régressif, -ive [regresif, -iːv], *a.* regressive; *Biol:* **forme régressive,** throwback; *Geol:* **érosion régressive,** headwater erosion; *Ling:* **dérivation régressive,** back formation.

régression [regrɛsjɔ̃], *s.f.* **1.** regression (towards point of departure); retreat, recession (of sea from the coast); *Mth:* **coefficient de r.,** regression coefficient. **2.** *Biol:* (*a*) retrogression; (*b*) throwback; regression; (*c*) *Psy:* regression. **3.** decline (in business, etc.); drop (in sales, etc.); **épidémie en r.,** epidemic on the decline.

regret [rəgrɛ], *s.m.* **1.** regret (**de,** of, for); (*a*) **exprimer le r. de ne pas être à même de . . .,** to express regret at not being in a position to . . .; **avoir du r.,** to feel regret; to be sorry; **avoir r. de qch.,** to regret sth.; **avoir r. que** + *sub.*, to regret that . . .; **j'ai r. de l'avoir trompé,** I regret having deceived him; **avoir du r. de ne pas avoir fait qch.,** to regret not having done sth., to be sorry not to have done sth.; **j'ai r. à vous quitter,** I am sorry to leave you; **j'ai le r. de vous annoncer que . . .,** I regret to have to tell, inform, you that . . .; **je leur exprimai mon r. qu'ils eussent sujet à mécontentement,** I expressed my regret that they had cause to be dissatisfied; **je suis aux regrets qu'il ait cru cela,** I am extremely sorry he should have believed it; **j'en suis au r.,** I am sorry; **faire, dire, qch. à r.,** to do, say, sth. with regret, regretfully, with reluctance, reluctantly; to be lo(a)th to do, say, sth.; **à r. je me vois forcé de . . .,** to my regret I find myself forced to . . .; **donner à r. son admiration,** to give grudging admiration; **à mon (grand) r. . . .,** to my (great) sorrow, (much) to my regret . . .; (*b*) **le r. de la patrie,** homesickness; **M. Martin a laissé, emporté, des regrets,** (the late) Mr Martin is sadly missed; **mourir sans laisser de regrets,** to die unmourned, unlamented, unregretted; (*c*) **cesser des regrets inutiles,** to desist from useless regrets. **2.** *Dial: A:* tolling (during funeral).

regrettable [rəgrɛtabl̩], *a.* regrettable; deplorable; unfortunate (mistake, etc.); **c'est d'autant plus r.,** the more's the pity; **c'est d'autant plus r. que** + *ind.*, it is all the more to be regretted as . . ., since . . .; **il est r. que** + *sub.*, it is regrettable, unfortunate, that. . . .

regrettablement [rəgrɛtabləmɑ̃], *adv.* regrettably.

regretté [rəgrete], *a.* **notre r. collègue,** our lamented colleague.

regretter [rəgrete], *v.tr.* **1. r. qn, qch.,** to regret s.o., sth.; **il mourut regretté de tous, par le peuple,** he died regretted by all, by the people; **r. d'avoir fait qch.,** to regret, be sorry for, having done sth., to be sorry to have done sth.; **je regrette de vous avoir fait attendre,** I'm sorry I kept you waiting; **si vous refusez vous le regretterez plus tard,** if you refuse you'll be sorry later on; **je regrette qu'il soit parti si tôt,** I regret, am sorry, that he left so early; I wish he hadn't left so early; **je regrette que le temps soit à la pluie,** I am so sorry it has turned out wet, that it's raining; **je regrette, mais . . .,** I'm sorry, but . . .. **2.** (*a*) **r. un absent,** to miss an absent friend; (*b*) **r. son argent,** to wish one had one's money back.

regrèvement [rəgrɛvmɑ̃], *s.m.* tax increase.

regrimper [rəgrɛ̃pe], *v.tr. & i.* to climb (up) (sth.) again; **r. l'escalier, r. à l'arbre,** to climb the stairs, the tree, again.

regros [rəgro], *s.m.* tanner's bark, tanbark.

regrossir [rəgrosiːr]. **1.** *v.tr. Engr:* ton, coarse broaden (lines of engraving). **2.** *v.i.* to put on weight again, to grow fatter again.

regroupement [rəgrupmɑ̃], *s.m.* (*a*) regrouping; (*b*) rallying; (*c*) *Fin: Com:* amalgamation; **r. d'actions,** regrouping of shares; (*d*) *Agr:* **r. parcellaire,** consolidation (of land holdings); (*e*) *Elcs:* (*computers*) (i) regrouping, gathering; (ii) connector (on a flow chart); (*f*) *Atom.Ph:* rearrangement (of nuclear particles); **r. nucléaire,** nuclear rearrangement.

regrouper [rəgrupe], *v.tr.* (*a*) to regroup; *Mil:* **se r. avant une attaque,** to regroup, re-form, in order to attack; (*b*) to rally; (*c*) to amalgamate; to consolidate; *Ind: etc:* **se r.,** to merge; (*d*) *Elcs:* (*computers*) (i) to gather; (ii) to implode.

régul [regyl], *a. P:* regular, straight.

régulage [regylaːʒ], *s.m. Metall:* babbit(t)ing.

régularisation [regylarizasjɔ̃], *s.f.* (*a*) regularization, regularizing; making (sth.) regular; putting in order; equalization (of dividends); *Fin:* **fonds de r.,** equalization fund; (*b*) regulation, regulating (of a river, of a piece of mechanism); **r. de la circulation,** traffic control.

régulariser [regylarize], *v.tr.* (*a*) to regularize; to make (sth.) regular; to put (document) into proper form; to put (sth.) in order; to equalize (dividends, etc.); to straighten out (irregular business); **r. la pente d'une route,** to grade a road; (*b*) **r. la marche d'une machine,** to regulate, steady, the running of a machine; **r. un fleuve,** to regulate the flow of a river; **r. la circulation (sur une route),** to regulate, control, the traffic (on a road).

régularité [regylarite], *s.f.* (*a*) regularity (of features, of geometrical figure, of habits); (*b*) steadiness, evenness, regularity (of motion, drive); consistency (of quality); *Aut: etc:* **épreuve de r.,** reliability trial; (*c*) **r. d'humeur,** equability of temper; (*d*) punctuality.

régulateur, -trice [regylatœːr, -tris]. **1.** *a.* regulating, regulative (force); *Mch:* regulating (mechanism); **soupape régulatrice,** governor valve; *Pol.Ec:* **stocks régulateurs,** buffer stocks. **2.** *s.m. Tchn:* regulator; (*a*) *Clockm:* regulator, governor, balance wheel (of watch, clock); (*b*) *Mec.E:* regulator, governor (of steam-engine, turbine, etc.); throttle valve (of steam engine); *Av:* governor, constant-speed unit (of propeller); *Nau:* governor (of log); **r. à boules, r. (à force) centrifuge,** (fly)ball governor, centrifugal governor; **masselotte de r.,** governor flyweight; **r. de débit,** flow regulator; **r. de débit du gaz,** gas governor; **r. d'eau d'alimentation,** feed-water regulator; **r. de pression,** pressure regulator; **r. de vitesse,** speed governor; *I.C.E:* **r. de pompe d'injection,** fuel governor (of reactor); *Typewr:* **r. de marge,** marginal stop; (*c*) *El:* **r. (automatique) de tension,** (automatic) voltage regulator; *Th:* **r. d'éclairage de scène,** stage dimmer; *Elcs:* (*computer*) **r. à fil pilote,** pilot-wire regulator. **3.** *s.m.* (*a*) *Rail: etc:* (*pers.*) controller, *U.S:* dispatcher; (*b*) *Navy:* guide (of the fleet).

régulation [regylasjɔ̃], *s.f.* **1.** *Nau:* regulation, readjustment (of compass). **2.** control, regulation; (*a*) *Adm: etc:* **r. des naissances,** birth control; **r. de la circulation (aérienne, ferroviaire, routière),** (air, rail, road) traffic control; **poste de r. du trafic, de la circulation,** traffic control post, point; (*b*) *Mec.E:* **dispositif, système, de r. (du carburant, de la pression, etc.),** (fuel, pressure, etc.) control system; **r. thermique,** thermal, temperature, control; *Av:* **système de r. électronique du moteur,** electronic engine control system; **r. par réaction,** feedback control; (*c*) *El:* **r. de la tension,** voltage regulation; **relais de r.,** regulation relay; **schéma de r.,** wiring diagram; (*d*) *Ind:* **r. d'un procédé,** process control; (*e*) *Rail:* control system, *U.S:* dispatching; **poste de r.,** control office.

régule [regyl], *s.m.* **1.** *F: A:* petty king. **2.** *Mec.E:* white metal, antifriction metal, babbit(t) metal. **3.** *Ch: A:* regulus.

régulé [regyle], *a. Mec.E:* babbit(t)-lined.

réguler [regyle], *v.tr. Mec.E:* to babbit(t) (a bearing).

régulidés [regylide], *s.m.pl. Orn:* Regulidae.

régulier, -ière [regylje, -jɛːr]. **1.** *a.* (*a*) regular (features, geometrical figure, habits, etc.); valid (passport); **quittance régulière,** receipt in due form; proper receipt; *Gram:* **verbe r.,** regular verb; **trouver qch. r.,** to find sth. in order, all right; **ce n'est pas r.,** that's not businesslike; *Sp:* **avoir un jeu r.,** to play, have, a steady game; *P:* **c'est un homme r.,** he's a straight sort (of chap); (*b*) steady (pulse, increase); even (motion); **vie régulière,** regular, steady, ordered, life; **être r. dans ses actions,** to be exact, punctual, in one's actions; (*c*) **humeur régulière,** equable temper. **2.** *a. & s.m. Ecc: Mil:* regular (priest, soldier); **le clergé r.,** the regular clergy; **troupes régulières,** regular troops; regulars. **3.** *s.f. P:* **ma régulière,** (i) the wife, the missus; (ii) the woman I live with.

régulièrement [regyljɛrmɑ̃], *adv.* (*a*) regularly; in accordance with the regulations; **membres r. désignés,** properly elected members; members duly appointed; (*b*) steadily, evenly; (*c*) punctually.

régulin [regylɛ̃], *Ch:* **1.** *a. A:* reguline. **2.** *s.m.* reguline.

Régulus [regylys], *Pr.n.m. Rom.Hist: Astr:* Regulus.

régur [regyːr], *s.m. Geol:* regur, black cotton soil.

régurgitation [regyrʒitasjɔ̃], *s.f.* regurgitation.

régurgiter [regyrʒite], *v.tr.* to regurgitate (food).

réhabilitable [reabilitabl̩], *a.* fit, deserving, to be rehabilitated, suitable for rehabilitation.

réhabilitant [reabilitɑ̃], *a. Jur:* rehabilitating (order, etc.).

réhabilitation [reabilitasjɔ̃], *s.f.* **1.** rehabilitation; recovery of civil rights; discharge (of bankrupt); re-establishment (of s.o.'s memory, good name, etc.). **2.** cleaning and renovating (of old buildings); rehabilitation (of slum district).

réhabilitatoire [reabilitatwaːr], *a. Jur:* rehabilitating.

réhabilité, -ée [reabilite], *s. Jur:* discharged bankrupt.

réhabiliter [reabilite], *v.tr.* **1.** to rehabilitate (s.o., s.o.'s memory, s.o.'s good name); to discharge (bankrupt); **r. qn dans ses droits,** to reinstate s.o. in his rights; **r. qn dans l'opinion,** to rehabilitate, re-establish, s.o. in the public esteem. **2.** to clean and renovate (old buildings); to rehabilitate (slum district).

réhabilitoire [reabilitwaːr], *a. Jur:* rehabilitating (decree, etc.).

réhabituer [reabitɥe], *v.tr.* to reaccustom (à, to); **se r. à un travail,** to get used, accustomed, to doing a job again.

rehaussage [rəosaːʒ], *s.m. Art:* heightening, touching up (of colour, etc.).

rehausse [rəoːs], *s.f. Rail: Av:* raising block.

rehaussé [rəose], *a. Cu:* highly seasoned.

rehaussement [rəosmɑ̃], *s.m.* **1.** (*a*) raising (of wall, of picture on wall, etc.); (*b*) **r. des monnaies,** appreciation of the coinage. **2.** heightening, enhancing, setting off (of colour, beauty, etc.); touching up (of colour).

rehausser [rəose], *v.tr.* **1.** (*a*) to raise; to make (construction, etc.) higher; **r. une maison d'un étage,** to raise a house (by) one storey; **r. le courage de qn,** to increase s.o.'s courage; *Typ:* **r. la composition,** to underlay the type; (*b*) **r. les monnaies,** to appreciate the coinage; **r. le prix du pain,** to raise the price of bread; **le prix du blé est rehaussé,** wheat has gone up (in price). **2.** to heighten, enhance, set off (beauty, merit, a colour, complexion); to touch up (a colour); **le vernis rehausse la peinture,** paint comes up when varnished; **description qui se rehausse d'une pointe de satire,** description set off with a touch of satire; **r. un détail,** to accentuate a detail.

rehaut [rəo], *s.m.* **1.** *Fin:* appreciation (of money). **2.** *Art:* touch-up (to a picture, etc.); **les rehauts,** the high lights.

rehbok [rebɔk], *s.m. Z:* reebok, rehbok.

réhydration [reidrasjɔ̃], *s.f.* rehydration; reconstitution (of dehydrated foods).

réification [reifikasjɔ̃], *s.f. Phil:* reification.

réifier [reifje], *v.tr.* (*p.d. & pr.sub.* **n. réifiions, v. réifiiez**) *Phil:* to reify.

reillère [rɛjɛːr], *s.f. Hyd.E:* channel, head race (of overshot weir).

réimperméabilisation [reɛ̃pɛrmeabilizasjɔ̃], *s.f.* reproofing (of raincoat, etc.).

réimperméabiliser [reɛ̃pɛrmeabilize], *v.tr.* to reproof (raincoat, etc.).

réimplantation [reɛ̃plɑ̃tasjɔ̃], *s.f. Surg: Dent:* reimplantation.

réimplanter [reɛ̃plɑ̃te], *v.tr. Surg: etc:* to reimplant.

réimportation [reɛ̃pɔrtasjɔ̃], *s.f.* **1.** reimportation, reimporting. **2.** reimport.

réimporter [reɛ̃pɔrte], *v.tr.* to reimport.

réimposer [reɛ̃poze], *v.tr.* **1.** (*a*) to tax (s.o.) again; (*b*) to reimpose (tax). **2.** *Typ:* to reimpose.

réimposition [reɛ̃pozisjɔ̃], *s.f.* **1.** further taxation; reimposition (of tax). **2.** *Typ:* reimposition.

réimpression [reɛ̃prɛsjɔ̃], *s.f.* **1.** reprinting. **2.** reprint, reimpression.

réimprimer [reɛ̃prime], *v.tr.* to reprint.

Reims [rɛ̃ːs], *Pr.n.m. Geog:* Rheims.

rein [rɛ̃], *s.m.* **1.** *Anat:* kidney; *Med:* **r. mobile, flottant,** floating kidney; **r. artificiel,** kidney machine. **2.** *pl.* (*a*) loins, back; *B:* reins; **la chute, le creux, des reins,** the small of the back; **douleur aux reins,** pain in the small of the back; backache; **casser les reins à qn,** to kill s.o.; **se casser les reins,** to break one's back; *F:* **il ne se casse pas les reins,** he doesn't break his back over his work; **mal de reins,** lumbago; **ceindre ses reins,** to gird (up) one's loins; **Monsieur le maire, l'écharpe tricolore autour des reins,** the Mayor, with the tricolor sash round his waist; **il a les reins solides,** (i) he has a strong back; he is a sturdy fellow, a stout fellow; (ii) *F:* he is a man of substance; (*b*) *Arch:* sides, reins, haunches (of an arch).

réincarnation [reɛ̃karnasjɔ̃], *s.f.* reincarnation.

réincarné [reɛ̃karne], *a.* reincarnate.

réincarner [reɛ̃karne], *v.tr.* to reincarnate.

réincorporer [reɛ̃kɔrpɔre], *v.tr.* to reincorporate; to re-embody (militia, etc.).

reine [rɛn], *s.f.* **1.** (*a*) Queen; **la r. Anne,** Queen Anne; **r. mère,** queen mother; **port de r.,** queenly bearing; **elle veut faire la r.,** she wants to queen it; (*b*) **r. (des abeilles),** queen (bee); (*c*) *Chess: Cards:* queen; (*d*) *Ich:* **r. des carpes,** queen carp; (*e*) *Bot:* **r. de la nuit,** queen of the night (cactus); **r. des bois,** woodruff; **r. des prés,** meadow sweet; (*f*) *A:* **la petite r.,** bicycle. **2. la presse, r. de l'opinion,** the press, that rules, governs, opinion; **la r. du bal,** the belle of the ball.

reine-claude [rɛnkloːd], *s.f. Hort:* greengage; *pl. reines-claudes.*

reine-des-prés [rɛndepre], *s.f. Bot:* meadowsweet; *pl. reines-des-prés.*

reine-marguerite [rɛnmargərit], *s.f. Bot:* china-aster; *pl. reines-marguerites.*

reinette [rɛnɛt], *s.f. Hort:* rennet, pippin (apple); **r. grise,** russet; **r. du Canada,** reinette du Canada.

réinfecter [reɛ̃fɛkte], *v.tr. & pr.* to reinfect; **la plaie s'est réinfectée,** the wound has become infected again.

réinhumation [reinymasjɔ̃], *s.f.* reinterment.

réinhumer [reinyme], *v.tr.* to reinter.

reinite [rɛnit], *s.f. Miner:* iron tungstate.

réinscription [reɛ̃skripsjɔ̃], *s.f.* (*a*) inscribing again; (*b*) re-registration.

réinscrire [reɛ̃skriːr], *v.tr.* (*conj. like* INSCRIRE); (*a*) to inscribe again; (*b*) to re-register.

réinsérer [reɛ̃sere], *v.tr.* (*conj. like* INSÉRER) to reinsert; **r. des handicapés dans la vie sociale,** to rehabilitate handicapped people.

réinsertion [reɛ̃sɛrsjɔ̃], *s.f.* reinsertion; reintegration; rehabilitation (of the handicapped, etc.).

réinstallation [reɛ̃stalasjɔ̃], *s.f.* reinstalment, fresh installation; **depuis sa r. à Paris,** since he came back to live in Paris.

réinstaller [reɛ̃stale], *v.tr.* to reinstall; **au lieu de se r.,** instead of settling down again.

réinstituer [reɛ̃stitɥe], *v.tr.* to re-establish.

réinstitution [reɛ̃stitysjɔ̃], *s.f.* re-establishment.

reinté [rɛ̃te], *a.* **bien r.,** broad-backed, strong-backed.

réintégrable [reɛ̃tegrabl̩], *a.* that can be reinstated, restored, rehabilitated.

réintégrande [reɛ̃tegrɑ̃ːd], *s.f. Jur:* action of recovery (of land, etc.); action of ejectment.

réintégration [reɛ̃tegrasjɔ̃], *s.f.* **1.** (*a*) reinstatement, readmission (of official, etc.); restoration; (*b*) **r. des démobilisés dans la vie civile,** rehabilitation of ex-servicemen. **2.** *Adm:* return to store (of articles on loan or unexpended). **3. r. de domicile,** resumption of residence; *Jur:* **r. du domicile conjugal,** restitution of conjugal rights. **4.** *Mth:* reintegration.

réintégrer [reɛ̃tegre], *v.tr.* (*conj. like* INTÉGRER) **1. r. qn (dans ses fonctions),** to reinstate s.o.; to restore s.o. to his position, his office; *Fb: etc:* **r. un joueur à son ancien poste,** to put a player back in, to restore a player to, his former position; **r. qn dans ses possessions,** to reinstate s.o. in his possessions; **r. des employés,** to take employees on again; to re-engage employees. **2.** *Adm:* to return to store, to take back into store (articles on loan or unexpended). **3. r. son domicile,** to resume possession of one's domicile; to return to one's home, one's domicile. **4.** *Mth:* to reintegrate.

réinterprétation [reɛ̃tɛrpretasjɔ̃], *s.f.* reinterpretation; new interpretation.

réinterpréter [reɛ̃tɛrprete], *v.tr.* (*conj. like* INTERPRÉTER) to reinterpret.

réinterroger [reɛ̃tɛrɔʒe, -te-], *v.tr.* (*conj. like* INTERROGER) to reinterrogate; to question (s.o.) again.

réintroduction [reɛ̃trɔdyksjɔ̃], *s.f.* reintroduction.

réintroduire [reɛ̃trɔdɥiːr], *v.tr.* (*conj. like* INTRODUIRE) to reintroduce.

réinventer [reɛ̃vɑ̃te], *v.tr.* to reinvent.

réinvestir [reɛ̃vɛstiːr], *v.tr.* to reinvest; *Ind: etc:* **r. les bénéfices,** to plough back the profits.

réinviter [reɛ̃vite], *v.tr.* to reinvite; to invite (s.o.) again.

réitérateur, -trice [reiteratœːr, -tris], *a.* repeating (theodolite, etc.).

réitératif, -ive [reiteratif, -iːv], *a.* reiterative; **sommation réitérative,** second summons.

réitération [reiterasjɔ̃], *s.f.* reiteration.

réitérer [reitere], *v.tr.* (**je réitère, n. réitérons; je réitérerai**) to reiterate, repeat; **demandes réitérées,** repeated requests.

reithrodontomys [rɛtrodɔ̃tɔmis], *s.m. Z:* (American) harvest mouse; (*genus*) Reithrodontomys.

reître [rɛtr̥], *s.m.* (*a*) *Hist:* reiter; (*b*) ruffianly soldier; (*c*) *F: A:* **vieux r.,** crafty old fellow, rough and tough old customer.

rejaillir [rəʒajiːr], *v.i.* (*a*) *A:* (*of solid body*) to rebound, to fly back; (*b*) (*of water, blood*) to spurt back, to gush out (**sur,** on); to spurt up, out; to spout (up, out); (*of light*) to be reflected, to flash, glance, back; **la honte en rejaillira sur vous,** the disgrace will affect you; **sa honte a rejailli sur nous,** we were involved in his disgrace; **tout ceci rejaillit sur moi,** all this sort of thing is a reflection on me; **sa gloire a rejailli sur sa famille,** some of his fame was shared by his family; **l'honneur de cette découverte rejaillit sur X,** the honour of this discovery must be attributed to X.

rejaillissant [rəʒajisɑ̃], *a.* gushing, spurting.

rejaillissement [rəʒajismɑ̃], *s.m.* (*a*) *A:* rebound(ing) (of a solid body); (*b*) reflection (of light, glory, etc.); springing (up), gushing (out), spurting (back, up, out), spouting (up, out) (of liquid).

réjection [reʒɛksjɔ̃], *s.f.* rejection.

rejet [rəʒɛ], *s.m.* **1.** (*a*) throwing out (of earth from trench, etc.); throwing up (of food); casting up (of object from the sea); evacuation (of water); (*b*) material thrown out; spoil (earth); (*c*) *Geol:* throw (of fault); **r. horizontal,** heave; **rejets (d'une éruption),** ejectamenta. **2.** rejection (of proposal, etc.); *Med:* rejection (of transplant); *Jur:* setting aside (of claim, etc.); disallowance (of expenses); **r. de pourvoi,** dismissal of an appeal. **3.** *Ap:* cast, after-swarm (of bees). **4.** *Hort:* (= REJETON) shoot; sprout. **5.** *Pros:* enjambment. **6.** *Gram: etc:* end positioning (of verb, significant word, etc.).

rejetable [rəʒ(ə)tabl̥], *a.* rejectable; that can, should, be cast aside, rejected.

rejéteau, -eaux [rəʒeto], *s.m. Const:* drip moulding; flashing board (of door, window); **joint à r.,** flashed joint.

rejeter [rəʒ(ə)te], *v.tr.* (*conj. like* JETER) **1.** to throw (sth.) again. **2.** (*a*) to throw, fling, (sth.) back; to return (ball); **r. un poisson à la mer,** to throw a fish back into the sea; **r. l'ennemi,** to hurl, fling, back the enemy; **r. ses cheveux en arrière,** to brush one's hair back; **r. son chapeau en arrière,** to tilt one's hat back; **r. qn dans l'incertitude,** to throw s.o. back into a state of uncertainty; (*b*) to throw up, cast up; **débris rejetés par la mer,** wreckage cast up by the sea; **il rejette tout ce qu'il mange,** he throws up, brings up, vomits up, all he eats; (*c*) *abs. Geol:* (*of a fault*) to throw. **3.** to transfer; (*a*) **r. la faute, le blâme, sur d'autres,** to shift, cast, lay, the blame on others; **r. la responsabilité sur qn,** to throw, shift, the responsibility on s.o.; **r. un crime sur quelqu'un d'autre,** to lay a crime at some one else's door; (*b*) to carry on (word to next line); to transfer (notes to the end of volume). **4.** to reject, set aside (sth.); to refuse to acknowledge (s.o.); **r. une offre,** to reject, dismiss, turn down, an offer; **r. un projet de loi,** to reject, throw out, a bill; **la motion a été rejetée,** the motion was lost; **r. un conseil,** to spurn a piece of advice; **r. une pensée,** to dismiss a thought; **r. une responsabilité, etc.,** to disclaim a responsibility, etc.; *Jur:* **r. un pourvoi,** to dismiss an appeal; **r. une réclamation,** to overrule an objection; **r. une candidature,** to turn down an application; **r. une dépense,** to disallow an expense. **5.** *Arb:* to throw out (new shoots); *abs.* to shoot out, to shoot from the base; to sucker. **6.** *Knitting:* **r. les mailles,** to cast off.

se rejeter. **1.** to fall back (**sur,** on); **se r. sur les circonstances,** to lay the blame on circumstances. **2. se r. en arrière,** to leap, dart, spring, back(wards); to dodge; (*of horse*) to shy; to start back.

rejeton [rəʒtɔ̃], *s.m.* **1.** *Hort:* shoot, sucker (of plant); **émettre des rejetons,** to sprout from the base; to sucker; **rejetons de framboisier,** raspberry canes. **2.** (*a*) descendant, offspring (of a family); **dernier r. d'une race illustre,** last representative of an illustrious race; (*b*) *F: Hum:* **mon r.,** my child, the offspring.

rejetonner [rəʒtɔne], *v.i. Hort:* (*of plant*) to sucker; to sprout from the base.

rejetteau, -eaux [rəʒɛto], *s.m.* = REJÉTEAU.

rejettement [rəʒɛtmɑ̃], *s.m.* **1.** throwing back; flinging back. **2.** rejecting, rejection.

rejoindre [rəʒwɛ̃ːdr̥], *v.tr.* (*conj. like* JOINDRE) **1.** to rejoin, reunite; to join (things, persons) (together) again; to connect; **rues latérales qui vont r. les grandes voies,** side streets which connect with the main arteries; **sa pensée rejoint celles des plus grands philosophes,** his ideas are akin to, link up with, those of the greatest philosophers; **cela rejoint ce que je disais hier,** that links up, ties up, with what I was saying yesterday. **2. r. qn,** to rejoin s.o.; to overtake s.o.; to catch s.o. up (again); **je vous rejoindrai à Lille,** I'll join you, pick you up, at Lille; *Mil:* **r. son régiment,** to join one's regiment; *Nau:* **être rejoint par un navire,** to be approached by a ship.

se rejoindre. **1.** to meet; **routes qui se rejoignent à Pontoise,** roads that meet at Pontoise. **2.** to meet again.

rejointoiement [rəʒwɛ̃twamɑ̃], *s.m. Const:* (re)jointing, (re)pointing.

rejointoyer [rəʒwɛ̃twaje], *v.tr.* (*conj. like* JOINTOYER) *Const:* to (re)joint, (re)point (walls).

rejouer [rəʒwe], *v.tr.* to replay (a match, etc.); to play off (a draw); to play (a piece of music) again; to act (a play) again.

réjoui [reʒwi], *a.* jolly, cheerful, cheery, merry (person); **air réjoui,** happy look, delighted expression; **mine réjouie,** cheerful, beaming, face.

réjouir [reʒwiːr], *v.tr.* (*a*) to delight, gladden, cheer (s.o.); **cela me réjouit le cœur de l'entendre,** it makes my heart glad, it does my heart good, to hear him; **r. l'œil de qn,** to delight s.o.'s eye; *Lit:* **le vin réjouit le cœur,** wine maketh glad the heart of man; (*b*) **r. la compagnie,** to amuse, divert, entertain, the company.

se réjouir. **1.** to rejoice (**de,** at, in); to be glad (**de,** of); **se r. de qch.,** to be delighted at sth.; **se r. d'une nouvelle,** to welcome a piece of news; to be delighted to hear a piece of news; **je me réjouis de le revoir,** I am delighted to see him again; **je me réjouis qu'ils soient réconciliés, de ce qu'ils se sont réconciliés,** I am so glad that they are reconciled; **il se réjouit du malheur d'autrui,** he rejoices in the misfortunes of others. **2.** to enjoy oneself; **ils se réjouissent à vos dépens,** they are enjoying themselves at your expense.

réjouissance [reʒwisɑ̃ːs], *s.f.* **1.** rejoicing; **des réjouissances publiques,** public rejoicings, public festivities; **les navires furent pavoisés en signe de r.,** ships were dressed in token of rejoicing; *F:* **quel est le programme des rejouissances?** what's on the agenda? **2.** *Com: A:* makeweight (in bones, added to meat sold).

réjouissant [reʒwisɑ̃], *a.* **1.** cheering, heartening. **2.** amusing, diverting.

réjuvénescence [reʒyvenɛs(s)ɑ̃ːs], *s.f. Biol:* rejuvenescence.

relâchant [rəlaʃɑ̃]. **1.** *a.* relaxing; *Med: A:* laxative. **2.** *s.m. Med: A:* laxative.

relâche [rəlɑːʃ]. **1.** *s.m.* (*a*) slackening, loosening (of rope, etc.); (*b*) relaxation, respite, rest (from regular work); breathing space; **travailler sans r.,** to work without respite, without intermission; to work without interruption; (*c*) *Th:* **il y a r. ce soir,** there is no performance this evening; *P.N:* **relâche,** closed; **les théâtres font r. le vendredi saint,** theatres close on Good Friday. **2.** *s.f. Nau:* (*a*) call; putting in; **faire r. dans un port, faire une r.,** to call at, put into, a port; **faire r. à Brest,** to put in at Brest; **r. forcée,** forced putting in to port; **en r. forcée,** (i) storm bound; (ii) held up in port (by breakdown, etc.); (*b*) port of call; place of call.

relâché [rəlaʃe], *a.* relaxed; (*a*) slack (rope, etc.); (*b*) loose, lax (morals, conduct); (*c*) **ventre r.,** loose bowels.

relâchement [rəlaʃmɑ̃], *s.m.* (*a*) relaxing, slackening (of muscle, cord, etc.); slackening off; *Mec.E:* **r. par cliquet,** ratchet release (of spring, etc.); (*b*) relaxation, falling off (of discipline, of zeal); abatement (of severe weather); looseness (of the bowels); looseness, laxity (of morals, conduct, etc.); *Med:* relaxation (of muscle); (*c*) relaxation (from work); easing off.

relâcher [rəlaʃe]. **1.** *v.tr.* (*a*) to loosen, slacken, ease, release (cord, bonds, spring, etc.); *Mch:* **r. la pression,** to slack off the pressure; **le vent du sud a relâché le temps,** the weather has turned milder with the south wind; (*b*) to relax (discipline, morals, one's mind); to abate (one's zeal); to loosen (the bowels); **se r. l'esprit,** to give the mind some relaxation; (*c*) *Cu:* to thin (down) (sauce, etc.); (*d*) *A:* **je ne veux rien r. de la dette,** I will not remit a penny of the debt. **2. r. un prisonnier, un oiseau,** to release a prisoner, a bird; to set a prisoner at liberty; to let a bird go; **relâché sous caution,** let out on bail. **3.** *v.i. Nau:* to put into port; **r. pour se mettre à l'abri,** to put into harbour for shelter.

se relâcher. **1.** (*of violin string, rope*) to slacken; (*of shoelace*) to get loose; (*of fever*) to abate; (*of pers.*) to become slack; *F:* to sit back; (*of zeal*) to flag, to abate, to fall off; (*of affection*) to grow less; (*of morals*) to grow lax, loose; *Med:* (*of muscle*) to become relaxed; **se r. dans sa vigilance,** to relax one's vigilance; **après avoir si bien travaillé, il ne faut pas vous r.,** after doing so well you must not get slack; **vos élèves se relâchent,** your pupils are slacking; **pendant la morte saison l'atelier se relâche un peu,** during the dead season the workers ease off a little. **2.** (*of the weather*) to grow milder; (*of pain*) to grow less acute; to abate.

relais[1] [rəlɛ], *s.m.* **1.** (*a*) *Geol:* exposed channel bank, sandbank (along a river); sand flats (along the shore); silt, warp; (*b*) **r. de mer,** foreshore. **2.** *Jur:* derelict land.

relais[2], *s.m.* **1.** (*a*) relay (*A.Trans:* of horses, *Ven:* of hounds); *Ind:* shift; **chevaux de r.,** relay, post, horses; **travail sans r.,** unrelieved (spell of) work; *Sp:* **course de, à, r.,** relay race; **prendre le r.,** to take over; (*b*) stage; coaching inn; **r. gastronomique,** restaurant with a reputation for good food; *Aut:* **r. routier,** service station (with restaurant, etc.). **2.** relay; (*a*) *Mec.E:* **r. pneumatique,** pneumatic relay; **r. de mise en marche, de mise en route,** starting relay; *I.C.E:* **r. de boîte (de vitesses) auxiliaire,** transfer-unit relay; **r. de carter de volant,** belt-housing relay; **r. de commande des gaz,** throttle relay; **r. de réversion,** reverse-pitch relay, reversing relay; **transmission par r.,** transmission by relay; (*b*) *El:* **r. électrique, électromagnétique, magnétique,** electric electromagnetic, magnetic, relay; **r. instantané,** instantaneous relay; **r. retardé, r. temporisé,** time-lag, time-delay, relay; **r. à deux seuils, à double effet,** two-step relay; **r. à armature, sans armature,** armature, armature-free, relay; **r. détecteur,** sensing relay; **r. différentiel,** differential relay; **r. polarisé,** biased relay; **r. de contrôle,** alarm, pilot, relay; **r. de protection, r. protecteur,** protective relay; **r. de tension,** voltage relay; (*c*) *Tp:* **r. téléphonique,** telephone relay; **r. d'appel, de sonnerie,** calling relay; **r. d'occupation,** holding relay; **r. amplificateur téléphonique,** telephone repeater; **r. de délestage,** relief relay; **r. de coupure,** cut-off relay; **r. d'amovibilité,** changeover switch; **système automatique tout à r.,** relay automatic system, *U.S:* all-relay system; (*d*) *Elcs: W.Tel:* **r. hertzien,** microwave relay, radio repeater; **r. de prodiffusion, r. transhorizon,** forward-scatter radio link; **r. par bande perforée,** tape relay; **station r.,** relay station; **émetteur de station r.,** relay transmitter; **r. de radio-diffusion,** relay broadcasting station.

relaissé [rəlese], *a. Ven:* (*of quarry*) exhausted; driven, run, to a standstill.

relaisser (se) [sərəlɛse], *v.pr. Ven:* (*of quarry*) to come to a halt, a standstill.

relance [rəlɑ̃ːs], *s.f.* (*a*) *Cards:* (*poker*) raise; **poker sans maximum de r.,** roofless poker; (*b*) boost; fresh start; **r. économique,** economic revival; **mesures de r. de l'activité économique,** economic pump priming; (*c*) *Ind: etc:* follow up (of work in hand); *Com:* following up (of customer); (*d*) *Com: Journ:* subscription renewal notice; **lettre de r.,** reminder letter, follow-up letter.

relancement [rəlɑ̃smɑ̃], *s.m.* **1.** throwing back; throwing again. **2.** (*a*) restarting (of stag, of machine, etc.); boosting (production, etc.); (*b*) bothering, *F:* badgering (s.o.).

relancer [rəlɑ̃se], *v.tr.* (*conj. like* LANCER) **1.** to throw (sth.) again; to throw (sth.) back; *Ten:* **r. la balle,** to return the service, a stroke. **2.** (*a*) *Ven:* to start (the quarry) again; (*b*) **r. l'industrie, l'agriculture,** to give a new impetus to industry, agriculture; to put industry, agriculture, on its feet again; (*c*) *Const:* to replace, renew (faulty stonework, etc.); (*d*) *Ind: etc:* to check the progress of (the work in hand); (*e*) *Aut: etc:* **r. le moteur,** to restart the engine; (*f*) *v.i. Cards: etc:* to increase the stake, to raise.

relanceur, -euse [rəlɑ̃sœːr, -øːz], *s. Ten:* striker.
relancis [rəlɑ̃si], *s.m. Const:* replacement, renewing (of beam, etc.).
relaps, -e [rəlaps], *Theol:* **1.** *a.* relapsed (heretic, etc.). **2.** *s.* relapsed heretic; apostate; backslider.
relargage [rəlargaːʒ], *s.m. Ind:* salting out (of soap).
rélarge [relarʒ], *s.m. Dressm: etc:* turnings, extra width (left to allow for modifications).
rélargir [relarʒiːr], *v.tr. A:* to widen; to make (sth.) wider; **r. ses habits,** to let out one's clothes.
rélargissement [relarʒismɑ̃], *s.m. A:* widening; letting out (of garment).
relarguer [rəlarge], *v.tr. Soapm:* to salt out (soap).
relater [rəlate], *v.tr.* to relate, state (facts); to report (fact).
relateur [rəlatœːr], *s.m. A:* relater.
relatif, -ive [rəlatif, -iːv], *a.* **1.** (*a*) relative (position, value); *Gram:* **pronom r., proposition relative,** relative pronoun, clause; *Mus:* **tons relatifs,** related keys; (*b*) **questions relatives à un sujet,** questions related to, connected with, a subject; (*c*) comparative; partial, incomplete, limited; **période de repos r.,** period of comparative rest; **silence r.,** relative silence; **vivre dans un luxe r.,** to live in comparative luxury; **tout est r.,** everything is relative; **elle est belle!—c'est r.,** she's beautiful!—that depends on what you mean by beautiful; **il est d'une honnêteté toute relative,** he's honest up to a point; (*d*) (*in computer work*) **adresse relative,** relative address; **code r.,** relative code. **2.** *s.m. Phil:* **le r.,** the relative.
relation [rəlasjɔ̃], *s.f.* relation. **1.** connection; (*a*) (*between persons*) **les relations humaines,** human relations; **nos relations avec la Hollande,** our relations with Holland; **entamer des relations, se mettre, entrer, en relations avec qn,** to enter into relations, get into touch, with s.o.; to communicate with s.o.; **établir des relations étroites entre deux services,** to bring two services into close relationship; **avoir, entretenir, des relations avec qn,** to be in touch, to have dealings, relations, with s.o.; **être en r. avec qn,** to be in communication, in touch, with s.o.; **être en relations suivies,** to be in close communication with one another, to hear regularly from one another; **être en relations d'amitié avec qn,** to be on friendly terms with s.o.; **relations tendues entre deux pays,** strained relations between two countries; **relations d'affaires,** business connection; **être en relations d'affaires avec qn,** to have business relations, to have dealings, with s.o.; **entrer en relations d'affaires avec une maison,** to open up a business connection with a firm; *Tp:* **être mis en r. avec qn,** to be put through to s.o.; **il a des, de belles, relations,** (i) he is well connected; (ii) he has influential friends; (iii) *Iron:* he's got fine friends! **faire jouer ses relations,** to pull strings; **être éloigné de toutes ses relations,** to be far from all friends; **étendre le cercle de ses relations,** to enlarge one's circle of acquaintance; **rompre toutes relations, cesser ses relations, avec qn,** to break off all relations, all connection, all dealings, with s.o., *F:* to drop s.o.; **chef du service des relations avec le public, des relations publiques,** public relations officer; (*computers*) **opérateur de r.,** relational operator; (*b*) (*between things*) **r. entre la cause et l'effet, r. de cause à effet,** relation, connection, between cause and effect; **r. étroite entre deux faits,** close connection between two facts; **faits reliés par une r. directe,** facts closely bound up with one another; *Rail:* **r. entre Paris et Lille,** service between Paris and Lille; **relations directes,** through connections; *Gram:* **accusatif de r.,** accusative of respect; (*c*) **avoir des relations (sexuelles) avec une femme,** to have (sexual) intercourse with a woman; (*d*) *Anat:* **relations de deux organes,** relative positions of two organs. **2.** account, report, narrative, statement; **faire la r. de qch.,** to give an account of sth.; **il a donné une r. de son voyage,** he has given us an account of his journey.
relationnel, -elle [rəlasjɔnɛl], *a. Phil:* relational.
relativement [rəlativmɑ̃], *adv.* (*a*) relatively (**à,** to); **moteur puissant r. à son poids,** engine that is powerful relatively to, in relation to, its weight; (*b*) **il est r. pauvre,** he is comparatively poor; (*c*) **je n'ai rien appris de nouveau r. à cette affaire,** I have learnt nothing new about this matter, with reference to this matter.
relativisme [rəlativism], *s.m. Phil:* relativism.
relativiste [rəlativist]. **1.** *a.* relativistic; *Ph:* **masse r.,** relativistic mass. **2.** *s.m. & f.* relativist.
relativité [rəlativite], *s.f.* relativity; **théorie de la r.,** theory of relativity; **théorie de la r. restreinte,** restricted theory of relativity, special theory of relativity.
relavage [rəlavaːʒ], *s.m.* rewashing; *Min:* second washing (of ore, etc.).
relaver [rəlave], *v.tr.* to rewash (sth.), to wash (sth.) again.
relax [rəlaks], *a. & s.m.* **(fauteuil) r.,** reclining chair.
relaxant [rəlaksɑ̃], *a.* relaxing (atmosphere).
relaxation [rəlaksasjɔ̃], *s.f.* **1.** relaxation. **2.** *Jur:* (*a*) reduction (of a sentence); (*b*) release, discharge (of prisoner). **3.** *Tchn:* **r. des aciers,** loss of tensile stress; *Ph:* **oscillation de r.,** relaxation oscillation.
relaxe [rəlaks], *s.f.* **1.** *Jur:* (*a*) release (of prisoner); (*b*) order of *nolle prosequi.* **2.** relaxation.
relaxer [rəlakse], *v.tr.* **1.** to relax. **2.** *Jur:* to release, set at large (prisoner); **r. l'accusé des fins de toute poursuite,** to discharge the accused on every count.
se relaxer, to relax.
relaxine [rəlaksin], *s.f. Physiol:* relaxin.
relayé, -ée [rəleje], *s. Sp:* (*in relay race*) runner, etc., who hands over.
relayer [rəleje], *v.* (**je relaie, je relaye, n. relayons; je relaierai, je relayerai**) **1.** *v.i. A.Trans:* to relay; to change horses. **2.** *v.tr.* (*a*) to relay, relieve, take turns with, change with (s.o.); *Sp:* (*in relay race*) to take over from (s.o.); **les deux équipes se relayent,** (i) the two teams, (ii) the two shifts, take over from each other; (*b*) *El: Tp: W.Tel: etc:* to relay (telephone message, etc.).
relayeur [rəlejœːr], *s.m.* **1.** *A:* postmaster (at a posting station). **2.** *Sp:* (*in relay race*) runner, etc., who takes over; **les relayeurs,** the relay team.
relecture [rəlɛktyːr], *s.f.* re-reading, second reading.
relégable [rəlegabl̩], *a. Jur:* (*of convict*) liable to hard labour for life.
relégation [rəlegasjɔ̃], *s.f.* (*a*) *Jur:* relegation (to a penal colony); transportation for life; (*b*) police translocation.
relégué [rəlege]. **1.** *a.* relegated, isolated; **village r. au fond de la vallée,** village tucked away at the far end of the valley. **2.** *s.m. Jur:* convict (sentenced to transportation).
reléguer [rəlege], *v.tr.* (*conj. like* LÉGUER) to relegate; (*a*) *Jur:* to transport (convict); (*b*) **r. un tableau au grenier,** to relegate, consign, a picture to the attic; **r. un fonctionnaire en Corse,** to relegate an official to Corsica; **il a relégué son fils à la campagne,** he has packed his son off to the country; **se trouver relégué au deuxième rang,** to find oneself pushed into the background; to be made to take a back seat.
relent [rəlɑ̃], *s.m.* musty smell, taste; unpleasant smell; **r. de bière, d'alcool,** stale smell of beer, of spirits; **attraper un r. des égouts,** to get a whiff from the sewers.
relevable [rəlvabl̩], *a.* that can be raised; (*ship*) that can be refloated; hinged (counter flap, etc.); *Av:* **train d'atterrissage r.,** retractable undercarriage.
relevage [rəlvaːʒ], *s.m.* **1.** raising, lifting (of object); raising, salving (of submarine); **dock, navire, de r.,** (submarine) salvage vessel; **dispositif de r. d'une grue,** luffing gear, luff tackle, of a crane; *Mch:* **barre de r.,** reversing rod, weigh shaft (of a locomotive). **2.** *Post:* collection (of letters).
relevailles [rəlvɑːj], *s.f.pl.* (*a*) churching (of a woman after childbirth); **faire ses r.,** to be churched; (*b*) **repas de r.,** dinner given after the churching.
relevant [rəlvɑ̃], *a. Jur: etc:* dependent, depending (**de,** on); within the jurisdiction (**de,** of); **terres relevantes de la Couronne,** Crown lands; **r. directement de qn,** directly responsible to s.o.
relève [rəlɛːv], *s.f.* **1.** (*a*) *Mil: etc:* relief (of troops, sentry, etc.); **troupes de r.,** *abs.* **la relève,** relieving troops; draft of reliefs; **la r. de la garde,** the changing of the guard; **sentinelle de r.,** *abs.* **relève,** relief (man); **prendre la r.,** to go on guard; **opérer la r.,** to carry on; (*b*) *Nau:* relief (of the watch); (*c*) *Hist:* levy of French ("voluntary") workers sent to Germany (1940-1943). **2. r. des blessés,** picking up of the wounded. **3.** locating (of mechanical defect).
relevé [rəlve]. **1.** *a.* (*a*) raised, erect (head, etc.); turned up (collar, sleeve); stand-up (collar); **chapeau r.,** off-the-face hat; **pantalon à bords relevés,** turn-up trousers, *U.S:* cuff trousers; **ouvrage r. en bosse,** raised work; work in relief; *Equit:* **cheval qui marche d'un pas r.,** high-stepping horse; high-stepper; **airs relevés,** airs above the ground; (*b*) exalted, high (position); noble (sentiment); lofty (style); (*c*) highly-seasoned, spicy (sauce, anecdote). **2.** *s.m.* (*a*) abstract, summary, account, statement; **r. de consommation (du gaz),** meter reading; **jour du r.,** meter-reading day; **r. des naissances,** table, summary, of births; **relevés officiels,** official returns; *Com:* **r. de compte(s),** statement (of account); **r. remis,** account tendered; (*b*) survey; (*by aerial photography*) mosaic; **faire le r. d'un terrain,** to survey, plot, a piece of land; *Mch:* **r. d'un diagramme,** taking of a diagram; (*c*) (*radar*) plot, plotting; (*d*) (*computer*) chart, record; **r. de connexions,** plugging chart; (*e*) *Cu:* next course after the soup; remove; (*f*) *N.Arch:* rise, upsweep (of timber, etc.); (*g*) tuck (in a dress); (*h*) *Farr:* reseating, refitting (of horseshoe).
relevée [rəlve], *s.f. A. & Adm:* afternoon; **à une heure de r.,** at one p.m.
relève-jupe [rəlɛvʒyp], *s.m.inv. A:* dress-holder.
relèvement [rəlɛvmɑ̃], *s.m.* **1.** (*a*) raising up or again, setting up again (of fallen object); setting (of chair, child) on its feet again; rebuilding (of wall, etc.); (*b*) picking up (of object); *Mil:* picking up, collection (of the wounded); (*c*) raising (of picture, wall, to greater height); re-establishment, restoration (of fortunes, etc.); retrieval (of fortunes); recovery, revival (of business); increase (in wages); raising (of tariff, tax, etc.); **r. du taux officiel de l'escompte,** raising of, rise in, the bank rate. **2.** *Com:* (*a*) making out of a statement; (*b*) statement. **3.** (*a*) relieving (of sentry, etc.); (*b*) *Navy:* **ligne de r.,** quarter line. **4.** *Nau: Surv:* bearing (by compass); position; *Surv:* resection; **r. croisé,** cross bearing; **r. gonio,** loop bearing; **r. radio(goniométrique),** radio bearing; *F:* fix; **r. vrai,** true bearing; **relèvements réciproques,** reciprocal bearings; **faire, prendre, un r.,** to take a bearing; to take the bearings (of a coast, etc.); **porter un r. (sur la carte),** to prick a bearing (on the chart); to lay off a bearing; **faire le point par relèvements,** to take cross bearings; **cercle de r.,** azimuth circle. **5.** rise; **r. sensible de la température,** perceptible rise in temperature. **6.** *Geol:* upcast (fault). **7.** *N.Arch:* rise, sheer (of bows); *Artil:* jump; **angle de r.,** angle of jump.
relever [rəlve], *v.* (*conj. like* LEVER) **I.** *v.tr.* **1.** (*a*) to raise, lift, set, (s.o., sth.) up again; to set (s.o., chair, horse) on his, its, feet again; **r. un mur,** to rebuild a wall; *Nau:* **r. un navire,** to right a ship; (*b*) to pick up (object, from the ground); *Mil:* to pick up, collect (the wounded); **r. le gant,** to pick up, take up, the gauntlet; to accept the challenge; (*c*) to raise (picture, etc., to a greater height); to turn up (one's collar, etc.); to tuck up (one's skirt, one's sleeves); to take up, pick up (a stitch); **r. un mur,** to raise a wall; **r. sa moustache,** to turn up one's moustache; **r. son voile,** to push up, raise, one's veil; **r. ses cheveux,** to put one's hair up; **r. ses lunettes sur son front,** to push up one's spectacles; **r. la tête,** to hold up one's head (again); to look up; **r. le menton à qn,** to chuck s.o. under the chin; **r. les salaires, les prix, le cours du franc,** to raise, increase, wages, prices; to raise the value of the franc; **r. les espérances de qn,** to raise, revive, s.o.'s hopes; **r. la conversation,** to revive the conversation; **r. la fortune, de qn,** to restore s.o.'s fortunes; *Jur:* **r. (un titre),** to call (a title) out of abeyance; *Nau:* **r. une ancre, une torpille, une bouée,** to pick up an anchor, a torpedo; to take up a buoy; **r. une mine,** to fish up, raise, a mine; **r. un navire coulé, un sous-marin,** to refloat, raise, salve, a sunken ship, a submarine; **r. la sonde,** to haul in the line; (*d*) *Farr:* **r. un fer à cheval,** to reseat a shoe; (*g*) *Tp: etc:* **r. un dérangement,** to clear a fault. **2.** (*a*) to call attention to (sth.); to note, notice; **r. les fautes d'un ouvrage,** to point out, criticize, the defects of a work; **r. une affirmation,** to take up, challenge, a statement; (*b*) **r. qn,** to take s.o. up sharply. **3.** (*a*) to bring into relief; to enhance, heighten, set off (colour, etc.); to exalt, extol (a deed, s.o.'s merit); **ces pierreries relèvent sa beauté,** these jewels set off her beauty; **action qui a relevé sa gloire,** action that increased his fame; (*b*) *Cu:* to season, to add condiments to (sauce, etc.); **prudence relevée d'une certaine audace,** prudence tinged with audacity, boldness. **4.** (*a*) to relieve (troops, a sentry); *Nau:* **r. au quart,** to relieve the watch; (*b*) **r. qn,** to take s.o.'s place (on duty); to take

over; **r. une tranchée,** to take over a trench. **5.** (*a*) **r. qn de ses vœux,** to release s.o. from his vows; (*b*) **r. qn de ses fonctions,** to relieve s.o. of his office; to dismiss s.o. **6.** to take down (statement, etc.); to record (temperature, pressure, etc.); *Com:* to make out (account); to read (electric meter, etc.); *Sch:* **r. les notes,** to take in the marks; **r. des empreintes digitales,** to take fingerprints. **7.** (*a*) *Nau:* (i) to take the bearing(s) of (a place); (ii) to lay down (a coast); **comment relève-t-on la terre?** how does the land bear? **le lendemain nous relevâmes la terre par tribord devant,** the next day we sighted land on our starboard bow; *Surv:* **r. un terrain,** to survey, plot, a piece of land; (*b*) *Mth:* to plot (a graph). **8.** *Jur:* **r. une charge contre qn,** to bring, lay, a charge against s.o.

II. relever, *v.i.* **1. r. de maladie,** to have (only) just recovered from an illness; **elle relève de (ses) couches,** she has just been confined. **2. r. de qn, de qch.,** to be dependent on, answerable to, responsible to, s.o., sth.; **les gouvernements dont nous relevons,** the governments to which we belong; **je ne relève que de mon mari,** I am answerable only to my husband; **r. de l'article 7,** to come under article 7. **3. cela relève de la démence,** this is utter madness.

se relever. 1. (*a*) to rise to one's feet (again); to get up from one's knees; to pick oneself up; **se r. du lit,** to get out of bed again; (*b*) **le navire se releva lentement,** the ship slowly righted (itself); (*c*) (*of ground*) to rise. **2.** (*of trade, courage*) to revive; **les cours se relèvent,** prices are recovering; **les affaires se relèvent,** business is looking up. **3.** (*a*) to rise again (in public estimation); (*b*) **se r. de qch.,** to recover from sth.; **il ne s'en relèvera pas,** he will never get over it. **4.** *Nau:* (*of ship*) **se r. de la côte,** to bear off from the shore.

relève-rail [rəlɛvrɑ:j], *a.inv.*, **relève-voie** [rəlɛvvwa], *a.inv. Rail:* rail-lifting (jack) (for track levelling).

releveur, -euse [rəlvœ:r, -ø:z]. **1.** *a. & s.m. Anat:* **(muscle) r.,** levator (muscle). **2.** *s.m.* (*a*) *Mec.E:* raising lever, raising device; (*b*) *Engr:* (*tool or pers.*) chaser, embosser; (*c*) *Surg:* **r. de paupière,** eyelid retractor. **3.** meter reader, *F:* gas, electricity, etc. man.

reliage [rəlja:ʒ], *s.m.* hooping (of casks).

relicte [rəlikt], *s.f. Biol:* relic(t).

relief [rəljɛf], *s.m.* **1.** (*a*) *Sculp: etc:* relief; relievo; *Geog:* relief; **carte en r.,** raised relief map; three-dimensional, 3-D, map; **plan en r.,** raised relief model; **le r. de la Suisse est très accidenté,** Switzerland is very mountainous; **la Bretagne a moins de r.,** Brittany is less mountainous, has a less strongly marked relief; **télévision en r.,** stereoscopic television; **voix sans r.,** monotonous voice; **mettre qch. en r., donner du r. à qch.,** to throw sth. into relief; to bring out (contrast(s)); to set off (beauty, etc.); **occuper une position très en r.,** to hold a prominent position; to be very much in the public eye; (*b*) *Tchn:* embossing; *Typ:* **r. du blanchet,** embossing of the blanket. **2.** *pl. A:* scraps, leavings (from a meal).

relier [rəlje], *v.tr.* (*p.d. & pr.sub.* **n. reliions, v. reliiez**) **1.** to bind, tie, (sth.) again; to refasten. **2.** (*a*) to connect, link, bind, join, couple (things, persons); **un réseau de voies ferrées relie Paris à toutes les grandes villes,** a system of railways connects, links, Paris with all the large towns; **traditions qui relient le présent au passé,** traditions that connect the present with the past; **r. les bords d'une brèche,** to bridge a gap; *El:* **r. à la terre, au sol,** to connect to earth, to earth, *U.S:* to ground; (*b*) to bind (book); **r. un livre de nouveau,** to rebind a book; **relié en veau,** bound in calf, calf-bound; **machine à r.,** binding machine; (*c*) to hoop (cask).

relieur, -euse [rəljœ:r, -ø:z], *s.* **1.** (*pers.*) (book)-binder. **2.** *s.m.* letter file; spring-back binder.

religieusement [rəliʒjøzmɑ̃], *adv.* **1.** religiously, piously; **vivre r.,** to lead a pious, religious, life. **2.** religiously, scrupulously; **elle polissait r. tous les meubles même quand la famille était absente,** she used to polish all the furniture scrupulously, religiously, even when the family was away; **écouter r. un orateur,** to listen religiously to a speaker, to drink in a speaker's words.

religieux, -euse [rəliʒjø, -ø:z]. **1.** *a.* (*a*) religious; sacred; **persécution religieuse,** religious persecution; **fanatisme r.,** religious fanaticism; **mariage r.,** church wedding; **art r., musique religieuse,** sacred art, music; **magasin d'articles r.,** repository; shop selling devotional objects; (*b*) **vie religieuse,** religious life; **communauté religieuse,** religious community; **r. par nature,** religious by nature; (*c*) **silence r.,** religious silence; **soin r.,** religious, scrupulous, care; (*d*) *Ent:* **mante religieuse,** praying mantis. **2.** *s.* religious; *m.* monk, friar; *f.* nun. **3.** *s.f. Orn:* **religieuse,** saddleback, hooded, crow. **4.** *s.f. Cu:* **religieuse,** (type of) chocolate éclair; **religieuse au café,** coffee éclair.

religion [rəliʒjɔ̃], *s.f.* (*a*) religion; **avoir de la r.,** to be religious; **mourir en r.,** to die in the faith; **entrer en r.,** to enter into religion, to take the vows; **elle s'appelle en r. sœur Marthe,** her name in religion is Sister Martha; **minorités de r.,** religious minorities; *Rel.H:* **la r. réformée,** Calvinism; **les guerres de r.,** wars of religion; (*b*) **se faire une r. de qch.,** to make a religion of sth.; to consider sth. one's (bounden) duty; to make sth. a point of conscience; **forfaire à la r. du serment,** to violate the sanctity of the oath; *A:* **surprendre la r. de qn,** to impose upon s.o.'s good faith.

religionnaire [rəliʒjɔnɛ:r], *s.m. & f. A:* Calvinist.

religiosité [rəliʒjozite], *s.f.* religiosity.

relimer [rəlime], *v.tr. Tchn:* to file (sth.) again.

reliquaire [rəlikɛ:r], *s.m.* reliquary; shrine.

reliquat [rəlika], *s.m.* (*a*) remainder, residue; unexpended balance; (*b*) **r. d'un compte,** balance of an account; (*c*) **r. d'une maladie,** after effects of an illness.

relique [rəlik], *s.f.* **1.** relic (of saint, etc.); **garder qch. comme une r.,** to treasure sth. **2.** *Biol:* relict.

relire [rəli:r], *v.tr.* (*conj. like* LIRE) to re-read; to read (sth.) (over) again; **j'ai lu et relu sa lettre,** I have read his letter over and over again; **je n'ai pas eu le temps de me r.,** I hadn't time to read over what I had written.

reliure [rəljy:r], *s.f.* **1.** bookbinding; **atelier de r.,** bindery. **2.** binding (of book); **r. anglaise, en toile,** cloth binding; **r. pleine,** (full) leather binding; **r. (d')amateur,** library binding; half-leather binding; **r. sans couture, r. arraphique,** perfect binding; **r. à dos brisé,** bastard leather binding, binding with a loose back; **r. à dos fixe, plein,** binding with a tight back; **r. à tiges,** loose-leaf, inter-screw, binding; **r. hélicoïdale,** spiral binding; **r. électrique,** spring binding (for holding papers, MSS).

relogeable [rəlɔʒabl̩], *a. Elcs:* (*computers*) relocatable; **liste d'adresses relogeables,** relocation dictionary; **sous-programme r.,** open, inline, direct-insert, subroutine.

relogement [rəlɔʒmɑ̃], *s.m.* rehousing.

reloger [rəlɔʒe], *v.tr.* (*conj. like* LOGER) (*a*) to rehouse; (*b*) (*computers*) to relocate.

relouer [rəlue], *v.tr.* **1.** to relet (house, etc.). **2.** to take a new lease of (house, etc.).

reluctance [rəlyktɑ̃:s], *s.f. El:* magnetic resistance; reluctance.

reluctivité [rəlyktivite], *s.f. El:* reluctivity.

reluire [rəlɥi:r], *v.i.* (*conj. like* LUIRE) to shine (by reflected light); to glitter, glisten, gleam; **faire r. qch.,** to polish, brighten, sth. up; **le soleil faisait r. la mer,** the sun cast a shimmer, threw a sheen, over the sea, made the sea shimmer; *Prov:* **tout ce qui reluit n'est pas or,** all that glisters, glitters, is not gold; **brosse à r.,** polishing brush (for shoes); *F:* **passer la brosse à r.,** to soft-soap s.o.

reluisant [rəlɥizɑ̃], *a.* shining, glittering; glossy; well-groomed (horse); **r. de propreté,** spick and span; **visage r. de propreté,** scrubbed and shining face; *F:* **cela n'est pas très r.,** it's not all that wonderful.

reluquer [rəlyke], *v.tr. F:* **1.** to eye, leer at, s.o.; **il aime r. les filles,** he's got an eye for a skirt. **2.** to covet, have one's eye on (sth.).

rem [rɛm], *s.m. Atom.Ph:* rem.

remâchement [rəmɑʃmɑ̃], *s.m.* chewing (sth.) over; turning (sth.) over in one's mind.

remâcher [rəmɑʃe], *v.tr.* (*a*) to chew (sth.) again; (*b*) to ruminate on, over (sth.); to turn (sth.) over in one's mind; **r. le passé,** to brood over the past.

remaçonner [rəmasɔne], *v.tr.* to rebuild, to reface (wall, etc.).

remaillage [rəmɑja:ʒ], *s.m.* mending the meshes (of net); mending of ladders (in stockings).

remailler [rəmɑje], *v.tr.* to mend the meshes of, to re-mesh (net); **r. un bas,** to mend a ladder in a stocking; *Const:* **r. un mur,** to repair the surface of a wall (before roughcasting).

remailleuse [rəmɑjø:z], *s.f. Needlew:* (*pers. or tool*) ladder mender.

remake [rimek], *s.m. Cin: Rec:* remake.

rémanence [remanɑ̃:s], *s.f. Magn:* remanence, retentivity, residual magnetism; *Opt:* **r. des images visuelles,** persistence of vision; **r. de l'écran radar,** radarscope afterglow.

rémanent [remanɑ̃], *a. El: Magn:* residual, remanent (current, magnetism); *Opt:* **image rémanente,** persistent image; *Elcs:* (*computers*) **mémoire rémanente, non rémanente,** non-volatile, volatile, store.

remanger [rəmɑ̃ʒe], *v.* (*conj. like* MANGER) **1.** *v.tr.* to eat (the same sort of food) again; **j'en ai remangé,** I had some more. **2.** *v.i.* to eat again, to have another meal.

remaniable [rəmanjabl̩], *a.* that can be altered, adapted; adaptable.

remaniage [rəmanja:ʒ], *s.m. A:* = REMANIEMENT.

remaniement, *A:* **remanîment** [rəmanimɑ̃], *s.m.* **1.** rehandling; repairing; altering; changing, reshaping; *Typ:* overrunning; **r. d'une canalisation,** relaying of a main; *Agr:* **r. parcellaire,** consolidation (of land holdings). **2.** alteration, modification, change; **apporter des remaniements à un travail,** to alter, recast, a work; *Pol:* **r. ministériel,** cabinet reshuffle, *U.S:* shake-up.

remanier [rəmanje], *v.tr.* (*p.d. & pr.sub.* **n. remaniions, v. remaniiez**) (*a*) to rehandle (material); to relay (pavement, etc.); to alter (building); to retile (roof); *Typ:* to overrun (matter); (*b*) to recast, reshape, alter, adapt (literary work, etc.) **pièce remaniée d'après le français,** play adapted from the French.

remanieur, -euse [rəmanjœ:r, -ø:z], *s.* remodeller, recaster, adapter.

remariage [rəmarja:ʒ], *s.m.* remarriage.

remarier [rəmarje], *v.tr.* **r. sa fille,** to remarry one's daughter; to marry one's daughter again.

se remarier, to remarry; to marry again, a second time; **il s'est remarié avec une Japonaise,** he got married again, this time to a Japanese woman.

remarquable [rəmarkabl̩], *a.* (*a*) remarkable (**par,** for); noteworthy (**par,** for); distinguished (**par,** by); **faits remarquables (de la semaine),** outstanding events, highlights (of the week); **une petite robe r. seulement par la façon,** a little dress, distinguished only by its cut, by the way in which it was made; **personne r. par sa laideur,** remarkably ugly person; **chose r., il était à l'heure,** extraordinary thing, he was on time; (*b*) **homme r.,** remarkable man; **un des hommes les plus remarquables de notre temps,** one of the most distinguished, remarkable, men of our time; **orateur r.,** remarkable, outstanding, speaker; (*c*) strange, astonishing; **il est r. qu'il n'ait rien entendu,** it's a wonder that he heard nothing; (*d*) *Surv:* **objet, point, r.,** conspicuous object, point; landmark.

remarquablement [rəmarkabləmɑ̃], *adv.* remarkably; **il a réussi r.,** he succeeded remarkably well; he had a remarkable success.

remarque [rəmark], *s.f.* **1.** remark; **faire une r.,** (i) to make, pass, a remark; (ii) to make a critical observation, remark; **faire la r. que . . .,** to remark that . . .; **faire la r. de qch.,** (i) to make a note of sth., to notice sth.; (ii) to remark on sth.; **vous vous souvenez que j'en ai fait la r.,** you remember that I remarked on it; **digne de r.,** noteworthy; **accompagner un texte de remarques,** to annotate a text, to make notes on a text, to edit a text; **texte accompagné de remarques,** annotated text, text with comments; **des remarques?** any comments? **2.** inset engraving. **3.** *Nau: A:* landmark, beacon.

remarqué [rəmarke], *a.* **il a prononcé un discours très r.,** he made a speech that attracted considerable attention, notice; **cette différence essentielle et si peu remarquée,** this essential difference which is so rarely noticed, observed.

remarquer [rəmarke], *v.tr.* **1.** to re-mark; to mark (linen, etc.) again. **2.** to remark, observe, notice; **nous ne remarquons, chacun, que ce qui nous intéresse,** we all of us notice only the things that interest us; **je n'ai pas remarqué son absence,** I didn't notice his absence, that he wasn't there; **détails qui se remarquent à peine,** hardly noticeable details; **cette tache ne se remarque pas,** this stain doesn't show; **vous remarquerez qu'il y a erreur dans le compte,** you will observe, you will note, that there is a mistake in the account; **faire r. qch. à qn,** to point sth. out to s.o., to call s.o.'s attention to sth.; **nous ferons r. que . . .,** attention must be drawn to the fact that . . .; **permettez-moi de vous faire r. qu'il en est tout autrement,** may I point out to you that it is not at all like that; **r. qn dans la foule,** to notice s.o. in the crowd; **il entra sans être remarqué,** he came in without being observed, noticed; **se faire r.,** to attract attention, notice; to make oneself conspicuous; **se faire r. par qch.,** to distinguish oneself by sth., to be noticeable on account of sth.; (*b*) to remark, observe, say; **tu es idiot, remarqua son frère,** "you're an idiot," his brother remarked.

remâter [rəmɑte], *v.tr.* to remast (ship).

remballage [rɑ̃bala:ʒ], *s.m.* repacking, re-baling (of goods).

remballer [rɑ̃bale], *v.tr.* to repack; to pack (goods) (up) again; to rebale.

rembarquement [rɑ̃barkəmɑ̃], *s.m.* re-embarking, re-embarkation (of persons or goods); reshipping, reshipment (of goods).

rembarquer [rɑ̃barke]. **1.** *v.tr.* to re-embark; to re-ship (goods); **r. une embarcation,** to hoist in a boat. **2.** *v.i. & pr.* (*a*) to re-embark; to go on board again; (*b*) to go to sea again; (*c*) **se r. dans une entreprise,** to take up a business again.

rembarrer [rɑ̃bɑre, -ar-], *v.tr.* **1.** to bring (the enemy, etc.) to a dead stop; to bar the way to (s.o.). **2.** *F:* (*a*) to rebuff, snub (s.o.); to put (s.o.) in his place; (*b*) to go for (s.o.); to jump down (s.o.'s) throat; to bite (s.o.'s) head off.

remblai [rɑ̃blɛ], *s.m. Civ.E: etc:* **1.** (*a*) filling up, filling in, packing (with earth, etc.); backfilling; *Min:* stowing (of old workings, etc.); (*b*) embanking; banking (up). **2.** filling (material); earth. **3.** (*a*) embankment, mound, bank; **route en r.,** embanked road; (*b*) fill; **remblais et déblais,** cuts and fills; (*c*) *Ind:* slag dump.

remblaiement [rɑ̃blɛmɑ̃], *s.m. Geol:* aggradation; accretion.

remblayage [rɑ̃blɛja:ʒ], *s.m.* = REMBLAI 1.

remblayer [rɑ̃bleje], *v.tr.* (**je remblaie, je remblaye, n. remblayons; je remblaierai, je remblayerai**) *Civ.E: Min: etc:* (*a*) to fill (up), pack (sunk part of ground, etc.); to backfill; *Min:* to stow (old workings, etc.); (*b*) to embank, to bank (up) (road, railway line, snow, etc.).

remblayeur [rɑ̃blɛjœ:r], *s.m.* (*pers.*) *Civ.E: etc:* filler up; backfiller; packer.

remblayeuse [rɑ̃blɛjø:z], *s.f. Civ.E: etc:* (*machine*) backfiller.

rembobinage [rɑ̃bəbina:ʒ], *s.m. Cin: Typewr: etc:* rewinding (film, ribbon, etc.).

rembobiner [rɑ̃bəbine], *v.tr. Cin: Typewr: etc:* to rewind (film, ribbon).

remboîtage [rɑ̃bwata:ʒ], *s.m.* re-casing (of a book).

remboîtement [rɑ̃bwatmɑ̃], *s.m.* **1.** re-casing (of book). **2.** (*a*) reassembling (of piece of furniture, etc.); (*b*) *Surg:* setting (of bone in its socket); reducing, reduction (of dislocation).

remboîter [rɑ̃bwate], *v.tr.* **1.** to re-case (book). **2.** (*a*) to reassemble; to fit (pieces) together again; (*b*) *Surg:* to set (bone in its socket); to reduce (dislocation).

rembord [rɑ̃bɔ:r], *s.m. Bookb:* turn-in (of paper or cloth in order to cover boards).

rembourrage [rɑ̃bura:ʒ], *s.m.* **1.** stuffing, padding, upholstering (of chair, mattress, etc.). **2.** stuffing (material); padding, upholstery.

rembourré [rɑ̃bure], *a.* (*a*) padded; **porte rembourrée,** baize-covered door; (*b*) *F:* (*of pers.*) **bien r.,** plump; chubby.

rembourrer [rɑ̃bure], *v.tr.* to stuff, pad, upholster (chair, mattress, etc.).

rembourrure [rɑ̃bury:r], *s.f.* padding, stuffing (for chains, etc.).

remboursable [rɑ̃bursabl̥], *a. Com: Fin:* repayable, reimbursable, refundable; redeemable (annuity, etc.).

remboursement [rɑ̃bursəmɑ̃], *s.m. Com: Fin:* reimbursement, repayment, refunding; redeeming, redemption (of annuity, etc.); **emprunt de r.,** refunding loan; **r. d'un capital,** return of a capital sum; **r. d'un effet,** retiral, retirement, of a bill; **livraison contre r.,** payment on delivery, cash on delivery, C.O.D.

rembourser [rɑ̃burse], *v.tr.* **1.** to repay, refund (expenses, etc.); to redeem, pay off (annuity, bond); **r. un emprunt,** to return a loan; **r. un effet,** to retire a bill; **registre des chèques à r.,** in book; **commis chargé d'inscrire les chèques à r.,** in-clearer. **2. r. qn de qch.,** to reimburse, repay, s.o. for sth.; **on m'a remboursé,** I got my money back; *Th: F:* **remboursez!** give us our money back!

rembranesque [rɑ̃branɛsk], *a. Art:* Rembrandtesque.

rembrayer [rɑ̃breje], *v.i.* **1.** *Aut:* to let the clutch in again. **2.** *F:* to start work again.

rembrunir [rɑ̃bryni:r], *v.tr.* **1.** to make (sth.) dark(er); to darken (sth.). **2.** to cast a gloom over (the company); to make (s.o.) sad.

se rembrunir, (*of the sky*) to cloud over, to grow dark; (*of pers.*) to become gloomy.

rembuché [rɑ̃byʃe], *a. Ven:* (*of quarry*) gone to cover(t), to earth.

rembuchement [rɑ̃byʃmɑ̃], *s.m. Ven:* reimbushment; return to cover(t).

rembucher [rɑ̃byʃe], *v.tr. Ven:* to reimbush, to drive (stag, etc.) to cover(t); **r. le gibier,** to track up the game.

remède [rəmɛd], *s.m.* remedy, cure (**à, pour, contre,** for); **r. contre les cors,** corn cure; **r. de bonne femme,** old wives' remedy; *O:* **r. guérit-tout,** panacea; **r. de charlatan,** nostrum, quack remedy; **administrer un r. à qn,** to give s.o. a dose of physic; **(ap)porter r. à un mal,** to remedy an evil; **le r. est pire que le mal,** the cure is worse than the evil, trouble; **tout est perdu à moins d'un prompt r.,** all is lost without an immediate remedy, unless remedial measures are taken at once; **r. héroïque,** heroic remedy, kill-or-cure remedy; *Prov:* **aux grands maux les grands remèdes,** desperate ills call for desperate remedies; **c'est sans r.,** it is past, beyond, remedy; it's beyond hope; there's nothing that can be done about it; *A:* **il y a r. à tout, fors à la mort,** there is a cure for everything but death; **à chose faite point de remède,** it's no use crying over spilt milk; **il n'y a pas de r.,** there's no help for it; *P:* **r. d'amour, contre l'amour,** (i) excessively ugly woman, fright; (ii) (old) bitch.

remédiable [rəmedjabl̥], *a.* remediable.

remédiement [rəmedimɑ̃], *s.m.* remedying (**à qch.,** sth.).

remédier [rəmedje], *v.ind.tr.* (*p.d. & pr.sub.* **n. remédiions, v. remédiiez**) **r. à qch.,** to remedy, cure, sth.; **r. à un inconvénient,** to meet, cope with, a difficulty; **r. à un mal,** to cure an evil; to put a trouble right; **r. à des abus,** to eliminate abuses; **r. à l'usure,** to make good the wear and tear; *Nau:* **r. à une voie d'eau,** to stop a leak; **un expédient ne remédie jamais à rien,** a compromise never works, is never satisfactory.

remêler [rəmele], *v.tr.* to mix again; **r. les cartes,** to reshuffle the cards.

remembrance [rəmɑ̃brɑ̃:s], *s.f. A. & Lit:* (= SOUVENIR) **c'est une curieuse r.,** it is a curious fact to look back upon.

remembrement [rəmɑ̃brəmɑ̃], *s.m. Adm: Agr:* **r. des terres,** re-allocation, regrouping, of land.

remembrer [rəmɑ̃bre], *v.tr. Adm: Agr:* to re-allocate, regroup (land).

remémorateur, -trice [rəmemɔratœ:r, -tris]. **1.** *a.* recalling, reminding; reminiscent (**de,** of). **2.** *s.* recaller (of the past).

remémoratif, -ive [rəmemɔratif, -i:v], *a.* commemorative (festival, etc.).

remémoration [rəmemɔrasjɔ̃], *s.f. A:* (*a*) reminding, recalling; (*b*) remembrance.

remémorer [rəmemɔre], *v.tr.* **r. qch. à qn,** to remind s.o. of sth.; to recall sth. to s.o.'s mind; **se r. qch.,** to remember sth., to call sth. to mind; **r. d'anciens scandales,** to rake up old scandals.

remenée [rəmne], *s.f. Const:* (window, door,) arch.

remener [rəmne], *v.tr.* (*conj. like* MENER) to lead, take, back.

remérage [rəmera:ʒ], *s.m. Ap:* replacement of the queen, requeening.

remerciement, *A:* **remercîment** [rəmɛrsimɑ̃], *s.m.* thanks, acknowledgement; **faire ses remerciements à qn (pour qch.),** to thank s.o. (for sth.); **exprimer, présenter, ses remerciements sincères à qn,** to express, to offer, one's sincere thanks to s.o.; to thank s.o. sincerely; **se confondre en remerciements,** to thank s.o. effusively; **voter des remerciements à qn,** to pass a vote of thanks to s.o.; **nous exprimons nos plus vifs remerciements à tous ceux qui . . .,** we wish to extend our (sincere) thanks to all those who . . ..

remercier [rəmɛrsje], *v.tr.* (*p.d. & pr.sub.* **n. remerciions, v. remerciiez**) **1.** (*a*) to thank; **r. qn de, pour, qch.,** to thank s.o. for sth.; **je vous remercie de m'avoir aidé,** thank you very much for helping me; **je vous remercie de faire cela pour elle,** I should be grateful if you would do that for her; **remerciez-les bien de ma part,** give them my best thanks; **il me remercia d'un salut, d'un sourire,** he bowed, smiled, his thanks; **il me remercia d'un coup de chapeau,** he lifted his hat in acknowledgement; **voulez-vous du café?—je vous remercie,** will you have some coffee?—no, thank you; (*b*) *abs.* to decline. **2.** to dismiss, discharge (servant, employee).

réméré [remere], *s.m. Com: Jur:* **faculté de r.,** option of repurchase; **vente à r.,** sale subject to right of vendor to repurchase, with privilege of repurchase.

remettage [rəmɛta:ʒ], *s.m. Tex:* looming.

remettant, -ante [rəmɛtɑ̃, -ɑ̃:t], *s. Post: Com:* sender (of money).

remetteur, -euse [rəmɛtœ:r, -ø:z]. **1.** *a.* remitting (banker, bank, etc.). **2.** *s.* (*a*) sender (of money, etc.); (*b*) *Tex:* **r. de chaînes,** warp drawer, warper.

remettre [rəmɛtr̥], *v.tr.* (*conj. like* METTRE) **1.** to put (sth.) back (again); (*a*) **r. son chapeau, son habit,** to put one's hat, one's coat, on again; **r. un livre à sa place,** to replace a book; to put a book back in its place; to return a book to its place; *F:* **r. qn à sa place,** to put s.o. in his place; to take s.o. down (a peg); to snub s.o.; **r. qn sur le trône,** to restore s.o. to the throne; **r. les ennemis en déroute,** to beat back the enemy; *Fb:* **r. le ballon en jeu,** to throw the ball in; *Ten:* **(balle) à r.,** let (ball); **r. son épée (au fourreau),** to sheathe one's sword; to put up one's sword; *Mil: A:* **r. le sabre,** to return swords; **r. une locomotive sur les rails,** to re-rail a locomotive; **remettez cela!** put that away! **r. un os,** to set a bone; **r. qn dans son chemin,** to set s.o. on his way again; **r. qn dans ses droits, dans ses biens,** to restore s.o. to his rights; to restore his property to s.o.; **r. qch. en question,** to call sth. in question again; **r. qch. en usage,** to bring sth. into use again; **r. un manche à un balai,** to put a new handle on a broom; to rehandle a broom; **r. une doublure à un habit,** to reline a coat; **r. un fond à un pantalon,** to reseat a pair of trousers; **r. en état,** to repair, to overhaul; to recondition; (*in computer work*) **r. à l'état initial,** to reset, restore; **r. à zéro,** to zeroize, to clear; **r. en marche,** to restart (engine, etc.); **r. une pièce au théâtre,** to put on a play again; to revive a play; **je vais lui r. sous, devant, les yeux les dangers qu'il court,** I will point out to him the dangers he is running; *abs.* **r. à la voile,** to put to sea again, to set sail again; (*b*) **r. l'esprit de qn,** to calm, compose, s.o.'s mind; **r. qn de sa frayeur,** to calm s.o.'s fears; **r. qn (sur pied),** (i) to restore s.o. to health; (ii) to bring s.o. round (after a faint); **l'air de la campagne l'a remis,** the country air has set him up again, has put him on his feet again; (*c*) **(se) remettre qch., qn,** to recall, recollect, sth., s.o.; **je ne vous remets pas,** I do not remember, recognize, you; I can't place you; **vous ne me remettez pas?** don't you remember me? (*d*) **r. bien ensemble des personnes brouillées,** to bring together, to reconcile, people who have quarrelled; **se r. bien ensemble,** to make it up again; to become reconciled. **2.** (*a*) to hand over, deliver (up); to send in (application); **r. une dépêche à qn,** to deliver, hand, a telegram to s.o.; **r. des fonds à qn,** to entrust money to s.o.; **r. des documents à qn,** to lodge documents with s.o.; **r. de l'argent à qn,** to hand over money to s.o.; **r. un prisonnier à la justice,** to hand over a prisoner to justice; **le voleur fut remis entre les mains de la police,** the thief was turned over to the police; **r. une affaire entre les mains de qn,** to place a matter in s.o.'s hands; **r. une affaire au jugement de qn,** to refer a matter to s.o.'s judgment; **r. son âme à Dieu,** to commit one's soul to God; **je remets mon sort entre vos mains,** I place my fate in your hands; **r. le commandement à qn,** to hand over the command to s.o.; to place s.o. in command; (*b*) **r. une charge,** to hand over one's duties (to s.o. else) **3.** (*a*) to remit, pardon; **r. une peine, des péchés,** to remit a penalty, sins; **r. une offense à qn,** to pardon, forgive, s.o. an offence; (*b*) *Com:* to allow (discount); **r. 5% sur le montant d'une facture,** to allow 5% on the amount of an invoice. **4.** to postpone; **r. une affaire au lendemain,** to put off, postpone, defer, a matter till the next day; **r. une cause à huitaine,** to postpone, adjourn, remand, a case for a week; **r. une question à plus tard,** to allow a question to stand over; **est-ce que cela ne peut pas se r. à plus tard?** couldn't we do that another time? *Chess: etc.* **partie remise,** drawn game; **c'est partie remise,** we'll put it off for the time being; it's only a pleasure deferred. **5.** *F:* (*a*) **remettons ça!** (i) let's have another try! let's begin again! (ii) let's have another drink; *P:* **voilà qu'elle remet ça,** she's at it again! (*b*) **en r.,** to lay it on thick.

se remettre. 1. (*a*) **se r. au lit,** to go back to bed again; **se r. en route,** to start off on one's way again; **se r. en voiture,** to get into one's car again; **se r. à table,** to sit down at, to, table again; **le temps se remet au beau,** *abs.* **le temps se remet,** the weather is clearing up (again); (*b*) **se r. au travail, à travailler,** to start work again; to set to work again; **se r. au français,** to take up French again; to brush up one's French; **se r. à pleurer,** to start crying again. **2. se r. d'une maladie, d'une alerte,** to recover from, get over, an illness, an alarm; **il se remet lentement,** he is recovering, mending, slowly; **j'attendrai que vous vous**

remettiez, I shall wait till you are yourself again; **voyons, remettez-vous!** come, pull yourself together! **3. s'en r. à qn (de qch.),** to rely on s.o. (for sth.); to leave it to s.o.; **je m'en remets entièrement à vous,** I'm completely in your hands; **s'en r. à la générosité de qn,** to throw oneself on s.o.'s generosity; **je veux bien m'en r. à votre sentiment,** I am prepared to fall in with your way of thinking; **remettez-vous-en à moi,** leave it to me.

remeubler [rəmœble], *v.tr.* to refurnish (house).

Remi, Remy [remi], *Pr.n.m.* (Saint) Remigius.

rémige [remiːʒ], *s.f. Orn:* remex, wing quill; flag; **les (plumes) rémiges,** the remiges.

remilitarisation [rəmilitarizasjɔ̃], *s.f.* remilitarization.

remilitariser [rəmilitarize], *v.tr.* to remilitarize.

reminéralisation [rəmineralizasjɔ̃], *s.f. Med:* making good of mineral deficiency.

réminiscence [reminisɑ̃ːs], *s.f.* **1.** reminiscence. **2.** vague recollection.

remiremontais, -aise [rəmirmɔ̃tɛ, -ɛːz], *a. & s. Geog:* (native, inhabitant) of Remiremont.

remisage [rəmizaːʒ], *s.m.* putting up (of vehicle); putting (of vehicle, engine) into a shed, etc.; garaging (a car).

remise [rəmiːz], *s.f.* **1.** (*a*) putting back (of sth. into its place); **r. d'une locomotive sur les rails,** re-railing of an engine; *Fb:* **r. en jeu,** throw-in; (*b*) **r. en état,** repairing; overhauling; **r. à neuf,** doing up; **r. en ordre,** putting in order; **r. en marche,** restarting; (*c*) revival (of a play). **2.** (*a*) restoration (of lost property); delivery (of letter, parcel, etc.); remitting (of money); **réclamer la r. d'un navire,** to demand the surrender of a ship; **r. d'un navire aux armateurs,** delivery of a ship to the owners; **payable contre r. du coupon,** payable on presentation of the coupon; (*b*) remission (of penalty, debt, tax); **faire r. d'une dette,** to remit, cancel, a debt; (*c*) handing over (of one's duties); demission (of an office); **r. des clefs,** handing over of keys (of flat, etc. to purchaser, tenant). **3.** *Com: Fin:* (*a*) remittance; **faire une r. (de fonds) à qn,** to send s.o. a remittance; to remit a sum to s.o.; (*b*) commission (paid to agent); (*c*) discount, rebate, allowance; **r. sur marchandises,** trade discount; **faire une r. sur un article,** to allow a discount, make a reduction, on an article; **r. de 10%,** discount of 10%; 10% off. **4.** *A:* postponement, putting off; *still so used in* **je partirai demain sans r.,** I shall start tomorrow without fail. **5.** (*a*) *A:* coachhouse; **(voiture de) r.,** hired carriage, livery carriage; (*modern use*) **voiture de (grande) r.,** hired car (with chauffeur); *F:* **être sous la r.,** to be on the shelf; (*b*) shed, outhouse; *Rail:* engine shed, *U.S:* roundhouse; *Th:* **r. à décors,** scene dock. **6.** *Ven:* cover(t) (of birds, game).

remiser[1] [rəmize], *v.tr.* **1.** (*a*) to put up (vehicle); to garage (car); to put (engine) in the shed, *U.S:* the roundhouse; **r. sa voiture,** to put one's car away; **r. sa valise,** to put one's case away; (*b*) to throw (sth.) away, to get rid of (sth.). **2.** *P:* to take (s.o.) down a peg or two; to tell (s.o.) where he gets off.

se remiser, *Ven:* (*of winged game*) to alight, to take cover.

remiser[2], *v.i.* (*gaming, etc.*) to make a new stake.

remiseur [rəmizœːr], *s.m.* keeper of a livery stable; jobmaster.

remisier [rəmizje], *s.m. St.Exch:* intermediate broker, half-commission man.

remisse [rəmis], *s.m. Tex:* heald.

rémissibilité [remisibilite], *s.f.* remissibility (of sin, penalty).

rémissible [remisibl̩], *a.* remissible.

rémission [remisjɔ̃], *s.f.* **1.** remission (of sin, of debt, *A:* of penalty); **sans r.,** (i) unremitting(ly); (ii) relentless(ly); **travailler sans r.,** to work without a break. **2.** *Med:* remission, intermission, abatement (of fever, etc.).

rémissorial, -aux [remisɔrjal, -o], *a. Jur:* remissory.

rémittence [remitɑ̃ːs], *s.f. Med:* remittence, remittency.

rémittent [remitɑ̃], *a. Med:* remittent (fever, etc.).

rémiz [remiːz], *s.m. Orn:* **r. penduline,** penduline tit.

remmaillage [rɑ̃majaːʒ], *s.m.* **1.** *Knitting: etc:* grafting. **2.** mending the meshes (of net); mending (ladder in stocking).

remmailler [rɑ̃maje], *v.tr.* **1.** *Knitting: etc:* to graft. **2.** to mend the meshes of (net); to mend a ladder in (stocking).

remmailleuse [rɑ̃majøːz], *s.f.* **1.** (*pers.*) *Knitting: etc:* grafter; mender (of ladders in stockings). **2.** grafting machine.

remmancher [rɑ̃mɑ̃ʃe], *v.tr.* **1.** to put a new handle on (sth.); to rehandle (tool, etc.). **2.** to secure the handle of (tool, etc.) (again).

remmener [rɑ̃mne], *v.tr.* (*conj. like* MENER) to lead (s.o., animal, cart) away (again); to take back (**à, en, to**); **il fut remmené en prison,** he was taken back to prison.

remmoulage [rɑ̃mulaːʒ], *s.m. Metall:* coring up (of mould).

remmouler [rɑ̃mule], *v.tr. Metall:* **r. un moule,** to core up a mould.

remodelage [rəmɔdlaːʒ], *s.m.* remodelling; **r. du nez par la chirurgie esthétique,** remodelling the nose by plastic surgery; *Town P:* **r. d'un quartier, etc.,** replanning, making a new layout for, a district, etc.

remodeler [rəmɔdle], *v.tr.* (*conj. like* MODELER) *Art: Surg:* to remodel; *Adm:* **on a remodelé les départements de la région parisienne,** the departments of the Paris region have been reorganized.

rémois, -oise [remwa, -waːz], *a. & s. Geog:* (native, inhabitant) of Rheims.

remontage [rəmɔ̃taːʒ], *s.m.* **1.** going up; ascending (of stream). **2.** winding up (of clock); **pendule à r. automatique,** self-winding clock. **3.** *Com:* fortifying (of wine). **4.** putting together, setting up (of piece of furniture, etc.); (re)-assembling, refitting (of parts of machinery, of rifle, etc.); vamping (of boots, shoes). **5.** restocking (of a shop).

remontant [rəmɔ̃tɑ̃]. **1.** *a.* (*a*) ascending; **le train r.,** the down train; (*b*) stimulating, strengthening, tonic (drink, etc.); (*c*) *Hort:* remontant (rose, raspberry); **rosiers non remontants,** summer roses. **2.** *s.m.* (*a*) *Med:* stimulant, tonic; (*b*) *F:* pick-me-up.

remonte [rəmɔ̃ːt], *s.f.* **1.** (*a*) ascent (of salmon, etc.) from sea to river; (*b*) run (of fish). **2.** *Mil:* (*a*) remounting (of cavalry); remount; **cheval de r.,** remount; **officier de r.,** remount officer; (*of officer*) **aller en r.,** to buy remounts; **établissement, dépôt, de r.,** remount depot; (*b*) **r. d'un officier,** mounting of an officer; (*c*) *P:* procuring girls for brothels.

remonté [rəmɔ̃te], *a.* **épaules remontées,** high shoulders.

remontée [rəmɔ̃te], *s.f.* **1.** climb (of road, etc., after running down hill); *Av:* upward motion, climbing (following on a dive); **des sourcils à la r. un peu satanique,** eyebrows with a somewhat satanic upward curve; *Sp:* **une belle r.,** a good pull-up; a good recovery (after bad start, etc.): **r. mécanique,** ski lift; **r. du visage,** face lift. **2.** *Min:* raising (of the men, of the coal, the ore).

remonte-pente [rəmɔ̃tpɑ̃ːt], *s.m.* ski-lift; *pl. remonte-pentes.*

remonter [rəmɔ̃te]. **1.** *v.i.* (*the aux. is usu.* **être,** *occ.* **avoir**) (*a*) to go up again; **r. à, dans, sa chambre,** to go up to one's room again; **je suis remonté lui parler,** I went upstairs again to speak to him; **r. sur le trône,** to re-ascend the throne; **r. à cheval, sur son cheval,** to remount one's horse; **r. en voiture,** to get into one's car again; **r. vers la source de la rivière,** to proceed, sail up, row up, towards the source of the river; **r. sur l'eau,** to come (up) to the surface again; *abs.* **le baromètre remonte,** the glass is rising, is going up; **le soleil remonte,** the sun is getting higher; the days are growing longer; **les actions pétrolières ont remonté,** oil shares, oils, have gone up again; *F:* (*of pers.*) **ses actions remontent,** things are looking up for him; the tide has set in his favour; **votre cravate remonte par derrière,** your tie is riding (up); (*b*) to go back; **r. plus haut,** to go further back; **r. à l'origine, à la cause, de qch.,** to go back to the origin, to the cause of sth.; **notre connaissance remonte aux premiers jours de ma jeunesse,** our acquaintance goes back to, dates from, the earliest days of my youth; **tout cela remonte loin,** all that goes back a long way, a long time; **faire r. qn dans le passé,** to carry s.o. back (in memory); **il fait r. sa famille aux Croisades,** he traces back his family to the Crusades; **r. à la source du mal,** to trace an evil to its source; **cette dette remonte à plusieurs années,** this debt dates back several years; *Ven: etc:* **r. sur la piste du gibier, etc.,** to back trail game, etc.; **à quand remonte votre dernier repas?** when did you last eat? (*c*) *Med:* (*of gout*) to retrocede; (*d*) *Nau:* (*of the wind*) to come round; (*of the tide*) to flow. **2.** *v.tr.* (*a*) to go up, climb up (hill, stairs, etc.) again; **r. la rue,** to go, walk, drive, ride, up the street; **r. le fleuve, la rivière,** (i) to go, row, sail, swim, upstream; (ii) (*of fish*) to run up; **r. le courant,** (i) to stem the current; (ii) to fight one's way back again; (iii) (*after illness*) to get on one's feet again; *Nau:* **r. le vent,** to beat up to windward; **r. la pente,** (i) to climb up the slope again; (ii) to get on one's feet again; (iii) to make up lost ground; *Sp:* (*of score*) **nous allons r. ça,** we'll pull up, catch up; (*b*) to take, carry, raise, (sth.) up again; *Min:* to raise (the men, coal, ore); **r. une malle au grenier,** to take a trunk back to the attic; **r. la mèche d'une lampe,** to turn up the wick of a lamp; **r. ses chaussettes,** to pull up one's socks; **r. son pantalon,** to hitch up one's trousers; **se faire r. les bajoues,** to have one's face lifted; **r. un mur,** to raise a wall; (*c*) **r. un officier, un regiment de cavalerie,** to remount an officer, a regiment; to provide remounts for a cavalry regiment; (*d*) **r. une horloge, un ressort,** to wind (up) a clock, a spring; **l'horloge a besoin d'être remontée,** the clock needs winding; *F:* **être remonté,** to be wound up; **r. le courage de qn,** *F:* **r. qn,** to revive s.o.'s courage, to cheer, *F:* buck, s.o. up; **r. (les forces de) qn,** to put new life into s.o.; **un verre de vin vous remontera,** a glass of wine do you good, set you up, put you right; **voilà qui vous remonte!** that's something to put you right! (*e*) **r. un vin en alcool,** to fortify a wine; (*f*) to refit; to reassemble (mechanism, etc.); to vamp, new-front (shoes); **to restring** (violin, etc.); to remount (map); to reset (jewel); (*g*) **r. une ferme, un magasin,** to restock a farm, a shop; **r. sa garde-robe,** to replenish one's wardrobe; **r. sa maison,** to refurnish, re-staff, one's house; (*h*) *Th:* to re-stage (a play); to put (a play) on again.

se remonter, to recover one's strength, one's spirits; **aller à la mer pour se r.,** to go to the sea(side) to recover one's health, to convalesce; **prendre qch. pour se r.,** to take a tonic.

remonteur, -euse [rəmɔ̃tœːr, -øːz], *s.* **1.** fitter, assembler (of sth.). **2.** winder (of clocks).

remontoir [rəmɔ̃twaːr], *s.m.* **1.** (*a*) winder, button (of watch); **montre à r.,** stem winder; (*b*) *A:* keyless watch. **2.** (watch, clock) key; key (of toy engine, etc.).

remontrance [rəmɔ̃trɑ̃ːs], *s.f.* remonstrance; **faire des remontrances à qn,** to remonstrate with s.o., to admonish s.o. (**au sujet de,** about).

remontrant [rəmɔ̃trɑ̃], *s.m. Ecc.Hist:* Remonstrant.

remontrer [rəmɔ̃tre], *v.tr.* **1.** to show, demonstrate (sth.) again. **2.** (*a*) **r. à qn sa faute, son devoir,** to point out to s.o. his error, his duty; **r. à qn qu'il a tort,** to point out to s.o. that he is wrong; (*b*) **(en) r. à qn,** to give advice to s.o.; to remonstrate with s.o.; **ce n'est pas à vous de nous en r.,** you have no business to try to put us right; **une créature du diable qui en remontrerait au diable,** a child of the devil, who could teach the devil a trick or two.

remontreur, -euse [rəmɔ̃trœːr, -øːz], *s.* remonstrator.

rémora [remɔra], *s.m. Ich:* remora, sucking fish.

remordre [rəmɔrdr̩]. **1.** *v.tr.* (*a*) to bite (s.o., sth.) again; (*b*) *A:* **sa conscience le remord,** his conscience pricks him; (*c*) *Engr:* to re-etch (a plate). **2.** *v.i.* **r. à qch.,** to bite at sth. again; to have another bite, another go, at sth.; **r. à l'hameçon,** (i) to nibble at the bait again; (ii) to be taken in again by the same trick; **y r.,** to try again; to tackle it again; **il ne veut pas r. au travail,** he doesn't want to get down to work again.

remords [rəmɔːr], *s.m.* remorse, self-reproach, compunction; **un r.,** a feeling, a twinge, of remorse; **des r. cuisants,** bitter remorse; **éprouver du, des, r. d'avoir fait qch.,** to be smitten with remorse, to feel remorse, at having done sth.; **r. de conscience,** twinges of conscience; **être pris de r.,** to be smitten with remorse; **atteint de r., bourrelé de r.,** conscience-stricken; **sans r.,** (i) remorseless; (ii) remorselessly.

remorquage [rəmɔrkaːʒ], *s.m.* (*a*) towage, haulage; towing; *Aut:* **r. suspendu,** suspended towing; *Av:* **barre de r.,** tow bar (of glider); (*b*) **(droit, frais, de) r.,** towage dues; towage; *Aut:* towing charge; *Nau:* **indemnité de r.,** salvage (paid to salvage tug).

remorque [rəmɔrk], *s.f.* **1.** towing; **prendre un navire, une voiture, en, à la, r.; donner la r. à un navire, etc.,** to take a ship, a car, in tow; to tow a ship, etc.; **croc de r.,** tow hook; *Veh:* **timon de r.,** tow bar, towing pole; **être à la r.,** to be in tow; **se mettre à la r.,** to be taken in tow; **sortir du port à la r.,** to be towed out of harbour; **se mettre, être, à la r. de qn,** to follow in s.o.'s wake; to follow s.o.'s lead; **politique à la r.,** follow-my-leader policy; **il est toujours à la r.,** he's always trailing behind. **2. (câble de) r.,** tow line, tow rope, tow; *Nau:* **donner la r.,** to give the tug a rope; to give, pass, a tow line; **prendre la r.,** to haul the tow rope aboard. **3.** (*a*) tow; vessel towed; (*b*) *Veh:* trailer; **r. citerne,** tank trailer; **r. (de) camping,** caravan, *U.S:* camping trailer; (*c*) *Rail:* **rame r.,** slip portion; **voiture r.,** slip coach. **4.** *Av:* trolley; **r. pour hydroplanes,** seaplane beaching trolley.

remorquer [rəmɔrke], *v.tr.* to tow (ship, car); to haul, tug (ship); to haul (trailer); to pull, draw (train); *Nau:* **r. en arbalète,** to tow astern; **r. en flèche,** to tow ahead; **r. un navire à couple,** to tow a ship alongside; *Aut:* **dépanneuse qui remorque une voiture en panne,** breakdown lorry, *U.S:* wrecker, towing a car that has broken down.

remorqueur, -euse [rəmɔrkœːr, -øːz]. **1.** *a.* (*a*) towing (boat, etc.); (*b*) *Rail:* relief (engine). **2.** (*a*) *s.m.* tug; tow boat; **r. à vapeur,** steam tug; **r. de haute mer,** ocean-going tug; *Navy:* fleet tug; **r. de mer,** sea-going tug; **r. de port,** harbour tug; **r. de bassin,** port tug; **r. d'assistance, r. de sauvetage,** salvage tug; **r. fluvial,** river tug; (*b*) *s.m. or f.* traction engine, tractor. **3.** *s.m.* member of a tug's crew.

remorsure [rəmɔrsyːr], *s.f. Engr:* re-etching (of plate).

remoudre [rəmudr̥], *v.tr.* (*conj. like* MOUDRE) to regrind; to grind (corn, coffee) again.

rémoudre [remudr̥], *v.tr.* (*conj. like* MOUDRE) to resharpen; to regrind (knife, tool).

remouiller [rəmuje], *v.tr.* **1.** to wet, moisten (sth.) again; **ne va pas te r. les pieds!** don't go and get your feet wet again! **2.** *Nau:* to cast anchor again.

rémoulade [remulad], *s.f. Cu:* remoulade sauce (made with mustard, oil, etc.).

remoulage[1] [rəmulaːʒ], *s.m.* **1.** remoulding. **2.** *Metall:* coring up (of a mould).

remoulage[2], *s.m.* **1.** regrinding, remilling (of cereals). **2.** bran; *Mill:* **r. mêlé,** middlings, pollards.

remouler [rəmule], *v.tr.* **1.** to remould; to mould (sth.) anew. **2.** *Metall:* to core up (a mould).

rémouleur [remulœːr], *s.m.* (knife-and-scissors-) grinder.

remous [rəmu], *s.m.* **1.** (*a*) eddy (water or wind); wash (of ship); swirl (of the tide); backwash; boil (in a stream); **r. de courant,** eddy current; **r. d'eau,** whirlpool; *Nau:* **r. de sillage,** dead water; *Av: Aut: etc:* **r. d'air,** (i) slip stream; (ii) eddy (current); **chambre, banc, aérodynamique pour étude des r.,** eddy chamber; **il y a eu un r. dans la foule,** there was a movement in the crowd; **dans les r. de la foule,** in the milling crowd; (*b*) *F:* public unrest; **ce livre va provoquer des r.,** this book is going to cause a stir. **2.** rise in level (of river above dam).

rempaillage [rɑ̃pɑjaːʒ], *s.m.* **1.** recovering, repacking, restuffing (of sth.) with straw. **2.** reseating, re-bottoming (of rush-bottomed chairs).

rempailler [rɑ̃pɑje], *v.tr.* **1.** to re-cover, repack, re-stuff, (sth.) with straw. **2.** to re-seat, re-bottom (rush-bottomed chair).

rempailleur, -euse [rɑ̃pɑjœːr, -øːz], *s.* chair bottomer, chair mender.

rempaquement [rɑ̃pakmɑ̃], *s.m.* packing (of herrings in a barrel).

rempaquer [rɑ̃pake], *v.tr.* to pack (herrings in a barrel).

rempaqueter [rɑ̃pakte], *v.tr.* (*conj. like* PAQUETER) to pack, wrap, (sth.) up again.

remparé [rɑ̃pare], *a. A:* provided with ramparts, ramparted.

remparer (se) [sərɑ̃pare], *v.pr.* **se r. de qn, de qch.,** to take possession of, to seize, s.o., sth., again; to recapture s.o., sth.

rempart [rɑ̃paːr], *s.m.* **1.** rampart; **les remparts de la ville,** the ramparts, walls, battlements, of the town; *Lit:* **le r. de nos libertés,** the bulwark of our liberties; **un r. de cyprès qui m'abritent du vent,** a screen, rampart, of cypress trees that protect me from the wind. **2.** outer wall (of volcano).

rempiétement [rɑ̃pjɛtmɑ̃], *s.m. Const:* underpinning (of wall, etc.).

rempiéter [rɑ̃pjete], *v.tr.* (**je rempiète, n. rempiétons; je rempiéterai**) **1.** *Const:* to underpin (wall, etc.). **2.** to refoot (stocking).

rempilé [rɑ̃pile], *s.m. Mil: F:* re-engaged soldier, N.C.O.

rempiler [rɑ̃pile]. **1.** *v.tr.* to stack, pile up, again. **2.** *v.i. Mil: F:* to re-engage.

remplaçable [rɑ̃plasabl̥], *a.* replaceable.

remplaçant, -ante [rɑ̃plasɑ̃, -ɑ̃ːt], *s.* (*pers.*) (*a*) substitute, replacement; proxy; deputy; locum (tenens) (of doctor, clergyman); (*b*) *s.m. Mil: A:* substitute.

remplacement [rɑ̃plasmɑ̃], *s.m.* replacing, replacement; substitution; **en r. de qch.,** in (the) place of sth.; as a substitute for sth.; in lieu of sth.; as a replacement for sth.; **en r. de qn,** in place of s.o.; in succession to s.o.; **faire un r.,** to act as replacement, as locum (for s.o.); to stand in (for s.o.); **institutrice qui fait des remplacements,** supply teacher; **dactylo qui fait des remplacements,** temporary, supply, typist; *F:* temp.; (*b*) **pile de r.,** (torch) refill; **pneu de r.,** spare tyre; **aliment de r.,** substitute food; **installations de r.,** substitute installations; alternative facilities; *Av:* **terrain d'atterrissage de r.,** alternative landing field; *Com:* **débouchés, marchés de r.,** replacement, alternative, markets; *Ins:* **valeur de r.,** replacement value (of lost or damaged property).

remplacer [rɑ̃plase], *v.tr.* (*conj. like* PLACER) to replace; to take the place of (s.o., sth.); to deputize for (s.o.); **r. une cuisinière à gaz par une cuisinière électrique,** to replace a gas cooker by an electric one; **la traction électrique remplace de plus en plus la vapeur,** electric traction is more and more taking the place of steam; **pendant la guerre la margarine a remplacé le beurre,** during the war margarine was used as a substitute for butter; **on ne détruit réellement que ce qu'on remplace,** the only things really destroyed are those replaced by others; **r. une vitre cassée,** to replace a broken pane; **cette assiette peut se r. facilement,** it will be easy to replace this plate, to find another plate like this one; **je l'ai remplacé pendant sa maladie,** I took his place, deputized for him, during his illness; **r. qn (à une cérémonie, etc.),** to deputize, stand proxy, for s.o. (at a ceremony, etc.); **un homme comme vous ne se remplace pas facilement,** it isn't easy to replace a man like you; **r. un ambassadeur,** to appoint a successor to an ambassador; *abs. Nau:* **r. au quart,** to relieve the watch; **la nouvelle génération qui va nous r.,** the young generation that will take our place; **les modes sont sans cesse remplacées par d'autres,** fashions are for ever changing.

remplage [rɑ̃plaːʒ], *s.m.* (*a*) *Civ.E: Const:* rubble filling (between walls); backing; (*b*) *Arch:* (window) tracery.

rempli [rɑ̃pli]. **1.** *a.* (*a*) full; **journée bien remplie,** full, busy, day; **sac bien r. de pommes de terre,** sack bulging with potatoes; **texte r. d'erreurs,** text full of mistakes; **être r. de soi-même,** to be full of one's own importance; (*b*) (*of promise, etc.*) fulfilled. **2.** *s.m. Needlew:* (*a*) tuck (in a dress); **faire un r.,** to make, take up, a tuck (**à,** in); (*b*) turning (for a seam or hem in a garment).

remplier [rɑ̃plije], *v.tr. Needlew:* (*a*) to make, put, a tuck in (garment, etc.); (*b*) to turn in, lay (hem, etc.).

remplir [rɑ̃pliːr], *v.tr.* **1.** (*a*) to fill up, refill (glass, lamp, etc.) (**de,** with); to fill in (gap, space); **je voudrais r. un peu ma cave,** I want to stock up my cellar a bit; **elle remplit mon assiette de cerises,** she heaped my plate with cherries; (*for a toast*) **remplissez vos verres!** (please) fill up your glasses! **une vague remplit d'eau notre embarcation,** a wave swamped our boat; **la lecture remplit toutes mes soirées,** reading fills up all my evenings; **cela a rempli mon temps,** it occupied, took up, all my time; **r. une place,** to fill, occupy, a situation; **r. les fonctions de . . .,** to serve in the capacity of . . .; (*b*) to sew over, to darn (hole in a sail, in a sock). **2.** to fill; **les étrangers remplissaient la ville,** the town was filled with strangers; **r. l'air de ses cris,** to fill the air with one's cries. **3.** to fill up, fill in, complete (a form, etc.); *U.S:* to fill out (a blank); (*computers*) **r. de zéros,** to zerofill. **4.** to fulfil (an expectation, promise, order, etc.); **r. les instructions de qn,** to fulfil, carry out, s.o.'s instructions; **r. une formalité,** to comply with a formality; **r. le but,** to serve, answer, the purpose; **r. son devoir,** to do, perform, one's duty; **r. une mission,** to perform, carry out, a mission; *Th:* **r. un rôle,** to fill, sustain, a part.

remplissage [rɑ̃plisaːʒ], *s.m.* **1.** filling (up) (of cask, reservoir, etc.); **stylo à r. automatique,** self-filling fountain pen; **robinet de r.,** feed-water cock. **2.** (*a*) filling (in) (of a piece of masonry, of hole in a sail, of embroidery, etc.); *Min:* infilling (of vein); (*b*) padding (of literary work, etc.); overloading (of a painting); *W.Tel: F:* fill-up; *Mus: A:* **parties de r.,** filling-in parts; (*c*) (*in computer work*) padding; **caractère de r. (de temps),** pad character; **caractère de r. (d'espace ou de temps),** null, throw-away, character; **chiffres de r.,** gap digits; **instruction de r.,** dummy instruction; **zone de r.,** filler.

remplisseur, -euse [rɑ̃plisœːr, -øːz]. **1.** *s.* filler (in). **2.** *s.m. Ind:* charging hopper. **3.** *s.f. Ind:* **remplisseuse,** bottle-filling machine.

remplissure [rɑ̃plisyːr], *s.f.* **1.** filling (in). **2.** space filled in.

remploi [rɑ̃plwa], *s.m.* **1.** (*a*) re-employment; (*b*) using again; **église romane où on constate le r. de colonnes romaines,** romanesque church in the construction of which Roman columns have been used. **2.** *Jur:* re-investment (of the proceeds of a sale of property, etc.); **le r. des biens dotaux est stipulé dans le contrat de mariage,** in a marriage under the dotal regime, the proceeds of the sale of any of the wife's property must be re-invested.

remployable [rɑ̃plwajabl̥], *a.* **1.** (*a*) re-employable; (*b*) that can be used again. **2.** *Fin:* that can be re-invested; (funds) for re-investment.

remployer [rɑ̃plwaje], *v.tr.* (*conj. like* EMPLOYER) **1.** (*a*) to employ (s.o.) again; (*b*) to make use of (sth.) again. **2.** to re-invest (money).

remplumer [rɑ̃plyme], *v.tr.* to feather (sth.) again.

se remplumer. **1.** (*of bird*) to get new feathers, new plumage. **2.** *F:* (*of pers.*) (*a*) to become solvent again; to recover one's fortune; (*b*) to put on weight again; (*c*) to recover (one's health), to get better.

rempocher [rɑ̃pɔʃe], *v.tr.* to pocket (sth.) again; to repocket (sth.); to put (sth.) back in(to) one's pocket.

rempoigner [rɑ̃pwaɲe], *v.tr.* to grasp, catch hold of, (sth.) again.

rempoissonnement [rɑ̃pwasɔnmɑ̃], *s.m.* restocking (of pond) with fish.

rempoissonner [rɑ̃pwasɔne], *v.tr.* to restock (pond) with fish.

remporter [rɑ̃pɔrte], *v.tr.* **1.** to carry, take, (sth.) back; to carry, take, (sth.) away. **2.** to win, carry off, (prize); to achieve (success); to win, reap, gain (victory, advantage) (**sur,** over); **ne r. que du ridicule,** to gain, achieve, nothing but ridicule; **r. la première place (dans un concours, etc.),** to get first place (in a competition).

rempotage [rɑ̃pɔtaːʒ], *s.m. Hort:* repotting; potting on.

rempoter [rɑ̃pɔte], *v.tr.* to repot, to pot on (plant).

remprisonner [rɑ̃prizɔne], *v.tr.* to reimprison.

remprunter [rɑ̃prœ̃te], *v.tr.* to borrow (sth.) again.

remuable [rəmɥabl̥], *a.* movable; **une gigantesque armoire à peine r.,** a huge wardrobe that could scarcely be moved.

remuage [rəmɥaːʒ], *s.m.* **1.** moving (of object to another place). **2.** agitating, shaking, stirring (up); *Wine-m:* working of the deposit down on to the cork; champagnization (of wine).

remuant [rəmɥɑ̃], *a.* **1.** restless, bustling (person); restless, turbulent (spirit); **personne toujours remuante,** person always on the go, on the move. **2.** *A:* moving (spectacle).

remue [rəmy], *s.f. Husb: Dial:* (*a*) transhumance; (*b*) seasonal pasture; (*c*) mountain hut (for shepherds, etc.).

remué [rəmɥe], *a.* (*a*) agitated; moved (by event); (*b*) *F:* **cousin r. de germain,** second cousin, first cousin once removed.

remue-ménage [rəmymenaːʒ], *s.m.inv.* stir, bustle, confusion, upset, hullabaloo, hubbub; **il y eut un grand r.-m.,** there was a great to-do, a great stir.

remuement, *A:* **remûment** [rəmymɑ̃], *s.m.* **1.** (*a*) moving, stirring; (*b*) removing, removal (of furniture, etc.); **r. des terres,** removal of earth. **2.** stir, disturbance.

remuer [rəmɥe]. **1.** *v.tr.* to move, stir, agitate; (*a*) **r. la tête,** to move one's head; **ne r. ni pied ni patte,** not to move hand or foot; (*b*) **r. de la terre,** to remove, transport, shift, earth; (*c*) **r. son café,** to stir one's coffee; **r. la terre,** to turn up, turn over, disturb, the ground; **r. les masses,** to stir up, rouse, the masses; **r. ciel et terre, r. toutes choses,** to move heaven and earth, to leave no stone unturned; **ne remuez pas le passé,** don't rake up the past; **ne remuez pas le fer dans la plaie,** don't rub it in; **r. une question,** to investigate a question; **r. beaucoup d'idées,** to be full of ideas; **r. beaucoup d'argent,** to handle a lot of money; (*d*) **r. qn, le cœur de qn,** to stir, move, s.o., s.o.'s heart; **événements qui remuent l'âme,** events that stir the soul; soul-stirring events. **2.** *v.i.* (*a*) to move, stir, *F:* budge; (*to child*) **ne remue pas tout le temps!** don't fidget! **ne remuez pas!** don't move! don't budge! (*b*) **dent qui remue,** loose tooth.

se remuer, to move, stir; to bustle about; to be active; **remuez-vous un peu!** get on with it! get stirring! look alive! get a move on!

remueur, -euse [rəmɥœːr, -øːz]. **1.** *a.* active, bustling. **2.** *s.* (*a*) *O:* mover; shifter (of furniture, etc.); (*b*) stirrer up (of trouble, etc.); disturber; (*c*) **r. d'idées,** introducer of new ideas; **remueurs d'affaires,** go-ahead business men. **3.** (*a*) *s.m.* stirrer, stirring device; (*b*) *s. A:* (*pers.*) rocker (of child in cradle).

remugle [rəmygl̩], *s.m.* mustiness, musty smell.

rémunérateur, -trice [remyneratœːr, -tris]. **1.** *a.* remunerative (work, price, freight, etc.); paying, profitable; **ce travail n'est pas r.,** this work doesn't pay; **peu r.,** unremunerative. **2.** *s.* remunerator, rewarder; **Dieu r. de la vertu,** God, who rewards virtue.

rémunération [remynerasjɔ̃], *s.f.* remuneration, payment (**de,** for); consideration (for services rendered); **en r. de vos services,** as payment for your services; in consideration of your services; **r. du capital,** return on capital.

rémunératoire [remyneratwaːr], *a. Jur:* (legacy, etc.) in consideration of services rendered; (sum) granted as a recompense.

rémunérer [remynere], *v.tr.* (**je rémunère, n. rémunérons; je rémunérerai**) **1.** *O:* to remunerate, to reward (s.o.). **2.** to pay for (services); **collaborateurs rémunérés,** paid helpers.

Rémus [remys], *Pr.n.m. Rom.Hist:* Remus.

renâcler [rənɑkle], *v.i.* (*a*) (*of horse*) to snort; (*of pers.*) to sniff, snort; *F:* **r. à un plat,** to sniff, turn up one's nose, at a dish; (*b*) to show reluctance (in doing sth.); to hang back; **r. à la besogne,** to shirk, fight shy of, one's job; to jib at one's work; to be workshy; **il a accepté en renâclant,** he accepted grudgingly.

renâcleur [rənɑklœːr], *s.m.* (*a*) shirker, hanger back; (*b*) grumbler.

renaissance [rənesɑ̃ːs], *s.f.* **1.** (*a*) rebirth; (*b*) revival, renewal; **r. des lettres,** revival of letters; **r. du printemps,** reappearance of spring; *Tex:* **(drap de) laine (de) r.,** shoddy. **2.** *Art: Lit:* **la R.,** the Renaissance; **style de la R.,** *a.inv.* **style R.,** Renaissance style; **les châteaux R. des bords de la Loire,** the Renaissance châteaux of the Loire valley.

renaissant [rənesɑ̃], *a.* **1.** renascent; reviving (strength, hope); (vegetation) that springs up again; **querelles sans cesse renaissantes,** ever-recurring quarrels. **2.** *F:* (of the) Renaissance.

renaître [rənɛtr̩], *v.i.* (*conj. like* NAÎTRE, *but p.p.* **rené** *and comp. tenses are not in use, and p.h.* **je renaquis** *is rare*) **1.** to be born again; **ville qui renaît de ses cendres,** town that is rising again from its ashes; **r. à l'espérance,** to feel one's hopes reviving; to take heart again; **r. à la vie,** to take on a new lease of life. **2.** to return, reappear; (*of plants, etc.*) to grow again, to spring up again; (*of nature, hope, of the arts*) to revive; **le jour renaît,** a fresh day is dawning; **faire r. les espérances de qn,** to revive s.o.'s hopes; **voir r. le calme,** to see calm restored.

rénal, -aux [renal, -o], *a. Anat: Med:* renal; **calcul r.,** renal calculus, stone in the kidneys; **artères, veines, rénales,** renal arteries, veins; **plexus r.,** renal plexus.

renard [rənaːr], *s.m.* **1.** (*a*) *Z:* fox; **r. argenté,** silver fox; **r. polaire, r. bleu,** white fox, arctic fox; **r. des sables, r. famélique,** sand fox; **la chasse au r.,** (fox) hunting; **une chasse au r.,** a (fox) hunt, a meet; *Lit:* **compère le R., Maître R.,** Reynard (the Fox); **se confesser au r.,** to betray oneself; **c'est un fin r.,** he's as sly as a fox; *Prov:* **mettre le r. avec les poules,** to set the cat among the pigeons; **le r. est pris, lâchez vos poules,** the danger's over now; **vendre la poule au r.,** to betray one's side, one's friends; **prendre martre pour r.,** to mistake one thing for another; **tirer au r.,** (i) to refuse to go on; to dig one's heels in; (ii) to try to back out; *P:* **aller au r., écorcher un r., piquer un r.,** to be sick, to throw up, to cat; (*b*) *Cost:* fox (fur); fox collar; (*c*) *Ind: O:* (i) non-union man; (ii) strike breaker, blackleg, *U.S:* scab. **2.** *Ich:* **r. marin, r. de mer,** fox shark, sea fox, sea ape, thresher. **3.** *Tchn:* (*a*) *Nau: etc:* dog(-hook); (*b*) *Const:* blind wall; (*c*) *N.Arch:* traverse board (of ship's helm); (*d*) leak, fissure, gap (in boiler, dam, etc.); (*e*) *Metall:* bloom, loop.

renarde [rənard], *s.f. Z:* vixen.

renardeau, -eaux [rənardo], *s.m.* fox cub.

renarder [rənarde], *v.i.* **1.** *F:* to fox; to play the fox. **2.** *P:* to be sick, to throw up, to cat.

renardier, -ière [rənardje, -jɛːr]. **1.** *a.* of, pertaining to, foxes. **2.** *s.m.* fox catcher. **3.** *s.f.* **renardière** (*a*) fox's hole, fox's earth, fox earth; (*b*) *Metall:* refinery, refining furnace.

renardite [rənardit], *s.f. Miner:* renardite.

Renaud [rəno], *Pr.n.m.* **1.** *Medieval Lit:* Rinaldo. **2.** Reginald.

renaud [rəno], *s.m. P:* **1. être en r.,** to be furious, in a foul temper; to see red. **2.** violent protest; row; **y a du r.,** there's a hell of a row, a shindy; **chercher du r. à qn,** to pick a quarrel with s.o.

renauder [rənode], *v.i. P:* to grumble, complain, bellyache, beef.

renaudeur [rənodœːr], *s.m. P:* grumbler, bellyacher, beefer.

renaudin, -ine [rənodɛ̃, -in], *a. & s. Geog:* (native, inhabitant) of Châteaurenault.

rencaissage [rɑ̃kɛsaːʒ], *s.m.,* **rencaissement** [rɑ̃kɛsmɑ̃], *s.m.* **1.** putting (of plants) in boxes or tubs again. **2.** receiving back (of money).

rencaisser [rɑ̃kese], *v.tr.* **1.** *Hort:* to put (plants) in boxes or tubs again; to re-box (orange trees, etc.). **2.** to receive back (money); to have (money) refunded.

rencard [rɑ̃kaːr], *s.m. P:* dope, gen, information.

rencarder [rɑ̃karde], *v.tr. P:* to fill (s.o.) in, to give (s.o.) the dope, the gen, the information.

rencart [rɑ̃kaːr], *s.m.* **1. mettre qch. au r.,** to put sth. on one side; to shelve sth. **2.** *P:* (*a*) date, rendezvous; (*b*) dope, gen, information.

renchaîner [rɑ̃ʃene]. **1.** *v.tr.* to chain (dog, etc.) up again. **2.** *v.i. F:* to carry on (a conversation where it was broken off).

renchéri, -ie [rɑ̃ʃeri], *a. & s. A: F:* particular, fastidious, fussy (person); **ne faites pas tant le r.,** (i) don't be so squeamish, so fastidious; (ii) don't put on such airs.

renchérir [rɑ̃ʃeriːr]. **1.** *v.tr.* to make (sth.) dearer; to raise the price of (sth.). **2.** *v.i.* (*a*) (*of goods, etc.*) to get dearer; to increase, rise, in price; **tout renchérit,** everything is going up (in price); (*b*) (*of person*) **r. sur qn,** (i) to outbid s.o.; (ii) to outdo s.o.; to go further than s.o., to go one better than s.o.; **r. sur une histoire,** to improve on a story; **r. sur une citation,** to cap a quotation; **le mot "vénération" renchérit sur le mot "respect"** the word "veneration" is stronger than, implies more than, the word "respect."

renchérissement [rɑ̃ʃerismɑ̃], *s.m.* rise, advance, increase, in price.

renchérisseur, -euse [rɑ̃ʃerisœːr, -øːz], *s.* **1.** (*a*) outbidder; (*b*) outdoer. **2.** runner up of prices.

rencogner [rɑ̃kɔɲe], *v.tr.* to push, drive, (s.o.) into a corner; **il s'est rencogné contre sa mère,** he huddled up against his mother; *F:* **rencogné dans un fauteuil,** huddled, curled up in an armchair.

rencontre [rɑ̃kɔ̃ːtr], *s.f.* **1.** (*a*) meeting, encounter (of persons); meeting (of streams); **faire la r. de qn, faire une r.,** to meet s.o.; **aller, venir, à la r. de qn,** to go, come, to meet s.o.; **faire une mauvaise r.,** to come up against something unpleasant; to have an unpleasant experience; to be held up (by brigands, etc.); **gouvernement de r.,** makeshift government; **c'est un bibelot de r.,** it is a curio that I came across, that I picked up; **connaissance de r.,** chance acquaintance; **vol à la r.,** unpremeditated theft; *F:* **le faire à la r.,** to pretend that it is a chance meeting; *P:* **faire qn à la r.,** to butt s.o. in the chest; *Clockm:* **roue de r.,** balance wheel; (*b*) **r. de deux automobiles,** collision between two cars; (*c*) **r. d'or dans une veine,** occurrence of gold in a vein; **r. de pétrole,** strike, striking, of oil; (*d*) *Mth:* **point de r.,** meeting point (of curves). **2.** encounter (of adversaries, opposing forces, etc.); duel; skirmish; *Sp:* match, meeting; *Box:* fight; **une r. avec l'ennemi,** a brush with the enemy; *Mil:* **bataille de r.,** encounter battle. **3.** (*a*) *A: & Lit:* occasion, conjuncture; (*b*) **par r.,** by chance. **4.** *Book-k:* posting folio. **5.** *Her:* beast's head caboched.

rencontrer [rɑ̃kɔ̃tre], *v.tr.* **1.** to meet, to fall in with (s.o., sth.); to come upon, to light upon (sth.); **r. par hasard . . .,** to stumble upon . . .; **r. un vieil ami,** to meet, chance upon, an old friend; **r. qn sur son chemin,** to run across s.o.; **je viens de le r. qui traversait la rue,** I have just met him as he was crossing the street; **à Paris le hasard me fit r. X,** in Paris I came across X; **le hasard m'a fait le r.,** chance brought us together; **r. l'ennemi,** to encounter the enemy; *Nau:* **r. un navire,** (i) to meet a ship; (ii) to run foul of a ship; **r. les yeux de qn,** to meet s.o.'s glance; **ses yeux rencontrèrent les miens,** his eyes caught mine; **de tels hommes se rencontrent souvent,** one often meets, comes across, such men; **r. un obstacle,** to meet with an (unexpected) obstacle, to encounter a difficulty; **le tramway a rencontré un autobus,** the tram collided with, ran into, a bus; **la balle a rencontré un os qui l'a fait dévier,** the bullet struck, met, a bone that deflected it; **ses yeux rencontrèrent le tableau,** his eyes lighted on the picture; **r. un indice,** to hit upon a clue; **r. le bonheur auprès de qn,** to find happiness with s.o.; *abs.* **vous avez bien rencontré, vous avez rencontré juste,** you've made a lucky hit; you've guessed right; *Ven:* **les chiens ont rencontré,** the hounds have found (the scent). **2.** (*a*) **r. un argument,** to refute an argument; (*b*) *Nau:* **r. (l'embardée) avec la barre, r. la barre,** to meet her with the helm, to meet the helm; **rencontrez!** meet her!

se rencontrer. 1. to meet; (*a*) **leurs yeux se rencontrèrent,** their eyes met; **je dois me r. avec lui à six heures,** I am to meet him (by appointment) at six o'clock; **se r. en duel,** to meet (in a duel); (*b*) (*of vehicles*) to collide, to run into each other; (*of ships*) to run foul of one another; (*c*) (*of substance, etc.*) to occur, to be found; **comme cela se rencontre!** how lucky! how things do happen! **2.** (*of ideas*) to agree, tally; (*of persons*) to be of the same mind.

rencourager [rɑ̃kuraʒe], *v.tr.* (*conj. like* ENCOURAGER) to restore the courage of (s.o.); to put new heart into (s.o.).

rendage [rɑ̃daːʒ], *s.m.* difference between the face value and real value (of coinage).

rendant, -ante [rɑ̃dɑ̃, -ɑ̃ːt]. *Jur:* **1.** *a.* **parties rendantes,** parties tendering accounts. **2.** *s.* **r. (compte),** person rendering an account.

rendement [rɑ̃dmɑ̃], *s.m.* **1.** (*a*) produce, yield (of piece of ground, tax, etc.); return, profit (of transaction); *Pol.Ec:* **loi du r. non-proportionnel,** law of diminishing returns; **actions à gros r.,** shares that bear, yield, high interest; (*b*) *Trans:* capacity (of port, dock, railway, road network, etc.); (*c*) *Ind: etc:* output (of worker); output, production (of works, mine, etc.); throughput (of computer); yield (of mine, oil well, ore, etc.); **r. à l'heure, r. horaire,** output per hour; **r. journalier moyen,** average daily output; **r. du personnel,** output of the staff; **r. individuel,** output per man; **r. du geste,** motion efficiency (in chain production); **r. d'ensemble, r. total,** aggregate output; **augmentation, diminution, du r.,** rise, fall, in output; **travailler à plein r.,** (i) (*of works*) to work to full capacity; (ii) (*of workers*) to work full out; (iii) (*of machine*) to work at full load; **le haut fourneau travaille à plein r.,** the furnace is working at full blast; (*d*) *Mec.E:* efficiency, duty, performance (of engine, machine, etc.); efficiency (of computer); **r. apparent,** apparent efficiency; **r. effectif,** performance rating; **r. économique,** commercial efficiency; **r. d'appropriation,** performance, duty, under service conditions; **r. calorifique, r. thermique,** heat efficiency, thermal efficiency; **r. énergétique,** energy efficiency, yield; **r. mécanique,** mechanical efficiency; **r. global,** overall efficiency; *I.C.E:* **r. volumétrique,** volumetric, volume, efficiency; **machine à bas r.,** low-efficiency, low-speed, machine; **machine à bon, à grand, r.,** efficient machine; high-efficiency, high-speed, machine; heavy-duty machine; **meilleur r. du moteur,** optimum engine performance; *Aut:* **r. des différentes vitesses,** speed in various gears; *Av: Nau:* **r. de l'hélice,** propeller efficiency; **r. propulsif,** propulsive efficiency; *Nau:* **r. de carène,** hull efficiency; (*e*) *El:* efficiency (of transformer, etc.); volt efficiency (of storage battery); **r. énergétique d'un accumulateur,** watt-hour efficiency of a storage battery; *W.Tel:* **r. à l'antenne,** aerial efficiency; *Elcs:* **r. quantique,** quantum efficiency; (*f*) *Atom.Ph:* yield (of reaction, fission, etc.); **r. en rayonnement, en radiations,** yield of radiation; **r. en neutrons,** neutron yield; **r. ionique,** ion yield; **r. du produit appauvri,** stripped output; **r. du produit enrichi,** enriched output. **2.** *Rac:* **r. de temps,** time allowance; time handicap.

rendetter (se) [sərɑ̃detɛ], *v.pr.* to run into debt again.

rendeur, -euse [rɑ̃dœːr, -øːz], *s.* person who returns, gives back.

rendez-moi [rɑ̃demwa], *s.m.inv. P:* **vol au r.-m.,** ringing the changes.

rendez-vous [rɑ̃devu], *s.m.inv.* **1.** rendezvous; appointment; **donner (un) r.-v., fixer un r.-v., à qn,** to make, fix, an appointment with s.o., to arrange to meet s.o.; *F:* to make a date with s.o.; **prendre r.-v. avec qn pour trois heures,** to make, accept, an appointment with s.o. for three o'clock; to arrange to meet s.o. at three o'clock; **se rencontrer avec qn sur r.-v.,** to meet s.o. by appointment; **je serai exact au r.-v.,** I shall keep the appointment punctually; **le médecin ne reçoit que sur r.-v.,** the doctor sees patients by appointment only; **r.-v. d'affaires,** business appointment; **r.-v. spatial, orbital,**

rendezvous in space, orbital rendezvous; **manœuvres de r.-v. orbital,** orbital rendezvous operations; **r.-v. amoureux, galant,** (lovers') date; **maison de r.-v.,** assignation hotel; **avoir r.-v. avec la chance,** to meet with a piece of luck, to strike lucky; *F:* **toutes les laideurs s'étaient donné r.-v.,** it was a collection of all the ugliest people possible. **2.** place of meeting, rendezvous; resort, haunt (of boon companions); **r.-v. de chasse,** venue of the meet; place of meeting (of the hunt or of the shooting party); **ce café est le r.-v. des artistes à la mode,** this cafe is the rendezvous, meeting place, of fashionable artists.

rendition [rɑ̃disjɔ̃], *s.f.* returning of pawned articles to their owners; **salle de r.,** room where pawned articles may be redeemed.

rendormir [rɑ̃dɔrmiːr], *v.tr.* (*conj. like* DORMIR) to send, lull, (s.o.) to sleep again.

se rendormir, to fall asleep again; to go to sleep again; to go back to sleep; to drop off to sleep again.

rendosser [rɑ̃dose], *v.tr.* **r. son manteau,** to put one's coat on again; **r. l'uniforme,** to put on one's uniform again, to return to military life.

rendre [rɑ̃ːdr̥], *v.tr.* **1.** (*a*) to give back, return, restore; **r. un dépôt, un livre prêté,** to return a deposit, a book one has borrowed; **r. de l'argent,** to repay, pay back, money; **r. son salut à qn,** to return s.o.'s greeting; *A:* (*of army*) **r. le combat,** to stand its ground; to engage in combat; **r. les clefs de la ville,** to give up the keys of the city; **r. son équipement en quittant l'armée,** to turn in one's equipment on leaving the army; *Equit:* **r. la bride, la main (à un cheval),** to ease both reins; **r. la santé, la liberté, à qn,** to give s.o. back, restore to s.o., his health, his liberty; **r. qn à la santé, à la liberté,** to restore s.o. to health, to liberty; **il le lui rend en affection,** in return he gives him his affection; he repays him in affection; **rendu à la liberté, il voyagea,** once he was free again he travelled; **r. la monnaie d'un billet de cent francs,** to give change for a hundred franc note; *Turf:* **Éclipse rend 10 livres à Astérix,** Eclipse gives 10 pounds to Asterix; **r. le bien pour le mal,** to return good for evil; *F:* **je le lui rendrai!** I'll be even with him yet! *Ecc: A:* (*of parishioner*) **r. le pain bénit,** to provide (in rotation) the bread for consecration; (*b*) to render, give, pay; **r. hommage à qn,** to pay homage to s.o.; **r. grâce à qn,** to give, render, thanks to s.o.; **r. service à qn,** to render, do, s.o. a service; **r. la justice,** to dispense, administer, justice; **r. compte de qch.,** to render an account of sth.; to account for sth.; **r. une moyenne de . . .,** to give an average of . . ., to average . . .; (*c*) to yield (produce, etc.); (*of flower*) to give out (scent); (*of musical instrument*) to emit (sound); (*of land, taxes, etc.*) to give, produce, yield (so much); *abs.* **le moteur rend bien,** the engine runs, works, well; **sa physionomie rend bien en photographie,** his face comes out well in photographs; **placement qui rend 10%,** investment that brings in 10%; **terre qui ne rend rien,** *abs.* **terre qui ne rend pas,** land that yields no return; unproductive land; **blé qui rend beaucoup de farine,** wheat that yields a large amount of flour; *Games: etc:* **billard qui ne rend pas, qui rend bien,** slow, fast, billiard table; (*d*) *abs.* (*of rope*) to stretch. **2.** (*a*) to convey, deliver; **montez dans ma voiture, et je vous rendrai chez vous,** get in the car and I'll take you home; **r. des marchandises à destination,** to deliver goods (to their destination); **rendu à bord,** delivered on board; **rendu franco à bord,** (delivered) free on board; **rendu (à l')usine,** free factory; **prix rendu,** delivery price; (*b*) *abs. A:* (= MENER) **chemin qui rend au village,** road which leads to the village. **3.** (*a*) (*of pers.*) to bring up, throw up (medicine, food, etc.); *abs.* to vomit, to be sick; *P:* **r. tripes et boyaux,** to be as sick as a dog; to throw up everything; **r. qch. avec les selles,** to pass sth. with the stools; **r. l'âme, la vie,** to breathe one's last, to give up the ghost, to die; (*b*) *Jur:* **r. un arrêt,** to issue, pronounce, a decree; **r. un jugement,** to deliver a judgment; **r. un verdict,** to bring in, return, a verdict. **4.** to render up, give up, surrender, yield (fortress, etc.); **r. les armes,** (i) to surrender, give up, one's arms; (ii) to acknowledge oneself beaten; **r. son âme à Dieu,** to commit one's soul to God; to die. **5.** to reproduce, render, express; **r. l'aspect de qch.,** to render the appearance of sth.; **r. le sens de l'auteur,** to express, convey, the author's meaning; **r. un passage,** to translate, render, a passage; **le peintre a bien rendu vos traits,** the painter has reproduced, portrayed, your features well; **elle rend très bien Chopin,** she plays Chopin very well. **6.** to make, render; **la nouvelle l'a rendue heureuse,** the news has made her happy; **le homard me rend malade,** lobster makes me ill; **il se rend ridicule,** he is making himself ridiculous; **vous me rendez fou!** you're driving me mad, driving me crazy! **r. une rivière navigable,** to make a river navigable; **r. une maison impossible à cambrioler,** to make a house burglar-proof.

se rendre. 1. to go, make for (a place); **nous voilà rendus (à destination)!** here we are! we've arrived! **les fleuves se rendent à la mer,** rivers run into the sea; **se r. en toute hâte à un endroit,** to hurry to a place; **se r. chez qn,** to call on s.o.; to call at s.o.'s house. **2.** (*a*) to surrender; to give in, to yield; *Mil:* **se r. par capitulation,** to surrender on terms; **se r. prisonnier,** to give oneself up; **rendez-vous!** hands up! (*b*) **se r. à la raison,** to yield to reason; **se r. à l'opinion de qn,** to defer to s.o.'s opinion; *A:* **se r. à son devoir,** (i) to answer the call of duty; (ii) to mend one's ways; to return to the path of duty.

rendu. 1. *a.* (*a*) **r. (de fatigue),** exhausted, all in, knocked up, dead beat; (*b*) (*of tackle*) taut, home. **2.** *s.m.* (*a*) *Art:* rendering (of subject); **r. exact des couleurs,** exact reproduction of colour; (*b*) *Com:* returned article; return; **faire un r.,** (i) to return an article; (ii) to exchange an article; (*c*) *A:* **c'est un r.,** it's tit for tat.

rendurcir [rɑ̃dyrsiːr], *v.tr.* to harden; to make (s.o., sth.) harder.

rendurcissement [rɑ̃dyrsismɑ̃], *s.m.* hardening.

rendzine [rɑ̃dzin], *s.f. Geol:* rendsina, rendzina.

rêne [rɛn], *s.f. usu. pl.* rein; **fausses rênes, r. d'enrênement,** bearing rein, check rein; **rênes de bride,** bit reins; **rênes de mors,** curb reins; **rênes de filet,** snaffle reins; **à bout de rênes,** with reins slack; **lâcher les rênes,** to loosen, slacken, the reins; to give a horse his head; **prendre, tenir, les rênes du gouvernement,** to assume, hold, the reins of government.

René [rəne], *Pr.n.m.* (*a*) Renatus; (*b*) *Fr.Hist:* René; **R. d'Anjou, le Bon roi R.,** René of Anjou, René the Good.

Renée [rəne], *Pr.n.f.* Renée.

renégat, -ate [rənega, -at], *s.* renegade, turncoat.

rêner [rene], *v.tr.* to bridle; to put the reins on (horse).

rénette [renɛt], *s.f. Tls:* **1.** *Farr:* paring knife. **2.** *Carp: etc:* tracing iron. **3.** *Leath:* race knife.

rénetter [renete], *v.tr. Farr:* to pare (horse's hoof).

renfaîtage [rɑ̃fɛtaːʒ], *s.m. Const:* new-ridging, repair (of roof).

renfaîter [rɑ̃fɛte], *v.tr.* to new-ridge, repair (roof).

renfermé [rɑ̃fɛrme]. **1.** *a.* uncommunicative, close (person). **2.** *s.m. used in the phrs.* **odeur de r.,** close smell, fusty smell, stale smell (of room, etc.); **sentir le r.,** to smell close, stuffy, fusty, fuggy, musty.

renfermement [rɑ̃fɛrməmɑ̃], *s.m. A:* shutting up, locking up, enclosing, enclosure, confinement; **ma vie de r.,** my secluded, cloistered, existence.

renfermer [rɑ̃fɛrme], *v.tr.* **1.** to shut up, lock up, (s.o., sth.) again. **2.** (*a*) to shut, lock, (sth., s.o.) up; **voyager renfermés dans un compartiment,** to travel boxed up in a compartment; **se r. dans le silence,** to withdraw into silence; **r. ses chagrins dans son cœur,** to lock one's griefs up in one's heart; *El:* **fusible renfermé,** enclosed fuse; (*b*) to confine, restrict; **se r. dans ses instructions,** to confine oneself to one's instructions. **3.** to contain, comprise, include, enclose; **livre qui renferme des idées nouvelles,** book that contains new ideas; **le crâne renferme le cerveau,** the skull encloses the brain; **le genre renferme l'espèce,** the genus includes the species; **article qui renferme les dispositions suivantes,** article that embodies the following regulations. **4.** *Equit:* to have (horse) well under the control of the hands and legs.

renfiler [rɑ̃file], *v.tr.* (*a*) to thread, string, (pearls, etc.) again; (*b*) *F:* **r. qch. à sa place,** to slip sth. back into place.

renflammer [rɑ̃flame], *v.tr.* to rekindle.

se renflammer, to take fire again; to flame up, flare up, blaze up, again; **son cœur se renflamma,** his love was rekindled.

renflé [rɑ̃fle], *a.* swelling (pillar, etc.); *Arch:* (pillar) with entasis; *Conch: etc:* ventricose (shell, etc.); **menton r.,** full chin; *Nau:* **navire à proue renflée, navire r.,** bluff-headed ship, bluff-bowed ship.

renflement [rɑ̃fləmɑ̃], *s.m.* **1.** swelling, bulging, enlargement. **2.** bulge, boss; swell (of gun); *Arch:* entasis.

renfler [rɑ̃fle], *v.tr. & i.* to swell (out); to enlarge, to (re)inflate; (*of dough*) to rise; **r. un tube de chaudière,** to expand a boiler tube.

renflouage [rɑ̃fluaːʒ], *s.m.*, **renflouement** [rɑ̃flumɑ̃], *s.m.* **1.** *Nau:* heaving off, floating off, refloating (of stranded ship); **matériel de r.,** salvage plant. **2.** *Aer:* reinflation, topping up (of gas of balloon after ascent).

renflouer [rɑ̃flue], *v.tr.* **1.** *Nau:* to heave off, float off, get off, refloat, set afloat (stranded ship); *Com:* **r. une entreprise,** to set a business afloat, on its feet, again; *F:* **r. qn,** to keep s.o. afloat (financially). **2.** *Aer:* to replenish the gas of (balloon, after ascension); to reinflate, top up (balloon).

renfoncé [rɑ̃fɔ̃se], *a.* deep-set; sunken (eyes).

renfoncement [rɑ̃fɔ̃smɑ̃], *s.m.* **1.** knocking in (of sth.) again; driving in (of sth.) deeper; **r. d'un chapeau,** (i) pulling down of a hat (over the eyes); (ii) *F:* bashing in of a hat. **2.** (*a*) hollow, recess, cavity, dent; bruise (on metal); **r. d'une porte,** doorway; (*b*) *Geol:* downcast fault; (*c*) *Typ:* indention, indentation (of line). **3.** *Art:* receding of the background; effect of depth.

renfoncer [rɑ̃fɔ̃se], *v.tr.* (*conj. like* ENFONCER) **1.** to knock in, drive in; to drive (sth.) further in; **r. son chapeau,** (i) to pull down one's hat; (ii) *F:* to bash in one's hat; **r. ses larmes, son chagrin,** to choke back one's tears, one's grief. **2.** (*a*) *Const:* to recess, set back (façade, etc.); (*b*) *Typ:* to indent (line). **3.** *Coop:* to new-bottom (cask).

se renfoncer, to sink in; *Art:* (*of background*) to recede.

renforçage [rɑ̃fɔrsaːʒ], *s.m.* **1.** strengthening, reinforcing. **2.** *Phot:* intensification.

renforçateur [rɑ̃fɔrsatœːr]. **1.** *s.m. Ph:* reinforcer, magnifier (of sound); *Phot:* intensifier; intensifying agent. **2.** *a.* **écran r.,** intensifying screen (for X-rays).

renforcé [rɑ̃fɔrse], *a.* (*a*) stout, strong (cloth, etc.); *Mec.E:* reinforced, strengthened, strong; braced; trussed (girder, etc.); **cheval r.,** thickset, strong, horse; *Tls:* **tour r.,** strong lathe; *Tex:* **nylon r.,** spliced, reinforced, nylon; *O: F:* **sot, âne, r.,** downright, out and out, idiot, ass; **bourgeois r.,** out and out bourgeois; (*b*) *Phot:* intensified.

renforcement [rɑ̃fɔrsəmɑ̃], *s.m.* (*a*) strengthening, reinforcement, stiffening, bracing (of beam, etc.); backing (of wall, map, etc.); trussing (of beam, of motor car chassis, etc.); *Mec.E:* **nervure de r.,** stiffening rib; (*b*) intensifying, reinforcing (of sound); *Phot:* intensification; (*c*) reinforcement (of army, security measures, etc.); **le r. des régimes capitalistes,** the strengthening of capitalist regimes; (*d*) *Psy:* **r. négatif, positif,** negative, positive, stimulus; **r. verbal,** word(s) of encouragement.

renforcer [rɑ̃fɔrse], (*conj. like* FORCER) **1.** *v.tr.* (*a*) to reinforce (garrison, etc.); (*b*) to strengthen, reinforce, stiffen, brace (wall, beam, etc.); to truss (girder, etc.); to back (wall, map); to strengthen (a law); *Nau:* to line (sail); to prick (the seam of a sail); **malle à coins renforcés,** trunk with strengthened corners; **citer des faits pour r. son dire,** to quote facts to back up one's assertion; (*c*) to reinforce, magnify (sound); to intensify (colour, *Phot:* negative or print); (*d*) **r. la dépense,** to increase the expenditure; **r. la paix,** to consolidate the peace; **cela m'alarma et renforça mes soupçons,** that alarmed me and increased my suspicions. **2.** *v.i.* (*of wind*) to grow stronger.

se renforcer, to grow stronger, more vigorous; to gather strength; **son esprit s'était renforcé par l'étude,** his mind had improved through study.

renforcir [rɑ̃fɔrsiːr], *v.i. F: Dial:* to grow stronger.

renformer [rɑ̃fɔrme], *v.tr.* to stretch (gloves).

renformir [rɑ̃fɔrmiːr], *v.tr. Const:* to repair and roughcast (a wall).

renformis [rɑ̃fɔrmi], *s.m. Const:* repairing and roughcasting (a wall).

renformoir [rɑ̃fɔrmwaːr], *s.m.* glove stretcher.

renfort [rɑ̃fɔːr], *s.m.* **1.** *Mil: etc:* reinforcement(s); **nouveaux renforts,** fresh supply of troops; **éléments, troupes, de r.,** reinforcing elements, troops; **amener des renforts,** to bring up reinforcements; **envoyer des renforts,** to dispatch, send, reinforcements; **envoyer un r. de cinq mille hommes, cinq mille hommes en r.,** to send five thousand men as a reinforcement; **envoyer deux divisions en r. de la première armée,** to send up two divisions in support of the first army; **envoyé en r.,** sent up to reinforce; *El:* **batterie de r.,** booster battery; **cheval de r.,** extra horse, trace horse; *Rail:* **machine de r.,** bank engine;

engager deux ouvriers, deux serveurs, en r., to engage two additional workers, waiters; **ajuster une robe à grand r. d'épingles,** to adjust a dress with a copious supply of pins; *Cu: A:* **r. de potage,** side-dishes (to the soup); *F:* **pour r. de potage,** to make matters worse. **2.** *Mec.E: etc:* reinforcement; strengthening piece; reinforce (of gun); stiffener, backing, lining (of sail, etc.); **plaque, tôle, de r.,** stiffening piece of plate; *Bootm:* **pièce de r.,** stiffening tip; (toe-)cap; **bande de r.,** foxing; *Carp:* **r. de tenon,** tusk, haunch; **tenon à r.,** tusk tenon; **r. carré,** square haunch; *Nau:* **bande de r.,** strengthening band, strain band; **r. d'ancre,** billboard.

renfrogné [rɑ̃frɔɲe], *a.* frowning (brow, face); sullen, scowling, (person, face); glum (look).

renfrognement [rɑ̃frɔɲmɑ̃], *s.m.* knitting (of the brows); frowning, scowling.

renfrogner (se) [sərɑ̃frɔɲe], *v.pr.* to frown, scowl; to look glum.

rengagé [rɑ̃gaʒe], *a. & s.m. Mil:* re-engaged, re-enlisted (man, N.C.O.).

rengagement [rɑ̃gaʒmɑ̃], *s.m.* **1.** *Mil: etc:* re-engagement, re-joining; *Mil:* re-enlistment. **2.** pledging, pawning, (of sth.) again.

rengager [rɑ̃gaʒe], *v.tr.* (*conj. like* ENGAGER) **1.** (*a*) to re-engage; to engage (s.o.) again; (*b*) **r. le combat,** to renew the combat; (*c*) *v.i. & pr. Mil:* **(se) r.,** to re-enlist; (*d*) *v.i.* to begin again; **quant à ça, je n'ai aucune envie de r.,** as far as that's concerned I've no desire to begin (all over) again. **2.** to pledge, pawn, (sth.) again.

rengaine [rɑ̃gɛːn], *s.f.* catchword; catchy tune; **vieille r.,** (i) old refrain; (ii) old tag, old story; threadbare story; **c'est toujours la même r., la vieille r.,** it's always the same old story; **c'est sa r.,** he's always harping on that subject.

rengainer[1] [rɑ̃gene], *v.tr.* to sheathe, put up (one's sword); **il rengaina son revolver,** he put his revolver back into its holster; *F:* **r. son compliment,** to shut up, to say no more (from Molière's *Mariage Forcé*).

rengainer[2], *v.tr. F:* **r. toujours la même histoire,** to be always harping on the same string.

rengorgement [rɑ̃gɔrʒəmɑ̃], *s.m.* strut (of peacock); swagger.

rengorger (se) [sərɑ̃gɔrʒe], *v.pr.* (*conj. like* ENGORGER) (*of bird*) to strut; (*of pers.*) to strut, swagger; to give oneself airs; **il se rengorge depuis que . . .,** he's very pleased with himself, full of himself, since . . ..

rengraisser [rɑ̃grese]. **1.** *v.tr.* to fatten (animal) (up) again. **2.** *v.i. & pr.* to grow fat, stout, again; to put on weight.

rengrégement [rɑ̃greʒmɑ̃], *s.m. A: & Lit:* increase, aggravation (of trouble, difficulty, etc.).

rengréger [rɑ̃greʒe], *v.tr. & i.* **(je rengrège, n. rengrégeons, je rengrégeai(s), je rengrégerai),** *A: & Lit:* to increase, augment, aggravate (trouble, difficulty, etc.); **cet esprit caustique le poussait à r. sur la misère,** this caustic outlook led him to exaggerate trouble, misfortune.

rengrènement [rɑ̃grɛnmɑ̃], *s.m. Mec.E:* throwing (part) into gear again; re-engaging (pinion, etc.).

rengrener [rɑ̃grəne], **rengréner** [rɑ̃grene], *v.tr.* **(je rengrène, n. rengrenons, n. rengrénons; je rengrènerai, je rengrénerai) 1.** *Mill:* to feed (hopper, threshing machine) with fresh corn. **2.** *Mec.E:* to re-engage (part); to throw (part) into gear again.

renhardir [rɑ̃ardiːr], *v.tr.* to put fresh courage into (s.o.); **il s'est renhardi,** he has plucked up courage.

reniable [rənjabl̩], *a. A:* deniable.

renié [rənje], *a. A:* **chrétien r.,** renegade (Christian); **moine r.,** (i) renegade monk; (ii) ex-monk.

reniement, *A:* **renîment** [rənimɑ̃], *s.m.* **1.** disowning, betrayal (of friend, etc.); repudiation (of opinion); denial (of Christ). **2.** (*a*) disavowal (of action); (*b*) abjuration (of one's faith).

renier [rənje], *v.tr.* (*conj. like* NIER) **1.** to disown, renounce (friend, opinion); to betray (friend, etc.); to repudiate (opinion); to deny (Christ); **être renié de Dieu et des hommes,** to be rejected of God and of men; **r. Dieu,** to utter a profane oath, to swear; **ils se renient entre eux,** they disown, repudiate, each other. **2.** (*a*) to disavow (action); (*b*) to abjure (one's faith).

reniffe [rənif], *s.f. coll. P:* the police, the cops.

reniflage [rəniflaːʒ], *s.m. I.C.E:* popping back.

reniflant [rəniflɑ̃], *s.m. P:* nose, smeller.

reniflard [rəniflaːr], *s.m.* **1.** *Mch:* snifting valve; air valve, breather; blow valve (of steam boiler). **2.** strainer, rose; *Min:* wind bore, snore piece (of pump). **3.** *I.C.E:* breather (pipe) (of crank case).

reniflement [rənifləmɑ̃], *s.m.* **1.** (*a*) sniffing, snuffling, snorting; (*b*) snivelling. **2.** sniff, snort. **3.** *Vet:* snuffles, bullnose (of pig).

renifler [rənifle]. **1.** *v.i.* (*a*) to sniff, snort, snuffle; **r. sur qch.,** to sniff at, turn up one's nose at, sth.; *F:* (*of horse, pers.*) **r. sur l'avoine,** to be off his feed; (*b*) to snivel; (*c*) *I.C.E:* to pop back; (*d*) (*of mine pump*) to be in fork, to have the water in fork. **2.** *v.tr.* (*a*) to sniff (up) (sth.); **il sait r. une bonne affaire,** he's got a (good) nose for a bargain; (*b*) to sniff, smell (flower, etc.).

reniflerie [rənifləri], *s.f.* sniffing.

reniflette [rəniflɛt], *s.f. F:* **avoir la r.,** to sniff, to be sniffly.

renifleur, -euse [rəniflœːr, -øːz]. **1.** *s.* sniffler; *a.* **des enfants renifleurs,** sniffing, sniffly, children. **2.** *s.m. I.C.E:* breather (pipe) (of crank case).

réniforme [renifɔrm], *a. Nat.Hist: etc:* reniform, kidney-shaped.

rénine [renin], *s.f. Bio-Ch:* renin.

reniquer [rənike], *v.i. O: P:* to grumble, object; **il renique,** his monkey's up.

rénitence [renitɑ̃ːs], *s.f. Med:* resistance to pressure (of tumour, etc.), renitency.

rénitent [renitɑ̃], *a. Med:* resisting pressure; renitent (tumour, etc.).

reniveler [rənivle], *v.tr.* (*conj. like* NIVELER) (*a*) to level (sth.) again; to re-level; (*b*) to top up (accumulator).

renivellement [rənivɛlmɑ̃], *s,m.* (*a*) re-levelling; (*b*) topping up (of accumulator).

renjamber [rɑ̃ʒɑ̃be], *v.tr.* to stride, step, over (sth.) again.

rennais, -aise [rɛnɛ, -ɛːz], **rennois, -oise** [rɛnwa, -waːz], *a. & s. Geog:* (native, inhabitant) of Rennes.

renne [rɛn], *s.m. Z:* reindeer; **r. mâle,** bull; **r. femelle,** cow.

renom [rənɔ̃], *s.m.* renown, fame; **en r.,** famous, celebrated, well known; **médecin en grand r.,** doctor with a great reputation; **auteur sans r.,** unknown author; **se faire un mauvais r.,** to get a bad name.

renommé [rənɔme], *a.* renowned, famous, well-known, celebrated; **région renommée pour ses vins,** region famous, well-known, for its wines; **elle était renommée pour sa cuisine,** she was famous, had a great reputation, for cooking.

renommée [rənɔme], *s.f.* **1.** (*a*) renown, fame; good name; reputation; **sa r. s'étendait au loin,** his fame extended over a wide area; *Prov:* **bonne r. vaut mieux que ceinture dorée,** a good name, a fair name, is better than riches; (*b*) **avoir la r. de diplomate habile,** to have the reputation of being a clever diplomatist; **connaître qn de r.,** to know s.o. by repute; (*c*) *Myth:* **la R.,** Fame. **2.** *A: & Lit:* rumour, report; *Jur:* **(preuve par) commune r.,** hearsay evidence; common report.

renommer [rənɔme], *v.tr.* **1.** to re-elect, re-appoint. **2.** *A:* to praise, extol, celebrate (s.o.); **se faire r.,** to make oneself renowned famous; **se r. de qn,** to use s.o.'s name as a reference, as an introduction.

renonçant, -ante [rənɔ̃sɑ̃, -ɑ̃ːt], *Jur:* **1.** *a.* renouncing. **2.** *s.* renouncer.

renonce [rənɔ̃ːs], *s.f. Cards:* **1.** renounce; inability to follow suit; **avoir une r. à cœur,** to be short of hearts; **(se) faire une r. à cœur,** to clear one's hand of hearts, to discard hearts. **2. fausse r.,** revoke; **faire une fausse r.,** to revoke.

renoncement [rənɔ̃smɑ̃], *s.m.* **1.** renouncing, renouncement (à, of). **2.** (*a*) self-denial; (*b*) renunciation; **mener une vie de r.,** to live a life of renunciation; *Jur:* **lettre de r.,** letter of renunciation.

renoncer [rənɔ̃se], *v.* **(je renonçai(s); n. renonçons) 1.** *v.ind.tr.* (*a*) **r. à qch.,** to renounce, give up, forgo, sth.; **r. au monde,** to renounce the world; **r. au tabac,** to give up tobacco, to give up smoking; **r. à qch. pour autre chose,** to give up sth. for something else; **r. à faire qch.,** (i) to give up, forgo, doing sth.; (ii) to give up, drop, the idea of doing sth., to give sth. up as a bad job; **r. à un avantage, à un droit,** to waive an advantage, a right; **r. à une réclamation, à une prétention,** to renounce, withdraw, waive, a claim; *Jur:* **r. à des poursuites,** to abandon a prosecution; **r. à un projet,** to give up, abandon, a project; *F:* to cry off; **r. à la lutte,** to give up the struggle, *F:* to throw up the sponge, *U.S:* to quit; **y r.,** to abandon the attempt, the idea; to give it up (as a bad job); to throw in one's cards; *abs.* **j'ai envie de r.,** I feel like giving up; **deux des coureurs ont renoncé,** two of the runners dropped out; *O:* (*of woman*) **r. à quarante ans,** to give up trying to look young at forty; (*b*) **r. à ses dieux, à sa religion,** to renounce one's gods, to abnegate one's religion; (*c*) *abs. Cards:* (i) to renounce, to fail to follow suit; (ii) to revoke. **2.** *v.tr.* (*a*) *A:* to renounce, disown, repudiate, to disclaim (s.o.); **r. sa foi,** to renounce, abnegate, one's faith; *B:* **avant que le coq chante vous me renoncerez trois fois,** before the cock crow thou shalt deny me thrice; (*b*) **r. sa patrie,** to renounce one's country, to defect.

renonciataire [rənɔ̃sjatɛːr], *s.m. & f.* **1.** *Jur:* releasee. **2.** *Mil:* man who surrenders his dispensation from military service.

renonciateur, -trice [rənɔ̃sjatœːr, -tris], *s.* **1.** *Jur:* releasor. **2.** renouncer.

renonciatif, -ive [rənɔ̃sjatif, -iːv], *a.* renunciative, renunciatory.

renonciation [rənɔ̃sjasjɔ̃], *s.f.* **1.** *Jur:* **r. à un droit,** renunciation, disclaimer, waiver, of a right. **2.** renunciation, abnegation.

renonculacées [rənɔ̃kylase], *s.f.pl. Bot:* Ranunculaceae.

renoncule [rənɔ̃kyl], *s.f. Bot:* ranunculus; **r. âcre,** tall crowfoot, tall buttercup; **r. bulbeuse,** bulbous buttercup; **r. rampante,** creeping buttercup, creeping crowfoot; **r. glaciaire,** glacier crowfoot; **r. langue,** spearwort; **r. flammule,** lesser spearwort; **r. à tête d'or,** goldilocks; **r. des champs,** corn crowfoot, hunger-weed; **r. double,** bachelor's buttons; **r. à feuilles d'aconit,** fair-maid-of-France; garden buttercup; **r. flottante,** water crowfoot; **r. aquatique,** water buttercup; **r. des marais,** marsh marigold; **fausse r.,** lesser celandine.

renonculier [rənɔ̃kylje], *s.m. Hort:* double-flowered gean, (ornamental) cherry tree.

renoper [rənɔpe], *v.tr. Tex:* to burl (cloth).

renouée [rənwe], *s.f. Bot: F:* polygonum, knot grass, knot weed; **r. traînasse,** hogweed, knot grass; **r. des oiseaux,** knot grass; **r. amphibie,** amphibious bistort; **r. maritime,** seaside knot grass; **r. vivipare,** serpent grass.

renouement [rənumɑ̃], *s.m.* renewal (of friendship, etc.).

renouer [rənwe], *v.tr.* (*a*) to tie (up), knot, (sth.) again; to join (thgs) again; to put (thgs) together again; (*b*) to renew, resume (conversation, correspondence, etc.); **r. (amitié) avec qn,** to renew one's friendship with s.o.

renoueur, -euse [rənwœːr, -øːz], *s. A. & Dial:* bone setter.

réno-urétéral, -aux [renoyreteral, -o], *a. Anat:* reno-ureteral.

renouveau [rənuvo], *s.m.* (*the pl.* **renouveaux** *is rarely used*) (*a*) *A. & Lit:* springtide; spring (of the year); (*b*) **r. de jeunesse, d'amour,** renewal of youth, renewed love; **r. de vie,** new lease of life; **r. religieux,** religious revival; **r. des arts,** artistic revival; (*c*) *Pol.Ec:* resurgence.

renouvelable [rənuvlabl̩], *a.* renewable.

renouvelant, -ante [rənuvlɑ̃, -ɑ̃ːt], *s. R.C.Ch:* communicant who formally renews his or her first Communion.

renouvelé [rənuvle], *a.* **r. de,** borrowed from; **jeux olympiques modernes renouvelés des jeux grecs,** the modern Olympic games borrowed from the Greeks; *F:* **c'est r. des Grecs,** that was new when Adam was a boy; *F:* that's old hat now.

renouveler [rənuvle], *v.tr.* **(je renouvelle, n. renouvelons; je renouvellerai) 1.** (*a*) to renew, renovate (one's wardrobe, etc.); **r. ses pneus,** to get a new set of tyres; **r. l'air d'une salle,** to air a room; (*b*) **r. sa maison, son service,** to make a complete change of servants; **r. son personnel,** to renew one's staff; (*c*) **r. la face du pays,** to alter the whole appearance of the country; to transform the country. **2.** (*a*) to renew (promise, treaty, alliance, passport, etc.); to revive (custom, etc.); **r. connaissance avec qn,** to renew acquaintance with s.o.; **r. un procès, une querelle,** to reopen a lawsuit, a quarrel; **r. son attention,** to pay still greater attention; **r. le souvenir de qch.,** to refresh one's memory about sth.; *Com:* **r. une commande,** to repeat an order; **commandes renouvelées,** repeat orders; (*b*) *Ecc:* to renew (one's vows); *abs.* to renew (formally) one's first Communion. **3.** *v.i.* (*a*) **la lune vient de r.,** the moon is new; (*b*) **renouveler de zèle,** to act with renewed zeal; **r. d'appétit,** to eat with renewed appetite; to eat more heartily than ever; *O:* **r. de jambes,** to step out with renewed vigour.

se renouveler. 1. to be renewed. **2.** to recur, to happen again; **le lendemain les plaintes se renouvelèrent,** the next day the complaints were repeated; **il ne se renouvelle pas,** it's always the same old story with him.

renouvellement [rənuvɛlmɑ̃], *s.m.* **1.** (*a*) renovation (of garment, house, etc.); **le r. de l'air d'une chambre,** the airing of a room; (*b*) complete change (of staff, servants); (*c*) *Ind:* replacement (of equipment); **r. échelonné du matériel,** phasing out of equipment; **programme de r. du matériel,** equipment replacement schedule. **2.** renewing, renewal (of treaty, lease, etc.); increase (of zeal, attention, etc.); **à moins de r.,** unless renewed; *Ins:* **prime de r.,** renewal premium. **3.** *Theol:* **r. de l'âme,** renovation of the soul.

rénovateur, -trice [renɔvatœːr, -tris]. **1.** *a.* renovating. **2.** *s.* renovator, restorer. **3.** *s.m. Dom.Ec:* (paint, surface, etc.) restorer.

rénovation [renɔvasjɔ̃], *s.f.* **1.** renovation, restoring, restoration (of morals); (religious) revival. **2.** renewing, renewal (of a vow, *Jur:* of a title). **3.** *Alch:* perfecting.

rénover [renɔve], *v.tr.* (*a*) to renovate, restore (morals, etc.); *Jur:* to renew (a title); (*b*) to revive; **r. un genre littéraire,** to revive a literary genre.

renquiller [rɑ̃kije], *v.tr. F:* **1.** to pocket, to put away; **renquille ton argent, c'est moi qui paie,** put away your money, it's on me. **2. r. son compliment,** to say no more, to shut up.

renrailleur [rɑ̃rɑjœːr], *s.m. Rail:* (*machine*) re-railer.

renrouler [rɑ̃rule], *v.tr.* to rewind (electric coil).

renseigné [rɑ̃sɛɲe], *a.* well-informed (person); **être (bien) r. sur qch.,** to be well informed on sth., well posted (up) in sth.; **peu r. des questions de l'art,** ill informed about artistic questions.

renseignement [rɑ̃sɛɲmɑ̃], *s.m.* (*a*) (piece of) information, (piece of) intelligence; indication; *Tp: etc:* **renseignements,** inquiries; **donner des renseignements sur qch.,** to give information, particulars, on, about, sth.; **prendre des renseignements sur qch.,** to make inquiries about sth.; to inquire about sth.; **renseignements pris . . .,** upon inquiry . . .; **aller aux renseignements,** to make inquiries; **demande de renseignements,** inquiry; **bons renseignements sur qn,** favourable report on s.o.; **il m'a demandé des renseignements sur elle,** he asked me for particulars about her; **prendre un domestique sans renseignements,** to engage a servant without references; **bureau de renseignements,** information bureau, inquiry office; *F:* **c'est un vrai bureau de renseignements,** he is a regular mine of information, a walking encyclopedia; **pour plus amples renseignements s'adresser à . . .,** for further information, for further particulars, apply to . . .; **à titre de r.,** by way of information; for information only; **pour tous renseignements complémentaires adressez-vous à votre fournisseur habituel,** for further particulars apply to your usual supplier; (*b*) **renseignements (techniques),** data; **renseignements statistiques,** statistical data; *Mapm:* **renseignements marginaux,** marginal data; (*c*) *Mil: etc:* **r. (brut),** information; **r. (exploitable),** intelligence; **r. faux, digne, de foi,** false, reliable, information; **service de r.,** intelligence branch, service, department; **organes de renseignements et de sécurité,** security; **réseau de r.,** intelligence net; **source de r.,** source of information; **agent de, du, r.,** (intelligence) agent; **officier de r.,** intelligence officer; **plan de r.,** intelligence plan; **tenir une carte de r.,** to keep an intelligence map; **bulletin de r.,** intelligence bulletin; **compte rendu de r.,** intelligence report; **résumé de r.,** intelligence summary; **synthèse de r.,** intelligence estimate; **recherche, recueil, des renseignements,** collecting of information; **organes de recherche de renseignements,** information-collecting agencies; **évaluation, critique, du r.,** evaluation of information; **recoupement du r.,** checking of information; **interprétation du r.,** interpretation of information; **exploitation du r.,** processing of information; **diffusion des renseignements,** dissemination of information; **recueillir, évaluer, recouper, interpréter, un r.,** to collect, evaluate, check, interpret, an (item of) information; **exploiter et diffuser un r.,** to process and disseminate an (item of) information.

renseigner [rɑ̃sɛɲe], *v.tr.* **1. r. qch. à qn,** to teach s.o. sth. again. **2. r. qn sur qch.,** to inform s.o., give s.o. information about sth., to put s.o. right about sth.; **on me renseigna bien,** the information I received was correct; **on vous a mal renseigné,** (i) you have been misinformed; (ii) you were given wrong directions; **par qui vous êtes-vous fait r.?** whom did you ask about it? who did you get the information from? **je vais vous r. sur lui,** I'll tell you sth. about him; **document qui renseigne utilement,** document containing useful information.

se renseigner sur qch., to get information, make inquiries, find out, about sth.; to inquire, ask, about sth.; **renseignez-vous avant d'entreprendre quoi que ce soit,** you should get information, make inquiries, before undertaking anything.

rensselaerite [rɛnselerit], *s.f. Miner:* rensselaerite.

rentabilisation [rɑ̃tabilizasjɔ̃], *s.f. Com:* making (sth.) pay, show a profit.

rentabiliser [rɑ̃tabilize], *v.tr.* **l'industrie exige de gros investissements longs à rentabiliser,** the industry demands heavy investments which take a long time to produce a profit.

rentabilité [rɑ̃tabilite], *s.f.* profitability, profit-earning capacity; economy of operation (of equipment); *Pol.Ec:* **taux de r.,** rate of profitability; **limite de r.,** limit of profitability.

rentable [rɑ̃tabl̩], *a.* profitable; profit-earning; paying (proposition); **ce n'est pas r.,** it isn't profitable, it doesn't pay; **loyer r., peu r.,** economic, uneconomic, rent; **la publicité est r.,** it pays to advertise.

rentamer [rɑ̃tame], *v.tr.* to start (conversation, etc.) again.

rentasser [rɑ̃tɑse], *v.tr.* to heap, pile, (sth.) up again.

rente [rɑ̃ːt], *s.f.* **1.** *A. & Pol.Ec:* revenue, rent; **r. foncière,** ground rent. **2.** *usu. pl.* (unearned) income; **avoir cent mille francs de rente(s),** to have a private income of a hundred thousand francs; to have a hundred thousand francs a year; **vivre de ses rentes,** to live on one's (private) income. **3.** annuity, pension, allowance; **r. viagère,** life annuity, life interest; **r. perpétuelle,** perpetual annuity; perpetuity; **r. sur l'État,** government annuity; **faire une r. de mille francs à qn,** to allow s.o. a thousand francs a year; **on lui a fait une r.,** he has been pensioned off; **r. à terme,** terminable annuity; **r. à paiement différé,** reversionary annuity. **4. rente(s) (sur l'État),** (government) stock(s), funds, bonds; **rentes, actions et obligations,** stocks and shares; **biens en rentes,** funded property.

renté [rɑ̃te], *a. O:* (*a*) endowed (hospital, etc.); (*b*) (person) of independent means; **être bien r.,** to be well off, well-to-do; to have a large income.

renter [rɑ̃te], *v.tr. O:* (*a*) to endow (hospital, school, etc.); (*b*) to assign a yearly income to (s.o.).

renterrement [rɑ̃tɛrmɑ̃], *s.m.* reinterment.

renterrer [rɑ̃tere], *v.tr.* to reinter; to bury (s.o., sth.) again.

rentier, -ière [rɑ̃tje, -jɛːr], *s.* (*a*) *Fin:* stockholder; shareholder; *esp.* holder of government stocks; (*b*) **r. viager,** annuitant; (*c*) person of independent means, who lives on his (unearned) income; *Pol.Ec:* rentier; **petit r.,** small investor.

rentoilage [rɑ̃twalaːʒ], *s.m.* (*a*) remounting (of map, etc.); (*b*) backing (of a painting with new canvas).

rentoiler [rɑ̃twale], *v.tr.* (*a*) to remount (map, etc.); (*b*) to put a new canvas to (a painting); to back (a painting).

rentrage [rɑ̃traːʒ], *s.m.* (*a*) taking in, housing, cellaring (of firewood, etc.); (*b*) *Nau:* unshipment, unshipping (of oars); (*c*) *Tex:* looming, drawing in.

rentraire [rɑ̃trɛːr], *v.tr.* (*p.p.* **rentrait;** *no other parts*) *A:* to mend (invisibly); to make good (defects in cloth, etc.).

rentraiture [rɑ̃trɛtyːr], *s.f. A:* invisible mending (of garment, tapestry, etc.).

rentrant, -ante [rɑ̃trɑ̃, -ɑ̃ːt]. **1.** *a.* (*a*) re-entering; re-entrant (angle, curve); *Mth:* **angle r.,** reflex angle; (*b*) *Phot:* **monture rentrante,** sunk mount; *Mec.E:* **coussinet r.,** inset bearing; (*c*) *Av:* **train d'atterrissage r.,** retractable undercarriage; (*d*) *Elcs:* (*computers*) **programme r.,** re-entrant programme. **2.** *s. Games:* new player; *Cards:* cutter in. **3.** *s.m. Const:* recess (in wall, etc.).

rentrayage [rɑ̃trɛjaːʒ], *s.m. A:* invisible mending (of tapestry, etc.); making good the defects (in leather surface, etc.).

rentrayer [rɑ̃treje], *v.tr. A:* = RENTRAIRE.

rentrayeur, -euse [rɑ̃trɛjœːr, -øːz], *s. A:* invisible mender (of tapestry, etc.); adjuster of defects (in cloth, etc.).

rentré [rɑ̃tre]. **1.** *a.* (*a*) hollow, sunken (eyes, cheeks, etc.); (*b*) repressed (feelings, etc.); suppressed (laughter, etc.); **rage rentrée,** suppressed rage; **je suis un comédien r.,** I ought to have been an actor. **2.** *s.m.* (*a*) *Needlew:* hem, turn in; (*b*) *Typ:* indent.

rentrée [rɑ̃tre], *s.f.* **1.** (*a*) return, return home, homecoming; **à sa r. en France,** on his return to France; *Nau:* **r. au port,** putting back, return, to port; (*of spacecraft*) **r. atmosphérique,** re-entry into the atmosphere; **effectuer la r., les opérations de r.,** to perform the re-entry; **course de r.,** re-entry run; **manœuvre de r.,** re-entry steering; **trajectoire, vitesse, de r.,** re-entry trajectory, speed; *Mus:* **r. du motif principal,** re-entry of the original theme; **r. d'un instrument,** re-entry of an instrument; (*of instrument*) **faire une r.,** to re-enter; (*b*) re-opening (of schools, law courts, theatres, etc.); re-assembly (of Parliament); return to the stage, reappearance (of actor after absence); *Sch:* **la r. des classes,** the beginning of term; **à la r. de septembre,** at the beginning of the autumn term; *Publ:* **la r. littéraire,** this autumn's new books. **2.** (*a*) taking in, receipt, encashment (of money); getting in, collection (of taxes); **opérer une r.,** to collect a sum of money; **faire des rentrées d'argent,** to get some money in; **j'attends des rentrées,** I am expecting to receive payments; **impôts d'une r. difficile,** taxes difficult to get in; (*b*) *pl. Bank:* bills and cheques paid in; (*c*) collecting, getting in (of crops). **3.** coming in; (*a*) *Aer:* **r. d'air,** penetration of air (into balloon); *Av:* **r. du train (d'atterrissage) et des volets,** raising of the (landing) gear and flaps; *Mch:* **r. d'eau,** priming; (*b*) *Typ:* indention, indentation (of line); (*c*) *N.Arch:* tumble home, tumbling home (of upper works); (*d*) *Tex:* shrinkage, shrinking. **4.** *Fb:* **r. en touche,** throw-in.

rentrer [rɑ̃tre]. **I.** *v.i.* (*the aux. is* être) **1.** (*a*) to re-enter; to come; go, in again; to return (to); (*of spacecraft*) to re-enter (the atmosphere); **il ne rentra jamais dans cette maison,** he never re-entered that house; **r. dans sa chambre,** to return to, go back into, one's room; **lorsqu'il rentra en France, à Paris,** when he returned to France, to Paris; *Nau:* **r. au port,** to return, put back, to port; **r. dans l'armée,** to go back into the army; to rejoin the army; **r. en faveur,** to return to favour; **r. dans les bonnes grâces de qn,** to regain favour with s.o.; **r. dans ses droits,** to recover one's rights; **r. dans ses avances,** to recover money advanced; **r. dans ses frais,** to be reimbursed (for one's expenses); to recover one's outlay; **r. dans une catégorie,** to fall into a category; **r. dans son sujet,** to return to one's subject; **r. en correspondance avec qn,** to resume correspondence with s.o.; **faire r. qn dans l'ordre,** to reduce s.o. to order again; **r. en fureur,** to fly into a rage again; **r. dans son bon sens,** to recover one's senses; **r. dans le bon chemin,** to mend one's ways, to turn over a new leaf; *Th:* (*of actor*) **r. en scène,** to come on again; **Macbeth rentre,** re-enter Macbeth; **r. en danse, en lice,** to return to the fray; (*b*) to return home, come home, come in again; **il est l'heure de r.,** it's time we went home; **je rentre préparer le dîner,** I'm going home to get (the) dinner ready; **r. dîner,** to go home to dinner, for dinner; **faire r. les enfants,** to call the children in; **elle rentre de l'église, de Paris,** she is just home from church, from Paris; **r. de chasse,** to come back from a day's shooting; **r. de récréation,** to come in from play; **r. de son travail, r. de travailler,** to come home from work; *Nau:* **r. à bord,** to come back on board; (*c*) (*of school, law courts, etc.*) to re-open, to resume; (*of Parliament*) to re-assemble; (*of schoolboy*) to return to school; (*of actor after period of absence*) to return to the stage, to make a re-appearance; (*of official, etc.*) **r. en fonction(s),** to resume duty, to resume his duties; (*d*) (*of thgs*) to go back, go in; **faire r. qch. dans sa boîte,** to put sth. back into its box; *Nau:* (*of gun*) **r. en batterie,** to return to firing position, to run up; (*e*) (*of money, etc.*) to come in; **faire r. ses fonds,** to call in one's money; **cet argent vous rentrera bientôt,** this money will soon be repaid to you; (*f*) *Med:* (*of gout*) to retrocede, strike in. **2.** (*intensive form of* **entrer**) (*a*) to enter, go in; *Cards:* to cut in; **r. en soi-même,** to retire into oneself, to examine one's conscience; **r. dans le néant,** to be defeated; to lapse into obscurity; **r. dans sa coquille,** to retire into one's shell; *F:* **les jambes me rentrent dans le corps,** I'm tired out, I can't stand on my feet any longer; *F:* **faire r. qn dans la poussière, en terre, cent pieds sous terre,** (i) to reproach s.o. severely; to tell s.o. where he gets off; to tear a strip off s.o.; (ii) to humiliate s.o., to take s.o. down a peg or two; *P:* **r. dans qn, r. dans le mou à qn,** to pitch into s.o.; **ils se sont rentrés en plein dedans,** they ran slap (bang) into each other; (*b*) **tubes qui rentrent les uns dans les autres,** tubes that fit into one another; (*c*) **cela ne rentre pas dans mes fonctions,** that doesn't come within my province, that's not (part of) my job; **le différend rentre dans les dispositions de l'article . . .,** the dispute comes within the provisions of article . . .; (*d*) (*of* *material*) (*the aux. is* **avoir**) to shrink; (*e*) *Mil: etc:* (*of soldier in line*) to dress back; (*f*) *Typ:* **faire r. une ligne,** to indent a line.

II. **rentrer,** *v.tr.* (*the aux. is* **avoir**) **1.** to take in, bring in, get in, draw in, pull in (sth.); *Tex:* to draw in (warp); to put away (instrument); to heave in, haul in (rope); to haul down, strike (the colours); *Artil:* to run in (gun); *Nau:* to lay in, ship, unship (the oars); **rentrez!** unship oars! **r. l'ancre,** to take the anchor aboard; **r. une embarcation,** to get in, haul up, a boat; **r. les amarres,** to heave in the lines; **r. le loch,** to haul in the log; *Av:* **r. le train (d'atterrissage),** to retract, raise, the (landing) gear; **r. le train et les volets,** to raise the gear and flaps; **r. la récolte,** to get, gather, in the harvest; **qui va rentrer les chaises?** who's going to carry in the chairs, to take the chairs in? **r. sa chemise,** to tuck in one's shirt; **le chat rentra ses griffes,** the cat drew in its claws; **r. un désir,** to repress a desire; **r. le corps,** to draw back the body; *Mil: etc:* to dress back; **r. le ventre,** to pull in one's stomach; (*of snail*) **r. les cornes,** to draw in its horns; **r. une robe à la taille,** to take in a dress at the waist. **2.** to take (s.o., sth.) home; **c'est l'heure où les mamans rentrent les enfants,** it is the time when the mothers take their children home; **comment puis-je r. ce paquet chez moi?** how am I to get this parcel home? **3.** *Book-k:* **r. un article sur un compte,** to re-enter an item in an account.

rentr'ouvrir [rɑ̃truvriːr], *v.tr.* (*conj. like* OUVRIR) to half-open (door, eyes) again.

renumérotage [rənymerɔtaːʒ], *s.m.* renumbering.

renuméroter [rənymerɔte], *v.tr.* to renumber.

renvahissement [rɑ̃vaismɑ̃], *s.m.* fresh, new, invasion, reinvasion.

renvelopper [rɑ̃vlɔpe], *v.tr.* to wrap (sth.) up again.

renvenimer [rɑ̃vnime], *v.tr.* to inflame (quarrel, wound) anew.

renvers [rɑ̃vɛːr], *s.m. Const:* ridge covering, capping (of slate roof).

renversable [rɑ̃vɛrsabl̩], *a.* **1.** reversible. **2.** that can be upset, overthrown; capsizable (boat, etc.).

renversant [rɑ̃vɛrsɑ̃], *a. F:* astounding, staggering (news, etc.).

renverse [rɑ̃vɛrs], *s.f.* **1.** *Nau:* shift, turn (of tide, current); change round (of the wind). **2.** *adv. phr.* **tomber à la r.,** (i) to fall backwards, on one's back, head over heels; (ii) to be staggered, bowled over (by piece of news, etc.).

renversé [rɑ̃vɛrse], *a.* **1.** inverted, reversed (image, etc.); *Her:* reversed, renversé; *Mus:* inverted (interval, chord); *Navy:* **ordre r.,** inverse order (of the line); **écriture renversée,** backhanded writing, backhand; *Arch:* **arc r.,** inverted arch; *Cu:* **crème renversée,** custard mould, custard shape; (*of horse*) **encolure renversée,** ewe neck; **cheval à encolure renversée,** ewe-necked horse; *Mch:* **bielle renversée,** back-acting connecting rod; *Nau:* **compas r.,** hanging compass; *F:* **c'est le monde r.!** it's preposterous! what's the world coming to! *Golf:* **crosse à face renversée,** lofted club. **2.** (*a*) overturned, upset; overthrown, thrown down (wall, etc.); (*b*) *F:* **il avait le visage r.,** he looked terribly upset; **j'en suis r.,** I'm amazed, staggered.

renversement [rɑ̃vɛrsəmɑ̃], *s.m.* **1.** (*a*) reversal; inversion (*Opt:* of image; *Log:* of proposition, etc.); *Mus:* inversion (of interval, chord); **r. des valeurs,** inversion of values; **r. de situation,** reversal of a situation; *Ph:* **r. de polarité,** reversal of polarity; (*b*) *Mch:* **r. de la vapeur,** reversing (of engine); **mécanisme de r.,** reversing gear; *Typewr:* **r. automatique du ruban,** automatic ribbon reverse; (*c*) turn(ing) (of the tide); shift(ing), backing (of the wind); changing (of the monsoon). **2.** (*a*) turning (of sth.) upside down; overturning, upsetting; throwing down (of wall); *Metall:* rolling over; **charrette à r.,** tip-up cart; *Mec:* **couple de r.,** torque reaction; torque; (*b*) *A:* confusion, disorder; **r. d'esprit,** madness; (*c*) overthrow, ruin (of a state, of one's fortunes, etc.).

renverser [rɑ̃vɛrse]. **1.** *v.tr.* (*a*) to reverse, invert (*Opt:* image; *Log:* proposition); *Mus:* to invert (interval, chord); *Mil:* **r. les fusils,** to reverse arms; **marcher armes renversées,** to march with reversed arms; *Navy:* **r. la ligne,** to turn the line; **r. un levier,** to throw over a lever; **r. la marche,** *Mch:* to reverse (the engine); *Aut:* to go into reverse; **r. la vapeur,** (i) to reverse steam; (ii) to go back on one's decision; *El:* **r. le courant,** to reverse the current; (*in restaurant*) **r. une chaise pour un habitué,** to turn down a chair for a regular customer; **r. les rôles,** to turn the tables on s.o.; (*b*) to turn (glass, etc.) upside down; *Com:* **ne pas r.,** this side up; **tout r.,** to turn everything upside down, topsy-turvy; **r. l'esprit à qn,** to send s.o. out of his wits; (*c*) to knock, throw, (s.o., sth.) over, down; to throw down (wall); to overturn, upset (pail, etc.); to capsize (boat); to spill (liquid); **r. qn d'un coup de poing,** to strike s.o. down; **le vent a renversé un arbre,** the wind has blown down a tree; **r. les quilles (avec la boule),** to knock down, bowl over, the skittles; **il fut renversé par une auto,** he was knocked down by a car; *F:* **une odeur à vous r.,** a smell fit to knock you down; *Mil: A:* **r. un corps de troupes,** to defeat a body of troops; (*d*) to overthrow (a state, a system, a theory, etc.); (*e*) *F:* to astound, astonish, amaze; **son impudence me renversa,** his impudence staggered me, bowled me over. **2.** *v.i.* (*of vehicle, etc.*) to overturn, upset; (*of boat*) to capsize; (*of liquid*) to spill.

se renverser. 1. to fall over, fall down; to upset, overturn; to capsize; (*of projectile*) to tumble; **se r. sur sa chaise,** (i) to lean back, lie back, loll back, in one's chair; (ii) to tilt one's chair back; **le chien se renversa sur le dos,** the dog turned over on to its back. **2.** *Mil: A:* to fall back in disorder.

renvi [rɑ̃vi], *s.m. Cards: etc:* increased stake.

renvidage [rɑ̃vidaːʒ], *s.m. Tex:* winding on (of cops).

renvider [rɑ̃vide], *v.tr. Tex:* to wind on (cops).

renvideur, -euse [rɑ̃vidœːr, -øːz], *Tex:* **1.** *s.* (*pers.*) winder. **2.** mule (jenny); **r. automatique,** self-acting mule.

renvier [rɑ̃vje], *v.i. Cards: etc:* to increase the stake.

renvoi [rɑ̃vwa], *s.m.* **1.** sending back, return(ing) (of goods, etc.); throwing back (of ball, of sound); reverberation (of sound); reflecting (of light); (*computers*) feedback; *Rugby Fb:* drop-out (from the 25); *Ten:* return. **2.** dismissal (of servant, etc.); discharge (of troops); expulsion (of pupil). **3.** putting off, postponement; adjournment; *Parl:* **r. à la suite,** adjournment (of debate). **4.** (*a*) referring, reference (of a matter to some authority); **r. devant un Conseil de guerre,** reference (of a case) to a Court Martial; *Pol:* **r. d'un projet à une commission,** sending of a bill to a committee; committing of a bill; (*b*) *Jur:* transfer (of case to another court). **5.** (*a*) *Typ:* reference (mark); cross reference; (*b*) caret, insertion mark; **r. en marge,** marginal alteration; **parafer un r.,** to initial an alteration; (*c*) *Mus:* repeat (mark). **6.** *Mec.E:* (*a*) **r. de mouvement,** counter gear(ing), counter motion, reverse motion; **r. d'angle,** bevel gear; **r. de commande,** shafting; **r. de sonnette, r. par levier coudé,** bell-crank lever; **levier de r.,** (i) reversing lever; (ii) bell-crank lever; **mécanisme, tringlerie, de r.,** bell-crank linkage; **r. de raccordement,** connecting gear; *Mch:* **r. du tiroir,** (slide-) valve gear; **arbre de r.,** countershaft, intermediate shaft, outrigger shaft, idler shaft; **engrenage de r.,** reversing gear; **galet de r.,** sheave pulley; **poulie de r.,** guide pulley, idler pulley, intermediate pulley; (*b*) **r. d'huile,** oil deflector, oil thrower. **7.** *El.E:* transfer; **circuit, jack, de r.,** transfer line, jack. **8.** *N.Arch:* flare (of ship's sides at bow). **9.** *Nau:* (*a*) backwater (of sea); (*b*) **r. de vent,** eddy wind; **r. de courant,** cross current. **10.** *Med:* eructation, belch; *F:* (*of food*) **donner des renvois,** to repeat.

renvoler (se) [sərɑ̃vɔle], *v.pr.* to fly away again.

renvoyer [rɑ̃vwaje], *v.tr.* (*conj. like* ENVOYER) **1.** (*a*) to send (s.o., sth.) back; to return (sth.); to throw back, re-echo, reverberate (sound); to reflect (heat, light); *Cards:* to play (the same suit) again; to return (suit); **r. un homme à son poste,** to order a man back to his post; **se r. des reproches,** to bandy reproaches; **être renvoyé de Caïphe à Pilate,** to be driven from pillar to post; **je l'ai renvoyé (pour) acheter un journal,** I sent him back to buy a paper; (*b*) *Mec.E:* **r. le mouvement,** to counter the motion; **les câbles sont renvoyés sur leurs parcours par des poulies,** the cables return over pulleys. **2.** (*a*) to send, turn, (s.o.) away; *Jur:* to discharge (defendant); **r. des troupes, des réservistes, dans leurs foyers,** to dismiss troops, reservists (after service or training); **r. qn tout penaud,** to send s.o. away thoroughly crestfallen; *F:* **r. qn bien loin,** to send s.o. packing; to send s.o. about his business; *Jur:* **r. le plaideur de sa demande,** to nonsuit the plaintiff; (*b*) to dismiss, *F:* sack (employee); to send (s.o.) down (from university); **r. un élève de l'école,** (i) to send a boy home from school; (ii) to expel a boy from school; *Mil: Navy:* **être renvoyé du service,** to be dismissed (from) the service. **3.** to put off, postpone, defer, adjourn (a matter, debate, etc.); *Jur:* **r. le prévenu à une autre audience,** to remand the prisoner. **4.** to refer; **je l'ai renvoyé au préfet,** I referred him to the prefect; **r. une question à une juridiction,** to refer, entrust, a question to a court; *Pol:* **r. un projet à une commission,** to send a bill to a committee; to commit a bill; *abs:* **les numéros renvoient aux notes,** the numbers refer to the notes. **5.** *abs.* (*of ship*) (i) to heel; (ii) to pitch.

réoccupation [reɔkypasjɔ̃], *s.f.* reoccupation, reoccupying (of territory, etc.).

réoccuper [reɔkype], *v.tr.* to re-occupy; *Adm:* **r. une fonction,** to resume an office.

réolais, -aise [reɔlɛ, -ɛːz], *a. & s. Geog:* (native, inhabitant) of La Réole.

réopérer [reɔpere], *v.tr. Surg:* to reoperate.

réorchestration [reɔrkɛstrasjɔ̃], *s.f. Mus:* reorchestration.

réorchestrer [reɔrkɛstre], *v.tr. Mus:* to rescore (opera, etc.); to reorchestrate.

réordination [reɔrdinasjɔ̃], *s.f. Ecc:* reordination.

réordonner [reɔrdɔne], *v.tr.* **1.** *Ecc:* to reordain (priest). **2. r. à qn de faire qch.,** to order s.o. again to do sth. **3.** to resequence.

réorganisateur, -trice [reɔrganizatœːr, -tris]. **1.** *a.* reorganizing. **2.** *s.* reorganizer.

réorganisation [reɔrganizasjɔ̃], *s.f.* reorganization; reorganizing; re-arrangement; *Agr:* **r. foncière,** consolidation (of land holdings).

réorganiser [reɔrganize], *v.tr.* to reorganize.

réorientation [reɔrjɑ̃tasjɔ̃], *s.f.* reorientation.

réorienter [reɔrjɑ̃te], *v.tr.* to reorient, reorientate.

réouverture [reuvɛrtyːr], *s.f.* reopening (of theatre, etc.); resumption.

rep [rɛp], *s.m. Atom.Ph:* rep.

repaire [rəpɛːr], *s.m.* den (of lions, thieves); lair (of wild beasts, of robbers); nest (of pirates); haunt (of criminals).

repairer [rəpɛre], *v.tr. Ven:* (*of game*) to be in its den, lair; to have gone to earth; to be in cover(t).

repaître [rəpɛtr̩], *v.* (*pr.p.* **repaissant;** *p.p.* **repu;** *pr.ind.* **je repais, il repait, n. repaissons;** *pr.sub.* **je repaisse;** *p.d.* **je repaissais;** *p.h.* **je repus;** *fu.* **je repaîtrai**) **1.** *v.tr.* (*a*) to feed (animals); (*b*) *Lit:* **r. qn d'espérances,** to feed s.o. on hopes; **r. ses yeux de (la vue de) qch.,** to feast one's eyes on (the sight of) sth. **2.** *v.i. A:* (*of animal or pers.*) to feed.

se repaître, (*a*) (*of animal*) to eat it's fill; (*b*) *Lit:* **se r. de qch.,** to feed on, eat one's fill of, sth.; to batten, raven, on sth.; **se r. de sang,** to wallow in blood; **se r. de chimères,** to indulge in vain imaginings, to feed one's mind on fancies.

répandage [repɑ̃daːʒ], *s.m.* spreading (of tar on road, etc.).

répandeur [repɑ̃dœːr], *s.m. Civ.E:* (concrete, macadam) spreader.

répandeuse [repɑ̃døːz], *s.f. Civ.E:* (tank) sprayer (for tar).

répandre [repɑ̃ːdr̩], *v.tr.* **1.** to pour out; to spill, drop, shed; **r. du sel, du vin,** to spill salt, wine; **r. des larmes, son sang,** to shed tears, one's blood; **r. son cœur,** to open one's heart. **2.** to spread, diffuse, scatter (light, etc.); to give off, give out (heat, scent, etc.); **le fleuve répandit ses eaux dans la campagne,** the river spread its waters over the countryside, flooded the countryside; **on répandait des fleurs sur son passage,** they strewed flowers in his path; they strewed his path with flowers; **on répandit du sable sur le plancher, sur le sang,** they sprinkled the floor with sand; they sprinkled sand over the blood; **le soleil répand la lumière,** the sun sheds light; **les fleurs répandaient un doux parfum,** the flowers gave out a delicate scent; **r. une forte odeur,** to give off a strong smell; **r. la terreur,** to spread terror; **cette nouvelle répandit la tristesse dans la ville,** this news cast a gloom over the town; **r. une nouvelle,** to spread, circulate, broadcast, a piece of news; **r. une découverte,** to circulate a discovery. **3.** to scatter, distribute, lavish (money, alms, etc.).

se répandre. 1. (*of pers.*) (*a*) **se r. dans le monde,** to go a great deal into society; **il se répand beaucoup,** he goes out a great deal; he leads a very social life; **il faut vous r.,** you should go about more; (*b*) **se r. en un long discours, en invectives contre qn,** to launch into a long speech, into abuse of s.o.; **se r. en éloges sur qn,** to be full of praise of s.o.; **se r. en explications,** to break forth, burst forth, launch forth, into explanations; **se r. en excuses,** to apologize profusely; **se r. en jurons,** to let fly a volley of oaths; **se r. en menaces,** to burst out into threats; to pour out a stream of threats; **se r. sur un sujet,**

to spread oneself on a subject. 2. (*a*) (*of liquid*) to spill; to run out; to run over; **le vin se répandit sur la table,** the wine ran (all) over the table; *F:* se **r. sur le tapis,** to fall flat on the carpet; (*b*) to spread; **l'odeur s'en répand partout,** the smell of it spreads everywhere; **la terreur se répandit parmi les peuples,** terror spread among the nations; **les envahisseurs s'étaient répandus sur le pays,** the invaders had overrun the country; **les touristes se répandent dans le ville,** tourists are invading, overruning, the town; **sa chevelure se répandit, était répandue, sur ses épaules,** her hair fell loose, came down, over her shoulders; **une pâleur mortelle se répandit sur son visage,** her face went as pale as death, deathly pale; **une rougeur subite se répandit sur son visage,** a sudden flush spread over her face; **cette opinion se répand,** this opinion is gaining ground, is spreading; **un bruit s'est répandu,** a rumour has spread (abroad); **la nouvelle s'est répandue par degrés, peu à peu,** the news trickled out; *impers.* **il s'est répandu que . . .,** there is a rumour spread around that . . .; **l'usage de cet article s'est répandu,** this article is now widely used.

répandu [repɑ̃dy], *a.* **1.** (*of thg*) widespread, widely distributed, prevalent, in general use; **journal r.,** widely-read paper; **opinion répandue,** widely-held opinion. **2.** (*of pers.*) widely known, much in evidence; **il est très r. dans les milieux politiques,** he is well known in political circles; **il est très r. dans le monde,** he goes about a great deal, he leads a very social life.

repapilloter [rəpapijɔte], *v.tr.* **1.** to put (one's hair) in curlers again. **2.** *F:* to reconcile (people); to make it up between (people).

se repapilloter, *F:* **1. se r. avec qn,** to make it up with s.o. **2. les affaires se repapillotent,** business is looking up, is improving.

réparable [reparabl̩], *a.* (*a*) reparable; repairable, mendable; (*b*) **erreur r.,** mistake that can be rectified, put right.

réparage [repaRaːʒ], *s.m.* repairing, repair (of work of art).

reparaître [rəparɛtr̩], *v.i.* (*conj. like* PARAÎTRE; *the aux. is usu.* **avoir**) **1.** to reappear; to make one's appearance again; **il reparaîtra un de ces jours,** he will turn up one of these days. **2.** (*of disease, etc.*) to recur.

réparateur, -trice [reparatœːr, -tris]. **1.** *a.* repairing, restoring; **sommeil r.,** refreshing sleep; **accomplir un geste r.,** (i) to make amends; (ii) to make a peace offering. **2.** *s.* repairer, mender; **r. de bicyclettes,** bicycle repairer.

réparation [reparasjɔ̃], *s.f.* **1.** repair; repairing (of equipment, house, machine, etc.); mending (of clothes, shoes, etc.); **r. courante,** maintenance, running, repair, *Nau:* voyage repair; **r. d'entretien,** maintenance; **r. provisoire,** temporary repair; **r. de fortune,** temporary, makeshift, repairs; emergency repairs; *Aut:* roadside repairs; **grosse r., r. importante,** major repair; *Nau: etc:* **grosses réparations,** capital repairs; **petite, légère, menue, r.,** minor, slight, repair; *Av:* line repair; *Nau:* **r. d'avarie,** damage repair; (**être**) **en r.,** (to be) under repair; **faire, effectuer, des réparations,** to make repairs; **entretenir un immeuble en r.,** to keep a building in repair; **des réparations s'imposent (pour l'immeuble),** the house is in urgent need of repair; **atelier de r.,** repair(ing) shop; *Mil:* **base, dépôt, de r.,** repair base, depot; **équipe de r.,** repair team; **nécessaire, outillage, de r.,** repair(ing) outfit; **trousse de r.,** repair(ing) kit; **durée de r.,** repair time, down time. **2.** atonement, reparation, amends, redress; **en r. d'un tort,** in reparation of, in atonement for, as amends for, a wrong; **r. par les armes,** duel; **réparations de guerre,** war reparations; *Hist:* **la Commission des Réparations,** the Reparations Commission; *Jur:* **r. légale,** legal redress; **r. civile,** compensation; **r. des maladies professionnelles,** compensation for industrial diseases; *Fb:* **coup de pied de r.,** penalty kick; **surface, point, de r.,** penalty area, spot.

réparatoire [reparatwaːr], *a.* reparative.

reparcourir [rəparkuriːr], *v.tr.* (*conj. like* PARCOURIR) to go over (piece of ground) again; to glance through (book) again.

réparer [repare], *v.tr.* **1.** to repair, mend (shoe, bridge, machine, etc.); to overhaul (machine); to refit (ship); **r. ses forces,** to restore one's strength; **r. le désordre,** to put things in order; to make order out of chaos; **r. ses pertes,** to retrieve, make good, one's losses; **r. l'usure,** to make good the wear and tear; **la maison a besoin d'être réparée,** the house is in need of repair; *Cin:* **r. un film cassé,** to splice a broken film. **2.** to make atonement, make amends, for (misdeed); to rectify (mistake), to put (mistake) right; *abs.* to make an honest woman of s.o.; **r. une omission, un oubli, une injustice,** to rectify, to make good, an omission, an oversight, an injustice; **r. un tort, un dommage,** to redress a wrong, an injury; **r. les dégâts,** to make good the damage; **r. le temps perdu,** to make up for lost time; **r. le mal,** to undo the mischief; *Prov:* **faute avouée est à demi réparée,** a fault confessed is half redressed.

répareur, -euse [reparœːr, -øːz], *s.* repairer.

reparler [rəparle]. **1.** *v.i.* (*a*) **r. de qch.,** to speak about sth. again; **il ne faut plus en r.,** it must not be referred to, mentioned, again; (*b*) **r. à qn,** to speak to s.o. again; **ils se reparlent,** they are on speaking terms again. **2.** *v.tr.* to speak (a language) again.

repartager [rəpartaʒe], *v.tr.* (*conj. like* PARTAGER) to share (sth.) out, to divide (sth.), again.

repartie [rəparti], *s.f.* repartee; retort, rejoinder (**à**, to); pat answer; **avoir l'esprit de r., avoir la r. prompte, des reparties spirituelles,** to be quick at repartee; **c'est lui, sans r., qui a raison,** he's undoubtedly right, there's no doubt (about the fact) that he's right.

repartir [rəpartiːr], *v.i.* (*conj. like* PARTIR) **1.** (*aux.* **être**) (*a*) to set out again, start off again; **je repars pour Paris,** I'm off to Paris again; **il est reparti à Paris pour deux mois,** he has gone back to Paris for two months; **il est reparti hier,** he left (again) yesterday; **il est reparti les mains pleines,** he came, went, away with his hands full; **r. à zéro,** to start from scratch again; to go back to the beginning again; **r. à rire,** to burst out laughing again; **nous repartirons à 8 heures demain matin,** we shall set out again at 8 o'clock tomorrow morning; (*b*) (*computers*) to restart. **2.** (*aux.* **avoir**) to retort, reply.

répartir [repartiːr], *v.tr.* (**je répartis, n. répartissons**) **1.** to distribute, divide, share out (**entre,** among); **r. un dividende,** to distribute a dividend; **versements répartis sur plusieurs années,** payments, spread over several years; **touristes répartis en cinq groupes,** tourists divided into five parties, groups; **charge uniformément, mal, répartie,** evenly, unevenly, distributed load; *El.E:* **inductance répartie,** distributed inductance; *Dressm:* **r. le surplus du col,** to ease the collar. **2.** to apportion, assess; **r. des impôts,** to assess taxes; **r. des frais par parts égales,** to divide expenses in equal proportions; *Fin:* **r. des actions,** to allot, allocate, shares; *M.Ins:* **r. une avarie,** to adjust an average.

répartissable [repartisabl̩], *a.* that can be distributed, divided, apportioned, assessed; divisable, dividable, distributable, apportionable, allottable, assessable.

répartiteur [repartitœːr], *s.m.* **1.** distributer, divider, apportioner; *Mil:* billet master; *Nau:* adjuster, stater (of average); *Adm:* **(commissaire) r.,** assessor of taxes. **2.** *Elcs: Tp:* dispatcher; distribution frame; **r. d'entrée,** main distribution frame; *El:* **r. de charge,** load dispatcher.

répartitif, -ive [repartitif, -iːv], *a.* dividing, demarcation (line); *Ind: etc:* **conflit au sujet des limites répartitives,** demarcation dispute.

répartition [repartisjɔ̃], *s.f.* **1.** distribution (of persons, animals, things, wealth, etc.); *Ph: Mec:* distribution (of energy, power, light, etc.); *Atom.Ph:* distribution (of velocity), traverse (of flux, neutrons, etc.); **r. de la population de la région parisienne,** distribution of the population in the Paris region; **r. de la population par groupes d'âge,** breakdown of the population by age groups; **r. de la flore d'une région,** distribution of the flora of a region; **r. des eaux et des terres à la surface du globe,** repartition of land and water on the surface of the globe; *Mil:* **r. générale des forces,** general distribution, disposition, of forces; *Mec:* **r. des forces,** stress distribution; *El:* **r. de charge,** load distribution; *Mth:* **r. des erreurs,** frequency of errors. **2. r. (de qch. entre plusieurs personnes),** distribution (of sth. among several persons); (*a*) dividing up, sharing out (of expenses, responsibilities, work, etc.); distribution, appropriation (of profit); distribution, allotment (of functions, tasks); allotment (of land, votes); *War Adm:* (rationing) allocation; *Mil:* distribution (of means available), allotment (of missions), assignment (of targets); **nouvelle r.,** redistribution; *Jur:* **r. entre créanciers,** distribution among creditors; (*b*) (*pro rata distribution*) apportionment, allocation (of expenses, losses, property, resources, rights, liabilities, etc.); assessment (of taxes); *Book-k:* apportionment (of costs, expenses, to different accounts); **r. d'une somme entre les ayants droit,** apportionment of a sum among the persons entitled; **r. proportionnelle des pertes entre les commanditaires,** (pro rata) apportionment of losses among the sleeping partners; *M.Ins:* **r. d'avarie,** adjustment (of average); (*c*) *Fin:* (i) allotment (of shares); **(lettre d')avis de r.,** letter of allotment; **versement de r.,** allotment money; **libération, versement intégral, à la r.,** payment in full on allotment; (ii) dividend, distribution; **première et unique r.,** first and final dividend, distribution; **nouvelle r.,** second dividend, distribution; **dernière r.,** final dividend, distribution; (*d*) *Elcs:* (*computers*) **r. des groupes primaires, secondaires,** group, supergroup, allocation.

réparton [repartɔ̃], *s.m. Min:* slab (of slate).

répartonneur [repartɔnœːr], *s.m. Tchn:* slate splitter.

repas [rəpɑ], *s.m.* meal; (*of animal*) feed, feeding; **r. de noce** = wedding breakfast; *Mil:* **r. de corps,** regimental dinner; **faire un r.,** to have a meal; **pour une fois nous fîmes un vrai r.,** for once we had a proper sit-down meal; *A:* **faire un r. de mouton, de brebis,** to have a meal without drinking; **léger r., petit r.,** light meal; snack; **r. complet, ample r.,** square meal, full meal; **r. froid,** cold meal; (*in restaurant*) **prendre un r. à la carte, à prix fixe,** to take an à-la-carte meal, the menu; **petit r. (à un bar, etc.),** quick lunch; **aux heures de r.,** at meal times; **prendre ses r. chez qn,** to board with s.o.; **prière avant le r.,** grace before meat.

repassage [rəpɑsaːʒ], *s.m.* **1.** (*a*) repassing; recrossing (of river, etc.); (*b*) going over (lessons, etc.). **2.** sharpening, whetting, grinding (of knife, etc.); stropping (of razor). **3.** (*a*) ironing (of clothes); **ne nécessitant, n'exigeant, aucun r.,** non-iron; (*b*) raking (over) (of path). **4.** *P:* murder, bumping off, doing in.

repasser [rəpɑse]. **1.** *v.i.* (*the aux. is usu.* **être**) (*a*) to repass; to pass (by) again, go by again, come by again; **r. chez qn,** to call on s.o. again; **l'employé du gaz a dit qu'il repasserait jeudi,** the gas man said he would call again on Thursday; **r. en Angleterre,** to cross over to England again; **une idée me repasse dans l'esprit,** an idea keeps running through my mind; *F:* **vous repassez!** you've got another think coming; (*b*) *Elcs:* (*computer*) to rerun; *Rec:* **faites r. la dernière phrase,** play back the last sentence. **2.** *v.tr.* (*a*) to repass; to pass by, pass over, cross (over), (sth.) again; **r. la mer,** to cross the sea again; (*b*) to go over, look over, say over, (sth.) (again); **r. qch. dans son esprit,** to go over sth. in one's mind; **r. un compte,** to go through an account again; to re-examine an account; **r. une leçon, un rôle,** to look over, go over, a lesson, a part; **r. une bande, un disque,** to replay, to play back, a tape, a record; *Nau:* **r. le gréement,** to overhaul the rigging; (*c*) to take, convey, (sth., s.o.) over again; **le batelier nous repassera,** the boatman will take us back; **r. un plat à qn,** to pass s.o. a dish again; **repassez-moi du pain,** pass me some (more) bread (please); **repassez-moi cette lettre,** let me see that letter again; *F:* **r. une fausse pièce à qn,** to palm off, foist, unload, a dud coin on s.o.; (*d*) to sharpen, whet, grind (knife, tool, etc.); to set (razor); **r. un outil sur la meule,** to grind a tool; **r. un outil sur la pierre,** to whet a tool; **r. un rasoir sur le cuir,** to strop a razor; *Metalw:* **r. les filets (d'une vis),** to chase (screw threads); (*e*) to iron (clothes, etc.); **fer à r.,** (laundry) iron; **planche à r.,** ironing board; **machine à r.,** ironing machine; (*f*) **r. une allée,** to rake (over) a path; (*g*) *P:* to murder, bump off, do in (s.o.).

repasserie [rəpɑsri], *s.f.* ironing room.

repasseur, -euse [rəpɑsœːr, -øːz], *s.* **1.** *Ind:* (*a*) finisher; (*b*) **r. de déchets,** waste sorter; (*c*) examiner; *Tex:* **r. d'écheveaux,** skein examiner. **2.** *s.m.* grinder (of knives, etc.); **r. ambulant,** itinerant grinder. **3.** *s.f.* **repasseuse,** ironer (person or machine); **repasseuse de linge fin,** fine ironer; laundress.

repatriage [rəpatrijaːʒ], *s.m.* repatriation.

repatriement [rəpatrimɑ̃], *s.m.* **1.** repatriation. **2.** *Dial:* reconciliation.

repatrier [rəpatrije], *v.tr.* (*p.d. & pr.sub.* **n. repatriions, v. repatriiez**) **1.** to repatriate. **2.** *Dial:* to reconcile.

repavage [rəpavaːʒ], *s.m.*, **repavement** [rəpavmɑ̃], *s.m.* repaving.

repaver [rəpave], *v.tr.* to repave.

repayement [rəpɛ(j)mɑ̃], *s.m.* paying (over) again.

repayer [rəpeje], *v.tr.* (*conj. like* PAYER) to pay (over) again.

repêchage [rəpɛʃa:ʒ], *s.m.* (*a*) fishing up (again), fishing out (again); picking up (of torpedo, etc.); *Min:* fishing up (broken drill, etc.); (*b*) helping, lending a hand to, rescuing (s.o. in difficulties); *Sch:* supplementary, second chance, examination (for candidates who have failed); **épreuve de r.,** (i) second chance; (ii) *Sp:* repêchage.

repêcher [rəpeʃe], *v.tr.* (*a*) to fish (sth.) up, out, (again); **r. un cadavre,** to fish out a body; **r. une torpille,** to pick up a torpedo; (*b*) to rescue; **r. un noyé,** to save, *F:* to fish out, a drowning man; **r. un candidat à l'oral,** to give a candidate a chance of scraping through at the viva; **ceux qui ont échoué au mois de juillet peuvent se r. en octobre,** those who failed in July get a second chance in October; **r. un parent dans l'embarras,** to come to the rescue of a relative in difficulties.

repeindre [rəpɛ̃:dr̥], *v.tr.* (*conj. like* PEINDRE) **1.** to repaint; to paint (sth.) again. **2.** *Lit:* **se r. un événement passé,** to recall to mind, to revisualize, a past event.

repeint [rəpɛ̃], *s.m. Art:* touching-up.

repenser [rəpɑ̃se], *v.i.* **1.** to think again (**à**, of, about); **j'y repenserai,** I shall think it over; **je n'y ai pas repensé,** (i) I did not give it another thought; (ii) I forgot all about it. **2.** *v.tr.* **r. une question,** to reconsider a problem.

repentance [rəpɑ̃tɑ̃:s], *s.f. Lit:* repentance; contrition.

repentant [rəpɑ̃tɑ̃], *a.* repentant, repenting (person, soul).

repenti, -ie [rəpɑ̃ti], *a. & s.* repentant; (**fille**) **repentie,** Magdalen(e); **maison des filles repenties, les Repenties,** rescue home for unfortunates, Magdalen hospital; **les justes et les repentis,** the righteous and the repentant.

repentir (se) [sərəpɑ̃ti:r]. I. *v.pr.* (*pr.p.* **se repentant;** *p.p.* **repenti;** *pr.ind.* **je me repens, il se repent;** *pr.sub.* **je me repente;** *p.d.* **je me repentais;** *p.h.* **je me repentis;** *fu.* **je me repentirai**) **se r.** (**de qch.**), to repent (sth.); to be sorry (for sth.); **je m'en repens amèrement,** I repent it bitterly; **se r. d'avoir fait qch.,** to repent having done sth.; to be sorry for having done sth.; **faire r. qn,** to make s.o. repent; **laisser r. qn, laisser qn se r.,** to allow s.o. to repent.

II. **repentir,** *s.m.* **1.** repentance; remorse. **2.** *Art:* alteration, second thought. **3.** *A:* ringlet.

repérable [rəperabl̥], *a.* locatable; that can be located, pin-pointed.

repérage [rəpera:ʒ], *s.m.* **1.** (*a*) marking (of instrument, etc.) with guide marks, with reference marks; *Typ:* marking the lay (on page). *W.Tel:* logging (of station); **numéros de r. (sur une carte),** key numbers (on a squared map); *Mec.E:* **r. des pièces du moteur,** marking of engine parts; **r. mécanique,** mechanical indexing; (*b*) adjusting, fixing, setting (of instrument, etc.) by reference marks, guide marks; *Mec.E: Civ.E:* lining up (of component parts of machine, structure, etc.); (*c*) *Typ: Engr:* **r. (du tirage),** registering (of the impression); **bon r.,** good lay, good register; **mauvais r.,** bad lay, bad register; **défaut de r.,** misregister, lack of register; **châssis de r.,** register frame; **règle de r.,** registering gauge; **travail de grand r.,** close-register job; **gravures en couleurs tirées au grand r.,** close-registered, carefully registered, colour prints; (*d*) *Cin:* synchronizing (of picture and sound track). **2.** (*a*) locating (of imperfection, fault, source of rumour); *Av:* identification; *Mil:* locating (of target, enemy, etc.), *F:* spotting (of enemy gun, aircraft, etc.); **r. de l'origine d'un bruit,** locating (of) the source of a noise; **r. à distance,** remote locating; **r. au radar,** radar locating, positioning; **r. radio,** radio location, radio fix; **r. de précision, r. ponctuel,** pinpointing; (*b*) *Artil:* ranging, registration; **r. au, par le, son,** sound ranging or registration; **appareil de r. par le son,** sound locator; **r. aux, par les, lueurs,** flash ranging or registration; **r. des distances,** taking of key ranges.

repercer [rəpɛrse], *v.tr.* (*conj. like* PERCER) **1.** to pierce, bore, perforate (sth.) again. **2.** to pierce (metal).

répercussif, -ive [repɛrkysif, -i:v], **répercutant** [repɛrkytɑ̃], *a.* repercussive.

répercussion [repɛrkysjɔ̃], *s.f.* (*a*) repercussion; backlash (of an explosion); reverberation (of sound); (*b*) repercussion; impact; consequential effects (of an action).

répercuté [repɛrkyte], *a. Elcs:* (*computers*) **erreur répercutée,** propagated error.

répercuter [repɛrkyte], *v.tr.* **1.** to reverberate, reflect back (sound); to reflect (light, heat). **2.** (*a*) **r. un ordre,** to pass on an order, a command; **la taxe sera répercutée sur les consommateurs,** the tax will be passed on to the consumers; (*b*) **les effets de la fatigue se répercutent sur le moral,** the effects of fatigue have repercussions, react, on the morale.

reperdre [rəpɛrdr̥], *v.tr.* **1.** to lose again; **le temps gagné est reperdu,** the time gained has been lost again. **2.** *O:* to lead (s.o.) astray again.

repère [rəpɛ:r], *s.m.* (*a*) reference (to datum line, etc.); *Mth:* reference system, frame; frame of reference; *Surv:* **ligne de r.,** datum line; *Tg:* **chiffre de r.,** test number (of telegram); (*b*) (**marque, point de**) **repère,** reference mark, guide mark, guiding mark (on instrument, object, etc.); fiducial mark, point (on scale); *Civ.E: Surv: etc:* bench mark, datum point; *Mec.E:* index mark (on machine part); *Typ: Engr:* lay mark; **r. topographique,** landmark; **trait de r.,** guiding line, datum line; *Mec.E:* **r. de calage,** setting mark; *Mec.E: Civ.E:* **r. de montage, d'ajustage,** assembly mark, line-up mark, match mark; *I.C.E.:* **r. de (réglage de la) distribution,** timing mark; *Civ.E: Surv: Artil:* **r. de distance,** range mark; (*of graduated measure, instrument*) **affleurer à un trait de r.,** to coincide with a gauge mark; (*c*) *Aut:* wing indicator, feeler.

repérer [rəpere], *v.tr.* (**je repère, n. repérons; je repérerai**) **1.** (*a*) to mark (instrument, etc.) with guide marks, reference marks; *Typ:* to mark the lay on (page); *W.Tel:* to log (station); (*b*) to adjust, fix, set, (instrument, etc.) by guide marks, by reference marks; *Typ:* **r. une impression,** to register an impression; *v.i.* **épreuve qui repère bien,** proof that falls, registers, well; (*c*) *Cin:* to synchronize the clapstick signals (on picture film and sound track). **2.** (*a*) to locate (imperfection, fault, etc.); *Av:* to identify (aircraft); *Mil:* to locate (target, etc.); *F:* to spot (gun, aircraft, etc.); **r. des distances,** to take key ranges; **r. le point de chute d'un obus,** to mark the fall of a shell; **r. l'origine d'une rumeur,** to locate the source of a rumour; (*b*) *F:* to spot, pick out; **après avoir repéré mon wagon,** after making sure which was my carriage; **r. qn dans la foule,** to spot s.o., pick s.o. out, in the crowd; *Turf: etc:* **il a le flair pour r. les gagnants,** he knows how to pick the winners; **tu vas nous faire r.,** you'll get us caught.

se repérer, (*a*) to take one's bearings; (*b*) *F:* **se r. dans une ville,** to find one's way about in a town; **je n'arrive pas à me r. dans ce problème,** I can't find my way round, make head or tail of, this problem.

reperforateur [rəpɛrfɔratœ:r], *s.m. Elcs:* (*computers*) **r. imprimeur,** printing reperforator, *U.S:* printer perforator.

reperforateur-transmetteur [rəpɛrfɔratœrtrɑ̃smɛtœ:r], *s.m.* perforated-tape retransmitter; *pl. reperforateurs-transmetteurs.*

répertoire [repɛrtwa:r], *s.m.* **1.** (*a*) index, table, list, catalogue; **r. à onglets,** thumb index, thumb register; **r. d'adresses,** (i) directory; (ii) address-book; *Jur:* **r. de jurisprudence,** summary of leading cases and decisions; (*b*) (*computer*) directory, repertory; **r. d'instructions,** instruction repertory set. **2.** repertory, repository (of information, etc.); referencing; **c'est un vrai r. d'anecdotes,** he is a perfect mine of stories. **3.** *Th: etc:* repertoire, repertory; **pièce de, du, r.,** stock piece; **il a un r. de trois discours,** he has three stock speeches; **tout un r. d'injures,** a whole repertory of insults.

répertorier [repɛrtɔrje], *v.tr.* (*p.d. & pr.sub.* **n. répertoriions, v. répertoriiez**) **1.** to index (file, etc.); to make a reference table for (sth.). **2.** to index (item); to enter (item) in an index.

repeser [rəpəze], *v.tr.* (*conj. like* PESER) to re-weigh.

répéter [repete], *v.tr.* (**je répète, n. répétons; je répéterai**) **1.** (*a*) to repeat; to say or do (sth.) (over) again; **r. un vers,** to repeat a line; **r. un secret,** to repeat a secret; **ne le répétez pas,** don't repeat it; (i) don't do it again; (ii) don't say it again; **chose qui se répète souvent,** thing that happens over and over again; **j'espère que cela ne se répétera pas,** I hope it will not be repeated, will not occur again; **des assauts répétés,** charge after charge; **faire r. qch.,** to have sth. repeated; *Sch: A:* **faire r. sa leçon à qn,** to make s.o. repeat his lesson, to hear s.o. his lesson; **je ne me le ferai pas r.,** I shall not need to be told twice; (*b*) *Th:* to rehearse (play); (*c*) to learn (part, lesson); (*d*) (*of mirror, etc.*) to reflect (image). **2.** *Jur:* to ask back, claim back (money, goods).

se répéter, (*of pers.*) to repeat oneself; (*of event, etc.*) to recur, to happen again.

répéteur [repetœ:r], *s.m. Elcs: etc:* repeater; **r. d'impulsions, de ligne,** pulse, line, repeater; **r. de câble,** cable repeater; **r. téléphonique,** telephone repeater, amplifier; **station de répéteurs,** repeater station.

répétiteur, -trice [repetitœ:r, -tris], *a. & s.* **1.** (*a*) *Sch: A:* (**maître**) **r.,** (**maîtresse**) **répétitrice,** assistant (in boarding school) in charge of preparation, etc.; (*b*) private tutor, coach; (*c*) *Th:* chorus master, répétiteur. **2.** (*a*) *s.m. Navy:* repeater, repeating ship; (*b*) *s.m. Nau: Av: etc:* indicator; *Nau:* **r. d'angle de barre,** helm indicator, rudder-angle indicator, rudder telltale; **r. de cap,** heading repeater; (*c*) *a. Nau:* **compas r.,** repeater compass; *Nau: Surv:* **cercle r.,** repeating circle; *Surv:* **théodolite r.,** repeating theodolite.

répétitif, -ive [repetitif, -i:v], *a.* repetitive.

répétition [repetisjɔ̃], *s.f.* **1.** (*a*) repetition (of word, action, etc.); **fusil à r.,** repeating rifle; **montre à r.,** repeater (watch); *Med:* **bronchite à r.,** recurrent, *F:* chronic, bronchitis; (*b*) *Elcs:* (*computers*) **instruction de r.,** repetition instruction; **système détecteur d'erreurs avec demande de r.,** error-detecting and feedback system; (*c*) reproduction, duplicate, replica. **2.** (*a*) *Th:* rehearsal (of play); **r. générale, r. en costume,** dress rehearsal; **mettre une pièce en r.,** to put a play into rehearsal; **la pièce est en r.,** the play is in rehearsal; (*b*) (band, choral) practice; (*c*) learning (of part, lesson). **3.** *Sch:* (coach's) lesson; **donner des répétitions,** to give private lessons, private coaching. **4.** *Jur:* claiming back; **r. d'indu,** recovery of payment made by mistake.

repeuplée [rəpœple], *s.f. For:* replanting.

repeuplement [rəpœpləmɑ̃], *s.m.* repeopling, repopulation (of country); restocking (of river, pond); *For:* replanting.

repeupler [rəpœple], *v.tr.* to repeople, repopulate (country); to restock (river, pond); to replant (forest); **la ville se repeuple,** the population of the town is increasing again.

repic [rəpik], *s.m. Cards:* (*at piquet*) repique; *A:* **faire qn r. (et capot),** to outwit s.o.

repincer [rəpɛ̃se], *v.tr.* (*conj. like* PINCER) **1.** to pinch, nip (sth., s.o.) again; *Bookb:* **volume repincé,** cased book. **2.** to catch (s.o.) again; *F:* **on ne m'y repincera pas,** you won't catch me at it again.

repiocher [rəpjɔʃe], *v.tr.* **1.** to dig (earth) again. **2.** *F:* to work hard at (sth.) again, to swot up (subject) again.

repiquage [rəpika:ʒ], *s.m.* **1.** pricking, piercing, (of sth.) again. **2.** *Civ.E:* mending, repairing (of road). **3.** *Hort:* pricking out, planting out (of seedlings). **4.** *Phot:* = REPIQUE. **5.** *Typ:* overprinting. **6.** *Bac:* sub(-)culture. **7.** *Rec:* re-recording.

repique [rəpik], *s.f. Phot:* spotting (of negatives or prints).

repiquement [rəpikmɑ̃], *s.m.* = REPIQUAGE.

repiquer [rəpike]. **1.** *v.tr.* (*a*) to prick, pierce, (sth.) again; (*b*) *Civ.E:* to mend, repair (road); (*c*) *Dom.Ec:* to restitch; (*d*) *Hort:* to prick out, plant out (seedlings); **plant à r.,** bedding plant; (*e*) *Phot:* to spot (negative or print); (*f*) *Typ:* to overprint; (*g*) *Stonew:* to dress (millstone); (*h*) *Bac:* to sub(-)culture; (*i*) *Rec:* to re-record. **2.** *v.i.* (*a*) *F:* to pick up again (in health); (*b*) *F:* **r. au plat,** to have a second helping; *P:* **r. au truc,** (i) to begin again, to start afresh; (ii) to go back to one's old ways; (iii) to re-enlist; (*c*) *Nau:* **r. dans le vent,** to haul the wind again.

repiqueur, -euse [rəpikœ:r, -ø:z], *s. Hort: etc:* **1.** (*pers.*) planter out (of seedlings, etc.). **2.** *s.f.* (*machine*) **repiqueuse,** planter.

répit [repi], *s.m.* respite; breathing space; *Com:* **jours de r.,** days of grace; **laisser un moment de r. à qn,** to give s.o. some breathing space, a breather; **prendre un moment de r.,** to take a bit of time off (from work); **les douleurs ne lui laissent pas un moment de r.,** he is never free from pain; **souffrir sans r.,** to have no respite from pain; **ne laisser à l'ennemi aucun r.,** to keep the enemy on the run, on the alert.

replacage [rəplaka:ʒ], *s.m.* replating (of copper sheet).

replacement [rəplasmɑ̃], *s.m.* **1.** (*a*) replacement, replacing; putting, setting, (of sth.) in place again; putting back (of sth.) in its proper place; (*b*) reinvestment (of funds). **2.** settling (of s.o.) in a new situation, job.

replacer [rəplase], *v.tr.* (*conj. like* PLACER) **1.** (*a*) to replace; to put, set, (sth.) in place again; to put (sth.) back; *Mil:* **r. l'arme,** to recover arms; (*b*) to reinvest (funds). **2.** to allocate (s.o.) to a new job; **r. ses employés,** (i) to reallocate the work of one's staff; (ii) to find fresh employment, fresh jobs, for one's staff; **domestique qui se replace,** maid who finds a new job.

replaider [rəplede], *v.tr. Jur:* to plead (case) again.

replain [rəplɛ̃], *s.m.* (cultivated) terraces (on hillside).

replanir [rəplaniːr], *v.tr. Carp:* to give a final planing, finish, to (woodwork).

replanissage [rəplanisaːʒ], *s.m. Carp:* final planing (of woodwork).

replantage [rəplɑ̃taːʒ], *s.m.*, **replantation** [rəplɑ̃tasjɔ̃], *s.f.* replanting.

replanter [rəplɑ̃te], *v.tr.* **1.** to replant. **2.** *F:* **jamais je ne replanterai les pieds chez lui,** I shall never set foot in his house again.

replaquer [rəplake], *v.tr.* to replate (copper sheet).

replat [rəpla], *s.m.* (*a*) *Geog:* shoulder; (*b*) *Mount:* shelf.

replâtrage [rəplɑtraːʒ], *s.m.* **1.** (*a*) replastering, plastering up (of a wall, etc.); (*b*) tinkering up, patching up (of sth. radically unsound). **2.** (*a*) superficial repair; (*b*) superficial reconciliation; patched-up peace.

replâtrer [rəplɑtre], *v.tr.* **1.** to replaster, plaster up (wall). **2.** to patch up, tinker up (sth. radically unsound); to patch up (quarrel).

replet, -ète [rəplɛ, -ɛt], *a.* stoutish, *F:* podgy (person); **petit homme r.,** dumpy little man.

réplétif, -ive [repletif, -iːv], *a.* repletive.

réplétion [replesjɔ̃], *s.f.* **1.** (*a*) repletion; (*b*) surfeit (of food). **2.** *A:* plethoric condition (of body); corpulence.

repleuvoir [rəplœvwaːr], *v.impers.* (*conj. like* PLEUVOIR) to rain again; **voilà qu'il repleut!** the rain's started again! here's the rain again!

repli [rəpli], *s.m.* **1.** fold, crease, turn, plait (in cloth, etc.); **replis du terrain,** folds in the ground; **les plis et les replis du cœur,** the innermost recesses, the secret places, of the heart. **2.** winding, bend, sinuosity (of river, etc.); coil (of rope, of serpent); **les replis d'une rivière,** the meanders of a river. **3.** (*a*) *Mil:* falling back, withdrawal; (*b*) *St.Exch:* recession, set back, fall, drop (in the value of shares).

repliable [rəplijabl̩], *a.* that may be folded (up), turned up, bent back; folding; *Av:* **ailes repliables,** folding wings; *Nau:* **berthon r.,** collapsible Berthon boat.

replicatif, -ive [rəplikatif, -iːv], *a. Bot:* replicative, replicate.

replié [rəplije], *a.* (*a*) turned in; doubled up; folded again; **unité économique repliée sur elle-même,** self-sufficient economic unit; (*b*) (*of pers.*) withdrawn.

repliement [rəplimɑ̃], *s.m.* **1.** folding (of sth.) again, folding up, turning up, bending back. **2.** *Mil:* falling back, withdrawal (of troops). **3.** (*of pers.*) withdrawal; withdrawing (into one's shell).

replier [rəplije], *v.tr.* (*conj. like* PLIER) **1.** to fold (sth.) up (again); to coil (sth.) up; to double (sth.) up; to bend (sth.) back; to turn in, tuck in (edge of garment, etc.); **r. un parapluie,** to fold up, close, an umbrella; *Mil:* **r. un pont,** to haul in each half of a pontoon bridge to the bank. **2.** *Mil:* (*a*) to drive back, force back (troops); (*b*) to draw in (outposts, advanced troops).

se replier. 1. (*a*) (*of object*) to fold up, turn up, coil up, bend back; (*of pers.*) to double up, coil up; (*of serpent*) to coil up; *Equit:* (*of horse*) to turn suddenly round; (*b*) (*of stream, path*) to wind, turn, twist, bend; (*of stream*) to meander. **2.** se **r. sur soi-même,** to fall back upon one's own thoughts; to retire within oneself. **3.** *Mil:* (*a*) (*of outposts*) to fall back; to retire, withdraw; (*b*) (*of troops in combat*) to give ground; to fall back. **4.** *Fin: St.Exch:* to fall back.

réplique [replik], *s.f.* **1.** (*a*) retort, rejoinder; pat answer; **avoir la r. prompte,** to be ready with an answer; **preuve, argument, qui ne souffre aucune r.,** incontrovertible proof; unanswerable argument; **un argument sans r.,** an unanswerable argument; **obéir sans r.,** to obey without a word; **r. impertinente,** impertinent remark; back answer; *F:* **et pas de r.!** don't you dare answer me back! (*b*) *Jur:* (i) replication; (ii) **droit de r.,** right to compel the insertion of a further answer (in newspaper). **2.** *Th:* cue; **donner la r. à qn,** (i) give s.o. his cue; (ii) to play up to s.o.; (iii) to answer s.o. pat; (iv) *Sp:* to play a return match; *Th:* **donner la r. à un acteur,** (i) to feed an actor; (ii) to play opposite an actor; **manquer la r.,** to miss one's cue. **3.** *Art:* replica (of statue, etc.); counterpart. **4.** *Mus:* (*a*) replicate (at octave); (*b*) (*in counterpoint*) answer. **5.** second striking (of clock with double chime). **6.** *Meteor:* aftershock (of earthquake). **7.** *Cin:* retake (of a scene).

répliquer [replike], *v.i.* to retort, to answer back; **r. avec aigreur,** to answer tartly, acrimoniously; **il répliqua sur le champ,** he answered without hesitation, his answer came pat; **r. à qn,** to answer s.o. back; **ne répliquez pas!** don't answer back! **à cette objection on réplique que . . .,** the answer to this objection is that . . .; (*with cogn.acc.*) **r. une insolence,** to make an insolent retort.

répliqueur, -euse [replikœːr, -øːz], *a.* & *s.* (person) given to answering back; cheeky (child).

replissage [rəplisaːʒ], *s.m.* re-folding; re-pleating (of a skirt, etc.).

replisser [rəplise], *v.tr.* to re-fold; to re-pleat; **faire r. une jupe,** to have a skirt re-pleated.

reploiement [rəplwamɑ̃], *s.m. Lit:* (*a*) folding up, folding again, bending back; (*b*) (*of pers.*) withdrawal; withdrawing (into one's shell).

replonger [rəplɔ̃ʒe], *v.* (*conj. like* PLONGER) **1.** *v.tr.* to plunge, dip, immerse, (sth.) again; to replunge (sth.) (**dans,** into). **2.** *v.i.* to dive in again; (of waterfowl) to duck again, to dive again.

se replonger dans l'eau, dans l'étude, to immerse oneself once more in the water, in study; **il se replongea dans sa lecture,** he went back to his reading.

reployer [rəplwaje], *v.tr.* (*conj. like* PLOYER) **1.** *A:* to fold up (again); to bend back; to coil up. **2.** *Lit:* **elle était encore reployée sur sa douleur,** she was still withdrawn in her grief.

repluire [rəplɥiːr], *s.f. Metall:* surface defect (of casting).

repolir [rəpɔliːr], *v.tr.* to repolish; to reburnish (metal); to rub up (spoon); **r. un ouvrage,** to polish up, touch up, a work again.

repolissage [rəpɔlisaːʒ], *s.m.* repolishing; reburnishing; rubbing up.

reponchonner [rəpɔ̃ʃɔne], *v.tr. Dy:* to renew (exhausted bath) by adding fresh dye.

répondant [repɔ̃dɑ̃], *s.m.* **1.** *Ecc:* server (at mass). **2.** *Jur:* surety, security, referee, reference, guarantor, warrantor; *esp.* bail(sman); *F:* **avoir du r.,** to have money to pay. **3.** *A:* candidate (in an examination); respondent.

répondeur, -euse [repɔ̃dœːr, -øːz]. **1.** *a.* & *s.* (person) fond of answering back; cheeky (child). **2.** (*a*) *s.m. Elcs:* responder, transponder; **r. actif,** active responder, responder beacon; **r. passif,** passive responder; *Tp:* **r. téléphonique,** telephone answerer; (*b*) *a. Av: etc:* **balise répondeuse** responder beacon.

répondeur-enregistreur [repɔ̃dœrɑ̃rəʒistrœːr], *s.m. Tp:* automatic message recorder; (*R.t.m.*) Ansaphone; *pl. répondeurs-enregistreurs.*

repondre [rəpɔ̃ːdr̥], *v.tr.* to lay (an egg, eggs) again; **poule qui commence à r.,** hen beginning to lay again.

répondre [repɔ̃ːdr̥]. **1.** *v.tr.* to answer, reply, respond; (*a*) *A:* **r. une lettre,** to answer a letter; *still so used in F:* **lettres répondues,** letters answered; **lettres à r.,** letters to be answered; (*b*) **répondre qch.,** to make some reply; **je n'ai rien répondu,** I made no reply; I gave no answer; **qu'avez-vous à r.?** what have you to say in reply? **r. des mensonges,** to answer with lies; *O:* **ne r. ni œuf ni bœuf,** not to answer a syllable; **il répondit que j'avais tort,** he answered that I was wrong; **il répondit n'en rien savoir,** he answered that he knew nothing about it; *Ecc:* **r. la messe,** to make the responses at Mass; (*c*) *v.ind.tr.* **r. à qn, à une question,** to answer s.o.; to reply to s.o., to a question; **r. au salut de qn,** to return, acknowledge, s.o.'s greeting; **r. à l'appel,** to answer the roll, to answer one's name; **r. à une lettre,** to answer, acknowledge, a letter; **r. à une accusation,** to answer a charge; **r. au feu de l'ennemi,** to reply to the enemy's fire; **r. à une demande,** to comply with, fall in with, a request; **r. à un coup de sonnette,** to answer the bell; **r. à l'amour de qn,** to return s.o.'s love; **ne pas r. aux avances de qn,** to fail to respond to s.o.'s advances; **ne pas r. à une invitation,** (i) to fail to answer an invitation; (ii) to ignore an invitation; **c'est mal r. à ses bontés,** that is a poor return for his kindness; *Fin:* **r. à une prime,** to declare an option; (*d*) *abs.* **r. par écrit,** to write back; to reply in writing; **la sonnette répond dans la cuisine,** the bell rings in the kitchen; *W.Tel:* (*used for conversations*) **répondez!** over! **2.** *v.i.* (*a*) to answer, correspond to, come up to (a standard, etc.); **cela ne répond pas à mes besoins,** it does not meet, answer, my requirements; **r. à l'attente de qn,** to answer, satisfy, come up to, be equal to, s.o.'s expectations; **ne pas r. à l'attente,** to fall short of expectation; **r. à la formule,** to comply with, agree with, the formula; **r. au but,** to answer the purpose; **son succès ne répondit pas à ses efforts,** his success was not commensurate with his efforts; **les deux ailes de l'édifice ne se répondent pas,** the two wings of the building do not correspond; (*b*) **allées qui répondent à un bassin,** paths that lead to a pond. **3.** *v.i.* **r. de qn, de qch.,** to answer for s.o., for sth.; to be answerable, accountable, responsible, for s.o., for sth.; **je réponds de son obéissance,** I guarantee his obedience; **il va revenir, je vous en réponds,** he will come back, I assure you, (you may) take my word for it; **j'en répondrais,** I'd take my oath on it; *F:* **je vous en réponds!** you bet! rather! **il faisait chaud, je vous en réponds!** it *was* warm, I can tell you, and no mistake! **je ne réponds pas que vous l'aurez cette semaine,** I can't answer for your getting it this week.

répons [repɔ̃], *s.m. Ecc:* response.

réponse [repɔ̃ːs], *s.f.* **1.** (*a*) answer, reply; **avoir, trouver, r. à tout,** to have, find, an answer for everything; never to be at a loss for an answer; **rendre r. à qn,** to return s.o. an answer, to reply to s.o.; **faire, donner, envoyer, un mot de r. à qn,** to drop s.o. a line in reply; **argument sans r.,** unanswerable argument; **en r., il nous montra la porte,** by way of answer, he pointed to the door; **pour toute r., elle éclata en sanglots,** her only answer was to break into sobs; *Com:* **en r. à votre lettre du 20 ct . . .,** in answer to your letter of the 20th inst . . .; (*of letter, etc.*) **rester sans r.,** to be left unanswered; **r., s'il vous plaît,** an answer is requested; *Post:* **r. payée,** reply paid; *Jur:* **droit de r.,** right to reply (in the public press to a public privileged statement reprinted in the paper concerned); (*b*) response; **son appel resta sans r.,** there was no response to his appeal; (*c*) *Physiol:* responsiveness, response (to stimulus); **r. motrice,** motor response; **r. instinctive, naturelle,** native response; **r. réflexe,** reflex response; **temps de r.,** reaction time; (*d*) *Ph: Elcs:* response; (*computers*) answer, answering, answer-back; **courbe de r.,** response curve; **r. en amplitude, en fréquence,** amplitude, frequency, response; **r. thermique,** thermal response; (*computers*) **r. automatique,** unattended answering; **r. de, en, fréquence,** frequency response; **jack de r.,** answering jack; **lampe de r.,** answer lamp; **signal de r.,** answer signal; **temps de r.,** response time; *Phot:* **r. de l'émulsion,** response of the emulsion; (*e*) *Mus:* real answer (in fugue). **2.** *Fin:* **r. des primes,** declaration of options. **3.** *Jur:* **réponses de droit,** judicial decisions.

repopulation [rəpɔpylasjɔ̃], *s.f.* repopulation, repopulating; restocking (of river, etc.).

report [rəpɔːr], *s.m.* **1.** *Com: Book-k:* (*a*) carrying forward, bringing forward; (*b*) amount carried forward; carry forward, carry over; **r. des exercices antérieurs,** amount brought in; **r. à nouveau,** amount carried forward, balance to next account; **r. du folio . . .,** brought forward from folio . . .; (*c*) posting (of journal entries to the ledger accounts). **2.** *Jur:* antedate (of a bankruptcy, etc.). **3.** *St.Exch:* (*a*) contango(ing), continuation; **prendre des actions en r.,** to take in stock; **titres en r.,** stock taken in, stock carried over; (*b*) (**taux de**) **r.,** contango (rate), continuation rate; (*c*) difference between cash and settlement prices. **4.** *Phot: Lith: etc:* transfer; **papier (à) r.,** transfer paper; **r. à la machine, à la main,** machine, hand, transferring; **r. de pierre à pierre,** re-transfer; **r. de texte,** type-transfer; **r. photo(graphique),** phototransfer; **épreuve à r.,** transfer impression; **tirer une épreuve à r.,** to pull a transfer; **tirage d'une épreuve à r.,** transfer pulling; **machine à r.,** transferring machine, step and repeat machine. **5.** *Typ:* lines carried over. **6.** *Elcs:* (*a*) (*radar, etc.*) plot(ting); **table de r.,** plotting board; (*b*) (*computers*) carry; **r. bloqué sur neuf,** standing-on-nines carry; **r. en boucle,** end-around carry; **r. rapide,** high-speed carry, ripple-through carry; **addition sans report(s),** false add; **registre de r.,** carry register; **signal de fin de r.,** carry-complete signal.

reportable [rəpɔrtabl̩], *a. St.Exch:* contangoable, continuable.

reportage [rəpɔrta:ʒ], *s.m. Journ:* **1.** reporting; *s.a.* FILM. **2.** (newspaper) report; **r. sensationnel (qu'on est le premier à publier),** scoop. **3.** set of (contributed) articles (on a topical subject). **4.** *W.Tel:* running commentary (on a match, etc.).

reporté [rəpɔrte], *s.m. St.Exch:* giver (of stock); payer (of contango).

reporter[1] [rəpɔrte], *v.tr.* **1.** *(a)* to carry back; to take (sth.) back; **r. un livre à qn,** to take a book back to s.o.; *(b)* **r. qn au temps de son enfance,** to take, carry, s.o. back (in thought) to the time of his childhood; **r. l'origine de l'homme à un passé très lointain,** to trace the origin of man back to a remote past. **2.** *(a)* **r. qch. à plus tard,** to postpone, defer, sth. until later, to a later date; *(b) Com: Book-k:* (i) to carry forward, bring forward, carry over (total); (ii) to post (up) (sum to ledger accounts); **à r.,** (carried) forward; *(c) St.Exch:* to continue, contango; to carry over; **(faire) r. des titres,** to take in, borrow, carry, stock; **(faire) r. un emprunteur,** to take in stock for a borrower; **se faire r.,** to be carried over, to lend stock; *(d) (computers)* to carry. **3.** *Lith: Phot: etc:* to transfer.

se reporter. 1. se r. à un document, to refer, turn, to a document; **se r. à . . .,** the reader is referred to . . .; "see . . ." **2. se r. au passé,** to go back to, look back to, the past. **3.** *St.Exch:* **personne ne veut se r. sur cette valeur,** there are no givers on the stock.

reporter[2] [rəpɔrtɛ:r], *s.m. Journ:* reporter; **il est r. d'un journal du soir,** he is a reporter on an evening paper; **r. photographe,** press photographer.

reporteur [rəpɔrtœ:r], *s.m.* **1.** *St.Exch:* taker (of stock); receiver (of contango). **2.** *Phot: Lith:* transferrer; **r. lithographe,** transfer printer.

reporteuse [rəpɔrtø:z], *s.f. Elcs:* transfer interpreter (of computer).

repos [rəpo], *s.m.* **1.** *(a)* rest, repose (after movement or exertion); **au r., en r.,** at rest; *(of the sea, etc.)* in repose; **se tenir au r., en r.,** to keep quiet, still; not to move, *F:* budge; **se donner, prendre, du r.,** to take a rest; **il n'eut de r. que l'on ne lui eût accordé sa demande,** he never rested till his request was granted; *Lit:* **le r. éternel,** the last sleep; *Lit:* **le champ de r.,** the churchyard, God's acre; *Agr:* **terre au r.,** fallow land; *Chess:* **coup de r.,** waiting move; *(b) Mil:* **repos!** stand at ease! **r. (à volonté),** stand easy! **être, se tenir, au r.,** to stand at ease; **mettre la troupe au r.,** to order troops to stand at ease (or to stand easy); *(c) Sm.a:* (of rifle, pistol, etc.); **(être) au r.,** (to be) at halfcock, halfcocked; **mettre une arme au r.,** to set an arm at halfcock; **cran de r.,** halfcock; *(d) Tchn:* **(être) au r.,** (i) *Mec.E: etc: (of mechanism)* (to be) in neutral position; (ii) *Mec.E: (of machine)* (to be) out of gear; *(of boiler)* (to be) laid off, standing by; **position de r.,** (i) *Mec.E:* rest position (of machine), neutral position (of mechanism); off position; (ii) *El:* home position (of contact); *Elcs:* **fréquence de r.,** non-operating frequency; *Tp:* **contact repos-travail,** make-and-break contact; *Atom.Ph:* **énergie au r.,** rest energy; *(e)* pause, rest (in a verse); *Mus:* pause, hold. **2.** peace, tranquillity (of mind); **r. public,** public peace, tranquillity; **avoir l'esprit en r.,** to enjoy peace of mind; **être en r. au sujet de qn,** to feel easy in one's mind about s.o.; not to be anxious about s.o.; **laisser qn en r.,** to leave s.o. in peace; to leave s.o. alone; **que Dieu donne le r. à son âme!** God rest his soul! **de tout r.,** absolutely safe, reliable; **valeur de tout r.,** (perfectly) safe investment, gilt-edged security. **3.** *(a)* resting place; seat (in garden, etc.); landing (on stair); *(b)* stop (in lock, etc.).

reposant [rəpozɑ̃], *a.* **1.** restful (spot, occupation); refreshing (sleep). **2. hypothèse bien reposante,** well-founded hypothesis.

repose [rəpo:z], *s.f. Tchn:* re-laying, re-fixing.

reposé [rəpoze], *a.* **1.** rested, refreshed (look, etc.); fresh (complexion); **s'éveiller bien r.,** to awake refreshed. **2.** sedate, quiet, calm; **paysage r.,** restful country scene; **à tête reposée,** (i) deliberately, coolly; (ii) at leisure; **laissez-moi y réfléchir à tête reposée,** give me time to think it over.

reposée [rəpoze], *s.f.* **1.** *Ven:* lair (of wild beast). **2.** *A:* **voyager à reposées,** to travel with occasional rests, halts.

repose-fer [rəpozfɛ:r], *s.m. Dom.Ec:* iron(ing) stand; *pl. repose-fers.*

repose-pied [rəpozpje], *s.m.inv.* foot rest (of motor cycle, chair).

reposer [rəpoze]. I. *v.tr.* **1.** *(a)* to put, place, lay, set (sth.) back (in its place); to replace (sth.); **r. un livre sur la table,** to put a book back on the table; *Mil:* **r. l'arme,** to return to the "order" (from the "slope"); to order arms; **reposez arme!** order arms! **r. le sabre,** to slope swords; *(b) Rail: etc:* **r. une voie ferrée, une voie de tramway,** to re-lay a railway line, tram lines. **2.** *(a)* **r. ses regards sur qch.,** to let one's glance rest on sth.; *(b)* to rest; **r. sa tête sur un coussin,** to rest one's head on a cushion; **r. l'esprit,** to rest, refresh, the mind; **r. qn de qch.,** to give s.o. a rest from sth.; **couleur qui repose les yeux,** colour that rests, is restful to, the eyes; **le sommeil repose le teint,** sleep freshens the complexion. **3. r. le problème en termes différents,** to restate the problem in different terms; **r. une question,** to ask a question, the same question, again.

II. **reposer,** *v.i.* to lie, rest; *(a)* **le corps reposait sur son lit de parade,** the body was lying in state; **cet espoir repose dans notre cœur,** we cherish this hope in our hearts; **ici repose . . .,** here lies (buried) . . .; **qu'ils reposent en paix!** may they rest in peace! *(b)* **fondations qui reposent sur le roc,** foundations built on a rock; **le commerce repose sur le crédit,** commerce is based on credit; **bruit qui ne repose sur rien,** groundless report, unfounded report; **ce roman repose sur les événements de 1939,** this novel is based on the events of 1939.

se reposer. 1. to alight, settle, again; **l'oiseau se reposa sur la branche,** the bird settled on the bough again. **2.** *(a)* to rest, to take a rest; **travailler sans se r.,** to work without resting, without relaxing; **se r. d'un travail par un autre,** to seek relaxation from a task by working at something else; **journée sur laquelle mon souvenir aime à se r.,** day on which my memory loves to dwell; **faire r. ses chevaux, laisser r. ses chevaux,** to rest one's horses; **laisser r. une terre,** to let a piece of ground rest, lie fallow; **se r. sur ses lauriers,** to rest on one's laurels; *(b)* **se r. sur qn, sur qch.,** to rely upon, put one's trust in, s.o., sth.; **se r. sur qn du soin de qch.,** to rely upon s.o. to take charge of sth.; *Lit:* **chacun se dit ami, mais fou qui s'y repose,** everyone professes friendship, but he is a fool who trusts in it; *(c)* **laisser r. une solution, du vin,** to allow a solution, wine, to settle.

repose-tête [rəpoztɛt], *s.m.inv. Aut:* headrest.

reposoir [rəpozwa:r], *s.m.* **1.** resting place; *(a) A:* wayside shelter; cold harbour; *(b) Ecc:* wayside altar; temporary altar. **2.** *Dy: etc:* settling vat, tub.

repoudrer [rəpudre], *v.tr.* to powder again.

repous [rəpu], *s.m. Civ.E:* crushed brick, rubble, hard core (to consolidate roads, etc.).

repoussage [rəpusa:ʒ], *s.m.* **1.** repelling, driving back. **2.** *Tchn:* chasing, embossing, repoussé work(ing); *Metalw:* snarling; (cold) spinning; **r. au tour,** floturning, hydro spinning. **3.** *Typ:* lettering by hand, hand stamping.

repoussant [rəpusɑ̃], *a.* repulsive, repellent, loathsome (appearance, etc.); offensive (smell, etc.); **il est d'une laideur repoussante,** he is repulsively ugly; his ugliness is repulsive, repellent.

repousse [rəpus], *s.f.* **1.** growing again. **2.** fresh growth (of hair, etc.).

repoussé [rəpuse], *a.* chased (silver); embossed, tooled (leather); repoussé (work); *Metalw:* **cuivre r.,** spun copper; *s.m.* **(travail de) r.,** chasing, embossing, repoussé (work); snarling; **travailler une aiguière d'argent au r.,** to snarl a silver ewer.

repoussement [rəpusmɑ̃], *s.m.* **1.** repulse (of person); rejection, voting down (of motion) rejection (of idea). **2.** recoil, kick (of firearm). **3.** dislike, disinclination; **éprouver du r. à faire qch.,** to dislike the idea of doing sth.; to feel disinclined to do sth.

repousse-peaux [rəpuspo], *s.m.inv. Toil:* cuticle pen.

repousser [rəpuse]. **1.** *v.tr.* *(a)* to push back, push away, drive off, thrust aside, repulse, repel; **r. les volets,** to push back, throw back, the shutters; **il repoussa violemment la porte,** he flung back, open, the door; **r. un assaut,** to repulse, repel, beat off, an attack; **r. une offre,** turn down, to reject, decline, an offer; **r. la tentation,** to thrust aside temptation; **r. du pied les dons offerts,** to spurn the gifts offered; **r. qn, les avances de qn,** to spurn s.o., s.o.'s advances; **être repoussé de tout le monde, par ses amis,** to be spurned by all, by one's friends; **r. une accusation,** to deny a charge; **r. un projet de loi,** to throw out a bill; **r. une mesure,** to reject, vote down, a measure; **r. un amendement,** to negative an amendment; *Tchn:* **r. un rivet,** to drive out, knock out, a rivet; *(b)* **r. une conférence à plus tard,** to postpone a conference; *(c)* to be repellent to (s.o.); to repel; *(d) Tchn:* to emboss (leather); to chase (metal); to work (metal) in repoussé; *(e) Typ:* to stamp in by hand; *(f) abs. (of firearm)* to recoil, kick; *(of spring)* to resist. **2.** *(a)* *v.tr.* *(of tree, plant etc.)* to throw out (branches, shoots) again; *(b) v.i. (of tree, plant)* to shoot (up) again, spring (up) again, sprout again; *(of hair)* to grow again. **3.** *v.tr.* **r. un cri,** to utter a cry again; to utter a fresh cry; to cry out again.

repousseur [rəpusœ:r], *s.m. Metalw: (pers.)* spinner.

repoussoir [rəpuswa:r], *s.m.* **1.** *(a) Tls:* driving bolt, starting bolt, drift (bolt); pin drift, starter rammer; *(b)* embossing punch; snarling iron; *(c) Toil:* cuticle pen. **2.** *Hyd.E:* fender pile. **3.** *(a) Art:* strong piece of foreground; *(b)* set-off, foil; **servir de r. à la beauté de qn,** to set off s.o.'s beauty; to serve as a foil to s.o.'s beauty; *F: (of woman)* **c'est un r.,** she won't spoil the home with her beauty; she's got a face to stop a clock.

répréhensible [repreɑ̃sibl̥], *a.* reprehensible.

répréhensiblement [repreɑ̃sibləmɑ̃], *adv.* reprehensibly.

répréhensif, -ive [repreɑ̃sif, -i:v], *a.* reprehensive.

répréhension [repreɑ̃sjɔ̃], *s.f.* reprehension.

reprendre [rəprɑ̃:dr̥], *v.* (*conj. like* PRENDRE) **1.** *v.tr.* *(a)* to take again, retake, recapture; **r. un prisonnier évadé,** to recapture an escaped prisoner; **r. une ville à, sur, l'ennemi,** to retake, recapture, a town from the enemy; *(b)* **r. du pain,** to take, have, some more bread; **r. les armes,** to take up arms again; **r. sa canne,** to pick up one's stick again; **je suis allé r. mon parapluie,** I went to recover, retrieve, my umbrella; **j'ai repris mon pardessus d'hiver,** I have gone back to my winter overcoat; **r. sa place,** to resume one's seat; **dans ce chapitre l'auteur reprend l'histoire de son héros,** in this chapter the author takes up the story of his hero again; **je vous reprendrai en passant,** I'll pick you up again as I go by; **la goutte l'a repris,** he has, has had, another attack of gout; **la fièvre l'a repris, lui a repris,** he has (had) another bout of fever; **sa timidité l'a repris,** his shyness got the better of him again; he was overcome by shyness again; **r. ses esprits, ses sens,** to recover consciousness; to come to; **r. froid,** to catch cold again; *Ten:* **r. une volée,** to take a volley; *F:* **on ne m'y reprendra plus,** I shan't be had again, another time; **que je ne vous y reprenne plus!** don't let me catch you at it again; *(c)* to take back; **r. un cadeau,** to take back a gift; **r. un employé,** to take back, re-engage, an employee; **r. des invendus,** to take back unsold copies, etc.; **nous reprendrons les invendus,** you can take the goods on sale or return; **r. sa promesse, sa parole,** to take back, retract, one's promise to go back on one's word; *(d)* to resume, take up again (conversation, sittings, work, etc.); **r. une tâche,** to return to a task; **r. ses habitudes,** to resume one's habits; **r. les travaux,** to restart work; to resume operations; **il reprit tout le travail,** he went over, did, the whole work again; **reprenons les faits,** let us recapitulate (the facts); **r. un procédé,** to employ a method again; to go back to a method of working; **r. l'affaire à son origine,** to go back to the beginning (of the matter); **r. les faits de plus haut,** to go further back into the matter, to investigate the facts more thoroughly; **r. du goût pour qch.,** to recover one's taste for sth.; **r. une ancienne mine,** to rework an old mine; **r. la route,** to take (to) the road again; **r. le chemin de la maison,** to set out for home again; **r. la mer,** to put out to sea again; **r. le lit,** to take to one's bed again; *Th:* **r. une pièce,** to revive a play; **r. des forces,** to regain strength; **r. courage,** to take courage again; **r. le dessus,** to get the upper hand again; to recover a lost advantage; **r. le vent,** to get one's bearing(s); **r. la parole,** (i) to find one's speech, one's tongue, again; (ii) to resume, go on; *abs.* **oui, madame, reprit-il,** yes, madam, he replied; **il reprit après un instant,** he went on again after a moment; *(e)* **r. une maison de commerce,** to take over a business; *(f) A:* to repair, mend (wall, stocking, etc.); *still so used in* **r. un mur en sous-œuvre,** to underpin a wall; *(g)* to reprove, admonish; to find fault with (s.o., sth.); **r. qn de ses fautes,** to reprove, reprimand, s.o. for his faults; **il l'en avait reprise avec douceur,** he had remonstrated gently with her; **r. qn aigrement,** to take s.o. up sharply; **son affirmation était fausse et je le repris aussitôt,** his statement was false and I took him up at once; *(h) Nau:* **r. un palan,** to fleet a block. **2.** *v.i.* *(a)* to recommence, return, revive; **le froid a repris,** cold weather has set in again; **cette mode**

reprend, this fashion is coming in again; **le malade reprend,** the patient is recovering, is picking up again; **sa santé reprend,** his health is improving; **les affaires reprennent,** business is improving, is looking up; **si les hostilités reprenaient,** if hostilities should be resumed; *Aut:* (*of engine*) **r. (vivement),** to pick up (smartly); (*b*) (*of liquid*) to freeze, set, again; (*c*) (*of plant*) to take root again; to strike root, *abs.* to strike; (*of wound*) to heal up again.

se reprendre. **1.** to recover, to pull oneself together; **donnez-moi le temps de me r.,** give me time to collect myself, to collect my thoughts. **2.** to correct oneself (in speaking). **3.** *A:* **se r. à espérer, à pleurer,** to begin to hope, to cry, again; **il se reprit à espérer,** his hopes revived; **se r. à l'entreprise,** to tackle the job again; to go back to the job again; **se r. à ses occupations ordinaires,** to resume, to go back to, one's usual occupations; **se r. à la vie,** to take a new lease of life. **4. s'y r. à plusieurs fois (pour faire qch.),** to make several attempts (before succeeding in sth.); to have several goes at sth. (before succeeding); **il ne s'y reprend jamais à deux fois,** he never needs to have two shots at it.

représailles [rəpreza:j], *s.f.pl.* reprisals, retaliation; **en r. pour, de,** as a reprisal for; **user de r.,** to make reprisals; to retaliate (**envers,** on); **faire qch. par r.,** to do sth. by way of reprisal; **expédition de r.,** punitive, punitory, expedition; *Hist:* **lettres de r.,** letters of marque and reprisal.

représentable [rəprezɑ̃tabl̩], *a.* (*a*) representable; (*b*) *Th:* performable.

représentant, -ante [rəprezɑ̃tɑ̃, -ɑ̃:t]. **1.** *a.* representative (body, etc.). **2.** *s.* (*a*) representative (of the people, etc.); official; **notre r. (à la Chambre),** our member (of Parliament); *Dipl:* **r. du Saint-Siège,** representative of the Holy See; *F:* **r. de la loi,** policeman, arm of the law; (*b*) *Com:* (i) agent; (ii) representative, (commercial) traveller; **r. exclusif de . . .,** sole agent for . . .; **r. en dentelles,** traveller in lace; (*c*) *Jur:* representative (heir).

représentatif, -ive [rəprezɑ̃tatif, -i:v], *a.* representative.

représentation [rəprezɑ̃tasjɔ̃], *s.f.* **1.** (*a*) *Art: Pol: Jur: etc:* representation; *Pol:* **r. proportionnelle,** proportional representation; *Jur:* **venir par r. à une succession,** to inherit by right of representation; (*b*) *Com:* agency; **r. exclusive d'une maison,** sole agency for a firm; **avoir la r. exclusive de . . .,** to be sole agents for . . .; (*c*) *Psy:* **faculté de la r. spatiale,** space perception; (*d*) (*computers*) **r. analogique,** analogue representation; **r. discrète,** discrete representation. **2.** *Jur:* production, exhibition (of documents, etc.). **3.** *Th:* performance (of a play); **r. en matinée,** matinée; **r. à bénéfice,** charity performance; **r. extraordinaire,** benefit performance; **troupe en r.,** company on tour; **droit de r.,** right of performance; **droits de r.,** dramatic fees; **la pièce a eu deux cents représentations,** the play ran for, had a run of, two hundred nights. **4.** *Adm:* (official) state, display; dignity (of state official); **frais de r.,** entertainment allowance; *F:* **être toujours en r.,** to be always showing off. **5.** remonstrance, protest; **faire des représentations à qn,** to make representations to s.o., to remonstrate with s.o.

représentativement [rəprezɑ̃tativmɑ̃], *adv.* representatively.

représentativité [rəprezɑ̃tativite], *s.f.* representativeness; **r. d'un échantillon,** representativeness of a sample.

représenter [rəprezɑ̃te], *v.tr.* **1.** (*a*) to present (sth.) again; (*b*) to introduce (s.o.) again; to reintroduce (s.o.). **2.** *Jur:* to produce, exhibit (documents). **3.** to represent; to symbolize; (*a*) *Art:* to depict, portray; **tableau représentant un moulin,** picture representing a mill; picture of a mill; **plusieurs artistes ont représenté cet incident,** several artists have portrayed this incident; **M. Martin veut que je le représente en sénateur romain,** Mr Martin wants me to paint, portray, him as a Roman senator; *Th:* **la scène représente une rue,** the scene represents a street; **représentez-vous mon étonnement,** just imagine, picture, my astonishment; **je n'arrive pas à me r. . . .,** I can't visualize . . .; **qui est-ce que cela représente?** who is this supposed to be? **r. qn comme un imposteur,** to represent s.o. as an impostor; **r. sous forme de tableau,** to tabulate; (*b*) to recall (s.o., sth.) to mind; **il me représente son père,** he puts me in mind of his father; (*c*) *Com: Jur: Pol:* to represent, stand for, act for (s.o.); **se faire représenter,** to appoint, send, a representative, a deputy, a proxy; **inviter qn à se faire r.,** to invite s.o. to be represented; **r. une circonscription,** to sit for a constituency; **nous représentons la maison X et Cie,** we are agents for, we represent, Messrs. X & Co.; (*of lawyer*) **r. qn en justice,** to hold a brief for s.o., to appear for s.o.; (*d*) to correspond to, account for; **ceci représente 10% du budget,** this accounts for 10% of the budget; **la mise au point d'un ordinateur représente de nombreuses heures de travail,** many man-hours go into the developing of a computer. **4.** *Th:* (*a*) to perform, act, produce, give (a play); to put on (a play); (*b*) to act (part); to take the part of (Hamlet, etc.). **5. r. qch. à qn,** to represent, point out, sth. to s.o.; **je lui ai représenté qu'il y aurait avantage à . . .,** I represented, put it, to him that it would be advantageous to . . .; **6.** *abs.* (*a*) to have a good presence; **c'est un homme qui représente (bien),** he has a fine presence; **il ne représente pas bien,** he is not very impressive; he doesn't cut a very impressive figure; **il ne représente pas au physique,** he's not very impressive physically, *F:* he isn't much to look at; (*b*) to maintain the dignity of one's (official) position.

se représenter. **1.** (*a*) (*of pers.*) to introduce oneself again; to present oneself again (for an examination, etc.); to offer oneself again as a candidate; (*b*) to reappear; to turn up again; (*c*) (*of an occasion*) to occur again; to recur. **2. se r. comme acteur, comme officier,** to represent, describe, oneself as an actor, as an officer.

repressage [rəprɛsa:ʒ], *s.m. Cer:* re-pressing.

represser [rəprese], *v.tr. Cer:* to re-press.

répresseur [represœ:r], *s.m. Biol:* repressor.

répressible [represibl̩], *a.* repressible (offence, etc.).

répressif, -ive [represif, -i:v], *a.* repressive (law, etc.).

répression [represjɔ̃], *s.f.* repression; *Psy:* conscious repression.

reprêter [rəprete], *v.tr.* to lend (sth.) again.

réprimable [reprimabl̩], *a.* repressible; (offence) to be repressed.

réprimandable [reprimɑ̃dabl̩], *a.* deserving of reproof, of censure; blameworthy.

réprimande [reprimɑ̃:d], *s.f.* reprimand, rebuke, reproof; *F:* talking-to, telling off; **faire une r. à qn,** to reprimand s.o., *F:* to tell s.o. off; *Mil:* **r. prononcée par un conseil de discipline,** reprimand by a court martial.

réprimander [reprimɑ̃de], *v.tr.* to reprimand, rebuke, reprove; to take (s.o.) to task, *F:* to give (s.o.) a (good) talking to, to tell (s.o.) off; **être réprimandé par qn pour avoir fait qch.,** to be reprimanded by s.o. for having done sth., for doing sth.

réprimant [reprimɑ̃], *a.* repressing; repressive.

réprimer [reprime], *v.tr.* to repress; (*a*) to check, curb (desires, etc.); to strangle (sneeze); **r. sa colère,** to check, hold back, one's anger; (*b*) to quell, put down (revolt).

repris, -ise [rəpri, -i:z]. **1.** *a.* (*a*) retaken, recaptured; taken up again; (*b*) *Com:* **emballage non repris,** non-returnable packing. **2.** *s.* **r. de justice,** habitual criminal; old offender; former convict, *F:* man who has done time; old lag.

reprisage [rəpriza:ʒ], *s.m.* darning, mending (of stockings, etc.).

reprise [rəpri:z], *s.f.* **1.** (*a*) (i) retaking, recapture, recovery (of position, etc.); (ii) ship recaptured; (*b*) taking over (of fittings, etc., with house); **louer un appartement avec une r. de meubles,** to rent a flat and take over the furniture; (*c*) *Com:* **r. des invendus,** taking back of unsold goods; **marchandises en dépôt avec r. des invendus,** goods on sale or return; **r. d'une voiture,** trade-in (allowance) of a car; (*d*) *Jur:* **reprises,** claims (preliminary to a division of property); **droit de r.,** right to recover possession; **reprises matrimoniales,** division of assets (on liquidation of a *régime communautaire*); **r. des propres,** recovery of individual assets (by husband and wife). **2.** (*a*) resumption, renewal (of negotiations, etc.); **r. de travail,** return to work (after absence); **r. des travaux,** resumption of work, restarting work; **r. d'une pièce,** revival of a play; **r. d'un film,** rerun (of a film); *Mil:* **r. en main,** rally; regaining of control; (*b*) **r. d'activité,** renewal of activity; **r. du froid,** new spell of cold (weather); **r. de la fièvre,** fresh attack, bout, of fever; **r. des cours, du crédit international,** recovery of prices, of international credit; **r. des affaires,** recovery, revival, of business; **mouvement de r.,** upward movement; *Hort:* **r. (d'une bouture, etc.),** striking (root) (by a slip, etc.); (*c*) *I.C.E:* pick-up, acceleration (of engine); (*d*) *Elcs:* (*computers*) rerun, restart; **point de r.,** rerun, restart, point; checkpoint; **programme de r.,** rerun, rollback, routine; **temps de r.,** makeup time; (*e*) (*one of several stages*) *Box:* round; *Fenc:* bout; *Equit:* (i) part of riding lesson; (ii) riding squad; *Artil:* **r. du tir,** period of fire; **faire qch. par reprises,** to do sth. in successive stages; **à diverses reprises,** at different, various, times; on several (different) occasions; **à maintes reprises,** over and over again; **à deux reprises,** twice (over); **à trois reprises,** three times running; **faire qch. à plusieurs reprises,** to do sth. (i) several times, (ii) on several occasions; (*f*) *Mus:* (i) repeat; **points de r.,** double bars (in a piece of music); **chanson à reprises,** catch (song); (ii) re-entry (of subject in fugue). **3.** (*a*) *Needlew:* (i) darning, mending; (ii) darn; **point de r.,** darning stitch; **r. perdue,** fine-drawn mend; **faire une r. perdue à une déchirure, à un vêtement,** to fine-draw, invisibly mend, a tear, a garment; (*b*) *Const:* repairing (of a building); **r. en sous-œuvre,** underpinning (of a wall). **4.** *Bot:* stonecrop. **5.** (car, etc., taken in) part exchange, trade-in.

repriser [rəprize], *v.tr.* to mend, darn (stockings, etc.); **boule, œuf, à r.,** darning ball, egg, mushroom.

repriseuse [rəprizø:z], *s.f.* (*pers.*) mender, darner.

réprobateur, -trice [reprɔbatœ:r, -tris], *a.* reproachful; reproving, reprobatory; **regard r.,** look of reproach; reproachful, reproving, look.

réprobation [reprɔbasjɔ̃], *s.f.* reprobation; censure; (severe) disapproval.

reprochable [rəprɔʃabl̩], *a.* (*a*) reproachable; (*b*) *Jur:* **témoin r.,** witness to whom exception can be taken.

reproche [rəprɔʃ], *s.m.* **1.** reproach; **mériter des reproches,** to deserve blame, censure; **faire des reproches à qn,** to reproach, s.o. (**au sujet de,** about); **je ne vous fais pas de reproches,** I am not blaming you; **je ne lui ai pas fait le moindre r.,** I didn't reproach him in the slightest; **ton de r.,** reproachful, reproving, tone; **d'un ton de r.,** reproachfully, reprovingly; **s'attirer des reproches,** to incur reproaches; **homme, vie, sans r.,** blameless man, life; **sans r., je vous ferai observer que . . .,** without meaning to reproach you, I must point out that . . .; **qui n'est pas à l'abri du r.,** not beyond reproach. **2.** *Jur:* **r. de témoins,** impeachment of witnesses; **témoin sans r.,** unimpeachable, reliable, witness; **reproches,** exceptions taken (to witness).

reprocher [rəprɔʃe], *v.tr.* **1.** to reproach; **r. ses fautes à qn,** to reproach, taunt, s.o. with his faults; **il me reproche cela à tout moment,** he is always reproaching me for that, *F:* is always on at me for that; **on lui reproche la moindre peccadille,** he is taken to task for the merest trifle; **il nie les faits qu'on lui reproche,** he denies the actions for which he is blamed, of which he is accused; **r. qn d'avoir fait qch.,** to reproach, blame, s.o. for doing sth., for having done sth.; **je me reprocherai cela tout ma vie,** I shall blame, reproach, myself for it all my life; **je n'ai rien à me r.,** I have nothing to reproach myself with, blame myself for; **je n'ai, je ne trouve, rien à lui r.,** I have nothing to reproach him with; **qu'est-ce que vous reprochez à ce livre?** what do you find wrong with this book? **2. r. un plaisir, un succès, à qn,** to grudge s.o. a pleasure, a success; **r. les morceaux à qn,** to (be)grudge s.o. every bite he eats, the bread he eats. **3.** *Jur:* **r. un témoin, un témoignage,** to take exception to a witness, to evidence.

reproducteur, -trice [rəprɔdyktœ:r, -tris]. **1.** *a.* reproductive (organ, etc.); reproducing. **2.** *s.m.* **(animal) r.,** animal kept for breeding purposes, breeder; **r. d'élite,** pedigree sire. **3.** *s.m.* (*a*) *Elcs: Rec:* reproducer; **r. de bande,** tape reproducer; (*b*) *El:* **r. de charge,** replenisher. **4.** *s.f. Elcs:* (*computers*) **reproductrice (de cartes),** (card) reproducer, reproducing punch.

reproductibilité [rəprɔdyktibilite], *s.f.* reproducibility.

reproductible [rəprɔdyktibl̩], *a.* reproducible.

reproductif, -ive [rəprɔdyktif, -i:v], *a.* reproductive.

reproduction [rəprɔdyksjɔ̃], *s.f.* **1.** (*a*) reproduction; **les organes de la r.,** the reproductive organs; **animaux élevés en vue de la r.,** breeding stock; *Biol:* **r. sexuée, asexuée,** sexual, asexual, reproduction; **taux brut, net, de r.,** crude, net, reproduction rate; (*b*) reproduction, reproducing; duplicating (of documents, etc.); *Publ:* **tous droits de r. et de traduction réservés pour tous pays,** (all) reproduction and translation rights reserved for all countries; *Journ:* **droits de r. en feuilleton,** serial rights; (*c*) (*computers*) **r. de constantes,** gang punch; **code de r.,** reproduction code. **2.** copy, reproduction.

reproductivité [rəprɔdyktivite], *s.f.* reproductiveness.

reproduire [rəprɔdɥiːr], *v.tr.* (*conj. like* PRODUIRE) (*a*) to reproduce; **r. les mêmes arguments,** to reproduce, bring up again, the same arguments; **l'art qui veut r. la nature,** art which attempts to reproduce nature; **l'écho reproduit les sons,** an echo reproduces sounds; **l'orthographe ne reproduit pas exactement la langue parlée,** spelling does not give an exact image of the spoken language; **r. les gestes d'un comédien,** to reproduce, give a faithful imitation of, the gestures of an actor; (*b*) to reproduce, duplicate, copy (document, etc.); **tableau reproduit à des milliers d'exemplaires,** a picture of which thousands of reproductions have been made; **modèle reproduit en grande série,** model that has been mass produced; (*c*) *Publ: etc:* to reprint, republish (article, etc.); *abs. Journ:* **les journaux australiens sont priés de r.,** Australian (news)-papers please copy.

se reproduire. 1. (*a*) (*of events, etc.*) to recur, to happen again; (*b*) (*of pers.*) to appear again (after absence). 2. to reproduce, breed, multiply.

reprogrammation [rəprɔgramasjɔ̃], *s.f.* reprogramming (of computer).

reprogrammer [rəprɔgrame], *v.tr.* to reprogram(me) (computer).

reprographie [rəprɔgrafi], *s.f. Com: etc:* reproduction, duplicating (of documents).

reprographique [rəprɔgrafik], *a.* reprographic.

réprouvable [repruvabl̩], *a.* reprovable, blamable; that deserves blame.

réprouvé, -ée [repruve]. 1. *s.* outcast (of society); reprobate. 2. *a. Theol:* condemned (by God's decree); damned.

reprouver [rəpruve], *v.tr.* to prove (sth.) again.

réprouver [repruve], *v.tr.* 1. to condemn (crime); to reject (doctrine); to disapprove of (s.o., sth.). 2. *Theol:* (*of God*) to reprobate, damn.

reps [rɛps], *s.m. Tex:* rep(s), repp; **r. de laine,** woollen rep.

reptation [rɛptasjɔ̃], *s.f.* (*a*) *Z:* reptation; creeping; (*b*) *Geol:* creep.

reptatoire [rɛptatwaːr], *a. Z: etc:* reptatory, reptant; creeping.

reptile [rɛptil]. 1. *a. Z:* reptile, reptant; creeping; *Lit:* **âmes reptiles,** grovelling souls. 2. *s.m.* reptile.

reptilien, -ienne [rɛptiljɛ̃, -jɛn], *a. Z:* reptilian.

repu [rəpy], *a.* satiated, full; **lion r.,** sated lion; **je suis r. du théâtre,** I have had my fill of the theatre; *A:* **r. de fatigue,** dog-tired.

républicain, -aine [repyblikɛ̃, -ɛn]. 1. *a. & s.* republican. 2. *s.m. Orn:* sociable weaver bird, republican grosbeak.

républicaniser [repyblikanize], *v.tr.* to republicanize.

républicanisme [repyblikanism], *s.m.* republicanism.

republier [rəpyblije], *v.tr.* (*conj. like* PUBLIER) to republish.

république [repyblik], *s.f.* (*a*) republic; **la R. française,** the French Republic; *F:* **je m'en fiche de la R.,** I don't give a damn, care two hoots, for anyone; (*b*) commonwealth, community; **la r. des lettres,** the republic of letters, the world of letters.

répudiable [repydjabl̩], *a.* repudiable.

répudiation [repydjasjɔ̃], *s.f.* 1. repudiation (of wife, contract, debt, etc.). 2. *Jur:* renunciation (of succession); relinquishment.

répudiatoire [repydjatwaːr], *a.* repudiatory.

répudier [repydje], *v.tr.* (*p.d. & pr.sub.* **n. répudiions, v. répudiiez**) 1. to repudiate (wife, opinion, etc.). 2. *Jur:* to renounce, relinquish (succession).

repue [rəpy], *s.f. A:* 1. feeding. 2. meal, repast; **r. franche,** free meal.

répugnance [repyɲɑ̃ːs], *s.f.* 1. repugnance; (*a*) dislike (**pour, à,** to, of, for); aversion (**pour, à,** to, from, for); (*b*) loathing (**pour, à,** of, for); **éprouver de la r. pour qn, qch.,** to hate, loathe, feel an aversion for, s.o., sth. 2. **r. à faire qch.,** reluctance to do sth.; **quelque r. qu'il eût à écrire,** however reluctant, loath, he was to write; however repugnant writing was to him; **faire qch. avec r.,** to do sth. reluctantly, unwillingly. 3. *A:* contradiction.

répugnant [repyɲɑ̃], *a.* 1. repugnant, loathsome, offensive (**à,** to); disgusting. 2. *A:* **r. à qch.,** contrary, contradictory, to (reason, etc.).

répugner [repyɲe], *v.i.* 1. (*of pers.*) **r. à qch.,** to feel repugnance to, to revolt at, sth.; **r. à,** *occ.* **de, faire qch.,** to feel repugnance to doing sth.; to feel reluctant, lo(a)th, to do sth.; **la raison y répugne,** reason revolts at it. 2. (*a*) (*of thg, pers.*) **r. à qn,** to be repugnant, distasteful, to s.o.; **ces créatures me répugnent,** I loathe these creatures; (*b*) *impers.* **il me répugne de le faire,** it is repugnant to me, it goes against me, I am reluctant, to do it; I shrink from doing it; I am lo(a)th to do it; I loathe doing it; **il ne me répugnerait pas de l'épouser,** I should not be averse to marrying him, her; I wouldn't mind marrying him, her. 3. *A:* **cela répugne à la raison,** it is contrary to reason.

répulsif, -ive [repylsif, -iːv], *a.* repulsive, repellent (force, manners, etc.).

répulsion [repylsjɔ̃], *s.f.* repulsion; (*a*) *Ph:* **r. mutuelle des corps électrisés,** mutual repulsion of electrified bodies; (*b*) **éprouver de la r. pour qn,** to feel repulsion, an aversion, for s.o.; to be repelled by s.o.; **inspirer de la r. à qn,** to repel s.o.

réputation [repytasjɔ̃], *s.f.* reputation, repute; good or bad name; character; **jouir d'une bonne r.,** to have a good reputation; **les vins de Bourgogne sont en r.,** burgundies are held in high repute, are highly esteemed, have a good reputation; **cela a fait sa r.,** it made his name, his reputation; **avoir la r. d'être riche,** to have the reputation of being wealthy; **sa r. de chirurgien,** his reputation as a surgeon; **se faire une r.,** to make a name for oneself; to achieve a reputation (**de, as**); **il s'était fait une r. d'oracle du temps,** he had made a name, had become famous, as a weather prophet; **avoir la r. de médecin habile,** to have the reputation of being a skilful doctor; **avoir une r. de courage et d'adresse,** to have a reputation for courage and skill; **connaître qn de r.,** to know s.o. by reputation, by repute; **il a (une) bonne r.,** he has a good name; he is well spoken of; **il a (une) mauvaise r.,** he has a bad reputation, a bad character; **maison de mauvaise r.,** house in ill repute; disreputable house; **perdre qn de r., ruiner la r. de qn,** to ruin s.o.'s reputation, s.o.'s character; **se perdre de r., perdre sa r.,** to forfeit one's good name, to lose one's character; **cette marque a perdu sa r.,** this brand has fallen into discredit, into disrepute.

réputé [repyte], *a.* well-known, famous (expert, etc.); (doctor) with a high reputation; **vin r.,** highly considered wine; **un des restaurants les plus réputés de la ville,** one of the most famous, the best-known, restaurants in the town; **r. pour qch.,** well known for sth.

réputer [repyte], *v.tr. A:* to consider, think; **on les réputait riches, amis,** they were thought, considered, to be rich, to be friends; **r. qn médecin habile,** to consider s.o. a skilful doctor; **se r. heureux,** to consider, think, oneself lucky; *now used esp. in the passive:* **il est réputé ne rien ignorer de cette science,** he is reputed to know everything about this science; **être réputé innocent,** to be considered innocent; **l'intention est réputée pour le fait,** we take the will for the deed; **Chicago était réputée une ville de gangsters,** Chicago had the reputation of being a city of gangsters.

requérable [rəkerabl̩], *a. Jur:* demandable; liable to be requisitioned.

requérant, -ante [rəkerɑ̃, -ɑ̃ːt], *Jur:* 1. *a.* **partie requérante,** applicant, claimant. 2. *s.* plaintiff, petitioner, applicant. 3. *s.m. Ven:* (*of gun dog, etc.*) good finder.

requérir [rəkeriːr], *v.tr.* (*conj. like* ACQUÉRIR). 1. *A:* **venir, aller, r. qn, qch.,** to come, go, for s.o., sth.; **je viens vous r. d'un bon office,** I have come to ask you to do me a service; **on me requit de l'aller trouver,** I was asked to go to him; (*b*) to ask for (sth.); **r. une grâce,** to solicit a favour; **r. la présence de qn,** to ask, request, s.o. to attend. 2. (*a*) to demand, claim; **r. aide et assistance,** to demand assistance; **r. qn,** to call upon s.o. to give assistance; **r. la force armée,** to requisition troops (in aid of the civil power); **opération qui requiert des mains habiles,** operation that calls for skilled hands; **la cour requiert que vous comparaissiez,** the court requires you to attend; (*b*) **r. qn de faire qch.,** to call upon, summon, s.o. to do sth.; to require s.o. to do sth.; (*c*) to requisition. 3. *v.i. Jur:* **le Procureur de la République requiert contre X,** the Public Prosecutor demands a penalty against X.

requête [rəkɛt], *s.f.* 1. request, suit, petition; **je viens à la r. de . . .,** I have come at the request of . . .; **adresser une r. à qn,** to petition s.o.; *Jur:* **r. civile,** extraordinary procedure against a judgment (in case of gross miscarriage of justice); **Maître des Requêtes au Conseil d'État,** rapporteur of the Council of State; **à la r. de . . .,** at the suit of . . . . 2. *Ven:* new search.

requiem [rekɥi(j)ɛm], *s.m. Ecc:* prayer for the dead; **messe de r.,** requiem mass; requiem.

requienia [rekjenja], *s.m. Paleont: Moll:* Requienia.

requimpette [rəkɛ̃pɛt], *s.f. P:* (short) jacket.

requin [rəkɛ̃], *s.m.* 1. *Ich:* shark; **r. marsouin,** mackerel shark; porbeagle; **r. bleu,** requin, blue shark; **r. blanc, r. carcharadonte,** white shark, *F:* man-eating shark; **r. bouclé,** bramble shark; **r. de sable,** sand shark; **r.(-)tigre,** tiger shark; **r. zébré, r.(-)tapis,** carpet shark; **peau de r.,** shagreen. 2. *F:* shark, swindler.

requin-baleine [rəkɛ̃balɛn], *s.m. Ich:* whale shark; *pl. requins-baleines.*

requin-marteau [rəkɛ̃marto], *s.m. Ich:* hammerhead (shark); *pl. requins-marteaux.*

requin-pèlerin [rəkɛ̃pɛlrɛ̃], *s.m. Ich:* basking shark; *pl. requins-pèlerins.*

requinquant [rəkɛ̃kɑ̃], *a. F:* that puts you to rights, bucks you up.

requinquer [rəkɛ̃ke], *v.tr. F:* (*a*) to repair; to put (sth.) to rights; (*b*) to smarten (s.o.) up.

se requinquer. *F:* 1. to smarten, spruce, oneself up; to renew one's wardrobe, to get a new rig-out. 2. to recover, pick up, perk up (after illness).

requis [rəki]. 1. *a.* required, requisite, necessary; **les qualités requises pour ce poste,** the qualities required, the requisite qualities, for this post; **avec tout le soin r.,** with all due care. 2. *s.m.* (*a*) labour conscript (1939-1945 war); (*b*) (*in wartime, etc.*) conscript allocated for civilian duties, for a public service.

réquisition [rekizisjɔ̃], *s.f.* 1. (*a*) requisitioning; commandeering; *Adm:* **r. civile,** conscription for a public service; (*b*) requisition, levy; **mettre en r.,** to requisition, to levy; to put into requisition; **cheval de r.,** horse registered for requisition; **imposer des réquisitions à un village,** to levy requisitions on a village; (*c*) requisition, demand; **agir sur, à, la r. de qn,** to act on s.o.'s requisition. 2. *pl. Jur:* address of the Public Prosecutor to the Court.

réquisitionnaire [rekizisjɔnɛːr], *s.m. Mil.Hist:* man called up (by a decree of the *Convention*).

requisitionné [rekizisjɔne], *s.m. Adm:* person conscripted for a public service.

réquisitionnement [rekizisjɔnmɑ̃], *s.m.* requisitioning; commandeering.

réquisitionner [rekizisjɔne], *v.tr.* to requisition; to commandeer (provisions, etc.); *A:* to impress (men of military age).

réquisitoire [rekizitwaːr], *s.m. Jur:* (Public Prosecutor's) charge, indictment.

réquisitorial, -aux [rekizitɔrjal, -o], *a. Jur:* **plaidoyer r.,** Public Prosecutor's charge, indictment.

résazurine [rezazyrin], *s.f. Ch:* resazurin.

rescapé, -ée [rɛskape], *a. & s.* (person) rescued; survivor (of disaster, shipwreck, etc.).

rescellement [rəsɛlmɑ̃], *s.m.* resealing.

resceller [rəsele], *v.tr.* to reseal; to seal (up) again.

rescié [rəsje], *a.* **bois r.,** resawn timber.

rescindable [resɛ̃dabl̩], *a.* rescissible, rescindable.

rescindant [resɛ̃dɑ̃], *Jur:* 1. *a.* rescissory. 2. *s.m.* application to rescind (contract, etc.).

rescindement [resɛ̃dmɑ̃], *s.m.* rescindment, rescinding.

rescinder [resɛ̃de], *v.tr. Jur:* to rescind, annul, cancel; to avoid (contract).

rescision [resizjɔ̃], *s.f. Jur:* rescission, annulment; avoiding (of contract, owing to mistake or misrepresentation).

rescisible [resizibl̩], *a.* rescissible.

rescisoire [resizwaːr], *Jur:* 1. *a.* rescissory (action, etc.). 2. *s.m.* rescissory action.

rescousse [rɛskus], *s.f. A:* rescue; *still used in* **aller, venir, à la r. de qn,** to go, come, to the rescue of s.o.

rescrit [rɛskri], *s.m. Ecc: etc:* rescript.

resculpturage [rəskyltyraːʒ], *s.m. Aut: Adm:* retreading (of tyre).

réseau, -eaux [rezo], *s.m.* 1. (*a*) *A:* net; (spider's) web; (*b*) netting, network (for lace, etc.); réseau; (*c*) *Cost: O:* hairnet; (*d*) *Arch:* tracery; (*e*) *Anat:* plexus (of nerves, etc.); *Biol:* **r. nucléaire,** nuclear meshwork; (*f*) *Opt:* diffraction grating; *Astr:* réseau (of small squares); (*g*) *Phot:* (*in colour photography*) **plaque à r. mosaïque polychrome,** screen plate; (*h*) *Atom. Ph:* lattice (of reactor); **r. cristallin,** crystal lattice; **r. en graphite et uranium,** graphite-uranium lattice; **r. modérateur,** moderator lattice. 2. (*a*) *Trans:* network, system (of roads, railways, etc.); **r. fluvial,** river system; **r. de canalisations, de conduites, pour transporter du combustible liquide,** system of pipelines, of pipes, for conveying liquid fuel; r. aérien, air-line network, system; (b) r. électrique, electric system, network; r. (électrique) national, national grid system; r. de distribution, distribution network; r. de distribution urbain, town mains; r. d'éclairage, lighting system; r. d'énergie, power-supply system; r. d'équilibrage, balancing network; r. haute tension, high-tension network; r. dipole, quadripole, two-terminal, four-terminal, network; r. diphasé, two-phase, quarter-phase, network; r. triphasé, three-phase network; *Av:* r. de bord, aircraft mains; (c) (*for gas, etc.*) r. collecteur, gathering system; r. d'alimentation, feeder system; (d) r. télégraphique, téléphonique, telegraph, telephone, system; r. télégraphique, téléphonique, filaire, telegraph wire, telephone wire, system; r. aérien de fils télégraphiques, téléphoniques, overhead system of telegraph wires, of telephone wires; *Tp:* r. automatique, automatic, dial (telephone), system; r. téléphonique privé, house-exchange system; r. d'abonné, individual trunk; r. urbain, local area, local network; r. interurbain, trunk circuit; r. régional, inter-office trunk; le r. de Paris, de Londres, the Paris, London, area; (e) *Elcs:* r. d'antenne, aerial array; *U.S:* antenna array; r. de guide d'ondes, wave-guide array; *W.Tel:* station hors r., off-net station; (*of computer*) r. analogique, analog(ue) network; r. d'étude analogique, network analog(ue) (device); simulateur (d'étude) de réseaux, network analyser; station de coordination de r., net control station; (f) r. d'espionnage, spy ring, network; (*World War II*) r. de résistance, resistance network; (g) *Mil:* réseaux de fil de fer, barbed wire entanglements; r. dangereux, electrified wire entanglement.

résécable [resekabl̩], *a. Surg:* resectable.

résecteur [resɛktœːr], *s.m. Surg:* resectoscope.

résection [resɛksjɔ̃], *s.f. Surg:* resection.

réséda [rezeda], *s.m.* (a) *Bot:* reseda; r. gaude, r. des teinturiers, yellow weed, dyer's weed; (b) *Hort:* r. odorant, mignonette.

résédacées [rezedase], *s.f.pl. Bot:* Resedaceae, the mignonette family.

resemer [rəsəme], *v.tr.* to sow again, to resow.

reséquent [rəsekɑ̃], *a. Geol:* resequent (river, valley); resequent, re-consequent (drainage).

réséquer [reseke], *v.tr.* (je résèque, n. réséquons; je réséquerai) *Surg:* to resect.

réserpine [rezɛrpin], *s.f. Pharm:* reserpine.

réservat [rezɛrva], *s.m. Ecc:* (papal) reservation (of a benefice).

réservataire [rezɛrvatɛːr], *a. Jur:* héritier r., heir who cannot be totally disinherited.

réservation [rezɛrvasjɔ̃], *s.f.* (a) reservation, reserving; r. faite de tous mes droits, without prejudice to my rights; (b) (hotel, plane, rail, etc.) reservation.

réserve [rezɛrv], *s.f.* 1. *A:* reserving, reservation; *Rail: etc:* r. de places, reservation, booking, of seats. 2. (a) reserve, reservation; *Jur:* protest in writing; faire des réserves, to make reserves, reservations; apporter une r. à un contrat, to enter a reservation in respect of an agreement; à la réserve de . . ., except for . . ., with the reservation of . . .; à la réserve que + *ind.*, except that . . .; sous (la) r. de qch., subject to, contingent on, sth.; *Jur:* sous r., without prejudice; sous ces réserves, with these reserves; sous r. que . . ., provided that . . .; sous toutes réserves, without committing oneself; publier une nouvelle sous toutes réserves, to publish a piece of news without vouching for its accuracy; ces prix sont sous r. d'une remise de 5%, these prices are subject to a discount of 5%; sans r., without reservation, unreservedly; éloges sans r., unqualified praise; se rallier sans r. à une décision, to give one's unqualified, unhesitating, approval to a decision; non sans réserves, avec quelques réserves, not without reservation, with some reservation; *Com:* reçu sans r., clean receipt; (b) reserve, guardedness, caution (in speech, conduct, etc.); se tenir, demeurer, sur la r., to refuse to commit oneself; être sur la r., to be on one's guard; observer une sage, une prudente, r., to maintain a wise reserve; to be very non-committal (in answering); quand il sort de sa r., when he breaks through his reserve. 3. (a) reserve (of provisions, water, energy, etc.); *pl.* reserves (of ore, petroleum, etc.); *Min:* réserves prouvées, known reserves; le paysan a toujours des réserves, the countryman has always something put by; *Mch: etc:* r. de puissance, d'énergie, reserve power, reserve energy; *Ph: N.Arch:* r. de flottabilité, reserve buoyancy; (b) *Mil: etc:* reserve (of men, ammunition, equipment); r. de l'armée active, reserve of the regular army; officier de r., reserve officer; bataillon d'élèves officiers de r., reserve officers' training battalion; lieutenant, capitaine, de r., lieutenant, captain, of the reserve (army); r. générale, general reserve; r. stratégique, strategic reserve; r. mobile, mobile reserve; r. mobile d'approvisionnements, mobile supply reserve; en r. d'unité, in local reserve; (c) *Fin:* réserves bancaires, bank reserves; r. de prévoyance, contingency reserve; r. latente, occulte, hidden, secret, reserve; r. visible, visible reserve; r. liquide, liquid assets; r. légale, legal reserve; r. statutaire, statutory reserve, reserve provided by the articles; r. pour créances douteuses, bad debts reserve; affecter une somme à la r. de prévoyance, to allocate, appropriate, a sum to the contingency reserve; puiser dans les réserves, to draw on the reserves; (d) *Jur:* r. légale, legal share; portion (of inheritance) that must devolve upon the heirs; (e) en r., in reserve; *attrib.* de r., reserve, standby; mettre qch. en r., to reserve sth.; to put sth. by; mettre de l'argent en r. (pour l'avenir), to put money by; mettre un navire en r., to put a ship out of commission; to put a ship in reserve (with maintenance party); tenir qch. en r., to keep sth. in reserve, in store; *Fin:* fonds de r., reserve fund; (*computers*) bloc de r., standby block; matériel en r., standby equipment; registre de r., standby register; mettre en r., to preserve, to dump; *Mil:* vivres de r., reserve, emergency, rations; iron rations; *Mec.E:* pièces de r., spare parts; machine de r., standby engine, spare engine, reserve engine; *Nau:* soute de r., spare bunker; (f) *Ecc:* la sainte Réserve, the Reservation (of the Sacrament). 4. (a) *For: Ven:* preserve; reserve; r. naturelle, nature reserve; r. zoologique, wild life sanctuary; (*in U.S:*) réserves (indiennes), (Indian) reservation; (b) *Com. etc:* store; (*in library, museum, etc.*) storeroom, reserve. 5. *Engr: Dy: etc:* resist; r. contre l'action de l'acide, acid resist; r. colloïdale, colloid resist; encre de r., developing ink; couverture bleue avec titre en r. blanche, blue cover with title left in white.

réservé [rezɛrve], *a.* reserved; (a) guarded, cautious (person, conduct, etc.); (b) shy; être r. avec qn, to be reserved with s.o.; (c) stand-offish; ne faites pas le r., don't be so stand-offish; ne faites pas la réservée, don't pretend to be shy; (d) (*computers*) mot r., reserved word; zone réservée, reserved area; (e) quartier r., red-lamp district.

réserver [rezɛrve], *v.tr.* (a) to reserve; to set (sth.) aside; to put, lay, (sth.) by; to save (sth.) up; to keep (sth.) back; to keep (sth.) in store; r. une place à qn, to reserve a seat for s.o.; place réservée, reserved seat; r. une danse à qn, to save a dance for s.o.; r. du bois pour l'hiver, to store wood for the winter; je lui réserve un accueil cordial, I shall give him a hearty welcome; se r. un droit, to reserve oneself a right; tous droits réservés, all rights reserved; se r. le droit de faire qch., to reserve the right to do sth.; ce que l'avenir nous réserve, what the future holds in store for us; les déceptions qui nous sont réservées, the disappointments lying in store for us; r. qch. à demain, to keep sth. for tomorrow; je me réserve, I shall wait and see; I'll bide my time; *impers.* il lui était réservé de réussir, success was in store for him; he was destined to succeed; *Ecc:* cas réservé, reserved sin; *Jur:* biens réservés de la femme mariée, married woman's separate estate; *P.N:* pêche réservée, private fishing; *For:* r. un arbre, to leave a tree standing; (b) to set apart, put aside, earmark (money for a purpose); je vais r. demain matin pour terminer ce travail, I am going to keep tomorrow morning free for finishing this work.

reservir [rəsɛrviːr], *v.* (*conj. like* SERVIR) 1. *v.i.* to serve again (in the army). 2. = RESSERVIR.

réserviste [rezɛrvist], *s.m. Mil:* reservist.

réservoir [rezɛrvwaːr], *s.m.* 1. (a) *Hyd.E:* reservoir; r. de barrage, storage basin; r. de compensation, de purge, surge tank; (b) fish pond, fish tank. 2. (a) *Ind:* tank, holder, container; r. compartimenté, segmental tank; r. à eau, water tank, (water) reservoir; r. d'eau chaude, hot-water tank; r. d'alimentation, supply tank; *Mch:* feed tank; r. d'alimentation en eau, water-feed tank; r. à gaz, gas holder, gasometer; *Gasm:* r. amortisseur, surge tank; r. flexible géant, banana bag; r. à grains, grain feeder (on docks, etc.); r. à minerai, ore bin, ore bunker; r. de stockage, d'emmagasinage, storage tank; r. à pétrole, à mazout, petroleum, fuel-oil, tank; r. de fonctionnement, working tank; r. de vide-vite, blow-down tank; parc de réservoirs, tank farm, tank park; prix de cession en r., tank cession price; (b) r. de thermomètre, thermometer bulb; (c) *Mec.E:* tank, reservoir, drum; cistern, well (of pump); r. à graisse, grease box; r. à huile, oil reservoir, tank; r. d'air (comprimé), air reservoir, air drum (of locomotive, railway carriage, etc.); air receiver (of air compressor); air chamber (of torpedo); r. d'eau, flume, forebay (of turbine); water space (of boiler); *Mch:* r. d'alimentation, hot well (of condenser); r. de vapeur, steam drum; steam space (of boiler); r. d'expansion, expansion tank; (d) *I.C.E:* r. de carburant, de combustible, fuel tank; r. d'essence, petrol tank, *U.S:* gas tank; r. (de carburant) en charge, gravity(-feed) (fuel) tank; r. (de carburant) sous pression, force-feed (fuel) tank; r. à liquide pour freins, brake-fluid reservoir; orifice de remplissage du r., tank filler neck; bouchon de r., tank cap; *Av:* r. d'aile, wing tank; r. de bout d'aile, tip tank; r. incorporé, r. de structure, r. structural, built-in tank, integral tank; r. d'aile incorporé, r. structural de voilure, wing-integral (fuel) tank; r. de fuselage, fuselage tank; r. ventral, belly tank, ventral tank; r, d'assiette, d'équilibrage, trim tank; r. de transfert, transfer tank; r. auto-étanche, self-sealing tank; r. largable, droppable, detachable, tank; jettison(able) tank; drop tank, slip tank; (e) *Elcs:* (*computers*) r. à mercure, mercury tank.

réservoir-nourrice [rezɛrvwarnuris], *s.m. I.C.E:* feed tank; *pl. réservoirs-nourrices.*

résidant, -ante [rezidɑ̃, -ɑ̃ːt]. 1. *a.* resident, residing; *Ecc:* residentiary (canon). 2. *s.* resident.

résidence [rezidɑ̃ːs], *s.f.* 1. (a) residence; residing; fonctionnaire pour qui la r. est obligatoire, tenu à la r., official of whom residence is required; lieu de r., place of residence; en r. surveillée, under house arrest; (b) residence; home; r. secondaire, secondary residence (in the country), cottage in the country, weekend cottage; changer de r., to change one's residence; to move; (c) *Adm:* r. (administrative), (administrative) headquarters; residency (in a protectorate, etc.). 2. *Adm:* residentship, inhabitancy.

résident, -ente [rezidɑ̃, -ɑ̃ːt]. 1. (a) *a. & s. Dipl:* resident; ministre r., minister resident; la résidente, the resident's wife; (b) *s.m. Hist:* R. général en Tunisie, Resident General in Tunisia. 2. *s. Adm:* (*alien living in a country*) resident.

résidentiel, -elle [rezidɑ̃sjɛl], *a.* residential; quartier r., residential district.

résider [rezide], *v.i.* 1. (a) to reside, live (à, dans, at, in); (b) *abs.* les chanoines ne résidaient pas, the canons were non-resident. 2. toute la difficulté réside en ceci, all the difficulty rests, lies, consists, in this; la souveraineté réside dans le peuple, sovereign power resides in the people; la force du style réside dans les images, strength of style lies in similes.

résidu [rezidy], *s.m.* 1. *Ch: Ind: etc:* residue, residuum; *Artil: etc:* r. de la poudre, fouling; résidus urbains, town refuse; r. de carrière, quarry spalls; *Petroleum Ind:* résidus de distillation, tower bottoms, still residue; r. de goudron, dry run tar; *Atom.Ph:* résidus de fission, radioactive waste. 2. (a) *Mth:* residue (of a function); *Ar: A:* (= RESTE) remainder; (b) *Com: A:* (= RELIQUAT) r. de compte, amount still owing; balance; (c) *Fin:* fraction (of stock, share).

résiduaire [rezidɥɛːr], *a.* waste; *Ind:* eaux résiduaires, waste water, process water.

résiduel, -elle [rezidɥɛl], *a.* residual; *Physiol:* air r., supplemental air (in the lungs); *El:* électricité résiduelle, electric residuum; charge résiduelle, residual charge; *Elcs:* bande résiduelle, vestigial sideband; transmission avec bande latérale résiduelle, vestigial-sideband transmission; erreur résiduelle, residual error; *Geol:* argile résiduelle, residual clay.

résignant, -ante [reziɲɑ̃, -ɑ̃ːt], *s.* resigner (of living, of office).

résignataire [reziɲatɛːr], *s.m.* resignatary, resignee, one in whose favour a resignation is made.

résignateur [reziɲatœːr], *s.m.* resigner (of office).

résignation [reziɲasjɔ̃], *s.f.* resignation. 1. handing over, giving up (of a living, etc.). 2. submissiveness (to God), meekness of spirit; resignedness; avec r., resignedly.

résigné, -ée [reziɲe], *a. & s.* resigned (à, to); meek, submissive, uncomplaining; d'un air r., resignedly.

resigner [rəsiɲe], *v.tr.* to sign (sth.) again; to re-sign (sth.).

résigner [reziɲe], v.tr. to resign (a possession, etc.); to give (sth.) up (à, to); r. son âme à Dieu, to commit one's soul to God; r. un bénéfice, to resign a living; r. sa charge, ses fonctions, to give up, relinquish, one's appointment; to resign; r. le pouvoir, to lay down office; (of monarch) to abdicate.

se résigner (à qch., à supporter qch.), to resign oneself, to submit (to sth., to enduring sth.); se r. à ce que qch. se fasse, to resign oneself to sth. being done.

résiliable [reziljabl̩], a. that may be annulled, cancelled.

résiliation [reziljasjɔ̃], s.f. Com: Jur: cancelling, cancellation, annulling, annulment, termination, avoidance (of contract, etc.).

résiliement, résilîment [rezilimɑ̃], s.m. = RÉSILIATION.

résilience [reziljɑ̃:s], s.f. Mec: resilience, impact strength; essai de r., impact test.

résilient [reziljɑ̃], a. resilient.

résilier [rezilje], v.tr. to annul, cancel, terminate; Jur: avoid (agreement, etc.).

résille [rezi:j], s.f. 1. hairnet. 2. cames, lattice (of stained-glass window).

résinage [rezina:ʒ], s.m. For: resin tapping.

résinate [rezinat], s.m. Com: resinate.

résine [rezin], s.f. resin; r. vierge, crude turpentine; r. acrylique, acrylic plastic; r. polyvinylique, polyvinyl resin; r. végétale, natural resin; r. thermodurcissable, thermo-setting resin; r. photosensible, photosensitive resin.

résiné [rezine], a. & s.m. (vin) r., retsina, wine containing resin.

résiner [rezine], v.tr. 1. to resin; to dip (firewood, etc.) in resin. 2. to tap (trees) for resin.

résinerie [rezinri], s.f. 1. resin industry. 2. resin factory.

résineux, -euse [rezinø, -ø:z]. 1. a. resinous, resinaceous; forêt résineuse, coniferous forest. 2. s.m.pl. les r., conifers.

résinier, -ière [rezinje, -jɛ:r]. 1. a. resin (industry, etc.). 2. s.m. (a) For: resin tapper; (b) worker in a resin factory

résinifère, [rezinifɛ:r], a. resiniferous, resin-producing (tree); Arb: canal r., resin duct, canal.

résinifiable [rezinifjabl̩], a. resinifiable.

résinification [rezinifikasjɔ̃], s.f. resinification.

résinifier [rezinifje], v.tr. to resinify.

résiniforme [rezinifɔrm], a. resiniform.

résinique [rezinik], a. Ch: resinic; acide r., resin, resinic, acid.

résinite [rezinit], s.m. Miner: resinite, wax opal.

résinocyste [rezinɔsist], s.m. Bot: resin canal, duct.

résinoïde [rezinɔid], a. & s.m. resinoid.

résipiscence [resipisɑ̃:s], s.f. Lit: resipiscence; venir à r., to show repentance, to return to a better frame of mind; recevoir qn à r., to forgive and forget.

résistance [rezistɑ̃:s], s.f. 1. (a) resistance, opposition (à, to); r. passive, passive resistance; r. acharnée, désespérée, desperate resistance; r. à outrance, all-out resistance; r. fanatique, farouche, fanatical, wild, resistance; r. obstinée, opiniâtre, stubborn resistance; r. passive, passive resistance; r. sporadique, sporadic resistance; n'offrir, n'opposer, aucune r., to offer, make, no opposition, no resistance; offrir, opposer, une faible, une forte, r., to offer, make, a weak, a strong, resistance; to offer light, strong, opposition; opposer une vive r. à l'avance ennemie, to offer strong opposition to the advance of the enemy; ne rencontrer aucune r., to meet with no resistance, no opposition; rencontrer une faible, vive, r., to meet with a weak, a strong, resistance; to meet with light, strong, opposition; (b) Hist: la Résistance, the Resistance (movement); il a fait (partie) de la R., he was a member of the Resistance (movement), was in the Resistance; (c) r. à la maladie, à la contagion, resistance to disease, to contagion; r. (d'un virus) à un antibiotique, immunity (of a virus) to an antibiotic; r. de la peau, dermal resistance; (d) r. aérodynamique, aerodynamic force, drag; r. aux forces aérodynamiques, aerodynamic damping; r. hydrodynamique, water resistance; r. à l'air, air resistance; r. de l'air, air friction; r. de frottement, frictional resistance; r. résiduaire, residuary resistance; Av: Nau: r. à l'avancement, drag, Av: head resistance; r. due au frottement, frictional drag or resistance, skin resistance; Av: r. du moteur, engine drag; r. nuisible, deadhead resistance, parasite resistance; Nau: r. de carène, r. à l'avancement, tow-rope resistance; r. à la dérive, lateral resistance; r. de remous, wake resistance; r. due aux vagues, wave resistance; Aut: etc: r. au dérapage, skid resistance; (e) (i) El: (electric) resistance; r. d'amortissement, damper resistance; r. d'entrée, input resistance; r. de capacité, capacitance; r. spécifique, resistivity; r. de contact, contact resistance; r. de fuite, leakage resistance; r. de terre, earth resistance; r. du primaire, du secondaire, primary, secondary, resistance; (ii) El: Elcs: resistant element, resistor; boîte de résistances, resistor box; r. chauffante, heater element; r. de chauffage, heating resistor; r. de charge, load resistor; r. d'équilibrage, ballast resistor; r. régulatrice de tension, bleeder resistor; r. à curseur, sliding-contact resistor; rheostat; r. en série, series resistor; r. de champ, field rheostat; r. de démarrage, starting rheostat; W.Tel: etc: r. du circuit de la grille, r. de fuite de la grille, grid leak, grid(-leak) resistor. 2. (a) resistance, strength, toughness (of materials); r. à la flexion, bending strength; r. à l'éclatement, bursting strength; r. à la corrosion, resistance to corrosion; r. à la déformation permanente, r. élastique, yield strength, stress; r. à la fatigue, fatigue strength; r. à la flexion, bending strength; r. à la torsion, torsional strength; r. au cisaillement, shear(ing) strength; r. au flambage, buckling strength; r. au déchirement, tearing strength; r. à l'arrachement, resistance to tearing; r. à l'écrasement, crushing strength, compressive strength; r. à la tension, tensile strength; r. au choc, impact strength; resilience; r. élastique, yield stress; limite de la r. (élastique), yield point; r. vive, resilience; r. de rupture, ultimate stress; acier à haute r., high-resistance, high-tensile, steel; métal de haute r., hard-drawn metal; tissu qui n'a pas de r., flimsy material; (b) resistance, staying power, stamina, endurance (of pers., animal); pièce de r., pièce de résistance; (i) Cu: principal dish; (ii) principal feature, item (of entertainment, etc.); Cu: plat de r., principal dish, main course.

résistant, -ante [rezistɑ̃, -ɑ̃:t]. 1. a. (a) resistant (medium, etc.); strong, stout, resistant (material); tough (wood, etc.); couleur résistante, fast colour; virus r. à un antibiotique, virus immune to an antibiotic; r. à l'acide, acid-proof; r. aux intempéries, weatherproof; r. à la chaleur, heatproof; r. à l'écrasement, au choc, crash-proof, shockproof; r. à l'usure, strong, hard-wearing; resistant to wear; Bot: r. au froid, frost-hardy; l'acier est plus r. que le fer, steel is more resistant, has a greater resistance, than iron; (b) (of pers.) strong, resistant; (c) Pol: etc: rebellious; ils se sont montrés résistants, they protested; they were up in arms. 2. s. Pol: etc: (a) rebel; contestant; insurgent; (b) (1939-45 war) resister, member of the Resistance movement.

résister [reziste], v.ind.tr. to resist; (a) r. à qn, à la justice, to resist, offer resistance to, s.o., the law; (b) r. à (qch.), to resist (temptation); to hold out against (attack); to bear (up against), to withstand (pain); Mec: to take, support (a stress); Nau: r. à une tempête, to weather a storm; si l'on pouvait r. à l'action de la vieillesse, if one could resist the onslaught of old age; (c) r. à faire qch., to show reluctance to do sth.; to refuse to do sth.; F: to kick at doing sth., to jib at doing sth.; (d) ces couleurs ne résistent pas, these colours are not fast, resistant; (e) St.Exch: les pétroles résistent mal, oils, oil shares, tend to sag.

résistible [rezistibl̩], a. resistible.

résistivité [rezistivite], s.f. El: resistivity.

résistor [rezistɔ:r], s.m. El: resistor.

résite [rezit], s.f. resite, C-stage resin.

résitol [rezitɔl], s.m. resitol, B-stage resin.

resnatron [rɛsnatrɔ̃], s.m. Elcs: resnatron.

résol [rezɔl], s.m. resol(e), A-stage resin.

résolu [rezɔly], a. 1. resolute, determined (person). 2. r. à faire qch., resolved, determined, to do sth.

résolubilité [rezɔlybilite], s.f. resolvability.

résoluble [rezɔlybl̩], a. 1. solvable, resoluble (problem). 2. Jur: annullable, cancellable, terminable (contract, agreement).

résolument, A: **résolûment** [rezɔlymɑ̃], adv. resolutely, determinedly.

résolutif, -ive [rezɔlytif, -i:v], a. & s.m. Med: resolvent, discutient.

résolution [rezɔlysjɔ̃], s.f. 1. (a) Ch: Mth: Mus: etc: resolution (of substance, of dissonance); solution (of problem, of equation); r. de l'eau en vapeur, resolution of water into steam; Opt: limite de r., limit of resolution; pouvoir de r., resolving power; photographie à haute r., high-resolution photograph; (computers) r. d'opérations logiques, logical resolution; erreur de r., resolution error; (b) Jur: avoidance, termination, cancellation, annulment (of agreement, owing to breach, etc.); cancelling (of sale); action en r., action for rescission of contract. 2. resolution, determination; (a) resolve; prendre la r. de faire qch., to resolve to do sth., to determine to do sth.; (b) resoluteness; manquer de r., to lack determination, strength of will; s'armer de r., to make up one's mind to go through with it; (c) (of meeting) prendre, adopter, une r., to pass, carry, adopt, a resolution; soumettre, proposer, une r. à l'assemblée, to put a resolution to the meeting.

résolutoire [rezɔlytwa:r], a. Jur: condition r., condition of avoidance (in contract); resolutory condition.

résolvant [rezɔlvɑ̃], a. & s.m. Med: resolvent.

résonance [rezɔnɑ̃:s], s.f. 1. (a) Ph: etc: resonance; corde qui vibre par r., string that vibrates sympathetically; sympathetic string; Mus: caisse de r., sound box, chest; resonance box; (b) r. atomique, nuclear resonance; neutron de r., resonance neutron; (c) repercussion; responsiveness. 2. W.Tel: etc: resonance, tuning; mettre le poste en r., to tune the set; to tune in; être en r., to be in tune.

résonateur [rezɔnatœ:r]. 1. a. Ph: resonating. 2. s.m. Ac: El: resonator; r. d'entrée, input resonator, buncher; r. de sortie, output resonator, catcher.

résonnant [rezɔnɑ̃], a. resounding, resonant, sonorous; Elcs: circuit r., resonant circuit.

résonnement [rezɔnmɑ̃], s.m. A: resounding, resonance, re-echoing, reverberation.

résonner [rezɔne], v.i. to resound, re-echo, reverberate; (of metal, etc.) to ring, clang, clank; (of string) to twang; le timbre électrique résonna, the electric bell rang, sounded; l'air résonnait de leurs cris, the air rang with their cries; faire insonoriser une pièce qui résonne trop, to insulate a room that has too much resonance.

résorbant [rezɔrbɑ̃], a. & s.m. Med: absorbefacient.

résorber [rezɔrbe], v.tr. to reabsorb; to be absorbed; Med: to resorb; mesures prises pour r. les excédents de blé, measures taken to absorb the surplus wheat; mesures prises en vue de r. la crise économique, measures taken with a view to solving the economic crisis from within.

se résorber, Med: le point de congestion se résorbe, the pneumonia is resolving.

résorcine [rezɔrsin], s.f., **résorcinol** [rezɔrsinɔl], s.m. Ch: resorcin, resorcinol.

résorcyclique [rezɔrsiklik], a. Ch: resorcyclic.

résorption [rezɔrpsjɔ̃], s.f. Med: resorption, reabsorption.

résorufine [rezɔryfin], s.f. Ch: resorufin.

résoudre [rezudr̥], v.tr. (pr.p. résolvant; p.p. (i) résolu, (ii) Ph: résous, -oute; pr.ind. je résous, il résout, n. résolvons; p.d. je résolvais; p.h. je résolus; fu. je résoudrai) 1. (a) r. qch. en qch., to resolve, dissolve, break up, sth. into sth.; la vapeur que le froid avait résoute en eau, the steam that the cold had resolved into water; le brouillard s'est résous en pluie, the fog resolved itself into rain; (b) Jur: to annul, cancel, avoid, terminate, rescind (contract, etc.). 2. to resolve, clear up (a difficulty); to solve (equation, problem); to work out (problem); to settle (a question); r. une objection, to remove an objection; r. une équation par rapport à x, to solve an equation for x; Mus: r. une dissonance, to resolve a discord. 3. (a) r. qn à, de, faire qch., to induce, persuade, prevail upon, s.o. to do sth.; (b) r. qch., to decide on, determine on, sth.; on a résolu la guerre, war has been decided upon; r. de partir, to decide to go; on a résolu que nous resterions, it has been decided that we should stay; il faut nous y r., we must bring ourselves, make up our minds to do it, accept it.

respect [rɛspɛ], s.m. respect, regard; avoir du r. pour qn, to respect s.o.; avoir le r. des lois, to respect the law; parler avec r., to speak respectfully; Ecc: tu ne prononceras le nom de Dieu qu'avec r., thou shalt not take the name of the Lord thy God in vain; traiter qn avec r., to show deference to s.o.; to show regard for s.o.; r. de soi, self-respect; r. humain [rɛspɛkymɛ̃], (i) deference to public opinion; (ii) undue deference to public opinion; fear of what people may say; faire qch. par r. pour qn, to do sth. out of respect for s.o., out of regard for s.o.; il a su se faire porter du r., he knew how to make himself respected; manquer de r. à, envers, qn, to be disrespectful to s.o.; **tenir qn en r.,** (i) to keep s.o. at a respectful distance, at arm's length; (ii) to hold s.o. in check; (iii) to keep s.o. in awe; **sauf le r. que je vous dois, sauf votre r.,** with all due respect, with all due deference (to you); **rendre ses respects à qn,** to pay one's respects to s.o.; **veuillez bien présenter mes respects à mademoiselle votre fille,** please give my regards to your daughter.

respectabilité [rɛspɛktabilite], *s.f.* respectability.

respectable [rɛspɛktabl̩], *a.* **1.** respectable, worthy of respect. **2.** respectable, fairly large; **somme r.,** respectable sum of money; **pièce de dimension r.,** reasonably large room, room of respectable dimensions; **il y en avait un nombre r.,** there were a respectable, reasonable, number of them.

respectablement [rɛspɛktabləmɑ̃], *adv.* respectably.

respecter [rɛspɛkte], *v.tr.* to respect, have regard for (sth., so.); **r. une clause dans un contrat,** to respect, comply with, a clause in a contract; **r. la tradition,** to respect tradition; **r. la loi, une décision,** to respect, abide, by the law, to abide by a decision; **faire r. la loi,** to enforce the law; **tout le monde le respecte,** everybody looks up to him, respects him; se **faire r.,** to make oneself respected, to command respect; **le feu ne respecta rien,** the fire spared nothing; **la mort le respecta,** death spared him; **un homme qui se respecte ne saurait que refuser,** a man who has any respect for himself, any self-respecting man, can only decline; **je me respecte trop pour faire cela,** I respect myself too much to do that.

respectif, -ive [rɛspɛktif, -iːv], *a.* respective; **nos demeures respectives,** our respective homes; **nos obligations respectives,** our several obligations.

respectivement [rɛspɛktivmɑ̃], *adv.* respectively.

respectueusement [rɛspɛktɥøzmɑ̃], *adv.* respectfully.

respectueux, -euse [rɛspɛktɥø, -øːz]. **1.** *a.* respectful; **r. des lois,** respectful of thel aw, law-abiding; **il ne se montre guère r. envers ses parents,** he shows little respect for his parents; **dire en termes r. que . . .,** to say with all due respect that . . .; **silence r.,** respectful silence; **se tenir à distance respectueuse,** to keep at a safe, respectful, distance; *Corr:* **veuillez agréer mes sentiments r.,** yours sincerely. **2.** *s.f. P:* **respectueuse,** prostitute, tart.

respirable [rɛspirabl̩], *a.* respirable, breathable; **l'atmosphère n'est pas r. ici,** you (just) can't breathe here.

respirateur, -trice [rɛspiratœːr, -tris]. **1.** *a.* respiratory (organ, nerves, etc.). **2.** *s.m. Med: Mil: etc:* respirator.

respiration [rɛspirasjɔ̃], *s.f.* respiration, breathing; **r. par la bouche,** mouth breathing, breathing through the mouth; **r. artificielle,** artificial respiration; **r. artificielle bouche à bouche,** mouth-to-mouth insufflation, *F:* the kiss of life; **couper la r. à qn,** (i) to wind s.o.; to hit, catch, s.o. in the wind; (ii) to take s.o.'s breath away, to flabbergast s.o.; **la r. commençait à nous manquer,** our breath was beginning to fail; **la respiration lui manqua,** he caught his breath; **avoir la r. difficile,** to breathe with difficulty; **avoir la r. coupée,** (i) to be short of breath; (ii) to be flabbergasted; *Physiol:* **air de r.,** tidal air.

respiratoire [rɛspiratwaːr], *a.* respiratory, breathing (organ, etc.); **appareil r.,** (i) *Anat:* respiratory system, organs; (ii) *Min: etc:* breathing apparatus; **casque r.,** (fireman's) smoke helmet, breathing helmet; **masque r.,** oxygen mask.

respirer [rɛspire]. **1.** *v.i.* to breathe, respire; **r. longuement,** to draw a long breath; **r. court,** to be short-winded; **r. péniblement,** to breathe heavily; **j'ai de la difficulté à r.,** I find it hard to get my breath; **donnez-moi le temps de r.,** give me time to breathe, to take breath; give me breathing time; **"n'est-ce que cela?" je respirai,** "Is that all?" I breathed again; *A:* **r. après qch.,** to hanker, sigh, after sth. **2.** *v.tr.* (*a*) to breathe, inhale; **r. son air natal,** to breathe (in) one's native air; **aller r. un peu d'air,** to go for a breather; **r. la vengeance,** to breathe (out, forth) vengeance; (*b*) **ici tout respire la paix,** here everything breathes, denotes, peace; **ses yeux respiraient la franchise,** his open nature could be read in his eyes; **visage respirant la bonté,** face that radiates goodness.

resplendir [rɛsplɑ̃diːr], *v.i.* to be resplendent, to shine, to glitter; **les cieux resplendissaient d'étoiles,** the heavens were resplendent with stars; **visage qui resplendit de santé,** face shining, glowing, aglow, with health.

resplendissant [rɛsplɑ̃disɑ̃], *a.* resplendent, shining; glittering (uniform, etc.); **visage r. de santé,** face shining, glowing, aglow, with health; **resplendissante de jeunesse et de beauté,** resplendent in her youth and beauty; **r. de lumière, de couleur,** ablaze with light, with colour.

resplendissement [rɛsplɑ̃dismɑ̃], *s.m.* resplendence, brightness, splendour.

responsabilité [rɛspɔ̃sabilite], *s.f.* responsibility, accountableness, accountability, liability (**de,** for); **r. de l'employeur,** employer's liability; **la r. incombe au locataire de s'assurer . . .,** the responsibility rests with, devolves on, the tenant to make sure . . .; **accepter une r.,** to assume, accept, a responsibility; **décliner toute r.,** to refuse to accept any responsibility; **la r. qui m'est imposée,** the responsibility that is laid upon me; **j'ai la r. de l'entretien de la maison,** I am responsible for the upkeep of the house; **engager la r. de qn,** to involve s.o.'s responsibility; **engager sa r. personnelle en ce qui concerne qch.,** to assume personal responsibility for sth.; **faire qch. sous sa (propre) r.,** to do sth. on one's own responsibility; **r. civile,** civil liability (for damages caused by an agent); **sens des responsabilités,** sense of responsibility; **responsabilités d'État,** cares of state.

responsable [rɛspɔ̃sabl̩]. **1.** *a.* responsible, accountable, answerable (**envers,** to; **devant,** before); **r. pour ses enfants, pour ses serviteurs,** answerable for one's children, for one's servants; **r. vis-à-vis de l'opinion publique,** responsible before public opinion; **le ministre est r. aux Chambres, devant, envers, les Chambres, vis-à-vis des Chambres,** the Minister is responsible to Parliament; **tenir qn (pour) r. de qch.,** to hold s.o. responsible for sth.; **les autorités sont responsables de l'exécution du décret,** the authorities are responsible for the carrying out of the order; **rendre qn r. d'un malheur,** to blame s.o. for a misfortune; **être r. du dommage,** to be liable for the damage. **2.** *s.* (*a*) person responsible (**de,** for); (*b*) responsible person; person authorized to take decisions.

responsif, -ive [rɛspɔ̃sif, -iːv], *a. Jur:* in reply.

resquillage [rɛskijaːʒ], *s.m.*, **resquille** [rɛskiːj], *s.f.* *F:* (*a*) gatecrashing; (*b*) wangling.

resquiller [rɛskije], *v.tr. and abs.* (*a*) *F:* to wangle; (*b*) to avoid paying (for); to gatecrash.

resquilleur, -euse [rɛskijœːr, -øːz], *s. F:* (*a*) uninvited guest, gatecrasher; **roi des resquilleurs,** champion gatecrasher; (*b*) wangler; (*c*) queue jumper; (*d*) cheat.

ressac [rəsak], *s.m. Nau:* **1.** underset, undertow. **2.** surf. **3.** (= BRISANTS) breakers.

ressaigner [rəseɲe]. **1.** *v.i.* (*of wound, etc.*) to bleed again. **2.** *v.tr.* to bleed (s.o.) again.

ressaisir [rəseziːr], *v.tr.* **1.** to seize again; to recapture; to recover possession of (s.o., sth.). **2.** (*a*) **r. qn de qch.,** to put s.o. back in possession of sth., to restore sth. to s.o.; (*b*) **r. le tribunal d'une cause,** to bring a case back before the court.

se ressaisir. 1. to regain one's self-control; to recover; to collect one's wits; to pull oneself together. **2.** to recover one's balance (after stumbling).

ressassage [rəsɑsaːʒ], *s.m.*, **ressassement** [rəsɑsmɑ̃], *s.m.* **1.** (*a*) re-sifting, re-bolting (of flour); (*b*) **r. de ses malheurs,** dwelling on, harking back to, one's misfortunes. **2.** *A:* re-examining, re-investigation.

ressasser [rəsɑse], *v.tr.* **1.** (*a*) to re-sift, re-bolt (flour); (*b*) **toujours r. la même histoire,** to be for ever going back over, harking back to, dwelling on, the same old story; **r. un argument,** to hack an argument to death. **2.** *A:* **r. un compte,** to re-examine, scrutinize, an account.

ressasseur, -euse [rəsɑsœːr, -øːz], *s.* person who constantly repeats the same ideas, tells the same old story; bore.

ressaut [rəso], *s.m.* **1.** (*a*) *Arch:* projection, set-off, offset, ressaut; *Mec.E:* swell, lug; *Civ.E:* shelf, ledge (along track); *Geol:* rock step; *Artil:* **r. d'un projectile,** shoulder of a projectile; **faire r.,** to project; (*b*) **r. de terrain,** sharp rise in the ground; (*c*) *Hyd.E:* jump. **2.** (*a*) *Equit:* rise (in the saddle); (*b*) (i) *A:* sudden movement, leap (of indignation, astonishment); *F: A:* **mettre qn à r.,** to rouse s.o.'s ire, to make s.o. indignant; (ii) *P:* **faire du r.,** to revolt, to be up in arms; **mettre qn à r.,** to get on s.o.'s nerves; (*c*) **les sauts et ressauts de sa conversation,** the disconnectedness of his conversation; the way he jumps from one subject to another.

ressauter [rəsote]. **1.** *v.i.* (*a*) to start, jump (with fear, etc.); to be tossed about; (*b*) *P:* (i) to jib; to revolt; to be up in arms; (ii) to fly into a rage. **2.** *v.tr. & i.* (*a*) to jump again; (*b*) to jump back. **3.** *v.i. Const:* to project.

ressauteur [rəsotœːr], *s.m. P:* rebel, agitator; contestant.

ressayer [rɛsaje], *v.tr.* (*conj. like* ESSAYER) to try (sth.) again, to have another try, go, at (sth.); to try (garment) on again; to sit (examination) again.

resseller [rəsele], *v.tr.* to re-saddle (horse, etc.).

ressemblance [rəsɑ̃blɑ̃ːs], *s.f.* resemblance, likeness; **avoir, offrir, de la r. avec qn, à, avec, qch.,** to bear, show, a resemblance to s.o., to sth.; to be like s.o., sth.; *Lit: Cin: etc:* **toute r. avec des personnages réels ne peut être que fortuite,** any resemblance to any person living or dead is purely accidental.

ressemblant [rəsɑ̃blɑ̃], *a.* like, alike; **portrait bien r.,** portrait very like the original; good likeness; **portrait peu r.,** poor likeness; **frères ressemblants,** brothers who are very much alike; **une pitié ressemblante au mépris,** a pity akin to contempt.

ressembler [rəsɑ̃ble], *v.ind.tr.* **r. à qn, à qch.,** to resemble, to be like, to look like, s.o., sth.; **ce portrait vous ressemble,** this portrait is like you; **il ressemble à un hibou,** he looks like an owl; **sa maison ressemble assez à la nôtre,** his house is not (terribly) unlike ours; **il a pu m'échapper quelque chose qui ressemblât à une promesse,** some words may have escaped me that sounded like a promise; **il n'y eut rien qui ressemblât à une émeute,** there was nothing that resembled a riot; **cela ne vous ressemble pas du tout,** it isn't a bit like you; **il vous ressemble par les yeux, par le courage,** his eyes are like yours; he has your courage; **comment vous intéressez-vous à des gens qui vous ressemblent si peu?** how can you be interested in people so unlike yourselves? **qui ressemble à . . ., . . . -like; qui ressemble aux brutes,** brute-like; *F:* **cela ne ressemble à rien,** (i) it's like nothing on earth; (ii) it just doesn't make sense.

se ressembler, to be (a)like; **ils se ressemblent comme deux gouttes d'eau, comme deux œufs,** they are as like as two peas; **vous vous ressemblez tous!** you are all alike! *Prov:* **les jours se suivent et ne se ressemblent pas,** tomorrow is another day.

ressemelage [rəsəmlaːʒ], *s.m.* re-soling (of shoes).

ressemeler [rəsəmle], *v.tr.* (*conj. like* SEMELER) to re-sole (shoes).

ressemer [rəsme], *v.tr.* (*conj. like* SEMER) to sow (seeds, field) again; to resow; **r. du blé après une gelée,** to resow wheat after a frost; **le cerfeuil se ressème et produit des plants nouveaux,** chervil seeds itself and produces a new crop.

ressenti [rəsɑ̃ti], *a.* deeply felt; *Art:* strongly expressed.

ressentiment [rəsɑ̃timɑ̃], *s.m.* **1.** resentment (**de,** at; **contre,** against); **il m'en a parlé avec r.,** he spoke to me resentfully about it. **2.** *A:* (*a*) feeling, sense (of good, evil, etc.); (*b*) slight return, fresh touch (of pain, disease).

ressentir [rəsɑ̃tiːr], *v.tr.* (*conj. like* SENTIR) (*a*) to feel (pain, emotion, etc.); **elle ne ressentait pas de joie de ce qu'il revenait,** she felt no joy at his coming back; **r. de l'affection pour qn,** to be fond of s.o.; **r. vivement la perte de qn,** to feel deeply, to be deeply affected by, the loss of s.o.; (*b*) to resent (an injury, etc.); **r. vivement une injure,** to feel an insult keenly; (*c*) to feel, experience (shock, etc.); **la secousse s'est ressentie très loin,** the shock was felt at a great distance.

se ressentir d'un accident, d'une maladie, etc., to feel the effects of an accident, of an illness, etc.; **il s'en ressentira longtemps,** he will feel the effects for a long time; it will take him a long time to get over it; **il se ressent à peine, ne se ressent pas du tout, de son aventure,** he is very little, none, the worse for his experience; **je me ressens de l'insulte que j'ai reçue,** I feel deeply the insult I have received; *F:* **une maison qui diminue sa publicité ne tarde pas à s'en r.,** a firm that reduces its advertising soon knows it, soon feels the difference; **on se ressentait de plus en plus du manque de bière,** the lack of beer was making itself increasingly felt; *P:* **s'en r. pour qch.,** to feel fit for, up to, sth.; **tu t'en ressens pour le championnat de France?** d'you feel up to tackling the French championship? **je ne m'en ressens pas,** I don't feel like it, up to it; **s'en r. pour qn,** to have a liking for, be keen on, s.o.

resserrant [rəsɛrɑ̃], *a.* tightening, contracting; constricting, gripping; *Med:* constipating.

resserre [rəsɛːr], *s.f.* **1.** (*a*) *A:* storage, safe keeping; **armoire de fer pour la r. des objets précieux,** safe for storing, keeping, valuables; (*b*) holding up (of food stuffs, etc.); **pratiquer la r. (du blé, etc.),** to hold up, hoard (wheat, etc.). **2.** (*a*) *A:* (storage) yard, shed; store room; **r. de transit,** quay-side cold-room; (*b*) *A:* secret niche, cupboard; (*c*) (garden) tool shed; (*d*) rack; **r. à légumes,** vegetable rack.

resserré [rəsere], *a.* **1.** narrow, confined, cramped, shut in; **espace r.,** confined space; **propriété resserrée entre les montagnes,** estate boxed, shut, in by the mountains. **2.** *Med: A:* costive, constipated (person).

resserrement [rəsɛrmɑ̃], *s.m.* **1.** (*a*) contracting, contraction, tightening, narrowing; constriction, closing up, pinch(ing); *Med: A:* costiveness, constipation; (*b*) *Pol.Ec:* **r. du crédit,** credit squeeze. **2.** (*a*) tightness, scarceness (of money); (*b*) **r. de l'esprit,** narrowness of mind; **r. de cœur,** heaviness of heart.

resserrer [rəsere], *v.tr.* **1.** to put away (sth.) again; to put back (sth.); **r. ses bijoux dans son bureau,** to lock up one's jewels in one's desk again. **2.** (*a*) to contract, restrain, confine, narrow, shrink, constrict, pinch; *Mil: Navy:* **r. une ligne de bataille,** to close up a line of battle; **r. les colonnes,** to close the columns; **le froid resserre les pores,** cold closes the pores; *A:* **r. un récit,** to condense, compress, a story; **rivière resserrée dans son lit,** river confined within its bed; **r. ses besoins,** to restrict one's wants; (*b*) *A:* **r. un prisonnier,** to confine a prisoner more closely. **3.** (*a*) to tie (up) again; to draw (sth.) tighter; to tighten; **r. les liens de l'amitié,** to draw the bonds of friendship closer; (*b*) *Med: A:* (*of food*) **r. le ventre,** to be constipating.

se resserrer. **1.** (*of thgs*) (*a*) to contract, shrink; to become closer, narrower, tighter; (*b*) *A:* (*of the weather*) to grow cooler. **2.** *A:* (*of pers.*) to retrench; to curtail one's expenses.

resservir [rəsɛrviːr], *v.tr. & i.* (*conj. like* SERVIR) **1.** to serve again, to re-serve; **r. un plat,** to serve up a dish again. **2. billet qui ne peut r.,** ticket that cannot be used again.

ressort [rəsɔːr], *s.m.* **1.** (*a*) elasticity, springiness; **corps à r.,** elastic, springy, body; **faire r.,** to be elastic, springy; to spring back, fly back; **avoir du r.,** (i) to be resilient; (ii) (*of pers.*) to be full of buoyancy; **le marché a du r.,** the market is buoyant; **se sentir sans r.,** to feel slack; (*b*) *Mec.E: etc:* spring; **r. à boudin, à spires, en spirale,** coil spring, spiral spring; **r. en volute, r. spiral,** volute spring, hair spring; **r. à feuilles, à lames (étagées),** leaf spring, laminated spring, plate spring; **lame de r.,** spring leaf, plate; **r. cantilever,** cantilever spring; **r. (semi-)elliptique,** (semi-)elliptic spring; **r. hélicoïdal,** helical spring; **r. hydraulique,** liquid spring; **r. amortisseur,** buffer spring, shock-absorbing spring; **r. d'asservissement,** follow-up spring; **r. de compression,** compression spring; **r. de rappel,** release spring, return spring, restoring spring; **r. de suspension,** suspension spring (of vehicle, mechanical part, etc.); bearing spring (of locomotive, railway carriage); **r. de tension,** tension spring; **r. de torsion,** torsion spring, torsional spring; **r. de traction,** draw, draft, spring; drag spring; **r. moteur, grand r.,** main spring; **r. récupérateur,** recoil spring, return spring (of machine gun, etc.); *Sm.a:* **r. de gâchette, petit r.,** sear spring; **r. régulateur,** constant-effort spring; **bride de r.,** spring bridle, buckle; **flèche de r.,** spring camber; **guide de r.,** spring guide; **tube guide de r.,** spring-guide tube; **jumelle, étrier, de r.,** spring shackle; **logement, boîtier, de r.,** spring seat, clamp; **support de r.,** spring bracket; **à r.; actionné, mû, par r.,** spring-actuated; spring-driven; spring-loaded; **commutateur à r.,** snap switch; **verrou à r.,** spring-loaded latch, spring bolt; **moteur à r.,** clockwork motor; *Cin:* **caméra avec moteur à r.,** clockwork-driven cine camera; *Veh: etc:* **suspension à ressort(s),** spring suspension, springing, springs; **suspendu à ressort(s),** sprung; **(suspendu) sans ressort(s),** unsprung; **r. de voiture,** carriage spring; **r. sous l'essieu,** underslung spring; **r. de sommier,** bed spring; **r. de montre,** watch spring; **comprimer, tendre, un r.,** to compress, set, a spring; **détendre un r.,** to relax, release, a spring; **faire jouer un r.,** to work a spring; **faire r.,** to act as a spring; **faire jouer tous les ressorts,** to pull all the strings, to leave no stone unturned; **le véritable r. de la recherche scientifique,** the true incentive to scientific research; **l'intérêt est un puissant r.,** (self-)interest is a powerful motive, stimulus, incentive; (*c*) *Mus:* bass bar (of violin, etc.); (*d*) *Tp:* spring band (of head phone). **2.** *Jur:* (*a*) province, scope, competence; (extent of) jurisdiction; **être du r. de la cour,** to be, fall, within the province, the competence, of the court; **cela n'est pas de son r.,** that does not fall within his province; that's not in his line; **ressorts judiciaires d'une région,** judicial areas of a district; (*b*) **prononcer un jugement en premier r.,** to pass judgment with possibility of appeal; **en dernier r.,** (i) without appeal; (ii) in the last resort.

ressortir [rəsɔrtiːr], *v.i.* (*conj. like* SORTIR, *except in* 3) **1.** (*a*) (*aux.* **être**) to come, go, out again; (*b*) *v.tr.* **r. les chaises,** to bring out the chairs again; **pourquoi r. cette vieille histoire,** why drag up that old story? **2.** (*aux. usu.* **être**) (*a*) to stand out (in relief); to be evident; **faire r. vivement un visage,** to bring out a face in strong relief; to throw a face into strong relief; **faire r. des couleurs, etc.,** to bring out, set off, colours, etc.; **faire r. un fait,** to refer particularly to a fact; to dwell on, emphasize, accentuate, lay stress on, a fact; **faire r. le sens de qch.,** to bring out the meaning of sth.; **faire r. de gros bénéfices,** to show large profits; (*b*) to result, follow, be deduced (**de,** from); **de ce que j'ai dit il ressort que . . .,** from what I have said it follows that . . ., it is apparent that . . .; **comme il ressort de la lettre ci-jointe,** as will be gathered, as appears, from the enclosed letter; **de ces faits il ressort que . . .,** from these facts it emerges that . . .; **le prix moyen ressort à vingt francs,** the average price works out at twenty francs; (*c*) *v.tr. Book-k:* to bring out, show (totals, etc.); **sommes ressorties à l'encre rouge,** amounts shown in red ink. **3.** (*aux.* **avoir**) (*pr.p.* **ressortissant;** *pr.ind.* **il ressortit;** *p.d.* **il ressortissait**) (*a*) *Jur: A:* to appeal (**à,** to); (*b*) **r. à qn, à qch.,** to be under the jurisdiction of, to be amenable to (a court, a country); **ces affaires ressortissent à la justice de paix,** these cases belong to, come before, a conciliation court; (*c*) **concepts qui ressortissent à la géométrie,** concepts that belong to geometry; **ce sujet ressortit à la rhétorique,** this subject comes under the heading of rhetoric.

ressortissant [rəsɔrtisɑ̃]. **1.** *a. Jur:* under the jurisdiction (**à,** of); amenable (to a jurisdiction); belonging (to a country, etc.). **2.** *s.m.* **les ressortissants d'un pays,** the nationals of a country.

ressoudage [rəsudaːʒ], *s.m. Metalw:* resoldering; rewelding; *Med:* mending (of broken bones); joining together again.

ressouder [rəsude], *v.tr. Metalw:* to resolder; to reweld.

se ressouder, (*of bone*) to knit again, to join again, to mend.

ressoudure [rəsudyːr], *s.f.* (*rare*) = RESSOUDAGE.

ressource [rəsurs], *s.f.* **1.** (*a*) resource; resourcefulness; **personne de r.,** person of resource, resourceful person; (*b*) (*possibility of aid*) **ville de r.,** well-supplied town; **être ruiné sans r.,** to be irretrievably, irremediably, ruined; **sans r. et sans espoir,** helpless and hopeless. **2.** expedient, shift; **avoir mille ressources,** to be full of expedients; to be very resourceful; **il me reste encore une r.,** I have still one string to my bow; **je n'avais d'autre r. que la fuite,** there was no course open to me but flight; **faire r. de tout,** to turn all one's possessions into ready cash; **nous sommes à notre dernière r.,** we are at the end of our resources, at our last shift; **en dernière r.,** in the last resort. **3.** *pl.* resources, means; **quelles sont nos ressources en chevaux?** how do we stand in the matter of horses? **être à bout de ressources,** to be at the end of one's resources, *F:* on one's last legs, on one's beam ends; **être sans ressources,** (i) to be penniless, without means of support; (ii) *Com:* to be bankrupt; **ressources personnelles,** private means. **4.** *Av:* flattening out, pull-out (from dive).

ressouvenance [rəsuvnɑ̃ːs], *s.f. A. & Lit:* recollection, remembrance.

ressouvenir [rəsuvniːr]. I. *v.* (*conj. like* VENIR) to remember (again). **1.** *v.impers. A:* **il me ressouvient de . . .,** I have a distant memory of . . .; **il me ressouvient que . . .,** I seem to remember that . . .. **2.** *v.pr.* **se r. de qch.,** to remember sth. (from long ago); **je me ressouviens avec tristesse du passé,** I look back with regret to the past; **faire r. qn de qch.,** to remind s.o. of sth.

II. **ressouvenir,** *s.m. A: & Lit:* remembrance, memory.

ressuage [rəsɥaːʒ], *s.m.* **1.** (*a*) sweating (of walls, etc.); (*b*) cooling off (of new-baked bread). **2.** *Metall:* (*a*) sweating, roasting (of lead and silver ore); crack detection; (*b*) shingling (of puddle ball).

ressuer [rəsɥe], *v.i.* **1.** (*a*) (*of walls, etc.*) to sweat; (*b*) **laisser r. le pain,** to let bread cool off. **2.** *Metall:* (*a*) **faire r.,** to sweat, roast (lead and silver ore); (*b*) **faire r. une loupe,** to shingle a puddle ball.

ressui [resɥi], *s.m.* (*a*) **vent du r.,** drying wind; (*b*) *Ven:* (stag's, etc.) cover(t), refuge (where it retires to dry itself); **donner du r.,** to supply (game birds) with sand (for dusting themselves); (*c*) *Cer:* (*defect of pottery*) dull surface.

ressuiement [resɥimɑ̃], *s.m. Agr:* drying out (of soil by the wind); drying (of hay, etc. in the open air).

ressuivage [resɥivaːʒ], *s.m. Rail:* maintenance work, minor overhaul (of rolling stock).

ressure [rəsyːr], *s.f. Fish:* salted cod roe (used as bait).

ressurgir [rəsyrʒiːr], *v.i.* = RESURGIR.

ressuscitable [resysitabl̩], *a.* that can be resuscitated, restored to life.

ressuscitation [resysitasjɔ̃], *s.f.* resuscitation.

ressuscité, -ée [resysite], *a. & s.* resuscitated, revived (person); **Jésus r.,** the risen Christ.

ressusciter [resysite]. **1.** *v.tr.* (*a*) to resuscitate; to restore (s.o.) to life; **r. les morts,** to raise the dead; **ce vin me ressuscite,** this wine is putting new life into me; (*b*) to revive (quarrel, fashion, etc.). **2.** *v.i.* to resuscitate, revive, come to life again; to return from the dead; **r. des morts, d'entre les morts,** to rise from the dead; **ressuscité d'entre les morts,** risen from the dead.

ressuyage [resɥijaːʒ], *s.m. Hort:* cleaning (of vegetables for market).

ressuyé [resɥije], *a.* **1.** *Lit. or Dial:* dried (by the sun, etc.). **2.** restored, re-established, put in order again. **3.** *Cer:* **glaçure ressuyée,** (defectively) dull glaze.

ressuyer [resɥije], *v.tr.* (*conj. like* ESSUYER) to dry (lime, etc.); *Lit. or Dial:* **le soleil a ressuyé la route, la route s'est ressuyée au soleil,** the sun has dried the road.

restanque [rɛstɑ̃ːk], *s.f.* (*S. of Fr.*) terraced field.

restant, -ante [rɛstɑ̃, -ɑ̃ːt]. **1.** *a.* (*a*) remaining, left; **les héritiers restants,** the remaining heirs; (*b*) **poste restante,** poste restante, *U.S:* general delivery; **adresser une lettre poste restante, bureau r.,** to address a letter poste restante. **2.** *s.* remaining person, person left behind; **il est le seul r. de sa famille,** he is the sole survivor of his family, the only one of his family left. **3.** *s.m.* (= RESTE) remainder, rest; **si j'avais un r. d'appétit,** if I had any appetite left; *Com:* **r. d'un compte,** balance of an account; **je trouvai quelques restants de nourriture,** I found a few remains of food.

restapler [rɛstaple], *v.tr. Min:* (*N.Fr.*) to backfill, stow (old workings).

restaurant [rɛstɔrɑ̃]. **1.** *a. A:* restoring, restorative (food, etc.). **2.** *s.m.* (*a*) *A:* restorative; (*b*) restaurant; **r. gastronomique,** restaurant with a reputation for its cuisine; **r. libre-service,** cafeteria; **r. universitaire,** university canteen; **r. routier** = transport café; **r. communautaire,** civic restaurant; *A:* **r. social** = British restaurant.

restaurateur, -trice [rɛstɔratœːr, -tris], *s.* **1.** (*a*) restorer (of buildings, works of art, etc.); **r. de tableaux,** picture restorer; (*b*) *Lit:* restorer (of a régime, the monarchy, etc.). **2.** *s.m.* restaurateur; proprietor, manager, of a restaurant.

restauratif, -ive [rɛstɔratif, -iːv], *a.* restorative (medicine, etc.).

restauration [rɛstɔrasjɔ̃], *s.f.* **1.** restoration (of decayed building, statue, etc.; of dynasty; of finances); restoring, re-establishment (of discipline, etc.); *Hist:* **la R.,** the Restoration. **2.** (*a*) catering; (*b*) *Sw.Fr:* restaurant. **3.** *Elcs:* (*computers*) regeneration.

restaurer [rɛstɔre], *v.tr.* (*a*) to restore (building, dynasty, finances, one's health, etc.); **r. la discipline, l'autorité,** to re-establish discipline, authority; (*b*) **r. qn,** to refresh, s.o., to set s.o. up again (in vigour); **nourriture qui restaure,** satisfying food; (*c*) (*computers*) to reset, to restore.

se restaurer, to take some refreshment, to have sth. to eat.

reste [rɛst], *s.m.* **1.** rest, remainder, remains; **le r. de la vie,** the rest, remainder, of one's life; **avoir un r. d'espoir,** to have still some hope left; to have a remnant of hope; **un r. de confiance,** a vestige of confidence; **elle a de beaux restes, des restes de beauté,** she still has traces of beauty; **jouir de son r.,** to make the most of what is left, of one's remaining time; **être en r.,** (i) to be in arrears, behindhand; (ii) to lag behind; **être en r. avec qn,** to be indebted to s.o.; **je ne veux pas**

être en r. de générosité, I don't want to be indebted to anyone; to be behindhand, backward, in generosity; **jouer le r. de son argent,** to stake what money one has left; **jouer son r.,** to play one's last stake; *F:* **donner son r. à qn,** to finish s.o. off, to settle s.o.; **ne pas demander son r.,** to have had enough of it; not to wait for anything more; to decamp; **je ferai le r.,** I shall do the rest; **et le r.,** and everything else; and so on; and so forth; *F:* **il lui faut tout et le r.,** he wants the lot and then some; *Elcs:* (*computers*) **contrôle sur r.,** residue check, modulo N check; *Ar:* **division sans r.,** division with no remainder; *Com:* **payer le r. par acomptes,** to pay the balance in instalments; *adj.phr.* **de r.,** (to) spare; left (over); over and above; **quand j'ai du temps de r.,** when I have time to spare; **avoir de l'argent de r.,** to have more than enough money, to have money and to spare; **je sais de r. quelle patience cela exige,** I know only too well what patience it requires; *adv.phr.* **au r.,** *or more usu.* **du r.,** besides, moreover; **du r., j'ai appris que . . .,** moreover, I learnt that . . .. **2.** *pl.* (*a*) remnants, remains, leavings, scraps, left-overs (of a meal, etc.); **je trouvai quelques restes de nourriture,** I found some remains of food; **on donne les restes aux chiens,** the scraps, the left-overs, are given to the dogs; (*b*) *Com:* left-overs; (*c*) **restes mortels,** mortal remains (of s.o.); (*d*) *Poet:* **les restes d'Ilion,** the remnant from Ilium; all that were left from Ilium.

rester [rɛste], *v.i.* (*the aux. is* **être**) **1.** to remain, to be left; **les cinq francs qui restent,** the remaining five francs; **voilà tout ce qui lui reste de ses cinq livres,** that's all that remains, all that is left, of his five pounds; **le seul espoir qui nous reste,** our only remaining hope; **elle était restée veuve à trente ans,** she had been left a widow at thirty; *impers.* **il me reste cinq francs,** I have five francs left; **il reste beaucoup à faire,** much remains to be done; **il ne me reste qu'à vous remercier,** it only remains for me to thank you; **(il) reste à savoir si . . .,** it remains to be seen whether . . .; *Ar:* **dix-neuf divisé par cinq, je pose 3, reste 4,** nineteen divided by five makes 3, and 4 over. **2.** (*a*) to remain; to stay; **il est resté à travailler,** he stayed behind to work; **je vais r. faire le guet,** I will stay here and keep watch; **il est resté à Paris,** he stayed, remained, stopped, behind in Paris; (*of thg*) **r. à la même place,** to remain in the same place, *F:* to stay put; **les mots lui restèrent dans la gorge,** the words stuck in his throat; **la victoire resta aux mains du prince Eugène,** the victory remained with Prince Eugene; **il restait là à me regarder,** he remained, sat, stood, there looking at me; **restez où vous êtes,** keep, stay, where you are; **r. en bonne santé,** to remain, keep, in good health; **r. assis, debout, à genoux,** to remain sitting, standing, kneeling; **r. au lit,** to stay in bed; **r. (à) dîner,** to stay to dinner; **vous nous restez jusqu'à dimanche?** you will stay until Sunday, won't you? **r. en arrière,** to fall, lag, behind; **r. en route,** to stop on the way; *F:* **il est resté en route,** he stuck; he came to a full stop; **elle est restée court,** she stopped short; **ne restez pas sous la pluie,** don't stay (there, out) in the rain; **r. sur place,** to stay where one is, *F:* to stay put; *F:* **j'y suis, j'y reste,** here I am and here I stay, stick; *F:* **y r.** to be killed (on the spot); *Mil:* **r. sur le champ d'honneur,** to be killed in action; **en r. là,** to stop at that point; to proceed no further in the matter; **où en sommes-nous restés (de notre lecture, etc.)?** where did we leave off? **la chose en resta là,** there the matter rested, remained; **que cela reste entre nous,** this is strictly between ourselves; **la mémoire de cet homme restera,** this man's memory will last, endure; **cela restera,** it will last, it's here to stay; **livre qui restera,** book that has come to stay; (*b*) **r. tranquille, calme,** to stay still; to remain calm; **r. fidèle,** to remain faithful; **ils sont restés amis,** they remained friends, kept up the friendship; **r. bien avec qn,** to remain, keep, on good terms with s.o. **3.** to stay (in hotel, etc.); **où restez-vous?** where are you staying?

restiacées [rɛstjase], *s.f.pl. Bot:* Restionaceae.

restiforme [rɛstifɔrm], *a. Anat:* restiform (bodies).

restio [rɛstjo], *s.m. Bot:* rope grass, cordleaf; (*genus*) Restio.

restituable [rɛstitɥabl̩], *a.* **1.** returnable, repayable. **2.** restorable (to original condition).

restituant [rɛstitɥɑ̃]. **1.** *a.* returning, refunding. **2.** *s.* refunder.

restituer [rɛstitɥe], *v.tr.* **1.** (*a*) to restore (building, text, etc.); (*b*) *Jur:* to reinstate, rehabilitate (s.o.). **2.** to restore (**à,** to); to hand (sth.) back over; to return, refund (money); to turn in; to make restitution of (sth.). **3.** *Surv:* to plot (district, with stereoautograph).

restituteur [rɛstitytœːr], *s.m.* **1.** restorer (of mutilated text). **2.** *Surv:* plotter (with stereoautograph).

restitution [rɛstitysjɔ̃], *s.f.* **1.** restoration (of text, building). **2.** restitution; (*a*) *Jur:* **r. d'indu,** return of payment made in error; (*b*) *Mec:* **coefficient de r.,** coefficient of restitution; (*c*) *Elcs:* (*computers*) **r. isochrone,** isochronous restitution; **mise en mémoire et r. de l'information,** storage and read-out of information. **3.** *Surv:* plotting (with stereoautograph).

restitutoire [rɛstitytwaːr], *a.* restitutory.

Restoroute [rɛstɔrut], *s.m. R.t.m:* (motorway, roadside) restaurant (with service station).

restreindre [rɛstrɛ̃ːdr̥], *v.tr.* (*pr.p.* **restreignant;** *p.p.* **restreint;** *pr.ind.* **je restreins, il restreint, n. restreignons, ils restreignent;** *p.d.* **je restreignais;** *p.h.* **je restreignis;** *fu.* **je restreindrai**) to restrict, to curb; **r. les dépenses,** to restrict, curtail, expenses; to retrench; **r. la production,** to restrict, cut down, production; **r. l'autorité de qn,** to restrict, limit, s.o.'s authority; **r. ses désirs,** to limit, curb, one's desires.

se restreindre. 1. to cut down expenses; to retrench. **2. se r. au strict nécessaire,** to limit oneself to essential necessities, to essentials; **se r. à faire qch.,** to limit oneself, confine oneself, to doing sth.

restreignant [rɛstrɛɲɑ̃], *a.* restricting (clause, etc.).

restreint [rɛstrɛ̃], *a.* restricted; **dans un sens r.,** in a restricted, limited, qualified, sense; **espace r.,** confined space; **limites restreintes,** narrow limits; **édition à tirage r.,** limited edition; **nombre r.,** small, limited, number; **le nombre d'adhérents reste r.,** there is still a restricted membership.

restrictif, -ive [rɛstriktif, -iːv], *a.* restrictive (term, clause); limitative (clause).

restriction [rɛstriksjɔ̃], *s.f.* restriction; limitation (of authority); **r. mentale,** mental restriction, mental reservation; **apporter des restrictions à . . .,** to place restrictions on . . .; **r. apportée à une promesse,** limitation of a promise; **consentir, se soumettre, sans r.,** to consent, submit, unreservedly.

restringent [rɛstrɛ̃ʒɑ̃], *a. & s.m. Med:* astringent, styptic.

restructuration [rəstryktyrasjɔ̃], *s.f.* reorganizing the structure (of an industry, etc.).

restructurer [rəstryktyre], *v.tr.* to reorganize the structure of, to restructure.

resucé, -ée [rəsyse], *F:* **1.** *a.* (*a*) stale (news, etc.); (*b*) faded, wishy-washy. **2.** *s.f.* **resucée** (*a*) rehash (of book, etc.); (*b*) **une resucée,** a drop more; **une petite resucée?** (how about) another little drink? shall we have another?

résultant, -ante [rezyltɑ̃, -ɑ̃ːt]. **1.** *a.* (*a*) resultant; resulting (**de,** from); consequent (**de,** upon); (*b*) *Elcs:* (*computers*) **programme r.,** object program(me), object routine. **2.** *s.f. Mec: Mth:* **résultante,** resultant.

résultat [rezylta], *s.m.* result (of mathematical operation, of measurement); result, outcome (of action, decision, investigation, work, etc.); result, effect (of disease, treatment, etc.); *pl.* **résultats,** (i) results (of examination, contest, race, etc.); (ii) data (of scientific analysis); (iii) *Pol.Ec:* outcome variables (of market analysis); **sans r.,** without result; inconclusive (experiment, observation, etc.); ineffective (remedy); *Med:* **traitement sans r.,** ineffective, ineffectual, treatment; *Sp:* **match, compétition, sans r.,** draw; **r. d'observation,** observed result; *Com:* **résultats de l'exercice, de l'exploitation,** trading results; **avoir, obtenir, un r.,** to get, obtain, a result; **avoir pour r. de . . .,** to result in . . .; to lead to . . .; **ces révélations eurent pour r. la chute du Ministère,** these revelations led to, resulted in, the fall of the Government; **donner des résultats,** to yield results; **aboutir à un r. favorable,** to reach a favourable result, a favourable issue.

résultatif, -ive [rezyltatif, -iːv], *a. Ling:* resultative.

résulter [rezylte], *v.i.* (*used only in the third pers. & pr.p. the aux. is usu.* **être**) to result, follow, arise (**de,** from); **les maux qui résultent de l'intempérance,** the evils that result, ensue, follow, from intemperance; **qu'en est-il résulté?** what was the result of it? what came of it? **je ne sais pas ce qui en résultera,** I don't know what the outcome will be; **voilà ce qui en a résulté, ce qu'il en est résulté,** that is what it resulted in; that is what it led to; that was the effect it had; **les avantages économiques qui en résultent,** the accompanying, resultant, economic benefits; **il en est résulté beaucoup de mal,** much harm resulted from this; **il en résulte que + *ind.*,** consequently . . ., the result is that . . .; it follows from this that . . .; **il n'en résulte pas que + *sub.*,** it does not follow that . . .; *Jur:* **les faits qui résultent des informations,** the facts established by the inquiry; **réclamation résultant de la perte de . . .,** claim for the loss of . . ..

résumé [rezyme], *s.m.* (*a*) summary, abstract, epitome, résumé, abridgement; abridged version; *Journ:* **r. des chapitres précédents,** (summary of) the story so far; (*b*) *Elcs:* (*computers*) abstract; **r. automatique,** auto-abstract; **r. succinct,** compendium; (*c*) *Jur:* **r. des débats,** summing up; *adv.phr.* **au r., en r.,** in short, to sum up, in brief, after all.

résumer [rezyme], *v.tr.* (*a*) to summarize; to give a summary of (sth.); to sum up (an argument, etc.); *Jur: etc:* **r. les débats,** to sum up; **pour résumer les faits . . ., pour me r.,** to sum up . . .; **voilà toute l'affaire résumée en un mot,** that's the whole thing in a nutshell; **voilà à quoi tout cela se résume,** that's what it all amounts to, comes down to, *F:* boils down to; **le risque se résume à l'avarie du moteur,** the risk is reduced, limited, to damage to the engine; (*b*) *Elcs:* (*computers*) to abstract.

résupination [resypinasjɔ̃], *s.f. Bot:* resupination.

résupiné [resypine], *a. Bot:* resupinate.

resurchauffe [rəsyrʃof], *s.f.* re-superheating (of steam).

résure [rezyːr], *s.f. Fish:* salted cod roe (used as bait).

résurgence [rezyrʒɑ̃ːs], *s.f.* **1.** *Phil:* resurgence. **2.** *Geog:* resurgence, reappearance (of subterranean river).

résurgent [rezyrʒɑ̃], *a. Geog:* resurgent (stream).

resurgir [rəsyrʒiːr], *v.i.* to re-appear; to rise up (again) (above the surface of the water, etc.).

résurrection [rezyrɛksjɔ̃], *s.f.* **1.** resurrection; **la r. des morts,** the resurrection of the dead. **2.** revival, restoration, resurrection (of the arts, etc.).

résurrectionnel, -elle [rezyrɛksjɔnɛl], *a.* resurrectional.

résurrection(n)iste [rezyrɛksjɔnist], *s.* **1.** resurrectionist; resuscitator, resurrecter (of dead theories, etc.). **2.** *Eng.Hist:* resurrectionist, body-snatcher, resurrection man.

retable [rətabl̩], **rétable** [retabl̩], *s.m. Ecc.Arch:* retable, reredos, altar piece.

rétablir [retabliːr], *v.tr.* to re-establish, restore, set up again; (*a*) **r. l'ordre, la discipline,** to restore public order, discipline; **r. un budget déficitaire,** to balance an adverse budget; *Mil:* **r. la bataille,** to restore the battle; **r. sa position,** (i) to retrieve one's position; (ii) to regain the upper hand; **r. sa fortune, sa réputation,** to retrieve one's fortune, one's good name; **r. sa santé,** to recover one's health; **r. un malade,** to restore a patient to health; (*b*) **r. un texte,** to restore a text; **r. les faits,** to set the facts in their true light; (*c*) to reinstate (official, etc.); **r. un officier dans son commandement,** to restore an officer to his command; **r. un roi sur son trône,** to re-establish a king on his throne; **r. les fonctions de représentant,** to re-appoint a representative; (*d*) **r. une loi,** to bring a law into force again; (*e*) **r. le niveau,** to top up (a battery, storage tank, etc.); (*f*) *Elcs:* (*computers*) to reset.

se rétablir. 1. (*a*) to recover; to get well again; to pick up again; **il est rétabli,** he is better, has got over it; **je me sens bien rétabli,** I feel myself again; **il est allé dans le Midi pour achever de se r.,** he has gone to the South of France to finish convalescing; (*b*) **l'ordre se rétablit,** public order is being restored; there is a return to public order; *Fin:* **le crédit se rétablit,** credit is reviving. **2. se r. dans les bonnes grâces de qn,** to re-establish oneself in s.o.'s good graces.

rétablissement [retablismɑ̃], *s.m.* **1.** re-establishment; restoration (of order, of peace, of a dynasty); reinstatement (of an official); retrieval (of fortune, of one's good name); **r. d'un édifice,** repair, restoration, of a building; **r. de la religion,** religious revival. **2.** recovery (after illness); **j'attends le r. de ma santé,** I am waiting until I have recovered my health, until I am better. **3.** *Gym:* pull up; **faire un r.,** to heave oneself up (on to *e.g.* a ledge above). **4.** *Elcs:* (*computers*) **r. automatique,** automatic reset; **impulsion de r.,** reset pulse.

retaillement [rətajmɑ̃], *s.m.* cutting again; recutting; *Hort:* repruning.

retailler [rətɑje], *v.tr.* to cut (sth.) again; to recut (file, etc.); **r. un arbre,** to reprune a tree, prune a tree again; **r. un crayon,** to sharpen a pencil again, to re-sharpen a pencil.

retailles [rətɑːj], *s.f.pl. Tail:* cabbage; *Furs:* fur scraps.

rétamage [retamaːʒ], *s.m.* **1.** re-tinning. **2.** re-silvering.

rétamer [retame], *v.tr.* **1.** to re-tin (pots, pans). **2.** to re-silver (mirror). **3.** *F:* **être rétamé,** (i) to be drunk, tight; (ii) to be worn out, tired out; (iii) to be broke.

rétameur [retamœːr], *s.m. Tchn:* **1.** tinsmith, tinner. **2.** silverer.

retapage [rətapaːʒ], *s.m.* doing up; retouching; recasting (of speech, play); **r. rapide d'un lit,** quick making up of a bed; **cela ira, après un bon r.,** it will do, when we have given it a good touching up, when we've put it in order properly.

retape [rətap], *s.f.* **1.** *F:* (*of woman*) **faire la r.,** to solicit; to walk the streets. **2.** *F:* vulgar publicity.

retaper [rətape], *v.tr. F:* **1.** (*a*) to repair, mend, patch up, do up; to straighten (bed); to retouch, touch up, recast (speech, play); **r. une vieille maison,** to patch up an old house; **se r. le moral,** to buck up; **aller en Suisse pour se r. les poumons,** to go to Switzerland to patch up one's lungs; **prenez ça, ça vous retapera,** drink that, it will set you up, buck you up; (*b*) **se r. les cheveux,** to put one's hair straight. **2.** *A:* to plough, fail (candidate at examination).

retard [rətaːr], *s.m.* **1.** (*a*) delay, slowness; backwardness (of harvest, of child); **une heure de r.,** an hour's delay; *Artil:* **fusée à court r.,** fuse with short delay action; **agir sans retard,** to act without delay; **ces paiements ont subi un long r.,** these payments have been long delayed; **le train a du r.,** the train is late; **apporter du r. à (faire) qch.,** to be slow, behindhand, to delay, in doing sth.; **le r. prolongé que vous avez apporté à répondre,** your long delay in replying; **il a un fort r. à rattraper,** he has considerable leeway to make up; **le r. dont souffre le pays,** the backward state of the country; *Mil:* **r. dans le domaine des fusées,** missile gap; **en r.,** late, behindhand; *For:* **arbre en r.,** laggard; *Com:* **commandes en r.,** back orders; **mettre qn en r.,** to make s.o. late; to delay s.o.; **être en r.,** (i) to be late; (ii) to be behindhand, in arrears; (iii) (*of schoolboy*) to be behind the others; **je serai en r. à ma leçon,** I shall be late for my lesson; **être en r. pour ses études, dans son travail,** to be behind in one's studies, with one's work; **les élèves en r.,** the backward pupils; **en r. de dix minutes,** ten minutes late; **navire en r.,** ship overdue; **qu'est-ce qui vous a mis en r.?** (i) what made you late? (ii) what put you in arrears? **moisson en r.,** backward harvest; **être en r. sur son siècle, sur la mode,** to be behind the times, behind the fashion; **ma montre est en r.,** my watch is slow; **ma montre est en r. sur l'horloge de la ville,** my watch is slow by the town clock; **contribuable en r.,** ratepayer in arrears; **je suis en r. de trois mois pour mon terme,** I am three months behind with the rent; **compte en r.,** account outstanding, overdue; **mesures en r. sur les événements,** belated measures; **le train a dix minutes de r., est en r. de dix minutes, a un r. de dix minutes,** the train is ten minutes late, overdue, behind time; **votre montre a dix minutes de r.,** your watch is ten minutes slow; *Sp:* **ils ont deux buts de r., ils ont un r. de deux buts,** they are two goals behind; (*b*) *Tchn:* retardation, lag; **r. diurne de la marée,** lag(ging) of the tides; *Mch:* **r. à l'admission,** retarded admission, late admission; admission lag; *I.C.E:* **r. à la fermeture de l'admission,** late cut-off (of the admission); **r. à l'allumage,** late ignition, post ignition; *El:* **r. d'aimantation,** magnetic lag; **être en r. de phase,** to lag in phase; *W.Tel:* **angle de r.,** angle of lag; *Elcs:* (*computers*) **r. différentiel,** differential delay; **r. d'exploitation,** operating delay; **ligne à r.,** delay line; **mémoire, registre, à ligne à r.,** delay-line store, register. **2.** *Mus:* suspension, retardation.

retardataire [rətardatɛːr]. **1.** *a.* (*a*) late, behind time; behindhand, in arrears; (*b*) backward (pupil, race, etc.). **2.** *s.* (*a*) latecomer; (*b*) loiterer; laggard; (*c*) *Mil: etc:* soldier, sailor, who overstays his pass, who overstays pass; (*d*) tenant, etc., in arrears (with the rent, with the rates and taxes).

retardateur, -trice [rətardatœːr, -tris]. **1.** *a.* retarding, retardative; delaying (tactics). **2.** *s.m.* (*a*) *Phot:* restrainer, retarder; (*b*) (cement-setting) retarder; (vulcanization) retarder.

retardation [rətardasjɔ̃], *s.f. Mec:* retardation, negative acceleration.

retardé, -ée [rətarde]. **1.** *a.* delayed (departure, etc.); **ouverture retardée,** delayed opening (of parachute). **2.** *a. & s.* **(enfant) r.,** backward, retarded, child.

retardement [rətardəmɑ̃], *s.m.* **1.** retardment, retarding. **2.** (*a*) delay, putting off; **spéculation à r.,** speculation with a view to the future, the results of which will be deferred; (*b*) delayed action; *Mil:* **action de r.,** delaying action; **bombe à r.,** delayed-action bomb, time bomb; **mine à r.,** delayed-action mine; **fusible à r.,** delayed-action fuse.

retarder [rətarde]. **1.** *v.tr.* (*a*) to retard, delay, hold up, *F:* hang up, (s.o., sth.); to make (s.o.) late; **navire retardé par le mauvais temps,** ship delayed by bad weather; (*b*) to delay, put off (an event); **r. un payement,** to defer a payment; (*c*) **r. la pendule,** to put back, set back, the clock. **2.** *v.i.* (*a*) to be late, slow, behindhand; **l'horloge retarde,** the clock (i) loses (time), (ii) is slow; **ma montre retarde,** *F:* **je retarde de dix minutes,** my watch is ten minutes behind the time, ten minutes slow; *F:* I am ten minutes slow; **pendule qui retarde de dix minutes par jour,** clock that loses ten minutes a day; **les fleurs des champs retardent sur celles des jardins,** wild flowers are later than garden ones; **il retarde sur son siècle,** he is behind the times; (*b*) *Tchn:* (*of tides, etc.*) to lag; *El:* **courant retardé,** lagging current.

retartiner [rətartine], *v.tr. El: A:* to re-paste (accumulator plates).

retassure [rətɑsyːr], *s.f. Metall:* shrinkage hole, pipe.

retâter [rətɑte]. **1.** *v.tr.* (*a*) to touch, feel, (sth.) again; (*b*) to sound (s.o.) again (**sur une affaire,** on a matter); **se r.,** to think it over again. **2.** *v.ind.tr.* **r. de qch.,** to try, taste, sth. again; to have another taste of sth.; *F:* **r. de la prison,** to go to prison again; to have another spell of prison.

reteindre [rətɛ̃ːdr], *v.tr.* (*conj. like* TEINDRE) to redye; to dye (sth.) again; to dye (sth.) another colour.

retéléphoner [rətelefɔne], *v.tr.* to ring (s.o.) up again, *U.S:* to call (s.o.) again; **je vais r. ce soir,** I'll ring back again, *U.S:* call back, this evening.

retenage [rətnaːʒ], *s.m. Leath:* second racking (of skin).

retendoir [rətɑ̃dwaːr], *s.m.* piano tuning key.

retendre [rətɑ̃ːdr], *v.tr.* **1.** to stretch (sth.) again; to tighten (strings of an instrument) again; to set (trap) again, to reset (trap); to bend (a bow) again; to retighten (belt); to spread (sail) again. **2.** to hold out (one's hand, etc.) again.

rétène [retɛn], *s.m. Ch:* retene.

retenir [rətniːr], *v.tr.* (*conj. like* TENIR) **1.** (*a*) to hold (s.o., sth.) back; to hold up, keep back (from falling, etc.); to detain; **r. qn,** (i) to keep hold of s.o.; (ii) to detain, delay, s.o.; **r. qn de force,** to detain s.o. forcibly; **je le retins au moment où il allait tomber,** I caught him as he was falling; **r. l'attention,** to hold, arrest, the attention; **cette question ne nous retiendra pas,** this question need not detain us; **r. qn au lit,** to keep s.o. in bed; to confine s.o. in bed; **r. qn à dîner,** to make s.o. stay to dinner; to keep s.o. for dinner; **on m'a retenu pour ce soir,** I'm engaged, booked, for this evening; **r. la foule,** to keep back, hold back, the crowd; **r. qn prisonnier,** to keep s.o. prisoner; **r. qn en otage,** to hold s.o. as hostage; **je suis retenu ici par mes affaires,** I am kept here by business; **il ne faut pas que je vous retienne, je ne vous retiens pas,** I mustn't detain you, don't let me keep you; **qu'est-ce qui vous retient?** what prevents, hinders, you? what's keeping you? **être retenu par un charme,** to be bound by a charm; to be spellbound; *Nau:* **retenu par les glaces, par la marée,** ice-bound, tide-bound; (*b*) to hold (sth.) in position, to secure (sth.); **r. une poutre,** to cramp down a beam; (*c*) **r. l'eau,** to be water-tight; **nos citernes ne retenaient plus l'eau,** our supply tanks were leaking; (*d*) *Hyd.E:* to impound (water). **2.** to retain; (*a*) **r. une somme sur le salaire de qn,** to keep back so much from s.o.'s wages; **r. qch. par cœur,** to remember sth. by heart; **cet enfant ne retient rien,** this child can't remember anything, can't keep a thing in his head; *Com:* **r. l'escompte,** to deduct the discount; (*b*) **r. un domestique,** to engage a servant; **r. des places (dans un train), des chambres (à un hôtel),** to make (train, hotel) reservations; to book rooms in an hotel; **r. une place au théâtre,** to book a seat at the theatre; **je vous retiens à dîner pour mercredi,** keep Wednesday free to have dinner with us; *F:* **je vous retiens!** (i) I won't forget! I'll watch it next time; (ii) you're a (fat) lot of use! (*c*) *Ar:* to carry (a figure); **je pose 2 et je retiens 5,** put down 2 and carry 5; *F:* **je pose zéro et je retiens tout,** I'm hanging on to this and you can whistle for the change; (*d*) *Jur:* (*of judge*) **r. une cause,** to declare his competency in a given case; **l'autre chef d'accusation n'a pas été retenu,** the other charge has not been proceeded with; (*e*) **r. une candidature, une proposition,** to short-list a candidate, an application; to consider a proposal; *Com: etc:* **r. une offre,** to accept an offer. **3.** to restrain, curb, check (one's anger, etc.); **r. un cri,** to stifle a cry; **r. son souffle,** to hold one's breath; **r. ses larmes,** to keep back, hold back, check, restrain, one's tears; **avoir peine à r. ses larmes,** to find it difficult to restrain one's tears; **r. son cheval,** to hold in, rein in, one's horse; **r. sa langue,** to put a curb on one's tongue; to bridle one's tongue; **r. qn de faire qch.,** *A:* **qu'il ne fasse qch.,** to restrain s.o., hold s.o. back, from doing sth.

se retenir. 1. se r. à qch., to catch hold of, cling to, clutch at, sth.; **un homme qui se noie se retient à tout,** a drowning man catches at every straw. **2. se r. au milieu de sa course,** to check oneself, to stop, in the middle of one's course. **3.** to restrain, control, contain, oneself; to hold oneself in; **il se retint,** he held himself back; **se r. sur la boisson,** to drink in moderation, to be careful not to drink too much; **se r. de faire qch.,** to refrain from doing sth.; **se r. de pleurer,** to keep back, check, restrain, one's tears; **se r. de rire,** to restrain one's mirth; **je ne pus me r. de lui exprimer mon admiration,** I could not refrain from expressing my admiration; **se r. pour ne pas parler,** to put a curb on one's tongue.

retenter [rətɑ̃te], *v.tr.* to reattempt; to try (sth.) again.

réteneur, -trice [retɑ̃tœːr, -tris]. **1.** *a.* retaining (force, etc.); *Anat:* **muscle r.,** retentor (muscle). **2.** *s.m. Jur:* lienor.

rétentif, -ive [retɑ̃tif, -iːv], *a. Anat: Physiol:* retentive.

rétention [retɑ̃sjɔ̃], *s.f.* **1.** *Med:* retention (of urine, bile); *Obst:* **r. intra-utérine de l'œuf mort,** missed abortion. **2.** *Jur:* reservation; retaining (of pledge); **droit de r. de marchandises,** lien on goods. **3.** *Ar:* carrying (of a figure). **4.** *Jur:* **r. d'une cause,** retention of a case (by a judge).

rétentionnaire [retɑ̃sjɔnɛːr], *s. Jur:* lienor.

rétentionniste [retɑ̃sjɔnist], *s.m. & f. Med:* patient suffering from retention of urine.

retentir [rətɑ̃tiːr], *v.i.* to (re)sound, echo, ring, reverberate; **un klaxon retentit,** a hooter sounded; **le couloir retentit du son de sa voix,** the passage rang with his voice; **les bois retentissent du chant des oiseaux,** the woods resound with the songs of the birds; **la forge retentit du son du marteau,** the smithy rings with the clang of the hammer; **l'enclume retentit sous le marteau,** the anvil clangs under the hammer; **faire r. l'air de ses cris,** to make the air re-echo with one's cries; **la fanfare fit r. une marche,** the band blared out a march; **choc qui retentit dans tout l'organisme,** shock that causes repercussions throughout the organism.

retentissant [rətɑ̃tisɑ̃], *a.* resounding, ringing, loud (voice, noise); **discours r.,** speech that aroused world-wide interest; **succès r.,** astounding, overwhelming, success; **échec r.,** abysmal, dismal, failure.

retentissement [rətɑ̃tismɑ̃], *s.m.* resounding, echoing, sound or noise; reverberation; repercussions (of an event, etc.); **discours, procès, qui a eu un grand r.,** speech, lawsuit, that excited universal interest, that was greatly talked of, that created a great stir; **avoir peu de r.,** to create little stir, to pass almost unnoticed.

rétentivité [retɑ̃tivite], *s.f.* **1.** retentiveness; **manque de r.,** irretentiveness. **2.** *Ph:* retentivity (of magnetism).

retenu [rət(ə)ny], *a.* prudent, circumspect, cautious (person, mind).

retenue [rət(ə)ny], *s.f.* **1.** (*a*) deduction, stoppage, docking (of pay, etc.); **faire une r. de 5% sur les salaires,** to stop, deduct, 5% from the wages; **traitement soumis à r.,** salary subject to superannuation contributions; *Adm:* **r. à la source** = pay as you earn; (*b*) sum kept back, stoppage (from wages, etc.); (*c*) *Ar:* carry over; (*computers*) borrow; **deux de r. et sept font neuf,** carry two and seven are nine. **2.** *Sch:* detention, keeping in; **mettre un élève en r.,** to keep a pupil in; to give a boy detention; to put a boy in detention. **3.** reserve, discretion (in conduct, bearing); restraint (in one's words or actions); **manger avec r.,** to eat sparingly. **4.** (*a*) holding back; **clapet, soupape, de r.,** back-pressure valve, non-return valve, check valve; (*b*) damming (of water); (*c*) holding up, staying; **pieu, piquet, de r.,** anchor stake (of flagstaff, etc.); (*d*) holding down; **goupille de r.,** hold-down cotter. **5.** *Hyd.E:* (*a*) dam; reservoir (for town supply); (*b*) water gate; (*c*) reach (between two gates); (*d*) water level (in reach). **6.** *Nau: etc:* guy; **(aussière de) r.,** check rope; **r. de basse voile,** midship tack; **r. de bossoir,** davit guy; **r. de mât de charge,** derrick guy, vang, boom guy; *W.Tel:* **retenues de mât d'antenne,** stays of an aerial mast. **7.** *Hyd.E:* **r. d'air,** air pocket (in pipe, etc.).

rétépore [retepɔːr], *s.m. Z:* retepore; (*genus*) Retepora.

reterçage, retersage [rətɛrsaːʒ], *s.m.* reploughing (of vineyard).

retercer, reterser [rətɛrse], *v.tr.* **(retercer: n. reterçons, je reterçai(s)),** to replough (vineyard).

rethélois, -oise [rətɛlwa, -waːz], *a. & s.* (native, inhabitant) of Rethel.

rétiaire [resjɛːr], *s.m. Rom.Ant:* retiarius, retiary.

réticence [retisɑ̃ːs], *s.f.* reticence, reserve; *Jur:* non-disclosure, concealment, misrepresentation; **sans r.,** unreservedly; wholeheartedly.

réticent [retisɑ̃], *a.* (*a*) reticent; hesitant; (*b*) unwilling; grudging.

réticulaire [retikylɛːr], *a.* reticular; *Anat:* **substance r. grise,** reticular formation (of the brain).

réticulation [retikylasjɔ̃], *s.f.* reticulation; *Phot:* **r. de la gélatine,** reticulation, wrinkling, of the gelatine.

réticule [retikyl], *s.m.* **1.** (small) handbag; dorothy bag. **2.** *Opt:* reticle, graticle, cross wires, cross hairs, spider lines (of optical instrument); **fil de r.,** hair; **fils d'araignée d'un r.,** spider lines.

réticulé [retikyle], *a. Nat.Hist: etc:* reticulate(d), cancellate(d) (leaf, etc.); *Mth:* latticed; *Arch:* **appareil r.,** reticulated, reticular, (masonry) work.

réticuline [retikylin], *s.f. Physiol:* reticulin.

réticulite [retikylit], *s.f. Vet:* reticulitis.

réticulocyte [retikylɔsit], *s.m. Biol:* reticulocyte.

réticulo-endothélial, -aux [retikylɔɑ̃dɔteljal, -o], *a.m. Anat:* reticulo-endothelial (system).

réticulo-endothéliose [retikylɔɑ̃dɔteljoːz], *s.f. Med:* reticuloendotheliosis.

réticulo-sarcome [retikylɔsarkoːm], *s.m. Med:* reticulosarcoma; *pl. réticulo-sarcomes.*

réticulose [retikyloːz], *s.f. Med:* reticulosis.

réticulum [retikylɔm], *s.m. Z:* reticulum.

rétif, -ive [retif, -iːv], *a.* restive, stubborn, disobedient, mulish (animal, person); **cheval r.,** stubbornly disobedient horse; **paysans rétifs aux achats,** farmers unwilling to buy.

rétiforme [retifɔrm], *a.* retiform, netlike.

rétinacle [retinakl̩], *s.m. Bot: Ent:* retinaculum.

rétinal [retinal], *s.m. Bio-Ch:* retinene.

rétinalite [retinalit], *s.f. Miner:* retinalite.

rétinasphalte [retinasfalt], *s.m. Miner:* retinasphalt(um).

rétine [retin], *s.f. Anat:* retina (of the eye).

rétinène [retinɛn], *s.m. Bio-Ch:* retinene.

rétinerve [retinɛrv], **rétinervé** [retinɛrve], *a. Bot:* retinerved, net-veined, netted-veined.

rétinien, -ienne [retinjɛ̃, -jɛn], *a.* retinal; *Ent: etc:* **cellules rétiniennes,** retinula cells, retinulae.

rétinite[1] [retinit], *s.f. Miner:* pitchstone, retinite, cyanite.

rétinite[2], *s.f. Med:* retinitis.

rétinopathie [retinɔpati], *s.f. Med:* **r. diabétique,** diabetic retinopathy.

rétinoscopie [retinɔskɔpi], *s.f. Opt:* retinoscopy.

rétinule [retinyl], *s.f. Ent:* retinula.

retirable [rətirabl̩], *a.* withdrawable; that can be withdrawn, removed.

retirade [rətirad], *s.f. A.Fort:* retirade.

retirage [rətiraːʒ], *s.m.* **1.** withdrawing, retiral. **2.** subsidence, falling (of waters); receding (of sea). **3.** *Publ: etc:* reprint.

retiration [rətirasjɔ̃], *s.f. Typ:* printing of verso, reiteration, backing up, perfecting; **mettre une feuille en r.,** to perfect, back up, a sheet; **presse, machine, à r.,** perfecting machine.

retiré [rətire], *a.* **1.** (*a*) retired, solitary, secluded, remote (place); retired, solitary (life); (*b*) **vivre r.,** to live in retirement, in seclusion. **2. être r. des affaires,** to have retired from business.

retire-botte [rətirbɔt], *s.m.* bootjack; *pl. retire-bottes.*

retirement [rətirmɑ̃], *s.m.* **1.** *A:* (= CONTRACTURE) contraction (of a muscle). **2.** *Cer:* crawling (of the glaze).

retirer [rətire], *v.tr.* **1.** (*a*) to pull, draw, take, (sth., s.o.) out; to withdraw (sth.); **r. qn de l'eau,** to pull s.o. out of the water; **r. un enfant du collège,** to remove a child, take a child away, from school; **r. son argent d'une banque,** to withdraw one's money from a bank; **r. la clef de la serrure,** to take the key out of the lock; **r. des marchandises de la douane,** to take goods out of bond; to clear goods; **r. des bagages de la consigne,** to take out, check out, one's luggage from the cloakroom; **r. son manteau,** to take off one's coat; **r. un bouchon,** to draw a cork; **r. une balle d'une plaie,** to extract a bullet from a wound; **r. ses mains de ses poches,** to take one's hands out of one's pockets; (*b*) *A:* **r. qn de la misère, de l'erreur,** to deliver, rescue, s.o. from poverty, from error; (*c*) *A:* **r. qn chez soi,** to give shelter to s.o.; to make a home for s.o.; (*d*) **r. un profit de qch.,** to derive, draw, get, a profit from sth.; to derive a benefit from sth.; **qu'a-t-il retiré de mes conseils?** how did he benefit by my advice? (*e*) to obtain, extract; **r. du sucre de la betterave,** to obtain sugar from beet; *A.Min:* **r. de l'huile du schiste,** to extract oil from shale. **2.** (*a*) **r. qch. à qn,** to withdraw sth. from s.o.; to pull, draw, take, snatch, sth. back from s.o.; **r. sa chaise à qn,** to pull away s.o.'s chair; **r. sa main,** to draw one's hand away; **r. une arme à un enfant,** to take a weapon away, remove a weapon, from a child; **r. le permis de conduire à qn,** to disqualify, ban, s.o. from driving; **se voir r. son permis de conduire,** to have one's (driving) licence taken away; to be disqualified, banned, from driving; (*b*) **r. sa parole, sa promesse,** to take back, withdraw, one's word; *F:* to back out; **r. un mot injurieux,** to withdraw an insulting remark; **je retire ce que j'ai dit,** I take back what I said; **r. sa candidature,** to withdraw one's candidature; to stand down; **r. son amitié à qn,** to withdraw one's friendship from s.o.; *Jur:* **r. une plainte,** to withdraw an action; (*c*) **retirer une monnaie de la circulation,** to call in a currency; *Com:* **r. un effet,** to retire, withdraw, take up, a bill; (*d*) **r. une sentinelle,** to withdraw a sentry. **3.** (*a*) *Typ:* to reprint (book); (*b*) to hold another draw of (a lottery); (*c*) to fire off (gun, etc.) again; to fire a second shot.

se retirer. 1. (*a*) to retire, withdraw; **se r. dans sa chambre,** to retire to one's bedroom; **vous pouvez vous r.,** you may go; **se r. à la campagne,** to retire into the country; **se r. d'une entreprise,** to withdraw from an undertaking; to back out of an undertaking; **se r. de la lutte, du combat,** to retire from the field; to withdraw from the fight; to beat a retreat; (*of candidate*) **se r. en faveur de qn,** to stand down; **un des candidats se retire,** one of the candidates is dropping out; (*b*) **se r. des affaires,** to retire (from business); to give up business. **2.** (*of parchment, etc.*) to contract, shrink. **3.** (*of waters*) to fall, subside; (*of sea*) to recede; (*of tide*) to ebb; **ici la mer se retire très loin,** here the tide goes out a long way.

retirons [rətirɔ̃], *s.m.pl. Tex:* combings (left in the carder).

retirure [rətiryːr], *s.f. Metall:* hollow (in casting).

rétiveté [retivte], *s.f.,* **rétivité** [retivite], *s.f.* obstinacy; stubbornness.

retombant [rətɔ̃bɑ̃], *a.* drooping (lips, etc.); hanging (draperies, etc.).

retombe [rətɔ̃ːb], *s.f.* **1.** *Adm:* **feuilles de r.,** sheets attached (to document for remarks, to plan showing possible modifications, etc.). **2.** *Arch:* spring(ing) (of arch of vault).

retombée [rətɔ̃be], *s.f.* **1.** (*a*) *Arch:* spring(ing) (of arch of vault); **assise de r.,** springing course; (*b*) *Const:* whitened frieze (round room); (*c*) **la r. du lierre sur les ruines,** the ivy overhanging the ruins. **2.** fall (of bullets, etc., fired at aircraft, etc.). **3.** (*a*) **retombées radioactives,** radioactive fallout; (*b*) **les retombées civiles des recherches nucléaires militaires,** the repercussions on civilian life of military nuclear research; **la grève aura des retombées sur les prix,** the strike will have repercussions on prices.

retombement [rətɔ̃bmɑ̃], *s.m.* falling down (again); collapse; falling back; relapse; *Lit:* **j'étais trahi; mon r. fut atroce,** I had been betrayed; I felt bitter disillusionment.

retomber [rətɔ̃be], *v.i.* (*the aux. is usu.* **être**) **1.** (*a*) to fall down again; (*of child learning to walk*) **il tombe, se relève, retombe,** he falls down, picks himself up, and falls down again; **la cuillère est retombée dans la soupe,** the spoon has fallen into the soup again; (*b*) to land (after a jump, etc.); **un chat retombe presque toujours sur ses pattes,** cats nearly always land on their feet; (*of pers.*) **il retombe toujours sur ses pieds,** he always falls, lands, on his feet; (*c*) **r. dans la misère,** to be reduced to poverty again; **r. dans le vice,** to relapse into vice; **r. dans le chaos,** to fall back into chaos; **r. dans l'oubli,** to fall into oblivion, to be forgotten; *abs.* **l'intérêt du lecteur ne doit pas r.,** the reader's interest should not be allowed to flag; **r. malade,** to fall, become, ill again; **la conversation retombe toujours sur le même sujet,** the conversation always comes back to the same subject, comes round to the same subject again. **2.** (*a*) to fall back; **r. dans son fauteuil,** to fall back, sink back, into one's armchair; **les vagues s'élevaient et retombaient,** the waves were rising and falling; **le brouillard retomba,** the fog came down again; (*b*) **faire r. un store,** to let down, pull down, a blind; **laisser r. ses bras,** to drop one's arms; **il laissa r. son regard sur l'enfant qui jouait sur la pelouse,** he looked down again at the child who was playing on the lawn; (*c*) **r. sur qn,** to fall back on s.o.; **le blâme retombera sur lui,** the blame will fall on him; **faire r. le blâme sur qn,** to lay the blame on s.o.; **toute la responsabilité retombe sur moi,** all the responsibility devolves, falls, on me; it is I who am saddled, landed, with all the responsibility; **son crime retomba sur lui-même,** his guilt was on his own head; *F:* **tout ça retombera sur moi, me retombera sur le nez,** it'll all come back on me, catch up with me; I'll have to stand the racket, carry the can. **3.** to hang down; **draperies qui retombent,** hanging draperies; **ses cheveux lui retombaient sur les épaules,** her hair hung down on her shoulders.

retondeur [rətɔ̃dœːr], *s.m. Tex:* (*pers.*) shearer, cropper.

retondre [rətɔ̃ːdr̩], *v.tr.* **1.** to shear (sheep, cloth) again. **2.** to recut, clean off (stonework).

retoquer [rətɔke], *v.tr. F:* to plough, fail (candidate at an examination).

retorcher [rətɔrʃe], *v.tr. Metall: Cer:* to fettle (hearth of furnace, pottery, etc.).

retordage [rətɔrdaːʒ], *s.m.,* **retordement** [rətɔrdəmɑ̃], *s.m. Tex:* twisting (of thread, yarn, *esp.* of silk).

retorderie [rətɔrdəri], *s.f. Tex:* twist mill; **r. de soie,** silk-twisting mill.

retordeur, -euse [rətɔrdœːr, -øːz], *Tex:* **1.** *s.* (*pers.*) twister. **2.** *s.f.* **retordeuse,** twister, twisting machine.

retordre [rətɔrdr̩], *v.tr.* **1.** to wring out (the washing) again. **2.** *Tex:* to twist (thread, yarn, silk); **machine à r.,** twisting machine; twister; *F:* **il vous donnera du fil à r.,** he will give you trouble, you have your work cut out with him; **vous avez là du fil à r.,** you have your work cut out (to do it).

retordu [rətɔrdy], *a. Tex:* twisted; **tissu corde retordue,** twisted cord fabric.

rétorquer [retɔrke], *v.tr.* (*a*) to retort; **il rétorqua que cette raison n'était pas valable,** he retorted that this argument was not valid; (*b*) to cast back, hurl back (accusation); **r. un argument contre qn,** to turn s.o.'s argument against himself.

retors, -orse [rətɔːr, -ɔrs], *a.* **1.** (*a*) *Tex:* twisted (thread, silk, cord, etc.); (*b*) **oiseau au bec r.,** bird with a curved beak. **2.** crafty, wily, intriguing, devious (person); pettifogging, rascally (lawyer); **c'est un r.,** he's a slippery customer.

rétorsion [retɔrsjɔ̃], *s.f.* (*a*) retorting; throwing back (of an argument); (*b*) *Jur:* retortion (as a form of retaliation); **mesures de r.,** retaliatory measures.

retouche [rətuʃ], *s.f.* (*a*) slight alteration (à, in), retouching (à, of) touching up, touch up; *Art:* retouch (to painting, etc.); *Ind:* dressing, finishing; **faire des retouches à un travail,** to retouch a piece of work; **faire des retouches à un vêtement,** to make alterations to a garment; **boutique de retouches,** shop that does alterations (to customer's garments); (*b*) *Phot:* retouching; **pupitre à retouche(s),** retouching desk.

retoucher [rətuʃe]. **1.** *v.tr.* (*a*) to retouch, touch up, improve (picture, photograph, etc.); *Ind:* to dress, finish (work); *Dressm: etc:* to alter (garment); (*b*) *F:* **r. la même corde,** to harp back on the same string. **2.** *v.ind.tr.* **r. à qch.,** to touch sth., meddle with sth., again; **votre article est bien, n'y retouchez pas,** your article is a good one, don't alter a word of it, leave it alone.

retoucheur, -euse [rətuʃœːr, -øːz], *s.* **1.** *Art: Phot:* retoucher. **2.** *s.f. Dressm:* **retoucheuse,** finisher.

retouchoir [rətuʃwaːr], *s.m.* retouching brush, instrument.

retour [rətu:r], *s.m.* **1.** (*a*) twisting, winding; **tours et retours,** twists and turns; (*b*) turn (of rope); lead (of tackle); (*c*) *Arch:* return, turn, bend, angle (of wall, etc.); **en r. d'équerre,** at right angles; (*d*) turn, vicissitude, reversal (of fortune, of opinion, etc.); **r. d'opinion en faveur de qn,** revulsion of feeling in favour of s.o.; **r. de conscience,** qualms of conscience; **faire un r. sur soi-même,** to indulge in serious reflexions on one's conduct; **faire un r. sur le passé,** to look back on the past; **par un juste r. des choses d'ici-bas,** by one of time's revenges; (*e*) recurrence; **le r. fréquent de ces accès,** the frequent recurrence of these attacks. **2.** return, going back, coming back (in space or time); (*a*) **de r.,** just back, back (again); **être de r.,** to be back again; **(de) r. du travail,** back from work; **un journaliste (de) r. de Paris,** a reporter just back from Paris; **je pense qu'il sera de r. demain,** I expect him back tomorrow; **de r. chez moi, je lui écrivis,** on my return home I wrote to him; **être sur son r.,** to be about to return, on the point of returning; **à mon r.,** on my return; **je vous verrai à, dès, mon r.,** I shall see you as soon as I am back, immediately I return; **il est temps de songer au r.,** it's time we thought about going back; **partir sans r.,** to depart for ever; **être perdu sans r.,** to be irretrievably lost, past praying for; *F:* **cheval de r.,** old offender, old lag; (*b*) *Trans:* **(voyage de) r.,** (i) *Rail: etc:* return journey, return trip; (ii) *Nau:* return or homeward voyage, return or homeward passage; (iii) *Av:* return flight or voyage; **billet de r.,** return ticket; **coupon de r.,** return half; **train de r.,** (i) up train; (ii) the train home, back; **navire sur le r.,** ship homeward bound; **navire affrété pour voyage à Lisbonne avec r. sur Londres,** ship chartered to Lisbon and back to London; *Nau: etc:* **cargaison, chargement, frêt, de r.,** return cargo, freight; homeward(-bound) cargo, freight; *Rail: etc:* **r. à vide, en charge,** empty, loaded, return; **(wagon, etc.) vide en r.,** (of truck, etc.) returned empty; **chargé en r.,** returned loaded, back loading; *Av:* **r. à la base, au terrain,** return to base; **r. à l'aire de stationnement,** return to ramp; **r. en vol,** return to station; *Av: etc:* **point de non r.,** point of no return; (*c*) *Post:* **par r. (du courrier),** by return of post; (*d*) *Mil:* **r. offensif,** counter attack, counter stroke; (*e*) *Row:* **le r. sur l'avant,** the recover, the swing forward; (*f*) *Cin: Th:* **r. en arrière,** flashback; **r. sur l'avant-guerre,** flashback to pre-war times; (*g*) *Biol:* **r. à un type,** reversion to (a) type; (*h*) *Physiol: etc:* **être sur le r.,** to be on the decline (of life); to be past middle age, past one's prime; **beauté sur le r.,** beauty on the wane; **le r. d'âge,** the critical age, the turn, change, of life. **3.** *Tchn:* (*a*) *Mec.E:* backlash (of mechanism); return (of machine part, etc.); **non r.,** failure to return (of machine part, etc.); **choc en r.,** return stroke; **r. d'huile,** return oil flow; *Av:* **circuit de r. hydraulique,** hydraulic return system; *Mch:* **course de r. (d'un piston),** back stroke (of a piston); *Artil:* **r. en batterie (du tube de pièce),** run-up (of gun barrel); *I.C.E:* **r. de carburateur,** backfire; **avoir des retours,** to backfire; *Aut:* **r. de manivelle,** backfire kick; **manivelle à r. empêché,** non-return handle; *Tp:* **r. du cadran,** return of dial; *Typewr: etc:* **r. de chariot,** carriage return; **r. arrière,** backspace; **r. automatique de ruban,** automatic ribbon reverse; (*computers*) **r. d'information,** information, message, feedback; **r. à zéro, non r. à zéro,** return, non-return, to zero; **code de r.,** return code; **point de r.,** re-entry point; **voie de r.,** backward channel; (*b*) *Mch.-Tls:* return (of tool); **r. à vide, à blanc,** idle return; **r. rapide,** quick return; **vitesse de r.,** return speed; (*c*) *El:* **conducteur de r.,** return conductor; **courant de r.,** return current; **tension de r.,** return voltage; **r. par la masse, par la terre,** earth return, earth circuit; **r. à la terre, à la masse,** earth connection, *U.S:* ground connection; earthing; **choc en r.,** return shock; (*d*) *Hyd.E:* **r. de courant,** eddy; **r. d'eau,** retaining valve; back pressure valve. **4.** (*a*) *Com: Fin: etc:* return (of goods, of dishonoured bill, etc.); **marchandises de r.,** *F:* **retours,** returnable goods, returns; **vendu avec faculté de r.,** on sale or return; **territoires qui ont fait r. à la France,** territories returned to France; *Fin:* **lettre d'avis de r. de souscription,** letter of regret (to applicant for shares); (*b*) dishonoured bill, bill returned dishonoured; (*c*) *Jur:* reversion (of an inheritance, etc.); **droit de r.,** right of reversion; (*of estate*) **faire r. à un ascendant,** to revert to an ascendant. **5.** return (for a kindness, service, etc.); **devoir du r. à qn,** to owe s.o. some return; **payer qch., qn, de r.,** to requite sth., s.o.; to reciprocate (feeling); **payer de r. l'affection de qn,** to return s.o.'s affection; **aimer qn en r.,** to return s.o.'s love; **en r. de . . .,** in return for . . ., in exchange for . . .; **en r. d'une somme de . . .,** in consideration of a sum of . . .; **à beau jeu beau r.,** one good turn deserves another; *Sp:* **match r.,** return match. **6.** turn-back, turnover, turndown (of sheet, in making bed).

retournage [rəturna:ʒ], *s.m.* **1.** *Tail:* turning (of coat). **2.** *Mec.E:* reshaping (on lathe).

retourne [rəturn], *s.f.* **1.** *Cards:* turned-up card, turn-up; **la r. est de pique,** the turn-up is spades; spades are trumps. **2.** upheaval; turning inside out, upside down; *P:* **les avoir à la r.,** to be bone idle. **3.** *Journ:* continuation, turnover, runover (of an article to another page).

retournement [rəturnəmɑ̃], *s.m.* turning; turning round; turning over; turning inside out; reversal; *Wr:* **r. de bras,** hammer lock; *Av:* **r. sur l'aile,** wing over.

retourner [rəturne]. **1.** *v.tr.* (*a*) to turn (a skin, etc.) inside out; **la bourrasque retourna mon parapluie,** the gust turned my umbrella inside out; **r. un habit,** (i) to turn a coat inside out; (ii) *Tail:* to turn a coat; **retournez vos poches,** turn out your pockets; (*b*) to turn (sth.) over; to turn (sth.) up, down, back; **r. le sol,** to turn over turn up, the soil; to plough up the soil; **on avait retourné la pièce pour trouver la lettre,** they had ransacked the room, turned the room upside down, to find the letter; **r. une idée,** to turn over an idea; **r. le foin, une omelette,** to turn the hay, an omelette; **r. la salade,** to mix the salad; **r. une carte,** to turn up a card; **r. qch. dans tous les sens,** to turn sth. over and over (again); **r. une question dans tous les sens,** to thrash out a question; **r. le fer dans la plaie,** to turn the knife in, rub salt into, the wound; *F:* **c'est votre récit qui m'a retourné les sangs, qui m'a tout retourné,** it was your story that upset me, that gave me quite a turn; (*c*) to turn (sth.) round; **r. la tête,** to turn one's head; to look round; **r. le bras à qn,** to twist s.o.'s arm; *F:* **avoir les bras retournés,** to be lazy; *Nau:* **r. un navire,** to bring a ship about; **r. un argument contre qn,** to turn an argument against s.o.; to turn the tables on s.o.; **r. les rires contre qn,** to turn the laughter against s.o.; **r. une situation,** to reverse, upset, a situation; to turn the tables; **r. qn,** to make s.o. alter his views. **2.** *v.tr.* **r. qch. à qn,** to return sth. to s.o., to give, send, sth. back to s.o.; **je vous retourne votre livre,** I am returning your book to you; **r. le compliment,** to return the compliment; *Fin:* **r. un effet impayé,** to return a bill dishonoured. **3.** *v.i.* (*the aux. is usu.* **être**) (*a*) to return; to go back; to drive, fly, ride, sail, walk, back; to make one's way back; **r. dans sa patrie, à sa place,** go back to one's native land, to one's seat; **r. en toute hâte,** to hurry, rush, back; **sa fortune retourne à sa famille,** his fortune reverts to his family; **r. attendre qn,** to go back to wait for s.o.; **r. déjeuner chez soi,** to go home to lunch; **ne retournons pas sur le passé,** we won't go back to the past; we won't revert to the past; **r. en arrière,** (i) to turn back, go back; (ii) to retrograde; *A: F:* **n'y retournez plus,** don't you do it again; **il retourna en France ambassadeur,** he returned to France as ambassador; *Biol:* **r. à un type,** to revert to a type; *Pol:* **r. devant les électeurs,** to go back to the country; (*b*) (*of a crime, mistake, etc.*) **r. sur qn,** to return, come back, recoil, upon s.o.; to come home to roost. **4.** *impers.* **de quoi retourne-t-il?** (i) *Cards:* what are trumps? (ii) *F:* what's it all about? what's up? **savoir de quoi il retourne,** (i) to know how matters stand, what it's all about, what's going on, what's afoot; (ii) to know what's what.

se retourner. 1. (*a*) to turn (round); to turn over; **je sentais mon estomac,** *P:* **mes tripes, se r.,** I felt my stomach heaving; *F:* **avoir le temps de se r.,** to have time to look round; **il sait se r.,** he's never at a loss, he knows how to get out of a difficulty; **il saura bien se r.,** he'll manage all right; (*b*) turn round, to look round, to look back; **se r. vers qn,** to turn round towards s.o.; **se r. sur qn,** to turn round and stare at s.o.; (*c*) to round (**contre qn,** on s.o.); **quand je voulus m'interposer, ils se retournèrent tous les deux contre moi,** when I tried to intervene, they both rounded on me. **2.** to turn round, veer (in one's opinion); *St.Exch:* to go on the other tack (*e.g.* to change from bear to bull). **3.** *F:* **s'en r.** (**à un endroit**), to return, go back (to a place); to make one's way back; **il s'en retourna sans dire un mot,** he went off without saying a word.

retracer [rətrase], *v.tr.* (*conj. like* TRACER) **1.** to retrace (a line); to trace (sth.) again; **r. une allée,** to mark out a path again. **2.** to recall, recount; **r. les événements de la semaine,** to go over the events of the week; **tout ici me retrace ma jeunesse,** everything here recalls my youth to me, reminds me of my youth; **se r. qch.,** to recall sth. to mind.

rétractable [retraktabl̩], *a.* retractable.

rétractation [retraktasjɔ̃], *s.f.* retractation, recantation; *Jur:* rescinding (of sentence, of decree).

rétracter[1] [retrakte], *v.tr.* to retract, to draw in, pull back; **le colimaçon rétracte ses cornes,** the snail retracts, draws in, its horns.

se rétracter, (*of materials*) to shrink; *Anat:* (*of muscle*) to retract.

rétracter[2], *v.tr.* to retract; to withdraw, recant, unsay; to go back on (opinion, etc.); **r. ses paroles,** to eat one's words; **r. une décision, un don,** to withdraw a decision, a gift; *Jur:* **r. un arrêt,** to rescind, retract, a decree.

se rétracter, (*a*) to retract, recant, to eat one's words; (*b*) to withdraw a charge.

rétracteur [retraktœ:r], (*a*) *a.* & *s.m.* *Anat:* **(muscle) r.,** retractor (muscle); (*b*) *s.m.* *Surg:* (*instrument*) retractor.

rétractibilité [retraktibilite], *s.f.* retractibility.

rétractible [retraktibl̩], *a.* retractile.

rétractif, -ive [retraktif, -i:v], *a.* retractive.

rétractile [retraktil], *a.* retractile (organ, etc.).

rétractilité [retraktilite], *s.f.* retractility.

rétraction [retraksjɔ̃], *s.f.* **1.** *Med:* retraction (of muscle, etc.). **2.** contraction, shortening; *Med:* **r. de l'aponévrose palmaire,** Dupuytren's contracture, contracture of palmar fascia.

retraduire [rətradɥi:r], *v.tr.* (*conj. like* TRADUIRE) to retranslate; to translate again.

retraire [rətrɛ:r], *v.tr.* (*conj. like* TRAIRE, *but rarely used except in inf. and in p.p.* **retrait**) *Jur:* to redeem, repurchase (estate, etc.).

retrait[1] [rətrɛ], *a.* contracted, shrunken; warped.

retrait[2], *s.m.* **1.** (*a*) shrinkage, shrinking, contraction (of wood, metal, cement, etc.); (*of wood*) **prendre du r.,** to shrink; **caler (une frette, etc.) à r.,** to shrink on (a ring, etc.); **calage à r.,** shrinking on; shrunk-on fit; (*b*) retirement (of the waters); retreat (of a glacier) (*c*) withdrawal (during sexual intercourse). **2.** (*a*) withdrawal (of order, of bill, of licence, of troops, etc.); cancelling (of licence); scratching (of horse in a race); **r. du permis de conduire,** suspension of driving licence; **r. de fonds,** withdrawal of capital; **r. d'un ordre de grève,** calling off a strike; *Mil:* **r. d'emploi,** deprivation of office; **mettre qn en r. d'emploi,** to retire s.o. (from his employment); *Fin:* **lettre de r.,** letter of withdrawal; **r. de monnaies,** withdrawal of currency from circulation, calling in of currency; (*b*) *Jur:* redemption, repurchase (of estate, etc.). **3.** recess (in wall, etc.); step (of seaplane float, etc.); **rayons de livres dans les retraits,** bookshelves in the recesses; *adv.phr.* **en r.,** recessed (shelves, etc.); pocketed (electrode, etc.); **panneau en r.,** sunk panel; **devant en r.,** recessed front; **maison en r.,** house standing back, set back (from the road); **bâtir une maison en r.,** to set back a house (from the road); (*of pers.*) **être en r.,** to be, stay, in the background; *Typ:* **ligne en r.,** indented line.

retraitant [rətrɛtɑ̃], *s.m.* *Ecc:* retreatant.

retraite[1] [rətrɛt], *s.f.* **1.** (*a*) *Mil: etc:* retreat, withdrawal, retirement; **battre en r.,** to beat a retreat; to retire; **couper la r. à une armée,** to cut off an army's retreat; to head back, head off, an army; **battre, sonner, la r.,** to beat, to sound, the retreat; (*b*) *Navy:* **en r.,** on the quarter; **tirer en r.,** to fire on the quarter or to fire astern; **pièce de r.,** stern chaser (gun); after gun; **en ordre de r.,** in retiring order; *Lit: Hist:* **la r. des Dix Mille,** Anabasis; (*c*) (*in argument, etc.*) **faire r.,** to withdraw. **2.** (*a*) tattoo; **battre, sonner, la r.,** to beat, sound, the tattoo; *Navy:* **coup de canon de r.,** evening gun; (*b*) *Mil.Hist:* (*19th cent.*) (*in garrison towns*) (evening) retreat (with march through the town); *Mil:* **r. aux flambeaux,** torchlight tattoo; torchlight procession. **3.** (*a*) retirement (from working life); **r. par limite d'âge,** retirement on account of age; **caisse de r.,** superannuation fund, pension fund; **pension de r., r. de vieillesse,** retirement pension; **r. des cadres** = (i) graduated pension; (ii) top hat insurance scheme; *Mil: etc:* retired pay; **être en r.,** to be on the retired list; **officier en r.,** retired officer; **militaire en r.,** army pensioner; **mettre qn à la r.,** to retire s.o., pension off s.o.; superannuate s.o.; **être mis à la r. sur sa demande,** to retire, to be placed on the retired list, at one's own request; **prendre sa r.,** to retire (on a pension); **être en r.,** to have retired; **service qui compte pour la r.,** service that counts towards pension; (*b*) *Ecc:* retreat; **faire une r. de huit jours,** to go into retreat for a week; **maison de r.,** retreat house; (*c*) **vivre dans la r.,** to live in retirement; **maison de r. (pour les vieillards, les personnes âgées)** = old people's home. **4.** (*a*) retreat, place of retirement; (*b*) (place of) shelter; refuge; lair, haunt (of wild beasts); (thieves') hideout. **5.** shrinking. **6.** *Arch:* offset (of wall, from storey to storey); recess (in wall).

retraite[2], *s.f. Com:* re-draft, re-exchange; renewed bill; **faire r. sur qn,** to re-draw on s.o.

retraité, -ée [rətrete]. **1.** *a.* retired; pensioned; *Mil:* (*of officer*) on the retired list; **soldat r.,** army pensioner. **2.** *s.* pensioner; person retired on a pension.

retraiter[1] [rətrete], *v.tr.* to pension (s.o.) (off); to retire, superannuate (s.o.); to place (officer) on the retired list.

retraiter[2], *v.tr.* **1.** to treat, handle, (subject) again. **2.** to process again, to reprocess.

retranché [rətrɑ̃ʃe], *a. Mil:* **camp r.,** (i) entrenched camp; (ii) fortified area; (iii) fortress.

retranchement [rətrɑ̃ʃmɑ̃], *s.m.* **1.** cutting off; stopping (of a ration, etc.); docking (of pension etc.); **r. d'un mot,** excision of a word; **r. des abus,** suppression of abuses. **2.** *Mil:* retrenchment, entrenchment; **forcer l'ennemi dans ses derniers retranchements,** to carry the enemy's last positions; **forcer qn dans ses (derniers) retranchements,** to leave s.o. without a leg to stand on; **il est acculé dans ses derniers retranchements,** he is fighting with his back to the wall.

retrancher [rətrɑ̃ʃe], *v.tr.* **1.** (*a*) **r. qch. de qch.,** to cut off sth. from sth.; **r. un passage d'un livre,** to cut, strike, a passage out of a book; **r. un nombre d'un autre,** to subtract, take, a number from another; **r. qch. sur une somme,** to deduct sth. from a sum (of money); (*b*) *O:* **r. qch. à qn,** to dock s.o. of sth.; **le médecin m'a retranché le café,** the doctor has forbidden me to drink coffee, has cut off my coffee; **on lui a retranché sa pension,** his pension has been taken away from him; **se r. tout luxe,** to cut out all luxuries; **r. le superflu,** to cut out everything unnecessary, superfluous. **2.** *Mil:* to entrench, retrench (post).

se retrancher. 1. *A:* **se r. à faire qch.,** to confine oneself to doing sth.; **se r. dans les faits,** to confine oneself to facts. **2.** *A:* to retrench; to curtail one's expenses. **3.** *Mil:* to entrench oneself; to dig in; **il se retrancha dans le silence,** he took refuge in silence; **se r. derrière les ordres reçus,** to take refuge behind one's instructions.

retransmetteur [rətrɑ̃smɛtœːr], *s.m. Elcs: Tg: etc:* retransmitter; **r. à bande perforée,** perforated-tape retransmitter.

retransmettre [rətrɑ̃smɛtr̥], *v.tr.* (*conj. like* TRANSMETTRE) to retransmit.

retransmission [rətrɑ̃smisjɔ̃], *s.f. Elcs: W.Tel: etc:* retransmission; **r. automatique par bande perforée,** automatic tape relay.

retravailler [rətravaje]. **1.** *v.tr.* to work (sth.) over again; to touch up (piece of work). **2.** *v.i.* **r. à qch.,** to work at sth. again.

retraverser [rətravɛrse], *v.tr.* to recross, retraverse; to cross (road, river) again.

retrayant, -ante [rətrɛjɑ̃, -ɑ̃ːt], *s. Jur:* repurchaser, redemptor (of property).

retrayé, -ée [rətreje], *s. Jur:* seller (against whom right of redemption is exercised).

retread [ritred], *s.m. Civ.E:* resurfacing (road) with re-used materials.

rétréci [retresi], *a.* **1.** narrow, contracted, restricted; **esprit r.,** narrow mind; *Aut:* **cadre r. à l'avant,** inswept frame. **2.** *Med:* strictured.

rétrécir [retresiːr]. **1.** *v.tr.* (*a*) to narrow (a street, the mind); to contract, straiten; to shrink (garment); (*b*) to take in (garment, etc.). **2.** *v.i. & pr.* (*a*) to contract; to narrow, to grow narrow; **la lutte s'est rétrécie entre le socialisme et le radicalisme,** the struggle has narrowed down to a fight between socialism and radicalism; (*b*) (*of garment, etc.*) to shrink.

rétrécissable [retresisabl̥], *a.* shrinkable.

rétrécissement [retresismɑ̃], *s.m.* **1.** (*a*) narrowing, contracting; **r. de la pupille,** contraction of the pupil; *Aut:* **r. du cadre,** insweeping of the frame; (*b*) shrinking (of cloth); **tissu qui n'a pas été soumis au r.,** unshrunk material. **2.** (*a*) narrow part, neck (of tube, etc.); (*b*) *Med:* stricture.

rétreigneur [retrɛɲœːr], *s.m. Metalw:* hammerman, hammerer.

rétreindre [retrɛ̃dr̥], *v.tr.* (*conj. like* ÉTREINDRE) *Metalw:* to hammer (out).

rétreint [retrɛ̃], *s.m.*, **rétreinte** [retrɛ̃ːt], *s.f. Metalw:* hammering (out).

retrempe [rətrɑ̃ːp], *s.f.* retempering (of steel).

retremper [rətrɑ̃pe], *v.tr.* **1.** to soak, steep, (linen, etc.) again. **2.** (*a*) to retemper (steel, etc.); (*b*) to tone, brace, (s.o.) up; to reinvigorate (s.o.); (*c*) *Lit:* to retemper (the soul, the mind); **il s'est retrempé dans l'adversité,** he has gone through the fires of adversity.

rétribuer [retribɥe], *v.tr.* to remunerate, pay (employee, service); **travail rétribué,** paid work; **fonctionnaires bien rétribués,** highly paid officials.

rétributeur [retribytœːr], *s.m.* remunerator.

rétribution [retribysjɔ̃], *s.f.* **1.** remuneration, reward, payment (for services rendered); salary; **fonctions sans r.,** unsalaried office; honorary duties. **2.** compensation.

retrier [rətrije], *v.tr.* to re-sort.

rétro- [retrɔ], *pref.* retro-.

rétro [retro], *a. & s.m.* (*a*) *Bill:* pull-back, screw-back (stroke); (*b*) *Cy:* back-pedal (brake).

rétroactif, -ive [retrɔaktif, -iːv], *a.* retroactive, retrospective, (law, etc.); *Jur:* ex post facto; **augmentation avec effet r. au 1er juillet,** increase backdated to July 1st.

rétroaction [retrɔaksjɔ̃], *s.f.* **1.** retroaction, retrospective effect. **2.** *Elcs: W.Tel:* feedback; back coupling.

rétroactivement [retrɔaktivmɑ̃], *adv.* retroactively, retrospectively.

rétroactivité [retrɔaktivite], *s.f.* retroactivity, retrospective effect; **traitement avec r. au 1er mars,** salary with arrears as from March 1st.

rétroagir [retrɔaʒiːr], *v.i.* to retroact, to be retroactive.

rétrocédant, -ante [retrɔsedɑ̃, -ɑ̃ːt], *s. Jur:* party who retrocedes, reconveys, reassigns (right, etc.).

rétrocéder [retrɔsede], *v.tr.* (*conj. like* CÉDER) **1.** *Jur:* to retrocede; to redemise, reconvey, reassign (right, etc.). *Com:* **r. une commission,** to return a commission. **2.** *Med:* to retrocede.

rétrocessif, -ive [retrɔsesif, -iːv], *a.* retrocessive.

rétrocession [retrɔsesjɔ̃], *s.f.* **1.** *Jur:* retrocession, reconveyance, redemise. **2.** *Med:* retrocession (of eruption, etc.).

rétrocessionnaire [retrɔsesjɔnɛːr], *s. Jur:* cessionary, assignee.

rétrodéviation [retrɔdevjasjɔ̃], *s.f. Med:* retrodeviation.

rétrodiffusé [retrɔdifyze], *a. Atom.Ph: Elcs:* backscattered (radiation, etc.).

rétrodiffusion [retrɔdifyzjɔ̃], *s.f. Atom.Ph:* backward diffusion, back-scatter(ing) (of particles).

rétrofléchi [retrɔfleʃi], *a.* retroflected, retroflexed.

rétroflexe [retrɔflɛks], *a. Ling:* cerebral (consonant).

rétroflexion [retrɔflɛksjɔ̃], *s.f. Med:* retroflexion, retroversion (*esp.* of the womb).

rétrofusée [retrɔfyze], *s.f.* retro rocket.

rétrogradation [retrɔgradasjɔ̃], *s.f.* **1.** (*a*) *Astr:* retrogradation, retrogression; (*b*) going back (in knowledge, etc.); **r. morale,** moral lapse. **2.** (*a*) *Mil:* reduction (of N.C.O.) to lower rank; *Navy:* disrating; (*b*) *Sp:* penalty classification (for hindering an opponent).

rétrograde [retrɔgrad]. **1.** *a.* retrograde, backward, reversed (motion); *Bill:* **effet r.,** pull back, screw back, check side; **faire de l'effet r.,** to put bottom on the ball; *Med:* **amnésie r.,** retrograde amnesia. **2.** *a. & s.* reactionary.

rétrograder [retrɔgrade]. **1.** *v.i.* to retrogress; to move backwards, to go back; (*of planet, glacier*) to retrograde; *Mil: etc:* to fall back, to retreat; *Aut: etc:* to change down, *U.S:* to shift down. **2.** *v.tr.* (*a*) *Mil:* to reduce (N.C.O.) to a lower rank; *Navy:* to disrate (petty officer); (*b*) *Sp:* to penalize (player, horse) (for hindering opponent).

rétrogressif, -ive [retrɔgresif, -iːv], *a.* retrogressive.

rétrogression [retrɔgresjɔ̃], *s.f.* retrogression.

rétromammaire [retrɔmamɛːr], *a. Anat:* retromammary.

rétromoteur [retrɔmɔtœːr], *s.m.* retro rocket.

rétropédalage [retrɔpedalaːʒ], *s.m. Cy:* back pedalling; **frein à r.,** back-pedal brake.

rétropédaler [retrɔpedale], *v.i.* to back-pedal.

rétropéritonéal, -aux [retrɔperitɔneal, -o], *a. Anat:* retroperitoneal.

rétropharyngien, -ienne [retrɔfarɛ̃ʒjɛ̃, -jɛn], *a. Anat:* retropharyngeal.

rétropropulsion [retrɔprɔpylsjɔ̃], *s.f. Av: etc:* reverse thrust.

rétroposition [retrɔpɔzisjɔ̃], *s.f. Anat:* retroposition.

rétropubien, -ienne [retrɔpybjɛ̃, -jɛn], *a. Anat:* retropubic.

rétropulsion [retrɔpylsjɔ̃], *s.f. Med:* retropulsion.

rétrospectif, -ive [retrɔspɛktif, -iːv], (*a*) *a.* retrospective; **vue rétrospective,** retrospect; (*b*) *s.f.* **rétrospective,** retrospect; *Art:* retrospective (exhibition).

rétrospection [retrɔspɛksjɔ̃], *s.f.* retrospection; *Phil:* looking backward.

rétrospectivement [retrɔspɛktivmɑ̃], *adv.* retrospectively.

rétrosternal, -aux [retrɔstɛrnal, -o], *a. Anat:* retrosternal.

rétrotuyère [retrɔtɥijɛːr], *s.f. Av: etc:* retrorocket.

retroussage [rətrusaːʒ], *s.m.*, **retroussement** [rətrusmɑ̃], *s.m.* turning up, tucking up; **retroussement des lèvres,** curling of the lips.

retroussé [rətruse], *a.* turned up; (*a*) tucked up, bunched up (dress, etc.); turned up (sleeves); (*b*) **nez r.,** snub nose; turned-up, up-tilted, tip-tilted, nose; (*of horse*) **avoir les flancs retroussés,** to be hollow-flanked; (*c*) *Const:* **cintre r.,** cocked centre.

retrousser [rətruse], *v.tr.* to turn up, roll up (one's sleeves, trousers, etc.); to tuck up, pull up, bunch up (one's skirt, etc.); to turn up, twist up (one's moustache, etc.); to curl (up) (one's lip); to cock (one's hat); **quand on porte une robe longue il faut se r. pour monter l'escalier,** if you wear a long dress you have to pull up your skirt to go upstairs.

retroussis [rətrusi], *s.m.* **1.** *A:* cock (of wide-brimmed hat); turned-back facings or lappet (of uniform); **bottes à r.,** top-boots. **2.** curling up (of hair, lips, etc.).

retrouvable [rətruvabl̥], *a.* that may be found again; recoverable; retrievable; **classeur où les dossiers sont aisément retrouvables,** cabinet in which the files can easily be found.

retrouvaille [rətruvaːj], *s.f.* finding (of sth.) again; rediscovery; *usu. pl.* meeting (of s.o.) again.

retrouver [rətruve], *v.tr.* (*a*) to find (sth., s.o.) (again); to meet (with) (sth., s.o.) (again); to rediscover (sth.); **r. son chemin,** to find one's way again; **la clef a été retrouvée,** the key has been found; **que je ne vous retrouve plus ici!** don't let me find you here again! **r. la parole, sa santé,** to recover one's speech, one's health; **r. ses forces,** to regain one's strength; to pick up again (after illness); **on retrouve chez le fils le nez du père,** the son has his father's nose, has a nose like his father's; **le récit fait un retour en arrière pour r. les personnages principaux,** the narrative goes back to pick up the story of the principal characters; **on retrouve dans ce film la même préoccupation avec la mort,** we find (once more) in this film the same preoccupation with death; **on ne retrouve plus cet auteur dans son dernier roman,** this author's last novel is completely uncharacteristic; (*b*) **aller r. qn,** to go and join s.o.; **je vous retrouverai ce soir,** I shall see you again this evening; **venez donc nous r. au Sénégal,** do come out to Senegal to see us; (*c*) *Elcs:* (*computers*) to retrieve.

se retrouver. 1. se r. dans la même position, to find oneself, to be, in the same position again; **si un jour je me retrouve à Paris . . .,** if ever I am back in Paris . . .. **2.** to be oneself again; to find one's bearings; **je ne puis m'y r.!** I can't make it out! **3.** to meet again; to fall in with one another again; **nous nous retrouverons à Paris,** we shall meet again in Paris; **comme on se retrouve!** how small the world is! how easy it is to run across people! *F:* **on se retrouvera!** I'll get my own back! I'll be even with you yet! **4.** *F:* **s'y r.,** (i) to cover one's expenses, to break even; (ii) to make a profit out of sth.; to derive benefit from sth.; to make something out of sth.

rétrovaccin [retrɔvaksɛ̃], *s.m. Med:* retrovaccine.

rétrovaccination [retrɔvaksinasjɔ̃], *s.f. Med:* retrovaccination.

rétroversé [retrɔvɛrse], *a.* retroverse, retroverted.

rétroversion [retrɔvɛrsjɔ̃], *s.f. Med:* retroversion (of womb, tooth).

rétroviseur [retrɔvizœːr], *s.m. Aut:* **(miroir) r.,** driving mirror, rearview mirror, *U.S:* rearvision mirror.

rets [rɛ], *s.m. Ven: A: & Lit:* net; **poser les r.,** to net (a wood, etc.); *Lit:* **prendre qn dans ses r.,** to catch s.o. in one's toils.

retubage [rətybaːʒ], *s.m.* re-tubing (of boiler).

retuber [rətybe], *v.tr.* to re-tube (a boiler).

retziane [rɛtzjan], *s.f. Miner:* retzian.

réuni [reyni], *a.* united; joined together; **les Allemands sont plus forts que nous et les Anglais réunis,** the Germans are stronger than us and the English together; **vingt petites boutiques réunies,** twenty small shops all in one.

réunification [reynifikasjɔ̃], *s.f. Pol:* reunification.

réunifier [reynifje], *v.tr.* (*conj. like* UNIFIER) *Pol:* to reunify.

réunion [reynjɔ̃], *s.f.* reunion. **1.** (*a*) bringing together, reuniting; junction; joining up again; connection; connecting; *Surg:* (re-)union; **r. d'une province à la France,** union of a province with France; (*b*) *Elcs:* (*computers*) **r. logique,** disjunction OR; (*c*) *A:* reconciliation. **2.** (*a*) coming together; **droit de r.,** right of assembly; **salle de r.,** assembly room; **lieu de r.,** place of assembly; (*b*) assembly, gathering, meeting; **réunions d'une commission,** sessions, sittings, of a commission; **c'est arrivé dans une r.,** it happened at a meeting; **r. publique,** public meeting; (*c*) social gathering, party; *F:* function; **la petite r. s'est très bien passée,** the little party went off very well.

Réunion (La) [lareynjɔ̃], *Pr.n.f. Geog:* Reunion.

réunionnais, -aise [reynjɔnɛ, -ɛːz], *a. & s. Geog:* (native, inhabitant) of Reunion.

réunir [reyniːr], *v.tr.* to re-unite; (*a*) to join (things) together; **r. les morceaux,** to bring, put, the pieces together; **r. qch. à qch.,** to join sth. to, with, sth.; **r. la force du corps à celle de l'âme,** to unite, combine, strength of body with strength of mind; **r. une somme,** to collect, get together, a sum of money; **r. une armée,** to raise an army; **r. une assemblée, un comité,** to convene an assembly, a committee; to call a committee together; (*b*) *A:* to reconcile; *Hist:* **Réunis,** Protestants who turned Catholic after the revocation of the Edict of Nantes.

se réunir, (*a*) to meet, to gather together; (*of water*) to collect; **les Chambres se réunissent demain,** Parliament meets tomorrow; (*b*) *Com: Fin:* (*of banks, etc.*) to amalgamate; (*c*) (*of churches, etc.*) to unite; (*d*) **se r. contre qn,** to join forces against s.o.; **se r. pour faire qch.,** to join together to do sth.; **tout se réunissait contre nous,** everything combined against us.

réunissage [reynisaːʒ], *s.m. Tex:* doubling (thread).

réunisseuse [reynisøːz], *s.f. Tex:* doubling frame.

réussi [reysi], *a.* successful, successfully done, well performed; **la soirée a été très réussie,** the evening was a great success; **mal r.,** unsuccessful, badly done, spoilt; **photographie mal réussie,** blurred, spoilt, photograph; *F:* **c'est r., ça!** a nice mess you've made of that!

réussinite [reysinit], *s.f. Miner:* reussinite, fossil resin.

réussir [reysiːr]. **1.** *v.i.* (*a*) to turn out (well or badly); **le projet avait mal réussi,** the plan had proved a failure; **cela lui a mal réussi,** it turned out badly for him; **ce traitement ne m'a pas réussi,** this treatment did not agree with me, suit me; *F:* **le homard ne me réussit pas,** lobster doesn't agree with me, I'm allergic to lobster; (*b*) to succeed; **r. dans qch.,** to succeed, be successful, at, in, sth.; **r. à un examen,** to pass an examination; *F:* **si tu continues comme ça tu vas r. à te faire recaler,** if you go on in that way you'll end up by being failed (in your exam); **r. à faire qch.,** to succeed in doing sth.; to manage to do sth.; **c'est un garçon qui réussira,** he's a boy who will do well; **r. dans la vie,** to get on in life; **ne pas r.,** to fail; **je n'ai pas réussi à le convaincre,** I failed to convince him; **je réussis à aller jusqu'à Paris, à me rendre à Paris,** I managed to get as far as Paris; **si jamais elle réussit à se faire épouser,** if ever she succeeds in getting a husband; **tout lui réussit,** he is successful in everything; he carries everything off; everything comes out right for him; (*c*) **la pièce a réussi,** the play is a success, has taken; **si l'entreprise réussit,** if the undertaking prospers, is a success; **ce truc-là ne réussira pas,** that trick won't work, won't come off; (*d*) (*of plants*) to thrive. **2.** *v.tr.* to make a success of (sth.); to carry out (sth.) well; **X a réussi un but magnifique,** X scored a fine goal; **elle réussit bien les omelettes,** she's a good hand at (making) an omelette, she makes very good omelettes; **ce qu'il réussit le mieux, c'est le paysage,** he is best at landscape painting; *Cards:* **r. son contrat,** to make one's contract; **petit chelem demandé et réussi,** little slam bid and made; *F:* **r. le coup,** to do the trick; **je n'ai pas réussi le coup,** I didn't bring it off.

réussite [reysit], *s.f.* **1.** issue, result, upshot; **bonne r.,** successful outcome; **mauvaise r.,** unfortunate result. **2.** success, successful result; **je crois à sa r.,** I believe he will be successful. **3.** *Cards:* patience; **faire une r.,** to work out, to do, a patience.

revaccination [rəvaksinasjɔ̃], *s.f.* revaccination.

revacciner [rəvaksine], *v.tr.* to revaccinate.

revalidation [rəvalidasjɔ̃], *s.f.* revalidation.

revaloir [rəvalwaːr], *v.tr.* (*conj. like* VALOIR; *used chiefly in the fu.*) to return, pay back, (*esp.* evil) in kind; **je vous revaudrai cela!** (i) I'll be even with you yet! I'll pay you out, serve you out, for that! (ii) I shall do as much for you another time.

revalorisation [rəvalɔrizasjɔ̃], *s.f.* (*a*) *Fin:* revalorization (of the franc, etc.); (*b*) **depuis la r. du caoutchouc,** as rubber becomes more valuable.

revaloriser [rəvalɔrize], *v.tr.* **1.** (*a*) *Fin:* to revalorize (currency); (*b*) to give a new value to (idea, etc.); to bring (idea, etc.) into favour, currency, again. **2.** to stabilize (prices) at a higher level.

revanchard, -arde [rəvɑ̃ʃaːr, -ard], *a. & s. Pol: Pej:* revanchist.

revanche [rəvɑ̃ːʃ], *s.f.* **1.** (*a*) revenge; **prendre sa r. sur qn,** to get one's own back on s.o., to get even with s.o.; **c'était sa r.,** it was a bit of his own back; **je prendrai ma r. un jour,** it will be my turn one day; (*b*) *Games:* **jouer la r.,** to play the return match, game; **quand nous donnerez-vous notre r.?** when will you give us our revenge? **2.** requital, return service; **en r.,** (i) in return, in compensation; to make up for it; (ii) on the other hand; **faible en mathématiques, mais en r. très bon latiniste,** weak in mathematics, but on the other hand very good at Latin; **à charge de r.,** on condition that I do the same for you (one day). **3.** *Nau: Hyd.E: etc:* safety margin.

revancher (se) [sərəvɑ̃ʃe], *v.pr.* to revenge oneself, to be revenged, get one's own back (for an insult); *A:* **se r. d'un bienfait,** to requite a good turn.

rêvasser [rɛvase], *v.i.* **1.** to dream of one thing and another. **2.** to muse; to indulge in day dreaming; to be wool gathering; **r. à l'avenir,** to muse on the future; to make day dreams about the future.

rêvasserie [rɛvasri], *s.f.* **1.** musing, day dreaming. **2.** *pl.* day dreams.

rêvasseur, -euse [rɛvasœːr, -øːz], *s.* (day) dreamer.

rêve [rɛːv], *s.m.* **1.** dream; **faire un r.,** to (have a) dream; **voir qch en r.,** to see sth. in a dream, in one's dreams; **le monde des rêves,** the world of dreams; **sortir d'un r.,** to come to one's senses; **c'est un r. que de vous voir ici!** I should never have dreamt of meeting you here! **2.** day dream; **caresser un r.,** to cherish a dream; **rêves de gloire,** dreams of glory; **la maison de nos rêves,** the house of our dreams, our dream house, our ideal house; **c'est le r.!** it's everything one could desire; it's ideal; **clerc d'avoué dans un petit trou, ce n'était pas le r.,** to be a solicitor's clerk in a small country town was not all that I had dreamt of, was not the height of my ambition; **porté au r. et à la paresse,** given to day dreaming.

revêche [rəvɛʃ], *a.* **1.** harsh, rough (cloth, wine, etc.); (stone, wood) difficult to work. **2.** bad-tempered, cantankerous (person); sour (face). **3.** short, brittle (iron).

réveil [revɛːj], *s.m.* **1.** (*a*) waking, awakening; **à mon r., je me souvins . . .,** on waking, I remembered . . .; **le r. de la nature, de l'opinion,** the awakening of Nature, of public opinion; **avoir un fâcheux r.,** to have a rude awakening; (*b*) *Mil:* reveille; rouse; **sonner le r.,** to sound reveille; (*c*) *Rel:* revival. **2.** alarm (clock); **r. de voyage,** travelling alarm clock; **mettre le r. sur, à, six heures,** to set the alarm for six o'clock.

réveille-matin [revɛjmatɛ̃], *s.m.inv.* **1.** alarm (clock). **2.** *Bot: F:* sun spurge, wart weed, milk-weed.

réveiller [reveje], *v.tr.* **1.** to awake, awaken, wake, waken (s.o.); to wake (s.o.) up; to rouse (s.o.); to (a)rouse (s.o.) from his sleep; *Mil:* to turn out (men); **réveillez-moi à sept heures,** wake me up, call me, give me a call, a knock, at seven o'clock; knock me up at seven o'clock; **r. le chat qui dort,** to rouse the sleeping lion; **ne réveillez pas le chat qui dort,** let sleeping dogs lie. **2.** to awaken, stir up, rouse (feelings, memories); to revive (memory, courage).

se réveiller. **1.** (*of pers.*) to awake; to wake (up); **se r. célèbre,** to wake up to find oneself famous; **se r. d'un sommeil agité,** to wake out of, from, a troubled sleep; **se r. en sursaut,** to wake up with a start. **2.** (*a*) (*of feelings*) to be awakened, roused, stirred up; to revive; **son amour, son courage, se réveilla,** his love, his courage, revived; **sa jalousie se réveilla,** his jealousy was aroused afresh; (*b*) (*of nature, vegetation, etc.*) to revive.

réveilleur [revɛjœːr], *s.m. Orn:* currawong, bell magpie.

réveillon [revɛjɔ̃], *s.m.* **1.** midnight feast, supper (*esp.* after midnight mass on Christmas Eve, and on New Year's Eve); **r. de la Saint-Sylvestre,** seeing the New Year in; New-Year's Eve celebration, party; **faire r.,** to have a midnight supper; to see Christmas, the New Year, in. **2.** *Art:* high light, point of high colour (in a picture); **obscurité trouée de réveillons,** darkness broken, relieved, by patches of light.

réveillonner [revɛjɔne], *v.i.* to have, give, a midnight supper; to see Christmas, the New Year, in.

réveillonneur, -euse [revɛjɔnœːr, -øːz], *s.* **à Noël les restaurants de Paris sont pleins de réveillonneurs,** at Christmas, the Paris restaurants are full of people having midnight supper.

révélateur, -trice [revelatœːr, -tris]. **1.** *a.* revealing, disclosing, tell-tale (sign, etc.) *Ch:* **substance révélatrice,** tracer (substance). **2.** *s.* revealer, discoverer, discloser (of plot, etc.). **3.** *s.m.* (*a*) *Phot:* developer; **r. à base de sels de soude,** soda developer; **r. à l'acide pyrogallique,** pyrosoda developer; **r. au métol-hydroquinone,** metol and hydroquinone developer; (*b*) *Tchn:* detector, indicator (of leakages, etc.).

révélation [revelasjɔ̃], *s.f.* **1.** revelation, disclosure (of secret, plot, etc.); betrayal (of one's ignorance); *Jur:* breach of secrecy; **ce fut une r.!** that was an eye-opener! **c'est toute une r.,** that throws a light on, explains, many things. **2.** *Theol:* (*a*) revelation; **la r. divine,** the revealed religion; (*b*) **les Révélations de saint-Jean,** the Book of Revelation; the Apocalypse of St John.

révélatoire [revelatwaːr], *a.* revelatory.

révélé [revele], *a. Theol:* revealed (religion, doctrine).

révéler [revele], *v.tr.* (**je révèle, n. révélons; je révélerai**) **1.** (*a*) to reveal, disclose; *F:* to let out (fact, secret); **il révéla maladroitement la vérité,** he blurted out the truth; **somme dont le montant n'a pas été révélé,** undisclosed amount; (*b*) to show; to reveal (kindness, good humour); to bring to the forefront; to betray, reveal (faults, neglect). **2.** *Phot:* to develop (plate, image).

se révéler. **1.** (*a*) to reveal oneself, one's character; **il s'est révélé excellent chef, comme excellent chef,** he showed himself a first-rate leader; **se r. utile, difficile,** to prove, show oneself, helpful, difficult; (*b*) to come to the front. **2.** to be revealed; **le fait se révéla alors que . . .,** the fact then came to light that . . .; **la vérité se révéla tout à coup à mon esprit,** the truth burst (in) upon me.

revenant [rəvnɑ̃]. **1.** *a. O:* pleasing, prepossessing (face, manners, etc.). **2.** *s.m.* (*a*) ghost; **histoire de revenants,** ghost story; **croire aux revenants,** to believe in ghosts; (*b*) *F:* (*s.o. whom one has not seen for a long time*) stranger; **quel r. vous faites!** you're quite a stranger!

revenant-bon [rəvnɑ̃bɔ̃], *s.m.* **1.** *Fin: Com:* surplus, bonus; unexpected balance; casual profit. **2.** perquisite(s); **c'est le r.-b. du métier,** these are the perquisites of the trade; *pl. revenants-bons.*

revendeur, -euse [rəvɑ̃dœːr, -øːz], *s.* (*a*) retailer, middleman; (*b*) secondhand dealer; *A:* **revendeuse à la toilette,** wardrobe dealer.

revendicable [rəvɑ̃dikabl̩], *a.* claimable.

revendicateur, -trice [rəvɑ̃dikatœːr, -tris]. **1.** *a.* demanding, claiming; **paroles revendicatrices,** assertive words; **lettre revendicatrice pour affirmer ses droits,** letter in claim of one's rights. **2.** *s.* claimant, claimer.

revendicatif, -ive [rəvɑ̃dikatif, -iːv], *a.* demanding, claiming; **une journée revendicative,** a day of protest; **mouvements revendicatifs,** protest movements; **lutte revendicative,** (wage) claims dispute.

revendication [rəvɑ̃dikasjɔ̃], *s.f.* **1.** claiming. **2.** (*a*) claim, demand (**sur,** on); **les revendications ouvrières,** the demands of labour; (*b*) *Jur:* (**action en**) **r.,** action for recovery of property; **action en r. immobilière,** action for declaration of title (to land); **r. de brevet,** patent claim; **actionner qn en r.,** to lodge a claim against s.o.; **émettre une r.,** to set up a claim; (*c*) (diplomatic) revendication.

revendiquer [rəvɑ̃dike], *v.tr. Jur:* (*a*) to claim, demand; **r. ses droits,** to assert, insist on, one's rights; *F:* to push one's demands; **r. un honneur,** to claim an honour; **r. le mérite d'une découverte,** to claim (the) credit for a discovery; **r. un livre,** to lay a claim to the authorship of a book; **r. Gibraltar à l'Angleterre,** to claim back Gibraltar from England; (*b*) **r. une responsabilité,** to assume a responsibility.

revendre [rəvɑ̃:dr̩], *v.tr.* to resell; to sell (sth.) again; *F:* **avoir de qch. à r.,** to have enough and to spare of sth.; **en r. à qn,** to outwit s.o.; **il vous en revendrait,** he is too much for you; he is more than a match for you; *Fin:* **r. des titres,** to sell out stock; **bonne occasion pour r.,** good occasion for selling out; *Jur:* **r. à la folle enchère,** to put (sth.) up for auction again after a bid that cannot be made good.

revenez-y [rəvnezi], *s.m.inv. F:* **1.** *O:* going back, return (to the past, to a habit, etc.); repetition; **il m'a joué un tour, mais je l'attends au r.-y,** he has played me a trick, but wait till he does it again! **un r.-y de tendresse,** a return, renewal, of affection. **2.** (*of child*) afterthought. **3.** appetizing dish; cut and come again; **ce gâteau a un goût de r.-y,** this cake makes you want a second helping, is very more-ish, morish.

revenger (se) [sərəvɑ̃ʒe], *v.pr.* (**je me revengeai(s); n.n. revengeons**) *A. & Dial:* = SE REVANCHER.

revenir [rəvni:r], *v.i.* (*conj. like* VENIR, *the aux. is* être) **1.** to return; to come back, come again; to walk, ride, drive, sail, fly, back; **r. à la hâte,** to hurry back; to rush back; **l'employé du gaz a dit qu'il reviendrait jeudi,** the gasman said he would call again on Thursday; **je l'ai rencontré en revenant de l'église,** I met him on my way back, on my way home, from church; (**de la main**) **il me fit signe de r.,** he waved me back, beckoned me back; **je reviens à Paris,** I am returning to Paris; **on revient au chemin de fer,** we are coming back, reverting, to travel by rail; **je suis revenu par chemin de fer,** I came back by rail, by train; **il revient de Paris le dix,** he is coming back, returning, from Paris on the 10th; **il est en route pour r.,** he is on his way back; **le temps passé ne revient plus,** time that is past will never come again; **l'herbe reviendra, vos cheveux reviendront,** the grass, your hair, will come, will grow, again; **fête qui revient tous les dix ans,** festival that occurs, recurs, comes round, every ten years; **esprit qui revient,** ghost that walks; *impers.* **il revient (des esprits) dans le château,** the castle is haunted; **je suis revenu au régime lacté,** I have gone back to a milk diet. **r. à la charge,** to return to the charge; **r. sur ses aveux,** to retract one's confession; *F:* **n'y revenez plus,** don't (you) do it again; **r. sur ses pas,** to retrace one's steps, to turn back; **pas sur lequel il n'y a pas à r.,** irretrievable step; **la machine revient sur le train,** the engine is backing down; **r. sur une promesse, une décision,** to go back on a promise, on a decision; **r. sur son opinion,** to reconsider one's opinion; **r. sur le compte de qn,** to reconsider one's opinion of s.o.; **cadavre qui revient sur l'eau,** corpse that comes, floats, to the surface; *F:* **le voilà revenu sur l'eau,** he has found his feet, come to the front, again; **cette question est revenue sur l'eau, sur le tapis,** this question has come up, cropped up, again; **r. sur un sujet,** to hark back to, bring up, a subject again; **r. sur le passé,** to rake up the past; **ne revenons plus sur le passé,** let bygones be bygones; **il n'y a pas à y r.,** there is no going back on it, the question cannot be reopened; **aliments qui reviennent,** food that repeats (on the stomach); *F:* **tissu qui revient bien au lavage,** material that comes up well in the wash; *Mil:* **revenez!** as you were! **2.** **revenir à qn;** (*a*) to return, come back, to s.o.; **il revint à moi,** he came back to me; **je suis sûre qu'il me reviendra,** I am sure he will come back to me; **mes partisans me reviennent,** my party is rallying round me again; **revenez-nous bientôt,** come back (to us) soon; **la mémoire me revient,** my memory is coming back; **les forces me reviennent,** I am recovering my strength; **il me revient (encore) dix francs,** I have (still) ten francs to get; **honneur qui me revient,** honour that falls to me by right; **succession qui revient à l'État,** succession that reverts to the State, that escheats; **quel profit vous en reviendra-t-il?** what will you make by it? **à chacun ce qui lui revient,** to each (one) his due; **il me revient (la tâche) de le renvoyer,** it's fallen to me to sack him, I've got the job of sacking him; **si nous avons réussi, c'est à vous**

qu'en revient le mérite, if we were successful, it is entirely thanks to you; (*b*) **son visage, son nom, me revient,** I am beginning to recall his face, his name; **cela me revient à la mémoire,** it's coming back to me; **votre nom ne me revient pas,** your name has slipped from my memory; I can't think of your name; **il me revient que . . .,** it comes back to my mind, I recollect, that . . .; (*c*) **son visage ne me revient pas,** I don't like, don't fancy, his looks; (*d*) *impers.* **il me revient que vous dites du mal de moi,** I hear, I have been told, that you are saying unkind things about me. **3.** (*a*) to recover; **r. de ses craintes, de sa surprise, d'une maladie,** to recover from, get over, one's fears, one's surprise, an illness; **r. de ses préjugés,** to shake off one's prejudices; **r. d'une théorie,** to abandon a theory; **r. d'une erreur,** to realize one's mistake; **être revenu de qch.,** to have lost one's infatuation, to no longer care, for sth.; **vous en reviendrez,** you'll get over it, you won't always be so keen; **je suis revenu de toutes mes illusions,** I have lost all my illusions; **je n'en reviens pas!** it's amazing! I can't get over it! **je n'en reviens pas qu'il ait perdu, de ce qu'il a perdu,** I can't get over his having lost; **en r. d'une belle,** to have had a narrow escape; **r. à la santé,** to recover one's health; to be restored to health; **il revient de loin,** he has been at death's door; he has looked death in the face; it was touch and go with him; **il n'en reviendra pas,** he won't get over it, he won't recover; he'll never pull through; **r. à soi,** to recover consciousness; *F:* to come round, to come to; (*b*) *Cu:* **faire r.,** to brown (in a pan); (*c*) *Metalw:* **faire r. un outil,** to let down the temper of, to temper, to draw (the temper of), a tool. **4.** **en r. à qch., y r.,** to revert, hark back, to sth.; **on en revient aux jupes longues,** we are going back to long skirts; **pour en r. à la question,** to revert, come back, to our subject; **nous reviendrons là-dessus,** we'll come back to that; **il y revient toujours,** he keeps coming back to it; **vous y reviendrez plus tard,** you will come back to your first opinion by and by; **j'en reviens toujours à dire que . . .,** I always come back to the same conclusion that . . . **5.** (*a*) to cost; **sa maison lui revient à 50 000 francs,** his house has cost him 50,000 francs; *Com:* **cet article vous reviendra à 50 francs,** this article comes out at 50 francs; (*b*) to amount; **cela revient au même,** it amounts, comes, to the same thing; **cela revient à dire que . . .,** that amounts to saying, is tantamount to saying, that . . ., it amounts to this, that . . . **6.** *P:* (= VENIR) **je reviens de le voir,** I've just seen him.

s'en revenir, *F:* to return; to go back home; **s'en r. tout doucement chez soi,** to wander back home.

revente [rəvɑ̃:t], *s.f.* **1.** resale; **objet de r.,** secondhand article; **marché de r.,** secondhand market. **2.** selling out; *esp. Fin:* **r. de titres,** selling out of stock; **occasion de r.,** chance of selling out.

revenu [rəvny]. **1.** *a.* **homme r. de bien des choses,** man who has lost most of his illusions, man without many illusions; **r. de tout,** disillusioned, cynical. **2.** *s.m.* (*a*) income (of pers.); revenue (of the State); **valeur à r. fixe,** fixed-interest security; **valeurs à r. variable,** determinable interest securities, equities; *Pol.Ec:* **politique des revenus,** (prices and) incomes policy; **r. national brut,** gross national income; **impôt sur le r.,** income tax; **déclaration de revenus,** income-tax return; **r. imposable,** taxable income; **dépenser tout son r.,** to live up to one's income; **dépenser plus que son r.,** to exceed, outrun, one's income; to live beyond one's income; (*b*) *Com:* (i) yield (of investment, etc.); (ii) *pl.* incomings; (*c*) *Metall:* drawing the temper, tempering (of steel); process annealing; **r. isotherme,** austempering; **bain de r.,** tempering bath, annealing bath; **couleur de r.,** tempering colour; (*d*) *Ven:* new growth (on animals).

revenue [rəvny], *s.f.* **1.** *A:* (*a*) return; homecoming; (*b*) way back; **la r. est longue,** it is a long way back. **2.** *For:* new growth; young wood.

rêver [reve]. **1.** *v.i.* to dream; (*a*) **r. toute la nuit,** to dream all night; **r. de qch.,** to dream (in one's sleep) about sth.; (*b*) **r. à, sur, de, qch.,** to muse on, ponder over, sth.; **il ne vous entend pas, il rêve,** he doesn't hear you, he's dreaming, he's wool gathering; (*c*) **r. tout éveillé,** to be full of idle fancies, of impossible schemes; **vous rêvez!** you're dreaming! **on croirait r.,** you'd think you were dreaming. **2.** *v.tr.* to dream of

(sth.); **r. la gloire,** to dream of glory; **r. mariage,** to dream of marriage; **c'était pour elle le mari rêvé,** he was the husband of her dreams; **c'est le chapeau rêvé,** it's a dream of a hat; **qu'avez-vous rêvé cette nuit?** what did you dream (of) last night? **vous l'avez rêvé!** you must have dreamt it! it is pure imagination on your part! **partout on rêvait voir des espions,** everywhere people imagined they saw spies; **r. sa jeunesse,** to dream of, to see in imagination, one's youth; **ce n'est pas là le résultat que j'avais rêvé,** that's not the result which I had hoped for, expected; **il rêvait de faire un long voyage,** he was dreaming of a long journey.

réverbérant [reverberɑ̃], *a.* reverberating, reverberant (light, sound); **salle réverbérante,** echo chamber.

réverbération [reverberasjɔ̃], *s.f.* reverberation, reflection (of light, heat); re-echoing (of sound).

réverbère [reverbɛ:r], *s.m.* **1.** *A.Tchn:* (*a*) reverberator, reflector (of heat); **four à r.,** reverberatory furnace; (*b*) baffle plate. **2.** (*a*) reflector, reflecting mirror (of Argand lamp, etc.); (*b*) street lamp; *P:* (*of woman*) **être sous les réverbères,** to be on the streets.

réverbérer [reverbere], *v.* (**il réverbère; il réverbérera**) to reverberate. **1.** *v.tr.* to reflect, throw back (heat, light); to re-echo (sound); to make (sth.) reverberate. **2.** *v.i.* to be reverberated, reflected.

reverdir [rəvɛrdi:r]. **1.** *v.i.* (*of plants, etc.*) to grow, turn, green again; *Lit:* (*of pers.*) to grow young again. **2.** *v.tr.* (*a*) to paint or make (sth.) green again; **le printemps reverdit les champs,** spring makes the fields green again. (*b*) *Leath:* to soak, soften (hides).

reverdissage [rəvɛrdisa:ʒ], *s.m. Leath:* soaking, softening (of hides).

reverdissant [rəvɛrdisɑ̃], *a.* **arbres reverdissants,** trees that are turning green again; **une revue littéraire sans cesse reverdissante,** a literary review always full of life.

reverdissement [rəvɛrdismɑ̃], *s.m.* growing green again; new life.

reverdisseur [rəvɛrdisœ:r], *s.m. Leath:* softener (of hides).

révéremment [reveramɑ̃], *adv.* reverently.

révérence [reverɑ̃:s], *s.f.* **1.** (*a*) reverence (**envers, pour,** for); **sauf r., r. parler,** with all due respect; (*b*) *A:* (*to ecclesiastic*) **Votre R.,** your Reverence. **2.** bow; curtsey; **faire la r. à qn,** **tirer une, sa, r. à qn,** (i) to make a bow to s.o.; to bow to s.o.; (ii) to make, drop, s.o. a curtsey; (iii) to say no to s.o.; to refuse; **tirer sa r. (à la compagnie),** to bow oneself out; to make one's bow; **je vous tire ma r.,** I must go; **faire force révérences,** to bow and scrape.

révérenciel, -ielle [reverɑ̃sjɛl], *a.* reverential (respect or awe); **il m'inspire une crainte révérencielle,** I live in holy fear of him.

révérencieusement [reverɑ̃sjøzmɑ̃], *adv.* with much ceremony, ceremoniously.

révérencieux, -euse [reverɑ̃sjø, -ø:z], *a.* overpolite, (fussily) ceremonious (person); ceremonious (compliment).

révérend, -ende [reverɑ̃, -ɑ̃:d]. **1.** *a. Ecc:* reverend; **le r. père Martin, le R. P. Martin,** Reverend Father Martin; **la révérende mère supérieure,** the Reverend Mother Superior; **très r.,** very reverend. **2.** *s. A. & Hum:* **oui, mon r.,** yes, your Reverence.

révérendissime [reverɑ̃disim], *a.* most reverend, right reverend (cardinal, archbishop, or abbot).

révérer [revere], *v.tr.* (**je révère, n. révérons; je révérerai**) to revere; to reverence; **révéré de tous,** held in reverence by all.

rêverie [revri], *s.f.* reverie; dreaming, musing; **plongé dans de vagues rêveries,** in a brown study.

revérification [rəverifikasjɔ̃], *s.f.* reverification, re-check(ing).

revérifier [rəverifje], *v.tr.* (*conj. like* VÉRIFIER) to reverify, re-check, check again.

revernir [rəvɛrni:r], *v.tr.* to revarnish (furniture, etc.).

revernissage [rəvɛrnisa:ʒ], *s.m.* revarnishing.

revers [rəvɛ:r], *s.m.* **1.** (*a*) reverse (side) (of coin, etc.); wrong side (of material, etc.); other side (of page, etc.); **r. de la main,** back of the hand; **donner un (coup de) r., donner un r. de main, à qn,** to deal s.o. a backhanded blow, *F:* a backhander; (**coup de**) **r.,** (i) *Ten: etc:* backhand stroke; *Ten:* **servir sur le r. adverse,** to serve on one's opponent's backhand; (ii) *Fenc:* reverse; (iii) *Row:* back stroke; *Ten:* **reprendre la balle en r.,** to take the ball on the backhand; *s.a.* MÉDAILLE 1; *Mil:* **r. d'une tranchée,** outside edge of a trench; **prendre une position à r.,** to take a position in reverse, in the rear; *Nau:* **l'amure de r.**, the opposite tack; the lee tack; (*b*) facing, lapel, revers (of coat, etc.); turnover (of sock); boot top; **r. de pantalon**, trouser turn-up; **habit à r. de velours**, coat faced with velvet; **à r. de soie**, silk-faced; **bottes à r.**, top boots. **2.** reverse (of fortune); setback; **les succès et les r. de la vie**, the ups and downs of life; **essuyer un r.**, to suffer a reverse, a setback.

réversal, -aux [reversal, -o], *a. Jur:* relating to mutual concessions; *esp.* **lettres réversales**, *s.f.pl.* **réversales**, letters of mutual concessions.

reverseau, -eaux [rəverso], *s.m. Const:* flashing board, weather board (of door, window).

reversement [rəversmɑ̃], *s.m. Fin:* transfer (of funds from one account to another).

reverser [rəverse], *v.tr.* **1.** (*a*) to pour (sth.) out again; **il me reversa à boire**, he poured me out another glass; (*b*) to pour (sth.) back. **2.** (*a*) to shift (blame, responsibility) (**sur**, on to); (*b*) *Com:* to transfer, carry (an item from one account to another); (*c*) to pay back; (*d*) *A:* to trans-ship.

reversi(s) [rəversi], *s.m. Cards: A:* reversi(s).

réversibilité [reversibilite], *s.f.* **1.** reversibility. **2.** *Jur:* revertibility.

réversible [reversibl̩], *a.* **1.** reversible; **hélice à pas r.**, reversible (pitch) propeller; *Ch:* **réaction r.**, reversible reaction; *Elcs:* **transformation magnétique r.**, reversible magnetic process; *Phot:* **arrière-cadre r.**, reversing back (of camera); **manteau r.**, reversible coat; **l'histoire n'est pas r.**, you can't put the clock back. **2.** *Jur:* revertible (succession, etc.) (**à, sur**, to).

réversif, -ive [reversif, -iːv], *a.* reversive.

réversion [reversjɔ̃], *s.f.* (*a*) *Jur:* reversion (**à**, to); **rente viagère avec r.**, reversionary annuity; (*b*) *Biol:* reversion (to type).

reversoir [rəverswaːr], *s.m. Hyd.E:* (*a*) barrage; weir; (*b*) sluice.

revêtement [rəvɛtmɑ̃], *s.m.* (*a*) (*general sense*) coating, covering; **matière de r.**, coating compound, material; **r. de renforcement**, backing; **r. de protection, r. protecteur**, protective coating; **r. en contreplaqué**, plywood covering; **r. en toile**, fabric or canvas covering; **r. en émail**, enamel coating; **r. métallique**, metal coating, covering; *Tchn:* **r. par immersion**, dip-coating; **r. antirouille**, rustproofing; **r. antiabrasif**, hard surfacing; (*b*) (*metal coating*) plating, cladding, sheathing; **r. électrolytique**, electro-plating; **r. en aluminium**, aluminium cladding; **r. en cuivre**, copper sheathing; **r. en plaques de métal**, plating; **r. en plaques d'acier**, steel-plate cladding; (*c*) (*exterior covering*) *Const:* facing (of tiles on wall, of masonry on surface of slope, etc.); casing (of masonry); *Join:* veneer; *Civ.E: Fort: etc:* revetment (of stone, concrete, fascines, etc., to maintain an embankment); *Civ.E:* surface, carpet (of road); (*outer layer*) investment; **r. routier**, road metal; **mur de r.**, revetment wall; **r. calorifuge**, lagging (of duct, pipe, boiler, etc.); **r. réfractaire**, refractory investment, lining; **r. pour soudure**, soldering investment; *Nau:* **r. de pont**, decking, deck covering; *El:* **câble à r. en caoutchouc**, rubber-covered cable; (*d*) (*interior coating*) lining; *Metall:* **r. acide, basique**, acid, basic, lining; **r. en caoutchouc**, rubber lining; *Min:* **r. d'un puits**, lining (of shaft); **r. de boisage**, framework (of pit shaft); (*e*) *Av: Nau:* skin(ning) (of aircraft, ship); *Nau:* serving (of cable); *Av:* **r. en alliage léger**, light-alloy skin; **r. d'aile**, wing skin; **r. inférieur, r. d'intrados**, bottom skin; **r. supérieur, r. d'extrados**, top skin; **r. travaillant**, stressed skin; **poser le r.**, to skin; **pose du r.**, skinning; (*f*) *Z:* vestiture.

revêtir [rəvetiːr], *v.tr.* (*conj. like* VÊTIR) **1.** to clothe (s.o.) again; to reclothe. **2.** (*a*) to clothe, dress; **r. qn de qch.**, to dress s.o. in sth.; **revêtus de leurs habits des dimanches**, dressed in their Sunday best; **r. qn d'une dignité**, to invest s.o. with a dignity; **r. un document d'une signature, un effet de l'acceptation**, to appose a signature to a document, to provide a bill with acceptance; **pièce revêtue de votre signature**, document bearing your signature; *Lit:* **champs revêtus de verdure**, verdure-clad fields; **pensées revêtues d'une forme précise**, thoughts clothed in exact terms; (*b*) *Const: etc:* to face, coat, cover, case, line, sheathe; *Fort:* to revet *Mch:* to lag (boiler); *N.Arch:* to skin (ship); **murs revêtus de boiseries**, walls lined with wooden panelling; panelled walls. **3. r. un habit, un uniforme**, to don, put on, a coat, a uniform; **r. la pourpre**, to assume the purple; **r. son armure**, to buckle on one's armour; **r. la forme humaine**, to assume, put on, human shape; **r. un personnage**, to assume a character; **la pensée a besoin de r. une forme spéciale: le langage**, thought must take on a special form, language.

se revêtir. 1. to put on one's clothes again. **2. se r. de qch.**, to clothe oneself in sth., to put on sth.; to assume (a dignity, etc.).

rêveur, -euse [rɛvœːr, -øːz]. **1.** *a.* dreaming, dreamy, musing; **d'un air r.**, dreamily, musingly; **yeux d'une douceur rêveuse**, soft and dreamy eyes; **son succès laisse r.**, his success makes you wonder. **2.** *s.* dreamer, muser; stargazer.

rêveusement [rɛvøzmɑ̃], *adv.* dreamily.

revidage [rəvidaːʒ], *s.m.* **1.** re-emptying. **2.** *Com:* knock-out (after auction sale).

revider [rəvide], *v.tr.* **1.** to re-empty. **2.** *Com:* to knock-out (after auction sale).

revient [rəvjɛ̃], *s.m.* **1.** *Com:* (**prix de**) **r.**, cost price, manufacturing cost, prime cost; **établir le prix de r. d'un article**, to cost an article; **établissement des prix de r.**, costing. **2.** *Metalw:* drawing the temper, letting down the temper, tempering.

revif [rəvif], *s.m.* **1.** *Oc:* rising of water (between low and high tide). **2.** *Lit:* renewal of life; revival.

revigoration [rəvigɔrasjɔ̃], *s.f.* renewal of vigour.

revigorer [rəvigɔre], *v.tr.* to reinvigorate.

revigorisation [rəvigɔrizasjɔ̃], *s.f.* reinvigoration.

revirement [rəvirmɑ̃], *s.m.* **1.** *Nau: A:* tacking about, going about. **2.** sudden change (of fortune); revulsion, reversal (of feeling); sudden turn (of the market, etc.); **revirements d'opinion**, veerings of opinion. **3.** *Com:* transfer, making over (of a debt, etc.).

revirer [rəvire], *v.i.* **1.** *Nau: A:* **r.** (**de bord**), to tack (about), to go about. **2. r. de bord**, to turn round, to change sides; *F:* to rat.

révisable [revizabl̩], *A:* **revisable** [rəvizabl̩], *a. Jur:* revisable, reviewable (case); *Com:* **prix r.**, price (i) subject to alteration, to modification, (ii) open to offer; **prix non r.**, (i) firm, fixed, price; (ii) (*in advertisement of house for sale, etc.*) no offers.

réviser [revize], *A:* **reviser** [rəvize], *v.tr.* **1.** (*a*) to revise (text, proof, etc.); **les textes de nos traducteurs sont toujours révisés**, the texts of our translators are always (carefully) checked, revised; (*b*) to audit (accounts); (*c*) *Jur:* to review, reconsider (lawsuit, sentence). **2.** (*a*) to examine, inspect (sth.) (again); (*b*) *Sch:* to revise (sth. for an examination); (*c*) to overhaul (car, etc.); *Aut: etc:* **moteur révisé**, reconditioned engine.

réviseur [revizœːr], *A:* **reviseur** [rəvizœːr], *s.m.* reviser; examiner; reviewer, checker; *Typ:* proof reader; *Com:* **r.** (**comptable**), auditor.

révision [revizjɔ], *A:* **revision** [rəvizjɔ̃], *s.f.* **1.** (*a*) revision, examination (of list, account, translation, etc.); *Typ:* proof reading; (*b*) auditing (of accounts); (*c*) *Sch:* revision (for examination); (*d*) review, reconsideration (of sentence, lawsuit); revision (of dictionary, etc.); *Com:* **formule de r. de prix**, price variation clause; escalation clause; **horaire soumis à des révisions périodiques**, timetable subject to periodic alterations; **r. déchirante**, agonizing re-appraisal. **2.** (*a*) inspection, testing (of engines, boilers, etc.); (*b*) overhaul (of car, etc.); **r. générale**, general servicing; (*computers*) **périodicité moyenne des révisions**, mean time between overhauls (m.t.b.o.); (*c*) *Mil: etc:* medical examination (of recruits); **conseil de r.**, (army) medical board (for recruiting); (*d*) *Nau:* **révisions**, survey repairs.

révisionnel, -elle [revizjɔnɛl], *a.* revisional, revisionary.

révisionnisme [revizjɔnism], *s.m. Pol:* revisionism.

révisionniste [revizjɔnist]. **1.** *a.* revisory; **parti r.**, revisionist party. **2.** *s.m. & f.* revisionist.

revisiter [rəvizite], *v.tr.* to revisit (place, patient).

revisser [rəvise], *v.tr.* to screw up, tighten up (part).

revitalisation [rəvitalizasjɔ̃], *s.f.* revitalization; revitalizing.

revitaliser [rəvitalize], *v.tr.* to revitalize.

revivaliste [rəvivalist], *s.m. & f. Rel:* revivalist.

revivification [rəvivifikasjɔ̃], *s.f.* **1.** revivification. **2.** *Ch: etc:* reactivation.

revivifier [rəvivifje], *v.tr.* (*p.d. & pr.sub.* **n. revivifions, v. revivifiiez**) to revivify, revive, regenerate, revitalize.

reviviscence [rəvivisɑ̃ːs], *s.f.* reviviscence.

reviviscent [rəvivisɑ̃], **reviviscible** [rəvivisibl̩], *a.* reviviscent.

revivre [rəviːvr̥], *v.i.* (*conj. like* VIVRE) (*a*) to live again, to come to life again; **se sentir r.**, to feel oneself restored to life; **faire r. qn**, to bring s.o. to life again; to revive s.o.; **faire r. une coutume**, to revive a custom; **l'industrie commence à r.**, industry is reviving; (*b*) *with cogn. acc.* to relive (the past, etc.); **si je pouvais r. ma vie**, if I could live my life over again.

révocabilité [revɔkabilite], *s.f.* revocability.

révocable [revɔkabl̩], *a.* **1.** revocable, subject to repeal. **2.** removable (official); subject to dismissal.

révocablement [revɔkabləmɑ̃], *adv.* revocably.

révocation [revɔkasjɔ̃], *s.f.* **1.** revocation (of testament); repeal, revocation (of edict, etc.); cancellation, rescinding, countermanding (of an order). **2.** removal, dismissal (of an official).

révocatoire [revɔkatwaːr], *a.* revocatory.

revoici [rəvwasi], *prep. F:* **me r.!** here I am again! **me r. riche**, once more I am rich; **nous r. à Noël**, here we are at Christmastime again.

revoilà [rəvwala], *prep. F:* **le r.!** there he is again! **r. le chien qui hurle**, there's that dog howling again!

revoir[1] [rəvwaːr], *v.tr.* (*conj. like* VOIR) **1.** to see (s.o., sth.) again; to meet (s.o.) again; **on se reverra!** we shall meet again! **avec quelle netteté je revois ce spectacle!** how vividly I recall the scene! **2.** (*a*) to revise, re-examine; to inspect, to look over, (accounts, manuscript, etc.) again; to read (proofs); **à r.**, for revision, to be revised; (*b*) *Jur:* to review (lawsuit); to reconsider (sentence).

revoir,[2] *s.m.* **1.** (*a*) seeing (s.o.) again; **le dialogue du r.**, the conversation on meeting again; (*b*) *s.m.inv.* **au r.**, goodbye; **ce furent des au r. sans fin**, the goodbyes seemed endless, seemed to go on for ever; **accompagner un ami pour lui dire au r.**, to see a friend off. **2.** *Ven:* trace, track (of quarry).

revoler[1] [rəvɔle], *v.tr.* to steal (sth.) again.

revoler[2], *v.i.* **1.** to fly again. **2.** to fly back (**à**, to).

revolin [rəvɔlɛ̃], *s.m. Nau:* **1.** eddy wind. **2.** back current, reverse current; eddy; **r. de lame**, cross ripple.

révoltant [revɔltɑ̃], *a.* revolting, sickening, shocking (sight, etc.); outrageous (behaviour, etc.).

révolte [revɔlt], *s.f.* **1.** revolt, rebellion; **région en r. ouverte**, district in open rebellion. **2.** *Mil: Navy:* mutiny.

révolté, -ée [revɔlte], *s.* **1.** rebel, revolter, insurgent. **2.** *Mil: Navy:* mutineer.

révolter [revɔlte], *v.tr.* (*a*) to induce (s.o.) to revolt; to rouse, to stir up (the people); **r. des sujets contre leur roi**, to urge subjects to revolt, to rebel, against their king; (*b*) to revolt; **ses procédés me révoltent**, his business methods disgust me, sicken me; **ce spectacle m'a révolté**, I was shocked at the sight.

se révolter. 1. (*a*) to revolt, rebel (**contre**, against); (*b*) **le bon sens se révolte contre une telle supposition**, common sense revolts at, against, such a supposition. **2.** *Mil: Navy:* to mutiny.

révolu [revɔly], *a.* (*of time*) completed; **quand le mouvement diurne de la terre est r.**, when the diurnal revolution of the earth is completed; **avoir quarante ans révolus**, to have completed one's fortieth year; **quand le temps sera révolu**, in the fullness of time; **les jours de l'individualisme sont révolus**, the time of individualism has gone; **le siècle n'était pas encore r.**, the wheel had not yet come full circle.

révoluté [revɔlyte], *a. Bot:* revolute (leaf).

révolutif, -ive [revɔlytif, -iːv], *a. Mec: etc:* rotational.

révolution [revɔlysjɔ̃], *s.f.* (*a*) *Astr: Geom: etc:* revolution; rotation, revolution (of a wheel); **les révolutions du globe terrestre**, the revolutions of the earth; (*b*) *Pol: etc:* revolution; upheaval; *Hist:* **la R.**, the (French) Revolution; **r. de l'opinion**, revulsion of feeling; **tout le quartier, est en r.**, the whole district is up in arms, is in revolt.

révolutionnaire [revɔlysjɔnɛːr], (*a*) *a. & s.* revolutionary; (*b*) *s.* revolutionist.

révolutionnairement [revɔlysjɔnɛrmɑ̃], *adv.* in a revolutionary spirit, in a spirit of protest.

révolutionnarisme [revɔlysjɔnarism], *s.m.* revolutionariness; advocacy of revolutionary principles.

révolutionner [revɔlysjɔne]. **1.** *v.tr.* (*a*) to revolutionize (a country, manners, etc.); **r. la face du monde**, to change the face of the world; **invention qui a révolutionné l'industrie**, invention that revolutionized industry; (*b*) to upset (s.o.'s) equanimity. **2.** *v.i.* to revolve, to turn.

révolvant [revɔlvɑ̃], *a. Tchn:* revolving.

revolver [revɔlvɛːr], *s.m.* **1.** revolver, *F:* gun; **r. à six coups,** six-chambered revolver, *F:* six-shooter; **r. d'abattage,** humane killer (for slaughtering). **2.** (*a*) *Mec.E:* **(porte-outils) r.,** revolving tool holder; turret, capstan; **tour (à) r.,** turret lathe, capstan lathe; (*b*) revolving nose piece (of microscope); set of revolving eye-pieces (of prismatic field glass).

revomir [rəvɔmiːr], *v.tr.* **1.** to vomit (up); to throw up (food); *abs.* to vomit, be sick, again. **2. r. des injures,** to pour out another flood of abuse.

révoquer [revɔke], *v.tr.* **1.** (*a*) to revoke, repeal, cancel, rescind (decree, etc.); to countermand (an order, etc.); **r. un ordre de grève,** to call off a strike; (*b*) **r. qch. en doute,** to call sth. in question; to question (statement, evidence). **2.** to dismiss; to remove (official) from office; to recall (ambassador).

revouloir [rəvulwaːr], *v.tr.* (*conj. like* VOULOIR) to wish, desire, (sth.) again; **en reveux-tu?** would you like some more?

revoyeur [rəvwajœːr], *s.m.* canal dredge boat.

revoyure [rəvwajyːr], *s.f. P:* **à la r.** (= **au revoir**)! so long! cheerio!

revue [rəvy], *s.f.* **1.** review, looking over, survey, inspection; *Mil:* review; muster, inspection; **passer qch. en r.,** (i) to review, survey, run over, sth.; (ii) (*computers*) to browse; **faire la r. de ses factures,** to go through, look over, one's bills; *Mil:* **r. de détail,** checking of kit, stores, etc., in detail; **r. de casernement,** barrack-room inspection; **r. de literie, de matériel de couchage,** bunk inspection; **r. de santé,** medical inspection; **r. d'incorporation,** medical inspection of recruits; **passer les troupes en r.; faire, passer, la r. des troupes,** to review, inspect, the troops; to take the salute at the march past; **passer une r.,** to hold a review, an inspection; *Navy:* **r. d'effets** kit inspection; *Journ:* **r. de presse,** press review; *F:* **je suis encore de la r.,** (i) I'm in for it, in trouble again! just my luck! I've been done down! (ii) I've had all this trouble for nothing; I've had it! **2.** (*a*) *Publ:* review, magazine; journal; **r. scientifique,** scientific journal; (*b*) *Th:* revue. **3.** *F:* **nous sommes de r., des gens de r.,** (i) we shall meet again; (ii) we often meet.

revue-féerie [rəvyfeeri], *s.f.* pantomime; *pl. revues-féeries.*

revuette [rəvɥɛt], *s.f. Th:* short revue.

revuiste [rəvɥist], *s.m. & f. Th:* composer of revues, revuist.

révulsé [revylse], *a.* **l'œil r.,** with turned-up eyes.

révulser [revylse], *v.tr.* **1.** *Med:* to counter-irritate. **2.** (*as result of illness, terror, etc.*) **son regard se révulsa,** he showed the whites of his eyes.

révulsif, -ive [revylsif, -iːv], *a. & s.m. Med:* revulsive; counter-irritant.

révulsion [revylsjɔ̃], *s.f. Med:* revulsion; counter-irritation.

rex [rɛks], *attrib. a. Z: Bot:* **lapin r.,** rex; **bégonia r.,** begonia rex.

rexisme [rɛksism], *s.m. Belgian Pol:* Rexism.

rexiste [rɛksist], *a. & s.m. & f. Belgian Pol:* Rexist.

rez [re, rɛ], *prep. A: also prep.phr.* **à r. de,** (on a) level with; even with; *still occ. in* **voler r. terre, à r. de terre,** to fly along the ground; to skim the ground; (*more usu.* **à ras de terre**).

rez-de-chaussée [redʃose], *s.m.inv.* (*a*) ground level, street level; (*b*) ground floor, *U.S:* first floor; **au r.-de-c.,** on a level with the ground, on the ground floor; *Th:* **r.-de-c. de la salle,** stalls and pit, *U.S:* parquet, of the house.

rez-de-jardin [redʒardɛ̃], *s.m.inv.* ground floor flat (opening on to a garden).

rez-terre [retɛːr], *s.m.inv.* (*a*) *Const: etc:* uniformly level surface; (*b*) *For:* felling (tree) at ground level.

rezzou [redzu], *s.m.* (*in North Africa*) **1.** raiding party (of Arabs). **2.** incursion, raid, razzia.

rhabdite [rabdit], **rhabditis** [rabditis], *s.m. Ann:* rhabditis.

rhabdocèles [rabdɔsɛl], *s.m.pl. Ann:* Rhabdocoelida.

rhabdolite [rabdɔlit], *s.m. Prot:* rhabdolith.

rhabdomancie [rabdɔmɑ̃si], *s.f.* rhabdomancy.

rhabdomancien, -ienne [rabdɔmɑ̃sjɛ̃, -jɛn], *s.,* **rhabdomant, -ante** [rabdɔmɑ̃, -ɑ̃ːt], *s.* rhabdomancer.

rhabdome [rabdɔm], *s.m. Ent:* rhabdom(e).

rhabdomyome [rabdɔmjoːm], *s.m. Med:* rhabdomyoma.

rhabdophane [rabdɔfan], *s.f. Miner:* rhabdophane, rhabdophanite.

rhabdopleura [rabdɔplœra], *s.m. Z:* rhabdopleura.

rhabillage [rabijaːʒ], *s.m.* **1.** repairing, overhaul, putting in order; **r. de meules,** dressing of millstones. **2.** tinkering, patching up; **ce n'est qu'un r.,** it's only been tinkered up.

rhabiller [rabije], *v.tr.* **1.** to repair, overhaul, mend; to put (watch, etc.) in order; **r. une meule,** to dress a millstone. **2.** (*a*) to reclothe (s.o.); to provide (s.o.) with new clothing; **r. ses domestiques,** to put one's servants into a new livery; **r. une vieille idée,** to dress up an old idea in new, modern, terms; (*b*) to dress (s.o.) again; to put (child's) clothes on again; (*c*) *Const:* to coat.

se rhabiller, (*a*) to put on one's clothes again; to dress again; *F: Sp: Th: etc:* (*of poor player, actor, etc.*) **il peut aller se r.,** he'd better give up! *P:* **va te r.!** wrap up! shut up! *U.S:* get lost! (*b*) to buy a new outfit.

rhabilleur [rabijœːr], *s.m.* **1.** repairer; *esp.* (*a*) **(horloger) r.,** clock and watch repairer; (*b*) dresser (of millstones, of emery wheels). **2.** *F:* bonesetter.

rhabituer [rabitɥe], *v.tr.* **r. qn à qch.,** to accustom s.o. to sth. again; to reaccustom s.o. to sth.

se rhabituer, to become reaccustomed, rehabituated (**à,** to); **je commence à me r. ici,** I am beginning to settle down again here.

rhacophore [rakɔfɔːr], *s.m. Amph:* flying frog; (*genus*) Rhacophorus, Polypedates.

rhacophoridés [rakɔfɔride], *s.m.pl. Amph:* Rhacophoridae.

Rhadamante [radamɑ̃ːt], *Pr.n.m. Gr.Myth:* Rhadamanthus; **jugement de R.,** Rhadamanthine judgment.

rhagade [ragad], *s.f. Med:* rhagades (*pl.*).

rhagie [raʒi], *s.f. Ent:* rhagium.

rhagionidés [raʒjɔnide], *s.m.pl. Ent:* Rhagonidae.

rhagite [raʒit], *s.f. Miner:* rhagite.

rhagoletis [ragɔletis], *s.m. Ent:* cherry fruit fly; (*genus*) Rhagoletis.

rhagonyque [ragɔnik], *s.f. Ent:* soldier beetle.

rhamnacées [ramnase], *s.f.pl. Bot:* Rhamnaceae.

rhamnite [ramnit], **rhamnitol** [ramnitɔl], *s.m. Ch:* rhamnitol.

rhamnose [ramnoːz], *s.m. Ch:* rhamnose.

rhamnoside [ramnɔzid], *s.m. Ch:* rhamnoside.

rhamphastidés [ramfastide], *s.m.pl. Orn:* Rhamphastidae.

rhamphocèle [ramfɔsɛl], *s.m. Orn:* scarlet-rumped tanager.

rhamphorhynque [ramfɔrɛ̃k], *s.m. Paleont:* rhamphorhynchid.

rhamphothèque [ramfɔtɛk], *s.f. Orn:* rhamphotheca.

rhantus [rɑ̃tys], *s.m. Ent:* r(h)antus.

rhaphidioptères [rafidjɔptɛːr], *s.m.pl. Ent:* Raphidioptera.

rhapis [rafis], *s.m. Bot:* fan palm.

rhapontic [rapɔ̃tik], **rhaponticum** [rapɔ̃tikɔm], *s.m. Bot:* rhapontic; knapweed.

rhapsode [rapsɔd], *s.m.* rhapsode, rhapsodist.

rhapsoder [rapsɔde], *v.tr. A:* (*a*) to rhapsodize (a tale); (*b*) to repair, to put in order.

rhapsodie [rapsɔdi], *s.f.* rhapsody.

rhapsodique [rapsɔdik], *a.* rhapsodique.

rhapsodiste [rapsɔdist], *s.m.* rhapsodist.

rhé [re], *s.m. Ph:* rhe.

Rhée [re]. **1.** *Pr.n.f. Myth:* Rhea. **2.** *s.f. Orn:* rhea, nandu.

rheedia [redja], *s.m. Bot:* Spanish plum tree.

rhéidés [reide], *s.m.pl. Orn:* Rheidae, the rheas.

rhénan, -ane [renɑ̃, -an], *Geog:* **1.** *a.* Rhenish, (of the) Rhine; **les pays rhénans,** the Rhineland. **2.** *s.* Rhinelander.

Rhénanie (la) [larenani], *Pr.n.f. Geog:* the Rhineland.

rhénique [renik], *a. Ch:* rhenic.

rhénium [renjɔm], *s.m. Ch:* rhenium.

rhénois, -oise [renwa, -waːz], *Geog:* **1.** *a.* of the Rhineland. **2.** *s.* Rhinelander.

rhéobase [reɔbaːz], *s.f. Ph:* rheobase.

rhéographe [reɔgraf], *s.m. El:* rheograph.

rhéolaveur [reɔlavœːr], *s.m. Min:* rheolaveur.

rhéologie [reɔlɔʒi], *s.f. Ph:* rheology.

rhéomètre [reɔmɛtr], *s.m.* **1.** *El: A:* rheometer. **2.** *Hyd.E:* rheometer.

rhéométrie [reɔmetri], *s.f. Tchn:* magna flux (testing); *Hyd.E:* rheometry.

rhéophile [reɔfil], *a. Z:* rheophil(e), rheophilous.

rhéophore [reɔfɔːr], *s.m. El:* rheophore.

rhéoscopique [reɔskɔpik], *a. El:* rheoscopic.

rhéostat [reɔsta], *s.m. El:* rheostat; variable resistance; *El.E:* **r. de démarrage,** starting rheostat; rheostatic starter (of electric motor); **r. de champ,** field resistance, field rheostat; **r. de réglage,** regulating resistance; **r. à commande par servo-moteur,** motor-controlled rheostat; **r. à compression de charbon,** carbon rheostat; **r. à curseur,** slide-wire, slider, rheostat; **r. d'excitation,** field regulator; **r. de charge, d'absorption,** load rheostat; **r. de glissement,** slip regulator; **r. de réglage de vitesse,** shunt speed regulating rheostat; **r. en pont, potentiométrique,** potentiometer rheostat.

rhéostatique [reɔstatik], *a. El.E:* rheostatic; *Rail:* **freinage r.,** rheostatic braking.

rhéostriction [reɔstriksjɔ̃], *s.f. Elcs:* pinch effect, rheostriction.

rhéotaxie [reɔtaksi], *s.f. Biol:* rheotaxis.

rhéotaxique [reɔtaksik], *a. Biol:* rheotactic.

rhéotome [reɔtɔm], *s.m. Med:* rheotome.

rhéotropisme [reɔtrɔpism], *s.m. Biol:* rheotropism.

rhésus [rezys], *s.m.* **1.** *Z:* **(macaque) r.,** rhesus (monkey), bandar. **2.** *Physiol:* **facteur r.,** Rh, rhesus, factor; **r. positif, négatif,** Rh positive, negative.

rhétais, -aise [retɛ, -ɛːz], *a. & s.* (native, inhabitant) of the île de Ré.

rhéteur [retœːr], *s.m.* (*a*) *A:* rhetor, teacher of rhetoric; (*b*) orator; (*c*) *Pej:* mere talker.

Rhétie [reti], *Pr.n.f. A.Geog:* Rhaetia.

rhétien, -ienne [retjɛ̃, -jɛn]. **1.** *a. & s. A.Geog:* Rhaetian. **2.** *a. & s.m. Geol:* Rhaetic.

rhétique [retik]. **1.** *a. Geog:* Rhaetian; **les Alpes rhétiques,** the Rhaetian Alps. **2.** *s.m.* Rhaetian (language).

rhétoricien, -enne [retɔrisjɛ̃, -jɛn], *s.* **1.** (*a*) rhetorician; (*b*) *Pej:* great talker. **2.** *Sch: A:* = sixth former.

rhétorique [retɔrik], *s.f.* (*a*) rhetoric; **figure de r.,** figure of speech; (*b*) *Sch: A:* **(classe de) r.,** (now *classe de première*) = sixth form; **r. supérieure,** higher classical form (*preparing for the* **École normale supérieure,** *q.v.* under NORMAL 1).

rhétoriqueur [retɔrikœːr], *s.m.* **1.** *Lit.Hist:* **les grands rhetoriqueurs,** school of poets of the XVth and XVIth centuries. **2.** *occ.* = RHÉTORICIEN.

rhéto-roman, -ane [retɔrɔmɑ̃, -an], *a. & s. Ling:* Rhaeto-Romanic.

rheum [reɔm], *s.m.inv. Bot:* rheum.

rhexia [rɛksja], *s.m. Bot:* deer grass, meadow beauty; (*genus*) Rhexia.

Rhin (le) [lərɛ̃], *Pr.n.m. Geog:* the Rhine; **vin du R.,** Rhine wine, hock; **caillou du R.,** rhinestone.

rhinanthe [rinɑ̃ːt], *s.m. Bot:* rhinanthus, yellow rattle; **r. crête-de-coq,** (corn-)rattle.

rhinanthées [rinɑ̃te], *s.f.pl. Bot:* Rhinanthoideae.

rhinarium [rinarjɔm], *s.m. Z: Ent:* rhinarium.

rhinencéphale [rinɑ̃sefal], *s.m.* **1.** *Anat:* rhinencephalon. **2.** *Ter:* rhinencephalus.

rhingrave [rɛ̃graːv], **1.** *Hist: s.m.* Rhinegrave; *s.f.* Rhinegravine. **2.** *s.m. A.Cost:* petticoat-breeches (as introduced by the Rhinegrave of Salm).

rhingraviat [rɛ̃gravja], *s.m. Hist:* rhinegraviate.

rhinite [rinit], *s.f. Med: Vet:* rhinitis, coryza; **r. périodique,** hay fever; **r. atrophique du porc,** atrophic swine rhinitis.

rhinobatidés [rinɔbatide], *s.m.pl. Ich:* Rhinobatidae.

rhinobatos [rinɔbatɔs], *s.m. Ich:* rhinobatos; guitarfish.

rhinocéphale [rinɔsefal], *s.m. Ter:* rhinencephalus, rhinocephalus.

rhinocéros [rinɔserɔs], *s.m.* **1.** *Z:* rhinoceros. **2.** *Ent:* rhinoceros beetle.

rhinocérotidés [rinɔserɔtide], *s.m.pl. Z:* Rhinocerotidae.

rhinochète [rinɔkɛt], *s.m. Orn:* kagu.

rhinoderme [rinɔdɛrm], *s.m. Amph:* **r. du Chili,** Darwin's frog.

rhinolalie [rinɔlali], *s.f. Med:* rhinolalia.

rhino-laryngite [rinɔlarɛ̃ʒit], *s.f. Med:* rhinolaryngitis.

rhinologie [rinɔlɔʒi], *s.f. Med:* rhinology.

rhinolophe [rinɔlɔf], *s.m. Z:* rhinolophid; *F:* horseshoe, leaf-nosed, bat.

rhinolophidés [rinɔlɔfide], *s.m.pl. Z:* Rhinolophidae.

rhinométrie [rinɔmetri], *s.f. Med:* measurement of the degree of nasal obstruction.

rhinoncus [rinɔ̃kys], *s.m. Ent:* rhinoncus.

rhinonécrose [rinɔnekroːz], *s.f. Med:* rhinonecrosis.

rhino-pharyngien, -ienne [rinɔfarɛ̃ʒjɛ̃, -jɛn], *a. Med:* rhinopharyngeal.

rhinopharyngite [rinɔfarɛ̃ʒit], *s.f. Med:* rhynopharyngitis, nasal catarrh.

rhino-pharynx [rinɔfarɛ̃ks], *s.m. Anat:* nasopharynx; nose and throat; rhinopharynx.

rhinophonie [rinɔfɔni], *s.f. Med:* rhinophonia.

rhinophore [rinɔfɔːr], *s.m. Moll:* rhinophore.

rhinophylle [rinɔfil], *s.m. Z:* South American leaf-nosed bat.

rhinophyma [rinɔfima], *s.m. Med:* rhinophyma.

rhinopithèque [rinɔpitɛk], *s.m. Z:* snub-nosed monkey.

rhinoplastie [rinɔplasti], *s.f. Surg:* rhinoplasty.

rhinoplastique [rinɔplastik], *a.* rhinoplastic.

rhinopome [rinɔpɔm], *s.m. Z:* mouse-tailed bat.

rhinoptera [rinɔptera], *s.f. Ich:* rhinoptera.

rhinorragie [rinɔraʒi], *s.f. Med:* rhinorrhagia, nosebleed.

rhinorrhée [rinɔre], *s.f. Med:* rhinorrhea, rhinorrhoea.

rhino-salpingite [rinɔsalpɛ̃ʒit], *s.f. Med:* rhino-salpingitis.

rhinosclérome [rinɔskleroːm], *s.m. Med:* rhinoscleroma.

rhinoscopie [rinɔskɔpi], *s.f. Med:* rhinoscopy.

rhinosime [rinɔzim], *s.m. Ent:* rhinosimus.

rhinothèque [rinɔtɛk], *s.f. Orn:* rhinotheca.

rhinotomie [rinɔtɔmi], *s.f. Surg:* rhinotomy.

rhipidoglosses [ripidɔglɔs], *s.m.pl. Moll:* Rhipidoglossa.

rhipiphore [ripifɔːr], *s.m. Ent:* wasp fan beetle.

rhipiphoridés [ripifɔride], *s.m.pl. Ent:* Rhipiphoridae.

rhipiptères [ripiptɛːr], *s.m.pl. Ent:* Rhipiptera.

rhipsalis [ripsalis], *s.m. Bot:* mistletoe cactus.

rhizalise [rizaliːz], *s.f. Dent:* killing of nerve root.

rhizine [rizin], *s.m. Moss:* rhizine.

rhizo- [rizɔ], *pref.* rhizo-.

rhizobium [rizɔbjɔm], *s.m. Bac:* rhizobium.

rhizobius [rizɔbjys], *s.m. Ent:* rhizobius.

rhizocarpé, -ée [rizɔkarpe], *Bot:* **1.** *a.* rhizocarpous, rhizocarpic. **2.** *s.f.* **rhizocarpée,** rhizocarp.

rhizocarpes [rizɔkarp], *s.f.pl.* Rhizocarpeae.

rhizocarpien, -ienne [rizɔkarpjɛ̃, -jɛn], **rhizocarpique** [rizɔkarpik], *a. Bot:* rhizocarpous, rhizocarpic, rhizocarpian.

rhizocéphale [rizɔsefal], *Z:* **1.** *a.* rhizocephalous. **2.** *s.m.* rhizocephalan; *pl.* **rhizocéphales,** Rhizocephala.

rhizocrinus [rizɔkrinys], *s.m. Z:* rhizocrinus.

rhizoctone [rizɔktɔn], *s.m.*, **rhizoctonie** [rizɔktɔni], *s.f. Fung:* rhizoctonia.

rhizoflagellé [rizɔflaʒɛle], *a. & s.m. Prot:* rhizoflagellate; *s.m.pl.* **rhizoflagellés,** Rhizoflagellata.

rhizogène [rizɔʒɛn], *a. Bot:* rhizogenic, rhizogenous.

rhizoglyphe [rizɔglif], *s.m. Ent:* rhizoglyphus.

rhizoïde [rizɔid], *s.f. Bot:* rhizoid.

rhizomastigines [rizɔmastiʒin], *s.f.pl. Bot:* Rhizomastigina.

rhizomateux, -euse [rizɔmatø, -øːz], *a. Bot:* rhizomatic, rhizomatous.

rhizome [rizoːm], *s.m. Bot:* rhizome.

rhizomélique [rizɔmelik], *a. Anat:* rhizomelic.

rhizomorphe [rizɔmɔrf]. **1.** *a.* rhizomorphous. **2.** *s.m. Fung:* rhizomorph.

rhizomucor [rizɔmykɔːr], *s.m. Med:* rhizomucor.

rhizomyidés [rizɔmjide], *s.m.pl. Z:* Rhizomyidae.

rhizomys [rizɔmis], *s.m. Z:* rhizomys.

rhizoperthe [rizɔpɛrt], *s.m. Ent:* lesser grain borer; (*genus*) Rhizopertha.

rhizophage [rizɔfaːʒ], *a.* rhizophagous (animal, etc.).

rhizophora [rizɔfɔra], *s.m.*, **rhizophore** [rizɔfɔːr], *s.m. Bot:* mangrove (tree), mangle; (*genus*) Rhizophora.

rhizophoracées [rizɔfɔrase], *s.f.pl. Bot:* Rhizophoraceae.

rhizoplaste [rizɔplast], *s.m. Biol:* rhizoplast.

rhizopode [rizɔpɔd]. **1.** *a.* rhizopodous, rhizopod. **2.** *s.m. Prot:* rhizopod; *pl.* **rhizopodes,** Rhizopoda.

rhizopus [rizɔpys], *s.m. Fung:* rhizopus.

rhizosphère [rizɔsfɛːr], *s.f. Bot:* rhizosphere.

rhizostome [rizɔstoːm], *s.m. Coel:* rhizostome.

rhizostomidés [rizɔstɔmide], *s.m.pl. Coel:* Rhizostomae, Rhizostomata.

rhizotaxie [rizɔtaksi], *s.f. Bot:* rhizotaxis.

rhizotome [rizɔtɔm], *s.m. Agr:* root slicer.

rhizotomie [rizɔtɔmi], *s.f. Surg:* rhizotomy, cutting of nerve roots.

rhizotrogue [rizɔtrɔg], *s.m. Ent:* garden chafer.

rhô [ro], *s.m. Gr.Alph:* rho.

rhod(o)- [rɔd(ɔ)], *pref.* rhod(o)-.

rhodalose [rɔdaloːz], *s.f. Miner:* red vitriol, bieberite.

rhodamine [rɔdamin], *s.f. Ch:* rhodamin(e).

rhodanate [rɔdanat], *s.m. Ch:* rhodanate.

rhodane [rɔdan], *s.m. Ch:* thiocyanogen.

rhodanien, -ienne [rɔdanjɛ̃, -jɛn], *a. Geog:* of, pertaining to, the Rhone; **la vallée rhodanienne,** the Rhone valley.

rhodante [rɔdɑ̃ːt], *s.m. Bot:* rhodanthe.

rhodéose [rɔdeoːz], *s.m. Ch:* rhodeose.

Rhodes [rɔd], *Geog:* **1.** *Pr.n.f.* Rhodes (the island). **2.** *Pr.n.f.pl.* **les R. intérieures, extérieures,** the Inner, Outer, Rhodes (of Switzerland).

Rhodésie [rɔdezi], *Pr.n.f. Geog:* Rhodesia; *Paleont:* **l'homme de R.,** Rhodesian man.

rhodésien, -ienne [rɔdezjɛ̃, -jɛn], *a. Geog:* Rhodesian.

rhodeus [rɔdeys], *s.m. Ich:* bitterling; (*genus*) Rhodeus.

rhodiage [rɔdjaːʒ], *s.m.* rhodium plating.

rhodié [rɔdje], *a.* of, containing, rhodium; rhodium (alloy).

rhodien, -ienne [rɔdjɛ̃, -jɛn], *a. & s. Geog:* Rhodian.

rhodier [rɔdje], *v.tr.* to plate with rhodium.

rhodinol [rɔdinɔl], *s.m. Ch:* rhodinol.

rhodiola [rɔdjɔla], *s.m. Bot:* sedum, orpine.

rhodique [rɔdik], *a. Ch:* rhodic.

rhodite[1] [rɔdit], *s.m. Ent:* cynips; gall wasp.

rhodite[2], *s.f. Miner:* rhodite.

rhodium [rɔdjɔm], *s.m. Ch:* rhodium.

rhodizionique [rɔdizjɔnik], *a. Ch:* **acide r.,** rhodizionic acid.

rhodizite [rɔdizit], *s.f. Miner:* rhodizite.

rhodizonique [rɔdizɔnik], *a. Ch:* rhodizonic (acid).

rhodochrosite [rɔdɔkrozit], *s.f. Ch:* rhodochrosite.

rhododendron [rɔdɔdɛ̃drɔ̃], *s.m. Bot:* rhododendron.

rhodographie [rɔdɔgrafi], *s.f. Bot:* treatise on roses.

Rhodoïd [rɔdɔid], *s.m. R.t.m:* Rhodoid.

rhodolite [rɔdɔlit], *s.f. Miner:* rhodolite.

rhodonite [rɔdɔnit], *s.f. Miner:* rhodonite, red manganese.

rhodophycées [rɔdɔfise], *s.f.pl. Algae:* Rhodophyceae.

rhodopsine [rɔdɔpsin], *s.f. Bio-Ch:* rhodopsin.

rhodosperme [rɔdɔspɛrm], *a. Bot:* rhodospermous.

rhodostéthie [rɔdɔsteti], *s.m. Orn:* wedge-tailed, Ross's, gull.

rhodotypos [rɔdɔtipɔs], *s.m. Bot:* rhodotypos.

rhodyménia [rɔdimenja], *s.m.*, **rhodyménie** [rɔdimeni], *s.f. Algae:* (*genus*) Rhodymenia; **r. palmée,** water leaf.

rhœadales [røadal], *s.f.pl. Bot:* Rhoeadales.

rhombe [rɔ̃ːb]. **1.** *s.m.* (*a*) *Cryst:* rhomb; (*b*) *Geom:* rhombus. **2.** *a.* rhombic.

rhombencéphale [rɔ̃bɑ̃sefal], *s.m. Anat:* rhombencephalon.

rhombiforme [rɔ̃bifɔrm], *a. Cryst:* rhombiform.

rhombique [rɔ̃bik], *a.* rhombic.

rhomboèdre [rɔ̃bɔɛdr], *s.m. Cryst:* rhombohedron.

rhomboédrique [rɔ̃bɔedrik], *a.* rhombohedral.

rhomboïdal, -aux [rɔ̃bɔidal, -o], *a.* rhomboidal.

rhomboïde [rɔ̃bɔid], *s.m. & a.* (*a*) *Mth:* rhomboid; (*b*) *Anat:* rhomboid (muscle); *s.m.* rhomboideus.

rhombus [rɔ̃bys], *s.m. Mth:* rhombus.

rhonc(h)us [rɔ̃kys], *s.m. Med:* rhonchus, râle.

Rhône (le) [lərɔːn], *Pr.n.m. Geog:* the (river) Rhone.

rhopalie [rɔpali], *s.f. Coel:* rhopalium.

rhopalocère [rɔpalɔsɛːr], *Ent:* **1.** *a.* rhopalocerous, rhopaloceral. **2.** *s.m.pl.* **rhopalocères,** Rhopalocera.

rhotacisme [rɔtasism], *s.m. Ling:* rhotacism.

rhubarbe [rybarb], *s.f. Bot:* rhubarb; **r. des paysans, des pauvres,** meadow rue; **r. de Chine,** Chinese rhubarb; **r. des Indes,** East Indian rhubarb; **r. de Moscovie,** Russian rhubarb; **r. de Turquie,** Turkey rhubarb; **r. batave,** Batavian rhubarb; *Prov:* **passez-moi la r. et je vous passerai le séné,** claw me and I'll claw thee; you scratch my back and I'll scratch yours.

rhum [rɔm], *s.m.* rum.

rhumatisant, -ante [rymatizɑ̃, -ɑ̃ːt], *a. & s. Med:* rheumatic (patient, subject); *F:* rheumaticky (person).

rhumatisé [rymatize], *a. F:* rheumaticky.

rhumatismal, -aux [rymatismal, -o], *a. Med:* rheumatic (pain, fever).

rhumatisme [rymatism], *s.m.* (*a*) *Med:* rheumatism; **r. articulaire,** rheumatism in the joints, rheumatoid arthritis, arthritis deformans, nodose rheumatism, osseous rheumatism; **r. goutteux,** rheumatic gout; **r. articulaire aigu,** rheumatic fever; **j'ai un peu de r.,** I have a touch of rheumatism; (*b*) *pl. F:* **être perclus de rhumatismes,** to be crippled with rheumatism.

rhumatoïde [rymatɔid], *a. Med:* rheumatoid.

rhumatologie [rymatɔlɔʒi], *s.f. Med:* rheumatology.

rhumatologue [rymatɔlɔg], *s.m. & f. Med:* rheumatologist.

rhumb [rɔ̃ːb], *s.m. Nau:* rhumb.

rhumbatron [rɔ̃batrɔ̃], *s.m. Elcs:* rhumbatron.

rhume [rym], *s.m. Med:* cold; **gros r.,** heavy, bad, violent, cold; **r. de poitrine,** cold on the chest; **r. de cerveau,** cold in the head; **r. des foins,** hay fever; **prendre, attraper, un r.,** to catch (a) cold; **j'ai attrapé un r. de cerveau,** I caught a cold in the head; **nourrir un r.,** to feed a cold; *P:* **prendre qch. pour son r.,** to get hauled over the coals.

rhumer [rɔme], *v.tr.* to add rum to (a cake, a drink, etc.); **eau de vie rhumée,** brandy and rum.

rhum(m)erie [rɔmri], *s.f.* rum distillery.

rhumier, -ière [rɔmje, -jɛːr], *a.* rum (industry, etc.).

rhus [rys], *s.m. Bot:* rhus.

rhyacophile [riakɔfil], *s.m. Ent:* rhyacophilia.

rhynchite [rɛ̃kit], *s.m. Ent:* rhynchites; **r. conique,** common vine grub.

rhynchobdellidés [rɛ̃kɔbdɛlide], *s.f.pl. Z:* Rhynchobdellida.

rhynchocéphales [rɛ̃kɔsefal], *s.m.pl. Rept:* Rhynchocephalia.

rhynchocyon [rɛ̃kɔsjɔ̃], *s.m. Z:* rhynchocyon.

rhynchonelle [rɛ̃kɔnɛl], *s.f. Paleont:* rhynchonellid; (*genus*) Rhynchonella.

rhynchope [rɛ̃kɔp], **rhynchops** [rɛ̃kɔps], *s.m. Orn:* skimmer, scissor-bill.

rhynchophore [rɛ̃kɔfɔːr], *s.m. Ent:* rhynchophoran; *pl.* **rhynchophores,** Rhynchophora.

rhynchospores [rɛ̃kɔspɔːr], *s.m.pl. Bot:* R(h)ynchospora.

rhynchotes [rɛ̃kɔt], *s.m.pl. Ent:* Rhynchota.

rhynia [rinja], *s.f. Bot: Paleont:* rhynia.

rhyolit(h)e [rijɔlit], *s.f. Miner:* rhyolite.

rhyparographe [riparɔgraf], *s.m. Ant:* rhyparographer.

rhyparographie [riparɔgrafi], *s.f. Ant:* rhyparography.

rhysse [ris], *s.f. Ent:* rhyssa.

rhythme [ritm], *s.m.* = RYTHME.

rhytidome [ritidoːm], *s.m. Arb:* rhytidome, scale bark, shell bark.

rhytine [ritin], *s.f. Z:* **r. de Steller,** Steller's sea cow, rhytina.

ria [ria], *s.f. Ph.Geog:* ria; **côte à rias,** ria coast.

riant [rijɑ̃], *a.* **1.** smiling (face, person, etc.). **2.** cheerful, agreeable, pleasant (prospect, thought, etc.); **les riantes campagnes,** the smiling countryside.

ribambelle [ribɑ̃bɛl], *s.f. F: usu. Pej:* long string (of animals, insults); **r. d'enfants,** swarm, whole lot, of brats; **il y avait là une r. d'enfants,** there were lots of children; **et toute la r.,** and the whole boiling.

ribaud, -aude [ribo, -oːd], *a. & s.* **1.** *A:* ribald. **2.** *s.f. Tex:* **ribaude,** ridge (in material due to fault in manufacture).

ribaudequin [ribodkɛ̃], *s.m. A.Arms:* ribaudequin.

ribauderie [ribodri], *s.f. A:* ribaldry.

ribaudure [ribodyːr], *s.f. Tex:* ridge (in material) due to fault in manufacture.

ribbonisme [ribɔnism], *s.m. Irish Hist:* ribbonism.

ribboniste [ribɔnist], *s.m. Irish Hist:* ribbon-man.

ribes [ribɛs], *s.m. Bot:* ribes.

ribésiacées [ribezjase], **ribésiées** [ribezje], *s.f.pl. Bot:* Saxifragaceae.

ribler [rible], *v.tr. Mill:* to true up, dress (millstone).

riblette [riblɛt], *s.f. Cu:* slice of meat grilled *à la minute.*

riblon [riblɔ̃], *s.m. usu. pl.* (iron or steel) scrap; swarf.

ribocétose [ribɔsetoːz], *s.m. Ch:* pentose.

riboflavine [ribɔflavin], *s.f. Ch:* riboflavin(e), vitamin B_2.

ribonique [ribɔnik], *a. Ch:* ribonic.

ribonucléase [ribɔnykleaːz], *s.f. Ch:* ribonuclease.

ribonucléique [ribɔnykleik], *a. Ch:* **acide r.,** ribonucleic acid.

ribonucléoprotéide [ribɔnykleɔprɔteid], *s.m. Ch:* ribonucleoprotein.

ribord [ribɔːr], *s.m. N.Arch:* bottom planking (above garboard strakes).

ribordage [ribɔrdaːʒ], *s.m. Nau:* (expenses **for**) damages caused by running foul.

ribose [riboːz], *s.m. Ch:* ribose.

ribosome [ribozoːm], *s.m. Bio-Ch:* ribosome.

ribote [ribɔt], *s.f. F:* drunken bout; binge; **faire (la) r.,** to booze; to have a drinking bout; **être en r.,** (i) to be tipsy, tight; (ii) to be on the spree, on the binge.

riboter [ribɔte], *v.i. F:* to booze; to have a drinking bout.

riboteur, -euse [ribɔtœːr, -øːz]. **1.** *s. F:* regular tippler; toper, boozer. **2.** *a.* boozy.

ribouis [ribwi], *s.m. P:* (*a*) boot or shoe (*esp.* of poor quality or the worse for wear); (*b*) cobbler.

ribouldingue [ribuldɛ̃:g], *s.f. P:* spree; **faire la r.,** to be, go, on the spree.

ribouler [ribule], *v.i. F:* **r. des yeux,** to roll one's eyes (with amazement).

ricain, -aine [rikɛ̃, -ɛn], *a. & s. F:* American, Yank.

ricanement [rikanmɑ̃], *s.m.*, **ricanerie** [rikanri], *s.f.* unpleasant, grating, sneering, derisive, laugh; *pl.* derisive laughter.

ricaner [rikane], *v.i.* to laugh unpleasantly, derisively; to indulge in mocking, sneering, laughter.

ricaneur, -euse [rikanœ:r, -ø:z]. **1.** *a.* derisive (air, etc.). **2.** *s.* sneerer, derider.

ric-à-rac [rikarak], *adv.*, **ric-à-ric** [rikarik], *adv.* = RIC-RAC.

riccie [riksi], *s.f. Moss:* riccia.

ricciocarpus [riksjɔkarpys], *s.m. Bot:* ricciocarpus.

rice-rat [raisrat], *s.m. Z:* rice rat, rice mouse; *pl. rice-rats.*

ricercare [ritʃɛrkare], *s.m. Mus:* ricercar(e).

richard[1], **-arde** [riʃa:r, -ard], (*a*) *s.* rich person; **c'est un r.,** he's rolling (in it), he's got lots of money; (*b*) *s.m. Ent: F:* buprestid.

Richard[2], *Pr.n.m.* Richard; *Hist:* **R. Cœur de Lion,** Richard Lion Heart.

richardia [riʃardja], *s.m.*, **richardie** [riʃardi], *s.f. Bot:* calla; (*genus*) richardia.

richardsonia [riʃardsɔnja], *s.m. Bot:* richardsonia.

riche [riʃ], *a.* **1.** (*a*) rich, wealthy; opulent; well-off; **se trouver r. d'un million de francs,** to find oneself worth a million francs; **il était très r.,** he was a man of wealth; **j'étais peu r. alors,** I was anything but well-off in those days; **être r. à millions,** to be worth millions; *F:* **r. à crever,** rolling in money; **être r. de qch.,** to possess sth.; **r. d'espérances,** rich in hope; **livre r. de faits,** book rich in, crammed with, information; **musée r. en tableaux,** museum rich in paintings; **pays r. en blé,** country rich, abounding, in cereals; **langue r.,** rich language; *Pros:* **rime r.,** rich rhyme; **végétation r.,** rich, exuberant, vegetation; (*b*) *Lit:* **jeune homme r. de mine,** handsome-looking young man. **2.** valuable; **r. cadeau,** valuable, handsome, gift; **minerai r.,** rich ore; **r. moisson,** rich, abundant, harvest; **faire un r. mariage,** to marry into a wealthy family; *F:* to marry money; *Com:* **article r.,** superior article; **r. en protéine,** with a high protein content; *I.C.E: etc:* **mélange r.,** rich mixture. **3.** *F:* **une r. idée,** a splendid idea; **rater une r. occasion,** to miss a rare opportunity; **c'est une r. nature,** (i) he, she, is full of energy and promise; (ii) he, she, is goodlooking and generous; (iii) *Iron:* he, she, is well-upholstered, fat; **ce n'est pas r.,** it's not up to much. **4.** *s.* rich person; **les riches,** the rich, the wealthy; **nouveau r.,** nouveau-riche; **on ne prête qu'aux riches,** only the rich can borrow (money); *B:* **le mauvais r.,** Dives.

richelieu [riʃəljø], *s.m.* **(soulier) r.,** lace-up shoe, Oxford (shoe); *pl. richelieu(s).*

richellite [riʃəlit], *s.f. Miner:* richellite.

richement [riʃmɑ̃], *adv.* **1.** richly; (*a*) abundantly; **pourvoir r. ses enfants,** to make abundant provision for one's children; (*b*) wealthily, sumptuously, opulently; **appartement r. meublé,** sumptuously furnished flat. **2.** *F:* **on s'est r. amusé,** we had a great time; it was tremendous fun; **r. mérité,** richly deserved.

richesse [riʃɛs], *s.f.* **1.** wealth; (*a*) **la r. publique,** public wealth; **r. en matières premières,** resources in raw materials; **arriver à la r.,** to achieve wealth; (*b*) riches; **amasser de grandes richesses,** to amass great wealth, great riches; *s.a.* CONTENTEMENT. **2.** object of value; **musée plein de richesses,** gallery full of valuable exhibits. **3.** richness; fertility (of soil); exuberance (of vegetation); sumptuousness (of furniture); exuberant colouring (of picture); *I.C.E:* richness (of mixture); **commande de r. (de mélange),** mixture control; **richesses des possibilités,** versatility (of machine, etc.).

richi [riʃi], *s.m. Hindu Rel:* rishi, rsi.

richissime [riʃisim], *a. F:* extremely rich, ultra-wealthy, rolling in wealth; *s.m.* multi-millionaire.

ricin [risɛ̃], *s.m.* **1.** *Bot:* castor-oil plant, ricinus, palma Christi; **huile de r.,** castor oil; **graine de r.,** castor(-oil) bean. **2.** *Arach: F:* dog tick.

riciné [risine], *a. Med: Ch:* impregnated with castor oil.

ricinoléate [risinɔleat], *s.m. Ch:* ricinoleate.

ricinoléine [risinɔlein], *s.f. Ch:* ricinolein.

ricinoléique [risinɔleik], *a. Ch:* **acide r.,** ricinoleic acid.

ricinuléides [risinyleid], *s.m.pl. Arach:* Ricinulei.

rickardite [rikardit], *s.f. Miner:* rickardite.

rickettsie [rikɛtsi], *s.f. Med: Biol:* rickettsia.

rickettsiose [rikɛtsjo:z], *s.f. Med:* rickettsiosis.

ricocher [rikɔʃe], *v.i.* (*a*) to rebound; to glance off; (*b*) (*of bullet, shell, etc.*) to ricochet.

ricochet [rikɔʃɛ], *s.m.* (*a*) rebound; **faire des ricochets (sur l'eau),** to make ducks and drakes; (*b*) ricochet; *Artil:* **tir à r., feu par r.,** ricochet fire; *F:* **apprendre qch. par r.,** to hear of sth. indirectly, in a roundabout way.

ric-rac [rikrak], *adv. F:* strictly, rigorously, punctually; **payer qch. r.-r.,** to pay sth. to the very last farthing; *occ. a.* **il est r.-r.,** he is very strict.

rictus [riktys], *s.m.* **1.** rictus. **2. r. (moqueur, etc.),** grin.

ridage [rida:ʒ], *s.m.* **1.** *Nau:* setting up, tightening (of the shrouds). **2.** *Paint:* shrinking.

ride[1] [rid], *s.f.* **1.** wrinkle (on the face); **les rides du front,** the lines of the forehead; **front creusé de rides profondes,** deeply lined brow; **front sans rides,** smooth, unwrinkled, brow. **2.** ripple (on water, sand, etc.); ridge (of sand); *Metall:* surface folding; *Geol:* (i) fold (in the ground); (ii) ripple mark; *Ph:* **rides de l'espace einsteinien,** crumplings, puckerings, in the Einsteinian space. **3.** *Bot:* girdle scar, scale-leaf scar.

ride[2], *s.f. Nau:* (shroud) lanyard; **nœud de r.,** Matthew Walker knot.

ridé [ride], *a.* **1.** wrinkled; *Bot:* rugose, rugous; **pomme ridée,** shrivelled apple. **2.** ribbed, corrugated, fluted; **tôle ridée,** corrugated iron. **3.** *Ven:* **fumées ridées,** dung, fumet, of old deer.

rideau, -eaux [rido], *s.m.* **1.** (*a*) screen, curtain (of trees, etc.); **r. d'incendie,** fire screen; *Const:* **r. ondulé,** corrugated screen; *Mil:* **r. de troupes,** screen of troops; *Mil:* **r. de feu,** fire curtain; *Mil: Navy:* **r. de fumée,** smoke screen; *Navy:* **r. d'éclairage,** scouting screen (of cruisers, etc.); *For:* **r. forestier,** protective belt; *Pol:* **R. de Fer,** Iron Curtain; **pays au-delà du R. de Fer,** Iron-Curtain countries; (*b*) *Fort:* rideau. **2.** (*a*) curtain, *U.S:* drape; **rideaux de lit, de fenêtre,** bed, window, curtains; *Nau:* **rideaux de tentes,** awning curtains; **garni de rideaux,** hung with curtains; **lit garni de rideaux,** curtained bed; **rideaux de lit,** bed hangings; **tirer les rideaux,** to draw the curtains; *F:* **tirer le r. sur . . .,** to draw a veil over . . .; *A:* **se tenir derrière le r.,** to pull the strings; **doubles rideaux,** draw curtains; (*b*) *Th:* (drop) curtain; **r. d'entr'acte,** act drop; **r. de fer,** safety curtain; **r. de réclame,** advertisement curtain; **r. à la grecque, à l'allemande,** draw-type curtain; **r. à la guillotine, à la romaine,** drop-type curtain; **r. à l'italienne,** tableau-, tab-, type curtain; **r. à huit heures précises,** the curtain rises at eight sharp; *P:* **r.!** let's call it a day! let's pack it in! *s.a.* LEVER II, 2; (*c*) **r. de cheminée,** register, blower, of a fireplace; **r. de bureau,** roll top of a desk; **classeur à r.,** roll-shutter cabinet; *Phot:* **r. de châssis,** dark-slide shutter; *Const:* **r. ondulé,** rolling shutter; **r. à enroulement,** roller curtain; **r. de palpanches,** pile planking, sheet piling; *Tchn:* **r. de fermeture,** shutter; *Hyd.E:* slide (of slide valve); *Civ.E:* **r. d'étanchéité,** cut-off; (*d*) *Civ.E:* embankment wall; (*e*) *Elcs: etc:* **r. d'antennes,** aerial array, antenna array.

ridectomie [ridɛktɔmi], *s.f.* face lifting.

ridée [ride], *s.f.* lark net.

ridelage [ridla:ʒ], *s.m. Leath:* (*glovemaking*) sizing, measurement (of pieces of leather on the rack).

rideleuse [ridlø:z], *s.f. Leath:* (*glovemaking*) glove sizer.

ridelle [ridɛl], *s.f.* **1.** (*a*) rack, rail (of cart, lorry); **fausses ridelles,** (cart) ladders, floating raves; (*b*) *Leath:* (*glovemaking*) rack. **2.** *pl.* oaken saplings (reserved for wheelwright's work).

ridement [ridmɑ̃], *s.m.* **1.** (*a*) wrinkling, lining (of forehead); shrivelling (of skin, etc.); (*b*) corrugating, fluting, ribbing (of metal, etc.). **2.** rippling (of water, etc.).

ridenne [ridɛn], *s.f. Orn:* gadwall.

rider[1] [ride], *v.tr.* **1.** (*a*) to wrinkle, line (the forehead, etc.); to shrivel (skin, etc.); (*b*) to corrugate, flute, rib (metal, etc.). **2.** to ripple, ruffle (the water, etc.).

se rider. 1. to wrinkle; (*of forehead, etc.*) to become lined; (*of apple*) to shrivel up. **2.** (*of water*) to ripple.

rider[2], *v.tr. Nau:* to set up, tighten (the shrouds); to haul (the shrouds) taut.

rider[3] [raidœ:r], *s.m. Equit: Turf:* **(gentleman) r.,** amateur rider.

ridicule[1] [ridikyl]. **1.** *a.* ridiculous, laughable, ludicrous, absurd; **se rendre r.,** to make oneself ridiculous, to make a fool of oneself. **2.** *s.m.* (*a*) ridiculousness, the ridiculous, absurdity; **le r. de la situation,** the ridiculous side, the absurdity, of the situation; **c'est d'un r. achevé,** it is perfectly ridiculous, the height of absurdity; **tomber dans le r.,** to make oneself ridiculous; **tourner qn, qch., en r.,** to hold s.o., sth., up to ridicule; to poke fun at s.o., sth.; **couvrir qn de r.,** to make s.o. look ridiculous; **se couvrir de r.,** to make a fool of oneself; (*b*) ridicule; **craindre le r.,** to fear ridicule; **prêter au r.,** to give cause for ridicule; to be open to ridicule; **s'exposer au r.,** to lay oneself open to ridicule; **braver le r.,** to defy ridicule; (*c*) ridiculous habit; **se moquer des ridicules de qn,** to make fun of s.o.'s ridiculous ways, absurd behaviour; **les ridicules de notre époque,** the absurdities of our time.

ridicule[2], *s.m. A. & F:* = RÉTICULE.

ridiculement [ridikylmɑ̃], *adv.* ridiculously, laughably, ludicrously; **chiffres r. bas,** absurdly, ridiculously, farcically, low figures.

ridiculiser [ridikylize], *v.tr.* to ridicule; to make (s.o., sth.) ridiculous; to hold (s.o., sth.) up to ridicule; **se r.,** to make oneself ridiculous, to make a fool of oneself.

ridoir [ridwa:r], *s.m. Nau:* (rigging-)stretching device; **r. à vis,** stretching screws; **r. à fourreau,** bottle (rigging) screw; *Nau: Av:* turnbuckle.

ridule [ridyl], *s.f.* small wrinkle.

riebeckite [ribɛkit], *s.f. Miner:* riebeckite.

Riedel [ridəl], *Pr.n. Med:* **maladie de R.,** Riedel's disease, ligneous thyroiditis.

riel [rjɛl], *s.m. Num:* riel.

rien [rjɛ̃]. I. *pron.indef.m.* **1.** anything; (*a*) (*in questions* **rien** *is preferred to* **quelque chose** *when a negative answer is expected or implied, cf.* AUCUN) **avez-vous jamais r. vu d'aussi drôle?** did you ever see anything so funny? **y a-t-il r. de plus triste?** is there anything more depressing? (*b*) **s'il y a r. que vous désiriez,** if there is anything that you want. **2.** nothing, not anything; (*a*) (*with* **ne** *expressed*) **r. ne l'intéresse,** nothing interests him; **r. ne presse,** there's no hurry; **je n'ai r. vu,** I saw nothing; **je n'ai r. à faire,** I have nothing to do; **il n'y a r. à faire,** there is nothing to be done; it can't be helped; I am helpless in the matter; **on ne veut r. lui donner,** they won't give him anything; **il ne faut r. lui dire,** he must not be told anything; **personne n'osa lui r. dire, r. lui dire,** nobody ventured to say anything to him; **n'en dites r.,** say nothing about it; **(il n'est) r. de tel que de se bien porter,** there is nothing like health; **r. de tel que de savoir écouter,** there's nothing like knowing how to listen; **je n'ai r. d'autre, r. de nouveau, à vous dire,** I have nothing else, nothing new, to tell you; **il ne vous faut r. d'autre?** do you require anything else? **nous n'avions plus r., r. de plus, à nous dire,** we had nothing more to say to each other; **il ne fait r.,** (i) he is out of work; he doesn't do, hasn't got, a job; (ii) he doesn't do a thing; (iii) (*of tradesman*) he is not doing well; **tout le reste n'est r.,** nothing else matters; **cela ne fait r.,** that doesn't matter, it makes no difference; *F:* **ça ne fait r.,** it's no odds; **cela ne fait r. à l'affaire,** that is nothing to do with it; **si cela ne vous fait r.,** if you have no objection, if you don't mind; **cela ne sert à r., de r.,** it's no use; **elle ne lui ressemble en r.,** she is not at all, not a bit, like him; **comme si de r. n'était,** as if nothing had happened; **il n'en est r.!** nothing of the kind! **je n'en ferai r.,** I shall do nothing of the sort, nothing of the kind; **il n'y avait r. dans la bourse,** the purse had nothing in it; **il n'a r. d'un héros,** there is nothing of the hero, nothing heroic, about him; **sa fille n'a r. de lui,** his daughter doesn't take after him in any way; **il n'était pour r. dans l'affaire,** he had nothing to do with, had no hand in, the matter; *F:* **il ne sait r. de r., il sait deux fois r.,** he knows nothing whatever, nothing at all; he knows nothing about anything; **il n'y connaît r.,** *P:* **il n'y pige r.,** he knows damn all; **il ne comprend r. à r.,** he is a complete fool, he doesn't understand a single thing; **il ne sera jamais r.,** he will never be anybody; *s.a.* DIRE I. 4, MOINS 1, MONDE[1] 1, PARLER I, 2; (*b*) (*with* **ne** *understood*) **que faites-vous?—r., presque r.,** what are you doing?—nothing, hardly anything; **r. du tout,** nothing at all; **passer le jour à (ne) r. faire,** to spend the day doing nothing; **se réduire à r.,** to come to nothing; **avoir, obtenir, qch. pour r.,** to get sth. for next to nothing, for a mere song, dirt cheap; **la vie est pour r. ici,** one can live here for next to nothing; **parler pour r.**, to waste one's breath, to waste words; **se fâcher de r.**, to get angry about nothing; **merci, madame—de r., monsieur,** thank you (so much)—I'm glad I could help; it was a pleasure; oh please . . .! **en moins de r.**, in less than no time, in no time; **une affaire de r. du tout,** an insignificant matter; **une petite maison de r. du tout,** a poky, wretched, little house; **une petite pièce de r. du tout,** a poky little room; **un (homme de) r. du tout,** a man of no account, a nobody; **il m'a donné un couteau de r. du tout,** he gave me a measly knife; **fréquenter les femmes de r.**, to associate with cheap prostitutes; **r. de plus beau que . . .,** nothing could be finer than . . .; **allez-vous à Londres ce soir?—pourquoi?—oh, pour r.!** are you going to London to-night?—why?—oh, I just wondered; **pour trois fois r.**, for next to nothing; *Ten:* **quinze à r., r. à quinze,** fifteen love, love fifteen; (*c*) (*the negation is expressed or implied in some other part or word of the sentence*) **non qu'il y connaisse r.**, not that he knows anything about it; **il est inutile de r. dire,** you needn't say anything; **sans r. faire,** without doing anything; **sans r. d'autre que . . ., sans r. autre chose que . . .,** without anything but . . .; (*d*) *adv.phr.* **r. que,** nothing but, only, merely; **r. que ce silence le condamne,** his silence alone is sufficient proof against him; **je frémis r. que d'y songer,** the very thought (of it) makes me shudder, I shudder at the mere thought, at the bare idea; **il tremblait r. qu'en le racontant,** only, merely, to tell of it made him tremble; **il faut le respecter r. que pour sa probité,** we must respect him if only for his honesty; **ils font cinquante kilomètres r. que pour aller à un bal,** they will travel fifty kilometres just to go to a dance; **il m'a confié le secret, r. qu'à moi,** he told me the secret, just to me; **r. que cela!** *F:* **ça!** is that all? (*e*) (*with* **ne . . . pas**) **on ne peut pas vivre de r.**, you can't live on nothing; **ce n'est pas r.!** that's something! **ce n'est pas pour r. que . . .,** it is not without good reason that . . .; **la ville n'est pas r. qu'un port de mer,** the town is not merely a seaport. **3.** *P:* (*intensive*) **elle est r. chic!** she isn't half smart! **on a r. rigolé!** didn't we just enjoy ourselves! you should have heard us laugh!

II. **rien,** *s.m.* **1.** trifle, mere nothing; **se piquer d'un r.**, to take offence at the slightest thing; **s'amuser à des riens,** to trifle; **perdre son temps, son argent, à des riens,** to trifle away one's time, one's money; **passer une heure à dire des riens,** to spend an hour in small talk; **il le fera en un r. de temps,** he'll do it in no time; **un r. l'habille,** she looks good in anything. **2.** just a little; **ajouter un r. d'ail,** to add just the smallest piece of garlic, to add a touch of garlic; **donnez-moi un r. de fromage,** give me just a taste of cheese; **il y avait dans son sourire un r. de jalousie,** in his smile there was just a shade, a tinge, a hint, of jealousy; **un r. de fille,** a slip of a girl; **un r. de femme,** a tiny little woman. **3.** a trifle; **il est un r. pédant,** he is a trifle pedantic; **il est un r. menteur,** he's a bit of a liar.

rien-du-tout [rjɛ̃dytu]. **1.** *s.f.inv. F:* woman of easy virtue, tart. **2.** *s.m.inv.* (i) a nobody; (ii) a rotter.

riesling [rislinŋ], *s.m. Vit:* (*also* **vin de R.**) Riesling.

rietbok [ritbɔk], *s.m. Z:* rietbok, reitbok.

rieur, -euse [rijœːr, -øːz]. **1.** *a.* laughing; fond of laughter; merry. **2.** *s.* laugher; **avoir les rieurs de son côté, pour soi,** to have the laugh on one's side; **il avait maintenant les rieurs contre lui,** the laugh was now against him. **3.** *a. & s.f. Z:* **(mouette) rieuse,** black-headed gull.

Rif (le) [lərif], *Pr.n.m. Geog:* the Rif(f).

rif, riffe [rif], *s.m. Mil: P:* (*a*) front; firing line; (*b*) revolver; (*c*) fight, brawl.

rifain [rifɛ̃], *Geog:* **1.** *a.* belonging to the Rif(f), Riffian. **2.** *s.* Rif(f), Riffian, native, inhabitant, of the Rif(f).

riffauder [rifode], *v.tr. A: P:* to burn.

rif(f)le [rifl̥], *s.m. Gold Min:* riffle.

rififi [rififi], *s.m. P:* (*a*) money, dough; (*b*) scuffle, brawl, free-for-all.

riflard[1] [riflaːr], *s.m. Tls:* **1.** coarse file (for metals). **2.** paring chisel (for masonry). **3.** jack-plane. **4.** plastering trowel.

riflard[2], *s.m.* longest wool, most valuable part of fleece.

riflard[3], *s.m. F:* umbrella, *F:* brolly, gamp.

rifle [rifl̥], *s.m.* (*a*) *Gold Min:* riffle; (*b*) *Sm.a:* rifle; **une carabine de 22 long r.**, *F:* **un two-two long r.**, a ·22 long rifle; (*c*) *Mil:* rifle.

rifleman [rifləman], *s.m. Mil:* rifleman; *pl. riflemen.*

rifler [rifle], *v.tr. Tchn:* (*a*) to plane; (*b*) to pare; (*c*) to file.

riflette [riflɛt], *s.f. Mil: P:* war; front; **partir pour la r.**, to go off to war, to the front.

rifloir [riflwaːr], *s.m. Tls:* riffler.

rift [rift], *s.m. Geol:* rift valley, graben.

Riga [riga], *Pr.n. Med:* **maladie de R.**, Riga's disease.

rigadeau, -eaux [rigado], *s.m. Moll: Com:* cockle.

rigaud [rigo], *s.m. Const:* stone, hard lump (in lime).

rigaudon [rigodɔ̃], *s.m. A:* = RIGODON.

rigide [riʒid], *a.* (*a*) rigid (object, virtue, etc.); tense (muscle, etc.); inflexible (system, etc.); **visage aux traits rigides,** set face; **étiquette r.**, rigid, *F:* cast-iron, hidebound, etiquette; **essieu r.**, fixed axle; (*b*) *a. & s.m. Aer:* rigid (airship).

rigidement [riʒidmɑ̃], *adv.* rigidly; tensely.

rigidifier [riʒidifje], *v.tr.* (*p.d. & pr.sub.* **n. rigidifiions, v. rigidifiiez**) to rigidify, to make rigid.

rigidité [riʒidite], *s.f.* rigidity, rigidness, stiffness; tenseness (of muscles, etc.); inflexibility (of system, etc.); *Med:* **r. cataleptique,** cataleptic rigor; **r. cadavérique,** rigor mortis, cadaveric rigidity; *El:* **r. diélectrique,** dielectric strength; *Tchn:* **module de r.**, rigidity modulus; **coefficient de r.**, stiffness coefficient; *Magn:* **r. magnétique,** magnetic rigidity; *Ball:* **r. de la trajectoire,** rigidity of the trajectory.

rigodon [rigodɔ̃], *s.m.* **1.** *Danc: Mus: A:* rigadoon. **2.** *Mil:* (*from drum-signal given*) **faire un r.**, to score, make, a bull's eye.

rigolade [rigɔlad], *s.f. P:* fun; lark, spree; **tout ça, c'est de la r.**, it's all a huge joke; that's all fun; **il prend tout à la r.**, he won't take anything seriously; **le problème de maths?—c'était de la r.**, the maths problem?—it was child's play.

rigolage [rigɔlaʒ], *s.m. Hort:* trenching (for setting young plants).

rigolard, -arde [rigɔlaːr, -ard], *P:* **1.** *a.* (*a*) fond of a lark, a joke; full of fun; (*b*) = RIGOLO. **2.** *s.* merry person; jolly dog; joker.

rigolboche [rigɔlbɔʃ], *a. P: A:* = RIGOLO 1 (*a*).

rigole [rigɔl], *s.f.* drain, furrow drain, trench, gutter, channel, ditch; *Metall:* sow channel; **r. de captage, d'écoulement,** catch drain; **r. (de fenêtre),** condensation groove; **r. d'assèchement,** drainage channel, drainage ditch, gutter; *Min:* **r. de chargement,** loading trough, conveyor trough; *Const:* **r. de déversement,** chute.

rigoler[1] [rigɔle], *v.i. F:* (*a*) to laugh; **histoire de r. un coup!** it's good for a laugh! **tu rigoles!** you're joking! (*b*) to have some fun, to enjoy oneself.

rigoler[2], *v.tr.* to make furrow drains in (field, etc.); to trench (field).

rigoleur[1], **-euse**[1] [rigɔlœːr, -øːz]. **1.** *a.* fond of fun; jolly, jovial. **2.** *s.* (*a*) laugher; (*b*) joker; **c'est un r.**, he's always ready (i) for, (ii) with, a joke.

rigoleur[2], *s.m. Agr:* drill hoe.

rigoleuse[2], *s.f.* trench plough; *For:* tree plough.

rigollot [rigɔlo], *s.m. Pharm: O:* **(papier) r.**, mustard leaf paper, plaster (*from the chemist of that name,* 1810-73).

rigolo, -ote [rigɔlo, -ɔt], *F:* **1.** *a.* (*a*) comic, laughable, funny; **c'était d'un r.!** it was too funny for words! it was screamingly funny! a perfect scream! **ce n'est pas r.**, it's no joke; (*b*) surprising, queer, odd. **2.** *s.m.* joker; *Pej:* **c'est un (petit) r.**, he can't stop trying to be funny. **3.** *s.m.* revolver or pistol; gun.

rigorisme [rigɔrism], *s.m.* rigorism, strictness, austerity.

rigoriste [rigɔrist]. **1.** *a.* rigorous (person, discipline, etc.); strict (code of morals); **je ne suis pas r. à l'égard des convenances,** I'm not a stickler for propriety. **2.** *s.* rigorist; rigid moralist.

rigoureusement [rigurøzmɑ̃], *adv.* rigorously. **1.** **punir qn r.**, to punish s.o. rigorously; to inflict rigorous punishment upon s.o. **2.** strictly; **r. parlant, à parler r., ce n'est pas vrai,** strictly speaking, it is not true; **r. exact,** absolutely correct; **je n'ai r. rien compris,** I understand absolutely nothing, I haven't understood a thing.

rigoureux, -euse [rigurø, -øːz], *a.* rigorous. **1.** severe, harsh; **sentence rigoureuse,** severe sentence; **règlements r.**, stringent measures; **climat r.**, severe, rigorous, climate; **hiver r.**, hard winter; **sort r.**, hard lot. **2.** strict, close; **ordres r.**, strict orders; **observer une neutralité rigoureuse,** to observe strict neutrality; **raisonnement r.**, close reasoning; **au sens r. du mot,** in the strict sense of the word.

rigueur [rigœːr], *s.f.* **1.** rigour, harshness, severity; **il y aurait quelque r. à exiger . . .,** it would appear somewhat exacting to demand . . .; **les rigueurs du sort,** the hardships of fate; **j'ai connu les rigueurs de la pauvreté,** I have known the rigours of poverty; **prendre des mesures de r.**, to take rigorous, severe, measures; **les rigueurs que vous avez provoquées,** the severe measures which you have brought upon yourselves; **r. du temps, du climat,** severity of the weather, of the climate; **avant les rigueurs de l'hiver,** before the severe part of the winter sets in; **user de r. avec qn,** to be severe, hard, on s.o.; **tenir r. à qn,** to refuse to relent towards s.o.; to keep up a grudge against s.o.; to refuse to be mollified; **elle vous tient r. de l'avoir fait attendre,** she has not forgiven you for keeping her waiting; *s.a.* ARRÊT 4. **2.** strictness; **appliquer la loi dans toute sa r.**, to put the law in operation in all its rigour; **la r. des règles,** the strictness of the rules; **la r. d'un raisonnement,** the closeness, exactness, of a piece of reasoning; (*of thg*) **être de r.**, to be indispensable, compulsory, obligatory, de rigueur; **délai de r.**, deadline (date); **l'habit n'est pas de r.**, evening dress is optional; *adv.phr.* **à la r.**, (i) *A:* rigorously, strictly; (ii) if need be, if really necessary, at the worst, *F:* at a pinch; *A:* **observer les lois à la r.**, to observe the laws to the letter; **à la r. on peut se servir de . . .,** at a pinch one may use . . .; **à la r. on pourra se passer de viande,** if the worst comes to the worst we can do without meat.

Rig-Véda [rigveda], *Pr.n.m. Hindu Rel:* Rig-veda.

rikiki [rikiki], *s.m.* = RIQUIQUI.

rillauds [rijo], *s.m.pl. Cu:* pork cut up into small pieces and cooked in lard for a long time.

rillettes [rijɛt], *s.f.pl. Cu:* rillettes; potted mince (of pork, etc.).

rill-marks [rilmarks], *s.f.pl.* rill marks (on a beach).

rillons [rijɔ̃], *s.m.pl. Cu:* greaves.

rimaille [rimɑːj], *s.f. F: A:* bad poetry.

rimailler [rimɑje], *v.i. F:* to string rhymes together, to dabble in verse-making.

rimaillerie [rimɑjri], *s.f. F:* (*a*) dabbling in poetry; (*b*) doggerel.

rimailleur [rimɑjœːr], *s.m. F:* rhymester, would-be poet.

rimaye [rimɑːj], *s.f. Mount:* bergschrund, rimaye.

rime [rim], *s.f. Pros:* rhyme; **rimes masculines, féminines,** masculine, feminine, rhymes; **rimes plates, suivies,** alternate masculine and feminine couplets, couplet rhymes; **rimes croisées, alternées,** alternate rhymes; **r. riche,** rich, perfect, rhyme; **r. pour l'œil,** eye, sight, rhyme; printer's rhyme; *s.a.* EMBRASSÉ, MARIÉ 3; **dictionnaire de rimes,** rhyming dictionary; **cheviller pour la r.**, to tag one's verse for the sake of rhyme; *F:* **sans r. ni raison,** without rhyme or reason; **cela n'a ni r. ni raison,** there's neither rhyme nor reason in it; **n'entendre ni r. ni raison,** not to listen to reason.

rimé [rime], *a. Pros:* rhymed.

rimer [rime]. **1.** *v.tr.* to versify, to put (tale, etc.) into rhyme. **2.** *v.i.* (*a*) (*of verses, words*) to rhyme (**avec,** with); **r. à, pour, l'oreille,** to rhyme; **r. aux, pour les, yeux,** to be composed of eye rhymes, to rhyme on paper; *F:* **à quoi cela rime-t-il?** what sense, what meaning, is there in that? **cela ne rime à rien,** there's no sense, neither rhyme nor reason, in it; **ces deux choses ne riment pas ensemble,** these two things do not go together, have no connections with each other; (*b*) (*of pers.*) (i) to write verses, poetry; (ii) to find rhymes (for a word).

rimeur [rimœːr], *s.m. Pej:* rhymer, rhymester, versifier; **ce sont des rimeurs, pas de vrais poètes,** they're only versifiers, not real poets.

rimeux, -euse [rimø, -øːz], *a. Nat.Hist:* rimose.

rimmel [rimɛl], *s.m.* mascara.

rinçage [rɛ̃saːʒ], *s.m.* rinsing; *Hairdr:* (colour) rinse.

rinceau, -eaux [rɛ̃so], *s.m.* **1.** *Arch: Sculp:* (ornamental) foliage; foliated scroll. **2.** *Her:* branch. **3.** *Furn:* (curtain) loop hook.

rince-bouche [rɛ̃sbuʃ], *s.m.inv.*, **rince-doigts** [rɛ̃sdwa], *s.m.inv.* finger bowl.

rince-bouteilles [rɛ̃sbutɛːj], *s.m.inv.* bottle-washing machine, bottle washer.

rincée [rɛ̃se], *s.f.* **1.** *O: P:* drubbing, thrashing. **2.** downpour; **j'ai pris une r.**, I got caught in a downpour.

rincer [rɛ̃se], *v.tr.* (**je rinçai(s); n. rinçons**) **1.** to rinse (clothes, etc.); to rinse out (glass); **se r. la bouche,** to rinse one's mouth; *P:* **se r. le gosier, la dalle,** to wet one's whistle; *P:* **se r. l'œil,** to get an eyeful. **2.** *P:* (*a*) (*of rain*) to drench (s.o.);

(*b*) to stand drinks to (s.o.); **se faire r.**, to sponge on others for drinks; (*c*) **se faire r.**, to be cleaned out (gambling). **3.** *O: P:* to drub, thrash (s.o.).

rince-tonneau [rɛ̃stɔno], *s.m.inv.* barrel-washing machine.

rincette [rɛ̃sɛt], *s.f. P:* nip (of spirits, after coffee).

rinceur, -euse [rɛ̃sœr, -øz]. **1.** *s.* (*pers.*) rinser. **2.** *s.f.* **rinceuse,** (*machine*) (*a*) rinser; (*b*) bottle-washing machine.

rinçoir [rɛ̃swaːr], *s.m.* **1.** rinsing bowl. **2.** rinsing sink.

rinçure [rɛ̃syːr], *s.f.* (*a*) rinsings, slops; (*b*) *F:* poor wine; *P:* hogwash.

rinforzando [rinfɔrdzando], *adv. Mus:* rinforzando.

ring [riŋ], *s.m. Box:* ring; **monter sur le r.,** to get into the ring, to climb into the ring; **manquer de r.,** to have been out of the ring for a long time.

ringard [rɛ̃gaːr], *s.m.* **1.** (furnace) fire iron, clinkering iron, tapping iron, poker, clinker bar, slice bar, prick bar, pricker; **r. à crochet,** rake. **2.** *Metall:* rabble, rabbler. **3.** *Metalw:* porter.

ringardage [rɛ̃gardaːʒ], *s.m.* raking out, clinkering (of furnace).

ringarder [rɛ̃garde], *v.tr.* **1.** to poke, to rake the clinker of (furnace fire). **2.** to rabble (molten metal).

ringente [rɛ̃ʒɑ̃ːt], *a.f. Bot:* ringent (corolla).

ringot [rɛ̃go], *s.m. Nau:* becket (on pulley).

ringoule [rɛ̃gul], *s.f. Bot: agaricus pleurotus.*

riodinides [riɔdinid], *s.m.pl. Ent:* Riodinidae, Erycinidae, the metalmarks.

riol(l)e [rjɔl], *s.f. Lit:* feasting, carousal, revelry.

riomois, -oise [rjɔmwa, -waːz], *a. & s. Geog:* (native, inhabitant) of Riom.

riot [rjo], *s.m. Dial:* stream.

riotte [rjɔt], *s.f. Lit:* row, quarrel.

ripage [ripaːʒ], *s.m.* **1.** scraping, polishing (of stones). **2.** sliding along, shifting (of heavy box, railway track, etc.). **3.** (*a*) (*of hawsers, etc.*) (i) scraping, rubbing; (ii) slipping (on the capstan); (*b*) (*of wheels*) skidding; (*c*) (*of cargo*) shifting.

ripagérien, -ienne [ripaʒerjɛ̃, -jɛn], *a. & s. Geog:* (native, inhabitant) of Rive-de-Gier.

ripaille [ripɑːj], *s.f. F:* feasting, carousal, revelry; *F:* blowout; **faire r.,** to feast, to have a good blowout.

ripailler [ripɑje], *v.i. F:* to feast, carouse, revel; to have a good blowout.

ripailleur, -euse [ripɑjœːr, -øːz], *s. F:* feaster, carouser, reveller.

ripainsel [ripɛ̃sɛl], *s.m. Mil: A:* soldier or officer in the French Army Service Corps.

ripaton [ripatɔ̃], *s.m. P:* **1.** boot. **2.** foot; **jouer des ripatons,** to beat it, to decamp.

ripatonner [ripatɔne], *v.tr. O: P:* to mend; to patch (sth.) up; to botch (sth.) up.

ripatonneur [ripatɔnœːr], *s.m. O: P:* botcher up (of sth.).

rip [rip], *s.f.* **1.** *Sculp: etc:* scraper. **2.** *Fr.C:* wood shavings.

ripement [ripmɑ̃], *s.m.* = RIPAGE.

riper [ripe]. **1.** *v.tr.* to scrape, polish (stone). **2.** *v.tr.* (*a*) to slip, let slip (chain on capstan, etc.); (*b*) to slide (heavy box, etc.) along; to shift (load, etc.); (*c*) *Rail:* to shift (the track). **3.** *v.i.* (*a*) (*of hawser*) (i) to scrape, rub; (ii) to slip (on the capstan); (*b*) (*of wheels*) to skid; (*c*) (*of cargo, etc.*) to shift; (*d*) *Av:* **atterrissage ripé,** lateral drift landing; (*e*) *P:* to clear off.

ripeur [ripœːr], *s.m.* (*at les Halles*) (market) porter.

ripicole [ripikɔl], *a. Geol:* riparian, riparial.

ripidolite [ripidɔlit], *s.f. Miner:* ripidolite.

ripiéniste [ripjenist], *s.m. & f. Mus:* ripienist.

ripieno [ripjeno], *s.m. Mus:* ripieno.

Ripolin [ripɔlɛ̃], *s.m. R.t.m:* Ripolin enamel paint.

ripoliner [ripɔline], *v.tr.* to (paint with) Ripolin enamel.

ripopée [ripɔpe]. *s.f. O: F:* slops, lap; heel-taps (of wine); **r. de vieilles théories,** hash-up, hotch-potch, of old theories.

riposte [ripɔst], *s.f.* riposte. **1.** *Box: Fenc:* return, counter; *Fenc:* answer; *Mil:* **r. graduée,** flexible response. **2.** (*a*) retort; pat answer; (*b*) counter-stroke.

riposter [ripɔste], *v.i.* **1.** (*a*) *Box: Fenc:* to riposte, counter; **je riposterai,** I'll give as good as I get; (*b*) **r. à une influence,** to counteract an influence. **2.** to retort; to answer pat; **r. par un défi,** to fling back, flash back, defiance; *with cogn. acc.* **r. qch. de désagréable,** to retort sth. unpleasant; to fling back an ungracious retort.

ripper [ripœːr], *s.m. Civ.E:* ripper, scarifier.

ripple [ripḷ], *s.m. Geog:* ripple.

ripple-mark [riplmark], *s.f. Geol:* tide mark, ripple mark.

ripuaire [ripɥɛːr], *a. & s. Hist:* Ripuarian; **les (Francs) ripuaires,** the Ripuarian Franks (who dwelt on the banks of the Rhine).

riquet [rikɛ], *s.m. Ent: F:* cricket.

riquiqui [rikiki], *s.m. F:* **1.** (*a*) the little finger; (*b*) undersized person, little squirt. **2.** (*a*) brandy of poor quality; rotgut; (*b*) **un petit verre de r.,** a little drop of spirits. **3.** *a.* small, puny; measly (little); undersized.

rire [riːr]. I. *v.i.* (*pr.p.* **riant**; *p.p.* **ri**; *pr.ind.* **je ris, n. rions, ils rient**; *pr.sub.* **je rie**; *p.d.* **je riais, n. riions**; *p.h.* **je ris**; *fu.* **je rirai**) **1.** to laugh; **se tenir les côtes de r., r. comme un bossu,** to be doubled up, convulsed, with laughter; to shake with laughter; **r. bruyamment,** to guffaw; **r. en soi-même, r. tout bas,** to laugh to oneself; to chuckle; **r. en dedans,** to laugh up one's sleeve; to snigger; **r. de bon cœur,** to laugh heartily; **r. faux, pointu,** to give a forced laugh; to force a laugh; **r. bêtement,** to give a stupid laugh, (i) to haw-haw; (ii) to giggle, titter; **dire qch. en riant,** to say sth. laughingly, with a laugh; **r. dans le dos de qn,** to laugh at s.o. behind his back; *s.a.* ANGE 1, BARBE[1] 1, CAPE 1, DENT 1, ÉCLAT 2, ÉCLATER 2, FOU 1, GORGE 2, GOSIER, JAUNE 2, LÈVRE 1, PINCER 1, TAS 1, SE TORDRE; **il a ri (jusqu')aux larmes,** he laughed till he cried; **c'était à mourir de r.,** *P:* **à crever de r.,** it was killingly funny; we nearly died with laughter; **ne pas avoir le cœur à r.,** not to be in a laughing mood; **il n'y a pas de quoi r.,** it's no laughing matter; **faire r. qn,** to make s.o. laugh, to set s.o. laughing; **cela fait r.,** it, that, makes you laugh; **cela nous a souvent fait r.,** we have had many a laugh over it; **cela fit r. toute la salle,** it made the audience roar with laughter; **il nous faisait tordre, mourir, de r.,** he convulsed us with laughter, he made us split our sides laughing; **l'enfant rit à ses parents,** the child greets his parents with a laugh; **r. de qn,** to laugh, mock, at s.o.; **ne riez pas de lui,** don't make fun of him; **r. d'une histoire,** to laugh over a story; **c'est à faire r. les pierres,** it is enough to make a cat laugh; **il rit de vos menaces,** he laughs at, makes light of, your threats; *s.a.* NEZ 1; **il prête à r.,** he makes himself a laughing-stock; **j'ai peur de prêter à r.,** I am afraid of being laughed at, of making myself ridiculous; **sa toilette prête à r.,** the way she dresses make you want to laugh; **cela ne prête pas à r.,** it is no laughing matter; *Prov:* **tel qui rit vendredi dimanche pleurera,** laugh on Friday, cry on Sunday; **rira bien qui rira le dernier,** he laughs longest who laughs last; **nous allons r.!** we'll have some fun! **r. franchement de . . .,** to laugh out at . . .; **vous me faites r.!** nonsense! are you trying to be funny? **laissez-moi r.! ne me faites pas r.!** don't make me laugh! **2.** to jest, joke; **vous voulez r.!** you mean that for a joke! are you joking? do you really mean it? **dire, faire, qch. en riant,** to say, do, sth. for a joke; **prendre qch. en riant,** to laugh sth. off; **pour r.,** for fun, for a joke; **cela a été dit pour r.,** it was said by way of a joke; *P:* **c'était pour de r.,** it was only my fun; *A:* **journal pour r.,** comic paper; **roi pour r.,** sham king, mock king; **soldats pour r.,** make-believe soldiers; **enchères pour r.,** spoof auction (at bazaar, etc.); **je l'ai fait, histoire de r.,** I did it for a joke, for fun, for the fun of the thing. **3.** to smile; (*a*) *Lit: A:* **r. à qn,** to smile to s.o., to greet s.o. with a smile; **r. d'une oreille à l'autre,** to grin from ear to ear; (*b*) **l'espoir riait dans ses yeux,** hope was smiling in his eyes; *Poet:* **tout rit dans ce séjour,** all is pleasant in this abode; (*c*) to be favourable, propitious (à, to); **la fortune lui rit,** fortune smiles on him; **les heureux du monde à qui tout rit,** the fortunate of this world for whom everything is pleasant. **4.** *F:* **habit qui rit par toutes les coutures,** coat that gapes at every seam.

se rire, (*a*) **se r. de qn,** to laugh at, mock, s.o.; to make fun of, poke fun at, s.o.; *F:* to have s.o. on a string; to laugh s.o. to scorn; (*b*) **se r. de qch.,** to laugh at, make light of, sth.

II. **rire,** *s.m.* (*a*) laughter, laughing; **le r. aide à digérer,** laughter is good for the digestion; **éclat de r.,** burst of laughter; **il eut un court éclat de r.,** he gave a short laugh; **partir d'un (grand) éclat de r.,** to burst out laughing, to burst into a loud laugh, into loud laughter; **avoir un accès de fou r.,** to be overcome with uncontrollable laughter; (*b*) **un r.,** a laugh; **provoquer, exciter, les rires,** to cause laughter; **cette pièce est un fou r.,** this play is a screaming farce; **arracher un r. à l'auditoire,** to draw a laugh from the audience; **un r. moqueur,** a sneer; **il eut un r. d'incrédulité,** he laughed incredulously; **un gros r. (bruyant),** a horse laugh; a guffaw; **un r. bête,** a stupid laugh, (i) a haw-haw; (ii) a giggle, a titter; **il eut un r. gras,** (i) he gurgled with laughter; (ii) he gave a dirty laugh.

ris[1] [ri], *s.m. A. & Poet:* laugh, laughter; **les Jeux et les R.,** Sport and Mirth.

ris[2], *s.m. Nau:* reef (in sail); **prendre un r.,** to take in a reef; **prendre un r. à une voile,** to reef a sail; **prendre un r. à l'irlandaise,** to slash a sail (in an emergency); **prendre les r.,** to reef the sails; **voile au bas r.,** close-reefed sail; **mettre les huniers au bas r., prendre le bas r.,** to full reef the topsails; **avec deux r.,** double-reefed; **larguer un r.,** to shake out a reef; **bande de r.,** reef band; **garcettes de r.,** reef points; **œillet de r.,** eyelet hole of reef; **raban de r.,** reef earing.

ris[3], *s.m. Cu:* **r. de veau, d'agneau,** calf's, lamb's, sweetbread.

risberme [risbɛrm], *s.f. Civ.E:* berm (of a dam).

rise [riːz], *s.f. Min:* small channel (to drain water); *For:* wooden chute (for conveying logs).

risée [rize], *s.f.* **1.** (*a*) jeer, mockery, derision; **s'exposer à la r. publique, aux risées,** to expose oneself to public scorn, derision; (*b*) laughing-stock, butt; **être la r. de toute la ville,** to be the laughing-stock of the whole town; (*c*) *A:* outburst of laughter. **2.** *Nau:* light squall; flurry (of wind).

riser [rize], *v.i. Min:* to make a small channel (to drain water).

risette [rizɛt], *s.f.* **1.** (child's) pretty laugh, smile; **fais (la) r. à papa!** now smile for daddy! **2.** *Nau:* cat's paw (of wind).

rishi [riʃi], *s.m.inv. Hindu Rel:* rishi, rsi.

risibilité [rizibilite], *s.f.* **1.** *A:* risibility; ability, inclination, to laugh. **2.** laughableness.

risible [riziblḷ], *a.* **1.** *A:* risible; disposed to laugh. **2.** ludicrous, laughable (mistake); ridiculous (person).

risiblement [rizibləmɑ̃], *adv. O:* ludicrously, laughably.

risorius [rizɔrjys], *s.m. Anat:* risorius.

risotto [rizɔto], *s.m. Cu:* risotto.

risquable [riskabḷ], *a.* that may be risked; that may be ventured upon; **une affaire r.,** a possible venture.

risque [risk], *s.m.* (*a*) risk; **courir un r.,** to run, incur, a risk; **vous courez un grand r.,** you are running a great risk; **il court le r. d'être arrêté,** he runs the risk of being arrested; **à tout r.,** at all hazards; **c'est un r. à courir,** it's a risk worth running; **prendre un r., des risques,** to take a risk, risks; **vous le faites à vos risques et périls,** you do it at your own risk; *Com:* **aux risques et périls du destinataire,** at owner's risk; **risques de mer,** sea perils; **sans r. de naufrage,** with no risk of shipwreck; **au r. de sa vie,** at the risk, peril, of his life; **au r. de manquer le train,** at the risk of losing the train; **il y a du r. à attendre,** there is some risk in waiting; *F:* **r. à faire qch.,** with the ultimate possibility of doing sth., with a view to doing sth.; **risques de guerre,** war risks, hazards of war; **risques du métier,** occupational hazards; *Pol: etc:* **r. calculé,** calculated risk; *Golf:* **r. de jeu,** rub of, on, the green; (*b*) *Ins:* (i) (*danger*) risk; **r. assuré,** risk subscribed, taken up; **r. collectif,** collective risk; **police tous risques,** comprehensive, all-in, all-risks, policy; **r. d'incendie,** fire risk; **r. de casse,** breakage risk; **r. de perte,** loss risk; **r. de vol,** theft risk; **r. du recours de tiers,** third-party risk; **r. locatif,** tenant's third-party risk; **r. maritime, r. de mer,** maritime risk, sea risk; **r. d'allèges,** craft risk; **r. de port,** port risk; **r. de port sur corps,** hull port risk; **r. de guerre,** war risk; **couvrir un r.,** to cover a risk; **souscrire un r.,** to underwrite a risk; (ii) (*pers. or thg considered as a hazard*) **un bon, un mauvais, r.,** a good, a bad, risk.

risqué [riske], *a.* risky; **une affaire très risquée,** a risky, hazardous, business; **chanson risquée,** risky, risqué, off-colour, song; **votre conversation, votre conduite, est un peu risquée,** you're sailing rather close to the wind.

risquer [riske], *v.tr.* to risk, venture, chance; **r. sa vie,** to risk, venture, one's life; **il risquait la mort,** he was carrying his life in his hands; **vous risquez beaucoup, vous ne risquez rien, à attendre,** you are running a great risk, you risk nothing, by waiting; **il faut r. le combat,** we must risk a battle; **je ne veux rien r.,** I am not taking any risks, any chances; **r. gros,** to play for heavy stakes; *Prov:* **qui ne risque rien n'a rien,** nothing venture, nothing win; **r. le coup,** to chance it; **il risquait de tout perdre,** he risked, ran the risk of, losing everything; **vous risquez qu'on vous**

aperçoive, you are running the risk of being seen; **risquons!** let's chance it! *F:* **r. le paquet,** to chance it; **il a risqué le tout pour le tout,** (i) he pinned everything on it; (ii) he risked his neck; *F:* **j'ai risqué de me faire tuer en rentrant,** I nearly got killed on my way home; **la grève risque de durer longtemps,** the strike may (well) go on for a long time; *F:* **il risque de gagner,** he has a good chance of winning, he's likely to win; **ma tante risque de venir,** I'm very much afraid my aunt may come; *F:* **r. un œil,** to peep out.

se risquer, to take a risk; to take risks; **se r. à faire qch.,** to venture, to make bold, to do sth.; **se r. à sortir,** to venture out of doors; **trop agité pour se r. à parler,** too excited to trust himself to speak.

risque-tout [riskətu], *s.m.inv.* desperado, dare-devil.

riss [ris], *s.m. Geol:* Riss.

risse [ris], *s.f.* **1.** *Nau:* lashing rope. **2.** *Orn:* kittiwake.

risser [rise], *v.tr. Nau:* to lash, secure (small boat, etc.).

rissien, -ienne [risjɛ̃, -jɛn], *a. Geol:* Riss, Rissian.

rissoa [risɔa], *s.f. Moll:* rissoa.

rissoïdés [risɔide], *s.m.pl. Moll:* Rissoidae.

rissole[1] [risɔl], *s.f. Cu:* (meat, etc.) patty.

rissole[2], *s.f. Fish:* (*in the Mediterranean*) anchovy net, sardine net.

rissoler [risɔle], *v.tr. & i. Cu:* to brown (*esp.* in the oven); *F:* **visage rissolé,** sunburnt face; **se laisser r. au soleil,** to roast in the sun.

rissolette [risɔlɛt], *s.f. Cu:* mince on toast baked in the oven.

rissolier [risɔlje], *a. & s.m. Fish:* (*in the Mediterranean*) **(bateau) r.,** fishing boat equipped with an anchovy net, a sardine net.

ristocétine [ristɔsetin], *s.f. Pharm:* ristocetin.

ristourne [risturn], *s.f.* **1.** (*a*) *Adm: Fin:* refund; return (of amount overpaid); rebate; (*b*) *Ins:* cancelling, annulment (of policy); repayment (to party insured); (*c*) *Com:* discount; commission; **timbre r.,** coupon redeemable for cash. **2.** *O: Book-k:* transfer(ring), writing back (of item to another account).

ristourner [risturne], *v.tr.* **1.** (*a*) to refund, return (amount overpaid); (*b*) *Ins:* to cancel, annul (policy); (*c*) *F:* to give (s.o.) a discount (on sth.). **2.** *Book-k: O:* to transfer, to write back (an article to another account).

rit [rit], *s.m. A:* = RITE; *pl. rites.*

rita [rita], *s.m. Bot:* soapnut tree.

Rital [rital], *s.m. P:* Italian, Eyetie; Wop.

ritardando [ritardando], *adv. & s.m. Mus:* ritardando.

rite [rit], *s.m.* rite; **le r. de l'Église romaine,** the Roman rite; **Congrégation des Rites,** Congregation of Sacred Rites; **les rites de la franc-maçonnerie,** the rites of freemasonry; **les rites de la vie quotidienne,** the ritual of everyday life; **pratiquer un r.,** to practise a rite; **r. de passage,** rite of passage; (*b*) *R.C.Ch:* rank (of feast); **r. simple,** simple, simplex; **r. double,** double, duplex.

ritologique [ritɔlɔʒik], *a.* **l'étude r.,** the study of rites.

ritonis [ritɔnis], *s.m. Fish:* (type of) pound net.

ritournelle [riturnɛl], *s.f. Mus:* ritornelle; ritornello; *F:* **c'est toujours la même r.,** (i) he's always harping on the same subject, on the same string; (ii) it's always the same old story; *Com:* **r. publicitaire,** (advertising) jingle.

rittingérite [ritɛ̃ʒerit], *s.f. Miner:* rittingerite.

rituale [ritɥal], *s.m. R.C.Ch:* rituale.

ritualisme [ritɥalism], *s.m. Ecc:* ritualism; *Pej:* ceremonialism.

ritualiste [ritɥalist]. **1.** *a.* ritualistic. **2.** *s.m. & f.* ritualist; *Pej:* ceremonialist.

rituel, -elle [ritɥɛl]. **1.** *a.* ritual (service, etc.); **on but les toasts rituels,** the customary toasts were drunk. **2.** *s.m.* (*a*) ritual; *R.C.Ch:* ceremonial; (*b*) ritual (book).

rituellement [ritɥɛlmɑ̃], *adv.* ritually.

rivage[1] [rivaːʒ], *s.m.* bank, side (of river); shore, beach (of lake, sea); *Geol:* **r. fossile,** abandoned shoreline; **maison bâtie sur le r.,** house built on the waterside; **pousser un bateau au r.,** to run a boat inshore; *Lit:* **de lointains rivages,** distant shores; **droits de r.,** mooring dues, moorage dues (in river).

rivage[2], *s.m.* riveting.

rivagérien, -enne [rivaʒerjɛ̃, -jɛn], *a. & s. Geog:* (native, inhabitant) of Rive-de-Gier.

rival, -ale, -aux [rival, -o], *a. & s.* rival; **sans r.,** unrivalled; **puissances rivales,** rival powers.

rivaliser [rivalize]. **1.** *v.i.* **r. avec qn,** (i) to rival s.o.; (ii) to compete; vie, with s.o.; (iii) to emulate s.o.; **il peut r. avec les meilleurs,** he can hold his own, compare, with the best; **r. d'efforts avec qn,** to vie with s.o.; **r. d'adresse avec qn,** to vie in skill with s.o.; **ils rivalisent à qui fera le mieux,** they are all anxious to outdo one another. **2.** *occ. v.tr.* **r. qn,** to rival s.o.

rivalité [rivalite], *s.f.* rivalry, competition.

rive [riːv], *s.f.* **1.** (*a*) bank, side (of river); shore, side (of lake); waterside; margin (of glacier); skirt, edge (of a wood); verge (of road); **la r. droite, gauche,** (i) (*of the Seine, Rhine, etc.*) the right, the left, bank; (ii) (*of the Thames*), the south, the north, bank; south of the river, north of the river; the south, north, side; **arche de r.,** end arch (of a bridge); *Mil:* **première r.,** near bank (in bridge building); **seconde r.,** further bank; **c'est un problème sans fond ni r.,** it's an unfathomable problem; (*b*) *Lit: A:* seashore. **2.** *Tchn:* edge, edging; border (of horseshoe); lip (of oven); edge (of paper); margin (of sprocket-punched continuous paper); thickness of edge (of plank); *Bak:* **pain de r.,** bread baked at one side of the oven; *Const:* **r. de tête,** top side (of hipped roof); **poutre de r.,** edge beam; **r. latérale,** side (of hipped roof).

rivelaine [rivlɛn], *s.f. Min:* pick.

rivelles [rivɛl], *s.f.pl. For:* oak saplings (reserved for wheelwright's work).

rivement [rivmɑ̃], *s.m.* = RIVETAGE.

river [rive], *v.tr.* (*a*) to rivet (sheet of iron, etc.); **machine à r.,** riveting machine; **rivé à couvre-joint,** butt-riveted; (*b*) to clinch (nail); *F:* **ils sont rivés l'un à l'autre,** they're inseparable; *F:* **r. son clou à qn,** (i) to give s.o. a clincher; to leave s.o. without a leg to stand on; to score off s.o.; (ii) to give s.o. a piece of one's mind; **ma réponse lui a rivé son clou,** my retort cut the ground from under his feet; **ses yeux étaient rivés sur la photographie,** his eyes were riveted on the photograph.

riverage [rivraːʒ], *s.m.* toll for the upkeep of the towpath.

riverain, -aine [rivrɛ̃, -ɛn]. **1.** *a.* (*a*) riparian, riverside, waterside, riverain (owner, property, etc.); **propriétés riveraines de la Loire,** estates bordering on the Loire; *Min:* **concession riveraine,** bank claim; (*b*) bordering on a road, on a wood, etc.; wayside (property, etc.); **boutiques riveraines des trottoirs,** shops along the pavement. **2.** *s.* (*a*) riverside resident; riverain; *Jur:* riparian proprietor; adjacent owner, abutter; (*b*) borderer (upon a place) resident; **les riverains de cette route,** the people who live along this road; the residents of this road; *P.N:* **route interdite sauf aux riverains,** residents' cars only; access only.

riveraineté [rivrɛnte], *s.f. Jur:* riparian rights.

rivereux, -euse [rivərø, -øːz], *a.* (*of falcon*) (specially) trained to fly over water.

rivesaltais, -aise [rivsaltɛ, -ɛːz], *a. & s. Geog:* (native, inhabitant) of Rivesaltes.

rivet [rivɛ], *s.m.* (*a*) rivet; **r. à fût droit,** straight-neck, straight-shank, rivet; **r. à fût renflé,** swell-neck, tapered-neck, rivet; **r. à tête affleurée,** flush-head rivet; **r. à tête bombée, à tête hémisphérique, à tête ronde; r. à tête bouterollée, à tête en goutte de suif,** button-head rivet, snap-head rivet; *Av:* brazier-head rivet; **r. à tête conique,** conical-head, steeple-head, rivet; **r. à tête fraisée,** counter-sunk rivet; **r. à tête noyée, à tête perdue,** flush rivet; **r. à tête plate,** flat-head, pan-head, rivet; **r. creux, r. forcé,** hollow rivet; **r. plein,** solid rivet; **r. tubulaire,** tubular rivet; **r. bifurqué,** slotted rivet; **tête de r.,** rivet head; **tige de r.,** rivet shaft, shank; **trou de r.,** rivet hole; **r. à trou conique,** taper-bore rivet; **assemblage à rivets,** rivet joint, riveted joint; **sans r.,** rivetless; **poser un r.,** to lay, drive, a rivet; **enlever un r.,** to drive out a rivet; (*b*) clinch.

rivetage [rivtaːʒ], *s.m.* (*a*) riveting; **r. au marteau,** hammer riveting; **r. mécanique,** machine riveting; **r. à chaud, à froid,** hot, cold, riveting; **r. à fleur,** flush riveting; **r. à recouvrement,** *Nau:* **r. à clins,** lap riveting; **r. des abouts,** *Nau:* **r. à franc bord,** butt riveting; **r. en quinconce,** staggered riveting; (*b*) clinching.

riveter [rivte], *v.tr.* (**je rivette, n. rivetons; je rivetterai**) to rivet.

riveteur [rivtœːr], *s.m.,* **riveur** [rivœːr], *s.m. Metalw:* riveter.

riveteuse [rivtøːz], *s.f.,* **riveuse** [rivøːz], *s.f. Tls:* riveting machine; riveter; **r. hydraulique,** hydraulic riveter, riveting machine; **r. pneumatique,** rivet gun, compression riveter.

Riviera [rivjera], *s.f. Geog:* the Eastern, Italian, Riviera.

rivière [rivjɛːr], *s.f.* **1.** (*a*) river; stream; **fausse r.,** overflow arm (of river); **tomber à, dans, la r.,** to fall into the river; *s.a.* EAU 2, RUISSEAU 1; (*b*) *Rac:* water jump; (*c*) **des rivières de feu coulaient du Vésuve,** streams of fire flowed down from Vesuvius. **2.** *Geog:* **la Rivière (de Gênes),** the (Eastern) Riviera. **3. r. de diamants,** diamond rivière. **4.** *Needlew:* row of openwork; openwork, hemstitch.

riviérette [rivjerɛt], *s.f. Geog:* small river, stream.

riviéreux, -euse [rivjerø, -øːz], *a.* (*of falcon*) (specially) trained to fly over water.

rivina [rivina], *s.m. Bot:* rivina.

rivoflavine [rivɔflavin], *s.f. Ch:* riboflavin(e), lactoflavin.

rivoir [rivwaːr], *s.m.* **1.** riveting hammer. **2.** riveting machine; riveter.

rivois [rivwa], *s.m.* riveting hammer.

Rivoli [rivɔli], *Pr.n. Geog:* Rivoli; *F:* **rue de R.,** the French *Ministère des Finances* (whose offices are in the rue de Rivoli in Paris).

rivolin [rivɔlɛ̃], *s.m. Nau:* = REVOLIN.

rivotter [rivɔte], *v.tr. Agr:* **r. la charrue,** to alter the axle height of the wheels of a plough.

rivulaire [rivylɛːr]. **1.** *a.* riverine. **2.** *s.f. Algae:* rivularia.

rivularia [rivylarja], *s.m. Algae:* rivularia.

rivulariacées [rivylarjase], *s.f.pl. Algae:* Rivulariaceae.

rivure [rivyːr], *s.f.* **1.** riveting; **r. sur un rang, r. simple,** single riveting; **r. sur deux rangs, r. double,** double riveting; **r. sur trois rangs, r. triple,** triple riveting; **r. étanche,** close riveting. **2.** (*a*) rivet(ed) joint; (*b*) rivet head; **r. bouterollée,** snap head; **r. écrasée,** battered head; (*c*) = CONTRE-RIVURE. **3.** (*a*) pin joint; (*b*) hinge pin, pintle.

rixdale [riksdal], *s.f. Num: A:* rix-dollar.

rixe [riks], *s.f.* brawl, scuffle; **r. de cabaret,** public-house brawl, row.

riz [ri], *s.m.* **1.** rice; **r. en paille,** paddy; **r. décortiqué,** husked rice; **r. blanc,** milled, whitened, rice; **r. glacé,** polished, bright, rice; **eau de r.** rice water; *Cu:* **r. au lait** [riolɛ], (milky) rice pudding; **gâteau de r.,** rice shape; *Orn:* **oiseau de r.,** Java sparrow; *s.a.* PAPIER 1, POUDRE 2. **2.** *Bot:* **r. du Canada,** zizania, Canadian (wild) rice, Indian rice. **3.** *Astr:* **grains de r.,** (solar) granulation; *Cer:* **décoration en grain de r.,** rice-grain decoration.

rizaire [rizɛːr], *a. Agr:* (*of land*) suitable for growing rice.

rizerie [rizri], *s.f.* rice mill.

rizicole [rizikɔl], *a.* **production r.,** rice output.

riziculteur [rizikyltœːr], *s.m.* rice grower.

riziculture [rizikyltyːr], *s.f.* rice growing.

rizier, -ière [rizje, -jɛːr]. **1.** *a.* of rice; **contrée rizière,** rice-growing country. **2.** *s.f.* **rizière,** rice plantation; rice field(s), paddy field(s). **3.** *s.m.* (*pers.*) **r. glacier,** rice polisher.

riziforme [rizifɔrm], *a.* **1.** riziform. **2.** *Med:* **selles riziformes,** rice-water evacuations.

rizon [rizɔ̃], *s.m.* husked rice, rice in its husk.

rizot [rizo], *s.m.* low-quality rice.

riz-pain-sel [ripɛ̃sɛl], *s.m.inv. A: Mil: Hum:* the Commissariat.

rô [ro], *s.m. Gr.Alph:* rho.

road-oil [roudɔil], *s.m. Civ.E:* bitumen road emulsion; *U.S:* road oil.

roadster [roːdstɛːr], *s.m. Aut:* roadster.

roannais, -aise [rɔanɛ, -ɛːz; rwa-], *a. & s. Geog:* (native, inhabitant) of Roanne.

rob[1] [rɔb], *s.m. Cards:* rubber.

rob[2], *s.m. Pharm:* syrup; **r. de belladone,** belladonna syrup.

robage [rɔbaːʒ], **robelage** [rɔblaːʒ], *s.m.* **1.** wrapping (of cigar in its wrapper leaf). **2.** stripping (of madder for processing).

robe [rɔb], *s.f.* **1.** (*a*) (lady's) dress; *Com:* gown; (*esp.* child's) frock; **r. décolletée, montante,** low-neck(ed), high-neck(ed), dress; **r. du soir,** evening dress; **se mettre en r. du soir pour dîner,** to dress for dinner; **r. de mariée,** wedding dress; **r. d'intérieur,** (i) *A:* tea-gown; (ii) house-coat; **r. de cocktail,** cocktail dress; **r. d'après-midi,** afternoon dress, day dress; **r. de plage,** sun dress, beach dress; **r. chemise,** shift; **elles portent la r. courte,** they wear short dresses; (*b*) **r. de chambre,** dressing gown; *Cu:* **pommes de terre en r. de chambre, en r. des champs,** potatoes in their jackets, jacket potatoes; (*c*) (long) robe, gown (of professor, lawyer, etc.); **avoué en r.,** gowned solicitor; **les gens de r., la r.,** *A:* **les gens de r. longue,** the gentlemen of the robe, the legal profession, the lawyers; *A:* **les gens de r. courte, the military, the soldiers;** (*c*)

Fr.Hist: **noblesse de r.**, people who owed their patents of nobility to administrative or legal posts they or their ancestors had bought. **2.** (*a*) skin (of an onion, sausage, etc.); husk (of a bean); wrapper (leaf), outside leaf, outer leaf (of cigar); (*b*) coat (of horse, dog, etc.); fleece (of sheep); *Orn:* **r. de noces,** courting plumage; (*c*) **vin avec une belle r.,** wine of a rich brilliant ruby.

robe-manteau [rɔbmɑ̃to], *s.f. Cost:* coat dress; *pl. robes-manteaux.*

rober [rɔbe], *v.tr.* to wrap (cigar in its wrapper leaf).

Robert [rɔbɛːr]. **1.** *Pr.n.m.* Robert, *F:* Rob, Bob; **métal du prince R.,** prince's metal; *Bot:* **herbe à R.,** herb Robert. **2.** *s.m.pl. P:* breasts; *Cost: P:* **Roberts de chez Michelin,** falsies.

robertine [rɔbɛrtin], *s.f. A:* thesis (for the *baccalauréat*).

robert-le-diable [rɔbɛrlədjabl], *s.m.inv. Ent:* comma moth.

Roberval [rɔbɛrval], *Pr.n.* **balance de R.,** Roberval's balance, Roberval counter machine.

robette [rɔbɛt], *s.f.* woollen shirt worn by Carthusian monks.

robeuse [rɔbøːz], *s.f.* (*a*) (*machine*) cigar roller; (*b*) (*woman*) (cigar) roller.

robière [rɔbjɛːr], *s.f.* (*a*) *Ecc:* wardrobe sister; (*b*) wardrobe (for nuns' clothes).

robigalia [rɔbigalja], *s.f.pl. A.Rom:* Robigalia.

robin[1] [rɔbɛ̃], *s.m. Lit: Pej:* gentleman of the robe; lawyer; *a. A:* **la petite noblesse robine,** the families qualifying as noble by holding a legal appointment.

Robin[2], *Pr.n.m. F:* (*dimin. of Robert*) Robin; *A:* **un plaisant R.,** a sorry clown; **vivre ensemble comme R. et Marion,** to be like Darby and Joan; *Prov:* **toujours souvient à R. de ses flûtes,** old habits die hard, once a rustic always a rustic; **R. des Bois,** Robin Hood.

robine [rɔbin], *s.f.* **1.** *Tchn:* caster's hammer. **2.** *Fr.C: P:* rubbing alcohol, surgical spirit; methylated spirits. **3.** *Dial:* (*S. of Fr.*) small canal.

robinet [rɔbinɛ], *s.m.* **1.** (*a*) *Plumb: Hyd.E: etc:* cock, tap, faucet, spigot; **r. à bec courbe,** bib-cock; **r. à bec droit,** straight-nose cock; **r. à col de cygne,** swan-neck cock; **r. à clef,** plug cock; **r. tournant,** taper-plug cock; **r. d'arrêt, r. de fermeture,** stopcock, shut-off (valve); **r. à boisseau,** cock valve, plug valve; **r. à vanne,** valve tap; **r. à guillotine,** gate valve; **r. à soupape,** globe valve, screw-down valve; **r. de branchement (pour bouche à incendie),** hose valve; **r. d'incendie armé,** permanent fire-hose point; **r. à deux, à trois, voies,** two-way, three-way, cock; **r. d'alimentation, de remplissage,** feed cock; **r. de trop-plein,** overflow cock; **r. de vidange, de purge,** drain cock; **r. d'extraction à la surface, r. de purge,** scum cock; **r. (de réglage) à flotteur,** ballcock; *Nau:* **r. de prise d'eau à la mer,** sea cock; **r. de noyage,** flooding cock; **r. d'eau chaude, froide,** hot tap, cold tap; **r. mélangeur,** mixing tap, mixer; **ouvrir, fermer, le r.,** to turn on, turn off, the tap, the water, etc.; *Fin:* **fermer le r.,** to freeze credits; *F:* **tenir le r.,** to hold the purse strings; *Ar: F:* **problèmes de r.,** sums about filling a bath, a tank; (*b*) *Mec.E: Mch:* valve, cock; **r. modérateur,** throttle valve; **r. à piston,** piston valve; **r. de refoulement,** feed cock; **r. chef,** king valve, master valve; *Mec.E:* **r. à débit constant,** constant-flow valve; **r. à papillon,** plug-type valve; butterfly valve; **r. à pointeau,** needle valve; **r. de commande,** control valve; **r. d'isolement, r. coupe-feu,** shut-off valve; **r. de vérification,** test cock; *Mch:* **r. d'arrêt,** stop valve; **r. de prise d'eau,** water valve; **r. de prise de vapeur,** steam valve; **r. de purge, r. d'extraction, r. purgeur,** blow-off cock, blow-through cock, waste cock; bleeder valve, bleeding cock (of air reservoir); **r. de vidange, de décharge,** drain valve, pet cock; *I.C.E:* **r. de distribution,** selector valve; **r. d'arrivée d'essence,** petrol tap; **r. d'entrée, r. de sortie,** inlet valve, outlet valve; **r. d'entrée d'air,** air cock; **r. de vidange de radiateur,** radiator drain cock; *Av:* **r. vide-vite,** jettison valve; *Rail:* **r. de mécanicien,** brake valve; (*c*) *F:* (*pers.*) **r. d'eau tiède,** old bore. **2.** key, plug (of a cock); **tourner le r.,** to turn (on, off) the tap.

robinetier [rɔbin(e)tje], *s.m.* **1.** brass founder and finisher; brass-smith. **2.** (i) manufacturer, (ii) seller, of taps, cocks and fittings, of valves and fittings.

robinetterie [rɔbinɛtri], *s.f.* **1.** (*a*) brass founding and finishing; (*b*) brass foundry. **2.** (*a*) taps, cocks and fittings; valves and fittings; **bruits de r.,** plumbing noises; *F:* French plumbing; (*b*) taps, cocks and fittings, valves and fittings, (i) industry, manufacture, (ii) factory, works, (iii) installation, (iv) shop.

robinet-vanne [rɔbinɛvan], *s.m. Hyd.E:* water gate, gate valve, sluice valve; *pl. robinets-vannes.*

robineux [rɔbinø], *s.m. Fr.C: P:* surgical spirits, methylated spirits, drinker.

robinier [rɔbinje], *s.m. Bot:* robinia; false acacia, (common) locust tree.

robinson [rɔbɛ̃sɔ̃], *s.m. F: A:* gamp, umbrella (by allusion to that of Robinson Crusoe).

roble [rɔbl], *s.m. Bot:* roble.

Roboam [rɔbɔam], *Pr.n.m. B.Hist:* Rehoboam.

roboratif, -ive [rɔbɔratif, -iːv], *a. & s.m. Med: A:* (= FORTIFIANT) fortifying, strengthening, tonic (medicine).

robot [rɔbo], *s.m.* robot; **avion r.,** pilotless plane; *Adm:* **portrait r.,** composite picture, artist's impression, sketch impression; mind picture, identikit (picture).

robotisation [rɔbɔtizasjɔ̃], *s.f.* robotization.

robotiser [rɔbɔtize], *v.tr.* to robotize; to turn (s.o.) into a robot.

robre [rɔbr], *s.m. Cards:* rubber; **faire un r.,** to play a rubber.

roburite [rɔbyrit], *s.f. Exp:* roburite.

robuste [rɔbyst], *a.* robust (person, health); rugged; able-bodied (person); sturdy (child); stout (faith); hardy (plant); strongly built (bicycle); **r. de corps et d'esprit,** vigorous in body and mind.

robustement [rɔbystəmɑ̃], *adv. O:* robustly, lustily, sturdily, stoutly.

robustesse [rɔbystɛs], *s.f.* robustness, sturdiness, hardiness, strength, ruggedness.

roc[1] [rɔk], *s.m.* (*esp. as a geological formation*) rock; **bâti sur le r.,** built on rock; **ferme comme un r.,** as firm as a rock.

roc[2], *s.m. Chess: A:* rook, castle; *Her:* **r. (d'échiquier),** chess rook.

rocade [rɔkad], *s.f.* **1.** *Chess:* **ligne de r.,** castling base. **2.** *Mil: Civ.E:* lateral, transversal road; by-pass; *Mil:* **voie de r.,** strategic route behind the front and running parallel to it; **chemin de fer, ligne, de r.,** strategic railway behind the front and parallel to it; **mouvement de r., des armées,** movement of forces in the rear of the theatre of operations and parallel to the front.

rocaillage [rɔkɑjaːʒ], *s.m. Const:* rubble filling, ornamentation.

rocaille [rɔkɑːj], *s.f.* **1.** (*a*) rock work; grotto work; **jardin de r.,** rockery; rock garden; (*b*) rubble. **2.** *Furn: A:* rocaille, rococo. **3.** *Cer:* flux; base of an enamel.

rocailleur [rɔkɑjœːr], *s.m. Const:* worker in reinforced concrete who specializes in rock work.

rocailleux, -euse [rɔkɑjø, -øːz], *a.* (*a*) rocky, pebbly, stony, flinty; (*b*) rugged, harsh (style, etc.).

rocambeau, -eaux [rɔkɑ̃bo], *s.m. Nau:* **1.** traveller (ring). **2.** boom iron.

rocambole [rɔkɑ̃bɔl], *s.f.* **1.** (*a*) *Bot:* rocambole, Spanish garlic, *F:* sand leek; (*b*) *A:* (i) spice, zest, attraction; (ii) mere nothing; (iii) stale joke. **2.** (*from Rocambole, hero of Ponson du Terrail's extravagant romances*) traveller's tale, cock-and-bull story.

rocambolesque [rɔkɑ̃bɔlɛsk], *a.* fantastic, incredible (adventures, etc.); *cf.* ROCAMBOLE 2.

roccella [rɔksɛla], **rocelle** [rɔsɛl], *s.f. Bot:* **orchil;** dyer's moss.

roccelline [rɔksɛlin], *s.f. Ch:* roccelline.

roccellique [rɔksɛlik], *a. Ch:* **acide r.,** roccellic acid.

rochage [rɔʃaːʒ], *s.m.* **1.** *Metalw:* fluxing (of a welding). **2.** (*a*) frothing, foaming (of fermenting beer); (*b*) *Metall:* vegetation, spitting, sprouting (of molten silver or platinum).

rochassier, -ière [rɔʃasje, -jɛːr], *s. Mount:* rock climber.

roche [rɔʃ], *s.f.* (*a*) rock; boulder; *Rom.Ant:* **la R. tarpéienne,** the Tarpeian Rock; *Lit:* **la route se dessinait à travers les éboulis de roches,** the road wound its way across a scree of boulders; **il y a anguille sous r.,** there's something afoot, something in the wind; I smell a rat; (*b*) *Geol:* rock; **roches ignées, sédimentaires, métamorphiques,** igneous, sedimentary, metamorphic, rocks; **roches volcaniques, basaltiques,** volcanic, basaltic, rocks; **r. (à structure) alvéolaire,** honeycomb rock; **cristal de r.,** rock crystal; quartz; **r. mère,** mother rock, parent rock; matrix; gangue; **r. mère (de pétrole),** (oil) source rock; *Min:* **r. de filon,** vein stone; **r. de fond,** bedrock; *Nau:* **fond de r.,** rocky bottom; **eau de r.,** clear spring water; **clair comme de l'eau de r.,** as clear as crystal; **avoir un cœur de r.,** to have a heart of stone; **homme de la vieille r.,** one of the old school; (*c*) *Ich:* **poisson de r.,** rockfish; *Orn:* **coq de r.,** rockbird.

roché [rɔʃe], *s.m. Lap:* gangue, matrix (of precious stone).

rochechouart, -arte [rɔʃ(ə)ʃwaːr, -art], *a. & s. Geog:* (native, inhabitant) of Rochechouart.

rochefortais, -aise [rɔʃfɔrtɛ, -ɛːz], **rochefortain, -tine** [rɔʃfɔrtɛ̃, -tin], *a. & s. Geog:* (native, inhabitant) of Rochefort.

rochelle [rɔʃɛl], *s.f.* small rock, small rocky eminence; *Geog:* **(La) Rochelle,** (La) Rochelle.

rochelais, -aise [rɔʃəlɛ, ɛːz], **rochelois, -oise** [rɔʃəlwa, -waːz], *a. & s.* (native, inhabitant) of La Rochelle.

roche-magasin [rɔʃmagazɛ̃], *s.f. Geol:* reservoir, carrier, container, rock; *pl. roches-magasins.*

rocher[1] [rɔʃe], *s.m.* **1.** (*a*) rock; crag; boulder; **r. isolé,** rock island; **r. branlant,** rocking stone, logan stone; **côte hérissée de rochers,** rockbound coast; **à flanc de r.,** on the rock face; **alpiniste qui fait du r.,** rock climber; *Geog:* **le r. de Gibraltar,** the Rock of Gibraltar, *F:* the Rock; *Myth:* **le r. de Sisyphe,** the rock of Sisyphus; *Lit:* **quel r. de Sisyphe!** what a Sisyphean, never-ending task! **c'est comme si on parlait à des rochers,** it's like talking to a stone wall; *attrib.* **papier r.,** stiff brown paper (used for the Christmas crib scene); (*b*) **r. artificiel,** rockery. **2.** *Anat:* petrosal (bone); otic bone. **3.** *Moll:* **r. épineux,** sting winkle, murex.

rocher[2]. **1.** *v.tr. Metalw:* to flux (a welding). **2.** *v.i.* (*a*) (*of fermenting beer*) to froth, foam; (*b*) *Metall:* (*of silver, etc.*) to vegetate, spit, sprout.

roche-réservoir [rɔʃrezɛrvwaːr], *s.f.* = ROCHE-MAGASIN; *pl. roches-réservoirs.*

rochet[1] [rɔʃɛ], *s.m.* **1.** *Mec.E:* ratchet; **roue à r.,** ratchet wheel; **vilebrequin à r.,** ratchet brace. **2.** *Tex:* (large) bobbin. **3.** *A.Arms:* rebated lance-point.

rochet[2], *s.m. Ecc.Cost:* rochet.

rocheux, -euse [rɔʃø, -øːz], *a.* (*a*) rocky, stony; **masse rocheuse,** rock mass; *Geog:* **les montagnes Rocheuses,** *s.* **les Rocheuses,** the Rocky Mountains, the Rockies; (*b*) *s.m. Sculp:* **le r. du travail,** the ruggedness of the execution.

rochier [rɔʃje], *s.m. Ich:* **1.** wrasse. **2.** dogfish.

rochoir [rɔʃwaːr], *s.m. Metalw:* borax box.

rock [rɔk], *s.m.* the roc (in the Arabian Nights).

rock-bit [rɔkbit], *s.m.* rock drill; *pl. rock-bits.*

rocket [rɔkɛt], *s.f.* rocket.

rocking [rɔkiŋ], *s.m.* **rocking chair** [rɔkiŋtʃɛːr], *F:* rocking chair; *pl. rocking-chairs.*

rococo [rɔkɔko]. **1.** *a.inv. or F: with f.* **rococote;** (*a*) *Art: Lit:* rococo; (*b*) antiquated, old-fashioned (furniture, etc.). **2.** *s.m.* **le r.,** rococo.

rocou [rɔku], *s.m. Dy:* annatto, roucou.

rocouer [rɔkwe], *v.tr. Dy:* to dye (cloth, etc.) with annatto.

rocouyer [rɔkuje], *s.m. Bot:* annatto tree, arnotto (tree); roucou (tree).

rocque [rɔk], *s.m. Chess:* (*a*) *A:* rook, castle; (*b*) castling.

rocquer [rɔke], *v.i. Chess:* to castle.

rocroien, -ienne [rɔkrwajɛ̃, -jɛn], *a. & s. Geog:* (native, inhabitant) of Rocroi.

rodage [rɔdaːʒ], *s.m.* grinding. **1.** lapping, polishing (of shaft, gem); grinding in (of glass stopper, *Mch:* of valve parts); running in (of engine); **en r.,** running in. **2.** wearing (of badly lubricated parts).

rôdailler [rodɑje], *v.i. F:* = RÔDER.

rodéo [rɔdeo], *s.m.* rodeo.

roder [rɔde], *v.tr.* to grind; (*a*) to lap, polish (metal part, gem); to grind in (glass stopper, valve, etc.); **r. le piston dans le cylindre,** to grind in the piston; *I.C.E:* **r. le siège d'une soupape,** to reseat a valve; **poudre à r.,** abradant; **machine à r.,** lapping machine; *El.E:* **r. les balais (d'une dynamo),** to bed the brushes; (*b*) *Aut:* to run in; **moteur encore mal rodé,** engine not yet run in; (*c*) to wear (down) (surface); (*d*) (*of organization, theatrical production, etc.*) to get into its stride; *F:* (*of pers.*) to be broken in (to a job).

rôder [rode], *v.i.* **1.** to prowl (with ill intent); to be on the prowl; to hang about; to loiter; *with cogn.acc.* **r. les rues,** to prowl about, hang about, the streets. **2.** (*a*) *A:* to roam; (*b*) (*of machine parts*) to have play; (*c*) (*of ship*) **r. sur son ancre,** to veer at anchor.

Roderic [rɔdrik], *Pr.n.m.* Roderick.

rodeur [rɔdœːr], *s.m.*, **rode-soupapes** [rɔdsupap], *s.m.inv. Aut:* valve-grinding tool.

rôdeur, -euse [rodœːr, -øːz]. **1.** *a.* prowling. **2.** *s.* prowler; **r. de nuit,** night prowler; **r. de grève,** (i) riverside prowler, loafer; (ii) beachcomber; *s.a.* BARRIÈRE 2.
rodeuse [rɔdøːz], *s.f. Tchn:* grinding machine.
Rodilard [rɔdilaːr], *Pr.n.m.* the Cat (in Rabelais and La Fontaine).
rodoir [rɔdwaːr], *s.m.* **1.** grinding tool, grinder; lapping tool, lap, polisher, hone; **r. à l'émeri,** emery stick. **2.** *Tan:* (tanning) vat.
Rodolphe [rɔdɔlf], *Pr.n.m.* Rudolph, Ralph.
rodolphin [rɔdɔlfɛ̃], *a. Astr:* **tables rodolphines,** Rudolphine tables.
Rodomont [rɔdɔmɔ̃]. **1.** *Pr.n.m. Lit:* Rodomont, Rodomonte (in Ariosto's *Orlando Furioso*). **2.** *s.m. A:* swashbuckler, braggart, swaggerer, blusterer, *A:* **faire le r.,** to brag; to rant; to bluster; *A:* to rodomontade.
rodomontade [rɔdɔmɔ̃tad], *s.f.* bluster, braggadocio, swagger.
rodonticide [rɔdɔ̃tisid], *a.* (*a*) rodenticidal; (*b*) *s.m.* rodenticide.
Rodrigue [rɔdrig], *Pr.n.m.* Roderigo, Roderick.
rœblingite [rœblɛ̃ʒit], *s.f. Miner:* rœblingite.
rœmérie [rœmeri], *s.f. Bot:* roemeria.
rœmérite, römérite [rœmerit], *s.f. Miner:* roemerite.
rœntgen [rœntgɛn], *s.m. Ph:* roentgen.
rœntgenthérapie [rœntgɛnterapi], *s.f. Med:* roentgenotherapy, röntgenotherapy.
roffrir [rɔfriːr], *v.tr.* (*conj. like* OFFRIR) to offer (sth.) again.
Rogations [rɔgasjɔ̃], *s.f.pl. Ecc:* rogation days; **la semaine des Rogations,** rogation week, procession week.
rogatoire [rɔgatwaːr], *a. Jur:* rogatory; **commission r.,** rogatory commission; commission (from foreign tribunal) to take evidence.
rogatoirement [rɔgatwarmɑ̃], *adv. Jur:* through a rogatory commission.
rogaton [rɔgatɔ̃], *s.m.* **1.** scrap (of food), leftover; throwout. **2.** *A: Lit:* (*a*) humble request; (*b*) **rogatons,** scribblings. **3.** *A:* **rogatons,** scraps of news; tittle-tattle.
Roger [rɔʒe], *Pr.n.m.* **1.** Roger; **un R. Bontemps,** a happy-go-lucky fellow, a jolly fellow, a jovial soul (as sung by Béranger). **2.** *Med:* **maladie de R.,** Roger's disease. **3.** *Lit:* Ruggiero (in Ariosto's *Orlando Furioso*).
rognage [rɔɲaːʒ], *s.m.,* **rognement** [rɔɲmɑ̃], *s.m.* clipping, trimming, paring; *Bookb:* cutting.
rogne[1] [rɔɲ], *s.f.* **1.** *Bookb:* cutting. **2.** *Bootm:* clogmaker's knife, stock; hollower.
rogne[2], *s.f. F: O:* scab (of plants); mange, itch (of animals).
rogne[3], *s.f. F:* bad temper; **être en r.,** to be cross, in a temper; to be ratty; **se ficher en r.,** to get hot under the collar; **ça vous fiche en r.,** that makes you see red; **chercher r., des rognes, à qn,** to look for a squabble.
rogné [rɔɲe], *s.m. Leath:* (act of) trimming leather articles.
rogne-pied [rɔɲpje], *s.m.inv. Tls:* (farrier's) paring knife.
rogner[1] [rɔɲe], *v.tr.* to clip, trim, pare, cut, cut down; **r. les tranches (d'un livre),** to cut, trim, the edges (of a book); *Bookb:* **trop r. (un volume),** to bleed (a book); **r. une pièce de monnaie,** to clip a coin; *F:* **r. les ailes à qn,** to clip s.o.'s wings; **on lui a rogné les griffes,** his claws have been pared, clipped; **r. la pension de qn,** to whittle down s.o.'s allowance; *F:* **r. les morceaux à qn,** to cut down s.o.'s allowance, profits; **r. les dépenses,** to cut down, curtail, reduce, expenses; *s.a.* ONGLE 1, PRESSE 1.
rogner[2], *v.i. F:* to be cross, in a temper; to grumble, to grouse.
rogneur, -euse[1] [rɔɲœːr, -øːz], *s.* **1.** (*a*) *A:* clipper (of coins); (*b*) trimmer, cutter (of paper, books, sheet iron, etc.). **2.** *s.f.* **rogneuse,** trimming machine.
rogneux[1], **-euse**[2] [rɔɲø, -øːz], *a. F: O:* scabby, mangy.
rogneux[2], **-euse**[3], *F:* (*a*) *a.* in a bad temper, furious; (*b*) *s.* bad-tempered person.
rognoir [rɔɲwaːr], *s.m.* paring tool, parer, clipper, trimmer, scraper.
rognon [rɔɲɔ̃], *s.m.* **1.** *esp. Cu:* kidney (of animals) **rognons à la diable,** devilled kidneys; *Vet:* **mal de r.,** saddle gall. **2.** *Geol:* (*a*) rognon; **r. de silex,** flint module, kidney stone; (*b*) rocky island (in the middle of a glacier or snowfield). **3.** *Furn:* **(table en) r.,** kidney(-shaped) table.
rognonnade [rɔɲɔnad], *s.f. Cu:* loin of veal cooked with its kidneys.
rognonnement [rɔɲɔnmɑ̃], *s.m. F:* grumbling, muttering, growling.
rognonner [rɔɲɔne], *v.i. F:* to grumble, mutter, growl; to grouse.
rognure [rɔɲyːr], *s.f.* cutting, clipping, shaving, paring; trimming; scrap; **rognures d'ongles,** nail clippings; **rognures de peaux,** clippings of hides (for making glue); *Glassm:* **rognures de verre,** cullet.
rogomme [rɔgɔm], *s.m.* (*a*) *P: A:* spirits, liquor; (*b*) *F:* **voix de r.,** husky voice (of a drunkard).
rogommeux, -euse [rɔgɔmø, -øːz], *a.* **voix rogommeuse,** husky (and vulgar) voice; drunkard's voice.
rogue[1] [rɔg], *a.* (*a*) arrogant, haughty, offensive (voice, bearing); (*b*) **cheval r.,** rogue (horse); **éléphant r.,** rogue elephant.
rogue[2], *s.f. Fish:* salted cod's roe (used as bait).
rogué [rɔge], *a.* roed (herring, etc.).
roguement [rɔgmɑ̃], *adv.* arrogantly, haughtily.
rohart [rɔaːr], *s.m.* walrus or hippopotamus ivory.
roi [rwa], *s.m.* (*a*) king; **le r. est mort, vive le r.!** the King is dead, long live the King! **r. de droit divin,** king by divine right; **r. absolu,** absolute monarch; **r. constitutionnel,** constitutional monarch; **le r. de Suède,** the King of Sweden; **le r. des Belges,** the King of the Belgians, of Belgium; **les rois de France,** the kings of France, the French kings; **le r. Louis XIII,** King Louis XIII (the thirteenth); *Hist:* **le r. soleil,** the sun king (Louis XIV); **le R. de Rome,** the King of Rome (Napoleon II); (*as title*) **le Roi Très-Chrétien,** his Most Christian Majesty, the King of France; **le R. Catholique,** his Catholic Majesty, the King of Spain; **les rois catholiques,** the catholic monarchs (Ferdinand and Isabella); *B:* **les rois (mages),** the three kings, the Magi; **jour, fête, des Rois,** Twelfth Day; Twelfth Night; **fêter les Rois,** to celebrate Twelfth Night, Epiphany; **galette des Rois,** Twelfth-night cake; **tirer les rois,** to (pass round the cake to) find the (bean) king; **la Maison du roi,** the Royal Household; **r. d'armes,** King of, at, Arms; **de par le r.,** in the king's name; **vivre en r.,** to live like a king; **action digne d'un r.,** kingly action; action worthy of a king; **plaisir, morceau, de r.,** pleasure, dish, fit for a king; *F:* **morceau de r.,** pretty woman; **heureux comme un r.,** as happy as a king; supremely happy; **le r. n'est pas son oncle, son cousin,** he wouldn't call the king his cousin; **travailler pour le r. de Prusse,** to get nothing for one's pains, one's efforts; *F:* **aller où le r. va à pied, va seul,** to go to the lavatory, the loo; (*b*) *attrib.inv.* **bleu r.,** royal blue; **des uniformes bleu r.,** royal blue uniforms; (*c*) **l'homme, r. de l'univers,** man, the master of the universe; **un r. du pétrole,** an oil magnate; **un millionnaire, roi du cuivre ou de la viande en conserve,** a millionnaire, some copper or canned-meat king; (*d*) *Lit:* **le r. des animaux,** the king of beasts (the lion); **le r. des oiseaux, de l'air,** the king of birds, of the air (the eagle); **le r. de la forêt,** the king of the forest (the oak); *Nat.Hist:* **r. des cailles,** landrail, corncrake; **r. des harengs,** garfish, king of the herrings; **r. des rougets,** cardinal fish, king of the mullets; **r. des vautours,** king vulture; *F:* **le r. des fromages, des vins,** a superlative cheese, wine; a cheese, wine, that has all the others beat; *F:* **tu es le r. (des imbéciles),** you're a complete fool; as far as stupidity goes, you're a past-master; (*e*) *Astr:* **les Trois Rois,** Orion's belt; (*f*) *Cards: Chess:* king; **r. de trèfle, de cœur,** king of clubs, of hearts; **faire les rois** = to cut, draw, for partners.
roide [rɛd, *occ. in verse* rwad *for the sake of the rhyme*], *a.,* **roideur** [rɛdœːr, rwa-], *s.f.,* **roidir** [rɛdiːr, rwa-], *v.tr.,* **roidissement** [rɛdismɑ, rwa-], *s.m. See* RAIDE, RAIDEUR, RAIDIR, RAIDISSEMENT.
roine [rwan], *s.f. Tex:* upright supports (of a loom).
roitelet [rwatlɛ], *s.m.* **1.** kinglet, petty king. **2.** *Orn:* wren, *U.S:* winter wren; **r. huppé,** gold(en)-crested wren; gold crest; **r. à triple bandeau,** firecrest.
rôlage [rolaːʒ], *s.m.* twisting (of tobacco).
Roland [rɔlɑ̃], *Pr.n.m.* (*a*) *Fr.Lit:* Roland; (*b*) *Italian Lit:* **R. Furieux,** Orlando Furioso.
rolandique [rɔlɑ̃dik], *a. Anat:* rolandic; **région r.,** rolandic area.
rôle [roːl], *s.m.* **1.** (*a*) roll (of parchment, etc.); (*b*) *Jur: etc:* roll (of court); list; register; roster; **à tour de r.,** in turn, by turns, in rotation; turn and turn about; **faire qch. à tour de r.,** to take turns in doing sth.; *Mil:* **les rôles de l'armée active,** the active list; **r. des malades,** sick report, sick list; *Nau:* **r. de l'équipage,** list of the crew; muster roll, book; (ship's) articles; **r. des quarts,** watch bill; **r. de combat,** quarter bill; **r. de manœuvre,** station bill; *Adm:* **r. des impôts,** assessment book. **2.** *Th:* part, role; **premier r.,** leading part; lead; leading man; leading lady; **r. sérieux,** heavy part; **second r.,** supporting part, rôle; **Mme X dans le r. de la Tosca,** Mme X as Tosca; **jouer un r.,** to play a part; **créer un r.,** to create a rôle; **assigner un r. à qn,** to cast s.o. for a part; **distribution des rôles,** (i) casting, (ii) cast (of a play); **jouer le r. de Macbeth,** to play, take the part of, Macbeth; **jouer des rôles de femme, d'enfant,** to play women's parts, children's parts; **jouer des petits rôles,** to play small parts, bit parts; **jouer un r. secondaire,** to play a secondary part; to play second fiddle; **prendre un r. accessoire,** to take a back seat; **il a bien joué, bien rempli, son r. dans cette affaire,** he played his part well in this matter; **jouer un r. important dans une affaire,** to play, take, a prominent part in a matter; to be instrumental in carrying sth. through; **sortir de son r.,** (i) to go beyond one's part; (ii) to take too much upon oneself; **ce n'est pas mon r. de les avertir,** it is not my part, not my business, to warn them. **il a soutenu son r. jusqu'au bout,** he kept up his part, his character, to the end; *Cin:* **r. de composition,** character; *Psy:* **test du jeu de r.,** role playing; *s.a.* RENVERSER 1. **3.** (*a*) billet, round log; (*b*) roll, twist (of tobacco).
rôler [role], *v.tr.* to twist (tobacco).
rôleur [rolœːr], *s.m.* twister (of tobacco).
rolle[1] [rɔl], *s.m. Tchn:* (lime-burner's) poker.
rolle[2], *s.m. Orn:* dollar bird.
roller-gin [rɔlɔrdʒin], *s.m. Tex:* roller gin.
rollier [rɔlje], *s.m. Orn:* **r. (d'Europe),** roller.
rolling [rɔliŋ], *s.m.* rotary file.
rollinia [rɔlinja], *s.m. Bot:* rollinia.
rollmops [rɔlmɔps], *s.m.inv. Cu:* rollmops.
Rollon [rɔlɔ̃], *Pr.n.m. Hist:* Rollo.
roloway [rɔlɔwɛ], *s.m. Z:* roloway, Diana monkey.
Romagne (la) [laromaɲ], *Pr.n.f. Geog:* the Romagna.
romagnol, -ole [rɔmaɲɔl], *a. & s.* (*a*) Romagnese, Romagnol(e); (*b*) *s.m. Ling:* Italian dialect of the Romagna.
romaillet [rɔmajɛ], *s.m. Nau:* graving piece.
romain, -aine[1] [rɔmɛ̃, -ɛn]. **1.** *a. & s.* Roman; (*a*) **l'Empire r.,** the Roman Empire; **chiffres romains,** Roman figures, numerals; *Typ:* **(caractère) r.,** roman type; **gros r.,** great primer; **petit r.,** bourgeois; *Rel.H:* **Sainte Françoise Romaine,** St Frances of Rome; **travail de R.,** vast undertaking; long and difficult job; **le** *Standard Dictionary* **est un travail de R.,** the *Standard Dictionary* is a vast undertaking; (*b*) *Orn:* **pigeon r.,** French giant pigeon. **2.** *s.f. Hort:* **romaine,** cos lettuce; *P: A:* **bon comme la romaine,** (too) good-natured; *P:* **s'il l'apprend, je suis bon comme la romaine,** if he finds out I'm in dire straits, I've had it.
romaine[2], *s.f.* steelyard; *s.a.* BALANCE 1, BASCULE 1.
romaïque [rɔmaik], *a. & s.m. Ling: etc:* Romaic; modern Greek.
roman[1] [rɔmɑ̃], *s.m.* **1.** (*a*) novel; **r. policier,** detective novel; *F:* **r. à, de, quatre sous,** penny dreadful; **r. noir,** thriller; **r. à thèse,** roman à thèse, tendenz novel; **r. d'aventures,** adventure story; **r. de mœurs,** social novel; **r. personnel, autobiographique,** autobiographical novel; **r. cyclique,** saga (novel); *F:* **il se prend pour un héros de r.,** he's a bit of a day-dreamer; **votre histoire, c'est du r.,** your story is just a fairy tale; **ses aventures ont tout l'intérêt d'un r.,** his adventures read like a novel; *s.a.* ROSE[1] 1, 2; (*b*) **l'histoire de notre rencontre est tout un r.,** the story of our meeting is quite a romance; (*c*) **le r., les romans,** (prose) fiction; **il n'écrit que des romans, il ne fait que du r.,** he writes only fiction. **2.** *Medieval Lit:* romance; **le R. de la Rose,** the Romaunt of the Rose.
roman[2], **-ane** [rɔmɑ̃, -an], *a. & s.m.* **1.** *Ling:* Romance, Romanic. **2.** *Arch:* romanesque; (*in Eng.*) (i) Saxon; (ii) Norman.
romanais, -aise [rɔmanɛ, -ɛːz], *a. & s. Geog:* (native, inhabitant) of Romans.
romance [rɔmɑ̃ːs], *s.f. Mus:* (sentimental) song, drawing-room ballad; love song; **r. sans paroles,** song without words.
romancé [rɔmɑ̃se], *a.* **biographie romancée, vie romancée,** biography in the form of a novel, of fiction; biographical novel.
romancer [rɔmɑ̃se], *v.tr.* to fictionalize.
romancero [rɔmɑ̃sero], *s.m. Spanish Lit:* romancero, collection of romances.
romanche [rɔmɑ̃ːʃ], *a. & s.m. Ling:* Romanche, Romans(c)h.

romancier, -ière [rɔmɑ̃sje, -jɛːr], *s.* 1. novelist; writer of fiction. 2. *s.m. Medieval Lit:* writer of romances. 3. *a.* fictitious.
romancine [rɔmɑ̃sin], *s.f. A:* 1. complaint. 2. reproof.
romanciser [rɔmɑ̃size], *v.tr. O:* to romanticize (idea, incident).
roman-cycle [rɔmɑ̃sikl], *s.m.* saga (novel); *pl. romans-cycles.*
romand [rɔmɑ̃], *a. Geog:* **la Suisse romande, les cantons romands,** French Switzerland, the French(-speaking) cantons.
Romandie [rɔmɑ̃di], *Pr.n.f.* French(-speaking) Switzerland.
romandisme [rɔmɑ̃dism], *s.m. Ling:* Swiss-French expression, turn of phrase.
romanesque [rɔmanɛsk], *a.* 1. romantic (idea, etc.); **jeune fille r.,** romantic young woman; *s.* **donner dans le r.,** to lean to romance. 2. **technique r.,** technique of the novel; **ouvrages romanesques et non romanesques,** works of fiction and non-fiction.
romanesquement [rɔmanɛskəmɑ̃], *adv.* romantically.
roman-feuilleton [rɔmɑ̃fœjtɔ̃], *s.m. Journ:* serial (story); *pl. romans-feuilletons.*
roman-fleuve [rɔmɑ̃flœːv], *s.m.* saga (novel); *pl. romans-fleuves.*
romani [rɔmani], *s.inv.,* **romanichel, -elle** [rɔmaniʃɛl], *s.* 1. (*a*) gipsy, romany; (*b*) vagrant. 2. *s.m. Ling:* Romany.
romanisant, -ante [rɔmanizɑ̃, -ɑ̃ːt], *Rel:* 1. *a.* Romanizing. 2. *s.* Romanizer.
romanisation [rɔmanizasjɔ̃], *s.f. Hist:* Romanization.
romaniser [rɔmanize], *v.tr. & i.* 1. to Romanize; **se r.,** to become a Roman Catholic. 2. *A:* to romanticize.
romanisme [rɔmanism], *s.m.* Romanism, *Pej:* popery.
romaniste [rɔmanist], *s.m.* 1. *Ecc:* Romanist. 2. *Ling:* Romanist; student of the Romance languages. 3. *A:* novelist.
romanité [rɔmanite], *s.f. Rom.Hist:* Romanity, Romanism.
romano-gallican [rɔmanogalikɑ̃], *a. Ecc:* Romano-gallican; *pl. romano-gallicans.*
roman-photos [rɔmɑ̃fɔtɔ], *s.m.inv.* story told in photographs.
romanticisme [rɔmɑ̃tisism], *s.m. Lit: A:* romanticism.
romantique [rɔmɑ̃tik]. 1. *a.* romantic; (*a*) *Lit. Hist:* belonging to the romantic school of literature; (*b*) **le public est peu r.,** the public has little imagination. 2. *s. Lit.Hist:* romanticist; *s.a.* CLASSIQUE 3.
romantiquement [rɔmɑ̃tikmɑ̃], *adv.* romantically.
romantiser [rɔmɑ̃tize], *v.tr.* to romanticize.
romantisme [rɔmɑ̃tism], *s.m. Lit.Hist:* romanticism.
romarin [rɔmarɛ̃], *s.m. Bot:* rosemary.
rombière [rɔ̃bjɛːr], *s.f. P:* pretentious and ridiculous (middle-aged) woman; **vieille r.,** old hag, old trout.
Rome [rɔm], *Pr.n.f. Geog:* Rome; *Prov:* **tous les chemins mènent à R.,** all roads lead to Rome; **à R. il faut vivre comme à R.,** when in Rome do as the Romans do; *F: A:* **si jamais cela arrive, je l'irai dire à R.,** if ever that happens, I shall be very much surprised, *F:* I'll eat my hat; *F: A:* **s'il n'est pas content, qu'il aille le dire à R.,** if he isn't pleased, let him say what he likes; if he doesn't like it, he can lump it.
roméine [rɔmein], **roméite** [rɔmeit], *s.f. Miner:* romeite.
roumérage [rɔmeraːʒ], *s.m.* (*in Provence*) saint's day celebration.
romérie [rɔmeri], *s.f.* Spanish village fête.
römérite [rœmerit], *s.f. Miner:* roemerite.
romillon, -onne [rɔmijɔ̃, -ɔn], *a. & s. Geog:* (native, inhabitant) of Romilly-sur-Seine.
romorantinois, -oise [rɔmɔrɑ̃tinwa, -waːz], *a. & s. Geog:* (native, inhabitant) of Romorantin.
rompement [rɔ̃pmɑ̃], *s.m. A:* breaking (off, up, asunder); *used esp. in* **r. de tête,** deafening (of s.o.); worrying (of s.o.) to death.
rompis [rɔ̃pi], *a. & s.m.* 1. *For:* **(bois) r.,** group of broken trees. 2. *Agr:* **(pré) r.,** ploughed-up meadow.
rompre [rɔ̃ːpr], *v.* (*pr.ind.* **je romps, il rompt, ils rompent**) 1. *v.tr.* to break; (*a*) to break in two (with an effort); to snap (stick, bough); **r. un morceau de pain,** to break a piece of bread; **se r. le cou,** to break one's neck; *A:* **r. un condamné,** to break a condemned man on the wheel; *O:* **r. la paille,** to break, quarrel, with s.o.; *Lit:* **r. ses chaînes, ses fers,** to burst asunder one's fetters, to escape from bondage; (*b*) to disrupt; **r. une coalition, l'unité nationale,** to break up, disrupt, a coalition, national unity; (*of stream*) **r. ses digues,** to burst its banks; **se r. une artère,** to burst, rupture, an artery; *Th: etc:* **applaudir à tout r.,** to bring down the house; *A:* **il y en avait six à tout r.,** there were six (of them) at the most; *A:* **r. sa maison, son train, son ménage,** to dispense with one's servants; *A:* **r. sa table,** to stop giving dinner parties; *F:* **r. la tête, les oreilles, à qn,** (i) to make a deafening noise; (ii) to drive s.o. crazy (with questions, etc.); **ils vous rompent les oreilles,** they'll talk your head off; **se r. la tête,** to cudgel one's brains; *F:* **cette course m'a rompu,** I'm absolutely all in after that race; *Mil:* **r. une armée,** (i) *A:* to disband an army; (ii) to disrupt, scatter, an army; *Mil:* **r. le camp,** to break camp; **r. le combat,** to break off a fight; **r. le pas,** to break step; **r. les rangs,** to disperse, to dismiss; **rompez!** dismiss! *Mil: Navy:* **r. les postes de combat,** to disperse; *s.a.* CONTACT 1, FAISCEAU, OS; (*c*) **r. le silence,** to break the silence; **r. une promesse,** to break a promise; **r. la paix,** to break the peace; **r. une habitude,** to break a habit; *A:* **r. sa prison,** to break (out of) prison; (*d*) to deaden; to bring to nought; **r. un coup, un choc,** to deaden the force of a blow; to deaden a shock; **r. une attaque,** to break up, stop, an attack; (*e*) to break off, interrupt; **r. une conversation,** to break off a conversation; **r. un tête-à-tête,** to interrupt, break in on, a private conversation; **r. un marché,** to call off a deal; **le mariage est rompu, les fiançailles sont rompues,** the engagement has been broken off; *F:* the engagement is off; **r. les relations diplomatiques,** to break off diplomatic relations; *El:* **r. un circuit,** to break, disconnect, open, a circuit; (*f*) to interfere with (sth.); **r. l'équilibre de qch., de qn,** to upset the equilibrium, the balance, of sth., of s.o.; **r. les desseins de qn,** to upset s.o.'s plans; **r. un cours d'eau,** to divert a stream; **r. les chiens,** (i) *Ven:* to call off the hounds; (ii) to change the subject; (iii) to put an end to the conversation; (*g*) **r. un cheval,** to break in a horse; **r. le caractère de qn,** to break s.o.'s temper; **r. qn à la discipline, aux affaires,** to break s.o. in to discipline, to train s.o. in business, to get s.o. accustomed to business; **r. qn à la fatigue,** to inure s.o. to fatigue; (*h*) *Agr:* **r. (une prairie),** to plough (a meadow); (*i*) *Art:* **r. les couleurs,** to tone colours down; **r. la laine,** to mix wool of different colours. 2. *v.i.* (*a*) to break (off, up, in two); **r. avec qn, avec la vie traditionnelle,** to break with s.o., with traditional ways of living; **r. avec une habitude,** to break (oneself of) a habit; **r. avec sa vie passée,** to break away from one's past life; (*b*) (*of troops*) **r. devant l'ennemi,** to break before the enemy; (*c*) *Box: etc:* to retreat; *Fenc:* to break; **r. la mesure,** to retire while parrying; **r. la mesure à son adversaire,** to keep, ward, off one's opponent.
se rompre. 1. to break (in two); (*of branch*) to snap, break off; (*of ice*) to break (up); **se r. en trois morceaux,** to break into three pieces; **son cœur battait à se r.,** his heart was throbbing violently, *F:* fit to burst. 2. **se r. à qch.,** to break oneself in to sth., to accustom oneself to sth.; **se r. au travail,** to inure oneself to work.
rompri [rɔ̃pri], *a. & s.m.* = ROMPIS 2.
rompu [rɔ̃py]. 1. *a.* (*a*) broken; **chemin r.,** road with a broken surface, full of potholes; **être r. de fatigue,** to be worn out, tired out, knocked up; to be done up; *Mec.E:* **banc r.,** gap bed (of lathe); **tour à banc r.,** gap lathe; *Nau:* **vaisseau r.,** hogged ship; **couleur rompue,** colour with a shot effect; *s.a.* BÂTON[1] 1, JAMBE 1; (*b*) broken-in; **être r. aux affaires,** to be experienced in business; **r. au travail,** used, inured, to work. 2. *s.m.* (*a*) fraction (of share, stock); (*b*) gap (of lathe bed).
romsteck [rɔmstɛk], *s.m. Cu:* rump steak.
ronce [rɔ̃ːs], *s.f.* 1. *Bot:* bramble; blackberry-bush; **r. bleue,** dewberry; **couvert de ronces, plein de ronces,** brambly. 2. *F:* thorns; **ronce(s) artificielle(s),** barbed wire; *F:* **les ronces de la vie,** the trials and troubles of life. 3. curl (in grain of wood); **r. de noyer,** bur walnut, figure(d) walnut.
ronce-framboise [rɔ̃sfrɑ̃bwaːz], *s.f. Hort:* loganberry; *pl. ronces-framboises.*
ronceraie [rɔ̃srɛ], *s.f.* bramble patch.
roncet [rɔ̃sɛ], *s.m. Bot:* degeneration disease of the vine.
ronceux, -euse [rɔ̃sø, -øːz], *a.* 1. overgrown with brambles, brambly. 2. **acajou r.,** curly(-grained), figured, mahogany.
Roncevaux [rɔ̃s(ə)vo], *Pr.n.m.* 1. *Geog:* Roncevaux (in the Pyrenees). 2. *Lit: Hist:* Roncesvalles; the Vale of Thorns.
ronchon [rɔ̃ʃɔ̃], *a. & s.inv. in f. F:* **il est r., c'est un r.,** he's a grumbler, a grouser; **elle est r., c'est une r.,** she's a grumbler; she a bit of a scold.
ronchonnement [rɔ̃ʃɔnmɑ̃], *s.m. F:* grumbling, grousing.
ronchonner [rɔ̃ʃɔne], *v.i. F:* to grumble, grouse.
ronchonneur, -euse [rɔ̃ʃɔnœːr, -øːz], *s. F:* grumbler, grouser; *f.* scold.
ronchonot [rɔ̃ʃɔno], *s.m. F:* 1. grumbler. 2. old crock (as referring to old officers, from C. Leroy's *Colonel Ronchonot*).
ronchus [rɔ̃kys], *s.m. Med:* rhonchus, râle.
roncier [rɔ̃sje], *s.m.,* **roncière** [rɔ̃sjɛːr], *s.f.* 1. thick bramble bush. 2. **roncier,** barbed-wire maker.
roncinée [rɔ̃sine], *a.f. Bot:* runcinate (leaf).
roncus [rɔ̃kys], *s.m. Med:* rhonchus, râle.
rond, ronde [rɔ̃, rɔ̃ːd]. 1. *a.* (*a*) round (ball, table, etc.); rounded (arm, etc.); plump (person, figure); **bourse ronde,** well-lined purse; **fortune ronde,** considerable, *F:* tidy, fortune; **écriture ronde,** round hand; **écouter, les yeux ronds,** to listen in round-eyed amazement; *Anat:* **ligament r.,** *ligamentum teres femoris;* **ligament r. du foie,** *ligamentum teres hepatis;* **ligament r. de l'utérus,** *ligamentum teres uteri;* **muscle r. pronateur,** *musculus pronator teres;* (*b*) **voix ronde,** full voice; **vent r.,** brisk wind; **en chiffres ronds,** in round figures; **compte r.,** round sum, even money; (*of actor*) **il a un jeu r.,** his acting is free, spontaneous; *F:* **homme tout r.,** straightforward, bluff, man; **c'est une intelligence ronde,** he is gifted with plain common sense; **il est r. en affaires,** he does a straight deal; (*c*) *P:* tipsy, drunk; **il est r. comme une bille, comme une barrique,** he's as high as a kite, as tight as a drum. 2. *adv.* **tourner r.,** (i) (*of wheel*) to run true; (ii) (*of engine, factory, etc.*) to run smoothly; **ne pas tourner r.,** to run out of true; *F:* **cela ne tourne pas r.,** it's not working properly; *F:* **elle ne tourne plus r.,** she's off her head; **ça ne tourne pas r. dans son ménage,** things are not going well for him at home. 3. *s.m.* (*a*) round, circle; *Veh:* fifth wheel; **faire un r.,** to draw a circle; **le chat se met en r.,** the cat curls up, coils itself up; **danser en r.,** to dance in a ring; **tourner en r.,** (i) to go round in a circle; (ii) to get nowhere, to go round in circles; **courir, voler, en r.,** to run, fly, round and round; *Danc:* **r. de jambe,** sweep of the leg; *F:* **faire les ronds de jambe,** to be obsequious; *Equit:* **couper le r.,** to cut a volt; **r. de serviette,** napkin ring; **r. à patiner,** skating rink; *Fb:* **r. central,** centre circle; *Tchn:* **mise au r.,** first stage in the peeling of logs (to make plywood); *Bot:* **r. de sorcières,** fairy ring; *s.a.* EMPÊCHEUR, GENOU 1; (*b*) disc; **r. de saucisson,** slice, round of sausage; **r. de beurre,** pat of butter; **r. de cuir,** (round leather) chair cushion (formerly used in offices, etc.); *P:* **(en) être, rester, comme deux ronds de flan, de frites,** to be flabbergasted, struck all of a heap. *P:* **il n'a pas un r.,** he's hard up; he hasn't a brass farthing; he hasn't a penny; *P:* **il a des ronds,** he's rolling in it; (*c*) *Arch:* rounded moulding; round; **quart de r.** quarter-round; (*d*) *Const:* **r. à béton,** concrete bar; (*e*) *Anat:* (*muscles*) **petit r.,** *teres minor;* **grand r.,** *teres major;* (*f*) *pl. Com:* bar iron. 4. *s.f.* **ronde:** (*a*) round (dance); *Mus:* round, roundelay; (*b*) *Mil: etc:* round(s); (*of policeman*) beat; **faire la ronde,** to go the rounds; **service de ronde,** rounds (as duty); *A:* **la ronde de nuit,** (i) the watch patrol; (ii) the watch; **contrôleur de ronde,** watchman's clock; *Fort:* **chemin de ronde,** wall walk, parapet walk, rampart walk; (*c*) round hand (writing); (*d*) *Mus:* semibreve; (*e*) *adv.phr.* **à la ronde,** around; **à dix lieues à la ronde,** for thirty miles round; within a range, radius, of thirty miles; **(faire) passer le vin à la ronde,** to pass the wine round, to hand round the bottle; **boire à la ronde,** to drink in turn.
rondache [rɔ̃daʃ], *s.f. A.Arms:* rondache, roundel.
rondachier [rɔdaʃje], *s.m. A.Mil:* rondacher, rondellier.
rondade [rɔ̃dad], *s.f. Gym:* take off, spring.
rond-de-cuir [rɔ̃dkɥiːr], *s.m. F:* (*a*) clerk (*esp.* in government service); pen-pusher; (*cf.* ROND 3); **vieux r.-de-c.,** old stick-in-the-mud; (*b*) bureaucrat; *pl. ronds-de-cuir.*
rondeau, -eaux [rɔ̃do], *s.m.* 1. *Fr.Lit:* rondeau. 2. *Mus:* rondo. 3. *Agr: etc:* roller. 4. baker's peel. 5. *Tchn:* disc.

ronde-bosse [rɔ̃dbɔs], *s.f. Art:* (sculpture in) the round; **figures de r.-b., en r.-b.,** figures (modelled) in the round.

rondel [rɔ̃dɛl], *s.m. Fr.Lit:* rondel.

rondelet, -ette [rɔ̃dlɛ, -ɛt]. **1.** *a.* roundish, plump-ish (person); **doigts rondelets,** podgy fingers; **somme rondelette,** good round sum; nice, tidy, little sum. **2.** *s.f.* **rondelette;** (*a*) *Dressm:* silk cord; (*b*) dishcloth, floorcloth, duster, material; (*c*) *Bot:* ground ivy. **3.** *s.m. Harn:* stick used for stuffing a harness.

rondelle [rɔ̃dɛl], *s.f.* **1.** (*a*) small round; disc (of cardboard, etc.); **r. de cornichon,** slice of gherkin; *Fr.C:* **r. (de hockey),** (ice hockey) puck; (*b*) *Sm.a:* wad (of cartridge); (*c*) *Mch:* **r. fusible,** fusible plug (of boiler). **2.** (*a*) ring; **r. de parapluie,** umbrella ring; **r. de fourneau,** stove ring; *Mec.E:* **r. de butée,** thrust collar; (*b*) washer; **r. de robinet,** tap washer; **r. de garniture,** packing washer; **r. à ressort,** spring washer; **r. Belleville,** conical washer; **r. Grower,** (helical) spring washer, split washer; **r. éventail,** star, fan-lock, washer; **r. biaise,** tapered washer; **r. à collerette,** flanged washer; **r. d'appui, de butée,** thrust washer; **r. d'arrêt, de blocage, de frein,** lock washer, stop washer; **r. frein à ergots, à pattes, à languettes,** tab washer; **r. d'écartement, d'espacement,** spacing washer; **r. d'épaisseur, de calage,** shim; **r. plate, r. ordinaire,** plain washer, flat washer; **r. d'étanchéité,** sealing washer; **r. de friction,** friction washer; **portée de r.,** washer seat; (*c*) ring (of ski stick). **3.** (*a*) *A.Arms:* vamplate (of lance); (*b*) round hand-guard (of sword). **4.** *Sculp:* round-nosed chisel.

rondelote [rɔ̃dlɔt], *s.f. Bot:* ground ivy.

rondement [rɔ̃dmɑ̃], *adv.* (*a*) roundly, briskly, promptly, smartly; **mener r. une affaire,** to lose no time over a piece of business; to dispatch a piece of business promptly, quickly; **mener r. les choses,** to hustle things on; to make short work of it; (*b*) **il nous a dit r. que . . .,** he told us straight, bluntly, that . . ..

rondet [rɔ̃dɛ], *s.f. Fr.Lit:* rondeau.

rondeur [rɔ̃dœːr], *s.f.* **1.** (*a*) roundness, rotundity; (*b*) fullness (of shape); *pl.* rounded forms, lines; (*of woman*) curves. **2.** (*a*) frankness, straightforwardness, plain dealing, outspokenness; roundness (of style); (*b*) (*of actor*) **jouer avec r.,** to act spontaneously, with freedom and vigour.

rondi [rɔ̃di], *a.* (*of slate*) trimmed.

rondie [rɔ̃di], *s.f. Tchn:* wooden mandrel used for shaping lead pipes.

rondier[1] [rɔ̃dje], *s.m. Bot:* palmyra.

rondier[2], *s.m.* roundsman.

rondin [rɔ̃dɛ̃], *s.m.* **1.** (*a*) (round) billet; log (of firewood); **chemin de rondins,** corduroy road; (*b*) thick stick (*esp.* as weapon); (*c*) round bar (of iron); (*d*) cylindrical object. **2.** *Fr.Lit:* rondeau.

rondine [rɔ̃din], *s.f.* = RONDIE.

rondir [rɔ̃diːr], *v.tr.* to make (sth.) round; to trim (slates); (*of cat, etc.*) **rondissant le dos,** arching its back.

rondis [rɔ̃di], *s.m. Lap:* girdle.

rondissage [rɔ̃disaːʒ], *s.m.* trimming (of slates).

rondisseur [rɔ̃disœːr], *s.m.* (*pers.*) slate trimmer.

rondisseuse [rɔ̃disøːz], *s.m.* slate-trimming machine.

rondo [rɔ̃do], *s.m. Mus:* rondo.

rondoir [rɔ̃dwaːr], *s.m.* bung.

rondou [rɔ̃du], *s.m. Ich:* flying fish.

rondouillard [rɔ̃dujaːr], *a.* plump, fat.

rond-point [rɔ̃pwɛ̃], *s.m.* **1.** (*a*) circus (where several roads meet); (*b*) **r.-p. (à sens giratoire),** roundabout, *U.S:* traffic circle. **2.** *A:* = ABSIDE; *pl. ronds-points.*

Ronéo [rɔneo], *R.t.m:* **1.** *s.f.* Roneo(graph). **2.** *s.m.* roneoed document.

ronéotyper [rɔneɔtipe], *F:* **ronéoter** [rɔneɔte], *v.tr.* to roneo.

ronflant [rɔ̃flɑ̃], *a.* **1.** (*a*) snoring (person); (*b*) *Med:* **râle r.,** rhonchus. **2.** (*a*) roaring, rumbling, booming, humming, whirring, throbbing (noise, etc.); (*b*) **voix ronflante,** booming voice; **titres ronflants,** sonorous titles; **tirade ronflante,** bombastic, high-sounding, tirade.

ronflement [rɔ̃fləmɑ̃], *s.m.* **1.** (*a*) snoring; (*b*) snore. **2.** roaring, rumbling, booming, humming, whirring; *W.Tel:* buzzing; hum (in loudspeaker); *W.Tel:* **r. du secteur,** mains hum; **le r. des machines, de l'avion, d'une toupie,** the hum, whirr, of the machinery, of the aircraft; the hum of a top; the throbbing of machinery; **le r. de la contrebasse, de l'orgue,** the booming note of the double-bass, of the organ.

ronfler [rɔ̃fle], *v.i.* **1.** to snore. **2.** (*of wind, fire, etc.*) to roar; (*of organ*) to boom; (*of top*) to hum; (*of engine*) to whirr; **faire r. les r,** to roll one's r's; **acteur qui sait faire r. les vers,** actor who knows how to boom out his lines; *P:* **ça ronfle, les affaires,** we are doing a roaring trade; **il faut que ça ronfle,** we must get a move on, speed things up.

ronflette [rɔ̃flɛt], *s.f. P:* sleep, snooze.

ronfleur, -euse [rɔ̃flœːr, -øːz], *s.* **1.** snorer. **2.** *s.m. El: etc:* buzzer; **r. à interruption,** rhythmic buzzer.

ronflot(t)er [rɔ̃flɔte], *v.i.* to snore gently.

rongeage [rɔ̃ʒaːʒ], *s.m. Tex:* discharge printing.

rongeant [rɔ̃ʒɑ̃]. **1.** *a.* (*a*) corroding (acid, etc.); rodent (ulcer); (*b*) gnawing (anxiety). **2.** *s.m. Tex:* (*printing*) discharge.

rongement [rɔ̃ʒmɑ̃], *s.m.* **1.** gnawing; **il écoutait avec un r. de cœur,** he listened with a gnawing at his heart. **2.** eating away, corroding.

ronger [rɔ̃ʒe], *v.tr.* (**je rongeai(s); n. rongeons**) **1.** to gnaw, nibble; **r. un os,** (*of dog*) to gnaw a bone; (*of pers.*) to pick a bone; **les vers rongent les fruits, le bois,** worms eat into fruit, into wood; **se r. le cœur, les foies, les sangs,** to eat, fret, one's heart out; to worry; **les soucis qui lui rongent le cœur,** the cares that are gnawing at him; **il se rongeait les poings de dépit,** he was gnawing his knuckles with rage; **donner à qn un os à r.,** to give s.o. sth. to do to tide him over, to keep him occupied; *s.a.* FREIN 1, ONGLE 1, VER 2. **2.** (*of acid, rust, etc.*) to corrode; to pit, to eat away (metal); **r. un métal à l'acide,** to etch a metal; **falaises rongées par la mer,** cliffs eaten away, eroded, by the sea; *Phot:* **fixateur qui ronge les détails,** fixing solution that eats into, eats away, the detail; **être rongé de chagrin,** to be consumed, tormented, with grief; **visage rongé par les soucis,** careworn face. **3.** *Ven:* (*of stag, hart*) to ruminate.

se ronger, to worry; **se r. de chagrin, d'ennui,** to eat one's heart out with sorrow, boredom.

rongeur, -euse [rɔ̃ʒœːr, -øːz]. **1.** *a.* rodent, gnawing (animal); rodent (ulcer); gnawing (anxiety); *s.a.* VER 2. **2.** *s.m. Z:* rodent; *pl.* **rongeurs,** Rodentia, rodents.

rongeure [rɔ̃ʒyːr], *s.f.* part eaten away.

rônier [ronje], *s.m. Bot:* palmyra.

ronron [rɔ̃rɔ̃], *s.m.* **1.** purr(ing); **faire r.,** (i) (*of cat*) to purr; (ii) (*of pers.*) to sleep, snooze. **2.** *F:* hum, whirr.

ronronnant [rɔ̃rɔnɑ̃], *a.* (*a*) purring; (*b*) humming, whirring (wheel).

ronronnement [rɔ̃rɔnmɑ̃], *s.m.* (*a*) purring; (*b*) *Mch: W.Tel: etc:* humming; **le r. du moteur (de l'avion),** the drone of the engine.

ronronner [rɔ̃rɔne], *v.i.* (*a*) to purr; (*b*) *Mch: W.Tel: etc:* to hum.

ronsardiste [rɔ̃sardist], *s.m. Fr.Lit.Hist:* follower of Ronsard.

Röntgen [rœntgen]. **1.** *Pr.n. Ph:* **rayons R.,** Röntgen rays. **2.** *s.m. Rad.-A:* röntgen.

röntgenthérapie [rœntgenterapi], *s.f.* röntgen(o)therapy.

rookerie, rookery [rukri], *s.f. Orn:* (penguin) rookery.

rooter [rutœːr], *s.m. Mec.E:* rooter, heavy excavator.

roquage [rɔkaːʒ], *s.m.,* **roque**[1] [rɔk], *s.m. Chess:* castling; **petit r.,** king-side castling; **grand r.,** queen-side castling.

roque[2], *s.f.* (*a*) *A.Cost:* tunic; (*b*) working garment worn by monks in the middle ages.

roquefort [rɔkfɔːr], *s.m.* Roquefort (cheese); **aussi fort que le r.,** (i) very tasty; (ii) very smelly.

roquelaure [rɔklɔːr], *s.f. A.Cost:* roquelaure (cloak).

roquentin [rɔkɑ̃tɛ̃], *s.m. F: A:* old fop, old beau.

roquer [rɔke], *v.i.* **1.** *Chess:* to castle. **2.** *Croquet:* to (loose-)croquet (the ball); to roquet-croquet; **coup roqué,** croquet.

roquet[1] [rɔkɛ], *s.m.* (*a*) pug (dog); (*b*) cur, mongrel.

roquet[2], *s.m. Tex:* (large) bobbin.

roquetin [rɔktɛ̃], *s.m. Tex:* (*a*) silk spool; (*b*) (large) bobbin.

roquette[1] [rɔkɛt], *s.f.* **1.** *Bot:* rocket; **r. des champs, fausse r.,** corn rocket; **r. des jardins,** winter-cress; **r. blanche,** wall rocket; **r. de mer,** sea rocket, cakile; **r. d'orient,** hare's ear; *s.a.* CHOU 1. **2.** *Orn:* partridge.

roquette[2], *s.f.* enamelling flux.

roquette[3], *s.f. Tex:* silk spool.

roquette[4], *s.f. Ball:* rocket.

rouille [rɔkiːj], *s.f.* orange marmalade.

rorqual [rɔrkwal], *s.m. Z:* rorqual; fin-back (whale); **r. de Rudolphi, r. du nord,** sei whale, *F:* sei; **petit r.,** lesser rorqual, *F:* minke; **r. à bec,** doegling; **huile du r. à bec,** doegling oil; *pl. rorquals.*

Rorschach [rɔrʃak], *Pr.n. Psy:* **test de R.,** Rorschach test.

ros [ro], *s.m. Tex:* reed, slay.

rosace [rozas], *s.f. Arch:* (*a*) rose (window); (*b*) **r. de plafond,** ceiling-rose; rosette; (*c*) *Tchn:* rosette; (*d*) *Mus:* rose (soundhole) (of lute, etc.).

rosacé [rozase], *a. Bot:* rosaceous, rose-like.

rosacée [rozase], *s.f. Med:* acne rosacea.

rosacées [rozase], *s.f.pl. Bot:* Rosaceae.

rosage [rozaːʒ], *s.m. Bot:* (*a*) rhododendron; (*b*) golden-flowered rhododendron; (*c*) rusty-leaved rhododendron; alpine rose.

rosagine [rozaʒin], *s.f. Bot:* rusty-leaved rhododendron; alpine rose.

rosaire [rozɛːr], *s.m. Ecc:* rosary (of 165 beads); **dire le r.,** to go through the rosary; to tell one's beads; **confrérie du r.,** Confraternity of the Rosary.

rosalbin [rozalbɛ̃], *s.m. Orn:* (Australian) rose-breasted cockatoo.

rosales [rozal], *s.f.pl. Bot:* Rosales.

Rosalie[1] [rozali]. **1.** *Pr.n.f.* Rosalie. **2.** *s.f. Mil: P:* bayonet; toothpick; *A:* (*1914–18 war*) **y aller avec R.,** to charge with the bayonet.

rosalie[2], *s.f.* **1.** *Ent:* Alpine longhorn. **2.** *Z:* marikina, silky tamarin. **3.** *Mus:* rosalia.

Rosalinde [rozalɛ̃ːd], *Pr.n.f.* Rosalind.

rosaniline [rozanilin], *s.f. Ch:* rosaniline.

rosarium [rozarjɔm], *s.m. Hort:* rosarium.

rosat [roza], *a.inv.* **1.** *Pharm:* (*of oils, pomade, etc.*) prepared with roses. **2.** *Bot:* **géranium r.,** rose geranium.

rosâtre [rozɑːtr], *a.* pinkish; of a dirty pink.

rosbif [rɔzbif], *s.m.* (*a*) roast beef; **r. de mouton,** leg and loin of mutton; (*b*) *P: A:* Englishman.

roscoélite [rɔskɔelit], *s.f. Miner:* roscoelite.

roscovite [rɔskɔvit], *a. & s.m. & f.* (native, inhabitant) of Roscoff.

rose[1] [roːz]. **1.** *s.f. Bot:* rose; (*a*) **r. incarnate,** damask rose; **r. mousseuse,** moss rose; **r.-thé,** tea rose; **r. pompon,** fairy rose; **r. des quatre saisons,** monthly rose; Indian or China rose; **r. sauvage, r. de cochon, r. de chien,** wild rose, dog rose; **eau de r.,** rosewater; *F:* **sentimentalité à l'eau de r.,** sugary sentiment; goo; gooey sentimentality; **roman à l'eau de r.,** penny novelette; **essence de roses,** attar of roses, otto of roses; *Lit:* **les roses de son teint,** her rosy complexion; **lèvres de r.,** rosy lips; *F:* **cela ne sent pas la r.,** it doesn't smell sweet; **être (couché) sur des roses, être sur un lit de roses,** to be on a bed of roses; **tout n'est pas rose dans ce monde,** life is not a bed of roses; *F:* life isn't all beer and skittles; **(il n'est) pas de r. sans épines,** no rose without a thorn; *F:* **découvrir le pot aux roses** [pɔtoroːz], to find out the secret; to fathom the mystery; *F:* **envoyer qn sur les roses,** to send s.o. packing; *Her:* **r. héraldique,** rose; (*b*) **r. de Noël,** Christmas rose; **r. de Notre-Dame,** peony; **r. pivoine,** double peony; **r. trémière,** hollyhock, rose-mallow; **r. de Jéricho,** rose of Jericho; **r. d'Inde,** African marigold; **faux bois de r.,** Portia tree; **bois de r.,** tulip wood, rosewood; *s.a.* GUELDRE 3. **2.** (*a*) *a.* pink (dress); rosy (complexion); **des rubans roses,** pink ribbons; (*inv. in compounds*) **des rubans rose pivoine, r. tendre,** peony-red ribbons, pale pink ribbons; *F:* **ce n'est pas bien r., cette histoire-là,** it's a pretty grim story; *F:* **elle n'avait pas la vie bien r., elle ne l'avait pas bien r.,** she didn't have an easy time of it, her life wasn't a bed of roses; **roman r.,** milk-and-water novel; (*b*) *s.m.* rose (colour); pink; **robe d'un joli r.,** pretty pink dress; **le r. monta à ses joues,** her cheeks flushed pink; *Lit:* **l'aurore aux doigts de r.,** rosy-fingered Dawn; **voir tout en r., voir tout couleur de r.,** to see everything through rose-coloured spectacles. **3.** *s.f.* (*a*) *Arch:* rose window; (*b*) *Nau:* **r. des vents,** compass card, dial; mariner's card; **dire la r.,** to box the compass; *Nau:* **r. mobile,** floating dial; (*c*) *Lap:* rose (diamond), rose-cut diamond; rosette; (*d*) *Mus:* sound hole (of guitar); (*e*) *Metall:* irisated spot (in steel); (*f*) *Miner:* **r. des sables, r. des déserts,** gypsum flower.

Rose[2], *Pr.n.f.* Rose.

Rose[3], *Pr.n.m. Med:* **position de R.,** Rose's position.

rosé [roze], *a.* rosy, rose-pink; pale pink; **vin r.,** rosé wine.

roseau, -eaux [rozo], *s.m.* (*a*) *Bot:* reed; **r. aromatique,** sweet calamus, sweet flag, sweet rush; **r. des sables,** beach grass; **r. panaché,** ribbon grass; **r. de la Passion, des étangs,** cat-tail; **s'appuyer sur un r.,** to lean on a broken reed; *O:* **c'est un r. peint en fer,** he is a lath painted to look like iron, a broken reed; (*b*) *Arch:* cabling.

rose-croix [rozkrwa], *s.m.inv.* member of the Rosicrucian brotherhood; Rosicrucian.
rosé-des-prés [rozedepre], *s.m. Fung:* meadow agaric; *pl. rosés-des-prés.*
rosée [roze], *s.f.* **1.** dew; **la r. de mai,** the may-dew; **il tombe de la r.,** dew is falling; **goutte de r.,** dewdrop; **couvert, humecté, de r.,** dewy; *Ph:* **point de r.,** dew point. **2.** *(a) Bot:* **r. du soleil,** sundew; *(b) Vit:* **r. de farine,** mildew, brown rot. **3.** *Tex:* pile warp.
rose-gorge [rozgɔrʒ], *s.m.inv. Orn:* rose-breasted grosbeak.
roselet [rozlɛ], *s.m. Com:* ermine.
roselier, -ière [rozəlje, -jɛːr]. **1.** *a.* reed-bearing, reed-producing (marsh, etc.). **2.** *s.f.* **roselière,** reed bed.
roselin [rozlɛ̃], *s.m. Orn:* **r. cramoisi,** scarlet grosbeak; **(martin) r.,** rose-coloured starling; **r. rose,** rose finch.
rosélite [rɔzelit], *s.f. Miner:* roselite.
roselle [rozɛl], *s.f. Orn:* red-winged thrush.
Rosemonde [rozmɔ̃ːd], *Pr.n.f.* Rosamond.
Rosenbach [rozənbak], *Pr.n. Med:* **syndrome de R.,** Rosenbach's syndrome.
rosenbuschite [rozənbuʃit], *s.m. Miner:* rosenbuschite.
Rosenmüller [rozənmylɛːr], *Pr.n. Anat:* **fosses de R.,** Rosenmüller's fossa; **organe de R.,** Rosenmüller's organ.
roséocobaltique [rozeɔkɔbaltik], *a. Ch:* roseocobaltic.
roséole [rozeɔl], *s.f. Med:* roseola, rose rash.
roser [roze], *v.tr.* to make (sth.) pink, rosy; **la longue promenade avait rosé ses joues,** the long walk had made her cheeks pink.
roseraie [rozrɛ], *s.f.* rosary, rosery; rose garden.
rosetier [roztje], *s.m. Tls: Metalw:* rose punch.
rosette[1] [rozɛt], *s.f.* **1.** *A:* small rose. **2.** *(a)* bow (of ribbon); *(b)* rosette; *esp.* **la r. de la Légion d'honneur,** the rosette of the Legion of Honour; *(c) Bot:* rosette; *(d) (on a watch)* fast and slow dial. **3.** *(a)* rose pink; *(b)* red ink; *(c)* red chalk; *(d) Cu:* (kind of) salami. **4. (cuivre de) r.,** rose copper, rosette copper. **5.** *Metalw:* burr, rivet washer. **6.** clout nail. **7.** *Dial: Ich:* red eye, rudd. **8.** *Pr.n.f.* **Rosette,** *(diminutive of* ROSE[2]*)* = Rosie. **9.** *Arch: Sculp:* rosette. **10.** *Arb:* rosette (disease).
Rosette[2], *Pr.n. Geog:* Rosetta; **la pierre de R.,** the Rosetta stone.
rosettier [rozɛtje], *s.m. Tls: Metalw:* rose punch.
roseur [rozœːr], *s.f.* pinkness, rosiness.
rosicrucien, -ienne [rozikrysjɛ̃, -jɛn], *a.* Rosicrucian.
rosier[1] [rozje], *s.m.* rose tree, rose bush; **r. sur tige,** standard rose; **r. nain,** bush rose; **r. grimpant,** rambler; **r. sauvage, de chien,** dog rose; briar; **r. du Japon,** Japan rose, camellia.
rosier[2], *s.m. Tex:* reed maker.
rosière[1] [rozjɛːr], *s.f.* *(a)* maiden to whom the wreath of roses (and a small dowry) was awarded for virtuous conduct; **(le couronnement de la Rosière** *was an annual event in certain French villages)*; *(b) F:* innocent, artless, girl.
rosière[2], *s.f. Ich:* bitterling.
rosiériste [rozjerist], *s.m. & f.* rose grower, rosarian.
rosir [roziːr]. **1.** *v.tr.* to turn (s.o., sth.) rosy. **2.** *v.i.* *(a)* to become, turn, rosy; *(b)* to blush; to go pink.
rosminien, -ienne [rɔsminjɛ̃, -jɛn], *a. & s. Rel:* Rosminian.
rosolique [rozɔlik], *a. Ch:* rosolic.
rossard [rɔsaːr]. **1.** *s.m. P:* idler, lazybones. **2.** *a. P:* spiteful, catty, bitchy.
rosse[1] [rɔs]. **1.** *s.f.* *(a) F: (horse)* nag; *(b) P:* objectionable, ill-natured, person; skunk; **le patron est une r.,** the boss is a swine; *(of a woman)* **c'est une petite r.,** she's a little bitch. **2.** *a. P:* objectionable, ill-natured; nasty (person, song, etc.); low-down (trick); **question r.,** tough question; *P:* snorter; **professeur r.,** perfect beast of a master; *A: Lit:* **comédie r.,** drama in which virtue goes unrewarded and vice unpunished; cynical comedy.
rosse[2], *s.f. Ich: F:* red eye, rudd.
rossée [rɔse], *s.f. F:* beating, thrashing, licking, lathering; **administrer une bonne r. à qn,** to give s.o. a sound beating, a good hiding.
rosser [rɔse], *v.tr. F:* to give (s.o.) a beating, a thrashing, a licking; to lather (s.o.); **r. qn d'importance,** to give s.o. a sound thrashing, a good beating.
rosserie [rɔsri], *s.f. F:* **1.** nastiness (of conduct, of speech). **2.** *(a)* nasty, dirty, trick; **faire une r. à qn,** to put it across s.o.; *(b)* nasty story, scurrilous expression; *(c)* spiteful, catty, remark.
rossette [rɔsɛt], *s.f. Ich: Dial:* red eye, rudd.
rossia [rɔsja], *s.f. Moll:* (large) type of sepiola.
rossignol [rɔsiɲɔl], *s.m.,* **rossignole** [rɔsiɲɔl], *s.f.* **1.** *(a) Orn:* nightingale, **rossignole,** hen nightingale; **r. progné,** thrush nightingale; **r. à flancs roux,** red-flanked bluetail; **r. du Japon,** Japanese nightingale; **r. des murailles,** redstart; *F:* **j'ai des rossignols,** there are funny noises in the car; *(b) F: A:* **r. d'Arcadie,** ass, *F:* Jerusalem pony. **2.** *Nau:* whistle (for commands). **3.** picklock, skeleton key. **4.** *Carp:* mortise wedge. **5.** *F:* old unsaleable article (in shop); piece of junk; **vieux rossignols,** old stock; **on vous a refilé un r.,** you've been had; they've sold you a pup.
rossinante [rɔsinɑ̃ːt], *s.f. F:* Rosinante, old worn-out hack *(from Don Quixote's horse).*
rossite [rɔsit], *s.f. Miner:* rossite.
rossolis[1] [rɔsɔli], *s.m. Bot:* sundew, drosera.
rossolis[2], *s.m.* rosolio (cordial).
rostein [rɔstɛ̃], *s.m. Tex:* large bobbin.
rostelle [rɔstɛl], *s.f. Bot:* rostellum (of orchid).
rostellé [rɔstɛle], *a. Bot:* rostellate.
rostral, -aux [rɔstral, -o], *a. Rom.Ant: Z:* rostral; *Rom.Ant:* **couronne rostrale,** rostral crown, naval crown; **colonne rostrale,** rostral column.
rostre [rɔstr̥], *s.m.* **1.** *Bot: Z: etc:* rostrum; *Rom.Ant:* **les Rostres,** the Rostra. **2.** *Paleont:* guard (of belemnite).
rostré [rɔstre], *a. Bot: Z: etc:* rostrate(d).
rostrifère [rɔstrifɛːr], *a. Z: Bot:* rostriferous.
rostriforme [rɔstrifɔrm], *a. Nat.Hist:* rostriform.
rot[1] [ro], *s.m. P:* belch; burp; **faire un r.,** to bring up wind; to burp; **faire faire son r. à un bébé,** to bring up a baby's wind, *U.S:* to burp a baby.
rot[2], *s.m. Tex:* reed, slay.
rot[3], *s.m. Agr: Hort:* rot.
rôt [ro], *s.m. Lit: A:* *(a)* roast (meat); *(b)* roast meat course; *A:* **le gros r.,** the roast joint; **le menu, petit, r.,** roast chicken, game; *F:* **être à pot et à r.,** to be bosom friends.
rotacé [rɔtase], *a. Bot:* rotate (corolla).
rotacteur [rɔtaktœːr], *s.m. T.V:* iron-cored choke.
rotang [rɔtɑ̃], *s.m. Bot:* rattan.
rotangle [rɔtɑ̃ːgl̥], *s.m. Ich:* red eye, rudd.
rotarien [rɔtarjɛ̃], *s.m.* rotarian, member of a rotary club.
rotary [rɔtari], *s.m.* **1.** *Tchn:* rotary rig, drill. **2.** *Tp:* rotary switch; *pl. rotarys.*
rotateur, -trice [rɔtatœːr, -tris]. **1.** *a.* rotative, rotatory (force, etc.); *Anat:* **muscle r.,** *s.m.* **rotateur,** rotator. **2.** *s.m. Biol:* rotifer, rotator.
rotatif, -ive [rɔtatif, -iːv], *a.* rotary, rotating, rotative (pump, *Mch:* valve); *Av:* **moteur r.,** rotary engine; *(of computers)* **cadran r.,** rotary dial; **commutateur r.,** uniselector, rotary switch.
rotation [rɔtasjɔ̃], *s.f.* **1.** *Mec: Ph:* rotation; spin (of projectile); revolution; **mouvement de r.,** rotational motion; **corps en r.,** rotating body; **pièce à r.,** revolving part (of mechanism); **r. à droite, r. dans le sens des aiguilles d'une montre,** right-hand rotation, clockwise rotation; **r. à gauche, r. en sens inverse des aiguilles d'une montre,** left-hand rotation, anti-clockwise rotation; **axe de r.,** axis of rotation; **inertie de r.,** rotational inertia; **moment de r.,** rotating moment; **sens de (la) r.,** direction of rotation; **vitesse de r.,** rotation speed; *Mth:* **faire faire une r. de 90° à une droite,** to rotate a line through an angle of 90°; *Fort: Mil: Navy:* **mécanisme de r. de tourelle,** turret traversing mechanism; *Swim:* **r. du corps,** rolling of the body. **2.** *(a) Agr:* **r. des cultures,** rotation of crops; *(b) Trans:* turn-round, *U.S:* turn around (of ship, vehicle, aircraft, train); **durée de r.,** turn-round time, schedule; *Nau:* **installations permettant la r. des navires,** turn-round facilities; *(b) Com: etc:* turnover (of stocks); **r. des capitaux,** turnover of capital; **r. des stocks,** inventory turnover; **r. du personnel,** turnover of staff; **taux de r.,** rate of turnover; *(c) Psy:* **r. des axes,** rotation of the factor axes. **3.** *Aer:* helicopter flight.
rotationnel, -elle [rɔtasjɔnɛl], *Ph:* **1.** *a.* rotational, vortical. **2.** *s.m.* vorticity; **r. absolu, relatif,** absolute, relative, vorticity.
rotative [rɔtatiːv], *s.f. Typ:* rotary printing-press.
rotativiste [rɔtativist], *s.m.* rotary printer.
rotatoire [rɔtatwaːr], *a.* **1.** *Mec:* rotatory (movement); rotative, rotational (force). **2.** *Ph:* rotary (polarization); **pouvoir r.,** rotatory power (of a crystal, etc.); *Opt:* **pouvoir r.,** chirality (of a solution).
rotavator [rɔtavatɔːr], *s.m. Agr:* rotary cultivator.
rote[1] [rɔt], *s.f.* **1.** *Ecc:* rota (Romana). **2.** *A.Mus:* *(a)* rota, round; *(b)* rota, hurdy-gurdy.
rote[2], *s.f. A.Mus:* rote, crowd, crwth.
rotengle [rɔtɑ̃ːgl̥], *s.m. Ich:* red eye; rudd.
roténone [rɔtenɔn], *s.f.* rotenone (insecticide).
roter [rɔte], *v.i.* **1.** *Ven:* to troat. **2.** *P:* to belch, to burp, to bring up wind, have the wind; *(of sth. disagreeable)* **en r.,** to put up with it, to swallow it; to work like a slave (at sth.).
roteur, -euse [rɔtœːr, -øːz], *s. P:* belcher.
rothoffite [rɔtɔfit], *s.f. Miner:* rothoffite.
rothschild [rɔtʃild], *s.m. A:* low easy-chair with padded headrest.
rôti [roti, rɔ-], *s.m.* roast (meat); **r. de mouton, de porc, etc.,** (joint of) roast mutton, roast pork, etc.; *F:* **ne vous endormez pas sur le r.,** don't dawdle; get on with it.
rôtie [roti, rɔ-], *s.f.* round of toast; **rôties au beurre,** buttered toast; **r. à l'anglaise,** Welsh rabbit, Welsh rarebit.
rotier [rɔtje], *s.m. Tex:* reed maker.
rotifère [rɔtifɛːr], *s.m. Biol:* rotifer; rotator; *pl.* **rotifères,** Rotifera.
rotiforme [rɔtifɔrm], *a.* rotiform, rotate; wheel-shaped.
rotin[1] [rɔtɛ̃], *s.m.* **1.** *Bot:* rattan; calamus; **sièges en r.,** cane chairs; **meubles en r.,** cane, basket-work, furniture. **2.** rattan cane, switch, or walking-stick.
rotin[2], *s.m.* = penny; **rien! pas un r.!** nothing (at all)! not a penny! not a brass farthing!
rotine [rɔtin], *s.f. Mount:* rimaye.
rotinier [rɔtinje], *s.m.* cane worker.
rôtir [rotiːr, rɔ-]. **1.** *v.tr.* *(a)* to roast (meat); to toast (bread); to roast (chestnuts); **porc rôti,** roast pork; **pain rôti,** toast; **r. un bœuf tout entier,** to barbecue an ox; **une cheminée à r. un bœuf,** a fireplace large enough to roast an ox; **il attend que les alouettes lui tombent toutes rôties,** he wants everything on a plate; *F:* **feu à r. un bœuf,** fire fit to roast an ox; *(b) F: (of the sun)* to scorch, dry up (grass, etc.); **se r. au soleil,** to roast in the sun; *s.a.* BALAI 1. **2.** *v.i.* to roast; to toast; to scorch; *F:* **on rôtit ici,** it's scorching hot here.
rôtissage [rotisaːʒ, rɔ-], *s.m.* roasting.
rôtisserie [rotisri, rɔ-], *s.f.* *(a) A:* cook-shop; eating-house; *(b)* grill room; *(in proper names)* = restaurant.
rôtisseur, -euse [rotisœːr, -øːz, rɔ-], *s.* *(a) A:* cook-shop proprietor; *(b)* grill-room proprietor.
rôtissoire [rotiswaːr, rɔ-], *s.f.* **r. (électrique),** (electric) spit-roaster.
roto [rɔto], *s.f. Typ: F:* = ROTATIVE.
rotobineuse [rɔtɔbinøːz], *s.f. Agr:* rotary hoe.
rotocalcographique [rɔtɔkalkɔgrafik], *a. Typ:* **impression r.,** offset (process).
rotogravure [rɔtɔgravyːr], *s.f. Typ:* rotogravure.
rotonde [rɔtɔ̃ːd], *s.f.* **1.** *(a) Arch:* rotunda, circular hall; *(b) Rail:* (circular) engine shed; round-house. **2.** *(a) Veh: A:* boot (of stagecoach); *(b) Aut:* rear part of the body. **3.** *A.Cost:* (long sleeveless) cloak.
rotondité [rɔtɔ̃dite], *s.f.* *(a)* rotundity; roundness; **je n'ai jamais conçu comme ce soir-là la r. de la terre,** I had never been aware, as I was that evening, of how the earth was round; *(b) F: (of pers.)* rotundity, plumpness, stoutness; **les rotondités d'une femme,** a woman's curves.
rotor [rɔtɔːr], *s.m.* *(a) El:* rotor (of dynamo, alternator); **r. bobiné,** wound rotor; **bobinage, enroulement, de r.,** rotor-winding; *(b) Mec.E:* rotor, impeller (of turbine, compressor, supercharger); **aube de r.,** rotor vane, blade; **aubage de r.,** rotor vanes, blades; *(c) Av:* rotor (of helicopter); **rotors en tandem,** tandem rotors; **r. principal,** main rotor; **r. de queue,** tail rotor; **mât de r.,** rotor pylon, mast; **pale de r.,** rotor blade; **vitesse circonférentielle du r.,** rotor-tip velocity; **appareil à r. flexible, à r. rigide,** flexible-rotor, rigid-rotor, aircraft.
rotorique [rɔtɔrik], *a. El.E:* rotor (circuit, etc.).
rototo [rɔtɔto], *s.m. F:* (baby's) burp.
rotoviscosimètre [rɔtɔviskɔzimɛtr̥], *s.m. Tchn:* torsion visco(si)meter.
rottain [rɔtɛ̃], *s.m. Bot:* rattan.
rottbœllia [rɔtbølja], *s.m. Bot:* hard grass.
rotte [rɔt], *s.f. A.Mus:* *(a)* rota, round; *(b)* rota, hurdy-gurdy; *(c)* rote, crowd.
rotule [rɔtyl], *s.f.* **1.** *Anat:* kneecap, patella; *F:* **être sur les rotules,** to be fagged out, on one's last legs. **2.** *Mec.E:* knee joint; ball(-and-socket) joint, swivel joint, toggle joint; **corps de r.,** ball-head; **r. d'attache,** trunnion; *Aut:* **r. de direction,** steering knuckle.
rotulien, -ienne [rɔtyljɛ̃, -jɛn], *a. Anat:* patellar (ligament, etc.), rotulian; **réflexe r.,** knee jerk, reflex.
roture [rɔtyːr], *s.f.* **1.** commoner's condition; *A:* **terre en r.,** land held by a commoner. **2.** *coll.* commonalty, commons.

roturier, -ière [rɔtyrje, -jɛːr]. 1. *a.* common, of the common people; unrefined (manners). 2. *s.* (*a*) commoner; **les roturiers,** the commonalty; (*b*) self-made man.
rouable [rwabl̩], *s.m.* 1. fire rake. 2. salt rake.
rouage [rwaːʒ], *s.m.* 1. wheels, wheelwork, mechanism (of a machine); gear work; *Clockm:* **rouage(s) d'une montre,** works, train of wheels, of a watch; **r. d'horloge,** clockwork; **pont de r.,** (watch)cock; **les rouages de l'administration,** the wheels of government, the intricate machinery of government; **je ne suis qu'un r. de la machine,** I am only a cog in the machinery. 2. (toothed) wheel, gear wheel, cog wheel.
rouan, -anne[1] [rwɑ̃, -an], *a.* roan (horse, cow).
rouanne[2] [rwan], **rouannette** [rwanɛt], *s.f. Tls:* 1. (*a*) marking tool, rasing knife (for marking barrels, etc.); (*b*) scribing compass. 2. carpenter's auger. 3. *Tchn:* paring-knife.
rouant [rwɑ̃], *a.m. Her:* (*of peacock*) in pride.
roubaisien, -ienne [rubɛzjɛ̃, -jɛn], *a. & s.* (native, inhabitant) of Roubaix.
roublard, -arde [rublaːr, -ard], *a. & s. F:* foxy, wily, artful, crafty (person); **un fin r.,** an old fox; **elle est roublarde,** she's up to every trick.
roublarder [rublarde], *v.i. F:* to finesse; to cheat.
roublarderie [rublardəri], *s.f. F:* = ROUBLARDISE 1.
roublardise [rublardiːz], *s.f. F:* 1. cunning, foxiness, craftiness. 2. piece of trickery.
rouble [rubl̩], *s.m. Num:* rouble.
roucaou [rukau], *s.m. Ich:* labrus, wrasse.
roucherolle [ruʃrɔl], *s.f. Orn:* redwing.
rouchi [ruʃi], *s.m.* dialect of Valenciennes and its surroundings.
roucou [ruku], *s.m. Dy:* annatto, roucou.
roucoulade [rukulad], *s.f. Iron:* cooing.
roucoulant [rukulɑ̃], *a.* cooing; **un petit rire r.,** a low gurgling laugh.
roucoulement [rukulmɑ̃], *s.m.* cooing.
roucouler [rukule], *v.i. & tr.* to coo; *F:* **r. une chanson,** to warble a song.
roucoulis [rukuli], *s.m.* cooing sound.
roucouyer [rukuje], *s.m.* = ROCOUYER.
roudoudou [rududu], *s.m. Sch: F:* (kind of) toffee.
roue [ru], *s.f.* wheel; (*a*) **r. motrice,** driving wheel (of a vehicle); **r. arrière,** back wheel; **r. avant,** front wheel; **r. de secours,** spare wheel; **voiture à quatre roues,** four-wheeled carriage; four-wheeler; **r. de charrette,** cart wheel; *Artil: etc:* **sur roues,** wheeled; *Aut:* **r. indépendante,** independent wheel; **suspension à quatre roues indépendantes,** four-wheel independent suspension; **r. à fils, à rayons métalliques,** wire wheel; **r. pleine,** spokeless wheel, solid wheel; **rouler en r. libre,** to coast; *Cy: F:* **prendre la r. de qn, être dans la r. de qn,** to follow s.o. closely; **gagner d'une r.,** to win by a wheel's length; *Rail:* **roues porteuses,** carrying wheels; *Av:* **roues de train, roues porteuses,** landing wheels, ground wheels; **r. de nez, r. avant,** nose wheel; **roues rentrées, roues sorties,** wheels up, wheels down; *Navy:* **roues d'un affût,** trucks of a gun mounting; *F:* **la cinquième r. du carosse,** *P:* **de la charrette,** an entirely useless person, thing; **pousser à la r.,** to put one's shoulder to the wheel, to lend a helping hand, to work hard (in support of an undertaking); **sans roues,** wheelless; **faire la r.,** (i) (*of peacock, turkey, etc.*) to spread (out) its tail; (ii) to strut, to swagger; (iii) *Gym:* to turn cartwheels, Catherine wheels; (iv) *Mil:* to wheel about; **paon qui fait la r.,** peacock in his pride; *s.a.* BATON[1] 1; (*b*) *Mec.E:* pulley; **r. à gorge,** grooved wheel, sheave; **r. à corde,** cable pulley; **r. à courroie,** belt pulley; **r. à chaîne,** chain pulley, chain sheave; chain wheel; **r. pour bobiner un câble,** drum wheel; (*c*) **r. à aile, r. volante,** flywheel; (*d*) wheel, pinion; **r. dentée, r. d'engrenage,** toothed wheel, cogwheel, rack wheel, gear (-wheel); **r. dentée conique, r. d'angle,** bevel wheel, mitre wheel; **r. droite,** spur wheel; **r. dentée d'entraînement, r. à cames, à picots,** sprocket wheel; **r. à rochet, r. d'encliquetage, r. à cliquet,** ratchet wheel, click wheel; **r. de champ,** face wheel; **r. de friction,** friction wheel; **r. hyperbolique,** skew (bevel) gear; **r. (d'engrenage) à vis,** worm wheel; **r. de commande, de transmission, r. motrice,** driving wheel, pinion; **r. intermédiaire,** intermediate wheel; **r. planétaire,** planet wheel, planetary pinion; **r. calée, r. fixe,** fast wheel, fixed wheel; **r. décalée, r. folle,** loose wheel, idle wheel; **r. parasite,** idle wheel, idler; **r. à patin(s),** caterpillar wheel; *Clockm:* **r. de rencontre,** swing wheel; **r. de compte,** chime barrel; (*e*) wheel, impeller (of turbine, compressor, supercharger); **r. de turbine à deux étages,** two-stage turbine wheel, impeller; **r. simple, double, de compresseur,** supercharger single-sided, double-sided, wheel; **r. d'admission,** rotating guide vane; **r. directrice d'entrée,** guide-vane rotor (of compressor); **r. d'entrée,** impeller intake guide vane; (*f*) *Hyd.E:* **r. à eau, r. hydraulique,** water wheel, hydraulic wheel; **r. élévatoire,** water-raising wheel, elevating wheel; **r. à aubes, à palettes,** paddle wheel; **r. à augets, à godets,** bucket wheel; **r. de côté,** breast (water) wheel; **r. en dessous,** undershot (water)wheel; **r. en dessus,** overshot (water)wheel; **r. de moulin,** mill wheel; **r. à meuler,** grinding wheel (of flour mill); *Nau:* **bateau à roues,** paddle boat; (*g*) **r. à vent,** wind wheel; (*h*) *Nau:* **r. du gouvernail,** steering wheel, the wheel; (*i*) **r. de câble,** coil of rope; (*j*) *Pyr:* **r. à feu,** Catherine wheel; (*k*) *A:* **condamner un criminel à la r.,** to condemn a criminal to the wheel; *P:* **être à la r.,** to be knowing, to know the ropes; (*l*) **la r. de la fortune,** the wheel of fortune; (*m*) *Cost:* false hem (on a skirt, etc.).
roué, -ée [rwe]. 1. *s.m.* rake, profligate; roué (originally of the Regency period). 2. *a. & s.* cunning, sly, artful (person). 3. *a. Farr:* **encolure rouée (d'un cheval),** arched neck.
rouelle [rwɛl], *s.f.* 1. round slice (of bread, apple, lemon, leather, etc.); round (of beef, etc.); **r. de veau,** fillet of veal; *s.a.* SÉTON. 2. *Arm:* kneecap, elbow cap.
Rouen [rwɑ̃], *Pr.n.* 1. *Pr.n. Geog:* Rouen; *F: A:* **aller à R.,** to come a cropper, *Th:* to get the bird; *Com: P: A:* **faire un R.,** to miss a sale. 2. *s.m. A:* = ROUENNERIE.
rouennais, -aise [rwanɛ, -ɛːz], *a. & s.* (native, inhabitant) of Rouen.
rouennerie [rwanri], *s.f. Tex:* printed cotton goods.
rouennier [rwanje], *s.m.* (i) manufacturer, (ii) seller, of printed cotton goods.
rouer [rwe]. 1. *v.tr.* to coil (rope). 2. *v.tr.* (*a*) *A:* to break (s.o.) on the wheel; (*b*) *F:* **r. qn de coups,** to thrash s.o. soundly; to beat s.o. black and blue; *A:* **roué de fatigue,** spent, worn-out, *F:* knocked up, with fatigue. 3. *v.i.* (*of peacock*) to spread its tail, to display.
rouergat, -ate [ruɛrga, -aːt], **rouergois, -oise** [ruɛrgwa, -waːz], *a. & s. Geog:* (native, inhabitant) of the Rouergue.
Rouergue [rwɛrg], *Pr.n.m. Geog:* the Rouergue.
rouerie [ruri], *s.f.* trick; piece of trickery; (artful) dodge; piece of sharp practice.
rouet [rwɛ], *s.m.* 1. spinning wheel; *Med:* **bruit de r.,** venous hum; **r. d'arpenteur,** surveyor's measuring wheel; *Ven:* (*of hunted hare*) **se mettre en r.,** to run round in a circle (to try to escape from the hounds). 2. (*a*) sheave (of pulley); pulley wheel; **r. à chaîne,** chain sheave; **r. de pompe,** pump impeller; (*b*) *Nau:* gin; (*c*) winding block (for gold wire). 3. (*a*) curb (supporting the lining of a well); (*b*) *Const:* framework of flèche, lantern. 4. scutcheon (of lock). 5. *A:* wheel-lock (of gun).
rouette [rwɛt], *s.f.* osier band (for tying up faggots, etc.).
rouf [ruf], *s.m.* (*a*) *Nau:* deck house (of ship); **r. central, r.-passerelle,** bridge house; (*b*) cuddy (of barge).
rouffion, -ionne [rufjɔ̃, -jɔn], *s. P:* (*a*) apprentice; (*b*) good-for-nothing.
rouflaquette [ruflakɛt], *s.f. F:* (*a*) kiss curl, lovelock; (*b*) *pl.* sidewhiskers, sideburns.
roufle [rufl̩], *s.m.* = ROUF.
rouge [ruːʒ]. 1. *a.* red; (*a*) **fer r.,** red-hot iron; **être r. de honte,** to be red, to blush, with shame; **devenir r. comme une pivoine,** to turn as red as a peony; **r. comme une tomate, comme une guigne, comme un homard, comme une écrevisse,** as red as a beetroot; **r. comme un coq,** as red as a turkey cock; **r. comme du sang,** blood-red; **r. de colère,** crimson with rage; **visage r. de santé,** face glowing with health; *F: A:* **marquer qn à l'encre r.,** to swear vengeance against s.o.; **le chapeau r.,** the cardinal's (red) hat; *Pol:* **le drapeau r.,** the red flag; **l'Armée r.,** the Red Army; (*of albinos*) **yeux rouges,** pink eyes; *Geog:* **la mer Rouge,** the Red Sea; **la promotion r.,** the list of nominations to the Legion of Honour; **porto r.,** ruby port; *Orn:* **canard aux pattes rouges,** musk duck; *Vet:* **maladies rouges,** pigs' diseases (including swine fever, swine erysipelas and salmonellosis); *adv.* **se fâcher tout r.,** to lose one's temper completely; **voir r.,** see red; *Pol:* **voter r.,** to vote communist; to vote for the Reds; *s.a.* ÂNE 1; (*b*) (*inv. in compounds*) **rouge sang,** blood-red; **des rubans rouge cerise,** cherry-red ribbons; **des joues rouge brique,** brick-red cheeks; **r. drapeau,** pillar-box red. 2. *s.m.* (*a*) red (colour); **le r. de la colère lui monta au visage,** his face flushed, he flushed, an angry red; **porter le fer au r.,** to make the iron red-hot, to raise the iron to a red heat; **tissonier chauffé au r.,** red hot poker; **r. blanc,** white heat, welding heat; *Hist: Pol:* **les Rouges,** the Reds; **c'est un r.,** he's a Red, a Communist; *Prov:* **r. le soir, espoir,** red sky at night (is the) shepherd's delight; *F:* **c'est le r. pour les taureaux,** it's like a red rag to a bull; (*b*) *Toil:* rouge; **r. à lèvres, bâton de r.,** lipstick; **r. à lèvres rose,** pink lipstick; **(se) mettre du r.,** (i) to rouge (one's face); (ii) to put on (some) lipstick; (*c*) **r. à polir, rouge d'Angleterre, de Prusse,** (jewellers') rouge; crocus; **r. d'Andrinople,** Turkey red; (*d*) *Geol:* **r. antique,** rosso antico; (*e*) red wine; **gros r.,** coarse red wine; *F:* **un coup de r.,** a glass, drink, of red wine.
rougeâtre [ruʒɑːtr̩], *a.* reddish.
rougeau [ruʒo], *s.m. Vit:* rougeot.
rougeaud, -eaude [ruʒo, -oːd]. 1. *a. & s.* red-faced (person); high in colour; **un gros r.,** a big red-faced man. 2. *s.m. Vit:* rougeot.
rouge-gorge [ruʒgɔrʒ], *s.m. Orn:* robin, (robin) redbreast; **r.-g. mâle, femelle,** cock robin, jenny robin; *pl. rouges-gorges.*
rougeoiement [ruʒwamɑ̃], *s.m.* reddish glare, glow.
rougeole [ruʒɔl], *s.f.* 1. (*a*) *Med:* measles; (*b*) *Vet: F:* **r. des moutons,** sheep pox. 2. *Bot: F:* field cow-wheat.
rougeoleux, -euse [ruʒɔlø, -øːz], *a. & s.* measles (patient).
rougeot [ruʒo], *s.m.* 1. *Orn:* pochard. 2. *Vit:* rougeot.
rougeotte [ruʒɔt], *s.f. Bot:* purple cow-wheat.
rougeoyant [ruʒwajɑ̃], *a.* (*a*) reddening, turning red; (*b*) glowing; lurid (flame, etc.).
rougeoyer [ruʒwaje], *v.i.* **(il rougeoie; il rougeoiera)** (*of thgs*) (*a*) to turn red; (*b*) to glow red.
rouge-queue [ruʒkø], *s.m. Orn:* **r.-q. (à front blanc, de muraille),** redstart; **r.-q. noir,** black redstart; **r.-q. de Moussier,** Moussier's redstart; *pl. rouges-queues.*
rouget, -ette [ruʒɛ, -ɛt]. 1. *A: a.* reddish. 2. *s.m.* (*a*) *Ent: F:* harvest bug, mite; harvester; (*b*) *Ich:* **r. (barbet),** (i) red mullet; (ii) surmullet; **r. grondin,** gurnard, red-fish; **r. volant,** flying gurnard, sea bat; (*c*) *Vet:* swine, *U.S:* hog, erysipelas, diamond skin disease. 3. *s.f. Bot:* **rougette blanche,** (corn) rattle.
rougeur [ruʒœːr], *s.f.* 1. redness. 2. blush; flush; **ces mots lui firent monter la r. au visage,** these words brought a flush to his face, made him flush. 3. red spot, red patch, blotch (on the skin); **couvert de rougeurs,** blotched, blotchy.
rougi [ruʒi], *a.* reddened; turned red; **yeux rougis de pleurs,** eyes reddened by tears; **feuilles rougies,** leaves that have turned red; **eau r.,** water slightly coloured with red wine; wine with water.
rougir [ruʒiːr]. 1. *v.tr.* (*a*) to redden; to turn (sth.) red; to tinge (sth.) with red; **je ne fais que r. mon eau,** I drink water with just a little wine; **r. ses mains de sang,** to stain one's hands with blood; (*b*) to bring (metal) to a red heat; **fer rougi au feu,** iron heated red-hot; **r. le fer au blanc,** to make iron white-hot; (*c*) to flush (the face); **visage rougi par l'exercise, par la boisson,** face flushed with exercise, with drink, wine. 2. *v.i.* (*a*) to redden, to turn red; (*b*) **faire r. un métal,** to heat a metal red-hot; (*c*) (*of pers.*) to turn, go, red; to colour; to blush; to flush (up); **faire r. qn,** (i) to make s.o. blush; (ii) to put s.o. to shame; **cela l'a fait r.,** that made her blush, brought a blush, the colour, to her cheeks; *F:* **tenir des propos à faire r. un singe,** to say things that would make a sailor blush; **r. de colère,** to flush with anger; **r. jusqu'aux oreilles,** to flush up to the ears; **r. comme une pensionnaire,** to blush like a schoolgirl; **r. comme une pivoine,** to turn as red as a peony, as a turkey cock; *s.a.* BLANC II 2.
rougissant [ruʒisɑ̃], *a.* (*a*) reddening, turning red; (*b*) blushing.
rougissement [ruʒismɑ̃], *s.m.* (*a*) reddening, turning red; (*b*) (*of pers.*) blushing, going red.
roui [rwi], *s.m.* 1. retting, steeping (of flax). 2. *F:* (*of food*) **sentir le r.,** to taste of dishwater.
rouille [ruːj], *s.f.* 1. (*a*) rust; **tache de r.,** iron stain, iron mould; (*of leak*) **s'obstruer par la r.,** to rust up; (*b*) *A:* **r. de cuivre,** verdigris; **r. de plomb,** white lead, ceruse. 2. *Agr:* rust, mildew, blight; *Vit:* **r. des feuilles,** brown rot; leaf blight; **r. blanche,** white rust; *For:* **r. du pin,** pine-blister. 3. *Cu:* mayonnaise flavoured with pimento. 4. *Dy:* rouille. 5. *a.inv.* rust-coloured, rusty; rust, reddish-brown.

rouillé[1] [ruje], *a.* **1.** (*a*) rusted, rusty (metal, etc.); *Gold Min:* **or r.,** rusty gold; (*b*) rust-coloured, rusty; (*c*) rusty; out of practice; **je suis r. en latin, mon latin est un peu r.,** my Latin is a bit rusty; **mes vieilles jambes sont rouillées,** my old legs are stiff in the joints; (*c*) (*of sound*) grating (like a rusty hinge). **2.** mildewed (plant).

rouillé[2], *s.m. Ich: F:* wrasse.

rouiller[1] [ruje], *v.tr.* **1.** to rust; to make (iron, etc.) rusty; **l'oisiveté rouille l'esprit,** idleness rusts the mind. **2.** to mildew, blight (plant).

se rouiller. 1. (*a*) to rust (up); to get rusty; **l'écrou s'est rouillé avec le boulon,** the nut has rusted on to the bolt; (*b*) **laisser r. ses connaissances,** to allow one's knowledge to get rusty; **je me rouille,** I am getting rusty, getting out of practice; **je fais une partie tous les jours pour ne pas me r.,** I play a game every day to keep my hand in. **2.** (*of plant*) to become mildewed.

rouiller[2], *v.i. Min:* to kerf.

rouilleuse[1] [rujø:z], *s.f. Min:* kerfing machine.

rouilleux, -euse[2] [rujø, -ø:z], *a. A:* rust-coloured; rusty (black, etc.).

rouillure[1] [rujy:r], *s.f.* **1.** rustiness. **2.** (*of plants*) rust, blight.

rouillure[2], *s.f. Min:* kerf.

rouir [rwi:r]. **1.** *v.tr.* to steep, ret (flax, etc.); **r. le lin sur pré,** to dew-ret flax. **2.** *v.i.* (*of flax, etc.*) to steep, ret.

rouissage [rwisa:ʒ], *s.m.* steeping, retting (of flax).

rouisseur, -euse [rwisœ:r, -ø:z], *s.m.* retter (of flax).

rouissoir [rwiswa:r], *s.m. Tex:* retting pit, rettery.

roukerie [rukri], *s.f. Orn:* (penguin) rookery.

roulade [rulad], *s.f.* **1.** roll (in the dust, downhill, etc.); **faire une r.,** to roll downhill. **2.** *Mus:* roulade, run, vocal flourish. **3.** *Cu:* (*a*) beef, etc. olive; (*b*) jam roll; (*c*) collar (of meat or fish).

roulage [rula:ʒ], *s.m.* **1.** (*a*) rolling (of ploughed land, of metal, etc.); (*b*) easy rolling (of vehicle). **2.** carriage, cartage (of goods); haulage, trucking (of coal); **entreprise de r.,** carrying company; forwarding agent; **commissionnaire, entrepreneur, de r.,** carrier; haulage contractor; **cheval de r.,** cart horse, draught horse; **voitures de r.,** haulage vehicles; **matériel de r.,** haulage plant; *Mil:* **police de r.,** flying column. **3.** road traffic.

roulance [rulɑ̃:s], *s.f. Typ: P:* jerry (as a send-off, as a form of protest).

roulant, -ante [rulɑ̃, -ɑ̃:t]. **1.** *a.* (*a*) rolling; sliding (door); moving (staircase); travelling (crane, etc.); portable (vice-stand); **allure roulante,** rolling gait; **voiture bien roulante,** smooth-running (i) carriage, (ii) car; **voiture accidentée roulante,** damaged car that can still run, that will still go; *Rail:* **matériel r.,** rolling stock; **personnel r.,** train, lorry, bus, etc. crews; *s.a.* FEU[1] 3, TAPIS 3, TROTTOIR 2; (*b*) smooth; **chemin bien r.,** good road, easy(-running) road. **2.** *a. Com:* **affaire roulante,** going concern; **fonds r.,** working capital; *Fin:* **capitaux roulants,** circulating, floating, capital; *Typ:* **presse roulante,** working press. **3.** *a. P:* side-splitting, killing (sight, joke); **c'est r.!** it's a scream! **4.** *s.m.* patent topsail (of yacht, etc.). **5.** *s.m.* (*pers.*) letter sorter (in train), *U.S:* railway mail clerk; *F:* **les roulants,** (i) *Rail:* train crews; (ii) *Trans:* lorry, bus, etc., crews. **6.** *s.f. F: Mil:* **roulante,** field kitchen. **7.** *s.f. Mth:* **roulante,** rolling circle.

roule [rul], *s.m. For:* **1.** tree trunk. **2.** roller (for shifting heavy weights).

roulé [rule]. **1.** *a.* (*a*) rolled; *Cost:* **col r.,** roll collar; polo neck; *US:* turtle neck; *Cu:* **épaule roulée,** rolled shoulder; (*b*) *Ling:* **consonne roulée,** trilled consonant; **r roulé,** rolled r; **le chant r. du courlis,** the bubbling, trilling, song of the curlew; (*c*) *F:* (*of woman*) **bien roulée,** with a well-rounded figure, with good curves; *F:* who comes out in the right places; (*d*) (*of timber*) with ring shake, cup shake. **2.** *s.m.* (*a*) *Cu:* rolled joint; **r. de veau,** rolled veal; (*b*) *Civ.E:* small rounded stones (used for road foundations).

rouleau, -eaux [rulo], *s.m.* **1.** roller; (*a*) **roulements à rouleaux,** roller bearings; **r. de tension,** tension roller; idle(r) roller (of caterpillar); (*b*) **r. compresseur,** road roller; **r. à vapeur,** steam roller; *Civ.E:* **r. à pieds de mouton,** sheep's foot roller, sheep's foot tamper; *Agr:* **r. à dents,** toothed roller; **r. squelette,** Cambridge roller; **r. pour gazon,** garden roller; **r. brise-mottes,** clod crusher; **passer le gazon au r.,** to roll the grass; (*c*) **r. pour essuie-mains, r. porte-serviettes,** towel roller; *Typwr:* **r. porte-papier,** impression roller; platen; cylinder; *Tchn:* **transporteur à rouleaux,** roller conveyor; **r. (de caisse enregistreuse),** tally roll; **r. d'impression,** print roll; *Rec:* **r. pinceur,** pinch roller; *Nau:* **voile à r.,** rolling reef; **r. du gui,** rolling-gear of the boom (of yacht); **carte sur r.,** roller map; **(store sur) r.,** roller-blind; (*d*) (i) *Typ:* (ink) roller; **r. chargeur,** rider roller; **r. de bassin de mouillage,** water-fountain roller; **r. mouilleur,** damper roller; **r. preneur,** ductor roller, ink-feed roller; **r. toucheur,** inking roller; **encrer au r.,** to roll up; **coup de r.,** roller mark(ing); **faire un nouveau r.,** to break a new roller; **régler un r.,** to set a roller; (ii) *Phot:* roller (squeegee); (iii) *Cu:* **r. à pâtisserie,** rolling pin; (iv) **r. à peinture,** paint roller; (*e*) **rouleaux concasseurs de coke,** coke-crushing rolls; (*f*) *Tex:* beam (of loom); (*g*) *Paperm:* **rouleaux d'immersion, dipping rolls; r. d'entrée,** entering reel; **r. de sortie,** delivery reel; **r. égoutteur,** dandy roll, dandy roller; (*h*) *Veh:* **r. de ressort,** spring eye. **2.** roll (of paper, etc.); roll, web (of news-print); roll, spool (of cinematograph film); coil (of rope, wire); *A:* scroll (of parchment, etc.); *Arch:* (i) curve of arch; (ii) volute of modillion; *F:* **je suis au bout de mon, du, r.,** I am at the end of my tether, at my wits' end; **r. à musique,** music roll, holder; **r. hygiénique,** toilet roll; **r. de tabac,** twist of tobacco; **tabac en r.,** twist tobacco; **r. d'or,** rouleau (of gold). **3.** *A:* phonograph record. **4.** *Z:* roller, coral snake. **5.** *Oc:* billow, roller. **6.** *Sp:* (*high jump*) roll; **r. ventral,** straddle; **r. costal,** western roll; **sauter en r.,** to do a roll; **sauter en r. ventral,** to straddle.

roulé-boulé [rulebule], *s.m. Av:* roll ball; **technique du r.-b.,** roll-ball technique.

roulée [rule], *s.f. P:* (*a*) thrashing, licking; (*b*) ready-made cigarette.

roulement [rulmɑ̃], *s.m.* **1.** (*a*) rolling (of ball, etc.); **r. d'yeux,** rolling of the eyes; (*b*) rolling (of vehicle); *Aut: etc:* **bande de r.,** tread (of tyre); **r. anti-dérapant,** non-skid tread; **chemin de r.,** treadway (of bridge); (*c*) *Av:* (i) run (at take-off or landing), roll (at landing); (ii) taxying (from one place to another on airfield); **roulements très courts au décollage et à l'atterrissage,** very short runs at take-off and landing; **chemin de r.,** taxiway; (*d*) running, working (of a machine, etc.); **r. silencieux,** smooth running; (*c*) working season (of blast furnace). **2.** rumbling (of waggon, of thunder); rattle (of vehicle on stones); roll(ing) (of drum); **j'entendis un r. de tambour,** I heard a roll on the drum. **3.** (*a*) *Mec:* rolling; **frottement de r.,** rolling friction; (*b*) *Mec.E:* bearing; **r. à aiguilles,** needle bearing; **r. à billes,** ball bearing; **r. à billes renforcé,** heavy-duty (ball) bearing; **r. à galets, à rouleaux,** roller bearing; **r. à galets, à rouleaux, coniques,** tapered roller bearing; **chemin de r. (à galets),** roller track; **r. à rotule, r. oscillant,** self-aligning bearing; **r. auto-centrant,** self-centring bearing; **r. de butée,** thrust bearing; **r. de butée à billes,** ball-thrust bearing; **r. fixe,** radial bearing; **r. lisse,** plain-journal bearing; **r. à rattrapage de jeu,** pre-loaded bearing; **r. annulaire d'embrayage,** radial clutch bearing (*c*) *Veh:* running gear, carriage (of car, locomotive, railway carriage, etc.). **4.** *Veh:* **train de r.,** bogie; **galet de r.,** bogie wheel; **glissière guide du train de r.,** bogie guide slide; **chariot de galet de r.,** bogie bracket; *Rail:* **table, surface, plan, de r. du rail,** running surface of the rail, tread of rail. **5.** (*a*) *Com:* **r. de fonds,** circulation of capital; *s.a.* FONDS 3; (*b*) alternation, taking turns (in duties, etc.); rotation-roll; **par r.,** in rotation; **les après-midi libres sont distribuées par r.,** free afternoons are allotted in rotation.

rouler [rule]. **1.** *v.tr.* (*a*) to roll (stone, cask, etc.) (along, about); *Games:* to cast (dice), to roll; **r. les yeux,** to roll one's eyes; **r. un projet (dans sa tête),** to revolve, turn over, a plan (in one's mind); **r. de mauvaises pensées,** to think evil thoughts; *Min:* **r. le charbon,** to haul, wheel, tram, truck, coal; *Golf:* **coup roulé,** putt; **long coup roulé,** approach putt; (*at bowls*) **Monsieur X fit r. la premiere boule,** Mr X sent down the first wood; *s.a.* BOSSE 1, CARROSSE 1; (*b*) *F:* **r. qn,** (i) to diddle s.o.; to take s.o. in; to do s.o.; to swindle s.o.; (ii) to beat, lick, s.o.; **il m'a roulé de deux mille francs,** he has done me out of two thousand francs; (*c*) to roll up (map, etc.); to roll (meat, fish); **r. une cigarette,** to roll a cigarette; **r. une voile, un parapluie,** to roll up, furl, a sail, an umbrella; *Tchn:* **machine à r. les filets,** thread rolling machine; (*d*) **r. la terre, un champ, un tennis,** to roll the ground, a field, a tennis court; (*e*) **r. les r,** to roll one's r's; (*f*) **r. qn dans une couverture,** to roll, wrap, s.o. up in a blanket; (*g*) **r. une feuille de papier, une pièce d'étoffe,** to roll (up) a sheet of paper, a piece of cloth; (*h*) *Ven:* to shoot (ground game) dead; (*i*) *P:* **se les r.,** not to work at all; to have a cushy time. **2.** *v.i.* (*a*) to roll (over, along, about); **r. sur le sol,** to roll over on the ground; **r. sur une pente,** to roll down a slope; **r. (en voiture),** to drive; **r. sur une route,** to travel along a road; **nous avons roulé toute la nuit,** we travelled all night; **cette voiture n'a pas beaucoup roulé,** this car hasn't done many miles; (*in advertisement*) **peu roulé,** low milage; *Av:* **r. sur le sol,** to taxi; *F:* **ça roule,** everything's fine, O.K.; **ça roule, les affaires,** business is good; *F:* **je ne roule pas sur l'or,** I'm not exactly rolling in money; *Fin:* **l'argent roule,** money is circulating freely; **ces idées lui roulaient dans la tête,** his brain was busy with these ideas; these ideas were turning round and round in his head; **la conversation roulait sur le sport,** the talk ran, turned, on sport; **tout roule sur lui,** everything turns on him; **toute la vie humaine roule sur des probabilités,** the whole of human life hangs on probabilities, depends on chance; the life of man is a perpetual balancing of probabilities; **r. dans tous les pays, r. par le monde,** to travel all over the world; to knock about the world; *F:* **ce que j'ai roulé!** what a rolling stone I've been! (*with cogn.acc.*) *F:* **r. les cafés,** to spend one's day(s) loafing from one café to another, pub-crawling; *Prov:* **pierre qui roule n'amasse pas mousse,** a rolling stone gathers no moss; (*b*) (*of thunder, etc.*) to roll, rumble; (*c*) (*of locomotive, etc.*) to run, work; **auto qui roule bien,** car that runs well; (*d*) *Nau:* (*of ship*) to roll; **r. bas, lourdement,** to roll heavily; (*of small boat*) to broach to and capsize; **r. à bord, sur bord,** to roll gunwale under; (*e*) to rotate, to take turns (in the performance of a duty, etc.); **r. ensemble,** to take duty by turns on the same roster, to take it in turns; (*f*) to fluctuate, vary; **revenu qui roule entre 10,000 et 15,000 francs,** income that fluctuates between 10,000 and 15,000 francs.

se rouler. 1. (*a*) to roll, to turn over and over (in the grass, etc.); (*b*) **le hérisson se roule en boule,** the hedgehog rolls up, rolls itself, into a ball. **2.** *F:* **se r. (par terre),** to be convulsed with laughter; **il y a de quoi se r. (de rire),** it's enough to make you split your sides, die of laughing.

roule-ta-bille [rultabi:j], **roule-ta-bosse** [rultabɔs], *s.m.inv. F:* rolling stone.

roulette [rulɛt], *s.f.* **1.** (*a*) caster; roller; small wheel; truck wheel (of gun carriage); **chaise à roulettes,** chair on casters; **patins à roulettes,** roller skates; **r. du trolley,** trolley-wheel (of tram car); *F:* **ça marche, va, comme sur des roulettes,** everything is working smoothly; things are going like clockwork; (*b*) *Av:* **r. de nez,** nose wheel; **r. de queue,** tail wheel; (*c*) *Tls:* (bookbinder's) fillet; (shoemaker's) pricking wheel; *Dressm: Harn:* tracing wheel, tracer; *Engr:* roulette; *Dom.Ec:* pastry wheel, jagger; (*d*) (spring) tape measure; **r. d'arpenteur,** surveyor's tape; (*e*) *F:* dentist's drill. **2.** (*a*) *A:* wheeled chair; (*b*) truckle bed. **3.** (game of) roulette; **r. russe,** Russian roulette. **4.** *Geom:* cycloid, roulette, trochoid.

rouleur, -euse[1] [rulœ:r, -ø:z], *s.* **1.** (*a*) workman who rolls (barrels, etc.) who wheels (barrow, etc.); *Min:* trammer, wheeler, drawer, roller, haulage-man; (*b*) *F:* **c'est un r.,** he's a man who always gets the better of people, the best of the bargain. **2.** (*a*) travelling journeyman; (*b*) *O:* workman, workwoman, who never remains long on the same job; rolling stone; *F:* **r. de cabarets,** pub crawler; (*c*) *Sp: Cy:* **un bon r.,** a tireless cyclist on the flat. **3.** *s.m.* (*a*) *Nau:* ship that rolls heavily; (*b*) *Av:* ground machine; (*c*) *Aut:* **(cric) r.,** mobile car jack; (*d*) *Ent:* vine weevil; (*e*) *Z:* tumbler pigeon, roller; **pigeon r. oriental,** Oriental roller. **4.** *s.f.* **rouleuse:** (*a*) *Ent:* leaf roller, leaf crumpler (caterpillar); *a.* **insecte rouleur,** leaf-rolling insect; (*b*) *F:* gutter prostitute; (*c*) cigarette-making machine.

rouleux, -euse[2] [rulø, -ø:z], *a. Nau:* unsteady, cranky (ship).

roulier, -ière [rulje, -jɛ:r]. **1.** *a.* carrying (trade, etc.). **2.** *A: s.m.* carter, waggoner; carrier. **3.** *s.f. A:* **roulière,** waggoner's overall.

roulis [ruli], *s.m. Nau: Av:* roll(ing); **coup de r.,** roll, lurch; **r. du bord du vent,** weather lurch; **quille de r.,** rolling chock, bilge keel; **table à r.,** fiddle; **planche à r.,** bunk board; **palan de r.,** rolling tackle; **avoir du, un mouvement de, r.,** to roll; **aller au r.,** to fetch way; *Nau: Av:* **ampleur de r.,** roll rate; **angle de r.,**

angle of roll; *Av:* **balance de r.,** rolling balance; **moment de r.,** rolling moment; **contrôle en r.,** lateral control; *F:* (*of pers.*) **marcher avec un r. prononcé,** to walk with a rolling gait.

roulisse [rulis], *s.f. Min:* curb, crib (bed).

rouloir [rulwaːr], *s.m.* **1.** (candle maker's) rolling board. **2.** *Tex:* roller, cylinder, (for smoothing cloth).

roulon [rulɔ̃], *s.m.* rung, round (of ladder, chair, manger-rack).

roulottage [rulɔtaːʒ], *s.m.* stealing from parked vehicles.

roulotte [rulɔt], *s.f.* (*a*) (gipsies') caravan; **r. (de camping),** (touring) caravan, *U.S:* trailer; (*b*) **vol à la r.,** stealing from parked vehicles.

roulotté [rulɔte], *a. & s.m. Needlew:* **ourlet r.,** rolled hem; **faire un r.,** to make a rolled hem (on scarf, handkerchief, etc.).

roulotter [rulɔte], *v.tr. Needlew:* to roll a hem on (an edge, etc.).

roulottier [rulɔtje], *s.m.* **1.** caravanner. **2.** thief (who steals from parked vehicles).

roulure [rulyːr], *s.f.* **1.** rolled edge (of sheet metal, etc.). **2.** *Arb:* cup shake, ring shake (in timber). **3.** *P:* gutter prostitute.

roumain, -aine [rumɛ̃, -ɛn], *a. & s. Geog: Ling:* Rumanian, Romanian, Roumainian.

roumanche [rumɑ̃ʃ], *s.m.* = ROMANCHE.

Roumanie [rumani], *Pr.n.f. Geog:* Rumania, Romania, Roumania.

Roumélie (Orientale) [rumeli(ɔrjɑ̃tal)], *Pr.n.f. A.Geog:* (Eastern) Rumelia.

rouméliote [rumeljɔt], *a. & s. A.Geog:* Roumeliote.

roumi [rumi], *s.m.* Christian (in the language of Arabs and Moslems).

round [rawnd, rund], *s.m. Box:* round.

roupala [rupala], *s.m. Bot:* stink-albe, fireproof tree.

roupettes [rupɛt], *s.f.pl. P:* (= *testicules*) balls.

roupie[1] [rupi], *s.f. Num:* rupee.

roupie[2], *s.f.* **1.** *F:* snivel; drop (of running mucus); *P:* dewdrop; **avoir la r.,** to have a drippy nose; **roupies de café,** coffee-slops, -drips; **c'est pas de la r. de sansonnet,** there's nothing wrong with that; it's not bad. **2.** *P:* **une vieille r.,** an old hag, an old trout.

roupieux, -euse [rupjø, -øːz], *A:* **1.** *a. & s.* snotty-nosed (person). **2.** *a. & s.m.* snotty (nose).

roupiller [rupije], *v.i. F:* to sleep; to snooze; to take a nap; to doze.

roupilleur, -euse [rupijœːr, -øːz], *s. F:* snoozer.

roupillon [rupijɔ̃], *s.m. F:* nap, snooze; **piquer un r.,** to snooze.

roupillonner [rupijɔne], *v.i. F:* = ROUPILLER.

rouquier [rukje], *s.m. Ich:* wrasse.

rouquin, -ine [rukɛ̃, -in]. **1.** *a. & s. F:* red-haired, ginger-haired, carroty-haired, sandy-haired (person); *s.* redhead. **2.** *s.m. P:* rough red wine.

roure [ruːr], *s.m.* = ROUVRE.

rouscaille [ruskɑːj], *s.f. P:* complaint, grouse; bellyaching.

rouscailler [ruskɑje], *v.i. P:* to complain, to grouse; to bellyache.

rouscailleur, -euse [ruskɑjœːr, -øːz], *s. P:* grouser; bellyacher.

rouspétance [ruspetɑ̃ːs], *s.f. F:* resistance, opposition; griping, grousing, bellyaching; **faire de la r.,** to be obstreperous; to kick over the traces.

rouspéter [ruspete], *v.i.* (**je rouspète, n. rouspétons; je rouspéterai**) *F:* to resist, grumble, gripe, grouse, bellyache, protest; to show fight; to kick; **il n'a pas rouspété,** he went like a lamb.

rouspéteur, -euse [ruspetœːr, -øːz], *F:* **1.** *a.* quarrelsome, grumbling, grouchy; **il est gentil mais un peu r.,** he's all right, but a bit inclined to grouse. **2.** *s.* fighter; quarrelsome person; grumbler, griper, grouser.

roussable [rusabl̩], *s.m. Fish Ind:* herring smoke-house.

roussard [rusaːr], *s.m. Orn:* (breed of) pigeon.

roussâtre [rusɑːtr̩], *a.* reddish (hair); brownish (water).

rousse[1] [rus], *s.f.* **1.** *Dial:* (*in W. of Fr.*) polled willow. **2.** *P: coll.* **la r.,** the police, the cops, the fuzz.

rousseau, -eaux [ruso], *a. & s.m.* **1.** = ROUSSOT. **2.** *s.m. Ich:* sea bream.

rousselé [rusle], *a.* marked with red or brown spots.

rousselet [ruslɛ], *s.m.* russet pear.

rousseline [ruslin], *s.f. Orn:* tawny pipit.

rousser [ruse], *v.i. P:* = ROUSPÉTER.

rousserolle [rusrɔl], *s.f. Orn:* **r. (effarvatte),** reed warbler; **r. des buissons,** Blyth's reed warbler; **r. isabelle,** paddyfield warbler; **r. turdoïde,** great reed warbler; **r. verderolle,** marsh warbler.

roussette [rusɛt], *s.f.* **1.** *Ich:* spotted dog-fish; roussette. **2.** *Orn: F:* (*a*) reed bunting; (*b*) wood warbler. **3.** *Z: F:* flying fox, fox-bat; roussette. **4.** *Cu:* fried cake; fritter; *U.S:* cruller. **5.** russet pear. **6.** white wine from Savoie and Jura.

rousseur [rusœːr], *s.f.* redness (of hair, etc.); **tache de r.,** freckle; **couvert de taches de r.,** freckled.

roussi[1] [rusi], *s.m. Tan: A:* Russia(n) leather.

roussi[2] [rusi]. **1.** *a.* browned; scorched. **2.** *s.m.* **cela,** *F:* **ça, sent le r.,** (i) there's a smell of something burning; (ii) *F:* there's trouble ahead; we're in for a bad time; *A:* (*of pers., of opinions*) **sentir le r.,** to be in danger of burning at the stake; to smack of heresy.

roussiller [rusije], *v.tr.* to singe.

roussillonnais, -aise [rusijɔnɛ, -ɛːz], *a. & s. Geog:* (native, inhabitant) of Roussillon.

roussin[1] [rusɛ̃], *s.m.* cob; plough horse, carthorse; *F: A:* **r. d'Arcadie,** ass, Jerusalem pony.

roussin[2], *s.m. P: A:* policeman; police spy.

roussir [rusiːr]. **1.** *v.tr.* (*a*) to turn (sth.) russet or brown; to redden; *Cu:* to brown (meat); **viande roussie,** meat done brown; (*b*) to scorch, singe (linen); **se r. les cheveux,** to singe one's hair. **2.** *v.i.* (*a*) to turn brown, to turn russet, to redden; (*of wig, etc.*) to turn a rusty brown; (*b*) *Cu:* **faire r. du beurre, une sauce,** to brown butter, a sauce; (*c*) to scorch, singe; to get scorched.

roussissage [rusisaːʒ], *s.m.* dyeing (of sth.) russet.

roussissement [rusismɑ̃], *s.m.*, **roussissure** [rusisyːr], *s.f.* **1.** turning brown, russet; reddening. **2.** scorching, burning.

roussot, -ot(t)e [ruso, -ɔt], *a. & s. F:* red-haired (man, girl); *s.* redhead.

rouste [rust], *s.f. P:* **flanquer une r. à qn,** to thrash s.o., to beat s.o. up.

rouster [ruste], *v.tr.* **1.** *Nau:* to woold (yard, etc.). **2.** *F:* **r. qn,** to thrash s.o.

roustir [rustiːr], *v.tr.* **1.** *Cu: Dial:* to roast. **2.** *P:* to cheat (s.o.); to do (s.o.) down; **être rousti,** to be done for.

roustisseur, -euse [rustisœːr, -øːz], *s. P: A:* cheat; sponger.

roustissure [rustisyːr], *s.f. A:* **1.** *Th: F:* (*a*) worthless play; (*b*) poor part. **2.** *P:* trash; tripe.

roustons [rustɔ̃], *s.m.pl. P:* (= *testicules*) balls.

rousture [rustyːr], *s.f. Nau:* woolding; **faire une r. à une vergue,** to woold a yard.

rousturer [rustyre], *v.tr. Nau:* to woold (yard, etc.).

routage [rutaːʒ], *s.m. Post:* sorting and routing of second class mail.

route [rut], *s.f.* **1.** road; (*a*) **r. nationale, r. de grande communication, grande r.** = A road, first-class road, main road, major road, *U.S:* highway; **r. départementale,** road (*usu.* secondary road) maintained by the *département*; **r. secondaire** = B road, secondary road, second-class road; **r. cantonale, r. vicinale, r. d'intérêt local,** local road, minor road; **r. à grande circulation,** road with heavy traffic; busy road; **r. de ceinture,** orbital road, ring road, *U.S:* belt highway; **r. internationale,** international road; **r. à péage,** toll road; **r. d'accès,** approach road; **r. muletière,** mule track; **la r. de Paris, de la fortune,** the road to Paris, to fortune; **la r. de Paris à Bordeaux,** the road from Paris to Bordeaux; **prendre la r. de Paris,** to take the road for Paris; **au bord de la r.,** on the roadside; **hors de la r.,** clear of the road; **r. à sens unique,** one-way road; **r. à deux sens,** two-way road; **r. à voie unique,** single-track road; **r. à deux voies,** double-track, two-lane, road; **r. à trois voies,** three-lane road; **r. à chaussées séparées, à deux voies séparées,** dual carriageway; **r. à flanc de coteau,** road that follows the hillside; **r. en corniche,** cornice road; **r. en encorbellement,** overhanging road; **r. en déblai, r. encaissée,** sunken road, road in cutting, road with high banks; **r. en remblai,** road on an embankment, embanked road; **r. en chaussée,** road on an embankment; **r. surélevée,** elevated highway, *U.S:* skyway; **r. asphaltée, bitumée, goudronnée,** tarred road; **r. macadamisée,** macadam road; **r. empierrée,** metalled road; **r. non empierrée,** unmetalled road; **r. pavée,** paved road; **code de la r.,** highway code; **l'état des routes,** road conditions; **r. carrossable,** road suitable for motor vehicles; **r. praticable,** passable road; **r. impraticable,** unpassable road; **r. de viabilité douteuse,** unreliable road; **r. cahoteuse,** bumpy road; **r. raboteuse,** rugged road; **r. défoncée,** broken road; **r. interdite,** forbidden road; **r. désaffectée,** abandoned road; **r. en réparation,** road under repair; (*b*) *Mil:* **r. militaire,** military road; **r. d'étapes,** main communication road; **r. stratégique,** strategic road; **r. à circulation libre,** open road; **r. à circulation réglementée,** supervised road; **r. gardée,** reserved road, dispatch road. **2.** route, way; course; (*a*) **r. du soleil,** path of the sun; (*b*) **en r.!** (i) let's go! en route! (ii) off you go! (iii) *Rail:* right away! (iv) *Nau:* full speed ahead! **être en r.,** (i) to be on the way; (ii) (*of commercial traveller*) to be out; to be on the road; **être en r. pour . . ., être sur la r. de . . .,** to be on one's way, on the way, on the road, to . . .; **navire en r. pour l'étranger,** ship outward bound; **faire r. avec qn,** to go along with s.o.; to travel with s.o.; **faire r. ensemble,** to travel together; **faire, refaire, la r. à pied, en voiture,** to walk, drive, all the way, all the way back; **mettre en r. un convoi,** to start, dispatch, a convoy; **mise en r.,** starting, dispatch(ing); starting up; **se mettre en r.,** to start on one's way, to set out; (*of ship*) to get under way; **mettre des travaux en r.,** to set work going, to start operations; **mettre en r. la machine, le moteur,** to start (up) the engine; **se remettre en r., reprendre sa r.,** to resume one's journey; **s'attarder en r.,** to linger on the way, the journey; **marchandises avariées en cours de r.,** goods damaged in transit; (*of ship*) **relâche forcée en cours de r.,** forced call during the voyage; **frais de r.,** travel(ling) expenses or allowances; *Mil:* **chanson de r.,** marching song, **barrer la r. à qn,** to bar s.o.'s way; **montrer la r. à qn,** to show s.o. the way; (*of ship*) **s'écarter de la r. d'un autre navire,** to keep out of the way of another ship; (*c*) **r. aérienne,** (i) air route; (ii) airway (with navigational aids); **r. de mer, r. maritime,** sea route; *Nau:* **r. de navigation,** (shipping) lane, ocean lane; **r. terrestre,** (over)land route; **r. commerciale,** commercial route, trade route; **par la r. habituelle,** by the customary, usual, route; **par n'importe quelle r.,** by any route; **c'est sur la r. du trolleybus,** it is on the trolleybus route; (*d*) *Nau: Av:* **r. (à suivre),** course; **r. (suivie),** track; **angle de r.,** track angle; **r. apparente,** steered course; **r. à suivre, à donner,** required track, course to steer; **r. suivie,** track (made good); **la bonne r.,** the proper course; **r. à l'estime,** dead reckoning; **r. au compas,** compass route; **compas de r.,** steering compass; **r. magnétique,** magnetic course; **r. vraie,** true course; **r. estimée,** estimated course; **r. corrigée,** course made good; corrected course; **r. à relèvement constant,** constant-bearing course; **r. loxodromique,** rhumb-line course, *Nau:* rhumb sailing; **r. par arc de grand cercle,** great-circle course; **carte de la r. à suivre,** route chart; **carte de la r. suivie,** track chart; **tracer la r.,** to set, shape, the course (on the chart); **suivre une r.,** to steer a course; **suivre la même r.,** to steer the same course; **faire r. sur . . .,** to steer, make, for . . .; to shape one's course for . . .; **faire r. au sud,** to steer south; **revenir en r. au sud,** to steer once more to the south; **se soutenir sur sa r., ne pas dévier de sa r.,** to keep one's course; **dévier de sa r.,** not to keep one's course; to deviate (from one's course); **changer de, la, r.,** to alter (the) course; **hors de sa, de la, r.,** off (one's) course; *Nau:* **r. moyenne, résolution de routes,** traverse sailing; **faire r.,** (i) to go ahead; (ii) to steer the course; **faire r. dans les eaux de . . .,** to steer astern of . . .; **en r., faisant r.,** underway; **navire en r.,** ship on her course, underway; **faire mauvaise r.,** to be on a bad course; **traceur de r.,** course-recording machine; *Av:* **indicateur de r.,** course indicator; **intégrateur de r.,** course computer; **sélecteur de r.,** course selector; *Artil:* **r. de l'objectif,** target course.

router [rute], *v.tr. Post:* to sort and route second class mail.

routier[1], **-ière** [rutje, -jɛːr], *a. & s.* **1.** *a. & s.m. Nau: Av:* **(livre) r.,** track chart, route chart; *Av:* **r. automatique,** moving map. **2.** (*relating to roads*) (*a*) *a.* **carte routière,** road map; **le budget r.,** the road budget; (*b*) *a.* **voie routière,** highway; **réseau r.,** network of roads; **police routière,** traffic police; **pont r.,** road bridge; (*c*) *a. & s.* **routier, (bicyclette) routière,** roadster; **(locomotive) routière,** traction engine, road engine; **transports routiers,** road transport, road haulage; **gare routière,** (i) bus, coach, station; (ii) road haulage depot; (*d*) *s.m.* **gros r.,** heavy (goods) lorry, long-distance lorry, *U.S:* heavy truck; (*e*) *s.m.* long-distance lorry driver, *U.S:* truck driver, teamster; **restaurant des routiers** = transport café; (*f*) *s.m. Cy: Rac:* (*pers.*) road racer; **r.-sprinter,** road-race cyclist noted for his finishing sprint; (*g*) *s.f. Aut:* **routière,** tourer; (*h*) *s.f. P:* **routière,** tart, floozy.

routier[2], *s.m.* (*a*) *Mil: A:* free companion; mercenary; (*b*) *F:* **vieux r.,** old campaigner; old stager; (*c*) *Scouting:* rover.

routin [rutɛ̃], *s.m. Ven:* drive.

routine [rutin], *s.f.* (*a*) routine; **examen de r.,** routine examination; *Av:* **mission de r.,** routine flight; (*b*) routinism; **faire qch. par r.,** (i) to do sth. by rule of thumb, by rote; (ii) to do sth. out of sheer habit; **travail de r.,** routine work; *F:* donkey work; (*c*) red tape; (*d*) (*computers*) routine.

routiner [rutine], *v.tr. A: & Dial:* **r. qn à qch., à faire qch.,** to get s.o. into the routine of sth., of doing sth.

routinier, -ière [rutinje, -jɛːr]. **1.** *a.* (*a*) routine (duties, etc.); (*b*) (person) who follows a routine; routinish; *F:* stuck in a groove. **2.** *s.* slave to routine; **c'est un parfait r.,** he's a regular stick-in-the-mud.

routoir [rutwaːr], *s.m. Tex:* retting pit, retting ground; rettery.

rouverain, rouverin [ruvrɛ̃], *a.m. Metalw:* **fer r.,** hot-short iron; red-short, brittle, iron.

rouvet [ruvɛ], *s.m. Bot:* poet's cassia.

rouvieux [ruvjø], *Vet:* **1.** *s.m.* (horse, dog) mange. **2.** *a.* **cheval, chien, r.,** mangy horse, dog.

rouvraie [ruvrɛ], *s.f.* plantation of (Austrian, Russian) oaks.

rouvre [ruːvr̥], *a. & s.m. Bot:* (**chêne**) **r.,** robur.

rouvrir [ruvriːr], *v.* (*conj. like* OUVRIR) **1.** *v.tr.* to reopen, to open again; **r. une plaie,** (i) to reopen a wound; (ii) to reopen an old sore. **2.** *v.i.* **le théâtre rouvrira le quinze,** the theatre will reopen on the fifteenth.

se rouvrir, (*of door, etc.*) to open again; to reopen; **sa blessure s'est rouverte,** his wound has reopened, has broken out afresh.

roux, rousse[2] [ru, rus]. **1.** (*a*) *a.* (russet-)red, (reddish-)brown; (*of hair*) red, *F:* carroty; **vents r.,** the nipping winds of April; *s.a.* LUNE 1; *inv.* in compounds; **chevaux r. alezan,** red bays; **chevelure blond r.,** sandy hair; (*b*) *s.* red-haired, sandy-haired, person; redhead; *Hist:* **Guillaume le R.,** William Rufus. **2.** *s.m.* (*a*) russet, reddish-brown (colour); (*b*) *Cu:* roux; (*c*) *Bot: F:* Sicilian sumac, tanner's sumac; *s.a.* ROUSSE[1].

rowlandite [rɔlɑ̃dit], *s.f. Miner:* rowlandite.

Roxane [rɔksan], *Pr.n.f.* Roxana.

royadère [rwajadɛːr], *a. & s.m. & f. Geog:* (native, inhabitant) of Royat.

royal, -aux [rwajal, -o]. **1.** *a.* royal; regal, kingly; **la famille royale,** the royal family; **prince r.,** crown prince, heir presumptive (to the throne); *A:* **chemin r.,** national road; *Nau:* **pompe royale,** main pump (of ship); *A:* (**barbe à la**) **royale,** beard, whiskers, trimmed like the reigning king's; **prestance royale,** kingly bearing, regal bearing; *Cards:* **quinte royale,** royal flush. **2.** *s.m. Fung:* royal agaric. **3.** *s.f. Cu:* **royale,** royale.

royalement [rwajalmɑ̃], *adv.* royally, regally; in a kingly manner; *F:* **s'amuser r.,** to enjoy oneself immensely, hugely; **je m'en fiche r.,** I couldn't care less about it.

royalisme [rwajalism], *s.m.* royalism.

royaliste [rwajalist], *a. & s.m. & f.* royalist; **être plus r. que le roi,** to out-Herod Herod.

royalties [rwajaltiːz], *s.f.pl.* royalties ((i) on patent, (ii) on oil or for use of pipeline).

royan [rwajɑ̃], *s.m.* (type of) small sardine.

royannais, -aise [rwajanɛ, -ɛːz], *a. & s. Geog:* (native, inhabitant) of Royan.

royaume [rwajoːm], *s.m.* kingdom, realm; **le r. des cieux,** the kingdom of heaven; **le r. des glaces,** the realm(s) of ice; **je ne le ferais pas pour un r.,** I wouldn't do it for a kingdom.

Royaume-Uni [rwajomyni], *Pr.n.m.* **le R.-U.,** the United Kingdom.

royauté [rwajote], *s.f.* **1.** royalty; kingship; **les insignes de la r.,** the regalia. **2. royautés,** royalties.

royen, -enne [rwajɛ̃, -jɛn], *a. & s. Geog:* (native, inhabitant) of Roye.

royena [rwajena], *s.m. Bot:* African bladder nut.

royer [rwaje], *v.tr.* to crisscross (a field) with irrigation channels.

royes [rwa], *s.f.pl. Fish:* nets forming the leader of a pound net.

ru [ry], *s.m.* channel, watercourse; bed (of brook); gully.

rû [ry], *s.m. Geol:* (*in Jura*) cataclinal, dip-slope, ravine.

ruade [rɥad], *s.f.* lashing out, fling out, buck, kick (of horse); **allonger, décocher, lancer, une r.,** to lash out (**à,** at).

rubace [rybas], *s.f.*, **rubacelle** [rybasɛl], *s.f.* (*a*) red topaz; (*b*) rubicelle, red quartz.

ruban [rybɑ̃], *s.m.* **1.** (*a*) ribbon, band; **attacher ses cheveux avec un r.,** to tie up one's hair with a ribbon; **r. de chapeau,** hatband; **rubans de décorations,** medal ribbons; **le r. rouge,** the red ribbon (of the Legion of Honour); **le r. violet,** the purple ribbon (of the *palmes académiques*); *Nau:* **le r. bleu,** the blue ribbon; **un long r. de route blanche,** a long ribbon of white road; *s.a.* MÖBIUS; (*b*) **r. de fil, de coton,** tape; **mètre à r., en r., r.-mesure,** measuring tape; **r. adhésif, autocollant,** self-adhesive (cellulose) tape; **r. d'arpenteur,** surveyor's tape; **r. magnétique,** magnetic, recording, tape; **r. perforé,** punched (paper) tape, perforated tape; *Bookb:* **coudre sur r.,** to tape (sheets of a book); *Rac:* **les rubans,** the tapes (at starting gate); *Typwr:* **r. encreur,** inking ribbon; *El.E:* **r. isolant,** insulating tape; **fil sous r.,** taped wire; (*c*) *Tex:* top; **r. converti,** converted top; **r. peigné,** combed top. **2.** metal strip; **r. d'acier,** (i) steel band; (ii) steel tape-measure; *El.E: Mec.E:* **r. de contact,** bonding strip; (*a*) *Sm.a:* riband, strip (for the manufacture of gun barrels); (*b*) *Com:* **fer à r.,** hoop-iron; (*c*) *Tls:* **scie à r.,** band-saw, belt-saw; (*d*) **r. d'un frein,** strap of a brake, brake-band. **3. r. roulant, transporteur,** belt conveyor. **4.** *Ich:* red band-fish, red snake-fish. **5.** *Bot: F:* **r. de bergère,** gardener's garters; **r. d'eau,** bur-reed.

rubanage [rybanaːʒ], *s.m. El.E:* taping (of wire).

rubanaire [rybanɛːr], *a.* ribbon-like.

rubané [rybane], *a.* **1.** *Nat.Hist: etc:* ribboned, striped. **2.** *Miner:* banded, taped; **agate rubanée,** ribbon agate, banded agate; **jaspe r.,** ribbon jasper. **3. canon r.,** strip-wound gun barrel. **4.** *Glassm:* **verre à pied r.,** wine glass with an enamel-twist stem.

rubanement [rybanmɑ̃], *s.m. Geol:* **r. concrétionné,** crustified banding.

rubaner [rybane], *v.tr.* **1.** (*a*) to ribbon, to trim (sth.) with ribbon; (*b*) *El.E:* to tape (wire). **2.** to ribbon (sth.); to cut (sth.) into ribbons, into strips.

rubanerie [rybanri], *s.f.* **1.** ribbon manufacture, ribbon trade. **2.** ribbon factory.

rubaneur, -euse[1] [rybanœːr, -øːz], *a. Tex:* ribbon making.

rubaneux, -euse[2] [rybanø, -øːz], *a.* ribbon-like.

rubanier, -ière [rybanje, -jɛːr]. **1.** *a.* pertaining to ribbons; **marchand r.,** dealer in ribbons; ribbon dealer. **2.** *s.* (*a*) ribbon maker; (*b*) ribbon seller; (*c*) *s.m. Bot:* branched bur-reed.

rubasse [rybaːs], *s.f. Miner: Lap:* rubasse, rubicelle, Mont Blanc ruby.

rubato [rubato], *adv. & s.m. Mus:* rubato.

rubéfaction [rybefaksjɔ̃], *s.f. Med: Geol:* rubefaction.

rubéfiant [rybefjɑ̃], *a. & s.m.* rubefacient.

rubéfier [rybefje], *v.tr. Med:* to rubefy.

rubellite [rybɛl(l)it], *s.f. Miner:* rubellite.

Ruben [rybɛn, -bɛ̃], *Pr.n.m. B.Hist:* Reuben.

Rubens [rybɛ̃ːs], *Pr.n.m.* Rubens; *a.inv.* **chapeau Rubens,** Gainsborough hat.

rubéole [rybeɔl], *s.f.* **1.** *Bot:* crosswort, squinancy wort. **2.** *Med:* rubella; German measles.

rubéoleux, -euse [rybeɔlø, -øːz], *a. & s. Med:* **1.** *a.* concerning, related to, German measles. **2.** *s.* German measles patient.

rubéoliforme [rybeɔlifɔrm], *a.* resembling German measles.

rubéolique [rybeɔlik], *a.* = RUBÉOLEUX.

rubéroïde [rybərɔid], *s.m. Const:* rubberoid.

rubérythrique [ryberitrik], *a. Ch:* **acide r.,** ruberythric acid.

rubescent [rybɛs(s)ɑ̃], *a.* rubescent.

rubia [rybja], *s.m. Bot:* rubia, madder.

rubiacé [rybjase]. **1.** *a. Bot:* rubiaceous. **2.** *s.f.pl.* **rubiacées,** Rubiaceae.

rubican [rybikɑ̃], *a.* **cheval r.,** black, bay, chestnut, roan.

rubicelle [rybisɛl], *s.f.* = RUBACE.

rubicole [rybikɔl], *a. Ent:* **abeille r.,** carpenter bee.

Rubicon [rybikɔ̃]. **1.** *Pr.n.m. A.Geog:* the Rubicon; **franchir le R.,** to cross the Rubicon. **2.** *s.m. Cards:* rubicon.

rubicond [rybikɔ̃], *a.* rubicund, florid (complexion).

rubidine [rybidin], *s.f. Ch:* rubidium hydroxide.

rubidium [rybidjɔm], *s.m. Ch:* rubidium.

rubiette [rybjɛt], *s.f. Orn:* **r. de Moussier,** Moussier's redstart.

rubigineux, -euse [rybiʒinø, -øːz], *a.* rubiginous, rusty, rust-coloured.

rubine [rybin], *s.f. Ch: A:* ruby, rubin(e); **r. d'arsenic,** ruby of arsenic.

rubinspath [rybinspat], *s.m. Miner:* rhodonite.

rubis [rybi], *s.m.* **1.** ruby; **r. oriental,** true, oriental, ruby; **r. balais,** balas ruby; **r. spinelle,** spinel ruby; **r. blanc,** leuco-sapphire; **r. de Bohème,** rose quartz; **r. du Brésil,** burnt topaz; **r. de Sibérie,** siberite; **faux r.,** (variety of) fluorite; **r. d'arsenic,** ruby of arsenic, red arsenic; *Glassm:* **verre r.,** ruby glass; **r.** (**d'une montre**), jewel (of a watch); **montée sur r.,** jewelled (watch); *F:* **faire r. sur l'ongle,** to drink to the last drop; **payer r. sur l'ongle,** to pay to the last farthing, *U.S:* to the last cent. **2.** *P: A:* pimple, red blotch (on the nose, etc.). **3.** *Orn:* **r.-émeraude,** ruby; **r.-topaze,** ruby-and-topaz hummingbird; **petit r. de la Caroline,** ruby-throated hummingbird.

rubricaire [rybrikɛːr], *s.m. Ecc:* rubrician.

rubrique [rybrik], *s.f.* **1.** *A:* red chalk, red ochre, ruddle. **2.** (*a*) *Ecc: Jur:* rubric; (*b*) imprint (of book); (*c*) *Journ: etc:* heading; item; **il tient la r. de la mode au Figaro,** he writes the fashions columns in the *Figaro*; **sous la même r. vous lirez . . .,** under the same heading you may read . . .; **vous trouverez cela sous la r. "divers",** you will find it under "miscellaneous"; (*d*) (*computers*) record. **3.** *A:* **savoir toutes sortes de rubriques,** to be up to all sorts of dodges.

rubriquer [rybrike], *v.tr.* **1.** to rubricate (titles on vellum, etc.). **2.** to provide (text, etc.) with rubrics, with headings.

rubriqueur [rybrikœːr], *s.m. Journ:* columnist; **r. aux sports,** sports columnist.

ruby [rybi], **ruby-spaniel** [rybispanjɛl], *s.m. Z:* ruby(-)spaniel; *pl. rubies, ruby-spaniels.*

ruche [ryʃ], *s.f.* **1.** (bee)hive; **r. en paille,** straw hive, bee-skep; **r. démontable,** frame hive; *F:* **r. d'industrie,** regular hive of industry. **2.** *Needlew:* ruche, ruching; *Cost:* ruff. **3.** *Ost:* cultch; *Fish:* fish pot.

ruché [ryʃe], *s.m. Needlew:* ruching; flounce.

ruchée [ryʃe], *s.f.* hiveful.

rucher[1] [ryʃe], *s.m.* apiary.

rucher[2], *v.tr.* **1.** *Needlew:* to ruche; to quill; to make ruches in (material). **2.** *Agr:* **r. le foin,** to make haycocks.

ruck-sack [ryksak], *s.m.* rucksack; *pl. ruck-sacks.*

rudanier [rydanje], *a. A:* uncouth.

rudbeckia [rydbɛkja], **rudbeckie** [rydbɛki], *s.f. Bot:* rudbeckia, cone flower.

rude [ryd], *a.* **1.** (*a*) uncouth, unpolished, primitive (people, manners); untaught (people); (*b*) rough (skin, cloth, wine, etc.); stiff, hard (brush); harsh, grating (voice); **sentier r.,** rough, rugged, path; **mer r.,** rough sea; **barbe r.,** stubby, bristly, beard; *s.a.* ESPRIT 3. **2.** (*a*) hard, arduous, severe; **temps rudes,** hard times; **il a été à r. école,** he had a strict upbringing; **hiver r., r. hiver,** hard, severe, inclement, winter; **froid r.,** bitter cold; **r. épreuve,** severe trial; **r. tâche, tâche r.,** stiff, arduous, task; **r. secousse,** rude shock; **coup r.,** heavy, severe, hard, blow; **r. montée, montée r.,** stiff, steep, climb; (*b*) gruff, ungracious, brusque (voice or manner); **maître r. à, envers, ses domestiques,** master rough, harsh, unkind, to(wards) his servants; hard taskmaster. **3.** *F:* (*intensive*) **r. appétit,** hearty appetite; **r. adversaire,** tough, doughty, formidable, opponent; **faire une r. gaffe,** to put one's foot in it in no uncertain manner.

rudement [rydmɑ̃], *adv.* **1.** (*a*) roughly, harshly, severely; **être r. éprouvé,** to be severely tried; **parler r. à qn,** to speak harshly to s.o.; **travailler r.,** to work hard; (*b*) roughly, coarsely; **frapper r. à la porte,** to knock loudly at the door. **2.** *F:* (*intensive*) **dîner r. bon,** jolly good, damn good, dinner; **je suis r. fatigué,** I'm awfully tired, tired out; **vous avez été r. bête,** you were an awful fool; **vous avez r. bien fait,** you certainly did (the) right (thing).

rudenté [rydɑ̃te], *a. Arch:* cabled (column).

rudenter [rydɑ̃te], *v.tr. Arch:* to cable (a column).

rudenture [rydɑ̃tyːr], *s.f. Arch:* cabling.

rudérale [ryderal], *a.f. Bot:* ruderal (plant); growing in rubbish.

rudération [ryderasjɔ̃], *s.f. Civ.E:* cobble paving.

rudesse [rydɛs], *s.f.* **1.** uncouthness, primitiveness (of savages, etc.). **2.** roughness, ruggedness (of a surface, of style); coarseness (of material); roughness (of wine); harshness (of voice); **rudesses de caractère,** asperities of character. **3.** (*a*) severity (of winter, work, task); (*b*) ungraciousness (of voice or manner); brusqueness, abruptness; bluntness; gruffness (**envers,** towards); **traiter qn avec r.,** to treat s.o. roughly; to browbeat s.o.; to ride roughshod over s.o.

rudiment [rydimɑ̃], *s.m.* **1.** *Biol:* rudiment; **r. de pouce, de queue,** rudiment of a thumb, of a tail. **2.** (*a*) *pl.* rudiments, smattering, (of knowledge); **il possède bien les rudiments de . . .,** he has been well grounded, has a good grounding in . . .; (*b*) *sg. A:* primer (of Latin grammar, etc.).

rudimentaire [rydimɑ̃tɛ:r], *a.* rudimentary (organ, civilization).

rudimentairement [rydimɑ̃tɛrmɑ̃], *adv.* rudimentarily.

rudistes [rydist], *s.m.pl. Paleont:* Rudista.

rudoiement [rydwamɑ̃], *s.m.* browbeating; bullying.

rudoyer [rydwaje], *v.tr.* (**je rudoie, n. rudoyons; je rudoierai**) to treat (s.o.) roughly; (*a*) to browbeat, bully (s.o.); (*b*) to knock (s.o.) about; to give (s.o.) a rough house; **r. un cheval,** (i) to ill-treat a horse; (ii) to be rough with a horse.

rue[1] [ry], *s.f.* **1.** street, thoroughfare; **r. principale,** main thoroughfare; **la grande r.,** the high street, the main street; **petite r. écartée,** back street; **r. à sens unique,** one-way street; **descendre dans la r.,** to come down into the street; **le peuple descendit dans la r.,** the street fighting began; *F:* **être à la r.,** to find oneself out on the street, homeless; **jeter qn à la r.,** to put s.o. out into the street; **il demeure r. de Tournoi,** he lives in the Rue de Tournoi; **histoire vieille comme les rues,** story as old as the hills; **courir les rues,** (i) to run about the streets; (ii) (*of news, etc.*) to be common talk, to be in everyone's mouth; (*of rumour*) to be rife; **les bons domestiques ne courent pas les rues,** good servants are not found every day; *F:* **les rues en sont pavées,** it is as common as dirt, they are as common as blackberries; **l'homme de la r.,** the man in the street; **fille des rues,** prostitute; **le français de la r.,** everyday French. **2.** (*a*) space (in a quarry); (*b*) *pl. Th:* slips. **3.** *Typ:* river (of white down the page).

rue[2], *s.f. Bot:* rue; **r. odorante,** common rue.

rue-des-murailles [rydemyra:j], *s.f. Bot:* wall rue; *pl. rues-des-murailles.*

ruée[1] [rɥe], *s.f.* rush, onrush; *Hist:* **la r. sur Verdun,** the onslaught on Verdun; **la r. sur, vers, les plages de la Côte d'Azur,** the rush for, descent on, the Riviera; **la r. vers l'or,** the gold rush.

ruée[2], *s.f. Agr:* rotting strawstack.

ruelle[1] [rɥɛl], *s.f.* **1.** lane; alley; *Mil:* (small) street (in camp). **2.** (*a*) *A:* space between the bedside and the wall; ruelle; (*b*) *A:* (*time of Louis XIV*) (lady's) "alcove" (for reception); ruelle; *hence* (*c*) *A:* literary clique or coterie.

ruelle[2], *s.f. Tls:* croze.

ruellois, -ois [rɥɛlwa, -wa:z], *a. & s. Geog:* (native, inhabitant) of Rueil.

ruement [rymɑ̃], *s.m. A:* **1.** kicking (of animal); fling-out. **2.** onrush (of crowd, etc.).

ruer [rɥe], *v.i.* (*a*) (*of animal*) to kick, to fling out, to lash out; *Equit:* **r. en vache,** to give a cow-kick; **r. à la botte,** (i) to try to kick the rider's boot; (ii) to be bad-tempered; *s.a.* BRANCARD 1; (*b*) (*of gun carriage*) to jump (on recoil).

se ruer sur qn, sur qch., to hurl, fling, oneself at s.o., at sth.; **se r. à l'attaque,** to throw oneself into the attack; to rush, dash, at s.o., at sth.; **se r. à la fenêtre,** to rush to the window.

rueur, -euse [rɥœ:r, -ø:z]. **1.** *a.* kicking (horse, etc.). **2.** *s.* kicker.

ruffian, rufian [ryfjɑ̃], **rufien** [ryfjɛ̃], *s.m. A:* (i) procurer; (ii) bully, pander, debauchee, ruffian.

Rufin [ryfɛ̃], *Pr.n.m.* Rufinus.

rufi- [ryfi], *comb.fm.* rufi-, reddish brown.

ruficaude [ryfikod], *a.* ruficaudate.

ruficorne [ryfikɔrn], *a.* ruficornate.

rufimorique [ryfimɔrik], *a.* rufimoric.

rugby [rygbi], *s.m.* Rugby (football); **r. à quinze,** Rugby Union; **r. à treize,** Rugby League.

rugbyman, *pl.* **-men** [rygbiman, -mɛn], *s.m.* Rugby player.

rugination [ryʒinasjɔ̃], *s.f. Surg:* scraping (of bone).

rugine [ryʒin], *s.f.* (*a*) *Surg:* xyster; (*b*) *Dent:* scaler.

ruginer [ryʒine], *v.tr. Surg:* to scrape (bone).

rugir [ryʒi:r], *v.i.* to roar; (*of wind*) to howl; **r. des menaces,** to roar out, bellow out, threats.

rugissant [ryʒisɑ̃], *a.* roaring (lion); howling (wind); (*of pers.*) roaring, bellowing.

rugissement [ryʒismɑ̃], *s.m.* **1.** roaring (of lion, etc.); howling (of storm). **2.** roar, bellow.

rugosimètre [rygozimɛtr̥], *s.m. Metall: etc:* surface-finish tester; *Elcs:* roughometer.

rugosité [rygozite], *s.f.* **1.** rugosity, ruggedness, roughness. **2.** wrinkle, corrugation.

rugueux, -euse [rygø, -ø:z]. **1.** *a.* (*a*) rugose; rugged, rough; gnarled (tree, bark); *Phot:* **papier r.,** rough-surface paper; (*b*) wrinkled, corrugated. **2.** *s.m. Artil:* striker, percussion pin (of fuse).

Ruhr (la) [laru:r], *Pr.n.f. Geog:* the Ruhr.

ruilée [rɥile], *s.f. Const:* cement, weather, mortar, fillet.

ruiler [rɥile], *v.tr. Const:* to fillet (with cement, mortar, etc.).

ruine [rɥin], *s.f.* ruin. **1.** (*a*) downfall; decay (of building, etc.); **la r. de Troie,** the fall of Troy; **tomber en ruine(s),** to fall in(to) ruin(s); to tumble to pieces; **rien que quelques maisons qui tombent en ruine(s),** nothing but a few tumble-down houses; **tout tombe en r.,** everything is going to (w)rack and ruin; **vieilles maisons qui menacent r.,** decaying, tumbledown, old houses; *Artil:* **battre un fort en r.,** to batter down a fort; **le bombardement mit la ville en r.,** the bombardment laid the town in ruins; *Bot:* **r. de Rome,** ivy-leaved toad-flax, mother of thousands; (*b*) downfall (of pers., society, etc.); **achever la r. de qn, de qch.,** to bring about the downfall, ruin, of s.o., of sth.; **aller, courir, à la r.,** to be on the road to ruin; **être à deux doigts de la r., à la veille de la r.,** to be on the brink of ruin; **la r. se dressait devant moi,** ruin was staring me in the face; **ce sera sa r.,** it will be the ruin, the ruination, of him; **cela fera sa fortune ou sa r.,** this will either make or break him; **c'est la r.,** it's all up with me; **cette mesure causa la r. des provinces de l'est,** this measure brought ruin upon the eastern provinces; **s'enrichir par la r. d'autrui,** to grow rich through the ruination of others; **le jeu, c'est la r.,** gaming spells ruination. **2.** (*usu. in pl.*) ruins; **les ruines de Troie,** the ruins of Troy; **leur château est une vieille r.,** their castle is an old ruin; *F:* (*of pers.*) **n'être plus qu'une r.,** to be only a ruin, to be but a shadow of one's former self.

ruiner [rɥine], *v.tr.* **1.** to ruin, destroy; to spoil utterly; to blast (reputation); **r. une doctrine,** to disprove a theory; **r. qn,** to bankrupt s.o.; **se r. la santé,** to ruin one's health; **avoir la santé ruinée,** to be broken down in health; **son commerce est ruiné,** his trade is ruined, gone; **ces pertes le ruinèrent,** these losses broke him; **un homme ruiné,** a broken man; **cheval ruiné,** broken-down horse; *F:* **tu vas nous r. en chiffons,** we'll be broke if you go on buying so many clothes. **2.** *Carp:* to groove, notch (post or beam, where it is to bed).

se ruiner. 1. (*of pers.*) to ruin oneself; **se r. à jouer,** to ruin oneself gambling. **2.** (*of thg*) to fall into ruins; to crumble to pieces.

ruineusement [rɥinøzmɑ̃], *adv.* ruinously.

ruineux, -euse [rɥinø, -ø:z], *a.* ruinous. **1.** *A:* falling into ruin; crumbling, tottering (wall); dilapidated (building). **2.** (*a*) disastrous (war, etc.); (*b*) expensive, ruinous; **ce n'est pas r.,** it won't ruin us, break us (to buy it).

ruiniforme [rɥinifɔrm], *s. Geol:* ruiniform.

ruiniste [rɥinist], *s.m.pl. Art:* painter of ruins.

ruinure [rɥiny:r], *s.f. Carp:* groove, notch, housing (of a post or beam).

ruisseau, -eaux [rɥiso], *s.m.* **1.** (*a*) brook, (small) stream, streamlet, rivulet; *Prov:* **les petits ruisseaux font les grandes rivières,** little streams make great rivers; many a little makes a mickle; many a mickle makes a muckle; (*b*) stream (of blood, etc.); *Lit:* **verser des ruisseaux de sang,** to shed rivers of blood. **2.** (street) gutter, runnel, kennel; *F:* **calomnie ramassée dans le r.,** slander picked up in the gutter; **laisser ses parents dans le r.,** to leave one's relatives in the gutter, in abject poverty.

ruisselant [rɥislɑ̃], *a.* (*a*) streaming; dripping (wet); **parquet r.,** floor streaming, running, with water; **une soirée ruisselante,** a pouring wet evening; **visage r. de larmes, de sang,** face streaming with tears, with blood; **front r. de sueur,** forehead dripping with perspiration; **eaux ruisselantes,** (i) running waters; (ii) trickling water; (*b*) *F:* flashy.

ruisseler [rɥisle], *v.i.* (**il ruisselle; il ruissellera**) **1.** (*of liquid*) (*a*) to stream (down), run (down); **l'eau ruisselait par la porte,** the water was streaming in (or out) at the door; (*b*) to trickle; **l'eau ruisselle à travers la roche,** the water trickles through the rock. **2.** (*of surface*) to run, to drip, to trickle; **le parquet ruisselait,** the floor was running with water; **son visage ruisselait de sueur,** his face was streaming, running, with sweat; *with cogn.acc.* **ses vêtements ruisselaient la pluie,** his clothes were dripping with rain; **livre qui ruisselle d'esprit,** book brimming over with wit.

ruisselet [rɥislɛ], *s.m.* brooklet, streamlet, rivulet, rill.

ruisselis [rɥisli], *s.m. Lit:* trickle, trickling; tinkle (of a fountain).

ruissellement [rɥisɛlmɑ̃], *s.m.* **1.** (*a*) streaming, running (of water, etc.); *Hyd.E: Geog:* runoff; *Geol:* **terre de r.,** alluvium; **r. diffus, (transport par) r.,** rainwash; (*b*) trickling, dripping. **2. r. de pierreries,** play of light on jewellery; shimmer of jewellery.

ruisson [rɥisɔ̃], *s.m.* small drainage channel (in marshy land).

rumb [rɔ̃:b], *s.m. Nau:* r(h)umb; **ligne de r.,** rhumb line.

rumba [rumba], *s.f. Danc:* rumba.

rumen [rymɛn], *s.m. no pl. Z:* rumen; paunch (of ruminant).

rumeur [rymœ:r], *s.f.* **1.** (*a*) confused or distant murmur; hum (of traffic, etc.); (*b*) din, clamour, uproar; **tout est en r.,** everything is in an uproar. **2.** rumour; **de vagues rumeurs de défaite,** vague rumours of defeat; **la r. court que . . .,** it is rumoured that . . ., rumour has it that . . ..

rumex [rymɛks], *s.m. Bot:* rumex.

rumilien, -ienne [rymiljɛ̃, -jɛn], *a. & s. Geog:* (native, inhabitant) of Rumilly.

ruminant [ryminɑ̃], *a. & s.m. Z:* ruminant; *F:* **mener une vie de r.,** to lead a cabbage-like existence; *pl.* **les ruminants,** the Ruminantia.

rumination [ryminasjɔ̃], *s.f.* rumination, ruminating; pondering.

ruminé [rymine], *a. Bot:* ruminate.

ruminement [ryminmɑ̃], *s.m.* rumination, pondering.

ruminer [rymine], *v.tr.* **1.** *abs.* (*of animal*) to ruminate; to chew the cud. **2.** (*of pers.*) **r. une idée,** to ruminate about, on, over, an idea; to ponder an idea, on an idea; to chew over an idea; to turn an idea over in one's mind.

rumsteck [rɔmstɛk], *s.m.* rump steak.

runabout [rynabu], *s.m. Nau:* runabout; speed-boat.

rune [ryn], *s.f.* rune.

runiforme [rynifɔrm], *a.* runiform.

runique [rynik], *a.* runic (letters, verse).

runologue [rynɔlɔg], *s.m. & f.* runologist.

runway [rœnwei], *s.f. Mil.Av:* taxi track, taxi strip, taxiway.

ruolz [rɥɔls, ryɔls], *s.m.* electroplated ware.

rupélien [rypeljɛ̃], *a. & s.m. Geol:* Rupelian.

rupelle [rypɛl], *s.f. Bot:* ruppia.

Rupert [rypɛ:r], *Pr.n.m.* Rupert.

rupestre [rypɛstr̥], *a.* (*a*) *Bot:* rupestral, rupestrine, rupicolous; (*b*) **dessins rupestres,** rock drawings; **art r.,** cave art; **peintures rupestres,** cave paintings.

rupia [rypja], *s.m. Med:* rupia.

rupicole [rypikɔl]. **1.** *a. Bot:* rupicolous. **2.** *s.m. Orn:* cock-of-the-rock.

rupin, -ine [rypɛ̃, -in], *a. P:* (*a*) fine, first-rate; (*b*) (*of pers.*) wealthy, rolling in it; *s.* **les rupins,** the rich.

rupiner [rypine], *v.i. P:* to do well (in an examination); *P:* **ça rupine,** everything's O.K.; *Sch: P:* **il a rupiné,** he's done a good paper, given a good answer.

ruppia [rypja], *s.m.,* **ruppie** [rypi], *s.f. Bot:* ruppia; **ruppie (maritime),** sea grass.

rupteur [ryptœ:r], *s.m. El: I.C.E:* interrupter, contact breaker, circuit breaker; **r. distributeur,** make-and-break.

rupture [rypty:r], *s.f.* breaking, rupture; (*a*) breaking down (of beam, etc.); bursting (of dam, etc.); **r. de canalisation,** pipe breakage; *Mec:* **point de r.,** breaking-down point; **charge de r., tension de r.,** breaking load or stress; (*b*) breaking (in two); rupture (of blood vessel, of ligament, etc.); fracture (of bone); parting (of hawser); *Mec.E:* **r. d'un arbre,** breakage of a shaft; (*c*) breaking-up; **r. d'une route par un torrent,** cutting up, destruction, of a road by a torrent; *Artil:* **obus de r.,** armour-piercing shell; **r. de l'équilibre,** upsetting of the equilibrium; (*d*) breaking off, breach, discontinuance; **r. de combat,** breaking off of a battle; **r. des négociations,** breaking off, rupture, of negotiations; **r. du marché,** calling off of the deal; **r. de fiançailles,** breaking off of an engagement; **r. de contrat, de promesse de mariage,** breach of contract, of promise of marriage; **état en r. de pacte,** covenant-breaking state; *Com:* **magasin en r. de stock,** shop that is out of stock; **r. d'amitié,** breach of friendship; **il y a eu r. entre eux,** they've quarrelled; there's been a split between them; *s.a.* BAN 2; *El:* **r. du courant, du circuit,** breaking of the current, of the circuit; break in the circuit; **dispositif, levier, de**

r., contact-breaker, make-and-break; **étincelle de r.,** break spark; (*e*) **r. de pente,** change of slope; (*f*) **r. de charge,** (i) *Rail:* dividing of load; (ii) *Trans:* trans-shipment (of cargo); (*g*) (*computers*) change.

rural, -aux [ryral, -o]. **1.** *a.* rural; **vie rurale,** country life; **chemin r.,** country lane; **facteur r.,** country postman. **2.** *s.m.* (*a*) **un r.,** a rustic; a countryman; **les ruraux,** country dwellers, country people; (*b*) **le r.** (*short for* **le facteur rural**), the country postman.

ruralement [ryralmɑ̃], *adv.* rurally.

ruralisme [ryralism], *s.m.* the art of rural living, of living in the country.

ruralité [ryralite], *s.f.* rurality, ruralism.

rusa [ryza], *s.m. Z:* rusa; sambur.

ruse [ryːz], *s.f.* (*a*) ruse, trick, wile, dodge; **r. de guerre,** stratagem (of war); **obtenir qch. par r.,** to obtain sth. by trickery, by guile, by cunning; **user de r. dans une négociation,** to show wiliness in a negotiation; *Prov:* **en amour la r. est de bonne guerre,** all is fair in love and war; (*b*) *Ven:* double, doubling (of the quarry).

rusé [ryze], *a. & s.* artful, crafty, sly, sharp, astute, wily, deep; **il est r. comme un vieux renard,** he's as sly as an old fox; **un air r., une mine rusée,** a sly, cunning, expression; **un tour r.,** a crafty trick; **ce r. d'avocat,** that wily lawyer; *s.* **c'est une petite rusée,** she's a sly, cunning, little thing.

ruser [ryze], *v.i.* (*a*) to use craft, trickery; **r. avec qn,** to try to diddle s.o.; (*b*) *Ven:* (*of fox, etc.*) to double.

ruseur [ryzœːr], *s.m.* trickster, deceiver.

rush [rœʃ], *s.m.* (*a*) *Sp:* sprint, spurt (at end of race); (*b*) *F:* rush; (*c*) *pl. Cin:* **rushes,** rushes.

russe [rys], *a. & s.* Russian; **R. Blanc,** White Russian; **Petit Russe,** Little Russian; Ruthenian, Russniak; *s.a.* CHAUSSETTE; *Z:* **lévrier r.,** Russian wolfhound.

Russie [rysi], *Pr.n.f. Geog:* Russia; **R. Blanche,** White Russia; *Hist:* **la retraite de R.,** the retreat from Moscow; *s.a.* CUIR 2, PIN.

russification [rysifikasjɔ̃], *s.f.* Russianization, Russification.

russifier [rysifje], *v.tr.* (*pr.sub. & p.d.* n. **russifiions,** v. **russifiiez**) to Russify, Russianize.

russo- [ryso], *pref.* Russo-.

russophile [rysɔfil], *a. & s.m. & f.* Russophile.

russophobe [rysɔfɔb], *a. & s.m. & f.* Russophobe.

russule [rysyl], *s.f. Fung:* russula; **r. cyanoxante, charbonnière,** blue and yellow russula; **r. amère,** geranium-scented russula; **r. verdoyante,** greenish russula.

rustaud, -aude [rysto, -oːd]. **1.** *a.* boorish, uncouth (appearance, person). **2.** *s.* boor; bumpkin, *U.S:* hick; **un gros r.,** a great lout (of a fellow); **une grosse rustaude,** a hefty country girl.

rustauderie [rystodri], *s.f.* boorishness, uncouthness.

ruste [ryst], *s.f. Her:* rustre, voided lozenges.

rusticage [rystikaːʒ], *s.m. Const:* light mortar (used to roughcast a wall).

rusticité [rystisite], *s.f.* **1.** rusticity; (*a*) rural character (of neighbourhood, etc.); (*b*) uncouthness, boorishness. **2.** (*a*) primitiveness, simplicity (of machine, etc.); (*b*) hardiness (of plant).

Rustine [rystin], *s.f. R.t.m:* rubber (puncture) patch.

rustique [rystik], *a.* (*a*) rustic; **danse r.,** country dance; **mœurs rustiques,** (i) rustic, country, manners; (ii) unpolished manners; **accent r.,** broad accent, speech; (*b*) *Const:* **ouvrage r.,** rustic work; (**marteau r.,** (mason's) bush hammer; (*c*) *Th:* rustic (scenery); (*d*) hardy (plant).

rustiquement [rystikmɑ̃], *adv.* rustically.

rustiquer [rystike], *v.tr. Arch:* to rusticate, give a rustic appearance to (stonework, building).

rustre [rystr̩]. **1.** *a.* boorish, loutish. **2.** *s.m.* boor, lout; bumpkin, clodhopper. **3.** *s.f. Her:* = RUSTE.

rustré [rystre], *a. Her:* rustred.

rustrerie [rystrəri], *s.f.* boorishness, loutishness.

rusturer [rystyre], *v.tr. Nau:* to woold (yard, etc.).

rut [ryt], *s.m.* (*of animals*) rut(ting); **saison du r.,** rutting season; **être en r.,** (*of male*) to rut; (*of female*) to be on heat.

rutabaga [rytabaga], *s.m.* Swedish turnip, swede.

rutacé [rytase], *Bot:* **1.** *a.* rutaceous. **2.** *s.f.pl.* **rutacées,** Rutaceae.

Ruth [ryt], *Pr.n.f.* Ruth.

Ruthène [ryten], *a. & s.m. & f. Hist:* Ruthenian, Ruthene, Russniak; Little Russian.

Ruthénie [ryteni], *Pr.n.f. Hist:* Ruthenia.

ruthénique [rytenik], *a. Ch:* ruthenic.

ruthénium [rytenjɔm], *s.m. Ch:* ruthenium.

ruthénois, -oise [rytenwa, -waːz], *a. & s. Geog:* (native, inhabitant) of Rodez.

rutherford [ryθərfɔrd], *s.m. Atom.Ph:* rutherford.

rutherfordite [ryθərfɔrdit], *s.f. Miner:* rutherfordite, rutherfordine.

rutilance [rytilɑ̃ːs], *s.f.* glow(ing) (of colour).

rutilant [rytilɑ̃], *a.* (*a*) glowing red, rutilant, gleaming (in the red of the sun); **uniforme r. de décorations,** uniform glittering with decorations; (*b*) *Ch:* (*of fumes*) rutilant.

rutilation [rytilasjɔ̃], *s.f.* glow(ing).

rutile [rytil], *s.m. Miner:* rutile.

rutilement [rytilmɑ̃], *s.m.* glow(ing), gleam(ing).

rutiler [rytile], *v.i.* to glow; to gleam red; **tout l'horizon rutilait,** along the west (or east) lay a flush of crimson, of gold; the whole horizon was aflame.

rutilisme [rytilism], *s.m. Physiol:* rutilism.

rutine [rytin], *s.f.,* **rutinoside** [rytinɔzid], *s.m.,* **rutoside** [rytɔzid], *s.m. Bio-Ch:* rutin.

ruz [ry], *s.m. Geol:* (*in Jura*) cataclinal, dip-slope, ravine.

rynchée [rɛ̃ʃe, -ke], *s.f. Orn:* painted snipe.

ryot [rjo], *s.m.* ryot; Indian peasant.

rythme [ritm], *s.m.* (*a*) *Pros: Mus: etc:* rhythm; **le cortège avançait au r. de deux tambours,** the procession moved forwards to the rhythm, beat, of two drums; (*b*) **r. respiratoire,** rate of respiration; **r. cardiaque,** rate of heart beat; (*c*) rhythm; tempo; **le r. de la vie moderne,** the tempo of modern life; *Com:* **r. des livraisons,** delivery rate; **pannes qui interrompent le r. de la production,** breakdowns that upset the tempo of production; *I.C.E:* **r. d'allumage,** order of firing (of cylinders).

rythmé [ritme], *a.* rhythmed; rhythmic(al).

rythmer [ritme], *v.tr.* to put rhythm into (a motion).

rythmeur [ritmœːr], *s.m. Elcs:* (*computers*) interval timer.

rythmicien [ritmisjɛ̃], *s.m.* rhythmologist.

rythmique [ritmik]. **1.** *a.* rhythmic(al); *Ling:* **groupe r.,** rhythmic group. **2.** *s.f.* rhythmics.

S

S, s [ɛs], s.m. & f. (the letter) S, s; Tp: S comme
Suzanne, S for Sammy; F: faire des s., to zig-
zag; sentier en s., winding path; Const: etc: fer
en S, S-shaped wall-anchor; s de suspension,
S(-shaped) hook; s . . ., usual abbreviation for
SACRÉ 3.

Saba [saba], Pr.n. Geog: Sheba; la reine de S., the
Queen of Sheba.

Sabaoth [sabaɔt], Pr.n.m. B.Hist: Sabaoth;
Jéhovah S., the Lord of Sabaoth.

sabaye [sabɛ:j], s.f. Nau: (a) mooring rope; (b)
towline.

sabayon [sabajɔ̃], s.m. Cu: zabaglione.

sabbat [saba], s.m. 1. (Jewish) Sabbath; jour du
s., Sabbath day; observer, violer, le s., to keep,
break, the Sabbath; violation du s., Sabbath
breaking; chemin du s., Sabbath day's journey.
2. (witches') midnight revels; (witches') sabbath;
F: faire un s. de tous les diables, to make a
frightful row, a terrible racket; s. de chats,
caterwauling; c'est le s. déchaîné, it's hell let
loose.

sabbataire [sabatɛ:r], s.m. Rel.H: Sabbatarian.

sabbatia [sabasja], s.m. Bot: Sabbatia.

sabbatine [sabatin], a.f. Rel.H: Sabbatine
(bull).

sabbatique [sabatik], a. sabbatic(al) (year, etc.);
le repos s., the rest of the Sabbath.

sabbatiser [sabatize], v.i. A: to keep the Sabbath;
to sabbatize.

sabbatisme [sabatism], s.m. keeping of the
Sabbath; sabbatarianism.

sabéen, -enne [sabeɛ̃, -ɛn], a. & s. A.Geog:
Sab(a)ean.

sabéisme [sabeism], s.m. Rel.H: Sabaism.

sabellaria [sabɛlaria], s.m. Ann: sabellaria.

sabellariens [sabɛlarjɛ̃], s.m.pl. Ann: Sabellariidae.

sabelle [sabɛl], s.f. Ann: Sabella.

sabellien, -ienne [sabɛljɛ̃, -jɛn], a. & s. 1. Rom.
Hist: Ling: Sabellian. 2. Rel.H: follower of
Sabellius; Sabellian.

sabellidés [sabɛlje], s.m.pl. Ann: Sabellidae.

sabellique [sabɛl(l)ik], a. Rom.Hist: Sabellian.

sabia [sabja], s.m. Bot: sabia.

sabicu [sabiky], s.m. sabicu (wood).

sabin, -ine¹ [sabɛ̃, -in], a. & s. A.Hist: Sabine;
l'enlèvement des Sabines, the rape of the Sabines,
of the Sabine women.

Sabine², Pr.n.f. Sabina.

sabine³, s.f. Bot: savin(e).

sabir [sabi:r], s.m. Ling: lingua franca; sabir;
pidgin.

sablage [sabla:ʒ], s.m. 1. Ind: sand blasting (of
casting). 2. spreading of sand, grit (on icy
roads); sanding (of a path).

sablais, -aise [sablɛ, -ɛ:z], a. & s. Geog: (native,
inhabitant) of les Sables-d'Olonne.

sable¹ [sɑ:bl], s.m. 1. sand; s. bitumineux, bituminous sand; sables mouvants, boulants, A:
flottants, quicksands; répandre du s. sur le
plancher, to sand the floor; Const: s. liant, s.
mordant, sharp sand; s. gras, loamy sand;
Metall: s. vert, s. humide, glauconieux, green
sand; s. sec, s. à saupoudrer, parting sand; s. de
moulage, fire sand, moulding sand; Civ.E:
couche de s., blinding (of road); Nau: fond de s.,
sandy bottom; Mil: boîte à s., sand table; Ch:
Med: bain de s., sand bath; F: être (mis) sur le s.,
to be left high and dry; F: être sur le s., to be
broke; to be down and out; avoir du s. dans les
yeux, to be sleepy; le marchand de s. est passé,

the sandman has gone by; bâtir sur le s., to build
on sand; horloge à, de, s., sand glass, hour glass;
s.a. CHAUX, JET 2. 2. Med: gravel; urinary sand;
arena. 3. s. de fer, fine iron filings.

sable², s.m. 1. A: (a) Z: sable; (b) sable (fur). 2.
Her: sable, black.

sablé [sɑble]. 1. a. (a) sanded, gravelled (path,
etc.); verre s. d'or, glass flecked with gold; (b)
moulded, cast, in sand; (c) fontaine sablée,
sand filter. 2. s.m. Cu: (sort of) shortbread.

sabler [sɑble], v.tr. 1. to sand, gravel (path, etc.);
to spread sand, grit (on icy roads). 2. (a) to
cast (medal, etc.) in a sand mould; (b) F: A: to
swig, knock back (wine, etc.); s. le champagne,
to celebrate in, with, champagne. 3. to sand-
blast (casting). 4. F: A: to sandbag (s.o.).

sablésien, -ienne [sɑblezjɛ̃, -jɛn], a. & s. (native,
inhabitant) of Sablé.

sableur, -euse¹ [sɑblœ:r, -ø:z], s. 1. maker of sand
moulds, sand moulder. 2. F: A: hard drinker.
3. s.f. sableuse, sand blast, jet; sand-blasting
machine; sand spreader.

sableux, -euse² [sɑblø, -ø:z], a. sandy (ground,
salt, etc.).

sablier¹ [sɑblje], s.m. 1. sandman, sand dealer.
2. (a) A: sand box (holding fine sand for drying
ink); (b) Bot: sand-box tree. 3. sand glass, hour
glass; Cu: egg timer.

sablier², s.m. = SABLIÈRE² 1.

sablière¹ [sɑbljɛ:r], s.f. 1. sand pit, gravel pit.
2. (a) sand sprayer; (b) sand box (of a locomotive).

sablière², s.f. 1. (lengthwise) beam, stringer,
templet; esp. Const: s. de comble, wall plate (of
roof truss); s. basse, ground plate, (ground) sill
(of frame); s. haute, head plate (of frame); a.
panne s., eaves purlin. 2. Nau: s. de lancement,
sliding way.

sabline [sɑblin], s.f. Bot: sandwort; s. péploïde,
sea purslane.

sablon [sɑblɔ̃], s.m. 1. fine sand; scouring sand;
welding sand. 2. A: sandhill.

sablonner [sɑblɔne], v.tr. 1. to scour with sand;
to sand. 2. Metall: to sprinkle (iron) with
welding sand.

sablonneux, -euse [sɑblɔnø, -ø:z], a. sandy (shore,
plain); gravelly (path); gritty (fruit).

sablonnier [sɑblɔnje], s.m. dealer in fine sand;
sandman.

sablonnière [sɑblɔnjɛ:r], s.f. 1. sand pit, gravel
pit. 2. Metall: sand box.

sabolien, -ienne [sɑbɔljɛ̃, -jɛn], a. & s. Geog:
(native, inhabitant) of Sablé-sur-Sarthe.

sabord [sabɔ:r], s.m. Nau: port(hole); s. d'aération,
air port; s. d'évacuation, freeing port; s. à
charbon, coaling port; s. de charge, cargo door;
s. de batterie, gun port, embrasure; s. de lancement, port (of torpedo tube); faux s., deadlight;
P: mille sabords! shiver my timbers! P: les
sabords, the peepers.

sabordage [sabɔrda:ʒ], s.m., sabordement [sabɔr-
dəmɑ̃], s.m. Nau: scuttling.

saborder [sabɔrde], v.tr. 1. Nau: to scuttle (ship,
plan, etc.). 2. to ruin, destroy.

se saborder. Nau: to scuttle one's ship; Adm:
etc: to wind up; plusieurs journaux se sont
sabordés sous l'occupation, several newspapers
wound up their affairs under the occupation.

sabot [sabo], s.m. 1. (a) wooden shoe, clog,
sabot; F: il est venu à Londres en sabots, he
came to London with only a few pence in his

pocket; je vous entends, vois, venir avec vos
gros sabots, it's easy to see what your little
game is; I can see what you're after; on dit
qu'ils mêlent leurs sabots, people say they are
living together; (baignoire) s., slipper bath; (b)
P: any bad, worn out, or antiquated article; dud
violin; old tub (of a ship); ramshackle old
(motor) car; (c) F: A: bungler; (d) F: jouer,
chanter, comme un s., to play, sing, very badly;
F: travailler comme un s., to botch things up;
(e) (at baccarat) slipper, sabot. 2. hoof (of
horse, etc.). 3. Tchn: shoe, sabot (of pile, lance,
etc.); ferrule (of picket, etc.); caster socket (of
furniture); saddle (of vertical girder); Artil:
sabot (of projectile); Agr: s. séparateur (de
moissonneuse), track clearer; Sm.a: s. anti-recul,
anti-recoil shoe; s. d'enrayage, drag, skid, shoe,
U.S: trig (of wheel); s. d'arrêt, scotch; s. de
frein, brake block, brake shoe; s. de pompe,
pump piston, bucket; Trans: s. de prise de
courant, plough collector (of tram); contact
shoe; Rail: s. de remise, re-railing ramp; Aut:
s. (de pare-chocs), overrider; El.E: s. de balai,
brush clamp. 4. whip(ping) top; s.a. DORMIR 1.
5. Bot: s. de Vénus, lady's slipper. 6. Conch:
turban shell. 7. Tls: curved plane.

sabotage [sabota:ʒ], s.m. 1. sabot making. 2.
Rail: chairing (of sleepers). 3. F: (a) scamping,
botching, bungling (of work); (b) scamped,
botched, piece of work. 4. (a) sabotage,
malicious destruction (of machinery, tools,
etc.); Typ: intentional garbling (of copy); (b) act
of sabotage.

sabot-cale [sabokal], s.m. Rail: (brake) skid; pl.
sabots-cales.

saboter [sabɔte]. 1. v.i. (a) to clatter (with one's
sabots); (b) to whip a top; (c) F: to botch one's
work. 2. v.tr. (a) Tchn: to shoe (a pile, etc.); (b)
Rail: to chair (sleeper); (c) F: to botch, bungle,
scamp (a piece of work); to make a bad job of
(sth.); to murder (song, recitation, etc.); to do
(work) all anyhow; (d) to do wilful damage to
(machinery, etc.), to sabotage (a job); Typ: to
garble (copy, with malicious intent).

saboterie [sabɔtri], s.f. sabot factory.

saboteur, -euse [sabɔtœ:r, -ø:z], s.m. F: 1.
bungler, botcher. 2. saboteur.

sabotier [sabɔtje], s.m. maker of sabots.

sabotière [sabɔtjɛ:r], s.f. 1. sabot-maker's workshop. 2. dance in sabots; clog dance. 3. slipper
bath.

saboulade [sabulad], s.f., saboulage [sabula:ʒ],
s.m., saboulement [sabulmɑ̃], s.m. F: A: 1.
pulling-about, jostling, jostle. 2. dressing down,
scolding, ticking-off.

sabouler [sabule], v.tr. F: A: 1. to jostle; to pull
(s.o.) about. 2. to jump on (s.o.); to haul (s.o.)
over the coals; to give (s.o.) a ticking-off. 3.
A: = SABOTER 2 (c).

sabre [sɑ:br], s.m. 1. (a) sabre, (cutting) sword,
broadsword; en s., sabre-like; traîner, faire
sonner, son s., to rattle one's sabre; Navy: A: s.
d'abordage, cutlass; hussard à s., sabred hussar;
coup de s., sabre cut, sabre wound; slash (from
a sword); coup de plat de s., blow with the flat
of the sword; s. au clair, (i) drawn sword; (ii)
with drawn swords; Mil: s. à la main! draw
swords! s. de bois, (i) (Harlequin's) lath; (ii) (as
a mild oath) hell! s.a. GOUPILLON 1, TIRER I. 4,
TRAÎNEUR 1; (b) V: penis. 2. Ich: swordfish.
3. Glassm: sabre.

S:1

sabre-baïonnette [sɑbrəbajɔnɛt], *s.f.* sword-bayonet, sabre-bayonet; *pl. sabres-baïonnettes.*

sabre-briquet [sɑbrəbrikɛ], *s.m. A:* short sword; *pl. sabres-briquets.*

sabrement [sɑbrəmɑ̃], *s.m.* cutting down (with the sword); sabring.

sabrer [sɑbre], *v.tr.* **1.** (*a*) to sabre; to cut down (s.o.) with the sword; to slash; (*b*) *F:* to make drastic cuts in (a MS., a play); (*c*) *F:* to criticize (s.o.), to run (s.o.) down; (*d*) *P:* **s. une fille,** to sleep with a girl. **2.** *F:* to botch, scamp (a piece of work).

sabretache [sɑbrətaʃ], *s.f. A.Mil:* sabretache.

sabreur [sɑbrœːr], *s.m.* **1.** swordsman; dashing cavalry officer (but no strategist). **2.** *F:* **s. de besogne,** slapdash worker.

sabrure [sɑbryːr], *s.f.* slash.

saburral, -aux [sabyral, -o], *a. Med:* saburral; **langue saburrale,** coated tongue.

saburre [sabyːr], *s.f. A.Med:* saburra.

sac[1] [sak], *s.m.* **1.** (*a*) sack, bag, pouch; **s. de, en, papier,** paper bag; **s. à blé,** corn sack; **s. de blé,** sack of wheat, corn; **s. à main,** handbag, *U.S:* purse; **s., à, en, bandoulière,** shoulder bag; **(petit) s. de soirée,** vanity bag; *A:* **s.-jumelle,** Gladstone bag; *A:* **s. de toilette,** dressing case; **s. à ouvrage,** workbag; **s. à outils,** tool bag, wallet; **s. à blanchissage, à linge,** washbag, laundry bag; **s. de voyage, de nuit,** travel bag, overnight bag; **s. d'alpiniste, de campeur, de camping,** knapsack, rucksack; **s. tyrolien, de montagne, à dos,** rucksack; **s. alpin (de boy-scout),** knapsack; **sacs d'écus,** money bags; **course en sacs,** sack race; **mettre qch. en s.,** to sack, bag, sth.; **mise en s.,** sacking, bagging; *Com:* **s. filet,** mesh bag; **charbon en sacs,** coal in bags; *Mil:* **s. de fantassin, de soldat,** (soldier's) pack, knapsack; **s. de grande monture, s. de paquetage,** kitbag; **s. au dos!** put on packs! **s. à terre!** packs off! **s. à munitions,** cartridge pouch; **s. de couchage,** *F:* **s. à viande,** sleeping bag; **s. à terre,** sandbag; *Nau:* **s. (de) marin,** sea bag, kitbag, *F:* dunnage; *F:* **s. d'os,** bag of bones; *F:* **donner à qn le s.,** to sack s.o., to give s.o. the sack; *F:* **un s. (de nœuds),** a muddle; *Box: F:* **travailler le sac,** to practise with the punchball; **s. à fourrages,** nosebag; **s. à poussières,** dustbag (for vacuum cleaner, etc.); **s. de sauvetage,** canvas chute (for escaping from a fire); *Adm:* **s. de dépêches, s. postal,** mailbag, postbag; **par sacs postaux,** per bulk post; *Med:* **s. à glace,** icebag; *F:* **s. percé,** spendthrift; **s. à vin,** toper, boozer; *P:* **il en a plein son s.,** he's got a skinful, he's tight; **homme de s. et de corde,** out-and-out scoundrel, gallowsbird; *P:* **avoir le s., être au s.,** to be rich, to have a well-lined purse; **ils ont le s., il y a le s.,** they've got pots of money; **faire, gagner, son s.,** to make one's pile; **épouser le (gros) s.,** to marry money; *F:* **prendre qn la main dans le s.,** to catch s.o. in the (very) act (of stealing); to catch s.o. red-handed; **vider son s.,** (i) to clear one's bowels; (ii) to get it off one's chest; to come clean; **ils sont tous à mettre dans le même s.,** they're all tarred with the same brush; **voir le fond du s.,** to get to the bottom of sth.; *P:* **remplir son s.,** to fill one's belly; *F:* **mettez ça dans votre s.,** put that in your pipe and smoke it! *F:* **l'affaire est dans le s.,** it's in the bag, it's as good as settled; (*of sail, etc.*) **faire s.,** to bag, to belly; *int. A:* **s. à papier! veux-tu te taire!** hang it all! damn it! will you shut up! *s.a.* MALICE 2, QUILLE[1] 1; (*b*) *F:* a thousand francs; (*c*) (i) *Anat:* sac; (ii) *Bot:* **s. embryonnaire,** embryo sac; (*d*) pouch (of kangaroo, etc.); (*e*) *Fish:* poke-net; (*f*) *Av:* **s. à vent,** wind cone; (*g*) **s. de minerai,** pocket of ore. **2.** sackcloth; **sous le s. et la cendre,** in sackcloth and ashes.

sac[2], *s.m.* sacking, pillage; **mettre à s. une ville,** to sack a town; to pillage, plunder, a town; **faire le s. d'une maison,** to ransack a house.

saccade [sakad], *s.f.* **1.** jerk, start, shake, jolt; violent pull; *Mec.E:* backlash; **s. de bride,** sharp jerk of the bridle; **arracher une dent d'une s.,** to jerk out a tooth; *F:* to yank out a tooth; **par saccades,** in jerks; by fits and starts. **2.** *F: A:* sharp rebuke, reprimand.

saccadé [sakade], *a.* jerky, abrupt (movement, style); **marcher d'un pas s.,** to walk with a jerky stride; **d'une voix saccadée,** in a jerky, staccato, voice; **style s.,** jerky style; **respiration saccadée,** irregular breathing; gasping breath; gasping; **courbe saccadée,** curve showing jumps, violent fluctuations.

saccader [sakade], *v.tr.* to jerk (a horse's rein).

saccage [sakaːʒ], *s.m.* (*a*) havoc; (*b*) confusion, upset.

saccagement [sakaʒmɑ̃], *s.m. O:* sacking, pillaging (of a town).

saccager [sakaʒe], *v.tr.* **(je saccageai(s); n. saccageons)** (*a*) to sack, pillage (town); to ransack (house, etc.); (*b*) to throw (contents of a room, etc.) into disorder, into confusion.

saccageur, -euse [sakaʒœːr, -øːz], *s.* pillager, plunderer; ransacker.

saccharase [sakaraːz], *s.f. Physiol:* saccharase, invertase.

saccharate [sakarat], *s.m. Ch:* saccharate.

saccharide [sakarid], *s.m. Ch:* saccharide.

saccharifère [sakarifɛːr], *a.* sacchariferous; containing sugar.

saccharifiable [sakarifjabl̩], *a. Ch:* saccharifiable.

saccharifiant [sakarifjɑ̃], *a.* saccharifying.

saccharification [sakarifikasjɔ̃], *s.f.* saccharification.

saccharifier [sakarifje], *v.tr.* (*pr.sub. & p.d.* **n. saccharifiions, v. saccharifiiez**) *Ch:* to saccharify.

saccharimètre [sakarimɛtr̩], *s.m.* **1.** *Ch:* saccharimeter. **2.** *Brew:* saccharometer.

saccharimétrie [sakarimetri], *s.f.* saccharimetry.

saccharin [sakarɛ̃], *a.* saccharine.

saccharine [sakarin], *s.f. Ch: etc:* saccharin(e).

saccharique [sakarik], *a. Ch:* saccharic (acid).

saccharoïde [sakarɔid], *a.* saccharoid (gypsum); **calcaire s.,** metamorphic limestone.

saccharolé [sakarɔle], *s.m. Pharm:* sugar-based medicine, syrup, powder.

saccharomètre [sakarɔmɛtr̩], *s.m.* saccharometer.

saccharomyces [sakarɔmisɛs], *s.m.* saccharomyces, yeast fungus; **les s.,** the Saccharomycetes, the yeasts.

saccharose [sakaroːz], *s.m. Ch:* saccharose, sucrose.

saccharure [sakaryːr], *s.m. Pharm:* sugar-based solid medicine, pill.

sacciforme [saksifɔrm], *a. Bot:* sacciform, saccular, bag-shaped.

saccophore [sakɔfɔːr], *s.m. Z:* saccophore, gopher.

saccule [sakyl], *s.m. Anat:* saccule.

sacculine [sakylin], *s.f. Crust:* sacculina; parasitic barnacle.

sacerdoce [sasɛrdɔs], *s.m.* **1.** priesthood; ministry (of the Church); **pour lui, c'est un s.,** he is dedicated; **le s. de la médecine,** dedication to medicine. **2.** *coll.* the ecclesiastical body, the priesthood.

sacerdotal, -aux [sasɛrdɔtal, -o], *a.* sacerdotal (function, garment, dignity); priestly (garb, caste); priestlike (demeanour); *s.a.* VÊTEMENT.

sacerdotalisme [sasɛrdɔtalism], *s.m.* sacerdotalism.

sachée [saʃe], *s.f.* sackful, bagful.

sachem [saʃɛm], *s.m.* (*N. American Indian chief*) sachem.

sacherie [saʃri], *s.f.* **1.** sack and bag trade. **2.** sacks.

sachet [saʃɛ], *s.m.* **1.** (*a*) sachet, small bag; **s. à graines,** seed bag; **s. d'aiguilles,** packet of needles; **s. à aiguilles,** needle case; (*b*) *Artil:* cartridge bag. **2. s. à parfums,** scent bag; sachet.

sacoche [sakɔʃ], *s.f.* **1.** (*a*) satchel, wallet; money bag (of bank messenger, bus conductor, etc.); (*b*) *Mil:* **s. d'état-major,** dispatch case; **s. de selle,** saddlebag; **s. d'arçon,** wallet. **2.** (*a*) *Cy:* saddlebag; (*b*) tool bag; (*c*) (*in Belgium*) handbag.

sacoléva [sakɔleva], *s.f.*, **sacolève** [sakɔlɛːv], *s.m. Nau:* small Levantine sailing boat.

sacquer [sake], *v.tr. F:* = SAQUER[2].

sacral, -als [sakral], *a.* **1.** sacral (formula, etc.). **2.** *Anat:* sacral, of the sacrum.

sacralisation [sakralizasjɔ̃], *s.f.* **1.** *Surg:* sacralization. **2.** *Phil:* action of sacralizing.

sacraliser [sakralize], *v.tr.* to make (sth., s.o.), sacred; to consider (sth., s.o.) sacred.

sacramentaire [sakramɑ̃tɛːr], *s.m.* **1.** *Ecc: A:* sacramentary (book of prayer). **2.** *Rel.H:* sacramentarian, sacramentary (Calvinist or Zwinglian).

sacramental, -aux [sakramɑ̃tal, -o], *a.* = SACRAMENTEL.

sacramentalement [sakramɑ̃talmɑ̃], *adv.* sacramentally.

sacramentel, -elle [sakramɑ̃tɛl], *a.* (*a*) *Ecc:* sacramental; (*b*) decisive, binding; **prononcer les paroles sacramentelles,** to utter the ritual words, the fateful words.

sacramentellement [sakramɑ̃tɛlmɑ̃], *adv.* sacramentally.

sacrarium [sakrarjɔm], *s.m. Rom.Ant:* sacrarium.

sacre[1] [sakr̩], *s.m.* anointing, crowning, coronation, sacring (of king); consecration (of bishop).

sacre[2], *s.m.* **1.** (*a*) *Orn:* saker; (*b*) *F: A:* blackguard, scoundrel; bandit; *A:* **jurer comme un s.,** to swear like a trooper. **2.** *A.Arms:* saker (cannon).

sacré [sakre], *a.* **1.** holy (scripture, etc.); sacred, consecrated (vessel, place, etc.); **art s.,** sacred art; **les ordres sacrés,** holy orders; *Rom.Ant:* **la Voie Sacrée,** the Sacred Way, the Via Sacra (this name was given also in 1916 to the road from Bar-le-Duc to Verdun, which was the sole means of communication left between Verdun and the rest of France); **pour ces gamins rien n'est s.,** to these youngsters nothing is sacred; **il a le feu s.,** he is truly inspired; **il n'a pas le feu s.,** his heart isn't in it; *s.m.* **le s. et le profane,** things sacred and profane. **2.** sacred, inviolable (trust, law, etc.); **mon devoir s.,** my bounden duty. **3.** *P:* damn(ed), bloody; **votre s. chien,** your damn, bloody, dog; **s. imbécile,** bloody fool; **il a une sacrée chance,** he's damn lucky, he's got the devil's own luck; **elle a une sacrée allure,** she's damn(ed) attractive; **s. nom de Dieu! d'un chien!** damn and blast it! **4.** *Anat:* pertaining to the sacrum; **la région sacrée,** the sacral region; **les vertèbres sacrées,** the sacral vertebrae.

sacrebleu [sakrəblø], *int.* (*oath*) good Lord!

Sacré-Cœur [sakrekœːr], *s.m. Ecc:* **fête du S.-C.,** feast of the Sacred Heart (of Jesus); **église du S.-C.,** church of the Sacred Heart.

sacredieu [sakrədjø], **sacredié** [sakrədje], *Dial: int.* good God!

sacrement [sakrəmɑ̃], *s.m. Ecc:* **1.** (*a*) sacrament; **les sacrements,** the sacraments; the means of grace; **le saint S. (de l'autel),** the Blessed Sacrament (of the altar); **s'approcher des sacrements,** to partake of the Sacrament; **fréquenter les sacrements,** to be a regular partaker of the Sacrament, a regular communicant; **décédé muni des sacrements de l'Église,** died fortified with the rites of the Church; *F:* **avoir tous les sacrements,** to have full official blessing; (*b*) the marriage tie. **2.** *F:* **un saint s.,** a monstrance.

sacrément [sakremɑ̃], *adv. P:* damn(ed); **il fait s. chaud,** it's damn hot.

sacrer [sakre]. **1.** *v.tr.* (*a*) to anoint, crown (a king); to consecrate (a bishop); (*b*) **s. qn roi,** to anoint, crown, s.o. king. **2.** *v.i. F:* to curse and swear.

sacret [sakrɛ], *s.m. Orn:* sakeret (male of the saker).

sacrifiable [sakrifjabl̩], *a.* that can be sacrificed; *Mil: etc:* expendable.

sacrificateur, -trice [sakrifikatœːr, -tris], *s.* sacrificer; **grand s.,** (Jewish) High Priest.

sacrificatoire [sakrifikatwaːr], *a.* sacrificial.

sacrificature [sakrifikatyːr], *s.f. A.Rel:* priesthood.

sacrifice [sakrifis], *s.m.* sacrifice; **offrir un s.,** to offer up a sacrifice; **offrir qch. en s.,** to offer up sth. as a sacrifice; **faire à qn le s. de sa vie,** to sacrifice one's life for s.o.; **ses parents ont fait de grands sacrifices pour lui faire faire ses études,** his parents made every sacrifice to give him an education; *Ecc:* **le saint s.,** the celebration of mass; the Blessed Sacrament; *B:* **s. de prospérités,** peace offering; **faire, offrir, un s. de louanges à Dieu,** to offer the sacrifice of praise to God.

sacrifier [sakrifje], *v.tr.* (*p.d. & pr.sub.* **n. sacrifiions, v. sacrifiiez**) (*a*) to sacrifice (victim); to offer (sth.) in sacrifice; *abs.* **s. aux idoles,** to sacrifice to idols; **s. à la mode,** to conform to fashion; **s. aux préjugés de l'époque,** to make concessions to the prejudices of the time; *Com:* **s. des marchandises,** to sacrifice goods; to sell goods at a loss; **article sacrifié,** loss leader; (*b*) to sacrifice, give up, devote (time, money, comfort, etc.) (à, to); **elle a sacrifié sa fortune à votre éducation,** she sacrificed, gave up, her fortune to, for, your education; **il a réussi en sacrifiant sa santé,** he succeeded at the sacrifice of his health; **elle s'est sacrifiée pour vous,** she sacrificed herself for you; **s. sa vie pour son pays,** to lay down one's life for one's country; **s. sa vie à une cause,** to devote one's (entire) life to a cause; (*c*) **s. ses intérêts à son inclination,** to sacrifice one's interests to one's inclination; **s. ses amis à son ambition,** to sacrifice one's friends to one's ambition.

sacrilège[1] [sakrilɛːʒ], *s.m.* sacrilege; **ce serait un s. que de . . .,** it would be sacrilege to . . . .

sacrilège[2]. **1.** *a.* sacrilegious (action, thought, etc.); **porter une main s. sur qch.,** to lay a sacrilegious, an impious, hand upon sth. **2.** *s.* sacrilegious person.

sacrilègement [sakrilɛʒmɑ̃], *adv.* sacrilegiously, impiously.

sacripant [sakripɑ̃], *s.m.* (*a*) *A:* braggart, hector, swaggerer, bully, (*from the character Sacripant in Tassoni's Rape of the Bucket*); (*b*) rascal, scoundrel, knave.
sacristain [sakristɛ̃], *s.m.* **1.** *Ecc:* sacristan; sexton. **2.** *Cu:* (kind of) small flaky pastry.
sacristi [sakristi], *int. A:* **1.** the devil! devil take it! **2.** good Lord!
sacristie [sakristi], *s.f. Ecc:* **1.** sacristy, vestry. **2.** church plate and raiment (kept in the vestry). **3.** *A:* (priest's) perquisites (from special masses, etc.).
sacristine [sakristin], *s.f.* vestry nun, sacristine.
sacro- [sakrɔ], *pref.* sacro-.
sacro-coccygien, -ienne [sakrɔkɔksiʒjɛ̃, -jɛn], *a. Anat:* sacro-coccygeal; *pl. sacro-coccygiens, -iennes.*
sacro-épineux, -euse [sakrɔepinø, -øːz], *a. Anat:* sacro-spinal; *pl. sacro-épineux, -euses.*
sacro-iliaque [sakrɔiljak], *a. Anat:* sacro-iliac (ligament); *pl. sacro-iliaques.*
sacro-lombaire [sakrɔlɔ̃bɛːr], *a. Anat:* sacro-lumbal (muscle); *pl. sacro-lombaires.*
sacro-saint [sakrɔsɛ̃], *a.* sacrosanct; **les sacro-saintes frites des Belges,** the Belgians and their sacrosanct chips; *pl. sacro-saint(e)s.*
sacro-sciatique [sakrɔsjatik], *a. Anat:* sacro-sciatic; *pl. sacro-sciatiques.*
sacro-vertébral, -aux [sakrɔvɛrtebral, -o], *s. Anat:* sacro-vertebral.
sacrum [sakrɔm], *s.m. Anat:* sacrum.
sadique [sadik]. **1.** *a.* sadistic. **2.** *s.m. & f.* sadist.
sadisme [sadism], *s.m.* sadism.
sadiste [sadist], *s.m. & f.* sadist.
sadomasochisme [sadɔmazɔʃism], *s.m. Psy:* sado-masochism.
sadomasochiste [sadɔmazɔʃist], *Psy:* **1.** *a.* sado-masochistic. **2.** *s.m. & f.* sadomasochist.
saducéen, -enne [sadyseɛ̃, -ɛn], *Rel.H:* **1.** *a.* Sadducean. **2.** *s.* Sadducee.
saducéisme [sadyseism], *s.m.* Sadduceeism.
safari [safari], *s.m.* safari; **en s.,** on safari.
safflorite [saflɔrit], *s.f. Miner:* safflorite.
safran[1] [safrɑ̃], *s.m.* **1.** *Bot:* (*a*) saffron, crocus; **s. cultivé, officinal,** autumn crocus; (*b*) **s. bâtard,** safflower; bastard saffron; **s. marron,** Indian shot; **s. des Indes,** turmeric. **2.** *Cu: A.Dy: A.Pharm: etc:* saffron; **essence de s.,** saffron oil; *a.inv.* **gants safran,** saffron(-coloured) gloves.
safran[2], *s.m. Nau:* rudder blade; **s. du gouvernail,** after piece, back piece, cheek, of the rudder.
safrané [safrane], *a.* **1.** saffron(-coloured), yellow (complexion, etc.). **2.** *Cu: Pharm:* flavoured with saffron; saffroned.
safraner [safrane], *v.tr. Cu:* to flavour (rice, etc.) with saffron; to saffron.
safranière [safranjɛːr], *s.f.* saffron plantation.
safranine [safranin], *s.f. Ch: Ind:* safranin; saffron yellow.
safranum [safranɔm], *s.m. Dy:* safflower.
safre [safr̥], *s.m. Ch: Ind:* zaffre, zaffer.
safrol(e) [safrɔl], *s.m. Ch:* safrol.
saga [saga], *s.f. Lit:* saga.
sagace [sagas], *a.* sagacious, acute, shrewd.
sagacement [sagasmɑ̃], *adv.* sagaciously, shrewdly.
sagacité [sagasite], *s.f.* sagacity, shrewdness; **avec s.,** sagaciously; **vous devriez avoir plus de s. à votre âge,** you ought to know better at your age.
sagaie [sagɛ], *s.f.* assegai.
sagard [sagaːr], *s.m. For: Dial:* sawyer (in a forest sawmill).
sagartia [sagartja], *s.f.,* **sagartie** [sagarti], *s.f. Coel:* sagartia.
sage [saːʒ], *a.* **1.** wise; **Alphonse le S.,** Alfonso the Learned; *s.m.* **les sept Sages,** the Seven Sages; the Seven Wise Men; **le S.,** Solomon; *Lit:* **le S. de Ferney,** the Sage of Ferney (Voltaire); *Pol:* **le comité des sages,** the wise men; *Prov:* **un fou avise bien un s.,** a wise man can learn from a fool. **2.** judicious, prudent, wise, sage (policy, etc.); sapient, sober-minded (person); discreet (behaviour); **les esprits sages,** sensible people; **politique peu s.,** unwise policy. **3.** well-behaved, well-mannered, steady (person); good (child); quiet, docile (animal); well-mannered (horse); **femme s.,** modest, chaste, woman; **sois s.!** be a good child! be good! **s. comme une image,** as good as gold; **cheval s. au feu,** horse steady under fire.
sage-femme [saʒfam], *s.f.* midwife; *pl. sages-femmes.*
sagement [saʒmɑ̃], *adv.* **1.** wisely, sagely, prudently. **2.** steadily, soberly.
sagénite [saʒenit], *s.f. Miner:* sagenite.
sagesse [saʒɛs], *s.f.* **1.** (*a*) wisdom; **s. du monde, s. humaine,** worldly wisdom; *s.a.* ARBRE 2; (*b*) prudence, discretion; **agir avec s.,** to act wisely; **dent de s.,** wisdom tooth; **ce serait une s. d'attendre,** it would be wise to wait. **2.** (*a*) steadiness, good behaviour; quietness (of horse, etc.); *Sch:* **prix de s.,** good-conduct prize; (*b*) modesty, chastity (of a woman).
sagette [saʒɛt], *s.f.* **1.** *A:* arrow. **2.** *Bot:* arrowhead.
sagien, -ienne [saʒjɛ̃, -jɛn], *a. & s. Geog:* (native, inhabitant) of Sées.
sagine [saʒin], *s.f. Bot:* pearlwort, pearlgrass, pearlweed.
sagittaire [saʒitɛːr]. **1.** *s.m. Rom.Ant:* archer; *Astr: Her:* Sagittarius. **2.** *s.f. Bot:* sagittaria, arrowhead.
sagittal, -aux [saʒital, -o], *a. Anat:* sagittal (suture, section).
sagittariidés [saʒitariide], *s.m.pl. Orn:* Sagittariidae, the secretary birds.
sagitté [saʒite], *a. Bot:* sagittate, arrow-shaped (leaf).
Sagonte [sagɔ̃ːt], *Pr.n.f.* (*a*) *A.Geog:* Saguntum; (*b*) *Geog:* Sagunto.
sagontin, -ine [sagɔ̃tɛ̃, -in], *a. & s. A.Geog:* Saguntine.
sagou [sagu], *s.m.* sago.
sagouin [sagwɛ̃], *s.m.* **1.** *Z:* squirrel-monkey, sagouin. **2.** *F:* (*f.* **sagouine**) sloven; slovenly, dirty, fellow; *f.* slattern, slut; **ce vieux s. de père Marchal,** that foul old man Marchal.
sagoutier [sagutje], *s.m. Bot:* sago palm, sago tree.
Sahara (le) [ləsaara], *Pr.n.m. Geog:* the Sahara (Desert).
saharien, -ienne [saarjɛ̃, -jɛn], *a.* (*a*) Saharan, Saharian, Saharic; *Mil:* **les compagnies sahariennes,** the camel corps, the camelry; (*b*) *s.f.* **saharienne,** bush shirt.
Sahel (le) [ləsaɛl], *Pr.n.m. Geog:* the Sahel; **S. algérien,** Sahel of Algeria, Algerian Sahel.
sahélien, -ienne [saeljɛ̃, -jɛn], **1.** *a. & s. Geog:* (native, inhabitant) of the Sahel. **2.** *a. & s.m. Geol:* Sahelian.
sahib [saib], *s.m.* sahib.
saï [sai], *s.m. Z:* capuchin monkey.
saie[1] [sɛ], *s.f.* **1.** *Rom.Ant:* sagum. **2.** *Tex:* fine woollen lining.
saie[2], *s.f.* (goldsmith's) bench brush.
saietter [sɛjete], *v.tr.* to clean up with a (goldsmith's) bench brush.
saïga [saiga], *s.m. Z:* saiga antelope.
saignant [sɛɲɑ̃], *a.* **1.** bleeding, raw (wound, etc.); **blessure toujours saignante,** ever-open wound. **2.** *Cu:* lightly done, red, rare (meat).
saignée [sɛɲe], *s.f.* **1.** (*a*) *Med:* bleeding, blood-letting; **faire une s. à qn,** (i) to bleed s.o.; (ii) *F:* to extort money from s.o.; to bleed s.o.; **faire une s. dans un arbre,** to tap a tree (for gum, etc.); (*b*) *F:* **s. continuelle,** constant drain (on one's resources); (*c*) *Ent:* **s. réflexe,** auto-h(a)emorrhage. **2.** bend of the arm, the knee. **3.** (*a*) (drainage) trench, ditch; **s. d'irrigation,** surface drain (of a field); (*b*) *Mch: Mec.E:* cut, groove (for oil, etc.); (*c*) *El.E:* **conducteur à saignées,** tapped conductor; (*d*) *Const:* **faire une s. dans un mur,** to make a hole in a wall (for pipe, cable, etc.).
saignement [sɛɲmɑ̃], *s.m.* bleeding (of wound, etc.); **s. de nez,** nosebleed, bleeding at, from, the nose; *Med:* **temps de s.,** length of bleeding time (before coagulating).
saigner [sɛɲe]. **1.** *v.i.* (*of pers., wound, etc.*) to bleed; **s. du nez,** (i) to bleed at, from, the nose; (ii) *P: A:* to funk, to back out ignominiously; **je saigne du nez,** my nose is bleeding; **faire s. qn du nez,** to make s.o.'s nose bleed; **le cœur m'en saigne,** it makes my heart bleed; **c'est une plaie qui saigne encore,** the wound still rankles. **2.** *v.tr.* (*a*) to bleed; (i) *Med:* to draw, let, blood from (s.o.); (ii) *F:* to extort money from (s.o.); **s. un porc, un poulet,** to bleed, stick, a pig; to bleed a chicken; **s. un animal à blanc,** to bleed an animal white; *F:* **ils l'ont saigné à blanc,** they have cleaned him out, bled him white; **se s. aux quatre membres pour qn,** to make every sacrifice, to pinch and scrape, for s.o.; **se s. aux quatre veines pour payer,** to bleed oneself white in order to pay; (*b*) **s. un arbre,** to tap a (gum) tree; **s. un fossé,** to drain a ditch; **s. une rivière,** to divert water from a river; to tap a stream.
saigneur [sɛɲœːr], *s.m.* (*a*) bleeder (of pigs, etc.); pigsticker, pig slaughterman; (*b*) *Med: A:* blood-letter; (*c*) collector of rubber (in rubber plantation).
saigneux, -euse [sɛɲø, -øːz], *a.* bloody; blood-stained (handkerchief, etc.); **bout s.,** scrag end (of veal, mutton, etc.).
Saïgon [saigɔ̃], *Pr.n.m. Geog:* Saigon.
saïgonnais, -aise [saigɔnɛ, -ɛːz], *a. & s. Geog:* (native, inhabitant) of Saigon.
saillant [sajɑ̃]. **1.** *a.* (*a*) *A:* leaping; *Her:* salient; (*b*) projecting, jutting out (roof, cornice, balcony, etc.); **pommettes saillantes,** prominent, high, cheek bones; **muscles saillants,** muscles that stand out; **dents saillantes,** protruding teeth; buck teeth; *Const:* **assise saillante,** projecting course; *Fort: etc:* **angle s.,** salient angle; (*c*) salient, striking, outstanding, remarkable (feature, etc.); **faits saillants,** (i) salient facts; (ii) outstanding facts; highlights. **2.** *s.m. Mil:* salient.
sailler [saje], *Nau:* **1.** *v.tr.* **s. le bout-dehors,** to rig out the studding-sail boom. **2.** *v.i.* **le navire saille de l'avant,** the ship is making good headway.
saillie [saji], *s.f.* **1.** (*a*) spurt, spirt, spring, bound; **avancer par (bonds et) saillies,** to advance by leaps and bounds; **couler par saillies,** to flow in spurts; *A:* **s. de sang,** spurt, issue, of blood; (*b*) *Breed:* covering (by male); lining (of bitch); **faire saillies,** to be at stud; (*c*) *Mil: A:* sally; (*d*) (i) sally, flash of wit; (ii) outburst (of passion, of high spirits). **2.** protrusion; (*a*) *Arch: Const:* projection, ledge, set-off; **pierre en s.,** projecting stone; **fenêtre en s.,** bay window; **maison en s. sur la rue,** house jutting out over the street; **s. du mollet,** swell of the calf; **faire s.,** to project, jut out; **toit qui fait s.,** roof that overhangs the street; jutting out roof; **menton qui fait s.,** protruding chin; *F:* **pantalon qui fait s. au genou,** trousers baggy at the knee; **les balcons portent en s.,** the balconies are corbelled out; *Art:* **figure qui n'a pas assez de s.,** figure that does not stand out sufficiently, that does not come forward enough; (*b*) *Carp: Mec.E:* lug, flange; **s. d'arrêt,** stop shoulder; *Mec.E:* **s. de denture,** addendum (of gear tooth); (*c*) *Carp:* rabbet.
saillir [sajiːr], *v.* **1.** (*pr.p.* **saillissant;** *p.p.* **sailli;** *pr.ind.* **je saillis, n. saillissons;** *fu.* **je saillirai**) (*a*) *v.i. A:* (*of liquid*) to gush out, spurt out, spirt out; *A:* (*of besieged troops*) to (make a) sally; (*b*) *v.tr. Breed:* (*of stallion*) to cover (mare). **2.** *v.i.* (*used only in pr.p.* **saillant;** *p.p.* **sailli;** *pr.ind.* **il saille, ils saillent;** *fu.* **il saillera**) to jut out, stand out; **la poutre saille de 25 cm.,** the beam projects 10 inches; **balcon qui saille sur la rue,** balcony projecting over the street; **les traits qui le font s. dans la foule,** characteristics that make him stand out in the crowd; *Art:* **figure qui saille trop,** figure that stands out too much (in relief).
saïmiri [saimiri], *s.m. Z:* squirrel monkey.
sain, saine [sɛ̃, sɛn], *a.* (*a*) healthy, hale (person); sound (fruit, timber, paper, etc.); sound, sane (judgement); sound (doctrine); wholesome (food); **climat, exercice, s.,** healthy climate, exercise; **écurie propre et saine,** clean and sweet stable; **s. et sauf,** safe and sound; **ils s'en tirèrent sains et saufs,** they came out of it in one piece; *Jur:* **s. d'esprit,** of sound mind, sound in mind; **s. de corps et d'esprit,** sound in body and mind; **jugement s.,** sound judgement; **politique saine,** sound policy; **avoir la peau saine,** to be clean-skinned; **avoir le corps s.,** to be sound in wind and limb; **cheval s. et net,** horse sound and free from vice; horse sound in wind and limb; (*b*) *Nau:* clear, safe (coast, anchorage); fair (channel).
sainbois [sɛ̃bwa], *s.m. Bot:* spurge flax.
saindoux [sɛ̃du], *s.m.* **1.** *Cu:* lard. **2.** *Mil: P: A:* corporal.
sainement [sɛnmɑ̃], *adv.* **1.** healthily, wholesomely; soundly. **2.** sanely.
sainfoin [sɛ̃fwɛ̃], *s.m.* **1.** *Bot: Agr:* sainfoin. **2.** *Bot: F:* **s. d'hiver,** whin, furze, gorse; **s. oscillant,** telegraph plant.
saint, sainte [sɛ̃, sɛ̃ːt]. **1.** *a.* holy; (*a*) *Ecc:* **la Sainte Trinité,** the Holy Trinity; **la Sainte Église,** the Holy Church; **les saintes Écritures,** Holy Writ; **le S. sépulcre,** the Holy Sepulchre; **guerre sainte,** holy war; **semaine sainte,** Holy Week; **le Vendredi s.,** Good Friday; *s.a.* JEUDI, SAMEDI; (*b*) saintly, saint-like, godly (person, life); (*c*) sanctified, consecrated, sainted; **terre sainte,** hallowed, consecrated, ground; **la Terre sainte,** the Holy Land; **lieu s.,** holy place; *F:* **toute la sainte journée,** the whole blessed day; *Bot:* **bois s.,** lignum vitae; *Bot: F:* **arbre s.,** pride of India, of China; bead tree; (*d*) saint; **faire une prière à s. Pierre, à s. Antoine, à sainte Catherine,** to say a prayer to St Peter, to St Anthony, to St Catherine; **l'église S.-Pierre,** St Peter's (church); **la Sainte-Catherine,** Saint Catherine's day; the feast of Saint Catherine; **la rue, la place, S.-Georges,** the

Rue Saint-Georges, the Place Saint-Georges. **2.** *s.* saint; **saint d'une ville,** patron saint of a town; **fête de s.,** saint's day; *Ecc:* **mettre qn au nombre des saints,** to canonize s.o.; *F:* **prendre un air de petit s.,** to put on a saintly air; **c'est un petit s. (de bois),** he's a little prig, he's a little plaster saint; **il lasserait la patience d'un s.,** he would try the patience of a saint; **chacun prêche pour son s.,** everyone has an eye to his own interest; **il prêche pour son s.,** he has his own (particular) axe to grind; **ne savoir plus à quel s. se vouer,** to be at one's wits' end; **à chaque s. sa chandelle,** honour where honour is due; *F:* **un s. du jour,** a leading light of the day; *Rel:* **les Saints du dernier jour,** the Latter-day Saints. **3.** *s.m.* **le S. des Saints,** the Holy of Holies.

saint-Aignanais, -aise [sɛ̃tɛɲanɛ, -ɛːz], *a. & s. Geog:* (native, inhabitant) of Saint-Aignan.

saintais, -aise [sɛ̃tɛ, -ɛːz], *a. & s. Geog:* (native, inhabitant) of Saintes.

saint-Affricain, -aine [sɛ̃tafrikɛ̃, -ɛn], *a. & s. Geog:* (native, inhabitant) of Saint-Affrique.

Saint-Ange [sɛ̃tɑ̃ːʒ], *Pr.n.m.* **le Fort Saint-A.,** the Castle of Sant'Angelo.

Saint-Barthélemy (la) [lasɛ̃bartelemi], *s.f.* (i) St Bartholomew's Day; (ii) massacre of St Bartholomew (1572).

saint-bernard [sɛ̃bɛrnaːr], *s.m.inv.* St Bernard (dog); *F:* **c'est un vrai s.-b.,** he's a good Samaritan.

saint-Chamonais, -aise [sɛ̃ʃamɔnɛ, -ɛːz], *a. & s. Geog:* (native, inhabitant) of Saint-Chamond.

saint-Claudien, -ienne [sɛ̃klodjɛ̃, -jɛn], *a. & s. Geog:* (native, inhabitant) of Saint-Claude.

saint-crépin [sɛ̃krepɛ̃], *s.m. no pl. A:* (*a*) shoemaker's tools; grindery; (*b*) **porter tout son s.-c. sur son dos,** to carry all one's worldly goods on one's back.

Saint-Cyr [sɛ̃siːr], *Pr.n.m.* Saint-Cyr military school (infantry and cavalry); *F:* **il ne faut pas être sorti de S.-C. pour . . .,** you don't have to be a genius to . . ..

Saint-Cyrien [sɛ̃sirjɛ̃], *s.m.* cadet training at Saint-Cyr; *pl. Saint-Cyriens.*

Saint-Domingue [sɛ̃dɔmɛ̃ːg], *Pr.n.m.* Santo Domingo.

Sainte-Anne [sɛ̃tan], *s.f. formerly* a lunatic asylum in Paris; *hence:* **il est bon à enfermer à S.-A.,** he ought to be in a lunatic asylum, he's raving mad.

sainte-barbe [sɛ̃tbarb], *s.f.* **1.** *Nau: A:* powder magazine; gunners' store room. **2.** *F:* **c'est la S.-B.,** it's an awful bore; *pl. saintes-barbes.*

Sainte-Croix [sɛ̃tkrwɑ], *Pr.n. Geog:* **l'île S.-C.,** Santa Cruz Island.

Sainte-Hélène [sɛ̃telɛn], *Pr.n. Geog:* Saint Helena.

Saint-Elme [sɛ̃tɛlm], *Pr.n.m.* **feu S.-E.,** corposant, Saint-Elmo's fire, dead fire.

Sainte-Lucie [sɛ̃tlysi], *Pr.n. Geog:* St Lucia; *Com:* **bois de S.-L.,** mahaleb cherry wood.

saintement [sɛ̃tmɑ̃], *adv.* holily; **vivre s.,** to live righteously, to lead a godly life; **mourir s.,** to die a godly death.

sainte-nitouche [sɛ̃tnituʃ], *s.f. See* NITOUCHE.

Saint-Esprit [sɛ̃tɛspri], *Pr.n.m. Ecc:* **le S.-E.,** the Holy Ghost, the Holy Spirit.

sainteté [sɛ̃tte], *s.f.* holiness, saintliness (of a person); sanctity (of the law, of a vow); *Art:* **sujet de s.,** religious subject; *Ecc:* **sa, votre, S.,** His Holiness, Your Holiness (the Pope); *s.a.* ODEUR 1.

Sainte-Touche [sɛ̃ttuːʃ], *s.f. F:* pay day.

saint-frusquin [sɛ̃fryskɛ̃], *s.m. no pl. P:* all the worldly goods (of a person); **et tout le s.-f.,** and the whole caboodle; and the whole damn lot.

saint-Gallois, -oise [sɛ̃galwa, -waːz], *a. & s. Geog:* (native, inhabitant) of Saint-Gall; *pl. saint-Gallois(es).*

saint-Gaudinois, -oise [sɛ̃godinwa, -waːz], *a. & s. Geog:* (native, inhabitant) of Saint-Gaudens; *pl. Saint-Gaudinois(es).*

Saint-Georges [sɛ̃ʒɔrʒ], *Pr.n.m. Geog:* **le canal de S.-G.,** Saint George's Channel.

Saint-Germain [sɛ̃ʒɛrmɛ̃], *Pr.n.m.* **1.** *Cu:* **potage S.-G.,** pea soup. **2.** *s.m. Hort:* (type of) sweet eating pear.

saint-Germinois, -oise [sɛ̃ʒɛrminwa, -waːz], *a. & s. Geog:* (native, inhabitant) of Saint-Germain; *pl. saint-Germinois(es).*

saint-Gironnais, -aise [sɛ̃ʒirɔnɛ, -ɛːz], *a. & s. Geog:* (native, inhabitant) of Saint-Girons.

Saint-Glinglin [sɛ̃glɛ̃glɛ̃], *used in F:* **jusqu'à la S.-G.,** till the cows come home; till doomsday; **à la S.-G.,** tomorrow come never.

Saint-Graal (le) [ləsɛ̃grɑːl], *s.m., A:* **Saint-Gréal (le)** [ləsɛ̃greal], *s.m. Lit:* the (holy) Grail.

Saint-Guy [sɛ̃gi]. *See* DANSE.

saint-honoré [sɛ̃tɔnɔre], *s.m.* (type of) cream tart.

saint-hubert [sɛ̃tybɛːr], *s.f. Ven:* fanfare (sounded on St Hubert's day).

Saint-Jean (la) [lasɛ̃ʒɑ̃], *s.f.* Midsummer Day; **feu de la S.-J.,** Midsummer's eve bonfire; *A:* **herbes de la S.-J.,** magic herbs cut on midsummer morning; *F:* **employer toutes les herbes de la S.-J.,** to use every possible means to succeed.

Saint-Jean d'Acre [sɛ̃ʒɑ̃dakr̥], *Pr.n. Geog:* Acre.

saint-Jean-de-Luzien, -ienne [sɛ̃ʒɑ̃dəlyzjɛ̃, -jɛn], *a. & s. Geog:* (native, inhabitant) of Saint-Jean-de-Luz; *pl. saint-Jean-de-Luzien(ne)s.*

Saint-Laurent (le) [ləsɛ̃lɔrɑ̃], *Pr.n.m. Geog:* the Saint Lawrence (river).

saint-Lois, -oise [sɛ̃lwa, -waːz], *a. & s.* (native, inhabitant) of Saint-Lo; *pl. saint-Lois(es).*

saint-Louisien, -ienne [sɛ̃lwizjɛ̃, -jɛn], *a. & s. Geog:* (native, inhabitant) of Saint-Louis (Senegal); *pl. saint-Louisien(ne)s.*

Saint-Lundi [sɛ̃lœ̃di], *used in F:* **faire la S.-L.,** to take Monday off.

saint-Maixentais, -aise [sɛ̃mɛksɑ̃tɛ, -ɛːz]. **1.** *Geog: a. & s.* (inhabitant, native) of Saint-Maixent. **2.** *s.m.* infantry officer promoted from the ranks after passing through the military school of Saint-Maixent; *pl. saint-Maixentais(es).*

Saint-Marin [sɛ̃marɛ̃], *Pr.n. Geog:* (the Republic of) San Marino.

Saint-Martin (la) [lasɛ̃martɛ̃], *s.f.* Saint Martin's day; Martinmas; **été de la S.-M.,** Saint Martin's summer.

Saint-Michel (la) [lasɛ̃miʃɛl], *s.f.* the feast of Saint Michael; Michaelmas; **à la S.-M.,** on Michaelmas Day.

Saint-Office [sɛ̃tɔfis], *s.m.* **1.** *R.C.Ch:* the Holy Office. **2.** *Ecc.Hist:* the Inquisition.

saintongeais, -aise [sɛ̃tɔ̃ʒɛ, -ɛːz], *a. & s. Geog:* (native, inhabitant) of (the province of) Saintonge.

Saint-Père (le) [ləsɛ̃pɛːr], *s.m. Ecc:* the Holy Father, the Pope.

Saint-Pétersbourg [sɛ̃petɛrzbuːr], *Pr.n.f. Geog: A:* St Petersburg.

Saint-Pierre [sɛ̃pjɛːr], *s.m.inv. Ich:* John Dory.

saint-Ponais, -aise [sɛ̃pɔnɛ, -ɛːz], *a. & s. Geog:* (native, inhabitant) of Saint-Pons; *pl. saint-Ponais(es).*

saint-Quentinois, -oise [sɛ̃kɑ̃tinwa, -waːz], *a. & s. Geog:* (native, inhabitant) of Saint-Quentin.

saint-Rémois, -oise [sɛ̃remwa, -waːz], *a. & s. Geog:* (native, inhabitant) of Saint-Remy; *pl. saint-Rémois(es).*

saint-sépulcre [sɛ̃sepylkr̥], *s.m. Art:* entombment of Christ; *pl. saint-sépulcres.*

saint-Servantin, -ine [sɛ̃sɛrvɑ̃tɛ̃, -in], *a. & s. Geog:* (native, inhabitant) of Saint-Servan; *pl. saint-Servantin(e)s.*

Saint-Siège (le) [ləsɛ̃sjɛːʒ], *s.m. Ecc:* the Holy See.

saint-simonien, -ienne [sɛ̃simɔnjɛ̃, -jɛn], *a. & s. Hist. of Pol.Ec:* Saint-Simonian (doctrine, disciple); Saint-Simonist; *pl. saint-simonien(ne)s.*

saint-simonisme [sɛ̃simɔnism], *s.m. Pol.Ec:* Saint-Simonianism; Saint-Simonism.

saint-sulpicien, -ienne [sɛ̃sylpisjɛ̃, -jɛn], *a. F:* **l'art s.,** the art of plaster saints; *pl. saint-sulpiciens, -iennes.*

Saint-Sylvestre (la) [lasɛ̃silvɛstr̥], *s.f.* New Year's Eve; **faire la veillée de la S.-S.,** to see the new year in; **du premier janvier à la S.-S.,** all the year round.

saïque [saik], *s.f.* (Levantine) sailing ship; saic.

saïs[1] [sais], *s.m.* syce, sice.

Saïs[2], *Pr.n.f. A.Geog:* Sais.

saisi [sezi], *s.m. Jur:* distrainee, person distrained.

saisie [sezi], *s.f.* (*a*) seizure (of contraband goods, of neutral vessel, etc.); **opérer la s. de marchandises de contrebande,** to seize contraband goods; **s. conservatoire,** seizure, by a court, of goods the ownership of which is under dispute; seizure for security; (*b*) *Jur:* distraint, execution; *Nau:* embargo; **s. immobilière,** seizure, attachment, of real property; **s. foraine,** distraint upon the goods of a person of no fixed abode; **s. pour loyer,** distress; **s. d'une hypothèque,** foreclosure, foreclosing, of a mortgage; **opérer une s.,** to levy a distress; (*c*) *Elcs:* (*computers*) **s. de données,** data acquisition.

saisie-arrêt [seziarɛ], *s.f. Jur:* attachment, garnishment; *Scot:* arrestment; **ordonnance de s.-a.,** garnishee order; *pl. saisies-arrêts.*

saisie-brandon [sezibrɑ̃dɔ̃], *s.f. Jur:* distraint by seizure of crops; *pl. saisies-brandons.*

saisie-exécution [seziɛgzekysjɔ̃], *s.f. Jur:* distress, execution (by sale of debtor's chattels); *pl. saisies-exécutions.*

saisie-gagerie [sezigaʒri], *s.f. Jur:* writ of execution (on tenant's furniture and chattels); *pl. saisies-gageries.*

saisie-revendication [sezirəvɑ̃dikasjɔ̃], *s.f. Jur:* seizure under a prior claim; *pl. saisies-revendications.*

saisine [sezin], *s.f.* **1.** *Jur:* livery of seisin; *Scot:* sasine. **2.** *Nau: etc:* lashing (of gun, etc.); **saisines d'un canot,** slings of a boat; boat-gripes.

saisir [seziːr], *v.tr.* **1.** to seize; (*a*) to grasp; to lay hold, take hold, catch hold, of (s.o., sth.); **s. qn par le bras, au collet,** to seize, catch, grab, s.o. by the arm, by the collar; *Jur:* **s. qn au corps,** to apprehend s.o.; **il saisit un revolver sur la table,** he seized, grabbed, snatched up, a revolver from the table; **s. un trône, une ville,** to seize, take possession of, a throne, a town; **s. un prétexte,** to seize upon a pretext; **s. l'occasion (de faire qch.),** to seize, grasp, avail oneself of, snatch at, the opportunity (to do sth.); **la peur le saisit,** fear gripped him, he took fright; **saisi de crainte,** struck with fear; **être saisi (d'étonnement),** to be startled, staggered; **dès l'entrée une odeur de choux saisit l'odorat,** at the very door we were met by a smell of cabbage; (*b*) *Jur:* to seize, attach (real estate); to distrain upon (goods); to lay an embargo on (ship); to attach (ship); **s. une hypothèque,** to foreclose a mortgage; **faire s. qn,** *F:* to sell s.o. up; **on a saisi trois journaux nationalistes,** three nationalist papers were sequestrated, seized; (*c*) *Nau:* to stow, secure, lash (the anchors); to stow, secure, gripe (the boats); (*d*) to perceive, discern, apprehend; **s. la vérité de qch.,** to recognize, grasp, the truth of sth.; **s. le raisonnement de qn,** to catch s.o.'s point; **je n'ai pas saisi son nom,** I didn't catch his name; **je ne saisis pas,** I don't get the idea; **je ne saisis pas bien,** I don't quite get your meaning; **mal s. qch.,** to misapprehend sth., to understand sth. wrongly; **l'artiste a bien saisi la ressemblance,** the artist has caught the likeness; **il n'a pas saisi le rôle,** he has not caught the spirit of the part; **il saisit vite,** he's got a quick mind, he's quick in the uptake. **2.** *Jur:* (*a*) **s. qn d'un héritage,** to vest s.o. with, put s.o. in possession of, an inheritance; (*b*) **s. un tribunal d'une affaire,** to refer a matter to a court, to lay a matter before a court; **le tribunal est saisi d'une demande de discussion,** application has been made to the court for an inquiry into the debtor's assets; **nous sommes saisis de deux questions,** we have two questions before us; **s. la chambre d'un projet de loi,** to table a bill. **3.** *Cu:* to seal (steak, etc.) by exposure to a fierce heat.

se saisir de qn, de qch., to seize on s.o., sth.; to lay hands on sth.; **se s. d'un prétexte,** to seize on a pretext.

saisir-arrêter [sezirarete], *v.tr.* (*used only in inf. and p.p.* **saisi-arrêté**) *Jur:* to garnish, distrain upon (debtor); *cf.* SAISIE-ARRÊT; *thus also* **saisir-brandonner, saisir-exécuter, saisir-gager, saisir-revendiquer;** *cf.* SAISIE-BRANDON, etc.

saisissabilité [sezisabilite], *s.f.* liability to distraint or attachment.

saisissable [sezisabl̥], *a.* **1.** seizable (object, etc.); **murmure à peine s.,** hardly distinguishable murmuring; **crime difficilement s.,** crime difficult to trace. **2.** *Jur:* distrainable, attachable; subject to seizure or to attachment.

saisissant, -ante [sezisɑ̃, -ɑ̃ːt], *a.* **1.** *Jur:* (*a*) seizing, distraining (party); (*b*) *s.* distrainer, garnisher, arrester. **2.** (*a*) piercing, biting (cold); (*b*) startling, striking (resemblance); gripping (words, scene); thrilling (spectacle).

saisissement [sezismɑ̃], *s.m.* seizure; (*a*) sudden chill; (*b*) **s. de joie,** access, thrill, of joy; (*c*) shock; **il mourut de s.,** he died of the shock; the shock killed him.

saison [sɛzɔ̃], *s.f.* season; (*a*) **les quatre saisons,** the four seasons; **rose des quatre saisons,** monthly rose; **en cette s.,** at this time of year; **en toute(s) saison(s),** all the year round; **très tôt en s.,** very early in the season; *s.a.* MARCHAND 1; **la s. nouvelle,** spring (tide); **la mauvaise s.,** the winter months; **la belle s.,** the summer months; (*b*) (*in the tropics*) **la s. des pluies,** the rainy season; **la belle s.,** the dry season; (*c*) time (of year, etc.); **la s. des semailles,** sowing time; **fruits en pleine s.,** fruit in season; **la haute s., la s. touristique,** the tourist season; **Londres pendant la s.,** London during the season; **la s. bat son plein,** it is the height of the season; **la fin de s.,** the end of the season; **la s. de grand travail, le fort de la**

s., the busy season; **la s. creuse**, the slack season; the off season; *Sp:* **la s. de piste**, the running season; **de s.**, (i) in season, seasonable; (ii) timely; **légumes de s.**, vegetables in season; **les huîtres sont de s., hors de s.**, oysters are in season, out of season; **la prudence est toujours de s.**, prudence is always timely; **propos hors de s.**, ill-timed, inopportune, remarks; **plaisanteries, temps, hors de s.**, unseasonable jokes, weather; **cela se fera en temps et s.**, it shall be done in due course; (*d*) **s. thermale**, spell of treatment at a spa; **faire une s. de trois semaines à Vichy**, to take a three weeks' cure at Vichy; *F:* **faire les saisons**, to do seasonal work (in resorts).

saisonner [sezɔne], *v.i. Hort:* (*of tree*) to bear abundant fruit; to fruit well.

saisonnier, -ière [sezɔnje, -jɛːr], (*a*) *a.* seasonal (disease, employment, etc.); **chômage s.**, seasonal unemployment; (*b*) *s.m.* seasonal worker.

saisonnièrement [sezɔnjɛrmɑ̃], *adv.* seasonally.

Saïte [sait], *a. A.Geog:* Saitic.

sajou [saʒu], *s.m. Z:* sajou, sapajou (monkey); capuchin monkey.

saké [sake], *s.m.*, **saki**[1] [saki], *s.m.* saké (brewed with fermented rice).

saki[2], *s.m. Z:* saki (monkey); couxia.

salabre [salabr̥], *s.m. Fish:* **1.** hand-net. **2.** drag-net.

salace [salas], *a.* salacious.

salacité [salasite], *s.f.* salaciousness, salacity.

salade[1] [salad], *s.f.* **1.** (*a*) salad; **faire, fatiguer, touiller, la s.**, to mix the salad; **panier à s.**, (i) salad shaker; (ii) *F:* = Black Maria; (*b*) **s. de fruits**, fruit salad; **s. de homard**, lobster salad; **s. russe**, (i) Russian salad; (ii) *F:* jumble, miscellany, hotchpotch; *F:* **mettre tout en s.**, to throw everything into confusion; to jumble everything up; **elle fait une s.!** she gets everything mixed up! **quelle s.!** what a mess! *Mch: F:* **s. d'aubes**, smash-up of turbine vanes; (*c*) *pl. P:* (i) lies; (ii) nonsense; **arrête tes salades!** stow it! shut up! **2.** *Hort: Cu:* (*the word* **salade** *is commonly used with the meaning of "lettuce", "endive", etc.*) green salad; *Bot: F:* **s. de blé, de chanoine**, corn salad, lamb's lettuce.

salade[2], *s.f. Arm:* sallet, salade.

saladelle [saladɛl], *s.f. Bot:* red behen.

saladier [saladje], *s.m.* salad bowl; **un s. de laitue**, a salad bowl full of lettuce.

salage [salaːʒ], *s.m.* **1.** (*a*) salting (of fish, meat, etc.); curing; (*b*) *Phot:* salting (of paper); (*c*) *Cer:* **vernissage par s.**, salt glazing. **2.** *A:* salt-tax.

salaire [salɛːr], *s.m.* wage(s); **1.** pay (of manual worker); **s. à la tâche, aux pièces**, piece wage(s); **s. à forfait**, job wages; **s. à la journée**, day wages; **s. journalier**, earnings per day; **s. au rendement**, efficiency wages, *U.S:* incentive wages; **s. au temps**, time wages; **s. indexé**, index-linked wages; **s. de base**, basic wage; **s. légal**, legal rate of pay; **s. minimum interprofessionnel de croissance (S.M.I.C.)**, *O:* **s. minimum interprofessionnel garanti (S.M.I.G)** = guaranteed minimum wage; **s. indirect**, fringe benefits; *Prov:* **toute peine mérite s.**, the labourer is worthy of his hire. **2.** reward, recompense, retribution; **le s. du péché**, the wages of sin.

salaison [salɛzɔ̃], *s.f.* **1.** (*a*) salting (of fish, etc.); curing (of bacon); (*b*) *Phot:* salting (of paper); (*c*) (degree of) salinity (of the sea). **2.** salt provisions; **marchand de s.**, salt-provision dealer, *U.S:* drysalter.

salamalec [salamalɛk], *s.m. F:* salaam, bowing and scraping; **faire des salamalecs à qn**, to bow and scrape to s.o.; to kowtow to s.o.

salamandre [salamɑ̃ːdr̥], *s.f.* **1.** *Amph:* (*a*) salamander; **s. du Japon**, giant salamander; **s. tachetée**, (European) spotted salamander; **s. tigrée**, (American) tiger salamander; **s. des grottes (nord-américaines)**, (North American) grotto salamander; **salamandres géantes américaines**, giant American salamanders, *F:* mud-puppies, hellbenders; **s. alpestre**, alpine salamander; (*b*) **s. aquatique**, newt, eft; **s. aquatique de Californie**, Californian newt. **2.** salamander stove; slow-combustion stove.

salamandridés [salamɑ̃dride], *s.m.pl. Amph:* Salamandridae.

Salamanque [salamɑ̃ːk], *Pr.n.f. Geog:* Salamanca.

salami [salami], *s.m. Comest:* salami (sausage).

Salamine [salamin], *Pr.n.f. Geog:* Salamis.

salaminien, -ienne [salaminjɛ̃, -jɛn], *a. & s.* (native, inhabitant) of Salamis.

salangane [salɑ̃gan], *s.f. Orn:* salangane.

salanque [salɑ̃ːk], *s.f.* (*a*) salt marsh, salt pans; (*b*) (*in Roussillon*) alluvial plain.

salant [salɑ̃], *a.m.* salt, saline; **marais s.**, salt marsh, salt pans, saltern, saline, salina.

salarial, -aux [salarjal, -o], *a.* pertaining to wages; **masse salariale**, total wages, the aggregate of wages.

salariat [salarja], *s.m.* **1.** wage-earning. **2.** *coll.* the wage earners.

salarié, -ée [salarje]. **1.** *a.* (*a*) wage-earning; (*b*) paid (work). **2.** *s.* (*a*) wage earner; (*b*) *Pej:* hireling.

salarier [salarje], *v.tr.* (*p.d. & pr.sub.* **n. salariions, v. salariiez**) **1.** to pay a wage to (s.o.). **2.** *A:* to reward (**de**, for).

salaud, -aude [salo, -oːd], *s. P:* (*a*) filthy beast; *f.* slut; **petit s.!** you dirty little beast! (*b*) (dirty) bastard, swine, louse; son of a bitch; **ça c'est un tour de s.!** that's a dirty, low, mean, trick!

salauderie [salodri], *s.f.* (*a*) dirty trick; (*b*) filthy language.

salbande [salbɑ̃ːd], *s.f. Geol:* selvage, selvedge (of vein).

salde [sald], *s.m. Ent:* salda.

sale [sal], *a.* dirty. **1.** (*a*) unclean, filthy; (*of ship's bottom*) foul; **enfant s.**, dirty child; **linge s.**, soiled linen; **s. comme un peigne**, filthy; **couleur s.**, dull, dingy, dirty, colour; *P:* (*in neg.*) **c'était pas s.!** it was pretty good! it was quite something! (*b*) **mot s.**, offensive, filthy, coarse, word. **2.** *F:* (*always before the noun*) **s. individu, s. type**, rotter, *P:* louse; **s. bête**, dirty dog; **s. fasciste!** filthy Fascist! **s. coup**, (i) nasty blow; (ii) low, dirty, trick; **c'est une s. affaire**, it's a low-down, dirty, business; **il m'a joué un s. tour**, he did the dirty on me; **s. temps**, (i) *Nau:* foul weather; (ii) *F:* rotten, beastly, weather. **3.** *s.m. F:* **mettre du linge au s.**, to put washing in the dirty clothes basket; to put dirty clothes in the wash.

salé [sale], *a.* **1.** salt (fish, butter, etc.); salted (almonds); *Poet:* briny (waves); **eau salée**, (i) salt water; (ii) brine; *Geog:* **le Grand Lac S.**, the Great Salt Lake; **bœuf s.**, salt beef; *Nau:* junk; **le potage est trop s.**, the soup is too salt(y); *Leath:* **peau salée**, cured skin; *Husb:* **pain s.**, lick, *U.S:* salt lick; *s.a.* BEC 2; *Husb:* **prés salés**, saltings, salt meadows; *s.a.* PRÉ-SALÉ; *s.m.* **du s.**, salt pork; **petit s.**, pickled pork; *P:* **un (petit) s., un morceau de s.**, a (newborn) child, baby, brat. **2.** (*a*) keen, biting (epigram, etc.); (*b*) broad, spicy (tale, joke); **en raconter de salées**, to tell spicy, smutty, stories; (*c*) *F:* exorbitant, stiff (price); stiff, unduly severe (sentence).

salègre [salɛgr̥], *s.m.* **1.** *Husb:* piece of rock salt (for cattle to lick). **2.** saltcat (for pigeons, etc.).

salement [salmɑ̃], *adv.* **1.** dirtily, filthily, nastily, disgustingly; **se conduire s.**, to behave in a low manner. **2.** *P:* (very) badly; **être s. touché**, to be terribly badly wounded; **être s. fatigué**, to be dog tired; **s. difficile**, bloody difficult; **ça va nous rendre s. service**, it'll be damn useful.

salep [salɛp], *s.m. A.Pharm:* salep.

saler [sale], *v.tr.* to salt. **1.** (*a*) to season (sth.) with salt; (*b*) *F:* to charge exorbitantly for (sth.); to fleece (customers); **s. la note**, to stick it on (to the bill); **on nous a salés**, we had to pay through the nose, we were stung; **on l'a salé**, he got a tough sentence. **2.** to salt, pickle (pork, herrings, etc.); to salt, cure (bacon); *Leath:* to cure (a skin); *Phot:* to salt (paper).

Salerne [salɛrn], *Pr.n.f. Geog:* Salerno; *Med:* **l'école de S.**, the Salernitan school.

salernitain, -aine [salɛrnitɛ̃, -ɛn], *a. & s. Geog:* Salernitan.

saleron [salrɔ̃], *s.m.* (bowl of) salt cellar.

salésien, -ienne [salezjɛ̃, -jɛn]. **1.** *a.* concerning, connected with, St François de Sales; **l'école salésienne**, the Salesian School. **2.** *s.m.* **un s.**, a Salesian (member of the Society of St François de Sales).

saleté [salte], *s.f.* **1.** (*a*) dirtiness, filthiness (of person, street, clothes, etc.); (*b*) dirt, filth; **ôtez toute cette saleté!** take away all this dirt, filth, mess! (*c*) bit of dirt; **faire des saletés partout**, to make a mess everywhere; **enlever une s. sur un vêtement**, to remove a bit of dirt from a garment; **enlever les saletés du perroquet**, to clear up, away, the mess made by the parrot; (*d*) trashy goods, trash, rubbish. **2.** (*a*) nastiness, obscenity; beastliness (of mind); **s. d'une chanson**, coarseness, indecency, of a song; (*b*) nasty, coarse, remark, joke; **dire, raconter, des saletés**, to talk smut, to tell dirty stories; (*c*) low, mean, dirty, trick; **faire une s. à qn**, *F:* to do the dirty on s.o.

saleur, -euse [salœːr, -øːz]. **1.** *s.* salter, dry-curer (of meat, fish, etc.). **2.** *s.f.* **saleuse**; *Rail: etc:* salt truck (for melting the snow).

salicacées [salikase], *s.f.pl. Bot:* Salicaceae.

salicaire [salikɛːr], *s.f. Bot:* (spiked purple) loosestrife.

salicine [salisin], *s.f. Ch:* salicin.

salicinées [salisine], *s.f.pl. Bot:* Salicaceae.

salicional [salisjɔnal], *s.m. Organ:* salicional, salicet (stop).

salicole [salikɔl], *a.* **1.** pertaining to salt; **industrie s.**, salt industry. **2.** saliferous. **3.** *Bot:* salsuginous, halophytic (plant).

salicoque [salikɔk], *s.f. Crust:* **(grande crevette) s.**, palaemon, *F:* prawn.

salicorne [salikɔrn], *s.f.*, **salicornia** [salikɔrnja], *s.m. Bot:* (jointed) glasswort, saltwort; marsh-samphire; **s. herbacée**, sea-grass.

salicoside [salikɔzid], *s.m. Ch:* salicin.

saliculteur [salikyltœːr], *s.m.* salt producer.

saliculture [salikyltyːr], *s.f.* exploitation of a salt marsh, of a saline; salt production.

salicylate [salisilat], *s.m. Ch:* salicylate.

salicyle [salisil], *s.m. Ch:* salicyl.

salicyler [salisile], *v.tr.* to salicylate (beer, etc.).

salicyline [salisilin], *s.f. Ch:* salicylic acid.

salicylique [salisilik], *a.m. Ch:* salicylic (acid); **aldéhyde s.**, salicylaldehyde.

salicylol [salisilɔl], *s.m. Ch:* salicylic aldehyde.

salien[1] [saljɛ̃], *Rom.Ant:* **1.** *a.m.* Salian; of the Salii. **2.** *s.m.pl.* **les Saliens**, the Salii.

salien[2], *Hist:* **1.** *a.m.* Salian, of the Salians. **2.** *s.m.pl.* **Les (Francs) Saliens**, the Salian Franks.

salière [saljɛːr], *s.f.* **1.** (*a*) salt cellar; **s. saupoudroir**, salt shaker; (*b*) (kitchen) salt box. **2.** (*a*) eye socket (of horse); (*b*) *F:* (*hollow above the collar bone*) salt cellar.

salifère [salifɛːr], *a.* saliferous (ground, etc.).

saliférien, -ienne [saliferjɛ̃, -jɛn], *a. Geol:* saliferous (system).

salifiable [salifjabl̥], *a. Ch:* salifiable.

salification [salifikasjɔ̃], *s.f.* salification.

salifier [salifje], *v.tr.* (*p.d. & pr.sub.* **n. salifiions, v. salifiiez**) *Ch:* to salify.

saligaud, -aude [saligo, -oːd], *s. P:* (*a*) dirty beast; *f.* slut; (*b*) bastard, swine; *f.* bitch.

salignon [saliɲɔ̃], *s.m.* cake of salt.

saligot [saligo], *s.m. Bot: F:* saligot, water chestnut.

salin, -ine [salɛ̃, -in]. **1.** *a.* saline, briny; salty (taste); **air s.**, (salt) sea air. **2.** *s.m.* (*a*) salt marsh; (*b*) *Ch: Ind:* salin(e); (crude, red) potash. **3.** *s.f.* **saline**; (*a*) salt works, salt pan, salina; brine pit; (*b*) rock-salt mine; (*c*) *A:* salted provisions, *esp.* salt fish; (*d*) *pl.* fish-curing establishment.

salinage [salinaːʒ], *s.m. Salt Ind:* **1.** salt mine; salt marsh; salt works. **2.** (*a*) concentrating of the brine; (*b*) saturated solution of salt.

salingue [salɛ̃ːg], *P:* **1.** *a.* filthy. **2.** *s.* filthy, disgusting, person.

salinier, -ière [salinje, -jɛːr]. **1.** *a.* relating to salt production; **industrie salinière**, salt industry. **2.** *s.m.* (*a*) salt-mine owner; (*b*) salt merchant; salter.

salinité [salinite], *s.f.* saltness, salinity (of sea water, etc.).

salinois, -oise [salinwa, -waːz], *a. & s. Geog:* (native, inhabitant) of Salins.

salinomètre [salinɔmɛtr̥], *s.m.* salinometer, brine gauge.

salique [salik], *a. Hist:* Salic (law).

salir [saliːr], *v.tr.* to dirty, soil (one's hands, linen, etc.); to make (ship's bottom, etc.) foul; to corrupt (the imagination); **se s. la figure**, to dirty one's face; *P:* **se s. le nez**, to get drunk; **s. le plancher**, (i) to make the floor dirty; (ii) (*of animal*) to make a mess on the floor; **c'est un vilain oiseau que celui qui salit son nid**, it's a dirty bird that fouls its own nest; **s. sa réputation**, to tarnish one's reputation.

se salir. **1.** to get dirty, soiled; **étoffe qui se salit facilement**, material that soils easily. **2.** (*a*) to soil, dirty, one's clothes; (*b*) to tarnish one's reputation; to degrade oneself.

salisien, -ienne [salizjɛ̃, -jɛn], *a. & s. Geog:* (native, inhabitant) of Salies-de-Béarn.

salissant [salisɑ̃], *a.* **1.** soiling, that dirties; **travail s.**, dirty, messy, work. **2.** easily soiled (material, etc.); **teinte peu salissante**, shade that does not show the dirt.

salisson [salisɔ̃], *s.f. Dial: F:* dirty, untidy, little girl.

salissure [salisyːr], *s.f.* stain, dirty mark.

salivaire [salivɛːr], *a.* salivary (gland, etc.).

salival, -aux [salival, -o], *a.* salival, salivary.

salivard [salivaːr], *s.m. F:* chatterbox, windbag.

salivation [salivasjɔ̃], *s.f. Med:* salivation.

salive [sali:v], *s.f.* saliva, spittle; *F:* **perdre sa s.,** to waste one's breath; *F:* **avaler, ravaler, sa s.,** to be stumped for an answer; *F:* **dépenser beaucoup de s.,** to talk nineteen to the dozen.

saliver [salive], *v.i.* to salivate.

sallanchard, -arde [salɑ̃ʃa:r, -ard], **sallanchois, -oise** [salɑ̃ʃwa, -wa:z], *a. & s. Geog:* (native, inhabitant) of Sallanches.

salle [sal], *s.f.* **1.** hall; (*usu.* large) room; (*a*) **s. de séjour,** living room; **s. commune,** (i) living room; (ii) *Sch:* common room; (iii) *Mil:* day-room; **s. à manger,** (i) dining room; *Mil:* mess (room); *Nau:* dining saloon; (ii) *Furn:* dining-room suite; *Fr.C:* **s. à dîner,** dining room; **s. de bain(s),** (i) bathroom; (ii) bathroom suite; **s. d'eau,** shower room; *A:* **s. du commun,** servants' hall; *Sch:* **s. de classe,** classroom; **s. de cours, s. de conférences,** lecture room; **s. des professeurs,** staff room; (*b*) (*recreational premises, etc.*) **s. des fêtes** = hall (of community centre, etc.); village hall; **s. d'œuvres de la paroisse,** parish hall, church hall; **s. de récréation,** recreation room; **s. de spectacles,** auditorium; concert hall; *Sp:* **partie en s.,** indoor game; **les salles du Louvre,** the galleries of the Louvre; (*c*) (*professional, commercial, etc. premises*) **s. d'accueil, de visite,** reception room; **s. d'attente,** waiting room; **s. de repos (du personnel),** rest room; *Jur:* **s. d'audience,** courtroom; **s. du conseil,** council room, chamber; *Ind: etc:* boardroom; **s. des dactylo(graphe)s,** typing pool; *Com: etc:* **s. de démonstration,** demonstration room, showroom; **s. d'exposition,** showroom; **s. de ventes,** saleroom; auction room; *Ind:* **s. de dessin,** drawing office; **s. d'essais,** testing room; **s. de décapage,** pickling room; **s. des accumulateurs,** accumulator room; **s. des chaudières,** boiler room; **s. des machines,** engine room; plant room; *N.Arch:* **s. à tracer,** mould loft; **s. des gabarits,** template room; **s. d'exploitation radar,** radar operations room; (*of spacecraft*) **s. de contrôle,** control room; *Cin: T.V:* **s. de régie,** control room; *Cin:* **s. de projection, de vision,** viewing room; *Trans:* **s. d'enregistrement des bagages,** luggage registration office; **s. des pas perdus,** waiting hall (of law courts, railway station, etc.); lobby (of Houses of Parliament); **s. d'hôpital,** (hospital) ward; **s. d'opérations,** (operating) theatre; *Mil:* **s. de garde,** guardroom; **s. de police,** (i) prisoners' room; (ii) guardroom; **s. de service,** orderly room; **s. des opérations,** operations room. **2.** *Th: etc:* auditorium, house; **s. pleine,** full house; **toute la s. applaudit,** the whole house, audience, applauded. **3.** *Z:* cheek pouch (of monkey).

Salluste [salyst], *Pr.n.m. Lt.Lit:* Sallust.

Salmanasar [salmanaza:r], *Pr.n.m. A.Hist:* Salmanasar, Shalmaneser.

salmigondis [salmigɔ̃di], *s.m.* **1.** *Cu:* salmagundi; ragout (of various meats). **2.** medley, miscellany, hotchpotch.

salmine [salmin], *s.f. Bio-Ch:* salmine.

salmis [salmi], *s.m.* **1.** *Cu:* salmi; ragout (of roasted game). **2.** *A:* = SALMIGONDIS 2.

salmonella [salmɔnela], *s.f.inv.*, **salmonelle** [salmɔnɛl], *s.f. Bac:* salmonella.

salmonellose [salmɔnɛlo:z], *s.f. Med: Vet:* salmonellosis.

salmoniculteur [salmɔnikyltœ:r], *s.m.* (*a*) salmon breeder; (*b*) trout breeder.

salmoniculture [salmɔnikylty:r], *s.f.* salmon breeding.

salmonidé [salmɔnide], *s.m. Ich:* salmonid; *pl.* **salmonidés,** Salmonidae.

saloir [salwa:r], *s.m.* **1.** salting tub, powdering tub. **2.** *Dom.Ec:* salt sprinkler.

salol [salɔl], *s.m. Pharm:* salol.

Salomé [salɔme], *Pr.n.f. B.Hist:* Salome.

Salomon [salɔmɔ̃], *Pr.n.m.* Solomon; *s.a.* SCEAU; *Geog:* **les îles S.,** the Solomon Islands.

salomonien, -ienne, [salɔmɔnjɛ̃, -jɛn], *Geog:* **1.** *a.* of the Solomon Islands. **2.** *s.* Solomon Islander.

salon [salɔ̃], *s.m.* (*a*) drawing room; sitting room; **petit s.,** (i) morning room; (ii) *Furn:* three-, five-piece suite; (*in hotel, etc.*) **s. réservé,** private room; **jeux de s.,** parlour games; *s.a.* COMÉDIE 1; *F:* **héros de s.,** carpet knight; **fréquenter les salons,** to move in fashionable circles; (*b*) saloon, cabin (in ship, etc.); saloon car (in train); *Mil:* anteroom (of officers' mess); (*c*) *A:* **s. de pose,** (photographer's) studio; **s. de thé,** tea room(s); **s. de coiffure,** hairdressing salon; **s. de modiste,** milliner's showroom; (*d*) **le S.,** the Salon (annual art exhibition in Paris); **le S. de l'automobile,** the (French) Motor Show; **le S. nautique,** the Boat Show; **s. dentaire,** dental trade exhibition; *s.a.* MÉNAGER² 1; (*e*) *Fr.Lit. Hist:* salon (of the marquise de Rambouillet, etc.).

salon(n)ard, -arde [salɔna:r, -ard], *s. Pej:* social climber; person who frequents social gatherings in the hope of making profitable contacts.

Salonique [salɔnik], *Pr.n.f. Geog:* Salonika, Saloniki.

salonnier [salɔnje], *s.m.* **1.** critic (of the *Salon*); art critic. **2.** hairdresser's assistant (for men).

salonnière [salɔnjɛ:r], *s.f. Dressm:* (*haute couture*) head receptionist.

salop, -ope [salo, -ɔp], *s. P:* (*a*) (dirty) bastard; swine, louse; son of a bitch; *f.* bitch; slut; (*b*) *s.f.* **salope,** prostitute, tart.

salopard, -arde [salɔpa:r, -ard], *s. P:* **1.** dirty bastard; shyster; *f.* (dirty) bitch. **2.** *Hist:* rebel fighter.

saloper [salɔpe], *v.tr. P:* to botch (a piece of work).

saloperie [salɔpri], *s.f. P:* **1.** (*a*) filthiness, filth; (*b*) trashy goods; trash, rubbish; (*c*) botched piece of work. **2.** (*a*) **faire une s. à qn,** to play a dirty trick on s.o.; (*b*) **dire des saloperies,** to talk smut.

salopette [salɔpɛt], *s.f.* (*a*) (workman's, child's, etc.) overall(s); (*b*) (engineer's) dungarees; (*c*) rough holland trousers or breeches (for shooting, etc.).

salopiat [salɔpja], *s.m.*, **salopiaud** [salɔpjo], *s.m. P:* = SALAUD.

salpe [salp], *s.m. Moll:* salpa.

salpêtrage [salpetra:ʒ], *s.m.* **1.** *Tchn:* manufacturing of saltpetre, potassium nitrate. **2.** (*a*) formation of saltpetre (on walls, etc.); (*b*) treating (of soil, etc.) with saltpetre.

salpêtre [salpɛtr̥], *s.m.* (*a*) saltpetre, potassium nitrate; **s. du Chili,** Chile saltpetre; sodium nitrate; *F: A:* **c'est un vrai s.,** he flares up at the slightest provocation; (*b*) saltpetre rot (on walls); calcium nitrate.

salpêtrer [salpetre], *v.tr.* **1.** to cover, treat (ground) with saltpetre. **2. l'humidité salpêtre les murs,** damp rots the walls.

se salpêtrer, (*of wall*) to become covered with saltpetre.

salpêtrerie [salpɛtrəri], *s.f.* saltpetre works.

salpêtreux, -euse [salpɛtrø, -ø:z], *a.* saltpetrous (wall, etc.).

salpêtrier [salpɛtri(j)e], saltpetre worker.

salpêtrière [salpɛtri(j)ɛ:r], *s.f.* **1.** *A:* saltpetre works. **2. la S.,** (*in Paris*) home for aged and mentally sick women, originally also for former prostitutes.

salpêtrisation [salpɛtrizasjɔ̃], *s.f.* **1.** covering, treating (of ground) with saltpetre. **2.** rotting (of walls, pictures).

salpicon [salpikɔ̃], *s.m. Cu:* filling for vol-au-vent, etc.

salpidés [salpide], *s.m.pl. Moll:* Salpidae.

salpiglossis [salpiglɔsis], *s.m. Bot:* salpiglossis.

salpingectomie [salpɛ̃ʒɛktɔmi], *s.f. Surg:* salpingectomy.

salpingien, -ienne [salpɛ̃ʒjɛ̃, -jɛn], *a. Anat:* salpingian.

salpingite [salpɛ̃ʒit], *s.f. Med:* salpingitis.

salpingo-ovarite [salpɛ̃gɔɔvarit], *s.f. Med:* salpingo-ovaritis.

salpingostomie [salpɛ̃gɔstɔmi], *s.f. Surg:* salpingostomy.

salpingotomie [salpɛ̃gɔtɔmi], *s.f. Surg:* salpingotomy.

salpinx [salpɛ̃:ks], *s.m. Gr.Ant:* salpinx, trumpet.

salse [sals], *s.f. Geol:* salse, mud volcano.

salsepareille [salsəparɛ:j], *s.f. Bot: Pharm:* sarsaparilla.

salsifis [salsifi], *s.m. Bot: Cu:* salsify; purple goat's beard; *F:* oyster plant; **s. d'Espagne, s. noir,** black salsify, viper's grass, scorzonera; **s. des prés,** Jack-go-to-bed-at-noon.

salsola [salsɔla], *s.m. Bot:* salsola, saltwort.

salsolacées [salsɔlase], *s.f.pl. Bot:* Chenopodiaceae, Salsolaceae.

saltarelle [saltarɛl], *s.f.* saltarello (dance).

saltateur, -trice [saltatœ:r, -tris]. **1.** *a.* dancing. **2.** *s. Rom.Ant:* dancer; acrobat.

saltation [saltasjɔ̃], *s.f.* **1.** *Rom.Ant:* saltation. **2.** (*a*) *Bot: Biol:* saltation, discontinuous variation; saltatory evolution; (*b*) *Geol:* saltation.

saltatoire [saltatwa:r], *a.* **1.** *Ent:* saltatory, saltatorial. **2.** *Med:* **chorée s.,** saltatory spasm.

salticidés [saltiside], *s.m.pl. Arach:* Salticidae.

saltigrade [saltigrad], *a. & s.m.* saltigrade (spider); *pl.* **saltigrades,** Saltigradae.

saltimbanque [saltɛ̃bɑ̃:k], *s.m.* **1.** (*a*) *A:* tumbler; (*b*) member of travelling circus; showman; **voiture de saltimbanques,** showmen's caravan. **2.** *Pol: etc:* mountebank, charlatan.

saltique [saltik], *s.f. Arach:* jumping spider.

salubre [saly:br̥], *a.* salubrious, healthy (air, climate); wholesome (food, water).

salubrement [salybrəmɑ̃], *adv.* salubriously, healthily; wholesomely.

salubrité [salybrite], *s.f.* salubrity, salubriousness, healthiness (of climate, etc.); wholesomeness (of food); **s. publique,** public health; sanitation.

saluer [salɥe], *v.tr.* **1.** (*a*) to salute; to bow to (s.o.); to greet (s.o.); *abs. Av:* to dip; **s. qn d'un coup de chapeau,** to raise one's hat to s.o.; **s. qn de la main,** (i) to wave to s.o.; (ii) to touch one's hat, one's cap, to s.o.; **nous nous saluons,** I have a nodding acquaintance with him; **il sortit en saluant,** he bowed himself out; **passer qn sans le s.,** to cut s.o. (dead); *Bill:* **s. la bille,** to miss; *Mil: etc:* **s. qn du sabre,** to salute s.o. with the sword; **s. du drapeau,** to lower the colour; *U.S:* to droop the colour; *Nau:* **s. du pavillon,** *abs.* **s.,** to dip the flag, *abs.* to dip; **s. du canon,** to fire a salute; **s. de vingt coups,** to fire a salute of twenty guns, to fire a twenty gun salute; **s. qn par un vivat,** to cheer s.o.; (*b*) to greet, to hail; **saluez-le de ma part,** give him my kind regards; *Corr: A:* **j'ai (bien) l'honneur de vous s.,** I am yours very truly; **s. une démarche, une décision, une occasion,** to welcome a step, a decision, an opportunity; **son entrée fut saluée par de longs applaudissements,** his appearance was hailed, greeted, with prolonged applause; **je vous salue, Marie . . .,** hail, Mary . . .; *A:* **s. qn roi,** to hail, acclaim, s.o. king. **2.** *Nau:* **s. un grain,** to reduce sail for a squall.

salueur, -euse [salɥœ:r, -ø:z], *s.* one who bows and scrapes; ceremonious person.

salure [saly:r], *s.f.* (*a*) saltness, salinity; (*b*) **la s. de l'air de la mer,** the tang of the sea air.

salut [saly], *s.m.* **1.** (*a*) safety; *Hist:* **Comité de s. public,** Committee of Public Safety (1793); **chercher son s. dans la fuite,** to seek safety in flight; to fly for one's life; **port de s.,** haven of refuge; *s.a.* PLANCHE 1; (*b*) salvation; **faire son s.,** to find salvation; **travailler à son s.,** to work out one's own salvation; *B:* **quiconque aime Dieu fera son s.,** whosoever loveth God shall be saved; **hors de là point de s.,** without that there is no hope of salvation; **l'Armée du S.,** the Salvation Army; (*c*) saving (of lives, souls). **2.** (*a*) bow, salutation, greeting; **adresser un s. à qn,** (i) to bow to s.o.; (ii) to raise one's hat to s.o.; **faire un grand, un profond, s. à qn,** to bow low to s.o.; **adresser de la tête, de la main, un s. à qn,** to nod to s.o.; to touch one's hat to s.o.; to wave to s.o.; **prendre congé de qn avec force saluts,** to bow oneself out; **s. à tous!** (i) greeting(s) to all! (ii) *F:* hullo, everybody! (iii) *F:* (*on leaving*) so long, everybody! *F:* **bonjour, s.!** hullo, how are you? *Jur: etc:* **à tous ceux qui ces présentes verront, s.,** to all to whom these presents may come, greeting; *s.a.* ENTENDEUR; (*b*) *Mil: etc:* salute; **faire un s.,** to give a salute; **faire le s. militaire,** to salute; **rendre un s.,** to return a salute; **échanger le s.,** to exchange salutes; **s. du drapeau,** lowering of the colour; **s. au drapeau,** (i) saluting the colours; (ii) *Mus:* (salute to the) colours; *Nau:* **s. du pavillon,** dipping of the flag; **s. des armes,** (i) *Mil:* military salute; (ii) *Fenc:* salute with the foils; *s.a.* SALVE. **3.** *R.C.Ch:* (*evening service*) Benediction (of the Holy Sacrament), Salut.

salutaire [salytɛ:r]. **1.** *a.* salutary, beneficial, beneficient; wholesome; **innovation s.,** salutary innovation; **exercer une influence s.,** to exert a salutary influence; to be a power for good. **2.** *s.m. A:* **le S.,** the Saviour.

salutairement [salytɛrmɑ̃], *adv.* wholesomely; beneficially, beneficently.

salutation [salytasjɔ̃]. *s.f.* salutation, greeting; **faire une profonde s. à qn,** to give s.o. a low bow; **salutations à votre famille,** kind regards to your family; (*at end of a letter*) **agréez mes meilleures salutations, mes salutations très respectueuses,** yours sincerely; *s.a.* ANGÉLIQUE 1, EMPRESSÉ.

salutiste [salytist], *s.m. & f.* Salvationist; member of the Salvation Army.

Salvador [salvadɔ:r], *Pr.n.m. Geog:* El Salvador.

salvadoracées [salvadɔrase], *s.f.pl. Bot:* Salvadoraceae.

salvarsan [salvarsɑ̃], *s.m.* arsphenamine; *R.t.m:* Salvarsan.

salvatelle [salvatɛl], *s.f. Anat:* salvatella.

salvateur, -trice [salvatœ:r, -tris], *a.* saving.

salve [salv], *s.f.* **1.** *Artil: Sm.a:* salvo, volley; **tirer une s.,** to fire a salvo, a volley; **tirer par salves,** to fire salvoes; **feu de, par, salves,** volley firing; *Artil:* **s. d'essai,** trial salvo; **s. de réglage,** ranging salvo; **s. efficace,** bracketing salvo; **s. encadrante,** straddle. **2.** *Artil:* salute; **s. d'honneur,** saluting fire, gun salute; **tirer une s. (d'honneur),** to fire a salute.

Salvé [salve], *s.m. Ecc:* Salve Regina (prayer, antiphon, or anthem).

Salvien [salvjɛ̃], *Pr.n.m. Ecc.Hist:* Salvianus.

salviniacées [salvinjase], *s.f.pl. Bot:* Salviniaceae.

Salzbourg [salzbuːr], *Pr.n.m. Geog:* Salzburg.

Samarcande [samarkɑ̃ːd], *Pr.n.f. Geog:* Samarkand.

samare [samaːr], *s.f. Bot:* samara, key, winged seed (of ash, sycamore, etc.).

Samarie [samari], *Pr.n.f. Hist: Geog:* Samaria.

samaritain, -aine [samaritɛ̃, -ɛn]. **1.** *a. & s. Hist: Geog:* Samaritan; *B:* **le bon S.,** the good Samaritan; **Jésus et la Samaritaine,** Jesus and the woman of Samaria. **2.** *s.m. Ling:* Samaritan.

samarium [samarjɔm], *s.m. Ch:* samarium.

samarskite [samarskit], *s.f. Miner:* samarskite.

samba [sɑ̃ba], *s.f. Danc:* samba.

sambar [sɑ̃baːr], *s.m. Z:* sambar, sambur.

sambleu [sɑ̃blø], *int. A:* (*attenuated form of* **sang Dieu**) 'sblood! zounds.

sambuque [sɑ̃byk], *s.f.* **1.** *Mus: A:* (*a*) sambuca, sambuke; (*b*) *B.Lit:* sackbut. **2.** *Rom.Ant:* sambuca (war engine).

sambur [sɑ̃byːr], *s.m. Z:* sambur, sambar.

samedi [samdi], *s.m.* Saturday; **le S. saint,** (the) Saturday before Easter, Holy Saturday.

samien, -ienne [samjɛ̃, -jɛn], *a. & s. Geog:* Samian.

samirésite [samirezit], *s.f. Miner:* samiresite.

samit [sami], *s.m. Tex: A:* samite.

Samnite [samnit], *a. & s. Rom.Hist:* Samnite.

samoan, -ane [samɔɑ̃, -an], *a. & s. Geog:* Samoan.

samole [samɔl], *s.m. Bot:* water pimpernel, brookweed.

Samosate [samɔzat], *Pr.n.f. A.Geog:* Samosata.

samosaténien, -ienne [samɔzatenjɛ̃, -jɛn], *a. & s. A.Geog:* Samosatenian.

samosatien, -ienne [samɔzatjɛ̃, -jɛn], *a. & s. Rel.H:* Samosatenian.

samothracien, -ienne [samɔtrasjɛ̃, -jɛn], *a. & s. Geog:* Samothracian.

samouraï, samurai [samuraːj], *s.m. Japanese Hist:* samurai.

samovar [samɔvaːr], *s.m.* samovar.

samoyède [samɔjɛd]. **1.** *a.* Samoyed; **chien s.,** Samoyed. **2.** (*a*) *s. Ethn:* Samoyed; (*b*) *s.m. Ling:* Samoyed.

sampan(g) [sɑ̃pɑ̃], *s.m.* sampan.

Samson [sɑ̃sɔ̃], *Pr.n.m.* Samson.

Samuel [samɥɛl], *Pr.n.m.* Samuel.

sana [sana], *s.m. F:* sanatorium.

sanatoire [sanatwaːr], *a. A:* curative, healing (ointment, etc.).

sanatorium [sanatɔrjɔm], *s.m.* sanatorium (for tubercular patients).

san-benito [sɑ̃benito], *s.m. Rel.H:* sanbenito; *pl. san-benitos.*

sancerrois, -oise [sɑ̃sɛrwa, -waːz], *a. & s. Geog:* (native, inhabitant) of Sancerre.

Sanche [sɑ̃ːʃ], *Pr.n.m. Spanish Hist:* Sancho.

Sancho Pança [sɑ̃ʃopɑ̃sa], *Pr.n.m. Lit:* Sancho Panza.

sancir [sɑ̃siːr], *v.i. Nau:* to founder head down.

sanctifiant [sɑ̃ktifjɑ̃], *a.* sanctifying (grace).

sanctificateur, -trice [sɑ̃ktifikatœːr, -tris]. **1.** *a.* sanctifying. **2.** *s.* sanctifier; le S., the Holy Ghost, the Sanctifier.

sanctification [sɑ̃ktifikasjɔ̃], *s.f.* (*a*) sanctification; (*b*) **s. du dimanche,** keeping of the Sabbath (day); observance of the Sabbath.

sanctifier [sɑ̃ktifje], *v.tr.* (*p.d. & pr.sub.* **n. sanctifiions, v. sanctifiiez**) to sanctify; to make holy; to hallow; **que Ton nom soit sanctifié,** hallowed be Thy Name; s. **le dimanche,** to keep (holy) the Sabbath (day); to observe the Sabbath.

sanction [sɑ̃ksjɔ̃], *s.f.* sanction. **1.** approbation, assent; **s. royale,** royal assent; **s. de l'usage,** sanction, authority, of custom. **2.** (*a*) **s. (pénale),** penalty; vindicatory, punitive, sanction; coercive weapon; **s. disciplinaire,** summary punishment; **loi qui comporte des sanctions (pénales) pour . . .,** law providing punishment for . . .; (*b*) *Pol:* **prendre des sanctions contre un pays,** to impose sanctions on a country; **prendre des sanctions contre des grévistes,** to take action against strikers; (*c*) **l'échec est la s. de la paresse,** failure is the consequence of, a retribution for, laziness.

sanctionner [sɑ̃ksjɔne], *v.tr.* to sanction. **1.** to approve, ratify, countenance; to give official recognition to; **sanctionné par l'usage,** sanctioned by custom; **s. une théorie de son autorité,** to support a theory with one's authority. **2.** (*a*) to sanction, attach a penalty to (decree); (*b*) to penalize (an offence); (*c*) to penalize (person).

sanctionniste [sɑ̃ksjɔnist], *a. & s.m. & f.* sanctionist.

sanctissime [sɑ̃ktisim], *a.* very holy, most holy, holiest.

sanctuaire [sɑ̃ktɥɛːr], *s.m.* (*a*) *Ecc.Arch:* sanctuary; (*in Jewish Temple*) Sanctuary, Holy of Holies; (*b*) sanctuary, holy place; **Lourdes est un s. très fréquenté,** Lourdes is a shrine visited by many people; (*c*) (wild-life, etc.) sanctuary; (*d*) *Lit:* **dans le s. de mon cœur,** in my heart of hearts, in my inmost heart; **il s'est trouvé un s. loin du bruit de la ville,** he has found a sanctuary, a refuge, far away from the noise of the town.

sanctus [sɑ̃ktys], *s.m. Ecc: Mus:* Sanctus (as part of the Mass).

sandal [sɑ̃dal], *s.m. A:* = SANTAL[1].

sandale [sɑ̃dal], *s.f.* (*a*) sandal; *B:* **secouer la poussière de ses sandales,** to shake off the dust of one's feet; (*b*) fencing shoe, gym shoe; sand-shoe.

sandalette [sɑ̃dalɛt], *s.f.* light sandal.

sandalier, -ière [sɑ̃dalje, -jɛːr], *s.* sandal maker.

sandaraque [sɑ̃darak], *s.f.* **1.** *A:* sandarac, realgar. **2.** (gum) sandarac; **poudre de s.,** (gum-sandarac) pounce.

sandastre [sɑ̃dastr̥], *s.f.,* **sandastros** [sɑ̃dastrɔs], *s.m. Lap:* sandastra, sandastros.

sanderling [sɑ̃dɛrlɛ̃], *s.m. Orn:* **s. (des sables),** sanderling.

sandhi [sɑ̃di], *s.m.inv. Ling:* sandhi.

sandjak [sɑ̃dʒak], *s.m. Turkish Hist:* sanjak.

sandow [sɑ̃dɔːv, sɑ̃do], *s.m. R.t.m:* **1.** *Gym:* chest expander. **2.** *Mec.E: Av: etc:* rubber extensible spring; *Av:* bungee cord.

sandr(e[1]) [sɑ̃ːdr̥], *s.m. Geol:* sandr, sandur.

sandre[2] [sɑ̃ːdr̥], *s.f. Ich:* pike perch; sauger.

sandwich [sɑ̃dwi(t)ʃ]. **1.** *s.m.* sandwich; **homme(-) s.,** sandwich man; *attrib.* **verre s.,** laminated glass; *F:* **pris en s.,** caught, stuck, jammed, sandwiched (between two thgs, pers.). **2.** *Tchn:* **matériaux sandwichs à couches multiples, à trois couches,** multi-layer, three-layer, sandwich materials; *El:* **bobiné en s.,** sandwich-wound. **3.** *Geog:* **les îles S.,** the Sandwich Islands.

sandwicher [sɑ̃dwi(t)ʃe], *v.tr. F:* to sandwich; **les deux dames entre qui j'étais sandwiché,** the two ladies I was sandwiched between.

sanflorain, -aine [sɑ̃flɔrɛ̃, -ɛn], *a. & s. Geog:* (native, inhabitant) of Saint-Flour.

sang [sɑ̃], *s.m.* **1.** blood; **animaux à s. chaud, froid,** warm-blooded, cold-blooded, animals; **coup de s.,** apoplectic fit, *F:* stroke; **yeux injectés de s.,** bloodshot eyes; **répandre, verser, le s.,** to shed blood; **verser son s. pour sa patrie,** to shed one's blood for one's country; **il y a du s. versé entre eux,** there's a blood feud between them; **effusion de s.,** (i) bleeding; (ii) bloodshed; **victoire sans effusion de s.,** bloodless victory; **le prix du sang,** blood money; **écoulement de s.,** bleeding, haemorrhage; **je n'arrive pas à arrêter le s.,** I cannot stop the bleeding; **il était tout en s.,** he was covered with blood; **mains souillées de s., mouchoir taché de s.,** bloodstained hands, handkerchief; **fouetter qn jusqu'au s.,** to flog s.o. till one draws blood; *A:* **se battre au premier s.,** to fight until blood is drawn (and no longer); **avoir le s. chaud,** to be quick-tempered; **le s. lui monta au visage,** the blood rushed to his face; he flushed up; **le s. me bouillait,** I was boiling with impatience; **cela fait bouillir le s.,** it makes one's blood boil; **cela me glace le s.,** it makes my blood run cold; **vent d'est qui vous fouette le s.,** east wind that makes the blood tingle; **il n'a pas de s. dans les veines,** nothing will rouse him; he will stand any insult; **se faire du mauvais s., se manger les sangs,** to fret (and fume); to worry; **ne vous faites pas de mauvais s. à mon sujet,** don't bother your head about me; **se faire du bon s.,** (i) to laugh heartily; (ii) to enjoy oneself, to enjoy life; **je donnerais le plus pur de mon s. pour . . .,** I would give my life's blood to . . .; **son s. soit sur lui,** his blood be on his own head; **ne faites pas retomber sur nous le s. de ces hommes,** do not lay the blood of these men at our door; **se faire un s. d'encre,** to worry oneself sick; *P:* **pisser du s.,** to sweat one's guts out; **suer s. et eau** [sɑ̃keo], to sweat blood; **conte à tourner les sangs,** bloodcurdling tale; **vous m'avez tourné les sangs,** you gave me such a turn! **tout mon s. n'a fait qu'un tour,** my heart leapt into my mouth; **buveur de s.,** bloodthirsty man; *Ind: etc:* **apport en s. frais,** (i) new blood; (ii) fresh, additional, capital; **ces immigrants constituent un apport de s. frais,** these immigrants are bringing fresh, new, blood, into the country; *P:* **bon s. (de bon s.)! bon s. de bon Dieu!** damn and blast it! *P:* **bon s. d'imbécile!** you bloody fool! **2.** (*a*) blood, race, lineage; **Indiens pur s.,** full-blooded Indians; **(homme de) s. mêlé,** half-caste; (*of horse*) **avoir du s.,** to be blooded; **cheval de s.,** blood-horse; **cheval pur s.,** full-bred horse; thoroughbred (horse); **ils sont tous marins; c'est dans le s.,** they are all sailors; it runs in the blood; **s. royal, illustre, bleu,** blue blood; *Prov:* **bon s. ne peut mentir,** blood, breed, will tell; (*b*) blood, kinship, relationship; **les liens du s.,** the ties of kindred; **son propre s.,** one's own flesh and blood; **droit du s.,** birthright; **prince du s.,** prince of the blood; **proximité de s.,** blood relationship; **la voix du s.,** the call of blood, of kinship.

sang-dragon [sɑ̃dragɔ̃], *s.m.,* **sang-de-dragon** [sɑ̃d(ə)dragɔ̃], *s.m.inv.* **1.** dragon's blood (resin). **2.** *Bot: F:* bloodwort, bloody dock.

sang-froid [sɑ̃frwɑ], *s.m. no pl.* coolness, composure, sang-froid; **garder, conserver, son s.-f.,** (i) to keep cool (and collected); (ii) to keep one's temper; **garder un s.-f. imperturbable,** to keep one's sang-froid; to keep cool, as cool as a cucumber; **perdre son s.-f.,** to lose (i) one's self-control, one's self-possession, (ii) one's temper, (one's) patience; *adv.phr.* **de s.-f.,** deliberately; **commettre un crime de s.-f.,** to commit a crime in cold blood.

sanglade [sɑ̃glad], *s.f.* cut (with a whip); lash.

sanglage [sɑ̃glaːʒ], *s.m.* **1.** girthing (of horse); strapping (of packet, etc.); tacking the webbing to (chair, etc.). **2.** lashing, whipping (of s.o.).

sanglant [sɑ̃glɑ̃], *a.* **1.** (*a*) bloody (wound, battle, tale); sanguinary (battle); bloodstained (handkerchief, etc.); (face) covered with blood; (*b*) blood-red. **2.** (*a*) cruel, cutting, bitter (reproach, etc.); **larmes sanglantes,** bitter tears, tears of blood; **soumettre une pièce à une critique sanglante,** to write a scathing criticism of a play; to cut a play to pieces; (*b*) **affront s.,** deadly, outrageous, unforgivable, damnable, insult.

sangle [sɑ̃ːgl̥], *s.f.* **1.** strap, band, webbing; **s. de selle,** (saddle) girth; **lit de s.,** camp bed, trestle bed; **s. dossière,** back strap (of stretcher, etc.); *Aut: Rail:* **s. de portière,** check strap; *Av:* **s. d'ancrage,** mooring band; **s. de sûreté,** safety belt. **2.** *Nau:* (*a*) *pl.* gripes (of a small boat); (*b*) *pl.* gaskets (of furled sails); (*c*) breast rope (for leadsman). **3.** *Nau:* chafing mat.

sangler [sɑ̃gle], *v.tr.* **1.** (*a*) to girth (horse); to strap (parcel, etc.); **s. un fauteuil,** to tack the webbing straps to an armchair; (*b*) **sanglé dans son uniforme,** buttoned up tight in his uniform. **2.** *A:* to thrash, lash (s.o.); **s. un coup de fouet à qn,** to give s.o. a cut with one's whip.

sanglier [sɑ̃gli(j)e], *s.m.* **1.** *Z:* (*a*) wild boar; **chasse au s.,** boar hunting; (*b*) **s. d'Amérique,** peccary; (*c*) **s. d'Afrique,** warthog. **2.** *Ich:* **s. de mer,** boar fish. **3.** *Her:* sanglier.

sanglon [sɑ̃glɔ̃], *s.m. Fish:* gill net.

sanglot [sɑ̃glo], *s.m.* sob; **pousser un s.,** to give a sob; **pousser des sanglots,** to sob; **elle pleurait à gros sanglots,** she was sobbing her heart out, crying fit to break her heart; **elle accepta d'un s.,** she accepted with a sob; **les plaintes et les sanglots des femmes,** the wailing and sobbing of the women; **d'une voix pleine de sanglots elle avoua . . .,** in a sobbing voice she confessed . . . .

sanglotant [sɑ̃glɔtɑ̃], *a.* sobbing (voice, etc.).

sangloter [sɑ̃glɔte], *v.i.* to sob; *with cogn.acc.* **s. des excuses, un aveu,** to sob out an apology, a confession.

sang-mêlé [sɑ̃mele], *s.m.inv.* person of mixed blood; (*outside Europe*), half-caste; (*S. Africa*) coloured person.

sangsue [sɑ̃sy], *s.f.* **1.** (*a*) *Ann:* leech; *Med:* **mettre, poser, des sangsues à qn,** to apply leeches to s.o.; (*b*) *F:* leech, bloodsucker, extortioner; **2.** *A.Med:* **sangsue artificielle,** wet cup.

sanguin, -ine [sɑ̃gɛ̃, -in]. I. *a.* **1.** (*a*) *Anat:* sanguineous; of blood; **émission sanguine,** flow of blood; **groupe s.,** blood group; **transfusion sanguine,** blood transfusion; **les vaisseaux sanguins,** the blood vessels; **le système s.,** the circulatory system; (*b*) *Miner:* **jaspe s.,** bloodstone. **2.** full-blooded, sanguineous (person); **tempérament s.,** sanguine temperament; **un gros homme s.,** a big red-faced man. **3.** *s.m.* dogwood.

II. **sanguine,** *s.f.* **1.** (*a*) red hematite, red chalk; **esquisses à la s.,** sketches in red chalk; *Metalw:* **s. à brunir,** polishing stone; (*b*) red chalk drawing, sanguine. **2.** bloodstone. **3.** blood orange.

sanguinaire [sɑ̃ginɛːr]. **1.** *a.* sanguinary; bloodthirsty (man); bloody (fight). **2.** *s.f. Bot:* bloodroot; sanguinaria; red puccoon.

sanguinelle [sɑ̃ginɛl], *s.f. Bot:* dogwood.

sanguinivore [sɑ̃ginivɔːr], *a. Nat.Hist:* sangui(ni)vorous.

sanguinolent [sãginɔlã], *a.* **1.** sanguinolent, tinged with blood; *Med:* **crachats sanguinolents,** sanguinolent sputa. **2.** *Nat.Hist:* blood-red.

sanguisorbe [sãgųisɔrb], *s.f. Bot:* burnet, bloodwort; (*genus*) Sanguisorba.

sanhédrin [sanedrɛ̃], *s.m. Jewish Ant:* Sanhedrin, Sanhedrim.

san-heen [sanen], *s.m.inv. Mus:* samisen.

sanicle [sanikl], *s.f.,* **sanicule** [sanikyl], *s.f. Bot:* sanicle; **s. d'Europe,** wood sanicle.

sanidine [sanidin], *s.f. Miner:* sanidine, glassy feldspar.

sanie [sani], *s.f. Med:* sanies, pus, matter.

sanieux, -euse [sanjø, -ø:z], *a. Med:* sanious (matter, ulcer).

sanitaire [sanitɛ:r]. **1.** *a.* (*a*) medical; **personnel s.,** medical staff, personnel; **matériel s.,** medical stores, equipment; **propagande s.,** hygiene propaganda; *Mil: etc:* **formation s.,** hospital unit; **voiture s.,** ambulance; **compagnie s. auto-(mobile),** ambulance company; **point de chargement en voitures sanitaires,** ambulance loading point; **avion s.,** ambulance plane, aircraft; **planeur s.,** ambulance glider; **train s.,** hospital, ambulance, train; *Nau:* **déchargement s.,** unloading (of ship) with special sanitary precautions; (*b*) *Plumb:* sanitary; **matériel s.,** sanitary ware, equipment; **technicien en équipement s.,** sanitary engineer; **technique s., constructions et matériel sanitaires,** sanitary engineering; **système s.,** sanitation; *Nau:* **eau s.,** sanitary water; **pompe s.,** sanitary pump. **2.** *s.m.* **le s.,** *F:* **les sanitaires,** sanitary ware, equipment, installations; *F:* (the) plumbing. **3.** *s.f. Mil: etc:* (motor) ambulance.

sanité [sanite], *s.f. A:* healthiness.

sans [sã], *prep.* **1.** (*a*) without; **partez s. moi,** go without me; **il est revenu s. argent,** he came back without any money; **il est revenu s. l'argent,** he came back without the money; **il est revenu s. un sou, s. le sou,** he came back without a penny; **il arriva s. argent ni bagages,** he arrived without either money or luggage; **je ne l'ai jamais vue sans son chapeau,** I have never seen her without her hat off; **s. naissance,** of humble birth; **s. faute,** without fail; **il a été un bon gradé, s. plus,** he was a good N.C.O., nothing more; **s. parler,** without speaking; **cela va s. dire,** (it's a matter) of course; **s. être belle, elle plaisait,** although (she was) not beautiful, she was attractive; **s. mentir,** to tell the truth; **vous n'êtes pas s. le connaître,** you cannot fail to know him; **ces questions n'étaient pas s. m'embarrasser,** these questions were naturally somewhat embarrassing; **non s. difficulté,** not without difficulty; **non s. éprouver quelques inquiétudes,** not without experiencing a few qualms; *F:* **pourquoi porter des lunettes si vous y voyez s.?** why wear spectacles if you can see, can do, without? *P:* **des lettres de lui? voila trois mois qu'on est s.,** letters from him? we haven't had any for three months; *Com:* (**on bill of exchange) s. frais, s. protêt, s. compte de retour,** no expenses; *conj.phr.* **s. que** + *sub.,* without + *ger.;* **s. que nous le sachions,** without our knowing it; **il ne parlait jamais s. qu'on lui parlât,** he never spoke unless he was spoken to; **il ne se passe jamais une année s. qu'il nous écrive,** a year never passes without his writing to us; *s.a.* PLUS 2; (*b*) -less, -lessly, -free; **plaintes s. fin,** endless complaints; **se plaindre s. fin,** to complain endlessly; **homme s. peur,** fearless man; **agir s. peur,** to act fearlessly; **plaine s. arbres,** treeless plain; **jour s. pluie,** rainless day; **être sans le sou,** *F:* **être s. un sou,** to be broke, to be penniless; **elle mourut s. enfants,** she died childless; **régime s. sel,** salt-free diet; **baignade s. danger,** safe bathing; (*c*) **un-; plaintes s. fin,** unending complaints; **courage s. exemple,** unexampled courage; **parler s. cesse,** to talk unceasingly; **sans hésiter,** unhesitatingly. **2.** but for, were it not for; **s. vous je ne l'aurais jamais fait,** but for you I should never have done it; **s. cela, s. quoi,** otherwise, else, had it not been for that.

sans-abri [sãzabri], *s.m.inv.* homeless (person).

sans-atout [sãzatu], *s.m.inv. Cards:* **demander s.-a.,** to call no trumps.

sans-cœur [sãkœ:r], *s.m. & f.inv. F:* heartless person.

sanscrit [sãskri], *a. & s.m. Ling:* Sanskrit.

sanscritique [sãskritik], *a.* Sanskritic.

sanscritiste [sãskritist], *s.m.* Sanskrit scholar; Sanskritist.

sans-culotte [sãkylɔt], *s.m. Hist:* (*Fr. Revolution*) sansculotte, sansculottist; extreme republican; *pl. sans-culottes.*

sans-culottide [sãkylɔtid], *a. & s.f. Hist:* (jours) **sans-culottides,** sansculottides.

sans-culottisme [sãkylɔtism], *s.m.* sansculottism.

sansevière [sãsəvjɛ:r], *s.f. Bot:* sansevieria.

sans-façon [sãfasɔ̃]. **1.** *s.m.* (*a*) honesty, straightforwardness, bluntness (of speech, etc.); (*b*) unceremoniousness; (*c*) off-handedness. **2.** *a. & s.m. & f.inv.* (*a*) homely, unpretentious, informal (person); (*b*) offhand (person).

sans-famille [sãfami:j], *s.m.pl.* (the) homeless.

sans-faute [sãfo:t], *s.m.inv. Equit:* clear round.

sans-fil [sãfil], *s.inv. O:* **1.** *s.f.* wireless (telegraphy). **2.** *s.m.* (**dépêche par) s.-f.,** radio, wireless, message.

sans-filiste [sãfilist], *s.m. & f. O:* **1.** wireless, radio, enthusiast. **2.** wireless, radio, operator. **3.** *attrib.* **électricien s.-f.,** wireless, radio, engineer; *pl. sans-filistes.*

sans-gêne [sãʒen]. **1.** *s.m.* (offensive) off-handedness, over-familiarity; *F:* cheek. **2.** (*a*) *a.inv.* unceremonious; (*b*) *s.m. & f.inv.* unceremonious person; **en voilà un s.-g.!** well, that's a cool customer!

sans-gîte [sãʒit], *s.m.pl.* (the) homeless.

sanskrit [sãskri], *a. & s.m. Ling:* Sanskrit.

sanskritique [sãskritik], *a.* Sanskritic.

sanskritiste [sãskritist], *s.m.* Sanskrit scholar; Sanskritist.

sans-le-sou [sãlsu], *s.m. & f.inv. F:* penniless, destitute, person.

sans-logis [sãlɔʒi], *s.m. & f.inv.* homeless person.

sansonnet [sãsɔne], *s.m.* **1.** *Orn:* starling; *F:* **c'est de la roupie de s.,** it's rubbish, *U.S:* it's for the birds. **2.** *Fish: Dial:* small mackerel.

sans-parti [sãparti], *s.m. & f.inv. Pol:* **les membres du parti (communiste) et les s.-p.,** members of the Party and non-Party members.

sans-patrie [sãpatri], *s.m. & f.inv.* stateless person.

sans-soin [sãswɛ̃], *s.m. & f.inv. F:* careless person.

sans-souci [sãsusi], *s.inv.* **1.** *s.m. & f.* happy-go-lucky kind of person; easy-going, carefree, individual. **2.** *s.m.* carefree manner, state of mind; unconcern; insouciance; **il est d'un s.-s. inconcevable,** he is inconceivably easy-going.

sans-travail [sãtrava:j], *s.m. & f.inv.* unemployed (person).

santal¹ [sãtal], *s.m. Bot: Com:* sandal(wood); (*a*) **s. blanc, s. citrin,** sandalwood (proper); white sandalwood; *Pharm:* **essence de s. citrin,** sandalwood oil; (*b*) **s. citrin (de Cochinchine),** yellow sandalwood, yellow-wood; (*c*) **s. rouge (des Indes),** red sandalwood, red sanders; African rosewood.

Santal², -als [sãtal], *s.m.* **1.** *Ethn:* Santal. **2.** *Ling:* Santali.

santé [sãte], *s.f.* (*a*) health; **s. physique, morale,** physical, moral, well-being; **s. mentale,** mental health; **être en bonne s.,** to be well, in good health; **être en parfaite s.,** to be in perfect health, in the best of health; **s. de fer, de cheval,** iron constitution; **ne pas avoir de s.,** to be in poor health; **avoir une s. fragile, une s. délicate,** *F:* **avoir une petite s.,** to be delicate; **jeune homme à l'air plein de s.,** healthy-looking young man; **respirer la s.,** to look the picture of health; **absent pour raison de s.,** absent on account of illness, on medical grounds; **rendre la s. à qn, rendre qn à la s.,** to restore s.o. to health; **maison de s.,** (private) nursing home; *Prov:* **s. passe richesse,** health before wealth; **boire à la s. de qn, porter la s. de qn,** to drink s.o.'s health; **à votre s.!** your health! *F:* cheers! *Sw.Fr:* *F:* (*when s.o. sneezes*) **s!** (God) bless you! *F:* **et les santés? et ces petites santés?** how's everybody? *P:* **vous en avez une s.!** you've got a nerve! *P:* **tu lui as fait son travail? tu en as une s.!** you did his work for him? you are a fool, a sucker! (*b*) *Adm:* **Ministère de la S. publique,** Ministry of Health; **médecin de la s.,** medical officer of health; **directeur de la s.,** chief medical officer of health; **le service de (la) s.,** (i) *Mil:* the medical service, staff, corps, department; (ii) *Nau:* the quarantine service; (iii) *F:* the port doctor; **école du service de s. militaire** = Army Medical College; **la S. = la prison de la s.** (a Paris prison); **bureau de s.,** (i) board of health; (ii) health officer's office; *Nau:* **agent de (la) santé,** quarantine officer; *Navy:* **conseil de santé,** medical board; **officier de s.,** (i) *Nau:* health officer (of port); (ii) *A:* medical practitioner authorized to practise without a degree.

santoline [sãtɔlin], *s.f. Bot:* santolina, lavender cotton; **s. cyprès,** ground cypress.

santon¹ [sãtɔ̃], *s.m.* santon. **1.** Mohammedan monk. **2.** (*in Algeria*) tomb of a saint. **3.** (*in Provence*) clay, carved wood, figure (in Christmas crib).

santon², -onne [sãtɔ̃, -ɔn], *a. & s. Geog:* (native, inhabitant) of Saintes.

santonine [sãtɔnin], *s.f.* **1.** (*a*) *Bot:* santonica; (*b*) *Pharm:* santonica; Levant wormseed. **2.** *Ch:* santonin.

santonique [sãtɔnik], *a. Ch:* santonic (acid).

santonnier [sãtɔnje], *s.m.* (*in Provence*) maker of santons.

sanve [sã:v], *s.f. Bot:* charlock, wild mustard.

saoul [su], **saoulard, saouler** = SOÛL, SOÛLARD, SOÛLER.

sapaie [sapɛ], *s.f.* forest of fir trees.

sapajou [sapaʒu], *s.m.* (*a*) *Z:* sapajou; (*b*) *F: A:* mischievous little monkey (of a child).

sapan [sapã], *s.m. Bot: Dy:* sapan wood.

sape [sap], *s.f.* **1.** (*a*) undermining (of wall, tower, etc.); *Mil:* sapping; (*b*) sap, trench; **s. debout,** direct double sap; **s. en zigzag,** zigzag sap; **s. en galeries de mine,** underground sap; **exécuter une s.,** to drive a sap; **faire déboucher une s.,** to break out a sap; **travail en s.,** sapping; **tête de s., saphead;** (*c*) *F:* army engineers, sappers. **2.** (*a*) mattock; (miner's) hoe; (*b*) (Flemish) short-handled scythe; (*c*) **s. d'un piolet,** adze of an ice axe. **3.** *P:* conviction, sentence; **s. de gonzesse,** light sentence. **4.** *pl. P:* **sapes,** clothes, togs.

sapé [sape], *a. P:* **bien s.,** well-dressed.

sapement [sapmã], *s.m.* **1.** sapping, undermining, undercutting. **2.** *P:* conviction, sentence.

sapèque [sapɛk], *s.f. Num:* sapek, sapeque.

saper [sape], *v.tr.* **1.** to sap, undermine (foundations, etc.); **s. un principe à la base,** to undermine a principle. **2.** *Dial:* (*a*) to cut, excavate, (coal) with a hoe; (*b*) to cut (wheat). **3.** *P:* to convict, sentence (s.o.). **4.** *P:* to dress; **être bien sapé,** to be well dressed.

saperlipopette [saperlipɔpɛt], **saperlotte** [saperlɔt], *int. F:* good heavens! heavens above!

saperde [saperd], *s.f. Ent:* saperda.

sapeur [sapœ:r], *s.m. Mil:* sapper; pioneer; **s. du génie,** engineer sapper; *A:* **s. du régiment,** regimental sapper, infantry sapper; *F:* **fumer comme un s.,** to smoke like a chimney, to smoke one's head off.

sapeur-aérostier [sapœraerɔstje], *s.m. A: Mil:* soldier of a balloon unit; balloon man; *pl. sapeurs-aérostiers.*

sapeur-cycliste [sapœrsiklist], *s.m. A: Mil:* sapper cyclist; *pl. sapeurs-cyclistes.*

sapeur-mineur [sapœrminœ:r], *s.m. A:* sapper and miner; *pl. sapeurs-mineurs.*

sapeur-pompier [sapœrpɔ̃pje], *s.m. Adm:* fireman; **les sapeurs-pompiers,** the fire brigade.

sapeur-télégraphiste [sapœrtelegrafist], *s.m. A: Mil:* telegraph operator; **les sapeurs-télégraphistes,** the signal corps; *F:* signals.

saphène [safɛn], *s.f. Anat:* saphena (vein); **grande s.,** long, internal, saphena; **petite s.,** short, posterior, external, saphena.

saphique [safik], *a.* **1.** *Pros:* sapphic (stanza, etc.); **vers saphiques,** sapphics. **2.** lesbian.

saphir [safi:r], *s.m.* **1.** *Orn:* sapphire; *Miner:* **s. mâle,** indigo-blue sapphire; **s. femelle,** blue fluorspar; **s. du Brésil,** blue tourmaline, indicolite; **s. faux,** sapphire quartz; **s. blanc, s. d'eau,** white sapphire, water sapphire. **2.** *Rec:* sapphire. **3.** *a.inv. & s.m.* (the colour of) sapphire.

Saphire [safi:r], *Pr.n.f. B.Hist:* Sapphira.

saphirin, -ine [safirɛ̃, -in]. **1.** *a.* sapphirine. **2.** *s.f. Miner:* saphirine, sapphirine.

saphisme [safism], *s.m.* sapphism; lesbianism.

Sapho [safo], *Pr.n.f. Gr.Lit:* Sappho.

sapide [sapid], *a.* sapid; savoury; palatable.

sapidité [sapidite], *s.f.* sapidity; savouriness; palatability.

sapience [sapjã:s], *s.f. A:* sapience, wisdom.

sapiential, -aux [sapjãsjal, -o], *a. B:* **les livres sapientiaux, s. les sapientiaux,** the books of Wisdom.

sapin [sapɛ̃], *s.m.* **1.** (*a*) *Bot:* fir (tree); **s. argenté, blanc, pectiné, des Vosges,** silver fir, Swiss pine; **s. baumier,** balsam fir, silver pine, Canada balsam fir; **s. du Nord, de la Baltique, d'Écosse,** northern pine, Baltic pine, Scotch fir, Scotch pine; **s. de Norvège, s. blanc,** Norway spruce, Norway fir, white fir; **s. de Nordmann,** Nordmann's fir; **s. de Douglas,** Douglas fir, Douglas pine, red fir; **s. épicéa,** spruce; **faux s.,** pitchpine; (*b*) *Com:* (**bois de) sapin,** deal; **s. rouge,** red deal. **2.** *F: A:* cab, four-wheeler; (*b*) coffin; **sentir le s.,** to have one foot in the grave; **toux qui sent le s.,** churchyard cough.

sapinages [sapina:ʒ], *s.m.pl. Fr.C:* fir bush; fir branches.
sapindacé [sapɛ̃dase], *Bot:* **1.** *a.* sapindaceous. **2.** *s.f.pl.* **sapindacées,** Sapindaceae.
sapindé [sapɛ̃de], *a. Bot:* sapindaceous.
sapine [sapin], *s.f.* (*a*) fir plank; deal board; (*b*) *Const:* crane tower; (*c*) *Vit:* deal tub.
sapineau, -eaux [sapino], *s.m. Bot:* young fir.
sapinette [sapinɛt], *s.f.* **1.** *Bot:* (hemlock) spruce; **s. blanche, noire,** white, black, spruce. **2.** spruce beer.
sapinière [sapinjɛ:r], *s.f.* **1.** fir plantation; pinetum. **2.** deal coffin.
sapiteur [sapitœ:r], *s.m. M.Ins:* valuer (of cargo).
sapogénine [sapɔʒenin], *s.f. Ch:* sapogenin.
saponacé [sapɔnase], *a.* saponaceous, soapy.
saponaire [sapɔnɛ:r], *s.f. Bot:* saponaria; **s. d'Orient,** soap root; **s. officinale,** soapwort, saponary.
saponase [sapɔna:z], *s.f. Bio-Ch:* lipase.
saponifiable [sapɔnifjabl̩], *a.* saponifiable.
saponifiant [sapɔnifjɑ̃], *Ch:* **1.** *a.* saponifying. **2.** *s.m.* saponifier, saponifying agent.
saponification [sapɔnifikasjɔ̃], *s.f.* saponification; **indice de s.,** saponification number.
saponifier [sapɔnifje], *v.tr.* (*p.d. & pr.sub.* **n. saponifiions, v. saponifiiez**) to saponify.
saponine [sapɔnin], *s.f. Ch:* saponin(e).
saponite [sapɔnit], *s.f. Miner:* saponite, soapstone.
sapotacées [sapɔtase], *s.f.pl. Bot:* Sapotaceae.
sapote [sapɔt], *s.f. Bot:* mammee sapota, marmalade plum.
sapotier [sapɔtje], *s.m. Bot:* (*a*) marmalade tree, sapote; (*b*) sapodilla (tree), naseberry.
sapotille [sapɔti:j], *s.f. Bot:* sapodilla (plum); **s. mamey,** mammee sapota, marmalade plum.
sapotillier [sapɔtije], *s.m. Bot:* sapodilla (tree), naseberry.
sapotoxine [sapɔtɔksin], *s.f. Ch:* sapotoxin.
sappan [sapɑ̃], *s.m. Bot:* sapan wood.
saprelotte [saprəlɔt], *int. F:* good heavens!
saprémie [sapremi], *s.f. Med:* sapraemia, septicaemia.
sapristi [sapristi], *int. F:* good heavens! heavens above!
saprobionte [saprɔbjɔ̃:t], *s.m. Biol:* saprobe, saprobiont.
saprogène [saprɔʒɛn], *a. Med:* saprogenic, saprogenous.
saprolégniales [saprɔleɲjal], *s.f.pl. Fung:* Saprolegniales.
saprolégnie [saprɔleɲi], *s.f. Fung:* saprolegnia.
sapropel, sapropèle [saprɔpɛl], *s.f. Geol:* sapropel.
sapropélique [saprɔpelik], *a.* sapropelic.
saprophage [saprɔfa:ʒ], *a. Ent:* saprophagous.
saprophyte [saprɔfit], *s.m. Biol:* saprophyte.
saprophytique [saprɔfitik], *a. Bot:* saprophytic.
saprophytisme [saprɔfitism], *s.m. Bot:* saprophytism.
saprozoïte [saprɔzɔit], *a. Biol:* saprozoic.
sapucaia [sapykaja], *s.m. Bot:* sapucaia (tree).
saqueboute [sakbut], **saquebute** [sakbyt], *s.f. Mus: A:* sackbut.
saquer[1] [sake], *v.tr. Nau:* to jerk (heavy body) along.
saquer[2], *v.tr. P:* to sack (s.o.); to give (s.o.) the sack, the boot; to fire (s.o.); **être saqué,** to get the sack, the boot; to be fired.
Sara(h) [sara], *Pr.n.f.* Sara(h); *Th: F: O:* **faire sa S.,** to make the most of a stage death (like Sarah Bernhardt).
sarabande [sarabɑ̃:d], *s.f. Danc: Mus:* (*a*) saraband; (*b*) *F:* (i) wild dancing; (ii) uproar, bedlam.
saragossain, -aine [saragɔsɛ̃, -ɛn], *a. & s. Geog:* (native, inhabitant) of Saragossa.
Saragosse [saragɔs], *Pr.n.f. Geog:* Saragossa.
sarbacane [sarbakan], *s.f.* **1.** (*a*) blowtube, blowpipe, sarbacand, sarbacane (for killing birds, etc.); (Malay's) sumpitan; (child's) peashooter; (*b*) *Glassm:* blowpipe. **2.** *A:* speaking tube.
sarcasme [sarkasm], *s.m.* (piece of) sarcasm; sarcastic remark; taunt, gibe; **essuyer les sarcasmes de qn,** to put up with s.o.'s sarcasm; **c'est un s. à votre adresse,** that's a dig at you.
sarcastique [sarkastik], *a.* sarcastic.
sarcastiquement [sarkastikmɑ̃], *adv.* sarcastically, in a sarcastic manner, tone.
sarcelle [sarsɛl], *s.f. Orn:* **s. d'hiver,** teal; **s. d'été,** garganey; **s. élégante,** Baikal teal; **s. marbrée,** marbled duck; **s. soucrourette,** blue-winged teal; **s. à faucilles,** falcated teal.
sarcelline [sarsɛlin], *s.f. Orn:* (**sarcelle**) **s.,** teal.
sarcine[1] [sarsin], *s.f. Bac:* sarcina.
sarcine[2], *s.f. Ch:* sarcine, sarkine, hypoxanthine.
sarclage [sarkla:ʒ], *s.m.* weeding.
sarcler [sarkle], *v.tr.* **1.** to clean (a field); to weed (garden, etc.); to hoe, spud (turnips, vine). **2.** to hoe up, out (weeds).
sarclet [sarklɛ], *s.m.,* **sarclette** [sarklɛt], *s.f.* (weeding) hoe.
sarcleur, -euse [sarklœ:r, -ø:z]. **1.** *s.* weeder. **2.** *s.f.* **sarcleuse,** weeding machine, weeder.
sarcloir [sarklwa:r], *s.m.* (weeding) hoe; spud.
sarclure [sarkly:r], *s.f.* (uprooted) weeds; weedings.
sarco- [sarkɔ], *pref.* sarco-.
sarcoblaste [sarkɔblast], *s.m. Biol:* sarcoblast.
sarcocarpe [sarkɔkarp], *s.m. Bot:* sarcocarp.
sarcocèle [sarkɔsɛl], *s.f. Med:* sarcocele.
sarcocollier [sarkɔkɔlje], *s.m. Bot:* sarcocolla.
sarcocyste [sarkɔsist], *s.m. Vet:* sarcocyst.
sarcode [sarkɔd], *s.m. Biol:* sarcode.
sarcoderme [sarkɔdɛrm], *s.m. Bot:* sarcoderm.
sarcoïde [sarkɔid], *a. & s.f. Med:* sarcoid.
sarcolactique [sarkɔlaktik], *a. Ch:* sarcolactic (acid).
sarcolemme [sarkɔlɛm], *s.m. Anat:* sarcolemma.
sarcolite [sarkɔlit], *s.f. Miner:* sarcolite.
sarcologie [sarkɔlɔʒi], *s.f.* sarcology.
sarcomateux, -euse [sarkɔmatø, -ø:z], *a. Med:* sarcomatous.
sarcomatose [sarkɔmato:z], *s.f. Med:* sarcomatosis.
sarcome [sarko:m], *s.m. Med:* sarcoma.
sarcophage [sarkɔfa:ʒ]. **1.** *s.m.* sarcophagus. **2.** *s.f. Ent:* fleshfly.
sarcophile [sarkɔfil], *s.m. Z:* sarcophile, Tasmanian devil; (*genus*) Sarcophilus.
sarcoplasma [sarkɔplasma], *s.m.,* **sarcoplasme** [sarkɔplasm], *s.m. Anat:* sarcoplasm(a).
sarcoplastique [sarkɔplastik], *a. Anat:* sarcoplastic.
sarcopte [sarkɔpt], *s.m. Arach:* sarcoptid; (*genus*) Sarcoptes; **s. de la gale,** itch mite.
sarcoptidés [sarkɔptide], *s.m.pl. Arach:* Sarcoptidae.
sarcoramphe [sarkɔrɑ̃:f], *s.m. Orn:* sarcoramphus.
sarcosine [sarkɔzin], *s.f. Ch:* sarcosin(e).
sarcose [sarko:z], *s.f. Med:* sarcosis.
sarcosome [sarkozo:m], *s.m. Anat:* sarcosome, sarcosoma.
sarcosporidies [sarkɔspɔridi], *s.f.pl. Prot:* Sarcosporidia.
sarcosporidiose [sarkɔspɔridjo:z], *s.f. Vet: Med:* sarcosporidiosis.
Sardaigne [sardɛɲ], *Pr.n.f. Geog:* Sardinia.
Sardanapale [sardanapal]. **1.** *Pr.n.m. A.Hist:* Sardanapalus. **2.** *s.m. Lit:* (type of) effeminate and dissolute monarch.
sardanapalesque [sardanapalɛsk], *a. Lit:* Sardanapalian (life, etc.).
sardane [sardan], *s.f. Mus: Danc:* (Catalonian) sardana.
sarde [sard]. **1.** *a. & s. Geog:* Sardinian. **2.** *s.m. Lap: A:* sard. **3.** *s.f. Ich:* bonito.
Sardes [sard], *Pr.n.f. A.Geog:* Sardis.
sardien, -ienne [sardjɛ̃, -jɛn], *a. & s. A.Geog:* Sardian.
sardine [sardin], *s.f.* **1.** (*a*) *Ich:* sardine; (young) pilchard; (*b*) *Com:* sardine; **sardines à l'huile,** tinned sardines; *F:* **serrés comme des sardines,** packed like sardines. **2.** (*a*) *Mil: F:* N.C.O.'s stripe; (*b*) *P:* **les sardines,** the fingers.
sardinerie [sardinri], *s.f.* sardine curing and packing establishment.
sardinier, -ière [sardinje, -jɛ:r]. **1.** *s.* (*a*) sardine fisher; (*b*) sardine curer, packer. **2.** *s.m.* (*a*) sardine net; (*b*) sardine boat.
Sardique [sardik], *Pr.n.f. A.Geog:* Sardica (today Sofia).
sardoine [sardwan], *s.f. Lap:* sard.
sardonien [sardɔnjɛ̃], *a.m. Med:* sardonic (laughter, rictus).
sardonique [sardɔnik], *a.* sardonic (smile, grin).
sardoniquement [sardɔnikmɑ̃], *adv.* sardonically; in a sardonic manner, tone.
sardonyx [sardɔniks], *s.f. Miner:* sardonyx.
sargasse [sargas], *s.f.* sargasso, gulf weed; *Geog:* **la mer des Sargasses,** the Sargasso Sea.
sargue [sarg], *s.m. Ich:* sar, sargus, sargo.
sari [sari], *s.m. Cost:* sari.
sariette [sarjɛt], *s.f. Bot:* savory.
sarigue [sarig], *s.m.* (*the female is* **la sarigue**) *Z:* sarigue; (South American) opossum; quica.
sarisse [saris], *s.f. Gr.Ant:* sarissa, Macedonian spear.
sarkinite [sarkinit], *s.f. Miner:* sarkinite.
sarladais, -aise [sarladɛ, -ɛ:z], *a. & s. Geog:* (native, inhabitant) of Sarlat.
Sarmates [sarmat], *s.m.pl. A.Hist:* Sarmatians.
Sarmatie [sarmati], *Pr.n.f. A.Geog:* Sarmatia.
sarmatien, -ienne [sarmatjɛ̃, -jɛn], **sarmatique** [sarmatik], *a. A.Geog:* Sarmatian, Sarmatic.
sarment [sarmɑ̃], *s.m.* (*a*) vine shoot; *P:* **jus de s.,** wine; (*b*) (any) woody climbing stem; bine.
sarmenter [sarmɑ̃te], *v.i.* to gather up the shoots (after pruning vines).
sarmenteux, -euse [sarmɑ̃tø, -ø:z], *a.* (*a*) *Hort:* sarmentous, sarmentose; **rosier s.,** rambler; (*b*) **vigne sarmenteuse,** climbing vine; vine long in the stalk; (*c*) gnarled (limb, etc.).
Saron [sarɔ̃], *Pr.n.m. Geog:* Sharon.
sarong [sarɔ̃], *s.m. Cost:* sarong.
saros [saros], *s.m. Astr:* saros.
Sarpédon [sarpedɔ̃], *Pr.n.m. Gr.Lit:* Sarpedon.
sarracéniacées [sarasenjase], *s.f.pl. Bot:* Sarraceniaceae.
sarracéniales [sarasenjal], *s.f.pl. Bot:* Sarraceniales.
sarracénie [saraseni], *s.f. Bot:* sarracenia, pitcher plant.
sarracénique [sarasenik], *a. Hist:* Saracenic.
sarraf [saraf], *s.m.* shroff; money-changer (in the East).
sarrasin, -ine [sarazɛ̃, -in]. **1.** *Hist:* (*a*) *a.* Saracenic, Saracen; (*b*) *s.* Saracen. **2.** *s.m.* (*a*) *Agr:* buckwheat; Saracen corn; (*b*) *Metall:* waste, sweepings; (*c*) *pl. Nau:* brash ice; (*d*) *Typ: P:* non-union workman. **3.** *s.f.* **sarrasine,** portcullis.
sarrasinière [sarazinjɛ:r], *s.f.* barn, grange (for storing buckwheat).
sarrasinois, -oise [sarazinwa, -wa:z], *a. & s. Hist:* Saracen.
sarrau [saro], *s.m. Cost:* overall, smock; *pl. sarraus, sarraux.*
Sarre (la) [lasa:r], *Pr.n.f. Geog:* (i) the (river) Saar; (ii) the Saar Basin; (iii) Saarland, the Saar; **en Sarre,** in the Saar (region).
Sarrebourg [sarbu:r], *Pr.n.m. Geog:* Sarrebourg, Saarebourg.
sarrebourgeois, -oise [sarburʒwa, -wa:z], *a. & s. Geog:* (native, inhabitant) of Sarrebourg.
Sarrebruck [sarbryk], *Pr.n.m. Geog:* Saarbrücken.
sarrebruckois, -oise [sarbrykwa, -wa:z], *a. & s.* (native, inhabitant) of Saarbrücken.
sarregueminois, -oise [sargəminwa, -wa:z], *a. & s. Geog:* (native, inhabitant) of Sarreguemines.
Sarrelouis [sarlwi], *Pr.n.m. Geog:* Saarlouis.
sarrette [sarɛt], *s.f. Bot:* sawwort.
sarriette [sarjɛt], *s.f. Bot: Cu:* savory; **essence de s.,** savory oil; **s. des jardins,** summer savory; **s. des montagnes,** winter savory.
sarrois, -oise [sarwa, -wa:z], *a. & s. Geog:* (native, inhabitant) of the Saar; Saarlander.
sarrussophone [sarysɔfɔn], *s.m. Mus:* sarrusophone.
sartenais, -aise [sartənɛ, -ɛ:z], *a. & s. Geog:* (native, inhabitant) of Sartène.
sarthois, -oise [sartwa, -wa:z], *a. & s. Geog:* (native, inhabitant) of the department of Sarthe.
sartinois, -oise [sartinwa, -wa:z], *a. & s. Geog:* (native, inhabitant) of Sartène.
sartorite [sartɔrit], *s.f. Miner:* sartorite.
sartorius [sartɔrjys], *s.m. Anat:* sartorius (muscle).
sas[1] [sɑ, sas], *s.m.* sieve, bolter, screen, riddle; **s. mobile,** cradle rocker; **passer qch. au s.,** to sift, bolt, sth.; *A:* (**faire**) **tourner le s.,** to turn, cast, the riddle (and shears) (in divination).
sas[2], *s.m.* (*a*) *Hyd.E:* lock chamber; coffer; (*b*) lock; *Civ.E: Nau: etc:* **s. à air, s. pneumatique,** air lock (of boiler room, etc.); (*c*) flooding chamber (of submarine).
sassafras [sasafrɑ(s)], *s.m. Bot:* sassafras.
sassage[1] [sɑsa:ʒ], *s.m.* (*a*) sifting, bolting, screening (of flour, etc.); (*b*) *Min:* jigging (of ore); (*c*) polishing (of precious metals by rubbing in sand).
sassage[2], *s.m.* passing (of a boat) through a lock; locking (of a boat).
Sassanide [sasanid], *a. & s. A.Hist:* Sassanid, Sassanian.
sasse[1] [sɑ:s], *s.f. Nau:* bailing scoop, bailer.
sasse[2], *s.f. Mill:* (flour) bolter.
sassement[1,2] [sɑsmɑ̃], *s.m.* = SASSAGE[1,2].
sasser[1] [sɑse], *v.tr.* (*a*) to sift, bolt, screen (flour, plaster); to winnow (grain); *Min:* to jig (ore); (*b*) *Lit:* **s.** (**et ressasser**), to sift, scrutinize (evidence); to examine minutely (pros and cons); to go over (a matter) again and again.
sasser[2], *v.tr.* to pass (a boat) through a lock; to lock (a boat).
sasseur, -euse [sɑsœ:r, -ø:z]. **1.** *s. Mill: etc:* sifter; winnower. **2.** *s.m.* (*a*) sifting machine; winnower; (*b*) *Min:* (dry) jigger; jig.
sassoire [saswa:r], *s.f. Veh:* slider; sway bar.
sassoline [sasɔlin], *s.f. Miner:* sassoline, native boracic acid.

sassure [sɑsyːr], *s.f. Mill: etc:* siftings.
Satan[1] [satɑ̃], *Pr.n.m.* Satan.
satan[2], *s.m. Z:* satan monkey.
satané [satane], *a. F:* (*intensive, always before the noun*) devilish, confounded; **s. temps!** beastly weather! **ah, le s. farceur!** the devil take him and his jokes! **c'est un s. menteur,** he's the devil of a liar.
satanique [satanik], *a.* satanic; fiendish (cruelty); diabolical (idea, grin, etc.).
sataniquement [satanikmɑ̃], *adv.* satanically; fiendishly; diabolically.
satanisme [satanism], *s.m.* satanism.
satellisable [satɛl(l)izabl̥], *a. Space:* **ce n'est pas s. avec ce type de fusée,** it cannot be put into orbit with this type of rocket.
satellisation [satɛl(l)izasjɔ̃], *s.f.* (*a*) putting into orbit, orbiting, (of satellite, spacecraft); **programme de s.,** space programme; (*b*) *Pol:* (*of country*) becoming a satellite.
satelliser [satɛl(l)ize], *v.tr.* (*a*) to put (satellite, spacecraft, man, etc.) into orbit; (*b*) *Pol:* to make (a country) into a satellite.
satellite [satɛllit]. **1.** *s.m.* (*a*) *A:* satellite, henchman; (*b*) *Astr:* satellite, secondary planet; **s. artificiel,** artificial satellite; **s. porteur d'êtres vivants,** biosatellite; **s. habité (par l'homme),** manned satellite; **s. non habité,** unmanned satellite; **s. auxiliaire,** subsatellite; **s. stationnaire, synchrone,** stationary, synchronous, satellite; **s. terrestre, lunaire,** earth-orbiting, moon-orbiting, satellite; **s. de collecte de données, s. de renseignement,** data-gathering satellite; **s. de détection nucléaire,** nuclear-detection satellite; **s. de détection, s. recenseur, des ressources naturelles, s. de prospection,** earth-resources satellite, resource-census satellite; **s. géodésique, géophysique,** geodetic, geophysical, satellite; **s. de navigation,** navigation(al) satellite; **s. de télécommunications,** (tele)communications satellite, comsat; **s. militaire de télécommunications,** military (tele)communications satellite; **s. météorologique,** weather satellite, meteorological satellite, metsat; **lancer un s. en orbite autour de la terre, de la lune,** to launch a satellite into orbit around the earth, the moon; (*c*) *a. & s.m. Pol:* **(pays) s.,** satellite (state); (*d*) *Tchn:* planet wheel, bevel gear; **engrenage à satellites,** planet gear, sun-and-planet gear; (*e*) *Bot:* trabant, satellite. **2.** *a.* (*a*) *Anat:* **veines satellites,** companion veins; (*b*) **agglomération s.,** satellite town.
satellitisme [satɛl(l)itism], *s.m.* satellitism.
sâti [sɑti], *Hindu Rel:* **1.** *s.m.* suttee, sutteeism. **2.** *s.f.* suttee (widow).
satiété [sasjete], *s.f.* satiety; surfeit; **manger jusqu'à s.,** to eat to repletion, to eat one's fill.
satin [satɛ̃], *s.m.* **1.** *Tex:* satin; **s. de laine,** calamanco; **s. à effet de chaîne,** warp sateen; **ruban (de) s.,** satin ribbon; **drap s.,** satin cloth; **une peau de s.,** a smooth and delicate skin. **2.** (*a*) **bois de s.,** satinwood; (*b*) *Bot:* **s. blanc,** honesty, white satin, satin flower.
satinade [satinad], *s.f. Tex:* satinet(te).
satinage [satinaːʒ], *s.m.* (*a*) satining (of ribbon, cloth); glazing (of leather); hot pressing (of paper, linen); surfacing (of paper); (*b*) *Phot:* burnishing, enamelling (of print).
satinaire [satinɛːr], *s.m. Tex:* satin weaver.
satiné [satine]. **1.** *a.* satiny, satin-like; **spath s.,** satin gypsum; **cuir s.,** glazed leather; **papier s.,** hot-pressed paper, glazed paper. **2.** *s.m.* (*a*) gloss; (*b*) *a. & s.m. Bot:* **(bois) s.,** satinwood; (*c*) *Furn:* gold embroidery; (*d*) **le s. de la peau,** the satin of the skin. **3.** *s.f. Bot:* **satinée,** honesty, satin flower.
satiner [satine]. **1.** *v.tr.* (*a*) to satin, give a glossy surface to (material, etc.); to glaze (leather); to surface (paper); **s. du linge, du papier (à chaud),** to (hot-)press linen, paper; **s. à froid,** to cold-press; **cylindre à s.,** glazing roll; (*b*) *Phot:* to burnish, enamel (print); **presse à s.,** burnisher, enameller. **2.** *v.i.* (*of fruit*) to take on a satiny appearance, become satiny.
satinette [satinɛt]. **1.** *s.f. Tex:* sateen, satinet(te). **2.** *a. Orn:* **pigeon s.,** satinette.
satineur, -euse [satinœːr, -øːz]. **1.** *s.* satiner, glazer (of cloth, paper, etc.). **2.** *s.f.* **satineuse,** satining machine, glazing machine.
satire [satiːr], *s.f.* **1.** satire **(contre,** on); **s. personnelle,** lampoon; **trait de s.,** epigram. **2.** satirizing; **faire la s. de son époque,** to satirize one's times.
satirique [satirik]. **1.** *a.* satiric(al). **2.** *s.m. & f.* satirist.
satiriquement [satirikmɑ̃], *adv.* satirically.
satiriser [satirize], *v.tr.* to satirize.
satiriste [satirist], *s.m.* satirist.
satisfaction [satisfaksjɔ̃], *s.f.* **1.** satisfaction, contentment; **s. de ses appétits,** gratification of one's appetites; **donner de la s. à qn,** to give s.o. cause for satisfaction; **enfant qui donne de la s. à sa mère,** child who is a joy to his mother; **donner s. aux vœux de qn,** to satisfy s.o.'s desires; **avoir la s. de faire qch.,** to have the satisfaction of doing sth.; **vos désirs ont reçu s.,** your desires have been met, have been complied with; **témoignage de s.,** expression of commendation (by the authorities); **s. de soi-même,** (i) sense of duty done; (ii) self-satisfaction, self-complacency. **2.** reparation, amends **(pour, de,** for); *Theol:* atonement (for); **demander à qn s. (d'une offense),** to demand from s.o. satisfaction (for an insult), *A:* to challenge s.o.; **donner s. à qn,** to give s.o. satisfaction.
satisfactoire [satisfaktwaːr], *a. Theol:* atoning, satisfactory (act, alms).
satisfaire [satisfɛːr], *v.* (*conj. like* FAIRE) to satisfy. **1.** *v.tr.* (*a*) to satisfy, please; to give satisfaction to (s.o.); **s. ses maîtres,** to satisfy, please, one's masters; **s. sa curiosité,** to gratify, satisfy, one's curiosity; **s. le désir de qn,** (i) to meet, grant, (ii) to carry out, (iii) to gratify, s.o.'s wish; **s. une rancune personnelle,** to gratify a personal grudge; **s. l'attente de qn,** to answer, come up, to, s.o.'s expectation; **je ne me satisfais pas de conjectures,** I am not content with guesses; **le travail sera fait de manière à vous s.,** the work will be done to your satisfaction; *abs. Com:* **s. pour qn,** to meet s.o.'s liabilities; (*b*) to make amends to (s.o.); *abs. Theol:* to make atonement; (*c*) **se s. de peu,** to be satisfied, contented, with very little; *abs.* **se s.,** (i) to relieve oneself; (ii) to satisfy one's sexual desires. **2.** *v.ind.tr.* (*a*) *A:* **s. à qn,** to give s.o. satisfaction; to meet s.o.'s challenge; (*b*) **s. (à qch.),** to meet (demands); to answer, meet, satisfy (condition, objection); to carry out (undertaking); to fulfil, carry out (one's desires); to comply with (regulation, etc.); **s. à un examen,** to satisfy the examiners (at an examination); *Mth:* **s. à une équation,** to satisfy an equation.
satisfaisant [satisfəzɑ̃], *a.* satisfying; satisfactory; **réponse satisfaisante, travail s.,** satisfactory reply, work; **repas s.,** satisfying meal; **d'une manière satisfaisante,** satisfactorily; **peu s.,** unsatisfactory; **d'une manière peu satisfaisante,** unsatisfactorily.
satisfait, -aite [satisfɛ, -ɛt], (*a*) *a.* satisfied, contented; comfortable; **s'estimer s.,** to consider oneself lucky; **tenez-vous pour s.,** rest content(ed); *Iron:* **vous voilà s.!** well, you asked for it! **je suis très s. de son travail,** I'm very pleased with his work; **je n'en suis pas s.,** I'm not pleased with it, not happy about it; *Com:* **j'espère que vous en serez entièrement s.,** I hope it will meet with your entire approval, will give you complete satisfaction; **mal s.,** dissatisfied **(de,** with); (*b*) *s.* satisfied, contented, person; **les hommes les plus riches ne sont pas des satisfaits,** the richest men are not contented.
satisfecit [satisfesit], *s.m.inv. Sch:* good mark; good report.
satrape [satrap], *s.m.* (*a*) *A.Hist:* satrap; (*b*) despot.
satrapie [satrapi], *s.f.* (*a*) satrapy; (*b*) despotic government.
satrapique [satrapik], *a.* satrapic, despotic.
Satsoma [satsɔma], **Satsuma** [satsyma]. **1.** *Pr.n. Geog:* Satsuma; *Cer:* **faïence de S.,** *s.m.* **le satsuma,** Satsuma ware. **2.** *s.f.* **satsuma,** satsuma (orange).
saturabilité [satyrabilite], *s.f.* saturability.
saturable [satyrabl̥], *a.* saturable.
saturant [satyrɑ̃], *a.* saturating, saturant; *Ph:* **vapeur saturante,** saturated vapour.
saturateur [satyratœːr], *s.m.* (*a*) *Ch: Ind:* saturator; (*b*) humidifier.
saturation [satyrasjɔ̃], *s.f.* (*a*) saturation; **dissoudre un sel jusqu'à s.,** to dissolve a salt to saturation; **s. en eau, gaz, huile,** water, gas, oil, saturation; *Elcs:* **caractéristiques de s.,** bottoming characteristics (of transistor); (*b*) (*in advertising*) **campagne de s.,** all-out (publicity) campaign.
saturé [satyre], *a.* saturated (solution, compound); *Com:* **le marché est s.,** the market has reached saturation point; **il a trop lu de romans policiers; il en est s.,** he has read too many detective stories and has had enough of them, and doesn't want to read any more; **le stationnement est impossible dans les villes saturées,** parking is impossible in overcrowded cities.
saturer [satyre], *v.tr.* (*a*) to saturate (solution, acid) **(de,** with); **l'air est saturé de vapeur d'eau,** the air is saturated with vapour; (*b*) **cette propagande exagérée a fini par s. le public,** the public has had enough of, has got fed up with, this exaggerated propaganda.
saturnales [satyrnal], *s.f.pl.* (*a*) *Rom.Ant:* Saturnalia; (*b*) (*occ.* **la saturnale**) debauch.
Saturne [satyrn]. **1.** *Pr.n.m. Myth: Astr:* Saturn. **2.** *s.m. A.Ch:* lead, saturn; *Pharm: A:* **extrait de S.,** Goulard's extract.
saturnides [satyrnid], *s.m.pl. Ent:* Saturniidae, Saturniids, the emperor moth family.
saturnie [satyrni], *s.f. Ent:* emperor moth; (*genus*) Saturnia.
saturnien, -ienne [satyrnjɛ̃, -jɛn], *a.* **1.** *Pros:* saturnian (metre, etc.). **2.** *A: & Lit:* saturnine (disposition).
saturnin [satyrnɛ̃], *a.* saturnine. **1.** pertaining to lead; **intoxication saturnine,** lead poisoning; **paralysie saturnine,** lead palsy. **2.** *A:* gloomy (disposition).
saturnisme [satyrnism], *s.m. Med:* lead poisoning, saturnism, plumbism.
saturomètre [satyrɔmɛtr̥], *s.m.* brine gauge.
satyre[1] [satiːr], *s.m.* **1.** (*a*) satyr; (*b*) *F:* sex maniac. **2.** *Ent:* satyr butterfly. **3.** *Fung:* phalloid; **s. puant,** stinkhorn.
satyre[2], *s.f. Gr.Lit:* satyric drama.
satyresse [satirɛs], *s.f. Lit:* she-satyr.
satyriasis [satirjazis], *s.m. Med:* satyriasis.
satyrides [satirid], *s.m.pl. Ent:* Satyridae, the satyrids.
satyrion [satirjɔ̃], *s.m. Bot:* orchid, *A:* satyrion.
satyrique [satirik], *a. Gr.Ant:* **1. drame s.,** satyric drama. **2. danse s.,** dance of satyrs.
satyrisme [satirism], *s.m.* satyrism.
sauce [soːs], *s.f.* **1.** sauce; **s. blanche, s. béchamel,** white sauce; melted butter sauce; **s. aux câpres,** caper sauce; **s. aux champignons,** mushroom sauce; **s. d'un rôti,** sauce from the roast; gravy; **s. courte,** sauce in small quantity; thick sauce. **rallonger la s.,** (i) to thin out the sauce; (ii) *F:* to pad out a book; to spin out a story; *Prov:* **il n'est s. que d'appétit,** hunger is the best sauce; *F:* **accommoder un même sujet à toutes les sauces,** to dish up the same subject in every shape; **on le met à toutes les sauces,** he is put to every kind of work; **la s. vaut mieux que le poisson, la s. fait manger, passer, le poisson,** the accessory is better than the principal; **à quelle s. sera-t-il mangé?** how shall we deal with it, him? **on ne sait à quelle s. le mettre,** one doesn't know what use to make of it, of him; *A:* **vous ne sauriez faire, mettre, une bonne s. à cela,** you can't do much with that; *A:* **faire sa s. à qn,** to give s.o. a good blowing-up; *F:* **un repas à vingt francs sans la s.,** a twenty franc meal without extras; **gâter la s.,** to spoil the whole business; **qu'il en boive la s.,** he must put up with the consequences; *F:* **être dans la s.,** to be in the soup; *Av: Aut: F: O:* **mettre toute la s.,** to open the throttle, to give full throttle, to step on the gas. **2.** (*a*) *Draw:* soft black crayon, black chalk, lamp black; (*b*) *Tobacco Ind: Gilding:* sauce. **3.** *F:* shower.
saucé [sose], *a. A.Num:* dipped, (thinly) silver-plated (coins).
saucée [sose], *s.f. F:* **1.** (*a*) downpour; (*b*) **recevoir une s.,** to get a wetting, a soaking. **2.** scolding, dressing down, blowing-up.
saucer [sose], *v.tr.* **(je sauçai(s); n. sauçons) 1.** (*a*) to dip, sop, steep (one's bread, etc.) in the sauce; (*b*) to souse, drench (sth. in a liquid); **s. des feuilles de tabac,** to damp tobacco leaves with sauce; *F:* **l'orage nous a saucés,** we got drenched, wet through, in the storm. **2.** *F:* to scold; to give (s.o.) a blowing-up.
saucier [sosje], *s.m.* **1.** sauce cook. **2.** *Nau:* socket, saucer (of the capstan).
saucière [sosjɛːr], *s.f. Dom.Ec:* sauceboat.
sauciflard [sosiflaːr], *s.m. P:* sausage, banger.
saucisse [sosis], *s.f.* **1.** (*a*) *A:* (large preserved) sausage (ready for eating); (*b*) (fresh) sausage (that requires cooking); *F:* **il n'attache pas ses chiens avec des saucisses,** he's very mean; (*c*) *P:* idiot, nit. **2.** *Mil: F:* (*a*) observation balloon; barrage balloon; (*b*) trench-mortar shell.
saucisson [sosisɔ̃], *s.m.* **1.** (*a*) (large) sausage; cold sausage; **s. à l'ail,** garlic sausage; (*b*) *P:* idiot, nit; (*c*) cylindrical loaf. **2.** (*a*) *Exp:* powder hose; saucisse; (*b*) *Mil:* (long) fascine. **3.** *Av: F:* aerial torpedo.
saucissonner [sosisɔne], *F:* **1.** *v.tr.* to tie up like a sausage. **2.** *v.i.* to picnic, to eat a snack; **nous avons saucissonné dans le train,** we ate a snack meal in the train.

saucissonneur, -euse [sosisɔnœːr, -øːz], *s. F:* picnicker.

sauf¹, sauve [sof, soːv], *a.* safe, unscathed, unhurt; **sain et s.,** safe and sound; **l'honneur est s.,** honour is saved; **s'en tirer la vie sauve,** to get off with one's life, with a whole skin; **ils obtinrent la vie sauve,** they obtained an assurance that their lives would be spared.

sauf², *prep.* save, but, except; **tout son bien fut vendu s. une terre,** all his property was sold except (for) one estate; **il est indemne s. une écorchure au bras,** he is unhurt except for a grazed arm; **il n'a rien s. ses gages,** he has nothing except, beyond, his wages; **s. correction,** subject to correction; *A:* **s. votre respect,** saving your presence; **s. avis contraire (de votre part), s. contrordre,** unless I hear to the contrary, *Com:* failing your advice to the contrary; **s. indication contraire,** unless otherwise stated, specified; **s. décision contraire du conseil,** unless the council decides to the contrary; **s. disposition expressément contraire,** except where otherwise expressly provided; **s. convention contraire entre les parties,** unless otherwise agreed by the parties; **s. de rares exceptions,** with very few exceptions; **s. accidents, s. imprévu,** barring accidents, unless anything unforeseen occurs; **s. erreur ou omission,** errors and omissions excepted; **je consens, s. à revenir sur ma décision,** I consent, but I reserve the right to reconsider my decision; **je vous ai griffonné qch., s. à corriger plus tard,** I've scribbled sth. down for you, subject to correction later; **s. à la rendre malheureuse,** short of making her unhappy; **s. s'il pleut,** unless it rains, if it doesn't rain; **s. d'user de violence,** short of (using) violence; **je n'ai rien fait, s. d'écrire des lettres,** I haven't done anything, except for, apart from, writing some letters; *conj.phr. F:* **sauf que** + *ind.,* except, that; **il en est sorti indemne, s. qu'il a perdu son chapeau,** he came out of it unscathed, except for losing his hat; **tout se passa bien s. que la mariée arriva en retard,** everything went off well, apart from the fact that the bride was late.

sauf-conduit [sofkɔ̃dɥi], *s.m.* safe conduct, pass; *pl. sauf-conduits.*

sauge [soːʒ], *s.f.* (*a*) *Bot: Cu:* sage; **s. sauvage, s. des prés,** meadow sage; **s. amère, s. des bois,** bitter sage, wood sage; **s. sclarée,** clary; (*b*) *Bot:* salvia.

saugé [soʒe], *s.m.,* **sauget** [soʒɛ], *s.m. Bot:* (variety of) lilac.

saugrenu [sogrəny], *a.* absurd, preposterous, ridiculous (question, answer, idea).

saugrenuité [sogrənɥite], *s.f.* absurdity, preposterousness, ridiculousness.

saugue [soːg], *s.f.* Mediterranean fishing boat.

Saül [sayl], *Pr.n.m. B.Hist:* Saul.

saulaie [solɛ], *s.f.* willow plantation.

saule [soːl], *s.m. Bot:* willow; **s. pleureur,** weeping willow; **s. blanc,** white willow, swallow-tail willow; *Com:* bat willow; **s. des vanniers,** velvet osier; **s. pourpre,** red osier.

saulée [sole], *s.f.* row of willows.

saulet [solɛ], *s.m. Orn: F:* tree sparrow.

saulsaie [solsɛ], *s.f.* willow plantation.

saumâtre [somɑːtr], *a.* **1.** brackish, briny (taste, water). **2.** *F:* (*a*) (*of pers.*) bitter, sour; (*b*) **je la trouve s.,** I think it's a bit thick.

saumier [somje], *s.m.* salmon gaff.

saumon [somɔ̃], *s.m.* **1.** *Ich:* salmon; **s. de fontaine,** brook trout, speckled trout; **rivière pleine de saumons,** river full of salmon; *a.inv.* **rubans saumon,** salmon-pink ribbons. **2.** *Metall:* ingot (of tin, etc.); pig (of lead, etc.); **s. de fonte,** pig (iron); *Nau:* kentledge; **plomb en s.,** pig lead. **3.** *Av:* detachable wing tip; **s. de dérive,** vertical stabilizer tip; **s. de plan fixe,** horizontal stabilizer tip.

saumoné [somɔne], *a. used esp. in* **truite saumonée,** salmon trout.

saumoneau, -eaux [somɔno], *s.m. Ich:* young (salmon-) peel; samlet, parr, pink.

saumonelle [somɔnɛl], *s.f. Fish:* (*a*) small fry; (*b*) whitebait.

saumoner [somɔne], *v.tr.* to colour (sth.) salmon-pink.

saumur [somyːr], *s.m.* (*also* **vin de S.**) Saumur (wine); **s. mousseux,** sparkling Saumur (wine).

saumurage [somyraːʒ], *s.m.* pickling (in brine).

saumure [somyːr], *s.f.* (pickling) brine; pickle; **conserver de la viande dans la s.,** to pickle meat; **anchois conservés dans la s.,** anchovies in brine.

saumuré [somyre], *a.* pickled (in brine); brined (anchovies, meat).

saumurer [somyre], *v.tr.* to pickle; **s. des harengs,** to pickle, marinate, herrings.

saumurien [somyrjɛ̃], *s.m. Mil:* cadet at the cavalry school of Saumur.

saumurois, -oise [somyrwa, -waːz], *a. & s. Geog:* (native, inhabitant) of Saumur.

sauna [sona], *s.m.* sauna.

saunage [sonaːʒ], *s.m.,* **saunaison** [sonɛzɔ̃], *s.f.* **1.** salt making; *Hist:* **faux saunage,** breaking of the salt laws, illicit salt making. **2.** salt trade. **3.** time, season, for salt making.

sauner [sone]. **1.** *v.i.* (*a*) to make salt; (*b*) (*of salt marsh*) to deposit its salt. **2.** *v.tr.* **s. un marais salant,** to extract the salt from a salt marsh.

saunerie [sonri], *s.f.* **1.** salt works, saltern. **2.** *A:* salt market.

saunier [sonje], *s.m.* **1.** salt maker. **2.** salt merchant; *Hist:* **faux s.,** maker of, dealer in, contraband salt.

saunière [sonjɛːr], *s.f.* **1.** salt box. **2.** *Husb:* salt lick.

saupe [soːp], *s.f. Ich: F:* Mediterranean bream.

saupiquet [sopikɛ], *s.m. Cu:* sharp, spiced sauce for meat stews.

saupoudrage [sopudraːʒ], *s.m.* **1.** powdering, sprinkling, dusting, dredging (with sugar, salt, flour, etc.). **2.** *Adm: Fin:* allocation (of small amounts of credit to a large number of recipients); **le s. aboutit à un gaspillage énorme,** the division of credit leads to enormous waste (of money).

saupoudrer [sopudre], *v.tr.* **1.** *A:* to sprinkle (sth.) with salt. **2.** (*a*) to sprinkle, powder, dust, dredge (de, with); **s. un gâteau de sucre,** to dust a cake with sugar; **se s. de talc,** to dust oneself (over) with talcum powder; (*b*) **s. un discours de citations latines,** to sprinkle, interlard, a speech with Latin quotations.

saupoudreuse [sopudrøːz], *s.f.,* **saupoudroir** [sopudrwaːr], *s.m.* dredger, sprinkler; castor; sugar sifter.

saur [sɔːr], *a.m.* **hareng s.,** red herring.

saure [sɔːr], *a.* yellowish-brown; (*a*) (*of horse*) sorrel; **jument s.,** sorrel mare; (*b*) unfledged, callow (bird); *esp.* **faucon s.,** red hawk.

saurel [sɔrɛl], *s.m. Ich:* horse mackerel; scad.

saurer [sɔre], *v.tr.* to kipper (herrings); to smoke (fish, bacon).

saurésie [sɔrezi], *s.f. Rept:* West Indian slow worm.

sauret [sɔrɛ], *a.m. & s.m. O:* **(hareng) s.,** red herring.

sauriasis [sɔrjazis], *s.m. Med:* sauriosis, sauriasis.

saurien [sɔrjɛ̃], *a. & s.m. Rept:* saurian; *s.m.pl.* **sauriens,** Sauria.

saurin [sɔrɛ̃], *s.m.* freshly smoked herring, bloater.

saurir [sɔriːr], *v.tr.* (*a*) to smoke (fish, etc.); (*b*) to pickle (fish, etc.).

sauris [sɔri], *s.m. Cu:* (pickling) brine.

saurissage [sɔrisaːʒ], *s.m.* (*a*) bloating, curing, kippering (of herrings); (*b*) pickling (of fish, meat).

saurisserie [sɔrisri], *s.f.* herring-curing establishment.

saurisseur [sɔrisœːr], *s.m.* (*pers.*) herring curer.

sauroïde [sɔrɔid], *a. & s.m. Z:* sauroid.

sauropodes [sɔrɔpɔd], *s.m.pl. Paleont:* Sauropoda.

sauropsidés [sɔrɔpside], *s.m.pl. Z:* Sauropsida.

sauroptérygien [sɔrɔpteriʒjɛ̃], *s.m. Paleont:* sauropterygian; *pl.* **sauroptérygiens,** Sauropterygia.

saururés [sɔryre], *s.m.pl. Orn: Paleont:* Saururae.

saussaie [sosɛ], *s.f.* willow plantation.

saussurite [sosyrit], *s.f. Miner:* saussurite.

saussuritisation [sosyritizasjɔ̃], *s.f.* saussuritization.

saut [so], *s.m.* **1.** (*a*) jump; leap; vault; *Sp:* **s. en longueur, en hauteur,** long jump, high jump; **triple s.,** triple jump; **s. de pied ferme, sans élan,** standing jump; **s. précédé d'une course,** running jump; **s. à la perche,** pole vault, pole jump; **s. d'obstacles, de barrière, de haie,** obstacle jumping, hurdle jumping, hurdling; **s. de côté avec appui des mains,** (side) vaulting; **s. en skis,** ski jump; **s. en parachute,** parachute drop; *Swim:* **s. de l'ange,** swallow dive; **faire un s.,** to take a leap; (*of horse*) **faire des sauts,** to curvet; **se lever d'un s.,** (i) to leap up (out of a chair, etc.); (ii) to leap out of bed; **au s. du lit,** on getting up; on getting out of bed; **franchir un fossé de plein s.,** to clear a ditch at one bound; *P:* **le grand s.,** the final plunge, death; **faire le s.,** (i) to take a decision, the plunge; (ii) to give in, give way; *F:* **faire le s. en l'air,** to be hanged, to swing for it; **faire le s. périlleux,** (i) to (do a) somersault; (ii) to make a decision, to take the plunge; *Wr:* **s. de Breton,** Breton fall; *O:* **faire le s. de Breton à qn,** to wreck s.o.'s plans; **avancer par sauts et par bonds,** to skip, hop, along; **aller par sauts et par bonds, to speak,** write, disjointedly, disconnectedly, in a jerky manner; **travailler par sauts et par bonds,** to work spasmodically, by fits and starts; **la nature procède parfois par sauts,** nature sometimes advances by leaps and bounds; **arriver à une dignité d'un (plein) s.,** to reach a high position straight away, *F:* at one go; **faire un s. (jusqu')en ville, (jusqu')à Paris,** to pop into town, over to Paris; **faites donc un saut chez le boulanger,** just slip round, pop over, to the baker's; **il a fait un s. vers la porte,** he made a beeline for the door; **il n'y a qu'un s. d'ici là,** it's only a stone's throw (away); (*b*) **s. de température,** sudden rise, jump, in temperature; **s. d'un cordage,** surge, jerk, of a rope; **s. brusque d'une courbe,** kick-up of a curve; (*c*) *Mus:* skip; disjunct interval; (*d*) *Elcs:* (*computers*) **instruction de s.,** jump instruction; branch instruction; skip instruction; (control) transfer instruction; **s. conditionnel,** conditional branch; conditional control transfer; **s. de bande,** tape skip; **s. après impression,** tape slew; **s. de papier,** paper throw, slew; (*e*) *Breed:* covering. **2.** waterfall; **le s. du Doubs,** the falls on the Doubs; **s. de moulin,** fall between the leat and the water wheel. **3.** *Nau:* **s. d'un palan,** thorough foot in a tackle.

sautage [sotaːʒ], *s.m.* **1.** *A:* (*a*) blowing up, explosion (of mine, etc.); (*b*) blasting. **2.** *Typwr:* skipping (of space); **dispositif de s.,** tabulating key.

sautant [sotɑ̃], *a. Her:* saltant.

saut-de-lit [sodli], *s.m.* (light) dressing gown; *pl. sauts-de-lit.*

saut-de-loup [sodlu], *s.m.* (*a*) ha-ha, sunk fence; (*b*) (basement) area; *pl. sauts-de-loup.*

saut-de-mouton [sod(ə)mutɔ̃], *s.m. Civ.E:* flyover, *U.S:* overpass; *pl. sauts-de-mouton.*

saut-de-ski [sod(ə)ski], *s.m.* (*a*) *Sp:* ski-jump; (*b*) *Civ.E:* ski-jump, spillway.

saute [soːt], *s.f.* (sudden) change (of temperature); jump (in temperature, price); *esp. Nau:* **s. de vent,** shift, change, of wind; **s. d'humeur,** (sudden) change of mood; *El:* **s. d'intensité, de tension,** surge.

sauté [sote]. **1.** *a. & s.m. Cu:* sauté. **2.** *a. Tex:* **maille sautée,** drop stitch.

sautée [sote], *s.f.* leap; **ce ruisseau est d'une s.,** you can clear this stream in one leap.

sauteler [sotle], *v.i.* to hop (like a sparrow); to skip, jump (about).

sautelle [sotɛl], *s.f.* layered vine shoot.

saute-mines [sotmin], *s.m.inv. Mil:* mine exploder, mine-exploding device.

saute-mouton [sotmutɔ̃], *s.m. no pl.* (*a*) *Games:* leapfrog; (*b*) *Elcs:* (*computers*) **test s.-m.,** leapfrog test.

saute-moutonner [sotmutɔne], *v.i.* to play leapfrog.

sauter [sote]. **1.** *v.i.* (*the aux. is* **avoir**) (*a*) to jump; to leap; to skip; **les chiens sautaient après moi,** the dogs were jumping up at me; **s. de joie,** to leap for joy; **s. à la perche,** to pole-vault; **s. à la corde,** to skip (with a skipping rope); **s. du lit,** to leap out of bed; **s. à cheval, s. en selle,** to spring, leap, on to one's horse, into the saddle; **s. à terre,** (i) to jump down; (ii) *Equit:* to dismount; **s. en parachute,** to parachute (out); to bale out; **s. d'un sujet à un autre, du coq à l'âne,** to skip from one subject to another; **s. du rire aux larmes,** to pass suddenly from laughter to tears; **s. aux yeux, au collet, à la gorge, de qn,** to fly at s.o., at s.o.'s throat; **cela saute aux yeux,** it's obvious; *F:* **et que ça saute!** and make it snappy! step on it! **s. sur son adversaire,** to fling, hurl, oneself at one's opponent; **s. au cou de qn,** to fling one's arms round s.o.'s neck; **reculer pour mieux s.,** (i) to step back in order to have a better take-off; (ii) *Iron:* to procrastinate (only to find one's difficulties increased); **s. au plafond,** (i) to jump out of one's skin; (ii) to be overjoyed, to leap for joy; **s. sur une offre,** to leap, jump, at an offer; **s. sur l'occasion,** to jump at the opportunity; (*b*) (*of mine*) to explode; (*of powder magazine, etc.*) to blow up; (*of bank, etc.*) to go smash; (*of ministry*) to fall; (*of business*) to go bankrupt, to fail; (*of button, etc.*) to come off, to fly off; (*of rivet*) to start; *El:* (*of fuse*) to blow, *F:* to go; (*c*) *Nau:* (*of the wind*) to change, shift; to chop round; to veer; **vent qui ne fait que s.,** baffling wind; (*d*) **faire s.,** to make (s.o., sth.) jump; to blast (rock); to blow up (bridge, etc.); to explode (mine); to burst (boiler); to wreck (plan, etc.); to bring down (government, etc.); to sack, fire (official); *Cu:* to sauté (potatoes, etc.); *Agr:* to ted (hay); to toss (in the air); **faire s. un enfant sur ses genoux,** to bounce a child up and down on one's knees, one's lap; *Cu:* **faire s. une crêpe,** to toss a pancake; **le prix qu'il a demandé nous a fait s.**, the price he asked made us jump; **faire s. une serrure**, to burst a lock (open); **faire s. l'argent**, to make the money fly; **faire s. la caisse**, to rob the till; **faire s. un piège**, to spring a trap; **faire s. un bouton**, to burst a button; **faire s. le bouchon**, to pop the cork (of a bottle); **il lui a fait s. le revolver des mains**, he knocked the revolver out of his hands; *Nau:* **se faire s.**, to blow up one's ship; **se faire s. la cervelle**, to blow one's brains out; *Gaming:* **faire s. la banque**, to break the bank; *Bill:* **faire s. une bille**, to jump a ball off the table; *Typ:* **faire s. un mot, une lettre**, to turn a word, a letter, over (to the next line); *El:* **faire s. les plombs**, to blow the fuses. **2.** *v.tr.* (*a*) to jump over, leap over, clear (ditch, fence, etc.); **s. le pas**, to take a decision; to take the plunge; (*b*) to skip (pages in reading); to leave out (line in copying, etc.); to drop (a stitch); **s. une danse**, to sit out a dance; *Sch:* **s. une classe**, to skip a form; *Typ:* **s. un mot**, to make an out; *F:* **je la saute**, (i) I've got to skip the meal; (ii) I'm ravenous; (*c*) (*of stallion*) to cover (mare); *P:* **s. une fille**, to have a girl.

sautereau, -eaux [sotro], *s.m.* jack (of harpsichord).

sauterelle [sotrɛl], *s.f.* **1.** (*a*) *Ent:* grasshopper; **grande s. d'Orient**, locust; (*b*) *Crust:* **s. de mer**, squill(-fish). **2.** (*a*) bird trap, springe; (*b*) *Carp: etc:* (shifting) bevel, bevel square; (*c*) catch of a swinging bail (in stable); (*d*) *Ind:* portable conveyor; (*e*) *Av:* snap fastener, toggle fastener.

sauteriau, sauteriot [sot(ə)rjo], *s.m. Dial:* **1.** grasshopper. **2.** small active child.

sauterie [sot(ə)ri], *s.f.* **1.** *A:* jumping, hopping. **2.** private dance; informal dance, *F:* hop.

sauternais, -aise [sotɛrnɛ, -ɛ:z], *a. & s. Geog:* (native, inhabitant) of Sauternes.

sauternes [sotɛrn], *s.m.* (*also* **vin de S.**), Sauterne (wine).

saute-ruisseau [sotrɥiso], *s.m.inv. A: F:* (*a*) errand boy (in lawyer's office); (*b*) underling.

sauteur, -euse [sotœ:r, -ø:z]. **1.** *a.* leaping, jumping (insect, etc.). **2.** *s.* (*a*) leaper, jumper; **s. de corde**, skipper; **s. de cirque**, tumbler; *Equit:* (*of a horse*) **grand s.**, high-jumper; (*b*) *Equit:* bucking horse (in riding school); (*c*) *F:* weathercock; waverer; unreliable person. **3.** *s.f.* **sauteuse**; (*a*) (shallow) frying pan; (*b*) jigsaw; (*c*) *P:* prostitute, tart.

sautillage [sotija:ʒ], *s.m. A:* hopping, skipping.

sautillant [sotijɑ̃], *a.* hopping (bird); skipping (child); **style s.**, jerky style.

sautillement [sotijmɑ̃], *s.m.* **1.** = SAUTILLAGE. **2.** hop, skip.

sautiller [sotije], *v.i.* (*a*) to hop (like a sparrow); to skip, jump (about); **les moineaux s'approchent en sautillant**, the sparrows come hopping up; **s'en aller en sautillant**, to skip off; **son cœur sautillait**, her heart was throbbing; (*b*) *Pej:* to jump from one thing to another (in conversation, writing); **son style sautille**, his style is jerky.

sautoir [sotwa:r], *s.m.* **1.** (*a*) St Andrew's cross; *Her:* saltire; **en s.**, crosswise; (*of rope*) with a cross seizing; *Her:* in saltire, saltirewise; **écartelé en s.**, party per saltire; **étai en s.**, diagonal stay; **porter un baudrier en s.**, to wear a belt crosswise, over the shoulder; **porter un ordre en s.**, to wear an order on a ribbon round the neck; **porter un havresac en s.**, to carry a haversack with the straps crossed over one's chest; (*b*) locket (and chain); (*c*) *A.Cost:* fichu. **2.** *Dom.Ec:* (shallow) frying pan. **3.** *Sp:* jumping area.

sauvable [sovabl̩], *a.* **1.** salvable. **2.** savable.

sauvage [sova:ʒ]. **1.** *a.* (*a*) primitive, uncivilized (people, etc.); wild, untamed (animal); *Nat. Hist:* feral (beast, plant); barbarous, brutal (nature, custom); **chat s.**, (i) wild cat; (ii) raccoon; **olivier s.**, wild olive; **soie s.**, wild silk; **lieu s.**, wild, uninhabited, spot; wilderness; **forêt s.**, primeval forest; trackless forest; *Geog:* **eaux sauvages**, run-off; **tribu s.**, primitive tribe; **état s.**, savage, wild, state; (*of plants*) **retourner à l'état s.**, to revert to type; to return to the wild state; **cet enfant est complètement s.**, this child is quite uncivilized, uncouth, has no manners, doesn't know how to behave (in company); (*b*) *Rac:* **cheval s.**, loose, riderless, horse; (*c*) unsociable, averse to society; shy, retiring; (*d*) unauthorized; **grève s.**, wild-cat strike; **amour s.**, free love; (*e*) **soldes sauvages**, slashed prices. **2.** *s.* (*f. occ.* **sauvagesse**) (*a*) savage; *Her:* savage man; *Fr.C:* (American) Indian; **une sauvagesse**, a savage; *Fr.C:* a squaw; an Indian girl; **pays peuplé de sauvages**, country inhabited by primitive people; (*to child*) **tu te conduis comme un s.!** have you no manners? don't you know how to behave? (*b*) unsociable, retiring, person; **vivre en s.**, to lead an unsociable existence; to refuse to mix with people; (*c*) *P:* (*of criminal*) lone wolf.

sauvagement [sovaʒmɑ̃], *adv.* wildly; savagely; **il l'a tué s.**, he killed him savagely; **l'enfant s'est jeté à mon cou et m'a embrassé s.**, the child flung himself round my neck and gave me a wild hug.

sauvageon, -onne [sovaʒɔ̃, -ɔn]. **1.** *s.m. Arb:* (*a*) wild stock (for grafting); (*b*) sucker; (*c*) wilding, seedling. **2.** *a. & s.* uncouth and shy (child).

sauvagerie [sovaʒri], *s.f.* **1.** (*a*) (*rare*) primitive, uncivilized, state; (*b*) savagery, brutality, bestiality; barbarity; **il était rempli d'horreur devant la s. de l'assassin**, the brutality of the murderer filled him with horror; **ça, c'est de la s.!** that's downright barbarity. **2.** unsociability; shyness; **il allait rarement dans le monde, mais non par s.**, he went very little into society, but not because he was unsociable.

sauvagin, -ine [sovaʒɛ̃, -in]. **1.** *a. & s.m.* **goût s., odeur sauvagine, le sauvagin**, taste, (characteristic) smell, of wildfowl, of waterfowl. **2.** *s.f.* **sauvagine**; (*a*) *coll.* wildfowl; waterfowl; **chasse à la sauvagine**, wildfowling; (*b*) *Com:* common pelts; (strong-smelling) furs (of foxes, badgers, etc.).

sauvaginier [sovaʒinje], *s.m. Com:* dealer in common pelts.

sauvegarde[1] [sovgard], *s.f.* **1.** safeguard, safe keeping; safety; **s. de la vie humaine en mer**, safety of life at sea; **sous la s. de qn**, under s.o.'s protection; *Jur:* **mise sous la s. de la justice**, placing under the protection of the Court. committing to the care of the Court; **les bonnes mœurs sont la s. de la société**, good morals are the safeguard of society; **l'obscurité fut sa s. contre la persécution**, obscurity was his safeguard against persecution; **clause de s.**, saving clause; *Pol.Ec:* **droits de s.**, safeguarding duties. **2.** *A:* safe conduct. **3.** *A:* bodyguard (of prince, etc.). **4.** *Nau:* (*a*) lifeline, man rope; (*b*) oar lanyard; (*c*) rudder chain, rudder pendant.

sauvegarde[2], *s.m. Rept:* teju.

sauvegarder [sovgarde], *v.tr.* to safeguard, protect; to watch over (the interests, honour, etc., of s.o.); **s. les apparences**, to save appearances.

sauve-qui-peut [sovkipø], *s.m.inv.* stampede, helter-skelter flight, headlong flight, panic flight; **ce fut un s.-q.-p. général**, there was a general stampede.

sauver [sove], *v.tr.* (*a*) to save, rescue (s.o.); *Ecc:* to save (s.o., s.o.'s soul); **un rédempteur qui sauverait son peuple**, a Redeemer who would save his people; **circonstances qui ont contribué à s. le pays d'une invasion**, circumstances that helped to save the country from invasion; **s. qn du naufrage, du désespoir**, to save s.o. from shipwreck, from despair; **s. la vie à, de, qn**, to save s.o.'s life; **s. un malade**, to save, cure, a patient; **il est sauvé**, he's saved, out of danger; **Dieu sauve le roi!** God save the King! **nous sommes sauvés!** we are saved! we are safe! **s. les apparences**, to save, preserve, appearances; (*b*) to salve, salvage (ship, goods); **s. des meubles de l'incendie**, to salvage furniture from the fire, from the burning house; *F:* (*after financial disaster, etc.*) **s. les meubles**, to salvage enough to live on; to salvage, save, sth. from the wreck; *F:* **s. sa peau, sa tête**, to save one's skin; to get away with one's life.

se sauver. 1. (*a*) **se s. d'un péril**, to escape, make one's escape, from a danger; **sauve qui peut!** (i) every man for himself! (ii) *Navy:* signal to ships' captains to take independent action; (*b*) *A:* to take refuge (in church, etc.); (*c*) **se s. sur qch.**, to indemnify oneself, make it up, on sth.; **vendre à bas prix et se s. sur la quantité**, to sell at a low price and recoup oneself by large sales. **2.** (*a*) to run away, to be off; *F:* to clear out; **se s. de prison**, to escape from prison; **se s. à toutes jambes**, to make off, *F:* to cut and run; **il se fait tard, je me sauve**, it's getting late, I'm off, I must hurry away, must fly; (*b*) (*of liquid in saucepan, etc.*) to boil over.

sauvetage [sovta:ʒ], *s.m.* (*a*) life saving; rescue (of pers. from drowning, from fire); **s. aérien en mer**, air-sea rescue; **il a fait plusieurs sauvetages en mer**, he has saved several lives at sea; **guide qui a effectué le s. d'un alpiniste en danger**, guide who rescued a mountaineer in danger; **appareil de s.**, life-saving apparatus, rescue apparatus; **médaille de s.**, life-saving medal; **ceinture, gilet, de s.**, lifebelt; **bouée de s.**, lifebuoy; **ligne de s.**, lifeline; **canot, embarcation, de s.**, (coastal, ship's) lifeboat; **poste de s.**, lifeboat station; **exercices de s.**, life-saving drill; **échelle de s.**, fire escape; **la Société de s. des naufragés** = the Royal National Lifeboat Institution; (*b*) salvage, salving (of ship, goods); **remorqueur de s.**, salvage tug; **frais de s.**, salvage expenses; **droits de s.**, salvage dues; **société de s.**, salvage company.

sauveté [sovte], *s.f.* **1.** *Hist:* (*S. of Fr.*) rural township (founded in feudal times by monasteries as a sanctuary for fugitives). **2.** *Ap:* **cellules de s.**, queen cells; **reine de s.**, replacement queen.

sauveter [sovte], *v.tr.* (*hardly used except in inf. and p.p.*) *Nau: A:* to salve, salvage (ship, goods).

sauveteur [sovtœ:r]. **1.** *s.m.* (*a*) rescuer, lifesaver; **équipe de sauveteurs**, rescue party; (*b*) lifeboatman; (*c*) salvor, salvager. **2.** *a.m.* **bateau s.**, (i) (coastal) lifeboat; (ii) salvage vessel.

sauvette (à la) [alasovɛt], *adv.phr.* (i) on the run, *F:* ready to beat it quickly; (ii) illicitly; (iii) furtively, stealthily; (iv) hastily; with undue, suspicious, haste; **vendeur, marchand, à la s.**, illicit street vendor; **décision prise à la s.**, hasty decision; **moments de liberté à la s.**, moments of stolen liberty.

sauveur, salvatrice [sovœ:r, salvatris]. **1.** *s.* saver, preserver, deliverer; *Theol:* **le S.**, the Saviour, the Redeemer. **2.** *a.* saving; **remède s.**, healing remedy.

sauve-vie [sovvi], *s.f.inv. Bot:* wall rue.

sauvignon [soviɲɔ̃], *s.m.* (variety of) white grape.

savacou [savaku], *s.m. Orn:* boatbill.

savamment [savamɑ̃], *adv.* (*a*) learnedly; (*b*) knowingly, wittingly; **j'en parle s.**, I speak with full knowledge; I know what I'm talking about.

savane [savan], *s.f.* **1.** *Geog:* savanna(h). **2.** *Fr.C:* swamp, swampy ground.

savane-parc [savanpark], *s.f. Geog:* savanna park; *pl. savanes-parcs.*

savant, -ante [savɑ̃, -ɑ̃:t]. **1.** *a.* (*a*) learned (en, in); erudite, scholarly, well-informed, knowledgeable; **très s. en histoire**, well versed in history; **un s. ouvrage sur Platon**, a masterly work, an erudite work, on Plato; **vous paraissez bien s. sur ce chapitre**, you seem well informed on this subject; *Mil:* **les armes savantes**, the artillery and the engineers; (*b*) skilful, clever, able; **panser une plaie d'une main savante**, to dress a wound with a skilful hand; **chien s.**, performing dog; **s. à faire qch.**, clever at doing sth.; skilful performer of sth. **2.** *s.* scientist; scholar; *A:* **s. en us** [ɑ̃nys], sesquipedalian pedant.

savantas [savɑ̃ta], **savantasse** [savɑ̃tas], *s.m. A: & Lit: Pej:* pedant; sciolist; man who has an inflated opinion of his (own) erudition.

savantissime [savɑ̃tisim], *a. F: Hum:* most learned.

savarin [savarɛ̃], *s.m. Cu:* savarin.

savate [savat], *s.f.* **1.** old, worn-out, shoe; *F:* **traîner la s.**, to be down at heel, poverty-stricken; **en savates**, down at heel; slipshod (person); *F:* **jouer comme une s.**, to play very badly, to be a shocking player. **2.** *Games: A:* hunt-the-slipper. **3.** sole plate (of stanchion, etc.); sole (of sheers, rudder); shoe (of anchor). **4.** foot boxing; French boxing; **tirer la s.**, to go in for foot boxing. **5.** *F:* bungler, clumsy person; **quelle s.!** what a clumsy clot!

savetier[1] [savtje], *s.m.* **1.** *A:* cobbler. **2.** *F:* botcher, bungler, clumsy workman.

savetier[2], *s.m. Ich: F:* stickleback.

savernois, -oise [savɛrnwa, -wa:z], *a. & s. Geog:* (native, inhabitant) of Saverne.

saveur [savœ:r], *s.f.* **1.** savour, taste, flavour; **plein de s.**, full-flavoured; **sans s.**, tasteless, insipid. **2.** pungency (of style, etc.); **conte qui manque de s.**, flat, lifeless, story; **observations pleines de s.**, pungent remarks.

savinier [savinje], *s.m. Bot:* savin(e).

Savoie [savwa], *Pr.n.f. Geog:* Savoy; *Cu:* **biscuit de S.** = sponge cake.

savoir [savwa:r]. **I.** *v.tr.* (*pr.p.* **sachant**; *p.p.* **su**; *pr.ind.* **je sais, il sait, n. savons, ils savent**; *pr.sub.* **je sache, n. sachions, ils sachent**; *imp.* **sache, sachons, sachez**; *p.d.* **je savais**; *p.h.* **je sus**; *fu.* **je saurai**) to know. **1.** (*to know through having learnt*) **s. qch. par cœur**, to know sth. by heart; **s. une langue**, to know a language; **s. sa leçon**, to know one's lesson; **vous savez le chemin?—oui, je le connais bien**, you know the way!—yes, I know it well; **cet élève ne sait rien de rien!** this boy's ignorance is phenomenal! *cf.* 2; **s. le, son, monde**, to know how to behave in company, to have savoir faire; **il en sait plus d'une**, he knows a thing or two; *Prov:* **s. c'est pouvoir**, knowledge is power. **2.** to be aware of (sth.); (*a*) **je ne savais pas cela,** I did not know, was not aware of, that; **vous n'êtes pas sans s. que . . .,** you are not unaware that . . .; **savez-vous qu'il est midi?** do you know, are you aware, that it is twelve o'clock? **je (le) sais bien!** I know! **elle est jolie, et elle le sait bien,** she's pretty, and well she knows it! and doesn't she know it! *F:* **je sais ce que je sais,** I know what I know; **il ne sait rien de rien,** he knows nothing at all about it; he's entirely in the dark; *cf.* 1; **ce n'est pas bien, tu sais!** it isn't right, you know! **vous ne savez pas! nous allons nous cacher,** I'll tell you what, let's hide; **j'en sais moins que vous,** I know less about it than you; **s. mieux qu'on ne dit,** to know more than one says; **je n'en sais rien,** I know nothing about it; I don't know, I can't tell; **personne n'en sait rien,** (i) nobody knows anything about it; (ii) (*esp. of future event*) nobody can tell; **en savoir trop,** to know too much; **je n'en sais trop rien, je ne sais trop,** I'm not (very) sure; **comment le saurais-je? qu'est-ce j'en sais?** how can I tell? how should I know? **peut-on s.?** what's it (all) about? may I know, can you tell me, sth. about it? **je n'en sais pas plus long pour cela,** I'm none the wiser; **je ne veux pas s.,** I don't want to know (anything about it); I don't want (to hear) any explanations, any excuses; *F:* **je n'ai pas à le s., je ne veux pas le s.,** that's nothing to do with me; I don't want to know anything about that; *F:* **est-ce que je sais, (moi)?** I haven't a clue! don't ask me! **des stylos, des crayons, est-ce que je sais, moi?** pens, pencils—anything you like, —what have you; *F:* **tu ne sais pas, je ne peux pas me passer de toi,** d'you know, I can't do without you; *F:* **il en sait des choses,** he knows a thing or two, knows what's what; he's got his wits about him; *F:* **comme si je n'étais pas payé pour le s.!** don't I know it! *Lit:* **je ne sais,** I do not know; **sans le s.,** unwittingly, unconsciously; without being aware of it; **pas que je sache,** not that I know of, not that I am aware of, not to my knowledge; **il n'est venu personne (à ce) que je sache,** nobody came so far as I know; **(pour) autant que je sache,** (i) to the best of my knowledge; as far as I know; as far as I am aware; (ii) for all I know; as likely as not; **autant que je sache, voilà deux ans que je n'ai pris le car,** I don't suppose I have ridden in a bus for two years; **la question est de s. si elle viendra,** the question is whether she will come; **on ne sait pas ce que cela peut être,** there is no saying what it may be; **on ne sait jamais,** one never knows; you never can tell; **si jeunesse savait!** if youth but knew! **si j'avais su,** had I known; (*b*) to know of (s.o.); **je sais un habile horloger,** I know (of) a good watchmaker; *Lit:* **je sais un paysan qu'on appelait Gros-Pierre,** I have heard of a peasant whose name was Gros-Pierre; (*c*) *Lit:* (*in first pers. only*) **je ne sache pas l'avoir froissée,** I am not aware of having offended her; **je ne sache pas qu'on vous y ait autorisé,** I am not aware that you have been allowed to do so; (*d*) **je la sais intelligente,** I know her to be intelligent; **je me savais très malade,** I knew I was very ill; **je vous savais à Paris,** I knew you to be in Paris, I knew you were in Paris; **des parents que je sais venir de Londres,** relatives who I know come from London; (*e*) *Lit:* (*with dat. pron.*) **je lui savais une grande fortune,** I knew him to be wealthy; **on lui sait des parents,** he is known to have relatives. **3.** to understand; **il sait ce qu'il veut,** he knows what he wants; he knows his own mind; **je ne sais (pas) où le trouver,** I don't know where to find him; **ne s. que faire, que dire,** not to know, to be at a loss, what to do, to say; **il ne savait que faire pour s'excuser,** he was at a loss how to apologize, he did not know how to make his apologies; **je ne sais que penser,** I do not know, I am at a loss, what to think; **je ne sais trop que répondre,** I don't quite know what to answer; **sachez que . . .,** I would have you know that . . .; **sachez bien que . . .,** (you should) understand, bear in mind, be assured, that . . .. **4.** to be well informed of (sth.); (*a*) **on a su la nouvelle à quatre heures, la nouvelle s'est sue à quatre heures,** the news came out, became known, at four o'clock; **la nouvelle se sait déjà,** the news is already known; **tout se sait tôt ou tard,** everything gets known sooner or later; **comment cela s'est-il su?** how did it leak out? **il n'en a rien su,** he never knew of it; he was none the wiser; **vous n'êtes pas sans s. que . . .,** you probably know, you must be aware, that . . .; *Prov:* **ce que trois personnes savent est public,** what three people know the whole world knows; **il est difficile de s. si . . .,** it is difficult to ascertain whether . . .; **c'est à s.,** that remains to be seen; **reste à s. si . . .,** it remains to be seen whether . . ., if . . .; **je voudrais bien savoir s'il est parti,** I wonder whether he has gone; **je crois s. qu'il est ici,** I understand he is here; **je voudrais bien s. pourquoi,** I wonder why; **il n'a rien voulu s.,** he wouldn't listen to us, *F:* there was nothing doing; (*b*) **faire s. qch. à qn,** to let s.o. know sth.; to inform s.o. of sth.; to tell s.o. sth.; **vous auriez dû le lui faire s.,** you should have let him (or her) know; **on lui fit s. que . . .,** he was informed, told, that . . .; **on fait s. que . . .,** notice is hereby given that . . .; *Jur:* **s. faisons par les présentes que . . .,** know all men by these presents that . . .; (*c*) *conj.phr.* **(à) s.,** to wit, namely, viz., that is to say; **à vendre trois immeubles, à s. . . .,** to be sold three houses, viz. . . .. **5.** (*a*) to know how, to be able (to do sth.); **il faut s. obéir pour s. commander,** one must know how to obey in order to know how to command; **savez-vous nager?** can you swim? **je sais y aller,** I know how to go, get, there; **elle ne sait rien faire,** she is quite untrained; *A:* **nous avons su leur faire croire que . . .,** we managed, were able, to persuade them that . . .; **je crois que je saurai le faire,** I think I can manage it; **s. vivre,** to know how to behave; to be well-bred; (*b*) (*in careful speech*) **je ne saurais dire pourquoi,** I cannot say, have no idea, why; **je ne saurais guère vous le dire,** I'm afraid I can't tell you; **on ne saurait penser à tout,** one can't think of everything; (*polite refusal*) **je ne saurais permettre cela,** I cannot allow that. **6.** (*a*) *pron.phrs.* **(un) je ne sais qui nous a écrit,** we had a letter from somebody or other; somebody or other wrote to us; **donner la main de ma fille à je ne sais qui!** let my daughter marry a perfect stranger! any Tom, Dick or Harry! **je ne sais qui de ses amis lui a fait croire que . . .,** some friend or other of his has made him think that . . .; **un je ne sais quoi de déplaisant,** sth. vaguely unpleasant; **elle a lu je ne sais quoi,** she has read some rubbish or other; **c'est je ne sais quoi qu'elle a mangé,** it's something she's eaten; **un je sais tout,** a know-all; (*b*) *adj.phr.* **il est mort de je ne sais quelle maladie,** he died of some disease or other; **une ville abandonnée à la suite d'on ne savait quel sinistre,** a town abandoned after some unknown disaster; (*c*) *adv.phr.* **je suis tout je ne sais comment,** I feel so queer; I'm feeling completely under the weather; **il y a je ne sais combien de temps,** ages ago, heaven knows how long ago; (*d*) *exclam.phrs.* **des robes, des chapeaux, des gants, que sais-je?** dresses, hats, gloves, and goodness knows what else; **il a des amis, Dieu sait,** God knows, he has plenty of friends! **Dieu sait quand je serai de retour,** heaven knows when I shall get back; **on s'en est tiré Dieu sait comment!** we got out of it heaven knows how!

II. **savoir,** *s.m.* knowledge, learning, scholarship; **un homme d'un grand s.,** a man of great learning, a great scholar.

savoir-faire [savwarfɛːr], *s.m.inv.* savoir-faire; ability; know-how; **le s.-f. vaut souvent mieux que le savoir,** knowing how (to tackle things) is often more valuable than (sheer) knowledge.

savoir-vivre [savwarvivr̥], *s.m.inv.* savoir-vivre; (good) breeding; good manners; tact; **manquer de s.-v.,** to have no manners; to be ill-bred; **les règles du s.-v.,** social conventions.

savoisien, -ienne [savwazjɛ̃, -jɛn], *a. & s. Geog:* Savoyard; (native, inhabitant) of Savoy.

savon [savɔ̃], *s.m.* **1.** soap; **pain de s.,** cake of soap; **s. à barbe,** shaving soap, stick; **s. noir, s. vert, s. mou,** soft soap; **s. de Marseille,** = household soap; **s. blanc,** Castile soap; **s. ponce,** pumice soap; **s. minéral,** sand soap; **s. de selle,** saddle soap; leather soap; **eau de s.,** soap suds; **bulle de s.,** (soap) bubble; **fabricant de s.,** soap boiler, maker; *F:* **donner, flanquer, passer, un s. à qn,** to give s.o. a good talking-to, a good dressing-down; to haul s.o. over the coals; **recevoir un s.,** to catch it. **2.** *Mch: etc:* **s. métallique,** antifriction grease; *Ind:* **s. d'aluminium, de plomb, etc.,** aluminium, lead, etc., soap; **s. des verriers,** glass soap (manganese dioxide); *Miner:* **s. blanc, s. minéral, s. de montagne,** mountain soap, rock soap; **s. naturel, s. des soldats,** smectic clay; **pierre de s.,** soapstone; talc; steatite.

Savonarole [savonarɔl], *Pr.n.m. Hist:* Savonarola.

savonnage [savonaːʒ], *s.m.* (*a*) soaping, washing (of clothes, etc.); **faire un petit s.,** to wash a few things; to do a little washing; (*b*) *Tchn:* grinding, rubbing (of surface of glass with emery paste).

savonner [savɔne], *v.tr.* (*a*) to soap; to wash clothes, etc.) in soap and water; **se s. le menton,** to lather one's chin (before shaving); *F:* **s. (la tête à) qn,** to blow s.o. up; to haul s.o. over the coals; *A:* **tissu qui se savonne bien,** material that washes well; *Aut:* **piste savonnée,** skidpan; *Lit:* **la pente savonnée,** the slippery slope; (*b*) *Tchn:* to rub, to grind (glass with glass soap).

savonnerie [savɔnri], *s.f.* **1.** soap works, factory. **2.** soap making, boiling. **3.** soap trade. **4.** (*from factory established on site of former soap works*) **tapis, tapisserie, de la S.,** Savonnerie carpet, tapestry.

savonnette [savɔnɛt], *s.f.* **1.** cake, tablet, of (toilet) soap; cake of shaving soap; **s. sautoir,** shower soap. **2.** *A:* shaving brush. **3.** *A:* **(montre à) savonnette(s),** hunter (watch). **4.** *A:* **s. à vilain,** title purchased by a commoner.

savonneux, -euse [savɔnø, -øːz], *a.* **1.** soapy (water, etc.). **2.** *Miner:* **terre savonneuse,** fuller's earth; **pierre savonneuse,** soapstone.

savonnier, -ière [savɔnje, -jɛːr]. **1.** (*a*) *a.* of soap; **industrie savonnière,** soap industry; (*b*) *s.m.* soap maker, boiler. **2.** *s.m. Bot:* soapberry (tree).

savorée [savɔre], *s.f. Bot:* savory.

savourer [savure], *v.tr.* to relish, enjoy (one's food, cup of coffee, piece of flattery, etc.); **s. une pipe,** to sit, linger, over a pipe, to enjoy a pipe; **s. une plaisanterie, un spectacle, sa vengeance,** to gloat over a joke, a sight, one's revenge.

savouret [savurɛ], *s.m. Cu: A:* marrow-bone (of beef, pork); bone for stock.

savoureusement [savurøzmɑ̃], *adv.* with relish, with gusto.

savoureux, -euse [savurø, -øːz], *a.* savoury, tasty (dish); pleasant (perfume); racy (anecdote); **vin s.,** full-flavoured wine; **sensation savoureuse,** enjoyable sensation; **une savoureuse lecture,** delectable reading; **peu s.,** (i) unsavoury; (ii) insipid.

savoyard, -arde [savwajaːr, -ard]. **1.** (*a*) *a. & s. Geog:* Savoyard; (native, inhabitant) of Savoy; (*b*) *Cu:* **à la savoyarde,** cooked with grated cheese. **2.** *s.m. A:* **petit s.,** little chimney-sweep; climbing-boy.

saxatile [saksatil], *a. Nat.Hist:* saxatile.

Saxe [saks], *Pr.n.f. Geog:* **1.** Saxony; **porcelaine de S.,** *s.m.* **saxe,** Dresden china. **2.** (*in compounds*) Saxe(-Weimar, etc.).

saxhorn [saksɔrn], *s.m. Mus:* saxhorn; **s. basse,** euphonium.

saxicave [saksikaːv], *Moll:* **1.** *a.* saxicavous, rock-boring. **2.** *s.f.* stone borer; (*genus*) Saxicava.

saxicole [saksikɔl]. **1.** *a. Nat.Hist:* saxicolous, saxicoline. **2.** *s.m.pl. Orn:* Saxicolinae.

saxifragacées [saksifragase], **saxifragées** [saksifraʒe], *s.f.pl. Bot:* Saxifragaceae.

saxifrage [saksifraːʒ], *s.f. Bot:* saxifrage. **1. s. granulée,** white meadow saxifrage; **s. tridactyle, à trois doigts,** rue-leaved saxifrage; **s. hypnoïde, mousseuse,** mossy saxifrage; **s. d'automne,** yellow saxifrage; **s. ombreuse,** London pride; **s. cunéiforme,** wood saxifrage. **2. s. dorée,** golden saxifrage.

saxo [sakso], *s.m. F:* saxophone, *F:* sax.

saxon, -onne [saksɔ̃, -ɔn]. **1.** *a. & s. Hist: Geog:* Saxon. **2.** *a. & s.m. Ling:* Saxon.

saxonien, -ienne [saksɔnjɛ̃, -jɛn], *a. & s.m. Geol:* Saxonian.

saxophone [saksɔfɔn], *s.m. Mus:* **1.** saxophone. **2.** saxophonist.

saxophoniste [saksɔfɔnist], *s.m. & f. Mus:* saxophonist.

saxotromba [saksɔtrɔ̃ba], *s.m. Mus:* saxotromba.

sayette [sɛjɛt], *s.f. Tex: A:* (*a*) sagathy; (*b*) light Flanders serge; sayette.

sayetterie [sɛjɛtri], *s.f. Tex: A:* **1.** sayette weaving. **2.** light Flanders serges.

saynète [sɛnɛt], *s.f. Th:* playlet, sketch, short comedy, comedietta.

sayon [sɛjɔ̃], *s.m. A.Cost:* (peasant's, soldier's, sleeveless) tunic; sayon.

sayornis [sɛjɔrnis], *s.m. Orn:* phoebe (bird); (*genus*) Sayornis.

sbaïkien, -ienne [zbaikjɛ̃, -jɛn], *a. & s.m. Prehist:* Sbaikian.

sbire [zbiːr], *s.m.* **1.** sbirro. **2.** *F: Pej:* (officious) policeman.

scabieux, -ieuse [skabjø, -jøːz]. **1.** *a.* scabby, scabious (eruption, etc.). **2.** *s.f. Bot:* **scabieuse,** scabious; **scabieuse des champs,** field, meadow, scabious; **scabieuse tronquée, succise,** blue scabious, devil's bit scabious; **scabieuse fleur de veuve,** purple, sweet, scabious; **scabieuse colombaire,** small scabious; **fausse scabieuse,** sheep's bit.

scabre [skɑːbr̥], *a. Bot:* scabrous (leaf, etc.); rough to the touch.

scabreux, -euse [skabrø, -øːz], *a.* **1.** *A:* rugged, rough (path, etc.). **2.** difficult, dangerous, risky, ticklish (work); *Mus:* **un passage s.,** a tricky passage. **3.** indelicate (allusion); delicate, embarrassing (question); risqué, improper, obscene (story); scandalous (behaviour); **il a eu quelques affaires scabreuses,** he has lived through a few scandals.

scacchite [skakit], *s.f. Miner:* scacchite.

scaferlati [skafɛrlati], *s.m.* (standard quality of) cut tobacco (issued by the French State factories).

scagliola [skaljɔla], *s.f. Const:* scagliola.

scalaire[1] [skalɛːr], *s.f. Moll:* **s. (précieuse),** wentletrap, *F:* staircase shell.

scalaire[2], *s.f. Ich:* scalare, (Brazilian) angel fish.

scalaire[3], *a. & s.m. Mth:* scalar; **matrice s., produit s.,** scalar matrix, product; **grandeur s.,** scalar quantity; *El:* **champ s.,** scalar field.

scalariforme [skalarifɔrm], *a. Biol: etc:* scalariform; *Bot:* **vaisseaux scalariformes,** scalariform vessels.

scalariidés [skalariide], *s.m.pl. Moll:* Scalariidae.

scald [skald], *s.m. Hort: (disease of apples)* scald.

scalde [skald], *s.m.* (ancient Scandinavian) scald, skald, bard.

scaldique [skaldik], *a.* scaldic (poetry).

scalène [skalɛn]. **1.** *a.* scalene (triangle). **2.** *a. & s.m. Anat:* scalenus (muscle).

scalénoèdre [skalenɔɛdr̥], *Cryst:* **1.** *a.* scalenohedral. **2.** *s.m.* scalenohedron.

scalidés [skalide], *s.m.pl. Moll:* Scalariidae.

scalimétrie [skalimetri], *s.f. Ich:* scale measurement.

scalope [skalɔp], *s.m. Z:* scalops, scalopus; (American) mole.

scalp(e) [skalp], *s.m.* scalp; **danse du s.,** scalp dance.

scalpel [skalpɛl], *s.m. Surg:* scalpel.

scalpement [skalpəmɑ̃], *s.* scalping.

scalper [skalpe], *v.tr.* to scalp.

scalpeur [skalpœːr], *s.m.* scalper.

Scamandre (le) [ləskamɑ̃ːdr̥], *Pr.n.m. A.Geog:* the (river) Scamander, Xanthus.

scammonée [skamɔne], *s.f. Bot: Pharm:* scammony.

scandale [skɑ̃dal], *s.m.* **1.** *A:* evil example; *A:* **pierre de s.,** stumbling-block; *B:* **si votre main droite vous est un sujet de s., coupez-la,** if thy right hand offend thee cut it off. **2.** scandal; (cause of) shame; **c'est un s.,** it's a scandal; **faire un s., causer du s.,** to create a scandal; **livre qui fait s.,** book that is shocking the public, is causing a scandal; **éviter le s.,** to avoid public exposure; **au grand s. des gens de bien,** to the indignation, disgust, of decent people; **crier au s.,** to cry shame.

scandaleusement [skɑ̃daløzmɑ̃], *adv.* (*a*) scandalously; disgracefully; **vivre s.,** to lead a life of scandal, a scandalous life; (*b*) **être s. riche,** to be enormously, disgustingly, terrifically, rich; *F:* **elle est s. laide,** she's abominally, dreadfully, ugly.

scandaleux, -euse [skɑ̃dalø, -øːz], *a.* scandalous, shameful, disgraceful, notorious, discreditable; **des abus s.,** glaring abuses; **il est s. qu'il soit en liberté,** it is disgraceful that he is allowed to go free; **conduite scandaleuse,** scandalous, shameful, behaviour; **cette élection a été scandaleuse,** that election was a dirty, shocking, piece of work; *F:* **prix s.,** scandalous price; **mauvais goût s.,** shockingly bad taste; **c'est s.!** it's scandalous, shocking, terrible!

scandalisateur, -trice [skɑ̃dalizatœːr, -tris], *s. A:* person who scandalizes, who causes offence; scandalizer.

scandaliser [skɑ̃dalize], *v.tr.* **1.** *A:* to lead (s.o.) astray (by one's bad example). **2.** to scandalize, shock; to cause offence to (s.o.); **il est scandalisé que nous nous soyons conduits ainsi, de ce que nous nous sommes conduits ainsi,** he is disgusted that we should have behaved in this way; **il ne se scandalise de rien,** nothing shocks him; *abs.* **il a le désir de s.,** he's all out for, seems bent on, making a scandal. **3.** *Y:* **s. le pic,** to lower the peak.

scander [skɑ̃de], *v.tr. Pros:* to scan (verse); *Mus:* to mark, stress (a phrase); **s. ses phrases de coups de poing sur la table,** to punctuate one's sentences with thumps on the table; *A:* **aiguille qui scande les secondes,** hand that marks the seconds; **s. gaiement le pas,** to swing merrily along; **marche scandée,** measured, rhythmical, tread; **s. un slogan,** to chant a slogan.

scandinave [skɑ̃dinaːv], *a. & s. Geog:* Scandinavian.

Scandinavie [skɑ̃dinavi], *Pr.n.f. Geog:* Scandinavia.

scandinavisme [skɑ̃dinavism], *s.m.* Scandinavianism.

scandium [skɑ̃djɔm], *s.m. Ch:* scandium.

scandix [skɑ̃diks], *s.m. Bot:* scandix, *F:* shepherd's needle.

scansion [skɑ̃sjɔ̃], *s.f.* scansion, scanning (of verse).

scape [skap], *s.m. Bot: Ent:* scape; peduncle.

scaphandre [skafɑ̃ːdr̥], *s.m.* **1.** *A:* cork jacket. **2.** (*a*) diving suit; **s. autonome,** aqualung, scuba; **s. métallique,** metallic diver's suit; **casque de s.,** diver's helmet; **pompe de s.,** diving pump; (*b*) **s. (d'un cosmonaute),** space suit. **3.** *Moll:* scaphander.

scaphandridés [skafɑ̃dride], *s.m.pl. Moll:* Scaphandridae.

scaphandrier [skafɑ̃dri(j)e], *s.m.* diver (in diving suit).

scaphirhynque [skafirɛ̃ːk], *s.m. Ich:* scaphyrhinchid; *pl.* **scaphirhynques,** Scaphyrhinchidae.

scaphite [skafit], *s.m. Paleont:* scaphite.

scaphocéphale [skafɔsefal], *a. Anthr:* scaphocephalic, scaphocephalous.

scaphocéphalie [skafɔsefali], *s.f. Anthr:* scaphocephaly.

scaphoïde [skafɔid]. **1.** *a. Nat.Hist:* scaphoid, boat-shaped. **2.** *a. & s.m. Anat:* scaphoid.

scaphopodes [skafɔpɔd], *s.m.pl. Moll:* Scaphopoda.

scapolite [skapɔlit], *s.f. Miner:* scapolite.

scapulaire [skapylɛːr]. **1.** *s.m.* (*a*) *Ecc:* scapular, scapulary; (*b*) *Surg:* scapular (bandage). **2.** *a. Anat:* scapular (artery, etc.).

scapulalgie [skapylalʒi], *s.f. Med:* scapulalgia.

scapulectomie [skapylɛktɔmi], *s.f. Surg:* scapulectomy.

scapulo-huméral, -aux [skapylɔymeral, -o], *a. Anat:* scapulohumeral.

scarabée [skarabe], *s.m.* **1.** *Ent:* (*a*) (scarabaeid) beetle; **s. sacré,** scarabaeus; (*b*) **s. à ressort,** skipjack, click beetle, elater. **2.** *Egyptian Ant:* scarab.

scarabéidé [skarabeide], *s.m. Ent:* scarabaeid; *pl.* **scarabéidés,** Scarabaeidae.

scarabéoïde [skarabeɔid]. **1.** *a. & s.m. Ant:* scaraboid. **2.** *a. Ent:* scaraboid, scarabaeoid.

scare [skaːr], *s.m. Ich:* parrot fish, scar.

scaridé [skaride], *s.m. Ich:* scarid; parrot fish; *pl.* **scaridés,** Scaridae.

scarieux, -ieuse [skarjø, -jøːz], *a. Bot:* scarious, scariose (bracts, etc.).

scarifiage [skarifjaːʒ], *s.m. Agr:* scarifying (of the soil).

scarificateur [skarifikatœːr], *s.m.* (*a*) *Agr:* harrow, scarifier; (*b*) *Surg:* scarificator.

scarification [skarifikasjɔ̃], *s.f. Agr: Surg:* scarification.

scarifier [skarifje], *v.tr.* (*p.d. & pr. sub.* **n. scarifiions, v. scarifiiez)** *Agr: Surg:* to scarify; *Biol: U.S:* to abrade.

scarlatine [skarlatin], *s.f. Med:* scarlatina, scarlet fever.

scarlatineux, -euse [skarlatinø, -øːz], *Med:* **1.** *a.* suffering from scarlatina, scarlet fever. **2.** *s.* scarlatina, scarlet-fever, patient.

scarlatiniforme [skarlatinifɔrm], *a. Med:* scarlatiniform, scarlatinoid.

scarole [skarɔl], *s.f. Bot:* endive.

scatol(e) [skatɔl], *s.m. Ch:* skatol(e).

scatologie [skatɔlɔʒi], *s.f.* scatological humour, literature.

scatologique [skatɔlɔʒik], *a.* scatological (literature).

scatophage [skatɔfaːʒ]. **1.** *a.* scatophagous (fish, insect). **2.** *s.m. Ent:* scatophage; dung fly.

scatophagie [skatɔfaʒi], *s.f.* scatophagy.

scatophile [skatɔfil], *a.* dung-loving (insect, etc.); (plant) that grows on dung.

scatopse [skatɔps], *s.m. Ent:* scatopsid.

scatopsidés [skatɔpside], *s.m.pl. Ent:* Scatopsidae.

sceau, sceaux [so], *s.m.* seal; (*a*) **S. de l'État,** State seal; **mettre, apposer, son s. à un document,** to affix, set, put, one's seal to a document; **mettre le s. à la réputation de qn,** to set the seal on, to stamp, crown, s.o.'s reputation; **sous le s. du secret, du silence,** under the seal of secrecy, of silence; **s. du génie,** mark, stamp, of genius; **marquer qn du s. de l'infamie,** to brand s.o. with infamy; *Adm:* **les Sceaux** = the Great Seal; (*b*) *Bot:* **s. de Salomon,** Solomon's seal; **s. de la Vierge, de Notre-Dame,** black bryony.

sceau-cylindre [sosilɛ̃dr̥], *s.m. Hist: Archeol:* cylinder seal; *pl. sceaux-cylindres.*

scéen, -enne [seɛ̃, -ɛn], *a. & s. Geog:* (native, inhabitant) of Sceaux.

scélérat, -ate [selera, -at]. **1.** *a.* (*a*) wicked, nefarious (person, action); (*b*) crafty, cunning. **2.** *s.* (*a*) scoundrel; villain; (*b*) *F:* **petit(e) scélérat(e)!** you little rascal! **ma scélérate de jambe me fait mal,** my confounded leg is hurting. **3.** *s.f. Bot:* **scélérate,** celery-leaved crowfoot.

scélératement [seleratmɑ̃], *adv.* (*a*) wickedly; nefariously; villainously; (*b*) with low cunning.

scélératesse [seleratɛs], *s.f. A: & Lit:* **1.** (*a*) wickedness; villainy; (*b*) low cunning. **2.** wicked action; piece of low cunning.

scelidosaurus [sɛlidɔzɔrys], *s.m. Z: Paleont:* scelidosaur; (*genus*) Scelidosaurus.

scelidotherium [sɛlidɔtɛrjɔm], *s.m. Z: Paleont:* scelidotherium.

scélionides [seljɔnid], *s.m.pl. Ent:* Scelionidae.

scellage [sɛlaːʒ], *s.m.* sealing; affixing of seals.

scellé [sele]. **1.** *a.* sealed; under seal. **2.** *s.m. Jur:* (imprint of official) seal; **apposer les scellés (à un meuble), mettre (un meuble) sous le s.,** to affix the seals (to furniture); **lever les scellés,** to remove the seals; **bris de scellé(s),** breaking of seals; **sous scellés,** under seal.

scellement [sɛlmɑ̃], *s.m. Const:* (*a*) sealing, setting, fixing, bedding (of a post in stone, in concrete); **bloc de s.,** foundation block; **vis de s.,** concrete screw; **pistolet de s.,** stud driver; **patte de s.,** expansion bolt, *U.S:* expansion anchor; (*b*) sealing socket (for post in stone, etc.); plug (in wall, for nail); (*c*) end (of post, etc., fitting in socket).

sceller [sele], *v.tr.* **1.** (*a*) to seal (letter, etc.); to seal up (test tube); *Jur:* to affix an official seal to (box, door); **scellé en cire rouge,** sealed with red wax; **signé et scellé par moi,** given under my hand and seal; (*b*) to ratify, confirm (a privilege, a friendship); to seal (an alliance, etc.). **2.** *Const:* to bed, fasten, fix in (a post, an iron bar, etc.); to plug (nail in wall, etc.).

scénario [senarjo], *s.m. Th:* scenario; *Cin:* film script; **s. découpé,** shooting script; **recevoir une pièce sur s.,** to accept a play from an outline of the plot; *F:* **les policiers ont reconstitué le s. de l'attentat,** the police have made a reconstruction of the crime; *F:* **le ministre a bien rempli son s.,** the minister did exactly what everyone thought he would.

scénariste [senarist], *s.m. & f.* scenario writer; *Cin:* script writer.

scène [sɛn], *s.f. Th:* **1.** (*a*) stage; (*of actor*) **entrer en s.,** to appear, come on; **alors, mon frère entra en s.,** then my brother came, appeared, on the scene; **liste des acteurs par ordre d'entrée en s.,** cast in order of appearance; (*of actor*) **être en s.,** to be on; **en s. pour le un!** beginners please! **mise en s.,** (i) staging, production; (ii) mise en scène, setting (of a play); **l'art de la mise en s.,** stagecraft; **metteur en s.,** producer; **mettre qch. en s.,** to stage sth.; **porter qch. à la s.,** to adapt sth. for the stage, for the theatre; **adapter un roman à la s.,** to stage a novel; **elle a la folie de la s.,** she's stagestruck, mad to go on the stage; **quitter la s.,** to retire from the stage, from acting; (*b*) the theatre, drama; dramatic art; **les chefs-d'œuvre de la s. française,** the masterpieces of the French theatre; **la s. est un tableau des passions humaines,** the theatre depicts human passions; (*c*) **la s. politique,** the political scene; **occuper le devant de la s.,** to hold an important position; to be in the limelight. **2.** scene; (*a*) (*scene of action*) **changement de s.,** change of scene; **la s. représente une forêt,** the scene represents a forest; **la s. est à Paris,** the action takes place in Paris; **la s. se passe au moyen âge,** the action takes place in the middle ages; **revoir les scènes de sa jeunesse,** to revisit the scenes of one's youth; (*b*) (*subdivision of a play*) **troisième s. du second acte,** act two scene three; **la grande scène, la s. à faire,** the big scene (of the play); (*c*) **ce fut une s. pénible,** it was a painful scene; **scènes de la vie des camps,** scenes of camp life; (*d*) *F:* scene, row; **faire une s.,** to make a scene; **faire une s. d'indignation,** to make a scene, show, of indignation; **s. de ménage,** squabble between husband and wife.

scène-raccord [sɛnrakɔːr], *s.f. Cin:* insert; intercut; *pl. scènes-raccords.*

scénique [senik], *a.* scenic; theatrical; of the stage; **éclairage s.,** stage lighting; **indications scéniques,** stage directions; **l'art s.,** stagecraft; **jeux scéniques, représentations scéniques,** pageant; **la valeur s. d'une pièce,** the stage potentialities of a play.

scéniquement [senikmɑ̃], *adv.* from the theatrical point of view; theatrically speaking.

scénographe [senɔgraf], *s.m. & f.* scenographer.

scénographie [senɔgrafi], *s.f.* 1. *Art: etc:* scenography. 2. *Th:* scenography; scenecraft.

scénographique [senɔgrafik], *a.* scenographic.

scénologie [senɔlɔʒi], *s.f.* scenography; scenecraft.

scénopégies [senɔpeʒi], *s.f.pl. Jewish Rel:* Feast of Tabernacles.

scepticisme [sɛptisism], *s.m.* scepticism, *U.S:* skepticism.

sceptique [sɛptik]. 1. *a.* sceptical, *U.S:* skeptical. 2. *s.m. & f.* sceptic, *U.S:* skeptic.

sceptiquement [sɛptikmɑ̃], *adv.* sceptically, *U.S:* skeptically.

sceptre [sɛptr̥], *s.m.* sceptre; **tenir le s.,** to hold, wield, the sceptre; **vivre sous un s. de fer,** to be ruled with a rod of iron.

schabraque [ʃabrak], *s.f.* = CHABRAQUE.

Schaffhouse [ʃafu:z], *Pr.n. Geog:* Schaffhausen.

schaffhousois, -oise [ʃafuzwa, -wa:z], *a. & s. Geog:* (native, inhabitant) of Schaffhausen.

schah [ʃa], *s.m.* Shah.

schako [ʃako], *s.m.* shako.

schampooing [ʃɑ̃pwɛ̃], *s.m.* = SHAMPOOING.

schappe [ʃap], *s.f. or m. Text:* silk waste, floss silk.

schappiste [ʃapist], *s.m. & f.* floss silk manufacturer, worker.

scheelisation [ʃelizasjɔ̃], *s.m.* adulterating of wines with glycerine, glycerining of wines.

scheelite [ʃelit], *s.f. Miner:* scheelite.

schefférite [ʃɛferit], *s.f. Miner:* schefferite.

scheidage [ʃɛda:ʒ], *s.m. Min:* hand sorting (of ore); cobbing; *Min:* **minerai de s.,** cobbed ore; **marteau de s.,** cobbing hammer.

scheider [ʃede], *v.tr. Min:* to hand-sort (ore); to cob.

scheik [ʃɛk], *s.m.* sheik.

schelem [ʃlɛm], *s.m. Cards:* slam; **petit, grand, s.,** little, grand, slam.

schéma [ʃema], *s.m.* 1. (*a*) diagram; (sketch) plan; **s. de principe,** schematic, simplified, diagram; *El: etc:* **s. de connexion, de câblage,** connection, wiring, diagram; *Elcs:* (*computers*) **s. de connexions,** plugging chart; **s. synoptique,** block diagram; *Mec.E:* **s. de fonctionnement,** functional diagram; **s. de graissage,** lubrication chart; *Dent:* **s. dentaire,** odontogram; **dessiner un s. de la coupe transversale d'une racine,** to make a sketch (diagram) of the transverse section of a root; (*b*) project, plan (for a book, etc.); scheme, arrangement; *Mil:* **s. du commandement,** scheme of command; **s. du tir,** scheme of fire; *Atom.Ph:* **s. de désintégration,** decay scheme; **s. du fonctionnement d'un système électoral,** plan to show how an electoral system works. 2. *Phil: Psy:* schema.

schématique [ʃematik], *a.* (*a*) diagrammatic; schematic; **coupe s.,** diagrammatic section; **dessin s.,** diagram; draft; **plan s.,** outline plan; **organisation s.,** skeleton organization; (*b*) *Pej:* over-simplified (interpretation, etc.).

schématiquement [ʃematikmɑ̃], *adv.* (*a*) schematically, diagrammatically; (*b*) in outline; in a simplified manner.

schématisation [ʃematizasjɔ̃], *s.f.* schematization; reduction to essentials.

schématiser [ʃematize], *v.tr.* to schematize; to make a diagram of; to simplify.

schématisme [ʃematism], *s.m.* (*a*) *Phil:* schematism; (*b*) *often Pej:* simplification.

schème [ʃɛm], *s.m.* (*a*) *Phil: Psy:* schema; (*b*) *Art: etc:* design; **le peintre plie la réalité à ses schèmes,** a painter bends, adapts, reality to his design.

schénanthe [skenɑ̃:t], *s.m. Bot:* lemon grass, sweet rush, sweet calamus, camel's hay.

schéol [ʃeɔl], *s.m. Jewish Rel:* Sheol.

scherzando [skɛrtsando, skɛrdz-], *adv. Mus:* scherzando.

scherzo [skɛrtso, -dzo], *Mus:* 1. *s.m.* scherzo. 2. *adv.* scherzando.

Schéveningue [skevnɛ̃:g], *Pr.n. Geog:* Scheveningen.

schibboleth [ʃibɔlɛt], *s.m. B.Hist: etc:* shibboleth.

schiedam [skidam], *s.m.* Hollands (gin).

schilling [ʃiliŋ], *s.m. Num:* (Austrian) schilling.

schipperke [ʃipɛrk], *a. & s.m. & f.* schipperke (dog).

schismatique [ʃismatik], *a. & s.m. & f.* schismatic.

schisme [ʃism], *s.m.* schism.

schiste [ʃist], *s.m. Geol:* schist, shale; **s. micacé, s. lustré,** mica schist; **s. ardoisier,** slate; **schistes alunifères,** alum shales; **s. bitum(in)eux,** oil shale; **huile de s.,** shale oil.

schisteux, -euse [ʃistø, -ø:z], *a. Geol:* schistose, schistous; **houille schisteuse,** foliated coal; slaty coal.

schistification [ʃistifikasjɔ̃], *s.f. Min:* sterilization (of coal dust in mine).

schistifier [ʃistifje], *v.tr. Min:* to sterilize (coal dust in mine).

schistocarpe [ʃistɔkarp], *a. Bot:* schizocarpous.

schistoïde [ʃistɔid], *a.* schistoid.

schistosité [ʃistozite], *s.f. Geol:* schistosity.

schistosome [ʃistɔzo:m], *s.m. Ann:* schistosome, schistosoma.

schistosomiase [ʃistɔzomja:z], *s.f. Med:* schistosomiasis.

schizanthe [skizɑ̃:t], *s.m. Bot:* schizanthus.

schizocœle [skizɔkel], *s.m. Biol:* schizocoele.

schizogamie [skizɔgami], *s.f. Biol:* schizogamy.

schizogénèse [skizɔʒenɛ:z], *s.f. Biol:* schizogenesis.

schizogone [skizɔgɔn], *a. Biol:* schizogonous.

schizogonie [skizɔgɔni], *s.f. Biol:* schizogony.

schizogonique [skizɔgɔnik], *a. Biol:* schizogonic.

schizoïde [skizɔid], *a. & s.m. & f. Psy:* schizoid.

schizoïdie [skizɔidi], *s.f. Psy:* schizoidism; schizothymia.

schizoïdique [skizɔidik[, *a. Psy:* schizoid.

schizolite [skizɔlit], *s.f. Miner:* schizolite.

schizomycète [skizɔmisɛt], *s.m. Biol:* schizomycete.

schizonte [skizɔ̃:t], *s.m. Prot:* schizont.

schizophasie [skizɔfazi], *s.f. Psy:* schizophasia.

schizophrène [skizɔfrɛn], *a. & s.m. & f.* schizophrenic; *s.* schizophrene.

schizophrénie [skizɔfreni], *s.f. Psy:* schizophrenia.

schizophrénique [skizɔfrenik], *a. & s.m. & f. Psy:* schizophrenic; *s.* schizophrene.

schizophycées [skizɔfise], *s.f.pl. Bot:* Schizophyceae.

schizophyte [skizɔfit], *s.m. Bot:* schizophyte; *pl.* **schizophytes,** Schizophyta.

schizopode [skizɔpɔd], *s.m. Crust:* schizopod.

schizostélie [skizɔsteli], *s.f. Bot:* schizostely.

schizothyme [skizɔtim], *s.m. & f. Psy:* schizothyme.

schizothymie [skizɔtimi], *s.f. Psy:* schizothymia.

schizothymique [skizɔtimik], *a. Psy:* schizothymic.

schlague (la) [laʃlag], *s.f. Mil: A:* flogging.

schlaguer [ʃlage], *v.tr. A:* to flog.

schlamm [ʃlam], *s.m. Min:* sludge, tailings, slime.

schlammeux, -euse [ʃlamø, -ø:z], *a. Min:* sludgy, slimy.

schlass [ʃlɑ:s], *a. P:* the worse for drink, sozzled.

schlich [ʃlik], *s.m. Metall:* crushed ore, schlich, slick.

schlinguer [ʃlɛ̃ge], *v.i. P:* to stink, to pong.

schlittage [ʃlita:ʒ], *s.m.* transporting of lumber on a *schlitte.*

schlitte [ʃlit], *s.f.* (timber) sledge (for transporting lumber down the mountain side); *U.S:* dray; **chemin de s.,** dray road.

schlitter [ʃlite], *v.tr.* to transport (lumber) on a *schlitte.*

schlitteur [ʃlitœ:r], *s.m.* lumberman (in charge of a *schlitte*).

schloff [ʃlɔf], *P: O: used in the phr.* **faire s.,** to sleep; to go to sleep; to go to bed.

schnaps [ʃnaps], *s.m.* schnapps.

schnau(t)zer [ʃnotzɛ:r], *s.m.* (*dog*) schnauzer.

schnick [ʃnik], *s.m. A: P:* (inferior) brandy, spirits, *P:* rot-gut.

schnock, schnoque [ʃnɔk], *P:* 1. *a.* (*of pers.*) batty, crazy, loopy. 2. *s.* idiot, nit.

schnorchel, schnorkel [ʃnɔrkɛl], *s.m. N.Arch:* snorkel.

schnouff [ʃnuf], *s.f. P:* (*narcotic*) dope, junk.

schofar [ʃɔfa:r], *s.m. Jewish Rel: Mus:* shophar.

schooner [skunœ:r, ʃunɛ:r], *s.m. Nau:* schooner.

schoopage [ʃupa:ʒ], *s.m. Metalw:* schoop process.

schorl [ʃɔrl], *s.m. Miner:* schorl, shorl, schorlite.

schorlacé [ʃɔrlase], *a. Miner:* schorlaceous, schorlous.

schorlomite [ʃɔrlɔmit], *s.f. Miner:* schorlomite.

schorre [ʃɔ:r], *s.m.* salt meadow.

schpromm [ʃprɔm], **schproom** [ʃprum], **schproum(e)** [ʃprum], *s.m. P:* row; **faire du s.,** to kick up a row, to make a shindy.

schungite [ʃœ̃ʒit], *s.f. Miner:* schungite.

schuss [ʃus], *s.m. Ski:* schuss.

schwitzois, -oise [ʃvitswa, -wa:z], *a. & s. Geog:* (native, inhabitant) of Schwyz.

sciable [sjabl̥], *a.* (*of timber*) fit for sawing.

sciaenidés [sjenide], *s.m.pl. Ich:* Sciaenidae.

sciage [sja:ʒ], *s.m.* sawing (of wood, or stone); **bois de s.,** sawn timber.

sciagraphie [sjagrafi], *s.f.*, **sciagraphique** [sjagrafik], *a.* = SCIOGRAPHIE, SCIOGRAPHIQUE.

scialytique [sjalitik], *a. & s.m. R.t.m:* Scialytic (light); **(réflecteur) s.,** shadowless lamp.

sciant [sjɑ̃], *a. P:* boring; **il est s.,** (i) he's a damn nuisance; (ii) he bores me stiff.

sciaphile [sjafil], *a. Biol:* shade-loving; **plante s.,** shade plant, sciophyte.

sciapode [skjapɔd], *s.m. & f. Myth:* sciapod.

sciatalgie [sjatalʒi], *s.f. Med:* sciatalgia.

sciatique [sjatik]. 1. (*a*) *a. Anat:* sciatic (nerve, artery, etc.); (*b*) *s.m.* sciatic nerve. 2. *s.f. Med:* sciatica.

scie [si], *s.f.* 1. saw; (*a*) *Tls:* **s. à bois,** wood saw; **s. à placage,** veneer saw; **s. à métaux,** metal saw, hacksaw; **s. à pierre,** stone saw; **s. de tailleur de pierre,** stonecutter's saw; **s. à marbre,** marble saw; **s. à main,** handsaw; **s. égoïne,** small handsaw; **s. mécanique,** machine saw, power saw, sawing machine; **s. alternative,** alternating, reciprocating, saw; **s. alternative à plusieurs lames, s. multiple,** gang saw, stock saw; **s. à ruban, s. sans fin,** band saw, belt saw, ribbon saw; **s. circulaire,** circular saw, *U.S:* buzz saw; **s. articulée, s. à chaîne(tte),** chain saw; **s. à dos,** back saw, carcase saw; **s. à châssis, à cadre,** frame saw; **s. de long,** long saw, pit saw; **s. de travers,** cross-cut(ting) saw; **s. passe-partout,** felling saw, cross-cut saw; **s. à bûches,** bucksaw; **s. à chantourner,** (i) (*handsaw*) bow saw, turning saw; (ii) (*machine*) jigsaw, scroll saw; **s. à découper, s. anglaise,** (i) (*handsaw*) fretsaw; (ii) (*machine*) jig saw; **s. à guichet,** compass saw, keyhole saw; **s. à guichet démontable, s. à manche,** pad saw; **s. à refendre,** (framed) rip saw, split saw; **s. à tenon,** tenon saw; **trait de s.,** saw cut; kerf; **en dents de s.,** serrate(d); (*b*) *Games:* **jeu de la s.,** cat's cradle; (*c*) *Med:* **bruit de s.,** rasping murmur. 2. *Ich:* **(poisson) s.,** sawfish; *Ent:* **mouche à s.,** sawfly. 3. *F:* (*a*) bore, nuisance; **quelle s.!** damn! what a nuisance! what a bore! **monter une s. à qn,** to play the same practical joke on s.o. again and again; (*b*) catch phrase (of comic song); catchword, gag; (*c*) hit tune; **la s. du jour,** the hit tune of the day.

sciemment [sjamɑ̃], *adv.* knowingly, wittingly; **il ne vous a pas offensé s.,** he did not mean to offend you.

science [sjɑ̃:s], *s.f.* 1. knowledge, learning; skill; ability; **la s. du monde, du cœur,** knowledge of the world, of the heart; *Theol:* **s. infuse,** intuition; mystical vision; *F:* **il croit qu'il a la s. infuse,** he thinks he knows it all by intuition; **il vous égale en s.,** he is your equal in learning; **être un puits de science,** to be a well of knowledge, extremely learned; **montrer toute sa s.,** to show all one's skill, ability; *A:* **savoir qch de s. certaine,** to know sth. for a fact; *B:* **l'arbre de la s. du bien et du mal,** the tree of knowledge of good and evil. 2. (*a*) science; **la s. n'a pas de patrie,** science knows no frontiers; **homme de s.,** scientist; (*b*) *pl.* **élève doué pour les sciences,** pupil who is good at science; **préparer une licence de sciences,** to study for a degree in science; **les sciences exactes,** the exact sciences; **sciences physiques,** physical science; **sciences naturelles,** natural science; **sciences appliquées,** applied science; **sciences humaines,** humanities; **sciences sociales,** social science(s); **les sciences occultes,** the occult sciences.

science-fiction [sjɑ̃sfiksjɔ̃], *s.f.* science fiction; **romans de s.-f.,** science-fiction stories, novels.

sciène [sjɛn], *s.f. Ich:* sciaena.

sciénidé [sjenide], *s.m. Ich:* sciaenid; *pl.* **sciénidés,** Sciaenidae.

scientifique [sjɑ̃tifik]. 1. *a.* scientific; **recherche s., ouvrage s.,** scientific research, work. 2. *s.m. & f.* scientist.

scientifiquement [sjɑ̃tifikmɑ̃], *adv.* scientifically.

scientisme [sjɑ̃tism], *s.m.* (*a*) scientism; (*b*) (doctrines of) Christian Science.

scientiste [sjɑ̃tist]. 1. *a.* scientistic. 2. *s.m. & f.* (*a*) (*adept of scientism*) scientist; (*b*) **s. chrétien(ne),** Christian Scientist.

scier¹ [sje], *v.tr.* (*pr.sub. & p.d.* **n. sciions, v. sciiez**) 1. to saw (wood, stone); **s. de long,** to rip; to saw with the grain; *Equit:* **s. du bridon,** to saw a horse's mouth; *F:* **s. le dos à qn,** to bore s.o. stiff. 2. (*a*) to saw off (branch, etc.); (*b*) *A:* to cut down, reap (corn with a sickle).

scier², *v.i. Row:* to back water, to back the oars; **sciez partout!** back together! back water!

scierie [siri], *s.f.* 1. sawmill, sawyard. 2. (*a*) power saw, sawmill; (*b*) gang of saws.

scieur [sjœ:r], *s.m.* 1. sawyer; **s. de long,** (pit)-sawyer. 2. *A:* **s. de blé,** reaper.

scieuse [sjø:z], *s.f.* mechanical saw.

scille [sil], *s.f.* (*a*) *Bot:* scilla, squill; **s. maritime,** sea onion; **s. blanche,** sea daffodil; (*b*) *Pharm:* squills; **sirop de s. composé,** compound syrup of squills, hive syrup.
scillitique [sil(l)itik], *a. Pharm:* squillitic; containing squills.
scincidés [sɛ̃side], **scincoïdes** [sɛ̃kɔid], *s.m.pl. Rept:* Scincidae, the skinks.
scindement [sɛ̃dmɑ̃], *s.m.* dividing, splitting up (of a question, of a political party).
scinder [sɛ̃de], *v.tr.* to divide, split up (proposition, question, *Pol:* party); **le parti s'est scindé après l'élection du président,** the party split after the election of the president; *Fin:* **stocks scindés,** split stocks.
scinque [sɛ̃:k], *s.m. Rept:* skink; **s. des apothicaires, s. du Sahara,** medicinal skink; **s. à langue bleue (d'Australie),** (Australian) blue-tongued skink; **s. officinal, s. des boutiques,** adda.
scintillant [sɛ̃tijɑ̃]. **1.** *a.* scintillating, scintillant; twinkling (star, *Nau:* light); sparkling (wit, style). **2.** *s.m.* sparkling, tinsel, ornament (for Christmas tree, etc.).
scintillateur [sɛ̃tijatœ:r], *s.m. Ph:* scintillation counter; *Atom.Ph:* scintillator; **s. liquide, organique,** liquid, organic, scintillator.
scintillation [sɛ̃tijasjɔ̃], *s.f.*, **scintillement** [sɛ̃tijmɑ̃], *s.m.* (*a*) scintillation (of star, luminous body, etc.); **temps de croissance, de décroissance, d'une s.,** scintillation rise, decay, time; **compteur de s., à scintillations,** scintillation counter; **spectromètre à scintillations,** scintillation spectrometer; (*b*) *Cin: T.V:* flicker(ing); **bruit de s.,** flicker noise; **effet de s.,** flicker effect; (*c*) **scintillement (des yeux, des étoiles, des bijoux, etc.),** sparkling, twinkling (of eyes, stars, jewellery, etc.).
scintiller [sɛ̃tije], *v.i.* to scintillate; to sparkle; (*of star*) to twinkle; *Elcs: T.V: Cin:* to flicker; **lumières lointaines qui scintillent,** lights flickering in the distance; **esprit qui scintille,** sparkling wit.
scintillomètre [sɛ̃tijɔmɛtr̥], *s.m. Tchn:* scintillometer, scintillation meter; flicker meter.
sciographie [sjɔgrafi], *s.f.* **1.** *Astr:* sciagraphy, skiagraphy. **2.** *Arch: etc:* sciograph, skiograph, vertical section.
sciographique [sjɔgrafik], *a.* (drawing, plan) in vertical section.
scion [sjɔ̃], *s.m.* **1.** *Hort:* scion, shoot. **2.** top (-piece), tip (of fishing rod); **pointe de s.,** tip.
scioptique [sjɔptik], *a.* scioptic.
sciotte [sjɔt], *s.f.* (stonecutter's) hand saw; gauge saw.
sciotter [sjɔte], *v.tr.* to saw (stone, marble).
sciotteuse [sjɔtø:z], *s.f.* (mechanical) saw (for cutting marble).
Scipion [sipjɔ̃], *Pr.n.m.A.Hist:* Scipio; **les Scipions,** the Scipios; **S. l'Africain,** Scipio Africanus; **S. Émilien,** Scipio Æmilianus.
scirpe [sirp], *s.m. Bot:* club rush, bulrush; (*genus*) Scirpus.
scissile [sisil], *a.* (*a*) scissile (rock); (*b*) *Atom.Ph:* fissile, fissionable (material).
scission [sisjɔ̃], *s.f.* (*a*) scission, division, split (in assembly, political party, etc.); secession; **faire s.,** to secede; **la s. de l'Église d'Angleterre,** the secession of the Church of England; (*b*) *Ch:* scission, cleavage; (*c*) *Atom.Ph:* fission, splitting; **s. nucléaire,** nuclear fission, splitting of atomic nucleus; **s. de l'uranium,** uranium fission.
scissionnaire [sisjɔnɛ:r]. **1.** *a.* seceding. **2.** *s.m. & f.* seceder.
scissionnisme [sisjɔnism], *s.m. Pol:* tendency to split, to divide.
scissionniste [sisjɔnist], *a. & s.m. or f.* secessionist.
scissipare [sisipa:r], *a. Biol:* fissiparous, scissiparous; reproduced by segmentation.
scissiparité [sisiparite], *s.f. Biol:* scissiparity, schizogenesis, fissiparity.
scissure [sisy:r], *s.f. Anat: etc:* fissure, cleavage, cleft; **s. de Rolando,** fissure of Rolando; **s. de Sylvius,** fissure of Sylvius; **s. de Glaser,** Glaserian, petrotympanic, fissure; **grande s., s. interhémisphérique,** interhemispheric fissure.
scissurelle [sisyrɛl], *s.f. Moll:* scissurellid; (*genus*) Scissurella.
scissurellidés [sisyrɛlide], *s.m.pl. Moll:* Scissurellidae.
scitaminé [sitamine], *Bot:* **1.** *a.* scitamineous. **2.** *s.f.pl.* **scitaminées,** Scitamineae.
sciure [sjy:r], *s.f.* **s. (de bois),** sawdust; **s. de marbre,** marble dust.
sciuridés [sjyride], *s.m.pl. Z:* Sciuridae.
sciuromorphes [sjyrɔmɔrf], *s.m.pl. Z:* Sciuromorpha.
scléral, -aux [skleral, -o], *a. Anat:* scleral, sclerotic.
scléranthe [sklerɑ̃:t], **scléranthus** [sklerɑ̃tys], *s.m. Bot:* scleranth(us).
sclérectasie [sklerɛktazi], *s.f. Med:* sclerectasia.
sclérectomie [sklerɛktɔmi], *s.f. Surg:* sclerectomy.
sclérème [sklerɛm], *s.m. Med:* sclerema.
sclérenchyme [sklerɑ̃ʃim], *s.m. Nat.Hist:* sclerenchyma.
scléreux, -euse [sklerø, -ø:z], *a. Med:* sclerous, sclerosed, hard (tissue).
sclériase [skleria:z], *s.f. Med:* scleriasis, scleroma.
sclérifié [sklerifje], *a. Nat.Hist:* sclerosed, sclerified, hardened (tegument, etc.).
sclérite [sklerit], *s.f.* **1.** *Nat.Hist:* sclerite. **2.** *Med:* sclerotitis, scleritis.
sclér(o)- [skler(ɔ)], *pref.* scler(o).-
sclérobase [sklerɔba:z], *s.f. Z:* sclerobase.
scléro-choroïdite [sklerɔkɔrɔidit], *s.f. Med:* sclerochoroiditis.
scléro-conjonctivite [sklerɔkɔ̃ʒɔ̃ktivit], *s.f. Med:* scleroconjunctivitis.
sclérodactylie [sklerɔdaktili], *s.f. Med:* sclerodactylia, sclerodactyly.
scléroderme [sklerɔdɛrm], *s.m.* **1.** *Ich:* scleroderm; *pl.* **sclérodermes,** Sclerodermi. **2.** *Fung:* false truffle; (*genus*) Scleroderma.
sclérodermé [sklerɔdɛrme], *a. Z:* sclerodermatous, sclerodermic.
sclérodermie [sklerɔdɛrmi], *s.f. Med:* scleroderma, sclerodermia.
sclérogène [sklerɔʒɛn], *a. Med:* sclerogenic.
sclérokératite [sklerɔkeratit], *s.f. Med:* sclerokeratitis.
sclérome [sklero:m], *s.m. Med:* scleroma.
scléromètre [sklerɔmɛtr̥], *s.m. Ph:* sclerometer.
sclérophtalmie [sklerɔftalmi], *s.f. Med:* sclerophthalmia.
sclérophylle [sklerɔfil], *Bot:* (*a*) *a.* sclerophyllous; (*b*) *s.m.* sclerophyll.
scléroprotéine [sklerɔprɔtein], *s.f. Bio-Ch:* scleroprotein.
scléroscope [sklerɔskɔp], *s.m. Ph:* scleroscope.
sclérose [sklero:z], *s.f.* (*a*) *Med:* sclerosis; **s. vasculaire, des artères,** arterio-sclerosis; **s. en plaques,** multiple, disseminated, sclerosis; (*b*) lack of adaptability; ossification; mental sclerosis; **la s. de cette organisation est incroyable,** this organization has become incredibly ossified.
sclérosé [skleroze], *a.* (*a*) *Med:* sclerosed; (*b*) rigid, seized up; hidebound; immobilized, ossified; **une industrie sclérosée,** an industry that has ground to a standstill.
scléroser [skleroze], *v.tr.* (*a*) *Med:* to sclerose, harden; **l'alcool sclérose les vaisseaux,** alcohol hardens the blood vessels; (*b*) **l'administration se sclérose,** the administration is losing its adaptability, is growing (too) rigid, is becoming hidebound.
sclérostome [sklerɔstɔm], *s.m. Ann:* sclerostoma.
sclérote [sklerɔt], *s.m. Fung:* sclerotium, sclerote.
scléro(tico)tomie [sklerɔ(tikɔ)tɔmi], *s.f. Surg:* sclerotomy.
sclérotinia [sklerɔtinja], *s.m. Fung:* sclerotinia.
sclérotique [sklerɔtik], *Anat:* **1.** *a.* sclerotic. **2.** *s.f.* sclerotic, sclera (of the eye).
sclérotite [sklerɔtit], *s.f. Med:* sclerotitis.
scolaire [skɔlɛ:r], *a.* (*a*) scholastic, relating to schools; **vie s.,** school life; **année s.,** school, academic, year; **enfant d'âge s.,** child of school age; **frais scolaires,** school fees; **livres scolaires,** school books; text books; **réformes scolaires,** educational reforms; **organisation s.,** educational organization; **groupe s.,** school block, school buildings; **assurance s.,** school insurance; (*b*) *Pej:* bookish; lacking in originality; pedestrian; **roman qui a un caractère s.,** laboured, pedestrian, novel; novel that reads like a school exercise; (*c*) *occ.* **s. un, une, s.,** a (school) pupil.
scolairement [skɔlɛrmɑ̃], *adv.* like a schoolboy, schoolgirl.
scolarisation [skɔlarizasjɔ̃], *s.f.* **1.** school attendance; **taux de s.,** percentage of children attending school. **2.** education; schooling.
scolariser [skɔlarize], *v.tr.* to provide education for (children); to equip, provide (a country, an area) with schools, educational establishments.
scolarité [skɔlarite], *s.f. Sch:* (*a*) *A:* status of a student; **privilège de s.,** (university) student's right to be tried by a special tribunal; (*b*) **s. obligatoire,** compulsory school attendance; **prolongation de la s.,** raising of the school-leaving age; **taux de s.,** percentage of children (of a given age) attending school; **s. à temps partiel** = day release classes; **années de s.,** number of years' study (at school, university, etc.); (*c*) *pl.* school fees; **payer les scolarités,** to pay the school fees.
scolasticat [skɔlastika], *s.m.* **1.** theological college. **2.** period of theological training. **3.** theological course.
scolastique [skɔlastik]. **1.** *a.* scholastic (philosophy, etc.). **2.** *s.m.* schoolman, scholastic. **3.** *s.f.* scholasticism, school theology.
scolastiquement [skɔlastikmɑ̃], *adv.* in a scholastic, formal, manner; **le général imita s. une manœuvre de Napoléon,** the general copied one of Napoleon's manœuvres to the letter, *F:* straight out of the book.
scolasticisme [skɔlastisism], *s.m.* scholasticism.
scolécite[1] [skɔlesit], *s.f. Miner:* scolecite, scolezite.
scolécite[2], *s.m. Fung:* scolecite.
scolécospore [skɔlekɔspɔ:r], *s.f. Bot: Fung:* scolecospore.
scolésite, scolézite [skɔlezit], *a.f. Miner:* scolecite, scolezite.
scolex [skɔlɛks], *s.m.inv.* scolex, head (of tapeworm).
scoliaste [skɔljast], *s.m.* scholiast.
scolie[1] [skɔli]. **1.** *s.f.* (commentator's) scholium (to classical text). **2.** *s.m.* (mathematician's) scholium (to Euclid's Elements).
scolie[2], *s.m. Gr.Ant:* scolion (sung at a banquet).
scolie[3], *s.f. Ent:* scolia.
scoliidés [skɔliide], *s.m.pl. Ent:* Scoliidae.
scoliose [skɔljo:z], *s.f. Med:* scoliosis, lateral curvature of the spine.
scoliotique [skɔljɔtik], *a. Med:* scoliotic.
scolopacidés [skɔlɔpaside], *s.m.pl. Orn:* Scolopacidae.
scolopaciné [skɔlɔpasine], *s.m. Orn:* scolopacine.
scribomanie [skribɔmani], *s.f.* graphomania.
scolopendre[1] [skɔlɔpɑ̃:dr̥], *s.f. Myr:* scolopendra, centipede.
scolopendre[2], *s.f. Bot:* hart's tongue, scolopendrium.
scolopendridés [skɔlɔpɑ̃dride], *s.m.pl. Myr:* Scolopendridae.
scolopidie [skɔlɔpidi], *s.f. Biol: Ent:* scolopidium.
scolyte [skɔlit], *s.m. Ent:* scolytid, bark beetle, shot-hole borer.
scolytidés [skɔlitide], *s.m.pl.* Scolytidae.
scombéroïde [skɔ̃berɔid], *s.m. Ich:* scombroid.
scombre [skɔ̃:br̥], *s.m. Ich:* scombrid; *esp.* mackerel.
scombrésoce [skɔ̃bresɔs], *s.m. Ich:* saury; (*genus*) Scombresox.
scombrésocidés [skɔ̃bresɔside], *s.m.pl. Ich:* Scombresocidae.
scombridés [skɔ̃bride], *s.m.pl. Ich:* Scombridae.
sconce, sconse [skɔ̃:s], *s.m. Z:* skunk; *Com:* skunk (fur).
scooter [skutɛ:r], *s,m.* (motor) scooter.
scootériste [skuterist], *s.m. & f.* scooter rider, scooterist.
scopèle [skɔpɛl], *s.m.*, **scopélide** [skɔpelid], *s.m. Ich:* scopelid, lantern fish.
scopélidés [skɔpelide], *s.m.pl. Ich:* Scopelidae, Myctophidae.
scopidés [skɔpide], *s.m.pl. Orn:* Scopidae.
scopie [skɔpi], *s.f. F:* radioscopy.
scopolamine [skɔpɔlamin], *s.f. Ch: Pharm:* scopolamine; hyoscine.
scops [skɔps], *s.m. Orn:* scops owl.
scorbut [skɔrbyt], *s.m. Med:* scurvy, scorbutus; **s. infantile,** Barlow's disease.
scorbutigène [skɔrbytiʒɛn], *a. Med:* scurvy-producing (diet).
scorbutique [skɔrbytik], *a. & s. Med:* scorbutic.
score [skɔ:r], *s.m. Psy: Sp: Fb:* score.
scoriacé [skɔrjase], *a. Metall: etc:* slaggy; scoriaceous; *Geol:* **laves scoriacées,** scoria, slaggy lava.
scorie [skɔri], *s.f. usu. pl.* **1.** *Metall:* slag, cinders, scoria; (iron) dross; **scories de déphosphoration,** basic slag; **scories vitreuses,** clinker; **s. de forge,** scale, hammer scale; **scories de laminoir,** roll scale, mill scale. **2.** *Geol:* **scories (volcaniques),** scoria; cellular, slaggy, lava; volcanic slag. **3.** mediocre, inferior, part (of sth.); *Lit:* **cette masse de scories qui, chez les écrivains non artistes, souillent les meilleures intentions,** all these inferior, poorly written, passages with which writers lacking any artistic sense ruin their best projects.
scorifère [skɔrifɛ:r], *a.* **charbon s.,** clinkering coal.
scorifiant [skɔrifjɑ̃], *a. Metall:* slag-forming.
scorification [skɔrifikasjɔ̃], *s.f. Metall:* scorification; slagging.
scorifier [skɔrifje], *v.tr. Metall:* to scorify; to slag.
scoriforme [skɔrifɔrm], *a.* scoriform.
scorodite [skɔrɔdit], *s.f. Miner:* scorodite.
scorpène [skɔrpɛn], *s.f. Ich:* scorpene, scorpaenid, scorpion fish; (*genus*) Scorpaena.
scorpénidés [skɔrpenide], *s.m.pl. Ich:* Scorpaenidae.

scorpioïde [skɔrpjɔid], *a. Bot:* scorpioid.
scorpion [skɔrpjɔ̃], *s.m.* **1.** (*a*) *Arach:* scorpion; **s. des livres,** book scorpion; (*b*) *Astr:* **le S.,** Scorpio, the Scorpion; **le Cœur du S.,** the Scorpion's heart; Antares. **2.** (*a*) *Ent:* **s. aquatique, d'eau,** water scorpion; (*b*) **s. de mer,** scorpion fish.
scorpionidés [skɔrpjɔnide], *s.m.pl. Arach:* Scorpionida.
scorsonère [skɔrsɔnɛːr], **scorzonère** [skɔrzɔnɛːr], *s.f. Bot:* scorzonera, viper's grass, black salsify.
scotch [skɔtʃ], *s.m.* **1.** scotch (whisky); **commander un double s.,** to order a double scotch; **baby s.,** small, single, scotch; *pl. scotches.* **2.** *R.t.m:* **Scotch,** self-adhesive (cellulose) tape, Scotch tape.
scotch-terrier [skɔtʃtɛrje], *s.m. Z:* Scottish, Scotch, terrier; *pl. scotch-terriers.*
scotie [skɔti], *s.f. Arch:* scotia (of pillar).
scotisme [skɔtism], *s.m. Rel.H:* Scotism.
scotiste [skɔtist], *s.m. & f. Rel.H:* Scotist; follower of Duns Scotus.
scotodinie [skɔtɔdini], *s.f. Med:* vertigo.
scotome [skɔtoːm], *s.m. Med:* scotoma, scotomy.
scotopique [skɔtɔpik], *a. Med:* scotopic.
scottish [skɔtiʃ], *s.f. Danc: Mus:* schottische.
scottish-terrier [skɔtiʃtɛrje], *s.m. Z:* Scottish, Scotch, terrier; *pl. scottish-terriers.*
scout [skut]. **1.** *s.m.* (boy) scout; **Scouts de France,** (Roman) Catholic scouts. **2.** *a.* scout; **le mouvement s.,** the scout movement.
scoutisme [skutism], *s.m.* scouting.
scramasaxe [skramasaks], *s.m. A.Arms:* scramasax.
scraper [skrepœːr, skra-], *s.m. Civ.E:* scouring machine, drag scraper.
scratch [skratʃ], *s.m. Sp:* scratch; *Rac:* scratch line; **partir s.,** to start (at) scratch; **(course) s.,** scratch race; **(joueur) s.,** scratch player; **avoir un adversaire s.,** to be up against a scratch player.
scratcher [skratʃe], *v.tr. Turf: etc:* to scratch (horse, competitor).
scribe [skrib], *s.m.* (*a*) *Ant:* scribe; (*b*) *Pej:* copyist, pen-pusher.
scriblage [skriblaːʒ], *s.m. Tex:* scribbling (of wool).
scribler [skrible], *v.tr. Tex:* to scribble (wool).
scribouillage [skribujaːʒ], *s.m. F:* (*a*) scribbling, writing in poor style; (*b*) work written in poor, slapdash, style; scribble.
scribouillard, -arde [skribujaːr, -ard], *s. F: Pej:* clerk, pen-pusher.
scribouiller [skribuje], *v.i. F:* (*a*) to be a clerk, a pen-pusher; (*b*) to scribble; to write in poor, slapdash, style.
scribouilleur [skribujœːr], *s.m.* scribbler ((i) person who is always writing, (ii) writer who writes in poor, slapdash, style).
script[1] [skript], *s.m. Fin:* scrip.
script[2], *s.m.* **1.** script (writing); **écrire en s.,** to write in script, to print; *attrib.* **écriture s.,** script, printing. **2.** *F:* film script. **3.** *s.f. Cin: F:* continuity girl, script girl.
scripteur [skriptœːr], *s.m.* **1.** (*a*) writer (*i.e.* in respect of the handwriting); (*b*) writer of the Pope's bulls. **2.** *W.Tel: T.V:* script writer.
script-girl [skriptgœrl], *s.f. Cin:* continuity girl, script girl; *pl. script-girls.*
scriptuaire [skriptɥɛːr], *a. Fin:* **monnaie s.** (*general term describing all papers* (*apart from banknotes*) *representing money, such as cheques, postal orders, bearer bonds, etc.*), negotiable instrument.
scriptural, -aux [skriptyral, -o], *a.* (*a*) scriptural; (*b*) *Bank:* **monnaie scripturale,** bank or other forms of financial credit.
scrobe [skrɔb], *s.m. Ent:* scrobe.
scrobiculaire [skrɔbikylɛːr], *s.f. Moll:* scrobicularia.
scrobiculé [skrɔbikyle], *a. Physiol:* scrobicular, scrobiculate.
scrofulaire [skrɔfylɛːr], *s.f. Bot:* figwort; **s. aquatique,** water betony.
scrofulariacées [skrɔfylarjase], *s.f.pl. Bot:* Scrophulariaceae.
scrofule [skrɔfyl], *s.f. Med:* scrofula; *A.Med:* **les scrofules,** scrofula; the king's evil.
scrofuleux, -euse [skrɔfylø, -øːz], *Med:* **1.** *a.* scrofulous (person); strumous (tumour). **2.** *s.* patient suffering from scrofula.
scrofulisme [skrɔfylism], *s.m.* scrofulism.
scro(n)gneugneu, -eux [skrɔɲøɲø]. **1.** *s.m.* cantankerous old soldier; Colonel Blimp. **2.** *int: Hum:* damme, sir!
scrotal, -aux [skrɔtal, -o], *a. Anat:* scrotal.
scrotiforme [skrɔtifɔrm], *a.* scrotiform.
scrotocèle [skrɔtɔsɛl], *s.f. Med:* scrotocele.
scrotum [skrɔtɔm], *s.m. Anat:* scrotum.
scrubber [skrœbœːr], *s.m. Ch: Ind: O:* scrubber (of coal gas, etc.); gas-scrubbing apparatus.
scrupulard [skrypylaːr], *s.m. Pej: esp. Pol:* person who makes a parade of his scruples.
scrupule [skrypyl], *s.m.* **1.** *A.Meas:* scruple (weight). **2.** scruple, (conscientious) doubt (**sur,** about); **homme sans scrupules,** man of no scruples; unscrupulous man; **j'ai quelque s. à intervenir,** I hardly like to intervene; **se faire (un) s. de faire qch., avoir des scrupules à faire qch.,** to have scruples, qualms (of conscience), about doing sth.; **il ne se fait pas s. d'emprunter à la caisse,** he makes nothing of borrowing from the till; **il ne s'embarrasse d'aucun s.,** he is not troubled by any scruples; he sticks at nothing; **lever les scrupules de qn,** to put an end to s.o.'s scruples; **avoir le s. de l'exactitude,** to make a point of accuracy; **avoir des scrupules dans le choix des mots,** to be meticulous in the choice of words; **n'ayez aucun s. à accepter mon aide,** have no scruples about accepting my help; **exact jusqu'au s.,** scrupulously exact; *Med:* **maladie du s.,** morbid irresolution.
scrupuleusement [skrypyløzmɑ̃], *adv.* scrupulously; **payer s. ses dettes,** to be scrupulous about paying one's debts; **traduire s.,** to make a faithful, exact, translation.
scrupuleux, -euse [skrypylø, -øːz], *a.* scrupulous (**sur,** about, over, as to); **peu s.,** unscrupulous; **s. jusqu'à l'excès,** over-scrupulous; scrupulous to a fault; **s. à remplir ses devoirs,** scrupulous, punctilious, in the performance of one's duties; *s.* **faire le s.,** to pretend to have scruples.
scrupulosité [skrypylozite], *s.f.* scrupulousness, scrupulosity.
scrutateur, -trice [skrytatœːr, -tris]. **1.** *a.* searching (mind, look); scrutinizing (curiosity); **regarder qn d'un œil s.,** to look searchingly at s.o. **2.** *s.* (*a*) scrutinizer, scrutator, investigator; (*b*) teller, scrutineer (of a ballot or poll).
scruter [skryte], *v.tr.* to scrutinize; to scan; to examine closely; **s. le visage de qn,** to scan s.o.'s face; **s. qn du regard,** to take a good look at s.o.; to give s.o. a searching look; **s. sa mémoire,** to search one's memory; **s. la nuit,** to peer (out) into the night.
scrutin [skrytɛ̃], *s.m.* **1.** poll; **la veille du s.,** the day before the poll; **s. d'arrondissement** = constituency poll; **s. de liste,** voting for several members (out of a list); **s. majoritaire,** election by absolute majority; **s. secret,** *A:* **s. couvert,** secret vote; **s. découvert,** open vote; **dépouiller le s.,** to count the votes; **proclamer le résultat du s.,** to declare the poll. **2. tour de s.,** ballot; **voter au s.,** to ballot; **élire qn au s.,** to ballot for s.o.; **élection au s.,** balloting; **deuxième tour de s.,** second ballot(ing). **3.** voting (in an assembly); (parliamentary) division; **procéder au s.,** to take the vote; (*in Engl. Parliament*) to divide; **demander le s.,** to ask for a count; **projet adopté sans s.,** bill passed without a division.
scrutiner [skrytine], *v.i.* (*a*) to poll, vote; to go to the poll; (*b*) to ballot.
scull [skyl, skœl], *s.m. Sp: Nau:* (*a*) scull, skiff; (*b*) sculling.
sculptable [skyltabl], *a.* (subject) that can be represented in sculpture, in carving.
sculptage [skyltaːʒ], *s.m.* (*a*) sculpturing, sculpting; carving; (*b*) *Cer:* hand finishing (of design in relief).
sculpter [skylte], *v.tr.* to sculpture, sculpt; to carve; **bois sculpté,** carved wood; **s. une statue dans la pierre,** to sculpture a statue out of stone, in stone; **un amour sculpté,** a carved cupid.
sculpteur [skyltœːr], *s.m.* (*with occ. f.* **sculptresse** [skyltrɛs]) sculptor; **femme s.,** woman sculptor, sculptress; **s. sur bois,** wood-carver.
sculptural, -aux [skyltyral, -o], *a.* sculptural (art); statuesque (figure); **elle a une beauté sculpturale,** she has a statuesque beauty, is worthy of a statue.
sculpture [skyltyːr], *s.f.* (*a*) sculpture; **s. sur bois,** wood-carving; (*b*) **une s.,** a statue; a (piece of) carving; **une petite s.,** a small statue, a statuette; a small, carved figure; (*c*) *Aut:* **s. de la bande de roulement,** tread design (of tyre).
scurrile [skyr(r)il], *a. A:* scurrilous.
scurrilité [skyr(r)ilite], *s.f. A:* scurrility, scurrilousness.
scutellaire [skytɛl(l)ɛːr]. **1.** *a. Ent:* scutellar. **2.** *s.f. Bot:* scutellaria, skull cap.
scutelle [skytɛl], *s.f. Nat.Hist:* scutellum.
scutelliforme [skytɛl(l)ifɔrm], *a. Nat.Hist:* scutelliform.
scutifolié [skytifɔlje], *a. Bot:* scutifoliate.
scutiforme [skytifɔrm], *a. Anat: Ent: etc:* scutiform, shield-shaped.
scutigère [skytiʒɛːr], *s.f. Myr:* scutiger.
scutigéridés [skytiʒeride], *s.m.pl. Myr:* Scutigeridae.
scutum [skytɔm], *s.m. Rom.Ant: Nat.Hist:* scutum.
scybales [sibal], *s.f.pl. Med:* scybala.
scyliorhinidés [siljɔrinide], *s.m.pl. Ich:* Scyl(l)iorhinidae.
Scylla [sil(l)a], *Pr.n.m. Myth:* Scylla; *s.a.* CHARYBDE.
scyllare [silaːr], *s.m. Crust:* scyllarian.
scyllaridés [silaride], *s.m.pl. Crust:* Scyllaridae.
scyllée [sile], *s.f. Moll:* scyllaea.
scylléidés [sileide], *s.m.pl. Moll:* Scyllaeidae.
scyphistome [sifistɔm], *s.m. Coel:* scyphistoma.
scyphoméduse [sifɔmedyːz], *s.f. Coel:* scyphomedusan; *pl.* **scyphoméduses,** Scyphomedusae.
scyphozoaires [sifɔzɔɛːr], *s.m.pl. Coel:* Syphozoa.
scytale [sital]. **1.** *s.f. Gr.Ant:* scytale. **2.** *s.m. Rept:* scytale.
scythe [sit], *a. & s. A.Geog:* Scythian.
Scythie [siti], *Pr.n.f. A.Geog:* Scythia.
scythique [sitik], *a. A.Geog:* Scythic, Scythian.
scytodepsique [sitɔdɛpsik], *a. Leath:* scytodepsic.
se, *before a vowel sound* **s'** [s(ə)], *pers. pron. acc. & dat. unstressed, attached to the verb or its adjuncts.* **1.** (*a*) (*reflexive*) oneself; himself, herself, itself, themselves; **se flatter,** to flatter oneself; **il se venge,** he avenges himself; **elle s'est coupée au doigt, s'est coupé le doigt,** she has cut her finger; **s'attribuer qch.,** to attribute sth. to oneself; **il se parle (à lui-même),** he's talking to himself; **ils se font mal,** they hurt themselves; (*b*) (*reciprocal*) each other, one another; **se nuire (l'un à l'autre),** to hurt one another; **elles se disent des injures,** they abuse one another; **il est dur de se quitter,** it is hard to part. **2.** (*giving passive meaning to active vbs*) **la clef s'est retrouvée,** the key has been found; **cet article se vend partout,** this article is sold everywhere; **la porte s'est ouverte,** the door opened; the door came open; **l'anglais se parle presque partout,** English is spoken nearly everywhere. **3.** (*in purely pronom. conjugation*) *See* S'EN ALLER, SE BATTRE, SE DÉPÊCHER, SE FÂCHER, etc. NOTE: **se** *is often omitted before an infinitive dependent on* **faire, laisser, mener, envoyer, voir**; *e.g:* **se taire: faire taire les enfants; s'envoler: faire envoler les oiseaux; s'invétérer: laisser invétérer une habitude; se promener: mener promener les enfants; je l'ai envoyé promener; se coucher: envoyer coucher les enfants; se lever: nous avons vu lever le soleil.**
sea-line [silin], *s.m. Petroleum Ind:* sea line, ship-to-shore pipeline; *pl. sea-lines.*
séamment [seamɑ̃], *adv. A: & Lit:* becomingly, fittingly.
séance [seɑ̃ːs], *s.f.* **1.** *A:* seat; **prendre s.,** to take one's seat (at a council table, in the Academy, etc.); **avoir s. à un conseil,** to be entitled to, to have, a seat on a committee or board. **2.** sitting, session, meeting; (*of parliament*) **être en s.,** to be sitting, in session; *St.Exch:* **s. de clôture,** closing session; **la s. s'ouvrira à huit heures,** the meeting will open at eight; **déclarer la s. ouverte,** to open the meeting; **lever la s.,** (i) to dissolve the meeting, to leave the chair; (ii) to adjourn; **la s. fut levée dans le tumulte,** the meeting broke up in confusion; **tenir une s. publique,** to have, hold, an open meeting; **en s. publique,** at an open meeting; *Jur:* in open court; **à la s. tenue à Londres,** at a meeting (held) in London; **s. d'information,** briefing; *s.a.* TENANT. **3.** performance (at cinema, etc.); **s. de cinéma,** film show; **s. de prestidigitation,** conjuring performance; **s. de spiritisme,** seance. **4.** (*a*) sitting (for one's portrait, etc.); **peindre un portrait en une s.,** to paint a portrait at one sitting; **faire une longue s. à table,** to sit a long time over one's meal; **aller faire un traitement de trois séances chez le médecin,** to take a course of three treatments at the doctor's; (*b*) period; **s. de travail, d'entraînement,** working, training, period, session.
séant [seɑ̃], *a.* **1.** (*a*) sitting, in session; **assemblée séante à Versailles,** assembly sitting at Versailles; (*b*) *s.m.* **se mettre, se dresser, sur son s.,** to sit up (in bed); **être sur son s.,** to be in a sitting position; **tomber sur son s.,** to sit down with a bump. **2.** *A: & Lit:* becoming (**à,** to); fitting, proper, seemly; **cette robe ne lui est pas séante,** this dress does not become her; **il n'est pas s. qu'elle sorte seule,** it is not proper, not seemly, that she should go out alone; **les sourcils noirs sont très séants aux blondes,** dark eyebrows are very attractive on fair-haired women. **3.** *Her:* sejant.

seau, pl. **seaux** [so], s.m. pail, bucket; **s. à traire,** milking pail; **s. à glace, à rafraîchir,** ice bucket; **s. à incendie,** fire bucket; **s. à charbon,** coal scuttle; Nau: **s. à escarbilles,** ash bucket; **s. de toilette, de ménage,** slop pail; **s. hygiénique,** sanitary slop pail; commode pan; **s. tamiseur,** cinder sifter; **s. à biscuits,** biscuit barrel; Fish: **s. à vif,** bucket, container, for live bait; **apporter un s. d'eau, plein un s. d'eau,** to bring a pailful of water; F: **il pleut à seaux,** it's pouring down in buckets full; F: **être dans le s.,** to be in the cart, in a fix, in the soup.

seau-pompe [sopɔ̃p], s.m. stirrup pump (and bucket); pl. **seaux-pompes.**

sébacé [sebase], a. sebaceous (gland).

sébacique [sebasik], a. Ch: sebacic (acid).

sébaste [sebast], s.m. Ich: Norway haddock, rose-fish.

Sébastien [sebastjɛ̃], Pr.n.m. Sebastian.

sébeste [sebɛst], s.m. A.Pharm: sebestan, sebesten (plum).

sébestier [sebɛstje], s.m. Bot: sebestan (tree), sebesten (tree).

sébifère [sebifɛːr], a. Anat: Bot: sebiferous.

sébile [sebil], s.f. 1. wooden bowl; A: **tendre la s.,** to beg; A: **s. à aiguilles,** needle-box (of gramophone). 2. Gold Min: abacus, pan, batea.

sebk(h)a [sɛpka], s.f. Geog: sebk(h)a.

séborrhée [sebɔre], s.f. Med: seborrh(o)ea.

séborrhéique [sebɔreik], a. Med: seborrh(o)eic.

sébum [sebɔm], s.m. Anat: sebum.

sec, sèche [sɛk, sɛʃ]. 1. a. (a) dry; **temps s.,** dry weather; **orage s.,** rainless storm; **les rues sont sèches,** the streets have dried up; **voici du linge s.,** here is some dry linen; **terrain s.,** dry, arid, ground; Cr: Golf: fiery pitch, green; **gorge sèche,** parched throat; **avoir la gorge sèche,** F: **le gosier s.,** to be thirsty; to feel dry; F: **j'ai le gosier d'un s.! je l'ai s.!** I'm parched! I'm so dry, so thirsty! **regarder d'un œil s.,** to look on dry-eyed; **mettre un enfant au pain s. et à l'eau,** to put a child on bread and water; Mch: etc: **joint s.,** face-to-face joint; **mur de pierres sèches,** drystone wall; **pointe sèche,** (etcher's) point, etching needle; Aut: **être en panne sèche,** to have run out of petrol; **traverser un torrent à pied s.,** to cross a torrent dryshod; **s. comme une allumette,** bone dry, as dry as tinder; Adm: **le régime s.,** the dry regime; prohibition; **les États-Unis ont eu le régime sec,** the United States was dry; **pays secs,** prohibitionist countries; dry countries; (b) dried (cod, fruit, etc.); seasoned, matured (wood, cigar); dry (wine); **pois secs,** dried peas; (c) **perte sèche,** dead loss; P: **consultation sèche,** free consultation; (d) Cards: **roi s.,** unguarded king; **as s., rois.,** ace bare, king bare. 2. a. (a) spare, gaunt (person); lean (figure, horse); **s. et nerveux,** wiry; **s. comme un échalas, comme un pendu, comme un coucou, comme un coup de trique,** as thin as a lath; s. **un vieux s.,** a wizened old man; (b) sharp, dry, curt (remark, answer); incisive (tone); **donner un coup s. à qch.,** to give sth. a sharp blow, tap; **casser qch. d'un coup s.,** to snap sth. off; to break sth. with a snap; Golf: **coup s.,** stab shot; **il refusa mon offre d'un ton s.,** he met my offer with a curt refusal; **faire un accueil très s. à qn,** to give s.o. a very cool, curt, reception; **mine sèche,** sour face; **un merci tout s.,** a bare thank you; (c) unsympathetic, unfeeling (heart, etc.); (d) barren; meagre; dry, bald (narrative, etc.); bald (style); (e) Cards: etc: **partie sèche,** one game (without revenge); **on va faire un écarté en cinq s.,** we'll have one game at écarté; F: **faire qch. en cinq sec(s).,** to do sth. in (less than) no time, without hesitation; (f) Nau: **vergue sèche,** bare yard. 3. adv. (a) **boire s.,** (i) to drink one's spirits neat, straight; (ii) to drink hard; **brûler s.,** to burn like tinder; (b) **la voiture vira très s.,** the car made a very sharp turn, swung round sharply; (of coin) **sonner s.,** to chink; **fermer s. le couvercle,** to slam down the lid; **parler s.,** not to mince one's words, to rap out one's words; **apostropher qn s.,** to bite s.o.'s head off; (c) **rire s.,** to give a harsh, dry, laugh. 4. adv.phr. (a) **à s.,** (i) dry; (ii) dried up; (iii) F: hard up, broke, on the rocks; **puits à s.,** well that has run dry; **cours d'eau à s.,** dry river bed; **les sources sont complètement à s.,** the springs are bone dry, have completely dried up; F: **au bout de cinq minutes il était à s.,** at the end of five minutes he had nothing to say, he had dried up; **mettre une mare à s.,** to drain a pond; F: **mettre qn à s.,** to win all s.o.'s money; F: to clean s.o. out; (b) **remettre un cheval à s.,** to take a horse off the grass; (c) Min: etc: **broyage à s.,** dry crushing; Const: **maçonnerie à s.,** dry masonry; Tex:

filature à s., dry spinning; (d) Nau: **navire à s., au s.,** ship aground, high and dry, sewed up, sued up; **laisser un navire au s.,** to sew, sue, a vessel; **tirer, haler, un bateau à s.,** to draw up, haul up, a boat (on a beach); to draw a boat high and dry; (e) (of ship) **filer, courir, fuir, à s.** (de toile), to run, scud, under bare poles; to run ahull; (f) **tout s.,** only, merely; P: **aussi s.,** at once, straight away; right away; **il a reçu un télégramme et il est reparti aussi s.,** he received a telegram and left straight away, at once. 5. s.m. (a) dryness; drought; **ce mélange du s. et de l'humide,** this mixture of dryness and humidity; (b) **tenir au s.,** keep in a dry place; Tex: **filature au s.,** dry spinning; (c) Husb: dry fodder; **mettre un cheval au s.,** to put a horse on dry fodder. 6. s.f. **sèche,** (a) Nau: dry shelf, flat (left at low tide); (b) P: cigarette, fag; (c) Sch: F: O: **piquer une sèche,** to be stumped, to dry up (at an oral).

sécable [sekabl], a. sectile, divisible, that can be cut.

sécale [sekal], s.m. Bot: secale.

secam [sekam], a. & s.m. T.V: secam.

sécant, -ante [sekɑ̃, -ɑ̃ːt], Geom: 1. a. secant, cutting (line, surface). 2. s.f. **sécante,** secant.

sécateur [sekatœːr], s.m. 1. secateur(s); pruning shears. 2. A: net cutter (of torpedo).

seccotine [sɛkɔtin], s.f. 1. R.t.m: Seccotine. 2. F: (pers.) bore.

sécession [sesɛsjɔ̃], s.f. secession; **faire s.,** to secede (de, from); U.S.Hist: **la Guerre de S.,** the War of Secession.

sécessionnisme [sesɛsjɔnism], s.m. secessionism.

sécessionniste [sesɛsjɔnist], a. & s.m. & f. secessionist.

séchage [seʃaːʒ], s.m. 1. (a) drying (of hay, clothes, etc.); seasoning (of wood); **s. à l'air,** drying in the open air; seasoning (of wood); **s. par le vide,** vacuum drying; **s. à l'étuve,** stove drying; (b) P: cutting (of lectures). 2. drying factory (for fruit, etc.).

sèche-cheveux [sɛʃʃəvø], s.m.inv. hair drier.

sèche-cliché [sɛʃkliʃe], s.m. Phot: plate drier; pl. **sèche-clichés.**

séchée [seʃe], s.f. (a) drying process; (b) period of drying.

sèche-linge [sɛʃlɛ̃ːʒ], a.inv. Dom.Ec: armoire s.-l., drying cupboard.

sèchement [sɛʃmɑ̃], adv. 1. curtly, tartly. 2. **peindre s.,** to paint with a hard touch; **écrire s.,** to write in a bald style; **traiter un sujet s.,** to treat a subject baldly.

sécher [seʃe], v. (je **sèche,** n. **séchons;** je **sécherai**) 1. v.tr. (a) to dry (clothes, etc.); **s. ses larmes,** to dry one's tears; **séché à l'air,** air-dried, air-dry; seasoned (wood); **séché au soleil,** sun-dried; **séché à l'étuve,** oven-dried; kiln-dried; **s. le houblon au four,** to kiln the hops; **s. au ventilateur,** to fan dry; **s. au buvard,** to blot (off); Paperm: **papier séché à la machine,** cylinder-dried paper; **la chaleur a séché le ruisseau,** the heat has dried up the stream; **il s'est séché devant le feu,** he dried himself in front of the fire; (b) F: **s. un verre,** to knock back a glass (of whisky, etc.); (c) F: Sch: etc: **s. un cours, une réunion,** to cut a lecture, a meeting; (d) A: **s. un candidat,** to fail a candidate; (e) P: **s. un type,** to kill s.o., to bump s.o. off. 2. v.i. (a) to dry; to become dry; **faire s. du bois,** (i) to dry, (ii) to season, wood; **faire s. du linge,** to dry the linen; Husb: **faire s. une vache,** to dry (off) a cow; (b) **s. d'impatience,** to be consumed with impatience; **s. sur pied,** (i) (of plant) to wilt; to wither; (ii) (of pers.) to wilt; to be pining away, wasting away; (c) F: not to know what to say, to dry up; Sch: to be stumped (by an examiner); (d) P: (pers.) to smoke.

sécheresse [seʃrɛs, sɛ-], s.f. 1. (a) dryness (of the air, ground, throat, etc.); (b) drought. 2. (a) leanness, spareness (of the figure); (b) curtness (of manner, etc.); (c) coldness, unfeelingness (of heart, etc.); (d) barrenness, meagreness, baldness (of style, of work of art); jejuneness (of a subject).

sécherie [seʃri, sɛ-], s.f. 1. drying room, ground, yard, floor. 2. For: Hort: seed kiln. 3. drying machine, drier.

sécheron [seʃrɔ̃, sɛ-], s.m. 1. Dial: (in E. of Fr.) dry meadow. 2. F: A: lean, lank, spare, dried-up, person.

sécheur [seʃœːr], s.m. Tchn: drying apparatus, chamber; drier (for tobacco, etc.); Mch: **s. de vapeur,** steam drier; **s. à vide,** vacuum drier.

sécheuse [seʃøːz], s.f. Laund: steam drier.

séchoir [seʃwaːr], s.m. Tchn: 1. drying place, room, loft, ground; **s. à houblon,** oasthouse. 2.

(a) drier, drying apparatus; desiccator; **s.** (à cheveux), (hairdresser's) hair drier; Ind: **s. à vapeur,** steam drier; (b) clothes horse, towel rail; **s. de plafond,** (ceiling) clothes drier and airer.

seclinois, -oise [səklinwa, -waːz], a. & s. Geog: (native, inhabitant) of Seclin.

second, -onde [səgɔ̃, zgɔ̃, -ɔ̃ːd]. 1. a. second; (a) **une seconde fois,** a second time; twice; **en s. lieu,** in the second place; **l'habitude est une seconde nature,** habit is second nature; a. & s.m. **habiter au s.** (étage), to live on the second, U.S: third, floor; **votre ami est un s. Sherlock Holmes,** your friend is another, a second, Sherlock Holmes; Mus: **les seconds violons,** the second violins; Gram: **la seconde personne du singulier, du pluriel,** the second person singular, plural; **de seconde main,** secondhand; **entendre une nouvelle de seconde main,** to hear a piece of news secondhand, from a third party; **au s. plan,** in the background; **être relégué au s. plan,** to be relegated into the background; to be forced to take a back seat; **le s. fils du maire, s. le s. des fils du maire,** the mayor's second son; **le don de seconde vue,** the gift of second sight; Mth: n **seconde,** n double dash (n"); (b) (taking second place; inferior) Com: **s. associé,** junior partner; **passer s.,** to take second place; Sp: **finir bon s.,** to come in a good second; **l'équipe seconde,** the second team; **ouvrage de s. ordre,** inferior, second-rate, (piece of) work; **article de s. choix,** inferior, second-grade, article; Th: **jouer les seconds rôles,** to play the supporting parts; Lit: **sans s.,** matchless, peerless, unparalleled; **audace sans seconde,** unparalleled audacity; **beauté à nulle autre seconde,** peerless, matchless, beauty; Ch: A: **eau seconde,** lye water, weak nitric acid; (c) Phil: etc: **causes secondes,** second causes; Gr.Gram: **temps seconds,** secondary, historic, tenses; (d) Med: **état s.** (d'un somnambule), semi-conscious state (of a sleepwalker); **les jeunes dansaient dans un état s.,** the young people were dancing in a state of trance. 2. s.m. (a) principal assistant; second (in command); Nau: first mate, first officer, chief officer (of ship); Navy: **commandant, officier, en s.,** F: **le s.,** executive officer; **s. maître,** petty officer; **commander en s.,** to be second in command; Jur: (of notary) **signer en s.,** to countersign (deed); (b) second (in a duel, of boxer). 3. s.f. **seconde:** (a) Typ: second proof, revise; Fenc: **seconde** (parry); Rail: etc: second (class); **voyager en seconde,** to travel second (class); **les voyageurs de seconde,** the second-class passengers; Sch: (**classe de**) **seconde** = fifth form; **élève de seconde** = fifth-former; Mus: **seconde majeure, mineure,** major, minor, second; Aut: **rouler en seconde,** to drive in second (gear); (b) second (of time, arc, angle); **ponctualité à la seconde,** punctuality to the second; **aiguille des secondes,** second hand (of a watch); **je reviens dans deux secondes,** I'll be back in two seconds; **attendez une seconde! une seconde!** just a second! just a moment! **en un quart, une fraction, de seconde,** in a split second, in no time.

secondaire [səgɔ̃dɛːr, zgɔ̃-], a. 1. (a) secondary (planet, circuit, haemorrhage, etc.); (b) Atom. Ph: secondary (radiation, electron); (c) Elcs: (computers) **voie s.,** secondary route; **défaillance s.,** secondary failure; **liaison en groupe s.,** super-group link; (d) **enseignement s.,** secondary education; **établissement d'enseignement s.,** secondary school; **centre d'études secondaires** = comprehensive school. 2. subordinate, of minor importance; **question d'importance s.,** question of minor interest; side issue; Rail: **voie s.,** side track; Ling: **accent s.,** secondary accent, secondary stress; Mus: **temps s.,** weak beat; Th: Lit: **intrigue s.,** sub plot. 3. (a) s.m. El.E: secondary winding; W.Tel: secondary (of transformer); (b) a. & s.m. Geol: **l'ère s., le s.,** the secondary (era); (c) a. & s.m. Pol.Ec: secondary (activities).

secondairement [səgɔ̃dɛrmɑ̃, zgɔ̃-], adv. secondarily.

secondement [səgɔ̃dmɑ̃, zgɔ̃-], adv. secondly, in the second place.

seconder [səgɔ̃de, zgɔ̃-], v.tr. 1. to second, back up, support (s.o.); to help (s.o.); **grâce à l'équipe qui me secondait . . .,** thanks to the team that was helping, assisting, me . . .; **s. effectivement qn,** to lend effective help to s.o.; **secondé par le sort,** helped, favoured, by fortune. 2. to forward, further, promote (s.o.'s interests, plans, etc.).

secondine [səgɔ̃din], s.f. 1. Bot: secundine. 2. pl. Obst: A: secundines, afterbirth.

secondipare [səgɔ̃dipaːr], a. secundiparous.

sécot [seko], *a. P:* lank, lanky, lean, skinny; **un petit s.,** a wiry fellow.

secouage [səkwa:ʒ], *s.m.*, **secouement** [səkumɑ̃], *s.m.* **1.** shaking; **répondre d'un secouement de tête,** to answer with a shake of the head. **2.** shaking, shake-up; jolting, jolt.

secouée [səkwe], *s.f. F:* **1.** (*a*) shaking, jolt; (*b*) *P:* scolding, blowing-up. **2.** fall of apples, etc. (when tree is shaken); *P:* **il y en avait une s.,** there were heaps, tons, of them.

secouer [səkwe], *v.tr.* **1.** (*a*) to shake (tree, one's head, etc.); to plump up, shake up (a pillow); **être secoué de sursauts dans son lit,** to toss about in bed; **il a été bien secoué par sa maladie,** he is much shaken by his illness; **il resta là, le cœur secoué,** he stood there, shaken at heart; *abs.* **voiture qui secoue,** bumpy, jolting, car; **navire secoué rudement par le vent,** ship buffeted by the wind; **nous avons été secoués pendant la traversée,** we were tossed about during the crossing; we had a bumpy crossing; **j'ai dû le s. pour le réveiller,** I had to shake him to wake him up; (*b*) **il est impossible de s. son indifférence,** it is impossible to rouse him from, shake him out of, his indifference; **il nous faut nous s.,** we must get down to things, get a move on; *F:* **secouez-vous!** pull yourself together! get down to it! get a move on! snap out of it! *F:* **s. (les puces à) qn,** (i) to give s.o. a good talking to; to tell s.o. off; (ii) to rouse s.o. to action; to stick a few pins into s.o. **2.** (*a*) to shake down (fruit, etc.); (*b*) **s. le joug,** to shake off the yoke; **s. la poussière de qch.,** to shake the dust off sth.; **s. la poussière de ses souliers,** to shake the dust from one's feet; to depart indignantly; **s. les cendres de sa pipe,** to knock the ashes out of one's pipe.

secoueur, -euse [səkwœ:r, -ø:z], *s.* **1.** shaker (of sth.). **2.** *s.m.* (*a*) form-breaker, mallet (to break up moulds after casting); (*b*) *Agr:* shaker (of thresher).

secourable [səkurabl], *a.* **1.** helpful, willing to help; **elle fut toujours s. aux pauvres,** she was always ready to help the poor; **tendre une main s. à qn,** to lend s.o. a helping hand; **peu s.,** unhelpful. **2.** *Mil:* (*of fortified place*) relievable, that can be relieved; **place s. par mer,** place relievable by sea.

secoureurs [səkurœ:r], *s.m.pl. Ecc.Hist:* relievers.

secourir [səkuri:r], *v.tr.* (*conj. like* COURIR) to help, aid; **s. une entreprise,** to back up an undertaking; **s. les pauvres,** to help the poor.

secourisme [səkurism], *s.m. Med:* first aid.

secouriste [səkurist], *s.m. & f.* member of a first-aid association; first-aid worker; relief worker; **les secouristes arrivèrent sur les lieux de l'accident,** first-aid workers arrived at the scene of the accident.

secours [səku:r], *s.m.* help, relief, aid, assistance; **crier au s.,** to call for help; **appel au s.,** call for help; **au s.!** help! **porter, prêter, (du) s. à qn,** to give, lend, assistance to s.o., to help s.o.; *Med:* **premiers s.,** first aid; **poste de s.,** first-aid post; *Mil:* dressing station; **société de s.,** first-aid association; **boîte, trousse, de s.,** first-aid box, outfit; **s. en montagne,** mountain rescue (work, service); **caravane de s.,** rescue party; **comité de s.,** relief committee; **demander (du) s.,** to ask for help; **aller, se porter, au s. de qn,** to go to s.o.'s aid; *Mil: Navy:* **se porter au s. d'un bataillon, d'un navire,** to go in support of a battalion, of a ship; **venir au s. de qn, rendre s. à qn,** to come to s.o.'s help; **cela m'a rendu grand s., cela m'a été d'un grand s.,** it has been very helpful to me; it has been a great help; it has stood me in good stead; **puis-je vous être d'aucun s.?** can I be of help? **s. d'argent,** financial assistance; *Adm: A:* **s. aux pauvres,** relief of the poor; **s. à domicile,** outdoor relief; **le s. aux enfants,** child-welfare work; **caisse de s.,** relief fund; **crédits de s.,** relief credits; **société de s. mutuels,** benefit society, friendly society; **sortie, porte, de s.,** emergency exit; *Fort:* **porte de s.,** sally port; *Aut:* **roue de s.,** spare wheel; *Av:* **terrain de secours,** emergency landing-ground; emergency airstrip; **éclairage de s.,** emergency lighting system; *Ecc: A:* **(chapelle de) s.,** chapel of ease; *Mec.E: etc:* **machine de s.,** stand-by engine, reserve engine; *Mil:* **troupes de s.;** *s.m.pl.* **des secours,** relief troops, relieving force; *Rail:* **convoi, corvée, de s.,** breakdown train, gang; **locomotive, train, de s.,** relief engine, train; *Th:* **grand s.,** fire hydrant.

secousse [səkus], *s.f.* shake, shaking; jolt, jerk; shock; **s. sismique,** earth tremor; **s. prémonitoire,** warning tremor (before earthquake); **les secousses de la route,** the jolts, bumps, of the road; **les secousses de la voiture,** the jolting of the car; **imprimer une (brusque) s. à qch.,** to jolt sth.; to make (table, etc.) jump; **se lever d'une s.,** to spring to one's feet; **sa santé a reçu une s.,** his health has been shaken; **se dégager d'une s.,** to jerk, wrench, shake, oneself free; **arriver à ses fins sans s.,** to attain one's ends smoothly, without great exertion; **respirer par secousses pénibles,** to breathe in painful gasps; **s. politique,** political upheaval; **se remettre d'une s.,** to recover from a shock; *Ind:* **tamis à secousses,** jigging sieve; **couloir à secousses,** shaker conveyor, shaking shoot; *Physiol:* **s. musculaire,** (muscle) jerk; **travailler par secousses,** to work in fits and starts; *F:* **en donner une s.,** to work hard; to get down to it; *F:* **il n'en fait, fiche, pas une s.,** he doesn't do a thing.

secret[1], **-ète**[1] [səkrɛ, -ɛt], *a.* (*a*) secret (orders, signal, treaty, etc.); hidden (feelings); occult (science); *Adm:* **très s., ultra-s.,** top secret; **il y a une raison secrète derrière tout cela,** there's sth. behind all that; **escalier s.,** secret stair; **invention secrète,** secret invention; **influence secrète,** secret, backstair, influence; **la police secrète,** *s.* **la secrète** = the Criminal Investigation Department, the C.I.D.; **fonds secrets,** secret-service funds; **tenez, gardez, cela s.!** keep it secret! *F:* keep it dark! (*b*) reticent, close (person); *Ven:* **chien s.,** mute hound.

secret[2], *s.m.* **1.** secret; **garder un s.,** to keep a secret; **garder le s. au sujet de qch.,** to keep sth. secret; **gardez le s.!** keep it dark! **mettre qn dans le s.,** to let s.o. into the secret; **être du s., dans le s.,** to be in the secret, *F:* in the know; **le s. de la famille,** the skeleton in the cupboard; **n'avoir point de s. pour qn,** to have no secrets from s.o.; **trahir un s.,** to betray a secret, *F:* to let the cat out of the bag; **le s. de son succès,** the secret of his success; **trouver le s. de faire qch.,** to find the knack of doing sth.; **s. d'un mécanisme,** secret spring; **bureau à s.,** desk with a secret compartment; **faire jouer le s.,** to touch, press, the secret spring (of desk, etc.). **2.** secrecy, privacy; **promettre le s.,** to promise secrecy; **dire qch. à qn sous le sceau du s., en grand s.,** to tell s.o. sth. under pledge of secrecy, as a great secret; **en s.,** in secrecy, in secret, privily, privately; **abuser du, trahir le, s. professionnel,** to commit a breach of confidence; *Ecc:* **le s. de la confession,** the seal of confession; **dépôt de brevet au s. d'un an,** patent application with one year's secrecy provision; *Jur:* **s. des lettres,** secrecy of correspondence. **3.** solitary confinement; **mettre qn au s.,** to put s.o. in solitary confinement.

secrétage [səkreta:ʒ], *s.m. Leath:* carroting (of pelts).

secrétaire [səkretɛ:r]. **1.** *s.m. or f.* secretary; **s. particulier,** private secretary; **s. médicale,** (i) doctor's, (ii) dentist's, secretary; **s. d'État,** Secretary of State; *Dipl:* **s. d'ambassade,** (first, second, third) secretary; *Journ:* **s. de la rédaction,** sub-editor; *Mil:* **s. d'état-major,** staff clerk; **s. général des Nations-Unies,** Secretary General to the United Nations; *Adm:* **s. de direction,** executive secretary; principal assistant; **s. d'administration** = assistant principal; **s. de mairie** = town clerk (not *usu.* a lawyer); (*in village*) secretarial assistant to the mayor. **2.** *s.m. Orn:* secretary bird. **3.** *s.m.* secretaire, writing desk. **4.** *s.m. A:* collection of model letters; letter-writer's guide.

secrétairerie [səkretɛr(ə)ri], *s.f.* **1.** registry, chancery (of a State department). **2.** secretary's (office) staff; secretariat(e).

secrétariat [səkretarja], *s.m.* **1.** secretaryship. **2.** secretary's office; secretariat.

secrète[2] [səkrɛt], *s.f. Ecc:* secret; priest's private prayer before the preface.

secrètement [səkrɛtmɑ̃], *adv.* secretly, covertly; in secret.

secréter [səkrete], *v.tr.* **(je secrète, n. secrétons; je secréterai)** *Leath:* to carrot (pelts).

sécréter [sekrete], *v.tr.* **(il sécrète; il sécrétera)** *Physiol:* (*of gland, etc.*) to secrete; **s. des hormones,** to discharge hormones.

sécréteur, -trice, *occ.* **-euse** [sekretœ:r, -tris, -ø:z], *a. Physiol:* secreting, secretory (gland, etc.).

sécrétine [sekretin], *s.f. Physiol:* secretin.

sécrétion [sekresjɔ̃], *s.f. Physiol:* secretion; **glande à s. externe,** exocrine gland.

secrétivité [sekretivite], *s.f.* secretiveness.

sécrétoire [sekretwa:r], *a. Physiol:* secretary (process, etc.).

sectaire [sɛktɛ:r]. **1.** *s.m.* sectary, sectarian. **2.** *a.* sectarian (worship, etc.).

sectarisme [sɛktarism], *s.m.* sectarianism.

sectateur, -trice [sɛktatœ:r, -tris], *s.* follower, disciple (of s.o.); member, adherent (of a sect, etc.).

secte [sɛkt], *s.f.* sect; **faire s.,** to form a party; **ils font s. à part,** they form a sect, a party, of their own; **esprit de s.,** sectarian, parochial, mind.

secteur [sɛktœ:r], *s.m.* **1.** (*a*) *Astr: Geom:* sector; *Mth:* **s. circulaire,** sector of a circle; **s. sphérique,** spherical sector; *Draw:* **graphique à secteurs,** pie chart; (*b*) *Mec.E: Mch:* sector, quadrant, arc; **s. denté,** toothed arc, segment, sector; notched, toothed, quadrant; segment gear; **cran d'un s.,** tooth, notch, of a sector, of a quadrant; **guide de s.,** quadrant guide; **levier s'actionnant sur un s.,** quadrant-type lever; **vis sans fin et s.,** worm and segment; *Aut: etc:* **s. de direction,** steering sector; **s. de frein,** quadrant, ratchet, of the handbrake; *I.C.E:* **s. de commande (des gaz),** (control) quadrant; *Nau:* **s. de barre,** *Av:* **s. de gouverne, de direction,** rudder quadrant; *Nau:* **s. dangereux,** dangerous quadrant (of storm); *Artil:* **s. de pointage en hauteur,** elevating rack, elevation sector; **s. de pointage en direction,** traversing arc; **s. fileté (de culasse),** threaded sector (of breech block); **s. interrompu (de culasse),** interrupted screw (of breech block). **2.** area, district; (*a*) *Com:* **s. de vente,** sales area, trading area; (*b*) *Mil:* (i) division sector, division(al) area; (ii) **secteur (affecté à une unité),** area, sector, of responsibility; **s. d'attaque,** area, sector, of attack; **s. de défense,** area, sector, of defence; defensive area; **s. de tir,** firing area, area to be covered by fire; **s. battu par les feux,** area, sector, covered by fire; **s. privé de, non battu par les, feux,** area, sector, not covered by fire; *Mil.Adm:* **s. postal,** postal sector, area handled by army post office; (*c*) **s. de surveillance,** (i) (*radar, etc.*) surveillance sector, area; (ii) (policeman's) beat; (*d*) *El:* **secteur (de distribution électrique),** mains; **s. aller,** mains out; **s. retour,** mains in; **s. lumière,** lighting mains; **brancher sur le s.,** to take power from the mains; *W.Tel:* **poste s.,** mains set; **poste s. tous courants,** all-mains set. **3.** (*a*) *Pol.Ec: etc:* field (of activity); **s. de produits,** field of products; **s. primaire, secondaire, tertiaire,** primary, secondary, tertiary, activities; **s. économique,** economic sector; **s. industriel,** industrial sector; **le s. privé,** the private sector, private enterprise; **le s. public,** the public sector, state enterprise; *F:* **ce n'est pas mon s.,** that's not my line; (*b*) *Elcs:* (*computers*) **le s.,** the field.

section [sɛksjɔ̃], *s.f.* **1.** section, cutting; **s. des tendons,** cutting of the tendons; **s. de la queue,** docking of the tail (of a horse). **2.** (*a*) section (of chapter, building, etc.); (*b*) *Nat.Hist:* section (of a genus); (*c*) *Adm:* branch (of a department, political party, etc.); (electoral) division; **s. de vote,** polling station; (*d*) *Mil:* platoon (of infantry); section (of artillery); **chef de s.,** platoon commander; **S. Géographique de l'Armée** = Geographical Section General Staff; *Artil:* **s. de munitions,** ammunition column; *Hist:* **sections d'assaut,** storm troops; (*e*) *Navy:* sub-division (of fleet); (*f*) *Mil.Av:* **s. de bombardiers,** bomber flight. **3.** (*a*) *Mth:* (i) section; (ii) intersection; **sections coniques,** conic sections; **sections carrées,** square sections; **point de s.,** point of intersection; (*b*) *Arch: Const:* section, profile; **s. droite, s. transversale,** cross-section, transverse section; **s. longitudinale,** longitudinal section, *N.Arch:* buttock line; **s. horizontale,** horizontal section; **s. plane,** plane section; **s. oblique,** oblique section, *N.Arch:* diagonal line; *N.Arch:* **s. hors bordé,** outer section; **s. sur membre,** inner section; (*c*) *El:* **s. morte,** idle coil; (*d*) (*computers*) bay, section; **s. de contrôle,** control section; **s. d'essais,** test section; **s. de groupe primaire,** group section; **s. de groupe secondaire,** supergroup section; **s. de groupe tertiaire,** mastergroup section; (*e*) *Atom.Ph:* **s. efficace,** cross-section; **s. efficace d'un noyau,** nuclear cross-section; **s. efficace de choc,** collision cross-section; **s. efficace de diffusion, de fission, de réaction,** diffusion, fission, reaction, cross-section; **s. efficace d'ensemble,** bulk cross-section; (*f*) *Hyd.E:* **s. mouillée,** wetted section. **4.** (*a*) stage (on bus, etc. route); **changement de s.,** fare stage; (*b*) *Rail:* **s. de block,** block section; **s. bloquée,** line blocked; **s. débloquée,** line clear; **s. horizontale, s. en palier,** level length.

sectionnaire [sɛksjɔnɛ:r], *s.m. Hist:* member of the National Guard; National Guard(sman).

sectionnel, -elle [sɛksjɔnɛl], *a.* sectional.

sectionnement [sɛksjɔnmɑ̃], *s.m.* **1.** division into sections. **2.** cutting, severing.
sectionner [sɛksjɔne], *v.tr.* **1.** to divide (district, etc.) into sections; to section. **2.** (*a*) to cut (off), sever; *Surg:* to amputate; (*b*) to cut into pieces; to dissect.
sectionneur [sɛksjɔnœːr], *s.m. El.E:* disconnecting switch, isolating switch.
sectoriel, -ielle [sɛktɔrjɛl], *a.* sectorial.
séculaire [sekylɛːr], *a.* **1.** (*a*) occurring once in a hundred years; secular (games, jubilee); *Pol.Ec:* **mouvement s. des prix,** secular trend of prices; (*b*) **année s.,** last year of a century; (*c*) *Astr:* secular. **2.** (*a*) century-old, secular (tree, monument); (*b*) age-long, time-honoured (custom).
séculairement [sekylɛrmɑ̃], *adv.* from century to century, from age to age.
sécularisation [sekylarizasjɔ̃], *s.f.* secularization; conversion (of church, etc.) to secular uses; deconsecration.
séculariser [sekylarize], *v.tr.* to secularize; to convert (church property, etc.) to secular uses; to deconsecrate (church).
sécularisme [sekylarism], *s.m. Eng.Phil:* secularism.
sécularité [sekylarite], *s.f.* **1.** secularity. **2.** secular jurisdiction (of a Church).
séculier, -ière [sekylje, -jɛːr]. **1.** *a.* (*a*) secular (clergy, jurisdiction); **le bras s.,** the secular arm; **institut s.,** secular institute; (*b*) laic; (*c*) *A:* mundane, worldly. **2.** *s.* layman; **les séculiers,** the laity.
séculièrement [sekyljɛrmɑ̃], *adv.* secularly; from a secular, worldly, point of view; in a secular way.
secundo [səgɔ̃do, sek-], *Lt.adv.* secondly, in the second place.
sécuriforme [sekyrifɔrm], *a. Bot: Ent: etc:* securiform, axe-shaped.
sécurité [sekyrite], *s.f.* **1.** security, secureness; freedom from apprehension; reliability (of statistics); **être en s. contre le danger,** to be secure against, from, danger; *Ind: etc:* **s. du fonctionnement,** reliability, dependability (of machinery); **s. d'exploitation,** operational reliability (of engine, apparatus, etc.); *Com:* **société de s.,** guarantee society; **s. de l'emploi,** security of employment, guaranteed employment; *Adm:* **S. sociale** = National Health (Service). **2.** (*a*) safety; **s. de la route,** road safety; *Adm:* **direction de la s. publique,** department of public safety; **compagnies républicaines de sécurité** (C.R.S.), riot police; **services de s.,** (i) *Mil:* security forces; (ii) stewards (at demonstration, etc.); security police (in firm, etc.); *U.S:* vigilantes; *Nau:* **officier de s.,** officer in charge of fire precautions; (*b*) *Mec.E: Civ.E: Ind:* **coefficient de s.,** security factor; **marge de s.,** security margin; **règles de s.,** safety rules or code; *El.E:* **s. intrinsèque,** total security; *Rail:* safety of traffic; **dispositif de s.,** safety device; **les divers dispositifs de s.,** the various safety arrangements; **verrouillage de s.,** interlocking device; *Ind: etc:* **verre de s.,** safety glass, splinterproof glass; *El:* **éclairage de s.,** emergency lighting.
sedan [sədɑ̃], *s.m. Tex:* sedan cloth.
sedanais, -aise [sədanɛ, -ɛːz], *a. & s. Geog:* (native, inhabitant) of Sedan.
sédatif, -ive [sedatif, -iːv], *a. & s.m. Med:* sedative; *Pharm:* **eau sédative,** lotion of ammonia; camphorated alcohol, salt and water.
sédation [sedasjɔ̃], *s.f. Med:* sedation.
Sédécias [sedesjɑːs], *Pr.n.m. B.Hist:* Zedekiah.
sédentaire [sedɑ̃tɛːr]. **1.** *a.* (*a*) sedentary (occupation, life); (*b*) **os s.,** protuberance of the ischium. **2.** *a.* fixed, stationary, settled; (*a*) **troupes sédentaires,** sedentary, non-mobile, troops; garrison troops; *Mil.Av:* **cadre s.,** ground personnel; *Hist:* (*during the siege of Paris*) **garde nationale s.,** militia; *s.m.* **un s.,** a militiaman; (*b*) *Fish:* **rets s.,** anchored net, fixed net; (*c*) **oiseau s.,** non-migrant bird. **3.** *s.m. & f.* sedentary. **4.** *s.f.pl. Ann:* **sedentaires,** Sedentaria.
sédentairement [sedɑ̃tɛrmɑ̃], *adv.* sedentarily.
sédentarité [sedɑ̃tarite], *s.f.* sedentariness, sedentary life, lack of exercise.
séderbande, séder-bande [sedɛrbɑ̃ːd], *s.f.* (*in marquetry*) border between sections.
sédiment [sedimɑ̃], *s.m.* sediment, deposit; *Geol:* **sédiments lacustres,** lacustrine sediments; **sédiments marins,** marine deposits; **sédiments vaseux,** ooze; *Petroleum Ind:* **sédiments et résidus,** bottom settlings.
sédimentaire [sedimɑ̃tɛːr], *a. Geol: etc:* sedimentary (stratum, etc.); sedimental (matter); **roche s.,** sedimentary rock.
sédimentation [sedimɑ̃tasjɔ̃], *s.f.* sedimentation; *Med:* **vitesse de s. globulaire,** sedimentation test.
sédimenter (se) [səsedimɑ̃te], *v.pr.* to (form a) deposit.
sédimentologie [sedimɑ̃tɔlɔʒi], *s.f.* sedimentology.
sédimentologique [sedimɑ̃tɔlɔʒik], *a.* sedimentological.
sédimentologiste [sedimɑ̃tɔlɔʒist], *s.m. & f.* sedimentologist.
séditieusement [sedisjøzmɑ̃], *adv.* seditiously.
séditieux, -euse [sedisjø, -øːz]. **1.** *a.* (*a*) seditious (speech, assembly); **tenir des propos s.,** to talk treason; (*b*) mutinous, rebellious. **2.** *s.m.* fomenter of sedition, mutineer.
sédition [sedisjɔ̃], *s.f.* sedition; mutiny; **être en s.,** to be in revolt.
séditionner [sedisjɔne], *v.tr. A:* to incite (the people) to sedition, to revolt.
se séditionner, *A:* to rise (in revolt).
Sedlitz [sedlits], *Pr.n. Geog:* Seidlitz; *Pharm:* **sel de S.,** Seidlitz powder.
séducteur, -trice [sedyktœːr, -tris]. **1.** *s.* (*a*) tempter, beguiler, enticer, inveigler; (*b*) *s.m.* seducer; abuser (of young women). **2.** *a.* tempting, enticing (word, look); seductive, fascinating, alluring (charm, grace); **l'Esprit s.,** the Tempter.
séductible [sedyktibl̩], *a.* seducible.
séduction [sedyksjɔ̃], *s.f.* **1.** (*a*) seduction; enticement, leading astray; *Jur:* **rapt par s.,** abduction (with consent); **s. de témoins,** subornation of witnesses; **user de s. pour faire faire qch. à qn,** to entice s.o. into doing sth.; **il est à l'épreuve de toute s.,** he is proof against all enticements; (*b*) *Jur:* seduction; **s. dolosive,** deceitful enticement of woman to sexual relations. **2.** seduction, charm, allurement, attraction, seductiveness; **séductions physiques,** physical attractions; **la s. des richesses,** the allurement of wealth; **succomber aux séductions de qn,** to fall a victim (i) to the wiles of s.o., (ii) to the charms of s.o.
séduire [sedɥiːr], *v.tr.* (*pr.p.* **séduisant;** *p.p.* **séduit;** *pr.ind.* **je séduis, n. séduisons, ils séduisent;** *pr.sub.* **je séduise;** *p.d.* **je séduisais;** *p.h.* **je séduisis;** *fu.* **je séduirai**) **1.** to seduce; to lead astray; **s. une femme,** to seduce a woman; **s. des témoins,** to bribe, suborn, witnesses; *A:* **se laisser s. à la tentation,** to yield to temptation; **se laisser s. à faire qch.,** to allow oneself to be tempted into doing sth. **2.** to fascinate, captivate, lure, allure, charm; to please (s.o.'s) fancy; to attract s.o.; **cela m'a séduit du premier coup,** it took my fancy at once; **s. l'imagination,** to appeal to the imagination; **voilà qui le séduira!** *F:* that will fetch him!
séduisant [sedɥizɑ̃], *a.* **1.** seductive, tempting, alluring (plan, offer, etc.). **2.** fascinating, charming, taking, engaging, captivating (manner, person); **jeune fille séduisante,** attractive girl; **sourire s.,** captivating smile.
sédum, sedum [sedɔm], *s.m. Bot:* sedum.
sédunois, -oise [sedynwa, -waːz], *a. & s.* (native, inhabitant) of Sion (Switz.)
Seeland [selɑ̃ːd], *Pr.n. Geog:* **l'île de Seeland,** the Island of Zealand.
ségala [segala], *s.m. Agr: Dial:* land planted, sown, with rye.
ségestain, -aine [seʒɛstɛ̃, -ɛn], *a. & s. A.Geog:* Segestan.
Ségeste [seʒɛst], *Pr.n. A.Geog:* Segesta.
ségétal, -aux [seʒetal, -o], *a.* segetal; growing in cornfields.
ségétière [seʒetjɛːr], *s.f. Fish:* large, *esp.* Mediterranean, trammel-net.
segment [sɛgmɑ̃], *s.m.* **1.** (*a*) *Geom:* segment (of line, sphere, etc.); **s. circulaire, s. de cercle,** segment of a circle; **s. linéaire, s. de droite,** segment of a line; (*b*) segment (of worm, insect, etc.); *Med:* **s. interannulaire,** interannular segment; **s. inférieur,** lower uterine segment; **s. musculaire de Krause,** sarcomere; *Exp:* **obus à segments,** segment shell; (*c*) *Aut:* joint (of caterpillar tyre). **2.** *I.C.E: Mch: etc:* **s. de piston,** piston ring, packing ring; **s. à joint en sifflet,** oblique-slotted ring; **s. à joint à baïonnette,** ring with stopped ends; **s. d'étanchéité,** ring seal, compression ring, sealing ring; **s. (d'étanchéité) de culasse,** junk ring; **s. de frein,** brake shoe; **frein à segments,** segmented brake; **s. racleur,** scraper ring; oil scraper; *El:* **s. de collecteur,** commutator, bar, segment; (*computers*) **s. principal,** root segment; **s. de recouvrement,** overlay.
segmentaire [sɛgmɑ̃tɛːr], *a.* **1.** *Geom:* segmentary (solid). **2.** *Anat: Arch:* segmental (organ, vault).
segmentarité [sɛgmɑ̃tarite], *s.f.* segmentary nature (of sth.).
segmentation [sɛgmɑ̃tasjɔ̃], *s.f.* (*a*) segmentation; **divisé par s.,** segmented; (*b*) *Biol:* cleavage of cells; (*c*) (*computers*) partitioning.
segmenter [sɛgmɑ̃te], *v.tr.* to segment; to divide into segments; (*computers*) to partition, section, segment.
se segmenter, to segment; to undergo segmentation, cleavage.
segmentina [sɛgmɑ̃tina], *s.m. Moll:* segmentina.
Ségovie [segɔvi], *Pr.n.f. Geog:* Segovia.
ségrairie [segrɛri], *s.f. For:* (*a*) joint ownership of woodland; (*b*) woodland which is owned jointly.
ségrais [segrɛ], *s.m. For:* isolated woodland (exploited separately).
ségrayer [segrɛje], *s.m. For:* joint owner of woodland.
segréen, -enne [səgreɛ̃, -ɛn], *a. & s. Geog:* (native, inhabitant) of Segré.
ségrégabilité [segregabilite], *s.f. Tchn:* tendency to segregation.
ségrégatif, -ive [segregatif, -iːv], *a.* segregative, segregating.
ségrégation [segregasjɔ̃], *s.f.* segregation; setting apart; isolation; **s. raciale,** colour bar, *U.S:* color line; apartheid; *Geol:* **gîte de s. magmatique,** magmatic segregation deposit.
ségrégationisme [segregasjɔnism], *s.m. Pol:* (policy of) racial segregation.
ségrégationiste [segregasjɔnist], *a. & s.m. & f. Pol:* segregationist.
séguedille [segədiːj], *s.f. Danc: Mus:* seguidilla.
séguia [segja], *s.f.* (*in North Africa*) irrigation channel.
seiche[1] [sɛʃ], *s.f. Moll:* cuttlefish, sepia; **os de s.,** cuttlebone.
seiche[2], *s.f.* seiche, tidal wave.
séid [seid], *s.m. Moslem Civ:* say(y)id; lord.
séide [seid], *s.m. Lit:* devoted follower, blind supporter; henchman; blind tool (of his master) (*from the character in Voltaire's Mahomet*).
seigle [sɛgl], *s.m.* **1.** rye; **faire les seigles,** to harvest the rye; **pain de s.,** rye bread; *s.a.* ERGOTÉ 2. **2.** **faux s.,** rye grass; **s. bâtard,** fescue grass.
seigneur [sɛɲœːr], *s.m.* **1.** (*a*) lord; **notre s. suzerain,** our sovereign lord; *F:* **le s. et maître d'une femme,** a woman's lord and master; **à tout s. tout honneur,** (i) honour to whom honour is due; (ii) give the devil his due; *Th: A:* **s., le carrosse attend,** the carriage waits, my lord; (*b*) lord of the manor; squire; *A:* seignior; **le s. de Sercq,** the seigneur, *f.* the dame, of Sark; (*c*) nobleman, noble; *Hist:* **les seigneurs,** the nobility; **petit s.,** lordling; **des grands seigneurs et des petits seigneurs,** lords and lordlings; **mener une vie de grand s.,** to live like a lord; **faire le grand s., trancher du grand s.,** to lord it (**avec,** over); to put on airs, give oneself airs; **ne faites pas le grand s.,** don't be so high and mighty; don't try and lord it over us; **il nous a reçus en grand s.,** we were received in grand style; **les grands seigneurs de la littérature,** the great names in literature. **2.** **le S.,** God; the Lord; **Notre-S.,** our Lord; **le jour du S.,** the Lord's day; *F:* **S.! S. Dieu!** good Lord! **3.** *Ich:* lumpfish, lumpsucker. **4.** *Astrol:* lord.
seigneuriage [sɛɲœrjaːʒ], *s.m. A:* seigniorage.
seigneurial, -aux [sɛɲœrjal, -o], *a. A:* seigniorial, manorial (rights, etc.); **demeure seigneuriale,** baronial hall; **maison seigneuriale,** manor house.
seigneurie [sɛɲœri], *s.f.* (*a*) *A:* seigniory; *Fr.Hist:* lordship; seigneury; *Italian Hist:* seigniory; (*b*) domain, manor; (*c*) (*as a title*) **votre s.,** your Lordship; *Iron:* **à la porte apparaît sa s. elle-même!,** who should walk in but his lordship, *P:* his nibs!
seille [sɛːj], *s.f.* (wooden) pail; bucket; **s. à traire,** milking pail.
seillette [sɛjɛt], *s.f.* small pail.
seillon [sɛjɔ̃], *s.m. Dial:* (*a*) small wooden tub; (*b*) *Winem:* oval tub (for catching drips under the spigot).
seime [sɛm], *s.f. Vet:* sand-crack (on horse's hoof).
sein [sɛ̃], *s.m.* **1.** (*a*) breast, bosom; *Lit:* **il présenta son s. à l'épée,** he bared his breast to the sword; *B:* **le s. d'Abraham,** Abraham's bosom; **donner le s. à un enfant,** to give the breast to a child; to suckle a child; **cacher qch. dans son s.,** to hide sth. in one's brassière; **faux seins, seins postiches,** *F:* falsies; *s.a.* BOUT 2, RÉCHAUFFER 1; **au s. de la famille,** in the bosom of the family; **au s. du luxe,** in the lap of luxury; **au s. de la commission,** within the committee; **le conseil élit le président dans son s.,** the council elects the president from amongst its members; **le s. de l'Église,** the bosom of the Church; (*b*) **s. d'une voile,** belly of a sail; (*c*) *A:* land-locked bay; gulf. **2.** *Lit:*

womb; **enfant que j'ai porté dans mon s.,** child that I carried in my womb; **porter qn dans son s.,** to cherish s.o.; **le s. de la terre,** the bowels of the earth.

seine [sɛn], *s.f. Fish:* seine, drag-seine; beach seine; **pêcher des maquereaux à la s.,** to seine mackerel.

seiner [sene], *v.tr. Fish:* to seine (mackerel, etc.).

seineur [sɛnœːr], *s.m. (pers.)* seiner.

seing [sɛ̃], *s.m. A:* sign manual; *still used in Jur:* **acte sous s. privé,** simple contract; private agreement; contract in writing, signed but not sealed or witnessed.

séismal, -aux [seismal, -o], *a.* seismal.

séisme [seism], *s.m. (a)* earthquake, seism; **s. par effondrement,** earthquake due to underground subsidence; *(b) Lit:* upheaval.

séismicité [seismisite], *s.f.* seismicity.

séismique [seismik], *a.* seismic.

séismo- [seismo], *comb.fm.* seismo-; *for* **séismographe, séismologie,** *etc. see* **sismo-,** *which is the more usual spelling.*

séismonastie [seismɔnasti], *s.f. Bot:* seismonasty.

séismonastique [seismɔnastik], *a. Bot:* seismonastic.

seisonides [seizɔnid], *s.m.pl. Z:* Seisonacea, Seisonidea.

seissette [sɛsɛt], *s.f. Bot:* (type of) soft wheat.

seizain [sɛzɛ̃], *s.m. (a) Num:* quarter of a crown; *(b) Pros:* poem of sixteen lines.

seizaine [sɛzɛn], *s.f. A:* (approximate) sixteen, some sixteen; **une s. de francs,** sixteen francs or so.

seize [sɛːz], *num.a.inv. & s.m.inv.* sixteen; **Louis S.,** Louis the Sixteenth; **le s. mai,** (on) the sixteenth of May; **demeurer au numéro s.,** to live at number sixteen; **au chapitre s. de . . .,** in the sixteenth chapter of. . . .

seizième [sɛzjɛm]. 1. *num.a. & s.* sixteenth. 2. *s.m.* sixteenth (part); **trois seizièmes,** three sixteenths. 3. *s.f. Cards:* run of six cards (in piquet).

seizièmement [sɛzjɛmmɑ̃], *adv.* sixteenthly, in the sixteenth place.

Séjan [seʒɑ̃], *Pr.n.m. Rom.Hist:* Sejanus.

séjour [seʒuːr], *s.m.* 1. *(a)* stay, sojourn; *Lit:* delay; **s. de quinze jours,** fortnight's stay; **bête de s.,** sick horse (kept in the stable); *Mil:* **camp de s.,** camp for one day or night only; *s.a.* PERMIS 2, INTERDICTION 1; *(b) F:* living room. 2. (place of) abode; residence, resort; **le s. des bienheureux,** the home, abode, of the blessed; *Poet:* **l'infernal s.,** the infernal regions; **le noir, sombre, ténébreux, s.,** Hades, the inferno.

séjournement [seʒurnəmɑ̃], *s.m.* 1. sojourning. 2. lying (of water, etc.).

séjourner [seʒurne], *v.i.* 1. to stay, stop, sojourn, reside (in a place). 2. to remain, stop; **les eaux séjournent dans les fossés,** the water lies stagnant in the ditches.

sel [sɛl], *s.m.* 1. salt; *(a)* **s. blanc,** table salt; **s. gris, s. marin, s. de cuisine,** kitchen salt; **s. fin,** fine salt; **gros s.,** coarse salt; **s. gemme,** rock-salt; *(of meat, etc.)* **prendre le s., son s.,** to take the salt; **jambon d'un bon s.,** well-cured ham; **régime sans s.,** salt-free diet; **mettre un grain de s. sur la queue d'un oiseau,** to put a pinch of salt on a bird's tail; **manger du pain et du s. avec qn,** to eat salt with s.o.; *s.a.* MINOT[1]; *B:* **vous êtes le s. de la terre,** ye are the salt of the earth; *A:* **faux s.,** contraband salt; *F:* **il met son grain de s. dans tout,** he's a meddler; **mettre son grain de s.,** to pass uncalled-for remarks, to chip in; *(b) Pharm:* **s. anglais, d'Angleterre, d'Epsom,** Epsom salts; *Toil:* **s. pour bains,** bath salts; *Alch:* **s. des philosophes,** mercury; *(c) pl.* **sels (volatils) anglais,** smelling-salts; **flacon de sels,** (bottle of) smelling-salts; *(d) Ch:* salt; **s. double,** double salt; **s. de Mohr,** Mohr's salt; **s. de potasse,** potassium salt; **s. ammoniac,** salammoniac; **s. de Seignette,** Rochelle salt; *s.a.* ESPRIT 2. 2. piquancy, wit; **conversation pleine de s.,** witty conversation; **plaisanteries sans s.,** pointless jokes; **satire, plaisanterie, au gros s.,** coarse satire, joke; *F: Iron:* **c'est fin comme du gros s.,** very clever! **s. attique,** Attic salt, Attic wit.

sélacien, -ienne [selasjɛ̃, -jɛn], *Ich:* 1. *a.* selachian. 2. *s.m.pl.* **sélaciens,** selachians, Selachii.

sélaginelle [selaʒinɛl], *s.f. Bot:* selaginella.

Seldjoukides [sɛldʒukid], **Seldjoucides** [sɛldʒusid], *Pr.n.m.pl. Turk.Hist:* the Seljuks, the Seljukians.

select, sélect [selɛkt], *a. (f.* **sélect** *or* **sélecte)** *F:* choice, select (gathering); **le monde s.,** high society.

sélecter [selɛkte], *v.tr. Com: F:* to choose.

sélecteur, -trice [selɛktœːr, -tris]. 1. *a.* selecting; *attrib:* selector; *Phot:* **écran s.,** selective filter, separation filter; *El:* **commutateur s.,** selector switch; *(computers)* **impulsion sélectrice,** gating pulse; *Mec.E:* **robinet s.,** selector valve. 2. *s.m.* selector; *(a) Elcs:* **s. stroboscopique périodique,** chopper; **s. d'amplitude (des impulsions),** pulse-amplitude, pulse-height, selector; **s. de mode,** mode selector; *(computers)* **s. de perforation,** digit selector, digit filter; *(b) Tp:* **s. à relais,** relay group; **s. de commutation,** selector switch; **s. à panneau,** panel switch; **s. d'écoute,** audio switch; **s. de fiche,** plug selector; **s. répéteur,** selector repeater; **bloc de sélecteurs,** selector unit; **monture de s.,** selector shelf; *(c) Atom.Ph:* **s. à coïncidences,** coincidence selector; **s. à anticoïncidences,** anticoincidence selector; **s. de neutrons,** neutron chopper; *(d) Av:* **commande à s.,** selective control; *(e) Aut: etc:* selector, automatic gear-shift lever.

sélectif, -ive [selɛktif, -iːv], *a. (a)* selective; **classement s.,** selective classification; *(b) W.Tel: etc:* selective; *(computers)* **accès s.,** random access; **vidage dynamique s.,** snapshot dump.

sélection [selɛksjɔ̃], *s.f.* 1. selection, choice; *F:* weeding out; **s. professionnelle,** professional aptitude test; *Sp:* **match de s.,** trial game, selection match; *Phot:* **écran de s.,** selective filter; *Biol:* **s. naturelle,** natural selection; **opérer une s.,** to exercise selection; *Tp:* **s. pas à pas,** step by step selection; *(computers)* **s. au cadran,** dialling, dial, operation; **s. d'une fréquence,** frequency discrimination; **code de s.,** dialling code; **numéro de s.,** dialling number; **signal de s.,** dialling signal; **dispositif automatique de s.,** automatic dialling unit. 2. *Mus:* selection (sur, from).

sélectionné [selɛksjɔne], *a. & s.* selected (player, etc.); *(computers)* **élément s.,** selected cell; *Sp:* **voici les noms des sélectionnés pour le match de dimanche,** these are the players chosen for Sunday's match.

sélectionner [selɛksjɔne], *v.tr.* to choose, select; *(computers)* (i) to dial; (ii) to pick, to select.

sélectionneur, -euse [selɛksjɔnœːr, -øːz], *s. (a)* selector; *(b) Agr:* seed selector.

sélectivement [selɛktivmɑ̃], *adv.* selectively.

sélectivité [selɛktivite], *s.f.* selectivity.

selen(o)- [selen(ɔ)], *pref.* selen(o)-.

Séléné, Selênê [selene], *Pr.n.f. Gr.Myth:* Selene.

séléniate [selenjat], *s.m. Ch:* selen(i)ate.

selenicereus [seleniseréys], *s.m. Bot:* selenicereus.

sélénié [selenje], *a. Ch:* selenious, selenous.

sélénien, -ienne [selenjɛ̃, -jɛn]. 1. *a.* selenian, pertaining to the moon. 2. *s.m.* selenite, inhabitant of the moon.

sélénieux [selenjø], *a.m. Ch:* selenious (acid).

sélénifère [seleniféːr], *a. Miner:* seleniferous.

selenipedium [selenipedjɔm], *s.m. Bot:* selenipedium.

sélénique[1] [selenik], *a. Ch:* selenic (acid).

sélénique[2], *a. Astr:* selenic, selenian; relating to the moon.

sélénite[1] [selenit], *s.m. Ch:* selenite.

sélénite[2], *s.m.* selenite, inhabitant of the moon.

sélénite[3], *s.f. Miner:* selenite; crystalline or foliated gypsum; **s. fibreuse,** satin spar, satin stone.

séléniteux, -euse [selenitø, -øːz], *a. Ch:* selenitic.

sélénium [selenjɔm], *s.m. Ch:* selenium.

sélén(o)- [selen(ɔ)], *pref.* selen(o)-.

sélénocentrique [selenɔsɑ̃trik], *a. Astr:* selenocentric.

sélénocyanique [selenɔsjanik], *a. Ch:* **acide s.,** selenocyanic acid.

sélénodonte [selenɔdɔ̃ːt], *a. Z:* selenodont.

sélénodésie [selenɔdezi], *s.f. Astr:* selenodesy.

sélénographe [selenɔgraf], *s.m.* selenographer.

sélénographie [selenɔgrafi], *s.f.* selenography.

sélénographique [selenɔgrafik], *a.* selenographic(al) (map, etc.).

sélénolite [selenɔlit], *s.f. Miner:* selenolite.

sélénologie [selenɔlɔʒi], *s.f. Astr:* selenology.

sélénologue [selenɔlɔg], *s.m. Astr:* selenologist.

sélestadien, -ienne [selɛstadjɛ̃, -jɛn], *a. & s. Geog:* (native, inhabitant) of Sélestat.

séleucide[1] [seløsid], *s.m. Orn:* **s. multifil,** twelve-wired bird of Paradise.

Séleucide[2], *A.Hist:* *(a)* Seleucid; *(b)* **les Séleucides,** Seleucidae.

Séleucie [seløsi], *Pr.n.f. A.Geog:* Seleucia.

self [sɛlf]. 1. *s.f. El:* **(bobine de) self(-induction),** inductance coil; **s. de filtrage,** smoothing coil, choke; **s. protectrice,** air choke; **s. d'antenne,** aerial inductance; **s. d'accord,** variable inductance, tuning coil. 2. *s.m. P:* self-service restaurant.

self-acting [sɛlfaktiŋ], *s.m. Tex:* self-acting mule.

self-inductance [sɛlfɛ̃dyktɑ̃ːs], *s.f. El:* self inductance.

self-induction [sɛlfɛ̃dyksjɔ̃], *s.f. El:* self induction; inductance; **s.-i. de fermeture, d'ouverture,** self induction on closure, on opening; **circuit à s.-i.,** self-induction circuit; **coefficient de s.-i.,** inductance.

selfique [sɛlfik], *a. El:* (self-)inductive.

self-service [sɛlfsɛrvis], *s.m. F:* self-service store; **manger au s.-s.,** to eat in the cafeteria; *pl. self-services.*

seligmannite [sɛligmanit], *s.f. Miner:* seligmannite.

Sélinonte [selinɔ̃ːt], *Pr.n.f. A.Geog:* 1. Selinus (in Sicily); Selinunte. 2. Selinus (in Asia Minor); Selinti; Trajanopolis.

sellaïte [sɛlait], *s.f. Miner:* sellaite.

sellage [sɛlaːʒ], *s.m.* saddling.

selle [sɛl], *s.f.* 1. *(a) A:* seat, stool; *F:* **demeurer entre deux selles (le cul à terre),** to fall between two stools; *(b) Med:* motion of the bowels; stool; **aller à la s.,** to go to stool; **pousser une s.,** to have a motion; **deux selles par jour,** two (easy) motions daily; **selles abondantes,** copious stools; **examen des selles,** examination of fæces; *(c) Tchn:* (caulker's) seat, cradle. 2. *(a)* saddle; **s. de dame,** lady's saddle, side saddle; **s. anglaise,** hunting saddle; *Mil:* **s. d'armes,** service saddle; **bois de s.,** saddle tree; **cheval de s.,** saddle horse; **mulet de s.,** riding mule; **cheval qui va mal à la s.,** horse not good under the saddle; **se mettre, sauter, en s.,** to mount, to vault into the saddle; **se remettre en s.,** (i) to remount; (ii) to get into the saddle again (after a failure); **être bien en s.,** (i) to have a good seat; (ii) to be firmly established; **aider qn à monter en s.,** (i) to help s.o. into the saddle; (ii) *F:* to give s.o. a leg up, a helping hand; **monter sans s.,** to ride bareback; *(b)* (bicycle) saddle; **s. de passager, s. tandem,** pillion seat (of motor cycle). 3. *Cu:* **s. de mouton,** saddle of mutton; **s. de bœuf,** baron of beef. 4. (cooper's) bench; (modeller's) turntable; (wheelwright's) nave-block. 5. *Mch: I.C.E:* saddle, seat (of cylinder); *Rail:* **s. d'appui, d'arrêt,** tie plate, packing plate. 6. *Geol:* anticline. 7. *Anat:* **s. turcique,** sella turcica.

sellée [sɛle], *s.f.* row of ceramic tiles ready for baking.

seller[1] [sele], *v.tr.* to saddle (horse).

seller[2] **(se),** *v.pr. Agr: (of land)* to harden at the surface.

sellerie [sɛlri], *s.f.* 1. saddlery; saddler's (i) trade, (ii) shop. 2. harness room, saddle room. 3. *coll. (= saddles and harnesses)* saddlery.

sellerie-bourrellerie [sɛlriburɛlri], *s.f. (= manufacture and repair of saddles and harness)* saddlery and harness making.

sellerie-garniture [sɛlrigarnityːr], *s.f.* car upholstery and fittings (industry).

sellerie-maroquinerie [sɛlrimarɔkinri], *s.f.* fancy leather-goods, travel-goods, (i) manufacture, (ii) shop.

sellette [sɛlɛt], *s.f.* 1. *(a) A:* stool of repentance; *F:* **tenir, mettre, qn sur la s.,** to cross-examine s.o.; to call s.o. to account; *F:* to have s.o. on the mat, on the carpet; **être sur la s.,** to be under cross-examination, to be on the carpet; *(b)* (small) seat, stool; *esp.* caulker's or painter's slung cradle; bosun's chair; **s. à traire,** milking stool; *(c)* (modeller's) turntable; (bootblack's) foot rest; *(d) Rail:* bed-plate, bolster; *(e) Veh:* lower bolster, axle tree bolster (of wag(g)on); *Artil:* limber bolster. 2. saddle (of draught horse).

sellier [selje], *s.m.* saddler, harness maker (and repairer).

sellier-bourrelier [seljeburəlje], *s.m.* saddler and harness maker; *pl. selliers-bourreliers.*

sellier-garnisseur [seljegarnisœːr], *s.m.* maker of car upholstery and fittings; *pl. selliers-garnisseurs.*

sellier-maroquinier [seljemarɔkinje], *s.m.* maker of fancy leather goods and travel goods; *pl. selliers-maroquiniers.*

selon [s(ə)lɔ̃], *prep. (a)* according to; **contribuer s. ses moyens,** to contribute according to one's means; **s. toute apparence,** to all appearance(s); **l'Évangile s. Saint Luc,** the Gospel according to Saint Luke; **s. moi,** in my opinion, as I see it; **s. lui,** according to him; **s. les termes de cet article . . .,** by the terms of this article . . .; **c'est s.,** that's as may be, that depends (on circumstances); it all depends; *(b) conj.phr.* **s. que** + *ind.,* according as to whether; depending on whether; **on voit les choses différemment, s. qu'on est riche ou pauvre,** we see things differently according to whether we are rich or poor.

seltz [sɛls], *s.m.* **eau de s.,** soda water.

seltzogène [sɛlsɔʒɛn], *s.m.* seltzogene.

selva [sɛlva], **selve** [sɛlv], *s.f. Geog:* selva; **s. obscure,** dark (virgin) forest.

Sem [sɛm], *Pr.n.m. B.Hist:* Shem.

semailler [səmɑje], *v.tr.* to sow.

semailles [səmɑːj], *s.f.pl.* **1.** sowing; **le temps des s.,** sowing time, seedtime. **2.** *coll.* seeds.

semaine [səmɛn], *s.f.* (*a*) week; **deux fois par s.,** twice a week, twice weekly; **une s. de vacances,** a week's holiday; **fin de s.,** weekend; **jour de s.,** weekday; *O:* **vêtements de s.,** everyday, weekday, clothes; **la s. seulement,** weekdays only; **il est toujours à Paris en s.,** he is always in Paris during the week; **la s. sainte,** Holy Week; *Sch:* **pensionnaire à la s.,** weekly boarder; *F:* **politique à la petite s.,** shortsighted policy; **gouverner à la petite s.,** to govern by means of expedients; *F:* **escroc à la petite s.,** petty crook; *A:* **prêter à la petite s.,** to make a short-term loan at a high rate of interest; *F:* **la s. des quatre jeudis,** never; when pigs fly; **il vous remboursera la s. des quatre jeudis,** you'll never see your money back; (*b*) working week; week's work; **s. anglaise,** five-day week; **faire la s. anglaise,** to work a five-day week; to have Saturday off; (*c*) *Mil: etc:* week's duty; **officier de s.,** duty officer for the week; **prendre la s., être de s.,** to go, be, on duty, for the week; (*d*) week's pay, wages; **toucher sa s.,** to get one's week's wages; (*e*) set of seven (objects); **une s. de pipes,** a set of seven pipes.

semainier, -ière [səmɛnje, -jɛːr]. **1.** *s.* person on duty for a week; duty officer for the week; (*in convent*) hebdomadary. **2.** *s.m.* (*a*) *O:* case of seven razors; seven-day case of razors; (*b*) (workmen's) time sheet; (*c*) *Furn:* semainier; (*d*) desk diary (with sections for each day of the week). **3.** *a.* weekly, week's (output, issue, etc.); hebdomadal (council).

semaison [səmɛzɔ̃], *s.f.* **1.** sowing time, seedtime. **2.** self-seeding (of plants).

sémantème [semɑ̃tɛm], *s.m. Ling:* semanteme.

sémanticien, -ienne [semɑ̃tisjɛ̃, -jɛn], *s.*, **sémantiste** [semɑ̃tist], *s.m. & f.* semantician, semanticist.

sémantique [semɑ̃tik], *Ling:* **1.** *a.* semantic; **champ s.,** area of meaning. **2.** *s.f.* semantics.

sémaphore [semafɔːr], *s.m.* semaphore; *Rail:* semaphore signal; *Nau:* signal station (on land).

sémaphorique [semafɔrik], *a.* semaphoric.

sémaphoriste [semafɔrist], *s.m.* semaphorist.

sémasiologie [semazjɔlɔʒi], *s.f.* semasiology, semantics.

semblable [sɑ̃blabl̥]. **1.** *a.* (*a*) alike; similar (**à,** to); like; **deux cas tout à fait semblables,** two cases absolutely alike; **votre cas est s. au mien,** your case is similar to mine; **s. à son père,** like his father; **les universités sont restées semblables à elles-mêmes au cours des siècles,** the universities have remained unchanged throughout the centuries; *Geom:* **triangles semblables,** similar triangles; *Alg:* **termes semblables,** like terms; (*b*) such; **de semblables projets demandent du temps,** such plans require time; **quand j'entends des choses semblables . . .,** when I hear things like that . . .; **en s. occasion,** on such an occasion; **je n'ai rien dit de s.,** I said nothing of the sort, no such thing; **boutiquiers et petits fermiers, et autres gens semblables,** shopkeepers and small farmers, and people like that, of that sort. **2.** *s.* fellow; (*a*) like, equal, counterpart; **vous ne trouverez pas son s.,** you will not find his like, his equal; (*b*) **nos semblables,** our fellowmen, fellow-creatures.

semblablement [sɑ̃blabləmɑ̃], *adv.* similarly, likewise; in a similar, the same, way; **j'aurais agi s.,** I should have done the same.

semblance [sɑ̃blɑ̃ːs], *s.f. Poet:* resemblance.

semblant [sɑ̃blɑ̃], *s.m.* semblance, appearance; (outward) show; **faux s.,** pretence, sham; **sous un s. d'amitié, sous de faux semblants d'amitié,** under the mask, the cover, of friendship; **elle portait un s. de jupe,** she was wearing an apology for a skirt; **faire un s. de résistance,** to make a show of resistance; **semblants de repentir,** show, pretence, of repentance; **faire s. de faire qch.,** to pretend to be doing sth.; to make a pretence of doing sth.; **il fit s. de monter se coucher,** he pretended to go up to bed; **il fit s. de vouloir me frapper,** he made as if to strike me; he looked as if he were going to hit me; **faire s. d'être malade,** to sham illness; to pretend to be ill; **sans faire s. de rien,** (i) surreptitiously; (ii) without seeming to take any notice, as if nothing had happened; **sans faire s. de rien il glissa la lettre sous le livre,** he slipped the letter surreptitiously under the book.

sembler [sɑ̃ble], *v.i.* (*the aux. is* **avoir**) (*a*) to seem, to appear; **elle semblait malade,** she seemed (to be) ill; **le soldat semblait les prendre en pitié,** the soldier seemed to take pity on them; **ma pitié semblerait un effet de ma peur,** pity on my part would look as if it were dictated by fear; **voilà, ce me semble, un avis excellent,** that, to my mind, is excellent advice; (*b*) *impers.* **il me semblait rêver,** it seemed to me, I thought, that I was dreaming; **il me semble entendre un cri,** I think I (can) hear a cry, a shout; **il me semble l'entendre encore,** I can hear him still; **il me semble avoir entendu son nom,** I seem to have heard his name; **à ce qu'il me semble,** it strikes me that; I think; **ils pourront, quand bon leur semblera . . .,** they may, at any time . . .; **faites comme bon vous semble(ra), ce que bon vous semble(ra), ce qu'il vous semble bon,** do as you think best, as you think fit, as you please; **que vous semble(-t-il) de ce vin?** how do you like this wine? **que vous en semble?** what do you think of it? **il semble qu'il ne veut, ne veuille, pas y aller,** it looks as if he wouldn't go; **il me semble que** + *ind.*, it seems to me that . . .; **ne vous semble-t-il pas que** + *ind.*, does it not strike you that . . .? **il ne me semble pas que** + *sub.*, it does not look to me as if . . .; **il me semble que c'est un songe,** it seems to me like a dream; **il me semble que c'est hier,** it seems to me like yesterday.

sème [sɛm], *s.m. Ling:* sememe.

semé [səme]. **1.** *a.* (*a*) strewn, sprinkled; **ciel s. d'étoiles,** star-spangled, starry, sky; **s. de citations,** with quotations scattered throughout; **pelouse semée de pâquerettes,** lawn sprinkled, dotted, with daisies; (*b*) *Ven:* **tête mal semée,** stag with uneven antlers. **2.** (*a*) *a. & s.m. Her:* **(écu) s. de fleurs de lis,** (shield) semé of fleurs-de-lis; (*b*) *s.m. Bookb:* semé.

séméiologie [semejɔlɔʒi], *s.f. Med:* sem(e)iology, symptomatology.

séméiologique [semejɔlɔʒik], *a. Med:* sem(e)iological.

séméiologue [semejɔlɔg], *s.m. & f. Med:* sem(e)iologist.

séméiotique [semejɔtik]. **1.** *a. Mth: Log:* semiotic. **2.** *s.f.* (*a*) *Mth: Log:* semiotics; (*b*) *Med:* sem(e)iology.

Sémélé [semele], *Pr.n.f. Gr.Myth:* Semele.

semelle [səmɛl], *s.f.* **1.** (*a*) sole (of shoe); foot (of stocking); **chaussures à s. simple, double,** shoes with a single, double, sole; **s. intérieure (de liège, de feutre),** (cork)sole, (felt) sock (inserted in the shoe); (cork, felt) insole; **chaussures à semelles épaisses, à semelles de caoutchouc,** thick-soled, rubber-soled, shoes; **s. compensée,** wedge heel; **remettre une s. à une chaussure,** to re-sole a shoe; **battre la s.,** (i) to be on the tramp; (ii) to stamp one's feet (to warm them); (iii) to kick one's heels; (*b*) foot's length; **ne pas avancer d'une s.,** to make no progress; not to move a step forward; **il ne reculera pas d'une s.,** he won't give (way) an inch; **il ne me quitte pas d'une s.,** he's always at my heels; (*c*) **s. de frein,** brake shoe; (*d*) *Bot:* **s. du pape,** nopal. **2.** (*a*) *Const: Min: etc:* ground sill, sole piece; sleeper; sill (of a stay); footing (of an upright); **s. de comble,** pole plate; **s. d'ancrage,** stay block (for rigging); (*b*) **s. de poutre,** girder flange; boom (of built-up girder); **s. (d'encastrement de porte),** corbel (block); **s. de coussinet de rail,** chair foot; (*c*) bed plate (of machine, lathe); (*d*) shoe (of anchor, sledge); (*e*) *Tls:* face (of plane); (*f*) tread (of tyre, stirrup). **3.** *Nau:* **s. de dérive,** leeboard; **s. de lancement,** skid. **4.** *Metalw:* file blank. **5. s. à fruits,** punnet.

semence [səmɑ̃ːs], *s.f.* **1.** (*a*) seed; **blé de s.,** seed corn; **semences de discorde,** seeds of discord; **malentendus, s. de guerre,** misunderstandings that breed war; *B:* **la s. d'Abraham,** the seed of Abraham; (*b*) *Physiol:* semen. **2.** (*a*) **s. de perles,** seed pearls; **s. de diamants,** diamond sparks; seed diamonds; (*b*) **semence(s) (de tapissier),** (tin)tacks, sprig nails; **clouer qch. avec de la s., avec des semences,** to tack sth. (down).

semenceau [səmɑ̃so], *s.m. Agr:* seed beet, beet grown for seed.

semencier [səmɑ̃sje], *a. For:* (*tree*) seed-bearer.

semen-contra [semɛnkɔ̃tra], *s.m. Pharm:* santonica.

semer [səme], *v.tr.* (**je sème, n. semons; je sèmerai**) **1.** to sow (seeds); **s. un champ,** to sow a field; *abs.* **s. à tout vent, à la volée,** to sow broadcast; **s. en terre ingrate,** to sow on stony ground; *Prov:* **on recueille ce qu'on a semé; on ne récolte que ce qu'on sème,** we reap as we sow. **2.** to spread, strew, scatter (flowers, etc.); to disseminate, spread abroad (doctrines, news, etc.); to set (rumour) afloat; **s. la terreur, la discorde,** to spread, sow, terror, discord; **s. le mécontentement,** to sow the seeds of discontentment; **s. de l'argent,** to spend money recklessly, to throw money about. **3.** *F:* (*a*) to shake off, get rid of, shed (uncongenial member of the party, etc.); **s. une connaissance,** to drop an acquaintance; **s. un concurrent,** to leave a rival behind; (*b*) **s. une valise,** to lose, *F:* shed, a suitcase.

semestre [səmɛstr̥], *s.m.* **1.** half-year; **s. de janvier, d'hiver,** first half of the year; first half-year; **s. de juillet, d'été,** second half-year. **2.** six months' pay, income. **3.** six months' duty; **être de s.,** to be on duty (for six months). **4.** *A: Mil:* six months' leave of absence; **être en s.,** to be on six months' leave or furlough. **5.** *Sch:* semester; term (of six months). **6.** *a.* (*a*) *A:* of six months' duration; (*b*) *A:* **accouchement s.,** premature delivery at the sixth month.

semestriel, -elle [səmɛstrijɛl], *a.* **1.** half-yearly, semi-annual, six-monthly. **2.** of six months' duration.

semestriellement [səmɛstrijɛlmɑ̃], *adv.* semi-annually, half-yearly, every six months.

semeur, -euse [səmœːr, -øːz], *s.* **1.** (*a*) sower (of wheat, etc.); (*b*) disseminator, spreader (of doctrines, false news, disease). **2.** *s.f.* **semeuse,** (*a*) *Agr:* drill (for sowing seed); (*b*) *Orn:* wagtail.

semi- [səmi], *pref.* semi-; Note: *For the plural of compound words prefixed by* **semi-**, **semi-** *remains invariable and the following noun or adj. takes the sign of the plural.*

semi-adhérent [səmiaderɑ̃], *a.* semi-adherent, semi-attached.

semi-amplexicaul [səmiɑ̃plɛksikol], *a. Bot:* semi-amplexicaul.

semi-annuel, -elle [səmianɥɛl], *a.* semi-annual.

semi-argenté [səmiarʒɑ̃te], *a.* semi-silvered (mirror, etc.).

semi-aride [səmiarid], *a. Geog:* semi-arid; semi-desertic.

semi-arien, -ienne [səmiarjɛ̃, -jɛn], *a. & s. Rel.H:* semi-Arian.

semi-automatique [səmiɔtɔmatik], *a.* semi(-)automatic.

semi-autopropulsé [səmiɔtɔprɔpylse], *a.* semi-self-propelled.

semi-autopropulsion [səmiɔtɔprɔpylsjɔ̃], *s.f.* semi-self-propulsion.

semi-balistique [səmibalistik], *a.* semi-ballistic (missile, etc.).

semi-brève [səmibrɛːv], *s.f. Mus: A:* semibreve.

semicarbazone [səmikarbazɔn], *s.f. Ch:* semicarbazone.

semi-centrifuge [səmisɑ̃trifyːʒ], *a.* semi-centrifugal.

semi-chenillé [səmiʃ(ə)nije], *a. & s.m.* half-track (vehicle).

semi-circulaire [səmisirkylɛːr], *a.* semicircular.

semi-coke [səmikɔk], *s.m.* semi-coke; *R.t.m.:* Coalite.

semi-conducteur [səmikɔ̃dyktœːr], *s.m. El:* semi(-)conductor; **s.-c. extrinsèque, intrinsèque,** extrinsic, intrinsic semiconductor; **s.-c. intermétallique,** intermetallic semiconductor.

semi-conductivité [səmikɔ̃dyktivite], *s.f. El:* semi(-)conductivity.

semi-conserve [səmikɔ̃sɛrv], *s.f.* semi-preserved food; **semi-conserves,** semi-preserved goods.

semi-consonantique [səmikɔ̃sɔnɑ̃tik], *a.* semi-consonantal.

semi-consonne [səmikɔ̃sɔn], *s.f.* semi-vowel, semi-consonant.

semi-continu [səmikɔ̃tiny], *a. Mth:* semi-continuous.

semi-cristal [səmikristal], *s.m.* crown glass, soda-lime glass.

semi-cristallin [səmikristalɛ̃], *a. Geol:* semicrystalline, hemicrystalline.

semi-cubique [səmikybik], *a. Mth:* semicubical.

semi-déployé [səmideplwaje], *a. Mil: etc:* semi-deployed.

semi-déponent [səmidepɔnɑ̃], *a. Lt.Gram:* semi-deponent.

semi-diesel [səmidjezɛl], *s.m. I.C.E:* semi-diesel engine, hot-bulb engine.

semidine [səmidin], *s.f. Ch:* semidin(e).

semi-distillation [səmidistilasjɔ̃], *s.f.* semi-coking (to produce smokeless fuel).

semi-double [səmidubl̥], *a. Bot: etc:* semi-double.

semi-duplex [səmidyplɛks], *a. & s.m.* semi-duplex, half-duplex; **exploitation, fonctionnement, en s.-d.,** semi-duplex operation.

semi-elliptique [səmieliptik], *a.* semielliptic, half-elliptic.

semi-fini [səmifini], *a. Ind: etc:* semi-finished (product).

semi-fixe [səmifiks], *a.* semi-fixed; semi-portable (apparatus).
semi-flosculeux, -euse [səmifləskylø, -øːz], *a. Bot:* semiflosculous, semiflosculose, semi-floscular, ligulate.
semi-fluide [səmiflɥid], *a. & s.m.* semi-fluid.
semi-hebdomadaire [səmiɛbdəmadɛːr], *a.* half-weekly, semi-weekly, bi-weekly (periodical, etc.).
semi-historique [səmiistərik], *a.* semi-historical.
semi-illettré [səmiil(l)ɛtre], *a.* semi-literate, half-literate.
semi-intégré [səmiɛ̃tegre], *a.* half-integrated; *Elcs:* (*computers*) **circuit s.-i.,** hybrid integrated circuit.
semi-liquide [səmilikid], *a.* semi-fluid.
sémillance [semijɑ̃ːs], *s.f.* sprightliness (of the mind); brightness (of a glance).
sémillant [semijɑ̃], *a.* sprightly, bright (child, wit); bright, engaging (glance).
sémiller [semije], *v.i. A:* to show sprightliness.
semi-logarithmique [səmilɔgaritmik], *a.* semi-logarithmic.
semi-lunaire [səmilynɛːr], *a.* semilunar, semi-lunate; half-moon shaped.
semi-mensuel, -elle [səmimɑ̃sɥɛl], *a.* half-monthly, semi-monthly, fortnightly, bi-monthly (periodical, etc.).
séminaire [seminɛːr], *s.m.* seminary. **1.** (*a*) **grand s.,** (Roman Catholic) seminary; training college (for the priesthood); **s. de missionnaires,** missionary college; **petit s.,** secondary school (staffed by priests); (*b*) *Sch:* seminar; (*c*) seminary, training centre; **cette école fut un s. de bons officiers,** this school trained many good officers; (*d*) conference. **2.** *Husb:* fattening coop.
séminal, -aux [seminal, -o], *a.* seminal.
séminariste [seminarist], *s.m.* seminarist.
séminase [seminaːz], *s.f. Bio-Ch:* seminase.
sémination [seminasjɔ̃], *s.f. Bot:* semination.
séminifère [seminifɛːr], *a. Bot:* seminiferous; *Anat:* **conduits séminifères,** seminiferous tubules.
Séminoles [seminɔl], *s.m.pl. Ethn:* Seminoles.
semi-nomade [səminəmad], **1.** *a.* seminomadic. **2.** *s.m. & f.* seminomad.
semi-nomadisme [səminəmadism], *s.m.* semino-madism.
séminome [seminəm], *s.m. Med:* seminoma.
semi-nymphe [səminɛ̃ːf], *s.f. Ent:* semi-nymph.
semi-officiel, -ielle [səmiəfisjɛl], *a.* semi(-)official.
sémiologie [semjɔlɔʒi], *s.f. Med:* sem(e)iology.
sémiologique [semjɔlɔʒik], *a. Med:* sem(e)iological.
sémiologue [semjɔlɔg], *s.m. & f. Med:* sem(e)iologist.
semi-opale [səmiəpal], *s.f.* semi(-)opal.
sémioticien, -ienne [semjɔtisjɛ̃, -jɛn], *s.m. & f.* semiotician.
sémiotique [semjɔtik]. **1.** *a. Mth: Log:* semiotic. **2.** *s.f.* (*a*) *Mth: Log:* semiotics; (*b*) *Med:* sem(e)iology.
semi-ouvré [səmiuvre], *a. Ind: etc:* semi-finished, semi-manufactured (product).
semi-palmé [səmipalme], *a. Orn:* semipalmate(d).
semi-pélagianisme [səmipelaʒjanism], *s.m. Rel. H:* Semi-Pelagianism.
semi-perforant [səmiperfɔrɑ̃], *a.* semi-armour-piercing (shell, etc.).
semi-perméable [səmipɛrmeabl], *a.* semiper-meable, partially permeable.
semi-polaire [səmipəlɛːr], *a. Ch:* semi-polar.
semi-portique [səmipərtik], *s.m.* semi-portal bridge crane.
semi-précieux, -ieuse [səmipresjø, -jøːz], *a.* semi-precious (stone).
semi-preuve [səmiprœːv], *s.f. Jur:* half-proof.
semi-produit [səmiprədɥi], *s.m. Ind:* semi-finished product.
semi-public, -ique [səmipyblik], *a.* semi(-)public.
sémique [semik], *a.* semic.
semi-remorque [səmirəmərk], *s.f. Veh:* (*a*) trailer (of articulated vehicle); (*b*) articulated vehicle; semitrailer; **béquille à roulettes de s.-r.,** semi-trailer landing gear.
semi-rigide [səmiriʒid], *a.* semi-rigid (airship).
semi-rupture [səmiryptyːr], *s.f.* semi-armour-piercing effect; **(projectile, etc.) de s.-r.,** semi-armour-piercing (projectile, etc.).
semis [səmi], *s.m. Agr: Hort:* **1.** sowing; **s. à la volée,** broadcast sowing; **s. en lignes,** sowing in drills; **s. en terrines,** sowing in seed pans; **s. par trous,** dibbling; **terrine, boîte, à s.,** seed pan, seed tray; **fleurs qui proviennent de s.,** flowers raised from seed; **les plantes annuelles ne se multiplient guère que par s.,** it is rare for annuals to grow again without (re-)sowing. **2.** seed bed. **3.** seedlings; **fonte des s.,** damping off. **4.** *Bookb:* semis.
semi-solide [səmisəlid], *a. Ch: etc:* semi-solid.
Sémites [semit], *s.m.pl. Ethn:* Semites.
sémitique [semitik], *a.* Semitic.
sémitisant, -ante [semitizɑ̃, -ɑ̃ːt], *s.,* **sémitiste** [semitist], *s.m. & f.* Semitic scholar, Semitist.
sémitisme [semitism], *s.m.* Semitism.
semi-ton [səmitɔ̃], *s.m. Mus:* semitone.
semi-transparence [səmitrɑ̃sparɑ̃ːs], *s.f.* semi-transparency.
semi-transparent [səmitrɑ̃sparɑ̃], *a.* semi-trans-parent.
semi-tubulaire [səmitybylɛːr], *a.* semitubular.
semi-voyelle [səmivwajɛl], *s.f. Ling:* semivowel.
semnopithèque [sɛmnəpitɛk], *s.m. Z:* langur, leaf monkey.
semoir [səmwaːr], *s.m. Agr:* **1.** seed lip. **2.** sowing machine, seeder; **s. à la volée,** broadcast seeder; **s. en lignes,** drill; **s. en poquets,** drop drill.
semonce [səmɔ̃ːs], *s.f.* **1.** (*a*) summons, invitation (to meeting, wedding, etc.); (*b*) *Navy:* call (to a ship to show her flag, to heave to); **coup de s.,** warning shot. **2.** reprimand, scolding, lecture, dressing-down; **verte s.,** good talking-to, good dressing-down; **faire à qn une s. paternelle,** to give s.o. a talking-to, to talk to s.o. like a Dutch uncle; **s. conjugale,** (wifely) nagging.
semoncer [səmɔ̃se], *v.tr.* **(je semonçai(s); n. semonçons) 1.** (*a*) *A:* to summon, invite (to meeting, etc.); (*b*) *Nau:* to call upon (ship) to show her flag or to heave to. **2.** to lecture, scold, reprimand, sermonize; *F:* to blow s.o. up; **je l'ai semoncé d'importance,** *F:* I gave it him hot, I gave him a good dressing-down, a good blowing-up, a good ticking-off.
semondre [səmɔ̃ːdr], *v.tr. A:* **1.** = SEMONCER. **2. s. qn de sa parole,** to call upon s.o. to implement his promise.
semoule [səmul], *s.f.* semolina; **sucre s.,** caster sugar.
semoulerie [səmulri], *s.f.* (*a*) semolina factory; (*b*) semolina industry.
semoulier, -ière [səmulje, -jɛːr], *s.* semolina manufacturer; worker in a semolina factory.
semper virens [sɛ̃pɛrvirɛ̃ːs], *Bot:* **1.** *a.inv.* ever-green (plant). **2.** *s.m. A:* evergreen honeysuckle.
sempervivum [sɛ̃pɛrvivəm], *s.m.inv. Bot:* semper-vivum, houseleek.
sempiternel, -elle [sɛ̃pitɛrnɛl], *a.* sempiternal, never-ceasing.
sempiternellement [sɛ̃pitɛrnɛlmɑ̃], *adv.* sempiter-nally; **répéter s. les mêmes choses,** to go on repeating, never to stop repeating, the same things.
semple [sɑ̃ːpl], *s.m. Tex:* simple (of loom).
Sempronie [sɛ̃prəni], *Pr.n.f. Rom.Hist:* Sem-pronia.
semurois, -oise [səmyrwa, -waːz], *a. & s.* (native, inhabitant) of Semur.
sénaire [senɛːr], *a. Mth:* senary (scale, division).
senaïte [senait], *s.f. Miner:* senaite.
sénarmontite [senarmɔ̃tit], *s.f. Miner:* senarmon-tite.
sénat [sena], *s.m.* **1.** senate. **2.** senate house.
sénateur [senatœr], *s.m.* (*a*) senator; **s. inamovible,** life senator; *F:* **aller son train de s.,** to walk at a snail's pace, at a funereal pace, slowly and majestically; (*b*) *F:* (*pers. firmly implanted in a job, etc.*) fixture; (*c*) *Orn: F:* **(mouette) s.,** ivory gull.
sénatorial, -aux [senatərjal, -o], *a.* senatorial (dignity, etc.).
sénatorien, -ienne [senatərjɛ̃, -jɛn], *a.* senatorial, senatorian, senator's (house, family, etc.).
sénatrice [senatris], *s.f. Hist:* senator's wife (in Poland, Sweden, etc.).
sénatus-consulte [senatyskɔ̃sylt], *s.m.* senatus consult(um); *pl. sénatus-consultes.*
senau [səno], *s.m. Nau:* **1.** *A:* snow. **2.** trysail; **mât de s.,** trysail mast.
séné [sene], *s.m.* senna; **tisane, infusion, de s.,** senna tea.
senebière [sənbjɛːr], *s.f.,* **senebiérie** [sənbjeri], *s.f. Bot:* senebiera, *F:* wort-cress.
sénéchal, -aux [seneʃal, -o], *s.m. Hist:* seneschal.
sénéchale [seneʃal], *s.f. Hist:* seneschal's wife.
sénéchaussée [seneʃose], *s.f. Hist:* (*a*) seneschalsy, seneschal's jurisdiction; (*b*) seneschal's court.
seneçon [sənsɔ̃], **séneçon** [sɛnsɔ̃], *s.m. Bot:* groundsel; **s. en arbre, s. arborescent,** arbores-cent, tree, groundsel.
Sénégal [senegal], *Pr.n.m. Geog:* Senegal.
sénégalais, -aise [senegalɛ, -ɛːz], *a. & s. Geog:* Senegalese.
sénégali [senegali], *s.m. Orn:* waxbill.
sénégalien, -ienne [senegaljɛ̃, -jɛn], *a.* of, pertain-ing to, Senegal; Senegalese.
Sénégambie [senegɑ̃bi], *Pr.n.f. Geog:* Senegam-bia.
sénégambien, -ienne [senegɑ̃bjɛ̃, -jɛn], *a. & s. Geog:* Senegambian.
sénegré [sɛngre], *s.m. Bot:* fenugreek.
Sénèque [senɛk], *Pr.n.m. Lt.Lit:* Seneca.
sénescence [senɛs(s)ɑ̃ːs], *s.f. Biol:* senescence.
sénescent [senɛs(s)ɑ̃], *a. Biol:* senescent.
senestre [sənɛstr], **sénestre** [senɛstr], *a. A:* left; *Her:* sinister; *Moll:* **coquille s.,** sinistral shell.
senestré [sənɛstre], **sénestré** [senɛstre], *a. Her:* **pal s. d'une croix,** pale having on its sinister side a cross.
sénestrochère [senɛstrəkɛːr], *s.m. Her:* left arm.
sénestrogyre [senɛstrəʒiːr], *a. Ch:* laevorotatory.
senestrorsum [sənɛstrərsəm], **sénestrorsum** [senɛstrərsəm], *a.inv. & adv.* anticlockwise, counter-clockwise; sinistrorse; sinistrorsally.
sénevé [senve], *s.m.* **1.** *Bot:* mustard. **2.** mustard seed.
sénile [senil], *a.* (*a*) *Med:* senile (gangrene, etc.); **démence s.,** senile dementia; **dégénérescence s.,** senile degeneration; (*b*) senile, of an elderly person; **il parlait d'une voix s. mais encore bien accentuée,** his voice was that of an old man, but his enunciation was still clear; *F:* **il n'est pas du tout s.,** he's not at all gaga.
sénilité [senilite], *s.f.* **1.** senility; senile decay. **2.** *Geog:* (*in cycle of erosion*) old age.
senior [senjɔːr], *a. & s. Sp:* (*usu. = competitors over 20*) senior.
séniorat [senjəra], *s.m.* seniority.
senlisien, -ienne [sɑ̃lizjɛ̃, -jɛn], *a. & s. Geog:* (native, inhabitant) of Senlis.
Sennaar [sɛnnaːr], *Pr.n.m. B:* Shinar.
senne [sɛn], *s.f. Fish:* seine, draw net.
senneur [sɛnœːr], *s.m. Fish:* (*boat*) seiner.
sénonais, -aise [senənɛ, -ɛːz], *Geog:* **1.** *a. & s.* (native, inhabitant) of (i) Sens, (ii) Senones, (iii) the Sens region. **2.** *Pr.n.m.* **le Senonais,** the Sens region.
sénonien, -ienne [senənjɛ̃, -jɛn], *a. & s.m. Geol:* Senonian.
sénonois, -oise [senənwa, -waːz], *a. & s. Geog:* (native, inhabitant) of Senones.
senorita [senjərita], *s.m.* small cigar, whiff.
sens [sɑ̃ːs], *s.m.* **1.** (*a*) sense (of touch, sight, etc.); **les cinq s.,** the five senses; **le sixième s.,** the sixth sense; **perdre, reprendre, ses s.,** to lose, regain, consciousness; **s. moral,** moral sense; conscience; **avoir le s. du beau,** to have a sense of beauty; **avoir le s. de l'heure,** to have a sense of time; **avoir le s. des affaires,** to have a good business sense, head; **avoir le s. de l'air,** to be air-minded; **il n'avait nul s. du comique, de l'humour,** he had no sense of humour; he was completely unable to see a joke; **il tombe sous le s. que . . .,** it is obvious, self-evident, it stands to reason, that . . .; **cela tombe sous le s.,** it's self-evident, obvious; (*b*) **plaisir des s.,** sensual pleasures; **éveiller les s.,** to rouse the sexual instinct. **2.** sense, judgement; intelligence; understanding; **avoir le s. droit,** to have clear judgement; **s. commun, bon s.,** common sense, good sense; **un homme de bon s.,** a sensible man; **bon s. natif,** mother wit; **gros, robuste, bon s.,** elementary common sense; **cela n'a pas de s. commun, de bon s.,** there's no sense in it; **agir, faire qch. en dépit du bon s.,** to go against all the criteria of common sense; to do something stupid; to make a mess of things; **vous avez perdu le s. commun,** you've taken leave of your senses; you're not in your right mind; **tout homme jouissant de son bon s., qui est dans son bon s.,** any man in his senses; **rentrer dans son bon s.,** to come to one's senses again; **le bon s. veut que . . .,** it stands to reason that . . .; **s. rassis,** sane, well-balanced, judgement; **s. pratique,** practical (common) sense; **il n'a aucun s. pratique,** he's completely unpractical; **à mon s.,** in my opinion; **il n'y a, à mon s., rien de plus intéressant que . . .,** in my opinion, in my mind, to my way of thinking, there is nothing more interesting than . . .; **j'abonde dans votre s.,** I am entirely of your opinion, I entirely agree with you. **3.** sense, meaning (of a word, etc.); **s. propre,** literal, basic meaning; **s. figuré,** figurative meaning; **au s. ordinaire du mot,** in the ordinary meaning of the word; **mot à double s.,** word with a double meaning; **attacher un s. à un passage,** to give a certain interpretation to a passage; **faire un faux s.,** to misinterpret, to misunderstand (a passage, a word); **ces paroles n'ont pas de s. pour moi,** these words mean, convey, nothing to me; **s'exprimer, parler, dans le même s.,** to express the same views; **en ce s. que . . .,** in that . . .. **4.** direction, way; **dans le bon s.,** in the right

direction; the right way (round, up); **dans le mauvais s.**, in the wrong direction; the wrong way (round, up); **vous tournez le bouton dans le mauvais s.**, you're turning the knob the wrong way; **prendre une rue dans le mauvais s.**, to go up a (one-way) street the wrong way; **en s. inverse**, in the opposite direction; **dans le s. du courant**, with the current, with the stream; **dans le s. de la longueur**, lengthwise; **dans le s. de la largeur**, breadthwise; across; **dans les deux s.**, both ways; **tailler dans le s. du bois**, to cut wood with the grain; **dans le s. inverse du grain**, against, across, the grain; **tissu qui n'est pas coupé dans le bon s.**, cloth cut the wrong way; **dans le s. des aiguilles d'une montre**, clockwise; **dans le, en, s. inverse des, contre le s. des, dans le s. opposé aux, aiguilles d'une montre**, anti-clockwise; **courir dans tous les s.**, to run in all directions; to run here, there and everywhere; **s. de la circulation**, direction of the traffic; **rue à double s.**, street with two-way traffic; *P.N:* **s. unique**, one-way street; *P.N:* **s. interdit**, no entry; **route divisée en six pistes, trois dans chaque s.**, road with three lanes in each direction; *Rail:* **voyager dans le s. de la marche**, to travel with one's face to, facing, the engine; *Mth:* **s. direct**, positive direction; **s. rétrograde**, negative direction; *Elcs:* (*computers*) **s. de déroulement**, flow direction; **s. de déroulement bidirectionnel**, bidirectional flow; **nous avons pris des dispositions dans ce s.**, we have made our plans with this end in view; *adv.phr.* **s. dessus dessous** [sɑ̃tsytsu], (i) upside down, the wrong way up; (ii) in a mess, in a muddle, topsy-turvy; **le salon était s. dessus dessous**, the drawing room was in confusion, all upside down; **cet accident m'a mis s. dessus dessous**, the accident left me in a state of confusion; *F:* all turned up; **s. devant derrière**, back to front; **mettre son pull-over s. devant derrière**, to put one's pullover on back to front.

sensas(s) [sɑ̃sas], *a. F:* stupendous, smashing, superb.

sensation [sɑ̃sasjɔ̃], *s.f.* sensation. **1.** feeling; **s. de chaleur, de froid**, feeling of warmth, of cold; **s. agréable de chaleur**, pleasant sense of warmth; **cela donne la s. de . . .**, it feels like . . .; **je n'aimais pas la s. de sa main froide et moite**, I didn't like the feel of his clammy hand; *Psy:* **s. de l'odeur**, olfaction. **2.** excitement; **roman à s.**, sensational novel; **nouvelles à s.**, sensational news; **faire s.**, to create, make, a sensation; *F:* to make news; **la pièce a fait s.**, the play was a hit.

sensationnel, -elle [sɑ̃sasjɔnɛl], *a.* (*a*) sensational (news, novel, etc.); *s.m.* **à l'affût du s.**, (i) all out to cause a sensation; (ii) on the lookout for something sensational; (*b*) *F:* superb (of its kind); stupendous; **avec une mauvaise foi sensationnelle**, with remarkable dishonesty.

sensationnisme [sɑ̃sasjɔnism], *s.m. Phil:* sensationalism.

sensationniste [sɑ̃sasjɔnist], *s.m. & f. Phil:* sensationalist.

sensé [sɑ̃se], *a.* sensible, judicious (person, action, answer).

sensément [sɑ̃semɑ̃], *adv.* sensibly.

senseur [sɑ̃sœːr], *s.m. Elcs:* sensor, sensing device, sensing unit; **s. solaire**, sun sensor; **s. d'étoiles, s. stellaire**, star sensor; **s. de Canope**, star-Canopus sensor.

sensibilisable [sɑ̃sibilizabl̩], *a. Phot:* sensitizable (paper, etc.).

sensibilisateur, -trice [sɑ̃sibilizatœːr, -tris], *Phot: etc:* **1.** *a.* sensitizing. **2.** *s.m.* sensitizer, sensitizing bath. **3.** *s.f. Biol:* **sensibilisatrice**, sensitizer.

sensibilisation [sɑ̃sibilizasjɔ̃], *s.f.* **1.** *Phot:* sensitizing, sensitization. **2.** *Med:* sensitization. **3.** **leur but est la s. de l'opinion à ce problème**, their aim is to make (public) opinion sensitive to, aware of, this problem.

sensibiliser [sɑ̃sibilize], *v.tr.* **1.** *Phot:* to sensitize (paper, collodion); **bain à s.**, sensitizing bath. **2.** *Med: etc:* to sensitize. **3.** to make (s.o.) sensitive to, aware of (sth.).

sensibilité [sɑ̃sibilite], *s.f.* (*a*) sensitiveness, sensitivity (of a person); **la s. qui les rend humains**, that sensitiveness that makes them human; **la s. de l'artiste**, the sensitive nature of the artist; **enfant d'une grande s.**, extremely sensitive child; *Psy:* **s. différentielle**, differential sensibility; (*b*) compassion, feeling; **avoir de la s.**, to be soft-hearted; (*c*) sensitiveness (of skin, balance, film, etc.); sensitivity (of an instrument); **défaut de s. d'une boussole**, sluggishness of a compass; **s. au choc**, sensitiveness to shock; *Tchn:* **s. à la rupture**, susceptibility to rupture, to breaking; *Petroleum Ind:* **s. au plomb**, lead susceptibility; *Ph:* **s. chromatique, s. spectrale**, colour sensitivity, colour response, spectral sensitivity; **s. thermique**, thermal response; *Exp: Phot: etc:* **réducteur de s.**, desensitizer; *El: W.Tel: Elcs:* **s. de déviation**, deflection sensitivity; *Elcs:* **s. dynamique**, dynamic sensitivity; **s. statique**, static sensitivity; *Elcs: W.Tel:* **s. aux parasites**, sensitivity to interference.

sensible [sɑ̃sibl̩], *a.* **1.** (= SENTANT) sentient. **2.** (*a*) sensitive, susceptible, impressionable, responsive; **être peu s.**, to be insensitive, *F:* to have a thick skin, a thick hide; **avoir l'oreille s.**, to have a sensitive ear, a keen sense of hearing; **avoir la peau s.**, (i) to have a sensitive skin; (ii) *F:* to be thin-skinned; **toucher, ouïe, peu s.**, dull sense of touch, dull hearing; **être s. au froid**, to feel the cold; *Hort:* to be frost-tender; **être très s. à la douleur**, to be very susceptible to pain; **être s. au ridicule**, to be sensitive to ridicule; **très s. aux mauvaises influences**, very susceptible to evil influences; **devenir s. au danger**, to awake to the danger; *Equit:* (*of horse*) **s. à l'éperon, aux rênes**, spur-wise, bridle-wise; **s. sur l'honneur**, sensitive about honour; **je suis profondément s. à cet honneur**, I am fully alive to the honour you have done me; **être s. aux bontés de qn**, to appreciate s.o.'s kindness; **être s. à la musique**, to have a feeling for music; **c'était sa seule œuvre à laquelle je n'ai pas été s.**, this was the only work of his to which I did not respond, that left me cold; *Mus:* **la note s.**, *s.f.* **la sensible**, the leading note, tone; the sensible note; si (in the movable Do system); **toucher la note, la corde, s.**, to appeal to the emotions, to touch the sensitive chord; (*b*) sympathetic; **homme s.**, man of active sympathies; **cœur s.**, tender heart; **se montrer s. aux malheurs, à la douleur, de qn**, to sympathize with s.o.; **peu s.**, callous; impervious (**à**, to); (*c*) sensitive (plate, balance, thermometer, etc.); **balance s. au milligramme**, balance sensitive to a milligramme; **compas peu s.**, sluggish compass; *Phot:* **papier s.**, sensitive, sensitized, paper; *W.Tel:* **détecteur s.**, responsive detector; (*d*) painful, sore (when touched); sensitive, tender (tooth, etc.); **je me chausse difficilement, car j'ai les pieds sensibles**, I find it difficult to buy shoes as I have tender feet, as my feet tend to hurt me; **s. au toucher**, tender to the touch; **l'endroit s.**, the tender spot, the sore point; **toucher qn à un endroit s.**, to touch s.o. on a tender spot, on the raw; **blesser qn à l'endroit s.**, to tread on s.o.'s pet corn. **3.** sensible; tangible, perceptible; **différence s.**, sensible, considerable, difference; palpable difference; **le monde s.**, the tangible world; **d'une manière s.**, perceptibly, appreciably; **dommages sensibles**, serious damage; **faire des progrès sensibles**, to make appreciable, considerable, progress; **un vide s.**, a noticeable gap; **éprouver un plaisir s.**, to feel a keen, lively, pleasure; **une hausse s. des prix**, a considerable rise in prices. **4.** *s.m. Phil:* **le s.**, the tangible (world); *Psy:* **s. commun**, common sensibility, coenaesthesia.

sensiblement [sɑ̃sibləmɑ̃], *adv.* **1.** appreciably, perceptibly; obviously; to a considerable extent; **augmenter s. qch.**, to increase sth. materially; **s. plus âgé**, considerably, appreciably, older. **2.** acutely, keenly, deeply (affected, touched). **3.** *F:* approximately, roughly, nearly.

sensiblerie [sɑ̃sibləri], *s.f.* sentiment(ality), sentimentalism, mawkishness, *F:* slip-slop, sob stuff; **faire de la s.**, to make an excessive display of emotion.

sensille [sɑ̃siːj], *s.f. Ent:* sensillum, sensilla; **s. campaniforme**, campaniform sensillum; bell-shaped sense organ.

sensitif, -ive [sɑ̃sitif, -iːv]. **1.** *a.* (*a*) sensitive, having the faculty of feeling; (*b*) sensory, sensorial; **nerf s.**, sensory nerve; (*c*) *Tls:* **perceuse sensitive**, sensitive drill. **2.** (*a*) *s.* sensitive person; (*b*) *s.f. Bot:* **sensitive**, sensitive plant, mimosa pudica.

sensitivité [sɑ̃sitivite], *s.f.* sensitivity.

sensitivo-moteur [sɑ̃sitivɔmɔtœːr], *a.m. Anat:* sensorimotor (nerve); *pl. sensitivo-moteurs.*

sensitomètre [sɑ̃sitɔmɛtr̩], *s.m. Opt: Phot:* sensitometer.

sensitométrie [sɑ̃sitɔmetri], *s.f.* sensitometry.

sensitométrique [sɑ̃sitɔmetrik], *a.* sensitometric.

sensoriel, -ielle [sɑ̃sɔrjɛl], *a.* sensorial, sensory; **erreurs sensorielles**, sensorial errors.

sensorimétrie [sɑ̃sɔrimetri], *s.f. Psy:* sensorimetry.

sensorimétrique [sɑ̃sɔrimetrik], *a. Psy:* sensorimetric.

sensori-moteur, -trice [sɑ̃sɔrimɔtœːr, -tris], *a. Med:* sensorimotor, sensimotor, sensomotor; *pl. sensori-moteurs, -trices.*

sensorium [sɑ̃sɔrjɔm], *s.m. Anat: Biol:* sensorium.

sensualiser [sɑ̃sɥalize], *v.tr.* to sensualize (thought, ideas).

sensualisme [sɑ̃sɥalism], *s.m.* **1.** sensualism. **2.** *Phil:* sensationalism.

sensualiste [sɑ̃sɥalist]. **1.** *s.m. & f.* sensualist. **2.** *a.* sensual (philosophy, etc.).

sensualité [sɑ̃sɥalite], *s.f.* (*a*) sensuality; carnality; (*b*) voluptuousness.

sensuel, -elle [sɑ̃sɥɛl]. **1.** *a.* sensual, sensuous; carnal. **2.** *s.* (*a*) sensualist; (*b*) voluptuary.

sensuellement [sɑ̃sɥɛlmɑ̃], *adv.* sensually; carnally.

sentant [sɑ̃tɑ̃], *a.* sentient.

sent-bon [sɑ̃bɔ̃], *s.m.inv. F:* scent.

sente [sɑ̃ːt], *s.f.* footpath; track.

sentence [sɑ̃tɑ̃ːs], *s.f.* **1.** maxim; **homme qui ne parle que par sentences**, sententious person; man who always talks sententiously, pedantically. **2.** (*a*) sentence, judgment; **s. de mort**, sentence of death; **prononcer une s.**, to pass a sentence; (*b*) decision, award; **rendre une s. (arbitrale)**, to make an award.

sentencieusement [sɑ̃tɑ̃sjøzmɑ̃], *adv.* sententiously.

sentencieux, -ieuse [sɑ̃tɑ̃sjø, -jøːz], *a.* sententious (style, writer).

senteur [sɑ̃tœːr], *s.f.* **1.** *Ven:* scent. **2.** *Lit:* (= ODEUR) scent, perfume. **3.** *Bot:* **pois de s.**, sweet pea.

senti [sɑ̃ti]. **1.** *a.* well-expressed, strong (dramatic, situation, etc.); true to life; **paroles bien senties**, heartfelt words; **vérités bien senties**, home truths. **2.** *s.m. Psy:* sense-datum; that which is felt.

sentier [sɑ̃tje], *s.m.* (foot)path; **s. à mulets, s. muletier**, mule track; **s. pour cavaliers**, bridle path; **le s. de la gloire**, the path of glory; **s'écarter des sentiers battus**, to turn aside from the beaten track.

sentiment [sɑ̃timɑ̃], *s.m.* **1.** (*a*) sensation, feeling (of joy, relief, hunger, etc.); **contenir ses sentiments**, to repress one's feelings, to keep one's feelings under control; (*b*) sense, consciousness; **avoir le s. que . . .**, to have a feeling that . . ., to be conscious that . . .; **privé de s.**, devoid of feeling; numb (limb, etc.); **posséder un haut s. du devoir, de ses devoirs**, to have a high, lofty, sense of duty, of one's duties; **s. très vif, très fin, de l'humour**, keen, delicate, sense of humour; **elle a le s. très vif du beau**, she has a very keen sense of beauty; **juger par s.**, to judge by one's impressions; (*c*) **faire appel aux bons sentiments de qn**, to appeal to s.o.'s better feelings. **2.** (*a*) sentiment, sensibility, feeling; **le s. de la nature**, a feeling for nature; **ses sentiments vis-à-vis de moi**, his feelings towards me; **jouer avec s.**, to play (the piano, etc.) with feeling; **se permettre de grands sentiments**, to indulge in high-flown sentiments; **faire du s.**, to sentimentalize; **je ne fais pas de s. en affaires**, I don't let sentiment interfere with business; *F:* **le faire au s.**, to appeal to the emotions; (*b*) **avoir du s. pour qn**, to be drawn to s.o., to feel attracted to s.o.; (*c*) *Corr:* **veuillez agréer (l'expression de) mes sentiments distingués**, yours faithfully; **veuillez bien recevoir l'expression de mes sentiments les meilleurs**, yours sincerely. **3.** opinion; **au s. de mon père**, in my father's opinion; **au s.**, (i) by judgment, by guess(work); (ii) at will; **partager les sentiments de qn**, to share s.o.'s views, feelings; **voilà mon s.**, those are my sentiments, those are my feelings; that is how I feel; **parler à sentiments ouverts**, to speak one's mind, to be quite frank. **4.** *Ven:* (*a*) scent (of quarry); (*b*) sense of smell (of hound).

sentimental, -ale, -aux [sɑ̃timɑ̃tal, -o], *a.* (*a*) **intrigue sentimentale**, love affair; (*b*) sentimental; (*c*) **attachement s. pour son pays natal**, sentimental attachment to one's native land; *s.* **c'est un s., une sentimentale**, he, she, is very sentimental.

sentimentalement [sɑ̃timɑ̃talmɑ̃], *adv.* sentimentally.

sentimentaliser [sɑ̃timɑ̃talize], *v.tr. & i.* to sentimentalize.

sentimentalisme [sɑ̃timɑ̃talism], *s.m.* sentimentalism, sentimentality.

sentimentaliste [sɑ̃timɑ̃talist], *a. & s.m. & f.* sentimentalist.

sentimentalité [sɑ̃timɑ̃talite], *s.f.* sentimentality.

sentine [sɑ̃tin], *s.f. Nau:* bilge, well (of ship); *Lit:* **s. de tous les vices**, sink of iniquity.

sentinelle [sɑ̃tinɛl], *s.f. Mil:* 1. sentry; poser, (re)lever une s., to post, relieve, a sentry. 2. guard(ing), watch; faire (la) s., (i) to mount guard, to stand sentry; (ii) to be on the watch; en s., on sentry duty, on post. 3. *Elcs:* (*computers*) sentinel, mark, marker. 4. *P:* turd; déposer une s. sur le pas de la porte, to leave one's card on the doorstep.

sentir [sɑ̃tiːr], *v.* (*pr.p.* sentant; *p.p.* senti; *pr.ind.* je sens, il sent, n. sentons, ils sentent; *pr.sub.* je sente; *p.d.* je sentais; *p.h.* je sentis; *fu.* je sentirai) 1. *v.tr.* (*a*) to feel (pain, hunger, cold, joy, sorrow, etc.); je sentais trembler le plancher, I could feel the floor trembling; je sens l'hiver qui vient, I can feel winter coming; il y a des gens qui ne sentent rien, there are some people who feel nothing, who do not seem to feel anything; je sens vivement qu'il ne m'écrive plus, I feel very hurt that he has stopped writing to me; je me sentais presser dans ses bras, I felt his arms round me; s. qch. pour qn, to feel affection for s.o., to feel drawn towards s.o.; je ne sens rien pour lui, I have no particular feelings for him (one way or the other); he leaves me cold; *F:* s. ses bras, ses jambes, to feel pains in one's arms, one's legs; je ne sens plus mes jambes, mes pieds, I can hardly feel my legs, my feet (for tiredness, for the cold); (*b*) to be conscious of, to feel (insult, one's strength, etc.); s. un danger, to be conscious of danger; il en sent toute l'importance, he is fully alive to, aware of, the importance of it; il ne sent pas les affronts, he doesn't mind being insulted; he's (completely) thick-skinned; s. grandir son influence, to feel one's influence growing; je sens que vous avez raison, I have a feeling that you are right; s. son cheval dans la main, to have one's horse well in hand; (*of ship*) s. la barre, to answer to the helm; il m'a fait s. que . . ., he gave me to understand that . . .; faire s. son autorité, to make one's authority felt; faire s. la mélodie, to stress, bring out, the melody; l'effet se fera s., the effect will be felt; l'effet de ces drogues se fait s. à la longue, these drugs tell upon one in time; l'effet de chaque coup se faisait s., every blow told; se s. dix ans de moins, to feel ten years younger; se s. beaucoup d'amitié pour qn, to be very fond of s.o.; se s. du courage, to feel full of courage; je ne m'en sens pas le courage, I don't feel equal to it; (*c*) to smell (odour, flower); sentez cette rose, just smell this rose; avec mon rhume je ne sens rien, with my cold I can't smell anything; *F:* je ne peux pas le s., I can't bear him, can't stand him (at any price); I hate the sight of him; s. le cadavre, to scent disaster, to smell ruin; s. qch. de loin, to be aware of sth. a long way off; to feel sth. coming; s. qn de loin, (i) to have a feeling that s.o. is coming; (ii) to see through s.o. 2. *v.i.* (*a*) (*with cogn.acc.*) to taste of, smell of (sth.); cela sent le brûlé, there's a smell of burning; vin qui sent le bouchon, corked wine; la pièce sent l'humidité, the room smells, feels, damp; pièce qui sent le renfermé, stuffy room; la salle sentait le tabac à plein nez, the room was reeking of tobacco; il sentait l'acteur à plein nez, he had actor written all over him; il sent le cadavre, he looks as if he were not long for this world; toux qui sent le sapin, churchyard cough; s. le fagot, to savour of heresy; ouvrage qui sent la lampe, qui sent l'huile, work that savours, smells, of midnight oil; s. le terroir, to smack of the soil; il sent la potence, he'll end his days on the gallows; (*b*) s. bon, mauvais, to smell good, bad; l'air sentait bon le printemps, there was a pleasant smell of spring in the air; ça sent bon le pain frais, there's a delicious smell of fresh bread; fleurs qui sentent bon, sweet-smelling flowers; *F:* ça ne sent pas bon, that seems a bit unsavoury, a bit fishy; (*c*) *abs. F:* to smell bad, to stink; cette viande sent, this meat smells; il sent des pieds, his feet smell; il sent de la bouche, he's got bad breath, his breath smells; le cadavre commence à s., the corpse is beginning to smell, to stink.

se sentir. 1. vous vous sentez bien? are you feeling well? se s. mal, to be feeling ill; je me sens fatigué, I feel tired; *Iron:* tu ne te sens pas bien? tu te sens bien, oui? are you feeling all right; *F:* tu ne te sens plus? have you taken leave of your senses? 2. (*a*) elle se sentait mourir, she felt she was dying; il ne se sent pas de joie, he is beside himself with joy; *A:* je suis dans une colère que je ne me sens pas! I'm too angry for words! (*b*) se s. de qch., to be affected by sth.; on se sent toujours d'une bonne éducation, one always feels the benefit of a good education; chacun se sent de ces améliorations, everyone benefits from these improvements; je me sens encore de ma blessure, I still feel the effects of my wound. 3. (*of pers.*) to be conscious of one's own strength, one's capabilities; artiste qui commence à se s., artist who is beginning to find his feet.

seoir [swaːr], *v.i.* 1. (*hardly used except in inf. and pr.p.* séant, *p.p.* sis) (*a*) *A:* to sit; sieds-toi, sit (thee) down; (*b*) *Jur:* to be situate(d); maison sise rue Saint-Honoré, house situate(d) in the Rue Saint-Honoré. 2. (*used only in pr.p.* seyant, séant; *pr.ind.* il sied, ils siéent; *pr.sub.* il siée, ils siéent; *p.d.* il seyait, ils seyaient; *fu.* il siéra, ils siéront) to suit, become; cette robe vous sied bien, that dress suits you, is very becoming, attractive; il lui sied mal de parler ainsi, it ill becomes him to talk in that strain; cette vanité ne sied pas bien avec la piété, such vanity does not go well with piety.

sep [sɛp], *s.m.* 1. *Nau: etc:* cleat. 2. slade, sole (of plough).

sépalaire [sepalɛːr], *a. Bot:* sepalous.

sépale [sepal], *s.m. Bot:* sepal.

sépaloïde [sepalɔid], *a. Bot:* sepaloid.

séparabilité [separabilite], *s.f.* separability, separableness.

séparable [separabl̥], *a.* separable (de, from); liberté politique difficilement s. des notions d'égalité, political liberty which it is difficult to separate, differentiate, from ideas of equality.

séparateur, -trice [separatœːr, -tris]. 1. *a.* separating, separative; *Opt:* pouvoir s., resolution, resolving power. 2. *s.m. Dent: Tchn:* separator; s. centrifuge, centrifugal separator; s. d'huile, oil separator; s. de suie, soot remover; s. d'eau de condensation, steam trap; s. à chicanes, baffle separator; (*computers*) s. d'enregistrements, d'unités, record, unit, separator; *Atom.Ph:* s. d'isotopes, isotope separator; s. d'épuisement, d'extraction, stripper.

séparatif, -ive [separatif, -iːv], *a.* separative, separating; separatory; dividing (wall, etc.).

séparation [separasjɔ̃], *s.f.* 1. (*a*) separation, severance, severing, parting; s. d'avec qn, (i) separation from s.o.; (ii) parting with s.o.; la s. de l'erreur et de la vérité, discrimination between error and truth; s. de la tête du corps, severance of the head from the body; s. judiciaire, judicial separation (of husband and wife); s. de fait, s. amiable, *de facto* separation (of husband and wife, without legal settlement); *Jur:* s. de biens, (i) (conventionnelle) marriage settlement under which husband and wife administer their separate properties; (ii) (judiciaire) settlement by court order under which the wife administers her property separately (on account of the husband's mismanagement); s. de l'Église et de l'État, disestablishment (of the church); (*b*) *Ph:* s. par fractionnement, momentum separation; *Mch:* s. (de l'eau de la vapeur) par heurtement, par choc, baffle separation; *Petroleum Ind:* s. à sec, dry separation; s. des produits de tête, topping; s. du propane, depropan(iz)ation; s. par barbotage, bubble-type separation; (*computers*) s. de colonne, column split; *Atom.Ph:* s. isotopique, s. des isotopes, isotope separation; (*c*) partition, division; mur de s., partition wall, dividing wall; établir une s. entre deux champs, to set up a boundary between two fields; surface de s., interface (of two liquids flowing in the same pipe); (*d*) *Ac: W.Tel:* (*in stereo sound equipment*) separateness. 2. breaking up, dispersal (of meeting, of a family).

séparatisme [separatism], *s.m. Pol:* separatism, separationism.

séparatiste [separatist]. 1. *s.m. & f.* separatist, seceder, secessionist. 2. *a.* separatist, seceding.

séparé [separe], *a.* 1. separate, different, distinct; *Mec.E:* commande séparée, individual drive. 2. separated, apart; vivre s. de sa femme, to live apart from one's wife.

séparément [separemɑ̃], *adv.* separately; individually; vivre s., to live apart.

séparer [separe], *v.tr.* 1. (*a*) to separate (de, from); to disunite, part; s. les bons d'avec les mauvais, to separate, set apart, the good from the bad; s. la tête du corps, to sever the head from the body; s. les cheveux sur le front, to part the hair on the forehead; s. une chambre en trois, to divide a room into three; s. deux combattants, to part, separate, two fighters; *Box:* séparez! break (away)! personne ne peut nous s., no one can come between us; *Jur:* s. des époux, to separate judicially a married couple; *Ecc:* s. qn des sacrements, to exclude s.o. from the sacraments; (*b*) *Petroleum Ind:* s. l'huile de l'eau, to knock down oil; s. le propane du pétrole, to depropanize oil; s. par distillation, to distil out; (*c*) *Elcs:* (*computers*) to unpack. 2. to divide, keep apart; mur qui sépare deux champs, wall dividing two fields; une table le séparait de la porte, a table was between him and the door; la raison sépare l'homme des bêtes, reason distinguishes man from beasts; la ligne qui sépare le sublime du boursouflé, the line that divides the sublime from the bombastic; deux mille ans nous séparent des Romains, there are two thousand years between us and the Romans.

se séparer. 1. to separate, part (de, from); to part company; nous ne nous séparerons jamais, we shall never part; se s. de sa femme, d'avec sa femme, to separate from one's wife; se s. du monde, to detach oneself from the world; il n'y a si bonne compagnie qui ne se sépare, the best of friends must part; l'armée se sépara, the army disbanded. 2. (*of river, road, etc.*) to divide, branch off; là où les routes se séparent, at the parting of the ways; ici je me sépare entièrement de vous, here I disagree, part company, with you; *Ch:* (*of salt*) se s. à l'état cristallin, to crystallize out; se s. par précipitation, to precipitate out. 3. (*of crowd, assembly, etc.*) to break up, disperse; l'assemblée s'est séparée dans le tumulte, the meeting broke up in disorder.

sépédon [sepedɔ̃], *s.m. Rept:* ringhals, spitting snake.

sépia [sepja], *s.f.* 1. *Moll:* sepia, cuttlefish. 2. sepia (colour); (dessin à la) s., sepia drawing.

sépiole [sepjɔl], *s.f. Moll:* sepiola.

sépiolidés [sepjɔlide], *s.m.pl. Moll:* Sepiolidae.

sépiolite [sepjɔlit], *s.f. Miner:* sepiolite.

sépion [sepjɔ̃], *s.m.* cuttlebone.

sépoule [sepul], *s.f. Tex:* pirn.

seps [sɛps], *s.m. Rept:* seps; serpent-lizard.

sept [sɛt], *num.a.inv. & s.m.inv.* seven; le s. mai, the seventh of May; Édouard Sept, Edward the Seventh; *Cards:* le s. de cœur, the seven of hearts; bottes de s. lieues, seven-league boots.

septain [sɛtɛ̃], *s.m.* 1. *Pros:* seven-line stanza. 2. seven-strand(ed) rope.

septal, -aux [sɛptal, -o], *a. Bot:* septal.

septantaine [sɛptɑ̃tɛn], *s.f. Belg: Sw.Fr:* about seventy; le vieux n'avait encore que la s., the old man was still in his seventies.

septante [sɛptɑ̃ːt], *num.a.inv. & s.m.inv.* 1. *A:* (*still used in S.-E. of Fr., in Belg. and Switz.*) seventy; *B:* pardonner jusqu'à s. fois sept fois, to forgive until seventy times seven. 2. les S., the Seventy (translators of the Old Testament into Greek); la version des S., *s.f.* la Septante, the Septuagint (version of the Bible); the Alexandrian version.

septantième [sɛptɑ̃tjɛm], *num.a. Belg: Sw.Fr:* seventieth.

septe [sɛpt], *s.m.* septum (of coral, of chambered shell).

septembre [sɛptɑ̃bŗ], *s.m.* September; en s., in September; au mois de s., in the month of September; le premier, le sept, s., (on) the first, the seventh, of September, (on) September (the) first, (the) seventh.

septembrisades [sɛptɑ̃brizad], *s.f. pl. Fr.Hist:* September Massacres (1792).

septembriseur [sɛptɑ̃brizœːr], *s.m. Fr.Hist:* (1792) Septembrist, Septembrizer.

septemvir [sɛptɛmviːr], *s.m. Rom.Hist:* septemvir.

septemvirat [sɛptɛmvira], *s.m.* septemvirate.

septénaire [sɛptenɛːr], *a. & s.m.* septenary.

septennal, -aux [sɛptennal, -o], *a.* septennial, seven-year (period, parliament).

septennalité [sɛptɛn(n)alite], *s.f.* septennial, seven-year, system (of electing President, etc.).

septennat [sɛptɛn(n)a], *s.m.* (*a*) septennium; (*b*) septennate (of Fr. President).

septentrion [sɛptɑ̃tri(j)ɔ̃], *s.m. Poet: Lit:* 1. north; au s., in the north; au s. de . . ., to the north of . . .. 2. *Astr:* le S., Septentrion, the Little Bear.

septentrional, -aux [sɛptɑ̃tri(j)ɔnal, -o]. 1. *a.* septentrional; northern (country, etc.). 2. *s.m.pl.* northerners.

septicémie [sɛptisemi], *s.f. Med:* septicaemia, sepsis; blood-poisoning; *Vet:* s. hémorragique, haemorrhagic septicaemia, shipping fever, septic pneumonia.

septicémique [sɛptisemik], *a. Med:* septicaemic.

septicide [sɛptisid], *a. Bot:* septicidal.

septicité [sɛptisite], *s.f. Med:* septicity.

septicolore [sɛptikɔlɔːr], *a.* septicoloured.

septicopyoémie [sɛptikɔpjɔemi], *s.f. Med:* septicopyaemia.

septidi [sɛptidi], *s.m. Fr.Hist:* (*Republican Calendar*) seventh day of the decade.

septième [sɛtjɛm]. **1.** *num.a. & s.* seventh; **être au s. ciel,** to be in the seventh heaven (of delight); **demeurer au s. (étage),** to live on the seventh, *U.S:* eighth, floor. **2.** *s.m.* seventh (part); **trois septièmes,** three sevenths. **3.** *s.f.* (*a*) seventh; (*b*) *Mus:* (i) subtonic; (ii) leading note; (*c*) *Sch:* **(classe de) s.** = top form of primary school.

septièmement [sɛtjɛmmɑ̃], *adv.* seventhly, in the seventh place.

septifère [sɛptifɛːr], *a. Nat.Hist:* septiferous.

septiforme [sɛptifɔrm], *a. Nat.Hist:* septiform, septum-like.

septillion [sɛptiljɔ̃], *s.m.* **1.** (*since 1948*) septillion (10^{42}). **2.** (*before 1948*) quadrillion (10^{24}), *U.S:* septillion.

septime[1] [sɛptim], *s.f. Fenc:* septime.

Septime,[2] *Pr.n.m.* Septimus.

septimo [sɛptimo], *adv.* in the seventh place, seventhly.

septique [sɛptik], *a. Med:* septic; *Hyg:* **fosse s.,** septic tank.

septivalent [sɛptivalɑ̃], *a. Ch:* septivalent, heptavalent.

sept-mâts [sɛtmɑ], *s.m.inv.* seven-masted sailing ship; seven-master.

septuagénaire [sɛptɥaʒenɛːr]. **1.** *a.* septuagenarian, seventy-year old. **2.** *s.m. & f.* septuagenarian.

septuagésime [sɛptɥaʒezim], *s.f.* Septuagesima (Sunday).

septum [sɛptɔm], *s.m. Anat: Bot:* septum, dissepiment.

septuor [sɛptɥɔːr], *s.m. Mus:* septet(te).

septuple [sɛptypl̩], *a. & s.m.* septuple, sevenfold; **au s.,** sevenfold; **quatorze est (le) s. de deux,** fourteen is seven times (as much as) two.

septupler [sɛptyple], *v.tr. & i.* to increase sevenfold; to multiply by seven; to make seven times larger, seven times as big.

sépulcral, -aux [sepylkral, -o], *a.* sepulchral (stone, voice); **figure sépulcrale,** lugubrious face.

sépulcre [sepylkr̩], *s.m.* sepulchre; **le saint s.,** the Holy Sepulchre; *B:* **sépulcres blanchis,** whited sepulchres.

sépulture [sepyltyːr], *s.f.* **1.** burial, sepulture, interment; **refuser la s. à qn,** to refuse Christian burial to s.o.; **corps restés sans s.,** bodies that had lain unburied; **le lieu de s. de nos rois,** the burial place of our kings. **2.** burial place; **violer une s.,** to despoil, rifle, a tomb; **sépultures militaires,** war cemeteries.

séquanais, -aise [sekwanɛ, -ɛːz]. *A.Hist:* **1.** *a.* Sequanian. **2.** *s.m.pl.* **les Séquanais** (*also* **les Séquanes, les Séquaniens**), the Sequani.

séquanien, -ienne [sekwanjɛ̃, -jɛn], *a. & s.m. Geol: A.Hist:* Sequanian.

séquelle [sekɛl], *s.f.* **1.** *Pej:* (*a*) gang, set, crew (of persons); **toute la sainte s.,** the whole blessed lot; (*b*) string (of oaths, insults). **2.** *pl. Med:* **séquelles,** sequelae; after-effects (of illness, accident, etc.).

séquence [sekɑ̃ːs], *s.f. Ecc: Mus: Cin: Cards: etc:* sequence; *T.V:* **s. d'entrelacement,** sequence of interlace; **séquences de réserve,** stock shots; *El:* **s. de phase,** phase sequence; *Elcs:* (*computers*) **s. d'appel,** calling sequence; **s. (d'exécution) des instructions,** control sequence; **s. d'interclassement,** collating, collation, sequence; **s. de nombres aléatoires,** random-number sequence; *Cards:* **s. de trois,** run of three; **s. flush,** straight flush.

séquentiel, -ielle [sekɑ̃sjɛl], *a.* sequential.

séquestrant [sekɛstrɑ̃], *a. Med:* sequestrum-producing.

séquestration [sekɛstrasjɔ̃], *s.f.* **1.** *Jur:* sequestration (of goods). **2.** isolation (of infected animals, etc.). **3.** seclusion (of s.o.); *esp. Jur:* illegal restraint; false imprisonment. **4.** *Med:* formation of a sequestrum.

séquestre[1] [sekɛstr̩], *s.m.* **1.** *Jur:* (*a*) sequestration; embargo (on ship); **en, sous, s.,** sequestered; **mettre en, sous, s. les biens de qn,** to sequester, sequestrate, s.o.'s property; **s. (judiciaire),** writ of sequestration; **ordonnance de mise sous s.,** receiving order (in bankruptcy proceedings); (*b*) *A:* **jeune fille mise en s. dans un couvent,** girl relegated to a convent. **2.** property sequestrated. **3.** *Sch: A:* detention room. **4.** *Med:* sequestrum.

séquestre[2], *s.m. Jur:* receiver, depositary, trustee, administrator (of sequestrated property); sequestrator; **(administrateur) s.,** assignee.

séquestrectomie [sekɛstrɛktɔmi], *s.f. Surg:* sequestrectomy.

séquestrer [sekɛstre], *v.tr.* **1.** to sequester, sequestrate (property); *Nau:* to lay an embargo upon (ship). **2.** to isolate, seclude (lepers, etc.); to relegate (s.o.) **(dans,** to); *Jur:* to confine (s.o.), shut (s.o.) up, illegally; to put (s.o.) under illegal restraint; **il était arrivé véritablement à s. sa femme,** he had literally come to the point of keeping his wife shut up; **il semblait vouloir se s.,** he seemed to want to cut himself off from the world, from society.

sequestrotomie [sekɛstrɔtɔmi], *s.f. Surg:* sequestrotomy.

sequin [səkɛ̃], *s.m. Num: Cost:* sequin.

sequoia [sekɔja], *s.m. Bot:* sequoia; **s. géant,** giant sequoia, *F:* big tree (of California); **s. toujours vert,** redwood.

sérac [serak], *s.m.* **1.** *Geol:* serac. **2.** (*in Switz. Alps*) cottage cheese.

sérail [seraːj], *s.m.* seraglio; *pl. sérails.*

séran [serɑ̃], *s.m. Tex:* flax comb, hackle, heckle, hatchel.

sérançage [serɑ̃saːʒ], *s.m. Tex:* hackling, heckling.

sérancer [serɑ̃se], *v.tr. Tex:* to hackle, heckle.

séranceur [serɑ̃sœːr], *s.m. Tex:* hackler, heckler.

serançoir [serɑ̃swaːr], *s.m. Tex:* flax comb, hackle, heckle, hatchel.

sérapéion [serapejɔ̃], *s.m.,* **sérapéum** [serapeɔm], *s.m. Egyptian Ant:* serapeum, temple of Serapis.

séraphin [serafɛ̃], *s.m.* (*a*) seraph; **les séraphins,** the seraphs, the seraphim; (*b*) *Fr.C: F:* **c'est un s.,** he's mean, stingy.

séraphique [serafik], *a.* seraphic, angelic; *Ecc. Hist:* **le docteur s.,** the Seraphic Doctor (St Bonaventura); **l'ordre s.,** the Franciscan order.

sérapion [serapjɔ̃], *s.m.* = SÉRAPÉION.

séraskier, sérasquier [seraskje], *s.m. Hist:* seraskier; (Turkish) commander-in-chief.

serbe [sɛrb], *a. & s. Geog:* Serb, Serbian.

Serbie [sɛrbi], *Pr.n.f. Geog:* Serbia.

serbo-croate [sɛrbɔkrɔat]. **1.** *a. & s.m. & f. Geog:* Serbo-Croat(ian). **2.** *s.m. Ling:* Serbo-Croat.

Sercq [sɛrk], *Pr.n.m. Geog:* (the island of) Sark.

serdar [sɛrdaːr], *s.m. Hist:* sirdar.

serein[1] [sərɛ̃], *a.* **1.** serene, calm (sky, weather); **jours sereins,** halcyon days, cloudless days. **2.** (*of pers.*) serene; calm and collected; tranquil; **visage s.,** calm, composed, serene, face. **3.** *Med:* **goutte sereine,** amaurosis.

serein[2], *s.m.* (precipitation of) evening dew; (*in tropical countries*) serein; **prendre froid au s., prendre le s.,** to catch a chill in the evening damp.

sérénade [serenad], *s.f.* serenade; **donner une s. à qn,** to serenade s.o.

sérénissime [serenisim], *a.* **Son Altesse S.,** His, Her, Serene Highness; *Hist:* **la s. république,** *s.f.* **la S.,** the Serene Republic, the Venetian Republic.

sérénité [serenite], *s.f.* **1.** serenity, calmness (of the sky, of the mind); **troubler la s. de qn,** to disturb s.o.'s equanimity; **avec s.,** serenely. **2.** serenity (title of honour); *Hist:* **Sa S. le Doge,** his Serenity the Doge.

Sérès [serɛs], *Pr.n. Geog:* Seres, Serres.

séreux, -euse [serø, -øːz]. **1.** *a. Anat: Med:* serous (fluid, etc.); **membrane séreuse,** *s.f.* **séreuse,** serous membrane, serosa. **2.** *s.f. Ent:* **séreuse,** serosa.

serf, serve [sɛrf, sɛrv]. **1.** *s.* (*a*) *Hist:* serf; (*b*) *F: Pej:* slave, dogsbody. **2.** *a.* (*a*) *Hist:* **condition serve,** serfdom; (*b*) (*of land*) in bondage, in villein tenure; (*c*) servile (outlook, etc.).

serfouage [sɛrfwaːʒ], *s.m.* hoeing.

serfouette [sɛrfwɛt], *s.f. Hort:* combined hoe and fork.

serfouir [sɛrfwiːr], *v.tr. Hort:* to hoe (vegetables, etc.); to loosen (the soil).

serfouissage [sɛrfwisaːʒ], *s.m. Hort:* hoeing.

serge[1] [sɛrʒ], *s.f. Tex:* (woollen) serge; *occ.* silk serge; **manteau en s.,** serge coat.

Serge[2], *Pr.n.m.* Sergius; Serge.

sergé [sɛrʒe]. **1.** *a.* serge-like; woven in twill weave on eight or more shafts. **2.** *s.m.* cotton serge.

sergent[1] [sɛrʒɑ̃], *s.m.* **1.** sergeant; (*a*) **s. d'armes,** (i) *A:* sergeant-at-arms; (ii) *Navy:* = ship's corporal; *A:* **sergent de ville,** policeman; *A:* **s. à verge,** tipstaff; **s. de nuit,** sergeant of the watch; (*b*) *Mil:* sergeant (infantry, air force); **s. fourrier, s. comptable,** quartermaster sergeant; **s. major** = senior quartermaster sergeant; **plume s. major,** steel nib; **s. instructeur,** drill sergeant. **2.** (*a*) *Ent:* ground-beetle; (*b*) *Dial:* (in *S. of Fr.*) = ROTENGLE.

sergent[2], *s.m. Tchn:* (= SERRE-JOINT) cramp, screw frame, holdfast; (carpenter's) clamp; (cooper's) dog.

sergent-chef [sɛrʒɑ̃ʃɛf], *s.m. Mil:* quartermaster-sergeant; staff sergeant (in certain corps); *Mil. Av:* flight-sergeant; *pl. sergents-chefs.*

serger [sɛrʒe], *s.m.,* **sergier** [sɛrʒje], *s.m.* serge maker.

sergerie [sɛrʒəri], *s.f.* serge (i) manufacture, (ii) trade, (iii) (wholesale) warehouse.

sergette [sɛrʒɛt], *s.f. Tex:* sergette.

sergot [sɛrgo], *s.m. A: P:* policeman, copper, bobby.

sérialisme [serjalism], *s.m. Mus:* dodecaphony, serialism.

sériation [serjasjɔ̃], *s.f.* seriation.

séricicole [serisikɔl], *a.* seri(ci)cultural.

sériciculteur [serisikyltœːr], *s.m.* seri(ci)culturist, silkworm breeder.

séri(ci)culture [seri(si)kyltyːr], *s.f.* seri(ci)culture, silkworm breeding.

séricigène [serisiʒɛn], *a. Ent:* silk-producing (organ, insect); **glande s.,** silk gland.

séricine [serisin], *s.f. Bio-Ch:* sericin.

séricite [serisit], *s.f. Miner:* sericite.

séricitеux, -euse [serisitø, -øːz], *a. Miner:* sericitic.

séricitisation [serisitizasjɔ̃], *s.f. Miner:* sericitization.

séricole [serikɔl], *a.* seri(ci)cultural.

série [seri], *s.f.* **1.** (*succession of numbers, events, etc.*) (*a*) *Mth:* series; **la loi des séries,** the law of series; **s. convergente, divergente,** convergent, divergent, series; **s. exponentielle,** exponential series; **s. infinie,** infinite series; **s. de Fourier,** Fourier series; **développer en s.,** to expand; (*b*) series, succession (of events, accidents, etc.); **s. chronologique,** time series; **s. de catastrophes, s. noire,** series, chapter, of accidents; run of bad luck; **faire une s. de visites,** to go on a round of visits; **s. de jours chauds,** spell of hot weather; **s. de conférences,** series, course, of lectures; *W.Tel: T.V:* **s. (d'émissions),** (radio, television) series; *Med:* **une s. de piqûres,** a course of injections; *Tchn:* **s. d'opérations,** sequence (of operations); *Elcs:* **s. d'impulsions,** pulse train; (*c*) *Bill: etc:* break; *Bill:* run (of cannons); **s. de vingt,** run of twenty; (*d*) *Sp:* heat; **s. éliminatoire,** qualifying heat. **2.** (*series, group, set, of thgs*) (*a*) series (of topics, press articles, postage stamps, etc.); set (of documents, instruments, tools, weights, etc.); range (of colours, sizes, samples, etc.); **en, par, série(s),** in series, serially; **valeurs remboursables par séries,** securities redeemable in series; **s. complète de factures,** full set of invoices; **publier une s. de volumes sur la préhistoire,** to issue a series (of volumes) on prehistory; **numéro de s.,** running, serial, number; *Nau:* **s. de pavillons,** set of flags; *Pol.Ec:* **s. économique,** economic batch; **amplitude, éventail, de s. économique,** economic batch range; (*b*) *Ind: Com:* range, line (of goods, etc.); **fabrication, production, en (grande(s)) série(s),** mass production; **fabrication en petite(s) série(s),** small-scale manufacture; batch production; **chaîne de fabrication en s.,** production line; **fabriquer en s.,** to mass produce; **voiture de s.,** series car; *Adm: etc:* **prix de s.,** contract price (for public works, etc.); *Com:* **fins de séries,** ends of lines, oddments, remnants; *Publ:* remainders; **article hors s.,** specially manufactured article; custom-made, custom-built, article; **c'est tout à fait hors s.,** it's quite exceptional, out of the ordinary; *Nau:* **bâtiments de même s.,** sister ships; (*c*) *Ch: Atom.Ph: etc:* series; **s. éthylénique,** ethylene series; **s. collatérale,** collateral series; **s. homologue, hétérologue,** homologous, heterologous, series; **s. des tensions,** electromotive or electrochemical series; *Atom.Ph:* **s. de désintégration,** decay chain; **s. radioactive,** radioactive series; **s. de l'uranium,** uranium series; *Geol:* **s. sédimentaire,** sedimentary series; **s. pliocène,** pliocene series; **s. carbonifère,** carboniferous series; (*d*) *El.E:* **en s.,** in series; **enroulement en s.,** series winding; **excité en s.,** series-wound; **montage en s.,** series connection; **monter, brancher, en s.,** to connect in series; (*e*) group, category; *Sp:* rating; *Box:* **s. poids plumes,** featherweight rating; *Cin:* **film de s. B.,** B-category film; *Pej:* **film de s. Z.,** n^{th} grade film.

sérié [serje], *a.* seriate(d).

sériel, -ielle [serjɛl], *a.* serial; *Mus:* twelve-tone, serial, dodecaphonic.

série-parallèle [seriparal(l)ɛl], *s.f. El.E:* series parallel, multiple winding; **monté en s.-p.,** connected in series parallel.

sérier [serje], *v.tr.* (*p.d. & pr.sub.* **n. sériions, v. sériiez**) to arrange in series, to seriate; **s. les questions,** to take the questions one by one; **sérions les questions!** first things first!

sérieusement [serjøzmɑ̃], *adv.* (*a*) seriously, gravely, with gravity, solemnly; (*b*) seriously, in earnest, genuinely; **travailler s.,** to work in real, good, earnest; **parlez-vous s.?** are you serious? do you really mean it? **il l'a dit s.,** he meant what he said; **il ne l'a dit qu'à moitié s.** he was only half in earnest; (*c*) seriously, gravely (ill, wounded).

sérieux, -euse [serjø, -øːz]. **1.** *a.* (*a*) serious, grave, sober; *F:* **sérieux comme un pape, comme un âne qu'on étrille,** as solemn as a judge; **porter un costume s.,** to be quietly, soberly, dressed; (*b*) serious-minded (person); (*c*) serious, earnest, genuine; **êtes-vous s.?** are you serious, in earnest? do you mean it? **d'un ton, d'un air, s.,** earnestly; **homme s.,** responsible, steady, reliable, man; **offre sérieuse,** bona-fide offer; **acheteur s.,** genuine purchaser; **peu s.,** irresponsible (person); **ce n'est pas de la finance sérieuse,** it isn't sound finance; (*d*) serious, important (matter, etc.); **maladie sérieuse,** serious illness; **c'est tout ce qu'il y a de plus s.,** (i) it is extremely serious; (ii) I mean it in all seriousness; *Com:* **client s.,** good customer; **maison sérieuse,** reliable firm; **2.** *s.m.* (*a*) seriousness, gravity; **garder son s.,** to preserve one's gravity, to keep one's countenance, to keep a straight face; **prendre qch. (trop) au s.,** to take sth. (too) seriously; **se prendre au s.,** to take oneself seriously; **je vous ai pris au s.,** I thought you were serious, I thought you meant it; **manque de s.,** (i) levity; (ii) irresponsibility; (*b*) *Th:* serious parts; **il joue surtout dans le s.,** he usually takes serious parts; (*c*) *F:* large glass of beer (half litre).

sérigraphie [serigrafi], *s.f.* **1.** silk-screen printing, serigraphy; **à la s.,** by the silk-screen process. **2. une s.,** a serigraph.

serin, -ine [s(ə)rɛ̃, -in]. **1.** (*a*) *s. Orn:* **s. (domestique),** canary; *s.f.* **serine,** hen canary; **s. cini,** serin; (*b*) *a.inv.* **des gants jaune s.,** canary-yellow gloves; **jaune queue de s.,** bright canary-yellow. **2.** *a. & s. F:* silly, stupid, idiotic (person); *s.* idiot, nit.

serinage [s(ə)rinaːʒ], *s.m.* (*a*) *O:* teaching a canary to sing (by playing a bird organ); (*b*) teaching by dint of repeating; cramming; indoctrinating.

sérine [serin], *s.f.* **1.** *Ch:* serine. **2.** *Physiol:* serum albumin; blood albumin.

seriner [s(ə)rine], *v.tr.* (*a*) **s. un serin; s. un air à un serin,** to teach a canary to sing by means of the bird-organ; (*b*) *F:* **s. un air,** to grind out a tune; to tootle a tune (on the flute, etc.); to thump out a tune (on the piano); (*c*) **s. qn; s. qch. à qn,** to teach s.o. sth. (by constant repetition), to drum sth. into s.o.; **s. un rôle à qn,** to din a part into s.o.; (*d*) *P: O:* to bore (s.o.); (*e*) *A: P:* to be unfaithful to, to cuckold, one's husband.

serinette [s(ə)rinɛt], *s.f.* (*a*) bird-organ; (*b*) *F: A:* expressionless singer.

seringa(t) [s(ə)rɛ̃ga], *s.m. Bot:* seringa, mock orange.

seringage [s(ə)rɛ̃gaːʒ], *s.m. Hort:* syringing, spraying.

seringue [s(ə)rɛ̃ːg], *s.f.* **1.** syringe, squirt; *Hort:* sprayer; **s. de jardin,** garden syringe; **s. bruineuse,** fine-spraying syringe; *Med:* **s. à injections, s. de Pravaz,** hypodermic syringe; **s. à lavement,** enema syringe; *Aut:* **s. à graisse,** grease-gun. **2.** *P:* (*a*) trombone; (*b*) rifle, pistol; (*c*) (*of pers.*) bore.

seringuer [s(ə)rɛ̃ge], *v.tr.* **1.** (*a*) to syringe (wound, ear, etc.); (*b*) to squirt (liquid); **s. de la morphine,** to inject morphia; (*c*) *Hort:* to water (leaves of plants) with a syringe or pump. **2.** to spray (with machine-gun fire); *F: Nau:* to rake (a ship) fore and aft (with shot); *P:* **s. qn,** to shoot s.o.

sérinurie [serinyri], *s.f. Med:* serinuria.

sériole [serjɔl], *s.f. Ich:* seriola.

sérique [serik], *a. Med:* **exanthème s.,** serum rash; **réaction s.,** serum sickness.

serment [sɛrmɑ̃], *s.m.* (solemn) oath; **prêter s. (entre les mains de qn),** to take an oath, to be sworn (before s.o.); (of jury, etc.) to be sworn in; **faire prêter s. à qn,** to administer the oath to s.o.; to put s.o. on oath; **déclarer sous s.,** to state, declare, under oath; *Pol:* **s. politique,** *U.S:* oath of office; *Adm:* **s. professionnel,** swearing in (of magistrates, lawyers, police, etc.); *Jur:* **s. supplétoire, supplétif,** suppletory oath; *Hist:* **s. civique,** oath of allegiance (taken by public servants during the French Revolution); **s. de fidélité,** oath of allegiance; *s.a.* HIPPOCRATE; **le s. de fidélité à lui prêté par eux,** the allegiance which they had sworn to him; **déférer le s. à qn,** to administer, tender, an oath to s.o.; (i) to swear s.o., (ii) to swear s.o. in; **rendre son s. à qn; délier, relever, qn de son s.,** to release, relieve, s.o. from his oath; to give s.o. back his promise; **violer un s.,** to break an oath; **être sous la foi du s.,** to be on oath; **faire s. de faire qch.,** to swear that one will do sth.; **faire s. de se venger sur qn,** to swear vengeance upon s.o.; **certifier qch. sous s.,** to declare sth. on oath; **elle déclara sous s. l'avoir payé,** she swore that she had paid for it; **déclaration sous s.,** sworn statement; **faire un faux s.,** to commit perjury.

sermon [sɛrmɔ̃], *s.m.* (*a*) sermon; **prêcher un s. sur . . .,** to preach, deliver, a sermon on . . .; *s.a.* MONTAGNE 1; (*b*) *F:* talking-to, lecture; **pas de sermons!** no sermonizing! **faire un s. à qn,** to tell s.o. off.

sermonnade [sɛrmɔnad], *s.f. F: O:* reprimand, admonition, dressing-down.

sermonnaire [sɛrmɔnɛːr], *s.m.* **1.** collection of sermons. **2.** writer of sermons.

sermonner [sɛrmɔne], *F:* **1.** *v.i.* to sermonize, preach; to preachify. **2.** *v.tr.* to sermonize, lecture, reprimand (s.o.), to take (s.o.) to task, to give (s.o.) a talking-to; to expostulate, remonstrate, with (s.o.); to read (s.o.) a lecture.

sermonneur, -euse [sɛrmɔnœːr, -øːz], *F:* **1.** *a.* sermonizing; fault-finding. **2.** *s.* sermonizer; fault-finder.

sermontain [sɛrmɔ̃tɛ̃], *s.m. Bot: F:* laserwort.

sérodiagnostic [serɔdjagnɔstik], *s.m. Med:* sero-diagnosis.

sérologie [serɔlɔʒi], *s.f. Med:* serology.

séro-réaction [serɔreaksjɔ̃], *s.f. Med:* sero-reaction; *pl. séro-réactions.*

sérosité [serozite], *s.f.* serosity.

sérothérapie [serɔterapi], *s.f.* serotherapy.

sérothérapique [serɔterapik], *s.f.* serotherapeutic.

sérotine[1] [serɔtin], *a.f. & s.f. Obst:* **(membrane) s.,** decidua basalis.

sérotine[2], *s.f. Z:* serotine (bat).

sérotonine [serɔtɔnin], *s.f. Ch:* serotonin.

sérovaccination [serɔvaksinasjɔ̃], *s.f. Med:* serovaccination.

seroual [serwal], *s.m.* (*N.Africa*) trousers.

serpe[1] [sɛrp], *s.f.* bill hook, hedging bill, *U.S:* bush hook; **fait, taillé, à la s., à coups de s.,** roughly made, hacked out.

serpe[2], *s.f. Mec.E:* worm (screw).

serpent [sɛrpɑ̃], *s.m.* **1.** (*a*) serpent, snake; **s. femelle,** female snake; **s. d'eau,** grass-snake; **s. de verre,** slow-worm, blind-worm; **s. à coiffe, à lunettes,** (Indian) cobra; **s. à grosse tête,** thirst snake; **s. arc-en-ciel,** rainbow snake; **s. à sonnettes,** rattlesnake; **s. à sonnettes cornu,** horned rattlesnake; *U.S: F:* sidewinder; **s. à sonnettes des bois,** timber rattlesnake; **s. à sonnettes des prairies,** Prairie rattlesnake; **s. à sonnettes pygmée,** pygmy rattlesnake; **s. cornu,** horned viper; **s. cracheur,** spitting cobra; **s. de mort,** Australian death adder; **s. devin,** boa constrictor; **s. arlequin, s. corail commun,** common coral snake; **s. corail de Wied,** Wied's coral snake; **s. corail d'Arizona,** Sonoran coral snake; **s. tigre,** tiger snake; **s. brun d'Australie,** Australian brown snake; **s. noir d'Australie,** Australian black snake; **s. d'arbre à long nez,** long-nosed tree snake; **s. d'arbre noir et or,** black and gold tree snake; **s. lime,** file snake; **s. royal,** king snake; **s. mangeur d'œufs,** (African) egg-eating snake; **s. mangeur de poules,** chicken snake; **s. ratier,** (Indian) rat snake; **serpents marins,** sea-snakes; **serpents pêcheurs,** fishing snakes; **serpents taureaux,** bull snakes; **serpents volants,** flying snakes; **s. de mer,** (i) *Myth:* sea serpent; (ii) pipe fish; (iii) *Journ:* stock article; *B:* **s. d'airain,** serpent of brass; *Pyr:* **s. de Pharaon,** Pharaoh's serpent; **langue de s.,** (i) *F:* venomous tongue; (ii) *Bot:* adder's tongue; *s.a.* RÉCHAUFFER 1; (*b*) (i) snake-like object; (ii) *F:* treacherous person. **2.** *Mus: A:* (*a*) serpent; (*b*) serpent-player. **3.** *Aer:* thick rope (used in balloon manœuvres). **4.** *Bot: Com:* **bois de s.,** snake wood. **5.** *Astr:* **le S.,** Serpens; the Serpent. **6.** *Alch:* mercury.

serpentage [sɛrpɑ̃taːʒ], *s.m. Av:* snaking.

serpentaire[1] [sɛrpɑ̃tɛːr], *s.f. Bot: Pharm:* serpentaria; **s. de Virginie,** Virginia snake-root.

serpentaire[2], *s.m. Orn:* serpent eater, secretary bird.

Serpentaire[3] **(le),** *Pr.n.m. Astr:* Ophiuchus, Serpentarius.

serpentant [sɛrpɑ̃tɑ̃], *a.* winding, snaky (curve, road); meandering (stream).

serpent-corail [sɛrpɑ̃kɔraːj], *s.m. Rept:* coral snake; *pl. serpents-corail.*

serpente [sɛrpɑ̃ːt]. **1.** *Hist: s.f.* **(papier) s.,** tissue paper (with snake as a water-mark); silver paper. **2.** *s.m. Nau:* snaking.

serpenteau, -eaux [sɛrpɑ̃to], *s.m.* **1.** young snake. **2.** *Pyr:* serpent, squib. **3.** *Nau:* snaking line.

serpentement [sɛrpɑ̃tmɑ̃], *s.m.* winding, curving (of a road, line); meandering (of river); turn (in coil); *Mth:* **point de s.,** point of inflection.

serpenter [sɛrpɑ̃te]. **1.** *v.i.* (*of river, road, etc.*) to wind, curve, meander; **rivière qui serpente dans la vallée,** river that meanders through the valley; **le chemin monte, descend, en serpentant,** the road winds up, down, the hill. **2.** *v.tr. Nau:* to snake (two ropes).

serpentiforme [sɛrpɑ̃tifɔrm], *a.* serpentiform, snakelike; **anneaux serpentiformes,** snake rings (of fishing rod).

serpentin, -ine [sɛrpɑ̃tɛ̃, -in]. **1.** *a.* (*a*) serpentine (line, dance, etc.); *F:* **langue serpentine,** scandal-monger, backbiter; *Equit:* (*of horse*) **avoir la langue serpentine,** to roll the tongue; (*b*) **marbre s.,** serpentine (marble), ophite. **2.** *s.m.* (*a*) worm (of still, etc.); coil (of tubing); **s. métallique,** coil of metal piping; *Ind:* **s. plat,** pancake coil; **s. plafonnier,** overhead coil; **s. de réchauffage,** heating coil; *Petroleum Ind:* **s. de craquage,** cracking coil; **roue serpentine,** worm wheel; (*b*) paper streamer (as used at fêtes); (*c*) *A.Artil:* serpentine; **orgue à serpentins,** organ gun; (*d*) *A.Sm.a:* (lever) serpentine. **3.** *s.f.* **serpentine:** (*a*) *Geol:* serpentine (marble, stone); *Miner:* serpentine, ophite; (*b*) *Bot:* snake wood; (*c*) *Equit:* serpentine.

serpentineux, -euse [sɛrpɑ̃tinø, -øːz], *a. Geol:* serpentinous.

serpentinisation [sɛrpɑ̃tinizasjɔ̃], *s.f. Geol:* serpentinization.

serpentueux, -euse [sɛrpɑ̃tɥø, -øːz], *a. A:* serpentiform, snakelike.

serper [sɛrpe], *v.tr. & i. Nau:* to heave up the anchor (by hand or by means of pulley blocks).

serpette [sɛrpɛt], *s.f. Hort:* (*a*) pruning knife; (*b*) billhook.

serpiérite [sɛrpjerit], *s.f. Miner:* serpierite.

serpigineux, -euse [sɛrpiʒinø, -øːz], *a. Med:* serpiginous.

serpigo [sɛrpigo], *s.m. A.Med:* serpigo.

serpillière [sɛrpijɛːr], *s.f.* **1.** (*a*) *Tex:* packing cloth; sacking; (*b*) *Dom.Ec:* floorcloth. **2.** (tradesman's) apron. **3.** winding sheet (made of sacking).

serpillon [sɛrpijɔ̃], *s.m.* = SERPETTE.

serpolet [sɛrpɔlɛ], *s.m. Bot:* wild thyme; mother of thyme.

serpule [sɛrpyl], *s.f. Ann:* serpula.

serradelle [sɛradɛl], *s.f. Bot:* serradilla, serradella.

serrage [sɛraːʒ], *s.m. Tchn:* **1.** securing, tightening (of knot, screw, etc.); screwing tight (of nut, etc.); screwing down (of packing); clamping (of joint, etc.); driving in (of screw); grip, holding (of chuck); *Rail:* accidental application of automatic brake; **s. des freins,** application of the brakes; braking; **s. à chaud,** shrinking on (of tyre on wheel, etc.); *Typ:* **s. des formes,** locking up of the formes; **outil de s.,** holding device; **clef de s.,** wedge key; **collier de s.,** clamping-band; *Aut:* hoseclip; **vis de s.,** set-screw, clamping-screw, locking-screw; **écrou de s.,** adjusting-nut; hold-down nut. **2.** *Tchn:* depth of cut (in one rotation of the workpiece). **3.** *Min:* balk.

serran [sɛrɑ̃], *s.m. Ich:* serranid, sea bass.

serranides [sɛranid], *s.m.pl.*, **serranidés** [sɛranide], *s.m.pl. Ich:* Serranidae.

serrasalme [sɛrasalm], *s.m. Ich:* serrasalmo, serrasalmus.

serrate [sɛrat], *a. Num:* deeply indented, serrate; **monnaie s.,** serrated (Roman) coins.

serration [sɛrasjɔ̃], *s.f. Mec.E:* serration (on shaft and collar).

serratule [sɛratyl], *s.f. Bot:* saw-wort, serratula.

serre [sɛːr], *s.f.* **1.** (*a*) greenhouse, conservatory, glasshouse; **s. chaude,** hothouse; **grande s.,** winter garden; **s. de palmiers,** palm house; **plantes de s. chaude,** hothouse plants, stove plants; **plantes sous s.,** plants under glass; (*b*) woodshed. **2.** pressing, squeezing (of grapes, etc.). **3.** (*a*) grip; **avoir la s. bonne,** (i) to have a strong grip; (ii) to be close-fisted; (iii) (*of spiteful pers.*) to have sharp claws; (*b*) *pl.* claws, talons (of bird of prey); (*c*) clip; *Surg:* **s. fine,** suture forceps; clip. **4.** *N.Arch:* (*a*) stringer; (*b*) beam clamp. **5.** *Metall:* (*a*) mould press; (*b*) (*action of*) ramming (the sand of a mould). **6.** *Fish:* crawl, pen. **7.** *Ph.Geog:* long narrow ridge.

serré [sere, se-], *a.* (*a*) tight (boots, clothes, knot, screw, etc.); close (texture); compact, serried, dense (ranks); narrow (defile, pass); **s. à la main,** hand-tight; **tissu s.,** closely woven fabric; **bois s.,** close-grained wood; **ressort (à boudin) à spires serrées,** close-wound spring; **pluie serrée,** teeming rain; **deux pages d'une écriture serrée,** two closely written pages; **oignons plantés en rangs serrés,** close-set onions; *For:* **peuplement s.,** dense crop; **dents serrées,** close-set teeth; **les dents serrées, les lèvres serrées,** with clenched teeth, with tight lips; **maisons serrées,** houses huddled together; **voyager serrés dans une voiture,** to travel boxed up in a carriage; **serrés comme des harengs, des sardines,** packed (in) like sardines; **avoir le cœur s.,** to be sad at heart, to have a heavy heart; *s.a.* GORGE 2, VENTRE 1; **surveillance serrée,** close supervision; **logique, traduction, serrée,** close reasoning, close translation; **étude serrée (d'un texte),** intensive study (of a text); **style s.,** concise style; *Mil:* **en ligne serrée,** in close order; *Navy:* **à distance serrée,** in close order; *s.a.* COURIR 1; **lutte serrée,** close struggle; *Rac: etc:* **arrivée serrée,** close finish; *W.Tel:* **accord s.,** sharp tuning; (*b*) *O:* close-fisted, avaricious (person); (*c*) *Equit:* **cheval s. du devant,** knock-kneed horse; **cheval s. du derrière,** cow-hocked horse; *Ven:* **cerf à tête serrée,** stag with narrow span (between beams); *Vet:* (*of horse*) **être atteint de pied s.,** to suffer from binding. **2.** *adv.* (*a*) *O:* **mordre s.,** to bite hard; **geler s.,** to freeze hard; **mentir s.,** to lie consistently, unblushingly; (*b*) **jouer s.,** to play a cautious game; to take no chances.

serre-bauquière [sɛrbokjɛːr], *s.m. N.Arch:* beam clamp; *pl. serre-bauquières.*

serre-bosse [sɛrbɔs], *s.m. Nau:* shank-painter; *pl. serre-bosses.*

serre-câble [sɛrkɑːbl̩], *s.m. Nau: Tchn:* cable clamp, wire-rope clip; *pl. serre-câbles.*

serrée [sere], *s.f. Min:* nip.

serre-écrou [sɛrekru], *s.m.inv. Tls:* bolt spanner; nut setter.

serre-file [sɛrfil], *s.m.* **1.** *Mil:* (*a*) file closer; (*b*) serrefile; **marcher en s.-f.,** to march serrefile; **officiers en s.-f.,** serrefile officers. **2.** *Navy:* sternmost ship, rear ship (of a line ahead); *pl. serre-files.*

serre-fils [sɛrfil], *s.m.inv. El:* binding-screw (of terminal); clamp; binding-post; *Tg:* connector.

serre-fine [sɛrfin], *s.f. Surg:* suture forceps; *pl. serre-fines.*

serre-flan [sɛrflɑ̃], *s.m. Mec.E:* blank holder; *pl. serre-flans.*

serre-frein [sɛrfrɛ̃], *s.m.*, **serre-freins,** *s.m.inv.* **1.** *Rail:* brakesman. **2.** *Mec.E:* brake tightener, brake adjuster; *pl. serre-freins.*

serre-garniture [sɛrgarnityːr], *s.m. Mch: etc:* gland (of packing box); *pl. serre-garnitures.*

serre-joint(s) [sɛrʒwɛ̃], *s.m.inv. Tls:* (joiner's) cramp, cramp frame; screw clamp; (shipwright's) wring bolt; *pl. serre-joints.*

serre-livres [sɛrliːvr], *s.m.inv.* book ends.

serrement [sɛrmɑ̃], *s.m.* **1.** squeezing, pressure; **s. de main,** hand pressure, hand squeeze; handshake, grip of the hand; **s. de cœur,** pang. **2.** *Min:* dam, partition (to keep out water).

serrément [seremɑ̃], *adv. A:* stingily, parsimoniously.

serre-nez [sɛrne], *s.m.inv. Vet:* twitch (for horse).

serre-nœud [sɛrnø], *s.m. Surg:* (*a*) *A:* ligature tightener; (*b*) (nasal polypus) snare; *pl. serre-nœud(s).*

serre-papiers [sɛrpapje], *s.m.inv. A:* **1.** file (for papers); filing cabinet. **2.** (set of) pigeonholes. **3.** paper holder, paper clip. **4.** paperweight.

serrer [sɛre, se-], *v.tr.* **1.** to put away, stow away (sth. in drawer, cupboard, etc.); to house (corn); **s. qch. sous clef,** to lock sth. up; to lock sth. away. **2.** to press, squeeze, clasp; **s. la main à, de, qn,** to clasp s.o.'s hand, to shake hands with s.o.; **tenir qch. sans s.,** to hold sth. loosely; **s. qn entre ses bras,** to clasp s.o. in one's arms; to hug s.o.; **s. le cou à qn,** to strangle s.o.; **s. qch. dans sa main,** to grip, grasp, sth.; **s. son corset, se s. dans son corset,** to lace one's corset up tight; to squeeze one's figure; **serrée dans son corset,** tight-laced; **la taille serrée par une ceinture,** tightly belted; **se s. la ceinture,** (i) to tighten one's belt; (ii) to go without food; *F:* **tu peux te s. la ceinture,** you've had it, you can whistle for it; (*of tree*) **serré dans son écorce,** bark-bound; (*of a dog*) **s. la queue,** to hold its tail between its legs; **cela me serre le cœur,** it wrings my heart; *Equit:* **s. un cheval,** to keep a horse well in hand; *s.a.* FESSE 1, PINCE 4, POUCE 1. **3.** to tighten (knot, joint, screw, etc.); to take in (sleeve, etc.); to furl, take in (sails); to screw up, tighten (nut); to screw down (packing); to drive in (screw); to drive (on) (barrel hoop); **s. les freins,** to apply, put on, the brakes; to brake; **s. qch. dans un étau,** to grip sth. in a vice; **s. (les cordons de) sa bourse,** to tighten one's purse strings; **s. les sourcils,** to knit one's brows; **s. les dents,** to clench, set, one's teeth; *Equit:* **s. les bottes,** to grip the horse close; **s. les côtes à son cheval,** to keep a tight grip on one's horse; to urge one's horse on; *F:* **s. les côtes à qn,** to prod, jog, s.o. on; to keep s.o. at it; to keep s.o. up to scratch; **s. l'éperon à un cheval,** to put spurs to a horse; *Mus:* **en serrant,** stringendo; *s.a.* POING, VENTRE 1. **4.** to close, close up, press close together; **s. son style,** to aim at concision, to condense one's style; **s. son jeu,** (i) (at draughts) to keep one's men in close formation; (ii) *F:* to play a close game, to take no risks; *Mil:* **s. (les rangs),** to close the ranks; to close up; *Navy:* **s. la ligne,** to close the line; *Typ:* **s. les formes,** to lock up the formes; **s. une ligne,** to reduce the spaces in a line; **s. la mesure, la botte,** (i) *Fenc:* to press one's opponent; (ii) *F:* to browbeat one's opponent in an argument. **5.** to keep close to (s.o., sth.); **s. la muraille,** to hug, skirt, the wall; *Nau:* **s. la côte, la terre,** to sail along the land, to hug the shore, to keep close inshore; **s. le vent,** to haul, hug, the wind; **s. le vent de plus près (qu'un autre vaisseau),** to keep the better wind; **s. qn de près,** to follow s.o. closely; **nous étions serrés de près,** we were hard pressed; **s. une question de près,** to go closely into a question; **s. le texte de près,** to keep close to the text, to the original; **s. qn de questions,** to ply s.o. with searching questions; *Sp: Rac:* **s. un concurrent,** to jostle a competitor; *Aut:* **s. le plus près possible du trottoir,** to hug the near-side, the kerb; *P.N:* **serrez à droite!** = keep to nearside (lane)! *F:* **se s. les coudes,** to back one another up (in the face of danger).

se serrer. 1. to stand, sit, close together; to crowd; **les enfants se serrent autour de leur mère,** the children press, crowd, round their mother; **serrez-vous!** close up! sit closer! **se s. les uns contre les autres,** to huddle together; **se s. contre qn,** to snuggle up to s.o.; to cling close to s.o. **2.** to tighten, to become tighter; **ses lèvres se serrèrent,** his lips tightened; **mon cœur se serra,** my heart sank; my heart jumped into my mouth. **3.** (*a*) to squeeze, pull in, one's figure, one's waist; (*b*) *F:* to reduce one's expenses; to cut down on inessentials.

serre-rail(s) [sɛrrɑːj], *s.m.inv. Rail:* rail plate; clip.

serre-rayons [sɛrrɛjɔ̃], *s.m.inv. Tls:* (bicycle) spoke setter.

serre-tête [sɛrtɛt], *s.m.inv.* **1.** (*a*) headband; hairband; *Sp:* ear protector; scrum cap; (*b*) scarf (tied over the hair). **2.** leather helmet.

serrette [sɛrɛt], *s.f. Bot:* saw-wort.

serre-tube(s) [sɛrtyb], *s.m.inv. Mch: etc:* tube wrench, riveting clamp.

serricorne [sɛr(r)ikɔrn], *a. & s.m. Ent:* serricorn.

serriforme [sɛr(r)ifɔrm], *a.* serriform.

serron [sɛrɔ̃], *s.m. A:* seron, seroon, bale (of exotic products).

serrulé [sɛr(r)yle], *a. Nat.Hist:* serrulate(d).

serrure [sɛryːr, se-], *s.f.* lock; **s. à entailler, s. encastrée, s. à encastrer,** flush lock; **s. à larder, s. à mortaiser,** mortise lock; **s. à pêne dormant,** dead-lock; **s. à deux pênes,** two-bolt lock; **s. à ressort,** spring lock; **s. bec-de-cane,** (i) spring lock; (ii) slide-bolt; (iii) lever-handle lock; **s. demi-tour,** type of spring lock operated by means of a key from one side and a lever from the other; **s. camarde,** drawback lock; **s. à broche,** piped-key lock; **s. à combinaisons, s. secrète, à secret,** combination lock; **s. de sûreté,** safety lock; **poser une s. à une porte,** to put a lock on a door; **brouiller la s.,** to tamper with the lock; to spoil the lock; **trou de la s.,** keyhole; **faire jouer la s.,** to unlock a door, a box, etc.; *s.a.* BÉNARDE, PALASTRE, POMPE[2], 3.

serrurerie [sɛryrri, se-], *s.f.* **1.** (*a*) locksmithing, locksmithery, locksmith's trade; (*b*) the locksmith's (shop); (*c*) mechanism of a lock. **2.** (*a*) iron work, metal work; (*b*) iron working, metal working; **s. d'art,** (i) art metal-work; (ii) art metal trade; **s. de bâtiment** (i) builder's hardware; (ii) builder's hardware trade; **s. en charronnage,** (i) coachsmith work; (ii) coachsmithing; **grosse s.,** (i) heavy iron-work; (ii) heavy smithing.

serrurier [sɛryrje, se-], *s.m.* **1.** locksmith. **2.** metal worker, iron worker, ironsmith, whitesmith; **s. d'art,** art metal-worker; **s. en bâtiments,** builder's hardware merchant, iron-work contractor; **s. charron,** coachsmith.

serte [sɛrt], *s.f.* setting (of precious stones) in a bezel.

sertir [sɛrtiːr], *v.tr.* (*a*) to set (precious stone) in a bezel; (*b*) **vitres serties de plomb,** panes set in lead; (*c*) *Metalw:* to crimp; **s. une cartouche de chasse, une capsule de bouteille, etc.,** to crimp a sporting cartridge, a bottle cap, etc.; **s. à chaud,** to shrink on; **pinces à s.,** crimping pliers; **presse à s.,** crimping press.

sertissage [sɛrtisaːʒ], *s.m.* (*a*) setting (of jewels); (*b*) setting (of glass) in lead; (*c*) *Opt:* glazing; (*d*) crimping (of cartridge, tin, etc.).

sertisseur, -euse [sɛrtisœːr, -øːz]. **1.** *s.m.* (*a*) setter (of jewels); (*b*) crimping tool; (*c*) (*pers.*) crimper. **2.** *s.f. Ind:* **sertisseuse,** sealer (for tins, etc.); **sertisseuse automatique,** automatic crimper (for tinning food, etc.).

sertissure [sɛrtisyːr], *s.f.* (*a*) setting (of precious stone); bezel; (*b*) *Sm.a:* crimp, crimped rim (of sporting cartridge).

sertule [sɛrtyl], *s.m. Bot:* sertulum.

sérulé [seryle], *a. Bot:* serrulate, denticulate.

sérum [serɔm], *s.m.* (*a*) serum; **s. sanguin,** blood serum; **maladie du s.,** serum-sickness; **s. physiologique,** physiological salt solution, saline; *Med:* **s. de vérité,** truth serum, *F:* truth drug; (*b*) **s. (lactique),** whey.

sérumthérapie [serɔmterapi], *s.f.* = SÉROTHÉRAPIE.

servage [sɛrvaːʒ], *s.m.* serfdom, serfage; bondage, thraldom; bondservice.

serval [sɛrval], *s.m.* serval, bush cat, tiger cat; *pl. servals.*

servant, -ante [sɛrvɑ̃, -ɑ̃ːt]. **1.** *a.* serving; **frère s.,** lay brother; **gentilhomme s.,** gentleman-in-waiting; *s.a.* CAVALIER 2, CHEVALIER 1. **2.** *s.m.* (*a*) *Artil:* gunner; "number" (of gun crew); **s. de hausse,** sight setter; **les servants,** the gun crew; (*b*) *Ten:* server; (*c*) **s. (de messe),** server. **3.** *s.f.* **servante,** (*a*) (maid)servant, servant (girl); (**je suis votre**) **servante,** (i) (I am) at your service; (ii) *Lit: Iron:* no, thank you; I would rather not; (*b*) (i) dinner waggon; (ii) butler's tray; (iii) dumb waiter; (*c*) *Tchn:* (i) prop, support (of carriage pole, etc.); *Th:* prop; (ii) **servante d'établi,** bench vice.

serve[1] [sɛrv], *s.f. See* SERF.

serve[2], *s.f.* drinking-pond (for cattle).

Servet [sɛrvɛ], *Pr.n.m. Rel.H:* Servetus.

serveur, -euse [sɛrvœːr, -øːz], *s.* **1.** (*a*) carver (at hotel, etc.); (*b*) barman, *f.* barmaid; (*c*) (*in restaurant*) waiter, *f.* waitress. **2.** *Cards:* dealer. **3.** *Ten:* server.

serviabilité [sɛrvjabilite], *s.f.* obligingness, willingness to help.

serviable [sɛrvjabl̩], *a.* obliging, willing to help.

serviablement [sɛrvjablmɑ̃], *adv.* obligingly, willingly.

service [sɛrvis], *s.m.* **1.** (*a*) (domestic, etc.) service; **entrer en s.,** to go into service; **se mettre, entrer, au s. de qn,** to go into s.o.'s service; **prendre qn à son s.,** to take s.o. into one's service; **gens de s.,** domestic staff; **être au s. de qn,** to be in s.o.'s service, in attendance on s.o.; to attend s.o. (**en qualité de,** as); to be under s.o.; **mourir au s. du roi,** to die in the king's service; **escalier de s.,** backstairs; **porte de s.,** tradesmen's entrance, back door; (*b*) attendance, service (in hotel, restaurant, etc.); **s. compris,** service included, inclusive of service; **s. non compris,** service not included, exclusive of service; **ajouter à la note 10% pour le s.,** to add 10% to the bill for service; **libre s.,** self-service (in restaurant, shop, etc.); *Com:* **s. après vente,** after-sales service; (*c*) *Adm:* **s. contractuel,** contract service; **indications de s.,** service instructions; **nécessités de s.,** service requirements; *Adm: Mil:* **états de s.,** service record; *Tp:* **communication, conversation, de s.,** service call; *Mil: Navy:* **s. militaire (obligatoire),** (compulsory) military service; **s. volontaire,** voluntary service; **s. armé,** general service, combatant service; **s. auxiliaire,** limited service, non-combatant service; **s. actif,** service with the colours; **en s. actif, en activité de s.,** on the active list; **service(s) de guerre,** active service; **en s. aux armées,** on active service; **s. dans la, les, réserve(s),** service in the reserve; **être apte au, bon pour le, s.,** to be fit for service; **être inapte au s.,** to be unfit for service; **être libéré du s.,** to be discharged; **libération du s.,** army discharge; **faire son (temps de) s.,** to do one's national, military, service; **s. à bord, s. à la mer,** service afloat, sea service; **s. au port,** harbour service; **avoir du s.,** to have seen service; **avoir vingt ans de service(s),** to have served twenty years; **au s.,** in the service; **être appelé au s.,** to be called up; **entrer au s.,** to enter the service, to go into the army; **prendre du s. dans l'armée,** to enlist (in the army); (*d*) *Jur:* **s. foncier,** easement charge (on real estate); *Fin:* **s. des intérêts,** interest charges; *Publ:* **faire à qn le s. d'une publication,** to put s.o. on the free list for a publication; (*e*) (religious) service; (*f*) *Sp:* (i) *Cr:* bowling; (ii) *Ten:* service; **s. au-dessus de la**

tête, overhand service; s. par en dessous, underhand service; s. coupé américain, American service; s. canon, cannon-ball service; au s., Martin, Martin to serve. 2. duty; *Adm:* s. actif, outdoor duty; s. sédentaire, indoor duty; *Adm: Mil:* s. courant, current, routine, duty; normal, ordinary, routine; daily, everyday, routine; s. de jour, day duty; s. de nuit, night duty, *Navy:* orders for the night; être de s., to be on duty; ne pas être de s., to be off duty; être exempt de s., to be excused from duty; tableau de s., duty chart, list, roster; tour de s., tour of duty; à quelle heure prenez-vous, quittez-vous, votre s.? at what time do you go on duty; off duty? en dehors du s. je suis libre, when I am off duty I am free; *Mil: Navy:* s. commandé, duty covered by orders; en s. commandé, (when) on duty; mort en s. commandé, killed on active service; s. de corvée, *Mil:* fatigue duty; *Navy:* duty; s. de garde, guard duty; s. de veille, watch duty; s. de garnison, garrison duty; s. intérieur, service in barracks and quarters; planton de s., duty orderly; officier, sous-officier, de s., duty officer, non-commissioned officer; *F:* être s. s., to be a stickler for rules and regulations. 3. branch, department, service; (a) *Adm:* s. administratif, (i) administrative service; (ii) administrative, public, authority; services administratifs, administrative department; chef de s., head of department, *U.S:* executive; s. central, headquarters; s. du personnel, personnel department; appointments department; les services actifs, outdoor staff, establishment; les services sédentaires, indoor staff, establishment; s. de renseignements, enquiry office, department, *Tp:* directory enquiries; les services publics, public utilities, *U.S:* utilities; entreprise de s. public, public utility undertaking; s. des eaux, water supply; s. de fourniture du courant électrique, electric supply service; s. des postes, s. postal, postal service, mail service; s. des douanes, s. douanier, customs service; s. gouvernemental, government agency; correspondance de s., official correspondence; *Sw.Fr:* s. du feu, fire service; (b) *Mil:* s. de l'intendance = Royal Army Service Corps (R.A.S.C.), *U.S:* quartermaster corps; s. de l'habillement, army clothing department; s. de la solde = Royal Army Pay Corps (R.A.P.C.), *U.S:* finance department; s. des fournitures, procurement or supply service; s. de la poste aux armées, army postal service; s. du matériel = Royal Army Ordnance Corps (R.A.O.C.), *U.S:* ordnance service; *Mil: etc:* s. des renseignements, intelligence (service); *Navy:* bureau du s. intérieur, commander's office; (c) *Med: etc:* services sociaux, services d'assistance sociale, the social services; s. de (la) santé, s. médical, medical service, health service; s. de santé publique, public health service; s. de santé militaire, army medical corps, service; s. hospitalier, hospital service, department, ward; s. de chirurgie, surgical department; s. de pédiatrie, pediatric service; s. des contagieux, isolation ward; s. d'hygiène, health service; les services d'hygiène (publique), administrative health authorities; s. dentaire, dental service, department; s. dentaire scolaire, school dental service, department; s. dentaire militaire, army dental corps, service; (d) *Com:* department (of firm); s. de la comptabilité, accounting, accounts, department; s. du contentieux, solicitor's department, law department; s. des expéditions, forwarding service department; dispatch department; s. de groupage (des expéditions), joint-cargo service, department; s. de livraison, delivery service; s. des achats, purchasing department; *Fin:* s. des émissions, issue department; *Ind: etc:* s. commercial, commercial department; s. technique, technical branch; engineering department; s. de préparation des fabrications, pre-production department; s. du matériel, supply, equipment, department, *Rail:* rolling-stock department; *Tp: Trans:* s. de l'exploitation, traffic department; *Rail:* s. de la traction, loco(motive) department; s. de la voie, permanent way department; *Journ:* s. des informations (d'un journal), information service (of a newspaper). 4. (a) running (of machine, etc. by operator); s. à bras, s. manuel, hand, manual, operation; *Artil:* s. de la pièce, service of the gun; (b) use (of machine, etc.); en s., in service, in use, in operation; (*of aircraft, ship*) in commission; non en s., not in use, not in commission; aptitude au s., serviceability; en (bon) état de s., propre au s., in (good) running, working, order, fit for service, fit for use, serviceable; hors (de) s., (*of thg*) out of use, out of service, unserviceable; (*of machine, mechanism*) not working, out of gear, dead; (*of gun, etc.*) out of action; disabled (ship, etc.); *Ind:* mise hors s., outage; durée de s., service time; taux de s., service rate; mettre en s., to bring, put, introduce, into service; (*of aircraft, ship*) to put into commission; retirer du s., to withdraw from service, from use; retirer graduellement du s., to phase out; *El:* s. intermittent, permanent, intermittent, permanent, duty; ses jambes refusaient le s., his legs refused to obey him; (c) *Trans:* service (of train, liner, aircraft, etc.); assurer, faire, le s. entre . . . et . . ., to run between . . . and . . .; s. de navette, shuttle service; s. de voyageurs, de passagers, passenger service; s. aérien de voyageurs, air passenger service; s. automobile de voyageurs, motor passenger service; mettre un autobus en s., to put a bus into service; s. de chemin de fer, s. ferroviaire, railway service; s. train auto-couchettes, motorail service; car sleeper service; s. d'autorail, rail-car service; s. de paquebots, liner service; s. de cargos, de navires de charge, cargo service; s. assuré toute l'année, all the year round service; s. de marchandises, goods, freight, service; s. express, s. rapide, express service; s. de camionnage, de factage, cartage service. 5. (*service rendered*) rendre (un) s. à qn, to do s.o. a service, a good turn; rendre un bon, un mauvais, s. à qn, to do s.o. a good, a bad, turn; voulez-vous me rendre un grand s.? will you do me a great service, a great favour? les services qu'il a rendus à l'enseignement, his services to education; à votre s., at your service; qu'y a-t-il pour votre s.? can I be of any use to you? what can I do for you? cet habit m'a fait un bon s., this coat has worn well; ce livre m'a rendu grand s., this book was very useful to me; *O:* vêtements de bon s., hard-wearing clothes, serviceable clothes. 6. *Breed:* service (of stallion). 7. (a) course (of a meal); (b) *Rail: etc:* premier s., first lunch, dinner; dernier s. à deux heures, last sitting, service, at two o'clock. 8. set (of utensils, etc.); s. de table, dinner service, dinner set; s. à découper, set of carvers; s. à dessert, dessert service; s. américain, set of table mats.

servier-boy [sɛrvjebɔi], *s.m.*, **servier-table** [sɛrvjetabl̩], *s.f. Sw.Fr:* (tea) trolley; *pl. servier-boys, -tables.*

serviette [sɛrvjɛt], *s.f.* 1. (a) (table) napkin; serviette; s. de plateau, traycloth; s. d'enfant, feeder; *F:* il ne faut pas mêler les torchons avec les serviettes, oil and water won't mix; (b) s. de toilette, towel; s. sans fin, roller towel; s. hygiénique, sanitary towel, *U.S:* napkin; (c) *Arch:* s. repliée, linenfold. 2. briefcase.

serviette-éponge, *s.f.* Turkish towel; *pl. serviettes-éponges.*

servile [sɛrvil], *a.* servile. 1. *Rom.Hist:* les guerres serviles, the servile wars. 2. (a) servile, dependent (condition); (b) menial (duties); (c) cringing, base, abject; subservient; (d) slavish (imitation, imitator). 3. *Gram:* lettres serviles, servile letters.

servilement [sɛrvilmɑ̃], *adv.* servilely, abjectly, cringingly; slavishly; subserviently.

servilisme [sɛrvilism], *s.m.* servilism.

servilité [sɛrvilite], *s.f.* servility; slavishness; cringing.

servir [sɛrviːr], *v.* (*pr.p.* servant; *p.p.* servi; *pr.ind.* je sers, il sert, n. servons; *pr.sub.* je serve; *p.d.* je servais; *p.h.* je servis; *fu.* je servirai) to serve. 1. *v.i.* (a) to be useful (à qn, to s.o.); to be in use; machine qui sert depuis dix ans, machine that has been in use for ten years; la machine peut encore s., the machine is still fit for use; cela peut s. un de ces jours, it may come in handy one day; ces gants ont l'air d'avoir déjà servi, these gloves look as though they had already been worn; ce livre lui a beaucoup servi, the book has been of great use to him; appareil (de photo) toujours prêt à s., camera always ready for use; *Nau:* faire s. une voile, to fill a sail; (b) s. à qch., à faire qch., to be useful for sth., for doing sth.; le chlore sert au blanchiment de la toile, chlorine is used for bleaching linen; outil qui sert à beaucoup de choses, tool that is useful for many purposes; ne s. à rien, *A:* ne s. de rien, to be of no use; to serve no purpose; to be useless; à quoi cela sert-il? what is the good, the use, of that? *F:* à quoi sert ce truc-là? what's that gadget for? ça ne servira pas à grand-chose, that won't be much good, much use; cela ne sert qu'à l'irriter, it only irritates him; je ne vois pas à quoi sert d'apprendre ces futilités, I do not see the good of learning such rubbish; cela ne sert à rien de pleurer, it's no good crying; à un sot l'expérience ne sert à rien, *A:* ne sert de rien, experience is wasted on a fool; il fit s. les lois à l'injustice, he used the law as a cover for injustice; (c) s. à qn à, pour, faire qch.; ce canif me sert à me faire les ongles, I use this penknife to do my nails; ces bottines me servent pour patiner, these are my skating boots; (d) s. de, to serve as, be used as (s.o., sth.); les pupitres servent de tables, the desks are used as tables; les châteaux servaient d'hôpitaux, the country houses were used as hospitals; s. de prétexte, to serve as a pretext; elle lui a servi de mère, she has been a mother to him; sa fille lui sert de secrétaire, his daughter acts as his secretary; (e) *impers.* il ne sert à rien de pleurer, rien ne sert de pleurer, it is no good crying; *Prov:* rien ne sert de courir, il faut partir à point, it is no good hurrying, you must start punctually; à quoi sert de pleurer? what is the use of crying? à quoi sert qu'on l'attende? what is the use of waiting for him? 2. *v.tr.* (a) to be a servant to (s.o.); to serve (s.o.); s. Dieu, to serve God; s. sa patrie, une cause, to serve one's country, a cause; *abs.* (*motto*) "servir!", "service"; vous avez l'air d'être très bien servi, you seem to be very well looked after; je me sers moi-même, I am my own servant; ce cours d'eau sert le moulin, this stream drives the mill; (b) *abs.* to serve (in army, navy); il avait servi sous La Fayette, he had served under La Fayette; en âge de s., of military age; j'ai servi pendant la guerre, I was in the forces during the war; (c) to serve, wait on, attend to (customer, etc.); est-ce qu'on vous sert? are you being attended to? pour vous s., monsieur, at your service, sir; au dîner nous étions servis par trois domestiques, at dinner we were waited on by three servants; madame est servie, *F:* c'est servi, dinner is served, madam; *abs.* s. à table, to wait at table; *F:* en fait de pluie, nous sommes servis, as far as rain goes, we get plenty, we get all we want and more; (d) (*of tradesman*) to serve, supply (s.o. with goods); s. une livre de beurre à qn, to serve s.o. with a pound of butter; s. une rente à qn, to pay an annuity to s.o.; (*in bus*) tout le monde est servi? any more fares please? (e) to serve up, dish up, bring in (dinner, etc.); to serve (the cheese, fruit, etc.); s. un mets à qn, to set a dish before s.o., to serve s.o. with a dish; s. qch. chaud, to serve sth. up hot; nous trouvâmes un souper froid tout servi, we found a cold supper ready laid out; (f) to serve out (the fish, etc.); s. à qn d'un plat, to help s.o. to a dish; s. à boire à qn, to fill s.o.'s glass; servez-vous, help yourself; il se servit un bon quart du pâté, he helped himself to a good quarter of the pâté; *s.a.* CUILLER 1; (g) to help, assist, be of service to (s.o.); *Lit:* il m'a servi auprès du roi, he was of service to me with the king; en quoi puis-je vous s.? what can I do for you? sa mémoire l'a mal servi, his memory served him ill, played him false; s. les intérêts de qn, to further s.o.'s interests; (h) to serve (gun), to work, operate (gun, pump); (i) *Ecc:* s. la messe, to serve at mass; (j) *Ten:* to serve; s. la balle belle à qn, to serve an easy ball to s.o.; *s.a.* HAUT III, 2; *Cr:* servir la balle, to bowl; *Cards:* à vous de s., (it's) your deal; (k) *Breed:* (*of stallion*) to serve, cover (mare), (l) *Ven:* s. un animal au couteau, to dispatch an animal.

se servir. 1. se s. chez qn, to buy one's provisions, supply oneself with goods at a shop; nous nous servons toujours chez Potin, we always deal with Potin. 2. se s. de qch., de qn, to use sth., s.o.; to make use of sth., of s.o.; vous servez-vous de votre plume? are you using your pen? se s. de qn pour parler anglais, to practise one's English on s.o.; savoir se s. de . . ., to be handy with . . .; savoir, ne pas savoir, se s. de ses mains, to be good, no good, with one's hands.

serviteur [sɛrvitœːr], *s.m.* servant; *A:* s. à gages, hired servant; s. de l'État, civil servant; *A: & Lit:* votre s., (i) (*in speaking*) your servant, sir! (ii) (*in writing*) your obedient servant; personne ne le sait mieux que votre s., no one knows it better than your humble servant, than yours truly; *Lit: Iron:* (je suis votre) s., no, thank you; I would rather not.

servitude [sɛrvityd], *s.f.* 1. (a) servitude; (i) bondservice; (ii) slavery; réduire un peuple en s., to reduce a people to bondage; (b) constraint; la s. de la mode, the tyranny of fashion. 2. (a) *Jur:* easement, charge (on real estate); disability; les servitudes s'éteignent par le non-usage pendant trente ans, easements are extinguished by non-user during thirty years; servitudes défensives, militaires, conditions attaching to the ownership of land in the vicinity of military defences; **s. apparente,** apparent servitude, apparent easement; **s. de passage,** right of way; **s. de vue,** (i) = ancient lights; (ii) right to light; *F:* **servitudes d'ordre moral,** moral obligations; (b) **affranchir un appareil de la s. de qch.,** to free an apparatus from the limitations of sth.; (c) **bâtiment de s.,** (i) *Nau:* harbour craft; (ii) *Navy:* tender; *Nau:* **canot de s.,** tender; (d) *Adm:* **les servitudes,** the public utility services. **3.** *Av:* **servitudes au sol,** ground hauling services; *Aer:* **groupe de s.,** auxiliary power unit.

servo- [sɛrvo], *pref.* servo-.

servocommande [sɛrvokɔmɑ̃d], *s.f. Av: Aut: etc:* servo(-control); **excitation d'une s.,** servo input; **réponse d'une s.,** servo output; **attaqué, mû, par servocommandes hydrauliques,** operated by hydraulic servos.

servofrein [sɛrvofrɛ̃], *s.m. Aut: etc:* servo-brake.

servograisseur [sɛrvogrɛsœːr], *s.m. Aut: etc:* pressure oiler.

servomécanisme [sɛrvomekanism], *s.m. Tchn:* servomechanism; servo system; (*computers*) multiplicateur à s., servo multipler.

servomoteur [sɛrvomotœːr], *s.m. Mch:* servomotor, auxiliary motor; thrustor; **s. de gouvernail,** steering engine or gear.

sésame [sezam], *s.m. Bot:* sesame, sesamum; **s. d'Orient, de l'Inde,** gingili; *Com:* **huile de s.,** gingili oil; *Lit:* (in the "*Arabian Nights*") **s., ouvre-toi!** open, sesame!

sésamées [sezame], *s.f.pl. Bot:* Sesameae.

sésamie [sezami], *s.f. Ent:* sesamia.

sésamoïde [sezamɔid], *a. & s.m. Anat:* sesamoid (bone).

sésamoïdien, -ienne [sezamɔidjɛ̃, -jɛn], *a. Anat:* with sesamoid bones.

sesbania [sɛsbanja], **sesbanie** [sɛsbani], *s.f. Bot:* sesban, daincha, Colorado River hemp.

séséli [sezeli], *s.m. Bot:* seseli, meadow saxifrage.

sésie [sezi], *s.f. Ent:* **s. apiforme,** hornet clearwing moth; *pl.* **sésies,** the wasp moths.

sesleria [sɛslɛrja], *s.m.,* **seslérie** [sɛsleri], *s.f. Bot:* moorgrass.

sesqui- [sɛskɥi], *pref.* sesqui-.

sesquialtère [sɛskɥialtɛːr]. **1.** *a. Mth:* sesquialter(al). **2.** *s.m. or f. Mus:* sesquialtera (organ stop).

sesquibasique [sɛskɥibazik], *a. Ch:* sesquibasic.

sesquicarbonate [sɛskɥikarbɔnat], *s.m. Ch:* sesquicarbonate.

sesquifluorure [sɛskɥiflɥɔryːr], *s.m. Ch:* sesquifluoride.

sesquiiodure [sɛskɥijɔdyːr], *s.m. Ch:* sesquiiodide.

sesquioxyde [sɛskɥiɔksid], *s.m. Ch:* sesquioxide.

sesquipédale [sɛskɥipedal], *a.* sesquipedalian (word).

sesquiplan [sɛskɥiplɑ̃], *s.m. Av:* sesquiplane.

sesquisel [sɛskɥisɛl], *s.m. Ch:* sesquisalt.

sesquisulfure [sɛskɥisylfyːr], *s.m. Ch:* sesquisulfide.

sesquiterpène [sɛskɥitɛrpɛn], *s.m. Ch:* sesquiterpene.

sesquitierce [sɛskɥitjɛrs], *a. Mth: A:* sesquitertial.

sessile [sɛs(s)il], *a.* sessile (leaf, horn, tumour, etc.).

sessilifolié [sɛs(s)ilifɔlje], *a. Bot:* sessile-leaved.

sessiliventres [sɛs(s)ilivɑ̃tr], *s.m.pl. Ent:* Sessiliventres.

session [sɛsjɔ̃, se-], *s.f.* **1.** session, sitting (of Parliament, etc.). **2.** *Jur: Sch:* session, term (at law courts, universities); *Sch:* **première s., s. de juin,** summer, June, examination period; **deuxième s.,** second examination period (of the year); **s. de repêchage,** re-sits.

sesterce [sɛstɛrs], *s.m. Rom.Ant:* sestertius, sesterce; **grand s.,** sestertium.

seston [sɛstɔ̃], *s.m. Biol:* seston.

set [sɛt], *s.m.* **1.** *Ten:* set. **2.** *Cin:* set. **3.** *Dom.Ec:* **s. de table,** set of table mats.

sétacé [setase], *a.* setaceous, bristly.

sétaire [setɛːr], *s.f. Bot:* setaria.

séteux, -euse [setø, -øːz], *a. Nat.Hist:* setose.

setier [s(ə)tje], *s.m. A: Meas:* setier.

sétifère [setifɛːr], *a.* setiferous, setigerous, bristly.

sétiflore [setiflɔːr], *a. Bot:* having bristle-like petals.

sétiforme [setifɔrm], *a. Bot:* setiform; bristle-shaped.

sétigère [setiʒɛːr], *a.* = SÉTIFÈRE.

setim [setim], *s.m. B:* bois de s., shittim wood.

sétois, -oise [setwa, -waːz], *a. & s. Geog:* (native, inhabitant) of Sète.

séton [setɔ̃], *s.m.* (a) *Surg: Vet:* **s. à mèche,** seton; *Vet:* **s. en rouelle, s. à rouelle, s. anglais,** rowel; (b) **blessure en s.,** flesh wound; *s.a.* HERBE 4; (c) *Mec.E:* **coupure en s.,** skewered cut.

---

sétophage [setɔfaːʒ], *s.m. Orn:* fly-catching warbler.

setter [sɛtɛːr], *s.m. Z:* (dog) setter.

sétule [setyl], *s.f. Bot:* seta; setula.

seuil [sœːj], *s.m.* **1.** threshold; door sill, door step; **franchir le s.,** to cross the threshold; **sur le s., au s.,** on the threshold; **s'arrêter au s. du crime,** to pause on the threshold of crime, to stop short of crime; **être au s. de la célébrité,** to stand on the threshold of fame; **au s. de l'hiver,** on the edge of winter; *Pol.Ec:* **s. de rentabilité,** break-even point; *Com:* **s. de réapprovisionnement,** re-order point; *Physiol:* **s. d'élimination,** renal threshold; *Psy:* **s. de l'excitation** (d'un muscle, etc.)**, s. absolu,** stimulus threshold; threshold of response; **s. de sensibilité,** threshold of sensitivity, of response; **s. différentiel,** differential threshold; **s. de la conscience, d'excitation, s. électrique,** limen. **2.** *Geog:* (a) shelf (of ocean bed); **s. continental,** continental shelf; **s.** (sous-marin), rise; (b) sill; **le s. du Poitou,** the Poitou gate. **3.** *Hyd.E:* sill (of dry dock, lock). **4.** *Tex:* shuttle race, lay race. **5.** *Elcs:* **s. de commutation,** switching threshold; **s. de sensibilité,** input-signal threshold.

seuillet [sœje], *s.m. Tex:* shuttle race, lay race.

seul [sœl], *a.* **1.** (**seul** *preceding the noun*) only, sole, single; **un s. homme,** one man only, only one man; **il faut qu'un s. homme commande,** it is essential for one single man to command; **le gouvernement d'un s.,** absolute monarchy; **avancer comme un s. homme,** to advance as one man; **son s. exécuteur testamentaire,** his sole executor; **son s. souci,** his one, only, sole, care; **il ne suffit pas d'un s. exemple,** a single example will not suffice, no single example will suffice; **mon s. et unique faux col,** my one and only collar; **un s. mot, et je te quitte,** one word from you and I'll go; **pas un s.,** not a single one, not one, none whatever; **pas un s. n'en réchappa,** not a single person survived; **vous êtes le s. qui puissiez m'aider,** you alone can help me; **il fut le s. à nous encourager,** he was the only one who encouraged us, he alone encouraged us; *Fin:* **un s. et même emprunt,** a single loan; *s.f. Com:* **seule de change,** sole of exchange; (b) **la seule pensée m'effraie,** the thought alone frightens me; **the bare, mere, very, thought frightens me. 2.** (**seul** *following the noun or used predicatively*) alone, by oneself; on one's own; **un homme s.,** a man alone, by himself; **Hamlet s.,** Hamlet alone; **se sentir très s.,** to feel very lonely, very lonesome; (of bachelor) **être garçon s.,** to be unattached; **les jeunes filles étaient censées ne pas voyager seules,** young ladies were not supposed to travel alone, unchaperoned, without an escort; **il peut marcher tout s. maintenant,** he can walk by himself now; **parler s. à s. à qn,** to speak to s.o. alone; **ils en parlaient parfois seul à seul,** they sometimes spoke of it when alone together; **il était s. à s. avec soi-même,** he was alone with his thoughts; *Prov:* **un malheur ne vient jamais s.,** misfortunes never come singly; it never rains but it pours; **l'œuvre seule de . . .,** the exclusive work of . . .; **j'ai une cachette que moi s. connais,** I have a hiding-place which I alone know; **je l'ai fait tout s., à moi s.,** I did it (by) myself, alone, single-handed; **il dirige l'usine s.,** he manages the factory single-handed; **il est s. de son opinion,** he stands alone in his opinion; **cela va tout s.,** it is plain sailing; **cela ne va pas tout s.,** it isn't easy; things are not going smoothly; it isn't all plain sailing; **le miracle s'est fait tout s.,** the miracle came about of itself; **parler, chanter, etc., tout s.,** to talk, sing, etc., to oneself; *Mus:* **passage pour violon s.,** passage for an unaccompanied violin. **3.** (**seul** *following the noun or preceding the article or poss. adj.*) alone (*after noun*); only; **s. un homme pourrait l'entreprendre,** only a man could undertake it; **la violence seule, seule la violence, le contraindrait,** only violence, violence alone, nothing, short of violence, would compel him; **seule la chasse les fait vivre,** hunting is their only source of food; **s. un expert pourrait nous conseiller,** only an expert could advise us; **nous sommes seuls à le savoir,** we are the only people who know of it.

seulement [sœlmɑ̃], *adv.* **1.** (a) only; **nous sommes s. deux,** there are only two of us; **venir s. de faire qch.,** to have only just done sth.; **non s. . . ., mais aussi . . ., mais encore . .,** not only . . ., but also . . .; (b) solely, merely; **il y va s. pour vous faire plaisir,** he is going merely to please you; (c) *F:* **faites s.,** please do; **entrez s.,** do come in. **2.** even; **sans s. me regarder,** without even looking at me; **il ne m'a pas s. regardé,** he didn't

---

even look at me; **si s. il m'avait regardé!** if only he had looked at me! **si je pouvais s. la voir,** if I could only see her; **je n'ai pas s. le prix de mon voyage,** I haven't so much as my fare; *s.a.* SI[1]. **3.** (*with conj. force*) **je viendrais bien, s. . . .,** I should like to come, but . . ., only . . .

seulet, -ette [sœlɛ, -ɛt], *a. esp. f. Lit:* alone, lonely, lonesome; *F:* **tu es bien seulette,** you are all alone.

sève [sɛːv], *s.f.* (a) *Bot:* sap (of plant); **plein de s.,** full of sap; sappy; **sans s.,** sapless; **teneur en s.,** sappiness; (b) vigour, go; **la s. de la jeunesse,** the vigour of youth; **plein de s.,** full of vigour; (c) aromatic savour (of wine); sève.

sévère[1] [sevɛːr], *a.* severe. **1.** stern, hard, harsh (judge, etc.); **regard s.,** severe, stern, look; **beauté s.,** severe beauty; **climat s.,** hard climate; **visage froid et s.,** dour countenance; **être s. envers qn, pour qn, avec qn, pour les fautes de qn,** to be hard, on s.o., on s.o.'s failings; **mener un train s.,** to set a gruelling pace. **2.** strict, rigid (fast, censorship, discipline); **mœurs sévères,** strict morals; **architecture, style, s.,** severe architecture, style; **morale peu s.,** lax morals.

Sévère[2], *Pr.n.m. Rom.Hist:* Severus.

sévèrement [sevɛrmɑ̃], *adv.* **1.** severely, sternly, harshly; **ne le jugez pas si s.,** do not think so hardly of him; do not be so hard on him. **2.** strictly, rigidly.

Séverin [sevrɛ̃], *Pr.n.m. Ecc.Hist:* Severinus.

sévérité [severite], *s.f.* **1.** (a) severity (of sentence, punishment); sternness (of face, look); strictness (of discipline); **traiter qn avec s.,** to treat s.o. harshly, severely; (b) severity (of style, line, taste, dress). **2.** **les sévérités seraient mal venues,** any acts of severity would be ill-advised; **les sévérités de ce juge,** the harsh sentences of this judge.

séveux, -euse [sevø, -øːz], *a. Bot:* sappy, full of sap.

sévices [sevis], *s.m.pl. Jur:* maltreatment (**envers,** of); brutality, cruelty (**envers,** to(wards)) (*usu.* within the home circle).

sévillan, -ane [sevijɑ̃, -an], *a. & s. Geog:* Sevill(i)an.

Séville [sevil], *Pr.n. Geog:* Seville.

sévir [seviːr], *v.i.* **1.** **s. contre qn,** to deal severely with s.o.; to treat s.o. rigorously; **s. contre un abus,** to deal severely with an abuse. **2.** (of war) to rage; (of poverty, heresy) to be rife, rampant; **la crise qui sévit actuellement,** the present acute crisis; **le froid sévissait,** the cold was severe; **le froid qui sévit en ce moment,** the prevailing cold spell.

sevrage [səvraːʒ], *s.m.* **1.** weaning; *Med:* **symptômes de s.,** withdrawal symptoms. **2.** *Hort:* separating, (of layer, scion, from plant in grafting by approach).

sevrer [səvre], *v.tr.* (je sèvre, n. sevrons; je sèvrerai) **1.** to wean (child, lamb); **s. qn de ses droits, de distractions,** to deprive s.o. of his rights, of amusements. **2.** *Hort:* to separate (layer, scion, from plant in grafting by approach).

Sèvres [sɛːvr]. **1.** *Pr.n. Geog:* Sèvres. **2.** *s.m. Cer:* **du s., service de s.,** (set of) Sèvres porcelain; **vieux s.,** old Sèvres; pre-Revolution Sèvres porcelain.

sevreuse [səvrøːz], *s.f. A:* weaning nurse, dry nurse.

sévrien, -enne [sevri(j)ɛ̃, -(j)ɛn]. **1.** *a. & s. Geog:* (native, inhabitant) of Sèvres. **2.** *s.f.* **sévrienne,** student at or former student of the *École normale de Sèvres*.

sexage [sɛksaːʒ], *s.m.* sorting (of poultry) according to sex.

sexagénaire [sɛgazenɛːr], *a. & s.m. & f.* sexagenarian.

sexagésimal, -aux [sɛgazezimal, -o], *a.* sexagesimal; *Mth:* **fractions sexagésimales,** sexagesimal fractions, astronomical fractions; sexagesimals.

Sexagésime [sɛgazezim], *s.f.* Sexagesima (Sunday).

sex-appeal [sɛksapil], *s.m. F:* sex appeal.

sexdigitaire [sɛksdiʒitɛːr], *a.,* **sexdigital, -aux** [sɛksdiʒital, -o], *a.* sexdigital, sexdigitate, six-fingered, six-toed (hand, foot).

sexdigité [sɛksdiʒite], *a.* sexdigitate, sexdigitated.

sexdigitisme [sɛksdiʒitism], *s. Ter:* sexdigitism.

sexe [sɛks], *s.m.* **1.** sex; **le s. fort,** the strong sex, the male sex; **enfant du s. masculin, féminin,** male child, female child; **le (beau) s., le s. faible,** the fair sex; the weaker sex. **2.** external sex organs; genitals.

sexennal, -aux [sɛksɛn(n)al, -o], *a.* sexennial.

sexfide [sɛksfid], *a. Bot:* sex(i)fid.

sexifère [sɛksifɛːr], *a. Bot:* sexiferous.
sexjugué [sɛksʒyge], *a. Bot:* sejugous.
sexloculaire [sɛkslɔkylɛːr], *a. Bot:* sexlocular.
sexologie [sɛksɔlɔʒi], *s.f.* sexology.
sexologique [sɛksɔlɔʒik], *a.* sexological.
sexologue [sɛksɔlɔg], *s.m. & f.* sexologist.
sexonomie [sɛksɔnɔmi], *s.f. Biol:* study of sex determination.
sexpartite [sɛkspartit], *a. Arch:* **voûte s.,** sexpartite vault.
sex-ratio [sɛksrasjo], *s.f.* sex ratio.
sextans [sɛkstɑ̃ːs], *s.m. Rom.Num:* sextans.
sextant [sɛkstɑ̃], *s.m.* **1.** *Mth: Nau:* sextant. **2.** *Astr:* **le S.,** Sextans.
sexte [sɛkst], *s.f. Ecc:* sext.
sextidi [sɛkstidi], *s.m. Fr.Hist:* (Republican calendar) sixth day of a decade.
sextil [sɛkstil], *a. Astrol:* sextile (aspect, etc.).
sextillion [sɛkstiljɔ̃], *s.m.* **1.** (*since 1948*) sextillion (10^{36}); *U.S:* decillion. **2.** (*before 1948*) a thousand trillions (10^{21}); *U.S:* sextillion.
sextine [sɛkstin], *s.f. Pros:* sestina.
sexto [sɛksto], *adv.* (*in a series*) sixthly.
sextolet [sɛkstɔlɛ], *s.m. Mus:* sextuplet.
sextuor [sɛkstɥɔːr], *s.m. Mus:* sextet(te).
sextuple [sɛkstypl̩], *a. & s.m.* sextuple; sixfold; **il me l'a rendu au s., he repaid me sixfold; douze est le s. de deux,** twelve is six times as much as two.
sextuplé, -ée [sɛkstyple], *s.* sextuplet.
sextupler [sɛkstyple]. **1.** *v.tr.* to sextuple (a number). **2.** *v.tr. & i.* to increase sixfold.
sexualiser [sɛksɥalize], *v.tr.* to sexualize.
sexualisme [sɛksɥalism], *s.m.* sexualism.
sexualité [sɛksɥalite], *s.f.* sexuality.
sexué [sɛksɥe]. **1.** *a.* sexed (plant, statue, etc.). **2.** *s.m.pl. Ent:* (*of termites, etc.*) **les sexués,** the royal pair.
sexuel, -elle [sɛksɥɛl], *a.* sexual; **caractères sexuels,** sexual characteristics; **rapports sexuels illicites,** unlawful sexual relations.
sexupare [sɛksypaːr], *a. Ent:* sexuparous.
sexvalent [sɛksvalɑ̃], *a. Ch:* hexavalent, sexivalent.
sexy [sɛksi], *a.inv. P:* sexy.
seyant [sɛjɑ̃], *a.* becoming (garment, colour); **coiffure très seyante,** very becoming hair style.
seymouria [semurja], *s.m. Rept:* seymouria.
sézigue [seziːg], *s.m. P:* oneself, him(self), her(self).
sfakiote [sfakjɔt], *a. & s.m. & f. Geog:* (native, inhabitant) of Sfax [sfaks].
sfumato [sfumato], *s.m. Art:* sfumato.
Sganarelle [sganarɛl], *s.m. Lit:* cuckold (*from character in several of Molière's plays*).
sgraffite [sgrafit], *s.m. Art:* (s)graffito.
shaddock [ʃadɔk], *s.m. Bot:* shaddock tree.
shah [ʃa], *s.m.* shah.
shake-hand [ʃɛk(h)ɑ̃d], *s.m.inv. A:* handshake; **il distribua des s.,** he shook hands all round.
shaker [ʃɛkɛːr, -œːr], *s.m.* cocktail shaker.
shak(e)spearien, -ienne [ʃɛkspirjɛ̃, -jɛn], *a.* Shakespearian.
shako [ʃako], *s.m. Mil:* shako.
shama [ʃama], *s.m. Orn:* shama.
shamisen [ʃamizɛn], *s.m. Mus:* samisen, shamisen.
shampooing [ʃɑ̃pwɛ̃], *s.m.* **1.** (*action*) shampoo; **faire, donner, un s. à qn,** to shampoo s.o.'s hair; **s. et mise en plis,** shampoo and set; **se faire un s.,** to shampoo one's hair; to wash one's hair. **2.** (*product*) shampoo; **s. liquide,** liquid shampoo; **s. en poudre,** shampoo powder; **s. sec,** dry shampoo.
shampouineuse [ʃɑ̃pwinøːz], *s.f.* shampooer.
Shanghaï [ʃɑ̃gai], *Pr.n.m. Geog:* Shanghai.
shanghaier [ʃɑ̃gaje], *v.tr.* to shanghai.
shant(o)ung [ʃɑ̃tuŋ], *s.m. Tex:* shantung.
sharpie [ʃarpi], *s.m. Nau:* sharpie, sharpy.
shaving [ʃɛviŋ], *s.m. Metalw:* shaving.
shed [ʃɛd], *s.m. Const:* (**toit en**) **s.,** saw-tooth roof (of factory, etc.).
sheik [ʃɛk], *s.m.* sheik.
shellac [ʃɛlak], *s.m. Ch:* shellac(k).
shepherdia [ʃɛfɛrdja], *s.m. Bot:* buffalo berry, buffalo bush.
shérardie [ʃerardi], *s.f.*, **shérarde** [ʃerard], *s.f. Bot:* sherardia; **s. des champs,** field madder.
shérardisation [ʃerardizasjɔ̃], *s.f. Metalw:* sherardizing.
shérardiser [ʃerardize], *v.tr. Metalw:* to sherardize (with zinc dust).
shérif [ʃerif], *s.m.* (*a*) *Eng.Adm:* sheriff; (*b*) *U.S:* sheriff.
sherpa [ʃɛrpa], *s. Ethn:* Sherpa.
Shetland [ʃɛtlɑ̃ːd], *Pr.n.m.* **1.** *Geog:* **les (îles) S.,** the Shetland Islands, the Shetlands. **2.** *s.m. Tex:* Shetland.
shetlandais, -aise [ʃɛtlɑ̃dɛ, -ɛːz], *Geog:* **1.** *a.* Shetland(ic); **poney s.,** Shetland pony. **2.** *s.* Shetlander.
shibboleth [ʃibɔlɛt], *s.m.* shibboleth.
shift [ʃift], *s.m.* (*esp. for dockers*) shift; **le premier s. va de sept heures à midi,** the first shift is from seven o'clock to midday.
shilling [ʃiliŋ], *s.m.* shilling.
shimmy [ʃimi], *s.m.* **1.** *Danc:* shimmy (shake). **2.** *Aut:* (front-wheel) wobble; shimmy.
shinto [ʃɛ̃to], *s.m.* Shintoism.
shintoïque [ʃɛ̃tɔik], *a.* Shinto, Shintoistic.
shintoïsme [ʃɛ̃tɔism], *a.m.* Shintoism.
shintoïste [ʃɛ̃tɔist]. **1.** *a.* Shinto, Shintoistic. **2.** *s.m. & f.* Shintoist.
shirting [ʃirtɛ̃ːg], *s.m. Tex:* shirting.
shoddy [ʃɔdi], *s.m. Tex:* shoddy.
shogoun [ʃɔgun], *s.m. Japanese Hist:* shogun.
shogounal, -aux [ʃɔgunal, -o], *a. Japanese Hist:* shogunal (dynasty, etc.).
shogunat [ʃɔguna], *s.m. Japanese Hist:* shogunate.
shoot [ʃut], *s.m. Fb:* shot; **s. au but,** shot (at goal).
shooter [ʃute], *v.i. Fb:* to shoot.
shooting [ʃutiŋ], *s.m. Sp:* (pigeon, etc.) shooting, shoot.
shopping [ʃɔpiŋ], *s.m.* shopping; **faire du s.,** to go shopping.
shorea [ʃɔrea], *s.m. Bot:* shorea.
short [ʃɔrt], *s.m. Cost:* shorts.
shortia [ʃɔrtja], *s.m. Bot:* shortia.
show [ʃo], *s.m.* music-hall, cabaret, show featuring one artist in particular.
shrapnel(l) [ʃrapnɛl], *s.m. Mil:* shrapnel shell.
shunt [ʃœ̃ːt], *s.m.* (*a*) *El:* shunt; **s. de masse,** ground shunt; *W.Tel:* **s. de grille,** grid leak; (*b*) *Surg:* shunt.
shuntage [ʃœ̃taːʒ], *s.m. El:* shunting.
shunter [ʃœ̃te], *v.tr. El:* to shunt (circuit, ammeter); **condensateur shunté (par une résistance),** condenser with a shunt resistance.
si[1] [si], *conj.* (*by elision* **s'** *before* **il, ils**) **1.** if; (*a*) **je ne sortirai pas s'il pleut,** I shall not go out if it rains; **j'irai avec toi, si tu crois que je le doive,** I will go with you if you think I ought to; **si on ne le surveille pas, il s'échappera,** unless he is watched he will escape; **s'il n'avait pas plu, nous serions partis,** if it had not rained, had it not rained, we should have started; **s'il avait vécu,** *Lit:* **s'il eût vécu, de notre temps, il eût été sénateur,** if he had lived in our time, he would have been a senator; **s'il vient, vous m'avertirez,** if he comes, you will let me know; **s'il venait, vous m'avertiriez,** if he should come, you would let me know; **j'aurais été soldat, si je n'étais poète,** I would have been a soldier, if I were not, were I not, a poet; **si j'avais su,** had I but known; **il l'aurait fait s'il n'eût manqué de courage,** he would have done it if he had not lacked courage; **si ce n'est toi, c'est donc ton frère,** if it is not you, then it is your brother; **qui le fera si ce n'est moi?** who will do it unless I do? **votre article est très bien si ce n'est qu'il pourrait être un peu plus court,** your article is very good except that it might be a little shorter; **si ce n'était que je l'ai vu moi-même . . .,** if I hadn't seen it myself . . .; **si ce n'était mon rhumatisme, je vous accompagnerais,** were it not, if it weren't, for my rheumatism, I would go with you; **s'ils avaient un chef qui eût de l'énergie . . .,** if they had a leader with some energy . . .; **s'ils avaient un chef capable et qui eût de l'énergie . . .,** if they had a capable leader, and a man of energy . . .; **s'il fait beau et si je suis libre je sortirai; s'il fait beau et que je sois libre je sortirai,** if the weather is fine and (if) I am free, I shall go out; **s'il m'a oublié et refuse de me recevoir . . .,** if he has forgotten me and refuses to see me . . .; *s.a.* DE II 2, QUE[3] 6, TANT 1; **si je ne me trompe,** if I am not mistaken; **si seulement je pouvais . . .!** if only I could . . .! **si seulement j'avais un véritable chez-moi!** if only I had a real home! **si seulement j'étais à Paris!** if only I were in Paris! **si tant est que** + *sub.*, if so it be that . . .; *B:* **si le grain ne meurt . . .,** except a corn of wheat die . . .; *A. & Lit:* **que si je vous ai offensé, j'en ai un profond regret,** if I have offended you, I regret it deeply; (*b*) (*concessive*) **s'il fut sévère, il fut juste,** if he was severe, he was just; **si je me plains, c'est que j'en ai sujet,** if I complain, I have good cause; **s'il est malheureux et s'il a des ennuis, c'est bien de sa faute,** if he is unhappy and in trouble, it is entirely his own fault; **si ce n'est pas le navire le plus grand du monde, ce n'en est pas moins le plus connu,** while it isn't the largest ship in the world, it is none the less the most famous; **ce fut à peine s'il put distinguer l'heure à sa montre,** he could scarcely see the hands of his watch; **c'est tout au plus si l'on peut compter jusqu'à vingt femmes dans la salle,** at the most there are only about twenty women in the hall; **le père Martin, (un) brave homme s'il en fut,** old Martin, a worthy man if ever there was one. **2.** whether, if; **je me demande si c'est vrai, s'il viendra,** I wonder whether, if, it is true, whether, if, he will come; **je lui demandai s'il était marié et s'il avait des enfants,** I asked him whether he was married, and if he had a family; *Lit:* **est-ce bien lui? ou si mes yeux me trompent!** is it he, or do my eyes deceive me? *F:* **vous connaissez Paris?—si je connais Paris!** you know Paris?—of course, I know Paris! don't I just know Paris! *P:* **si c'est pas malheureux de voir ça!** isn't it dreadful to see that! **3.** how, how much; **pensez si j'étais furieux!** you can imagine how angry I was! **vous savez si je vous aime,** you know how I love you. **4.** what if, suppose; **et si elle l'apprend,** and what if she hears of it? **si nous changions de sujet?** suppose we change the subject? **si on faisait une partie de bridge?** what do you say to a game of bridge? what about a game of bridge? **5.** *s.m.* **tes si et tes mais,** your ifs and buts; **c'est un homme qui n'a ni si ni mais,** he's a plain downright fellow; *Prov:* **avec des si on mettrait Paris en bouteille,** if ifs and ands were pots and pans there'd be no use, no need, no trade, for tinkers.
si[2], *adv.* **1.** so, so much; (*a*) **ne courez pas si vite,** don't run so fast; **il est si faible que . . .,** he is so weak that . . .; so weak is he that . . .; **un si bon dîner,** such a good dinner, so good a dinner; **de si bons dîners,** such good dinners; **il n'est pas si à plaindre que cela,** he is not so much to be pitied as all that; **il n'est pas si sévère qu'il en devienne cruel,** he is not so severe as to become cruel; **il n'est si bonne compagnie qui ne se sépare** (*sub.*), the best of friends must part; **ce n'est pas si facile,** it's not so easy; *Iron:* **il n'est pas vraiment riche—si peu!** he isn't really rich—not much! (*b*) (= AUSSI *in negative clause*) **il n'est pas si beau que vous,** he is not as handsome, not so handsome, as you; (*c*) (*still used* = AUSSI *in affirmative clause in the phrs.*) **donnez-m'en si peu que vous voudrez, si peu que rien,** give me the smallest little bit (or drop); give me just a (very) little; (*d*) **si bien que . . .,** with the result that . . .; **il dépensa sans regarder, si bien qu'en fin de compte il fut ruiné,** he spent recklessly so that in the end he was ruined. **2.** (*concessive*) **si . . . que** + *sub.*, however; **si jeune qu'il soit,** however young he may be; young as he is; **aucun médecin, si habile soit-il . . .,** no doctor, however capable he is . . .; **si peu que ce soit,** (i) however little it may be; (ii) ever so little; **votre méthode, si parfaite soit-elle . . .,** your method, however perfect in itself . . .; **si bien qu'il s'y prenne . . .,** however skilfully he sets about it . . . . **3.** (*a*) (*in answer to a neg. question*) yes; **si fait,** yes indeed; **ne m'avez-vous pas entendue?—si (fait), madame,** didn't you hear me?—yes, I did, ma'am; **ça ne fait rien.—si, ça fait quelque chose,** it doesn't matter.—it *does* matter! **il n'est pas parti?—si, je crois que si,** he hasn't gone?—yes, he has; yes, I think he has; **mais si, je l'ai vu,** I *did* see him; **vous n'y parviendrez pas—je parie que si!** you won't manage it—I bet you I do! **il ne s'en remettra pas—que si!** he will not get over it—of course, he will! yes, he will! (*b*) *F:* (*after expression of doubt*) **tu t'en souviens, je pense?—oui, peut-être . . .—mais si, bien sûr . . .,** you remember it, I should think?—yes, perhaps . . .—yes, of course; (*to stress affirmative after a negation*) **vous en voulez?—non—mais si—**do have some?—no, thank you—oh, do. **4.** *A:* (= AINSI) **si veut le roi,** such is the will of the king; **si veut le roi, si veut la loi,** the king's will is law.
si[3], *s.m.inv. Mus:* **1.** (the note) B; **morceau en si,** piece in B; **en si bémol,** in B flat. **2.** si (in the fixed do system).
sial [sjal], *s.m. Geol:* sial.
sialadénite [sjaladenit], *s.f. Med:* sialadenitis.
sialagogue [sjalagɔg], *a. & s.m. Pharm:* sialagogue, sialagogic.
sialie [sjali], *s.f. Orn:* (American) bluebird.
sialidés [sjalide], *s.m.pl. Ent:* Sialidae.
sialis [sjalis], *s.m. Ent:* sialid; (*genus*) Sialis.
sialisme [sjalism], *s.m. Med:* sialorrhoea.
sialo- [sjalɔ], *pref. Med:* sialo-.
sialodochite [sjalɔdɔkit], *s.f. Med:* sialodochitis.
sialographie [sjalɔgrafi], *s.f. Med:* sialography.
sialorrhée [sjalɔre], *s.f. Med:* sialorrhoea, slavering.

Siam [sjam], *Pr.n.m. Geog:* Siam; **le haut, le bas, S.,** Upper, Lower, Siam; **le golfe de S.,** the Gulf of Siam.
siamang [sjamɑ̃], *s.m. Z:* **(gibbon) s.,** siamang.
siamois, -oise [sjamwa, -waːz]. **1.** *a. & a. Geog:* Siamese; **chat s.,** Siamese cat; **s. bleu,** blue-point Siamese; **frères s., sœurs siamoises,** Siamese twins. **2.** *s.f. Furn:* **siamoise,** conversation chair. **3.** *s.m. Ling:* **le s.,** Siamese.
Sibérie [siberi], *Pr.n.f. Geog:* Siberia; **chien de S.,** Siberian dog.
sibérien, -ienne [siberjɛ̃, -jɛn], *a. & s. Geog:* Siberian.
sibérite [siberit], *s.f. Miner:* siberite.
sibiche [sibiʃ], *s.f. P:* cigarette, fag.
sibilance [sibilɑ̃ːs], *s.f. Med:* sibilance, sibilancy.
sibilant [sibilɑ̃], *a. esp. Med:* sibilant, hissing; **râle s.,** sibilant râle.
sibilation [sibilasjɔ̃], *s.f.* sibilation.
sibylle [sibil]. **1.** *s.f.* Sibyl; **feuilles de la s.,** sibylline leaves; *F:* **une vieille s.,** an old hag. **2.** *Pr.n.f.* Sibylle, Sibyl, Sybil.
sibyllin [sibil(l)ɛ̃], *a.* (*a*) sibylline (books, etc.); (*b*) cryptic, enigmatic.
sibyllique [sibil(l)ik], *a.* sibylline, sybilline (inspiration, etc.).
sic [sik], *adv.* (*a*) sic; (*b*) *F:* **la sincérité-s., le socialisme-s.,** so-called sincerity, socialism.
sicaire [sikɛːr], *s.m.* bravo, hired assassin.
Sicambres [sikɑ̃ːbr̥], *s.m.pl. Hist:* Sicambri, Sicambrians.
siccatif, -ive [sikatif, -iːv]. **1.** *a.* (quick-)drying, siccative (oil, varnish). **2.** *s.m.* drying substance; (*a*) siccative, drier (as used by painters); **s. en pâte,** paste drier; **s. liquide,** liquid drier; (*b*) (quick-drying) polish; **passer le carrelage au s.,** to polish the tiles (of the floor).
siccativant [sikativɑ̃], *s.m. Paint:* siccative.
siccativité [sikativite], *s.f.* drying property (of a siccative).
siccité [siksite], *s.f.* **1.** dryness; **évaporer une solution jusqu'à s.,** to evaporate a solution to dryness. **2.** *A: Const:* weatherboard, drip moulding (of window).
Sicile [sisil], *Pr.n.f. Geog:* Sicily.
sicilien, -ienne [sisiljɛ̃, -jɛn]. **1.** *a. & s. Geog:* Sicilian; *Hist:* **les Vêpres siciliennes,** the Sicilian Vespers. **2.** *s.f. Mus: Danc:* **sicilienne,** Siciliana.
sicklémie [siklemi], *s.f. Med:* sickl(a)emia.
sicle[1] [sikl̥], *s.m.* **1.** *B:* shekel; **le s. royal, du sanctuaire,** the shekel of the sanctuary. **2.** *A.Num:* shekel.
sicle[2], *s.m. Cards:* (*in tarok*) coat card, court card.
sicula [sikyla], *s.f. Paleont:* sicula.
Sicules [sikyl], *s.m.pl. A.Geog:* Siculi.
Sicyone [sisjɔn], *Pr.n.f. A.Geog:* Sicyon.
sicyonien, -ienne [sisjɔnjɛ̃, -jɛn], *a. & s. A.Geog:* Sicyonian.
sida [sida], *s.m. Bot:* sida (weed).
sidalcea [sidalsea], *s.m. Bot:* sidalcea.
sidecar, side-car [sidkaːr], *s.m.* motor-cycle and sidecar, motor-cycle combination; sidecar.
sidéral, -aux [sideral, -o], *a.* **1.** *Astr:* sidereal (day, year, etc.). **2.** *Agr:* **culture sidérale,** manure crop.
sidéralité [sideralite], *s.f. Psychics:* astral state.
sidérant [siderɑ̃], *a. F:* flabbergasting, shattering, staggering; **nouvelle sidérante,** staggering piece of news.
sidération [siderasjɔ̃], *s.f.* **1.** *Astrol:* sideration. **2.** *Med: O:* sudden stroke (of apoplexy). **3.** *O:* blasting (of tree by lightning). **4.** *Agr:* fertilization (of ground) by manure crops; sideration.
sidérazote [siderazɔt], *s.f. Miner:* siderazot(e).
sidéré[1] [sidere], *a. Miner:* siderous.
sidéré[2], *a.* (*a*) *O:* struck dead (by lightning, apoplexy); (*b*) *F:* struck dumb (with astonishment, etc.); thunderstruck, flabbergasted, staggered.
sidérer [sidere], *v.tr.* (**il sidère; il sidérera**) **1.** (*of lightning, apoplexy, etc.*) *O:* to strike (s,o.) dead, to strike (s.o.) down. **2.** *F:* to strike (s.o.) dumb; to flabbergast, stagger (s.o.); to strike (s.o.) all of a heap.
sidérique [siderik], *a. Miner:* sideritic.
sidérite [siderit], *s.f.* **1.** *Miner:* siderite. **2.** *Bot:* ironwort.
sideritis [sideritis], *s.m. Bot:* sideritis.
sidérochrome [siderɔkroːm], *s.m. Miner:* chromite, chrome iron.
sidérographie [siderɔgrafi], *s.f.* siderography.
sidérolithe [siderɔlit], *s.f. Miner:* siderolite; meteoric iron.
sidérolithique [siderɔlitik], *a. Miner:* siderolithic.
sidéromélane [siderɔmelan], *s.f. Miner:* sideromelane.
sidéronatrite [siderɔnatrit], *s.f. Miner:* sideronatrite.
sidéroscope [siderɔskɔp], *s.m. El:* sideroscope.
sidérose [sideroːz], *s.f.* **1.** *Miner:* siderite. **2.** *Med:* siderosis.
sidérostat [siderɔsta], *s.m. Astr:* siderostat.
sidérotechnie [siderɔtɛkni], *s.f. O:* siderotechny, the metallurgy of iron and steel.
sidérotyl [siderɔtil], *s.m. Miner:* siderotil.
sidéroxyle [siderɔksil], *s.m.*, **sideroxylon** [siderɔksilɔ̃], *s.m. Bot:* sideroxylon, ironwood.
sidérurgie [sideryrʒi], *s.f.* the metallurgy of iron and steel.
sidérurgique [sideryrʒik], *a.* **industrie s.,** iron and steel industry; **usine s.,** iron and steel works; ironworks; steel works, plant.
sidérurgiste [sideryrʒist], *s.m.* iron and steel metallurgist.
sidi [sidi], *s.m.* **1.** sidi, sayyid. **2.** *P:* (*a*) *O:* Arab (*esp.* living in France); wog; (*b*) *A:* bloke; **drôle de s.,** funny, odd, sort of bloke.
Sidoine Apollinaire [sidwanapɔl(l)inɛːr], *Pr.n.m. Hist:* Sidonius Apollinaris.
Sidon [sidɔ̃], *Pr.n. A.Geog:* Sidon.
sidonien, -ienne [sidɔnjɛ̃, -jɛn], *a. & s. A.Geog:* Sidonian.
Sidre [sidr̥], *Pr.n.f. Geog:* **le golfe de la S.,** the Gulf of Sidra.
siècle [sjɛkl̥], *s.m.* **1.** century; **au vingtième s.,** in the twentieth century; **lit vieux d'un bon s.,** bed at least a hundred, a good hundred, years old. **2.** age, period (of time); **le s. d'Auguste,** the Augustan age; **le s. de Louis XIV, le grand s.,** the age of Louis XIV; **notre s.,** the age we live in, the present time; **c'est un homme de son s.,** he's a man of his times; **ils sont d'un autre s.,** they belong to another age, another century; **jusqu'à la fin des siècles,** to the end of (all) time; *Ecc:* **pour les,** *O:* **dans tous les, siècles des siècles,** world without end; *F:* **il y a un s. que je ne vous ai vu,** I haven't seen you for ages. **3.** (*with religious connotation*) the world; things mundane; **se séparer du s.,** to withdraw from the world, from worldly life.
siège [sjɛːʒ], *s.m.* **1.** (*a*) seat, centre (of learning, of activity, etc.); **s. social,** head office, registered office (of a company); **le s. du gouvernement,** the seat of government; *Min:* **s. (d'exploitation, d'extraction),** workings, works; **chef de s.,** engineer in charge (of mine, etc.); *Med:* **découvrir le s. du mal,** to locate the seat of the disease; (*b*) *Ecc:* **s. épiscopal,** see. **2.** (*a*) *Mil:* siege; **s. en règle, en forme,** regular siege; **artillerie, pièce, de s.,** siege artillery, siege gun; **mettre le s. devant une ville, faire le s. d'une ville,** to lay siege to a town; **lever le s.,** (i) to raise the siege; (ii) *F:* to get up and go; **déclarer l'état de s. (dans une ville),** to declare a state of siege (in a town); to declare martial law; **mon s. est fait,** (i) *Hist:* (Abbé Vertot) I have written my history of the siege (and I do not intend to begin again); (ii) that's my last word on the subject; (*b*) *Bot: F:* **herbe de s.,** water betony. **3.** seat, chair; (coachman's) box; **s. au parlement,** seat in parliament; **ce parti a gagné 30 sièges aux dernières élections,** this party gained 30 seats at the last election; **le s. du juge,** the judge's bench; *Jur:* **jugement rendu sur le s.,** judgement delivered from the bench (without leaving the court); *Veh:* **s. avant,** front seat; **s. arrière,** back seat; **prenez un s.,** take a seat; (do) sit down; **il occupe le s. de président,** he acts as chairman (of the meeting, etc.); **il occupe un s. important,** he holds an important position. **4.** (*a*) seat (of chair, etc.); **fauteuil à s. de cuir,** leather-seated chair; *Av:* **s. éjectable,** ejection, ejector, seat; (*b*) (*in certain expressions*) seat (of pers.); **bain de s.,** sitz bath; hip bath; *Obst:* **accouchement par le s.,** *F:* **un s.,** breech delivery; **présentation par le s.,** *F:* **un s.,** breech presentation; **s. complet,** full breech presentation; **s. décomplété,** frank presentation; (*c*) *Hyg:* (lavatory) seat; **s. à l'anglaise,** standard type lavatory pan (with seat); (*d*) seating (of valve, etc.); **s. du pointeau,** needle-valve seating.
siège-baquet [sjɛʒbakɛ], *s.m. Aut:* bucket seat; *pl. sièges-baquets.*
siegénite [siʒenit], *s.f. Miner:* siegenite.
siéger [sjeʒe], *v.i.* (**je siège, n. siégeons; je siégeai(s); je siégerai**) **1.** (*of company, etc.*) to have its head office, headquarters; **association siégeant à . . .,** association with headquarters at . . .; *Ecc:* **Pape qui a siégé vingt ans,** Pope who held office, who occupied the Holy See, for twenty years; (*of bishop*) **après avoir siégé à Bayeux pendant dix ans,** having held the see of Bayeux for ten years . . .; *Med:* **c'est là que siège le mal,** that is the seat of the trouble. **2.** (*of court of law, judge, assembly, etc.*) to sit. **3.** (*a*) **s. à la Chambre, au Parlement,** to have a seat, to sit, in Parliament; **s. à droite, à gauche,** to sit on the right, on the left (of the Chamber); (*b*) *Jur:* **s. au tribunal,** to be on the bench.
siège-tonneau [sjɛʒtɔno], *s.m. Aut:* bucket seat; *pl. sièges-tonneaux.*
siemens [simɛns, sjemɛ̃ːs], *s.m. El.Meas:* mho, reciprocal ohm.
sien, sienne[1] [sjɛ̃, sjɛn], his, hers, its, one's. **1.** *poss.a.* **adopter qch. comme s.,** to adopt sth. as one's own; **faire sien,** to accept as one's own; *A: & Lit:* **un s. oncle,** a cousin of his, of hers. **2.** **le s., la sienne, les siens, les siennes:** (*a*) *poss. pron.* **ma sœur est plus jolie que la sienne,** my sister is prettier than his, than hers; **il prit mes mains dans les deux siennes,** he took my hands in both of his; **ton courage n'est pas comparable au s.,** your courage cannot compare with his; **mes intérêts sont les siens,** my interests are his, hers; (*b*) *s.m.* (i) one's own, his own (property, etc.); **à chacun le s.,** to each one his own, let each have what belongs to him; **y mettre du s.,** to contribute to an undertaking; **il n'y met pas du s.,** he does not pull his weight, do his share; **ajouter du s. à un récit,** to improve upon a tale; (ii) *pl.* his own, her own, one's own (family, friends, etc.); *B:* **les siens ne l'ont point reçu,** his own received him not; (iii) **faire des siennes,** to be up to one's tricks; **il a encore fait des siennes,** he's been up to his tricks again.
Sienne[2] [sjɛn], *Pr.n.f. Geog:* Sienna; *Com:* **terre de S. naturelle, brûlée,** raw, burnt, sienna.
siennois, -oise [sjɛnwa, -waːz], *a. & s. Geog:* Sien(n)ese.
sierra [sjɛr(r)a], *s.f. Geog:* sierra.
sieste [sjɛst], *s.f.* siesta, nap; **faire la s.,** to take a siesta; to take a nap (after lunch); **faire une courte s.,** to take a short siesta, *F:* to have forty winks.
siester [sjɛste], *v.i.* (*rare*) to take one's siesta, take a nap.
sieur [sjœːr], *s.m. A: & Jur:* Mr; *Pej:* **un s. Martin,** some Mr Martin or other.
sifflage [siflaːʒ], *s.m. Vet:* wheezing, whistling.
sifflant, -ante [siflɑ̃, -ɑ̃ːt]. **1.** *a.* hissing (sound); whistling (note); wheezing, wheezy (breath); sibilant (consonant). **2.** *s.f. Ling:* **sifflante,** sibilant.
sifflement [sifləmɑ̃], *s.m.* **1.** whistling, whistle (of s.o., the wind, etc.); hissing (of serpent, goose, steam); whirr (of missile); swish(ing) (of whip); whizz (of bullet, arrow); singing (of arrow); wheezing (of asthmatic person); singing, hissing, sizzling (of food in the frying pan, of arc lamp); **le s. plaintif des obus,** the whining of the shells; **le s. du gaz,** the hiss of the gas. **2.** whistling, hissing, booing.
siffler [sifle]. **1.** *v.i.* (*a*) (*of pers., bird, engine, ship, the wind*) to whistle; (*of serpent, goose, etc.*) to hiss; (*of missile*) to whirr, whizz; (*of asthmatic pers.*) to wheeze; (*of food frying, of arc lamp*) to sizzle; *Navy:* to pipe (an order); **s. à dîner,** to pipe dinner; (*b*) to blow a whistle; to blow the whistle. **2.** *v.tr.* (*a*) to whistle (a tune); *Nau:* to pipe (a command); *Sp:* **s. une faute, la mi-temps,** to blow the whistle for a foul, for half time; (*b*) to whistle for, whistle up (a taxi, etc.); to whistle to, for, after (a dog, etc.); *Aut: F:* **je me suis fait s. (par la police),** I've been pulled up (by the police); *F:* **s. une fille,** to wolf-whistle; (*c*) *A:* **s. un oiseau,** to train a bird to sing (by whistling to it); (*d*) *Th: etc:* to hiss, boo, hoot; *F:* to give the bird to (actor, etc.); **être sifflé,** to be hissed (off the stage, etc.), to get the bird; *P:* **sifflé!** rubbish! boo! yah! (*e*) *Equit:* **s. sa gaule,** to make one's switch whistle (through the air); (*f*) *P:* to swig, toss off (a glass of beer, etc.).
sifflerie [sifləri], *s.f. O:* whistling, *esp.Th:* hissing, booing, hooting.
sifflet [siflɛ], *s.m.* **1.** whistle (instrument); *Navy:* (boatswain's) pipe; **s. à roulette,** "pea" whistle; **coup de s.,** blast of the whistle; whistle; *Mil:* call; *Navy:* pipe; **donner un coup de s.,** to whistle, to blow the whistle; *Navy:* to pipe; *Sp:* **coup de s. final,** final whistle; *Mch:* **s. à vapeur,** steam whistle; *Nau:* **s. de brume,** fog whistle; *Mil:* **commandement avec le s.,** whistle signal; call; *P:* **couper le s. à qn,** (i) to cut s.o.'s throat; (ii) to cut s.o. off, to shut s.o. up; (iii) to take s.o.'s breath away; *P:* **serrer le s. à qn,** to strangle s.o., to wring s.o.'s neck; *Row:* **attaquer en s.,** to catch a crab; *Carp:* **assemblage en s.,** scarf joint; **couper en s.,** to skew, bevel, splay; to cut slantwise; *Petroleum Min:* **s. de déviation,** whip-stock. **2.** (*sound*) whistle; *Th: etc:* catcall hiss. **3.** *P:* clawhammer coat. **4.** *Ich:* small pike.

sifflet-avertisseur [siflɛavɛrtisœːr], *s.m. Mch:* **s.-a. de bas niveau,** low-water alarm; *pl. sifflets-avertisseurs.*

sifflet-déviateur [siflɛdevjatœːr], *s.m. Petroleum Min:* whipstock; *pl. sifflets-déviateurs.*

siffleur, -euse [siflœːr, -øːz]. **1.** *s.* whistler; *Th:* hisser, booer. **2.** *s.m.* (*a*) *Orn:* widgeon; (*b*) *Z:* whistler, Canadian marmot. **3.** *a.* whistling (bird, duck); hissing (serpent); wheezy (horse, etc.); *Orn:* **canard s.,** baldpate.

siffleux [siflø], *s.m. Fr.C: Z:* ground hog, whistler, woodchuck.

sifflotement [siflɔtmɑ̃], *s.m.* whistling (softly, to oneself).

siffloter [siflɔte], *v.i.* **1.** to whistle to oneself, under one's breath. **2.** to whistle in snatches; to whistle away.

sifilet [sifilɛ], *s.m. Orn:* bird of paradise; paradise whydah.

sigillaire [siʒi(l)ɛːr]. **1.** *a.* relating to seals, sigillary; **anneau s.,** signet ring. **2.** *s.f. Paleont:* sigillaria.

sigillation [siʒil(l)asjɔ̃], *s.f.* sigillation, affixing of seals.

sigillé [siʒil(l)e], *a. Bot: Cer: etc:* sigillate(d) (stem, pottery).

sigillographe [siʒil(l)ɔgraf], *s.m.* sigillographer.

sigillographie [siʒil(l)ɔgrafi], *s.f.* sigillography.

sigillographique [siʒil(l)ɔgrafik], *a.* sigillographical.

sigisbée [siʒisbe], *s.m. A: & Lit:* cicisbeo, attendant gallant (to a woman).

Sigismond [siʒismɔ̃], *Pr.n.m.* Sigismund.

siglaison [siglɛzɔ̃], *s.f.* making words from initials (*e.g.* UNESCO, NATO, WREN).

sigle [sigl], *s.m.* **1.** *Pal:* siglum. **2.** (*in stenography*) outline. **3.** set of initials; **le s. de l'U.N.E.S.C.O.,** the U.N.E.S.C.O. initials; **langage des sigles,** *F:* initialese; **abus des sigles,** *F:* alphabet soup.

sigma [sigma], *s.m. Gr.Alph:* sigma.

sigmatique [sigmatik], *a. Gr.Gram:* sigmatic (future, aorist).

sigmatisme [sigmatism], *s.m. Ling:* sigmatism.

sigmodonte [sigmɔdɔ̃ːt], *s.m. Z:* sigmodont.

sigmoïde [sigmɔid], *a. Anat:* sigmoid (cavity, etc.); **anse s.,** sigmoid flexure (of the colon).

sigmoïdectomie [sigmɔidɛktɔmi], *s.f. Surg:* sigmoidectomy.

sigmoïdien, -ienne [sigmɔidjɛ̃, -jɛn], *a. Anat:* sigmoid; **tumeur sigmoïdienne,** tumour of the sigmoid flexure.

sigmoïdite [sigmɔidit], *s.f. Med:* sigmoiditis.

sigmoïdostomie [sigmɔidɔstɔmi], *s.f. Surg:* sigmoidostomy.

signal, -aux [siɲal, -o], *s.m.* (*a*) signal; **donner, faire, un s.,** to give, make, a signal; **faire des signaux,** to make signals, to signal; **envoyer, lancer, un s.,** to send a signal; **recevoir un s.,** to receive a signal; **capter un s. (à l'improviste),** to catch a signal; **le s. du départ,** the signal for departure; **donner le s. du départ,** to give (a) signal for departure; *Rail: Sp:* **s. de départ,** starting signal (of train, race, etc.); **au s. donné, tous se levèrent,** on a gesture of command, they all stood up; *Mil:* **le s. d'ouverture de feu,** the signal to open fire; **donner le s. de l'ouverture du feu,** to give (the) signal to open fire; **s. à vue, s. optique,** visible signal, visual signal; **s. à bras,** hand signal, *Mil: Navy:* semaphore signal; **s. sémaphorique,** semaphore signal; *Mil:* **s. par fanions,** *Nau:* **s. à pavillons,** flag signal; *Mil: Av:* **s. par panneaux,** panel signal; **s. lumineux,** light signal; *Adm:* **signaux lumineux,** traffic lights; **s. à éclats, s. clignotant,** flash signal; **s. optique Morse,** blinker signal; **s. à fanaux,** lantern signal; **s. par projecteur, par voyant lumineux,** lamp signal; **s. par artifices, s. pyrotechnique,** firework signal, pyrotechnic signal flare; **s. à fusée,** rocket signal; **s. acoustique,** acoustic, audible, signal; **s. sonore, s. phonique,** sound signal; **s. tactile,** touch signal; **s. avertisseur, s. d'avertissement, s. d'alerte,** warning signal; **s. d'alerte aérienne,** air-raid warning (signal), air-alarm signal; **s. de fin d'alerte (aérienne, etc.),** all-clear (signal); **s. d'alarme,** alarm signal; **s. de danger,** danger signal; **s. d'incendie,** fire alarm; **s. d'aperçu,** answering signal; **s. de reconnaissance, d'identification,** recognition signal, identification signal; *Nau:* **s. de brume,** fog signal; **s. de détresse,** distress, S.O.S., signal; **signaux de port,** harbour or port signals; **signaux de mouvements de port,** harbour, port, traffic signals; **signaux d'entrée, de sortie, de port,** entering, leaving, signals; **signaux de marée,** tide signals; *Nau: W.Tel:* **s. horaire,** time signal; **ballon de s. horaire,** time ball; *Navy:* **le journal des signaux,** the signal log; *Rail:* **s. à distance, s. avancé,** distant (block) signal; **s. rapproché, s. d'entrée,** home signal; **s. détonant,** detonator, fog signal; **s. de cantonnement,** block signal; **s. de protection,** covering, protection, signal; **s. de ralentissement,** slacken-speed signal, warning signal; **s. d'arrêt,** danger signal; **s. à l'arrêt,** signal at danger; **s. d'arrêt absolu,** stop signal; **s. de voie fermée, s. fermé,** "on", stop, signal; **s. de voie libre, s. effacé,** "off", clear, signal; **ouvrir un s.,** to throw a signal "off"; **fermer un s.,** to pull a signal "on"; **guérite à signaux,** signal cabin; **poste de signaux,** signal tower; *Aut:* **signaux routiers,** road signs; (*b*) *Tp:* **s. d'appel,** calling signal; **s. de début de communication,** clear-down signal; **s. de fin de communication,** clearing signal; **s. d'occupation, s. "pas libre",** "line engaged" signal, *U.S:* busy tone; **s. de ligne libre,** "disengaged-line" signal, *U.S:* free-line signal; **s. de numérotation,** dialling tone; **s. d'essai,** test tone; (*c*) *Elcs: W.Tel:* signal; (*radar*) trace, signal; **s. simple,** single-component signal; **s. complexe,** multi-component signal; **s. de ré(tro)action,** feedback signal; *T.V: etc:* **s. d'image, s. video,** picture signal, video signal; **signaux parasites,** clutter, *F:* hash; (*computers*) **s. d'invitation à transmettre,** proceed-to-send, proceed-to transmit, signal, *U.S:* start dialling signal; **s. de (sortie) lecture,** sense signal, read output (signal); **s. de début de bloc,** start-of-block signal, *U.S:* synch; **s. binaire,** bit stream; **s. parasite,** interfering signal, parasitic signal, drop-in; **émetteur de signaux,** digit emitter; (*d*) *Surv:* target (over a bench mark).

signalé [siɲale], *a.* **1.** *Trans: etc:* **virage s., passage à niveau s.,** bend, level crossing, indicated by a warning sign. **2.** (*a*) signal, outstanding, (service); remarkable, conspicuous (bravery); **auteur s.,** well-known, prominent, author; (*b*) *Pej:* notorious (criminal, etc.).

signalement [siɲalmɑ̃], *s.m.* description (of pers. on passport, of criminal, of lost article, etc.); **s. d'une voiture,** particulars of a car.

signaler [siɲale], *v.tr.* **1.** (*a*) *O:* to make (sth.) conspicuous; **de grandes victoires signalèrent son règne,** his reign was marked by great victories; (*b*) to point out; to call, draw, attention to (sth.); to signal (s.o., sth.) out; **s. qch. à l'attention de qn,** to point out sth. to s.o.; to draw s.o.'s attention to sth.; **se s. à l'attention de qn,** to catch s.o.'s eye; **s. un livre à qn,** to recommend a book to s.o.; **s. un fait,** to refer, make reference, to a fact; **résultat qui mérite d'être signalé,** result worth recording; (*c*) to notify; to report; **le comité signale que . . .,** the committee reports that . . .; **rien à s.,** nothing to report; *Nau:* **date à laquelle un navire a été signalé pour la dernière fois,** date when a ship was last spoken. **2.** (*a*) to signal (train, ship, etc.); *abs.* to signal; *Av:* **les balises servent à s. l'emplacement d'une piste,** beacons are used to indicate the position of a runway; (*b*) *Elcs:* (*computers*) to post.

se signaler, to distinguish oneself (**par,** by); to have a reputation (for); **se s. dans les sciences,** to have reputation as a scientist; **se s. par son courage,** to be of outstanding courage.

signalétique [siɲaletik], *a.* (*a*) *Adm:* descriptive (of a person); **fiche s.,** description (in police records); *Mil:* **état s.,** descriptive return; **état s. et des services (d'un homme),** soldier's history sheet; (*b*) *El: etc:* **plaque s.,** rating plate.

signaleur [siɲalœːr], *s.m.* (*a*) *Mil: etc:* signaller, sender (of signals); **école des signaleurs,** signalling school; (*b*) *Rail:* signalman.

signalisateur, -trice [siɲalizatœːr, -tris]. **1.** *a. Ind:* **lampe signalisatrice,** telltale lamp. **2.** *s.m. O: Aut:* traffic indicator; **s. anti-vol,** burglar alarm.

signalisation [siɲalizasjɔ̃], *s.f.* **1.** signalling; **s. optique,** visual signalling; **s. à bras,** arm signalling; **lampe, projecteur, de s.,** signal(ling) lamp; **miroir de s.,** heliograph (signalling mirror). **2.** (*a*) (road, etc.) signs; **s. routière internationale,** international (system of) road signs; **panneau de s.,** direction indicator; **poteau de s.,** signpost; **route dont la s. est défectueuse,** road inadequately signposted; **feux de s.,** *Adm:* **appareil de s. à feux multiples,** traffic lights; (*b*) *Av:* beaconing (of landing ground); (*in cinema, etc.*) **la s. lumineuse des sorties est obligatoire,** the exits must be clearly indicated by illuminated signs; (*c*) *Psy:* **système de s.,** set of conditioned stimuli.

signaliser [siɲalize], *v.tr.* to signpost (road).

signataire [siɲatɛːr], *s.m. & f.* signer, signatory, subscriber; **gouvernements signataires d'une convention,** governments signatories to a convention.

signation [siɲasjɔ̃], *s.f. R.C.Ch:* signation.

signature [siɲatyːr], *s.f.* **1.** signing; *Publ: Lit:* **séance de s.,** signing party. **2.** signature; **apposer sa s. à un acte,** to sign a document; *Jur:* to set one's hand to a deed; **mettre sa s. au bas d'un document,** to put one's name to a document; **s. autographiée,** facsimile signature; **présenter un décret à la s. du président,** to submit a decree to the president for signature; **la lettre portait la s. de . . .,** the letter was signed by . . .; *Com:* **pour s.,** for signature; **la s. sociale,** the signature of the firm; **avoir la s.,** to be authorized to sign (on behalf of the firm, etc.); **jeton de s.,** signing fee (of company director, etc.); **livre de signatures,** autograph book. **3.** *Typ:* signature.

signe [siɲ], *s.m.* **1.** (*a*) sign; indication (of rain, etc.); symptom (of illness); mark, token (of friendship, etc.); **ne donner aucun s. de vie, ne pas donner s. de vie,** (i) to show no sign of life; (ii) to send no news (of oneself); **c'est un s. des temps,** it's a sign of the times; **la réunion a eu lieu sous le s. de la cordialité,** cordiality was the keynote of, presided over, the proceedings; **le congrès est sous le s. des engins intercontinentaux,** intercontinental missiles are the theme of the conference; **c'est bon s., mauvais s.,** it's a good, bad, sign; that looks good, bad; (*b*) *R.C.Ch:* **s. sensible,** sensible sign. **2.** sign, symbol, mark; **s. algébrique,** algebraical sign; **signes astronomiques,** astronomical signs; **les signes de (la) ponctuation,** the punctuation marks; *Mil:* **s. de grade,** insignia of rank; *Typ:* **signes de correction,** proof-correction marks; *Mus:* **signes constitutifs,** key signature; **s. du zodiaque,** sign of the zodiac; **s. de chance,** lucky sign; (*computers*) **chiffre de s.,** sign digit; **bit de s.,** sign bit; **amplificateur inverseur de s.,** sign-reversing, sign-changing, amplifier; inverting amplifier. **3.** (distinctive) mark (on the body); *Adm:* **signes particuliers,** special peculiarities (of a person). **4.** sign, gesture, motion; **les muets parlent par signes,** the dumb talk by signs; **il nous fit un signe d'adieu,** he waved us goodbye; **il me congédia d'un s. de la main,** he dismissed me with a wave of the hand; **s. de tête,** nod; **s. de l'œil,** wink; **faire s. à qn,** (i) to motion to s.o., to make a sign to s.o.; (ii) to beckon to s.o.; (iii) to get in touch with s.o.; **faire s. à qn de faire qch.,** to signal to s.o. to do sth.; **je lui fis s. de venir,** I beckoned to him to come; **il fit s. de se taire,** he gave a signal for silence; **le pilote fit s. d'enlever les cales (de l'avion),** the pilot gave the signal to remove the chocks; **faire s. à qn de la main de reculer, de s'écarter, de partir,** to wave s.o. back, aside, off, away; **faire s. que oui,** to nod in agreement; **faire s. que non,** to shake one's head (in dissent); **en s. de respect,** as a token of respect.

signer [siɲe], *v.tr.* **1.** to sign; **s. un document,** to sign a document; to put, set, one's name to a document; *Jur:* **ordonnance signée par . .,** ordinance under the hand of . . .; *v.ind.tr.* **s. à un document,** to witness a document, to subscribe one's name to a document; **s. (à) un contrat,** to become a party to an agreement; **s. un chèque,** to sign a cheque; *F:* **je te signerai un chèque,** I'll write you a cheque; **un correspondant qui signe "Viator,"** a correspondent who signs himself "Viator"; *Com:* **s. à l'arrivée,** to check in; to sign for (goods); *Nau:* **s. l'engagement,** to sign on; **s. qch. de son sang,** to sign sth. with one's own blood; *F:* **je vous le signerais de mon sang,** I'll swear to it on my life; *F:* **c'est signé,** it's easy to guess who did that; **c'était bien Arsène Lupin-c'est signé!** it must have been Arsène Lupin—he's left his trademark! **c'est signé Paul,** that's just like Paul, it's typical of Paul. **2.** *Tchn:* (*a*) to stamp, mark (jewellery, etc.); (*b*) *Glassm:* **s. une pièce de verre,** to mark a piece of glass (for cutting).

se signer, to cross oneself.

signet [siɲɛ], *s.m.* **1.** *A:* (*a*) signet; (*b*) signet ring. **2.** *Boobk:* bookmark(er), tassel, register.

signifiant [siɲifjɑ̃]. **1.** *a.* (*a*) meaningful, expressive; (*b*) *Theol:* significant (signs of grace). **2.** *s.m. Ling:* significans.

significatif, -ive [siɲifikatif, -iːv], *a.* significant; **regard s.,** significant look; look of deep significance; meaning look; **s'en tenir aux faits significatifs,** to stick to the relevant facts; *Ar:* **chiffre s.,** significant figure.

signification [siɲifikasjɔ̃], *s.f.* **1.** meaning, significance, sense, acceptation (of a word, symbol); import (of a ceremony); *Pol.Ec:* **test de s.,** significance test; **seuil de s.,** level of significance (of given data). **2.** *Jur:* notification; service, serving (of writ); **s. à personne,** personal service.

significativement [siɲifikativmɑ̃], *adv.* significantly.
signifié [siɲifje], *s.m. Ling:* signification.
signifier [siɲifje], *v.tr.* (*p.d. & pr.sub.* **n. signifiions, v. signifiiez**) **1.** (*a*) to mean, signify; **que signifie ce mot?** what does this word mean? what is the meaning of this word? **que signifie cette cérémonie?** what is the significance of this ceremony? **cela ne signifie rien,** (i) it doesn't mean anything; (ii) it's of no consequence, no importance; **des remarques qui ne signifient rien,** meaningless remarks; (*b*) *F:* (*denoting indignation*) **qu'est-ce que cela signifie? que signifie?** what's the meaning of this? what do you mean by this? (*c*) **liberté ne signifie pas nécessairement anarchie,** liberty need not mean anarchy; **la moindre imprudence signifierait la mort pour eux,** the slightest imprudence would mean death for them. **2.** to intimate clearly; **s. ses intentions à qn,** to notify s.o. of one's intentions; **je lui signifiai qu'il eût à faire face à ses créances,** I intimated to him that he must meet his debts; **on lui signifia de partir sur le champ,** he was notified that he must depart at once; **s. son congé à qn,** (i) to give s.o. notice to quit; to serve a notice upon (tenant); (ii) to give s.o. notice of dismissal; *Jur:* **s. un arrêt à qn,** to serve a notice on s.o.
signol(le) [siɲɔl], *s.f. Tchn:* windlass crank.
sikh, -e [sik], *a. & s. Indian Rel: Ethn:* Sikh.
sikimi [sikimi], *s.m. Bot:* (Japanese sacred) anise tree.
sil [sil], *s.m. Cer: Ant:* ochreous (pottery) clay.
silane [silan], *s.m. Ch:* silane.
silaus [silos], *s.m. Bot:* (pepper) saxifrage.
silence [silɑ̃:s], *s.m.* **1.** silence; *Rec:* pause; **il se fit un s. subit,** there was a sudden silence, a sudden hush; **s. absolu,** unbroken silence; dead silence; **un s. de mort,** a deathlike silence; **un s. ému, anxieux,** a breathless silence; **imposer s. à qn, réduire qn au s.,** to put, reduce, s.o. to silence; to silence s.o.; **imposer s. à ses passions,** to still one's passions; **rompre le s.,** to break (the) silence; **garder, observer, le s.,** to keep silent (**sur,** about); to hold one's peace; **être engagé au s.,** to be tongue-tied; **faire s.,** to stop talking; **il y eut un s.,** there was a pause (in the conversation, etc.); **s.! du s.!** silence! hush! be quiet! **souffrir en s.,** to suffer in silence, silently; **passer qch. sous s.,** to pass over sth. in silence; to ignore sth.; to gloss over sth.; to hush sth. up; to keep sth. secret; **écrire à qn après un s. de deux ans,** to write to s.o. after a break, a silence, of two years; **préparer qch. dans le s.,** to prepare sth. in secrecy; **faire jurer le s. à qn,** to swear s.o. to secrecy; **le s. de la nuit,** the silence, stillness, of the night; (*b*) *Aer:* **cône de s.,** cone of silence; *Elcs:* **zone de s.,** silent zone. **2.** *Mus:* rest.
silenciaire [silɑ̃sjɛ:r], *s.m.* **1.** *Hist:* silentiary (of the Byzantine court). **2.** *Ecc:* member of a silent order; silentiary.
silencieusement [silɑ̃sjøzmɑ̃], *adv.* silently.
silencieux, -ieuse [silɑ̃sjø, -jø:z]. **1.** *a.* (*a*) silent; taciturn (person); (*b*) noiseless (typewriter, etc.); **des pas s.,** silent footsteps; (*c*) still, peaceful (woods, evening); (*d*) *Med:* painless; *Dent:* **ce stade de début de la carie est en général s.,** this early stage of decay is generally painless. **2.** (*a*) *s.m. I.C.E:* silencer, *U.S:* muffler; (*b*) *Sm.a:* silencer; (*c*) *W.Tel:* squelch.
Silène [silɛn]. **1.** *Pr.n.m. Myth:* Silenus. **2.** *s.m.* (*a*) *Bot:* catch-fly; **s. enflé,** frothy poppy, bladder campion, white behen; **s. maritime,** sea campion; **s. nocturne,** night-flowering campion; (*b*) *Z:* Silenus ape.
silentiaire [silɑ̃sjɛ:r], *s.m.* = SILENCIAIRE.
Silésie [silezi], *Pr.n.f. Geog:* Silesia.
silésien, -ienne [silezjɛ̃, -jɛn]. **1.** *a. & s. Geog:* Silesian. **2.** *s.f. Tex:* **silésienne,** silesia (used for dress linings).
silex [silɛks], *s.m.inv.* **1.** silex, flint; **s. corné,** horn flint; **s. noir,** chert, rock flint, hornstone; **s. taillés,** chipped flint implements; **platine à s.,** flint lock (of gun); **fusil à s.,** flint-lock (gun). **2.** (*a*) **s. molaire,** travertin(e), sinter; (*b*) **s. volcanique,** obsidian.
silexiforme [silɛksifɔrm], *a.* flint-shaped.
silhouettage [silwɛta:ʒ], *s.m. Phot: etc:* blocking out.
silhouette [silwɛt], *s.f.* (*a*) silhouette; (*b*) silhouette, outline, form (of person, building, etc.); profile; (*c*) *Mil:* silhouette target, figure target; (*d*) profile of cross section (of key bit).
silhouetter [silwete], *v.tr.* (*a*) to silhouette; to outline; (*b*) *Phot:* to block out.
se silhouetter, to stand out, show up (against the horizon, etc.).
silhouetteur [silwɛtœ:r], *s.m.* silhouettist (**de,** of).
silicatage [silikata:ʒ], *s.m.* silicification.
silicate [silikat], *s.m. Ch:* silicate; **s. d'aluminium,** aluminium silicate; **s. double,** bisilicate, metasilicate; **s. de potasse,** waterglass.
silicater [silikate], *v.tr.* to silicate; to treat with silicate.
silicatisation [silikatizasjɔ̃], *s.f. Tchn:* silicating, silicification (of wood, stone, etc.).
silicatiser [silikatize], *v.tr.* to silicate, silicify (wood, stone); to treat (road, etc.) with silicate.
silice [silis], *s.f. Ch:* silica; silicon dioxide.
siliceux, -euse [silisø, -ø:z], *a.* siliceous; **bronze s.,** silicon bronze.
silicicole [silisikɔl], *a. Bot:* silicicolous.
silicié [silisje], *a. Ch:* combined with silicon; **hydrogène s.,** silicon hydride.
silicifère [silisifɛ:r], *a.* siliciferous.
silicification [silisifikasjɔ̃], *s.f.* silicification.
silicifier [silisifje], *v.tr.* to silicify.
silicique [silisik], *a. Ch:* silicic (acid).
silicium [silisjɔm], *s.m. Ch:* silicon.
siliciure [silisjy:r], *s.m. Ch:* silicide, siliciuret.
silico- [silikɔ], *pref.* silico-.
silicocalcaire [silikɔkalkɛ:r], *a.* silicocalcareous, silicicalcareous.
silicochloroforme [silikɔklɔrɔfɔrm], *s.m.* silicochloroform.
silicoflagellés [silikɔflaʒɛle], *s.m.pl. Prot: Paleont:* Silicoflagellata.
silicomanganèse [silikɔmɑ̃ganɛ:z], *s.m.* silicomanganese.
silicone [silikɔn], *s.f. Ch:* silicone.
siliconer [silikɔne], *v.tr. Tchn:* to coat with silicone.
silicose [siliko:z], *s.f. Med:* silicosis.
silicotique [silikɔtik], *a. & s.m. & f. Med:* silicotic.
silicotitanate [silikɔtitanat], *s.m. Ch:* silicotitanate.
silicotungstate [silikɔtœ̃gstat], *s.m. Ch:* silicotungstate.
silicule [silikyl], *s.f. Bot:* silicle, silicula, silicule.
siliculeux, -euse [silikylø, -ø:z], *a. Bot:* siliculose.
silique [silik], *s.f.* **1.** *Rom.Ant: Meas:* siliqua. **2.** *Bot:* silique; pod.
siliqueux, -euse [silikø, -ø:z], *a. Bot:* siliquose, siliquous.
siliquiforme [silikifɔrm], *a.* siliquiform.
Silistrie [silistri], *Pr.n.f. Geog:* Silistria.
sill [sil], *s.m.* (*a*) *Geol:* laccolite, laccolith; (*b*) *Min:* sill, bed vein.
sillage [sija:ʒ], *s.m.* **1.** (*a*) wake, wash, track, furrow (of ship); *Fish:* drag; **couper, franchir, le s. d'un vaisseau,** to cross the track of a ship; **marcher dans le s. de qn,** to follow in s.o.'s wake; *F:* **il fait plus de remous que de s.,** he makes a great commotion about very little work; (*b*) *Av: etc:* slip stream; **s. aérodynamique,** aerodynamic drag. **2.** seaway, headway, speed (of ship); **doubler le s. d'un navire,** to make twice as much way as another ship. **3.** *Min:* continuation of a vein (of coal).
sille [sil], *s.m. Gr.Lit:* satirical poem.
siller[1] [sije], *v.i. Nau: O:* (*of ship*) to make headway.
siller[2], *v.* = CILLER.
sillet [sijɛ], *s.m.* nut (of stringed instruments); **grand s.,** tail-piece nut; **petit s.,** nut at the neck.
sillomètre [sijɔmɛtr̥], *s.m. Nau:* speed indicator; patent log.
sillon [sijɔ̃], *s.m.* **1.** (*a*) *Agr:* furrow; **mener droit son s.,** to plough a straight furrow; **faire, creuser, son s.,** to plough one's own furrow, to hoe one's own row; (*b*) *Agr:* (= *small furrow*) drill; **semer la graine par sillons,** to sow the grain in drills; (*c*) *pl. Lit: Poet:* fields, country; **le sang inonda nos sillons,** our fields ran with blood; (*d*) line (on the forehead, etc.); wrinkle; *Geol:* **s. ondulé,** ripple mark; (*e*) *Geol:* trench; **s. prélittoral,** offshore bar. **2.** track, trail (of wheel); wake (of ship); path (of projectile); **s. de lumière, de feu,** streak of light, of fire (of rocket, etc.); **éclairs en sillons,** forked lightning. **3.** (*a*) *Anat:* sulcus, groove; **s. primitif,** primitive groove; (*b*) groove, spiral (of gramophone); **s. initial,** lead-in groove, spiral; **s. de sortie,** lead-out groove, spiral; **s. intermédiaire,** crossover groove, spiral. **4.** *Rail:* **s. d'un train,** calculated time interval between trains (following each other on a busy line).
sillonner [sijɔne], *v.tr.* **1.** (*a*) to furrow; to plough (the seas); **flanc de montagne sillonné par les torrents,** mountain side grooved, scored, by torrents; **bois sillonné de nombreux sentiers,** wood crossed by numerous paths; (*b*) (*of light, lightning, etc.*) to streak (the sky); **ciel sillonné d'étoiles filantes,** sky streaked with shooting stars; (*c*) **nous avons sillonné la rade sans rien trouver,** we scoured the roadstead without finding anything; (*d*) *Lit:* to wrinkle, furrow (the brow, etc.); **l'âge a sillonné son visage,** age has furrowed his face, has left its mark on his face. **2.** *Nau:* (*of ship*) to scrape (the sea bottom).
sillonneur [sijɔnœ:r], *s.m. Agr:* drill plough.
silo[1] [silo], *s.m.* (*a*) *Agr:* silo; clamp; store pit; **s. (temporaire) de pommes de terre,** clamp of potatoes; **mettre en s.,** to silo, to bury; (*b*) silo, elevator; **s. à blé,** grain elevator; **silos coopératifs,** grain-storage cooperatives; (*c*) **s. à ciment,** cement bin; (*d*) *Ball:* **s. de lancement,** launching silo.
Silo[2], *Pr.n. B.Geog:* Shiloh.
Siloé [silɔe], *Pr.n. B.Geog:* **la fontaine de S.,** the pool of Siloam.
silotage [silɔta:ʒ], *s.m. Agr: etc:* ensilage.
siloxane [silɔksan], *s.m. Ch:* siloxane.
silphe [silf], *s.m. Ent:* silpha, carrion beetle.
silphidés [silfide], *s.m.pl. Ent:* Silphidae.
silphion [silfjɔ̃], **silphium** [silfjɔm], *s.m. Bot:* silphium, cup plant.
silure [sily:r], *s.m. Ich:* silurus, sheat fish, catfish; **s. électrique,** thunder fish (of the Nile); **s. cuirassé,** armoured catfish; **s. à nez de renard,** fox-snouted catfish.
Silures [sily:r], *Pr.n.m.pl. A.Geog:* Silures.
silurides [silyrid], **siluridés** [silyride], *s.m.pl. Ich:* Siluridae, the catfishes.
silurien, -ienne [silyrjɛ̃, -jɛn], *a. & s.m. Geol:* Silurian; **s. inférieur,** Ordovician.
Silvain [silvɛ̃], *Pr.n.m. Rom.Myth:* Sylvanus.
silveroïd(e) [silverɔid], *s.m.* cupro-nickel.
silvestre [silvɛstr̥], *a.* woodland, *Lit:* sylvan.
silvestrite [silvɛstrit], *s.f. Miner:* siderazote.
silybe [silib], *s.m.,* **silybium** [silibjɔm], *s.m. Bot:* milk thistle.
sima [sima], *s.m. Geol:* sima.
simagrée [simagre], *s.f.* (*a*) pretence; **faire la s. de refuser,** to go through the form of refusing; (*b*) *usu. pl.* affected airs; grimaces; affectation; **simagrées de politesse,** smirks and smiles; affected politeness; **faire des simagrées,** to smirk; **ne fais pas tant de simagrées,** don't make so much fuss.
simar(o)uba [simaruba], *s.m. Bot:* simar(o)uba; *Pharm:* **écorce de s.,** simar(o)uba bark.
simar(o)ubacées [simarubase], *s.pl. Bot:* Simar(o)ubaceae.
simarre [sima:r], *s.f.* (*a*) *A.Cost:* (woman's) simar; (*b*) *A:* magistrate's cassock (as worn under gown); *Lit: F:* **ambitionner la s.,** to aim at high judicial office; (*c*) *Ecc:* (bishop's) chimere.
simbleau, -eaux [sɛ̃blo], *s.m.* (*a*) *Artil:* (breech) bore sight; (*b*) *Tchn:* (i) centring bridge (for finding the centre of hollow cylinder structure); (ii) cord (for drawing circles).
Siméon [simeɔ̃], *Pr.n.m.* Simeon; **S. Stylite,** Simeon Stylites.
simien, -ienne [simjɛ̃, -jɛn], *Z:* **1.** *a.* simian. **2.** *s.m.pl.* **simiens,** Simiidae, the simians.
simiesque [simjɛsk], *a.* simiesque; monkey-like, ape-like, apish (face, grimace).
simiidés [simiide], *s.m.pl.* Simiidae, the higher apes.
similaire [similɛ:r]. **1.** *a.* similar (**à,** to); like; of the same kind; **cannes et objets similaires,** walking sticks and like objects. **2.** *s.m. Nau:* sister ship.
similairement [similɛrmɑ̃], *adv.* similarly.
similargent [similarʒɑ̃], *s.m.* imitation silver.
similarité [similarite], *s.f.* similarity, likeness.
simili[1] [simili]. **1.** *pref.* imitation; artificial. **2.** *s.m. F:* imitation; *Tex:* silk-finished cotton; *Phot:* half tone; **bijoux en s.,** imitation, costume, jewellery. **3.** *s.f. F:* process engraving, half-tone engraving, block.
simili[2], *a.m.pl. Mus:* simili; repeat in every bar bearing the sign.
similibois [similibwɑ], *s.m.* artificial wood.
similibronze [similibrɔ̃:z], *s.m.* imitation bronze.
similicuir [similikɥi:r], *s.m.* artificial leather, imitation leather; leatherette.
simili-écaille [similieka:j], *s.m.inv.* imitation tortoiseshell.
similigraveur [similigravœ:r], *s.m.* process-engraver, half-tone engraver.
similigravure [similigravy:r], *s.f.* process-engraving, half-tone (engraving, block); **s. en couleur,** colour screen process; **chambre noire pour s.,** screen camera; **cliché de s.,** half-tone plate, block; **trame de s.,** half-tone screen.
similimarbre [similimarbr̥], *s.m.* imitation marble.
similipierre [similipjɛ:r], *s.f.* imitation stone.
similisage [similiza:ʒ], *s.m. Tex:* silk finish; schreinering (of cottons).
similiser [similize], *v.tr. Tex:* to silk-finish, schreiner (cotton).

similiste [similist], *s.m. Phot.Engr:* half-tone etcher; fine etcher.

similitude [similityd], *s.f.* similitude. **1.** resemblance, likeness (of two people, things); similarity (of ideas, expressions); *Geom:* similarity (of triangles); *Med:* **loi de s.,** law of similars. **2.** *Rh:* simile.

similor [similɔːr], *s.m.* imitation gold; similor, pinchbeck.

Simoïs [simɔis], *Pr.n.m. A.Geog:* (the river) Simois.

Simon [simɔ̃], *Pr.n.m.* Simon; **S. le Magicien,** Simon Magus.

simoniaque [simɔnjak], *Ecc:* **1.** *a.* simoniac(al). **2.** *s.m.* simoniac, simonist.

Simonide [simɔnid], *Pr.n.m. Gr.Lit:* Simonides.

simonie [simɔni], *s.f. Ecc:* simony.

simoon, simoun [simun], *s.m.* simoon (wind).

simple [sɛ̃ːpl̩], *a.* simple. **1.** (*a*) single (flower, ticket, etc.); **soulier à semelle s.,** shoe with single sole; *Ecc:* **l'œil s.,** the single eye; *Cr:* **s. guichet,** single wicket; *s.m. Ten:* **jouer un s.,** to play a single; **s. messieurs,** men's singles; **s. dames,** ladies' singles; *Nau:* **ordre s.,** order in single line; *Mec.E: etc:* **à s. effet,** single-acting; (*b*) (*not compound*) **avoir une chance s.,** to have an even chance; *Turf:* **faire un pari s.,** to back a horse to win; *Gram:* **temps s.,** simple tense; **passé s.,** past historic (tense); *Ch:* **corps s.,** elementary body, element; *Mth:* **équation s.,** simple equation. **2.** (*a*) ordinary, common; **un s. particulier,** a private citizen; **s. soldat,** private (soldier); **s. matelot,** ordinary seaman; (*b*) **condamner qn sur un s. soupçon,** to condemn s.o. on a mere, bare, suspicion; **c'est une s. question de temps,** it is simply a matter of time; **la vérité pure et s.,** the plain truth; the truth pure and simple; **c'est de la folie pure et s.,** it is sheer madness; **croire qn sur sa s. parole,** to believe s.o. on his word alone; **ne vous fâchez pas d'une s. remarque,** don't take offence at a mere remark; **la s. prudence veut que . . .,** ordinary, elementary, prudence demands that . . .; **les faits tout simples,** the broad facts; the plain facts; (*c*) plain, simple, (dress, food, truth); **gens simples,** simple, unpretentious, people; *s.* **c'est un s.,** he's a plain man; **avoir des goûts simples,** to have simple tastes; **modestie s.,** unaffected, natural, modesty; (*d*) easy, straightforward; **méthode s.,** simple, easy, method; **c'est simple comme bonjour,** it's as easy as A.B.C., as winking, as falling off a log; **d'où il est s. à déduire que . . .,** from which it is easy to deduce that . . .. **3.** (*a*) simple-minded; **il est un peu s. d'esprit,** he's half-witted, not all there; *s.m.* **c'est un s. (d'esprit),** he's a moron, a half-wit; (*b*) ingenuous; credulous; *F:* green; **je ne suis pas assez s. pour . . .,** I'm not so green as to . . .; I know better than to . . .. **4.** *s.m. usu. pl.* simples, medicinal herbs.

simplement [sɛ̃pləmɑ̃], *adv.* simply. **1.** plainly (dressed, etc.); **vivre s.,** to live in a plain way. **2.** naturally, unaffectedly; **le plus s. du monde,** without any fuss. **3.** with a simple mind; ingenuously. **4.** just, merely; **j'ai fait s. remarquer que . . .,** I merely observed that . . .; **purement et s.,** purely and simply.

simplesse [sɛ̃plɛs], *s.f. A: & Lit:* simpleness, artlessness.

simplet, -ette [sɛ̃plɛ, -ɛt], *a. F:* rather silly, stupid; rather green; dop(e)y.

simplex [sɛ̃plɛks], *s.m. Elcs:* (*computers*) simplex; **communication s.,** simplex circuit.

simplicidentés [sɛ̃plisidɑ̃te], *s.m.pl. Z:* Simplicidenta.

simplicifolié [sɛ̃plisifɔlje], *a. Bot:* having simple leaves.

simplicité [sɛ̃plisite], *s.f.* **1.** (*a*) simplicity (of dress, manners, etc.); **vêtue avec une s. de bon goût,** simply dressed in exquisite taste; **en toute s.,** without affectation; simply; naturally; **venez en toute s.,** (i) come as you are; (ii) come and take pot luck; (*b*) elementary nature (of atoms, etc.). **2.** artlessness, simpleness; simple-mindedness; *O:* **dire des simplicités,** to make naive remarks.

simplifiable [sɛ̃plifjabl̩], *a.* that can be simplified, capable of simplification.

simplificateur, -trice [sɛ̃plifikatœːr, -tris]. **1.** *a.* simplifying (method). **2.** *s.m.* simplifier.

simplification [sɛ̃plifikasjɔ̃], *s.f.* simplification; *Mth:* cancelling, cancelling out; **apporter des simplifications à un procédé,** to simplify a process; *Ind: etc:* **s. du travail,** systemization of work, (application of) time and motion study.

simplifier [sɛ̃plifje], *v.tr.* (*p.d. & pr.sub.* **n. simplifiions, v. simplifiiez**) to simplify; **s. une fraction,** to reduce a fraction to its lowest terms; *abs.* **tout ce qui simplifie éclaircit,** simplification makes things clearer.

simplisme [sɛ̃plism], *s.m.* over-simplification (of an argument); begging the question; superficial approach (to a subject).

simpliste [sɛ̃plist]. **1.** *a.* simplistic, over-simple (theory, explanation); **esprit s.,** superficial mind; mind incapable of seeing below the surface (of a problem). **2.** *s.* **c'est un s.,** he can only see one side of the question; he has a superficial mind.

simulacre [simylakr̥], *s.m.* (*a*) simulacrum, image; (*b*) semblance, show; *Mil:* dummy (grenade, tank, etc.); **s. de résistance,** show of resistance; **faire le s. de faire qch.,** to pretend to do sth., to make a show of doing sth.; *Mil:* **s. de combat,** sham fight; **son procès ne fut qu'un s.,** his trial was a mere mockery.

simulateur, -trice [simylatœːr, -tris], (*a*) *s.* simulator, shammer; malingerer; (*b*) *s.m. Tchn:* simulator; *Av:* **s. de vol,** flight simulator; **expérience acquise sur s.,** simulation experience; *Elcs:* (*computers*) **s. (d'étude) de réseaux,** network analyser; **s. mathématique de calculateur,** Turing machine; *Atom.Ph: etc:* **s. analogique, numérique,** analogue, digital, simulator.

simulation [simylasjɔ̃], *s.f.* (*a*) simulation; pretence; malingering; (*b*) *Av:* **s. de vol,** flight simulation; (*computers*) **s. en temps réel,** real-time simulation; *Atom.Ph: etc:* **s. analogique, numérique,** analogue, digital, simulation.

simulé [simyle], *a.* feigned (illness); sham (fight); fictitious, bogus (sale); **facture simulée,** pro forma invoice.

simuler [simyle], *v.tr.* to simulate; to feign, counterfeit, sham; **s. une maladie,** to feign illness, to pretend to be ill; to malinger.

simulides [simylid], *s.m.pl. Ent:* Simuliidae.

simulie [simyli], *s.f. Ent:* simulid, sandfly; (*genus*) Simulium.

simuliidés [simyliide], *s.m.pl. Ent:* Simuliidae.

simultané [simyltane], *a.* simultaneous; *Mth:* **équations simultanées,** simultaneous equations; *W.Tel:* **position en s.,** connection for simultaneous relay; **accès s.,** simultaneous access; **transmission non simultanée,** non-simultaneous transmission; **traduction simultanée,** simultaneous translation; **personnalité simultanée,** dual personality.

simultanéité [simyltaneite], *s.f.* simultaneousness, simultaneity; (*computers*) overlap; **erreur de s.,** coincidence error.

simultanément [simyltanemɑ̃], *adv.* simultaneously.

Sinaï [sinai], *Pr.n.m. Geog:* Sinai.

sinaïtique [sinaitik], *a. Geog:* Sinaitic.

sinanthrope [sinɑ̃trɔp], *s.m. Anthr:* Sinanthropus, Pekin man.

sinapine [sinapin], *s.f. Ch:* sinapine.

sinapique [sinapik], *a. Ch:* sinapic (acid).

sinapiser [sinapize], *v.tr.* to add mustard to (bath, poultice); **bain, cataplasme, sinapisé,** mustard bath, poultice.

sinapisme [sinapism], *s.m. Med:* (*a*) mustard plaster; sinapism; (*b*) mustard poultice.

sincère [sɛ̃sɛːr], *a.* **1.** sincere, frank, candid (person); candid (opinion); **homme s.,** plain-spoken man. **2.** (*a*) sincere, genuine, honest (person); (*b*) genuine, sincere (joy, sorrow, etc.); sincere, earnest (effort, etc.); **regrets sincères,** sincere regrets; **vœux, remerciements, sincères,** heartfelt wishes, thanks; **agréez mes sincères salutations,** yours sincerely; (*c*) (*of document, etc.*) authentic.

sincèrement [sɛ̃sɛrmɑ̃], *adv.* sincerely. **1.** frankly, candidly; **nous espérons bien s. que . . .,** we earnestly hope that . . .. **2.** genuinely (glad, etc.).

sincérité [sɛ̃serite], *s.f.* (*a*) sincerity, frankness, candour; **en toute s. . . .,** speaking in all sincerity . . .; honestly . . .; (*b*) genuineness (of regret, etc.).

sincipital, -aux [sɛ̃sipital, -o], *a. Anat:* sincipital.

sinciput [sɛ̃sipyt], *s.m. Anat:* sinciput; calvarium.

Sind (le) [ləsɛ̃ːd], *Pr.n.m. Geog:* **1.** the (river) Indus, the (river) Sind. **2.** the (province) Sind.

sindon [sɛ̃dɔ̃], *s.m.* **1.** (Christ's) shroud, winding-sheet, sindon. **2.** *Surg:* pledget.

sinécure [sinekyːr], *s.f.* sinecure; *F:* **ce n'est pas une s.,** it's not exactly a rest cure.

sinécurisme [sinekyrism], *s.m.* sinecurism.

sinécuriste [sinekyrist], *s.m. & f.* sinecurist.

sine die [sinedje], *adv.phr.* sine die.

sine qua non [sinekwanɔn], *adj.phr.* sine qua non.

sinfonietta [sɛ̃fɔnjɛta], *s.f. Mus:* sinfonietta.

singalais, -aise [sɛ̃galɛ, -ɛːz], *a. & s. Geog:* Singhalese.

singalette [sɛ̃galɛt], *s.f. Bookb:* mull.

Singapour [sɛ̃gapuːr], *Pr.n.m. Geog:* Singapore.

singe [sɛ̃ːʒ], *s.m.* **1.** (*a*) monkey; ape; **s. araignée,** spider monkey; coaita; **s. cochon,** pigtailed monkey; **s. laineux,** woolly monkey; **s. moine,** hairy saki; **s. lion,** wanderoo; **s. rouge, s. pleureur,** patas monkey, red monkey; **s. hurleur,** howler (monkey); **s. nocturne,** night ape, douroucouli; **malin comme un s.,** as artful as a cartload of monkeys; **laid comme un s.,** as ugly as sin; *Prov:* **on n'apprend pas à un vieux s. à faire des grimaces,** don't teach your grandmother to suck eggs; *s.a.* MONNAIE 1; (*b*) *F:* ape, imitator; (*c*) *F:* ugly person; fright; scarecrow. **2.** *Cu: P:* **du s.,** bully beef. **3.** *P:* **le s.,** the boss. **4.** *Tchn:* (*a*) hoist, windlass, winch, crab; (*b*) monkey (of pile driver); (*c*) *O:* pantograph. **5.** *a.inv.* imitative, apish.

singer [sɛ̃ʒe], *v.tr.* (**je singeai(s); n. singeons**) **1.** to ape, mimic (s.o.); to take (s.o.) off. **2.** *Tchn:* **tour à s.,** copying lathe.

singerie [sɛ̃ʒri], *s.f.* **1.** (*a*) grimace, apish antic, monkey trick; (*b*) = SIMAGRÉE; (*c*) (monkey-like, grotesque) imitation. **2.** (*a*) monkey house; apery; (*b*) *A:* caricatural drawing in which men were represented as apes.

singesse [sɛ̃ʒɛs], *s.f.* (*a*) female monkey, ape; (*b*) *F: Pej:* ugly girl, woman; fright; scarecrow.

singeur, -euse, -eresse [sɛ̃ʒœːr, -øːz, sɛ̃ʒrɛs], *A:* **1.** *a.* aping, imitating. **2.** *s.* imitator, ape.

singhalais, -aise [sɛ̃galɛ, -ɛːz], *a. & s. Geog:* Singhalese.

single [siŋgl̩], *s.m.* **1.** *Ten:* singles (game). **2.** single-berth compartment (in wagon lit).

singleton [sɛ̃glətɔ̃], *s.m. Cards:* singleton.

sing-sing [siŋsiŋ], *s.n. Z:* sing-sing; *pl. sing-sings.*

singulariser [sɛ̃gylarize], *v.tr.* to make (s.o.) conspicuous; **ses chapeaux la singularisent,** her hats make her conspicuous.

se singulariser, to attract attention, to make oneself conspicuous (by one's oddity); **se s. par son costume,** to make oneself conspicuous by the way one dresses; **l'envie de se s.,** the desire to be different.

singularité [sɛ̃gylarite], *s.f.* singularity. **1.** (*a*) peculiarity, special feature (of a belief, a character, etc.); (*b*) **la s. de ces faits,** the unusualness of these facts. **2.** oddness, oddity, eccentricity (of dress, speech, conduct, etc.); **faire qch. par esprit de s.,** to do sth. out of a desire to be different from other people. **3.** *Gram:* singular connotation (of an ending, etc.).

singulier, -ière [sɛ̃gylje, -jɛːr], *a.* singular. **1.** (*a*) (*referring to one*) **combat s.,** single combat; *s. Gram:* **(nombre) s.,** singular (number); **au s.,** in the singular; *Mth:* **points singuliers d'une courbe,** singular points in a curve; (*b*) peculiar (**à,** to); **cette fermeté d'âme, à vous si singulière,** this firmness of spirit, so peculiar to yourself. **2.** peculiar, remarkable, uncommon (merit, virtue, etc.). **3.** (*a*) odd, curious, strange, queer (person, method, custom, fact); **par un hasard s. je le rencontrai à Londres,** oddly enough I came across him in London; **il est s. qu'il ne soit pas encore arrivé,** it is strange that he has not arrived yet; (*b*) conspicuous; like nobody else; **elle affiche ces chapeaux par désir d'être singulière,** she flaunts these hats in order to make herself conspicuous; **son envie d'être singulière,** her desire to be different from other people.

singulièrement [sɛ̃gyljɛrmɑ̃], *adv.* **1.** singularly; **il s'est conduit s. dans cette affaire,** he behaved in a peculiar manner in this business. **2.** (*a*) oddly, uncommonly, strangely, queerly; **s'habiller s.,** to dress in a strange way, in an odd fashion; **vous êtes s. distrait aujourd'hui,** you are uncommonly, singularly, absent-minded today; (*b*) conspicuously. **3.** specially, in particular, particularly, mainly.

sinisation [sinizasjɔ̃], *s.f.* sinicization, sinification.

siniser [sinize], *v.tr.* to sinicize.

sinistre [sinistr̥]. **1.** *a.* (*a*) sinister, fatal, ominous, of evil omen; **de s. mémoire,** of evil memory; **symptômes sinistres,** ominous symptoms; **événement s.,** fatal occurrence; **sourire s.,** sinister smile; **lueur s.,** lurid light; **chercher à tout de sinistres interprétations,** to look for an evil intention in everything; (*b*) *F:* dull; catastrophic. **2.** *s.m.* (*a*) disaster, catastrophe, calamity (*esp.* fire, earthquake, or shipwreck); **s. en mer,** catastrophe at sea; (*b*) loss (through disaster); **évaluer le s.,** to estimate the damage, the loss; *Ins:* **bonification pour non-s.,** no-claims bonus.

sinistré, -ée [sinistre]. **1.** *a.* that has suffered a disaster, fire, shipwreck, etc.; **zone sinistrée,** distressed area; disaster area. **2.** *s.* victim of, sufferer from, a disaster; **indemniser les sinistrés,** to compensate the victims.

sinistrement [sinistrəmɑ̃], *adv.* sinisterly, ominously; in a sinister manner.
sinistrogyre [sinistroʒiːr], *a.* sinistrogyric, sinistrogyrate, back-handed (hand-writing).
sinistrorse [sinistrɔrs], *a. Nat.Hist:* sinistrorse (stem, etc.).
sinistrorsum [sinistrɔrsɔm]. **1.** *a.inv.* sinistral, sinistrorsal (whorl, etc.). **2.** *adv.* sinistrally, sinistrorsally, counter-clockwise, from right to left.
sinistrose [sinistroːz], *s.f. Med:* sinistrosis.
sinn fein [sinfɛn], *s.m. Pol.Hist:* Sinn Fein.
sinn-feiner [sinfɛnɛːr], *s.m. & f. Pol.Hist:* Sinn Feiner.
sino- [sinə], *comb.fm.* Sino-.
sino-japonais, -aise [sinəʒapɔnɛ, -ɛːz], *a.* Sino-Japanese.
sinologie [sinɔlɔʒi], *s.f. Ling: etc:* sinology.
sinologique [sinɔlɔʒik], *a.* sinological.
sinologue [sinɔlɔg], *s.m. & f.* sinologue, sinologist; Chinese scholar.
sinon [sinɔ̃], *conj.* **1.** otherwise, (or) else, if not; **il faut obéir, s. gare!** you must obey, or else look out! *F:* **rendez-moi ma canne, s. je ne peux pas marcher,** give me my walking stick back, or I can't walk. **2.** except, unless; **il ne fait rien s. manger et boire,** he does nothing except eat and drink; **pour être heureux que faut-il s. de ne rien désirer?** the only condition for achieving happiness is to have no desires; **s. que,** except that; **rien n'y fut décidé, s. que la paix était impossible,** nothing was decided except that peace was impossible.
Sinop [sinɔp], *Pr.n.f. Geog:* Sinope.
sinople [sinɔpl̩], *s.m.* **1.** *Miner:* sinople. **2.** *Her:* vert, sinople.
sinoque [sinɔk], *a. P:* crackers, bats, mad.
sintoïsme [sɛ̃tɔism], *s.m.* Shintoism.
sintoïste [sɛ̃tɔist], *s.m. & f.* Shintoist.
sinué [sinɥe], *a. Bot:* sinuate.
sinueux, -euse [sinɥø, -øːz], *a.* sinuous; circuitous, tortuous, winding (path); meandering (stream); **pensée sinueuse,** devious way of reasoning.
sinuosité [sinɥozite], *s.f.* (*a*) sinuosity, winding; meandering; (*b*) deviousness. 2. bend, loop (of river, etc.).
sinus[1] [sinys], *s.m. Anat:* sinus; **les s. frontaux,** the frontal sinuses; **s. maxillaire,** maxillary sinus; antrum (of Highmore); **s. du cœur,** sinus of the aorta.
sinus[2], *s.m. Mth:* sine.
sinusal, -aux [sinyzal, -o], *a. Anat:* sinusal.
sinusite [sinyzit], *s.f. Med:* sinusitis.
sinusoïdal [sinyzɔidal], *a. Mth:* sinusoidal (function); **onde sinusoïdale,** sine wave, sinusoid; *Elcs:* **potentiomètre à variations sinusoïdales,** sine-cosine, resolving, potentiometer.
sinusoïde [sinyzɔid], *s.f. Mth:* sinusoid, sine curve.
Sion [siɔ̃, sjɔ̃], *Pr.n. B.Geog:* Zion, Sion.
sionisme [sjɔnism], *s.m.* Zionism.
sioniste [sjɔnist], *a. & s.* Zionist.
sioux [sju], *a. & s.inv. Ethn:* Sioux; **s'avancer avec des ruses de S.,** to proceed stealthily.
siphoïde [sifɔid], *a.* siphonal, siphoniform.
siphon [sifɔ̃], *s.m.* **1.** (*a*) *Ph: etc:* siphon; *Tg:* **s. recorder,** siphon recorder; (*b*) **s. (d'eau de Seltz),** (soda water) siphon; (*c*) *Const: etc:* trap (of sink pipe, drain, etc.); **s. d'égout,** interceptor; **s. de fermeture hydraulique,** liquid seal; **s. isolateur,** water seal; (*d*) *Geol:* siphon. **2.** *Z:* siphon, siphuncle. **3.** *Nau: A:* waterspout.
siphonage [sifɔnaːʒ], *s.m.* siphonage, siphoning.
siphonal, -aux [sifɔnal, -o], *a.* siphonal (tube).
siphonaptères [sifɔnaptɛːr], *s.m.pl. Ent:* Siphonaptera.
siphonariidés [sifɔnariide], *s.m.pl. Moll:* Siphonaridae.
siphonné [sifɔne], *a. F:* crazy, bats, loopy.
siphonnement [sifɔnmɑ̃], *s.m.* siphoning, siphonage.
siphonner [sifɔne], *v.tr.* to siphon.
siphonogamie [sifɔnɔgami], *s.f. Biol:* siphonogamy.
siphonophore [sifɔnɔfɔːr], *s.m. Coel:* siphonophore; *pl.* **siphonophores,** Siphonophora.
siphonostome [sifɔnɔstoːm], *Ich:* **1.** *a.* siphonostomatous. **2.** *s.m.* siphonostoma, pipe fish; *pl.* **siphonostomes,** Siphonostomata.
Sirbon [sirbɔ̃], *Pr.n. Geog:* **le lac de S.,** the Serbonian Lake; *Lit:* the Serbonian Bog.
sirdar [sirdaːr], *s.m.* sirdar.
sire [siːr], *s.m.* **1.** (*a*) *A:* lord, sir; **beau s.,** fair sir; (*b*) *Pej:* **un triste s.,** a sad specimen (of humanity). **2.** (*title of address to emperor or king*) Sire.
sirène [sirɛn], *s.f.* **1.** (*a*) *Myth:* siren, mermaid; **chant de s.,** siren song; (*b*) *A: F:* siren, *P:* vamp. **2.** *Nau: Ind:* (*a*) siren, hooter, buzzer; (*b*) fog horn; **un coup de s.,** a blast on the siren. **3.** (*a*) *Rept:* siren; (*b*) *Z:* **les sirènes,** the Sirenia (dugong, manatee, etc.).
siréner [sirene], *v.i.* (**je sirène, n. sirénons; je sirénerai**) *Nau: A:* to blow the siren.
sirénidés [sirenide], *s.m.pl. Amph:* Sirenidae.
sirénien [sirenjɛ̃], *a. & s.m. Z:* sirenian; *pl.* **siréniens,** Sirenia.
sirex [sirɛks], *s.m. Ent:* sirex.
siricidés [siriside], *s.m.pl. Ent:* Siricidae.
sirli [sirli], *s.m. Orn:* **s. des déserts,** bifasciated lark; **s. de Dupont,** Dupont's lark.
siroc(c)o [sirɔko], *s.m.* siroc(c)o (wind).
sirop [siro], *s.m.* syrup; *Med:* linctus; **s. de sucre,** golden syrup; **s. de groseille(s),** red-currant syrup; *P:* **s. de grenouille(s),** water; **tomber au s.,** to fall into the water, the river, etc.; *P:* **avoir un coup de s.,** to be slightly tipsy; to have had a drop too much; *P:* **je l'ai eu au s.,** I led him up the garden path, put one over on him.
siroter [sirɔte], *v.tr.* (*a*) *F:* to sip (one's wine, etc.); (*b*) *abs. P:* to tipple.
siroteur, -euse [sirɔtœːr, -øːz], *s. F:* tippler.
sirupeux, -euse [sirypø, -øːz], *a.* (*a*) syrupy; (*b*) (*of pers.*) sentimental, sloppy.
sirvente [sirvɑ̃ːt], **sirventès** [sirvɑ̃tɛs], *s.m. Hist. of Lit:* sirvente (a form of Provençal lay).
sisal [sizal], *s.m. Bot:* sisal; **(fibre de) s.,** sisal hemp, grass, fibre.
Sisara [sizara], *Pr.n.m. B.Hist:* Sisera.
sismal, -aux [sismal, -o], *a.* seismal.
sismicité [sismisite], *s.f.* seismicity.
sismique [sismik], *a.* seismic (movement).
sismo- [sismɔ], *pref.* seismo-.
sismogénique [sismɔʒenik], *a.* that causes an earthquake.
sismogramme [sismɔgram], *s.m.* seismogramme.
sismographe [sismɔgraf], *s.m.* seismograph.
sismographie [sismɔgrafi], *s.f.* seismography.
sismographique [sismɔgrafik], *a.* seismographic (-al).
sismologie [sismɔlɔʒi], *s.f.* seismology.
sismologique [sismɔlɔʒik], *a.* seismological.
sismologiste [sismɔlɔʒist], **sismologue** [sismɔlɔg], *s.m. & f.* seismologist.
sismomètre [sismɔmɛtr̥], *s.m.* seismometer.
sismoscope [sismɔskɔp], *s.m.* seismoscope.
sismothérapie [sismɔterapi], *s.f. Med:* **1.** vibromassage. **2.** shock therapy.
sisteronais, -aise [sistərɔnɛ, -ɛːz], *a. & s. Geog:* (native, inhabitant) of Sisteron.
sistre [sistr̥], *s.m. A.Mus:* sistrum.
sisymbre [sizɛ̃br̥], *s.m.,* **sisymbrium** [sizɛ̃brjɔm], *s.m. Bot:* sisymbrium; **sisymbre officinal,** hedge mustard.
Sisyphe [sizif], *Pr.n.m. Myth:* Sisyphus; **un travail de Sisyphe,** Sisyphean labour; **c'est le rocher de Sisyphe,** it's a never-ending job.
sita [sita], *s.m.inv.* (*from* **Société industrielle de transports automobiles**) *F:* (*in Paris*) dust cart.
sitar [sitaːr], *s.m. Mus:* sitar.
site [sit], *s.m.* **1.** (*a*) (picturesque) site; beauty spot; (*b*) (building, etc.) site; **s. archéologique,** archaeological site. **2.** (*a*) *Civ.E: Mil:* lie of the ground; (*b*) *Artil: Surv: etc:* **(angle de) site,** angle of sight; **(angle de) s. positif,** (angle of) elevation; **(angle de) s. négatif,** (angle of) depression; *Artil:* **s. négatif 10°,** depression 10°; **ligne de s.,** line of sight.
sitiologie [sitjɔlɔʒi], *s.f.* sit(i)ology; dietetics.
sitogoniomètre [sitɔgɔnjɔmɛtr̥], *s.m. Ball:* sitogoniometer.
sitôt [sito], *adv.* (*a*) (= AUSSITÔT) as soon, so soon; **je ne serai pas de retour s. que vous,** I shall not be back as soon as you; **s. le soleil couché,** as soon as the sun was set; **s. après l'école, il entra dans le commerce,** on leaving school he went straight into business; **s. dit s. fait,** no sooner said than done; *conj.phr.* **s. que** + *ind.,* as soon as . . .; **s. que la nouvelle se sut . . .,** the minute the news became known . . .; (*b*) (*with neg.*) **vous ne le reverrez pas de s.,** it will be a long time, it will be a good while, before you see him again.
sittelle [sitɛl], *s.f. Orn:* sitta; **s. (torche-pot),** nuthatch; **s. corse,** Corsican, *U.S:* red-breasted, nuthatch; **s. des rochers,** rock nuthatch.
situable [sitɥabl̩], *a.* that can be situated; **événement s.,** event that can (easily) be placed, situated.
situation [sitɥasjɔ̃], *s.f.* **1.** (*a*) situation, position, site (of a town, etc.); (*b*) *Nau:* bearing. **2.** *A:* attitude, posture, position (of the body). **3.** (*a*) state, condition; **être en s. de faire qch.,** to be in a position to do sth.; **exposer la s.,** to explain the situation, the state of affairs; **j'exposerai clairement la s.,** I will put the case clearly; **je lui ai exposé ma s.,** I explained to him how I was placed, how I stood; **s. sociale,** station in life; **je voudrais améliorer ma s.,** I want to better my circumstances; **quelle est sa s. de fortune?** what is his financial position? **quelle est la s. (des affaires) de cette maison?** what is the position of the firm? how is the firm placed? **elle est dans une s. intéressante,** she is pregnant, in an interesting condition; **s. difficile,** difficult situation; predicament; **l'homme de la s.,** the right man in the right place; **s. financière d'une maison,** financial standing of a house; **s. de la caisse,** cash position; **s. en banque d'un client,** customer's position at the bank; (*b*) **mot de s.,** appropriate word; *adv.phr.* **en s.,** in the right place, appropriate; (*c*) *Adm: Mil: etc:* report, return; **s. de la banque,** bank return, bank statement; *Mil:* **s.-rapport,** daily return of strength. **4. il a une belle s.,** he has a good job; **se faire une belle s.,** to work one's way up into a good position; *Journ:* **situations vacantes,** appointments, situations, vacant.
situé [sitɥe], *a.* (*of town, house, etc.*) situate(d) (**à,** at); **cette maison est bien située,** this house has a good situation, is well placed.
situer [sitɥe], *v.tr.* to place, situate, locate (a house, etc.); **s. un ouvrage dans l'ensemble de l'œuvre de qn,** to allocate, assign, a place to a work within s.o.'s literary productions; *F:* **s. qn,** to make s.o. out, size s.o. up; *Th: etc:* **l'action se situe à Rome en 1516,** the action takes place in Rome in 1516; **son œuvre se situe à l'aube du romantisme,** his work belongs to the early days of romanticism; **je n'arrive pas à me s. (par rapport à ce groupe),** I can't find my feet (in this circle).
situtounga [sitytungə], *s.m. Z:* situtunga.
sium [sjɔm], *s.m. Bot:* sium; (*a*) caraway; (*b*) skirret.
six, *num.a.inv. & s.m.* (*before noun beginning with consonant* [si]; *before noun beginning with vowel sound* [siz]; *otherwise* [sis]) six. **1.** *card.a.* **s. hommes** [sizɔm], six men; **s. petits enfants** [siptizɑ̃fɑ̃], six little children; **à s. heures** [asizœːr], at six o'clock; **j'en ai s.** [sis], I have six. **2.** (*a*) *s.m.* **s. et demi** [sisedmi], six and a half; (*b*) (*ordinal use, etc.*) **le s. mai** [simɛ], the sixth of May; **Charles Six,** [sis], Charles the Sixth; **le numéro s.** [sis], number six; **le s.** [sis] **de cœur,** the six of hearts; **le double s.,** the double six (at dominoes); (*c*) (*in dicing*) sice; **amener s. et cinq,** to throw sice cinque.
sixain [sizɛ̃], *s.m.* **1.** group of six (objects); packet of six packs (of cards, etc.). **2.** *Pros:* sextain, six-line stanza. **3.** *Cr:* over. **4.** *Mus:* sextolet.
sixaine [sizɛn], *s.f.* (*rare*) half (a) dozen.
six-huit [sisɥit], *s.m. Mus:* **1. (mesure à) s.-h.,** six-eight time. **2.** piece in six-eight time.
sixième [sizjɛm]. **1.** *num.a. & s.* sixth; **le, la, s. de sa classe,** the sixth in his, her, class; **demeurer au s. (étage),** to live on the sixth floor, *U.S:* seventh floor. **2.** *s.m.* sixth (part); **cinq sixièmes,** five sixths. **3.** *s.f. Sch:* **(classe de) s.** (*approx.* =) first form (of grammar school).
sixièmement [sizjɛmmɑ̃], *adv.* sixthly, in the sixth place.
six-mâts [simɑ], *s.m.inv.* six-masted vessel; six-master.
six-quatre [siskatr̥], *s.m. Mus:* **1. (mesure à) s.-q.,** six-four time. **2.** piece in six-four time.
six-quatre-deux (à la) [alasiskatdø], *adv.phr. F:* **faire qch. à la s.-q.-d.,** to do sth. in a slapdash manner; to dash sth. off; to do sth. all anyhow.
sixte[1] [sikst], *s.f.* **1.** *Mus:* sixth; **accord de s.,** chord of the sixth. **2.** *Fenc:* **parer en s.,** to parry in sixte.
Sixte[2], *Pr.n.m. Ecc.Hist:* Sixtus; **S. Quint,** Sixtus the Fifth.
Sixtine [sikstin], *a.f.* **la chapelle S.,** the Sistine Chapel.
sizain [sizɛ̃], *s.m.* **1.** packet of six packs (of cards, etc.). **2.** *Pros:* sextain, six-line stanza.
sizaine [sizɛn], *s.f. Scouting:* (cub, brownie) six.
sizerin [siz(ə)rɛ̃], *s.m. Orn:* **s. flammé,** redpoll; **s. blanchâtre,** arctic, *U.S:* hoary, redpoll; **s. du Groënland,** greater redpoll; **s. cabaret,** lesser redpoll; **s. boréal,** mealy redpoll.
skénite [skenit], *s.f. Med:* inflammation of Skene's glands.
sketch [skɛtʃ], *s.m. Th:* sketch; *pl. sketches.*
ski [ski], *s.m.* **1.** ski; **descendre à, en, skis,** to ski down, to come down on skis; **saut en, à, ski(s),** ski jump, ski jumping; **mettre, attacher, ses skis,** to put on one's skis. **2.** skiing; **faire du s.,** to ski; to go in for skiing; **il aime faire du s.,** he is fond of skiing; **chaussures de s.,** ski boots; **bâton de s.,** ski stick; **station de s.,** ski resort; **piste de s.,** ski slope; **saut de s.,** (i) ski jump; (ii) *Civ.E:* ski jump, spillway. **3. s. nautique,** water skiing; **faire du s. nautique,** to water-ski.

skiable [skjabl̩], *a.* **neige s.,** good skiing snow; **piste s.,** slope fit for skiing; **domaine s.,** skiing area.
skiagramme [skjagram], *s.m.* sciagraph, skiagram, radiograph.
skiagraphie [skjagrafi], *s.f.* sciagraphy, radiography.
skiascopie [skjaskɔpi], *s.f. Opt:* skiascopy, sciascopy.
skiatron [skjatrɔ̃], *s.m. Elcs:* skiatron.
skier [skje], *v.i.* to ski.
skieur, -euse [skjœːr, -øːz], *s.* skier; *Mil:* **éclaireurs skieurs,** ski troops.
skiff [skif], *s.m. Nau:* skiff.
skip [skip], *s.m. Ind:* skip; **s. à déversement automatique,** self-dumping skip; **s. basculant,** tilting skip.
skungs [skœ̃ːgz], **skunks** [skœ̃ːks], *s.m. Com:* skunk (fur).
skuttérudite [skyterydit], *s.f. Miner:* skutterudite.
slacks [slak(s)], *s.m.pl. Cost:* slacks.
slalom [slalɔm], *s.m.* (*a*) *Skiing:* slalom; (*b*) *F:* **faire du s. entre les voitures,** to dodge in and out among the cars; **conduire à Paris c'est un drôle de s.,** driving in Paris is a hell of an obstacle race.
slave [slaːv]. **1.** *a.* Slav, Slavonic. **2.** *s.m. & f.* Slav. **3.** *s.m. Ling:* **le slave,** Slavonic; **vieux-s. (d'Église),** Palaeoslavonic, Church Slavonic.
slavisant, -ante [slavizɑ̃, -ɑ̃ːt], *s.,* **slaviste** [slavist], *s.m. & f.* student of Slavonic languages, history, customs, etc.; Slavist.
slavon, -onne [slavɔ̃, -ɔn]. **1.** *a. & s. Geog:* Slavonian, Slavonic. **2.** *s.m. Ling:* **le s.,** Palaeoslavonic, Church Slavonic.
Slavonie [slavɔni], *Pr.n.f. Geog:* Slavonia.
slavophile [slavɔfil], *a. & s.m. & f.* Slavophile.
slavophobe [slavɔfɔb], *a. & s.m. & f.* Slavophobe.
sleeping [slipiŋ], *s.m. Rail: F:* (*a*) sleeping car; (*b*) berth.
Slesvig (le) [ləslɛzvig], *Pr.n.m. Geog:* Schleswig.
slikke [slik], *s.f. Geog:* mud flat, tidal flat.
slip [slip], *s.m.* **1.** *Cost:* briefs; (*for man*) slip; **s. minimum,** bikini briefs; **s. de bain,** bathing slip, briefs; **s. de soutien (pour sportifs),** athletic support, *F:* jock strap. **2.** *Sp:* (*coursing*) slip. **3.** *Nau:* slipway; *Av:* launching ways (of seaplane).
slogan [slɔgɑ̃], *s.m. Com: Pol:* slogan.
sloop [slup], *s.m. Nau:* sloop; **s. à tape-cul,** yawl.
sloughi [slugi], *s.m.* saluki; Arabian gazelle hound.
slovaque [slɔvak], *a. & s.m. & f. Geog: Ling:* Slovak.
Slovaquie [slɔvaki], *Pr.n.f. Geog:* Slovakia.
slovène [slɔvɛn]. **1.** *a. & s. Ethn:* Slovene, Slovenian. **2.** *s.m. Ling:* **le s.,** Slovenian.
Slovénie [slɔveni], *Pr.n.f. Geog:* Slovenia.
slow [slo], *s.m. Danc: F:* slow foxtrot.
sluice [slɥis], *s.m. Gold Min:* sluice.
smala(h) [smala], *s.f.* (*a*) (Arab chief's) retinue; (*b*) *F:* large family, household; **partir au bord de la mer avec toute sa s.,** to go off to the seaside with all one's tribe.
Smalkalde [smalkald], *Pr.n. Geog:* Schmalkalden; *Hist:* **la ligue de S.,** the Schmalkaldic League; *Rel.H:* **articles de S.,** Schmalkaldic articles.
smalt [smalt], *s.m. Ch: Glassm: etc:* smalt.
smaltine [smaltin], *s.f.,* **smaltite** [smaltit], *s.f. Miner:* smaltine, smaltite.
smaragd [smaragd], *s.m. Miner:* smaragd.
smaragdin [smaragdɛ̃], *a.* emerald green, smaragdine (stone, etc.).
smaragdite [smaragdit], *s.f. Miner:* smaragdite.
smash [smaʃ], *s.m. Ten: etc:* smash.
smasher [smaʃe], *v.tr. Ten: etc:* to smash (the ball).
smectique [smɛktik], *a.* **argile s.,** fuller's earth; smectite.
smectite [smɛktit], *s.f. Miner:* smectite.
smegma [smɛgma], *s.m. Physiol: Vet:* smegma.
smeltage [smɛltaːʒ], *s.m. Metall:* smelting.
smérinthe [smerɛ̃ːt], *s.m. Ent:* hawk moth.
smigard, -arde [smigaːr, -ard], *s. F:* worker on minimum basic wage.
smilax [smilaks], *s.m. Bot:* smilax; **s. de Chine,** China root.
smillage [smilaːʒ], *s.m. Const: Min:* spalling, scabbling.
smille [smiːj], *s.f. Tls:* spalling hammer.
smiller [smije], *v.tr. Const: Min:* to spall, scabble; *Const:* **moellon smillé,** spalled stone, scabbled stone; **appareil en moellons smillés,** spalled rubble.
sminthure [smɛ̃tyːr], *s.m. Ent:* sminthurid.
sminthuridés [smɛ̃tyride], *s.m.pl. Ent:* Sminthuridae.
smithsonite [smitsɔnit], *s.f. Miner:* smithsonite.
smock [smɔk], *Needlew:* **1.** *a.inv.* **fronces s.,** smocking. **2.** *pl.* **smocks,** smocking.
smogler [smɔgle], *v.tr. F:* to smuggle.
smogleur [smɔglœːr], *s.m. F:* smuggler.
smoking [smɔkiŋ, -iŋ], *s.m.* dinner jacket, *U.S:* tuxedo.
smolt [smɔlt], *s.m. Pisc:* smolt.
Smyrne [smirn], *Pr.n.f. Hist:* Smyrna; *Cu:* **raisins de S.,** sultanas.
smyrnéen, -enne [smirneɛ̃, -ɛn], *a. & s.,* **smyrniote** [smirnjɔt], *a. & s. Hist:* Smyrniote, Smyrnean.
snack(-bar) [snak(baːr)], *s.m. F:* snack bar; *pl. snack(-bars).*
snob [snɔb]. **1.** *a. & s.m. & f.* (*a*) pretentious person; (*b*) snob. **2.** *a. F:* smart; **ça fait très s.,** that's very smart, very U.
snobard, -arde [snɔbaːr, -ard], *s. F: Pej:* snob.
snober [snɔbe], *v.tr. F: Pej:* to despise, look down on (s.o.); to cold-shoulder, cut (s.o.).
snobinard, -arde [snɔbinaːr, -ard], *s.* a bit of a snob.
snobinette [snɔbinɛt], *s.f. F: Pej:* pretentious young woman.
snobisme [snɔbism], *s.m.* **1.** infatuation for anything that is all the rage; (vulgar) desire to be in the swim; devotion to fashion. **2.** snobbery; **s. à rebours,** inverted snobbery; **s. intellectuel,** intellectual snobbery.
snow-boot [snobut], *s.m. O:* snow boot; galosh; *pl. snow-boots.*
sobre [sɔbr̩], *a.* **1.** temperate, abstemious (person); moderate (meal); **c'est un homme s.,** he's a sober, abstemious, man; *F:* **il est s. comme un chameau,** he never drinks. **2. s. de paroles, de louanges,** sparing of words, chary of praise; **homme s. de paroles,** man of few words; **dépêche s. de renseignements,** dispatch sparing of information, reticent dispatch; *A:* **homme s. à louer,** man chary of praise. **3. dessin très s.,** sober drawing, drawing showing great economy of line; restrained drawing.
sobrement [sɔbrəmɑ̃], *adv.* soberly. **1.** temperately, moderately, frugally, abstemiously. **2.** quietly, unostentatiously (dressed).
sobriété [sɔbri(j)ete], *s.f.* **1.** temperateness, abstemiousness, sobriety (in food and drink); moderation (in speech, etc.); **habitudes de s.,** temperate habits; **s. de parole,** sobriety of speech; **s. de style,** restraint (in style); **manger et boire avec s.,** to eat and drink in moderation, temperately. **2.** discreetness.
sobriquet [sɔbrikɛ], *s.m.* nickname, so(u)briquet; **connu sous le s. de Bossu,** nicknamed, dubbed, the Hunchback.
soc [sɔk], *s.m.* **1.** ploughshare. **2.** (*a*) shoe, socket (of lance, colour staff); (*b*) *Artil:* blade portion (of trail spade).
socage [sɔkaːʒ], *s.m. Hist:* soc(c)age.
sochet [sɔʃɛ], *s.m.* swing plough.
sociabilité [sɔsjabilite], *s.f.* sociability, sociableness.
sociable [sɔsjabl̩]. **1.** *a.* sociable, companionable; **peu s.,** unsociable. **2.** *s.m. A.Veh:* sociable.
sociablement [sɔsjabləmɑ̃], *adv.* sociably.
social, -ale, -aux [sɔsjal, -o]. **1.** *a.* social; (*a*) of society; **l'ordre s.,** the social order; **science sociale,** social science, sociology; **œuvres sociales,** welfare activities; **guerre sociale,** class war; *A.Hist:* **les guerres sociales,** the social wars; **service s. de l'armée,** army welfare service, *U.S:* special service; **atteindre le sommet de l'échelle sociale,** to reach the top of the social ladder; *Z:* **abeilles, fourmis, sociales,** social bees, ants; (*b*) *Com:* **nom s., raison sociale,** name, style, of the firm, of the company; **siège s.,** head office; **capital s.,** registered capital; **année sociale,** company's (trading) year. **2.** *s.f. A:* **la Sociale, the** Social State. **3.** *s.m. F:* social news.
social-démocrate [sɔsjaldemɔkrat], *a. & s.m. & f. Pol:* social democrat; *pl. sociaux-démocrates.*
social-démocratie [sɔsjaldemɔkrasi], *s.f. Pol:* social democracy.
socialement [sɔsjalmɑ̃], *adv.* socially, with reference to society; **son mariage l'a tuée s.,** her marriage finished her off socially.
socialisant, -ante [sɔsjalizɑ̃, -ɑ̃ːt], *a. & s. Pol:* (person) with socialist tendencies.
socialisation [sɔsjalizasjɔ̃], *s.f. Pol.Ec:* socialization, collectivization (of capital, industries).
socialiser [sɔsjalize], *v.tr. Pol.Ec:* to socialize, collectivize (property, etc.).
socialisme [sɔsjalism], *s.m.* socialism; **s. d'État,** State socialism; **s. chrétien,** Christian socialism.
socialiste [sɔsjalist]. **1.** *a.* (*a*) socialistic (doctrine, etc.); socialist (doctrine, M.P.); (*b*) *Lit:* social. **2.** *s.m. & f.* socialist.
sociétaire [sɔsjetɛːr]. **1.** *s.m. & f.* (*a*) (full) member (of corporate body); **carte de s.,** membership card; (*b*) **s. d'une société anonyme,** shareholder, stockholder; (*c*) *Th:* actor who has a share in the profits of the company (*esp.* Comédie Française). **2.** *s.m.pl. Z:* **(animaux) sociétaires,** sociable, gregarious, animals.
sociétariat [sɔsjetarja], *s.m.* full membership (*esp.* of the Comédie-Française).
société [sɔsjete], *s.f.* **1.** (*a*) society; community; **devoirs envers la s.,** duty to society, to the community; (*b*) company, gathering, group, circle; **un nouveau venu à notre s.,** a newcomer to our circle, our group; **ça ne se fait pas dans la bonne s.,** that is not done in the best society; **nous étions une s. nombreuse,** we were a large gathering, a large group; (*c*) **animaux qui vivent en s.,** social animals. **2.** (*a*) society, association; *Hist:* **la S. des Nations,** the League of Nations; **s. de gymnastique,** gymnastics club; **s. de tir,** rifle club; **s. de secours aux blessés,** first-aid association; (*b*) *Com: Ind:* company, firm; partnership; **s. mère,** parent company; **s. filiale,** subsidiary company; branch; **s. par actions,** joint-stock company; *U.S:* incorporated company; **s. anonyme,** public company; **s. à responsabilité limitée** = limited (liability) company; **s. en commandite,** limited partnership; **s. d'économie mixte,** semi-public corporation, semi-nationalized industry; **s. constituée,** incorporated company; **s. d'exploitation minière,** mining company; **s. immobilière,** real estate company; *Nau:* **s. d'armement, de navigation, de transports maritimes,** shipping, navigation, company; **s. de classification (de navires),** ships' classification society; **s. d'utilité publique,** public utility company, *U.S:* utility; **s. d'exploitation,** development company; **s. concessionnaire,** statutory company; **s. coopérative,** co-operative society; **s. de crédit mutuel,** friendly society; **s. en nom collectif,** firm, (general) partnership, private company; **acte de s.,** (i) deed of partnership; (ii) memorandum of association; *Fin:* **s. à portefeuille,** holding company; **s. de placement,** investment trust; *Mth:* **règles de s.,** rules of proportionate division, distribution. **3.** (*a*) company (of one's fellows); **il aime la s.,** he likes company; (*b*) (fashionable) society; **femmes de s.,** society women; *A:* **homme de s.,** man about town; **talents de s.,** social gifts; (*c*) **jeux de s.,** parlour games. **4.** *Geog:* **archipel de la S.,** Society Islands.
Socin [sɔsɛ̃], *Pr.n.m. Rel.H:* Socinus.
socinianisme [sɔsinjanism], *s.m. Theol:* Socinianism.
socinien, -ienne [sɔsinjɛ̃, -jɛn], *a. & s. Theol:* Socinian.
sociocentrisme [sɔsjɔsɑ̃trism], *s.m.* sociocentrism.
sociocratie [sɔsjɔkrasi], *s.f.* sociocracy.
socio-culturel, -elle [sɔsjɔkyltyrɛl], *a.* sociocultural; *pl. socio-culturel, -elles.*
sociodrame [sɔsjɔdram], *s.m. Psy:* sociodrama.
socio-économique [sɔsjɔekɔnɔmik], *a.* socio-economic; *pl. socio-économiques.*
sociogénèse [sɔsjɔʒenɛːz], *s.f.* sociogenesis.
sociogénétique [sɔsjɔʒenetik], *a.* sociogenetic.
socio-géographie [sɔsjɔʒeɔgrafi], *s.f.* sociogeography.
sociogramme [sɔsjɔgram], *s.m. Psy:* sociogram.
sociologie [sɔsjɔlɔʒi], *s.f.* sociology.
sociologique [sɔsjɔlɔʒik], *a.* sociological.
sociologisme [sɔsjɔlɔʒism], *s.m.* sociologism.
sociologiste [sɔsjɔlɔʒist]. **1.** *a.* sociologistic. **2.** *s.m. & f.* sociologist.
sociologue [sɔsjɔlɔg], *s.m. & f.* sociologist.
sociométrie [sɔsjɔmetri], *s.f.* sociometry.
sociométriste [sɔsjɔmetrist], *s.m. & f.* sociometrist.
socle [sɔkl̩], *s.m.* socle, base, bottom, pedestal, plinth (for statue, column); stand (for apparatus); footing (of wall); base, socket (for mast, etc.); bed plate (of engine); concrete bed (for heavy ordnance); *Geol:* insular shelf; base, substratum; **le s. de la société française demeure toujours paysan,** the basis of the French social system is still the farmer; *Const:* **s. de lambris,** skirting board; *El:* **s. isolant,** insulating base; **s. à bornes,** terminal plate.
Socotora [sɔkɔtɔra], **Socotra** [sɔkɔtra], *Pr.n. Geog:* Socotra, Sokotra.
socque [sɔk], *s.m.* **1.** clog, patten. **2.** *A: Th:* (comedian's) sock; *Lit:* **le s. et le cothurne,** comedy and tragedy.
socquette [sɔkɛt], *s.f.* ankle sock, *U.S:* bobby sock.
Socrate [sɔkrat], *Pr.n.m.* Socrates.
socratique [sɔkratik], *a.* Socratic (method, irony); *Lit:* **mœurs socratiques,** pederasty.

soda [sɔda], *s.m.* **1.** *Miner:* soda. **2.** *Com:* soda water.
sodalite [sɔdalit], *s.f. Miner:* sodalite.
sodalité [sɔdalite], *s.f. A: & Lit:* **1.** sodality. **2.** good fellowship, conviviality.
soddite [sɔdit], *s.f.*, **soddyite** [sɔdjit], *s.f. Miner:* sodd(y)ite.
sodé [sɔde], *a.* containing soda.
sodique [sɔdik], *a. Ch:* (of) sodium, containing soda, sodic; **sel s.,** soda salt, sodium salt.
sodium [sɔdjɔm], *s.m. Ch:* sodium.
sodoku [sɔdɔky], *s.m. Med:* sodoku, rat-bite fever.
Sodome [sɔdɔm], *Pr.n. B.Hist:* Sodom.
sodomie [sɔdɔmi], *s.f.* sodomy.
sodomiser [sɔdɔmize], *v.i.* to practise sodomy, to sodomize.
sodomite [sɔdɔmit], *s.m.* sodomite.
sœur [sœːr], *s.f.* **1.** sister; *Jur:* **s. de père et mère, s. germaine,** sister german, own sister, full sister; **s. consanguine, de père,** half sister (on father's side); **s. utérine, de mère,** half sister (on mother's side), uterine sister; **s. de lait,** foster sister; **baiser de s.,** sisterly kiss; *Lit:* **les neuf sœurs,** the nine muses; *P:* **et ta s.!** tell that to the marines! **2.** *Ecc:* sister, nun; **les petites Sœurs des Pauvres,** the Little Sisters of the Poor; **la s. Ursule,** Sister Ursula; **entrez, ma s.,** come in, sister.
sœurette [sœrɛt], *s.f. Lit:* little sister.
sofa [sɔfa], *s.m.* sofa, settee.
soffite [sɔfit], *s.m. Arch:* soffit.
sofi [sɔfi], *s.m.* Sufi ((i) Mohammedan mystic; (ii) ancient title of Persian monarch).
sofisme [sɔfism], *s.m. Rel.H:* Sufiism, Sufism.
software [sɔftwɛːr], *s.m. Elcs:* (*computers*) software.
Sogdiane [sɔgdjan], *Pr.n.f. A.Geog:* Sogdiana.
soi [swa], *pers.pron.*(*stressed, usually, but not always, referring to an indef. subject*) oneself; himself, herself, itself, etc. **1.** (*reflexive or reciprocal*) **on doit rarement parler de s.,** one should avoid speaking too much of oneself; **chacun pour s.,** everyone for himself; **la vertu est aimable en soi, de s.,** virtue is lovable in itself, per se; **article en s. inoffensif,** article inoffensive in itself; **il va de s. que . . .,** it stands to reason, goes without saying, that . . .; **penser à s.(-même),** to think of oneself; **avoir la loi pour s.,** to have the law on one's side; **il n'est plus maître de s.,** he is no longer master of himself; **elle traînait derrière s. sa poupée cassée,** she was dragging her broken doll behind her; **se parler à s.-même,** to talk to oneself; **petits services qu'on se rend entre s.,** small mutual services; (*often useful to discriminate between complements*) **l'avare qui a un fils prodigue n'amasse ni pour s. ni pour lui,** the miser who has a prodigal son collects neither for himself nor for that son. **2.** (*emphatic*) **pour s'assurer qu'une chose sera bien faite, il faut la faire s.-même,** if you want a thing well done, you must do it yourself.
soi-disant [swadizɑ̃]. **1.** *a.inv.* (*a*) self-styled, would-be; **une s.-d. comtesse,** a self-styled countess; a *soi-disant* countess; (*b*) so-called; **les arts s.-d. libéraux,** the so-called liberal arts. **2.** *adv.* supposedly, ostensibly; **il est parti s.-d. pour revenir,** he went away, supposedly with the intention of coming back.
soie [swa, swɑ], *s.f.* **1.** (*a*) bristle (of pig, wild boar, caterpillar, etc.); **couvert de soies,** bristled; bristly; *Moll: F:* **s. marine,** byssus (of pinna); (*b*) **coton à longues soies,** long-yarn cotton. **2.** (*a*) silk; **s. filée,** spun silk; **robe de s.,** silk dress; **s. végétale,** vegetable silk; *O:* **s. artificielle,** artificial silk; **papier de s.,** tissue paper; *Lit:* **jours filés d'or et de s.,** life of happiness and prosperity; (*b*) **s. de verre,** fibre glass. **3.** *Bot:* (*a*) awn; (*b*) **plante à s.,** silkweed, swallow wort. **4.** *Tchn:* (*a*) tang, tongue, fang (of tool, sword, blade, etc.); (*b*) *Mch:* pin (of crank, etc.). **5.** *Vet:* toe crack (of horse).
soierie [swari], *s.f.* **1.** silk fabric, silk fabrics; silk goods; silks; **marchand de soieries,** silk mercer. **2.** (*a*) silk factory; (*b*) silk trade.
soif [swaf], *s.f.* thirst; (*a*) **avoir s.,** to be thirsty; dry; **les rosiers ont s., il faut les arroser,** the rose trees are dry, we must water them; **boire à sa s., étancher sa s.,** *F:* **boire jusqu'à plus s.,** to drink one's fill; to slake one's thirst; **cela me donne s.,** it makes me thirsty; **je meurs de s.,** I'm dying of thirst; **rester sur sa s.,** (i) to remain thirsty; (ii) to remain unsatisfied; to want more (of sth.); **garder une poire pour la s.,** to put sth. aside for a rainy day; *Prov:* **on ne saurait faire boire un âne qui n'a pas s.,** you can lead a horse to the water but you can't make him drink; (*b*) **la s. de connaître,** the thirst for knowledge; **la s. de l'or,** the thirst for gold; **la s. du pouvoir, de la vengeance,** hankering after, craving for, power, revenge; **avoir s. de sang,** to be bloodthirsty; **avoir la s. des louanges, avoir s. de louanges,** to have a craving for praise.
soiffard, -arde [swafaːr, -ard], *a. & s. P:* (person) who is (i) always ready for a drink, (ii) who drinks too much, lifts the elbow; *s.* drunk(ard), boozer, tippler.
soiffer [swafe], *v.i. P:* to booze, to soak, to tipple.
soiffeur, -euse [swafœːr, -øːz], *s. P:* toper, soaker, boozer, tippler.
soigné [swaɲe]. **1.** *a.* (*a*) well finished, carefully done; **repas s.,** carefully prepared meal; **style s.,** polished style; **chevaux bien soignés,** well-groomed horses; **mains soignées,** well-kept hands; **air s.,** well-groomed, spruce, appearance; **elle est très soignée de sa personne,** she is very careful, particular, about her appearance; **peu s. dans sa mise,** dressed in a slovenly manner; ill-groomed; **moustache soignée,** neat, trim, moustache; (*b*) *P:* first-rate, first-class; **une raclée soignée,** a sound thrashing, the hell of a thrashing; **un rhume s.,** a hell, a stinker, of a cold. **2.** *a. Art:* **faire s.,** to paint with a care for detail. **3.** *s.m. F: Iron:* **voilà du s.!** that's a nice, fine, bit of work!
soigner [swaɲe], *v.tr.* to look after, take care of (s.o., sth.); to attend to (sth.); (*a*) **s. un malade,** to nurse, look after, a patient; (*of doctor*) to attend a patient; **s. une maladie,** to treat an illness; **se s.,** (i) to take care of, look after, oneself; (ii) *F:* to coddle oneself; (iii) *F:* to do oneself well; **se s. à la quinine,** to treat, dose, oneself with quinine; **le paludisme se soigne à la quinine,** malaria is treated with quinine; **cette maladie ne se soigne pas bien,** there is no successful treatment for this disease; this disease is very difficult to cure; **il faut vous faire s. par un médecin,** you should have medical treatment, see a doctor; **il va se faire s. dans une clinique,** he is going to have treatment in a nursing home; *F:* **il faut te faire s.!** you must be mad! *F:* **soignez-le bien (pas d'indulgence),** give him the full treatment, the works; **vous avez l'air d'être très bien s.,** you appear to be very well looked after; (*b*) **s. son ménage,** to be a good housekeeper; to keep one's house in good order; **s. ses outils,** to look after one's tools, keep one's tools in good order; **s. un travail,** to do a piece of work carefully; **s. son style,** to polish one's style; **s. sa popularité,** to nurse one's public; **s. sa toilette, sa mise,** to dress with care; to be careful, particular, about one's appearance; **s. sa ligne,** to think about one's figure; to watch one's waistline.
soigneur [swaɲœːr], *s.m.* **1.** *Cy: Rac: etc:* second; bottle holder, welfare man. **2.** *Ind:* (machine) minder, tenter.
soigneusement [swaɲøzmɑ̃], *adv.* carefully, with care.
soigneux, -euse [swaɲø, -øːz], *a.* (*a*) careful, painstaking (worker, etc.); careful, tidy (pers.); **peu s.,** careless, untidy; **s. dans sa tenue,** careful, particular, about one's appearance; *A:* **s. de faire qch.,** careful to do sth.; (*b*) careful (work, etc.); **recherches soigneuses,** careful research.
soi-même [swamɛm]. *See* SOI *and* MÊME.
soin [swɛ̃], *s.m.* (*a*) care; **le s. des enfants,** the care of children; looking after children; **avoir, prendre, s. de qn, de qch.,** to look after, take care of, s.o., sth.; **avoir s. de sa réputation,** to take care of one's reputation; **confier qch. aux soins de qn,** to place sth. in s.o.'s care; to entrust s.o. with sth.; to ask s.o. to mind sth.; (*on letters etc.*) **aux (bons) soins de . . .,** care of . . ., c/o; **par les soins de . . .,** by courtesy of . . .; thanks to . . .; **les soins du ménage,** household duties; housekeeping; **il prend peu de s. de sa personne,** he is very careless, slovenly, about his appearance; (*b*) care, trouble; attention; **avoir s., grand s., bien s., de faire qch.,** to take (particular) care to do sth.; to make a point of doing sth.; **j'ai eu s. de lui rappeler que . . .,** I was careful to remind him that . . .; I made a point of reminding him that . . .; **avoir s. que** (+ *sub.*), to see that (sth. is done, etc.); to make a point of (sth. being done, etc.); **j'aurai s. que cela se fasse,** I shall see that it is done; I shall attend to it; **mettre un s. infini, tous ses soins, à faire qch.,** to put oneself to great trouble, take great pains; to do sth.; **mettre tous ses soins à ce qu'une chose soit bien faite,** to take great care, great pains, to see that sth. is properly done; **apporter tous ses soins, un s. extrême, à qch., à faire qch.,** to take great care over sth.; **confier à qn le s. de faire qch.,** to entrust s.o. with (the task of) doing sth.; **je vous laisse le s. de décider,** I leave it to you to decide; **je leur ai laissé le s. de la distraire,** I left it to them to entertain, amuse, her; (*c*) **avoir beaucoup de s.,** to be very tidy, orderly; **avec s.,** carefully; with care; **avec beaucoup de s.,** with great care; **il faut s'en servir avec s.,** one must use it with care; one must take precautions when using it; **sans s.,** (i) *adj.* careless, untidy; slovenly; slipshod; (ii) *adv.* carelessly, untidily; in a slipshod manner; **s. c'est un vrai sans s.,** he's very slipshod, slovenly; **manque de s.,** carelessness; (*d*) *pl.* care, attention; **soins médicaux,** medical care, aid; medical attendance; **premiers soins (aux blessés),** first aid (to the injured); **soins prénataux,** prenatal care; **soins pré-opératoires, post-opératoires,** pre-operative, post-operative, treatment; **il a reçu des soins à l'hôpital,** he was treated in hospital; **soins à domicile,** home nursing; **l'enfant a besoin des soins d'une mère,** a child needs a mother's care; **les soins des personnes âgées,** the care of the aged, of old people; **les soins dont il entoure sa femme,** the care he lavishes on his wife; **il faut voir de quels soins il entoure son jardin,** you should see the care he takes of his garden; **soins et traitements des animaux,** care and treatment of animals; **être aux petits soins pour, avec, qn,** to fuss over, make much of, s.o.; to wait hand and foot on s.o.; (*e*) *A:* anxiety, worry; **n'en soyez pas en s.,** have no anxiety about it.
soir [swaːr], *s.m.* (*a*) evening; **ce s.,** this evening, tonight; *Th: etc:* **représentations tous les soirs,** performances nightly, every evening; **à ce s.!** see you tonight, this evening! **il fait frais le s.,** it's cool in the evening; **que faites-vous le s.?** what do you do in the evening? **à dix heures du s.,** at ten (o'clock) in the evening; **demain (au) s.,** tomorrow evening, tomorrow night; **hier (au) s.,** yesterday evening; yesterday, last, night; **lundi (au) s.,** Monday evening; **tous les lundis s.,** every Monday evening; **le premier mai au s.,** on the evening of the first of May; **le lendemain s.,** the next evening; **la veille au s.,** the evening before, on the previous evening; **par un beau s. d'été,** on a fine summer evening; **un s. de fête,** (i) one evening of celebrating; (ii) in the evening on the day of a fair; **le s. de la fête,** the evening of the day of the fair; **le s. des noces,** in the evening after the wedding; **travailler du matin au s.,** to work from morning until night; *F:* **être du s.,** to stay up late (as a habit), *F:* to be a night bird; **robe du s.,** evening dress; *Lit:* **au s. de sa vie,** in the evening of one's life, towards the end of one's life; *Pol: O:* **le Grand S.,** the great social upheaval; (*b*) *A: & Dial:* afternoon; **à deux heures du s.,** at two o'clock in the afternoon.
soirée [sware], *s.f.* **1.** (duration of) evening; **pendant la s.,** during the evening; **passer la s. chez un ami,** to spend the evening at a friend's house; **les longues soirées d'hiver,** the long winter evenings; **bonne s.!** have a good evening (out)!, enjoy your evening! **2.** (*a*) (evening) party; **donner une s. dansante,** to give a dance; **s. musicale,** musical evening; **nous allons en, à une, s.,** we are going to an evening party, to a reception; **habit de s.,** dress suit; **tenue de s.,** evening dress; **en fin de s.,** (i) late in the evening; (ii) last thing in the evening; (*b*) *Th: etc:* **représentation de s., donnée en s.,** evening performance.
soissonnais, -aise [swasɔnɛ, -ɛːz], *a. & s. Geog:* (native, inhabitant) of Soissons.
soissons [swasɔ̃], *s.m.* (variety of) haricot bean (as grown at Soissons).
soit [swa; *before a vowel or as interjection:* swat]; (*third pers. of pr.sub. of* être) **1.** (*a*) *int.* all right! O.K.! agreed! **s., allez,** all right then, go; **vous proposez cette solution; eh bien, s.!** that's the solution you suggest; very well then; (*b*) (*retaining subjunctive value*) suppose; if for instance; **s. trois multiplié par six,** if three is multiplied by six; **s.** *ABC* **un triangle,** let *ABC* be a triangle; given a triangle ABC; **s. un cylindre creux rempli d'eau,** given a hollow cylinder filled with water; (*c*) (*conj. of co-ordination*) (that is to) say; **trois objets à dix francs, s. trente francs,** three articles at ten francs, that is to say thirty francs. **2.** (*a*) *conj.* **soit . . soit . . .; soit . . ou . . .,** either . . . or . . .; whether . . . or . . .; **s. l'un s. l'autre,** either one or the other; **s. maintenant ou demain, cela arrivera sûrement,** whether it happens today or tomorrow, it is bound to happen; **s. modestie, s. paresse, il n'a jamais rien écrit,** whether from modesty or through laziness, he has never written anything; (*b*) *conj.phr.* **s. qu'il vienne, s. qu'il ne vienne pas; s. qu'il vienne ou qu'il ne vienne pas,** whether he comes or not.

soit-communiqué [swakɔmynike], *s.m.inv. Jur:* **ordonnance de s.-c.,** order (of an examining magistrate) to send the papers relating to a case to the Public Prosecutor.

soixantaine [swasɑ̃tɛn], *s.f.* (approximately) sixty, about sixty; **une s. de francs,** some, about, sixty francs or so; **elle approche de la s.,** she is not far off, is getting on for, sixty; **il a passé la s.,** he's in his sixties.

soixante [swasɑ̃:t], *num.a.inv. & s.m.inv.* sixty; **page s.,** page sixty; **au chapitre s. de . . .,** in the sixtieth chapter of . . .; **s. et un,** sixty-one; **s. et onze,** seventy-one; **s. et onzième,** seventy-first.

soixante-dix [swasɑ̃tdis], *num.a.inv. & s.m.inv.* **1.** seventy. **2.** *Hist:* 1870.

soixante-dixième [swasɑ̃tdizjɛm]. **1.** *num.a. & s.* seventieth. **2.** *s.m.* seventieth (part).

soixante-quinze [swasɑ̃tkɛ̃:z]. **1.** *num.a.inv.* seventy-five. **2.** *s.m. Artil:* **un s.-q.,** a seventy-five (mm. field-gun).

soixantième [swasɑ̃tjɛm]. **1.** *num.a. & s.* sixtieth. **2.** *s.m.* sixtieth (part).

soja [sɔʒa], *s.m. Bot:* soya bean, soy.

sol[1] [sɔl], *s.m.* **1.** (*a*) ground, earth; **au s.,** at ground level; *El:* **relier un fil au s.,** to earth, *U.S:* ground, a wire; **conducteur au s.,** grounded conductor, earthed conductor; *Hyd.E:* **s. de fondation,** foundation stratum; **rester cloué au s.,** (i) (*of aircraft*) to be grounded; (ii) *F:* to stand rooted to the spot; *Av:* **se poser au s.,** to land (on the ground); **équipement de s.,** ground equipment; **(indicateur de) position s.,** ground position (indicator); *Aer:* **personnel au s.,** ground staff; *A:* **il ne faut pas bâtir sur le s. d'autrui,** one should not poach on other people's preserves; **le s. natal,** one's native soil; (*b*) *Geol: Agr:* soil; **s. sablonneux,** sandy soil; **s. aride, fertile,** arid, fertile, soil; (*c*) floor; **s. cimenté,** cement floor. **2.** *Her:* field. **3.** *Mil:* floor (of ditch, caponier).

sol[2], *s.m. A:* sou.

sol[3], *s.m.inv. Mus:* **1.** (*a*) (the note) G, **clef de s.,** treble clef, G clef; **morceau en s.,** piece in G; (*b*) the G string (of violin, etc.). **2.** sol, soh, (in the fixed do system).

sol[4], *s.m. & comb.fm.* sol.

sola [sɔla], *s.m. Bot:* sola; *Cost:* **casque colonial en s.,** pith helmet, sola topee.

sol-air [sɔlɛ:r], *a.inv. Mil:* ground-to-air; **engin s.-a.,** ground-to-air missile.

solaire [sɔlɛ:r], *a.* solar (system, eclipse, etc.); **rayons solaires,** solar rays; **cadran s.,** sundial; **lunettes solaires,** sun glasses; **crème s.,** sun lotion; *Med:* **traitement s.,** sunray treatment; *Astr:* **éruption s.,** solar flare; **taches solaires,** sunspots; **tour s.,** solar tower; **vent s.,** solar wind; *Ph:* **four s.,** solar furnace; **pile s.,** solar battery; *Anat:* **plexus s.,** solar plexus.

solamire [sɔlami:r], *s.f.* bolting cloth.

solanacé [sɔlanase], **solané** [sɔlane], *Bot:* **1.** *a.* solanaceous. **2.** *s.f.pl.* **solanacées, solanées,** Solanaceae.

solarigraphe [sɔlarigraf], **solarimètre** [sɔlarimɛtr], *s.m.* sunshine recorder.

solarisation [sɔlarizasjɔ̃], *s.f.* solarization.

solariser [sɔlarize], *v.tr. Phot:* to solarize (plate).

solarium [sɔlarjɔm], *s.m.* (*a*) *Med:* solarium (for sun baths); (*b*) suntrap; sun terrace.

solbatu [sɔlbaty], *a. Vet:* bruised in the hoof.

sol-ciment [sɔlsimɑ̃], *s.m. Const:* cement flooring; *pl. sols-ciments.*

soldanelle [sɔldanɛl], *s.f. Bot:* soldanella.

soldat, -ate [sɔlda, -at], *s.* **1.** (*a*) *s.m.* soldier; serviceman; **s. d'artillerie,** artilleryman; **s. de cavalerie,** cavalryman; **s. à cheval,** trooper, mounted soldier; **s. du génie,** engineer; **s. musicien,** bandsman; **s. d'ordonnance,** orderly; **s. secrétaire,** soldier clerk; **s. de marine,** marine; **soldat de 2e classe, simple s.,** private; **les simples soldats,** the rank and file; **s. de première classe,** lance-corporal; **s. mobilisable, non mobilisable,** trained, untrained, soldier; **école du soldat,** recruits' drill; **le S. inconnu,** the Unknown Warrior; **se faire s.,** to go into the army; **s. de fortune,** soldier of fortune; **vieux s.,** old campaigner; **lever des soldats,** to raise troops; *F: A:* **femme à soldats,** garrison hack; **digne d'un s.,** soldier-like; *F:* **jouer au petit s.,** to try to be smart; (*b*) *s.m. Av:* aircraftman; **s. de 2e classe,** aircraftman second-class; **s. de première classe,** aircraftman first-class; (*c*) *s.f.* **soldate,** servicewoman; (*d*) *adv.phr.* **à la soldate,** in a soldierly, soldier-like, way, fashion; (*e*) *s.m. Toys:* **s. de plomb,** tin soldier. **2.** *s.m.* (*a*) *Ent:* **s. des bois,** soldier (ant); (*b*) *Crust:* **s. marin,** soldier (crab).

soldatesque [sɔldatɛsk], *Pej:* **1.** *a.* of the soldiery; **expressions, manières, soldatesques,** barrack-room language, manners; **à la s.,** in barrack-room fashion. **2.** *s.f.* (undisciplined) soldiery.

solde[1] [sɔld], *s.f. Mil: Navy:* pay; **supplément de s.,** extra pay; *Mil: Ind:* **état de s.,** pay bill, pay sheet; **feuille de s.,** payroll; **soldes et indemnités,** ordinary pay and allowances; **s. d'activité, de présence; s. entière,** active-duty pay, full pay; **s. de non-activité, demi-s.,** unemployed pay, half-pay; **officier en demi-s.,** officer on half-pay; **s. de congé,** leave pay; **s. de retraite,** retiring pension; **s. de route,** allowance on a march; **cahier de s.,** ledger; **entrer en s.,** to begin to draw pay; *Pej:* **être à la s. de qn,** to be in s.o.'s pay.

solde[2], *s.m. Com:* **1.** balance; **s. de compte,** balance of account; balance due; **s. débiteur, s. déficitaire,** debit balance; **s. créditeur,** credit balance, balance in hand; **votre s. créditeur,** the amount standing to your credit; **s. d'ouverture,** opening balance; **s. de fin de mois,** end of the month balance; **s. à un moment donné,** outstanding balance; **s. non compensé, s. de clearing,** clearing balance; **paiement pour s.,** payment of balance, final instalment; **pour s.,** in settlement; **pour s. de tout compte,** in full settlement; to close the account; **pour s. à l'acquit,** in full settlement; **s. en caisse,** balance in hand; **s. de dividende,** final dividend; **livre de soldes,** trial-balance book. **2.** (*a*) surplus stock, job lot, remnant; (*b*) **(vente de) soldes,** (i) (clearance) sale; (ii) bargain counter; **courir les soldes,** to go round the sales; **soldes après inventaire,** stock-taking sale; **s. d'édition,** (i) remainder(s), remainder line (in books); (ii) remainder sale (of books); **(en) s.,** to clear; **je l'ai eu en s.,** I got it in a sale, the sales; I got it cheap; **prix de s.,** bargain prices.

solder[1] [sɔlde], *v.tr.* **1.** to pay (soldiers). **2.** to have (spies, etc.) in one's pay.

solder[2], *v.tr.* **1.** (*a*) *Com:* to balance (an account); **les comptes se soldent par un bénéfice net de . . .,** the accounts show a net profit of . . .; (*b*) *Com:* to settle, discharge, pay (off) (an account); **s. l'arriéré,** to make up back payments; (*c*) **la tentative d'envol s'était soldeé par un échec,** the launching attempt had ended in failure; **la quatrième croisade se solda par la conquête de . . .,** the fourth crusade came to an end with the conquest of . . .. **2.** to sell off, to clear (surplus stock); *Publ:* to remainder (book).

soldeur, -euse [sɔldœ:r, -ø:z], *s. Com:* end-of-season buyer of dress models, etc.; buyer of clearance lines; *Publ:* remainder buyer.

sole[1] [sɔl], *s.f.* sole (of animal's hoof); *Vet:* **s. battue,** bruised hoof, foot founder.

sole[2], *s.f.* **1.** (*a*) *Const:* sleeper, sill; (*b*) *Mec.E:* sole(plate), bed plate, base plate (of machine); (*c*) *Metall:* sole(plate), bed plate, hearth (of furnace); (*d*) *Min:* floor, pavement, sole, sill (of mine-level); **s. du chantier,** stope floor. **2.** *Nau:* flat bottom (of vessel).

sole[3], *s.f. Ich:* sole; **s. perdrix,** variegated sole.

sole[4], *s.f. Agr:* break; field (with regard to rotation of crops); **s. en jachère,** fallow break.

soléaire [sɔleɛ:r], *a. Anat:* soleus (muscle).

soléciser [sɔlesize], *v.tr. Lit:* to solecize.

solécisme [sɔlesism], *s.m.* (*a*) *Gram:* solecism; (*b*) **s. (de conduite),** solecism; blunder, gaffe.

soléidés [sɔleide], *s.m.pl. Ich:* Soleidae.

soleil [sɔlɛ:j], *s.m.* **1.** sun; (*a*) **lever du s.,** sunrise; **au lever du s.,** at sunrise; **coucher du s.,** sunset, sundown; **s. levant,** (i) rising sun; (ii) rising power; **adorer le s. levant,** to do worship to the rising sun, to the rising power; **s. couchant,** (i) setting sun; (ii) declining power; **d'un s. à l'autre, entre deux soleils,** between sunrise and sunset; **s. de minuit,** midnight sun; **s. d'eau,** watery sun; *B:* **le s. de justice,** the Sun of righteousness; **il n'y a rien de nouveau sous le s.,** there is nothing new under the sun; *Fr.Hist:* **le Roi S.,** the Sun King, Louis XIV; *Paperm:* **format s.,** 60 × 80 cm. format; *Cost:* **plissé s.,** sun-ray pleats; (*b*) *Astr:* **s. apparent, s. fictif,** fictitious sun; **s. moyen,** mean sun; (*c*) **faux s.,** parhelion, mock sun, sun dog. **2.** sunshine; **il fait du s.,** the sun is shining; it is sunny; **le s. dardait ses rayons sur la foule,** the sun was blazing down on the crowd; **dans le s.,** against the sun; **au (grand) s.,** in the (bright) sunshine, full in the sun; **avoir sa place au s.,** to have one's place in the sun; **avoir du bien au s.,** to have landed property; **endroit exposé au s.,** sunny spot; **se chauffer au s., prendre le s.,** to bask in the sun, to sun oneself; **prendre des bains de s.,** to sunbathe; **jour de s.,** sunny day; day of sunshine; **sans s.,** sunless; **coup de s.,** (i) *Med:* sunburn; (ii) *Med:* touch of sunstroke; siriasis, insolation, heat apoplexy; (iii) sunny interval; (iv) *F:* sudden blush, flush (of confusion); **prendre un coup de s.,** to get a touch of the sun, a touch of sunstroke; *F:* **piquer un s.,** to blush, to flush up; *P:* **avoir un coup de s.,** to be fuddled, tipsy; **ôte-toi de mon s.!** get out of my light! **3.** *Bot:* sunflower. **4.** *Ecc:* monstrance. **5.** *Gym:* **faire le grand s.,** to do the grand circle on the horizontal bar; *F:* **faire un s.,** to roll over and over. **6.** *Pyr:* Catherine wheel, *U.S:* pinwheel; **s. d'eau,** water wheel (for fireworks).

soleilleux, -euse [sɔlɛjø, -ø:z], *a. Lit:* sunny, sunshiny (spot).

solen [sɔlɛn], *s.m. Moll:* solen; razor fish, *U.S:* razor clam.

solénidés [sɔlenide], *s.m.pl. Moll:* Solenidae.

solennel, -elle [sɔlanɛl], *a.* solemn. **1.** (*a*) *Jur:* **contrat s.,** solemn agreement; *Ecc:* **fête solennelle,** high day; (*b*) official; **distribution solennelle des prix,** formal prize distribution; **réception solennelle d'un prince,** state reception of a prince. **2. parler d'un ton s.,** to speak in a solemn, grave, tone; **silence s.,** solemn, impressive, silence; *F:* **une occasion solennelle,** a special occasion.

solennellement [sɔlanɛlmɑ̃], *adv.* solemnly. **1.** with ceremony; **recevoir s. un ambassadeur,** to receive an ambassador in state. **2.** impressively.

solennisation [sɔlanizasjɔ̃], *s.f.* solemnization, solemnizing.

solenniser [sɔlanize], *v.tr.* to solemnize; to celebrate.

solennité [sɔlanite], *s.f.* **1.** (*a*) solemnity; (*b*) solemn ceremony; **les solennités de Pâques,** the Easter celebrations. **2. parler avec s.,** to speak impressively, solemnly.

soléno- [sɔlenɔ], *pref.* soleno-.

solénodon [sɔlenɔdɔ̃], *s.m. Z:* Cuban solenodon.

solénoglyphe [sɔlenɔglif], *Rept:* **1.** *a.* solenoglyphic. **2.** *s.m.* solenoglyph; *pl.* **solénoglyphes,** Solenoglypha.

solénoïdal, -aux [sɔlenɔidal, -o], *a. El:* solenoidal.

solénoïde [sɔlenɔid], *s.m.* (*a*) *El:* solenoid; (*b*) *Av:* **s. de blocage,** snubber.

solénopsis [sɔlenɔpsis], *s.m. Ent:* solenopsis.

soleret [sɔlrɛ], *s.m. A.Arm:* solleret; steel shoe (of armour).

Soleure [sɔlœ:r], *Pr.n. Geog:* Solothurn.

soleurois, -oise [sɔlœrwa, -wa:z], *a. & s. Geog:* (native, inhabitant) of Solothurn.

solfatare [sɔlfata:r], *s.f. Geol:* solfatara, sulphur spring.

solfatarien, -ienne [sɔlfatarjɛ̃, -jɛn], *a. Geol:* solfataric.

solfège [sɔlfɛ:ʒ], *s.m. Mus:* sol-fa; **apprendre le s.,** to learn the rudiments of music.

solfier [sɔlfje], *v.tr.* (*p.d. & pr.sub.* **n. solfiions, v. solfiiez**) *Mus:* to sol-fa (melody).

solidage [sɔlida:ʒ], *s.f.,* **solidago** [sɔlidago], *s.m. Bot:* solidago; golden rod.

solidaire [sɔlidɛ:r], *a.* **1.** *Jur:* joint and several; jointly liable, responsible; **responsabilité (conjointe et) s.,** joint and several liability; **vous êtes s. des dégâts,** you are jointly liable for the damage; **être s. des actes de qn,** to be responsible for s.o.'s acts; **il n'est s. de personne,** he is answerable to no one; **obligation s.,** obligation binding on all parties. **2.** interdependent, solidary; **nous sommes tous solidaires,** we are interdependent; **actions, faits, solidaires,** interdependent actions, facts; **la richesse privée est s. de la prospérité générale,** private wealth is bound up in general prosperity; **ses intérêts sont solidaires des nôtres,** his interests are bound up with ours; **être s. d'un mouvement,** to associate oneself with a movement; *Tchn:* **roue s. d'une autre,** wheel forming one piece with another; wheel rigidly locked with another; wheel integral, solid, with another.

solidairement [sɔlidɛrmɑ̃], *adv.* jointly; *Jur:* **conjointement et s.,** jointly and severally.

solidariser [sɔlidarize], *v.tr.* **1.** to render jointly liable, jointly responsible. **2.** *Tchn:* **mécanisme à action solidarisée,** interlocking gear.

se solidariser. 1. to join together in liability, in responsibility. **2.** to make common cause (**avec,** with).

solidarisme [sɔlidarism], *s.m. Pol.Ec:* solidarism.

solidariste [sɔlidarist]. **1.** *a.* solidaristic. **2.** *s.m. & f.* solidarist.

solidarité [sɔlidarite], *s.f.* **1.** *Jur:* joint and several obligation or liability; joint responsibility. **2.** (*a*) interdependence (of parts); (*b*) fellowship, solidarity; community of interests; **grève de s.,** sympathetic strike; *F:* **débrayer par s. (avec),** to come out (on strike) in sympathy (with).

solide [sɔlid]. **1.** *a.* (*a*) solid (body, food, earth); *Geom:* **angle s.,** solid angle; (*b*) solid, strong (wall, cloth); solid, secure (foundation); sound (argument); fast (colour); *Com:* sound, solvent (person); well-established (position, business); **peu s.,** weak; flimsy; **l'édifice n'est pas plus s. que le fondement,** a building cannot be stronger than its foundations; **avoir les bras solides,** to have strong arms; **un coup de poing s.,** a vigorous, hefty, blow; **qualités solides,** sterling qualities; **garantie s.,** reliable, trustworthy, guarantee; **ami s.,** staunch, reliable, trusty, friend; **réputation s.,** established reputation; **livre s.,** book of substance; substantial book; **faire un repas s.,** to make a hearty meal; **s. appétit,** hearty appetite; **elle a eu une s. éducation,** she has had a sound education; **avoir la tête s.,** to have a good head for drink, to hold one's drink; (*c*) **homme s.,** man of sound constitution; **un gaillard s., un s. gaillard,** a strong, stout, strapping, hefty, fellow; **être encore s. (comme un chêne),** to be still hale and hearty; **je suis encore peu s.,** I am still far from strong; **alors, toujours s. au poste?** still going strong (in the job)? **2.** *s.m.* (*a*) solid (body); *Geom:* **s. de révolution,** solid of revolution; (*b*) **bâtir sur le s.,** to build on solid foundations; **creuser jusqu'au s.,** to dig down to solid ground; *F:* **chercher le s., songer au s.,** to have an eye to the main chance, to look to the main chance.

solidement [sɔlidmɑ̃], *adv.* solidly, firmly, securely, stoutly, soundly; **s'établir s. dans une position,** to establish oneself firmly, securely, in a position; **raisonner s.,** to argue soundly.

solidification [sɔlidifikasjɔ̃], *s.f.* solidification, solidifying; **point, température, de s.,** setting point.

solidifier [sɔlidifje], *v.tr.* & *pr.* (*p.d.* & *pr.sub.* **n. solidifiions, v. solidifiiez**) to solidify.

solidité [sɔlidite], *s.f.* solidity; strength, security (of building, etc.); strength (of material); substantiality (of furniture, etc.); soundness (of a firm, of judgment); strength, stability (of friendship); *Paint: Dy:* **s. d'une couleur,** fastness of a colour; **c'est d'une s. à toute épreuve,** it stands up to anything.

solifluction, solifluxion [sɔliflyksjɔ̃], *s.f. Geol:* solifluction, solifluxion.

solifluer [sɔliflɥe], *v.i. Geol:* (*of surface deposits*) to creep; to be subject to solifluction.

solifluidal, -aux [sɔliflɥidal, -o], *a. Geol:* solifluctional.

soliloque [sɔlilɔk], *s.m.* soliloquy.

soliloquer [sɔlilɔke], *v.i.* to soliloquize; to talk to oneself.

Soliman [sɔlimɑ̃], *Pr.n.m. Hist:* Suleiman.

solin [sɔlɛ̃], *s.m. Const:* (*a*) space between two joists; (*b*) plaster filling (between joists); (*c*) joint filled with plaster; mortar bedding (of ridge tile, etc.); (*d*) **bande de s.,** flashing.

solipède [sɔlipɛd], *Z:* **1.** *a.* solidungulate, whole-hoofed. **2.** *s.m.* soliped; **les solipèdes,** the equine species.

solipsisme [sɔlipsism], *s.m.* solipsism.

solipsiste [sɔlipsist]. **1.** *a.* solipsistic. **2.** *s.m.* & *f.* solipsist.

soliste [sɔlist], *s.m.* & *f.* soloist; *a.* **violon s.,** solo violin.

solitaire [sɔlitɛːr]. **1.** *a.* (*a*) solitary, lonely, lonesome (person, life); **lieu s.,** lonely, deserted, desolate, spot; *Bot:* **fleur s.,** solitary flower; **pin s.,** lone, isolated, pine; **ver s.,** tapeworm; (*b*) **avoir l'humeur s.,** to be fond of solitude. **2.** *s.m.* (*a*) hermit, recluse; (*b*) solitaire (game); (*c*) solitaire (diamond); (*d*) (i) *Ven:* old boar; (ii) rogue elephant, buffalo, etc.; (*e*) **tour du monde en s.,** solo trip round the world.

solitairement [sɔlitɛrmɑ̃], *adv.* solitarily; alone.

solitude [sɔlityd], *s.f.* **1.** solitude, loneliness; **j'aime la s.,** I like being, living, alone; **vivre dans la s.,** to live in solitude, in seclusion; **se jeter dans la s.,** to retire from the world. **2.** (*usu. in pl.*) lonely spot; wilderness; solitude.

solivage [sɔlivaːʒ], *s.m.* **1.** *Const:* joisting. **2.** cutting of a log into beams.

solive [sɔliːv], *s.f. Const:* joist, beam, balk, rafter; **s. en fer,** iron beam; girder; **s. enchevêtrée, boiteuse,** trimmed joist; trimmer; **s. de remplissage,** intermediate joist; *F:* **Roi S.,** King Log.

soliveau, -eaux [sɔlivo], *s.m.* (*a*) *Const:* small joist; small girder; (*b*) *F:* **un Roi S.,** a King Log; a nonentity.

solivure [sɔlivyːr], *s.f.* beams and joists (of a building).

sollicitable [sɔlisitabl̩], *a.* that may be solicited.

sollicitation [sɔlisitasjɔ̃], *s.f.* **1.** solicitation, entreaty, earnest request; canvassing (**de,** for); *Jur:* application (to a judge); **c'est à votre s. que . . .,** it is at your request that . . .. **2.** *A:* care; **être chargé de la s. des affaires de qn,** to be entrusted with looking after, seeing to, s.o.'s affairs. **3.** attraction, pull (of magnet); stress (of attraction). **4. les sollicitations de la faim, de l'ambition,** the call of hunger, of ambition.

solliciter [sɔlisite], *v.tr.* **1.** (*a*) *A:* **s. qn à qch., à, de, faire qch.,** to incite s.o. to sth., to do sth.; **s. qn,** (i) to urge, tempt, s.o.; (ii) to canvass s.o.; **s. son cheval,** to urge on one's horse; (*b*) *A:* **médicament qui sollicite la transpiration,** medicine that induces perspiration. **2.** to solicit (s.o., sth.); to request earnestly, beg for (favour, interview, etc.); **s. un emploi (de qn),** to apply (to s.o.) for a job; **s. des voix,** to canvass for votes; **s. des votes dans une région,** to canvass a district; **s. son congé,** to ask for leave of absence; **s. l'attention du public,** to crave the attention of the audience; **s. qn à, de, faire qch.,** to ask, beg, s.o. to do sth.; **il est sollicité de toutes parts,** he is very much in demand. **3.** (*of magnet*) to attract; (*of spring*) to pull; **corps sollicité par une force,** body pulled, attracted, acted upon, by a force; **regard qui sollicite la pitié,** look that provokes pity.

solliciteur, -euse [sɔlisitœːr, -øːz], *s.* petitioner; solicitant; applicant (**de,** for); **s. de voix,** canvasser.

sollicitude [sɔlisityd], *s.f.* (*a*) solicitude, (tender) care; (*b*) anxiety, concern (**pour,** for); **causer beaucoup de s. à qn,** to cause s.o. much anxiety; **il demanda avec s. si . . .,** he enquired with concern whether . . ..

solmisation [sɔlmizasjɔ̃], *s.f. Mus:* solmization, sol-fa.

solmiser [sɔlmize], *v.tr. Mus:* to solmizate.

solo [sɔlo]. **1.** *s.m.* solo; *Mus:* **s. de violon,** violin solo; **jouer en s.,** to play solo; *pl. des solos, des soli.* **2.** *a.inv.* **violon s.,** solo violin; **motocyclette s.,** solo motor-bicycle; *Cards:* **jouer s.,** to go solo.

Sologne [sɔlɔɲ], *Pr.n.f. Geog:* the Sologne (region).

solognot, -ote [sɔlɔɲo, -ɔt], *a.* & *s.* (native, inhabitant) of the Sologne; belonging to the Sologne.

sol-sol [sɔlsɔl], *a.inv. Ball:* ground-to-ground; **engin s.-s.,** ground-to-ground missile.

solstice [sɔlstis], *s.m.* solstice; **s. d'été, d'hiver,** summer solstice, winter solstice.

solsticial, -aux [sɔlstisjal, -o], *a.* solstitial (point, period).

solubilisant [sɔlybilizɑ̃]. **1.** *a.* solubilizing; that makes, renders (sth.) soluble. **2.** *s.m.* solubilizer.

solubilisation [sɔlybilizasjɔ̃], *s.f.* solubilization.

solubiliser [sɔlybilize], *v.tr.* to solubilize, to render (sth.) soluble.

solubilité [sɔlybilite], *s.f.* **1.** solubility (of a body). **2.** solvability (of a problem).

soluble [sɔlybl̩], *a.* **1.** soluble (substance); **café s.,** instant coffee. **2.** solvable (problem).

solunaire [sɔlynɛːr], *a.* solunar.

soluté [sɔlyte], *s.m. Pharm:* aqueous solution.

solution [sɔlysjɔ̃], *s.f.* **1. s. de continuité,** (i) solution of continuity; gap; break; (ii) *El: etc:* break of continuity; fault; **il y a s. de continuité entre le présent et l'avenir,** there is a break, a gap, between the present and the future. **2.** *Ch: Ph: etc:* solution (of solid in liquid); **sel en s. (dans l'eau),** salt in solution (in water); **s. mère,** pregnant solution; **s. au titre, s. normale,** standard solution; **s. concentrée,** concentrated solution, stock solution; **s. saturée,** saturated solution; **s. diluée, étendue,** diluted solution; **s. diluée d'acide sulfurique,** diluted solution of sulphuric acid; **s. détergente,** cleaning solution; **s. de carbonate de soude,** solution of washing soda; **s. électrolytique,** electrolytic solution; **s. solide,** solid solution; **s. colloïdale,** colloidal solution; *Dy:* **s. de chlorure stanneux,** cotton spirits; *Engr:* **s. de morsure,** etching solution; **s. de mouillage,** damping solution; **s. d'enlevage,** wash-out solution; *Ind:* **s. de polissage,** bright dip; **s. mercurielle,** blue dip; **s. tampon,** buffer solution. **3.** solution (of, to, question, problem, equation); **s. de remplacement,** alternative solution; **s. de paresse, de facilité,** easy way out; **brusquer la s. d'une crise,** to find a quick way to end a crisis; *Mth:* **s. étrangère (d'une équation, d'un problème),** inapplicable, non-valid, solution; **collection de problèmes avec solutions,** collection of problems with answers. **4.** *Jur:* discharge (of obligation); **jusqu'à parfaite s.,** until discharged in full. **5.** *Med. A:* termination, solution, issue (of disease).

solutionner [sɔlysjɔne], *v.tr.* to solve (problem, difficulty).

solutréen, -enne [sɔlytreɛ̃, -ɛn], *a.* & *s.m. Prehist:* Solutrian.

solutréo-magdalénien, -ienne [sɔlytreɔmagdalenjɛ̃, -jɛn], *a. Prehist:* Solutreo-Magdalenian; *pl. solutréo-magdaléniens, -iennes.*

solvabilité [sɔlvabilite], *s.f.* solvency.

solvable [sɔlvabl̩], *a.* (financially) solvent.

solvant [sɔlvɑ̃], *s.m. Ch:* solvent.

solvatation [sɔlvatasjɔ], *s.f. Ch:* solvation.

solvate [sɔlvat], *s.m. Ch:* solvate.

solvatisation [sɔlvatizasjɔ̃], *s.f. Ch:* solvation (*esp.* of colloid).

solvatisé [sɔlvatize], *a. Ch:* solvated.

soma [sɔma], *s.m. Biol:* soma.

somali, -ie [sɔmali]. **1.** *a.* & *s. Geog:* Somali; **les Somalis,** the Somali; **Côte française des Somalis,** French Somaliland; **l'économie somalie,** the economy of Somalia. **2.** *s.m. Ling:* **le s.,** Somali.

Somalie [sɔmali], *Pr.n.f.* **1.** *Hist:* **S. britannique, S. italienne,** British, Italian, Somaliland. **2.** *Geog:* **(République démocratique de) S.,** Somalia.

somalien, -ienne [sɔmaljɛ̃, -jɛn], *a. Geog:* Somali; of Somalia.

somat(h)ormone [sɔmatɔrmɔn], *s.f.* somatotropic hormone.

somation [sɔmasjɔ̃], *s.f. Biol:* acquired characteristic.

somatique [sɔmatik], *a.* somatic.

somatisation [sɔmatizasjɔ̃], *s.f. Psy:* somatization.

somatiser [sɔmatize], *v.tr. Psy:* **il a somatisé son angoisse,** he has converted his anxiety into somatic symptoms.

somato- [sɔmatɔ], *comb.fm.* somato-.

somatocyte [sɔmatɔsit], *s.m. Biol:* somatic cell.

somatogène [sɔmatɔʒɛn], *a.* somatogenic, somatogenetic.

somatognosie [sɔmatɔgnozi], *s.f.* somatognosis.

somatologie [sɔmatɔlɔʒi], *s.f.* somatology.

somatologique [sɔmatɔlɔʒik], *a.* somatologic(al).

somatopleure [sɔmatɔplœːr], *s.f.* somatopleure.

somato-psychique [sɔmatɔpsiʃik], *a.* somatopsychic.

somatotrope [sɔmatɔtrɔp], *a.* somatotropic (hormone).

sombrage [sɔ̃braːʒ], *s.m.* first dressing (given to the soil of vineyard, etc.).

sombre [sɔ̃ːbr], *a.* dark, sombre, gloomy; (*a*) dark (colour); **religieuses qui portent l'habit s.,** nuns who wear sombre habits; *inv.* **des robes bleu sombre,** dark blue dresses; *Phot: Cin:* **photographie très s.,** photograph in a low key; (*b*) dim (forest, room, light, etc.); dull, overcast (sky); *s.a.* COUPE[2] 1; **il fait s.,** it is dark, dull, weather; **il faisait très s. dans la pièce,** it was very dark in the room; (*c*) dismal, melancholy (face, thoughts, character); saturnine (temperament); dark (despair); **peindre la situation sous les couleurs les plus sombres,** to paint a picture of the situation in the darkest colours; *s.* **avoir du s. dans l'âme,** (i) to feel gloomy; (ii) to have a streak of gloom in one's nature; to be of a saturnine disposition; *Th:* **les rôles sombres,** the heavy parts; **une s. histoire de s. assassinat,** a sinister tale of foul murder; *F:* **un s. imbécile,** a first-class imbecile, idiot.

sombrée [sɔ̃bre], *a.f. Mus:* **voix s.,** veiled voice.

sombrement [sɔ̃brəmɑ̃], *adv.* gloomily, sombrely; **songer s. à qch.,** to brood over sth.

sombrer[1] [sɔ̃bre], *v.i. Nau:* (*of ship*) to founder (in bad weather); to be engulfed, to go down; to sink (after striking a rock, etc.); **sa fortune sombrait,** he was on the brink of ruin; **le soleil sombra dans une mer de nuées,** the sun sank in a sea of cloud; **il vit s. sa fortune,** he saw his fortune engulfed; **il vit s. ses espérances,** he saw his hopes dashed; **sa raison sombra complètement,** his mind, his reason, gave way completely; **ce manque d'harmonie fit s. l'enterprise,** it was this lack of harmony that caused the undertaking to come to grief; **je me sentais s.,** I felt that this was the end of everything; **tout sombrait,** the bottom seemed to have dropped out of everything.

sombrer[2], *v.tr.* to give the first dressing to (soil of vineyard, etc.).

sombrero [sɔ̃brero], *s.m.* sombrero.

somite [sɔmit], *s.m. Z:* somite.

sommable [sɔm(m)abl̩], *a. Mth:* summable.

sommail [sɔmaːj], *s.m. Nau:* shoal (in fairway); sandbank.

sommaire [sɔm(m)ɛːr]. 1. *a.* (*a*) summary, succinct, concise; **exposé s.**, summary, succinct, brief, account; **tenue s.**, scant attire; (*b*) summary, hasty, improvised; **pansement s.**, first-aid dressing; **repas s.**, scanty meal; **dîner s.**, scratch dinner; **lit s.**, shakedown; (*c*) *Jur:* **statuer en procédure s.**, to sit in cases of summary procedure; **affaire s.**, summary proceedings. 2. *s.m.* summary, abstract, synopsis; *Typ:* **composition en s.**, reverse indention, hanging indention.

sommairement [sɔm(m)ɛrmɑ̃], *adv.* 1. summarily; **vêtu s.**, scantily dressed; *Jur:* **statuer s.**, to make a ruling by summary process. 2. **s. organisé**, hastily improvised.

sommateur, -trice [sɔm(m)atœːr, -tris], *s. Jur:* summoner.

sommation[1] [sɔm(m)asjɔ̃], *s.f.* 1. *Jur:* summons (**de faire qch.**, to do sth.); request, demand; notice (to perform contract); **faire les trois sommations légales**, to read the riot act; **s. respectueuse**, summons by son or daughter to obtain parents' consent to marriage; **s. réitérative**, second summons; **s. sans frais**, second demand (for income tax, not involving a fine). 2. (sentry's) challenge.

sommation[2], *s.f. Mth:* summation (of a series).

somme[1] [sɔm], *s.f.* (*a*) *A:* pack-saddle; (*b*) *A:* burden, load; *still used in* **bête de s.**, (i) beast of burden; (ii) drudge, *F:* dogsbody; *A:* **mulet, cheval, de s.**, pack-mule, -horse; **housse de bête de s.**, *A:* sumpter-cloth.

somme[2], *s.f.* 1. sum; total; amount; (*a*) *Mth: etc:* **s. algébrique**, algebraic sum; **s. factorielle**, factorial sum; **faire la s. de dix nombres**, to add (up) ten numbers; **la s. s'élève à 100 francs**, the total amounts to 100 francs; **s. générale, s. totale**, general total, total sum; **la s. des trois angles d'un triangle vaut deux angles droits**, the sum of the three angles of a triangle is two right angles, 180°; (*b*) **la s. des pertes humaines est incalculable**, the number of lives lost is incalculable; **si vous saviez la s. de travail qu'il est capable de fournir**, if you knew the amount of work he can do; **une s. donnée d'énergie**, a given amount of energy; **en s.**, on the whole; all things considered; in short; **c'est en s. assez facile**, on the whole it's quite easy; **s. toute**, altogether; when all is said and done; *in fine*; **c'était, s. toute, assez bien fait**, altogether it was quite well done; (*c*) **s. (d'argent)**, sum of money; **payer une s. de 200 francs**, to pay (a sum of) 200 francs; **payer une forte s.**, to pay a large sum of money; **payer la forte s.**, to pay top price; **dépenser des sommes folles**, to spend vast sums, a mint, of money; **être mis à l'amende pour la s. de 500 francs**, to be fined (a total of) 500 francs; **arrondir une s.**, to make the money up to an even sum; **sommes à verser et à recevoir**, sums payable and payments due, *U.S:* payables and receivables; **un million! c'est une s.!** a million! that's a lot of money! **il méprisait les gens pour qui 500 francs est une s.**, he despised people who think 500 francs a considerable amount of money. 2. epitome; outline; **la S. théologique**, the Summa Theologica (of St Thomas Aquinas).

somme[3], *s.m.* nap; short sleep; *F:* snooze; **faire un s.**, to take a nap; **faire un petit s.**, to have forty winks; **ne faire qu'un s., dormir d'un s.**, to sleep without waking, without a break; to sleep the night through.

somme[4], *s.f.* sandbank, sandbar (at mouth of river).

sommé [sɔme], *a. Her:* surmounted.

sommeil [sɔmɛːj], *s.m.* 1. sleep; slumber; **s. de mort, de plomb**, heavy sleep; **dormir d'un s. de plomb**, to sleep like a log; **avoir le s. léger, profond**, to be a light, a heavy, sleeper; **avoir le s. dur**, to be hard to wake; **arracher qn au s.**, to rouse s.o. from his sleep; **nuit sans s.**, sleepless night; **chercher le s.**, to try to sleep; **s'endormir d'un profond s.**, to fall into a deep, sound, sleep; **dormir du s. du juste**, to sleep the sleep of the just; **j'en perds le s.**, I lose sleep over it; (*of plants, etc.*) **en s.**, (lying) dormant; **s. hibernal** (**des animaux**), winter sleep; **s. de la mort**, *Lit:* **du trépas, de la tombe, éternel**; **dernier s.**, sleep of death, of the tomb; the last sleep. 2. sleepiness, drowsiness; **avoir s.**, to feel sleepy, drowsy; **le s. me gagne**, I'm beginning to fall asleep; **je tombe, je meurs, de s.**, I can't keep awake; I'm ready to drop with sleep; **il a cédé au s.**, he was overcome by sleep; *Med:* **maladie du s.**, sleeping sickness.

sommeiller [sɔmeje], *v.i.* 1. to sleep lightly; to doze; **s. dans son fauteuil**, to take a nap, doze off, in one's armchair; **il n'y a guère d'auteur qui ne sommeille quelquefois**, there is hardly an author who is never caught nodding. 2. (*of nature, one's intelligence, etc.*) to lie dormant; to be asleep.

sommeilleux, -euse [sɔmɛjø, -øːz]. 1. *a.* sleepy. 2. *s.* person suffering from sleeping sickness.

sommelier [sɔməlje], *s.m.* 1. *A:* butler. 2. (*a*) cellarman; *Ecc:* *A:* cellarer; (*b*) (*in restaurant*) wine waiter.

sommellerie [sɔmɛlri], *s.f.* 1. (*a*) *A:* butlership; (*b*) duties of wine waiter. 2. (*a*) *A:* (butler's) pantry; (*b*) wine cellar (of restaurant).

sommer[1] [sɔme], *v.tr. Mth:* to sum; to find the sum of (terms of a series, etc.).

sommer[2], *v.tr.* to summon; **s. qn de faire qch.**, to call on s.o. to do sth.; *A:* **s. qn de sa parole, s. qn de tenir sa promesse**, to call on s.o. to keep his promise; **on somma les mutins de se disperser**, the mutineers were called upon to disperse; *Mil:* **s. une place**, to summon a besieged town to surrender; *Jur:* **s. qn de, à, comparaître**, to summon s.o. to appear.

sommet [sɔmɛ], *s.m.* top, summit (of roof, hill); tip (of rifle sight, etc.); vertex, apex (of angle, curve); vertex (of trajectory, cone); crest (of wave); crown (of arch, of the head); zenith, pinnacle, acme (of power, fame); **être au s. de l'échelle**, to be at the top of the ladder; *Pol:* **conférence, réunion, rencontre, au s.**, summit meeting, conference; **après le s. américano-soviétique**, after the U.S.-Soviet summit meeting.

sommier[1] [sɔmje], *s.m.* 1. *A:* pack-animal; pack-horse; *A:* sumpter. 2. (*a*) *Furn:* **s. à ressorts**, box mattress; **s. métallique**, wire mattress; **s. en mousse**, foam rubber mattress; (*b*) wind chest (of organ); string plate, wrest plank (of piano); (*c*) (*part under load, under strain*) springer (of arch); transom, lintel, breastsummer (of door, etc.); binder, cross beam (of floor); stringer (of bridge); bearer, bearing bar (of furnace grate); lower crossbar (of iron gate, grating); stretcher (of frame saw); beam (of balance); stock (of heavy bell); double hoop (at end of barrel or cask); *Mec.E:* bed (of machine); *N.Arch:* upper sill (of port); (*d*) *Rail: Veh:* bolster.

sommier[2], *s.m.* 1. *Adm: etc:* register; **s. d'entrepôt**, register of goods in bond; *Jur:* **sommiers judiciaires**, (i) criminal records office; (ii) criminal records; **il n'y a rien sur lui au s.**, he's got a clean record. 2. *Com:* cash book.

sommier-divan [sɔmjedivɑ̃], *s.m. Furn:* divan (bed); *pl. sommiers-divans.*

sommière [sɔmjɛːr], *s.f.* (forest) glade, clearing.

sommital [sɔmital], *a.* **crête sommitale**, summit ridge.

sommité [sɔmite], *s.f.* 1. summit, top (of mountain); extremity, tip (of plant, branch); *Bot:* **s. fleurie**, flowering top; **s. fructifère**, fruiting top; **sommités de l'art**, leading people, persons of influence, in the world of art. 2. *Pharm:* **sommités d'origan**, marjoram tops.

somnambule [sɔmnɑ̃byl]. 1. *a.* (*a*) somnambulistic, somnambulant; (*b*) clairvoyant. 2. (*a*) *s.m. & f.* somnambulist, somnambulant, sleepwalker; **il est s.**, he walks in his sleep; (*b*) *s.f.* **somnambule lucide**, clairvoyant(e).

somnambulesque [sɔmnɑ̃bylɛsk], **somnambulique** [sɔmnɑ̃bylik], *a.* somnambulistic.

somnambuliquement [sɔmnɑ̃bylikmɑ̃], *adv.* like a sleepwalker; mechanically, automatically.

somnambulisme [sɔmnɑ̃bylism], *s.m.* 1. somnambulism, sleepwalking. 2. **s. provoqué**, hypnotic state; artificial somnambulism.

somnifère [sɔmnifɛːr]. 1. *a.* somniferous, sleep-inducing; *F:* **discours s.**, deadly dull, soporific, speech. 2. *a. & s.m. Med:* soporific, narcotic; (**comprimé**) **s.**, sleeping tablet, sleeping pill.

somniloque [sɔmnilɔk]. 1. *a.* somniloquous, somniloquent. 2. *s.m. & f.* somniloquist, sleep talker.

somniloquie [sɔmnilɔki], *s.f.* somniloquy, sleep talking.

somnolence [sɔmnɔlɑ̃ːs], *s.f.* somnolence; sleepiness, drowsiness.

somnolent [sɔmnɔlɑ̃], *a.* somnolent; sleepy, drowsy; **être s. après un bon repas**, to feel drowsy after a good meal.

somnoler [sɔmnɔle], *v.i.* to drowse, doze.

somnose [sɔmnoːz], *s.f.* 1. hypnotic sleep. 2 *Med:* sleeping sickness.

somptuaire [sɔ̃ptɥɛːr], *a.* (*a*) *A.Jur:* **loi s.**, sumptuary law; (*b*) *Fin:* **taxes somptuaires**, tax on luxury articles; **arts somptuaires**, luxury crafts; **dépenses somptuaires**, expenditure on luxuries.

somptueusement [sɔ̃ptɥøzmɑ̃], *adv.* sumptuously.

somptueux, -euse [sɔ̃ptɥø, -øːz], *a.* sumptuous; **cadeau s.**, sumptuous, magnificent, present; **repas s.**, lavish meal; **mener un train de vie s.**, to live extravagantly, in a lavish manner; *Lit:* **vêtements plus s. que choisis**, garments characterized by extravagance in style rather than good taste.

somptuosité [sɔ̃ptɥozite], *s.f.* sumptuousness.

son[1], **sa, ses** [sɔ̃, sa, se, sɛ], *poss.a.* (**son** *is used instead of* **sa** *before fem. nouns beginning with a vowel or* **h** *'mute'*); his, her, its, one's; **son père, sa mère, et ses enfants**, his, her, father, mother, and children; **tirer son épée**, to draw one's sword; **il tira son épée**, he drew his sword; **on ne connaît jamais son bonheur**, one never knows one's own happiness; **sa propre fille**, his, her, own daughter; **un de ses amis**, a friend of his, of hers; **un militaire de ses amis**, a soldier friend of his, hers; **ses père et mère**, his, her, father and mother; **ses date et lieu de naissance**, the date and place of his, her, birth; *F:* **il sent son policier d'une lieue**, you can tell he's a detective a mile away; there's detective written all over him.

son[2], *s.m.* (*a*) sound (of voice, instrument, etc.); **s. d'une cloche**, sound, ringing, tinkle, of a bell; **s. d'une grosse cloche**, clang of a big bell; **le s. profond de la cloche**, the deep tone of the bell; **s. du tambour, de la trompette**, beat of the drum, blare of the trumpet; **annoncer une nouvelle à s. de trompe**, to blare out a piece of news; **s. de l'or**, chink of gold; **la boîte rendit un s. creux**, the box gave a hollow sound, sounded, rang, hollow; *Nau:* **s. de sirène, de sifflet**, blast of the siren; (*b*) *Ac: Ph: Mus:* sound, tone; **s. aigu**, high-pitched sound, tone; **s. grave**, low-pitched sound, tone; deep tone; **s. différentiel**, difference tone; **s. musical**, musical sound, tone; **s. pur**, clean tone; **niveau du s.**, sound level; **timbre du s.**, quality, timbre, of sound, tone; **vitesse du s.**, sound velocity; *Av:* **mur du s.**, sonic wall, sound barrier; **atténuateur, affaiblisseur, de s.**, sound attenuator; **détecteur de s.**, sound detector; *Cin: Rec:* **enregistrement du s.**, sound recording; **appareil d'enregistrement du, enregistreur de, s.**, sound recorder; **prise de s.**, sound pick-up; **la prise de s. est bonne**, the recording is good; *W.Tel: etc:* **réception au s.**, aural reception; *Tp:* **signal s.**, aural signal; *Cin: etc:* **ingénieur du s.**, sound engineer; (**spectacle**) **s. et lumière**, son et lumière; *P:* (*of pers.*) **il est tout à fait s. et lumière**, he's a square, he's had it.

son[3], *s.m.* bran; **eau de s.**, bran water; *Husb:* **s. mouillé**, bran mash; *Mil: F:* **boule de s.**, ration loaf; **tache de s.**, freckle; **taché de s.**, freckled; *F:* **c'est moitié farine et moitié son**, it's mixed fat and lean; *F:* it's like the curate's egg—good in parts; *F:* **faire l'âne pour avoir du s.**, to play the simpleton, act the fool, in order to find sth. out.

sonar [sɔnaːr], *s.m. Nau: Navy:* sonar; **s. actif, passif**, active, passive, sonar; **s. de coque**, hull sonar; **s. remorqué**, towed sonar; **s. d'écoute**, monitoring sonar; *Navy:* **s. d'attaque**, hunter sonar; **s. de tir**, fire-control sonar; **s. de veille, de surveillance**, search sonar.

sonate [sɔnat], *s.f. Mus:* sonata.

sonatine [sɔnatin], *s.f.* sonantina.

sondage [sɔ̃daːʒ], *s.m.* 1. (*a*) *Nau: Av: etc:* sounding; probe; **faire des sondages**, to take soundings; **ballon de s.**, pilot balloon, sounding balloon; *Av:* **s. par fusée**, rocket sounding; **s. d'alimentation**, refuelling probe; (*b*) *Min:* boring; **faire des sondages**, to make borings; **s. d'exploration**, wildcat; **appareil de s.**, drilling rig; (*c*) *Metall:* **essai de s.**, probe test; **s. pyrométrique**, pyrometric, temperature, probing; (*c*) *Med:* probing (of wound); (*d*) **s. Gallup, s. d'opinion**, Gallup poll, public opinion poll; **enquête par s.**, sample survey; **contrôle par s.**, random check; **s. aléatoire**, random sampling; **sondages de paix**, peace feelers; **faire des sondages dans des titres**, to scrutinize, challenge, securities. 2. *Min:* borehole, drill hole.

sonde[1] [sɔ̃ːd], *s.f.* 1. (*a*) *Nau:* (sounding) lead, sounding line, plummet; **petite s.**, hand lead; **grande s.**, deep-sea lead; **jeter la s.**, to heave the lead; **naviguer à la s.**, to navigate by soundings, by the lead; **coup de s.**, cast of the lead; **être sur la s.**, to be in soundings; to have struck soundings; **être hors des sondes**, to be out of soundings; **sondes d'une carte**, soundings marked on a chart; (*b*) sounding rod (for pump, well, ship's hold); (*c*) (*of whale*) **faire la s.**, to sound; (*c*) *Meteor: Av:* **s. aérienne**, sounding balloon; **s. spatiale**, space probe; *Av:* **s. de réservoir**, tank probe; **s. à fil chaud**, hot-wire anemometer. 2. *Med:* sound, probe; **s. œsophagienne**, probang; **introduire une s. dans une plaie**, to probe a wound; **nourri à la s.**, tube-fed. 3. (*a*) taster (for cheese, etc.); (*b*) (grain) sampler. 4. *Min:* borer; drill; **tige de s.**, drill pipe; **train (des tiges) à s.**, (rotary) drilling string.

Sonde², *Pr.n.f. Geog:* **les îles de la S.,** the Sunda Islands.

sonder [sɔ̃de], *v.tr.* **1.** (*a*) *Nau:* to sound; **s. la côte,** to take soundings along the coast; **on n'a jamais sondé ce mystère,** this mystery has never been fathomed; (*b*) *v.i.* (*of whale*) to sound; (*c*) **s. l'atmosphère,** to make soundings in the atmosphere; (*d*) *Min:* **s. un terrain,** *abs.* **sonder,** to make borings. **2.** to sound, probe, examine, investigate, test; (*a*) **s. un fromage,** to probe, try, taste, a cheese; **s. une poutre,** to prove, examine, a beam (to see if it is sound); **s. un bois,** to explore a wood; **s. l'horizon,** to scan the horizon; **s. un gouffre (de l'œil),** to peer into a chasm; **s. les dépositions d'un témoin,** to go into the statements of a witness; **s. des bagages à la douane,** to go through luggage at the customs; **les coussins ont été sondés avec une longue et fine aiguille,** the cushions were examined with a long, fine needle; (*b*) **s. qn (relativement à qch.),** to sound s.o. (about sth.); **je l'ai sondé là-dessus,** I sounded him on the matter; **se s.,** to sound the depths of one's mind, to delve into the recesses of one's mind; **s. l'opinion,** to sound public opinion; to make a survey of public opinion; **s. le terrain,** to feel one's way, to see how the land lies. **3.** *Med:* to sound, probe (a wound); to sound (a patient).

sondeur, -euse [sɔ̃dœːr, -øːz]. **1.** *s.m.* (*a*) *Nau:* leadsman; (*b*) *Min:* borer, driller. **2.** *s.* prober (of secrets). **3.** *s.m. Nau:* sounder; depth finder; **s. acoustique, s. par le son,** echo sounder; **s. à ultra-sons,** supersonic sounder. **3.** *s.f. Min: etc:* **sondeuse,** borer, drill, driller; **s. à (pointe de) diamant,** diamond drill; **s. à grenaille,** shot drill; **s. à percussion,** impact drill.

sone [sɔn], *s.m. Ac:* sone.

songe [sɔ̃ːʒ], *s.m.* dream; **faire un s.,** to dream; to have a dream; **voir qch. en s.,** to see sth. in a dream; *Prov:* **mal passé n'est qu'un s.,** an ill that is past is but a bad dream; **clef des songes,** dream book.

songe-creux [sɔ̃ʒkrø], *s.m.inv. Lit:* dreamer, visionary; **air de s.-c.,** dreamy look.

songer [sɔ̃ʒe], *v.i.* **(je songeai(s); n. songeons) 1.** (*a*) to dream **(de,** of); (*b*) to muse **(à,** on); to daydream; **je ne songeais guère que . . .,** little did I dream that . . .; **personne n'aurait songé à le soupçonner,** no one would have dreamt of suspecting him; **je songeais en moi-même que . . .,** I thought to myself that . . .; *s.a.* CREUX 2. **2.** (*a*) **s. à qch.,** to think of sth.; to consider, think over, think of, sth.; **songez-y bien,** think it over carefully; **il ne faut pas y s.,** that's quite out of the question; **sans s. à mal,** without evil intent; without meaning any harm; without seeing any harm in it; **s. à faire qch.,** to contemplate doing sth.; to think of doing sth.; to have thoughts of doing sth.; to intend to do sth.; **elle ne songe qu'à danser,** she is entirely taken up with dancing; **elle ne songe qu'à se marier,** her one thought is to get married; **il ne songe qu'à gagner de l'argent,** he can't think of anything but making money; **s. à l'avenir,** to plan for the future; **je n'étais pas sans s. à l'avenir,** I was not without thought for the future; **sans y s.,** without thinking; **songez à ce que vous faites!** think what you're doing! (*b*) to imagine; **songez si j'étais furieux,** you can imagine how angry I was; **songez donc!** just think! just imagine! just fancy! (*c*) to remember; **on ne songe pas à tout,** one cannot think of, remember, everything; **songez à lui,** keep, bear, him in mind; **je ne songeais pas que j'étais déjà pris,** it never entered my mind, I had forgotten, that I already had an appointment; **songez à ne pas être en retard,** mind you're not late. **3.** *v.tr. A:* to think of, let one's thoughts run on (sth.); **j'avais songé une comédie,** I had a (possible) play in my mind.

songerie [sɔ̃ʒri], *s.f.* **1.** (day)dreaming, idle musing. **2.** (*a*) reverie; brown study; (*b*) *pl.* daydreams, waking dreams.

songeur, -euse [sɔ̃ʒœːr, -øːz]. **1.** *s. A. & B:* dreamer. **2.** *a.* (*a*) dreamy (person, nature); **esprit s.,** dreamer; (*b*) pensive, thoughtful; wrapped in thought; **d'un air s.,** pensively.

songeusement [sɔ̃ʒøzmɑ̃], *adv.* dreamily; pensively.

Songhaï [sɔ̃gaːj], *s.m.pl. Ethn:* Songhay, Surhai.

sonique [sɔnik], *a.* sonic; **mur s.,** sonic wall, sound barrier; **détonation, gong, s.,** supersonic boom, bang, sonic boom; **avion s.,** supersonic aircraft.

soniquement [sɔnikmɑ̃], *adv.* sonically.

sonnage [sɔnaːʒ], *s.m.* sounding (of metal to test for cracks).

sonnaille [sɔnaːj], *s.f.* cattle bell.

sonnailler¹ [sɔnaje], *s.m. Husb:* bell-wether.

sonnailler². **1.** *v.i.* to be for ever ringing the bell. **2.** *v.tr.* to ring continually for (one's maid, etc.).

sonnaillerie [sɔnajri], *s.f. coll. F:* ringing (of bells), noise of (bells) ringing.

sonnant [sɔnɑ̃], *a.* **1.** striking; **horloge sonnante,** striking clock; **à dix heures sonnant(es),** on the stroke of ten; *O:* **arriver à la seconde sonnant,** to arrive on the stroke of time. **2.** sounding, resounding; *Lit:* **l'airain s.,** the blare of the brass; **monnaie sonnante,** hard cash; *Jur: A:* **payer en espèces sonnantes et trébuchantes,** to pay in coin of the realm, in hard cash.

sonné [sɔne], *a.* **1. il est dix heures sonnées,** it is past ten, it's gone ten; **son heure est sonnée,** his hour has come, has struck; **elle a quarante ans sonnés,** she's on the wrong side of forty; she won't see forty again; **il n'y a pas loin de soixante ans bien sonnés que j'étais à l'école,** it's almost a full sixty years since I was at school. **2.** *F:* (*a*) *Box: etc:* groggy; punch-drunk; (*b*) barmy, cracked.

sonner [sɔne]. **1.** *v.i.* to sound; (*of clocks*) to strike; (*of bells*) to ring; to toll; **le cor anglais sonne une quinte plus bas que le hautbois,** the English horn speaks a fifth lower than the oboe; **s. creux,** to sound hollow; **argument qui sonne creux,** hollow, empty, argument; (*of coin*) **s. clair, faux,** to ring true, false; **sa réponse a sonné faux,** his answer did not ring true; **s. bien, mal,** to sound, not to sound, well; to make a good, a bad, impression; **l'italien sonne bien à l'oreille,** Italian is a pleasant-sounding language; **cela sonne bien,** it sounds well; **demeurer à une adresse qui sonne bien,** to live at a good address; **mot qui sonne mal,** word that offends the ear; **l'r sonne dans "mer,"** the r is sounded in "*mer*"; **faire s. les r.,** to roll one's r's; **faire s. un mot,** to emphasize a word; **faire s. son argent,** to chink, rattle, one's money; **faire s. une pièce d'argent,** to ring a coin (in order to test it); **faire s. ses clefs,** to jingle one's keys; **faire s. ses bottes sur le parquet,** to stamp one's boots on the floor; *Lit:* **faire s. (haut) une action, etc.,** to praise, extol, a deed, etc.; **six heures sonnèrent,** the clock struck six; **midi vient de s.,** twelve o'clock has just struck; it has just gone twelve; **six heures sonnent, sont sonnées,** it is striking, has struck, six; **les vêpres sonnent,** the bells are ringing for vespers; **son heure, sa dernière heure, a sonné,** his last hour has come, he is about to die; **la trompette sonne,** the trumpet is sounding; **les oreilles lui sonnaient,** his ears were buzzing. **2.** *v.tr.* (*a*) to sound; to cause (sth.) to sound; **s. la cloche,** to ring the bell; **s. le glas,** to toll the knell; *Prov:* **on ne peut s. les cloches et aller à la procession,** one can't do two things at once; one can't be in two places at the same time; *abs.* **on sonne,** the bell is ringing, there's a ring at the door; **horloge qui sonne les heures,** clock that strikes the hours; **ne (pas) s. mot,** not to utter a word; **s. la messe, l'office,** to ring for mass, for church; **s. pour les morts,** to toll for the dead; **la cloche sonnait matines, sonnait vêpres,** the bell was ringing for matins, for vespers; **s. le dîner** to ring the dinner bell; *v.ind.tr.* **s. du clairon, du cor,** to sound the bugle, to wind the horn; *Th:* **s. pour faire lever le rideau, pour faire baisser le rideau,** to ring up, ring down, the curtain; *Mil:* **s. la charge, la retraite,** to sound the charge, the retreat; *F:* **il va se faire s. (les cloches)!** he'll catch it! (*b*) to ring for (s.o.); **s. la femme de chambre,** to ring for the chambermaid; **s. pour avoir de l'eau,** to ring for water; *O:* **s. qn au téléphone,** to ring s.o. up, *U.S:* to call s.o.; *P:* **on ne vous a pas sonné!** mind your own business! (*c*) *P:* **s. qn,** (i) to knock s.o. flat, to bash s.o.'s head on the pavement; (ii) to beat s.o. up, to give s.o. the works; (*d*) *Tchn:* to sound (metal for cracks); to ring, test (coin); (*e*) **s. le fêlé,** (i) (*of vase, etc.*) to sound cracked; (ii) *F:* (*of pers.*) to sound loopy, cracked; **s. le creux,** to have a hollow ring.

sonnerie [sɔnri], *s.f.* **1.** (*a*) ringing (of bells); (*b*) (set of) bells, chimes (of church, etc.); **la grosse s.,** the heavy bells, the full chimes. **2.** (*a*) striking mechanism (of clock); **pendule à s.,** striking clock; **montre à s.,** repeating watch, repeater; (*b*) **s. électrique,** electric bell; **s. téléphonique,** telephone bell; **s. d'appel,** call bell; **s. d'alarme,** alarm bell; **bouton de s.,** bell-push; **fil à s.,** bell wire. **3.** *Mil:* (trumpet, bugle,) call; **s. aux morts,** last post.

sonnet [sɔnɛ], *s.m.* sonnet; **auteur, faiseur, de sonnets,** sonnet writer.

sonnette [sɔnɛt], *s.f.* **1.** (*a*) small bell; (*b*) handbell; (*c*) (house) bell; **agiter la s.,** to ring the bell; **tirer la s.,** to pull the bell; **cordon de s.,** bell pull; *Med:* **s. de nuit,** night bell; **s. d'alarme,** alarm bell; **coup de s.,** ring (at the door, etc.); **personne ne répondit à mon coup de s.,** no one answered the bell; **pose de sonnettes,** bellhanging; **poseur de sonnettes,** bellhanger; *O:* **être (assujetti) à la sonnette,** to be continually interrupted in one's work; to be at everybody's beck and call. **2.** pile-driving apparatus, pile driver; **s. à main, à tiraude,** hand pile driver; **mouton de s.,** monkey. **3.** *pl.* rattle (of rattlesnake); **serpent à sonnettes,** rattlesnake. **4.** *Tex:* mark on the selvedge (of fabric to indicate a fault).

sonnettiste [sɔnɛtist], *s.m. & f.* sonnet writer.

sonneur, -euse [sɔnœːr, -øːz]. **1.** *s.* (*a*) bellringer; *F:* **dormir comme un s. (de cloches),** to sleep like a log; **boire comme un s.,** to drink like a fish; (*b*) **s. de trompette, de clairon,** trumpeter, bugler; **s. de trompe (de chasse),** (hunting) horn blower. **2.** *s.m. Tg:* sounder (device). **3.** *s.m. Amph: F:* **s. à ventre jaune,** fire-belly toad, bombinator.

sono [sɔno], *s.f. Mus: F:* **la s. était pourrie,** the amplifiers weren't, the sound wasn't, working.

sonomètre [sɔnɔmɛtr], *s.m.* **1.** *Ph:* sonometer. **2. s. électrique,** audiometer.

sonore [sɔnɔːr], *a.* (*a*) resonant; echoing (vault, etc.); (*b*) sonorous; deep-toned, ringing (voice, etc.); clear-toned (bell, etc.); resounding (laughter, etc.); **intensité s.,** sound intensity; **niveau (d'intensité) s.,** sound (intensity) level; *Pej:* **phrases sonores,** high-sounding, bombastic, sentences; (*c*) *Ling:* **consonne s.,** *s.f.* **une sonore,** voiced consonant; (*d*) acoustic(al); **église s.,** church with good acoustics; **vibrations sonores,** acoustic resonance; **onde s.,** soundwave; *Cin:* **film s.,** sound film; **effets sonores,** sound effects; **bande, piste, s.,** sound track.

sonorisation [sɔnɔrizasjɔ̃], *s.f.* (*a*) *Ling:* voicing (of consonant); (*b*) *Cin:* (i) scoring; (ii) providing of sound effects; (*c*) wiring (of room) for sound.

sonoriser [sɔnɔrize], *v.tr.* (*a*) *Ling:* to voice; **f s'est sonorisé,** f became voiced; (*b*) **s. un film,** (i) to score a film; (ii) to add the sound effects to a film; (*c*) **s. une salle,** to wire a hall for sound.

sonorité [sɔnɔrite], *s.f.* (*a*) sonorousness, sonority; pleasing tone; **cette radio a une bonne s.,** this radio has a good tone; **sa voix avait des sonorités douces,** she had a harmonious voice; (*b*) resonance; (*c*) acoustics (of a room, etc.).

Sonrhaï [sɔ̃raːj], *s.m.pl.* = SONGHAÏ.

sopha [sɔfa], *s.m.* sofa.

Sophie [sɔfi], *Pr.n.f.* Sophia, Sophie; *F: O:* (*of girl*) **faire sa S.,** (i) to be goody-goody, behave prudishly; (ii) to put on airs, to swank.

sophisme [sɔfism], *s.m.* sophism; *Log:* fallacy.

sophiste [sɔfist]. **1.** *a.* sophistical. **2.** *s.m. & f.* sophist.

sophisterie [sɔfistəri], *s.f.* sophistry.

sophistication [sɔfistikasjɔ̃], *s.f.* **1.** *O:* adulteration (of wine, etc.). **2.** sophistication, use of sophistry. **3.** (*of pers.*) (over-) sophistication, artificiality, affectation.

sophistique [sɔfistik]. **1.** *a.* sophistic(al). **2.** *s.f.* sophistry. **3.** *Log: A:* the study of fallacies; sophistic(s).

sophistiqué [sɔfistike], *a.* **1.** *O:* adulterated (wine, etc.). **2. raisonnement s.,** sophistical, quibbling, argument. **3.** (*of pers.*) sophisticated, affected; **style s.,** affected style.

sophistiquement [sɔfistikmɑ̃], *adv.* sophistically.

sophistiquer [sɔfistike], *v.tr.* **1.** (*a*) to sophisticate (a subject); to involve (a subject) in sophistries; (*b*) *abs.* to indulge in sophistry; to quibble; to subtilize. **2.** *O:* to sophisticate, adulterate (wine, etc.).

sophistiqueur, -euse [sɔfistikœːr, -øːz], *s.* **1.** quibbler. **2.** *O:* adulterator.

Sophocle [sɔfɔkl], *Pr.n.m. Gr.Lit:* Sophocles.

sophocléen, -enne [sɔfɔkleɛ̃, -ɛn], *a.* Sophoclean.

Sophonie [sɔfɔni], *Pr.n.m. B.Lit:* Zephaniah; Sophonias.

Sophonisbe [sɔfɔnisb], *Pr.n.f.* Sophonisba.

sophora [sɔfɔra], *s.m. Bot:* sophora; **s. du Japon,** Japanese pagoda tree.

sopor [sɔpɔːr], *s.m. Med:* lethargic sleep; sopor; coma.

soporatif, -ive [sɔpɔratif, -iːv], *A:* **1.** *a.* soporiferous, sleep-inducing, soporific (medicine). **2.** *s.m. Med:* soporific.

soporeux, -euse [sɔpɔrø, -øːz], *a. Med:* comatose (sleep); coma-inducing (disease).

soporifique [sɔpɔrifik], *a. & s.m.* (*a*) soporific, sleep-inducing (drug); (*b*) *F:* **discours s., livre s.,** tedious, boring, speech, book; *s.m.* **ce livre est un vrai s.,** this book sends you to sleep.

sopranino [sɔpranino], *s.m. Mus:* sopranino.

sopraniste [sɔpranist], *s.m. Mus:* sopranist, male soprano singer.

soprano [sɔprano], *Mus:* (*a*) *s.m.* soprano voice; (*b*) *s.m. & f.* (*pers.*) soprano; (*c*) *a.* **saxophone s.,** soprano saxophone; *pl. soprani, sopranos (the form* **sopranos** *is now preferred).*

sorbe [sɔrb], *s.f.* sorb apple, service apple.

sorbet [sɔrbɛ], *s.m.* **1.** *A:* (oriental) sherbet. **2.** *Cu:* sorbet, water ice.

sorbetière [sɔrbətjɛːr], *s.f.* ice-cream freezer.

sorbier [sɔrbje], *s.m. Bot:* sorb, service tree; **s. sauvage, commun, des oiseaux, des oiseleurs,** rowan (tree), mountain ash.

sorbique [sɔrbik], *a. Ch:* sorbic (acid).

sorbite [sɔrbit], *s.f.,* **sorbitol** [sɔrbitɔl], *s.m. Ch:* sorbite, sorbitol.

sorboniste [sɔrbɔnist], *s.m. A:* graduate of the Sorbonne.

sorbonnard, -arde [sɔrbɔnaːr, -ard], *F: Pej:* (*a*) *s.* (i) student, (ii) lecturer, at the Sorbonne; (*b*) *a.* **esprit s.,** niggling turn of mind.

Sorbonne [sɔrbɔn]. **1.** *Pr.n.f.* the Sorbonne (seat of the University in Paris); **étudier à la S., en S.,** to study at the Sorbonne. **2.** *s.f. Ch:* fume cupboard, chamber. **3.** *s.f. P: O:* head; **je paumerai la S.,** I'll lose my head.

sorbose [sɔrboːz], *s.m. Ch:* sorbose.

sorcellerie [sɔrsɛlri], *s.f.* **1.** witchcraft, sorcery. **2.** piece of sorcery.

sorcier, -ière [sɔrsje, -jɛːr]. **1.** *s.* sorcerer, *f.* sorceress; wizard, *f.* witch; **s. guérisseur,** witch doctor, medicine man; **chasse aux sorcières,** witch hunt; *F:* **vieille sorcière,** old hag, old trout; **il ne faut pas être s. pour s'en apercevoir,** one needn't be a genius, it isn't very difficult, to see that; *a. F:* **ce n'est pas bien s.,** there's no magic about that; you couldn't call that difficult; *Bot: F:* **herbe des sorciers,** datura, thornapple, *U.S:* jimsonweed; **herbe aux sorcières,** vervain, enchanter's herb; **cercle, rond, de sorcières,** fairy ring. **2.** *s.m. Bot:* enchanter's nightshade, circaea. **3.** *s.f. Ent:* **sorcière noire,** black witch (moth).

sordide [sɔrdid], *a.* **1.** sordid, squalid, filthy; **vêtements sordides,** filthy (old) clothes; **habiter une pièce s.,** to live in a sordid, squalid, room. **2.** sordid, mean; vile; **crime s.,** sordid crime.

sordidement [sɔrdidmɑ̃], *adv.* sordidly; **vivre s.,** to live in squalor.

sordidité [sɔrdidite], *s.f.* sordidness, squalor.

sore [sɔːr], *s.m. Bot:* sorus.

sorédie [sɔredi], *s.f. Moss:* soredium, brood bud.

sorg(h)o [sɔrgo], *s.m. Bot:* sorghum, Indian millet; **s. sucré, à sucre,** sweet sorghum; African, Chinese, sugar cane.

soricidés [sɔriside], *s.m.pl. Z:* Soricidae, the shrews.

soricoïdes [sɔrikɔid], *s.m.pl. Z:* Soricoidea.

sorite [sɔrit], *s.m. Log:* sorites.

Sorlingues (les) [lesɔrlɛ̃ːg], *Pr.n.f.pl. Geog:* the Scilly Isles.

sorne [sɔrn], *s.f. Metall:* sinter slag.

sornette [sɔrnɛt], *s.f.* (*usu. pl.*) nonsense; idle talk; **conter, débiter, des sornettes,** to talk rubbish; to make idle conversation.

sororat [sɔrɔra], *s.m. Anthr:* sororate.

sororité [sɔrɔrite], *s.f. Sch: U.S:* sorority.

sorose [sɔroːz], *s.f. Bot:* sorosis.

Sorrente [sɔrɑ̃ːt], *Pr.n. Geog:* Sorrento.

sorrentin, -ine [sɔrɑ̃tɛ̃, -in], *a. & s. Geog:* (native, inhabitant) of Sorrento.

sort [sɔːr], *s.m.* **1.** (*a*) lot; condition in life; **être content de son s.,** to be content with one's lot; **assurer le s. de ses enfants,** *occ.* **faire un s. à ses enfants,** to settle the future of one's children; to provide for one's children; **il voulait faire qch. pour améliorer leur s.,** he wanted to do sth. to improve their condition; *F:* **faire un s. à qch., à qn,** to dispose of sth., s.o.; **faire un s. à un poulet, à une bouteille,** to polish off a chicken; to kill a bottle; (*b*) **il fait un s. à chaque phrase,** he emphasizes each sentence. **2.** destiny, fate; **ainsi le veut le s.,** such is fate; **abandonner qn à son s.,** to leave s.o. to his fate; **notre s. est décidé,** our fate is sealed; **l'artillerie fit le s. de la bataille,** the artillery decided the battle; **coup du s.,** stroke of fate; **ironie du s.,** irony of fate; **on ne lutte pas contre le s.,** there is no striving against fate. **3.** chance, fortune, lot; **tirer au s.,** (i) to draw lots; (ii) *Fb: etc:* to toss, to spin the coin; **tirer une place, etc., au s.,** to ballot for a place, etc.; **tiré au s. parmi . . .,** drawn by lot from amongst . . .; **tirage au s.,** (i) drawing of lots; balloting; *Adm: A:* drawing (of lots) for conscription; (ii) *Fb: etc:* toss; **le s. en est jeté,** the die is cast; **s'en remettre au s. des armes,** to resort to arms; *Prov:* **le s. est aveugle,** Fortune is blind. **4.** spell, charm; **jeter un s. à qn,** to cast a spell on, over, s.o.

sortable [sɔrtabl̩], *a.* (*a*) *A:* suitable (match, employment); eligible (young man); (*b*) *F:* **il n'est pas s.,** he's not fit to be invited anywhere; **je n'ai pas une seule robe s.,** I haven't a single decent dress, a dress fit to wear.

sortant, -ante [sɔrtɑ̃, -ɑ̃ːt], *a.* coming out; **numéro s.,** number (in a lottery) that is drawn; winning number; **membres (de comité) sortants,** retiring, outgoing, members (of a committee); **administrateurs sortants (d'une société),** retiring directors (of a company); **élèves sortants,** pupils in their last term (at school, at college); cadets passing out; **foule sortante,** out-going crowd; *Typ:* **ligne sortante,** line that overruns into the margin, that is out of alignment, that needs ranging; *s.* **les entrants et les sortants,** those going in and those coming out; the comers and goers.

sorte [sɔrt], *s.f.* **1.** manner, way; **ne parlez pas de la s.,** don't talk like that, in that way, in that fashion; *adv.phr.* **en quelque s.,** as it were, in a way; *A:* **traiter qn de la bonne s.,** to treat s.o., rigorously, severely; *conj.phr.* **de s. que, de telle s. que** + *ind.* (of consequence) or *sub.* (of purpose), so that; **il est sorti sans pardessus, de s. qu'il a attrapé un rhume,** he went out without his overcoat, so that, with the result that, he caught cold; **parlez de (telle) s. qu'on vous comprenne,** speak so as to be understood, so that you are understood; **en s. que** + *sub.*, so that, in such a manner that; **faites en s. que tout soit prêt à temps,** see to it that everything is ready in time; **j'ai fait en s. d'y arriver de bonne heure,** I managed, arranged, to get there early; **faites en s. d'être prêt,** try to be ready. **2.** sort, kind; **toute(s) sorte(s) de choses, des choses de toute(s) sorte(s),** all sorts, kinds, of things; **un homme de la s.,** a man of that sort, of that kind; **un homme de votre s.,** a man like you; **on éprouve une s. de plaisir à se dénigrer,** there is a kind of pleasure in speaking ill of oneself; *Lit:* **il n'est s. de soins qu'il n'ait pris,** he spared no pains; **je n'ai rien dit, rien fait, de la s.,** I said, did, no such thing, nothing of the kind; **j'ai une s. d'impression qu'il viendra,** I sort of feel, have a feeling, he'll come. **3.** *Typ:* sort; **s. surabondante,** superfluous sort; **s. manquante,** missing sort, short sort.

sortie [sɔrti], *s.f.* **1.** (*a*) going out; coming out; departure; exit; **à toutes mes sorties,** every time (i) I go out, (ii) I went out; **faire une s. pour prendre l'air,** to go out to get a breath of (fresh) air; **c'était ma première s. depuis mon accident,** it was my first time out after my accident; **à la s. du théâtre,** when the play is, was, over; at the end of the play; when the people were leaving the theatre; **à la s. des classes,** when the children come, came, out of school; when school is, was, over (for the day); **la s. des ouvriers se fait à 6 heures,** the workers knock off, leave work, at 6 o'clock; *F:* **se ménager une porte de s.,** to arrange a way out (of the difficulty) (for oneself); to arrange a bolt hole; *Th:* **fausse s.,** sham exit (from stage); offers to go; **dessiner une s.,** to offer to go; *Ind:* **s. d'usine,** roll-out (of aircraft, vehicle, etc.); **on a annoncé la s. d'un nouveau modèle de voiture,** a new model of car has been put on the market; *Nau:* **frêt de s.,** outward freight; (*b*) leaving (for good); retirement (of official, etc.); **à ma s. d'école,** on (my) leaving school, when I left school; **inventaire de s. (d'un immeuble),** outgoing inventory; **à la s. de l'hiver,** when winter is over; (*c*) flowing out (of liquid); *Hyd.E: Mec.E:* outlet (of fluid); **s. d'eau,** water discharge; **température, vitesse, à la s.,** outlet temperature, velocity; *Ind: Mch:* **tubulure de s.,** outlet piping; **tuyaux de s.,** outgoing pipes; *Atom.Ph:* **s. de réacteur,** downstream end of reactor; (*d*) *El: Elcs:* output; **s. de fils,** lead-out connection; **s. d'alimentation,** supply lead; **borne de s.,** output terminal; **circuit, courant, tension, de s.,** output circuit, current, voltage; **puissance de s.,** power output; *W.Tel:* **lampe, tube, de s.,** output valve (of receiving set); (*e*) (*computers*) (i) exit; **s. anormale,** abnormal exit, **s. différée,** deferred exit; **amplificateur à une s.,** single-ended amplifier; (ii) output; **s. en temps réel,** real-time output; **générateur de programmes de s.,** output-routine generator; (*f*) delivery (of pattern from mould, of sheets from printing press, etc.); *Typ:* **s. à chaîne,** chain delivery; **chaîne de s.,** delivery chain; **cylindre de s.** taking-off cylinder; **table de s.,** delivery table; (*g*) *Com:* export (of goods); **droit de s.,** export duty; **prohibition de s.,** prohibition of export; **déclaration de s.,** entry outwards; **sorties de fonds,** expenses, outgoings; **ce mois-ci il y a eu plus de sorties que de rentrées,** this month outgoings have exceeded payments received; *F:* we are down on this month's trading, takings; (*h*) *Fin:* **gold-point de s.,** export gold-point; **les sorties or,** the gold withdrawals; **s. de devises, de capitaux,** currency, capital, outflow; flight of currency, of capital; **freiner la s. des capitaux,** to curb the capital outflow; (*i*) *Adm:* issue (of stores); **bon, facture, de s.,** issue voucher; *Cust:* **s. d'entrepôt,** clearing from, taking out of, bond. **2.** (*a*) trip, excursion; leave; **faire une s. en mer,** to go for a short sea trip; **faire une s. le dimanche,** to go for an outing, a trip, on Sundays; **jour de s.,** day out, holiday; **avoir un jour de s. par semaine,** to have one free day a week; *Navy:* **s. à terre,** shore leave; *Nau:* **s. préliminaire,** preliminary run (of new ship); (*b*) **l'année dernière les canots de sauvetage ont fait cinquante sorties,** last year the lifeboats went out fifty times. **3.** (*a*) *Mil:* sally, sortie; *Fb:* run out (by goalkeeper), **fausse s.,** feint sortie, (*b*) *F.* outburst, tirade; **faire une s. à, contre, qn,** to launch out at, pitch into, s.o.; to lash out at s.o.; **elle est capable de n'importe quelle s. devant les gens,** she is capable of saying anything, terrible things, in front of people. **4.** (*a*) exit, way out; **maison à deux sorties,** house with two exits; **sorties d'un théâtre,** exits of a theatre; **s. de secours,** emergency exit; **il y a une s. sur la ruelle,** there is a way out into the lane; **à la s. de la gare,** at the station exit; **s. d'une mine,** outlet of a mine; **par ici la s.,** this way out; (*b*) **s. d'eau, de vapeur,** water outlet, steam outlet; *Metall:* **s. du laitier,** slag hole, cinder notch. **5. s. de bal, de théâtre,** (i) evening wrap, opera cloak; (ii) *P: O:* knuckle-duster, life preserver; **s. de bain,** bathwrap. **6.** *Ecc: Mus:* concluding voluntary, outgoing voluntary; **jouer la s.,** to play the congregation out of church.

sortilège [sɔrtilɛːʒ], *s.m.* piece of witchcraft, sorcery; spell, charm, sortilege.

sortir[1] [sɔrtiːr], *v.* (*pr.p.* **sortant;** *p.p.* **sorti;** *pr.ind.* **je sors, il sort, n. sortons, ils sortent;** *pr.sub.* **je sorte;** *p.d.* **je sortais;** *p.h.* **je sortis;** *fu.* **je sortirai)** I. *v.i.* (*aux.* **être**). **1.** (*a*) to go, come, out; to leave the room, house, etc.; **s. de la salle,** to go, walk, step, stride, out of the room; **faire s. qn,** (i) to take s.o., child, out (for a walk); (ii) to rout s.o. out; (iii) to order s.o. out of the room, out of the house; *F:* to chuck s.o. out; *Ven:* **faire s. un animal de son terrier,** to unearth, dislodge, a quarry; **laisser sortir qn,** to allow s.o. to go, to come, out; **ne le laissez pas s.,** don't let him (go) out; **il ne sort pas de chez moi,** he practically lives at my place, he's always on my doorstep; **entrer par une porte et s. par l'autre,** to go in at one door and out at the other; **s. de son lit,** (i) to get out of bed; (ii) to leave one's bed (after illness); (iii) (*of river*) to overflow its banks; *Th:* **Macbeth sort,** exit Macbeth; **il va pour s.,** (i) *Th:* he offers to go; (ii) *F:* he makes as if to go; *F:* **d'où sortez-vous?** where have you been all this time? (*cp.* 4) **le train sortit du tunnel,** the train emerged from the tunnel; **il ne faut pas que ce domaine vous sorte des mains,** this estate must not pass out of your hands; (*of ship*) **s. du port,** to leave harbour; (*of ship*) **s. de l'eau,** to rise, appear, on the horizon; **source qui sort de la terre,** spring that gushes, issues, from the earth; **le sang lui sortait de la bouche,** (the) blood was streaming from his mouth; **s. d'un emploi,** to leave a job; **il est sorti de l'hôpital hier,** he was discharged from, left, hospital yesterday; **faire s. du pus de la plaie,** to squeeze matter out of the wound; **s. de la vie,** to depart this life; **cela m'est sorti de l'esprit,** it has passed from my mind, dropped out of my mind; **cela m'est sorti de la mémoire, de la tête,** it has slipped my memory, gone out of my head; **que sortira-t-il de tout cela?** what will be the issue, the result, of it all? **il ne sortira pas grand-chose de tout cela,** little will result from all this; *Ind:* **s. de la chaîne de fabrication,** to come off the production line; **le premier numéro de cette revue sortira le 8 mars,** the first number of this review will come out on the 8th of March; *Sch: F:* **est-ce que je peux s.?** may I be excused? *Mil:* **s. des rangs,** to leave (one's place in) the ranks, to step out of the ranks; **la garde sort,** the guard is turning out; **faire s. la garde,** to turn out the guard; *Fin:* (*of bonds*) **s. au tirage,**

to be drawn; *Cards:* **le dix de carreau est sorti,** the ten of diamonds turned up; *(b) (of horseman)* to ride out; *(of driver or vehicle)* to drive out; *(of captain or ship)* to sail out; *(c)* **s. en courant,** to run out; **s. en dansant,** to dance out, to skip out; **s. précipitamment, à la hâte, en toute hâte; se hâter de s.,** to hurry out; to bolt out; to hurry from the room, from the house; **s. brusquement,** to fling out of the room, of the house; **s. furtivement, à pas de loup,** to steal, creep, out; **parvenir à s.,** to (manage to) get out; *(d) (of flowers, corn, etc.)* to come up, spring up; **il lui est sorti une dent,** he has cut a tooth; *F:* **la rougeole est sortie,** the rash has come out; *Sch:* **cette question est sortie (à l'examen),** this question was set (in the examination); *(e)* to have just come out; **je sors de table,** I have just finished eating, have just got up from table; **s. du collège,** to have just left school; **s. de l'enfance,** to emerge from childhood; **je sors d'une typhoïde,** I am just recovering from typhoid; **s. de prison,** to have just come out of prison; **on sortait de l'hiver,** winter was just over; **il sort d'ici,** he was here a minute ago, he has just left; **le pain sortait du four,** the bread was fresh from the oven; *(f) A: & F:* (= **venir de . . .**) **s. de faire qch.,** to have just done sth.; **je sors de le voir,** I have just seen him; *P:* **merci bien! je sors d'en prendre,** no thank you! you won't find me doing that again, going through that again; *(g)* to swerve, deviate (from one's duty, etc.); **s. de son sujet,** to depart, wander, from one's subject; *(of writer, artist)* **s. de son talent,** to go outside his range; **s. de la question,** to wander from the point; **cela sort de ma compétence,** that doesn't come within my scope; it's quite beyond me; **s. des bornes de la bienséance,** to overstep the bounds of decency; **s. d'une règle,** (i) to ignore, depart from, a rule; (ii) to transgress a rule; *(of train)* **s. des rails,** to jump the rails; **il ne sort pas de là, il n'en sort pas,** he sticks to his point; that is his firm conviction; *Danc: etc:* **s. de cadence,** to get out of step; *Mus:* **s. de mesure,** to be, get, out of time; **s. du ton,** to get out of tune. **2.** to go out, go from home; *F:* to go places; **Madame X est sortie; elle est sortie à trois heures,** Mrs X is out; she went out at three o'clock; **s. à cheval, à pied,** to go out riding, walking; **elle sort beaucoup,** she is out a great deal, she goes out a lot; **elle ne sort pas beaucoup,** she doesn't go out much, a great deal; *(of convalescent)* **il ne peut pas encore s.,** he's not allowed out yet; he can't get about yet. **3.** to get out of, extricate oneself from (a difficulty, danger); **aider qn à s. d'une difficulté,** to help s.o. out; **il n'y a pas à s. de là,** there is no way out; **soyez plus précis ou nous n'en sortirons pas,** be more precise or we shall never get to the end of it; **il sortit vainqueur,** he came off victorious; **il en est sorti les mains nettes,** he has come out of it with clean hands; **cinquante chances sur cent de vous en s.,** (i) you've a fifty-fifty chance of getting out of this mess; (ii) you've a fifty-fifty chance of surviving; *F:* **j'ai trop à faire, je n'en sors pas,** I've too much to do, I shall never get through it, I'm completely swamped. **4.** to spring, issue, descend (from a good family, etc.); **sorti du peuple,** sprung from the people; **ce livre sort de ma plume,** the book is one of mine, it is a book I have written; **robes qui sortent de chez les grands couturiers,** dresses from, made by, the great fashion houses; **de quel pays sortez-vous?** where do you come from? **elle sort du Conservatoire,** she studied at the Conservatoire; **les ingénieurs sortis de Centrale,** engineers who have been educated at the *École centrale*; **s. de l'université,** to graduate (from university); *F:* **d'où sortez-vous?** where are you from that you don't know that? *(cp.* **1.** *(a));* **cheval sorti d'un bon haras,** horse that comes from a good stud; **officier sorti du rang,** officer who has risen from the ranks, ranker, *U.S:* mustang. **5.** *(a)* to stand out, stick out, protrude, project; **pierre qui sort du mur,** stone that projects from the wall; **yeux qui sortent de la tête,** protruding eyes; **les yeux lui sortaient de la tête,** his eyes started out of his head; **un navire sortit du brouillard,** a ship loomed out of the fog; **il fut longtemps à s. de l'obscurité,** it was a long time before he emerged from obscurity; *(b) (of figure in picture, of thought, characteristic)* to stand out, to be prominent; *Th:* **le rôle du fils ne sort pas assez,** the son's part is not given enough prominence, does not stand out as it should; **faire s. un trait de caractère, un rôle,** to emphasize a characteristic, a part.

II. **sortir,** *v.tr. (the aux. is* **avoir***) (a)* to take out, bring out, pull out; **sortez-nous des chaises,** bring us out some chairs; **s. la voiture,** to get out the car; **sortez vos morts!** bring out your dead! **s. un interrupteur,** to throw, *F:* chuck, out an interrupter; *F:* **s. qn,** to expel s.o.; to dismiss s.o.; **s. un enfant,** to take a child out; **cela nous sortira de l'ordinaire,** that will make a change; **sortez-moi de cette affaire, de ce mauvais pas,** get me out of this business, out of this fix; **le malade s'en sortira,** the patient will pull through; **s. les mains de ses poches,** to take one's hands out of one's pockets; **il sortit sa pipe,** he brought out, took out, his pipe; **il sortit son carnet de chèques,** he pulled out his cheque book; **s. un revolver,** to produce a revolver, to whip out a revolver; **s. la tête à la portière,** to put one's head out of the carriage window; **l'escargot sort ses cornes,** the snail puts out its horns; *Publ:* **s. un ouvrage,** to publish, bring out, a book; **s. un livre de la bibliothèque,** to take a book out of the library; **il sortit une drôle d'expression,** he came out with a queer expression; *F:* **il nous en a sorti une bien bonne,** he came out with a good one; *Ind: etc:* **s. les feux,** to draw the fires; *Metall:* **s. un modèle du moule,** to deliver a pattern from the mould; *Typ:* **s. une ligne,** to run out a line (into the margin); *(b) Elcs: (computers)* to output.

III. **sortir,** *s.m.* **au s. du théâtre,** on coming out of the theatre; **au s. de l'école,** (i) when school ends, ended; when they, we, come, came, out of school; (ii) on leaving school (for good); **au s. du lycée il entra dans un bureau,** on leaving, when he left, school he went into an office; **au s. de la table,** at the end of the meal; when we, they, got up from table; **au s. de l'hiver,** at the end of winter; **au s. de l'enfance,** on emerging from childhood; **au s. de la réunion,** at the end of the meeting; when the meeting broke up.

sortir², *v.tr. (conj. like* FINIR; *used only in third pers.)* **1.** *A:* to obtain by lot. **2.** *Jur:* to obtain, have (effect); **cette sentence sortira son plein (et entier) effet,** this decision shall have full effect.

S.O.S. [ɛsoɛs], *s.m.* S.O.S.; **lancer un S.O.S.,** to send out an S.O.S.

Sosie [sɔzi, so-]. **1.** *Pr.n.m.* Sosia (in the *Amphitruo* of Plautus and *Amphitryon* of Molière); *hence* **2.** *s.m. F:* (s.o.'s) double, counterpart; **je viens de voir votre s.,** I have just met your double, a man who is the very image of you.

sot, sotte [so, sɔt]. **1.** *a. (a)* silly, stupid, foolish; **s. comme un panier (percé),** as stupid as an owl; **s. projet,** senseless, absurd, plan; **sotte réponse,** stupid, ridiculous, answer; *(b)* embarrassed, disconcerted; **rester tout s.,** to look sheepish; to feel foolish; to be taken aback. **2.** *s.* fool, idiot, ass; **c'est un s. en trois lettres,** in plain English, he's an ass; he's a downright fool, idiot; **c'est une petite sotte,** she's a little idiot, a silly little thing; *Prov:* **un s. a bientôt vidé son sac,** a fool's bolt is soon shot.

sotch [sɔtʃ], *s.m. Geol: (in the Causses)* uvala.

sotériologie [sɔterjɔlɔʒi], *s.f. Theol:* soteriology.

sothiaque [sɔtjak], *a. Chr:* sothic, sothiac (cycle, year).

Sotho(s) [sɔto], *s.m.pl. Ethn:* Basuto(s).

sotie [sɔti], *s.f. Lit.Hist:* satirical farce (of the 14th and 15th centuries).

sot-l'y-laisse [solilɛs], *s.m.inv. Cu:* oyster piece (of poultry).

sottement [sɔtmɑ̃], *adv.* stupidly, foolishly; **agir s.,** to make a fool, an ass, of oneself.

sottevillais, -aise [sɔtvilɛ, -ɛːz], *a. & s. Geog:* (native, inhabitant) of Sotteville-lès-Rouen.

sottise [sɔtiːz], *s.f.* **1.** stupidity, silliness, folly, foolishness; **il est d'une s. sans pareille,** he is incredibly stupid. **2.** *(a)* foolish act; stupid remark; **faire, dire, des sottises,** to do, say, silly things; **débiter des sottises,** to talk nonsense; *F:* to talk through one's hat; **ai-je dit une s.?** have I said sth. stupid? have I put my foot in it? **tâchez de ne pas faire des sottises,** try not to be a fool, to do anything stupid; *(b)* offensive remark, insult; **dire des sottises à qn,** to abuse, slang, s.o.

sottisier, -ière [sɔtizje, -jɛːr], *s.* **1.** *A:* ribald talker. **2.** *s.m.* collection of howlers.

sou [su], *s.m. (still used, esp. colloquially, though there is no longer a coin of that name) (a)* sou (= 5 centimes); *F:* **pièce de cent sous,** five-franc piece; *A:* **gros s.,** penny (piece); **une question de gros sous,** a question of pounds, shillings and pence; **des gens à gros sous,** (very) rich people; *A:* **le s. du franc,** the market penny; **être près de ses sous,** to be mean, avaricious; to count every penny; **prendre garde à un s.,** to look at every penny; **amasser une fortune s. par s.,** to scrape a fortune together; **payer s. à s.,** to pay in small instalments; **mettre s. sur s.,** to save every penny one can; **n'avoir pas le s., pas un s. vaillant; être sans le s., sans un s. vaillant,** to be penniless, not to have a penny to bless oneself with; **laisser qn sans le s.,** to leave s.o. destitute; **il n'a pas le s.,** he hasn't a penny (to bless himself with); **appareil, machine, à sous,** penny-in-the-slot machine; one-armed bandit; **cela vaut cent mille francs comme un s.,** it's worth a hundred thousand francs if it's worth a penny; *Prov:* **un s. amène l'autre,** money makes money; **manger ses quatre sous,** to squander one's small fortune; **affaire de quatre sous,** twopenny-halfpenny business; **je m'en moque comme de quatre sous,** I don't care a tuppenny damn (for it, about it); **on n'aurait pas donné deux sous de sa vie,** one wouldn't have given tuppence for his chance of living; **pas ambitieux pour deux sous, pour un s.,** not in the least ambitious; **il n'a pas pour deux sous de courage,** he hasn't a scrap of courage; **journaliste à deux sous la ligne,** penny-a-liner; **médecin de deux sous,** twopenny-ha'penny doctor; *A:* **distribuer les profits au s. la livre,** to distribute the profits according to the amounts of money contributed; *(b) Fr.C:* cent.

Souabe [swab], *Geog:* **1.** *Pr.n.f.* **la S.,** Swabia. **2.** *a. & s.* Swabian.

souahéli [swaheli], **souahili** [swahili]. **1.** *a. & s. Ethn:* Swahili. **2.** *s.m. Ling:* **le s.,** Swahili.

Souakin [swakin], *Pr.n.m. Geog:* Suakin, Suakim.

soua-soua [swaswa], *a.inv. P:* first-rate, out of this world.

souazi [swazi], *a. & s. Geog:* Swazi.

Souaziland (le) [ləswazilɑ̃ːd], *Pr.n.m. Geog:* Swaziland.

soubarbe [subarb], *s.m.* = SOUS-BARBE.

soubassement [subɑsmɑ̃], *s.m.* **1.** *(a) Arch:* sub-foundation, foundation mass; base, basement (of building); stylobate (of colonnade); **le s. social,** the social substructure; *(b)* base (plate) (of machine tool, etc.); *(c) Geol:* bed rock. **2.** (bed) valance. **3.** *Aut:* sub-frame; **s. de châssis,** underframe.

soubresaut [subrəso], *s.m. (a)* sudden start; bound, leap (of horse, etc.); jolt (of vehicle); **le marché a des soubresauts,** the market is unsteady; *(b)* sudden emotion, catch of the breath; gasp; **cette nouvelle m'a donné un s.,** the news made me gasp, gave me a start; *(c) pl.* trembling, convulsive movements (of the limbs).

soubresauter [subrəsote], *v.i. (of horse, etc.)* to leap, start, bound; *(of vehicle)* to jolt; *(of pers.)* to make a convulsive movement; to jump.

soubrette [subrɛt], *s.f. Th:* soubrette, waiting-maid.

soubuse [subyːz], *s.f. Orn: O:* hen harrier.

souche [suʃ], *s.f.* **1.** *(a)* stump, stub, stock (of tree, etc.); root stock (of iris, etc.); vine stock; **s. d'enclume,** anvil block; *F:* **rester (là) comme une s.,** to stand like a log; **dormir comme une s.,** to sleep like a log; *(b) F:* idiot, nit. **2.** *(a)* head, founder (of family); **faire s.,** to found a family; **chien de bonne s.,** pedigree dog; **il vient de bonne s.,** he comes of sound stock; **famille de vieille s.,** an old family; **français de s.,** French by blood, of French blood; *(b)* strain (of virus, etc.). **3.** *Com: (a)* counterfoil, stub, stump, butt (of cheque, ticket, etc.); tally counterpart (of receipt); **carnet, livret, à s.,** counterfoil book; *(b) A:* **s. de taille,** payer's half of tally. **4.** *(a)* shaft, stack (of chimney); *(b) Ecc:* candlestick. **5.** water pipe (of basin). **6.** end of horseshoe nail left in hoof.

soucherie [suʃri], *s.f.* frame of a tilt hammer.

souchet¹ [suʃɛ], *s.m.* **1.** *Bot: (a)* cyperus; **s. long, odorant,** sweet cyperus, sweet sedge, galingale; **s. comestible,** rush nut, tiger nut; *(b)* **s. d'Amérique,** rattan (cane); *(c)* **s. des Indes,** turmeric, curcuma. **2.** *Orn:* **(canard) s.,** shovel(l)er (duck).

souchet², *s.m.* ragstone (of quarry).

souchetage [suʃtaːʒ], *s.m. For: (a)* marking (of trees for felling); *(b)* verification (of number of trees felled).

soucheter [suʃte], *v.tr. For:* to verify (the number of trees felled).

souchette [suʃɛt], *s.f. Fung: F:* spindle shank.

souchevage [suʃəvaːʒ], *s.m.,* **souchèvement** [suʃɛvmɑ̃], *s.m. Min:* undercutting.

souchever [suʃəve], *v.tr.* **(je souchève, n. souchevons; je souchèverai)** *Min:* to undercut.

souchong [suʃɔ̃], *s.m.* souchong (tea).

souci¹ [susi], *s.m. Bot:* marigold; **s. d'eau** (= POPULAGE), marsh marigold.

souci[2], *s.m.* **1.** care; solicitude; preoccupation; **mon s. de votre bien-être,** my concern for your welfare; **avoir le s. de plaire,** to be anxious to please; **s. de la vérité,** regard for truth; **avoir le s. de la vérité, de l'exactitude,** to be meticulously truthful, accurate; to be a stickler for truth, accuracy; **ne prendre nul s. des conseils de qn,** to care nothing for, to take no notice of, s.o.'s advice; **il ne prend s. de rien,** he doesn't care about anything; **sans s. de l'opinion publique,** with no thought for public opinion; **c'est le moindre, le dernier, le cadet, de mes soucis,** it doesn't bother me in the slightest; I couldn't care less; that's the least of my worries. **2.** (*a*) anxiety, worry; **se faire du s.,** to worry; **il se fait des soucis à votre sujet, sur votre compte,** he worries about you; **donner bien des soucis à qn,** to cause s.o. great anxiety; *Lit:* **soucis rongeurs,** gnawing anxiety; **les noirs soucis,** overwhelming anxiety, *F:* the blues; **son visage portait l'empreinte de ses soucis,** she had a careworn expression; **cette affaire me tient en s.,** I keep worrying about this business; **chassons les soucis!** let us throw care to the winds! let's forget our worries! **sans s., libre de soucis,** carefree; free from anxiety; (*b*) **cet enfant est un perpétuel s. pour ses parents,** this child is a perpetual source of anxiety for his parents; **soucis d'argent, soucis financiers,** money troubles, financial worries.

souci[3], *s.m. Ent:* sulphur butterfly.

soucier [susje], *v.tr. & i.* (*p.d. & pr.sub.* **n. souciions, v. souciiez**) *A:* (*of thg*) to trouble, disturb (s.o.); **cela le, lui, soucie fort peu,** that does not trouble him much.

se soucier. (*a*) *A:* to worry; **quand vous vous soucieriez encore plus que vous ne faites, à quoi cela remédierait-il?** were you to worry even more than you are doing, what good would it do? (*b*) (*usu. neg.*) **se s. de qn, de qch., de faire qch.,** to be concerned about s.o., sth.; to worry about s.o., sth., doing sth.; to mind sth., doing sth.; **il se soucie toujours des autres,** he is always worrying about other people; **il ne se soucie guère de vos critiques,** he doesn't pay much attention to your criticism; your criticism doesn't worry, bother, him much; **ne se s. de rien,** not to worry, bother, about anything; **il ne se souciait pas de cela,** he didn't bother his head about that; *F:* **je m'en soucie comme de l'an quarante, de ma première chemise, d'une guigne, comme un poisson d'une pomme,** I don't care a damn, a hang, a rap, about that; a fat lot I care about that! **ne vous souciez pas du qu'en dira-t-on,** never mind what people say; **elle ne se soucie plus d'aller à Paris,** she doesn't care about going to Paris now; **elle se souciait fort peu de parler,** she didn't bother much about talking; (*c*) *Lit:* **je ne me soucie pas qu'il vienne,** I am not anxious that he should come.

soucieusement [susjøzmɑ̃], *adv.* (*a*) anxiously; (*b*) carefully, with care.

soucieux, -ieuse [susjø, -jøːz], *a.* (*a*) anxious, concerned (de, about); **être s. de faire qch.,** to be anxious to do sth.; **je suis s. avant tout d'assurer votre bien-être,** my main care is your well-being; **être s. de ses propres intérêts,** to be alive to one's own interest; **peu s. du lendemain,** unconcerned about, careless of, the morrow; **peu s. de se rencontrer avec elle,** not very anxious to meet her; (*b*) full of care, worried, bothered; **avoir un air s.,** to wear an anxious, a worried, look; to look careworn, anxious, worried; **un front s.,** a worried look.

soucoupe [sukup], *s.f.* (*a*) saucer; **elle faisait des yeux comme des soucoupes,** she was staring with eyes like saucers; (*b*) *Aer: F:* **s. volante,** flying saucer.

soucrourette [sukrurɛt], *s.f. Orn:* blue winged teal.

soudable [sudabl̩], *a.* **1.** that can be soldered. **2.** weldable; **acier s.,** welding steel.

soudage [sudaːʒ], *s.m.* **1. s. (hétérogène),** soldering. **2. s. (autogène)** (autogenous) welding, brazing (of metals); **s. continu, s. à (la) molette,** seam welding; **s. discontinu,** intermittent welding; **s. à la forge,** blacksmith welding; **s. à plat,** flat welding; **s. électrique par points,** spot welding; **machine à arc submergé pour s. sous conducteur,** subarc machine for electro-slag welding; **s. à l'arc électrique,** electric-arc welding; **s. automatique,** automatic welding; **s. sous-marin,** underwater welding; **s. à l'arc,** arc welding; **s. à franc-bord, par rapprochement,** butt welding; **s. par recouvrement,** lap welding; **s. par points,** tack welding; spot welding; **s. manuel,** manual welding; **s. au chalumeau,** torch welding; **s. en atmosphère de gaz inerte,** gas-shielded welding; mig welding; **s. à l'arc sous flux,** submerged-arc welding; **s. par résistance,** resistance welding; **s. par étincelage,** flash welding; **s. par pression,** pressure welding; **s. alumino-thermique,** thermit welding; **s. de goujons,** stud welding; **s. par fusion,** fusion welding; **s. par bossage circulaire,** projection welding; **s. à l'arc en cône,** cone-arc welding; **s. en cascade,** cascade welding; **s. par diffusion,** diffusion welding; **s. en atmosphère d'hélium,** heliwelding; **s. à l'arc au tungstène,** tig welding; **s. par percussion,** percussive welding; **s. par pression à froid,** cold pressure welding; **s. par refoulement,** upset welding; **s. à la pince,** pinch welding; **s. en bouchon,** plug welding; *Const etc:* **s. de charpente,** structural welding.

soudain [sudɛ̃]. **1.** *a.* sudden, unexpected; **sa mort a été soudaine,** he died suddenly. **2.** *adv.* suddenly, all of a sudden; **s. la porte s'ouvrit,** suddenly the door opened; *conj.phr. A:* **s. qu'elle m'a vu,** as soon as she saw me.

soudainement [sudɛnmɑ̃], *adv.* suddenly, unexpectedly; **il est mort s.,** he died suddenly; **la porte s'ouvrit s.,** the door suddenly opened; the door flew open.

soudaineté [sudɛnte], *s.f.* suddenness, unexpectedness.

soudan[1] [sudɑ̃], *s.m. A:* sultan (of Syria, Egypt); *A:* soldan.

Soudan[2] **(le),** *Pr.n. Geog:* the Sudan.

soudanais, -aise [sudanɛ, -ɛːz], *a. & s. Geog:* Sudanese.

soudanien, -ienne [sudanjɛ̃, -jɛn], *a. Geog:* of the Sudan; Sudanese.

soudant [sudɑ̃], *a. Metalw:* welding, brazing; **fer s.,** welding iron; **blanc s.,** welding heat.

soudard [sudaːr], *s.m. usu. Pej:* **(vieux) s.,** (hardened) old soldier, old trooper.

soude [sud], *s.f.* **1.** *Bot:* (*a*) saltwort, (prickly) glasswort; (*b*) barilla. **2.** *Ch: Ind:* soda; **s. des varechs,** kelp; **carbonate de s.,** *F:* **cristaux de s., s. ordinaire,** washing soda, common soda; **bicarbonate de s.,** bicarbonate of soda; **s. caustique,** caustic soda; **azotate de s.,** sodium nitrate; **s. carbonatée,** natron.

souder [sude], *v.tr.* **1.** (*a*) to solder; **s. au cuivre, au laiton,** to braze, to hard solder; **s. à l'étain,** to sweat, to soft solder; **s. au bain,** to solder by dipping; **eau à s.,** killed spirits; **fer à s.,** (i) soldering lamp, blowlamp; (ii) *Av: P:* jet plane, *U.S:* heat can; (*b*) to weld, braze; **s. à l'arc (électrique),** to arc weld; **machine à s.,** welding machine, welder; **s. par points,** to spot weld; **machine à s. par points,** spot welder; **soudé bord à bord, soudé bout à bout, soudé à franc-bord, soudé à, par, rapprochement, soudé en bout,** butt-welded; **soudé à, par, recouvrement, soudé en écharpe, soudé par amorces,** lap-welded, scarf-welded; **tuyau soudé,** lap-welded pipe; **soudé par étincelage,** flash-welded. **2.** to make fast; to join, unite (fractured bone, edges of wound, etc.); **pierres soudées entre elles sans ciment,** stones interlocked without cement; **ils étaient soudés autour de leur chef,** they were united around their leader.

se souder, (*a*) to join together; to weld, fuse, together; (*b*) (*of bones*) (i) to knit (together); (ii) to become anchylosed.

soudeur, -euse [sudœːr, -øːz]. **1.** *s.* (*pers.*) (*a*) solderer; (*b*) welder; **s. par points,** spot welder; **s. au chalumeau,** lamp, torch, welder. **2.** *s.f.* **soudeuse,** welder, welding machine; **s. par points,** spot welder.

soudier, -ière [sudje, -jɛːr]. **1.** *a.* soda (trade, industry, etc.). **2.** *s.m.* soda maker. **3.** *s.f.* **soudière,** soda works.

soudo-brasage [sudɔbrazaːʒ], *s.m.* braze welding; **s.-b. à l'arc,** arc brazing.

soudo-brasure [sudɔbrazyːr], *s.f.* bronze weld(ing); *pl. soudo-brasures.*

soudoir [sudwaːr], *s.m. Tls:* soldering iron; copper bit; **s. à, en, marteau,** soldering hammer.

soudoyer [sudwaje], *v.tr.* **(je soudoie, n. soudoyons; je soudoierai) 1.** *A:* to have (troops, etc.) in one's pay; to pay (mercenaries). **2.** (*a*) to hire (assassin, etc.); (*b*) *Pej:* to bribe, nobble (newspaper, officials, etc.).

soudure [sudyːr], *s.f.* **1.** (*a*) (= SOUDAGE 1) soldering; **s. au cuivre, au laiton,** brazing, hard soldering; **s. à l'étain,** sweating, soft soldering; **s. au chalumeau,** lamp, blowpipe, soldering; **s. par immersion,** dip soldering; (*b*) soldered joint; **s. à nœud,** wipe(d) joint; (*c*) (*metal alloy for soldering*) solder; **s. en baguettes,** solder in strips; **s. grasse, maigre,** fine, coarse, solder; **s. forte,** hard solder, brazing solder; **s. tendre,** soft solder; **s. enrobée,** cored solder; **s. de cuivre, de laiton,** brass solder; **s. d'étain,** tin solder; **s. à base de zinc,** spelter solder. **2.** (*a*) (= SOUDAGE 2) welding, brazing; **poste de s. (autogène),** welding set, welder generator; **s. par pression,** pressure welding; **s. (par pression) à froid,** cold welding; **s. par forgeage, s. à la forge,** forge welding, blacksmith welding, hammer welding; **s. au gaz à l'eau,** water gas welding; **s. électrique,** electric welding; **s. (électrique) par résistance,** resistance welding; **s. par courant pulsé,** pulsation welding; **s. par bombardement électronique,** electron beam welding; **s. par bossages,** projection welding; **s. par étincelage, par étincelles,** flash welding; **s. par percussion,** percussion, percussive, welding; **s. par refoulement,** upset welding; **s. en cascade,** cascade welding; **s. haute fréquence,** high-frequency welding; **s. par aluminothermie, s. aluminothermique, s. à la thermite,** aluminothermic welding, thermit welding; **s. par fusion,** fusion welding; **s. au chalumeau, s. oxyacétylénique,** blowpipe welding, oxyacetylene welding; **s. au gaz,** gas welding; **s. à l'arc (électrique),** arc welding; **s. à l'arc en cône,** cone-arc welding; **s. à l'arc (à électrode) en charbon,** carbon-arc welding; **s. (à l'arc) à électrode de charbon enrobée, nue,** shielded, unshielded, carbon-arc welding; **s. à l'arc (à électrode) métallique,** metal-arc welding; **s. (à l'arc) à électrode métallique enrobée, nue,** shielded, unshielded, metal-arc welding; **s. à l'arc au tungstène,** tig welding; **s. à l'arc à l'argon,** argon-arc welding; **s. à l'hydrogène atomique,** atomic-hydrogen-arc welding; **s. à l'arc en atmosphère inerte, en atmosphère réductrice,** inert-gas, reducing-gas, welding; **s. à l'arc en atmosphère d'hélium,** heliwelding; **s. sous l'eau,** underwater welding; **s. à l'arc immergé, s. à l'arc sous flux,** submerged-arc welding; **machine à arc immergé pour s. sous flux conducteur,** subarc machine for electro-slag welding; (*b*) (welded, brazed) seam; weld; **sans soudure(s),** seamless, weldless; (*in the following, "soudure" = weld and welding*) **s. bord à bord, s. bout à bout, s. à franc-bord, s. à, par, rapprochement, s. en bout,** butt weld(ing); **s. affleurée, s. arasée,** flush weld(ing); **s. à, par, recouvrement, s. à clin, s. en écharpe, s. par amorces,** lap weld(ing); **s. à plat,** flat weld(ing); **s. à droite, à gauche,** backhand, forehand, weld(ing); **s. en plafond,** overhead weld(ing); **s. continue, s. à la molette,** continuous weld(ing), seam weld(ing); **s. discontinue,** intermittent weld(ing); **s. en chaîne,** chain intermittent weld(ing); **s. par points,** spot weld(ing); **s. alternée,** staggered weld(ing); **s. à cordon longitudinal,** bead weld(ing); **s. en cordons parallèles déposés par passe longitudinale,** parallel beads, beading; **s. circulaire,** girth-seam weld(ing); **s. d'agrafage, d'assemblage,** tack weld(ing); temporary weld(ing); **s. en bouchon,** plug weld(ing); **s. d'angle,** fillet weld(ing); **s. montante,** vertical weld(ing). **3.** (*a*) union, join (of bones, etc.); *Med:* accretion; **s. des épiphyses,** epiphyseal closure; (*b*) *Hyd.E:* bonding; (*c*) *Pol.Ec:* **faire la s.,** to bridge the gap; to tide over; **stocker du blé pour la s. du printemps,** to stock up wheat to bridge the gap in the spring, to tide over the spring.

soue [su], *s.f.* pigsty.

soufflage [suflaːʒ], *s.m.* **1.** glass blowing. **2.** (*a*) sheathing (of ship's bottom); (*b*) *Mch:* **s. en planches,** cylinder jacket; (*c*) *Nau:* bill-board. **3.** blowing, blow, blast (of furnace); **s. sous grille,** under-grate blast; **s. par ventilateurs,** fan draught; *El:* **s. d'étincelles,** blowout; **parafoudre à s. magnétique,** lightning arrester with magnetic blowout.

soufflant, -ante [suflɑ̃, -ɑ̃ːt]. **1.** *a.* (*a*) blowing; **machine soufflante,** blowing engine, blast engine; (*b*) *Ling:* **consonne soufflante,** fricative, spirant, consonant; breath consonant; (*c*) *F:* **ça, c'est s.,** it's breathtaking. **2.** *s.f. Mec.E:* **soufflante,** blower, fan; **s. de sustentation (d'aéro-glisseur),** lift-fan (of hovercraft); **s. monoétage sans aubes de guidage,** single-stage fan with no intake guide-vanes; **soufflantes et ventilateurs,** blowers and fans; *Av:* **soufflante aval,** aft fan; *I.C.E: etc:* **soufflante de suralimentation,** supercharger.

soufflard [suflaːr], *s.m. Geol:* fumarole; mud volcano; *Min:* **s. de grisou,** blower gas vent.

souffle [sufl̩], *s.m.* breath. **1.** (*a*) puff, blast, breath (of air, wind); **le s. glacé du nord,** the icy blast of the north; **il y eut un s. d'air chaud,** there was a puff of warm air; **le moindre s. des vents,** the slightest breeze; the slightest puff of wind; **pas un s. de vent,** not a breath of air; (*b*) blast (of exploding shell); muzzle blast (of gun); (*c*) *Av:* slipstream, wash, wake (of propeller); **voilure soumise au s. des hélices,** wing blown by the propeller slipstream; wing in the slipstream, in the propeller's wake; (*d*) **le s. poétique,** poetic inspiration; (*of poet*) **manquer de s.,** to lack inspiration. 2. (*a*) respiration, breathing; **retenir son s.,** to hold one's breath; **éteindre une chandelle avec son s.,** to blow out a candle; **le s. ne suffit pas pour éteindre cette torche,** there is no blowing this torch out; **on le renverserait d'un s., au moindre s.,** the least puff would knock him over; **couper le s. à qn,** to take s.o.'s breath away; to flabbergast s.o.; **chose dite à peine dans un s.,** thing mentioned only in a whisper; **le s. vital, de la vie,** the breath of life; **dernier s.,** last breath; **exhaler son dernier s.,** to breathe one's last; **défendre qch. jusqu'à son dernier s.,** to defend sth. to the last gasp; **n'avoir plus que le s.,** to be at one's last gasp; **sa vie ne tient qu'à un s.,** his life hangs by a thread; *F:* **c'est à vous couper le s.,** it's breathtaking; *F:* **il ne manque pas de s.!** he's got a cheek, a nerve! *Med:* **s. amphorique,** amphoric breathing; (*b*) *Med:* **(bruit de) s.,** souffle, murmur, venous hum; **s. placentaire,** uterine souffle; (*c*) breath, wind (of runner, etc.); **être à bout de s.,** to be winded, out of breath, *F:* to be puffed; (*of runner*) **avoir beaucoup de s.,** to have plenty of wind; **manquer de s.,** to be short-winded; **il a trouvé son deuxième s.,** he has found his second breath, wind; *Sp:* **équipe bien en s.,** team in good training.

soufflé [sufle]. 1. *a.* (*a*) *Ling:* unvoiced (vowel); (*b*) puffed up, puffy (face, etc.); soufflé (omelette, potatoes); **les cours sont un peu soufflés,** prices are a bit inflated; *F:* **réputation soufflée,** exaggerated reputation; (*c*) *Av:* **aileron s., aile soufflée,** aileron, wing, in the slipstream, in the propellers' wake; **voilure soufflée sur toute sa surface,** wing fully in the slipstream, in the propellers' wake; (*d*) *F:* **être s.,** to be flabbergasted, taken aback. 2. *s.m. Cu:* soufflé; **moule à soufflés,** soufflé dish.

soufflement [sufləmɑ̃], *s.m.* blowing.

souffler [sufle]. 1. *v.i.* (*a*) to blow; (*of cat, etc.*) to spit; **le chat soufflait de colère,** the cat was spitting with rage; **s. dans ses doigts,** to blow on one's fingers; *F:* **tu peux s. dessus,** you can whistle for it! *F:* **il croit qu'il va y arriver en soufflant dessus,** he thinks he can do it as easy as winking, anything; *F:* **s. aux oreilles de qn,** to have a quiet, private, word with s.o.; (*b*) to recover one's breath; **laissez-moi le temps de s.,** leave me time to get my breath; **laisser s. un cheval,** to let a horse get its wind; to give a horse a breather; (*c*) to pant; to puff; **suant et soufflant,** puffing and blowing; *F:* **s. comme un bœuf, comme un phoque,** to blow like a grampus; (*d*) (*of the wind, etc.*) to blow; **le vent souffle en tempête,** it's blowing a gale; **il soufflait une brise du sud,** there was a southerly breeze (blowing); **regarder, voir, d'où, de quel côté, souffle le vent,** to see which way the wind is blowing; **un vent de révolte soufflait,** there was a spirit of revolt in the air; *B:* **l'Esprit souffle où il veut,** the Spirit bloweth where it listeth; (*e*) (*of buffalo*) to snort. 2. *v.tr.* (*a*) to blow (glass); to blow up (toy balloon, etc.); **s. un veau,** to blow up a calf (before skinning); (*b*) to blow (the organ); to blow up (the fire); to blow off (dust); to blow out (a candle); **s. la discorde,** to stir up discord; (*c*) to breathe, utter (a word, a sound); **ne pas s. mot de qch.,** not to breathe a word about sth.; **s. qch. à l'oreille de qn,** to whisper sth. to s.o.; (*d*) **s. son rôle à un acteur,** to prompt an actor; **s. un acteur, un élève,** to prompt an actor, a schoolboy; (*e*) *Games:* (*at draughts*) to huff (a man, an opponent); **s. n'est pas jouer,** huffing is not reckoned a move; *F:* **s. qch. à qn,** to trick s.o. out of sth.; to pinch sth. from s.o.; *A:* **s. une dépêche,** to keep back a dispatch (from the addressee); (*f*) *Nau:* to sheathe (ship's bottom); (*g*) (*of explosion*) to blast (building, etc.); *F:* (*of event, etc.*) to take (s.o.) aback; *F:* **son culot nous a soufflés,** his cheek took our breath away, knocked us flat.

soufflerie [sufləri], *s.f.* 1. bellows (of organ, forge); wind supply, bellows action (of organ). 2. (*a*) *Ind:* blowing engine, blast engine; blower; **air, vent, de la s.,** blast; *Av:* **s. carénée,** ducted fan; (*b*) wind tunnel.

soufflet [suflɛ], *s.m.* 1. (*a*) (pair of) bellows; **faire aller le s.,** to blow the bellows; *Med:* **bruit de s.,** blowing murmur; (*b*) blowing machine; (*c*) *Ind: etc:* fan, fanner. 2. (*a*) *A.Veh:* (extensible) hood (of carriage); **malle à soufflets,** portmanteau with expanding sides; (*b*) *Rail:* concertina vestibule (joining coaches); **wagon, train, à soufflets,** vestibule coach, train; (*c*) *Phot:* bellows (of camera); (*d*) *Dressm:* gusset, gore, inlay; **poche à s.,** gamekeeper's pocket; (*e*) *Mus:* swell (of organ). 3. *Lit:* (*a*) box on the ear, slap in the face; *hence* (*b*) affront, humiliation, snub.

souffleter [sufləte], *v.tr.* (**je soufflette, n. souffletons; je soufflletterai**) *Lit:* (*a*) **s. qn,** to box s.o.'s ears, to slap s.o.'s face; *hence* (*b*) to insult (s.o.); **s. qn de son mépris,** to treat s.o. with crushing contempt.

soufflette [suflɛt], *s.f.* 1. *Cer: Paperm:* blister. 2. *Metall:* blower.

souffleur, -euse [suflœːr, -øːz], *s.* 1. (*a*) (*pers.*) blower; **s. d'orgue,** organ blower; *Mus:* **les souffleurs,** the wind; **s. de verre,** glass blower; **s. de verre industriel,** power glassblower; (*b*) (i) *F:* puffer and blower; (ii) *Vet:* roaring horse; roarer; (*c*) *Th: etc:* prompter; **trou du s.,** prompt box, prompter's box (in front of stage); **l'exemplaire du s., le manuscrit du s.,** the prompt book, prompt copy; (*d*) *Const:* foreman mason. 2. *s.m.* (*a*) blower (of locomotive, for ventilation, etc.); *El:* **s. magnétique,** magnetic blow-out; (*b*) *Min:* blower, feeder (of fire damp). 3. *s.m. Ich:* blower (dolphin). 4. *s.f.* **souffleuse,** (*a*) snow-blower; (*b*) *Agr:* blower container (for seeds, etc.).

soufflure [suflyːr], *s.f.* (*a*) blister (in paint, etc.); **formation de soufflures,** blistering; (*b*) *Glassm:* bubble; (*c*) *Metall:* blister, blowhole, flaw (in casting); airhole, air pocket (in welding); (*d*) *Aut: etc:* bulge (in tyre).

souffrable [sufrabl̩], *a. A:* sufferable, tolerable.

souffrance [sufrɑ̃ːs], *s.f.* 1. (*a*) *Jur:* sufferance; **jour, vue, de s.** = ancient lights; (*b*) suspense; **en s.,** in suspense, in abeyance; **travail en s.,** work awaiting attention, pending; **candidats en s.,** candidates on the waiting list; **intérêts en s.,** interest in suspense; *Fin:* **coupons en s.,** outstanding, unpaid, coupons; **effets en s.,** bills held over; bills overdue, outstanding; **les colis en s.,** the parcels hung up in transit or awaiting delivery; **votre colis est en s. à la gare,** your parcel is waiting to be called for at the station; **ce procès a mis mes projets en s.,** all my plans are hung up, are at a standstill, pending decision of this lawsuit. 2. suffering, pain; **gai malgré ses souffrances,** cheerful in spite of his suffering.

souffrant [sufrɑ̃], *a.* 1. *A:* patiently abiding, long-suffering; **il n'est pas d'humeur souffrante,** he is short-tempered. 2. (*a*) suffering, in pain; *s.* sufferer; **l'humanité souffrante,** suffering humanity; **l'Église souffrante,** the souls in Purgatory; (*b*) unwell, poorly, indisposed; **il a l'air s.,** he doesn't look well.

souffre-douleur [sufrədulœːr], *s.m., occ.f., inv.* (*a*) drudge; (*b*) butt (of one's jokes, etc.); scapegoat.

souffreteux, -euse [sufrətø, -øːz], *a.* & *s.* 1. *A:* destitute, needy (person). 2. sickly, peaky, half-starved (child, etc.).

souffrir [sufriːr], *v.* (*pr.p.* **souffrant;** *p.p.* **souffert;** *pr.ind.* **je souffre, il souffre, n. souffrons, ils souffrent;** *p.d.* **je souffrais;** *p.h.* **je souffris;** *fu.* **je souffrirai**) to suffer. 1. *v.tr.* (*a*) to endure, undergo, bear, put up with (pain, fatigue, cold, loss, insult, etc.); *Mil:* **s. une attaque,** (i) to be attacked; (ii) to sustain, withstand, an attack; *F:* **je ne peux pas le s.,** I can't bear (the sight of) him; I can't stand him at any price; **ils ne peuvent pas se s.,** they can't stand each other; **je ne peux pas s. qu'on vienne me déranger,** I cannot bear to be disturbed; *A:* **le vaisseau a souffert désastre,** the ship met with disaster; *s.a.* PASSION 1; (*b*) to permit, allow; **je ne saurais s. cela,** I cannot allow that; **on lui souffre toutes sortes de fantaisies,** he is indulged in all sorts of fancies; **on ne lui souffre aucune fantaisie,** he is not allowed any whim; **il ne souffre aucune réplique,** he can't bear being contradicted; **souffrez que je vous dise la vérité,** allow me to tell you the truth; **situation qui ne souffre aucun retard,** situation that brooks no delay, that admits of no delay; **règle qui ne souffre pas d'exception,** rule which admits of no exception; **règle qui souffre des exceptions,** rule liable to exceptions; *A:* **souffrez à votre humble serviteur de s'expliquer,** allow your humble servant to explain; *Breed:* (*of mare*) **s. l'étalon,** to take the stallion. 2. *v.i.* (*a*) to feel pain; **souffre-t-il?** is he in pain? **s. de rhumatisme(s),** to suffer from rheumatism; **s. de la tête,** to suffer from headaches; **mon bras me fait s.,** my arm is giving me pain, is hurting me; **s. de la soif,** to be suffering from thirst; **je souffre de le voir si changé,** it pains, grieves, me to see him so changed; **nous avons beaucoup souffert de la guerre,** we were hard hit by the war; **je souffre à marcher,** I find walking painful; **avoir cessé de s.,** to be out of pain; (*b*) to suffer injury; (*of thgs*) to be injured, damaged (by frost, travel, etc.); **il a souffert dans sa réputation,** his reputation has suffered; **les vignes ont souffert de la gelée,** the vines have suffered from the frost; (*c*) (*of crops, trade, etc.*) to be in a bad way.

soufi [sufi], *s.m. Rel.H:* Sufi.

soufisme [sufism], *s.m. Rel.H:* Sufiism, Sufism.

soufrage [sufraːʒ], *s.m.* sulphuring (of matches, plants, etc.); sulphuration (of textiles); stumming (of wine).

soufre [sufr̩], *s.m.* 1. (*a*) sulphur; *U.S:* sulfur; **s. brut,** brimstone; **s. actif,** corrosive sulphur; **s. vierge, s. vif,** virgin sulphur; **s. de mine,** native sulphur; **fleur(s) de s., s. en fleur(s), s. pulvérulent, pulvérisé, en poudre, s. sublimé,** flowers of sulphur; **lait de s.,** milk of sulphur; **s. en canon, en bâtons,** roll sulphur, stick sulphur; **s. mou,** plastic sulphur; **opinions qui sentent le s.,** views that smack of heresy; (*b*) *a.inv.* **des gants s.,** yellow gloves. 2. **s. végétal,** vegetable sulphur; lycopodium.

soufré [sufre], *s.m. Ent:* sulphur (butterfly), brimstone (butterfly).

soufrer [sufre], *v.tr.* to sulphur; to treat (sth.) with sulphur; to dip (matches) in sulphur; to sulphurate (wool, etc.); to stum (wine); **allumette soufrée,** sulphur match, *A:* brimstone match; *Hort:* **bouillie soufrée,** lime sulphur.

soufreur, -euse [sufrœːr, -øːz]. 1. *s.* (*pers.*) (*a*) *Vit: etc:* person who treats vines etc. with sulphur; (*b*) *Ind:* worker in sulphur factory. 2. *s.f.* (*machine*) **soufreuse,** sulphurator, sulphur sprayer.

soufrière [sufri(j)ɛːr], *s.f.* 1. sulphur mine. 2. *Geol:* solfatara.

soufroir [sufrwaːr], *s.m. Tex: etc:* sulphuring chamber, room, stove.

souhait [swɛ], *s.m.* wish; desire; **souhaits de bonne année,** New Year's wishes; compliments of the season; **présenter ses souhaits à qn,** to offer s.o. one's good wishes; *adv.phr.* **à s.,** according to one's wishes, to one's liking; **avoir tout à s.,** to have everything one can wish for; **réussir à s.,** to succeed to perfection; *A:* **le temps est à s.,** the weather is all one could wish for; *F:* (*when s.o. sneezes*) **à vos souhaits!** (God) bless you!

souhaitable [swɛtabl̩], *a.* desirable, to be wished for; **il est s. que** + *sub.,* it is to be desired that . . ., to be hoped that . . .; **ce n'est guère s.,** one can hardly wish for, hope for, that.

souhaiter [swete], *v.tr.* to wish. 1. (*a*) **s. les richesses,** to wish for wealth, to want to be rich; **je souhaiterais (de) pouvoir vous aider,** I should like to be able to help you; **je souhaite que vous réussissiez, je vous souhaite de réussir,** I hope you will succeed; **je souhaite que vous ayez raison,** I hope you're right; (*b*) **je vous souhaite une bonne année,** I wish you, here's wishing you, a happy new year; **s. le bonsoir à qn,** to wish s.o. goodnight; **s. bon voyage à qn,** to wish s.o. a good journey; *F: Iron:* **je vous en souhaite!** you'll be lucky! 2. *A:* **s. qn,** to long for s.o.; **se faire s.,** to keep people waiting.

souillard [sujaːr], *s.m.* 1. (*a*) sinkhole (in a stone flag); (*b*) sink stone. 2. *Const:* strut, brace. 3. ice fender (of a bridge).

souillarde [sujard], *s.f.* (*a*) scullery; (*b*) wooden tube.

souille [suːj], *s.f.* 1. (wild boar's) wallow, *A:* soil; (*of boar*) **prendre s.,** to return to its wallow; *A:* to take soil. 2. (*a*) *Nau:* impression, bed (of ship's bottom in the mud); (*b*) *Const:* long underwater excavation (for placing foundation blocks); (*c*) *Artil:* strike (of low-range projectile).

souiller [suje], *v.tr.* 1. to soil, dirty (garments, etc.) (**de,** with); to foul (nest, etc.); **vêtements souillés de boue,** mudstained clothes. 2. to pollute; to contaminate; to taint; **s. ses mains de sang,** to stain one's hands with blood; to commit murder. 3. to tarnish, sully, dishonour (one's name, a memory, etc.); **son honneur était un peu souillé,** his honour had suffered somewhat; **s. la couche nuptiale, le lit nuptial,** to commit adultery.

souillon [sujɔ̃], *s.m.* & *f.* 1. sloven; *esp. f.* slut, slattern; **petite s.,** dirty, bedraggled, little girl. 2. *s.f.* scullery maid.

souillure [sujyːr], *s.f.* 1. (*a*) spot (of dirt); stain (on garment, etc.); (*b*) *Ch: etc:* impurity; contamination. 2. *Lit:* blot, blemish (on one's reputation, on one's honour); defilement; **sans s.,** unsullied, unblemished, undefiled.

souimanga [swimɑ̃ga], *s.m. Orn:* sunbird, sugar bird; **s. du Sénégal,** scarlet-breasted sunbird.

souk [suk], *s.m.* (*a*) (*in Middle East and N. Africa*) souk, market; (*b*) *P:* (*of place*) shambles.

souki [suki], *s.m. Bot:* vegetable marrow.

soûl [su]. 1. *a.* (*a*) *O:* glutted, surfeited, gorged (with food, drink, etc.); *Lit:* être s. de plaisir, de musique, to have had a surfeit of pleasure, of music; (*b*) *F:* drunk, tipsy, fuddled; s. comme un Polonais, comme un cochon, comme une bourrique, comme une vache, *O:* comme une grive, to be as drunk as a lord, as an owl; s. perdu, blind drunk. 2. *s.m. F:* boire, manger, rire, chanter, tout son s., to drink, eat, laugh, sing, to one's heart's content; to drink, eat, one's fill; s'amuser tout son s., to enjoy oneself to the full; en avoir tout son s., to have all that one wants; il s'est battu tout son s., he's had his bellyful of fighting.

soulagement [sulaʒmɑ̃], *s.m.* relief, alleviation, assuagement (of pain, grief); solace, comfort; apporter du s. à qn, to bring relief to s.o.; to comfort s.o.; *Mch:* soupape de s., relief valve.

soulager [sulaʒe], *v.tr.* (je soulageai(s); n. soulageons) to lighten the burden of (mule, etc.); to ease (pressure); to relieve, alleviate, allay (pain, grief); to soothe, comfort (s.o.'s mind, sorrow, conscience); s. le peuple d'un impôt, to relieve the people of a tax; on soulage ses maux à les raconter, it is a relief, a comfort, to speak of one's troubles; s. une poutre, to relieve the strain on, take the strain off, a beam; *Nau:* s. un palan, to ease up a tackle; s. le gui, to trip up, trice up, the boom; s. les soupapes, to blow off steam; soulage(z) la toile, les toiles! show a leg! cela me soulage l'esprit d'un grand poids, that is a great weight off my mind; *F:* s. qn de son portefeuille, to relieve s.o. of his wallet.

se soulager. 1. to work less, to ease up, to take things more easily; se s. d'un fardeau, to ease oneself of a burden. 2. to relieve one's feelings, one's mind. 3. *F:* to relieve nature.

soulane [sulan], *s.f.* (*in the Pyrenees*) sunny side (of mountain).

soûlant [sulɑ̃], *a.* (*a*) *A:* filling, over-satisfying; (*b*) *P:* boring; tedious; (*c*) il est s., his talking makes my head spin, whirl.

soûlard, -arde [sulaːr, -ard], **soûlaud, -aude** [sulo, -oːd], *s. P:* drunkard, soak; vieux s., old soak.

soulcie [sulsi], *s.m. Orn:* moineau s., rock sparrow.

soûler [sule], *v.tr.* 1. *O:* s. qn de viande, de boisson, to surfeit s.o., to fill s.o. to repletion, with meat, with drink; tout soûle à la fin, one can have too much of a good thing. 2. *F:* to make (s.o.) drunk; se s. de paroles, to get drunk with the sound of one's own voice.

soûlerie [sulri], *s.f.* 1. *O:* satiety; goûter un plaisir jusqu'à la s., to indulge in a pleasure to (the point of) satiety. 2. *P:* (*a*) drinking bout; (*b*) drunkenness.

soulevé [sulve], *s.m.* weight lifting.

soulèvement [sulɛvmɑ̃], *s.m.* (*a*) rising, heaving (of the ground, of the stomach); swell(ing) (of the waves); s. de cœur, nausea; (*b*) *Geol:* upheaval, upthrust, uplift (of the earth's surface); (*c*) revolt, rising (of a people); (*d*) burst of indignation, general protest.

soulever [sulve], *v.tr.* (je soulève, n. soulevons; je soulèverai) 1. (*a*) to raise (*usu.* with effort); to lift (up) (a weight); s. un malade, to lift a patient; grue qui soulève de lourdes charges, crane that takes heavy loads; la marée soulèvera le bateau, the tide will lift the boat, will float the boat off; poussière soulevée par le vent, dust raised by the wind; un soupir lui souleva la poitrine, her chest heaved (with a sigh); s. le porte-monnaie de qn, to steal, *F:* lift, s.o.'s purse; *Geol:* couches soulevées, raised, upheaved, beds; plage soulevée, raised beach; (*b*) to raise slightly; s. le rideau, to peep out under the curtain; *Lit:* s. le voile qui cache l'avenir, to raise a corner of the veil that hides the future; (*c*) s. une objection, to raise an objection; s. des doutes, to raise doubts; to give rise to doubts; s. une réclamation, to make, put in, a claim; la question fut soulevée, the question was raised, mooted, brought up. 2. (*a*) to rouse, stir up (people to revolt); une émotion intense souleva le pays, the country was stirred by a deep emotion; (*b*) to excite, provoke, rouse (passion, indignation).

se soulever. 1. (*a*) to rise; la mer se soulève, the sea is heaving, swelling, whipping up; tout mon être se soulève en colère contre lui, my whole being rises in anger against him; (*b*) (*of the stomach*) to heave, to turn. 2. (*a*) to raise oneself (with one's hands, etc.); (*b*) to revolt; to rise (in rebellion).

soulier [sulje], *s.m.* 1. shoe; souliers de marche, walking shoes; souliers ferrés, (i) hobnailed, (ii) spiked, shoes; souliers de toile, canvas shoes; souliers à bouts carrés, square-toed shoes; souliers richelieu, lace up, oxford, shoes; souliers bas, (oxford) shoes; gros souliers, heavy shoes; souliers à talons, shoes with a heel; souliers à talons hauts, high-heeled shoes; souliers de bal, (ladies') evening shoes; (men's) pumps; ne pas avoir de souliers aux pieds, to have no shoes to one's feet; *F:* être dans ses petits souliers, to be in an embarrassing, awkward, situation; to be ill at ease, on pins and needles; *Prov:* chacun sait où le s. le blesse, everyone knows best where his own shoe pinches; faute de souliers on va nu-pieds, beggars cannot be choosers. 2. *Bot:* souliers de Notre-Dame, lady's slipper.

soulignage [suliɲaːʒ], *s.m.*, **soulignement** [suliɲmɑ̃], *s.m.* (*a*) underlining; underscoring; (*b*) stressing (of a word).

souligner [suliɲe], *v.tr.* (*a*) to underline, underscore (word, passage); c'est moi qui ai souligné, the underlining is mine; (*b*) to emphasize, lay (an) emphasis on, lay stress on, accentuate (word, fact).

souliote [suljɔt], *a. & s. Ethn:* Suliote.

soûlographe [sulɔgraf], *s.m. P:* drunkard, soak.

soûlographie [sulɔgrafi], *s.f. P:* (*a*) drunkenness; (*b*) drinking bout; orgy.

souloir [sulwaːr], *v.i. A:* to be accustomed (to do sth.); (*still found in the p.d. as a humorous archaism*) une taverne qu'il soulait fréquenter, a tavern that he was wont to frequent.

Soulou [sulu], *Pr.n. Geog:* les îles S., the Sulu Islands.

soulte [sult], *s.f.* (*a*) *Jur:* balance (to equalize shares, etc.); (*b*) additional payment (over and above the legal price).

soumettre [sumɛtr], *v.tr.* (*conj. like* METTRE) 1. to subdue, to bring into subjection (people, province, one's passions). 2. to submit, refer, present, put (question, etc.); s. une demande à qn, to bring, lay, a request before s.o.; to refer a request to s.o.; s. ses projets à qn, to lay, put, one's plans before s.o. 3. (*a*) s. qch. à un examen, to subject sth. to an examination; s. qn à une épreuve, to put s.o. through a test; s. les enfants à la discipline, to put, keep, the children under discipline; to keep the children in order; (*b*) to bind; être soumis à des règles strictes, to be bound by strict rules.

se soumettre, to submit, give in, yield; se s. à l'autorité, to submit to authority; se s. aux volontés de qn, to comply with s.o.'s wishes; se s. à la décision de qn, to defer to s.o.'s decision; to abide by s.o.'s decision.

soumis [sumi], *a.* 1. submissive, obedient; dutiful. 2. subject, amenable (to law, authority, etc.); pays s. à l'influence française, country under French influence; peuples s. à Rome, peoples under the power of Rome; non s., unconquered; votes de crédit s. à des retards, votes of credit subject to delays; dividendes s. à l'impôt sur le revenu, dividends liable to income tax; s. au timbre, subject to stamp duty; fille soumise, registered prostitute.

soumission [sumisjɔ̃], *s.f.* 1. (*a*) submission (of rebels, etc.); faire (sa) s., to surrender, yield; (*b*) profession of allegiance; les ducs firent leur s. à Henri IV, the dukes made their submission to Henry IV; (*c*) obedience, submissiveness, amenableness (à, to); s. aux règlements, observance of the regulations. 2. (*a*) *Com:* tender (for public works, etc.); s. cachetée, sealed tender; faire une s. pour un travail, to send in a tender, to tender, for a piece of work; (*b*) *Jur:* undertaking, bond; acte de s., guarantee given (in lieu of bail) for an individual; (*c*) *pl. A:* excuses, apology.

soumissionnaire [sumisjɔnɛːr], *s.m.* (*a*) party tendering for work on contract; tenderer; (*b*) *Fin:* underwriter.

soumissionner [sumisjɔne], *v.tr.* (*a*) to tender for, put in a tender for (job, public works, etc.); *abs.* s. à une adjudication, to tender for a contract; (*b*) *Fin:* to underwrite (new issue, etc.).

Soungari [sungari], *Pr.n.m. Geog:* the (river) Sungari.

soupape [supap], *s.f. Tchn:* 1. valve; (*a*) s. à clapet, à charnière, clack valve, flap valve; s. en champignon, s. à déclic, poppet valve, mushroom valve; s. à boulet, ball valve; s. à pointeau, needle valve; s. à cloche, cup valve; s. à guide, spindle valve; s. à tiroir, slide valve; s. de sûreté, safety valve; blast gate (of turbojet); la liberté de la presse est une s. de sûreté, liberty of the press acts as a safety valve; s. d'étranglement, throttle valve; s. de réglage, à papillon, throttle valve; damper (of stove pipe); s. d'avertissement, sentinel valve; s. d'arrêt, stop valve; tide flap (of sewer); s. d'admission, d'arrivée, inlet valve, induction valve; s. d'échappement, s. de décharge, outlet valve, exhaust valve, escape valve; s. à flotteur, ballcock, *occ.* ball valve; s. commandée, mechanically operated valve; s. à levée automatique, automatically operated valve; *I.C.E:* soupapes en tête, en chandelle, overhead valve; soupapes latérales, en chapelle, side valves; s. de surpression, s. de décompression, relief valve (on oil pump); *Hyd.E:* s. de retenue, feed-check valve; back-pressure valve; s. de refoulement, forcing valve; s. de dérivation, by-pass valve; s. à ailettes, à brides, flanged valve; sans soupapes, valveless; (*b*) *El: Elcs:* s. électrique, (current-rectifying) valve; rectifier; s. électronique, electron valve, tube; s. ionique, gas-filled rectifier; s. à gaz, gas tube; s. à vide, vacuum tube. 2. plug (of bath, reservoir).

soupçon [supsɔ̃], *s.m.* 1. suspicion; distrust; s'exposer aux soupçons, to lay oneself open to suspicion; être l'objet de soupçons, to be under a cloud; devenir l'objet des soupçons, to fall under suspicion; sa conduite n'a éveillé aucun s., his conduct aroused no suspicions; pas l'ombre d'un s., not the shadow, not the ghost, of a suspicion; avoir des soupçons à l'endroit de qn, to feel suspicious about s.o., regarding s.o.; j'en avais le s.! I thought so! I suspected as much! concevoir des soupçons à l'égard de qn, to have suspicions about s.o.; to begin to suspect s.o.; il est au-dessus de tout s., not a breath of suspicion attaches to him; endormir les soupçons, to lull suspicion; faire naître les soupçons, to arouse suspicion; arrêter qn sur un s., to arrest s.o. on a mere suspicion. 2. suspicion, surmise, conjecture; je n'en avais pas le moindre s., I had no suspicion of it; I never suspected it for a moment, I never had the slightest inkling of it; si vous m'en aviez donné le moindre s., if you had given me the slightest hint, the slightest inkling, about it. 3. *F:* slight flavour, small quantity, dash, soupçon (of vinegar, garlic, etc.); touch (of fever, rouge, irony, etc.); pas un s. de preuve, not the slightest bit of evidence; pas un s. de chance, not the ghost of a chance; boire un s. de vin, to drink just a drop of wine.

soupçonnable [supsɔnabl̩], *a.* liable, open, to suspicion; il est difficilement s. avec un tel alibi, with an alibi like that he can hardly be suspected.

soupçonner [supsɔne], *v.tr.* 1. to suspect; sa conduite n'a pas été soupçonnée, his conduct aroused no suspicions; s. qn de qch., de faire qch., d'avoir fait qch., to suspect s.o. of sth., of doing sth., of having done sth.; la femme de César ne doit pas être soupçonnée, Caesar's wife must be above suspicion; (*with adv.*) s. juste, to be right in one's suspicions; je lui soupçonne un peu d'égoïsme, I suspect he is inclined to be selfish; *Lit:* je le soupçonne royaliste, I suspect him of royalism; *abs. Lit:* on soupçonne aisément quand on n'est pas heureux, we are apt to be suspicious when we are not happy. 2. to surmise, suspect, conjecture; livre que je soupçonne être mien, book which I suspect is mine; je ne soupçonnais pas que . . ., I had no suspicion, no idea, that . . .

soupçonneusement [supsɔnøzmɑ̃], *adv.* suspiciously, distrustfully; in a suspicious manner.

soupçonneux, -euse [supsɔnø, -øːz], *a.* (*a*) suspicious, distrustful; peu s. de caractère, unsuspicious by nature; naturally unsuspicious; (*b*) (*of horse*) shy, nervous.

soupe [sup], *s.f.* 1. (*a*) *O:* sop; soaked slice of bread; tailler la s., to cut up the bread for soup; s. au vin, *F:* s. au perroquet, bread soaked in wine; (*b*) s. au lait, bread and milk; *F:* il s'emporte, monte, comme une s. au lait, il est très s. au lait, c'est une s. au lait, he flares up very easily, he's always flying off the handle. 2. (*a*) soup; s. grasse, soup made with meat stock; s. aux pois, à l'oignon, pea soup, onion soup; s. populaire, *A:* s. à la Rumford, s. économique, soup for distribution to the poor, the destitute; *F:* venez manger la s. avec nous, come and have sth. to eat with us; come and take pot luck with us; *F:* (*of married couple*) manger la s. à la grimace, to sulk (after a quarrel); (*of husband*) recevoir la s. à la grimace, to get a poor welcome (from his wife); *F:* un gros plein de s., a great lump of a man; *F:* marchand de s., (i) poor restaurateur; (ii) headmaster of a poor boarding school; *Th:* servir la s., to take small parts, bit parts; *P:* par ici la bonne s.! that's the way to make money! (*b*) *Mil: F:* s. du matin, du soir, morning, evening, meal; être de s., to be on cookhouse fatigue, to be cookhouse orderly; à la s.! (i) *Mil:* come to the cookhouse door boys! (ii) grub's up! *Prov:*

la s. fait le soldat, there's nothing like plain food; (*c*) *Husb:* fodder soaked in water; (*d*) *Ski: F:* soft snow. **3. s. (populaire),** soup kitchen.

soupé [supe], *s.m.A:* = SOUPER II.

soupe-au-lait [supolɛ], **soupe-de-lait** [supdəlɛ], *a.inv.* cream-coloured (horse).

soupente [supɑ̃:t], *s.f.* **1.** (*a*) *A:* main braces, *U.S:* thorough brace (of coach); (*b*) supporting beam, support (of winch, pulley, etc.). **2.** (*a*) loft, garret; (*b*) closet; **s. d'escalier,** cupboard under the stairs.

souper [supe]. I. *v.i.* to have supper; **s. d'une salade,** *F:* **avec une salade,** to make one's supper of a salad; *F:* **j'en ai soupé,** I have had enough of it, I'm fed up with it.

II. **souper,** *s.m.* **1.** (*a*) (*now used rarely except in country districts and Fr.C:*) supper, evening meal; **on l'envoya coucher sans s.,** he was sent to bed supperless; (*b*) theatre supper. **2.** *Mil:* evening stables.

soupeser [supəze], *v.tr.* (**je soupèse, n. soupesons; je soupèserai**) to feel, try, the weight of (sth.); to weigh, poise (sth.) in the hand; *U.S:* to heft (packet, etc.); **s. les données d'un problème,** to weigh up the data of a problem.

soupeur, -euse [supœ:r, -ø:z], *s.* supper eater.

soupied [supje], *s.m.* = SOUS-PIED.

soupier, -ière [supje, -jɛ:r]. **1.** *F:* (*a*) *a.* soup-eating, fond of soup; **je ne suis pas très s.,** I'm not much of a soup eater, I'm not very fond of soup; (*b*) *s.* soup eater. **2.** *s.f.* **soupière,** soup tureen.

soupir [supi:r], *s.m.* **1.** sigh; **pousser un s.,** to sigh; to heave a sigh; **il poussa un s. de soulagement,** he breathed, heaved, a sigh of relief; **tirer des soupirs de ses talons,** to heave a great sigh; **un long s.,** a long-drawn sigh; **un gros s.,** a heavy sigh; **il poussa un long s.,** he gave a long sigh; **rendre le dernier s.,** to draw one's last breath, to breathe one's last, to pass away; **c'est moi qui ai reçu son dernier s.,** I was with him when he breathed his last; **jusqu'à mon dernier s.,** until my last breath; **le Pont des Soupirs,** the Bridge of Sighs; **s. du vent,** sighing, sough, of the wind. **2.** *Mus:* crotchet rest; **quart de s.,** semiquaver rest; **demi-quart de s.,** demisemiquaver rest.

soupirail, -aux [supira:j, -o], *s.m.* (*a*) air trap, air hole; (cellar) ventilator; vent (in air shaft, etc.); (*b*) small basement window.

soupirant [supirɑ̃]. **1.** *a.* sighing (lover). **2.** *s.m. A: & Hum:* suitor, admirer.

soupirer [supire], *v.i.* (*a*) to sigh; **en soupirant,** with a sigh; **il soupira longuement,** he gave a long sigh; (*b*) **s. après, pour, à, vers, qch.,** to long, yearn, sigh, for sth.; **s. après qch.,** to hanker after sth.; *A:* **il soupirait de partir,** he was longing to depart; (*c*) *with cogn. acc. Poet:* to breathe out, sigh out (one's woes, etc.).

soupireur [supirœ:r], *s.m. A:* love-sick swain.

souple [supl̩], *a.* supple; (*a*) pliant (willow); flexible, pliable (branch, etc.); lithe, lissom(e) (body, figure); flexible (voice); limp (binding); yielding (snow); **cuir s.,** soft leather; **cheveux souples,** soft hair; **esprit s.,** adaptable, versatile, mind; *I.C.E:* **moteur s.,** flexible engine; *Aer:* **dirigeable s.,** non-rigid airship; (*b*) docile, pliant, tractable, accommodating, easily moulded (nature); **s. à toutes les volontés de son maître,** ready to comply with his master's every wish; **s. comme un gant,** accommodating to the verge of servility; **s. comme une anguille,** slippery as an eel.

souplement [supləmɑ̃], *adv.* supply; flexibly.

souplesse [suplɛs], *s.f.* **1.** suppleness; flexibility; pliability; litheness (of body, movement, etc.); **en s.,** in a relaxed, easy, manner; **s. d'esprit,** adaptability of mind; versatility; **s. du style,** ease of style; **s. économique,** economic adaptability; *Tchn:* **s. de fonctionnement,** flexibility (of a machine, engine, etc.); **s. d'emploi,** versatility (of equipment). **2.** (*a*) pliability (of character); (*b*) **il a beaucoup de s.,** he knows how to be diplomatic.

souquenille [sukni:j], *s.f. O:* (*a*) smock (as worn by groom, etc.); (*b*) shabby old garment.

souquer [suke]. **1.** *v.tr.* (*a*) *Nau:* to haul (rope) taut; (*b*) *F:* to thrash, beat (s.o.). **2.** *v.i.* (*a*) **s. sur les avirons,** to pull away at the oars, to stretch out, to give way; **s. un coup,** to pull one stroke; (*b*) *F:* to work, do one's utmost, exert oneself.

Sourât [surat], *Pr.n. Geog:* Surat.

sourate [surat], *s.f.* sura(h) (of the Koran).

source [surs], *s.f.* source. **1.** (*a*) spring(head), fountain (head), well; **s. d'eau vive, s. vive,** living spring, gushing spring; *Lit:* **les sources vives de son influence ne sont pas taries,** the living springs of his influence have not run dry; **eau de s.,** spring water; **s. d'eau minérale,** mineral spring; **s. thermale,** hot spring; **rivière qui prend sa s. dans,** river that has its source in, that rises in; **remonter la rivière jusqu'à la s.,** to go up the river to its source; **couper une s.,** to intercept, divert, a spring; **son récit coule de s.,** he gives a straightforward account; *F:* **ça coule de s.,** it's obvious; (*b*) **s. de pétrole,** oil spring; **s. jaillissante,** gusher; **s. boueuse,** mud geyser, mud volcano; *Metall:* **coulée en s.,** bottom pouring; (*c*) *Opt:* **s. lumineuse,** light source; **s. de lumière,** illuminant; *El:* **s. d'énergie, s. d'alimentation,** power supply; *Elcs:* (*computers*) **s. de données,** data source; **code s.,** source code; **langage s.,** source language; **paquet de cartes en langage s.,** source deck. **2.** origin (of evil, wealth, news, etc.); *Fin:* **imposé à la s.,** taxed at source; **la s. de tous nos malheurs,** the source, cause, of all our troubles; **aller à la s. du mal,** to get to the root of the evil; **informations de s. américaine,** information from an American source; **emprunter des faits à de mauvaises sources,** to take facts from unreliable sources; **je le tiens de bonne s.,** I have it on good authority, from a trustworthy informant; **ce que je dis, je le sais de bonne s.,** I speak with inside knowledge; **remonter aux sources d'une tradition,** to trace a tradition back to its source(s); *F:* **faire un retour aux sources,** to return to nature; *Nau:* **s. du vent,** wind's quarter.

sourcer [surse], *v.tr. Dial:* to rinse (linen) in clean water.

sourcier, -ière [sursje, -jɛ:r], *s.* water diviner; dowser; **baguette de s.,** divining rod, dowsing rod.

sourcil [sursi], *s.m.* (*a*) eyebrow; **sourcils épais,** shaggy eyebrows; **aux sourcils épais, lourds, touffus,** beetle-browed, heavy-browed; **froncer le(s) sourcil(s),** to knit one's brow, to frown, to scowl; (*b*) *Anat:* supercilium (of cotyloid cavity).

sourcilier, -ière [sursilje, -jɛ:r], *a. Anat:* superciliary (muscle, artery, etc.); **les arcades sourcilières,** the superciliary arches, ridges; the brow ridges.

sourciller [sursije], *v.i.* **1.** to knit one's brows, to frown. **2.** to wince, flinch; **sans s.,** without wincing, without moving a muscle, without blenching, without turning a hair; **il n'a pas sourcillé,** he didn't turn a hair; *F:* he never batted an eyelid.

sourcilleusement [sursijøzmɑ̃], *adv.* superciliously; with a frown, frowningly.

sourcilleux, -euse [sursijø, -ø:z], *a.* **1.** (*a*) supercilious, haughty; (*b*) gathered, frowning (brow); beetling (brow); **il avait le front s.,** he looked worried. **2.** *Poet: A:* tall, lofty (tree, mountain).

sourd, sourde [su:r, surd]. **1.** (*a*) *a.* deaf; **s. d'une oreille,** deaf in one ear; *F:* **s. comme un pot, comme une bécasse,** as deaf as a post; **s. aux prières,** deaf, irresponsive, to entreaties; **rester s. aux prières,** to turn a deaf ear to entreaties; (*b*) *s.* deaf person; **crier comme un s.,** to yell, to squeal; **frapper qn comme un s.,** to beat s.o. unmercifully; **taper comme un s.,** to lay about one, to lash out wildly; **faire le s.,** (i) to sham deafness; (ii) to be deaf (to entreaties, etc.); **autant vaut parler à un s.,** you might as well talk to a brick wall; **un dialogue de sourds,** a dialogue of the deaf; *Prov:* **il n'est pire s. que celui qui ne veut point entendre,** there are none so deaf as those who don't want to hear; (*c*) *a. Orn:* **bécassine sourde,** jack snipe. **2.** *a.* (*a*) dull (tint, pain); dull, muffled (noise); muted (string); hollow (voice); secret (rumour, desire); **cri s.,** low, smothered, cry; **coup s.,** dull, muffled, blow; **cela tomba avec un bruit s.,** it fell with a thump, with a thud; **lanterne sourde,** dark lantern; **pierre sourde,** cloudy gem; **hostilité sourde,** undertone of hostility, veiled hostility, hostile mutterings; **haine sourde,** bottled-up hatred; *Ling:* **consonne sourde,** mute, voiceless, breathed, consonant; surd; *Mth: A:* **quantité, racine, sourde,** surd; (*b*) underhand (agitation, practices); *A:* **manière sourde,** underhand manner. **3.** *a.* soundproof; dead (room).

sourdement [surdəmɑ̃], *adv.* (*a*) dully, with a dull, hollow, sound; **le tonnerre grondait s.,** the thunder was rumbling, there was a rumble of thunder; (*b*) secretly; **agir s.,** to act in an underhand way; **on parlait s. de . . .,** there was mysterious, secret, talk of. . . ..

sourdière [surdjɛ:r], *s.f.* padded shutter.

sourdinage [surdina:ʒ], *s.m. Tg:* fitting of silencing devices (to cable supports).

sourdine [surdin], *s.f.* **1.** (*a*) *Mus:* mute, sordine (for violin, cornet, etc.); **mettre une s. à un violon,** to mute a violin; **violons en s.,** muted violins; **mettre une s. à ses plaintes,** to lower the tone of one's complaints; to soft-pedal one's complaints; *F:* **mettre la s.,** to pipe down; (*b*) *W.Tel: etc:* damper; (*c*) *Tg:* silencing device (for cable supports); (*d*) *Const:* padded shutter. **2. accompagnement (de voix) en s.,** hummed accompaniment; **jurer en s.,** to swear under one's breath; **entendre qch. en s.,** to hear sth. as a dull murmur; **tout se passait en s.,** it was all going on in secret, on the sly; **décamper en s.,** to clear out quietly, to flit.

sourdiner [surdine], *v.tr. Tg:* to fit silencing devices to (cable supports).

sourdingue [surdɛ̃:g], *a. & s.m. & f. P:* deaf (person).

surdité [surdite], *s.f. Ling:* voicelessness (of consonant).

sourd-muet, sourde-muette [surmɥɛ, surdmɥɛt]. **1.** *a.* deaf-and-dumb. **2.** *s.* deaf mute; *pl. sourds-muets, sourdes-muettes.*

sourdre [surdr̩], *v.i.* (*used only in third pers.* **il sourd, ils sourdent,** *and in inf.*; the past tenses are rare) **1.** (*of waters*) (*a*) to spring, to well (up); (*b*) **eaux qui sourdent de la roche,** waters that ooze (out), trickle, from the rock. **2.** *Lit:* to result, arise, spring; **que verra-t-on s. de ces événements?** what will spring, arise, from these events?

souriant [surjɑ̃], *a.* smiling; **elle était toute souriante,** she was all smiles; **l'avenir est s.,** the future is rosy; *F:* **un cadre s.,** pleasant surroundings; **un ciel s.,** a good, sunny, climate.

souriceau, -eaux [suriso], *s.m.* little mouse, young mouse.

souricier [surisje], *s.m.* (*of cat, etc.*) mouser.

souricière [surisjɛ:r], *s.f.* (*a*) mousetrap; (*b*) trap, snare; *esp.* police trap; **tendre une s.,** to set a trap (**à,** for); **se jeter dans la s.,** to fall into the trap; (*c*) *Min:* overshot.

sourire [suri:r]. I. *v.i.* (*conj. like* RIRE) **1.** (*a*) to smile; **s. à qn,** to smile to s.o.; **cette réponse fit s. tout le monde,** this answer provoked a general smile; **en souriant,** with a smile, smilingly; **la fortune lui sourit,** fortune smiles on him; *Phot:* **souriez!** smile please! say cheese! (*b*) *Pej:* to smirk, to simper. **2.** (*a*) (*of thgs*) to please; to prove attractive (**à qn,** to s.o.); **l'idée me souriait assez,** I was rather taken with the idea; **projet qui ne me sourit pas,** plan which does not appeal to me; **l'idée ne nous souriait pas,** we did not relish the idea; *impers. Lit:* **il nous eût souri de pénétrer plus avant dans le pays,** we should have liked to go further inland; (*b*) **tout lui sourit,** he, she, makes a success of everything; **en jardinage tout lui sourit,** he, she, has green fingers.

II. **sourire,** *s.m.* smile; **s. affecté,** smirk, simper; **s. de mépris,** scornful, smile; sneer; **s. de pitié,** pitying smile; **s. de découragement,** wintry smile; **large s.,** broad smile; grin; **son visage s'épanouit en un large s.,** he grinned broadly; his face broke into a broad grin; **approuver d'un large s.,** to show one's approval with a broad smile; **elle souriait de son plus gracieux s.,** she gave her most gracious smile; **elle eut un s. énigmatique,** she gave an enigmatic soile; she smiled enigmatically; **il nous reçut le s. aux lèvres,** he received us with a smile on his lips; **adresser un s. à qn,** to give s.o. a smile; **écarter d'un s. les craintes de qn,** to smile s.o.'s fears away; **garder le s.,** to keep smiling.

souris[1] [suri], *s.f.* **1.** (*a*) mouse; **s. de terre,** field mouse; **s. d'eau,** water shrew; **s. sauteuse, s. de montagne,** jerboa, jumping mouse; **s. des bouleaux,** birch mouse; **s. blanche,** white mouse; **s. à pattes blanches,** white-footed mouse; **s. glaneuse,** wild house mouse; **s. marsupiale australienne,** Australian marsupial mouse; **s. à miel,** honey possum; **s. arboricole papoue,** Papuan arboreal mouse; **guetter qn comme le chat fait de la s.,** to watch s.o. like a cat watching a mouse; **on aurait entendu trotter une s.,** you could have heard a pin drop; **marcher à pas de s.,** to pit-pat along; *a.inv.* **(couleur) gris (de) s.,** mouse colour; **cheval, fourrure, (gris) s.,** mouse-coloured horse, fur; *Prov:* **s. qui n'a qu'un trou est bientôt prise,** one must have more than one string to one's bow; (*b*) *Ich: F:* climbing perch; **s. de mer,** dragonet; (*c*) *Bot:* **s. végétale,** Chinese gooseberry; (*d*) *F:* **petite s.,** (i) busy little old lady; (ii) mousy little woman; *Pej:* **s. de sacristie,** bigoted churchwoman; (*e*) *P:* bird, dame; **s d'hôtel,** (female) hotel thief. **2.** (*a*) space between the thumb and index finger; (*b*) knuckle end (of leg of mutton). **3.** *Av:* nose cone, shock cone. **4.** *Pyr:* squib.

souris[2], *s.m. A. & Poet:* = SOURIRE II.

sourlit [surli], *s.m. A.Furn:* truckle bed.

sournois, -oise [surnwa, -waːz]. **1.** *a.* artful, sly, deep, crafty (person); cunning, shifty (look); underhand (person, dealings). **2.** *s.* sneak, underhand person.

sournoisement [surnwazmɑ̃], *adv.* cunningly, artfully, slyly; in an underhand manner.

sournoiserie [surnwazri], *s.f.* **1.** artfulness, slyness; (underhand) cunning; craftiness. **2.** underhand trick.

sous [su], *prep.* **1.** under(neath), beneath, below; (*a*) **s'asseoir s. un arbre,** to sit down under a tree; **tirer un tabouret de s. la table,** to pull out a stool from under the table; **disparaître, sombrer, s. les flots,** to sink beneath the waves; **s. terre,** underground, below ground; **s. clef,** under lock and key; **s. le sceau du secret,** under pledge of secrecy; **s. nos propres yeux,** under, before, our very eyes; **chercher un mot s. la lettre S,** to look up a word under (the letter) S; **avoir qch. s. la main,** to have sth. within (easy) reach; **regarder qn s. le nez,** to stare at s.o.; **soldat s. un uniforme de général,** soldier masquerading as a general; **paraître s. un jour favorable,** to appear in, under, a favourable light; **connu s. le nom de . . .,** known by the name of . . .; **travailler s. la pluie,** to work in the rain; **câble s. caoutchouc,** rubber-covered cable; *Mil:* **s. les armes,** under arms; fighting; **s. les drapeaux,** with the colours; **les combats s. Verdun,** the fights under the forts of Verdun; **s. le feu de . . .,** exposed to the fire of . . .; *Nau:* **s. pavillon anglais,** flying the English flag; **s. le vent,** under the lee; (*b*) **s. les tropiques,** in the tropics; **s. l'équateur,** at the equator; (*c*) **s. Louis XIV,** under Louis XIV; in the reign of Louis XIV; **s. peine de mort,** on pain of death; **s. un prétexte,** under a pretext; **écrire s. la dictée de qn,** to write at, from, s.o.'s dictation. **2.** within (the time of); **je répondrai s. trois jours,** I shall reply within three days; **s. peu,** before long.

sous- [su], *before vowel sound* [suz], *comb.fm.* sub-; under-.

sous-acétate [suzasetat], *s.m. Ch:* subacetate; *pl. sous-acétates.*

sous-affermer [suzafɛrme], *v.tr.* **1.** to sublet (land). **2.** to sublease (land).

sous-affluent [suzaflyɑ̃], *s.m. Geog:* tributary of a tributary; *pl. sous-affluents.*

sous-affrètement [suzafrɛtmɑ̃], *s.m.* sub-charter(ing); *pl. sous-affrètements.*

sous-affréter [suzafrete], *v.tr.* (*conj. like* FRÉTER) to sub-charter (ship, etc.).

sous-affréteur [suzafretœːr], *s.m.* sub-charterer; *pl. sous-affréteurs.*

sous-agence [suzaʒɑ̃ːs], *s.f.* sub-agency; *pl. sous-agences.*

sous-agent [suzaʒɑ̃], *s.m.* sub-agent; *pl. sous-agents.*

sous-aide [suzɛd], *s.m. & f.* junior assistant; *pl. sous-aides.*

sous-alimentation [suzalimɑ̃tasjɔ̃], *s.f.* malnutrition; undernourishment; underfeeding.

sous-alimenté, -ée [suzalimɑ̃te], *a. & s.* underfed, undernourished (person); *pl. sous-alimenté(e)s.*

sous-alimenter [suzalimɑ̃te], *v.tr.* to underfeed; to undernourish.

sous-amendement [suzamɑ̃dmɑ̃], *s.m.* amendment to an amendment; *pl. sous-amendements.*

sous-aponévrotique [suzaponevrɔtik], *a. Anat:* subaponeurotic; *pl. sous-aponévrotiques.*

sous-arachnoïdien, -ienne [suzaraknɔidjɛ̃, -jɛn]. *a. Anat:* subarachnoid; *pl. sous-arachnoïdiens, -iennes.*

sous-arbrisseau, -eaux [suzarbriso], *s.m. Bot:* sub-shrub, suffrutex.

sous-arrondissement [suzarɔ̃dismɑ̃], *s.m.* subdistrict (of naval administration); *pl. sous-arrondissements.*

sous-astragalien, -ienne [suzastragaljɛ̃, -jɛn], *a. Anat:* subastragalar, subastragaloid; *pl. sous-astragaliens, -iennes.*

sous-âtre [suzaːtr̥], *s.m.* hearthstone; *pl. sous-âtres.*

sous-axillaire [suzaksilɛːr], *a. Bot:* subaxillary; *pl. sous-axillaires.*

sous-azotate [suzazɔtat], *s.m. Ch:* subnitrate; *pl. sous-azotates.*

sous-bail [subaːj], *s.m.* sublease; *pl. sous-baux.*

sous-bailleur, -bailleresse [subajœːr, -baj(ə)rɛs], *s.* sub-lessor; *pl. sous-bailleurs, -bailleresses.*

sous(-)bande [subɑ̃ːd]. **1.** *s.m. Artil:* trunnion bed plate; **s. d'essieu,** axle-tree coupling band. **2.** *s.f. Elcs:* (*computers*) sub-band; *pl. sous(-) bandes.*

sous-bandé [subɑ̃de], *a. Civ.E: etc:* trussed (girder); *pl. sous-bandé(e)s.*

sous-barbe [subarb], *s.f.* **1.** chin groove (of horse). **2.** back stay (of bridle). **3.** *Nau:* bobstay; *pl. sous-barbes.*

sous-berme [subɛrm], *s.f.,* **sous-berne** [subɛrn], *s.f.* spate (of river).

sous-bibliothécaire [subibliɔtekɛːr], *s.m.* sub-librarian, assistant librarian; *pl. sous-bibliothécaires.*

sous-bock [subɔk], *s.m.inv.* beer mat.

sous-bois [subwɑ], *s.m.inv.* **1.** undergrowth; underwood. **2.** *Art:* picture of a forest interior.

sous-bout [subu], *s.m. Bootm:* lift (of heel); *pl. sous-bouts.*

sous-bras [subra], *s.m.inv. Dressm:* under arm part (of garment); *Cost:* dress shield.

sous-brigadier [subrigadje], *s.m.* lance-corporal (of excise officers, of police); *pl. sous-brigadiers.*

sous-calibré [sukalibre], *a. Artil:* subcalibre (projectile); *pl. sous-calibré(e)s.*

sous-cape [sukap], *s.f.* binder (of cigar); *pl. sous-capes.*

sous-capitalisation [sukapitalizasjɔ̃], *s.f.inv. Pol. Ec:* undercapitalization.

sous-carbonate [sukarbɔnat], *s.m. Ch:* subcarbonate; *pl. sous-carbonates.*

sous-caudal, -aux [sukodal, -o], *a. Z:* subcaudal; *Orn:* **plumes sous-caudales,** lower tail coverts.

sous-cavage [sukavaːʒ], *s.m. Min:* undercutting.

sous-cave [sukaːv], *s.f. Min:* undercut excavation; *pl. sous-caves.*

sous-caver [sukave], *v.tr. Min:* to undercut.

sous-centre [susɑ̃tr̥], *s.m. Elcs:* (*computers*) subcentre; *pl. sous-centres.*

sous-chantre [suʃɑ̃ːtr̥], *s.m. Ecc:* succentor, subchanter; *pl. sous-chantres.*

sous-chargé [suʃarʒe], *a. Mil: Min:* undercharged; *pl. sous-chargé(e)s.*

sous-charriage [suʃarjaːʒ], *s.m. Geol:* underthrust; *pl. sous-charriages.*

sous-chasse [suʃas], *s.f. Tls: Metalw:* counter flatter, bottom swage; *pl. sous-chasses.*

sous-chef [suʃɛf], *s.m.* **1.** deputy chief clerk. **2.** sub-manager, assistant manager; **s.-c. de gare,** deputy stationmaster. **3.** *Mus:* deputy conductor; *pl. sous-chefs.*

sous-chevron [suʃəvrɔ̃], *s.m. Const:* under-rafter; *pl. sous-chevrons.*

sous-chlorure [suklɔryːr], *s.m. Ch:* subchloride; *pl. sous-chlorures.*

sous-classe [suklɑːs], *s.f. Nat.Hist:* subclass; *pl. sous-classes.*

sous-claviculaire [suklavikylɛːr], *a. Anat:* subclavicular; *pl. sous-claviculaires.*

sous-clavier, -ière [suklavje, -jɛːr], *a. Anat:* subclavian (artery, muscle, etc.); *pl. sous-claviers, -ières.*

sous-comité [sukɔmite], *s.m.* sub-committee; *pl. sous-comités.*

sous-commissaire [sukɔmisɛːr], *s.m.* sub-commissioner; *Navy:* assistant paymaster; *pl. sous-commissaires.*

sous-commission [sukɔmisjɔ̃], *s.f.* **1.** sub-committee. **2.** sub-commission; *pl. sous-commissions.*

sous-compte [sukɔ̃ːt], *s.m.* subsidiary account; sub-account; *pl. sous-comptes.*

sous-conjonctival, -aux [sukɔ̃ʒɔ̃ktival, -o], *a. Anat:* subconjunctival.

sous-consommation [sukɔ̃sɔmasjɔ̃], *s.f.inv. Pol. Ec:* underconsumption.

sous-coracoïdien, -ienne [sukɔrakɔidjɛ̃, -jɛn], *a. Anat:* subcoracoid; *pl. sous-coracoïdiens, -iennes.*

sous-cortical, -aux [sukɔrtikal, -o], *a. Anat: Bot:* subcortical.

sous-costal, -aux [sukɔstal, -o], *a. Anat:* subcostal.

sous-couche [sukuʃ], *s.f.* **1.** substratum; underlying layer; **s.-c. de neige,** underlayer of snow (beneath the freshly fallen layer); *Metalw:* **s.-c. oxydée, d'oxydation,** subscale. **2.** *Paint:* primer; *pl. sous-couches.*

sous-crépitant [sukrepitɑ̃], *a. Med:* subcrepitant; *pl. sous-crépitant(e)s.*

souscripteur [suskriptœːr], *s.m.* **1.** *Fin:* (*a*) subscriber, applicant (for shares, etc.); (*b*) drawer (of cheque, etc.). **2.** subscriber (to new publication).

souscription [suskripsjɔ̃], *s.f.* **1.** (*a*) execution, signing (of deed); (*b*) subscription, signature; (*c*) underline, bibliographical note (printed at end of book). **2.** (*a*) *Fin: etc:* subscription, application (**à des actions,** for shares); **bulletin de s.,** allotment letter; **s. en titres,** subscription by conversion of securities; **lettre de s. éventuelle à forfait,** underwriting contract; (*b*) **bal par s.,** subscription dance. **3.** subscription, contribution (of sum of money); **monument élevé par s. publique,** monument erected by public subscription; **verser une s.,** to pay a subscription; **honoré d'une s. de . . .,** under the patronage of . . .; **lancer une s.,** to start a fund. **4.** *Rac:* entering (of horse for race).

souscrire [suskriːr], *v.tr.* (*conj. like* ÉCRIRE) **1.** to sign, execute (deed); to subscribe, sign (bond); to draw (cheque, etc.); **s. un chèque au porteur,** to draw a cheque to bearer; to make a cheque payable to bearer; **l'arrêté est souscrit du ministre, par le ministre,** the decree is signed by the minister. **2.** to subscribe; **s. un abonnement,** to take out a subscription (for library, etc.); **s. mille francs pour une œuvre de charité,** to subscribe a thousand francs to a charity; *Fin:* **s. des actions,** to subscribe, apply for, shares; **capital souscrit,** subscribed capital; *Ins:* **s. une police,** to take out a policy. **3.** *abs.* (*a*) **s. à une nouvelle édition, pour un journal,** to subscribe for a new edition, for a newspaper; *Fin:* **s. à une émission,** to apply for, subscribe to, an issue; **s. à titre irréductible,** to apply as of right for new shares; **s. à titre réductible,** to apply for excess shares; **s. à des actions,** to take up shares; (*b*) **s. pour (la somme de) mille francs,** to subscribe a thousand francs; **s. pour une œuvre de bienfaisance,** to subscribe to a charity; to patronize a charity; (*c*) **s. à une opinion,** to subscribe to an opinion; to endorse an opinion.

souscrit [suskri], *a. Gr.Gram:* (iota) subscript.

sous-critique [sukritik], *a. Atom.Ph: etc:* subcritical; *pl. sous-critiques.*

souscrivant [suskrivɑ̃], *s.m. A:* = SOUSCRIPTEUR.

sous-cul [sukyl], *s.m. Sch: P:* seat mat, bottom mat; *pl. sous-culs.*

sous-cutané [sukytane], *s.* subcutaneous; *pl. sous-cutané(e)s.*

sous-décanat [sudekana], *s.m.* subdeanery; *pl. sous-décanats.*

sous-décuple [sudekypl̥], *a. Mth:* subdecuple; *pl. sous-décuples.*

sous-délégation [sudelegasjɔ̃], *s.f.* subdelegation; *sous-délégations.*

sous-délégué, -ée [sudelege], *a. & s.* **1.** subdelegate. **2.** vice-president (of charity organization); *pl. sous-délégué(e)s.*

sous-développé, -ée [sudevlɔpe]. **1.** *a.* (*a*) *Pol.Ec:* underdeveloped; **pays sous-développés,** underdeveloped countries; (*b*) underequipped, undermechanized (factory, etc.). **2.** *s. F:* native, inhabitant, of an underdeveloped country; *pl. sous-développés, -ées.*

sous-développement [sudevlɔpmɑ̃], *s.f.inv. Pol. Ec:* underdevelopment.

sous-diaconat [sudjakɔna], *s.m.* subdeaconry, subdiaconate; *pl. sous-diaconats.*

sous-diacre [sudjakr̥], *s.m.* subdeacon; *pl. sous-diacres.*

sous-diaphragmatique [sudjafragmatik], *a. Anat:* subdiaphragmatic; *pl. sous-diaphragmatiques.*

sous-directeur, -trice [sudirɛktœːr, -tris], *s.* **1.** sub-manager, sub-manageress. **2.** vice-principal (of school); deputy headmaster, headmistress; *pl. sous-directeurs, -trices.*

sous-dirigé [sudiriʒe], *a. Aut:* (car) that understeers; *pl. sous-dirigé(e)s.*

sousdit, -ite [sudi, -it], *a. & s. Jur:* below-mentioned, under-mentioned.

sous-diviser [sudivize], *v.tr.* to subdivide.

sous-division [sudivizjɔ̃], *s.f.* subdivision; *pl. sous-divisions.*

sous-dominante [sudɔminɑ̃ːt], *s.f. Mus:* subdominant; fa (of Movable Do system); *pl. sous-dominantes.*

sous-double [sudubl̥], *a. Mth:* subduple (progression); *pl. sous-doubles.*

sous-doublé [suduble], *a. Mth:* subduplicate; *used only in* **en raison s.-doublée,** in subduplicate ratio.

sous-doyen [sudwajɛ̃], *s.m. Ecc:* subdean; *pl. sous-doyens.*

sous-doyenné [sudwajɛne], *s.m. Ecc:* subdeanery; *pl. sous-doyennés.*

sous-économe [suzekɔnɔm], *s.m.* assistant treasurer, assistant bursar; *pl. sous-économes.*

sous-embranchement [suzɑ̃brɑ̃ʃmɑ̃], *s.m. Nat. Hist:* subphylum; *pl. sous-embranchements.*

sous-emploi [suzɑ̃plwa], *s.m.inv. Pol.Ec:* underemployment.

sous-ensemble [suzɑ̃sɑ̃bl̥], *s.m. Mec.E:* subassembly, sub-system, sub-unit; *Mth:* subassembly; *Elcs:* (*computers*) subassembly, subset; *pl. sous-ensembles.*

sous-entendre [suzɑ̃tɑ̃ːdr̥], *v.tr.* to understand; not to express; to imply; *Gram:* **on sous-entend "pendant,"** "*pendant*" is understood.

sous-entendu [suzɑ̃tɑ̃dy], *s.m.* thing understood; implication; **suggérer qch. par sous-entendus,** to hint at sth.; *pl. sous-entendu(e)s.*

sous-entrepreneur [suzɑ̃trəprənœːr], *s.m. Const:* subcontractor; *pl. sous-entrepreneurs.*

sous-épidermique [suzepidɛrmik], *a.* subepidermic, subepidermal; *pl. sous-épidermiques.*

sous-épineux, -euse [suzepinø, -øːz], *a. Anat:* **1.** infraspinous (fossa, etc.). **2. muscle s.-é.,** infraspinator (muscle); *pl. sous-épineux, -euses.*

sous-équipé [suzekipe], *a. Pol.Ec:* under-equipped; *pl. sous-équipé(e)s.*

sous-équipement [suzekipmɑ̃], *s.m.inv. Pol.Ec:* under-equipment; *Civ.E:* underplanting.

sous-espace [suzɛspas], *s.m. Mth:* subspace; *pl. sous-espaces.*

sous-espèce [suzɛspɛs], *s.f.* subspecies; *pl. sous-espèces.*

sous-estimation [suzɛstimasjɔ̃], *s.f.*, **sous-évaluation** [suzevalɥasjɔ̃], *s.f.* undervaluation; *pl. sous-estimations, -évaluations.*

sous-estimer [suzɛstime], **sous-évaluer** [suzevalɥe], *v.tr.* to underestimate, undervalue, underrate.

sous-étage [suzetaːʒ], *s.m.* **1.** *Geol:* substage. **2.** *For:* **créer un s.-é. à une futaie,** to underplant a high forest; *pl. sous-étages.*

sous-exposer [suzɛkspoze], *v.tr. Phot:* to underexpose.

sous-exposition [suzɛkspozisjɔ̃], *s.f. Phot:* underexposure; *pl. sous-expositions.*

sous-faîte [sufɛt], *s.m. Const:* under ridgeboard; *pl. sous-faîtes.*

sous-famille [sufamiːj], *s.f. Nat.Hist:* subfamily; *pl. sous-familles.*

sous-ferme [sufɛrm], *s.f.* **1.** underlease (of land). **2.** *Hist:* sub-farm; *pl. sous-fermes.*

sous-fermer [sufɛrme], *v.tr.* to sublet, sublease (land).

sous-fermier, -ière [sufɛrmje, -jɛːr], *s.* underlessee, sub-lessee; *Hist:* sub-farmer; *pl. sous-fermiers, -ières.*

sous-fifre [sufifr̥], *s.m. F:* second fiddle; dogsbody; *pl. sous-fifres.*

sous-fluvial, -aux [suflyvjal, -o], *a. El:* **traversée sous-fluviale,** underwater river crossing (by cables).

sous-fréter [sufrete], *v.tr.* (**je sous-frète, n. sous-frétons; je sous-fréterai**) to under-freight, to underlet (a ship).

sous-fréteur [sufretœːr], *s.m. Com:* underletter (of ship); *pl. sous-fréteurs.*

sous-frutescent [sufrytes(s)ɑ̃], *a. Bot:* suffrutescent; **plante sous-frutescente,** sub-shrub; *pl. sous-frutescent(e)s.*

sous-gammes [sugam], *s.f.inv. Ph: etc:* subrange.

sous(-)garde [sugard], *s.f. Sm.a:* trigger guard; *pl. sous(-)gardes.*

sous-genre [suʒɑ̃ːr], *s.m. Nat.Hist:* sub-genus; *pl. sous-genres.*

sous-gérant, -ante [suʒerɑ̃, -ɑ̃ːt], *s.* assistant manager, manageress; *pl. sous-gérant(e)s.*

sous-glaciaire [suglasjɛːr], *a. Geog:* subglacial; *pl. sous-glaciaires.*

sous-gorge [sugɔrʒ], *s.m.inv. Equit:* throat lash (of bridle).

sous-gouverneur [suguvɛrnœːr], *s.m.* deputy governor, vice-governor; *pl. sous-gouverneurs.*

sous-groupe [sugrup], *s.m. Nat.Hist: Mth:* subgroup; *Elcs:* (*computers*) **tri par sous-groupes (d'indicatif),** block sort; *pl. sous-groupes.*

sous-gui [sugi], *s.m. Nau:* **bonnette de s.-g.,** ring tail.

sous-hépatique [suzepatik], *a. Anat:* subhepatic; *pl. sous-hépatiques.*

sous-homme [suzɔm], *s.m.* subman; *pl. sous-hommes.*

sous-hyoïdien, -ienne [suziɔidjɛ̃, -jɛn], *a. Anat:* subhyoid(ean); *pl. sous-hyoïdiens, -iennes.*

sous-inféodation [suzɛ̃feɔdasjɔ̃], *s.f. no pl. Hist:* subinfeudation.

sous-ingénieur [suzɛ̃ʒenjœːr], *s.m. Ind: etc:* assistant engineer; *pl. sous-ingénieurs.*

sous-inspecteur, -trice [suzɛ̃spɛktœːr, -tris], *s.* assistant inspector, inspectress; sub-inspector, sub-inspectress; *pl. sous-inspecteurs, -trices.*

sous-intendance [suzɛ̃tɑ̃dɑ̃ːs], *s.f. Hist:* understewardship, junior intendance; *pl. sous-intendances.*

sous-intendant [suzɛ̃tɑ̃dɑ̃], *s.m.* **1.** *A.Mil:* = Assistant Quartermaster-General. **2.** *Hist:* under-steward, junior intendant; *pl. sous-intendants.*

sous-jacent [suʒasɑ̃], *a.* subjacent, underlying; deep-seated; **idée sous-jacente,** idea at the back of one's mind; *pl. sous-jacents, -entes.*

sous-jupe [suʒyp], *s.f. Cost:* underskirt; waist slip, waist petticoat; *pl. sous-jupes.*

sous-lacustre [sulakystr̥], *a.* sublacustrine; *pl. sous-lacustres.*

Sous-le-vent [sulvɑ̃], *Pr.n. Geog:* **les îles S.-le-v.,** the Leeward Islands ((i) of French Oceania, (ii) of the West Indies).

sous-lieutenance [suljøtnɑ̃ːs], *s.f.* second-lieutenancy, sub-lieutenancy; *pl. sous-lieutenances.*

sous-lieutenant [suljøtnɑ̃], *s.m.* second lieutenant, sub-lieutenant; *Av:* **s.-l. (aviateur),** pilot officer; *pl. sous-lieutenants.*

souslik [sulik], *s.m. Z:* spotted souslik.

sous-lingual, -aux [sulɛ̃gɥal, -o], *a. Anat:* sublingual.

sous-lit [suli], *s.m. A.Furn:* truckle bed; *pl. sous-lits.*

sous-locataire [sulɔkatɛːr], *s.m. & f.* subtenant, sub-lessee; *pl. sous-locataires.*

sous-location [sulɔkasjɔ̃], *s.f.* **1.** (*a*) subletting; (*b*) sub-renting. **2.** sub-tenancy; sub-lease; *pl. sous-locations.*

sous-longeron [sulɔ̃ʒrɔ̃], *s.m. Civ.E:* auxiliary beam, girder; *pl. sous-longerons.*

sous-louer [sulwe], *v.tr.* **1.** to sub-let, sub-lease (house); **s. avec bail,** to underlease. **2.** to rent (house) from a tenant.

sous-main [sumɛ̃], *s.m.inv.* blotting pad; writing pad; desk pad; *F:* **en s.-m.,** behind the scenes.

sous-maître, -maîtresse [sumɛtr̥, -mɛtrɛs], *A:* **1.** (*a*) *s. Sch:* unqualified assistant (helping qualified teacher); (*b*) *s.f.* **sous-maîtresse,** chief assistant to brothel keeper. **2.** *Mil:* = assistant riding instructor.

sous-mammaire [sumamɛːr], *a. Anat:* submammary; *pl. sous-mammaires.*

sous-marin [sumarɛ̃]. **1.** *a.* (*a*) submarine (vessel, volcano, etc.); submerged (reef); **courant s.-m.,** deep-sea current; (*b*) underwater; **brise-roc s.-m.,** underwater rock breaker; **chasse sous-marine,** underwater fishing; undersea hunting; **masque s.-m.,** frogman's mask. **2.** *s.m.* submarine (boat); **s.-m. côtier,** coast-defence submarine; **s.-m. de croisière,** ocean-going submarine; **s.-m. allemand,** German submarine, U-boat; **s.-m. nucléaire,** nuclear-powered submarine; **s.-m. nucléaire lanceur de missiles,** nuclear-powered ballistic-missile-armed submarine; Polaris submarine; **s.-m. chasseur (de sous-marins),** hunter-killer submarine; **s.-m. de poche,** pocket submarine; *pl. sous-marins.*

sous-marinier [sumarinje], *s.m.* submariner; *pl. sous-mariniers.*

sous-maxillaire [sumaksilɛːr], *a. Anat:* submaxillary (glands, etc.); *pl. sous-maxillaires.*

sous-médiante [sumedjɑ̃ːt], *s.f. Mus:* supertonic; re (of Movable Do system); *pl. sous-médiantes.*

sous-mentionné [sumɑ̃sjɔne], *a.* undermentioned; *pl. sous-mentionné(e)s.*

sous-menton [sumɑ̃tɔ̃], *s.m. Ent:* submentum (of insect); *pl. sous-mentons.*

sous-mentonnière [sumɑ̃tɔnjɛːr], *s.f.* chin strap (of helmet, etc.); *pl. sous-mentonnières.*

sous-modèle [sumɔdɛl], *s.m.* sub-model; *pl. sous-modèles.*

sous-multiple [sumyltipl̥], *a. & s.m. Mth:* submultiple (**de,** of); *pl. sous-multiples.*

sous-muqueux, -euse [sumykø, -øːz], *a. Anat:* submucous; **tissu s.-m.,** submucous tissue, submucosa.

sous-nappe [sunap], *s.f.* underlay (for tablecloth); *pl. sous-nappes.*

sous-nasal, -aux [sunazal, -o], *a. Anat:* subnasal; **point s.-n.,** subnasal point.

sous-nitrate [sunitrat], *s.m. Ch:* subnitrate, basic nitrate; *pl. sous-nitrates.*

sous-noix [sunwa], *s.m.inv. Cu:* round (of beef).

sous-normale [sunɔrmal], *s.f. Mth:* subnormal (of curve); *pl. sous-normales.*

sous-occipital, -aux [suzɔksipital, -o], *a. Anat:* suboccipital.

sous-œuvre [suzœːvr̥], *s.m.* **1.** *Const: Civ.E:* underpinning; **reprendre un édifice en s.-o.,** (i) to underpin a building; (ii) to shore up a building; **reprise en s.-o.,** underpinning. **2.** under portion, underside; *pl. sous-œuvres.*

sous-off [suzɔf], *s.m. Mil: F:* N.C.O., non-com; *pl. sous-offs.*

sous-officier [suzɔfisje], *s.m.* **1.** *Mil:* non-commissioned officer; warrant officer. **2.** *Navy:* petty officer; *pl. sous-officiers.*

sous-ongulaire [suzɔ̃gylɛːr], *a. Anat:* subungual; *pl. sous-ongulaires.*

sous-orbitaire [suzɔrbitɛːr], *a. Anat:* suborbital; *pl. sous-orbitaires.*

sous-orbital [suzɔrbital], *a.* suborbital; **vitesse sous-orbitale,** suborbital velocity; **vol s.-o. d'un véhicule spatial habité,** manned suborbital flight; *pl. sous-orbitaux, -ales.*

sous-ordre [suzɔrdr̥], *s.m.* **1.** *inv. Pej:* subordinate, underling; **en s.-o.,** subordinate(ly); *A:* **commandant en s.-o.,** subordinate commander; **créancier en s.-o.,** creditor of a creditor (in bankruptcy). **2.** *Nat.Hist:* sub-order; *pl. sous-ordres.*

sousouc [susuk], *s.m. Z:* susu, platanist.

sous-oxyde [suzɔksid], *s.m.* suboxide; *pl. sous-oxydes.*

sous-palan (en) [ɑ̃supalɑ̃], *adv.phr. Com: Nau:* **livraison en s.-p.,** delivery (of goods) ready for shipping.

sous-parcelle [suparsɛl], *s.f. For:* sub-compartment (of forest); *pl. sous-parcelles.*

sous-payer [supeje], *v.tr.* (*conj. like* PAYER) to underpay; **ouvriers sous-payés,** underpaid workers.

sous-périosté [superjɔste], *a. Anat:* subperiosteal; *pl. sous-périostés.*

sous-péritonéal, -aux [superitɔneal, -o], *a. Anat:* subperitoneal.

sous-perpendiculaire [supɛrpɑ̃dikylɛːr], *s.f. Geom:* subperpendicular, subnormal; *pl. sous-perpendiculaires.*

sous-phrénique [sufrenik], *a. Anat:* subphrenic; *pl. sous-phréniques.*

sous-pied [supje], *s.m.* (*a*) under strap (of gaiters); (*b*) trouser strap; *pl. sous-pieds.*

sous-porteuse [supɔrtøːz], *a.f. & s.f. Elcs:* (**onde**) **s.-p.,** subcarrier; **s.-p. intermédiaire,** intermediate subcarrier; *pl. sous-porteuses.*

sous-poutre [suputr̥], *s.f. Const:* under girder; bolster; *pl. sous-poutres.*

sous-préfectoral, -aux [suprefɛktɔral, -o], *a.* subprefectoral.

sous-préfecture [suprefɛktyːr], *s.f.* sub-prefecture (district, functions, or residence); *pl. sous-préfectures.*

sous-préfet [suprefɛ], *s.m. Adm:* sub-prefect; *pl. sous-préfets.*

sous-préfète [suprefɛt], *s.f. F:* sub-prefect's wife; *pl. sous-préfètes.*

sous-preneur [suprənœːr], *s.m. Jur:* sub-lessee; *pl. sous-preneurs.*

sous-pression [suprɛsjɔ̃], *s.f. Civ.E:* (*in dam*) uplift; *pl. sous-pressions.*

sous-prieur, -eure [supri(j)œːr], *s. Ecc:* subprior, subprioress; *pl. sous-prieurs, -prieures.*

sous-principal, -aux [suprɛ̃sipal, -o], *s.m. Sch:* vice-principal.

sous-production [suprɔdyksjɔ̃], *s.f. Pol.Ec:* underproduction; *pl. sous-productions.*

sous-produit [suprɔdɥi], *s.m. Ind: etc:* by-product; secondary product; *pl. sous-produits.*

sous-programme [suprɔgram], *s.m. Elcs:* (*computers*) subroutine, subprogram(me); **s.-p. fermé,** closed, linked, subroutine; **s.-p. ouvert,** open subroutine; **sous-programmes emboîtés,** nesting subroutines; *pl. sous-programmes.*

sous-pubien, -ienne [supybjɛ̃, -jɛn], *a. Anat:* subpubic; *pl. sous-pubiens, -iennes.*

sous-quadruple [sukwadrypl̥], *a. & s.m. Mth:* subquadruple; *pl. sous-quadruples.*

sous-quintuple [suk(ɥ)ɛ̃typl̥], *a. & s.m. Mth:* subquintuple; *pl. sous-quintuples.*

sous-race [suras], *s.f. Z:* subrace; *pl. sous-races.*

sous-refroidi [surəfrwadi], *a. Ph:* supercooled; *pl. sous-refroidis.*

sous-refroidissement [surəfrwadismɑ̃], *s.m. Ph:* supercooling.

sous-répartition [surepartisjɔ̃], *s.f.* **1.** subdivision (of a share). **2.** second assessment (of a tax); *pl. sous-répartitions.*

sous-scapulaire [suskapylɛːr], *a. & s.m. Anat:* subscapular; **fosse s.-s.,** sub-scapular fossa; *pl. sous-scapulaires.*

Sousse [sus], *Pr.n. Geog:* Susa (in Tunis), Sousse.

sous-secrétaire [susəkretɛːr], *s.* under-secretary; **S.-s. d'État,** Under-secretary of State; *pl. sous-secrétaires.*

sous-secrétariat [susəkretarja], *s.m.* **1.** under-secretaryship. **2.** under-secretary's office, department; *pl. sous-secrétariats.*

sous-seing [susɛ̃], *s.m.* private agreement, private contract; *pl. sous-seings.*

sous-sel [susɛl], *s.m. Ch:* subsalt, basic salt; *pl. sous-sels.*

sous-septuple [susɛptypl̥], *a. & s.m. Mth:* subseptuple; *pl. sous-septuples.*

sous-séreux, -euse [suserø, -øːz], *a. Anat: Med:* subserous; *pl. sous-séreux, -euses.*

sous-sextuple [susɛkstypl̥], *a. & s.m. Mth:* subsextuple; *pl. sous-sextuples.*

soussien, -ienne [susjɛ̃, -jɛn], *a. & s. Geog:* (native, inhabitant) of Susa (Tunisia).

soussigné, -ée [susiɲe], *a. & s.* undersigned; **je s. déclare que . . .,** I the undersigned declare that . . .; **les soussignés déclarent que . . .,** the undersigned declare that . . ..
soussigner [susiɲe], *v.tr.* to subscribe, to sign, undersign (document).
sous-sol [susɔl], *s.m.* **1.** *Geol:* subsoil, substratum; *Min:* **travailleurs du s.-s.,** underground workers. **2.** *Const:* (*a*) basement; **garage en s.-s.,** basement (i) garage, (ii) car park; (*b*) basement flat; *pl. sous-sols.*
sous-solage [susɔlaːʒ], *s.m. Agr:* subsoiling; *pl. sous-solages.*
sous-soler [susɔle], *v.tr. Agr:* to subsoil.
sous-soleuse [susɔløːz], *s.f. Agr:* subsoil plough; *pl. sous-soleuses.*
sous-station [sustasjɔ̃], *s.f. El:* substation; *pl. sous-stations.*
sous-sternal, -aux [susternal, -o], *a. Anat: etc:* substernal.
sous-structure [sustryktyːr], *s.f.* substructure; *pl. sous-structures.*
sous-système [susistɛm], *s.m.* subsystem; *pl. sous-systèmes.*
sous-tangente [sutɑ̃ʒɑ̃ːt], *s.f. Geom:* subtangent; *pl. sous-tangentes.*
sous-tasse [sutɑːs], *s.f.* saucer; *pl. sous-tasses.*
sous-tenant [sutənɑ̃], *s.m. Hist:* subvassal; *pl. sous-tenants.*
sous-tendante [sutɑ̃dɑ̃ːt], *s.f. Geom:* subtense (of an arc); *pl. sous-tendantes.*
sous-tendre [sutɑ̃ːdr̥], *v.tr. Geom:* to subtend (an arc); **les axiomes qui sous-tendent la pensée humaine,** the axioms underlying human thought.
sous-tension [sutɑ̃sjɔ̃], *s.f. El:* undervoltage; **circuit s.-t.,** live circuit; *pl. sous-tensions.*
sous-titrage [sutitraːʒ], *s.m. no pl.*; *Cin:* subtitling.
sous-titre [sutitr̥], *s.m.* subtitle; *pl. sous-titres.*
sous-titrer [sutitre], *v.tr. Cin:* to subtitle; **film sous-titré en anglais,** film with English subtitles.
sous-titreur [sutitrœːr], *s.m. Cin:* writer of subtitles; *pl. sous-titreurs.*
soustracteur [sustraktœːr], *s.m. Mth: etc:* subtracter.
soustractif, -ive [sustraktif, -iːv], *a. Mth: Phot:* subtractive.
soustraction [sustraksjɔ̃], *s.f.* (*a*) removal, taking away, withdrawal, abstraction; **acte de s.,** (act of) purloining; *Jur:* **s. frauduleuse,** abstraction of documents; (*b*) *Mth: Elcs:* subtraction.
soustraire [sustrɛːr], *v.tr.* (*conj. like* TRAIRE) **1.** to take away, withdraw, abstract, purloin (document, etc.); **s. qn à une influence,** to withdraw s.o. from an influence; **s. une feuille d'un livre,** to tear a leaf out of a book. **2.** to screen, preserve, shield (s.o. from sth.); **s. qn à la colère de qn,** to protect s.o. from s.o.'s anger; **s. qn aux recherches de la justice,** to hide s.o. from justice; to convey s.o. beyond the reach of justice; **s. qn à la vengeance de qn,** to put s.o. out of reach of s.o.'s revenge. **3.** *Mth: etc:* to subtract (**de,** from); **quantité à s.,** subtrahend.
se soustraire à qch., to avoid, elude, escape, sth.; **se s. au châtiment, à l'attention,** to avoid punishment, publicity; **se s. aux regards,** to retire from sight; **je ne vois aucun moyen de m'y s.,** I see no means of escape, of getting out of it; **se s. à la justice,** to elude justice; to abscond; **se s. à une discussion, à une obligation,** to back out of a discussion, of an obligation; to shirk, evade, a discussion, an obligation.
sous-traitance [sutrɛtɑ̃ːs], *s.f.* subcontracting; *pl. sous-traitances.*
sous-traitant [sutrɛtɑ̃], *s.m.* subcontractor; *pl. sous-traitants.*
sous-traité [sutrete], *s.m.* subcontract; *pl. sous-traités.*
sous-traiter [sutrete], *v.tr.* **1.** to subcontract. **2.** sublet (a contract).
sous-triple [sutripl̥], *a. & s.m.* subtriple; in the ratio of 1 to 3; *pl. sous-triples.*
sous-triplé [sutriple], *a. Mth:* subtriplicate; expressed by the cube root; **en raison sous-triplée,** in subtriplicate ratio; *pl. sous-triplé(e)s.*
sous-trochantérien, -ienne [sutrɔkɑ̃terjɛ̃, -jɛn], *a. Anat:* subtrochanteric; *pl. sous-trochantériens, -iennes.*
soustylaire [sustilɛːr], *s.f.* substyle (of sundial).
sous-unguéal, -aux [suzɔ̃gɥeal, -o], *a. Anat:* subungual.
sous-variant [suvarjɑ̃], *s.m. Biol:* sub-variant; *pl. sous-variants.*
sous-variété [suvarjete], *s.f.* subvariety; *pl. sous-variétés.*
sous-vassal, -aux [suvasal, -o], *s.m. Hist:* undervassal, subvassal.
sous-vendre [suvɑ̃ːdr̥], *v.tr. Com:* to resell (portion of goods purchased to a third party).
sous-vente [suvɑ̃ːt], *s.f. Com:* resale (of goods to a third party); *pl. sous-ventes.*
sous-venter [suvɑ̃te], *v.i. Nau:* to blanket.
sous-ventrière [suvɑ̃tri(j)ɛːr], *s.f. Harn:* (*a*) belly-band (attached to shafts); (*b*) saddlegirth; (*c*) surcingle (securing blanket, etc.); *pl. sous-ventrières.*
sous-verge [suvɛrʒ], *s.m.inv.* **1.** (unridden) off-horse (of a pair); **s.-v. de derrière,** off-wheeler; **s.-v. de devant,** off-leader. **2.** *F:* underling, *F:* dogsbody.
sous-verre [suvɛːr], *s.m.inv.* passe-partout mounting.
sous-vêtement [suvɛtmɑ̃], *s.m.* undergarment; **sous-vêtements,** underclothing, underclothes, underwear.
sous-vêture [suvɛtyr], *s.f. Lit: Hum:* underclothes.
sous-vicaire [suvikɛːr], *s.m. Ecc:* = assistant curate; *pl. sous-vicaires.*
sous-virage [suviraːʒ], *s.m. Aut:* understeering.
sous-virer [suvire], *v.i. Aut:* to understeer.
sous-vireur, -euse [suvirœːr, -øːz], *a. Aut:* (car) which understeers; *pl. sous-vireurs, -euses.*
sous-voie [suvwa], *s.f. Elcs:* (*computers*) time-derived channel; *pl. sous-voies.*
sous-voltage [suvɔltaːʒ], *s.m. no pl. El:* undervoltage.
sous-volteur [suvɔltœːr], *s.m. El:* negative booster; *pl. sous-volteurs.*
soutache [sutaʃ], *s.f. Cost:* (*a*) (military) braid, frog; (*b*) *Dressm:* braid; **brodé en s.,** braided.
soutacher [sutaʃe], *v.tr. Cost:* to braid.
soutage [sutaːʒ], *s.m.* refuelling (of ship).
soutane [sutan], *s.f.* cassock, soutane; **prendre la s.,** to become a priest; to take (holy) orders; **prêtres en s.,** cassocked priests; **le respect dû à la s.,** the respect due to the cloth.
soutanelle [sutanɛl], *s.f.* **1.** *A:* short cassock. **2.** clerical frock-coat.
soutasse [sutɑːs], *s.f.* saucer.
Sou-Tchéou [sutʃeu], *Pr.n. Geog:* Soochow.
soute[1] [sut], *s.f. Jur: A:* balance (to equalize shares, etc.).
soute[2], *s.f. Nau:* store room; **s. à charbon,** coal bunker; **s. du charbon de réserve,** reserve coal bunker; **soutes fixes,** permanent bunkers; **soutes latérales,** side bunkers; **soutes de réserve,** cross bunkers; **mettre du charbon en s.,** to bunker coal; **s. à voiles,** sail locker; **s. à filin,** rope locker; **s. aux câbles,** cable tier, cable locker; **s. à eau,** water tank; **soutes à mazout, à pétrole,** oil(-fuel) tanks; **s. à munitions,** magazine; **s. aux poudres,** (powder) magazine; **s. à obus,** shell room; **s. à provisions,** store room, issue room; **s. à biscuit, s. au pain,** bread room; **s. aux bagages,** (i) *Nau:* luggage room, baggage room; (ii) *Av:* luggage compartment, *U.S:* baggage compartment; **s. à valeurs,** strongroom; bullion room; *Av:* **s. à essence,** refuelling point; *Mil.Av:* **s. à bombes,** bomb bay.
soutenable [sutnabl̥], *a.* (*a*) bearable, supportable (burden, existence, etc.); (*b*) tenable (opinion); arguable (theory); **opinion peu s.,** untenable opinion; opinion that cannot be maintained, upheld; (*c*) *Mil: A:* (= TENABLE) tenable (position).
soutenance [sutnɑ̃ːs], *s.f. Sch:* maintaining, defence (of a thesis).
soutenant, -ante [sutnɑ̃, -ɑ̃ːt]. **1.** *a.* sustaining (power). **2.** *s. Sch:* maintainer (of a thesis), student (defending thesis).
soutènement [sutɛnmɑ̃], *s.m.* **1.** supporting, support, propping, holding up; *Arch: Civ.E:* **arche de s.,** relieving arch; **mur de s.,** retaining, supporting, sustaining, wall; breast wall; *Min:* **bois de s.,** pit props. **2.** *Jur:* explanatory statement in writing.
souteneur, -euse [sutnœːr, -øːz]. **1.** *s.* upholder (of system, etc.). **2.** *s.m.* souteneur, pimp, ponce.
soutenir [sutniːr], *v.tr.* (*conj. like* TENIR) **1.** (*a*) to support, hold, prop, (s.o., sth.) up; to prevent (s.o., sth.) from falling; **cette colonne soutient tout le bâtiment,** this pillar supports, bears the weight of, the whole building; **l'espérance nous soutient,** it is hope that keeps us going; **aliments qui soutiennent,** sustaining food; **il ne peut plus s. le poids des affaires,** he is no longer equal to the strain of business; (*b*) to keep, maintain (parents, family); (*c*) to back (up) (undertaking, cause, person); to stand by, stand up for (s.o.); to back (s.o. financially); to be at the back of (s.o.); to be behind (s.o.); (*in games*) to back up (one's partner); *Mil:* to support (troops); **s. qn jusqu'au bout,** to see s.o. through; **sa banque le soutient,** his bank is backing him; **s. la motion** to support the motion; **voix soutenue par le piano,** voice supported by the piano; (*d*) to maintain, uphold (opinion, one's character); to affirm (fact); *Sch:* to defend (a thesis); **il soutient l'avoir vu,** he asserts, maintains, that he saw it; **il soutient que . . .,** he asserts that . . ., he will have it that . . .; **opinion qui ne peut pas se s.,** opinion that cannot be upheld; (*e*) to keep up, sustain, maintain (conversation, speed, one's rank, a part, one's credit); **pouvez-vous s. une conversation en anglais?** can you carry on a conversation in English? **s. la conversation,** to keep the conversation going; to keep the ball rolling; *Nau:* **s. la vitesse de la flotte,** to keep the speed of the fleet; **s. la chasse,** (i) to press the chase; (ii) to keep up a running fight; **s. une longue lutte,** to maintain a long struggle; **il ne soutient pas la boisson,** he can't take his drink; (*f*) *Equit:* **s. un cheval,** to hold a horse to the pace. **2.** (*a*) to bear, stand, endure (slight, reproach); to sustain, withstand, hold out against (siege, attack); (*b*) **s. une dépense,** to afford an expense; to meet an expense.
se soutenir. 1. (*a*) to support, maintain, oneself; **se s. sur ses pieds,** to stand on one's feet; **je ne me soutiens plus,** I'm ready to drop; *F:* **il a de la peine à se s.,** he finds it hard to keep his head above water; (*b*) *Nau:* **se s. dans sa route,** to keep the course. **2.** to last, continue; **vogue qui ne se soutiendra pas,** fashion that will not last; **cette amitié s'est soutenue,** this friendship has been maintained, *F:* has worn well; **l'intérêt se soutient,** the interest is kept up, does not flag; **femme qui se soutient bien,** woman who wears well; **le mieux se soutient,** the improvement continues.
soutenu [sutny], *a.* **1.** sustained (attention, effort); constant (effort); **unflagging,** unfailing, constant, continued (interest); **au trot s.,** at a steady trot; **marché s.,** steady market; **marché moins s.,** easier market. **2. style s.,** sustained style (of writing, etc.). **3.** firm (outline); solid, strong (colour).
souter [sute], *v.tr.* to refuel (ship).
souterrain [sutɛrɛ̃]. **1.** *a.* (*a*) underground, subterranean (water, passage); *El: etc:* **câble s.,** buried cable; **couloir, passage, s.,** subway; **chemin de fer s.,** underground railway, *U.S:* subway; **guerre souterraine,** underground warfare; mine warfare; (*b*) *F:* underhand (practices, ways); **employer des voies souterraines,** to have recourse to underhand methods. **2.** *s.m.* (*a*) (large) cavern; caves; (*b*) underground gallery, workings; (*c*) underground passage; tunnel; subway; **rue en s.,** underpass (street); (*d*) vault.
souterrainement [sutɛrɛnmɑ̃], *adv.* (*a*) underground; **mine exploitée s.,** mine worked underground; (*b*) **agir s.,** to act in an underhand manner.
soutien [sutjɛ̃], *s.m.* **1.** supporting; **en s.,** in support; *Mil:* **unité de s.,** support unit; **s. logistique,** (logistical) support; **matériel de s. logistique,** (logistical) support equipment; *Mil.Av:* **opération de s. aérien,** air strike. **2.** (*a*) support, prop; **il est sans s.,** he has nobody behind him; (*b*) supporter, upholder; mainstay; **s. de famille,** (i) breadwinner; (ii) *Mil:* man who has a family entirely dependent on him; *Mil:* **s. spécial,** special escort (of artillery).
soutien-gorge [sutjɛ̃gɔrʒ], *s.m. Cost:* brassière, *F:* bra; **s.-g. ampliforme,** padded brassière; **s.-g. corbeille,** sling, cradle, platform, brassière; **s.-g. préformé,** preformed brassière; *pl. soutiens-gorge.*
soutien-pieds [sutjɛ̃pje], *s.m.* **s.-p. d'une croix,** suppedaneum of a cross (of crucifixion).
soutien-vélo [sutjɛ̃velo], *s.m.* bicycle stand; *pl. soutien-vélos.*
soutirage [sutiraːʒ], *s.m.* drawing off, racking, clarifying (of wine, etc.); tapping (of electric supply, etc.); *Mec.E:* bleeding off (of pressure from a turbine); *Geog:* **s. karstique,** underground drainage (in karst country).
soutirer [sutire], *v.tr.* to draw off, rack (wine, etc.); to tap (electric supply, etc.); to bleed (steam); **s. de l'argent à qn,** to get, wheedle, squeeze, money out of s.o.; **fonds soutirés à des dupes,** funds extracted from dupes, suckers.
Soûtra [sutra], *s.m. Sanscrit Lit:* Sutra; **le S.,** the Sutras.
soutrage [sutraːʒ], *s.m. For:* clearing of undergrowth.
soutrager [sutraʒe], *v.tr.* (**je soutrageais; n. soutrageons**) *For:* to clear (forest) of undergrowth.
souvenance [suvnɑ̃ːs], *s.f. A: & Lit:* remembrance, recollection (**de,** of); *Lit:* **combien j'ai douce s. de . . .,** what sweet memories I have of . . ..

souvenir [suvniːr]. I. *v.impers. Lit:* (*conj. like* VENIR; *the aux. is* être) to occur to the mind; **il me souvient d'une histoire curieuse,** I remember a curious story; **c'est du plus loin qu'il me souvienne,** that dates from my earliest memories; **vous souvient-il que . . .?** do you remember that . . .? **autant qu'il m'en souvient, qu'il m'en souvienne,** to the best of my recollection; as far, as near, as I can remember; **du plus loin qu'il m'en souvienne,** as long, as far back, as I can remember.

se souvenir de qch., de qn, to remember, recall, sth., s.o.; **peu de gens se souviennent (d')avoir été jeunes,** few people remember that they were once young; **se s. de loin,** to be able to remember things that happened a long time ago; **je ne me souviens pas de son nom,** I don't remember his name; **je me souviendrai,** I shall not forget (this insult, etc.); **nous nous souviendrons de lui,** we shall remember him; **autant que je m'en souviens, que je m'en souvienne,** to the best of my recollection; if my memory serves me; **faire s. qn de qch.,** to remind s.o. of sth.; **cela me fait s. de ma jeunesse,** that carries me back to my youth; *B:* **souviens-toi que tu n'es que poussière,** remember that thou art but dust; **je tâcherai de m'en s.,** I shall try to bear it in mind.

II. **souvenir,** *s.m.* **1.** remembrance, recollection, memory; **avoir gardé un bon s. de qch.,** to have a pleasant recollection of sth.; **j'en ai un s. confus, un vague s.,** I have a dim, vague, recollection of it; **je n'en ai pas s.,** I have no recollection of it; **si mes souvenirs sont exacts,** if my memory serves me (well); **conserver un s. net de qch.,** to retain a clear memory of sth.; **il conserve, a conservé, de vous un excellent s.,** he has (i) very pleasant memories of you, (ii) a very favourable recollection of you; **souvenirs de ma jeunesse,** memories of my youth; **pays riche en souvenirs historiques,** country rich in historical associations; **veuillez me rappeler à son bon s.,** please remember me kindly to him; **ma mère vous envoie son affectueux s.,** mother sends her love; **faire qch. en s. de qn,** to do sth. in remembrance of s.o.; **en s. du passé,** for old times' sake. **2.** memorial, memento; **ses blessures sont de glorieux souvenirs de ses victoires,** his wounds are glorious mementoes of his victories. **3.** (*token of remembrance*) (*a*) keepsake, souvenir; **ce sera un s. de vous,** it will be something to remember you by; (*b*) **s. (offert à un fonctionnaire, etc.),** presentation; **remise d'un s. à qn,** presentation to s.o.; **offrir un s. à qn,** to make a presentation to s.o. **4.** *A:* memorandum book.

souvent [suvɑ̃], *adv.* often; **vient-il s.?** does he come often, frequently? **peu s.,** not often; seldom, infrequently; **il ne vient pas s. nous voir,** he doesn't often come and see us; **assez s.,** quite often; fairly often; **plus s.,** more often; **il est malade plus s. qu'à son tour,** he has more than his share of illness; **le plus s.,** usually; as often as not; more often than not; *P:* **plus s.!** no fear! not if I know it! some hope! **plus s. que j'irais!** no fear of my going! **plus s. que j'y en donnerais!** give some? me? not likely!

souventé [suvɑ̃te], *a. Nau:* blanketed.

souventefois, souventes fois [suvɑ̃tfwa], *adv. A:* oft, oft-times; many a time and oft.

souverain, -aine [suvrɛ̃, -ɛn]. **1.** *a.* sovereign (power, prince, remedy, etc.); **état s.,** sovereign state; **le s. pontife,** his Holiness (the Pope); **s. bonheur,** supreme happiness; **beauté souveraine,** sovereign beauty; *Lit:* **le s. bien,** the sovereign good; *Jur:* **cour souveraine,** final court of appeal; supreme court; **jugement s.,** judgment of the final court of appeal, final judgment; **avoir un s. mépris pour qn,** to hold s.o. in sovereign contempt, in supreme contempt. **2.** (*a*) *s.* sovereign; **Rübezahl, le s. de la montagne,** Rübezahl, the lord of the mountain; (*b*) *s.m. Num: A:* sovereign.

souverainement [suvrɛnmɑ̃], *adv.* **1.** supremely, superlatively, extremely; *Lit:* **l'esprit est s. maître,** the mind is sovereign master. **2.** *Jur:* **juger s.,** to judge without appeal.

souveraineté [suvrɛnte], *s.f.* sovereignty. **1.** (*a*) supreme authority; **droits de s.,** sovereign rights; **tenir un pays en s.,** to hold sovereign power over a country; (*b*) supremacy (of law, of right); **s. du but,** sovereignty of the end (which justifies the means). **2.** territory, dominion(s) (of sovereign prince).

soviet [sɔvjɛt], *s.m.* soviet.

soviétique [sɔvjetik]. **1.** *a.* soviet; **l'Union des Républiques socialistes soviétiques,** the Union of the Socialist Soviet Republics. **2.** *s.m. & f.* Soviet citizen.

soviétisation [sɔvjetizasjɔ̃], *s.f.* sovietization.

soviétiser [sɔvjetize], *v.tr.* to sovietize; to convert (a country) to the Soviet system.

sovkhoz(e) [sɔvkoːz], *s.m. Pol.Ec:* sovkhoz.

soya [sɔja], *s.m. Bot:* soya bean, soy.

soyer[1] [swaje], *s.m. A:* (type of) champagne sorbet.

soyer[2], **-ère** [swaje, -ɛːr]. **1.** *a.* of, pertaining to, silk; **les industries soyères,** the silk industries. **2.** *s.* silk mercer.

soyeux, -euse [swajø, -øːz]. **1.** *a.* silky. **2.** *s.f.* **soyeuse:** (*a*) *Bot:* silkweed, milkweed; (*b*) *Husb:* silky (fowl). **3.** *s.m.* (*in Lyon(s)*) silk manufacturer; silk merchant.

spacieusement [spasjøzmɑ̃], *adv.* spaciously; with plenty of room.

spacieux, -euse [spasjø, -øːz], *a.* spacious; roomy; capacious; **appartement s.,** spacious, roomy, flat, *U.S:* apartment; **voiture spacieuse,** roomy car.

spaciosité [spasjozite], *s.f.* spaciousness; roominess; capaciousness.

spadassin [spadasɛ̃], *s.m.* (*a*) *A:* bully, bravo; (*b*) **s. (à gages),** hired assassin, hired ruffian.

spadice [spadis], *s.m. Bot:* spadix.

spadicé [spadise], *a. Bot:* spadacious.

spadiciflore [spadisiflɔːr], *Bot:* **1.** *a.* spadicifloral. **2.** *s.f.pl.* **spadiciflores,** Spadiciflorae.

spadille [spadiːj], *s.m. Cards:* spadille; ace of spades (at ombre).

spadois, -oise [spadwa, -waːz], *a. & s. Geog:* (native, inhabitant) of Spa.

spaghetti [spageti, -ɛtti], *s.m.pl. Cu:* spaghetti.

spahi [spai], *s.m. Mil:* spahi.

spalacidés [spalaside], *s.m.pl. Z:* Spalacidae.

spalax [spalaks], *s.m. Z:* spalax; mole rat.

spallation [spalasjɔ̃], *s.f. Atom.Ph:* spallation (of nucleus).

spalme [spalm], *s.m. Nau: A:* **1.** coat of tallow and tar (for ship's bottom). **2.** coat of tallow (for racing boat's bottom).

spalmer [spalme], *v.tr. Nau: A:* to clean, tallow, pay (ship's bottom).

spalt[1] [spalt], *s.m. Metall:* spalt.

spalt[2], *s.m.* Jew's pitch; compact bitumen.

spalter [spaltɛːr], *s.m. Paint:* graining brush.

spangolite [spɑ̃gɔlit], *s.f. Miner:* spangolite.

spanopnée [spanɔpne], *s.f. Med:* spanopn(o)ea, slowing down of the respiration.

sparadrap [sparadra], *s.m.* adhesive plaster, sticking plaster.

sparaillon [sparajɔ̃], *s.m. Ich:* spargo.

spardeck [spardɛk], *s.m. N.Arch:* spar deck.

spare [spaːr], *s.m. Ich:* spar, sparid.

sparganier [sparganje], *s.m. Bot:* sparganium, bur reed.

spargoule [spargul], *s.f.*, **spargoute** [spargut], *s.f. Bot:* spergula, spurrey.

sparidés [sparide], *s.m.pl. Ich:* Sparidae.

sparnacien, -ienne [sparnasjɛ̃, -jɛn]. **1.** *a. & s. Geog:* (native, inhabitant) of Épernay. **2.** *a. & s.m. Geol:* Sparnacian.

sparoïde [sparɔid], *a. Ich:* sparoid.

sparring-partner [spariŋpartnɛːr], *s.m. Box: F:* sparring partner; *pl. sparring-partners.*

sparsiflore [sparsiflɔːr], *a. Bot:* sparsiflorous, with scattered flowers.

sparsifolié [sparsifɔlje], *a. Bot:* sparsifolious, with scattered leaves.

sparsile [sparsil], *a. Astr:* sparsile (star).

spart [spart], *s.m. Bot:* esparto (grass).

spartakisme [spartakism], *s.m. Pol.Hist:* Spartacism.

spartakiste [spartakist], *s.m. & f. Pol.Hist:* Spartacist; *a.* **groupe s.,** Spartacist group.

spartan [spartɑ̃], *s.m. Nau:* **1.** coir. **2.** bass (rope).

sparte[1] [spart], *s.m. Bot:* esparto (grass).

Sparte[2], *Pr.n.f. A.Geog:* Sparta.

spartéine [spartein], *s.f. Pharm:* spartein.

sparterie [spartri], *s.f.* **1.** esparto factory. **2.** *usu. pl.* esparto goods, ware.

spartiate [sparsjat]. **1.** (*a*) *s.m. & f. A.Geog:* Spartan; (*b*) *s.m.* (*man of endurance*) spartan. **2.** *a.* spartan; austere; **à la s.,** spartanly, in a spartan manner; severely; austerely. **3.** *s.f.* leather sandal.

spartina [spartina], *s.m. Bot:* spartina.

spartium [spartjɔm], *s.m. Bot:* spartium, Spanish broom.

spasme [spasm], *s.m.* spasm; **spasmes toniques,** tonic spasms; **spasmes cloniques,** clonic spasms; **spasmes fonctionnels,** functional spasms.

spasmodicité [spasmɔdisite], *s.f. Med:* spasticity.

spasmodique [spasmɔdik], *a. Med:* spasmodic; spastic; **paraplégie s.,** spastic paraplegia.

spasmodiquement [spasmɔdikmɑ̃], *adv.* spasmodically.

spasmolytique [spasmɔlitik], *a. Med:* spasmolytic.

spasmophilie [spasmɔfili], *s.f. Med:* spasmophilia.

spastique [spastik], *a.* spastic; spasmodic.

spatangide [spatɑ̃ʒid], *a. Echin:* spatangoid.

spatangue [spatɑ̃ːg], *s.m. Echin:* spatangus; *F:* heart urchin.

spath [spat], *s.m. Miner:* spar; **s. brunissant,** brown spar; ankerite; **s. calcaire,** calcite, calcspar, calcareous spar; **s. d'Islande,** Iceland spar; **s. fluor, s. fusible,** fluorspar, fluorite; **s. perlé,** pearl spar; **s. pesant,** heavy spar, barite; **s. schisteux,** argentine; slate spar.

spathacé [spatase], *a. Bot:* spathaceous.

spathe [spat], *s.f. Bot:* (*a*) spathe; (*b*) shuck (of maize).

spathé [spate], *a. Bot:* spathaceous, spathose.

spathelle [spatɛl], *s.f. Bot:* spathella.

spathifier [spatifje], *v.tr. Miner:* to transform into spar.

spathiforme[1] [spatifɔrm], *a. Miner:* spathiform.

spathiforme[2], *a. Bot:* spathose.

spathique [spatik], *a. Miner:* spathic, sparry; **fer s.,** spathic iron, sparry iron; siderite; **diamant s.,** adamantine spar.

spatial, -aux [spasjal, -o], *a.* spatial, relating to space; (*a*) **l'infinité spatiale,** the infinity of space; *Psy:* **perception spatiale,** space perception; (*b*) **engin s.,** spacecraft; **voyage s.,** journey in space; **la conquête spatiale,** the conquest of space; **combinaison spatiale,** spacesuit; *Elcs:* **charge spatiale,** space charge; **guerre spatiale,** space warfare; (*c*) *F:* astounding, astonishing.

spatialisation [spasjalizasjɔ̃], *s.f.* spatialization.

spatialiser [spasjalize], *v.tr.* **1.** to give a spatial character to (sth.); to locate, localize (sth.) in space; to spatialize. **2.** to send, project, into space; to put into orbit.

spatialité [spasjalite], *s.f.* spatiality, spatial quality.

spatio-temporel, -elle [spasjɔtɑ̃pɔrɛl], *a.* space-time; *pl. spatio-temporel(le)s.*

spatulaire [spatylɛːr], *s.m. Ich: F:* paddlefish, spoonbill, spadefish.

spatule [spatyl], *s.f.* **1.** (*a*) spatula; **s. à beurre,** butter pat; **doigts en s.,** spatulate fingers; (*b*) (moulder's) spoon tool; (*c*) ski tip. **2.** *Orn:* **s. blanche,** spoonbill. **3.** *Ich:* spadefish, paddle fish; Chinese sturgeon; **grande s.,** large paddle-fish, spoonbill.

spatulé [spatyle], *a.* spatulate.

spatuliforme [spatylifɔrm], *a.* spatuliform, spatulate.

speaker [spikœːr], *s.m. W.Tel: T.V:* announcer; *Sp:* megaphone steward.

speakerine [spik(ə)rin], *s.f. W.Tel: T.V:* (woman) announcer.

spécial, -aux [spesjal, -o], *a.* special, especial; particular; **faire une étude spéciale de qch.,** to make a special study of sth.; **je viens pour une affaire spéciale,** I have come about a special, particular, piece of business; **privilège s. aux militaires,** privilege reserved for, restricted to, military men; *Journ:* **notre envoyé s.,** our special correspondent; **revue spéciale pour l'histoire et la géographie,** periodical specially devoted to history and geography; **dictionnaires généraux et dictionnaires spéciaux,** general and specialized dictionaries; **hommes spéciaux,** specialists, professionals, experts; *Mil:* **armes spéciales,** technical arms; *Sch:* **mathématiques spéciales,** *s.f.* **la spéciale,** advanced mathematics class; *Elcs:* (*computers*) **caractère s.,** special, additional, character; **caractère de série spéciale,** shift-out character; **correction sans courants spéciaux,** correction from signals; **rien de s. à citer,** nothing special, out of the ordinary, to report; *F:* **c'est un peu s.,** it's rather odd, queer; *Pej:* **mœurs spéciales,** homosexuality.

spécialement [spesjalmɑ̃], *adv.* (e)specially, particularly; **s'intéresser s. à qch.,** to take a special interest in sth.; *F:* **pas s. beau,** not particularly beautiful.

spécialisation [spesjalizasjɔ̃], *s.f.* specialization, specializing.

spécialisé [spesjalize], *a.* specialized, special (work, materials, etc.); **ouvrier s.,** semi-skilled worker; **calculateur s.,** special-purpose computer.

spécialiser [spesjalize], *v.tr.* (*a*) *A:* to specify; *Fin:* **s. des fonds,** to earmark funds; (*b*) to specialize; **se s. dans qch.,** to specialize, be a specialist, in sth.; to make a special study of sth.

spécialisme [spesjalism], *s.m.* specialism.

spécialiste [spesjalist], *s.m. & f.* specialist; expert; *Mil: etc:* tradesman; *Med:* **s. du cœur, des maladies nerveuses,** heart specialist; specialist in nervous diseases; **s. du vol à voile,** gliding expert; **s. en vieux tableaux,** specialist in old paintings; **s. en botanique,** specialist in botany; *Iron: F:* **elle est s. de ce genre de gaffes,** she specializes, she's a specialist, in that sort of blunder.

spécialité [spesjalite], *s.f.* **1.** speciality, special feature, special function. **2.** specialty, speciality; special class of goods; special line of business; particular branch (of a service); **faire sa s. des mathématiques,** to specialize in, make a special study of, mathematics; **il a la s. de me taper sur les nerfs,** he has a knack of getting on my nerves; *Navy:* **les spécialités de la marine,** the specialized branches of the naval service; **homme de s.,** rating who has qualified for special duties. **3.** (*a*) **spécialités pharmaceutiques,** patent medicines; (*b*) *Cu:* **spécialités régionales,** local dishes.

spéciation [spesjasjɔ̃], *s.f. Biol:* speciation.

spécieusement [spesjøzmɑ̃], *adv.* speciously, plausibly.

spécieux, -euse [spesjø, -øːz], *a.* specious; that appears good, reasonable, on the surface; plausible (pretext, etc.).

spécificatif, -ive [spesifikatif, -iːv], *a.* specifying.

spécification [spesifikasjɔ̃], *s.f.* **1.** (*a*) specification; determination of species; (*b*) *Elcs:* (*computers*) **s. du programme,** program(me) specification. **2.** *Tchn:* working up (of material). **3.** *usu. in pl.* specifications, *F:* specs.

spécificité [spesifisite], *s.f. Med: etc:* specificity, specific character (of symptom, etc.).

spécifier [spesifje], *v.tr.* (*p.d. & pr.sub.* **n. spécifiions, v. spécifiiez**) **1.** to specify; to mention specially, to state definitely; **s. des fonctions,** to lay down duties; **s. que . . .,** to lay down that . . .; **compte spécifié,** detailed account, itemized account; *St.Exch:* **s. un cours,** to make a price. **2.** to determine (sth.) specifically; to distinguish (sth.) as belonging to a particular species.

spécifique [spesifik]. **1.** *a.* specific (function, remedy, germ, etc.); *Nat.Hist:* **nom s.,** specific name; **bacille s. de la tuberculose,** bacillus specific of tuberculosis; *Ph:* **poids s.,** specific gravity; **différence s.,** specific difference, difference in kind; *Elcs:* (*computers*) **équipement terminal s.,** job-oriented terminal. **2.** *s.m. Med:* specific (remedy) **(contre,** for).

spécifiquement [spesifikmɑ̃], *adv.* specifically.

spécimen [spesimɛn], *s.m.* specimen; *Publ:* free copy; inspection copy; *Pej:* **un drôle de s.,** an odd chap; *a.* **numéro s. d'un journal,** specimen number of a paper; **page s.,** specimen page.

spéciosité [spesjozite], *s.f.* speciousness.

spectacle [spɛktakl̩], *s.m.* **1.** spectacle, sight, scene; **s. charmant,** charming sight; **se donner en s., faire s.,** to make an exhibition of oneself; to make oneself conspicuous; **faire s. de qch.,** to show off, exhibit, advertise, sth. **2.** (*a*) *Th:* play, entertainment, *F:* show; **aller au s.,** to go to the theatre, to a show; **salle de s.,** (concert, etc.) hall; theatre; **taxe sur les spectacles,** entertainment tax; (*b*) **s. payant,** sideshow (at bazaar, exhibition, etc.); **spectacles forains,** shows, sideshows (at fair, etc.). **3.** show, display; *Th:* **pièce à grand s.,** spectacular play, lavish production; *Cin:* **film à grand s.,** epic.

spectaculaire [spɛktakyleːr], *a.* **1.** (*a*) spectacular; (*b*) dramatic. **2.** theatrical (guide, almanac, etc.).

spectateur, -trice [spɛktatœːr, -tris], *s.* spectator, onlooker, bystander; beholder; witness (of accident, etc.); **acteurs et spectateurs,** actors and audience; **les spectateurs sont priés de ne pas fumer,** patrons are requested not to smoke; **un général s. de la bataille,** a general who witnessed the battle; **elle a été spectatrice de tous ces événements,** she lived through, witnessed, all these events.

spectral, -aux [spɛktral, -o], *a.* spectral. **1.** ghostly, ghostlike (vision, etc.). **2.** *Opt:* pertaining to the spectrum; **couleurs spectrales,** colours of the spectrum; *Ch:* **analyse spectrale,** spectrum analysis, spectral analysis.

spectre [spɛktr̥], *s.m.* **1.** spectre, ghost, apparition; **évoquer des spectres,** to raise ghosts; *Lit:* **le s. rouge,** the ghost of revolution. **2.** spectrum; (*a*) *Opt:* **s. optique,** optical spectrum; **s. solaire,** solar spectrum; **s. de diffraction,** diffraction spectrum; **s. de réfraction,** refraction spectrum; (*b*) **s. du Brocken,** Brocken spectre; (*c*) *Ph:* **s. acoustique,** acoustic(al) spectrum, sound spectrum; **s. calorifique,** heat spectrum; **s. chimique,** chemical spectrum; **s. continu,** continuous spectrum; **s. de bandes,** band spectrum; **s. de raies,** line spectrum; **s. d'absorption,** absorption spectrum; **s. d'émission,** emission spectrum; **s. de fréquences,** frequency spectrum; **s. de masse,** mass spectrum; **spectres de vapeurs métalliques,** flame spectra of metals; (*d*) *Phot:* **s. secondaire,** ghost, flare (spot). **3.** *Magn:* magnetic tracing (in iron filings, etc.).

spectro- [spɛktrɔ], *comb.fm.* spectro-.

spectrogramme [spɛktrɔgram], *s.m.* spectrogram(me); **s. acoustique,** sound spectrogram(me), sonagram.

spectrographe [spɛktrɔgraf], *s.m.* spectrograph; **s. à rayons X,** X-ray spectrograph; **s. de masse,** mass spectrograph.

spectrographie [spɛktrɔgrafi], *s.f.* spectrography; **s. d'absorption,** absorption spectrography; **s. de masse,** mass spectrography; **s. d'émission,** emission spectrography; **appareil de s. acoustique,** sound spectrograph, sonagraph.

spectrographique [spɛktrɔgrafik], *a.* spectrographic.

spectrohéliographe [spɛktrɔeljɔgraf], *s.m. Phot:* spectroheliograph.

spectromètre [spɛktrɔmɛtr̥], *s.m.* spectrometer; **s. à réseau,** grating spectrometer; **s. de masse(s),** mass spectrometer; **s. à scintillation,** scintillation spectrometer.

spectrométrie [spɛktrɔmetri], *s.f.* spectrometry.

spectrométrique [spɛktrɔmetrik], *a.* spectrometric.

spectrophotographie [spɛktrɔfɔtɔgrafi], *s.f.* spectrophotography.

spectrophotomètre [spɛktrɔfɔtɔmɛtr̥], *s.m.* spectrophotometer.

spectrophotométrie [spɛktrɔfɔtɔmetri], *s.f.* spectrophotometry.

spectroscope [spɛktrɔskɔp], *s.m. Opt:* spectroscope; **s. à prismes,** prism spectroscope; **s. à réseau,** grating spectroscope; **s. à vision directe,** direct-vision spectroscope.

spectroscopie [spɛktrɔskɔpi], *s.f.* spectroscopy.

spectroscopique [spɛktrɔskɔpik], *a.* spectroscopic.

spectroscopiste [spɛktrɔskɔpist], *s.m. & f.* spectroscopist.

spectro-tubérantiel, -ielle [spɛktrɔtyberɑ̃sjɛl], *a.* pertaining to the solar prominences; *pl. spectro-tubérantiel(le)s.*

spéculaire [spekyleːr]. **1.** *a.* (*a*) specular (mineral); **fer s.,** specular iron ore; *A:* **pierre s.,** mica; (*b*) **objectif à lentilles spéculaires,** mirror lens; (*c*) *Med:* **écriture s.,** mirror writing (symptomatic of aphasia). **2.** *s.f. Bot:* specularia; **s. miroir de Vénus,** Venus's looking glass.

spéculateur, -trice [spekylatœːr, -tris], *s.* **1.** speculator, theorizer. **2.** *Fin:* speculator.

spéculatif, -ive [spekylatif, -iːv]. **1.** *a. & s.* speculative, contemplative (person). **2.** *a. Fin:* speculative (deal, etc.).

spéculation [spekylasjɔ̃], *s.f.* **1.** (*a*) speculation (sur, on); cogitation, pondering; (*b*) theory, hypothesis, conjecture. **2.** *Fin:* speculation; **s. à la baisse,** bear operations; **s. à la hausse,** bull operations; **pure s.,** pure gamble; **acheteur en s.,** speculative purchaser.

spéculativement [spekylativmɑ̃], *adv.* speculatively.

spéculer [spekyle], *v.i.* **1.** to speculate, cogitate **(sur,** on, about); to ponder **(sur,** over). **2.** *Fin:* to speculate; **s. sur le caoutchouc,** to speculate in rubber; **s. à la hausse,** to speculate for a rise; to go a bull; **s. à la baisse,** to speculate for a fall; to go a bear.

speculum, spéculum [spekylɔm], *s.m. Med:* speculum; **s. vaginal,** vaginal speculum.

speiskobalt [spɛskɔbalt], *s.m. Miner:* speiskobalt, speiss cobalt, smaltite.

speiss [spɛs], *s.m. Metall:* speiss.

spéléiste [speleist], *s.m. & f.* potholer, *U.S:* spelunker.

spéléologie [speleɔlɔʒi], *s.f.* spel(a)eology; cave hunting; potholing.

spéléologique [speleɔlɔʒik], *a.* spel(a)eological.

spéléologue [speleɔlɔg], *s.m. & f.* spel(a)eologist; potholer, *U.S:* spelunker.

spélonque [spelɔ̃ːk], *s.f.* **1.** cave. **2.** *Med:* pulmonary cavity.

spencer [spɛ̃sɛːr], *s.m. Cost:* **1.** (man's) short tight jacket; *A:* spencer; *Nau:* monkey jacket; *Mil:* mess jacket. **2.** (*a*) (woman's) short jacket; (*b*) *A:* (woman's) spencer.

spent [spɛnt], *s.f. Fish:* spent-gnat fly.

spéos [speos], *s.m. Egyptian Ant:* speos.

spergulaire [spɛrgyleːr], *s.f.,* **spergularia** [spɛrgylarja], *s.m. Bot:* spergularia, sand spurry.

spergule [spɛrgyl], *s.f. Bot:* spergula, spurr(e)y.

spermaceti [spɛrmasɛti], *s.m.* spermaceti; **huile de s.,** sperm oil, spermaceti oil.

spermaphytes [spɛrmafit], *s.f.pl. Bot:* Spermatophyta.

spermathèque [spɛrmatɛk], *s.f. Biol:* spermatheca.

spermaticide [spɛrmatisid], *a. Med: etc:* spermicidal.

spermatide [spɛrmatid], *s.f. Biol:* spermatid.

spermatie [spɛrmati], *s.f. Fung:* spermatium.

spermatique [spɛrmatik], *a. Anat:* spermatic (cord, etc.).

spermatisme [spɛrmatism], *s.m. Hist. of Med:* spermism.

spermato- [spɛrmatɔ], *comb.fm.* spermato-.

spermatoblaste [spɛrmatɔblast], *s.m. Biol:* spermatoblast.

spermatocèle [spɛrmatɔsɛl], *s.f. Med:* spermatocele.

spermatocystite [spɛrmatɔsistit], *s.f. Med:* spermatocystitis.

spermatocyte [spɛrmatɔsit], *s.f. Biol:* spermatocyte.

spermatogénèse [spɛrmatɔʒenɛːz], *s.f. Biol:* spermatogenesis.

spermatogonie [spɛrmatɔgɔni], *s.f. Anat:* spermatogonium.

spermatologie [spɛrmatɔlɔʒi], *s.f.* spermatology.

spermatophore [spɛrmatɔfɔːr], *s.m. Biol:* spermatophore.

spermatophytes [spɛrmatɔfit], *s.f.pl. Bot:* Spermatophyta.

spermatorrhée [spɛrmatɔre], *s.f. Med:* spermatorrhoea.

spermatothèque [spɛrmatɔtɛk], *s.f. Biol:* spermatheca, spermatotheca.

spermatozoaire [spɛrmatɔzɔɛːr], *s.m.,* **spermatozoïde** [spɛrmatɔzɔid], *s.m. Biol:* spermatozoon.

sperme [spɛrm], *s.m.* **1.** *Physiol:* sperm, semen. **2. s. de baleine,** spermaceti.

spermicide [spɛrmisid]. *Med: etc:* **1.** *a.* spermatocidal, spermicidal. **2.** *s.m.* spermicide.

spermiducte [spɛrmidykt], *s.m. Anat:* spermiduct, spermoduct.

spermine [spɛrmin], *s.f. Bio-Ch:* spermin(e).

spermiogénèse [spɛrmjɔʒenɛːz], *s.f. Biol:* spermiogenesis.

spermoderme [spɛrmɔdɛrm], *s.m. Bot:* spermoderm.

spermogonie [spɛrmɔgɔni], *s.f. Bot:* spermogonium, spermogone.

spermophile [spɛrmɔfil], *s.m. Z:* spermophile, gopher, (European) ground squirrel.

spermophore [spɛrmɔfɔːr]. **1.** *s.m. Bot:* spermophore, spermophyte. **2.** *a.* spermophytic.

spermotoxine [spɛrmɔtɔksin], *s.f. Bio-Ch:* spermotoxin.

sperrylite [spɛrilit], *s.f. Miner:* sperrylite.

spessartine [spɛsartin], *s.f. Miner:* spessartine, spessartite.

spet [spɛ], *s.m. Ich:* spet, sennet.

sphacélariales [sfaselarjal], *s.f.pl. Algae:* Sphacelariales.

sphacèle [sfasɛl], *s.m. Med:* sphacelus, gangrene.

sphacélé [sfasele], *a. Med:* sphacelate, gangrenous, mortified.

sphacéler [sfasele], *v.tr.* **(il sphacèle; il sphacélera)** *Med:* to sphacelate; to make gangrenous; to mortify.

sphacélie [sfaseli], *s.f. Fung:* sphacelia.

sphacélisme [sfaselism], *s.m. Med:* sphacelism; mortification.

Sphactérie [sfakteri], *Pr.n.f. Geog:* Sphagia, *A:* Sphacteria.

sphærite [sferit], *s.f. Miner:* sphaerite.

sphagnacées [sfagnase], *s.f.pl. Bot:* Sphagnaceae, peat mosses.

sphaigne [sfɛɲ], *s.f. Bot:* sphagnum, peat moss.

sphalérite [sfalerit], *s.f. Miner:* sphalerite, blende.

sphégidés [sfeʒide], **sphégiens** [sfeʒjɛ̃], *s.m.pl. Ent:* Sphecidae.

sphène [sfɛn], *s.m. Miner:* sphene.

sphéniscidés [sfeniside], *s.m.pl. Orn:* Spheniscidae.

sphénisciformes [sfenisifɔrm], *s.m.pl. Orn:* Sphenisciformes.

sphéno- [sfenɔ], *pref.* spheno-.

sphénodon [sfenɔdɔ̃], *s.m. Rept:* tuatara, tuatera; (*genus*) Sphenodon.

sphénoïdal, -aux [sfenɔidal, -o], *a.* **sphénoïdien, -ienne** [sfenɔidjɛ̃, -jɛn], *a. Anat:* sphenoidal (fissure, sinus, etc.).

sphénoïde [sfenɔid], *a. & s.m. Anat:* sphenoid.

sphénoïdite [sfenɔidit], *s.f. Med:* sphenoiditis.

sphéno-maxillaire [sfenɔmaksilɛːr], *a. Anat:* sphenomaxillary; *pl. sphéno-maxillaires.*

sphéno-palatin [sfenɔpalatɛ̃], *a. Anat:* sphenopalatine; *pl. sphéno-palatin(e)s.*

sphénophore [sfenɔfɔːr], *s.m. Ent:* sphenophorus.

sphère [sfɛːr], *s.f.* **1.** sphere; *Astr:* **la s. céleste,** the celestial sphere; *Geog:* **s. terrestre,** globe; *Sch: A:* **étude de la s.,** the use of the globes. **2. s. d'activité,** sphere of activity; **s. d'action,** sphere, field, of action; **s. d'influence,** sphere of influence; **être hors de sa s.,** to be out of one's sphere, one's element; **le bruit court dans certaines sphères,** it is rumoured in certain quarters.
sphéricité [sferisite], *s.f.* sphericity; *Opt:* **aberration de s.,** spherical aberration.
sphérique [sferik]. **1.** *a.* spherical, globe-shaped; **géométrie s.,** spherical geometry; **triangle, polygone, s.,** spherical triangle, polygon. **2.** *s.m. Aer:* balloon of globular type.
sphériquement [sferikmɑ̃], *adv.* spherically.
sphéro- [sferə], *pref.* sphaero-.
sphéroblaste [sferəblast], *s.m. Bot:* sphaeroblast.
sphérocobaltite [sferəkəbaltit], *s.f. Miner:* sphaerocobaltite.
sphéroïdal, -aux [sferəidal, -o], *a.* spheroid(al).
sphéroïde [sferəid], *s.m.* spheroid; **s. allongé,** prolate spheroid; **s. aplati,** oblate spheroid.
sphéroïdisation [sferəidizasjɔ̃], *s.f. Metall:* spheroidizing.
sphérolit(h)e [sferəlit], *s.m. Geol:* spherulite.
sphérolit(h)ique [sferəlitik], *a. Geol:* spherulitic.
sphéromètre [sferəmɛtr̥], *s.m.* spherometer.
sphérosidérite [sferəsiderit], *s.f. Miner:* sphaerosiderite.
sphérospore [sferəspɔːr], *s.f.* sphaerospore.
sphérulaire [sferylɛːr], *a.* spherular.
sphérule [sferyl], *s.f.* spherule, small sphere.
sphex [sfɛks], *s.m. Ent:* sphex(wasp).
sphincter [sfɛ̃ktɛːr], *s.m. Anat:* sphincter.
sphinctérien, -ienne [sfɛ̃kterjɛ̃, -jɛn], *a. Anat:* sphincteral, sphincteric.
sphinctérotomie [sfɛ̃kterətəmi], *s.f. Surg:* sphincterotomy.
sphinge [sfɛ̃ːʒ], *s.f. Myth:* female sphinx.
sphingidés [sfɛ̃ʒide], *s.m.pl. Ent:* Sphingidae, sphinxes, hawkmoths.
sphingomyéline [sfɛ̃gəmjelin], *s.f. Bio-Ch:* sphingomyelin.
sphingosine [sfɛ̃gəzin], *s.f. Bio-Ch:* sphingosine.
sphinx [sfɛ̃ːks], *s.m.* **1.** *Myth:* sphinx; **sourire de s.,** sphinx-like smile. **2.** *Ent:* sphinx, hawkmoth; **s. bélier,** burnet moth; **s. du caille-lait,** humming-bird hawkmoth; **s. du troène,** privet hawkmoth; **s. tête de mort,** death's-head hawkmoth.
sphragide [sfraʒid], *s.f.* **sphragidite** [sfraʒidit], *s.f. Miner:* sphragide.
sphragistique [sfraʒistik], *s.f.* sphragistics.
sphygmique [sfigmik], *a. Med:* sphygmic, of the pulse.
sphygmo- [sfigmə], *pref.* sphygmo-.
sphygmogramme [sfigməgram], *s.m. Med:* sphygmogram.
sphygmographe [sfigməgraf], *s.m. Med:* sphygmograph.
sphygmographie [sfigməgrafi], *s.f. Med:* sphygmography.
sphygmomanomètre [sfigməmanəmɛtr̥], *s.m. Med:* sphygmomanometer.
sphygmomètre [sfigməmɛtr̥], *s.m. Med:* sphygmometer.
sphygmoscope [sfigməskəp], *s.m. Med:* sphygmoscope.
sphygmotensiomètre [sfigmətɑ̃sjəmɛtr̥], *s.m. Med:* sphygmomanometer.
sphyrène [sfirɛn], *s.f. Ich:* sphyraenid, barracuda; (*genus*) Sphyraena; **s. barracuda,** becuna, great barracuda.
sphyrnidés [sfirnide], *s.m.pl. Ich:* Sphyraenidae.
spic [spik], *s.m. Bot:* spike lavender, French lavender; **essence de s.,** spike oil.
spica [spika], *s.m. Med:* spica (bandage).
spicanard [spikanaːr], *s.m. Bot:* spikenard.
spicifère [spisifɛːr], *Orn:* **1.** *a.* spiciferous. **2.** *s.m.* green peacock, Java peacock.
spiciflore [spisiflɔːr], *a. Bot:* spiciflorous.
spiciforme [spisifɔrm], *a. Bot:* spiciform, spike-like.
spiculaire [spikylɛːr], *a. Miner:* spicular.
spicule [spikyl], *s.m.* spicule, spikelet (in sponges, etc.); *Spong:* **s. à quatre points,** caltrop.
spiculé [spikyle], *a. Bot:* spiculate(d).
spider [spidɛːr], *s.m. Aut: A:* **1.** dickey (seat). **2.** two-seater with dickey.
spiegel [spigɛl], *s.m. Metall:* spiegeleisen, spiegel.
spigélie [spiʒeli], *s.f. Bot:* spigelia; **s. de Maryland,** Maryland pink root.
spilite [spilit], *s.f. Miner:* spilite.
spin [spin], *s.m. Atom.Ph:* spin; **s. de la voie d'entrée, de sortie,** entrance, exit, channel spin; **s. isobarique,** isobaric spin.
spina-bifida [spinabifida], *s.m. Med:* spina bifida.
spinacié [spinasje], *a. Bot:* spinaceous.
spinal, -aux [spinal, -o], *a. Anat:* spinal.
spinalien, -ienne [spinaljɛ̃, -jɛn], *a. & s. Geog:* (native, inhabitant) of Épinal.
spina-ventosa [spinavɑ̃toza], *s.m. Med:* tubercular osteitis (of the fingers).
spinelle[1] [spinɛl], *a. & s.m. Miner:* spinel.
spinelle[2], *s.f. Nat.Hist:* spinule.
spinellé [spinɛle], *a. Bot:* spinulose.
spinescence [spinɛs(s)ɑ̃ːs], *s.f. Bot:* spinescence.
spinescent [spinɛs(s)ɑ̃], *a. Bot:* spinescent.
spinifère [spinifɛːr], *a. Nat.Hist:* spiniferous; thorny, spiny.
spiniforme [spinifɔrm], *a. Nat.Hist:* spiniform.
spinigère [spiniʒɛːr], *a. Nat.Hist:* spinigerous.
spinnaker [spinakɛːr], *s.m. Nau:* spinnaker.
spinocarpe [spinəkarp], *a. Nat.Hist:* spinocarpous.
spinosisme, spinozisme [spinəzism], *s.m. Phil:* Spinozism.
spinosiste, spinoziste [spinəzist], *Phil:* **1.** *a.* Spinozistic. **2.** *s.m. & f.* Spinozist.
spinthariscope [spɛ̃tariskəp], *s.m.* spinthariscope.
spinthermètre [spɛ̃tɛrmɛtr̥], *s.m.* **spinthéromètre** [spɛ̃terəmɛtr̥], *s.m. El:* spark meter.
spinthéropie [spɛ̃terəpi], *s.f. Med:* spintherism.
spinule [spinyl], *s.f. Nat.Hist:* spinule, minute spine.
spinuleux, -euse [spinylø, -øːz], *a. Nat.Hist:* spinulescent, spiny.
spiquenard [spiknaːr], *s.m. Bot:* spikenard.
spiracle [spirakl̥], *s.m. Amph:* spiracle (of a tadpole).
spiral, -aux [spiral, -o]. **1.** *a.* spiral; **ressort s.,** spiral spring; **reliure spirale,** spiral binding. **2.** *s.m.* hairspring (of watch); coil spring, involute spring, spiral. **3.** *s.f.* **spirale,** spiral, helix; **en spirale,** (i) *adv.* in a spiral, spirally; (ii) *adj.* spiral; **aller en spirale,** to wind; **la fumée monte en spirales,** the smoke is curling, spiralling, upwards; **escalier en spirale,** winding staircase; *Av:* **descente en spirale,** spiral dive, glide; **montée en spirale,** spiral climb; **descendre, monter, en spirale,** to spiral down, up; *Ind:* **spirale transporteuse,** spiral conveyor, conveyor worm; *W.Tel:* **spirale métallique (du détecteur),** cat's whisker; *Fish:* **anneaux forme spirale,** snake rings (of fishing rod).
spiralé [spirale], *a.* spiral, spirated, helical.
spiralisation [spiralizasjɔ̃], *s.f.* spiralization.
spiraloïde [spiraləid], *a.* spiraloid.
spiranne [spiran], *s.m. Ch:* spiran.
spirant, -ante [spirɑ̃, -ɑ̃ːt], *Ling:* **1.** *a.* spirant. **2.** *s.f.* **spirante,** spirant.
spiration [spirasjɔ̃], *s.f. Theol:* spiration.
spire[1] [spiːr], *s.f.* single turn, whorl (of spiral, screw, helix); *Conch:* twirl; *El:* helix, spiral (of coil, of armature); **s. morte,** idle, dead, turn (of coil).
Spire[2], *Pr.n. Geog:* Speyer.
spirée [spire], *s.f. Bot:* spiraea; **s. ulmaire,** meadow sweet.
spirifer [spirifɛːr], *s.m. Paleont:* spirifer.
spiriféridés [spiriferide], *s.m.pl. Paleont:* Spiriferidae.
spiriforme [spirifɔrm], *a.* spiriform.
spirille [spiriːj, -ril], *s.m. Bac:* spirillum; thread-shaped bacterium.
spirillose [spiril(l)oːz], *s.f. Med:* spirillosis.
spirite [spirit], *Psychics:* **1.** *a.* spiritualistic, spiritistic (seance, etc.). **2.** *s.* spiritist, spiritualist.
spiritisme [spiritism], *s.m. Psychics:* spiritism; spiritualism.
spiritiste [spiritist], *Psychics:* **1.** *a.* spiritistic; spiritualistic. **2.** *s.m. & f.* spiritualist.
spiritualisation [spiritɥalizasjɔ̃], *s.f.* spiritualization.
spiritualiser [spiritɥalize], *v.tr.* **1.** to spiritualize. **2.** *Ch: A:* to distil; to convert (liquid, salt) into spirit.
spiritualisme [spiritɥalism], *s.m. Phil:* spiritualism; animism.
spiritualiste [spiritɥalist], *Phil:* **1.** *a.* spiritualistic (philosophy). **2.** *s.m. & f.* spiritualist.
spiritualité [spiritɥalite], *s.f. Phil:* spirituality.
spirituel, -elle [spiritɥɛl]. **1.** (*a*) *a.* spiritual (being, power, life, etc.); **exercices spirituels,** religious exercises; **lecture spirituelle,** reading of religious works; **père s., directeur s.,** spiritual father; **parents spirituels,** god-parents; **concert s.,** concert of sacred music; (*b*) *s.m.* **le s.,** (i) things spiritual; (ii) spiritual power. **2.** *a.* witty (person, answer, etc.); **physionomie spirituelle,** lively, humorous face.
spirituellement [spiritɥɛlmɑ̃], *adv.* **1.** spiritually. **2.** wittily.
spiritueux, -euse [spiritɥø, -øːz]. **1.** *a.* spirituous; alcoholic (drink). **2.** *s.m. Adm:* spirituous liquor; **les s.,** spirits.
spirivalve [spirivalv], *a. Moll:* spirivalve.
spirobactéries [spirəbakteri], *s.f.pl.* spirobacteria.
spirochète [spirəkɛt], *s.m. Bac:* spirochaeta, spirochaetes.
spirochétose [spirəketoːz], *s.f. Med:* spirochetosis.
spirodèle [spirədɛl], *s.f. Bot:* spirodela.
spirographe [spirəgraf], *s.m. Ann:* spirographis.
spirogyre [spirəʒiːr], *s.m. Algae:* spirogyra.
spiroïdal, -aux [spirəidal, -o], **spiroïde** [spirəid], *a.* spiroidal, spiroid; spiral.
spiromètre [spirəmɛtr̥], *s.m.* spirometer.
spirométrie [spirəmetri], *s.f. Physiol:* spirometry.
spirométrique [spirəmetrik], *a. Physiol:* spirometric(al).
spirorbe [spirərb], *s.m. Ann:* spirorbis.
spiroscope [spirəskəp], *s.m.* spiroscope.
spirule [spiryl], *s.f. Moll:* spirula.
Spitsberg, Spitzberg [spitzbɛrg], *Pr.n. Geog:* Spitzbergen.
splanchnicectomie [splɑ̃knisɛktəmi], *s.f.*, **splanchnicotomie** [splɑ̃knikətəmi], *s.f. Surg:* splanchnicectomy.
splanchnique [splɑ̃knik], *a. Anat:* splanchnic (nerve, etc.).
splanchnologie [splɑ̃knələʒi], *s.f. Anat:* splanchnology.
splanchnopleure [splɑ̃knəplœːr], *s.f. Biol:* splanchnopleure.
splanchnoptôse [splɑ̃knəptoːz], *s.f. Med:* splanchnoptosis.
splanchnoscopie [splɑ̃knəskəpi], *s.f. Rom.Ant:* splanchnoscopy.
spleen [splin], *s.m. Lit:* depression, lowness of spirits; **avoir le s.,** to be depressed, low, in the dumps.
spleenétique [splinetik], *a.* splenetic.
splénalgie [splenalʒi], *s.f. Med:* splenalgia; pain in the spleen.
splénalgique [splenalʒik], *a. Med:* splenalgic.
splendeur [splɑ̃dœːr], *s.f.* splendour; (*a*) brilliance, radiance, brightness (of the sun, etc.); (*b*) magnificence, grandeur, display; **l'Espagne, aux jours de sa s.,** Spain, in the days of her glory; **déchu de son ancienne s.,** fallen from a high position.
splendide [splɑ̃did], *a.* splendid. **1.** resplendent, brilliant (sun). **2.** magnificent (palace, victory); sumptuous, wonderful (meal); splendid, magnificent, (sunset).
splendidement [splɑ̃didmɑ̃], *adv.* splendidly; magnificently; wonderfully.
splénectomie [splenɛktəmi], *s.f. Surg:* splenectomy.
splénétique [splenetik], *a.* **1.** *Med:* splenetic (patient). **2.** splenetic, morose, in low spirits.
splénification [splenifikasjɔ̃], *s.f. Med:* splenization (of lungs or liver).
splénique [splenik], *a. Anat:* splenic (artery, disease).
splénisation [splenizasjɔ̃], *s.f. Med:* splenization.
splénite [splenit], *s.f. Med:* splenitis.
spléno- [splenə], *pref.* spleno-.
splénocèle [splenəsɛl], *s.f. Med:* splenocele, rupture of the spleen.
splénocyte [splenəsit], *s.m. Anat:* splenocyte.
splénographie [splenəgrafi], *s.f. Med:* splenography.
splénoïde [splenəid], *a.* splenoid.
splénome [splenom], *s.m. Med:* tumour of the spleen.
splénomégalie [splenəmegali], *s.f. Med:* splenomegaly.
splénopathie [splenəpati], *s.f. Med:* splenopathy.
splénopexie [splenəpɛksi], *s.f. Surg:* splenopexis.
splénopneumonie [splenəpnøməni], *s.f. Med:* splenopneumonia.
splénotomie [splenətəmi], *s.f. Surg:* splenotomy.
spodiosite [spədjozit], *s.f. Miner:* spodiosite.
spodite [spədit], *s.f.* volcanic ash.
spodumène [spədymɛn], *s.m. Miner:* spodumene, triphane.
spolétain, -aine [spəletɛ̃, -ɛn], *Geog:* (native, inhabitant) of Spoleto.
Spolète [spəlɛt], *Pr.n. Geog:* Spoleto.
spoliateur, -trice [spəljatœːr, -tris]. **1.** *s.* despoiler. **2.** *a.* (*a*) despoiling (robber, etc.); (*b*) spoliatory (law, etc.); **acte s.,** act of spoilation; **mesure spoliatrice,** spoliatory measure.
spoliatif, -ive [spəljatif, -iːv], *a. Med:* spoliative (treatment, etc.).

spoliation [spɔljasjɔ̃], *s.f.* **1.** spoliation; despoiling, robbing (of s.o.); despoiling, plundering, rifling (of tomb, house, etc.). **2.** *Post:* **s. d'une lettre chargée,** stealing of the contents of a registered letter; theft from a registered letter.

spolier [spɔlje], *v.tr.* (*p.d. & pr.sub.* **n. spoliions, v. spoliiez**) **1.** to despoil, rob (s.o.) (**de,** of); to despoil, plunder, rifle (tomb, house, etc.); **on l'a spolié de son héritage,** he was robbed, deprived, of his inheritance. **2.** *Post:* **s. une lettre chargée,** to steal the contents of a registered letter.

spondaïque [spɔ̃daik], *a. Pros:* spondaic.

spondée [spɔ̃de], *s.m. Pros:* spondee.

spondias [spɔ̃djas], *s.m. Bot:* spondias, *F:* hog plum.

spondylarthrite [spɔ̃dilartrit], *s.f. Med:* spondylarthritis; **s. ankylosante,** rheumatoid spondylitis, spondylitis deformans, Marie's disease.

spondyle [spɔ̃dil], *s.m.* **1.** *Anat: A:* spondyl, spondylus; vertebra. **2.** *Moll:* spondylus.

spondylite [spɔ̃dilit], *s.f. Med:* spondylitis; **s. tuberculeuse,** Pott's disease.

spondylolisthésis [spɔ̃dilɔlistezis], *s.m. Med:* spondylolisthesis.

spondylose [spɔ̃diloːz], *s.f. Med:* spondylosis; **s. rhizomélique,** spondylitis deformans.

spongiaires [spɔ̃ʒjɛːr], *s.m.pl.* Spongiae, Porifera.

spongiculture [spɔ̃ʒikyltyːr], *s.f.* cultivation of sponges.

spongieux, -ieuse [spɔ̃ʒjø, -jøːz], *a.* spongy; bibulous (paper); *Anat:* **os s.,** ethmoid bone.

spongiforme [spɔ̃ʒifɔrm], *a.* spongiform.

spongille [spɔ̃ʒiːj], *s.f.* spongilla, fresh-water sponge.

spongine [spɔ̃ʒin], *s.f. Bio-Ch:* spongin.

spongiole [spɔ̃ʒjɔl], *s.f. Bot:* spongiole, spongelet (of root).

spongioplasme [spɔ̃ʒjɔplasm], *s.m. Biol:* spongioplasm.

spongiosité [spɔ̃ʒjozite], *s.f.* sponginess.

spongoïde [spɔ̃gɔid], *a. Anat: Med:* spongoid, spungoid (tissue, bone, inflammation).

spontané [spɔ̃tane], *a.* spontaneous (movement, offer, etc.); self-sown (plant); **combustion spontanée,** spontaneous combustion; *I.C.E:* **allumage s.,** self-ignition; *Jur:* **aveu s.,** voluntary confession of guilt; **chambre des aveux spontanés,** room where prisoners are subjected to third degree questioning; *Biol:* **génération spontanée,** spontaneous generation, abiogenesis.

spontanéité [spɔ̃taneite], *s.f.* spontaneity, spontaneousness.

spontanément [spɔ̃tanemɑ̃], *adv.* spontaneously; **donner s. des renseignements,** to volunteer information.

spontanisme [spɔ̃tanism], *s.m.* (theory of) spontaneous generation.

sporadicité [spɔradisite], *s.f.* sporadic nature, sporadicalness (of disease, etc.).

sporadique [spɔradik], *a.* sporadic (disease, plant).

sporadiquement [spɔradikmɑ̃], *adv.* sporadically.

sporadosidérite [spɔradɔsiderit], *s.f. Miner:* sporadosiderite.

sporange [spɔrɑ̃ːʒ], *s.m. Bot:* sporangium, spore case.

sporangiole [spɔrɑ̃ʒjɔl], *s.m. Bot:* sporangiole.

sporangiophore [spɔrɑ̃ʒjɔfɔːr], *s.m. Bot:* sporangiophore.

spore [spɔːr], *s.f. Biol: Bot:* spore; **asque à huit spores,** eight-spored ascus; **s. d'un sporocarpe,** carpospore.

sporé [spɔre], *a.* having spores; spored.

sporée [spɔre], *s.f. Bot:* spurrey.

sporidie [spɔridi], *s.f. Biol: Bot:* sporidium.

sporifère [spɔrifɛːr], *a.* sporiferous.

sporo- [spɔrɔ], *pref.* sporo-.

sporoblaste [spɔrɔblast], *s.m. Prot:* sporoblast.

sporobolus [spɔrɔbɔlys], *s.m. Bot:* dropseed; (*genus*) Sporobolus.

sporocarpe [spɔrɔkarp], *s.m. Bot:* sporocarp.

sporocyste [spɔrɔsist], *s.m. Bot: Z:* sporocyst.

sporoducte [spɔrɔdykt], *s.m. Z:* sporoduct.

sporogone [spɔrɔgɔn], *s.m. Moss:* sporogonium.

sporogonie [spɔrɔgɔni], *s.f. Biol:* sporogony.

sporophore [spɔrɔfɔːr], *s.m. Bot:* sporophore.

sporophylle [spɔrɔfil], *s.m. Bot:* sporophyl(l).

sporophyte [spɔrɔfit], *s.m. Bot:* sporophyte.

sporotriche [spɔrɔtriʃ], *s.m. Fung:* sporothrix; (*genus*) Sporotrichum.

sporotrichose [spɔrɔtrikoːz], *s.f. Med: Vet:* sporotrichosis.

sporotrichosique [spɔrɔtrikozik], *a. Med: Vet:* sporotrichotic.

sporozoaire [spɔrɔzɔɛːr], *s.m. Prot:* sporozoan, sporozoon; *pl.* **sporozoaires,** Sporozoa.

sporozoïte [spɔrɔzɔit], *s.m. Prot:* sporozoite.

sport [spɔːr]. **1.** *s.m.* (*a*) sport (*usu.* not including hunting, fishing, or horse racing); games; **sports athlétiques,** athletics (and gymnastics); **sports d'équipe,** team games; **sports d'hiver,** winter sports; **s'adonner aux sports,** to go in for sport; *F:* **vous allez voir du s.,** now you're going to see things; something's going to happen now; (*b*) *Biol:* sport. **2.** *a.inv.* (*a*) **vêtements s., costume s.,** casual clothes, clothes for casual wear; **voiture s.,** sports car, sports model; (*b*) (*of pers.*) sporting.

sportif, -ive [spɔrtif, -iːv]. **1.** *a.* (*a*) sporting; (of) sport; devoted to sport, athletic; **les quotidiens sportifs,** the sporting dailies; **rédacteur s.,** (i) sporting editor; (ii) sports editor; **édition sportive,** sports edition (of paper); **réunion sportive,** athletic meeting; **ils n'ont pas l'esprit s.,** they've no sporting spirit; they're no sportsmen; they're bad losers; **être très s.,** to be a good loser; **la foule, sportive pour une fois, applaudit,** the crowd, sporting for once, applauded; (*b*) *Biol:* **variation sportive,** sport, *F:* freak (of nature). **2.** *s.* sportsman; games player; athlete; **je suis un vieux s.,** I went in for athletics, games, in my day.

sportivement [spɔrtivmɑ̃], *adv.* in a sporting spirit; sportively.

sportivité [spɔrtivite], *s.f.* sportsmanship; **il eut la s. de . . .,** he was sporting enough to . . ..

sport(s)man [spɔrt(s)man], *s.m.* **1.** *A:* = SPORTIF 2. **2.** *Lit:* patron of the turf, racegoer; *pl. sport(s)-men* [spɔrt(s)mɛn].

sportule [spɔrtyl], *s.f. Rom.Ant:* sportula.

sporulation [spɔrylasjɔ̃], *s.f. Bot:* sporulation, sporation.

sporule [spɔryl], *s.f. Bot:* sporule, spore.

sporulé [spɔryle], *a.* sporulated.

sporuler [spɔryle], *v.i. Biol:* to sporulate.

spot [spɔt], *s.m. T.V: Elcs: etc:* spot; blip (on radar screen); **s. explorateur,** scanning spot; **s. lumineux,** light spot (of recording apparatus, etc.); tip (of light pencil); **s. mobile,** flying spot.

spoutnik [sputnik], *s.m.* sputnik, artificial satellite.

sprat [sprat], *s.m. Ich:* sprat.

spring [spriŋ], *s.m. Nau:* spring towline.

springbok [spriŋbɔk], *s.m. Z:* springbok.

springer [spriŋœːr], *s.m. Ven: Z:* springer (spaniel)

sprint [sprint], *s.m. Sp:* sprint; **piquer un s.,** (i) to make a final sprint; (ii) to make a dash.

sprinter[1] [sprintœːr], *s.m. Sp:* sprinter.

sprinter[2] [sprinte], *v.i. Sp:* to sprint.

sprue [spry], *s.f. Med:* sprue; psilosis.

spume [spym], *s.f. Med: A:* (frothy) spume (at the mouth).

spumescent [spymɛs(s)ɑ̃], *a.* spumescent, foaming.

spumeux, -euse [spymø, -øːz], *a.* spumy, spumous, foamy, frothy (blood, saliva, etc.).

spumosité [spymozite], *s.f.* spumescence.

squale [skwal], *s.m. Ich:* dogfish (shark); *pl.* **squales,** Squali, sharks.

squalide [skwalid], *a. & s.m. Ich:* squaloid.

squalidés [skwalide], *s.m.pl. Ich:* Squalidae.

squalidien, -ienne [skwalidjɛ̃, -jɛn], *a. Ich:* squaloid.

squaloïdes [skwalɔid], *s.m.pl. Ich:* Squaloidea.

squamaire [skwamɛːr], *s.f. Bot:* squamaria.

squame [skwam], *s.f. Anat: Bot: etc:* squama; scale (of skin); exfoliation (of bone).

squamé [skwame], *a.* squamate.

squamelle [skwamɛl], *s.f. Bot:* squamella, squamule.

squamellifère [skwamɛlifɛːr], *a.* squamulose, squamelliferous.

squameux, -euse [skwamø, -øːz], *a. Anat: Med: etc:* squamous, scaly (skin, bone); *Bot:* squamose, squamous (bulb).

squamifère [skwamifɛːr], *a.* squamiferous (catkin, fish).

squamifolié [skwamifɔlje], *a. Bot:* squamifoliate.

squamiforme [skwamifɔrm], *a. Miner:* squamiform.

squamipennes [skwamipɛn], *s.m.pl. Ich:* Squamipennes.

squamosité [skwamozite], *s.f.* squamation, squamousness.

squamule [skwamyl], *s.f. Biol:* squamula.

square [skwaːr], *s.m.* (public) square (with garden).

squarreux, -euse [skwarø, -øːz], *a. Bot: Ent:* squarrose.

squatine [skwatin], *s.m. Ich:* squatina, angelfish.

squatinidés [skwatinide], *s.m.pl. Ich:* Squatinidae.

squatter [skwatɛːr], *s.m.* squatter.

squaw [skwo], *s.f.* (Indian) squaw.

squeeze [skwiːz], *s.m. Cards:* (*at bridge*) squeeze.

squeezer [skwize], *v.tr. Cards:* (*at bridge*) to squeeze.

squelette [skəlɛt], *s.m.* (*a*) skeleton (of animal, leaf); **c'est un vrai s.,** he's a living skeleton; (*b*) carcass, skeleton, framework (of ship, etc.); skeleton, outline (of play, novel, etc.).

squeletté [skəlete], *a. Const:* (steel, etc.) framed.

squelettique [skəletik], *a.* (*a*) skeletal (arch, muscles); (*b*) skeleton-like; **maigreur s.,** extreme thinness; (*c*) *Geol:* **sol s.,** skeletal soil.

squelettisation [skəletizasjɔ̃], *s.f.* skeletonizing (of leaf).

squelettiser [skəletize], *v.tr.* to skeletonize (a leaf).

squelettogène [skəletɔʒɛn], *a. Biol:* skeletogenous.

squilidés [skilide], *s.m.pl. Crust:* Squillidae.

squille [skiːj], *s.f.* **1.** *Bot:* squill. **2.** *Crust:* squill(fish); squilla, mantis shrimp.

squine [skin], *s.f. Bot: Pharm:* China root.

squirr(h)e [skiːr], *s.m. Med:* scirrhus.

squirr(h)eux, -euse [skirø, -øːz], *a. Med:* scirrhous, scirrhoid.

squirrosité [skirozite], *s.f. Med:* scirrhosity.

st [st], *int.* psst! here! you there!

stabat [stabat], *s.m. Ecc.Mus:* Stabat Mater.

Stabies [stabi], *Pr.n.m. A.Geog:* Stabiae.

stabilisant [stabilizɑ̃], *s.m. Ch:* stabilizer, stabilizing agent.

stabilisateur, -trice [stabilizatœːr, -tris]. **1.** *a.* stabilizing; *attrib:* stabilizer; **appareil s.,** stabilizing device, stabilizer gear; **gyroscope s.,** stabilizing gyro(scope); *Av:* **plan s.,** stabilizer fin; *Nau:* **aileron s. de roulis,** roll-damping fin; *El:* **circuit s.,** stabilizer circuit; *Elcs:* **tube s.,** stabilizer tube; *Pol.Ec:* **exercer une action stabilisatrice sur les prix,** to have, exert, a stabilizing action on prices. **2.** *s.m.* (*a*) *Aer: Mec.E: etc:* stabilizer; *Av:* tail-plane, stabilizer; *Av:* **s. fixe,** fixed horizontal tail-plane; **s. mobile,** trimming tail-plane; *Av: Ball: Nau:* **s. gyroscopique,** gyro(scopic) stabilizer; *Nau:* **s. à aileron,** fin stabilizer; **s. de roulis,** roll damper; **s. de cap,** heading hold; *El.E:* **s. de fréquence,** frequency monitor; **s. de tension,** voltage stabilizer, equalizer; (*b*) *Ch:* stabilizer.

stabilisation [stabilizasjɔ̃], *s.f.* **1.** *Mec: Ch: etc:* stabilization, stabilizing (of mechanical system, of ship, of aircraft, of projectile, of chemical preparation, of foodstuff by chemical treatment, etc.); *Pol.Ec:* stabilization (of currency); stabilization, pegging (of prices, market, etc.); *Mil:* stabilization (of the front); standstill (in operations); *Biol:* balancing; *Mec.E:* **s. gyroscopique,** gyro(scopic) stabilization; **s. par (gradient de) gravité,** gravity(-gradient) stabilization; **s. par rotation,** spin stabilization; *El:* **s. de la tension,** voltage stabilization; *Pol.Ec:* **fonds de s.,** stabilization fund, equalization fund; *Civ.E:* **s. du sol,** soil stabilization, solidification. **2.** *Metalw:* annealing (of finished piece after hammering, etc.).

stabilisé [stabilize], *a.* **1.** *Mec: Ch: Pol.Ec: etc:* stabilized; *Biol:* balanced; *Mec.E:* **s. par gyroscope,** gyro-stabilized; **s. par (gradient de) gravité,** gravity-(gradient) stabilized; **s. par rotation,** spin-stabilized; *Av: Ball: etc:* **plate-forme stabilisée,** stabilized, inertial, platform; *Elcs:* **antenne stabilisée,** stabilized antenna. **2.** *Metalw:* annealed.

stabiliser [stabilize], *v.tr.* **1.** *Mec: Ch: etc:* to stabilize (mechanical system, ship, aircraft, projectile, chemical preparation, foodstuff by chemical treatment, etc.); *Pol.Ec:* to stabilize (currency, prices, market, employment, etc.); **les prix se sont stabilisés,** prices have stabilized; *Mec.E:* **s. la marche d'une machine,** to steady the running of a machine; *Aut:* **s. la direction,** to balance the steering gear. **2.** *Metalw:* to anneal (finished piece after hammering, etc.).

stabilité [stabilite], *s.f.* **1.** *Mec: Ch: etc:* stability (of mechanical system, aircraft, projectile, chemical preparation, etc.); stability, stiffness (of ship); firmness, stability (of building, etc.); stability, steadiness (of prices, political institutions, etc.); *Av: Nau:* **s. dynamique, statique,** dynamic, static, stability; *Av:* **s. automatique,** automatic stability; **s. inhérente, s. propre,** inherent stability; **s. latérale,** lateral, rolling, transversal, stability; **s. longitudinale,** longitudinal, spiral, stability; **s. de route, s. par rapport à l'axe de lacet,** directional stability; *Nau:* **s. de route,** stability of motion; **s. initiale,** initial stability; **s. négative,** negative stability; **s. sous voiles,** sail-carrying power; *Ch: Ph:* **s. chimique,** chemical stability; **s. nucléaire,** nuclear stability; **s. physique, structurale,** physical, structural, stability; **s. thermique,** thermal stability; **la s. politique engendre souvent l'immobilisme,** political stability often engenders stagnation; **la s.**

économique est une assurance contre la récession, economic stability is a security against recession. **2.** permanence (of a conquest, of the law); durability; **s. d'emploi,** security of tenure.

stable [stabl̩], *a.* **1.** stable, firm, steady; balanced; **son caractère n'est pas s.,** he hasn't a very firm, stable, character; *Ch:* **corps s.,** stable substance; *Mec:* **équilibre s.,** stable equilibrium; **peu s.,** unstable. **2.** durable, permanent, stable; **paix s.,** enduring peace; lasting peace.

stablement [stabləmɑ̃], *adv.* stably.

stabulation [stabylasjɔ̃], *s.f.* **1.** (*a*) keeping (of cattle) in sheds; stalling (of cattle); stabling (of horses); **mettre les bêtes en s.,** to bring in the cattle for the winter; (*b*) *Pisc: Ost:* storing in tanks. **2.** *Med:* rest cure.

stabuler [stabyle], *v.tr.* (*a*) to stall (cattle); to bring (cattle) in for the winter; to stable (horses); (*b*) to store (fish, oysters) in tanks.

staccato [stakato], *adv. & s.m. Mus:* staccato.

Stace [stas], *Pr.n.m. Lt.Lit:* Statius.

stachyose [stakjoːz], *s.m. Ch:* stachyose.

stachys [stakis], *s.m. Bot:* stachys.

stacté [stakte], *s.m. Ant:* stacte (spice).

stade [stad], *s.m.* **1.** (*a*) *Gr.Ant:* stadium; (*b* stadium, sports ground; **s. olympique,** olympic stadium. **2.** (*a*) stage (of evolution, development, disease, etc.); **s. clef,** crucial, key, step; (*b*) *Ent:* instar (of caterpillars, etc.); **deuxième s. (de mue),** second instar.

stadia [stadja], *s.m. Surv:* stadia, stadium.

stadimètre [stadimɛtr̥], *s.m. Surv:* stadimeter.

stadiomètre [stadjɔmɛtr̥], *s.m. Surv:* stadiometer.

staff [staf], *s.m. Const:* (*building material*) staff.

staffélite [stafelit], *s.f. Miner:* staffelite.

staffer [stafe], *v.tr. Const:* to construct in staff.

staffeur [stafœːr], *s.m. Const:* mason specializing in decorative staff work.

stage [staːʒ], *s.m.* period of probation, instruction, training; course of instruction; **faire son s.,** (*of law student*) to keep one's terms; (*of barrister*) = to eat one's dinners; (*of teacher*) to do one's teaching practice; (*of nurse*) to do one's probationary period; (*of trainee*) to attend a (training) course; *Jur:* **conférence du s.,** barrister's training course; *Mil:* **faire un s. dans l'armée française,** to serve an attachment with, to be attached (temporarily) to, the French army.

stagiaire [staʒjɛːr]. **1.** *a.* training (period); (period) of instruction, of probation; **officier s.,** (i) officer attached for instruction; (ii) officer on probation; **interprète s.,** trainee interpreter; **avocat s.,** advocate going through his three years' probation. **2.** *s.m. & f.* trainee; (*esp. nurse*) probationer.

Stagire [staʒiːr], *Pr.n. A.Geog:* Stagira, Stagirus.

Stagirite (le) [ləstaʒirit], *s.m.* the Stagirite (Aristotle).

stagnant [stagnɑ̃], *a.* stagnant (water, business, etc.); standing (water); *Lit:* **les mares stagnantes de la littérature,** literary backwaters.

stagnation [stagnasjɔ̃], *s.f.* stagnation; stagnancy (of water); (*of trade, etc.*) **en s.,** at a standstill, stagnant; *Nau:* **s. du compas,** slowness, torpidity, of the compass.

stagner [stagne], *v.i.* (*of water, trade*) to stagnate.

stagnicole [stagnikɔl], *a. Nat.Hist:* stagnicolous.

stakhanovisme [stakanɔvism], *s.m.* stakhanovism.

stakhanoviste [stakanɔvist], *a. & s.m. & f.* stakhanovite.

stalactifère [stalaktifɛːr], *a.* stalactited (grotto, etc.).

stalactite [stalaktit], *s.f. Geol:* stalactite.

stalactitique [stalaktitik], *a. Geol:* stalactitic.

stalagmite [stalagmit], *s.f. Geol:* stalagmite.

stalagmitique [stalagmitik], *a. Geol:* stalagmitic.

stalagmomètre [stalagmɔmɛtr̥], *s.m. Pharm: etc:* stactometer, stalagmometer.

stalagmométrie [stalagmɔmetri], *s.f. Pharm: etc:* stalagmometry.

stalagmométrique [stalagmɔmetrik], *a. Pharm: etc:* stalagmometric.

Staline [stalin], *Pr.n.m.* Stalin.

stalinien, -ienne [stalinjɛ̃, -jɛn], *a. & s.* Stalinist.

stalinisé [stalinize], *a.* Stalinized.

stalinisme [stalinism], *s.m.* Stalinism.

stalle [stal], *s.f.* **1.** stall (in cathedral); (numbered) seat (in the theatre); **stalles d'orchestre,** orchestra stalls. **2.** stall, box (in stable).

Stamboul [stɑ̃bul]. **1.** *Pr.n. Geog: A:* Stambul; (old) Constantinople. **2.** *s.m. Tex:* thick woollen cloth (made in the Levant).

staminaire [staminɛːr], **staminal, -aux** [staminal, -o], *a. Bot:* staminal.

staminé [stamine], *a. Bot:* staminate, stamened.

stamineux, -euse [staminø, -øːz], *a. Bot:* stamineous, stamineal.

staminifère [staminifɛːr], *a. Bot:* staminiferous.

staminiforme [staminifɔrm], *a.* shaped like a stamen.

staminode [staminɔd], *s.m. Bot:* staminode, staminodium.

stamino-pistillé [staminɔpistile], *a. Bot:* hermaphrodite, bisexual; *pl. stamino-pistillé(e)s.*

stamnos [stamnɔs], *s.m. Gr.Ant:* stamnos.

stampe [stɑ̃ːp], *s.f. Min:* country rock (between lodes).

stampien, -ienne [stɑ̃pjɛ̃, -jɛn], *a. & s.m. Geol:* Stampian.

stance [stɑ̃ːs], *s.f. Pros:* stanza.

Stanco [stɑ̃ko], *Pr.n. Geog:* Stanchio.

stand [stɑ̃ːd], *s.m.* **1.** stand (on racecourse); stand, stall (at exhibition, etc.); **tenir un s.,** to have (i) a stand (at exhibition), (ii) a stall (at fête); *Rac: Aut:* **les stands de ravitaillement,** the pits. **2. s. (de tir),** (i) shooting stand, shooting gallery; (ii) rifle range. **3.** stand, rest (for typewriter, etc.).

standard [stɑ̃daːr], *s.m.* **1.** (*a*) standard; (*b*) **s. de vie,** standard of living. **2.** *Tp:* (house, office) switchboard. **3.** *attrib.* standard.

standardisation [stɑ̃dardizasjɔ̃], *s.f. Ind: etc:* standardization.

standardiser [stɑ̃dardize], *v.tr. Ind: etc:* to standardize.

standardiste [stɑ̃dardist], *s.m. & f. Tp:* switchboard operator.

standing [stɑ̃diŋ], *s.m. F:* high standard of living; standing; **immeuble, appartements, de grand s.,** prestige, luxury, flats; **quartier de grand s.,** select district; desirable residential district; **s. de vie,** status.

standolie [stɑ̃dɔli], *s.f. Paint:* stand oil, bodied oil.

stangue [stɑ̃ːg], *s.f. Her:* shank (of anchor).

stanhope [stanɔp]. **1.** *s.m. A: Veh:* stanhope; high buggy. **2.** *s.f. Typ:* stanhope press.

Stanislas [stanislɑːs], *Pr.n.m.* Stanislaus, Stanislas.

stannage [stan(n)aːʒ], *s.m. Tex:* mordanting (with a stannic mordant).

stannate [stan(n)at], *s.m. Ch:* stannate.

stanneux, -euse [stan(n)ø, -øːz], *a.* (*a*) *Ch:* stannous (oxide); (*b*) **une odeur stanneuse,** a tinny smell.

stannichlorure [stan(n)iklɔryːr], *s.m. Ch:* stannic chloride.

stannifère [stan(n)ifɛːr]. **1.** *a.* stanniferous, tin-bearing; **gîte s.,** tin deposit. **2.** *s.f.pl. Fin: O:* **stannifères,** tin shares.

stannine [stan(n)in], *s.f. Miner:* stannite.

stannique [stan(n)ik], *a. Ch:* stannic (acid).

stannite [stan(n)it], *s.f. Miner:* stannite.

stannochlorure [stan(n)ɔklɔryːr], *s.m. Ch:* stannous chloride.

stannolite [stan(n)ɔlit], *s.f. Miner:* cassiterite, tinstone.

stapéal [stapeal], *s.m. Anat:* stapes, stirrup bone.

stapédien [stapedjɛ̃], *Anat:* **1.** *a.m.* stapedial. **2.** *s.m.* stapedius (muscle) (of the inner ear).

stapélie [stapeli], *s.f. Bot:* stapelia.

staphisaigre [stafizɛgr̥], *s.f. Bot:* staphisaigra, *F:* lousewort.

staphylier [stafilje], *s.m. Bot:* **s. pinné,** bead tree.

staphylin[1] [stafilɛ̃], *s.m. Ent:* staphylinid, cocktail (beetle), rove beetle, *F:* devil's coach horse.

staphylin[2], *a. Anat:* staphyline.

staphylinidés [stafilinide], *s.m.pl. Ent:* Staphylinidae.

staphylinoïdes [stafilinɔid], *s.m.pl. Ent:* Staphylinoidea.

staphylococcie [stafilɔkɔksi], *s.f. Med:* staphylococcia.

staphylococcique [stafilɔkɔksik], *a. Med:* staphylococcic.

staphylocoque [stafilɔkɔk], *s.m. Bac:* staphylococcus.

staphylomateux, -euse [stafilɔmatø, -øːz], *a. Med:* staphylomatous.

staphylome [stafiloːm], *s.m. Med:* staphyloma.

staphyloplastie [stafilɔplasti], *s.f. Surg:* staphyloplasty.

staphylorraphie [stafilɔrafi], *s.f. Surg:* staphylorr(h)aphy.

staphylotomie [stafilɔtɔmi], *s.f. Surg:* staphylotomy.

stappe [stap], *s.m. Min:* pillar (left to support roof).

star [staːr], *s.f. Cin: F:* star.

starie [stari], *s.f. Jur: Nau:* **jours de s.,** lay days.

starique [starik], *s.m. Orn:* parrakeet auklet.

starlette [starlɛt], *s.f. Cin: F:* starlet.

staroste [starɔst], *s.m. Hist:* (*in Russia, Poland*) starosta.

starostie [starɔsti], *s.f. Hist:* starosty (in Poland).

starter [startɛːr, -œːr], *s.m.* **1.** *Rac:* starter (who gives the signal). **2.** *Aut:* choke.

starting-block [startiŋblɔk], *s.m. Sp: F:* starting block; *pl. starting-blocks.*

starting-gate [startiŋgɛt], *s.m. Rac:* starting gate; *pl. starting-gates.*

stase [stɑːz], *s.f. Med:* stasis.

stater, statère [statɛːr], *s.m. Num:* stater.

stathouder [statudɛːr], *s.m. Hist:* stad(t)holder.

stathoudérat [statudera], *s.m. Hist:* stad(t)holderate, stad(t)holdership.

statice [statis], *s.m. Bot:* statice, sea lavender, sea thrift, sea pink.

statif [statif], *s.m.* stand (of microscope).

station [stasjɔ̃], *s.f.* **1.** (*a*) standing; stationary position; **en s. derrière un arbre,** on the lookout behind a tree; *Rail:* **wagons en s. sur une voie de garage,** trucks standing in a siding; (*b*) position; **s. debout,** standing position; upright posture; **cela me fatigue de faire des stations debout,** standing tires me; **s. verticale,** vertical position; **mettre un théodolite en s., faire la mise en s. d'un théodolite,** to set up a theodolite; (*c*) attitude (of horse); **s. libre,** free attitude. **2.** (*a*) break (in journey); halt, stop; **faire une s. à . . .,** to halt, stop, at . . .; **faire des stations devant toutes les vitrines,** to stop at every shop window; (*b*) *Ecc:* **les quatorze stations,** the (fourteen) stations of the Cross. **3.** (*a*) *Rail:* halt; small station; **s. de métro,** underground, tube, station; **s. d'autobus,** bus stop; **s. de taxis,** taxi rank, cab rank; (*b*) **s. d'hiver, de ski,** winter resort, ski resort; **s. d'été,** summer resort; **s. balnéaire,** seaside resort; **s. climatique,** health resort; **s. thermale,** spa; (*c*) **s. agronomique,** agricultural research establishment; (*d*) **s. radio,** radio station; *Av:* ground station; **s. de radiodiffusion,** broadcasting station; **s. de télévision,** television broadcast station; **s. d'émission, s. émettrice,** sending, transmitting, station; **s. réceptrice,** receiving station; **s. à grande puissance,** super-power station; **s. asservie,** slave station; **s. mère,** parent, key, station; **s. relais,** relay station, repeater station, radio link; **s. de bord,** ship station; **s. côtière,** coast station; (*e*) *El:* **s. centrale,** power station; **s. auxiliaire,** booster station; *Hyd.E:* **s. de pompage,** pumping station; (*f*) *Mil: etc:* post, station; *Navy:* cruising ground; station; **s. de garde-côte,** coastguard station; **s. de sauvetage,** lifeboat station; **navire en s.,** ship on station; (*g*) *Ecc: O:* **donner une s. de carême à un prédicateur,** to assign a church to a (special) preacher for the Lenten addresses.

stationnaire [stasjɔnɛːr]. **1.** *a.* stationary; (*a*) **rester s.,** to remain stationary; to stand still; **baromètre s.,** steady barometer; *Av: etc:* **vol s.,** hovering (flight); **orbite s.,** synchronous orbit; (*b*) **chaudière s.,** fixed boiler, stationary boiler; (*c*) *Med:* **maladie s.,** stationary disease; **son état est s.,** his condition remains unchanged. **2.** *s.m. Navy:* guardship, station ship; **le dragueur Narvik, s. de Dakar,** the minesweeper *Narvik,* station ship at Dakar.

stationnale [stasjɔnal], *a.f. Ecc:* stational (church, mass).

stationnement [stasjɔnmɑ̃], *s.m.* **1.** (*a*) stopping, parking (of cars, etc.); *Geol:* **s. d'un glacier,** halt of a glacier; **auto en s.,** stationary car, parked car; **s. interdit,** no parking; no waiting; **route à s. interdit,** clearway; **s. en oblique, en épi, en talon,** angle parking; **s. en batterie,** parking at right angles to the kerb; **s. en double file,** double parking; **compteur de s.,** parking meter; (*b*) *Mil:* stationing, quartering; halt (for a considerable time). **2.** (*a*) **s. (de taxis),** taxi rank, cab rank; (*b*) **(parc de) s.,** car park; (*c*) *Av:* **aire, piste, parc, de s.,** (airfield) apron; (*d*) *Mil:* quarters.

stationner [stasjɔne], *v.i.* **1.** to stop; to take up one's position; to halt. **2.** (*of car, etc.*) to park (in street, etc.); *P.N:* **défense de s.,** no parking; no waiting. **3.** (*a*) (*of troops*) to be stationed; (*b*) (*of ships*) to be on station; **flotte stationnée à l'étranger,** fleet stationed abroad.

station-service [stasjɔ̃sɛrvis], *s.f. Aut:* service station (for petrol, etc.); *pl. stations-service.*

statique [statik]. **1.** *a.* static (electricity, etc.); statical (fan); *Av:* **essais statiques,** static testing (of aircraft).

statiquement [statikmɑ̃], *adv.* statically.

statisticien, -ienne [statistisjɛ̃, -jɛn], *s.* statistician.

statistique [statistik]. **1.** *a.* statistical. **2.** *s.f.* (*a*) statistics; **commission de s.,** statistical commission; **spécialiste en matière de statistique(s),** statistical expert; *Cust:* **droit de s.,** small duty on all goods cleared either inwards or outwards (to cover the cost of trade statistics); (*b*) *pl.* statistical tables; **statistiques pour 1971,** statistics, figures, for 1971.

statistiquement [statistikmɑ̃], *adv.* statistically.

statocyste [statɔsist], *s.m. Coel:* statocyst.

stator [statɔːr], *s.m. Mch: El:* stator (of turbine, of electric motor); field winding.

statoréacteur [statɔreaktœːr], *s.m. Av:* ramjet (engine).

statoscope [statɔskɔp], *s.m. Av:* statoscope.

statuaire [statɥɛːr]. **1.** *a.* statuary (art, marble, etc.). **2.** *s.m. & f.* sculptor, sculptress. **3.** *s.f.* (art of) statuary.

statue [staty], *s.f.* statue; image; *Arch:* **s. persique,** caryatid; telamon; **droit comme une s.,** as stiff as a statue; frozen like a statue.

statue-menhir [statymɛniːr], *s.f. Prehist:* inscribed menhir; *pl. statues-menhirs.*

statuer [statɥe], *v.tr.* **1.** to decree, enact, ordain, rule; **s. une enquête,** to order an enquiry; **s. que** + *ind.*, to rule, ordain, that . . . . **2.** *abs.* **s. sur une affaire,** to pronounce judgment in, give a decision on, deal with, decide, a matter; **s. sur un litige,** to settle a dispute; **s. sommairement** to make a ruling by summary process.

statuette [statɥɛt], *s.f.* statuette.

statufier [statyfje], *v.tr.* (*p.d. & pr.sub.* **n. statufiions, v. statufiiez**) *F:* to erect a statue to (s.o.); **personnage statufié,** person commemorated by a statue.

statu quo [statyk(w)o], *s.m.* status (in) quo; **in s. q.,** in statu quo.

stature [statyːr], *s.f.* stature, height (*esp.* of person); **il est de grande s.,** he is very tall; **un lion d'immense s.,** a huge lion.

statut [staty], *s.m.* **1.** statute, ordinance, article (of society, company, etc.); rule, regulation, by(e)-law; **les statuts de l'Académie française,** the statutes of the French Academy; **statuts d'une société,** (memorandum and) articles (of association) of a company; **s. local,** local by(e)-law; **le S. international des marins,** the International Seamen's Code. **2.** *Dipl: etc:* status (of country, port, etc.); constitution; **le S. de Tanger,** the status of Tangiers; **s. personnel,** personal status; **le s. économique de la France,** the economic constitution of France.

statutaire [statytɛːr], *a.* statutory, statutable; *Fin:* **réserve s.,** reserve provided by the articles; **gérant s.,** manager appointed according to the articles; **actions statutaires,** qualifying shares.

statutairement [statytɛrmɑ̃], *adv. Fin: etc:* in accordance with the articles; under the articles.

staurolite [stɔrɔlit], *s.f. Miner:* staurolite.

stauroscope [stɔrɔskɔp], *s.m. Opt:* stauroscope.

staurotide [stɔrɔtid], *s.f. Miner:* staurolite, staurotide.

stayer [stɛjœːr], *s.m. Sp:* long-distance runner, cyclist; stayer.

stéarate [stearat], *s.m. Ch:* stearate.

stéarine [stearin], *s.f. Ch:* stearin.

stéarinerie [stearinri], *s.f.* stearin factory.

stéarinier [stearinje], *s.m.* stearin manufacturer, worker in a stearin factory.

stéarique [stearik], *a.* **1.** *Ch:* stearic (acid). **2.** *Ind:* **bougie s.,** stearin candle.

stéaryle [stearil], *s.m. Ch:* stearyl.

stéaschiste [steaʃist], *s.m.*, **stéatite** [steatit], *s.f. Miner:* steatite, soapstone.

stéatiteux, -euse [steatitø, -øːz], *a.* steatitic.

stéatocèle [steatɔsɛl], *s.f. Med:* steatocele.

stéatome [steatoːm], *s.m. Med:* steatoma.

stéatopyge [steatɔpiːʒ], *a. Anthr:* steatopygous.

stéatopygie [steatɔpiʒi], *s.f. Anthr:* steatopygia, steatopygy.

stéatornithidés [steatɔrnitide], *s.m.pl. Orn:* Steatornithidae.

stéatose [steatoːz], *s.f. Med:* steatosis, fatty degeneration.

steeple-chase [stipləʧɛːs], *s.m. F:* **steeple** [stipl], *s.m. Rac:* steeplechase; *pl. steeple-chases.*

stégocéphales [stegɔsefal], *s.m.pl. Paleont:* Stegocephalia.

stégocéphalien, -ienne [stegɔsefaljɛ̃, -jɛn], *a. & s. Paleont:* stegocephalian.

stégodon [stegɔdɔ̃], *s.m. Paleont:* stegodon.

stégomyie [stegɔmii], *s.f. Ent:* yellow-fever mosquito.

stégosaure [stegɔsɔːr], **stegosaurus** [stegɔsɔrys], *s.m. Paleont:* stegosaur; (*genus*) Stegosaurus.

steinbock [stɛ̃bɔk], *s.m. Z:* steinbok, steenbok.

Steinkerque [stɛ̃kɛrk]. **1.** *Pr.n. Hist:* Steinkirk. **2.** *s.f. Cost: A:* (*also* **cravate à la S.**) steenkirk.

stèle [stɛl], *s.f.* **1.** stele (bearing inscription); *Moslem Rel:* **s. turbanée,** turban stone. **2.** *Bot:* stele.

stellage [stelaːʒ, stɛ-], *s.m. Fin:* double option, put and call.

stellaire [stelɛːr, stɛ-]. **1.** *a.* stellar (light, etc.). **2.** *s.f. Bot:* stellaria; starwort; **s. holostée,** stitchwort.

stellère [stelɛːr, stɛ-], *s.m. or f. Z:* Steller's sea cow.

stellérides [stelerid, stɛ-], *s.m.pl. Echin:* Stelleroidea, Stelliformia.

stelliforme [stelifɔrm, stɛ-], *a.* stelliform, star-shaped.

stellinervé [stelinɛrve, stɛ-], *a. Bot:* star-ribbed (leaf).

stellion [steljɔ̃, stɛ-], *s.m. Rept:* stellion.

stellionat [steljɔna, stɛ-], *s.m. Jur:* fraudulent misrepresentation as to mortgages on a property; stellionate.

stellionataire [steljɔnatɛːr, stɛ-], *a. & s.m. & f.* (person) guilty of stellionate.

stellite [stelit, stɛ-], *s.f. R.t.m: Metall:* Stellite.

stelliter [stelite, stɛ-], *v.tr. Metall:* to coat with Stellite.

stellulé [stelyle, stɛ-], *a.* stellular, stellulate.

stembogen [stɛmbogen], *s.m. Ski:* stembogen; stem(m)turn.

stem(m) [stɛm], *s.m. Ski:* stem(ming).

stemmate [stɛmat], *s.m. Z:* stemma; simple eye.

stencil [stɛnsil], *s.m.* stencil.

stenciliser [stɛnsilize], *v.tr.* to stencil.

stenciliste [stɛnsilist], *s.m. & f.* stencil(l)er.

sténo [steno], *F:* **1.** *s.f.* stenography, shorthand writing; **s. mécanique,** typed shorthand stenotypy. **2.** *s.m. & f.* stenographer; shorthand writer, shorthand reporter.

sténocardie [stenɔkardi], *s.f. Med:* stenocardia.

sténodactylo [stenɔdaktilo], *s.m. & f.*, **sténodactylographe** [stenɔdaktilɔgraf], *s.m. & f.* shorthand typist.

sténodactylo(graphie) [stenɔdaktilɔ(grafi)], *s.f.* shorthand typing.

sténoderme [stenɔdɛrm], *s.m. Z:* stenoderm.

sténogramme [stenɔgram], *s.m.* **1.** *Shorthand:* outline (used as a sign); logograph, logogram; short form. **2. s. des débats,** verbatim report of proceedings.

sténographe [stenɔgraf], *s.m. & f.* stenographer; shorthand writer, shorthand reporter.

sténographie [stenɔgrafi], *s.f.* stenography; shorthand (writing).

sténographier [stenɔgrafje], *v.tr.* (*pr.sub. & p.d.* **n. sténographiions, v. sténographiiez**) to write, take down, (speech, etc.) in shorthand.

sténographique [stenɔgrafik], *a.* stenographic, shorthand (writing, etc.).

sténographiquement [stenɔgrafikmɑ̃], *adv.* stenographically.

sténohalin [stenɔalɛ̃], *a. Biol:* stenohaline.

sténohalinité [stenɔalinite], *s.f. Biol:* stenohaline conditions, habits.

sténopé [stenɔpe], *s.m. Phot:* pinhole.

sténopéique [stenɔpeik], *a. Opt:* stenopeic (slit, etc.).

sténopéphotographie [stenɔpefɔtɔgrafi], *s.f.* pinhole photography.

sténophage [stenɔfaːʒ], *a. Ent:* stenophagous (caterpillar, insect).

sténophylle [stenɔfil], *a. Bot:* stenophyllous, narrow-leaved (plant).

sténosage [stenozaːʒ], *s.m. Text: Paperm:* hardening of cellulose fibres (by immersion in formol).

sténoscope [stenɔskɔp], *s.m. Phot:* pinhole camera.

sténose [stenoːz], *s.f. Med:* stenosis.

sténotherme [stenɔtɛrm], *a. Biol:* stenothermal, stenothermic.

sténothermie [stenɔtɛrmi], *s.f. Biol:* stenothermy.

sténotyper [stenɔtipe], *v.tr.* to stenotype, to take down (speech, etc.) on a shorthand typewriter.

sténotyper [stenɔtipe], *v.tr.* to stenotype, to use a shorthand typewriter.

sténotypie [stenɔtipi], *s.f.* stenotypy; typed shorthand.

sténotypiste [stenɔtipist], *s.m. or f.* stenotypist.

Stentor [stɑ̃tɔːr]. **1.** *Pr.n.m. Gr.Lit:* Stentor; **voix de S.,** stentorian voice. **2.** *s.m.* (*a*) *Prot:* stentor; (*b*) *Z:* stentor (monkey); howler.

stéphanien, -ienne [stefanjɛ̃, -jɛn], *a. & s.m. Geol:* Stephanian.

stéphanion [stefanjɔ̃], *s.m. Anthr:* stephanion.

stéphanite [stefanit], *s.f. Miner:* stephanite, black silver.

stéphanois, -oise [stefanwa, -waːz], *a. & s. Geog:* (native, inhabitant) of Saint-Étienne.

steppe [stɛp], *s.f. Geog:* steppe; **s. tropicale désertique,** tropical desert steppe.

stepper[1] [stepe], *v.i.* (*of horse*) to step well; to step high.

stepper[2], **steppeur** [stɛpœːr], *s.m.* (*of horse*) high-stepper.

steppique [stepik], *a. Geog:* **paysage s.,** steppe-like country; **population s.,** people of the steppes.

stéradian [steradjɑ̃], *s.m. Meas: Geom:* steradian.

stérage [steraːʒ], *s.m.* measuring, measurement (of firewood).

stercoraire [stɛrkɔrɛːr]. **1.** *Med: a.* stercoraceous; stercoral (ulcer, fistula). **2.** *s.m.* (*a*) *Ent:* dung beetle; dor; (*b*) *Orn:* skua; **s. parasite,** Arctic skua; **s. cataracte,** great skua.

stercoral, -aux [stɛrkɔral, -o], *a.* stercoral (matter, etc.).

stercorariidés [stɛrkɔrariide], *s.m.pl. Orn:* Stercorariidae, the skuas.

stercorite [stɛrkɔrit], *s.f. Miner:* stercorite.

sterculiacées [stɛrkyljase], *s.f.pl. Bot:* Sterculiaceae.

stère [stɛːr], *s.m. Meas:* stere, cubic metre (of firewood); **bois de s.,** cord wood.

stéréo- [stereɔ], *pref.* stereo-.

stéréo [stereo], *a.inv. & s. F:* **1.** *a.* stereo, stereophonic. **2.** *s.f.* stereo, stereophony.

stéréoautographe [stereɔotɔgraf], *s.m. Surv:* stereoautograph.

stéréobate [stereɔbat], *s.m. Arch:* stereobate.

stéréochimie [stereɔʃimi], *s.f.* stereochemistry.

stéréochromie [stereɔkrɔmi], *s.f.* stereochromy.

stéréocomparateur [stereɔkɔ̃paratœːr], *s.m. Astr: Phot:* stereocomparator, stereocomparagraph, stereoscopic plotter.

stéréognosie [stereɔgnozi], *s.f. Physiol:* stereognosis.

stéréogramme [stereɔgram], *s.m. Opt: Phot:* stereogram, stereograph; stereoscopic image or slide; (block) diagram.

stéréographe [stereɔgraf], *s.m. Opt: Phot:* stereograph (instrument).

stéréographie [stereɔgrafi], *s.f. Geom:* stereography.

stéréographique [stereɔgrafik], *a.* stereographic(al).

stéréographiquement [stereɔgrafikmɑ̃], *adv.* stereographically.

stéréomètre [stereɔmɛtr], *s.m.* stereometer (to measure capacity of a vessel, etc.).

stéréométrie [stereɔmetri], *s.f.* stereometry.

stéréométrique [stereɔmetrik], *a.* stereometric.

stéréon [stereɔ̃], *s.m. Fung:* **s. pourpre,** stereum purpureum, silver leaf.

stéréophonie [stereɔfɔni], *s.f.* stereophony.

stéréophonique [stereɔfɔnik], *a.* stereophonic.

stéréophotographie [stereɔfɔtɔgrafi], *s.f.* stereophotography.

stéréoplasme [stereɔplasm], *s.m.* stereoplasm.

stéréorama [stereɔrama], *s.m.* relief map.

stéréoscope [stereɔskɔp], *s.m. Opt:* stereoscope.

stéréoscopique [stereɔskɔpik], *a.* stereoscopic (effect, telescope).

stéréoscopiquement [stereɔskɔpikmɑ̃], *adv.* stereoscopically.

stéréostatique [stereɔstatik], *s.f.* stereostatics.

stéréotélémètre [stereɔtelemɛtr], *s.m.* stereoscopic telemeter.

stéréotomie [stereɔtɔmi], *s.f. Geom: Arch:* stereotomy.

stéréotomique [stereɔtɔmik], *a.* stereotomic(al).

stéréotypage [stereɔtipaːʒ], *s.m. Typ:* stereotyping; stereotype printing.

stéréotype [stereɔtip]. *Typ:* **1.** *a.* stereotype (printing); stereotyped (edition). **2.** *s.m.* stereotype plate.

stéréotyper [stereɔtipe], *v.tr. Typ:* to stereotype; to print from stereotyped plates; **expression stéréotypée,** stereotyped phrase, hackneyed phrase; **sourire stéréotypé,** fixed smile.

stéréotypeur [stereɔtipœːr], *s.m. Typ:* stereotyper, stereotypist.

stéréotypie [stereɔtipi], *s.f.* **1.** *Typ:* stereotypy. **2.** stereotype foundry. **3.** *Med: Psy:* stereotypy.

stérer [stere], *v.tr.* (**je stère, n. stérons; je stérerai**) to measure (wood) by the stere.

stéride [sterid], *s.m. Ch:* sterid, steroid.

stérile [steril], *a.* sterile, unfruitful; barren (female, land); sterile (flower); childless (marriage); unproductive (land); fruitless (efforts); unprofitable (work); **vie s. en bonnes œuvres,** life barren of good works; **esprit s. en idées,** mind barren of ideas; *Med: etc:* **instruments stériles,** sterile, sterilized, instruments; *s.m.pl. Min:* **stériles,** deads.

stérilement [sterilmɑ̃], *adv.* barrenly, unfruitfully, fruitlessly, unprofitably.

stérilet [sterilɛ], *s.m. Hyg:* (*for birth control*) coil, loop.

stérilisant [sterilizɑ̃], *a. & s.m.* sterilizing (agent).

stérilisateur [sterilizatœːr], *s.m.* sterilizer.

stérilisation [sterilizasjɔ̃], *s.f.* sterilization; *Hyg: etc:* **étuve à s.,** sterilizing closet; sterilizer.
stériliser [sterilize], *v.tr.* to sterilize.
stérilité [sterilite], *s.f.* sterility, barrenness, unfruitfulness, unproductiveness; **mouvement frappé de s.,** movement that led to no results; abortive movement; **il y a s. de nouvelles,** there is a paucity, a dearth, of news.
stérique [sterik], *a. Ch:* steric.
sterlet [stɛrlɛ], *s.m. Ich:* sterlet.
sterling [stɛrliŋ], *a.m.inv.* sterling; **dix livres s.,** ten pounds sterling.
sternal, -aux [stɛrnal, -o], *a. Anat:* sternal.
sternbergite [stɛrnbɛrʒit], *s.f. Miner:* sternbergite.
sterne [stɛrn], *s.f. Orn:* tern; **s. bridée,** bridled tern; **s. caspienne,** Caspian tern; **s. voyageuse,** lesser crested tern; **s. arctique, paradis,** arctic tern; **s. Pierre-Garin,** common tern; **s. hansel,** gull-billed tern; **s. naine, au front blanc,** little, *U.S:* least, tern; **s. de Dougall,** roseate tern; **s. caugek,** sandwich, *U.S:* Cabot's, tern; **s. fuligineuse,** sooty tern.
stern(o)- [stɛrn(ə)], *comb.fm.* stern(o)-.
sterno-claviculaire [stɛrnɔklavikylɛːr], *a. Anat:* sterno-clavicular; *pl. sterno-claviculaires.*
sterno-cléido-mastoïdien [stɛrnɔkleidɔmastɔidjɛ̃], *Anat:* **1.** *a.m.* sternomastoid, sternocleidomastoid. **2.** *s.m.* sternocleidomastoidus, sterno-(cleido)mastoid (muscle); *pl. sterno-cléido-mastoïdiens.*
sterno-costal, -aux [stɛrnɔkɔstal, -o], *a. Anat:* sternocostal.
sternothère [stɛrnɔtɛːr], *s.m. Rept:* Sternotherus, the (N. American) musk turtle.
sternum [stɛrnɔm], *s.m. Anat:* sternum, breastbone; *Box:* **la pointe du s.,** the mark.
sternutatif, -ive [stɛrnytatif, -iːv], *a. Med:* sternutatory, sternutative; sneezing (powder, etc.).
sternutation [stɛrnytasjɔ̃], *s.f.* sternutation, sneezing.
sternutatoire [stɛrnytatwaːr], *a. & s.m. Med:* sternutatory; sneezing(-powder); sternutative.
stéroïde [sterɔid], *s.m. Biol: Med:* steroid.
stérol [sterɔl], *s.m. Ch: Physiol:* sterol.
stertor [stɛrtɔːr], *s.m. Med:* stertor; stertorous breathing.
stertoreux, -euse [stɛrtɔrø, -øːz], *a. Med:* stertorous (breathing).
stéthomètre [stetɔmɛtr], *s.m. Med:* stethometer.
stéthoscope [stetɔskɔp], *s.m. Med:* stethoscope; **s. bi-auriculaire,** binaural stethoscope.
stéthoscopie [stetɔskɔpi], *s.f. Med:* stethoscopy.
stéthoscopique [stetɔskɔpik], *a. Med:* stethoscopic.
steward [stiwar(d)], *s.m. Nau: Av:* steward.
stewardess [stiwardɛs], *s.f. Nau: Av:* stewardess; *Av:* air hostess.
sthène [stɛn], *s.m. Meas:* sthene.
sthénique [stenik], *a. Med:* sthenic (symptom, etc.).
stibial, -iaux [stibjal, -jo], *a.* stibial, antimonial (sulphur, etc.).
stibié [stibje], *a. Pharm:* impregnated with antimony; stibiated; **tartre s.,** tartrate emetic, tartar emetic.
stibieux, -ieuse [stibjø, -jøːz], *a. Ch:* stibious, antimonious.
stibine [stibin], *s.f. Ch: Miner:* stibnite.
stibique [stibik], *a. Ch:* stibic, antimonic.
stibnite [stibnit], *s.f. Ch: Miner:* stibnite.
stichomythique [stikɔmitik], *a. Gr.Lit:* **vers stichomythiques,** amoebaean verse.
stick [stik], *s.m.* **1.** (soldier's) swagger-stick. **2.** (riding-) switch; riding-whip. **3.** *Sp: (hockey)* (*a*) stick; (*b*) stick fault, sticks. **4.** *Av: Mil:* stick (of parachutists).
stigmate [stigmat], *s.m.* **1.** *A:* (*a*) stigma, brand (on slave, etc.); (*b*) stigma, brand of infamy, stain (on character). **2.** (*a*) mark, scar (of wound); pit (of smallpox); pock-mark; (*b*) *Med:* stigma (of hysteria, etc.); (*c*) *pl. Rel.H:* stigmata. **3.** (*a*) *Bot:* stigma; (*b*) *Ent:* spiracle, stigma.
stigmatique [stigmatik], *a.* **1.** *Nat.Hist:* stigmatic. **2.** *Opt:* (ana)stigmatic.
stigmatisation [stigmatizasjɔ̃], *s.f.* stigmatization.
stigmatisé, -ée [stigmatize]. **1.** *a.* stigmatized. **2.** *s. Rel.H:* stigmatist; stigmatic.
stigmatiser [stigmatize], *v.tr.* **1.** (*a*) *A:* to brand (slave, animal); (*b*) to stigmatize (**de,** with); to brand (s.o.) with infamy; to set the stamp of shame on (sth.). **2.** to pock-mark (s.o.).
stigmule [stigmyl], *s.m. Bot:* stigmula.
stilb [stilb], *s.m. Ph:* stilb.
stilbite [stilbit], *s.f. Miner:* stilbite, desmine.
stil-de-grain [stildəgrɛ̃], *s.m. Paint:* yellow lake.
Stilicon [stilikɔ̃], *Pr.n.m. Rom.Hist:* Stilicho.

stillant [stil(l)ɑ̃], *a.* (*of water*) that drips; that falls drop by drop; dripping, oozing.
stillation [stil(l)asjɔ̃], *s.f.* dripping; falling drop by drop; oozing (from rock, etc.).
stillatoire [stil(l)atwaːr], *a.* filtering, oozing.
stilligoutte [stil(l)igut], *s.m.* dropping tube, dropper (for bitters, etc.).
stilpnosidérite [stilpnɔsiderit], *s.f. Miner:* stilpnosiderite, limonite.
stimulant [stimylɑ̃]. **1.** *a.* stimulating, stimulative. **2.** *s.m.* (*a*) *Med: etc:* stimulant; **s. de l'appétit,** whet to the appetite; (*b*) stimulus, spur, incentive, inducement.
stimulateur, -trice [stimylatœːr, -tris], (*a*) *a.* stimulative; (*b*) *s.m. Surg:* **s. électrique du cœur,** pacemaker.
stimulation [stimylasjɔ̃], *s.f.* stimulation.
stimule [stimyl], *s.m. Bot:* stimulus, stinging hair; sting.
stimuler [stimyle], *v.tr.* to stimulate. **1.** to incite; to spur (s.o.) on; **s. qn au travail,** to incite s.o. to work; **il a de bonnes intentions, mais il faut le s.,** he is well-intentioned, but he needs to be prodded; **stimulé par l'ambition,** stimulated by ambition. **2. s. la digestion,** to stimulate the digestion; **s. l'appétit,** to whet the appetite; **s. les affaires,** to give a stimulus, a fillip, to business; **s. l'amitié entre les peuples,** to foster friendship between peoples.
stimuleux, -euse [stimylø, -øːz], *a. Bot:* stimulose (leaf).
stimuline [stimylin], *s.f. Biol: Physiol:* **1.** stimuline. **2.** hormones from the pituitary glands.
stimulus [stimylys], *s.m.inv. Biol: Med:* stimulus.
stinkal [stɛ̃kal], *s.m. Miner:* stinkstone; *esp.* anthraconite.
stipe[1] [stip], *s.f. Bot:* feather-grass.
stipe[2], *s.m. Bot:* (*a*) stipe(s) (of fern, of fungus); culm; (*b*) stem (of palm tree).
stipelle [stipɛl], *s.f. Bot:* stipel, stipella.
stipellé [stipe(ɛl)le], *a. Bot:* stipellate.
stipendiaire [stipɑ̃djɛːr], *a. & s.m. usu. Pej:* (*a*) (*of soldier*) mercenary; (*b*) hireling; *Iron:* **les stipendiaires de la loi,** the myrmidons of the law.
stipendié [stipɑ̃dje]. **1.** *a.* mercenary, hired (ruffian, etc.). **2.** *s.m.* = STIPENDIAIRE.
stipendier [stipɑ̃dje], *v.tr.* (*pr.sub. & p.d.* **n. stipendiions, v. stipendiiez**) (*a*) *A:* to keep (troops, etc.) in one's pay; (*b*) *Pej:* to keep (ruffians, politicians, etc.) in one's pay.
stipiforme [stipifɔrm], *a. Bot:* stipiform.
stipité [stipite], *a. Bot:* stipitate, stalked.
stipulacé [stipylase], *a. Bot:* stipulaceous.
stipulaire [stipylɛːr], *a. Bot:* stipular.
stipulant [stipylɑ̃], *Jur:* **1.** *a.* stipulating. **2.** *s.m.* stipulator.
stipulation [stipylasjɔ̃], *s.f.* stipulation; **s. particulière,** special provision; **stipulations d'un contrat,** articles, specifications, of a contract; conditions laid down in an agreement.
stipule [stipyl], *s.f. Bot:* stipule.
stipulé [stipyle], *a. Bot:* stipulate, stipuled.
stipuler [stipyle], *v.tr.* to stipulate; to lay down (that . . .); **il est stipulé que la livraison devra être faite cette année,** it is stipulated that delivery shall be effected this year; **s. une récompense de cent livres,** to stipulate for a reward of a hundred pounds; **s. que toutes les réparations seront à la charge du locataire,** to stipulate that the tenant shall be responsible for all repairs.
stipuleux, -euse [stipylø, -øːz], *a. Bot:* stipulose.
stirator [stiratɔːr], *s.m. A:* drawing-board (with stretching reglets); stretching-frame.
stochastique [stɔkastik], *a.* **1.** at random; resulting from guesswork. **2.** *Mth: etc:* stochastic; **variation s.,** stochastic variation.
stock [stɔk], *s.m. Com:* stock (of goods), *U.S:* inventory; **s. en début d'exercice, s. initial,** opening stock; **s. en fin d'exercice, s. final,** closing stock; **s. en magasin, s. existant,** stock in, on, hand; **avoir en s.,** to have in stock; **s. de dépannage, de sécurité,** safety stock; **constituer des stocks,** to build up stocks; **constitution de stocks,** stock building; **gestion des stocks,** stock control; *U.S:* inventory control management; **entamer, prélever sur, les stocks,** to tap, draw on, the stocks; **épuiser les stocks,** to consume, exhaust, stocks; **nos stocks s'épuisent,** our stocks are running out; **épuisement des stocks,** depletion, exhaustion, of stocks; **liquider un s.,** to sell off, clear, a stock; **liquidation du stock, des stocks,** stock clearance; liquidation of stock; **renouvellement des stocks,** re-stocking; **rotation des stocks,** stock turnover; *F:* **gardez-le, j'en ai tout un s., un vrai s.,** keep it, I've a whole stock of them, plenty of them.

stockage [stɔkaːʒ], *s.m.* **1.** (*a*) stocking, keeping in stock (of goods); storage; (*computers*) **s. de données,** data storage; **installations de s.,** storage installations, facilities; **matériel de s.,** storage equipment; *Petroleum Ind: etc:* **parc de s.,** storage plant, tank farm; **réservoir de s.,** storage tank; (*b*) **s. artificiel de gaz,** artificial reservoir. **2.** (*a*) stocking, building up of stocks; (*b*) stockpiling.
stock-car [stɔkkaːr], *s.m. Aut:* stock car; **course de stock-cars,** stock-car race; *pl. stock-cars.*
stocker [stɔke], *v.tr.* (*a*) to stock (goods); (*b*) to stockpile; (*c*) *Elcs:* (*computers*) to store (data).
stockfisch [stɔkfiʃ], *s.m.* stockfish.
stockiste [stɔkist], *s.m. Com:* wholesale warehouseman; stockist; *Aut: etc:* agent.
stœchiométrie [stœkjɔmetri], *s.f. Ch:* stoich(e)iometry.
stœchiométrique [stœkjɔmetrik], *a. Ch:* stoech(e)iometric; **rapport s.,** equivalence ratio.
stoff [stɔf], *s.m. Tex:* light woollen material.
stoïcien, -ienne [stɔisjɛ̃, -jɛn]. **1.** *a.* stoical, stoic. **2.** *s.* stoic.
stoïcisme [stɔisism], *s.m.* **1.** *A.Phil:* stoicism. **2.** stoicism, impassiveness.
stoïcité [stɔisite], *s.f.* stoicalness, stoicism.
stoïque [stɔik]. **1.** *a.* stoic, stoical. **2.** *s.* stoic.
stoïquement [stɔikmɑ̃], *adv.* stoically.
stoker [stɔkœːr], *s.m. Rail:* (mechanical) stoker.
stola [stɔla], *s.f. Rom.Ant:* stole; *pl. stolae.*
stolon [stɔlɔ̃], *s.m.,* **stolone** [stɔlɔn], *s.f. Bot:* stolon, offset; runner, sucker (of strawberry, etc.); *Biol:* stolon.
stolonifère [stɔlɔnifɛːr], *a. Bot:* stolonate, stoloniferous.
stolzite [stɔlzit], *s.f. Miner:* stolzite.
stomacal, -aux [stɔmakal, -o]. **1.** *a.* stomachal, gastric. **2.** *a. & s.m. Anat: Med:* stomachic.
stomate [stɔmat], *s.m.* **1.** *Anat:* stoma. **2.** *Bot:* stoma, stomate.
stomatite [stɔmatit], *s.f. Med:* stomatitis.
stomato- [stɔmatɔ], *comb.fm.* stomato-.
stomato-gastrique [stɔmatɔgastrik], *a. Anat:* stomatogastric; *pl. stomato-gastriques.*
stomatologie [stɔmatɔlɔʒi], *s.f.* stomatology.
stomatologiste [stɔmatɔlɔʒist], *s.m.* stomatologist.
stomatoplastie [stɔmatɔplasti], *s.f. Surg:* stomatoplasty.
stomatopode [stɔmatɔpɔd], *s.m. Crust:* stomatopod.
stomatoscope [stɔmatɔskɔp], *s.m. Surg:* stomatoscope.
stomiatidés, stomiatides [stɔmjatide, -tid], *s.m.pl. Ich:* Stomiatidae, Stomiatids, stomiatoid fishes.
stomoxe [stɔmɔks], *s.m.,* **stomoxys** [stɔmɔksis], *s.m. Ent:* stomoxys calcitrans; *F:* stable fly.
stop [stɔp]. **1.** *int. Nau: Equit: Aut: Mch:* stop! **2.** *s.m. Aut:* (*a*) stoplight; (*b*) **brûler un s.,** to jump, shoot, the (traffic) lights. **3.** *s.m. F:* **faire du s.,** to hitch-hike; **aller à Paris en s.,** to hitch-hike to Paris; **un camion nous a pris en s.,** we hitched a ride on a lorry, *U.S:* a truck.
stoppage[1] [stɔpaːʒ], *s.m.* **1.** stoppage, stopping (of machine, etc.); countering (of motion). **2.** *A:* obstruction, stoppage (in pipe, etc.). **3.** *Adm. A:* **s. à la source,** deduction (of tax) at the source.
stoppage[2], *s.m.* invisible mending (of garment): fine darning.
stopper[1] [stɔpe]. **1.** *v.i.* (*of ship, train, car, mechanism*) to stop; to come to a stop. **2.** *v.tr.* (*a*) to stop (train, etc.); to check (chain or cable); (*b*) to stop (payment of cheque); (*c*) *Adm: A:* to deduct (tax) at the source.
stopper[2], *v.tr.* to repair (garment) by invisible mending; to fine-darn.
stoppeur[1] [stɔpœːr], *s.m. Nau: etc:* compressor (on chain or cable); chain-stopper.
stoppeur[2], **-euse** [stɔpœːr, -øːz], *s.* invisible mender.
storax [stɔraks], *s.m. Pharm:* storax.
store [stɔːr], *s.m.* (inside or outside window) blind; carriage blind; **s. à rouleaux,** roller blind; **s. à l'italienne,** awning blind; **s. vénitien,** Venetian blind; **s. de serre,** greenhouse shade.
stovaïne [stɔvain], *s.f. Pharm:* stovaine.
stovaïner [stɔvaine], **stovaïniser** [stɔvainize], *v.tr. Med:* to anaesthetize with stovaine.
strabique [strabik]. **1.** *a.* (*a*) strabismic; squint-eyed, *F:* cross-eyed; (*b*) **angle s.,** angle of squint. **2.** *s.m. & f.* squinter.
strabisme [strabism], *s.m.* strabism(us); squinting.
Strabon [strabɔ̃], *Pr.n.m. Gr.Lit:* Strabo.
strabotomie [strabɔtɔmi], *s.f. Surg:* strabotomy.
stradivarius [stradivarjys], *s.m.* Stradivarius (violin); *F:* Strad.

stramoine [stramwan], *s.f.*, **stramonium** [stramənjəm], *s.m. Bot:* stramonium, stramony, thorn-apple.

stramonine [stramənin], *s.f. Pharm:* stramonium.

strangulation [strɑ̃gylasjɔ̃], *s.f.* strangulation. **1.** *Jur:* strangling, throttling. **2.** *Med: etc:* constriction.

strangulé [strɑ̃gyle], *a. Med: etc:* strangulated, strangled; **voix strangulée**, strangled voice.

strangurie [strɑ̃gyri], *s.f. Med:* strangury.

strapasser [strapase], **strapassonner** [strapasəne], *v.tr. Art:* to paint (sth.) in a slapdash manner.

strapontin [strapɔ̃tɛ̃], *s.m.* **1.** *(a) Aut: Th: etc:* flap seat, folding seat; tip-up seat; cricket-seat (of taxi); *(b) F:* temporary job (at conference, etc.). **2.** *A:* narrow bed, mattress. **3.** *Cost: P: A:* (lady's) bustle.

Strasbourg [strazbu:r], *Pr.n. Geog:* Strasbourg, *occ.* Strasburg, Strassburg.

strasbourgeois, -oise [strazburʒwa, -wa:z], *a. & s. Geog:* (native, inhabitant) of Strasbourg; *s. occ.* Strasburger.

strass [stras], *s.m.* strass; paste (jewellery) (from the name of the inventor).

strasse [strɑs], *s.f.* **1.** *(a)* floss silk; *(b)* waste silk. **2.** coarse packing-paper.

stratagème [strataʒɛm], *s.m.* *(a) Mil: A:* stratagem, artifice of war; *(b)* stratagem, ruse, scheme.

strate [strat], *s.f. Geol:* stratum, layer.

stratège [stratɛ:ʒ], *s.m.* **1.** *Gr.Ant:* strategus. **2.** strategist.

stratégie [strateʒi], *s.f.* strategy; generalship.

stratégique [strateʒik], *a.* strategic(al) (point, line, etc.).

stratégiquement [strateʒikmɑ̃], *adv.* strategically.

stratégiste [strateʒist], *s.m.* strategist.

stratification [stratifikasjɔ̃], *s.f.* **1.** *Geol: Bot: Physiol:* stratification; *Geol:* bedding; **concordance de s.**, concordant bedding; **s. entrecroisée**, diagonal stratification; cross bedding. **2.** *Agr:* storing (of seeds) between layers of earth or sand.

stratifié [stratifje]. **1.** *a.* stratified; *Geol:* **s. en couche**, bedded. **2.** *s.m.* laminated wood, plastics, glass.

stratifier [stratifje], *v.tr.* **1.** to stratify. **2.** *Agr:* to store (seeds) between layers of earth or sand.

stratiforme [stratifɔrm], *a. Anat: etc:* stratiform.

stratigraphe [stratigraf], *s.m. & f. Geol:* stratigrapher.

stratigraphie [stratigrafi], *s.f. Geol:* stratigraphy.

stratigraphique [stratigrafik], *a.* stratigraphic.

stratiome [stratjəm], **stratiomys** [stratjəmis], *s.m. Ent:* stratiomyi(i)d; *F:* soldier fly.

stratiomyide [stratjəmiid], *Ent:* **1.** *a.* stratiomyi(i)d (insect). **2.** *s.m.* stratiomyi(i)d (fly); *F:* soldier fly.

stratiote [stratjət], *s.f. Bot:* stratiotes; **s. faux aloès**, water-soldier.

stratocratie [stratəkrasi], *s.f.* stratocracy; military government.

strato-cumulus [stratəkymylys], *s.m.inv. Meteor:* stratocumulus.

Straton [stratɔ̃], *Pr.n.m. Gr.Ant:* Strato.

stratonaute [stratono:t], *s.m.* stratosphere explorer, balloonist.

stratopause [stratəpo:z], *s.f. Meteor:* stratopause.

stratosphère [stratəsfɛ:r], *s.f. Meteor:* stratosphere.

stratosphérique [stratəsferik], *a.* stratospheric; **avion (de ligne) s.**, stratoliner, stratocruiser.

stratus [stratys], *s.m. Meteor:* stratus (cloud).

strepsiptères [strepsiptɛ:r], *s.m.pl. Ent:* Strepsiptera.

streptococcémie [strɛptəkəksemi], *s.f. Med:* streptoseptic(a)emia.

streptococcie [strɛptəkəksi], *s.f. Med:* streptococcosis.

streptococcique [strɛptəkəksik], *a. Bac:* streptococcic.

streptocoque [strɛptəkək], *s.m. Bac:* streptococcus.

streptomycine [strɛptəmisin], *s.f. Bac:* streptomycin.

stress [strɛs], *s.m. Med:* stress.

strette [strɛt], *s.f. Mus:* stretto.

striage [strija:ʒ], *s.m. Civ.E:* indenting, crimping (of asphalted, etc., road surface).

striation [strijasjɔ̃], *s.f.* striation.

strict [strikt], *a.* strict; *(a) (precisely defined)* **obligation stricte**, strict obligation; **le s. nécessaire**, the bare essentials; **le s. minimum**, the strict, bare, minimum; *(b)* severe, exact (person); **s. en affaires**, strict, exact, in business matters; *(c)* plain, severe (suit, etc.); **coiffure stricte**, severe hairstyle.

strictement [striktəmɑ̃], *adv.* strictly; *(a)* **s. parlant**, strictly speaking; to be exact; **il est s. interdit de fumer**, smoking is strictly forbidden; **se soumettre s. à un emploi du temps**, to adhere strictly to a timetable; **s. confidentiel**, strictly, highly, confidential; *(b)* **être habillé s.**, to be dressed severely, in a severe style, formally.

striction [striksjɔ̃], *s.f.* **1.** *Geom:* **ligne de s.**, curve, line, of striction. **2.** *Metalw:* contraction of cross section; necking (down) (of bar under tension test); reduction of area. **3.** *Med:* constriction.

stricturotomie [striktyrətəmi], *s.f. Surg:* stricturotomy.

stridemment [stridamɑ̃], *adv.* stridently, shrilly.

stridence [stridɑ̃:s], *s.f.* *(a)* harshness (of sound); stridency; shrillness; *(b)* shrill, strident, sound; **la s. des sauterelles**, the shrill noise of the grasshoppers.

strident [stridɑ̃], *a.* strident, shrill, harsh, grating (noise, voice); **grincement s.**, harsh grating noise; **le sifflet s. d'une locomotive**, the shrill whistle of a locomotive.

strideur [stridœ:r], *s.f. A: & Lit:* piercing, strident, noise.

stridor [stridɔ:r], *s.m. or f. Med:* stridor.

stridulant [stridylɑ̃], *a.* stridulant, chirring (insect).

stridulation [stridylasjɔ̃], *s.f.* stridulation, chirring.

stridulatoire [stridylatwa:r], *a.* stridulatory.

striduler [stridyle], *v.i.* to chirr, to stridulate.

striduleux, -euse [stridylø, -ø:z], *a. Med:* stridulous; **laryngite striduleuse**, false croup.

strie [stri], *s.f.* **1.** score, scratch; *Anat: Bot: Geol:* stria; *Geol:* **stries glaciaires**, glacial striae; **stries de froissement**, slickensides. **2.** *(a)* rib ridge; *Arch:* (= LISTEL) fillet, stria (between flutings); *(b)* streak (of colour). **3.** *Av:* **méthode des stries**, Schlieren photography technique.

strié [strije], *a.* **1.** scored, scratched; *Bot: Geol:* striated; *Anat:* striped, striated (muscle); **carte striée de traits rouges et bleus**, card striped with red and blue lines. **2.** *(a)* fluted, grooved (column); ribbed (glass); corrugated (sheet iron); **tôle striée**, chequered plate; *(b)* streaked (marble).

strier [strije], *v.tr.* (*p.d. & pr.sub.* **n. striions, v. striiez**) **1.** to striate, score, scratch. **2.** *(a)* to flute, groove, rib, corrugate; *(b)* to streak.

strige [stri:ʒ], *s.f.* vampire, ghoul.

strigidés [striʒide], *s.m.pl. Orn:* Strigidae.

strigiformes [striʒifɔrm], *s.m.pl. Orn:* Strigiformes.

strigile [striʒil], *s.m. Gr. & Rom.Ant:* strigil.

strigops [strigɔps], *s.m. Orn:* kakapo, owl parrot, night parrot.

strigovite [strigəvit], *s.f. Miner:* strigovite.

striole [strijəl], *s.f. Biol:* striola, minute stria.

striolé [strijəle], *a.* striolate.

striomètre [strijəmɛtr̥], *s.m. Opt:* striometer, flow visualization system, Schlieren measuring equipment.

strioscope [strijəskəp], *s.m. Opt:* strioscope, Schlieren set-up.

strioscopie [strijəskəpi], *s.f. Opt:* strioscopy, streak photography, Schlieren photography.

strioscopique [strijəskəpik], *a.* Schlieric; *attrib.* Schlieren; **méthode s.**, Schlieren method.

stripper[1] [stripe], *v.tr. Petroleum Ind: F:* to strip.

stripper[2] [stripɛ:r], *s.m. Surg: (instrument)* stripper.

strippeuse [stripø:z], **stripteaseuse** [striptizø:z], *s.f. F:* stripper, strip-tease artiste.

stripping [stripiŋ], *s.m.* **1.** *Atom.Ph: Petroleum Ind:* stripping. **2.** *Surg:* stripping.

striptease [stripti:z], *s.m.* strip-tease.

striquer [strike], *v.tr.* *(a) Tex:* to finish (cloth); *(b)* to sew on (appliqué).

striqueur, -euse [strikœ:r, -ø:z]. **1.** *(pers.)* *(a) s. Tex:* finisher; *(b) s.f.* appliqué-lace maker. **2.** *s.f. Tex:* **striqueuse**, finishing machine.

striure [strijy:r], *s.f.* striation. **1.** *(a)* score, scratch, groove; *(b)* streak; stripe. **2.** scoring, scratching, grooving.

strobilacé [strəbilase], *a. Bot:* strobilaceous.

strobilation [strəbilasjɔ̃], *s.f. Biol:* strobilation (of tapeworms, etc.).

strobile [strəbil], *s.m.* **1.** *Bot:* strobile, strobilus, cone (of pine, hops, etc.). **2.** *Ann:* strobila, strobilus (of tapeworm).

strobilifère [strəbilifɛ:r], *a. Bot:* strobiliferous, cone-bearing.

strobiliforme [strəbilifɔrm], *a. Nat.Hist:* strobiliform, cone-shaped.

stroboscope [strəbəskəp], *s.m. Opt:* stroboscope.

stroboscopie [strəbəskəpi], *s.f. Opt:* stroboscopy.

stroboscopique [strəbəskəpik], *a. Opt:* stroboscopic.

strobosique [strəbəzik], *a. Opt:* strobic.

stroma [strəma], *s.m. Nat.Hist:* stroma.

stromatée [strəmate], *s.m. Ich:* stromateus, *F:* pomfret.

stromatique [strəmatik], *a.* stromatic.

stromatoporidés [strəmatəpəride], *s.m.pl. Paleont:* Stromatoporidae.

strombe [strɔ̃:b], *s.m. Moll:* stromb; wing shell; **s. géant**, fountain shell.

strombidés [strɔ̃bide], *s.m.pl. Moll:* Strombidae.

strombolien, -ienne [strɔ̃bəljɛ̃, -jɛn], *a. Geog:* Strombolian.

stromeyérite [strəmejerit], *s.f. Miner:* stromeyerite.

strongle [strɔ̃:gl], *s.m.*, **strongyle** [strɔ̃ʒil], *s.m.* strongyle (thread worm); **s. géant**, palisade worm.

strongyloïdés [strɔ̃ʒiləide], *s.m.pl. Ann:* Strongylidae.

strongylose [strɔ̃ʒilo:z], *s.f. Vet:* strongylosis, strongyhydrosis.

strontiane [strɔ̃sjan], *s.f. Ch:* strontia; *Miner:* **s. carbonatée**, strontianite.

strontianite [strɔ̃sjanit], *s.f. Miner:* strontianite, strontian.

strontique [strɔ̃tik], *a. Ch:* strontic.

strontium [strɔ̃sjəm], *s.m. Ch:* strontium; **s. radioactif**, radioactive strontium, radiostrontium.

strophaire [strəfɛ:r], *s.m. Fung:* stropharia.

strophantine [strəfɑ̃tin], *s.f. Pharm:* strophanthin.

strophe [strəf], *s.f.* **1.** *Gr.Lit:* strophe. **2.** *Pros:* stanza, verse; **s. saphique**, sapphic stanza.

strophiole [strəfjəl], *s.m. Bot:* strophiola, strophiole.

strophisme [strəfism], *s.m. Bot:* strophism.

strophoïde [strəfəid], *s.f. Geom:* strophoid; strophoidal curve.

strophulus [strəfylys], *s.m. Med:* strophulus, red gum or white gum; tooth rash.

stropiat [strəpja], *s.m. P:* cripple (real or sham).

Strouma [struma], *Pr.n.f. Geog:* the (river) Struma.

structural, -aux [stryktyral, -o], *a.* *(a)* structural; *Ling:* **modèle s.**, pattern; *(b) Mec.E:* integral; *Av:* **réservoirs structuraux de voilure**, integral wing fuel tanks.

structuralement [stryktyralmɑ̃], *adv.* structurally.

structuralisme [stryktyralism], *s.m. Psy: Ling:* structuralism.

structuraliste [stryktyralist], *a. & s.m. & f. Psy: Ling:* structuralist.

structuration [stryktyrasjɔ̃], *s.f.* *(a)* structuration; *(b)* structuralization, structuration; *(c) Ling:* patterning.

structure [strykty:r], *s.f.* structure, construction (of edifice, human body, poem, etc.); structure (of matter, atom, etc.); *Atom.Ph:* **s. du noyau**, structure of nucleus; **s. du réseau**, lattice structure (of reactor); *(computers)* **s. logique**, logical design; *Geol:* **s. à, en, écailles**, imbricate structure; **s. alliotriomorphe**, alliotriomorphic structure (in igneous rocks); **s. linéaire dans des roches plissées**, mullion structure; *Cryst:* **s. crystalline**, space lattice; **s. hypidiomorphe**, subhedral, hypidiomorphic, structure; *St.Exch:* **s. des taux de change**, cross-rate structure; *Pol. Ec:* **s. des prix**, price structure, set-up.

structurel, -elle [stryktyrɛl], *a.* structural; **déséquilibre s.**, structural disequilibrium.

structurellement [stryktyrɛlmɑ̃], *adv.* structurally.

structurer [stryktyre], *v.tr.* *(a)* to give a structure to sth., to structure; *F:* **s. une histoire**, to build up a story; *(b)* to structuralize; *(c) Ling:* to pattern.

structurologie [stryktyrələʒi], *s.f. Geol:* study of structure.

strudel [strudɛl], *s.m. Cu:* **s. (aux pommes)**, (apple) strudel.

strume [strym], *s.f. Med:* **1.** struma, scrofula. **2.** goitre.

strumeux, -euse [strymø, -ø:z], *a. Med:* strumous, scrofulous.

struthidea [strutidea], *s.m. Orn:* apostle bird.

struthionidés [strytjənide], *s.m.pl. Orn:* Struthionidae, the ostriches.

struthioniformes [strytiənifɔrm], *s.m.pl. Orn:* Struthioniformes.

struvite [stryvit], *s.f. Miner: etc:* struvite.

strychnine [striknin], *s.f. Ch: Pharm:* strychnin(e).

strychnique [striknik], *a. Med:* strychnic.

strychniser [striknize], *v.tr. Med:* to strychnine; to treat (patient) with strychnine.

strychnisme [striknism], *s.m. Med:* strychn(in)ism.

strychnos [striknəs], *s.m. Bot:* strychnos; **s. bois de couleuvre**, snakewood.

stuc [styk], *s.m. Const:* stucco.

stucage [styka:ʒ], *s.m. Const:* stucco work; **enduire de s.**, to stucco.

stucateur [stykatœ:r], *s.m.* stucco worker.

stucatine [stykatin], *s.f. Const:* fine stucco.
studette [stydɛt], *s.f. Com:* studio flat, one-roomed flat.
studieusement [stydjøzmɑ̃], *adv.* studiously.
studieux, -ieuse [stydjø, -jø:z], *a.* studious; **passer des vacances studieuses,** to spend one's vacation studying.
studio [stydjo], *s.m.* **1.** (*a*) (photographer's, etc.) studio; (*b*) *Cin:* (film) studio; (*c*) *W.Tel:* **s. d'émission,** broadcasting studio; **s. d'enregistrement,** recording studio. **2.** (*a*) one-roomed flat (with bathroom, etc.); (*b*) (suite of) furniture for a one-roomed flat.
studiosité [stydjozite], *s.f.* studiousness.
stupéfaction [stypefaksjɔ̃], *s.f.* stupefaction, (*usu.* in the sense of) amazement.
stupéfait [stypefɛ], *a.* stupefied, amazed, aghast, astounded, dumbfounded; **s. que** + *sub.*, **de ce que** + *ind. or sub.*, astounded that . . ..
stupéfiant [stypefjɑ̃]. **1.** *a.* (*a*) *Med:* stupefying, stupefacient (drug); (*b*) amazing, astounding (news). **2.** *s.m. Med:* narcotic, stupefacient; *F:* drug; **faire usage de, s'adonner aux, stupéfiants,** to take drugs, to drug oneself; **trafic des stupéfiants,** drug traffic; **trafiquer en stupéfiants,** to traffic in drugs.
stupéfier [stypefje], *v.tr.* (*p.d. & pr.sub.* **n. stupéfiions, v. stupéfiiez**) (*a*) *Med: etc:* to stupefy; (*b*) to astound, amaze, dumbfound.
stupeur [stypœ:r], *s.f.* stupor. **1.** dazed state. **2.** amazement; **muet de s.,** dumbfounded; **être frappé de s.,** to be struck with astonishment; **la nouvelle le frappa de s.,** he was dumbfounded at the news; **écouter avec s.,** to listen in amazement.
stupide [stypid]. **1.** *a.* (*a*) *A:* stupid; stunned with surprise; dazed; (*b*) stupid, dull-witted; (*c*) silly, stupid, foolish. **2.** *s.* stupid person; blockhead; *F:* idiot, clot.
stupidement [stypidmɑ̃], *adv.* stupidly.
stupidité [stypidite], *s.f.* **1.** stupidity; foolishness. **2.** piece of stupidity; **répondre par une s.,** to give a silly, foolish, stupid, answer.
stuporeux, -euse [stypɔrø, -ø:z], *a. Med:* stuporous.
stupre [stypr̥], *s.m.* **1.** (act of) rape; indecent assault. **2. plongé dans le s.,** sunk in debauchery.
stuquer [styke], *v.tr. Const:* to stucco.
stygien, -ienne [stiʒjɛ̃, -jɛn], *a.* Stygian (darkness, etc.).
stylaire [stilɛ:r], *a. Bot:* stylar.
sturnelle [styrnɛl], *s.f. Orn:* sturnella, meadow lark.
sturnidés [styrnide], *s.m.pl.* Sturnidae.
style [stil], *s.m.* **1.** (*a*) *Ant:* stylus, style (as writing implement); (*b*) stylus, graver, etching needle; *Rec:* **s. (d'enregistrement),** record cutter; (*c*) style, pin, gnomon (of sundial); hand (of barometer); (*d*) *Bot:* style. **2.** *Lit: Arch: etc:* style; **s. de l'Écriture, s. biblique,** biblical style; **s. du palais, s. judiciaire,** judicial style; **écrivain qui n'a pas de s.,** writer who lacks style; **écrit d'un, dans un, s. peu original,** written in an unoriginal style; **dans le s. de Rubens,** in the style of Rubens, after the Rubens manner; **s. gothique, byzantin,** Gothic, Byzantine, style; **meubles s. Empire,** furniture in the Empire style, Empire furniture; **meubles de s.,** period furniture; **robe de s.,** period dress; *Chr:* **vieux s., nouveau s.,** Old Style, New Style (of calendar).
stylé[1] [stile], *a. Nat.Hist:* stylate.
stylé[2], *a.* trained, schooled (**à,** in); **domestique, cheval, bien s.,** well-schooled servant, horse.
styler [stile], *v.tr.* to train, form; *F:* to put a polish on (s.o.); **s. qn aux usages du monde,** to instruct s.o. in the ways of society.
stylet [stilɛ], *s.m.* **1.** stiletto, stylet. **2.** *Surg:* stylet, probe. **3.** *Z:* stylet. **4.** (*computers*) **s. lumineux,** light pen, light gun.
styliforme [stilifɔrm], *a. Bot: etc:* styliform, style-shaped.
stylisation [stilizasjɔ̃], *s.f.* stylization.
styliser [stilize], *v.tr. Art:* to stylize, conventionalize (form, design); **fleurs stylisées,** conventionalized flowers.
stylisme [stilism], *s.m. Lit: Cost: Com:* stylism.
styliste [stilist], *s.m. & f. Lit: Cost: Com:* stylist.
stylisticien, -ienne [stilistisjɛ̃, -jɛn], *s.* expert in stylistics.
stylistique [stilistik]. **1.** *a.* stylistic. **2.** *s.f.* stylistics.
stylite [stilit], *a. & s.m. Rel.H:* stylite; **Saint Siméon S.,** Saint Simeon Stylites.
stylo [stilo], *s.m. F:* fountain pen; **s. à bille,** ballpoint pen.
stylo- [stilɔ], *pref.* styl(o)-.
stylobille [stilobi:j], *s.m. F:* ballpoint pen.
stylobate [stilɔbat], *s.m. Arch:* stylobate.
stylo-glosse [stilɔglɔs], *Anat:* **1.** *a.* styloglossal. **2.** *s.m.* styloglossus; *pl. stylo-glosses.*
stylographe [stilɔgraf], *s.m.* (*a*) stylograph (pen); (*b*) fountain pen.
stylographique [stilɔgrafik], *a.* stylographic; **encre s.,** fountain-pen ink.
stylo-hyoïdien, -ienne [stilɔiɔidjɛ̃, -jɛn], *a. & s.m. Anat:* stylohyoid (muscle); *pl. stylo-hyoïdien(ne)s.*
styloïde [stilɔid], *a. Anat:* styloid (process, etc.).
stylolite [stilɔlit], *s.m. Geol:* stylolite.
stylo-mastoïdien, -ienne [stilɔmastɔidjɛ̃, -jɛn], *a. Anat:* stylomastoid (foramen); *pl. stylo-mastoïdien(ne)s.*
stylo-maxillaire [stilɔmaksil(l)ɛ:r], *a. Anat:* stylo-maxillary (ligament); *pl. stylo-maxillaires.*
stylométrie [stilɔmetri], *s.f.* stylometry.
stylomine [stilɔmin], *s.m. R.t.m:* propelling pencil.
stylommatophores [stilɔm(m)atɔfɔ:r], *s.m.pl. Moll:* Stylommatophora.
stylospore [stilɔspɔ:r], *s.f. Bot:* stylospore.
Stymphale [stɛ̃fal], *Pr.n. A.Geog:* Stymphalus; *Myth:* **les oiseaux du lac S.,** the Stymphalian birds.
stypa [stipa], *s.m. Bot:* stipa.
styphnate [stifnat], *s.m. Ch:* styphnate.
styptique [stiptik], *a. & s.m. Med:* styptic, astringent.
styracacées [stirakase], *s.f.pl.*, **styracées** [stirase], *s.f.pl. Bot:* Styraceae.
styrax [stiraks], *s.m. Bot:* styrax; **s. benzoin,** benzoin laurel, benjamin tree.
styrène [stirɛn], *s.m. Ch:* styrene.
Styrie [stiri], *Pr.n.f. Geog:* Styria.
styrien, -ienne [stirjɛ̃, -jɛn], *a. & s. Geog:* Styrian.
styrol [stirɔl], *s.m. Ch: A:* styrol.
styrolène [stirɔlɛn], *s.m. Ch:* styrene, styrolene.
Styx [stiks], *Pr.n.m. Myth:* the (river) Styx; **visiter les bords du S.,** to visit the Stygian shores.
su [sy], *s.m.* knowledge; *used in the phr.* **au su de . . .,** to the knowledge of . . .; **au su de tout le monde il avait . . .,** it was common knowledge that he had . . .; **à mon vu et su,** to my certain knowledge.
suage[1] [sɥa:ʒ], *s.m.* sweating, oozing (of wall, timber, etc.).
suage[2], *s.m. Metalw:* **1.** *Tls:* (*a*) swage; (*b*) creasing hammer, creasing tool. **2.** fillet(-border) (of candlestick, of silver plate).
suage[3], *s.m. Nau:* **1.** paying, tallowing (of vessel). **2.** paying stuff; tallow.
suager[1] [sɥaʒe], *v.tr.* (**je suageai(s); n. suageons**) *Tchn:* to swage, crease (tin-plate, etc.).
suager[2], *v.tr. Nau:* to pay, tallow (vessel).
suaire [sɥɛ:r], *s.m.* **1.** winding-sheet; shroud; **le saint S.,** the Sindon (of Christ). **2.** *Rel.H:* sudarium, veronica.
suant [sɥɑ̃], *a.* **1.** sweating; (*a*) (*of people, animals*) in a sweat; sweaty (hands, etc.); (*b*) (*of walls, wood*) oozing moisture; (*c*) *P:* boring. **2.** *Metalw:* **chaleur suante, blanc s.,** welding heat, white heat.
suave [sɥa:v], *a.* (*a*) sweet, pleasant (music, scent, etc.); soft (shade); mild (cigar); (*b*) suave, bland (tone, manner).
suavement [sɥavmɑ̃], *adv.* (*a*) sweetly, pleasantly, softly; (*b*) suavely, blandly.
suavité [sɥavite], *s.f.* (*a*) sweetness, softness (of perfume, melody); (*b*) suavity, blandness (of tone, manner).
sub- [syb], *pref.* sub-.
subaérien, -ienne [sybaerjɛ̃, -jɛn], *a.* subaerial (denudation, etc.); exposed to the air; **plantes subaériennes,** subaerial plants.
subaigu, -uë [sybegy], *a. Med:* subacute.
subalaire [sybalɛ:r], *a. Orn:* subalary.
subalcalin [sybalkalɛ̃], *a. Ch: Geol:* subalkaline.
subalpin [sybalpɛ̃], *a.* subalpine.
subalternation [sybalternasjɔ̃], *s.f. Log:* subalternation.
subalterne [sybaltɛrn]. **1.** *a.* subordinate, minor (official, position, part); **les esprits subalternes,** inferior minds; **employé s.,** junior employee; employee in a minor position, underling. **2.** *s.m.* (*a*) underling, subaltern; (*b*) *Mil:* **(officier) s.,** subaltern (officer) or captain.
subaquatique [sybakwatik], *a.* subaqueous (light); subaquatic (exploration); **pêche s.,** underwater fishing.
subatomique [sybatɔmik], *a.* subatomic.
subbitumineux, -euse [syb(b)ityminø, -ø:z], *a.* subbituminous.
subcaudal, -aux [sybkodal, -o], *a. Z:* subcaudal.
subconsciemment [sybkɔ̃sjamɑ̃], *adv.* subconsciously.
subconscience [sybkɔ̃sjɑ̃:s], *s.f.* subconsciousness.
subconscient [sybkɔ̃sjɑ̃], (*a*) *a.* subconscious; (*b*) *s.m. Psy:* **le s.,** the subconscious.
subcortical, -aux [sybkɔrtikal, -o], *a. Bot:* subcortical.
subcostal, -aux [sybkɔstal, -o], *a. Anat: Ent:* subcostal.
subcritique [sybkritik], *a. Atom.Ph: etc:* subcritical.
subculture [sybkylty:r], *s.f.* subculture.
subdélégation [sybdelegasjɔ̃], *s.f.* subdelegation.
subdélégué, -ée [sybdelege], *s.* subdelegate.
subdéléguer [sybdelege], *v.tr.* (*conj. like* DÉLÉGUER) to subdelegate.
subdésertique [sybdezɛrtik], *a. Geog:* semi-desert, semi-arid (climate).
subdiviser [sybdivize], *v.tr.* to subdivide, to split up (**en,** into).
subdivisible [sybdivizibl̥], *a.* subdivisible.
subdivision [sybdivizjɔ̃], *s.f.* subdivision.
subdivisionnaire [sybdivizjɔnɛ:r], *a. Adm:* subdivisional, subdivisionary.
subéquatorial, -aux [subekwatɔrjal, -o], *a. Geog:* subequatorial.
suber [sybɛ:r], *s.m. Bot:* suber.
subérate [syberat], *s.m. Ch:* suberate.
subéreux, -euse [syberø, -ø:z], *a. Bot:* suberous, suberose; corky (layer, etc.); **enveloppe subéreuse,** cortex; epiphloem.
subérification [syberifikasjɔ̃], *s.f. Ch:* suberification.
subérine [syberin], *s.f. Ch:* suberin.
subérique [syberik], *a. Ch:* suberic (acid).
subériser [syberize], *v.tr. Bot:* to suberize.
subérosité [syberozite], *s.f. Bot:* corky character.
subfébrile [sybfebril], *a. Med:* subfebrile.
subgranulaire [sybgranylɛ:r], **subgranuleux, -euse** [sybgranylø, -ø:z], *a.* subgranular.
subgronde [sybgrɔ̃:d], *s.f. Const:* eaves (of roof).
subincision [sybɛ̃sizjɔ̃], *s.f.* subincision.
subintrant [sybɛ̃trɑ̃], *a. Med:* subintrant (fever, etc.), proleptic.
subir [sybi:r], *v.tr.* to undergo, go through (operation, trial, examination, etc.); to come under (an influence); to suffer, sustain (defeat, casualties, loss); to submit to, suffer, put up with (punishment, one's fate); *A:* **s. la question,** to undergo torture; **s. la peine de mort,** to suffer death; **s. son jugement, sa peine,** to serve one's sentence; **s. une complète métamorphose,** to undergo a complete metamorphosis; **s. la loi de qn,** to be dominated, ruled, by s.o.; **le peuple subissait un joug écrasant,** the people were under a crushing yoke; **faire s. un examen à qn,** to put s.o. through, to subject s.o. to, an examination; **faire s. une peine, des cruautés, à qn,** to inflict a penalty, cruelties, on s.o.; *Jur:* **s. un interrogatoire,** to undergo examination, to be closely questioned; **ce projet pourra s. des modifications,** the plan is liable to, subject to, modifications.
subirrigation [sybir(r)igasjɔ̃], *s.f.* subirrigation.
subit [sybi], *a.* sudden, unexpected (death, change).
subitement [sybitmɑ̃], *adv.* suddenly; all at once; all of a sudden.
subito [sybito], *adv. F: O:* (*a*) all of a sudden; (*b*) at once.
subjacent [sybʒasɑ̃], *a. Lit:* subjacent, underlying.
subjectif, -ive [sybʒɛktif, -i:v], *a. Phil: Gram:* subjective; *Gram:* **cas s.,** nominative case.
subjectile [sybʒɛktil], *s.m. Art:* support (beneath paint, etc.).
subjectivement [sybʒɛktivmɑ̃], *adv.* subjectively.
subjectivisme [sybʒɛktivism], *s.m. Phil:* subjectivism.
subjectiviste [sybʒɛktivist], *a. & s.m. & f. Phil:* subjectivist.
subjectivité [sybʒɛktivite], *s.f. Phil:* subjectivity.
subjonctif, -ive [sybʒɔ̃ktif, -i:v], *Gram:* **1.** *a.* subjunctive (mood). **2.** *s.m.* subjunctive mood, subjunctive; **verbe au s.,** verb in the subjunctive.
subjugation [sybʒygasjɔ̃], *s.f.* subjugation; bringing into subjection.
subjuguer [sybʒyge], *v.tr.* to subjugate, subdue; to bring (people, nation) into subjection; **s. un cheval,** to subdue, master, a horse; to get the upper hand of a horse; **s. tous les cœurs,** to captivate, conquer, all hearts; **se laisser s. par ses domestiques,** to allow one's servants to get the upper hand.
sublétal, -aux [sybletal, -o], *a.* sublethal.
sublimable [syblimabl̥], *a. Ch:* sublimable.
sublimat [syblima], *s.m. Ch:* sublimate.
sublimation [syblimasjɔ̃], *s.f. Ch: Psy:* sublimation.
sublimatoire [syblimatwa:r], *Ch:* **1.** *a.* sublimatory. **2.** *s.m.* sublimating vessel; sublimatory.
sublime [syblim], *a.* **1.** sublime; lofty, exalted; *s.* **le s.,** the sublime. **2.** *Anat:* sublime (muscle).

sublimé [syblime]. 1. *a.* sublimated. 2. *s.m. Ch:* sublimate; *Pharm:* **s. corrosif,** corrosive sublimate; **gaze au s.,** (corrosive) sublimate gauze; *A:* **s. doux,** calomel.

sublimement [syblimmɑ̃], *adv.* sublimely.

sublimer [syblime], *v.tr.* (*a*) *Ch:* to sublimate, to sublime (solid); (*b*) to purefy, refine; (*c*) *Psy:* to sublimate.

subliminal, -aux [sybliminal, -o], *a.*, **subliminaire** [sybliminɛːr], *a. Psy:* below the threshold; subliminal (consciousness, memory); **publicité subliminale,** subliminal advertising.

sublimiser (se) [səsyblimize], *v.pr. Psy:* (*of instinct*) to become sublimated.

sublimité [syblimite], *s.f.* sublimity (of thought, language).

sublinéaire [sylineɛːr], *a.* sublinear.

sublingual, -aux [syblɛ̃gwal, -o], *a. Anat:* sublingual (gland, etc.); *Pharm:* **comprimé s.,** pill to be placed under the tongue.

sublunaire [syblynɛːr], *a.* 1. sublunary. 2. *Lit:* pertaining to this world, mundane.

subluxation [syblyksasjɔ̃], *s.f. Med:* subluxation.

submarginal, -aux [sybmarʒinal, -o], *a. Z: Ent:* submarginal.

submental, -aux [sybmɑ̃tal, -o], *a. Anat:* submental.

submerger [sybmɛrʒe], *v.tr.* (**je submergeai(s); n. submergeons**) 1. to submerge; to put under water; (*a*) to flood (meadow, village); (*b*) to swamp (boat); (*c*) to plunge (object) into water; to immerse (object). 2. to overwhelm; **être submergé de besogne,** to be snowed under with work.

submersibilité [sybmɛrsibilite], *s.f.* submersibility.

submersible [sybmɛrsibl̩]. 1. *a.* (*a*) sinkable; submersible (boat); (*b*) *Bot:* submersed, submerged (plant); (*c*) **terrain facilement s.,** ground easily flooded. 2. *s.m. Navy:* submarine.

submersion [sybmɛrsjɔ̃], *s.f.* submersion, submergence. 1. immersion; **mort par s.,** death by drowning; *Nau: M.Ins:* **s. sans possibilité de renflouement,** permanent sinking. 2. *Vit:* **s. des vignes,** flooding of the vineyards.

subminiature [sybminjatyːr], *a. Elcs:* subminiature.

subminiaturisation [sybminjatyrizasjɔ̃], *s.f. Elcs:* subminiaturization.

subnormal, -aux [sybnɔrmal, -o], *a.* subnormal.

suboccipital, -aux [sybɔksipital, -o], *a. Anat:* suboccipital (nerve, etc.).

subodorer [sybɔdɔre], *v.tr.* (*of dog*) to scent out (game); *F:* (*of pers.*) to suspect, scent, have a presentiment of (danger, etc.); *F:* **il a subodoré quelque chose,** he smelt a rat.

suborbital, -aux [sybɔrbital, -o], *a.* suborbital.

subordination [sybɔrdinasjɔ̃], *s.f.* subordination (à, to); *Gram:* **conjonctions de s.,** subordinating conjunctions.

subordonnant [sybɔrdɔnɑ̃], *a. Gram:* subordinating (conjunction, etc.).

subordonné, -ée [sybɔrdɔne]. 1. *a. Gram:* subordinate (clause). 2. (*a*) *s.* subordinate; (*b*) *s.f. Gram:* subordinate clause. 3. (*a*) (*computers*) **s. au temps de calcul,** compute(r)-limited; **s. au temps d'entrée, de sortie,** input, output-limited; **s. au temps d'entrée, de sortie (sur bande),** tape-limited.

subordonnément [sybɔrdɔnemɑ̃], *adv.* subordinately.

subordonner [sybɔrdɔne], *v.tr.* to subordinate (à, to); **s. ses dépenses à son revenu,** to cut one's coat according to one's cloth; **le service est subordonné au nombre des voyageurs,** the service depends on the number of travellers.

se subordonner, to submit to authority.

subornation [sybɔrnasjɔ̃], *s.f. Jur:* intimidation or bribing (of witnesses); subornation; **s. d'un juré,** embracery.

suborner [sybɔrne], *v.tr.* 1. to suborn, instigate (criminal, etc.). 2. *Jur:* to suborn, to tamper with; *F:* to get at (witness, etc.); to embrace (member of jury).

suborneur, -euse [sybɔrnœːr, -øːz]. 1. *s. Jur:* suborner, briber, embracer (of witnesses, etc.). 2. *a.* persuasive, seductive (person, oratory).

subpolaire [sybpɔlɛːr], *a.* sub-polar (climate, etc.).

subrécargue [sybrekarg], *s.m. Nau:* supercargo.

subreptice [sybrɛptis], *a.* surreptitious; clandestine.

subrepticement [sybrɛptismɑ̃], *adv.* surreptitiously; clandestinely; stealthily.

subreption [sybrɛpsjɔ̃], *s.f. Jur:* subreption.

subrogateur [sybrɔgatœːr], *Jur:* 1. *s.m.* judge-advocate substitute. 2. *a.* **acte s.,** act of subrogation, of substitution (of guardian, etc.).

subrogation [sybrɔgasjɔ̃], *s.f. Jur:* 1. subrogation, substitution. 2. delegation (of powers, rights).

subrogatoire [sybrɔgatwaːr], *a. Jur:* **acte s.,** act of subrogation, of substitution (of guardian, etc.).

subrogé, -ée [sybrɔʒe]. 1. *a.* subrogated; **s. tuteur,** deputy guardian; surrogate guardian; **demeurer s. aux droits d'un créancier,** to enter into the rights of a creditor. 2. *s. Ecc: Jur:* surrogate, deputy.

subroger [sybrɔʒe], *v.tr.* (**je subrogeai(s); n. subrogeons**) *Jur:* to subrogate; to substitute; to appoint (s.o.) as deputy, as surrogate.

subséquemment [sypsekamɑ̃], *adv.* subsequently; in due course.

subséquence [sypsekɑ̃ːs], *s.f.* subsequence.

subséquent [sypsekɑ̃], *a.* subsequent. 1. ensuing. 2. later (testament, etc.). 3. *Geog:* **cours d'eau s.,** subsequent stream.

subside [sypsid, sybz-], *s.m.* subsidy; **fournir des subsides à une puissance,** to subsidize a power.

subsidence [sypsidɑ̃ːs, sybz-], *s.f.* subsidence.

subsidiaire [sypsidjɛːr, sybz-], *a.* subsidiary, auxiliary, additional, accessory (à, to); *Parl:* **amendement s.,** minor amendment.

subsidiairement [sypsidjɛrmɑ̃, sybz-], *adv.* subsidiarily, in addition (à, to).

subsidier [sypsidje, sybz-], *v.tr.* (*p.d. & pr.sub.* **n. subsidiions, v. subsidiiez**) to subsidize.

subsistance [sybzistɑ̃ːs], *s.f.* 1. subsistence, sustenance, maintenance; (one's) keep; *Mil:* **être mis en s.,** to be attached for rations to some unit other than one's own. 2. *pl.* provisions; **subsistances militaires,** military supplies.

subsistant [sybzistɑ̃]. 1. *a.* subsisting, existing, still extant. 2. *s.m. Mil:* soldier attached (to a unit) for rations; soldier on the ration strength (of a unit).

subsister [sybziste], *v.i.* to subsist. 1. to (continue to) exist; to be still extant, in existence; **traité qui subsiste toujours,** treaty that still holds good; **cette objection subsiste,** the objection stands, remains, holds. 2. to live (**de,** upon), to have means of living; **moyens de s.,** means of subsistence; **s. d'aumônes,** to subsist on charity.

subsomption [sypsɔ̃psjɔ̃], *s.f. Phil:* subsumption.

subsonique [sypsɔnik], *a. Av:* subsonic.

substance [sypstɑ̃ːs], *s.f.* substance. 1. **s. d'un article, d'un argument,** gist of an article, of an argument; **arguments sans s.,** insubstantial arguments; **en s.,** in substance, substantially; **conditions contenues en s., sinon formellement, dans un contrat,** conditions laid down substantially, if not formally, in an agreement. 2. matter, material, stuff; **s. étrangère,** extraneous substance; *El:* **s. isolante,** insulating material; *Metall:* **substances rebelles,** refractory ores.

substantialisme [sypstɑ̃sjalism], *s.m. Phil:* substantialism.

substantialiste [sypstɑ̃sjalist], *a. & s.m. & f. Phil:* substantialist.

substantialité [sypstɑ̃sjalite], *s.f.* substantiality.

substantiel, -ielle [sypstɑ̃sjɛl], *a.* substantial (food, book, etc.); **quelque chose de s.,** something substantial, something to get one's teeth into.

substantiellement [sypstɑ̃sjɛlmɑ̃], *adv.* substantially; in substance.

substantif, -ive [sypstɑ̃tif, -iːv]. 1. *a.* substantive; *A:* **le verbe s.,** the substantive verb; the verb "to be." 2. *s.m. Gram:* substantive, noun.

substantification [sypstɑ̃tifikasjɔ̃], *s.f.* substantification.

substantifier [sypstɑ̃tifje], *v.tr.* to substantify.

substantival, -aux [sypstɑ̃tival, -o], *a. Gram:* substantival.

substantivation [sypstɑ̃tivasjɔ̃], *s.f. Gram:* substantiv(iz)ation.

substantivement [sypstɑ̃tivmɑ̃], *adv. Gram:* substantively, substantivally.

substantiver [sypstɑ̃tive], *v.tr. Gram:* to use (word, phrase) as a noun; to substantivize.

substituant [sypstitɥɑ̃], *s.m.* 1. *Mil: A:* substitute (for service). 2. *Ch:* substituent.

substitué, -ée [sypstitɥe]. 1. *a. Jur:* **enfant s.,** suppositious child. 2. *s. s. Jur:* heir appointed in succession to another or failing another.

substituer [sypstitɥe], *v.tr.* 1. to substitute (à, for); **s. l'acier à la pierre,** to substitute steel for stone, in the place of stone; to replace stone by steel. 2. *Jur:* (*a*) **s. un héritier,** to appoint an heir (grandchild or grand-nephew) in succession to another or failing another; (*b*) **s. un héritage,** to entail an estate (to grandchildren or grand-nephews).

se substituer à qn, à qch., to serve as a substitute for s.o., for sth.; to take the place of s.o., sth.; **se s. à la justice,** to take the law into one's own hands.

substitut [sypstity], *s.m.* substitute; assistant or deputy (to official); locum tenens (of doctor); *Jur:* deputy public prosecutor.

substitution [sypstitysjɔ̃], *s.f.* 1. (*a*) substitution; **s. de la margarine au beurre,** substitution of margarine for butter; *Mec.E:* **appareil de s.,** change-over mechanism; (*b*) *Alg:* substitution; (*c*) *Geol:* metasomatism; (*d*) *Psy:* **activité de s.,** displacement activity; (*e*) (*computers*) **s. d'adresse,** address substitution; **caractère de s.,** substitute character. 2. *Jur:* entail (to grandchildren or grand-nephews).

substitutionnaire [sypstitysjɔnɛːr], *s.m. & f.* substitute; person substituted.

substrat [sypstra], *s.m.*, **substratum** [sypstratɔm], *s.m. Geol: Ling: Phil:* substratum; *Phot: Biol: Elcs:* (*computers*) substrate.

substruction [sypstryksjɔ̃], *s.f.* 1. (*a*) substruction, substructure, foundation; (*b*) underlying ruins of ancient buildings (that have since been built over). 2. underpinning.

substructural, -aux [sypstryktyral, -o], *a.* substructural.

substructure [sypstryktyːr], *s.f.* substructure.

subsumer [sypsyme], *v.tr. Phil:* to subsume.

subterfuge [syptɛrfyːʒ], *s.m.* subterfuge; **user de s.,** to resort to subterfuge; to evade the issue, to quibble.

subterminal, -aux [syptɛrminal, -o], *a.* subterminal.

subterrané [syptɛrane], *a.* subterranean; underground.

subtil [syptil], *a.* subtle. 1. (*a*) tenuous, thin (matter); fine (dust); rarefied (air); (*b*) pervasive (poison, scent, etc.). 2. (*a*) acute, keen (sense of smell, hearing, etc.); discerning, shrewd (mind, leader); (*b*) delicate, nice, fine (distinction, etc.); (*c*) *Pej:* artful, crafty, cunning (mind, etc.); fine-spun (argument).

subtilement [syptilmɑ̃], *adv.* (*a*) subtly; (*b*) craftily.

subtilisation [syptilizasjɔ̃], *s.f.* subtilization; *Ch:* volatilization.

subtiliser [syptilize], *v.tr.* 1. to subtilize; (*a*) to refine (a substance); (*b*) to make (an argument, an answer) too subtle; *abs.* **s. sur une question,** to subtilize on a question. 2. *F:* (*a*) to take in, cheat (s.o.); (*b*) to sneak (s.o.'s watch, etc.); to pinch (s.o.'s money); **on m'a subtilisé ma montre,** someone has pinched my watch.

subtiliseur, -euse [syptilizœːr, -øːz], *s. A:* (*a*) subtilizer; hairsplitter; (*b*) sneak-thief.

subtilité [syptilite], *s.f.* 1. subtlety (of matter, poison, etc.); fineness (of dust); rarefied state (of air). 2. (*a*) acuteness, quickness (of hearing, etc.); shrewdness (of mind); (*b*) subtlety, niceness, over-nicety, fineness (of distinction); (*c*) subtlety (of argument); (*d*) artfulness, craftiness. 3. subtle argument, distinction.

subtropical, -aux [syptrɔpikal, -o], *a.* subtropical.

subulé [sybyle], *a. Nat.Hist:* subulate(d), awl-shaped (leaf, antenna).

subulifolié [sybylifɔlje], *a. Bot:* with subulate leaves.

suburbain [sybyrbɛ̃], *a.* suburban.

suburbicaire [sybyrbikɛːr], *a. Ecc.Adm:* suburbicarian, suburbican (diocese).

Subur(r)e (la) [lasybyːr], *Pr.n.f. Rom.Ant:* the Subur(r)a.

subvenir [sybvəniːr], *v.ind.tr.* (*conj. like* VENIR) (*the aux. is* **avoir**) **s. à qn,** to come to the aid of s.o.; **s. à l'entretien de qn,** to support s.o.; **s. aux besoins de qn,** to supply, provide for, the needs of s.o.; **s. aux frais d'une maladie,** to meet, defray, the expenses of an illness; **s. à la détresse, de qn,** to relieve s.o.'s distress; **il a subvenu à tout,** he provided for everything; he met all expenses.

subvention [sybvɑ̃sjɔ̃], *s.f.* subsidy, subvention, grant (of money); **recevoir une s. de l'État,** to be subsidized by the state.

subventionnel, -elle [sybvɑ̃sjɔnɛl], *a.* subventionary (payment).

subventionner [sybvɑ̃sjɔne], *v.tr.* to subsidize; to grant financial aid to (undertaking, institution, etc.); **être subventionné par l'État,** to be subsidized by the State, to receive a State grant, to be State-aided; **industries subventionnées,** subsidized industries; **subventionné par la municipalité, par la commune,** rate-aided; **école subventionnée,** maintained school; **étudiants subventionnés,** grant-aided students.

subversif, -ive [sybvɛrsif, -iːv], *a.* subversive (**de,** of); **doctrines subversives de tout patriotisme,** doctrines subversive of all patriotism.

subversion [sybvɛrsjɔ̃], *s.f.* subversion (of morality); overthrow (of the State, etc.).

subversivement [sybvɛrsivmɑ̃], adv. subversively.

subvertir [sybvɛrtiːr], v.tr. to subvert (order, morality, etc.).

suc[1] [syk], s.m. (a) juice; Bot: sap; s. de citron, de viande, lemon juice, meat juice; s. gastrique, gastric juice; (b) pith, essence, quintessence (of a book, poem, etc.); tirer tout le s. de qch., to extract all the goodness from sth.

suc[2], s.m. Geol: (a) (volcanic) cone; (b) phonolitic dike.

succédané [syksedane]. 1. a. Pharm: succedaneous, substitute (remedy). 2. s.m. substitute (de, for); les succédanés de l'absinthe, substitutes for absinthe.

succéder [syksede], v.ind.tr. (je succède, n. succédons; je succéderai) 1. s. à qn, à qch., to succeed, follow after, s.o., sth.; les vivants succèdent aux morts, the living replace the dead, step into the shoes of the dead; au potage succéda la viande, meat followed the soup; un sentiment de pitié succéda à sa rage, his anger gave place to a feeling of pity; s. au trône, to succeed to the throne; s. à une fortune, to inherit, come in for, a fortune; il est pharmacien et il veut que son fils lui succède, he is a chemist and wants his son to succeed him in, to take over, the business; les années se succèdent, the years follow one another; les révolutions se sont succédé au Pérou, revolution followed revolution in Peru; Peru has had a succession of revolutions. 2. A: (a) (of activity) to be successful; tout leur rit, tout leur succède, everything is favourable to them, they are successful in everything; (b) to happen, occur; qui sait ce qui pourra s.? who knows what may happen?

succenteur [syksɑ̃tœːr], s.m. Ecc: succentor.

succenturié [syksɑ̃tyrje], a. Z: succenturiate; Orn: ventricule s., succenturiate lobe; crop.

succès [syksɛ], s.m. 1. A: result, issue (of an undertaking, etc.); bon s., mauvais s., favourable, unfavourable, issue. 2. success, favourable result; la vie est remplie de s. et d'échecs, life is full of ups and downs; avoir du s., (of undertaking) to turn out a success; (of article of commerce) to be a success, to catch on; remporter de grands s., to achieve great triumphs; remporter un s. complet, to be entirely successful; F: to sweep the board; il s'en est tiré avec s., he got through successfully; tentative sans s., unsuccessful attempt; il essaya sans s. de . . , he tried unsuccessfully to . . .; une seconde tentative n'eut pas plus de s., a second attempt met with no better success; un facteur de s., a factor for, in, success; c'est un (grand) s. de librairie, it's a best-seller; livre à s., best-seller; auteur à s., best-selling author, F: best-seller; avoir grand s., to be a great, a huge, success; Th: décrocher le grand s., to make a big hit, a great hit; c'est un s. fou, it's a great success, Th: a smash hit; pièce à s., hit; s. d'estime, succès d'estime, success with a limited public; s. de scandale, succès de scandale; durée du s. d'une pièce, run of a play.

successeur [syksesœːr], s.m. successor (de, to, of); Com: ancienne maison Martin; Thomas s., Thomas late Martin.

successibilité [syksesibilite], s.f. 1. Pol: successiveness. 2. Jur: right of succession to an inheritance.

successible [syksesibl̥], a. Jur: 1. (of relation) entitled to inherit, to succeed. 2. parenté au degré s., degree of relationship entitling to a share in the estate of an intestate.

successif, -ive [syksesif, -iːv], a. 1. successive; trois jours successifs, three days running; après des pertes successives, after a succession of losses; rires et pleurs successifs, alternate laughter and tears; Nav: mouvement s., alteration of course (16 points) in succession. 2. Jur: (a) droit s., law of succession, of inheritance; (b) droits successifs, right to succeed, right of succession.

succession [syksesjɔ̃], s.f. 1. succession; (a) series, sequence (of ideas, sounds, days, etc.); s. de mésaventures, chapter of accidents; par s. de temps, in course of time; (b) s. à la couronne, à la présidence, succession to the crown, to the presidency; prendre la s. d'une maison de commerce, to take over a business. 2. codage en s., straight-line coding. 3. Jur: inheritance, succession; (a) inheriting, coming into (property); droits de s., probate duty; estate duties; death duties; (b) estate; laisser une s. considérable, to leave a large estate; recueillir une s., to come into an inheritance, into an estate.

successivement [syksesivmɑ̃], adv. successively, in succession; one after another; in turn.

successivité [syksesivite], s.f. successiveness, successivity.

successoral, -aux [syksesɔral, -o], a. Jur: relating to a succession, to an inheritance; successional; taxes successorales, death duties; estate duties.

succin [syksɛ̃], s.m. succin, succinite; yellow amber; vernis au s., amber varnish.

succinamide [syksinamid], s.m. Ch: succinamide.

succinate [syksinat], s.m. Ch: succinate.

succinct [syksɛ̃, syksɛ̃ːkt], a. 1. succinct, brief, concise (statement, etc.); F: repas s., scanty meal; short commons. 2. (computers) résumé s., compendium.

succinctement [syksɛ̃tmɑ̃, -ɛ̃ktəmɑ̃], adv. succinctly, briefly, concisely; F: dîner s., to have a meagre dinner, a scanty meal.

succinique [syksinik], a. Ch: succinic (acid).

succinite [syksinit], s.f. Miner: succinite.

succinyle [syksinil], s.m. Ch: succinyl.

succion [syksjɔ̃], s.f. 1. suction; sucking (of a wound); pratiquer la s. d'une plaie, to suck a wound. 2. down draught (of sinking ship).

succomber [sykɔ̃be], v.i. to succumb. 1. s. sous le poids de qch., to sink under the weight of sth.; je succombe au sommeil, I can't stay awake. 2. (a) to be overpowered, defeated; s. sous le nombre, to succumb to odds, to force; to be overpowered by numbers; (b) to yield (to grief, etc.); s. à l'émotion, to be overcome by emotion; s. à la tentation, to succumb to temptation; ne nous laissez pas s. à la tentation, lead us not into temptation; s. aux séductions de qn, to fall a victim to the wiles of s.o.; il succombe toujours à l'attrait d'un joli minois, he always falls for a pretty face; (c) to die; s. à une maladie, to succumb to an illness; s. au poison, to die of poison; il succomba sous les coups, he was beaten to death.

succube [sykyb], s.m. succubus, succuba.

succulence [sykylɑ̃ːs], s.f. 1. succulence; juiciness. 2. A: succulent morsel; toothsome morsel.

succulent [sykylɑ̃], a. succulent (food); morceau s., succulent, tasty, morsel; Bot: feuille succulente, succulent, fleshy, leaf; plante succulente, succulent.

succursale [sykyrsal], s.f. (a) branch (establishment) (of stores, etc.); branch (of bank); sub-office; (b) Ecc: also a. (église) s., chapel of ease, succursal chapel.

succursaliste [sykyrsalist], s.m. 1. priest in charge (of a chapel of ease). 2. Com: (a) branch manager; (b) chain of stores.

succussion [sykysjɔ̃], s.f. Med: succession.

sucement [sysmɑ̃], s.m. sucking.

suce-pierre [syspjɛːr], s.m.inv. Ich: lamprey.

sucer [syse], v.tr. (je suçai(s); n. suçons) to suck (milk, orange, bone, etc.); s. une plaie, to suck a wound; se s. les doigts, to suck one's fingers; s. de bons principes avec le lait, to acquire sound principles from infancy; F: s. qn jusqu'au dernier sou, jusqu'à la moelle des os, to suck s.o. dry; to take s.o.'s last farthing; to bleed s.o. white; P: s. la pomme à qn, to kiss s.o.

sucette [syset], s.f. 1. Sug.-R: sucker (to drain off the syrup); Paperm: suction box (under the machine wire). 2. (a) (baby's) comforter, dummy; (b) lollipop, F: lollie, lolly; s. glacée, ice-lolly.

suceur, -euse [sysœːr, -øːz]. 1. s. (a) sucker; (b) s.m. Ich: sucker, sucking fish; (c) s.m.pl. Z: Suctoria. 2. (a) s.m. nozzle (of vacuum cleaner); (b) s.f. suceuse, suction dredger. 3. a. (a) sucking (child, etc.); (b) Z: suctorial.

suçoir [syswaːr], s.m. suctorial organ; Ent: etc: sucker.

suçon [sysɔ̃], s.m. F: 1. mark made (on skin) by sucking, by a kiss. 2. (a) stick of barley sugar; (b) A: crust (wrapped in a rag, to be sucked by infant); (c) Dressm: dart.

suçotement [sysɔtmɑ̃], s.m. sucking.

suçoter [sysɔte], v.tr. F: to suck away at (a sweet).

sucrage [sykraːʒ], s.m. sugaring, sweetening (of wines, etc.).

sucrase [sykrɑːz], s.f. Ch: invert sugar.

sucrate [sykrat], s.m. sucrate, saccharate.

sucre [sykr̥], s.m. sugar; (a) s. de canne, cane sugar; s. de betterave, beet sugar; s. en pains, loaf sugar; pain de s., sugar-loaf; montagne en pain de s., sugar-loaf mountain; s. en poudre, s. semoule, caster sugar; s. cristallisé, granulated sugar; s. farine, s. glace, s. à glacer, icing sugar; s. vanillé, vanilla sugar; s. en morceaux, A: en tablettes; A: s. cassé, lump sugar; s. brut, crude sugar; s. d'orge, barley sugar; F: s. noir, liquorice; des sucres de pomme, sticks of sugar candy; pince à s., sugar tongs; fabricant de s., sugar maker, boiler; faire sa fortune dans les sucres, to make one's fortune in sugar; F: il a été tout s. et tout miel, he was all honey; F: casser du s. sur le dos de qn, to run s.o. down; to make a scurrilous attack on s.o.; A: brûler du s., to burn sugar (in a spoon, etc., in order to disinfect a room); F: A: toutes les fois que je vais le voir il brûle du s., he can't bear the sight of me; P: c'est un vrai s., he's a poppet; Fr.C: partie de s., sugaring party; (b) Ch: s. de gélatine, glycocoll, glycin; gelatine sugar; s. de lait, lactose; s. de fruit, fructose, levulose; s. de raisin, grape sugar; glucose; s. de saturne, sugar of lead.

sucré [sykre], a. 1. sugared, sweetened (coffee, etc.); sweet (fruits, etc.); le gâteau est trop s., the cake has too much sugar in it, is too sweet; mon thé est trop s., my tea is too sweet; eau sucrée, sugar and water. 2. sugary (words, manner, smile); elle fait la sucrée, butter wouldn't melt in her mouth; elle fait la sucrée quand vous êtes là, she's all sweetness when you are there.

sucrer [sykre], v.tr. to sugar; to sweeten; F: sucrez-vous, help yourself to sugar (in your tea, etc.); P: se s., to line one's own pockets, to make a good thing out of something; to take the lion's share; F: s. les fraises, (i) to tremble; (ii) to be an old dotard, in one's dotage.

sucrerie [sykrəri], s.f. 1. (a) sugar works, mill; (b) sugar refinery. 2. pl. sweetmeats, sweets, confectionery; aimer les sucreries, to have a sweet tooth. 3. Fr.C: maple tree grove.

sucrier, -ère [sykrije, -ɛːr]. 1. a. (of) sugar; industrie sucrière, sugar industry. 2. s. sugar manufacturer, sugar boiler. 3. s.m. sugar basin. 4. s.m. Orn: sunbird.

sucrin [sykrɛ̃], a. & s.m. (melon) s., sugary melon.

sud [syd]. 1. s.m. no pl. (a) south; un vent du s., a southerly wind; le vent du s., the south wind; maison exposée au s., house with a southern exposure, house that faces south; demeurer dans le s. de l'Angleterre, to live in the south of England; au s., in the south; borné au s. par . . ., bounded on the south by . . .; Orléans est au s. de Paris, Orleans lies, is, (to the) south of Paris; l'Amérique du S., South America; Astr: La Croix du S., the Southern Cross; Nau: faire le s., to steer a southerly course; vers le s., southward; (b) Nau: le s., the south wind. 2. a.inv. south, southerly (wind); southern (part, latitude); Nau: chemin s., southing; le pôle s., the south pole; le côté s., the south side (of house, wall, etc.).

sud-africain, -aine [sydafrikɛ̃, -ɛn], a. & s. Geog: South(-)African; la République sud-africaine, the Republic of South Africa; Hist: l'Union Sud-africaine, the Union of South Africa; pl. sud-africain(e)s.

sud-américain, -aine [sydamerikɛ̃, -ɛn], a. & s. Geog: South(-)American; pl. sud-américain(e)s.

sudamina [sydamina], s.m.pl. Med: sudamina (of typhoid fever, etc.); prickly heat.

sudation [sydasjɔ̃], s.f. Med: etc: sudation. sweating.

sudatoire [sydatwaːr]. 1. a. sudatory. 2. s.m. hot-air bath; sweating-room; Rom.Ant: sudatorium.

sud-coréen, -éenne [sydkɔreɛ̃, -eɛn], a. & s. South Korean; pl. sud-coréens, -ennes.

sud-est [sydɛst]. 1. s.m. no pl. south east; vent du s.-e., south-east wind, south-easter; vers le s.-e., south eastward. 2. a.inv. south-east, south-easterly (wind); south-eastern (region).

sud-est-quart-est [sydɛstkarɛst, Nau: syrɛkarɛ], s.m. & a.inv. south-east by east.

sud-est-quart-sud [sydɛstkarsyd, Nau: syrɛkarsy], s.m. & a.inv. south-east by south.

Sudètes [sydɛt], Pr.n.m.pl. Geog: les Allemands des S., the Sudeten Germans; les monts S., the Sudeten Mountains.

sudiste [sydist], s.m. Geog: Hist: (in the American Civil War) southerner; a. southern (army, troops).

sudorifère [sydɔrifɛːr], a. = SUDORIPARE.

sudorifique [sydɔrifik], a. & s.m. Pharm: sudorific (drug).

sudoripare [sydɔripaːr], a. Anat: sudoriferous, sudoriparous, perspiratory; glande s., sweat gland.

sud-ouest [sydwɛst, Nau: syrwɛ, syrwa]. 1. s.m. no pl. (a) south-west; du s.-o., south-westerly, south-western; vers le s.-o., south-westward; (b) south-west wind, south-wester. 2. a.inv. south-westerly (wind); south-western (region).

Sud-Ouest Africain (le) [ləsydwɛstafrikɛ̃], Pr.n.m. Geog: South-West Africa.

sud-ouest-quart-ouest [sydwɛstkarwɛst, Nau: syrwakarwa], s.m. & a.inv. Nau: south-west-by-west.

sud-ouest-quart-sud [sydwɛstkarsyd, *Nau:* syd-wakarsy], *s.m. & a.inv. Nau:* south-west-by-south.

sud-quart-sud-est [sydkarsydɛst, *Nau:* sykarsyɛ], *s.m. & a.inv. Nau:* south-by-east.

sud-quart-sud-ouest [sydkarsydwɛst, *Nau:* syk-arsyrwa], *s.m. & a.inv.* south-by-west.

sud-sud-est [sydsydɛst, *Nau:* sysyɛ], *s.m. & a.inv.* south-south-east.

sud-sud-ouest [sydsydwɛst, *Nau:* sysyrwa], *s.m. & a.inv.* south-south-west.

sud-vietnamien, -ienne [sydvjɛtnamjɛ̃, -jɛn], *a. & s.* South Vietnamese; *pl. sud-vietnamiens, -iennes.*

suécoman, -ane [sɥekɔmɑ̃, -an], *Pol.Hist:* (in Finland). **1.** *a.* pro-Swedish. **2.** *s.* pro-Swede.

Suède [sɥɛd], *Pr.n.f. Geog:* Sweden; **gants de s.,** suède gloves.

suédé [sɥede], *s.m. Tex:* suède cloth, imitation suède.

suédine [sɥedin], *s.f.* suedine, suedette, suède cloth.

suédois, -oise [sɥedwa, -waːz]. **1.** *a.* Swedish; *Metall:* **fonte suédoise,** Swedish pig; *Gym:* **la gymnastique suédoise,** *s.f.* **la suédoise,** Swedish gymnastics, exercises; *s.a.* ALLUMETTE 1. **2.** *s.* Swede. **3.** *s.m. Ling:* Swedish.

suée [sɥe], *s.f.* **1.** *Med: Vet: etc:* sweating, sweat; **une bonne s.,** a good sweat. **2.** *P:* (*a*) start, fright, scare; (*b*) hard job; sweat; fag; grind.

suer [sɥe], *v.* to sweat. **1.** *v.i.* (*a*) to perspire, sweat; **s. à grosses gouttes,** to sweat profusely; *F:* **s. comme un phoque,** to sweat like a bull, horse, pig; **faire s. qn,** (i) to make s.o. sweat; (ii) *F:* to annoy, sicken, s.o.; **tu me fais s.!** you make me sick! I'm tired of you! (*b*) (*of walls, etc.*) to ooze weep; *Tchn:* **faire s. une peau,** to sweat a skin; (*c*) to labour, toil, drudge. **2.** (*with cogn. acc.*) (*a*) to exude (poison, etc.); (*b*) **s. du sang,** to sweat blood; **s. la piété,** to ooze piety; **s. l'égoïsme,** to be steeped in selfishness; **maison qui sue la misère, le crime,** house that bears every mark of poverty, that reeks of crime. **3.** *v.tr.* (*a*) **s. un cheval,** to sweat a horse; (*b*) *Metall:* **s. le fer,** to sweat iron.

suerie [syri], *s.f.* **1.** *A:* = SUÉE. **2.** drying barn, sweat house (for tobacco).

Suétone [sɥetɔn], *Pr.n.m. Rom.Hist:* Suetonius.

suette [sɥɛt], *s.f.* **1.** *Med:* **s. miliaire,** miliary fever. **2.** *Hist:* **s. anglaise,** sweating sickness.

sueur [sɥœːr], *s.f.* sweat, perspiration; **être en s.,** to be sweating, in a sweat; **avoir des sueurs froides,** to be in a cold sweat; **gagner son pain à la s. de son front,** to live by the sweat of one's brow; to toil and moil; **le fruit de mes sueurs,** the fruits of my labour.

Suèves [sɥɛːv], *s.m.pl. Hist:* Suevi, Suevians; *Geog: A:* **la mer des S.,** the Baltic Sea.

Suez [sɥɛːz], *Pr.n. Geog:* Suez; **le canal de S.,** the Suez Canal.

suffètes [syf(f)ɛt], *s.m.pl. A.Hist:* Suffetes.

suffire [syfiːr], *v.i.* (*pr.p.* **suffisant;** *p.p.* **suffi;** *pr.ind.* **je suffis, n. suffisons, ils suffisent;** *pr.sub.* **je suffise;** *p.d.* **je suffisais;** *p.h.* **je suffis;** *fu.* **je suffirai**) (*a*) to suffice; to be sufficient; **un rien suffit à l'inquiéter,** he worries about trifles; **cela ne me suffit pas,** that's not enough, that won't do, for me; **cela ne me suffit pas pour vivre,** that is not enough for me to live upon; **quelle somme suffira pour vous contenter?** what amount will (be sufficient to) satisfy you? **cela suffit pour qu'on ne puisse se méprendre sur . . .,** that is enough to prevent, exclude, the possibility of any misapprehension about . . .; *Prov:* **à chaque jour suffit sa peine, sa tâche, son mal,** sufficient unto the day is the evil thereof; *impers.* **il suffit de quelques mots pour le persuader,** a few words were enough to persuade him; **il suffit de l'écouter, pour . . .,** one only has to, one need only, listen to him to . . .; **il suffit qu'il le dise,** (it is) enough for him to say so; **il suffit d'un coup d'œil pour se rendre compte que . . .,** a mere glance will show that . . .; *F:* **(il) suffit! ça suffit!** enough! that'll do! **suffit que je n'en ai rien obtenu,** suffice it to say that I got nothing out of him; **il suffit d'une heure pour . . .,** it only takes an hour to . . .; (*b*) **s. à qch., à faire qch.,** to be equal, adequate, to sth., to doing sth.; **moi seul je suffis à toutes les dépenses,** I am myself equal to, can meet, all the expenses; **s. à ses besoins,** to satisfy one's requirements; **il ne peut pas s. à tout,** he can't cope with everything; **je n'y suffis plus,** it's too much for me; *F:* I can't cope; **il s'est toujours suffi,** he has always supported himself, paid his way, made his own living; **à l'âge qu'il a, il devrait se s. (à lui-même),** at his age he ought to be able to fend, to shift, for himself, to keep himself, to pay his way; **industries qui se suffisent à elles-mêmes,** self-contained industries; **pays qui se suffisent à eux-mêmes,** self-supporting countries.

suffisamment [syfizamɑ̃], *adv.* sufficiently, enough, adequately; **j'ai s. de bien,** I am well enough off; **agir sans avoir s. réfléchi,** to act without due reflection.

suffisance [syfizɑ̃ːs], *s.f.* **1.** (*a*) sufficiency, adequacy; **avoir s. de qch.,** to have enough of sth.; **manger à sa s.,** to eat one's fill; **avoir de qch. à s., en s.,** to have plenty of sth.; (*b*) *A:* competence; **homme de s.,** competent man. **2.** self-complacency; self-importance; self-conceit; **il est d'une s. insupportable,** he is unbearably conceited, priggish.

suffisant [syfizɑ̃], *a.* **1.** (*a*) sufficient, adequate, enough; *Phil:* **raison suffisante,** sufficient reason; *Theol:* **grâce suffisante,** sufficient grace; **c'est plus que s.,** that is more than enough; **connaissance suffisante de l'anglais,** competent, adequate, knowledge of English; **quantité suffisante de vivres,** adequate supply of food; **c'est s. pour le voyage,** that is enough, sufficient, for the journey; (*b*) *A:* **lui seul est s. pour cela, pour faire cela,** he alone is equal to that. **2.** self-satisfied, self-important, bumptious, conceited (air, tone); *s.m.* conceited person; prig; **faire le s.,** to give oneself airs; to be self-important.

suffixal, -aux [syfiksal, -o], *a. Gram:* suffixal.

suffixation [syfiksasjɔ̃], *s.f. Gram:* suffixation.

suffixe [syfiks], *Gram:* **1.** *s.m.* suffix. **2.** *a.* **particule s.,** suffixed particle.

suffixer [syfikse], *v.tr. Gram:* to suffix.

suffocant [syfɔkɑ̃], *a.* (*a*) suffocating, stifling; **gaz s.,** semi-asphyxiating gas; (*b*) stunning; **nouvelles suffocantes,** stunning, overwhelming, news.

suffocation [syfɔkasjɔ̃], *s.f.* suffocation, choking.

suffoquer [syfɔke]. **1.** *v.tr.* (*a*) *A:* to suffocate; smother, choke (s.o. to death); (*b*) (*of smell, etc.*) to suffocate, stifle; **les sanglots la suffoquaient** she was choking with sobs; **ce secret le suffoque,** he can bear this secret no longer; *F:* **un sans-gêne qui suffoque,** a coolness that takes one's breath away. **2.** *v.i.* to choke; **s. de colère,** to choke with anger.

suffragant [syfragɑ̃], *a. & s.m. Ecc:* (*a*) suffragan (bishop); **diocèse s. de . . .,** diocese suffragan to . . .; (*b*) (*in the Protestant Church*) probationer.

suffrage [syfraːʒ], *s.m.* **1.** *Pol:* suffrage, vote; **dix mille suffrages,** ten thousand votes; **s. universel,** universal franchise or suffrage; **s. restreint,** limited franchise; *A:* **s. censitaire,** vote the qualification for which is by ownership of property, by tax assessment; **s. universel pur et simple,** one-man-one-vote suffrage; **mériter le(s) suffrage(s) du public,** to earn the approbation of the public. **2.** *Ecc:* suffrage, (short) intercessory prayer.

suffragette [syfraʒɛt], *s.f. Pol:* suffragette.

suffragiste [syfraʒist], *s.m. & f. Pol:* suffragist.

suffrutescent [syf(f)rytɛs(s)ɑ̃], *a. Bot:* suffrutescent.

suffusion [syf(f)yzjɔ̃], *s.f. Med:* suffusion (*esp.* of blood); flush.

suggérer [syɡʒere], *v.tr.* (**je suggère, n. suggérons; je suggérerai**) to suggest (à, to); **s. de faire qch.,** to suggest doing sth.; **suggérer à qn de faire qch.,** to suggest to s.o. that he should do sth.; **s. de fixer la réunion au 9 juin; s. que la réunion soit fixée au 9 juin,** to suggest that the meeting be fixed for June 9th; **s. une réponse à qn,** to prompt s.o. with an answer; *Jur:* **s. un testament,** to use undue influence with the maker of a will.

suggestibilité [syɡʒɛstibilite], *s.f.* suggestibility; susceptibility, susceptivity (to impressions, suggestions, hypnotic influences).

suggestible [syɡʒɛstibl], *a.* suggestible.

suggestif, -ive [syɡʒɛstif, -iːv], *a.* (*a*) suggestive; (*b*) evocative; (*c*) **plaisanterie suggestive,** suggestive joke.

suggestion [syɡʒɛstjɔ̃], *s.f.* suggestion; (*a*) (evil) suggestion, incitement; *Lit:* **les suggestions du démon,** the suggestions of the Evil One; (*b*) **suggestions en vue d'une amélioration,** suggestions for improvement; **pas la moindre s. de . . .,** not the slightest hint of . . .; **conclusion donnée à titre de s.,** tentative conclusion; (*c*) **s. hypnotique,** hypnotic suggestion.

suggestionner [syɡʒɛstjɔne], *v.tr.* to produce an effect of suggestion on (s.o.); **se laisser s.,** to succumb to suggestion.

suggestionneur [syɡʒɛstjɔnœːr], *s.m. Med:* suggestionist.

suggestivité [syɡʒɛstivite], *s.f.* suggestive character, tendencies (of s.o., sth.); suggestiveness.

sugillation [syʒil(l)asjɔ̃], *s.f. Med:* suggillation.

suicidaire [sɥisidɛːr]. **1.** *a.* suicidal (tendencies, etc.), suicide-prone (pers.). **2.** *s.m. & f.* person haunted by the idea of committing suicide; suicidomaniac; suicidal, suicide-prone person.

suicidant [sɥisidɑ̃], *a.* suicidal; **mélancolie non suicidante,** melancholy that stops short of suicide.

suicide[1] [sɥisid], *s.m.* suicide; **faux s.,** attempted suicide; *a. Hist:* **avion s.,** suicide plane.

suicide[2]. **1.** *s.m.* = SUICIDÉ. **2.** *a.* suicidal.

suicidé, -ée [sɥiside], *a. & s.* (*pers.*) suicide; *Jur:* felo de se.

suicider [sɥiside], *v.tr. F:* (*a*) to murder (s.o.) and make it look like suicide; **il ne s'est pas suicidé; on l'a suicidé,** he didn't commit suicide; it was just made to look like it; (*b*) to drive (s.o.) to suicide.

se suicider, to commit suicide; **se s. politiquement,** to commit political suicide.

suicidomane [sɥisidɔman], *s.m. & f.* suicidal maniac.

suicidomanie [sɥisidɔmani], *s.f. Med:* suicidal mania.

suidés [sɥide], *s.m.pl. Z:* Suidae, swine.

suie [sɥi], *s.f.* **1.** soot, **murs noirs de s.,** sooty walls. **2.** *Agr:* smut (of cereal).

suif [sɥif], *s.m.* **1.** (*a*) tallow; *F:* candle grease; **s. de mouton,** mutton fat; **chandelle de s.,** tallow candle; **huile de s.,** oleine; *s.a.* BOULE 1; *Tchn:* **mettre une peau en s.,** to tallow a skin; **cuir en s.,** tallowed leather; (*b*) *Nau:* paying stuff; **donner du s. à un navire,** to pay, tallow, a ship; *P: A:* **recevoir un s.,** to get a wigging, a dressing-down; *P:* **faire du s.,** to kick up a row; *P:* **chercher du s.,** to be out for a fight. **2.** (*a*) *Miner:* **s. minéral,** mineral tallow, mountain tallow, hatchettite; (*b*) **s. végétal,** vegetable tallow; **arbre à s.,** Chinese tallow tree. **3.** *Nau:* arming (of the deep-sea lead).

suiffard, -arde [sɥifaːr, -ard], *s. P:* **1.** *A:* toff, swell. **2.** *A:* cheat (at cards). **3.** quarrelsome person.

suiffée [sɥife], *s.f. P:* thrashing.

suiffer [sɥife], *v.tr.* (*a*) to tallow (leather, etc.); to grease (a pole); *Nau:* **s. la sonde,** to arm the lead; (*b*) *Nau:* to pay (ship); (*c*) *P:* to give (s.o.) a good dressing-down; (*d*) *I.C.E:* **bougie suiffée,** sooted sparking plug.

suiffeux, -euse [sɥifø, -øːz], *a.* tallowy; greasy.

suiformes [sɥifɔrm], *s.m.pl. Z:* Suiformes.

suin(t) [sɥɛ̃], *s.m.* **1.** yolk, suint, (natural) grease (of wool); wool fat, wool grease; **laines en s.,** greasy wool, wool in the yolk, in (the) grease. **2.** *Glassm:* sandiver; glass gall.

suintant [sɥɛ̃tɑ̃], *a.* oozing, dripping; sweating (wall, etc.).

suintement [sɥɛ̃tmɑ̃], *s.m.* oozing, seeping, trickling, dripping; sweating (of water, of rock, wall); running, weeping (of wound); leaking (of boiler).

suinter [sɥɛ̃te]. **1.** *v.i.* (*a*) (*of water, wall, rock*) to ooze, seep, sweat, drip, trickle; (*b*) (*of vessel*) to leak; (*of wound*) to run, to weep. **2.** (*with cogn. acc.*) to exude; *F:* **s. la haine,** to ooze hatred.

Suisse[1] [sɥis], *Pr.n.f. Geog:* Switzerland; **la S. alémanique,** German Switzerland; **la S. romande,** French-speaking Switzerland; **la S. italienne,** Italian-speaking Switzerland.

suisse[2]. **1.** *a.* Swiss; **femme s.,** Swiss woman. **2.** *s.m.* (*a*) **un S.,** a Swiss (man); **les Suisses,** the Swiss; (*b*) *Hist:* (i) Swiss mercenary, Switzer (in the service of France); (ii) Swiss guard (at the Vatican); *F:* **boire en s.** *A:* **faire s.,** to drink or eat on one's own (without treating the company); (*c*) *Ecc:* verger (in full regalia); (*d*) **petit s.,** small cream cheese; petit suisse; (*e*) *Fr.C: Z:* **s. (rayé),** chipmunk.

Suissesse [sɥisɛs], *s.f.* (*often Pej:*) Swiss (woman).

suite [sɥit], *s.f.* **1.** (act of) following, pursuit; **droit de s.,** (i) *Hist:* (lord's) right of pursuit (of a serf); (ii) *Com:* stoppage in transitu; (iii) *Nau:* right of pursuit; **être à la s. de qn,** to be in pursuit of s.o.; *F:* to be after s.o. (*cp.* 3). **2.** (*a*) continuation, following up; (*in restaurant*) **apportez-nous la s.,** may we have the next course please? **j'oublie la s. de l'air,** I forget how the tune goes on; **faire s. à qch.,** to be a continuation of sth.; to follow up sth.; **le salon fait s. à la salle à manger,** the drawing room leads out of the dining room; *Corr:* **comme s. à notre lettre d'hier,** in further reference to, further to, referring to, our letter of yesterday; **à la s. de votre demande,** referring to, in reply to, with reference to, your request; **sous s. de tous**

frais, all charges will follow; *Com:* **donner s. à une commande**, to deal with, carry out, an order; **pour s. à donner**, (passed to you) for action; (*of article*) **sans s.**, cannot be repeated; **donner s. à une décision**, to give effect to a decision; **prendre la s. des affaires d'une maison**, to succeed to, take over, a business; **à la s. les uns des autres**, one after another; **nous marchions à sa s.**, we followed in his wake; **nous pénétrâmes à sa s. dans la salle**, we followed him into the room; **les historiens venus à sa s.**, the historians who came after him; **les maux que la guerre traîne à sa s.**, the evils that war brings in its train; *Mil:* **être mis à la s.**, to be discharged with a pension; **officier à la s.**, supernumerary officer; **à la s. de la décision prise**, following the decision made; *adv.phr.* **de s.**, (i) in succession; (ii) consecutively; **dix camions de s.**, ten lorries one after another, in a line; **dix heures de s.**, ten hours on end; **dix jours de s.**, ten days running; **il reste souvent ici pendant plusieurs semaines de s.**, he is often here for several weeks at a time; **et ainsi de s.**, and so on; *adv.phr.* **tout de s.**, *F:* **de s.**, at once, immediately, without delay; **je vais m'y mettre tout de s.**, I shall do it right away; I shall do it first thing; **dans la s.**, subsequently, in process of time; **par la s.**, later on, afterwards, eventually; **il fera mieux par la s.**, he will do better after a while, from now on; (*b*) sequel (of book, tale, etc.) (**de**, of; **à**, to); **s. au prochain numéro**, to be continued in our next; *Journ:* **s. à la page 30**, continued on page 30; **s. et fin**, concluded; (*c*) coherence, consistency (in reasoning); **sans s.**, (i) incoherent, disconnected (words, thoughts); (ii) brokenly, disconnectedly, incoherently; **propos sans s.**, desultory remarks; **s. dans les idées**, singleness of mind; **manquer (d'esprit) de s.**, (i) not to stick at anything for long; (ii) to lack method. **3.** (*a*) those coming after; tail (of procession, etc.); (*b*) suite, retinue, train, attendants (of monarch, etc.); **être à la s. de qn**, to be in s.o.'s train; (*cp.* 1); (*c*) *A:* **n'avoir point de s.**, to have no descendants or relatives; to have neither kith nor kin. **4.** (*a*) series, sequence, succession (of events, etc.); **s. de malheurs**, run of misfortunes, chapter of accidents; **longue s. d'ancêtres**, long line of ancestors; **la s. des temps**, the sequence of time; **dans la s. des siècles**, in the course of time, of centuries; **s. d'estampes**, set of prints; *Typ:* **tirage à la s.**, run-on printing; *Hyd.E:* **s. de biefs**, ladder of locks; (*b*) *Mth:* series; (*c*) *Mus:* **s. d'orchestre**, orchestral suite. **5.** consequence, result, issue; **cette affaire aura des suites graves**, this business will have serious consequences; **mourir des suites d'une blessure**, to die (as the result) of a wound; **se ressentir des suites d'une pneumonie**, to feel the after-effects of pneumonia; *s.a.* COUCHE 1; *adv.phr.* **par s. . . .**, consequently . . .; *prep.phr.* **par s. de**, **en s. de**, **s. à**, in consequence of, through, on account of; **absent par s. de maladie**, absent owing to, in consequence of, through, on account of, illness; **par s. de l'urgence de . . .**, in view of the urgency of . . .; **par s. d'une erreur**, by, through, an error; **par s. de sa blessure**, as a result of his wound, owing to his wound.

suitée [sɥite], *a.f.* **bête s.**, mare and foal; **laie s.**, wild sow with her young.

suivant[1] [sɥivɑ̃], *prep.* **1.** in the direction of; **marcher s. l'axe de la vallée**, to walk along the line of the valley; **coupe s. la ligne M N**, section along the line M N. **2.** according to, in accordance with (one's means, taste, etc.); in accordance with, following (instructions); **s. lui**, in his opinion, according to him; *Com:* **s. inventaire**, according to stock-list, as per list; *conj.phr.* **s. que** + *ind.*, depending on whether . . ., according as . . .; **s. qu'on m'aime ou qu'on me hait, j'aime ou hais à mon tour**, according to whether I am loved or hated, I also love or hate.

suivant[2], **-ante** [sɥivɑ̃, -ɑ̃:t]. **1.** *a.* (*a*) next, following (page, day, etc.); **au chapitre s.**, in the following chapter; **voir page 6 et suivantes**, see page 6 *et seq*; **les trois jours suivants**, the next three days; **pas dimanche prochain mais le dimanche s.**, not this Sunday but the next one, the one after; **notre méthode est la suivante**, our method is as follows; **au suivant! next (person) please!** (*b*) (*computers*) **caractère de mise en début de ligne suivante**, new line character. **2.** *s.m.* (*a*) follower, attendant; (*b*) *A:* **n'avoir ni enfants ni suivants**, to have neither kith nor kin. **3.** *s.f. Th:* **suivante**, waiting-maid; attendant.

suiveur, -euse [sɥivœ:r, -ø:z], (*a*) *s.m.* follower (de, of); (*b*) *a.* **voiture suiveuse**, car following a cycle race, etc.

suivez-moi-jeune-homme [sɥivemwaʒœnɔm], *s.m. inv. A.Cost:* follow-me-lads.

suivi [sɥivi]. **1.** *a.* connected (speech); sustained, coherent (reasoning); close (business relations); steadfast, unwavering (policy); continuous (work); *Com:* steady, persistent (demand); **correspondance suivie**, close, uninterrupted, correspondence. **2.** *a.* (*a*) well-attended, popular (course of lectures, etc.); **ce cours est très s.**, attendance at this class is very large; (*b*) **prédicateur très s.**, preacher who has a large following. **3.** *s.m.* follow-up; **faire le s. de qch.**, to keep track of sth.

suivisme [sɥivism], *s.m. Pol: etc:* tagging along.

suiviste [sɥivist], *a. & s.* tag-along.

suivre [sɥi:vr̩], *v.tr.* (*pr.p.* suivant; *p.p.* suivi; *pr.ind.* je suis, il suit, n. suivons, ils suivent; *pr.sub.* je suive; *p.d.* je suivais; *p.h.* je suivis; *fu.* je suivrai) to follow. **1.** (*a*) to go after, behind (s.o., sth.); **s. qn de près**, to follow close on s.o.'s heels; **s. qu pas à pas**, to dog s.o.'s footsteps; **être suivi par un chien**, to be followed by a dog; **partez, je vous suis**, you go on, I'm just coming, I'll follow on, I'll follow suit; **s. qn des yeux**, (i) to stand and follow s.o.'s progress (with one's eyes); (ii) not to lose sight of s.o.; **faire s. une lettre**, to forward, to redirect, a letter; (*on letter*) (*prière de*) **faire s.**, please forward; **ne pas faire s.**, not to be forwarded; *Typ:* (faire) **s.**, run on; (*in serial stories*) **à . . . s.**, to be continued; **arguments qui se suivent bien**, arguments that are connected, coherent; *Com:* **s. une affaire**, to follow up business; *Com:* **nous n'avons pas suivi cet article**, we have given up, discontinued, are not going on with, this line; (*b*) to understand; **je ne vous suis pas**, (i) I don't see your point; I don't follow you; *F:* I'm not with you; (ii) I don't agree with you; **je ne vous suis pas sur ce terrain**, I can't follow you when you get on to that; *Ten:* **s. la balle**, to follow through; (*c*) to escort, attend, accompany (s.o.); **être suivi de ses gens**, to be followed by one's attendants; to be attended by one's servants; **s. qn à cheval**, to ride behind s.o.; to escort s.o. on horseback; (*d*) to pursue (animal, enemy); **le remords le suit partout**, he is pursued by remorse; (*e*) to pay heed to, be attentive to (sth.); **il parle si vite que je ne peux pas le s.**, he talks so quickly that I cannot follow him; **suivez attentivement**, pay great attention; *Mus:* **suivez le chant**, colla parte, colla voce; *Sch: etc:* (*in reading*) **s. les lignes avec son doigt**, to follow the lines with one's finger; **s. avec qn**, to follow from s.o. else's book; (*f*) to watch (over), observe (s.o.'s progress, course of events, etc.); *Turf:* **chevaux à s.**, horses to follow; (*g*) **s. une piste, une indication**, to follow up a clue. **2.** (*a*) to succeed; to come, happen, after (sth.); **le printemps suit l'hiver**, spring follows winter; **winter is succeeded by spring; ces deux mots se suivent**, these two words are consecutive; **ça se suit bien**, it reads very well; **événements qui se suivent de près**, events that follow each other in quick succession; **conditions ainsi qu'il suit**, terms as follows; **les personnes dont les noms suivent**, the following persons; (*b*) to result from, be the consequence of (sth.); **la peine suit le crime**, punishment follows crime; *impers.* **il suit de là que . . .**, it follows (from this) that . . .; **que s'en est-il suivi?** what came of it? what was the consequence? **3.** (*a*) to go, proceed, along (road, train of thought, etc.); **s. son chemin**, to go on one's way; to pursue one's way; **suivez le bord de la rivière**, keep along the river; **la rivière suit son cours**, the river follows its course; **la justice suivra son cours**, justice will take its course; (*b*) to obey, conform to (fashion, law, etc.); to follow, act upon (advice); **s. son penchant**, to follow one's bent; **s. un dessin**, to follow, imitate, copy, a plan; **s. un mode de procédure**, to carry out a procedure; **s. une ligne de conduite**, to pursue a line of conduct. **4.** (*a*) to attend (series of concerts, etc.) (regularly); **s. des conférences**, to attend, hear, lectures; **s. un cours**, to take a course (of study); *Med:* **s. un traitement**, to follow a course of treatment; (*b*) to practise, exercise (profession, calling); **s. la profession de son père**, to follow one's father's profession; (*c*) to be a disciple of (s.o.); (*d*) **s. son temps**, to keep abreast of the times.

sujet[1], **-ette** [syʒɛ, -ɛt]. **1.** *a.* subject; (*a*) *A:* dependent; **être s. aux lois**, to be subject, amenable, to law; **je suis s. à l'heure**, my time is not my own; I must be there at the right time; **provinces sujettes**, subject provinces; **tenir qn très s.**, (i) to keep s.o. well under one's thumb; (ii) to keep s.o. very much tied; (*b*) liable, prone, exposed (à, to); **s. à la mort**, mortal;

s. à l'erreur, liable to, capable of, error; **s. au vice**, prone to vice; **être s. à la goutte**, to be subject, a martyr, to gout; **à mon âge on est s. au rhumatisme**, at my age one is liable, subject, to rheumatism; **votre ami paraît très s. à s'endetter**, your friend appears to be very good at running into debt; **s. à oublier, à mentir**, apt to forget, given to lying; *s.a.* CAUTION 1; (*c*) **contrat s. au droit de timbre**, agreement subject to stamp duty; **marchandises sujettes à un droit de . . .**, goods subject to a duty of . . . **2.** *s.* subject (of a state); *A:* **à nos féaux sujets**, to our trusty lieges.

sujet[2], *s.m.* **1.** subject; (*a*) cause, reason, object, ground (of complaint, anxiety, quarrel, etc.); **s. d'étonnement**, matter of astonishment; **être un s. de pitié**, to be an object of pity; **le Déluge avait été le s. de ses études**, the Flood had been the object of his studies; **j'ai tout s. d'espérer**, I have every reason to hope; **je ne vois là aucun s. de désaccord**, I can see no ground for dispute; **je n'ai aucun s. de plainte, de me plaindre**, I have no grounds for complaint, no reason to complain, nothing to complain about; **si je me plains c'est que j'en ai s.**, if I complain I have good cause; **agir avec s.**, to act with good reason; **avoir s. à mécontentement**, to have cause for dissatisfaction; *prep.phr.* **au s. de qn, de qch.**, relating to, concerning, about, s.o., sth.; **au s. de votre lettre**, with reference to your letter; **éprouver des craintes au s. de qch.**, to have fears about sth.; (*b*) subject matter (of speech, book, etc.); theme (of play, picture, discussion, etc.); topic (of conversation); *Mus:* subject (of fugue, etc.); **un beau s. de roman**, a fine subject for a novel; **c'est un de ses sujets préférés**, it is a favourite topic of his; **pendant que nous sommes sur ce s.**, while we are on this subject; **tous renseignements à ce s.**, all relevant information; (*c*) *Gram:* **s. du verbe**, subject of the verb; (*d*) *Psy: Med: etc:* subject (of an experiment); **servir de s. d'expérience**, to be a subject of experiment, *F:* to act as a guinea-pig. **2.** work of art; (finished) production; *Com:* **beau s. en faïence**, fine china statuette or group. **3.** individual, fellow; **mauvais s.**, (i) ne'er do well, bad lot, scapegrace; (ii) *Sch:* unsatisfactory pupil; **bon s.**, (i) steady, reliable, person; (ii) *Sch:* good pupil. **4.** *Hort:* stock.

sujétion [syʒesjɔ̃], *s.f.* **1.** subjection (à, to); servitude; **vivre dans la s.**, to live in subjection, in bondage; **s. aux lois**, subservience to the laws; **une habitude devient vite une s.**, we soon become slaves to a habit. **2.** (*a*) constraint, obligation; **emploi d'une grande s.**, job that keeps one close tied; (*b*) *Jur:* = SERVITUDE 2 (*a*). **3.** putting down, laying (of gun platform, etc.).

Sulamite (la) [lasylamit], *Pr.n.f. B.Lit:* the Shulamite.

sulcature [sylkaty:r], *s.f.* furrow, groove, fissure, *esp: Anat:* sulcus (of the brain).

sulcifère [sylsifɛ:r], *a. Nat.Hist:* sulcate.

sulciforme [sylsifɔrm], *a. Anat:* sulciform.

sulf(o)- [sylf(ɔ)], *pref. Ch:* sulph(o)-, sulf(o); NOTE. *the spelling sulf(o)-, now largely U.S. usage, may gradually replace sulph(o)- in international scientific use.*

sulfacide [sylfasid], *s.m. Ch:* sulpho-acid; thioacid.

sulfadiazine [sylfadjazin], *s.f. Pharm:* sulphadiazine, sulfadiazine.

sulfaguanidine [sylfagwanidin], *s.f. Pharm:* sulphaguanadine, sulfaguanidine.

sulfamate [sylfamat], *s.m. Ch:* sulphamate.

sulfamide [sylfamid], *s.m. Ch:* sulphamide; sulphonamide, sulpha drug; **la série des sulfamides**, the sulpha series.

sulfamique [sylfamik], *a. Ch:* sulphamic (acid).

sulfanilamide [sylfanilamid], *s.m. or f. Pharm:* sulphanilamide.

sulfanilique [sylfanilik], *a. Ch:* sulphanilic (acid).

sulfarsénique [sylfarsenik], *a. Ch:* sulpharsenic, thioarsenic.

sulfarséniure [sylfarsenjy:r], *s.m. Ch:* sulpharsenide.

sulfatage [sylfata:ʒ], *s.m.* **1.** *Ch: Ind:* sulphating; *El:* **s. des bornes**, corrosion on battery terminals. **2.** *Vit:* treating, dressing, (of vines) with copper sulphate.

sulfatation [sylfatasjɔ̃], *s.f. El:* sulphating (of accumulator plates).

sulfate [sylfat], *s.m. Ch:* sulphate, *U.S:* sulfate; **s. ferreux**, ferrous sulphate; **s. de cuivre**, copper sulphate; **s. de soude**, sodium sulphate; *Com:* sulphate; **s. de zinc**, zinc sulphate.

sulfaté [sylfate], *a.* sulphated (lime, mineral water, etc.).

sulfater [sylfate], *v.tr.* **1.** *Ch: Ind:* to sulphate, *U.S:* sulfate; *Vit:* to treat, dress (vines) with copper sulphate. **2.** *P:* to shoot, kill, (s.o.) with a sub-machine-gun.
se sulfater, (*of accumulator plate*) to sulphate.
sulfateur, -euse [sylfatœːr, -øːz], *s.* **1.** *Vit:* person who treats vines with copper sulphate. **2.** *s.f.* **sulfateuse:** (*a*) *Vit:* sulphate sprayer; (*b*) *P:* sub-machine-gun.
sulfatisation [sylfatizasjɔ̃], *s.f.* sulphatization.
sulfhydrate [sylfidrat], *s.m.* *Ch:* sulphydrate, hydrosulphide.
sulfhydrique [sylfidrik], *a.* *Ch:* **acide s.,** hydrogen sulphide, sulphuretted hydrogen.
sulfine [sylfin], *s.f.* *Ch:* sulphonium, sulfonium.
sulfinisation [sylfinizasjɔ̃], *s.f.* *Metalw:* case hardening.
sulfinusation, sulfinuzation [sylfinyzasjɔ̃], *s.f.* *Metalw:* sulfinuzing.
sulfinyle [sylfinil], *s.m.* *Ch:* sulphinyl.
sulfitage [sylfitaːʒ], *s.m.* (*a*) sulphiting, sulfiting; (*b*) treatment (of wines) with a sulphite.
sulfitation [sylfitasjɔ̃], *s.f.* sulphitation, sulfitation.
sulfite [sylfit], *s.m.* *Ch:* sulphite.
sulfiter [sylfite], *v.tr.*(*a*) to sulphite, sulfite; (*b*) to treat (wines) with a sulphite.
sulfocalcique [sylfɔkalsik], *a.* *Hort:* **bouillie s.,** lime sulphur.
sulfocarbonate [sylfɔkarbɔnat], *s.m.* *Ch:* thiocarbonate; *A:* sulphocarbonate.
sulfocyanate [sylfɔsjanat], *s.m.* *Ch:* sulphocyanate.
sulfocyanique [sylfɔsjanik], *a.* *Ch:* thiocyanic; sulphocyanic.
sulfocyanure [sylfɔsjanyːr], *s.m.* *Ch:* sulphocyanide.
sulfonal [sylfɔnal], *s.m.* *Pharm:* sulphonal.
sulfonate [sylfɔnat], *s.m.* *Ch:* sulphonate, *U.S:* sulfonate.
sulfonation [sylfɔnasjɔ̃], *s.f.* *Ch:* sulphonation, *U.S:* sulfonation.
sulfoné [sylfɔne], *a.* *Ch:* sulphonated, *U.S:* sulfonated; sulphonic, *U.S:* sulfonic.
sulfones [sylfɔn], *s.f.pl.* *Ch:* sulphones, *U.S:* sulfones.
sulfonique [sylfɔnik], *a.* *Ch:* sulphonic, *U.S:* sulfonic; **acide s.,** sulphonic acid.
sulfonitrique [sylfɔnitrik], *a.* *Ch:* nitrosulphuric (acid).
sulfonyle [sylfɔnil], *s.m.* *Ch:* sulphonyl.
sulforicinate [sylfɔrisinat], *s.m.* *Ch:* sulphoricinate.
sulfosalicylate [sylfɔsalisilat], *s.m.* *Ch:* **s. de mercure,** mercury sulphosalicylate.
sulfosalicylique [sylfɔsalisilik], *a.* sulphosalicylic.
sulfosel [sylfɔsɛl], *s.m.* *Ch:* sulpho-salt, salt of a thio-acid.
sulfovinique [sylfɔvinik], *a.* *Ch:* sulphovinic, *U.S:* sulfovinic.
sulfurage [sylfyraːʒ], *s.m.* *Agr: Vit:* sulphiding; treating, dressing, (of vines) with sulphide.
sulfuration [sylfyrasjɔ̃], *s.f.* *Ch:* sulphur(iz)ation.
sulfure [sylfyːr], *s.m.* **1.** *Ch:* sulphide, sulphuret; **s. de plomb,** lead sulphide; **s. de zinc,** zinc sulphide; *Miner:* glance; **s. de fer,** iron pyrites; **s. de carbone,** carbon disulphide; *Phot:* **virage au s.,** sulphide toning. **2.** *Glassm:* (*a*) millefiori; (*b*) ornamental glass paperweight.
sulfuré [sylfyre], *a.* *Ch:* sulphuretted, sulphurated; **hydrogène s.,** hydrogen sulphide, sulphuretted hydrogen; *Miner:* **fer s.,** iron pyrites.
sulfurer [sylfyre], *v.tr.* to sulphurize, sulphurate (substance, ground); *Vit:* to treat, dress, (vines) with sulphide.
sulfureux, -euse [sylfyrø, -øːz], *a.* (*a*) sulphureous; (*b*) *Ch:* sulphurous; **eau, source, sulfureuse,** sulphur water, spring; **anhydride sulfureux,** sulphur dioxide.
sulfurique [sylfyrik], *a.* *Ch:* sulphuric, *U.S:* sulfuric (acid).
sulfurisation [sylfyrizasjɔ̃], *s.f.* *Ch:* sulphur(iz)ation.
sulfurisé [sylfyrize], *a.* sulphurized, *U.S:* sulfurized; **papier s.,** imitation parchment, butter-paper, greaseproof paper.
sulfuriser [sylfyrize], *v.tr.* *Ch:* to sulphurize, *U.S:* sulfurize.
sulfuryle [sylfyril], *s.m.* *Ch:* sulphuryl.
sulidés [sylide], *s.m.pl.* *Orn:* Sulidae, the gannets.
sulky [sylki], *s.m.* *Turf: Rac:* sulky.
Sulpice [sylpis], *Pr.n.m.* *Ecc.Hist:* (St) Sulpice; **S.-Sévère,** Sulpicius Severus.
Sulpicius [sylpisjys], *Pr.n.m.* *Rom.Hist:* Sulpicius.
sultame [syltam], *s.f.* *Ch:* sultam.
sultan [syltɑ̃], *s.m.* **1.** sultan. **2.** *A:* (*a*) silk-lined basket; (*b*) scent sachet.
sultanat [syltana], *s.m.* sultanate.
sultane [syltan], *s.f.* **1.** sultana, sultaness. **2.** *Orn:* **poule sultane,** purple gallinule; sultana (bird). **3.** *Furn:* sultane, ottoman.
sultone [syltɔn], *s.f.* *Ch:* sultone.
sulvanite [sylvanit], *s.f.* *Miner:* sulvanite.
sumac [symak], *s.m.* *Bot: Dy: Leath:* sumac(h); **s. blanc,** smooth sumac; **s. à perruque, s. fustet,** young fustic; Venetian sumac; **s. vénéneux,** poison-ivy, poison oak, poison sumac; **s. des corroyeurs, s. de Sicile,** Sicilian sumac, tanner's sumac; **s. vernis,** Japanese lacquer tree; **s. cirier,** Japanese wax tree.
sumatrien, -enne [symatrijɛ̃, -ɛn], *a.* & *s.* *Geog:* (native, inhabitant) of Sumatra; Sumatran.
sumérien, -ienne [symerjɛ̃, -jɛn]. **1.** *a.* & *s.* *A.Geog: Ethn:* Sumerian. **2.** *s.m.* *Ling:* **le s.,** Sumerian.
sumérologue [symerɔlɔg], *s.m.* & *f.* Sumerologist.
summum [sɔmmɔm], *s.m.* acme, height, summit (of civilization, etc.); *a.inv.* **chiffre s.,** top figure, highest price.
sunamite [synamit], *a.* & *s.* *B.Hist: Geog:* Shunammite.
Sund (le) [ləsœnd, ləsœːd], *Pr.n.m.* *Geog:* the Sound.
sunlight [sœnlait], *s.m.* *Cin:* sunlight lamp.
sunnite [syn(n)it], *s.m.* & *f.* Sunni, Sunnite, orthodox Mohammedan.
super- [sypɛːr], *pref.* super-.
super[1] [sypɛːr]. **1.** *a.* *F:* super. **2.** *s.m.* (*occ. esp. Belg. s.f.*) *F: Aut:* (*petrol*) super. **3.** *s.m.* *Rec:* **un s. 45 tours,** an extended-play record, *F:* an E.P.; **un s. 33 tours,** a long-playing record, *F:* an L.P.
super[2] [sype]. **1.** *v.tr.* (*a*) *Dial:* **s. un œuf cru,** to suck a raw egg; (*b*) *Nau:* (*of pump*) **s. l'eau,** *abs.* **s.,** to suck. **2.** *v.i.* (*a*) (*of pipe, etc.*) to get stopped (up), plugged up, juicy; (*b*) **navire supé,** vessel stuck in the mud.
superaérodynamique [sypɛraerɔdinamik], *s.f.* superaerodynamics.
superbe [sypɛrb]. **1.** *a.* (*a*) *A.* & *Lit:* proud, haughty, vainglorious, arrogant; (*b*) superb; stately (building); (*c*) magnificent (horse); splendid, marvellous (weather, show); **une femme s.,** a fine woman; **faire une affaire s.,** to do a first-rate deal; **il fait des affaires superbes,** he is doing magnificent business; (*in shop*) he is doing a roaring trade; **étalage s.,** magnificent display. **2.** *s.f.* *A.* & *Lit:* pride, haughtiness, vainglory, vaingloriousness.
superbement [sypɛrbəmɑ̃], *adv.* **1.** *A:* haughtily, arrogantly, vaingloriously. **2.** superbly, magnificently.
superbénéfices [sypɛrbenefis], *s.m.pl.* *Com: Ind:* excess profits, surplus profits.
supercarburant [sypɛrkarbyrɑ̃], *s.m.* high-grade, branded, premium-grade, petrol; *F:* super.
supercentrale [sypɛrsɑ̃tral], *s.f.* *El:* main generating station.
supercherie [sypɛrʃəri], *s.f.* (*a*) deceit, fraud; piece of trickery; swindle; (*b*) hoax; **s. littéraire,** literary fabrication, hoax.
superciment [sypɛrsimɑ̃], *s.m.* *Const:* rapid-hardening (Portland) cement.
superconjoncture [sypɛrkɔ̃ʒɔ̃ktyːr], *s.f.* *Pol.Ec:* boom.
supercritique [sypɛrkritik], *a.* *Atom.Ph:* supercritical.
superdividende [sypɛrdividɑ̃ːd], *s.m.* *Com: Ind:* bonus, surplus profit; *Fin:* surplus dividend.
supère [sypɛːr], *a.* *Bot:* superior (ovary, etc.).
supérette [syperɛt], *s.f.* *Com: F:* small supermarket.
superexcellence [sypɛrɛksɛlɑ̃ːs], *s.f.* superexcellence.
superfécondation [sypɛrfekɔ̃dasjɔ̃], *s.f.* *Vet: Physiol:* superfecundation.
superfétation [sypɛrfetasjɔ̃], *s.f.* (*a*) *Physiol:* superf(o)etation; (*b*) *Lit:* superfluity (of words, etc.); redundancy; supererogation; **ce serait une s. de . . .,** it would be supererogatory to . . ..
superfétatoire [sypɛrfetatwaːr], *a.* superfluous.
superficiaire [sypɛrfisjɛːr], (*a*) *a.* *Jur:* superficiary (ownership); **propriétaire s.,** superficiary; (*b*) *s.m.* *Jur:* superficiary.
superficialité [sypɛrfisjalite], *s.f.* superficiality.
superficie [sypɛrfisi], *s.f.* (*a*) surface; **la s. de la terre,** the earth's surface; (*b*) **s. d'un champ, d'un triangle,** area of a field, of a triangle; (*c*) (mere) surface (of things); **son savoir est tout en s.,** his knowledge is all on the surface, entirely superficial; **il s'arrête à la s.,** he does not probe beneath the surface (of things).
superficiel, -elle [sypɛrfisjɛl], *a.* superficial (area, wound, knowledge, observer); skin-deep (wound, beauty); shallow (mind); **connaissances superficielles,** sketchy, superficial, knowledge; *Ling:* **structure superficielle,** surface structure; *Geog:* **eau superficielle,** surface water; **la plante superficielle,** the part of the plant above ground; *El:* **effet s.,** skin effect; *Ph:* **tension superficielle,** surface tension.
superficiellement [sypɛrfisjɛlmɑ̃], *adv.* superficially; **pays s. plus grand que la France,** country larger in area than France; **la balle ne l'a touché que s.,** the bullet only grazed him; **il pense s.,** he is not a deep thinker; he is a shallow thinker.
superfin [sypɛrfɛ̃], *a.* *A:* superfine (cloth, etc.); of extra quality.
superfinir [sypɛrfiniːr], *v.tr.* *Metall: Tchn:* to superfinish.
superfinition [sypɛrfinisjɔ̃], *s.f.* *Metall: Tchn:* superfinish.
superflu [sypɛrfly]. **1.** *a.* (*a*) superfluous, unnecessary (ornaments, etc.); **il est s. de dire . . .,** it is superfluous to say . . .; (*b*) **regrets superflus,** vain, useless, regrets; (*c*) (*computers*) redundant. **2.** *s.m.* superfluity; possessions in excess; **donner de son s.,** to give of one's superfluity; **avoir du s. en main-d'œuvre,** to have too many employees; to be overstaffed.
superfluide [sypɛrflɥid], *a.* *Ph:* superfluid.
superfluidité [sypɛrflɥidite], *s.f.* *Ph:* superfluidity.
superfluité [sypɛrflyite], *s.f.* **1.** superfluity, superabundance. **2. se passer de superfluités,** to do without unnecessary things.
superforteresse [sypɛrfɔrtərɛs], *s.f.* *Av: A:* superfortress.
superhétérodyne [sypɛreterɔdin], *s.m.* *W.Tel:* superheterodyne.
supérieur, -eure [syperjœːr]. **1.** *a.* (*a*) upper (storey, limb, province); **dynamo (du) type s.,** over-type dynamo; **cours s. d'une rivière,** upper course of a river; *Typ:* **chiffre s.,** superior number (as a note reference); *Astr:* **les planètes supérieures,** the superior planets; (*b*) superior (**à,** to); **s. à la normale,** above normal; **s. à la moyenne,** above, better than, average; **lutter, combattre, contre des forces supérieures,** to fight against odds; **se montrer s. aux événements,** to rise above events; **courage s. au danger,** courage that rises above danger; **être s. à qn pour la taille,** to be taller than s.o.; **être s. à qn,** to rank above s.o.; **il est s. à sa place,** he is too good for his situation; **nommer qn à un emploi s.,** to appoint s.o. to a higher post; (*c*) higher, upper; *Mil: etc:* **un commandement s.,** a senior command; **classes supérieures,** (i) upper classes (of society); (ii) upper forms (in school); *Sch:* **cours s. (d'algèbre, etc.),** advanced course (in algebra, etc.); **mathématiques supérieures,** higher mathematics; **enseignement s.,** higher, university, education; **offre supérieure,** higher bid; **les animaux supérieurs,** the higher animals; *Jur:* **cour supérieure,** higher court; (*d*) *Com:* of superior quality; **nous ne vendons que des articles supérieurs,** we sell only articles of the highest quality; **combustible, carburant, de qualité supérieure,** high-grade fuel; (*e*) (*computers*) **portion des rangées supérieures (d'une carte),** upper curtate; **indice s.,** superscript; **total de niveau s.,** major total. **2.** *s.* superior; (*a*) one's better; **il est votre s.,** (i) he is your superior; (ii) he is a better man than you; **n'oubliez pas le respect dû à vos supérieurs,** do not forget the respect due to your superiors; **il est mon s. hiérarchique,** he is above me in rank; (*b*) head of a convent, monastery, seminary; **la Mère supérieure, la Supérieure,** the Mother Superior.
supérieurement [syperjœrmɑ̃], *adv.* **1.** superlatively well; **il a joué s.,** he played in a masterly fashion; **être s. doué,** to be exceptionally gifted; **chanter s.,** to sing superbly; **manier s. les armes,** *F:* to be a first-class fencer. **2. s. à . . .,** to a higher degree than . . ., better than . . ..
superinfection [sypɛrɛ̃fɛksjɔ̃], *s.f.* *Med: Vet:* superinfection.
supériorité [syperjɔrite], *s.f.* **1.** superiority; **s. de talent,** superiority in talent; **s. d'âge,** seniority; **un air de s.,** a superior air; **s. sur les marchés mondiaux,** command of the world-markets; **grâce à la s. de vos richesses,** thanks to your superior wealth; *Mil: etc:* **s. en hommes et en matériel,** superiority in men and material; **lutter contre une s. écrasante,** to fight against crushing odds. **2.** superiorship (of convent).
superlatif, -ive [sypɛrlatif, -iːv]. **1.** *a.* superlative (adjective, etc.). **2.** *s.m.* *Gram:* superlative (degree); **adjectif au s.,** adjective in the superlative; **laid au s.,** superlatively ugly; **s. absolu, relatif,** absolute, relative, superlative.
superlativement [sypɛrlativmɑ̃], *adv.* *F:* superlatively.

superléger [sypɛrleʒe], *a. & s.m. Box:* light welterweight.

superlifique [sypɛrlifik], *a. P: A:* splendiferous.

supermarché [sypɛrmarʃe], *s.m. Com:* supermarket.

supernova [sypɛrnɔva], *s.f. Astr:* supernova; *pl. supernovæ.*

super-ordre [sypɛrɔrdr̥], *s.m. Nat.Hist:* superorder; *pl. super-ordres.*

superovarié [sypɛrɔvarje], *a. Bot:* having a superior ovary.

superovulation [sypɛrɔvylasjɔ̃], *s.f. Biol:* superovulation.

superpanchromatique [sypɛrpɑ̃krɔmatik], *a. Phot:* superpanchromatic.

superphosphate [sypɛrfɔsfat], *s.m. Agr:* superphosphate.

superpolyamide [sypɛrpɔljamid], *s.m. Ch:* superpolyamide.

superposable [sypɛrpozabl̥], *a.* superposable, superimposable; *Furn:* **chaise s.,** stacking chair.

superposé [sypɛrpoze], *a. El: Elcs:* superposed; **circuit s.,** superposed, by-product, circuit.

superposer [sypɛrpoze], *v.tr.* to superpose (à, (up)on); to superimpose; *A:* **s. des gros sous,** to superpose pennies; **s. des couleurs,** to superimpose colours; *Geom:* **s. deux triangles,** to superpose two triangles; *Mch:* **machine superposée,** over-type engine (built over the boiler).

superposition [sypɛrpozisjɔ̃], *s.f.* superposition (of triangles, of geological strata, etc.); superimposition (of colours); *Cin:* superimposition.

superproduction [sypɛrprɔdyksjɔ̃], *s.f. Cin:* spectacular.

superrégénérateur [sypɛrreʒeneratœːr], *s.m. W.Tel:* superregenerative receiver.

supersonique [sypɛrsɔnik], *a.* supersonic, ultrasonic; **bombardier s.,** supersonic bomber.

superstitieusement [sypɛrstisjøzmɑ̃], *adv.* **1.** superstitiously. **2.** over-scrupulously; **s'attacher s. aux choses indifférentes,** to make too much of trifles.

superstitieux, -euse [sypɛrstisjø, -øːz], *a.* superstitious (person, rites, etc.).

superstition [sypɛrstisjɔ̃], *s.f.* **1.** superstition. **2. avoir la s. du passé,** to be foolishly attached to the past.

superstrat [sypɛrstra], *s.m. Ling:* superstratum.

superstructure [sypɛrstryktyːr], *s.f.* **1.** superstructure; upper works; deck erection, fittings (of ship); *Petroleum Ind:* **s. d'un derrick,** headgear. **2.** *Rail:* permanent way, superstructure.

supertanker [sypɛrtɑ̃kɛːr], *s.m. Nau:* supertanker.

superviser [sypɛrvize], *v.tr.* to supervise; (*computers*) to control.

superviseur [sypɛrvizœːr]. **1.** *a. Elcs:* (*computers*) **état s.,** supervisory state; **programme s.,** executive routine, executive programme, supervisory routine. **2.** *s.m.* supervisor; (*computers*) **s. de segments de recouvrement,** overlay supervisor.

supervision [sypɛrvizjɔ̃], *s.f.* supervision; (*computers*) **s. des travaux,** job management, task management; **relais de s.,** supervisory relay; **signal de s.,** supervisory signal; **voie de s.,** supervisory channel.

superwelter [sypɛrvɛltɛːr], *a. & s.m. Box:* light middleweight.

supin [sypɛ̃], *s.m. Lt.Gram:* supine; **s. actif,** first supine; **s. passif,** second supine; **au s.,** in the supine.

supinateur [sypinatœːr], *a. & s.m. Anat:* supinator (muscle).

supination [sypinasjɔ̃], *s.f.* supination; **en s.,** supine (patient).

supion [sypjɔ̃], *s.m. Moll:* (*S. of Fr.*) small calamary.

supplantateur, -trice [syplɑ̃tatœːr, -tris], *s.* supplanter.

supplantation [syplɑ̃tasjɔ̃], *s.f.,* **supplantement** [syplɑ̃tmɑ̃], *s.m.* supplanting, supplantation.

supplanter [syplɑ̃te], *v.tr.* to supplant, supersede, displace.

supplanteur, -euse [syplɑ̃tœːr, -øːz], *s.* supplanter.

suppléance [sypleɑ̃ːs], *s.f.* **1.** substitution, finding of a deputy. **2.** (*a*) deputyship, functions of a substitute; **obtenir la s. de qn,** to be appointed s.o.'s substitute; (*b*) temporary post (during holder's absence); post ad interim; supply (post); **remplir une s.,** to deputize, stand in, supply, for someone.

suppléant, -ante [sypleɑ̃, -ɑ̃ːt]. **1.** *s.* (*of pers.*) substitute (**de,** for); supply teacher; deputy, locum tenens; *Th:* understudy; *Artil: etc:* spare number (of gun's crew, etc.). **2.** *a.* (*a*) acting, temporary (official, etc.); surrogate (judge); **professeur s.,** (i) (assistant) lecturer; (ii) supply teacher; (*b*) *Gram:* substitute (verb, etc.).

suppléer [syplee]. **1.** *v.tr. A: & Lit:* (*a*) to supply, make up, make good (what is lacking); **s. la quantité par la qualité,** to make up for lack of quantity with quality; **la sollicitude maternelle ne se supplée pas,** nothing can replace a mother's care; (*b*) to take the place of, act as deputy for, deputize for, supply for (s.o.); **se faire s.,** to find a substitute, a deputy; to arrange for a supply. **2.** *v.i.* **s. à qch.,** to make up for, supply the deficiency of, compensate for, sth.; **s. au vin par le cidre,** to make up for (the lack of) wine with cider; to eke out the wine with cider; **s. à une vacance, à un poste vacant,** to fill a vacancy, a vacant post.

supplément [syplemɑ̃], *s.m.* (*a*) supplement, addition; **en s.,** additional; (*b*) extra, additional, payment; *Rail:* excess fare, extra fare; **s. de prix,** extra charge; **payer le s.,** to pay the additional charge, the extra; **on paye un s. pour déjeuner dans sa chambre,** meals taken in the bedroom are charged extra, are subject to an extra charge; **prendre un s.,** to transfer to a more expensive seat (at theatre, etc.); *Rail:* to pay the excess (on one's ticket); **percevoir un s.,** to make an extra charge; **percevoir un s. sur un billet,** to excess a ticket; **supplément de solde,** extra pay; **s. d'imposition,** additional tax; **renvoyer une question à une commission pour s. d'examen,** to refer a matter to a commission for further consideration; (*c*) supplement (to book, magazine, etc.); (*d*) (*in restaurant*) extra (dish); extra charge (for special dish); (*e*) *Geom:* supplement (of an angle); *a.* **angle s. d'un autre,** angle supplemental to another.

supplémentaire [syplemɑ̃tɛːr], *a.* supplementary, additional, extra, further; **port s.,** extra postage; **entretien s.,** supplementary maintenance; *Ind:* **heures supplémentaires (de travail),** overtime; **une heure s.,** an hour's overtime; **demander un crédit s.,** to ask for an additional credit, for a further credit; *Rail:* **train s.,** (*s.m.* **supplémentaire**), relief train; *Geom:* **angles supplémentaires,** supplementary angles; *Mus:* **lignes supplémentaires,** ledger lines, added lines; *Elcs:* (*computers*) **article s.,** addition record; **bit s.,** overhead bit; *Tp:* **installation d'abonné avec postes supplémentaires,** private branch exchange, P.B.X.

supplémentairement [syplemɑ̃tɛrmɑ̃], *adv.* in addition; furthermore.

supplémenter [syplemɑ̃te], *v.tr.* (*a*) to supplement; (*b*) to support; (*c*) **s. un billet,** to issue a supplementary ticket for an excess fare.

supplétif, -ive [sypletif, -iːv]. **1.** *a.* suppletive (word). **2.** (*a*) *a. & s.m. Mil:* auxiliary (troops); (*b*) *s.m. Adm:* = special constable.

supplétoire [sypletwaːr], *a. Jur:* **serment s.,** oath in supplement; suppletory oath.

suppliant, -ante [sypliјɑ̃, -ɑ̃ːt]. **1.** *a.* suppliant, supplicating, imploring, pleading, beseeching, entreating (look, etc.); **il me regarda d'un air s.,** he looked at me appealingly, beseechingly, imploringly, with a look of appeal, of entreaty, on his face. **2.** *s.* suppliant, supplicant; *Gr.Lit:* **les Suppliantes,** the Suppliants (of Aeschylus).

supplication [syplikasjɔ̃], *s.f.* supplication, beseeching, entreaty.

supplicatoire [syplikatwaːr], *a.* supplicatory (prayer).

supplice [syplis], *s.m.* (*a*) (severe corporal) punishment; torture; **le s. du fouet,** the penalty of the lash; **le dernier s.,** (i) *A:* execution after torture; (ii) capital punishment, the extreme penalty; (*b*) torment, anguish, agony; **la goutte est un s.,** gout is a real torture; **le s. de Tantale,** the torment of Tantalus; **mettre qn au s.,** (i) to torture s.o., to cause s.o. great pain; (ii) *F:* to make s.o. squirm; (iii) to keep s.o. on tenterhooks, to tantalize s.o.; **être au s.,** to be on the rack, on thorns; **j'étais au s. à l'idée que . . .,** I was agonized at the thought that. . . .

supplicié, -ée [syplisje], *s.* (i) executed criminal; criminal under torture and about to be executed; (ii) tortured prisoner, etc.

supplicier [syplisje], *v.tr.* (*p.d. & pr.sub.* **n. suppliciions, v. suppliciiez**) (*a*) *A:* to execute (criminal); (*b*) *Lit:* to torture, agonize (s.o.).

supplier [syplije], *v.tr.* (*p.d. & pr.sub.* **n. suppliions, v. suppliiez**) to beseech; to beg, implore; **s. qn pour obtenir qch.,** to beg s.o. for sth.; to implore sth. of s.o.; **s. qn de faire qch.,** to implore, entreat, beg, s.o. to do sth.; **il supplie qu'on veuille bien l'écouter,** he begs to be heard; **taisez-vous, je vous en supplie,** be silent, I beg you; *F:* **je supplie Dieu, le ciel, de ne pas avoir à rester longtemps ici,** I'm praying to God I won't have to stay here too long.

supplique [syplik], *s.f.* petition; *Lit:* **ayez égard à ma s.,** hear my prayer.

support [sypɔːr], *s.m.* **1.** support, prop, stay; *Carp:* strut; *Const:* **bois de s.,** putlog; *Sp:* **s. athlétique,** athletic support, *P:* jock-strap; **trouver un s. certain dans la religion,** to find a firm support in religion; **il est sans s.,** he has nobody to back him up. **2.** *Her:* supporter (of shield). **3.** *Tchn:* (*a*) rest (for tools, etc.); stand (for lamp, etc.); holder (for memo block, etc.); mount (of photograph); *Arch: Const:* support (of structure, arch, etc.); **s. à trois pieds,** tripod (stand); **s. d'abat-jour,** shade holder, carrier; **s. de bicyclette,** bicycle stand; **s. pour bicyclettes,** bicycle rack; *Ch:* **s. pour tube à essais,** test-tube stand; **s. à anneau, à pince (pour tube à essais),** stand with ring, with clamp (for test tube); **s. de toile métallique,** gauze frame (of filter); *Dent:* **s. pour fraise,** bur stand; *Bootm:* **s. plantaire,** arch support; *Veh:* **s. de timon,** pole yoke; *Rail:* **s. de caténaire,** catenary hanger; *Petroleum Ind:* **s. du balancier,** samson post; (*b*) *Mec.E:* bearer, bracket, support (of machine part); pedestal, pillow(block) (of journal, shaft, etc.); **s. amortisseur, s. antivibrateur, antivibratoire,** cushioned mounting, support; shock-absorbing mount(ing), support; rubber mounting; spring stand; **s. élastique,** elastic bracket, support; **s. à pivot,** pivoting support; **s. coulissant,** slide(r); **s. guide,** guide bracket; **s. libre,** loose, free, support; **s. fixe,** fixed base, support; **s. flottant,** floating base, support; **s. en équerre,** square support, bracket; **plaque s.,** support plate; **s. pendant,** bearer hanger; **s. d'étrier,** U-bracket; *Mch:* **s. d'arbre,** shaft bracket; **s. de culbuteur,** rocker (arm) shaft bracket; **s. de, du, moteur,** engine bearer, bracket; engine bed, mount; **s. de presse-étoupe,** gland support; *Machine-Tls:* **s. à chariot, s. porte-outils,** slide rest (of lathe); **s. porte-fraise,** overhanging arm (of milling machine); *Av:* **s. de fuseau-moteur,** nacelle pedestal; **s. de turboréacteur,** jet pedestal; **s. de train avant,** nose gear saddle; **s. de couple,** torque pin (of brake system); (*c*) *Metalw:* chaplet (of core); **s. de soudage,** backing; (*e*) *Nau:* bracket, crutch (of spar, appliances); **s. de bôme, de gui,** boom crutch, rest; **s. de mât de charge,** derrick crutch, stool; **s. d'arbre de couche,** propeller-shaft stay, shaft strut; **s. de barrot mobile,** beam shoe, beam socket, hatch carrier; **s. de gouvernail,** rudder carrier; **s. de bossoir,** davit socket; **s. d'embarcation,** boat stand; **s. (de bordée),** girder; **s. en caisson,** box girder; **s. central,** centre girder; **s. latéral,** side girder; **s. longitudinal,** longitudinal girder; (*f*) *El.E:* **s. d'électrode,** electrode support; **s. d'induit,** armature spider; *Elcs:* **s. de lampe, de tube,** valve holder, tube socket; *Tp:* **s. isolant,** insulating holder. **4.** *Phot: Cin:* backing (of emulsion); support (of sensitized layer); **s. du film, de l'émulsion,** base of the film; *Typ:* **s. d'impression,** material on which printing is done (paper, card, plastic, etc.); *Com:* **s. de publicité, s. publicitaire,** publicity medium, advertising medium (*i.e.* the particular newspapers, magazines which print an advertisement). **5.** (*computers*) **s. (d'information),** medium; **s. de données,** data carrier, data medium; **s. d'enregistrement magnétique,** magnetic recording medium; **s. exploitable sur machine,** machine-readable medium, automated data medium; **s. de mémoire,** storage medium, **s. vierge,** blank medium, empty medium, virgin medium; **caractère de fin de s.,** end of medium character.

supportable [sypɔrtabl̥], *a.* **1.** supportable, bearable, tolerable, endurable; **pas s.,** intolerable; unbearable. **2.** tolerably good, fair to middling; **acteur s.,** passable, tolerable, fair to medium, actor.

supportablement [sypɔrtabləmɑ̃], *adv.* fairly well; tolerably well.

supporter[1] [sypɔrte], *v.tr.* **1.** to support, prop, hold up, sustain, bear, carry (ceiling, arch); to support, back up (person, theory); **s. les frais de qch.,** to bear the cost of sth.; **il faut des mille et des cents pour supporter un train de maison pareil,** one must have tons of money to keep up such an establishment; (*of pillar, etc.*) **s. une grande charge,** to take a heavy load. **2.** (*a*) to endure, suffer, bear; to stand up to, withstand (heat, misfortune, etc.); **argument qui ne supporte pas l'examen,** argument that does not stand, bear, investigation; **il n'a pas supporté l'épreuve,** he was not equal to the test; he was tried and found wanting; **il ne supporte plus de se coucher tard,** he is no longer equal to staying up late; **il supporte bien le vin,** he carries his wine well;

Nau: **s. un coup de vent,** to weather a gale; (*b*) to tolerate, put up with, stand (rudeness, etc.); **s. l'humeur de qn,** to bear with s.o.'s temper; **j'ai supporté votre insolence pendant une heure,** I have put up with your insolence for an hour; **cela ne peut pas se s.,** that is intolerable; **je ne supporterai pas une pareille conduite,** I will not tolerate such behaviour; **ne pouvoir s. la vue de qn,** to be unable to bear the sight of s.o.; **je ne peux pas le s.,** I can't stand him; **ne pouvoir s. que qn fasse qch.,** to be unable to tolerate, stand, s.o.'s doing sth.

supporter[2] [sypɔrtɛːr], *s.m. Sp:* supporter.

supports-chaussettes [sypɔrʃosɛt], *s.m.pl.* sock suspenders.

supposé[1] [sypoze]. **1.** *a.* supposed, alleged (thief, etc.); assumed, false, fictitious (name, etc.). **2.** *prep.* **s. même sa conversion,** even if his conversion be assumed; *conj.phr.* **s. que** + *sub.*, supposing that . . ., on the supposition that . . .; **s. qu'il soit coupable,** supposing he is, were, guilty.

supposé[2], *a.* supposititious (child); forged (will).

supposer[1] [sypoze], *v.tr.* **1.** to suppose, assume, imagine; **l'auteur suppose tout et ne prouve rien,** the author assumes everything and proves nothing; **s. vrai ce qui est en question,** to beg the question; **en supposant que** + *sub.*, **à s. que** + *sub.*, supposing that . . ., suppose that . . .; **à s. qu'il soit coupable,** suppose he is, he be, guilty; **supposons que** + *sub.*, let us take it that . . ., let us presume that . . ., suppose that . . .; **on suppose que** + *ind.*, it is thought, inferred, that . . .; **elle lui supposait une grande fortune,** she credited him with a large fortune; **j'étais à mille lieues de s. que . . .,** I should never have dreamt that . . .; *abs.* **vous avez supposé juste,** you were right in your conjecture, you guessed right; **on le suppose à Paris, on suppose qu'il est à Paris,** he is supposed to be in Paris; **pourquoi irais-je s. cela?** why should I make such a supposition? **supposez-vous à Paris,** imagine yourself in Paris; **supposons que nous sommes des Indiens,** let's pretend we're Indians; **on le supposait riche,** he was supposed, thought, to be wealthy. **2.** to presuppose, imply; **les droits supposent les devoirs,** rights presuppose, imply, duties; **cela lui suppose du courage,** it implies courage on his part.

supposer[2], *v.tr. Jur:* to put forward (sth.) as genuine; **s. un testament,** to present, produce, a forged will; **s. un enfant,** to set up a child to displace the real heir.

suppositif, -ive [sypozitif, -iːv], *a.* suppositive.

supposition[1] [sypozisjɔ̃], *s.f.* supposition, conjecture, assumption; **s. gratuite,** gratuitous assumption, unfounded supposition; **si par s. il revenait,** supposing he came back; **dans la s. que** + *sub.*, suppose, supposing, that . . ..

supposition[2], *s.f. Jur:* production of forged document(s); forging (of will); assumption (of false name); impersonation (of party to contract); **s. d'enfant,** setting up of a supposititious child; *A:* supposition of a child.

suppositoire [sypozitwaːr], *s.m. Med: Pharm:* suppository.

suppôt [sypo], *s.m.* **1.** (*a*) *A:* member (of party, body) (performing certain duties); henchman; (*b*) (*of pers.*) tool, instrument (of another); **les suppôts de la loi,** the myrmidons of the law, *F:* **s. de Satan,** hell-hound, fiend; **s. de Bacchus,** henchman, votary, of Bacchus. **2.** *Phil:* suppositum.

suppresseur [sypresœːr], *s.m. W.Tel: etc:* suppressor; (*radar*) **s. d'échos fixes,** moving target indicator, M.T.I.; (*computers*) **s. d'espaces,** blank deleter.

suppressif, -ive [sypresif, -iːv], *a.* suppressive.

suppression [sypresjɔ̃], *s.f.* **1.** (*a*) suppression (of law, tax, journal, etc.); discontinuance (of a service, etc.); cutting out, removal (of difficulty); cancelling (of a passage, etc.); quelling (of revolt); **s. de solde,** stoppage of pay; **la Commission pour la s. du bruit,** the Noise Abatement Commission; *Jur:* **s. d'état,** destruction of the proofs of s.o.'s civil status; (*b*) *Med:* suppression, stoppage (of perspiration, or urine); (*c*) concealment (of a fact); *Jur:* **s. d'enfant,** concealment of birth. **2.** *Typ:* cancel-matter. **3.** (*computers*) delete, suppression; **s. d'espaces,** space suppression; **s. de zéros,** zero suppression; **caractère de s.,** delete character, rub-out character.

supprimable [syprimabl̩], *a.* suppressible.

supprimer [syprime], *v.tr.* **1.** (*a*) to suppress (newspaper, document, etc.); to put down (abuse); to abolish, do away with (law, tax, etc.); to put an end to (competition, etc.); to withdraw (credit); to omit, leave out, cut out (word, sentence); to dis(credit); to discontinue, cancel, take off (train, etc.); to remove (difficulty); to quell (revolt); (*computers*) to delete; **transmission avec bande latérale partiellement supprimée,** asymmetric(al) sideband transmission, transmission with partial sideband suppression; *Med:* **s. un cautère,** to dry up an issue; *F:* **s. qn,** to kill s.o., to make away, do away, with s.o., to bump s.o. off; *F:* **se s.,** to commit suicide; *El:* **s. le contrôleur,** to cut out the controller; **voilà qui supprime toutes les objections,** that disposes of all objections; *Typ:* **à s.,** delete; (*b*) *Jur:* to conceal (document, fact); to suppress, withhold, burke (fact). **2. s. qch. à qn,** to deprive s.o. of sth.; **s. les vivres à qn,** to cut off s.o.'s food supplies; **s. l'eau à un abonné,** to cut off a consumer's water supply; **s. le vin à qn,** to cut out wine from s.o.'s diet; *Mch:* **s. la vapeur,** to cut off steam.

suppurant [sypyrɑ̃], *a. Med:* suppurating, running (sore).

suppuratif, -ive [sypyratif, -iːv], *a.* & *s.m. Med: Pharm:* suppurative.

suppuration [sypyrasjɔ̃], *s.f.* suppuration, running (of sore, etc.).

suppurer [sypyre], *v.i.* (*of wound, sore*) to suppurate, run.

supputation [sypytasjɔ̃], *s.f.* computation, calculation, reckoning; working out (of interest, etc.).

supputer [sypyte], *v.tr.* to compute, calculate, reckon; to work out (interest, expenses).

supra- [sypra], *pref.* supra-.

supra, *adv.* supra.

supra-axillaire [sypraaksilɛːr], *a. Bot:* supra-axillary; *pl. supra-axillaires.*

supraconducteur, -trice [syprakɔ̃dyktœːr, -tris], *Ph: El:* **1.** *a.* supraconductive, superconductive; **métal s.,** supraconductor metal. **2.** *s.m.* supraconductor, superconductor.

supraconductibilité [syprakɔ̃dyktibilite], *s.f.*, **supraconduction** [syprakɔ̃dyksjɔ̃], *s.f.*, **supraconductivité** [syprakɔ̃dyktivite], *s.f. Ph: El:* supraconductivity, superconductivity, supraconduction, superconduction.

supraliminal, -aux [sypraliminal, -o], *a. Psy:* supraliminal; above the threshold.

supramondain [sypramɔ̃dɛ̃], *a.* supramundane.

supranational, -aux [sypranasjɔnal, -o], *a.* supranational, supernational.

suprasegmental, -aux [syprasɛgmɑ̃tal, -o], *a.* suprasegmental.

suprasensible [syprasɑ̃sibl̩], *a. Metaph:* suprasensible, supersensible.

suprastructure [syprastryktyːr], *s.f. Phil:* superstructure.

supraterrestre [sypratɛrɛstr̩], *a.* superterrestrial.

suprathoracique [sypratɔrasik], *a.* suprathoracic.

suprématie [sypremasi], *s.f.* supremacy; **disputer la s. à qn,** to compete for power with s.o.; *Hist:* **acte de S.,** Act of Supremacy; **le serment de s.,** the Test (prescribed by the Test Act of 1673); the Oath of Supremacy.

suprême [syprɛːm]. **1.** *a.* (*a*) supreme; highest (degree); crowning (effort); paramount (importance); **l'Être s.,** the Supreme Being; **le pouvoir s.,** sovereignty; **cour s.,** supreme court (of judicature); **au s. degré,** in the highest degree, eminently; (*b*) last (honours); **l'heure, le moment, s.,** the hour of death; **les volontés suprêmes,** the final requests. **2.** *s.m. Cu:* **s. de volaille,** suprême of chicken, chicken suprême.

suprêmement [syprɛmmɑ̃], *adv.* supremely; in the highest degree.

sur[1] [syr], *prep.* **1.** (*a*) on, upon; **assis s. une chaise,** sitting on a chair; **monter s. la table,** to get up on to the table; *Box: Wr:* **monter s. le ring,** to climb into the ring; **il lui donna un coup s. la tête,** he hit, struck, him on the head; **s. toute la ligne,** all along the line; *P.N:* **virages s. 2 kilomètres,** bends for 2 kilometres; **ville s. la Seine,** town on the Seine; **se promener s. l'avenue,** to walk in the avenue; **je suis venu s. le bateau,** I came by boat; **graveur s. bois,** engraver on wood; *F:* **la clef est s. la porte, s. la serrure,** the key is in the door, in the lock; **je n'ai pas d'argent s. moi,** I have no money on me; **défense de porter des armes s. soi,** it is forbidden to carry arms on one's person; **fenêtre qui donne s. le jardin,** window which looks on to the garden; **serrer qn s. son cœur,** to clasp s.o. to one's heart; **page s. page,** page after page; **faire sottise s. sottise,** to commit one blunder after another, blunder after blunder; **juger qn s. la mine,** to judge s.o. by appearances; **s. ma bonne réputation, j'eus tout de suite un bon poste,** I got a good job immediately on the strength of my good reputation; **faire qch. s. le désir de qn,** to do sth. by s.o.'s desire; **répondre s. un ton de reproche,** to reply in a reproachful tone; **chanter qch. s. un certain air,** to sing sth. to a certain tune; *Com:* **livraison s. stock,** available from stock; **vente s. catalogue,** mail-order, (i) sale, (ii) business; **rabais d'un tiers s. tous les articles,** a third off everything; all articles reduced by a third; **mis à mort s. une fausse accusation,** put to death on a false accusation; (*b*) **marcher, fonctionner, s.,** to work, operate, on, off; (*c*) towards; **avancer s. qn,** to advance on, against, s.o.; **tirer s. l'âge** to be growing old; **les trains s. Orléans,** the trains for Orleans; **la moitié du chiffre d'affaires est s. l'étranger,** half the turnover is with foreign countries; (*d*) over, above; **les astres s. nos têtes,** the stars above our heads; **dormir s. son travail,** to go to sleep over one's work; **être toujours s. les livres,** to be ever poring over books; **être s. un travail,** to be engaged in, on, a piece of work; **l'emporter s. qn,** to prevail over s.o.; **avoir autorité s. qn,** to have authority over s.o.; **s. toute(s) chose(s),** above all (things); **jeter un pont s. une rivière,** to throw a bridge across a river; to bridge a river; (*e*) about, concerning, respecting; **prendre des renseignements s. qch.,** to get information about sth.; **interroger qn s. ses motifs,** to question s.o. as to his motives; **il y a erreur s. ce point,** you are wrong about this. **2.** (*of time*) (*a*) about, towards; **s. le soir, s. le tard,** towards evening; **s. les trois heures,** about three o'clock; **je l'ai connu s. mes dix-huit ans,** I knew him when I was about eighteen; **s. mes vieux jours,** in my old age; **la pièce se termine, s'achève, s. la mort du colonel,** the play ends with the colonel's death; (*b*) **s. ce, s. quoi, il nous quitta,** thereupon, whereupon, he left us; **s. ce, je vous quitte,** and now I must leave you; **il est s. son départ,** he is on the point of departure, about to start. **3.** out of; (*a*) **un jour s. quatre,** one day out of four, every fourth day; **une fois s. deux,** every other time; **cela arrive une fois s. mille,** it happens once in a thousand times; (*b*) **vous vous payerez s. le surplus,** you will pay yourself out of what remains over; **on paye les pompiers s. les fonds de la ville,** the firemen are paid out of, from, the town funds; (*c*) (*in measurements*) by; **huit mètres s. six,** eight metres by six.

sur-, *pref.* **1.** super-. **2.** over-, to excess. **3.** supra-. **4.** sur-.

sur[2] [syːr], *a.* sour (fruit, etc.); tart.

sûr [syːr], *a.* sure. **1.** (*a*) safe, secure (locality, shelter, etc.); **plage sûre,** safe beach, safe bathing; *Nau:* **côte sûre,** bold shore; **quartier où il ne fait pas s. la nuit,** district in which it is not safe to go out at night; **peu s.,** insecure, unsafe; **jouer au plus s.,** to play a safe game; to play for safety; **le plus s. serait de . . .,** the safest course would be to . . .; **pour le plus s.,** to be on the safe side; (*b*) trustworthy, reliable (person, memory); trusty, true, staunch (friend); **temps s.,** settled weather; **le temps n'est pas s.,** the weather is threatening; we cannot rely on the weather; **machine d'un fonctionnement s.,** reliable machine; **coup d'œil s.,** unerring glance; **avoir le coup d'œil s.,** to have an accurate eye; **goût s.,** discerning taste; **j'ai la mémoire sûre,** my memory never plays me false; **avoir la main sûre, le pied s.,** to have a steady hand, to be sure-footed; **un poney au pied s.,** a sure-footed pony; **frapper un coup s., à coup s.,** to strike an unerring blow; **mettre son argent en mains sûres,** to put one's money into safe hands; *Com:* **maison sûre,** firm of good standing, of established standing. **2.** certain; **remède s., poison s.,** infallible remedy; unfailing poison; **c'est une affaire sûre,** it's a certainty, a sure thing, *F:* a dead cert; **être s. de réussir,** to be sure, assured, of success; **être s. de qch.,** to be sure, certain, of sth.; **je suis s. de mon fait,** I am sure of my facts, of what I am saying; **êtes-vous bien s. qu'il n'est pas encore parti?** are you quite sure he has not left yet? **je ne suis pas s. s'il est de mon avis (ou non, ou pas),** I am not sure whether he agrees with me or not; **je suis s. de lui,** I can depend on him; **s. de soi,** self-assured; **il est très s. de lui(-même),** he is very self-assured, self-confident; **s. et certain,** absolutely certain; **tireur s. de son coup,** dead shot; **parier à coup s.,** to make a safe bet; to bet on a certainty; *adv.phr.* **à coup s.,** assuredly, for certain; without fail, infallibly; **nous réussirons à coup s.,** we are bound to be successful, to succeed; **il viendra à coup s.,** he will come beyond (a) doubt, sure enough; **à coup s. il sera tué,** he will be killed for sure; *F:* **bien s.! pour s.!** to be sure! surely! of course! *U.S:* sure! *P:* **pour sûr que c'est pas facile!** of course it isn't easy! *F:* **bien s.?** you really mean it? **bien s. que non!** of course not! **3.** *adv. F:* surely; **pas s.!** perhaps not!

surabondamment [syrabɔ̃damɑ̃], *adv.* superabundantly; **démontrer s. que . . .,** to prove beyond doubt that . . ..

surabondance [syrabɔ̃dɑ̃:s], *s.f.* superabundance; *Com:* glut (of produce, etc.).

surabondant [syrabɔ̃dɑ̃], *a.* superabundant; superfluous.

surabonder [syrabɔ̃de], *v.i.* to superabound; **s. de, en, qch.,** to have a great store of, to overflow with, sth.; to be glutted with (goods).

suractiver [syraktive], *v.tr.* to increase the activity of (sth.).

suractivité [syraktivite], *s.f. Physiol:* abnormal activity, overactivity (of an organ).

suraffinage [syrafina:ʒ], *s.m.* over-refining (of metals).

suraffiner [syrafine], *v.tr.* to over-refine.

surah [syra], *s.m. Tex:* surah.

suraigu, -uë [syregy], *a.* **1.** (*a*) overshrill, high-pitched (voice, note); (*b*) *Mus:* above the usual range (of voice or instrument). **2.** *Med:* peracute (inflammation).

surajouter [syraʒute], *v.tr.* to superadd; to superinduce.

sural, -aux [syral, -o], *a. Anat:* sural (arteries, etc.).

suralimentation [syralimɑ̃tasjɔ̃], *s.f.* **1.** *Med:* feeding up. **2.** overfeeding; *F:* stuffing. **3.** *I.C.E:* supercharging; **pression de s.,** boost pressure; **s. par turbine,** turbocharging.

suralimenter [syralimɑ̃te], *v.tr.* **1.** *Med:* to feed up, overfeed (a person). **2.** *I.C.E:* to supercharge (engine).

suranal, -aux [syranal, -o], *a. Ent:* suranal.

surandouiller [syrɑ̃duje], *s.m. Ven:* bay (antler).

suranné [syrane], *a.* out of date. **1.** *A:* (= PÉRIMÉ) expired (season ticket, passport, etc.). **2.** antiquated, old-fashioned (coat, custom, language, etc.); **beauté surannée,** faded beauty.

suranner [syrane], *v.i. Jur: A:* (*of power of attorney, etc.*) to become stale by lapse of time; to superannuate.

surarbitre [syrarbitr̥], *s.m.* referee (deciding a tie between umpires).

surard [syra:r], *a. & s.m.* **(vinaigre) s.,** elder-flower vinegar.

surassurance [syrasyrɑ̃:s], *s.f.* over-insurance.

surate[1] [syrat], *s.f.* Sura(h) (of the Koran).

Surat(e)[2], *Pr.n. Geog:* Surat.

surbaissé [syrbese], *a.* **1.** *Arch:* depressed, flattened, surbased, segmental (arch, vault); **arc s.,** pointed obtuse arch, pointed segmental arch. **2.** *Aut: etc:* dropped (axle, frame, etc.); extra-low, underslung (chassis).

surbaissement [syrbɛsmɑ̃], *s.m. Arch:* surbasement.

surbaisser [syrbese], *v.tr.* **1.** *Arch:* to surbase, flatten, depress (arch, vault). **2.** *Aut: etc:* to drop, undersling (frame, etc.).

surbande [syrbɑ̃:d], *s.f.* bandage (over pad, etc.).

surbâtir [syrbɑti:r], *v.tr.* to overbuild.

surbau, -aux [syrbo], *s.m. Nau:* (hatchway) coaming; **s. transversal,** headledge.

surboucher [syrbuʃe], *v.tr.* to cap, put a capsule on (bottle).

surboum [syrbum], *s.f. F: A:* (young people's) party; surprise party.

surcalciner [syrkalsine], *v.tr.* to over-calcine.

surcapacité [syrkapasite], *s.f. Ind: etc:* surplus production capacity.

surcapitalisation [syrkapitalizasjɔ̃], *s.f.* over-capitalization.

surcapitalisé [syrkapitalize], *a.* over-capitalized.

surcharge [syrʃarʒ], *s.f.* **1.** overloading, overstressing, overworking; *Mch:* **s. d'épreuve,** test pressure (of boiler); **poids en s.,** overload. **2.** (*a*) overload, overstress; extra load; additional burden; *El:* overcharge (of accumulator); *Mec.E:* overload (of valves); *Ind:* **s. permise,** permissible overload; (*b*) excess weight (of luggage); (*c*) weight handicap (of racehorse). **3.** (*a*) overtax, overcharge; (*b*) additional charge (on account rendered); *Typ: etc:* extras. **4.** *Typ:* word written over another, interlineation. **5.** surcharge (on postage stamp).

surcharger [syrʃarʒe], *v.tr.* **(je surchargeai(s); n. surchargeons) 1.** (*a*) to overburden, overload, weigh down (vehicle, horse, one's stomach, etc.); *El:* to over-charge (accumulator); **s. ses employés de travail,** to overwork one's employees; **pour ne pas s. ce volume,** so as not to overweight this volume; *Fin:* **s. le marché,** to encumber, overload, glut, the market; *Nau:* **s. un bateau de gréement,** to overrig a boat; (*b*) to overtax, overcharge. **2.** (*a*) *Typ:* to write over (other words); to write between the lines of (MS. or proof); *Mapm:* to overlay; (*b*) to surcharge, overprint (postage stamp).

surchauffage [syrʃofa:ʒ], *s.m.* **1.** overheating (of oven). **2.** superheating (of steam).

surchauffe [syrʃo:f], *s.f.* **1.** = SURCHAUFFAGE. **2.** superheat (in steam). **3.** *Pol.E:* **s. (économique),** inflation, overheating.

surchauffer [syrʃofe], *v.tr.* **1.** to overheat (oven, etc.); *Metalw:* to burn (iron). **2.** to superheat (steam); **chaudière à vapeur surchauffée,** superheated steam boiler.

surchauffeur [syrʃofœ:r], *s.m. Mch:* (steam) superheater.

surchoix [syrʃwa], *s.m.* finest quality; *attrib.* **viande s.,** prime quality meat; **tabacs s.,** choice tobaccos; **dattes s.,** selected dates.

surclassement [syrklɑsmɑ̃], *s.m.* **le s. est lié au reclassement professionnel,** the employment of people with qualifications higher than the job requires is bound up with re-employment in new professions.

surclasser [syrklɑse], *v.tr.* to outclass (opponents, etc.).

surcompensation [syrkɔ̃pɑ̃sasjɔ̃], *s.f. Psy:* overcompensation.

surcompensé [syrkɔ̃pɑ̃se], *a. Psy:* overcompensated.

surcomposé [syrkɔ̃poze], *a.* **1.** *Bot:* supracomposite (leaf). **2.** *Gram:* double-compound (tense) (*e.g.* **lorsque j'ai eu fini**).

surcompresseur [syrkɔ̃prɛsœ:r], *s.m. I.C.E:* supercharger; **s. à soufflerie,** blower-type supercharger.

surcompression [syrkɔ̃presjɔ̃], *s.f. I.C.E:* supercharging.

surcomprimé [syrkɔ̃prime], *a.* pressurized; supercompressed; *I.C.E:* supercharged (engine).

surcomprimer [syrkɔ̃prime], *v.tr. I.C.E:* to pressurize; to supercharge.

surcongélation [syrkɔ̃ʒelasjɔ̃], *s.f.* deep freezing, *U.S:* quick freezing.

surcongelé [syrkɔ̃ʒle], *a.* deep-frozen, *U.S:* quick-frozen (food, etc.).

surconsommation [syrkɔ̃sɔmasjɔ̃], *s.f. Pol.Ec:* overconsumption.

surcontre [syrkɔ̃:tr̥], *s.m. Cards:* redouble.

surcontrer [syrkɔ̃tre], *v.tr. Cards:* to redouble.

surcorrection [syrkɔrɛksjɔ̃], *s.f.* over-correction; *Opt: Phot:* **s. chromatique,** chromatic over-correction.

surcostal, -aux [syrkɔstal, -o], *a. & s.m. Anat:* supercostal.

surcot [syrko], *s.m. A.Cost:* surcoat.

surcoter [syrkɔte], *v.tr.* to overestimate.

surcoupe [syrkup], *s.f. Cards:* overtrumping.

surcouper [syrkupe], *v.tr. Cards:* to overtrump.

surcreusement [syrkrøzmɑ̃], *s.m. Geol:* over-deepening (by glaciers).

surcritique [syrkritik], *a. Atom.Ph:* supercritical.

surcroissance [syrkrwasɑ̃:s], *s.f.* overgrowth.

surcroît [syrkrwa], *s.m.* addition, increase; **avoir un grand s. de travail,** to have a great deal of extra work; **il craint un s. de besogne,** he is afraid it means more work; **faire un s. d'effort,** to make an extra effort; **pour donner un s. d'effet à . . .,** to give an added effect to . . .; **par s.,** into the bargain, in addition, besides, further; **par s. de besogne,** to add to my work; **pour s. de bonheur,** as a crowning happiness, piece of good luck; **pour s. de malheur,** to make matters worse; **pour s. de sûreté,** to make assurance doubly sure.

surcuit [syrkɥi], *a. A: Cu:* overdone.

surdent [syrdɑ̃], *s.f. Vet:* irregular tooth; (*in horse*) wolf's tooth.

surdéveloppé [syrdevlɔpe], *a. Pol.Ec:* (*a*) highly developed (economy); (*b*) **un secteur s. de l'économie,** an over-developed sector of the economy.

surdéveloppement [syrdevlɔpmɑ̃], *s.m. Pol.Ec:* over-development, above-average development.

surdi-mutité [syrdimytite], *s.f.* deaf and dumbness, deaf-muteness.

surdirigé [syrdiriʒe], *a. Aut:* **voiture surdirigée,** car that oversteers.

surdité [syrdite], *s.f.* (*a*) deafness; **s. musicale,** tone deafness; *Med:* **s. verbale,** auditory asphasia, word deafness; **s. psychique,** psychic deafness; psychogenic deafness; *s.a.* APPAREIL 2; (*b*) unwillingness to hear or listen.

surdon [syrdɔ̃], *s.m. Com:* **1.** compensation (allowed to purchaser) for damage to goods. **2.** right of non-acceptance (of damaged goods).

surdoré [syrdɔre], *a.* double-gilt.

surdorer [syrdɔre], *v.tr.* to double-gild.

surdorure [syrdɔry:r], *s.f.* double-gilding.

surdos [syrdo], *s.m.* **1.** *Harn:* back band, back strap, loin strap. **2.** (porter's) carrying pad.

surdosage [syrdoza:ʒ], *s.m.* overdosage.

surdoué [syrdwe], *a.* exceptionally gifted (child).

sureau, -eaux [syro], *s.m.* **1.** elder (tree); **s. noir, s. proprement dit,** common elder, black-berried elder; **baie de s.,** elderberry; **s. hièble, petit s.,** bloodwort, danewort, dwarf elder; ground elder, *U.S:* **s. à grappes,** red-berried elder. **2. s. aquatique, s. d'eau,** wild guelder rose, marsh elder, water elder.

surécartement [syrekartəmɑ̃], *s.m. Rail:* gauge clearance; increase of gauge.

suréchauffé [syreʃofe], *a.* (*a*) overheated; (*b*) over-excited (person).

surélévation [syrelevasjɔ̃], *s.f.* **1.** (*a*) *Const:* heightening, raising (of wall, etc.); *Aut:* upsweep(ing) (of frame); (*b*) excessive increase, forcing up (of price, etc.). **2.** additional storey (to house, etc.).

surélevé [syrɛlve], *a.* **1.** elevated (railway); **cabine surélevée,** raised signal box. **2.** *Aut:* upswept (member of frame). **3.** *Arch:* surmounted, raised (arch, etc.).

surélever [syrɛlve], *v.tr.* (*conj. like* ÉLEVER) **1.** (*a*) to heighten, to raise (the height of) (wall, building); (*b*) *Aut: etc:* to upsweep (frame, etc.); (*c*) *Golf:* to tee (ball). **2.** (*a*) to raise (prices, tariff, etc.) higher; to force up (prices, etc.); (*b*) *El:* **s. le potentiel jusqu'à 1000 volts,** to boost the potential up to 1000 volts.

surelle [syrɛl], *s.f. Bot:* wood sorrel; sheep's sorrel.

sûrement [syrmɑ̃], *adv.* **1.** steadily, unhesitatingly, confidently. **2.** surely, certainly, assuredly; to be sure! **il réussira s.,** he is sure to succeed; **il va s. y avoir des changements,** there are sure to be (some) changes. **3.** (*a*) surely, securely, safely, reliably; (*b*) **frapper s.,** to strike an unerring blow.

suréminence [syreminɑ̃:s], *s.f.* supereminence.

suréminent [syreminɑ̃], *a.* supereminent.

surémission [syremisjɔ̃], *s.f.* over-issue (of paper money).

suremploi [syrɑ̃plwa], *s.m.* over-employment.

surenchère [syrɑ̃ʃɛ:r], *s.f.* (*a*) higher bid, further bid; outbidding; **faire une s. sur qn,** to outbid s.o.; **adjudication à la s.,** allocation to the highest bidder; (*b*) **une s. de violence,** ever-increasing violence; **faire de la s. électorale,** to make even more extravagant promises to catch the votes; (*c*) *F:* one-upmanship; **faire de la s.,** to go one better; to keep up with the Joneses.

surenchérir [syrɑ̃ʃeri:r]. **1.** *v.i.* (*a*) to bid higher; to overbid; **s. sur qn,** to bid higher than s.o.; to outbid s.o.; *F:* to go one better than s.o.; (*b*) to rise higher in price. **2.** *occ. v.tr.* **s. qch.,** to bid higher for sth.

surenchérissement [syrɑ̃ʃerismɑ̃], *s.m.* **1.** higher bidding. **2.** further rise in price.

surenchérisseur, -euse [syrɑ̃ʃerisœ:r, -ø:z], *s.* overbidder, outbidder.

surencombré [syrɑ̃kɔ̃bre], *a.* appallingly congested, overcongested (street, etc.).

surencombrement [syrɑ̃kɔ̃brəmɑ̃], *s.m.* severe congestion, overcongestion (of streets, etc.).

surentraînement [syrɑ̃trɛnmɑ̃], *s.m. Sp:* over-training.

surentraîner [syrɑ̃trɛne], *v.tr. Sp:* to over-train.

surépaisser [syrepɛse], *v.tr.* to give additional thickness to (sth.); *Metalw: etc:* **joint surépaissé,** reinforced seam.

surépaisseur [syrepɛsœ:r], *s.f.* (*a*) extra thickness; *Mec.E:* **s. pour ajustage,** allowance for machining; (*b*) *Med:* abnormal thickness (of the skin).

suréquipement [syrekipmɑ̃], *s.m. Pol.Ec:* over-equipment.

suréquiper [syrekipe], *v.tr. Pol.Ec:* to over-equip; **cette usine est suréquipée en raison de ses besoins économiques,** this factory is over-equipped for its economic needs.

surérogation [syrerɔgasjɔ̃], *s.f.* supererogation; *Theol:* **œuvres de s.,** works of supererogation.

surérogatoire [syrerɔgatwa:r], *a.* supererogatory (good works, etc.); (works) of supererogation.

suresnois, -oise [syrɛnwa, -wa:z], *a. & s. Geog:* (native, inhabitant) of Suresnes.

surestarie [syrɛstari], *s.f. Nau:* demurrage; **jours de s.,** extra lay days; **indemnité pour surestaries,** demurrage.

surestimation [syrɛstimasjɔ̃], *s.f.* over-estimate, overvaluation.

surestimer [syrɛstime], *v.tr.* to over-estimate, overvalue (price, cost); **s. qn,** to overrate s.o.

suret, -ette, -ète [syrɛ, -ɛt]. 1. *a.* sourish. 2. *s.f. Bot:* **surette,** wood sorrel, sheep's sorrel.

sûreté [syrte], *s.f.* 1. (*a*) safety, security, safe-keeping; **lieu de s.,** place of safety; **être en s.,** to be safe, in a safe place, out of harm's way; *O:* **être en s. de qch., de qn, contre qn,** to be safe from sth., from s.o.; **se mettre en s. (de qch.),** to make oneself safe (against sth.); to get out of harm's way; **mettre qn en (lieu de) s.,** (i) to put s.o. in prison; (ii) to put s.o. in safe keeping, out of harm's way; **pour plus de s., pour surcroît de s.,** for safety's sake; (in order) to make assurance doubly sure; **en s. de conscience,** with an easy conscience; **rasoir de s.,** safety razor; **allumette de s.,** safety match; **serrure de s.,** safety lock; **mécanisme de s.,** fool-proof mechanism; **mettre son fusil au cran de s.,** to put one's gun to safety, to half-cock; *s.a.* SOUPAPE 1; (*b*) security, protection; *Mil:* **s. en marche,** protection on the march; **s. en campagne,** field security; **service de s.,** protection; **détachement de s.,** protective detachment; (*Police*) **la S.** = Scotland Yard; **agent de la s.,** detective; **la police de s.,** the detective force. 2. sureness (of hand, foot); unerringness, soundness (of vision, taste, judgment); unerringness (of blow, stroke); **s. de soi,** self-confidence, self-assurance; **s. de mémoire,** reliability, retentiveness, of memory. 3. (*a*) *Com:* surety, security, guarantee; **s. d'une créance,** security, surety, for a debt; **prendre toutes ses sûretés,** to secure all guarantees; (*b*) measure of precaution; *Prov:* **deux sûretés valent mieux qu'une,** it is well to make assurance doubly sure.

surévaluation [syrevalɥasjɔ̃], *s.f.* overvaluation, over-estimate.

surévaluer [syrevalɥe], *v.tr.* to overestimate.

surexalter [syrɛgzalte], *v.tr.* to over-excite (the imagination, etc.).

surexcitable [syrɛksitabl̩], *a.* easily excited; excitable; **imagination s.,** over-fertile imagination).

surexcitant [syrɛksitɑ̃]. 1. *a.* strongly exciting, over-stimulating (drink, emotion). 2. *s.m. Med:* (strong) stimulant.

surexcitation [syrɛksitasjɔ̃], *s.f.* 1. excitement; **la s. du peuple,** the excitement among the people. 2. *Med: etc:* over-stimulation.

surexciter [syrɛksite], *v.tr.* (*a*) to over-stimulate; to over-excite; (*b*) to excite (s.o.); **tous les esprits étaient surexcités,** the people were seething with excitement.

surexploitation [syrɛksplwatasjɔ̃], *s.f.* over-exploitation, excessive exploitation (of natural resources, etc.).

surexposer [syrɛkspoze], *v.tr. Phot:* to over-expose.

surexposition [syrɛkspozisjɔ̃], *s.f. Phot:* over-exposure.

surf [sərf], *s.m. Sp:* surfing, surf riding.

surfaçage [syrfasa:ʒ], *s.m. Tchn:* surfacing; mechanical polishing; surface (flat) grinding.

surface [syrfas], *s.f.* surface; (*a*) outside; **s. unie, s. lisse,** even, smooth, surface; **s. rugueuse,** rough surface; **s. plane,** dead level; **s. gauchie,** warped surface; **la s. de la terre, la s. terrestre,** the earth's surface; **eau de s.,** surface water; *Geol:* **onde de s.,** surface wave (of earthquake); *Ph:* **tension de s.,** surface tension (of liquid); *Rec:* **bruit de s.,** surface scratching; (*of submarine*) **naviguer en s.,** to progress on the surface; **vitesse en s.,** surface speed; **faire s., revenir en s.,** (i) (*of submarine*) to (break) surface; (ii) *F:* (*of pers.*) to come to; to surface; **refaire s.,** to resurface; **ce problème est trop grave pour être traité en s.,** the problem is too serious to be treated superficially; **amitié de s.,** surface friendship; **tout en s.,** superficial; **sa politesse est toute en s.,** his politeness is all on the surface; **il s'arrête à la s. des choses,** he never goes below the surface; he's very superficial; (*b*) *Geom:* **s. de révolution, de rotation,** surface of revolution; (*c*) area; **s. d'appui, s. de portée, s. portante,** bearing area, surface; **s. utile,** useful, working, surface; **s. de frottement,** wearing, rubbing, surface; **s. de séparation,** (i) separation, separating, surface; (ii) boundary surface, interface (between two liquids); *Mch:* **s. de grille,** grate area; **s. de chauffe,** heating surface, fire surface; *Const:* **s. couverte,** floor area; **s. des étages,** floor space (of building); **s. corrigée,** real floor space; *Com:* **les grandes surfaces,** the hypermarkets, supermarkets, large stores, etc.; *Geol:* **s. d'érosion, s. d'aplanissement,** peneplain, peneplane; *Rail:* **s. de roulement,** wheel tread (of rail); *Av:* **s. portante, s. de sustentation,** lifting surface ((i) wing area; (ii) aerofoil, *U.S:* airfoil); **s. d'aile, s. des plans de sustentation,** wing area; **s. alaire,** design wing area; *Aer:* **s. tourbillonnaire,** vortex sheet; *Nau:* **s. des ailes (de l'hélice),** blade area; **s. de voilure,** sail area; (*d*) **il présente une s. financière suffisante,** his financial standing is satisfactory.

surfacer [syrfase], *v.tr.* (**je surfaçais, n. surfaçons**) *Tchn:* to surface; to plane, dress, the surface of; to grind, polish.

surfaceur, -euse [syrfasœ:r, -ø:z], *Tchn:* 1. *s.* (*pers.*) polisher; **s. de précision,** precision polisher. 2. *s.f.* (*machine*) **surfaceuse,** surfacer, planing machine, dressing machine.

surfactif [syrfaktif], *s.m. Ch: Ind:* surface active, compound, agent; surfactant.

surfaire [syrfɛ:r], *v.tr.* (*conj. like* FAIRE) *Lit:* (*a*) to overcharge; to ask too much for (sth.); **il n'a pas l'habitude de s., il n'est pas homme à s.,** he is not given to overcharging; **vous me l'avez surfait de cent francs,** you have overcharged me a hundred francs for it; (*b*) to over-estimate, overrate (person, talent, etc.); to overpraise; **on a surfait cet auteur,** this author has been praised too much, has been made too much of.

surfait [syrfɛ], *a.* **prix surfaits,** excessive prices; **réputation surfaite,** exaggerated, overrated, reputation.

surfaix [syrfɛ], *s.m. Harn:* surcingle.

surf-boat [sərfbout], *s.m.* surfboat; *pl. surf-boats.*

surf-casting [sərfkastiŋ], *s.m. no pl. Fish:* surf casting.

surfil [syrfil], *s.m. Dressm:* overcasting.

surfilage [syrfila:ʒ], *s.m.* 1. *Dressm: Needlew:* overcasting. 2. *Tchn: Text:* final twist, extra twist (given to a thread).

surfiler [syrfile], *v.tr.* 1. *Dressm: Needlw:* to overcast, to oversew. 2. *Text:* to give an extra twist to (the thread).

surfin [syrfɛ̃], *a. Com:* superfine, highest quality.

surfing [sərfiŋ], *s.m. Sp:* surfing; surf riding.

surfleurir [syrflœri:r], *v.i.* (*of tree*) to blossom, bloom, again (in the same year).

surfondre [syrfɔ̃dr̩], *v.tr. & i. Ph:* to superfuse; to supercool (a substance).

surfondu [syrfɔ̃dy], *a. Ph:* superfused, surfused; supercooled, undercooled (substance).

surforage [syrfɔra:ʒ], *s.m. Petroleum Ind:* wash-over.

surfusible [syrfyzibl̩], *a. Ph:* superfusible.

surfusion [syrfyzjɔ̃], *s.f. Ph:* superfusion, surfusion; supercooling, undercooling.

surge [syrʒ], *a.f. & s.f. Tex:* **(laine) s.,** raw wool.

surgé [syrʒe], *s.m. Sch: F:* vice-principal, deputy head.

surgélateur [syrʒelatœ:r], *s.m.* deep freeze(r).

surgélation [syrʒelasjɔ̃], *s.f.* deep freezing; *U.S:* quick freezing.

surgelé [syrʒəle], *a. & s.m.* deep-frozen; **(produits) surgelés,** deep-frozen foods, *U.S:* quick-frozen food.

surgeler [syrʒəle], *v.tr.* (*conj. like* GELER) to deep-freeze, *U.S:* to quick-freeze.

surgénérateur, -trice [syrʒeneratœ:r, -tris], *Atom. Ph:* (*a*) *s.m.* breeder; **s. rapide,** fast breeder; (*b*) *attrib.* breeder; **réacteur s.,** breeder reactor.

surgénération [syrʒenerasjɔ̃], *s.f. Atom.Ph:* breeding.

surgénérer [syrʒenere], *v.tr.* (*conj. like* GÉNÉRER) *Atom.Ph:* to breed.

surgeon [syrʒɔ̃], *s.m.* 1. *Hort:* sucker; **enlever les surgeons d'une plante,** to sucker a plant; (*of plant*) **pousser des surgeons,** to sucker. 2. *A:* scion (of royal stock, etc.).

surgeonner [syrʒɔne], *v.i. Hort:* (*of plant*) to put out suckers; to sucker.

surgir [syrʒi:r], *v.i.* (*the aux. is* **avoir,** *occ.* **être**) to rise; to come into view; to loom (up); **s. brusquement,** to appear suddenly; **une voile surgit dans l'ombre,** a sail loomed up in the darkness; **une forme surgit des ténèbres,** a figure loomed out of the darkness; **la fenaison faite, ces plantes surgissent pleines de vie,** once the hay is in, these plants crop up full of life; **de nouvelles difficultés ont surgi,** fresh difficulties have arisen, have cropped up, have come into view, emerged; *impers.* **plus on discuta plus il surgit de dissentiments,** the longer the discussion went on, the more differences of opinion cropped up; **faire s. des difficultés,** to give rise to difficulties.

surgissant [syrʒisɑ̃], *a.* (thoughts, difficulties, etc.) that arise.

surgissement [syrʒismɑ̃], *s.m.* (*a*) (sudden) appearance; looming up; (*b*) *Geol:* uplift, upthrow.

surglacer [syrglase], *v.tr.* (**je surglaçai(s); n. surglaçons**) 1. *Cu:* to ice (cake). 2. to glaze (paper).

surgraissage [syrgrɛsa:ʒ], *s.m.* superfatting (of soap).

surgreffage [syrgrɛfa:ʒ], *s.m. Hort:* double grafting.

surgreffer [syrgrɛfe], *v.tr. Hort:* to double-graft.

surhaussé [syrose], *a.* 1. *Arch: etc:* surmounted, raised, high-pitched (arch). 2. canted or banked (on the outer side).

surhaussement [syrosmɑ̃], *s.m.* 1. *Arch: etc:* superelevation, heightening, raising; *Rail:* cant, superelevation (of outer rail); *Civ.E:* banking (of one side of a road). 2. increase, forcing up (of prices).

surhausser [syrose], *v.tr.* 1. (*a*) to heighten, raise (wall, etc.); (*b*) *Rail:* to cant (outer rail); *Civ.E:* to bank (road at a corner). 2. to increase, force up, the price of (sth.).

surhomme [syrɔm], *s.m.* superman.

surhumain [syrymɛ̃], *a.* superhuman.

suricate [syrikat], *s.m. Z:* suricate; **les suricates,** the Suricata.

surimposer [syrɛ̃poze], *v.tr.* 1. to superimpose. 2. to increase the tax on (sth.). 3. to overtax.

surimposition [syrɛ̃pozisjɔ̃], *s.f.* 1. superimposition. 2. increase of taxation. 3. overtaxation. 4. *Geol:* pseudomorphism; superimposition.

surimpression [syrɛ̃prɛsjɔ̃], *s.f. Phot: Cin:* superimposition; **tirage par s.,** overprinting (of a film).

surimprimé [syrɛ̃prime], *a.* superimposed; *Cin:* **titre s.,** superimposed title.

surin[1] [syrɛ̃], *s.m.* young apple-tree stock.

surin[2], *s.m. P: O:* (apache's) knife, dagger.

surincombant [syrɛ̃kɔ̃bɑ̃], *a.* superincumbent.

surindustrialisation [syrɛ̃dystri(j)alizasjɔ̃], *s.f.* (i) overindustrialization; (ii) excessive concentration of industries (in one area).

suriner [syrine], *v.tr. P: O:* to knife (s.o.); to stab (s.o.) to death; to murder; to do (s.o.) in.

surineur [syrinœ:r], *s.m. P: A:* murderer.

surinfecté [syrɛ̃fɛkte], *a. Med:* **plaie surinfectée,** wound with a secondary infection.

surinfection [syrɛ̃fɛksjɔ̃], *s.f. Med:* 1. secondary infection. 2. superinfection.

surintendance [syrɛ̃tɑ̃dɑ̃:s], *s.f. Hist:* 1. superintendence, stewardship. 2. superintendent's offices.

surintendant [syrɛ̃tɑ̃dɑ̃], *s.m.* superintendent, overseer, steward; *Hist:* **s. des finances,** financial secretary (under the old regime); superintendent of finance.

surintendante [syrɛ̃tɑ̃dɑ̃:t], *s.f.* 1. (*a*) (woman) superintendent; (*b*) **s. (d'usine),** welfare officer. 2. *Hist:* (*a*) superintendent's wife; (*b*) chief lady-in-waiting. 3. headmistress (of a school for the daughters of members of the *Légion d'Honneur*).

surintensité [syrɛ̃tɑ̃site], *s.f. El:* overcurrent, excess current.

surinvestissement [syrɛ̃vɛstismɑ̃], *s.m. Fin:* over-investment.

surir [syri:r], *v.i.* (*of wine, soup, etc.*) to turn sour.

surjacent [syrʒasɑ̃], *a. Geol:* superjacent, overlying (rocks, etc.).

surjaler [syrʒale], *Nau:* 1. *v.tr.* to foul (the anchor stock); **l'ancre est surjalée,** the chain is round the stock. 2. *v.i.* (*of anchor*) to become unstocked.

surjet [syrʒɛ], *s.m.* (*a*) *Needlew:* overcasting, whipping (of seams); **faire un s.,** to overcast, whip, a seam; **point de s.,** overcast stitch, whip stitch; (*b*) overcast seam; (*c*) *Bookb:* overcast.

surjeter [syrʒəte], *v.tr.* (*conj. like* JETER) *Needlew:* to overcast, whip (seam).

surjeteuse [syrʒətø:z], *s.f.* 1. overcasting machine. 2. (*pers.*) overcaster.

surlargeur [syrlarʒœ:r], *s.f.* extra width (of rails or road on curve); *Adm:* **s. avant un virage,** added turning lane.

sur-le-champ [syrləʃɑ̃], *adv.* at once; on the spot; forthwith; there and then.

surlendemain [syrlɑ̃dmɛ̃], *s.m.* **le s.,** the day after the next; two days later; **le s. de son arrivée,** two days, the second day, after his arrival; **il arriva le s.,** he arrived two days later; **la cause fut renvoyée au s.,** the case was adjourned for two days.

surlier [syrlje], *v.tr.* (*p.d. & pr.sub.* **n. surliions, v. surliiez**) *Nau:* to whip (rope, etc.).

surliure [syrljy:r], *s.f. Nau:* serving, whipping.

surlonge [syrlɔ̃:ʒ], *s.f. Cu:* cut (of beef) between the clod and the chuck; chuck end of the clod.

surlouer [syrlwe], *v.tr.* (i) to let, (ii) to rent (house, etc.) at an excessive figure.

surloyer [syrlwaje], *s.m.* sum in addition to the rent fixed in the contract.

surmaturation [syrmatyrasjɔ̃], *s.f. Vit:* **s. du raisin,** over-ripening of grapes.

surmenage [syrməna:ʒ], *s.m.* overwork; over-exertion; **s. intellectuel,** mental strain; mental fatigue.

surmenant [syrmənɑ̃], *a.* exhausting (work, etc.).

surmené [syrməne], *a.* overworked; exhausted; jaded (horse, mind); stale (team).

surmener [syrməne], *v.tr.* (*conj. like* MENER) to overwork; to exhaust; to overtask (children); to override, overdrive (horse); *El:* to overrun (lamp); **s. ses employés,** to work one's employees too hard.

se surmener, to overwork; to exhaust oneself; to work too hard; to overtax one's strength; to overdo it; to overstrain oneself.

surmesure [syrməzyːr], *s.f. Jur:* overmeasure.

surmodulation [syrmədylasjɔ̃], *s.f. Elcs:* overmodulation.

sur-moi [syrmwa], *s.m. no pl. Psy:* **le s.,** the superego.

surmontable [syrmɔ̃tabl̩], *a.* surmountable, superable.

surmonter [syrmɔ̃te], *v.tr.* **1.** to surmount; to (over-)top; to rise above, higher than (sth.); **l'eau surmonta les maisons,** the water came up over the houses; **colonne surmontée d'une croix,** column surmounted, crowned, topped, by a cross. **2.** to overcome, surmount (obstacle, one's emotion); to get over (difficulty); to master, get the better of (one's anger, grief); to tide over; **cette somme nous permettra de s. nos difficultés,** this sum will tide us over; *Lit:* **s. ses ennemis,** to overcome one's enemies; **s. un chagrin avec le temps,** to live down a sorrow. **3.** (*of oil, etc.*) to rise above, float to the top of (water, etc.); *abs.* **l'huile surmonte toujours,** oil always comes to the top.

se surmonter, to master, control, one's feelings, one's passions.

surmoulage [syrmulaːʒ], *s.m.* (*a*) *Typ:* duplicating (of block); (*b*) *Typ:* cast, mould (from existing plate); *Metall:* mould.

surmouler [syrmule], *v.tr.* (*a*) *Typ:* to duplicate (block); (*b*) *Typ:* to cast, mould (from existing plate); *Metall:* to mould.

surmoût [syrmu], *s.m. Wine-m:* new must.

surmulet [syrmylɛ], *s.m. Ich:* surmullet.

surmulot [syrmylo], *s.m.* brown rat, wharf rat.

surmultiplication [syrmyltiplikasjɔ̃], *s.f. Aut:* overdrive (system).

surmultiplié [syrmyltiplije], *a. Aut:* **quatrième vitesse surmultipliée,** overgeared fourth, overdrive; *s.f.* **en surmultipliée,** in overdrive.

surnageant [syrnaʒɑ̃], *a.* (*of fluid, etc.*) floating on the surface.

surnager [syrnaʒe], *v.i.* (**je surnageai(s); n. surnageons**) (*a*) to float on the surface; (*b*) **ce qui avait surnagé au naufrage,** what had remained afloat from the wreck; **il a surnagé au krach,** he has survived the (financial) crash; (*c*) to survive, remain (in the mind, memory).

surnatalité [syrnatalite], *s.f.* excessively high birthrate.

surnaturaliser [syrnatyralize], *v.tr.* to supernaturalize.

surnaturalisme [syrnatyralism], *s.m.* supernaturalism; preternaturalism.

surnaturaliste [syrnatyralist], *a. & s.m. & f.* supernaturalist.

surnaturalité [syrnatyralite], *s.f.* supernaturality, supernaturalness; preternaturality.

surnaturel, -elle [syrnatyrɛl], *a.* (*a*) supernatural; preternatural; *s.* **le s.,** the supernatural; (*b*) extraordinary, inexplicable, out of the ordinary; uncanny.

surnaturellement [syrnatyrɛlmɑ̃], *adv.* supernaturally; preternaturally.

surneigé [syrneʒe], *a. Ven:* (*of track, scent*) covered with snow.

surnom [syrnɔ̃], *s.m.* **1.** *A:* surname. **2.** (*a*) *Rom. Ant:* agnomen; (*b*) appellation; **Robert II ne mérita guère son s. de Pieux,** Robert II hardly deserved his appellation of the Pious; (*c*) nickname.

surnombre [syrnɔ̃br̩], *s.m.* number over the regulation number; redundancy (of workers); **en s.** (i) supernumerary; (ii) (*of worker*) redundant; **rester en s.,** to be odd man out; **exemplaires en s.,** excess copies; **j'ai ces livres en s.,** I have spare copies of these books.

surnommer [syrnəme], *v.tr.* **s. qn, qch.,** (i) to name, call, s.o., sth.; **Jean surnommé sans Terre,** John called Lackland; (ii) to nickname s.o., sth.

surnourrir [syrnuriːr], *v.tr.* (*a*) to overfeed; (*b*) to feed (s.o.) up.

surnuméraire [syrnymerɛːr], *a. & s.m.* supernumerary.

surnumérariat [syrnymerarja], *s.m.* (*a*) post of supernumerary; (*b*) period during which one is a supernumerary.

suroffre [syrɔfr̩], *s.f.* better offer, better bid.

suroffrir [syrɔfriːr], *v.i.* (*conj. like* OFFRIR) to offer more; to make a higher bid.

suroît [syrwa, -waɛ], *s.m. Nau:* **1.** south-west. **2.** sou'wester (wind or hat).

suros [syro], *s.m. Vet:* splint, fusee (on the cannon-bone).

suroxydation [syrɔksidasjɔ̃], *s.f. Ch:* peroxydization.

suroxyde [syrɔksid], *s.m. Ch:* = PEROXYDE.

suroxyder [syrɔkside], *v.tr.* (*a*) *Ch:* to peroxidize; *A:* to superoxidize; (*b*) to overoxidize.

suroxygéner [syrɔksiʒene], *v.tr.* (**je suroxygène, n. suroxygénons; je suroxygénerai**) *Ch:* to superoxygenate; to overcharge with oxygen.

surpaie [syrpɛj, -pɛ], *s.f.* = SURPAYE.

surpassable [syrpɑsabl̩], *a.* surpassable.

surpasser [syrpɑse], *v.tr.* to surpass. **1.** to be higher than (s.o., sth.); to overtop (sth.); **s. qn de la tête,** to be a head taller than s.o. **2.** (*a*) to go beyond, to exceed; to outdo, to transcend (s.o.); to make obsolescent; **il a surpassé tous ses rivaux,** he outdid all his rivals; **le résultat a surpassé notre espoir,** the outcome exceeded all our hopes; **dépense qui surpasse mes moyens,** expense beyond my means; **s. qn par l'intelligence,** to surpass s.o. in intelligence, to be more intelligent than s.o.; **s. qn en éclat,** to outshine s.o.; **il a formé des élèves qui l'ont surpassé,** he trained pupils who outshone him; **s. une armée en nombre,** to outnumber an army; *F:* **cela me surpasse,** that beats me; **il s'est surpassé,** he has surpassed himself; (*b*) *Fin:* to oversubscribe (loan, etc.).

surpatte [syrpat], *s.f. F:* surprise party.

surpatter [syrpate], *v.tr. Nau:* to foul (the anchor fluke); **l'ancre est surpattée,** the chain is round the arms.

surpaye [syrpɛːj, -pɛ]. **1.** overpaying, overpayment. **2.** additional pay, extra pay; bonus.

surpayer [syrpeje], *v.tr.* (*conj. like* PAYER) to overpay (s.o.); to pay too much for (sth.).

surpeuplé [syrpœple], *a.* overpopulated; overcrowded.

surpeuplement [syrpœpləmɑ̃], *s.m.* overpopulation; overcrowding.

surplace, sur-place [syrplas], *s.m.* balance (of cyclist before starting a race); *Aut: F:* **faire du s.,** to crawl.

surplat [syrpla], *s.m.* upper face (of bolt).

surplatine [syrplatin], *s.f.* super-stage (of microscope).

surplis [syrpli], *s.m. Ecc:* surplice; **en s., vêtu d'un s.,** surpliced.

surplomb [syrplɔ̃], *s.m.* overhang (of wall, rock, etc.); **être en s.,** to overhang; **rocher, mur, en s.,** overhanging rock, wall.

surplombant [syrplɔ̃bɑ̃], *a.* overhanging (rock, etc.).

surplombement [syrplɔ̃bmɑ̃], *s.m.* overhanging, overhang.

surplomber [syrplɔ̃be]. **1.** *v.i.* (*of wall, rock, etc.*) to overhang. **2.** *v.tr.* to overhang, hang over (sth.); **rocher qui surplombe le ravin,** rock that projects, juts out, over the ravine.

surplus [syrply], *s.m.* surplus, overplus, excess; **vous garderez le s.,** you will keep the rest, the difference, what is over; **payer le s.,** to pay the difference; **au s.,** besides, after all, what is more; moreover, furthermore; **de s.,** over and above; **vivres de s., en s.,** provisions in excess; **les s. du gouvernement,** government surplus (stock).

surpoids [syrpwa], *s.m.* overweight, excess weight; **en s.,** in excess.

surpopulation [syrpɔpylasjɔ̃], *s.f.* overpopulation.

surprenant [syrprənɑ̃], (*a*) *a.* surprising, astonishing; **chose surprenante,** strange to relate, strange to say; for a wonder; **il est s. d'énergie,** his energy is surprising, astonishing, amazing; **rien de s. si . . .,** it wouldn't be surprising, I shouldn't be surprised, if . . .; **il est s. d'apprendre que . . .,** it is surprising to learn that . . .; **il est s. que vous le sachiez,** it is surprising that you should know of it; (*b*) *s.m.* **le s.,** (i) the astonishing (thing); (ii) the unexpected.

surprendre [syrprɑ̃ːdr̩], *v.tr.* (*conj. like* PRENDRE) to surprise. **1.** (*a*) to come upon (s.o., sth.) unexpectedly; to catch (s.o.) unawares; **aller s. un ami chez lui,** to pay a surprise visit to a friend, at a friend's house; to drop in unexpectedly on a friend; **la nuit nous surprit,** night overtook us; **être surpris par la pluie,** to be caught in the rain; **se laisser s. au charme de qn,** to fall a victim to s.o.'s charm; **s. qn en flagrant délit,** to catch s.o. in the act; **s. qn à faire qch.,** to catch s.o. (in the act of) doing sth.; **je me surpris à pleurer,** I found myself, caught myself, crying; **s. un larcin,** to catch s.o. pilfering; **s. une ville,** to take a town by surprise; **s. qn désarmé,** to catch s.o. unprepared; *Mil:* **s. une tranchée,** to rush a trench; (*b*) to intercept (letter, glance); to overhear (conversation, etc.); **s. le secret de qn,** to detect s.o.'s secret; (i) to ferret out s.o.'s secret; (ii) to come upon s.o.'s secret by chance; **je lui ai surpris un défaut,** I have detected a failing in him; (*c*) **s. la bonne foi de qn,** to abuse s.o.'s good faith; **s. la signature de qn,** to obtain s.o.'s signature by fraud, by a trick; to trick s.o. into signing. **2.** to astonish; **ce qui me surprend c'est que . . .,** what surprises me is that . . .; **cela me surprend beaucoup,** I am very much surprised by that; that surprises me very much; **cela me surprendrait qu'il revienne, s'il revenait,** I should be surprised if he came back; **ça a l'air de vous s.,** you seem to be taken aback; **cela ne me surprend pas,** I don't wonder at that; it's not to be wondered at; I'm not surprised; I'm not astonished; **cela ne me surprendrait pas s'il était,** *Lit:* **quand il serait, du complot,** I should not be surprised if he were in the plot; **ce n'est pas pour me s.,** it doesn't surprise me in the least.

surpressé [syrprese], *a.* under high compression; **lampe à gaz s.,** high-pressure (paraffin or spirit) lamp.

surpresseur [syrprɛsœːr], *s.m. Tchn:* booster.

surpression [syrprɛsjɔ̃], *s.f.* **1.** overpressure, excessive pressure; *Av:* boost pressure. **2.** high pressure. **3.** *Hyd:* boosting.

surprime [syrprim], *s.f. Ins:* extra premium; loaded premium.

surpris [syrpri], *a.* surprised; **vous avez l'air s.,** you seem to be taken aback; **il parut légèrement s.,** he seemed a little taken aback; **je m'arrêtai, s.,** I paused in surprise; **s., je les regardais,** I watched them in surprise; **être s. d'apprendre qch.,** to be surprised to hear of sth.; **s. que** + *sub.*, **si** + *ind.*, surprised that . . .; **je serais s. qu'il revienne, s'il revenait,** I should be surprised if he came back; **je ne serais pas s. qu'il revienne, s'il revenait,** *Lit:* **quand il revînt, quand il reviendrait,** I should not be surprised if he came back.

surprise [syrpriːz], *s.f.* **1.** surprise; **à sa grande s.,** to his great surprise, much to his surprise, to his astonishment; **s'emparer d'une ville par s., par un coup de s.,** to capture a town by surprise; *Mil:* **s'emparer d'une tranchée par s.,** to rush a trench; **il m'a fait sa demande par s.,** he sprang his request on me; **craindre une s.,** to fear a sudden attack; **quelle bonne s.!** what a pleasant surprise! **vous me mettez au comble de la s.,** well, I *am* surprised! **attendez-vous à une drôle de s.,** be prepared for a shock; *Toys:* **boîte à s.,** Jack-in-the-box. **2. pochette s.,** lucky dip; prize packet, surprise packet.

surprise-partie [syrprizparti], *s.f.* (*a*) *A:* surprise party (at friend's house); (*b*) (dancing) party; *pl. surprises-parties.*

surproduction [syrprɔdyksjɔ̃], *s.f.* overproduction.

surproduire [syrprɔdɥiːr], *v.tr. & i.* to overproduce.

surprofit [syrprɔfi], *s.m. Pol.Ec:* (i) abnormally high, (ii) excessive, profit.

surprotection [syrprɔtɛksjɔ̃], *s.f.* over-protection (of child); coddling.

surre [syːr], *s.m. Bot:* (*in S. of Fr.*) cork oak.

surréalisme [syr(r)ealism], *s.m.* surrealism.

surréaliste [syr(r)ealist], *a. & s.m. & f.* surrealist.

surrection [syr(r)ɛksjɔ̃], *s.f. Geol:* uplift (of mountains, sea floor).

surrède [syrɛd], *s.m.* (*in S. of Fr.*) cork-oak plantation.

surréel [syr(r)eɛl]. **1.** *a.* surreal, surrealistic. **2.** *s.m.* the surreal.

surrégénérateur, -trice [syr(r)eʒeneratœːr, -tris], *a. Atom.Ph:* **réacteur s.,** breeder reactor.

surrégénération [syr(r)eʒenerasjɔ̃], *s.f. Atom.Ph:* **réacteur à s.,** breeder reactor.

surremise [syr(r)əmiːz], *s.f. Com:* special discount; extra, additional, discount.

surrénal, -aux [syr(r)enal, -o], *a. Anat:* suprarenal, surrenal (artery, ganglion); adrenal (gland).

sursalaire [syrsalɛːr], *s.m.* supplementary wage, extra pay; bonus.

sursalé [syrsale], *a.* **les eaux sursalées de la Mer Morte,** the excessive salinity of the Dead Sea.

sursaturation [syrsatyrasjɔ̃], *s.f.* supersaturation.

sursaturer [syrsatyre], *v.tr.* to supersaturate.

sursaut [syrso], *s.m.* (involuntary) start, jump; **faire un s.,** to start, to give a jump; **il eut un s.,** he gave a start, started; **en s.,** with a start; **se lever en s.,** to start up; **réveiller qn en s.,** to startle s.o. out of his sleep; **se réveiller en s.,** to wake up with a start; to start out of one's sleep; **dans un s. d'énergie, elle sauta par-dessus la haie,** with a (final) burst of energy she jumped over the hedge; **il y a eu un s. de terrorisme,** there has been a new outburst of terrorism.

sursauter [syrsote], *v.i.* to start (involuntarily); to give a jump; **faire s. qn,** to startle s.o.; **vous m'avez fait s.,** you made me jump; **il sursauta en entendant frapper,** he gave a start on hearing a knock; **s. d'indignation,** to leap up with indignation.

surséance [syrseɑ̃:s], *s.f. Jur:* suspension, delay (of judgment or trial); stay of proceedings; arrest of judgment.

sursel [syrsɛl], *s.m. Ch:* supersalt, acid salt.

sursemer [syrsəme], *v.tr.* (*conj. like* SEMER) to oversow (land, seed).

surseoir [syrswa:r], *v.ind.tr.* (*pr.p.* **sursoyant;** *p.p.* **sursis;** *pr.ind.* **je sursois, n. sursoyons;** *pr.sub.* **je sursoie;** *p.d.* **je sursoyais;** *p.h.* **je sursis;** *fu.* **je surseoirai)** *Jur:* **s. à un jugement,** to suspend, delay, put off, stay, a judgment; to arrest judgment; to stay proceedings; **s. à une inhumation,** to postpone a burial; **s. à l'exécution d'un condamné,** to reprieve a condemned man; **ordonnance de s. (à un jugement),** stay of execution; *impers.* **il a été sursis à la vente,** the sale has been postponed, has been put off.

sursis [syrsi], *s.m. Jur:* delay; stay of proceedings; respite; reprieve (from execution); **s. à l'exécution d'un jugement,** arrest of judgment; **loi de s.,** First Offenders Act; **condamné à un an de prison avec s.,** given a suspended prison sentence of one year; **condamné à trois mille francs d'amende avec s.,** fined three thousand francs with suspended execution of sentence; *Mil:* **s. d'appel,** deferment (of call-up); **mettre un homme en s.,** to allow a man deferment (*e.g.* to complete his studies); **être en s.,** to be on deferment; **faire une demande de s.,** to apply for deferment (of call up).

sursitaire [syrsitɛ:r], *s.m. Mil:* conscript provisionally exempted.

sursomme [syrsɔm], *s.f.* overload; *Prov:* **la s. abat l'âne,** it's the last straw that breaks the camel's back.

sursoufflage [syrsufla:ʒ], *s.m. Metalw:* afterblow (in steel refining); overblowing.

surstock [syrstɔk], *s.m. Com:* overstock; surplus stock.

sursulfaté [syrsylfate], *a. Civ.E:* **ciment métallurgique s.,** supersulphated cement, metallurgical cement.

surtare [syrta:r], *s.f. Com:* extra tare.

surtaux [syrto], *s.m.* over-assessment; **présenter une réclamation en s.,** to claim a reduction of assessment.

surtaxe [syrtaks], *s.f.* **1.** supertax; surtax, extra tax; **s. d'une lettre, s. postale,** extra postage, surcharge, on a letter; **s. sur les marchandises,** surcharge on goods. **2.** excessive tax; over-assessment.

surtaxer [syrtakse], *v.tr.* **1.** to surtax, supertax. **2.** to over-tax; to over-assess.

surtemps [syrtɑ̃], *s.m. Ind:* overtime.

surtendre [syrtɑ̃:dr̥], *v.tr.* to overstretch, overstrain.

surtension [syrtɑ̃sjɔ̃], *s.f.* **1.** overpressure. **2.** *El:* overvoltage, surge (of voltage); **facteur de s.,** Q; **coefficient de s.,** Q factor; *T.V:* **s. de retour,** fly-back voltage.

surtondre [syrtɔ̃dr̥], *v.tr. Leath:* to clip (the hair, the wool, after washing the hides).

surtonte [syrtɔ̃t], *s.f. Leath:* close clipping (after washing the hides).

surtout[1] [syrtu], *adv.* particularly, especially, principally, above all (things); **ayez s. soin de . . .,** be specially careful to . . .; **s. n'oubliez pas de . . .,** above all, do not forget to . . .; **elle est s. timide,** it is shyness with her more than anything else; *conj.phr. F:* **s. que . . .,** especially as . . ..

surtout[2], *s.m.* **1.** *Cost: A:* overcoat, surtout. **2.** centrepiece (on dinner table), epergne. **3.** *A:* light handcart. **4.** *Metall:* outer mould; mantle.

sururbanisation [syryrbanizasjɔ̃], *s.f. Town P:* (*a*) extensive urbanization; (*b*) over-urbanization.

survaleur [syrvalœ:r], *s.f.* overvalue (of currencies).

surveillance [syrvɛjɑ̃:s], *s.f.* supervision, watching, superintendence, surveillance; *Mil:* observation (of enemy, ground, etc.); lookout; *Sch:* invigilation; *Elcs:* monitoring, supervision; **appareil de s.,** monitor; **dé de s.,** monitoring key; **commande de s.,** supervisory control; **voie de s.,** supervisory channel; **exercer la s.,** (i) to act as supervisor; (ii) to be on duty (in playground, factory, etc.); **exercer une s. discrète sur qn, sur qch.,** to keep a discreet watch on s.o., on sth.; **exercer une s. de tous les instants,** to keep (a) constant watch; **être sous la s. de la police,** to be under police supervision; **être en s.,** (i) to be under police supervision, under surveillance; (ii) *Artil: etc:* to be in observation; **comité de s.,** vigilance committee; *Ind: Rail: etc:* **personnel chargé de la s.,** maintenance staff.

surveillant, -ante [syrvɛjɑ̃, -ɑ̃:t], *s.* **1.** supervisor, superintendent, overseer; shopwalker; *Rail:* inspector; *Freemasonry:* warden; *Sch:* invigilator; **s. général,** vice-principal; deputy headmaster; senior master; **s., surveillante, des études,** master, mistress, on duty. **2.** keeper, guardian, watchman; **s. militaire,** military watchman; sentry (at palace gates, etc.); *Tp:* **s. de ligne,** lineman. **3.** *s.f. Med:* **surveillante,** (ward)sister.

surveille [syrvɛ:j], *s.f.* = AVANT-VEILLE.

surveiller [syrveje], *v.tr.* **1.** to supervise, oversee, superintend (work, workers); to tend (machine). **2.** to watch (over), observe, look after (s.o.); *Sch:* to invigilate; (*in primary schools*) **s. la cantine,** (*in secondary schools*) **s. au réfectoire,** to do dinner duty; **s. les enfants,** to look after, keep an eye on, give an eye to, the children; **s. qn de près,** to watch s.o. closely; to keep a sharp eye on s.o.; **s. la situation de près,** to keep a close eye on the situation; **il a besoin qu'on le surveille,** he needs looking after; *Jur:* **régime de la mise en liberté surveillée,** probation system; **en liberté surveillée,** on probation; **délégué à la liberté surveillée,** probation officer; **le français parlé surveillé,** careful French speech. **3.** *W.Tel:* to monitor; **station surveillée,** attended station.

se surveiller, to keep a watch on oneself, to be on one's guard; *F:* to mind one's p's and q's; **recommander à qn de se s.,** to put s.o. on his best behaviour.

survenance [syrvənɑ̃:s], *s.f.* **1.** unexpected arrival; supervention, supervening. **2.** *Jur:* unforeseen birth of issue (after donation of estate).

survenant, -ante [syrvənɑ̃, -ɑ̃:t], *Lit:* **1.** *a.* coming unexpectedly, supervening. **2.** *s.* chance comer.

survendre [syrvɑ̃:dr̥], *v.tr. A:* to charge too much for (sth.); to overcharge for (sth.).

survenir [syrvəni:r], *v.i.* (*conj. like* VENIR); *the aux. is* **être**) (*of events*) to supervene, happen, occur; *F:* to crop up; (*of difficulty*) to arise; (*of pers.*) to arrive unexpectedly, *F:* to turn up, to drop in; **la gelée survint,** frost set in; *impers.* **il lui est survenu un nouvel embarras,** fresh trouble has overtaken him; **il survint une tempête,** a storm arose; **s'il ne survient pas de complications,** if no complications set in.

survente[1] [syrvɑ̃:t], *s.f. A:* overcharge, sale at an exorbitant price.

survente[2], *s.f. Nau:* overblowing; increase of wind.

surventer [syrvɑ̃te], *v.i. Nau:* (*of wind*) to overblow.

survenue [syrvəny], *s.f.* unexpected arrival, chance coming; supervention, supervening.

surverse [syrvɛrs], *s.m. Dial:* (*S. of Fr.*) outlet, overflow.

survêtement [syrvɛtmɑ̃], *s.m.* (*a*) track suit; (*b*) waterproof overalls.

survider [syrvide], *v.tr. A:* to pour off some of the contents of (overfull receptacle).

survie [syrvi], *s.f. Jur:* **1.** presumption of survival (of one person to another in a catastrophe). **2.** survivorship; **gain de s.,** right of survivorship (as between husband and wife). **3.** survival; *Ins:* **tables de s.,** "expectation of life" tables. **4.** *Sociology:* **taux de s.,** reproduction rate. **5.** survival (of feeling, etc.).

survirer [syrvire], *v.i. Aut:* to oversteer.

survireur, -euse [syrvirœ:r, -ø:z], *a. Aut:* (car) that tends to oversteer.

survitesse [syrvitɛs], *s.f. Tchn:* overspeed.

survivance [syrvivɑ̃:s], *s.f.* **1.** (*a*) survival, outliving; *Biol:* **s. du plus apte, des mieux adaptés,** survival of the fittest; (*b*) reversion (of estate, office); **acheter la s. d'une charge,** to acquire the reversion of an office. **2. une s. des temps passés,** a survival, relic, of times past.

survivancier, -ière [syrvivɑ̃sje, -jɛ:r], *s.* reversioner (of estate, office).

survivant, -ante [syrvivɑ̃, -ɑ̃:t]. **1.** *a.* surviving. **2.** *s.* survivor.

survivre [syrvi:vr̥], *v.ind.tr.* (*conj. like* VIVRE; *the aux. is* **avoir**); **s. à qn, à qch.,** to survive, outlive, s.o., sth.; **il ne lui survécut que (de) six mois,** he survived him only (for) six months; **s. à la tempête,** to weather the storm.

se survivre. se s. dans son œuvre, to live on in one's works, to be perpetuated in one's works; **il s'est survécu,** he has outlived his day.

survol [syrvɔl], *s.m.* (*a*) *Av:* flight over (a region), overflight; **le s. de l'Atlantique,** the flight over the Atlantic; **zone de s. interdit,** prohibited flying area, prohibited air zone; (*b*) *Cin:* panning; (*c*) general view (of a problem).

survoler [syrvɔle], *v.tr.* (*a*) *Av:* to fly over (mountain, locality); (*b*) **s. une question,** to get a general view of a problem.

survoltage [syrvɔlta:ʒ], *s.m. El:* **1.** boosting (of alternating current). **2.** overrunning (of glowlamp). **3.** *Pol.Ec:* **s. de l'économie,** boom.

survolté [syrvɔlte], *a.* **1.** *El:* boosted. **2.** *F:* worked up, het up; excited.

survolter [syrvɔlte], *v.tr. El:* **1.** to boost, step up (current). **2.** to overload, to overrun (lamp). **3.** *F:* **s. une foule,** to get a crowd worked up.

survolteur, -trice [syrvɔltœ:r, -tris], *El:* (*a*) *s.m.* booster, step-up transformer; **s. d'induction,** induction regulator; **s. d'artère,** feeder booster; (*b*) *a.* **batterie survoltrice,** booster battery.

survolteur-dévolteur [syrvɔltœrdevɔltœ:r], *s.m. El:* reversible booster; *pl. survolteurs-dévolteurs.*

sus [sy(s)]. **1.** *adv. A:* (up)on, against; (*still used in*) **courir s. à son adversaire,** to rush upon, at, one's opponent; to charge one's opponent; **ils voulurent me courir s.,** they went for me; **en s.,** in addition, extra, to boot; *prep.phr.* **en s. de ses gages,** over and above one's wages; *s.m.* **toucher un en s.,** to be paid something over and above, in addition. **2.** *int.* come on! now then! **s. à l'ennemi!** at them! at 'em, boys!

sus- [sys], *before vowel or h "mute"* [syz], *a.pref.* **1.** above-. **2.** supra-.

susannite [syzanit], *s.f. Miner:* susannite.

sus-carpien, -ienne [syskarpjɛ̃, -jɛn], *a. Anat:* posterior carpal (artery); *pl. sus-carpiens, -iennes.*

sus-caudal, -aux [syskodal, -o], *a. Orn:* **plumes sus-caudales,** upper tail-coverts.

susceptance [sysɛptɑ̃s], *s.f. El:* susceptance.

susceptibilité [sysɛptibilite], *s.f.* **1.** susceptibility, sensitiveness; **blesser les susceptibilités de qn,** to wound s.o.'s feelings. **2.** touchiness, irritability. **3.** *Magn:* **s. magnétique,** magnetic susceptibility.

susceptible [sysɛptibl̥], *a.* susceptible. **1. s. de qch.,** capable of, admitting of, liable to, sth.; **s. d'être prouvé,** susceptible of proof; **marchandises susceptibles de se corrompre,** goods liable to go bad; **passage s. de plusieurs sens,** passage admitting of several interpretations; **la matière est s. de toutes sortes de formes,** matter is capable of assuming all kinds of forms; **s. d'amélioration,** open to improvement; **s. de se produire,** apt to occur; **s. d'être utilisé pour . . .,** adaptable to (a purpose); **s. d'être traité à profit,** amenable to profitable treatment; **les documents susceptibles de vous intéresser,** such documents as may be of interest to you, the documents likely to interest you; **incident s. d'entraîner une rupture,** incident likely to lead to a rupture. **2.** (*a*) sensitive, delicate (organ, substance); **marchandises susceptibles,** goods susceptible to infection; (*b*) touchy, thin-skinned, easily offended.

susception [sysɛpsjɔ̃], *s.f. Ecc:* **1.** taking, assumption (of holy orders). **2.** susception (of the crown, of the cross).

suscitateur, -trice [sys(s)itatœ:r, -tris], *s.* instigator, creator, maker (of difficulties, etc.).

suscitation [sys(s)itasjɔ̃], *s.f. A:* instigation.

susciter [sys(s)ite], *v.tr.* **1.** (*a*) to raise up; *Lit:* **Dieu suscita des libérateurs,** God raised up, set up, deliverers; (*b*) to create (enemies); to give rise to (difficulties); **s. de l'étonnement,** to cause astonishment; **s. de longues discussions,** to give rise to long discussions; **s. des ennuis à qn,** to create petty annoyances for s.o.; **se s. des ennemis,** to incur enmity, hostility. **2.** to (a)rouse (envy); to instigate, stir up (revolt, etc.).

suscription [syskripsjɔ̃], *s.f.* superscription, address (on letter).

suscrire [syskri:r], *v.tr.* to superscribe.

sus-dénommé, -ée [sysdenɔme], *a. & s. Jur:* above-named, aforenamed; *pl. sus-dénommé(e)s.*

susdit, -ite [sysdi, -it], *a. & s. Jur:* aforesaid, above-mentioned.

sus-dominante [sysdɔminɑ̃:t], *s.f. Mus:* sub-mediant; la (of movable do system); *pl. sus-dominantes.*

Suse [sy:z], *Pr.n.f. Geog:* **1.** *A:* Susa (in Persia); *B:* Shushan. **2.** Susa (in Italy).

sus-énoncé [sysenɔ̃se, syze-], *a. Jur:* enumerated above, above-mentioned; **les circonstances sus-énoncées,** the above circumstances.

sus-épineux, -euse [syzepinø, -øːz], *a. Anat:* supraspinal; *pl. sus-épineux, -euses.*
sus-hépatique [syzepatik], *a. Anat:* suprahepatic (vein); *pl. sus-hépatiques.*
Susiane (la) [lasyzjan], *Pr.n.f. A.Geog:* Susiana.
susien, -ienne [syzjɛ̃, -jɛn], *a. & s. Geog:* (native, inhabitant) of (i) Susiana, (ii) Susa.
sus-jacent [sysʒasɑ̃], *a. Geol:* overlying (rock); *pl. sus-jacent(e)s.*
sus-maxillaire [sysmaksil(l)ɛːr], *Anat:* **1.** *a.* supermaxillary. **2.** *s.m.* upper jawbone, supermaxilla; *pl. sus-maxillaires.*
susmentionné [sysmɑ̃sjɔne], *a. & s. Jur:* above-mentioned, aforesaid, afore-cited.
susnommé [sysnɔme], *a. & s. Jur:* above-named, aforenamed.
sus-occipital, -aux [sysɔksipital, -o], *a. Anat:* supraoccipital.
sus-orbitaire [syzɔrbitɛːr], *a. Anat:* supra-orbital; *pl. sus-orbitaires.*
suspect [syspɛ(kt)]. **1.** *a.* suspicious, doubtful, questionable, suspect; **cela m'est s.,** I don't like the look of it; **tenir qn pour s.,** to hold s.o. in suspicion; to be suspicious of s.o.; **devenir s.,** to become suspect, to arouse suspicion; **devenir s. à qn,** to incur s.o.'s suspicion; **être s. à qn de qch.,** to be suspected by s.o. of sth., of doing sth.; **magistrat s. de partialité,** magistrate under suspicion of partiality; **louanges aucunement suspectes de flatterie,** praise free from any suspicion of flattery; *Hyg:* **marchandises de provenance suspecte,** goods not hygienically safe. **2.** *s.m.* suspect; *Hist:* **la loi des suspects,** the law against suspects (1793); **la liste des suspects,** the black list; **inscrire qn sur la liste des suspects,** to black-list s.o.
suspecter [syspɛkte], *v.tr.* to suspect (s.o.); to question, doubt (sth.); **on l'avait suspecté d'hérésie,** he had been suspected of heresy; **s. la loyauté de qn,** to cast suspicion on s.o.'s good faith; **je le suspecte de faire des dettes; je suspecte qu'il fait des dettes,** I suspect him of running into debt; **se s.,** to be suspicious of one another.
suspendeur [syspɑ̃dœːr], *s.m.* bicycle-holder (fitted on wall).
suspendre [syspɑ̃ːdr̥], *v.tr.* to suspend. **1.** to hang up; **on le suspendit par les pieds,** he was hung up by the feet; **s. un cheval pour une opération,** to suspend a horse for an operation; **s. un hamac,** to sling a hammock. **2.** *(a)* to defer, stay (judgment, revenge); to leave (decree) in abeyance; to suspend, stop (payment); **s. son jugement,** to suspend (one's) judgment; **s. le travail pour deux jours,** to suspend work for two days; **s. le travail pour la journée,** to knock off work for the day; **les troupes ont suspendu leur marche,** the troops have halted; **la séance est suspendue,** we will now adjourn; **le juge suspend l'audience pour que le jury puisse délibérer,** the judge orders the jury to retire and consider their verdict; **les abonnements sont suspendus pour ce soir,** season tickets are not valid tonight; *Aut:* **s. un permis de conduire,** to suspend a driving licence; *(b)* **s. la solde d'un homme pour huit jours,** to deprive, mulct, a man of a week's pay; *(c)* **s. un fonctionnaire, un prêtre,** to suspend an official; to inhibit a priest; **s. un avocat du barreau,** to suspend a barrister temporarily from (practice at) the bar.
se suspendre, to hang; **se s. à une corde,** to hang by a rope, to hang on to a rope; **le paresseux se suspend aux arbres par ses quatre membres,** the sloth hangs from the trees by all four legs; **se s. aux lèvres de qn,** to hang on s.o.'s lips, on s.o.'s words.
suspendu [syspɑ̃dy], *a.* **1.** suspended, hanging; *(a)* **les jardins suspendus de Babylone,** the hanging gardens of Babylon; **pont s.,** suspension bridge; **véhicule s.,** vehicle on springs; **charrette suspendue,** spring cart, swing cart; *Aut:* **voiture bien suspendue,** well-sprung car; **poids s.,** sprung weight; **poids non s.,** unsprung weight; **charrette non suspendue,** cart without springs; *(b)* **chèvre suspendue aux flancs d'une roche,** goat hanging on to a rock; **lampe suspendue au plafond,** lamp hanging from the ceiling; **il était s. à une corde,** he was hanging on to a rope; **une épée était suspendue par un crin au-dessus de la tête de Damoclès,** a sword was suspended, was hanging, by a hair above the head of Damocles; **le danger s. sur nos têtes,** the danger hanging over our heads; **être s. aux lèvres de qn,** to be hanging on s.o.'s words, lips; **aqueduc s. sur un torrent,** aqueduct spanning a torrent; *Ph.Geog:* **vallée suspendue,** hanging valley; **cœur s. entre l'espérance et la crainte,** heart hovering between hope and fear. **2.** *Mus:* **cadence suspendue,** suspended cadence.
suspens [syspɑ̃]. **1.** *a.m. A:* suspended (official); inhibited (priest). **2.** *adv.phr.* **en s.,** in suspense; (i) *(of pers.)* in doubt, in uncertainty; (ii) *(of thg)* in abeyance; **tenir qn en s.,** to keep s.o. in suspense; *Com:* **effets en s.,** bills in suspense, held over, outstanding; **problème encore en s.,** problem not yet solved; **questions en s.,** outstanding questions; questions not yet settled. **3.** *s.m. Book-k:* suspense item. **4.** *s.m. Lit:* suspense.
suspense[1] [syspɑ̃ːs], *s.f. Ecc: A:* suspension, inhibition (of incumbent).
suspense[2] [syspɛns], *s.m. Cin: etc: F:* suspense.
suspenseur [syspɑ̃sœːr]. **1.** *a.m. Anat:* suspensory (ligament). **2.** *s.m.* *(a)* hanger (for cables, etc.); sling; *(b) Bot:* suspensor.
suspensif, -ive [syspɑ̃sif, -iːv], *a.* **1.** suspensive (veto, etc.); *Jur:* **un appel n'est pas s.,** an appeal is not a stay. **2.** *Gram:* **points suspensifs,** points of suspension.
suspension [syspɑ̃sjɔ̃], *s.f.* suspension. **1.** *(a)* hanging (up), swinging; *Ind:* **aimant de s.,** lifting magnet; *(b) Ch:* **en s.,** in suspension, suspended. **2.** *(a)* (temporary) discontinuance, interruption (of work, etc.); abeyance (of law); *Gram:* **points de s.,** points of suspension; dots; **s. des hostilités, d'armes,** suspension of hostilities; truce, armistice; **s. de paiements,** suspension of payment; **s. d'une banque,** stoppage, suspension, of a bank; **s. de la circulation,** hold-up, stoppage, of the traffic; *Aut:* **s. d'un permis de conduire,** suspension of a driving licence; **s. pour un an du permis de conduire,** a year's driving ban; *Jur:* **arrêt de s.,** injunction; *(b)* **s. d'un fonctionnaire,** suspension of an official; *(c) Mus:* suspension. **3.** *(a)* hanging lamp, light pendant; ceiling lamp; **s. réglable,** droplight; **s. à contrepoids,** counterpoise ceiling lamp; *(b) Furn:* springing; *Aer:* suspension, system of suspending cords; *Aut:* suspension, springing, springs (of a car); **s. à la Cardan,** Cardan, cardanic, suspension.
suspensoïde [syspɑ̃sɔid], *s.m. Ch:* suspensoid.
suspensoir [syspɑ̃swaːr], *s.m.* **1.** *Surg:* suspensory bandage. **2.** *Civ.E:* suspending rod (of suspension bridge). **3.** *Nau:* tricing line.
suspente [syspɑ̃ːt], *s.f.* **1.** *Nau:* sling (of yard, etc.); *Aer:* suspending ropes (of balloon car, parachute); rigging line (of parachute). **2.** *Civ.E:* suspending rod (of suspension bridge).
suspicion [syspisjɔ̃], *s.f. esp. Jur:* suspicion; **s. légitime,** suspicion that fair trial will not be given; **être en s.,** to be suspected; **cette s. de ta part me blesse,** I resent such suspicions from you.
suspied [sypje], *s.m.* instep strap (of spur).
suspubien, -ienne [sypybjɛ̃, -jɛn], *a. Anat:* suprapubian.
sussexite [sysɛksit], *s.f. Miner:* sussexite.
susrelaté [sysrəlate], *a. & s.m. Jur:* above-mentioned; above-related.
susseyement [sysɛjmɑ̃], *s.m.* lisping; lisp.
susseyer [syseje], *v.i.* to lisp.
sussultoire [sysyltwaːr], *a. Geol:* sussultatory.
sustentateur, -trice [systɑ̃tatœːr, -tris], *a. Av:* **1.** lifting (force, etc.); **effort s.,** lift; **surface sustentatrice,** aerofoil; **aile sustentatrice,** main wing. **2.** *s.m.* **s. rotatif,** rotor (of helicopter).
sustentation [systɑ̃tasjɔ̃], *s.f.* *(a) Med:* sustenance, sustentation; *(b)* support; **base, trapèze, de s.,** basis of support, of equilibrium (of animal or man); *(c) Aer:* lift; **s. aérodynamique,** aerodynamic lift; **force de s.,** lift force; **moteur de s.,** lift engine; **soufflante, ventilateur, de s.,** lift fan; **réacteur de s.,** (i) lift jet, lift engine; (ii) vertical jet, vertical engine (of VTOL aircraft).
sustenter [systɑ̃te], *v.tr.* *(a)* to sustain, feed, nourish, support; *(b) Aer:* **les ailes sustentent l'avion,** the wings lift the aircraft.
se sustenter, to sustain oneself; **il faut vous s.,** you must take plenty of food, keep up your strength.
sus-tonique [systɔnik], *s.f. Mus:* supertonic; re (of movable do system); *pl. sus-toniques.*
susucre [sysykr̥], *s.m. F:* *(in nursery language; to dog)* sugar.
susurration [sysyrasjɔ̃], *s.f.,* **susurrement** [sysyrmɑ̃], *s.m. Lit:* susurration, susurrus, whispering; murmuring (of sea); soughing (of wind); rustling (of trees).
susurrer [sysyre], *v.i. Lit:* to susurrate; to murmur, whisper; to buzz; *with cogn.acc.* **s. quelques mots à l'oreille de qn,** to whisper a few words in s.o.'s ear.
susvisé [sysvize], *a. Jur:* **l'article s.,** the article referred to above.
suttee, suttie [syti], *s.f.* suttee.
sutural, -aux [sytyral, -o], *a. Anat: etc:* sutural.
suture [sytyːr], *s.f.* *(a) Anat: etc:* suture, join, joining (of two parts); *Surg:* suture, stitching (of wound); **(point de) s.,** stitch; **s. à points passés,** glover's suture; *(b) Bot:* suture.
suturer [sytyre], *v.tr. Surg:* to sew, stitch up, suture (lips of wound, etc.).
suve [syːv], *s.m.* *(in S. of Fr.)* cork oak.
Suzanne [syzan], *Pr.n.f.* Susanna(h), Suzanne, Susan; *(in the Apocrypha)* Susanna.
suzerain, -aine [syzrɛ̃, -ɛn]. **1.** *a.* paramount, suzerain (lord, power). **2.** *s.* *(a)* suzerain, *f.* suzeraine; *(b) Jur: s.m.* suzerain (state).
suzeraineté [syzrɛnte], *s.f.* suzerainty; lordship.
Suzon [syzɔ̃], *Pr.n.f.* *(dim. of* **Suzanne***),* Susie, Sue.
svanbergite [svanbɛrʒit], *s.f. Miner:* svanbergite.
svastika [svastika], *s.m.* swastika; fylfot.
svelte [svɛlt], *a.* slender, svelte, slim, slight, willowy (figure).
sveltesse [svɛltɛs], *s.f.* slenderness, slimness.
swahéli [swaeli]. **1.** *a. & s. Ethn:* Swaheli. **2.** *s.m. Ling:* **le s.,** Swahili.
sweater [switœːr], *s.m. Cost:* sweater.
Swedenborgien, -ienne [svedɛnbɔrʒjɛ̃, -jɛn], *a. & s. Rel.H:* Swedenborgian.
sweepstake [swipstɛk], *s.m. Turf:* sweepstake.
swing [swiŋ], *(a) s.m. Box: Golf:* swing; *(b) s.m. Mus: F:* swing; *a. F:* **une jeune fille s.,** a girl who is with it; **une robe s.,** a fashionable dress.
sybarite [sibarit], *a. & s.* sybarite; voluptuary.
sybaritique [sibaritik], *a.* sybaritic, sybarite, self-indulgent.
sybaritisme [sibaritism], *s.m.* sybaritism, self-indulgence.
sycomore [sikɔmɔːr], *s.m. Bot:* **1. (érable) s.,** sycamore (maple), great maple. **2. figuier s.,** Egyptian sycamore, oriental sycamore, sycamore fig. **3. faux s.,** pride of India; pride of China.
sycone [sikɔn], *s.m. Bot:* syconium.
sycophante [sikɔfɑ̃ːt]. **1.** *s.m.* sycophant, *F:* toady. **2.** *a.* sycophantic.
sycophantisme [sikɔfɑ̃tism], *s.m.* sycophancy.
sycosis [sikozis], *s.m. Med:* sycosis, *F:* barber's itch.
syénite [sjenit], *s.f. Miner:* syenite.
syénitique [sjenitik], *a. Miner:* syenitic.
syl-. *See* SYN-.
syllabaire [sil(l)abɛːr], *s.m.* spelling-book; syllabary.
syllabation [sil(l)abasjɔ̃], *s.f.* syllabication.
syllabe [sil(l)ab], *s.f.* syllable; **mot de deux, trois, syllabes,** two-, three-syllabled word; **il ne répond pas une s.,** he doesn't say a word.
syllabique [sil(l)abik], *a.* syllabic.
syllabisation [sil(l)abizasjɔ̃], *s.f.* syllabi(fi)cation.
syllabiser [sil(l)abize], *v.tr.* to syllabize; to syllabify.
syllabisme [sil(l)abism], *s.m.* syllabism.
syllabus [sil(l)abys], *s.m. Ecc:* *(in R.C.Ch.)* syllabus *(esp.* that of 1864).
syllepse [sil(l)ɛps], *s.f.* *(a) Gram:* sense agreement; *(b) Rh:* syllepsis.
sylleptique [sil(l)ɛptik], *a.* sylleptic.
syllis [silis], *s.f. Ann:* syllid.
syllogiser [sil(l)ɔʒize], *v.i.* to syllogize.
syllogisme [sil(l)ɔʒism], *s.m.* syllogism; **argumenter par syllogismes,** to syllogize.
syllogistique [sil(l)ɔʒistik], *a.* syllogistic.
sylphe [silf], *s.m.,* **sylphide** [silfid], *s.f.* sylph; **taille de sylphide,** sylphlike waist.
Sylvain [silvɛ̃]. **1.** *Pr.n.m. Rom.Myth:* Silvanus. **2.** *Lit:* *(a) a.* *(f.* **sylvaine***)* silvan, sylvan; *(b) s.m.pl.* **les sylvains,** the genii of the woods, the sylvans. **3.** *s.m. Ent:* limenitis; **petit s.,** white admiral (butterfly).
sylvanite [silvanit], *s.f. Miner:* sylvanite.
sylvatique [silvatik], *a. Bot:* sylvan, woodland (plant).
sylvestre[1] [silvɛstr̥], *a. Bot:* *(a)* growing in the woods; *(b)* woodland (tree); **flore s.,** silva, sylva.
Sylvestre[2], *Pr.n.m.* Sylvester; *s.a.* SAINT-SYLVESTRE.
sylvestrène [silvɛstrɛn], *s.m. Ch:* sylvestrene.
sylvestrin [silvɛstrɛ̃], *s.m. Ecc.Hist:* Sylvestrian (Benedictine).
sylvicole [silvikɔl], *a.* **1.** silvicolous, woodland, dwelling in woods. **2.** relating to forestry.
sylviculteur [silvikyltœːr], *s.m.* sylviculturist.
sylviculture [silvikyltyːr], *s.f.* sylviculture, arboriculture, forestry.
Sylvie [silvi]. **1.** *Pr.n.f.* Sylvia. **2.** *s.f.* *(a) Orn:* warbler, sylvia; *(b) Bot:* wood anemone.
sylvien, -ienne [silvjɛ̃, -jɛn], *a. Anat:* sylvian (aqueduct, fissure, etc.).
sylviette [silvjɛt], *s.f. Orn:* sylviid.

sylviidés [silviide], *s.m.pl. Orn:* Sylviidae.
sylvine [silvin], *s.f. Miner:* sylvite, sylvine.
sylvinite [silvinit], *s.f. Agr:* sylvinite.
symbiose [sɛ̃bjo:z], *s.f.* (*a*) *Biol:* symbiosis; (*b*) *F:* partnership.
symbiote [sɛ̃bjɔt], *s.m. Biol:* symbiont, symbion; **associé en s.,** symbiotic.
symblépharon [sɛ̃blefarɔ̃], *s.m. Med:* symblepharon.
symbole [sɛ̃bɔl], *s.m.* **1.** (*a*) symbol; conventional sign; (*b*) (*computers*) **s. littéral,** literal; **s. de contrôle,** check symbol; **chaîne de symboles,** symbol string; **ligne de jonction de symboles,** flowline; (*c*) *Navy:* **s. d'identification du convoi,** convoy designator. **2.** *Ecc:* creed; **le s. des Apôtres,** the Apostles' Creed.
symbolique [sɛ̃bɔlik]. **1.** *a.* (*a*) symbolic(al); **paiement s.,** token payment; (*b*) *Elcs:* (*computers*) **adressage s.,** symbolic addressing; **adresse s.,** symbolic address; **codage s.,** symbolic coding; **code s.,** symbolic code; **instruction s.,** symbolic instruction; **langage s.,** symbolic language; **logique s.,** symbolic logic; **nombre s.,** symbolic number; **notation s.,** symbolic notation; **programmation s.,** symbolic programming. **2.** *s.f.* (*a*) symbolics; (*b*) system of symbols; (*c*) **la s. des rêves,** the interpretation of dreams.
symboliquement [sɛ̃bɔlikmɑ̃], *adv.* symbolically.
symbolisation [sɛ̃bɔlizasjɔ̃], *s.f.* symbolization, symbolizing.
symboliser [sɛ̃bɔlize], *v.tr.* to symbolize.
symbolisme [sɛ̃bɔlism], *s.m.* symbolism.
symboliste [sɛ̃bɔlist]. **1.** *a.* symbolistic. **2.** *s.m. & f.* symbolist.
symbranchidés [sɛ̃brɑ̃ʃide], *s.m.pl. Ich:* Symbranchidae, Synbranchidae.
symétrie [simetri], *s.f.* symmetry; **axe de s.,** symmetry axis; **plan de s.,** plane of symmetry; **s. par rapport à un plan (donné),** plane symmetry; **sans s.,** unsymmetrical.
symétrique [simetrik], *a.* symmetrical; **s. par rapport à un point,** symmetrical about a point; *Elcs:* **amplificateur s.,** push-pull, double-ended, amplifier; **circuit s.,** balanced circuit; **magnétisation cyclique s.,** symmetrical cyclically magnetized condition; **montage s.,** push-pull circuit.
symétriquement [simetrikmɑ̃], *adv.* symmetrically.
symétrisation [simetrizasjɔ̃], *s.f.* symmetrization.
symétriser [simetrize]. **1.** *v.i.* to be arranged symmetrically (**avec,** with). **2.** *v.tr.* to symmetrize.
symistor [simistɔ:r], *s.m. Elcs:* symmetrical thyristor.
Symmaque [sim(m)ak], *Pr.n.m. Rom.Hist:* Symmachus.
sympa [sɛ̃pa], *a. F:* likeable, attractive.
sympathicectomie [sɛ̃patisɛktɔmi], *s.f.,* **sympathectomie** [sɛ̃patɛktɔmi], *s.f. Surg:* sympathectomy.
sympathie [sɛ̃pati], *s.f.* sympathy; (*a*) instinctive attraction, fellow feeling, congeniality; **avoir de la s. pour qn,** to feel drawn to s.o.; to like s.o.; **concevoir de la s. pour qn, se prendre de s. pour qn,** to take a liking to s.o.; to take to s.o.; to warm to s.o.; **sympathies et antipathies,** likes and dislikes; (*b*) **idées qui ne sont pas en s.,** conflicting ideas; (*c*) *Med: Physiol:* sympathy (between organs).
sympathique [sɛ̃patik], *a.* **1.** sympathetic; **être s. aux idées de qn,** to be in sympathy with s.o.'s ideas; **ressentir un mouvement s. pour qn,** to feel attracted to s.o. **2.** likeable, attractive (personality); **c'est un garçon s.,** he is a likeable young man; **être très s.,** to be a very likeable person; **personnalité peu s.,** unattractive personality; **il me fut s. par, à cause de, son courage,** I warmed to him for his courage; **il me fut tout de suite s.,** I took to him at once; **il me devint s.,** I came to like him; **elle ne m'est pas du tout s.,** she doesn't appeal to me, I don't feel drawn to her, in the least; **il avait l'abord peu s.,** one didn't take to him at first; **Paul est fort s. à ma mère,** my mother is very fond of Paul; **il savait se rendre s. dans tous les milieux,** he was a good mixer in company of all sorts; **travail, entourage, s.,** congenial work, surroundings. **3. encre s.,** sympathetic ink, invisible ink. **4.** *Anat: Physiol: etc:* sympathetic (nerve, action, ophthalmia); *Anat:* **le (nerf) grand s.,** the sympathetic nerve.
sympathiquement [sɛ̃patikmɑ̃], *adv.* sympathetically.
sympathisant, -ante [sɛ̃patizɑ̃, -ɑ̃:t]. **1.** (*a*) sympathizing. **2.** *s.* (*a*) sympathizer; well-wisher; (*b*) *Pol:* **s. communiste,** fellow-traveller.
sympathiser [sɛ̃patize], *v.i.* (*a*) to sympathize (**avec,** with); (*b*) to harmonize, (*of two persons*) to be friendly; **deux femmes, deux qualités, qui ne sympathisent pas,** two women who have nothing in common; two qualities that do not blend.
sympétalique [sɛ̃petalik], *a. Bot:* sympetalous.
symphonie [sɛ̃fɔni], *s.f.* **1.** *A:* harmony, consonance. **2.** *Mus:* symphony. **3.** *A:* instrumental accompaniment. **4.** (*a*) orchestra; (*b*) strings of the orchestra.
symphonique [sɛ̃fɔnik], *a. Mus:* symphonic (form, poem).
symphoniste [sɛ̃fɔnist], *s.m.* **1.** symphonist, composer of symphonies. **2.** orchestral player.
Symphorien [sɛ̃fɔrjɛ̃], *Pr.n.m.* (Saint) Symphorian.
symphorine [sɛ̃fɔrin], *s.f. Bot:* symphoricarpos; **s. boule-de-neige,** snowberry, waxberry.
symphyse [sɛ̃fi:z], *s.f. Anat:* symphysis.
sympiézomètre [sɛ̃pjezɔmɛtr], *s.m. Meteor:* sympiesometer.
symplectique [sɛ̃plɛktik], *s.m. Anat:* symplectic.
sympode [sɛ̃pɔd], *s.m. Bot:* sympode, sympodium.
sympodique [sɛ̃pɔdik], *a. Bot:* sympodial.
symposiarque [sɛ̃pɔziark], *s.m. Gr.Ant:* symposiarch.
symposium [sɛ̃pɔzjɔm], *s.m. Gr.Lit: etc:* symposium; *pl. symposiums.*
symptomatique [sɛ̃ptɔmatik], *a.* symptomatic.
symptomatiquement [sɛ̃ptɔmatikmɑ̃], *adv.* symptomatically.
symptomatologie [sɛ̃ptɔmatɔlɔʒi], *s.f. Med:* symptomatology.
symptôme [sɛ̃pto:m], *s.m.* (*a*) symptom; **s. prémonitoire,** premonitory symptom; (*b*) sign, token, indication.
syn- [sin, sɛ̃]; (*before* **l**) **syl-** [sil]; (*before* **b, m, p**) **sym-** [sɛ̃]; (*before* **r**) **syr-** [sir]; (*before* **s** *not followed by a consonant*) **sys-** [sis]; (*before* **s** *followed by a consonant or before* **z**) **sy-** [si], *pref.*; syn-, syl-, sym-, syr-, sy-.
synagogal, -aux [sinagɔgal, -o], *a.* synagogal, synagogical.
synagogue [sinagɔg], *s.f.* synagogue; *F: A:* **enterrer la s. avec honneur,** to end sth. well.
synalèphe [sinalɛf], *s.f. Gram:* synaloepha.
synallagmatique [sinal(l)agmatik], *a. Jur:* synallagmatic; **contrat s.,** bilateral contract; indenture.
synanthé [sinɑ̃te], *a. Bot:* synanthous.
synanthéré [sinɑ̃tere], *Bot:* **1.** *a.* (*of plant*) synanthereous; (*of stamens*) syngenesious. **2.** *s.f.pl.* **synanthérées,** Compositae.
synanthérie [sinɑ̃teri], *s.f. Bot:* syngenesia.
synapse [sinaps], *s.f.* **1.** *Anat:* synapse. **2.** *Biol:* synapsis.
synaptique [sinaptik], *a. Anat:* synaptic.
synarchie [sinarʃi], *s.f.* joint sovereignty, joint rule; synarchy.
synarchique [sinarʃik], *a.* synarchical.
synarthrodial, -iaux [sinartrɔdjal, -jo], *a. Anat:* synarthrodial.
synarthrose [sinartro:z], *s.f. Anat:* synarthrosis.
synbactéries [sɛ̃bakteri], *s.f.pl.* slime bacteria.
syncarpe [sɛ̃karp], *s.m. Bot:* syncarp.
syncarpé [sɛ̃karpe], *a. Bot:* syncarpous; **fruit s.,** syncarp.
synchondrose [sɛ̃kɔ̃dro:z], *s.f. Anat:* synchondrosis.
synchrocyclotron [sɛ̃krɔsiklɔtrɔ̃], *s.m. Atom.Ph:* synchrocyclotron.
synchroflash [sɛ̃krɔflaʃ], *s.m. Phot:* synchroflash.
synchrone [sɛ̃kro:n], *a.* synchronous (**de,** with); *El:* in step; *Elcs:* **calculateur s.,** synchronous computer; **fonctionnement s.,** synchronous working; **système s.,** synchronous system; **transmission s.,** synchronous transmission; *Space:* **orbite s.,** synchronous orbit (of satellite).
synchronie [sɛ̃krɔni], *s.f. Ling: etc:* synchrony.
synchronique [sɛ̃krɔnik], *a.* synchronic, synchronous, synchronistic, synchronological (table of events).
synchroniquement [sɛ̃krɔnikmɑ̃], *adv.* synchronically.
synchronisateur [sɛ̃krɔnizatœ:r], *s.m.* synchronizer; *Aut:* synchromesh device.
synchronisation [sɛ̃krɔnizasjɔ̃], *s.f.* synchronization, synchronizing; *Cin: T.V:* synchronization (of sound and image); *Mil: Av:* **mécanisme de s. de la mitrailleuse,** gun synchronizer; *Elcs:* **dispositif de s.,** timing mechanism, synchronizer; **bits de s.,** sync-bits, framing bits; **impulsion de s.,** clock, synchronizing, pulse; **marque de s.,** timing mark; **onde pilote de s.,** synchronizing pilot.
synchronisé [sɛ̃krɔnize], *a.* synchronized; in step; **feux synchronisés,** linked (traffic) signals; *Elcs:* **coupleur s.,** torque amplifier.
synchroniser [sɛ̃krɔnize], *v.tr.* to synchronize; (**qch. avec qch.,** sth. with sth.); *El:* to parallel.
synchroniseur, -euse [sɛ̃krɔnizœ:r, -øz]. **1.** *s.m.* (*a*) *El: etc:* synchronizer; (*b*) *Aut:* synchromesh device. **2.** *s.f. Cin:* **synchroniseuse,** film synchronizer.
synchronisme [sɛ̃krɔnism], *s.m.* synchronism; **en s.,** in synchronism; in time; *El:* in step; **horloges qui marchent en s.,** clocks that synchronize; **hors de s.,** out of synchronism; out of parallel; out of step; *Ph: etc:* **perdre le s.,** to fall out of step; *Cin: etc:* **marque, signal, de s.,** synchrony mark.
synchronologie [sɛ̃krɔnɔlɔʒi], *s.f.* synchronology.
synchronoscope [sɛ̃krɔnɔskɔp], *s.m. Elcs:* synchronous machine, synchronoscope.
synchrotron [sɛ̃krɔtrɔ̃], *s.m. Atom.Ph:* synchrotron; **s. à électrons, à protons,** electron, proton, synchrotron; **s. à focalisation forte,** strong focusing synchrotron; **s. à gradient alterné,** alternating-gradient synchrotron.
synchyse [sɛ̃ki:z], *s.f. Gram:* synchysis.
synchysis [sɛ̃kizis], *s.m. Med:* synchysis; **s. étincelant,** sparkling synchysis.
synclase [sɛ̃klɑ:z], *s.f. Geol:* contraction joint.
synclinal, -aux [sɛ̃klinal, -o], *a. Geog:* synclinal (valley, etc.).
synclinorium [sɛ̃klinɔrjɔm], *s.m. Geol:* synclinorium.
syncopal, -aux [sɛ̃kɔpal, -o], *a. Med:* syncopal.
syncope [sɛ̃kɔp], *s.f.* **1.** *Med:* syncope; faint, fainting fit; **s. mortelle,** heart failure; **tomber en s.,** to faint. **2.** *Gram:* syncope. **3.** *Mus:* (*a*) syncopation; (*b*) syncopated note.
syncopé [sɛ̃kɔpe], *a.* syncopated (note, music).
syncoper [sɛ̃kɔpe], *v.tr.* **1.** *Gram: Mus:* to syncopate. **2.** *F: A:* to amaze, to dumbfound.
syncotylédoné [sɛ̃kɔtiledɔne], *a. Bot:* syncotyledonous.
syncrétique [sɛ̃kretik], *a. Phil:* syncretic.
syncrétisme [sɛ̃kretism], *s.m. Phil:* syncretism.
syncrétiste [sɛ̃kretist], *Phil:* **1.** *a.* syncretistic. **2.** *s.m. & f.* syncretist.
syncytium [sɛ̃sisjɔm, sɛ̃sitjɔm], *s.m. Biol:* syncytium.
syndactyle [sɛ̃daktil], *a. Z:* syndactyl(ous), webfingered, -toed.
syndactylie [sɛ̃daktili], *s.f. Z:* syndactylism, syndactyly.
synderme [sɛ̃dɛrm], *s.m.* synthetic leather, leather substitute.
syndesmose [sɛ̃dɛsmo:z], *s.f. Anat:* syndesmosis.
syndic [sɛ̃dik], *s.m.* syndic; **s. de faillite,** assignee, official receiver, public trustee (in bankruptcy).
syndic-agréé [sɛ̃dikagree], *s.m.* = official receiver; *pl. syndics-agréés.*
syndical, -aux [sɛ̃dikal, -o], *a.* **1.** syndical (chamber); **chambre syndicale (des agents de change)** = Stock Exchange Committee; **acte s.,** underwriting contract. **2. mouvement s.,** trade-union movement.
syndicalisme [sɛ̃dikalism], *s.m.* syndicalism; *esp.* **s. (ouvrier),** trade unionism.
syndicaliste [sɛ̃dikalist], (*a*) *a.* syndicalist(ic); (*b*) *s.m. & f.* syndicalist; *esp.* trade unionist.
syndicat [sɛ̃dika], *s.m.* **1.** trusteeship (in bankruptcy). **2.** syndicate; (*a*) **s. professionnel,** trade society, trade association; **s. de producteurs,** producers' association; **s. patronal,** employers' federation; **s. des marchands de vins en gros,** association of wholesale wine merchants; *Com:* **s. industriel,** pool; *Fin:* **s. financier,** financial syndicate; **s. de garantie,** underwriting syndicate; **s. de placement,** pool; **s. des propriétaires, des locataires,** householder's, tenants', association; **s. d'initiative,** tourist office, bureau; (*b*) **s. (ouvrier),** trade union.
syndicataire [sɛ̃dikatɛ:r]. **1.** *a.* of, pertaining to, a syndicate. **2.** *s.* (*a*) member of a syndicate; (*b*) *Fin:* underwriter.
syndiqué, -ée [sɛ̃dike]. **1.** *a.* associated, combined; (*a*) belonging to a syndicate; (*b*) **ouvriers syndiqués,** trade unionists; **ouvriers non syndiqués,** non-union men. **2.** *s.* trade unionist.
syndiquer [sɛ̃dike], *v.tr.* **1.** to syndicate (an industry). **2.** to form (workers, etc.) into a trade union, to unionize (an industry, etc.).
se syndiquer. **1.** to combine; to form a syndicate, to syndicate. **2.** to form a trade union; (*of worker*) to join a union.
syndrome [sɛ̃dro:m], *s.m. Med:* syndrome; **s. de vidange,** dumping syndrome; *s.a.* PHARYNGO-LARYNGÉ.
synecdoche, synecdoque [sinɛkdɔk], *s.f. Rh:* synecdoche.
synectique [sinɛktik], *s.f.* synectics.
synérèse [sinerɛ:z], *s.f. Ph: Ling:* synaeresis.
synergides [sinɛrʒid], *s.f.pl. Bot:* Synergidae.
synergie [sinɛrʒi], *s.f.* synergy.

synergique [sinɛrʒik], *a.* synergic; (*a*) *Med:* effet s., additive effect; (*b*) *Theol:* synergistic.

synergisme [sinɛrʒism], *s.m.* synergism.

synergiste [sinɛrʒist], *s.m.* synergist.

synesthésie [sinestezi], *s.f. Psy:* synesthesia, synaestheasia.

syngame [sɛ̃gam], *s.m. Husb:* s. trachéal, gapeworm.

syngamique [sɛ̃gamik], *a. Biol:* syngamous.

syngamose [sɛ̃gamoːz], *s.f. Husb:* (the) gapes (in poultry).

syngénésie [sɛ̃ʒenezi], *s.f.*, **syngénèse** [sɛ̃ʒenɛːz], *s.f.* 1. *Bot:* syngenesia. 2. *Biol:* syngenesis.

syngénésique [sɛ̃ʒenezik], *a. Biol:* syngenetic.

syngénite [sɛ̃ʒenit], *s.f. Miner:* syngenite.

syngnathe [sɛ̃gnat], *s.m. Ich:* syngnathid; pipefish; *pl.* syngnathes, Syngnathidae.

syngnathidés [sɛ̃gnatide], *s.m.pl. Ich:* Syngnathidae.

synnévrose [sin(n)evroːz], *s.f. Anat:* syndesmosis.

synodal, -aux [sinɔdal, -o], *a.* synodal (examiner); synodical (proceedings, conference).

synode [sinɔd], *s.m. Ecc:* synod.

synodique [sinɔdik], *a.* synodic(al); *Astr:* mois, révolution, s., synodic period.

synœcie [sinesi], *s.f. Nat.Hist:* synoecy; s. d'habitat, habitat synoecy.

synonyme [sinɔnim]. 1. *a.* synonymous (de, with). 2. *s.m.* synonym.

synonymie [sinɔnimi], *s.f.* synonymy, synonymity.

synonymique [sinɔnimik]. 1. *a.* synonymic. 2. *s.f.* synonymics, synonymy.

synopse [sinɔps], *s.f.* synoptic table of the Gospels; synopsis of the Gospels.

synopsis [sinɔpsis], *s.f.* synopsis.

synoptique [sinɔptik], *a.* synoptic(al); les Évangiles synoptiques, the Synoptic Gospels; tableau s., conspectus (of a science, etc.); *Elcs:* schéma s., block diagram.

synoque [sinɔk], *a. P:* crackers, mad.

synostéologie [sinɔsteɔlɔʒi], *s.f. Anat:* synosteology.

synostose [sinɔstoːz], *s.f. Anat:* synostosis, ankylosis.

synovectomie [sinɔvɛktɔmi], *s.f. Surg:* synovectomy.

synovial, -iaux [sinɔvjal, -jo], *a. Anat:* synovial (gland, etc.).

synovie [sinɔvi], *s.f. Anat: Physiol:* synovia; *Med:* épanchement de s., housemaid's knee.

synovite [sinɔvit], *s.f. Med:* synovitis.

syntacticien, -ienne [sɛ̃taktisjɛ̃, -jɛn], *s. Gram:* syntactician.

syntactique [sɛ̃taktik], *a. Gram:* syntactic(al).

syntagmatique [sɛ̃tagmatik], *a. Ling:* syntagmatic.

syntagme [sɛ̃tagm], *s.m. Ling:* syntagm, syntagma.

syntaxe [sɛ̃taks], *s.f. Gram: etc:* syntax.

syntaxique [sɛ̃taksik], *a.* = SYNTACTIQUE.

synthèse [sɛ̃tɛːz], *s.f.* synthesis; pierre de s., synthetic stone.

synthétique [sɛ̃tetik], *a.* synthetic(al); *Tex:* fibre s., synthetic fibre; *Med:* régime s., well-balanced diet; langage s., synthetic language.

synthétiquement [sɛ̃tetikmɑ̃], *adv.* synthetically.

synthétiser [sɛ̃tetize], *v.tr.* to synthesize.

synthétiseur [sɛ̃tetizœːr], *s.m. Elcs:* synthetizer; s. numérique, digital synthetizer; *Av:* s. de vol, flight director.

synthol [sɛ̃tɔl], *s.m. Ch:* synthol.

syntomides [sɛ̃tɔmid], *s.m.pl. Ent:* Syntomidae, Euchromiidae.

syntone [sɛ̃tɔn], *a. Psy:* syntone.

syntonie [sɛ̃tɔni], *s.f.* (*a*) *Psy:* syntomy; (*b*) *W.Tel:* syntonism, syntony.

syntonique [sɛ̃tɔnik], *a.* 1. *A.Mus:* syntonous (diatonic scale). 2. *W.Tel:* syntonic, tuned (transmitter, receiver).

syntonisateur, -trice [sɛ̃tɔnizatœːr, -tris], *W.Tel:* 1. *a.* bobine syntonisatrice, tuning coil. 2. *s.m.* tuning device; tuner.

syntonisation [sɛ̃tɔnizasjɔ̃], *s.f. W.Tel:* tuning, syntonization; bobine de s., tuning coil.

syntoniser [sɛ̃tɔnize], *v.tr. W.Tel:* to syntonize; to tune in (set).

syphilide [sifilid], *s.f. Med:* syphilide; s. pigmentaire, macular syphilide.

syphilis [sifilis], *s.f. Med:* syphilis; s. extra-génitale, occupational syphilis.

syphilisation [sifilizasjɔ̃], *s.f. Med:* syphilization.

syphiliser [sifilize], *v.tr. Med:* to syphilize.

syphilisme [sifilism], *s.m.* syphilosis.

syphilitique [sifilitik], *a. & s.* syphilitic.

syphiloïde [sifilɔid], *a.* syphiloid.

syphilome [sifilɔːm], *s.m. Med:* syphiloma.

syphilophobie [sifilɔfɔbi], *s.f.* syphilophobia.

Syracuse [sirakyːz], *Pr.n. Geog:* Syracuse.

syracusain, -aine [sirakyzɛ̃, -ɛn], *a. & s. Geog:* Syracusan.

syriaque [sirjak], *a. & s.m. Ling:* Syriac.

Syrie [siri], *Pr.n.f. Geog:* Syria.

syrien, -ienne [sirjɛ̃, -jɛn], *a. & s. Geog:* Syrian.

syringa [sirɛ̃ga], *s.m. Bot:* lilac; syringa vulgaris.

syringe [sirɛ̃ːʒ], *s.f.* 1. syrinx. 2. *Archeol:* rock-cut tomb (of ancient Egypt).

syringomyélie [sirɛ̃gɔmjeli], *s.f. Med:* syringomyelia.

syringomyélique [sirɛ̃gɔmjelik], *a. Med:* syringomyelic.

syringotomie [sirɛ̃gɔtɔmi], *s.f. Surg:* syringotomy.

syrinx [sirɛ̃ks], *s.f.* syrinx. 1. pan's pipes. 2. *Archeol:* rock-cut tomb (of Ancient Egypt). 3. *Orn:* lower larynx.

syro-chaldaïque [sirɔkaldaik], *a. & s.m. Ling:* Syrochaldaic, Aramaic; *pl.* syro-chaldaïques.

syrphe [sirf], *s.m. Ent:* syrphus (fly).

syrphidés [sirfide], *s.m.pl. Ent:* Syrphidae.

syrrhapte [sirapt], *s.m. Orn:* s. paradoxal, Pallas's sand grouse.

syrte [sirt], *s.f. A:* syrtis, quicksand (in Africa); *Geog:* les Syrtes, the Syrtes.

systaltique [sistaltik], *a. Physiol:* systaltic (pulsation).

systématique [sistematik]. 1. *a.* (*a*) systematic; (*b*) *F:* hide-bound (opinions, person); (*c*) *Med:* examen s., routine examination. 2. *s.f.* systematics.

systématiquement [sistematikmɑ̃], *adv.* systematically.

systématisation [sistematizasjɔ̃], *s.f.* system(at)ization, systemizing.

systématiser [sistematize], *v.tr.* to system(at)ize.

systématiseur [sistematizœːr], *s.m.* systematizer, system-maker.

système [sistɛm], *s.m.* 1. system; (*a*) method, scheme, plan; un nouveau s., a new system, device; s. absolu, absolute system; s. combinatoire, combinatorial system; s. de référence, s. référentiel, frame of reference, reference system, system of co-ordinates; s. fermé, ouvert, closed, open, system; s. quantifié, non quantifié, quantized, non-quantized, system; s. récurrent, recursive system; *Mth:* s. décimal, decimal system; s. métrique, metric system; adoption du s. métrique, metrication; *Elcs:* (*computers*) s. de perforation double par colonne, ducol (punched card) system; analyste de systèmes, systems analyst; *Hist:* s. féodal, feudal system; (*b*) *Mil:* s. d'armes, weapon system; *Mec.E:* s. de commandes, control system, actuation system; s. de refroidissement, cooling system; s. asservi, servo-system; *Av: Ball:* s. de guidage, guidance system; s. d'autoguidage, homing system; *Ill:* s. d'éclairage, lighting system, illumination system; *Opt:* s. optique, optical system; *Tchn:* s. numérique de comptage, register; (*c*) agir par s., to stick to a system; établir qch. d'après un s., to establish sth. according to a system; avoir l'esprit de s., to refuse to deviate from the (established) system; le s. D, resourcefulness, wangling; (*d*) set (of wheels, of valves, etc.); network (of roads); *Physiol:* s. lymphatique, lymphatic system; s. nerveux, nervous system; s. neuro-végétatif, vegetative-nervous system; *F:* il me tape sur le s., he gets on my nerves. 2. (*a*) fusils de divers systèmes, rifles of various makes, types; bouton de col à s., patent collar stud; cravate s., clip-on tie; (*b*) systèmes d'un bateau, swivel rowlocks of a boat; (*c*) *Phot:* s. antérieur, postérieur (d'un objectif), front, back, lens.

systémiques [sistemik], *s.m.pl.* pesticides; systemic insecticides.

systole [sistɔl], *s.f. Physiol:* systole.

systolique [sistɔlik], *a.* systolic.

systyle [sistil], *a. & s.m. Arch:* systyle (temple, etc.).

syzygie [siziʒi], *s.f. Astr:* syzygy; les marées de s., the spring tides.

T

T, t (te], s.m. the letter T, t; (a) Tp: T comme Thérèse, T for Tommy; (b) t euphonique forms a link between verbal endings -a, -e and the pronouns il, elle, on; va-t-il? ira-t-elle? donne-t-on? (c) (of T-shaped object) fer à, en, T, T-iron, T-bar, tee; poutre en double T, H beam; (beam of) I section; tube en T, T branch; three-limb tube; chaînette à T, (watch)chain and toggle; Av: T. d'atterrissage, landing T; W.Tel: antenne en T, T-shaped antenna, T aerial; (d) (in naval warfare) barrer le T, to cross the T; s.a. TÉ 1.

tabac¹ [taba], s.m. 1. Bot: tobacco (plant). 2. (a) t. haché, cut tobacco; t. en corde, pigtail; t. en carotte, twist; t. à chiquer, à mâcher, chewing tobacco; t. à fumer, smoking tobacco; blague à t., tobacco pouch; pot à t. [poataba], tobacco jar; F: c'est un pot à t., he's a tubby little man; débitant de t., tobacconist; débit, bureau, de t., tobacconist's (shop); passer devant le t., to go past the tobacconist's; F: A: je n'en donnerais pas une pipe de t., I wouldn't say thank you for it; F: c'est du même t., it's the same thing; (b) t. à priser, t. râpé, snuff; prendre du t., to take snuff; s.a. PRISE 4. 3. les Tabacs, the (State) Tobacco Department. 4. a.inv. tobacco-coloured, snuff-coloured.

tabac² [taba], s.m. F: (esp. of the police) passer qn à t., to handle s.o. roughly; to put s.o. through it, to give s.o. the third degree; il y a du t., we're up against it; F: we're for it; Mil: il y aura du t. ce soir, we're in for some hard fighting tonight; there'll be hell to pay tonight.

tabacomane [tabakɔman], s.m. hard smoker; F: tobacco fiend.

tabacomanie [tabakɔmani], s.f. excessive smoking.

tabacophobe [tabakɔfɔb], s.m. tobacco hater.

tabagie [tabaʒi], s.f. 1. A: smoking-room, -den; smoking-saloon. 2. F: place reeking of stale tobacco smoke. 3. Fr.C: tobacconist's (shop).

tabagique [tabaʒik], a. nicotinic.

tabagisme [tabaʒism], s.m. nicotinism, nicotine poisoning.

tabanidés [tabanide], s.m.pl. Ent: Tabanidae; F: the horseflies.

tabar(d) [tabaːr], s.m. (herald's) tabard.

tabarin [tabarɛ̃], s.m. A: buffoon; (from Jean Salomon Tabarin, 1584-1633).

tabarinade [tabarinad], s.f. A.Th: broad farce (in the manner of Tabarin, early 17th cent.).

tabas(c)hir [tabaʃiːr], s.m. tabasheer, bamboo salt, sugar of bamboo.

tabassage [tabasaːʒ], s.m. F: beating up (of s.o.); fight.

tabassée [tabase], s.f. F: beating, (good) thrashing.

tabasser [tabase], v.tr. F: to beat up.

tabatier, -ière [tabatje, -jɛːr]. 1. s. tobacco worker. 2. s.f. tabatière, (a) snuff-box; (b) Const: (fenêtre, lucarne, châssis, à) tabatière, hinged skylight; Sm.a: A: fusil à tabatière, early form of French breech-loading rifle.

tabellaire [tabel(l)ɛːr], a. Typ: A: impression t., printing from engraved plates.

tabellion [tabeljɔ̃], s.m. (a) Jur: A: tabellion, scrivener; (b) F: Hum: limb of the law; lawyer.

tabernacle [tabɛrnakl], s.m. 1. Ecc: etc: tabernacle; Jewish Rel: la fête des Tabernacles, the Feast of Tabernacles. 2. Nau: tabernacle. 3. Const: inspection, fitting, chamber (for underground tap, etc.).

tabes, tabès [tabɛs], s.m. Med: tabes.

tabescence [tabɛs(s)ɑ̃ːs], s.f. Med: tabescence, emaciation.

tabescent [tabɛs(s)ɑ̃], a. Med: tabescent; wasting away.

tabétique [tabetik], a. & s. Med: tabetic.

tabi(s) [tabi], s.m. Tex: tabby, watered silk.

tabiser [tabize], v.tr. Tex: to tabby, water (silk, etc.).

Tabithe [tabit], Pr.n.f. B: Tabitha.

tablature [tablatyːr], s.f. Mus: 1. A: tablature; F: donner de la t. à qn, to cause s.o. trouble or embarrassment; to give s.o. a difficult job; A: savoir, entendre, la t., to know a thing or two, to be wide awake. 2. fingering chart (of wind instrument).

table [tabl], s.f. table. 1. (a) t. de salle à manger, dining table; t. à rallonges, telescope table; t. (avec rallonges) à l'italienne, drawleaf table; t. à abattants, (i) dropleaf table; (ii) gateleg, gate-legged, table; t. de jeu, gaming table; card table; t. de billard, billiard table; t. (à thé) roulante, tea trolley; t. pliante, folding table; t. de salon, coffee table; t. de malade, bed table; t. de toilette, dressing table; t. de nuit, bedside table, night table, pedestal cupboard; t. à repasser, ironing table; t. à dessiner, draughtsman's table, board; t. de modeleur, modelling board; t. d'opération, operating table; Lit: la T. ronde, the Round Table; Pol: Ind: t. ronde, round-table conference; Psychics: (phénomène des) tables tournantes, frappantes, table turning, table rapping; (b) board; Lit: la t. du festin, the festive board; la t. d'honneur, the high table (at a college); the head table (at a banquet, wedding); mettre, dresser, la t., to lay, the table; aimer la t., to be fond of good living, of good fare, of the table; la t. est bonne, the food is good; bière de t., table beer; raisins de t., dessert grapes; propos de t., table talk; se mettre à t., (i) to sit down to table, to dinner, etc.; (ii) P: to confess, to come clean; nous allons passer à t. dans quelques minutes, we shall start eating in a few minutes; à t.! dinner, lunch, is ready! F: let's eat! être à t., to be at table, at dinner, etc.; se lever, sortir, de t., to rise from table, to leave the table; tenir t. ouverte, to keep an open board; to keep open house; avoir t. et logement chez qn, to have board and lodge with s.o.; A: mettre qn sous la t., to drink s.o. under the table; (service de) petites tables, separate tables (at a restaurant); Mil: Navy: frais de t., table money; Mil: t. d'officiers, officers' mess; manger à la même t., to mess together; P: manger à la grande t., to be a police spy; F: sous la t., secretly, under the table; Ecc: la Sainte T., the Lord's Table, the Communion table; s.a. DESSOUS-DE-TABLE, HÔTE 1. 2. (flat surface) (a) Dom.Ec: t. de cuisson, (cooking) top, boiling ring unit, hotplate (of kitchen unit); t. de travail, working surface, top; (b) Lap: table (of gem); diamant (taillé) en t., table(-cut) diamond; (c) Mus: lay (of clarinet mouthpiece); t. d'harmonie, sound board, belly (of piano, etc.); belly (of violin); t. du fond, back (of violin); (d) Her: t. d'attente, field; (e) face, plate (of hammer, etc.); flange (of girder); Farr: table (of worn tooth); Rail: t. de roulement, tread (of rail); Mch: t. du tiroir, valve face; t. de foyer, furnace dead-plate; Mec.E: t. de planeuse, bed of a planing machine; (f) Anat: t.

interne, t. vitrée, inner, vitreous, table (of the skull); (g) Geog: montagne de la T., Table Mountain; (h) Min: t. à secousses, à percussion, jigging table; (i) Tp: switchboard; t. interurbaine, trunk switchboard; t. d'écoute, listening table (used by police to tap phone conversations); (j) Elcs: table, board; t. de décision, decision table; t. des en-têtes, header table; t. d'essais, test board; t. de report, plotting board; t. des symboles, symbol table; t. traçante, plotting board, plotting table, output table; consultation de t., recherche dans une t., table look-up. 3. (a) slab (of stone, etc.); tablet; Prehist: cap stone (of a dolmen); Const: t. rustique, rustic table (of a wall, etc.); Glassm: t. à couler, casting slab, table; B.Hist: les tables de la loi, the Tables of the Law; s.a. RAS¹ 1; (b) list, catalogue; t. alphabétique, alphabetical list, table, index; t. de multiplication, multiplication table; t. de multiplication par 9, nine times table; t. de conversion, conversion table, conversion chart; t. de corrélation, correlation table; t. de correspondance, correspondence table; tables de mortalité, mortality tables; t. des matières, (table of) contents; t. de déviation, deviation table (of magnetic needle); t. de triangulation, triangulator table; Mil: etc: t. de tir, firing table, range table; valeur portée sur une t., tabulated value.

tableau, -eaux [tablo], s.m. 1. (a) board; t. d'annonces, notice board; afficher un avis sur le t., to put a notice on the board; t. d'affichage, (i) bill frame, poster frame; (ii) Sp: telegraph board, number board; scoring board; (iii) (in schools, clubs, etc.) notice board, U.S: bulletin board; Sch: t. noir, blackboard; El: Tp: t. de distribution, t. commutateur, switchboard; distribution board, panel; t. de charge, charging panel; Tp: t. indicateur, annunciator; indicator board; t. indicateur à volet, drop-type switchboard, drop indicator; t. de contrôle, (i) Mec.E: control panel; (ii) Tp: monitoring board; t. de marche, control board; El: etc: t. d'éclairage, lighting panel; t. de manœuvre, instrument board, panel; t. de bord, (i) Aut: dashboard; (ii) Av: instrument panel; (computers) t. de connexions, plugboard; t. de commande, control panel; t. de jacks, jack panel; t. d'opération booléenne, Boolean operation table; (b) Bill: scoring board; (c) Nau: name board, escutcheon (of ship); (d) (in hotel) key rack, board. 2. (a) picture, painting; t. de fleurs, flower piece; t. d'autel, altar-piece; t. des événements de l'époque, picturesque description of the events of the time; faire un t. saisissant de qch., to draw a striking picture of sth.; de la colline se découvre un magnifique t., one gets a beautiful view from the hill; F: vieux t., painted old hag; old frump; mutton dressed as lamb; (b) Th: tableau (at end of act, etc.); F: hier on l'a surprise assise sur les genoux du chauffeur; t.! yesterday she was caught sitting on the chauffeur's knee; tableau! (c) t. vivant, living picture, Th: tableau vivant; (d) Th: scene, group of scenes, acted in one setting; féerie en douze tableaux, fairy play in twelve scenes. 3. (a) list, table; t. comparatif, comparative table; t. récapitulatif, summary (table); t. synoptique, synoptic table; t. par doit et avoir, balance sheet; Fin: t. d'amortissement, redemption table; Adm: Mil: Navy: t. d'avancement, promotion list, promotion roster; t. de

T:1

service, duty chart, roster, list; *Navy:* (day's) routine; *Aut:* **t. de graissage,** lubrication chart; *Aut:* **t. de gonflage,** (tyre) inflation table; *Phot: Cin:* **t. de mise au point,** test (chart); *Ind:* **t. de charge,** planning; load schedule (of workshop, etc.); **t. de marche,** progress schedule; *Ind:* flow sheet (of production); *Rail:* (service) timetable; *Nau:* list of sailings; *Navy:* sailing list, order; **t. de travail,** timetable; work(ing) schedule, record; *Mec.E:* **t. d'épreuves,** testing schedule; *Rail:* **t. de contrôle optique,** visual control diagram (in signalling box); **t. indicateur du service des quais,** train indicator; *Mil:* **t. de dotations,** table of allowances; **t. de dotation en matériel,** table of equipment; **t. d'effectifs,** table of organization, manning table; **t. d'effectifs de paix, de guerre,** table of organization in peace, in war; **t. d'effectifs et de dotations,** table of organization and equipment; *Mapm:* **t. d'assemblage des feuilles,** index of adjoining sheets; **t. des signes conventionnels,** conventional sheet, characteristic sheet; *Med:* **t. clinique,** clinical picture; **sous forme de t.,** in tabular form; (in) tabulated (form); **mettre sous forme de t.,** to tabulate; *F:* **gagner sur tous les, sur les deux, tableaux,** to win all along the line, on all counts; (*b*) *Jur:* roll (of lawyers); panel (of jurymen, doctors, etc.); **former un t.,** to empanel a jury; **être rayé du t.,** to be struck off the rolls; **se faire inscrire au t.,** to be called to the bar; **inscription au t.,** call to the bar; **rayer un avocat du t.,** to disbar a barrister; (*c*) *Sch:* **t. d'honneur,** honours board; (*d*) *Typ:* (i) table; (ii) table work. **4.** *Ven:* bag (laid out for inspection after the shoot); **qu'y a-t-il au t.?** what's the bag? *F:* **au t.,** in the bag. **5.** *Arch:* **t. de pied-droit,** reveal (of window or door).

tableautier [tablotje], *s.m. Typ:* tabulator; compositor on table work.

tableautin [tablotɛ̃], *s.m.* small picture.

tablée [table], *s.f.* **1.** company at table; (full table of) guests. **2.** length of material covering a table.

tabler [table], *v.i. A:* **1.** (*at backgammon*) to arrange the board; *F:* **t. sur qch.,** to count, reckon, on sth.; **on avait tablé sur un gros succès,** they had counted on a big success; they had taken a big success for granted. **2.** to sit at table.

tabletier, -ière [tablətje, -jɛːr], *s.* maker of, dealer, in chessboards, fancy articles (of ebony, ivory, bone, etc.), and inlaid ware.

tablette [tablɛt], *s.f.* **1.** (*a*) shelf (of bookcase, etc.); **t. à coulisse,** pull-out slide (of table or desk); (*b*) flat slab, level top (of piece of furniture, of stone, etc.); coping stone, coping (of quay wall); **t. de cheminée,** mantelshelf, mantelpiece; **t. de fenêtre,** window sill; **t. de piano,** music rest; *El:* **t. à bornes,** terminal plate; (*c*) bearing surface (of joist); *Nau:* **t. de bôme, de mât de charge,** boom table, derrick stool. **2.** *pl. A:* writing-tablets; *F:* **mettre qch. sur ses tablettes,** to make a note of sth.; **rayez cela de vos tablettes,** you must no longer reckon on that; you may dismiss that from your mind. **3.** bar (of chocolate); cube (of concentrated soup); *Pharm:* tablet, lozenge, troche.

tabletterie [tablɛtri], *s.f.* (*a*) fancy-goods industry; (*b*) chessboards and indoor games, inlaid ware, knick-knacks, and fancy goods; **t. de nacre,** mother-of-pearl goods.

table-valise [tabləvaliːz], *s.f.* collapsible picnic table; *pl. tables-valises.*

tablier [tablije], *s.m.* **1.** (*a*) apron; **t. d'enfant,** pinafore; **t. blouse,** (lady's) overall; *F:* (*of servant*) **rendre son t.,** to leave (one's employment); to give notice; *Th:* **rôle à t.,** (i) (humorous) artisan or male servant part; (ii) soubrette part; (*b*) *Harn:* breast-band. **2.** (*a*) *Veh:* apron (of carriage); *Artil:* footboard (of limber); *Aut:* dashboard; foot rest (of scooter); (*b*) **t. en trapèze d'une cheminée,** hood of a fireplace. **3.** (*a*) register, blower (that can be let down in front of French fireplace); (*b*) **t. de tôle (d'un magasin),** sectional steel shutter. **4.** *Nau:* tabling, top lining (of sail). **5.** superstructure, flooring, deck, road(way) (of bridge); table (of weighbridge); *Mch:* footplate (of locomotive). **6.** *Metall:* (*a*) table (of rolling mill); apron (of lathe); *Ind:* **t. sans fin,** apron feed; (*b*) hearth (of forge). **7.** (*a*) *Ap:* stand (for hives); (*b*) *Chess: etc:* board. **8.** *Anat:* (Hottentot) apron.

tabloïde [tablɔid], *s.m. Pharm:* (compressed) tablet.

tabor [tabɔːr], *s.m. Mil: A:* corps of Moroccan troops.

taborites [tabɔrit], *s.m.pl. Rel.H:* Taborites.

tabou [tabu]. **1.** *s.m.* taboo. **2.** *a.* (*often inv.*) taboo(ed); **sujets tabou(s),** forbidden, taboo, subjects; *Mil:* **armes taboues,** forbidden weapons; **déclarer un sujet t.,** to taboo a subject.

tabouer [tabwe], **tabouiser** [tabwize], *v.tr.* to taboo; to declare (sth.) taboo.

tabouisation [tabwizasjɔ̃], *s.f.* tabooing, making (sth.) taboo.

tabouret [taburɛ], *s.m.* **1.** (*a*) high stool; **t. de piano,** piano stool; **t. de vacher,** milking stool; (*b*) footstool; (*c*) *Fr.Hist:* folding stool (of those who were privileged to sit in the presence of the King and Queen); **droit du t.,** privilege of the tabouret; (*d*) *A:* stocks (for offenders). **2.** *Bot:* thlaspi; **t. des champs,** pennycress.

tabourin [taburɛ̃], *s.m.* revolving chimney cowl; chimney jack.

tabulaire [tabylɛːr], *a.* tabular.

tabulateur [tabylatœːr], *s.m. Typewr:* tabulating device; tabulator, tab key; *Tp: A:* dial; **faire marcher le t.,** to dial.

tabulation [tabylasjɔ̃], *s.f.* tabulation; *Typewr: etc:* **taquet de t.,** tabulation stop; (*computers*) **caractère de t.,** tabulation character.

tabulatrice [tabylatris], *s.f.* tabulator, tabulating machine (in punched-card system, etc.); **t. numérique,** digital tabulator.

tac [tak], *s.m.* click (of steel); clack (of mill); **le t. t. d'une mitrailleuse,** the rattle of a machine gun; *Fenc:* **riposter du t. au t.,** to parry with the riposte; **riposter, répondre, du t. au t.,** to give tit for tat, to make a lightning retort.

tacaud [tako], *s.m. Ich:* whiting pout; bib.

tacca [taka], *s.m. Bot:* tacca.

tacet [tasɛt], *s.m. Mus:* tacet; *A:* **garder le t.,** to keep mum.

tachage [taʃaːʒ], *s.m.* staining.

tachant [taʃɑ̃], *a.* **1.** (*of material, colour*) easily stained, soiled. **2.** that stains, soils (other things).

tache [taʃ], *s.f.* (*a*) stain, spot (of grease, mud, etc.); blob (of colour, grease); flaw, blemish (in precious stone, work of art, etc.); bruise (on fruit); stigma, blot (on family record); **t. d'encre,** blot, blur; **petite t. d'encre,** speck of ink; **t. de suie,** fleck of soot; smut (on the face, etc.); **t. solaire, t. du soleil,** sun-spot; **une t. sombre à l'horizon,** a dark patch on the horizon; **t. de lumière,** *Th: Cin:* hot spot; *T.V:* shading; **enlever, effacer, faire disparaître, une t.,** to remove a stain; **c'est une t. à sa réputation,** it is a blot on his good name; **sans t.,** spotless; stainless; without blemish, undefiled; **réputation sans t.,** unblemished, stainless, reputation; **sa réputation était sans t.,** he had a blameless reputation; **la t. du péché,** the stain, taint, stigma, of sin; **faire t.,** to stand out as a blemish; **détail qui fait t. dans un tableau,** detail that mars a picture; **il faisait t. dans leur société,** *F:* he didn't fit in; (*b*) (*on human body*) **t. de rousseur,** freckle; **t. de vin,** strawberry mark; **chien blanc à taches feu,** white dog with reddish markings, patches, spots; *Anat:* **t. jaune (de la rétine),** yellow spot; **t. de Mariotte,** blind spot (of the eye); (*c*) *Bot: F:* **herbe à la t.,** water avens.

tâche [tɑːʃ], *s.f.* task; **travail à la t.,** work by the job, taskwork, piecework, jobbing (work); **ouvrier à la t.,** (i) jobbing workman; (ii) *Ind:* piece worker; (*computers*) **distributeur de tâches,** task dispatcher; **file d'attente des tâches,** task queue; **remplir sa t.,** to perform, carry out, one's task; to fulfil one's duty; **prendre à t. de faire qch.,** to make it one's duty, to make every endeavour, to do sth.; to undertake to do sth.; to make a point of doing sth.; **je pris à t. de découvrir la vérité,** I made it my business to find out the truth; **nous n'avons pas à t. de retracer leur histoire,** we are not particularly concerned with tracing their history; *s.a.* MOURIR, SUFFIRE.

taché [taʃe], *a.* **1.** *Nat.Hist:* spotted. **2. fruit t.,** bruised fruit.

tachéographe [takeɔgraf], *s.m. Surv: A:* recording tacheometer.

tachéomètre [takeɔmɛtr], *s.m. Surv:* tacheometer, tachymeter.

tachéométrie [takeɔmetri], *s.f. Surv:* tacheometry, tachymetry.

tacher [taʃe], *v.tr.* to stain, spot (garment, etc.); to sully, tarnish, blemish (honour, reputation); **table tachée d'encre,** ink-stained table; **deux points rouges lui tachent les joues,** he has two red patches on his cheeks.

se tacher. 1. to soil one's clothes. **2.** to stain, spot; **ne se tachant pas à la pluie,** not liable to be stained by rain.

tâcher [tɑʃe], *v.i.* (*a*) to try, endeavour; **t. de,** *occ.* **à, faire qch.,** to try, strive, attempt, to do sth.; **tâchez de ne pas oublier,** try not to forget; mind you don't forget; **j'y tâcherai,** I shall make every endeavour; I shall do my best; *A:* **il commande le respect sans y t.,** he commands respect naturally, without making any particular effort; **elle est toujours grande dame sans y t.,** she is always the great lady without giving it a thought; *F: A:* **il n'y tâchait pas,** he didn't mean it; he didn't do it on purpose; **tâchez qu'on n'en sache rien,** try to keep it quiet; try to keep it dark; **nous tâchons à ce que rien ne nous échappe,** we endeavour to let nothing escape us; (*b*) to work hard; **pendant deux ans j'ai tâché à défricher cette terre,** for two years I laboured, toiled away at, clearing this ground.

tâcheron [tɑʃrɔ̃], *s.m.* **1.** jobbing workman; piece-worker (on land); *F:* **c'est un honnête t.,** he's a good plodder. **2.** *Const: etc:* sub-contractor, jobber.

tacheté [taʃte], *a.* spotted, speckled, mottled; **chat t.,** tabby cat, brindled cat.

tacheter [taʃte], *v.tr.* (**je tachette; je tachetterai,** *usu. pronounced* [taʃtre]) to mark with spots; to speckle, fleck, mottle.

tacheture [taʃtyːr], *s.f.* spots, speckles, specks, mottle.

tachina, tachinaire [takina, takinɛːr], *s.m. occ. f. Ent:* tachina (fly), tachinid fly.

tachisme [taʃism], *s.m. Art:* tachism.

tachiste [taʃist], *a. & s. Art:* tachist.

tachistoscope [takistɔskɔp], *s.m.* tachistoscope.

Tachkent [taʃkɛnt], *Pr.n.m. Geog:* Tashkent.

tachycardie [takikardi], *s.f. Med:* tachycardia.

tachygénèse [takiʒenɛːz], *s.f. Biol:* tachygenesis.

tachygraphe [takigraf]. **1.** *s.m. & f.* shorthand writer, tachygraph (*esp.* of ancient Greece and Rome). **2.** *s.m. Mec.E:* tachograph, recording tachometer.

tachygraphie [takigrafi], *s.f. A:* tachygraphy, shorthand (*esp.* of the ancients).

tachylite [takilit], *s.f. Miner:* tachylyte, tachylite, basalt glass.

tachymètre [takimɛtr], *s.m. Mec.E: etc:* tachometer, speedometer; **t. enregistreur,** recording tachometer.

tachymétrie [takimetri], *s.f. Mec.E:* tachometry.

tachymétrique [takimetrik], *a. El:* tachometric.

tachyon [takjɔ̃], *s.m. Atom.Ph:* tachyon.

tachyphagie [takifaʒi], *s.f. Med:* tachyphagia.

tachyphémie [takifemi], *s.f. Med:* tachyphaemia.

tachysystolie [takisistɔli], *s.f. Med:* **t. auriculaire** auricular flutter.

tacite[1] [tasit], *a.* tacit (consent, etc.); implied, understood, implicit; *s.a.* RECONDUCTION.

Tacite[2], *Pr.n.m. Lt.Lit:* Tacitus.

tacitement [tasitmɑ̃], *adv.* tacitly.

taciturne [tasityrn], *a.* taciturn, silent; reserved; uncommunicative, close-mouthed; (man) of few words; *Hist:* **Guillaume le T.,** William the Silent; **il est très t.,** *F:* he's just like an oyster, a clam.

taciturnité [tasityrnite], *s.f.* taciturnity.

tacon [takɔ̃], *s.m. Ich:* parr; smolt.

tacot[1] [tako], *s.m. Tex:* driver, picker (of loom).

tacot[2], *s.m. Veh: F:* **1.** shandrydan, rattletrap. **2.** (*a*) engine of small local train, Puffing Billy; (*b*) small local train. **3.** heavy old aircraft. **4.** (*a*) old crock (of a car); (*b*) (motor) car.

tacotier [takɔtje], *s.m. Tex:* weaver.

tact [takt], *s.m.* **1.** *A:* (sense of) touch; **avoir une grande finesse de t.,** to have a delicate sense of touch; **choisir une étoffe au t.,** to choose a cloth by feel; *Mil:* **garder le t. des coudes,** to keep touch. **2.** tact; **avoir du t., être plein de t.,** to be tactful; **homme de t.,** tactful man; **faire preuve de t.,** to show tact; **dépourvu de t.,** tactless; **manque de t.,** tactlessness; **manquer de t.,** to show a lack of tact, to be tactless; **agir avec t., sans t.,** to act tactfully, tactlessly.

tacticien, -ienne [taktisjɛ̃, -jɛn], *s.* tactician.

tactile [taktil], *a.* tactile.

tactilité [taktilite], *s.f.* tactility.

tactique [taktik]. **1.** *a.* tactical; *Mil:* **appui t.,** tactical, close, support; **cadre, milieu, t.,** tactical setting. **2.** *s.f.* tactics; **t. navale,** naval tactics; **avoir recours à, appliquer, une t. nouvelle,** to resort to new tactics; *Mil: etc:* **t. d'attaque des points faibles,** soft spot tactics; **t. de harcèlement,** harassing tactics; **t. générale,** combined-arms tactics.

tactisme [taktism], *s.m. Biol:* tactism.

tactuel, -elle [taktɥɛl], *a.* tactile; tactual.

Tadjiks [tadʒik], *s.m.pl. Ethn:* Tajiks.

tadorne [tadɔrn], *s.m. Orn:* sheldrake; **t. de Belon,** sheld-duck; **t. casarca (roux),** ruddy sheld-duck.

tael [taɛl], *s.m. A.Num:* tael.

tænia [tenja], *s.m.* = TÉNIA.

tænite [tenit], *s.f. Miner:* taenite.
taf [taf], *s.m. P:* fear, funk; **avoir le t.,** to have, get, the wind up.
taffer [tafe], *v.i. P:* to be afraid, to get the wind up.
taffetas [tafta], *s.m.* (*a*) *Tex:* taffeta; (*b*) *Med: A:* **t. d'Angleterre,** court plaster; **t. anglais, gommé,** sticking plaster; **t. imperméable,** oiled silk.
taffeur, -euse [tafœːr, -øːz], *s. P:* funk(er).
taffouilleux [tafujø], *s.m. A:* riverside collector of flotsam (in Paris); rag-picker.
tafia [tafja], *s.m.* tafia (rum); **t. de laurier,** bay rum.
Tagals [tagal], *s.m.pl. Ethn:* Tagals.
Tage (le) [lətaːʒ], *Pr.n.m. Geog:* the (river) Tagus.
tagetes [taʒetɛs], *s.m.,* **tagète, tagette** [taʒɛt], *s.m. Bot:* tagetes; marigold.
tagliatelles [taljatɛl], *s.f.pl. Cu:* tagliatelli.
tagme [tagm], *s.m. Z:* tagma; (*of insects*) **t. céphalique,** cephalic tagma, *F:* head.
Tahiti [taiti], *Pr.n. Geog:* Tahiti; **les îles T.,** the Society Islands.
tahitien, -ienne [taisjɛ̃, -jɛn], *a. & s.* Tahitian.
tahr [taːr], *s.m. Z:* tahr, thar; **t. de l'Himalaya, des Nilgiris, d'Oman,** Himalayan, Nilgiri, Arabian, tahr, thar.
taïaut [tajo], *int. Ven:* tally-ho!
taïcoun [taikun], *s.m.* tycoon (of Japan).
taie [tɛ], *s.f.* **1. t. d'oreiller,** pillowcase, pillow slip; **t. portefeuille,** pillowcase housewife style. **2.** *Med:* albugo, leucoma; white speck on the eye; nubecula.
taïga [taiga], *s.f. Geog:* taïga.
taillable [tajabl̥, ta-], *a. Hist:* talliable; liable to tallage; **t. et corvéable à merci,** talliable and liable to forced labour at pleasure.
taillade [tajad, ta-], *s.f.* (*a*) cut, slash, gash; *A.Cost:* **pourpoint à taillades,** slashed doublet; (*b*) slit (in wall, for drawbridge chains, for shooting through, etc.); loophole.
taillader [tajade, ta-], *v.tr.* (*a*) to slash, gash; **joue tailladée,** gashed cheek; *Cost:* **jupe tailladée,** slashed skirt; (*b*) *F:* **t. un article (de journal),** to make cuts in an article.
tailladin [tajadɛ̃, ta-], *s.m.* (thin) slice of lemon or orange.
taillage [tajaːʒ, ta-], *s.m.* cutting; *esp.* **t. de limes,** file cutting.
taillanderie [tajɑ̃dri, ta-], *s.f.* **1.** edge-tool industry. **2.** *coll.* edge tools.
taillandier [tajɑ̃dje, ta-], *s.m.* maker of edge tools.
taillant [tajɑ̃, ta-], *s.m. A:* (cutting) edge (of sword, knife, tool).
taille [taːj, taːj], *s.f.* **1.** (*a*) cutting (of diamonds, garments, etc.); pruning, trimming (of shrubs); clipping (of hedge); dressing (of vine); (i) hewing, (ii) cutting, dressing (of stone); *Mount:* step cutting; **t. de cheveux,** haircutting; **une t. de cheveux,** a haircut; **t. ornementale des arbres,** topiary work; **bois de t.,** coppice wood; **pierre de t.,** (i) freestone; natural stone; (ii) ashlar; *Mec.E:* **t. d'engrenages,** gear milling, cutting; (*b*) *Surg:* lithotomy, *A:* cutting for stone. **2.** method of cutting, cut; (*a*) *A:* **je n'aime pas la t. de votre pantalon,** I don't like the cut of your trousers; (*b*) *Tls:* **lime à simple t., à t. double,** single-cut, double-cut, file; **grosse t.,** rough cut; **t. douce,** smooth cut; **t. demi-douce, seconde t.,** second cut; *Stonew:* **t. brute, plane,** rough, smooth, dressing; (*c*) *Engr:* **t. de bois, d'épargne,** (blackline method of) wood engraving; *s.a.* TAILLE-DOUCE. **3.** (*a*) edge (of sword, etc.); **coup de t.,** cut, slash; *s.a.* ESTOC 2; (*b*) *For:* **une jeune t.,** a coppice; (*c*) *Com:* tally (stick); (*d*) *Min:* (i) working face (of coal, etc.); (ii) stall; **(front de) t.,** coal face; **t. chassante,** drift stope; *Petroleum Ind:* **t. à mi-pente,** rill cut; **t. hélicoïdale,** helical cut; **t. remblayée,** filled stope; **t. sans remblayage,** open stope; (*e*) *Cost: A:* seam; **galonné sur toutes les tailles,** braided over every seam. **4.** (*a*) stature, height (of pers.); dimensions (of monument, etc.); **t. debout,** full height (of s.o.); **être de grande t., de t. moyenne,** to be very tall, of medium height; **cheval de petite t.,** small(-sized) horse; **avoir la t. courte,** to be short (of stature); **avoir une t. de deux mètres,** to be two metres tall, high; **par rang de t.,** in order of height; *Com:* **quelle est votre t.?** what size do you take? **pour les tailles exceptionnelles, pour les grandes tailles,** (for) outsize(s); *Com:* **je n'ai rien à votre t.,** I've nothing in your size; **il est de t. à se défendre, à vous battre,** he is big enough, strong, enough, to look after himself, to beat you; **il n'est pas de t. à être chef,** he is not cut out to be a leader; **il n'est pas de t. à lutter contre vous,** he is no match for you; he stands no chance against you; *F:* you are (one) too many for him; **le mensonge est de t.,** *F:* it's a thumping lie; (*b*) (*body between shoulders and hips*) figure, waist; **tour de t.,** waist measurement; **t. de guêpe,** wasp waist; **avoir la t. élégante, être bien pris de t., dans sa t.,** to have an elegant, a good figure; **long, court, de t.,** long-waisted, short-waisted; **robe (à) t. basse, (à) t. haute,** low-waisted, high-waisted, dress; **prendre qn par la t.,** (i) to seize, take, s.o. round the waist; (ii) to put an arm round s.o.'s waist; *Dressm:* **t. normale,** natural waistline; **pardessus à t.,** fitted overcoat; **vêtement qui prend bien la t.,** close-fitting garment; **en t.,** with no overcoat on; *A:* **femme en t.,** woman wearing no jacket or wrap. **5.** *Hist:* tall(i)age, tax, toll; **t. réelle,** property tax; **t. personnelle,** tax on income. **6.** *Mus: A:* tenor; *s.a.* BASSE-TAILLE 1, HAUTE-TAILLE.
taillé [taje], *a.* **1. homme bien t.,** well set-up man; **il est t. pour commander,** he is cut out to be a leader; **visage taillé à coups de serpe,** rugged face; *s.a.* COTE 1, COUDRE[2] 1. **2. cristal t.,** cut glass; *Prehist:* **pierre taillée,** chipped stone. **3.** *Her:* **(écu) t.,** party per bend sinister.
taille-buissons [tajbɥisɔ̃], *s.m.inv.* (large) pruning shears, hedge shears.
taille-crayon, taille-crayons [tajkrɛjɔ̃], *s.m.inv.* pencil sharpener.
taille-douce [tajdus], *s.f. Engr:* **(gravure en) taille-douce,** copper-plate engraving; *pl. tailles-douces.*
taille-doucier [tajdusje], *s.m.* copperplate printer; *pl. taille-douciers.*
taille-légumes [tajlegym], *s.m.inv.* vegetable cutter, slicer.
taille-mer [tajmɛːr], *s.m.inv.* **1.** *N.Arch:* (*a*) cut-water (of bow); (*b*) bobstay piece. **2.** *Orn:* lesser black-backed gull.
taille-ongles [tajɔ̃ːgl], *s.m.inv.* nail clipper(s).
taille-pain [tajpɛ̃], *s.m.inv.* (*a*) bread-knife; (*b*) breadcutting machine; bread-slicer.
taille-plume [tajplym], *s.m. A:* pen-knife, -cutter; quill-cutter; *pl. taille-plume(s).*
tailler [taje, taje], *v.tr.* **1.** (*a*) to cut (stone, diamond, grass, hair); to hew (stone); to mill (gear wheels); to prune (tree); to trim, clip (hedge, beard, etc.); to dress (vine); **t. un crayon,** to sharpen a pencil; **t. le pain,** to cut, slice, the bread; **t. une armée en pièces,** to cut up an army; to cut, hew, an army to pieces; **t. un chemin dans le roc,** to hew a road out of the rock; **se t. un chemin à travers . . .,** to carve one's way through . . .; **t. une pierre en forme de lion,** to carve a stone in(to) the shape of a lion; **lion taillé dans le roc,** lion carved in the stone; (*of ship*) **t. la lame,** to cleave the waves, to cut through the waves; **t. de l'avant,** to forge ahead; (*b*) **t. un vêtement,** to cut out a garment; **elle taille dans ses robes pour habiller la petite,** she cuts down her dresses for the child; **complet bien taillé,** well-cut suit; *F:* **on m'a taillé de la besogne,** I have my work cut out for me; **j'ai la besogne toute taillée,** my work is cut and dried; **il peut t. en plein drap,** he has ample material, ample means; he has plenty to go on with; *Prov:* **il faut t. la robe selon le corps,** you must cut your coat according to your cloth; (*c*) *abs. Mount:* to cut steps. **2.** *Surg:* to operate on (s.o.) for stone. **3.** *abs. Cards:* to hold the bank, to deal out the cards (at faro, etc.); *s.a.* BAC[2]. **4.** *Hist:* to tax, *A:* to tail.
se tailler, *P:* to buzz off.
taille-racines [tajrasin], *s.m.inv.* vegetable cutter.
taillerie [tajri], *s.f.* **1.** gem cutting. **2.** lapidary's workshop.
taillerol(l)e [tajrɔl], *s.f. Tex:* trivet (knife).
tailleur, -euse [tajœːr, -øːz], *s.* **1.** (*a*) cutter (of gems, trees, files, etc.); hewer, cutter (of stone); (*b*) tailor, tailoress; **"t. à façon,"** "customer's own material made up"; **s'asseoir en t.,** to sit cross-legged; (*c*) banker (at gaming-table); (*d*) *Y:* **t. de route,** long-distance yachtsman. **2.** *s.m.* **(costume) t.,** (woman's) tailored suit; **robe t.,** tailored dress; **elle sait faire le flou et le t.,** she does both dressmaking and tailoring.
tailleur-pantalon [tajœrpɑ̃talɔ̃], *s.m. Cost:* (woman's) trouser suit; *pl. tailleurs-pantalons.*
tailleuse-couturière [tajøzkutyrjɛːr], *s.f.* tailoress; *pl. tailleuses-couturières.*
taille-vent [tajvɑ̃], *s.m.inv. Nau:* lug mainsail; lug-sail.
taillis [taji], *s.m.* **1.** copse, coppice; *a.* **bois t.,** copsewood, underwood, brushwood; bush; **s'enfoncer dans les t.,** to make for the heart of the woods; to lose oneself in the woods, in the bush; **gagner le t.,** to take refuge in the woods; to take to the bush; *For:* **t. à écorce,** bark coppice; **t. sous futaie,** coppice with standards. **2.** *Mil:* brushwood entanglement.
tailloir [tajwaːr], *s.m.* **1.** trencher. **2.** *Arch:* abacus.
taillole [tajɔl], *s.f. Cost: A:* (*in Provence*) woollen trouser-belt or sash (worn by peasants).
taillon [tajɔ̃], *s.m.* **1.** *Hist:* tax additional to the tall(i)age. **2.** nib (of quill pen).
tain[1] [tɛ̃], *s.m.* **1.** silvering (for mirrors); foil, tain; **glace sans t.,** plate glass; **miroir sans t.,** two-way mirror. **2.** *Ind:* tin bath (for tinning iron).
tain[2], *s.m.* = TIN.
taipan [taipɑ̃], *s.m. Rept:* (Australian) taipan.
taïra [taira], *s.m. Z:* taira, tayra.
taire [tɛːr], *v.tr.* (*pr.p.* **taisant;** *p.p.* **tu;** *pr.ind.* **je tais, il tait, n. taisons, ils taisent;** *pr.sub.* **je taise;** *p.d.* **je taisais;** *p.h.* **je tus;** *fu.* **je tairai**) to say nothing about (sth.), to suppress, keep dark, hush up (sth.); **t. le nom de qn,** to keep s.o.'s name secret, not to mention s.o.'s name; **une dame dont je tairai le nom,** a lady who shall be nameless, who shall go unnamed; **t. qch. à qn,** to keep, hide, conceal, sth. from s.o.; **des secrets tus longtemps,** secrets long unrevealed; *F:* **t. sa langue** = SE TAIRE.
se taire, to hold one's tongue, to hold one's peace, to be silent; to become silent; to keep one's own counsel; **la douleur qui se tait n'en est pas moins sincère,** silent grief is none the less sincere; **toute la nature se tait,** all nature is hushed; **se t. sur, de, qch.,** to pass sth. over in silence; **il sait se t.,** he knows when to keep silent; **tais-toi!** hold your tongue! be quiet! *F:* shut up! dry up! **faire t. (qn),** to silence (s.o.) to reduce (s.o.) to silence; to hush (a child); to keep (a child) quiet; *P:* to shut (s.o.) up; **faire t. sa douleur,** to stifle one's grief; **faire t. le canon de l'ennemi,** to silence the enemy's guns; *Poet:* **faire t. les vents,** to hush, still, the winds; **s'il essaie du chantage, je saurai bien le faire t.,** if he tries blackmail; I'll soon stop his mouth; *Prov:* **mieux vaut se t. que mal parler,** least said soonest mended; **taisez-vous donc!** nonsense! fiddlesticks! don't talk rot!
Taïti [taiti], *Pr.n.* Tahiti.
taïtien, -ienne [taisjɛ̃, -jɛn], *a. & s.* Tahitian.
takin [takɛ̃], *s.m. Z:* takin.
tala [tala], *s.m. & f. Sch: F:* militant Roman Catholic student (*from "ceux qui vont à la messe"*).
talaire [talɛːr]. **1.** *a. Rom. & Gr.Ant:* (toga) reaching to the ankles; talaric (tunic, etc.). **2.** *s.f.pl. Myth:* **talaires,** (Mercury's) heel-wings; talaria.
talapoin [talapwɛ̃], *s.m.* **1.** *A:* talapoin (monk or priest). **2.** *Z:* talapoin (monkey).
talc [talk], *s.m. Miner:* talc; French chalk; soap-stone; *Toil:* **(poudre de) t.,** talcum powder, talc.
talcaire [talkɛːr], **talcique** [talsik], *a.* talcose, talcous.
talcite [talsit], *s.f. Miner:* talcite.
talco-micacé [talkɔmikase], *a. Miner:* talcomicaceous; *pl. talco-micacé(e)s.*
talé [tale], *a.* bruised (fruit, etc.).
talent [talɑ̃], *s.m.* **1.** *Gr.Ant:* talent (weight or coin); *B:* **la parabole des talents,** the parable of the talents; *A:* **enfouir son t.,** to hide one's light under a bushel. **2.** talent, aptitude, faculty, gift; high mental capacity; **avoir du t.,** to be talented; **homme de t.,** talented man; **il n'a aucun t.,** he has no gift (for singing, painting, etc.); **talents de société,** drawing-room accomplishments; gifts as an entertainer; **il avait un t. particulier pour aviser aux difficultés,** he had a singular aptitude for dealing with difficulties; **sans t.,** talentless; **une œuvre de t.,** an able piece of work; **avoir le t. des langues,** to have a gift for languages; **son t. de pianiste,** his talent as a pianist, for the piano; **il a le t. d'amuser l'auditoire,** he is a great hand at keeping the audience amused; **il n'a pas le t. de vous plaire,** he hasn't the gift of pleasing you; *Pol: etc:* **faire appel à tous les talents,** to call in the best brains (irrespective of party); to form an administration of all the talents.
talentueux, -euse [talɑ̃tɥø, -øːz], *a.* talented.
taler [tale], *v.tr.* **1.** to bruise (fruit, etc.). **2.** *Dial:* to annoy.
taleth [talɛt], *s.m. Jew.Rel:* tallith.
talève [talɛːv], *s.f. Orn:* **t. d'Allen,** Allen's gallinule; **t. bleue,** green-backed gallinule.
tali [tali], *s.m. Bot:* sasswood, sassywood.
talion [taljɔ̃], *s.m.* talion, retaliation; *used esp. in:* **la loi du t.,** the lex talionis; the law of retaliation; **appliquer à qn la loi du t.,** to retaliate on s.o.; to give s.o. tit for tat.
talipot [talipo], *s.m. Bot:* talipot.
talisman [talismɑ̃], *s.m.* talisman.

talismanique [talismanik], *a.* talismanic.

talitre [talitr̥], *s.m. Crust:* sand flea, sand hopper, shore skipper.

talkie-walkie [tokiwɑlki, tɑlkiwɑlki], *s.m. F:* walkie-talkie; *pl. talkie-walkies.*

tallage [talaːʒ], *s.m. Agr: Hort:* **1.** (*a*) throwing-out of suckers; (*b*) tillering. **2.** tillers; new shoots; stools.

talle [tal], *s.f. Agr: Hort:* (*a*) sucker; (*b*) tiller.

taller [tale], *v.i. Agr: Hort:* (*a*) to throw out suckers; to sucker; (*b*) to tiller; to stool; **les blés ont bien tallé,** the wheat has tillered well.

tallipot [talipo], *s.m. Bot:* talipot.

tallöl [talœl], *s.m.* tall oil.

talmouse [talmuːz], *s.f. A:* **1.** *Cu:* marzipan turnover. **2.** *F:* smack; punch on the nose.

talmouser [talmuze], *v.tr. F: A:* to knock (s.o.) about.

Talmud [talmyd], *Pr.n.m.* **le T.,** the Talmud.

talmudique [talmydik], *a.* Talmudic(al).

talmudiste [talmydist], *s.m.* Talmudist.

talochage [talɔʃaːʒ], *s.m.* **1.** plastering (of a wall, using a hawk). **2.** *F:* cuffing, clouting (on the head).

taloche [talɔʃ], *s.f.* **1.** (plasterer's) hawk. **2.** *F:* cuff; clout on the head; **flanquer une t. à qn,** to cuff, clout, s.o.; to box s.o.'s ears.

talocher [talɔʃe], *v.tr.* **1.** to plaster (wall, using a hawk). **2.** *F:* to cuff; to clout (s.o.) on the head; to box (s.o.'s) ears.

talon [talɔ̃], *s.m.* **1.** heel (of foot or shoe); **t. Louis XV,** Louis heel; **t. aiguille,** stiletto heel; *Geog: F:* **le t. de la botte,** the heel of Italy; **marcher sur les talons de qn,** to follow close behind s.o., close on s.o.'s heels; **être toujours sur les talons de qn,** to dog s.o.'s footsteps; to trail at s.o.'s heels; **donner du t. à son cheval,** to give one's horse the spur; to clap spurs to one's horse; **cheval qui connaît les talons,** spur-wise horse; **montrer les talons, jouer des talons,** to show a clean pair of heels; to take to one's heels; to cut and run; **tourner les talons,** to turn on one's heel and go; *A:* **quand verrons-nous ses talons?** when shall we be rid of him? when shall we see the last of him? **traîner ses talons par les rues,** to trail around the streets; *O:* **tirer sa voix de ses talons,** to fetch one's voice from one's boots; *s.a.* ESTOMAC 1; **t. de bas,** stocking heel; **bas troués aux talons,** stockings out at heel; **remettre des talons à . . .,** to re-heel . . .; *Hist:* **t. rouge,** (i) red heel; (ii) aristocrat, courtier; **t. d'Achille,** Achilles' heel, heel of Achilles. **2.** *Tchn:* (*a*) heel (of tool, lance, mast, golf club, rifle butt); heel, nut (of violin, bow); butt (of billiard cue); shoulder (of sword blade, bayonet, pulley block, axle); flange, collar (on axle); *Sm.a:* tang (of breech); (*welding*) **t. de soudure,** toe; (*b*) catch, clip, hook, stud; beading, bead (of pneumatic tyre); *A:* **pneu à talons,** beaded tyre; **t. à crochet,** clincherbead; (*c*) *N.Arch:* **t. du gouvernail,** sole of the rudder; **t. de quille,** heel, skeg, of a keel; *Nau:* **donner un coup de t.,** to touch (the bottom); to bump; *Artil:* **t. de flasque,** trail plate; *Sm.a:* **t. de la crosse,** heel of the (rifle) butt; *s.a.* COULÉE 2. **3.** (*a*) (*at cards, dominoes, etc.*) stock (not yet dealt out); reserve; talon; (*b*) fag-end, remnant (of bread, cheese); heel (of loaf); *Cu:* **t. de collier,** clod (of beef); (*c*) **t. de souche,** counterfoil, stub (of cheque, etc.); talon (of sheet of coupons). **4.** (*a*) *Arch:* ogee moulding; talon; (*b*) *Tls:* ogee-moulding plane.

talonique [talɔnik], *a. Ch:* talonic.

talonnage [talɔnaːʒ], *s.m.* (*a*) re-heeling (of footwear); (*b*) *Rugby Fb:* heeling (out).

talonnement [talɔnmɑ̃], *s.m.* **1.** following on the heels (of s.o.); pressing closely (after, upon, s.o.); dogging (of s.o.); dunning (of debtor). **2.** spurring on (of horse, etc.). **3.** *Nau:* striking, bumping, grounding (of ship).

talonner [talɔne]. **1.** *v.tr.* (*a*) to follow (s.o.) closely; to follow on the heels of (s.o.); to dog (s.o.'s) footsteps; *F:* to breathe down s.o.'s neck; **t. l'ennemi,** to pursue the enemy vigorously; to press the enemy (closely); (*b*) to dig one's heels into (one's horse); to spur on, urge (horse); *F:* **t. un élève,** to spur on a pupil; **être talonné par le désir de qch.,** to hanker after sth., for sth.; (*c*) *Rugby Fb:* to heel (out). **2.** *v.i. Nau:* (*of ship, boat*) to touch, to bump; to strike.

talonnette [talɔnɛt], *s.f.* **1.** heel-piece (of stocking, shoe); **t. en caoutchouc,** rubber heel. **2.** (rubber or cork) elevator (inside shoe). **3.** binding (to reinforce inside of trouser bottoms).

talonneur [talɔnœːr], *s.m. Rugby Fb:* hooker.

talonnier [talɔnje], *s.m.* heel maker.

talonnière [talɔnjɛːr], *s.f.* **1.** *Nau:* heel, sole (of rudder). **2.** *pl. Myth:* **talonnières,** (Mercury's) heel-wings; talaria.

talose [taloːz], *s.m. Ch:* talose.

talpa [talpa], *s.f. Med:* talpa, testudo, wen.

talpack [talpak], *s.m. Mil:* busby.

talpidés [talpide], *s.m.pl. Z:* Talpidae.

talpiforme [talpifɔrm], *a.* mole-shaped, talpoid.

talquer [talke], *v.tr.* to sprinkle with soap-stone, to chalk.

talqueux, -euse [talkø, -øːz], *a. Miner:* talcose, talcous.

talure [talyːr], *s.f.* bruise (on fruit); graze (on branch).

talus[1] [taly], *s.m.* **1.** slope, *Civ.E:* batter; **t. de remblai,** embankment slope; **aller en t.,** to slope, shelve, batter; **en t.,** sloping; battered. **2.** (*a*) embankment, slope, ramp; **t. gazonné,** turfed slope, bank; (*b*) *Geol:* talus; scree (slope); **t. continental,** continental slope. **3.** *Typ:* beard (of letter).

talus[2] [talys], *a.m. Med:* **pied bot t.,** talipes calcaneus; talus.

talutage [talytaːʒ], *s.m.* **1.** sloping (of embankment, etc.); embanking (of track); battering (of wall). **2.** = TALUS[1] 1.

taluter [talyte], *v.tr.* to slope (ditch, etc.); to embank (track); to batter (wall).

taluteuse [talytøːz], *s.f. Civ.E:* sloper.

talweg [talvɛg], *s.m. Geog: Geol:* thalweg.

tam [tam], *s.m. P:* row; shindy; **quel t.!** what a din! **faire du t. (au sujet de qch.),** to make a great fuss, a song and dance (about sth.).

tamandua [tamɑ̃dɥa], *s.m. Z:* tamandua, collared anteater.

tamanoir [tamanwaːr], *s.m. Z:* great anteater, ant bear.

tamaricacées [tamarikase], *s.f.pl. Bot:* Tamaricaceae.

tamarin[1] [tamarɛ̃], *s.m. Bot:* **1.** tamarind. **2.** tamarind tree.

tamarin[2], *s.m. Z:* silky marmoset; tamarin; pinche.

tamarinier [tamarinje], *s.m. Bot:* tamarind tree.

tamaris [tamaris], *s.m. Bot:* tamarisk, tamarix; *esp.* tamarisk salt tree.

tambouille [tɑ̃buːj], *s.f. Mil: P:* **1.** kitchen. **2.** kitchen staff. **3.** cookery, cooking; **faire la t.,** to do the cooking; *Pej:* **quelle t.!** what muck!

tambour [tɑ̃buːr], *s.m.* **1.** drum; **battre du t.,** to play the drum; to drum; (*of town crier, etc.*) **battre le t.,** to beat the drum; to drum; **annoncer un fait au son du t.,** to announce a fact by beat of drum; *A:* by tuck of drum; **bruit de t.,** drumming; **chasser un soldat au son du t.,** to drum a soldier out; **peau de t.,** drum-head; **t. de basque,** tambourine (with jingles); **coup de t.,** beat, roll, on the drum; **sans t. ni trompette,** quietly, without fuss; **corde qui sonne le t.,** jarring note, wolf (on 'cello, etc.); *s.a.* BATTANT I. 2, CORDE 1, DÉNICHER 2, FLÛTE[1] 1. **2.** drummer; **t. de ville,** town crier. **3.** *Tchn:* (*a*) (*cylindrical container*) barrel, cylinder, drum; *Ind: Min:* **t. à assortir, t. de triage,** sizing drum, cylinder; sorting drum, cylinder; **t. culbuteur, t. dessableur,** tumbling barrel, drum; tumbler, rumbler, scouring barrel; **t. laveur, laveur à t.,** drum washer; **t. débourbeur,** clearing cylinder; (*b*) (*disc-shaped box*) (vacuum)box (of aneroid barometer); *Arms:* **chargeur à t., t. chargeur,** drum magazine; (*c*) (*box-like passage*) vestibule (of church, etc.); revolving door (of vestibule); *N.Arch:* casing, trunk(way); **t. d'écoutille,** trunk hatch; **t. du puits des machines,** engine casing; (*d*) (*case*) *Mec.E:* drum (of compressor, turbine, etc.); **t. de frein,** brake drum; **bicyclette avec frein à t.,** bicycle with drum brake; *N.Arch:* **t. d'une roue à aubes,** paddle box; (*e*) (*cylinder*) (i) *Arch:* drum, tambour (of column, of newel); (ii) drum (of measuring or recording instrument); **t. de lecture,** reading drum; **lecture du t.,** drum reading; **t. micrométrique,** micrometer drum; **enregistreur à t.,** drum recorder; (*computers*) **t. magnétique,** magnetic drum, drum memory; **t. (de) programme,** program(me) drum; *Artil:* **t. de hausse,** elevation drum; **t. de portée,** range drum; (*f*) (*reel*) *Civ.E: El.E: Nau:* drum (of capstan, windlass, etc.); *El.E:* cylinder (of coil); **t. de câble,** cable drum; **t. d'enroulement,** winding drum; **enroulement, enroulé, en t.,** drum winding, drum-wound; **t. dérouleur,** *Civ.E: El.E:* paying-out drum, *Cin:* feed-sprocket; *El.E:* **induit à t.,** drum armature; (*g*) (*cylindrical wheel*) *Mec.E:* **commande par t.,** drum drive; **came à t.,** drum cam; *Ind:* **machine à t. ponceur,** drum sander; *Petroleum Min: etc:* **t. de forage,** bull wheel; **t. de levage,** calf wheel; (*h*) tambour; (embroidery) frame; **broder au t.,** to tambour, to do tambour work; (*i*) *Anat: A:* ear drum, tympanum. **4.** tambourine (pigeon).

tambourin [tɑ̃burɛ̃], *s.m.* **1.** long, narrow drum (of Provence); tambourin; *A:* tabor; *B:* timbrel. **2.** *Tex:* warp-folding drum. **3.** *Games:* circular parchment racquet, held by the rim. **4.** *Cost:* pill-box (hat).

tambourinage [tɑ̃burinaːʒ], *s.m.* **1.** (*a*) drumming; (*b*) knocking, hammering, drumming (of machine part). **2.** *F: A:* boosting, advertising (of s.o.).

tambourinaire [tɑ̃burinɛːr], *s.m.* (*in S. of Fr.*) (*a*) tambourin player; pipe and tabor player; (*b*) town crier.

tambourinement [tɑ̃burinmɑ̃], *s.m.* drumming.

tambouriner [tɑ̃burine]. **1.** *v.i.* to drum; (*a*) to beat a drum or a tambourin; (*b*) *F:* to drum, thrum (with the fingers); to beat the devil's tattoo (on table, window, etc.); **la pluie tambourine sur le toit,** the rain drums on the roof; (*c*) (*of machine, part*) to knock, hammer; (*of old car*) to drum. **2.** *v.tr.* (*a*) to drum on (sth.); (*b*) **t. une nouvelle, un objet perdu,** to announce a piece of news, the loss of an object; to make sth. known by the town crier, by beat of drum; (*c*) *F: A:* **t. qn,** to cry s.o. up, to boost s.o.

tambourineur [tɑ̃burinœːr], *s.m.* **1.** drummer; town crier. **2.** = TAMBOURINAIRE.

tambour-major [tɑ̃burmaʒɔːr], *s.m. Mil:* drum major; *pl. tambours-majors.*

Tamerlan [tamɛrlɑ̃], *Pr.n.m. Hist:* Tamerlane, Timour.

tamia [tamja], *s.m. Z:* chipmunk, ground squirrel.

tamier [tamje], *s.m. Bot:* black bryony.

tamil [tamil], *s.m. Ethn: Ling:* Tamil.

taminier [taminje], *s.m. Bot:* black bryony.

tamis [tami], *s.m.* (*a*) sieve, sifter; (*for liquids*) strainer, tammy; (*for flour*) bolter; *Ind:* riddle, screen; **t. de crin,** hair sieve; **t. à gaze métallique,** wire-gauze sieve; **t. à cendres, t.-crible à escarbilles,** cinder sifter; **t. oscillant, t. vibrant,** vibrating sieve; **toile à t.,** bolting cloth; **passer qch. au t.,** (i) to sift, to strain sth.; to tammy sth.; (ii) to sift, to examine, (evidence, etc.) thoroughly; *Min:* **t. de bocard,** grate of a stamp; **t. métallique pour entonnoir,** gauze strainer for funnel; *Aut: A:* **t. anti-poussière,** dust cap, air filter; (*b*) sound(ing)-board (of organ); (*c*) **t. d'une raquette,** strings of a racquet.

tamisage [tamizaːʒ], *s.m.* **1.** sifting (of sand, etc.); screening (of coal, etc.); bolting (of flour, meal); filtering, straining (of liquid); filtering (of air); subduing (of light). **2.** *Rail:* (*of carriages*) swaying, whipping.

tamisaille [tamizɑːj], *s.f. Nau:* sweep (of tiller).

Tamise[1] **(la)** [latamiːz], *Pr.n.f. Geog:* the (river) Thames.

tamise[2] [tamiːz], *s.f. Tex:* tammy (cloth).

tamiser [tamize]. **1.** *v.tr.* to pass (sth.) through a sieve; to sift, screen (gravel, etc.); to bolt (flour); to strain, to tammy, to filter (liquids); to filter (air); **rideaux qui tamisent la lumière,** curtains that let through a softened light, that soften, subdue, the light; *abs. Nau:* **voile qui tamise,** sail that lets the wind through. **2.** *v.i.* (*a*) (*of dust, light, etc.*) to filter through; (*b*) *Rail:* (*of carriages*) to sway, to whip.

tamiserie [tamizri], *s.f.* sieve factory.

tamiseur, -euse [tamizœːr, -øːz]. **1.** *s.* (*pers.*) sifter, screener; strainer, filterer (of liquids). **2.** *s.m.* cinder sifter.

tamisier [tamizje], *s.m.* (*a*) maker of sieves; (*b*) dealer in sieves.

tamoul [tamul], *a. & s.m. Ethn: Ling:* Tamil.

tampe [tɑ̃ːp], *s.f. Tex:* wedge (on friezing table).

tamper [tɑ̃pe], *v.tr. Tex:* to fix the wedge on (friezing table).

tampico [tɑ̃piko], *s.m.* tampico fibre, istle (fibre).

tampon [tɑ̃pɔ̃], *s.m.* **1.** (*a*) plug, stopper; waste plug (of bath, etc.); **t. de liège,** bung (of cask); *Metall:* clay plug, taphole plug; *Nau:* **t. d'écubier,** hawse-plug, buckler; (*b*) *Const:* wall plug; (*c*) **t. d'égout,** manhole cover; (*d*) **t. bague,** "GO-NO GO" ring gauge; *Av:* **t. "n'entre pas,"** "NO GO" plug gauge. **2.** *Mil:* (*a*) *A.Artil:* **t. de bouche,** (muzzle) tompion, tampion; **t. de lumière,** vent plug; (*b*) *A:* flat cap (worn by orderly); (*c*) *A:* orderly, batman. **3.** (*a*) *Surg: etc:* wad, pad, plug, tampon, tent (of cotton wool, etc.); (*b*) pad (of flute key, etc.); (*c*) *Engr: Typ: etc:* (inking pad; tampon; **t. à timbrer,** stamp pad; **t. perpétuel, inépuisable,** self-inking pad; (*d*) rubber stamp; *Post:* postmark; **apposer le t. "acquitté" sur une facture,** to stamp "paid" on a bill; to receipt a bill; (*e*) **t. buvard,**

hand blotter; (*f*) (French-polisher's) pad. **4. t. de choc,** buffer; **t. à ressort,** spring buffer; **t. hydraulique,** hydraulic buffer; **t. à air, t. atmosphérique, t. pneumatique,** air buffer, pneumatic buffer; **t. à air d'un marteau-pilon,** air cushion of a steam hammer; *Rail:* **t. d'attelage,** coupling buffer; **t. d'arrêt,** buffer stop; **coup de t.,** collision; *Aer:* **t. de nacelle,** bumper; *El.E:* **accumulateur en t.,** accumulator forming a buffer; **batterie t.,** balancing battery; *Mec.E:* **t. amortisseur,** bumper (of pedal, etc.); insulator (of engine, etc.); **t. obturateur,** sealing pad; **t. vérificateur,** cylindrical gauge, plug-gauge; (*computers*) **mémoire t.,** buffer; **assignation unique de tampons,** simple buffering; **calculateur à mémoire(s) tampon(s),** buffered computer; *Dipl:* **état t.,** buffer state; *F:* **servir de t. (entre deux personnes),** to act as a buffer (between two people). **5.** *Mus:* bass drumstick, *F:* **coup de t.,** thump, punch.

tamponnage [tɑ̃pɔnaːʒ], *s.m.*, **tamponnement** [tɑ̃pɔnmɑ̃], *s.m.* **1.** plugging (of wound, etc.); stopping up. **2.** dabbing (with pad). **3.** *Rail:* (*a*) (end-on) collision; (*b*) collision with a buffer. **4.** *Ch:* **tamponnage,** neutralizing, making into a neutral solution. **5.** *P:* beating (s.o.) up, knocking (s.o.) about.

tamponner [tɑ̃pɔne], *v.tr.* **1.** (*a*) to plug; to stop up; **t. une plaie,** (i) to put a wad over a wound; (ii) to plug, tent, tampon, a wound; (*b*) *Const:* to plug (wall); (*c*) to pad; **plateaux tamponnés,** padded keys (of flute, etc.). **2.** (*a*) to dab (with pad); to ink up (type, metal plate); to rubber-stamp; **se t. les yeux,** to dab one's eyes; *P:* **s'en t. le coquillard,** not to give a damn; **se t. le front,** to mop one's brow; (*b*) to French-polish (furniture); (*c*) *Metall:* **t. un moule,** to dust a mould; (*d*) *Ch:* to neutralize. **3.** *Aut: Rail:* (*of car, train*) to run into, come into collision with, collide with, to bump into (another car or train); *P.N: Rail:* **défense de t.,** shunt with care. **4.** *P:* to beat (s.o.) up; to knock (s.o.) about.

tamponneur, -euse [tɑ̃pɔnœːr, -øːz]. **1.** *a.* **train t.,** train that ran into another; **autos tamponneuses,** dodgems. **2.** *s.m.* man who plugs the holes (*e.g.* made by shots). **3.** *s.m.* official (who stamps documents, etc.). **4.** *s.m. El:* reactor (in a circuit).

tamponnoir [tɑ̃pɔnwaːr], *s.m. Tls:* wall drill, wall bit, plugging tool.

tam-tam [tamtam], *s.m.* **1.** (*a*) tom-tom; **t.-t. de guerre,** war drum, tom-tom; (*b*) *F:* vulgar, loud, publicity; *F:* **faire du t.-t. autour de qch., à propos de qch.,** to make a great song and dance about sth. **2.** (Chinese) gong; *pl. tam-tams.*

tan [tɑ̃]. **1.** *s.m.* tan, (tanner's) bark; **briquette de t., motte de t.,** tan turf, tan ball; **fosse à t.,** tan vat, tan pit; **moulin à t.,** bank mill. **2.** *a.inv.* tan(-coloured).

tanacetum [tanasetɔm], *s.m. Bot:* tanacetum.

tanagra [tanagra], *s.m. or f.* (*a*) *Archeol: Cer:* Tanagra (figurine); (*b*) beautiful, graceful, girl; *F:* **c'est un vrai t.,** she's got a perfect figure.

tanagréenne [tanagreen], *s.f. Archeol:* (Tanagra) figurine.

tanagridés [tanagride], *s.m.pl. Orn:* Tanagridae; Thraupidae, the tanagers.

tanaisie [tanezi], *s.f. Bot:* tansy.

Tananarive [tananariːv], *Pr.n. Geog:* (An)tananarivo.

tancer [tɑ̃se], *v.tr.* (**je tançai(s); n. tançons**) to rate, scold; **t. qn vertement,** to give s.o. a good talking-to; to haul s.o. over the coals; to blow s.o. up; to give s.o. a good blowing-up.

tanche [tɑ̃ːʃ], *s.f. Ich:* tench.

Tancrède [tɑ̃krɛd], *Pr.n.m. Hist:* Tancred.

tandem [tɑ̃dɛm], *s.m.* (*a*) *Veh:* tandem; **conduire en t.,** to drive tandem; **chevaux attelés en t.,** horses driven tandem; (*b*) *Cy:* tandem (bicycle); (*c*) *esp. Sp:* twosome; *F:* pair (of criminals); (*d*) *Mch:* **cylindres en t.,** tandem cylinders; **fonctionnement en t.,** tandem working; (*e*) (*computers*) **central t.,** tandem exchange, tandem central office.

tandémiste [tɑ̃demist], *s.m. & f.* tandem rider.

tandis [tɑ̃di(s)]. **1.** *adv. A:* meanwhile. **2.** *conj.phr.* **t. que** [tɑ̃di(s)kə] + *ind.* (*a*) *A:* so long as; (*b*) whereas, while; **lui s'amuse, t. que nous, nous travaillons,** he plays, whereas, while, we have to work; (*c*) (= **pendant que**) while, whilst; **il s'amuse t. que nous travaillons,** he plays while we work; **travaillons t. que nous sommes jeunes,** let us work while we are young.

tangage [tɑ̃gaːʒ], *s.m.* pitching (of ship, of aircraft); **angle de t.,** angle of pitch.

tangara [tɑ̃gara], *s.m. Orn:* tanager; **t. rouge, t. cardinal,** red-bird, scarlet tanager.

tangelo [tɑ̃ʒlo], *s.m. Hort:* tangelo, ugli.

tangence [tɑ̃ʒɑ̃ːs], *s.f. Geom:* tangency; **point de t.,** point of contact; tangential point (of a curve).

tangent, -ente [tɑ̃ʒɑ̃, -ɑ̃ːt]. **1.** *a. Geom:* tangential, tangent (à, to); *P:* **c'est t.,** (i) it's as near as dammit; (ii) it's touch and go. **2.** *s. F: Sch:* borderline failure. **3.** *s.f.* **tangente:** (*a*) *Geom:* tangent; *F:* **s'échapper par la tangente, prendre la tangente,** (i) to fly off at a tangent; to dodge the question; (ii) to slip away; (*b*) *Sch: F:* (college) porter; (*c*) *F:* sword (of student at the *École polytechnique*).

tangentiel, -ielle [tɑ̃ʒɑ̃sjɛl], *a. Geom:* tangential; *Mec.E:* **vis tangentielle,** tangent screw.

tangentiellement [tɑ̃ʒɑ̃sjɛlmɑ̃], *adv.* tangentially.

Tanger [tɑ̃ʒe], *Pr.n. Geog:* Tangier(s).

tangerine [tɑ̃ʒrin], *s.f. Hort:* tangerine.

tanghin, tanghen [tɑ̃gɛ̃], **tanghinia** [tɑ̃ginja], *s.m.* tanghin (tree, poison); tanguin; ordeal tree; ordeal bark.

tangibilité [tɑ̃ʒibilite], *s.f.* tangibility, tangibleness.

tangible [tɑ̃ʒibl], *a.* tangible.

tangiblement [tɑ̃ʒibləmɑ̃], *adv.* tangibly.

tangitan, -ane [tɑ̃ʒitɑ̃, -an], *a. & s. Geog:* Tangerine.

tango [tɑ̃go]. **1.** *s.m. Danc:* tango. **2.** *a.inv.* yellow-orange (colour); tango.

tangon [tɑ̃gɔ̃], *s.m.* **1.** *Navy:* (swinging) boom (projecting from ship's side); *occ.* outrigger; **s'amarrer au t.,** to secure to the boom; **larguer le t.,** to cast off from the boom. **2. t. de spinnaker,** spinnaker boom.

tangoter [tɑ̃gɔte], *v.i. Danc: F:* to tango.

tanguant [tɑ̃gɑ̃], *a.* pitching (ship).

tangue [tɑ̃ːg], *s.f.* (slimy) sea-sand (*esp.* of the Mont Saint-Michel bay, used as fertilizer).

tanguer[1] [tɑ̃ge], *v.i.* **1.** *Av: Nau:* (*of aircraft, ship*) to pitch; **t. dur,** to pitch heavily. **2.** to be down by the head; **t. en arrière,** to squat.

tanguer[2], *v.i.* to dance the tango; to tango.

tangueur [tɑ̃gœːr], *s.m. Nau:* ship that pitches heavily, *F:* piledriver, bruise-water.

tanière [tanjɛːr], *s.f.* (*a*) den, lair (of lion, etc.); hole, earth (of fox); **le renard a regagné sa t.,** the fox has gone to ground; (*b*) hovel; (*c*) retreat.

tanification [tanifikasjɔ̃], *s.f.* conversion into tannin.

tanin [tanɛ̃], *s.m. Ch: Ind:* tannin.

tanisage [tanizaːʒ], *s.m. Vit:* treatment of wine with tannin.

taniser [tanize], *v.tr.* to treat (sth.) with tannin.

tank [tɑ̃ːk], *s.m.* **1.** *Mil:* tank. **2.** *Nau:* tank (of an oil-tanker).

tanker [tɑ̃kɛːr], *s.m. Nau:* tanker.

tankiste [tɑ̃kist], *s.m. Mil:* member of a tank crew.

tannage [tanaːʒ], *s.m.* **1.** tanning, tannage; **t. à l'alun,** tawing; **t. des peaux,** dressing of skins. **2.** *Phot:* hardening (of plate).

tannant [tanɑ̃], *a.* **1.** tanning; **jus t.,** tan liquor, tan ooze, tan pickle. **2.** *P:* boring, tiresome; annoying; **il est t.!** he's a nuisance! he bores me stiff!

tannate [tanat], *s.m. Ch:* tannate.

tanne [tan], *s.f.* **1.** spot (on leather). **2.** blackhead (on face).

tanné [tane]. **1.** *a.* tanned. **2.** *s.m.* (*a*) tan (colour); (*b*) **gants en t.,** tan(ned) leather gloves.

tannée [tane], *s.f.* **1.** spent tan bark, spent tan; *Hort:* **couche de t.,** bark bed. **2.** *P:* thrashing, hiding, tanning.

tanner [tane], *v.tr.* **1.** to tan. **2.** *P:* (*a*) to tire, bore, irritate, pester (s.o.); **t. les oreilles à qn au sujet de qch.,** to din sth. into s.o.'s ears; (*b*) **t. (le cuir à) qn,** to thrash, s.o.; to tan s.o.'s hide.

tannerie [tanri], *s.f.* **1.** tannery, tanyard. **2.** tanning trade.

tanneur [tanœːr], *s.m.* tanner.

tannin [tanɛ̃], *s.m.*, **tannisage** [tanizaːʒ], *s.m.*, **tanniser** [tanize], *v.tr. See* TANIN, TANISAGE, TANISER.

tannique [tanik], *a. Ch:* tannic (acid).

tanrec [tɑ̃rɛk], *s.m. Z:* tanrec, tenrec, tendrac.

tan-sad [tɑ̃sad], *s.m.* pillion(-seat) (of a motor-cycle); *pl. tan-sads.*

tant [tɑ̃], *adv.* **1.** (*a*) so much; **ceux qui m'ont t. fait souffrir,** those who made me suffer so much; **t. de bonté,** so much, such, kindness; **il a t. bu que . . .,** he has drunk so much that . . .; **il fit t. qu'enfin la porte céda,** he worked to such good purpose that at last the door yielded; **ce n'est pas la peine de t. vous presser,** you needn't be in such a hurry; *B:* **Dieu a t. aimé le monde que . . .,** God so loved the world that . . .; **si vous faites t. que de . . .,** if you decide to . . .; **si vous vouliez nous faire t. d'honneur que de dîner avec nous . . .,** if you would do us so much honour as to dine with us . . .; **pour t. faire, à t. faire,** *F:* **t. qu'à faire, j'aimerais autant . . .,** while I am at it, about it, if it comes to that, I would just as soon . . .; **pour t. faire qu'acheter une maison, autant en acheter une belle,** if it comes to buying a house, one may as well buy a nice one; **t. pour cent,** so much per cent; *s.* **le t. pour cent sur . . .,** the percentage on . . .; **être t. à t.,** to be even (at play); **en l'an de grâce onze cent et t.,** in the year of grace eleven hundred and something; **d'ici à Paris il y a cent et t. de kilomètres,** from here to Paris is a hundred kilometres and a bit; **votre lettre du t.,** your letter of such and such a date; **il a t. et plus d'argent,** he has any amount of money, he has money and to spare; **ils tiraient t. et plus,** they were pulling for all they were worth; **je me suis ennuyé t. et plus,** I was bored to tears, to death; **faire t. et si bien que . . .,** to work to such good purpose that . . .; **j'ai crié t. et t. qu'il est parti,** I shouted so much that he went; **t. s'en faut,** far from it; **t. s'en faut que je ne fasse pas cas de son ouvrage,** I am very far from failing to appreciate his work; **t. soit peu,** a little; somewhat; **s'il est t. soit peu galant homme, il fera des excuses,** if he is anything of a gentleman, he will apologize; **un t. soit peu vulgaire,** just a little bit vulgar; somewhat vulgar; **dès qu'on est un t. soit peu connu,** as soon as one gets to be known a little; **il y a une école dans tout village t. soit peu considérable,** there is a school in every village of any importance; **ils sont t. soit peu cousins,** they are more or less cousins; **son salon était t. soit peu un sanctuaire,** her drawing room was something of a sanctuary; **un t. soit peu trop long,** a shade, a fraction, too long; **il est t. soit peu avare,** he's a bit of a miser; *A:* **t. (il) y a que** + *ind.*, but the fact remains that . . .; **si t. est que** + *sub.*, if indeed . . .; **si t. est qu'il vienne,** if indeed he does come (at all); **si t. est qu'il soit mort,** if he really is dead; **il y en a peu, si t. est qu'il y en ait du tout,** there is little, there are few, if any; *F:* **vous m'en direz t.!** (i) now I see! now I understand! (ii) you don't say (so)! (iii) who could stand out against such a temptation as that! *s.a.* SI[1] 1; (*b*) so many; as many; **t. de fois,** so many times, so often; **t. d'amis,** so many friends; **il a t. et plus d'amis,** he has plenty of friends; **on a t. commis d'erreurs,** so many mistakes have been made; **tous t. que vous êtes,** every one of you; the whole lot of you; (*c*) (= **autant que**) **je ne mange pas t. que vous,** I don't eat as much, so much, as you; **je n'ai pas tant d'amis que vous,** I haven't got as many, so many, friends as you; **vous pourrez jouer du piano t. que vous voudrez,** you may play the piano as much as you like; (*d*) so, to such a degree; **il ne peut pas se lever, t. il est malade,** he cannot get up, he is so ill; **t. était grande sa discrétion que . . .,** so great was his discretion that . . .; **il vous assommerait d'un coup de poing, t. il est fort,** he would fell you with one blow, such is his strength; **t. il est vrai que . . .,** so true is it that . . .; **elle est t. aimée,** she is so greatly, much, loved; **un homme t. célèbre,** such a famous man; **elle n'est pas t. sotte!** she is not so stupid! **n'aimer rien t. que . . .,** to like nothing so much as . . .; **en t. que,** in so far as; **je suis Russe en t. que je suis né en Russie,** I am a Russian in so far as I was born in Russia; **l'homme en t. qu' homme, en t. que tel,** man, qua man; **l'homme, en t. qu'animal,** man, considered as an animal; **l'homme en t. qu'il diffère des animaux,** man, as distinct from animals; **en t. que vieil ami de votre père . . .,** as a very old friend of your father('s) . . .; (*e*) (*concessive* = QUELQUE) **t. aimable qu'il soit,** however pleasant he may be; (*f*) *adv. phr.* **t. mieux,** so much the better; that's all to the good! I'm very glad! good! that's a good job! **t. pis!** so much the worse; that's that! it can't be helped! what a pity! hard lines! never mind! **t. pis t. mieux!** well, well, it might be worse! *F:* **un Docteur T. pis,** a pessimist; **un Docteur T. mieux,** an optimist; *s.a.* PLUS 1. **2.** (*a*) as much, as well (as); **j'ai couru t. que j'ai pu,** I ran as hard as I could; *F:* **il pleut t. qu'il peut,** it's raining like anything; **t. aux Indes qu'ailleurs,** both in India and elsewhere; **t. pour vous que pour moi,** as much for your sake as mine; **t. avec la maison qu'avec le bureau . . .,** what with the house and what with the office . . .; **t. bien que mal,** somehow or other, after a fashion; (*b*) as long, as far (as); **t. que je vivrai,** as long as I live, while I live; **t. que la vue s'étend,** as far as the eye can see; **t. que vous y êtes,** while you're at it; (*c*) so long (as); **il n'y a rien à faire t. qu'il ne sera pas là,** there is nothing to be done so long as he isn't there; **t. que la pluie ne s'arrêtera pas de tomber, nous ne pourrons pas sortir,** so long as it goes on raining, until it stops raining, we shan't be able to go out; (*d*) *A:* (= **jusqu'à ce que**) **versez toujours, t. qu'on vous dise assez,** go on pouring until we say enough. **3.** *P:* **t. qu'à** = **quant à.**

tantalate [tɑ̃talat], *s.m. Ch:* tantalate, tantalic acid salt.

Tantale[1] [tɑ̃tal]. **1.** *Pr.n.m. Myth:* Tantalus; *Ph:* **vase de T.,** Tantalus cup. **2.** *s.m. Orn:* tantalus, wood stork.

tantale[2], *s.m. Ch:* tantalum; *El:* **lampe au t., à filament de t.,** tantalum lamp.

tantalique [tɑ̃talik], *a. Ch:* tantalic.

tantaliser [tɑ̃talize], *v.tr. A:* to tantalize, tease, torment (s.o.).

tantalite [tɑ̃talit], *s.f. Miner:* tantalite.

tante [tɑ̃:t], *s.f.* **1.** aunt; **t. à la mode de Bretagne,** (i) first cousin once removed; (ii) very distant relative; **t. par alliance,** aunt by marriage; *P:* **chez ma t.,** at my uncle's; at the pawnbroker's; up the spout; *P:* **quelle t.!** what a nuisance he is! **2.** *P:* sodomite, queer.

tantet [tɑ̃tɛ], *s.m. A:* = TANTINET.

tantième [tɑ̃tjɛm]. **1.** *a.* given, such a (part, proportion, etc.); **soit à trouver la t. partie d'un tout,** to find the required part of a whole. **2.** *s.m. Com:* percentage, share, quota (of profits, etc.); **prélever un t. de 10%,** to deduct 10 per cent; **tantièmes des administrateurs,** directors' percentage of profit.

tantine [tɑ̃tin], *s.f. F:* auntie.

tantinet [tɑ̃tinɛ], *s.m. F:* tiny bit, least bit (of bread, etc.); small drop (of wine); dash, touch, hint (of irony); **être un t. indisposé,** to be rather, slightly, out of sorts; **il est un t. joueur,** he is a bit of a gambler; **je le voudrais un t. plus long,** I want it a shade, a fraction, longer; **critique un t. sévère,** criticism just a shade too severe.

tantôt [tɑ̃to], *adv.* **1.** soon, presently; **voici t. trois ans que . . .,** it will soon be three years since . . .; **il est t. minuit,** it will soon be midnight; **je reviens t.,** I'll be back (i) presently, soon, later, (ii) this afternoon; **il pleuvra, il a plu, t.,** it will rain, it rained, this afternoon; **à t.,** good-bye for the present; see you again soon! **sur le t.,** towards evening; *Dial:* **à deux heures du t.,** at two o'clock in the afternoon. **2.** just now, a little while ago. **3. tantôt . . ., tantôt . . .,** at one time . . ., at another time . . .; now . . ., now . . .; sometimes . . ., sometimes . . .; **t. triste, t. gai,** now sad, now gay; **je gagne t. plus, t. moins,** some days I earn more, some days less; **t. je suis à Paris, t. à Londres,** sometimes I am in Paris, sometimes in London. **4.** *A:* (= BIENTÔT) *Prov:* **mémoire du bien t. passe,** eaten bread is soon forgotten.

tantouse [tɑ̃tu:z], *s.f. P:* sodomite, pansy, queer.

Tanzanie [tɑ̃zani], *Pr.n.f. Geog:* Tanzania.

taôisme [taɔism], *s.m. Rel.H:* Taoism.

taôiste [taɔist], *Rel.H:* **1.** *a.* Taoist(ic). **2.** *s.* Taoist.

taon [tɑ̃], *P:* [tɔ̃], *s.m.* gad-fly, breeze, horse-fly, cleg.

Taormina [taɔrmina], **Taormine** [taɔrmin], *Pr.n. Geog:* Taormina.

tapabor(d) [tapabɔ:r], *s.m. A:* cap with ear-flaps and turn-down brim; deerstalker.

tapage [tapa:ʒ], *s.m.* **1.** (loud) noise; din; uproar; *F:* racket, row; *Jur:* **t. nocturne,** disturbance of the peace at night; **faire du t.,** to kick up a row, a rumpus; *F:* **faire du t. autour d'un roman,** to give a novel a lot of publicity; **cette pièce a fait du t.,** this play was the talk of the town, was the subject of a great deal of controversy; *F:* **bien du t. pour peu de chose,** a lot of fuss over nothing, much ado about nothing. **2.** *P:* tapping, touching (of s.o. for money).

tapager [tapaʒe], *v.i.* (**je tapageai(s); n. tapageons**) *F:* to make a noise; to kick up a rumpus, a row.

tapageur, -euse [tapaʒœ:r, -ø:z]. **1.** *a.* (*a*) noisy (child, etc.); rowdy, uproarious, *F:* rackety (revellers, etc.); **gaieté tapageuse,** boisterous spirits; **il a décrit le côté t. de la vie,** he has described the rollicking side of life; (*b*) loud, flashy, showy (dress, etc.); blustering (speech); **individu au vêtement t.,** flashily dressed individual. **2.** *s.* (*a*) roisterer, rowdy; disturber of the peace; brawler; (*b*) **petit t.,** noisy little brat; **petite tapageuse,** noisy little girl.

tapageusement [tapaʒøzmɑ̃], *adv.* (*a*) noisily; rowdily; (*b*) loudly, flashily, showily.

tapant [tapɑ̃], *a. F:* (*of the hour*) striking; **arriver à l'heure tapante,** to arrive on the stroke of the hour, exactly on time, *F:* on the dot; **à six heures tapantes,** on the stroke of six.

tape[1] [tap], *s.f.* **1.** tap, rap, pat, slap; **t. sur l'épaule,** slap on the shoulder; **il m'a donné une t. sur l'épaule, une petite t. sur la joue,** he slapped me on the shoulder; he patted my cheek. **2.** *P: O:* failure; **ramasser une t.,** (i) to come a cropper; (ii) *Th:* to get the bird.

tape[2], *s.f.* plug, stopper, bung; *Artil:* tompion, tampion; *Nau:* **t. d'écubier,** hawse plug, buckler.

tapé [tape], *a.* **1.** dried (pears, apricots, apples, figs). **2.** *P:* first-rate; **réponse tapée,** smart answer.

tape-à-l'œil [tapalœ:j]. **1.** *a.inv.* loud, gaudy, flashy. **2.** *s.m.* gimcrack goods, flashy stuff; **c'est du t.-à-l'o.,** it looks all right on the surface; it's just window-dressing.

tapecu(l), tape-cul [tapky], *s.m.* **1.** see saw, *U.S:* teeter. **2.** counterpoise swing-gate, counterpoise barrier. **3.** *Nau:* jigger (sail). **4.** *Veh:* (*a*) gig; (*b*) hard-sprung or springless carriage; rattletrap; (*c*) *Rail: F:* railcar that stops at every station; *pl. tape(-)culs.*

tapée [tape], *s.f. F:* great quantity; lots, tons, heaps; **t. de marmots,** swarm of brats; **j'en ai une t.,** I've got heaps.

tape-marteau [tapmarto], *s.m. Ent: F:* skipjack, spring beetle, click beetle; *pl. tape-marteaux.*

tapement [tapmɑ̃], *s.m.* **1.** tapping (of an object against sth.); **tapements de pied,** stamping of feet. **2.** laying on (of varnish).

taper[1] [tape], *v.tr.* **1.** to tap, smack, slap, hit; (*a*) **t. du tambour,** to beat the drum; **t. la porte,** to slam the door; **se t. les cheveux,** to pat one's hair; to put one's hair straight; **t. un cheval,** to put a horse's mane straight; to make a horse look trim; **t. une lettre (à la machine),** to type a letter; *abs.* **savoir t.,** to be able to type; **t. un message sur un clavier,** to tap out a message; **t. un air (au piano),** to thump out a tune (on the piano); *F:* **t. la carte,** to play cards; *P:* **se t. la cloche, se t. un bon gueuleton,** to have a good tuck in; **se t. un whisky,** to treat oneself to a whisky; **se t. le derrière par terre,** to split one's sides laughing; *F:* **se t. de qn,** to make fun of s.o.; **je ne veux pas me t. encore une promenade cet après-midi,** I don't want to have to go for another walk this afternoon; *Aut: F:* **t. le 160,** to get up to 160 kms an hour; (*b*) *v.i.* **t. sur qch.,** to tap, rap, bang, on sth.; **se t. sur la cuisse,** to slap one's thigh; *F:* **t. sur le ventre à qn,** to give s.o. a dig in the ribs (as a mark of familiarity); **le soleil nous tapait sur la tête,** the sun was beating down on us; *F:* **ça tape,** it's pretty hot; **t. sur le piano,** to strum (on) the piano; **t. de la grosse caisse,** to beat the big drum; **t. au toucher,** to touch-type; **dactylo qui tape au toucher,** touch-typist; **t. sur qn,** to abuse, slate, slang, s.o.; **on lui a tapé dessus,** they pitched into him; **t. du pied,** to stamp one's foot; **je les regardais se t.,** I watched them knocking each other about; *Mil: F:* **t. sur un objectif,** to give a target a pasting, to strafe an objective; **taper à côté,** to miss the target; (*of wine*) **t. à la tête,** to go to the head; *s.a.* ŒIL 1, 3; (*c*) (*of artist*) to knock (sth.) off, to paint (sth.) rapidly; (*d*) *F:* **t. qn de mille francs,** to touch s.o. for a thousand francs; *P:* **tu peux te t.!** you can whistle for it! nothing doing! **2.** to dab on (paint); to prime (frame, etc.); to lay on, spread (varnish). **3.** *v.i.* **le bateau tape,** the ship is lifting with every wave. **4.** *v.i. P:* to stink; **ça tape ici!** what a stink!

taper[2], *v.tr.* to plug, stop up (hole, etc.); *Artil:* to put a tampion in (gun).

tapes [tap], **tapès** [tapɛs], *s.m. Moll:* carpet shell; clam; (*genus*) Tapes.

tapeti [tapti], *s.m. Z:* tapeti, tapiti.

tapette [tapɛt], *s.f.* **1.** (*a*) mallet, bat (for driving in corks); (*b*) carpet beater; (*c*) (engraver's) pad, dabber; (*d*) flapper; fly swatter; (*e*) *P:* tongue, clapper; **elle a une fière t.,** she's a great chatterbox; she *can* talk! (*f*) mousetrap. **2.** gentle tap. **3.** game of wall marbles. **4.** *P:* homo, fairy, Nancy, queer, one of them.

tapeur, -euse [tapœ:r, -ø:z]. **1.** *s. F:* (*a*) pianist (at dance, etc.); (*b*) constant borrower; cadger. **2.** *s.m. W.Tg:* tapper.

taphophobie [tafɔfɔbi], *s.f. Psy:* taphophobia.

taphrina [tafrina], *s.m. Fung:* taphrina.

taphrinacées [tafrinase], *s.f.pl. Fung:* Taphrinaceae.

taphrinales [tafrinal], *s.f.pl. Fung:* Taphrinales.

tapin [tapɛ̃], *s.m.* (*a*) *F: A:* drummer; *esp.* poor performer on the drum; (*b*) *P:* prostitute, tart; **faire le t.,** to solicit, to walk the streets.

tapiner [tapine], *v.i. P:* to solicit, to walk the streets.

tapineuse [tapinœ:z], *s.f. P:* prostitute, tart.

tapinocéphale [tapinɔsefal], *a. & s.m. & f. Anthr:* tapeinocephalic.

tapinois, -oise [tapinwa, -wa:z]. **1.** *s. A:* slyboots. **2.** *adv.phr.* **en t.,** stealthily, on the sly; **partir en t.,** to slip away.

tapinomes [tapino:m], *s.m.pl. Ent:* Tapinoma.

tapioca [tapjɔka], *s.m.* **1.** tapioca. **2.** (*in restaurant*) **un t.,** one tapioca soup, *F:* one tapioca, one.

tapiolite [tapjɔlit], *s.f. Miner:* tapiolite.

tapir[1] [tapi:r], *s.m. Z:* tapir.

tapir[2], *s.m. Sch: F:* **1.** private lesson. **2.** pupil who takes private lessons.

tapir[3] **(se)** [sətapi:r], *v.pr.* to squat, cower, lurk; to ensconce oneself; *Ven:* (*of game*) to nestle, take cover (in snow, etc.); **se t. derrière la porte,** to crouch behind the door; **être tapi dans un coin, dans un trou,** to crouch in a corner, to lie snug in a hole; **petite villa tapie dans un bois,** small villa hidden, nestling, in a wood.

tapiridés [tapiride], *s.m.pl. Z:* Tapiridae.

tapis [tapi], *s.m.* **1.** cloth, cover; **t. de sol,** ground sheet; **t. de selle,** saddle cloth; *Rac:* **t. de plomb,** weight cloth; **t. (de table),** table cover; **t. de billard,** billiard cloth; **t. vert,** (i) gaming table; (ii) conference table; **le t. brûle!** put down your stakes! **lever un beau t.,** to make a scoop (at the gaming table); **mettre qch. sur le t.,** to bring sth. up for consideration, for discussion; **la question a été mise sur le t. à la dernière réunion,** the matter was brought forward at the last meeting; **être sur le t.,** to be the topic for discussion; **amuser le t.,** to keep the company amused (before main event); *s.a.* NET 1. **2.** (*a*) carpet; **t. de haute laine, de laine rase,** long-pile carpet, short-pile carpet; **t. d'Orient, de Turquie, de Smyrne,** Turkey carpet; **t. d'origine,** hand-woven carpet; **t. mécanique,** machine-made carpet; **t. à prière,** prayer mat; **recouvrir le plancher d'un t.,** to carpet the floor; **couvert d'un t.,** carpeted; **t. de pied,** rug; *F:* **discussion de marchands de t.,** haggling; **t. de verdure,** carpet (-ing) of green; *Hort:* **t. de gazon,** (green)sward; **terrain recouvert d'un t. de gazon,** ground carpeted with turf; (*b*) carpeting. **3.** *Ind: Min:* **t. roulant,** continuous, endless, belt; conveyor belt; erecting track (in mass production); *Const:* **t. d'embarcation,** conveyor belt. **4.** *Box: Wr:* canvas; *Wr:* mat; *Box:* **envoyer son adversaire au t.,** to put one's opponent on the canvas; **aller au t.,** to be knocked down. **5.** *P: A:* **t. (-franc),** bar, dive; joint. **6.** *Bot:* tapetum, nutritive layer (in the androecium).

tapis-brosse [tapibrɔs], *s.m.* coir mat, doormat, coconut-fibre mat; *pl. tapis-brosses.*

tapisser [tapise], *v.tr.* **1.** to hang (wall, etc.) with tapestry. **2.** to paper (room); **les murs sont tapissés de jaune, un papier jaune tapisse les murs,** the walls are papered in yellow; **mur tapissé d'affiches,** wall plastered (over), covered, with advertisements; **t. les rues pour une procession,** to decorate the streets with hangings for a procession; **t. une boîte de papier,** to line a box with paper; **une membrane tapisse l'estomac,** the stomach is lined with a membrane; **mur tapissé de lierre,** ivy-clad, ivy-mantled, wall; wall covered with ivy; **pente tapissée de fleurs,** slope carpeted with flowers.

tapisserie [tapisri], *s.f.* **1.** (*a*) tapestry making, weaving; (*b*) tapestry works. **2.** tapestry, hangings, *A:* arras; **chaise en t.,** chair upholstered with tapestry; *F: A:* **être derrière la t.,** to be behind the scenes; (*at a ball*) **faire t.,** to be a wallflower. **3.** tapestry work; crewel work; rug work; **t. au, sur, canevas,** crewel work; **pantoufles en t.,** carpet slippers. **4.** wallpaper. **5.** tapestry carpet. **6. t. de pierre,** (kind of) mosaic.

tapissier, -ière [tapisje, -jɛ:r], *s.* **1.** (*a*) tapestry maker; (*b*) crewel worker. **2. t. (garnisseur, décorateur),** upholsterer; *attrib.* **sommier t.,** box mattress. **3.** *s.f.* **tapissière:** (*a*) spring van, delivery van; (*b*) covered waggonette. **4.** *s.f.pl. Arach:* **tapissières,** tapestry weavers.

tapon [tapɔ̃], *s.m.* plug, stopper; **boucher un trou avec un t. de linge,** to stop up a hole with a screwed-up rag; *adv.phr.* **en t.** (i) (*of clothes, etc.*) bundled up; (ii) (*of hair*) screwed up into a bun, into a knot; **ma robe est tout en t.,** my dress looks like a rag.

taponnage [tapɔna:ʒ], *s.m. A:* screwing up (of hair) into a bun, into a knot.

taponner [tapɔne], *v.tr. A:* to screw up (handkerchief, etc.); to screw up (one's hair) into a bun, into a knot.

tapotage [tapɔta:ʒ], **tapotement** [tapɔtmɑ̃], *s.m.* **1.** tapping, strumming. **2.** *Med:* tapotement (in massage).

tapoter [tapɔte], *v.tr. F:* to pat (child's cheek, etc.); to strum on (the table, etc.); to tap (keyboard of typewriter, etc.); **t. un air (au piano),** to strum a tune (on the piano); **se t. le visage avec une houpette,** to dab one's face with a powder puff.

tapoteur, -euse [tapɔtœːr, -øːz], *s.* strummer (on the piano).

tapotis [tapɔti], *s.m.* rattle (of typewriter).

tapura [tapyra], *s.m. Bot:* tapura.

tapure [tapyːr], *s.f. Metall:* shrinkage crack; cooling crack.

taquage [takaːʒ], *s.m. Bookb:* jolting (of sheets of paper).

taque [tak], *s.f.* (*a*) *Ind:* cast-iron plate; **t. d'assise,** bed plate (of machine, etc.); (*b*) fireback.

taquer [take], *v.tr.* (*a*) *Typ:* to plane, plane down (form); (*b*) *Bookb:* to jolt, to jog (sheets).

taquerie [takri], *s.f. Metall:* fire door (of reverberatory furnace).

taquet [takɛ], *s.m.* **1.** (*a*) *Carp: etc:* angle block; **t. de soutien,** bracket; (*b*) flange (of casting box, etc.); lug. **2.** *Mec.E: etc:* stop(per), block; *pl. Min:* (landing) dogs (of cage or shaft); keeps; **t. de sûreté,** safety stop; **t. d'arrêt,** (i) *Veh:* scotch; (ii) *Rail:* stop block; (iii) *Mec.E:* retaining lug; *Typewr:* **poser un t. (de tabulateur),** to set a tab(ulator stop), a stop. **3.** *Agr: Surv:* small picket, peg (delimiting ground to be ploughed, etc.). **4.** *Nau:* (*a*) **t. de tournage,** (belaying) cleat; **t. de hauban,** shroud cleat; (*b*) *pl.* ribs, whelps (of capstan or windlass); (*c*) *pl.* cheeks (of bowsprit); (*d*) (leather) button (of an oar). **5.** (*a*) *Tex:* driver, picker (of loom); (*b*) *I.C.E: etc:* **t. de soupape,** valve tappet; tappet rod; (*c*) *Mec.E: etc:* cam. **6.** *F:* **prendre un t. dans les gencives,** to get a clout on the jaw.

taqueuse [takøːz], *s.f. Tchn:* jogger, jogging machine.

taquin, -ine [takɛ̃, -in]. **1.** *a.* (given to) teasing. **2.** *s.* tease; teasing person. **3.** *s.m. Games:* (type of) picture puzzle.

taquinage [takinaːʒ], *s.m.* teasing.

taquiner [takine], *v.tr.* (*a*) to tease (s.o.); to plague (s.o.); **ne taquine pas ta petite sœur,** don't tease your little sister; **t. un bouton du pouce,** to fiddle with a button; **t. la Muse,** to play at writing poetry; **t. le goujon,** to tempt the fishes; to go fishing; (*b*) **ça me taquine qu'il n'arrive pas,** I'm rather worried that he isn't here yet; **mon bébé tousse, cela me taquine,** (my) baby has a cough and it rather worries me, it makes me uneasy.

taquinerie [takinri], *s.f.* **1.** teasing disposition; **être d'une grande t.,** to be a great tease **2.** teasing; **faire des taquineries à qn,** to tease s.o.

taquoir [takwaːr], *s.m. Typ:* planer.

taquon [takɔ̃], *s.m. Typ:* (*a*) underlay; (*b*) overlay.

taquonner [takɔne], *v.tr. Typ:* (*a*) to underlay (type); (*b*) to overlay (type).

tarabiscot [tarabisko], *s.m.* **1.** *Arch: Carp:* groove, channel (between mouldings). **2.** moulding plane.

tarabiscotage [tarabiskɔtaːʒ], *s.m.* grooving (of mouldings, panels).

tarabiscoté [tarabiskɔte], *a.* **1.** grooved (panel, etc.). **2.** over-elaborate, finicky (style, etc.).

tarabiscoter [tarabiskɔte], *v.tr.* **1.** to groove (mouldings, panels). **2.** to over-decorate; to overload (with elaborate decorations).

tarabuster [tarabyste], *v.tr. F:* **1.** to worry, plague, pester (s.o.); to bully (s.o.); **se t. l'esprit,** to rack one's brains. **2.** (*a*) to snub (s.o.); (*b*) to blow (s.o.) up.

tarage [taraːʒ], *s.m.* **1.** *Com:* taring; allowance for tare. **2.** (*a*) calibration (of a spring); (*b*) *Mch: etc:* **t. d'une soupape, etc.,** adjusting, adjustment, of a valve, etc.

taranche [tarɑ̃ːʃ], *s.f.* screw bar (of press).

tarantulidés [tarɑ̃tylide], *s.m.pl. Arach:* Tarantulidae.

tarare[1] [taraːr], *int. A:* fiddlesticks! nonsense!

tarare[2], *s.m. Agr:* winnowing machine; winnower, fanner.

tararer [tarare], *v.tr. Agr:* to winnow.

tararien, -ienne [tararjɛ̃, -jɛn], *a. & s. Geog:* (native, inhabitant) of Tarare.

tarasconnade [taraskɔnad], *s.f. F:* (*from Daudet's Tartarin de Tarascon*) (*a*) boasting, bragging; (*b*) tall story.

tarasconnais, -aise [taraskɔnɛ, -ɛːz], *a. & s. Geog:* (native, inhabitant) of Tarascon.

Tarasque[1] [tarask], *Pr.n.f. Myth:* Tarasque (*amphibious monster, said to have haunted the Rhone near Tarascon, where its effigy is still carried in feast-day processions*).

Tarasque[2]. **1.** *s.m. & f. Geog:* Tarasco. **2.** *s.m. Ling:* **le t.,** Tarascan, Tarasco.

taratata [taratata], *int. & s.m.* **1.** tantara(ra) (of trumpets). **2.** *O:* fiddlesticks! bunkum!

taraud [taro], *s.m. Tls:* (screw) tap; **t. à machine,** machine tap; **t. à main,** hand tap; **t. aléseur,** reaming, reamer, tap; **t. mère,** master tap; **t. conique,** taper tap; **t. amorceur, t. ébaucheur,** entering tap; **t. finisseur,** bottoming, finishing, tap.

taraudage [tarodaːʒ], *s.m.* screw cutting; tapping, screwing, thread(ing) (of nut, rod, etc.).

tarauder [tarode], *v.tr.* **1.** *Tchn:* to tap, cut, screw, thread (rod, nut, etc.); **machine à t.,** tapping machine. **2.** *F:* (*a*) to thrash (s.o.); to give (s.o.) a good hiding; (*b*) to pester, plague (s.o.).

taraudeuse [tarodøːz], *s.f. Tls:* tapper, tapping machine; screwing machine; screw cutter; thread cutter.

taraud-mère [taromɛːr], *s.m. Metalw:* hob; master tap; *pl. tarauds-mères.*

taravelle [taravɛl], *s.f. Vit:* strong dibber (for planting vines).

taraxacum [taraksakɔm], *s.m. Bot:* taraxacum, dandelion.

tarbais, -aise [tarbɛ, -ɛːz]. **1.** *a. & s. Geog:* (native, inhabitant) of Tarbes. **2.** *s.m.* horse or mule bred in the Tarbes region (*esp.* as a light cavalry mount).

tarbouch(e) [tarbuʃ], *s.m. Cost:* tarboosh.

tarbuttite [tarbytit], *s.f. Miner:* tarbuttite.

tard [taːr], (*a*) *adv.* late; **il est rentré fort t.,** he came home very late; **un peu t.,** rather late; belatedly; **plus t.,** later; later on; **au plus t.,** at the latest; **à midi au plus t.,** by twelve at the latest; **tôt ou t.,** sooner or later; *impers.* **il est t., il se fait t.,** it is late; **je ne pensais pas qu'il fût si t.,** I did not think it was so late; **je me suis couché t.,** I went to bed late; I was late in going to bed; **il se couche t.,** he keeps late hours; **il se maria t.,** he married late in life; **deux minutes plus t. et je manquais le bateau,** another two minutes and I should have missed the boat; *Prov:* **mieux vaut t. que jamais,** better late than never; **il n'est jamais trop t. pour se corriger,** it is never too late to mend; **il est trop t. pour qu'il se corrige,** he'll never improve; he's past praying for; **il se fait t.,** it is getting late; **il est t. dans la nuit,** it is late (at night); **il travaillait t. dans la nuit,** he worked late (at night); **je le ferai et pas plus t. que ce soir,** I'll do it this very evening; **pas plus t. qu'hier,** only yesterday; (*b*) *s.m.* **sur le t.,** (i) late in the day; (ii) late in life; **enfant sur le t.,** afterthought.

tardenoisien, -ienne [tardənwazjɛ̃, -jɛn], *a. Prehist:* Tardenoisian.

tarder [tarde], *v.i.* **1.** (*a*) to delay; **pourquoi tarde-t-il?** why is he so long? **il ne tardera pas maintenant,** he won't be long now; **t. en chemin,** to loiter on the way; **t. à faire qch.,** (i) to put off, defer, doing sth., (ii) to be long in (starting, coming, etc.); to be slow in (paying, etc.); **il ne tarda pas à nous venir en aide,** he was not long, not slow, in coming to our help; **sans t.,** without delay; **sans plus t.,** without further delay; without further loss of time; (*b*) **nous ne tarderons pas à le voir venir,** it will not be long, we shall not have to wait long, before he appears. **2.** *impers.* **il lui tarde de partir, qu'elle revienne,** he is longing, anxious, to get away, for her to return.

tardif, -ive [tardif, -iːv], *a.* **1.** (*a*) tardy, belated (regrets, etc.); late (hour, fruit); backward (fruit, etc.); (*b*) **t. à . . .,** slow to . . .; overslow (in taking action). **2.** *A:* slow, sluggish (steps); backward (intelligence). **3.** later; **les siècles tardifs du moyen âge,** the later centuries of the Middle Ages.

tardiflore [tardiflɔːr], *a. Bot:* late-blooming, late-flowering.

tardigrade [tardigrad], *Z:* **1.** *a.* (*a*) tardigrade, slow-paced; (*b*) *F:* reactionary (politician). **2.** *s.m. Z:* tardigrade; *Arach:* tardigrade, water bear; **les tardigrades,** the Tardigrada.

tardillon, -onne [tardijɔ̃, -ɔn], *s.m. A:* latest born (lamb, etc.); *F:* last child, baby (of family).

tardivement [tardivmɑ̃], *adv.* **1.** tardily, belatedly. **2.** *A:* slowly; **agir t.,** to be slow to take action.

tardiveté [tardivte], *s.f.* lateness, backwardness (of fruit, etc.); *A:* slowness (of walk).

tardon [tardɔ̃], *s.m. A:* = TARDILLON.

tard-venu [tarvəny], *s.m.* latecomer; *pl. tard-venus.*

tare [taːr], *s.f.* **1.** (*a*) *Com:* depreciation, loss in value (owing to damage or waste); **t. de caisse,** allowance for bad coin, mistakes, etc.; shorts; shortage in the cash; (*b*) (physical, moral) defect, blemish, fault; defect amounting to unsoundness (in horse, etc.); **t. héréditaire,** taint (of insanity, etc.); **cheval sans t.,** sound horse; **bois sans t.,** sound timber; (*c*) stain of illegitimacy. **2.** (*a*) tare; **t. réelle,** actual tare; **t. par épreuve,** average tare; **faire la t.,** to ascertain, allow for, the tare; (*b*) **faire la t. d'un ressort,** to calibrate a spring.

taré [tare], *a.* **1.** (*a*) spoilt, tainted, (fruit, etc.); damaged (goods); **cheval t.,** unsound horse; (*b*) (*of pers.*) syphilitic. **2.** (*a*) depraved, corrupt; (*b*) of damaged reputation, of ill repute; (*c*) with (i) a taint, (ii) a blot or blemish, in the family history. **3.** *Her:* (*of helmet on shield*) posé.

Tarentaise [tarɑ̃tɛːz], *Pr.n.f. Geog:* Tarentaise (region).

Tarente[1] [tarɑ̃ːt], *Pr.n.f. Geog:* Taranto; *A:* Tarentum.

tarente[2], *s.f. Rept: Dial:* gecko.

tarentelle [tarɑ̃tɛl], *s.f. Danc: Mus:* tarantella.

tarentin, -ine [tarɑ̃tɛ̃, -in], *a. & s. Geog:* Tarentine.

tarentisme [tarɑ̃tism], *s.m.*, **tarentulisme** [tarɑ̃tylism], *s.m. A.Med:* tarantism.

tarentule [tarɑ̃tyl], *s.f. Arach:* tarantula.

tarer [tare], *v.tr.* **1.** to spoil, damage (goods, fruit, etc., by damp, etc.); (*of horse*) **se t.,** to become unsound. **2.** (*a*) *Com:* to tare, to ascertain the weight of (packing case, etc.); (*b*) to calibrate (spring); *Mch: etc:* to adjust (valve, etc.) (to a given pressure).

taret [tarɛ], *s.m. Moll:* teredo; ship worm; borer.

targe [tarʒ], *s.f. A.Arm:* targe, buckler.

targette [tarʒɛt], *s.f.* **1.** *A.Arm:* target. **2.** (*a*) flat door bolt; (*b*) sash bolt. **3.** *pl. P:* shoes.

targeur [tarʒœːr], *s.m. Ich:* topknot.

targuer (se) [sətarge], *v.pr.* (*a*) **se t. de qch., de faire qch.,** to pride, plume, oneself on sth., on doing sth.; (*b*) **se t. d'un privilège,** to claim a privilege.

targui, *pl.* **touareg** [targi, twarɛg], *a. & s.* Touareg.

targum [targɔm], *s.m. Rel.Lit:* Targum.

targumique [targymik], *a. Rel.Lit:* Targumic.

targumiste [targymist], *s.m. Rel.Lit:* Targumist.

taricheute [tarikøt], *s.m. Egyptian Ant:* embalmer.

tarier [tarje], *s.m. Orn:* **t. pâtre,** stonechat; **t. des prés,** whinchat.

tarière [tarjɛːr], *s.f.* **1.** *Tls:* (*a*) auger; (*b*) drill; *Min:* borer; **t. rubanée, torse, en hélice,** (i) screw auger; (ii) twist drill; **t. à vis, à filet,** screw auger; **t. creuse à bout rond, t. à cuiller,** spoon auger. **2.** *Ent:* (*ovipositor*) terebra.

tarif [tarif], *s.m.* (*a*) tariff, price list; *Cust:* **t. d'entrée,** import list; **t. de sortie,** export list; (*b*) tariff, rate; scale; schedule of charges; **taux indices des tarifs,** tariff-level indices; **t. en vigueur,** rate in force; **t. dégressif,** tapering charge, sliding-scale tariff; **t. forfaitaire, t. à forfait,** (i) tariff as by contract, fixed rate; (ii) *Tp:* inclusive charge; **t. réduit,** reduced rate; **t. uniforme,** standard rate; **abaissement, relèvement, des tarifs,** lowering, raising, of tariffs; **classe de t.,** tariff rate; *Cust:* **t. douanier,** customs tariff; **t. ad valorem,** ad valorem tariff; **t. différentiel,** discriminating duty; **t. (douanier) de faveur, t. préférentiel,** preferential rate, tariff; *Post:* **tarifs postaux,** postal, postage, rates; **t. (des) lettres,** letter rate; **t. (des) cartes postales,** postcard rate; **t. (des) imprimés,** printed-paper rate; **t. (des) périodiques,** newspaper rate; **t. (des) échantillons,** sample rate; **t. télégraphique,** telegraph rates; **t. (du régime) intérieur,** inland rate; **t. ordinaire,** ordinary rate; **t. d'urgence** = first-class rate; *Rail:* **t. des chemins de fer,** railway rates; **t. (des) voyageurs,** passenger rates; **t. (des) marchandises,** goods, freight, rates; **t. par kilomètre,** fare per kilometre; **plein t.,** (i) full fare, adult fare (for passengers); (ii) full tariff (for goods, etc.); (iii) *F:* maximum penalty (for crime, etc.); **billet (à) plein t.,** full-fare ticket; *El: Gasm:* **t. à dépassement,** overload tariff; **t. à tranches,** multi-rate tariff; **t. binôme,** two-part tariff; **t. de location de(s) compteur(s),** meter rental tariff; *Com:* **t. de courtage,** commission rates; *Journ:* **t. de la publicité, t. des (petites) annonces,** (i) advertisement, advertising, rates; (ii) charge for announcements (in personal column).

tarifaire [tarifɛːr], *a.* relating to tariffs; **lois tarifaires,** tariff laws.

tarif-album [tarifalbɔm], *s.m.* trade catalogue; *pl. tarifs-albums.*

tarifer [tarife], *v.tr.* to tariff; to fix the rate of duties, etc.), the price (of (goods, etc.); **Walpole avait tarifé les consciences,** Walpole had put a price on every man's conscience; *Iron:* **amours tarifés,** love at a price.

tarification [tarifikasjõ], *s.f.* tariffing; fixing the rate (of duties), the price (of goods, etc.).

tarin[1] [tarɛ̃], *s.m.* **1.** *Orn:* **t. (des aulnes),** siskin, aberdevine. **2.** *P:* nose, beak, conk.

tarin[2], **-ine** [tarɛ̃-, in], *a. & s.* (native, inhabitant) of Tarentaise; *a. Husb:* **race tarine,** Tarentaise breed (of cattle).

tarir [tariːr]. **1.** *v.tr.* (*a*) to dry up (spring, river, tears); (*b*) to dry (up, off) (a cow, etc.); **elle ne peut pas nourrir son bébé parce que son lait s'est tari,** she cannot feed her baby as her milk has dried up; (*c*) to exhaust (one's means, words). **2.** *v.i.* (*a*) (*of waters*) to dry up, run dry; **la source a tari,** the spring has dried up; **la source est tarie,** the spring is dry; **les sources vives de son influence ne sont pas taries,** the living springs of his influence have not run dry; (*b*) (*of conversation, flow of tears, etc.*) to cease, stop, be exhausted; to dry up; **ne pas t. d'éloges sur qch.,** to be for ever praising sth.; never to tire of praising sth.; **ne pas t. sur un sujet,** to be for ever expatiating on a subject; **une fois sur ce sujet il ne tarit pas,** once he is on this subject he never stops.

tarissable [tarisabl̩], *a.* liable to run dry, to dry up; (*of source of money, etc.*) liable to come to an end, to dry up.

tarissant [tarisɑ̃], *a.* (spring) running dry; (money) coming to an end.

tarissement [tarismɑ̃], *s.m.* drying up, running dry (of waters); exhausting, exhaustion (of resources, etc.).

tarlatane [tarlatan], *s.f. Tex:* tarlatan (muslin).

Tarmac [tarmak], *s.m. Civ.E: R.t.m:* Tarmac.

tarmacadam [tarmakadam], *s.m. Civ.E: A:* tarmacadam.

tarmacadamiser [tarmakadamize], *v.tr. A:* to tarmacadamize.

taro [taro], *s.m. Bot:* taro.

tarole [tarɔl], *s.f. Mus:* (flat, orchestral) side drum.

tarot [taro], *s.m. Cards:* **1.** (*a*) tarot pack; (*b*) *A:* back (of playing card). **2.** *pl.* tarots (pack or game).

taroté [tarɔte], *a. A:* (*of playing cards*) with a grilled or chequered back.

taroupe [tarup], *s.f.* hair growing between the eyebrows.

tarpan [tarpɑ̃], *s.m. Z:* (*horse*) tarpan.

tarpéienne [tarpejɛn], *a.f. Rom.Ant:* **la Roche t.,** the Tarpeian Rock.

tarpon [tarpɔ̃], *s.m. Ich:* tarpon.

Tarquin [tarkɛ̃], *Pr.n.m. Rom.Hist:* Tarquin(ius); **T. l'Ancien,** Tarquinius Priscus; **T. le Superbe,** Tarquinius Superbus.

tarragonais, -aise [taragɔnɛ, -ɛːz], *a. & s. Geog:* (native, inhabitant) of Tarragona.

Tarragone [taragɔn], *Pr.n. Geog:* Tarragona.

tarsal, -aux [tarsal, -o], *a. Anat: Z:* tarsal.

tarse[1] [tars], *s.m. Anat: Z:* tarsus; **(cartilage) t.,** tarsus, tarsal plate (of the eyelid).

Tarse[2], *Pr.n. A.Geog:* Tarsus.

tarsectomie [tarsɛktɔmi], *s.f. Surg:* tarsectomy.

tarsien, -ienne [tarsjɛ̃, -jɛn]. **1.** *a. Anat:* tarsal (bone). **2.** *s.m.pl. Z:* **tarsiens,** Tarsioidea.

tarsier [tarsje], *s.m. Z:* tarsier.

tarsipède [tarsipɛd], *s.m. Z:* honey possum; (*genus*) Tarsipes.

Tarsis [tarsis], *Pr.n. A.Geog:* Tarshish.

tarso-métatarse [tarsɔmetatars], *s.m. Anat:* tarsometatarsus, tarsus; *pl. tarso-métatarses.*

tarso-métatarsien, -ienne [tarsɔmetatarsjɛ̃, -jɛn], *a. Anat:* tarsometatarsal; *pl. tarso-métatarsien(ne)s.*

tarsoplastie [tarsɔplasti], *s.f. Surg:* tarsoplasty.

tarsoptose [tarsɔptoːz], *s.f. Med:* tarsoptosis, flat feet.

tarsorr(h)aphie [tarsɔrafi], *s.f. Med:* tarsorrhaphy.

tarsotomie [tarsɔtɔmi], *s.f. Surg:* tarsotomy.

tartan [tartɑ̃], *s.m.* tartan (cloth or plaid).

tartane [tartan], *s.f. Nau:* tartan, tartane (of the Mediterranean).

tartanelle [tartanɛl], *s.f. Tex:* plaid.

tartare[1] [tartaːr]. **1.** *Ethn:* (*a*) *a.* Ta(r)tar, Tartarian; (*b*) *s.* (*with occ. f.* **tartaresse**) Ta(r)tar. **2.** *a. Cu:* **sauce t.,** sauce tartare, tartare sauce; **(steak) t.,** steak tartare; (*of certain grilled meats, fish*) **à la t.,** served with cold mustard sauce.

Tartare[2] **(le),** *Pr.n.m. Myth:* Tartarus.

tartaréen, -enne [tartareɛ̃, -ɛn], *a. Myth:* tartarean (blackness, shades).

tartareux, -euse [tartarø, -øːz], *a.* **1.** tartarous (sediment etc.). **2.** *A:* tartaric.

Tartarie [tartari], *Pr.n.f. Geog:* Tartary.

tartarin [tartarɛ̃], **tartarini** [tartarini], *s.m. Z:* tartarin, sacred baboon, Arabian baboon.

tartarinade [tartarinad], *s.f. F:* boasting.

tartarique [tartarik], *a. A: Ch:* tartaric.

tartarisé [tartarize], *a. A: Pharm: etc:* (*a*) tartarized; (*b*) tartrated, tartarated.

tarte [tart]. **1.** *s.f. Cu:* (open) tart; flan; **t. aux pommes,** apple tart; **t. à la crème,** custard tart; *Cin: F:* custard pie (thrown at s.o.); (*in allusion to Molière*) **c'est sa t. à la crème,** he's, she's, always harping on it; *F:* **c'est de la t.,** it's easy, it's a piece of cake. **2.** *s.f. P:* slap. **3.** *a. F:* (*a*) (*of pers.*) stupid, ridiculous; (*b*) (*of thg*) ugly; lousy; ridiculous; **film t.,** rotten, stupid, film; **chapeau t.,** ridiculous hat.

tartelette [tartəlɛt], *s.f. Cu:* tartlet.

Tartempion [tartɑ̃pjɔ̃], *s.m. F:* thingummy, thingumbob; what's his name; so-and-so.

tartignole [tartiɲɔl], *a. P:* ugly; rotten, lousy; stupid, ridiculous.

tartine [tartin], *s.f.* **1.** slice of bread and butter, bread and jam, etc.; **t. de confitures,** bread and jam. **2.** *F:* long-winded speech; rambling article; screed, rigmarole, effusion; **il m'a débité toute une t.,** (i) he told me a long story; (ii) he lectured me at great length.

tartiner [tartine]. **1.** *v.tr.* (*a*) to spread (sth.) with butter, etc.; to butter (sth.); **fromage à t.,** cheese spread; (*b*) *El: O:* to paste (accumulator plates). **2.** *v.i. F:* to ramble, to be long-winded (in speech or writing).

tartinier [tartinje], *s.m. F:* long-winded, rambling, speaker or writer.

tartouillade [tartujad], *s.f. F:* daub.

tartouiller [tartuje], *v.tr. & i. F:* to daub.

tartouilleur [tartujœːr], *s.m. F:* daub(st)er.

tartrage [tartraːʒ], *s.m.* treatment (of wine) with tartaric acid or calcium tartrate.

tartrate [tartrat], *s.m. Ch:* tartrate; **t. de potasse et d'antimoine,** tartar emetic.

tartrazine [tartrazin], *s.f. Dy:* tartrazine.

tartre [tartr̥], *s.m.* **1.** *Ch: etc:* tartar; **crème de t.,** cream of tartar; **t. brut,** argol; **t. stibié,** tartar emetic; tartarated antimony. **2.** (*a*) *Mch:* scale, fur (of boiler, etc.); **tartres boueux,** sludge, mud; (*b*) *Dent:* tartar (on teeth).

tartré [tartre], *a.* tartrated.

tartreux, -euse [tartrø, -øːz], *a.* **1.** tartarous (sediment). **2.** scaly, furry (boiler).

tartricage [tartrikaːʒ], *s.m.* treatment (of wine) with tartaric acid.

tartrifuge [tartrifyːʒ], *s.m.* boiler compound, scale preventer.

tartrique [tartrik], *a. Ch:* tartaric (acid); *Pharm:* **émétique t.,** tartar emetic.

tartronique [tartrɔnik], *a. Ch:* tartronic.

tartronylurée [tartrɔnilyre], *s.f. Ch:* tartronylurea, dialuric acid.

tartuf(f)e [tartyf], *s.m. Lit:* tartuf(f)e; sanctimonious hypocrite; pecksniff (*from the character in Molière's Tartuffe*).

tartuf(f)erie [tartyfri], *s.f. Lit:* **1.** hypocrisy, cant; tartuf(f)ism. **2.** piece of hypocrisy; of cant.

tartufier [tartyfje], *A:* **1.** *v.i.* (*p.d. & pr.sub.* **n. tartufiions, v. tartufiiez**) to play the hypocrite. **2.** *v.tr.* to hoodwink (s.o.) by one's sanctimonious hypocrisy; to humbug (s.o.).

tas [tɑ], *s.m.* **1.** (*a*) heap, pile (of stones, mud, wood, etc.); **t. de foin,** haycock; **t. de blé,** stook, shock, of corn; **t. de fumier,** manure heap, dunghill; *s.a.* FAMINE; **prendre au t., piquer dans le t.,** to help oneself; **prendre qn sur le t.,** to catch s.o. in the act, redhanded; **mettre des objets en t.,** to heap up, pile up, things; *Min:* **t. de déblais,** dump; *F:* **il ferait rire un t. de pierres,** he'd make a cat laugh; (*b*) large quantity (of people, things); **un t. de détails inutiles,** a mass of useless details; **un t. de mensonges,** a pack of lies; *F:* **il y en a des t. (et des t.),** there are heaps of them; **j'ai un t. de choses à faire,** I've heaps, loads, of things to do; **il m'a écrit des t. de fois,** he's written to me scores of times; **j'ai des t. de choses à vous raconter,** I've heaps of things to tell you; *Pej: F:* **tout un t. de gens,** a whole gang (of people); **quel t. de gens!** what a crew! what a gang! **t. d'imbéciles!** bunch of fools! (*c*) *Ven: etc:* **tirer dans le t.,** to fire into the brown, to brown a covey, etc. **2.** *Metalw:* (*a*) stake (anvil); (*b*) **t. à planer,** face plate; (*c*) **t. à river,** dolly; **teneur de t.,** holder-on, holder-up (assisting riveter). **3.** (*a*) *Const:* building under construction; **tailler des pierres sur le t.,** to dress stones on the building site; (*b*) **être sur le t.,** to be at work, on the job; *Ind: etc:* **formation sur le t.,** on-the-job training; **il a fait son apprentissage sur le t.,** he started at the bottom; **grève sur le t.,** sit-down strike. **4.** *Arch: Civ.E:* **t. de charge,** tas-de-charge, springing stones (on pier).

tas-étampe [tɑetɑ̃ːp], *s.m. Metalw:* swage block; *pl. tas-étampes.*

tasien, -ienne [tazjɛ̃, -jɛn], *a. & s.m. Prehist:* Tasian.

tasimètre [tazimɛtr̥], *s.m. El:* tasimeter.

Tasmanie [tasmani], *Pr.n.f. Geog:* Tasmania.

tasmanien, -ienne [tasmanjɛ̃, -jɛn], *a. & s. Geog:* Tasmanian.

tasmanite [tasmanit], *s.f. Miner:* tasmanite, combustible shale.

tassage [tɑsaːʒ], *s.m.* **1.** *Civ.E: etc:* ramming, packing, consolidating (of earth, etc.). **2.** *Sp:* ramming, crowding (of opponent).

tasse[1] [tɑːs], *s.f.* (*a*) cup; **t. à café,** coffee cup; **t. de café,** cup of coffee; **t. en métal,** tin mug; *Com:* **paire t.,** cup and saucer; **boire dans une t.,** to drink out of a cup; *F:* **la grande t.,** the sea, Davy Jones's locker; the drink; **boire à la grande t.,** to get drowned (at sea); (*b*) cupful; **boire une, la, t.,** to get a mouthful (when swimming); *Com: etc: F:* **boire la t.,** to come a cropper, to go under; (*c*) *P:* glass of wine; (*d*) *P:* **les tasses,** street urinals.

Tasse[2] **(le),** *Pr.n.m. Lit:* Tasso.

tassé [tɑse], *a.* **1.** (*a*) squat, dumpy (figure, etc.); (*b*) **t. par l'âge,** shrunk with age; **t. (sur soi-même),** curled up, huddled up. **2.** *F:* (*a*) full, complete; **livre de 1500 pages bien tassées,** book of at least, a good, 1500 pages; **trois heures (bien) tassées,** three full, whole, hours; **un verre bien t.,** a good glassful; (*b*) **un grog bien t.,** a stiff grog.

tasseau[1], **-eaux** [tɑso], *s.m. Tchn:* (*a*) cleat, strip, batten (supporting shelf, etc.); (*b*) bracket; (*c*) lug (of casting); (*d*) *Const:* brace lath; (*e*) brick foundation (of shed, etc.); (*f*) *Mch:* slide block (of piston crosshead); (*g*) rib (of tread of comb escalator).

tasseau[2], *s.m.* = TAS 2.

tassée [tɑse], *s.f.* cupful.

tasselier [tɑslje], *s.m.* (*in salt-marsh*) platform where the salt is made into a heap.

tassement [tɑsmɑ̃], *s.m.* **1.** cramming, squeezing, compressing, (of objects) together; ramming, packing (of earth, etc.). **2.** (*a*) (i) settling, settling down, consolidation, setting, (ii) sinking, subsidence (of foundations, embankment, etc.); **t. de l'opinion publique,** consolidation of public opinion; (*b*) *Fin: St.Exch:* setback.

tasser [tɑse]. **1.** *v.tr.* (*a*) to compress, cram, squeeze, (objects) together; to ram, pack, tamp (earth, etc.); to shake down (objects in box, etc.); to firm (the soil); **t. la chaussée,** to consolidate the road surface; (*b*) *Sp:* to crowd (an opponent). **2.** *v.i.* (*of plants*) to grow thick(ly).

se tasser. **1.** (*of foundations, etc.*) (*a*) to settle, set; (*b*) to sink, subside; **les opinions se sont tassées,** opinions have consolidated; *F:* **ça se tassera,** things will settle down; it will all come out in the wash; (*c*) *Fin:* (*of the market, of stocks*) to weaken; (*d*) **il commence à se t.,** he is beginning to shrink (with age); *F:* **ne te tasse pas dans ton fauteuil!** don't sit huddled up in your armchair! **2.** to crowd (up) together; to huddle together; (*of troops*) to bunch; **tassez-vous un peu,** squeeze up a bit; sit a little closer; **les bateaux se tassent dans un coin du port,** the boats are gathered, crowded, together in a corner of the harbour.

tassergal, -aux [tɑsɛrgal, -o], *s.m. Ich: F:* bluefish.

tassetier [tɑstje], *s.m. A:* purse maker.

tassettes [tɑsɛt], *s.f.pl. A.Arm:* tasses, tassets, taces (of armour).

tasseur [tɑsœːr], *s.m. Agr:* binder (of reaper binder).

taste-vin [tastəvɛ̃], *s.m.inv.* wine taster (pers. or thg).

tata [tata], *s.f. F:* **1.** (*child's word*) Auntie. **2.** **Madame Tata,** Mrs Busybody. **3.** plump, middle-aged woman (who is rather dowdy). **4.** *P:* homo, queer, fairy.

tâtage [tɑtaːʒ], *s.m.* feeling, touching, fingering, prodding.

tatajuba [tataʒyba], *s.m. Arb:* tatajuba.

tatane [tatan], *s.f. P:* shoe.

tatar, -are [tataːr]. **1.** *a. & s. Ethn: O:* Ta(r)tar. **2.** *s.m. Ling:* **le t.,** Tatar.

tatasse [tatas], *a.* = TATILLON.

ta ta ta [ta ta ta], *int.* well, now! come, now!

tâte [tɑt], *s.m. Ind:* sample (for testing during manufacture).

tâte-au-pot [tɑtopo], *s.m.inv. F: O:* man who meddles in the housekeeping.

tâtement [tɑtmɑ̃], *s.m.* feeling, touching.

tate-minette [tatminɛt], *a.* = TATILLON.

tâter [tɑte]. **1.** *v.tr.* to feel, touch; **t. une étoffe,** to feel, finger, handle, a material; **t. qch. du bout du doigt,** to prod sth.; **t. le pouls à qn,** (i) to feel s.o.'s pulse; (ii) to sound s.o. (on a matter); **t. le terrain,** to explore the ground; to throw out a feeler; to see how the land lies; **t. les défenses,** to probe the defences; **t. (le courage de) qn,** to try a man's mettle; **t. l'ennemi,** to try to draw the enemy; **avancer en tâtant, t. le mur,** to grope one's way forward; **t. la porte pour trouver la poignée,** to feel for the door handle; *Nau:* **t. le vent,** to touch (the wind); to hug the wind. **2.** *v.ind.tr.* to taste, try; *(a)* **t. d'un mets,** to taste a dish; **t. à une sauce,** to try a sauce; *F:* **vous en tâterez,** it will come your way one of these days; *(b)* **t. d'un métier,** to try one's hand at a trade; *F:* **il a tâté de la prison,** he's done time.

se tâter. **1.** to feel one's muscle; to feel for a sore spot, etc. **2.** to think it over, to take stock of oneself (before taking a step); *F:* **se t. (avant de faire qch.),** to stop to look at the fence.

tâteur, -euse [tɑtœːr, -øːz], *s.* **1.** *(a)* groper; *(b) F:* wobbler, waverer. **2.** taster (of wine, tea). **3.** *s.m. Tex:* weft-replenishing control (of automatic loom).

tâte-vin [tɑtvɛ̃], *s.m.inv.* wine taster (pers. or thg).

Tatien [tasjɛ̃], *Pr.n.m. Rel.H:* Tatian.

tatillon, -onne [tatijɔ̃, -ɔn; tɑ-]. **1.** *a.* *(a)* meddlesome; *(b)* niggling, finicky. **2.** *s.* *(a)* busybody; *(b)* niggler.

tatillonnage [tatijɔnaːʒ; tɑ-], *s.m.* *(a)* meddling; *(b)* niggling, fussiness, finickiness.

tatillonner [tatijɔne; tɑ-], *v.i.* *(a)* to meddle; to be meddlesome; *(b)* to niggle; to be fussy (about details).

tâtonnement [tɑtɔnmɑ̃], *s.m.* **1.** groping (in the dark). **2.** tentative effort; **procéder par tâtonnements,** to proceed by trial and error.

tâtonner [tɑtɔne], *v.i.* **1.** to grope (in the dark); to feel one's way; **se diriger en tâtonnant vers . . .,** to grope one's way towards . . .; **t. en cherchant qch.,** to grope, fumble (about), for sth.; **peint d'un pinceau qui tâtonne,** painted with a hesitating brush. **2.** to proceed cautiously, tentatively.

tâtonneur, -euse [tɑtɔnœːr, -øːz], *a. & s.* groper, fumbler.

tâtons (à) [atɑtɔ̃], *adv.phr.* gropingly; **avancer, aller, à t.,** to grope, feel, one's way (along); to grope about in the dark; **chercher qch. à t.,** to grope, feel, for sth.; **entrer, sortir, à t.,** to grope one's way in, out.

tatou [tatu], *s.m. Z:* armadillo, tatu; **t. velu,** hairy armadillo; **t. géant,** giant armadillo; **t. à neuf bandes,** nine-banded armadillo; **t. poyou,** poyou, peludo.

tatouage [tatwaːʒ], *s.m.* **1.** tattooing. **2.** tattoo, tattooed design. **3.** *Med:* **t. de la cornée,** tattooing of the cornea.

tatouer [tatwe], *v.tr.* to tattoo (the body).

tatoueur [tatwœːr], *s.m.* tattooer, tattooist.

tatouille [tatuːj], *s.f. P: O:* thrashing, licking.

tatouiller [tatuje], *v.tr. P: O:* to thrash, lick (s.o.).

tattersall [tatɛrsal], *s.m. A:* horse mart.

tatty [tati], *s.m.* (Anglo-Indian) tatty; fibre screen.

tatus [tatys], *s.m.*, **tatusie** [tatyzi], *s.f. Z:* tatusia.

tau [to], *s.m. Gr.Alph: Her: Archeol:* tau; *pl. taus.*

taube [toːb], *s.m. Mil.Hist:* *(1914-18 war)* taube (aeroplane).

taud [to], *s.m. Nau:* rain awning; **t. d'embarcation,** boat cover.

tauder [tode], *v.tr. Nau:* to cover (deck, etc.) with a rain awning.

taudion [todjɔ̃], *s.m. F: A:* miserable hovel.

taudis [todi], *s.m.* miserable room; dirty hole; hovel; **les t. de Paris,** the slums of Paris; **abolir les t.,** to clear away the slums; **lutte contre les taudis,** slum-clearance campaign.

taulard, -arde [tolaːr, -ard], *P:* *(a) s.* prisoner, convict; old lag; *(b) a.* **mes Noëls taulards,** the Christmases I spent in prison, in clink.

taule [toːl], *s.f. P:* *(a)* house; *(b)* room; *(c)* prison; **faire de la t.,** to do a stretch; *Mil:* **six semaines de t.,** six weeks' detention.

taulier, -ière [tolje, -jɛr], *s. P:* *(a)* owner, keeper (of pub, lodging house, brothel, etc.); *f.* madam (of brothel); *(b)* boss; *(c) s.m. O:* prisoner, convict, old lag.

taupe [toːp], *s.f.* **1.** *Z:* mole; **t. étoilée,** starnose, starnosed mole; **t. marsupiale,** marsupial mole; **t. dorée africaine,** African golden mole; *Ich:* **t. de mer,** porbeagle; *A: F:* **il est parti pour le royaume des taupes,** he is dead and buried; **il est myope comme une t.,** he's as blind as a bat, as a mole; **noir comme une t.,** black as pitch; *Mil: F:* **guerre de taupes,** mine warfare; *Vet:* **mal de t.,** poll evil. **2.** moleskin. **3.** *Sch: F:* (i) time of preparation; (ii) second-year class preparing for the *École polytechnique*; (iii) special maths class; *cf.* CORNICHE[3]. **4.** *P:* *(a) A:* prostitute, tart; *(b)* **vieille t.,** old crone, old hag. **5.** *Med:* talpa, wen.

taupé [tope], *a.* **feutre t.,** velour(s) felt; **chapeau t.,** velour(s) hat.

taupe-grillon [topgrijɔ̃], *s.m. Ent:* mole cricket; *pl. taupes-grillons.*

taupier [topje], *s.m.* mole catcher.

taupière [topjɛːr], *s.f.* mole trap.

taupin [topɛ̃], *s.m.* **1.** *Mil: A:* sapper. **2.** *Sch: F:* *(a)* student reading for the *École polytechnique*; *(b)* student in special maths class. **3.** *Ent:* elater, spring beetle, click beetle, skipjack.

taupinée [topine], *s.f.*, **taupinière** [topinjɛːr], *s.f.* molehill, mole cast.

taure [toːr], *s.f.* heifer.

taureau, -eaux [tɔro], *s.m.* **1.** *(a)* bull; **t. reproducteur,** bull for service; **il a un cou de t.,** he has a neck like a bull; **pugiliste au cou de t.,** bull-necked pugilist; **course, combat, de taureaux,** bullfight; *F:* **prendre le t. par les cornes,** to take the bull by the horns; *(b)* **t. à bosse, du Canada,** bison; **t. des Indes,** zebu. **2.** *Astr:* **le T.,** Taurus, the Bull.

tauresque [tɔrɛsk], *a.* bull-like, taurine; **à la face t.,** bull-faced.

Tauride [tɔrid], *Pr.n.f. Geog:* Taurida; *A.Geog:* Tauris.

taurides [tɔrid], *s.f.pl. Astr:* taurides (meteors).

taurillon [tɔrijɔ̃], *s.m.* bull calf.

taurin, -ine [tɔrɛ̃, -in]. **1.** *a.* taurine; of, relating to, a bull. **2.** *s.f. Ch:* **taurine,** taurin(e).

taurocéphale [tɔrɔsefal], *s.m. Ant:* bull-headed monster; minotaur.

taurocholate [tɔrɔkɔlat], *s.m. Ch:* taurocholate.

taurocholique [tɔrɔkɔlik], *a. Ch:* taurocholic.

tauromachie [tɔrɔmaʃi], *s.f.* tauromachy; bull-fighting.

tauromachique [tɔrɔmaʃik], *a.* tauromachian.

taurotrague [tɔrɔtrag], *s.m. Z:* taurotragus, eland.

tauto- [tɔtɔ], *pref.* tauto-.

tautochrone [tɔtɔkrɔn], *a. Mth:* tautochronous; **courbe t.,** tautochrone.

tautologie [tɔtɔlɔʒi], *s.f.* tautology; redundancy.

tautologique [tɔtɔlɔʒik], *a.* tautological; redundant.

tautomère [tɔtɔmɛːr], *a.* *(a) Anat:* tautomeral (neuron); *(b) Ch:* tautomeric.

tautomérie [tɔtɔmeri], *s.f. Ch:* tautomerism.

tautophonie [tɔtɔfɔni], *s.f.* tautophony.

taux [to], *s.m.* **1.** *(a)* rate (of wages, of exchange); (established or standard) price (of commodities, shares, etc.); *Adm:* **t. du salaire,** rate of wages; **t. du salaire de base,** standard wage rate; **t. de pension,** pension scale; *Mil:* **t. de solde,** rate of pay; *Com:* **t. du blé,** standard price of wheat (as fixed by the authorities); **vendre qch. à un t. trop élevé,** to sell sth. above the established price; *Nau:* **t. du frêt,** rate of freight; *Fin:* **t. d'émission,** issue price (of shares, etc.); **t. du change,** rate of exchange; **fléchissement du t. du change,** deterioration of the rate of exchange; **t. de stabilisation du franc,** rate at which the franc has been stabilized; *(b)* proportion, ratio; *Mil:* scale (of rations); *Mec:* **t. de charge,** load per unit area; **t. de travail de sécurité,** safe working load; **t. de distorsion,** distortion factor; *Mec.E: Ind:* **t. de rendement,** coefficient of efficiency, utilization factor; percentage of efficiency, of utilization (of machine, equipment, etc.); *Mch:* **t. de vaporisation,** steam and fuel ratio; *I.C.E:* **t. de compression,** compression ratio; *Mec.E: Ind:* **t. nominal,** marked ratio; **t. effectif, t. réel,** effective, actual, ratio; *Ch:* **t. de mélange,** mixture ratio; **t. pour dix, pour cent, parties,** number of parts per ten, per hundred; *Ph:* **t. d'amplitude,** peak-to-valley ratio (of waves); *Atom.Ph:* **t. de combustion, d'épuisement, de consommation (du combustible),** burn-up ratio (of fuel); **t. d'enrichissement,** enrichment factor; **t. d'ionisation,** ionization rate; *(c)* percentage; rate; *Fin: Bank:* **t. d'intérêt,** rate of interest; **t. (d'intérêt) progressif,** graduated interest; **au t. de . . .,** at the rate of . . .; **prêter au t. légal,** to lend at the legal rate; **prêter au t. de 10%,** to lend at the rate of 10%; *Fin: Com: etc:* **t. de rendement,** rate of return; **t. d'amortissement,** amortisation quota; depreciation rate; *Adm: etc:* **t. de consommation,** consumption rate; **t. d'usure,** rate of wear (of equipment); attrition rate (of personnel or equipment); **t. de mortalité,** death rate; **t. des naissances,** birth rate; **t. de scolarisation,** rate of school attendance; *Mil:* **t. de pertes,** casualty rate; *Med:* **t. de cicatrisation,** degree of cicatrisation; **t. d'invalidité,** degree of disablement; **t. des hospitalisations,** admission rate (to hospital); *Rail: etc:* **t. de pente,** rate of grade, gradient; *(d) Elcs:* *(computers)* ratio; rate; **t. de modulation,** modulation factor; **t. d'erreurs,** error rate, ratio. **2.** *A:* assessment.

tauzin [tozɛ̃], *s.m. Bot:* *(in S.W. Fr.)* black oak.

tavaillon [tavajɔ̃], *s.m. Const:* **1.** sheeting plank (of roof); thatch. **2.** shingle.

tavaïole [tavajɔl], *s.f. Ecc:* *(a)* chrisom cloth; *(b)* napkin (for consecrated bread, etc.).

tavelage [tavlaːʒ], *s.m.* spotting, speckling (of fruit); scab.

tavelé [tavle], *a.* spotted, speckled; **fruit t.,** speckled fruit; **panthère tavelée,** spotted panther.

taveler [tavle], *v.tr.* **(il tavelle; il tavellera)** *(of damp, etc.)* to spot, speckle (fruit, etc.); **fruits qui se tavellent,** fruit that becomes spotted, speckled.

tavelure [tavlyːr], *s.f.* spots, speckles; *Hort:* scab.

taverne [tavɛrn], *s.f.* **1.** *A:* tavern; public house. **2.** *A:* café-restaurant.

tavernier, -ière [tavɛrnje, -jɛːr], *s. A:* tavern-keeper; publican, inn-keeper; landlord, landlady.

tavistockite [tavistɔkit], *s.f. Miner:* tavistockite.

taxable [taksabl], *a.* *(computers)* chargeable; *Jur:* **frais non taxables,** extra costs.

taxacées [taksase], *s.f.pl. Bot:* Taxaceae.

taxateur [taksatœːr]. **1.** *s.m.* taxer, assessor; *Jur:* taxing master. **2.** *a.m.* taxing (official); *Jur:* **juge t.,** taxing master.

taxatif, -ive [taksatif, -iːv], *a. Jur:* taxable.

taxation [taksasjɔ̃], *s.f.* **1.** fixing of prices, wages, etc.; *Jur:* taxing (of costs). **2.** *Adm:* *(a)* taxation; *(b)* assessment. **3.** *Tp:* **zone de t.,** charging area; *(computers)* **période de t.,** charging period. **4.** *pl.* additional fees (of certain civil officials).

taxaudier [taksodje], *s.m. Bot:* bald cypress, taxodium.

taxe [taks], *s.f.* **1.** *(a)* fixed price, official price; *A:* assize (of certain foodstuffs, etc.); fixed rate (of wages); **vendu à la t.,** sold at the controlled price; *(b)* charge (for service); rate; **t. postale, des lettres,** postage; **t. supplémentaire,** (i) surcharge; (ii) late fee; **t. de recommandation,** registration fee; **t. d'abonnement au timbre,** composition for stamp duty; **t. téléphonique, t. des conversations téléphoniques,** telephone charge, call charge; **taxes des chemins de fer,** railway rates. **2.** *(a)* tax, duty, rate; **t. à la production, à l'achat, de consommation,** purchase tax; **t. à la valeur ajoutée,** value-added tax, *U.S:* processing tax; **t. sur les chiens,** dog tax; **t. de séjour,** visitors' tax; **t. d'habitation,** inhabited house duty; **t. officielle,** assessment; **t. d'office,** arbitrary assessment (of income tax); *Th: etc:* **t. sur les spectacles,** entertainment tax; *(b)* **t. de port,** harbour dues. **3.** *Jur:* taxing, taxation (of costs).

taxer [takse], *v.tr.* **1.** *(a)* to regulate the price of (bread, etc.), the rate of (wages, postage); **t. une denrée,** to fix a controlled price for a food product; *(b)* to surcharge (letter); *(c) Tp:* to charge for (call). **2.** to tax, impose a tax on (s.o., luxuries, motor cars, etc.); **on ne peut pas t. le génie,** one cannot impose conditions on genius. **3.** *(a) Jur:* to tax (costs); **mémoire taxé,** taxed bill of costs; *(b) Com:* to bill. **4.** to tax, accuse; **t. qn de lâcheté,** to tax s.o. with, accuse s.o. of, cowardice; **on taxe d'erreur cette doctrine,** this doctrine is denounced as erroneous; **on vous taxe d'être avare,** you are taxed with avarice, with being mean; **je ne taxe personne,** I am not accusing anybody.

taxi [taksi], *s.m.* **1.** taxi (cab); **conducteur de t., chauffeur de t.,** taxi driver; **faire le t.,** to be a taxi driver; *F:* **il est t.,** he is a taxi driver; **station de taxis,** taxi rank; **faire avancer un t.,** to call a cab (off the rank). **2.** *F:* *(a) Av:* plane; *(b)* car.

taxiarque [taksiark], *s.m. Gr.Ant:* taxiarch.

taxidé [takside], *s.m. Z:* American badger; *(genus)* Taxidea.

taxidermie [taksidɛrmi], *s.f.* taxidermy.

taxidermique [taksidɛrmik], *a.* taxidermal.

taxidermiste [taksidɛrmist], *s.m.* taxidermist.

taxie [taksi], *s.f. Biol:* taxis.

taxiforme [taksifɔrm], *a. Bot:* arranged like the leaves of a yew.

taximètre [taksimɛtr], *s.m.* **1.** taximeter. **2.** *Nau:* dummy compass, pelorus.

taxinées [taksine], *s.f.pl. Bot:* = TAXACÉES.

taxinomie [taksinɔmi], *s.f.* = TAXONOMIE.

taxiphone [taksifɔn], *s.m. Tp:* public call box.

taxiphote [taksifɔt], *s.m. Phot:* automatic stereoscope and classifier; taxiphote.

taxis [taksis], s.m. Med: taxis; manual reduction of hernia.

taxodier [taksɔdje], **taxodium** [taksɔdjɔm], s.m. Bot: bald cypress, (genus) Taxodium.

taxodontes [taksɔdɔ̃:t], s.m.pl. Moll: Taxodonta.

taxologie [taksɔlɔʒi], s.f. = TAXONOMIE.

taxologique [taksɔlɔʒik], a. taxonomic(al).

taxologiste [taksɔlɔʒist], **taxologue** [taksɔlɔg], s.m. & f. taxonomist.

taxonomie [taksɔnɔmi], s.f. Nat.Hist: taxonomy, taxology; classification.

taxonomique [taksɔnɔmik], a. taxonomic(al).

taxonomiste [taksɔnɔmist], s.m. & f. taxonomist.

tayaut [tajo], int. Ven: tally-ho!

Taygète (le) [lətaiʒɛt], Pr.n.m. Geog: Taygetus (mountain).

taylorisation [tɛlɔrizasjɔ̃], s.f. Ind: Taylorization.

tayloriser [tɛlɔrize], v.tr. Ind: to Taylorize.

taylorisme [tɛlɔrism], s.m. Ind: Taylorism.

taylorite [tɛlɔrit], s.f. Miner: taylorite.

Tchad (le) [lətʃad], Pr.n.m. Geog: 1. Lake Chad. 2. the Republic of Chad.

tchadien, -ienne [tʃadjɛ̃, -jɛn], a. & s. (native, inhabitant) of the Republic of Chad.

tchécoslovaque [tʃekɔslɔvak], a. & s. Geog: Czech, Czechoslovak, Czechoslovakian.

Tchécoslovaquie [tʃekɔslɔvaki], Pr.n.f. Geog: Czechoslovakia.

Tchéka (la) [latʃeka], s.f. Russian Hist: the Cheka.

tchèque [tʃɛk]. 1. a. & s.m. & f. Czech. 2. s.m. Ling: le t., Czech.

tchernoziom [tʃɛrnozjɔm], s.m. Geol: chernozem.

te, before a vowel sound **t'** [t(ə)], pers.pron., unstressed, attached to the verb or its adjuncts; (for the use of te cf. TU) 1. (a) (acc.) you; il t'adore, he adores you; te voilà, there you are; (b) (dat.) (to) you; il t'a écrit, he wrote to you; il te l'a dit, he told you so; (ethic dat.) je te le lui ai renvoyé sur-le-champ, I sent it back to him at once, you may be sure; (c) (with pr.vbs.) yourself (or not rendered into English); tu te fatigues, you are tiring yourself; tu vas te faire mal, you will hurt yourself; à quelle heure t'es-tu levé(e)? (at) what time did you get up? souviens t'en, remember it; va-t'en, go away. 2. thee, thyself; (a) (in addressing the Deity) nous te magnifions, we magnify Thee; (b) (in some Quaker speech, in dialect) va-t'en, get thee gone.

té¹ [te], s.m. 1. (the letter) T, tee; en té, T-shaped (pipe, bandage, etc.); in the shape of a T; fer à té, T-iron. 2. (a) Mch: té du piston, cross-head of the piston; (b) Const: tee-iron; T-piece; Mec.E: etc: union T; té de raccordement, té fendu, split T; té oblique, Y-branch; té de réduction, three-way restrictor; (c) té (à dessin), équerre en té, tee-square, T-square.

té², int. Dial: (S. of Fr.) hullo! té, c'est Marius! why, it's Marius! je suis de Marseille, té! I'm from Marseilles, of course!

téallite [tealit], s.f. Miner: teallite.

team [tim], s.m. Sp: team.

técéfiste [tesefist], s.m. & f. member of the T.C.F. (Touring-Club de France).

technétium [tɛknesjɔm], s.m. Ch: technetium.

technicien, -ienne [tɛknisjɛ̃, -jɛn], s. technician; technical man.

technicité [tɛknisite], s.f. technicalness, technicality.

Technicolor [tɛknikɔlɔr], s.m. R.t.m: Cin: Technicolor.

technique [tɛknik]. 1. a. technical; raisons d'ordre t., technical reasons; détails techniques d'une question, technicalities of a question; termes techniques, technical terms; aide t., technical aid, assistance. 2. s.f. (a) (= TECHNOLOGIE) technics; t. de l'ingénieur, engineering; t. de la construction, structural engineering; t. de la production, production engineering; t. électrique, electrical engineering; t. électronique, electronic engineering; t. radioélectrique, radio engineering; t. nucléaire, nucleonics; t. du froid, refrigerating engineering; t. des ultrasons, ultrasonics; Com: t. de la vente, sales engineering; techniques commerciales, marketing; techniques marchandes, merchandising; (b) technique (of artist, specialist, etc.); chaque science a sa t. particulière, every science has its own special technique; t. opérationnelle, know-how; Surg: t. opératoire, operative technique.

techniquement [tɛknikmɑ̃], adv. technically.

technocrate [tɛknɔkrat], a. & s.m. & f. technocrat.

technocratie [tɛknɔkrasi], s.f. Pol.Ec: technocracy.

technocratique [tɛknɔkratik], a. technocratic.

technogénie [tɛknɔʒeni], s.f. engineering.

technogénique [tɛknɔʒenik], a. données technogéniques, engineering data.

technographie [tɛknɔgrafi], s.f. technography.

technographique [tɛknɔgrafik], a. technographic(al).

technologie [tɛknɔlɔʒi], s.f. technology; Elcs: t. des circuits logiques transistorisés, solid logic technology.

technologique [tɛknɔlɔʒik], a. technological; chômage t., unemployment resulting from automation, etc.

technologiste [tɛknɔlɔʒist], s.m. & f., **technologue** [tɛknɔlɔg], s.m. & f. technologist.

teck [tɛk], s.m. (a) Bot: teak; (b) Com: teak(-wood).

teckel [tɛkɛl], s.m. dachshund.

técoma [tekɔma], s.m. Bot: tecoma.

tectibranche [tɛktibrɑ̃:ʃ], a. Moll: tectibranch; s.m.pl. tectibranches, Tectibranchia.

tectite [tɛktit], s.f. Miner: tektite.

tectogène [tɛktɔʒɛn], Geol: 1. a. tectogenic. 2. s.m. tectogene.

tectologie [tɛktɔlɔʒi], s.f. Biol: tectology.

tectonique [tɛktɔnik]. 1. a. tectonic. 2. s.f. tectonics.

tectrice [tɛktris], a.f. & s.f. Orn: (plumes) tectrices, tectrices, (wing) coverts.

Te Deum [tedeɔm], s.m.inv. Te Deum.

tee [ti], s.m. Golf: tee.

teel [til], s.m. Bot: til, teel; sesame.

teesdalie [tisdali], s.f., **teesdalea** [tisdalea], s.m. Bot: teesdalia.

Téflon [teflɔ̃], s.m. R.t.m: Teflon.

téflonisé [teflɔnize], a. Teflon-coated, F: non-stick (saucepan, etc.).

tégénaire [teʒenɛ:r], s.f. Arach: house spider; (genus) Tegenaria.

tegmen [tɛgmɛn], s.m. Bot: Ent: tegmen.

tegminé [tɛgmine], a. Bot: provided with a tegmen.

tégula [tegyla], s.f., **tégule** [tegyl], s.f. Ent: tegula.

tégulaire [tegylɛ:r], a. Miner: etc: tegular, tegulated; ardoise t., roofing slate.

téguline [tegylin], a.f. argile t., tile clay.

tégument [tegymɑ̃], s.m. Nat.Hist: tegument; integument; Bot: seed coat.

tégumentaire [tegymɑ̃tɛ:r], a. tegumentary.

Téhéran [teerɑ̃], Pr.n. Geog: Teh(e)ran.

teigne [tɛɲ], s.f. 1. Ent: (a) tinea, moth; t. des draps, clothes moth; t. des tapisseries, black-cloaked clothes moth; t. des pelleteries, single-spotted clothes moth; (b) t. de la cire, fausse t., honeycomb moth; t. des grains, fausse t. des blés, corn moth; t. de la vigne, cochylis; t. du mélèze, larch-miner moth; t. de la graisse, tabby; (c) F: pest; shrew (of a woman). 2. (a) Med: tinea; scalp disease; t. faveuse, favus, scald-head, crusted ringworm, honeycomb ringworm; t. tonsurante, t. tondante, ringworm; t. pelade, alopecia; (b) Vet: thrush; (c) scurf, scale (on old trees). 3. Bot: F: (a) dodder; (b) bur (of burdock).

teigneux, -euse [tɛɲø, -ø:z], a. & s. 1. a. & s. Med: (person) suffering from tinea, from ringworm; P: j'en mangerais sur la tête d'un t., I adore it; P: il n'y a que trois t. et un pelé, there's only a handful of odds and sods. 2. s.m. P: (pers.) stinker. 3. a. Typ: pitted.

téiidés [teiide], s.m.pl. Rept: Teiidae, Tejidae, the teyon, teju, lizards.

teillage [tɛja:ʒ], s.m. Tex: stripping, scutching, swingling (of hemp, flax, etc.).

teille [tɛ:j], s.f. harl (of hemp).

teiller [teje], v.tr. to strip, scutch, swingle (hemp, flax, etc.).

teilleur, -euse [tejœ:r, -ø:z], Tex: 1. s. flax stripper, scutcher. 2. s.f. teilleuse, scutching machine, scutcher.

teindre [tɛ̃:dr], v.tr. (pr.p. teignant; p.p. teint; pr.ind. je teins, il teint, n. teignons; pr.sub. je teigne; p.d. je teignais; p.h. je teignis; fu. je teindrai) 1. to dye; t. qch. en rouge, to dye sth. red; Tex: t. avant filature, to dye in the wool, before spinning; t. en pièces, to piece-dye; faire t. une robe, to have a dress dyed. 2. to stain, tinge, colour; t. sa main du sang de qn, dans le sang de qn, to stain one's hand with s.o.'s blood.

se teindre. 1. to dye one's hair. 2. to be tinged (de, with).

teint [tɛ̃], s.m. 1. dye, colour; bon t., grand t., fast colour, fast dye; dyed in the wool; bon t., (i) lasting; (ii) genuine; authentic; (iii) staunch; catholique bon t., staunch catholic; faux t., mauvais t., dye that is not fast, that will not last. 2. complexion, colour; au t. frais, fresh-complexioned; au t. jaune, sallow(-complexioned); t. de jeune fille, schoolgirl complexion; au t. pâle, pale-faced; à ces mots son t. pâlit, s'anima, at these words she grew pale, she flushed.

teinte [tɛ̃:t], s.f. (a) tint, shade; t. de fond (back)-ground shade, ground colour; Art: etc: t. plate, flat tint; t. neutre, neutral tint; Mapm: t. hypsométrique, hypsometric layer, tint; système de teintes hypsométriques, layer colouring; équidistance des teintes hypsométriques, layer step; échelle des teintes, identifying chart, key to colours used; (b) (= COLORANT) t. à haute, à basse, fusion, high-fusing, low-fusing, stain; (c) (légère) t. de . . ., tinge of . . .; t. de malice, d'ironie, touch, tinge, of malice, of irony; chants qui ont une t. mélancolique, songs tinged with melancholy; récits d'une t. satirique, stories with a strain of satire; discours sans t. de pédanterie, speech without a hint of, free of, pedantry.

teinter [tɛ̃te], v.tr. (a) to tint; Phot: t. une épreuve, to tint a print; papier teinté, tinted, toned, paper; Opt: verres teintés, tinted glasses; (b) t. (légèrement), to tinge; ciel teinté de rose, sky tinged with pink; eau teintée de vin, water tinged with wine, water with a dash of wine.

teinture [tɛ̃ty:r], s.f. 1. (a) dyeing (of cloth, hair, etc.); t. en pièces, piece dyeing; t. en cuve, dip dyeing; (b) tinting (of a drawing, of lantern-slide, etc.). 2. (a) dye; tissu qui prend bien la t., material that takes the dye (well); material that dyes well; couvertures sans t., undyed blankets; (b) colour, hue, tinge, F: O: avoir une (légère) t. de latin, to have a superficial knowledge, a smattering, of Latin; quand on a été marin, il en reste toujours une t., when a man has been to sea, he always smacks of the sea; (c) Her: tincture. 3. Pharm: tincture; t. d'iode, tincture of iodine.

teinturerie [tɛ̃tyr(ə)ri], s.f. 1. dyeing; dyer's trade. 2. dye works. 3. dry cleaner's (undertaking dyeing).

teinturier, -ière [tɛ̃tyrje, -jɛ:r]. 1. s. dyer; t. dégraisseur, dyer and cleaner. 2. a. relating to dyeing; dyeing (industry).

teius [teiys], s.m., **teju** [teʒy], s.m. Rept: teyou, teju, lizard.

téjidés [teʒide], s.m.pl. Rept: Tejidae, Teiidae, the teyou, teju, lizards.

tek [tɛk], s.m. = TECK.

tel, telle [tɛl], a. 1. such; (a) un t. homme, such a man; de telles choses, such things; pour de telles transactions il faut des capitaux, such transactions require capital; (b) this; il vous dira qu'en t. ou t. cas il faut . . ., he will tell you that in this or that case you should . . .; telle et telle cause a t. et t. effet, such and such a cause has such and such an effect; en t. lieu, in such and such a place; dans telle et telle rue, in such and such a street; inutile de demander si t. ouvrage remplit son but mieux que t. autre, it is useless to ask whether one book achieves its aim better than another; je sais telle maison où . . ., I know a firm, a house, where . . .; assurer par tels moyens et dans telles circonstances qu'on le jugera convenable . . ., to ensure by such means and under such conditions as shall, may, be deemed suitable . . .; prendre telles mesures qui paraîtront nécessaires, to take such steps as shall be considered necessary; vous amènerez telle personne que vous voudrez, you may bring any person you like; (c) sa bonté est telle que . . ., such, so great, is her kindness that . . .; t. charlatan qu'il puisse être j'ai confiance en ses soins, no matter how much of a quack he may be I believe in him; à t. point, to such an extent, to such a pitch; de telle sorte que, (i) + ind. (of event realized), (ii) + sub. (of event to be realized), in such a way that; il parle de telle sorte que je ne le comprends pas, he speaks in such a way that I don't understand him; je m'arrangerai de telle sorte qu'elle puisse partir dimanche, I will arrange things so that she can leave on Sunday. 2. (a) like; as; t. père, t. fils, like father like son; telle vie, telle fin, as we live, so we shall end; t. font les parents, t. feront les enfants, as the parents do so will the children; what the parents do the children will do also; (b) t. que, such as, like; un homme t. que lui, a man like him; une lassitude telle qu'on en éprouve par un jour orageux, a tiredness such as one feels on a stormy day; les grandes villes telles que Londres, par exemple, large towns such as London; la clause telle qu'elle est, the clause as it stands; voir les hommes tels qu'ils sont, to see men as they are; je vois les choses telles qu'elles sont, I look the facts in the face; c'est après dîner qu'il se montre t. qu'il est, it is after dinner that he shows himself, comes out, in his true colours; *F:* **t. que,** straight out; that's how it is; (*c*) **il n'y a rien de t., il n'est rien t., que d'avoir . . .,** there is nothing like having . . .; **rien de t. qu'un bon cigare,** there's nothing like, you can't beat, a good cigar; **il n'est rien de t. que d'être jeune,** there's nothing like being young; (*d*) *Lit:* **t. un éclair, il s'élance,** like a flash, lightning, he rushes forward; **il allait et venait, telle une bête en cage,** he paced to and fro like a caged beast; **il se tenait debout, telle une statue de bronze,** he stood like a bronze statue; **une tragédienne telle Sarah Bernhardt,** a tragédienne such as Sarah Bernhardt; (*e*) **t. quel,** (i) just as it is; just as he is; **je vous achète la maison telle quelle,** I'll buy the house from you just as it is, just as it stands; **j'ai acheté les livres tels quels,** I bought the books as they were, for what they were worth; (ii) *O:* **c'est un homme t. quel,** he's just an ordinary person; **il faut prendre un parti t. quel,** we must come to some decision or other; **une paix telle quelle,** a makeshift peace, a peace of sorts; (iii) **tout laisser, tout retrouver, t. quel,** to leave, to find, everything unaltered, *in statu quo*; **j'ai retrouvé la maison telle quelle,** I found the house just as I left it; (*f*) *A:* (= QUEL); **un nombre, t. qu'il soit, peut être augmenté,** a number, whatever it be, may be increased. **3.** *pron.* (*a*) such a one; **t. l'en blâmait, t. l'en excusait,** one would blame him, another would excuse him; **t. qui,** he who, many a one who; **t. admire le père qui blâme le fils,** some who blame the son admire the father; *Prov:* **t. rit vendredi qui dimanche pleurera, t. qui rit vendredi, dimanche pleurera,** laugh on Friday, cry on Sunday; laugh today, cry tomorrow; (*b*) **t. fut son langage,** such were his words; **son langage fut t. . . .,** he spoke as follows . . .; **il n'est pas beau mais il se prend pour t.,** he is not handsome but he thinks himself so; **il est très crâne et très connu pour t.,** he is very gallant and very well known as such; *s.* **un t., une telle,** so-and-so; **Monsieur un t., un T.,** Mr So-and-so; **nous dînons chez les un t.,** we dine at the so-and-so's; **je n'ai pas besoin de l'opinion de M. un T.,** I don't want the opinion of Mr This or Mr That; **s'adresser à t. et t.,** to apply to this man and that, to one (man) and another; **t. ou t. vous dira que . . .,** some people will tell you that . . .; **je serais incapable d'attribuer l'article à t. ou t.,** I cannot attribute the article to any particular person.

télagon [telagɔ̃], *s.m. Z:* teledu; stinkard; stinking badger; Javanese skunk.

Télamon [telamɔ̃]. **1.** *Pr.n.m. Myth:* Telamon. **2.** *s.m. Arch:* telamon; *pl.* telamones, atlantes.

télangiectasie [telɑ̃ʒjɛktazi], *s.f. Med:* telangiectasis, telangiectasia.

télautographe [telɔtɔgraf], *s.m. O: Tg:* telautograph, telewriter.

télautographie [telɔtɔgrafi], *s.f. O:* telautography.

télautographique [telɔtɔgrafik], *a. O:* telautographic.

télé [tele], *s.f. T.V: F:* telly.

télé- [tele], *pref.* tele-.

téléaffichage [teleafiʃɑ:ʒ], *s.m. Elcs:* (*computers, radar*) remote setting-up (of data).

téléaste [teleast], *s.m. & f.* (*a*) worker in television; telecaster; (*b*) television producer.

téléautogramme [teleɔtɔgram], *s.m.* teleautogram.

téléautographe [teleɔtɔgraf], *s.m.* tel(e)autograph, telewriter.

téléautographie [teleɔtɔgrafi], *s.f.* teleautography.

téléautographique [teleɔtɔgrafik], *a.* **appareil t.,** teleautograph.

télébande [telebɑ̃:d], *s.f.* teletape.

télébenne [telebɛn], *s.f.,* **télécabine** [telekabin], *s.f.* telpher carrier, car.

télécinéma [telesinema], *s.m.* telecine, telecinema.

télécommande [telekɔmɑ̃:d], *s.f.* remote control; telecontrol; distant control, radio control; **dispostif de t.,** remote-control system, unit; telecontrol system, unit; *Nau:* **appareil de t.,** follow-up gear.

télécommander [telekɔmɑ̃de], *v.tr.* to operate by remote control, by telecontrol; to radio-control; **télécommandé,** remote-controlled; remotely operated; **avion, bateau, télécommandé,** drone.

télécommunication [telekɔmynikasjɔ̃], *s.f.* telecommunication.

télécran [telekrɑ̃], *s.m.* large-sized telescreen, television screen (for an auditorium).

télécuriethérapie [telekyriterapi], *s.f. Med:* telecurie therapy.

télédétruire [teledetrui:r], *v.tr.* to destroy by remote control.

télédiaphonie [teledjafɔni], *s.f. Elcs:* (*computers*) far-end crosstalk.

télédiffusé [teledifyze], *a.* televised (programme).

télédu [teledy], *s.m. Z:* teledu; Javanese skunk; stinkard; stinking badger.

télédynamie [teledinami], *s.f.* teledynamics.

télédynamique [teledinamik], *a.* teledynamic, telodynamic.

téléférique [teleferik], *a. & s.m.* telpher (railway); teleferic.

téléga [telega], *s.f. Veh:* telega.

télégénique [teleʒenik], *a.* telegenic, who televises well.

télégestion [teleʒɛstjɔ̃], *s.f. Elcs:* (*computers*) teleprocessing, remote processing.

télégonie [telegɔni], *s.f. Biol:* telegony.

télégramme [telegram], *s.m.* telegram; **t. sous-marin,** cable(gram); **t. multiple,** multiple-address telegram; **t. collationné,** repetition-paid telegram; **t. avec réponse payée,** reply-paid telegram; **t. téléphoné,** telephoned telegram; **t. limité,** telegram upon which a late fee is levied for priority of transmission; **envoyer un t. à qn,** to send s.o. a telegram; to wire (to) s.o.; **envoyer un t. pour faire venir qn, qch.,** to wire for s.o., for sth.

télégraphe [telegraf], *s.m.* **1.** (*a*) *A:* semaphore, telegraph; *F:* **faire le t.,** to fling one's arms about; to gesticulate; (*b*) *Tls:* bevel square. **2.** (electric) telegraph; *A:* **t. écrivant,** writing telegraph, ink writer; **t. enregistreur,** recording telegraph; **t. imprimeur,** teletypewriter, ticker; **t. sous-marin,** cable; **aviser qn par le t.,** (i) to wire, (ii) to cable, to s.o. **3.** *Fr.C: F:* person who votes illegally in place of s.o. else.

télégraphie [telegrafi], *s.f.* **1.** telegraphy; *O:* **t. sans fil,** wireless; **t. par courants porteurs,** carrier (current) telegraphy; **t. par déplacement de fréquence,** frequency-shift telegraphy; **t. harmonique,** voice-frequency (multichannel) telegraphy. **2. t. aérienne, optique,** visual signalling.

télégraphier [telegrafje], *v.tr. & i.* (*p.d. & pr.sub.* **n. télégraphiions, v. télégraphiiez**) to telegraph, to wire; to cable; **t. à Paris,** to wire, send a wire, to Paris.

télégraphique [telegrafik], *a.* telegraphic; **adresse t.,** telegraphic address; **dépêche t.,** telegram; **réponse t.,** reply (i) by wire, (ii) by cable; **bureau t.,** telegraph office; **style t.,** telegraphic style, *F:* telegraphese; **fil t.,** telegraph wire.

télégraphiquement [telegrafikmɑ̃]. *adv.* telegraphically.

télégraphiste [telegrafist], *s.m.* telegraphist; telegraph operator; **facteur t.,** telegraph messenger; **petit t.,** telegraph boy.

télègue [telɛg], *s.f. Veh:* (Russian) telega.

téléguidage [telegida:ʒ], *s.m.* radio(-)control; telecontrol; remote control; radio guidance; **t. par ondes haute-fréquence,** command guidance; **t. radio-inertial,** radio-inertial guidance.

téléguidé [telegide], *a.* (command-, radio-) guided; **engin t.,** guided missile.

téléguider [telegide], *v.tr.* to radio-control; to guide (aircraft, missile, etc.); to operate by command guidance, radio guidance, remote control.

téléimprimeur [teleɛ̃primœ:r], *s.m.* teleprinter, telewriter; (*R.t.m.*) Teletype; *U.S:* teletypewriter.

téléjournal, -aux [teleʒurnal, -o], *s.m.* (television) news.

télékinésie [telekinezi], *s.f. Psychics:* telekinesis.

téléloupe [telelup], *s.f. Opt:* telescopic magnifier.

télémanipulateur [telemanipylatœ:r], *s.m. Atom. Ph:* remote manipulator.

Télémaque [telemak], *Pr.n.m. Gr. & Fr.Lit:* Telemachus.

télémark [telemark], *s.m. Ski:* telemark.

télémécanicien [telemekanisjɛ̃], *s.m.* telecommunications engineer, technician.

télémécanique [telemekanik]. **1.** *a.* electrically controlled (at a distance); telemechanic. **2.** *s.f. R.t.m:* telemechanics, telemechanism.

télémesure [teleməzy:r], *s.f. Surv: Elcs:* telemetering, telemetry; **appareil de t.,** telemeter, telemetering system; **émetteur de t.,** telemetry transmitter; **système digital de t.,** digital telemetry system.

télémétacarpalien, -ienne [telemetakarpaljɛ̃, -jɛn], *a. Z:* telemetacarpal.

télémétrage [telemetra:ʒ], *s.m.* telemetering.

télémètre [telemɛtr̥], *s.m.* telemeter; *Mil: etc:* rangefinder; **t. à laser,** laser rangefinder; *Av:* **t. de plafond,** ceiliometer.

télémétrer [telemetre], *v.tr.* (*conj. like* MÉTRER) *Mil: etc:* to telemeter; to take the range of (sth.).

télémétreur /telemetrœ:r], *s.m.* telemetrist, range taker.

télémétrie [telemetri], *s.f.* telemetry; *Mil: etc:* range finding.

télémétrique [telemetrik], *a.* telemetric(al).

télémoteur [telemɔtœ:r], *s.m. Nau:* telemotor.

télencéphale [telɑ̃sefal], *s.m. Anat:* telencephalon.

téléneurone [telenørɔn], *s.m. Anat:* teleneuron.

téléobjectif [teleɔbʒɛktif], *s.m. Phot:* telephoto(graphic) lens, telelens, teleobjective; **photographie au t.,** telephotography.

teleoceras [teleɔseras], *s.m. Paleont:* Teleoceras.

téléologie [teleɔlɔʒi], *s.f. Phil:* teleology.

téléologique [teleɔlɔʒik], *a. Phil:* teleological (argument, etc.).

téléosaure [teleɔsɔ:r], **teleosaurus** [teleɔsɔrys], *s.m. Paleont:* teleosaur(us).

téléosauridés [teleɔsɔride], *s.m.pl. Paleont: Rept:* Teleosauridae.

téléostéen, -enne [teleɔsteɛ̃, -ɛn], *a. Ich:* teleost(ean); *s.m.pl.* teleosts, Teleostei.

téléostomes [teleɔstom], *s.m.pl. Ich:* Teleostomi; the true fish.

Téléoute [teleut], *a. & s.m. & f. Ethn:* Teleut.

télépathe [telepat], *Psychics:* **1.** *a.* telepathic. **2.** *s.m. & f.* telepath(ist).

télépathie [telepati], *s.f. Psychics:* telepathy.

télépathique [telepatik], *a.* telepathic.

téléphérage [telefera:ʒ], *s.m. Ind:* telpherage; overhead cable transport; **ligne de t.,** telpher, telpher way.

téléphérer [telefere], *v.tr.* (**je téléphère, je téléphérerai**) to telpher; to transport (goods, etc.) by telpherage.

téléphérique [teleferik], *a. & s.m.* (**ligne**) **t.,** telpher railway; teleferic; **cabine, nacelle, t.,** cable car.

téléphonage [telefɔna:ʒ], *s.m.* (*a*) *Tchn:* telephoning (of a telegram); (*b*) telephoning; telephone conversation.

téléphone [telefɔn], *s.m.* telephone, *F:* phone; **t. automatique,** automatic telephone, dial telephone, *F:* the automatic; **t. d'abonné,** subscriber's telephone (set); **t. intérieur,** house (tele)phone; interphone, intercom; **t. d'appartement,** room-to-room telephone; **t. bâtiment-terre,** ship to shore telephone; *Pol:* **t. rouge,** hot line (U.S.A. to Kremlin); **t. vert,** hot line (Élysée to Kremlin); *F:* **t. arabe,** bush telephone, grapevine; **être abonné au t.,** to have the telephone installed, to be on the phone; **avez-vous le t.?** are you on the phone? **coup de t.,** telephone call; **appeler qn au t., donner un coup de t. à qn,** to ring s.o. up, to phone s.o., *U.S:* to call s.o. (up); **parler à qn au t., par t.,** to speak to s.o. on the phone; **qui a répondu au t.?** who took the call? who answered the phone? **demander qch. par t.,** to phone for sth.; *F:* **je vais faire venir le gigot par t.,** I'll phone for the leg of lamb.

téléphoner [telefɔne], *v.tr. & i.* **1.** to telephone (a piece of news, etc.); to give (a piece of news, etc.) on the telephone, by (tele)phone. **2. t. à qn,** to ring s.o. up, to phone s.o., *U.S:* to call s.o. (up); **je vous téléphonerai,** I'll give you a ring, a call; I'll ring you up, phone you; **j'ai téléphoné au docteur de venir tout de suite,** I rang the doctor and asked him to come at once. **3.** *Sp:* **t. ses coups,** to telegraph one's strokes, one's punches; *Pol: etc:* **une manœuvre téléphonée,** an obvious manœuvre.

téléphonie [telefɔni], *s.f.* telephony; **t. par fil,** line, wire, telephony; **t. sans fil,** wireless telephony, radio telephony; **t. par courant porteur,** carrier-current telephony; **t. multiple à courants porteurs,** multiple carrier telephony; **t. multivoie par courants porteurs,** multicircuit carrier telephony; **t. par le sol,** ground telephony; **t. automatique,** automatic telephone system.

téléphonique [telefɔnik], *a.* telephonic; **combiné t.,** handset, *F:* receiver; **cabine t.,** telephone booth, call box; **appel t.,** telephone call; **fil t.,** telephone wire; **fréquence t.,** telephone, voice, frequency; **commande téléphonique,** order by telephone.

téléphoniquement [telefɔnikmɑ̃], *a.* telephonically, by (tele)phone.

téléphoniste [telefɔnist], *s.m. & f.* telephonist; telephone operator; *Mil:* telephone orderly; **appeler le, la, t.,** to call the operator.

téléphonomètre [telefɔnɔmɛtr̥], *s.m.* telephone meter.

téléphore [telefɔ:r], *s.m. Ent:* soldier beetle.

téléphote [telefɔt], *s.m. Tg:* telephote.

téléphotographie [telefɔtɔgrafi], *s.f.* **1.** *Tg:* phototelegraphy. **2.** *Phot:* (*a*) telephotography; (*b*) telephotograph.

téléphotographique [telefɔtɔgrafik], *a.* **1.** phototelegraphic. **2.** telephotographic.

téléplasme [teleplasm], *s.m. Psychics:* teleplasm, ectoplasm.

télépointage [telepwɛ̃ta:ʒ], *s.m. Navy:* directing of gunfire by means of a director theodolite; **hune de t.,** director top.
téléportation [teleportasjɔ̃], *s.f.* teleportation.
téléradar [telerada:r], *s.m.* combined use of radar and television; *Av:* **navigation par t.,** teleran.
téléradio [teleradjo], *s.f. Med: F:* teleradiography.
téléradiographie [teleradjɔgrafi], *s.f. Med:* (*a*) teleradiography, tele(o)roentgenography; (*b*) teleradiogram.
télérécepteur [telereseptœ:r], *s.m.* television set.
téléréglage [teleregla:ʒ], *s.m.* remote control, distant control, radio control.
téléréglé [teleregle], *a.* remote-controlled, radio-controlled.
télérégler [teleregle], *v.tr.* (*conj. like* RÉGLER) to operate by remote control, to radio-control.
télérelais [telerəlɛ], *s.m.* distance relay; **t. d'impédance, de réactance,** impedance, reactance, relay.
télérepérage [telerəpera:ʒ], *s.m.* remote location, radio location, remote marking.
télérepéré [telerəpere], *a.* remotely located; radio-located, remotely marked.
télérepérer [telerəpere], *v.tr.* (*conj. like* REPÉRER) to operate by remote location, radar location, remote marking.
téléreportage [telerəpɔrta:ʒ], *s.m.* television newscasting; television commentary (on sports event, etc.).
téléroman [telerɔmɑ̃], *s.m.* television serial.
télérupteur [teleryptœ:r], *s.m. El:* telebreaker.
télérupture [telerypty:r], *s.f. El:* telebreaking.
télescopable [telɛskɔpabl̥], *a.* collapsible, telescopic (drinking cup, etc.).
télescopage [telɛskɔpa:ʒ], *s.m.* **1.** telescoping (of parts, trains, etc.); *Aut:* **t. en série,** pile-up. **2.** *Gasm:* making (a gasholder) telescopic.
télescope [telɛskɔp], *s.m.* telescope; **t. à miroir, à réflexion,** reflecting telescope; **t. électronique,** electron telescope; **pièces assemblées en t.,** parts made to telescope; *Com:* **caisse t.,** telescope box.
télescoper [telɛskɔpe], *v.tr. & pr.* (*a*) (*of railway coaches, etc.*) to telescope; to crumple up; **le train a télescopé la voiture au passage à niveau,** the train crushed the car on the level crossing; **se t.,** to crumple up, to concertina; **voitures qui se sont télescopées,** cars that telescoped (each other); (*b*) *Ling:* to telescope (words).
télescopeur [telɛskɔpœ:r], *a.* (*of train, etc.*) telescoping; colliding; **le camion t. marchait à toute vitesse,** the lorry that caused the collision, the pile-up, was travelling at full speed.
télescopique [telɛskɔpik], *a.* (*a*) telescopic (observation, funnel, etc.); (*b*) telescopic, collapsible; **pied t.,** telescopic leg; **longeron-support t.,** telescopic tie rod.
téléscripteur [teleskriptœ:r], *s.m.* teleprinter, *U.S:* teletypewriter.
téléséisme [teleseism], *s.m. Geol:* teleseism, distant shock.
télésiège [telesjɛ:ʒ], *s.m.* chair lift.
téléski [teleski], *s.m.* drag lift, ski tow.
télésouffleur [telesuflœ:r], *s.m. T.V:* teleprompter.
téléspectateur, -trice [telespɛktatœ:r, -tris], *s.* televiewer, viewer.
téléspectroscope [telespɛktrɔskɔp], *s.m. Astr:* telespectroscope.
téléstéréographe [telestereɔgraf], *s.m.* Belin telephote.
téléstéréoscope [telestereɔskɔp], *s.m. Opt:* telestereoscope.
télesthésie [telɛstezi], *s.f.* telesthesia; telepathy.
télesthésique [telɛstezik], *a.* telesthetic.
télétraitement [teletrɛtmɑ̃], *s.m.* teleprocessing.
télétype [teletip], *a. & s.m.* **(appareil) t.,** teleprinter, (*R.t.m.*) Teletype, *U.S:* teletypewriter.
télétypie [teletipi], *s.f.* teleprinting.
télétypiste [teletipist], *s.m. & f.* teletypist; teletype(writer) operator, teleprinter operator.
téleutospore [teløtɔspɔ:r], *s.f. Fung:* teleutospore. teliospore.
téléviser [televize], *v.tr.* to televise; **journal télévisé,** television news.
téléviseur [televizœ:r], *s.m.* television set; **t. couleur,** colour television (set).
télévision [televizjɔ̃], *s.f.* (*a*) television; **t. en couleur(s),** colour television; **t. en circuit fermé,** closed-circuit television; **t. par antenne collective,** community television; **station de t.,** television broadcast station; **chaîne de t.,** television network; **caméra de t.,** telecamera; **écran de t.,** telescreen; **film de t.,** telefilm; **émettre, diffuser, par t.,** to telecast; **émetteur de t.,** telecaster; **émission de t. en direct,** live television programme; **t. scolaire,** television for schools; **à la t.,** on television; (*b*) *F:* television (set).
télévisuel, -elle [televizɥɛl], *a.* televisual; of, relating to, television; **forme télévisuelle d'une pièce de théâtre,** television version of a play.
Télex [telɛks], *s.m.* (*R.t.m.*) Telex (machine); **abonné du T.,** Telex subscriber; **être relié au (réseau) T.,** to be on the teleprinter.
télexer [telɛkse], *v.tr.* to send by Telex (machine).
télexiste [telɛksist], *s.m. & f.* Telex operator.
telfairia [tɛlfɛrja], *s.m. Bot:* telfairia, oyster nut.
telférage [tɛlfera:ʒ], *s.m.* = TÉLÉPHÉRAGE.
teli [tɛli], *s.m. Bot:* sasswood, sassywood.
tell [tɛl], *s.m.* (*a*) *Geog:* **le T.,** the Tell; (*b*) *Archeol:* tell, occupation site.
tellement [tɛlmɑ̃], *adv.* **1.** *A:* in such a manner, so; **conduisez-vous t. qu'on n'ait rien à vous reprocher,** behave in such a way that, so that, no one has anything to say against you. **2.** to such a degree, so; **c'est t. facile,** it is so very easy; **t. que** + *ind.*, to such an extent that . . .; so . . . that . . .; **il est t. sourd qu'il faut crier,** he is so deaf that one has to shout; *F:* **t. de,** so much, so many; *F:* **ce n'est pas t. beau,** it's not all that beautiful; *A:* **t. quellement,** after a fashion; tolerably well; so so.
tellière [tɛljɛ:r], *a.inv. & s.m.* foolscap (paper) (*from the Chancellor Le Tellier, 1603-85*).
telline [tɛlin], *s.f. Moll:* tellina, sunset shell.
tellinidés [tɛlinide], *s.m.pl. Moll:* Tellinidae.
tellurate [tɛlyrat], *s.m. Ch:* tellurate.
tellure [tɛlly:r], *s.m. Ch:* tellurium; *Miner:* **t. graphique,** graphic tellurium, sylvanite.
telluré [tɛlyre], *a. Ch:* **hydrogène t.,** hydrogen telluride, telluretted hydrogen.
tellureux, -euse [tɛlyrø, -ø:z], *a. Ch:* tellurous.
telluride [tɛlyrid], *s.m. Miner:* telluride.
tellurhydrique [tɛlyridrik], *a. Ch:* **acide t.,** telluretted hydrogen, hydrogen telluride, tellurhydric acid.
tellurien, -ienne [tɛlyrjɛ̃, -jɛn], *a.* tellurian; earth (current).
tellurifère [tɛlyrifɛ:r], *a.* telluriferous.
tellurine [tɛlyrin], *s.f. Miner:* tellurite.
tellurique[1] [tɛlyrik], *a. Ch:* telluric (acid).
tellurique[2], *a.* telluric (fever, etc.); arising from the soil; **secousse t.,** earth tremor; *Geol:* **courants telluriques,** telluric currents; earth, *U.S:* ground, currents; *Min:* **prospection t.,** electromagnetic prospecting; *Opt:* **raie t.,** telluric line.
tellurisme [tɛlyrism], *a.m. Anthr: Med:* tellurism.
tellurite [tɛlyrit], *s.f.* **1.** *Miner:* tellurite. **2.** *Ch:* tellurite.
tellurium [tɛlyrjɔm], *s.m. Miner:* tellurium.
tellurohmmètre [tɛlyrɔmmɛtr̥], *s.m. Elcs:* tellurohmmeter.
telluromètre [tɛlyrɔmɛtr̥], *s.m. Elcs:* tellurometer.
tellurure [tɛlyry:r], *s.m. Ch:* telluride.
téloblaste [telɔblast], *s.m. Biol:* teloblast.
télocentrique [telɔsɑ̃trik], *a. Biol:* telocentric.
télodynamique [telɔdinamik], *a.* telodynamic, teledynamic.
télolécithe [telɔlesit], *a. Biol:* telolecithal.
télophase [telɔfa:z], *s.f. Biol:* telophase.
télougou [telugu], *a. & s.m. Ling:* Telugu.
telphérage [tɛlfera:ʒ], *s.m.* = TÉLÉPHÉRAGE.
telphérer [tɛlfere], *v.tr.* = TÉLÉPHÉRER.
telson [tɛlsɔ̃], *s.m. Crust:* telson.
Telstar [tɛlsta:r], *Pr.n.m. Telecom:* Telstar.
téméraire [temerɛ:r]. **1.** *a.* (*a*) rash, reckless, headstrong, foolhardy, daring; *Hist:* **Charles le T.,** Charles the Bold; (*b*) rash (judgment, statement); reckless (statement). **2.** *s.m. & f.* rash person; daredevil.
témérairement [temerɛrmɑ̃], *adv.* rashly, recklessly, daringly; in a daredevil manner.
témérité [temerite], *s.f.* **1.** temerity, rashness, recklessness, foolhardiness. **2.** rash deed; piece of daring; bold, daring, speech.
temnospondyles [temnɔspɔ̃dil], *s.m.pl. Amph:* Temnospondyli.
témoignage [temwaɲa:ʒ], *s.m.* **1.** (*a*) testimony, evidence; **recueillir des témoignages,** to collect evidence; **porter t.,** to certify, bear witness, give evidence; **rendre t. de qch.,** (i) to give evidence about sth.; (ii) to bear testimony to sth.; **rendre t. à la vérité,** to bear testimony, bear witness, to the truth; **rendre t. à qn.,** to testify in s.o.'s favour; **je vous rends ce témoignage que . . .,** I will say this in your favour that . . .; **rendre t. à Dieu,** to testify; **appeler qn en t.,** to call s.o. as witness, in testimony; **invoquer le t. de qn,** to call s.o. to witness; **faux t.,** false witness, false evidence; perjury; (*b*) evidence; statement; **d'après son t.,** according to his statement; **être appelé en t.,** to be called upon to give evidence; **t. des sens,** evidence of the senses; **ne s'en rapporter qu'au t. de ses yeux,** to believe only what one sees; **donner des témoignages de sa compétence,** to give evidence of one's ability. **2.** *Jur:* hearing (of witnesses). **3. t. d'amitié,** token of friendship; **en t. de mon estime,** as a mark, a token, of my esteem.
témoigner [temwaɲe]. **1.** *v.i.* to testify; to bear witness; to give evidence; **t. en faveur de qn,** to give evidence in s.o.'s favour; **les faits témoignent en faveur de son dire,** the facts corroborate his statements; **t. contre qn,** to bear witness against s.o.; **tout témoignait contre lui,** everything told against him. **2.** *v.tr. or ind.tr.* **t. (de) qch.,** to show, prove, sth.; to bear testimony to, bear witness to, testify to, sth.; to give evidence of sth.; **t. sa bonne volonté, t. de bonne volonté,** to prove, give proof of, (one's) good will; **t. d'un goût pour . . .,** to show, display, a taste for . . .; **t. sa reconnaissance à qn,** (i) to give expression to, (ii) to give proof of, one's gratitude to s.o.; **t. de l'intérêt à qn,** to show an interest in s.o.; **t. du dédain à qn,** to show contempt for s.o.; **réponse qui témoigne un esprit juste,** answer that shows a judicious mind; **ses écrits témoignent de son travail acharné,** his writings bear witness to his strenuous efforts, his desperately hard work; **par leurs gestes ils témoignèrent qu'ils ne demandaient qu'à nous aider,** by their gestures they showed that they were only too anxious to help us.
témoin [temwɛ̃], *s.m.* **1.** (*a*) witness; **être t. d'un accident,** to witness an accident; *Jur:* **t. à un acte,** witness to a signature; **elle fut t. de son action,** she (actually) saw him do it; **parler à qn sans témoins,** to speak to s.o. in private, without witnesses; **mes yeux en sont témoins,** I saw it with my own eyes; (*b*) *Jur:* **t. à charge, à décharge,** witness for the prosecution, for the defence; **barre des témoins,** witness box; **le premier t. a été la femme de l'accusé,** the first witness was the wife of the accused; **t. oculaire,** eye witness; **citer qn comme t.,** to call s.o. as witness; **appeler, prendre, qn à t.,** to call, take, s.o. to witness; **je vous prends tous à témoin que . . .,** I take you all to witness that . . .; **Dieu m'est t. que . . .,** God is my witness that . . .; **Dieu m'est t. si je vous ai aimé!** God knows how much I loved you! **t. les coups que j'ai reçus,** witness the blows which I received; (*c*) second (in duel); **envoyer ses témoins à qn,** to send s.o. a challenge (by one's seconds). **2.** (= TÉMOIGNAGE) **témoins de la piété de nos aïeux,** proofs, evidences, of the piety of our ancestors; *Jur:* **en t. de quoi . . .,** in witness whereof. . . . **3.** (*a*) boundary mark; *For:* border tree left standing; *Aut:* **t. d'aile,** wing indicator; feeler; (*b*) sample; fag-end (of new rope); *Min:* sample core (of bore); *Civ.E:* old man, dumpling (left in excavation); *Geol:* outlier; *Metall:* test button; *Ch:* reference solution; **échantillon t.,** check sample; *Phot:* **plaque t.,** reference plate; **épreuve t.,** pilot print; (*c*) *El.E: Ind: etc:* **lampe t.,** telltale lamp, signal lamp, pilot light, warning light; (*d*) *Bookb:* (i) **laisser les témoins,** to leave proof (uncut); (ii) **laisser un témoin,** to leave a dog's ear (showing size before trimming); (*e*) *Sp:* baton, etc. (passed from hand to hand in relay race); (*f*) **denrée t.,** basic commodity; (*g*) **appartement t.,** show flat.
tempe[1] [tɑ̃:p], *s.f. Anat:* temple; **frappé à la t.,** struck on the temple.
tempe[2], *s.f. Tex:* temple, tenter, tension frame.
Tempé [tɛ̃pe, tɑ̃pe], *Pr.n.f. A.Geog:* **la vallée de T.,** the vale of Tempe.
tempera (a) [atɑ̃pera], *Art:* (*a*) *adj.phr.* **peinture a t.,** tempera painting; (*b*) *adv.phr.* **peindre a t.,** to paint in tempera.
tempérament [tɑ̃peramɑ̃], *s.m.* **1.** (*a*) (physical) constitution, temperament; **son t. de fer,** his iron constitution; **paresseux par t.,** constitutionally lazy; **se tuer le t.,** to ruin one's constitution; (*b*) (moral) temperament; **t. violent;** violent temper; **t. placide,** placid, easy-going, temperament; **il n'est pas d'un t. à se laisser duper,** he's not the sort of person who lets himself be tricked; (*c*) **avoir du t.,** to have character; (*d*) *A:* (amorous) temperament; **avoir du t.,** to be of an amorous disposition. **2.** (*a*) *A:* moderation, spirit of compromise, conciliatory spirit; **garder en tout un certain t.,** to observe a golden mean in all things, a certain measure in all things; **ne garder aucun t.,** to abandon all restraint; to ride roughshod over people; **circonstances où les règles doivent admettre quelque t.,** circumstances when rules should allow some modification; (*b*) *Mus:* temperament (of the intervals

of the scale); **accorder par t.**, to set the temperament (in piano tuning). **3.** *Com:* **à t.**, by instalments, on the instalment system, on the deferred payment system; **vente à t.**, hire purchase, sale on the deferred payment system; **crédit à t.**, instalment credit.

tempéramental, -aux [tɑ̃peramɑ̃tal, -o], *a.* temperamental, constitutional; **variations tempéramentales inhérentes**, inherent constitutional variations.

tempérance [tɑ̃perɑ̃:s], *s.f.* (*a*) temperance, moderation; (*b*) temperance; teetotalism; **société de t.**, temperance society.

tempérant [tɑ̃perɑ̃]. **1.** *a.* (*a*) temperate, moderate, (person); (*b*) temperate, abstemious. **2.** *a. & s.m. Med: A:* sedative.

température [tɑ̃peraty:r], *s.f.* temperature; **t. du corps humain**, temperature of the human body; **chauffer à la t. du corps humain**, to raise to blood heat; *Med: F:* **avoir, faire, de la t.**, to have a (high) temperature; *Ph:* **t. d'ébullition**, boiling point; **t. de la glace fondante**, freezing point (of water); **t. des couleurs**, colour temperature; **t. du rouge**, red heat; **t. ambiante**, room temperature; *F:* **prendre la t. de l'auditoire**, to sense the audience, to gauge the temperature of the audience, the meeting.

tempéré [tɑ̃pere], *a.* **1.** temperate, moderate (climate, speech); restrained, sober (style); **les zones tempérées**, the temperate zones; **monarchie tempérée**, constitutional monarchy. **2.** *Mus:* **gamme tempérée**, equally tempered scale.

tempérer [tɑ̃pere], *v.tr.* (**je tempère, n. tempérons; je tempérerai**) to temper, moderate (heat, passions, etc.); **les pins tempèrent le caractère du paysage**, the pinewoods soften the landscape; **t. l'âcreté d'une boisson**, to modify the bitterness of a drink.

se tempérer, (*of the wind, etc.*) to moderate; (*of pers.*) to keep one's temper; to calm down.

tempête [tɑ̃pɛt], *s.f.* storm (of wind); *Nau:* hurricane; (*on barometer*) **t.**, stormy; **dommage causé par la t.**, storm damage; **t. de neige**, blizzard, snowstorm; **le vent souffle en t.**, it's blowing a hurricane; *Nau:* it is blowing great guns; **essuyer une t.**, to weather a storm; **battu par la t.** storm-beaten (coast); storm-tossed (ship); **il faisait une t.**, a storm was raging; **une t. dans un verre d'eau**, a storm in a teacup; **gare la t.!** look out for squalls! **calmer la t.**, to pour oil on troubled waters; **t. d'injures, d'applaudissements**, storm of abuse, of applause; *Geog: A:* **le cap des Tempêtes**, the Cape of Good Hope.

tempêter [tɑ̃pete], *v.i.* (*of pers.*) to storm; to rage, fume; *F:* to let off steam; **il tempêtait contre son patron**, he was fulminating against his boss; **t. contre l'injustice**, to rage, storm, about injustice.

tempétueusement [tɑ̃petɥøzmɑ̃], *adv.* tempestuously; stormily.

tempétueux, -euse [tɑ̃petɥø, -ø:z], *a.* (*a*) tempestuous; stormy (wind, sea, etc.); **accueil t.**, boisterous welcome, reception; *Lit:* **dans le courant t. de la vie**, in the tempestuous stream of life; (*b*) (*of pers.*) violent; who is always raging, fuming, about sth.

tempia [tɑ̃pja], *s.m.*, **temple**[1] [tɑ̃:pl], *s.m.*, **templet** [tɑ̃plɛ], *s.m. Tex:* temple, tenter, tension frame.

temple[2], *s.m.* (*a*) (pagan) temple; (*b*) (protestant) church, chapel; (*c*) (freemasons') temple; (*d*) *Jewish Rel:* **le T.**, the Temple (of Jerusalem); (*e*) *Hist:* **le T.**, the Temple (of the Knights Templars); **les chevaliers du T.**, the Knights Templars, the Knights of the Temple; (*f*) *Hist:* **le T.**, the Temple (prison); (*g*) *Lit:* **votre maison est pour moi le t. de la vertu**, your house is for me a temple of virtue; **la Bourse est le t. de la spéculation**, the Stock Exchange is the holy of holies of the speculator.

templer [tɑ̃ple], *v.tr. Tex:* to tenter (cloth).

templier [tɑ̃plije], *s.m. Hist:* (Knight) Templar; *F:* **jurer comme un t.**, to swear like a trooper.

tempo [tɛ̃po, tɛmpo], *s.m.* (*a*) *Mus:* tempo; (*b*) tempo (of modern life, etc.).

temporaire [tɑ̃pɔrɛ:r], *a.* **1.** temporary (authority, employee, etc.); provisional; *Astr:* **étoile t.**, temporary star, nova; *Dent:* **dents temporaires**, milk teeth. **2.** *Mus:* **valeur t. d'une note**, time value of a note.

temporairement [tɑ̃pɔrɛrmɑ̃], *adv.* temporarily; provisionally; for the time being.

temporal, -ale, -aux [tɑ̃pɔral, -o], *Anat:* **1.** *a.* temporal (bone, artery). **2.** *s.m.* (*a*) temporal bone; (*b*) temporal muscle, temporalis. **3.** *s.f.* **temporale**, temporal (artery).

temporalité [tɑ̃pɔralite], *s.f.* (*a*) *Ecc:* temporality, temporalty; temporal power; (*b*) *Phil:* temporality; (*c*) *Gram:* temporality (of a clause).

temporel, -elle [tɑ̃pɔrɛl]. **1.** *a.* (*a*) temporal (as opposed to eternal); (*b*) temporal (as opposed to spiritual); **puissance temporelle**, temporal power; **pouvoir t.**, temporal power (of the Pope); (*c*) *Gram:* temporal (clause, etc.). **2.** *s.m.* (*a*) temporal power; (*b*) temporalities, temporalties, revenue (of benefice).

temporellement [tɑ̃pɔrɛlmɑ̃], *adv.* temporally.

temporisateur, -trice [tɑ̃pɔrizatœ:r, -tris]. **1.** *s.* temporizer; procrastinator. **2.** *a.* temporizing. **3.** *s.m.* (*a*) *El:* (automatic) time switch; (*b*) (*welding*) timer.

temporisation [tɑ̃pɔrizasjɔ̃], *s.f.* **1.** temporization, temporizing; calculated delay. **2.** *El: Ind: etc:* timing; fitting with a time-delay system.

temporisé [tɑ̃pɔrize], *a. El: Elcs:* time(-delay) (relay); time-lag (device).

temporiser [tɑ̃pɔrize], *v.i.* to temporize; to put off action deliberately; to play for time.

temporiseur [tɑ̃pɔrizœ:r], *s.m.* temporizer; procrastinator; *A.Hist:* **Fabius Maximus le T.**, Fabius Maximus Cunctator.

temporo- [tɑ̃pɔrɔ], *pref.* temporo-.

temporo-auriculaire [tɑ̃pɔrɔorikylɛ:r], *a. Anat:* temporo-auricular; *pl. temporo-auriculaires.*

temporo-facial, -aux [tɑ̃pɔrɔfasjal, -o], *a. Anat:* temporofacial.

temporo-mastoïdien [tɑ̃pɔrɔmastɔidjɛ̃], *a.m. & s.m. Anat:* temporomastoid; *pl. temporo-mastoïdiens.*

temporo-maxillaire [tɑ̃pɔrɔmaksilɛ:r], *a. Anat:* temporomaxillary; *pl. temporo-maxillaires.*

temporo-pariétal, -aux [tɑ̃pɔrɔparjetal, -o], *a. Anat:* temporoparietal.

temps [tɑ̃], *s.m.* **1.** (*a*) time; **mettre beaucoup de t. à faire qch.**, to take a long time over (doing) sth.; **rattraper le t. perdu**, to make up for lost time; **tuer le t.**, to kill time; **vous avez le t. voulu**, you have enough time, as much time as you need; **vous avez bien le t., vous avez tout le t.**, you have plenty of time; **on a tout le t.**, there's no (need to) hurry; **cela prend du t.**, it takes, requires, time; **prendre tout son t.**, to take one's time; **prenez votre t.**, take your time, don't hurry; **le t. de** + *inf.*, **le t. que** + *subj.*, (i) until; (ii) by the time that; (iii) while; **(donnez-moi) le t. de signer, que je signe, et je suis à vous**, just give me time, a minute, to sign my letters and I'll be with you; **je n'ai pas de t. à perdre avec des gens qui n'ont rien à faire**, I've no time for idlers; I've no time to chat with people who have nothing to do; **nous n'avons pas le t. à présent**, there's no time now; **nous n'avons que le t. de . . .**, we have only just time to . . .; **combien de t. faut-il pour . . .?** how long does it take to . . .? **mettre un t. interminable à faire qch.** to take an interminably long time, *F:* ages, years, doing sth.; **gagner du t.**, (i) to gain time; (ii) to temporize, to play for time; **qui gagne du t. gagne tout, tout est affaire de t.**, time is everything; **perdre du t.**, to waste time; **dans le cours du t., dans la suite du t., avec le t.**, in the process of time, in course of time, with time; **elle est devenue laide avec le t.**, in the course of time, as time went on, passed, she became ugly; **cela rapportera avec le t.**, it will pay in the long run; **usé par le t.**, worn by the passage of time; **de t. en t.**, now and then; from time to time; occasionally; every so often; **il nous fait de t. en t. une petite visite le soir**, he looks in, drops in, on us from time to time in the evening; **une fois de t. à autre**, once in a while; **en d'autres t.**, at any other time; **en tout t.**, at all times; **en même t.**, at the same time; **parler tous en même t.**, to speak all at once, at the same time; **courir les cent mètres dans le même temps que le champion**, to run the hundred metres in the same time as the champion; **emploi à plein t.**, full-time employment; **travailler à plein t.**, to work full time; **prendre, se donner, du bon t.**, to have a good time, to enjoy oneself; to lead a gay life; *Prov:* **le t., c'est de l'argent**, time is money; *Myth: etc:* **le T.**, (Father) Time; (*b*) time, period; **un (certain) t., quelque t.**, for a while, for a time; **cela ne durera qu'un t.**, it will only last for a time, a while; it won't last for ever; **tout n'a qu'un t.**, there is an end to everything; **il restera alité pendant quelque t.**, he will have to stay in bed for some time (yet); **chaque chose a son t.**, everything has its day; **en t. de guerre**, in wartime; **le t. de la moisson**, harvest time; **le t. des cerises**, the cherry season; **T. de l'Ascension**, Ascensiontide; *T.V:* **t. d'antenne**, viewing time; **il y a peu de t.**, a little while ago; not long ago; **peu de t. après**, not long after; **pendant quelque t.**, for a time, for a short while; **d'ici quelque t.**, for some time to come; **au bout de quelque t., d'un certain t.**, after a certain time, a certain while; **au bout de très peu de t.**, in a very short space of time; **entre t.**, meanwhile; **il est beau t. qu'il est parti**, he left a long time ago; **depuis beau t. les journaux protestent**, the papers have been protesting for a long time, *F:* for ages; **un t. de course suivi d'un t. de marche**, a period of running followed by a period of walking; **faire un t. de galop**, to have a short gallop, to gallop for a time; **t. d'arrêt**, pause, halt; **marquer un t.**, to pause; (*c*) term (of service, etc.); **faire son t.**, to serve one's time; (*of convict*) to serve one's sentence, to do one's time; **travaux forcés à t.**, term of penal servitude; **bannissement à t.**, banishment for a term of years; **soldat qui a fait son t.**, time-expired soldier; **cette théorie a fait son t.**, this theory is out of date, outdated; **mode qui a fait son t.**, fashion that has seen its day; out-of-date fashion; (*d*) *Mec.E:* **t. à vide**, off-load period (of machine, etc.); **t. de fonctionnement**, running time (of machine); **t. de bon fonctionnement**, operating time; **t. actif, inactif**, active, inactive, time (of system, etc.); **t. mort**, idle time, period (of machine, etc.); dead time; interruption; *Av:* **t. mort au sol**, turn-round time; time lag; *Ind:* **étude des temps et méthodes**, time and method engineering; **étude des temps et ordonnancements**, time and motion study; *El: Elcs:* **t. d'ouverture**, "on" period; **t. de fermeture**, "off" period, break time; **t. de parcours électronique**, electron transit time; (*computers*) **ordinateur travaillant en t. partagé**, time-sharing computer; **utilisation (d'un ordinateur) en t. partagé**, time sharing; **exploiter (un ordinateur) en t. partagé**, to time-share; **t. d'accélération**, acceleration time; **t. de décélération**, deceleration time, stop time; **t. d'accès**, access time, read time; **t. d'attente**, (i) idle time, waiting time; (ii) latency (time); **t. machine**, computer time; **t. de panne**, down time, fault time; **t. de préparation**, set-up time; **en t. réel**, real time; **base de t.**, time base; clock; **fréquence de (la) base de t.**, clock frequency; (*e*) age, days, time(s); **les t. préhistoriques**, prehistoric times; **les hauts t.**, remote antiquity; **le bon vieux t.**, the good old days; **ce pays n'est plus l'Angleterre des t. passés**, this country is no longer the England of the past; **dans le t., au t. jadis**, in times past, in the old days; **dans la suite des t.**, in the course of time; **en d'autres t.**, (i) formerly, in other times; (ii) in time to come; **dans ce t.-là**, at that time; **ces t.-ci**, these days; **ce fut un grand homme dans son t.**, he was a great man in his day; **elle a eu son t. de beauté**, she was a beauty in her day; **du t., au t., de Napoléon**, in Napoleon's time; **du t. de ma jeunesse, du t. où j'étais jeune**, when I was young; in my youth; **du t. où j'étais le maître d'hôtel du marquis**, when I was butler to his lordship; **sa pensée revenait sur le t. où il était encore jeune avocat**, his mind went back to (the time) when he was a young barrister; **les t. sont durs**, times are hard; **il fut un t. où . . .**, there was a time when . . .; **signe des t.**, sign of the times; **par le t. qui court, par les t. qui courent**, as things are at present; in these days; **être de son t., marcher, vivre, avec son t.**, to move with the times; to be up-to-date, *F:* with it; **vous n'êtes pas de votre t.**, you're behind the times; **de notre t.**, in our days; **il n'en était pas ainsi de mon t.**, it wasn't so in my day; **cela est arrivé de mon t.**, it happened in my time, within my memory; **de tout t., en tout t.**, at all times; **de tout t. il a été ainsi**, it has always been like that; (*f*) time; hour; **arriver à t.**, to arrive in (good) time; **arriver juste à t.**, to arrive just in time, in the nick of time; **je ne suis pas arrivé à t.**, I didn't arrive in time; I was too late; **je me suis échappé de la maison juste à t.**, I escaped from the house just in time, none too soon; **en t. voulu, utile**, in due time; **je serai de retour en t. voulu**, I shall be back in, on, time; **il est t. qu'elle descende**, it is time she came down; **il est t. de rebrousser chemin**, we had better be, it is time to be, going back; **il est t. pour le gouvernement de prendre une décision**, it is time the government reached a decision; **il est grand t. que . . .**, it's high time, about time, that . . .; **il se fait t., il est t., de partir**, it's about time to start; **il serait t.!** it's about time! **il n'est plus t.**, it is too late; **il n'était que t.**, it was only just in time; **il n'est que t. de faire cela**, it's high time to do this; **il était t.!** it was a narrow escape! (*of event*) **venir en son t.**, to be timely; (*g*) *Astr:* **t. apparent**, apparent time; **t. vrai**, true time; **t. moyen**, mean time; **t. moyen de Greenwich**,

Greenwich mean time; **t. moyen local,** local mean time; *Nau:* **t. moyen du bord,** ship's mean time; **t. astronomique,** astronomical time; **t. sidéral,** sideral time; **t. sidéral de Greenwich,** Greenwich sideral time; **t. sidéral local,** local sideral time; **t. solaire,** solar time; **équation du t.,** equation of time; *Nau:* **(table de la) connaissance des temps,** nautical almanac; (*h*) time, occasion, opportunity; **il y a t. pour tout,** there is a time for everything; **chaque chose en son t.,** everything in good time; that's a bridge we'll cross when we come to it; **en t. et lieu,** in the proper time and place; **prendre son t.,** to choose one's time; **faire chaque chose en son t.,** to do everything at the proper time; **je le ferai à mon t.,** I shall do it in my own time, when it suits me. 2. weather; **par tous les t.,** in all weathers; **vous sortez par un pareil t.! par le t. qu'il fait!** you're going out in such weather, in weather like this, in this weather! **quel t. fait-il?** what's the weather like? what sort of weather is it? **quelque t. qu'il fasse il ne manque jamais sa promenade,** whatever the weather (is like) he never misses his walk; si **le t. le permet,** weather permitting; **beau t.,** fine weather; *F:* **il fera beau t. quand je ferai cela,** it'll be a long time before I do that; *Nau:* **gros t.,** heavy weather; **forcé par le gros t. de . . .,** compelled by the stress of weather to . . .; **t. gris, t. couvert,** overcast weather; **t. brumeux,** misty, hazy, weather; **le t. est au brouillard,** it's foggy; **le t. est à la pluie,** it looks like rain; we're going to have rain; **le t. est au beau,** the weather is settled; we're in for a spell of fine weather; **un t. de saison,** seasonable weather, normal weather for the time of year; **prévision du t.,** weather forecast; **une robe couleur du t.,** a sky-blue dress. 3. *Gram:* (*a*) tense; **t. primitifs,** principal parts (of a verb); (*b*) **adverbes de t.,** adverbs of time. 4. (*a*) *Mus:* measure, beat; **mesure à quatre t.,** common time, four-four time; **mesure à trois t.,** three-part time, three-four time; (*b*) *Mil: etc:* **exercice en trois t.,** exercise in three motions; **au t.!** as you were! **au t. pour moi,** (i) I (have done something wrong and) shall have to start all over again; (ii) (sorry,) my mistake! *Fenc:* **coup de t.,** time thrust, feint; *F:* **je vais vous faire ça en deux t. trois mouvements,** I'll have it done in less than no time, in two shakes (of a lamb's tail); (*c*) *I.C.E:* **moteur à deux, à quatre, t.,** two-stroke, four-stroke, engine; (*d*) *Surg: etc:* **les t. successifs d'une opération,** the successive steps, stages, in an operation; **l'accouchement comprend trois t.,** labour has three phases.

tenable [tənabl̩], *a.* (*usu. with negation*) **1.** *Mil: etc:* tenable, defensible (position); **la position n'était plus t.,** the position was no longer tenable, it was impossible to hold out any longer. **2.** bearable (state of affairs); **par cette chaleur, le bureau n'est pas t.,** in this heat the office is unbearable.

tenace[1] [tənas], *a.* (*a*) tenacious; obstinate (pers.); adhesive (matter); clinging (perfume); tough, cohesive (metal); stiff (soil); fast (colour); dogged, stubborn (will, purpose); retentive (memory); persistent (prejudice, illness); **brillant t.,** lasting shine; **espoir t.,** fond hope; **les vieilles habitudes sont tenaces,** old habits die hard; (*b*) *Bot:* (i) clinging; (ii) resistant; (*c*) *A:* close-fisted, miserly.

tenace[2], *s.f. Cards:* tenace; **être t.,** to hold the tenace.

tenacement [tənasmɑ̃], *adv.* tenaciously.

ténacité [tenasite], *s.f.* **1.** tenacity; *Metall:* tensile strength; strength (of paper, etc.); toughness (of iron, hemp); adhesiveness, stickiness (of glue); retentiveness (of memory); stubbornness (of will); **t. de caractère,** steadfastness of purpose; **avec t.,** tenaciously. **2.** *A:* miserliness.

tenaille [tənɑːj], *s.f.* **1.** *Tls:* (*a*) **t. de forge,** blacksmith's tongs; **t. (de forge) creuse,** pincer tongs, anvil tongs; **t. à vis,** hand vice; **t. à chanfrein(er),** bevelled vice-clamp; **t. de cordonnier,** shoemaker's nippers; **t. continue,** (wire-)drawing pliers; (*b*) *pl.* **tenailles,** pincers (for drawing nails); *Mil:* **manœuvre en tenailles,** pincer movement. **2.** *Fort:* tenail(le); **double t.,** double tenail(le). **3.** *A.Arm:* martel-de-fer.

tenaillé [tənɑje], *a. Fort:* **tracé t.,** tenail(le) line.

tenaillement [tənɑjmɑ̃], *s.m. A:* torture with (red-hot) pincers.

tenailler [tənɑje], *v.tr.* (*a*) *A:* to tear (criminal's flesh) with (red-hot) pincers; (*b*) **tenaillé par le remords,** racked, tortured, by remorse; **tenaillé par la faim,** gnawed by hunger.

tenaillon [tənɑjɔ̃], *s.m. Fort:* tenaillon.

ténalgie [tenalʒi], *s.f. Med:* tenalgia.

tenancier, -ière [tənɑ̃sje, -jɛːr], *s.* **1.** *A:* holder (of land); **grand t.,** great vassal, feudatory, feudal lord; **franc t.,** freeholder, yeoman. **2.** tenant farmer. **3.** keeper (of gambling den); lessee (of bar, casino, etc.); proprietor, -tress (of bar); *s.f.* **tenancière,** madam (of brothel).

tenant, -ante [tənɑ̃, -ɑ̃ːt]. **1.** *a.* (*a*) *used in* **séance tenante,** (i) during the sitting; (ii) forthwith, then and there, on the spot; (*b*) *Cost:* attached; **chemise col t.,** shirt with collar attached. **2.** *s.* (*a*) champion, defender (of s.o., of an opinion); supporter (of government, etc.); taker (of a bet); (*b*) *Sp:* holder (of title); (*c*) *s.m. Her:* supporter (of shield, represented by human figure); *Arch:* supporting figure. **3.** *s.m.* (*of landed property*) **tout d'un t., d'un seul t.,** continuous; all in one block; lying together; *pl.* **tenants,** lands bordering on, marching with, an estate; (*cf.* ABOUTISSANT 2); **tenants et aboutissants,** (i) adjacent parts (of estate); (ii) ins and outs, full details (of an affair); **savoir, connaître, les tenants et aboutissants de l'affaire,** to know the ins and outs of the case.

Ténare [tenaːr], *Pr.n. A.Geog:* **le cap T.,** Cape Taenarus.

tendage [tɑ̃daːʒ], *s.m.* stretching (of rope, wire).

tendance [tɑ̃dɑ̃ːs], *s.f.* tendency, inclination, propensity, trend, turn; the trend of opinion; **tendances vers le communisme,** communist leanings; **la t. générale de son caractère,** the general bent of his character; **avoir (une) t. à qch., à faire qch.,** to be inclined to sth., to do sth.; to have a tendency to sth., to do sth.; to be apt, liable, to do sth.; **t. à se griser,** propensity for getting drunk; **livre à t.,** tendentious book; *Ph:* **t. des corps vers un centre,** tendency of bodies (to move) towards a centre.

tendanciel, -ielle [tɑ̃dɑ̃sjɛl], *a.* having a (particular) tendency.

tendancieusement [tɑ̃dɑ̃sjøzmɑ̃], *adv.* tendentiously.

tendancieux, -ieuse [tɑ̃dɑ̃sjø, -jøːz], *a.* tendentious, tendencious, tendential; *Jur:* **question tendancieuse,** leading question; **interprétation tendancieuse,** tendentious, biased, interpretation; forced interpretation.

tende [tɑ̃ːd], *s.f. Cu:* **t. de tranche,** topside (of beef).

tendelet [tɑ̃dlɛ], *s.m. A: Nau:* awning, tilt, canopy (of boat's stern); hood (of steam launch); *Veh:* awning; *Aut:* hood.

tendelin [tɑ̃dlɛ̃], *s.m. Vit:* wooden basket, pannier (for transporting grapes).

tendelle [tɑ̃dɛl], *s.f. Ven:* snare (for thrushes).

tender [tɑ̃dɛːr], *s.m. Rail: Nau:* tender.

tenderie [tɑ̃dri], *s.f.* **1.** setting of traps and snares (to catch birds). **2.** *A:* spreading of streets with carpets for a solemn entry (of king).

tenderolle [tɑ̃drɔl], *s.f. Nau:* mizzen topmast staysail.

tendeur, -euse [tɑ̃dœːr, -øːz]. **1.** *s.* (*a*) layer (of carpets); hanger (of tapestries); (*b*) setter, layer (of traps, snares); (*c*) *s.m.* poacher; bird-netter. **2.** *s.m. Tchn:* stretcher, tightener, tensioner, brace rod, tension rod; slack adjuster (for telephone wires); take-up; (*a*) **t. pour fil de fer,** wire strainer; turnbuckle; **t. de courroie,** belt tightener; stretcher pulley; *Tel: etc:* **t. de haubans,** stay tightener; *Aut:* **t. du châssis,** tension rod; *Cy:* **t. de chaîne,** chain adjuster, tightener; *Av: etc:* **t. automatique de câble,** cable tension compensator; **t. à vis,** turnbuckle; **t. jambe de force,** radius arm; **t. (de cordon de tente),** runner (of guy rope); *a.* **écrou t.,** adjusting nut; **fil t.,** bracing wire; **renvoi t., galet t.,** tension block, tension pulley; (*b*) tension (device) (of sewing machine); (*c*) **t. pour chaussures,** shoe tree; **t. de pantalon,** trouser stretcher.

tendières [tɑ̃djɛːr], *s.f.pl. Const:* horizontal scaffolding poles; (scaffolding) transoms.

tendineux, -euse [tɑ̃dinø, -øːz], *a. Anat:* tendinous; **réflexe t.,** tendon reflex; **viande tendineuse,** stringy meat.

tendinite [tɑ̃dinit], *s.f. Med:* tendinitis.

tendoir [tɑ̃dwaːr], *s.m.*, **tendoire** [tɑ̃dwaːr], *s.f.* (*a*) *Tex:* tenter; (*b*) *Dy:* drying-pole; (*c*) *O:* clothes-line, drying-line.

tendon [tɑ̃dɔ̃], *s.m. Anat:* tendon, sinew; **t. d'Achille,** Achilles tendon; **t. du jarret,** hamstring; **t. conjoint,** conjoint, conjoined, tendon.

tendre[1] [tɑ̃ːdr̥]. **1.** *a.* tender; (*a*) soft (stone, porcelain, wood, metal, grass, pencil, etc.); delicate (colour, etc.); new (bread); **viande t.,** tender meat; **peau t.,** sensitive, tender, skin; **avoir la peau t.,** to be thin-skinned, easily ruffled; to be touchy; *A:* **être t. à la tentation,** to be easily tempted; *Equit:* **cheval t. à l'éperon,** horse tender to the spur; **cheval à la bouche t.,** tender-mouthed horse; **être t. aux mouches,** (i) (*of horse*) to be sensitive to flies; (ii) *F: A:* (*of pers.*) to be thin-skinned; (*b*) early (age, childhood); **dès ma plus t. enfance,** from my earliest youth; (*c*) fond, affectionate, loving; **avoir le cœur t.,** to be tender-hearted; **paroles tendres,** fond words; **ne pas être t.,** to be hard, severe; **avoir le vin t.,** to be maudlin in one's cups. **2.** *s.m. F:* **avoir un t. pour qn,** to have a soft spot, a soft place in one's heart, for s.o. **3.** *s.m. Cu:* **t. de tranche,** topside (of beef).

tendre[2]. **1.** *v.tr.* (*a*) to stretch, tighten; **t. une corde (de violon),** to tighten a (violin) string; **t. une courroie,** to stretch, tighten, a belt; **t. la peau d'un tambour,** to brace a drum; **t. un arc,** to bend, draw, a bow; **t. un ressort, un piège,** to set a spring, a trap; **t. tous les ressorts du gouvernement,** to strain every resource of the Government; (*b*) to fix up (tent, net, ropes, etc.); to spread (sail, net, etc.); to lay (carpet); to hang (wallpaper, tapestry); to pitch (tent); **église tendue de noir,** church hung, draped, with black; **chambre tendue de (papier) bleu,** room papered in blue; **barques tendues de voiles blanches,** boats with a spread of white sails; (*c*) to stretch out, hold out; **t. la main,** (i) to hold out, offer, *Lit:* proffer, one's hand; (ii) to beg; **t. la main à qn,** (i) to hold out one's hand to s.o.; (ii) to offer s.o. a helping hand; **les nations doivent se t. la main et coordonner leurs efforts,** the nations must join hands and coordinate their efforts; **t. les lèvres,** to offer one's lips (for a kiss); **t. le cou,** to crane one's neck; **t. le dos à un coup,** to raise, hump, one's back (in anticipation of a blow); *s.a.* BRAS 1; (*d*) to (over)strain; to stretch; **t. les rapports entre deux nations,** to strain the relations between two nations; *s.a.* OREILLE 2. **2.** *v.i.* to tend, lead, conduce (**à**, to); **vos paroles ne tendent qu'à le fâcher,** your words only tend to annoy him; **où tendent ces questions?** what is the aim, the drift, of these questions? *F:* what is he, are you, driving at? **discours tendant à prouver qch.,** speeches tending to prove sth.; **nez tendant à l'aquilin,** nose inclined to be aquiline; (*of thg*) **t. à sa fin,** to be near its end; *Lit:* **la ville où tendent nos pas,** the town to(wards) which we are going; **les voyelles faibles tendent à disparaître,** there is a tendency for weak vowels to disappear.

se tendre, to become taut; (*of relations*) to become strained; (*of prices, etc.*) to harden, stiffen; **le papier s'est mal tendu,** the paper has not stretched properly.

tendrelet, -ette [tɑ̃drəlɛ, -ɛt], *a.* rather tender (meat, etc.); young and tender.

tendrement [tɑ̃drəmɑ̃], *adv.* **1.** tenderly, fondly, affectionately; **je l'aime t.,** I love him dearly. **2.** **peindre t.,** to paint with a delicate touch.

tendresse [tɑ̃drɛs], *s.f.* **1.** (*a*) tenderness; fondness, love; **avec t.,** fondly, lovingly; **soigner qn avec t.,** to bestow loving care on s.o.; (*b*) *pl.* tokens of affection, caresses. **2.** **être dans la t. de l'âge,** to be of tender age. **3.** *Hist:* **garder des tendresses orléanistes,** to have a tenderness, weakness, for the Orleanist party.

tendret, -ette [tɑ̃drɛ, -ɛt], *a.* rather tender.

tendreté [tɑ̃drəte], *s.f.* tenderness (of food).

tendrille [tɑ̃driːj], *s.f. Bot:* tender shoot.

tendron [tɑ̃drɔ̃], *s.m.* **1.** *Bot:* tender shoot. **2.** *Cu:* tendron, gristle (of veal). **3.** *F:* very young, innocent girl.

tendu [tɑ̃dy], *a.* (*a*) stretched, strained, tense, taut, tight; *Ball: etc:* flat (trajectory); **corde tendue,** (i) tautrope; (ii) *Gym:* tightrope; **chaîne mal tendue,** slack chain; **ventre t.,** distended stomach; **avoir les nerfs tendus,** to be tense, strung-up; to have one's nerves on edge; **rapports tendus,** strained relations; **situation tendue,** tense, critical, situation; **foule tendue dans l'attente du match,** crowd tensely awaiting the match; crowd keyed up for the match; **style t.,** strained, stilted, style; *St.Exch:* **prix tendus,** stiff, hard, firm, prices; (*b*) *Ling:* strong (sound); voiceless (consonant); (*c*) **main tendue,** outstretched hand; **politique de la main tendue,** policy of making friendly overtures.

tendue [tɑ̃dy], *s.f.* **1.** (*a*) setting of traps and snares, of an ambush; (*b*) area set with traps; (*c*) *coll.* snares, traps. **2.** **t. d'eau,** (artificially) flooded area; **faire une t. d'eau,** to flood an area. **3.** *Fish:* ground line.

Tène, la [latɛn], *Pr.n. Prehist:* La Tène (period).

ténèbres [tenɛbr̥], *s.f.pl.* **1.** darkness, gloom; **les t. de la nuit,** the shades of night; **dans les t.,** in the dark; **œuvre de t.,** deed of darkness; **le Prince des T.,** the Prince of Darkness; **les t. extérieures,** outer darkness; **t. de l'ignorance,** darkness of ignorance. **2.** *Ecc:* Tenebrae.

ténébrescence [tenebrɛs(s)ɑ̃s], *s.f.* tenebrescence.

ténébreusement [tenebrøzmɑ̃], *adv.* **1.** gloomily, darkly. **2.** mysteriously, in an underhand manner.

ténébreux, -euse [tenebrø, -ø:z], *a.* **1.** gloomy, dark, sombre (wood, prison, etc.). **2.** (*a*) mysterious, obscure; sinister; **les temps t. de l'histoire,** the obscure periods of history; **style t.,** obscure style; **une ténébreuse affaire,** a dark, mysterious, business; (*b*) *s. Lit:* **beau ténébreux,** hero wrapt in Byronic gloom. **3.** *Lit:* **l'Ange t.,** the dark angel, the devil; **le t. séjour,** the shades, the realm of the dead.

ténébrion [tenebriɔ̃], *s.m. Ent:* tenebrio; meal beetle, mealworm.

ténébrionides [tenebriɔnid], **ténébrionidés** [tenebriɔnide], *s.m.pl. Ent:* Tenebrionidae.

tènement [tɛnmɑ̃], *s.m.* (*a*) *Dial:* holding; (*b*) *A.Jur:* **franc t.,** free socage.

ténesme [tenɛsm], *s.m. Med:* tenesmus.

tenette [tənɛt], *s.f. Surg:* forceps (used in operation for calculus).

teneur[1], **-euse** [tənœ:r, -ø:z], *s.* **1.** holder; taker (of a bet); *Typ:* **t. de copie,** copy holder. **2. t. de livres,** book-keeper. **3.** *s.m. Ven:* third falcon (launched in pursuit of a heron).

teneur[2], *s.f.* **1.** (*a*) tenor, terms (of document, etc.); (*b*) **la t. de sa vie, de sa conduite,** the tenor of his life, of his conduct. **2.** *Tchn:* amount, content, percentage; (*a*) *Ind: etc:* **t. qualitative, quantitative,** qualitative, quantitative, content; **t. en eau,** water content, moisture content; **t. en humidité,** degree of humidity, moisture content; **t. en graisse d'un cuir,** percentage of grease in a leather; (*b*) *Miner: etc:* grade, tenor (of ore, metal, etc.); **t. moyenne,** average grade (of ore); **t. payante,** payable grade (of ore); **t. limite,** lowest payable grade; **t. en or,** gold content(s); **t. en soufre,** percentage of sulphur, sulphur content (in ore); **t. en uranium,** uranium content; **minerai, acier, de haute t.,** high-grade ore, steel; (*c*) *Ch:* (standard) strength, titration (standard) (of solution); (*d*) *Atom.Ph:* **t. isotopique,** isotopic abundance; **t. isotopique naturelle,** natural (isotopic) abundance; **rapport des teneurs,** abundance ratio.

teneurmètre [tənœrmɛtr̥], *s.m. Min:* content meter; **t. de minerai,** ore content meter; **t. en uranium,** uranium content meter.

ténia [tenja], *s.m.* taenia, tapeworm; **t. armé,** armed tapeworm.

téniasis [tenjazis], *s.m. Med:* taeniasis.

ténie [teni], *s.f. Arch:* taenia.

ténifuge [tenify:ʒ], *a. & s.m. Med:* **(médicament) t.,** taenifuge, taeni(i)cide.

ténioglosses [tenjɔglɔs], *s.m.pl. Moll:* Taenioglossa.

tenir [təni:r], *v.* (*pr.p.* **tenant;** *p.p.* **tenu;** *pr.ind.* **je tiens, il tient, n. tenons, v. tenez, ils tiennent;** *pr.sub.* **je tienne, n. tenions;** *p.d.* **je tenais;** *p.h.* **je tins, n. tînmes, v. tîntes, ils tinrent;** *p.sub.* **je tinsse, il tînt, n. tinssions;** *fu.* **je tiendrai**) **I.** *v.tr.* **1.** to hold; (*a*) to have hold of (s.o., sth.); **t. qch. à la main, entre ses mains, dans, entre, ses bras, sur ses genoux,** to hold sth. in one's hand, in one's hands, in one's arms, on one's lap; **ils se tenaient par la main, ils se tenaient la main,** they held each other's hands, they were holding hands, they were holding each other by the hand; **t. qn par le bras, au collet,** to hold s.o. by the arm, by the scruff of his neck; **il se tenait la tête dans les mains,** he held his head in his hands; **t. serré qch.,** to keep tight hold of sth.; **se t. les côtes de rire,** to hold one's sides with laughter; **il me tenait à la gorge,** he had me by the throat; **la fièvre le tient,** he is in the grip of a fever; **mon rhume me tient,** I can't get rid of, throw off, my cold; *F:* **t. un bon rhume,** to have a stinking cold; *P:* **t. une bonne cuite,** to be gloriously drunk; *v.i. P:* **qu'est-ce qu'il tient!** (i) he's completely sozzled! (ii) what an idiot! **je tiens mon homme,** I've got my man; **t. le mot de l'énigme,** to have, hold, the key to the puzzle; **nous tenons le succès,** we have success within our grasp; *F:* **je tiens mon article,** I have my paper all fixed, all written out, in my head; **t. tout dans un coup d'œil,** to take in everything at a glance; **t. qn de près,** to hold, keep, s.o. under strict control; *Aut:* **t. bien la route,** *F:* **t. la mer,** to hold the road well; *A:* **t. une terre (à foi et hommage) de qn,** to hold land from s.o.; *abs.* **t. de qn,** to owe allegiance to s.o. (*cp.* II. 5); *s.a.* CORDE 1; *Prov:* **un "tiens" vaut mieux que deux "tu l'auras"; mieux vaut t. que courir,** a bird in the hand is worth two in the bush; **faire t. qch. à qn,** (i) to make s.o. hold sth.; (ii) to put s.o. in possession of sth.; **je vous fais t. par la poste la somme de mille francs,** I am sending you by post the sum of one thousand francs; *abs. in the imp:* **tiens! tenez!** look! look here! **tenez, je vais tout vous dire,** look here, I'll tell you everything; **tenez, mon chien à moi . . .,** now, that dog of mine . . ., **tenez! (ceci est pour vous),** here you are! **tenez, ôtez-moi cela,** here, take this away; **et tenez!** and look! and see! *s.a.* DRAGÉE 1, QUATRE, TÊTE 1; (*b*) to contain, have capacity for (a certain quantity); **tonneau qui tient vingt litres,** cask that holds twenty litres; **voiture qui tient six personnes,** *v.i.* **voiture où l'on tient à six,** car that takes six people, that holds six; *v.i.* **on tient douze à cette table,** this table seats twelve; **on tenait tout juste,** it was a tight fit, a tight squeeze; **tous ces livres tiendront dans cette caisse,** all these books will easily fit, go, into this box; **tout ça tient en deux mots,** all that can be said in a couple of words; **faire t. beaucoup de faits en peu de lignes,** to crowd a great many facts into few lines; (*c*) to retain; **baril qui tient l'eau,** barrel that holds water, that is watertight; (*d*) **t. de,** to have, get, derive, (sth.) from; to owe (sth.) to (some source); **t. qch. de bonne source,** to have sth. on good authority; **j'en suis sûr; je le tiens de mon député,** I am sure of it; I have it from my M.P.; **il tient sa timidité de sa mère,** he gets his shy nature from his mother; he owes his shy nature to his mother; (*e*) to keep, stock (groceries, etc.); *s.a.* COMPTE, RIGUEUR 1; (*f*) **en t.** (*of partridge, etc.*) **elle en tient** (*i.e.* **du plomb**), she's winged; *F:* (*of pers.*) **il en tient,** he's had a nasty blow; *P:* **en t. une,** to be gloriously drunk. **2.** to keep, direct; **t. un magasin, une école,** to keep, run, a shop, a school; **t. la caisse,** to have charge of the cash; **chambre bien tenue,** well-kept, tidy, room; **tout est bien tenu,** everything is well kept; **t. l'harmonium,** to play, preside at, the harmonium; **Mlle X tenait le piano,** Miss X was at the piano; **t. une séance,** to hold a sitting; **le conseil se tient dans la grande salle,** the council is held in the great hall; **le marché se tient le samedi,** the market is held on Saturdays. **3.** (*a*) to hold, maintain (opinion, certain line of conduct); to keep (one's word, promise); **il tiendra sa promesse,** he will keep to his promise; **je tiens que mon opinion est la bonne,** I consider that I am right; **ces vues, nous les tenons pour justes,** these views we believe to be fair and true; **t. un pari,** to take (up) a bet; (*b*) **t. de grands discours,** to hold forth at great length; **t. des propos désobligeants pour qn,** to speak disparagingly of s.o.; (*c*) **t. son rang,** to keep up, uphold, one's position; (*d*) **t. qn en mépris, en grand respect,** to hold s.o. in contempt, in great respect. **4.** to hold back, restrain (one's tongue, one's impatience); **t. un cheval,** to control a horse, to keep a horse in hand, to keep up a horse; **on ne peut plus t. ces enfants,** these children are quite out of hand; **il ne sait pas t. ses élèves,** he cannot control his pupils. **5.** (*a*) to hold, keep, preserve (in a certain position); **cette poutre tient le plafond,** that beam holds up the ceiling; **mon rhume me tient à la maison,** my cold is keeping me indoors; **il nous a tenus debout pendant deux heures,** he kept us standing for two hours; **t. qch. en état, en bon état,** to keep sth. in good order; **t. qch. sous clef,** to keep sth. under lock and key; **t. (qn) à l'œil,** to keep an eye on (s.o.); **t. qn dans les fers,** to keep s.o. in irons; **cette visite m'a tenu longtemps,** this visit kept me a long time, kept me back for a long time; **t. son fils au collège,** to keep one's son at school; **t. un paquet au frais,** to keep a package in a cool place; *s.a.* CHAUD 2; **tenez votre gauche, votre droite,** keep to the left, to the right; *Nau:* **t. le vent,** to keep her to; (*b*) **t. la chambre,** to be confined to one's room (through illness); **être obligé de t. le lit,** to be confined to one's bed; (*c*) **t. la mer,** (i) (*of ship*) to keep the sea; to hold on (in heavy weather); (ii) (*of country*) to be master, mistress, of the seas; (iii) *Aut: F:* to hold the road (well); **le navire tenait la mer depuis trois semaines,** the ship had been at sea for three weeks; *s.a.* LARGE 2; (*of ship*) **bien t. la mer,** to be a good sea ship; **navire capable, incapable, de t. la mer,** seaworthy ship, unseaworthy ship. **6.** to occupy, take up (space); **vous tenez trop de place,** you are taking up too much room, space; **la table tient la moitié de la pièce,** the table occupies half the floor space; (*of car*) **t. toute la route,** to hog the road. **7. t. les yeux fermés,** to keep one's eyes shut; **t. qn captif,** to keep, hold, s.o. prisoner; **t. qn pour habile,** to think, consider, s.o. clever; **je le tiens pour (un) honnête homme,** I hold, consider, him to be an honest man; **t. une nouvelle pour vraie,** to believe a piece of news; **tenir qch. comme établi,** to assume sth.; **tenez cela pour fait,** look on that as done; consider it done; **il se le tint pour dit,** he took the lesson to heart; **tenez-vous-le pour dit,** I shall not tell, warn, you again; take that once and for all; *s.a.* DESHONNEUR, HONNEUR 1.

II. tenir, *v.i.* **1.** (*a*) to hold; to adhere, hold on firmly; **clou qui tient bien,** nail that holds well; **la porte tient,** the door won't open; **vêtements qui ne tiennent plus (ensemble),** garments that won't hold together, that are falling to pieces; *s.a.* FER[1], FIL 1; **la croûte tient à la plaie,** the scab sticks, adheres, to the wound; *F:* **cela tient comme poix,** it sticks like pitch; *F:* **ses pieds ne tiennent pas à la terre,** he is never still for a minute; *s.a.* CŒUR 2; (*b*) to border on; **sa terre tient à la mienne,** his estate borders on mine; **les écuries tiennent à la maison,** the stables are built on to the house; **dans le passé la France tenait à l'Angleterre,** in the past France was joined to England; (*c*) to remain; **il ne tient plus sur ses jambes,** he is ready to drop (with fatigue); **ne pas t. en place,** to be restless; **elle ne pouvait t. en place,** she couldn't keep still; **il ne tint pas en place que tout ne fût prêt,** he could not keep still until everything was ready; *s.a.* PEAU 1. **2.** (*a*) **t. (bon, ferme),** to hold out, to stand fast; to resist; to hold on; to hold one's own; (*of cable, etc.*) to stand the strain, to hold; **tenez bon!** hold on! **votre argumentation ne tient guère,** your argument hardly stands up; **t. contre l'ennemi,** to hold, keep, stand, one's ground; **pourvu que les civils tiennent,** if only the civilians hold out; **t. jusqu'au bout,** to hold out (to the end); *F:* to stick it out, to see it through; **tenez bon! ferme!** (i) hold tight! *Nau:* (a)vast! (ii) never say die! *Nau:* **tenez bon l'amarre de bout!** hold on the head line! *Nau:* **tiens bon virer!** (a)vast heaving! **je n'y tiens plus,** I can't stand it, *F:* stick it, any longer; **il ne pouvait plus y t.,** he could bear it no longer; (*b*) to last, endure; **ma mise en plis n'a pas tenu deux jours,** my set didn't last, stay in, two days; **le vent va t.,** the wind will last; **son commerce ne tiendra pas,** his business won't last; **couleur qui tient bien,** fast colour; **mon offre tient toujours,** my offer stands; **le pari tient,** the bet stands, holds good; **il n'est d'ordre qui tienne, faites ce que je vous dis,** never mind orders, do as I tell you; (*c*) **les tribunaux tiennent toute l'année,** the courts sit all the year round; **l'Académie tient les jeudis,** the Academy sits on Thursdays; **le marché tient tous les samedis,** the market is held on Saturdays. **3. t. pour,** to hold for, be in favour of, stand up for (s.o., sth.); **je tiens pour la liberté,** I am all for liberty; **en t. pour qn,** to be fond of s.o.; to be in love with s.o.; **en t. pour son idée,** to stick to one's idea. **4. t. à qch.,** (*a*) to value, prize, sth.; **t. à la vie,** to value one's life; to cling to life; **il tient à sa peau,** he thinks discretion is the better part of valour; **t. à faire qch.,** to be bent on doing sth.; **je n'y tiens pas,** (i) I don't care for it; (ii) I would rather not; *F:* **je n'y tiens pas plus que cela,** I'm not keen on it; **tenez-vous beaucoup à y aller?** are you very keen on going? **je tiens à vous le dire,** I am anxious to tell you, I am making a point of telling you; **il tient à vous voir,** he is bent on seeing you; **je tiens à savoir . . .,** I want to know, I insist on knowing . . .; **t. à ce qu'on fasse qch.,** to be anxious, insistent, that something should be done; **je tiens beaucoup à ce qu'il vienne,** I am very anxious that he should come, for him to come; **puisque vous y tenez . . .,** since you desire it . . .; since you are set upon it . . .; (*b*) to depend on, result from, sth.; to be due to sth.; **son autorité tient à votre appui,** his authority is due to your support, he owes his authority to your support; **cela tient à son éducation,** that's the result, the fault, of his education; **à quoi tient la popularité du cinéma?** what are the causes of the popularity of the cinema? **à quoi cela tient-il?** what's the reason for it? what is it due to? **cela tient à ce que vous êtes Écossais,** that comes of your being Scottish; **son originalité tient à ce qu'il ne fait aucune concession à . . .,** his originality lies in the fact that he makes no concession to . . .; *impers.* **il ne tient qu'à vous de le faire,** it rests, lies, entirely with you to do it; **il ne tient qu'à vous que cela se fasse,** it depends entirely on you whether it is done; **qu'à cela ne tienne,** never mind that, that need be no obstacle; **s'il ne tient qu'à cela,** if that is all (the difficulty); **il n'a tenu à rien qu'il ne se noyât,** he was as near as could be to getting drowned. **5. t. de qn,** to take after s.o. (*cp.* I. 1); **t. de qch.,** to partake of the nature of sth.; **t. de son père,** to take after, be like, one's father; to favour one's father; **passion qui tient de l'amour,** passion that savours of, is akin to, love; **cela tient du miracle,** there is something miraculous about it; it sounds like a miracle; **cela tient de (la) famille,** it runs in the family; **avoir de qui t.,** to be of good stock; **il a de qui t.,** (i) blood will tell; (ii) *often Pej:* what's bred in the bone will out in the flesh.

se tenir. 1. (*a*) to keep, be, remain, stand, sit; **ils se tiennent toujours dans la même salle,** they always sit in the same room; they keep to the same room; **se t. chez soi,** to stay, remain, at home; *s.a.* DEBOUT 1; **tenez-vous là!** stand there! stay where you are! don't move! **tenez-vous droit,** (i) sit up, sit straight; (ii) stand straight, stand upright; **se t. tranquille,** to keep quiet; **se t. à cheval,** (i) to be on horseback; (ii) *Equit:* to have a good seat; **se bien, mal, t. à cheval,** to sit a horse well, badly, to have a good, a poor, seat; **tiens-toi,** (i) be on your best behaviour; (ii) behave yourself; **recommander à qn de se bien t.,** to put s.o. on his best behaviour; *F:* **on sait se t. avec les femmes,** I, we, know how to behave in the presence of ladies; **tenez-vous bien! vous n'avez qu'à vous bien t.!** you'd better watch your step; **tenez-vous bien, votre fils a disparu,** prepare yourself for a shock; your son has disappeared; (*b*) **se t. à qch.,** to hold on to sth.; *Rail:* **se t. aux courroies,** to hold on to the straps, to strap-hang; (*on bus, etc.*) **tenez-vous bien!** hold tight! (*c*) **la boisson, la misère, le crime, tout cela se tient,** drink, poverty, crime, all these go together; **ses arguments se tiennent (bien),** his arguments hold together. **2.** to contain oneself; **il ne se tient pas de joie,** he cannot contain himself for joy; **je ne pouvais me t. de rire,** I couldn't help laughing; **je ne pus me t. de l'embrasser,** I couldn't resist giving her a kiss; **je ne pus me t. d'admirer,** I could not contain my admiration; I could not help admiring; *s.a.* QUATRE. **3. se, s'en, t. à qch.,** to keep to sth.; **se t. à ce qu'on a décidé,** to stick to, abide by, what was decided; *Cards:* **je m'y tiens,** I am satisfied; content! **s'en t. à qch.,** to confine oneself to sth.; to be satisfied, contented, with sth.; **s'en t. à des amitiés de longue date,** to stick to old friendships; **je m'en tiens à ce que j'ai dit,** I'll stand by, stick to, what I have said; **je m'en tiens à votre décision,** I adhere to, abide by, your decision; **nous nous en tenons à l'exécution du traité,** we abide by the treaty; **il ne s'en tint pas là,** he did not stop at that; **tenons-nous-en là,** let it go at that; let us go no further; **je ne sais pas à quoi m'en t.,** I don't know what to believe; I don't know where I am, how I stand.

ténite [tenit], *s.f. Miner:* taenite.

tennantite [tɛnɑ̃tit], *s.f. Miner:* tennantite.

tennis [tenis], *s.m.* **1.** (lawn) tennis; **t. de table,** table tennis. **2. (court de) t.,** (lawn) tennis court. **3.** *Tex:* flannel with narrow stripes.

tennisman, *pl.* **tennismen** [tenisman, tenismɛn], *s.m. F:* tennis player.

ténodèse [tenɔdɛːz], *s.f. Surg:* tenodesis.

tenon¹ [tənɔ̃], *s.m.* **1.** *Carp:* tenon; **t. passant,** through tenon; **t. en about,** end tenon; *N.Arch:* **t. d'emplanture,** heel tenon (of wooden mast); **assembler à tenons,** to tenon. **2.** *Mec.E:* lug; shoulder, stud, tenon; **t. arrêtoir,** stop lug; **t. d'assemblage,** assembly stud; **t. de fixation,** retaining lug; **t. de guidage,** guide lug, guide pin; *Sm.a:* **t. de recul,** recoil shoulder; **t. de fermeture, de verrouillage,** locking lug. **3.** nut (of anchor). **4.** *Dent:* **dent à t.,** pivot tooth; **couronne à t.,** pivot crown; **t. dentaire,** pivot of crowned tooth.

Tenon², *Pr.n. Anat:* **capsule de T.,** Tenon's capsule; **cavité, espace, de T.,** Tenon's space.

tenonnage [tənɔnaːʒ], *s.m.* tenoning.

tenonner [tənɔne], *v.tr. Carp:* to tenon.

tenonneuse [tənɔnøːz], *s.f. Carp:* tenoning machine, tenoner.

ténoplastie [tenɔplasti], *s.f. Surg:* tenoplasty.

ténor [tenɔːr], *s.m.* (*a*) *Mus:* tenor; **voix de t.,** tenor voice; **t. léger,** light tenor; **fort t., t. de grand opéra,** operatic tenor; (*b*) *F: Pol: etc:* star performer.

tenorino [tenɔrino], *s.m. Mus:* tenorino; falsetto tenor.

ténorisant [tenɔrizɑ̃], *a. Mus:* **baryton t.,** high baritone.

ténoriser [tenɔrize], *v.i. Mus:* to sing like a tenor, in the tenor register.

ténorite [tenɔrit], *s.f. Miner:* tenorite, melaconite.

ténorrhaphie [tenɔrafi], *s.f. Surg:* tenorrhaphy.

ténosite [tenɔzit], *s.f. Med:* tendinitis, tenositis.

ténosynovite [tenɔsinɔvit], *s.f. Med:* tenosynovitis.

ténotome [tenɔtɔm], *s.m. Surg:* tenotomy knife; tenotome.

ténotomie [tenɔtɔmi], *s.f. Surg:* tenotomy.

tenrec [tɑ̃rɛk], *s.m. Z:* tenrec, tanrec.

tenrécidés [tɑ̃reside], *s.m.pl. Z:* Tenrecidae.

tenseur [tɑ̃sœːr], *a. & s.m.* **1.** (*a*) *Anat:* **(muscle) t.,** tensor; (*b*) *s.m. Mth:* tensor. **2.** *Tchn:* = TENDEUR 2.

tensif, -ive [tɑ̃sif, -iːv], *a. Med:* tensive (sensation, pain).

tensimètre [tɑ̃simɛtr̥], *s.m.*, **tensiomètre** [tɑ̃sjɔmɛtr̥], *s.m.* (*a*) *Med:* sphygmomanometer; (*b*) *Ph:* (i) tensimeter, manometer; (ii) tensiometer.

tensimétrie [tɑ̃simetri], *s.f. Ph:* measurement of the surface tension of liquids.

tensio-actif, -ive [tɑ̃sjɔaktif, -iːv], *Ch:* **1.** *a.* surface-active. **2.** *s.m.* (*a*) surface-active agent, surfactant; **t.-a. cationique,** cationic surface-active agent; (*b*) wetting agent; *pl. tensio-actifs, -ives.*

tension [tɑ̃sjɔ̃], *s.f.* **1.** (*a*) tension; stretching (of muscles, etc.); tightening (of guyrope, etc.); **écrou à t.,** tightening nut; **la t. d'esprit requise pour . . .,** the close application required for . . .; (*b*) *Mec:* **t. de rupture,** breaking strain, stress; *Metall:* **t. de cisaillement,** shear stress. **2.** (*a*) tightness (of rope, etc.); tenseness (of relations, etc.); flatness (of trajectory); *Ph:* **t. superficielle,** surface tension; *Mec.E:* **t. de courroie,** belt tension; **chaîne de t. réglable,** adjustable tension chain; **tensions d'un corps qui se refroidit,** (internal) tensile stresses of a cooling body; **acier à haute t.,** high-tensile steel; **période de t. internationale,** period of international tension; **cette t. des esprits pourrait amener une rupture,** this tenseness of attitude might bring about a rupture; (*b*) *St.Exch:* hardness, stiffness, firmness (of prices). **3.** (*a*) pressure (of steam, etc.); *Med:* **t. du pouls,** tightening of the pulse; **t. artérielle, t. du sang,** blood pressure; *F:* **avoir, faire, de la t.,** to suffer from high blood pressure; (*b*) *El: Elcs:* voltage; tension; **basse, haute, t.,** low, high, voltage; **t. à haute fréquence,** high frequency voltage; **t. nulle,** zero voltage; zero potential; **déclenchement à t. nulle,** no-volt release; **sans t.,** dead; **t. anodique,** anode voltage, potential; plate voltage; **t. anodique d'amorçage,** anode breakdown voltage; **t. aux bornes,** terminal tension, voltage; pole voltage; **t. cathodique,** cathode tension; **t. continue,** direct current voltage; **t. de contrôle,** test(ing) voltage, testing potential; **t. d'amorçage,** ignition voltage; sparking voltage; starting voltage; **t. d'entrée, de sortie,** input, output, voltage; **t. d'émission,** transmitting voltage; **t. de service, de régime, de fonctionnement,** working, operating, service, voltage; **t. nominale,** rated voltage; **t. induite,** induced, induction, voltage; **t. minimum, t. moyenne,** minimum, mean, voltage; **t. résiduelle,** residual voltage; backlash potential; **t. triphasée,** three-phase, delta, mesh, voltage; **t. d'entretien,** sustained voltage; **t. d'équilibrage,** phase-balance voltage; **t. de polarisation,** polarization, bias, voltage; **t. de polarisation de grille,** grid-bias voltage; **t. effective, t. efficace,** effective voltage, root-mean-square voltage; **régulateur de t.,** voltage regulator; **transformateur de t.,** voltage transformer; **stabilisateur de t.,** voltage stabiliser; **chute de t.,** decrease in voltage; potential drop; **augmentation, élévation, de (la) t.,** increase, rise, in voltage; **mettre sous t.,** to apply the voltage to, to switch on (circuit, etc.); **fil sous t.,** live, charged, wire; **montage des piles en t.,** connection of batteries in series; **induit enroulé en haute t.,** intensity armature; **nœud de t.,** potential node; **ventre de t.,** antinode, loop, of potential.

tensionnage [tɑ̃sjɔnaːʒ], *s.m. Tchn:* tensioning (of saw, etc.).

tensionner [tɑ̃sjɔne], *v.tr. Tchn:* to tension (saw, etc.).

tenson [tɑ̃sɔ̃], *s.f. Provençal Lit:* tenson.

tensoriel, -ielle [tɑ̃sɔrjɛl], *a. Mth:* tensorial.

tentaculaire [tɑ̃takylɛːr], *a. Z:* tentacular; **villes tentaculaires,** sprawling towns.

tentacule [tɑ̃takyl], *s.m. Z: Bot:* tentacle; *F:* tentacle (of town, etc.).

tentaculé [tɑ̃takyle], *a. Nat.Hist:* tentacled, tentaculate.

tentaculifères [tɑ̃takylifɛːr], *s.m.pl. Prot:* Tentaculifera.

tentaculites [tɑ̃takylitɛs], *s.m.pl. Paleont:* tentaculite; (*genus*) Tentaculites.

tentant [tɑ̃tɑ̃], *a.* tempting, alluring, enticing; **l'occasion était bien tentante,** I was greatly tempted; **le sujet est t.,** the subject is inviting.

tentateur, -trice [tɑ̃tatœːr, -tris]. **1.** *s.* tempter, temptress; **le T.,** the Tempter. **2.** *a.* tempting; **l'esprit t.,** the Tempter, the Devil.

tentatif, -ive [tɑ̃tatif, -iːv]. **1.** *a.* tentative. **2.** *s.f.* **tentative,** attempt, endeavour, bid; **échouer dans une t. auprès de qn,** to fail to win s.o. over; to fail to gain s.o.'s consent; **t. d'évasion,** attempt to escape; escape bid; **t. de violence,** attempt at violence; **t. d'assassinat,** attempted murder; **t. de résistance,** attempt to resist.

tentation [tɑ̃tasjɔ̃], *s.f.* temptation **(de faire qch.,** to do sth.); **succomber, céder, à la t.,** to succumb, yield, to temptation; to fall; **résister à la t.,** to resist temptation; **je ne pus résister à la t. de lui faire la grimace,** I couldn't resist making a face at him; **éviter les tentations,** to avoid temptation.

tente¹ [tɑ̃ːt], *s.f.* (*a*) tent; **t. conique,** bell tent; **t. de plage,** bathing tent; *Mil:* **t. individuelle,** *F:* bivvy; *Med:* **t. de vapeur(s),** tent (bed), steam tent; **t. à oxygène,** oxygen tent; **monter, dresser, les tentes,** to pitch (the) tents; **démonter, abattre, plier, les tentes,** to strike tents; **coucher sous la t.,** to sleep under canvas; **matériel de t.,** tentage; **se retirer dans, sous, sa t.,** to sulk in one's tent (like Achilles); (*b*) **les tentes de la foire, du marché,** the booths at the fair, in the market place; (*c*) *Nau:* awning; **faire les tentes,** to spread the awning.

tente², *s.f. Surg: A:* tent, (linen) probe; **introduire une t. dans une plaie,** to tent a wound.

tente-abri [tɑ̃tabri], *s.f. Mil:* shelter tent; *pl. tentes-abris.*

tenter¹ [tɑ̃te], *v.tr.* **1.** (*a*) *A: & B:* to tempt, prove, try; to put (s.o.) to the test; **Dieu tenta Abraham,** God tempted Abraham; (*b*) **t. la chance, la fortune,** to try one's luck; **t. Dieu, la Providence,** to risk one's life; to tempt Providence. **2.** to tempt (s.o.); **ce fut en vain qu'il tenta le geôlier,** he tried in vain to bribe the gaoler; **t. la fidélité de qn,** to tempt s.o. to be disloyal; **se laisser t.,** to allow oneself to be tempted; to yield to temptation; **je fus tenté d'essayer,** I was tempted to try. **3.** to attempt, try; **t. d'inutiles efforts pour . . .,** to make useless attempts to . . .; **t. des efforts surhumains,** to make superhuman efforts; **t. mille efforts,** to make countless efforts; **t. une expérience,** to try an experiment; **t. de,** *occ.* **à, faire qch.,** to try, endeavour, to do sth.

tenter², *v.tr.* to erect an awning over (court, boat, etc.).

tenthrède [tɑ̃trɛd], *s.f. Ent:* saw-fly; (*genus*) Tenthredo.

tenthrédinidés [tɑ̃tredinide], *s.m.pl. Ent:* Tenthredinidae.

tentiste [tɑ̃tist], *s.m. & f.* camper (in tent).

tenture [tɑ̃tyːr], *s.f.* **1.** hanging (of tapestry, etc.). **2.** (*a*) hangings, tapestry; *A:* arras; **t. de deuil,** funeral hangings; (*b*) **(papier-)t.,** wallpaper; (*c*) *Fr.C:* curtain, *U.S:* drape.

tenu [təny]. **1.** *a. & p.p.* (*a*) kept; **bien t.,** well-kept (child, etc.); tidy, well-kept (house, etc.); neat, trim (garden, etc.); **mal t.,** ill-kept, neglected, uncared-for (child, garden, etc.); untidy (house, etc.); (*b*) **être t. de, à, faire qch.,** to be bound, obliged, to do sth., to be held responsible for doing sth.; **vous n'êtes aucunement t. de me dédommager,** I have no claim on you; **les passants sont tenus de marcher sur le trottoir,** pedestrians must walk on the pavement; **le médecin est t. au secret professionnel,** the doctor is bound by professional secrecy; **les devoirs auxquels je suis t. envers lui,** the duties I owe him; *Jur:* **être t. à restitution,** to be bound to make restitution; (*c*) *St.Exch:* firm, hard (prices); (*d*) (*of a bet*) **tenu!** done! I take you! **2.** *s.m. Box:* hold; *Sp:* holding (of the ball).

ténu [teny], *a.* **1.** tenuous, thin; slender; fine (thread, etc.); subtle, fine (distinction); thin, watery (fluid, etc.); attenuated (air, gas); low (diet). **2.** *Ling:* **consonne ténue,** tenuis.

tenue [təny], *s.f.* **1.** (*a*) (manner of) holding (pen, etc.); keeping, holding (of position in convoy, etc.); **selle (de cheval) qui n'a pas de t.,** badly shaped, ill-fitting, saddle; (*of horse*) **avoir de la t.,** to have staying power, to be a stayer; *Nau:* **t. de l'ancre,** hold, holding (of the anchor); **fond de bonne t., de mauvaise t.,** good holding-ground; bad holding-ground; loose bottom; (*b*) sitting, session, holding (of an assembly, of assizes, etc.); (freemasons') lodge (meeting); (*c*) keeping, managing, running (of shop, house, etc.); **t. des livres,** book-keeping; *Com:* **pour la bonne t. de**

nos écritures . . ., in order to keep our accounts, our books, in order . . .; *Fin:* (*Giro account*) **t. de compte**, service charge; *Mch:* **t. des chaudières**, care of the boilers; (*d*) *Tchn:* **t. en fatigue, à la corrosion**, resistance to fatigue, to corrosion; (*e*) holding; **terres toutes d'une t., d'une seule t.**, lands in a continuous stretch. **2.** (*a*) bearing, behaviour, carriage; **avoir de la t.**, (i) to behave oneself; to have good manners; (ii) to have dignified manners, a sense of decorum, a good bearing; **Paul, de la t.!** Paul, behave yourself! **un peu de t.!** mind your manners! **la haute t. de ce périodique**, the high standard maintained by this periodical; *Equit:* **avoir une bonne, mauvaise, t.**, to have a good, poor, seat; **ne pas avoir de t.**, to have no seat; (*b*) **acier dont la t. est bonne aux hautes températures**, steel that stands up well to high temperatures; *Aer:* **t. en l'air, t. aéronautique**, behaviour in the air; airworthiness; *Av:* **t. en vol**, attitude of flight; **t. par rapport au vent**, attitude relative to wind; *Aut:* **t. en côte**, climbing ability; **t. de route**, road-holding qualities. **3.** dress; *Mil: Navy:* **t. de soirée**, mess dress; **t. de ville**, (i) (woman's) town clothes; (ii) (man's) lounge suit; **en t. de soirée**, in evening dress; **elle était en t. de ville**, she was dressed for going out; **il avait pris la t. d'un cheminot**, he had rigged himself out as a railwayman; **être dans une t. très soignée**, to be well-groomed; **t. de loisirs, de tous les jours**, casuals; *F:* **je vais me mettre en t.**, I'm going to change; *Mil: etc:* **en t.**, in uniform; *Navy:* **t. numéro un**, number one (uniform); **en grande t.**, in full dress (uniform), in review order, in gala order; **t. de sortie, de ville**, walking-out dress; **petite t.**, undress; **t. de campagne**, (i) field-service uniform; (ii) heavy marching order; **t. de combat**, battledress; **t. d'exercice**, drill uniform; **t. de corvée**, fatigue dress; **t. (de) fantaisie**, uniform not of regulation pattern; **t. civile, bourgeoise**, plain clothes, civilian clothes, *F:* civvies, mufti. **4.** *Mus:* (*a*) holding note, sustained note; (*b*) organ point. **5.** (*a*) steadiness, firmness (of prices); tone (of the market); (*b*) **tissu qui a de la t.**, firm material.

ténuiflore [tenɥiflɔːr], *a. Bot:* tenuiflorous.

ténuifolié [tenɥifɔlje], *a. Bot:* tenuifolious.

ténuirostre [tenɥirɔstr̥], *Orn:* **1.** *a.* tenuirostrate. **2.** *s.m.pl. A:* Tenuirostres.

ténuité [tenɥite], *s.f.* tenuity, tenuousness; thinness; slenderness; fineness (of sand, of distinction, etc.); wateriness (of liquid).

tenure [tənyːr], *s.f.* **1.** tenure; **t. à bail**, leasehold; *A:* **t. censuelle**, copyhold. **2.** holding, estate. **3.** *Tex:* waste thread of silk.

téorbe [teɔrb], *s.m. Mus: A:* theorbo.

téosinte [teɔsɛ̃ːt], *s.m. Bot: Agr:* teosinte.

tépale [tepal], *s.m. Bot:* tepal.

téphilin [tefilɛ̃], **tephillim** [tefilim], *s.m.pl. Jewish Rel:* tephillin, tefillin.

téphrite [tefrit], *s.f.* **1.** *Miner:* tephrite. **2.** *Ent:* tephritis.

téphroïte [tefrɔit], *s.f. Miner:* tephroite.

téphromyélite [tefrɔmjelit], *s.f. Med:* tephromyelitis.

tephrosia [tefrozja], *s.m.*, **téphrosie** [tefrozi], *s.f. Bot:* tephrosia.

tépide [tepid], *a. Lit:* tepid.

ter [tɛːr], *Lt.adv.* (*a*) three times; *Mus:* ter; (*b*) for the third time; **numéro 5 ter**, No. 5b, *occ.* 5c.

téra- [tera], *pref. Mth:* tera- (10^{12}).

téraphim [terafim], *s.m.pl. B.Lit:* teraphim.

téraphose [terafoːz], *s.f. Arach:* theraphose, bird spider.

téraspic [teraspik], *s.m. Hort:* candytuft.

tératogène [teratɔʒɛn], *a. Med:* teratogenic, teratogenetic.

tératogénèse [teratɔʒenɛːz], **tératogénie** [teratɔʒeni], *s.f. Med:* teratogenesis, teratogeny.

tératogénique [teratɔʒenik], *a. Med:* teratogenic, teratogenetic.

tératoïde [teratɔid], *a.* teratoid (tumour).

tératologie [teratɔlɔʒi], *s.f.* teratology.

tératologique [teratɔlɔʒik], *a.* teratological.

tératologiste [teratɔlɔʒist], **tératologue** [teratɔlɔg], *s.m.* teratologist.

tératome [teratoːm], *s.m. Med:* teratoma.

tératopage [teratɔpaːʒ], *s.m. Med:* (pair of) Siamese twins.

tératoscopie [teratɔskɔpi], *s.f.* teratoscopy.

terbine [tɛrbin], *s.f. Ch:* terbium hydroxide.

terbique [tɛrbik], *a. Ch:* terbic.

terbium [tɛrbjɔm], *s.m. Ch:* terbium.

tercer [tɛrse], *v.tr. Agr:* to plough (field) for the third time.

tercet [tɛrsɛ], *s.m. Pros:* tercet, triplet.

tère [tɛːr], *s.f. Ich:* eagle ray.

térébelle [terebɛl], *s.f.*, **terebellum**[1] [terebɛlɔm], *s.m. Ann:* terebella.

terebellum[2] [terebɛlɔm], *s.m. Moll:* terebellum.

térébellidés [terebelide], **térébelliens** [terebɛljɛ̃], *s.m.pl. Ann:* Terebellidae.

térébène [terebɛn], *s.m. Pharm:* terebene.

térébenthène [terebɑ̃tɛn], *s.m. Ch:* terebenthene.

térébenthinage [terebɑ̃tinaːʒ], *s.m.* turpentining (of resin).

térébenthine [terebɑ̃tin], *s.f.* turpentine; **essence de t.**, (oil of) turpentine; *F:* turps; **t. de Bordeaux**, galipot; **t. de Judée**, true balsam, Mecca balsam, balm of Gilead; **t. de Chio**, Chian turpentine.

térébenthiné [terebɑ̃tine], *a. Pharm:* terebinthinate, terebinthine.

térébinthacées [terebɛ̃tase], *s.f.pl. Bot:* Terebinthaceae.

térébinthe [terebɛ̃ːt], *s.m. Bot:* terebinth; turpentine tree.

térébique [terebik], *a. Ch:* terebic.

terebra [terebra], *s.m. Moll:* auger shell; (*genus*) Terebra.

térébrant [terebrɑ̃]. **1.** *a.* (*a*) terebrant, boring (insect, etc.); (*b*) *Med:* **douleur térébrante**, probing, boring, pain; **ulcération térébrante**, deep ulceration; **souci t.**, piercing anxiety. **2.** *s.m.pl. Ent:* **térébrants**, Terebrantia.

térébration [terebrasjɔ̃], *s.f.* terebration. **1.** boring (of resinous tree, etc.). **2.** *Surg:* trephining.

térébratule [terebratyl], *s.f. Moll:* lamp shell; (*genus*) Terebratula.

térébrer [terebre], *v.tr.* (**je térèbre, n. térébrons; je térébrerai**) to bore; to terebrate.

térébridés [terebride], *s.m.pl. Moll:* Terebridae.

térédinidés [teredinide], *s.m.pl. Moll:* Teredinidae.

térékie [tereki], *s.f. Orn:* terek.

Térence [terɑ̃ːs], *Pr.n.m. Lt.Lit:* Terence.

téréphtalate [tereftalat], *s.m. Ch:* terephthalate.

téréphtalique [tereftalik], *a. Ch:* terephthalic.

terfèze [tɛrfɛːz], *s.m. Fung:* terfez.

tergal[1], **-aux** [tɛrgal, -o], *a. Z:* tergal.

tergal[2], *s.m. R.t.m:* = TÉRYLÈNE.

tergéminé [tɛrʒemine], *a. Bot:* tergeminate, tergeminal.

tergite [tɛrʒit], *s.m. Z:* tergite.

tergiversateur, -trice [tɛrʒivɛrsatœːr, -tris], *s.* tergiversator, shuffler, wriggler.

tergiversation [tɛrʒivɛrsasjɔ̃], *s.f.* tergiversation, shuffling; beating about the bush; evasiveness.

tergiverser [tɛrʒivɛrse], *v.i.* to tergiversate, to equivocate; to shuffle; to beat about the bush; to wriggle; to dodge the issue.

tergum [tɛrgɔm], *s.m. Z:* tergum.

terlinguaïte [tɛrlɛ̃gait], *s.f. Miner:* terlinguaite.

terme[1] [tɛrm], *s.m.* **1.** (*a*) *Rom.Ant:* boundary stone; terminus; (*b*) *Sculp:* terminal (statue), term, terminus; *A:* **il ne bouge pas plus qu'un t.**, he stands like a statue; he never stirs. **2.** term, end, limit (of life, journey, race, etc.); **l'athéisme est le t. logique de cette doctrine**, atheism is the logical outcome of this doctrine; **arriver au t. de ses espérances**, to attain one's hopes; **toucher à son t.**, to be near one's end; **t. d'un mandat**, date of completion of a mandate; **être arrivé au t. de son mandat**, to have exhausted one's mandate; **mettre un t. à qch.**, to put a term, an end, a stop, to sth.; **il y a t. à tout**, there is an end to everything; **mener qch. à bon t.**, to bring sth. to a successful conclusion; to carry sth. through. **3.** (*a*) (appointed) time; (*of pregnant woman*) **être à t.**, to have reached her time; **accoucher avant t.**, to be delivered prematurely; **accouchement avant t.**, premature labour; *Mil: Navy:* **engagement à long t.**, long service; **engagés à long t.**, long-service men; **remplir un engagement dans le t. de trois mois**, to fulfil a contract within three months; **t. de rigueur**, latest time, latest date; **qui a t. ne doit rien**, a debt cannot be claimed before it is due; **marché à t.**, (i) *Com:* terminal market; *St.Exch:* settlement market; (ii) transactions on credit; *Com:* forward, terminal, transaction; *St.Exch:* settlement bargain; **avance à long t.**, long-term advance; (*of bills*) **à court t., à long t.**, short-dated, long-dated; **argent à court t.**, money at short notice, at call; *St.Exch:* **le t.**, the settlement; **valeurs à t.**, securities dealt in for the account; **acheter à t.**, (i) *Com:* to buy on credit; (ii) *St.Exch:* to buy for the settlement, for the account; **opérations à t.**, buying and selling at a date future and certain; forward deals; **taux pour les opérations à t.**, forward rates; **livrable à t.**, for future delivery; **livraisons à t.**, futures; *Ind: etc:* **prévisions à court t., à long t.**, short-range, long-range, forecasts; (*b*) delay (for payment); **demander un t. de grâce**, to ask for time to pay; *Com:* **octroi de termes et délais**, attermining, atterminement; (*c*) instalment; **payable à deux termes**, payable in two instalments. **4.** (*a*) quarter (of rent); term; **louer un appartement pour un t.**, to rent a flat for one quarter; (*b*) quarter's rent; *F:* **je suis un t. en retard**, I owe a quarter's rent; **payer le t.**, to pay the rent; (*c*) quarter day.

terme[2], *s.m.* **1.** term, expression; **t. de métier**, technical term; **t. de médecine, de droit**, medical term, legal term; **en termes de pratique**, in legal parlance; **employer les termes propres**, to use the appropriate terms; **il m'a dit en termes propres, en termes exprès, que . . .**, he told me in so many words that. . .; **en d'autres termes**, in other words; **il s'exprima ensuite en ces termes . . .**, he then spoke as follows . . .; **je répète ses propres termes**, I am repeating his very words; **peser, mesurer, ses termes**, to weigh one's words; **il n'a pas ménagé ses termes**, he didn't mince his words; **il m'a parlé de vous en très bons termes**, he spoke very well, favourably, of you; **dans toute la force du t.**, in the full sense of the word; *Log:* **termes d'un syllogisme**, terms of a syllogism; **termes contradictoires**, contradiction in terms; *Mth:* **t. d'une progression**, term of a progression; **termes d'une équation**, terms of an equation. **2.** *pl.* wording (of clause, etc.); terms, conditions; **termes d'un contrat**, terms of a contract; **aux termes de l'article 20 . . .**, by the terms of article 20 . . ., by, under, article 20 . . .; **aux termes de la décision . . .**, in accordance with the decision . . .. **3.** *pl.* terms, footing; **être en bons termes avec qn**, to be on good terms, on friendly terms, with s.o.; **être dans les meilleurs termes avec qn**, to be on the best of terms with s.o.; **en quels termes êtes-vous avec lui?** on what terms are you with him? **l'affaire est en termes d'accommodement**, negotiations are in hand for an amicable settlement.

terminable [tɛrminabl̥], *a.* terminable (annuity, etc.).

terminaison [tɛrminɛzɔ̃], *s.f.* termination, ending; *Anat:* insertion (of a muscle); *Gram:* **t. masculine**, masculine termination, ending; *Elcs:* (*computers*) **programme de lancement et de t.**, initiator/terminator.

terminal, -ale, -aux [tɛrminal, -o]. **1.** *a.* (*a*) terminal, final; *Sch:* **les classes terminales** = the sixth forms; (*b*) *Nat.Hist:* terminal (flower, etc.); **pousse terminale**, leading shoot, leader; terminal, apical, growth; (*c*) *El: Elcs:* **impédance terminale**, terminal impedance; (*computers*) **marque terminale**, end mark. **2.** *s.f. Sch: F:* **terminale** = sixth form. **3.** *s.m. Elcs:* (*computers*) terminal (unit); **t. spécifique**, job-oriented terminal. **4.** *s.m. Petroleum Ind:* pipeline terminal.

terminateur, -trice [tɛrminatœːr, -tris], *a. Astr:* **cercle t., ligne terminatrice (de la lumière)**, terminator (of moon's disc, etc.).

terminatif, -ive [tɛrminatif, -iːv], *a. Ling:* terminational (change, accent, etc.).

terminer [tɛrmine], *v.tr.* to terminate. **1.** to bound, limit (country, estate); **contours terminés**, well-marked outlines. **2.** to end, finish, to bring (war, speech, etc.) to an end, to a close; to settle, conclude (bargain, etc.); to complete (piece of work); **t. un différend**, to end a disagreement; **la mort termina les conquêtes d'Alexandre**, death put an end to the conquests of Alexander; **t. ses jours en paix**, to end one's days in peace; **t. une discussion par . . .**, to wind up a debate with . . .; **t. la soirée par l'hymne national**, to wind up the evening with the national anthem; **il faut en t.**, we must make an end; **nous en avons terminé avec ça**, we have finally finished with it; **t. court**, to come to an abrupt ending; *W.Tel:* **terminé!** out!

se terminer, to end, to come to an end; **la soirée se termina par des chants patriotiques**, the evening concluded with patriotic songs; **la guerre venait de se t.**, the war was just over; **mot qui se termine par une voyelle**, word that ends in a vowel; **le siècle d'Auguste se termine à, avec, Ovide**, the age of Augustus ends with Ovid; **cette affaire se termine mal**, this business is turning out badly.

termineur [tɛrminœːr], *s.m. Elcs:* four-wire terminating set.

terminisme [tɛrminism], *s.m. Theol:* terminism.

terministe [tɛrminist], *s.m. & f. Theol:* terminist.

terminologie [tɛrminɔlɔʒi], *s.f.* terminology.

terminologique [tɛrminɔlɔʒik], *a.* terminological.

termino-terminal, -aux [tɛrminɔtɛrminal, -o], *a. Surg:* end-to-end (union of parts).

terminus [tɛrminys]. **1.** *s.m.* (railway, coach, etc.) terminus. **2.** *a.inv.* **gare t.,** terminus; **les gares t. de Paris,** the Paris railway termini.

termite [tɛrmit], *s.m. Ent:* termite, white ant; *F:* **travail de t.,** destructive activities carried on in secret.

termitidés [tɛrmitide], *s.m.pl. Ent:* Termitidae.

termitière [tɛrmitjɛːr], *s.f. Ent:* termitary, termitarium.

termitophage [tɛrmitɔfaːʒ], *a. Z:* termitophagous.

termitophile [tɛrmitɔfil], *s.m. Ent:* termitophile.

ternaire [tɛrnɛːr], *a. Mth:* **numéraire t.,** ternary numeration; **forme t.,** ternary form; *Ch:* **composé t.,** ternary compound; *Mus:* **mesure t.,** triple time.

terne[1] [tɛrn], *a.* dim, dull, lustreless, leaden, tarnished (colouring, metal); **yeux ternes,** dull, lustreless, lack-lustre, eyes; **voix t.,** flat voice, colourless voice; **vie t.,** drab existence; **style t.,** dull, flat, lifeless, style; **ce chapitre est plutôt t.,** this chapter is rather flat, dull.

terne[2], *s.m.* **1.** (*a*) (*at dice*) two treys; (*b*) (*in lottery*) tern; (*c*) (*at bingo*) three numbers in one (horizontal) line. **2.** *El:* (set of) three conductors (of three-phase system).

terné [tɛrne], *a. Bot:* ternate; trifoliate.

terniflore [tɛrniflɔːr], *a. Bot:* ternately triflorous.

ternifolié [tɛrnifɔlje], *Bot:* ternate, trifoliate.

ternir [tɛrniːr], *v.tr.* to tarnish (metal); to dull, dim, deaden (colour, etc.); **t. un miroir de son haleine,** to cloud a mirror with one's breath; **les cuivres se sont ternis,** the brasses have got tarnished; **yeux ternis de pleurs,** eyes dimmed with tears; **t. une réputation,** to damage a reputation; **t. l'honneur de qn,** to tarnish s.o.'s honour; **le temps fait t. la beauté,** time makes beauty fade; **dès que ternit la nouveauté,** as soon as the novelty faded, wore off.

ternissement [tɛrnismɑ̃], *s.m.* tarnishing (of metals); clouding (of glass); fading (of colouring).

ternissure [tɛrnisyːr], *s.f.* (*a*) tarnished appearance; dull spot or patch (on metal, etc.); blur (on print, etc.); (*b*) blemish, stain (on reputation, etc.); **il n'aurait pas accepté de t.,** he would have accepted nothing that dishonoured him.

ternstrœmiacées [tɛrnstremjase], *s.f.pl. Bot:* Ternstroemiaceae.

Terpandre [tɛrpɑ̃ːdr], *Pr.n.m. Gr.Ant:* Terpander.

terpène [tɛrpɛn], *s.m. Ch:* terpene.

terpénique [tɛrpenik], *a. Ch:* terpenic.

terpine [tɛrpin], *s.f. Ch: Pharm:* terpin, terpinol.

terpinène [tɛrpinɛn], *s.m. Ch:* terpinene.

terpinéol [tɛrpineɔl], *s.m. Ch:* terpineol.

terpinol [tɛrpinɔl], *s.m. Ch:* terpinol, terpin.

terpinolène [tɛrpinɔlɛn], *s.m. Ch:* terpinolene.

Terpsichore [tɛrpsikɔːr], *Pr.n.f. Myth:* Terpsichore.

terra-cotta [tɛrakɔta], *s.f.* terra-cotta.

terrade [tɛrad], *s.f.* town wastes (used as fertilizer).

terrafungine [tɛrafɔ̃ʒin], *s.f. Pharm:* oxytetracycline; *R.t.m:* Terramycin.

terrage [tɛraːʒ], *s.m.* **1.** *A:* claying (of sugar). **2.** *Agr:* warping (of land); spreading of mould (on land). **3.** *Hist:* tithe (on produce).

terrailler [tɛrɑje], *v.tr. Agr:* to spread mould over (meadow, etc.), to cover (ground) with soil.

terrain [tɛrɛ̃], *s.m.* **1.** (*a*) ground; piece of ground, plot of land; **terrains à bâtir,** development site; **un t. à bâtir,** a building plot; **terrains vagues,** waste ground; (*b*) *Geog: etc:* country, ground; **relief du t.,** relief; **t. accidenté,** hilly ground, country; **t. couvert,** close country; **t. découvert** open country; **t. en pente,** sloping ground; **t. onduleux, t. vallonné,** undulating ground; **t. plat,** flat country; (*c*) soil, ground; **t. ferme,** firm ground, soil; **t. glaiseux,** loamy ground; **t. gras,** rich ground, soil; **t. mou,** soft soil; *Min: etc:* **terrains de couverture, de recouvrement,** overburden; (*d*) (*scene of action*) (duelling) ground; (cricket, football) field; (golf) course, links; *Mil:* terrain; **t. de jeux,** (i) playground; (ii) playing field; *Av:* **t. d'atterrissage,** landing strip, airstrip; *Mil:* **t. militaire,** military reservation; **compartimentage du t.,** dividing of the terrain into compartments; **utilisation du t.,** fieldcraft; **t. d'exercice,** training ground; **t. de manœuvres,** drill ground, parade ground; *Husb:* **t. d'exercice (d'un poulailler),** chicken run; **ménager le t.,** to make the most of one's resources; **aller sur le t.,** to fight a duel; **appeler qn sur le t.,** to call s.o. out (to fight a duel); **rester sur le t.,** (i) to be killed (in a duel); (ii) to be defeated; *Mil: etc:* **gagner du t.,** to gain ground; **perdre, céder, du t.,** to lose ground; **se disputer le t.,** to dispute the ground; **sonder, tâter, le t.,** to test the ground; to see how the land lies; **être sur son t.,** to be on familiar ground, in one's element; **connaître le t.,** to be sure of one's ground; to know the ropes; **je ne suis plus sur mon t.,** I am out of my depth; **préparer le t.,** to pave the way; *Cin:* **t. (de studio),** (studio) lot; *Ind: etc:* **sur le t.,** in the field; **travaux sur le t.,** fieldwork; *Av:* **entretien d'un hélicoptère sur le t.,** servicing a helicopter in the field. **2.** *Geol:* formation, (system of) rocks; terrane.

terral [tɛral], *s.m. Nau:* land breeze, terral.

terramare [tɛramaːr], *s.f. Agr:* terramare (fertilizer).

terramycine [tɛramisin], *s.f. Pharm: R.t.m:* Terramycin.

terrapène [tɛrapɛn], *s.m. Rept:* box turtle, box tortoise; (*genus*) Terrapene; **t. des Carolines,** (American) box turtle.

terrapin [tɛrapɛ̃], *s.m. Rept:* (diamond-back) terrapin.

terraqué [tɛrake], *a.* terraqueous (globe, planet).

terrarium [tɛrarjɔm], *s.m.* terrarium.

terra-rossa [tɛrarɔsa], *s.f. Geol:* terra rossa.

terrassant [tɛrasɑ̃], *a.* crushing (news, answer); overwhelming (evidence).

terrasse[1] [tɛras], *s.f.* **1.** (*a*) terrace; bank; **jardin en t.,** terraced garden, embanked garden; *Geog:* **cultures en terrasses,** terrace cultivation; **t. marine,** marine terrace, wave-built terrace; (*b*) **t. d'un café,** pavement in front of a café; **nous étions assis à la t.,** we were sitting outside (the café); (*c*) *Const:* verandah, terrace, balcony; **nous étions assis sur la t.,** we were sitting on the terrace, the balcony; **(toit en) t.,** flat roof, terrace roof. **2.** (*a*) *Art:* foreground (of landscape); (*b*) low pedestal (for statue); (*c*) *Her:* soil, earth. **3.** terrace, flaw (in marble).

terrasse[2], *s.f.* = TERRASSEMENT.

terrassé [tɛrase], *a. Her:* growing in soil.

terrassement [tɛrasmɑ̃], *s.m.* **1.** banking, digging (of earth); **travaux de t.,** navvying; **wagons de t.,** ballast trucks. **2.** earthwork, embankment; **entrepreneur de terrassements,** earthwork contractor.

terrasser [tɛrase], *v.tr.* **1.** (*a*) *A:* to bank up, embank (wall, road); (*b*) *Agr:* to work the soil of (vineyard, etc.). **2.** (*a*) to lay (s.o.) low; *F:* to down (s.o.); **t. un adversaire,** to floor, bring down, *Wr:* to throw, an opponent; (*b*) to overwhelm, dismay, crush; **être terrassé par le chagrin,** to be crushed, prostrated, with grief.

se terrasser, *Mil:* to dig oneself in.

terrassette [tɛrasɛt], *s.f. Geog:* terracette.

terrasseur [tɛrasœːr], *s.m. Const:* rubble worker, pugger.

terrasseux, -euse [tɛrasø, -øːz], *a.* earthy (stone, marble).

terrassier, -ière [tɛrasje, -jɛːr]. **1.** *s.m.* (*a*) navvy, digger; **travaux de t.,** navvying; (*b*) earthwork contractor. **2.** *s.m. A:* **t. à vapeur,** steam-navvy. **3.** *a. Ent:* **guêpe terrassière,** digger wasp.

terrasson [tɛrasɔ̃], *s.m. Const:* (*a*) small terrace; (*b*) top slope of mansard roof.

terrassonnais, -aise [tɛrasɔnɛ, -ɛːz], *a. & s. Geog:* (native, inhabitant) of Terrasson-Villedieu.

terrat [tɛra], *s.m. Cer:* water trough (used by potter to keep his hands wet).

terre [tɛːr], *s.f.* **1.** earth; (*a*) the world; **jusqu'au bout de la t.,** to the world's end; far and wide; **être seul sur (la) t.,** to be alone in the world, to have neither kith nor kin; **être encore sur t.,** to be still in the land of the living, still above ground; **revenir sur t.,** (i) to come back to earth (from a daydream, etc.); (ii) (*to be practical*) to come down to earth; **qui a les pieds sur t.,** down-to-earth; **tenir trop à la t.,** to be too much attached to this world; *s.a.* REMUER 1; (*b*) ground, land; **t. ferme,** continent, mainland; **armée, forces, de t.,** land forces; **pénétrer dans les terres,** to go, march, inland; *Geog:* **basses terres,** lowlands; **hautes terres,** highlands; **tremblement de t.,** earthquake; **aller par t.,** to go by land, overland; **à t., par t.,** on the ground, to the ground; **frapper qn à t.,** to strike s.o. when he is down; **tirer sur une perdrix à t.,** to shoot a partridge sitting; **tomber par t.,** to fall down (from standing position); **tomber à t.,** to fall down (from height); **être assis, couché, par t.,** to sit, lie, on the ground; *Nau: F:* **nous avions un mât par t.,** one of our masts was down; **mettre un tyran par t.,** to overthrow a tyrant; **mettre pied à t.,** to set foot to ground; to dismount (from horse); *Mil: etc:* **mettre sac à t.,** to make a halt; **attaquer une ville par t. et par mer,** to attack a town by land and sea; **tactique, politique, de la t. brûlée,** scorched-earth policy; **grand voyageur sur t. comme sur mer,** great traveller by land and sea; **appuyer son oreille contre t.,** to put one's ear to the ground; **habitation sous t.,** underground dwelling; **être sous t., en t.,** to be in one's grave; **porter qn en t.,** to bear s.o. to his grave; **t. sainte,** consecrated ground; (*c*) *El:* **mettre, relier, raccorder, à la t.,** to earth, *U.S:* to ground; **mise à la t.,** (i) earthing; (ii) earth contact, connection, wire, lead; **prise de t.,** earth (wire), *U.S:* ground connection; **câble de mise à la t.,** ground bus; **contact avec la t.,** earth fault; **pertes à la t.,** leakage of current; **circuit à retour par la t.,** earth, *U.S:* ground, return circuit; **fil de t.,** ground conductor; **plaque de t.,** ground plate; *Nau:* (*of ship*) **être à t.,** to be aground, ashore; **mettre qn à t.,** to land s.o.; to put s.o. ashore; **descendre à t., prendre t.,** to land, disembark, go ashore; *Nau:* **perdre t.,** to lose sight of land; **t. (en vue!),** land ho! **naviguer t. à t.,** to coast along; *adj.phr.* **t. à t.,** matter-of-fact, commonplace; *s.* **le t. à t. de sa pensée, de son style,** the lack of any elevation in his thought; the commonplace, pedestrian, nature of his thought, of his style. **2.** soil, land; **cultiver la t.,** to cultivate the soil; **ligue de retour à la t.,** "back to the land" league; *Prov:* **tant vaut l'homme, tant vaut la t.,** a good farmer makes a good farm; **t. grasse,** rich soil; *s.a.* SEMER 1. **3.** (*a*) estate, property; *Prov:* **qui t. a guerre a,** he that has land has trouble at hand; **il a une t. en Normandie,** he has an estate in Normandy; **venez chasser sur mes terres,** come and shoot over my property, over my land; (*b*) territory; **terres étrangères,** foreign countries, lands; **la T. Sainte,** the Holy Land; *Geog:* **la T. de Feu,** Tierra del Fuego; **les terres arctiques,** the arctic regions. **4.** (*a*) loam, clay, **t. végétale, franche, naturelle,** mould, loam; **t. jaune,** loess; **sol en t. battue,** mud floor; *Metall:* **t. de coulage,** casting loam; **t. à potier,** potter's clay; **t. de pipe,** pipeclay; **pipe en terre,** clay pipe; **t. cuite,** (i) baked clay; (ii) terra-cotta; *Art:* **une t. cuite,** a terra-cotta; **cruche de, en, t.,** earthenware jar; **t. de Chine, à porcelaine,** kaolin; **t. à casettes, cazettes,** sagger, saggar, clay; **t. réfractaire,** chamotte, grog; *Com:* **t. de montagne,** yellow ochre; **t. pourrie d'Angleterre,** rotten-stone, tripoli powder; **t. à poêle,** fireclay; (*b*) *Ch:* **terres rares,** rare earths.

terreau, -eaux [tɛro], *s.m. Hort:* (vegetable) mould; **t. de feuilles,** leaf mould; compost.

terreautage [tɛrotaːʒ], *s.m. Hort:* composting.

terreauter [tɛrote], *v.tr. Hort:* to treat (plant, ground) with mould; to compost (bed).

terrée [tɛre], *s.f. Agr:* raised field (made with soil from surrounding ditch).

Terre-ferme (la) [latɛrfɛrm], *Pr.n.f. Hist:* (*a*) the Spanish Main, the north-east coast of S. America; (*b*) **(États de) T.-f.,** Terra Firma, the Venetian mainland territories.

terrement [tɛrmɑ̃], *s.m. Agr:* warping (of land).

terre-mérite [tɛrmerit], *s.f. Bot:* turmeric.

terre-neuvas [tɛrnœvɑ], *s.m.inv. Dial:* (*in Brittany*) **1.** Newfoundland fisher. **2.** Newfoundland fishing boat.

Terre-Neuve [tɛrnœːv]. **1.** *Pr.n.f. Geog:* New foundland. **2.** *s.m.inv.* **un t.-n.,** a Newfoundland (dog); **il a un dévouement de t.-n.,** he has the devotion of a Newfoundland.

terre-neuvien, -ienne [tɛrnœvjɛ̃, -jɛn]. **1.** *Geog:* (*a*) *a.* (of) Newfoundland; (*b*) *s.* Newfoundlander, *F:* Newfie. **2.** *s.m.* (*a*) Newfoundland dog; (*b*) Newfoundland fisherman; (*c*) Newfoundland fishing vessel; banker; Newfoundlander; *pl. terre-neuviens, -iennes.*

terre-neuvier [tɛrnœvje]. **1.** *a.* Newfoundland (fisherman, etc.). **2.** *s.m.* (*a*) Newfoundland dog; (*b*) Newfoundland fisherman; (*c*) Newfoundland fishing vessel, banker; Newfoundlander; *pl. terre-neuviers.*

terre-noix [tɛrnwɑ], *s.f.inv. Bot:* earthnut, pignut.

terre-plein [tɛrplɛ̃], *s.m.* **1.** *Fort:* terreplein (of bastion or rampart). **2.** (*a*) earth platform; terrace; *Rail:* road bed; (*b*) raised strip of ground (with trees, etc.); *U.S:* boulevard (running along a street, etc.); (*c*) (any) strip of horizontal ground; (*d*) (*on road*) **t.-p. de stationnement,** layby; **t.-p. central,** central reservation, *U.S:* median strip, mall; **t.-p. circulaire,** central island (of roundabout); *pl. terre-pleins.*

terrer [tɛre], *v.tr.* **1.** *Hort:* to earth up (tree, plant). **2.** *Agr:* (*a*) to warp (field); (*b*) to spread mould over (meadow, etc.); to cover, fill up, (ground) with earth. **3.** *Tex:* to full (cloth). **4.** *A:* to clay (sugar).

se terrer. 1. (*a*) (*of rabbit, etc.*) to burrow; (*of fox*) to go to earth, to ground; *F:* **on dit qu'il s'est terré dans un monastère,** they say he has buried himself in a monastery; (*b*) (*of rabbit, partridge, etc.*) to squat. 2. *Mil:* (*a*) to entrench oneself, *F:* to dig oneself in; (*b*) to lie down.

terrestre [tɛrɛstr], *a.* (*a*) terrestrial (animal, plant); ground (plant); land (animal); earthly, worldly (thoughts, etc.); (*b*) **rotation t.,** rotation of the earth; **la pesanteur t.,** the earth's weight; (*c*) **paradis t.,** earthly paradise; *Mil:* **effectifs terrestres,** land forces; *Navy:* land-based; shore-based (installation, etc.); *Ins:* **assurance t.,** land insurance; (*d*) **exhalations terrestres,** exhalations from the ground.

terrestrement [terɛstrəmɑ̃], *adv.* terrestrially.

terrette [tɛrɛt], *s.f. Bot:* ground ivy.

terreur [tɛrœːr], *s.f.* 1. (*a*) terror; (intense) fear; dread; **fou de t.,** wild with fear; frightened out of one's wits; **être dans la t.,** to be in terror; **frapper qn d'une t. mystérieuse,** to strike s.o. with awe; **t. du noir,** fear of the dark; (*b*) **gouverner par la t.,** to rule by terror; *Fr.Hist:* **la T.,** the (Reign of) Terror (1793); **la T. blanche,** the White Terror (1815). 2. (*a*) object of dread; **il est la t. de ses ennemis,** he is a terror, an object of dread, to his enemies; **la t. de la famille,** the nightmare of the family; (*b*) *F:* gangster, thug; (*as nickname*) **Jo la T.,** Joe the Terror.

terreux, -euse [tɛrø, -øːz]. 1. *a.* (*a*) earthy (matter, taste, smell); (*b*) dull (colour); grubby, dirty (hands, etc.); **visage t.,** unhealthy, ashy, ashen, sickly, face, complexion; **peindre de terreuses ruines antiques,** to paint muddy-coloured ancient ruins; **sable t.,** muddy sand; **laitue terreuse,** badly, inadequately, washed lettuce; (*c*) *P:* **elle a le cul t.,** (she's nobody in particular but) she has a great many acres. 2. *s.m.* countryman, yokel, clodhopper.

terri [tɛri], *s.m. Min:* = TERRIL.

terrible [tɛribl̥], *a.* (*a*) terrible, terrifying; **cauchemar t.,** terrifying dream; **une t. catastrophe,** an appalling catastrophe; *Hist:* **Ivan le T.,** Ivan the Terrible; (*b*) **froid t.,** dreadful, extreme, cold; **orage t.,** terrific thunderstorm; **un temps t.,** awful weather; **enfant t.,** enfant terrible, little terror; *Lit:* **l'enfant t. du Romantisme,** the enfant terrible of the Romantic movement; **d'une humeur t.,** in a very bad temper; **bruit t.,** infernal din; (*c*) *F:* **un t. avantage,** a terrific advantage; **c'est un type t.,** he's terrific, incredible.

terriblement [tɛribləmɑ̃], *adv.* (*a*) terribly, dreadfully; (*b*) *F:* (*intensive*) **aimer t. qch.,** to be terribly, frightfully, fond of sth.; **il y avait t. d'étrangers,** there were a frightful, terrible, tremendous, lot of foreigners; **nous arrivons t. en retard,** we're shockingly, terribly, late.

terricole [tɛr(r)ikɔl]. 1. *a. Z:* terricolous, terricole. 2. *s.m.pl. Ann:* **terricoles,** Terricolae.

terrien, -ienne [tɛrjɛ̃, -jɛn]. 1. *a.* (*a*) possessing land; **propriétaire t.,** landed proprietor; **la persistance de l'esprit t. en France,** the Frenchman's enduring attachment to the land; (*b*) inland; terrestrial; **les origines terriennes des phoques,** the terrestrial origin(s) of seals; (*c*) country; rural; (*d*) Terran, of the earth. 2. *s.* (*a*) landowner; landed proprietor; (*b*) *Nau:* landsman, *F:* landlubber; (*c*) countryman, countrywoman; (*d*) earthman, earthwoman, Terran.

terrier[1] [tɛrje], *s.m.* burrow, hole (of rabbit, etc.); earth (of fox); set (of badger); **sortir de son t.,** to break cover; *F:* **vivre dans son t.,** to live on one's own; to bury oneself.

terrier[2], *a. & s.m.* relating to lands; *Hist:* **(papier) t.,** terrier; register of landed property; *Civ.E:* **plan t.,** land-use plan.

terrier[3], *a. & s.* **(chien, chienne) t.,** terrier (dog, bitch).

terrifiant [tɛr(r)ifjɑ̃], *a.* terrifying, awe-inspiring; **roman t.,** thriller.

terrifier [tɛr(r)ifje], *v.tr. & pr.sub.* **n. terrifiions, v. terrifiiez)** to terrify; *F:* to scare to death; **il était terrifié,** he was frightened out of his wits; he was in a state of terror.

terrifique [tɛr(r)ifik], *a. F:* terrifying.

terrigène [tɛr(r)iʒɛn], *a. Geol:* terrigenous.

terril [tɛri], *s.m. Min:* spoil heap, tip, dump; **mise à t.,** (i) tipping; (ii) (*mechanism*) tip, tipple.

terrine [tɛrin], *s.f.* 1. (*a*) earthenware vessel, pan (for milk, etc.); (*b*) (earthenware) pot (for pâté de foie, etc.); terrine; (*c*) *Hort:* seed pan. 2. potted meat; pâté, terrine.

terrinée [tɛrine], *s.f.* (*a*) panful; (*b*) potful; (*c*) *Cu:* (*in Normandy*) rice pudding flavoured with cinnamon.

terrir [tɛriːr], *v.i.* 1. (*of turtles*) to go ashore (to lay eggs). 2. *Nau: A:* (*a*) to make a landfall; (*b*) (*of boat*) to ground. 3. *Fish:* **poissons qui terrissent,** fish living in coastal waters.

territoire [tɛritwaːr], *s.m.* territory (of state, *Nat.Hist:* of bird, animal); district, area, or region under jurisdiction; *Geog:* **t. du Nord,** Northern Territory (of Australia); *Pol:* **t. sous mandat,** mandated territory; *Anat:* **territoires cérébraux,** areas of the brain.

territorial, -aux [tɛritɔrjal, -o]. 1. *a.* territorial (tax, army, etc.); **eaux territoriales,** territorial waters. 2. *Mil.Hist: F:* (*a*) *s.m.* territorial (soldier); (*b*) *s.f.* **la territoriale,** the territorial army.

territorialement [tɛritɔrjalmɑ̃], *adv.* territorially.

territorialité [tɛritɔrjalite], *s.f.* territoriality.

terroir [tɛrwaːr], *s.m. Agr:* soil; (*of wine, etc.*) **goût de t.,** tang of the soil, native tang; **sentir le t.,** to smack of the soil of one's locality; **mots de t.,** local words, sayings, expressions.

terroriser [tɛrɔrize], *v.tr.* (*a*) to terrorize; (*b*) to terrify.

terrorisme [tɛrɔrism], *s.m.* (*a*) terrorism; (*b*) terrorist régime.

terroriste [tɛrɔrist], *a. & s.m. & f.* terrorist; *Fr.Hist.* **le despotisme t.,** the despotism of the Terror.

terrure [tɛryːr], *s.f. Agr:* = TERRAGE 2.

terser [tɛrse], *v.tr. Agr:* to plough (field) for the third time.

terson, -onne [tɛrsɔ̃, -ɔn], *s. Husb: Dial:* three year old (cow, bull).

tertiaire [tɛrsjɛːr]. 1. *a.* tertiary; *Pol.Ec:* **secteur t.,** tertiary industries; *Med:* **syphilis t.,** tertiary syphilis; *Elcs:* (*computers*) **groupe t.,** master group. 2. *s.m. Geol:* **le T.,** the Tertiary. 3. *s.m. & f. R.C.Ch:* tertiary.

tertio [tɛrsjo], *adv.* thirdly.

tertre [tɛrtr̥], *s.m.* hillock, mound, knoll; **t. de fleurs,** bank of flowers; *Golf:* **t. de départ,** teeing ground; *Archeol:* **t. funéraire,** barrow, tumulus; **t. tumulaire allongé,** unchambered long barrow.

Tertullien [tɛrtyljɛ̃], *Pr.n.m. Rel.H:* Tertullian.

Tervagant [tɛrvagɑ̃], *Pr.n.m. Lit:* Tervagant, Termagant.

térylène [terilɛn], *s.m. R.t.m:* Terylene.

terza rima [tɛrzarima], **terzina** [tɛrzina], *s.f. Pros:* terza rima.

teschémachérite [tɛskemakerit], *s.f. Miner:* teschemacherite.

téséfiste [tesefist], *s. F: A:* wireless fan.

teskra [tɛskra], *s.f. Bot:* globe thistle.

Tesla [tɛsla], *Pr.n.* 1. *El:* **bobine de T.,** *F:* **une T.,** Tesla coil. 2. *s.m. Ph.Meas:* tesla.

tesselle [tɛsɛl], *s.f.* tessera (of mosaic).

tessellé [tɛsɛlle], *a.* tessellated.

tesséral, -aux [tɛs(s)eral, -o], *a. Cryst:* tesseral; isometric.

tessère [tɛsɛːr], *s.f. Rom.Ant:* tessera.

Tessin (le) [lətesɛ̃], *Pr.n.m. Geog:* 1. the (river) Ticino. 2. the Ticino (canton of Switzerland).

tessinois, -oise [tɛsinwa, -waːz], *a. & s. Geog:* (native, inhabitant) of the Ticino.

tessiture [tɛs(s)ityːr], *s.f. Mus:* tessitura.

tesson[1] [tɛsɔ̃], *s.m.* potsherd, fragment of earthenware or glass, shard; **t. de bouteille,** piece of broken bottle.

tesson[2], *s.m. A:* badger.

test[1] [tɛ(st)], *s.m.* 1. *Bot:* testa, episperm. 2. *Z:* test (of echinoderm, etc.).

test[2] [tɛst], *s.m. Med: etc:* test, trial; *Z:* **t. de la descendance,** progeny test; *Psy:* **t. de capacité intellectuelle,** intelligence test; **t. d'intelligence pratique,** aptitude test; **t. professionnel,** vocational, trade, occupational, test; (*Statistics*) **t. de signification,** significance test; *Ph:* **t. nucléaire,** nuclear test; *Elcs:* (*computers*) **t. de marges,** marginal check, test; high-low bias test; **t. d'occupation,** engaged, *U.S:* busy, test; **programme de t. sélectif,** leapfrog test.

testa [tɛsta], *s.m. Bot:* testa, episperm.

testabilité [tɛstabilite], *s.f. Psy:* testability, susceptibility to testing.

testacé [tɛstase]. 1 *a. Z:* testaceous, shelled. 2. *s.m.* shellfish, mollusc; testacean.

testacelle [tɛstasɛl], *s.f. Z:* testacella.

testage [tɛstaːʒ], *s.m. Husb:* progeny testing.

testament[1] [tɛstamɑ̃], *s.m.* will, testament; **absence de t.,** intestacy; **mettre qn sur son t.,** to mention s.o. in one's will; **ceci est mon t.,** this is my last will and testament; **mourir sans t.,** to die intestate; **t. (h)olographe,** holograph will; **t. noncupatif,** nuncupative will, testament; **t. authentique, (par acte) public,** will dictated by the testator, executed by two *notaires,* in the presence of two witnesses, or by one *notaire* with four witnesses; **t. mystique, t. secret,** will written or dictated by testator and sealed and handed to the *notaire* by him in the presence of at least six witnesses; *F:* **il peut faire son t.,** he'd better make his will, he won't last much longer; *Hist:* **t. politique,** statesman's declaration of political principles.

testament[2], *s.m. B:* Testament; **l'ancien, le nouveau, T.,** the Old, the New, Testament.

testamentaire [tɛstamɑ̃tɛːr], *a.* testamentary; **disposition t.,** clause (of a will); devise; **héritier t.,** devisee; **exécuteur, -trice, t.,** executor, executrix.

testateur, -trice [tɛstatœːr, -tris], *s.* testator, testatrix; *Jur:* devisor.

tester[1] [tɛste], *v.i.* to make one's will.

tester[2], *v.tr.* to test; *Husb:* to progeny-test.

testicardines [tɛstikardin], *s.f.pl. Biol:* Testicardines, Articulata.

testiculaire [tɛstikylɛːr], *a. Anat:* testicular.

testicule [tɛstikyl], *s.m. Anat:* testicle; testis.

testiculé [tɛstikyle], *a.* testiculate.

testif [tɛstif], *s.m. Com:* camel's hair.

testimonial, -aux [tɛstimɔnjal, -o], *a.* (*a*) *Jur:* deponed to by witness; **preuve testimoniale,** proof by witnesses, oral evidence; (*b*) **lettre testimoniale,** testimonial; certificate (of good conduct, etc.).

testimonialement [tɛstimɔnjalmɑ̃], *adv.* **prouver t.,** to prove by testimony, by witnesses.

test-objet [tɛstɔbʒɛ], *s.m. Opt:* test object; *pl. test-objets.*

teston [tɛstɔ̃], *s.m. Num: A:* testo(o)n, tester; *A:* **je n'en donnerais pas un t.,** I wouldn't give sixpence for it.

testostérone [tɛstɔsterɔn], *s.f. Biol: Physiol:* testosterone.

testu [tɛsty], *s.m. Ich: F:* bullhead, miller's thumb.

testudinaire [tɛstydinɛːr], *s.f.,* **testudinaria** [tɛstydinarja], *s.m. Bot:* testudinaria, *F:* Hottentot's bread; **t. pied d'éléphant,** elephant's foot; tortoise plant.

testudiné [tɛstydine], *Rept:* 1. *a.* testudinate. 2. *s.m.* testudinate; *pl.* **testudinés,** Testudinata.

testudinidés [tɛstydinide), *s.m.pl. Rept:* Testudinidae.

testudo [tɛstydo], *s.m.* 1. *Rept:* land tortoise; (*genus*) Testudo. 2. *Med:* testudo, talpa.

têt [tɛ], *s.m.* 1. (*a*) *A:* potsherd; (*b*) *pl. Metall:* cast-iron scrap; (*c*) *Ven: A:* skull (of stag). 2. (*a*) *Z:* test, shell (of sea urchin, etc.); (*b*) *Bot:* testa, skin (of seed). 3. *Ch:* small fireclay cup; (*a*) **t. de coupellation,** cupel, *A:* test; (*b*) **t. à gaz,** beehive shelf; (*c*) **t. à rôtir,** roasting crucible.

tétanie [tetani], *s.f. Med:* tetany; *Vet:* **t. d'herbage,** grass tetany, grass staggers.

tétaniforme [tetanifɔrm], *a.* tetaniform.

tétanine [tetanin], *s.f.* tetanine.

tétanique [tetanik], *a. Med:* 1. *a.* tetanic; **bacille t.,** tetanus bacillus; **médicament t.,** tetanic. 2. *s.* (*pers.*) tetanus subject.

tétanisation [tetanizasjɔ̃], *s.f.* tetanization.

tétaniser [tetanize], *v.tr. Med:* to tetanize (s.o.).

tétanisme [tetanism], *s.m. Med:* tetanic state, tetanism.

tétanolysine [tetanɔlizin], *s.f.* tetanolysin.

tétanomoteur [tetanɔmɔtœːr], *s.m. Physiol:* tetanomotor.

tétanos [tetanoːs, -ɔs], *s.m. Med:* tetanus, lockjaw; *Vet:* stag-evil; *Physiol:* **t. physiologique, musculaire,** tetanus (of a muscle).

tétanotoxine [tetanɔtɔksin], *s.f.* tetanotoxin.

têtard [tɛtaːr], *s.m.* 1. (*a*) tadpole; (*b*) *P:* child, son. 2. *Arb:* pollard. 3. *Ich:* (*a*) bullhead, miller's thumb; (*b*) chub. 4. *Veh:* squared end of carriage pole. 5. *Leath:* sucking lamb, kid, skin (for gloves).

tétartoèdre [tetartɔɛdr̥], *Cryst:* 1. *a.* tetartohedral. 2. *s.m.* tetartohedron.

tétartoédrie [tetartɔedri], *s.f. Cryst:* tetartohedrism.

tétartoédrique [tetartɔedrik], *a. Cryst:* tetartohedral.

tétasses [tetas], *s.f.pl. P:* pendulous breasts.

tête [tɛt], *s.f.* head. 1. (*a*) **de la t. aux pieds,** from head to foot, from top to toe; **elle se jette à votre t.,** she's terribly gushing; **marcher la t. haute,** to carry one's head high; **t. basse,** with a hang-dog look; **dépasser qn de la t.,** to stand head and shoulders above s.o.; *Turf:* **son cheval ne l'a emporté que d'une t.,** his horse won only by a head; **être t. nue,** to be bare-headed; **vieillard à t. grise,** grey-headed old man; **homme à grosse t.,** large-headed man; *F:* **une grosse t.,** an intellectual, a highbrow; *P:* **faire à qn une grosse t.,** to box s.o.'s ears; **monstre à deux**

têtes, two-headed monster; **corps sans t.,** headless body; *F:* **faire la, sa, t.,** to sulk; *F:* **faire sa t.,** to give oneself airs; *Ven:* **faire t.,** to stand at bay; **faire, tenir, t. à qn,** to hold one's own against s.o., to stand up to s.o.; to oppose s.o.; **faire, tenir, t. au malheur,** to bear up against misfortune; **tenir t. à l'orage,** to confront the storm; *F:* to face the music; **nous avons tenu t. à toutes les tempêtes,** we have stood four-square to every storm; **les nuages qui flottent sur nos têtes,** the clouds overhead; **endetté par-dessus la t.,** up to the eyes, over head and ears, in debt; **j'en ai par-dessus la t.,** I can't stand it any longer; *F:* I'm fed up; **(la) t. baissée,** head down; **la t. en bas,** head downwards; (*of thg*) upside down; **la t. la première,** head foremost; head first; **tomber sur la t.,** (i) to fall flat on one's face; (ii) *P:* to go mad, crackers; *P:* **il est tombé sur la t.,** he's mad, he was dropped on the head when he was young; **ne (pas) savoir où donner de la t.,** not to know which way to turn; **t. couronnée,** crowned head; **payer tant par t.,** *F:* **par t. de pipe,** to pay so much a head; **dîner t. à t.,** to dine tête-à-tête; **mettre tous ses biens sur la t. de sa femme,** to settle all one's property on one's wife; (*for annuity, etc.*) **sur une t., sur deux têtes,** on one life, on two lives; **son sang retombera sur votre t.,** his blood will be upon your head; **sa t. fut mise à prix,** a price was put on his head; **il y va de votre t.,** your life is at stake; **ça va lui en coûter la t.,** it is going to cost him his life; **j'en donnerais ma t. à couper que . . .,** I'll bet anything you like that . . .; **j'en donnerais ma t. à couper, j'en gagerais ma t. à couper,** I'd stake my life on it; **signe de t.,** nod (of the head); **mal de t.,** headache; **avoir mal à la t.,** to have a headache; **t. chauve,** bald head; **t. ronde,** bullet head; **à t. ronde,** bullet-headed; *Hist:* **t. ronde,** Roundhead; *Fb:* **faire une t.,** to head the ball; *Swim:* **piquer une t.,** to take a header, to dive; *Gym: Mil:* **t. (à) droite!** eyes right! *Num:* **t. d'une médaille,** obverse of a medal; *A:* **t. ou pile?** heads or tails? *s.a.* BAISSER I. 1, BONNET 1, COUP 1, HAUT I. 1, LAVER 1, LEVER I. 1, MORT[1] 2, PERRUQUE, TOURNER 2, TURC[1] 2, VOIX 1; (*b*) head of hair; **se laver la t.,** to wash one's hair; (*c*) face, appearance; *Th:* **se faire la t. d'un rôle,** to make up for a part; *P:* **t. à l'huile,** super; *F:* **faire une t.,** to pull a long face, to look glum; **il en fit une t.!** he did look sick! **je ne sais pas quelle t. il fera,** I don't know how he will take it; *s.a.* PAYER; **faire la t. à qn,** (i) to frown at s.o.; (ii) to be sulky with s.o.; **faire une t. de circonstance,** to put on a look, a face, to suit the occasion; **je connais cette t.-là,** I know that face; **il a une bonne t.,** (i) he looks a decent fellow, (ii) he looks a bit of a mug; *cf.* 2; *P:* **t. d'imbécile!** you idiot! you clot! (*d*) head (of animal, fish, bird, etc.); jowl (of fish); *Vet:* **t. noire,** blackhead; *Mec.E:* **t. de cheval,** swing frame (of screw-cutting lathe); *s.a.* ALOUETTE 2, ANE 4; (*e*) *Nau:* (*of ship*) **faire t. sur son ancre,** to be brought up by her anchor; (*f*) *Art: Sculp:* **t. plate,** beakhead; (*g*) *Cost:* fancy headdress. **2.** headpiece, brains, mind; **une pareille idée ne me serait jamais passée par la t.,** such an idea would never have entered my head, have come into my head; **se creuser la t.,** to rack one's brains; **avoir de la t.,** to have a good head on one's shoulders; **il n'a pas de t.,** he has no head; **c'est une femme de t.,** she's a capable woman; **avoir la t. légère,** to be irresponsible, feather-headed; **avoir la t. dure,** to be (i) stupid, dull-witted, thick-headed, wooden-headed, (ii) pigheaded; *F:* **c'est une t. de bois,** he's a blockhead; **c'est une t. de mule,** *F:* **de pioche, de cochon,** *P:* **de lard,** he's, she's, pig-headed, as stubborn as a mule; *F:* **c'est une t. à gifles, à claques,** he's asking for it; **se mettre en t. de faire qch.,** to take it into one's head to do sth.; **se mettre dans la t. que . . .,** to get it, the idea, into one's head that . . .; **il s'est mis dans la t. qu'on le persécute,** he has got it into his head that he is persecuted; **il s'est mis dans la t. d'écrire un roman,** he has set his mind on writing a novel; **avoir qch. dans la t.,** to have sth. on the brain; **je l'ai en t.,** I'm bearing it in mind; **ça m'est sorti de la t.,** I've forgotten, it's gone out of my head; **il a quelque chose en t.,** he is planning something, *F:* he's up to something; **qu'est-ce que vous avez en t.?** what are you up to? **bonne t.,** clever head; **forte t.,** strong-minded person; **mauvaise t.,** person refractory to discipline; unruly (boy, etc.); **faire la mauvaise t.,** to be a rebel; **t. chaude,** hothead; **c'est une t. brûlée,** he has a bit of the devil in him; **travail de t.,** brainwork; **calculer de t.,** to reckon in one's head; **calcul de t.,** mental arithmetic; **en faire à sa t.,** to have one's way, to go one's own way, to please oneself; **il n'en fait qu'à sa t.,** he does just what he pleases, he will take nobody's advice; **avoir sa petite t. à soi,** to like to have one's own way; to have a will of one's own; **idée de derrière la t.,** idea at the back of one's mind; **où ai-je la t.!** what am I thinking about! what am I doing! **conserver sa t.,** to keep one's head; to retain one's presence of mind; to remain calm and collected; **la t. lui manqua,** his presence of mind failed him; **perdre la t.,** to lose one's head, to lose one's self-possession; **est-ce que vous perdez la t.?** have you taken leave of your senses? **ne perdez pas la t.,** don't get flurried, excited; **faire perdre la t. à un candidat,** to fluster a candidate; **c'était à perdre la t.,** it was bewildering; **avoir toute sa t.,** to be quite rational, completely *compos mentis*; **j'ai toute ma t.,** I've got my wits about me; **il a encore toute sa t.,** his faculties are unimpaired; **il n'avait plus sa t. à lui,** he was off his head, no longer in his right mind, in his senses; he was half crazy; **il a la t. montée,** his blood is up; **à t. reposée,** at one's leisure; **il faut ne rien faire qu'à t. reposée,** we must do nothing without thinking it out carefully; *Prov:* **autant de têtes autant d'avis,** so many men so many minds. **3.** (*a*) leader (of society, establishment); (*b*) summit, crown, top (of volcano, tree, etc.); head, top (of book); *Nau: Oc:* **t. de roche,** rock summit; *I.C.E:* **soupapes en t.,** overhead valves; *Bookb:* **doré en t.,** gilt-topped; *Typ:* **blanc de t.,** margin at the head of a book; **ligne de t.,** head-line; **t. de chapitre,** chapter heading; (*c*) loaf, head (of cabbage); (*d*) *Anat:* **t. du fémur,** apophysis of the femur; **t. de l'humérus,** head of the humerus; **t. du condyle,** condyle head; (*e*) *Tchn:* head (of violin, mast, nail, pin, rivet, screw, etc.); butt (of a plank); *Furn:* **t. de lit,** bed head; **t. (de rivet) ronde, cylindrique, plate,** cheese-head (of rivet); **t. (de rivet) hémisphérique,** cup head (of rivet); *Tls: Mec.E:* **t. d'un marteau,** (i) head, (ii) face, of a hammer; **t. de hache,** axe head; **t. de benne,** grab head; **t. de cabestan,** drum head; **t. de flèche,** jib head (of crane); *Mch.Tls:* **t. porte-outil,** tool head; **t. porte-foret, t. de perçage,** drill(ing) head; **t. porte-fraise, t. de fraisage,** cutter head, milling head; **t. porte-segments,** grinding attachment (of grinding machine); **t. filière,** die head (of threading machine); *Min:* **t. de sonde,** casing head; *Petroleum Ind:* **t. d'injection,** swivel; **t. inclinable,** tilting head (of machine tool, of camera or instrument stand); **t. orientable, t. pivotante,** swivelling head; *s.a.* BIELLE 1; *Sm.a:* **t. mobile,** bolt head (of rifle); **tige de t. mobile,** obturator spindle; *N.Arch:* **t. de bossoir,** davit head; **t. d'épontille,** pillar head; **t. de mât de charge, t. de corne,** derrick head; **t. de mèche,** rudder head; **t. de varangue,** floor head; (*f*) *El.E:* **t. d'électrode,** electrode tip; **t. de câble,** cable terminal; **t. de disjoncteur,** cross-head; *Elcs:* **t. d'effacement,** erasing head (of tape recorder, etc.); **t. d'enregistrement, t. enregistreuse,** record(ing) head (of computer, tape recorder, record player); **t. de lecture,** (i) *Cin:* sound head; (ii) reading, read, play-back, head (of computer); (iii) *Rec:* tape reader; **t. magnétique,** magnetic head; **t. sonore,** sound head; (*computers*) **t. d'écriture,** writing, write, head; **t. de programme,** interlude; **ligne des "Y" en t.,** Y-edge leading; (*g*) *Ball:* **t. (de fusée),** warhead; **t. nucléaire,** nuclear warhead; **t. chercheuse,** seeker, homing device, homing head (of missile, etc.); (*h*) front place; head (of sap, vanguard, column, etc.); **colonne de t.,** leading column; **taxi en t. de file,** taxi at the head of the rank; *Rail:* **voiture de t.,** front carriage; **voiture en t. du train,** carriage at the front of the train; **je me trouvais en t. du train,** I was in the front part of the train; **à la t. du régiment,** at the head of the regiment; **marcher en t.,** to lead the way, to lead the van; **marcher à la t., en t., du cortège,** to head the procession; **venir tout en t.,** to come foremost; **venir en t. du scrutin,** to head the poll; **s'inscrire en t. de la liste,** to head the list; **être à la t. de la classe,** to be at the top of the form; *Ten:* **têtes de série,** seeded players; **être à la t. d'une fortune,** to be in possession of a fortune; *s.a.* SE PORTER 1, QUEUE[1] 3; *Rac: etc:* **prendre la t.,** to take the lead; *Mil:* **t. de pont,** (i) bridge-head; (ii) beach head; *Rail: etc:* **t. de ligne,** (i) starting point; terminus; (ii) railhead.

tête-à-queue [tɛtakø], *s.m.inv.* slew round, slue round; **faire (un) t.-à-q.,** (i) *Aut:* to slew round; (ii) (*of horse*) to whip round; (iii) *Nau:* to turn 16 points.

têteau [tɛto], *s.m. Arb:* main branch.

tête-à-tête [tɛtatɛt], *s.m.inv.* **1.** private interview, confidential conversation, tête-à-tête; **en t.-à-t.,** in private; **en t.-à-t. avec,** alone with; **dîner, conversation, en t.-à-t.,** tête-à-tête dinner, talk. **2.** (*a*) sofa, settee (for two); tête-à-tête; (*b*) tea, coffee, breakfast, set for two.

tête-bêche [tɛtbɛʃ], *adv.* (*of two pers. or thgs*) head to foot (alongside one another); head to tail; top to bottom; *Typ:* tumble style; **timbres t.-b.,** tête-bêche stamps.

têtebleu, tête-bleu [tɛtblø], *int. A:* 'zounds! 'sblood!

tète-chèvre, tette-chèvre [tɛtʃɛvr̥], *s.m. Orn: F:* nightjar, goatsucker; *pl. tète-chèvres, tette-chèvres.*

tête-de-chat [tɛtdəʃa], *s.f. Geol:* cathead; *pl. têtes-de-chat.*

tête-de-clou [tɛtdəklu], *s.m. Arch:* nail-head(ed) moulding; *pl. têtes-de-clou.*

tête-de-loup [tɛtdəlu], *s.f.* ceiling brush, Pope's head, Turk's head brush (with long handle); wall broom; *pl. têtes-de-loup.*

tête(-)de(-)maure [tɛtdəmɔːr], *s.f.* Dutch cheese; *pl. têtes-de-maure.*

tête-de-méduse [tɛtdəmedyːz], *s.f. Fung:* honey mushroom, honey fungus, honey agaric, shoe-string fungus; *pl. têtes-de-méduse.*

tête(-)de(-)moineau [tɛtdəmwano], *s.m.* **1.** *Min:* small coal, nuts. **2.** *Bot: F:* brown knapweed; *pl. têtes-de-moineau.*

tête-de-mort [tɛtdəmɔːr], *s.f.* **1.** death's-head; **pavillon à t.-de-m. des pirates,** skull-and-cross-bones pirate flag, Jolly Roger. **2.** *Ent:* death's-head moth. **3.** *Bot:* snapdragon. **4.** Dutch cheese; *pl. têtes-de-mort.*

tête-de-nègre [tɛtdənɛgr̥], *a. & s.m.inv.* dark brown; (*not used in U.S.*) nigger-brown (colour).

tête-Dieu [tɛtdjø], *int. A:* 'zounds! 'sdeath!

tétée [tete], *A:* **tetée** [təte], *s.f.* **1.** suck; amount of milk taken by a baby at one feed. **2.** (action of) suckling by baby; **l'heure de la t.,** (infant's) feeding time.

téter [tete], *v.tr.* **(il tète, il tètera)** (*a*) (*of infant or young*) to suck; **donner à t. à un enfant,** to suckle a child; to give suck to a child; **enfant qui a tété plusieurs laits,** child who has had several wet-nurses; **enfant qui tète son pouce,** child sucking its thumb; **avoir tété du bon, du mauvais lait,** to have very good, bad health; (*b*) to drink (alcohol), to soak.

teter [təte], *v.tr.* **(il tette, il tettera)** *A:* = TÉTER.

téterelle [tetrɛl], *s.f. A:* **1.** breast pump. **2.** breast reliever.

Téthys [tetis]. **1.** *Pr.n.f. Myth:* Tethys. **2.** *s.f. Moll:* tethys, aplesia, sea hare.

têtier [tɛtje], *s.m.* **1.** *Ind:* header (workman who fixes heads on pins, etc.). **2.** *Row:* bow (oarsman).

têtière [tɛtjɛːr], *s.f.* **1.** (*a*) infant's cap; (*b*) (monk's) cowl. **2.** *Harn:* headstall. **3.** (*a*) head (of bed); (*b*) antimacassar, chair back; **t. de canapé,** (sofa) runner. **4.** *Nau:* head (of sail); **ralingue de t.,** head rope. **5.** *Fish:* **t. (de filet),** balk. **6.** *Typ:* furniture at the head of the forme.

tétin [tetɛ̃], *s.m., A:* **tetin** [tətɛ̃], *s.m.* **1.** nipple, pap (of man or woman); teat (of woman); dug (of cow, etc.). **2.** *A:* breast.

tétine [tetin], *s.f., A:* **tetine** [tətin], *s.f.* **1.** dug (of animal); (*a*) udder; (*b*) teat. **2.** *pl. P:* pendulous breasts. **3.** **(rubber)** nipple, teat (of feeding bottle); **t. sur anneau,** baby's comforter; dummy. **4.** *Cu:* breast (of lamb, etc.).

téton [tetɔ̃], *s.m.,* **teton** [tətɔ̃], *s.m. A:* **1.** *F:* (woman's) breast. **2.** *Tchn:* vis à t., teat-screw; **t. de blocage,** locking stud.

tétonnière [tetɔnjɛːr], *s.f., A:* **tetonnière** [tətɔnjɛːr], *s.f.* **1.** *A.Cost:* bust-support. **2.** *s.f. & a.f. F:* big-bosomed (woman).

Tétouan [tetwɑ̃], *Pr.n.m. Geog:* Tetuan.

tétrabasique [tetrabɑzik], *a. Ch:* tetrabasic.

tetrabelodon [tɛtrabelədɔ̃], *s.m. Paleont:* Tetrabelodon, Trilophodon.

tétraborate [tetrabɔrat], *s.m. Ch:* tetraborate.

tétrabranche [tetrabrɑ̃ːʃ], *Moll:* **1.** *a.* tetrabranch(iate). **2.** *s.m.* tetrabranch; *pl.* Tetrabranchia(ta).

tétrabrométhane [tetrabrɔmetan], *s.m. Ch:* tetrabromoethane.

tétrabrométhylène [tetrabrɔmetilɛn], *s.m. Ch:* tetrabromoethylene.

tétrabromure [tetrabrɔmyːr], *s.m. Ch:* tetrabromide.

tétracaïne [tetrakain], *s.f. Pharm:* tetracaine.

tétracarbonyle [tetrakarbɔnil], *s.m. Ch:* tetracarbonyl.

tétracère [tetrasɛ:r]. 1. *a.* four-horned. 2. *s.m. Z:* four-horned antelope, bekra, bhokra, doda; (*genus*) Tetracerus.
tétrachloréthane [tetraklɔretan], *s.m. Ch:* tetrachlor(o)ethane.
tétrachloréthylène [tetraklɔretilɛn], *s.m. Ch:* tetrachloroethylene.
tétrachlorométhane [tetraklɔrɔmetan], *s.m. Ch:* tetrachloromethane, carbon tetrachloride.
tétrachlorure [tetraklɔry:r], *s.m. Ch:* tetrachloride; **t. de carbone,** carbon tetrachloride, tetrachloromethane.
tétracoque [tetrakɔk], *s.m. Bac:* tetracoccus.
tétracoralliaires [tetrakɔraljɛ:r], *s.m.pl. Paleont:* Tetracoralla.
tétracorde [tetrakɔrd], *s.m. A.Mus:* tetrachord.
tétractinellidés [tetraktinɛlide], *s.m.pl. Spong:* Tetractinellida.
tétracycline [tetrasiklin], *s.f. Pharm:* tetracycline.
tétradactyle [tetradaktil], *a. Z:* tetradactyl(ous); four-toed.
tétrade [tetrad], *s.f. Biol:* tetrad.
tétradrachme [tetradrakm], *s.m. Gr.Ant:* tetradrachm.
tétradymite [tetradimit], *s.f. Miner:* tetradymite.
tétradyname [tetradinam], **tétradynamique** [tetradinamik], *a. Bot:* tetradynamous.
tétraédral, -aux [tetraedral, -o], *a. Geom:* tetrahedral.
tétraèdre [tetraɛdr̥], *Geom:* 1. *a.* tetrahedral. 2. *s.m.* tetrahedron.
tétraédrique [tetraedrik], *a. Geom:* tetrahedral.
tétraédrite [tetraedrit], *s.f. Miner:* tetrahedrite.
tétraédroïde [tetraedrɔid], *s.m. Geom:* tetrahedroid.
tétraéthyle [tetraetil], *a. Ch:* tetraethyl; **plomb t.,** tetraethyl lead.
tétragène [tetraʒɛn], *s.m. Bac:* tetragenous bacterium, tetracoccus.
tétragone [tetragɔn], *Geom:* 1. *a.* tetragonal. 2. *s.m.* tetragon, quadrilateral. 3. *s.f. Bot:* tetragonia; **t. étalée,** New Zealand spinach.
tétragonie [tetragɔni], *s.f. Bot:* tetragonia.
tétragramme [tetragram], *s.m.* 1. tetragram. 2. *Rel.H: etc:* **le Tétragramme,** the Tetragrammaton.
tétragyne [tetraʒin], *a. Bot:* tetragynous.
tétrahexaèdre [tetraɛgzaɛdr̥], *s.m. Mth:* tetrahexahedron.
tétrahydrobenzène [tetraidrɔbɛ̃zɛn], *s.m. Ch:* tetrahydrobenzene.
tétrahydronaphtalène [tetraidrɔnaftalɛn], *s.m. Ch:* tetrahydronaphthalene, tetralin.
tétraïodofluorescéine [tetrajɔdɔflyɔresein], *s.f. Ch:* tetraiodofluorescein.
tétraline [tetralin], *s.f. Ch:* tetralin, tetrahydronaphthalene.
tétralogie [tetralɔʒi], *s.f.* 1. *Lit: Th:* tetralogy; *Mus:* **la Tétralogie (de Wagner),** The Ring. 2. *Med: s.m.* **t. (de Fallot),** congenital cyanosis.
tétramère [tetramɛ:r], *Ent: Bot: a.* tetramerous.
tétraméthylène [tetrametilɛn], *s.m. Ch: Ind:* tetramethylene.
tétramètre [tetramɛtr̥], *s.m. Pros:* tetrameter.
tétrandre [tetrɑ̃:dr̥], *a. Bot:* tetrandrous.
tétranitraniline [tetranitranilin], *s.f. Ch:* tetranitroaniline.
tétranitrométhane [tetranitrɔmetan], *s.m. Ch:* tetranitromethane.
tétraogalle [tetraɔgal], *s.m. Orn:* snow cock; (*genus*) Tetraogallus.
tétraonidés [tetraɔnide], *s.m.pl. Orn:* Tetraonidae, the grouse (family).
tétrapétale [tetrapetal], *a. Bot:* tetrapetalous.
tétraphasé [tetrafɑze], *a. El:* four-phase (current).
tétraphyllidiens [tetrafilidjɛ̃], *s.m.pl. Ann:* Tetraphyllidea.
tétraplégie [tetrapleʒi], *s.f. Med:* tetraplegia.
tétraploïde [tetraplɔid], *a. & s.m. & f. Biol:* tetraploid.
tétraploïdie [tetraplɔidi], *s.f. Biol:* tetraploidy.
tétrapneumone [tetrapnømɔn], *a. Arach:* tetrapneumonous.
tétrapode [tetrapɔd], *a. & s.m. Z: esp. Ent:* tetrapod.
tétrapolaire [tetrapɔlɛ:r], *a. El:* four-pole (motor).
tétraptère [tetraptɛ:r]. 1. *a. Ent: Bot:* tetrapterous. 2. *s.m. Ent:* tetrapteron.
tétrapyle [tetrapil], *s.m. Arch:* tetrapylon.
tétrarcat, tétrarchat [tetrarka], *s.m. A.Hist:* tetrarchate.
tétrarchie [tetrarʃi], *s.f. A.Hist:* tetrarchy.
tetrarhynques [tetrarɛ̃:k], *s.m.pl. Ann:* Tetrarhyncidea.
tétrarque [tetrark], *s.m.* tetrarch.
tétras [tetrɑ:s], *s.m. Orn:* grouse; **t. lyre,** black grouse; *f.* grey hen; **grand t., t. urogalle,** capercaillie, capercailzie; **t. obscur,** dusky grouse; **t. à fraise,** ruffed grouse; **t. centrocerque,** sage grouse; **t. cupidon,** pinnated grouse, prairie chicken.
tétrasépale [tetrasepal], *a. Bot:* tetrasepalous.
tétrasomie [tetrasɔmi], *s.f. Biol:* tetrasomy; *Alch:* the four elements.
tétrasomique [tetrasɔmik], *a. Biol:* tetrasomic.
tétrasporange [tetraspɔrɑ̃:ʒ], *s.m. Bot:* tetrasporangium.
tétraspore [tetraspɔ:r], *s.m. Bot:* tetraspore.
tétrastique [tetrastik], *a. Bot:* tetrastichous.
tétrastyle [tetrastil], *a. & s.m. Arch:* tetrastyle.
tétrasubstitué [tetrasypstitɥe], *a. Ch:* tetrasubstituted.
tétrasulfure [tetrasylfy:r], *s.m. Ch:* tetrasulphide.
tétrasyllabe [tetrasil(l)ab], **tétrasyllabique** [tetrasil(l)abik], *a. Gram:* tetrasyllabic; **mot t.,** tetrasyllable.
tétrathionique [tetratjɔnik], *a. Ch:* tetrathionic (acid).
tétratomique [tetratɔmik], *a. Ch:* tetratomic.
tétravalence [tetravalɑ̃:s], *s.f. Ch:* tetravalence, quadrivalence.
tétravalent [tetravalɑ̃], *a. Ch:* tetravalent, quadrivalent.
tétrazène [tetrazɛn], *s.m. Ch:* tetrazene.
tétrazine [tetrazin], *s.f. Ch:* tetrazine.
tétrazole [tetrazɔl], *s.m. Ch:* tetrazole.
tétréhexaèdre [tetreeksaɛdr̥], *s.m. Mth:* tetrahexahedron.
tétréthyle [tetretil], *s.m. Ch:* tetraethyl; **plomb t.,** tetraethyl lead.
tétrigidés [tetriʒide], *s.m.pl. Ent:* Tetrigidae.
tétrix [tetriks], *s.m. Ent:* grouse locust; (*genus*) Tetrix.
tétrode [tetrɔd], *s.f. W.Tel:* tetrode (valve).
tétrodon [tetrɔdɔ̃], *s.m. Ich:* globe fish; (*genus*) Tetr(a)odon.
tétrolique [tetrɔlik], *a. Ch:* tetrolic.
tétrose [tetro:z], *s.m. Ch:* tetrose.
tétroxyde [tetrɔksid], *s.m. Ch:* tetroxide.
tétryl [tetril], *s.m. Exp:* tetryl.
tette [tɛt], *s.f. A:* (*a*) dug, teat (of animal); (*b*) *F:* nipple, teat (of woman).
tettigoniidés [tɛtigɔniide], *s.m.pl. Ent:* Tettigoniidae.
têtu [tety, tɛ-]. 1. *a.* stubborn, obstinate; mulish; *F:* pig-headed; *F:* **t. comme un mulet, comme une mule,** as stubborn, as obstinate, as a mule. 2. *s.m. Stonew:* granite-hammer; (stoneworker's) sledge-hammer.
têtuer [tetɥe], *v.tr.* to shape (stone) with hammer.
teuf-teuf [tœftœf], *s.m. F: A:* (*child's word*) 1. puff-puff, train. 2. (motor) car.
teugue [tø:g], *s.f. N.Arch:* (i) anchor deck, donkey forecastle (for anchor and anchor gear); (ii) raised foredeck, forecastle deck; **t. d'avant,** topgallant forecastle; **navire à t.,** raised-foredeck-type ship, stepped-deck-type ship.
teuton, -onne [tøtɔ̃, -ɔn]. 1. *a.* Teuton(ic). 2. *s.* Teuton. 3. *s.m. Ling:* **le t.,** Germanic, Teutonic.
teutonique [tøtɔnik], *a.* Teutonic; *Hist:* **l'ordre t.,** the Teutonic Order (of Knights); **Hanse t.,** (German) Hansa.
texan, -ane [tɛksɑ̃, -an], *a. & s. Geog:* Texan.
Texas (le) [lətɛksɑ:s], *Pr.n.m. Geog:* Texas; *Vet:* **fièvre du T.,** Texas fever, tick pest.
texte [tɛkst], *s.m.* 1. (*a*) text (of author, book, sermon, etc.); **erreur de t.,** textual error; **critique des textes,** textual criticism; **revenons à notre t.,** let us return to our subject; *Th:* **il ne sait pas son t.,** he doesn't know his lines; **prendre t. d'une affirmation,** to found on a statement; *Bookb:* **gravure hors t.,** plate; full-page engraving; *Sch:* **cahier de textes,** homework, prep, book; (*b*) letterpress (to illustration); (*c*) *Elcs:* (*computers*) **début de t.,** start of text; **mode de t.,** text mode; **caractère (de) fin de t.,** end-of-text character. 2. *Typ: A:* **petit t.,** brevier, 7½-point type; **gros t.,** two-line brevier, great primer, 14 to 16-point type.
textile [tɛkstil]. 1. *a.* textile. 2. *s.m.* (*a*) textile; **textiles artificiels,** synthetic textiles; (*b*) **le t.,** the textile industries; **grève du t.,** strike in the textile trades.
texto [tɛksto], *adv. P:* word for word.
textuaire [tɛkstɥɛ:r]. 1. *a.* relating to the text; textuary; textual. 2. *s.m.* bare text (of the Bible, of the Law).
textuel, -elle [tɛkstɥɛl], *a.* textual; **citation textuelle,** textual quotation; word-for-word quotation.
textuellement [tɛkstɥɛlmɑ̃], *adv.* textually; word for word.
texture [tɛksty:r], *s.f.* (*a*) texture (of cloth, bone etc.); (*b*) texture (of play, novel, etc.).
Thabor [tabɔ:r], *Pr.n.m. Geog:* **le mont T.,** Mount Tabor (i) in Syria, (ii) in the Alps.
Thaddée [tade], *Pr.n.m. B.Hist:* Thaddeus.
thaï [taj]. 1. *a. Geog:* Thailand, Siamese. 2. *s.m. Ling:* (*a*) Thai, Siamese; (*b*) Thai (group).
thaïlandais, -aise [tailɑ̃dɛ, -ɛ:z], *Geog:* 1. *a.* Thailand, Siamese. 2. *s.* Thai, Thailander, Siamese.
Thaïlande (la) [latailɑ̃:d], *Pr.n. Geog:* Thailand, Siam.
Thaïs [tais], *Pr.n.f. A.Hist:* Thais.
thala [tala], *a. & s.m.f. Sch: F:* = TALA.
thalame [tala:m], **thalamus** [talamys], *s.m. Anat: Bot:* thalamus.
thalamencéphale [talamɛ̃sefal], *s.m. Anat:* thalamencephalon.
thalamiflore [talamiflɔ:r], *a. Bot:* thalamifloral, thalamiflorous.
thalamique [talamik], *a. Anat:* thalamic.
thalassémie [talasemi], *s.f. Med:* thalass(a)emia, thalassan(a)emia.
thalassidrome [talasidrɔm], *s.m. Orn:* storm petrel.
thalassine [talasin], *s.f. Bio-Ch:* thalassin.
thalassique [talasik], *a.* thalassic.
thalassocratie [talasɔkrasi], *s.f.* thalassocracy, thalattocracy; maritime supremacy.
thalassographie [talasɔgrafi], *s.f.* thalassography, oceanography.
thalassométrie [talasɔmetri], *s.f.* thalassometry.
thalassophobie [talasɔfɔbi], *s.f. Med:* thalassophobia.
thalassothérapie [talasɔterapi], *s.f. Med:* thalassotherapy; (i) salt-water cure; (ii) sea-air cure.
thalassotoque [talasɔtɔk], *a. Ich:* ocean-spawning, katadromous.
thalénite [talenit], *s.f. Miner:* thalenite.
thaler [talɛ:r], *s.m. Num:* thaler; **t. de Marie-Thérèse,** Maria Theresa thaler, dollar.
Thalès [talɛs], *Pr.n.m. Gr.Phil:* **T. de Milet,** Thales of Miletus.
thaliacés [taljase], *s.m.pl. Z:* Thaliacea.
thalidomide [talidɔmid], *s.f. Pharm:* thalidomide.
Thalie [tali]. 1. *Pr.n.f. Myth:* Thalia. 2. *s.f. Bot:* thalia.
thalle [tal], *s.m. Bot:* thallus.
thalleux, -euse [talø, -ø:z], **thallieux, -ieuse** [taljø, -jø:z], *a. Ch:* thallous.
thallique [talik], *a. Ch:* thallic.
thallium [taljɔm], *s.m. Ch:* thallium.
thallome [talo:m], *s.m. Bot:* thallome.
thallophytes [talɔfit], *s.m.pl. Bot:* thallophytes.
thallospore [talɔspɔ:r], *s.f. Fung:* thallospore.
thalweg [talvɛg], *s.m. Geol:* t(h)alweg.
Thamar [tama:r], *Pr.n.f. B:* Tamar; *Hist:* T(h)amara.
thameng [tamɛ̃g], *s.m. Z:* thameng, thamin.
thamnophile [tamnɔfil], *s.m. Orn:* ant shrike; (*genus*) Thamnophilus.
thanatologie [tanatɔlɔʒi], *s.f. Biol:* thanatology.
thanétien [tanesjɛ̃], *a.m. Geol:* Thanet (sandstone).
thapsia [tapsja], *s.m.* 1. *Bot:* thapsia. 2. *Pharm: O:* thapsia plaster.
thapsie [tapsi], *s.f. Bot:* thapsia; **t. garganique,** deadly carrot.
thaumalée [tomale], *s.m. Orn:* **t. d'Amherst,** Lady Amherst's pheasant; **t. doré,** golden pheasant.
thaumasite [tomazit], *s.f. Miner:* thaumasite.
thaumaturge [tomatyrʒ]. 1. *a.* thaumaturgic. 2. *s.m. & f.* thaumaturge, thaumaturgist; miracle worker.
thaumaturgie [tomatyrʒi], *s.f.* thaumaturgy.
thaumaturgique [tomatyrʒik], *a.* thaumaturgic(al).
thaumétopée [tometɔpe], *s.f. Ent:* processionary moth; (*genus*) Thaumetopoea.
thé [te], *s.m.* 1. (*a*) tea; **t. de Ceylan** = Indian tea; **t. de Chine,** China tea; **négociant en t.,** tea merchant; **c'est l'heure du t.,** it's teatime; **prendre le t. avec qn,** to take, have, tea with s.o.; (*for breakfast, etc.*) **t. complet,** tea with rolls and butter; continental breakfast with tea; **boîte à t.,** (i) tea caddy; (ii) tea canister; *a.inv.* **rose t.,** tea(-scented) rose; (*b*) **t. du Paraguay, t. des Jésuites,** maté; **t. en brique,** brick tea; **t. poudre à canon,** gunpowder tea; **t. de Bourbon,** Bourbon tea, faham; **t. de bœuf,** beef tea. 2. (*a*) tea party; **t. musical,** musical afternoon; (*b*) **salon de t.,** teashop, tearoom(s). 3. *Bot:* **t. d'Europe,** (i) common speedwell; (ii) gromwell; **t. de campagne,** ironwort; **t. du Labrador,** Labrador tea; **t. du Mexique,** Mexican tea; *Fr.C:* **t. des bois,** wintergreen. 4. *Husb:* **t. de foin,** mash of hay (for livestock).
Théatin, -ine [teatɛ̃, -in], *s. Ecc:* Theatine.

théâtral, -aux [teɑtral, -o], *a.* theatrical; *Pej:* stagy; **récit poussé à l'effet t.,** story told with a view to dramatic effect; **représentation théâtrale,** stage performance.
théâtralement [teɑtralmɑ̃], *adv.* theatrically.
théâtralisation [teɑtralizasjɔ̃], *s.f. Th:* dramatizing (of a novel, etc.).
théâtraliser [teɑtralize], *v.tr. Th:* to dramatize (a novel, etc.).
théâtralité [teɑtralite], *s.f.* theatricalness.
théâtre [teɑːtr̥], *s.m.* 1. (*a*) theatre, playhouse; **t. de verdure,** open-air theatre; **t. en rond,** arena theatre; (*b*) *Mil:* **t. des opérations,** theatre of operations; **t. de la guerre,** theatre of war; **t. de l'accident,** scene of the accident; (*c*) **t. d'eau,** group of ornamental fountains. 2. stage, scene; **paraître sur le t.,** to appear on the stage; **mettre une pièce au t.,** to stage, put on, a play; **se retirer du t.,** to give up the stage. 3. (*a*) dramatic art; **pièce de t.,** play; **écrire pour le t.,** to write for the stage; **costumier de t.,** theatrical costumier; **faire du t.,** to be an actor, be on the stage; **héros de t.,** (i) stage hero; (ii) *F:* tin god; **coup de t.,** dramatic, sensational, turn (to events); **en coup de t.,** with startling suddenness; (*b*) plays, dramatic works (of s.o.); **le t. anglais,** English drama.
théâtreuse [teɑtrøːz], *s.f. F: Pej:* actress (of sorts); showgirl (with little talent); woman who acts now and then.
théâtricule [teɑtrikyl], *s.m.* very small theatre.
Thébaïde (la) [latebaid]. 1. *Pr.n.f. A.Geog:* Thebaid. 2. *s.f. A:* hermitage, solitary retreat; **se retirer dans une t.,** to withdraw from the world.
thébain, -aine [tebɛ̃, -ɛn], *a.* & *s. Hist: Geog:* Theban.
thébaïne [tebain], *s.f. Pharm:* thebaine.
thébaïque [tebaik], *a. Ch: Pharm:* thebaic; **extrait t.,** opium extract.
thébaïsme [tebaism], *s.m. Med:* thebaism, opium poisoning.
Thèbes [tɛb], *Pr.n.f. Hist: Geog:* Thebes.
thécamœbiens [tekamebjɛ̃], *s.m.pl. Prot:* Thecamoebae, Thecamoebaea.
Thécel [tesɛl], *B:* **Mané, T., Pharès,** mene, tekel, upharsin.
thecla [tekla], *s.m.*, **thècle** [tɛkl̥], *s.m. Ent:* hairstreak butterfly; thecla, strymon.
théclines [teklin], *s.m.pl. Ent:* theclans, hairstreak butterflies.
thécodontes [tekodɔ̃ːt], *s.m.pl. Paleont:* Thecodontia.
thécophores [tekɔfɔːr], *s.m.pl. Rept:* Thecophora.
thécosomes [tekɔzoːm], *s.m.pl. Moll:* Thecosomata.
théerie [teri], *s.f.* 1. tea factory. 2. tea plantation.
théier, -ière [teje, -jɛːr]. 1. *a.* tea (industry), etc. 2. *s. F:* tea drinker, tea lover. 3. *s.m. Bot:* tea (tree). 4. *s.f.* **théière,** teapot.
théiforme [teifɔrm], *a.* theiform; resembling tea; prepared like tea.
theilériose [telerjoːz], *s.f. Vet:* theileriosis, theileriasis; east coast fever.
théine [tein], *s.f. Ch:* theine.
théisme[1] [teism], *s.m. Med:* theism; tea poisoning.
théisme[2], *s.m. Theol:* theism.
théiste [teist]. 1. *a.* theistic. 2. *s.* theist.
thek [tɛk], **théka** [teka], **thekka** [tɛka], *s.m. Bot:* teak.
Thélème [telɛm]. 1. *Pr.n. Lit:* **l'abbaye de T.,** the Abbey of Thélème. 2. *s.f.* community where all forms of pleasure are cultivated.
thélémite [telemit], *s.m.* & *f.* Thelemite; libertine.
thélite [telit], *s.f. Med:* thelitis.
thélyphonidés [telifɔnide], *s.m.pl. Arach:* Thelyphonidae.
thélytoque [telitɔk], *a. Biol:* thely(o)tokous.
thélytoquie [telitɔki], *s.f. Biol:* thely(o)toky, thelytocia.
thématique [tematik], *a.* thematic.
thème [tɛm], *s.m.* 1. (*a*) theme, topic; subject (of discourse, musical composition, etc.); **cet incident, t. à développements ingénieux,** this incident, a theme for ingenious developments; **t. d'actualité,** topic of the day; **thèmes littéraires,** literary subject matter; (*b*) *Mus:* antecedent, subject (of fugue); (*c*) *Sch:* prose; **t. latin,** Latin (prose) composition, Latin prose; **t. grec,** Greek prose; **t. d'imitation,** retranslation; *F:* **fort en t.,** very good and hard-working (but not necessarily brilliant) pupil; (*d*) *Mil: Navy:* **t. tactique,** tactical problem, scheme; **t. des manœuvres,** scheme, general idea, of the manœuvres. 2. *Gram:* stem, theme (of verb, noun).
Thémis [temis], *Pr.n.f.* 1. *Gr.Myth:* Themis; *Lit:* **le temple de T.,** the law courts. 2. *Astr:* Themis.
Thémistocle [temistɔkl], *Pr.n.m. Gr.Hist:* Themistocles.
thénar [tenaːr], *a.* & *s.m. Anat:* **(éminence) t.,** thenar eminence; ball of the thumb.
thénardite [tenardit], *s.f. Miner:* thenardite.
théo- [teɔ], *pref.* theo-.
theobroma [teɔbrɔma], **théobrome** [teɔbroːm], *s.m. Bot:* theobroma.
théobromine [teɔbrɔmin], *s.f. Ch:* theobromine.
théocrate [teɔkrat], *s.m.* theocrat.
théocratie [teɔkrasi], *s.f.* theocracy.
théocratique [teɔkratik], *a.* theocratic.
Théocrite [teɔkrit], *Pr.n.m. Gr.Lit:* Theocritus.
théodicée [teɔdise], *s.f. Phil:* theodicy.
théodolite [teɔdɔlit], *s.m. Surv:* theodolite; **t. à boussole,** transit theodolite.
Théodora [teɔdɔra], *Pr.n.f.* Theodora.
Théodore [teɔdɔːr]. 1. *Pr.n.m.* Theodore. 2. *Pr.n.f.* **(Sainte) T.,** (St) Theodora.
Théodoric [teɔdɔrik], *Pr.n.m. Hist:* Theodoric.
théodoricien, -ienne [teɔdɔrisjɛ̃, jɛn], *a.* & *s. Geog:* (native, inhabitant) of Château-Thierry.
Théodose [teɔdoːz], *Pr.n.m. Rom.Hist:* Theodosius.
théodosien, -ienne [teɔdozjɛ̃, -jɛn], *a.* Theodosian (code).
théogonie [teɔgɔni], *s.f.* theogony.
théogonique [teɔgɔnik], *a.* theogonic.
théogoniste [teɔgɔnist], *s.m.* theogonist.
théologal, -aux [teɔlɔgal, -o]. 1. *a.* **les trois vertus théologales,** the three theological virtues. 2. *s.m. Ecc:* theologal, theologus. 3. *s.f.* **théologale,** living (of a theologal).
théologie [teɔlɔʒi], *s.f.* theology; **cours de t.,** divinity course; **docteur en t.,** doctor of divinity, D.D.
théologien, -ienne [teɔlɔʒjɛ̃, -jɛn], *a.* & *s.* (*a*) theologist, theologian; divine; (*b*) theological student; *R.C.Ch:* (*in seminary*) theologian.
théologique [teɔlɔʒik], *a.* theological (discussion, sin).
théologiquement [teɔlɔʒikmɑ̃], *adv.* theologically.
théologiser [teɔlɔʒize], *v.i.* to theologize.
théologisme [teɔlɔʒism], *s.m. Pej:* theologizing.
théomythologie [teɔmitɔlɔʒi], *s.f.* theomythology.
théophanie [teɔfani], *s.f.* theophany.
théophilanthrope [teɔfilɑ̃trɔp], *s.m.* & *f. Fr.Hist:* theophilanthropist.
théophilanthropie [teɔfilɑ̃trɔpi], *s.f.*, **théophilanthropisme** [teɔfilɑ̃trɔpism], *s.m. Fr.Hist:* theophilanthropy, theophilanthropism.
théophilanthropique [teɔfilɑ̃trɔpik], *a. Fr.Hist:* theophilanthropic, theophilanthropist (movement, etc.).
Théophile [teɔfil], *Pr.n.m.* Theophilus.
Théophraste [teɔfrast], *Pr.n.m. Gr.Phil:* Theophrastus.
théophylline [teɔfilin], *s.f. Ch:* theophylline.
théopneustie [teɔpnøsti], *s.f.* theopneusty.
théorbe [teɔrb], *s.m. A.Mus:* theorbo.
théorématique [teɔrematik], *a.* theorematic.
théorème [teɔrɛm], *s.m.* theorem; **le t. de Newton,** the binomial theorem.
théorétique [teɔretik], *Phil:* 1. *a.* theoretic(al). 2. *s.f.* theoretics.
théoricien, -ienne [teɔrisjɛ̃, -jɛn], *s.* theor(et)ician, theorist.
théorie[1] [teɔri], *s.f.* 1. theory; **ce plan est excellent en t.,** this plan is a good one in theory; *Geol:* **t. cataclysmique,** catastrophism; *Mth: Elcs:* (*computers*) **t. des probabilités,** theory of probability; **t. de la décision,** decision theory; **t. de l'information,** information theory; **t. des automates,** automata theory; **t. des ensembles,** set theory; **t. des files d'attente,** queueing theory; **t. des graphes,** graph theory. 2. *Mil:* (*a*) theoretical instruction (as part of training); (*b*) training manual; **conforme à la t.,** (strictly) according to the book.
théorie[2], *s.f.* 1. *Gr.Ant:* theory, theoria. 2. *Lit:* procession, string, file (of persons, vehicles, etc.).
théorique[1] [teɔrik], *a.* theoretic(al).
théorique[2], *a. Gr.Ant:* theoric (tax, money).
théoriquement [teɔrikmɑ̃], *adv.* theoretically.
théoriser [teɔrize], *v.tr.* & *i.* to theorize.
théoriste [teɔrist], *s.m.* & *f.* theorist, theorizer.
théosophe [teɔzɔf], *s.m.* & *f.* theosophist.
théosophie [teɔzɔfi], *s.f.* theosophy.
théosophique [teɔzɔfik], *a.* theosophical.
thèque[1] [tɛk], *s.f. Anat: Bot:* theca; *Fung:* theca, ascus.
thèque[2], *s.f. Sp:* (*a*) rounders; (*b*) rounders bat.
théralite [teralit], *s.f. Miner:* theralite.
Théramène [teramɛn], *Pr.n.m. Gr.Hist:* Theramenes.
thérapeute [terapøːt], *s.m.* 1. *Rel.H:* therapeutic monk; **les thérapeutes,** the Therapeutae. 2. *Med:* therapeutist.
thérapeutique [terapøtik]. 1. *a.* therapeutic; **dose t.,** therapeutic dose. 2. *s.f.* therapeutics, therapy.
thérapeutiste [terapøtist], *s.m.* therapeutist.
théraphose [terafoːz], *s.f. Arach:* theraphose, bird spider.
théraphosidés [terafozide], *s.m.pl. Arach:* Theraphosidae.
thérapie [terapi], *s.f. Med:* therapy; **spécialiste de t. rééducative,** occupational therapist.
thérapsidés [terapside], *s.m.pl. Palaeont:* Therapsida.
therblig [tɛrblig], *s.m. Ind: etc:* therblig.
thérébinte [terebɛ̃ːt], *s.m. Bot:* terebinth.
Thérèse [terɛːz], *Pr.n.f.* Theresa; **Sainte T. d'Avila,** Saint Teresa of Avila.
thereva [tereva], *s.m. Ent:* stiletto fly; (*genus*) Thereva.
thérévidés [terevide], *s.m.pl. Ent:* Therevidae.
thériacal, -aux [terjakal, -o], *a. A.Pharm:* theriacal.
thériaque [terjak], *s.f. A.Pharm:* theriaca, *A:* (Venice) treacle.
théridiidés [teridiide], *s.m.pl. Arach:* Theridiidae.
théridion [teridjɔ̃], *s.m. Arach:* net weaver; (*genus*) Theridion.
thériodontes [terjɔdɔ̃ːt], *s.m.pl. Paleont: Rept:* Theriodont(i)a, theriodonts.
thermal, -aux [tɛrmal, -o], *a.* thermal; **eaux thermales,** thermal springs, hot springs; **établissement t.,** hydropathic (establishment); **station thermale,** spa.
thermalisme [tɛrmalism], *s.m.* (*a*) organization and running of spas; (*b*) hydrotherapy; spa bathing; (*c*) balneology; hydrotherapeutics.
thermalité [tɛrmalite], *s.f.* characteristics of hot springs.
thermes [tɛrm], *s.m.pl.* 1. *Gr.* & *Rom.Ant:* thermae, public baths. 2. thermal baths.
thermesthésie [tɛrmɛstezi], *s.f.* therm(a)esthesia.
thermicien, -ienne [tɛrmisjɛ̃, -jɛn], *s.* heat engineer.
thermicité [tɛrmisite], *s.f. Ph:* **t. positive,** exothermicity.
thermidor [tɛrmidɔːr], *s.m. Fr.Hist:* Thermidor; eleventh month (July-August) in the Fr. Republican calendar.
thermidorien, -ienne [tɛrmidɔrjɛ̃, -jɛn], *a.* & *s.m. Fr.Hist:* Thermidorian; of the 9th Thermidor (1794).
thermie [tɛrmi], *s.f. Ph:* thermal unit (= *1000 great calories*).
thermionique [tɛrmjɔnik], *a.* thermionic.
thermique [tɛrmik]. 1. *a. Ph:* thermic, thermal; **moteur t.,** heat engine; **écran t.,** heat screen; **traitement t.,** heat treatment; **rendement t.,** heat efficiency; *El:* **centrale t.,** thermal power station; *Aer:* **courant t.,** thermal current, thermal; *Elcs:* **relais t.,** thermorelay; *Ch:* **analyse t.,** thermal analysis, thermoanalysis; *Geog:* **régime t.,** temperature regime, pattern; **gradient t.,** temperature gradient; **amplitude t.,** range of temperature; *Physiol:* **sensibilité t.,** temperature sense; *Biol:* **preferendum t.,** temperature preference range. 2. *s.m. Aer:* thermal. 3. *s.f.* thermology, science of heat (production and utilization).
thermistance [tɛrmistɑ̃ːs], *s.f.*, **thermisteur** [tɛrmistœːr], *s.m.*, **thermistor** [tɛrmistɔːr], *s.m. El:* thermistor.
thermite[1] [tɛrmit], *s.f. Metalw:* thermit(e).
thermite[2], *s.f. Med:* heat dermatosis.
thermo- [tɛrmɔ], *Pref.* thermo-.
thermo-algésique [tɛrmɔalʒezik], *a. Path:* **sensibilité t.-a.,** thermalgesia.
thermo-anesthésie [tɛrmɔanɛstezi], *s.f. Med:* thermanaesthesia, thermo-anaesthesia.
thermo-avertisseur [tɛrmɔavɛrtisœːr], *s.m.* alarm thermometer; thermal alarm device; *pl. thermo-avertisseurs.*
thermobalance [tɛrmɔbalɑ̃ːs], *s.f. Ph:* thermobalance.
thermo-baromètre [tɛrmɔbarɔmɛtr̥], *s.m. Meteor: Surv:* thermobarometer; hypsometer; *pl. thermo-baromètres.*
thermo-cautère [tɛrmɔkotɛːr], *s.m. Surg:* thermocautery; *pl. thermo-cautères.*
thermochimie [tɛrmɔʃimi], *s.f.* thermochemistry.
thermochimique [tɛrmɔʃimik], *a.* thermochemical.
thermochroïque [tɛrmɔkrɔik], *a. Ph:* thermochroic (heat rays).
thermochrose [tɛrmɔkroːz], *s.f. Ph:* thermochrosy.
thermoclimatique [tɛrmɔklimatik], *a.* **camp t.,** (children's) camp at a spa.
thermocline [tɛrmɔklin], *s.f. Oc:* thermocline.
thermocollage [tɛrmɔkɔlaːʒ], *s.m.* heat sealing.

thermocolorer [tɛrməkɔlɔre], *v.tr. Glassm:* to strike.

thermocouple [tɛrməkupḻ], *s.m. El:* thermocouple.

thermocouverture [tɛrməkuvɛrtyːr], *s.f.* electric blanket.

thermodurcissable [tɛrmədyrsisabḻ], *a. & s.m.* heat setting, thermosetting, thermohardening (composition, plastic).

thermodynamique [tɛrmədinamik]. 1. *a.* thermodynamic. 2. *s.f.* thermodynamics.

thermoélectricité [tɛrmoelɛktrisite], *s.f.* thermoelectricity.

thermoélectrique [tɛrmoelɛktrik], *a. Ph:* thermoelectric(al); **pince t.**, thermocouple; **couple t.**, thermoelectric couple; **pile t.**, thermopile.

thermoélectronique [tɛrmoelɛktrɔnik], *a. Ph:* thermoelectronic.

thermo(-)esthésie [tɛrmoɛstezi], *s.f. Med:* therm(a)esthesia, thermo-(a)esthesia.

thermo(-)esthésiomètre [tɛrmoɛstesjɔmɛtr̩], *s.m. Physiol:* therm(a)esthesiometer.

thermogène [tɛrmoʒen], *a. Physiol:* thermogenic, thermogenous, thermogenetic; heat-producing (foods, etc.); *Med:* **ouate t.**, thermogene (wool).

thermogénèse [tɛrmoʒenɛːz], *s.f. Physiol:* thermogenesis.

thermogénie [tɛrmoʒeni], *s.f. Ph: Ch:* thermogenesis.

thermogramme [tɛrmogram], *s.m. Ph:* thermogram.

thermographe [tɛrmograf], *s.m. Ph:* thermograph.

thermographie [tɛrmografi], *s.f. Ph:* thermography.

thermo(-)ionique [tɛrmojɔnik], *a. W.Tel:* thermionic (valve, etc.).

thermolabile [tɛrmolabil], *a. Physiol: Ch:* thermolabile.

thermologie [tɛrmolɔʒi], *s.f. Ph:* thermology.

thermologique [tɛrmolɔʒik], *a. Ph:* thermologic(al).

thermoluminescence [tɛrmolyminɛs(s)ɑ̃s], *s.f. Ph:* thermoluminescence, thermophosphorescence.

thermoluminescent [tɛrmolyminɛs(s)ɑ̃], *a. Ph:* thermoluminescent.

thermolyse [tɛrmoliːz], *s.f. Physiol:* thermolysis.

thermomagnétique [tɛrmomaɲetik], *a. Ph:* thermomagnetic.

thermomagnétisme [tɛrmomaɲetism], *s.m. Ph:* thermomagnetism.

thermomécanique [tɛrmomekanik], *a. Ph:* thermomechanical.

thermomètre [tɛrmomɛtr̩], *s.m.* thermometer; **t. à mercure, à alcool,** mercury, alcohol, thermometer; **t. médical, de clinique,** clinical thermometer; **t. à maxima et minima,** maximum and minimum thermometer; **t. enregistreur,** recording thermometer; **t. sec, à boule sèche,** dry-bulb thermometer (of hygrometer); **t. mouillé, à boule mouillée,** wet-bulb thermometer; **t. centigrade,** centigrade thermometer; **t. de Celsius,** Celsius thermometer; **t. à gaz,** gas thermometer; **t. différentiel,** differential thermometer; *Mch:* **t. à cadran,** heat gauge; **le t. indique 10°,** the thermometer stands at, registers, 10°(C).

thermomètre-fronde [tɛrmomɛtr̩(ə)frɔ̃ːd], *s.m. Meteor:* sling thermometer, whirled thermometer.

thermométrie [tɛrmometri], *s.f. Ph:* thermometry.

thermométrique [tɛrmometrik], *a.* thermometric(al).

thermométrographe [tɛrmometrograf], *s.m. Ph:* (self-)recording thermometer; thermometrograph.

thermonastie [tɛrmonasti], *s.f. Bot:* thermonasty; floral movements due to temperature variations.

thermonastique [tɛrmonastik], *a. Bot:* thermonastic.

thermonatrite [tɛrmonatrit], *s.f. Miner:* thermonatrite.

thermoneutralité [tɛrmonøtralite], *s.f. Ch:* thermoneutrality.

thermonucléaire [tɛrmonykleɛːr], *a. Atom.Ph:* thermonuclear.

thermopériodisme [tɛrmoperjɔdism], *s.m. Bot:* thermoperiodism; daily temperature alterations.

thermophile [tɛrmofil], *a. Biol:* thermophil(e), thermophilic, thermophilous.

thermophone [tɛrmofɔn], *s.m.* thermophone.

thermopile [tɛrmopil], *s.f. El:* thermopile.

thermoplaste [tɛrmoplast], *s.m.* thermoplastic.

thermoplasticité [tɛrmoplastisite], *s.f. Ch:* thermoplasticity.

thermoplastique [tɛrmoplastik], *a. & s.m.* thermoplastic.

thermoplongeur [tɛrmoplɔ̃ʒœːr], *s.m.* immersion heater.

thermopompe [tɛrmopɔ̃ːp], *s.f.* heat pump.

thermopropulsé [tɛrmoprɔpylse], *a.* **fusée thermopropulsée,** thermopropulsion rocket.

thermopropulsif, -ive [tɛrmoprɔpylsif, -iːv], *a. Av:* thermopropulsive (nozzle, etc.); **tuyère thermopropulsive,** propulsive duct (of ramjet).

thermopropulsion [tɛrmoprɔpylsjɔ̃], *s.f. Av:* thermopropulsion.

thermopside [tɛrmopsid], *s.f.,* **thermopsis** [tɛrmopsis], *s.m. Bot:* bush pea; *(genus)* Thermopsis.

Thermopyles (les) [letɛrmopil], *Pr.n.f.pl. Geog:* (the Pass of) Thermopylae.

thermorégulateur [tɛrmoregylatœːr], *s.m.* thermoregulator, thermostat.

thermorégulation [tɛrmoregylasjɔ̃], *s.f.* thermoregulation.

thermorésistant [tɛrmorezistɑ̃], *a.* heat-resisting.

Thermos [tɛrmɔs], *s.m. or f. Min:* trade mark applied to vacuum flasks and other articles manufactured by Thermos (1925) Limited;* **bouteille T.,** Thermos flask.

thermoscope [tɛrmoskɔp], *s.m. Ph:* thermoscope.

thermoscopique [tɛrmoskɔpik], *a. Ph:* thermoscopic.

thermosiphon [tɛrmosifɔ̃], *s.m. Ph:* thermosiphon; *Aut:* **refroidissement par t.,** thermosiphon cooling.

thermostabile [tɛrmostabil], **thermostable** [tɛrmostabḻ], *a. Ch: Med:* thermostable.

thermostat [tɛrmosta], *s.m.* thermostat; **réglage par t.,** thermostatic control.

thermostatique [tɛrmostatik]. 1. *a.* thermostatic. 2. *s.f.* thermostatics.

thermotactisme [tɛrmotaktism], *s.m. Bot:* thermotropism.

thermotaxie [tɛrmotaksi], *s.f. Biol:* thermotaxis.

thermotéléphone [tɛrmotelefɔn], *s.m. Elcs:* thermophone.

thermothérapie [tɛrmoterapi], *s.f. Med: Vet:* heat cure, heat treatment, thermotherapy.

thermotropique [tɛrmotrɔpik], *a. Biol:* thermotropic.

thermotropisme [tɛrmotrɔpism], *s.m. Biol:* thermotropism.

théromorphes [teromɔrf], *s.m.pl. Paleont: Rept:* Theromorpha, Pelycosauria.

théromorphie [teromɔrfi], *s.f. Biol:* theromorphia, theromorphism.

thérophyte [terofit], *s.f. Bot:* therophyte.

théropodes [terɔpɔd], *s.m.pl. Paleont: Rept:* Theropoda.

Thersite [tɛrsit], *Pr.n.m. Gr.Lit:* Thersites.

thésard, -arde [tezaːr, -ard], *s. Sch: F:* student preparing a thesis.

thésaurisation [tezorizasjɔ̃], *s.f.* piling up, hoarding, of money, of treasure.

thésauriser [tezorize]. 1. *v.i.* to hoard (up); to amass treasure. 2. *v.tr.* **t. des capitaux,** to hoard, pile up, money.

thésauriseur, -euse [tezorizœːr, -øːz]. 1. *s.* hoarder of treasure, of money. 2. *a.* acquisitive (propensity, etc.).

thesaurus [tezɔrys], *s.m.* thesaurus.

thèse [tɛːz], *s.f.* 1. thesis, proposition, argument; **soutenir, défendre, une t.,** to uphold, to defend, a thesis; **poser en t. que . . . ,** to submit that . . . ; **sa t. est qu'il faudrait abolir l'or,** his argument is that gold should be done away with; **la t. de la France sur le problème de la bombe atomique,** the French approach to the question of the atom bomb; *Log:* **la t., l'antithèse et la synthèse,** thesis, antithesis and synthesis; **pièce à t.,** (i) propaganda play; (ii) problem play, drama of ideas; **roman à t.,** thesis novel, novel with a message; **en t. générale,** as a general principle, generally speaking; *Lit:* **voilà qui change la t.!** that alters the case, that makes all the difference. 2. *Sch:* thesis (submitted for degree); **soutenance de t.,** upholding, defending, of a thesis.

Thésée [teze], *Pr.n.m. Myth:* Theseus.

thésium [tezjɔm], *s.m. Bot:* bastard toadflax; *(genus)* Thesium.

thespesia [tɛspezja], *s.m. Bot:* portia tree, bendy tree, seaside mahoe; *(genus)* Thespesia.

thespien, -ienne [tɛspjɛ̃, -jɛn], *a. & s. A.Geog:* Thespian.

Thespies [tɛspi], *Pr.n.pl. A.Geog:* Thespiae.

Thespis [tɛspis], *Pr.n.m. Gr.Lit:* Thespis.

Thessalie [tesali], *Pr.n.f. Geog:* Thessaly.

thessalien, -ienne [tesaljɛ̃, -jɛn], *a. & s.* Thessalian.

Thessalonicien, -ienne [tesalonisjɛ̃, -jɛn], *a. & s. A.Geog:* Thessalonian.

Thessalonique [tesalɔnik], *Pr.n.f. A.Geog:* Thessalonica (= modern Salonika).

thêta [tɛta], *s.m. Gr.Alph:* theta.

thétique [tetik], *a. Phil:* thetic.

Thétis [tetis], *Pr.n.f. Gr.Myth: Astr:* Thetis.

théurgie [teyrʒi], *s.f.* theurgy.

théurgique [teyrʒik], *a.* theurgic(al).

thévétine [tevetin], *s.f. Min:* thevetin.

thial [tjal], *s.m. Ch:* thial, thioaldehyde.

thialdine [tjaldin], *s.f. Ch:* thialdine.

thiamine [tjamin], *s.f. Bio-Ch:* thiamin(e), aneurin(e).

thianthrène [tjɑ̃trɛn], *s.m. Ch:* thianthrene.

thiazine [tjazin], *s.f. Ch:* thiazine.

thiazinique [tjazinik], *a. Ch:* **colorant t.,** thiazine dye.

thiazole [tjazɔl], *s.m. Ch:* thiazole.

thiazoline [tjazɔlin], *s.f. Ch:* thiazoline.

thibaude [tibod], *s.f.* (a) *Tex:* (cow-)haircloth; coarse haircloth; (b) carpet felt.

Thibau(l)t [tibo], *Pr.n.m.* Theobald.

thierne [tjɛrn], *s.f. Min:* slant; diagonal heading.

thiernois, -oise [tjɛrnwa, -waːz], *a. & s. Geog:* (native, inhabitant) of Thiers.

Thierry [tjeri], *Pr.n.m. Fr.Hist:* Theodoric.

thiers [tjɛr], *s.m. Metalw:* cutlery made at Thiers.

thigmonastie [tigmonasti], *s.f. Bot:* thigmonasty, seismonasty.

thigmotactique [tigmotaktik], *a.* thigmotactic.

thigmotaxie [tigmotaksi], *s.f. Biol:* stereotaxy, thigmotaxy; stereotaxis, thigmotaxis.

thigmotropisme [tigmotrɔpism], *s.m. Biol:* thigmotropism, stereotropism.

thinite [tinit], *a. Archeol:* Thinite (monument, etc.).

thinocore [tinɔkɔːr], *s.f. Orn:* seed snipe; *(genus)* Thinocorus.

thinocoridés [tinɔkɔride], **thinocorythidés** [tinɔkɔritide], *s.m.pl. Orn:* Thinocoridae.

thioacétique [tjoasetik], *a. Ch:* thioacetic.

thioacide [tjoasid], *s.m. Ch:* thio acid.

thioalcool [tjoalkɔl], *s.m. Ch:* thioalcohol.

thioaldéhyde [tjoaldeid], *s.m. Ch:* thioaldehyde, thial.

thioamide [tjoamid], *s.m. Ch:* thioamide.

thiobactériales [tjobakterjal], *s.f.pl. Bac:* Thiobacteriales.

thiocarbamide [tjokarbamid], *s.m. Ch:* thiocarbamide.

thiocarbanilide [tjokarbanilid], *s.m. Ch:* thiocarbanilide.

thiocarbonate [tjokarbɔnat], *s.m. Ch:* thiocarbonate.

thiocarbonique [tjokarbɔnik], *a. Ch:* thiocarbonic.

thiocétone [tjosetɔn], *s.f. Ch:* thioketone.

thiocyanate [tjosjanat], *s.m. Ch:* thiocyanate; **les thiocyanates alcalins,** the sodium thiocyanates.

thiodiphénylamine [tjodifenilamin], *s.f. Ch:* thiodiphenylamine, phenothiazine.

thioéther [tjoetɛːr], *s.m. Ch:* thioether.

thiofène [tjofɛn], *s.m. Ch:* thiophene.

thioflavine [tjoflavin], *s.f. Ch:* thioflavin(e).

thioglycolique [tjoglikɔlik], *a. Ch:* thioglycolic.

thiogomme [tjogɔm], *s.f. Ind:* thioplast.

thio-indamine [tjoɛ̃damin], *s.f. Ch:* thioindamine.

thio-indigo [tjoɛ̃digo], *s.m. Ch:* thioindigo.

Thiokol [tjokɔl], *s.m. R.t.m:* Thiokol.

thiol [tjɔl], *s.m. Ch:* thiol.

thionaphtène [tjonaftɛn], *s.m. Ch:* thionaphthene.

thionate [tjonat], *s.m. Ch:* thionate.

thione [tjon], *s.f. Ch:* thione.

thionine [tjonin], *s.f. Ch:* thionine.

thionique [tjonik], *a. Ch:* thionic.

thionvillois, -oise [tjɔ̃vilwa, -waːz], *a. & s. Geog:* (native, inhabitant) of Thionville.

thionyle [tjonil], *s.m. Ch:* thionyl.

thiophène [tjofɛn], *s.m. Ch:* thiophene.

thiophénol [tjofenɔl], *s.m. Ch:* thiophenol.

thiophosgène [tjofɔsʒɛn], *s.m. Ch:* thiophosgene.

thiosinamine [tjosinamin], *s.f. Pharm:* thiosinamine.

thiosulfate [tjosylfat], *s.m. Ch:* thiosulphate.

thiosulfurique [tjosylfyrik], *a. Ch:* thiosulphuric.

thio(-)urée [tjoyre], *s.f. Ch:* thiourea.

thioxanthone [tjoksɑ̃tɔn], *s.f. Ch:* thioxanthone.

Thisbé [tizbe], *Pr.n.f. Lit:* Thisbe.

thixotrope [tiksotrɔp], **thixotropique** [tiksotrɔpik], *a. Ch: Ph:* thixotropic.

thixotropie [tiksotrɔpi], *s.f. Ch: Ph:* thixotropy.

thlaspi [tlaspi], *s.m.* 1. *Bot:* thlaspi; **t. des champs,** pennycress. 2. *Hort:* candytuft; **t. jaune,** rock alyssum.

tholos [tolɔs], *s.f. Archeol:* tholos.

Thomas [toma]. 1. *Pr.n.m.* Thomas; **Saint Thomas d'Aquin,** St Thomas Aquinas. 2. *s.m. P: O:* chamber-pot, jerry.

thomise [tomiːz], *s.m. Arach:* crab spider, thomisid; *(genus)* Thomisus.

thomisidés [tomizide], *s.m.pl. Arach:* Thomisidae.

thomisme [tomism], *s.m. Theol:* Thomism.

thomiste [tɔmist], *a. & s.m. & f. Theol:* Thomist.

thomomys [tɔmɔmis], *s.m. Z:* pocket gopher; (*genus*) Thomomys.

thomsenolite [tɔmsenɔlit], *s.f. Miner:* thomsenolite.

thomsonite [tɔmsɔnit], *s.f. Miner:* thomsonite.

thon [tɔ̃], *s.m. Ich:* tunny(fish), tuna(fish); **t. blanc,** albacore, germon; **t. rouge,** bluefin tuna, tunny.

thonaire [tɔnɛːr], *s.f. Fish:* tunny net.

thonides [tɔnid], *s.m.pl. Ich:* the tuna family, the tunnies, Thunnidae.

thonier, -ière [tɔnje, -jɛːr], *Fish:* **1.** *a.* **l'industrie thonière,** the tunny industry. **2.** *s.m.* (*a*) tunny boat; (*b*) tunny fisherman.

thonil [tɔnil], **thonilaud** [tɔnilo], *s.m. Fish:* sturgeon net.

thonine [tɔnin], *s.f. Ich:* bluefin tunny, tuna.

thoracentèse [tɔrasɑ̃tɛːz], *s.f. Surg:* thoracentesis.

thoracique [tɔrasik]. **1.** *a.* (*a*) *Anat:* thoracic; **cage t.,** rib cage; **canal t.,** thoracic duct; (*b*) *Ich:* thoracic (pelvic fin). **2.** *s.m.pl. Crust:* **thoraciques,** Thoracica.

thoracocentèse [tɔrakɔsɑ̃tɛːz], *s.f. Surg:* thora(co)centesis.

thoracopage [tɔrakɔpaːʒ], *s.m. Ter:* thoracopagus.

thoracoplastie [tɔrakɔplasti], *s.f. Surg:* thoracoplasty.

thoracoscopie [tɔrakɔskɔpi], *s.f. Med:* thoracoscopy.

thoracostracés [tɔrakɔstrase], *s.m.pl. Crust:* Thoracostraca.

thoracotomie [tɔrakɔtɔmi], *s.f. Surg:* thoracotomy.

thorax [tɔraks], *s.m.* **1.** *Anat:* thorax, chest. **2.** *Ent: etc:* thorax.

thorianite [tɔrjanit], *s.f. Miner:* thorianite.

thorine [tɔrin], *s.f. Ch:* thoria, thorium oxide.

thorique [tɔrik], *a. Ch:* thoric.

thorite [tɔrit], *s.f. Miner:* thorite.

thorium [tɔrjɔm], *s.m. Ch:* thorium.

thorogummite [tɔrɔgymit], *s.f. Miner:* thorogummite.

thoron [tɔrɔ̃], *s.m. Atom.Ph:* thoron.

thortveitite [tɔrtvetit], *s.f. Miner:* thortveitite.

thouarsais, -aise [twarsɛ, -ɛːz], *a. & s.* (native, inhabitant) of Thouars.

Thoune [tun], *Pr.n. Geog:* Thun; **le lac de T.,** the Lake of Thun.

Thrace [tras], *A.Geog:* **1.** *Pr.n.f.* **la Thrace,** Thrace. **2.** *a. & s.* Thracian. **3.** *s.m. Ling:* **le t.,** Thracian.

thran [trɑ̃], *s.m.* train oil.

Thrasybule [trazibyl], *Pr.n.m. Gr.Hist:* Thrasybulus.

thrène [trɛn], *s.m.*, **thrénodie** [trenɔdi], *s.f. A:* threnody.

thréose [treoːz], *s.m. Ch:* threose.

thridace [tridas], *s.f. Pharm:* thridace, lactucarium.

thrill [tril], *s.m. Path:* thrill (in circulatory system).

thrips [trips], *s.m. Ent:* thrips, thysanopter.

thrombase [trɔ̃bɑːz], *s.f. Bio-Ch:* thrombin.

thrombasthénie [trɔ̃basteni], *s.f. Med:* thrombasthenia, pseudohaemophilia.

thrombine [trɔ̃bin], *s.f. Bio-Ch:* thrombin.

thrombo-angéite [trɔ̃bɔɑ̃ʒeit], *s.f. Med:* thromboangiitis; *pl. thrombo-angéites.*

thrombocyte [trɔ̃bɔsit], *s.m. Physiol:* thrombocyte.

thrombocytopénie [trɔ̃bɔsitɔpeni], *s.f. Med:* thrombocytopenia.

thrombocytopénique [trɔ̃bɔsitɔpenik], *a. Med:* **purpura t.,** thrombocytopenic purpura.

thrombo-embolique [trɔ̃bɔɑ̃bɔlik], *a. Med:* thromboembolic; *pl. thrombo-emboliques.*

thrombokinase [trɔ̃bɔkinɑːz], *s.f. Bio-Ch:* thrombokinase.

thrombopénie [trɔ̃bɔpeni], *s.f. Med:* thrombopenia.

thrombophlébite [trɔ̃bɔflebit], *s.f. Med:* thrombophlebitis.

thromboplastine [trɔ̃bɔplastin], *s.f. Bio-Ch:* thromboplastin.

thromboplastique [trɔ̃bɔplastik], *a.* thromboplastic.

thrombose [trɔ̃boːz], *s.f. Med:* thrombosis.

thrombosé [trɔ̃boze], *a. Med:* thrombosed.

thrombus [trɔ̃bys], *s.m. Med:* thrombus.

thryonomidés [triɔnɔmide], *s.m.pl. Z:* Thryonomyidae.

thryonomys [triɔnɔmis], *s.m. Z:* ground pig, cane rat; (*genus*) Thryonomys.

thryothore [triɔtɔːr], *s.m. Orn:* Carolina wren; (*genus*) Thryothorus.

Thucydide [tysidid], *Pr.n.m. Gr.Lit:* Thucydides.

thug [tyg], *s.m.* thug.

thuggisme [tygism], *s.m.* thuggee, thuggism, thuggery.

thuia [tyja], *s.m. Bot:* thuja, thuya.

thuie [tɥi], *s.f. Dial:* **1.** furze, gorse. **2.** scrub, brushwood (cut for manure).

Thulé [tyle], *Pr.n.f. A.Geog:* (Isle of) Thule.

thulite [tylit], *s.f. Miner:* thulite.

thulium [tyljɔm], *s.m. Ch:* thulium.

thunbergia [tynbɛrʒja], *s.m.*, **thunbergie** [tynbɛrʒi], *s.f. Bot:* thunbergia; **t. alata,** black-eyed Susan.

thune [tyn], *s.f. P:* (*a*) *A:* five-franc piece; (*b*) **je me suis retrouvé sans une t.,** I found myself without a penny to bless my name with; **je n'en donnerais pas deux thunes,** I wouldn't give tuppence for it.

Thurgovie [tyrgɔvi], *Pr.n.f. Geog:* Thurgau.

thurgovien, -ienne [tyrgɔvjɛ̃, -jɛn], *a. & s. Geog:* Thurgovian.

thuriféraire [tyriferɛːr], *s.m.* (*a*) *Ecc:* (i) thurifer, incense bearer; (ii) boat-bearer, -boy; (*b*) *F:* flatterer (of s.o.); fawner (on s.o.); **entouré de thuriféraires,** surrounded by devotees.

thurifère [tyrifɛːr], *a. Bot:* thuriferous.

Thuringe [tyrɛ̃ːʒ], *Pr.n.f. Geog:* Thuringia.

thuringien, -ienne [tyrɛ̃ʒjɛ̃, -jɛn], (*a*) *a. & s. Geog:* Thuringian; (*b*) *a. & s.m. Geol:* Thuringian.

thuringite [tyrɛ̃ʒit], *s.f. Miner:* thuringite.

thuya [tyja], *s.m. Bot:* thuja, thuya, arbor vitae; **t. de Barbarie,** sandarac (tree); **bois de t.,** citronwood.

thuyène [tyjɛn], *s.m. Ch:* thujene.

thuylique [tyilik], *a. Ch:* **alcool t.,** thujyl alcohol.

thuyol [tyjɔl], *s.m. Ch:* thujyl alcohol.

thuyone [tyjɔn], *s.f. Ch:* thujone, thuyone.

thyade [tjad], *s.f. Gr.Ant:* thyiad.

Thyeste [tjɛst], *Pr.n.m. Gr.Lit:* Thyestes.

thylacine [tilasin], *s.m. Z:* thylacine; Tasmanian wolf.

thylacoleo [tilakɔleo], *s.m. Paleont:* thylacoleo.

thylle [til], *s.f. Bot:* tylose, tylosis, thylosis.

thyllose [tiloːz], *s.f. Bot:* **t. parasitaire de l'orme,** Dutch elm disease.

thylogale [tilɔgal], *s.m. Z:* scrub wallaby, pademelon; (*genus*) Thylogale.

thym [tɛ̃], *s.m. Bot:* thyme; **t. bâtard,** wild thyme, shepherd's thyme.

thymectomie [timɛktɔmi], *s.f. Surg:* thymectomy.

thyméléa [timelea], *s.m.*, **thymélée** [timele], *s.f. Bot:* thymelaea.

thyméléacées [timelease], *s.f.pl. Bot:* Thymelaeaceae.

thymique[1] [timik], *a. Anat: Med:* thymic (asthma, etc.).

thymique[2], *a. Ch:* thymic.

thymol [timɔl], *s.m. Pharm:* thymol.

thymolphtaléine [timɔlftalein], *s.f. Ch:* thymolphthalein.

thymonucléique [timɔnykleik], *a. Bio-Ch:* thymonucleic.

thymus [timys], *s.m. Anat:* thymus, thymus gland.

thyratron [tiratrɔ̃], *s.m. El:* thyratron.

thyréogène [tireɔʒɛn], *a. Physiol:* thyrogenic, thyrogenous.

thyréoglobuline [tireɔglɔbylin], *s.f. Bio-Ch:* thyroglobuline.

thyréoprive [tireɔpriːv], *a. Path:* thyroid-deprived (experimental animal).

thyréose [tireoːz], **thyréotoxicose** [tireɔtɔksikoːz], *s.f. Med:* thyrotoxicosis, hyperthyroidism.

thyréotrope [tireɔtrɔp], *a. Physiol:* thyreotropic, thyrotrop(h)ic.

thyridides [tiridid], *s.m.pl. Ent:* Thyrididae.

thyro- [tirɔ], *pref.* thyro-.

thyroaryténoïdien, -ienne [tirɔaritenɔidjɛ̃, -jɛn], *a. Anat:* thyroarytenoid.

thyro-épiglottique [tirɔepiglɔtik], *a. Anat:* thyroepiglottic; *pl. thyro-épiglottiques.*

thyroglobuline [tirɔglɔbylin], *s.f. Bio-Ch:* thyroglobulin.

thyrohyoïdien, -ienne [tirɔiɔidjɛ̃, -jɛn], *a. Anat:* thyrohyoid.

thyroïde [tirɔid], *a. Anat:* thyroid (cartilage, gland); *Pharm:* **extrait t.,** thyroid (gland extract).

thyroïdectomie [tirɔidɛktɔmi], *s.f. Surg:* thyroidectomy.

thyroïdectomiser [tirɔidɛktɔmize], *v.tr. Surg:* to thyroidectomize.

thyroïdien, -ienne [tirɔidjɛ̃, -jɛn], *Anat:* **1.** *a.* thyroid; **hormone thyroïdienne,** thyroid hormone. **2.** *s.f.* **thyroïdienne,** thyroid artery; thyroid vein.

thyroïdisme [tirɔidism], *s.m. Med:* thyroidism.

thyroïdite [tirɔidit], *s.f. Med:* thyroiditis.

thyronine [tirɔnin], *s.f. Bio-Ch:* thyronine.

thyropharyngien, -ienne [tirɔfarɛ̃ʒjɛ̃, -jɛn], *a. Anat:* thyropharyngean.

thyroptère [tirɔptɛːr], *s.m. Z:* disk bat, disk-wing bat; (*genus*) Thyroptera.

thyroxine [tirɔksin], *s.f. Bio-Ch:* thyroxin(e).

thyrse [tirs], *s.m.* **1.** *Gr.Ant:* thyrsus, thyrse. **2.** *Bot:* thyrse, thyrsus (of lilac, etc.).

thysanoptère [tisanɔptɛːr], *s.m. Ent:* thysanopter (on); *pl.* **thysanoptères,** Thysanoptera.

thysanoptéroïdes [tisanɔpterɔid], *s.m.pl. Ent:* Thysanopteroidea.

thysanoures [tisanuːr], *s.m.pl. Ent:* thysanura.

tiare [tjaːr], *s.f. A.Cost: Ecc:* tiara; **aspirer à la t.,** to aspire to the papacy.

tiarella [tjarɛla], *s.m. Bot:* foamflower, false mitrewort; (*genus*) Tiarella.

tiaris [tjaris], *s.m. Orn:* grassquit; (*genus*) Tiaris.

Tibère [tibɛːr], *Pr.n.m. Rom.Hist:* Tiberius.

Tibériade [tiberjad], *Pr.n.f. Geog:* Tiberias; **lac de T.,** Lake of Tiberias.

tibérien, -ienne [tiberjɛ̃, -jɛn], *a.* Tiberian.

Tibet (le) [lətibɛ]. **1.** *Pr.n.m. Geog:* Tibet; *Z:* **dogue du T.,** Tibetan mastiff; **griffon du T.,** Tibetan terrier, chrysanthemum dog. **2.** *s.m., Tex:* thibet, tibet.

tibétain, -aine [tibetɛ̃, -ɛn]. **1.** *a. & s. Geog:* Tibetan. **2.** *s.m. Ling:* Tibetan.

tibia [tibja], *s.m.* (*a*) *Anat:* tibia; **s'érafler le t.,** to bark one's shin; (*b*) *Ent:* tibia.

tibial, -iaux [tibjal, -jo], *a. Anat:* tibial (artery, etc.).

tibio-tarsien, -ienne [tibjɔtarsjɛ̃, -jɛn], *a. Anat:* tibiotarsal; *pl. tibio-tarsien(ne)s.*

tibouchina [tibuʃina], *s.m. Bot:* glory-bush, spiderflower; (*genus*) Tibouchina.

Tibre (le) [lətibr̥], *Pr.n.m. Geog:* the (river) Tiber.

Tibulle [tibyl], *Pr.n.m. Rom.Lit:* Tibullus.

tic [tik], *s.m.* (*a*) *Med:* tic; spasmodic tic; twitching; **il a un t.,** he has a tic; his face twitches; **t. douloureux,** facial neuralgia; (*b*) *Farr:* vicious habit, stable vice (of horse, etc.); **t. en l'air,** wind sucking; **t. rongeur,** crib biting; (*c*) *F:* (unconscious) habit; mannerism; trick (of doing sth.); **c'est un t. chez lui,** he's always doing it, it's a trick of his.

tichodrome [tikɔdrɔm], *s.m. Orn:* **t. échelette,** wall creeper.

ticker [tikɛːr], *s.m. Tg:* ticker.

ticket [tikɛ], *s.m.* (*a*) ticket (*esp.* on bus, underground, at swimming pool, etc.); numbered slip, check (at restaurant, cloakroom, etc.); *Rail: etc:* **t. de réservation,** reserved-seat ticket; **t. d'appel,** (numbered) call slip (at bus stops in Paris); *Rail:* **t. de quai,** platform ticket; *War Adm: A:* **t. de pain,** bread coupon; *Ins:* **t. modérateur,** quota, portion, of the cost of treatment paid by the insured (in Fr.); (*b*) *Elcs:* (*computers*) tag; (*c*) *P:* 1,000 (old) franc note; (*d*) *P:* **avoir un t. avec qn,** to click with s.o.

ticket-repas [tikɛrəpa], *s.m.*, **ticket-restaurant** [tikɛrɛstɔrɑ̃], *s.m.* = luncheon voucher; *pl. tickets-repas, -restaurant.*

tic(-)tac [tiktak], *s.m.* tick-tock; ticking (of clock); click-clack (of mill, loom); pit-a-pat (of heart); **faire t.-t.,** to go tick-tock, pit-a-pat, etc.

tictaquer [tiktake], *v.i.* (*of clock*) to tick, to tick-tock; (*of loom, etc.*) to go click-clack; (*of heart*) to go pit-a-pat.

tiédasse [tjedas], *a. F:* lukewarmish.

tiède [tjɛd], *a.* tepid; lukewarm (bath, friendship); (*of air*) mild; *adv.* **je bois toujours t.,** I always take the chill off my drink.

tièdement [tjɛdmɑ̃], *adv.* lukewarmly, half-heartedly.

tiédeur [tjedœːr], *s.f.* tepidity, tepidness; lukewarmness (of water, friendship, etc.); *F:* **agir avec t.,** to do things halfheartedly.

tiédir [tjediːr]. **1.** *v.i.* to become tepid, lukewarm; (*of friendship, etc.*) to cool off. **2.** *v.tr.* to make tepid, lukewarm; to take the chill off, to warm (water, etc.).

tiédissement [tjedismɑ̃], *s.m.* **1.** cooling (off). **2.** warming (up).

tiemannite [tjemanit], *s.f. Miner:* tiemannite.

tien, tienne [tjɛ̃, tjɛn], yours; thine; (*for the use of* **tien** *as opp. to* **votre,** *cf.* TU; *in Eng.* "*thine*" *is used only in prayers, occ. in Quaker speech, in dialect, and in literature*) **1.** *occ. poss. a. pred.* **mes intérêts sont tiens,** my interests are yours. **2. le t., la tienne, les tiens, les tiennes,** (*a*) *poss. pron.* **ma sœur se promène avec la tienne,** my sister is out walking with yours; **ses enfants ressemblent aux tiens,** his children are like yours; (*b*) *s.m.* (i) your own (property, etc.); yours, thine; **si tu veux du mien, donne-moi du t.,** if you want to have some of mine, give me some of yours; **le t. et le mien engendrent de nombreux procès,** questions of mine and thine, questions about property, lead to a great many lawsuits;

y mettre du t., to contribute money, your share; to make concessions, to give up something on your side; to touch up, to add to (a story); (ii) *pl.* your own (friends, etc.); **les tiens t'ont renié**, your own (people) have disowned you; (iii) *F:* **tu as encore fait des tiennes**, you have been up to your old tricks again.

tiens [tjɛ̃], *int.* **1.** hullo! **t., c'est vous!** hullo, is that you! **2.** look! hey! **t., c'est Philippe!** look, it's Philip! **t.! je te rapporte ton livre,** here, I've brought your book back. **3. t., t.!** indeed? well, well! you don't say! *U.S:* my! **t., t.! c'est curieux,** hullo! that's curious.

tierçage [tjɛrsaːʒ], *s.m. I.C.E:* **t. des segments,** spacing of the gaps in the piston rings 120° apart.

tierce[1] [tjɛrs]. **1.** *See* TIERS. **2.** *s.f.* (*a*) *Astr: Mth:* third (= sixtieth part of a second); (*b*) *Fenc:* tierce; (*c*) *Ecc:* terce, tierce; (*d*) *Mus:* third; **t. majeure,** major third; (*e*) *Typ:* final revise, press-proof; (*f*) *Cards:* tierce; **t. majeure,** tierce major.

tiercé [tjɛrse], *a.* **1.** *Agr:* ploughed for the third time. **2.** *Her:* tierced, tiercé. **3.** *Pros:* **rimes tiercées,** terza rima. **4.** *Turf:* **pari t.,** *s.m.*, **le t.,** forecast of the first three horses, **avoir le t. dans l'ordre,** to forecast the horses in order; **avoir le t. dans le désordre,** to name the placed horses not in order; **un beau t.,** a good win on the *tiercé*.

tiercée [tjɛrse], *s.f. Const:* slate roofing with a gauge of one-third of the slate.

tierce(-)feuille [tjɛrsfœːj], *s.f. Her:* trefoil.

tiercelet [tjɛrs(ə)lɛ], *s.m. Ven:* tercel, tercelet, male falcon.

tiercelin, -ine [tjɛrslɛ̃, -in], *s. R.C.Ch:* Franciscan tertiary.

tiercement [tjɛrs(ə)mɑ̃], *s.m.* **1.** increase (of price) by a third. **2.** division into three. **3.** *Agr:* third ploughing.

tiercer [tjɛrse], *v.tr.* (**je tierçai(s); n. tierçons**) **1.** to raise the price of (sth.) by one third. **2.** *Agr:* to plough (land) for the third time. **3.** *I.C.E:* **t. les segments,** to space the gaps in the piston rings 120° apart. **4.** *Const:* **t. le pureau des ardoises,** to reduce the gauge of slates to a third. **5.** *v.i. Typ:* to check a press-proof.

tierce-rime [tjɛrs(ə)rim], *s.f. Pros:* terza rima.

tierceron [tjɛrs(ə)rɔ̃], *s.m. Arch:* tierceron (rib).

tierceur [tjɛrsœːr], *s.m. Typ:* checker of press-proofs.

tierçon [tjɛrsɔ̃], *s.m. Com: A:* tierce (wooden cask or case).

tiers, tierce[2] [tjɛːr, tjɛrs]. **1.** *a. A:* third (person, power, etc.) *still used in the following: Hist:* **le t. état,** the third estate, the commonalty; *Ecc:* **t. ordre (de Saint-François, etc.)** Third Order of St Francis, etc.); (Franciscan, etc.) Tertiaries; **t. ordre régulier,** Third Order Regular; *Jur:* **en main tierce,** in the hands of a third party; **t. porteur,** second endorser (of bill); **tierce caution.** contingent liability; **tierce opposition,** opposition by third party to a judgment in a suit to which he is not a party but by which he suffers a prejudice; **t. opposant,** third party (in such a suit); *Pol: A:* **t. parti,** middle party, centre party; *A.Med:* **fièvre tierce,** tertian ague; *Mth:* **n tierce,** n triple dash (n‴). **2.** *s.m.* (*a*) third (part); **dormir le t. de la nuit,** to sleep a third of the night; **remise d'un t. (du prix),** discount of a third; *F:* a third off; **perdre les deux t. de son argent,** to lose two thirds of one's money; (*b*) third person, third party; **être en t.,** to be present as a third party, to make a third; **se trouver en t. avec des amoureux,** to play gooseberry to a pair of lovers; *F: A:* **le t. et le quart,** everybody, anybody; **devoir au t. et au quart,** to owe money right and left; **consulter le t. et le quart,** to consult all and sundry; **prendre le parapluie d'un t.,** to take a perfect stranger's umbrella; *Ins:* **assurance au t.,** third party insurance; (*c*) *Log:* **principe du t. exclu,** principle of the excluded middle. **3.** *s.f.* tierce, chaperon, companion, attending a nun who receives a visit.

tiers-an [tjɛrsɑ̃], *s.m. Ven:* three-year-old wild boar.

tiers-arbitre [tjɛrarbitr̥], *s.m.* referee (in case of tie between arbitrators or umpires); *pl. tiers-arbitres.*

tiers-monde [tjɛrmɔ̃ːd], *s.m. Pol:* **le t.-m.,** the uncommitted countries; the third world.

tiers-point [tjɛrpwɛ̃], *s.m.* **1.** *Geom: Arch:* tierce-point; **arc en t.-p.,** pointed equilateral arch. **2.** *Tls:* triangular file; three-cornered file; *pl. tiers-points.*

tiers-saisi [tjɛrsezi], *s.m. Jur:* garnishee; *pl. tiers-saisis.*

tieulet [tjølɛ], *s.m. Com:* small bundle of firewood.

tifomycine [tifəmisin], *s.f. Pharm:* chloromycetin (manufactured in France).

tifs, tiffes [tif], *s.m.pl. P:* hair, thatch.

tiga [tiga], *s.m. Orn:* three-toed woodpecker.

tige [tiːʒ], *s.f.* **1.** (*a*) stem, stalk (of plant); scape (of feather); *Tex:* **t. ligneuse,** boon (of hemp, etc.); (*b*) trunk, bole (of tree); **(arbre à) haute t.,** tall standard; (*c*) stock (of family); *Lit:* **faire t.,** to found a family, a house; **Saint Louis, t. de la branche des Bourbons,** Saint Louis, common ancestor of the Bourbons. **2.** (*a*) shaft (of column); stem (of candlestick, etc.); arm (of coke-oven ram, etc.); shank (of rivet, key, anchor, *Typ:* of letter); body (of penholder); stick (of violin bow); matchstick; **t. d'un guéridon,** leg of pedestal table **t. de soupape,** valve stem, spindle; *El:* **t. d'isolateur,** insulator spindle; *Typewr:* **t. à caractères,** type bar; (*b*) rod; **t. filetée, à vis,** threaded rod; *Mch:* **t. du piston,** piston rod; **t. de tiroir,** slide rod; *Mec.E:* **t. directrice,** slide rod; **t. de foret,** boring bar; **t. de commande de clapet,** push rod of a valve; **t. de pompe,** pump rod, spear; **t. de traction,** tie rod; **t. de réglage,** adjusting rod; *Petroleum Ind:* **t. de forage,** drill(ing) pipe; **t. faussée,** bent rod; **t. voleuse,** thief rod (for storage tank sampling); *I.C.E:* etc: **t. de jauge,** dipstick; **t. de paratonnerre,** lightning rod; *Cy:* **t. de selle,** saddle pin; saddle pillar; *Veh:* **t. de frein,** brake rod; **t. à vis du frein,** brake screw; (*c*) leg (of stocking); leg, upper (of boot); **bottes à tiges,** top boots; (*d*) *Av: F:* **les vieilles tiges,** pilots who got their licence before 1914; (*e*) *P:* cigarette, *P:* fag; (*f*) *P:* policeman.

tigelle [tiʒɛl], *s.f. Bot:* tigelle, tigella, tigel.

tigellé [tiʒɛle], *a. Bot:* tigellate.

tige-poussoir [tiʒpuswaːr], *s.f. I.C.E:* tappet-rod; *pl. tiges-poussoirs.*

tigette [tiʒɛt], *s.f. Arch:* caulicole, caulicolo.

tiglique [tiglik], *a. Ch:* tiglic (acid).

tiglon [tiglɔ̃], *s.m. Z:* tigon.

tignasse [tiɲas], *s.f.* (*a*) *A:* scrubby wig; (*b*) shock, mop (of hair); **t. mal peignée,** unkempt head of hair; shock of tousled hair.

tignonner [tiɲɔne], *v.tr. A:* (*a*) to curl the hair of (s.o.); (*b*) **elles se sont tignonnées,** they had a set-to; they clawed each other's hair.

Tigrane [tigran], *Pr.n.m. A.Hist:* Tigranes.

tigre[1], **tigresse** [tigr̥, tigrɛs]. **1.** *s.* (*a*) *Z:* tiger, tigress; **t. d'Amérique,** American tiger; **jaloux comme un t., jalouse comme une tigresse,** as jealous as hell; *F:* **c'est une vraie tigresse,** she's a jealous cat; (*b*) *F:* **t. de papier,** paper tiger (*the U.S.A. in Chinese view*). **2.** *s.m.* (*a*) small groom; tiger; (*b*) *Ent:* **t. du poirier,** pear tingis, pear lace bug.

Tigre[2] **(le),** *Pr.n.m. Geog:* **1.** the (river) Tigris. **2.** the (river) Tigre.

tigré [tigre], *a.* striped (fur); tigrine, speckled, spotted (skin); **chat t.,** tabby cat; **cheval t.,** leopard-spotted horse; *Bot:* **lis t.,** tiger lily.

tigrer [tigre], *v.tr.* to stripe, speckle; **bateaux qui tigrent le sable,** boats dotted about on the sand.

tigridie [tigridi], *s.f. Bot:* tiger flower.

tigron [tigrɔ̃], *s.m.* tigon.

tikker [tikeːr], *s.m. W.Tel: A:* tikker, ticker.

tilapie [tilapi], *s.m. Ich:* tilapia.

tilasite [tilazit], *s.f. Miner:* tilasite.

tilbury [tilbyri], *s.m. A.Veh:* tilbury, gig.

tilde [tild], *s.m. Typ: etc:* tilde.

tildé [tilde], *a.* (*of n*) having a tilde, with a tilde.

tiliacé [tiljase], *Bot:* **1.** *a.* tiliaceous. **2.** *s.f.pl.* **tiliacées,** Tiliaceae.

till[1] [til], *s.m. Bot:* til, sesame.

till[2], *s.m. Geol:* till, boulder clay.

tillac [tijak], *s.m. Nau:* deck; **franc t.,** flush deck, main deck.

tillage [tijaːʒ], *s.m. Tex:* stripping, scutching, swingling (of hemp, flax).

tillandsie [tijɑ̃dzi], *s.m. Bot:* tillandsia.

tille[1] [tiːj], *s.f.* **1.** bast, bass; **paillasson de t.,** bass(-mat). **2.** harl (of hemp).

tille[2], *s.f. Nau:* cuddy (of half-decked boat).

tille[3], *s.f. Tls:* (*a*) (cooper's) adze; (*b*) (ship's carpenter's) adze.

tiller [tije], *v.tr. Tex:* to strip, scutch, swingle (hemp, flax).

tilleul [tijœl], *s.m.* **1.** *Bot:* lime (tree); **t. à grandes feuilles,** broadleaved lime; **t. d'Amérique,** basswood, bass, linden. **2.** (*a*) lime blossom (used medicinally); (*b*) **(infusion de) t.,** lime-blossom tea.

tilleur, -euse [tijœːr, -øːz], *s. Tex:* **1.** *s.* flax stripper, scutcher. **2.** *s.f.* **tilleuse,** scutching machine, scutcher.

tillite [tijit], *s.f. Geol:* tillite.

tillodontes [tijɔdɔ̃ːt], *s.m.pl. Paleont:* Tillodontia, tillodonts.

tillotte [tijɔt], *s.f. Tex:* scutching machine, scutcher.

tillotter [tijɔte], *v.tr. Tex:* to strip, scutch, swingle (hemp, flax).

tiloptéridales [tilɔpteridal], *s.f.pl. Algae:* Tilopteridales.

timalie [timali], *s.f. Orn:* babbler; (*genus*) Timalia.

timaléidés [timaleide], **timaliidés** [timaliide], *s.m.pl. Orn:* Timaliidae, Timeliidae.

timbale [tɛ̃bal], *s.f.* **1.** (*a*) *Mus:* kettle drum; **battre des timbales, blouser les timbales,** to play the kettle drums, (*in orchestra*) the timpani; (*b*) *Games:* (kind of) battledore without a handle, and held by the rim; (*c*) *Ent:* timbale (of cicada). **2.** metal drinking cup, mug; **t. de voyage articulée,** telescopic drinking cup; *F:* **décrocher la t.,** to win the prize (originally from the top of the greasy pole); *F:* to bring home the bacon. **3.** *Cu:* (*a*) timbale mould; (*b*) **t. de langouste,** lobster timbale.

timbalier [tɛ̃balje], *s.m. Mus:* timpanist.

timbrage [tɛ̃braːʒ], *s.m.* **1.** stamping (of passport, letter, etc.). **2.** testing (of boiler).

timbre [tɛ̃ːbr̥], *s.m.* **1.** (*a*) (fixed) bell (with striking hammer); gong (of clock); spring bell (of bicycle, etc.); **t. électrique,** electric bell; *Ind: Navy: etc:* electric gong; **t. d'appel,** call bell; telephone bell; **t. avertisseur,** alarm bell, gong; **t. de table,** table bell; **coup de t.,** stroke of the bell; stroke on the gong; **presser le t.,** to press, ring, the (electric) bell; *F:* **avoir le t. fêlé,** *A:* **avoir un coup de t.,** to be cracked, daft; to have a screw loose; *O:* **ce malheur lui a brouillé le t.,** this misfortune has unhinged his mind; (*b*) shell (of helmet); (*c*) *Mus:* snare (of drum); (*d*) timbre, quality in tone (of voice, instrument); *Ling:* tamber; **voix sans t.,** toneless voice. **2.** (*a*) stamp (on document, etc.); **t. fixe, t. sec, à empreinte,** impressed stamp, embossed stamp; **t. du jour,** date (stamped on document); **t. de la poste,** postmark; *Adm:* **t. proportionnel,** stamp (on letter of exchange) according to amount payable; *ad valorem* stamp; (*b*) **t.(-poste),** (postage) stamp; **collection de timbres,** stamp collection; **t. mobile,** adhesive stamp; **t. d'effets,** duty stamp; **t. de dimension,** stamp (on posters, etc.) according to size; (*c*) stamp(ing instrument); **t. sec,** embossing press; **t. humide,** rubber stamp, pad stamp; **t. à date, t. dateur,** date stamp; **t. à encrage automatique,** self-inking stamp; (*d*) stamp duty; (*e*) **le Timbre,** the Stamp Office. **3.** *Mch:* (*a*) test plate (of boiler); (*b*) test pressure. **4.** (*a*) *Her:* timbre, timber; *esp.* helmet (surmounting the shield) (*b*) *Com:* crest, mark (of firm). **5. t. d'office,** (i) *Dom.Ec:* small washing-up sink; (ii) *Th:* old tune to which new words are fitted; **t. à (la) glace,** small icebox.

timbré [tɛ̃bre], *a.* **1.** sonorous (voice). **2.** *F:* cracked (brain), crack-brained (person); **il est t.,** he's dotty, cracked, off his head, off his nut. **3.** stamped (paper, document); *F:* **vous allez encore recevoir du papier t.,** you'll be getting another summons, another unpleasant communication. **4.** *Her:* timbred (shield).

timbre-épargne [tɛ̃breparɲ], *s.m.* savings(-bank) stamp; *pl. timbres-épargne.*

timbre-poste [tɛ̃br(ə)pɔst], *s.m.* postage stamp; *pl. timbres-poste.*

timbre-prime [tɛ̃br(ə)prim], *s.m. Com:* trading stamp; *pl. timbres-prime.*

timbre-quittance [tɛ̃br(ə)kitɑ̃ːs], *s.m.* receipt stamp; *pl. timbres-quittance.*

timbrer [tɛ̃bre], *v.tr.* **1.** (*a*) to stamp (passport, etc.); to stamp the postmark on (letter); **lettre timbrée de Paris,** letter with a Paris postmark; (*b*) **papier timbré au chiffre de qn,** paper stamped with s.o.'s arms; (*c*) **t. une lettre,** to stick a postage stamp on a letter, to stamp a letter. **2.** to put (boiler) through its test; **chaudière timbrée à . . .,** boiler tested at . . . . **3.** *Her:* to timbre, timber; **écu timbré d'un heaume couronné,** shield surmounted with a crowned helmet.

timbre-retraite [tɛ̃br(ə)rətrɛt], *s.m. A:* old-age pension stamp; *pl. timbres-retraite.*

timbre-taxe [tɛ̃br(ə)taks], *s.m.* postage-due stamp; *pl. timbres-taxe.*

timbreur, -euse [tɛ̃brœːr, -øːz], *s.* stamper.

timbrologie [tɛ̃brɔlɔʒi], *s.f. F:* stamp collecting.

timbrologique [tɛ̃brɔlɔʒik], *a. F:* philatelic.

Timée [time], *Pr.n.m.* Timaeus.

timéliidés [timeliide], *s.m.pl. Orn:* Timeliidae, Timaliidae.

timide [timid], *a.* timid; (*a*) timorous, apprehensive; (*b*) shy, bashful; diffident (**envers**, with); **un garçon d'aspect t.**, a shy-looking boy; **il est t. à se faire entendre**, he is shy of making himself heard; **pinceau, style, t.**, diffident brush, style; **peu t.**, not at all shy; bold; (*c*) *s.* **c'est un grand t.**, he's very shy.

timidement [timidmɑ̃], *adv.* timidly; (*a*) timorously, apprehensively; (*b*) shyly, bashfully, diffidently.

timidité [timidite], *s.f.* timidity; (*a*) timorousness; (*b*) shyness, bashfulness, diffidence; **t. à faire qch.**, (i) lack of courage to do sth.; (ii) diffidence in doing sth.

timocratie [timɔkrasi], *s.f.* timocracy.

timocratique [timɔkratik], *a.* timocratic.

timon[1] [timɔ̃], *s.m.* **1.** (*a*) pole (of vehicle); beam (of plough); (*b*) *occ. pl.* shafts (of vehicle). **2.** *Nau: A:* tiller; *Lit:* **prendre le t. des affaires**, to take the helm; to take the direction of affairs; **le t. de l'État**, the helm of State.

Timon[2], *Pr.n.m. Gr.Ant:* Timon.

timonerie [timɔnri], *s.f.* **1.** *Nau:* (*a*) steering (of ship); (**kiosque de**) **t.**, wheelhouse, pilot house; (*b*) (naval) signalling; **poste de t.**, signal station; **maître de t.**, (*in the navy*) yeoman of signals, (*in the merchant service*) quartermaster; **chef de t.**, chief yeoman of signals; *Navy:* **mousse de t.**, signal boy. **2.** *Aut:* (*a*) steering gear; (*b*) brake gear.

timonier [timɔnje], *s.m.* **1.** *Nau:* (*a*) helmsman, man at the wheel; (*b*) quartermaster; (*c*) *Navy:* signalman; **t. coureur**, messenger. **2.** *Veh:* wheelhorse; wheeler.

timoré [timɔre], *a.* timorous, fearful; **d'un air t.**, timorously; **conscience timorée**, easily alarmed conscience; over-scrupulous conscience.

Timothée [timɔte], *Pr.n.m.* **1.** *Gr.Hist:* Timotheus. **2.** *B.Hist: etc:* Timothy.

tin [tɛ̃], *s.m.* **1.** block; (boat) chock; *pl. N.Arch:* keel blocks (in dry dock); stocks (on slip). **2.** barrel chock.

tinamidés [tinamide], *s.m.pl. Orn:* Tinamidae, the tinamous.

tinamiformes [tinamifɔrm], *s.m.pl. Orn:* Tinamiformes, the tinamous.

tinamou [tinamu], *s.m. Orn:* tinamou.

tincal, tinkal [tɛ̃kal], *s.m. Miner:* tincal.

tincalconite [tɛ̃kalkɔnit], *s.f. Miner:* tincalconite.

tinctorial, -iaux [tɛ̃ktɔrjal, -jo], *a.* tinctorial (plant, process); **bois tinctoriaux**, dye woods; **matières tinctoriales**, dyestuffs.

tine [tin], *s.f.* butt; water cask; *Min:* kibble, tub.

tinée [tine]. *s.f. P: O:* lots, any amount; **il y en a une t.**, there's tons of it.

tinéides [tineid], **tinéidés** [tineide], *s.m.pl. Ent:* Tineidae.

tinet [tinɛ], *s.m.* (butcher's) gambrel.

tinette [tinɛt], *s.f.* **1.** tub. **2.** *Hyg:* (sanitary) soil tub.

tingidés [tɛ̃ʒide], *s.m.pl. Ent:* Tingidae.

tingis [tɛ̃ʒis], *s.m. Ent:* lace bug; (*genus*) Tingis.

tinier [tinje], *s.m. Bot:* cembra pine, Swiss (stone) pine, arolla (pine).

tinion [tinjɔ̃], *s.m. Bot: F:* couch grass, twitch.

tinne [tin], *s.f. Brickm:* clay crusher.

tinois, -oise [tinwa, -waːz], *a. & s. Geog:* (native, inhabitant) of Tain-l'Hermitage.

tintamarre [tɛ̃tamaːr], *s.m. F:* (*a*) din, racket, noise; (*b*) *O:* mock serenade; (*c*) **faire du t. autour d'un roman**, to give a novel wide publicity; to make a lot of fuss about a novel.

tintamarrer [tɛ̃tamare]. **1.** *v.i. A:* to make a din. **2.** *v.tr. F: O:* **t. qn**, to treat s.o. (unpopular) to a mock serenade, *U.S:* to shivaree s.o.

tintamarresque [tɛ̃tamarɛsk], *a. F:* loud, noisy (entertainment, humour); *O:* **succès t.**, resounding success.

tintement [tɛ̃t(ə)mɑ̃], *s.m.* **1.** ringing (of bell); **t. funèbre**, tolling. **2.** tinkling, tinkle (of small bells, glasses, etc.); jingling, jingle (of sleigh bells, keys); chink(ing) (of coins, glasses). **3.** buzzing, singing (in the ears); *Med:* tinnitus.

tinter[1] [tɛ̃te]. **1.** *v.tr.* to ring, toll (bell); **t. la messe**, to ring for mass. **2.** *v.i.* (*a*) (*of bell*) to ring; to toll; (*of small bells, etc.*) to tinkle; (*of coins*) to chink; (*of sleigh bells, keys*) to jingle; (*of glasses*) to clink; **faire t. les verres**, to clink glasses; (*b*) (*of the ears*) to buzz, tingle; **les oreilles me tintaient**, my ears were tingling, buzzing; **les oreilles doivent vous avoir tinté, ont dû vous t., hier soir**, your ears must have tingled, burned, last night (*i.e.* you were talked about).

tinter[2], *v.tr.* to support, chock up, block up (ship on stocks, barrel, etc.).

tintia(t) [tɛ̃tja], *s.m. Min:* temporary pitprop.

tintin [tɛ̃tɛ̃]. **1.** *s.m.* tinkle, chink, clink (of glasses, etc.); *F:* (se) **faire t.**, to go without sth.; to be done out of sth. **2.** *int. F:* no go! nothing doing!

tintinnabulement [tɛ̃tinabylmɑ̃], *s.m.* jingle, tintinnabulation.

tintinnabuler [tɛ̃tinabyle], *v.i. Lit:* (*of bells*) to tintinnabulate, tinkle, jingle; *F:* **faire t. un trousseau de clefs**, to jingle a bunch of keys.

Tintoret (le) [lətɛ̃tɔrɛ], *Pr.n.m. Hist. of Art:* Tintoretto.

tintouin [tɛ̃twɛ̃], *s.m.* **1.** *A:* singing, buzzing (in the ears). **2.** (*a*) din, racket; (*b*) trouble, worry; **quel t. il s'inflige!** what trouble he gives himself! **quel t. ces gosses!** what a worry the kids are! **donner du t.**, to give trouble; **c'est la main-d'œuvre qui nous donne le plus de t.**, most of our trouble is with the operatives; **elle me donne bien du t.**, she is very trying.

Tippoo Sahib, Tippou-Saïb [tipusaib], *Pr.n. Hist:* Tipu Sahib.

tipule [tipyl], *s.f. Ent:* tipula; *F:* daddy-long-legs, cranefly.

tipulides [tipylid], *s.m.pl. Ent:* Tipulidae.

tique [tik], *s.f. Arach:* tick, cattle tick; **t. du chien**, dog tick; **fièvre à tiques**, tick fever; *F:* **être comme une t. après qn**, (i) to pester s.o.; (ii) to batten on s.o.

tiquer [tike], *v.i.* **1.** *F:* (*a*) to twitch one's face, eyelids, etc.; (*b*) to wince; to show a slight sign of emotion, interest; **ne tiquez pas!** you needn't jump! **il n'a pas tiqué**, he didn't turn a hair; **il a tiqué**, he looked as if he didn't like it; **ça m'a fait t.**, it gave me a jolt; **c'est la chose qui m'a toujours fait t.**, that's the thing I've always jibbed at. **2.** *Vet:* (*of horse*) to have a stable vice; to suck wind, to crib, crib-bite, etc.

tiquet [tikɛ], *s.m. Ent:* flea-beetle.

tiqueté [tikte], *a.* speckled, mottled, variegated (flower, plumage, etc.).

tiqueture [tiktyːr], *s.f.* mottlings, speckles (on plumage, etc.).

tiqueur, -euse [tikœːr, -øːz]. **1.** *a. & s. Vet:* (horse, mare) with a stable vice; crib biter, wind sucker. **2.** *s. Psy:* person with a nervous tic.

tir [tiːr], *s.m.* **1.** (*a*) shooting; *Mil:* musketry; *Artil:* gunnery; **t. aux pigeons**, pigeon shooting; **médaille de t.**, medal for shooting; **concours de t.**, shooting match; **carnet de t.**, score book; *Mil:* **instructeur de t.**, musketry instructor; **effectuer un t.**, to carry out a shoot, a gunnery practice; **pratique du t.**, firing practice, range practice; (*b*) shooting match, competition. **2.** (*a*) fire, firing; **champ de t.**, range; **stand de t.**, shooting gallery, range; **butte de t.**, firing mound, target butt; **tranchée de t.**, fire trench, fire bay; **banquette de t.**, fire step; **exercice de t.**, firing drill, target practice; **t. d'instruction**, instruction, practice, firing; **t. réduit**, miniature-range shooting, sub-calibre, gallery, practice; **t. à distance réduite**, firing practice at reduced range; **stand de t. réduit**, miniature range; **cartouche de t. réduit**, gallery-practice cartridge; **t. réel**, fire, practice, under service conditions; **t. à distance réelle**, firing practice at normal range; **t. de combat**, battle practice; fire, practice, under active service conditions, *U.S:* combat firing; **t. à blanc**, fire, practice, with blank cartridges, with blank ammunition; **t. individuel**, individual firing, individual target practice; **t. collectif**, class firing, group target practice; **t. au commandement**, fire by order; **t. à volonté**, fire at will; **t. inopiné**, snap firing; **t. au jugé**, guess firing; **t. sur cible**, target shooting; **t. sur cible à éclipse**, fire at disappearing, at vanishing, target; **t. sur cible remorquée**, towed-target firing; **t. sur but fixe, mobile**, fire at fixed, at moving, target; **t. au but**, precision firing; **t. de groupement**, grouping practice; **t. précis**, well-grouped firing; **t. au fusil**, rifle shooting; **t. à bras francs**, offhand firing; **t. sur appui**, fire from a rest; **appui de t.**, elbow, rifle, rest; **t. debout**, fire, practice, in standing position; **t. à genoux**, fire, practice, in kneeling position; **t. couché**, fire, practice, in prone position; **t. de la hanche**, hip firing; **habileté au t.**, marksmanship; *Artil: etc:* **champ de t. (d'une arme)**, field of fire (of weapon); **dégager le champ de t.**, to clear the field of fire; **cadence, régime, vitesse, du t.**, rate of fire; **conduite du t.**, conduct of fire; **direction du t.**, fire control; **officier directeur du t.**, fire-control officer; **déclenchement du t.**, opening of fire; **déclencher le t.**, to open fire; **allonger, raccourcir, le t.**, to increase, reduce, the range; **t. de fonctionnement**, gun-testing fire; **t. direct, t. à vue directe**, direct fire; **t. indirect**, indirect fire; **t. d'après la carte**, map firing, predicted shooting; **t. de fauchage, t. fauchant**, traversing fire, sweeping fire; **t. sans fauchage**, fire without sweeping; **t. à couvert**, fire from cover; **t. à défilement**, fire from a defiladed position; **t. masqué**, fire from behind a mask, a ridge; **t. en marche**, firing on the move; **t. en station**, stationary fire; **t. bloqué**, fire with gun locked in direction; **t. débloqué**, fire with gun unlocked in direction; **t. coup par coup**, fire shot by shot; **t. par rafales**, fire by gusts, by bursts; **t. d'artillerie**, artillery fire; **t. de batterie**, battery fire; **éléments du t.**, firing data; **relever les éléments du t.**, to register fire; **observation du t.**, observation of fire; **plan de t.**, plan of fire; **table de t.**, firing table, range table; **t. à la demande**, fire on call; **t. suivant horaire**, schedule fire; **t. sur zones**, zone fire; **t. sur objectif de circonstance, sur objectif inopiné**, fire on target of opportunity; **t. par-dessus les troupes (amies)**, overhead fire; **t. d'accord**, calibration fire; **t. d'appui**, supporting fire; **t. d'appui immédiat**, close-support fire; **t. d'arrêt**, standing barrage; **t. de contre-batterie**, counter-battery fire; **t. de contre-préparation**, counter-preparation fire; **t. de destruction**, demolition fire; **t. d'efficacité**, fire for effect; **t. de harcèlement**, harassing fire; **t. d'encadrement**, bracketing fire; **t. d'encagement**, box fire; **t. de neutralisation**, neutralizing fire; **t. de préparation**, preparation fire; **t. de ratissage**, raking fire; **t. d'usure**, attrition fire, wearing-down fire; *Navy:* **t. en chasse**, bow fire; **t. en retraite**, stern fire; **reporter le t.**, to shift, switch, transfer, fire; **transport de t.**, shift, switch, transfer of fire; (*b*) *Min:* blasting; (*c*) *Fb:* **t. au but**, shot (at goal). **3.** (*a*) rifle range; (*b*) (**jeu de**) **t.**, shooting gallery.

tirade [tirad], *s.f.* **1.** *A:* pull, jerk; *A:* **tout d'une t.**, at one go. **2.** (*a*) *Th:* declamatory speech (of some length); (*b*) tirade, vituperative speech; **débiter une longue t. à qn**, to lecture s.o. at great length; **débiter des tirades contre qn**, to tirade against s.o.; **t. d'injures**, tirade of invectives, long string of insults. **3.** *Mus:* tirade, run (between two notes).

tirage [tiraːʒ], *s.m.* **1.** (*a*) pulling, hauling (of carriages, etc.); **il y a beaucoup de t. sur le caillou**, it is hard pulling over the cobblestones; **cheval de t.**, draught horse; *El:* **interrupteur à t.**, pull-and-push switch; *Aut:* **le t. (par opposition à la poussée)**, traction (as opposed to pulsion); **cordon de t.**, cord for drawing curtains, etc.); (*b*) *F:* trouble, difficulty; **il y a du t. entre eux**, there's friction between them; they don't get on well together; (*c*) (i) towing (of barges); (ii) towpath; (*d*) *Metalw:* wire drawing; (*e*) quarrying, extraction (of stone); **t. à la poudre**, blasting. **2.** *Phot:* extension, *A:* focal length (of camera); **chambre à double t.**, double-extension camera. **3.** draught (of flue); **t. forcé, soufflé**, forced draught, artificial draught; **t. renversé, inverti**, back draught; *I.C.E:* **carburateur à t. en bas**, down-draught carburettor. **4.** drawing (of lottery, of bonds); **les obligations sont rachetées par voie de t.**, the debentures are redeemed by lot; **bons sortis au t.**, drawn bonds. **5.** *Typ: Phot: etc:* (*a*) printing (off); **t. à part**, offprinting (of magazine, article, etc.); *Phot:* **t. par contact**, contact printing; *Bookb:* **t. à froid**, blind stamping; (*b*) number printed, printing, edition (of book, engraving, etc.); edition (of recording); **un mille de t.**, run, printing, of a thousand; **t. à part**, offprint; **journal à gros t.**, paper with a wide circulation; **le t. du journal baisse**, the circulation of the paper is falling off; **édition à t. limité**, limited edition; (*c*) *Typ:* **t. héliographique**, arc print; *Cin:* **t. en surimpression**, overprint. **6.** *Bank: etc:* drawing, emission (of cheque, bill of exchange); **t. en blanc, en l'air**, emission of a dud cheque, etc.

tiraille [tirɑːj], *s.f. Mch:* connecting rod.

tiraillement [tirɑjmɑ̃], *s.m.* **1.** tugging (on rope, etc.). **2. t. d'estomac**, gnawing at, of, the stomach; pangs of hunger. **3.** *F:* disagreement, wrangling, friction.

tirailler [tirɑje], *v.tr.* **1.** (*a*) to pull (s.o., sth.) about; **on le tiraillait par le bras**, they pulled him about by the arm; *F:* **tiraillé entre deux émotions**, torn between two opposing feelings; **je suis tiraillé de tous les côtés**, everybody wants me at once; **se faire tirailler**, to need a lot of asking; (*b*) *F:* to plague, pester (s.o.). **2.** *abs.* (*a*) to shoot aimlessly, desultorily; (*b*) *A:* to fire in skirmishing order.

se tirailler, *Fr.C:* to tussle; to scuffle.

tiraillerie [tirɑjri], *s.f.* **1.** (*a*) wrangling, friction; (*b*) pestering. **2.** wild firing; aimless firing, desultory firing.

tirailleur [tirɑjœːr], *s.m.* **1.** *Mil:* rifleman, skirmisher, sharpshooter, tirailleur; *A:* **tirailleurs algériens, sénégalais,** native Algerian, Senegalese, infantry; **trou de t.,** rifle pit; shelter trench; **en tirailleurs,** in skirmishing, in extended order. **2.** *F:* freelance journalist.

tirant [tirɑ̃], *s.m.* **1.** purse string. **2.** (*a*) boot strap; (*b*) boot tag; (*c*) *pl.* braces (of drum); (*d*) **t. de fourreau,** scabbard loop; (*e*) *Aut:* **t. de portière,** check strap; (*f*) *Cu:* sinew (in meat); **enlever les tirants,** to trim the meat. **3.** (*a*) *Const:* tie beam (of roof); tie, tie bolt, tie rod, cramp, truss rod; (*b*) *Tchn:* stay, brace; stay rod, stay bar, brace rod (of boiler, machine); **t. de frein,** brake rod; (*c*) *Mus:* **t. à accoupler,** coupler (of organ). **4.** *Nau:* **t. d'eau,** (ship's) draught, *U.S:* draft; **t. d'eau en charge,** loaded draught; **t. d'eau (à) lège,** light draught; **avoir dix pieds de t. d'eau,** to draw ten feet of water; **navire à faible t. d'eau,** shallow-draught ship; **différence du t. d'eau,** trim; **sans différence de t. d'eau,** on an even keel; **échelle de t. d'eau,** draught marks, numbers; *Civ.E: etc:* **t. d'air,** head room.

tirasse [tiras], *s.f.* **1.** *Ven:* draw net; clap net. **2.** *Mus:* pedal coupler (of organ).

tirasser [tirase]. **1.** *v.tr.* to catch (partridges, etc.) with a draw net. **2.** *v.i.* **t. aux cailles,** to go quail netting.

tiraude [tiroːd], *s.f. Civ.E:* **1.** lifting rope (of hand piledriver). **2.** hand piledriver.

Tircis [tirsis], *Pr.n.m. Lt.Lit:* Thyrsis.

tire [tiːr], *s.f.* **1.** *A:* pull(ing); **tout d'une t.,** without stopping, at one go; with one jerk; *still used in the phr.* **voleur à la t.,** pickpocket; **(vol à) la t.,** pickpocketing. **2.** row, line (*e.g. Her:* of vair). **3.** *Fr.C:* molasses toffee, *U.S:* molasses candy, taffy; *U.S:* taffy pull; **t. d'érable,** maple taffy. **4.** *Tex:* **(métier à la) t.,** drawloom. **5.** *P:* car.

tiré, -ée [tire]. **1.** *a.* (*a*) drawn, worn-out, peaked, pinched, haggard (features); **avoir les traits tirés,** to look tired; *F:* peaky; **il avait les traits tirés,** his face was drawn; **traits tirés par la faim,** face pinched with hunger; **aux cheveux tirés,** with her hair scraped back; (*b*) **t. par les cheveux,** far-fetched; (*c*) *Golf:* **coup t.,** pulled shot; pull; (*d*) **broderie à fils tirés,** drawn-thread work; (*e*) *Com:* **nous vous avons fait le prix le plus t. possible,** we have quoted you the cheapest possible price. **2.** *s. Com:* drawee. **3.** *s.m.* (*a*) shooting preserve; shoot; (*b*) *A:* shoot, day's sport. **4.** *s.m. Typ:* **t. à part,** offprint. **5.** *s.f.* **tirée:** (*a*) *Mount:* pull up; (*b*) *F:* long distance, drag; **il y a encore toute une tirée,** there's still a long drag, long haul, ahead; (*c*) *F:* **une tirée de qch.,** loads of sth.

tire-à-barrer [tirabare], *s.m.inv. Coop:* hoop cramp.

tire-au-cul [tiroky], *s.m.inv. P:* **tire-au-flanc** [tiroflɑ̃], *s.m.inv. F: Mil: etc:* malingerer; lazy bastard.

tire-balle [tirbal], *s.m.* **1.** *Sm.a:* bullet extractor. **2.** *Surg:* crowbill; *A:* bullet-forceps; *pl. tire-balles.*

tire-bonde [tirbɔ̃ːd], *s.m.* bung drawer; *pl. tire-bondes.*

tire-botte [tirbɔt], *s.m.* (*a*) bootjack; (*b*) boot-hook; *pl. tire-bottes.*

tire-bouchon [tirbuʃɔ̃], *s.m.* **1.** corkscrew; **en t.-b.,** in a corkscrew, in corkscrews. **2.** *Hairdr:* corkscrew curl; *pl. tire-bouchons.*

tire(-)bouchonnant [tirbuʃɔnɑ̃], *a.* in corkscrews, twisted; *pl. tire(-)bouchonnant(e)s.*

tire(-)bouchonné [tirbuʃɔne], *a.* (*of hair*) in corkscrew curls; *F:* **mouchoir t.-b.,** screwed-up handkerchief; *pl. tire(-)bouchonné(e)s.*

tire-bouchonnement [tirbuʃɔnmɑ̃], *s.m.* corkscrewing, spiralling.

tire(-)bouchonner [tirbuʃɔne]. **1.** *v.i.* (*of smoke, steam*) to curl, spiral, up; to rise in spirals. **2.** *v.tr.* to twist (sth.) in spirals; **t. son mouchoir,** to screw up, twist up, one's handkerchief.

tire-bourre [tirbuːr], *s.m.inv.* **1.** *Sm.a: A:* wad-extractor; worm. **2.** *Mec.E: etc:* packing extractor.

tire-bouton [tirbutɔ̃], *s.m.* buttonhook; *pl. tire-boutons.*

tire-braise [tirbrɛːz], *s.m.inv.* (baker's) oven rake.

tire-cartouche [tirkartuʃ], *s.m.* cartridge extractor; *pl. tire-cartouches.*

tire-cendre [tirsɑ̃ːdr], *s.m.inv. Miner:* tourmaline.

tire-clous [tirklu], *s.m.inv.* nail puller; nail wrench.

tire-d'aile (à) [atirdɛl], *adv.phr.* **s'envoler à t.-d'a.,** to fly swiftly away.

tire-douille [tirduːj], *s.m.* cartridge extractor; *pl. tire-douilles.*

tire-fesses [tirfɛs], *s.m.inv. F:* drag lift, ski tow.

tire-feu [tirfø], *s.m.inv. Artil:* **(cordon) t.-f.,** (firing) lanyard.

tire-fiacre [tirfjakr], *s.m.inv. F: A:* old cab-horse.

tire-filet [tirfilɛ], *s.m. Tls:* screw-cutting, thread-cutting tool; threader; *pl. tire-filets.*

tire-fond [tirfɔ̃], *s.m.inv.* **1.** long bolt, screw spike, foundation bolt; *Carp:* wood screw, coach screw, lag screw; *Rail:* sleeper screw. **2.** hook, ring (screwed into ceiling); eye bolt.

tirefonner [tirfɔne], *v.tr.* to bolt, to fasten by means of a *tire-fond.*

tirefonneuse [tirfɔnøːz], *s.f. Rail:* sleeper-screw driver.

tire-goupille [tirgupiːj], *s.m. Tls:* pin extractor; *pl. tire-goupilles.*

tire-hélice [tirelis], *s.m.inv. Av:* propeller remover.

tire-joint [tirʒwɛ̃], *s.m.inv. Const:* (*tool*) jointer.

tire-jus [tirʒy], *s.m.inv. P:* nosewipe, snot rag.

tire-laine [tirlɛn], *s.m.inv. A:* robber, coat-snatcher.

tire-lait [tirlɛ], *s.m.inv.* breast reliever.

tire-larigot (à) [atirlarigo], *adv.phr. F: O:* **boire à t.-l.,** (i) to drink by pouring wine from a height into the mouth; (ii) to drink deep, *F:* like a fish; **s'en donner à t.-l.,** to drink, eat, to one's heart's content; to have one's fill.

tire-ligne [tirliɲ], *s.m.* **1.** (*a*) drawing pen; **compas à t.-l.,** pen compass; **t.-l. à pointiller,** wheel pen, pricker; (*b*) *F:* uninspired architect. **2.** *Tls:* scriber, scribing awl, tool; scratch awl; *pl. tire-lignes.*

tire(-)lire[1] [tirliːr], *s.f.* **1.** money box; (*en forme de cochon*) piggy bank; *F:* **bascule à t.-l.,** slot weighing-machine. **2.** *P:* (*a*) face, *P:* mug; (*b*) belly.

tire-lire[2], *s.m.* (lark's) carol, tirralirra.

tire-lirer [tirlire], *v.i.* (*a*) (*of lark*) to carol; (*b*) to sing like a lark.

tire-l'œil [tirlœːj], *s.m.inv. F:* distinguishing feature; *F:* eye-catcher.

tire-moelle [tirmwal], *s.m.inv.* (*a*) marrow scoop, spoon; (*b*) *P:* nosewipe, snot rag.

tire-nerf [tirnɛːr, -nɛrf], *s.m. Dent:* barbed broach; *pl. tire-nerfs.*

tire-pied [tirpje], *s.m.* **1.** (shoemaker's) stirrup. **2.** shoehorn; *pl. tire-pieds.*

tire-pognon [tirpɔɲɔ̃], *s.m. F:* one-arm(ed) bandit, fruit machine; *pl. tire-pognons.*

tire-point [tirpwɛ̃], *s.m. Tls:* pricker, stabbing awl (for stitching leather); *pl. tire-points.*

tirer [tire]. **I.** *v.tr.* **1.** (*a*) to pull out, lengthen (out), stretch; **t. des fils métalliques,** to draw wire; **t. ses chaussettes,** to pull up one's socks; **t. une affaire en longueur,** to spin out a piece of business; *F:* **encore une heure à t. d'ici le déjeuner!** still another hour to get through before lunch! *P:* **t. cinq ans,** to get five years, a five-year stretch; *abs. F:* **t. à la ligne,** to eke out, pad out, a chapter or an article; (*b*) *Dial:* **t. une vache, etc.,** to milk a cow, etc. **2.** to pull, tug, draw, drag, haul; **t. qn par la manche,** to pluck s.o.'s sleeve; **il s'est fait t. pour payer, pour consentir,** he paid up, consented, very reluctantly; **t. les cheveux à qn,** to pull s.o.'s hair; **t. la jambe,** *F:* **t. la patte,** (i) to limp; (ii) to lag behind; **t. les rideaux,** to draw the curtains (to or apart); **t. le verrou,** to draw, pull back, the bolt; **il tira la porte sur lui,** he pulled the door to after him; *F:* **t. la couverture à soi,** to take the largest share of the blanket; to want more than one's share; *abs.* **cheval qui tire bien,** horse that is a good puller; **on aura bien à t. dans cette affaire,** it will be a stiff job to see this business through; *F:* **ça tire!** it's stiff going! **tableau qui tire l'œil,** arresting picture; *A:* **t. un criminel à quatre (chevaux),** to (hang,) draw and quarter a criminal; *F:* **être tiré à quatre,** to be worried on every side; *Mus:* (*violin*) **tirez!** down bow! **3.** (*a*) to pull off (shoes, stockings); **t. les bottes à qn,** to pull off s.o.'s boots; (*b*) **t. son chapeau à qn,** to raise, lift, one's hat to s.o.; **là-dessus il nous tira son chapeau,** thereupon he (lifted his hat and) departed; *A:* **t. sa révérence à qn,** (i) to bow oneself out; (ii) to say no to s.o. **4.** to pull out, draw out, take out, extract; **t. un journal de sa poche,** to pull a paper out of one's pocket; **de sa poche il tira une petite poupée,** he produced a little doll from his pocket; **t. une dent à qn,** to pull out, draw, s.o.'s tooth; **t. son épée, t. l'épée, t. sabre au clair,** to draw one's sword; **t. vivement un couteau,** to whip out a knife; **t. de l'eau,** to draw water; **souliers qui tirent l'eau,** shoes that let in water; **t. du vin d'un tonneau,** to draw wine from a cask; **t. des sons d'un instrument,** to draw, extract, sounds from an instrument; **t. des étincelles d'un silex,** to strike sparks from a flint; **t. des larmes des yeux de qn,** to draw tears from s.o.'s eyes; **t. les cartes,** to tell fortunes by cards; *Cards:* **t. pour la donne,** to cut for deal; **t. vanité de qch.,** to take pride in sth.; **t. plaisir de qch.,** to derive pleasure from sth.; **t. un bon revenu d'une propriété,** to derive a good income from an estate; **t. une règle générale de . . .,** to infer a general rule from . . .; **t. de l'argent de qn,** to get money out of s.o.; to extract money from s.o.; **t. de la pierre d'une carrière,** to quarry stone; *A:* **t. la pierre à la poudre,** to blast the stone; **c'est de la houille qu'on tire le gaz,** gas is extracted from coal; **l'huile se tire des olives,** oil is extracted from olives; **mot tiré du latin,** word derived from Latin; **t. la racine carrée d'un nombre,** to extract the square root of a number; **de son travail on peut t. encore d'autres preuves,** other evidence may be deduced from his work; **t. qn d'un mauvais pas,** to extricate s.o. from a difficulty; to get s.o. out of a fix; **t. qn de son lit,** to drag s.o. out of bed; **t. qn de son sommeil,** to drag s.o. from his sleep; **t. qn de prison,** to get s.o. out of prison; **il n'y a qu'un médecin qui puisse vous t. d'affaire,** only a doctor can pull you through. **5.** (*a*) to draw (line); to delineate (plan); (*b*) to pull, print (off), strike off (engraving, proof); **t. une circulaire à la Ronéo,** to roneo a circular; **donner le bon à t. d'un volume,** to pass a book for press; **épreuve en bon à t.,** press-proof, -revise; *abs.* **auteur qui tire à vingt mille,** author whose first editions run to twenty thousand; **ce journal tire à cent mille exemplaires,** this paper has a circulation of a hundred thousand; **t. une épreuve d'un cliché,** to take a print from a negative; **t. un plâtre d'une médaille,** to take a cast of a medal; (*c*) *Com:* to draw (bill of exchange); **t. un chèque sur une banque,** to draw a cheque on a bank; **t. à vue sur qn,** to draw on s.o. at sight. **6.** (*a*) to shoot, fire, let off (firearm, etc.); **t. un coup de revolver sur qn,** to fire, shoot, at s.o. with a revolver; *F:* **t. un coup de pied à qn,** to kick s.o.; **t. une flèche sur qn,** to shoot an arrow at s.o.; **il s'est tiré une balle dans la tête,** he shot himself in the head; **t. un feu d'artifice,** to let off fireworks; **t. un lièvre,** to shoot a hare; (*b*) *abs.* to shoot; (*of firearm*) to go off; **t. au canon, au fusil, au revolver,** to fire, shoot, with a gun, with a rifle, a shotgun, with a revolver; **t. au hasard, au jugé,** to fire at random, without aiming; **t. à couvert,** to fire from behind cover; **t. debout, à genoux, couché,** to fire standing, kneeling, from a prone position; **t. sur appui,** to fire from a rest; **t. d'après la carte,** to fire by the map; **t. tous azimuts,** to fire all round; **t. à blanc,** to fire (off) blank (cartridge); **nous tirions tant que nous pouvions,** we were firing, blazing, away as hard as we could go; **t. sur qn, sur qch.,** to shoot, fire, at s.o., at sth.; **t. sur une cible,** to fire at a target; **on tirait sur nous,** we were under fire; **le navire ennemi tirait sur nous,** the enemy ship was firing on us; *Fb:* **t. au but,** to shoot (at goal); (*c*) *Fenc:* **t. (des armes),** to fence; **t. sur le temps,** to make a time thrust; **t. en tierce, en quarte,** to thrust in tierce, in quarte; (*d*) *Phot: A:* to snap (s.o., sth.); **t. le portrait de qn,** to take s.o.'s photo(graph); **se faire t.,** to have one's portrait taken. **7.** *Nau:* **navire qui tire vingt pieds,** ship that draws twenty feet (of water).

II. tirer, *v.i.* **1.** to pull (on cable, reins, etc.); **t. sur sa barbiche,** to tug at one's beard; **t. sur sa pipe,** to have a pull, a draw, at one's pipe; to suck one's pipe. **2.** (*a*) to tend (to), incline (to); to verge (on); **couleur qui tire sur le rouge,** colour verging, bordering, on red; **bleu tirant sur le vert,** blue verging on, tending to, green; shading into green; greenish blue; **le jour tire à sa fin,** the day is drawing to its close; **le bonhomme tire à sa fin,** the old man's life is drawing to a close; **nos provisions tirent à leur fin,** our stores are running low, are giving out; **t. sur la soixantaine,** to be getting on for sixty; (*of doctor*) **t. à la visite,** to call on one's patient(s) more often than is necessary; (*of lawyer*) **t. à la consultation,** to seize every opportunity to advise one's client(s); (*b*) **t. sur la gauche,** to pull to the left; *O:* **t. vers la maison familiale,** to make for home; **t. au large,** (i) *Nau:* to stand out to sea; (ii) *F:* to scram, to beat it. **3.** (*of chimney, etc.*) to draw.

se tirer. 1. (*a*) **se t. d'un mauvais pas,** to extricate oneself from a difficulty; to get out of a fix; **vous ne vous en tirerez pas avec cette excuse-là,** you won't get away with that excuse; **s'en t. sans aucun mal,** to escape uninjured; **s'en t. sain**

et sauf, avec quelques égratignures, to come off with a whole skin, with a few scratches; **s'en t. tout juste,** to escape by the skin of one's teeth; **il s'en est bien tiré,** he came off well, got well out of it; **voyons comment il va se t. de son nouvel emploi,** let's see how he shapes up in his new job; **on s'en tire, voilà tout!** we just manage to make both ends meet, to scrape along; we just get by; **se t. d'affaire,** (i) to tide over a difficulty; to manage; (ii) to get out of trouble, *F:* to save one's bacon; **se t. d'affaire le mieux possible,** to make the best of a bad job; to make the best of it; (*b*) *F:* to come to an end; **ça se tire,** it'll soon be done now; **ça s'est bien tiré?** did it come off all right? **2.** *P:* (*of pers.*) to be off, to make tracks, to beat it.

tire-racine(s) [tirrasin], *s.m.inv. Dent:* stump forceps.

tirerie [tir(ə)ri], *s.f. A:* (*a*) wire drawing; (*b*) wire-drawing shop or mill.

tire-sac [tirsak], *s.m.* sack hoist, sack lift; *pl. tire-sacs.*

tire-sève [tirsɛːv], *s.m.inv. Hort:* bud-bearing branch.

tire-sou [tirsu], *s.m. P: A:* (*a*) tax collector; (*b*) usurer; (*c*) moneygrubber; (*d*) sponger; *pl. tire-sous.*

tiret [tirɛ], *s.m.* **1.** *A:* (parchment) latchet (holding deeds, etc., together). **2.** *Typ:* (*a*) hyphen; (*b*) dash, rule; (*c*) **ligne de tirets,** pecked line.

tiretaine [tirtɛn], *s.f. Tex: A:* linsey-woolsey; wincey.

tireté [tirte], *s.m. Typ:* broken line.

tirette [tirɛt], *s.f.* **1.** (*a*) curtain(-drawing), blind (-drawing), cords; (*b*) skirt, etc., loops (for hanging). **2.** (*a*) writing slide (of desk); (*b*) leaf (of table); (*c*) **boîte à t.,** slide box. **3.** *Mec.E:* pull handle, pull knob; flue damper (of furnace, etc.); *Aut: etc:* (pull-out) knob. **4.** *Aut: A:* **t. de fermeture,** bonnet fastener.

tirette-éclair [tirɛteklɛːr], (*in Belg.*) zip fastener; *pl. tirettes-éclair.*

tireur, -euse [tirœːr, -øːz], *s.* **1.** one who draws, drawer; (*a*) *Tchn:* **t. de soie,** silk reeler; *A:* **t. de fils métalliques,** wire-drawer; *Typ:* **t. d'épreuves,** proof puller; (*b*) (wine, beer) drawer; (*c*) *Com:* drawer (of bill of exchange, of cheque); (*d*) **t. de cartes,** fortune teller; (*e*) *Mil: etc: P:* **t. au flanc,** malingerer, shirker, lazy bastard. **2.** *Phot:* (*a*) printer; (*b*) *s.f.* **tireuse,** printing box, printer; **tireuse par contact,** contact printer. **3.** (*a*) shooter; firer; marksman; **c'est un bon t., un t. d'élite,** he's a good shot, a crack shot; **mauvais t.,** bad shot; **t. isolé, t. d'élite embusqué,** sniper; **essuyer les coups de feu de tireurs isolés,** to be sniped at; (*b*) **t. d'armes,** fencer; (*c*) pickpocket; *A:* **t. de laine,** robber, coat snatcher. **4.** *s.f. Winem:* **tireuse,** bottle filler, bottle-filling machine.

tire-v(i)eille [tirv(j)ɛːj], *s.f. Nau:* **1.** man rope, side rope; ladder rope. **2.** *pl.* yoke lines (of rudder); **barre à tire-veilles,** yoke.

tiroir [tirwaːr], *s.m.* **1.** drawer (of table, etc.); **tiroirs pleins de linge,** drawers filled with linen; *Lit:* **roman, comédie, à tiroir(s),** episodic novel, play; *Mil:* **mouvement en t.,** movement in echelon. **2.** *Mec.E:* slide, slide valve (of steam engine); **t. en D., t. de Watt, t. à garnitures,** D-valve; **t. cylindrique tournant,** segment valve (of Corliss engine, etc.); **boîte à t.,** steam chest; **t. compensé,** balanced slide valve; **t. à coquille, à trois ouvertures,** three-port slide valve; *Hyd.E:* **t. de soutirage,** weirbox. **3.** *Rail:* extension of the track beyond terminus (for crossover). **4.** *Ven:* lure (for hawk).

tiroir-caisse [tirwarkɛs], *s.m. Com:* till; *pl. tiroirs-caisses.*

Tiron [tirɔ̃], *Pr.n.m. Rom.Hist:* Tiro.

tironien, -ienne [tirɔnjɛ̃, -jɛn], *a. Rom.Ant:* Tironian; **notes tironiennes,** Tironian notes.

tirtifeu, -eux [tirtifø], *s.m. A:* poker.

Tirynthe [tirɛ̃ːt], *Pr.n.m. A.Geog:* Tiryns.

tisane [tizan], *s.f.* **1.** infusion, decoction, tea (of herbs, etc.); **t. de camomille,** camomile tea; **t. d'orge,** barley water. **2.** *Winem:* **t. de champagne,** light champagne. **3.** *P:* thrashing.

tisanerie [tizanri], *s.f. A:* kitchen (in hospital) where *tisanes* are prepared; patients' kitchen.

tisard, tisart [tizaːr], *s.m. Glassm:* stokehole.

tiser [tize], *v.tr. Glassm:* to stoke (furnace).

tiseur [tizœːr], *s.m. Glassm:* (*pers.*) stoker.

tisoir [tizwaːr], *s.m. Glassm:* furnace fireiron.

tison [tizɔ̃], *s.m.* **1.** (fire)brand; half-burned log; *F:* dregs, remains (of passion); **prendre le t. par où il brûle,** to take the bull by the horns; to grasp the nettle; **garder, être toujours sur, avoir toujours le nez sur, les tisons,** (*of old pers.*) **cracher sur les tisons,** to stick to one's chimney corner; to keep the fire warm; *Lit:* **prendrons-nous le café près des tisons?** shall we have coffee over the fire? *Lit:* **un t. arraché du feu,** a brand (snatched) from the burning; **t. de discorde,** mischief maker, firebrand. **2.** fusee (match).

tisonné [tizɔne], *a.* (*of horse's coat*) with black spots.

tisonnement [tizɔnmɑ̃], *s.m.* poking (of fire).

tisonner [tizɔne]. **1.** *v.i.* (*a*) to poke the fire; (*b*) to meddle with the fire. **2.** *v.tr.* to poke (the fire); **t. une querelle,** to fan a quarrel.

tisonnier [tizɔnje], *s.m.* **1.** poker. **2.** *pl. Mch: Ind:* firing tools (in general).

tissage [tisaːʒ], *s.m. Tex:* **1.** weaving; **t. à la main, à bras,** handloom weaving; **t. mécanique,** power-loom weaving. **2.** cloth mill, works.

Tissapherne [tisafɛrn], *Pr.n.m. A.Hist:* Tissaphernes.

tisser [tise], *v.tr.* (*a*) to weave; **métier à t.,** (weaving) loom; (*b*) *F:* to concoct a string of, to fabricate (lies, etc.).

tisserand, -ande [tisrɑ̃, -ɑ̃ːd]. **1.** *s.* weaver; **t. drapant,** cloth weaver; **t. en soie,** silk weaver. **2.** *s.m. Orn:* weaver (bird).

tisseranderie [tisrɑ̃dri], *s.f.* weaver's business; weaving (trade).

tisserin [tisrɛ̃], *s.m. Orn:* weaver(bird); **t. bicolore,** dark-backed weaver; **t. à capuchon,** village weaver; **t. républicain (d'Afrique du Sud),** (South African) sociable weaver(bird).

tisseur, -euse [tisœːr, -øːz], *s.* weaver.

tissu [tisy]. **1.** *a.* (*a*) *A:* woven (material, etc.); (*b*) *Lit:* **jours tissus de regrets et d'alarmes,** days made up of regrets and alarms. **2.** *s.m.* (*a*) texture; **vêtement d'un t. serré,** closely-woven garment, garment of a close weave; (*b*) fabric, tissue, textile; **gants en t.,** fabric gloves; **t. pour pantalon,** trousering; **t. de crin,** haircloth; **t. chauffant,** heating fabric; **t. de verre,** glass cloth, fabric; **t. de verre imprégné,** bonded-glass cloth; **t. métallique,** wire gauze; **t. de mensonges, d'absurdités,** string, tissue, of lies, of absurdities; (*c*) *pl. Com:* (i) suitings; (ii) soft goods; (*d*) *Biol:* (organic, cellular) tissue.

tissu-éponge [tisyepɔ̃ːʒ], *s.m. Tex:* sponge cloth; towelling; *pl. tissus-éponges.*

tissulaire [tisylɛːr], *a. Biol:* of tissue; tissual; **fragment t.,** fragment of tissue; **système t.,** tissue system.

tissure [tisyːr], *s.f. A:* tissue, texture (of material, of speech, poem); **t. lâche,** loose texture.

tissuterie [tisytri], *s.f. A:* making of ribbons and trimmings.

tissutier [tisytje], *s.m. A:* maker of ribbons and trimmings.

tistre [tistr̥], *v.tr. A:* (*used only in p.p.* **tissu** *and compound tenses*) to weave; **c'est lui qui a tissu cette intrigue,** it was he who wove this plot.

Titan [titɑ̃], *Pr.n.m. Myth: Astr:* Titan; **travail de T.,** titanic work; gigantic work; *Ind:* **grue T.,** giant crane, Titan crane.

titanate [titanat], *s.m. Ch:* titanate.

titane [titan], *s.m. Ch:* titanium; *Miner:* **t. oxydé,** titania; **t. oxydé ferrifère,** ilmenite; **t. silico-calcaire,** titanite.

titané [titane], *a. Ch: Miner:* titanic, titaniferous; **fer t.,** titanic, titaniferous, iron ore; ilmenite.

titanesque [titanɛsk], *a.* titanesque, titanic.

titaneux [titanø], *a.m. Ch:* titanous.

titanifère [titanifɛːr], *a. Miner:* titaniferous.

titanique[1] [titanik], *a. A:* titanic, titanesque.

titanique[2], *a. Ch:* titanic (acid).

titanite [titanit], *s.f. Miner:* titanite.

titanium [titanjɔm], *s.m. Ch:* titanium.

titanothéridés [titanɔteride], *s.m.pl. Paleont:* Titanotheridae.

titanyle [titanil], *s.m. Ch:* titanyl.

Tite [tit], *Pr.n.m.* Titus.

Tite-Live [titliːv], *Pr.n.m. Lt.Lit:* Livy.

Tithon [titɔ̃], *Pr.n.m. Myth:* Tithonus.

titi[1] [titi], *s.m. P:* street arab, cheeky urchin.

titi[2], *s.m. Z:* titi (monkey), teetee.

titianesque [tisjanɛsk], *a. Art:* Titianesque.

Titien (le) [lətisjɛ̃], *Pr.n.m. Hist. of Art:* Titian.

titillant [titillɑ̃], *a.* titillating, tickling.

titillateur [titillatœːr], *s.m. I.C.E:* tickler (of carburettor).

titillation [titillasjɔ̃], *s.f.* titillation, tickling.

titiller [titille], *v.tr.* to titillate; to tickle; *Aut: A:* **t. le carburateur,** to tickle the carburettor.

titisme [titism], *s.m. Pol:* Titoism.

titiste [titist], *a. & s.m. & f. Pol:* Titoist.

titrable [titrab̥l], *a. Metall:* assayable.

titrage [titraːʒ], *s.m.* **1.** (*a*) *Ch: Ind:* titration, titrating; standardizing (of a solution); assaying (of ore, etc.); determination of the strength (of alcohol, wine, etc.); (*b*) sizing, numbering (of cotton, wire, etc.); determination of the blend (of textile material). **2.** *Cin:* insertion of the titles.

titration [titrasjɔ̃], *s.f. Ch: Ind:* titration.

titre [titr̥], *s.m.* **1.** (*a*) title (of nobility, honour); official title; form of address; **avoir un t. (de noblesse),** to have a title, to be titled, *F:* to have a handle to one's name; **avoir ses titres de noblesse,** (i) to have a patent of nobility; (ii) to bear the stamp of respectability; (iii) to have made one's name, one's mark; **porter le t. de duc,** to bear the title of duke; **se donner le t. de . . .,** to style oneself . . .; **la Commission prendra le t. de . . .,** the Commission shall be entitled . . .; (*b*) **sans t. officiel,** without any official status; *adj.phr.* **en t.,** titular; on the regular staff; **professeur en t.,** titular professor; *F:* **la maîtresse en t. du roi,** the King's acknowledged mistress; *Jur:* **propriétaire en t.,** legal owner; (*c*) **titres à un emploi de fonctionnaire,** qualifications of an official for an appointment; (*d*) *Sp:* title; *Box:* **combat comptant, ne comptant pas, pour le t.,** title, non-title, fight. **2.** (*a*) *Sch: etc:* diploma, certificate; **pourvu de tous ses titres,** fully qualified; (*b*) voucher; *Rail:* **t. de transport,** ticket; **t. de réduction,** reduced-rate card; *Mil:* **t. de permission,** pass (for leave); (*c*) *Jur:* any instrument or document embodying a transaction in real estate; title deed; **t. de propriété,** title to property, title-deed; (*d*) **t. de créance,** proof of debt; evidence of indebtedness; (*e*) *Fin: Com:* warrant, bond, certificate; *pl.* stocks and shares, securities, *F:* scrip; **t. de rente,** government bond; **t. à lots,** lottery-loan bond; **t. au porteur,** bearer bond, negotiable instrument; **titres nominatifs,** registered securities, registered scrip; **certificat de titres,** share-certificate; **t. provisoire,** scrip (certificate); **t. de prêt,** loan certificate; **prendre livraison des titres,** to take delivery of stock. **3.** title, claim, right; **titres de gloire,** titles to fame; **t. juridique à qch.,** legal claim to sth.; **ses titres à notre amitié,** his claims to our friendship; **nommé chevalier de la Légion d'honneur au t. du Ministère de la Guerre,** made a Chevalier of the Legion of Honour at the instance of the Ministry of War; **à t. de,** by way of, as a, by right of, by virtue of, on the score of; **à t. d'office,** ex officio; **à t. de précaution,** just in case; **à t. d'ami,** as a friend; **à t. d'indication, à t. indicatif,** as a guide, for your, my, guidance; **à t. d'essai,** as a trial measure, experimentally; **envoi à t. d'essai,** trial lot; **montre envoyée à t. d'essai,** watch sent on approval; **à t. de faveur,** as a favour; **à bon t., à juste t.,** fairly, rightly; **à quel t.?** by what right? upon what score? upon what grounds? **X vient aussi—à quel t.?** X is coming too—what as? **à plus d'un t.,** for more than one good reason; **au même t.,** for the same reason; **à ce double t.,** on both these grounds; **à t. confidentiel,** in confidence; **à t. gratuit,** free of charge; *Jur:* **à t. onéreux,** for valuable consideration. **4.** (*a*) title (of book, song, etc.); **(page du) t.,** title-page; **faux t.,** half title, bastard title; **t. abrégé (d'un ouvrage catalogué),** catch title; (*b*) heading (of chapter, page); *Typ:* **t. courant,** running headline; **les gros titres,** the large headlines; (*c*) part, section (of regulations, of the Code). **5.** *Ecc:* **titres des cardinaux,** Titles (*i.e.* parish churches) of the cardinals. **6.** (*a*) title, titre (of gold); grade, content (of ore); fineness (of coinage); *Ch:* strength, titre (of solution); **t. d'eau,** degree of humidity; **or au t.,** standard gold; (*b*) size, number (of cotton, wire); grist (of yarn); specification of the blend (of textile).

titré [titre], *a.* **1.** titled; **il est t.,** he has a title, *F:* a handle to his name. **2.** *Sch:* qualified (teacher). **3.** *Ch:* titrated, standard (solution).

titrer [titre], *v.tr.* **1.** to give a title to (s.o., sth.); *Cin:* to insert the titles in (a film); *abs.* **la presse titrait en énormes manchettes,** the press printed in enormous headlines. **2.** *Tchn:* (*a*) *Ch: Ind:* to titrate; to standardize (solution); to make a standard solution of (liquor); to assay (ore, etc.); to determine the strength of (alcohol, wine, etc.); (*b*) to size, number (cotton, wire, etc.); to determine the blend of (textile material). **3.** (*of ore, etc.*) **t. tant % de métal,** to assay so much % of metal.

titreur [titrœːr], *s.m.* headline writer.

titreuse [titrøːz], *s.f. Cin:* (*device*) titler.

titrimètre [titrimɛtr̥], *s.m.* titrimeter.

titrimétrie [titrimetri], *s.f.* titrimetry.

titubant [titybɑ̃], *a.* reeling, lurching, staggering.

titubation [titybasjɔ̃], *s.f.* reeling, lurching, staggering; *Med:* titubation.

tituber [titybe], *v.i.* to reel (about); to lurch; to stagger, totter; **marcher, entrer, sortir, en titubant,** to stagger, lurch, along, in, out.

titulaire [titylɛ:r]. **1.** *a.* titular (bishop, professor, etc.); **patron t. d'une église,** titular saint, patron saint, of a church; **juge t.,** regular judge; **professeur t.,** titular, full, professor; **membre t.,** regular member. **2.** *s.* holder, titular (of right, title, certificate, etc.); bearer (of passport); occupant (of office); *Ecc:* incumbent (of parish); **être t. d'une médaille,** to hold a medal; **cours donné par un suppléant en l'absence du t.,** course given by a substitute in the absence of the regular professor; **t. d'une pension,** pensioner; *Tp:* **t. d'un abonnement,** telephone subscriber; **il est déjà t. de plusieurs condamnations,** he already has several convictions recorded against him.

titulariat [titylarja], *s.m.* titularity.

titularisation [titylarizasjɔ̃], *s.f. Adm:* establishment (of civil servants, etc.); **en stage de t.,** on probation.

titulariser [titylarize], *v.tr. Adm: etc:* to put (s.o.) on the establishment; to confirm (s.o.) in his post, appointment; to establish (s.o.); **fonctionnaires titularisés,** established civil servants; **fonctionnaires non titularisés,** non-established civil servants.

titulateur [titylatœ:r], *s.m. A: Cin:* caption writer; titler.

titulature [titylaty:r], *s.f.* titles borne, carried (by pers. or firm); style.

Titus [titys], *Pr.n.m.* Titus; *A:* **coiffure à la T.,** Titus crop; **être coiffé à la T.,** to have a pudding-basin haircut, to be cropped à la Titus.

titys [titis], *s.m. Orn:* black redstart.

tjaële, tjäle [tjɛl], *s.m. Geog:* tjaele, taele.

tlemcénien, -ienne [tlɛmsenjɛ̃, -jɛn], *a. & s. Geog:* (native, inhabitant) of Tlemcen.

tmèse [tmɛ:z], *s.f. Gram:* tmesis.

toast [tost], *s.m.* toast. **1. porter un t.,** to propose a toast; **porter un t. à qn,** to propose the health of s.o.; to drink s.o.'s health, to toast s.o. **2. t. beurré,** piece of buttered toast.

toaster[1] [toste], *v.tr. O:* to toast (s.o.); to drink (s.o.'s) health.

toaster[2] [tostɛ:r], **toasteur** [tostœ:r], *s.m.* (electric) toaster.

tobera [tɔbɛra], *s.m. Bot:* tobira.

Tobie [tɔbi], *Pr.n.m.* Tobias; Tobiah; Toby.

toboggan [tɔbɔgɑ̃], *s.m.* **1.** (*a*) toboggan; **piste de t.,** toboggan run; (*b*) chute (in swimming bath); (fairground) slide; (*c*) *Com: etc:* parcels, goods, chute. **2.** *Civ.E:* overpass.

tobogganiste [tɔbɔganist], *s.m. & f.* tobogganist, tobogganer.

Tobrouk [tɔbruk], *Pr.n. Geog:* Tobruk.

toc [tɔk]. **1.** (*a*) *int.* tap, tap! **entendre t., t., à sa porte,** to hear a knock knock, tap tap, rat-tat, at one's door; (*b*) *s.m.* tap, rap (on door, etc.). **2.** *F:* (*a*) *s.m.* imitation, sham, gold; faked stuff; **en t.,** pinchbeck; **bijoux, articles, en t.,** imitation jewellery; (*b*) *a.inv.* **être un peu t.,** to be a bit crazy, dotty, touched. **3.** *s.m. Mec.E:* (*a*) (lathe) carrier; dog; **t. d'entraînement,** driving dog; (*b*) stop; catch; *Nau:* **à t. de toile,** with every stitch of canvas set. **4.** *s.m. Fish:* bite.

tocade [tɔkad], *s.f. F:* (passing) craze; infatuation.

tocan [tɔkɑ̃], *s.m. Ich:* parr, smolt.

tocane [tɔkan], *s.f. Winem:* new champagne.

tocante [tɔkɑ̃:t], *s.f. P:* ticker, watch.

tocard [tɔka:r], *P:* **1.** *a.* (i) worthless, trashy, of poor quality; (ii) ugly. **2.** *s.m.* (*a*) *Rac:* (rank) outsider; (*b*) (*pers.*) hopeless case, dead loss.

tocasson [tɔkasɔ̃], *s.m. & f. O: P:* (i) ugly, (ii) silly, person; **quel t.!** (i) what a fright! (ii) isn't he a mug!

toccata [tɔkata], *s.f. Mus:* toccata.

tock [tɔk], *s.m. Orn:* **t. à bec rouge,** (African) red-billed hornbill.

tocoférol, tocophérol [tɔkɔferɔl], *s.m. Bio-Ch:* tocopherol.

tocologie [tɔkɔlɔʒi], *s.f.* tocology; obstetrics.

tocotechnie [tɔkɔtɛkni], *s.f.* midwifery.

tocsin [tɔksɛ̃], *s.m.* tocsin ((i) alarm signal; (ii) alarm bell); **sonner le t. contre, sur, qn,** to raise a hue and cry against s.o.

toc-toc [tɔktɔk], *a.inv. F:* daft, dotty.

todidés [tɔdide], *s.m.pl. Orn:* Todidae.

todier [tɔdje], *s.m. Orn:* tody; (*genus*) Todus.

toge [tɔ:ʒ], *s.f.* (*a*) *Rom.Ant:* toga; (*b*) gown, robe (of judge, etc.); **t. universitaire,** (college) gown.

Togo (le) [lətɔgo], *Pr.n.m. Geog:* Togoland; **République du T.,** Republic of Togo.

togolais, -aise [tɔgɔlɛ, -ɛz], *a. & s. Geol:* Togolese.

tohu-bohu [tɔybɔy], *s.m.* (*a*) *B:* the earth without form; chaos; (*b*) *F:* confusion, medley; hurly-burly; hubbub.

toi [twa], *stressed pers.pron.* (*for the use of* **toi,** *cf.* TU); (*a*) you (*subject or object*) **c'est t.,** it's you; **t. et moi nous irons ensemble,** you and I will go together; **il est plus âgé que t.,** he is older than you; **il n'aime que t.,** he loves only you; **tu as raison, t.,** you are right; **avec t.,** with you; **ce livre est à t.,** this book is yours, belongs to you; **tu le vois par t.-même,** you can see for yourself; **moi, je reste, et t., tu pars,** I'll stay and you go; **à tu et à t.,** *see* TU[1]; (*after the imp.*) **tais-t.!** hold your tongue, be quiet, *F:* shut up! (*b*) (*to the Deity, in dialect and literature*) thou, thee; **t. et ta postérité après t.,** thou and thy seed after thee; **assieds-t.,** sit thee down; **connais-t. t.-même,** know thyself.

toilage [twala:ʒ], *s.m. Lacem:* foundation, ground (of lace).

toile [twal], *s.f.* **1.** (*a*) linen, linen cloth; **t. bise, écrue,** unbleached linen; holland; **t. pour draps de lit,** sheeting; **t. à chemises,** shirting; **t. à matelas,** tick, ticking; **t. ouvrée,** huckaback; **t. à patrons,** leno; **t. de Jouy,** (kind of) cretonne print, toile; **drap de t.,** linen sheet; *F:* **se mettre dans les toiles,** to go to bed; **pantalon de t.,** duck trousers; **marchand de t.,** linen draper; (*b*) cloth; **t. de crin,** horsehair cloth; **t. de coton,** calico; **t. peinte,** print; **t. cirée,** (i) American cloth, oilcloth, (oil) baize; (ii) *Nau:* oilskin; **t. vernie,** oilskin; **t. à calquer, t. d'architecte,** tracing cloth; *Nau:* **t. abri,** weather-cloth; (bridge or hatchway) screen; **t. à voiles,** canvas, sailcloth; **t. fine pour voiles,** duck; **t. à bâches,** tarpaulin; **t. d'emballage,** pack-cloth; **t. à sac, t. à serpillières,** sackcloth, sacking, bagging; **t. à sangles,** webbing; **t. caoutchoutée,** rubberized cloth; **reliure en t.,** cloth binding; **t. de sauvetage,** jumping sheet, life net; (*c*) canvas; **t. de tailleur,** tailor's canvas; **toiles d'un pneu,** canvas of a tyre; **coucher sous la t., sous la même t.,** to sleep under canvas, under the same tent; **seau en t.,** canvas bucket; **collé sur t.,** mounted on canvas; **papier collé sur t.,** linen-backed paper; (*d*) **t. métallique,** wire gauze; **t. (d')émeri,** emery cloth; **t. d'amiante,** asbestos; (*e*) **t. d'araignée,** cobweb; spider's web. **2.** (*a*) oil painting (on canvas); canvas; (*b*) *Th:* curtain; **t. de fond,** back drop, back cloth, drop scene; **derrière la t.,** behind, off; *F:* **la toile!** up with the curtain! make a start! **3.** (*a*) *Nau:* sail; **augmenter de t.,** to make more sail; **forcer, diminuer, de t.,** to crowd, shorten, sail; **couvert de t., à toc de t.,** with every stitch of canvas set; cracking on; **à sec de t.,** under bare poles; (*b*) **toiles d'un moulin à vent,** sails of a windmill. **4.** *pl. Ven:* toils; *Lit:* **tendre ses toiles, sa t.,** to lay one's snares (for s.o.).

toilé [twale]. **1.** *a.* **papier t.,** linen (finish) paper, linen-faced paper. **2.** *s.m. Lacem:* (*a*) ground (net); (*b*) very close blond lace.

toilerie [twalri], *s.f.* **1.** (*a*) linen industry, trade; (*b*) the textile trade (excluding wool and silk). **2.** linen warehouse. **3.** (*a*) linen goods; (*b*) goods of linen, cotton, or hemp.

toilettage [twalɛta:ʒ], *s.m.* grooming and trimming (of pets, domestic animals, etc.).

toilette [twalɛt], *s.f.* **1.** (*a*) *O:* (tailor's, dressmaker's) wrapper (for garments, etc.); (*b*) *Cu:* caul (of mutton, etc.); crow (of pig). **2.** *A:* dressing-table cover. **3.** (*a*) wash-stand; (*b*) dressing table; make-up table; (*c*) *O:* toilet service (jug, wash-basin, etc.). **4.** (*a*) toilet, washing and dressing; **faire sa t.,** to wash and dress; **faire un bout, un brin, de t.,** to have a wash and brush up; to tidy oneself; **faire la t. d'un mort,** to lay out a corpse; **le chat fait sa t.,** the cat is washing; **faire la t. d'une voiture,** to clean a car; **faire la t. d'un arbre de Noël,** to decorate a Christmas tree; **cabinet de t.,** dressing room (with wash-basin); **trousse, nécessaire, de t.,** dressing case, toilet case; **gant de t.** = (face) flannel; **savon de t.,** toilet soap; (*b*) *P.N:* **toilettes,** toilets; public conveniences; *U.S:* comfort station. **5.** (*a*) (woman's) dress, clothes; **aimer la t.,** to be fond of dress, clothes; **être en (grande) t.,** to be in formal dress; **t. de bal,** ball dress; **faire t. pour qn,** to dress up for s.o.'s benefit; to put on one's smartest clothes for s.o.; *A:* **marchande, revendeuse, de t.,** wardrobe dealer; (*b*) *A:* set of (woman's) collar and cuffs.

toiletter [twalete], *v.tr.* to trim and groom (a domestic animal, a pet).

toilier, -ière [twalje, -jɛ:r], **1.** *a.* linen, (industry, etc.). **2.** *s.m.* (*a*) linen manufacturer; (*b*) linen dealer.

toi-même [twamɛ:m], *pers.pron. See* TOI *and* MÊME.

toise [twa:z], *s.f.* **1.** *A:* fathom; *F:* **mots longs d'une t.,** words as long as one's arm, a yard long. **2.** (*a*) measuring apparatus; **passer sous la t.,** to be measured (for height); **je mesure 1 m. 78 à, sous, la t.,** my official height is 1 m. 78; **faire passer sous la t.,** to examine minutely; (*b*) standard (of comparison); **mesurer les hommes à la t.,** to judge people by appearances; **ne mesurez pas tous les hommes à la même t., à votre t.,** don't judge all men by the same standard, by your own standard. **3.** *Civ.E:* gauged pile (of road metal). **4.** *P:* **flanquer une t. à qn,** to give s.o. a (good) thrashing.

toisé [twaze], *s.m.* **1.** measuring (up); measurement; *Civ.E: O: Const:* quantity surveying; **faire le t. d'un immeuble,** to survey a building for quantities. **2.** mensuration.

toiser [twaze], *v.tr.* **1.** (*a*) to measure (conscript, piece of ground, etc.); (*b*) *Civ.E: Const: O:* to survey for quantities, for work done. **2.** to take stock of (s.o.); to eye (s.o.) from head to foot, all over; **t. qn d'un air de dédain,** to look s.o. up and down contemptuously; **c'est un homme toisé,** everybody knows what he is!

toiseur [twazœ:r], *s.m. O:* surveyor, *esp.* quantity surveyor.

toison[1] [twazɔ̃], *s.f.* **1.** (*a*) fleece; *Myth:* **la T. d'or,** the Golden Fleece; *Hist:* **(ordre de) la T. (d'or),** (Order of) the Toison d'Or; (*b*) *Her:* toison, fleece. **2.** *F:* mop, shock (of hair).

toison[2], *s.f.* = TOISE 3.

toit [twa], *s.m.* **1.** roof; **t. à deux pentes, à deux égouts,** ridge roof; **t. en croupe,** hip roof; **t. à un égout,** lean-to roof; *Ind:* **t. en dents de scie,** saw-tooth roof (of factory, etc.); **t. d'ardoises, de tuiles, de chaume,** slated roof, tiled roof, thatched roof; **paysage de toits,** roofscape; **des ruines sans toits,** roofless ruins; *F:* **habiter sous les toits,** to live in a garret; **le Philosophe sous les toits,** the Attic Philosopher; **publier, crier, qch. sur les toits,** to proclaim sth. from the housetops, to noise, trumpet, sth. abroad; **ce n'est pas une chose à crier sur les toits,** it isn't the sort of thing to be blazed abroad; *Aut:* **t. découvrable, t. ouvrant,** sliding roof, sunshine roof; (*of tent*) **double t.,** flysheet. **2.** (*a*) house; **le t. paternel,** the home, the paternal roof; (*b*) **t. à porcs,** pigsty; (*c*) lean-to roof; shed. **3.** *Min:* top, roof (of mine); hanging wall (of lode).

toiture [twaty:r], *s.f.* roofing, roof.

toiture-terrasse [twatyrtɛras], *s.f. Const:* flat roof, terrace; *pl. toitures-terrasses.*

tokai, tokay [tɔkɛ], *s.m.* tokay (wine).

tokeh [tɔke], *s.m. Rept:* tokay; Malaysian gecko; **t. à taches rouges,** red-spotted tokay.

tokharien, -ienne [tɔkarjɛ̃, jɛn], *a. & s.m.* Tocharian, Tokharian.

tola [tɔla], *s.m. Bot:* agba wood.

tôlage [tola:ʒ], *s.f.* covering with sheet metal.

tolane [tɔlan], *s.m. Ch:* tolan(e).

tôlard [tola:r], *s.m. Mil: P:* prisoner (soldier sentenced to imprisonment for breach of discipline, etc.).

tôle[1] [to:l], *s.f.* **1.** sheet metal; (*a*) sheet iron; **t. d'acier,** sheet steel; **t. étamée,** tinned sheet; **t. galvanisée,** galvanized iron; **t. ondulée, ridée,** corrugated iron; **t. émaillée,** enamelled iron; **t. vernie,** japanned iron; **t. cintrée,** curved sheet; **t. d'emboutissage,** stamping sheet; **t. décapée, t. automobile,** bright-steel sheet; **t. laminée,** rolled plate; **malle de t.,** tin trunk; (*b*) **t. de cuivre,** copper sheets. **2.** (steel, iron) plate (for boilers, etc.); boiler plate; **tôles de fond,** bottom plates (of boiler); *N.Arch:* **t. de bordé,** shell plate; **t. de pavois,** bulwark plate; **t. de voûte,** oxter plate; **t. de blindage,** armoured plate; **t. plombée,** terne plate; **t. gouttière,** stringer plate; **t. pare-feu,** fire bulkhead. **3. t. d'enveloppe,** casing. **4.** *Dom.Ec:* baking tin, baking sheet.

tôle[2], *s.f. P:* = TAULE.

tôlé [tole], *a.* (*a*) built of, covered with, sheet metal; **panneau t.,** metal panel; (*b*) *Mount: Skiing:* **neige tôlée,** *s.f.* **tôlée,** crusted snow.

tolédan, -ane [tɔledɑ̃, -an], *a. & s. Geog:* Toledan.

Tolède [tɔlɛd], *Pr.n. Geog:* Toledo; **épée de T.,** Toledo blade; *A:* Toledo.

tôle-gouttière [tolgutjɛ:r], *s.f. N.Arch:* stringer plate; *pl. tôles-gouttières.*

tolérable [tɔlerabl̩], *a.* bearable, tolerable; *Mec.E:* **jeu t.,** permissible clearance.

tolérablement [tɔlerabləmɑ̃], *adv.* (*a*) tolerably, bearably; (*b*) tolerably well, reasonably well.

tolérance [tɔlerɑ̃:s], *s.f.* tolerance. **1.** toleration (in religious matters, etc.); **par t.,** on sufferance; **maison de t.,** licensed brothel. **2.** *Tchn:* (*a*) (*in coinage*) tolerance, remedy (of the Mint); (*b*) *Mec.E:* margin, limits, tolerance; **t. nulle,** zero allowance; **tolérances maxima et minima,** plus and minus limits; **t. sur l'épaisseur, sur la longueur,** thickness margin, length margin;

calibre de t., limit gauge; t. d'ajustage, tolerance on fit; t. de fabrication, factory limit, tolerance; t. de fonctionnement, operational tolerance; *Elcs:* t. de fréquence, frequency tolerance; (*c*) *Cust:* t. (permise), tolerance, allowance; il y a une t. d'un demi-litre, you are allowed to bring in half a litre free of duty; (*d*) concession. 3. *Med:* (*of patient*) tolerance (of a drug, etc.); *Bot:* (*of plant*) tolerance (of parasites).

tolérant, -ante [tɔlerɑ̃, -ɑ̃:t]. 1. *a.* tolerant; *Bot:* resistant, tolerant (plant). 2. *s.* tolerant person; person who shows religious tolerance.

tolérantisme [tɔlerɑ̃tism], *s.m.* religious toleration; latitudinarianism; **partisan du t.**, latitudinarian.

tolérer [tɔlere], *v.tr.* (je tolère, n. tolérons; je tolérerai) (*a*) to tolerate (opinions, religions, etc.); *F:* **je ne peux pas t. ce mioche,** I can't bear, endure, put up with, that brat; **t. qu'on fasse qch.,** to allow sth. to be done, to tolerate having sth. done; **ce que je ne peux t. chez lui c'est . . .,** the thing I can't bear about him is that . . .; (*b*) to allow tacitly, wink at (abuses, etc.); (*c*) *Med:* to tolerate (drug).

tôlerie [tolri], *s.f.* 1. sheet-iron and steel-plate trade. 2. rolling mills; sheet-iron works; boiler-plate works. 3. sheet iron and steel plate goods; *Aut: etc:* steelwork.

tolet [tɔlɛ], *s.m. Nau:* thole pin; **t. à fourche,** swivel rowlock.

toletière [tɔltjɛ:r], *s.f. Nau:* 1. strengthening plate (on gunwale, to receive rowlock). 2. rowlock.

tôle-varangue [tolvarɑ̃:g], *s.f. N.Arch:* floor plate; *pl. tôles-varangues.*

tôlier[1] [tolje], *s.m.* 1. sheet-iron merchant. 2. sheet-iron worker; *Aut:* panel beater.

tôlier[2], *s.m. P:* = TAULIER.

tolite [tɔlit], *s.f. Exp:* tolite.

tollé [tɔlle], *s.m.inv.* outcry of indignation; **crier t. contre qn,** to raise a hue and cry against s.o.; **soulever un t. général,** to raise a general outcry.

tollet [tɔlɛ], *s.m. Nau:* = TOLET.

toltèque [tɔltɛk], *Ethn:* 1. *a.* Toltecan. 2. *s.* Toltec.

Tolu [tɔly], *Pr.n. Geog:* Tolu; *Pharm: etc:* **baume de T.,** balsam of Tolu; tolu.

toluate [tɔlɥat], *s.m. Ch:* toluate.

toluène [tɔlɥɛn], *s.m. Ch:* toluene, methyl benzene; *Ch.Ind:* **t. pour nitration,** nitration grade toluene.

toluidine [tɔlɥidin], *s.f. Ch:* toluidine.

toluifera [tɔlɥifɛra], *s.m. Bot:* Toluifera, myroxylon.

toluique [tɔlɥik], *a. Ch:* toluic (acid).

toluol [tɔlɥɔl], *s.m. Ch:* toluol, toluene.

tolyle [tɔlil], *s.m. Ch:* tolyl.

tolypeute [tɔlipøt], *s.m. Z:* mataco armadillo.

tomahawk [tɔmaɔk], *s.m.* tomahawk.

tomaison [tɔmɛzɔ̃], *s.f. Typ:* volume number (on each signature).

tomate [tɔmat], *s.f.* (*a*) *Bot:* tomato; **t. groseille à grappes,** currant tomato; **sauce t.,** tomato sauce; *F:* **être (rouge) comme une t.,** to be as red as a beetroot; *O:* **en rester comme une t.,** to be flabbergasted; (*b*) *P:* pastis (or absinthe) with grenadine.

tomatier [tɔmatje], *s.m.* tomato grower.

tombac [tɔ̃bak], *s.m. Metall:* tombac(k).

tombal, -aux [tɔ̃bal, -o], (*a*) *a.* relating to tombs; **pierre tombale,** tombstone, gravestone; ledger; (*b*) *s.f.* **tombale,** ledger; slab (of vault).

tombant [tɔ̃bɑ̃]. 1. *a.* (*a*) falling; **dynastie tombante,** dynasty tottering to its fall; **à la nuit tombante,** at nightfall; (*b*) flowing (hair); drooping (branch, moustache); **robe à lignes tombantes,** dress falling freely, in straight lines; **épaules tombantes,** sloping shoulders, drooping shoulders. 2. *s.m.* (*a*) fringe (of epaulet); (*b*) *Dressm:* hang (of a dress); *O:* fall (of collar); (*c*) submerged part of cliff.

tombe [tɔ̃:b], *s.f.* 1. (*a*) tomb, grave; **t. collective,** mass grave; **être dans la t.,** to be dead; **être au bord de la t.; avoir un pied dans la t.,** to be on the point of death, on the edge of the grave; to have one foot in the grave; to be at death's door; (*b*) tombstone. 2. *Hort:* bed of leaf mould (for salads, etc.).

tombé [tɔ̃be], *a.* fallen; **roi t.,** fallen king; *Danc:* **pas t.,** tombé; *Rugby Fb:* **coup de pied t.,** drop-kick.

tombeau, -eaux [tɔ̃bo], *s.m.* tomb; monument (over grave or vault); *Lit: Mus:* commemorative poem, work; **t. de famille,** family vault; **fidèle jusqu'au t.,** true till death, faithful unto death; **être aux portes du t.,** to be at death's door, to have one foot in the grave; **mettre un corps au t.,** to entomb a body; **mise au t.,** entombment; *F:* **il me mettra, conduira, au t.,** (i) he will outlive me; (ii) he'll be the death of me; **galoper, rouler, conduire, à t. ouvert,** to ride, drive, at breakneck speed; *Lit:* **descendre au t.,** to die; *Lit:* to go down into the tomb; **à t., en t.,** tomb-shaped, tomblike; **brosse en t.,** brush with curved bristle surface, stove-shape brush; **c'est le t. des secrets,** he is an absolutely discreet person; he's as silent as the grave; **se creuser un t.,** to make one's own bed, to be responsible for one's own ruin; *Archeol:* **t. de forme allongée,** long barrow; **t. de forme arrondie,** round barrow.

tombée [tɔ̃be], *s.f.* 1. fall (of rain, night, etc., *cf.* CHUTE); **quelle t. de pluie!** what a downpour! **t. du jour, de la nuit,** nightfall; **à la t. de la nuit,** at nightfall, when night closes in; *Meteor: A:* **t. de pluie,** rainfall. 2. (*a*) calming, subsiding (of the sea); (*b*) subsidence (of underground gallery, etc.). 3. *F:* **t. (de tissu),** odd-come-short.

tomber [tɔ̃be]. I. *v.i.* (*the aux. is usu.* être) 1. to fall, fall down, tumble down, drop down; (*of aircraft*) to crash; **on l'enterra à la place où il était tombé,** they buried him where he fell; **le plafond est tombé,** the ceiling has come down; **tout tombe en pièces,** everything is falling to pieces; **la maison tombe de vieillesse,** the house is falling to pieces with old age; **tout tombe en poussière,** everything is crumbling to dust; **la neige tombe,** snow is falling; **la pluie a tombé, est tombée, à torrents,** rain fell in torrents; *impers.* **il tombe de la pluie, de la grêle,** it is raining, hailing; **il a tombé de l'eau,** it has been raining; **j'ai vu t. la foudre,** I saw the lightning strike; **le sort tomba sur lui,** the lot fell on him; **t. à bas de l'échelle,** to fall off the ladder, to the foot of the ladder; **t. de cheval,** to fall off a horse; to take a fall, a toss; to come a cropper; **t. la tête la première,** to fall headlong, head first, head foremost; **t. sur ses pieds,** to fall on one's feet; **t. aux pieds de qn,** to fling oneself at s.o.'s feet; to prostrate oneself before s.o.; *F:* **t. dans les pommes,** to pass out, to faint; **t. de fatigue, de sommeil,** to be ready to drop (with fatigue, with sleep); **faire t. qn, qch.,** (i) to knock over, push over, s.o., sth.; (ii) to bring about the fall of (the government, etc.); (iii) *Rel:* to lead s.o. into sin, lead s.o. astray; **faire t. qch. de la main de qn,** to knock sth. out of s.o.'s hand; **faire t. la tête de qn,** (i) to bring s.o. to the scaffold; (ii) to behead s.o.; **laisser t. qch.,** (i) to drop sth.; (ii) to allow sth. to fall; *Nau:* **laisser t. l'ancre,** to drop anchor; **laisser t. un droit,** to allow a right to lapse; *F:* **laisser t. qn,** (i) to drop s.o.; (ii) to let s.o. down; **se laisser t. dans un fauteuil,** to drop, sink, *F:* flop, into an armchair; *F:* (*of pers.*) **t. comme une masse,** to fall all of a heap; to collapse; to fall flop; **laisser t. ce qui n'est pas essentiel,** to discard the unessential; **mes cheveux commencent à t.,** my hair is beginning to come out; **t. à l'eau,** to fall in; *Cards:* **espérant faire t. le roi,** in the hope of dropping the king; *Journ:* **le journal est tombé,** the paper has gone to bed; *F:* **les bras m'en tombent,** I'm dumbfounded; **fruits qui tombent des branches,** fruit that drops off the branches; **fruits tombés,** windfalls; **les feuilles tombent,** the leaves are falling, dropping off. 2. (*of wind, anger, fever, etc.*) to drop, abate, subside, die down; (*of conversation*) to flag; *Cu:* to sink; **l'art de la biographie est tombé bien bas,** the art of biography has sunk low; **laisser t. sa voix,** to drop one's voice; **la nuit, le jour, tombe,** night is falling, closing in; **une fois la nuit tombée,** after dark; **le feu tombe,** the fire is dying down; *Nau: etc:* **laisser t. les feux,** to let the fires die out; **le vent, la conversation, tomba,** there was a lull in the wind, in the conversation; **le vent tomba,** the wind died away; **mode qui tombe,** fashion that is going out. 3. **t. entre les mains, aux mains, sous la main, sous la patte, sous la coupe, de qn,** to fall into s.o.'s hands, s.o.'s clutches; **t. dans un piège,** to fall into a trap; **t. dans l'erreur, t. en faute,** to fall into error; **t. dans la misère,** to fall into poverty; **t. en disgrâce,** to fall into disgrace; **t. dans le trivial,** to lapse into vulgarity; **rivière qui tombe dans un lac,** river that flows, runs, into a lake; *Nau:* **t. sous le vent,** to fall off; to fall to leeward; **t. sur un autre navire,** to drive on to another ship; to foul another ship; *Med:* (*of cold*) **t. sur la poitrine,** to go to the chest; *Ven:* **t. en défaut,** to be at fault; (*of hound*) **t. en arrêt,** to be at a standstill (before the quarry). 4. **t. sur l'ennemi,** to attack, fall on, the enemy; *F:* **t. sur qn,** to pitch into s.o. 5. **t. sur qn, sur qch.,** to come across, upon, s.o., sth.; to fall in with s.o.; **je suis tombé par hasard dans leur société,** I was thrown by accident into their company; **ce livre m'est tombé sous la main,** I came across this book; **un rayon de soleil tomba dessus,** a sunbeam lighted on it; **t. sur qn à l'improviste,** to drop in on s.o. unexpectedly; **il va nous t. sur le dos d'un moment à l'autre,** he'll be bursting in on us any moment; *abs.* **Noël tombe un jeudi cette année,** Christmas falls, is, on a Thursday this year; **vous tombez bien,** (i) you've come at the right moment, in the nick of time; (ii) you've guessed right; **vous êtes mal tombé,** you've come at the wrong time, just when you shouldn't; *F:* you've come to the wrong shop; **comme ça tombe!** what a coincidence! **t. juste,** (i) (*of thg*) to happen at the right time, just when you want it; (ii) (*of pers.*) to come at the right moment; (iii) *Ar:* to come out exactly; **cet argent lui tombe du ciel,** this money is a godsend to him; **t. sous le sens,** to be clear, obvious. 6. to fail; *Th:* **la pièce est tombée (à plat),** the play flopped, was a failure; **t. dans le troisième, le trente-sixième, dessous,** (i) to fail (in a part); (ii) (*of play*) to be a total flop. 7. (*of hair, drapery, etc.*) to fall, hang down; **ses cheveux lui tombent dans le dos,** her hair hangs down her back; **jupe qui tombe bien,** skirt that hangs, sits, well; **vêtement qui tombe jusqu'au genou,** garment that comes down to the knee. 8. **t. amoureux de qn,** to fall in love with s.o.; **t. malade,** to fall ill; **t. mort,** to fall dead. 9. *v.tr.* (*a*) *Wr:* **t. un adversaire,** to throw, give a fall to, an opponent; *P:* **t. une femme,** to get a woman; *Th:* **t. une pièce,** to bring about the failure of a play; (i) to hoot a play off the stage; (ii) to slash a play; (*b*) *Metalw:* to flange; **t. un collet (sur une tôle),** to turn up a flange (on a sheet); **t. le bord d'une tôle,** to turn down the edge of a sheet; **tôle à bord tombé,** flanged plate; (*c*) *F:* **t. la veste,** to take off one's jacket.

II. **tomber,** *s.m.* 1. **au t. du jour,** at nightfall. 2. *Wr:* fall.

tombereau, -eaux [tɔ̃bro], *s.m.* 1. (*a*) tip-cart; **t. à ordures,** dustcart; dung cart; **un t. de fumier,** a cartload of manure; **porter du charbon dans un t.,** to cart coal; **emporter, enlever, qch. dans un t.,** to cart sth. away; (*b*) *A:* tumbril. 2. *Rail:* (*a*) open truck; (*b*) truckload.

tomberelle [tɔ̃brɛl], *s.f.* partridge net.

tombeur [tɔ̃bœ:r], *s.m.* 1. *Const:* housebreaker. 2. (professional) wrestler. 3. *A:* tumbler, acrobat. 4. *F:* **t. (de femmes),** lady-killer; **t. de bourgeois,** opponent of the bourgeoisie.

tombisseur [tɔ̃bisœ:r], *s.m. Ven:* second hawk (flown at a heron).

tombola [tɔ̃bɔla], *s.f.* tombola, charity lottery, raffle; **tirer une t.,** to draw a lottery.

tombolo [tɔ̃bɔlo], *s.m. Geog:* tombolo.

Tombouctou [tɔ̃buktu], *Pr.n.m. Geog:* Timbuctoo, Timbuktu.

tome[1] [to:m, tɔm], *s.m.* (heavy) volume; tome; **ouvrage en plusieurs tomes,** work in several volumes; *Nau:* **t. des signaux,** signal book.

tome[2], [tɔm], *s.f.* cheese (made in Savoie and Dauphiné).

tomenteux, -euse [tɔmɑ̃tø, -ø:z], *a. Biol: Bot:* tomentose, tomentous, downy (leaf, body).

tomer [tɔme], *v.tr. Typ:* to divide into volumes; **t. les feuilles,** to mark the pages with a volume number.

tomette, tommette [tɔmɛt], *s.f.* (*in S. of Fr.*) floor tile.

tomme [tɔm], *s.f.* cheese (made in Savoie and Dauphiné).

tomogramme [tɔmɔgram], *s.m. Med:* tomogram.

tomographie [tɔmɔgrafi], *s.f. Med:* 1. tomography. 2. tomogram.

tom-pouce [tɔmpus], *s.m.* 1. (*a*) Tom Thumb, dwarf; midget; (*b*) *F:* insignificant person. 2. stumpy umbrella, Tom-Thumb umbrella; *pl. tom-pouces.*

ton[1], **ta, tes** [tɔ̃, ta, te, tɛ], *poss.a.* (**ton** *is used instead of* **ta** *before fem. words beginning with a vowel or* h *"mute"; for the use of* **ton** *as opp. to* **votre,** *cf.* TU). 1. your; **t. ami, t. amie,** your friend; **un de tes amis,** a friend of yours; **ta propre fille,** your own daughter; **c'est t. affaire à toi,** that's your business; **tes père et mère,** your father and mother. 2. (*in Biblical style; in addressing the Deity; in dialect and literature*) thy; **que ta volonté soit faite,** Thy will be done; **tes père et mère honoreras,** honour thy father and thy mother.

ton[2], *s.m.* 1. (*a*) tone, intonation; **parler d'un t. doux, sur un t. amical,** to speak gently, in a gentle tone, in a friendly tone; **hausser le t.,** to raise (the tone of) one's voice; **forcer le t.,** to speak more loudly and more urgently; **entre deux tons,** in undertones, in an undertone; **parler d'un t. dur,** to speak in a hard tone, harshly; **les**

employés prennent le t. du chef, the employees take their tone from the boss; **ce n'est pas ce qu'il dit mais le t. dont il le dit,** it isn't what he says, but the way he says it; **changer de t.,** to change one's tone; *F:* **vous changerez bientôt de t.!** you'll soon change your tune! **faire baisser le t. à qn,** to take s.o. down a peg (or two); **écrire sur un t. de plaisanterie,** to write in a humorous tone, style; **vous le prenez sur un t.!** you *are* uppish about it! **elle le prend sur ce t.?** is that how she speaks to you? (*b*) tone, manners, breeding; **le bon t.,** good form; **c'est de mauvais t.,** it is bad form, bad manners, vulgar; **gens du bon t.,** well-bred people; **son costume n'est pas tout à fait dans le t.,** his (or her) dress is not quite the thing; (*c*) *Mus:* tone (of instrument); **t. bouché,** stopped tone (on horn). **2.** *Mus:* (*a*) **(hauteur du) t.,** pitch; **donner le t.,** (i) to give (an orchestra) the tuning A; (ii) *F:* to set, lead, the fashion; **sortir du t.,** to be out of tune; **se mettre dans le t.,** to tune up; (*b*) key; **le t. d'ut,** the key of C; **t. relatif mineur,** relative minor key; **t. d'église,** church mode; *F:* **chanter sur un autre t.,** to change one's tune; **parler d'un t. bas,** to speak in a low key; (*of voice*) **monter de t.,** to rise in pitch; (*c*) **tons et demi-tons,** tones and semi-tones; **t. entier,** whole tone; (*d*) **t. de rechange,** crook (of horn, trumpet). **3.** *Ling:* pitch, accent. **4.** *Art: Phot:* tone, tint, colour; **tons chauds,** warm tints; **tapis assorti de ton avec les rideaux, tapis dans le ton des rideaux,** carpet toning with the curtains; **peindre ton sur ton,** to paint tint upon tint; **peinture, voiture, deux tons,** two-tone paint, car; **procurable dans n'importe quel t.,** obtainable in any shade. **5.** *Med: A:* tone; **médicament qui donne du t.,** medicine that tones you up, that tunes you up; tonic; **l'air de la mer vous donne du t.,** the sea air braces you up. **6.** *Ven:* **t. de chasse,** hunting call (to hounds).

ton³, *s.m. Nau:* masthead.

tonal, -als [tɔnal], *a. Mus:* tonal.

tonalement [tɔnalmɑ̃], *adv. Mus:* tonally.

tonalité [tɔnalite], *s.f. Art: Phot: Mus:* tonality; **paysage d'une t. claire,** landscape in a light key; *Tp:* **t. (continue),** dialling tone; **t. d'appel,** ringing tone.

tonaphasie [tɔnafasi], *s.f. Med:* sensory aphasia.

tonca [tɔ̃ka], *s.m.* = TONKA.

tondage [tɔ̃da:ʒ], *s.m.* (*a*) *Tex:* shearing, cropping (of cloth); (*b*) *O:* clipping (of dogs, horses).

tondaille [tɔ̃dɑ:j], *s.f. Dial: or A:* **1.** sheep-shearing time. **2.** the sheep-shearing festivities.

tondaison [tɔ̃dɛzɔ̃], *s.f. A:* = TONTE.

tondant [tɔ̃dɑ̃], *a. Med:* **teigne tondante,** ringworm.

tondeur, -euse [tɔ̃dœ:r, -ø:z]. **1.** *s.* shearer (of cloth, sheep); cropper (of cloth); clipper (of horses, dogs, hedge). **2.** *s.f.* **tondeuse,** (*a*) *Husb: Tex:* shearing machine; shears (for cloth, sheep); clippers (for human hair, for animal's coat); (*b*) **tondeuse (à gazon),** lawn mower; **tondeuse (à gazon) automobile, à moteur,** motor mower.

tondin [tɔ̃dɛ̃], *s.m.* **1.** *Arch:* torus (at foot of column). **2.** *Const:* (plumber's) mandrel.

tondre¹ [tɔ̃:dr̥], *v.tr.* **1.** to shear (cloth, sheep); to crop (cloth); to clip (hair, horse, hedge); **t. le gazon,** to mow the lawn; *Const:* **t. une pierre,** to shave the facing of a stone; **t. qn,** (i) to clip, crop, s.o.'s hair; (ii) *F:* to fleece s.o.; **t. le contribuable,** to skin the taxpayers; *F:* **il tondrait, trouverait à t. sur, un œuf,** he would skin a flint, he's a real moneygrubber; *F:* **avoir d'autres chiens à t.,** to have other fish to fry; *s.a.* LAINE. **2. les brebis tondaient l'herbe,** the sheep were cropping the grass.

tondre², *s.f.* touchwood; *Nau: A:* tinder box.

tondu [tɔ̃dy]. **1.** *a.* mown (grass); clipped (hedge); shorn (sheep); *F:* (*of pers.*) shorn. **2.** *s.m. Ecc:* monk; *Hist: F:* **le petit t.,** Napoleon (Bonaparte); *s.a.* PELÉ¹.

tondure [tɔ̃dy:r], *s.f. Tex:* (*a*) shearing, clipping (of cloth, etc.); (*b*) flock; clippings.

tonétique [tɔnetik], *a. Ling:* pertaining to stress; *s.f.* **la t. anglaise,** the laws of stress in English.

Tonga [tɔ̃ga]. **1.** *Pr.n.m. Geog:* **l'archipel de T.,** the Tonga Islands, the Friendly Islands. **2.** *s.m.* (*a*) *Ling:* **le t.,** Tongan; (*b*) *Med: Dial:* (*esp. in New Caledonia*) framboesia, yaws.

tongan, -ane [tɔ̃gɑ̃, -an], *a. & s. Geog:* Tongan.

Tongouses [tɔ̃gu:z], *s.m.pl. Ethn:* Tunguses.

tongrien, -ienne [tɔ̃grijɛ̃, -jɛn], *a. & s.m. Geol:* Tongrian.

tonicardiaque [tɔnikardjak], *a. & s.m.* cardiotonic; heart stimulant.

tonicité [tɔnisite], *s.f. Med:* tonicity, elasticity (of the muscles, etc.); tonus.

tonifiant [tɔnifjɑ̃], *a.* bracing, tonic.

tonification [tɔnifikasjɔ̃], *s.f.* toning up.

tonifier [tɔnifje], *v.tr.* (*p.d. & pr.sub.* **n. tonifiions, v. tonifiiez**) to brace, to tone up (the nervous system, a patient, etc.); to give tone to (the skin, etc.); to invigorate.

tonilière [tɔniljɛ:r], *s.f.* shrimp net.

tonique [tɔnik], *a.* **1.** *Med:* (*a*) **convulsion t.,** tonic spasm, tonus; (*b*) **médicament t.,** *s.m.* **tonique,** tonic (medicine); (*c*) *s.m. F:* tonic water; (*d*) stimulating, revivifying. **2.** *Ling:* tonic (accent); accented, stressed (syllable); **l'accent t. tombe sur . . .,** the stress falls on . . .. **3.** *Mus:* **note t.,** *s.f.* **tonique,** tonic, keynote; do (of movable-do system).

tonisme [tɔnism], *s.m. Med:* tonic spasm, convulsion.

tonitruant [tɔnitryɑ̃], *a.* like thunder, thundering, resounding (voice); *A:* violent, blustering (wind).

tonitruer [tɔnitrye], *v.i.* to thunder, resound.

tonka [tɔ̃ka], *s.m. Bot:* tonka bean (plant); dipteryx odorata; **fève t.,** *s.f.* tonka, tonka bean.

Tonkin (le) [lətɔ̃kɛ̃], *Pr.n.m. Geog:* Tonkin.

tonkinois, -oise [tɔ̃kinwa, -wa:z], *a. & s. Geog:* Tonkinese.

tonlieu [tɔ̃ljø], *s.m. A.Jur:* tax levied on fair-grounds, stallholders; *Hist:* tax on goods transported by land or water.

tonnage [tɔna:ʒ], *s.m. Nau:* **1.** tonnage, burthen (of ship); *N.Arch:* displacement (of warship); **t. brut,** gross tonnage; **t. net,** register tonnage; **t. réel,** deadweight tonnage. **2.** tonnage (of a port); **t. actif, en service,** active tonnage; **t. désarmé,** idle shipping. **3. (droit de) t.,** (duty based on) tonnage.

tonnant [tɔnɑ̃], *a.* thundering; **d'une voix tonnante,** with a voice of, like, thunder; **donner un ordre d'une voix tonnante,** to thunder out an order; **Jupiter t.,** Jupiter Tonans, Thundering Jove.

tonne [tɔn], *s.f.* **1.** (*a*) tun; (large) cask; **une t. de vin,** a tun of wine; (*b*) *Arm:* **armure à t.,** tonlet suit. **2.** (*a*) *Meas:* (metric) ton (= 1000 kilogrammes); **t. courte,** short ton (= 907.185 kg); **t. forte,** long ton, gross ton (= 1016.06 kg); *U.S:* **t. de réfrigération,** ton of refrigeration; **t. kilométrique,** ton kilometre; *F:* **des tonnes de,** tons of; (*b*) *Nau:* **t. d'arrimage, d'encombrement,** measurement ton; **t. de déplacement,** ton of displacement; **t. de jauge,** gross ton, register ton; **t. de pontée,** ton burden. **3.** *Nau:* nun-buoy. **4.** *Min:* kibble, skip.

tonneau, -eaux [tɔno], *s.m.* **1.** (*a*) cask, tun, barrel; **un t. de vin,** a barrel of wine, a cask of wine; **bière au t.,** beer from the wood; draught beer; *F:* **être d'un bon t.,** to be of first-rate quality; **du même t.,** of the same kind; alike; **t. pour l'eau de pluie,** rainwater butt; **petit t.,** keg; (*b*) **t. à mortier,** mortar mixer; **t. mélangeur à béton,** concrete-mixing drum; *Dy:* **t. de vaporisage,** steaming drum; *Metall:* **t. à dessabler,** tumbling drum; rumbling mill; rumble; **polissage au t.,** (abrasive) tumbling; *Hist:* **le t. de Diogène,** Diogenes' tub; *F:* **rouler son t.,** to make a show of activity (like Diogenes rolling his tub); (*c*) **t. d'arrosage,** water(ing) cart; (*d*) **(jeu de) t.,** (game of) toad in the hole; (*e*) *P:* drunkard; (*f*) *Tan:* tub-wheel. **2.** *Nau:* **t. de jauge,** gross ton, register ton; **t. d'affrètement, t. de mer,** freight ton; **navire de 500 tonneaux,** 500-tonner, ship of 500 tons burden. **3.** *Veh: A:* (*a*) governess-cart; (*b*) tonneau (of motor car). **4.** (*a*) *Av:* horizontal spin; roll; **t. déclenché,** flick roll; **t. lent,** aileron roll; **t. en descendant,** aileron turn; **demi-t.,** half-roll manœuvre; (*b*) **faire un t.** to flip, roll, over; **la voiture a fait trois tonneaux,** the car turned over three times. **5.** *Moll:* tun shell.

tonneau-brouette [tɔnobruɛt], *s.m.* water barrow; *pl. tonneaux-brouettes.*

tonneinquais, -aise [tɔnɛ̃kɛ, -ɛ:z], *a. & s. Geog:* (native, inhabitant) of Tonneins.

tonnelage [tɔnla:ʒ], *s.m.* cooperage; **marchandises de t.,** goods in barrels.

tonneler [tɔnle], *v.tr.* **(je tonnelle, n. tonnelons; je tonnellerai)** *Ven: A:* to tunnel (partridges).

tonnelet [tɔnlɛ], *s.m.* **1.** small cask; keg (of brandy, etc.); drum (of oil, etc.); *Nau:* keg (for drinking water). **2.** *Ent:* pupa. **3.** *A.Cost:* short, full, trunk hose.

tonnelier [tɔnəlje], *s.m.* wet cooper.

tonnelle [tɔnɛl], *s.f.* **1.** (*a*) arbour; bower; *Lit:* **déjeuner sous la t.,** to lunch al fresco; (*b*) *Arch:* semicircular arch, perfect arch. **2.** *Ven: A:* tunnel-net (for catching partridges). **3.** *A:* crupper armour (of horse).

tonnellerie [tɔnɛlri], *s.f.* **1.** cooperage; coopery; **bois de t.,** cooper's wood. **2.** cooper's shop.

tonner [tɔne], *v.i.* **1.** to thunder; *impers.* **il tonne,** it is thundering; *F:* **on n'entendrait pas Dieu t.,** the noise is deafening; *F:* **t. sur les choux,** to break a butterfly on the wheel. **2.** (*of cannon, etc.*) to sound like thunder; to thunder, to boom; *F:* **t. contre qn, contre qch.,** to thunder, thunder out, against s.o., sth.

tonnerre [tɔnɛ:r], *s.m.* **1.** (*a*) thunder; **coup de t.,** (i) clap, peal, of thunder; thunder clap; (ii) bombshell; **cet événement fut un coup de t.,** this event came like a bombshell; *F:* **être fait comme un coup de t.,** to be badly made; **roulement de t.,** roll of thunder; **t. d'applaudissements,** thunderous applause, thunder of applause; **(voix de) t.,** voice of, like, thunder; **le bruit de t. de la mer,** the booming, thundering, of the sea; *Bot: F:* **herbe du t.,** houseleek; (*b*) thunderbolt; lightning; **le t. est tombé sur une maison,** a house was struck by lightning; *Prov:* **toutes les fois qu'il tonne le t. ne tombe pas,** not all threats are carried out; (*c*) *int.* **t. (de Dieu, de Brest)!** I'm damned! heavens above! *Nau:* shiver my timbers! *attrib. F:* **du t.,** wonderful, terrific; **il fera un marin du t. (de Dieu),** he'll make a thundering good, a hell of a good, sailor; **un dîner du t. de Dieu,** a stupendous dinner. **2.** *A:* breech (of firearm); cartridge chamber. **3.** *Ich:* thunder fish (of the Nile).

tonnerrois, -oise [tɔnɛrwa, -wa:z], *a. & s.* (native, inhabitant) of Tonnerre.

tonofibrille [tɔnɔfibri:j], *s.f. Anat:* tonofibril(la).

tonomètre [tɔnɔmɛtr̥], *s.m.* tonometer.

tonométrie [tɔnɔmetri], *s.f.* tonometry.

tonométrique [tɔnɔmetrik], *a.* tonometric.

tonsillaire [tɔ̃sil(l)ɛ:r], *a. Anat:* tonsillar; **angine t.,** tonsillitis.

tonsille [tɔ̃si:j], *s.f.* (= AMYGDALE) tonsil.

tonsillectomie [tɔ̃sil(l)ɛktɔmi], *s.f. Surg:* tonsillectomy.

tonsillite [tɔ̃sil(l)it], *s.f.* (= AMYGDALITE) tonsillitis.

tonsillitome [tɔ̃sil(l)itɔm], *s.m.*, **tonsillotome** [tɔ̃sil(l)ɔtɔm], *s.m. Surg:* tonsillotome.

tonsurant [tɔ̃syrɑ̃], *a. Med:* **herpès t.,** ringworm.

tonsure [tɔ̃sy:r], *s.f.* tonsure; **recevoir, prendre, la t.,** to submit to the tonsure (as a first step towards taking holy orders); to enter the priesthood; *F: A:* **avocat, médecin, à simple t.,** mere tyro in his profession.

tonsurer [tɔ̃syre], *v.tr.* to tonsure (a cleric); **tête tonsurée,** shaven head; *s.m.* **un tonsuré,** a cleric; a priest; *A:* a shaveling.

tontaine [tɔ̃tɛn], *int.* (*refrain used in old songs*) = tra-la-la!

tonte [tɔ̃:t], *s.f.* **1.** *Husb:* (*a*) sheep shearing; clipping; (*b*) clip; (*c*) shearing time. **2.** *Tex:* shearing, cropping (of cloth). **3.** *Hort:* (*a*) mowing (of lawn); (*b*) clipping (of trees, hedge, etc.).

tontine¹ [tɔ̃tin], *s.f. Ins:* tontine.

tontine², *s.f.* protective sacking (round roots of trees to be transplanted).

tontiner [tɔ̃tine], *v.tr. Hort:* to ball and burlap.

tontinier, -ière [tɔ̃tinje, -jɛ:r], *a.* **pacte t.,** tontine agreement, arrangement (among joint owners).

tontisse [tɔ̃tis], *a. & s.f. Tex:* **(bourre) t.,** cropping flock; *Paperm:* **papier t.,** flock paper (for papering walls).

tonton¹ [tɔ̃tɔ̃], *s.m. F: A:* teetotum.

tonton², *s.m. F:* Uncle, Nunky.

tonture¹ [tɔ̃ty:r], *s.f.* **1.** (*a*) *Tex:* shearing, cropping (of cloth); (*b*) mowing (of lawn); clipping (of hedge). **2.** (*a*) *Tex:* shearings, croppings, flock; (*b*) cut grass, hay; clippings (from lawn, hedge).

tonture², *s.f. N.Arch:* sheer, camber.

tonturer [tɔ̃tyre], *v.tr. N.Arch:* to build (ship) with a sheer.

tonus [tɔnys], *s.m.* (*a*) *Med:* tonicity (of muscle), tonus, tone; (*b*) (*of pers.*) energy, dynamism; **manquer de t.,** to lack dynamism; (*c*) *F:* gay party (of medical students).

top [tɔp], *s.m. W.Tel: T.V:* time signal; **les tops,** the pips; *Elcs:* **t. d'écho,** blip, *U.S:* pip; **t. de synchronisation,** synchronizing signal; *int.* **un, deux, trois, t.!** one, two, three, now!

toparchie [tɔparʃi], *s.f. Ant:* toparchy.

toparchique [tɔparʃik], *a.* toparchical.

toparque [tɔpark], *s.m. Ant:* toparch.

topaze [tɔpa:z], *s.f.* topaz; **t. orientale,** oriental topaz, Indian topaz; **t. enfumée,** smoky topaz; **t. brûlée,** pink topaz; **t. occidentale,** false topaz.

topazolit(h)e [tɔpazɔlit], *s.f. Miner:* topazolite.

topectomie [tɔpɛktɔmi], *s.f. Surg:* topectomy.

toper [tɔpe], *v.i.* (*a*) *Gaming: A:* to cover the adversary's stake, to accept the challenge; (*b*) *F:* to agree, consent; to shake hands on it; **tope! tope là!** done! agreed! shake! **il dit tope à tout,** he accepts everything without a murmur.

topette [tɔpɛt], *s.f.* (*a*) phial, sample bottle; small flask (of wine, etc.); (*b*) **boire une t.,** to have a drink.

tophacé [tɔfase], *a. Med:* tophaceous, tophous (concretion).

topholipome [tɔfɔlipoːm], *s.m. Med:* topholipoma.

tophus [tɔfys], *s.m. Med:* toph, tophus, chalkstone.

topi [tɔpi], *s.m.inv. Z:* topi.

topiaire [tɔpjɛːr], *a.* topiary (art, garden).

topinambour [tɔpinɑ̃buːr], *s.m. Bot: Cu:* Jerusalem artichoke.

topique [tɔpik], *a.* **1.** (*a*) *A:* local; *Myth:* **divinité t.,** local divinity; (*b*) *Med:* topical, local (complaint, etc.); **remède t.,** *s.m.* **topique,** local remedy; topical remedy; *A:* topic. **2.** *Phil:* (*a*) **lieu t.,** *s.m.* **topique,** topic, commonplace; (*b*) **argument t.,** argument to the point; **exemple t.,** case in point; (*c*) *s.f.* (science of) topics.

topo [tɔpo], *s.m. F:* **1.** (*a*) *Journ:* popular article; (*b*) *Sch:* lecture, demonstration (by master or pupil); **faire un t. sur . . .,** to hold forth on . . .; (*c*) plan; sketch. **2.** *Mil:* staff officer, *F:* brass hat.

topochimique [tɔpɔʃimik], *a.* topochemical.

topographe [tɔpɔgraf], *s.m. & f.* topographer.

topographie [tɔpɔgrafi], *s.f.* **1.** topography. **2.** topographical map, plan (of district, etc.).

topographique [tɔpɔgrafik], *a.* topographic(al); **le service t.** = the Ordnance Survey; **carte t.,** topographical map; **instruments topographiques,** surveying instruments.

topographiquement [tɔpɔgrafikmɑ̃], *adv.* topographically.

topologie [tɔpɔlɔʒi], *s.f.* topology.

topologique [tɔpɔlɔʒik], *a.* topologic(al).

topométrie [tɔpɔmetri], *s.f.* topometry; plotting of points.

toponomastique [tɔpɔnɔmastik], *s.f. A:* = TOPONYMIE.

toponyme [tɔpɔnim], *s.m.* toponym, place name.

toponymie [tɔpɔnimi], *s.f.* toponymy; toponymics.

toponymique [tɔpɔnimik], *a.* toponymic.

toponymiste [tɔpɔnimist], *s.m. & f.* toponymist.

topophobie [tɔpɔfɔbi], *s.f. Med:* topophobia.

toquade [tɔkad], *s.f. F:* (passing) craze, fancy, infatuation; **avoir une t. pour qn,** to be infatuated with s.o.

toquante [tɔkɑ̃ːt], *s.f. F:* watch.

toquard [tɔkaːr]. **1.** *a. F:* ridiculous; ugly. **2.** *s.m.* (*a*) *Rac: F:* (rank) outsider; (*b*) *P:* (*pers.*) hopeless case, dead loss.

toque [tɔk], *s.f. Cost:* (*a*) cap (of a chef, of French magistrate); (*b*) jockey's cap; (*c*) (woman's) toque; (*d*) *A:* **la t. de Gessler,** Gessler's hat.

toqué [tɔke], *a. F:* **1.** crazy, cracked, round the bend; **il est un peu t.,** he's a bit off his head, a bit cracked. **2. être t. de qn,** to be infatuated, madly in love, with s.o.; **il est t. de la télé,** he has got the telly on the brain.

toquer [tɔke], *v.tr.* **1.** *Dial: & F:* to knock, rap (at door, etc.); to knock, touch (s.o.); *O:* **qui toque l'un toque l'autre,** if you offend one of them you offend the other. **2.** *F:* to send (s.o.) off his head, round the bend.

se toquer (de qn), *F:* to become infatuated (with s.o.), to lose one's head (over s.o.).

toquet [tɔkɛ], *s.m. A:* (*a*) (child's) brimless cap; (*b*) mob-cap, dust-cap.

toraille [tɔrɑːj], *s.m.* natural coral.

torbanite [tɔrbanit], *s.f. Miner:* torbanite.

torbernite [tɔrbɛrnit], *s.f. Miner:* torbernite, chalcotite.

torche [tɔrʃ], *s.f.* **1.** (*a*) torch; **t. électrique,** electric torch; *N.Am:* flashlight; **t. de discorde,** torch of discord; firebrand; (*of parachute*) **se mettre en t.,** to snake; (*b*) *Petroleum Min:* flare (bleeder), torch; **gaz de t.,** flare gas. **2.** (*a*) straw mat; straw band; twist of straw; (*b*) **t. d'osier,** rope border (of basket); (*c*) pad on (head, to carry loads) **3.** (painter's) rag (for cleaning brushes).

torché [tɔrʃe], *a. F:* (*a*) **bien t.,** well done, (pretty) good; **mal t.,** botched, scamped; **ça c'est un morceau t.,** that's a pretty good bit of work; (*b*) (*of pers.*) **bien, mal, t.,** well-dressed, badly dressed.

torche-cul [tɔrʃky], *s.m.inv. P:* (*not used in polite conversation*) (*a*) loo paper, bumf; (*b*) trashy book, article (fit only for use as loo paper).

torchée [tɔrʃe], *s.f. P:* good thrashing, good hiding.

torche-nez [tɔrʃne], *s.m.inv.* = TORD-NEZ.

torchepin [tɔrʃpɛ̃], *s.m. Bot:* mugho pine.

torche-pinceau [tɔrʃpɛ̃so], *s.m.* (painter's) rag (for cleaning brushes and palette); *pl. torche-pinceaux*).

torche-pot [tɔrʃpo], *s.m. Orn: F:* nuthatch; *pl. torche-pots.*

torcher[1] [tɔrʃe], *v.tr.* **1.** *F:* to wipe (sth.) clean (with rag, etc.); **t. le plat,** to lick the platter clean; **se t.,** (i) to dry oneself, (ii) *P:* to fight, to have a scrap; *P:* (*not used in polite conversation*) **se t. (le derrière, le cul),** to wipe oneself, one's backside; *P:* **je m'en torche,** I don't care a damn; *P:* **tu peux te t.!** you've had it! **2.** *F:* to knock off (sth.); to do (sth.) in a hurry; **elle a bientôt torché sa lessive,** she soon got through, polished off, her washing; *P:* **ce bouquin est drôlement bien torché,** this book's damn well written. **3.** *Const:* (*a*) to build, cover, (wall or floor) with cob mortar; (*b*) to daub (a wall). **4.** (*a*) *Basket-making:* to twist a rope border on (basket); (*b*) *Tex:* to bundle (yarn) into hanks.

torcher[2], *s.m. Const:* worker in cob.

torchère [tɔrʃɛːr], *s.f.* (*a*) *A:* cresset; (*b*) floor lamp, standard lamp; (*c*) candelabrum, candelabra, torchère; (*d*) *Petroleum Ind:* (*surplus gas*) flare.

torchette [tɔrʃɛt], *s.f.* **1.** (*a*) wisp of straw (for cleaning); (*b*) *Tex:* hank (of yarn). **2.** *A:* clout, house flannel. **3.** *F:* **papier t.,** toilet paper.

torche-tubes [tɔrʃtyb], *s.m.inv.* (*a*) tube brush; (*b*) flue brush.

torcheuse [tɔrʃøːz], *s.f. Tex:* (*pers.*) hank knotter.

torchis [tɔrʃi], *s.m. Const:* cob, daub; **mur de, en, t.,** cob wall, mud wall; **mur enduit de t.,** wall daubed with clay.

torchon [tɔrʃɔ̃]. **1.** *s.m.* (*a*) twist, plait, mat of straw (to protect cut stone during transport, etc.); (*b*) (kitchen) cloth; floorcloth; dishcloth; duster; *F:* **le t. brûle chez eux,** there are squalls in the home; they lead a cat and dog life; *P:* **se flanquer un coup de t.,** to fight, to have a scrap; *F:* **être fait comme un t.,** to be dressed in a slatternly way; to wear dirty clothes; **il ne faut pas mélanger les torchons et les serviettes,** we mustn't get our values mixed; (*c*) *A:* **t. végétal,** loofah; vegetable sponge; (*d*) *P: O:* (*woman*) slattern, slut; (*e*) *F:* badly-written article; badly presented text; (*newspaper*) rag. **2.** *a.inv.* (*a*) **dentelle t.,** torchon lace; (*b*) **édition t.,** cheap edition (of book); (*c*) *Art:* **papier t.,** torchon paper.

torchonner [tɔrʃɔne], *v.tr.* **1.** to wipe, rub clean (plates, pots and pans, etc.). **2.** *F:* to scamp, botch (piece of work).

torcol [tɔrkɔl], *s.m.,* **torcou** [tɔrku], *s.m. Orn:* **t. (fourmilier),** wryneck.

tordage [tɔrdaːʒ], *s.m.* **1.** twisting. **2.** twist (of hemp, silk).

tordant [tɔrdɑ̃], *a. F:* screamingly funny, side-splitting, killing (story, joke).

tord-boyau(x) [tɔrbwajo], *s.m. P:* **1.** (*poor quality brandy*) rotgut. **2.** *A:* rat poison.

tordeur, -euse [tɔrdœːr, -øːz]. **1.** *s. Tex:* twister (of hemp, wool); throwster (of silk). **2.** *s.f.* **tordeuse:** (*a*) cable-twisting machine; (*b*) *Ent:* tortrix; leaf-roller; **tordeuse des chênes,** oak moth.

tord-nez [tɔrne], *s.m.inv. Vet:* twitch (for keeping horse under control during operation).

tordoir [tɔrdwaːr], *s.m.* **1.** rope twister, rope tightener, rack stick. **2.** cable-twisting machine. **3.** *Laund: O:* mangle, wringer. **4.** oil press, oil mill.

tordre [tɔrdr̥], *v.tr.* to twist (hemp, wool, wire, etc.); to wring (clothes, etc.); **t. de la soie,** to throw silk; **t. ses cheveux en chignon,** to twist one's hair into a knot; **t. le cou à un poulet,** to wring a chicken's neck (to kill it); *F:* **t. le cou à qn,** to wring s.o.'s neck; to kill s.o.; **t. la bouche,** to pull a wry face; *F:* **t. les boyaux (à qn),** to give (s.o.) stomach ache; *F:* **bâiller à se t. la bouche,** to yawn one's head off; **t. le bras à qn,** to twist s.o.'s arm; **se t. le pied,** to twist one's ankle; **se t. les mains, les bras,** to wring one's hands; *A:* **t. le cœur à qn,** to wring s.o.'s heart; **t. une plaque de métal,** to buckle a metal plate; *F: A:* **ne faire que t. et avaler,** to eat ravenously; to bolt, gulp, one's food; **cheval qui tord les autres concurrents,** horse that beats the others hollow.

se tordre, to writhe, twist; **se t. de douleur,** to writhe with pain; *F:* **se t. (de rire), se t. comme une baleine, rire à se t.,** to be convulsed with laughter, to split one's sides laughing; **il y a de quoi se t.,** it's enough to make a cat laugh.

tordu, -ue [tɔrdy], *a.* **1.** twisted, wrung; (*of metal plate, etc.*) buckled; **châssis t.,** bent chassis; **nerfs tordus,** nerves on edge; **cheval tordu,** dead-beat horse; **traits tordus,** distorted features; *P:* **avoir la gueule tordue,** to be as ugly as sin; **des tordus sans intérêt,** a bunch of dreary frights, of ridiculous dowdies. **2.** (*a*) **esprit t.,** warped mind; (*b*) *F:* **être (complètement) t.,** to be mad, cracked, round the bend; *s.* **c'est un t., une tordue,** he's, she's, (quite) mad; **les tordus,** the lunatic fringe.

tore [tɔːr], *s.m. Arch: Bot:* torus; *Geom:* tore, torus, (anchor-)ring, annulus; *Elcs:* **t. (magnétique),** (magnetic) core (of computer); **t. de commutation,** switch core; **t. enroulé,** tape (-wound) core; **t. de ferrite,** ferrite core, ferrite bead; **t. à plusieurs trous,** multiple-aperture core.

toréador [tɔreadɔːr], *s.m.* toreador, bullfighter.

toréer [tɔree], *v.i.* to fight (in the bullring).

toreutique [tɔrøtik], *s.f.* toreutics.

torgn(i)ole [tɔrɲɔl], *s.f. P:* blow, cuff, slap (on head or face).

torgn(i)oler [tɔrɲɔle], *v.tr. P:* to slap (s.o.) in the face; to hit (s.o.) on the head; to give (s.o.) a clout over the head.

toril [tɔril], *s.m.* bull pen.

torique [tɔrik], *a. Mth: etc:* toric; annular; *Opt:* **verre t.,** toric lens; **aimant t.,** annular magnet; *Mch: I.C.E:* **joint t.,** O ring.

tormentille [tɔrmɑ̃tiːj], *s.f. Bot:* tormentil, shepherd's knot.

tormineux, -euse [tɔrminø, -øːz], *a. Med:* torminous, torminal.

tornade [tɔrnad], *s.f.* tornado; **déchaîner une t. (d'injures, etc.),** to let loose a hurricane (of abuse, etc.); **entrer comme une t.,** to come in like a whirlwind.

toroïdal, -aux [tɔrɔidal, -o], *a.* toroidal.

toron[1] [tɔrɔ̃], *s.m.* **1.** strand (of rope); **à trois torons,** three-stranded; **t. à fils métalliques,** wire strand. **2.** wisp (of straw).

toron[2], *s.m. Arch:* lower torus.

toronnage [tɔrɔnaːʒ], *s.m.* cord threading, fore-turn, lay.

toronner [tɔrɔne], *v.tr.* to strand (rope).

toronneuse [tɔrɔnøːz], *s.f. Ropem:* stranding machine.

torpédinidés [tɔrpedinide], *s.m.pl. Ich:* Torpedinidae.

torpédo [tɔrpedo], *s.f. Aut: A:* **1.** torpedo (body). **2.** open touring-car, open tourer.

torpeur [tɔrpœːr], *s.f.* torpor; **sortir de sa t.,** to arouse oneself from one's torpor; **je voulus le faire sortir de sa t.,** I tried to rouse him.

torpide [tɔrpid], *a.* torpid.

torpillage [tɔrpijaːʒ], *s.m. Navy: Petroleum Min:* torpedoing; **t. d'un projet,** torpedoing, shooting down, destroying, a plan.

torpille [tɔrpiːj], *s.f.* **1.** *Ich:* torpedo (ray), electric ray, cramp fish, numb fish. **2.** *Navy: etc:* (*a*) torpedo; **t. d'avion,** aerial torpedo; **attaquer à la t.,** to carry out a torpedo attack; **incidence d'entrée d'une t.,** angle of entry of a torpedo; **équipement de commande et de contrôle de déviation de t.,** torpedo order and deflection control; **manœuvre d'auto-protection contre les torpilles,** torpedo evasion; **vedette lance-torpilles,** torpedo craft, motor torpedo boat; (*b*) *A:* **t. portée,** spar torpedo; (*c*) *occ.* mine; **t. dormante, de fond,** ground mine; **t. vigilante,** contact mine; **t. sèche,** landmine; (*d*) **sac t.,** barrel-shaped handbag.

torpiller [tɔrpije], *v.tr.* **1.** to torpedo (ship, oil well, *F:* project). **2.** to mine (harbour); **zone torpillée,** mined area.

torpillerie [tɔrpijri], *s.f.* torpedo store, torpedo racks; torpedo gear.

torpilleur [tɔrpijœːr], *s.m. Navy:* **1.** torpedo man; **officier t.,** torpedo officer; **quartier-maître t.,** torpedo petty officer. **2. (bateau) t.,** (small) destroyer, *A:* torpedo-boat.

torque [tɔrk]. **1.** *s.m.* (*a*) *A.Cost:* torque(s), torc (of ancient Gauls); (*b*) *Dial:* ring-shaped loaf. **2.** *s.f.* coil ((i) of wire, (ii) of chewing tobacco). **3.** *s.f. Her:* crest wreath; torse, torce (of helmet).

torquer [tɔrke], *v.tr.* to twist (tobacco).

torquet [tɔrkɛ], *s.m. A:* snare, trap; **donner le, un, t. à qn,** to cheat, gull, s.o.; **donner dans le t.,** to fall into the trap.

torquette [tɔrkɛt], *s.f.* **1.** fish basket, hamper; game hamper. **2.** twist, roll (of tobacco). **3.** *Cu:* ring-shaped cake.

torréfacteur [tɔr(r)efaktœːr], *s.m.* roaster (for coffee, etc.); coffee burner.

torréfaction [tɔr(r)efaksjɔ̃], *s.f.* torrefaction.

torréfiant [tɔr(r)efjɑ̃], *a.* torrefying; roasting; *F:* scorching (heat, sun).

torréfier [tɔr(r)efje], *v.tr.* (*p.d. & pr.sub.* **n. torréfiions, v. torréfiiez**) to torrefy; to roast (coffee, maize, etc.); (*of sun, etc.*) to scorch.

torréfieur [tɔr(r)efjœːr], *s.m.* (*pers.*) (coffee, etc.) roaster.

torrent [tɔr(r)ɑ̃], *s.m.* torrent, mountain stream; **il pleut à torrents,** it's raining in torrents, in sheets; **t. de larmes,** flood, flow, of tears; **t. de lumière,** flood of light; **t. d'injures,** stream, torrent, of abuse; **le t. des affaires,** the rush of business; **laisser passer le t.,** to wait until the storm has blown over.

torrenticole [tɔr(r)ɑ̃tikɔl], *a. Nat.Hist:* living in torrents, mountain streams.

torrentiel, -ielle [tɔr(r)ɑ̃sjɛl], *a.* torrential; **nous avons eu une pluie torrentielle,** we have had torrential rain.

torrentiellement [tɔr(r)ɑ̃sjɛlmɑ̃], *adv.* torrentially, like a torrent.

torrentueux, -euse [tɔr(r)ɑ̃tɥø, -øːz], *a.* (*a*) torrent-like (river, etc.); (*b*) **existence torrentueuse,** tempestuous, stormy, life.

Torricelli [tɔr(r)isɛlli, -iʃɛlli], *Pr.n.m. Ph:* **(expérience, tube) de T.,** Torricellian (experiment, tube).

torride [tɔr(r)id], *a.* torrid (zone, etc.); scorching (heat, etc.); **nous avons eu une chaleur t.,** we have had scorchingly hot weather.

tors, torse[1], **torte** [tɔːr, tɔrs, tɔrt]. **1.** *a.* (*a*) twisted (thread, etc.); thrown (silk); **bois à fibres torses,** cross-grained, spiral-grained, wood; *Arch:* **colonne torse,** wreathed column; (*b*) (*f. occ.* **torte**), twisted, crooked, contorted; **jambes torses,** crooked, bandy, legs; **cou t.,** (i) *O:* wry neck; (ii) *F: A:* hypocrite. **2.** *s.m.* (*a*) twist, lay (of rope, etc.); (*b*) *Furn:* twisted cord. **3.** *s.f. Tls:* **torse,** twist bit; screw auger.

torsade [tɔrsad], *s.f.* **1.** (*a*) twisted fringe, twisted cord, torsade; **t. de cheveux,** twist, coil, of hair; **cheveux en t.,** twisted hair; coiled hair; *Knitting:* **(point) t.,** cable stitch; (*b*) *Mil: Navy:* thick bullion (of epaulet); **les torsades,** the bullion fringe. **2.** twist joint (of wires). **3.** *Arch:* rope moulding, cable moulding.

torsadé [tɔrsade], *a. El: Tp:* **paire torsadée,** twisted pair; **raccord t.,** twist joint.

torsader [tɔrsade], *v.tr.* **1.** to twist (rope, wire, withes, etc.); **cheveux torsadés,** coiled hair, coils of hair. **2.** to twist (wires, etc.) together.

torse[2] [tɔrs], *s.m.* torso, trunk (of statue, of person); **nous travaillions le t. nu,** we worked stripped to our waists; *F:* **bomber le t.,** to stick out one's chest.

torseur [tɔrsœːr], *s.m. Mec:* torque.

torsiomètre [tɔrsjɔmɛtr], *s.m. Mec.E:* torsion meter, torquemeter.

torsion [tɔrsjɔ̃], *s.f.* torsion; twisting (of rope, wire, etc.); *Ph:* **balance de t.,** torsion balance; *Mec:* **effort de t.,** torsional stress, strain; twist; torque reaction; **moment de t.,** torque; **essai de t.,** torsion, twist, test; **rigidité, raideur, à la t.,** torsional stiffness; *Aut:* **barre de t.,** torsion bar (spring).

torsk [tɔrsk], *s.m. Ich:* torsk, cusk, tusk.

tort [tɔːr], *s.m.* wrong. **1.** error, fault; **avouer ses torts,** to confess one's faults; **avoir t., être dans son t.,** to be wrong, in the wrong; **lequel des deux a t.?** which of them is wrong? **vous avez t. de vous moquer de lui,** you shouldn't laugh at him; **il a eu le t. de ne pas demander de reçu,** he made the mistake of not asking for a receipt; **les absents ont toujours t.,** the absent are always in the wrong; **se mettre dans son t.,** to put oneself in the wrong; **avouer être dans son t.,** to acknowledge one's mistake, to eat humble pie; **donner t. à qn,** to decide against s.o.; to lay the blame on s.o.; **avoir des torts envers qn,** to have behaved badly to(wards) s.o.; **il a tous les torts,** he is entirely to blame; *adv.phr.* **à t.,** wrongly; **à t. ou à raison,** rightly or wrongly; **à t. et à travers,** at random, without rhyme or reason. **2.** injury, harm, detriment, hurt; (*a*) **la grêle a fait beaucoup de t. dans cette région,** the hail has done a great deal of damage, has made havoc, in this district; **faire (du) t. à qn,** (i) to wrong s.o.; to do s.o. an injustice; (ii) to damage s.o.'s cause, business, reputation; **quel t. cela peut-il vous faire?** what harm can it do you? **cette campagne de presse a fait un t. irréparable à notre cause,** this press campaign has done our cause irreparable harm; **faire t. à la réputation de qn,** to injure s.o.'s reputation; **vous vous faites du t. par votre manque de . . .,** you are doing yourself harm by your lack of . . .; *F:* **ça lui fait t.,** it spoils her, him; **il ne fait de t. qu'à lui-même,** he is nobody's enemy but his own; (*b*) **faire t. à qn de qch.,** to defraud s.o. of sth.; **je ne vous ai jamais fait t. d'un sou,** I've never cheated you of a penny.

torte [tɔrt]. *See* TORS 1.

tortelle [tɔrtɛl], *s.f. Bot:* treacle mustard.

torticolis [tɔrtikɔli], *s.m. Med:* crick, (w)rick, in the neck; stiff neck; wryneck; torticollis.

tortil [tɔrtil], *s.m. Her:* baron's coronet.

tortillage [tɔrtijaːʒ], *s.m. F: A:* **1.** (*a*) involved phraseology; (*b*) quibbling, wriggling, squirming. **2.** underhand intrigue, trickery.

tortillard, tortillart [tɔrtijaːr]. **1.** *a.* (*a*) cross-grained (wood); (*b*) *Bot:* **orme t.,** dwarf elm. **2.** *s.m.* (*a*) *P:* deformed cripple; (*b*) (i) *A:* twisting, meandering, railway; small local railway; (ii) local train (on a narrow-gauge line).

tortille [tɔrtiːj], *s.f.* winding path (in wood, garden, etc.).

tortillé [tɔrtije], *a. Her:* tortilly.

tortillement [tɔrtijmɑ̃], *s.m.* **1.** twisting, twist, kink (of rope, etc.); wriggling (of worm). **2.** *F: A:* subterfuge, shuffling, quibbling, wriggling; squirming.

tortiller [tɔrtije]. **1.** *v.tr.* (*a*) to twist (up) (paper, ribbon, hair, etc.); to twirl, twiddle (one's moustache); (*b*) to kink (rope); (*c*) *P:* to wolf down, devour, make short work of (food); (*d*) *Carp:* to start (mortise) with an auger. **2.** *v.i.* (*a*) **t. des hanches,** to swing the hips (in walking); (*b*) *F:* to shuffle, prevaricate, quibble, wriggle; to use subterfuges; **il n'y a pas à t.,** it's no use shilly-shallying; there's no getting out of it; **je le lui ai dit sans t.,** I told him straight (out).

se tortiller, (*a*) (*of snake*) to wriggle, twist; (*b*) (*of pers.*) to writhe, squirm, wriggle; **se t. comme une anguille,** to wriggle like an eel; **il se tortillait à chercher du nouveau,** he was going out of his way, straining himself, to try to find sth. new.

tortillon [tɔrtijɔ̃], *s.m.* **1.** twist (of paper, hair, etc.); wisp (of straw); *Art:* tortillon; **l'enfant a défait le t. qui enveloppait le bonbon,** the child took the sweet out of its wrapper. **2.** pad (on head, for carrying loads). **3.** *Moll:* mantle (of gastropod).

tortillonner [tɔrtijɔne], *v.i. & tr.* (*a*) to twist and turn; (*b*) to quibble; to hedge; *F:* **répondez donc au lieu de chercher de t.,** for goodness' sake give a straight answer instead of trying to hedge.

tortionnaire [tɔrsjɔnɛːr]. **1.** *a.* (*a*) relating to torture; **appareil t.,** instrument of torture; (*b*) *Jur:* cruelly excessive; iniquitous (law, etc.); **rançon t.,** extortionate ransom. **2.** *s.m.* torturer.

tortis [tɔrti], *s.m.* (*a*) torsel, twisted threads; twisted chain; (*b*) *A:* wreath; (*c*) string of pearls (of baron's coronet).

tortoir [tɔrtwaːr], *s.m.* rack stick.

tortore [tɔrtɔːr], *s.f. P:* food, grub, nosh.

tortorer [tɔrtɔre], *v.tr. P:* to eat, to nosh.

tortricides [tɔrtrisid], **tortricidés** [tɔrtriside], *s.m.pl. Ent:* Tortricidae, the tortricid moths, the codling moths.

tortu [tɔrty], *Lit:* **1.** *a.* crooked (tree, body, nose, path, etc.); **avoir l'esprit t.,** to have a crooked, tortuous, mind; *Prov:* **le bois t. fait le feu droit,** the end justifies the means. **2.** *adv.* in a crooked manner.

tortue [tɔrty], *s.f.* **1.** tortoise; **t. de mer,** turtle; **t. éléphantine,** elephant tortoise; **t. grecque,** Greek tortoise; **t. des marais,** European pond tortoise; **t. léopard,** (African) leopard tortoise; **t. à carapace molle,** soft-shell turtle; **t. marine,** green turtle; **t. alligator,** snapping turtle; **t. des fissures,** crevice tortoise; **t. d'eau saumâtre,** diamondback terrapin; **t. à écailles,** hawksbill turtle; **t. à gueule,** matamata (turtle); **t. luth, t. à cuir,** leathery turtle; **t. verte,** green turtle; **aller à pas de t.,** to go at a snail's pace; *Cu:* **soupe à la t.,** turtle soup; **tête de veau en t.,** mock turtle; **soupe à la fausse t.,** mock turtle soup; *N.Arch:* **pont en carapace de t.,** turtle(-back) deck; *F:* **c'est une vraie t.,** he's a real slowcoach. **2.** *Rom.Ant:* testudo, tortoise. **3.** *Ent:* tortoiseshell (butterfly); **grande, petite, t.,** large, small, tortoiseshell. **4.** *Mil: P: A:* hand grenade.

tortuer [tɔrtɥe], *v.tr. A:* to make crooked; to bend (needle, etc.).

se tortuer, *A:* to become crooked; to twist; to warp.

tortueusement [tɔrtɥøzmɑ̃], *adv.* crookedly, tortuously.

tortueux, -euse [tɔrtɥø, -øːz], *a.* tortuous, winding, meandering (river, street); twisted (tree); tortuous, crooked, underhand, devious (conduct); wily, scheming, crooked (person).

tortuosité [tɔrtɥozite], *s.f.* **1.** tortuosity; crookedness (of character, intrigue). **2.** *usu. pl.* windings (of maze, etc.); **la t. d'un cours d'eau,** the winding, meandering, course of a stream.

torturant [tɔrtyrɑ̃], *a.* torturing, tormenting (thoughts, etc.).

torture [tɔrtyːr], *s.f.* torture; **mettre qn à la t.,** to put s.o. to torture, to torture s.o.; **être à la t.,** to be on the rack, on thorns; **esprit à la t.,** tortured mind; **mettre son esprit à la t.,** to rack, cudgel, one's brains; **instruments de t.,** instruments of torture.

torturer [tɔrtyre], *v.tr.* **1.** (*a*) to torture (prisoner, etc.); (*b*) to torture; to cause (s.o.) intense suffering; **la jalousie le torturait,** he was tortured by jealousy; **se t. l'esprit, la cervelle,** *F:* **les méninges,** to rack one's brains. **2.** to strain, twist, pervert (meaning of words, etc.); **t. un texte,** to torture a text; **t. son style,** to strain one's style.

tortureur, -euse [tɔrtyrœːr, -øːz]. **1.** *a.* torturing, tormenting. **2.** *s.* torturer.

torula [tɔryla], *s.f. Biol:* torula.

torule [tɔryl], *s.m.* (*a*) *Ent:* torulus (of antenna); (*b*) *Fung:* torula.

toruleux, -euse [tɔrylø, -øːz], *a. Nat.Hist:* torulose, torulous.

torulose [tɔryloːz], *s.f. Med: Vet:* torulosis.

torve [tɔrv], *a.* **regard t.,** grim look; menacing look; **yeux torves,** glowering, scowling, eyes.

torysme [tɔrism], *s.m. Pol:* toryism.

toscan, -ane[1] [tɔskɑ̃, -an], *a. & s. Geog: Arch:* Tuscan.

Toscane[2], *Pr.n.f. Geog:* Tuscany.

toss [tɔs], *s.m. Fb: etc:* toss; **gagner, perdre, le toss,** to win, lose, the toss.

toste [tɔst], *s.f. Nau:* rower's seat, thwart.

tôt [to], *adv.* (*a*) soon; *A:* **faites t.,** do it soon, quickly; **le plus t. possible,** as soon as possible; **ce sera la semaine prochaine au plus t.,** it will be next week at the earliest; **le plus t. sera le mieux,** the sooner the better; **t. après,** soon after; **t. ou tard,** sooner or later; sometime or other; **plus t. que tard,** sooner rather than later; **ce sera t. fait,** it won't take long; **pas de si t.,** not as soon as (all) that; **nous n'étions pas plus t. rentrés que . . .,** we had no sooner returned than . . .; **revenez au plus t.,** come back as soon as possible; (*b*) early; **se lever t.,** to get up early; **très t. dans l'après-midi,** very early in the afternoon; **venez t.,** come early; **vous auriez dû me le dire plus t.,** you should have told me so before; *a.* **il est trop t. pour manger,** it's too early to have a meal; *P:* **c'est pas trop t.!** and about time too!

total, -aux [tɔtal, -o]. **1.** *a.* total, complete, entire, whole; **éclipse totale,** total eclipse; **ruine totale,** utter ruin; **somme totale,** sum total. **2.** *s.m.* whole, total; **t. global,** sum total, grand total; **faire le t. des sommes,** to add up, calculate the total of, the amounts; **ces armées s'élevaient à un t. de trois cent mille hommes,** these armies aggregated, totalled, three hundred thousand men; **au t.,** on the whole, all things considered; *F:* **ils se sont chamaillés et, t., les voilà brouillés,** they've had a quarrel and, to cut a long story short, they're no longer on speaking terms.

totalement [tɔtalmɑ̃], *adv.* totally, entirely; utterly, completely (ruined).

totalisateur, -trice [tɔtalizatœːr, -tris]. **1.** *a.* adding (machine, etc.). **2.** *s.m.* adding machine; *Turf:* totalizer, totalizator, *F:* tote; *Av:* **t. de débit,** integrating flowmeter.

totalisation [tɔtalizasjɔ̃], *s.f.* totalizing, totalization; adding up, summing up (of amounts).

totaliser [tɔtalize], *v.tr.* **1.** to totalize, total up, add up; **l'actif se totalise par deux millions,** the assets add up to two millions. **2.** to total, add up to; **la population totalise à peu près dix mille personnes,** the total population is about ten thousand; **il totalise 4.255 heures de vol,** he has done 4,255 hours flying, he has totted up 4,255 hours flying time.

totaliseur [tɔtalizœːr], *s.m.* = TOTALISATEUR 2.

totalitaire [tɔtalitɛːr], *a.* totalitarian.

totalitarisme [tɔtalitarism], *s.m.* totalitarianism.

totalité [tɔtalite], *s.f.* totality, whole; **la presque t. de . . .,** almost all . . .; **en t.,** wholly, as a whole; **pris dans sa t.,** taken as a whole; in the aggregate.

totane [tɔtan], *s.m. Orn:* sandpiper.

tôte [toːt], *s.f. Nau:* rower's seat, thwart.

totem [tɔtɛm], *s.m.* totem.

totémique [tɔtemik], *a.* totemic.

totémisme [tɔtemism], *s.m.* totemism.

totémiste [tɔtemist], *s.m. & f.* totemist.

totémistique [tɔtemistik], *a.* totemistic.

tôt-fait [tofɛ], *s.m. Cu:* = hasty pudding; *pl.* *tôt-faits.*

totipalme [tɔtipalm], *Orn:* **1.** *a.* totipalmate. **2.** *s.m.pl.* **totipalmes,** Totipalmatae, Pelecaniformes.

toto [toto], *s.m. P:* louse, cootie.

toton [tɔtɔ̃], *s.m.* teetotum; *O:* **elle le fait tourner comme un t.**, (i) she keeps him on the go; (ii) she can twist him round her little finger.

touage [twaːʒ], *s.m. Nau:* **1.** (*a*) warping; (*b*) kedging; (*c*) chain towing, towage (on rivers and canals). **2.** chain-towage dues. **3.** *Fr.C: Adm: Aut:* **zone de t.**, towing zone.

Touareg [twarɛg]. **1.** *s.m.* (*pl.*) *Ethn:* T(o)uareg; **les T.,** (*incorrectly*) **les Touaregs,** the T(o)uareg; NOTE: *the more correct sing. is* **Targui,** *f.* **Targuia. 2.** *s.m. Ling:* **le t.,** T(o)uareg.

toubib [tubib], *s.m. F:* doctor, quack, medico; *Mil:* M.O.

toubibaille [tubibɑːj], *s.f. F:* doctors, the medical fraternity.

toucan [tukɑ̃], *s.m. Orn:* toucan; **t. à bec vert,** green-billed toucan.

toucanet [tukanɛ], *s.m. Orn:* toucanet; **t. à bec tacheté,** spot-billed toucanet.

touchable [tuʃabl̩], *a.* (*a*) touchable; (*b*) (cheque) that can be cashed; collectable (bill).

touchant [tuʃɑ̃]. **1.** *a.* (*a*) touching, moving, affecting (sight, speech); *s.m.* **le t. de l'histoire,** the pathetic part of the story; (*b*) **faire feu à bout t.,** to fire point-blank. **2.** *prep.* touching, concerning, about, with regard to; **il m'a entretenu t. votre avenir,** he had a talk with me about your future.

touchatouisme [tuʃatuism], *s.m. F:* meddlesomeness, poking one's nose into things, nosiness.

touchau(d) [tuʃo], *s.m.* touch needle, test needle (for testing precious metals).

touche [tuʃ], *s.f.* **1.** (*a*) touch, touching; **pierre de t.,** touchstone; (*b*) *Art:* stroke (of the brush); **le peintre voit son tableau avant d'avoir posé une seule t. de couleur,** the painter can visualize his picture before he has painted a single stroke; **mettre la dernière t. à qch.,** to add the finishing touches to sth.; **comme t. finale,** as a finishing touch; (*c*) touch, manner (of painter); style (of writer); **avoir une t. légère,** to have a light touch; (*d*) *Bill: Fenc: Lit:* **manque de t.,** miss; (*e*) *Fish:* bite, nibble; *F:* **avoir, faire, une t. avec qn,** to make a hit with s.o. (of the opposite sex); to get off, click, with s.o.; **essayer de faire une t. avec qn,** to make a pass at s.o.; (*f*) *Sp:* (*hockey*) roll-in; *Fb:* throw-in; **ligne de t.,** touch line; **hors des touches,** out of touch; **envoi de t.,** kick into touch; **rester sur la t.,** to be out of the game; *F:* **ce mot est encore sur la t.,** this word is not yet generally accepted; (*g*) *P:* appearance, look(s); **il a une drôle de t.,** he's a queer-looking, peculiar, customer; **quelle (drôle de) t.! il en a une t.!** what a (queer-looking) guy! what a weirdie! (*h*) *P:* shot, jab (of narcotic, etc.). **2.** (*a*) key (of piano, typewriter, computer, etc.); *Typewr:* **t. de manœuvre,** shift key; **t. de blocage,** shift lock; **t. de dégagement de chariot,** carriage release (lever); (*of computer*) **t. d'effacement,** erase key; **t. de fonction,** function key; (*b*) finger board (of violin); *pl.* frets, stops (of mandolin, guitar); (*c*) tab (of alphabetical register); thumb index, thumb register (of dictionary, etc.); (*d*) *Games:* (spillikins) hook; (*e*) (i) stick, goad (for driving cattle); (ii) drove (of cattle). **3.** *El:* (*a*) contact; *Tg:* **t. d'interruption,** break key; (*b*) (commutator) segment.

touche-à-tout [tuʃatu], *F:* **1.** *a.inv.* (*a*) (*pers.*) who can't keep his hands off things; (*b*) meddling, meddlesome; interfering. **2.** *s.m. & f. inv.* (*a*) meddler, busybody; (*b*) Jack-of-all-trades.

toucheau [tuʃo], *s.m.* = TOUCHAU(D).

toucher [tuʃe]. I. *v.* to touch. **1.** *v.tr.* (*a*) **t. qn à l'épaule,** to touch s.o. on the shoulder; **je lui touchai l'épaule,** I tapped him on the shoulder; **t. qch. de la main, des doigts,** to handle, finger, sth.; **faire t. du doigt qch. à qn,** to point sth. out (emphatically) to s.o.; *F:* to rub s.o.'s nose in sth.; **je n'ai pas pu le t.,** I couldn't get hold of him, couldn't lay my hands on him; *F:* **touche du bois!** touch wood; *Fb: etc:* **t. le ballon,** to handle the ball; *Bill:* **t. une bille,** to hit a ball; *Artil: etc:* **t. le but,** to hit the mark; *Fenc:* **t. son adversaire,** to wound, hit, touch, pink, one's opponent; to score a hit; **votre observation l'a touché au vif,** your remark has touched him on the raw, has gone home; **t. les bœufs,** to goad the oxen; **t. un cheval (du fouet),** to whip up, touch up, a horse; *abs. A:* **touchez, cocher!** whip up, driver! *A:* **t. le piano, l'orgue,** *v.ind.tr.* **t. du piano, de l'orgue,** to play the piano, the organ; **il ne faut pas t. cette corde-là,** you must not harp on that string; *F:* (*to child*) **pas touche!** don't touch (it)! *A:* **touchez là!** your hand on it! *F:* put it there! **ils se sont touché dans la main,** they shook hands over the bargain; **t. ses appointements,** *abs.* **toucher,** to draw, receive, one's salary; to be paid; **t. un chèque,** to cash a cheque; **t. une traite,** to collect a bill; *Mil:* **t. des rations,** to draw rations; **on n'a pas encore touché de fusils,** no rifles have been issued yet; *Rugby Fb:* **t. dans les buts,** to touch down; (*b*) (i) to assay, test (precious metal with touchstone); (ii) *Surg:* to cauterize (ulcer); *Engr:* **t. à l'eau forte,** to etch off (blemish, etc.); (*c*) *Typ:* to ink (up) (the formes); **t. des couleurs,** to lay on colours; (*d*) to move, affect (s.o.); **t. le cœur de qn,** to touch s.o.'s heart; **le secret de plaire et de t.,** the secret of pleasing and of touching the emotions; **t. qn jusqu'aux larmes,** to move s.o. to tears; **être touché de, par, la bonté de qn,** to be touched by s.o.'s kindness; **ces démonstrations me touchent très peu,** these demonstrations move me very little; (*e*) to concern, affect; **cela ne me touche ni en bien ni en mal,** that does not affect me one way or the other; **en ce qui vous touche,** as far as you are concerned; **cela nous touche de (plus) près,** this comes (nearer) home to us; (*f*) *Nau:* **t. terre,** to touch land; *abs.* **t. à un port,** (*of ship*) to touch, call, at a port; (*g*) *Min:* **t. l'or, le pétrole, un filon,** to strike gold, oil, a seam; (*h*) *Nau:* **t. (le fond),** (i) to strike the bottom; to touch bottom; to bump; (ii) to be aground; **t. un écueil,** to strike a reef; (*i*) to reach; to get hold of; **ma lettre ne l'aura pas touché,** my letter can't have reached him; **je lui ai donné un coup de téléphone, mais je n'ai pas pu le t.,** I rang him up but I couldn't get hold of him. **2.** (*a*) *v.tr.* to touch on, dwell on, deal with (fact, subject); to touch (lightly) on, allude to (subject); **j'ai déjà touché ces questions,** I have already touched on these questions; **je lui en toucherai un mot, deux mots,** I shall mention it to him; I'll have a word with him about it; I shall drop him a hint (about it); **je ne lui en ai pas touché mot,** I didn't mention it to him; I kept off the subject; (*b*) *v.ind.tr.* to meddle, interfere; to tamper with (sth.); **ne touchez pas à ce qui est bien,** let well alone; **ne touchez pas à mes outils,** don't meddle with my tools; leave my tools alone; **n'y touchez pas!** (keep your) hands off! **on ne touche pas!** hands off! **t. à des sujets délicats,** to tread on delicate ground; **t. au gouvernement établi,** to interfere with established government; **ne pas t. à un plat,** to leave a dish untasted; **il n'avait pas touché à la nourriture,** he had left the food untouched; **sans avoir l'air d'y t.,** in a detached manner; as if quite unconsciously; **avoir l'air de ne pas y t., n'avoir pas l'air d'y t.,** to put on an innocent air; to look as if butter wouldn't melt in one's mouth. **3.** *v.i.* (*a*) **t. à qch.,** to be in touch, in contact, with sth.; to be near, close, to sth.; to border on sth.; **maison qui touche à la mienne,** house adjoining mine; **jardins qui se touchent,** adjoining gardens; **les pays qui touchent à l'Allemagne,** the countries that border on Germany; **économie qui touche à l'avarice,** thrift that borders on avarice, that is akin, next door, to miserliness; **avec Chateaubriand nous touchons à l'époque romantique,** with Chateaubriand we are approaching the Romantic period; **l'année touche à sa fin,** the year is drawing to a close; **t. à la quarantaine,** to be close on forty; **t. au terme de la vie,** to have reached the end of life; **nous touchons au but,** the goal is within our reach; the end is in sight; **les extrêmes se touchent,** extremes meet; (*b*) *A:* **t. de naissance à qn,** to be related to s.o.; **t. de près à qn,** to be nearly related to s.o.; **détail qui touche à l'événement,** detail relevant to the event; **cela touche de très près à mes intérêts,** it closely affects my interests; **en ce qui touche à cette question,** as far as this question is concerned; (*c*) **palmes qui touchent au plafond,** palms that touch, reach, the ceiling; **t. à terre,** to touch the ground; *Lit:* **il ne touche pas à terre,** he is treading on air; he is in the seventh heaven (of delight).

II. **toucher,** *s.m.* touch. **1.** feel; **reconnaître qch. au t.,** to know sth. by the touch, by the feel of it; **t. du cuir, du papier,** feel of leather, of paper; **étoffe rude au t.,** cloth that is rough to the touch; **le mur était chaud au t.,** the wall felt hot; **t. d'un piano,** touch of a piano; *Med:* **t. vaginal,** vaginal touch. **2. le t. délicat d'un pianiste,** a pianist's delicate touch.

touchette [tuʃɛt], *s.f.* fret (of mandolin, guitar).

toucheur, -euse [tuʃœːr, -øːz], *s.* **1.** (*a*) *Fenc:* scorer of a hit; (*b*) (cattle) drover. **2.** *s.m. Typ:* inking roller, inker.

toue [tu], *s.f. Nau:* **1.** (*a*) warping; (*b*) kedging. **2.** (flat-bottomed river) barge.

touée [twe], *s.f. Nau:* **1.** (*a*) warping; **sortir d'un port à la t.,** to warp out of port; (*b*) kedging; **ancre de t.,** kedge. **2.** scope (of cable, of tow line); (riding-)scope (of ship at anchor). **3.** warp, warping rope, cable; **filer une t.,** (i) to pay out a cable, a warp; (ii) *F: A:* to spin a (long, an endless) yarn.

touer [twe], *v.tr. Nau:* **1.** (*a*) to warp; (*b*) to kedge. **2.** to chain-tow. **3.** to tow; to take (ship) in tow; to track (barge).

toueur, -euse [twœːr, -øːz], *Nau:* **1.** *a.* warping; **ancre toueuse,** kedge anchor. **2.** *s.m.* (*a*) warper (*man who warps*); (*b*) tug, towboat (*esp.* on chain).

toufan [tufɑ̃], *s.m.* typhoon (off the Arabian coast).

touffe [tuf], *s.f.* tuft (of hair, grass, etc.); wisp (of hay, straw); clump, cluster (of trees); bunch (of flowers, ribbons, etc.); *Av:* **t. de déperditeur,** static discharge wick.

touffer [tufe]. **1.** *v.tr.* to arrange (trees, plants, etc.) in tufts, in clusters. **2.** *v.i.* to grow in tufts.

touffeur[1] [tufœːr], *s.f. A:* suffocating heat (of a room); *F:* fug; fugginess.

touffeur[2], *s.f.* **1.** bushiness. **2.** *A:* tuft (of hair).

touffu [tufy], *a.* bushy (beard, etc.); thick (wood, eyebrows); close (thicket); tufted, thickly wooded (hillside, etc.); **style t.,** involved style; **ouvrage t.,** work that is full of facts, that is heavy reading; abstruse work.

touggourtin, -ine [tugurtɛ̃, -in], *a. & s. Geog:* (native, inhabitant) of Touggourt [tugurt].

touillage [tujaːʒ], *s.m. F:* mixing (of salad, etc.); stirring (of sauce).

touille [tuːj], *s.f. Ich: F:* mackerel shark.

touiller [tuje], *v.tr. F:* to stir (up); to mix, toss (salad, etc.); to shuffle (cards).

touillon [tujɔ̃], *s.m. Tchn:* whisk.

toujours [tuʒuːr], *adv.* **1.** always; ever; **un ami de t.,** a lifelong friend; **il est t. sorti,** he is always out; **t. riant,** always smiling; **les enfants sont t. les enfants,** boys will be boys; **pour t., à t.,** for ever; *Lit:* **adieu pour t.!** farewell for ever! **2.** still; **il fait t. aussi chaud,** it is as hot as ever; **demeure-t-il t. là?** is he still living there? **il montait t.,** he went up and up; **cherchez t.,** go on looking; **allez t.!** go ahead! go on! **3.** nevertheless, all the same, anyhow, always; but; **je peux t. essayer,** anyhow I can try; I can always, at least, try; **on peut t. essayer,** one, I, we, can but try; **payez t., on verra après,** pay up now, we'll arrange things later; **entrez t.,** come in anyhow; **dites t. ce que vous savez,** anyhow tell us what you know; **toujours est-il que . . .,** the fact remains that. . .; anyhow . . .; **t. est-il que je l'ai vue,** nevertheless, all the same, I saw her; the fact remains that I saw her; **j'aurai t. fait mon devoir,** I did my duty at any rate; **c'est t. ça,** it's better than nothing at any rate; it's always something; **la maison est à vous, il vous reste t. un chez-vous,** the house is yours; at least you still have a home. **4.** *Elcs:* (*computers*) **branchement t.,** unconditional branch, jump, transfer.

touline [tulin], *s.f. Nau:* (*a*) boat rope; (*b*) heaving line.

toulois, -oise [tulwa, -waːz], *a. & s.* (native, inhabitant) of Toul.

toulonnais, -aise [tulɔnɛ, -ɛːz], *a. & s. Geog:* (native, inhabitant) of Toulon.

toulousain, -aine [tuluzɛ̃, -ɛn], *a. & s. Geog:* (native, inhabitant) of Toulouse.

toumané [tumane], *s.m.*, **tumani** [tumani], *s.m. Mil: P: A:* Senegalese sharpshooter.

toundra [tundra], *s.f. Geog:* tundra.

Toungouse, Toungouze [tunguːz]. **1.** *a. & s. Ethn:* Tunguse. **2.** *s.m. Ling:* Tunguse.

toupet [tupɛ], *s.m.* **1.** (*a*) tuft of hair, quiff; (*b*) forelock; *Hairdr:* **(faux) t.,** toupee, toupet; *F: O:* **elles se sont prises au t.,** they grabbed each other by the hair; (*c*) forelock (of horse). **2.** *F:* cheek, impudence, sauce; nerve; **quel t.!** what a cheek, a nerve! **il a eu le t. de . . .,** he had the cheek, the nerve, to . . .; **payer de t.,** to brazen it out.

toupie [tupi], *s.f.* **1.** (*toy*) top; **t. d'Allemagne, t. ronflante,** humming top; **jouer à la t., faire tourner une t.,** to spin a top; **ronfler comme une t.,** to snore like a pig; **tourner comme une t.,** (i) to spin round on one's heels; (ii) to be always changing one's mind. **2.** *Carp: etc:* (*a*) vertical shaper, milled cutter (of moulding machine); (*b*) spindle moulding machine; (*c*) *Furn:* moulded foot (Louis XVI style). **3.** (plumber's) turn pin. **4.** *Ind:* **t. mécanique,** hydro-extractor, centrifugal extractor. **5.** *Fish:* (large) pear-shaped float. **6.** (*a*) *Wr:* head spin; (*b*) *P: A:* head, nut. **7.** *F:* (*a*) *A:* (*of woman*) flighty piece; (*b*) weak-willed person; (*c*) **vieille t.,** old frump; old trout.

toupiller [tupije]. **1.** *v.i. F:* (*a*) to spin round (like a top); to twirl round; (*b*) to buzz round, bustle about (in the house). **2.** *v.tr. Tchn:* to shape (wood).
toupilleur [tupijœ:r], *s.m. Tchn:* (*pers.*) spindle moulder.
toupilleuse [tupijø:z], *s.f.* spindle moulding machine.
toupillon [tupijɔ̃], *s.m.* **1.** small tuft of hair, of feathers; tail tuft (of cow, etc.). **2.** irregular group of branches (on tree). **3.** *Dial:* (*Provence*) earthenware bowl.
touque [tuk], *s.f.* **1.** (small) drum (for carrying liquids). **2.** herring boat.
tour[1] [tu:r], *s.f.* tower. **1.** (*a*) *Arch: Const:* **t. à cheval,** ridge turret; **t. d'angle,** angle tower (of castle); **t. de moulin à vent,** tower of windmill; **t. de guet,** lookout tower; fire tower; **t. d'observation,** watchtower, observation tower; conning tower; *A:* **t. à feu,** lighthouse; **la Tour de Babel,** the Tower of Babel; **la Tour Eiffel,** the Eiffel Tower; *P: A:* **la Tour,** the lock-up (*at the Palais de Justice, in Paris*); (*b*) *Av:* **t. balise,** beacon tower; **t. de contrôle,** control tower; **t. d'instruction de parachutistes,** parachute tower; *Ball:* **t. de remplissage,** umbilical tower (for rocket fuelling); (*c*) *Ind: Ch:* **t. d'absorption,** absorber; **t. de fractionnement,** bubble tower, fractionating tower, fractionator; **t. de rectification,** stripping tower; **t. de réfrigération,** cooling tower; *Min:* **t. de lavage,** *Atom.Ph:* **t. d'épuration,** scrubber; *Petroleum Min:* **t. de sondage, de forage,** derrick; rig; *Ch:* **t. de Gay-Lussac,** Gay-Lussac tower; **t. de Glover,** Glover tower; (*d*) *F:* massively built person. **2.** *Chess:* castle, rook.
tour[2], *s.m.* **1.** (*a*) (turning) lathe; **fait au t.,** (i) machine-turned; (ii) *F:* shapely (leg, etc.); **enlever les inégalités au t.,** to turn off inequalities; **t. alésoir,** boring and turning mill; **t. à pédale,** foot lathe; **t. à archet,** (watchmaker's) turn bench; **t. marchant au moteur,** power lathe; **t. à grande vitesse,** high-speed lathe; **t. à pointes,** centre lathe; **t. revolver,** capstan lathe; **t. à tourelle,** turret lathe; **t. à profiler,** forming lathe; **t. à repousser,** spinning lathe; **t. à plateau horizontal, t. vertical,** vertical turning mill, machine; **t. à tablier,** apron lathe; **t. à décolleter,** slicing lathe; **t. à charioter, t. parallèle,** slide lathe; **t. à double outil,** duplex lathe; **t. en l'air, à plateau,** face lathe; **t. à guillocher,** rose engine; **atelier des tours,** turning shop; (*b*) **t. de potier,** potter's wheel; (*c*) turning box, turning wheel (of convent, etc.); (*d*) *Nau:* log reel. **2.** (*a*) circumference, circuit; **t. (d'une spirale),** whorl; **ville qui a dix kilomètres de t.,** town ten kilometres in circumference; **faire le t. du monde,** (i) to go, sail, fly, round the world; (ii) to go for a voyage round the world; **le t. du monde en 80 jours,** around the world in 80 days; **faire le t. de l'île (à la rame, à la voile, à la nage),** to row, sail, swim, round the island; **faire le t. du parc,** to go, walk, drive, etc., round the park; **on me fit faire le t. du jardin,** they took me round the garden; **faire faire à qn le t. du propriétaire,** to take s.o. round one's estate; **faire le t. d'une question,** to examine the main points of a question; **t. d'horizon politique,** political survey; **faire un t. d'horizon,** to make a general survey of the situation; *Sp:* **t. de piste, de circuit,** lap; **t. d'honneur,** lap of honour; **T. de France** (cycliste), Tour de France (cycle race); **prendre un t. à ses rivaux,** to lap one's opponents; **faire le t. du cadran,** (i) (*of clock hand, etc.*) to move round the dial; (ii) *F:* to sleep the clock round; **faire le grand t.,** to take the longest way round; **collier qui fait deux tours autour du cou,** necklace that goes twice round the neck; **avoir 75 cm. de t. de taille,** to have a waist measurement of 75 cm.; **t. de poitrine,** chest, bust, measurement; **t. de tête,** size in hats, head size; **arbre qui a deux mètres de t.,** tree with a girth of two metres; *Nau:* **prendre, donner, du t.,** to give a headland, etc., a wide berth; **prendre du t. en accostant,** to take a sweep in coming alongside; (*b*) **t. de lit,** bed valence; *Cost:* **t. de cou,** necklet (of fur, etc.); neck ribbon; (*c*) *Nau: etc:* **t. de bitte,** turn round the bitt; **prendre un t.,** to take a turn; **t. dans les chaînes, t. de chaîne,** elbow in the hawse, foul cable; **avoir des tours,** to have a foul hawse; (*d*) **tours et retours d'un chemin,** twists and turns of a road; (*e*) turn (of phrase); shape, contour (of face, etc.); course, direction (of business affair); **l'affaire prend un mauvais t.,** the matter is taking a bad turn; **donner un bon t. à qch.,** (i) to give sth. a favourable turn; (ii) to put sth. in a favourable light; **donner un autre t. à la conversation,** to turn the conversation; to give another turn to the conversation; **t. d'esprit,** turn of mind; (*f*) **t. de reins,** twist, strain, in the back; **se donner un t. de reins,** to strain, crick, (w)rick, one's back; (*g*) outline (of face); **elle avait le t. du visage délicat,** her face was delicately shaped. **3.** (*a*) round, revolution, turn; **t. d'une roue,** turn, revolution, of a wheel; **la machine fait 2000 tours à la minute,** the engine runs at 2000 revolutions a minute; **donner un t. de clef à la porte,** to turn the key in, to lock, the door; **fermer la porte à double t.,** to double-lock the door; **frapper à t. de bras,** to strike with all one's might; *F:* **le sang ne m'a fait qu'un t.,** my heart seemed to stop beating; **son sang n'a fait qu'un t.,** (i) he fired up in a moment; (ii) it gave him a dreadful shock; *Nau:* **faire le t.,** (i) (*of boat*) to capsize; (ii) to swing the ship (for compass adjustment); (*order to engine room*) **un t. en avant!** one turn ahead! one kick ahead! **un t. en arrière!** one kick astern! (*b*) stroll; **faire un t. de jardin, de ville,** to have, take, a turn, a stroll; round the garden, round the town; **(aller) faire un t.,** to go for a stroll, to take a walk; *F:* **faire un petit t.,** to go and see a man about a dog; to go and spend a penny; (*c*) trip, tour; **faire un t. sur le continent,** to go for a tour on the continent; (*d*) row (of crochet, knitting). **4.** (*a*) rotation, turn; **à qui le tour?** whose turn is it? **à votre t. de parler,** now *you* make a speech; **ce fut ensuite au t. de X à mourir,** the next man to die was X; *F:* **quand viendra mon t.,** when my number's up; **t. de service,** spell of duty; *Nau:* **t. de barre, tour à la barre,** trick at the wheel; **chacun à son t.,** each one in his turn; **il est entré tout de suite par t. de faveur,** he was allowed to go in out of his turn, before his turn; he passed before his turn; **t. à t.,** by turns, in turn(s); turn and turn about; **s'emporter et se calmer t. à t.,** to flare up one moment and calm down the next; **à tour de rôle,** in turn, in rotation; *Cr:* **le t. est à Jones,** Jones is in; (*b*) *Cards:* round; *Th: etc:* turn; number; **t. de chant,** vocal number. **5.** trick, feat; **je fis exécuter quelques tours à mes animaux,** I put my animals through some tricks; **faire, jouer, un mauvais t. à qn,** to play s.o. a nasty trick; **il médite quelque mauvais t.,** he is up to some mischief; **le t. est joué,** I've done the trick; the trick has come off; that's that; **un t. de main,** a flick of the wrist; *F:* **il peut faire ça en un t. de main,** he can do it standing on his head; **le t. de main,** the tricks of the trade; **je n'ai pas le t. de main,** I haven't the knack of it; **tours de main d'atelier,** shop practice; **t. d'adresse,** (i) sleight of hand; (ii) acrobatic feat; **t. de force,** feat of strength; **t. de cartes,** card trick; *F:* **avoir plus d'un t. dans son sac,** to have more than one trick up one's sleeve.
touraco [turako], *s.m. Orn:* touraco; *F:* plant cutter, plantain eater.
touraillage [turaja:ʒ], *s.m. Brew:* kilning (of malt).
touraille [tura:j], *s.f. Brew:* malt kiln.
tourailler [turaje], *v.tr. Brew:* to kiln (malt).
touraillon [turajɔ̃], *s.m. Brew:* malt combs, cummings.
tourangeau, -elle, -eaux [turɑ̃ʒo, -ɛl, -o], *a. & s. Geog:* (native, inhabitant) (i) of Tours, (ii) of Touraine.
touranien, -ienne [turanjɛ̃, -jɛn], *a. & s. Ethn:* Turanian.
tourbage [turba:ʒ], *s.m.* peat cutting.
tourbe[1] [turb], *s.f. O:* mob, rabble.
tourbe[2], *s.f.* **1.** peat, turf; **mettre une motte de t. sur le feu,** to put a peat on the fire; *Husb:* **litière de t.,** peat litter. **2.** *Fr.C: Hort:* turf (cut for a lawn).
tourber [turbe]. **1.** *v.i.* to dig, cut, peat. **2.** *v.tr.* **t. un marais,** to cut, take, peat out of a bog.
tourbeux, -euse [turbø, -ø:z], *a.* **1.** peaty, boggy (soil, etc.); **marais t.,** peat moor. **2.** (*of plants*) growing in peat bogs.
tourbier, -ière [turbje, -jɛ:r]. **1.** *a.* peaty (soil). **2.** *s.m.* (*a*) peat worker; (*b*) owner of peat bogs or of a peatery. **3.** *s.f.* **tourbière:** (*a*) peat bog, turf moor; **chêne de tourbière,** bog oak; (*b*) peatery.
tourbillon [turbijɔ̃], *s.m.* **1.** whirlwind; **t. de poussière,** swirl of dust; (*of dust*) **monter en tourbillons,** to swirl up; **t. de neige,** flurry of snow. **2.** (*a*) whirlpool; (*b*) eddy (of water, wind); (*c*) *Ph: etc:* vortex; **t. stationnaire,** stationary vortex; **t. en ligne,** point vortex; **t. libre,** trailing vortex; **t. de surface,** vortex sheet; **t. acoustique,** sound whirl; (*d*) whirl, bustle (of life, business, etc.); vortex, whirl (of pleasures, etc.). **3.** *Astr: Phil:* vortex. **4.** *Pyr:* tourbillion.
tourbillonnaire [turbijɔnɛ:r], *a.* vortical; swirling; **mouvement t.,** vortex, vortical, motion; **nappe t.,** vortex sheet.
tourbillonnant [turbijɔnɑ̃], *a.* whirling (wheels, senses, etc.); **les jupes tourbillonnantes des danseuses,** the swirling skirts of the dancers; *Fb: etc:* **ballon t.,** spinning ball.
tourbillonnement [turbijɔnmɑ̃], *s.m.* whirling; eddying; swirling; **le t. des affaires,** the whirl, bustle, of business.
tourbillonner [turbijɔne], *v.i.* to whirl (round); to eddy, swirl; **s'élever en tourbillonnant,** to swirl up; **ses pensées tourbillonnaient,** his thoughts went whirling round.
tourd [tu:r], *s.m.* **1.** *Orn:* = TOURDELLE. **2.** *Ich:* Mediterranean wrasse.
tourdelle [turdɛl], *s.f. Orn: A:* thrush, *esp.* mistle thrush or fieldfare.
tour-du-cou [turdyku], *s.m.* neckband (of shirt); *pl. tours-du-cou.*
tourelé [turle], *a. Her: etc:* turreted; **couronne tourelée,** mural crown.
tourelle [turɛl], *s.f.* (*a*) *Arch:* turret; **t. en encorbellement,** bartizan, bartisan; **remparts garnis de tourelles,** turreted ramparts; *N.Arch:* **t. de fanaux,** (bow) lighthouse, side-light castle; (*b*) *Fort: Mil: Navy:* (gun) turret; *Fort: etc:* **t. à éclipse,** disappearing turret; **t. mobile, pivotante,** revolving, rotating, turret; **pièce de t.,** turret gun; **vireur de t.,** turret turning gear; **t. de mitrailleuse,** machine-gun turret; **à défilement de t.,** turret down; *Navy:* **navire à tourelles,** turret ship; **t. à ciel ouvert,** open turret; **t. double, triple, quadruple,** double-gun, triple-gun, quadruple-gun, turret; **t. excentrique,** offset turret; **t. de chasse, de retraite,** forward, after, turret; **t. de contrôle, de veille,** conning tower; *Av:* **t. de mitrailleuse,** gun ring, gun turret; **t. de mitrailleuse inférieure,** *F:* dustbin; **t. en dessous,** blister; (*c*) *Opt: Phot:* **t. à objectifs,** lens turret; (*d*) *Mec.E:* capstan (head), turret (head) (of lathe); **t. carrée, hexagonale,** square, hexagonal, turret; **chariot porte-t.,** turret slide; **course de la t.,** turret travel.
tourelleau [turɛlo], *s.m.* cupola (of tank turret).
tourer [ture], *v.tr. Cu:* to fold and roll (pastry).
touret [turɛ], *s.m.* **1.** small wheel (for spinning, for diamond cutting, polishing, etc.); **t. à polir,** polishing lathe. **2.** (*a*) reel (for cables, ropes, fishing lines, etc.); (*b*) drum (of winch); *El:* cable drum. **3.** *Tls:* bow drill. **4.** *Nau:* thole pin.
tourie [turi], *s.f.* carboy.
tourier, -ière [turje, -jɛ:r], *a. & s. Ecc:* (*in convent*) extern; **sœur tourière,** extern sister, out sister.
tourillon [turijɔ̃], *s.m.* **1.** (*a*) pivot, swivel pin (of iron gate, etc.); **t. de pivotement,** pivot pin; (*b*) **t. de chaîne à rouleaux,** link pin of a roller chain; (*c*) (wheel) spindle. **2.** (*a*) journal (of shaft, axle); **t. à cannelures,** collar journal; **t. sphérique,** ball journal; **palier de t.,** journal bearing; (*b*) trunnion (of gun, oscillating cylinder); **tourillons de support,** mounting trunnions; **embase des tourillons,** trunnion shoulder; **logement des tourillons,** trunnion hole.
tourillonner [turijɔne], *v.i. Tchn:* to swivel, to pivot.
tourisme [turism], *s.m.* tourism; touring; tourist trade; **agence, bureau, de t.,** travel agency, tourist agency; **centre, ville, de t.,** tourist centre; **le t. apporte à ce pays des revenus considérables,** the tourist trade is a considerable source of income to this country; **profiter d'un voyage d'affaires pour faire du t.,** to make use of a business trip to do some sightseeing; **voiture, avion, de t.,** private car, plane.
touriste [turist], *s.m. & f.* tourist; (holiday) visitor; *Pej:* tripper; **cette ville reçoit beaucoup de touristes,** this town is visited by large numbers of tourists, has an important tourist trade; *attrib. Nau: Av:* **classe t.,** tourist class.
touristique [turistik], *a.* touristic; **ville t.,** tourist centre; **renseignements touristiques,** tourist information; **guide t.,** tourist guide; **menu t.,** (special) tourist menu; **route t.,** (i) tourist route; (ii) picturesque road.
tourlourou [turluru], *s.m.* **1.** *P: A:* foot-soldier; *esp.* merry and bright "soldier-boy." **2.** *Crust:* land crab.
tourmaline [turmalin], *s.f. Miner:* tourmaline.
tourment [turmɑ̃], *s.m.* (*a*) *A: & Lit:* torture (of prisoner, etc.); (*b*) torture, anguish; **les tourments de la jalousie,** the pangs, torments, of jealousy; **l'incertitude est de tous les tourments la plus difficile à supporter,** the anguish, torture, of uncertainty is the most difficult of all to bear;

éprouver les tourments de la faim, to suffer severe pangs of hunger, to be tormented by hunger; (c) (*of pers.*) cause of great anxiety; **il a été le t. de ma vie,** he has been the bane of my life; he has always been a source of great anxiety to me; *O:* **quel t. que cet enfant-là!** what a plague that child is!

tourmentant [turmɑ̃tɑ̃], *a. Lit:* tormenting (thoughts, etc.).

tourmente [turmɑ̃:t], *s.f.* (a) *Lit:* gale, tempest; **t. de neige,** blizzard; (b) (political, etc.) upheaval; **la t. révolutionnaire,** revolutionary upheaval; **la t. politique,** the turmoil of politics; **une t. politique,** a political storm, upheaval.

tourmenté [turmɑ̃te], *a.* (a) distorted, contorted; **côte tourmentée,** jagged, broken, coastline; **paysage t.,** wild and uneven landscape; tormented landscape; **branches tordues aux formes tourmentées,** branches twisted into distorted shapes; (b) tormented, tortured; **conscience tourmentée,** tortured conscience; **visage t.,** tortured, anguished, face; (c) **mer tourmentée,** turbulent, seething, sea; **vie tourmentée,** tumultuous life; **esprit t.,** agitated, seething, tormented, mind; (d) *Art: Arch: etc:* unnatural, exaggerated; over-elaborate; **statues aux poses tourmentées,** statues with forced, unnatural, attitudes; **maison prétentieuse, aux balcons tourmentés,** a pretentious house, with balconies of over-elaborate design.

tourmenter [turmɑ̃te], *v.tr.* **1.** *A:* to torture (prisoner, etc.). **2.** (a) to torture, harass (s.o.); **ce souvenir le tourmente,** he is tortured by this memory; **quelque chose le tourmente,** something is harassing him, causing him grave anxiety; **l'ambition tourmente l'homme,** man is tormented by ambition; **il est tourmenté par la goutte,** he is racked, tortured, with gout; (b) to harry, pester, plague (s.o.); **ses créanciers le tourmentent,** his creditors are dunning him; **enfant qui tourmente ses parents,** child that plagues, harasses, his parents; (c) to agitate; **vent qui tourmente l'eau,** wind that lashes up the water; **navire tourmenté par la mer,** ship tossed on the waves; (d) *Art: Lit:* to over-elaborate; **t. son style,** to write in an unnatural, over-elaborate, style.

se tourmenter. 1. (a) to be anxious, uneasy; to fret; to be in a constant state of worry; **être porté à se t.,** to be over-anxious, to be given to worrying, to have a worrying disposition; **que c'est bête de vous t. comme ça!** it's stupid of you to worry like that, to be so anxious! **il se tourmentait de mille scrupules,** he was tortured by, a prey to, endless scruples; **ne vous tourmentez pas!** don't worry! (b) *Lit:* to be on tenterhooks. **2.** (*of ship*) to labour. **3.** (*of wood*) to warp.

tourmenteur, -euse [turmɑ̃tœ:r, -ø:z]. **1.** *a.* tormenting. **2.** (a) *s.m. A:* torturer; (b) *s.* tormenter.

tourmenteux, -euse [turmɑ̃tø, -ø:z], *a. Nau:* stormy; storm-swept; gale-ridden.

tourmentin [turmɑ̃tɛ̃], *s.m.* **1.** *Nau:* storm jib. **2.** *Orn:* petrel.

tournage [turna:ʒ], *s.m.* **1.** (a) turning (on the lathe); lathe work; **t. conique,** taper turning; **t. sur bois,** wood turnery; (b) *Cer:* turning; shaping (on the wheel). **2.** *Nau:* belaying; **taquet de t.,** belaying cleat. **3.** *Rail:* turning round (of locomotive) on turntable. **4.** *Cin:* shooting.

tournailler [turnaje], *F:* **1.** *v.i.* (a) to keep wandering round and round; (b) to prowl (about); **t. autour d'une femme,** to dance attendance on, hover around, a woman. **2.** *v.tr.* to twiddle (sth.) round and round; **t. la clef dans la serrure,** to turn the key round in the lock.

tournaisien, -ienne [turnɛzjɛ̃, -jɛn], *a. & s. Geog:* (native, inhabitant) of Tournai.

tournant, -ante [turnɑ̃, -ɑ̃:t]. **1.** *a.* (a) turning; revolving (bookcase, etc.); slewing (crane, etc.); live (axle); **fauteuil t., siège t.,** swivel chair, swivel seat; **pont t.,** swing bridge; *Rail: etc:* **plaque tournante,** turntable; **plateau t.,** turntable (of record player); **mouvement t.,** turning movement; swing round (movement); **grève tournante,** staggered strike; (b) winding (road, etc.); **escalier t.,** spiral staircase; **quartier t.,** bend, angle (in staircase). **2.** *s.m.* (a) turning; bend (in road, river); (street) corner; *Aut:* **t. brusque,** sharp corner; dangerous bend; **voiture qui prend bien les tournants,** car that corners well, that takes the bends well; *F:* **savoir prendre le t.,** to know how to adapt oneself to a situation; *F:* **attendre un concurrent au t.,** to be waiting for (an opportunity to catch) a rival; *F:* **je l'aurai au t.!** I'll get him yet! *F:* **retrouver qn au t.,** to have one's revenge, get one's own back on s.o.; (b) turning point; **les tournants de l'histoire,** the turning points in history; **à un t. de sa carrière,** at a turning point in his career; **au t. du siècle,** at the turn of the century; (c) *A:* expedient; **prendre des tournants pour arriver à son but,** to resort to expedients, devious ways, in order to achieve one's end; (d) turning space (of vehicle); (e) whirlpool, eddy; (f) wheel (of water mill). **3.** *s.f. Pyr:* **tournante,** spinning rocket.

tournas(s)age [turnasa:ʒ], *s.m. Cer:* throwing (of pottery on the wheel).

tournasser [turnase], *v.tr. Cer:* to throw, shape (sth. on the wheel).

tournasseur [turnasœ:r], *s.m. Cer:* thrower.

tournassine [turnasin], *s.f. Cer:* (lump of) clay (prepared for throwing).

tourne [turn], *s.f.* **1.** (a) **la t. du lait,** the turning, going sour, of milk; (b) **la t. du vin,** the souring of wine. **2.** (a) *Bak:* division and shaping (of dough into loaves); (b) division (of clay into portions to place on the wheel); (c) *Journ:* continuation (of article on another page). **3.** *Cards: F:* turned-up card (indicating trumps).

tourné [turne], *a.* **1.** turned (on a lathe); fashioned, shaped, made; **articles tournés,** turnery; **bien t.,** well-made; **une petite brune bien tournée,** an attractive little brunette; a little brunette with a lovely figure; **phrase bien tournée,** neatly turned sentence; **mal t.,** (i) badly made; (ii) ugly; unattractive; **avoir l'esprit mal t.,** (i) to take things the wrong way; (ii) to put an unpleasant interpretation on things. **2.** (a) **esprit t. aux plaisirs,** mind set on pleasure; **avoir les pieds tournés en dedans,** to be pigeon-toed; (b) **église bien tournée,** properly oriented church. **3.** (a) sour (milk, etc.); spoilt, sour, (wine); (b) **avoir la tête tournée,** (i) to have one's head turned (by success, etc.); (ii) to be distracted (by fear, etc.). **4.** *prep.* **t. le coin c'est la deuxième maison,** when you have turned the corner it's the second house.

tourne-à-gauche [turnago:ʃ], *s.m.inv. Tls:* **1.** (a) wrench; **t.-à-g. pour filière,** tap wrench; (b) stock (for dies). **2.** saw set, saw wrench, swage.

tournebouler [turnəbule], *v.tr. F:* to upset (s.o.).

tournebout [turnəbu], *s.m. Mus: A:* krummhorn, cromorne.

tournebride [turnəbrid], *s.m. A:* = roadside inn.

tournebroche [turnəbrɔʃ], *s.m. Cu:* **1.** roasting jack. **2.** *A:* turnspit (dog or boy).

tourne-disque(s) [turnədisk], *s.m. Rec:* record player; *pl. tourne-disques.*

tournedos [turnədo], *s.m. Cu:* tournedos; fillet steak.

tournée [turne], *s.f.* **1.** round, tour (of official); round of visits (of doctor, etc.); circuit (of judge); **la t. du facteur,** the postman's round; **le gardien de nuit faisait sa t.,** the night watchman was going his round, was on his rounds; **t. d'inspection,** tour of inspection; **troupe en t.,** theatrical company on tour; **faire une t. (en province),** to tour (the provinces); **représentant, voyageur, en t.,** representative, traveller, on the road; **notre voyageur est en t.,** our traveller is out; **faire la t. des musées,** to go round, *F:* to do, the picture galleries; **faire une t. en France,** to go on a trip through France; **faire une t. électorale,** to canvass a constituency; **l'inspecteur est en t.,** the inspector is on his round; **t. de golf,** round of golf; *s.a.* VIRÉE 1. **2.** (a) *F:* **payer une t.,** to stand a round (of drinks), to pay for, stand, drinks all round; **commander une t. générale,** to call for glasses all round; **c'est la t. du patron,** it's on the house; **encore deux tournées de rhum,** two more goes of rum; (b) *P:* **flanquer une t. à qn,** to thrash s.o. **3.** (short-handled) pick, mattock. **4.** *Fish:* (a) seine, drawnet (drawn by two fishing boats); (b) enclosure (of oyster bed, etc.).

tourne-feuille(s) [turnəfœ:j], *s.m.* leaf turner (for music); *pl. tourne-feuilles.*

tourne-foin [turnəfwɛ̃], *s.m.inv. Agr:* hay maker, tedder.

tourne-gants [turnəgɑ̃], *s.m.inv.* glove stretcher.

tournelle [turnɛl], *s.f.* (a) small tower; (b) *A:* small castle; *Fr.Hist:* **la T. criminelle, la T. civile,** two Courts in Paris under the Old Régime.

tournemain [turnəmɛ̃], *s.m. used in the phr.* **en un t.,** in an instant, in the twinkling of an eye, in two shakes (of a lamb's tail).

tournement [turnəmɑ̃], *s.m. A: & Dial: used in the phr.* **t. de tête,** vertigo, giddiness.

tourne-oreille [turnɔrɛ:j], *s.m.inv. Agr:* **charrue t.-o.,** plough with a reversible mould board.

tourne-pierre [turnəpjɛ:r], *s.m. Orn:* **t.-p.** (**à collier**), turnstone; *pl. tourne-pierres.*

tourner [turne], *v.* to turn. **1.** *v.tr.* (a) to fashion, shape, turn (sth.) on lathe; *F:* **bien t. une phrase,** to give a neat turn to a phrase, to turn a phrase neatly; *Cer:* **t. un pot,** to throw a pot; (b) to revolve, turn round, rotate (wheel, etc.); **t. la clef dans la serrure,** to turn the key in the lock; *Av:* **t. l'hélice,** to swing the propeller; *F:* **t. qn à son gré,** to twist s.o. round one's little finger; **vous tournez les choses de telle manière qu'il semble que vous avez raison,** you put things in such a way that you seem to be right; **t. qch. autour de qch.,** to wind sth. round sth.; *Nau:* **t. une amarre autour d'une bitte,** to belay, make fast, a hawser to a bitt; **tournez au taquet!** take a turn round the cleat! **t. la tête, les yeux, vers qn,** to turn one's head, one's eyes, towards s.o.; to look in s.o.'s direction; **t. le dos à qn, à qch.,** (i) to turn one's back on s.o., on sth.; to turn away from s.o.; to give s.o. the cold shoulder; to cut s.o.; (ii) to have one's back turned to s.o., to sth.; to face the other way; **t. le dos à ses assaillants,** to turn tail; **t. ses souliers,** to tread, walk, one's shoes over (on one side); **t. les pieds en dedans, en dehors,** to turn in, turn out, one's toes; *s.a.* POUCE 1, TALON 1; **t. bride,** to turn one's horse's head (and gallop away); *Cin:* **t. un film,** (i) to take, shoot, a film; (ii) to direct a film; (iii) to play, star, in a film; **t. une scène, un roman,** to film a scene, a novel; *Cu:* **t. une crème,** to stir a custard; *Rugby Fb:* **t. la mêlée** to wheel the scrum; (c) to change, convert; **t. une phrase en latin,** to translate, turn, a sentence into Latin; **t. tout en bien, en mal,** to put a good, a bad, interpretation on everything; **t. qch. en plaisanterie,** to turn sth. into a joke; to laugh sth. off; **t. qn en ridicule,** to hold s.o. up to ridicule; **t. qch. à son avantage,** to turn sth. to one's own advantage; (d) to turn over (page, etc.); to turn up (card); **t. et retourner qch.,** to turn sth. over and over; **t. une affaire en tous sens,** to turn a matter over and over (in one's mind); (e) **t. un pardessus,** to turn an overcoat; *s.a.* CASAQUE 1; (f) to get round (corner, obstacle, etc.); (i) to outflank; (ii) to circumvent (enemy); to evade, get round, dodge (difficulty); **t. la loi,** to get round the law; **vous trouverez l'épicerie en tournant le coin,** you will find the grocer round the corner; *Nau:* **t. un promontoire,** to weather a headland; (g) *F:* **t. le lait,** to turn the milk sour; **l'ambition lui a tourné la tête,** ambition has turned his head; **il lui a tourné la tête,** she has become infatuated with him; **les honneurs ne lui ont pas tourné la tête,** his success hasn't gone to his head; *s.a.* SANG 1; **cela m'a tourné l'estomac,** it turned my stomach; it made my stomach heave. **2.** *v.i.* (a) to revolve; to go round; (*of machine*) to run; (*of top*) to spin; **t. comme une toupie,** to spin like a top; **la porte tourna sur ses gonds,** the door swung, turned, on its hinges; **la terre tourne autour du soleil,** the earth revolves round the sun; **l'enfant aime à voir t. les roues,** the child likes to see the wheels go round; **engrenages tournant dans un bain d'huile,** gears running in an oil bath; **machine qui tourne à plein,** machine in full action; *Nau:* **faire t. les bossoirs,** to swing the davits; *F: O:* **allons, l'heure tourne!** come on, time is getting on! **t. autour de qn, de qch.,** to move, turn, round s.o., sth.; *F:* **t. autour du pot,** to beat about the bush; **voilà huit jours qu'il tourne autour d'elle,** he's been hanging round her, about her, for a week; **tout tourne autour de lui, la tête lui tourne,** he feels giddy; his head is swimming, spinning; **le sentier tourne autour de la pelouse,** the path winds round the lawn; **faire t. la machine,** to set the machinery going; **faire t. la clef dans la serrure,** to turn the key in the lock; **faire t. une pièce de monnaie,** to spin a coin; **le pied lui a tourné,** he twisted his ankle; (b) to change direction; **tournez à gauche,** turn to the left; **t. court,** (i) to turn short, sharply, (ii) *F:* to make off; (iii) to stop abruptly, to end suddenly; **ne savoir de quel côté t.,** not to know which way to turn; to be at one's wits' end; **le vent a tourné à l'ouest,** the wind has changed, shifted, to the west; **le temps tourne au froid,** it is turning cold; **sa chance a tourné,** his luck has turned; **tout tourne contre lui,** everything is turning against him; **il a tourné contre moi,** he has turned against me; **son amour a tourné en haine,** his love has turned, changed, to hatred; (c) (*of fruit, etc.*) to colour, ripen; **le raisin commence à t.,** the grapes are taking on colour; (d) to turn out, result; **les choses tournent bien, mal,** things are turning out well, badly; (*of pers.*) **mal**

t., to go to the bad; **son fils a mal tourné,** his son has turned out a scamp, has gone wrong, gone to the bad; **cela tournait mal,** things were taking a bad turn; **cela tournera mal,** evil will come of it; **l'entreprise tourne bien,** the undertaking is proving successful, is shaping well; (*e*) to tend (**à,** to); to turn; **portraits qui tournent à la caricature,** portraits that are almost caricatures; **jeune fille qui tourne à la coquette,** girl who is turning into a flirt; **l'affaire tournait au tragique,** the matter was taking a tragic turn, was turning to tragedy; (*of wine*) **t. au vinaigre,** to turn acid; **lait qui tourne à l'aigre,** milk that is turning sour; *abs.* **lait qui tourne,** milk that is turning, curdling; **faire t. qch.,** to curdle sth., to turn sth. sour; (*f*) *Cin:* **t. dans un film,** to act in a film; to play in a film. 3. *impers. Cards:* **il tourne carreau,** the turn-up is diamonds.

se tourner. 1. (*a*) **se t. vers qn, du côté de qn,** to turn towards s.o.; **se t. vers Dieu,** to turn to God; **ses yeux se tournèrent vers la porte,** his eyes turned to the door; **je ne vois pas d'issue, de quelque côté qu'on se tourne,** I see no way out of it, whichever way we turn; (*b*) **se t. contre qn,** to turn against s.o.; **c'est sa femme qui l'a fait t. contre vous,** it was his wife who turned him against you; (*c*) **se t. du côté du peuple,** to side with the people; (*d*) to turn round; **tournez-vous un peu que je vous voie de côté,** turn round a little and let me see your profile. 2. **son amour se tourna en haine,** his love turned to hate; (*of wine*) **se t. en vinaigre,** to turn into vinegar.

tournerie [turnəri], *s.f.* turner's shop, turnery.

tournesol [turnəsɔl], *s.m.* 1. *Bot:* turnsole ((i) sunflower; (ii) chrozophora). 2. *Dy: Ch:* **papier (de) t.,** litmus paper; **teinture de t.,** litmus solution.

tournette [turnɛt], *s.f.* 1. reel; wool winder. 2. washer cutter; circular glass cutter; *Phot:* circular print trimmer. 3. (*a*) turntable (for small objects); (*b*) *Ind: Phot: etc:* (drying) whirler; (*c*) *Cer:* tournette. 4. squirrel's cage.

tourneur, -euse [turnœ:r, -ø:z]. 1. *a.* **derviche tourneur,** dancing, whirling, dervish. 2. *s.m.* (*a*) turner; *Cer:* thrower; **t. de buis,** turner in boxwood; **t. de vis,** screwcutter; (*b*) **t. de baguette,** water diviner; dowser; (*c*) *Th: etc:* **t. de spectacle,** show organizer. 3. *s.f. Tex:* **tourneuse,** (woman) reeler, winder (of silk).

tourne-vent [turnəvɑ̃], *s.m.inv.* chimney cowl, chimney jack.

tournevire [turnəvi:r], *s.m. Nau:* messenger (of capstan).

tournevis [turnəvis], *s.m. Tls:* screwdriver; turnscrew.

tournicoter [turnikɔte], *v.i. F:* to wander round and round.

tournière [turnjɛ:r], *s.f. Agr:* headland (for turning the plough).

tourniller [turnije], (*a*) *v.tr.* to twist, twiddle, twirl (sth.); (*b*) *v.i.* to turn round in a small circle; (*c*) *v.i.* **chemin qui tournille,** path that twists and turns.

tourniole [turnjɔl], *s.f. Med: F:* whitlow, *esp.* felon.

tourniquer [turnike], *F:* 1. *v.i.* (*a*) to wander round and round; (*b*) to hover (round). 2. *v.tr.* to twiddle (sth.) round and round.

tourniquet [turnikɛ], *s.m.* 1. (*a*) **t.(-compteur),** turnstile; *Mil: P:* **passer au t.,** to be court-martialled; (*b*) revolving stand (for picture postcards, etc.). 2. (*a*) roller (for ropes, etc., to pass over); (*b*) swivel; (*c*) button, turnbuckle (on shutter, etc.). 3. (*a*) *Toys:* whirligig; (*b*) *Pyr:* Catherine wheel; (*c*) *Gaming:* **jeu du t.,** game played with wheel like roulette; (*d*) *Ph:* **t. hydraulique,** reaction wheel; **t. électrique,** electric whirl, vane; (*e*) sprinkler (for watering plants). 4. *Surg:* tourniquet. 5. *Ent:* **t. aquatique,** whirligig beetle.

tournis [turni], *s.m.* (*a*) *Vet:* staggers, sturdy, gid, goggles; (*b*) **donner le t. à qn,** to make s.o. giddy.

tournisse [turnis], *s.f. Const:* stud (post) (in wooden framework).

tournoi [turnwa], *s.m.* (*a*) *Hist:* tournament, tourney; (*b*) *Sp: etc:* (tennis, etc.) tournament; **t. de bridge,** bridge tournament; **t. de whist,** whist drive; **t. par paires,** pairs tournament; (*c*) **t. d'éloquence,** contest of eloquence.

tournoiement [turnwamɑ̃], *s.m.* 1. turning round, twirling, whirling; spinning (of suspended object); wheeling (of birds); eddying, swirling (of water). 2. (*a*) giddiness, dizziness; (*b*) *Vet:* staggers, sturdy, gid, goggles.

tournois [turnwa], *a.inv. Num: A:* minted at Tours, tournois.

tournonais, -aise [turnɔnɛ, -ɛ:z], *a.* & *s. Geog:* (native, inhabitant) of Tournon.

tournoyant [turnwajɑ̃], *a.* turning, twirling, whirling; spinning; wheeling (birds); eddying, swirling (water).

tournoyer [turnwaje], *v.i.* (**je tournoie, n. tournoyons; je tournoierai**) 1. (*a*) to turn round and round, to whirl; (*of suspended object*) to spin; (*of birds*) to wheel; (*of water*) to eddy, swirl; **descendre en tournoyant,** to come whirling down; **faire t. qch.,** to twirl, whirl, sth.; (*b*) *F:* to shilly-shally; to quibble. 2. *Hist:* to compete in a tournament, a tourney.

tournure [turny:r], *s.f.* 1. *Metalw:* turning (from a lathe); turnings. 2. turn, direction, course; **les affaires prennent (une) meilleure t.,** things are taking a turn for the better; business is looking up; **les affaires prennent une mauvaise t., une vilaine t.,** things are shaping badly, are looking black; **donner une t. agréable à la conversation,** to give a pleasant turn to the conversation. 3. shape, form, figure, appearance; (*a*) **c'était quelqu'un avec votre t.,** it was some one with your figure; **t. d'esprit,** turn of mind; **sa singulière t. d'esprit,** his queer twist of mind; **t. d'une phrase,** turn of a sentence; **t. de phrase,** turn of phrase; **donner une autre t. à la chose,** to put a new face on the matter; **le travail prend t.,** the work is taking shape; (*b*) *A:* **avoir une belle t.,** to have a good figure; **que dites-vous de ma t.?** how do you think I look like this? 4. *A.Cost:* bustle; dress-improver.

tournusien, -ienne [turnyzjɛ̃, -jɛn], *a.* & *s. Geog:* (native, inhabitant) of Tournus.

tourquenois, -oise [turkənwa, -wa:z], *a.* & *s. Geog:* (native, inhabitant) of Tourcoing.

tourte [turt], *s.f.* 1. (*a*) *Cu:* (covered) tart; **t. aux pommes,** apple pie, apple tart; (*b*) *F:* idiot, clot; *a.* **elle est belle, mais plutôt t.** = she's a dumb blonde. 2. *Dial:* round loaf (of bread). 3. *Metall:* torta (of silver ore). 4. *Agr:* marc, cake (of linseed for manure).

tourteau, -eaux [turto], *s.m.* 1. (*a*) *A:* round loaf (of bread); (*b*) *Husb:* oilcake (for cattle); cattle cake, cow cake; **t. de lin,** linseed meal; (*c*) *Com:* **t. de graines oléagineuses,** expellers. 2. *Crust:* **t. (dormeur),** edible crab. 3. *Mec.E:* centre boss (of wheel, crank); **t. d'assemblage,** shaft coupling. 4. tumbler (of dredge). 5. *Her:* roundel; **t. de gueules,** torteau; a roundel gules; **t. de pourpre,** golpe; **t. d'azur,** hurt; **t. de sable,** pellet; **t. de sinople,** pomey.

tourtelet [turtəlɛ], *s.m. Cu:* (cream, jam) puff.

tourtelette [turtəlɛt], *s.f. Cu:* small (covered) tart; tartlet.

tourtereau, -eaux [turtəro], *s.m.* (*a*) young turtle-dove; (*b*) *F:* **des tourtereaux,** a young couple very much in love, *F:* lovebirds.

tourterelle [turtərɛl], *s.f. Orn:* **t. (des bois),** turtle-dove; **t. rieuse,** Barbary dove; **t. orientale,** rufous, Eastern, turtle-dove; **t. turque,** collared turtle-dove.

tourtière [turtjɛ:r], *s.f.* 1. tart plate (for baking tarts). 2. *Fr.C:* meat pie, minced-pork pie.

tous-courants [tukurɑ̃], *a.inv. W.Tel:* **poste tous-courants,** all-mains receiver, set.

touselle [tuzɛl], *s.f. Bot:* beardless wheat.

toussailler [tusɑje], *v.i.* to have a nervous little cough.

Toussaint (la) [latusɛ̃], *Pr.n.f.* All Saints' day; All Hallows' day, All Hallows; Hallowmas; **la veille de la T.,** Hallowe'en.

tousser [tuse], *v.i.* (*a*) to cough; *F:* **t. un coup,** to clear one's throat; **il toussa pour m'avertir,** he gave a cough to warn me; **t. gras,** to cough up phlegm; *Med:* **toussez!** = say ninety-nine! (*b*) **moteur qui tousse,** spluttering engine; **le moteur a toussé et s'est arrêté,** the engine gave a cough and stopped.

tousserie [tusri], *s.f. O:* (constant) coughing (*esp.* among audience, etc.).

tousseur, -euse [tusœ:r, -ø:z], *s.* cougher.

toussotement [tusɔtmɑ̃], *s.m.* slight cough; clearing of the throat.

toussoter [tusɔte], *v.i.* (*a*) to clear one's throat; to cough slightly; (*b*) to have a slight cough.

toussoterie [tusɔtri], *s.f. F:* constant slight coughing.

tous-temps [tutɑ̃], *a.* all-weather; *Av:* **chasseur, intercepteur, t.-t.,** all-weather fighter, interceptor.

tout, toute, *pl.* **tous, toutes** [tu, tut, tu, tut] (*when* **tous** *is a pronoun it is pronounced* [tu:s]), all. I. *a.* 1. (*noun undetermined*) any, every, all; **t. travail de bureau lui est interdit,** he is forbidden to do any office work; **toute profession est honnête,** any, every, calling is honest; **les conditions requises pour t. progrès,** the requisite conditions for all progress; **pour t. mobilier deux petits lits,** for sole furniture two small beds; **pour toute arme il avait une canne,** his only weapon was a walking-stick; **pour toute réponse il éclata de rire,** his only answer was to burst out laughing; **t. autre que vous,** anybody but you; **je vous donne toute liberté d'agir,** I give you full liberty to act; **j'ai toute raison de croire que . . .,** I have every reason to believe that . . .; **repas à toute heure,** meals served at any time. 2. (*intensive*) **de toute force il nous faut . . .,** it is essential for us to . . .; we absolutely must . . .; **dans sa toute jeunesse,** when he was quite a child, in his early youth; *Lit:* **le fait est faux, et de toute fausseté,** the statement is a downright lie; **il demeure à la toute extrémité de la ville,** he lives at the very end of the town; **à la toute dernière minute,** at the very last minute; **des arbres de toute beauté,** most beautiful trees; **à toute vitesse, à toute allure, à toute bride, à toute vapeur,** at full speed; **t., toute, à vous,** entirely yours; **de toute importance,** of the first importance, all-important; **il est de toute importance que** + *sub.*, it is of the utmost importance that . . .; *Nau:* **la barre toute!** hard over! **à gauche toute!** hard a-port! 3. (*noun particularized in sg.*) the whole, all; **t. le monde,** everybody, everyone; **toute la famille,** the whole family, all the family; **t. mon argent,** all my money; **t. le jour, toute la journée,** the whole day, all day long; **pendant t. l'hiver,** throughout the winter; all through the winter; **répéter t. le temps la même chose,** to keep on saying the same thing; **l'armée cédait sur toute la ligne,** the army was giving way all along the line; **au milieu de tout ça . . .,** in the midst of it all . . .; **t. Paris est en danger,** the whole of Paris is in danger; **t. La Haye se trouvait dans les rues,** the whole population of the Hague was in the streets; **t. mars se passa sans nouvelles,** the whole of March went by without news; **existence toute de travail,** life entirely given up to work. 4. (*noun particularized in pl.*) all, every; (*a*) **tous les invités,** all the guests; **tous ces livres,** all these books; **tous ceux qui l'ont entendu,** all those who heard him, everyone who heard him; **tous les jours,** every day; **tous les quarts d'heure,** every quarter of an hour; **toutes les fois que . . .,** whenever . . .; each time that . . .; **Stendhal, Anatole France, Balzac, Proust—toutes gens qui savent écrire,** Stendhal, Anatole France, Balzac, Proust—all (of them) people who know how to write; (*b*) (*phrases in which the article is or may be omitted*) **au-dessus de toutes choses,** above all; **de tous (les) côtés, de toutes parts,** on all sides; (from) everywhere; **de toutes (les) couleurs,** of all colours; of every (possible) colour; **de toutes sortes,** of every sort, kind; **toutes affaires cessantes,** immediately; **toutes proportions gardées,** making due allowance, all allowances; *Nau:* **toutes voiles dehors,** in full sail. 5. (*with numerals*) **tous (les) deux,** both; **tous (les) trois, (les) dix,** all three, all ten; **tous les deux jours,** every other day; **tous les trois jours,** every third day; **tous les deux ou trois jours,** every second or third day; **tous les huit jours,** every week; once a week. 6. (*with* **un**) **t. un quartier de la ville a été incendié,** a whole district of the town was burnt down; **c'est toute une histoire,** (i) it's a long story; (ii) it's quite a job, *F:* some job; **son histoire est t. un roman,** his story is quite a romance.

II. **tout,** *pron.* 1. *sg.neut.* all, everything; **l'argent n'est pas t.,** money isn't everything; **il faut t. lui montrer,** we must show him everything; **je crois que c'est t.,** I think that's about all; *F:* **et t. et t.,** and all the rest of it; **t. est bien qui finit bien,** all's well that ends well; **voilà t. ce que je sais,** that's all I know; **voilà t. ce que je peux faire,** that's all, as much as, I can do; **j'aime t. ce qui est français,** I love anything, everything, French; **t. ce qui vous plaira,** whatever you like; anything you like; **il avait perdu t. ce qu'il possédait,** he had lost all his possessions, everything; **t. ce qui est musique l'intéresse,** he is interested in anything to do with music; **c'est t. ce qu'il y a de plus beau, de plus drôle,** it is most beautiful; nothing could be funnier; **il a t. mangé,** he has eaten everything, the whole lot; **il mange de tout,** he eats anything (and everything); **vendre de t.,** to sell everything; to deal in all sorts of things; **on trouve de t. à Paris,** you find all sorts of things in Paris; **depuis lors j'ai fait de t.,** since then I've done a bit of everything, all sorts of different jobs; **il est capable de t.,** he is capable of anything, will stop at nothing; *F:* **il a t. du caissier,** he's the complete cashier, he's got all the defects of a cashier; **c'est t. dire,** I needn't say more; **c'est t. un,** it's all one; **un homme à t. faire,** an all-rounder; **en t. et pour t.,** first and last . . .; **à t. prendre . . .,** on the whole; taking it all in all; *F:* **drôle comme t.,** awfully funny; **rire comme t.,** to laugh like a drain; *note the following:* **femmes, moine, vieillards, tout était descendu,** the women, the monk, the old people, one and all had got out (of the coach). **2.** *pl.* **une (bonne) fois pour toutes,** once for all; **venez tous** [tu:s]! come along all of you! **ils sont tous là** [tusla], **elles sont toutes là,** they are all there, all of them are there; **il faut tous faire votre devoir,** all of you must do your duty; **le meilleur de tous,** the best of them all, the best of the bunch; **il est impossible de les nommer tous, de tous les nommer,** it is impossible to name them all; **elle voulait toutes les ouvrir, les ouvrir toutes,** she wanted to open them all; **on nous en offrit un verre à tous,** we were all offered a glass; **il y va de leur bonheur à tous,** the happiness of all of them is at stake; **ceci soit dit à notre louange à tous,** let this be said in praise of us all; **tous à la fois,** all together; **tous sans exception,** all without exception, one and all, every single one of them; *Navy:* **signal à tous,** general signal; *F:* **on l'aimait bien tous,** we were all very fond of him; **nous tous, vous tous, eux tous,** all of us, of you, of them; **combien d'argent ont-ils à eux tous?** how much money have they between them?

III. **tout,** *s.m.* **1. le t.,** the whole, the lot; **le t. est de réussir,** the main thing is to succeed; **il faut risquer le t. pour le t.,** we must stake everything, our all; *F:* it's neck or nothing; **jouer le t. pour le t.,** to stake everything; *F:* to put one's shirt on (a horse, etc.); **son fils est son t.,** her son is her all in all; *F:* **ce n'est pas le t., ça!** that's not getting us very far! *adv.phr.* **du t. au t.,** entirely; **différer du t. au t.,** to be entirely different; **la situation a changé du t. au t.,** the situation has entirely changed; **voilà qui change les choses du t. au t.,** that puts quite a new complexion on the matter; **en t.,** in all; **les indications manquent en t. ou en partie,** indications are wholly or partly lacking; **ces espèces diffèrent du t. au rien,** some of these species are completely different, while others are very similar; **(pas) du t.,** not at all; **pardon, madame!—du t., monsieur!** I beg your pardon!—that's quite all right! please . . .! **2.** *Mth:* (*pl.* **touts**) total; **plusieurs touts,** several totals; (*in charades*) **mon t.,** my all, my whole.

IV. **tout,** *adv.* (*intensive*) (*before a fem.adj. beginning with a consonant or* **h** "*aspirate*" **tout** *becomes* **toute**) **1.** quite, entirely, completely, very; **t. nouveau(x), toute(s) nouvelle(s),** quite new; **ils sont t. seuls, elles sont toutes seules,** they are (quite) alone; **elle était encore toute petite, toute jeune,** she was still quite little, quite young; **hommes t. bon(s) ou t. mauvais,** men entirely good or entirely bad; **t. de noir vêtue, toute vêtue de noir,** dressed all in black; **elle était toute honteuse,** she was utterly ashamed; **tout(e) tremblant(e), t. ému, t. émue,** all of a tremble; **des lutteurs de t. premier ordre,** wrestlers of the very first order; **une t. autre personne,** quite a different person; an entirely different person; **t. droit,** bolt upright; **t. neuf,** brand new; **t. nu,** stark naked; **t. éveillé,** wide awake; **vêtement t. fait,** ready-made garment; **viande toute cuite,** ready-cooked meat; **nous trouvâmes un souper froid t. servi,** we found a cold supper ready laid; **t. au bout,** right at the end, at the very end; **t. là-bas,** right over there, away in the distance; **t. contre le mur,** right against the wall; **mains t. en sang,** hands all covered with blood, all bloody; **c'est t. comme chez nous!** it's just like home; **il est t. à son commerce,** he is entirely absorbed in his business; **t. doux!** gently! *adv.phr.* **t. à fait,** quite, entirely, altogether; **cela me va t. à fait,** it suits me perfectly, down to the ground; **il lui ressemble t. à fait,** he is just like him; **soirée t. à fait assommante,** thoroughly boring evening; **t. au plus,** at the very most; **t. au moins, t. le moins,** at the very least; (*at end of letter*) **t. à vous,** yours ever; *s.a.* AUTANT 1, BON[1] I. 11, COUP 4, COURT[1] 2, 3, GO, HAUT II. 1, HEURE (*f*), LONG 2, MÊME 3, OUVERT 1, SUITE 2, UN 1. **2.** (*with gerund*) **t. en parlant,** while speaking. **3.** (*concessive*) **t. ignorant qu'il soit, qu'il est,** however ignorant he is; ignorant though, as, he is; ignorant though he may be; **t. Parisien, toute Parisienne, que je suis, cela m'est nouveau,** Parisian though I am, this is new to me; **t. père, toute mère, que je suis,** although I am a father, a mother. **4.** (*qualifying noun usu. invariable, but occ. agrees with noun esp. when it has some adjectival force*) **être t. yeux, t. oreilles,** to be all eyes, all ears; **elle est t. joie et t. amour,** she is all happiness and love; **il était toute crainte et toute haine,** he was all fear and hate; **elle était t. attention,** she was all attention; **elle est t. le portrait de sa mère,** she is the living image of her mother; **cet homme était toute sagesse,** this man was all wisdom, full of wisdom; **c'était dans nos t. commencements,** it was in our very early days, at the very start (of our career, etc.); **au t. début du mois,** right at the beginning of the month.

tout-à-l'arrière [tutalarjɛ:r], *a.inv. Aut:* rear-engined.

tout-à-l'avant [tutalavɑ̃], *a.inv. Aut:* front-wheel drive.

tout-à-l'égout [tutalegu], *s.m.inv.* mains drainage.

Toutankhamon [tutɑ̃kamɔ̃], *Pr.n.m. A.Hist:* Tutankhamun.

toute-bonne [tutbɔn], *s.f.* **1.** *Bot:* Good King Henry, wild spinach. **2.** *Hort:* variety of pear; *pl. toutes-bonnes.*

toute-bonté [tutbɔ̃te], *s.f. Theol:* infinite goodness (of God).

toute-épice [tutepis], *s.f. Bot:* allspice, pimento, Jamaica pepper; *pl. toutes-épices.*

toutefois [tutfwa], *adv.* yet, nevertheless, however, still; **je vais voir ce qu'il dit, si t. je peux le joindre,** I will see what he says, that is, if I can get in touch with him.

toutenague [tutnag], *s.f. Metall:* tutenag(ue).

toute-présence [tutprezɑ̃:s], *s.f. Theol:* omnipresence.

toute-puissance [tutpɥisɑ̃:s], *s.f.* (*a*) *Theol:* omnipotence; (*b*) *Pol: etc:* absolute power.

toute-saine [tutsɛn], *s.f. Bot:* tutsan.

toute-science [tutsjɑ̃:s], *s.f. Theol:* omniscience.

toute-vive [tutviv], *s.f. Orn: F:* corn bunting; *pl. toutes-vives.*

tout-fou [tufu], *F:* (*a*) *a.m.* mad, bats; (*b*) *s.m.* idiot, clot; *pl. tout-fous.*

toutim(e) [tutim], *s.m. P:* **(tout) le t.,** the lot, the whole shoot.

toutou [tutu], *s.m.* (*a*) (*esp. child's word*) doggie, bow-wow; **viens, viens, petit t. de sa mémère,** come on then, mummy's little doggie-woggie; (*b*) (*weak-willed person*) **filer comme un t.,** to let oneself be led; to drift along; *pl. toutous.*

tout-ou-rien [tuturjɛ̃], *s.m.inv. Clockm:* repeating spring; *Mec.E:* **régulateur par t.-ou-r.,** hit-or-miss governor.

Tout-Paris [tupari], *s.m.* all Paris, fashionable Paris; **il connaît son T.-P. à fond,** he knows everybody who is anybody in Paris.

tout-petit [tup(ə)ti], *s.m.* toddler; *pl. tout-petits.*

tout-puissant, *f.* **toute-puissante** [tupɥisɑ̃, tutpɥisɑ̃:t], *a.* almighty, omnipotent, all-powerful; **désir t.-p.,** overwhelming desire; overpowering desire; *s.m.* **le Tout-Puissant,** the Almighty; *pl. tout-puissants, toutes-puissantes.*

tout-terrain [tutɛrɛ̃], *a.* (*a*) cross-country; *s.* **faire du t.-t.,** to go, move, cross-country; (*b*) **véhicule t.-t.,** all-purpose vehicle; jeep; *pl. tous-terrains.*

tout-venant [tuvnɑ̃], *s.m. Com:* ungraded product; *esp.* unsorted coal, run of the mine, through (-and-through) coal.

toux [tu], *s.f.* cough; **accès, quinte, de t.,** fit of coughing; **t. sèche,** dry cough; **t. grasse,** loose cough; coughing up of phlegm; **t. d'irritation,** tickling cough.

toxalbumine [tɔksalbymin], *s.f. Bio-Ch:* toxalbumin.

toxémie, toxhémie [tɔksemi], *s.f. Med:* toxaemia, blood-poisoning; **t. gravidique,** toxaemia of pregnancy; *Vet:* **t. de gestation (de la brebis),** ketosis (of ewes).

toxicité [tɔksisite], *s.f.* toxicity, poisonousness.

toxicodendron [tɔksikɔdɛ̃drɔ̃], *s.m. Bot:* (*a*) poison ivy, rhus; (*b*) toxicodendron.

toxicogène [tɔksikɔʒɛn], *a.* toxicogenic.

toxicologie [tɔksikɔlɔʒi], *s.f.* toxicology.

toxicologique [tɔksikɔlɔʒik], *a.* toxicological.

toxicologiste [tɔksikɔlɔʒist], *s.m.* & *f.,* **toxicologue** [tɔksikɔlɔg], *s.m.* & *f.* toxicologist.

toxicomane [tɔksikɔman], *s.m.* & *f.* drug addict, dope addict.

toxicomanie [tɔksikɔmani], *s.f.* toxicomania, drug addition.

toxicophage [tɔksikɔfa:ʒ]. **1.** *a.* toxicophagous. **2.** *s.m.* & *f.* toxiphagus.

toxicophobie [tɔksikɔfɔbi], *s.f. Med:* toxiphobia, toxicophobia.

toxicophore [tɔksikɔfɔ:r], *a.* toxiphoric.

toxicose [tɔksiko:z], *s.f. Med:* toxicosis.

toxidermie [tɔksidɛrmi], *s.f. Med:* toxicoderm(i)a.

toxigène [tɔksiʒɛn], *a.* toxigenic.

toxi-infectieux, -euse [tɔksiɛ̃fɛksjø, -ø:z], *a. Med:* toxinfectious; *pl. toxi-infectieux, -euses.*

toxi-infection [tɔksiɛ̃fɛksjɔ̃], *s.f. Med:* toxinfection, toxi-infection; *pl. toxi-infections.*

toxine [tɔksin], *s.f. Physiol:* toxin.

toxinhémie [tɔksinemi], *s.f. Med:* toxin(a)emia.

toxique [tɔksik]. **1.** *a.* toxic; **gaz t.,** poison gas. **2.** *s.m.* poison.

toxodontes [tɔksɔdɔ̃:t], *s.m.pl. Paleont:* toxodonts, Toxodontia.

toxoglosses [tɔksɔglɔs], *s.m.pl. Moll:* toxoglossates, Toxoglossa.

toxoïde [tɔksɔid], *s.m. Med:* toxoid.

toxoplasme [tɔksɔplasm], *s.m. Bac:* toxoplasm.

toxoplasmose [tɔksɔplasmo:z], *s.f. Med:* toxoplasmosis.

toxote [tɔksɔt], *s.m. Ich:* archer, archerfish; (*genus*) Toxotes.

toxurie [tɔksyri], *s.f. Med:* ur(a)emia.

toxylon [tɔksilɔ̃], *s.m. Bot:* osage orange.

toyère [twajɛ:r], *s.f.* eye (of axe head, of hammer head).

toy-spaniel [tɔispaɲɔl], *s.m. Z:* English toy spaniel; *pl. toy-spaniels.*

trabac [trabak], *s.m.* **1.** trabacolo, two-masted ship (of the Adriatic). **2.** *Fish:* (type of) pound net.

traban [trabɑ̃], *s.m. A.Mil:* (*a*) halberdier (*b*) trabant; Swiss guard (in the service of a prince).

trabant [trabɑ̃], *s.m. Biol:* trabant, satellite.

trabe [trab], *s.f.* **1.** pole (of flag, banner). **2.** *Her:* anchor stock.

trabéation [trabeasjɔ̃], *s.f.* **1.** *A.Arch:* trabeation, entablature. **2.** *Theol:* incarnation (of Christ).

trabéculaire [trabekylɛ:r], *a.* **1.** *Anat:* trabecular. **2.** *Arch:* **construction t.,** construction in bays.

trabécule [trabekyl], *s.f. Anat:* trabecula.

trabée [trabe], *s.f.* **1.** *Rom.Ant:* trabea. **2.** *Arach:* wolf spider; (*genus*) Trabaea.

trac[1] [trak], *s.m. F:* funk, fright; *Th:* stage fright; **il a le t.,** he's in a funk; he's got the wind up; *Th:* he's got stage fright.

trac[2], *s.m. used only in the adv.phr.* **tout à t.,** thoughtlessly, without reflection, blindly; out of the blue, suddenly.

trac[3], *s.m. Bot:* blackwood, East Indian rosewood.

traçage [trasa:ʒ], *s.m.* **1.** (*a*) tracing (of diagrams, etc.); setting out (of curve); laying out (of roads, gardens, etc.); marking out (of tennis court); **outil de t.,** marking-off tool; (*b*) **faire un t. de qch.,** to make a tracing of sth. **2.** *Min:* opening up (of coal seam).

tracanage [trakana:ʒ], *s.m. Tex:* reeling.

tracaner [trakane], *v.tr. Tex:* to reel (silk).

tracanoir [trakanwa:r], *s.m. Tex:* (silk) reeler, reeling machine, reel.

traçant [trasɑ̃], (*a*) *a. Bot:* running, creeping (root); (*b*) *a.* & *s.* **un (obus) t.,** a tracer shell; **une (balle) traçante,** a tracer bullet; (*c*) *Elcs:* **table traçante,** plotting board, table; output table.

tracas [traka], *s.m.* **1.** worry, trouble, bother; **avoir du t.,** to be worried; **le t. des affaires,** the worries of business; **susciter des t. à qn,** (i) to put difficulties in s.o.'s way; (ii) to give s.o. sleepless nights. **2.** *Ind:* hoist hole, *U.S:* hoist way (through floors of warehouse or factory).

tracassant [trakasɑ̃], *a.* worrying, bothering, troublesome (business).

tracassement [trakasmɑ̃], *s.m.* worrying, bothering.

tracasser [trakase]. **1.** *v.i. A:* (*a*) to fuss (about); (*b*) to potter about. **2.** *v.tr.* to worry, bother, plague (s.o.).

se tracasser, to worry; **se t. pour rien, pour des riens,** to worry, fuss, about nothing; **ne vous tracassez pas,** don't worry; **sans plus se t.,** without bothering any further.

tracasserie [trakasri], *s.f.* **1.** worry, fuss (about nothing). **2.** pestering, worrying (of s.o.). **3.** *pl.* **tracasseries,** (ill-natured, troublesome) interference; **les tracasseries de l'administration,** the petty annoyances of the civil service; **quand cet enfant aura-t-il fini ses tracasseries?** when will this child stop plagueing, pestering, me, us?

tracassier, -ière [trakasje, -jɛ:r]. **1.** *a.* (*a*) annoying, troublesome (proceedings, etc.); (*b*) pestering, interfering, cantankerous, meddlesome (person); (*c*) fussy (person); **peu t.,** easy-going. **2.** *s.* (*a*) annoying, troublesome, person; (*b*) busybody, mischiefmaker; (*c*) fussy person.

tracassin [trakasɛ̃], *s.m. F:* state of worry; **avoir le t.,** to be moody, in a perpetual state of worry.

trace [tras], *s.f.* trace. **1.** (*a*) trail, track, spoor (of beast); footprint(s), trail (of person); (wheel) track (of vehicle); **t. de lumière,** trail of light; *Mount: Ski: etc:* **faire la t.,** to lead the way, to find the route, to break trail; *Ski:* **trace directe,** direct descent; **suivre la t.,** to follow the trail; **être sur la t. de qn, qch.,** to be on s.o.'s tracks; to be on the track of sth.; *Ven:* (*of hounds*) **perdre la t.,** to be thrown off the scent; to lose the trail; **retrouver la t.,** to pick up the scent, the trail; **marcher sur les traces de qn,** to tread in s.o.'s footsteps; **il suit les traces de son père,** he follows in his father's footsteps; **ses doigts avaient laissé leurs traces,** his fingers had left their mark; **laisser une t. profonde,** to leave a deep impression behind; **retrouver t. de qn, de qch.,** to find a trace of s.o., sth.; *F:* to get on s.o.'s track again; **on n'a plus retrouvé t. des explorateurs,** no trace was ever found of the explorers; the explorers were never heard of again; *Tchn:* **dispositif de lecture de traces,** trace reader; *Elcs:* **t. du spot,** trace (in cathode-ray tube); (*radar*) **t. repère,** strobe; (*b*) weal, scar, mark (of wound, burn, etc.); **porter sur son visage la t. de la souffrance,** to bear marks of suffering on one's face; *Geol:* **t. de ruissellement,** rill mark; (*c*) (slight) trace; **pas de traces de poison,** no traces of poison; **il y a en lui une t. de sang irlandais,** he has a trace, a streak, of Irish blood. **2.** *A:* (= TRACÉ 2) outline, layout (of ground plan, of design); **faire la t. d'un parterre,** to lay out a flower bed. **3.** *Geom:* **traces d'une droite,** traces of a straight line.

tracé [trase], *s.m.* **1.** (*a*) tracing, sketching (of figure, etc.); setting out, plotting (of curve, etc.); marking out (of tennis court); laying out (of road, etc.); **faire le t. de . . .,** to trace, sketch (figure); to set out, plot (curve); to lay out (road); (*b*) layout (of town, railway system, etc.); lie, alignment (of a road, etc.). **2.** (*a*) outline, sketch, diagram, drawing; *Fort:* **t. d'une œuvre,** trace, ground plan, of a work; (*b*) graph (of curve, etc.); (*radar*) plot.

tracelet [traslɛ], *s.m. Tls:* scriber, tracing awl.

tracement [trasmɑ̃], *s.m.* = TRAÇAGE.

tracer [trase], *v.* (**je traçai(s); n. traçons**) **1.** *v.tr.* to trace; (*a*) to lay out (road, railway, grounds); to mark out (tennis court); to plot (curve, graph, etc.); to map out (route); *Min:* to open up (coal seam); **réserves tracées,** known reserves; *Nau:* **t. la route,** to set the course (on the chart); **t. une ligne de conduite,** to trace out, map out, lay down, a line of conduct, a policy; **t. le chemin à qn pour faire qch.,** to show s.o. the way to do something; (*b*) to draw (a line); to sketch, draw, outline (plan, pattern, etc.); **aiguille à t.,** scriber; **t. quelques lignes,** to trace, write, pen, a few lines. **2.** *v.i.* (*a*) *Hort:* (*of roots*) to run out; to creep; (*b*) (*of moles*) to burrow; (*c*) *Dial: & P:* to move quickly, get a move on; (*of car*) to speed.

traceret [trasrɛ], *s.m.* = TRACELET.

traceur, -euse [trasœːr, -øːz], (*a*) *s. Ind: etc:* tracer; (*b*) *s.m. Rad.-A:* **t. (radio-actif),** tracer; (*c*) *s.m. Elcs:* (*computers*) **t. (de courbes),** plotter; (*d*) *a.* **projectile t., balle traceuse,** tracer shell, tracer bullet.

trachéal, -aux [trakeal, -o], *a. Anat:* tracheal.

trachéate [trakeat], *s.m.* tracheate (arthropod).

trachée [traʃe], *s.f.* (*a*) *Anat: Z:* trachea; (*b*) *Bot:* trachea, vessel, duct.

trachée-artère [traʃeartɛːr], *s.f. Anat:* trachea; *pl. trachées-artères.*

trachéen, -enne [trakeɛ̃, -ɛn], *a. Anat:* trachean.

trachéide [trakeid], *s.f. Bot:* tracheid.

trachéite [trakeit], *s.f. Med:* tracheitis.

trachélo- [trakelə], *comb.fm.* trachelo-.

trachélobranche [trakeləbrɑ̃ːʃ], *a.* trachelobranchiate.

trachélorraphie [trakelərafi], *s.f. Surg:* trachelorrhaphy.

trachéloscapulaire [trakeləskapylɛːr], *a. Anat:* tracheloscapular.

trachélospermum [trakeləspɛrməm], *s.m. Bot:* star jasmine, confederate jasmine; (*genus*) Trachelospermum.

trachéo- [trakeə], *comb.fm.* tracheo-.

trachéo-branchie [trakeəbrɑ̃ʃi], *s.f.* tracheobranchia, tracheal gill; *pl. trachéo-branchies.*

trachéo-bronchique [trakeəbrɔ̃ʃik], *a. Anat:* tracheobronchial; *pl. trachéo-bronchiques.*

trachéo-bronchite [trakeəbrɔ̃ʃit], *s.f. Med:* tracheobronchitis.

trachéocèle [trakeəsɛl], *s.f. Med:* tracheocele.

trachéole [trakeəl], *s.f. Ent:* tracheole.

trachéophone [trakeəfən], *s.m. Orn:* tracheophone; *pl.* **trachéophones,** Tracheophonae.

trachéoscopie [trakeəskəpi], *s.f.* tracheoscopy.

trachéosténose [trakeəstenoːz], *s.f. Med:* tracheostenosis.

trachéotomie [trakeətəmi], *s.f.* tracheotomy.

trachéotomiser [trakeətəmize], *v.tr. Surg:* to tracheotomize (s.o.).

Trachine [traʃin], *Pr.n. A.Geog:* Trachis.

Trachiniennes (les) [letraʃinjɛn], *s.f.pl. Gr.Lit:* the Trachinian women; the Trachiniae.

trachodon [trakədɔ̃], *s.m. Paleont:* trachodont; (*genus*) Trachodon.

trachomateux, -euse [trakəmatø, -øːz], *Med:* **1.** *a.* trachomatous. **2.** *s.* trachoma patient.

trachome [trakoːm], *s.m. Med:* trachoma, granular conjunctivitis.

trachure [trakyːr], *s.m. Ich:* horse mackerel; (*genus*) Trachurus.

trachyandésite [trakjɑ̃dezit], *s.f. Miner:* trachyandesite.

trachycarpus [trakikarpys], *s.m. Bot:* hemp palm; (*genus*) Trachycarpus.

trachylides [trakilid], *s.m.pl. Coel:* Trachylina, Trachylinae.

trachyméduses [trakimedyːz], *s.f.pl. Coel:* Trachymedusae, Trachomedusae.

trachyptère [trakiptɛːr], *s.m. Ich:* dealfish, ribbonfish, trachypteroid; (*genus*) Trachypterus.

trachyptéridés [trakipteride], *s.m.pl. Ich:* Trachypteridae.

trachystomates [trakistəmat], *s.m.pl. Amph:* sirens; (*family*) Sirenidae.

trachyte [trakit], *s.m. Miner:* trachyte.

trachytique [trakitik], *a.* trachytic.

traçoir [traswaːr], *s.m.* = TRACELET.

tract [trakt], *s.m.* **1.** tract. **2.** leaflet; **les avions ont jeté des tracts au-dessus des lignes ennemies,** the planes dropped leaflets over the enemy lines.

tractabilité [traktabilite], *s.f.* tractability, malleability.

tractable [traktabl̩], *a.* capable of being drawn, towed; towable.

tractarianisme [traktarjanism], *s.m. Rel.H:* Tractarianism.

tractarien, -ienne [traktarjɛ̃, -jɛn], *s. Rel.H:* Tractarian.

tractation [traktasjɔ̃], *s.f. often Pej:* deal; dealings; bargaining; *Pol:* **tractations ministérielles,** ministerial deals; **se livrer à de louches tractations,** to go in for shady dealings, transactions.

tracté [trakte], *a.* tractor-drawn; **artillerie tractée,** tractor-drawn artillery.

tracter [trakte], *v.tr.* to draw by tractor.

tracteur, -trice [traktœːr, -tris]. **1.** *s.m.* (*a*) tractor; *Mil:* (*wheel-type, personnel-carrier, tractor*) prime-mover; **t. à chenilles,** Caterpillar tractor (*R.t.m.*); **t. à roues,** wheel-type tractor; **t. de dépannage,** breakdown tractor; **t. et semi-remorque,** tractor and trailer; articulated vehicle; **t. chenille à grue,** boom cat; (*b*) traction engine; *Rail:* **t. électrique,** electric engine; (*c*) tractor (of obstetrical forceps). **2.** *a.* (*a*) **voiture tractrice d'une caravane,** towing vehicle of a caravan; (*b*) *Geog:* **force tractrice (d'un courant),** transport capacity (of a current).

tracteur-navette [traktœrnavɛt], *s.m. Agr:* tractor that can operate in reverse; *pl. tracteurs-navette.*

tractif, -ive [traktif, -iːv], *a. Mec.E:* tractive (effort, force); **roues tractives,** traction wheels (of locomotive, etc.); *Av:* **hélice tractive,** tractor propeller; **appareil à hélice tractive,** tractor-plane.

traction [traksjɔ̃], *s.f.* (*a*) traction; pulling; **effort de t.,** tractive effort, pull; **t. magnétique,** magnetic pull; **t. au crochet,** draw-bar pull; **séparer par t.,** to pull off; *Mec:* **résistance à la t.,** tensile strength; **essai de t.,** tensile test; *Med:* **t. rythmique de la langue,** rhythmical traction on the tongue; *Gym:* **faire une t.,** (i) to chin the bar; (ii) to do push-ups, press-ups; (*b*) traction, draught; **t. à bras (d'homme),** manual haulage; **t. animale,** animal draught; **t. mécanique, t. par moteur,** mechanical traction, motor traction; **véhicule à t. mécanique,** mechanically propelled vehicle; **t. par machine fixe et par câble,** haulage by stationary engine and cable; **t. en palier,** level traction, haulage; **t. sur rails,** track haulage; **t. en rampe,** up-grade traction, haulage; **t. électrique,** electric traction; **t. par accumulateurs,** accumulator system; **t. par trolley,** (overhead) trolley system; **t. (électrique) en caniveau,** conduit system; **t. (électrique) par troisième rail,** third-rail system; **t. à plots,** surface-contact system, stud system; *Rail:* **t. double,** double heading; **train à double t.,** double-header; **tige de t.,** draw-bar; **ressort de t.,** draw-spring; **service de la t.,** locomotive department; *Aut:* **t. avant,** front-wheel drive; **une t. (avant),** a front-wheel-drive car.

tractionner [traksjəne], *v.tr. Metall:* to tensile-test.

tractoire [traktwaːr]. **1.** *a.* tractive; traction (engine). **2.** *s.f. Mth:* tractrix, tractory.

tractoriste [traktərist], *s.m. & f.* tractor driver, operator; tractorist.

tractrice [traktris], *s.f. Mth:* tractrix, tractory.

tractus [traktys], *s.m. Anat:* tract, tractus; **t. digestif,** digestive tract, system; **t. urogénital,** urogenital system.

tradescantia [tradɛskɑ̃sja], *s.m.,* **tradescantie** [tradɛskɑ̃ti], *s.f. Bot:* tradescantia; **t. (de Virginie),** spiderwort.

traditeur [traditœːr], *s.m. Rel.H:* traditor.

tradition [tradisjɔ̃], *s.f.* **1.** (*a*) tradition; **de t.,** traditional; **il est de t. de . . ., que** + *sub.,* it is traditional to . . ., that . . .; *Th:* **ce jeu de scène est de t.,** this stage business is traditional; (*b*) folklore. **2.** *Jur:* delivery, handing over (of property, etc.).

traditionalisme [tradisjənalism], *s.m.* (*a*) *Theol:* traditionalism; (*b*) traditionalism, conservatism.

traditionaliste [tradisjənalist], *s.m. & f.* (*a*) *Theol:* traditionalist; (*b*) traditionalist, conservative.

traditionnaire [tradisjənɛːr], *a. & s.m. & f. Rel:* orthodox (Jew); conservative (Jew); traditionalist.

traditionnel, -elle [tradisjənɛl], *a.* traditional; usual, habitual; standard (excuse, etc.); standing (joke); **matériel t.,** conventional equipment; **table que recouvre le t. tapis vert,** table covered with the traditional, usual, green cloth.

traditionnellement [tradisjənɛlmɑ̃], *adv.* traditionally.

traduc [tradyk], *s.f. Sch: F:* crib.

traducteur, -trice [tradyktœːr, -tris]. **1.** *s.* (*pers.*) translator; **t. littéraire,** literary translator; **t. technique,** technical translator. **2.** *s.m.* (*a*) *Cin:* **t. phonique,** sound unit; (*b*) *Elcs:* (*computers*) **t. un(e) pour un(e),** one-for-one translator; **(programme) t.,** translating programme, routine; translator; interpreter; (*c*) *Tp:* **t. Baudot,** Baudot code. **3.** *s.f. Elcs:* (*computers*) **traductrice reporteuse,** transfer interpreter.

traduction [tradyksjɔ̃], *s.f.* **1.** translating; *Elcs:* (*computers*) **t. automatique,** machine translation; **t. algorithmique,** algorithm translation; **t. des informations,** data reduction. **2.** translation; **faire une t. de qch.,** to translate sth., to make a translation of sth.; **t. simultanée,** simultaneous translation; **t. automatique,** automatic translation; **t. inexacte,** inaccurate translation; mistranslation; **essai de t.,** proposed rendering; *Sch:* **se servir d'une t. pour faire un devoir,** to use a crib to do one's prep.

traduire [tradɥiːr], *v.tr.* (*pr.p.* **traduisant;** *p.p.* **traduit;** *pr.ind.* **je traduis, il traduit, n. traduisons, ils traduisent;** *p.d.* **traduisais;** *p.h.* **je traduisis;** *fu.* **je traduirai**) **1.** (*a*) *A:* to convey, transfer; (*b*) *Jur:* **t. qn en justice,** to sue, prosecute, indict, arraign, s.o.; **t. qn en conseil de guerre,** to summon s.o. before a court martial. **2.** (*a*) to translate; **t. qch. du latin en anglais,** to translate, turn, sth. from Latin into English; **livre traduit de l'allemand,** book translated from (the) German; (*b*) **t. un câblogramme,** to decode a cable; (*c*) *Elcs:* (*computers*) **t. (une carte),** to interpret (a card); (*d*) to represent; to result in; to interpret, explain, express (feeling, idea, etc.); **vous traduisez mal ma pensée,** you're misinterpreting me, my thoughts; **t. ses pensées sur le papier,** to express one's thoughts on paper; **ses paroles traduisent ses pensées,** his words reveal, reflect, betray, his thoughts; **sa douleur se traduisit par des larmes,** his grief found expression in tears; **cette maladie se traduira par un changement total de ses habitudes,** this illness will mean a complete change in his habits; **l'accroissement soudain de la population se traduit par une demande pressante d'instituteurs,** the population explosion has meant, has resulted in, an urgent demand for teachers; *Com:* **les comptes se traduisent par une perte de** ***x*** **francs,** the accounts show a loss of *x* francs.

traduisible [tradɥizibl̩], *a.* **1. t. en justice,** liable to prosecution; liable to be sued. **2.** translatable; **ce jeu de mots n'est pas t.,** this play on words cannot be translated; **il y a des œuvres qui ne sont guère traduisibles,** some books cannot really be translated.

Trafalgar [trafalgaːr], *Pr.n.m.* **1.** *Geog:* Trafalgar. **2.** *F:* **un coup de T.,** an unexpected disaster, a sudden catastrophe.

trafic [trafik], *s.m.* **1.** (*a*) *O:* trading, trade; **le t. des vins,** the wine trade; (*b*) *Pej:* traffic, illicit trading; **t. des stupéfiants,** drug traffic; **t. des armes,** traffic in arms; **t. d'influence,** corrupt practice; **faire t. de son influence,** to trade on one's influence; **faire t. de son honneur,** to barter away one's honour; *F:* **faire t. de ses charmes,** to be a prostitute; *F:* **un drôle de t.,** a queer sort of business. 2. (*a*) *Trans:* traffic; **t. ferroviaire,** rail(way) traffic; **t. routier, aérien,** road, air, traffic; **t. voyageurs,** passenger traffic; **t. marchandises,** goods traffic; **route sur laquelle se fait un t. important,** busy road, road with heavy traffic; (*b*) *Elcs:* **t. telex,** telex traffic; **capacité d'écoulement de t.,** traffic capacity.

traficoter [trafikɔte], *v.i. Pej: F:* to traffic (in).

trafiquant, -ante [trafikɑ̃, -ɑ̃:t], *s.* (*a*) *A:* trader; (*b*) *Pej:* trafficker; **t. de, en, stupéfiants,** drug trafficker; drug peddler, pedlar; dope peddler, pedlar; **t. du marché noir,** black marketeer.

trafiquer [trafike]. 1. *v.i.* (*a*) *A:* to deal, trade; **t. en cuirs,** to deal in skins; (*b*) *Pej:* **t. de, en, qch.,** to traffic in sth.; to make (illicit) profit out of sth.; **t. de sa conscience,** to sell one's conscience; **t. en, dans les, stupéfiants,** to be in the drug traffic; to peddle drugs, dope; *P:* **qu'est-ce que tu trafiques?** what the hell are you up to? 2. *v.tr.* (*a*) to negotiate (a bill, etc.); (*b*) *F:* **t. le vin,** to adulterate wine; **t. une boisson,** to doctor a drink; **voiture d'occasion dont le moteur a été trafiqué,** secondhand car whose engine has been made to look all right.

trafiqueur, -euse [trafikœ:r, -ø:z], *s. Pej:* trafficker (**de, en,** in).

tragacanthe [tragakɑ̃:t], *s.f. Bot:* tragacanth, milk vetch.

tragédie [traʒedi], *s.f.* tragedy. 1. (*a*) **les tragédies de Sophocle, de Racine,** the tragedies of Sophocles, of Racine; *F:* **jouer la t.,** to put on a tragic act; (*b*) **les sanglantes tragédies de la Révolution,** the bloody tragedies of the Revolution. 2. the art of tragedy.

tragédien, -ienne [traʒedjɛ̃, -jɛn], *s.* tragic actor, tragedian; *f.* tragic actress, tragedienne.

tragélaphe [traʒelaf], *s.m.* 1. *Myth:* tragelaph(us). 2. *Z:* harnessed antelope, tragelaph; (*genus*) Tragelaphus.

tragélaphinés [traʒelafine], *s.m.pl. Z:* Tragelaphinae.

tragi-comédie [traʒikɔmedi], *s.f.* tragi-comedy; *pl. tragi-comédies.*

tragi-comique [traʒikɔmik], *a.* tragi-comic; *pl. tragi-comiques.*

tragien, -ienne [traʒjɛ̃, -jɛn], *a. Anat:* tragal.

tragique [traʒik]. 1. (*a*) *a.* tragic (writer, play, event); *Th:* **les rôles tragiques,** the tragic roles; (*b*) *s.m.* tragicalness; tragic side (of an event); **cela tourne au t.,** the thing is becoming tragic, serious; **prendre qch. au t.,** to make a tragedy of sth.; **prendre les choses au t.,** to take things too seriously; to take a tragic view of things; **ne le prenez pas si au t.,** don't take it so much to heart, don't be so tragic about it; **le t. de l'histoire c'est que . . .,** the tragic side of the story is that. . . . 2. *s.m.* (*a*) tragedian, writer of tragedies; (*b*) *A:* tragedian, actor who plays tragic roles. 3. *s.m. Th:* **le t.,** tragedy.

tragiquement [traʒikmɑ̃], *adv.* tragically.

tragopan [tragɔpɑ̃], *s.m. Orn:* tragopan.

tragule [tragyl], *s.m. Z:* tragulid, tragule, chevrotain.

tragulidés [tragylide], *s.m.pl. Z:* Tragulidae.

tragus [tragys], *s.m. Anat:* tragus (of ear).

trahir [trai:r], *v.tr.* to betray. 1. (*a*) *A:* **t. qch., qn, à qn,** to betray sth., s.o., to s.o.; (*b*) to reveal, disclose, give away (secret); **il trahit maladroitement la chose,** he blurted out the truth; **je fus trahi par les aboiements d'un chien,** I was betrayed by a dog barking; **t. sa pensée, se t.,** to give oneself away; **amener qn à t. la vérité,** to wheedle, to get, the truth out of s.o.. 2. **t. qn,** to play s.o. false; to deceive s.o.; *F:* to let s.o. down; **ne me trahissez pas,** don't betray me; don't give me away; *F:* don't split on me; **t. la confiance de qn,** to betray s.o.'s confidence; **t. les intérêts de qn,** to betray s.o.'s interests; to let s.o. down; **t. ses serments,** to forswear one's oath; to go back on one's word; **les événements trahirent ses espérances,** events put an end to his hopes; **au premier pas ses jambes le trahirent,** at the first step his legs failed him; **déjà ses forces le trahissaient,** already his strength was failing.

trahison [traizɔ̃], *s.f.* 1. (*a*) treachery, perfidy; **c'est par t. qu'on a arraché mon consentement,** I was tricked into consenting; (*b*) *Jur:* treason; **haute t.,** high treason. 2. betrayal, betraying (**de,** of).

traie [trɛ], *s.f. Orn: F:* missel thrush.

traille [trɑ:j], *s.f.* 1. flying bridge (on suspension cable); trail bridge, ferry. 2. *Fish:* trawl (net); **pêcher à la t.,** to trawl.

trailler [trɑje], *v.tr. Fish:* to troll, trawl.

traillon [trɑjɔ̃], *s.m.* = TRAILLE 1.

traimois [trɛmwa], *s.m. Agr:* 1. spring wheat. 2. mixed fodder crop (of wheat, rye, oats and vetch).

train [trɛ̃], *s.m.* 1. (*a*) train, string, line (of pack animals, vehicles, etc.); series; set; **t. de péniches,** string of barges; **t. de bois,** timber raft, float; **t. de roues,** (i) set of wheels; (ii) *Mec.E:* gear wheel train; **t. d'engrenages,** gear train, train of gearing; **t. baladeur,** sliding gear; *Aut:* **t. avant,** front axle (assembly); **t. arrière,** back axle (assembly); **t. de pneus,** set of tyres; *Ph:* **t. d'ondes,** train of waves, wave train; *Min:* **t. de tiges de forage,** set, string, of drill pipes; *Elcs:* **t. d'impulsions,** pulse group, pulse train; **t. de pensées,** train of thought; (*b*) *Metall:* train, rolls, mill; **t. ébaucheur,** blooming mill; **t. duo,** two-high rolls; **t. dégrossisseur, gros t.,** roughing mill; **t. finisseur,** finishing mill; (*c*) *Rail:* train; **t. de voyageurs,** passenger train; **t. de marchandises,** goods train; **t. de grande ligne,** main-line train; **t. de petite ligne,** branch-line train; local train; **t. rapide,** (fast) express (train); **t. express,** fast train; **t. de luxe,** Pullman (express), *F:* crack train; **t. direct,** through train, direct train; non-stop train; **t. omnibus, t. semi-direct,** slow train, stopping train, *U.S:* accommodation train; **t. autos-couchettes,** motorail, autorail, car sleeper; **t. supplémentaire,** relief train; **t. dédoublé,** train running in two parts, portions; **t. de secours,** breakdown train; **t. d'excursion, t. à prix réduit, t. de plaisir,** excursion train; **t. de neige,** winter-sports train; **t. de pèlerinage,** pilgrimage train (to Lourdes, etc.); **t. militaire,** troop train; **t. blindé,** armoured train; **voyager en t., par le t.,** to travel by train; **monter dans le t.,** to get into the train; to board the train; **descendre du t.,** to get out of the train; to leave the train; **comme une vache qui regarde passer un t.,** passively; phlegmatically; in a bovine manner; *F:* **prendre le t. onze,** to go on foot, to foot it; (*d*) *Mil:* train (of transport); *A:* **t. d'artillerie,** artillery train; **le t.,** *A:* **t. des équipages,** *approx.* = transport branch of Army Service Corps; *U.S:* transportation company; (*e*) suite, attendants; train (of servants, etc.); (*f*) (i) quarters (of horse); **t. de derrière, de devant,** hindquarters, forequarters; (ii) *P:* backside, rear (of pers.); **un coup de pied dans le t.,** a kick in the rear; **se manier le t.,** to get a move on; (*g*) **t. de roulement,** undercarriage (of wheeled vehicle); suspension and tracks (of tracked vehicle); *Av:* **t. (d'atterrissage),** landing gear, undercarriage; **t. d'atterrissage fixe, escamotable, largable,** fixed, retractable, droppable, undercarriage; **t. (d'atterrissage) sans essieu,** split undercarriage; **t. (d'atterrissage) chenillé,** tread-type landing gear; **t. (d'atterrissage) à skis,** ski undercarriage; **t. (d'atterrissage) tricycle,** tricycle undercarriage; **t. avant,** nose gear, nose wheel; **t. avant orientable,** steerable nose gear; **rentrer le t. (d'atterrissage),** to retract the wheels, the undercarriage; **sortir le t. (d'atterrissage),** to let down the wheels, the undercarriage; (*h*) *Typ:* (press) carriage. 2. movement; (*a*) pace, rate; **t. d'un cheval,** action, gait, of a horse; **cheval au t. doux,** easy-paced horse; **mener un cheval, une voiture, bon t.,** to drive a horse, a car, at a good rate; to drive fast; **aller bon t.,** to go at a good (round) pace; **les langues allaient leur t.,** tongues were wagging; **avancer d'un t. de sénateur,** to advance, move forward (i) at a dignified pace, solemnly, (ii) pompously; **aller son petit t.,** to jog along; **à grand t.,** at a good rate, pace; **à fond de t.,** at full, top, speed; at full tilt; all out; at a breakneck speed; **au t. dont il va, à ce t.-là,** at the rate he's going, at that rate; **du t. dont vont les choses, au t. où vont les choses,** as things are going; at the rate at which things are progressing; **du t. dont vous allez,** at the rate you are going; **tout d'un t.,** without stopping; *Sp:* **meneur de t.,** pacemaker; **mener le t.,** to set the pace; **mise en t.,** warming-up; **faire tout le t.,** to make all the running; **gagner au t.,** to win at a steady pace; (*b*) **il y a qch. en t.,** there's sth. afoot, in the wind; **mettre qch. en t.,** to start sth.; to set sth. going; to get (negotiations, etc.) under way; *Typ:* **mettre en t.,** to make ready; **mise en t.,** (i) starting (of sth.); getting (sth.) under way; (ii) *Typ:* making ready; *F:* **mettre qn en t.,** to get s.o. going; **pour mettre tout le monde en t.,** in order to brighten up, liven up, the company; **c'est lui qui met tout en t.,** he's the life and soul of the party; *F:* **il était un peu en t.,** he'd had a drop (too much); **l'affaire est mal en t.,** the business is hanging fire, has had a bad start; **les négociations sont en bon t.,** the negotiations have started well, are making good progress; **le malade est en bon t.,** the patient is making a good recovery; **être en t. de faire qch.,** to be busy, in the act of, doing sth.; (*usu. translated simply by the present or past continuous*) **il est en t. d'écrire,** he is writing; **il était en t. de travailler,** he was (busy) working; **j'étais en t. de regarder la télévision quand le téléphone a sonné,** I was watching the television when the telephone rang; **le t. ordinaire des jours,** the daily routine; **demain je reprends le t. du bureau,** tomorrow I go back to my office routine; **les choses vont leur t.,** things are proceeding, going along, as usual; *O:* **être dans le t.,** to be in the swim, in the movement; **il n'est pas dans le t.,** he's not up to date, not abreast of the times; (*c*) **t. de vie,** way of life; **t. de maison,** style of living; **il faut des mille et des cents pour supporter un t. de maison pareil,** it needs a lot of money to keep up such an establishment; **mener grand t.,** to live on a grand scale; **mener un t. d'enfer,** to live it up; (*d*) *F:* noise, row; clatter; **faire du t., faire un t. de tous les diables,** to kick up (the hell of) a row. 3. mood; **être en t.,** to be in good spirits, in good form; **quand il est bien en t.,** when he's at his best; **il n'était pas en t. ce jour-là,** he was below par, wasn't at his best, that day; **être mal en t.,** to be out of sorts; to feel unwell; **je ne suis pas en t. pour travailler,** I'm not in a working mood.

traînage [trɛna:ʒ], *s.m.* (*a*) hauling; *esp.* sledging, sleighing; (*b*) *Min:* haulage (of trains); **câble de t.,** haulage rope; (*c*) sleigh transport; (*d*) (*of balloon on landing*) dragging; (*e*) *T.V:* streaking.

traînailler [trɛnɑje], *F:* 1. *v.tr.* (*a*) **t. la jambe,** to drag one's leg; (*b*) to go on repeating (sth.); to repeat (sth.) over and over again. 2. *v.i.* (*a*) to wander (aimlessly) about; to loaf around; (*b*) to lead a wretched existence; **il traînailla plusieurs mois et finalement mourut,** he dragged on for several months and finally died.

traînance [trɛnɑ̃:s], *s.f. Av:* drag (per unit area).

traînant [trɛnɑ̃], *a.* 1. dragging, trailing (on the ground); **robe traînante,** trailing dress; *Mil: A:* **piques traînantes,** trailing pikes, trailed pikes. 2. languid, listless (life); drawling (voice); shambling, shuffling, slouching (gait); droning (music); drifting (clouds); lifeless (style); **approcher qn d'un pas t.,** to shuffle up to s.o.; **entrer à pas traînants,** to shuffle in; **parler d'un ton t.,** to talk in a singsong voice.

traînard, -arde [trɛna:r, -ard]. 1. *s.* (*a*) straggler, laggard; (*b*) dawdler, *F:* slowcoach. 2. *s.m. Mec.E:* carriage, saddle (of lathe). 3. *a.* slow, dawdling; shuffling (step); drawling, lazy (voice).

traînasse [trɛnas], *s.f.* 1. *Bot:* (*a*) stolon, runner; (*b*) (i) knotgrass, hogweed; (ii) bent (grass). 2. *Ven:* dragnet (for partridges, etc.).

traînassement [trɛnasmɑ̃], *s.m.*, **traînasserie** [trɛnasri], *s.f.* (*a*) wandering (aimlessly) around; loafing; (*b*) spinning out (of business, etc.).

traînasser [trɛnase]. 1. *v.tr. A:* to draw out, spin out (business, speech); to drag out (colourless existence, etc.). 2. *v.i.* to loaf, loiter, trail, about; **t. au lit jusqu'à midi,** to laze in bed until twelve.

train-balai [trɛ̃balɛ], *s.m.* last night train (on surburban line); *pl. trains-balais.*

train-drapeau [trɛ̃drapo], *s.m.* prestige train, crack train; *pl. trains-drapeaux.*

traîne[1] [trɛ:n], *s.f.* 1. (*a*) (act of) being dragged; *Nau:* **à la t.,** (i) (small boat) in tow; (ii) astern; *F:* **être à la t.,** to lag behind; **avoir qch. à la t.,** to have sth. dragging behind one; (*b*) *Ven:* **perdreaux en t.,** unfledged partridges. 2. object, rope, bundle, etc., dragged behind; *esp.* train (of dress); **robe à t.,** dress with a train; **deux petits pages portaient sa t.,** two little pages carried her train. 3. (*a*) drag (of rope walk); (*b*) *Fish:* seine (net), drag net, trail net; **pêcher à la t.,** to troll; **pêche à la t.,** trolling. 4. *Fr.C:* **t. sauvage,** toboggan. 5. *Dial:* sunken road.

traîne[2], *s.f. Turf:* (*of horse*) **être en t.,** to be in training.

traîneau, -eaux [trɛno], *s.m.* 1. sledge, sleigh; **faire une promenade en t.,** to go sledging; **transporter ses vivres en t.,** to sled, sledge, one's provisions; **chien de t.,** sledge dog; husky. 2. *Fish:* = TRAÎNE[1] 3 (*b*). 3. *Agr:* = TRAÎNOIR.

traîne-bûches [trɛnbyʃ], *s.m.inv. Fish: F:* caddis worm, bait.

traîne-buisson [trɛnbɥisɔ̃], *s.m. Orn: F:* hedge warbler, hedge sparrow, dunnock; *pl. traîne-buissons.*

traîne-charrue [trɛnʃary], *s.f. Orn: F:* wheatear; *pl. traîne-charrues.*

traînée [trɛne, trene], *s.f.* 1. (*a*) trail (of smoke, blood, light; of a snail, etc.); train (of gunpowder); belt (of ore, coal); *Av:* t. (de condensation), vapour trail, condensation trail, contrail; semer une t. de persil, to sow a row of parsley; de longues traînées de verdure, long lines of greenery; se répandre comme une t. de poudre, to spread like wildfire; (*b*) *Av: etc:* (effort, force, de) t., drag; (*c*) *Ball:* air lag (of bomb); t. réelle, trail. 2. *Fish:* ground line, bottom line. 3. *Bot:* runner. 4. *P:* prostitute; promiscuous woman.

traîne-la-patte [trɛnlapat], *s.m.inv. F:* (*a*) tramp, *U.S:* hobo; (*b*) weary Willie, slacker.

traîne-lattes [trɛnlat], *s.m.inv. P:* person who lives miserably, wretchedly; tramp, *U.S:* hobo.

traînelle [trɛnɛl], *s.f. Bot: F:* white clover, Dutch clover.

traîne-malheur [trɛnmalœːr], *s.m.inv.*, **traîne-misère** [trɛnmizɛːr], *s.m.inv. F:* miserable wretch.

traînement [trɛnmɑ̃], *s.m.* dragging, trailing; drawling (of voice).

traîne-patins [trɛnpatɛ̃], *s.m.inv. P:* = TRAÎNE-LATTES.

traîne-pattes [trɛnpat], *s.m.inv. P:* = TRAÎNE-LA-PATTE.

traîner [trɛne, trene]. 1. *v.tr.* to drag, pull, trail, haul, draw, (s.o., sth.) along; to tow (barges); to drag on, drag out (one's existence); to spin out, drag out (speech, business, etc.); to drawl (one's words); la locomotive traînait vingt-cinq wagons, the locomotive was pulling, hauling, twenty-five trucks; elle traînait cinq enfants après elle, she was trailing five children after her; *Hist:* le chariot de la Liberté était traîné par quatre bœufs, the Car of Liberty was drawn by four oxen; t. une vie de misère, to drag out a wretched existence; pendant dix ans encore il traîna une vie pénible, he dragged out his life for another ten years; t. la jambe, (i) to shuffle, hobble, limp, along; (ii) to be lame, to have a limp; t. le pied, to lag behind; s'avancer en traînant le pas, to slouch, shuffle, along; la perdrix traînait l'aile, traînait de l'aile, the partridge was dragging a wing; t. qn en prison, to drag s.o. off to prison; t. qn dans la boue, dans la fange, to drag s.o., s.o.'s name, through the mud, through the mire. 2. *v.i.* (*a*) to trail, draggle (in the dust, etc.); votre robe traîne, your dress is trailing; (*b*) to lag behind; to trail behind; to straggle; (*c*) to linger, loiter, dawdle; il passe sa journée à t. dans la rue, par les rues, he spends his day loafing about the streets; ne traîne pas dans la rue en rentrant de l'école, don't loiter on your way home from school; (*with cogn.acc.*) t. la rue, t. les rues, to loaf about; il traîne dehors toutes les nuits, he is never in at night; (*d*) to lie about; laisser t. son argent, to leave one's money lying about; habits qui traînent sur le plancher, clothes littering the floor; il emploie de ces adjectifs qui traînent partout, he uses adjectives that are in everybody's mouth; (*e*) to flag, droop, languish; il traîne depuis longtemps, he has been in poor health, has been ailing, for some time; l'affaire traîne, the matter is hanging fire; intrigue, conversation, qui traîne, plot, conversation, that drags; (*of lawsuit, etc.*) t. en longueur, to go on very slowly, to drag (on); les choses ne traînent pas avec vous, you don't let the grass grow under your feet; *F:* allez mettre votre chapeau et que ça ne traîne pas! go and put your hat on and don't be half an hour about it! laisser t. un compte, to leave an account unpaid.

se traîner. 1. (*a*) to crawl (along); il se traîna jusqu'au fossé, he crawled to the ditch; (*b*) se t. aux genoux de qn, to go on one's knees to s.o.; to make a desperate appeal to s.o.. 2. to drag oneself along; to trail along; to move with difficulty; il se traîne sur des béquilles, he drags himself about on crutches; il se traînait à peine, he could hardly drag himself along; je ne peux pas me t. plus loin, I can't drag my feet another step; les heures se traînent lourdement, time drags (heavily); time hangs heavy; des fumées se traînent dans le ciel, trails of smoke are drifting across the sky; the sky is streaked with smoke.

traînerie [trɛnri], *s.f.* (*a*) delay; dawdling; (*b*) *Mus:* dragging.

traîne-sabots [trɛnsabo], **traîne-savates** [trɛnsavat], **traîne-semelles** [trɛnsəmɛl], *s.m.inv.* = TRAÎNE-LATTES.

traîneur, -euse [trɛnœːr, -øːz], *s.* 1. (*a*) dragger, trailer (of sth.); *Min:* t. de wagonnets, hauler, drawer (of hutches); hutch runner; barrow man; *F:* t. de sabre, (i) swaggerer, swashbuckler; (ii) *Pej: Mil:* officer (in the permanent army); (*b*) *Ven:* netter (of partridges). 2. (*a*) *O:* straggler, laggard; dawdler; (*b*) *F:* t. de cafés, pub crawler; (*c*) *Ven:* hound that fails to follow the pack. 3. sleigh driver.

trainglot [trɛ̃glo], *s.m. P:* soldier in the French Army Service Corps.

training [trɛniŋ], *s.m.* (*a*) *Sp:* training; (*b*) *Psy:* t. autogène, training by autosuggestion.

traînoir [trɛnwaːr], *s.m. Agr:* bush harrow, brush harrow.

train-paquebot [trɛ̃pakbo], *s.m. A:* boat train; *pl. trains-paquebots.*

train-parc [trɛ̃park], *s.m.* train equipped with living quarters and store rooms for linesmen; *pl. trains-parcs.*

train-poste [trɛ̃pɔst], *s.m.* mail train; *pl. trains-poste.*

train-train [trɛ̃trɛ̃], *s.m. F:* routine, daily round; le t.-t. quotidien de la vie, the ordinary humdrum daily routine; rien qui sort du t.-t. des événements ordinaires, nothing out of the ordinary; nothing to break the (monotomy of the) routine; s'en aller de son t.-t. habituel, to jog along.

traire [trɛːr], *v.tr.* (*pr.p.* trayant; *p.p.* trait; *pr.ind.* je trais, n. trayons, ils traient; *p.d.* je trayais; *fu.* je trairai; *no p.h.*) t. une vache, etc., t. le lait d'une vache, etc., to milk a cow, etc.; machine à t., milker, milking machine; vache mal traite, badly-milked cow.

trait[1] [trɛ]. 1. *a.* wire-drawn (gold, silver). 2. *s.m.* gold wire (for gold lace, etc.).

trait[2], *s.m.* 1. (*a*) pulling, pull (of cord, weight); *A:* donner le premier t., to set sth. going; to start up a business, begin a matter; (*at chess or draughts*) avoir le t., to have first move; donner deux traits à qn, to allow s.o. two moves at the start; tout d'un t., at one stretch; écrire deux chapitres d'un t., to write two chapters at one stretch, one sitting; t. de balance, turn of the scale; cheval de t., draught horse, carthorse; cheval de gros t., heavy draught horse; (*b*) trace (of harness); le cheval s'empêtra dans les traits, the horse got tangled in the traces; (*c*) avoir un faux t. dans les yeux, to have a cast in one eye. 2. (*a*) armes de t., missile weapons; (*b*) arrow, dart, *Poet:* shaft; partir comme un t., to be off like an arrow, like a shot; *Lit:* les traits de l'Amour, Cupid's darts; les traits de Jupiter, Jove's thunderbolts; t. de médisance, piece, stroke, of slander; t. de satire, stroke of satire; gibe; envoyer, lancer, un t. à qn, to have a dig at s.o.; (*c*) beam (of light); le soleil darde ses traits, the sun is darting its beams; (*d*) flash (of light); t. d'esprit, flash, stroke, of wit; witticism; (*e*) *Mus:* (i) brilliant passage; (ii) run; (iii) melodic passage; (*f*) stroke (of file, etc.). 3. draught, gulp; boire qch. à longs traits, to drink sth. in long draughts; to gulp down (beer, etc.); d'un (seul) t., at one gulp; *F:* at one go. 4. (*a*) stroke, mark, line, streak, bar; d'un t. de plume, with a stroke of the pen; t. plein, continuous line; t. discontinu, broken line; en traits mixtes, chain-dotted; largeur de t., stroke width; dessin au t., outline drawing; copier qch. t. pour t., to copy sth. line by line; to make an exact replica of sth.; gravure au t., line engraving; les grands traits de qch., the main outlines, main features, of sth.; décrire qch. à grands traits, to give a general outline of sth.; to make a rapid picture of sth.; vous feriez mieux de tirer un t. sur cette affaire, you'd better forget the incident; *Tg:* points et traits, dots and dashes; (*b*) t. d'union, hyphen; ligne qui sert de t. d'union entre deux villes, line that serves as a link between two towns, that links up two towns; (*c*) kerf, saw cut. 5. (*a*) feature, lineament (of face); traits réguliers, regular features; traits fins, delicate features; traits grossiers, coarse features; (*b*) trait (of character); characteristic touch (of writer, etc.). 6. act, deed (of courage, kindness, etc.); t. de génie, stroke of genius; ce sont là de ses traits, those are some of his tricks; *F:* homme qui fait des traits à sa femme, husband who deceives his wife; scapegrace husband. 7. reference, bearing, connection; avoir t. à qch., to have reference to sth.; to refer to sth.; convention ayant t. à . . ., agreement relating to . . .; cela n'a aucun t. à la question, that has no relation to, does not bear on, the question; that is irrelevant; note ayant t. à un contrat, note on a contract.

traitable [trɛtabl], *a.* (*a*) (*of pers.*) tractable, manageable, docile; accommodating; (*b*) treatable; *Ind: etc:* tractable, manageable, malleable (material); certains sujets sont difficilement traitables, it is difficult to treat certain subjects.

traitant [trɛtɑ̃]. 1. *a.* médecin t., attending physician, doctor in attendance; mon médecin t., my (usual) doctor. 2. *s.m.* (*a*) *Hist:* farmer of revenue, of taxes; (*b*) *A:* t. des blanches, white-slaver.

traite [trɛt], *s.f.* 1. stretch (of road); stage (of journey); j'ai fait une longue t., I have come a long way; (tout) d'une t., at a stretch, without interruption, straight off the reel. 2. transport (of goods), trading; la t. de l'ivoire, the ivory trade; *A:* la t. des noirs, des nègres, *abs.* la traite, the slave trade; t. des blanches, white-slave trade, white slavery; t. des femmes et des enfants, traffic in women and children. 3. *Fin:* (*a*) drawing (of a bill of exchange, etc.); (*b*) (banker's) draft; bill (of exchange); t. en l'air, fictitious bill, *F:* kite; faire t. sur qn, to draw (a bill) on s.o.; t. à courte, à longue, échéance, short-dated, long-dated, bill; t. avalisée, guaranteed bill; t. à vue, draft at sight; t. sur l'étranger, sur l'extérieur, foreign bill; t. sur l'intérieur, inland bill; envoyer une t. à l'encaissement, to send a bill for collection; présenter une t. à l'acceptation, to present a bill for acceptance; escompter une t. avant l'échéance, to discount a bill before it falls due; (*c*) (hire purchase) payment, instalment. 4. (*a*) milking; t. mécanique, machine milking; (*b*) (the milk of one) milking.

traité[1] [trɛte], *s.m.* 1. treatise (de, sur, on); *Sch:* t. élémentaire de physique, elementary physics. 2. treaty, compact, agreement; préparer, négocier, conclure, un t., to arrange, to negotiate, to conclude, a treaty (avec, with); t. d'alliance, de paix, treaty of alliance, of peace; t. de commerce, commercial treaty; t. d'arbitrage, arbitration treaty; le T. de Berlin, de Versailles, the Treaty of Berlin, of Versailles; être en t. avec qn pour . . ., to be in treaty, to be negotiating, with s.o. for . . .; passer un t. avec une compagnie, to conclude an agreement with a company.

traité[2], *a.* treated; processed; *Agr: Hort:* (*of vines, fruit trees, etc.*) treated, sprayed (with sulphur, etc.); *Elcs:* (*computers*) données non traitées, raw data; *Phot:* objectif t., coated lens.

traitement [trɛtmɑ̃], *s.m.* 1. treatment; (*a*) mauvais t., ill-usage, maltreatment; enfant qui a subi de mauvais traitements, child that has been ill-used, badly treated; t. brutal, rough treatment; *Med:* premier t., first aid; initial treatment; t. chirurgical, surgery; operation; t. orthopédique, orthopaedic treatment; t. thermique, heat treatment; malade en t., patient under(going) treatment; (*b*) processing, treatment (of raw materials); t. des minerais, treatment of ores; t. anodique, anodising (in electrolysis); t. chimique, chemical processing; t. par voie humide, sèche, wet, dry, treatment; t. thermique, heat treatment; *Metall: etc:* t. de surface, surface treatment, surfacing; *Civ.E: etc:* t. superficiel, surfacing (of road, etc.); *Av:* t. de stabilisation, stress relieving; *Ind:* capacité de t., handling capacity; (*c*) *Elcs:* (*computers*) t. (automatique) de l'information, (automatic) data processing; t. direct, immédiat, in-line processing; t. en différé, off-line processing; t. différé, batch processing; t. non ordonné, random processing; t. multi-tâches, multitask operation; t. multi-travaux, multijob operation; t. numérique, digital processing; données en t., capacité, débit, de t., throughput; unité centrale de t., central processing unit, *U.S:* main frame; unité de t., task, job; t. en temps partagé, time sharing; t. à distance, teleprocessing. 2. salary; (officers') pay; augmenter les traitements du corps enseignant, to raise the teachers' salaries; *Mil: Navy:* t. de table, table money; secrétaire sans t., honorary secretary; magistrats sans t., unsalaried magistrates.

traiter [trete], *v.tr.* to treat. 1. (*a*) to behave towards (s.o.); vous m'avez fort bien traité, you have treated me very kindly, very well; sa tante la traite mal, her aunt treats her badly, unkindly; her aunt is unkind, *F:* beastly, to her; t. qn avec civilité, to treat s.o. courteously, politely; t. qn de haut en bas, to be patronizing to s.o.; t. qn comme un chien, to treat s.o. like a dog; t. qn comme un ami, en ami, to treat s.o. like, as, a friend; t. qn en enfant, to treat s.o. like, as, a child; t. qn d'égal, to treat s.o. as an equal; (*b*) to call, style; t. qn de lâche, d'enfant, to call s.o. a coward, a child; ils se traitaient d'imbéciles, they called each other fools; (*c*) *Med:* t. un malade, une maladie, to treat a patient, a disease; se faire t. d'un cancer, to undergo treatment for cancer; (*d*) *Ind:* to process; t. le quartz par le mercure, to treat quartz with mercury; (*e*) *esp. Lit:* to entertain (s.o.); **il nous a traités magnifiquement,** he gave us a magnificent reception, a superb dinner; **restaurateur qui traite bien ses clients,** restaurateur who serves his customers well. **2.** (*a*) to negotiate (deal, marriage, etc.); to handle (business); **t. une opération avec qn,** to transact a piece of business with s.o.; **le blé se traitait à cent francs le quintal,** wheat was being dealt in at a hundred francs a quintal; (*b*) to discuss, handle, deal with (subject); **t. une question,** to treat, deal with, a question; **t. légèrement les choses,** to make light of things. **3.** *v.i.* (*a*) to negotiate, deal; **t. de la paix,** *abs. A:* **traiter,** to treat for peace; **t. avec ses créanciers,** to treat, negotiate, with one's creditors; **t. pour un nouveau local,** to negotiate, be in treaty, for new premises; (*b*) (*of book*) **t. d'un sujet,** to treat of, deal with, a subject; **chapitre qui traite de . . .,** chapter dealing with . . ..

traiteur [trɛtœːr], *s.m.* (*a*) *A:* restaurateur; (*b*) caterer.

traitoir [trɛtwaːr], *s.m.*, **traitoire** [trɛtwaːr], *s.f. Coop:* hoop cramp.

traître, traîtresse [trɛːtr, trɛtrɛs]. **1.** *a.* treacherous, traitorous, perfidious (person); vicious (animal); dangerous, treacherous (stair, crevasse, etc.); *Lit:* **t. à l'honneur,** false to honour; *F:* **il n'en a pas dit un t. mot,** he didn't breathe a word about it. **2.** *s.* (*a*) traitor, traitress; **en t.,** treacherously; **prendre qn en t.,** to attack s.o. when off his guard; to deal treacherously with s.o.; (*b*) *Th:* **le t.,** the villain.

traîtreusement [trɛtrøzmɑ̃], *adv.* treacherously perfidiously; **attaquer t. (qn),** to make a treacherous attack on (s.o.).

traîtrise [trɛtriːz], *s.f.* **1.** treachery, treacherousness. **2.** piece of treachery.

Trajan [traʒɑ̃], *Pr.n.m. Rom.Hist:* Trajan.

Trajane [traʒan], *a.f. Rom.Ant:* **la colonne T.,** Trajan's column.

trajectographie [traʒɛktɔgrafi], *s.f. Ball:* trajectory calculation.

trajectoire [traʒɛktwaːr]. **1.** *s.f.* (*a*) *Astr:* path (of star); trajectory (of comet, meteorite); *Space:* trajectory (of satellite); *Astr:* **t. apparente,** apparent path; *Space:* **satellite lancé sur une t. tenue secrète,** satellite launched into undisclosed trajectory; *Meteor:* **t. d'une dépression,** path of a depression; (*b*) *Ball:* trajectory (of projectile); **gerbe de trajectoires,** sheaf of trajectories; **t. courbe,** curved trajectory; **t. rasante, tendue,** flat, low, trajectory; *Artil:* **t. d'écrêtement,** mean grazing trajectory; (*c*) *Atom.Ph:* **t. électronique,** electron path; **t. ionique,** ion path; (*d*) *Av: etc:* path, course; **t. de vol,** flight path; **t. de collision,** collision course; **t. de poursuite,** pursuit course; **t. consécutive,** overshoot path; **t. rectiligne,** straight course. **2.** *a. Mth:* **ligne t.,** trajectory.

trajet [traʒɛ], *s.m.* (*a*) journey (by railway, etc.); (length of) ride, drive, flight, etc.; passage (*e.g.* of food through the alimentary tract); **t. de mer, par mer,** passage, crossing; **faire le t. de Calais à Douvres,** to cross, make the crossing, from Calais to Dover; **un t. de deux heures,** a two hour journey, run, ride, crossing; **parcourir un long t.,** to travel a long way; **le t. n'est pas long,** it is quite a short way, quite a short distance; **j'ai fait une partie du t. en avion,** I flew part of the way; **sur le t. du restaurant,** on the way to the restaurant; (*b*) *Tex:* passage (of the shuttle); (*c*) course (of artery, nerve, etc.; of fistula; of bullet through the body, etc.; of projectile through space); path (of projectile, etc.); *El:* **t. du courant,** current path; *Med:* **t. fistuleux,** sinus tract.

tralala [tralala], *s.m.inv.* **1.** tra-la-la, tol-de-rol (as song refrain). **2.** *F:* fuss; splash; **recevoir à dîner en grand t.,** to make a great splash about giving a dinner party; **être sur son t., en grand t.,** to be all dressed up, togged up.

trale [tral], *s.f. Fish:* dragnet, trawl.

tram [tram], *s.m. Trans: F:* tram; *U.S:* streetcar.

tramail [tramaːj], *s.m. Fish: Ven:* trammel (net); *pl. tramails.*

trame [tram], *s.f.* **1.** *Tex:* (*a*) woof, weft; *Lit:* **la t. de la vie, d'un discours,** the web, thread, of life; the texture of a speech; (*b*) union linen; (*c*) tram (silk). **2.** plot, conspiracy; **ourdir une t.,** to hatch, concoct, a plot. **3.** (*a*) *Phot.Engr:* (half-tone) screen; *Phot:* **effet de t.,** canvas effect; *Engr:* **t. fine,** fine screen; **grosse t.,** coarse screen; **t. lignée,** ruled screen, one-way screen; **lignage de t.,** screen ruling; **t. quadrillée,** square-ruled screen, cross-lined screen; **t. de soie,** silk-screen process; serigraphy; **angle de t.,** screen angle; **écart de t.,** screen distance; **ouverture de t.,** screen aperture; **porte-t.,** screen carrier; (*b*) *T.V:* raster; **t. (double),** frame.

tramer [trame], *v.tr.* **1.** (*a*) *Tex:* to weave; (*b*) **t. une action,** to weave the plot (of novel, play, etc.); (*c*) **t. un complot,** to hatch a plot; **il se trame quelque chose,** a plot (of some sort) is being hatched; there's something in the wind, something afoot. **2.** *Phot.Engr:* **t. un cliché,** to take a negative through a (ruled half-tone) screen; **similigravure tramée,** half-tone process.

tramète [tramɛt], *s.m. Fung:* trametes.

trameur, -euse [tramœːr, -øːz], *s. Tex:* **1.** weft winder, weft-room hand. **2.** *s.f.* **trameuse,** weft-winding machine.

traminot [tramino], *s.m.* tramway employee, *U.S:* streetcar employee.

tramois [tramwa], *s.m. Agr:* **1.** spring wheat. **2.** mixed fodder crop (of wheat, rye, oats and vetch).

tramontane [tramɔ̃tan], *s.f.* **1.** (*a*) *A:* **la t.,** (i) the north; (ii) the north star, polestar; (*b*) **perdre la t.,** to lose one's bearings; to lose one's head. **2.** *Meteor:* (*in N. Mediterranean area*) tramontana.

tramp [trɑ̃ːp], *s.m. Nau:* tramp (steamer).

tramping [trɑ̃piŋ], *s.m. Nau:* tramping.

tramway [tramwɛ], *s.m.* **1.** tramway; **t. à câbles,** cable tramway; **t. aérien,** overhead tramway. **2.** tram, *U.S:* streetcar; **j'ai pris le t., je suis venu par le t.,** I came by tram.

tranchage [trɑ̃ʃaːʒ], *s.m.* cutting, slicing (of wood for veneer, etc.); slabbing (of marble, etc.).

tranchant [trɑ̃ʃɑ̃]. **1.** *a.* (*a*) cutting, sharp (tool, sword, etc.); keen (edge); **outil t.,** edge-tool; *Cr:* **coup t.,** cut; (*b*) trenchant, decisive (words, opinion); trenchant (argument); sharp, peremptory (tone); self-assertive (person); (*c*) sharply contrasted (colours); loud, glaring (colour); glaring (contradiction); (*d*) *Hist:* **écuyer t.,** gentleman carver; carver (to the King). **2.** *s.m.* (*a*) (cutting) edge (of knife, etc.); thin edge, end (of wedge); edge (of tennis racket); **mettre le t. à une lame,** to put an edge on a blade; to grind a blade; **épée, argument, à double t., à deux tranchants,** two-edged sword; double-edged argument; argument that cuts both ways; **se frayer un chemin du t. et de la pointe,** (i) *A:* to make one's way cutting and thrusting; (ii) to hack one's way through; **faux t. du sabre,** back of the sword; (*b*) *Leath:* fleshing knife.

tranche [trɑ̃ːʃ], *s.f.* **1.** (*a*) slice (of bread, melon, etc.); round (of beef, etc.); **t. de lard,** slice, rasher, of bacon; **t. de rôti,** cut off the joint; **en tranches,** in slices, sliced; **couper du jambon en tranches,** to slice (up) ham; **la t. des salariés moyens,** the middle-income bracket; *F:* **une t. de vie,** a slice of life; a cross-section of life; *F:* **se payer une t. de rire,** to have a good laugh; *F:* **s'en payer une t.,** (i) to have the time of one's life; (ii) to have a good laugh; (*b*) block, portion (of an issue of shares, etc.); *Adm:* **par t. de 1000 francs ou fraction de 1000 francs,** for every complete sum of 1000 francs or part thereof; **émettre un emprunt en tranches,** to issue a loan in instalments; *Ar:* **t. de trois chiffres,** group of three figures (in the decimal notation); *Rail:* **t. de voitures,** portion (of train). **2.** (*a*) slab (of marble, stone); *Cu:* **t. napolitaine,** Neapolitan ice (cream); (*b*) *Agr:* slab, slice, of earth (turned by the plough); ridge, furrow; (*c*) *Geol:* **t. de couche,** outcrop; (*d*) **t. grasse,** round, top rump (of beef). **3.** (*a*) face (of wheel, of gun muzzle, etc.); (*b*) edge (of coin, plank); **t. cannelée,** milling (of coin); (*c*) (cut) edge (of book); **livre doré sur t.,** gilt-edged book; (*d*) section; **t. verticale,** vertical section. **4.** *N.Arch:* **t. cellulaire,** cellular compartment (of ship). **5.** *Tls:* set, chisel; **t. à chaud, à froid,** hot set, cold set.

tranché [trɑ̃ʃe]. **1.** *a.* well-marked, distinct (colour, pattern, etc.); clear-cut (opinion); **refus t.,** blunt, categoric, refusal. **2.** *a. & s.m. Her:* tranché; party per bend.

tranchée [trɑ̃ʃe], *s.f.* **1.** (*a*) trench; *Agr:* drain; *Rail:* cutting; *Mil:* **guerre de tranchées,** trench warfare; **t. de première ligne,** first-line trench; **t. individuelle,** slit trench; rifle pit; **fausse t.,** dummy trench; **t. de départ,** jump-off trench; **t. de soutien,** support trench; **monter aux tranchées,** to go into the trenches; **descendre des tranchées,** to leave the trenches; (*b*) cutting (through forest); **t. garde-feu,** fire break. **2.** *pl.* colic, griping pains, tormina; *Obst:* **tranchées utérines,** after-pains; *Vet:* **tranchées rouges,** gripes, violent colic (in horses).

tranchée-abri [trɑ̃ʃeabri], *s.f. Mil:* shelter trench; *pl. tranchées-abris.*

tranchefil [trɑ̃ʃfil], *s.m. Harn:* curb chain.

tranchefile [trɑ̃ʃfil], *s.f. Bookb:* headband.

tranchefiler [trɑ̃ʃfile], *v.tr. Bookb:* to put a headband on (book).

tranche-gazon [trɑ̃ʃgazɔ̃], *s.m.inv. Hort:* (*a*) sod cutter, turfing-iron; (*b*) grass-edging iron, knife.

tranchelard [trɑ̃ʃlaːr], *s.m.* cook's knife.

tranchement [trɑ̃ʃmɑ̃], *s.m.* cutting; carving.

tranche-montagne [trɑ̃ʃmɔ̃taɲ], *s.m. F:* braggart, blusterer, fire-eater; **d'un air de t.-m.,** blusteringly; *pl. tranche-montagnes.*

tranche-pain [trɑ̃ʃpɛ̃], *s.m.inv.* bread cutter.

tranche-papier [trɑ̃ʃpapje], *s.m.inv.* paper knife.

trancher [trɑ̃ʃe]. **1.** *v.tr.* (*a*) to slice (bread, etc.); to cut; **couteau qui tranche comme un rasoir,** knife that cuts like a razor; **t. du bois,** to slice (off) wood; **t. du marbre,** to slab marble; **t. une peau,** to flesh a skin; **t. la tête à qn,** to cut off s.o.'s head; *abs.* **t. dans le vif,** (i) *Surg:* to use the knife; (ii) to adopt trenchant, drastic, uncompromising, measures; to have done with half measures; *Lit:* **la Parque a tranché ses jours,** fate cut the thread of his life; (*b*) to cut short (discussion, s.o.'s career); to settle (question) out of hand, once and for all; to make short work of (problem, difficulty); **t. le mot,** to speak plainly; to speak out; *abs.* **pour t. net,** to cut it short; **tranchons là,** that's enough; let us say no more; **il t. sur tout,** he is so positive, so dogmatic, so cocksure; he's always laying down the law; (*c*) *Cr:* to cut (ball); (*d*) to decide, settle, solve (difficulty, question); **t. un différend,** to settle (s.o. else's) quarrel. **2.** *v.i.* (*a*) (*of colours, characteristics, etc.*) to contrast strongly (**sur,** with); to stand out clearly; **t. sur le ciel,** to stand out against the sky; (*b*) **t. du bel esprit, du philosophe,** to set up for a wit, for a philosopher; (*c*) *A:* to carve (at table).

tranchet [trɑ̃ʃɛ], *s.m. Tls:* **1. t. (d'enclume),** anvil cutter. **2.** (shoemaker's, etc.) paring knife.

tranche-tête [trɑ̃ʃtɛːt], *s.m.inv. A:* headsman.

trancheur, -euse [trɑ̃ʃœːr, -øːz]. **1.** (*a*) *a. Hist:* **plat t.,** trencher; (*b*) *s.m. Fish:* cod knife. **2.** *s.m.* (*pers.*) (*a*) *Tchn: Min:* cutter; (*b*) carver (in restaurant, etc.); (*c*) *Fish:* cod gutter and preparer. **3** *s.f.* **trancheuse,** stone saw; **trancheuse verticale,** vertical saw.

tranchoir [trɑ̃ʃwaːr], *s.m.* **1.** *Dom.Ec:* trencher, chopping board. **2.** *Ich:* zanclus; Moorish idol. **3.** *Hort:* (*a*) turfing iron; (*b*) grass-edging iron.

tranquille [trɑ̃kil], *a.* tranquil; (*a*) calm, still, quiet (sea, etc.); steady (compass); quiet (horse); **cours d'eau t.,** placid stream; **il ne peut pas rester t.,** he can't keep still; he's a fidget; **se tenir t.,** (i) to keep still; (ii) to keep quiet; **nous nous tenons tranquilles aujourd'hui,** we are having a quiet day; **tenez-vous tranquilles!** be quiet! *Com:* **marché t.,** easy market; dull market; (*b*) quiet, peaceful (town, people, etc.); **un quartier t.,** a quiet, respectable, neighbourhood; **voisins tranquilles,** quiet neighbours; (*c*) undisturbed, untroubled, unruffled, easy (conscience, mind, etc.); *F:* **un père t.,** a placid sort of man; **vous pouvez dormir t.,** you can sleep in peace; **avoir l'esprit t.,** to be easy in one's mind; **ne pas avoir l'esprit t.,** to be uneasy, uncomfortable, in one's mind (**au sujet de,** about); **laissez-moi t.,** leave me alone; let me be; **soyez t. (là-dessus),** set your mind at rest, at ease, about that; **soyez t., il reviendra,** he'll come back, never fear! *F:* **il ne disait rien, mais il avait pris une décision, je suis t.,** he wasn't letting on, but he had made up his mind, I'm sure.

tranquillement [trɑ̃kilmɑ̃], *adv.* tranquilly, calmly, quietly, peacefully; **il a dormi t.,** he has had a quiet sleep.

tranquillisant [trɑ̃kilizɑ̃]. **1.** *a.* tranquillizing, reassuring (news, etc.); soothing (effect). **2.** *s.m. Med:* tranquillizer.

tranquillisation [trɑ̃kilizasjɔ̃], *s.f.* tranquillization; *Mec.E:* **chambre de t.,** plenum chamber.

tranquilliser [trɑ̃kilize], *v.tr.* to tranquillize; to reassure (s.o.) (**sur,** on, about); to set at rest, soothe, calm (the mind, etc.).

se tranquilliser. 1. (*of the sea, etc.*) to calm down. **2. tranquillisez-vous là-dessus,** don't be uneasy, set your mind at rest, about that; make yourself easy about that.

tranquillité [trɑ̃kilite], *s.f.* **1.** (*a*) tranquillity, calm(ness), peace, quiet, stillness; **troubler la t. publique,** to disturb the peace; **la t. de la mer,** the calmness of the sea; **la t. du soir,** the stillness, quiet, peace, of the evening; **vous pouvez partir en toute t.,** you can leave with an easy mind; (*b*) quietness (of horse). **2. t. d'esprit,** peace of mind.

trans [trɑ̃ːs], *a. Ch:* trans (isomer).

trans- [trɑ̃s-, trɑ̃z-], *pref.* trans-.

transaction [trɑ̃zaksjɔ̃], *s.f.* **1.** (*a*) *Com:* transaction; *pl.* dealings, deals; (*b*) *pl.* **transactions d'une société, etc.**, transactions, proceedings of a society. **2.** (*a*) *Jur:* settlement arrived at by parties *inter se*; arrangement, compromise; *Com:* composition; **accepter une t.**, to agree to a compromise; (*b*) *Pej:* **t. avec sa conscience, t. de conscience**, compromise with one's conscience.

transactionnel, -elle [trɑ̃zaksjɔnɛl], *a.* (*of agreement, etc.*) in the nature of a compromise; **arriver à une solution transactionnelle**, to effect a compromise.

transafricain [trɑ̃zafrikɛ̃]. **1.** *a.* transafrican. **2.** *A: s.m.* **le T.**, the Cape-to-Cairo railway.

transalpin [trɑ̃zalpɛ̃], *a.* transalpine ((i) from the Italian viewpoint; (ii) from the French viewpoint); *A.Hist:* **la Gaule transalpine**, Transalpine Gaul (north of the Alps).

transaméricain [trɑ̃zamerikɛ̃], *a.* transamerican.

transaminase [trɑ̃zaminaːz], *s.f. Bio-Ch:* transaminase.

transamination [trɑ̃zaminasjɔ̃], *s.f. Bio-Ch:* transamination.

transandin [trɑ̃zɑ̃dɛ̃], *a. Geog:* trans-Andean.

transat [trɑ̃zat], *F:* **1.** *s.m.* (*a*) liner; (*b*) deck chair. **2.** *s.f. Nau:* **la T.** (= *la Compagnie générale transatlantique*) = the French line.

transatlantique [trɑ̃zatlɑ̃tik]. **1.** *a.* transatlantic; **les câbles transatlantiques**, transatlantic cables. **2.** *s.m.* (*a*) (Atlantic) liner; (*b*) (hammock) deck chair.

transaustralien, -ienne [trɑ̃zostraljɛ̃, -jɛn]. **1.** *a.* trans-Australian. **2.** *s.m.* **le T.**, the trans-Australian railway.

transbahutement [trɑ̃sbaytmɑ̃], *s.m. F:* transferring; transporting; moving around; **épuisé par le t. de son bagage**, worn out with carting, humping, his luggage around.

transbahuter [trɑ̃sbayte], *v.tr. F:* (*a*) to transport, move, shift; **t. une armoire**, to move, shift, a wardrobe; **tout le bazar que j'ai à t.**, all the stuff I've got to shift, cart around; **si je n'avais pas à me t.!** if only I hadn't to move, to shift! (*b*) **t. des touristes d'un musée à l'autre**, to shepherd tourists from one museum to another.

Transbaïkalie [trɑ̃sbaikali], *Pr.n.f. Geog:* Transbaikalia.

transbordement [trɑ̃sbɔrdmɑ̃, trɑ̃z-], *s.m.* **1.** (*a*) transhipment (of cargo, passengers); **effectuer, opérer, un t.**, to tranship; (*b*) *Rail: etc:* transfer (of goods, passengers) from one train, plane, etc., to another; **frais de t.**, reloading charges. **2.** ferrying across. **3.** *Rail:* traversing (of trucks, etc.).

transborder [trɑ̃sbɔrde, trɑ̃z-], *v.tr.* **1.** (*a*) to tranship (cargo, passengers); (*b*) *Rail: etc:* to transfer (passengers, goods) from one train, plane, etc., to another. **2.** to convey, ferry, (passengers, etc.) across river, etc. **3.** *Rail:* to traverse (locomotive, etc.).

transbordeur [trɑ̃sbɔrdœːr, trɑ̃z-], *a. & s.m.* (**pont**) **t.**, transporter bridge; **bac t.**, transporter ferry, train ferry; *Rail:* (**chariot**) **t.**, traverser.

transcanadien, -ienne [trɑ̃skanadjɛ̃, -jɛn], *a.* trans-Canada; **route transcanadienne**, Trans-Canada Highway.

transcaspien, -ienne, [traskaspjɛ̃, -jɛn]. **1.** *a.* transcaspian. **2.** *s.m.* **le T.**, the Transcaspian railway.

Transcaucasie [trɑ̃skokazi], *Pr.n.f. Geog:* Transcaucasia.

transcaucasien, -ienne [trɑ̃skokazjɛ̃, -jɛn], *a.* Transcaucasian.

transcendance [trɑ̃s(s)ɑ̃dɑ̃ːs], *s.f. Phil: Theol: etc:* transcendency, transcendence.

transcendant [trɑ̃s(s)ɑ̃dɑ̃], *a.* **1.** transcendent (merit, genius, etc.); *Phil:* **idées transcendantes**, transcendent ideas; *F:* **il n'a rien de t.**, he's not much to write home about. **2.** *Mth:* transcendental (function, equation, etc.).

transcendantal, transcendental, -aux [trɑ̃sɑ̃dɑ̃tal, -o], *a. Phil:* transcendental.

transcendantalisme [trɑ̃s(s)ɑ̃dɑ̃talism], *s.m. Phil:* transcendentalism.

transcendantaliste [trɑ̃s(s)ɑ̃dɑ̃talist]. **1.** *a.* transcendental. **2.** *s.m.* transcendentalist.

transcender [trɑ̃s(s)ɑ̃de], *v.tr.* (*a*) *Phil:* to transcend; (*b*) *F:* to be superior to; to go beyond.

transcodage [trɑ̃skɔdaːʒ], *s.m. Elcs:* (*computers*) transcribing.

transcoder [trɑ̃skɔde], *v.tr. Elcs:* (*computers*) to transcribe.

transcontinental, -aux [trɑ̃skɔ̃tinɑ̃tal, -o], *a.* transcontinental.

transcripteur [trɑ̃skriptœːr], *s.m.* transcriber.

transcription [trɑ̃skripsjɔ̃], *s.f.* **1.** (*a*) transcription, transcribing; *Jur:* registration (of divorce, etc.); *Book-k:* posting (of journal); (*b*) **t. d'un alphabet en un autre**, transliteration (into phonetic script, etc.). **2.** (*a*) transcript, copy; (*b*) *Mus:* transcription (of song for violin, etc.).

transcrire [trɑ̃skriːr], *v.tr.* (*conj. like* ÉCRIRE) **1.** (*a*) to transcribe, write out (shorthand notes, etc.); (*computers*) to transcribe; **t. une lettre à la machine**, to type a letter; (*b*) *Jur:* to register (divorce, etc.); *Book-k:* **t. le journal au grand livre**, to post the journal into the ledger; to post up. **2. t. un texte (en caractères phonétiques, etc.)**, to transliterate a text; **t. un morceau pour le piano**, to make a transcription of a piece for the piano.

transdanubien, -ienne [trɑ̃sdanybjɛ̃, -jɛn], *a. Geog:* trans-Danubian.

transducteur [trɑ̃sdyktœːr], *s.m. Ph: Elcs:* transducer; **t. actif**, active transducer.

transduction [trɑ̃sdyksjɔ̃], *s.f. Biol:* transduction.

transe [trɑ̃ːs], *s.f.* **1.** *usu. pl.* fright, fear; **être dans des transes**, to be on tenterhooks, to be shivering in one's shoes. **2.** (hypnotic) trance.

transept [trɑ̃sɛpt], *s.m. Ecc.Arch:* transept.

transestérification [trɑ̃zɛsterifikasjɔ̃], *s.f. Ch:* cross esterification; transesterification.

transestérifier [trɑ̃zɛsterifje], *v.tr. & i. Ch:* to cross esterify.

transférabilité [trɑ̃sferabilite], *s.f.* transferability.

transférable [trɑ̃sferabl̩], *a.* transferable.

transfèrement [trɑ̃sfɛrmɑ̃], *s.m.* transferring, transference.

transférentiel, -ielle [trɑ̃sferɑ̃sjɛl], *a. Psy:* transferential, transference.

transférer [trɑ̃sfere], *v.tr.* (**je transfère, n. transférons; je transférerai**) (*a*) to transfer; to convey, remove (s.o., sth.) from one place to another; **t. un évêque**, to translate a bishop; **magasin transféré aux Champs-Élysées**, shop moved, transferred, to the Champ-Élysées; (*b*) **t. ses biens, etc., à qn**, to make over, assign, one's goods, etc., to s.o.; *Jur:* **t. une propriété**, to convey an estate; (*c*) to transfer (one's affections, etc.).

transfert [trɑ̃sfɛːr], *s.m.* **1.** (*a*) transferring, transfer (of persons, things, from one place or surface to another); **t. de population**, resettlement, transfer of population; *Phot:* **papier de t.**, transfer paper (in carbon process); **t. provisoire**, temporary transfer; (*b*) *Elcs:* (*computers*) **carte de t.**, transfer card; **t. de magnétisation**, magnetic printing; **clavier à t.**, storage keyboard; **durée de t.**, transfer time. **2.** making over; transfer, assignment (of stock, rights, etc.); demise, conveyance (of estate); *Fin:* **journal des transferts**, transfer register; *Jur:* **acte de t.**, deed of assignment (in favour of creditors); *Pol.Ec:* **t. de revenus**, shifting of income. **3.** *Psy:* transference.

transfert-paiement [trɑ̃sfɛrpɛmɑ̃], *s.m. Fin:* transfer of account (from one savings bank to another); *pl. transferts-paiements.*

transfert-recette [trɑ̃sfɛrrəsɛt], *s.m. Fin:* (*savings bank*) opening of transferred account; *pl. transferts-recettes.*

transfiguration [trɑ̃sfigyrasjɔ̃], *s.f.* (*a*) transfiguration; **la T. de Jésus-Christ**, the Transfiguration (of Jesus on the Mount); (*b*) **c'était moins un sourire qu'une t.**, it was not so much a smile as a transfiguration.

transfigurer [trɑ̃sfigyre], *v.tr.* to transfigure.

transfilage [trɑ̃sfilaːʒ], *s.m. Nau:* lacing (of sail); **t. avec demi-clef**, marling hitch.

transfiler [trɑ̃sfile], *v.tr. Nau:* **1.** to lace (sails, awnings, etc.). **2.** to snub (rope).

transfini [trɑ̃sfini], *a. Mth:* transfinite (number).

transfixiant [trɑ̃sfiksjɑ̃], *a.* **douleur transfixiante**, piercing pain.

transfixion [trɑ̃sfiksjɔ̃], *s.f. Surg:* transfixion (in amputation).

transfluxor [trɑ̃sflyksɔːr], *s.m. Elcs:* (*computers*) transfluxor.

transfo [trɑ̃sfo], *s.m. W.Tel: F:* transformer.

transformable [trɑ̃sfɔrmabl̩], *a.* transformable; *Aut:* **voiture t.**, convertible (car).

transformateur, -trice [trɑ̃sfɔrmatœːr, -tris], *El:* **1.** *a.* **station transformatrice**, transformer station. **2.** *s.m.* transformer; **t. rotatif**, rotary transformer, converter; **t. statique**, static transformer; **t. à champ tournant**, rotary-field transformer; **t. à noyau**, core transformer; **t. à huile**, oil transformer; **t. à air**, air-gap transformer; **t. élévateur**, step-up transformer; **t. abaisseur**, step-down transformer; **t. compensateur**, balancing transformer; **t. déphaseur**, quadrature transformer; **t. redresseur**, transformer rectifier; **poste, station, de transformateurs**, transformer station; *W.Tel:* **t. d'oscillations**, jigger; **t. d'antenne**, aerial, antenna, transformer; *Elcs:* **t. d'alimentation (secteur)**, mains transformer; **t. différentiel**, hybrid coil; (*radar*) **t. d'image**, picture transformer.

transformation [trɑ̃sfɔrmasjɔ̃], *s.f.* **1.** (*a*) transformation (**en**, into); **t. de l'énergie, d'une équation**, transformation of energy, of an equation; **acteur à transformations**, quick-change artist(e); **t. de l'enfant qui, en un jour, devient femme**, sudden transformation of a child into a woman; **nous avons fait beaucoup de transformations chez nous**, we have made a lot of alterations in the house; *Pol.Ec:* **industrie de t.**, processing industry; (*b*) *El:* **rapport de t.**, transformer ratio; *Elcs:* **t. de signaux**, signal transformation; **t. magnétique, irréversible, réversible**, irreversible, reversible, magnetic process; (*c*) *Mapm:* **t. conforme**, conformal mapping; (*d*) *Log:* conversion (of proposition); (*c*) *Rugby Fb:* **t. (d'un essai)**, conversion of a try. **2.** *Hairdr:* transformation; wig.

transformée [trɑ̃sfɔrme], *s.f. Mth:* transformed curve, transform.

transformer [trɑ̃sfɔrme], *v.tr.* (*a*) to transform, change; *Dressm:* to refashion, make over (a dress); **t. qch. en qch.**, to transform, convert, turn, sth. into sth.; *Mth:* **t. une équation**, to transform an equation; *Rugby Fb:* **t. un essai**, to convert a try; (*b*) *Elcs:* to transform, to map; (*c*) *Log:* to convert (proposition).

se transformer, to be transformed, to change, turn (**en**, into); **la chenille se transforme en papillon**, the caterpillar changes, turns, into a butterfly; **la neige tombante se transforma bientôt en pluie**, the falling snow soon turned to rain.

transformisme [trɑ̃sfɔrmism], *s.m. Phil: etc:* transformism.

transformiste [trɑ̃sfɔrmist], *a. & s.m. & f. Phil: etc:* transformist.

transfuge [trɑ̃sfyːʒ], *s.m. & f.* (*a*) *Mil:* deserter to the other side; defector; (*b*) turncoat; (*c*) *Com:* ex-employee, *F:* refugee (from firm).

transfuser [trɑ̃sfyze], *v.tr.* (*a*) to transfuse (*esp. Med:* blood); (*b*) to instil (**à**, into); **t. ses méthodes à un disciple**, to instil one's methods into a follower.

transfuseur [trɑ̃sfyzœːr], *s.m. Med:* **1.** transfuser (of blood). **2.** transfusionist.

transfusion [trɑ̃sfyzjɔ̃], *s.f.* transfusion (*esp.* of blood); *Bot:* **tissu de t.**, transfusion tissue.

transgangétique [trɑ̃sgɑ̃ʒetik], *a. Geog:* trans-Gangetic, beyond the Ganges; **l'Inde t.**, Further India.

transgresser [trɑ̃sgrese], *v.tr.* to transgress, contravene, break, infringe (the law, etc.); to disobey (orders).

transgresseur [trɑ̃sgrɛsœːr], *s.m. Lit:* transgressor; contravenor (**de**, of).

transgressif, -ive [trɑ̃sgrɛsif, -iːv], *a.* transgressive.

transgression [trɑ̃sgrɛsjɔ̃], *s.f.* (*a*) transgression (**de**, of); (*b*) *Geol:* **t. marine**, marine transgression.

transhorizon [trɑ̃zɔrizɔ̃], *attrib. W.Tel:* **câble hertzien t.**, forward-scatter radio link; **relais t.**, forward-scatter relay.

transhumance [trɑ̃zymɑ̃ːs], *s.f. Husb:* transhumance.

transhumant [trɑ̃zymɑ̃], *a. & s. Husb:* transhumant; (flocks, herds) on the move.

transhumer [trɑ̃zyme]. **1.** *v.tr.* (*a*) to move (flocks, herds) to or from mountain pastures; (*b*) *Hort:* to transplant (tree). **2.** *v.i.* (*a*) (*of flocks, herds*) to move to, from, mountain pastures; (*b*) *Ap:* (*of bees*) to move to, from, their seasonal areas.

transi [trɑ̃si, -zi], (*a*) *a.* chilled; perished with cold; **t. de peur**, paralysed, stiff, with fear; *F:* **amoureux t.**, bashful lover; (*b*) *s.m. Sculp:* recumbent effigy (of naked corpse).

transigeance [trɑ̃ziʒɑ̃ːs], *s.f.* transigence, willingness to compromise.

transiger [trɑ̃ziʒe]. **1.** *v.i.* (**je transigeai(s); n. transigeons**) to (effect a) compromise; **t. avec ses créanciers**, to come to terms, with one's creditors; **ne pas t.**, to be adamant. **2.** *v.tr.* to compromise (a dispute).

transigible [trɑ̃ziʒibl̩], *a.* (dispute) capable of accommodation.

transillumination [trɑ̃zil(l)yminasjɔ̃], *s.f. Med:* transillumination.

Transilvanie (la) [latrɑ̃silvani], *Pr.n.f. Geog:* Transylvania.

transir [trɑ̃siːr, -ziːr]. **1.** *v.tr.* (*a*) to chill, benumb (with cold); **ce froid me transit**, this cold goes right through me, chills me to the bone; (*b*) to paralyse, overcome (with fear); **cette nouvelle le transit de peur**, he was paralysed with fear at the news. **2.** *v.i. A:* (*a*) to be chilled, to be perishing with cold; (*b*) to be paralysed with fear.

transissement [trɑ̃sismɑ̃, -zi-], *s.m. A:* **1.** chill. **2.** fear and trembling; **attendre des nouvelles avec t.,** to await news in fear and trembling.

transistor [trɑ̃zistɔːr], *s.m. El:* (*a*) transistor; **à transistors,** transistorized; **poste à transistors,** transistor (radio, set); **t. au germanium,** germanium transistor; (*b*) *F:* transistor (radio).

transistorisation [trɑ̃zistɔrizasjɔ̃], *s.f. Elcs:* transistorization.

transistorisé [trɑ̃zistɔrize], *a.* (*a*) transistorized; **radiophare entièrement t.,** fully transistorized radio beacon; (*b*) **calculateur t.,** solid-state computer; **composant t.,** solid-state component; *Av:* **ensemble de navigation (entièrement) t.,** solid-state navigational equipment.

transistoriser [trɑ̃zistɔrise], *v.tr.* to transistorize, to equip with transistors.

transit [trɑ̃zit], *s.m.* **1.** *Cust:* transit; **marchandises en t.,** goods in transit; **marchandises de t.,** (warehoused) goods for transit; **maison de t.,** forwarding agency; **commerce de t.,** transit trade; *Cust:* **document de t.,** transit permit. **2.** *Rail:* through traffic. **3.** *Elcs:* **t. par bande perforée,** tape relay; **t. manuel par bande perforée,** manual tape relay, *U.S:* torn tape relay.

transitaire [trɑ̃zitɛːr]. **1.** *a.* relating to transit of goods; **pays t.,** country through which goods are conveyed in transit. **2.** *s.m.* forwarding agent, transport agent.

transiter [trɑ̃zite]. **1.** *v.tr.* to convey (goods) in transit; to forward (goods). **2.** *v.i.* (*of goods*) to be in transit.

transitif, -ive [trɑ̃zitif, -iːv], *a.* **1.** *Gram:* transitive (verb). **2.** *Geol:* transitional (stratum). **3.** *Phil:* transient (cause, etc.).

transition [trɑ̃zisjɔ̃], *s.f.* transition; **sans t.,** abruptly, without any transition; **chapitre qui fait t. entre . . . et . . . ,** chapter that effects the transition between . . . and . . .; **passer d'un état à un autre sans aucune t.,** to pass from one state to another without any intermediate stage; *Arch:* **style de t.,** transition style; *Geol:* **terrain de t.,** transitional stratum; *Ch:* **éléments de t.,** transition elements.

transitionnel, -elle [trɑ̃zisjɔnɛl], *a.* transitional.

transitivement [trɑ̃zitivmɑ̃], *adv. Gram:* transitively.

transitivité [trɑ̃sitivite], *s.f.* transitivity.

transitoire [trɑ̃zitwaːr], *a.* transitory, transient; **période t.,** period of transition; **mesure t.,** temporary measure; *Ling:* **son t.,** glide.

transitoirement [trɑ̃zitwarmɑ̃], *adv.* transitorily, transiently.

transitron [trɑ̃zitrɔ̃], *s.m. Elcs:* transitron.

Transjordanie [trɑ̃sʒɔrdani], *Pr.n.f. Hist:* Transjordan, Transjordania.

transjuran [trɑ̃sʒyrɑ̃], *a. Geog:* Transjuran, beyond the Jura Mountains.

Transkei (le) [lətrɑ̃skei], *Pr.n.m. Geog:* the Transkei.

translatable [trɑ̃slatabl̩], *a. Elcs:* (*computers*) relocatable; **adresse t.,** relocatable address.

translater [trɑ̃slate], *v.tr.* (*a*) *A:* to translate; (*b*) *Pej:* to translate indifferently; (*c*) *Elcs:* (*computers*) to relocate.

translateur [trɑ̃slatœːr], *s.m.* **1.** *A:* translator. **2.** (*a*) *Tg:* translator, repeater; **t. d'impulsions,** impulse repeater; (*b*) (*computers*) repeating coil.

translatif, -ive [trɑ̃slatif, -iːv], *a. Jur:* translative; **acte t. (de propriété),** conveyance, transfer.

translation [trɑ̃slasjɔ̃], *s.f.* **1.** *A:* (= TRADUCTION) translation. **2.** transfer(ring); *Ecc:* translation (of bishop, relics); *Jur:* transferring, conveyance (of property); *Tg:* retransmission, relaying, translation (of message); *Ecc:* **t. d'une fête,** transfer of a feast day (to another date). **3.** *Mec: etc:* **mouvement de t.,** motion, movement, of translation; **t. latérale,** side-travel (*e.g.* of ceiling crab).

transleithan [trɑ̃sletɑ̃], *a. Hist:* Transleithan.

Transleithanie (la) [latrɑ̃sletani], *Pr.n.f. Hist:* Transleithania.

translit(t)érer [trɑ̃slitere], *v.tr.* to transliterate.

translit(t)ération [trɑ̃sliterasjɔ̃], *s.f.* transliteration.

translocation [trɑ̃slɔkasjɔ̃], *s.f. Biol:* translocation.

translucide [trɑ̃slysid], *a.* translucent, translucid.

translucidité [trɑ̃slysidite], *s.f.* translucence, translucency; translucidity, translucidness; partial transparency.

transmanche [trɑ̃smɑ̃ːʃ], *a. Nau:* cross-Channel.

transmarin [trɑ̃smarɛ̃], *a. A:* oversea (region, goods).

transméditerranéen, -éenne [trɑ̃smediterraneɛ̃, -eɛn], *a. Geog:* Transmediterranean.

transméthylation [trɑ̃zmetilasjɔ̃], *s.f. Bio-Ch:* transmethylation.

transmetteur [trɑ̃smɛtœːr]. **1.** *s.m.* (*a*) *Tg: etc:* transmitter; *Ph: Elcs:* **t. (indirect),** transducer; *Elcs:* (*computers*) **t. de données,** data transmitter; *W.Tel:* **t. à étincelles,** spark transmitter; (*b*) *Nau:* **t. d'ordres,** (turret) telegraph, transmitter; (*c*) **(officier) t.,** signals officer. **2.** *attrib.* transmitting, sending (wire, etc.); *Elcs:* **distributeur t.,** transmitter distributor.

transmettre [trɑ̃smɛtr̩], *v.tr.* (*conj. like* METTRE) **1.** to transmit (light, heat, message); to pass on, convey (message, order, disease, etc.); to impart (the truth, energy); to hand (sth.) down (to posterity); *Tg: W.Tel:* to send, transmit (message); to broadcast (programme, etc.); *Elcs:* **signal d'invitation à t.,** proceed-to-send, proceed-to-transmit, signal, *U.S:* start dialling signal; **le son se transmet par vibration,** sound is transmitted by vibration. **2.** *Jur:* to transfer, convey, make over (property, etc.); to assign (shares, patents, etc.).

transmigration [trɑ̃smigrasjɔ̃], *s.f.* transmigration (of peoples, of the soul).

transmigré, -ée [trɑ̃smigre], *s.* transmigrant, transmigrator.

transmigrer [trɑ̃smigre], *v.i.* to transmigrate.

transmissibilité [trɑ̃smisibilite], *s.f.* (*a*) transmissibility; (*b*) transferability.

transmissible [trɑ̃smisibl̩], *a.* (*a*) transmissible, transmittable; **idées facilement transmissibles,** ideas that are easy to impart; (*b*) transferable (right, etc.).

transmission [trɑ̃smisjɔ̃], *s.f.* **1.** (*a*) transmission, transmittal (of heat, message, etc.); passing on (of message, order); imparting (of truth); handing down (of tradition, etc.); *Tg: W.Tel: T.V: etc:* transmission, sending (of message, programme, image, etc.); **t. optique,** visual transmission; **t. radioélectrique,** radio transmission; **t. aux ondes dirigées,** beam transmission; **t. par courants porteurs,** carrier transmission; **normes de t.,** standards of transmission; **vitesse de t.,** speed of transmission; *W.Tel: etc:* **antenne de t.,** sending aerial, transmitting aerial; *W.Tel: T.V:* **t. directe, en direct,** live broadcast, programme; **t. différée, en différé,** recorded broadcast, programme; **t. à plusieurs voies,** multi-channel transmission; **transmissions simultanées,** multiway transmission; **t. en série, en parallèle,** serial, parallel, transmission; **t. multiplex,** multiplex transmission; *Com:* **fiche de t.,** routing slip; *Mec.E:* **t. du mouvement,** transmission, conveying, of movement; **arbre de t.,** driving shaft; **les arbres de t.,** the shafting; **courroie de t.,** driving belt; **engrenage(s) de t.,** driving gear; *Navy: Mil:* **les transmissions,** signals; **officier de transmissions,** signal(s) officer; **commandant des transmissions,** chief signal(s) officer; **ordre pour les transmissions,** signal operating instructions; **t. par coureurs,** messenger communications; **axe des transmissions,** main line of signal communications; **centre de transmissions,** signal centre; (*b*) *Mec.E:* **la t.,** the transmission (gear); the shafting, belting, gearing, etc.; the drive; **t. principale,** main shafting; **t. secondaire, intermédiaire,** counter shafting; **t. par courroie,** belt transmission, belt drive; **t. par chaîne,** chain drive; **t. par câble,** rope gearing; **t. à cardan,** Cardan drive; universal-joint drive; **t. par balancier,** beam drive; **t. par engrenage,** gear drive; **t. par pignons,** bevel drive; **t. à friction,** friction drive, gear; *Aut:* **t. automatique,** automatic transmission, drive; **t. par vis en dessus,** overhead worm drive; *Nau:* **t. de barre hydraulique,** telemotor gear; **t. hydromécanique,** hydraulic coupling, hydraulic power transmitter; *Mec.E:* **t. flexible,** flexible shaft(ing); (*c*) *Elcs:* (*computers*) **t. arythmique,** start-stop transmission; **parasites de t.,** keying chirps; **voie de t.,** transmission channel; **unité de t.,** data set. **2.** (*a*) *Jur:* transfer(ence), making over, conveyance (of estate, privileges, etc.); assignment (of shares, patent, etc.); **t. d'un bien par succession,** descent of an estate; *Adm:* **t. des pouvoirs,** handing over; (*b*) *Fb:* **t. du ballon,** passing; (*c*) **t. de pensée,** thought transference.

transmittance [trɑ̃smitɑ̃ːs], *s.f. Elcs:* transmittance.

transmodulation [trɑ̃smɔdylasjɔ̃], *s.f. W.Tel: etc:* cross modulation, intermodulation.

transmontain [trɑ̃smɔ̃tɛ̃], *a. A:* tra(ns)montane, beyond the Alps ((i) as from France, (ii) as from Italy).

transmuable [trɑ̃smɥabl̩], *a.* transmutable (en, into).

transmuer [trɑ̃smɥe], *v.tr.* to transmute (en, into).

transmutabilité [trɑ̃smytabilite], *s.f.* transmutability.

transmutable [trɑ̃smytabl̩], *a.* transmutable.

transmutateur, -trice [trɑ̃smytatœːr, -tris], **1.** *a.* transmuting. **2.** *s.* transmuter.

transmutation [trɑ̃smytasjɔ̃], *s.f.* transmutation (en, into); *Atom.Ph:* **t. d'éléments,** transmutation of elements; **on entend par transmutations les transformations provoquées des noyaux,** transmutations are artificially produced nuclear transformations.

transmuter [trɑ̃smyte], *v.tr.* to transmute.

transneptunien, -ienne [trɑ̃snɛptynjɛ̃, -jɛn], *a. Astr:* trans-Neptunian.

transocéanien, -ienne [trɑ̃zɔseanjɛ̃, -jɛn], **transocéanique** [trɑ̃zɔseanik], *a.* transoceanic.

transpacifique [trɑ̃spasifik], *a.* transpacific.

transpadan [trɑ̃spadɑ̃], *a. Geog:* transpadane, beyond the (river) Po; *Hist:* **la République Transpadane,** the Transpadane Republic.

transparaître [trɑ̃sparɛːtr̩], *v.i.* (*conj. like* PARAÎTRE) to show through; *Lit:* **l'âme transparaît dans l'attitude et le geste,** through attitude and gesture one gets a glimpse of the soul.

transparence [trɑ̃sparɑ̃ːs], *s.f.* transparency (of air, water, etc.); *Art: etc:* **effet de t.,** transparent effect; **plaider pour la t.,** to plead for having things open and above board; **t. des salaires,** publication of wages paid.

transparent [trɑ̃sparɑ̃]. **1.** *a.* transparent; **tissu t.,** transparent material; **allusion transparente,** clear allusion, obvious reference (to sth.); **c'était un homme t.,** he was a man whose thoughts were easy to read; *F:* **tu n'es pas t.,** you make a better door than a window. **2.** *s.m.* (*a*) transparency (*i.e.* picture, print, etc., illuminated from behind); (*b*) underlines, *F:* guidelines (supplied with writing pad); (*c*) *pl. Tail:* vest slips; (*d*) *Cost:* thin material worn over a foundation; **t. de dentelle,** lace overlay.

transpercement [trɑ̃spɛrsəmɑ̃], *s.m.* piercing through; running, shooting, through (of the body); transfixion.

transpercer [trɑ̃spɛrse], *v.tr.* **(je transperçai(s); n. transperçons),** to (trans)pierce; to transfix; to stab, pierce (s.o., sth.) through; **transpercé d'un coup d'épée, d'une balle,** run through with a sword; shot through; **la pluie m'a transpercé,** I am soaked through (and through); **t. qn du regard,** to look s.o. through and through; **t. le cœur à qn, t. qn de douleur,** to pierce s.o. to the heart.

transpéritonéal, -aux [trɑ̃speritɔneal, -o], *a.* transperitoneal.

transpirant [trɑ̃spirɑ̃], *a.* perspiring, sweating; **doigts transpirants,** sweaty fingers.

transpiration [trɑ̃spirasjɔ̃], *s.f.* **1.** (*a*) perspiration, sweat; **être en t.,** to be perspiring, sweating; (*b*) *Bot:* transpiration. **2.** transpiring, coming to light (of a secret, etc.).

transpirer [trɑ̃spire], *v.i.* **1.** **(aux. avoir)** (*a*) to perspire, sweat; **je ne transpire pas des pieds,** my feet don't perspire; *Med:* **faire t. qn,** to sweat s.o.; **remède qui fait t.,** remedy that brings on perspiration; (*b*) *Bot:* to transpire; *v.tr.* to transpire (moisture). **2.** **(aux. avoir** *or* **être)** to transpire, to come to light; (*of news, etc.*) to leak out, to get abroad; **il n'en était rien transpiré,** nothing of it had transpired.

transplacentaire [trɑ̃splasɑ̃tɛːr], *a. Anat:* transplacental.

transplant [trɑ̃splɑ̃], *s.m. Surg:* transplant.

transplantable [trɑ̃splɑ̃tabl̩], *a.* transplantable.

transplantation [trɑ̃splɑ̃tasjɔ̃], *s.f., A:* **transplantement** [trɑ̃splɑ̃tmɑ̃], *s.m.* transplantation, transplanting; *Surg:* **transplantation cardiaque,** heart transplant.

transplanté, -ée [trɑ̃splɑ̃te], *s.* **1.** transplanted person. **2.** *Med:* **t. cardiaque,** patient who has had a heart transplant.

transplanter [trɑ̃splɑ̃te], *v.tr.* to transplant (trees, people, etc.); *Surg:* **t. un cœur,** to perform a heart transplant operation.

se transplanter, to settle elsewhere, to transplant oneself.

transplanteur [trɑ̃splɑ̃tœːr]. **1.** *s.m.* transplanter (of trees, etc.). **2.** *a.m.* **matériel t.,** transplanting equipment.

transplantoir [trɑ̃splɑ̃twaːr], *s.m. Hort: etc:* **1.** (garden) trowel. **2.** transplanter, transplanting machine.

transpleural, -aux [trɑ̃spløral, -o], *a. Surg:* transpleural (incision, etc.).

transpolaire [trɑ̃spɔlɛːr], *a.* transpolar.

transpondeur [trɑ̃spɔ̃dœːr], *s.m. Tg: Elcs:* transponder.
transpontin [trɑ̃spɔ̃tɛ̃], *a.* transpontine.
transport [trɑ̃spɔːr], *s.m.* **1.** (*a*) *Com: Trans:* transport, conveyance, carriage (of goods, passengers); haulage (of goods, materials); **capacité de t.,** transport capacity; **compagnie de t.,** transport company; carrying, forwarding, company; **contrat de t.,** carriage contract; **entrepreneur de t.,** haulage contractor; **frais de t.,** freight charges, carriage; **t. de marchandises,** (i) transport of goods; (ii) carrying trade; **les transports en commun,** public transport; *Ind:* **courroie de t.,** conveyor belt; *Mil:* **compagnie de t. auto(mobile),** mechanical transport company; **véhicule de t. de personnel,** personnel carrier; **t. de surface,** surface transport; **t. terrestre, t. par (voie de) terre,** land carriage, conveyance; **t. routier,** road transport; **t. par roulage,** cartage; haulage; **t. hippomobile,** horse-drawn transport; **t. auto(mobile),** motor transport, mechanical transport; **t. par (chemin de) fer, par voie ferrée,** transport by rail; railway carriage, transport; **t. (de pétrole, etc.) par canalisations,** conveying (of oil, etc.) by pipeline; piping (of oil); **canalisation(s) de t.,** conveyor pipeline; **t. par (voie d') eau,** (inland) water transport; **t. fluvial,** river transport; **t. maritime, t. par mer,** carriage by sea, marine transport; shipping; **t. mixte,** sea and land carriage; **t. aérien, t. par air, t. par avion(s),** air transport, conveyance by aircraft; airlift; **avion de t.,** transport aircraft; **avion de t. de passagers,** passenger (transport) aircraft; **avion de t. de frêt,** cargo aircraft; **avion de t. léger, moyen, lourd,** light, medium, heavy, transport aircraft; **avion de t. à courtes distances,** short-haul aircraft, short hauler; **avion de t. à moyennes distances,** medium-haul aircraft, medium hauler; **avion de t. à longues distances,** long-haul aircraft, long hauler; **cela permet de faire les transports urgents par avion,** this enables urgent freight to be sent by air; *El:* **t. d'énergie,** power transmission; **t. de force,** high-voltage power transmission; *Elcs:* **t. hertzien,** retransmission; (*b*) *Jur:* **t. (d'experts, etc.) sur les lieux,** visit (of experts, etc.) to the scene (of the accident, etc.); (*c*) *Geol:* **terrain de t.,** alluvial deposit; **t. glaciaire,** glacial drift. **2.** *Navy: etc:* transport (ship); *esp.* troop ship; **t. d'aviation,** aircraft transport; **t. de matériel,** store ship. **3.** (*a*) *Jur:* **t.(-cession),** transfer, assignment, making over, conveyance (of property, rights, etc.); (*b*) *Book-k:* (i) transfer (from one account to another); (ii) carrying out, extension (of balance to another column); (iii) balance brought forward; (*c*) *Lith:* transfer (on to the stone); **papier à t.,** transfer paper. **4.** transport, rapture; outburst of feeling; **dans un t. de joie,** in transports (of joy), in an ecstasy of joy; **dans un t. de colère,** in a burst of fury; **accueillir une nouvelle avec t.,** to receive news with (transports of) delight; *Med:* **t. au cerveau,** rush of blood to the brain ((i) lightheadedness; (ii) fit of delirium; brainstorm; (iii) stroke).
transportable [trɑ̃spɔrtabl̩], *a.* transportable; (patient, etc.) fit to be moved.
transportant [trɑ̃spɔrtɑ̃], *a.* exciting, thrilling.
transportation [trɑ̃spɔrtasjɔ̃], *s.f.* **1.** transport, *esp. U.S:* transportation, conveyance (of goods, etc.). **2.** (penal) transportation (of criminals).
transporté, -ée [trɑ̃spɔrte]. **1.** *s.* transported convict, transport. **2.** *a.* **t. de joie,** overjoyed, beside oneself with joy; **t. de fureur,** beside oneself with fury, with rage; **t. d'admiration,** carried away with admiration.
transporter [trɑ̃spɔrte], *v.tr.* **1.** (*a*) to transport, convey, remove, transfer, carry (goods, troops, etc., from one place to another); **t. qn à l'hôpital,** to take s.o. to hospital; **t. des marchandises (i) en camion, (ii) par chemin de fer, (iii) par eau,** to transport goods (i) by lorry, by road, *U.S:* by truck, (ii) by rail, *U.S:* by railroad, (iii) by water; **le courrier est transporté à Londres par avion,** letters are flown to London; **se t. dans l'avenir,** to project oneself into the future; (*of police, etc.*) **se t. sur les lieux,** to visit the scene of the crime, accident, etc.; (*b*) *Jur:* to transport (convict); (*c*) *Book-k:* (i) to carry over, (ii) to transfer, (iii) to carry out, extend (balance). **2.** *Jur:* **t. des droits, etc., à qn,** to transfer, make over, assign, rights, etc., to s.o. **3.** to transport, to carry away; to enrapture; **cette bonne nouvelle l'a transporté,** he was overjoyed by, carried away by, the good news.
transporteur [trɑ̃spɔrtœːr], *s.m.* **1.** carrier, forwarding agent. **2.** (*a*) *Ind:* conveyor; **t. à vis,** spiral conveyor, conveying screw; **t. à courroie mobile,** portable conveyor; *Rail:* **t. de wagons (plate-forme roulante),** tra(ns)verse table, traverse; **t. monorail,** telpher; **t. par câbles, t. aérien,** cableway, aerial ropeway, overhead runway; **t. à bande,** belt conveyor; **t. à augets, à godets,** bucket way, bucket conveyor; **(chariot) t.,** travelling crane, travelling platform; **t. à charbon,** coal conveyor; *Metall:* **t. à rouleaux,** live roller train (of rolling mill); (*b*) *Artil:* feeder, feed mechanism. **3.** *a.* (*f.* **transporteuse,** [trɑ̃spɔrtøːz]) **hélice transporteuse,** spiral conveyor; **bande, courroie, transporteuse,** belt conveyor.
transposable [trɑ̃spozabl̩], *a.* transposable.
transposer [trɑ̃spoze], *v.tr.* to transpose (two words, etc.); *Mus:* **t. un morceau d'ut en ré,** to transpose a piece from C to D.
transpositeur [trɑ̃spɔzitœːr], *Mus:* **1.** *a.m.* **piano t.,** transposing piano. **2.** *s.m.* transposing instrument.
transpositif, -ive [trɑ̃spɔzitif, -iːv], *a.* transpositive; transpositional.
transposition [trɑ̃spɔzisjɔ̃], *s.f.* (*a*) *Alg: Anat: Surg: Mus: etc:* transposition; *Bookb:* faulty assembling (of sheets); **t. du cœur et du foie,** transposition, transposed location, of the heart and liver; *Elcs:* **t. en fréquence,** frequency translation; (*b*) *Cin:* dubbing.
transpyrénéen,-éenne [trɑ̃spireneɛ̃, -eɛn], *a.* transpyrenean, beyond the Pyrenees.
transrhénan [trɑ̃srenɑ̃], *a.* beyond the Rhine, transrhenane.
transsaharien, -ienne [trɑ̃ssaarjɛ̃, -jɛn], *a. Geog:* Trans-Saharan.
transsibérien, -ienne [trɑ̃ssiberjɛ̃, -jɛn]. **1.** *a. Geog:* Trans-Siberian. **2.** *s.m.* **le T.,** the Trans-Siberian Railway.
transsonique [trɑ̃ssɔnik], *a. Ph:* trans-sonic, transonic.
transsubstantiation [trɑ̃ssypstɑ̃sjasjɔ̃], *s.f. Theol:* transubstantiation.
transsubstantier [trɑ̃ssupstɑ̃sje], *v.tr. Theol:* to transubstantiate.
transsudat [trɑ̃ssyda], *s.m. Physiol:* transudate.
transsudation [trɑ̃ssydasjɔ̃], *s.f.* transudation.
transsuder [trɑ̃ssyde]. **1.** *v.i.* (*of liquid*) to transude; to ooze through; *Ch: Ind:* to sweat. **2.** *v.tr.* to transude (liquid).
transtévérin, -ine [trɑ̃steverɛ̃, -in], *a. Geog:* transtiberine, transteverine (Rome).
transuranien, -ienne [trɑ̃syranjɛ̃, -jɛn], *a.* & *s.m. Ch:* **(élément) t.,** transuranic, transuranium, transuranian, element.
Transvaal (le) [lətrɑ̃sval, trɑ̃z-], *Pr.n.m. Geog:* the Transvaal.
transvaalien, -ienne [trɑ̃svaljɛ̃, trɑ̃z-, -jɛn], *Geog:* **1.** *a.* of the Transvaal. **2.** *s.* Transvaaler.
transvaluation [trɑ̃svalɥasjɔ̃], *s.f. Phil:* transvaluation.
transvasage [trɑ̃svɑzaːʒ], *s.m. Vit:* drawing off, racking, clarifying (of wine).
transvasement [trɑ̃svɑzmɑ̃], *s.m.* **1.** decanting (of liquid). **2.** *Ap:* transfer (of bees to another hive).
transvaser [trɑ̃svɑze], *v.tr.* to decant (wine, liqueurs, etc.); to transvase; to pour (liquid) into another container.
se transvaser, (*of water*) to siphon.
transvaseur [trɑ̃svɑzœːr], *s.m.* decanter (*pers. or apparatus*).
transverbération [trɑ̃svɛrberasjɔ̃], *s.f.* transverberation.
transverbérer [trɑ̃svɛrbere], *v.tr.* to transverberate.
transversal, -ale, -aux [trɑ̃svɛrsal, -o]. **1.** *a.* transverse, transversal; cross (section, gallery, artery, etc.); *Const:* **mur t.,** partition (wall); **poutre transversale,** cross girder; **route transversale,** crossroad; **rue transversale,** cross street; side street; *Anat:* **muscle t.,** *s.m.* **transversal,** transverse (muscle); *N.Arch:* **plan t.,** athwartship plane; **membrures transversales,** transverse frame; **dans le sens t.,** athwartship; **soutes transversales,** cross bunkers; *Mec.E:* **avance transversale,** *s.m.* **transversal d'alimentation,** cross feed; **vis d'avance transversale,** cross-feed screw (of lathe); *Elcs:* (*computers*) **contrôle t.,** transverse check; *Geog:* **vallée transversale,** transverse valley. **2.** *s.f.* **transversale:** (*a*) *Mth:* transversal (line); (*b*) crossroad; (*c*) (*at roulette*) transversale; **transversale pleine,** transversale pleine.
transversalement [trɑ̃svɛrsalmɑ̃], *adv.* transversely, crosswise, athwart; *Nau:* athwartship.
transverse [trɑ̃svɛrs]. **1.** *a. Mth:* **axe t.,** transverse axis; *Anat:* **apophyse t.,** transverse process; **artère t. de la face,** transverse facial artery; **muscle t. de l'abdomen,** transversus abdominis. **2.** *s.m. Anat:* transverse (muscle).
transvestisme [trɑ̃svɛstism], *s.m. Psy:* transvestism.
transvider [trɑ̃svide], *v.tr.* to pour (sth.) into another container.
transylvain, -aine [trɑ̃silvɛ̃, -ɛn], **transylvanien, -ienne** [trɑ̃silvanjɛ̃, -jɛn], *a.* & *s. Geog:* Transylvanian.
Transylvanie (la) [latrɑ̃silvani], *Pr.n.f. Geog:* Transylvania.
tran-tran [trɑ̃trɑ̃], *s.m.* = TRAIN-TRAIN.
trapa [trapa], *s.m. Bot:* water caltrop, water chestnut; (*genus*) Trapa.
trapan [trapɑ̃], *s.m.* top landing (of stair).
trapèze [trapɛːz], *s.m.* **1.** (*a*) *Geom:* trapezium (with two sides parallel); (*b*) *Gym:* trapeze; **faire du t. volant,** to perform on the flying trapeze; to do flying trapeze exercises. **2.** *a. Anat:* **muscle t.,** trapezius (muscle); **os t.,** trapezium (bone).
trapéziforme [trapezifɔrm], *a.* trapeziform.
trapéziste [trapezist], *s.m.* & *f. Gym:* trapezist, trapeze artist.
trapézoèdre [trapezɔɛdr̥], *s.m. Geom: Cryst:* trapezohedron.
trapézoïdal, -aux [trapezɔidal, -o], *a.* trapezoidal; **courroie trapézoïdale,** V(-shaped) (fan-)belt; *Elcs:* **intégration trapézoïdale,** trapezoidal integration.
trapézoïde [trapezɔid]. **1.** *a.* trapezoid(al); *Anat:* **os t.,** trapezium; trapezoid bone. **2.** *s.m. Geom:* trapezoid; trapezium.
trapézo-métacarpien, -ienne [trapezɔmetakarpjɛ̃, -jɛn], *a. Anat:* trapeziometacarpal; *pl. trapézo-métacarpiens, -iennes.*
trapillon [trapijɔ̃], *s.m.* **1.** catch, lock (of a trap door). **2.** *Th:* slot (for scenery).
trapp [trap], *s.m. Geol: A:* trap (rock).
trappe[1] [trap], *s.f.* **1.** *Ven:* trap, pitfall. **2.** (*a*) trap (door); **tomber dans une t.,** to fall through a trap door; (*b*) flap door; (*c*) register (of fireplace); (*d*) hatch; **t. de visites,** inspection hatch, trap; *Av:* **t. du train (d'atterrissage),** landing-gear hatch; **t. d'entretien et d'éjection,** ejection and maintenance hatch; **t. de la soute à bombes,** bomb door, hatch; **t. d'expansion,** high pressure spill vent; *Nau: etc:* **t. du compartiment moteur,** engine-compartment door.
Trappe[2] **(la),** *Pr.n.f. Ecc:* **1.** (*a*) the convent of La Trappe (in Normandy); (*b*) Trappist monastery. **2.** the Trappist order (of monks).
trappéen, -enne [trapeɛ̃, -ɛn], *a. Geol:* trappean (rock, etc.).
trapper [trape], *v.i.* to trap animals (for fur).
trappeur [trapœːr], *s.m.* trapper (of wild animals).
trappillon [trapijɔ̃], *s.m.* = TRAPILLON.
trappiste [trapist]. **1.** *a.* & *s.m. Ecc:* Trappist (monk). **2.** *s.m. Orn:* puffbird, barbet.
trappistine [trapistin], *s.f.* Trappistine (nun or liqueur).
trapu [trapy], *a.* (*a*) thick-set, dumpy, stocky (man, horse); squat (building, etc.); **sa petite personne trapue,** his compact little figure; (*b*) *Sch: F:* clever, bright, brainy (pupil); **être t. en math,** to be bright at, well up in, maths; **ce problème est t.,** that's a sticky problem; (*c*) *P:* (*pers.*) strong, tough.
traque [trak], *s.f. Ven:* beating for game.
traquenard [traknaːr], *s.m.* **1.** *Equit:* (*a*) racking gait (of horse); **aller le t.,** to rack; (*b*) racking horse. **2.** (*a*) trap, deadfall; **pris au t.,** caught in a trap; **pris dans son propre t.,** caught in his own trap, hoist with his own petard; **les traquenards d'une langue,** the pitfalls of a language; (*b*) ambush.
traquenarder [traknarde], *v.i.* (*of horse*) to rack, to amble.
traquer [trake], *v.tr. Ven:* **1.** to beat (wood, etc.) for game; to beat up (game). **2.** (*a*) to enclose, surround, hem in (quarry, bandits); (*b*) to track down, hunt down, run to earth (criminal). **3.** *v.i. F:* to get stage fright.
traquet[1] [trake], *s.m.* **1.** (mill) clapper, clack; *F: O:* **la langue lui va comme un t.,** her tongue's always going nineteen to the dozen. **2.** *Orn:* **t.(-)motteux,** wheatear; **t. noir, t. rieur,** black wheatear; **t. à tête blanche,** white-rumped black wheatear; **t. oreillard, t. stapazin,** black-eared wheatear; **t. leucomèle,** pied wheatear; **t. isabelle,** isabelline wheatear; **t. du désert,** desert wheatear; **t. pâtre,** stonechat; **t. tarier,** whinchat.
traquet[2], *s.m. A: Ven:* trap, snare; **donner dans le t.,** to fall into the trap.
traqueur[1] [trakœːr], *s.m. Ven:* beater.

traqueur², **-euse** [trakœːr, -øːz], *F:* **1.** *a.* cowardly, funky. **2.** *s.* coward, funk.

Trasimène [trazimɛn], *Pr.n.m. Geog:* **le lac T.,** Lake Trasimene; *A.Hist:* Lake Trasimenus.

trasle [trɑl], *s.m. Orn: F:* redwing.

trass [tras], *s. Miner:* trass.

traulet [trolɛ], *s.m.* dotting pen.

traulisme [trolism], *s.m.* traulism.

trauma [troma], *s.m. Med: Psy:* trauma.

traumaticine [tromatisin], *s.f. Pharm:* traumaticin(e).

traumatique [tromatik], *a. Med:* traumatic (fever, shock, etc.).

traumatisme [tromatism], *s.m. Med:* traumatism.

traumatologie [tromatɔlɔʒi], *s.f. Med:* traumatology.

traumatopnée [tromatɔpne], *s.f. Med:* traumatopn(o)ea.

travail¹ [travaːj], *s.m. Farr: Vet:* sling, frame (in which a horse is placed to be shod or to be operated upon); stocks, trave, travis; *pl. travails.*

travail², **-aux** [travaːj, -o], *s.m.* **1.** (*a*) *A:* suffering, pain; torment; **les voyages ont leur travaux comme leur plaisirs,** travel affords both pain and pleasure; (*b*) **femme en t.,** woman in labour, in childbirth; **arrêt du t.,** missed labour; (*in hospital*) **salle de t.,** labour room. **2.** (*a*) work; **dur t.,** hard, uphill, work; **division du t.,** division of labour; **organisation scientifique du t.,** organization and methods; *Ind:* **décomposition du t.,** job sequencing; **planification du t.,** job scheduling; **instruments de t.,** (i) tools; (ii) works of reference, reference books; **se mettre au t.,** to begin, start, set to, get down to, work; **allons, au t.!** come on, let's get down to work; **avoir le t. facile,** to work easily, to find one's work easy; **avoir le t. lent,** to work slowly; to be a slow worker; **cesser le t.,** (i) to stop work; to knock off (for the day); (ii) to down tools; **on a suspendu le t.,** work is suspended, in abeyance; **fournir un t. utile,** to do useful work; **à t. égal, salaire égal,** equal pay for equal work; **se débarrasser de sa graisse par le t.,** to work off one's fat; **vêtements de t.,** working clothes; *O:* **homme de t.,** labourer; **homme de grand t.,** hardworking man, hard worker; **séance de t. d'une association, etc.,** business meeting of an association, etc.; *Adm:* **admission des enfants au t.,** employment of children; **Ministère du T.** = Department of Employment; **Bureau International du T.,** International Labour Office; *Jur:* **t. disciplinaire,** *A:* **travaux forcés,** hard labour; *Myth:* **les douze travaux d'Hercule,** the twelve labours of Hercules; (*b*) **t. de tête, t. intellectuel,** intellectual work, brainwork; **t. manuel,** manual labour; *Sch:* **travaux manuels,** arts and crafts; **c'est du t. à la main,** it's handmade; **travaux des champs,** agricultural labour; *Ind:* **t. mécanique,** machine work; **t. de nuit,** night work; **t. à l'heure, à la journée,** work by the hour, by the day; **t. à la pièce, aux pièces,** piece work; job work; **t. à façon,** jobbing; **t. à domicile,** home industry; work done at home (outside office, etc., hours); **t. à l'entreprise,** contract work; **t. en série,** mass production; **t. noir,** black work; job outside the law; moonlighting; **t. à l'aiguille,** needlework; *O:* **travaux pour dames,** (ladies') fancy work; *Min:* **travaux de mines,** mining (work); **vieux travaux,** old workings; **t. à ciel ouvert,** (i) opencast mining; (ii) quarrying; **t. au tour,** lathe work; *Sch:* **travaux pratiques,** practical work, practicals; *Med:* tutorials; *F:* **quel t.!** what a mess! (*c*) *Elcs:* (*computers*) **t. principal,** main job; **élément de t.,** job; **étape de t.,** job step; **file d'attente des travaux,** task queue; **mémoire de t.,** working memory store; temporary storage; **ordre début des travaux,** job statement; (*d*) working, operation; **t. de la digestion,** working of the digestion; **le t. qui se fit dans son esprit,** the working out of things in his mind; **t. du vin,** working, fermenting, of wine; **t. des eaux,** action of water (on banks of stream, etc.); *Mec:* **t. mécanique, t. moteur,** mechanical energy; **t. à la tension,** tension stress; **t. au cisaillement,** shearing stress; **surface de t.,** working face (of valve, etc.); *Mch:* **pression de t.,** working pressure; (*e*) exercise, practice; **coup qui demande beaucoup de t.,** stroke that requires a lot of practice; *Mil:* **t. d'armes,** arms drill; (*f*) occupation, employment; **donner du t. à qn,** to give s.o. a job; **manque de t.,** lack of work; unemployment; **être sans t.,** to be out of work, unemployed; (*g*) (place of) work; **il est à son t.,** he's at work; **il est parti pour son t.,** he's left for work, he's (already) gone to work; **habiter loin de son t.,** to live a long way from one's work. **3.** (*a*) piece of work; **entreprendre un t.,** to undertake a piece of work, a job; **quel beau t.!** what fine work! what a fine piece of work! (*b*) (literary, etc.) work; **auteur d'un t. sur les métaux,** author of a work on metals; **travaux d'une société,** proceedings, transactions, of a society; (*c*) *Adm:* **travaux publics,** public works; *P.N:* **travaux,** road works ahead, men at work; *Mil:* **travaux de défense,** defensive works, outworks. **4.** workmanship; **bijou d'un beau t.,** jewel of fine workmanship.

travaillant [travajɑ̃], *a.* (*a*) working (surface, mechanism, etc.); (*b*) *Mec.E:* stress-bearing.

travaillé [travaje], *a.* (*a*) worked, wrought (iron, stone); **non t.,** unworked; (*b*) laboured, elaborate (style, etc.); (*c*) weathered (rock, etc.); (*d*) **l'opinion publique est très travaillée,** public opinion is very much worked up; **être t. par une idée,** to be obsessed by an idea.

travailler [travaje]. **1.** *v.tr.* (*a*) to torment, worry, obsess; **quelque chose le travaille,** something is preying on his mind; something is worrying him; **un désir le travaillait,** he was tormented, obsessed, with a desire; **l'ambition ne me travaille point,** I have no feeling of ambition; **être travaillé de, par, la goutte,** to be a martyr to, victim of, gout; **se t. l'esprit,** to worry; **se t. l'imagination,** to imagine all sorts of things; (*b*) to work (up)on (s.o., the feelings, etc.); to bring pressure to bear upon (s.o.); **le mécontentement travaille les masses,** the people are undermined by discontent; **t. l'armée,** to undermine the loyalty of the army; **t. des témoins,** to tamper with witnesses; (*c*) to overwork, fatigue (horse); (*d*) to work, fashion, shape (wood, iron, etc.); **t. la pâte,** to knead the dough; **t. son style,** to polish one's style; **de mes tragédies, voici celle que j'ai le plus travaillée,** this is the tragedy that gave me the hardest work, the greatest trouble; *Phot:* **t. un cliché,** to work up a negative; (*e*) to work at, study (one's part, music, etc.); **il faut t. votre anglais,** you must work hard at your English. **2.** *v.i.* (*a*) to work, labour, toil; **t. ferme pour nourrir sa famille,** to work hard to keep one's family; **t. à la terre,** to work on the land; **t. assidûment,** to plod, peg away (à, at); **t. dur,** to work hard; *F:* **t. comme un nègre, comme quatre, comme un cheval,** to work like a slave, a beaver, a Trojan, a horse; *P:* **t. du chapeau,** to have a screw loose; **le temps travaille pour nous,** time is on our side; **se tuer à (force de) t.,** to kill oneself with work; to work oneself to death; **t. pour le roi de Prusse,** to have one's trouble for nothing; to work for nothing; to get nothing out of it; **se rendre malade à force de t.,** to make oneself ill with work; **se mettre à t.,** to get down to work; **j'y ai travaillé jusqu'à minuit,** I was at it until midnight; **t. à l'aiguille,** to do needlework; **t. pour soi-même, pour, à, son compte,** to work, to be in business, for oneself, on one's own account; **t. pour le bien de qn,** to work for the good of s.o., in s.o.'s interest; **t. contre qn,** to work, intrigue, against s.o.; **t. à la perte de qn, à perdre qn,** to aim at ruining s.o.; **t. à un roman,** to work at, on, a novel; **t. à faire qch.,** to make an effort, exert oneself, to do sth.; **t. à produire de l'effet,** to strain after effect; (*b*) (*of performing animals, etc.*) to go through their performance, to perform; (*c*) (*of ship, cable, etc.*) to strain; (*of ship's sides*) to pant; (*of beam*) to be in stress, to be stressed; (*of wine*) to ferment, to work; (*of the mind*) to be in a ferment; (*of wood*) to warp, shrink; (*of walls*) to crack; (*of pigment*) to fade; (*of volcano*) to be active; (*d*) **faire t. une machine,** to work, run, an engine; **faire t. son argent,** to put one's money out at interest.

travailleur, **-euse** [travajœːr, -øːz]. **1.** *a.* (*a*) industrious, hard-working; **élève t.,** hard-working pupil; (*b*) **les masses travailleuses,** the workers, the working classes. **2.** *s.* worker; (*a*) **bon t.,** good, hard, worker; (*b*) **t. manuel,** manual worker; **t. de force,** heavy worker; **t. intellectuel,** intellectual, brain worker; **t. indépendant,** self-employed worker; **t. à domicile,** home worker; **t. ambulant, itinérant,** (i) itinerant worker; (ii) drifter; **t. en bâtiment,** building worker; **les travailleurs,** the workers, the working people; (*c*) *s.f.* **travailleuse familiale,** mother's help; (*d*) *s.f. Ent:* **travailleuse,** worker (bee). **3.** *s.f.* **travailleuse,** (lady's) work table.

travaillisme [travajism], *s.m. Pol:* (British) socialism, doctrine of the Labour Party.

travailliste [travajist], *Eng.Pol:* **1.** *s.m.* (*a*) member of the Labour Party; (*b*) Labour member (of Parliament). **2.** *a.* **parti t., député t.,** Labour Party, Labour member.

travail-repos [travajrəpo], *s.m.inv. Elcs:* **opération t.-r.,** make-break operation.

trave [traːv], *s.f. Carp:* notched joint.

traveau, -eaux [travo], *s.m. Const:* joist.

travée [trave], *s.f.* **1.** *Const: Arch:* bay. **2.** (i) span, bay (of bridge); (ii) independent girder (of bridge). **3.** *Av:* rib (of wing). **4.** bank (of seats, machines, etc.); series, tier (of bookshelves, etc.).

travelage [travlaːʒ], *s.m. Rail:* **le t.,** (i) the sleepers; (ii) the number of sleepers per kilometre.

travelling [travəliŋ], *s.m. Cin:* (*a*) dolly, travelling platform (for the camera); (*b*) **t. en poursuite,** dolly shot, follow shot, tracking shot.

travers [travɛːr], *s.m.* **1.** (*a*) breadth; **t. de doigt,** finger's breadth; *adv.phr.* **en t.,** across, athwart, crosswise, transversely; **autobus avec places disposées en t.,** bus with seats arranged crosswise; **profil en t.,** cross section; *prep.phr.* **en t. de,** across; **se mettre en t. du chemin, des volontés, de qn,** to stand in s.o.'s way, to thwart s.o.'s wishes; **à t. qch., au t. de qch.,** through sth.; **il lui passa son épée au t. du corps,** he ran him through (the body); **on étudie l'œuvre et on voit l'auteur à t.,** we study the work, and through it we imagine the author; **à t. le monde,** throughout the world; (*b*) *Nau:* beam, broadside (of vessel); **vent de t.,** wind abeam, on the beam; beam wind; **par le t.,** abeam, on the beam, on the broadside, athwartships; **droit par le t.,** right abeam; **mer, lame, de t.,** beam sea; **prendre, recevoir, la lame par le t.,** (i) to keep broadside on to the sea; (ii) to broach to; **cabine par le t.,** cabin amidships; **collision par le t.,** collision broadside-on; **présenter le t. à l'ennemi,** to turn broadside on to the enemy; **se canonner par le t.,** to exchange broadsides; **nous sommes par le t. du phare,** we are abeam, abreast, of the lighthouse; *F:* **prendre par le t.,** to take a short cut; **en t.,** athwart; **en t. du navire,** athwartship(s); **le courant est en t.,** the current is athwart; **tomber en t. du vent,** to fall off the wind; to fall off; **venir en t.,** to broach to; **mettre un navire en t.,** to bring a ship to; **être en t. de la lame,** to be in the trough of the sea; (*c*) *Elcs:* (*computers*) **correction de mise en t.,** deskew. **2.** (*a*) cross string (of racquet); (*b*) lintel (of mantelpiece). **3.** irregularity (of building, etc.) *adv.phr.* **de t.,** askew, the wrong way; **tout alla de t.,** everything went wrong; **regarder qn de t.,** to look askance, to scowl, at s.o.; **il a le nez de t.,** he has a crooked nose, his nose is askew; **il a la bouche de t.,** his mouth is crooked; **les tableaux pendaient de t.,** the pictures were hung crooked; **il a des idées tout(es) de t.,** his ideas are all wrong; **entendre, prendre, tout de t.,** to put a wrong construction on everything; to take things the wrong way; **vous avez compris de t. ce passage,** you have misunderstood this passage. **4.** (*a*) *A:* **t. (d'esprit),** eccentricity; **il a quelques petits t.,** he has some little oddities; (*b*) failing, bad habit, fault; **malgré tous ses t.,** in spite of all his faults. **5.** *pl. Metall:* cross cracks (in iron).

traversable [travɛrsabl], *a.* traversable (region, desert, etc.); fordable (river).

traversant [travɛrsɑ̃]. **1.** *a.* traversing; **boulon t.,** through bolt; **douleur traversante,** stabbing pain. **2.** *s.m.* beam (of balance).

traverse [travɛrs], *s.f.* **1.** (*a*) **(chemin de) t.,** cross road, short cut; **rue de t.,** cross street; **j'ai pris la t.,** I took the short cut; (*b*) *A:* **cela m'est venu de t.,** I heard of it indirectly. **2.** (*a*) **(barre de) t.,** cross bar, cross piece; traverse beam, girder; rail (of door); slat (of bed); rung (of ladder); *Artil:* cross bar (of sight); *Mil: etc:* ground sill (of trestle bridge); *Const:* transom; barge couple; *Rail:* sleeper, *U.S:* tie; *Tex:* headstock (of loom); *Veh:* (i) splinter bar, (ii) bolster (of carriage); *Aut: etc:* cross member (of frame); *Av:* compression strut; **t. arrière d'une locomotive,** tailpiece of a locomotive; **t. avant,** bumper (beam) (of locomotive); *Nau:* **t. de tente,** awning stretcher; (*b*) *Fort:* traverse; (*c*) *Mch:* crosshead; (*d*) *Nau:* bar (at harbour mouth); (*e*) *Her:* bendlet sinister. **3.** *F:* hitch, setback; **essuyer bien des traverses,** to meet with many setbacks; **se mettre, se jeter, à la t. des projets de qn,** to oppose s.o.'s plans; **se jeter à la t.,** to intervene.

traversée [travɛrse], *s.f.* **1.** (*a*) passage, (sea) crossing; **faire la t. de Douvres à Calais,** to cross from Dover to Calais; **nous avons eu, fait, une belle t., une mauvaise t.,** we had a fine, rough, crossing, passage; **la traversée sera bientôt faite,** we shall soon be across; **la longueur de la t.,** the distance across; (*b*) **faire la t. d'une ville,** to cross, pass through, a town; (*c*) *Mount:* traverse. **2.** *Rail:* **t. de voie,** railway crossing; crossover.

traversement [travɛrs(ə)mɑ̃], *s.m.* crossing.

traverser [travɛrse], *v.tr.* **1.** (*a*) to traverse (region); to cross, go across, step across (street, etc.); to go, pass, through (town, danger, crisis, etc.); to cross (a town); **t. la foule,** to make one's way through the crowd; **vous n'arriverez pas à t. la forêt,** you will never get through the forest; **il est arrivé à t. la rivière,** he got across the river; **t. la rivière à la nage, en bateau, par le bac,** to swim, row, ferry, across the river; **t. un pont,** to cross a bridge; **le pont qui traverse la rivière,** the bridge that crosses the river; **une planche traverse le ruisseau,** a plank bridges the stream, there is a plank across the stream; **un chemin étroit traverse la forêt,** a narrow path leads through the forest; **t. une forêt à cheval, à bicyclette, en auto,** to ride, cycle, drive, through a forest; **t. un désert en avion,** to fly across a desert; **il eut la jambe traversée par une balle,** he was shot through the leg; **la balle lui traversa le bras,** the bullet went through his arm; **la pluie avait traversé mon pardessus,** the rain had gone through my overcoat; **t. qch. de part en part,** to go right through sth.; **l'idée me traversa l'esprit comme un éclair,** the idea flashed through my mind; **ce reproche lui traversa le cœur,** this reproach pierced him to the heart; **un cri traversa le silence,** the silence was broken by a cry; (*b*) to cross-cut (stone). **2.** *A:* to cross, thwart (s.o.'s plans). **3.** *Nau:* (*a*) to fish (anchor); (*b*) to bear (sail) to the windward.

se traverser, (*of horse*) to traverse.

traversier, -ière [travɛrsje, -jɛːr]. **1.** *a.* cross, crossing; *A:* **rue traversière,** cross-street; *Const:* **poutre traversière,** bridging piece, straining piece; *A:* **barque traversière,** ferry (boat); *Nau:* **vent t.,** leading wind. **2.** *s.m.* (*a*) cross bar (of banner); (*b*) *Fr.C:* ferry (boat). **3.** *s.f.* **traversière:** (*a*) *Const:* bridging piece (between beams); collar beam (between rafters); (*b*) *Mil.E:* breast line (of pontoon bridge); (*c*) *Nau:* fish, fish tackle (of anchor).

traversin [travɛrsɛ̃], *s.m.* **1.** (*a*) *Carp: etc:* cross bar, cross piece, transom; thwart, stretcher (of rowing boat); *Nau:* **t. de panneau,** hatch carling; (*b*) *Nau:* cross tree; (*c*) beam (of balance). **2.** bolster (for bed).

traversine [travɛrsin], *s.f.* **1.** cross bar, cross beam, cross board, cross sleeper. **2.** (crossing) plank (between two ships); gang plank.

travertin [travɛrtɛ̃], *s.m. Geol:* travertine (stone); sinter; freshwater limestone; **barre de t.,** rimstone bar.

travesti, -ie [travɛsti]. **1.** *a.* (*a*) disguised; **bal t.,** fancy-dress ball, costume ball; *Th:* **rôle t.,** *s.m.* **travesti,** man's part taken by a woman, or vice versa; drag part; (*b*) travestied, burlesqued (play, etc.). **2.** *s.m.* fancy dress. **3.** *s.* transvestite.

travestir [travɛstiːr], *v.tr.* **1.** to disguise (*esp.* with ludicrous effect, or for fancy dress); **t. un homme en femme,** to disguise a man as a woman; **il s'était travesti en marin,** he had dressed himself up as a sailor. **2.** (*a*) to travesty, parody, burlesque (play, poem); *Th:* **t. un rôle,** to guy a part; (*b*) **t. la pensée de qn,** to misrepresent s.o.'s thoughts; to give a false representation of s.o.'s thoughts; **on a travesti ses défauts en vices,** his failings have been distorted into vices.

travestisme [travɛstism], *s.m. Psy:* transvestism; eonism.

travestissement [travɛstismɑ̃], *s.m.* **1.** (*a*) disguising; (*b*) disguise; *Th:* **rôle à travestissements,** quick-change part. **2.** (*a*) travesty (of play, etc.); (*b*) misrepresentation (of facts, etc.); **c'est un t. de la vérité,** it is a travesty of the truth. **3.** *Psy:* transvestism, eonism.

travestisseur, -euse [travɛstisœːr, -øːz]. **1.** *a.* parodying. **2.** *s.* parodist; misinterpreter.

traveteau, eaux [travto], *s.m.*, **travette** [travɛt], *s.f. Const:* joist.

traviole (de) [dətravjɔl], *adv.phr. P:* crooked, (all) on one side; **son chapeau était tout de t.,** his hat was all askew, all on one side; **le monde va de t.,** the world's all upside down.

travois [travwa], *s.m. Veh:* travois.

travon [travɔ̃], *s.m. Civ.E:* stringer (beam).

travure [travyːr], *s.f.* **1.** cookhouse (on river barge). **2.** *Const:* beams and joists (supporting a floor).

trayeur, -euse [trɛjœːr, -øːz]. **1.** (*a*) milking apparatus, etc.). **2.** *s.* (*pers.*) milker; *Med:* **nodule des trayeurs,** milkers' nodules. **3.** *s.f.* **trayeuse,** milking machine.

trayon [trɛjɔ̃], *s.m.* dug, teat (of cow, etc.).

Trébie (la) [latrebi], *Pr.n.f. Geog:* the (river) Trebbia.

Trébizonde [trebizɔ̃:d], *Pr.n. Geog:* Trebizond, Trabzon.

trébuchage [trebyʃaːʒ], *s.m.* testing (of coins) for weight.

trébuchant [trebyʃɑ̃]. **1.** *a.* staggering (along); stumbling; **voix trébuchante,** hesitating, quavering, voice. **2.** (*a*) *a. A:* (*of coin*) of full weight; (*b*) *s.m. A:* slight overweight (added to coins to provide against loss of weight by use).

trébuchement [trebyʃmɑ̃], *s.m.* stumbling; tripping up.

trébucher [trebyʃe]. **1.** *v.i.* (*the aux. is* **avoir,** *occ.* **être**) (*a*) *A:* to totter to one's fall; **il trébuchait déjà du faîte de sa gloire,** already he was tottering to his fall; (*b*) to stumble, trip, totter; **marcher en trébuchant,** to stumble along; **faire t. qn,** to trip s.o. up; **t. sur un mot,** to trip over a word; (*c*) (*of coin*) to turn the scale. **2.** *v.tr.* to test (coin) for weight.

trébuchet [trebyʃɛ], *s.m.* **1.** (*a*) bird trap; (*b*) trap, deadfall. **2.** (small) precision balance (for weighing gold, chemical ingredients, etc.); assay balance. **3.** *A.Arms:* trebuchet.

trécentiste [tresɑ̃tist], *s.m. Lit.Hist:* trecentist.

trêcheur [trɛʃœːr], *s.m. Her:* tressure.

trechmannite [trɛʃmanit], *s.f. Miner:* trechmannite.

trécorrois, -oise [trekɔrwa, -waːz], *a. & s. Geog:* (native, inhabitant) of Tréguier.

treedozer [tridozɛːr], *s.m. Civ.E:* treedozer.

tréfilage [trefilaːʒ], *s.m. Metalw:* wire drawing.

tréfiler [trefile], *v.tr. Metalw:* (*a*) to (wire)draw; **banc à t.,** wire-drawing bench; **presse à t.,** drawing press; (*b*) **métal tréfilé,** extruded metal.

tréfilerie [trefilri], *s.f. Metalw:* **1.** wire drawing. **2.** (wire-)drawing mill.

tréfileur [trefilœːr], *Metalw:* wire maker. **1.** *s.m.* (*pers.*) wire drawer; wire maker. **2.** *a.m.* **banc t.,** wire-drawing bench.

tréfileuse [trefiløːz], *s.f. Metalw:* wire-drawing machine.

tréfiloir [trefilwaːr], *s.m. Metalw:* (small) wire-drawing bench.

trèfle [trɛfl], *s.m.* **1.** *Bot:* (*a*) trefoil, clover; **t. blanc,** wild white clover; **t. rouge,** red clover; **t. incarnat, anglais, du Roussillon; t. farouche,** crimson clover, French clover; **t. rampant, petit t. blanc,** white clover, Dutch clover; (*in Ireland*) shamrock; **t. jaune,** kidney vetch, lady's fingers; **petit t. jaune,** nonsuch, black medick; **t. à quatre feuilles,** four-leaved clover; (*b*) **t. cornu,** bird's foot trefoil; **t. d'eau,** marsh trefoil, buckbean, bog bean, bog myrtle. **2.** *Arch: Her:* trefoil; *Civ.E:* **croisement en t.,** clover-leaf intersection. **3.** *Cards:* clubs; **jouer t.,** to play a club, clubs; **as de t.,** ace of clubs. **4.** *Mil:* (*a*) shoulder knot (of *gendarme*, etc.); (*b*) trefle, three-chamber mine. **5.** *Elcs:* **t. cathodique,** electron-ray tube, *F:* magic eye. **6.** *Nau:* spectacle clew (of square sail). **7.** *P:* crowd, mob.

tréflé [trefle], *a.* trefoil(ed); *Her:* treflé; *Arch:* **arc t.,** trefoil arch.

tréflière [trefljɛːr], *s.f.* clover field.

tréfoncier, -ière [trefɔ̃sje, -jɛːr]. **1.** *a.* of the subsoil; *Min:* **redevance tréfoncière,** royalty. **2.** *s.* owner of the soil and subsoil.

tréfonds [trefɔ̃], *s.m.* subsoil; minerals, etc., lying below the ground; **vendre le fonds et le t.,** to sell soil and subsoil; **t. d'un immeuble,** ground underneath a building; **le t. de l'âme,** the depths of the soul; **dans le t. de mon cœur,** in my heart of hearts; **le t. de notre être,** our innermost being; **savoir le fonds et le t. d'une affaire,** to have probed deeply into a matter; to know all about a matter.

trégorrois, -oise [tregɔrwa, -waːz], *a. & s. Geog:* (native, inhabitant) of Tréguier.

tréhala [treala], *s.m. Pharm:* trehala, tricala, Turkish manna.

tréhalase [trealaːz], *s.f. Bio-Ch:* trehalase.

tréhalose [trealoːz], *s.f. Ch:* trehalose.

treillage [trɛjaːʒ], *s.m.* trellis (work); lattice work; **t. métallique, en fil de fer,** (i) wire fencing; (ii) wire netting, *F:* chicken wire.

treillager [trɛjaʒe], *v.tr.* (**je treillageai(s); n. treillageons**) (*a*) to trellis, lattice (wall, etc.); **fenêtre treillagée,** lattice window; (*b*) to enclose with wire netting.

treillageur [trɛjaʒœːr], *s.m.*, **treillagiste** [trɛjaʒist], *s.m.* (i) manufacturer, (ii) seller, of trellis work or wire netting.

treille [trɛːj], *s.f.* **1.** (*a*) vine arbour; trellised vineyard, vines; **t. à l'italienne,** pergola; (*b*) (climbing) vine; *Lit:* **le dieu de la t.,** the god of wine, Bacchus; *F:* **le jus de la t.,** the juice of the grape; wine. **2.** *Fish:* shrimp net; prawn net.

treillis [trɛji], *s.m.* **1.** (*a*) trellis (work); lattice; **t. métallique,** wire netting, *F:* chicken wire; (*b*) *Civ.E:* **arc en t.,** trussed arch; **poteau en t.,** trellis-work post; *N.Arch:* **mât t.,** lattice mast; (*c*) *Her:* trellis. **2.** (*a*) grating; (*b*) *Mth:* lattice; *Mapm:* grid. **3.** *Tex:* (*a*) (coarse) canvas; sackcloth, sacking; (*b*) glazed calico; (*c*) *pl. Mil:* denims; dungarees, fatigue dress.

treillissé [trɛjise], *a.* **1.** (*a*) trellised, latticed (window, etc.); *Arm:* **cotte treillissée,** coat of trellised armour; (*b*) *Her:* fretty cloué. **2.** criss-cross (pattern, etc.); interlaced.

treillisser [trɛjise], *v.tr.* (*a*) to trellis, lattice; (*b*) to enclose with wire netting, to net.

treizaine [trɛzɛn], *s.f.* (approximately) thirteen, about thirteen; *A:* **vendre des œufs, des huîtres, par treizaines,** to sell eggs, oysters, in baker's dozens, by the baker's dozen.

treize [trɛːz], *num.a.inv. & s.m.inv.* thirteen; *Com:* **t. douze, t. à la douzaine,** thirteen as twelve; *F:* a baker's dozen; **le numéro t.,** number thirteen; **le t. mai,** the thirteenth of May; **Louis Treize,** Louis the Thirteenth; *Sp:* **jeu, rugby, à t.,** Rugby League football.

treizer [treze], *v.tr. F:* **t. la douzaine,** to make a baker's dozen.

treizième [trɛzjɛm]. **1.** *num.a. & s.* thirteenth. **2.** *s.m.* thirteenth (part). **3.** *s.f. Mus:* thirteenth.

treizièmement [trɛzjɛmmɑ̃], *adv.* thirteenthly, in the thirteenth place.

treiziste [trɛzist], *s.m. Sp: F:* Rugby League player.

trélingage [trelɛ̃gaːʒ], *s.m. Nau:* cat-harpings.

trélinguer [trelɛ̃ge], *v.tr. Nau:* to swifter (the shrouds, etc.).

tréma [trema]. **1.** *s.m.* diaeresis; *pl. trémas,* diaereses. **2.** *inv.* **des ë tréma,** e's with diaeresis.

trémail [tremaːj], *s.m. Fish:* trammel (net).

trémaillade [tremajad], *s.f. Fish:* large trammel (net).

trémat [trema], *s.m.*, **trémate** [tremat], *s.f.* sandbank (in river Seine).

trématage [tremataːʒ], *s.m. Nav:* (*a*) passing, steering round, sandbanks (in river); (*b*) **droit de t.,** priority of passage (at a lock).

trémater [tremate], *v.tr. & i. Nav:* (*in land waterways*) (*a*) to pass, overtake (another vessel); **il est interdit de t. aux abords des écluses,** overtaking is forbidden near a lock; (*b*) to pass, steer round (a sandbank); (*c*) to claim priority of passage (at a lock).

trématode [trematɔd], *s.m. Ann:* trematode (worm); fluke; *pl.* **trématodes,** Trematoda.

trématosaure [trematɔsɔːr], **trematosaurus** [trematɔsɔrys], *s.m. Paleont:* trematosaurus.

tremblaie [trɑ̃blɛ], *s.f.* aspen plantation; aspen grove.

tremblant, -ante [trɑ̃blɑ̃, -ɑ̃ːt]. **1.** *a.* trembling (knees, hand); quivering (face); shaky (bridge); quaking (ground); unsteady, flickering (light); trembling, tremulous, quavering, faltering (voice); **elle est toute tremblante,** she's trembling all over; **t. (de peur),** trembling, shaking, with fear. **2.** *s.m. Mus:* tremolo stop (of organ). **3.** *a. & s.f. Vet:* **(maladie) tremblante,** trembles (of sheep). **4.** *s.f. Ich:* **tremblante,** torpedo, electric ray.

tremble [trɑ̃ːbl], *s.m.* **1.** *Bot:* (*also* **peuplier t.**), aspen; trembling poplar. **2.** *Ich: F:* torpedo, electric ray.

tremblé [trɑ̃ble]. **1.** *a.* (*a*) shaky (handwriting, etc.); wavy (line); (*b*) *Mus:* **notes tremblées,** tremolo notes. **2.** *a. & s.m. Typ:* **(filet) t.,** waved rule.

tremblement [trɑ̃bləmɑ̃], *s.m.* **1.** trembling, quiver(ing), shaking (of body, hand, bridge, etc.); tremulousness, quavering (of voice), shuddering (with horror). **2.** (*a*) tremor; **un t. de peur, de joie, de colère,** a tremor of fear, of joy, of anger; **t. de fièvre,** fit of shivering (caused by fever); **t. de terre,** earth tremor; earthquake; *F:* **et tout le t.,** and all the rest of it; and the whole bag of tricks, and the whole lot, and the whole caboodle; (*b*) *Med:* tremor. **3.** *Mus:* tremolo. **4.** *Aer:* buffeting.

trembler [trɑ̃ble], *v.i.* **1.** (*a*) to tremble, quiver, shake, shiver; to quake; (*of light*) to quiver, flicker; (*of voice*) to quaver; (*of wings*) to flutter; **le pont, le sol, tremble,** the bridge, the earth, is shaking; **faire t. les vitres,** to make the windows shake, rattle; **la main lui tremblait,** his hand was shaking; **t. de colère, de froid, de fièvre,** to shake with anger, to shiver with cold, with fever; (*with cogn.acc*) **t. la fièvre,** to shake, shiver, with fever; (*b*) to tremble, quake, with fear; **t. de tout son corps, t. de tous ses membres,** to tremble in all one's limbs; to shake, tremble, all over; F: t. dans sa peau, to quake, shake, in one's shoes; t. devant qn, to stand in fear of s.o.; en tremblant, tremblingly, tremulously; je tremble à le voir, I tremble whenever I see him; je tremble de le rencontrer, I tremble at the thought of meeting him; je tremblais de le réveiller, I was fearful of awakening him; il tremblait à l'idée qu'on ne critiquât son œuvre, he trembled at the idea that his work might be criticized; elle tremblait qu'on (ne) la découvrît, she was in deadly fear of being discovered; she was terrified of being discovered; ça me fait t. quand j'y pense, it gives me the shivers to think of it; F: manger à faire t., to eat a tremendous amount, in terrific quantities. 2. Mus: to play tremolo; to quaver.

trembleur, -euse [trɑ̃blœːr, -øːz], s. 1. (a) trembler; (b) Rel.H: (i) Quaker; (ii) Shaker. 2. timid, apprehensive, person; rassurer les trembleurs, to reassure the anxious, the quaking spirits. 3. El: (a) s.m. trembler, vibrator (of coil); contact breaker, make-and-break; hammer break (of electric bell, etc.); Tg: Tp: buzzer, ticker; bobine à t., trembler coil; (b) a. sonnerie trembleuse, trembling electric bell. 4. s.f. Fish: pêche à la trembleuse, dapping; pêcher à la trembleuse, to dap.

trembleux [trɑ̃blø], s.m. Ich: F: torpedo, electric ray.

tremblotant [trɑ̃blɔtɑ̃], a. trembling (slightly); quivering, shivering (body); tremulous (smile); quavering (voice); flickering (light); fluttering (wings).

tremblote [trɑ̃blɔt], s.f. P: avoir la t., (i) to be all of a tremble, a dither; (ii) to have the jitters; (iii) to be all of a shiver.

tremblotement [trɑ̃blɔtmɑ̃], s.m. 1. trembling, quivering; quavering (of voice); shivering; fluttering (of wings). 2. quiver, shiver.

trembloter [trɑ̃blɔte]. 1. v.i. to tremble (slightly); to quiver; (of voice) to quaver, shake; (of light) to flicker; (of wings) to flutter; t. de froid, de peur, to shiver with cold, with fear; de timides lueurs tremblotent aux vitres du village, faint lights gleam unsteadily behind the village windows. 2. v.tr. t. une chanson, to quaver out a song.

trémellacées [tremɛl(l)ase], s.f.pl. Fung: Tremellaceae.

trémellales [tremɛl(l)al], s.f.pl. Fung: Tremellales.

trémelle [tremɛl], s.f. Fung: tremella.

tremex [tremɛks], s.m. Ent: wood wasp; (genus) Tremex.

trémie [tremi], s.f. 1. (a) (mill) hopper; boot (of grain elevator); loading funnel; cone (of blast furnace); (ore) bin; Civ.E: trémie, tremmie, U.S: treamie; (b) hopper (for chickens, etc.); feeding box (for pheasants, pigeons). 2. Const: hearth cavity. 3. (pyramidal) salt crystal formation.

trémière [tremjɛːr], a.f. & s.f. Bot: (rose) t., hollyhock.

trémois [tremwa], s.m. Agr: 1. spring wheat. 2. mixed fodder crop (of wheat, rye, oats and vetch).

trémolite [tremɔlit], s.f. Miner: tremolite, grammatite.

tremolo, trémolo [tremɔlo], s.m. Mus: 1. tremolo; avoir des tremolos dans la voix, to have a quaver in one's voice. 2. tremolo stop (of organ).

trémouline [tremulin], s.f. Ich: F: torpedo, electric ray.

trémoussement [tremusmɑ̃], s.m. (a) jigging up and down; danser avec des trémoussements de marionnettes, to dance as if hung on wires; (b) jerking, jerks (of a rope, etc.); (c) fluttering, flutter (of wings).

trémousser [tremuse], v.i. (of birds) t. des ailes, to flutter, flap, their wings.

se trémousser. 1. (a) to fidget; ne te trémousse pas sur ta chaise, don't fidget on your chair; (b) to jig up and down (in dancing, etc.); (c) (of birds) to flutter (about). 2. to make an effort, put oneself out (in order to achieve sth.); allons, trémoussez-vous! come on, get a move on!

trémoussoir [tremuswaːr], s.m. F: A: dance hall.

trempabilité [trɑ̃pabilite], s.f. Metall: hardening capacity, hardenability, (of steel and other alloys).

trempage [trɑ̃paːʒ], s.m. steeping, soaking (of skins, materials, grain, bricks, etc.); Typ: wetting, damping (of the paper); Cu: soaking (of dried vegetables, etc., before cooking, of babas, etc. in syrup).

trempant [trɑ̃pɑ̃], a. (of metal) capable of being tempered; acier t., hardening steel.

trempe [trɑ̃ːp], s.f. 1. steeping, dipping, soaking; Typ: damping, wetting (of the paper); mettre qch. en t., to steep sth.; to put sth. to soak. 2. Metall: hardening, quench(ing); t. et revenu, quenching and hardening; acier de t., hardening steel; agent de t., hardening agent; carbone de t., hardening carbon; atelier de t., hardening plant; t. superficielle, surface, face, hardening; t. à, au, cœur, through, full, hardening; t. à l'air, air hardening; t. à l'eau, water quenching, tempering; t. à l'huile, oil quenching; t. martensitique, martempering; t. martensitique incomplète, slack quench; t. bainitique (conjuguée), austempering; t. en dessous de zéro, chill hardening; t. par cémentation, t. de, en, surface, case hardening; t. au chalumeau, flame, torch, hardening; t. glacée, chilling (of cast iron); bain de t., hardening, quenching, bath; t. au bain de sel, free fall quench; t. en bains de sel par étapes, step quench; t. en vase clos, pot quenching; t. par induction, induction quench; vieillissement accéléré par t., quench ageing; t. différentielle, differential quench; t. à haute température, hot quench; t. interrompue, interrupted quench. 3. (a) temper, hardness (of steel); (b) quality, stamp; un homme de sa t., a man of his quality, stamp; a man of his kind, a man like him. 4. Brew: malting water. 5. P: shower of blows; (good) thrashing.

trempé [trɑ̃pe]. 1. a. (a) wet, soaked; t. jusqu'aux os, F: comme une soupe, wet through; soaked to the skin; drenched; like a drowned rat; t. de sueur, bathed in perspiration; streaming with perspiration; oreiller t. de pleurs, pillow drenched with tears; (b) hardened (steel, glass); tempered (steel); Metall: t. à l'huile, oil-tempered; t. revenu, quenched and tempered; t. à nouveau, rehardened; esprit bien t., well-tempered, resolute, mind; athlète bien t., athlete with plenty of stamina; (c) vin t., wine diluted with water. 2. s.m. Phot: etc: immersion; bathing (of plates).

trempée [trɑ̃pe], s.f. 1. steeping, soaking. 2. P: shower of blows; (good) thrashing.

tremper [trɑ̃pe]. 1. v.tr. (a) to mix, dilute, (wine) with water; (b) to soak, steep; to drench; t. qch. dans un liquide, to dip, soak, sth. in a liquid; se t. dans l'eau, to plunge into the water; se t. dans l'atmosphère du moyen âge, to steep oneself in the atmosphere of the Middle Ages; t. la soupe, to pour the soup on the bread; le terrain et les spectateurs étaient trempés, the ground was sodden and the spectators wet through; t. sa plume dans l'encre, to dip one's pen in the ink; t. ses lèvres dans son verre, to set, put, one's lips to one's glass; Tan: t. les peaux, to soak, steep, drench, the skins; Typ: t. le papier, to wet, damp, the paper; (c) Metall: to harden, quench (steel); to chill (cast iron); t. les muscles, to harden the muscles. 2. v.i. (a) (of skins, soiled linen, etc.) to soak, to steep, to lie in soak; (b) t. dans un complot, to have a hand in a plot; to be accessory to a plot; to be involved in a plot, a party to a plot; P: il trempe dans le bain, he's in it up to his neck.

tremperie [trɑ̃pri], s.f. Typ: wetting room.

trempette [trɑ̃pɛt], s.f. (a) sippet (of bread); (b) faire t., (i) to dip bread, etc., in coffee, wine, etc.; to dunk; (ii) F: to have a hasty dip, a quick bathe; il n'a fait qu'une petite t., he just about got wet; nous avons fait une bonne t., we had a good bathe.

trempeur [trɑ̃pœːr], s.m. Tchn: (pers.) 1. temperer, hardener (of metals). 2. dipper (in candle making, pottery glazing, etc.). 3. Typ: wetter.

trempis [trɑ̃pi], s.m. 1. acid bath (for dipping metals, etc.). 2. (a) bath (for desalting cod); (b) desalting room (for cod).

tremplin [trɑ̃plɛ̃], s.m. Sp: springboard; diving board; ski jump; faire le (saut du) t., (i) to jump off the springboard; (ii) to turn a somersault off the spring board; prendre un poste comme t., to take up a post as a stepping stone (to a better position); être sur le t., to be about to take the plunge.

trempoir [trɑ̃pwaːr], s.m. Tex: steeping room (of fulling mill).

trempoire [trɑ̃pwaːr], s.f. Ind: steeping trough, vat.

trémulation [tremylasjɔ̃], s.f. Med: tremor.

trémulent [tremylɑ̃], a. shimmering.

trémuler [tremyle]. 1. v.i. to tremble; to shiver, vibrate. 2. v.tr. t. les doigts, to twiddle, strum, one's fingers.

trenail [trənaːj], s.m. Rail: tre(e)nail.

trench-coat [trɛnʃkot], s.m. trench coat; pl. trench-coats.

trentain [trɑ̃tɛ̃], s.m. 1. Ten: (jeu de paume) thirty all. 2. Ecc: trental.

trentaine [trɑ̃tɛn], s.f. (about) thirty, some thirty; une t. de francs, thirty francs or so; il approche de la t., he's not far off thirty; he's getting on for thirty; avoir passé la t., to be in the thirties.

trente[1] [trɑ̃ːt], num.a.inv. & s.m.inv. thirty; t. jours, thirty days; le t. juin, (on) the thirtieth of June; les années t., the thirties (1930-1939); Hist: la Guerre de T. Ans, the Thirty Years' War; t. et un, thirty-one; F: se mettre sur son t. et un, to dress up; to put on one's best clothes; elle était sur son t. et un, she was all dressed up; Cards: t. et un, (game of) trente et un; t. et quarante, trente et quarante; rouge et noir; Ten: t. à, thirty all; Med: dites trente-trois = say ninety-nine.

Trente[2], Pr.n. Geog: Trent (in Italy); Ecc.Hist: le concile de T., the Council of Trent.

trente-deux-pieds [trɑ̃tdøpje], s.m.inv. Mus: thirty-two-foot stop (of organ).

trentenaire [trɑ̃tnɛːr], a. Jur: lasting thirty years; concession t., thirty years' lease (esp. of a grave); Jur: la possession t. opère la prescription, thirty years' possession founds prescription.

trente-six [trɑ̃tsi, -sis, -siz; for rules of pronunciation see SIX], num.a.inv. & s.m.inv. thirty-six; F: voir t.-s. chandelles, to see stars (after receiving a blow on the head); faire les t.-s. volontés de qn, to dance attendance on s.o., to be s.o.'s slave; il n'y va pas par t.-s. chemins, he doesn't beat about the bush; je le vois tous les t.-s. [trɑ̃tsis] du mois, I see him once in a blue moon; avoir t.-s. raisons de faire qch., to have umpteen reasons for doing sth.; il n'y a pas t.-s. façons de le faire, there are no two ways of doing it.

trente-sixième [trɑ̃tsizjɛm], num.a. & s.inv. thirty-sixth; être dans le t.-s. dessous, (i) to be dejected, in the dumps; (ii) to be down and out.

trentième [trɑ̃tjɛm]. 1. num.a. & s.inv. thirtieth. 2. s.m. thirtieth (part).

trentin [trɑ̃tɛ̃], Geog: 1. a. Trentine, Tridentine. 2. Pr.n.m. le T., the Trentino.

tréou [treu], s.m. Nau: storm lateen sail.

trépan [trepɑ̃], s.m. 1. Tls: (a) trepan, trepanning tool, boring bit; rock drill; ground auger; crown saw; Petroleum Ind: t. à deux étages à six lames, green head bit; t. à deux taillants, four-wing bit; t. à doigts, blue demon bit; t. d'attaque, spudding bit; affiler le t., to dress the bit; (b) Surg: trepan, trephine. 2. = TRÉPANATION.

trépanateur [trepanatœːr], s.m. Surg: trepanner.

trépanation [trepanasjɔ̃], s.f. Surg: trepanning, trephining.

trépaner [trepane], v.tr. 1. to bore, drill, into (rock, etc.). 2. Surg: to trepan; to trephine.

trépang [trepɑ̃], s.m. Echin: trepang, sea slug.

trépas [trepɑ], s.m. 1. Nau: A: narrow channel. 2. Poet: death, decease; passer, aller, de vie à t., to pass away; to depart this life.

trépassé, -ée [trepɑse], a. & s. dead, deceased (person); les trépassés, the dead, the departed; Ecc: le Jour, la Fête, des Trépassés, All Souls' Day; All Souls.

trépassement [trepɑsmɑ̃], s.m. A: death, passing (away).

trépasser [trepɑse], v.i. (the aux. is avoir, occ. être) A: & Lit: to die; to depart this life; to pass away; il a trépassé hier, he passed away yesterday.

trèpe [trɛp], s.m. P: crowd.

tréphine [trefin], s.f. Surg: trephine, perforator.

tréphocyte [trefɔsit], s.m. Med: trephocyte.

tréphone [trefɔn], s.f. Biol: trephone.

trépidant [trepidɑ̃], a. agitated, vibrating; vie trépidante, hectic life; quartier affairé et t., busy and bustling district.

trépidation [trepidasjɔ̃], s.f. 1. (ground) tremor; vibration, trepidation (of machinery, etc.); Metall: corrosion de t., vibration fretting. 2. (a) trepidation, quaking, trembling (of limbs); Med: clonus; (b) trepidation, agitation, state of alarm.

trépider [trepide], v.i. 1. (of machines, etc.) to vibrate, shake. 2. F: to be in a nervous, trembling, state; to be in a state of apprehension.

trépidomètre [trepidɔmɛtr], s.m. seismograph.

trépied [trepje], s.m. tripod; (a) three-legged stool, stand; (b) Ant: le t. de Delphes, the Tripod at Delphi, the Delphic oracle; (c) Cu: trivet; (d) (three-legged) brazier; (e) tripod mounting (of gun, rocket, theodolite, etc.).

trépignée [trepiɲe], s.f. P: O: thrashing, (good) hiding.

trépignement [trepiɲmɑ̃], s.m. stamping (with the feet); throbbing, vibration (of an engine, etc.).

trépigner [trepiɲe]. 1. *v.i.* t. de colère, de rage, to dance with rage; t. de joie, to jump for joy; t. d'impatience, to be like a cat on hot bricks; il trépignait de partir, he was itching to start. 2. *v.tr.* to trample down (earth).

trépigneuse [trepiɲø:z], *s.f.* treadmill (for horses, oxen).

trépointe [trepwɛ̃:t], *s.f.* welt (of shoe); mettre des trépointes à un soulier, to welt a shoe.

tréponématose [trepɔnemato:z], *s.f. Med:* treponematosis.

tréponème [trepɔnɛm], *s.m. Biol:* treponema.

tréponémicide [trepɔnemisid], *a. & s.m. Med:* treponemicide.

tréponémose [trepɔnemo:z], *s.f. Med:* treponematosis.

tréportais, -aise [trepɔrtɛ, -ɛ:z], *a. & s. Geog:* (native, inhabitant) of Le Tréport.

très [trɛ], *adv.* very, most; (very) much; t. bon, (i) very good, (ii) most kind; t. connu, very well known; il n'est pas t. lu, t. connu, aujourd'hui, he is not widely read, widely known, today, now; t. différent, very different, widely different; t. estimé, highly esteemed; t. vite, very quickly; il est soldat et t. soldat, he is a soldier and very much of a soldier; elle est t. femme, she is very feminine; un incident t. miracle de saint Hubert, an incident very like the miracle of St Hubert; prendre qch. t. au sérieux, to take sth. very seriously; *F:* avoir t. faim, t. soif, to be very hungry, very thirsty; avoir t. peur, to be very much afraid; j'ai eu t. honte, I was (very) much ashamed; ces robes sont t. portées, these dresses are very much in the fashion; est-ce-que je me suis fait t. remarquer?—très! did I attract very much notice?—you did! *F:* and how!

trésaille [treza:j], *s.f.* cross-piece, upper rail (of waggon body).

trésaillé [trezaje], *a.* crackled (surface of painting, china ware).

trésaillure [trezajy:r], *s.f.* crackle, minute crack (in picture, ceramics).

trescheur [treʃœ:r], *s.m. Her:* tressure.

très-fonds [trefɔ̃], *s.m. A:* = TRÉFONDS.

Très-Haut (le) [lətrɛo], *Pr.n.m.* The Almighty; God.

trésillon [trezijɔ̃], *s.m.* = ÉTRÉSILLON.

trésor [trezɔ:r], *s.m.* 1. (*a*) treasure; *F:* ma bonne est un t., my maid is a treasure; *F:* mon t., darling; (*b*) *Jur:* treasure trove; (*c*) *Ecc:* (collection of) relics and ornaments; (*d*) treasure house. 2. *pl.* riches, wealth; entasser des trésors, to accumulate, hoard, riches; les trésors de la terre, the treasures of the earth; *F:* il a dépensé des trésors pour cette affaire, he spent a fortune over this business; cela demanderait des trésors d'ingéniosité, it would require infinite ingenuity. 3. treasury; le T. (public), the (French) Treasury; le t. public, public moneys; bons du T., Treasury bills, bonds. 4. (*a*) *A:* t. de la langue grecque, thesaurus of the Greek language; (*b*) ce livre est un t. de faits, this book is a mine of facts.

trésorerie [trezɔrri], *s.f.* 1. treasury; la T. (britannique), the (British) Treasury; the Exchequer; t. générale, (i) office, function, (ii) offices, of a *trésorier général*; commis de t., clerk at a *trésorerie générale*. 2. (*a*) treasurership; (*b*) treasurer's office. 3. funds.

trésorier, -ière [trezɔrje, -jɛ:r], *s.* treasurer; paymaster, paymistress; *Adm:* t.(-payeur) général, chief treasurer and paymaster (of the *département*); commis t., treasury clerk; *Mil:* officier t., paymaster.

tressage [trɛsa:ʒ], *s.m.* braiding, plaiting.

tressaillant [tresajɑ̃], *a.* trembling, quivering (with fear, joy).

tressaillement [tresajmɑ̃], *s.m.* start (of surprise); quiver; shudder (of fear); wince (of pain).

tressaillir [tresaji:r], *v.i.* (*pr.p.* tressaillant; *p.p.* tressailli; *pr.ind.* je tressaille, n. tressaillons, ils tressaillent; *p.d.* je tressaillais; *p.h.* je tressaillis; *fu.* je tressaillirai) to start; to give a start, a jump (from surprise); to quiver; to shudder (with fear); to leap (with joy); (*of heart*) to throb, bound; t. de douleur, to wince; faire t. qn, to startle s.o.; faire t. le cœur de qn, to make s.o.'s heart flutter.

tressaillure [tresajy:r], *s.f. Cer:* crackle, minute crack.

tressaut [treso], *s.m.* (*a*) start, jump (of fear, surprise); (*b*) jolt.

tressautement [tresotmɑ̃], *s.m.* (*a*) starting jumping; (*b*) jolting.

tressauter [tresote], *v.i.* (*a*) to start, jump (with fear, surprise, etc.); (*b*) (*of thgs*) to jolt; to be jolted; to jump about, to be tossed about.

tresse [trɛs], *s.f.* 1. (*a*) plait (of hair); aux tresses d'or, goldenhaired; (*b*) braid (of yarn, etc.); plait (of straw, etc.); *Nau:* sennit, sinnet; *Dom.Ec:* t. de coton, cotton tape; *El:* fil conducteur sous t., braided conductor wire; t. de métallisation, de mise à la masse, bonding jumper; *Mec.E:* t. de garniture, gasket packing; t. en cuivre, stranded copper; (*c*) *Arch:* strap work. 2. thick brown wrapping paper.

tressé [trese], *a. Miner:* having interlaced fibres.

tresser [trese], *v.tr.* (*a*) to plait (hair, straw, etc.); to braid (yarn, etc.); to weave (basket); t. une guirlande, to weave a garland, to wreathe a garland; *F:* t. des couronnes à qn, to praise, flatter, s.o.; métier à t., braiding machine; (*b*) to braid (conductor wire, etc.).

tresseur, -euse [trɛsœ:r, -ø:z], *s.* 1. (*a*) braider; plaiter; (*b*) wig maker. 2. *s.f.* tresseuse, braiding machine.

tréteau, -eaux [treto], *s.m.* 1. trestle, support, stand, horse; t. de meule, rick stand. 2. *pl.* (mountebank's) stage, boards; monter sur les tréteaux, to go on the stage, on the boards.

treuil [trœ:j], *s.m.* (*a*) *Mec.E:* winch, windlass, winding drum; t. à bras, à manivelle, hand winch; t. à moteur, t. mécanique, motor winch; t. à vapeur, steam winch, donkey winch; t. électrique, hydro-électrique, electric, electro-hydraulic, winch; t. à adhérence, à friction, friction winch; t. à engrenages, t. composé, geared winch; t. à engrenages droits, spur-geared winch; t. à engrenages hélicoïdaux, worm-geared winch; t. à chaîne, chain hoist; t. à manège, gin; t. chariot, traveller (on gantry); t. roulant, t. portatif, crab; t. de levage, hoisting winch; t. de relevage, derricking winch; t. d'ascenseur, winding gear of a lift; *Min:* t. d'extraction, mine hoist, hoisting engine; *Nau:* t. de déhalage, mooring winch, warping winch; t. de remorquage, towing winch, towing engine; *Rail:* t. de manœuvre, shunting winch; *W.Tel:* t. d'antenne, aerial winch; (*b*) tread wheel.

treuillage [trœja:ʒ], *s.m.* winching; *Av:* launching (of glider) by winch.

treuiller [trœje], *v.tr.* to winch; *Av:* to launch (glider) by winch.

treuilliste [trœjist], *s.m.* winch operator, winchman, wincher.

trêve [trɛ:v], *s.f.* (*a*) truce; *Hist:* la t. de Dieu, the truce of God; *Pol:* *F:* t. des confiseurs, political truce in the Chamber at New Year; (*b*) respite, intermission; son mal de dents ne lui donne pas de t., his toothache gives him no respite; *F:* t. de bêtises, de plaisanteries! that's enough of, no more of, your nonsense, your joking! sans t., (i) truceless (war, etc.); (ii) unceasing(ly); without intermission.

Trèves [trɛ:v], *Pr.n. Geog:* Trier; *Hist:* Conseil de T., Council of Treves.

trévire[1] [trevi:r], *s.f. Nau: etc:* parbuckle.

Trévire[2]. 1. *s.m. & f. Geog:* native, inhabitant of Trier. 2. *A.Hist:* les Trévires, the Treviri.

trévirer [trevire], *v.tr.* 1. to parbuckle (cask, etc.). 2. to slue (topmast, etc.).

trévisan, -ane [trevizɑ̃, -an], *a. & s. Geog:* (native, inhabitant) of Treviso.

Trévise [trevi:z], *Pr.n. Geog:* Treviso.

tri[1] [tri], *s.m.* sorting (of letters, skills, etc.); classifying (of letters, skills, etc.); faire le t. de . . ., to sort out, arrange . . .; to set aside . . .; to pick out . . .; *Rail: etc:* bureau de tri, sorting office; *Elcs:* (*computers*) t. alphanumérique, alphanumeric sorting; programme de t., sorting programme; t. à quatre dérouleurs, four-tape sort; erreur de t., missort; indicateur de t., sort key; case de t., sorter pocket; faire un t. préalable, to screen.

tri[2], *s.m.* (*at bridge, whist*) odd trick.

tri- [tri], *pref.* tri-.

triable [trijabl], *a.* (*a*) sortable, that can be sorted; (*b*) worth sorting out; worth setting aside.

triacétine [triasetin], *s.f. Ch:* triacetin.

triacétonamine [triasetɔnamin], *s.f. Ch:* triacetonamine.

triacide [triasid], *a. & s.m. Ch:* triacid.

triacontaèdre [triakɔ̃taɛdr̥], *a. Cryst:* triacontahedral.

triade [triad], *s.f.* triad.

triadelphe [triadɛlf], *a. Bot:* triadelphous.

triadique [triadik], *a.* triadic.

triage [trija:ʒ], *s.m.* (*a*) sorting (of coal, letters, ores, etc.); t. à la main, hand picking, sorting; t. par voie humide, wet separation (of ores, etc.); *Rail:* manœuvres de t., shunting operations; t. sur pente, hump shunting; gare de t., marshalling yard; voie de t., siding; *Mil:* hôpital de t., clearing hospital; (*b*) selecting, picking out, sorting, setting aside (of the best, etc.); (*c*) grading (of ore); *Metall:* t. par courant gazeux, elutriation; (*d*) *For:* beat; area (covered by a forester, etc.).

trial [trial], *s.m. Mus:* comedy tenor.

trialisme [trialism], *s.m.* (*a*) *Phil: etc:* triadism; (*b*) *Hist:* trialism.

triandre [triɑ̃:dr̥], *a. Bot:* triandrous.

triandrie [triɑ̃dri], *s.f. A.Bot:* triandria.

triangle [triɑ̃:gl̥], *s.m.* 1. (*a*) *Geom: etc:* triangle; *Mec.E:* t. de sustentation, (i) three-point support; (ii) radius arms; *El:* roulé en t., wound in mesh; couplage en t., delta connection; *Navy:* fuir en t., to retire in triangular formation; *Astr:* le T., the Triangle (northern or southern); (*b*) *F:* l'éternel t., the eternal triangle. 2. (*a*) *Nau:* triangular flag; t. oui, affirmative signal; t. non, negative signal; (*b*) *Draw:* set square, *U.S:* triangle; (*c*) *Mus:* triangle; (*d*) *Th: Cost: F:* G-string.

triangulaire [triɑ̃gylɛ:r]. 1. *a.* triangular; *Nat. Hist:* triangulate; *Tchn:* (*of file, etc.*) three-square; *Nau:* voile t., leg-of-mutton sail; *Pol:* élection t., three-cornered election, fight. 2. *s.m. Anat:* triangularis (muscle).

triangulairement [triɑ̃gylɛrmɑ̃], *adv.* triangularly.

triangulateur [triɑ̃gylatœ:r], *a. & s.m.* (géomètre) t., surveyor (who makes triangulations).

triangulation [triɑ̃gylasjɔ̃], *s.f. Surv:* triangulation; faire, opérer, la t. d'une région, to triangulate a region; *Civ.E:* barre de t. (de poutre composée), lacing bar.

trianguler [triɑ̃gyle], *v.tr. Surv:* to triangulate.

triannuel, -elle [trianɥɛl], *a.* triennial.

trias [triɑ:s], *s.m. Geol:* Trias, Triassic.

triasique [triazik], *a. Geol:* triassic (rock, period, etc.).

triatome [triatom], *s.m. Ent:* conenose, assassin bug, triatomid; (*genus*) Triatoma.

triatomicité [triatɔmisite], *s.f. Ch:* triatomicity.

triatomique [triatɔmik], *a. Ch:* triatomic.

triaxonides [triaksɔnid], *s.m.pl. Spong:* Triaxonia, Triaxonida.

triazine [triazin], *s.f. Ch:* triazine.

triazole [triazɔl], *s.m. Ch:* triazole.

tribade [tribad], *s.f.* tribade, lesbian.

tribadisme [tribadism], *s.m.* tribadism, tribady, lesbianism.

tribal, -aux [tribal, -o], *a.* tribal (system, etc.).

tribalisme [tribalism], *s.m.* tribalism, tribal system.

triballe [tribal], *s.f. Leath:* tilt hammer.

triballer [tribale], *v.tr. Leath:* to stock.

tribart [triba:r], *s.m. Husb:* (triangular) clog; yoke, poke (to prevent passage of pigs, calves, etc., through fences).

tribasique [tribazik, -bɑ-], *a. Ch:* tribasic.

tribo-électricité [triboelɛktrisite], *s.f.* triboelectricity.

tribolium [tribɔljɔm], *s.m. Ent:* flour beetle; (*genus*) Tribolium.

tribologie [tribɔlɔʒi], *s.f. Tchn:* tribology.

triboluminescence [tribɔlyminɛs(s)ɑ̃:s], *s.f. Ph:* triboluminescence.

tribomètre [tribɔmɛtr̥], *s.m. Ph:* tribometer.

tribométrie [tribɔmetri], *s.f. Ph:* tribometry.

Tribonien [tribɔnjɛ̃], *Pr.n.m. Rom.Hist:* Tribonian.

tribord [tribɔ:r], *s.m. Nau:* starboard (side); à t., on the starboard side; to starboard; mettre la barre à t., to starboard the helm; la barre toute à t.! t. la barre toute! t. toute! hard-a-starboard! venez sur t.! port (the helm)! la terre par t.! land on the starboard (side)! par t. devant, on the starboard bow; faire feu de t. et de bâbord, to use every means in one's power; *Row:* aviron de t., bow-side oar.

tribordais [tribɔrdɛ], *s.m. Nau:* man of the starboard watch; les tribordais, the starboard watch.

triboulet[1] [tribulɛ], *s.m.* 1. *Metalw:* triblet, mandrel. 2. ring gauge.

Triboulet[2], *s.m.* (type of) tragic buffoon; (from V. Hugo's *Le Roi s'amuse*); un t. politique, a political buffoon.

tribractéolé [tribrakteɔle], *a. Bot:* tribracteolate.

tribractété [tribraktete], *a. Bot:* tribracteate.

tribraque [tribrak], *s.m. Pros:* tribrach.

tribromoéthanol [tribrɔmɔetanɔl], *s.m. Ch:* tribromoethanol.

tribromophénol [tribrɔmɔfenɔl], *s.m. Ch:* tribrom(o)phenol.

tribromure [tribrɔmy:r], *s.m. Ch:* tribromide.

tribu [triby], *s.f.* 1. tribe; membre d'une t., tribesman; *B:* la t. de Juda, the tribe of Judah. 2. *Nat.Hist:* tribe.

tribulation [tribylasjɔ̃], *s.f.* tribulation; trouble, trial; tout le monde a ses tribulations, everyone has his trials, tribulations.

tribulus [tribylys], *s.m. Bot:* burnut, caltrop; (*genus*) Tribulus.

tribun [tribœ̃], *s.m.* **1.** (*a*) *Rom.Hist: etc:* tribune; (*b*) popular orator, speaker. **2.** *Com: A:* ledger and invoice clerk.

tribunal, -aux [tribynal, -o], *s.m.* **1.** tribunal; (*a*) judge's seat, bench; (*b*) court of justice, law court; (the) magistrates; **en plein t.,** in open court; **t. civil,** civil court; **t. criminel,** criminal court; **t. d'instance,** *A:* **t. de simple police** = court of summary jurisdiction, magistrates' court, *F:* police court; **t. de grande instance,** *A:* **t. correctionnel** = county court; **t. d'enfants, t. pour enfants et adolescents,** juvenile court; **t. arbitral,** court of arbitration; **t. de commerce,** commercial court; **t. militaire,** military tribunal; **prendre la voie des tribunaux,** to take legal action; **comparaître devant un t.,** to appear before a tribunal; to stand one's trial; **le t. de l'opinion publique,** the tribunal, the bar, of public opinion; *Journ:* **gazette des tribunaux,** law reports; (*c*) *Navy:* **t. de prise,** prize court. **2.** *Ecc.Arch: A:* tribune (of basilica).

tribunat [tribyna], *s.m.* (*a*) *Rom.Hist: etc:* tribunate, tribuneship; (*b*) *Fr.Hist:* **le T.,** the Tribunate (1800-1807).

tribune [tribyn], *s.f.* **1.** tribune, rostrum, (speaker's) platform; **monter à la t.,** to go up to the tribune (in Fr. Parliament); to address the House; **éloquence de la t.,** parliamentary eloquence; **les luttes de la t.,** forensic contests; **la t. sacrée,** the pulpit. **2.** (*a*) gallery (in church, library, House of Parliament, etc.); **t. publique,** public gallery; (*in Parliament*) strangers' gallery; **t. des journalistes,** reporters' gallery; (*b*) *Sp:* **t. (d'honneur),** grandstand; **les tribunes,** the stands; (*c*) **t. d'orgues,** organ loft; **Mlle. X chantera à la t.,** Miss X will sing (from the organ loft) to an organ accompaniment. **3.** (*discussions on literature, politics, etc.*) forum.

tribunitien, -ienne [tribynisjɛ̃, -jɛn], *a.* (*a*) *Rom. Hist:* tribunician, tribunicial; (*b*) **éloquence tribunitienne,** mob oratory; *F:* tub-thumping.

tribut [triby], *s.m.* tribute; (*a*) *Hist:* tribute-money; **payer t.,** to pay tribute; (*b*) *A:* duty, tax; (*c*) **payer le tribut à la nature,** to pay the debt of nature; to die; **apporter son t. d'éloges,** to bring, offer, one's tribute of praise, one's contribution of praise; **tirer de son travail un t. légitime,** to obtain a fair reward for one's labour.

tributaire [tribytɛːr], *a. & s.m.* (*a*) tributary; *Hist:* **les Juifs furent faits tributaires des Romains,** the Jews were made tributaries of the Romans; **être t. de l'étranger,** to be dependent upon, to depend on, foreign supplies; to draw one's supplies from abroad; (*b*) tributary (river); **les tributaires du Danube,** the tributaries of the Danube; **fleuve t. de l'Atlantique,** river flowing into the Atlantic.

tributif, -ive [tribytif, -iːv], *a.* tribal.

tributyrine [tribytirin], *s.f. Ch:* (tri)butyrin.

tricâble [trikɑːbl̩], *a.* three-cable.

tricage [trikaːʒ], *s.m.* **1.** sorting, ranging (of timber). **2.** *N.Arch:* squaring (of timber).

tricalcique [trikalsik], *a. Ch:* tricalcic, tricalcium.

tricalcite [trikalsit], *s.f. Miner:* trichalcite.

tricapsulaire [trikapsylɛːr], *a. Bot:* tricapsular.

tricarballylique [trikarbalilik], *a. Ch:* tricarballylic.

tricaréné [trikarene], *a. Bot:* tricarinated.

tricénaire [trisenɛːr], *a.* tricenary.

tricennal, -aux [trisɛn(n)al, -o], *a. Jur:* tricennial (prescription).

tricentenaire [trisɑ̃tnɛːr]. **1.** *a.* tercentenary, tercentennial. **2.** *s.m.* tercentenary.

tricéphale [trisefal]. **1.** *a.* tricephalic, tricephalous (monster, etc.). **2.** *s.m.* tricephalus.

triceps [trisɛps], *s.m. Anat:* triceps (muscle); **t. brachial,** triceps brachii; **t. sural,** triceps surae.

tricératops [triseratɔps], *s.m. Paleont:* triceratops.

trich(o)- [trik(ɔ)], *comb.fm.* trich(o)-.

trichage [triʃaːʒ], *s.m.* cheating (at cards, etc.).

trichalcite [trikalsit], *s.f. Miner:* trichalcite.

triche [triʃ], *s.f.* **1.** *F:* trick, trickery; cheating (*esp.* at cards); **c'est de la t.,** that's cheating, that's not fair. **2.** *Cards:* tricon.

trichécidés [trikeside], *s.m.pl. Z:* Trichechidae.

tricher [triʃe], *v.i. & tr.* to cheat; to trick (s.o.); **t. sur le poids,** to give short weight; **t. sur sa date de naissance,** to lie about one's age; **en trichant un peu rien n'y paraîtra plus,** if you cover it up a bit nobody will notice.

tricherie [triʃri], *s.f.* cheating (at cards, etc.); trickery.

tricheur, -euse [triʃœːr, -øːz]. **1.** *a.* given to cheating. **2.** *s.* cheat; trickster; *Cards:* (card) sharper.

trichiasis [trikjazis], *s.m. Med:* trichiasis.

trichinal, -aux [triʃinal, trikinal, -o], *a. Vet: Med:* trichinal.

trichine [triʃin, trikin], *s.f. Ann:* trichina, threadworm; (*genus*) Trichinella.

trichiné [triʃine, trikine], *a.* trichinated, trichinous, trichinosed.

trichineux, -euse [triʃinø, trikinø, -øːz], *a.* trichinous.

trichinidés [triʃinide, trikinide], *s.m.pl. Ann:* Trichinellidae.

trichinoïde [triʃinɔid, trikinɔid], *a.* trichinoid.

trichinoscope [triʃinɔskɔp, trikinɔskɔp], *s.m.* trichinoscope.

trichinose [triʃinoːz, trikinoːz], *s.f. Med:* trichinosis.

trichion [trikjɔ̃], *s.m. Anat:* trichion.

trichite[1] [trikit], *s.f. Miner:* trichite; *Cryst:* whiskers.

trichite[2], *s.m. Prot:* trichite.

trichiure [trikjyːr], *s.m.* **1.** *Ent:* trichiura. **2.** *Ich:* trichiurus, hair-tail, *U.S:* silver eel.

trichiuridés [trikjyride], *s.m.pl. Ich:* Trichiuridae.

trichloracétique [triklɔrasetik], *a. Ch:* trichlor(o)-acetic.

trichloréthylène [triklɔretilɛn], *s.m. Ch:* trichlor-(o)ethylene.

trichlorure [triklɔryːr], *s.m. Ch:* trichloride.

trichobézoard [trikɔbezɔaːr], *s.m.* trichobezoar, hair ball.

trichobothrie [trikɔbɔtri], *s.f. Z:* trichobothrium.

trichocaule [trikɔkoːl], *a. Bot:* hairy-stemmed.

trichocéphale [trikɔsefal], *s.m. Ann: Med:* trichocephalus, trichuris, *F:* whip worm.

trichocéphalose [trikɔsefaloːz], *s.f. Med:* trichocephaliasis, trichuriasis.

trichocère [trikɔsɛːr], *s.f. Ent:* winter crane fly; (*genus*) Trichoceras.

trichocéridés [trikɔseride], *s.m.pl. Ent:* Trichoceratidae.

trichoclasie [trikɔklazi], *s.f. Med:* trichoclasis.

trichocyste [trikɔsist], *s.m.* trichocyst.

trichodecte [trikɔdɛkt], *s.m. Ent:* trichodectes, *F:* (animal) louse.

trichoglosse [trikɔglɔs], *s.m. Orn:* lorikeet, brush-tongued parrot.

trichoglossidés [trikɔglɔside], *s.m.pl. Orn:* Trichoglossidae.

trichoglossie [trikɔglɔsi], *s.f. Med:* trichoglossia.

trichogrammes [trikɔgram], *s.m.pl. Ent:* Trichogrammidae.

trichogyne [trikɔʒin], *s.f. Algae:* trichogyne.

trichologie [trikɔlɔʒi], *s.f.* trichology.

tricholome [trikɔloːm], *s.m. Fung:* tricholoma; **t. de la Saint-Georges,** St George's agaric.

trichoma [trikɔma], **trichome** [trikoːm], *s.m.* **1.** *Bot:* trichome. **2.** *Med:* plica, trichoma.

trichomanes [trikɔman], *s.m. Bot:* bristle fern; (*genus*) Trichomanes.

trichomonadines [trikɔmɔnadin], *s.m.pl. Prot:* Polymastigina.

trichomonas [trikɔmɔnas], *s.m. Prot:* trichomonad; (*genus*) Trichomonas.

trichomonase [trikɔmɔnaːz], **trichomonose** [trikɔmɔnoːz], *s.f. Med: Vet:* trichomoniasis; **t. vaginale,** trichomonadal vaginitis.

trichomycose [trikɔmikoːz], *s.f. Med:* trichomycosis.

trichomyctères [trikɔmiktɛːr], *s.m.pl. Ich:* Trichomycteridae.

trichonymphines [trikɔnɛ̃fin], *s.m.pl. Prot:* Hypermastigina.

trichophytie [trikɔfiti], *s.f. Med:* trichophytia, trichophytosis.

trichophyton [trikɔfitɔ̃], *s.m. Fung:* trichophyte; (*genus*) Trichophyton.

trichoptères [trikɔptɛːr], *s.m.pl. Ent:* Trichoptera, the caddis flies.

trichoptérygides [trikɔpteriʒid], *s.m.pl. Ent:* Trichopterygidae.

trichorhexis [trikɔrɛksis], *s.f. Med:* trichorrhexis.

trichosis [trikozis], *s.m. Med:* trichosis.

trichosure [trikɔzyːr], *s.m. Z:* (Australian) opossum.

trichotillomanie [trikɔtilɔmani], *s.f. Med:* trichotillomania.

trichotome [trikɔtoːm], *a.* trichotomic, trichotomous.

trichotomie [trikɔtɔmi], *s.f. Log: etc:* trichotomy.

trichotomique [trikɔtɔmik], *a.* trichotomic.

trichroïsme [trikrɔism], *s.m. Ph:* trichroism.

trichroïte [trikrɔit], *a. Ph:* trichroic.

trichrome [trikroːm], *a. Phot: Phot.Engr:* three-colour(ed), trichromatic (photography).

trichromie [trikrɔmi], *s.f. Phot: Phot.Engr:* three-colour process.

tricinate [trisinat], *s.m. Ch:* styphnate.

trick [trik], *s.m. Cards:* (*bridge, etc.*) odd trick.

triclades [triklad], *s.m.pl. Ann:* triclads, Tricladia.

triclinique [triklinik], *a. Cryst:* triclinic.

triclinium [triklinjɔm], *s.m. Rom.Ant:* triclinium.

tricoises [trikwaːz], *s.f.pl. Tls:* (smith's, farrier's) pincers.

tricolore [trikɔlɔːr], *a.* tricolour(ed); **le drapeau t.,** the French flag, the Tricolour; *Nau:* **fanal t.,** tricoloured lantern; *Adm:* **feux tricolores,** traffic lights, signals; *s.m.pl. Sp: F:* **les Tricolores,** the French team.

triconodon [trikɔnɔdɔ̃], *s.m. Paleont:* triconodont; (*genus*) Triconodon.

triconodontes [trikɔnɔdɔ̃ːt], *s.m.pl. Paleont:* Triconodonta.

tricoque [trikɔk], *a. Bot:* tricoccous (fruit).

tricorde [trikɔrd], *a. & s.m. Mus:* trichord; three-stringed (instrument).

tricorne [trikɔrn]. **1.** *a.* three-horned (animal, insect); tricorn, three-cornered (hat). **2.** *s.m.* (*a*) three-cornered hat; tricorn; (*b*) (lady's) hunt hat.

tricot[1] [triko], *s.m.* **1.** (*a*) knitting; knitted fabric; knitted wear; *Com:* knitwear, knit goods; **t. sport,** fisherman knit; **dentelle au t.,** knitted lace; **bas en, de, t.,** knitted stockings; **faire du t.,** to knit; (*b*) *Tex:* stockinet. **2.** (*a*) (knitted) jersey, jumper; *F:* woolly; (*b*) (under)vest.

tricot[2], *s.m. A:* stout stick; cudgel.

tricotage [trikɔtaːʒ], *s.m.* **1.** (*a*) knitting; (*b*) knitted work. **2.** *F:* rapid movement (of the legs); **il regardait le t. des coureurs cyclistes,** he watched the whirring legs of the racing cyclists.

tricotée [trikɔte], *s.f. P: A:* thrashing, cudgelling.

tricoter [trikɔte]. **1.** *v.tr.* to knit; **aiguilles à t.,** knitting needles; **machine à t.,** knitting machine. **2.** *v.i.* (*a*) *F:* to leg it, to stir one's stumps; *P:* **t. des jambes, des gambettes, des pincettes,** (i) to dance; (ii) to make off, scram; (iii) to race along (on a bicycle); (*b*) **cheval qui tricote,** horse with more action than pace.

tricoteur, -euse [trikɔtœːr, -øːz]. **1.** *s.* knitter; *Fr.Hist:* **les tricoteuses,** the stocking-knitters (of the French Revolution). **2.** *s.m.* knitting frame. **3.** *s.f.* **tricoteuse,** knitting machine; **tricoteuse mécanique,** power knitting-loom.

tricotin [trikɔtɛ̃], *s.m.* French knitting.

tricotoir [trikɔtwaːr], *s.m.* knitting-needle holder.

Tricouni [trikuni], *s.m. R.t.m: Mount:* Tricouni.

trictrac [triktrak], *s.m.* **1.** click, rattle (of dice, etc.). **2.** *Games:* (*a*) trick-track; backgammon; **faire un t.,** to play a game of backgammon; (*b*) backgammon board.

tricuspide [trikyspid], *a.* tricuspid, three-pointed; *Anat:* **valvule t.,** tricuspid valve (of the heart).

tricycle [trisikl̩]. **1.** *a. Av:* three-wheeled (undercarriage). **2.** *s.m.* (*a*) tricycle; **t. à moteur,** motor tricycle; (*b*) *A:* three-wheeled luggage truck.

tricyclecar [trisiklәkaːr], *s.m. Aut:* three-wheeler.

tricyclique [trisiklik], *a. Ch:* tricyclic.

tricycliste [trisiklist], *s.m. & f.* tricyclist.

tridacne [tridakn], *s.m. Moll:* giant clam; (*genus*) Tridacna.

tridactyle [tridaktil]. **1.** *a. Z:* tridactyl(ous). **2.** *s.m.* (*a*) *Ent:* mole cricket; (*b*) *Orn:* button quail.

tride [trid], *a. Equit:* quick and regular (movement of horse).

trident [tridɑ̃], *s.m.* **1.** (*a*) trident (of Neptune, etc.); (*b*) *Geom:* trident curve; (*c*) *Med:* **main en t.,** trident hand. **2.** (*a*) fish spear; (*b*) *Agr:* three-pronged (pitch)fork.

tridenté [tridɑ̃te], *a.* tridentate, tridental (leaf, etc.).

tridermique [tridɛrmik], *a. Biol:* tridermic.

tridi [tridi], *s.m. Fr.Hist:* third day of the decade (in the Republican Calendar).

tridimensionnel, -elle [tridimɑ̃sjɔnɛl], *a.* three-dimensional.

triduo [tridɥo], *s.m.,* **triduum** [tridɥɔm], *s.m. Ecc:* triduo, triduum; three days' service of prayer.

tridymite [tridimit], *s.f. Miner:* tridymite.

trie [tri], *s.f.* **1.** sorting out (of fish for market, etc.). **2.** pigeon house, loft.

trièdre [triɛdr̩]. **1.** *a. Geom:* trihedral. **2.** *s.m.* (*a*) *Geom:* trihedron; (*b*) *Av:* **t. de référence,** pitch, roll and yaw axes; **t. aérodynamique,** body axis; **t. de l'avion,** wind axis.

triennal, -aux [triɛn(n)al, -o], *a.* triennial. **1.** lasting three years; **magistrat t.,** magistrate appointed for a term of three years; **parlement t.,** triennial parliament. **2.** recurring every third year; (*a*) *Agr:* **assolement t.,** three-year rotation; (*b*) *A:* **office t.,** office held one year out of three, every three years.

triennat [triɛn(n)a], *s.m.* (*a*) triennium; (*b*) three-year period of office.

triennium [triɛnjɔm], *s.m. Rel.H:* triennium.

trier [trije], *v.tr.* (*p.d. & pr.sub.* **n. triions, v. triiez**) (*a*) to sort (letters, etc.); **t. sa garde-robe,** to go through one's wardrobe; *Rail:* **t. des wagons,** to marshal trucks; *Tex:* **t. la laine,** to pick the wool; *Min:* **minerai trié,** dressed ore; (*b*) to pick out, sort out, choose, select (the best, etc.); **t. à la main,** to hand-pick; *A:* **t. des pièces de monnaie,** to garble coin.
triérarchie [trierarʃi], *s.f. Gr.Ant:* trierarchy.
triérarque [trierark], *s.m. Gr.Ant:* trierarch.
trière [triɛːr], *s.f. Gr.Ant:* trireme.
triester [triɛstɛːr], *s.m. Ch:* triester.
triestin, -ine [triɛstɛ̃, -in], *a. & s. Geog:* (native, inhabitant) of Trieste.
triétéride [trieterid], *s.f. Gr.Ant:* (*a*) period of three years; (*b*) trieteric.
triétérique [trieterik], *a. Gr.Ant:* trieteric.
trieur, -euse [trijœːr, -øːz]. 1. *s.* sorter (of letters, etc.); **t. de laines,** wool picker. 2. *s.m. Ind:* screening machine; separator (for grain, ores, etc.). 3. *s.f.* **trieuse:** (*a*) wool-picking machine; (*b*) card sorter (for punch cards); card-sorting machine; sorter; **t. de documents,** document sorter; **case de réception de t.,** sorter pocket.
trieur-calibreur [trijœrkalibrœːr], *s.m. Ind:* grading machine; *pl. trieurs-calibreurs.*
trieuse-lectrice [trijøzlɛktris], *s.f. Elcs:* (*computers*) sorter reader; *pl. trieuses-lectrices.*
trifacial, -aux [trifasjal, -o], *a. & s.m. Anat:* (**nerf**) **t.,** trifacial (nerve), trigeminal (nerve).
trifide [trifid], *a. Bot: etc:* trifid, three-cleft.
trifilaire [trifilɛːr], *a. W.Tel:* three-wire (aerial).
triflore [triflɔːr], *a. Bot:* triflorous, three-flowered.
trifluvien, -ienne [triflyvjɛ̃, -jɛn], *a. & s.* (native, inhabitant) of Trois-Rivières.
trifolié [trifɔlje], *a. Bot:* trifoliate, three-leaved.
trifoliolé [trifɔljɔle], *a. Bot:* trifoliolate.
trifolium [trifɔljɔm], *s.m. Bot:* trifolium, clover.
triforium [trifɔrjɔm], *s.m. Arch:* triforium.
triforme [trifɔrm], *a.* triform; *Bot:* trimorphic; *Myth:* **Hécate t.,** triform Hecate.
trifouillage [trifujaːʒ], *s.m. F:* rummaging; fiddling about.
trifouillée [trifuje], *s.f. F:* 1. thrashing, flogging. 2. **(toute) une t. de . . .,** a (great) heap of . . ., a jumble of. . . .
trifouiller [trifuje], *v.tr. & i. F:* (*a*) to rummage (in); to fiddle about (with); to meddle (with); **t. dans un tiroir,** to rummage in a drawer; **ne trifouillez pas le mécanisme,** don't fiddle (about) with the mechanism; **t. dans la caisse,** to tamper with the cash; (*b*) to upset (s.o.).
trifouilleur, -euse [trifujœːr, -øːz], *s. F:* (*a*) rummager; meddler; (*b*) muddler; untidy person.
Trifouillis-les-Oies [trifujilezwa], *Pr.n.f. F:* Slocombe-on-the-Mud.
trifurcation [trifyrkasjɔ̃], *s.f.* trifurcation.
trifurqué [trifyrke], *a. Nat.Hist:* trifurcate; trichotomous; *Bot:* **orge trifurquée,** hooded barley.
trifurquer [trifyrke], *v.tr. & i.* to trifurcate, to divide into three branches.
trigame [trigam]. 1. *a. Jur: Bot:* trigamous. 2. *s. Jur:* trigamist.
trigamie [trigami], *s.f. Jur:* trigamy.
trigatron [trigatrɔ̃], *s.m. Elcs:* trigatron.
trigaud, -aude [trigo, -od], *s. F: A:* shuffler.
trige [triːʒ], *s.m.* 1. *Rom.Ant:* triga. 2. *attrib. Myth:* three-headed (cerberus, etc.).
trigémellaire [triʒemelɛːr], *a.* **accouchement t.,** birth of triplets.
trigéminé [triʒemine], *a.* 1. *Bot:* tergeminal, tergeminate. 2. (*a*) *Anat:* trigeminal (nerve); *Med:* trigeminal, intermittent (pulse); (*b*) *Biol:* trigeminous.
trigemme [triʒɛm], *a. Bot:* bearing three buds, three-budded.
trigle [trigḷ], *s.m. Ich:* triglid, gurnard; **t. hirondelle,** sapphirine gurnard; **t. lyre, t. cardinal,** piper gurnard; **t. pin,** red gurnard.
triglide [triglid], *a. & s.m. Ich:* triglid.
triglidés [triglide], *s.m.pl. Ich:* Triglidae.
triglochin [triglɔʃɛ̃]. 1. *a. Anat:* **valvule triglochine,** tricuspid valve. 2. *s.m. Bot:* arrowgrass; (*genus*) Triglochin; **t. maritime,** seaside arrowgrass.
triglotte [triglɔt], *A:* 1. *a.* trilingual; triglot (Bible, etc.). 2. *s.m. & f.* person who speaks three languages.
triglyphe [triglif], *s.m. Arch:* triglyph.
trigonal, -aux [trigɔnal, -o], *a.* trigonal.
trigone [trigɔn]. 1. *a.* trigonal, three-cornered. 2. *s.m.* (*a*) *Astrol:* trigon; (*b*) *Anat:* trigone; **t. cérébral,** fornix. 3. *s.f.* stingless (honey)bee; (*genus*) Trigona.
trigonella [trigɔnɛla], *s.f.*, **trigonelle** [trigɔnɛl], *s.f. Bot:* trigonella, *esp.* fenugreek.
trigonocéphale [trigɔnɔsefal], *s.m. Rept:* pit viper.
trigonocéphalie [trigɔnɔsefali], *s.f.* trigonocephaly.
trigonométrie [trigɔnɔmetri], *s.f.* trigonometry; **t. rectiligne,** plane trigonometry; **t. sphérique,** spherical trigonometry.
trigonométrique [trigɔnɔmetrik], *a.* trigonometric(al).
trigonométriquement [trigɔnɔmetrikmɑ̃], *adv.* trigonometrically.
trigramme [trigram], *s.m.* 1. (*inscription of three letters*) trigram. 2. (*vowel group, etc., of three letters*) trigraph, trigram.
trigrille [trigriːj], *s.f. W.Tel:* five-electrode valve.
trigyne [triʒin], *a. Bot:* trigynous; **plante t.,** trigyn; *A:* **plantes trigynes,** Trigynia.
trihebdomadaire [triɛbdɔmadɛːr], *a.* (*of newspaper, etc.*) triweekly; appearing, occurring, three times a week.
trihybride [triibrid], *a. & s.m. Biol:* trihybrid.
trihydrol [triidrɔl], *s.m. Ch:* trihydrol.
triiodure [trijɔdyːr], *s.m. Ch:* triiodide.
trijumeau, -elle, -eaux [triʒymo, -ɛl]. 1. *s.* triplet. 2. *a. & s.m. Anat:* (**nerf**) **t.,** trigeminal (nerve), trifacial nerve.
trilatéral, -aux [trilateral, -o], *a.* trilateral; three-sided.
trilinéaire [trilineɛːr], *a. Geom:* trilinear.
trilingue [trilɛ̃ːg], *a.* trilingual.
trilitéralité [triliteralite], *s.f. Ling:* triliterality, triliteralness.
trilithe [trilit], *s.m. Archeol:* trilith, trilithon.
trilit(t)ère [trilit(t)ɛːr], *a. Ling:* triliteral (language, etc.).
trille [triːj], *s.m. Mus:* trill.
triller [trije], *v.tr. Mus:* to trill (note, passage).
trillion [triljɔ̃], *s.m.* 1. (*since 1948*) trillion (10^{18}), *U.S:* quintillion. 2. (*before 1948*) billion (10^{12}), *U.S:* trillion.
trilobe [trilɔb], *s.m. Arch:* trefoil.
trilobé [trilɔbe], *a.* 1. *Arch:* three-cusped, trefoil (arch, etc.). 2. *Bot:* trilobate.
trilobite [trilɔbit], *s.m. Paleont:* trilobite; *pl.* (*class*) **trilobites,** Trilobita.
triloculaire [trilɔkylɛːr], *a. Bot: etc:* trilocular.
trilogie [trilɔʒi], *s.f.* 1. *Lit:* trilogy. 2. *Med:* triad (of symptoms).
trilogique [trilɔʒik], *a. Lit:* trilogic(al).
triloupe [trilup], *s.f.* magnifying glass with three lenses.
trimaran [trimarɑ̃], *s.m. Nau:* trimaran.
trimar(d) [trimaːr], *s.m. P:* 1. road; **battre le t., être sur le t.,** to be on the tramp, on the road. 2. (*pers.*) tramp.
trimarder [trimarde], *v.i. P:* to be on the tramp, on the road.
trimardeur [trimardœːr], *s.m. P:* tramp, *U.S:* hobo.
trimbal(l)age [trɛ̃balaːʒ], *s.m.*, **trimbal(l)ement** [trɛ̃balmɑ̃], *s.m. F:* dragging about, lugging about (of parcels, etc.); trailing about, around, (of children).
trimbal(l)ée [trɛ̃bale], *P: O:* whole lot; lots, quantities.
trimbal(l)er [trɛ̃bale], *v.tr. F:* to carry about; to drag, lug, about (parcels, etc.); to trail (children, etc.) about; **se faire t.,** to get a lift; **il trimbale toujours sa famille avec lui,** he always has his family in tow; **t. des cousins de province dans Paris,** to cart country cousins round Paris; *P:* **qu'est-ce qu'il trimbale!** what an idiot! what a clot!
se trimbal(l)er, *F:* to wander around; to drag oneself along.
trimer [trime], *v.i.* to work hard, slave away (at sth.); **quand on a trimé toute une vie,** when one has slaved hard all one's life; **faire t. qn,** to keep s.o. at it, on the go; to keep s.o.'s nose to the grindstone.
trimère [trimɛːr]. 1. *a.* (*a*) *Nat.Hist:* trimerous (tarsus, coleopter, plant, etc.); (*b*) *Ch:* trimeric. 2. *s.m.* (*a*) *Ent:* trimeran; **les trimères,** the Trimera; (*b*) *Ch:* trimer.
trimérite [trimerit], *s.f. Miner:* trimerite.
trimésique [trimezik], *a. Ch:* trimesic (acid).
trimestre [trimɛstr̥], *s.m.* 1. quarter; three months; trimester; *Sch:* term; *Sch:* **premier, deuxième, troisième, t.,** autumn, spring, summer, term; **par t.,** quarterly; *Sch:* every term; **abonnements au t.,** quarterly subscriptions. 2. quarter's salary, quarter's rent; *Sch:* term's fees.
trimestrialité [trimɛstrijalite], *s.f.* quarterly instalment, payment.
trimestriel, -elle [trimɛstrijɛl], *a.* quarterly (review, payment, account); trimestrial; *Sch:* **bulletin t.,** end-of-term school report.
trimestriellement [trimɛstrijɛlmɑ̃], *adv.* quarterly; every three months; once a term.
triméthylamine [trimetilamin], *s.f. Ch:* trimethylamine.
triméthylbenzène [trimetilbɛ̃zɛn], *s.m. Ch:* trimethylbenzene.
triméthylcarbinol [trimetilkarbinɔl], *s.m. Ch:* trimethylcarbinol.
triméthylène [trimetilɛn], *s.m. Ch:* trimethylene.
trimètre [trimɛtr̥], *Pros:* 1. *a.* trimeter, trimetric(al). 2. *s.m.* trimeter.
trimétrique [trimetrik], *a.* 1. *Pros:* trimetric(al). 2. *Cryst:* trimetric, orthorhombic.
trimmer [trimɛːr], *s.m.* 1. *Fish:* trimmer (used for catching pike). 2. *El:* trimmer (capacitor).
trimoléculaire [trimɔlekylɛːr], *a.* termolecular, trimolecular.
trimorphe [trimɔrf], *a. Cryst:* trimorphic, trimorphous.
trimorphisme [trimɔrfism], *s.m. Cryst: Nat.Hist:* trimorphism.
trimoteur [trimɔtœːr], *a. & s.m.* three-engined (aircraft).
trin [trɛ̃], **trine** [trin], *a.* 1. *Astrol:* trine; **trin(e) aspect,** trine aspect. 2. *Theol:* triune.
Trinacrie [trinakri], *Pr.n.f. A.Geog:* Trinacria.
trinaire [trinɛːr], *a.* trinary, ternary.
trinervé [trinɛrve], *a. Bot:* trinervate.
tringa [trɛ̃ga], *s.m. Orn:* tringa, sandpiper.
tringlage [trɛ̃glaːʒ], *s.m. Mec.E:* series, system, of rods.
tringle [trɛ̃ːgḷ], *s.f.* 1. (*a*) rod; **t. de, à, rideau,** curtain rod; tringle; **t. d'escalier,** stair rod; **t. d'un pneu,** wire of a tyre; *Mch:* **t. d'entraînement, de relevage,** drag link; *I.C.E: etc:* **t. de poussée,** radius arm; (*b*) bar; **t. de manœuvre,** (i) *Mch:* control rod; (ii) *Rail:* switch bar (of points); (*c*) *Mus:* beater (for triangle); (*d*) wooden lath, batten; *Nau:* **tringles de panneaux,** hatch battens, hatch bars. 2. *Const: etc:* line, mark (made by chalked string). 3. *Arch:* tringle; square moulding.
tringler [trɛ̃gle], *v.tr. Const: etc:* to line out (piece of wood, etc.); to chalk (a line).
tringlerie [trɛ̃gləri], *s.f. Mec.E:* (system of) rods, linkage; *I.C.E: etc:* **t. d'injecteur,** injector control linkage.
tringlette [trɛ̃glɛt], *s.f.* 1. small rod. 2. (glazier's) tringlette.
tringloir [trɛ̃glwaːr], *s.m.*, **tringloire** [trɛ̃glwaːr], *s.f. Engr:* graver.
tringlot [trɛ̃glo], *s.m. Mil: P: O:* soldier of the French Army Service Corps.
trinitaire [trinitɛːr]. 1. *s.m. or f.* (*a*) *Ecc:* Trinitarian, Redemptionist (monk or nun); (*b*) *Theol:* Trinitarian. 2. *s.f. Bot:* liverwort.
trinité [trinite], *s.f.* 1. *Theol:* Trinity; **la sainte T.,** the Holy Trinity; **(fête de) la T.,** Trinity Sunday; **les trinités païennes,** the pagan trinities. 2. *Geog:* **(île de) la T.,** Trinidad. 3. *Bot:* herb trinity.
trinitré [trinitre], *Ch:* 1. *a.* trinitrated, trinitro-. 2. *s.m.* trinitrate, trinitro-compound.
trinitrobenzène [trinitrɔbɛ̃zɛn], *s.m. Exp:* trinitrobenzene.
trinitrocrésol [trinitrɔkrezɔl], *s.m. Ch:* trinitrocresol.
trinitrophénol [trinitrɔfenɔl], *s.m. Ch:* trinitrophenol.
trinitrorésorcinate [trinitrɔrezɔrsinat], *s.m. Ch:* styphnate.
trinitrorésorcine [trinitrɔrezɔrsin], *s.f.*, **trinitrorésorcinol** [trinitrɔrezɔrsinɔl], *s.m. Exp:* trinitroresorcinol, styphnic acid.
trinitrotoluène [trinitrɔtɔlɥɛn], *s.m.*, **trinol** [trinɔl], *s.m. Exp:* trinitrotoluene, trinitrotoluol, trotyl, *F:* T.N.T.
Trinobantes [trinɔbɑ̃ːt], *s.m.pl. A.Geog:* Trinobantes.
trinôme [trinoːm], *a. & s.m. Mth:* trinomial.
trinquart [trɛ̃kaːr], *s.m. Fish:* herring boat.
trinquée [trɛ̃ke], *s.f. F:* drinking (in company); **j'aime la t. au bistro avec des camarades,** I like having a drink at the pub with friends.
trinquer [trɛ̃ke], *v.i.* 1. (*a*) to clink glasses (before drinking); **t. à qn, qch.,** to drink to s.o., sth.; (*b*) *F:* to drink, *esp.* to drink heavily, to booze; **on a trinqué ensemble,** we had a glass or two together. 2. (*a*) to bang about, knock together; **les bateaux trinquaient du ventre,** the boats were knocking against each other; (*b*) *P:* to get the worst of it, get it in the neck; **c'est le piéton qui trinque toujours,** it's always the pedestrian who gets the worst of it; **s'en tirer sans t.,** to get off scot-free; (*c*) *P:* to cop it; **t. de six mois de prison,** to get six months in prison.

trinquet[1] [trɛ̃kɛ], *s.m. Nau:* foremast (in lateen-rigged vessel).
trinquet[2], *s.m.* indoor pelota court.
trinquette [trɛ̃kɛt], *s.f. Nau:* **1.** storm jib. **2.** foretopmast staysail.
trinquette-ballon [trɛ̃kɛtbalɔ̃], *s.f. Nau:* balloon foresail; *pl. trinquettes-ballons.*
trinqueur [trɛ̃kœːr], *s.m. F:* drinker, tippler.
trinucléidés [trinykleide], *s.m.pl. Paleont:* Trinucleidae.
trio [trio], *s.m.* **1.** *Mus: etc:* trio. **2.** *Metall:* three-high mill.
triode [triɔd], *a. & s.f. Elcs: W.Tel:* **(lampe) t.,** three-electrode lamp, tube; triode; **monté en t.,** connected as a triode; **t. à gaz,** gas-filled triode; thyratron; **t. à forte pente,** high-slope triode; **t. de sécurité,** premium triode.
triodon [triɔdɔ̃], *s.m. Ich:* triodon, puff fish, puffer, globefish.
triol [triɔl], *s.m. Ch:* triol.
trioléine [triɔlein], *s.f. Ch:* triolein.
triolet [triɔlɛ], *s.m.* **1.** *Pros:* triolet. **2.** *Mus:* triplet. **3.** *Bot:* (*a*) Dutch clover; (*b*) black medick, nonsuch.
triomphal, -aux [trijɔ̃fal, -o], *a.* triumphal (car, progress, etc.).
triomphalement [trijɔ̃falmɑ̃], *adv.* triumphantly.
triomphant [trijɔ̃fɑ̃], *a.* triumphant (general, air, etc.); **l'Église triomphante,** the Church Triumphant.
triomphateur, -trice [trijɔ̃fatœːr, -tris]. **1.** *a.* triumphing (army, nation). **2.** *s.m.* (*a*) *Rom. Ant:* triumpher; (*b*) triumphant conqueror, conquering hero, victor.
triomphe[1] [trijɔ̃ːf], *s.m.* (*a*) triumph; **porter qn en t.,** to carry s.o. in triumph, shoulder high; to chair s.o.; **faire un t. à qn,** to give s.o. an ovation; **arc de t.,** triumphal arch; *Hist:* **le t. du Nord sur le Midi,** the triumph of the North over the South; (*b*) (*at Saint-Cyr*) passing-out ceremony.
triomphe[2], *s.f. A:* **1.** trump (card). **2.** (*card game*) triumph.
triompher [triɔ̃fe], *v.i.* **1.** (*a*) *Rom.Ant:* to triumph; to receive the honour of triumph; (*b*) to triumph (**de,** *occ.* **sur,** over); to get the better (of s.o.); **t. d'une difficulté,** to get over, overcome, master, a difficulty; **t. dans un art,** to excel in an art; **t. de tout, sur tout,** to carry all before one; **société où le vice triomphe,** society in which vice is triumphant. **2.** to exult, glory; **t. du malheur de qn,** to gloat over s.o.'s misfortune.
trional [triɔnal], *s.m. Pharm:* trional.
Triones [triɔn], *Pr.n.m.pl. Astr:* Triones.
triongulin [triɔ̃gylɛ̃], *s.m. Ent:* triungulin.
trionychidés [triɔnikide], *s.m.pl. Rept:* Trionychidae.
trionix, trionyx [triɔniks], *s.m. Rept:* soft-shelled turtle; (*genus*) Trionyx.
triostée [triɔste], *s.m. Bot:* feverwort, feverroot, horse gentian; (*genus*) Triosteum.
trioxyde [triɔksid], *s.m. Ch:* trioxide.
trioxyméthylène [triɔksimetilɛn], *s.m. Ch:* trioxymethylene, trioxane.
tripaille [tripɑːj], *s.f. F:* (*butchery*) offal; *Ven:* entrails.
tripale [tripal], *a.* **(hélice) t.,** three-bladed (propeller).
tripalmitine [tripalmitin], *s.f. Ch:* tripalmitin.
tripang [tripɑ̃], *s.m. Echin:* trepang, sea slug.
triparti [triparti], **tripartite** [tripartit], *a.* tripartite; *Dipl: Pol:* **conversations tripartites,** three-sided, three-party, conversations; **pacte tripartite,** three-power pact.
tripartisme [tripartism], *s.m. Pol: Dipl:* three-party government, three-party coalition.
tripartition [tripartisjɔ̃], *s.f.* tripartition.
tripatouillage [tripatujaːʒ], *s.m.* **1.** *F:* tampering, tinkering; gerrymandering; cooking of accounts. **2.** *P:* pawing, cuddling.
tripatouiller [tripatuje], *v.tr.* **1.** *F:* to tamper, tinker, with (literary work); to garble (news, etc.); to cook (accounts); to gerrymander (an election). **2.** *P:* to paw, cuddle (s.o.).
tripe[1] [trip], *s.f.* **1.** (*a*) *pl.* entrails (of animal); *Cu:* **tripes à la mode de Caen,** braised tripe; **œufs à la t., en tripes,** hard-boiled eggs fried with onions; (*b*) *usu. pl. P:* (*of pers.*) intestines, guts; **rendre tripes et boyaux,** to be horribly sick, to bring one's guts up; **mettre les tripes à l'air à qn,** to rip s.o. up (with a knife, etc.); *F:* **avoir la t. républicaine,** to be an out-and-out republican; **le mal du pays me saisit aux tripes,** I was gripped with a pang of homesickness. **2.** core, filling (of cigar). **3.** *Leath:* **peau en t.,** pelt.
tripe[2], *s.f. Tex:* **t. de velours,** mock velvet; velveteen.
tripée [tripe], *s.f.* = TRIPAILLE.
tripenné [tripɛn(n)e], *a. Bot:* tripinnate.
tripeptide [tripɛptid], *s.m. Bio-Ch:* tripeptide.
triperie [tripri], *s.f.* **1.** tripery; tripe shop. **2.** tripe trade.
tripétale [tripetal], **tripétalé** [tripetale], *a. Bot:* tripetalous.
tripette [tripɛt], *s.f. A:* small tripe; *F:* **ne pas valoir t.,** to be utterly worthless, not to be worth a damn.
triphane [trifan], *s.m. Miner:* triphane, spodumene.
triphasé [trifɑze], *a. El:* triphase, three-phase (current); **alternateur t., génératrice triphasée,** three-phase generator.
triphénylméthane [trifenilmetan], *s.m. Ch:* triphenylmethane.
triphtongue [triftɔ̃ːg], *s.f. Ling:* triphthong.
triphyline [trifilin], **triphylite** [trifilit], *s.f. Miner:* triphyline, triphylite.
triphylle [trifil], *a. Bot:* triphyllous.
tripier, -ière [tripje, -jɛːr]. **1.** *s.* tripe dealer, seller; tripe butcher. **2.** *s.f.* **tripière,** pot for cooking tripe.
triplace [triplas], *a. & s.m.* three-seater (aircraft).
triplan [triplɑ̃], *a. & s.m. Av:* triplane.
triple [tripl̩], *a. & s.m.* treble, threefold, triple; **une t. offense,** a treble offence; **fortune t. de la mienne,** fortune three times as large as mine; **attaqués par des forces triples des nôtres,** attacked by forces three times as great as ours; *F:* **t. menton,** triple chin; **six est le t. de deux,** six is the treble of two, is three times (as much as) two; **plier une feuille de papier en t.,** to fold a sheet of paper into three; **facture, contrat, en t. exemplaire, en t. expédition,** invoice, agreement, in triplicate; *Mth:* **raison t.,** triple ratio; *Elcs:* **fonctionnement en longueur t.,** triple-length working; *Mus:* **t. croche,** demi-semi-quaver; *Ch:* **sel t.,** triple salt; *Astr:* **étoile t.,** triple star; (*intensive*) *F:* **aller au t. galop,** to ride hell for leather; **un t. sot,** an out-and-out fool, a prize idiot.
triplé, -ée [triple]. **1.** *a.* (*a*) *Mth:* **raison triplée,** triplicate ratio; (*b*) *Mus:* **intervalle t.,** double octave. **2.** *s.pl.* triplets.
triplégie [tripleʒi], *s.f. Med:* triplegia.
triplement[1] [tripləmɑ̃], *adv.* trebly, triply; threefold.
triplement[2], *s.m.* trebling, tripling.
tripler [triple], *v.tr. & i.* (*a*) to treble, triple; to increase threefold; **depuis ce temps-là la population a triplé,** the population has trebled, has become three times as large, since that time; **t. sa fortune,** to treble one's fortune; (*b*) *v.i. Aut: Belg:* to overtake three abreast.
triplet [triplɛ], *s.m.* (*a*) *Arch:* triplet; (*b*) *Opt:* triplet lens; (*c*) (*pers.*) *occ.* triplet.
triplette [triplɛt], *s.f.* **1.** *A:* three-seater bicycle. **2.** *Sp:* threesome, team of three (players) (at bowls, etc.); *Fb:* **la t. centrale,** the three centre players.
Triplex [triplɛks], *s.m. R.t.m:* **(verre) T.,** Triplex (glass).
triplicata [triplikata], *s.m.inv.* triplicate; third copy.
Triplice [triplis], *s.f. Hist:* **la T.,** the Triple Alliance.
triplicité [triplisite], *s.f.* (*a*) triplicity (of God); (*b*) tripleness, trebleness.
triplinervé [triplinɛrve], *a. Bot:* triplinerved, triple-nerved.
triplique [triplik], *s.f. Jur: A:* (plaintiff's) surrejoinder.
triplite [triplit], *s.f. Miner:* triplite.
triploïde [triplɔid], *a. Biol:* triploid.
triploïdie [triplɔidi], *s.f. Biol:* triploidy.
triplure [triplyːr], *s.f. Tail:* buckram, stiffening.
tripode [tripɔd], *a. & s.m. Navy: etc:* **(mât) t.,** tripod mast.
tripodie [tripɔdi], *s.f. Lit:* tripody.
tripolaire [tripɔlɛːr], *a.* tripolar.
Tripoli [tripɔli]. **1.** *Pr.n. Geog:* Tripoli. **2.** *s.m.* tripoli (stone); **t. siliceux,** infusorial earth; **t. anglais,** rottenstone.
tripolir [tripɔliːr], **tripolisser** [tripɔlise], *v.tr.* to grind, polish, with rottenstone.
tripolitain, -aine [tripɔlitɛ̃, -ɛn], *Geog:* **1.** *a. & s.* Tripolitan. **2.** *Pr.n.f.* **la T.,** Tripolitania.
triporteur [triportœːr], *s.m.* **1.** carrier tricycle, box tricycle. **2.** (commercial) tri-car.
tripot [tripo], *s.m.* **1.** *A:* tennis-court; *F: A:* **battre un homme dans son t.,** to beat a man on his own ground. **2.** (*a*) gambling-den; **perdre son argent au t.,** to lose one's money gambling; (*b*) *A:* bawdy house.
tripotage [tripɔtaːʒ], *s.m. F:* **1.** (*a*) messing round; fiddling about; (*b*) odd jobs. **2.** underhand work; intrigue; **t. financier,** market jobbery; **tripotages de caisse,** tampering with the cash; cooking of accounts; **les tripotages des élections,** (shady) electioneering.
tripotailler [tripɔtaje], *v.tr. F: Pej:* = TRIPOTER.
tripotée [tripɔte], *s.f. P:* **1.** dressing down; thrashing, licking. **2.** large quantity; lots; crowds (of children, etc.).
tripoter [tripɔte], *F:* **1.** *v.i.* (*a*) to mess about, to fiddle about; **t. dans l'eau,** to dabble, mess about, in the water; **t. dans un tiroir,** to muddle up a drawer; to rummage in a drawer; (*b*) to engage in underhand dealings, in shady business; **t. dans la caisse,** to tamper with the cash; **t. sur les blés,** to gamble in wheat, to rig the wheat market. **2.** *v.tr.* (*a*) to finger, handle (s.o., sth.); to paw (s.o.); to meddle with (sth.); to mess (sth.) about; **t. son chapeau, sa cravate,** to fiddle with one's hat, with one's tie; **ne tripote pas mes outils!** don't meddle, mess around, with my tools! **ne me tripotez pas comme ça,** don't paw me like that; **qu'est-ce que vous tripotez là?** what are you up to? (*b*) to deal shadily, dishonestly, with (money); (*c*) to contrive, bring about (a marriage, etc.); *impers.* **il se tripote quelque chose,** there's something afoot, something cooking.
tripoteur, -euse [tripɔtœːr, -øːz], *s. F:* intriguer; mischief-maker; schemer; *esp.* shady speculator.
tripotier, -ière [tripɔtje, -jɛːr]. **1.** *s.* (*a*) keeper of a gambling house; (*b*) *A:* = TRIPOTEUR. **2.** *a.* scheming (person).
tripous, tripoux [tripu], *s.m.pl. Cu:* tripe cooked with sheep's trotters.
Triptolème [triptɔlɛm], *Pr.n.m. Gr.Myth:* Triptolemus.
triptyque [triptik], *s.m.* **1.** *Art:* triptych. **2.** *Aut:* triptyque (for international travel). **3.** *F:* three-part, three-phase, plan, etc.
trique [trik], *s.f.* **1.** *F:* cudgel, heavy stick; **donner des coups de t. à qn,** to thrash, beat, s.o.; **avoir recours à la t.,** to use big stick methods; **sec comme un coup de t., maigre comme une t.,** as thin as a rake. **2.** *Bot: F:* white stonecrop. **3.** *P:* prohibition from entering specified areas.
triqueballe [trikbal], *s.m. or f.* **1.** *Artil: etc:* sling-cart, devil-carriage. **2.** timber cart. **3.** logging wheels.
trique-madame [trikmadam], *s.f.inv. Bot:* white stonecrop.
triquer[1] [trike], *v.tr. F: A:* to cudgel; to beat, thrash (s.o.).
triquer[2], *v.tr.* **1.** to sort, range (timber). **2.** *N.Arch:* to square (timber).
triquet [trikɛ], *s.m.* **1.** *A:* tennis-bat (for *jeu de paume*). **2.** trestle. **3.** pair of steps.
triquètre [trikɛtr]. **1.** *a. Bot: etc:* triquetrous (stem, bone). **2.** *s.f. Num:* triskelion, triscele, triskele.
triquier, -ière [trikje, -jɛːr], *s.* rag-and-bone dealer.
triréacteur [trireaktœːr], *s.m. Av:* tri-jet.
trirectangle [trirɛktɑ̃ːgl̩], *a. Mth:* trirectangular.
trirègne [trirɛɲ], *s.m. Ecc:* (the Pope's) triple crown, tiara.
trirème [trirɛm], *s.f. Gr.Ant:* trireme.
trisaïeul, -e [trizajœl], *s.* great-great-grandfather; great-great-grandmother; *pl. trisaïeul(e)s.*
trisannuel, -elle [trizan(n)ɥɛl], *a.* triennial (event, plant).
trisecteur, -trice [trisɛktœːr, -tris], *Geom:* **1.** *a.* trisecting. **2.** *s.m.* trisector.
trisection [trisɛksjɔ̃], *s.f.* trisection.
trisépale [trisepal], *a. Bot:* trisepalous.
triséquer [triseke], *v.tr.* **(je trisèque; je triséquerai)** to trisect (angle, etc.).
trisme [trism], *s.m. Med:* trismus, lockjaw.
trismégiste [trismeʒist]. **1.** *a.m. Myth:* (Hermes) Trismegistus. **2.** *s.m. Typ:* three-line-pica.
trismus [trismys], *s.m. Med:* = TRISME.
trisoc [trisɔk], *s.m. Agr:* triple-furrow, three-shared, plough.
trisodique [trisɔdik], *a. Ch:* trisodium.
trisomie [trisɔmi], *s.f. Biol:* trisomy.
trisomique [trisɔmik], *a. Biol:* trisomic.
trisperme [trispɛrm], *a. Bot:* trispermous, three-seeded.
trissement [trismɑ̃], *s.m.* twitter(ing) (of swallows).
trisser[1] [trise], *v.i.* (*of swallow*) to twitter.
trisser[2], *v.tr. & i.* **1.** to encore (song, etc.) twice; to call for a second encore. **2.** *P:* **(se) t.,** to scram, to clear out, to beat it.
tris(s)yllabe [trisil(l)ab]. **1.** *s.m.* trisyllable. **2.** *a.* trisyllabic.
tris(s)yllabique [trisil(l)abik], *a.* trisyllabic.
Tristan [tristɑ̃], *Pr.n.m. Lit:* Tristram, Tristan.

triste [trist], *a.* **1.** (*a*) sad, sorrowful, miserable (person, face, etc.); woe-begone (face, expression); melancholy (news); **t. et abattu,** sad and downcast; **être tout t.,** to be (very) dejected; to be in low spirits, *F:* to be down in the mouth; **sourire t.,** sad, wan, smile; **vous nous trouvez tout tristes de la mort d'un ami,** you find us very sad at the death of a friend; **je fus (bien) t. d'apprendre que . . .,** I was (very) sorry, grieved, to hear that . . .; *F:* **c'est tout de même t.!** isn't it pathetic! (*b*) dreary, dismal, cheerless, gloomy, dull (life, weather, room); **campagne t.,** bleak, depressing, countryside; **faire t. mine à qn,** to receive s.o. without enthusiasm; to give s.o. a poor reception; **faire t. figure,** to pull a long face; **t. comme un jour de pluie, comme un bonnet de nuit,** dull as ditchwater. **2.** unfortunate, painful (news, duty, state); **en cette t. occasion,** on this sad occasion; **c'est une t. affaire,** it's a bad business, a sorry business, a bad job; **un t. sire,** a sordid character. **3.** *F:* poor, sorry, wretched (meal, excuse); **t. engeance!** what a crew! **faire t. figure,** to look out of place, out of one's element.

tristéarine [tristearin], *s.f. Ch:* tristearin.

tristement [tristəmɑ̃], *adv.* **1.** (*a*) sadly, mournfully, sorrowfully; (*b*) gloomily, dismally, cheerlessly. **2.** poorly, wretchedly; **mourir t. à l'hôpital,** to die a miserable death in hospital.

tristesse [tristɛs], *s.f.* (*a*) (feeling of) sadness; melancholy, gloom; **joie mêlée de t.,** joy not untinged with sadness; **jeter un voile de t. sur l'assemblée,** to throw a gloom over the meeting; **avec t.,** sadly; (*b*) dullness, dreariness, dismalness, cheerlessness (of a room, etc.); bleakness (of landscape).

tristique [tristik], *a. Bot:* tristichous.

tristouillard [tristujaːr], **tristouillet, -ette** [tristujɛ, -ɛt], *a. F:* rather sad.

trisubstitué [trisybstitɥe], *a. Ch:* trisubstituted.

trisulce [trizyls], *a. Z:* trisulcate.

trisulfure [trisylfyːr], *s.m. Ch:* trisulphide.

triterné [tritɛrne], *a. Bot:* triternate.

trithéisme [triteism], *s.m. Theol:* tritheism.

trithéiste [triteist], *s.m. Theol:* tritheist.

trithionique [tritjɔnik], *a. Ch:* trithionic.

trithrinax [tritrinaks], *s.m. Bot:* trithrinax, fan palm.

tritium [tritjɔm], *s.m. Ch:* tritium.

tritome [tritoːm], *s.m. Bot:* flame flower; *F:* red-hot poker.

tritomite [tritɔmit], *s.f. Miner:* tritomite.

Triton[1] [tritɔ̃]. **1.** *Pr.n.m. Myth:* Triton. **2.** *s.m.* (*a*) *Amph:* triton, water salamander, newt, eft; **t. crêté,** greater water newt, crested newt; **t. ponctué,** smooth newt; **t. marbré,** marbled newt; (*b*) *Moll:* trumpet shell; triton, triton shell.

triton[2], *s.m. Mus:* tritone; augmented fourth.

triton[3], *s.m. Atom.Ph:* triton.

tritonide [tritɔnid], *s.f.,* **tritonne** [tritɔn], *s.f. Myth:* tritoness.

tritonidés [tritɔnide], *s.m.pl. Moll:* Tritonidae.

tritonie[1] [tritɔni], *s.f. Bot:* tritonia, montbretia.

tritonie[2], *s.f. Moll:* triton (shell).

tritoxyde [tritɔksid], *s.m. Ch:* tritoxide.

tritri [tritri], *s.m. Orn: F:* corn bunting.

tritubercule [tritybɛrkyle], *a. Nat.Hist:* tritubercular, trituberculate.

triturable [trityrabl], *a.* triturable.

triturant [trityrɑ̃], *a. Anat:* **face triturante (d'une dent),** tritural surface (of a tooth).

triturateur [trityratœːr], *s.m. Ind:* triturator; triturating machine.

trituration [trityrasjɔ̃], *s.f.* trituration, grinding.

triturer [trityre], *v.tr.* (*a*) to triturate, grind, rub down, reduce to powder; (*b*) to masticate; *F: A:* **t. la besogne à qn,** to break the back of the work for s.o.

trityle [tritil], *s.m. Ch:* trityl.

tritylodon [tritilɔdɔ̃], *s.m. Paleont:* tritylodont; (*genus*) Tritylodon.

triumvir [triɔmviːr], *s.m. Rom.Hist:* triumvir.

triumviral, -aux [triɔmviral, -o], *a. Rom.Hist:* triumviral.

triumvirat [triɔmvira], *s.m. Rom.Hist:* triumvirate.

trivalence [trivalɑ̃ːs], *s.f. Ch:* trivalence, trivalency; tervalence.

trivalent [trivalɑ̃]. **1.** *a. Ch:* trivalent, tervalent; *Biol:* trivalent, triple. **2.** *s.m. Biol:* trivalent.

trivalve [trivalv], *a. Biol:* trivalvular, trivalve.

trivelin[1] [trivlɛ̃], *s.m. Dent:* elevator.

trivelin[2], *s.m. A.Th:* buffoon.

trivelinade [trivlinad], *s.f. A:* piece of buffoonery.

triviaire [trivjɛːr], *a.* **carrefour t.,** meeting of three roads, *Dial:* three-went-way.

trivial, -iaux [trivjal, -jo]. **1.** *a.* (*a*) *A:* trite, hackneyed, commonplace; **vérités triviales,** truisms; (*b*) vulgar, low, coarse (expression, etc.). **2.** *s.m.* (*a*) *A:* what is trite or hackneyed; (*b*) vulgarity, coarseness; **tomber dans le t.,** to lapse into vulgarity.

trivialement [trivjalmɑ̃], *adv.* vulgarly, coarsely, in a vulgar manner.

trivialiser [trivjalize], *v.tr.* **1.** *A:* to make (sth.) trite, commonplace; to trivialize. **2.** to vulgarize (one's style, etc.).

trivialité [trivjalite], *s.f.* **1.** (*a*) *A:* triteness; (*b*) vulgarity, coarseness. **2.** (*a*) *A:* truism, commonplace; (*b*) vulgarism, coarse expression.

trivium [trivjɔm], *s.m. Sch: A:* **le T.,** the trivium; the first three liberal arts.

Troade (la) [latrɔad], *Pr.n.f. A.Geog:* Troas; Troad.

troc [trɔk], *s.m.* truck; exchange (in kind); barter; *F:* swapping, swap; swopping, swop; **faire du t.,** to barter, *F:* to swap; **faire un t.,** to make an exchange in kind, *F:* to do a swop; *A:* **donner qch. en troc pour qch.,** to barter sth. for sth.; **t. pour t.,** even-handed, fair, exchange.

trocart [trɔkaːr], *s.m. Surg:* trocar.

trochaïque [trɔkaik], *a. & s.m. Pros:* trochaic.

trochanter [trɔkɑ̃tɛːr], *s.m. Anat: Ent:* trochanter; *Anat:* **le grand t.,** the great trochanter, trochanter major; **le petit t.,** the lesser trochanter, trochanter minor.

trochantérien, -ienne [trɔkɑ̃terjɛ̃, -jɛn], *a. Anat:* trochanteric.

trochantin [trɔkɑ̃tɛ̃], *s.m. Anat:* trochantin(e), lesser trochanter, trochanter minor; *Ent:* trochantin(e).

trochantinien, -ienne [trɔkɑ̃tinjɛ̃, -jɛn], *a. Anat:* trochantinal, trochantinian.

troche [trɔʃ], *s.f.* **1.** *A: & Dial:* bunch (of onions); cluster (of fruit, flowers). **2.** *pl. Ven:* fumet, dung (of deer, etc.). **3.** *Moll:* trochus, top shell.

trochée[1] [trɔʃe], *s.m. Pros:* trochee.

trochée[2], *s.f.* tuft of twigs (on tree stump).

trochereau, -eaux [trɔʃro], *s.m. Bot:* cluster pine, pinaster.

trochet[1] [trɔʃɛ], *s.m. Bot:* cluster (of fruit, flowers).

trochet[2], *s.m.* cooper's block.

trochéter [trɔketɛːr], *s.m. Anat:* great tuberosity (of the humerus).

trochidés [trɔkide], *s.m.pl. Moll:* Trochidae, trochids.

trochile [trɔkil], *s.m.* **1.** *Arch:* trochilus. **2.** *Orn:* (*a*) trochilus, crocodile bird; (*b*) (American) trochilus, humming bird.

trochilidés [trɔkilide], *s.m.pl. Orn:* Trochilidae, the humming birds.

trochin [trɔkɛ̃], *s.m.* lesser tuberosity (of the humerus).

trochisque [trɔʃisk], *s.m.* **1.** *Pharm:* troche, trochee; lozenge. **2.** (artist's) cake of paint.

trochiter [trɔkitɛːr], *s.m. Anat:* great tuberosity (of the humerus).

trochléaire [trɔkleɛːr], *a.* trochlear (muscle, surface).

trochlée [trɔkle], *s.f. Anat:* trochlea.

trochléen, -enne [trɔkleɛ̃, -ɛn], *a. Nat.Hist:* trochlear, pulley-shaped.

trochoïde [trɔkɔid]. **1.** *a.* (*a*) *Anat:* trochoid; (*b*) *Geom:* trochoidal. **2.** *s.m. Geom:* spherical lune. **3.** *s.f.* (*a*) *Anat:* trochoid, pivot joint; (*b*) *Geom:* (**courbe**) **t.,** cycloid, trochoid, roulette.

trochophore [trɔkɔfɔːr], **trochosphère** [trɔkɔsfɛːr], *s.f. Z:* trochophore, trochosphere.

trochure [trɔʃyːr], *s.f.* fourth tine (of stag's antlers).

trochus [trɔkys], *s.m. Moll:* top shell, trochus.

troctolite [trɔktɔlit], *s.f. Miner:* troctolite.

trœgérite [trœʒerit], *s.f. Miner:* troegerite, trögerite.

troène [trɔɛn], *s.m. Bot:* privet; **t. de la Chine,** wax tree.

troglobie [trɔglɔbi], *s.m. Biol:* troglobiont.

troglodyte [trɔglɔdit], *s.m.* **1.** *Anthr: Z:* troglodyte; *Anthr:* cave-dweller. **2.** *Orn:* troglodyte; **t. (mignon),** wren, *U.S:* winter wren.

troglodytidés [trɔglɔditide], *s.m.pl. Orn:* Troglodytidae.

troglodytique [trɔglɔditik], *a.* troglodytic.

trogne[1] [trɔɲ], *s.f. F:* bloated face; **il a une t. d'ivrogne,** he's got a beery face; he looks as if he drank too much.

trogne[2], *s.f. Dial:* pollard.

trognon [trɔɲɔ̃], *s.m.* **1.** core (of apple, etc.); stump (of cabbage, etc.); heel (of loaf); *F:* **jusqu'au au t.,** to the (bitter) end; completely, up to the neck; *F:* (*of child*) **un petit t. comme toi,** a nice little chap like you; *a.* **ce qu'il, qu'elle, est t.!** what a nice little boy, girl! **2.** *P:* head; **se fourrer une idée dans le t.,** to get an idea into one's head.

trogon [trɔgɔ̃], *Orn:* trogon; **t. d'Amérique, tropicale,** masked trogon.

trogonidés [trɔgɔnide], *s.m.pl. Orn:* Trogonidae, the trogons.

trogoniformes [trɔgɔnifɔrm], *s.m.pl. Orn:* Trogoniformes.

Troie [trwa], *Pr.n.f. A.Geog:* Troy; **la guerre de T.,** the Trojan War; **le siège de T.,** the siege of Troy; **le cheval de T.,** the Trojan horse.

troïka [trɔika], *s.f. Veh;* troika.

Troïle [trɔil], *Pr.n.m. Gr.Lit:* Troilus.

troïlite [trɔilit], *s.f. Miner:* troilite.

trois [trwa], *before a vowel sound in the same word group* [trwaːz], *num. a. & s.m. inv.* three; **t. enfants** [trwazɑ̃fɑ̃], three children; **trois hommes** [trwazɔm], three men; **à t. heures** [trwazœːr], at three o'clock; **j'en ai t.** [trwa], I have three; **deux ou t.** [døzutrwa], two or three; **t. et quatre** [trwa(z)ekatr̥] **font sept,** three and four are seven; **les t. quarts du temps,** most of the time; **il est en voyage les t. quarts du temps,** he spends most of his time travelling; **couper, diviser, une ligne, un angle, en t.,** to trisect a line, an angle; **entrer par t.,** to come in in threes, three at a time; **la vie à t.,** the eternal triangle; **le t. août** [lətrwa(z)u], the third of August; **Henri T.,** Henry the Third; **le t. de carreau,** the three of diamonds; *Ar:* **la règle de t.,** the rule of three; **je demeure au t.,** I live at number three; *Th:* **le décor du t.,** the scenery of the third act; **le t. pour cent,** the three per cent bonds; the three per cents; **il est arrivé t. ou quatrième,** he arrived, came in, third or fourth; *Elcs:* (*computers*) **à t. adresses,** three-address; **à t. adresses d'opérande et une adresse de commande,** three-plus-one address; **code "plus trois,"** excess-three code.

trois-balles [trwabal], *s.m.inv. Golf:* three-ball match.

trois-étoiles [trwazetwal], *s.m.* **cognac t.-é.,** three-star brandy; **hôtel t.-é.,** three-star hotel; *F: A:* **Madame T.-É., (Mme***),** Mrs X; *Mil: etc:* **un t.-é.,** (i) major general; (ii) vice-admiral.

trois-huit [trwaɥit], *s.m.inv. Mus:* **1.** three-eight (time). **2.** piece in three-eight time. **3.** *Ind:* **régime des t.-h.,** three-shift working, round-the-clock work in eight-hour shifts.

troisième [trwazjɛm]. **1.** *num.a. & s.* third; **demeurer au t. (étage),** to live on the third, *U.S:* fourth, floor; *Nau:* **faire la traversée en t. classe,** to go steerage; **il est arrivé t.,** he arrived, came in, third; **de t. ordre,** third-rate, third-class; *Pol.Ec:* **personnes du t. âge,** retired people. **2.** *s.m.* (*occ.* = TIERS) **deux troisièmes,** two thirds. **3.** *s.f.* (*a*) *Sch:* (**classe de**) **t.,** *approx.* = fourth form (of grammar school); (*b*) *Rail: O:* **voyager en t.,** to travel third(class).

troisièmement [trwazjɛmmɑ̃], *adv.* thirdly, in the third place.

trois-mâts [trwamɑ], *s.m.inv. Nau:* three-masted ship, three-master; **t.-m. carré,** fully-rigged ship, square-rigged three-master; **t.-m. barque,** three-masted barque; **t.-m. goélette,** three-masted schooner.

trois-pièces [trwapjɛs], *s.m.inv.* **1.** *Cost:* three-piece suit. **2.** three-roomed flat, *U.S:* apartment.

trois-ponts [trwapɔ̃], *s.m.inv. Nau: A:* three-decker.

trois-quarts [trwakaːr], *s.m.inv.* **1.** *Surg: A:* = TROCART. **2.** three-quarter violin. **3.** *Tls:* triangular rasp. **4.** *Rugby Fb:* **les t.-q.,** the three-quarters. **5.** *Cost:* three-quarter-length coat.

trois-quatre [trwakatr̥], *s.m.inv. Mus:* **1.** three-four (time). **2.** piece in three-four time.

trois-roues [trwaru], *s.m.inv.* three-wheeler.

trois-six [trwasis], *s.m. Dist:* proof spirit.

trôle[1] [troːl], *s.f. A:* **1.** open-air furniture market. **2.** furniture hawking (by the workman himself); so used in **ouvrier à la t.,** cabinet-maker who hawks his own wares from shop to shop.

trôle[2], *s.f. Fish:* dragging, trawling; **filet à la t.,** dragnet; trawl(net).

trôle[3], *s.f. Ven:* cast.

trôler [trole], *F: A:* **1.** *v.tr.* (*a*) to take, drag, (s.o.) about; to have (s.o.) in tow; (*b*) to trundle round (furniture) for sale; to hawk. **2.** *v.i.* to wander about, to loaf; *P:* to be on the tramp.

trôleur [trolœːr], *s.m.* (*a*) *A:* hawker; (*b*) *P:* vagrant, tramp.

troll [trɔl], *s.m. Norse Myth:* troll.

trolle[1] [trɔl], *s.m. Bot:* globe flower.

trolle[2], *s.f. Ven:* cast.

trolley [trɔlɛ], *s.m.* **1.** *Ind:* troll(ey), truck, runner (of aerial ropeway); **transport par t.,** overhead transport. **2.** (*a*) troll(e)y pole and wheel; **perche de t.,** trolley pole; (*b*) *F:* trolleybus.

trolleybus [trɔlɛbys], *s.m.* trolleybus.

trombe [trɔ̃:b], *s.f.* **1.** waterspout. **2. t. de vent,** whirlwind; **t. d'eau,** cloudburst; *F:* **entrer, sortir, en t.,** to burst in, out; to dash in, out; to sweep in, out, like a whirlwind. **3.** = TROMPE 5 (*b*).

trombidion [trɔ̃bidjɔ̃], **trombidium** [trɔ̃bidjɔm], *s.m. Ent:* trombidium.

trombidiose [trɔ̃bidjo:z], *s.f. Med: Vet:* trombidiasis.

trombine [trɔ̃bin], *s.f. P:* (*a*) head, nut; (*b*) face, mug.

trombinoscope [trɔ̃binɔskɔp], *s.m. F:* rogue's gallery.

tromblon [trɔ̃blɔ̃], *s.m.* **1.** blunderbuss. **2.** *Mil:* grenade sleeve (fitted to rifle).

trombone [trɔ̃bɔn], *s.m. Mus:* **1.** trombone (instrument or performer); **t. à coulisse,** slide trombone; **t. à pistons,** valve trombone; **t. alto, ténor, basse,** alto, tenor, bass, trombone. **2.** posaune (stop) (of organ). **3.** *F:* (wire) paper clip.

tromboniste [trɔ̃bɔnist], *s.m. & f. Mus:* trombonist; trombone player (by profession).

trommel [trɔmɛl], *s.m. Min: Civ.E:* revolving screen; **t. classeur,** sizing drum.

trompe [trɔ̃:p], *s.f.* **1.** (*a*) horn; **t. de chasse,** hunting horn; *F:* **publier qch. à son de trompe,** to trumpet sth. abroad; (*b*) hooter; (*c*) *Aut: A:* horn; **t. à poire,** bulb horn; (*d*) *A:* **t. de Béarn, à laquais,** jew's harp. **2.** proboscis (of animal, insect); trunk (of elephant); probe (of insect). **3.** *Anat:* **t. d'Eustache,** Eustachian tube; **les trompes de Fallope,** the Fallopian tubes. **4.** *Arch:* pendentive; squinch. **5.** (*a*) *Ind:* aspirator; siphon; *Ch:* **t. à vide,** filter pump; (*b*) *Metall:* blast pump; trompe; *Min:* water blast; (*c*) *Tchn:* nozzle.

trompe-la-mort [trɔ̃plamɔ:r], *s.m. & f.inv. F:* (*a*) death dodger; (*b*) daredevil.

trompe-l'œil [trɔ̃plœ:j], *s.m.inv.* **1.** (*a*) *Art:* trompe l'œil; (*b*) dummy window, etc. **2.** *Pej:* deceptive appearance, illusion; **projet de loi qui n'est qu'un t.-l'œ.,** bill that is only eyewash, window dressing, a piece of bluff, of camouflage.

tromper [trɔ̃pe], *v.tr.* to deceive. **1.** (*a*) to cheat; to impose upon, take in (s.o.); **t. le public,** to cheat, delude, the public; **se laisser t. aux apparences,** *occ.* **par les apparences,** to be taken in by appearances; **il est incapable de t.,** he is incapable of deception; (*b*) to betray, be unfaithful to (wife, husband); **t. une jeune fille,** to ruin a girl. **2.** (*a*) to mislead; **t. qn sur ses intentions,** to mislead s.o. as to one's intentions; **t. les espérances de qn,** to disappoint s.o.'s hopes; **le résultat a trompé notre calcul,** the result did not accord with our calculations; **c'est justement ce qui vous trompe,** that is just where you are mistaken, where you are wrong; **il ne faut pas se laisser t. par son apparence,** his appearance belies him; (*b*) to outwit, baffle, elude; **t. la vigilance de ses gardes,** to elude, balk, the vigilance of one's guardians; *A:* **t. la loi,** to elude the law; to get round the law; (*c*) to relieve, find relief for (grief, tedium); to while away (the time); **t. les longues heures de veille,** to while away the long night watches; **t. la faim,** to stave off one's hunger; **t. le chemin,** to while away the time on a journey.

se tromper, to be mistaken; to be wrong; to make a mistake; **si je ne me trompe,** if I am not mistaken; **se t. dans son calcul,** to be out in one's reckoning; **je me suis trompé de maison, de route,** I went to the wrong house, the wrong address, took the wrong road; **se t. de direction,** to go the wrong way; **se t. d'heure,** to mistake the time; **se t. de porte,** (i) to open the wrong door; (ii) to go to the wrong address; **se t. sur les intentions de qn,** to be mistaken regarding s.o.'s intentions; **elle ressemble à sa sœur à s'y t.,** you can't tell her from her sister; she is remarkably like her sister; **il n'y a pas à s'y t.,** there is no mistake about it; there is no possibility of a mistake; **que l'on ne s'y trompe pas,** let there be no misunderstanding, no mistake, about it; **vous m'avez fait t.,** you made me make a mistake; you put me off.

tromperie [trɔ̃pri], *s.f.* **1.** (*a*) deceit, deception, cheating, imposture, imposition, fraud; *Jur:* **t. sur la marchandise,** frauds relating to goods; (*b*) illusion; **la t. d'un songe agréable,** the illusions of a pleasant dream. **2.** piece of deceit; fraud.

trompeter [trɔ̃p(ə)te], *v.* (**je trompette, je trompetterai**) to trumpet. **1.** *v.tr.* (*a*) *A:* to publish, proclaim, summon, by trumpet; **t. une bague perdue,** to cry a lost ring; (*b*) *F:* to let out (secret); to trumpet (news) abroad. **2.** *v.i.* (*a*) to sound the trumpet; (*b*) (*of eagle*) to scream.

trompeteur [trɔ̃p(ə)tœ:r], *s.m.* **1.** trumpeter. **2.** *Anat:* buccinator (muscle).

trompette [trɔ̃pɛt]. **I.** *s.f.* **1.** (*a*) trumpet; *Mil:* **jouer de la t.,** to play the trumpet; **sonner de la t.,** to blow, sound, the trumpet; **sonnerie de t.,** trumpet call; *F:* **emboucher, entonner, la trompette,** to adopt a high-flown style, an epic style; **t. d'harmonie,** orchestral trumpet; **t. à pistons, chromatique,** valve trumpet; **t. à clefs,** keyed trumpet, keyed bugle; *Lit:* **la t. de la Renommée,** the trump of Fame; **la t. du jugement dernier,** the last trump, the trump of doom; **nez en t.,** turned up nose; *F:* **c'est la t. du quartier,** he's, she's, the town gossip; (*b*) *A:* **t. marine, parlante,** speaking trumpet; (*c*) *Mus: A:* (*monochord stringed instrument*) **t. marine,** trumpet marine; (*d*) *Mus:* (*organ stop*) trumpet; (*e*) *Aut:* **t. de pont,** rear axle flared tube. **2.** (*a*) *Conch:* trumpet shell; (*b*) *Ich:* trumpet fish; pipe fish; (*c*) *Orn:* **oiseau t.,** crowned crane, Balearic crane; (*d*) *Fung:* **t. de la mort, des morts,** craterellus.

II. **trompette,** *s.m. esp. Mil:* trumpeter, trumpet (player).

trompette-major [trɔ̃pɛtmaʒɔ:r], *s.m. Mil:* trumpet major; *pl. trompettes-majors.*

trompette-signal [trɔ̃pɛtsiɲal], *s.f. A:* horn, hooter (of tram); *pl. trompettes-signal.*

trompettiste [trɔ̃pɛtist], *s.m. & f. Mus:* trumpet (player).

trompeur, -euse [trɔ̃pœ:r, -ø:z]. **1.** *a.* (*a*) deceitful (person, words, etc.); **langue trompeuse,** lying tongue; (*b*) deceptive, delusive, misleading (appearance, symptom); *Prov:* **les apparences sont trompeuses,** appearances are deceptive. **2.** *s.* (*a*) deceiver, cheat(er); **le t. trompé,** the biter bit; *Prov:* **à t., t. et demi,** set a thief to catch a thief; (*b*) betrayer.

trompeusement [trɔ̃pøzmɑ̃], *adv.* (*a*) deceitfully; (*b*) deceptively.

trompillon [trɔ̃pijɔ̃], *s.m.* **1.** *Arch:* small pendentive, squinch. **2.** *Mch:* air hole (of water blast).

trona [trɔna], *s.m. Miner:* trona.

tronc [trɔ̃], *s.m.* **1.** (*a*) trunk (of tree, of body); bole, body, stem (of tree); barrel (of ox, cow, etc.); (*b*) *Arch:* trunk, drum (of column); (*c*) *Anat:* truncus, trunk, main stem (of artery, etc.); (*d*) parent stock (of family). **2.** collecting box (in church); **t. pour les pauvres,** poor-box, almsbox. **3.** *Geom:* **t. de cône, de pyramide, de prisme,** truncated cone, pyramid, prism; frustrum, frustum, of a cone, pyramid, prism.

troncation [trɔ̃kasjɔ̃], *s.f. Ling:* truncation, abbreviation (of a word).

troncature [trɔ̃katy:r], *s.f. Cryst: etc:* truncation; *Elcs:* **erreur de t.,** truncation error.

tronche [trɔ̃:ʃ], *s.f.* **1.** (*a*) *Dial:* log, *esp.* yule log; (*b*) *P:* head, nut. **2.** *For:* stem-pruned tree. **3.** end (of rope).

tronchet [trɔ̃ʃɛ], *s.m.* (cooper's, butcher's, etc.) block.

tronçon [trɔ̃sɔ̃], *s.m.* (*a*) section (of any roughly cylindrical object); length (of pipe); (broken) piece, end, stub, stump (of sword, lance, mast, etc.); frustrum (of column); **t. de bois,** log; **t. de rebut,** waste end; **t. d'anguille,** piece, slice, portion, of eel; **les deux tronçons du serpent continuaient à s'agiter,** the two portions of the serpent continued to wriggle; (*b*) dock (of horse's tail); (*c*) section (of railway, motorway, telegraph line, etc.); block (of railway track); **les tronçons d'arrière de la colonne,** the rear sections of the column; *Av:* **t. arrière,** afterbody (of aircraft); (*d*) part, fragment (of a sentence, a text, etc.); **sa phrase s'était débitée en trois tronçons,** his sentence came out in three separate fragments, *F:* he had three goes at finishing his sentence.

tronconique [trɔ̃kɔnik], *a. Geom:* in the shape of a truncated cone; **segment t.,** truncated segment.

tronçonnage [trɔ̃sɔna:ʒ], *s.m.,* **tronçonnement** [trɔ̃sɔnmɑ̃], *s.m.* cutting (of anything cylindrical) into lengths, into pieces.

tronçonner [trɔ̃sɔne], *v.tr.* to cut (anything of cylindrical shape) into pieces, into sections, into lengths; to cut up; **t. une anguille,** to chop an eel into pieces; to chop up an eel.

tronçonneur [trɔ̃sɔnœ:r], *s.m.* chain-saw operator.

tronçonneuse [trɔ̃sɔnø:z], *s.f.* **1.** motor chain saw; power-(driven) saw. **2.** cross-cut circular saw.

tronculaire [trɔ̃kylɛ:r], *a. Anat: etc:* truncal; *Dent:* **anesthésie t.,** block anaesthesis, conduction anaesthesis.

tron-de-l'air [trɔ̃dlɛ:r], *int. Dial: O:* (*in S. of Fr.*) by thunder! heavens above!

trône [tro:n], *s.m.* **1.** (*a*) throne; (*of monarch*) **monter sur le t.,** to come to the throne; **l'héritier du t.,** the heir to the throne; **placer, mettre, qn sur le t.,** to put s.o. on the throne; **perdre son t.,** to lose one's crown; **chasser un roi de son t.,** to dethrone a king; *Pol:* **discours du t.,** speech from the throne; king's, queen's, speech; *Ecc:* **le t. épiscopal,** the episcopal throne; (*b*) *F: Iron:* (= *lavatory*) throne; **il est sur le t.,** he's on the throne, in the loo, *U.S:* the john. **2.** *Theol:* (*order of Angels*) **les Trônes,** the Thrones.

trôner [trone], *v.i.* (*a*) *A:* (*of monarch*) to reign; (*b*) to sit enthroned; **dans le temple trône un Bouddha géant,** a huge Buddha sits enthroned in the temple; (*c*) to occupy a place of honour; (*d*) *Pej:* to lord it; **elle trônait à la caisse,** she was sitting in state, lording it, at the pay desk.

tronqué [trɔ̃ke], *a.* (*a*) truncated (tree, column, crystal, leaf, etc.); *Geom:* **cône t.,** truncated cone; **prisme t.,** truncated prism; *W.Tel: etc:* **mât t.,** stub mast; (*b*) **texte t., édition tronquée,** mutilated, abbreviated, text, edition.

tronquer [trɔ̃ke], *v.tr.* (*a*) to truncate (tree, etc.); to mutilate (statue, etc.); (*b*) *Elcs:* to truncate; (*c*) *Pej:* to curtail, cut down (novel, etc.).

troostite [trustit], *s.f. Metall:* troostite.

trop [tro]. **1.** *adv.* too; (*a*) (*with adj.*) too, over-; **c'est t. difficile,** it's too difficult; **un travail t. difficile,** too difficult a job; **t. aimable** [trɔpɛmabl̩], too, very, kind; **vous êtes t. aimable de le faire,** it is exceedingly kind of you to do it; **il est t. gentil pour le renvoyer,** he is too kind to sack him; **aliments t. riches,** over-rich food; **vous n'êtes que t. généreux,** you are all too generous; **t. fatigué,** overtired; **t. fatigué pour courir,** too tired to run; **vous n'êtes pas t. en avance,** you are none too early; **vous êtes t. grand pour qu'on puisse vous traiter en enfant,** you are too big to be treated as a child; **le trou était t. étroit pour qu'un rat entrât par là,** the hole was too narrow for a rat to come in by; (*b*) (*with vb*) too much, overmuch, unduly, over-; **t. travailler,** to overwork, to work too hard; **travailler t. ou t. peu,** to work too much or too little; **j'ai entendu des gens se plaindre que M. X ait t. écrit,** I have heard people complain that Mr X wrote too much; **boire t., t. boire,** to drink to excess, too much; **je l'ai t. aimé** [trɔpɛme], I loved him too well; **ne vous y fiez pas t., il ne faut pas t. vous y fier,** don't count on it too much; **ne faites pas t. le dégoûté,** don't be unduly squeamish, too squeamish; **il parle t.,** he is too talkative; **je l'ai t. écouté,** I have listened to him too long; **on ne saurait t. le répéter,** *A:* **le t. répéter,** it cannot be too often repeated; **je ne sais t. que dire,** I hardly know, I don't quite know, what to say; **je n'en sais t. rien,** I hardly know; **il a t. connu les hommes pour les mépriser,** he knew men too well to despise them. **2.** *s.m.* too much, too many; **il allait t. en dire, en dire t., en t. dire,** he was going to say too much; **le t. ne vaut rien; t. et t. peu n'est pas mesure, t. c'est t.,** too much is as bad as none at all; enough is as good as a feast; **elle n'a pas t. d'une heure pour s'habiller,** (i) she takes, (ii) she will need, a good hour to dress; **trop de bruit,** too much noise; **t. d'amis,** too many friends; **vous avez pris t. de précautions, vous avez t. pris de précautions,** you were overcautious; **je ne l'ai que t. dit, je ne l'ai dit que t.,** I've said it too many times already; **de t., en t.,** too much, too many; **j'ai une carte de t., en t.,** I have a card too many; **c'est une fois de t.,** that is once too often; **quand j'ai du temps de t.,** when I have time to spare; **payer en t.,** to overpay; **être de t.,** to be in the way, unwelcome, de trop; **ils sont t.!** they are too many! **ils sont de t.,** they are not wanted; **vous n'êtes pas de t.,** you're not at all in the way; we can do with your help; *F:* **travailler, boire, de t.,** to work too hard; to drink too much; *adv.phr.* **par t.,** (altogether) too (much); **être par t. généreux,** to be far too generous; **c'est t. fort,** *Lit:* **c'est par t. fort!** it is really too bad! it's a bit much! **c'en est t.!** this passes all bounds! *F:* this really is the limit!

tropane [trɔpan], *s.m. Ch:* tropane.

trope [trɔp], *s.m. Rh: A.Mus:* trope.

tropéolées [trɔpeɔle], *s.f.pl. Bot:* Tropaeolaceae.

tropéolum [trɔpeɔlɔm], *s.m. Bot:* tropaeolum.

tropézien, -ienne [trɔpezjɛ̃, -jɛn], *a. & s. Geog:* (native, inhabitant) of Saint-Tropez.

trophallaxie [trɔfalaksi], *s.f. Nat.Hist:* trophallaxis.

trophée [trɔfe], *s.m.* trophy (of war, of the chase, etc.); **dresser, ériger, un t. à qn,** to erect a trophy to s.o.; *A:* **faire t. de qch.,** to glory in sth.

trophie [trɔfi], *s.f.* trophism.

trophique [trɔfik], *a. Physiol:* trophic (nerves, etc.); **troubles trophiques,** digestive troubles.

trophisme [trɔfism], *s.m.* trophism.

tropho- [trɔfɔ], *comb.fm.* tropho-.

trophoblaste [trɔfɔblast], *s.m. Biol:* trophoblast.

trophocyte [trɔfɔsit], *s.m. Biol:* trophocyte.

trophœdème [trɔfedɛm], *s.m. Med:* trophœdema.

trophologie [trɔfɔlɔʒi], *s.f.* trophology.

trophonévrose [trɔfɔnevroːz], *s.f. Med:* trophoneurosis.

trophonucléus [trɔfɔnykleys], *s.m. Biol:* trophonucleus.

trophoplasma [trɔfɔplasma], *s.m. Biol:* trophoplasm.

trophosperme [trɔfɔspɛrm], *s.m. Bot:* trophosperm.

trophotaxie [trɔfɔtaksi], *s.f. Biol:* trophotaxis.

trophotropisme [trɔfɔtrɔpism], *s.m. Biol:* trophotropism.

tropical, -aux [trɔpikal, -o], *a.* tropical (plant, temperature, etc.).

tropicalisation [trɔpikalizasjɔ̃], *s.f. Com:* tropicalization.

tropicalisé [trɔpikalize], *a. Com:* tropicalized.

tropicaliser [trɔpikalize], *v.tr. Com:* to tropicalize.

tropidine [trɔpidin], *s.f. Ch:* tropidine.

tropique[1] [trɔpik]. **1.** *a.* tropical (year). **2.** *s.m.* (*a*) *Astr: Geog:* tropic; (*b*) *pl.* the tropics; **sous les tropiques,** in the tropics.

tropique[2], *a. Rh:* tropical, figurative.

tropisme [trɔpism], *s.m. Biol:* tropism.

tropologie [trɔpɔlɔʒi], *s.f.* tropology.

tropologique [trɔpɔlɔʒik], *a.* tropologic(al).

tropomètre [trɔpɔmɛtr̥], *s.m.* tropometer.

tropopause [trɔpɔpoːz], *s.f. Meteor:* tropopause.

tropophile [trɔpɔfil], *a. Bot:* tropophilous.

tropophyte [trɔpɔfit], *s.f. Bot:* tropophyte.

troposphère [trɔpɔsfɛːr], *s.f. Meteor:* troposphere.

trop-perçu [trɔpɛrsy], *s.m. Fin:* over-payment (of taxes); **rembourser le t.-p.,** to refund the over-payment; *pl. trop-perçus.*

trop-plein [trɔplɛ̃], *s.m.* overflow (of bath, reservoir, etc.); **(tuyau de) t.-p.,** waste pipe, overflow pipe; **t.-p. de tendresse,** overflowing wealth of affection; *pl. trop-pleins.*

troque [trɔk], *s.m. Moll:* trochus, common top shell.

troquer [trɔke], *v.tr.* to exchange, barter, truck, *F:* swap, swop (sth.); **t. qch. contre qch.,** to exchange, barter, sth. for sth.; *F:* **t. son cheval borgne contre un aveugle,** to exchange bad for worse, *abs.* **t. de monture,** to exchange mounts.

troquet[1] [trɔkɛ], *s.m. P:* (*a*) pub-keeper; (*b*) pub.

troquet[2], *s.m. Bot: F:* maize, *U.S:* corn.

troquet[3], *s.m. Const:* purlin support.

troqueur, -euse [trɔkœːr, -øːz], *a.* barterer.

troscart [trɔskaːr], *s.m. Bot:* arrow grass.

trot [tro], *s.m.* trot; **cheval de t.,** trotter; **t. assis,** close trot; bumping trot; **faire du t. assis,** to trot close; **t. enlevé,** rising trot, *U.S:* posting trot; **faire du t. enlevé,** to rise in the stirrups, *U.S:* to post; **au petit t.,** at a gentle, slow, controlled, trot; **au grand t.,** at a smart, brisk, trot; **faire le grand t.,** to trot out; **partir au t.,** to set off at a trot; **prendre le t.,** to break into a trot; **aller le t., au t.,** to trot; *F:* **aller au t. à tel endroit,** to hurry off, dash off, to such and such a place; *F:* **allez-y, et au t.!** go on, and be quick about it! **course de t.,** trotting race.

Trotskiste, Trotskyste [trɔtskist], *a. & s.m. & f.* Trotskyist, Trotskyite.

trotte [trɔt], *s.f. F:* (*a*) distance, stretch, run; **il y a une bonne t. d'ici là,** it is a good step from here; **faire une bonne t.,** to go a good long way (to see s.o., etc.); **tout d'une t.,** without stopping, at a stretch; (*b*) **cette t. perpétuelle,** this perpetual coming and going, moving around.

trotte-bébé [trɔtbebe], *s.m.inv.* go-cart, baby walker.

trotte-menu [trɔtməny], *a.inv.* (pitter-)pattering, scampering (steps of mice, etc.); (*in La Fontaine*) **la gent t.-m.,** the mouse tribe.

trotter [trɔte]. **1.** *v.i.* (*of horse or rider*) to trot; (*of mice*) to scamper; *Equit: O:* **t. à l'anglaise,** to rise in the saddle, *U.S:* to post; *F:* **elle est toujours à t.,** she is always trotting around, on the go; **on entendrait t. une souris,** you could hear a pin drop; **cette chanson me trotte par, dans, la tête,** that song keeps running through my head, is never out of my head; **air qui vous trotte par la tête,** haunting tune. **2.** *v.tr.* to put (horse) to the trot, to trot (horse).

se trotter, *P:* (*a*) to go, to be off; (*b*) to decamp.

trotteur, -euse [trɔtœːr, -øːz]. **1.** *s.* (*a*) *Equit:* trotter; trotting horse, mare; **ce cheval est bon t.,** this horse is a good trotter; (*b*) (*pers.*) great walker; quick walker. **2.** *s.f.* **trotteuse,** (*a*) seconds hand (of watch); **grande aiguille trotteuse centrale,** centre-seconds hand, sweep hand, seconds sweep (of chronometer, measuring instrument, etc.); **trotteuse double,** split-seconds hand; (*b*) go-cart, baby walker. **3.** *Cost:* (*a*) *a. & s.f. A:* **(jupe) trotteuse,** walking (skirt); (*b*) *a. & s.m.* walking (shoe).

trottin [trɔtɛ̃], *s.m. A:* (dressmaker's) errand girl.

trottinant [trɔtinɑ̃], *a.* toddling (gait).

trottinement [trɔtinmɑ̃], *s.m.* (*a*) jog trot; (*b*) trotting around; pitter-pattering; toddling.

trottiner [trɔtine], *v.i.* **1.** (*a*) *Equit:* to trot short; (*b*) *F:* to jog along (on one's horse). **2.** *F:* to trot about (from one room to another); to pitter-patter; (*of child*) to toddle.

trottinette [trɔtinɛt], *s.f.* (*a*) (child's) scooter; (*b*) *F:* small car.

trotting [trɔtiŋ], *s.m. Equit:* (*a*) (i) breeding, (ii) exercising, of trotting horses; (*b*) trotting races.

trottoir [trɔtwaːr], *s.m.* **1.** (*a*) footpath, pavement, *U.S:* sidewalk; **t. cyclable,** cycle track; **bordure du t.,** kerb(side); **glisser au défaut du t.,** to slip off the kerb; *Aut:* **heurter le t.,** to hit the kerb; **artiste de t.,** pavement artist; *F:* **fille de t.,** street-walker, tart; **faire le t.,** to solicit in the streets; *F:* to walk the streets; *Th: F:* **le grand t.,** the classical repertory (of the French stage); (*b*) *Rail: occ.* (station) platform; (*c*) *Geol:* erosion platform (at foot of cliff). **2. t. roulant,** travelator. **3.** *Rail:* side footplate (of locomotive).

trou [tru], *s.m.* hole. **1.** (*a*) **t. dans un bas,** hole in a stocking; **t. de clef,** keyhole (of clock, watch); **t. de serrure,** keyhole (of lock); **t. d'une aiguille,** eye of a needle; **trous d'une flûte,** ventages of a flute; **percer un t.,** to cut, bore, prick, a hole **(dans,** in); **découper des trous dans qch.,** to cut out, punch, holes in sth.; *F:* **faire son t.,** to come to the fore; to work oneself into a good position; **boucher un t.,** (i) to stop up a hole; (ii) to pay off a debt; **faire un t. pour en boucher un autre,** to rob Peter to pay Paul; *O:* **mettre la pièce à côté du t.,** to try a worse than useless expedient; **autant de trous, autant de chevilles,** he has an answer to everything; **t. de, du, chat,** (i) cat door (in house door, etc.); (ii) *Nau:* lubber's hole; *F:* **faire un t. à la lune,** to do a moonlight flit; to abscond; *Av: P:* **il a fait un t. dans l'eau,** he's gone for a Burton; *F:* **boire comme un t.,** to drink like a fish; *P:* **avoir un t. sous le nez,** to be over-fond of one's drink; to booze; (*b*) **t. dans une haie,** gap in a hedge; *Art:* **t. d'ombre,** packet of shadow; **t. de mémoire,** lapse of memory; **il y a un t. dans mes souvenirs,** there's a gap in my recollections; *Ten:* **laisser un t. dans son court,** to leave part of one's court unguarded; (*c*) *Anat:* foramen; **t. de conjugaison,** foramen invertebrale; **t. occipital,** occipital foramen, foramen magnum; **t. de Botal,** foramen ovale cordis; *Med: F:* **t. dans le cœur,** hole in the heart; *P:* (*not used in polite conversation*) **t. du cul, t. de balle,** arsehole; **petit t. du cul!** you bloody little fool! (*d*) **t. normand,** glass of Calvados (drunk between two courses of a meal). **2.** (*a*) **t. de souris,** mouse-hole; **les animaux rentrent dans leurs trous,** animals return to their holes; *Mil:* **t. individuel,** slit trench, foxhole; **t. d'obus,** shell hole; *Av:* **t. d'air,** air pocket; **t. (dans une route),** pothole (in a road); *P.N:* **trous en formation,** beware of potholes; *Th:* **t. du souffleur,** prompter's box; *Agr:* **t. au fumier,** manure pit; (*b*) *F:* place; **habiter un petit t. (mort, perdu),** to live in a dead-and-alive little hole, at the back of beyond; **je cherche un petit t. pas cher,** I'm looking for a little place that's not too expensive; (*c*) *Golf:* **envoyer la balle dans le t.,** to hole out; **pelouse du t.,** (putting) green; **partie par trous,** match play; **perdre sa balle au dixième t.,** to lose one's ball on the tenth; (*d*) *P:* (i) grave; (ii) prison; **on l'a mis dans le t.,** they buried him; **on l'a mis au t.,** he was jailed, given a stretch. **3.** (*a*) *Mch: etc:* **t. d'homme,** manhole; **t. de graissage,** oil hole; **t. de sel,** sludge hole, mud hole, wash-out hole; **t. borgne,** blind hole; **t. traversant,** through hole; **t. d'évidement,** recess; **t. de dégagement,** back-off hole; **t. de purge,** bleed hole; **t. d'aération,** air vent; *Metall:* **t. de coulée,** (i) runner, gate, sprue (of mould); (ii) taphole (of furnace); *Min:* **t. de mine,** blast hole, drill hole; *Min: Civ.E:* **t. de sondage, de sonde,** borehole; *Const:* **t. d'écoulement,** weep hole; (*b*) *Ph: Elcs:* hole; *Elcs:* **plaque à trous,** aperture plate; **tore à plusieurs trous,** multi-aperture core.

troubade [trubad], *s.m. F: A:* foot-soldier, Tommy.

troubadour [trubaduːr], *s.m. Lit.Hist:* troubadour.

troubadourisme [trubadurism], *s.m.* troubadourism.

troublant [trublɑ̃], *a.* disturbing. **1.** disquieting, disconcerting. **2.** perturbing; **lectures troublantes,** unsettling reading; **parfum t.,** heady perfume; **la singulière et troublante femme!** what a strange and disturbing woman!

trouble[1] [trubl̥], *a.* **1.** (*a*) turbid, cloudy, muddy (liquid); dim (light, eyes); murky (light); murky, overcast (sky); **avoir la vue t.,** to be dim-sighted; **aux yeux troubles,** bleary-eyed; **situation t.,** confused situation, situation that is far from clear; **pêcher en eau t.,** to fish in troubled waters; *adv.* **voir t.,** to be dim-sighted, to see things through a mist; **je vois t., mes yeux voient t.,** everything seems blurred; (*b*) **avoir une vue t. de qch.,** to have a blurred vision of sth. **2.** confused (mine); turbid (conscience); **joie t. et presque douloureuse,** uneasy and almost painful joy. **3.** *s.m. Ch:* **point de t.,** cloud point; *pl. A:* **troubles,** matter in suspension in liquid; turbidity, muddiness.

trouble[2], *s.m.* **1.** (*a*) confusion, disorder (in the ranks, in s.o.'s ideas, etc.); **porter le t. dans une cérémonie,** to disturb a ceremony; **apporter du t. dans une famille,** to cause trouble in a family; to make mischief; *Med:* **troubles de digestion,** digestive troubles; **troubles de vision,** eye trouble; (*b*) agitation, perturbation, uneasiness; **état de t.,** state of agitation; **cause de t.,** disturbing factor; **jeter le t. dans l'esprit de qn,** to disturb s.o.'s mind; to perturb s.o.; **un t. extrême s'empara de lui,** he became extremely perturbed; (*c*) *pl.* public disturbances; **troubles ouvriers,** labour disturbances. **2.** *Jur:* **t. de jouissance,** disturbance of possession; prevention of enjoyment of possession.

trouble[3], *s.f. Fish:* hoop net.

troubleau, -eaux [trublo], *s.m. Fish:* small hoop net.

trouble-fête [trubləfɛːt], *s.m.inv.* spoilsport, wet blanket, killjoy.

trouble-ménage [trubləmenaːʒ], *s.m.inv.* mischief-maker (between husband and wife).

troubler [truble], *v.tr.* **1.** to make (liquid, etc.) cloudy, thick, muddy; to muddy (water); **les malheurs lui ont troublé le cerveau,** misfortune has clouded his mind; **yeux troublés de larmes,** eyes blurred with tears, tear-dimmed eyes. **2.** to disturb (meeting, sleep, etc.); to interfere with, disturb (operations, activities); **t. le silence,** to break (in upon) the silence; **un vent léger troubla l'eau,** a slight wind ruffled the water; **rien ne troubla notre marche,** nothing interrupted, hampered, impeded, our march; **t. le bonheur de qn,** to spoil, mar, s.o.'s happiness; **événements qui ont troublé le pays,** events that have shaken the country; **t. le repos, l'ordre public,** to make, create, raise, a disturbance; *Jur:* to break the peace; **l'ordre public n'a été nullement troublé,** there has been no breach of the peace; **t. le repos de qn,** to disturb s.o.'s rest; to disturb s.o. from his rest; **t. la digestion de qn,** to upset s.o.'s digestion; **imagination troublée,** disordered imagination. **3.** to perturb; (*a*) to confuse, upset, discompose (s.o.); to disquiet (s.o.); to make (s.o.) uneasy; to put (s.o.) out; **ces incivilités ne le troublaient point,** he was not at all put out at this rudeness; **paraître troublé,** to look confused, flustered, upset; **elle était toute troublée,** she was completely flustered; (*b*) to agitate, excite, upset, stir; **elle n'était troublée d'aucune passion,** no passion disturbed her peace of mind; **il était encore troublé par elle, après tant d'années,** she still stirred his emotions after so many years; **leur voisinage le troublait profondément,** their proximity thrilled, excited, him; **parfums qui troublent les sens,** perfumes that stir the senses. **4.** *Jur:* **t. qn dans la jouissance d'un bien,** to disturb s.o.'s enjoyment of possession.

se troubler. 1. to become turbid; (*of wine, etc.*) to get cloudy; (*of sky*) to become overcast, to cloud over; (*of vision*) to become blurred, hazy, to grow dim; (*of voice*) to waver; to break (with emotion). **2.** to become perturbed, confused; **l'orateur se troubla,** the speaker got flurried, flustered; **sans se t.,** unconcerned, unruffled, without turning a hair.

trouée [true], *s.f.* gap, opening, breach (in hedge, wood, etc.); *Geog:* **la T. de Belfort,** the Belfort Gap; **faire sa t.,** to come to the fore; to make one's mark; **il est connu aujourd'hui, mais ç'a été une longue t.,** he is well known today, but it took him a long time to make his mark.

trouer [true], *v.tr.* to make a hole or holes in (wall, etc.); to make a breach in (enemy's lines, etc.); to wear, make, a hole in (garment); to perforate (zinc, etc.); **mur troué de meurtrières,**

loop-holed wall; **mes bas se trouent,** my stockings are wearing into holes; **avoir les bas troués,** to have holes in one's stockings; **troué aux coudes,** in holes at the elbows; out at elbows; **figure trouée de petite vérole,** pock-marked face; **de larges clairières trouent la forêt,** broad clearings form gaps in the forest; **les nuages commencent à se t.,** the clouds are beginning to break; *P:* **t. qn,** to shoot s.o.; **se faire t. la peau,** to be shot (dead).

troufignard, troufignon [trufiɲa:r, trufiɲɔ̃], *s.m. P:* arse-hole.

troufion [trufjɔ̃], *s.m. P:* (infantry) soldier, private.

trouillard, -arde [trujaːr, -ard], *P:* **1.** *a.* cowardly, jittery, funky. **2.** *s.* coward, funk.

trouille [tru:j], *s.f. P:* **avoir la t.,** to get the wind up; to be funky; **tu n'as pas la t.!** you've got some cheek! you've got a nerve! **flanquer, ficher, la t. à qn,** to give s.o. the jitters, to put the wind up s.o.

trouillomètre [trujɔmɛtr̥], *s.m. P:* **avoir le t. à zéro,** to be in a blue funk.

trou-madame [trumadam], *s.m. Games: A:* troll-madam, nine-holes, pigeon-holes; *pl. trous-madame.*

troun-de-l'air [trundəlɛ:r], *int. Dial: O:* (*in S. of Fr.*) by thunder! heavens above!

troupe [trup], *s.f.* **1.** (*a*) troop, band, company, group, (of people); gang, set (of thieves, etc.); (scout) troop; **la t. céleste,** the heavenly host; **errer en troupes,** to wander about in bands; (*b*) *Th:* troupe, (theatrical) company; (*c*) herd, drove (of cattle, deer); flock, gaggle (of geese); pride, flock, troop (of lions); flight, flock, (of birds); covey (of partridges); muster (of peacocks); **ces animaux vivent en t.,** these animals herd together, are gregarious. **2.** *Mil:* (*a*) troop; body of soldiers; regiment; **officier de t.,** regimental officer, line officer; (*b*) (i) *A:* N.C.O.s and men; (ii) men (as opp. to officers); **officiers et t.,** officers and other ranks; **la t. et les gradés,** the privates and the N.C.O.s; *O:* **enfant de t.,** army child, soldier's son or orphan (brought up and schooled in the barracks); **cigarettes de t.,** army issue cigarettes; *F:* **il fume la t.,** he smokes army tobacco; **voulez-vous une t.?** have one of my forces ones! (*c*) *F:* **voilà de la t. qui passe,** there are some soldiers, troops, going by; **chevaux de t.,** army remounts; (*d*) *pl.* troops, forces.

troupeau, -aux [trupo], *s.m.* herd, drove (of cattle); flock (of sheep, geese, etc.); **garder les troupeaux,** to tend the flocks; *P.N:* **passage de troupeaux,** cattle crossing; **le curé de la paroisse et son t.,** the parish priest and his flock; **un t. d'imbéciles,** a pack of fools.

troupiale [trupjal], *s.m. Orn:* troopial, troupial; **t. babillard,** bobolink; **t. baltimore,** Baltimore oriole.

troupier [trupje], *s.m. Mil: F:* soldier, private; **vieux t.,** old campaigner.

troussage [trusa:ʒ], *s.m.* **1.** trussing (of fowl, etc.). **2.** *Metall:* strickling, striking up (of mould). **3.** *Min:* airway.

trousse [trus], *s.f.* **1.** (*a*) bundle, package; truss (of hay); (*b*) roll, valise (carried behind saddle); *A:* **monter en t.,** to ride behind (on horse); (*c*) *Harn:* tail case (of horse). **2.** *pl. A.Cost:* trunk-hose; *F:* **être aux trousses de qn,** to be after s.o., on s.o.'s heels; **mettre la police aux trousses de qn,** to set the police after s.o.; **lancer le chien aux trousses de qn,** to set the dog at s.o.'s heels. **3.** case, kit (of instruments, tools, etc.); **t. (médicale) de première urgence,** first-aid kit, box; **t. de toilette,** dressing case; toilet case, bag; **t. d'écolier,** (pen and) pencil case; **t. d'outils,** tool kit, set of tools; **t. en toile pour outils,** canvas roll for tools; **t. à réparations,** repair outfit. **4.** *Metall:* (*a*) = TROUSSEAU 3; (*b*) (= PAQUET 3) faggot.

troussé [truse], *a.* **1.** bundled up; tucked-up (skirt, etc.); trussed (fowl, etc.). **2.** *F:* **bien t.,** well-arranged, neat (object); well-set up, dapper (individual); well-made (horse); well-prepared (meal); neatly turned (compliment).

trousseau, -eaux [truso], *s.m.* **1.** (*a*) bunch; **t. de clefs,** bunch of keys; (*b*) *Anat:* fasciculus (of blood vessels, etc.). **2.** (*a*) outfit (of clothing), *esp.* school outfit; **fournisseur de trousseaux,** general outfitter; (*b*) (bride's) trousseau; **voici quelque chose pour votre t.,** here's something for your bottom drawer. **3.** *Metall:* sweep(board), strickle; **mouler un noyau au t.,** to sweep a core.

trousse-étriers [trusetrie], *s.m.inv.* stirrup strap.

trousse-galant [trusgalɑ̃], *s.m.inv. A.Med:* sweating-sickness, stoop-gallant.

trousse-pet [truspɛ], *s.m.inv.* **trousse-pète** [truspɛt], *s.f.inv. P:* child, kid.

trousse-pied [truspje], *s.m.inv.* leg strap (for refractory horse).

trousse-queue [truskø], *s.m.inv. Harn:* tail case; **t.-q. de cuir,** tail leather.

troussequin [truskɛ̃], *s.m.* **1.** cantle (of saddle). **2.** = TRUSQUIN.

trousser [truse], *v.tr.* **1.** (*a*) *A:* to bundle up; *F: A:* **t. bagage,** to pack up one's luggage, to take oneself off, to decamp; (*b*) to tuck up, pin up (skirt, etc.); to turn up (one's trousers); *O:* **t. et fouetter un enfant,** to turn up a child's clothes and give him a whipping; *F:* **il est toujours à t. les filles, les jupons,** he's an inveterate skirt chaser; *abs.* **cheval qui trousse,** high-stepping horse, high-stepper; (*c*) *Cu:* to truss (fowl). **2.** *F:* (*a*) to dispatch, get through, (work, business) promptly; to polish off (meal); (*b*) *A:* **la fièvre jaune l'a troussé,** yellow fever did for him, carried him off. **3.** *Metall:* to sweep, strickle, strike up (mould).

se trousser, to tuck up one's clothes.

trousseur [trusœ:r], *s.m. F:* **t. de jupons,** skirt chaser.

troussis [trusi], *s.m. A:* tuck (to shorten a garment); **faire un t. à une jupe,** to make a tuck in a skirt.

trou-trou [trutru], *s.m. Needlew:* ribbon-leading, *U.S:* ribbon holes; *pl. trou-trous.*

trouvable [truvabl̥], *a.* findable, that can be found.

trouvaille [truvɑ:j], *s.f.* (*a*) find, lucky find, godsend, windfall; **votre bonne est une t.,** your maid is a treasure; (*b*) brainwave.

trouver [truve], *v.tr.* to find. **1.** (*a*) to find (sth. sought); **je ne peux pas t. mes clefs,** I can't find my keys; **où trouverai-je un taxi?** where can I get a taxi? **je lui trouve d'excellentes qualités,** I think he has excellent qualities; **je lui trouve mauvaise mine,** I think he looks ill, unwell; **où est-ce qu'on trouve cela? où cela se trouve-t-il?** where is that to be found? where can you, one, find that? **on trouve encore la miche croustillante,** you can still find crusty loaves; **ces plantes se trouvent partout,** these plants are to be found everywhere; **il trouve à redire à tout ce que je fais,** he finds fault with everything I do; **aller t. qn,** to go and (i) find, (ii) see, s.o.; **venir t. qn,** to come and (i) find, (ii) see, s.o.; **courir t. qn,** to run and find s.o.; **venez me t. demain matin,** come and see me tomorrow morning; **vous me trouverez ici à l'heure dite,** you'll find me here at the time arranged; *F:* **s'il ne m'avait pas cherché il ne m'aurait pas trouvé,** if he hadn't tried to pick a quarrel with me I wouldn't have done anything to him; (*b*) to discover, invent (a process, etc.). **2. t. (qch.) par hasard,** to discover, hit upon, come upon, come across (sth.); to find (sth.) out accidentally; **on l'a trouvé mort dans son lit,** he was found dead in bed; **t. qn en faute,** to catch s.o. out; **bureau des objets trouvés,** lost-property office; **t. un filon, une idée,** to strike upon a vein, an idea; **voilà un sujet de sermon tout trouvé,** there's a subject for a sermon ready to hand; **t. l'expression juste,** to hit upon, chance upon, light upon, the right phrase; **c'est bien trouvé!** happy thought! **exemple bien, mal, trouvé,** well chosen, badly chosen, example; **t. à placer son mot,** to find the opportunity to make an apt remark; **t. à qui parler,** to meet one's match; **il trouva la mort à . . .,** he met his death at . . .; **t. des détracteurs sur son chemin,** to meet with detractors; **il trouve du plaisir à lire,** he finds pleasure in reading, he enjoys reading; **il trouva enfin à s'en débarrasser,** at last he managed, contrived, to get rid of it. **3.** to think, consider; **je la trouve jolie,** I consider her pretty, I think she's pretty; **vous trouvez?** you think so? **comment trouvez-vous mon parapluie?** how do you like my umbrella? **je trouve mieux de ne pas . . .,** I think it better not to . . .. **4.** *Artil:* **t. la portée,** to work out the range.

se trouver. 1. (*a*) to be; **je me trouvais alors à Paris,** I was in Paris then; **il s'est trouvé à cette bataille,** he was present at this battle; **se t. en danger, dans la misère,** to be in danger, in want; **se t. pris,** to be caught; **trouvez-vous ici à quatre heures,** be here at four o'clock; **la maison se trouva vide pendant quelques minutes,** the house happened to be empty, was left empty, for a few minutes; (*b*) to feel; **je me trouve très bien ici,** I'm very comfortable here; **se t. bien de qch.,** to feel all the better for sth.; **comment vous êtes-vous trouvé de ce traitement?** how did the treatment work? **se t. bien d'avoir fait qch.,** to be glad to have done sth.; to feel all the better for having done sth.; **je me trouve mieux,** I feel better. **2.** to happen; to turn out; **cela se trouve bien,** this is most opportune; **je me trouve avoir du temps devant moi,** I happen to have some spare time; **la dame se trouva être sa propre femme,** the lady turned out to be his own wife; *impers.* **il se trouve que** + *ind.,* it happens that . . .; **il se trouve que j'ai une heure de libre,** it so happens that I have an hour to spare; **il se trouva que le chien m'appartenait,** the dog turned out to be mine; *F:* **si cela se trouve, il est déjà rentré,** maybe he's back.

trouvère [truvɛ:r], *s.m. Lit.Hist:* trouvere; *Th:* **le T.,** Il Trovatore (by Verdi).

trouveur, -euse [truvœ:r, -ø:z]. **1,** *s.* discoverer, inventor. **2.** *a.* inventive (mind, etc.).

trouvillais, -aise [truvilɛ, -ɛ:z], **trouvillois, -oise** [truvilwa, -wa:z], *a. & s. Geog:* (native, inhabitant) of Trouville.

troyen[1], **-enne** [trwajɛ̃, -ɛn], *a. & s.* Trojan; *Gr. Lit:* **les Troyennes,** Troades, the Trojan Women (by Euripides).

troyen[2], **-enne,** *a. & s. Geog:* (native, inhabitant) of Troyes.

truand, -ande [tryɑ̃, -ɑ̃:d], *s.* **1.** *A. & Hum:* sturdy beggar; vagrant. **2.** *P:* tough; ruffian; crook; **avoir une mentalité de t.,** to have a gangster mentality. **3.** *F:* swindler.

truander [tryɑ̃de]. **1.** *v.i. A:* to beg along the roads. **2.** *v.tr. F:* to swindle (s.o.).

truanderie [tryɑ̃dri], *s.f.* (*a*) *A:* vagabondage, vagrancy; (*b*) *coll.* toughs, gangsters.

truble [trybl̥], *s.f. Fish:* hoop net; shove net.

trubleau, -eaux [tryblo], *s.m. Fish:* small hoop net.

trublion [trybljɔ̃], *s.m.* trouble maker.

truc[1] [tryk], *s.m. F:* **1.** (*a*) knack; **avoir le t. pour faire qch.,** to have the knack of doing sth.; **saisir le t. pour faire qch.,** to get the hang of sth.; (*b*) trick, dodge; **connaître les trucs du métier,** to know the tricks of the trade; to be up to all dodges; *Th:* **pièce à trucs,** play with elaborate stage effects, devices; **t. d'optique,** optical illusion. **2.** (*a*) *F:* **Monsieur T.,** Mr what's his name; (*b*) *F:* thing, contraption, gadget.

truc[2], *s.m. Rail: etc:* truck.

trucage [tryka:ʒ], *s.m.* **1.** faking (of antiques, stamps, etc.); *F:* cooking (of accounts); cheating; *Mil:* dummy work; **t. électoral,** rigging the elections. **2.** fake; *Cin:* trick picture; **trucages,** special effects.

truchement [tryʃmɑ̃], *s.m.,* *A:* **trucheman** [tryʃmɑ̃], *s.m.* **1.** *A:* dragoman, interpreter. **2.** spokesman; **servir de t. à qn,** to act as spokesman for s.o.; **un chef-d'œuvre littéraire n'a besoin d'aucun t.,** a literary masterpiece needs no interpreter. **3.** go-between; intermediary; **par le t. de . . .,** through . . ..

trucidation [trysidasjɔ̃], *s.f. Hum: F:* killing, massacring.

trucider [tryside], *v.tr. Hum: F:* to kill, to massacre.

truck [tryk], *s.m. Rail: etc:* truck.

truculence [trykylɑ̃:s], *s.f.* (*a*) *A:* truculence truculency; (*b*) earthy realism.

truculent [trykylɑ̃], *a.* (*a*) *A:* truculent; (*b*) vigorous, earthy, realistic; *Th: etc:* **personnage t.,** (i) character larger than life; (ii) Rabelaisian character.

trudgeon [trœdʒɔn], *s.m. Swim: O:* trudgen stroke.

truellage [tryɛla:ʒ], *s.m.* trowel work.

truelle [tryɛl], *s.f.* **1.** trowel; **t. à mortier,** brick trowel; **t. brettée,** notched trowel. **2. t. à poisson,** fish slice.

truellée [tryɛle], *s.f.* trowelful.

truffage [tryfa:ʒ], *s.m.* **1.** *Cu:* stuffing (of sth.) with truffles. **2.** *Bookb:* grangerizing (of book); grangerism.

truffe [tryf], *s.f.* **1.** (*a*) truffle; (*b*) nose (of a dog); *P:* (*of pers.*) bulbous nose, bottle nose; (*c*) *P:* **quelle t.!** what an idiot! what a clot! what a sucker! **2.** *Bot:* **t. d'eau,** water caltrop.

truffer [tryfe], *v.tr.* **1.** *Cu:* to stuff (sth.) with truffles; **dinde truffée,** truffled turkey. **2.** *Bookb:* **t. un exemplaire d'un livre,** to grangerize a book. **3.** *F:* **truffé de balles,** riddled with bullets; **le sable est truffé de pierres noires,** the sand is full of black stones; **il a truffé son discours de citations,** he padded, stuffed, his speech with quotations; **traduction truffée d'erreurs,** translation riddled with mistakes.

trufficulteur, -trice [tryfikyltœ:r, -tris], *s.* truffle grower.

trufficulture [tryfikylty:r], *s.f.* cultivation of truffles, truffle growing.

truffier, -ière [tryfje, -jɛːr]. 1. *a.* relating to truffles; **terrain t.**, truffle(-producing) ground; **chien t.**, truffle hound; **chêne t.**, oak tree on the roots of which truffles grow. 2. *s.* = TRUFFICULTEUR. 3. *s.f.* **truffière,** truffle bed.
truie [tryi], *s.f.* 1. *Z:* sow; **jeune t.,** gilt; **peau de t.,** pigskin. 2. *Ich:* hogfish.
truisme [tryism], *s.m.* truism.
truite [tryit], *s.f. Ich:* trout; **rivière pleine de truites,** river full of trout; **t. saumonée, t. de mer,** salmon trout, sea trout; **t. de rivière,** brown trout; **t. arc-en-ciel,** rainbow trout; **t. à tête d'acier,** steelhead trout.
truité [tryite], *a.* red-spotted; speckled; spotted (dog, etc.); flea-bitten, trout-coloured (horse); mottled (pig iron); crackled (china).
truitelle [tryitɛl], *s.f. Ich:* troutlet, troutling.
truiticole [tryitikɔl], *a.* trout-breeding (industry, etc.).
truiticulteur [tryitikyltœːr], *s.m.* trout breeder.
truiticulture [tryitikyltyːr], *s.f.* trout breeding.
truiton [tryitɔ̃], *s.m. Ich:* troutlet, troutling.
trumeau, -eaux [trymo], *s.m.* 1. (*a*) *Arch:* pier; (*b*) *Furn:* pier glass; (*c*) *F:* **vieux t.,** old dodderer, *f.* old hag. 2. *Cu:* leg of beef; gravy beef.
truquage [trykaːʒ], *s.m.* = TRUCAGE.
truqué [tryke], *a. F:* faked; meretricious (style, etc.); **article t.,** fake; **match t.,** fixed fight, match.
truquer [tryke], *v.tr.* 1. (*a*) to fake (antiques, photograph, experiment, balance-sheet, etc.); to fix (match, fight, etc.); *F:* to cook (accounts); **t. une élection,** to manipulate, rig, *U.S:* gerrymander, an election; (*b*) *Min:* to salt (a mine, a mineral sample). 2. *abs.* to cheat; to sham.
truqueur, -euse [trykœːr, -øːz], *s.* 1. humbug, fraud, trickster. 2. faker (of jewellery, antiques, etc.). 3. *s.m.* male prostitute who blackmails his homosexual clients.
trusquin [tryskɛ̃], *s.m. Tls:* (*a*) (carpenter's) (i) marking gauge, (ii) mortise gauge; (*b*) *Metalw:* **t. à marbre,** surface gauge; (*c*) **compas à t.,** beam compass.
trusquinage [tryskinaːʒ], *s.m.* scribing, marking (timber, etc.).
trusquiner [tryskine], *v.tr.* to scribe, to mark, gauge (timber, etc.).
trust [trœst], *s.m. Fin:* trust; **t. vertical,** vertical trust; **t. de valeurs,** holding company; **législation anti-t.,** anti-trust legislation.
truster [tryste, trœste], *v.tr.* 1. to group into a trust. 2. *F:* to monopolize.
trusteur [trystœːr], *s.m.* organizer, administrator, of a trust; trustee.
trutticole [trytikɔl], *a.* trout-breeding (industry, etc.).
trutticulteur [trytikyltœːr], *s.m.* trout breeder.
trutticulture [trytikyltyːr], *s.f.* trout breeding.
truxillique [tryksilik], *a. Ch:* truxillic.
trypanocide [tripanɔsid], *Med:* 1. *a.* trypanocidal. 2. *s.m.* trypanocide.
trypanose [tripanoːz], *s.f.*, **trypanosomiase** [tripanɔzɔmjɑːz], *s.f.*, **trypanosomose** [tripanɔzɔmoːz], *s.f. Med: Vet:* trypanosomiasis; **t. africaine,** sleeping sickness.
trypanosome [tripanozoːm], *s.m. Prot:* trypanosome.
trypanosomidés [tripanɔzɔmide], *s.m.pl. Prot:* Trypanosomatidae.
tryparsamide [triparsamid], *s.f. Pharm:* tryparsamide.
trypeta [tripɛta], *s.f. Ent:* trypetid; (*genus*) Trypeta.
trypétidés [tripetide], *s.m.pl. Ent:* Trypetidae.
trypsine [tripsin], *s.f. Ch:* trypsin.
trypsinogène [tripsinɔʒɛn], *s.f. Bio-Ch:* trypsinogen.
trypsique [tripsik], *a. Ch:* tryptic.
tryptophane [triptɔfan], *s.m. Ch:* tryptophan.
tsar [tsaːr, dzaːr], *s.m.* tsar, czar.
tsarévitch [tsarevitʃ, dz-], *s.m.* tsarevitch, czarevitch.
tsarine [tsarin, dz-], *s.f.* tsarina, czarina.
tsarisme [tsarism, dz], *s.m. Hist:* tsarism.
tsariste [tsarist, dz-], *s.m.* & *f. Hist:* tsarist.
tscheffkinite [tʃɛfkinit], *s.f. Miner:* tscheffkinite.
tsé-tsé, tsétsé [tsetse], *s.f. Ent:* tsetse (fly).
tsoin-tsoin, tsouin-tsouin [tswɛ̃tswɛ̃]. 1. *int.* (*as refrain to song*) twing-twang. 2. *a. F:* first-rate.
tsunami [tsynami], *s.m. Oc:* tzunami.
tu [ty], *pers. pron., unstressed, subject of verb.* (*a*) (*usual form of address to relations, close friends, children and animals*) you; **tu as raison,** you are right; **qui es-tu?** who are you? **qui es-tu, toi?** and who are *you*? **tu veux sortir, minet?** d'you want to go out, puss? **ils se disent tu,** they call each other "tu"; **être à tu et à toi avec qn,** to be on terms of close friendship with s.o.; **être à tu et à toi avec tout le monde,** to be hail-fellow-well-met with everybody; (*b*) (*to the Deity*) Thou *or* You; *B:* **tu ne tueras point,** thou shalt not kill; (*c*) *P:* (*elided to* **t'** *before vowel or* **h** *mute*) **qu'est-ce que t'as?** what's up (with you)? **t'entends bien?** you understand?
tuable [tyabl], *a.* (*of animal*) fit for slaughter.
tuage [tyaːʒ], *s.m.* slaughter(ing), killing (of animals).
tuant [tyɑ̃], *a. F:* 1. killing, back-breaking (work, etc.); **mal de tête t.,** splitting headache. 2. boring (pers, etc.); exasperating.
tub [tœb], *s.m. Toil: O:* tub, bath; **prendre son t. tous les matins,** to tub every morning.
tuba [tyba], *s.m.* 1. *Mus:* (*a*) (sax-)tuba; bass tuba; (*b*) ophicleide (of organ). 2. (frogman's) breathing tube, snorkel.
tubage [tybaːʒ], *s.m.* 1. (*a*) *Civ.E: Min:* tubing (of borehole, well); casing (of shaft, well); (*b*) *Surg: Vet:* tubing, intubation (of larynx, etc.). 2. *coll. Mch:* tubing, tubes (of boiler).
tubaire [tybɛːr], *a. Med:* tubal; **grossesse t.,** tubal pregnancy; **souffle t.,** tubal, tubular, breathing.
tubard, -arde [tybaːr, -ard], *a.* & *s. F:* consumptive.
tubardise [tybardiːz], *s.f. F:* consumption.
tube [tyb], *s.m.* 1. tube, pipe; (*a*) *Metall: etc:* **t. étiré,** drawn tube; **t. étiré à froid,** cold-drawn tube; **t. laminé,** rolled tube; *Const:* **bâti en tubes d'acier,** tubular steel frame; *El:* **canalisations sous tubes,** conduit tubes; *Tls:* **clé à t.,** tubular spanner; (*b*) *Mec.E: etc:* **t. coudé,** bent tube, angle tube; **t. démontable,** assembled-parts tube; **t. de dégagement,** by-pass; **t. de graissage,** oil duct, way; **t. de guidage, t. guide,** guide tube; **t. de torsion,** torque tube; **t. entretoise,** spacer pipe; **t. raccord,** pipe connection; **t. télescopique,** draw tube, telescopic tube; **t. à flamme,** flame tube (of jet engine); *Aut:* **t. de direction,** steering column; *Av:* **t. de Pitot,** Pitot tube, static-pressure tube; *Mch:* **t. alimentaire, t. d'alimentation,** feeding tube, feed pipe; **t. de chaudière,** boiler tube; **chaudière à tubes,** tubular boiler; **t. de fumée,** fire tube; **chaudière à tubes de fumée,** fire-tube boiler; *F:* **à pleins tubes,** all out, at full blast; **t. de condenseur, t. à condensation,** condenser tube; **t. à ailettes (extérieures),** finned tube, gilled tube; **t. à ailettes intérieurs,** Serve tube; **t. de niveau d'eau,** water-gauge column; **t. indicateur de niveau,** gauge glass, glass gauge; *N.Arch:* **t. de sortie d'arbre, t. d'étambot,** stern tube; *Min:* **t. carrottier,** core barrel; **tubes d'exploitation, de pompage,** tubing; *El.E:* **t. guide-fils,** race track, race way (in building); (*c*) *Artil:* barrel; *F:* gun; **t. intérieur,** lining tube; **t. intérieur amovible,** removable liner; *Sm.a:* **t. réducteur,** Morris tube; *Navy:* **t. lance-torpille(s),** torpedo tube; **t. lance-torpille(s) aérien,** above-water torpedo tube; (*d*) *Opt:* **t. porte-lentille(s), t. porte-objectif,** lens holder, slide; **t. porte-oculaire,** eye tube; **t. de réglage, t. à tirage,** focusing slide, draw tube; (*e*) (i) **t. acoustique,** speaking tube; (ii) *P:* telephone, *P:* blower; **donner un coup de t. à qn,** to ring, *U.S:* call, s.o. up, to get through to s.o. on the blower; (*f*) *Surg: Vet:* **t. pour intubation,** intubation tube; **t. à laryngotomie, à trachéotomie,** laryngotomy, tracheotomy, tube; (*g*) *Anat:* tube, duct; **t. digestif,** digestive tract, alimentary canal; **t. bronchique,** bronchial tube; *Anat: Ph:* **t. capillaire,** capillary tube; *Ent:* **tubes de Malpighi,** Malpighian tub(ul)es, vessels; *Echin:* **tubes de Cuvier,** Cuvierian organs (of sea cucumber); (*h*) *Bot:* tube (of corolla or calyx); (*i*) *Turf: P:* tip; (*j*) *Th: etc: F:* smash hit; song hit. 2. (*container*) (*a*) **t. de dentifrice,** tube of toothpaste; **t. de peinture,** tube of colour; (*b*) *Ch:* **t. de verre gradué,** graduated glass tube; **t. pour dosage, t. doseur,** measuring tube; **t. à essais,** test tube; **t. de sûreté,** safety tube; **t. à boule,** safety tube with bulb; (*c*) *Ind:* **t. de maturation,** soaker tube; **t. pour distillation fractionnée,** fractional-distillation tube, fractionating tube, column. 3. *El: Elcs:* valve; tube; *El:* **t. au néon,** neon tube; **t. fluorescent,** fluorescent tube, lamp; *Elcs: W.Tel:* **t. de Branly,** (Branly) coherer; **t. cathodique,** cathode-ray tube; **t. électronique,** electron tube; **t. à faisceau électronique,** electron-beam valve; **t. à ondes progressives,** travelling-wave tube; **t. à gaz,** gas-filled tube, valve; **t. à vide,** vacuum valve; kenotron; **t. à grille,** grid valve; **t. à grilles multiples,** multi-grid valve; **t. à plusieurs électrodes,** multi-electrode valve; **t. amplificateur,** amplifier tube or valve; **t. redresseur,** rectifying valve, rectifier; **t. de balayage,** scanning tube; (*radar*) **t. d'affichage,** display tube; **t. phare,** lighthouse. 4. *pl. Dressm: A:* bugles. 5. *P: A:* top hat, topper.
tuber[1] [tybe], *v.tr.* 1. (*a*) *Civ.E:* to tube (borehole, well); to case (shaft, well); (*b*) *Surg: Vet:* to tube, intubate (larynx, etc.). 2. *Mch:* to tube (boiler).
tuber[2] [tœbe], *v.tr. F: O:* to tub, bath (s.o.); **se t.,** to have a bath.
tubéracé [tyberase], *Bot:* 1. *a.* tuberaceous. 2. *s.f.pl.* **tubéracées,** Tuberaceae.
tube-rallonge [tybralɔ̃ːʒ], *s.f. Phot: etc:* extension tube; *pl. tubes-rallonges.*
tuberculariacées [tybɛrkylarjase], *s.f.pl. Fung:* Tuberculariaceae.
tubercule [tybɛrkyl], *s.m.* 1. *Bot:* tuber. 2. *Med:* tubercle.
tuberculé [tybɛrkyle], *a. Biol:* tubercled, tuberculate, tuberculated.
tuberculeux, -euse [tybɛrkylø, -øːz]. 1. *a.* (*a*) *Bot:* tubercular (root); (*b*) *Med: Miner:* tuberculous (lung, chalk). 2. *s.* tubercular patient; consumptive.
tuberculide [tybɛrkylid], *s.f. Med:* tuberculid(e).
tuberculifère [tybɛrkylifɛːr], *a. Nat.Hist:* tuberculiferous, tuberiferous.
tuberculiforme [tybɛrkylifɔrm], *a. Nat.Hist:* tuberculiform, tuberiform.
tuberculination [tybɛrkylinasjɔ̃], *s.f. Vet:* tuberculinization, tuberculin testing.
tuberculine [tybɛrkylin], *s.f. Med:* tuberculin.
tuberculiner [tybɛrkyline], *v.tr. Med: Vet:* to tuberculinize; **troupeaux tuberculinés,** attested herds.
tuberculinique [tybɛrkylinik], *Med:* 1. *a.* tuberculinic. 2. *s.m.* & *f.* person predisposed to contract tuberculosis.
tuberculinisation [tybɛrkylinizasjɔ̃], *s.f. Med: Vet:* tuberculinization, tuberculin testing.
tuberculiniser [tybɛrkylinize], *v.tr. Vet: Med:* to tuberculinize, tuberculin test.
tuberculisation [tybɛrkylizasjɔ̃], *s.f.* 1. *Med:* tuberculization; **épreuve de t.,** tuberculin test. 2. *Bot:* tuberculation.
tuberculiser [tybɛrkylize], *v.tr. Med:* to tubercul(ar)ize.
se tuberculiser, *Med:* (*of lung, etc.*) to tuberculize, to become tubercular.
tuberculoïde [tybɛrkylɔid], *a.* tuberculoid.
tuberculome [tybɛrkyloːm], *s.m. Med:* tuberculoma.
tuberculose [tybɛrkyloːz], *s.f. Med:* tuberculosis; **t. pulmonaire,** pulmonary tuberculosis, phthisis, consumption.
tuberculostatique [tybɛrkylɔstatik], *Med:* 1. *a.* tuberculostatic. 2. *s.m.* tuberculostat.
tubéreux, -euse [tyberø, -øːz], *Bot:* 1. *a.* tuberous. 2. *s.f.* **tubéreuse,** tuberose, polianthes.
tubériforme [tyberifɔrm], *a.* tuberiform; truffle-shaped.
tubérisation [tyberizasjɔ̃], *s.f. Bot:* tuberization.
tubérisé [tyberize], *a. Bot:* tuberous; **racine tubérisée,** tuberous root.
tubérivore [tyberivɔːr], *a.* truffle-eating.
tubéroïde [tyberɔid], *a. Nat.Hist:* tuberoid.
tubérophage [tyberɔfaːʒ], *a.* truffle-eating.
tubérosité [tyberozite], *s.f.* tuberosity.
tube-tirage [tybtiraːʒ], *s.m. Opt:* draw tube; *pl. tubes-tirage.*
tubeuse [tybøːz], *s.f. Tchn:* cork-cutting machine.
tubi- [tybi], *comb.fm.* tubi-.
tubicole [tybikɔl]. 1. *a.* tubicolous. 2. *s.f.* tubicole; (*a*) *Ann:* tube worm; (*b*) *Moll:* tube shell.
tubicorne [tybikɔrn], *a. Z:* tubicorn (ruminant).
tubifère [tybifɛːr], *a.* tubiferous.
tubifex [tybifɛks], *s.m. Ann:* tubifex.
tubiflore [tybiflɔːr], *a. Bot:* tubiflorous, tubuliflorous.
tubiforme [tybifɔrm], *a.* tubiform, tubular.
tubipare [tybipaːr], *a. Ann:* tubiparous (gland).
tubipora [tybipɔra], *s.m.*, **tubipore** [tybipɔːr], *s.m. Coel:* tubipore, organ-pipe coral; (*genus*) Tubipora.
tubiporide [tybipɔrid], *s.m. Coel:* tubiporid.
tubiste [tybist], *s.m.* 1. *Civ.E:* worker in a caisson. 2. *Ind:* worker in a tube factory ((i) making metal tubes; (ii) making electronic tubes).
tubitélaires [tybitelɛːr], *s.m.pl.*, **tubitèles** [tybitɛl], *s.m.pl. Arach:* Tubitelae.
tubleu [tyblø], *int. A:* zounds!
tubo-ovarien, -ienne [tybɔovarjɛ̃, -jɛn], *a. Anat:* tubo-ovarian.

tubulaire [tybylɛ:r]. **1.** *a.* tubular (bridge, flower, boiler, etc.); cannular. **2.** *s.m. Fb:* teat (of football bladder). **3.** *s.m. Coel:* tubularia.
tubularidés [tybylaride], *s.m.pl. Coel:* Tubulari(d)ae, Anthromedusae.
tubule [tybyl], *s.m. Nat.Hist:* tubule, small tube.
tubulé [tybyle], *a.* tubulate (flower); tubulated (retort, etc.); tubular (boiler).
tubuleux, -euse [tybylø, -ø:z], *a.* tubulous.
tubulidentés [tybylidɑ̃te], *s.m.pl. Z:* Tubulidentata.
tubulifères [tybylifɛ:r], *s.m.pl. Ent:* Tubulifera.
tubuliflore [tybyliflɔ:r], *a. Bot:* tubuliflorous.
tubuliforme [tybylifɔrm], *a.* tubuliform.
tubulipore [tybylipɔ:r], *s.m. Biol:* tubulipore, tubuliporid; (*genus*) Tubulipora.
tubulure [tybyly:r], *s.f.* (*a*) *Hyd.E: etc:* tubulure; pipe(-run); neck; **flacon à trois tubulures,** three-neck bottle; **t. d'aspiration,** tail pipe, suction pipe (of a pump); **t. d'écoulement,** flow nipple; **t. sans bride,** pipe riser; *I.C.E:* **t. d'échappement,** exhaust manifold; **t. d'admission,** inlet manifold; *Av:* **t. d'évacuation,** tailpipe (of a jet engine); (*b*) *coll.* pipes, piping.
tuco(-)tuco [tykɔtyko], *s.m. Z:* tuco-tuco, tucutuco; **t.(-)t. fouisseur,** burrowing tuco-tuco.
tucum [tykɔm], *s.m. Bot:* tucum.
tudesque [tydɛsk]. **1.** *a.* (*a*) Teutonic, Germanic; (*b*) *F: A:* uncouth, boorish, coarse (manners). **2.** *s.m. Ling:* Teutonic, Germanic.
tudieu [tydjø], *int. A:* zounds! 'sdeath! by my halidom!
tue-cafards [tykafa:r], *s.m.inv.* beetle exterminator.
tue-chien [tyʃjɛ̃], *s.m.inv. Bot: F:* (*a*) meadow saffron; (*b*) black nightshade.
tue-diable [tydjabl̩], *s.m.inv. Fish:* (*bait*) wobbler.
tue-fourmis [tyfurmi], *s.m.inv.* ant exterminator, ant killer.
tue-loup [tylu], *s.m.inv. Bot: F:* wolf's bane.
tue-mouches [tymuʃ], *s.m.inv.* **1.** *Fung:* fly agaric. **2.** (i) fly swatter; (ii) fly killer; *a.* **papier t.-m.,** fly paper.
tue-punaises [typynɛ:z], *s.m.inv.* insect powder, bug killer.
tuer [tɥe], *v.tr.* to kill. **1.** to slaughter, butcher (animals, etc.); (*of butcher*) **t. deux fois par semaine,** to kill twice a week. **2.** (*a*) to kill (s.o.); **t. qn d'un coup de couteau, de poignard,** to stab s.o. to death; **t. qn d'un coup de revolver,** to shoot s.o. (dead) with a revolver; **il fut tué d'une balle au cœur,** he was shot through the heart; **tué d'un coup de corne,** gored to death; **Marius les attaqua et leur tua cent mille hommes,** Marius attacked them and killed a hundred thousand of their men; **t. qn raide,** (i) to kill s.o. on the spot; (ii) to shoot s.o. dead; **se faire t.,** (i) to seek death; (ii) to get killed; **ils se firent t. en braves,** they died like heroes; **tué à l'ennemi,** killed in action; **les tués et les blessés,** the killed and wounded; **t. une mouche, une chenille,** to kill a fly, a caterpillar; **le froid a tué les oliviers,** the cold has killed the olive trees; (*b*) **t. le temps,** to kill time; **avoir une heure à t.,** to have an hour on one's hands; (*c*) *Petroleum Min:* to kill (oil well, gas well); (*d*) *Ten:* **t. la balle,** to kill the ball. **3.** to tire (s.o.) to death; to bore (s.o.); **l'ennui le tue,** he's bored to death; **ces escaliers me tuent,** I find these stairs killing.
se tuer. **1.** (*a*) to kill oneself; to commit suicide; (*b*) to get killed. **2. se t. au travail, à travailler,** to work oneself to death; **se t. à force de boire,** to drink oneself to death; **je me tue à vous le dire,** I am sick and tired of telling you.
tuerie [tyri], *s.f.* **1.** slaughter, butchery, carnage. **2.** *A:* slaughterhouse.
tue-tête (à) [atytɛt], *adv.phr.* at the top of one's voice; **crier à t.-t.,** to bawl, yell, to shout at the top of one's voice.
tueur, -euse [tɥœ:r, -ø:z], (*a*) *s.* killer; murderer; **t. de lions,** lion killer; **t. à gages,** hired assassin; (*b*) *s.m.* butcher, slaughterman.
tue-vent [tyvɑ̃], *s.m.inv. Agr: etc:* wind break; wind screen.
tuf [tyf], *s.m.* **1.** *Geol:* (*a*) **t. volcanique,** tuff; **pierre de t.,** tuff-stone; (*b*) tufa, tophus; **t. calcaire,** calcareous tufa; chalky subsoil. **2.** *Lit:* bottom, bedrock, foundation (of one's mind, being); **le t. de son caractère,** the hidden part of his nature, his true nature; **descendre jusqu'au t.,** to get down to bedrock.
tufacé [tyfase], *a. Geol:* tufaceous, tuffaceous, tophaceous.
tufeux, -euse [tyfø, -ø:z], *a. Geol:* tuff (deposit, rock).
tuf(f)eau [tyfo], *s.m. Miner:* calcareous tufa, micaceous chalk.
tufier, -ière [tyfje, -jɛ:r], *a. Geol:* tufaceous.
tuie [tɥi], *s.f. Dial:* (*in S.W. Fr.*) **1.** furze, gorse. **2.** scrub, brushwood (cut for manure).
tuile [tɥil], *s.f.* **1.** (*a*) (roofing) tile; **t. flamande, en S.,** pantile; **t. plate,** flat tile, plain tile; **t. romaine,** half-round tile; **t. réfractaire,** fireproof tile; **t. creuse,** gutter tile; **t. faîtière,** ridge tile, crest tile; **couvrir un comble en tuiles,** to tile a roof; (*b*) *Cu:* **tuiles aux amandes,** almond slices. **2.** *F:* (piece of) bad luck; snag; **quelle t.!** what rotten luck! **t. sur t.,** one damn thing after another.
tuilé [tɥile], *a.* **vin t.,** raisin wine.
tuileau, -eaux [tɥilo], *s.m.* (piece of) broken tile; fragment of tile.
tuiler [tɥile], *v.tr.* (*freemasonry*) to tile (the lodge); to prove (a brother).
tuilerie [tɥilri], *s.f.* **1.** (*a*) tile works, tile field, tilery; (*b*) **les Tuileries,** the Tuileries ((i) *Hist:* palace, (ii) gardens, in Paris); *Hist:* **le cabinet des Tuileries,** the French Foreign Office. **2.** tile-kiln.
tuilette [tɥilɛt], *s.f.* small tile.
tuileur [tɥilœ:r], *s.m.* (*freemasonry*) tiler, tyler.
tuilier [tɥilje], *s.m.* (*a*) tile maker, tiler; (*b*) owner of tile works.
tularémie [tylaremi], *s.f. Vet: Med:* tularaemia.
tulipe [tylip], *s.f.* **1.** *Bot:* tulip; *Artil:* **bourrelet en t.,** swell of the muzzle. **2.** (tulip-shaped, bell-shaped) shade (for electric light, etc.). **3.** *Aut:* **volant en t.,** bowl-shaped steering wheel.
tulipier [tylipje], *s.m.* **1.** *Bot:* (*a*) tulip tree, liriodendron; (*b*) **(bois de) t.,** canary wood. **2.** tulip grower.
tulipiste [tylipist], *s.m.* tulip grower.
tulipomane [tylipɔman], *s.m.* tulipomaniac.
tulipomanie [tylipɔmani], *s.f.* tulipomania.
tulle [tyl], *s.m. Tex:* tulle; net (fabric); netting; **t. façonné, brodé,** figured net; **broderie sur t.,** tulle embroidery.
tullerie [tylri], *s.f.* **1.** tulle making. **2.** tulle factory.
Tullie [tyl(l)i], *Pr.n.f. Rom.Hist:* Tullia.
tullier, -ière [tylje, -jɛ:r], *a.* tulle, net (industry, etc.).
tulliste[1] [tylist], *s.* (i) maker of, (ii) dealer in, tulle, net.
tulliste[2], **tullois, -oise** [tylwa, -wa:z], *a.* & *s. Geog:* (native, inhabitant) of Tulle.
tuméfaction [tymefaksjɔ̃], *s.f. Med:* tumefaction, swelling; **t. des amygdales,** enlarged tonsils.
tuméfier [tymefje], *v.tr.* to tumefy; to cause (joint, etc.) to swell.
tumescence [tymes(s)ɑ̃:s], *s.f.* tumescence; swelling.
tumescent [tymes(s)ɑ̃], *a.* tumescent, swelling.
tumeur [tymœ:r], *s.f. Med:* **1.** tumour; *F:* growth; **t. dure,** indurated tumour; **t. bénigne, maligne,** benign, malignant, tumour. **2.** swelling; *F:* **t. blanche** (**tuberculeuse**), white swelling.
tumoral, -aux [tymɔral, -o], *a. Med:* tumoral.
tumulaire [tymylɛ:r], *a.* tumulary; sepulchral (stone, etc.); **pierre t.,** tombstone, gravestone.
tumulte [tymylt], *s.m.* tumult, hubbub, turmoil, uproar, commotion; **en t.,** in an uproar, in confusion; **un t. d'applaudissements,** a thunder of applause; **il y eut des tumultes,** there were riots; **le t. des armes,** the clash of arms; **le t. des affaires,** the hustle and bustle of business; **le t. de la politique, des passions,** the turmoil of politics, of the passions.
tumultuaire [tymyltɥɛ:r], *a. A:* tumultuary.
tumultueusement [tymyltɥøzmɑ̃], *adv.* tumultuously, noisily, boisterously.
tumultueux, -euse [tymyltɥø, -ø:z], *a.* tumultuous, noisy, riotous (gathering, etc.); **rues tumultueuses,** noisy streets; **vie tumultueuse,** stormy life; *Ch:* **réaction tumultueuse,** tumultuous reaction.
tumulus [tymylys], *s.m.* tumulus, barrow; burial mound; *pl. tumulus, tumuli.*
tuna [tyna], *s.m. Bot:* tuna, Indian fig, nopal.
tungar [tœ̃ga:r], *s.m. El:* tungar rectifier.
tungstate [tœ̃gstat], *s.m. Ch:* tungstate.
tungstène [tœ̃gstɛn], *s.m. Ch: Metall:* tungsten, wolfram; **acier au t.,** tungsten steel.
tungsténite [tœ̃gstenit], *s.f. Miner:* tungstenite.
tungstique [tœ̃gstik], *a. Ch:* tungstic (acid).
tungstite [tœ̃gstit], *s.f. Miner:* tungstite.
tungstosilicate [tœ̃gstɔsilikat], *s.m. Ch:* tungstosilicate.
tunicelle [tynisɛl], *s.f. Ecc.Cost:* tunicle.
tunicier [tynisje], *s.m. Z:* tunicate; *pl.* **tuniciers,** tunicates, Tunicata.
tunique [tynik], *s.f.* **1.** *Cost:* tunic ((i) of ancient Rome, (ii) military, etc.); *Ecc:* tunicle. **2.** *Biol: Bot:* tunic; coat, envelope, membrane (of an organ); coat (of bulb); skin (of seed).
tuniqué [tynike], *a. Nat.Hist:* tunicate(d).
Tunisie [tynizi], *Pr.n.f. Geog:* Tunisia.
tunisien, -ienne [tynizjɛ̃, -jɛn], *a.* & *s. Geog:* Tunisian.
tunisois, -oise [tynizwa, -wa:z], *a.* & *s. Geog:* Tunisian, (native, inhabitant) of Tunis.
tunnel [tynɛl], *s.m.* (*a*) tunnel; **percer un t. sous une montagne,** to tunnel a mountain; to drive a tunnel through a mountain; **percement d'un t.,** tunnelling; **t. routier,** road tunnel; **t. de chemin de fer,** railway tunnel; **le t. sous la Manche,** the Channel Tunnel; **le train s'est arrêté sous le t.,** the train stopped in the tunnel; *Aer:* **t. aérodynamique,** wind tunnel; (*b*) *Nau:* **t. de l'arbre de l'hélice,** propeller-shaft tunnel; (*c*) *El: etc:* **t. de câbles,** cable subway; (*d*) *Petroleum Ind:* **t. de ressuage,** sweating tunnel (for wax separator); (*e*) *attrib. Elcs:* **diode t.,** tunnel diode.
tupaïa, -aja [typaja], *s.m. Z:* tree shrew.
tupaiidés [typaide], *s.m.pl. Z:* Tupaiidae.
tuque [tyk], *s.f. Cost: Fr.C:* tuque, *F:* pompom hat, bobble cap.
turban [tyrbɑ̃], *s.m.* **1.** *Cost:* turban; *Lit:* **prendre le t.,** to go over to Islam. **2.** *Bot: F:* martagon, Turk's cap lily. **3.** *Crust:* **t. rouge,** acorn shell, barnacle. **4.** *Moll:* turban shell. **5.** *Cu:* turban.
turbané [tyrbane], *a.* turbaned.
turbellariés [tyrbɛlarje], *s.m.pl. Ann:* Turbellaria.
turbicole [tyrbikɔl], *a. Bot:* turbinaceous; pertaining to, growing in, peat bogs.
turbide [tyrbid], *a.* (*esp. of liquid*) turbid, muddy, cloudy.
turbi(di)mètre [tyrbi(di)mɛtr̥], *s.m.* turbidimeter.
turbi(di)métrie [tyrbi(di)metri], *s.f.* turbidimetry.
turbi(di)métrique [tyrbi(di)metrik], *a.* turbidimetric.
turbidité [tyrbidite], *s.f.* turbidity, turbidness, cloudiness, muddiness (of liquid).
turbin [tyrbɛ̃], *s.m. P:* work, grind, slog; **maison où il y a beaucoup de t.,** house where there is a lot to do; **le t. journalier,** the daily grind.
turbinage [tyrbina:ʒ], *s.m.* **1.** *Ind:* treatment (*esp.* of sugar) by centrifugal turbine action. **2.** *P:* working, slogging.
turbine [tyrbin], *s.f.* **1.** *Mec.E:* turbine; **t. à air,** air, wind, turbine; **t. à air dynamique,** ram-air turbine; **t. à eau, t. hydraulique,** water turbine, water wheel; **t. à gaz,** gas turbine; **t. à vapeur,** steam turbine; *Hyd.E:* **t. tangentielle,** tangential-flow turbine, Pelton wheel; *El:* **générateur à turbines,** turbine-driven, turbined, generator; **t. à action,** impulse turbine; **t. à réaction,** reaction turbine; **t. à écoulement axial, radial,** axial-flow, radial-flow, turbine; **t. à écoulement inverse,** contra-flow turbine; **t. centrifuge, centripète,** outward-flow, inward-flow, turbine; **t. à engrenage,** geared turbine; **t. multi-rotors,** compound turbine; **t. à hélice,** propeller turbine; **t. à pales mobiles,** feathering-propeller turbine; **t. à ventilateur auxiliaire,** ducted-fan turbine; **t. à étages, t. multiple, t. compound,** multi-stage turbine; **t. à étages de pression,** pressure-stage turbine; **t. à étages de vitesse,** velocity-stage turbine; **arbre de t.,** turbine shaft; **diffuseur annulaire de t.,** turbine nozzle ring; **disque de t.,** turbine disc; **roue de t.,** turbine wheel. **2.** (*a*) (rotary) fan (of vacuum cleaner, etc.); (*b*) *Exp:* acid wringer; (*c*) *Sug.R:* centrifugal separator.
turbiné [tyrbine], *a. Nat.Hist:* turbinate(d), turbiniform, whorled; **os t.,** scroll bone, turbinal bone; *Conch:* **coquille turbinée,** top (shell).
turbiner [tyrbine]. **1.** *v.tr. Hyd.E:* to harness water to rotate a turbine. **2.** *v.i. P:* to work, slog, grind; *Sch:* to swot.
turbineur [tyrbinœ:r], *s.m. P:* hard worker; *Sch:* swot.
turbinidés [tyrbinide], *s.m.pl. Moll:* Turbinidae.
turbitéen [tyrbiteɛ̃], *a.m. Orn:* turbiteen (pigeon).
turbith [tyrbit], *s.m.* **1.** *Pharm: A:* turpeth. **2. t. minéral,** turpeth mineral.
turbo[1] [tyrbo], *s.m. Moll:* turbo; turban shell.
turbo[2], *s.m. F:* (= *turbo-alternateur, etc.*) turbo.
turbo-alternateur [tyrbɔaltɛrnatœ:r], *s.m. El:* turbo-alternator; *pl. turbo-alternateurs.*
turbocompresseur [tyrbɔkɔ̃prɛsœ:r], *s.m. Mec.E: Av:* (*turbine-driven*) turbocompressor; (*exhaust-driven*) turbosupercharger, turbocharger.
turbodynamo [tyrbɔdinamo], *s.f. El.E:* turbodynamo.
turbo-électrique [tyrbɔelɛktrik], *a. Mch:* turbo-electric (drive, etc.); *pl. turbo-électriques.*
turboforage [tyrbɔfɔra:ʒ], *s.m. Min:* turbo-drilling.

turbogénérateur [tyrbɔʒeneratœːr], *s.m.*, **turbogénératrice** [tyrbɔʒeneratris], *s.f.* turbo-generator.

turbomachine [tyrbɔmaʃin], *s.f.* turboshaft engine; **t. à double flux,** bypass engine.

turbomoteur [tyrbɔmɔtœːr], *s.m. Mch:* turbo-motor; turboshaft engine.

turbo(-)nucléaire [tyrbɔnykleɛːr], *a.* turbonuclear.

turbopompe [trybɔpɔ̃ːp], *s.f. Mch:* turbo pump, turbine pump.

turbopropulsé [tyrbɔprɔpylse], *a.* turboprop (aircraft).

turbopropulseur [tyrbɔprɔpylsœːr], *s.m.* turbo-prop(eller); **avion à t.,** turboprop aircraft.

turboréacteur [tyrbɔreaktœːr], *s.m.* turbojet; **t. à simple flux,** (single-flow) turbojet; **t. à double flux,** turbofan, fan engine; bypass engine.

turboréaction [tyrbɔreaksjɔ̃], *s.f.* turboreaction.

turbosoufflante [tyrbɔsuflɑ̃ːt], *s.f.*, **turbosouffleuse** [tyrbɔsufløːz], *s.f.* turbo blower; blower (of submarines).

turbo-stato(-)réacteur [tyrbɔstatɔreaktœːr], *s.m. Av:* turbo ramjet (engine); *pl. turbo-stato(-) réacteurs.*

turbot [tyrbo], *s.m. Ich:* turbot; **t. épineux,** spiny turbot.

turbotière [tyrbɔtjɛːr], *s.f. Dom.Ec:* turbot kettle.

turbotin [tyrbɔtɛ̃], *s.m. Ich:* young turbot.

turbotrain [tyrbɔtrɛ̃], *s.m. Rail:* turbotrain.

turboventilateur [tyrbɔvɑ̃tilatœːr], *s.m.* turbo-ventilator.

turbulence [tyrbylɑ̃ːs], *s.f.* turbulence. **1.** (*a*) unruliness, insubordination; (*b*) boisterousness (of child, of wind or sea). **2.** *I.C.E:* **culasse à t.,** turbulent cylinder head.

turbulent [tyrbylɑ̃]. **1.** *a.* turbulent; (*a*) restless, unruly (population); (*b*) boisterous (child); boisterous, stormy (wind, sea). **2.** *s.m. Tan:* drum.

turc[1], *f.* **turque** [tyrk]. **1.** *a.* (*a*) Turkish; (*b*) *A:* harsh, cruel, piratical; **il est t. là-dessus,** he's an absolute Shylock in this matter; **à la turque,** (i) Turkish fashion, (ii) *A:* harshly, cruelly, roughly; **être assis à la turque,** to sit cross-legged; *Hyg:* **installation à la t.,** seatless lavatory, *F:* Turkish loo. **2.** (*a*) *s.* Turk; *F:* **fort comme un T.,** as strong as an ox; **tête de T.,** (i) try-your-strength machine (at fairs); hence (ii) butt; whipping-boy; (iii) *Nau:* Turk's head (knot); *A:* **traiter qn de t. à more,** to treat s.o. arrogantly, harshly; (*b*) *s.m. Ling:* **le t.,** Turkish.

turc[2], *s.m. Ent:* May-bug grub.

turcie [tyrsi], *s.f. A:* dyke, levee (along the Loire).

turco [tyrko], *s.m. Mil: F: A:* Turco, Algerian rifleman.

turco-balkanique [tyrkɔbalkanik], *a.* Turco-Balkan; *pl. turco-balkaniques.*

turcoin [tyrkwɛ̃], *s.m. Tex: A:* mohair.

turcoman [tyrkɔmɑ̃] = TURKMÈNE.

turcophile [tyrkɔfil], *a. & s.m. & f.* turcophile.

turcophobe [tyrkɔfɔb], *a. & s.m. & f.* turcophobe.

turde [tyrd], *s.m. Orn: (genus)* Turdus.

turdidés [tyrdide], *s.m.pl. Orn:* Turdidae.

turdoïde [tyrdɔid], *a. Orn:* turdoid, thrushlike; **rousserolle t.,** great reed warbler.

turelure [tyrlyːr], *s.f. F:* refrain (of song); fol-de-rol; *used in the phr. F: O:* **c'est toujours la même t.,** (i) it's the old story; (ii) he's always harping on the same string.

turf [tyrf], *s.m.* **1.** racecourse. **2. le t.,** racing; the turf; **habitué du t.,** race-goer; sporting man. **3.** *P:* (*a*) work; **allez! au t.!** come on, get down to it! (*b*) **elle fait le t.,** she's a tart, a prostitute.

turfiste [tyrfist], *s.m. & f.* race-goer; sporting man.

turgescence [tyrʒes(s)ɑ̃ːs], *s.f. Med: Bot:* turgescence, turgidity, turgor.

turgescent [tyrʒes(s)ɑ̃], *a.* turgescent.

turgide [tyrʒid], *a.* turgid, swollen.

turinois, -oise [tyrinwa, -waːz], *a. & s. Geog:* (native, inhabitant) of Turin.

turion [tyrjɔ̃], *s.m. Bot:* turion.

Turkestan [tyrkɛstɑ̃], *Pr.n.m. Geog:* Turkestan.

turkmène [tyrkmɛn]. **1.** *a. Geog:* Turkmenian, Turkmen. **2.** *s.m. & f. Geog:* Turkoman. **3.** *s.m. Ling:* **le t.,** Turkoman, Turkmen.

Turkménie [tyrkmeni], *s.f.*, **Turkménistan** [tyrkmenistɑ̃], *s.m. Geog:* Turkmenistan.

turlu(i) [tyrly, tyrlɥi], *s.m. Orn: F:* curlew jack, whimbrel.

turlupin [tyrlypɛ̃], *s.m. A:* (*actor's name in 17th cent. farcical comedy*) (*a*) clown, buffoon, merry-andrew; (*b*) scamp.

turlupinade [tyrlypinad], *s.f. A:* (*a*) low pun; (*b*) piece of clownery, of low buffoonery.

turlupiner [tyrlypine]. **1.** *v.i. A:* to act the buffoon. **2.** *v.tr. F:* to worry; **cette idée me turlupine,** this idea's bothering, worrying, me; **qu'est-ce qui vous turlupine?** what's eating you?

turlurette [tyrlyrɛt]. **1.** *s.f.* (*a*) *A:* (beggar's) guitar; (*b*) refrain, tol-de-rol. **2.** *int.* fiddle-de-dee!

turlutaine [tyrlytɛn], *s.f.* **1.** *A:* bird organ. **2.** *O:* everlasting theme; **c'est sa t.,** he's always harping on that, always harking back to that.

turluter [tyrlyte], *v.i. Fr.C: F:* to trill, to sing tra la la.

turlututu [tyrlytyty]. **1.** *s.m. F: & Dial:* eunuch flute, mirliton, kazoo. **2.** *int.* fiddlesticks! rot!

turne [tyrn], *s.f. P:* (*a*) hovel; (*b*) wretched, slummy, room; **quelle t.!** what a hole! (*c*) *Sch:* (student's) study bedroom.

turnep(s) [tyrnɛp(s)], *s.m. Agr:* turnip cabbage, kohl rabi.

turnicidés [tyrniside], *s.m.pl. Orn:* Turnicidae.

turnix [tyrniks], *s.m. Orn:* hemipode, button quail.

turonien, -ienne [tyrɔnjɛ̃, -jɛn], *a. & s.m. Geol:* Turonian.

Turons [tyrɔ̃], *s.m.pl. Hist:* Turon(e)s.

turpitude [tyrpityd], *s.f.* turpitude. **1.** depravity, baseness. **2.** (*a*) despicable, low, trick; (*b*) smutty talk, story; **débiter des turpitudes,** to talk smut; (*c*) skeleton in the cupboard.

turquerie [tyrk(ə)ri], *s.f.* (*a*) *A:* harshness, cruelty; rapaciousness; (*b*) Turkish scene, work of art, etc.

turquet [tyrkɛ], *s.m.* **1.** *Agr: F:* maize, *U.S:* corn. **2.** pug(dog).

turquette [tyrkɛt], *s.f. Bot:* smooth or glabrous rupturewort, burstwort.

Turquie [tyrki], *Pr.n.f. Geog:* Turkey; **T. d'Europe,** Turkey in Europe; **T. d'Asie,** Turkey in Asia; **tapis de T.,** Turkish carpet; **blé de T.,** Turkish wheat; maize, *U.S:* corn.

turquin [tyrkɛ̃], *a. used in* **bleu t.,** slate-blue, bluish-grey (marble, etc.).

turquoise [tyrkwaːz]. **1.** *s.f.* turquoise; (*a*) **t. de la vieille roche,** true oriental turquoise; (*b*) **t. osseuse, occidentale,** fossil turquoise; odontolite. **2.** *a.inv. & s.m.inv.* turquoise; turquoise blue.

turriculé [turikyle], *a. Conch:* turriculate(d), turreted.

turrilite [tyrilit], *s.m. Paleont:* turrilite.

turripinois, -oise [turipinwa, -waːz], *a. & s. Geog:* (native, inhabitant) of La Tour-du-Pin.

turritelle [tyritɛl], *s.f. Moll:* turritella, screw shell, auger (shell).

Tusculanes (les) [letyskylan], *s.f.pl. Rom.Lit:* the Tusculan Disputations.

tussack [tysak], *s.m. Bot:* tussock (grass).

tussah [tysa], *s.m.*, **tussau** [tyso], *s.m. Tex:* = TUSSOR(E).

tussilage [tysilaːʒ], *s.m. Bot:* coltsfoot; (*genus*) Tussilago.

tussor(e) [tysɔːr], *s.m. Tex:* tussore (silk).

tutélaire [tytelɛːr], *a.* tutelary (divinity, etc.); guardian (angel, etc.); **principe t. de . . .,** guardian principle of . . .; *Jur:* **gestion t.,** guardianship.

tutelle [tytɛl], *s.f.* **1.** *Jur:* (*a*) tutelage, guardianship; *Jur:* tutela; **rendre sa t.,** to give an account of one's guardianship; **enfant en t.,** child in tutelage, under guardianship; **enfant hors de t.,** child out of its pupilage; (*b*) *Pol:* trusteeship; **territoires sous t.,** trust territories; **droits de t. d'une commission,** rights of oversight of a commission. **2.** protection; **les citoyens sont sous la t. des lois,** citizens are under the protection of the law; **prendre qn sous sa t.,** to take s.o. under one's wing; **tenir qn en t.,** (i) to protect s.o.; (ii) to keep s.o. under one's thumb.

tuteur, -trice [tytœːr, -tris]. **1.** *s.* (*a*) *Jur:* guardian; tutor (of a minor); **t. d'un dément,** committee for a lunatic; (*b*) protector. **2.** *s.m. Hort:* prop, support, stake.

tuteurage [tytœraːʒ], *s.m. Hort:* staking (of plants).

tuteurer [tytœre], *v.tr. Hort:* to prop, support (young tree, etc.); to stake (plants).

tut(h)ie [tyti], *s.f. Metall: etc:* tutty; crude zinc oxide.

tutiorisme [tytjɔrism], *s.m. Theol:* tutiorism.

tutoi(e)ment [tytwamɑ̃], *s.m.* use of the familiar **tu** and **toi** in conversation (instead of the more formal **vous**).

tutoyer [tytwaje], *v.tr.* (**je tutoie, n. tutoyons; je tutoierai**) to address (s.o.) as **tu** and **toi** (instead of **vous**); to be on familiar terms with (s.o.); *Equit:* **t. un obstacle,** to graze an obstacle.

tutoyeur, -euse [tytwajœːr, -øːz], *s.* person who very readily uses **tu** and **toi.**

tutti [tyt(t)i], *s.m.inv. Mus:* tutti.

tutu [tyty], *s.m.* **1.** (*child's word*) bottom, behind, botty. **2.** tutu, ballet skirt.

tuyau, -aux [tɥijo], *s.m.* **1.** (*a*) pipe, tube; **t. normalisé,** standard pipe; **t. d'eau, de gaz,** water pipe, gas pipe; **t. de trop-plein,** overflow pipe; **t. d'évacuation,** discharge pipe; **t. d'aspiration,** sucking pipe; **t. de descente (d'une maison),** (i) rainwater pipe, down pipe, down-comer; (ii) soil pipe; **t. d'évent,** blow-off pipe (of cesspool); **t. vertical, t. de chute,** standpipe; **t. souple à gaz,** flexible gas pipe; **t. flexible, t. en caoutchouc,** (i) rubber tubing; (ii) hose(pipe); **t. d'incendie,** fire hose; **t. d'arrosage,** garden hose; **t. de cheminée,** chimney flue; **t. de poêle,** (i) stove pipe, flue pipe; (ii) *F: O:* stovepipe hat; **t. acoustique,** speaking tube; *Mus:* **t. d'orgue,** organ pipe; **t. à bouche,** fluepipe; **t. à anche,** reed pipe; **rangés en tuyaux d'orgue,** aligned in descending order of height; **tuyaux d'orgue** (i) *Dressm:* fluting; (ii) *Nau:* scupper-pipes; (iii) *Geol:* basalitic columns; *F:* **dire qch. à qn dans le t. de l'oreille,** to whisper sth. in s.o.'s ear (whence the meaning 2 below); *P:* **se rincer le t.,** to wet one's whistle; (*b*) stem (of tobacco pipe); nozzle (of bellows); (*c*) barrel (of quill); quill; (*d*) stalk (of corn, grass, etc.); (*e*) *Laund:* flute, goffer, quill. **2.** *F:* pointer, hint; gen, dope; (*esp. at races*) tip; **je faisais de mon mieux pour leur donner des tuyaux,** I did my best to give them a few tips, a bit of gen; **un t. crevé,** a rotten tip; **avoir des tuyaux,** to be in the know; **c'est un t. increvable,** it's straight from the horse's mouth.

tuyautage [tɥijotaːʒ], *s.m.* **1.** (*a*) piping, tubing; system of pipes, pipe work; tubing (of steam engine); **t. souple,** hose; **t. du gaz,** gas tubing; *I.C.E:* **t. d'échappement,** exhaust manifold; (*b*) canalization, pipeline; **t. de transport,** conveyor pipeline. **2.** *Laund:* fluting, goffering, quilling (of linen). **3.** *Rac: etc: F:* tipping; stable tips; putting (of s.o.) in the know. **4.** *Sch: F:* cribbing.

tuyauté [tɥijote], *s.m. Laund:* fluting, goffering, quilling.

tuyauter [tɥijote], *v.tr.* **1.** *Laund:* to flute, goffer, quill (linen); **fer à t.,** goffering tongs. **2.** (*a*) *Rac: etc: F:* to give a tip, a pointer to (s.o.); to put (s.o.) up to all the tips; to give (s.o.) the gen, the dope; **t. qn sur la Bourse,** to give s.o. a few tips on the Stock Exchange, the share market; (*b*) *abs. Sch: F:* to crib.

tuyauterie [tɥijotri], *s.f.* **1.** pipe and tube (i) factory, (ii) trade. **2.** tubing, pipes and fittings; **t. de prise d'eau,** feed pipes; **t. de refoulement,** outlet, exhaust, system; *P:* **s'envoyer un coup dans la t.,** to swill down a drink.

tuyauteur, -euse [tɥijotœːr, -øːz]. **1.** *s.m.* worker in pipe and tube factory; pipe fitter; pipeline man. **2.** *s. F:* tipster.

tuyère [tɥijɛːr], *s.f.* (*a*) *Metall:* tuyere, twyer, blast pipe, nozzle; *F:* snout (of blast furnace); tue-iron (of forge); **œil de t.,** tuyere hole; (*b*) *Mec.E: etc:* nozzle; **t. d'injecteur,** injector nozzle; **t. de détente, d'éjection,** discharge, exhaust, nozzle; **t. à rendement,** delivery pipe; *Av: etc:* **t. d'échappement,** jet pipe; **t. de post-combustion,** after burner; **t. à section variable,** variable-area nozzle; **t. orientable,** rotating nozzle, thrust-vectoring nozzle; **t. de propulsion,** thrust nozzle; **t. de sustentation,** lift nozzle; **t. d'éjection des gaz,** jet, exhaust, nozzle; **t. à déviation,** thrust reverser (of jet engine); **t. omnibus,** slave pipe (in test bed).

tweed [twid], *s.m. Tex:* tweed.

tweeter [twitœːr], *s.m. W.Tel:* tweeter (loud-speaker).

twill [twil], *s.m. Tex:* twill.

Tydée [tide], *Pr.n.m. Gr.Lit:* Tydeus.

tylenchus [tilɛ̃kys], *s.m. Ann:* tylench(id).

tylopodes [tilɔpɔd], *s.m.pl. Z:* Tylopoda.

tylose [tiloːz], *s.f. Med:* tylosis.

tympan [tɛ̃pɑ̃], *s.m.* **1.** *Anat:* tympanum, drum (of ear); **membrane du t.,** tympanic membrane, ear drum; **bruit à briser, crever, déchirer, rompre, le t.,** ear-splitting noise. **2.** *Typ:* tympan. **3.** *Arch:* (*a*) tympanum (of Greek temple); (*b*) (i) tympanum; (ii) spandrel (of cathedral door, etc.). **4.** die (of pedestal). **5.** *Hyd.E:* tympanum, scoop wheel. **6.** *Mec.E:* pinion (mounted on shaft). **7.** treadmill.

tympanal, -aux [tɛ̃panal, -o], *a. & s.m.* (**os**) **t.,** tympanic bone.

tympanique [tɛ̃panik], *a.* **1.** *Anat:* tympanic (membrane of the ear). **2.** *Med:* tympanitic (resonance on percussion).

tympaniser [tɛ̃panize], *v.tr. A:* (*a*) to advertise (by beat of drum); (*b*) to bring (s.o.'s) name before the public (favourably or unfavourably); to trumpet (s.o.'s) name abroad; (*c*) to plague, worry (s.o.).

tympanisme [tɛ̃panism], *s.m. Med:* **1.** tympanites, tympanitis, *F:* wind. **2.** tympanitic resonance (on percussion).

tympanite [tɛ̃panit], *s.f. Med:* **1.** = TYMPANISME 1. **2.** tympanitis (of the ear).

tympanon [tɛ̃panɔ̃], *s.m. Mus:* dulcimer.

tympe [tɛ̃ːp], *s.f. Metall:* tymp (of blast furnace).

tyndallisation [tɛ̃dalizasjɔ̃], *s.f.* tyndallization.

type [tip], *s.m.* **1.** type; standard model; *Z:* type, phylum; *Com:* sample piece; pattern; **t. de la beauté italienne**, typical Italian beauty; **le vrai t. français**, the true French type; the typical Frenchman; *Elcs:* **t. de circuit**, circuit grade; *attrib.* **maison t.**, show house; **motocyclette t.**, motor bicycle of standard design; **trois modes types de l'année**, three typical fashions of the year; *Nat.Hist:* **genre t.**, type genus; *For:* **arbre t.**, sample tree. **2.** *F:* (*a*) character, type; **c'est un vrai t.**, he's quite a character; (*b*) chap, type; **un drôle de t.**, a queer sort of chap, a weird specimen; **c'est un pauvre t.**, he's a poor sort of chap; **un t. à barbe**, a type, chap, with a beard; **t'es un chic t.!** you're a good sort! (*c*) *P:* (= AMANT) **elle se promenait avec son t.**, she was out with her chap, man. **3.** *Typ:* type; **types à distribuer**, dead matter.

typer [tipe], *v.tr.* to stamp, mark (sth.) (as belonging to a certain type); to typify.

typesse [tipɛs], *s.f. P:* woman, girl.

typha [tifa], *s.m. Bot:* typha, reed mace, cattail, cat's tail.

typhacées [tifase], *s.f.pl. Bot:* Typhaceae.

Typhée [tife], *Pr.n.m. Myth:* Typhoeus.

typhique [tifik], *a. Med:* typhous.

typhlite [tiflit], *s.f. Med:* typhlitis.

typhlomégalie [tiflomegali], *s.f. Med:* typhlomegaly.

typhlonecte [tiflonɛkt], *s.m. Amph:* caecilian.

typhlopexie [tiflopɛksi], *s.f. Surg:* typhlopexy.

typhlopidés [tiflopide], *s.m.pl. Rept:* Typhlopidae, the blind snakes.

typho-bacillose [tifobasiloːz], *s.f. Med: O:* typhobacillosis.

typhoïde [tifoid], *a. Med:* typhoid; **fièvre t.**, typhoid (fever); enteric fever.

typhoïdique [tifoidik], *a.* typhoidal; **bacille t.**, typhoid bacillus.

typhoïque [tifoik]. **1.** *a.* typhoidal. **2.** *s.m. & f.* patient with typhoid, typhoid case.

typhomalaria [tifomalarja], *s.f. Med:* typhomalaria.

typhomanie [tifomani], *s.f. Med:* typhomania.

typhon¹ [tifɔ̃], *s.m. Meteor:* typhoon.

Typhon², *Pr.n.m. Myth:* Typhon.

typhose [tifoːz], *s.f. Med:* typhosis; *Vet:* **t. aviaire**, fowl typhoid; **t. porcine**, hog cholera.

typhotoxine [tifotoksin], *s.f. Med:* typhotoxin.

typhus [tifys], *s.m. Med:* typhus (fever); *Vet:* **t. du chat**, (infectious) feline gastroenteritis.

typifié [tipifje], *a.* typical; standardized.

typifier [tipifje], *v.tr.* to typify.

typique [tipik], *a.* typical. **1.** symbolical. **2.** true to type, representative; **l'Anglais t.**, the typical ordinary, Englishman.

typiquement [tipikmɑ̃], *adv.* typically.

typo [tipo], *F:* **1.** *s.f.* typography. **2.** *s.m.* (*f. occ.* **typote**) (= TYPOGRAPHE) typo.

typo- [tipo], *comb.fm.* typo-.

typographe [tipograf]. **1.** *s.m.* typographer, printer. **2.** *a.* **ouvrier t.**, printer; **imprimeur t.**, letterpress printer.

typographie [tipografi], *s.f.* **1.** typography; (art of) letterpress printing. **2.** printing works.

typographier [tipografje], *v.tr.* (*pr.sub. & p.d.* **n. typographiions**, *v.* **typographiiez**) *Typ:* to set up, print (article, etc.).

typographique [tipografik], *a.* typographic(al); **erreur t.**, misprint.

typographiquement [tipografikmɑ̃], *adv.* typographically.

typolithographie [tipolitografi], *s.f.* typolithography.

typologie [tipoloʒi], *s.f.* typology.

typologique [tipoloʒik], *a.* typological.

typomanie [tipomani], *s.f.* typomania, craze to see oneself in print.

typomètre [tipomɛtr], *s.m. Typ:* typometer.

typon [tipɔ̃], *s.m. Typ:* offset film.

typophone [tipofon], *s.m. Mus:* dulcitone.

typotélégraphe [tipotelegraf], *s.m.* printing telegraph; typotelegraph.

typotélégraphie [tipotelegrafi], *s.f.* typotelegraphy.

Tyr [tiːr], *Pr.n. Hist: Geog:* Tyre.

tyran [tirɑ̃], *s.m.* (*with occ. f.* **tyranne** [tiran]) **1.** tyrant; **femme qui est un tyran domestique**, woman who is a domestic tyrant; **se conduire en t.**, to act tyrannically; **faire le t.**, to play the tyrant; **il est le t. de sa famille**, he tyrannizes his family. **2.** *Orn:* tyrant, king bird, field martin; **t. savanna**, fork-tailed flycatcher.

tyranneau, **-eaux** [tirano], *s.m.* petty tyrant.

tyrannicide¹ [tiranisid]. **1.** *a.* tyrannicidal. **2.** *s.* tyrannicide; killer of a tyrant.

tyrannicide², *s.m.* tyrannicide (as a crime).

tyrannidés [tiranide], *s.m.pl. Orn:* Tyrannidae.

tyrannie [tirani], *s.f.* tyranny; **la t. de la mode**, the tyranny of fashion.

tyrannique [tiranik], *a.* tyrannical, tyrannous; **autorité t.**, high-handed authority.

tyranniquement [tiranikmɑ̃], *adv.* tyrannically; with a high hand, high-handedly.

tyranniser [tiranize], *v.tr.* to tyrannize over (s.o.); to tyrannize (s.o.); to exercise mastery over (s.o.); to rule (s.o.) with a rod of iron; to treat (s.o.) high-handedly.

tyrannosaure [tiranozoːr], *s.m. Paleont:* tyrannosaur(us).

tyria [tirja], *s.f. Ent:* (*a*) cinnabar moth; (*b*) cinnabar caterpillar.

tyrien, **-ienne** [tirjɛ̃, -jɛn], *a. & s. A.Geog:* Tyrian.

Tyrol (le) [lətirɔl], *Pr.n.m. Geog:* (the) Tyrol.

tyrolien, **-ienne** [tiroljɛ̃, -jɛn]. **1.** *a. & s. Geog:* Tyrolese. **2.** *s.f. Mus:* tyrolienne, tyrolienne; yodelled song or melody.

tyrolite [tirolit], *s.f. Miner:* tyrolite.

tyrosinase [tirozinaːz], *s.f. Bio-Ch:* tyrosinase.

tyrosine [tirozin], *s.f. Bio-Ch:* tyrosin.

tyrothricine [tirotrisin], *s.f. Pharm:* tyrothricin.

tyrrhénien, **-ienne** [tirenjɛ̃, -jɛn], *a. Hist: Geog:* Tyrrhenian, Tyrrhene; **la Mer Tyrrhénienne**, the Tyrrhenian Sea.

Tyrtée [tirte], *Pr.n.m. Gr.Lit:* Tyrtaeus.

tysonite [tizonit], *s.f. Miner:* tysonite.

Tzar, **-évitch**, **-ine**, etc. = TSAR, etc.

tzigane [tsigan, dz-], *s.m. & f. & a.* tzigane; Hungarian gipsy.

tzingaro [tsɛ̃garo, dz-], *s.m.* gipsy, zingaro.

U

U, u [y], *s.m.* (the letter) U, u; *Tp:* **U comme Ursule,** U for Uncle; **fer, poutre, en U,** channel iron, girder; *Civ.E:* **poutre en U,** strut bracing; *Phot:* **porte-objectif en U,** stirrup lens front; *Geog:* **vallée (à profil) en U,** U-shaped valley.

ubac [ybak], *s.m. Geog:* ubac, shady side of a mountain.

ubiquisme [ybikɥism], *s.m. Rel.H:* Ubiquitarianism; Ubiquitism.

ubiquiste [ybikɥist]. **1.** *Rel.H:* (*a*) *a.* Ubiquitarian (doctrine); (*b*) *s.m. & f.* Ubiquitarian. **2.** *a. & s.m. & f.* ubiquitous (person).

ubiquitaire [ybikɥitɛːr]. **1.** *s.m. & f. Rel.H:* Ubiquitarian. **2.** *a.* ubiquitous; omnipresent.

ubiquité [ybikɥite], *s.f.* ubiquity; omnipresence; **avoir le don d'u.,** to have the gift of ubiquity.

ubuesque [ybɥɛsk], *a. Lit:* Ubuesque; ludicrous.

udomètre [ydɔmɛtr], *s.m.* udometer, pluviometer, rain gauge.

udométrique [ydɔmetrik], *a.* udometric, pluviometric.

ufologie [yfɔlɔʒi], *s.f.* ufoism.

ufologue [yfɔlɔg], *s.m. & f.* ufoist, ufologist.

Ugolin [ygɔlɛ̃], *Pr.n.m. Hist:* Ugolino.

uhlan [ylɑ̃], *s.m.* (*no liaison with preceding word*) *Mil.Hist:* uhlan; **les uhlans** [leylɑ̃], the uhlans.

uintatherium [ɥɛ̃taterjɔm], *s.m. Paleont:* Uintatherium.

ukase [ykɑːz, u-], *s.m.* ukase; edict (of Russian government); **u. paternel,** paternal fiat.

Ukraine (l') [lykrɛn], *Pr.n.f. Geog:* the Ukraine.

ukrainien, -ienne [ykrɛnjɛ̃, -jɛn], *a. & s. Geog:* Ukrainian.

ukulele [ykylele], *s.m. Mus:* ukulele.

ulcératif, -ive [ylseratif, -iːv], *a.* ulcerative.

ulcération [ylserasjɔ̃], *s.f.* **1.** ulceration. **2.** embitterment (of feelings, etc.).

ulcère [ylsɛːr], *s.m.* ulcer; sore; **u. rongeant, rongeur,** rodent, wasting, ulcer; hospital gangrene; **u. simple de l'estomac,** peptic ulcer; **u. d'Orient,** endemic ulcer.

ulcéré [ylsere], *a.* (*a*) ulcerated; (*b*) **avoir une conscience ulcérée,** to suffer pangs of conscience; **cœur u.,** embittered heart.

ulcérer [ylsere], *v.tr.* (il **ulcère**; il **ulcérera**) (*a*) *Med:* to ulcerate; (*b*) to wound, embitter (s.o.).

ulcéreux, -euse [ylserø, -øːz], *a. Med:* ulcerous; ulcerated (wound, etc.); covered with ulcers; *Vet:* **lymphangite ulcéreuse,** ulcerative lymphangitis, pseudoglanders.

ulcériforme [ylseriform], *a.* ulcer-like.

ulcérogène [ylserɔʒɛn], *s.m. Path:* ulcerogenic.

ulcéroïde [ylserɔid], *a. Path:* ulcer-like.

ulcéro-membraneux, -euse [ylserɔmɑ̃branø, -øːz], *a. Path:* ulceromembranous; *pl.* **ulcéro-membraneux, -euses.**

ulcus [ylkys], *s.m. Med:* ulcus.

uléma [ylema], *s.m. Moslem Rel:* ulema, ulama.

ulex [ylɛks], *s.m. Bot:* ulex, furze, gorse, whin.

ulexite [ylɛksit], *s.f. Miner:* ulexite.

uliginaire [yliʒinɛːr], **uligineux, -euse** [yliʒinø, -øːz], *a. Bot: etc:* uliginous; uliginal (plant); **terrain u.,** swampy ground; swamp, marshland.

ullmannite [ylmanit], *s.f. Miner:* ullmannite.

ulluco [ylyko], **ullucu** [ylyky], **ulluque** [ylyk], *s.m. Bot:* ullucu, olluco.

ulmacé [ylmase], *Bot:* **1.** *a.* ulmaceous (plant). **2.** *s.f.pl.* **ulmacées,** Ulmaceae.

ulmaire [ylmɛːr], *s.f. Bot:* (spiraea) ulmaria; meadow-sweet, goat's beard.

ulmanite [ylmanit], *s.f. Miner:* ullmannite.

ulmeau, -eaux [ylmo], *s.m. Bot:* (common) elm.

ulmine [ylmin], *s.f. Ch:* ulmin.

ulmique [ylmik], *a. Ch:* (*a*) ulmic (acid); (*b*) humic (acid).

ulmo [ylmo], *s.m. Bot:* ulmo, muermo.

ulnaire [ylnɛːr], *a. Anat:* ulnar.

uloboridés [ylɔbɔride], *s.m.pl. Arach:* Uloboridae.

ulotric [ylɔtrik], *s.m. Algae:* ulothrix.

ulotricales [ylɔtrikal], *s.f.pl. Algae:* Ulotrichales.

ulotrichacées [ylɔtrikase], *s.f.pl. Algae:* Ulotrichaceae.

ulotriche [ylɔtriʃ]. **1.** *a. Anthr:* ulotrichous. **2.** *s.m. Algae:* ulothrix.

ulotrique [ylɔtrik], *a. Anthr:* ulotrichous, woolly-haired.

Ulphilas [ylfilɑːs], *Pr.n.m. Lit.Hist:* Ulfilas.

Ulpien [ylpjɛ̃], *Pr.n.m. Rom.Hist:* Ulpian.

Ulrique [ylrik], *Pr.n.f.* Ulrica.

Ulster [ylstɛːr]. **1.** *Pr.n.m. Geog:* Ulster. **2.** *s.m. A.Cost:* ulster (overcoat).

ulstérien, -ienne [ylsterjɛ̃, -jɛn]. **1.** (*a*) *a. & s.m. Geog:* Ulsterman; (native, inhabitant) of Ulster; *attrib.* Ulster; (*b*) *s. Pol:* (i) Ulster Unionist; (ii) Orangeman. **2.** *a. & s.m. Geol:* Ulsterian.

ultérieur [ylterjœːr], *a.* **1.** *Geog:* farther. **2.** ulterior; subsequent (à, to); later (news, date, etc.); **dans une séance ultérieure,** at a subsequent, later, meeting; *Com:* **ordres ultérieurs,** further orders; orders to come.

ultérieurement [ylterjœrmɑ̃], *adv.* ulteriorly; later on, subsequently; **convention qui sera u. conclue,** convention hereafter to be agreed to; *Com:* **marchandises livrables u.,** goods for future delivery.

ultième [yltjɛm], *a.* = ULTIME.

ultimatif, -ive [yltimatif, -iːv], *a.* of the nature of an ultimatum.

ultimatum [yltimatɔm], *s.m.* ultimatum; **signifier un u. à un pays,** to deliver an ultimatum to a country; to present a country with an ultimatum; *pl.* **ultimatums.**

ultime [yltim], *a.* ultimate, final, last (syllable, symptom, etc.).

ultimo [yltimo], *adv.* lastly, finally.

ultimogéniture [yltimɔʒenityːr], *s.f.* ultimogeniture, postremogeniture.

ultra [yltra], *s.m. Pol:* ultra(ist), extremist.

ultra-, *pref.* ultra-.

ultrabasique [yltrabazik], *a. Geol:* ultrabasic.

ultrabasite [yltrabazit], *s.f. Miner:* ultrabasite.

ultracentrifugation [yltrasɑ̃trifygasjɔ̃], *s.f.* ultracentrifugation.

ultracentrifugeur [yltrasɑ̃trifyʒœːr], *s.m.,* **ultracentrifugeuse** [yltrasɑ̃trifyʒøːz], *s.f.* ultracentrifuge, high-speed centrifuge.

ultra-chic [yltraʃik], *a.inv.* ultra chic.

ultracisme [yltrasism], *s.m. Pol:* ultraism; *esp.* ultra-royalism.

ultra-court [yltrakuːr], *a. Ph:* **ondes ultra-courtes,** ultra-short waves.

ultrafiltration [yltrafiltrasjɔ̃], *s.f. Ch:* ultrafiltration.

ultrafiltre [yltrafiltr], *s.m. Ch:* ultrafilter.

ultrafiltrer [yltrafiltre], *v.tr.* to ultrafilter.

ultragerme [yltraʒɛrm], *s.m. Biol:* ultravirus.

ultraïsme [yltraism], *s.m. Pol:* ultraism; *esp.* ultra-royalism.

ultra-libéral, -ale [yltraliberal], *a. & s. Pol:* ultra-liberal; *pl.* **ultra-libéraux, -ales.**

ultra-marin, -ine [yltramarɛ̃, -in], *a.* ultramarine; overseas; *pl.* **ultra-marin(e)s.**

ultramarine [yltramarin], *s.f. Miner:* lapis lazuli, ultramarine.

ultramicromètre [yltramikrɔmɛtr], *s.m.* ultramicrometer.

ultramicroscope [yltramikrɔskɔp], *s.m.* ultramicroscope.

ultramicroscopie [yltramikrɔskɔpi], *s.f.* ultramicroscopy.

ultramicroscopique [yltramikrɔskɔpik], *a.* ultramicroscopic(al).

ultramoderne [yltramɔdɛrn], *a.* ultramodern.

ultramodernisme [yltramɔdɛrnism], *s.m.* ultramodernism.

ultramondain [yltramɔ̃dɛ̃], *a. A:* ultramundane.

ultramontain [yltramɔ̃tɛ̃]. **1.** *a.* ultramontane; beyond the Alps (as from France). **2.** *s. Theol: Pol:* ultramontanist, ultramontane.

ultramontanisme [yltramɔ̃tanism], *s.m. Theol: Pol:* ultramontanism.

ultra-petita [yltrapetita], *s.m. Jur:* (miscarriage of justice arising from) excessive award; **statuer u.-p.,** to adjudicate more than is asked for.

ultra-rapide [yltrarapid], *a.* high-speed; split-second; *pl.* **ultra-rapides.**

ultra-révolutionnaire [yltrarevɔlysjɔnɛːr], *a. & s.m. & f.* ultra-revolutionary; *pl.* **ultra-révolutionnaires.**

ultraroyaliste [yltrarwajalist], *a. & s.m. & f.* ultraroyalist.

ultra-secret, -ète [yltrasəkrɛ, -ɛt], *a.* top secret; *pl.* **ultra-secrets, -ètes.**

ultra-sensible [yltrasɑ̃sibl], *a.* ultra-sensitive (photography, etc.); *pl.* **ultra-sensibles.**

ultra(-)son [yltrasɔ̃], *s.m. Ph:* ultrasound; super-sound; **sondage sous-marin par ultra(-)sons,** supersonic sounding; *Med:* **traitement par les ultra(-)sons,** supersonic therapy; **à ultra(-)sons,** ultrasonic, supersonic; *Metall:* **essai à u.(-)s.,** ultrasonic testing; **science des ultra(-)sons,** ultrasonics.

ultrasonique [yltrasɔnik], *a.* ultrasonic, super-sonic.

ultrasonore [yltrasɔnɔːr], *a. Ph:* ultrasonic, super-sonic; super-audible (frequency, etc.).

ultrasonothérapie [yltrasɔnɔterapi], *s.f. Med:* ultrasound therapy, supersonic therapy.

ultrastructure [yltrastryktyːr], *s.f. Biol:* ultra-structure.

ultra-terrestre [yltraterɛstr], *a.* ultra-terrestrial; *pl.* **ultra-terrestres.**

ultravide [yltravid], *s.m.* ultra-high vacuum.

ultra(-)violet, -ette [yltravjɔlɛ, -ɛt]. **1.** *a.* ultra-violet; **lampe à rayons ultra-violets,** ultraviolet lamp. **2.** *s.m.* ultraviolet.

ultravirus [yltravirys], *s.m. Med:* ultravirus.

ultra-zodiacal [yltrazɔdjakal], *a. Astr:* ultra-zodiacal (planet); *pl.* **ultra-zodiacaux, -ales.**

ululation [ylylasjɔ̃], *s.f.,* **ululement** [ylylmɑ̃], *s.m.* (*usu. no liaison with preceding word*) ululation (of owls); tu-whit; tu-whoo; hoot(ing).

ululer [ylyle], *v.i.* (*of owl*) to ululate; to hoot.

ulve [ylv], *s.f. Algae:* sea lettuce, ulva.

Ulysse [ylis], *Pr.n.m.* Ulysses.

umangite [ymɑ̃ʒit], *s.f. Miner:* umangite.

umbilicus [ɔ̃bilikys], *s.m. Bot:* pennywort.

umbraculidés [ɔ̃brakylide], *s.m.pl. Moll:* Umbraculidae.

umbre [ɔ̃br], *s.m. Ich:* umbra, mud minnow.

umeau, -eaux [ymo], *s.m. Bot:* elm.

umiri [ymiri], *s.m. Bot:* umiri, umiry.

un, une [œ̃, yn]. 1. *num.a. & s.* (*a*) one; **des enfants de un à douze ans,** children aged from one to twelve; **il n'en reste qu'un,** there is only one left; **chambre à un lit,** single bedroom; **les Mille et Une Nuits,** the Thousand and One Nights; **vingt et une villes et villages** (*agreement with the nearest noun*), twenty-one towns and villages; **un à un** [œ̃naœ̃], **un par un,** one by one; *Mil:* **en colonne par un,** in single file; **une heure,** one o'clock; **travailler de une heure à deux,** to work from one to two; *F:* **sur, vers, les une** [leyn] **heure,** about one (o'clock); **je viendrai entre une et deux,** I shall come between one and two (o'clock); **page un,** page one, first page; **numéro un,** number one; **habiter au un,** to live at number one; **un et un** [œ̃eœ̃] **font deux,** one and one make two; **compter de un à dix** [œ̃adis], to count from one to ten; *Th:* **le un** [ləœ̃], the first act; **le un a gagné,** (i) *Rac:* number one was the winner; (ii) *Games:* one was the winning number; *Journ:* **la une** [layn], front page (of paper); *F:* **en savoir plus d'une,** to know a thing or two; *F:* **il était moins une,** it was a close thing, a close shave, it was a narrow escape; **de deux choses l'une, ou bien . . ., ou bien . . .,** it's one thing or the other—either . . ., or . . .; **il vient un jour sur deux,** *A:* **de deux jours l'un,** he comes every other day; **il est libre un dimanche sur trois,** he is free every third Sunday, one Sunday in, out of, three; **ces laitues coûtent un franc l'une,** these lettuces cost one franc apiece, one franc each; (*in gymnastics, sports, etc., usu.* **une**) **une, deux! une, deux!** *P:* **une, deusse! une, deusse!** one, two! one, two! **une, deux, trois, partez!** one, two, three, go! **il n'a fait ni une ni deux,** he didn't hesitate (for a moment); **sans faire ni une ni deux,** without the slightest hesitation; **et d'un dans nos filets!** that's one for us! **et d'un!, et d'une!** well, that's that! so much for that one! **il pensa à un moment que . . .,** he thought at one moment that . . .; *Elcs:* (*computers*) **état "un,"** one condition, one state; **assembleur pour un(e),** one-to-one assembler; (*b*) one (and indivisible); **Dieu est un,** God is one; **l'art est un,** art is one; **dans un poème l'action doit être une,** in a poem there must be unity of action; **c'est tout un** [tutœ̃], it's all one, all the same; it's as broad as it's long; it makes no difference; *F:* **ils ne font qu'un,** (i) they are indistinguishable; (ii) they're hand in glove; (iii) they are as one. 2. *indef.pron.* one; **un de ces jours, l'un de ces jours,** one of these days; **un que je plains, c'est . . .,** someone I do pity is . . .; **(l')un de nous, (l')un d'entre nous,** one of us; **un pour tous et tous pour un,** one for all and all for one; **les uns disent que . . .,** some say that . . .; **l'un et l'autre, ni l'un ni l'autre, l'un ou l'autre, l'un . . . l'autre, l'un l'autre, l'un dans l'autre,** *see* AUTRE 1; **pas un,** *see* PAS² 2; **un qui sera heureux c'est le père!** the one who'll be happy about it is the father! **il marchait comme un qui est fatigué,** he was walking like a tired man; *F:* **tu n'en as même pas une de voiture,** you haven't even got a car; *s.a.* POUSSER 1. 3. *indef.art.* (*pl.* **des,** *q.v. under* DE III); (*before a consonant*) a; (*before a vowel sound*) an (*pl.* some); (*a*) **un jour, une pomme, une heure,** a day, an apple, an hour; **un père et une mère,** a father and mother; **un père de famille,** the father of a family; **elle a osé te dire ça, une mère?** she, a mother, dared to tell you that? **une cravate et des chaussettes,** a tie and some socks; **venez me voir un lundi,** come and see me one Monday, some Monday; **dans un sens il a raison,** in a (certain) sense he is right; **pour une raison ou pour une autre,** for some reason or other; **la science est une chose, l'art en est une autre,** science is one thing, art is another; (*with a superlative*) **c'est une chose la plus aisée du monde,** it's one of the easiest things in the world; (*b*) such a one as; **quand on a été loué par un La Bruyère . . .,** when one has earned the praise of a La Bruyère . . .; **sans doute un Worth vous aurait-il mieux habillée,** no doubt a (firm like) Worth would have dressed you better; (*c*) (*intensive*) **j'ai eu un monde aujourd'hui!** I've had such a lot of people today! **il était d'une maladresse!** he was dreadfully clumsy! **l'effet était d'un réussi!,** the effect was one huge success; *F:* **il a fait une de ces têtes!** you should have seen his face! **c'est d'un médiocre,** it's thoroughly second-rate; **tu m'as fait une** (*F:* **de ces**) **peur(s)!** you gave me such a fright! **il fait un chaud là-dedans!** you should feel the heat in there! **il y a des années qu'il est mort,** he's been dead for (many) years; **pendant des heures et des heures,** for hours together, for hours and hours.

unaire [ynɛːr], *a.* unary.

unanime [ynanim], *a.* unanimous (**dans,** in); of one mind; **concert u. d'éloges,** unanimous concert of praise; **tous sont unanimes sur ce point,** all are unanimous on this point; **ils sont unanimes à vous accuser,** they are unanimous in accusing you; **nous avons été unanimes à, pour, reconnaître que . . .,** we expressed the unanimous opinion that . . ., we were at one in acknowledging that . . .

unanimement [ynanimmɑ̃], *adv.* unanimously; with one accord.

unanimisme [ynanimism], *s.m. Lit.Hist:* unanimism.

unanimiste [ynanimist], *a. & s.m. & f. Lit.Hist:* unanimist.

unanimité [ynanimite], *s.f.* unanimity; **à l'u.,** unanimously, with one consent; **à l'u. des voix,** without one dissentient voice; **voté à l'u. moins une voix,** passed with one dissentient vote; **la proposition a fait l'u.,** the proposal was accepted unanimously.

unau, -aux [yno], *s.m. Z:* unau.

uncaria [ɔ̃karja], *s.m. Bot:* uncaria.

uncial, -aux [ɔ̃sjal, -o], *a.* uncial (letter, MS.).

unciforme [ɔ̃sifɔrm], *a. Nat.Hist: Anat:* unciform, uncinate, hook-like; **éminence u.,** uncinate gyrus, uncinate convolution.

uncinaire [ɔ̃sinɛːr], *s.f. Ann:* hookworm.

uncinariose [ɔ̃sinarjoːz], *s.f. Med:* uncinariasis, ancylostomiasis, *F:* hookworm (disease).

unciné [ɔ̃sine], *a. Nat.Hist:* uncinate(d); *Psy:* **crise uncinée,** uncinate fit, seizure.

uncinula [ɔ̃sinyla], *s.m. Fung:* uncinula.

uncinule [ɔ̃sinyl], *s.f. Nat.Hist:* uncinus.

uncinulé [ɔ̃sinyle], *a. Nat.Hist:* unciform, uncinate, hook-like.

unda-maris [ɔ̃damaris], *s.m.inv. Mus:* unda maris.

undécanoïque [ɔ̃dekanɔik], *s.m. Ch:* undecanoic acid.

undécennal, -aux [ɔ̃desɛn(n)al, -o], *a.* undecennial, every eleven years.

undécylénique [ɔ̃desilenik], *a. Ch:* **acide u.,** undecylenic acid.

une-pièce [ynpjɛs], *s.m.inv. Cost:* one-piece swimsuit, bathing-suit.

Unesco [ynɛsko], *s.f.* Unesco (initials of United Nations Educational, Scientific and Cultural Organization).

ungémachite [ɔ̃ʒemakit], *s.f. Miner:* ungemachite.

unguéal, -aux [ɔ̃gɥeal, -o], *a. Anat:* ungual.

unguifère [ɔ̃gɥifɛːr], *a. Z:* unguiferous; clawed.

unguinal, -aux [ɔ̃gɥinal, -o], *Anat:* ungual.

unguis [ɔ̃gɥis], *s.m. Anat:* unguis, lachrymal bone.

uni [yni], *a.* 1. (*a*) united, harmonious (gathering, family, etc.); (*b*) **le Royaume-Uni,** the United Kingdom; **les États-Unis,** the United States; *Hist:* **les Provinces-Unies,** the United Provinces (of the Netherlands). 2. smooth, level, even (ground, etc.); **galop u.,** smooth gallop; **mer unie,** smooth sea; **chemin u.,** level, smooth, road; *A:* **à l'u.,** on a level; **vie unie,** regular, uneventful life; *adv.* **filer bien u.,** to spin an even yarn or thread. 3. (*a*) plain (material, colour, article, etc.); self-colour(ed) (material); solid (colour); simple (fashion, taste, etc.); **tulle u.,** plain net; **chat argenté u.,** self-silver Persian; *s.m.* **ne porter que de l'u.,** to dress in a plain style; (*b*) **un homme tout u.,** a plain man; a plain-living man.

uni- [yni], *pref.* uni-.

uniangulaire [yniɑ̃gylɛːr], *a.* having only one angle; *Bot:* uniangulate.

uniarticulé [yniartikyle], *a. Ent: etc:* uniarticulate.

uniate [ynjat], *s.m. & a. Rel.H:* Uniat(e).

uniatomique [yniatɔmik], *a. Ch:* monoatomic.

uniaxe [yniaks], *a. Cryst:* uniaxial.

unicapsulaire [ynikapsylɛːr], *a. Bot:* unicapsular.

unicaule [ynikoːl], *a. O: Bot:* uniaxial.

unicellulaire [yniselylɛːr], *a. Biol:* unicellular.

unicisme [ynisism], *s.m. Phil:* unicism; monism.

unicité [ynisite], *s.f.* 1. *Phil: etc:* oneness, unicity. 2. uniqueness, singleness.

unicolore [ynikɔlɔːr], *a.* unicolour(ed); one-coloured, whole-coloured (material, etc.).

unicorne [ynikɔrn]. 1. *a.* unicornous, one-horned, single-horned; *Anat:* **utérus u.,** one-horned uterus. 2. *s.m.* (*a*) *Myth: Her: Z:* unicorn; (*b*) *Z: O:* sea unicorn, narwhal.

unicursale [ynikyrsal], *a.f. Mth:* **(courbe) u.,** unicursal (curve).

unidimensionnel, -elle [ynidimɑ̃sjɔnɛl], *a.* unidimensional.

unidirectionnel, -elle [ynidirɛksjɔnɛl], *a.* one-way; unidirectional; simplex (circuit, etc.).

unième [ynjɛm], *num.a.* (*used only in compounds*) first; **trente et u.,** thirty-first; **cent u.** [sɑ̃ynjɛm], hundred and first.

unièmement [ynjɛmmɑ̃], *adv.* (*used only in compounds*) firstly; **vingt et u.,** twenty-firstly.

uniface [ynifas], *a.* unifacial.

unifeuillé [ynifœje], *a. Bot:* unifoliate.

unificateur, -trice [ynifikatœːr, -tris]. 1. *a.* unifying. 2. *s.* unifier.

unification [ynifikasjɔ̃], *s.f.* unification; consolidation (of ideas, loans, etc.); standardization (of weights and measures, of articles of commerce, etc.); *A:* **u. industrielle,** (i) amalgamating, amalgamation, of industries; (ii) industrial merger.

unifié [ynifje], *a.* unified; consolidated (debt, etc.); standard(ized) (weights, articles of commerce, etc.).

unifier [ynifje], *v.tr.* (*p.d. & pr.sub.* **n. unifiions, v. unifiiez**) to unify (ideas); to consolidate (loans, debt); to standardize (weights and measures, articles of commerce, etc.); to unify (a political party, etc.); *A:* to amalgamate (industries).

s'unifier, to become one, to become united.

unifilaire [ynifilɛːr], *a. El: etc:* unifilar; single wire (line); single-line (diagram).

uniflore [yniflɔːr], *a. Bot:* uniflorous, unifloral.

unifolié [ynifɔlje], *a. Bot:* unifoliate, one-leaved.

uniforme [ynifɔrm]. 1. *a.* uniform, unvarying (custom, practice, scene, colour, etc.); **vie u.,** uniform, regular, unvarying, life; **conduite u.,** uniform, consistent, conduct; **maisons uniformes,** uniform houses, houses all built to one type; **couleur u.,** uniform, even, colour; **allure u.,** even, uniform, unvarying, pace; **vitesse u.,** uniform velocity; **tarif kilométrique u.,** flat mileage rate. 2. *s.m. Mil: Sch: etc:* uniform; **grand u.,** full-dress uniform, regimentals; **culotte d'u.,** uniform breeches; **en u.,** in uniform, uniformed; *F:* **endosser l'u.,** to become a soldier, to enlist, to join up; **quitter l'u.,** to leave the service.

uniformément [ynifɔrmemɑ̃], *adv.* uniformly, unvaryingly; consistently; **colle étendue u.,** paste spread evenly; **vêtus u.,** all dressed alike.

uniformisation [ynifɔrmizasjɔ̃], *s.f.* standardization.

uniformiser [ynifɔrmize], *v.tr.* to make uniform; to standardize (methods, etc.).

uniformitarisme [ynifɔrmitarism], *s.m. Geol:* uniformitarianism.

uniformitariste [ynifɔrmitarist], *a. & s.m. & f.* uniformitarian.

uniformité [ynifɔrmite], *s.f.* uniformity.

unigemme [yniʒɛm], *a. Bot:* single-budded.

unigraphie [ynigrafi], *s.f. Book-k: A:* single-entry book-keeping.

unijambiste [yniʒɑ̃bist], *a. & s.m. & f.* one-legged (man, woman).

unijonction [yniʒɔ̃ksjɔ̃], *s.f. Elcs:* double-base diode.

unijugué [yniʒyge], *a. Bot:* unijugate.

unilabié [ynilabje], *a. Bot:* unilabiate.

unilatéral, -aux [ynilateral, -o], *a.* 1. *Bot: etc:* unilateral; *P.N:* **stationnement u.,** parking on one side only; **stationnement u. alterné,** parking on one side on alternate days, etc. 2. *Jur:* unilateral, one-sided (contract, information, etc.); *Pol: etc:* **décision unilatérale,** unilateral decision; *s.a.* ACTE 2.

unilatéralement [ynilateralmɑ̃], *adv.* unilaterally.

unilatère [ynilatɛːr], *a. Mth:* unilateral.

unilinéaire [ynilineɛːr], *a.* unilinear.

unilingue [ynilɛ̃ːg], *a.* unilingual (dictionary, etc.).

unilobé [ynilɔbe], *a. O: Nat.Hist:* unilobate.

uniloculaire [ynilɔkylɛːr], *a. Bot:* unilocular, one-celled (ovary).

unilocularité [ynilɔkylarite], *s.f.* unilocularity.

uniment [ynimɑ̃], *adv.* (*a*) smoothly, evenly; **fil filé u.,** evenly spun thread; **cheval qui galope u.,** horse that gallops steadily; horse with a smooth gallop; (*b*) **dire qch. tout u.,** to say sth. quite simply, plainly.

unimodal, -aux [ynimɔdal, -o], *a.* (*statistics*) unimodal.

uninervé [yninɛrve], *a. Bot:* (*of leaf*) uninervate uninerved, single-veined.

uninominal, -aux [yninɔminal, -o], *a.* 1. uninominal (species, etc.). 2. *Pol:* **scrutin u., votation uninominale,** uninominal voting; voting, ballot, for a single member, for one member only.

unio [ynjo], *s.m. Moll:* freshwater mussel.

unioculé [ynjɔkyle], *a. Z: etc:* uniocular; one-eyed.

union [ynjɔ̃], *s.f.* union. 1. junction, coalition, combination (of two or more things, parts, etc.); *Art: Mus:* blending (of colours, of registers of the voice); *Biol:* **u. sexuelle,** fertilization;

l'élection a imposé l'u. des gauches, the election has compelled the parties of the left to come together; *s.a.* TRAIT[2] 4. **2.** society, association; **l'U. américaine,** the American Union; *Hist:* **l'U. Sud-africaine,** the South African Union; *Hist:* **l'U. française,** the French Union; **U. de l'Europe Occidentale,** Western European Union; **l'U. soviétique,** the Soviet Union; *A:* **u. ouvrière,** trade union; *A:* **U. chrétienne de jeunes gens,** Young Men's Christian Association; **l'U. internationale de Berne,** the International Copyright Union; **U. postale universelle,** Universal Postal Union; **u. douanière,** customs union. **3.** marriage; **u. bien assortie,** well assorted union; **u. libre,** cohabitation (of unmarried couple). **4.** unity, concord, agreement; *Prov:* **l'u. fait la force,** unity is strength; united we stand, divided we fall; *Jur:* **contrat d'u.,** agreement (on the part of creditors) to take concerted action. **5.** *Tchn:* union, union joint, coupling; **u. à vis,** screw joint, screw coupling.

unionidés [ynjɔnide], *s.m.pl. Moll:* Unionidae.

unionisme [ynjɔnism], *s.m.* (*a*) *Pol:* unionism; (*b*) the scout movement (of the French Protestant churches).

unioniste [ynjɔnist]. **1.** *a.* (*a*) unionistic; (*b*) *Scouting:* **éclaireur u.,** scout (attached to a Protestant church). **2.** *s.* (*a*) *Pol:* Unionist; (*b*) *A:* member of the Young Men's Christian Association.

uniovulaire [yniɔvylɛːr], *a. Biol:* uniovular; **jumeaux uniovulaires,** identical twins.

uniovulé [yniɔvyle], *a. Bot:* uniovular, uniovulate.

unipare [ynipaːr], *a. Biol:* uniparous.

uniparité [yniparite], *s.f. Physiol:* single birth.

unipersonnel, -elle [ynipɛrsɔnɛl], *a. Gram:* **1.** unipersonal (verb). **2.** impersonal (verb).

unipétale [ynipetal], *a. Bot:* unipetalous.

uniphasé [ynifɑze], *a. El:* single-phase, uniphase, monophase.

unipolaire [ynipɔlɛːr], *a. El:* unipolar, homopolar, single-pole (dynamo, switch, etc.); *Biol:* **cellule u.,** unipolar cell; *Pol:* **coalition u.,** unipolar coalition.

unipolarité [ynipɔlarite], *s.f. El:* unipolarity.

unique [ynik], *a.* **1.** sole, only, single (specimen, etc.); **cas u.,** single case; unique, only, example; *Adm:* **allocation de salaire u.,** allowance paid to a man whose wife is not in employment; **fils u.,** only son; **le Fils u. du Père,** the only begotten Son of the Father; **exemplaire u.,** only copy extant; *Ins: etc:* **prime u.,** single premium; **associé u.,** sole partner; *Adm:* **(rue à) sens u.,** one-way road, street; **voie u.,** single-line traffic; **chemin de fer à voie u.,** single-track railway; *Mil: Pol:* **présenter un front u.,** to present a united front; **c'est ma seule et u. crainte,** it's my one and only fear. **2.** (*a*) unique, unrivalled, unparalleled (talent, etc.); (*b*) *F:* **il est u.,** he's priceless; *Pej:* **vous êtes u.!** you're the limit! **voilà qui est u.!** who ever heard of such nonsense?

uniquement [ynikmɑ̃], *adv.* solely, uniquely; **je viens u. pour vous voir,** I have come merely, simply, to see you; I have come just to see you.

unir [yniːr], *v.tr.* **1.** to unite, join, combine, link, connect; **lorsque la Bretagne fut unie à la France,** when Brittany was united to France; **u. les plaisirs aux affaires,** to combine business with pleasure; **faits étroitement unis,** facts closely linked together, closely bound together; **être uni par le mariage à . . .,** to be joined in wedlock to . . .; **u. le geste à la parole,** to suit the action to the word; **u. à nouveau,** to reunite. **2.** to smooth, level, make plane; **u. une pelouse,** to level a lawn.

s'unir. 1. to unite, join; **s'u. à qn,** (i) to join forces with s.o.; (ii) to marry s.o. **2.** to become smooth, level, even.

uniradiculaire [yniradikylɛːr], *a. Bot: Anat:* single rooted; uniradical.

uniréfringent [ynirefrɛ̃ʒɑ̃], *a.* monorefringent (crystal, etc.).

unisérié [yniserje], *a. Nat.Hist:* uniserial, uniseriate.

unisexualité [ynisɛksɥalite], *s.f.* unisexuality.

unisexué [ynisɛksɥe], *a. Biol:* unisexual, unisexed.

unisexuel, -uelle [ynisɛksɥɛl], *a.* (*a*) *Bot:* unisexual; (*b*) homosexual.

unisson [ynisɔ̃], *s.m. Mus:* unison; **à l'u.,** in unison (de, with); **goûts à l'u. des miens,** tastes attuned to mine, in harmony with mine; **sa maison est à l'u. de la rue,** his house is in character, in keeping, with the street; **se mettre à l'u. des circonstances,** to adapt oneself to the circumstances.

unissonnant [ynisɔnɑ̃], *a.* unisonant.

unitaire [ynitɛːr], *a.* **1.** *Rel.H:* Unitarian. **2.** unitary, unitarian (system, etc.); *Com:* **prix u.,** unit price; *Mth:* **vecteur u.,** unit vector; *Mec.E: etc:* **allongement u.,** elongation per unit length; **élément u.,** unit element; **intervalle u.,** unit interval; *Mth: etc:* **théorie du champ u.,** unified field theory.

unitairien, -ienne [ynitɛrjɛ̃, -jɛn], **unitarien, -ienne** [ynitarjɛ̃, -jɛn], *a. & s.* (*a*) *Pol:* unitarian; (*b*) *Rel:* Unitarian.

unitar(ian)isme [ynitar(jan)ism], *s.m.* (*a*) *Pol:* unitarianism; (*b*) *Rel:* Unitarianism.

unité [ynite], *s.f.* **1.** (*a*) *Mth: etc:* unity, one; *attrib. Biol:* **caractère u.,** unit character; *Com:* **prix de l'u.,** price of one (article), unit price; **chaque lot comprend une centaine d'unités,** each parcel contains a hundred units or so; *Fin:* **actions émises en unités et en coupures de 50 ou 100,** shares issued in ones and in denominations of 50 or 100; **la production a dépassé les 3.000 unités,** production has passed the 3,000 mark; (*b*) *Mil:* unit, formation; **grande u.,** major unit, larger unit, (higher) formation; **petite u.,** minor unit, smaller unit; **u. élémentaire,** basic unit; **u. autonome, u. formant corps,** self-contained unit; **u. cadre,** skeleton unit; **u. constitutive,** component unit; **u. organique,** organic unit; **u. subordonnée,** subordinate unit; **constituer, mettre sur pied, une u.,** to form, activate, a unit; **dissoudre une u.,** to disband, inactivate, a unit; **reconstituer, reformer, une u.,** to re-form, re-activate, a unit; **u. combattante,** fighting unit, *U.S:* combat unit; **u. tactique,** tactical unit; **u. tactique élémentaire,** basic tactical unit; **u. d'attaque,** attacking unit, unit told off for (the) attack; **u. de choc,** shock unit; **u. de premier échelon,** leading unit; **u. de première ligne,** front-line unit; **u. de deuxième échelon, u. de soutien, d'appui,** support unit; **u. de base,** directing unit; **unités encadrantes,** adjacent units; **unités réservées,** reserved units; *Av:* **u. aérienne, u. d'aviation,** air unit, aviation unit; **u. de l'armée de l'air, u. de l'aéronautique,** air force unit; (*c*) *Navy:* (i) (naval) unit, formation; (ii) ship; **grosse u.,** capital ship; (*d*) *Ind: Mec.E:* unit, plant; installation; **u. pilote,** pilot plant; *Petroleum Ind:* **u. de craquage,** cracking unit; **u. de craquage catalytique,** cat cracker; **u. combinée de distillation sommaire et de craquage,** combined topping and cracking unit; **u. de déparaffinage,** dewaxing plant, unit; **u. de forage mobile,** portable rig; (*e*) *Elcs:* (*computers*) unit, module; **u. arithmétique,** arithmetic unit, section; **u. centrale,** central processing unit, processor; **u. d'affichage,** display unit; **u. de disques,** disc (storage) unit; **u. de réponse vocale,** audio response unit; **u. périphérique,** peripheral unit; **u. de stockage,** cell; **u. de transmission,** data set; **u. de traitement,** task, job. **2.** unit (of measure, value, etc.); *Mth:* **u. arbitraire,** arbitrary unit; **u. fondamentale,** fundamental unit; **u. dérivée,** derived unit; **u. pratique,** practical unit; **u. d'angle,** unit of angle; **u. de capacité,** unit of capacity; **u. de longueur,** unit of length; **u. de poids,** unit of weight; **u. de surface,** unit of area, unit area; **u. de temps,** unit of time, unit time; **u. de volume,** unit of volume, unit volume; *Ph:* **u. physique,** physical unit; **u. de chaleur, u. thermique,** unit of heat, thermal unit; **u. de masse,** unit of mass; **u. optique,** optical unit; **u. d'éclairement,** unit of illumination; **u. d'intensité lumineuse,** unit of light; **u. électrique,** electrical unit; *El:* **u. de courant,** unit of current; *Atom.Ph:* **u. atomique,** atomic unit; **u. de rayonnement,** radiation unit; **u. d'irradiation,** irradiation unit; *Mec:* **u. mécanique,** mechanical unit; **u. d'accélération,** unit of acceleration; **u. d'énergie, u. de travail,** unit of energy, of work; **u. de force,** unit of force; **u. de puissance,** unit of power; **u. de vitesse,** unit of velocity; *Tp:* **u. de communication, de conversation,** unit call; *Pol. Ec:* **u. de consommation, de production,** unit of consumption, of production; **u. de travail,** man hour, man work unit; *Fin:* **u. de compte,** unit of account; **u. monétaire,** monetary unit; *F:* **une u.,** a million francs; *Artil:* **u. de feu,** unit of fire; *Mil:* **u. d'approvisionnement,** unit of supply; *Husb:* **u. fourragère,** fodder unit, feed unit; *attrib. Com:* **grandeur u.,** standard size. **3.** unity; (*a*) oneness (of God, etc.); (*b*) uniformity (of plan, action, etc.); **u. de style,** uniformity, consistency, of style; (*c*) *Lit:* **les trois unités,** the three unities; **u. de lieu,** unity of place.

unité-travailleur [ynitetravajœːr], *s.f. Pol.Ec:* man equivalent; *pl. unités-travailleur.*

unitif, -ive [ynitif, -iːv], *a.* unitive, uniting; *Theol:* **vie unitive,** life of perpetual communion with God.

univalence [ynivalɑ̃ːs], *s.f. Ch:* univalence, univalency, monovalency.

univalent [ynivalɑ̃], *a. Ch:* univalent, monovalent.

univalve [ynivalv]. **1.** *a.* (*a*) *Bot:* univalvular; (*b*) *Moll:* univalve. **2.** *s.m.pl. Moll: A:* **univalves,** Gastropoda.

univers [ynivɛːr], *s.m.* (*a*) universe; *Astr:* **la théorie de l'expansion de l'u,** the theory of the expanding universe; **tout l'u.,** the whole world; **par tout l'u.,** all over the world; **sa chambre et ses études, voilà tout son u.,** his whole world is limited to his room and his studies; (*b*) field, province; **l'u. mathématique,** the field of mathematics.

universalisation [ynivɛrsalizasjɔ̃], *s.f.* universalization.

universaliser [ynivɛrsalize], *v.tr.* to universalize, to make (sth.) universal; **s'u.,** to become universal, general.

universalisme [ynivɛrsalism], *s.m. Theol: etc:* universalism.

universaliste [ynivɛrsalist], *s.m. Theol: etc:* universalist.

universalité [ynivɛrsalite], *s.f.* **1.** universality (of the Church, of the English language, etc.). **2.** *A.* sum total; **léguer à qn l'u. de ses biens,** to bequeath to s.o. the whole of one's estate.

universaux [ynivɛrso], *s.m.pl. Log:* **les (cinq) u.,** the universals, the five predictables.

universel, -elle [ynivɛrsɛl]. **1.** *a.* universal (ruin, indignation, etc.); all-purpose, general-purpose (device); **réputation universelle,** world-wide reputation; **secousse universelle,** world commotion; **désarmement u.,** world disarmament; **savoir u.,** universal, all-embracing, knowledge; **homme u.,** versatile man, all-rounder; **je ne suis pas u.,** I can't know everything; *Mec.E:* **joint u.,** universal joint, coupling; **raccord u.,** universal adapter, coupling; **moteur u.,** universal motor; **fraiseuse universelle,** universal milling machine; **pinces universelles,** universal pliers; *El:* **courant u.,** all-mains current; *Mth:* **quantificateur u.,** universal quantifier; **calculateur u.,** general-purpose computer; **appareil de mesure u.,** all-purpose meter; *Log:* **proposition universelle,** *s.f.* **universelle,** universal proposition; *Jur:* **légataire u.,** residuary legatee. **2.** *s.m. Phil: Log:* universal.

universellement [ynivɛrsɛlmɑ̃], *adv.* universally; **fait u. reconnu,** fact universally admitted; **réputation u. reconnue,** world-wide reputation; *Log:* **les termes ne doivent pas être pris plus u. dans la conclusion qu'ils ne l'ont été dans les prémisses,** terms must not be given a wider extension in the conclusion than in the premisses.

universitaire [ynivɛrsitɛːr]. **1.** *a.* university (studies, body, town, etc.); **honneurs universitaires,** academic honours; **éducation u.,** university education; **la bibliothèque u.,** the university library; **cité u.** = (students') hall(s) of residence. **2.** *s.m. & f.* (*a*) member of the teaching profession; *a.* **le corps u.,** the (members of the) teaching profession; (*b*) **c'est un u.,** he's an academic.

université [ynivɛrsite], *s.f.* **1.** university (of Paris, Oxford, etc.); **il avait étudié à l'u.,** he had had a university education, been to a university. **2.** **l'U. (de France),** the teaching profession (including university staff, schoolmasters, inspectors, etc.); **entrer dans l'U.,** to enter the teaching profession.

univitellin [ynivitɛlɛ̃], *a. Biol:* monovular, monozygotic; **jumeaux univitellins,** identical twins.

univocation [ynivɔkasjɔ̃], **univocité** [ynivɔsite], *s.f.* univocity, univocality.

univoltin [ynivɔltɛ̃], *a.m. Ent:* univoltine (silkworm).

univoltinisme [ynivɔltinism], *s.m. Ent:* production of one brood (only) a year.

univoque [ynivɔk], *a.* (*a*) univocal; unequivocal; (*b*) *Med:* **signes, symptômes, univoques,** pathognomonic symptoms; **remède u.,** specific remedy.

Untel [œ̃tɛl], *s.m. Hum:* **M.U.,** Mr So-and-So; **la famille U.,** the So-and-So's; *cf.* TEL 3.

unterwaldien, -ienne [untɛrvaldjɛ̃, -jɛn], *a. & s. Geog:* (native, inhabitant) of Unterwalden.

upas [ypɑːs], *s.m.* **1.** *Bot:* upas (tree). **2.** upas (juice).

upérisation [yperizasjɔ̃], *s.f.* uperization.

upériser [yperize], *v.tr.* to uperize.

uppercut [ypɛrkyt], *s.m. Box:* uppercut.

Upsal [ypsal], *Pr.n. Geog:* Uppsala.

upsilon [ypsilɔn], *s.m. Gr.Alph:* upsilon.

upupidés [ypypide], *s.m.pl. Orn:* Upupidae, the hoopoes.

uracile [yrasil], *s.m. Ch:* uracil.

uræus [yreys], *s.m.inv. Egyptian Ant:* uraeus.

uramile [yramil], *s.m. Ch:* uramil.
uranate [yranat], *s.m. Ch:* uranate.
urane [yran], *s.m. Ch:* uranium oxide; **verre d'u.**, uranium glass.
uraneux, -euse [yranø, -ø:z], *a.* uranous.
Uranie[1] [yrani], *Pr.n.f. Myth: Astr:* Urania.
uranie[2], *s.f. Ent:* (*genus*) Urania; **u. de Madagascar,** urania moth.
uranien, -ienne [yranjɛ̃, -jɛn], *a. & s. Geog:* (native, inhabitant) of the Canton of Uri.
uranifère [yranifɛ:r], *a. Geol:* uraniferous, uranium-bearing.
uraniidés [yraniide], *s.m.pl. Ent:* Uraniidae.
uraninite [yraninit], *s.f. Miner:* uraninite.
uranique [yranik], *a. Ch:* uranic.
uranisme [yranism], *s.m. Med:* uranism.
uraniste [yranist], *a. & s.m. Med:* uranist.
uranite [yranit], *s.f. Miner:* uranite.
uranium [yranjɔm], *s.m. Ch:* uranium; **u. enrichi,** enriched uranium.
uranocircite [yranɔsirsit], *s.f. Miner:* uranocircite.
uranographe [yranɔgraf], *s.m. Astr:* uranographer.
uranographie [yranɔgrafi], *s.f. Astr:* uranography.
uranographique [yranɔgrafik], *a. Astr:* uranographic(al).
uranophane [yranɔfan], *s.f. Miner:* uranophane.
uranopilite [yranɔpilit], *s.f. Miner:* uranopilite.
uranoplastie [yranɔplasti], *s.f. Surg:* uranoplasty, uraniscoplasty.
uranoscope [yranɔskɔp], *s.m. Ich:* uranoscopus, *F:* stargazer.
uranosphérite [yranɔsferit], *s.f. Miner:* uranosph(a)erite.
uranospinite [yranɔspinit], *s.f. Miner:* uranospinite.
uranostaphylorraphie [yranɔstafilɔrafi], *s.f. Surg:* uranostaphylorrhaphy.
uranothallite [yranɔtalit], *s.f. Miner:* uranothallite.
uranothorite [yranɔtɔrit], *s.f. Miner:* uranothorite.
uranotile [yranɔtil], *s.f. Miner:* uranotil(e).
Uranus [yranys], *Pr.n.m. Myth: Astr:* Uranus.
uranyle [yranil], *s.m. Ch:* uranyl.
urao [yrao], *s.m. Miner:* urao.
urate [yrat], *s.m. Ch:* urate.
urazole [yrazɔl], *s.m. Ch:* urazole.
urbain[1] [yrbɛ̃], *a.* **1.** urban (population, administration, etc.); town (house); **architecture urbaine,** town planning; *A:* **la garde urbaine,** the town guard; the watch; *Tp:* **appel u.,** exchange call; **central u.,** local exchange; **communication urbaine,** local call. **2.** urbane.
Urbain[2], *Pr.n.m.* Urban.
urbanification [yrbanifikasjɔ̃], *s.f.* planning (of new urban area).
urbanifier [yrbanifje], *v.tr.* to plan (new urban area).
urbanisation [yrbanizasjɔ̃], *s.f.* urbanization.
urbaniser [yrbanize], *v.tr.* **1.** to urbanize (rural district, etc.); **zone urbanisée,** residential area. **2. s'u.,** to become (more) polite, polished.
urbanisme [yrbanism], *s.m.* town planning.
urbaniste[1] [yrbanist]. **1.** *a.* urban; **architecture u.,** town architecture. **2.** *s.m. & f.* town planner.
urbaniste[2]. **1.** *s.m. Rel.H:* Urbanist; partisan of Pope Urban VI. **2.** *s.f. Ecc:* Urbanist (nun).
urbanité [yrbanite], *s.f.* (*a*) urbanity; refined courtesy; **avec u.,** urbanely; (*b*) *Iron:* insult; **après cet échange d'urbanités, ils se sont séparés,** after calling each other names, they went their own ways.
Urbin [yrbɛ̃], *Pr.n.* **le duché d'Urbin,** the Duchy of Urbino.
urbinate [yrbinat], *a. & s.m. & f. Geog:* (native, inhabitant) of Urbino.
urcéole [yrseɔl], *s.m. Bot:* urceolus.
urcéolé [yrseɔle], *a. Bot:* urceolate; pitcher-shaped.
urdu [yrdy], *a. & s.m. Ling:* Urdu.
ure [y:r], *s.m. Z:* urus, aurochs.
uréase [yrea:z], *s.f. Bio-Ch:* urease.
urédinales [uredinal], *s.f.pl.*, **urédinées** [yredine], *s.f.pl. Fung:* Uredinales, Uredineae.
urédo [yredo], *s.m. Fung:* uredo.
urédospore [yredɔspɔ:r], *s.f. Fung:* ured(i)ospore.
urée [yre], *s.f. Ch:* urea.
uréide [yreid], *s.m. Ch:* ureid.
uréique [yreik], *a. Ch:* ureal, ureic.
urémie [yremi], *s.f. Med:* uraemia.
urémigène [yremiʒɛn], *a. Med:* uremigenic.
urémique [yremik], *a. Med:* uraemic.
urena [yrena], *s.m. Bot:* urena.
uréo- [yreɔ], *pref.* ure(o)-.
uréomètre [yreɔmɛtr̥], *s.m. Med:* ureameter, ureometer.
uréométrie [yreɔmetri], *s.f. Med:* ureametry, ureometry.
urétéral, -aux [yreteral, -o], *a. Anat:* ureteral, ureteric.
uretère [yrtɛ:r], *s.m. Anat:* ureter.
urétérectomie [yreterɛktɔmi], *s.f. Surg:* ureterectomy.
urétérique [yreterik], *a. Anat:* ureteric.
urétérite [yreterit], *s.f. Med:* ureteritis.
urétérocystonéostomie [yreterɔsistɔneɔstɔmi], *s.f. Surg:* ureterocystoneostomy.
urétéroentérostomie [yreterɔɑ̃terɔstɔmi], *s.f. Surg:* ureteroenterostomy.
urétérolithiase [ureterɔlitja:ʒ], *s.f. Med:* ureterolithiasis.
urétérolithotomie [yreterɔlitɔtɔmi], *s.f. Surg:* ureterolithotomy.
urétéropyélite [yreterɔpjelit], *s.f. Med:* ureteropyelitis.
urétéropyélographie [yreterɔpjelɔgrafi], *s.f. Med:* ureteropyelography.
urétéropyélostomie [yreterɔpjelɔstɔmi], *s.f. Surg:* ureteropyelostomy.
urétérorraphie [yreterɔrafi], *s.f. Surg:* ureterorrhaphy.
urétérosigmoïdostomie [yreterɔzigmɔidɔstɔmi], *s.f. Surg:* ureterosigmoidostomy.
urétérostomie [ureterɔstɔmi], *s.f. Surg:* ureterostomy.
urétérotomie [yreterɔtɔmi], *s.f. Surg:* ureterotomy.
uréthan(n)e [yretan], *s.m. Ch:* urethan(e).
urétral, -aux [yretral, -o], *a. Anat:* urethral.
urètre [yrɛtr̥], *s.m. Anat:* urethra, *F:* the passage.
urétrectomie [yretrɛktɔmi], *s.f. Surg:* urethrectomy.
urétrite [yretrit], *s.f. Med:* urethritis.
urétro-bulbaire [yretrɔbylbɛ:r], *a. Anat:* urethrobulbar; *pl. urétro-bulbaires.*
urétrocèle [yretrɔsɛl], *s.f. Med:* urethrocele.
urétro-périnéal, -aux [yretrɔperineal, -o], *a. Anat:* urethroperineal.
urétroplastie [yretrɔplasti], *s.f. Surg:* urethroplasty.
urétro-rectal, -aux [yretrɔrɛktal, -o], *a. Anat:* urethrorectal.
urétrorragie [yretrɔraʒi], *s.f. Med:* urethrorrhagia.
urétrorraphie [yretrɔrafi], *s.f. Surg:* urethrorrhaphy.
urétroscope [yretrɔskɔp], *s.m.* urethroscope.
urétroscopie [yretrɔskɔpi], *s.f. Med:* urethroscopy.
urétroscopique [yretrɔskɔpik], *a.* urethroscopic.
urétrostomie [yretrɔstɔmi], *s.f. Surg:* urethrostomy.
urétrotome [yretrɔto:m], *s.m.* urethrotome.
urétrotomie [yretrɔtɔmi], *s.f. Surg:* urethrotomy; **u. externe,** external, perineal, urethrotomy.
urétro-vésical, -aux [yretrɔvezikal, -o], *a. Anat:* urethrovesical.
urf [yrf], *a. A:* swell (society, etc.).
urgemment [yrʒamɑ̃], *adv. A:* urgently.
urgence [yrʒɑ̃:s], *s.f.* urgency; (*a*) (*urgent character of sth.*) **comme si l'u. de leur travail leur interdisait des politesses,** as if the urgent nature of their work prevented them from being polite; **il y a grande u. à ce qu'il revienne,** his return is most urgently required; **il y a u.,** it is a matter of urgency; **à cause de l'u. des affaires,** on account of the pressure of business; *Pol:* **demander l'u.,** to call for a vote of urgency; (*b*) (*necessity for acting quickly*) **en cas d'u.,** in an emergency; **état d'u.,** state of emergency; **billet d'u. (pour admission à l'hôpital),** emergency order (for admission to hospital); **salle d'u.,** emergency ward; **trousse d'u., de première u.,** first-aid kit; *Med:* **accidenté de première u.,** emergency (case); *Jur:* **réparations d'u.,** tenantable repairs; (*c*) *adv. phr.* **d'u.,** immediately; **à adresser d'u.,** to be sent immediately; **veuillez répondre d'u.,** please reply without delay, *Com:* at your earliest convenience; **convoquer d'u. les sociétaires,** to call an extraordinary meeting of the shareholders; **il a été appelé d'u.,** he received an urgent call, was sent for urgently; **transporter qn d'u. à l'hôpital,** to rush s.o. to hospital; (*d*) **une u.,** an emergency.
urgencer [yrʒɑ̃se], *v.tr. Tg:* **1.** to advise at once. **2.** to hurry up.
urgent [yrʒɑ̃], *a.* (*a*) urgent, pressing (matter, need, etc.); immediate (need); **c'est u.,** it's urgent, a matter of urgency; **rien d'u. ne l'obligeait à sortir,** there was nothing urgent to force him to go out; **cas u.,** urgent case; emergency; **réclamer de façon urgente une action immédiate,** to press the urgency of immediate action; (*b*) *Post:* urgent; for immediate delivery.
urger [yrʒe], *v.i. F:* to be urgent; **ça urge!** it's got to be done quickly! **rien n'urge,** there's no desperate hurry.
urginea [yrʒinea], *s.m. Bot:* urginea.
urgonien, -ienne [yrgɔnjɛ̃, -jɛn], *a. & s.m. Geol:* Urgonian.
urial [yrjal], *s.m. Z:* urial.
uricase [yrika:z], *s.f. Bio-Ch:* uricase.
uricémie [yrisemi], *s.f. Med:* uricacidaemia, uricaemia.
urico-éliminateur, -trice [yrikɔeliminatœ:r, -tris], **uricosurique** [yrikɔzyrik], *a. & s.m. Med:* uricosuric (substance).
Urie [yri], *Pr.n.m. B.Hist:* Uriah.
Uriel [yrjɛl], *Pr.n.m. B.Hist: Lit:* Uriel.
urinaire [yrinɛ:r], *a. Anat:* urinary; **les voies urinaires,** the urinary system; the urinary organs.
urinal, -aux [yrinal, -o], *s.m. Med:* urinal, *F:* bottle.
urine [yrin], *s.f.* urine; **évacuer l'u.,** to urinate, to pass water; **analyse d'u.,** urinalysis.
uriner [yrine], *v.i.* to urinate; to make water; *P.N:* **défense d'u.,** commit no nuisance.
urineux, -euse [yrinø, -ø:z], *a.* urinous.
urinifère [yrinifɛ:r], *a. Anat: Med:* uriniferous.
urinoir [yrinwa:r], *s.m.* **1.** (public) urinal. **2.** = URINAL.
urinomètre [yrinɔmɛtr̥], *s.m. Med:* urinometer.
urique [yrik], *a.* uric (acid, concretion, etc.).
urite [yrit], *s.m. Ent:* urite.
urne [yrn], *s.f.* (*a*) urn; **u. sépulcrale,** cinerary urn; (*b*) **u. de scrutin,** ballot box; **aller aux urnes,** to go to the polls; (*c*) *Mth:* (*statistics*) **schémas d'u.,** urn schemata; (*d*) *Bot:* capsule; (*e*) *Bot:* ascidium.
uro- [yrɔ], *pref.* ur(o)-.
urobiline [yrɔbilin], *s.f. Ch:* urobilin.
urobilinurie [yrɔbilinyri], *s.f. Med:* urobilinuria.
uroc(h)ordés [yrɔkɔrde], *s.m.pl. Biol:* Urochorda(ta).
urochrome [yrɔkro:m], *s.m. Physiol:* urochrome.
urocoptidés [yrɔkɔptide], *s.m.pl. Moll:* Urocoptidae.
urocyon [yrɔsjɔ̃], *s.m. Z:* American grey fox; (*genus*) Urocyon.
urocystis [yrɔsistis], *s.m. Fung:* urocystis.
urodèle [yrɔdɛl], *s.m. Amph:* urodele, tailed amphibian; *pl.* **urodèles,** Urodela, Caudata.
urodynie [yrɔdini], *s.f. Med:* urodynia.
urogastre [yrɔgastr̥], *s.m. Crust:* urogaster.
urogénital, -aux [yrɔʒenital, -o], *a. Anat:* urogenital.
urographie [yrɔgrafi], *s.f. Med:* urography.
uroïde [yrɔid], *a.* caudiform, tail-like.
urolagnie [yrɔlaɲi], *s.f. Med:* urolagnia.
urolithe [yrɔlit], *s.m. Med:* urolith, urinary calculus.
urologie [yrɔlɔʒi], *s.f.* urology.
urologique [yrɔlɔʒik], *a. Med:* urologic.
urologiste [yrɔlɔʒist], **urologue** [yrɔlɔg], *s.m. & f.* urologist.
uromastix [yrɔmastiks], *s.m. Rept:* mastigure.
uromère [yrɔmɛ:r], *s.m. Ent:* urite.
uromètre [yrɔmɛtr̥], *s.m. Med:* ureameter, ureometer.
uromyces [yrɔmisɛs], *s.m. Fung:* uromyces.
uromys [yrɔmis], *s.m. Z:* uromys.
uropeltidés [yrɔpeltide], *s.m.pl. Rept:* Uropeltidae, the Indian shield-tail snakes.
uropode [yrɔpɔd], *s.m. Crust:* uropod.
uropoïétique [yrɔpɔjetik], *a. Physiol:* uropoietic (function).
uroptère [yrɔptɛ:r], *s.m. Crust:* uropteran.
uropyge [yrɔpi:ʒ], *s.m. Orn:* uropygium.
uropygial, -aux [yrɔpiʒjal, -o], *a. Orn:* uropygial (gland, etc.).
uropygien, -ienne [yrɔpiʒjɛ̃, -jɛn], *a. Orn:* **glande uropygienne,** oil-gland (on bird), preen gland, uropygial gland.
uropygium [yrɔpiʒjɔm], *s.m. Orn:* uropygium.
uroscopie [yrɔskɔpi], *s.f. Med:* ur(in)oscopy.
urostyle [yrɔstil], *s.m. Amph:* urostyle.
urotoxie [yrɔtɔksi], *s.f. Med:* urotoxia, urotoxicity, urotoxy.
urotoxique [yrɔtɔksik], *a. Med:* urotoxic.
uroxanique [yrɔksanik], *a. Ch:* **acide u.,** uroxanic acid.
ursidés [yrside], *s.m.pl. Z:* Ursidae.
ursigramme [yrsigram], *s.m. Telecom:* ursigram.
ursin [yrsɛ̃], *a. Z:* ursine.
Ursule [yrsyl], *Pr.n.f.* Ursula.
ursuline [yrsylin], *s.f. Ecc:* Ursuline (nun); *F:* **les Ursulines,** Ursuline convent-school.

urticacées [yrtikase], *s.f.pl. Bot:* Urticaceae.
urticaire [yrtikɛːr], *s.f. Med:* urticaria, nettlerash.
urticales [yrtikal], *s.f.pl. Bot:* Urticales.
urticant [yrtikɑ̃], *a.* urticating, stinging, (larva, plant); **poil u.,** nettling hair.
urticarien, -ienne [yrtikarjɛ̃, -jɛn], *a. Med:* urticarial.
urtication [yrtikasjɔ̃], *s.f. Med:* urtication.
urubu [yryby], *s.m. Orn:* urubu, black vulture.
Uruguay [yrygwɛ, -gyɛ, -gɛ], *Pr.n.m. Geog:* Uruguay (river or state).
uruguayen, -enne [yrygwɛjɛ̃, -ɛn; g(y)ɛjɛ̃, -ɛn], *a. & s. Geog:* Uruguayan.
urunday [yrœ̃dɛ], *s.m. Bot:* urunday.
urus [yrys], *s.m. Z:* urus, aurochs.
urutu [yryty], *s.m. Rept:* urutu.
urva [yrva], *s.m. Z:* urva.
us[1] [y], *s.m.pl. A:* usages; (*still used in*) **les us et coutumes** [yzekutym] **d'un pays,** the ways and customs of a country.
us[2] [ys], (the Lt. ending) us; *F:* **mots en us,** learned words; **un savant en us,** a pedant (*A:* who Latinized his name).
usable [yzabl̩], *a.* liable to deteriorate through wear; liable to wear out.
usage [yzaːʒ], *s.m.* **1.** (*a*) use, using, employment; **mettre un article en u.,** to put an article into use; **faire u. de qch.,** to use, make use of, sth.; **faire u. d'un droit,** to avail oneself of a right; **faire bon u. de qch.,** to make good use of sth.; to put sth. to good use; **faire mauvais u. de qch.,** to make bad use of sth.; to put sth. to (a) bad use; to misuse sth.; *Pharm:* **pour l'u. externe,** for external application; **servir à plusieurs usages,** to have various uses; to answer various purposes; **article à mon u.,** article for my personal use; **à l'u. des écoles,** for the use of schools, for use in schools; **article d'u.,** article for everyday use; **article destiné à des usages pratiques,** article intended for practical purposes; **à usages multiples,** multi-purpose (equipment, etc.); versatile (tool, etc.); *attrib.* **véhicule tous usages,** all-purpose, general-purpose, vehicle; (*in advertisement*) (**à louer**) **local à u. de bureau,** office space available, to let; **s'améliorer à l'u.,** to improve with use; **avoir l'u. de,** to have the use of; **perdre, retrouver, l'u. de,** to lose, regain, the use of; **il a perdu l'u. de la parole,** he lost the power of speech; **hors d'u.,** (i) out of service; (ii) obsolete (word, etc.); **porte hors d'u.,** disused door; *Ling:* **coefficient d'u. d'un mot,** frequency index of a word, word-frequency index; **u. vicieux d'une locution,** wrong use of a phrase; **le bel u.** = the King's (Queen's) English; (*b*) wear, service (of garments, furniture, etc.); **de bon u.,** lasting; **biens, produits, d'u.,** durable goods; **faire un bon u., faire de l'u.,** to wear well, to do good service; **chaussettes d'u., de bon u.,** hard-wearing socks; **garanti à l'u.,** guaranteed to wear well. **2.** *Jur:* (*a*) **droit d'u. continu,** (right of) user; **se réserver l'u. de qch.,** to reserve the user of sth., the right to use sth.; **droit, clause, d'u.,** customary right, clause; (*b*) common of pasture; common of estovers. **3.** (*a*) usage; use (and wont); custom, practice; **usages locaux,** local customs; **coutume consacrée par l'u.,** time-honoured custom; **aller à l'encontre de l'u.,** to act unconventionally; **phrases, paroles, d'u.,** conversational commonplaces; *Sch:* **orthographe d'u.,** dictionary spelling (of words) (as opposed to the concords); **je peux vous fournir les références d'u.,** I can supply you with the usual references, with the customary references; **on me fit les compliments d'u.,** I was paid the habitual compliments; **comme d'u.,** as usual; **selon l'u., suivant l'u.,** according to custom; **il est d'u. de** + *inf.*, it is usual, customary, to . . .; **il est passé en u. que** (+ *sub.*), it has become the custom that . . .; (*b*) practice, experience; *Prov:* **u. rend maître,** practice makes perfect; **une langue ne s'apprend que par l'u.,** a language is learnt only by practice; **avoir l'u. de qch.,** to be experienced, used to, sth.; **l'u. du monde,** good breeding; **avoir de l'u., avoir l'u. du monde,** to have a knowledge of the ways of society; **manquer d'u.,** to lack breeding; **vieille famille où l'on a encore quelques usages,** old family in which a certain amount of formality has been retained; **c'est l'u.,** it's the done thing. **4.** *Ecc: A:* **les usages,** the church books (as a whole).
usagé [yzaʒe], *a.* **1.** (article) that has been used, worn; secondhand (car, etc.); **non u.,** new; **vêtement u.,** garment that has seen good service; **plaisanterie usagée,** well-worn joke; *F:* **elle a l'air u.,** she's looking jaded, tired. **2.** *A:* well-bred, well-mannered (person).
usager, -ère [yzaʒe, -ɛːr]. **1.** *s.* (*a*) *Jur:* commoner (*i.e.* one who enjoys right of common, common of pasturage); (*b*) user (of sth.); **les usagers de la route,** those who use the roads, road users. **2.** *a.* (*of articles*) of everyday use; *Cust:* **effets usagers,** articles for personal use; personal effects.
usance [yzɑ̃ːs], *s.f.* **1.** *Com:* usance; **lettre (de change) à une u., à deux usances,** bill payable in one, in two, months. **2.** *For:* time elapsed since the last cutting (of a coppice).
usant [yzɑ̃], *a.* **1.** wearing (life, work); abrading (powder, dust); **la vie sous les tropiques est très usante,** life in the tropics soon wears a man out. **2.** *Jur:* (*of son or daughter of full age and without parents*) **usant(e) et jouissant(e) de ses droits,** acting in his (or her) own right.
Usbek [yzbɛk]. **1.** *a. & s. Geog:* Uzbek. **2.** *s.m. Ling:* **l'u.,** Uzbek.
Uscoque [yskɔk], *s.m.* = USKOK.
usé [yze], *a.* (*of metal, stone, etc.*) worn; (*of garments*) worn (out); shabby, threadbare; (*of rope*) frayed; **personne usée par le travail, usée de corps,** person worn out by work; **visage u. par le chagrin,** careworn face; **u. par le temps,** time-worn; **sujet u.,** hackneyed, stale, threadbare, trite, trivial, subject; **c'est u.!** that's an old one! **cheval u.,** worn-out horse, overridden horse; **eaux usées,** waste water, discharge (of factory); **huile usée,** dirty oil; *Agr:* **terre usée,** exhausted land.
user [yze]. I. **1.** *v.ind.tr.* **u. de qch.,** to use sth., make use of sth.; **u. bien, mal, de qch.,** to make good use, bad use, of sth.; **u. d'une permission,** to avail oneself of a permission; **u. de son droit,** to exercise one's right; **u. de tous les artifices pour . . .,** to resort to every trick in order to . . .; **u. de force, de violence,** to resort to force, to violence; **u. de douceur,** to deal gently (with s.o.); **u. de son influence,** to use one's influence; **u. de moyens frauduleux,** to have recourse, to resort, to fraudulent means; **en bien u. avec qn,** to treat s.o. well; **en mal u. avec qn,** to treat s.o. badly; **en u. familièrement avec qn,** to treat s.o. with familiarity; to be on familiar terms with s.o.; **est-ce ainsi que vous en usez avec lui?** is that how you deal with him? how you treat him? **les diplomates en usent entre eux avec une extrême délicatesse,** diplomats act with extreme punctiliousness towards one another. **2.** *v.tr.* (*a*) to use (up), consume (sth.); **u. toutes ses provisions,** to use up all one's provisions; **ces vieilles machines usent beaucoup de charbon,** these old engines take, burn, a great deal of coal, are very heavy on coal, eat (up the) coal; (*b*) to wear (sth.) (out, away, down); to abrade; **u. ses vêtements,** to wear out one's clothes; **u. ses yeux à force de lire,** to spoil, ruin, one's eyes by reading; **u. sa jeunesse,** to waste one's youth; **s'u. de travail,** to wear oneself out with work; **il s'est usé à la tâche,** he wore himself out on the job; *Phot:* **u. un cliché,** to rub down a negative.
II. **user,** *s.m. A:* **étoffe d'un bon u.,** material that wears well; **homme bon à l'u.,** man (i) who improves on acquaintance, (ii) pleasant to deal with; **amitié que le temps et l'u. ont affermie,** friendship which time and habit have strengthened.
s'user, to wear (away); **mon habit s'use,** my coat is showing signs of wear; **ce tissu s'use vite,** this material wears out quickly; **ma vue s'use tous les jours,** my eyesight is growing worse every day; **sa résistance s'usera à la fin,** his resistance will wear down, break down, in due course.
useur, -euse [yzœːr, -øːz]. **1.** (*a*) *a.* that uses (sth.) up, wears (sth.) out; (*b*) *s.* pers. who uses (sth.) up, wears (sth.) out. **2.** *s. Cer: O:* grinder, polisher.
usinabilité [yzinabilite], *s.f. Ind:* suitability for machining.
usinage [yzinaːʒ], *s.m. Metalw:* machining, tooling (of castings, etc.); machine finishing; **u. chimique,** shaping of parts in a chemical bath; **cela compliquerait l'u.,** it would make manufacture difficult.
usine [yzin], *s.f.* works, factory, mill, plant; **établir une grande u.,** to set up a large factory; **u. à gaz,** gasworks; **u. marémotrice,** tidal power station; *El: A:* **u. centrale,** power station; *Tex:* **u. de tissage,** weaving mill; **u. hydraulique,** water-works; *Metalw:* **u. de laminage,** rolling mill; *Metall:* **u. d'affinage,** iron refinery; **u. de dosage (des agrégats de béton),** batching plant; **prix sortie d'u.,** price ex works; **u.-pilote,** pilot plant; **ouvrier d'u.,** factory worker, factory hand, mill hand; **ouvrière d'u.,** (female) factory hand; **directeur d'u.,** works manager; **apprentissage, formation, en u.,** in-plant training.
usiner [yzine]. **1.** *v.tr. Metalw:* to machine, to tool (castings, etc.); to machine-finish (parts); **parties usinées,** bright parts. **2.** *v.tr. A:* to manufacture. **3.** *v.i. F:* to work hard, to slog; **ça usine là-dedans,** they're hard at it.
usineur [yzinœːr], *s.m.* **1.** machine-tool operator; machinist. **2.** *F:* slogger.
usinier, -ière [yzinje, -jɛːr]. **1.** *s.m.* manufacturer; mill owner. **2.** *a.* relating to factories; **groupe u.,** group of factories.
usité [yzite], *a.* (*of customs, articles, etc.*) used; in use, current; **le mot n'est plus u.,** the word is obsolete; **mot très u.,** word in common use, in current use.
Uskok [yskɔk], *s.m. Hist:* Uskok; Serbian refugee.
usnée [ysne], *s.f. Moss:* tree moss; (*genus*) Usnea; **u. barbue,** greybeard lichen, beard lichen, beard moss.
usquebac [yskəbak], *s.m. Dist:* usquebaugh.
ussellois, -oise [ysɛlwa, waːz], *a. & s. Geog:* (native, inhabitant) of Ussel.
ustensile [ystɑ̃sil], *s.m.* utensil, implement, tool; **u. de ménage, de cuisine,** household utensil, kitchen utensil; **ustensiles de jardinage,** gardening tools, implements.
ustilaginales [ystilaʒinal], *s.f.pl. Fung:* Ustilaginales.
ustilaginées [ystilaʒine], *s.f.pl. Fung:* Ustilaginaceae.
ustilago [ystilago], *s.m. Fung:* ustilago.
ustion [ystjɔ̃], *s.f. Med: A:* burning; ustion; application of a cautery.
usucaper [yzykape], *v.tr. Jur:* to usucapt.
usucapion [yzykapjɔ̃], *s.f. Jur:* usucap(t)ion.
usuel, -elle [yzɥɛl], *a.* usual, customary, habitual, common, ordinary (remedy, term, expression, etc.); everyday; **l'anglais u.,** everyday English; **connaissances usuelles,** knowledge of everyday things. **2.** *s.m. F:* **les usuels,** reference books.
usuellement [yzɥɛlmɑ̃], *adv.* usually, habitually, commonly, ordinarily.
usufructuaire [yzyfryktɥɛːr], *a. Jur:* usufructuary (right, etc.).
usufruit [yzyfrɥi], *s.m. Jur:* usufruct, life interest; **plein u. de qch.,** full right of user of sth.
usufruitier, -ière [yzyfrɥitje, -jɛːr], *a. & s. Jur:* usufructuary; *s.* tenant for life; beneficial occupant.
usuraire [yzyrɛːr], *a.* usurious, exorbitant (interest, etc.); usurious (contract).
usurairement [yzyrɛrmɑ̃], *adv.* usuriously.
usure[1] [yzyːr], *s.f.* usury; (*a*) *A:* lending money at interest; (*b*) charging of illegal rates of interest; **pratiquer l'u.,** to practise usury; (*c*) exorbitant interest; *B:* **tu ne prêteras point à u. à ton frère,** thou shalt not lend upon usury to thy brother; (*d*) **rendre un bienfait avec u.,** to repay a service with interest.
usure[2], *s.f.* (*a*) wear (and tear) (of furniture, machinery, etc.); **u. unilatérale,** wearing one-sided; one-sided wear; *Tchn:* **pièce u.,** wearing part; *Aut:* (*of tyres*) **u. de roulement,** tread wear; *Com:* **u. en magasin,** shelf depreciation; *Phot:* **u. locale,** local rubbing down (of the negative); *Ling:* **u. phonique,** phonetic erosion; **u. naturelle,** (i) *Mec.E: etc:* normal wear; (ii) *Jur:* fair wear and tear; **résister à l'u.,** to stand wear and tear; **u. anormale, prématurée,** abnormal, premature, wear; **tissu qui résiste à l'u.,** material that wears well; **u. par frottement,** attrition; *Mil: Av: Navy:* **taux d'u.,** attrition rate; **tir d'u.,** attrition fire; **guerre d'u.,** war of attrition; **combat d'u.,** wearing down engagement; *F:* **je l'aurai à l'u.,** I'll wear him down; (*b*) *Geol: etc:* abrasion; erosion.
usurier, -ière [yzyrje, -jɛːr]. **1.** *s.* usurer; *F:* Shylock. **2.** *a.* usurious (moneylender, etc.); **banquier u.,** moneylender.
usurpateur, -trice [yzyrpatœːr, -tris]. **1.** *s.* usurper, *occ.f.* usurpress. **2.** *a.* (*a*) usurping; (*b*) encroaching.
usurpation [yzyrpasjɔ̃], *s.f.* (*a*) usurpation, unauthorized assumption (of right, etc.); (*b*) encroaching, encroachment (**de,** on).
usurpatoire [yzyrpatwaːr], *a.* usurpatory.
usurper [yzyrpe]. **1.** *v.tr.* (*a*) to usurp (throne, title of book, etc.) (**sur,** from); (*b*) to encroach upon, usurp (s.o.'s rights, etc.); **réputation usurpée,** usurped reputation. **2.** *v.i.* **u. sur les droits de qn, sur ses voisins,** to enroach, usurp, (up)on s.o.'s rights, upon one's neighbours.
ut [yt], *s.m.inv. Mus:* **1.** (the note) C; **ut dièse,** C sharp; **clef d'ut,** C clef; **clef d'ut quatrième ligne,** tenor clef; **morceau en ut,** piece in C. **2.** do(h) (in the fixed do system); (**do,** *and not* **ut,** *is used in solmization*).

uta [yta], *s.m. Med:* uta.

utérin [yterɛ̃], *a. Med:* uterine (complaint, etc.); *Jur:* **frère u., sœur utérine,** uterine brother, sister; half-brother, half-sister, on the mother's side.

utéromanie [yterɔmani], *s.f. Med:* nymphomania.

utéro-ovarien, -ienne [yterɔɔvarjɛ̃, -jɛn], *a. Anat:* utero-ovarian; *pl.* **utéro-ovarien(ne)s.**

utéro-placentaire [yterɔplasɑ̃tɛːr], *a. Obst:* utero-placental; *pl.* **utéro-placentaires.**

utéro-sacré [yterɔsakre], *a. Anat:* uterosacral; *pl.* **utéro-sacré(e)s.**

utéro-vaginal, -aux [yterɔvaʒinal, -o], *a. Anat:* uterovaginal.

utérus [yterys], *s.m. Anat:* uterus, womb.

utile [ytil], *(a) a.* useful, serviceable; **si je puis vous être u. en, à, quelque chose,** if I can be of any use, service, assistance, to you; **en quoi puis-je vous être u.?** what can I do for you? how can I help you? **puis-je être u. en rien?** can I do anything? can I be of any use? **il serait u. de l'avertir,** it would be as well to let him know; **ainsi qu'on le jugera u.,** as shall be deemed advisable; **cela m'a été bien u.,** it came in very handy, stood me in good stead; **en temps u.,** in (good) time; within the prescribed time; duly; **je vous répondrai en temps u.,** I shall answer you in due course; **prendre toutes dispositions utiles,** to make all necessary arrangements; **ne pas juger u. de (faire qch.),** to see no point in (doing sth.); **se rendre u.,** to make oneself useful; **qu'a-t-il fait d'u.?** what has he done that was of any use? **c'est un homme u. à connaître,** he is a useful man to know; **dictionnaire u. à consulter,** useful dictionary to consult; *Mec:* **effet u.,** useful effect, effective power; *Mec:* **charge u.,** useful load; *(b) s.m.* **joindre l'u. à l'agréable,** to combine business with pleasure; *A:* **je ferai l'u.,** I shall do whatever is required.

utilement [ytilmɑ̃], *adv.* usefully; serviceably; advantageously, with advantage; profitably; **intervenir u.,** to intervene effectively; **on pourrait u. écrire un livre sur . . .,** one might usefully write a book on . . .; **employer u. son temps,** to use one's time profitably; **pourrais-je u. lui écrire?** is it any use my writing to him?

utilisable [ytilizabl], *a.* utilizable, capable of being turned to account; usable, fit for use;

billet u. pour, dans, tous les trains, ticket available for all trains.

utilisateur, -trice [ytilizatœːr, -tris]. **1.** *a.* utilizing. **2.** *s.* user, utilizer.

utilisation [ytilizasjɔ̃], *s.f.* utilization (of sth.); turning (of sth.) to account, use; **u. en commun,** joint use; *Elcs:* (computers) **taux d'u.,** utilization ratio; **temps d'u.,** usage time.

utiliser [ytilize], *v.tr.* to use; to utilize; to make use of (sth.); to turn (sth.) to account; **j'ai utilisé l'argent à rebâtir ma maison,** I used the money to rebuild my house; **u. habilement qch.,** to make skilful use of sth.; to make the best of sth.

s'utiliser, to make oneself useful.

utilitaire [ytilitɛːr], *a. & s.m. & f.* utilitarian; *Aut:* **véhicules utilitaires,** commercial vehicles.

utilitairement [ytilitɛrmɑ̃], *adv.* from a utilitarian point of view.

utilitarisme [ytilitarism], *s.m.* utilitarianism.

utilitariste [ytilitarist], *a. & s.m. & f. Phil:* utilitarian.

utilité [ytilite], *s.f.* **1.** utility, use(fulness); useful purpose; service; **u. marginale,** marginal utility; **être d'une grande u.,** to be of great use, of great utility, to be; *F:* to come in, very useful; **outil de première u.,** essential tool; **cela ne m'est d'aucune u.,** it is no earthly use to me; **u. qu'il y aurait à faire qch.,** advisability of doing sth.; **sans u.,** useless(ly); **complication sans u.,** complication that serves no useful purpose; **s'entremettre sans grande u.,** to intervene to little purpose; *Adm: Com: A:* **articles d'u. sociale,** utility goods; *Jur:* **être d'u. publique,** to be in the public interest; **expropriation pour cause d'u. publique,** expropriation for public purposes. **2.** *Th:* utility actor, actress, utility man; **les utilités,** the small parts, minor parts; **jouer le utilités,** (i) to play small parts; (ii) *F:* to play second fiddle (in an enterprise, etc.). **3.** *Petroleum Ind:* **utilités,** utilities; **besoins en utilités,** utility requirements.

Utique [ytik], *Pr.n.f. A.Geog:* Utica; **Caton d'U.,** Cato of Utica.

uto-aztèque [ytɔaztɛk], *a. & s.m. Geog: Ling:* Uto-Aztecan; *pl.* **uto-aztèques.**

utopie [ytɔpi], *s.f.* utopia; **créer des utopies,** to create utopias, to build castles in Spain.

utopique [ytɔpik], **utopiste** [ytɔpist]. **1.** *s.m. & f.* utopian, utopist. **2.** *a.* utopian.

utraquisme [ytrakɥism], *s.m. Rel.H:* utraquism.

utraquiste [ytrakɥist], *s.m. Rel.H:* utraquist, Calixtin.

Utrecht [ytrɛk(t)], *Pr.n. Geog:* Utrecht; *Tex:* **velours d'U.,** Utrecht velvet.

utriculaire [ytrikylɛːr]. **1.** *a. Nat.Hist:* utricular. **2.** *s.f. Bot:* utricularia, bladderwort, pop-weed.

utriculariacées [ytrikylarjase], *s.f.pl. Bot:* Utriculariaceae.

utricule [ytrikyl], *s.m. Nat.Hist:* utricle.

utriculé [ytrikyle], **utriculeux, -euse** [ytrikylø, -øːz], *a. Bot:* utricular.

utriforme [ytrifɔrm], *a. O:* utriform, leathern-bottle shaped.

uva [yva], *s.m. Bot: Pharm:* uva.

uval, -aux [yval, -o], *a.* of, pertaining to, grapes; *Med:* **cure uvale,** grape cure.

uvarovite [yvarɔvit], *s.f. Miner:* uvarovite, uvarowite.

uva-ursi [yvayrsi], *s.m. Bot: Pharm:* uva ursi; bearberry.

uvéal, -aux [yveal, -o], *a. Anat:* uveal.

uvée [yve], *s.f. Anat:* uvea.

uvéite [yveit], *s.f. Med:* uveitis, iritis.

uvéoparotidite [yveɔparɔtidit], *s.f. Med:* uveo-parotitis.

uvette [yvɛt], *s.f. Bot:* ephedra, shrubby horsetail.

uvifère [yvifɛːr], *a. Bot:* grape-bearing.

uviforme [yvifɔrm], *a. Bot:* grape-shaped.

uviothérapie [yvjɔterapi], *s.f. Med:* ultra-violet therapy.

uvitique [yvitik], *a. Ch:* **acide u.,** uvitic acid.

uvulaire [yvylɛːr]. **1.** *a. (a) Anat:* uvular; *(b) Ling:* uvular. **2.** *s.f. Bot:* uvularia.

uvule [yvyl], *s.f. Anat:* uvula.

uvulite [yvylit], *s.f. Med:* uvulitis.

uxoricide [yksɔrisid], *s.m.* uxoricide.

uxorien, -ienne [yksɔrjɛ̃, -jɛn], *a.* **1.** uxorial. **2.** **neveu u.,** wife's nephew.

uzbek [yzbɛk]. **1.** *a. & s. Geog:* Uzbek. **2.** *s.m. Ling:* **l'u.,** Uzbek.

Uzbékistan [yzbekistɑ̃], *Pr.n.* **(République socialiste soviétique d')U.,** Uzbekistan, Uzbek Soviet Socialist Republic.

uzétien, -ienne [yzesjɛ̃, -jɛn], *a. & s. Geog:* (native, inhabitant) of Uzès [yzɛs].

V

V, v [ve], *s.m.* (the letter) V, v; **double v**(é), W, w.; *Tp:* **V comme Victor,** V for Victor; **rainure en V,** V-shaped groove; **support en V,** V-block; *I.C.E:* **moteur à cylindres en V,** V-type engine; *Geog:* **vallée (à profil) en V.,** V-shaped valley.

V-1, V-2 [veœ̃, vedø], *s.m. Mil: Ball:* (1939-45), V-1, V-2 (missiles).

vaalite [valit], *s.f. Miner:* vaalite.

vacance [vakɑ̃ːs], *s.f.* **1.** (*a*) vacancy; abeyance (of post); vacant office, post; **déclarer la v. d'une chaire,** to declare a (professorial) chair vacant; *O:* **j'ai à suppléer à deux vacances dans mes bureaux,** I have two vacancies, two vacant posts, to fill in my office; **chaque v. du trône était suivie d'une guerre civile,** every vacancy of the throne was the occasion for civil war; every time the throne was vacant a civil war followed; (*b*) **v. (de l'esprit),** vacuity. **2.** *pl.* vacation, holidays; (*of parliament*) recess; *Sch:* **les grandes vacances,** the summer holidays; (*of university*) the long vacation; **le moment des vacances,** holiday time; **nos vacances commencent, on entre en vacances, le quatre,** we break up on the fourth; **entrée en vacances,** breaking up; **la Chambre entre en vacances le quatre,** Parliament rises on the fourth; **vacances passées à pêcher, à excursionner à pied, à faire du camping, etc.,** fishing, hiking, camping, etc., holidays; **vacances de neige,** winter holiday; **en vacance(s), on holiday; un jour de vacance(s),** a (day's) holiday; **vacances judiciaires,** vacation, recess (of law courts).

vacancier, -ière [vakɑ̃sje, -jɛːr], *s.* holiday maker; *U.S.* vacationist.

vacant [vakɑ̃], *a.* **1.** vacant, unoccupied, tenantless (house, etc.); **place vacante,** (i) vacant seat; (ii) vacancy (of office); **trône v.,** vacant throne. **2.** *Jur:* **succession vacante,** estate in abeyance, without a claimant.

vacarme [vakarm], *s.m.* uproar, din, racket, hubbub; **faire du v.,** to create an uproar, a disturbance; *F:* to kick up a row, a shindy.

vacataire [vakatɛːr], *s.m. & f.* person employed for free-lance job.

vacation [vakasjɔ̃], *s.f.* **1.** *Jur:* (*a*) attendance, sitting (of officials); day's sale (at an auction); (*b*) *pl.* fees (of lawyer, etc.); **toucher de fortes vacations,** to pocket large fees; **vacations supplémentaires,** extra fees. **2.** *pl. Jur:* vacation, recess (of law courts); **chambre des vacations,** vacation court. **3.** abeyance (of succession, rights, etc.). **4.** *Adm:* period of duty; hours of service.

vaccaire [vakɛːr], *s.f. Bot:* vaccaria, *F:* cow-herb.

vaccin [vaksɛ̃]. **1.** (*a*) *s.m. Med:* vaccine; lymph; **v. antivariolique,** smallpox vaccine; **v. antiamaril,** yellow fever vaccine; **v. tétravalent,** tetravalent vaccine; (*b*) *F:* vaccination mark. **2.** *a.* vaccine (lymph, etc.).

vaccinable [vaksinabl], *a. Med:* vaccinable, who can be vaccinated.

vaccinal, -aux [vaksinal, -o], *a. Med:* vaccinal; **pustules vaccinales,** pustules of vaccinia, vaccine pustules; **réactions vaccinales,** vaccine reactions.

vaccinateur [vaksinatœːr], *s.m.* vaccinator.

vaccination [vaksinasjɔ̃], *s.f. Med:* (*a*) vaccination; (*b*) inoculation; **v. préventive, immunisante,** protective inoculation.

vaccine [vaksin], *s.f.* **1.** (*a*) *Vet:* vaccinia, cowpox; (*b*) *Med:* inoculated cowpox. **2.** *A:* = VACCINATION.

vaccinelle [vaksinɛl], *s.f. Med:* vacciniola, vaccinia, *F:* take.

vacciner [vaksine], *v.tr. Med:* (*a*) to vaccinate; **v. contre la diphtérie,** to immunize against diphtheria; (*b*) to inoculate; **se faire v.,** to get vaccinated, inoculated (**contre,** against); *F:* **être vacciné contre les désagréments du métier,** to become immune to the drawbacks of the job.

vaccinide [vaksinid], *s.f. Med:* vaccinid(e); generalized vaccinal rash.

vaccinier [vaksinje], *s.m. Bot:* vaccinium, blueberry.

vaccinifère [vaksinifɛːr], *a. Med: Vet:* vacciniferous.

vaccinogène [vaksinoʒɛn], *a.* vaccinogenic, lymph-producing.

vaccinoïde [vaksinoid], *a. & s.f. Med:* **1.** *s.f.* vacciniola, vaccinia. **2.** *a.* vacciniform, vaccinoid.

vaccinostyle [vaksinostil], *s.m. Med:* vaccinostyle.

vaccinothérapie [vaksinoterapi], *s.f. Med:* vaccinotherapy, vaccine therapy.

vache [vaʃ], *s.f.* **1.** (*a*) cow; **v. laitière, v. à lait,** milch cow; **vaches laitières,** dairy cattle; *P:* **v. à lait,** mug, sucker; **v. à eau,** canvas water carrier; *Lit:* **c'est la période des vaches maigres,** this is the time of the lean kine; *F:* **le grand chemin des vaches,** the beaten track; *F:* **le plancher des vaches,** dry land, terra firma; *P:* (*not used in polite conversation*) **il pleut comme v. qui pisse,** it's raining cats and dogs; *F:* **pleurer comme une v.,** to weep copiously; *P:* **prendre la v. et son veau,** to marry a woman made pregnant by another man; *F:* **parler français comme une v. espagnole,** to murder the French language; *F:* **manger de la v. enragée,** to rough it, to have a hard time of it; **coup de pied en v.,** (i) *Equit:* cow kick; (ii) *F:* underhand trick; stab in the back; *Metall: Com:* **côtes de v.,** slit iron; *Nau:* **nœud de v.,** granny (knot); (*b*) (i) *Z:* **v. de Tartarie,** yak; **v. marine** (= LAMANTIN, DUGONG, MORSE), sea cow (= manatee, dugong, walrus); (ii) *Ich:* **v. de mer,** cowfish, horned box fish; (*c*) *P:* (grosse) **v.,** (i) fat woman, great cow of a woman; old cow; (ii) *O:* loose woman; bitch; (iii) policeman; **à bas les vaches!** shoot the bloody cops! (iv) (*of man*) swine; (v) **j'ai une v. de faim,** I'm so hungry I could eat a horse; **c'est une v. de jolie fille,** she comes out in all the right places; (*d*) *A: P:* **coup v.,** dirty trick; (*of pers.*) **être v.,** (i) to be sarcastic; (ii) to be bloody-minded; **être v. avec qn,** to be a swine to s.o.; *Sch: etc:* **c'est drôlement v. ça,** that's a bastard! **allez, (ne) sois pas v.!** come on, be a sport! **2.** (*a*) cowhide; **cuir de v.,** neat's leather, cowhide; **valise en v.,** leather suitcase; (*b*) *A:* leather covering (on coach, to protect luggage); boot (of stage coach).

vachement [vaʃmɑ̃], *adv. P:* tremendously; **c'est v. difficile,** it's damned hard; **c'est v. bien,** it's dead good.

vacher [vaʃe], *s.m.* cowhand, cowherd, cowman; *U.S.:* cowboy.

vachère [vaʃɛːr], *s.f.* **1.** cow girl. **2.** cattle float.

vacherie [vaʃri], *s.f.* **1.** *A: & Dial:* (*a*) (cow) byre, cowshed; (*b*) dairy farm. **2.** *P:* (*a*) dirty trick; (*b*) **il ne dit que des vacheries,** he's always making stinging remarks, cracks.

vacherin [vaʃrɛ̃], *s.m.* **1.** sweet made with meringue and (ice) cream. **2.** cheese made in Franche-Comté.

vachette [vaʃɛt], *s.f.* (*a*) calf; (*b*) calfskin (leather).

vaciet [vasjɛ], *s.m. Bot:* bilberry, whortleberry.

vacillant [vasijɑ̃], *a.* **1.** unsteady (table, etc.); unsteady, flickering (flame, etc.); shaky (hand); uncertain, staggering (gait, etc.); **échelle vacillante,** wobbly ladder. **2.** vacillating; wavering, undecided (mind, etc.); uncertain (health). **3.** *Bot:* versatile (anther).

vacillation [vasijasjɔ̃], *s.f.* **1.** unsteadiness; wobbling (of table, ladder, etc.); flickering (of flame, etc.); bobbing up and down (of boat); (*radar*) jitter. **2.** vacillation, shilly-shallying; wavering (of opinion).

vacillatoire [vasijatwaːr], *a.* vacillatory.

vacillement [vasijmɑ̃], *s.m.* = VACILLATION 1.

vaciller [vasije], *v.i.* **1.** (*a*) to be unsteady; **v. en marchant,** to stagger, lurch, reel; **entrer sortir, en vacillant,** to stagger in, out; to lurch in, out; **table qui vacille,** wobbly table; **faire v. la table,** to shake the table; **il vacille sur ses jambes,** he is shaky, groggy, on his legs; **sa mémoire vacille,** his memory is uncertain; (*b*) (*of light*) to flicker; (*of stars*) to twinkle. **2.** to vacillate, waver; to be undecided; to shilly-shally.

va-comme-je-te-pousse [vakɔmʒtəpus], *s.m. & f. inv. F:* (*a*) easy-going person; (*b*) *adv.phr.* **à la va-comme-je-te-pousse,** haphazardly; in a happy-go-lucky way; **enfant élevé à la va-comme-je-te-pousse,** child that has been dragged up; **écrire à la va-comme-je-te-pousse,** to write in a slapdash manner, way.

vacuiste [vakɥist], *a. & s. Phil:* vacuist.

vacuité [vakɥite], *s.f.* vacuity, emptiness.

vacuolaire [vakɥolɛːr], *a.* **1.** *Biol:* vacuolar. **2.** *Bot: Geol:* vesicular.

vacuole [vakɥɔl], *s.f.* **1.** *Biol:* vacuole; **formation de vacuoles,** vacuolation, vacuolization. **2.** *Bot: Geol:* vesicle.

vacuolisation [vakɥɔlizasjɔ̃], *s.f. Biol:* vacuolation, vacuolization.

vacuoliser [vakɥɔlize], *v.tr. Biol:* to vacuolate.

vacuomètre [vakɥɔmɛtr], *s.m. Ph:* vacuum gauge.

vacuum [vakɥɔm], *s.m.* vacuum.

va-de-la-gueule [vadlagœl], *s.m. & f.inv. P:* (*a*) guzzler; (*b*) big mouth, loud mouth.

va-de-l'avant [vadlavɑ̃], *s.m.inv. F:* dynamic and unscrupulous man; thruster.

vade-mecum [vademekɔm], *s.m.inv.* vade mecum.

va-Dieu (à la) [alavadjø], *adv.phr. A:* in a happy-go-lucky way.

Vadius [vadjys], *s.m. Lit:* pedant (*from the character in Molière's les Femmes Savantes*).

vadrouillard, -arde [vadrujaːr, -ard], *F:* **1.** *a.* given to roving. **2.** *s.* = VADROUILLE 2 (*b*).

vadrouille [vadruːj], *s.f.* **1.** (*a*) *Nau:* pitch-mop; (*b*) *Nau:* (deck-) swab; (*c*) *Fr.C: Dom.Ec:* mop. **2.** *F:* (*a*) **faire une v., aller en v.,** to go on the spree, on the loose; to gallivant; (*b*) *A:* roving fellow or woman on the spree; gadabout; (*c*) *A:* party out on the spree.

vadrouiller [vadruje], *v.i. F:* (*a*) to gallivant; to go on the loose; (*b*) **v. de par le monde,** to roam, rove, about the world; to knock about the world.

vadrouilleur, -euse [vadrujœːr, -øːz], *s. P:* **1.** rollicker. **2.** roamer.

va-et-vient [vaevjɛ̃], *s.m.inv.* **1.** (*a*) movement to and fro; (i) backward and forward motion, reciprocating motion, *U.S:* back and forth motion; (ii) see-saw motion; (*of ferry boat, etc.*) **faire le va-et-vient entre . . . et . . .,** to ply between . . . and . . .; *a.inv.* **porte va-et-vient,** swing door; (*b*) coming and going (of persons); *Mil:* circulation from front to rear and vice versa. **2.** (*a*) *El:* two-way wiring (system); *a.inv.* **commutateur va-et-vient,** two-way switch; (*b*) *Mec.E:* reciprocating gear; (*c*) *Nau:* hauling line (*e.g.* between wreck and shore); (*d*) trail-bridge.

vagabond, -onde [vagabɔ̃, -ɔ̃:d]. **1.** *a.* vagabond, vagrant; **vie vagabonde,** wandering, roving, life; **pensées vagabondes,** wandering thoughts; **attention vagabonde,** wandering attention; **imagination vagabonde,** flighty, roving, imagination; (*croquet*) **balle vagabonde,** ball that has pegged out; *El:* **courant v.,** stray current. **2.** *s.* vagabond; vagrant, tramp.

vagabondage [vagabɔ̃da:ʒ], *s.m.* **1.** (*a*) vagrancy, vagabondage; (*b*) *Adm:* **(délit de) v. spécial,** (crime of) living on immoral earnings. **2.** truancy.

vagabonder [vagabɔ̃de], *v.i.* **1.** (*a*) to be a vagabond; **v. de par le monde,** to rove about the world; (*b*) to play truant. **2.** (*of the mind, etc.*) to wander.

vagal, -aux [vagal, -o], *a. Anat:* vagal.

vagin [vaʒɛ̃], *s.m. Anat:* vagina.

vaginal, -aux [vaʒinal, -o], *a. Anat:* vaginal; **douche vaginale,** vaginal douche.

vaginant [vaʒinɑ̃], *a.* vaginant.

vaginé [vaʒine], *a. Anat: etc:* vaginate, sheathed.

vaginicole [vaʒinikɔl], *s.f. Prot:* vaginicola.

vaginiforme [vaʒinifɔrm], *a.* vaginiform, sheath-like.

vaginisme [vaʒinism], *s.m. Med:* vaginismus, vulvismus.

vaginite [vaʒinit], *s.f. Med:* vaginitis.

vaginodynie [vaʒinɔdini], *s.f.* = VAGINISME.

vaginoscopie [vaʒinɔskɔpi], *s.f. Med:* examination of the vagina, vaginoscopy.

vagino-vésical, -aux [vaʒinɔvezikal, -o], *a. Anat:* vaginovesical.

vaginule [vaʒinyl], *s.f. Bot: etc:* vaginula, vaginule.

vagir [vaʒi:r], *v.i.* (*of new-born infant*) to cry, wail; (*of hare*) to squeak; (*of crocodile*) to whimper.

vagissant [vaʒisɑ̃], *a.* crying, wailing (infant).

vagissement [vaʒismɑ̃], *s.m.* vagitus, cry, wail(ing) (of new-born infant); squeak(ing) (of hare); whimper(ing) (of crocodile).

vagolytique [vagɔlitik], *a. Med:* vagolytic.

vago-sympathique [vagɔsɛ̃patik], *a. Physiol:* vagosympathetic; *pl. vago-sympathiques.*

vagotomie [vagɔtɔmi], *s.f. Surg:* vagotomy.

vagotonie [vagɔtɔni], *s.f. Med:* vagotony, vagotonia.

vagotonique [vagɔtɔnik], *a. Med: Psy:* vagotonic.

vaguage [vaga:ʒ], *s.m. Brew:* stirring (of mash).

vague[1] [vag], *s.f.* **1.** wave; (*a*) **grosse v.,** billow, sea; (*of sea*) **s'élever en vagues,** to billow; **soulevé par les vagues,** riding on the waves, on the billows; **une v. balaya le pont,** the deck was swept by a sea; a sea washed over the deck; **une v. déferla sur la plage,** a comber broke on the beach; a breaker swept over the beach; **v. de fond,** blind roller; **v. d'étrave,** bow wave; *s.a.* DÉFERLANT; **v. de chaleur,** heat wave; **v. de froid,** cold spell, spell of cold weather; **v. sismique,** seismic wave; **v. d'enthousiasme,** wave of enthusiasm; **v. de rire,** ripple of laughter; *Mil:* **v. d'assaut,** assaulting wave; *F:* **il y aura des vagues,** there'll be trouble; (*b*) *F:* generation; **la nouvelle v.,** the rising, new, generation; the new wave; *a.inv. Cin: Lit:* **les films, les romans, nouvelle v.,** the new wave films, novels. **2.** *Brew:* oar (for stirring mash).

vague[2]. **1.** *a.* (*a*) vague, indefinite; sketchy; dim (recollection); hazy (knowledge, recollection); looming (outlines of ships, etc.); **sourire v.,** shadowy smile, ghost of a smile; **notions plutôt vagues,** sketchy notions; **couleur v.,** indefinite, indeterminate, colour; *Cost:* **veste v.,** box jacket, boxy jacket; **quelque v. écrivain,** (i) a writer of some sort; (ii) some writer or other; (*b*) *a. & s.m. Anat: A:* **(nerf) v.,** vagus (nerve). **2.** *s.m.* vagueness, indefiniteness; **s'abandonner au v. de ses pensées,** to lose oneself in one's thoughts; **se sentir du v. à l'âme,** to have vague yearnings.

vague[3]. **1.** *a.* empty, vacant; *still so used in* **regard v.,** vacant stare; **regarder qn d'un air v.,** to gaze vacantly at s.o.; **terrain v.,** (piece of) waste land; vacant site; *U.S:* vacant lot; *F:* no man's land. **2.** *s.m.* empty space; **le v. des airs,** the vacant air; **fixer les yeux dans le v.,** to gaze into space; **regard perdu dans le v.,** abstracted look.

vaguelette [vaglɛt], *s.f.* wavelet.

vaguement [vagmɑ̃], *adv.* vaguely, dimly, indefinitely; **il était v. Américain,** he was vaguely American, an American of sorts; **comprendre v.,** to understand dimly; **j'ai v. l'intention de faire du droit,** I have some sort of intention of studying law; **j'avais v. l'idée qu'il était mort,** I had a vague idea that he was dead.

vaguemestre [vagmɛstr], *s.m.* **1.** *Mil: A:* baggage-master. **2.** (*a*) *Mil:* post orderly; (*b*) *Navy:* postman.

vaguer[1] [vage], *v.i.* to wander, roam, ramble (about); *F:* to moon about; **laisser v. ses pensées,** to let one's thoughts wander; to dream.

vaguer[2], *v.tr.* (*a*) *Brew:* to stir (mash) with the oar; (*b*) *P:* to frisk, search (s.o.).

vahiné [vaine], *s.f.* vahine, woman of Tahiti.

vaigrage [vɛgra:ʒ], *s.m. N.Arch:* ceiling, inner planking, inner plating, sheathing; **v. de fond,** floor ceiling; **v. plein,** casing; **v. à claire-voie,** cargo battens.

vaigre [vɛgr], *s.f. N.Arch:* ceiling plate, inner plank; **vaigres d'une embarcation,** bottom-boards of a small boat.

vaigrer [vɛgre], *v.tr. N.Arch:* to put in the ceiling of (ship); to sheathe.

vaillamment [vajamɑ̃], *adv.* valiantly, bravely, stoutly, courageously, gallantly; **se défendre v.,** to make a gallant fight of it; to offer, put up, a stiff, stout, resistance.

vaillance [vajɑ̃:s], *s.f.* valour, valiancy, bravery, courage, gallantry; **avec v.** = VAILLAMMENT.

vaillant [vajɑ̃]. **1.** *a.* (*a*) valiant, brave, courageous, spirited; stout (heart); *Mil:* gallant; (*b*) *F:* in fine fettle; **être v.,** to be well and strong; to be in good health; **je ne suis pas v.,** I'm not up to the mark; I'm pretty shaky; *A:* **cheval v.,** mettlesome horse. **2.** *adv. O:* **elle a cent mille francs v.,** she has a hundred thousand francs of her own, at her own disposal; *s.a.* SOU. **3.** *s.m. O:* (one's) substance; **perdre, dépenser, tout son v.,** to lose, spend, one's all.

vaillantise [vajɑ̃ti:z], *s.f. A. & Iron:* valiant deed; **raconter ses vaillantises,** to tell of one's deeds of derring-do.

vain [vɛ̃], *a.* **1.** (*a*) vain; sham, unreal, empty, pretended (title, etc.); **vaine gloire,** vainglory; **ce n'étaient pas là de vaines paroles,** these were no empty words, no idle words; **de vains amusements,** futile amusements; **vaines promesses,** hollow promises; **une ombre vaine,** an empty shadow; **de vaines excuses,** empty excuses; *adv.phr.* **en v.,** in vain; *B:* **prendre le nom de Dieu en v.,** to take God's name in vain; (*b*) ineffectual, vain, useless, fruitless (efforts, etc.); **s'épuiser en vains efforts,** *F:* to beat the air; *adv.phr.* **en v.,** in vain, vainly; **tous mes efforts furent en v.,** all my efforts were in vain, to no purpose; **en v. ai-je tâché de l'aider,** in vain I tried to help him; (*c*) **terres vaines et vagues,** waste land; **vaine pâture,** common (land); (*d*) **cheval v.,** horse easily knocked up. **2.** vain, conceited (person, etc.); *O:* **elle était vaine de sa beauté,** she was vain of her beauty; **très v. d'avoir réussi,** very vain of his success; very much puffed up by his success.

vaincre [vɛ̃:kr], *v.tr.* (*pr.p.* **vainquant;** *p.p.* **vaincu;** *pr.ind.* **je vaincs, il vainc, n. vainquons;** *pr.sub.* **je vainque;** *p.d.* **je vainquais;** *p.h.* **je vainquis;** *fu.* **je vaincrai**) **1.** (*a*) to vanquish, conquer, defeat, worst (adversary); (*b*) *Sp: etc:* to outdo, beat, excel (rival); **v. qn en générosité,** to outdo s.o. in generosity; **s'avouer vaincu,** to admit oneself beaten; *F:* to throw up the sponge; to throw in one's hand. **2.** to overcome, master, conquer, fight down, get the better of (feelings, disease, difficulties, etc.); **v. un cheval,** to master a horse; **v. sa frayeur,** to conquer one's fear; **v. toute opposition,** to break down all opposition; **v. toutes les résistances,** to carry all before one; *A:* **se laisser v. aux tentations,** to be overcome by temptation; to give way to temptation; **être vaincu par l'émotion,** to give way to one's feelings. **3.** *v.i.* **v. ou mourir,** to conquer or to die.

vaincu [vɛ̃ky], *s.m.* vanquished person; *Sp: etc:* loser; **malheur aux vaincus!** woe to the vanquished!

vainement [vɛnmɑ̃], *adv.* vainly, in vain; fruitlessly; to no purpose; **v. a-t-il crié au secours,** in vain he cried for help.

vainqueur [vɛ̃kœ:r]. **1.** *s.m.* (*a*) vanquisher (**de qn,** of s.o.); victor, conqueror; **Condé, le v. de Rocroi,** Condé, who was victorious at Rocroi; **sortir v. d'une épreuve,** to come through a test successfully; (*b*) *Sp: etc:* winner; **le v. des double-dames,** the winner of the ladies' doubles. **2.** *a.m.* vanquishing, conquering, victorious (hero, etc.); **air v.,** conquering air, air of victory.

vair [vɛ:r], *s.m.* **1.** *Her:* vair; **v. antique,** vair ancient; **v. en pal,** vair in pale. **2.** *Com:* (*a*) *O:* (whole-)squirrel fur; (*b*) (*usu. spelt* **verre** *by confusion of sounds, and wrongly translated traditionally in Eng.*) **la pantoufle de v. (de Cendrillon),** (Cinderella's) glass slipper.

vairé [vɛre], *a. Her:* vairy.

vairon [vɛrɔ̃]. **1.** *a.* (*a*) **aux yeux vairons,** with eyes of different colours; (*b*) wall-eyed (horse). **2.** *s.m. Ich:* minnow.

vaironner [vɛrɔne], *Fish:* **1.** *v.i.* to fish with a minnow. **2.** *v.i.* (*of trout*) to catch minnows. **3.** *v.tr.* **leurre vaironné,** artificial minnow.

vaisseau, -eaux [vɛso], *s.m.* **1.** (*a*) *A:* vessel, receptacle; **v. de terre,** earthenware pan; *Ch: etc:* **l'opération se fait en v. clos,** the operation is conducted in an airtight vessel; (*b*) *B:* vessel; **v. d'élection,** chosen vessel. **2.** (*a*) *Nau: A:* ship, vessel; **v. à voiles,** sailing vessel; **v. à vapeur,** steamship; **v. à moteurs,** motor ship; **v. à roues,** paddle-steamer; **v. de mer,** sea-going ship; **v. de guerre,** warship, man-of-war; **v. de ligne,** ship of the line; **v. amiral,** flagship; **v. marchand,** merchantman; merchant ship; **v. hôpital,** hospital ship; **v. rasé,** hulk; (*b*) **v. spatial, cosmique,** spacecraft, spaceship; **v. spatial habité,** manned spacecraft; (*c*) **le v. de l'État,** the ship of State; **conduire le v.,** to steer the ship; to be at the head of affairs; **brûler ses vaisseaux,** to burn one's boats. **3.** nave (of church); body, hall (of building). **4.** *Anat: Bot:* vessel, canal, duct; vas; **v. sanguin,** blood vessel; *Bot:* **vaisseaux primaires,** medullary sheath.

vaisseau-école [vɛsoekɔl], *s.m.* training ship; *pl. vaisseaux-écoles.*

vaisselier [vɛsəlje], *s.m. Furn:* dresser.

vaisselle [vɛsɛl], *s.f.* **1.** table service; plates and dishes; crockery; **v. de terre,** crockery, earthenware; **v. de porcelaine,** china; **v. d'étain,** pewter; **v. plate,** silver plate; **v. d'or,** gold plate; **laver, faire, la v.,** to wash up, to wash the dishes; **laveur, -euse, de v.,** washer-up; *U.S:* dishwasher; **machine à laver la v.,** washing-up machine, dishwasher; **eau de v.,** dishwater; **le potage a un goût d'eau de v.,** the soup is like dishwater; **c'est un marchand de v.,** he keeps a china shop. **2.** *Mil: P:* decorations; **étaler sa v.,** to display one's decorations, *F:* to show off all one's gongs.

vaissellerie [vɛsɛlri], *s.f.* **1.** crockery. **2.** manufacture of kitchenware and tableware.

val [val], *s.m. Geog: Poet:* narrow valley, vale; (*in the Jura*) synclinal valley; **le v. de Loire,** the Loire valley between Gien and Tours; *A:* **à v. de . . .,** down from; *the pl. is usu.* **vals** *except in the phrase* **par monts et par vaux** [vo], up hill and down dale.

valable [valabl], *a.* valid (title, testament, excuse, etc.); good (title, excuse); **billet v. pour deux mois,** ticket valid, good, for two months; **raison v.,** cogent, valid, good, reason; **interlocuteur v.,** authorized representative; *F:* **un roman v.,** a good novel; *Jur:* **effets valables,** personal estate of some value; **créances valables (à l'égard d'un établissement de crédit),** live claims.

valablement [valabləmɑ̃], *adv.* validly; **alléguer v. une excuse,** to offer a reasonable excuse, a good excuse.

Valachie (la) [lavalaʃi], *Pr.n.f. Geog:* Wallachia.

Valais (le) [ləvalɛ], *Pr.n.m. Geog:* (the canton of) Valais.

valaisan, -an(n)e [valɛzɑ̃, -an], *a. & s. Geog:* (native, inhabitant) of Valais.

valaque [valak], *a. & s. Geog:* Wallachian.

Valdemar [valdəma:r], *Pr.n.m. Hist:* Waldemar.

valdinguer [valdɛ̃ge], *v.i. P:* to come a cropper; **envoyer v. (qn),** to send (s.o.) packing; to fling (sth.) away; to send (s.o.) spinning.

valdisme [valdism], *s.m. Rel.H:* Vaudism.

valdotain, -aine [valdɔtɛ̃, -ɛn], *a. & s. Geog:* (native, inhabitant) of the Val d'Aosta.

valdrague (en) [ɑ̃valdrag], *adv.phr. Nau:* in disorder, in confusion.

Valence[1] [valɑ̃:s]. **1.** *Pr.n.f. Geog:* (*a*) Valencia (in Spain); (*b*) Valence (in France). **2.** *s.f.* Valencia orange.

valence[2], *s.f. Ch:* valence, valency; **électron de v.,** valency electron.
valencien, -ienne [valɑ̃sjɛ̃, -jɛn], *a. & s. Geog:* Valencian; of Valencia.
valenciennes [valɑ̃sjɛn], *s.f.* Valenciennes lace.
valenciennois, -oise [valɑ̃sjɛnwa, -waːz], *a. & s. Geog:* (native, inhabitant) of Valenciennes.
valentiel, -ielle [valɑ̃sjɛl], *a. Ch:* **électrons valentiels,** valency electrons, valence electrons.
Valentin[1], **-ine** [valɑ̃tɛ̃, -in], *Pr.n.* Valentine.
Valentin[2], *Pr.n.m. Rel.H:* Valentinus.
valentinien[1], **-ienne** [valɑ̃tinjɛ̃, -jɛn], *a. & s.m. Rel.H:* Valentinian.
Valentinien[2], *Pr.n.m. A.Hist:* Valentinian.
valentinite [valɑ̃tinit], *s.f. Miner:* valentinite.
valentinois, -oise [valɑ̃tinwa, -waːz]. **1.** *a. & s. Geog:* (native, inhabitant) of Valence. **2.** *Pr.n.m.* **le Valentinois,** the Valence region (of France).
valérate [valerat], *s.m.* = VALÉRIANATE.
Valère [valɛːr], *Pr.n.m.* **1.** Valerius; *Lt.Lit:* **V. Maxime,** Valerius Maximus. **2.** (*in Fr. comedy*) Valère.
valérianacées [valerjanase], *s.f.pl. Bot:* Valerianaceae.
valérianate [valerjanat], *s.m. Ch:* valerianate.
valériane [valerjan], *s.f. Bot:* (*a*) valerian; **v. rouge,** red valerian, spur valerian; (*b*) **v. grecque,** Greek valerian.
valérianelle [valerjanɛl], *s.f. Bot:* lamb's lettuce, corn salad.
valérianique [valerjanik], *a.* = VALÉRIQUE.
valéricain, -aine [valerikɛ̃, ɛn], *a. & s. Geog:* (native, inhabitant) of Saint-Valery-sur-Somme.
valéricais, -aise [valerikɛ, -ɛːz], *a. & s. Geog:* (native, inhabitant) of Saint-Valery-en-Caux.
Valérie [valeri], *Pr.n.f.* Valeria, Valerie.
Valérien [valerjɛ̃], *Pr.n.m. Rom.Hist:* Valerian.
valérique [valerik], *a. Ch:* valeric (acid).
valet [valɛ], *s.m.* **1.** (*a*) *A:* = VARLET; (*b*) *Cards:* knave, jack; **v. de carreau,** knave of diamonds; **v. quatrième,** guarded jack; **v. troisième, cinquième, etc.,** three, five, etc., cards to the jack. **2.** (*a*) manservant; **v. de chambre,** valet, manservant; **voyager avec son v.,** to travel with one's man; **v. de pied,** footman; *Mil:* **v. d'officier,** officer's servant; **v. d'écurie,** groom, ostler, stable boy; **v. de chenil,** kennelman; **v. de ferme,** farmhand; **maître v. (de ferme),** (farm) foreman; **v. de charrue,** ploughboy; *A:* **valets du bourreau,** executioner's assistants; *A:* **v. de place,** courier; **votre domestique est un vrai v. de comédie,** your man is full of resource, is up to every trick (like Scapin, etc., in old Italian comedy); *Prov:* **tel maître, tel v.,** like master, like man; (*b*) *Ven:* **v. de limier,** harbourer; **v. de chiens,** whipper-in; (*c*) *A. & Lit: Pej:* **âme de v.,** servile nature, cringing nature; **faire le plat v.,** to cringe, to toady, to fawn; **v. de carreau,** rogue, knave. **3.** *Tchn:* (*a*) door counterweight; (*b*) *Carp: etc:* clamp, holdfast, dog, claw; **v. d'établi,** dog, staple, of a bench; **v. de la platine d'un microscope,** clip of the stage of a microscope; (*c*) support, rest, stand (of mirror, photo frame, etc.); **v. de laboratoire,** stand for laboratory use; (*d*) *Surg:* **v. à Patin,** ligature forceps (as invented by Patin).
valetage [val(ə)taːʒ], *s.m. A:* (*a*) valeting; (*b*) servility; fetching and carrying.
valetaille [val(ə)tɑːj], *s.f. Pej:* varletry, menservants, flunkeys, menials.
valeter [valte], *v.tr.* (**je valette, n. valetons; je valetterai**) *A:* (*a*) to valet (s.o.); (*b*) to toady to (s.o.); *abs.* to fetch and carry.
Valette (la) [lavalɛt], *Pr.n. Geog:* Valetta.
valétudinaire [valetydinɛːr]. **1.** *a.* valetudinary, of feeble health. **2.** *s.m. & f.* valetudinarian.
valétudinarisme [valetydinarism], *s.m.* valetudinarianism; feeble health; invalidism.
valeur [valœːr], *s.f.* **1.** (*a*) (relative) value, worth; **attacher, attribuer, de la v. à qch., à qn,** to attach value to sth., s.o., to set value upon sth., s.o.; **v. de l'électrothérapie dans le traitement des maladies nerveuses,** value of electrotherapy in the treatment of nervous diseases; **v. d'une méthode, d'un système,** value, efficiency, of a method, of a system; **cela n'a pas grande v.,** it's not worth much; *Com:* **papier de v. douteuse,** dubious bills, unsafe paper; **homme de v.,** man (i) of real ability, (ii) of merit; **livre de véritable v.,** book of true merit; **de première v.,** (man) of outstanding merit; first-quality (article); **tôt ou tard la v. se fait jour,** sooner or later merit will tell, will out; *Mil:* **v. combative, v. militaire,** fighting efficiency, fighting qualities (of troops); **v. morale,** fighting spirit, morale; **v. nautique,** seaworthiness (of ship); *Navy:* **v. militaire d'un bâtiment,** fighting qualities of a ship; **mettre une terre en v.,** to increase the value of land; to develop land; **mettre un marais en v.,** to reclaim a marsh; **mettre en v. une chute d'eau,** to harness a waterfall; **il a su se mettre immédiatement en v.,** from the beginning he knew how to show himself to advantage; he made a good impression from the start; **mise en v.,** (i) development (of land, etc.); (ii) reclaiming (of marsh); (iii) harnessing (of waterfall); **mise en v. d'un site,** development of a beauty spot (for touristic purposes); **mise en v. des terres,** land utilization; **remise en v. des terres,** restoration of land to cultivation (after war, etc.); *Pol.Ec:* **v. ajoutée,** added value; **taxe à la v. ajoutée,** value-added tax; **v. d'échange,** exchange value; **v. d'usage,** value as a going concern; **v. marginale,** marginal value; (*b*) (monetary) value, worth; **v. marchande, v. vénale,** market(able) value, sale(able) value, commercial value; **article, objet, de v.,** article of value, valuable article; **objets de v., valeurs,** valuables; **bijou de grande v.,** jewel of great value; **attribuer une cote de v. à chaque objet,** to value each article; **estimer un objet au-dessus de sa v.,** to overvalue an object; **sans v.,** worthless, of no value; *Cust:* **v. en douane,** customs value; *Post:* **colis, paquet, avec v. déclarée,** insured parcel; **v. déclarée: cent francs,** insured for one hundred francs; *Com:* **v. comptable,** book value; **v. de facture,** invoice value; **v. reçue,** value received; **v. à l'échéance,** value at maturity; **v. au 15 prochain,** payable on the 15th prox; *Fin:* **v. boursière,** market value; **v. d'achat d'une action,** cost of a share; **v. de remboursement,** redemption value (of bond, etc.); *Ins:* **v. assurable,** insurable value; **v. assurée,** insured value; **v. de rachat (d'une police),** surrender value (of policy); (*c*) *Mus:* (time) value, length (of a note); (*d*) equivalent; **boire la v. d'un verre de vin,** to drink the equivalent of a glass of wine; (*e*) import, weight, value; **votre argument n'est pas sans v.,** there's something in what you say; **renseignements sans v.,** worthless information; **v. des mots,** import, full meaning, of words; **mettre un mot en v.,** to emphasize, give importance to, a word; **sentiment des valeurs,** sense of values; (*f*) *Mth: etc:* **attribuer une v. à x,** to give, attribute, a value to *x*; **v. absolue,** (i) absolute value; (ii) magnitude; **v. approximative,** approximate value, approximation; **v. efficace,** root-mean-square value; **v. positive, négative,** positive, negative, value; **valeurs naturelles des sinus, des cosinus,** natural sines, natural cosines; *Ph:* **v. calorifique,** heat value; **v. de crête, de pointe,** peak value; **v. de seuil,** threshold (value); (*g*) *Fr.C: F:* **c'est de v.,** it's unfortunate, it's a pity. **2.** *Fin:* (*a*) asset; **valeurs actives,** assets; **valeurs passives,** liabilities; (*of pers.*) *F:* **c'est une de nos valeurs,** he's one of our assets; *Bank:* **v. en compte,** value in account; **v. en capital,** capital value; **v. en espèces,** (i) cash; (ii) bullion; (*b*) *pl.* bills, shares, securities, stocks; **valeurs mobilières (négociables),** stocks and shares, transferable securities; **valeurs immobilières,** real property; **valeurs à revenu fixe, à revenu variable,** fixed-yield, variable-yield, securities; **valeurs au porteur,** bearer securities, shares; bearer bonds; **valeurs nominatives,** registered securities; **valeurs au comptant,** securities dealt in for cash; **valeurs à terme,** forward securities; **valeurs de coulisse, valeurs non cotées,** unquoted securities; **valeurs de parquet, valeurs cotées,** quoted securities; **valeurs de portefeuille, de placement,** investment securities, stocks; **valeurs à lot,** lottery bonds, prize bonds; **valeurs de père de famille, valeurs de tout repos, valeurs refuges,** gilt-edge(d) securities, safe investments; *F:* **valeurs de fantaisie,** bazaar shares. **3.** *O:* valour; gallantry; **se battre avec v.,** to fight gallantly.
valeureusement [valœrøzmɑ̃], *adv.* valorously, gallantly.
valeureux, -euse [valœrø, -øːz], *a.* valorous, brave, gallant (in battle).
valeur-or [valœrɔːr], *s.f. Fin:* value in gold currency; *pl. valeurs-or.*
valeur-seuil [valœrsœːj], *s.f. Elcs:* threshold value; *pl. valeurs-seuil.*
valgum [valgɔm], *a. & s.m.inv.,* **valgus** [valgys], *a. & s.m.inv. Surg:* valgus.
validation [validasjɔ̃], *s.f.* validation (of election, marriage, etc.); ratifying (of law); authentication (of document, signature, etc.); *Elcs:* **signal de v.,** enabling signal.
valide [valid], *a.* **1.** (*a*) valid (contract, marriage, reason, etc.); (*b*) (= VALABLE) **billet v. pour deux mois,** ticket available, good, for two months. **2.** *Mil: etc:* fit for service; able-bodied; **revenir du combat avec deux cents hommes valides,** to return from the fight with two hundred unwounded men; *F:* **être peu v.,** to be off colour, not up to the mark.
validement [validmɑ̃], *adv.* **1.** validly. **2.** vigorously.
valider [valide], *v.tr.* to validate (election, marriage); to ratify (contract, etc.); to authenticate (document, passport, etc.); to probate (a will).
validité [validite], *s.f.* validity (of contract, proof, title, election, passport, etc.); **durée de v. d'un billet,** period for which a ticket is available; availability of a ticket; **établir la v. d'un testament,** to prove a will; **établir la v. d'un argument,** to establish the validity of an argument; *Elcs:* **contrôle de v.,** validity check.
valine [valin], *s.f. Bio-Ch:* valin(e).
valise [valiːz], *s.f.* (*a*) *A:* (small) portmanteau; (*b*) suitcase; *U.S:* grip; **boucler sa v.,** to be ready to go; *F:* **faire sa, la, v.,** to beat it; (*c*) **v. diplomatique,** embassy dispatch bag, box; (diplomatic) bag; (*d*) *Fr.C:* boot, *U.S:* trunk (of a car).
valisolétain, -aine [valisɔletɛ̃, -ɛn], *a. & s.* (native, inhabitant) of Valladolid.
Valkyrie [valkiri], *s.f. Myth:* Walkyrie, Valkyrie.
vallécule [valekyl], *s.f. Bot:* vallecula, channel.
vallée [vale], *s.f.* **1.** valley; **la v. du Rhône,** the Rhone Valley; *B:* **la v. de Josaphat,** the Valley of Jehoshaphat; **cette v. de larmes,** this vale of tears; *Egyptian Archeol:* **la V. des Rois,** the Valley of the Kings; *Geog:* **v. noyée,** drowned valley. **2.** *Min:* inclined mother gate.
valleuse [valøːz], *s.f. Geog:* (*in Normandy, Picardy*) small dry (hanging) valley between cliffs.
vallisnérie [valisneri], *s.f. Bot:* (*genus*) Vallisneria; **v. spirale,** tape grass, eelgrass, wild celery.
valloirien, -ienne [valwarjɛ̃, -jɛn], *a. & s. Geog:* (native, inhabitant) of Saint-Vallier.
vallon [valɔ̃], *s.m.* small valley; dale, dell, vale; *Scot:* glen; *Myth:* **le sacré v.,** the Sacred Vale (abode of the Muses).
vallonée [valɔne], *s.f. Com: Tan: etc:* val(l)onia.
vallonné [valɔne], *a.* undulating (country); **pays très v.,** deeply undulated country.
vallonnement [valɔnmɑ̃], *s.m.* **1.** laying out (of park, etc.) in dells. **2.** foothills.
vallonner [valɔne], *v.tr.* to lay out (park, etc.) in dells.
vallum [val(l)ɔm], *s.m. Rom.Ant:* vallum.
valoche [valɔʃ], *s.f. P:* (suit)case.
valognais, -aise [valɔɲɛ, -ɛːz], *a. & s.* (native, inhabitant) of Valognes.
valoir [valwaːr], *v.tr. & v.i. with adverbial extension of value* (*pr.p.* **valant**; *p.p.* **valu**; *pr.ind.* **je vaux, il vaut, n. valons, ils valent**; *pr.sub.* **je vaille, n. valions, ils vaillent**; *p.d.* **je valais**; *p.h.* **je valus**; *fu.* **je vaudrai**) **1.** (*a*) to be worth (in money or quality); **tissu qui vaut dix francs le mètre,** material that is worth ten francs a metre; **deux maisons valant cent mille francs,** two houses worth one hundred thousand francs; **la somme qu'a valu cette propriété,** the sum which this property was worth; **combien,** *F:* **qu'est-ce que vaut le beurre aujourd'hui?** what is the price of butter today? **à v. sur (une somme),** on account of (a sum); **payer dix francs à v.,** to pay ten francs on account; **à v. sur qn,** on account of s.o.; for account of s.o.; **à v. sur votre facture,** set against your invoice; *s.m.* **un à v.,** *Com:* a sum on account; *Publ:* an advance; **v. son prix,** (i) to have a certain value, to be worth something; (ii) to be worth its price; **il ne vaut pas le pain qu'il mange,** he is not worth his salt; **ne pas v. grand-chose,** not to be worth much; **il ne vaut pas grand-chose,** he isn't up to much; **cela ne vaut pas grand-chose,** it's no great catch; **comme acteur il ne vaut pas cher,** as an actor he's not up to much, *F:* he's no great shakes; **vous valez mille fois mieux que lui,** you are a thousand times better than he is; **s'il n'est pas mort, il n'en vaut guère mieux,** if he is not dead, he is not far from it; **moins nous parlerons, mieux cela vaudra,** the less said the better; least said soonest mended; **cela vaut pour . . .,** that goes for . . ., that is true of . . .; **cela ne vaut rien,** that's no good; **ne rien v. pour la santé,** to be bad for the health; **ce climat ne vous vaut rien,** this climate is not good for you, is bad for you; **ce n'est rien qui vaille,** it isn't worth having, isn't of any value; **façade pauvre, sans un ornement qui vaille,** poor front with no ornament worth anything; **il ne fera jamais rien qui vaille,** he will never accomplish anything; **un, une, rien qui vaille,** a good-for-nothing, a bad lot; **son jeu ne vaut que par sa**

technique impeccable, his playing is remarkable only for its flawless technique; **cette remarque vaudra d'un bout à l'autre du voyage,** this remark will hold good from beginning to end of the journey; (*b*) to be equivalent to; **un franc vaut cent centimes,** a franc is equal to a hundred centimes; **le premier coup en vaut deux,** the first blow is half the battle; **c'est une façon qui en vaut une autre,** it's as good a way as any other; **sa famille vaut bien la vôtre,** his family is quite as good as yours; **l'un vaut l'autre,** one is as good, as bad, as the other; there's nothing to choose between them; **il ne vaut pas mieux que son frère,** he is no better than his brother; **la canaille de tous les pays se vaut,** there is nothing to choose between the riff-raff of one country and another; **rien ne vaut . . .,** you can't beat . . .; *F:* **ça se vaut,** it's the same either way; *A:* **cela vaut fait,** it is as good as done; (*c*) *impers:* **il vaut mieux, il vaudrait mieux, rester à la maison,** it is, would be, better to stay at home; **j'ai pensé qu'il valait mieux rester,** I thought it better to stay; **mieux vaudrait ne pas vous en mêler,** you had better not interfere; **il vaut mieux qu'il en soit ainsi,** it is better that it should be so; **il vaut mieux, mieux vaut + *inf.* que (de) + *inf.*,** it is better to + *inf.* than to + *inf.*; **mieux vaut se passer de thé que de manquer le train,** better do without tea than miss the train; **mieux vaut tard que jamais,** better late than never; **mieux vaut perdre sa fortune que son honneur,** better lose one's fortune than one's honour; **mieux vaut de . . .,** *is occ. met with:* **mieux vaut encore de penser que de lire,** it is even better to think than to read; **autant vaut rester ici,** we may as well stay here; **choses qu'il vaut autant ne pas rappeler,** things best forgotten; **c'est une affaire faite ou autant vaut,** it is as good as done; the business is settled to all intents and purposes; **il vaut la peine de vivre vieux,** it is worth living to a great age; **il ne vaut pas la peine de les mentionner,** they are not worth mentioning; (*d*) **faire v. qch.,** to make the most of sth.; to turn sth. to account; to put sth. forward; to set sth. off to advantage; to bring sth. out; to emphasize sth.; **costume qui fait v. son teint,** costume that sets off her complexion; **le fond en grisaille fait v. les personnages,** the shadowy background brings out the characters; **monture qui fait v. la pierre,** setting that shows off the stone; **faire v. ses opinions,** to command respect for one's opinions; **faire v. sa marchandise,** to make the most of one's wares; **faire v. ses droits à . . .,** to assert, enforce, one's claims to . . .; **faire v. son bon droit,** to vindicate one's rights; **faire v. ses raisons,** to put forward one's reasons; **j'ai fait v. que . . .,** I pointed out, urged, that . . .; I stressed the point that . . .; **faire v. le fond d'un ouvrage,** to bring out the inner meaning of a work; **se faire v.,** (i) to make the most of oneself; (ii) to push oneself forward; (iii) *F:* to put on side; **il ne sait pas se faire v.,** he doesn't know how to make the most of himself; **faire v. son argent,** to invest one's money to good account; **faire v. une terre,** to farm, develop, an estate. **2.** to be worth, to deserve, merit (sth.); **un service en vaut un autre; une amabilité en vaut une autre,** one good turn deserves another; **le livre vaut d'être lu,** the book is worth reading; **cela vaut la peine de faire le voyage,** it is worth making the journey; **cela vaut le voyage,** it's worth the journey, it's worth a special trip; **je viendrai si cela en vaut la peine,** I shall come if it is worth (my) while; **ce conseil vaut la peine qu'on s'en souvienne,** this advice is worth remembering; **cela ne valait pas qu'on s'en occupât,** it was not worth troubling about; *F:* **ça vaut le coup,** it's worth trying; **ça ne vaut pas le coup,** it isn't worth the trouble. **3.** *A:* **v. qch. à qn,** (*a*) to bring in, yield, fetch (so much); **cette terre lui vaut dix mille francs de rente,** this land brings him in an income of ten thousand francs; *adv.phr. F:* **vaille que vaille,** (i) for better for worse; (ii) at all costs, come what may; (iii) when all is said and done; **on vit vaille que vaille,** we manage to rub along; *A:* **continuons la partie, tout coup vaille,** let us go on with the game pending the umpire's decision; *F:* **tenter qch., tout coup vaille,** to attempt sth., hit or miss; (*b*) to obtain, win, gain; **cette action lui a valu d'être décoré,** this act won him a decoration; **cela ne me vaudra que des reproches,** I shan't get anything but blame for that; **les éloges que sa conduite lui a valus,** the praise which his conduct gained him; **qu'est-ce qui me vaut cet honneur?** to what do I owe this honour?

valorisation [valɔrizasjɔ̃], *s.f.* **1.** *Com: Fin:* valorization (of product, etc.); stabilization (of price of commodity). **2.** *Bank:* **v. (de chèques) sur Paris, sur Londres,** valuing (of cheques) on Paris, on London.

valoriser [valɔrize], *v.tr.* **1.** *Com: Fin:* (*a*) to valorize; to stabilize (price of commodity); (*b*) to raise the price of (a commodity). **2.** *Bank:* to value (cheques, etc.) **(sur Paris, sur Londres,** on Paris, on London).

valréassien, -ienne [valreasjɛ̃, -jɛn], *a. & s. Geog:* (native, inhabitant) of Valréas.

Vals [val(s)], *Pr.n.* **eau de V.,** mineral water from Vals-les-Bains.

valse [vals], *s.f.* waltz; **v. à trois temps,** trois-temps waltz; **v. à deux temps,** deux-temps waltz, quick waltz; **faire un tour de v.,** to waltz round the room; *F:* **on lui a fait faire un tour de v.,** he was given a diplomatic change of post, a change of air; **v. chantée,** waltz song; *F:* **la v. des étiquettes,** the spiralling up of prices.

valser [valse], *v.i.* **1.** to waltz; **j'ai fait v. Mlle X, I waltzed with Miss X; il ne faudra pas oublier de faire v. ta cousine,** you musn't forget to ask your cousin for a waltz; *with cogn.acc.* **v. une mazurka,** to waltz a mazurka; **toutes les compositions intitulées valses ne sont pas faites pour être valsées,** not all pieces called waltzes are intended to be waltzed. **2.** *F:* **faire v. qn,** (i) to lead s.o. a dance; to keep s.o. on the hop; (ii) to kick, boot, s.o. out; **envoyer qn v.,** to show s.o. the door; **faire v. l'argent,** to spend money like water; to play ducks and drakes with one's money; **quand ils se disputaient ils faisaient v. la vaisselle,** whenever they quarrelled, the dishes flew.

valseur, -euse [valsœːr, -øːz]. **1.** (*a*) *s.* waltzer; (*b*) *s.m. P:* buttocks; (*c*) *s.f.pl. V:* **valseuses,** testicles, balls. **2.** *a.* waltzing (doll, etc.).

valsois, -oise [valswa, -waːz], *a. & s. Geog:* (native, inhabitant) of Vals-les-Bains.

valtelin, -ine [valtəlɛ̃, -in], *a. & s. Geog:* (native, inhabitant) of Valtellina.

Valteline (la) [lavaltəlin], *Pr.n.f. Geog:* Valtellina.

value [valy], *s.f. A:* value, still used in MOINS-VALUE, PLUS-VALUE.

valvaire [valvɛːr], *a. Bot: etc:* valvar, valvate.

valve [valv], *s.f.* **1.** *Anat: Bot: Conch:* valve. **2.** *Mec.E: etc:* valve (*esp.* of clack valve or ball valve type); **v. de retenue,** non-return valve; **v. anti-retour,** check valve; *Metall:* **v. à vent chaud,** hot-blast valve; *Mch:* **v. tiroir,** slide valve; *Aut: Cy:* **v. de chambre à air,** tyre valve. **3.** *W.Tel:* valve (for rectification); **v. redresseuse,** rectifying valve; *s.a.* CUPROXYDE. **4. enregistrement par v. de lumière,** light-valve recording (of sound). **5.** *Surg:* (*a*) vaginal retractor; (*b*) **v. à bille,** artificial valve (in heart surgery).

valvé [valve], *a. Bot: etc:* valvate.

valviforme [valvifɔrm], *a.* valviform, valve-shaped.

valvulaire [valvylɛːr], *a.* **1.** valvular (lesion, etc.). **2.** *Nat.Hist:* valvulate.

valvule [valvyl], *s.f.* (*a*) *Nat.Hist:* valvule; (*b*) *Anat:* valve, valvula, valvule; **v. de Thébésius,** valve of Thebesius, coronary valve; **v. aortique,** aortic valve; **v. mitrale,** mitral, bicuspid, valve; **v. tricuspide,** tricuspid valve; **v. semi-lunaire,** semilunar valve.

valvulé [valvyle], *a. Nat.Hist:* valvulate.

valvulite [valvylit], *s.f. Med:* valvulitis.

valvuloplastie [valvyləplasti], *s.f. Surg:* valvuloplasty.

vamp [vɑ̃p], *s.f. F:* vamp.

vamper [vɑ̃pe], *v.tr. F:* to vamp; **elle essaya de le v.,** she had a go at vamping him.

vampire [vɑ̃piːr], *s.m.* **1.** (*a*) *Myth:* vampire; (*b*) *F:* vampire, extortioner, bloodsucker; (*c*) *F:* mass murderer. **2.** *Z:* vampire (bat); **v. spectre,** great vampire, false vampire.

vampirique [vɑ̃pirik], *a.* vampiric; bloodsucking.

vampirisme [vɑ̃pirism], *s.m.* vampirism. **1.** belief in vampires. **2.** *F:* bloodsucking; extortion.

van[1] [vɑ̃], *s.m.* **1.** *Agr:* (*a*) winnowing basket; sieve; (*b*) winnowing machine; fan; **passer du blé au v.,** to winnow corn; **v. mécanique,** aspirator. **2.** (*ore dressing*) van, vanning shovel.

van[2], *s.m. Veh:* horse box.

vanadate [vanadat], *s.m. Ch:* vanadate.

vanadeux, -euse [vanadø, -øːz], *a.*, **vanadié** [vanadje], *a. Metall:* vanadious (alloy, etc.).

vanadifère [vanadifɛːr], *a. Ch: Miner:* vanadiferous, vanadium-bearing (ore).

vanadinite [vanadinit], *s.f. Miner:* vanadinite.

vanadique [vanadik], *a. Ch:* vanadic (acid).

vanadium [vanadjɔm], *s.m. Ch:* vanadium; *Metall:* **acier au v.,** vanadium steel.

Vandale [vɑ̃dal], *s.m. & a.* **1.** *Hist:* Vandal. **2.** vandal, destroyer of works of art, etc.

vandalique [vɑ̃dalik], *a.* **1.** *Hist:* Vandalic (invasion, etc.). **2.** vandalistic.

vandalisme [vɑ̃dalism], *s.m.* vandalism; **acte de v.,** piece of vandalism.

vandoise [vɑ̃dwaːz], *s.f. Ich:* dace.

Van Dyck [vɑ̃dik], *Pr.n.m.* van Dyck, Vandyke.

vanesse [vanɛs], *s.f. Ent:* vanessa (butterfly), tortoiseshell butterfly; **v. de l'ortie,** small tortoiseshell.

vanille [vaniːj], *s.f. Bot: Cu:* vanilla; **gousse de v.,** vanilla bean; **glace à la v.,** vanilla ice.

vanillé [vanije], *a. Cu:* flavoured with vanilla; **crème vanillée,** vanilla custard.

vanillerie [vanijri], *s.f.* vanilla plantation.

vanillier [vanije], *s.m. Bot:* vanilla plant.

vanilline [vanijin, -ilin], *s.f. Ch: Ind:* vanillin.

vanillisme [vanijism], *s.m. Med:* vanillism.

vanillon [vanijɔ̃], *s.m. Com:* vanillon.

vanisé [vanize], *Com: Tex:* (*a*) *a.* cotton yarn mixed with wool, silk or nylon; (*b*) *s.m.* article made with this yarn.

vanité [vanite], *s.f.* vanity. **1.** futility (of worldly pleasures, etc.); *Lit:* **tout est v.,** all is vanity. **2.** conceit, self-sufficiency; egotism; **faire v., tirer v., de qch.,** to take an empty pride in sth.; to be unduly proud of sth.; **tirer v. de sa connaissance de l'anglais,** to pride oneself on one's knowledge of English; **faire qch. par v.,** to do sth. out of vanity; **sans v. . . .,** with all due modesty . . ., without wishing to boast . . . .

vaniteusement [vanitøzmɑ̃], *adv.* conceitedly, egotistically.

vaniteux, -euse [vanitø, -øːz], *a.* vain, conceited; egotistical; *s.* **c'est un v.,** he's full of self-conceit, he's (very) conceited.

vannage[1] [vanaːʒ], *s.m.* **1.** (*a*) *Agr:* fanning, winnowing, sifting (of grain); (*b*) vanning (of ore). **2.** *P:* fatigue, exhaustion.

vannage[2], *s.m.* **1.** *Hyd.E:* (*a*) gating (of turbine); (*b*) sluicing (of water gate). **2.** *Hyd.E:* (system of) sluice gates. **3.** *Mec.E:* regulation (of a valve).

vanne[1] [van]. **1.** (*a*) *Hyd.E:* sluice (gate), water (gate), shut-off; **v. de décharge,** overflow weir; **v. plongeante,** floodgate; **v. de communication,** sluice valve; **v. mélangeuse,** mixing valve; **lever les vannes,** to open the floodgates; **mettre les vannes,** to close the floodgates; *N.Arch:* **v. à glissière,** sluice valve; **v. de sabordage,** scuttle valve; (*b*) *Mch: Mec.E: etc:* valve; **v. à boisseau,** plug valve; **v. à obturateur, à opercule,** gate valve; **obturateur de v.,** valve shutter; **v. à papillon,** butterfly valve; **v. à plusieurs voies,** multi-way valve, star valve; **v. à trois voies,** three-way valve; **v. à gaz,** gas valve; **v. d'eau,** water valve; **v. régulatrice de débit,** flow-regulating valve; **v. d'arrêt,** check valve, non-return valve; stop valve, shut-off valve; **v. de vapeur,** steam valve; **v. de dérivation,** by-pass valve; **v. de réglage,** regulating valve; expansion valve (of refrigerator); **v. de sectionnement,** isolating valve, shut-off valve; *I.C.E:* **v. d'entrée,** inlet valve; *Metall:* **v. de réglage du vent,** blast gate (of furnace); (*c*) gate (of turbine); (*d*) *Agr:* shutter (of fan); (*e*) blade (of blower); (*f*) *Nau:* cock. **2.** *a.* **eaux vannes,** waste water (from factories, etc.); sewage water (from houses, etc.).

vanne[2], *s.m. or f. P:* **1.** witty (but sarcastic) remark; unkind reflection; (nasty) crack. **2.** dirty trick. **3.** spot of bother.

vanneau, -eaux[1] [vano], *s.m.* **1.** *Orn:* **v. (huppé),** lapwing, peewit, green plover; **v. éperonné, armé, épineux,** spur-winged plover; *Cu:* **œufs de v.,** plovers' eggs. **2.** *Moll:* queen.

vanneaux[2] [vano], *s.m.pl. Com: F: A:* goods sold under cost price, at a loss.

vannée [vane], *s.f. Agr:* winnowings.

vannelle [vanɛl], *s.f. Hyd.E:* sluice valve, paddle.

vanner[1] [vane], *v.tr.* **1.** (*a*) to winnow, fan, sift (grain); (*b*) to van (ore). **2.** *P:* to tire out, exhaust; **être vanné,** to be dead beat, played out, done up, all in.

vanner[2], *v.tr.* **1.** *Hyd.E:* (*a*) to fit sluices in, to sluice (water gate); (*b*) to gate (turbine). **2.** *Mec.E:* to regulate (a valve).

vannerie [vanri], *s.f.* **1.** basket making, basket trade; *Needlew:* **point de v.,** basket stitch. **2.** basketwork, wickerwork; **v. d'ameublement,** basket furniture; **chaises (de jardin) en v.,** wicker (garden) chairs.

vannet [vanɛ], *s.m. Fish:* (kind of) stownet (spread on a beach at low tide).
vannetais, -aise [vantɛ, -ɛːz], *a. & s. Geog:* (native, inhabitant) of Vannes.
vannette [vanɛt], *s.f.* winnowing basket (for sifting oats).
vanneur, -euse [vanœːr, -øːz]. **1.** *s.* (*a*) winnower; (*b*) (*ore-dressing*) vanner. **2.** *s.m.* vanner (for ore); vanning machine. **3.** *s.f.* **vanneuse,** winnowing machine.
vannier [vanje], *s.m.* basket worker; basket maker.
vannure [vanyːr], *s.f. Agr:* husks, chaff; winnowings.
vantail, -aux [vɑ̃taːj, -o], *s.m.* leaf (of door, shutter, sluice gate); folding panel (of triptych); **porte à deux vantaux,** folding door.
vantard, -arde [vɑ̃taːr, -ard]. **1.** *a.* boasting, boastful, bragging (person, air). **2.** *s.* braggart, boaster; *F:* bragger; *U.S: P:* blowhard.
vantardise [vɑ̃tardiːz], *s.f.* **1.** bragging, boastfulness; braggadocio. **2.** boast, brag.
vantelle [vɑ̃tɛl], *s.f. Hyd.E:* sluice valve, paddle.
vanter [vɑ̃te], *v.tr.* to praise (s.o., sth.); to speak highly of (sth.); *F:* to crack up (s.o., sth.); **on m'a beaucoup vanté vos mérites,** I have heard great things about you; *s.a.* MARCHANDISE.
se vanter. 1. to boast, brag; **sans me v.,** without boasting, without wishing to boast; **il n'y a pas de quoi se v.,** that's nothing to boast about, *F:* nothing to make a song (and dance) about, nothing to write home about; *F:* **il ne s'en est pas vanté,** he took care to keep quiet about it; he kept very quiet about it; **se v. d'être . . .,** to pride oneself on being . . .; **se v. que** + *ind.* or *sub*; **se v. de ce que** + *ind.,* to boast that . . .. **2. se v. de faire qch.,** to undertake to do sth.; **nul ne peut se v. de se passer de . . .,** nobody can claim to be able to do without . . ..
vanterie [vɑ̃tri], *s.f.* **1.** bragging, boasting. **2.** boast; piece of brag.
vanthoffite [vɑ̃tɔfit], *s.f. Miner:* vanthoffite.
va-nu-pieds [vanypje], *s.m. & f.inv.* barefoot tramp, beggar; **petit v.-n.-p.,** ragamuffin.
vanviste [vɑ̃vist], *a. & s.m. & f. Geog:* (native, inhabitant) of Vanves.
vapeur[1] [vapœːr], *s.f.* **1.** vapour; **vapeurs du matin,** morning mist, haze; **la v. de l'encens,** the fumes of incense; **la v. du rôti,** the fumes from the roast. **2.** *Ph: etc:* (*a*) **v. d'éther, d'alcool,** ether vapour, alcoholic vapour; **v. d'iode,** vapour of iodine; (*b*) **v. (d'eau),** (i) (water-)vapour; (ii) steam; **machine à v.,** steam engine; **bateau à v.,** steamer, steamship; **marchant à la v.,** steam-driven; **injection de v.,** steaming; **chauffer, développer, la v.,** to get up, raise, steam; *Mch:* **v. vierge, vive,** live steam; **v. d'échappement, v. épuisée,** exhaust steam; **mettre la v.,** to put steam on; **navire sous v.,** ship under steam; **à toute v.,** (at) full steam, at full speed; *Nau:* full steam ahead; *F: A:* **faire qch. à v.,** to do sth. with all speed; to scamp (a job); **casernes bâties à toute v.,** hurriedly built, rushed-up, barracks; (*c*) *Cu:* **cuire (des légumes, etc.) à la v.,** to steam (vegetables, etc.). **3.** *pl.* (*a*) fumes (of wine, petrol, etc.); (*b*) *usu. pl. A.Med:* vapours; **Mme X a des vapeurs,** Mrs X has the vapours; **il lui prit une v.,** she had a fit of dizziness.
vapeur[2], *s.m.* steamer, steamship; **v. à roues, à aubes,** paddle steamer; **v. à hélice(s),** screw steamer; **v. de charge,** cargo boat; **v. de cabotage,** coasting steamer.
vaporeusement [vapɔrøzmɑ̃], *adv. Lit:* vaporously.
vaporeux, -euse [vapɔrø, -øːz], *a.* **1.** (*a*) vaporous, vapourish, vapoury, misty (light, sky, etc.); steamy (atmosphere); (*b*) filmy, hazy (ideas, etc.); (*c*) nebulous, vaporous (style); (*d*) *Cost: F:* **dessous v.,** flimsies. **2.** *A:* vapourish (person, condition).
vaporimètre [vapɔrimɛtr̥], *s.m.* vaporimeter.
vaporisable [vapɔrizabl̥], *a.* vaporizable.
vaporisage [vapɔrizaːʒ], *s.m. Tex:* steaming process.
vaporisateur [vapɔrizatœːr], *s.m.* (*a*) vaporizer, atomizer; *Hort:* sprayer; **passer un arbre au v.,** to spray a tree; (*b*) scent spray.
vaporisation [vapɔrizasjɔ̃], *s.f.* vaporization; evaporation; atomization; *Mch:* **chaleur de v.,** steam-generating heat.
vaporiser [vapɔrize], *v.tr.* **1.** (*a*) to vaporize, volatilize (liquid); (*b*) to atomize, spray (liquid). **2.** to steam (cloth, etc.). **3.** *F:* to spray (sth.) with scent.
se vaporiser. 1. to become vaporized, to vaporize. **2.** to spray oneself.
vaquer [vake], *v.i.* **1.** (*a*) (*of situation*) to be vacant; *impers.* **hôpital où il vaque un lit,** hospital with a vacant bed; (*b*) (*of parliament, law courts*) to be in recess, not to be sitting; **les tribunaux vaquent au mois d'août,** the courts do not sit in August. **2. v. à qch.,** to attend to sth.; to be occupied with, concern oneself with, sth.; **v. aux soins du ménage,** to see to the household duties; **le matin je vaque à mes affaires,** in the morning I go about my work, I am busy with my work.
var [vaːr], *s.m. El: etc:* var (reactive volt-ampere unit).
varactor [varaktɔːr], *s.m. Elcs:* varactor.
varaigne [varɛɲ], *s.f.* tide gate (of salt pans).
varaire [varɛːr], *s.m. or f. Bot:* hellebore.
varan [varɑ̃], *s.m. Rept:* varanian (lizard); varan; monitor; water lizard; **v. de Komodo, v. géant,** Komodo monitor, dragon; **v. des déserts,** desert monitor; **v. à bandes,** Kabara goya.
varangue [varɑ̃ːg], *s.f.* **1.** *N.Arch:* floor timber, floor frame; **v. de fond,** flat; **v. de porque,** floor rider; **fausse v.,** filling floor; **haute v.,** deep floor. **2.** veranda(h) (in former French territories in India).
varanidés [varanide], *s.m.pl. Rept:* Varanidae.
varappe [varap], *s.f. Mount:* **1.** cliff, rock-face (to be climbed). **2.** rock climbing. **3.** rope-soled shoe.
varappée [varape], *s.f. Mount:* rock-climbing expedition.
varapper [varape], *v.i. Mount:* to climb (a rock face).
varappeur [varapœːr], *s.m. Mount:* rock climber; cliffsman.
varec(h) [varɛk], *s.m.* wrack, seaweed, varec(h); kelp; **ramasseur de v.,** kelp gatherer.
Varègues [varɛg], *Pr.n.m.pl. Hist:* Varangians.
varenne [varɛn], *s.f.* waste land; game preserve.
vareuse [varøːz], *s.f.* **1.** *Nau:* (*a*) (sailor's) jersey, jumper; (*b*) pilot coat, pea jacket. **2.** *Mil:* field-service tunic, fatigue jacket; *U.S:* blouse. **3.** loose-fitting jacket.
varheure [varœːr], *s.m. El:* reactive volt-ampere-hour.
varheuremètre [varœrmɛtr̥], *s.m. El:* reactive volt-ampere-hour meter.
varia [varja], *s.m.pl. Lit:* literary miscellany, varia.
variabilité [varjabilite], *s.f.* (*a*) *Biol: Gram: etc:* variability; (*b*) changeableness (of mood, weather).
variable [varjabl̥]. **1.** *a.* (*a*) *Biol: Gram: Mth:* variable; *Elcs:* **aiguillage v.,** variable connector, programmed switch; **calculateur à valeurs variables,** incremental computer; **données variables,** transaction data; **format en longueur v.,** V format; **représentation à virgule v.,** variable-point representation; (*b*) changeable, altering (mood, etc.); unsteady (barometer); varying (speed); **temps v.,** changeable, variable, unsettled, broken, weather; (*on barometer*) "**variable,**" "change"; **le baromètre est à v., s. au v.,** the barometer is at change; *Med:* **pouls v.,** unequal pulse; *Astr:* **étoile v.,** variable star. **2.** *s.f. Mth:* variable; **v. dépendante,** dependent variable; **v. indépendante,** independent variable, argument; *Elcs:* **v. binaire,** binary, two-state, variable; *Pol.Ec: etc:* **v. aléatoire,** random variable; **v. fictive,** shadow variable; **analyse à plusieurs variables,** multi-variate analysis.
Variagues [varjag], *Pr.n.m. pl. Hist:* Varangians.
variance [varjɑ̃ːs], *s.f.* variance; **v. de l'échantillon, de l'erreur,** sampling variance, error variance; **rapport des variances,** variance ratio.
variant, -ante [varjɑ̃, -ɑ̃ːt]. **1.** *a.* variable, fickle (character, etc.). **2.** *s.m. Nat.Hist:* variant, mutant. **3.** *s.f.* **variante:** (*a*) variant (reading of text, spelling of word); various reading; **voici les variantes du plan de la maison,** here are the alternative plans for the house; (*b*) *pl. Com:* (mixed) pickles.
variantement [varjɑ̃tmɑ̃], *s.m. Mil.Trans:* diversion (of an itinerary).
varianter [varjɑ̃te], *v.tr. Mil.Trans:* to divert (an itinerary).
variateur [varjatœːr], *s.m. Mec.E:* variable transmission; **v. de vitesse,** speed variator.
variation [varjasjɔ̃], *s.f.* **1.** variation; **v. du temps,** change in the weather; **variations du cours du franc,** fluctuations of the franc; **variations cycliques,** cyclic variations; *Nat.Hist:* **v. des espèces,** variation of species; divergence from type; *Mth:* **calcul des variations,** calculus of variations; *Ph: etc:* **v. aléatoire, v. erratique,** random variation; **v. lente et progressive,** drift; **v. de la vitesse en fonction de l'accélération,** acceleration dependence of velocity; **v. en fonction du temps,** time dependence; *Atom.Ph:* **v. de réactivité,** reactivity drift; **v. brusque de réactivité,** prompt jump of reactivity; *Artil:* **v. de hausse,** change in range; *Nau:* **v. d'assiette,** change of trim; *El:* **v. de courant,** current variation; **v. de fréquence,** frequency variation, shift; **v. de phase,** phase variation, shift; **v. de potentiel,** potential variation; **v. brusque de potentiel,** potential drop; **v. de charge, de régime,** load variation; *Elcs:* **v. discrète,** step change; *Magn:* **v. du magnétisme terrestre,** fluctuation, variation, of terrestrial magnetism; **v. du compas,** compass error; **compas à v.,** variation compass; *Astr:* **la v. de la lune est fonction de sa distance angulaire par rapport au soleil,** the variation of the moon depends on its angular distance from the sun. **2.** *Mus:* variation (**sur,** on); **air avec variations,** theme with variations.
variationel, -elle [varjasjɔnɛl], *a.* variational.
varice [varis], *s.f.* **1.** *Med:* varix, varicosity; varicose vein. **2.** *Conch:* varix.
varicelle [varisɛl], *s.f. Med:* varicella, chicken-pox.
varicocèle [varikɔsɛl], *s.f. Med:* varicocele.
varié [varje], *a.* varied; varying, diversified (types, etc.); miscellaneous (news); variegated (colours, plumage, etc.); **existence variée,** chequered existence; *Mus:* **air v.,** air with variations; *Mec:* **mouvement v.,** variable motion.
varier [varje], *v.* (*p.d. & pr.sub.* **n. variions, v. variiez**) **1.** *v.tr.* to vary; to diversify (occupations, expressions, etc.); to variegate (colours); *Mus:* **v. un air,** to make variations on an air. **2.** *v.i.* (*of wind, opinions, etc.*) to vary, change; (*of markets*) to fluctuate; **v. en qualité,** to vary in quality; **v. entre . . . et . . .,** to range between . . . and . . .; **v. dans ses réponses,** to be inconsistent in one's replies; **les auteurs varient souvent,** authors often differ, are often at variance; **les auteurs varient sur la date de . . .,** authors are not agreed as to the date of . . .; **v. de méthode,** to vary one's methods; *Mth:* **lorsque *y* vaire dans le même sens que et proportionnellement à *x*,** when *y* varies as *x*; **si *y* varie en raison directe de *x*,** if *y* varies directly as *x*; **l'on voit que *y* varie en raison inverse de *x*,** it is apparent that *y* varies inversely as *x*.
variétal, -aux [varjetal, -o], *a. Biol:* varietal.
variété [varjete], *s.f.* **1.** variety (**de,** of); diversity (of occupations, opinions, etc.); variedness (of landscape, etc.); *Com:* **grande v. de rayons,** wide range of departments; **donner de la v. au menu, au programme,** (i) to vary the menu, the programme; (ii) to lend variety to the menu, to the programme. **2.** *Nat.Hist:* variety (of flower, etc.). **3. spectacle de variétés,** variety show. **4.** *pl. Lit: Publ:* **variétés,** miscellanea.
variocoupleur [varjɔkuplœːr], *s.m. W.Tel:* vario-coupler.
variolaire [varjɔlɛːr], *a. Med:* variolar.
variole [varjɔl], *s.f.* **1.** *Med:* variola, smallpox; **v. discrète,** discrete smallpox; **v. confluente,** confluent smallpox. **2.** *Vet:* **v. des moutons,** sheep pox; **v. des vaches,** cowpox; **v. aviaire,** fowlpox.
variolé [varjɔle], *a.* pock-marked.
varioleux, -euse [varjɔlø, -øːz]. **1.** *a. Med:* variolous (pustules, patient, etc.). **2.** *s.* smallpox patient, sufferer from smallpox.
varioliforme [varjɔlifɔrm], *a.* resembling variola, varioloid.
variolique [varjɔlik], *a.* variolous (eruption, pustule, etc.).
variolisation [varjɔlizasjɔ̃], *s.f. A.Med:* variolization.
variolite [varjɔlit], *s.f. Miner:* variolite.
varioloïde [varjɔlɔid], *s.f. Med:* varioloid.
variomètre [varjɔmɛtr̥], *s.m.* (*a*) *El:* variometer; **v. à bobines plates,** disc-coil variometer; (*b*) *Av:* variometer, rate-of-climb indicator.
varioplex [varjɔplɛks], *s.m. Elcs:* varioplex.
variqueux, -euse [varikø, -øːz], *a.* **1.** varicose (vein, ulcer). **2.** varicated (shell).
variscite [varisit], *s.f. Miner:* variscite; utahlite; *Lap:* amatrice.
varistance [varistɑ̃ːs], *s.f. Elcs:* varistor.
varistor [varistɔːr], *s.m. Elcs:* varistor.
varlet [varlɛ], *s.m. Hist:* varlet, page.
varlope [varlɔp], *s.f. Tls:* trying plane, jointer; **v. à équarrir,** shooting plane.
varloper [varlɔpe], *v.tr. Carp:* to try up (plank).
varlopeuse [varlɔpøːz], *s.f. Carp:* planing machine.
varlot [varlo], *s.m. P: A:* fool, fathead.
varois, -oise [varwa, -waːz], *a. & Pr.n. Geog:* (native, inhabitant) of the department of Var.
varon [varɔ̃], *s.m.* = VARRON[2].
varonné [varɔne], *a.* = VARRONNÉ.
varoque [varɔk], *s.f.* rack-stick.

Varron[1] [varɔ̃], *Pr.n.m. Lt.Lit:* Varro.
varron[2] [varɔ̃], *s.m.* (*a*) *Ent:* warble (maggot); (*b*) *Vet:* warble (tumour).
varronné [varɔne], *a. Vet: Leath:* warbled (animal, hide).
varsoviana [varsɔvjana], *s.f. A.Danc: Mus:* varsovienne, varsoviana.
Varsovie [varsɔvi], *Pr.n.f. Geog:* Warsaw.
varsovien, -ienne [varsɔvjɛ̃, -jɛn]. **1.** *a. & s. Geog:* Varsovian. **2.** *s.f.* **varsovienne** = VARSOVIANA.
varus [varys], *Med:* **1.** *s.m.* varus. **2.** *a.* (*f.* **vara**) inturned (club-foot, etc.).
varve [varv], *s.f. Geol:* varve; **argile à v.,** varved clay.
vas [vaːs], *s.m. Anat: Med:* vas, canal, duct; *pl. vasa.*
vasard [vɑzaːr]. **1.** *a.* mud-bound (river, etc.). **2.** *s.m.* mud bottom.
Vascons [vaskɔ̃], *s.m.pl. A.Hist:* Vascones.
vasculaire [vaskylɛːr], **vasculeux, -euse** [vaskylø, -øːz], *a. Bot: Physiol:* vascular (tissue, vessels etc.); *Med:* **pression v.,** blood pressure.
vascularisation [vaskylarizasjɔ̃], *s.f. Physiol:* vascularization.
vascularisé [vaskylarize], *a. Bot: Physiol:* vascularized.
vascularité [vaskylarite], *s.f. Physiol:* vascularity.
vasculo-nerveux, -euse [vaskylɔnɛrvø, -øːz], *a.* composed of vessels and nerves.
vasculose [vaskyloːz], *s.f. Bot: Ch:* vasculose.
vase[1] [vɑːz], *s.m.* **1.** (*a*) vase, vessel, receptacle; **v. à fleurs,** flower vase; **v. de nuit,** chamber (pot); *s.a.* DÉBORDER 1; *Ch:* **v. gradué,** graduated vessel; **v. clos,** retort; airtight chamber; *F:* **vivre en v. clos,** to live in isolation; *Fin:* **la période du v. clos,** the period of isolation (during 1939-45 war); **v. à filtrations chaudes,** beaker; **v. d'expansion,** expansion chamber; *Ph:* **vases communicants,** communicating vessels; **v. évaporateur,** evaporating basin; *El:* **v. d'un élément de pile,** battery jar; **v. poreux,** porous cell; **v. de Klein,** Klein bottle; (*b*) *B:* **v. d'élection,** chosen vessel; **v. de colère,** vessel of wrath. **2.** (*a*) *Arch:* bell, vase (of capital); *Archeol:* **vases caliciformes, campaniformes,** beaker, bell-beaker, pottery; (*b*) *Bot:* calyx, vase (of tulip, etc.). **3.** *P:* **avoir du v.,** to be lucky; **manque de v.!** hard luck!
vase[2], *s.f.* mud, silt, slime, ooze, sludge; **banc de v.,** mudbank; **fond de v.,** muddy bottom.
vase[3], *s.f. P:* **1.** water. **2.** rain.
vasé [vɑze], *a.* covered with mud, with silt.
vasectomie [vɑsɛktɔmi], *s.f. Surg:* vasectomy.
vaseline [vazlin], *s.f.* (*a*) Vaseline (*R.t.m.*); petroleum jelly; *U.S:* petrolatum; **enduire qch. de v.,** to smear sth. with Vaseline; *Pharm:* **huile de v., v. liquide,** liquid paraffin; (*b*) *P:* flattery, soft soap.
vaseliner [vazline], *v.tr.* to (smear with) Vaseline.
vaser [vɑze], *v.i. P:* **1.** to rain. **2.** (*a*) to do nothing, to loaf; (*b*) to do badly (at an exam.)
vaseux, -euse [vɑzø, -øːz]. **1.** *a.* muddy, slimy (river bank, etc.). **2.** *a.* (*a*) *P:* seedy, out-of-sorts; droopy; off-colour; **il a l'air v.,** he looks a bit washed-out, under the weather; **excuse vaseuse,** lame excuse; **argument v.,** weak argument; shaky argument; (*b*) *F:* woolly; **des idées vaseuses,** woolly ideas; *s.m.* **pour excuser le v. de mes propos,** to excuse the woolliness, muddle-headedness, of what I say. **3.** *s.m. Fish:* maggot.
vasier, -ière [vɑzje, -jɛːr]. **1.** *a.* **bateau v.,** dredger, mud-lighter. **2.** *s.f.* **vasière,** (i) mudhole; muddy ground; (ii) (*salt marshes*) tidal reservoir.
vasistas [vazistɑːs], *s.m.* opening window frame, fanlight (over a door or window); ventilator (in window, over door).
vaso- [vazɔ], *pref.* vaso-.
vaso-constricteur, -trice [vazɔkɔ̃striktœːr, -tris]. **1.** *a.* vasoconstrictive. **2.** *s.m.* vasoconstrictor; *pl. vaso-constricteurs, -trices.*
vaso-constriction [vazɔkɔ̃striksjɔ̃], *s.f. no pl. Med:* vasoconstriction.
vaso-dilatateur, -trice [vazɔdilatatœːr, -tris], *a. & s.m. Anat: Med:* vasodilator; *pl. vaso-dilatateurs, -trices.*
vaso-dilatation [vazɔdilatasjɔ̃], *s.f. no pl. Med:* vasodilation, vasodilatation.
vaso-formatif, -ive [vazɔfɔrmatif, -iːv], *a.* vasoformative; *pl. vaso-formatifs, -ives.*
vaso-moteur, -trice [vazɔmɔtœːr, -tris], *a. & s.m. Anat:* vasomotor (nerve centre); *pl. vaso-moteurs, -trices.*
vaso-presseur [vazɔprɛsœːr], *s.m. Med:* vasopressor, vasoconstrictor; *pl. vaso-presseurs.*
vasopressine [vazɔprɛsin], *s.f. Med:* vasopressin.
vasotomie [vazɔtɔmi], *s.f. Surg:* vasectomy, vasotomy.
vasouillard [vɑzujaːr], *a. P:* woolly, muddle-headed.
vasouiller [vɑzuje], *v.i. P:* to be stumped; to be at sea; to be floored (at an examination); to make a mess of sth.
vasque [vask], *s.f.* **1.** basin (of fountain). **2. v. (lumineuse) en albâtre,** alabaster bowl (for electric light). **3.** *Geol:* shallow basin.
vassal, -ale, -aux [vasal, -o], *s. & a.* (*a*) vassal; (*b*) **région vassale de . . .,** region under the suzerainty of . . ..
vassaliser [vasalize], *v.tr.* to reduce to vassalage, to vassalize.
vassalité [vasalite], *s.f.,* **vasselage** [vaslaːʒ], *s.m.* **1.** vassalage. **2.** bondage, vassalage.
vassiveau, -eaux [vasivo], *s.m. Husb: Dial:* yearling lamb.
vassole [vasɔl], *s.f. Nau:* rabbet, groove, of hatch cover.
vaste [vast], *a.* **1.** vast, immense, spacious; of wide extent; **v. empire,** far-flung empire; **les vastes mers,** the spacious seas; **v. étendue de blé,** broad expanse of wheat; **v. érudition,** wide, comprehensive, all-embracing, learning; **une v. entreprise,** a vast undertaking; *F:* **les méthodes audio-visuelles sont une v. plaisanterie,** audio-visual methods are one big joke. **2.** *Anat:* **le muscle v. externe,** *s.* **le v. externe,** the vastus externus; **le (muscle) v. interne,** the vastus internus.
vastement [vastəmɑ̃], *adv.* vastly, spaciously, comprehensively.
Vasthi [vasti], *Pr.n.f. B.Hist:* Vashti.
vastité [vastite], *s.f.,* **vastitude** [vastityd], *s.f.* vastitude. **1.** vastity, vastness. **2.** vast expanse (of desert, etc.).
vastringue [vastrɛ̃ːg], *s.f. Carp:* spokeshave.
vat [vɑ(t)]. *See* À-DIEU-VAT.
Vatel [vatɛl], *s.m. F:* first-class chef (comparable to the famous *maître d'hôtel* of the Prince de Condé in the reign of Louis XIV).
va-t-en-guerre [vatɑ̃gɛːr], *s.m.inv. F:* sabre-rattler.
Vatican (le) [ləvatikɑ̃], *Pr.n.m.* the Vatican; *F:* **les foudres du V.,** the Papal interdicts; *Hist:* **le concile du V.,** the Vatican Council; *F:* **V. II,** Vatican II, the second Vatican Council.
vaticane [vatikan], *a.f.* of the Vatican; *esp.* **la bibliothèque v.,** *s.* **la Vaticane,** the Vatican Library.
vaticinant [vatisinɑ̃], *a. Pej:* prophetic.
vaticinateur, -trice [vatisinatœːr, -tris], *Pej:* **1.** *a.* vaticinal, prophetic. **2.** *s.m.* vaticinator, prophet.
vaticination [vatisinasjɔ̃], *s.f. Pej:* vaticination, prophecy.
vaticiner [vatisine], *v.i. Pej:* to vaticinate, to prophesy.
va-tout [vatu], *s.m.inv. Gaming:* the whole of one's stakes; *F:* **jouer son va-t.,** to stake one's all, one's last farthing.
vau (à) [avo], *adv.phr.* **à v.-l'eau,** downstream, with the stream; **tout va à v.-l'eau,** everything is being neglected, is going to rack and ruin, is left to drift, *F:* is going to the dogs; *A:* **à v.-deroute,** in disorder, in utter confusion, helter-skelter; *Ven:* **chasser à v.-vent,** to hunt or shoot down (the) wind; (*of the game*) **aller à v.-vent,** to run, fly, before the wind.
vauchérie [voʃeri], *s.f. Algae:* vaucheria.
vauclusien, -ienne [voklyzjɛ̃, -jɛn], *a. & s. Geog:* (native, inhabitant) of Vaucluse; *Geol:* **source vauclusienne,** Vauclusian spring.
vaudeville [vodvil], *s.m.* **1.** *Lit.Hist:* topical, satirical, song (with refrain). **2.** *Th:* vaudeville, light comedy (*usu.* with occasional song).
vaudevillesque [vodvilɛsk], *a.* Gilbertian, vaudevillian (situation, etc.).
vaudevilliste [vodvilist], *s.m.* vaudevillist, vaudevillian, writer of vaudevilles.
vaudois, -oise[1] [vodwa, -waːz], *a. & s.* **1.** *Geog:* (native, inhabitant) of Vaud (Swiss canton); Vaudois. **2.** *Rel.H:* Waldensian; **les V.,** the Waldenses.
vaudoise[2], *s.f. Ich:* (= VANDOISE) dace.
vaudou [vodu], *s.m.* voodoo, hoodoo, voodou; voodooism, voodouism; *a.inv.* **culte v.,** voodoo cult.
Vaugelas [voʒlɑ], *s.m. F: A:* **parler V.,** to speak French correctly, grammatically (according to the precepts of Vaugelas, the Fr. grammarian of the 17th century).
vauquelinite [vok(ə)linit], *s.f. Miner:* vauquelinite.
vauréen, -enne [voreɛ̃, -ɛn], *a. & s. Geog:* (native, inhabitant) of Lavaur.
vaurien, -ienne [vorjɛ̃, -jɛn], *s.* (*a*) loafer, good-for-nothing, *F:* layabout, yob, rotter, bad lot; **c'est une vaurienne,** she's a bad lot; (*b*) *F:* **petit v.!** you little scamp! you little rascal!
vaurienner [vorjɛne], *v.i. F: A:* to be up to every kind of mischief; to loaf.
vauriennerie [vorjɛnri], *s.f. F: A:* rascality.
vautour [votuːr], *s.m.* **1.** *Orn:* vulture; **v. fauve, v. griffon,** griffon vulture; **v. moine,** black vulture; **v. oricou,** sociable vulture; **v. arrian,** cinereous vulture. **2.** (*a*) *F:* usurer, shark; (*b*) *P:* landlord.
vautour-pêcheur [voturpɛʃœːr], *s.m. Orn:* vulturine fish-eagle; *pl. vautours-pêcheurs.*
vautrait [votrɛ], *s.m. Ven:* pack (of boar hounds).
vautre [voːtr̥], *s.m.* boarhound.
vautrement [votrəmɑ̃], *s.m.* (*a*) wallowing; (*b*) sprawling.
vautrer (se) [səvotre], *v.pr.* (*a*) (*of pig, etc.*) to wallow (in mud); **se. v. dans la débauche,** to wallow in debauch; (*b*) *F:* to sprawl (on grass, on a sofa).
vauvert [vovɛːr]. *See* DIABLE 1.
vauvertois, -oise [vovɛrtwa, -waːz], *a. & s. Geog:* (native, inhabitant) of Vauvert.
vaux [vo], *s.m.pl. See* VAL.
vavain [vavɛ̃], *s.m. Nau:* hawser.
vavassal, -aux [vavasal, -o], *s.m.,* **vavasseur** [vavasœːr], *s.m. Hist:* vavasour.
vavassorie [vavasɔri], *s.f. Hist:* vavasory.
va-vite (à la) [alavavit], *adv.phr.* **travail fait à la va-vite,** scamped work, rushed work.
vayvode [vɛvɔd], *s.m. Hist:* voivode, vaivode.
vayvodie [vɛvɔdi], *s.f. Hist:* voivodeship.
veau, -eaux [vo], *s.m.* **1.** (*a*) calf; **v. de lait.,** sucking calf; **le v. gras,** the fatted calf; *F:* **faire le v., s'étendre comme un v.,** to loll, sprawl; *F:* **pleurer comme un v.,** to cry one's eyes out; (*b*) **v. marin,** sea calf, seal; (*c*) *F:* (i) fool, clot; (ii) lout; (*d*) *P:* stubborn horse; *Turf:* dud horse, rank outsider; (*e*) *P:* unresponsive, sluggish, gutless, car. **2.** *Cu:* veal; **côtelette de v.,** veal cutlet; *F:* **v. blanc,** battery veal; **gelée de pied de v.,** calf's foot jelly; **ris de v.,** sweetbread; **tête de v.,** (i) calf's head; (ii) *F:* (*bald head*) billiard ball. **3.** calf (leather); calfskin; **v. chromé,** box calf; **reliure en v.,** calf binding.
vécés [vese], *s.m.pl. F:* toilet, loo.
vecteur, -trice [vɛktœːr, -tris]. **1.** *a. Mth:* **rayon v.,** radius vector; *Med:* **agent v.,** vehicle of disease, vector. **2.** *s.m. Space: Ball:* vehicle (of satellite, atomic warhead, etc.).
vectocardiogramme [vɛktɔkardjɔgram], *s.m. Med:* vectocardiogram.
vectocardiographie [vɛktɔkardjɔgrafi], *s.f. Med:* vectocardiography.
vectocardiographique [vɛktɔkardjɔgrafik], *a. Med:* vectocardiographic.
vectogramme [vɛktɔgram], *s.m. Med:* vectocardiogram.
vectographie [vɛktɔgrafi], *s.f. Med:* vectocardiography.
vectographique [vɛktɔgrafik], *a. Med:* vectocardiographic.
vectoriel, -ielle [vɛktɔrjɛl], *a. Mth:* vectorial (geometry, etc.); **calcul v.,** vector calculus; **fonction, quantité, vectorielle,** vector function, vector quantity; **produit v.,** vector product; *El:* **puissance vectorielle,** vectorial power, vector volt-amperes.
vécu [veky], *a.* **1. choses vécues,** things which have been lived through; actual experiences; *s.m.* **ce qui va suivre est du v.,** what follows is an account of actual experience; *Phil:* **durée vécue, temps v.,** time as experienced. **2.** (play, novel, etc.) true to life, founded on fact.
védas [veda], *s.m.pl. Rel.H:* **les V.,** the Veda(s).
vedettariat [vədɛtarja], *s.m. Cin: etc:* stardom.
vedette [vədɛt], *s.f.* **1.** *Mil:* vedette, mounted sentry; **être en v.,** to be on vedette duty. **2.** (*a*) *Navy:* vedette boat, scout; *A:* **v. à vapeur,** picket boat; **v. à moteur,** motor boat; **v. de port,** harbour motorboat; **v. des permissionnaires,** *F:* liberty boat; **v. de défense côtière,** coastal motorboat; **v. de défense côtière vers le large,** seaward defence boat; **v. lance-torpilles, v. porte-torpilles,** motor torpedo boat, M.T.B; **v. de la marine,** patrol boat; (*b*) *Nau:* small motorboat (on cross-harbour service, etc.); **v. de la police,** police launch; **v. de la douane,** patrol boat; **v. rapide,** fast patrol boat; (*c*) *Aer:* **v. aérienne,** blimp. **3.** (*a*) **écrire, imprimer, qch. en v.,** to write, print, sth. in a line by itself; to make (title, etc.) stand out; **mots en v.,** (i) words displayed in bold type; (ii) salutation (in a

letter); *Th:* **v. américaine** = curtain raiser; (*of actor*) **se trouver, être mis, en v. sur l'affiche,** to head, top, the bill; **bien en v.,** conspicuously displayed, in evidence, in the fore; **être en v.,** to be in the limelight; **faire v.,** to be in the forefront; **mettre en v.,** to highlight; **remporter la v.,** to steal the show; **faire la, sa, v., jouer les vedettes,** to hog the limelight; *Journ:* **partager la v.,** to share the top of the bill; **le problème de l'unité européenne retrouve la v.,** the problem of a united Europe is hitting the headlines again; *Fb: etc:* **club v.,** crack club; *Cost: Furn:* **coloris v.,** with-it colour; (*b*) *Th: Cin:* star; leading man, lady; **v. de l'écran,** film star.

védique [vedik], *a. Rel.H:* Vedic.

védisme [vedism], *s.m. Rel.H:* Vedism.

Véga [vega], *Pr.n.f. Astr:* Vega.

Végèce [veʒɛs], *Pr.n.m. Lit:* Vegetius.

végétal, -aux [veʒetal, -o]. **1.** *a.* plant (life, etc.); vegetable (kingdom); **beurre v.,** vegetable butter. **2.** *s.m.* plant.

Végétaline [veʒetalin], *s.f. R.t.m:* (*brand of*) vegetable fat.

végétalisme [veʒetalism], *s.m.* strict vegetarianism.

végétalité [veʒetalite], *s.f.* vegetable life.

végétant [veʒetɑ̃], *a.* vegetating.

végétarianisme [veʒetarjanism], *s.m.* vegetarianism.

végétarien, -ienne [veʒetarjɛ̃, -jɛn], vegetarian.

végétarisme [veʒetarism], *s.m.* vegetarianism.

végétatif, -ive [veʒetatif, -iːv], *a.* vegetative, vegetable-like, cabbage-like (existence).

végétation [veʒetasjɔ̃], *s.f.* **1.** vegetation; **arbres en pleine v.,** trees in full growth. **2.** *pl. Med:* vegetations; **végétations dans le nez, végétations adénoïdes,** adenoid growths, *F:* adenoids.

végétativement [veʒetativmɑ̃], *adv. Biol:* vegetatively, by vegetative propagation.

végéter [veʒete], *v.i.* (**je végète, n. végétons; je végéterai**) **1.** (*of plant*) to vegetate, grow. **2.** to vegetate; to lead an aimless, uneventful life; to jog along.

végéto- [veʒeto], *pref.* vegeto-.

végéto-animal, -aux [veʒetoanimal, -o], *a.* vegeto-animal.

végéto-minéral, -aux [veʒetomineral, -o], *a.* vegeto-mineral.

végéto-sulfurique [veʒetosylfyrik], *a.* vegeto-sulphuric; *pl. végéto-sulfuriques.*

veglione [vɛljone], *s.m.* carnival dance, fancy-dress ball; *pl. veglioni.*

véhémence [veemɑ̃ːs], *s.f.* vehemence (of speech, wind, etc.); **avec v.,** vehemently.

véhément [veemɑ̃], *a.* vehement, violent (speech, etc.).

véhémentement [veemɑ̃tmɑ̃], *adv.* vehemently, violently.

véhiculaire [veikylɛːr], *a.* vehicular; **langue v.,** common language; **au moyen âge, le latin était la langue v. acceptée par tous,** in the Middle Ages Latin was the universally accepted common tongue.

véhicule [veikyl], *s.m.* **1.** (*a*) vehicle; conveyance; **v. terrestre,** land vehicle; **v. à roues,** wheeled vehicle; **v. à chenilles, v. chenillé,** (full-)tracked vehicle; **v. semi-chenillé,** half-tracked vehicle, half-track; **v. tous terrains,** cross-country vehicle; **v. sur coussin d'air,** air-cushion vehicle; **v. amphibie,** amphibious vehicle; **v. à traction animale,** animal-drawn vehicle; **v. hippomobile,** horse-drawn vehicle; **v. à propulsion, à traction, mécanique,** mechanically-propelled vehicle; **v. automobile, v. à moteur,** motor vehicle, self-propelled vehicle; **colonne de véhicules en marche,** line, convoy, of moving traffic; **v. de transport de passagers, de marchandises,** passenger vehicle; freight vehicle, goods vehicle; **v. à toutes fins, v. tous usages,** general-purpose vehicle; **v. (à usage, à châssis) spécial,** special-purpose vehicle; **v. de dépannage,** breakdown vehicle; **v. de dépannage et de sauvetage,** recovery vehicle; **v. de servitude,** service vehicle; *Av:* **v. de servitude d'aérodrome,** line service vehicle; *Adm:* **v. articulé,** articulated vehicle; **véhicules commerciaux,** commercial vehicles; *Mil:* **v. administratif,** administrative vehicle; **v. de commandement,** command vehicle; **v. de combat,** fighting vehicle, *U.S:* combat vehicle; **v. blindé de transport de troupe, de transport de personnel,** armoured troop-carrier, armoured personnel-carrier; **v. blindé du génie,** armoured engineer vehicle; **v. de transport d'armement,** weapon carrier; **v. porte-mortier,** mortar carrier; **v. porte-munitions,** ammunition carrier; **v. démineur,** mine-sweeping vehicle; **v. poseur de pont,** bridge-laying vehicle; (*b*) **v. spatial,** spacecraft; **v. spatial habité, inhabité,** manned, unmanned, spacecraft; *Ball:* **v. de lancement,** launching vehicle (of nuclear bomb, satellite, etc.). **2.** (*a*) *Med:* carrier, vector; **servir de v. à (la contagion d') une maladie,** to convey, to be the carrier or vector of, a disease; **l'air, l'eau et les aliments peuvent être des véhicules d'infection,** air, water, and food may be the vehicles of infection; (*b*) **le langage est le v. de la pensée,** speech is the vehicle of thought; **l'orgue est, par excellence, le v. de la musique sacrée,** the organ provides an unrivalled medium for sacred music. **3.** (*a*) *Ch: Pharm: Art:* vehicle, medium (for mixing chemical substance, pigment, etc.); *Ph:* **l'air est le v. du son,** the air is the medium, the vehicle, of sound; (*b*) *Art:* carrier (for colours). **4.** *Rel:* Vehicle (of Buddhist salvation); **Grand V.,** Great Vehicle, Mahayana; **Petit V.,** Little Vehicle, Hinayana.

véhiculer [veikyle], *v.tr.* **1.** to convey, carry (by vehicle); to cart (sth.). **2. le langage véhicule les idées entre les hommes,** language is the vehicle of ideas, language transmits ideas between men.

Vehme [vɛm], *Pr.n.f. Hist:* **la sainte V.,** the Vehmgericht.

vehmique [vemik], *a. Hist:* Vehmic (tribunal, etc.).

véien, -ienne [vejɛ̃, -jɛn], *a.* & *s. A.Geog:* Veientian.

Véies [vei, vɛːj], *Pr.n.f. A.Geog:* Veii.

veille [vɛːj], *s.f.* **1.** (*a*) sitting up, staying up (at night); watching (by night); **être accoutumé aux veilles,** to be accustomed to late nights; **usé par les veilles,** worn out by long vigils; **consacrer ses veilles à qch.,** to give up one's nights' rest to sth; (*b*) vigil (of nun, etc.); *A:* **la v. des armes,** the vigil of arms (before entering the order of knighthood); (*c*) *Mil:* (night) watch; *Nau:* lookout; *Nau:* **homme de v.,** look-out (man); *Nau:* **chambre de v.,** chart house; **ancre de v.,** sheet anchor; **chaîne de v.,** sheet cable; *A:* **ancre en v.,** anchor a-cock-bill; **mettre l'ancre en v.,** to cockbill the anchor; (*d*) wakefulness; **entre la v. et le sommeil,** between waking and sleeping; **causer à qn bien des veilles,** to cause s.o. many a sleepless night; *Med:* **suggestion à l'état de v.,** suggestion in the waking state. **2.** (*a*) eve, preceding day; **la v. de Noël,** Christmas Eve; **la v. du jour de l'an,** New Year's Eve; **la v. de la bataille,** the day before the battle; **je l'avais vu la v.,** I had seen him the day before; **la v. au soir,** the evening before; (*b*) **être à la v. de la ruine, d'une guerre,** to be on the brink, on the verge, of ruin, of a war; **être à la v. de se marier,** to be on the eve, on the point, of getting married; **à la v. d'être emprisonné,** on the eve of his imprisonment; **à la v. de la réunion,** just before the meeting; *F:* **c'est pas demain la v.!** not likely!

veillée [veje], *s.f.* **1.** (*a*) night nursing (of the sick); **v. de corps,** watching, vigil (by dead body); (*esp. in Ireland*) wake; (*b*) *A:* **la v. des armes, une v. d'armes,** vigil of arms; *Pol:* **tous les partis tiennent ce soir leur v. d'armes,** tonight all the parties are holding their eve-of-election meetings. **2.** evening (spent in company) sitting up over the fire; **faire la v. chez des voisins,** to spend the evening socially with neighbours (*esp.* among country people during the winter months).

veiller [veje]. **1.** *v.i.* (*a*) to sit up, stay up, keep awake; **je veillerai jusqu'à leur retour,** I shall sit up for them; **il a veillé très tard,** he sat up very late; **v. fort avant dans la nuit,** to burn the midnight oil; (*b*) *Mil: Nau: etc:* to watch, be on the lookout; to keep a good lookout; to stand by; (*c*) *Ecc:* to keep vigil; (*d*) **v. sur qn, qch.,** to look after s.o., sth., to take care of s.o., sth.; (*e*) **v. à qch.,** to watch over, see to, sth; **v. au salut de l'État,** to watch over the safety of the State; **v. aux intérêts de qn,** to attend to, look after, s.o.'s interests; **v. à ses intérêts,** to be alive to one's interests; *Jur:* **v. (en justice) aux intérêts de qn,** to watch a case; to hold a watching brief for s.o.; **v. à la besogne,** to give an eye to the work; to keep an eye on the work; **v. à faire qch.,** to be careful to do sth.; **veillez à ce que vos outils soient en bon état,** look to your tools; **v. à l'hygiène publique,** to protect public health; **v. à ce que qch. se fasse,** to take care that sth. is done; to see to it that sth. is done; **veillez à ce qu'il ait tout ce qu'il lui faut,** see (to it) that he has everything he needs; *Nau:* **veillez aux écoutes!** stand by the sheets! *F:* **v. au grain,** to look out for squalls; to keep one's weather eye open. **2.** *v.tr.* (*a*) to sit up with, look after, watch over, attend (to) (sick person, etc.); **v. un mort,** to keep vigil over a dead body; to watch, wake, a corpse; (*b*) *Ven:* to watch (falcon).

veilleur, -euse [vɛjœːr, -øːz]. **1.** (*a*) *s.m.* watcher (by night); keeper of a vigil; *Ind: etc:* **v. de nuit,** nightwatchman; (*b*) *s.f.* **veilleuse,** nun keeping vigil (beside the dead). **2.** *s.f.* **veilleuse:** (*a*) night-light; **lumière en veilleuse,** light turned low; **mettre le gaz en veilleuse,** to turn down the gas to a pin point; **mettre l'électricité en veilleuse,** to dim the lights; *Aut: O:* **mettre les phares en veilleuse,** to dim the headlights; *attrib.* **ampoule veilleuse,** dimmer-bulb; *F:* **mettre une entreprise, une usine, en veilleuse,** to reduce output to a minimum; **mettre un projet en veilleuse,** to put a project off temporarily, *F:* to shelve a project, to put a project on ice; *P:* **la mettre en veilleuse,** to shut up, keep mum (about sth.); (*b*) by-pass (of gas-burner); pilot (burner, light); (*c*) *Bot:* meadow saffron.

veilloir [vɛjwaːr], *s.m.* saddler's bench.

veillotte [vɛjɔt], *s.f.* **1.** *Bot: F:* meadow saffron. **2.** *Agr:* (hay)cock.

veinage [vɛnaːʒ], *s.m.* veining, graining (of wood, etc.).

veinard, -arde [vɛnaːr, -ard], *a.* & *s. F:* (*a*) *a.* lucky (person, player, etc.); (*b*) *s.* lucky person, lucky dog; **c'est un v.,** he has all the luck; **(sacré) v.!** you lucky devil!

veine [vɛn], *s.f.* **1.** (*a*) *Anat: Bot:* vein; *F:* **tant que le sang coulera dans mes veines,** so long as I live; *s.a.* SAIGNER 2, SANG 1; *Anat:* **v. cave,** vena cava; (*b*) (underground) stream, rivulet; *Ph:* **v. fluide,** jet (of water, gas, etc.); *Aer:* jet stream; (*c*) vein (in wood, marble, etc.). **2.** (*a*) *Geol:* vein; lode (of ore); seam (of coal); (*b*) vein, inspiration, humour; **la v. poétique,** the poetic vein, poetic inspiration; **être en v. de faire qch.,** to be in the mood, in the humour, to do sth., for doing sth.; **être en v. de générosité,** to be in a giving humour, in a generous mood; (*c*) *F:* luck; **être en v., avoir de la v.,** to be in luck('s way); *F:* **avoir une v. de cocu, de cornard, de pendu,** to have the devil's own luck; **porter v. à qn,** to bring s.o. good luck; **je n'ai pas eu de v.,** I drew a blank; **coup de v.,** (i) stroke of luck; lucky strike; (ii) fluke; **jour de v.,** good day (at races, etc.); **quelle v.!** my luck's in! **pas de v.!** rotten luck! **c'est bien ma v.,** just my luck!

veiné [vene], *a.* veined (marble, etc.); grained (door, etc.).

veiner [vene], *v.tr.* to vein, grain (door, etc.).

veinette [vɛnɛt], *s.f.* veining brush, graining brush.

veineux, -euse [vɛnø, -øːz], *a.* **1.** (*a*) *Physiol:* venous (system, blood); (*b*) *Bot:* venose, veiny (leaf). **2.** veiny (wood, etc.); full of veins.

veinule [vɛnyl], *s.f.* **1.** veinlet; *Ent:* venule (of wing). **2.** *Min:* thread (of ore).

veinulé [vɛnyle], *a.* **des yeux veinulés,** bloodshot eyes.

veinure [vɛnyːr], *s.f.* veining (of wood, marble, etc.).

Vélabre (le) [ləvelaːbr], *Pr.n.m. Rom.Ant:* the Velabrum (district of Rome).

vêlage [vɛlaːʒ], *s.m.* (*of cow*) calving, freshening.

vélaire [velɛːr], *a.* & *s.f. Ling:* velar (guttural); back (consonant).

velaisien, -ienne [vəlɛzjɛ̃, -jɛn], *a.* & *s. Geog:* (native, inhabitant) of the Velay (region).

vélanède [velanɛd], *s.f.*, **vélani** [velani], *s.m. Bot: Com: Tan: etc:* val(l)onia (oak tree).

vélar [velaːr], *s.m. Bot:* hedge mustard.

vélarisation [velarizasjɔ̃], *s.f. Ling:* velarization.

vélariser [velarize], *v.tr. Ling:* to velarize; **consonne vélarisée,** velar consonant.

vélarium [velarjɔm], *s.m. Rom.Ant:* velarium.

vélaunien, -ienne [velonjɛ̃, -jɛn], *a.* & *s. Geog:* (native, inhabitant) of the Velay (region).

velche [vɛlʃ] = WELCHE.

Vel'd'Hiv' [vɛldiːv], *s.m. A: F:* = **Vélodrome d'Hiver** (the Paris cycle-racing track, often used for political meetings).

veld(t) [vɛlt], *s.m.* veldt.

vélelle [velɛl], *s.f. Coel:* velella.

vêlement [vɛlmɑ̃], *s.m.* (*of cow*) calving, freshening.

vêler [vele], *v.i.* (*of cow*) to calve, freshen.

vélie [veli], *s.f. Ent:* water flea.

véliforme [velifɔrm], *a. Nat.Hist:* veliform.

véligère [veliʒɛːr], *Z:* **1.** *a.* veligerous. **2.** *s.f.* veliger.

vélin [velɛ̃]. **1.** (*a*) *s.m.* vellum (parchment); (*b*) *a.m.* (*with occ. f.* **véline**) **(papier) v.,** wove paper; *Paperm:* **toile véline,** wirecloth (of mould). **2.** *s.m.* fine Alençon lace.

vélique [velik], *a. Nau:* **point v.,** centre of effort (of sails).

vélite [velit], *s.m. Rom.Ant:* velite, light-armed soldier; *pl. Hist:* **vélites,** light infantry (created by Napoleon).

vélivéliste [velivelist], *s.m. & f.*, **vélivole** [velivɔl], *s.m. & f. Aer:* (*pers.*) glider.

vélivoler [velivɔle], *v.i. Aer:* to glide.

velléitaire [vɛlleitɛːr, vele-]. **1.** *a.* impulsive, erratic, weak-willed (person). **2.** *s.* worker by fits and starts; trifler.

velléité [vɛlleite, vele-], *s.f.* slight desire, inclination; stray impulse; *Phil:* velleity; **avoir des velléités de travail,** to toy with the idea of work; **avoir des velléités de résistance,** to put up a show, some sort, of resistance.

vellèle [velɛl], *s.f. Coel:* velella, *F:* by-the-wind-sailor.

vélo [velo], *s.m.* bicycle, (push-)bike; *U.S: F:* wheel; **aller à, en, v.,** to cycle; *F:* to ride a bike; **faire du v.,** to go in for cycling; *P:* **est-ce que je te demande si ta grand-mère fait du v.?** mind your own business!

vélocar [velɔkaːr], *s.m.* pedal-car.

véloce [velɔs], *a. Lit:* swift (runner, etc.).

vélocifère [velɔsifɛːr], *s.m. A.Veh:* (*a*) fast stage-coach; (*b*) dandy horse.

vélocimane [velɔsiman], *s.m. A:* (*a*) hand-propelled tricycle (for invalids, etc.); (*b*) *Toys:* hand-propelled horse on wheels.

vélocimètre [velɔsimɛtr̥], *s.m. Ball: etc:* velocimeter.

vélocipède [velɔsipɛd], *s.m.* **1.** *A:* velocipede; **v. à bandages de fer,** bone-shaker. **2.** *Adm:* cycle (of any type).

vélocipédie [velɔsipedi], *s.f. A:* cycling.

vélocipédiste [velɔsipedist], *s.m. & f. A:* cyclist; *A:* velocipedist.

vélocité [velɔsite], *s.f.* speed, velocity, swiftness.

vélodrome [velɔdrɔm], *s.m.* cycle-racing track; cycling track.

vélomoteur [velɔmɔtœːr], *s.m.* lightweight motor cycle.

vélo-pousse [velɔpus], *s.m. Veh:* trishaw, bicycle rickshaw, pedicab; *pl. vélo-pousses.*

velot [vəlo], *s.m.Leath:* calf skin (of still-born calf).

vélotaxi [velɔtaksi], *s.m.* tandem, with passenger trailer, for hire (1939-45 war).

velours [v(ə)luːr], *s.m.* **1.** *Tex:* (*a*) velvet; **v. uni, v. plain,** plain velvet; **v. frappé,** raised, stamped, velvet; **v. broché,** brocaded velvet; **v. façonné,** figured velvet; **v. imprimé,** printed velvet; **v. glacé,** shot velvet; **v. bouclé, frisé, épinglé,** uncut velvet, terry (velvet); **v. ras, à fils courts,** short-nap velvet; **v. côtelé, à côtes, coulissé, de chasse,** ribbed velvet, corduroy velvet; **v. mille-raies,** needlecord; **v. de coton,** cotton velvet, velveteen; **v. de laine,** velour(s); *Prov:* **habit de v., ventre de son,** clothe the back and starve the belly; **v. de la pêche,** the downy skin of a peach; *s.a.* PATTE 1; (*b*) *pl. Com:* velvetings. **2.** *Lit:* **le chemin de v.,** the primrose path; **être sur le v.,** *F:* to be on velvet; *Golf:* to be dormy (2, 3, *etc.*); **jouer sur le v.,** to be on velvet; *F:* **c'est du v.,** it's easy, it's a piece of cake; *Th: F:* **faire rire le v.,** to play to an empty house. **3.** *F:* incorrect liaison consisting of an epenthetic [z], as; **j'ai été** [ʒezete], **il leur a dit** [ilœrzadi]; *cf. also* **entre quat'zyeux** (*under* ŒIL 1), which is sanctioned by use; **faire des velours,** to make incorrect liaisons; *cf.* CUIR 4.

velouté [v(ə)lute]. **1.** *a.* velvety; velvet-like; soft as velvet; downy (peach, cheeks); **vin v.,** velvety, mellow, wine; *Phot:* **papier v.,** velvet-surface paper. **2.** *s.m.* (*a*) velvetiness, softness (of material, voice, etc.); bloom (of peach, etc.); (*b*) *Cu:* thick cream soup, sauce; (*c*) *Tex:* **v. de laine,** velour(s) (cloth); (*d*) velvet braid.

veloutement [v(ə)lutmɑ̃], *s.m. Lit:* velvety aspect, touch, shade of colour.

velouter [v(ə)lute], *v.tr.* to give a velvety, soft, downy, appearance to (sth.); (*of shade, etc.*) to soften (contour); **vin qui se veloute,** wine which is getting mellow.

velouteux, -euse [v(ə)lutø, -øːz], *a.* velvety, soft.

veloutier [v(ə)lutje], *s.m.* velvet maker.

veloutine [v(ə)lutin], *s.f. Tex:* flannelette.

velpeau [vɛlpo], *s.m.* **bande de V., un v.,** crêpe bandage (as introduced by the surgeon Velpeau).

veltage [vɛltaːʒ], *s.m.* gauging (of casks).

velte [vɛlt], *s.f.* **1.** *A.Meas:* = approx. 7½ litres. **2.** gauging stick (for casks).

velter[1] [vɛlte], *v.tr.* to gauge (casks).

velter[2], *v.tr. Nau:* to woold, seize.

velture [vɛltyːr], *s.f. Nau:* woolding, seizing; **faire une v. à un espar,** to woold, seize, a spar.

velu [vəly]. **1.** *a.* (*a*) hairy (skin, etc.); villous (leaf, etc.); *Bot:* pubescent; (*b*) *Const:* **pierre velue,** rough, uncut, stone. **2.** *s.m.* villosity (of plant, etc.).

vélum, velum [velɔm], *s.m.* awning.

velvantine, velventine [vɛlvɑ̃tin], *s.f. Tex:* velveteen.

velvote [vɛlvɔt], *s.f. Bot: F:* toadflax.

venaison [vənɛzɔ̃], *s.f. Cu:* venison; **basse v.,** hare, rabbit.

venaissin [vənɛsɛ̃], *a.* of (the) Venasque (region); *s.a.* COMTAT.

vénal, -als, -aux [venal, -o], *a.* **1.** venal, purchasable (office, privilege, etc.); *Com:* **valeur vénale,** market value; **poids v.,** conventional selling weight. **2.** *Pej:* venal, mercenary, corruptible (person); corrupt (press); *A:* **juge v.,** barrator.

vénalement [venalmɑ̃], *adv.* venally, in a mercenary manner.

vénalité [venalite], *s.f.* venality; barratry (of a judge).

venant [vənɑ̃]. **1.** *a.* (*of child, plant, etc.*) thriving; **arbres bien venants,** trees that are coming on well; *A:* **deux mille livres de rente bien venantes,** a regular income of two thousand pounds. **2.** *s.m.* **à tout v., à tous venants,** to all comers, to all and sundry; **à tout v. beau jeu,** I am ready to take on all comers; *s.a.* ALLANT 3.

Venceslas [vɛ̃sɛslaːs], *Pr.n.m. A:* Wencesla(u)s.

vendable [vɑ̃dabl̥], *a.* saleable, vendible, marketable; **peu v.,** hard to sell; unsaleable.

vendange [vɑ̃dɑ̃ːʒ], *s.f.* **1.** (*often in pl.*) vintage (season). **2.** (*a*) vintage; grape gathering, vine harvest, wine harvest, grape harvest; *Lit:* **adieu, paniers, vendanges sont faites,** the business is over (and done with); (*b*) the grapes.

vendangeoir [vɑ̃dɑ̃ʒwaːr], *s.m.* grape basket.

vendangeon [vɑ̃dɑ̃ʒɔ̃], *s.m. Ent:* harvest bug.

vendanger [vɑ̃dɑ̃ʒe], *v.tr. & i.* (**je vendangeai(s); n. vendangeons**) (*a*) to vintage; to gather (the grapes); to gather the grapes of (vineyard); **le mauvais temps avait tout vendangé,** the bad weather had destroyed everything; (*b*) *F: A:* to make illicit profits; to feather one's nest.

vendangeron [vɑ̃dɑ̃ʒrɔ̃], *s.m. Ent:* harvest bug.

vendangerot [vɑ̃dɑ̃ʒ(ə)ro], *s.m. Vit:* wicker grape-basket.

vendangette [vɑ̃dɑ̃ʒɛt], *s.f. F:* thrush.

vendangeur, -euse [vɑ̃dɑ̃ʒœːr, -øːz], *s.* **1.** vintager; wine-harvester. **2.** *s.f. Bot: F:* **vendangeuse,** aster.

vendéen, -enne [vɑ̃deɛ̃, -ɛn], *a. & s. Geog: Hist:* Vendean; of the Vendée.

vendémiaire [vɑ̃demjɛːr], *s.m. Fr.Hist:* first month of the Fr. Republican calendar (Sep.-Oct.).

venderesse [vɑ̃drɛs], *s.f. Jur:* vendor.

vendetta [vɑ̃dɛtta, -eta], *s.f.* vendetta.

vendeur, -euse [vɑ̃dœːr, -øːz], *s.* **1.** (*a*) *Com:* seller, vendor (of goods); (*in shop*) salesman, saleswoman; assistant; shopman; counter hand; *U.S:* (sales) clerk; **v. à domicile, v. porte-à-porte,** door-to-door salesman; home-service salesman; (*b*) *B:* **les vendeurs du temple,** those that bought and sold in the temple; (*c*) *St.Exch:* **v. à découvert,** bear seller, short seller; **v. d'une prime directe,** taker for a call, seller of a call option; **v. d'une prime indirecte,** giver for a put, buyer of a put option. **2.** *Jur:* (*f.* **venderesse**) vendor.

vendômois, -oise [vɑ̃domwa, -waːz], *a. & s. Geog:* (native, inhabitant) of Vendôme.

vendre [vɑ̃ːdr̥], *v.tr.* **1.** to sell; **v. qch. à qn,** to sell s.o. sth.; to sell sth. to s.o.; **v. à terme,** to sell on credit; **v. comptant,** to sell for cash; **v. à perte,** to sell at a loss, under cost price; **v. en gros et en détail,** to sell wholesale and retail; (*esp. of manufacturer*) **v. à l'unité,** to sell articles singly; **v. cher, (à) bon marché,** to sell dear, cheap; **v. moins cher que qn,** to undersell s.o.; **v. chèrement sa vie,** to sell one's life dearly; **v. un objet trois francs,** *occ.* **pour trois francs,** to sell an object for three francs; **ces cuillers se vendent à dix francs pièce,** these spoons are going for ten francs each; **nous les avons tous vendus,** (i) we sold them all; (ii) we are sold out of them; **v. qch. au plus offrant,** to knock sth. down to the highest bidder; **article qui se vend cher, à un haut prix,** article that commands, fetches, a high price; **articles qui se vendent bien,** ready sellers, articles that sell well; *F:* **cela se vend comme des petits pains,** it's selling like hot cakes; **ces choses-là ne se vendent pas,** those things are not for sale, are not to be bought; **marchandises qui ne se vendent pas, qui se vendent mal,** slow sellers, goods that are a drug on the market; **maison à v.,** house for sale; **l'art de v.,** salesmanship; **v. sa conscience, son honneur,** to sell one's conscience, one's honour; **v. ses droits, sa liberté,** to barter away one's rights, one's liberty; **v. qn comme esclave,** to sell s.o. for a slave, into slavery; *s.a.* OURS, MÈCHE. **2. v. qn,** to sell s.o. up (for debt). **3. v. qn,** to betray s.o., *F:* to rat on s.o.; *P:* **v. ses complices,** to squeal; **v. un secret,** to betray a secret; **se v. au diable,** to sell oneself, one's soul, to the devil; **homme vendu au gouvernement,** creature of the government, government minion. **4.** *v.i. Com:* **affiche qui vend,** poster that sells (goods advertised).

vendredi [vɑ̃drədi]. **1.** *s.m.* Friday; **le v. saint,** Good Friday; *s.a.* RIRE I. 1. **2.** *Pr.n.m.* Man Friday (in *Robinson Crusoe*).

vendu [vɑ̃dy], *s.m.* **1.** traitor. **2.** *P: A:* re-enlisted soldier.

vené [vəne], *a.* high (meat).

Vénèdes [venɛd], *Pr.n.m.pl. A.Geog:* Veneti.

venelle [vənɛl], *s.f.* alley; *Scot:* vennel; *O: F:* **enfiler la v.,** to slip away; to take to one's heels; *O:* **ne prenez pas par la v.!** don't dodge the issue!

vénéneux, -euse [venenø, -øːz], *a.* poisonous (plant, food, chemical).

vénénifère [venenifɛːr], *a.* veneniferous, poison-bearing (glands, etc.).

vénénifique [venenifik], **vénénipare** [venenipaːr], *a. Z:* venenific, poison-producing (glands, etc.).

vener [vəne], *v.i.* (**je vène, n. venons; je vènerai**) **faire v. de la viande,** to hang meat (until it is high).

vénérabilité [venerabilite], *s.f.* venerability.

vénérable [venerabl̥]. **1.** *a.* venerable (old man, custom, etc.). **2.** *s.m.* worshipful master (of masonic lodge).

vénérablement [venerabləmɑ̃], *adv.* venerably.

vénérateur, -trice [veneratœːr, -tris], *s.* venerator, reverencer.

vénération [venerasjɔ̃], *s.f.* veneration, reverence; **avoir de la v. pour qn,** to hold s.o. in veneration.

vénéréologie [venereɔlɔʒi], *s.f. Med:* venereology.

vénéréologue [venereɔlɔg], *s.m. & f. Med:* venereologist.

vénérer [venere], *v.tr.* (**je vénère, n. vénérons; je vénérerai**) (*a*) to venerate, reverence, revere; (*b*) to worship (saint, relics, etc.).

vénéricarde [venerikard], *s.f. Moll:* heart cockle, heart shell.

vénerie [vɛnri], *s.f.* **1.** venery; (science of) hunting; **termes de v.,** hunting terms; **bête de v.,** beast hunted with hounds (stag, boar, etc.). **2.** *Hist:* care and management of the royal hunts.

vénérien, -ienne [venerjɛ̃, -jɛn], *a. Med:* venereal.

venet [vənɛ], *s.m. Fish:* semi-circular moored tide net.

Vénètes [venɛt], *Pr.n.m.pl. A.Geog:* Veneti.

Vénétie [venesi], *Pr.n.f. Geog:* Venezia.

venette [vənɛt], *s.f. P: O:* funk; **avoir la v.,** to be in a blue funk; to have, get, the wind up; **donner la v. à qn,** to put s.o. in a funk; to give s.o. the shivers; to put the wind up s.o.

veneur [vənœːr], *s.m. Ven:* huntsman; **les veneurs,** the hunt, the field; *Hist:* **le Grand V.,** the Master of the Royal Hunt.

vénézolan, -ane [venezɔlɑ̃, -aːn], *a. & s.* Venezuelan.

Vénézuéla (le) [ləvenezɥela], *Pr.n. Geog:* Venezuela.

vénézuélien, -ienne [venezɥeljɛ̃, -jɛn], *a. & s. Geog:* Venezuelan.

venez-y-voir [vnezivwaːr], *s.m.inv. Iron: A:* sight; fine thing to see; **voilà un beau v.-y-v.!** just look at it!

vengeance [vɑ̃ʒɑ̃ːs], *s.f.* **1.** revenge; **par v.,** out of revenge, vengefully; **esprit de v.,** vengefulness, spirit of revenge; **il avait toujours la v. dans le cœur,** he was still harbouring thoughts of revenge; **avoir soif de v.,** to be thirsting for revenge; **tirer v. d'une injure,** to be revenged for an insult; **tirer, prendre, v. de qn, exercer sa v. sur qn,** to be avenged on s.o.; to have one's revenge on s.o.; to wreak one's vengeance on s.o. **2.** vengeance, retribution, requital; **la v. de Dieu,** the vengeance of God; **crime qui crie v.,** crime that cries for vengeance.

venger [vɑ̃ʒe], *v.tr.* (**je vengeai(s); nous vengeons**) to avenge (insult, insulted person); **v. qn d'une injure,** to avenge s.o. for an insult; **v. une injure sur qn,** to take it out on s.o. for an insult.

se venger, to be revenged, to have one's revenge; **se v. d'une injure,** to take vengeance for an insult; to requite an insult; **se v. de ses ennemis,** to be avenged, revenged, to wreak vengeance on, one's enemies; **se v. sur qn (de qch.),** to have one's revenge on s.o. (for sth.); to pay s.o. out.

vengeur, -eresse [vɑ̃ʒœːr, -rɛs]. **1.** *s.* avenger, revenger; **Dieu, le v. du crime,** God, the Avenger of crime; **sa mort trouvera des vengeurs,** his death will be avenged. **2.** (i) *Lit:* avenging, vengeful (sword, etc.).

véniel, -ielle [venjɛl], *a.* venial (sin).

véniellement [venjɛlmɑ̃], *adv.* (to sin) venially.

venimeux, -euse [vənimø, -øːz], *a.* venomous; (*a*) poisonous (bite, animal, *esp.* serpent); (*b*) spiteful, malignant, virulent (critic, tongue).

venimosité [vənimozite], *s.f.* venomousness (of sting, of criticism, etc.).

venin [vənɛ̃], *s.m.* venom; (*a*) poison (of adder, etc.); **glandes à v.,** poison glands; (*b*) spite, malice, virulence; **homme sans v.,** man who bears no malice; **jeter tout son v.,** to vent all one's spleen; *s.a.* MORT[1] 1.

venir [v(ə)niːr]. I. *v.i.* (*pr.p.* **venant;** *p.p.* **venu;** *pr.ind.* **je viens, il vient, n. venons, ils viennent;** *pr.sub.* **je vienne, n. venions, ils viennent;** *p.d.* **je venais;** *p.h.* **je vins, n. vînmes, v. vîntes, ils vinrent;** *p.sub.* **je vinsse;** *fu.* **je viendrai;** *the aux. is* **être**) to come. **1.** (*a*) **je viens!** I'm coming! **ne faire qu'aller et v.,** to be always on the move, on the go; **je ne ferai qu'aller et v.,** I shall be back in a minute, I shall come straight back; **mais venez donc!** do come along! **venez par ici,** come this way; **d'où venez-vous?** where have you come from? where have you been? **il vint à moi, vers moi,** he came up to me, stepped up to me; *B:* **laissez v. à moi les petits enfants,** suffer the little children to come unto me; **il vint sur moi,** he advanced on me (threateningly); **v. au monde,** to be born; **l'été viendra,** summer will soon come round; **ces bruits vinrent jusqu'à moi,** these rumours reached me, came to my ears; **l'année qui vient,** next year; **ses succès à v.,** his future successes; **dans les temps à v.,** in the days to come; **il faut prendre les choses comme elles viennent,** we must take things as they come; we must take the rough with the smooth; **vienne un peu de soleil et tout le monde est gai,** the minute the sun comes out everyone is cheerful; *Lit:* **il aura dix ans vienne (la) Noël,** he will be ten come Christmas; **faire v. qn,** to send for, call in, fetch, s.o.; **faire v. ses robes de Paris,** to get one's dresses from Paris; **vous ferez v. un tonneau de bière,** you must order, send for, a barrel of beer; **monuments romains qui sont venus jusqu'à nous,** Roman monuments that have come down to us; **je préfère voir v.,** I prefer to wait and see; **voir v. qn,** to see s.o. coming; *F:* **je vous vois v.!** I see what you are driving at, what you are getting at; **le voici v., le voici qui vient,** here he comes; **se faire bien v. de qn,** to ingratiate oneself with s.o.; to get into s.o.'s good books; **être bien, mal, venu,** to be welcome, unwelcome; **son discours était mieux venu que les précédents,** his speech was more acceptable than the previous ones; **vous seriez bien venu à les aider,** they would welcome your help; **je serais mal venu à . . .,** it would be ungracious of me to . . .; **vous êtes mal venu à, de, me faire des reproches,** (i) it is not for you, (ii) this is no time, to reproach me; *impers.* **il vient ici toutes sortes de gens,** all sorts of people call here; **est-il venu quelqu'un?** has anyone called? has anybody been? *Nau:* **v. dans le vent,** to come round; **v. sur bâbord, sur tribord,** to alter course, to port, to starboard; **v. de cinq quarts sur tribord,** to alter (one's) course five points to port; **v. en grand sur la droite,** to alter course smartly to starboard; (*b*) **venir** + *inf.* (i) **il vint tomber à mes pieds,** he fell at my feet; **le hasard vient souvent faire échouer les meilleurs projets,** chance often wrecks the best plans; (ii) **venez me trouver à quatre heures,** come and see me at four o'clock; **je viens vous voir,** I have come to see you; **venez me voir demain,** come and see me tomorrow; **v. chercher qch., qn, v. prendre qch., qn,** to come and fetch sth.; to call for s.o.; (*c*) **v. de faire qch.** (*pr. & p.d.* only), to have (only) just done sth; **il vient, venait, de sortir,** he has just, had just, gone out; **je viens de passer ma journée à lire,** I have been reading all day; **je viens de le voir,** I have just seen him. **2.** (*denoting origin*) (*a*) **il vient d'Amérique,** he comes from America; **blé venu de Russie,** wheat from Russia; **v. de bonne souche,** to come, to be descended, from good stock; **mot qui vient du latin,** word derived from Latin; **la confiance vient du savoir,** confidence is born of knowledge; **ce bien lui est venu de famille,** this property was a family inheritance; **ce mobilier lui vient de sa mère,** he inherited this furniture from his mother; **tout cela vient de ce que . . .,** all this is the result of . . .; (*b*) *impers.* **d'où vient(-il) que . . .?** how is it that . . .? how comes it that . . .? **d'où vient(-il) qu'il m'ait refusé ce qu'il a accordé aux autres?** why (on earth) should he have refused me what he granted to others? **3.** (*a*) to occur, to come; **le premier exemple venu,** the first example that comes to mind; **je dis les choses comme elles me viennent,** I say things as they occur to me; **la pitié lui vient parfois,** now and again he is moved to pity; **l'idée me vient que . . ., il me vient à l'esprit que . . . il me vient l'idée que . . .,** the thought strikes me, it comes to my mind, that . . .; it occurs to me that . . .; (*b*) **v. à faire qch.,** to happen to do sth., to chance to do sth.; **s'il venait à mourir,** if he should happen to die; **toute somme qui viendrait à être allouée,** any sum that may be allocated. **4.** (*a*) to attain, reach; **il ne vient pas à l'épaule de son frère,** he doesn't come up to his brother's shoulder; **l'eau leur venait aux genoux,** the water reached, was up to, their knees; (*b*) **v. à rien,** to come to nothing; **v. à bien,** to succeed, prosper; *s.a.* BOUT 1; (*c*) **en v. à qch., à faire qch.,** to come to sth., to the point of doing sth.; **en v. aux coups, aux mains, à la violence,** to come to blows; **j'en suis venu aux reproches, à le gronder,** in the end I had to reproach him, to scold him; **il en était venu à mendier,** he had come down, was reduced, to begging; **les choses en sont-elles venues là?** have things come to such a pass? **venons-en maintenant au verbe,** let us now come to the verb; **il faudra bien en v. là,** it must come to that; **je comprends où vous voulez en v.,** I understand, I see what you are driving at; I see what you are at, what you are after; **où voulez-vous en v.?** what are you driving at? what are you getting at? what's your little game? **j'en suis venu à votre manière de penser,** I've come round to your way of thinking; **on en est venu à considérer ce reproche comme justifié,** the reproach has come to be considered as justified. **5.** (*of plants, teeth, children, etc.*) to come up, grow, grow up; **bien v.,** to thrive; **arbre mal venu,** stunted tree; **jeune homme mal venu,** weedy, puny, youth; **faire v. du blé,** to grow corn; **les dents commencent à v. à cet enfant,** the child is beginning to cut his teeth; **il lui est venu une tumeur,** he developed a tumour; *F:* **éternuements qui ne viennent pas,** sneezes that don't materialize; *Phot:* **voici le détail qui vient,** the detail is coming out, coming up; (*of photograph, engraving, etc.*) **être bien venu,** to be successful; **édition bien, mal, venue,** well, poorly, produced edition; **photographie mal venue,** unsuccessful print; *Metall:* **venu de forge, de fonte, de tour, avec . . .,** forged, cast, turned, in one piece with . . ..

s'en venir. *F:* to come along; **venez-vous-en avec moi,** come along with me; **un paysan s'en venait au village,** a peasant was going to the village.

II. **venir,** *s.m.* (*Rare*) *used in* **l'aller et le v.,** the coming and the going.

Venise [vəniːz], *Pr.n.m. & f. Geog:* Venice; *Needlew:* **point de V.,** Venetian lace.

vénitien, -ienne [venisjɛ̃, -jɛn], *a. & s.* Venetian ((i) of Venice, (ii) of Venezia); **store v.,** Venetian blind; *s.a.* BLOND 3, LANTERNE 1.

vénosité [venozite], *s.f. Anat: Med:* venosity.

vent [vɑ̃], *s.m.* **1.** (*a*) wind; **le v. du nord, du sud,** the north, south, wind; **le v. d'est, d'ouest,** the east, west, wind; **le v. du nord-est,** the north-east wind; **un v. de nord-est,** a north-east wind; *Nau:* **v. frais,** strong breeze; **v. grand frais,** moderate gale; **grand v., v. fort,** high wind; gale; **journée de grand v.,** gusty, windy, day; **la palissade fut renversée par le v.,** the fence was blown over, blown down (by the wind); **coup de v.,** (i) gust of wind, squall; (ii) *Nau:* whole gale; **fort coup de v.,** strong gale; *F:* **entrer, sortir, en coup de v.,** to dash in, out; to bounce in, out; **elle courait la chevelure au v.,** she ran with her hair streaming in the wind; *A: F:* **jeter la plume au v.,** to trust to chance; **v. de mer,** sea wind, sea breeze; **endroit exposé au v.,** windy place; **à l'abri du v.,** (i) sheltered from the wind; (ii) *Nau:* under the wind; under the lee; *Mus:* **instrument à v.,** wind instrument; *Mus: pl.* **les vents,** the wind; *Mec.E: Ind:* **machine à v.,** blower; *s.a.* MOULIN 1; **il fait du v.,** it is windy (weather); **faire du v. avec un éventail,** to create a wind, make a draught, with a fan; **pression du v.,** (i) wind pressure; (ii) *Metall:* blast pressure; **aller comme le v.,** to go like the wind; *Nau:* **avoir bon v.,** to have a fair wind; **aller selon le v.,** (i) *Nau:* to sail according to the wind; (ii) *F:* to drift with the current; **avoir le v. en poupe, entre deux écoutes,** to have the wind right aft, dead aft; *F:* **il a le v. en poupe,** he is sailing with wind and tide; he is on the high road to success; **v. portant,** leading, fair, wind; **v. arrière,** down wind, following wind; *Av:* tail wind; **aller v. arrière,** to sail, run before the wind; **v. avant,** head wind; *Av:* **v. de travers,** cross wind; **v. debout,** upwind; **contre le v.,** against the wind, in the teeth of the wind; *Nau:* **tenez le v.!** keep her to! **sous le v.,** alee, (to) leeward; **tomber sous le v.,** to drop to leeward; **sous le v. de . . .,** to leeward of . . .; **passer sous le v. de . . .,** to pass to leeward of . . .; **au v.,** (i) a-weather; (ii) (to) windward; **au v. de . . .,** to windward of . . .; **être au v. de sa bouée,** (i) to be to windward of one's moorings; (ii) *F:* to be on the right side; to be all right; **mettre la barre au v.,** to put the helm up, alee; **la barre au v. toute!** hard up with the helm! **côté du v.,** weather side; **côté sous le v.,** lee side; **courant portant au v.,** weather current; **courant portant sous le v.,** lee current; *Nau:* **v. dessus v. dedans,** backing and filling; **avoir le v. dessus,** to be aback; **être pris v. dessus,** to be caught, to be taken, aback; **avoir l'avantage du v., gagner le dessus du v.,** to have, get, the weather gauge; **prendre le v.,** to get the weather gauge (sur, of), **regarder de quel côté vient le v., de quel côté souffle le v.,** to watch which way the wind is blowing; **il sait d'où vient le v.,** he knows which way the wind blows; he knows on which side his bread is buttered; *Pol: F:* **tendre les voiles du côté d'où vient le v.,** to trim; to hedge; to play for safety; *Prov:* **selon le v. la voile,** we must trim our sails to the wind; we must adapt ourselves to circumstances; *F:* **tourner, virer, à tout v., à tous les vents, au moindre v.,** to be a weathercock; **quel bon v. vous amène?** what good wind, what lucky chance, brings you here? *F: Iron:* **bon v.!** goodbye (*with the implication* and good riddance); *P:* **du v.!** get out! scram! **le v. de l'adversité,** the chill wind of adversity; *Prov:* **qui sème le v. récolte la tempête,** he who sows the wind shall reap the whirlwind; (*of horse, F: of pers.*) **porter la tête au v.,** to carry the head high; (*of horse*) **tirer au v.,** to hold its head high; *F:* **être dans le v.,** to be up-to-date, to be with it; to be in; *s.a.* ABATTRE 5, ALIZÉ, AUTANT 1, BREBIS 2, COULIS[1], DEBOUT 3, DEVANT 2, ÉCORNER 1, HERBE 4, MARÉE 1; *Geog:* **les îles du V.,** the Windward Islands; (*b*) **aire de v.,** point of the compass; **les quatre vents,** the four cardinal points; **logé aux quatre vents,** exposed to the four winds of heaven; exposed to every wind that blows; **prendre le vent,** (i) (*of sails*) to catch the wind, to take; (ii) *F:* to see how the land lies; *s.a.* REPRENDRE 1; (*c*) air; **ballon plein de v.,** ball full of air; **en plein v.,** in the open air; **marché, assemblée, en plein v.,** open-air market, meeting; *s.a.* ARBRE 1; **mettre qch. au v.,** to hang sth. out to air, to dry; **donner v. à un tonneau,** to make a vent in a barrel; *F:* **donner v. à sa colère,** to give vent to one's anger; (*d*) blast (of bellows, gun); *Av:* **v. de l'hélice,** propeller slip, slipstream; (*e*) wind, breath, breathing; *A:* **prendre v.,** to recover one's wind, one's breath; **cheval qui a du v.,** short-winded horse; (*f*) *Med: F:* flatulence, wind; **avoir des vents,** to suffer from wind; **lâcher un v., faire des vents,** to break wind; (*g*) *F:* **ce n'est que du v.,** it's all (so much) hot air; *F:* **il déplace beaucoup de v.,** he makes a lot of fuss and bother. **2.** *Artil: Sm.a:* windage (between projectile and bore); *Mch:* clearance (of piston). **3.** *Ven:* scent; **avoir le v. de son gibier,** to have the wind of one's game; **avoir v. de qch.,** to get wind of sth.; to get scent of sth.; to have an inkling of sth.

ventage [vɑ̃taːʒ], *s.m. Agr:* winnowing, fanning (of corn).

ventail [vɑ̃taːj], *s.m.,* **ventaille** [vɑ̃taːj], *s.f. Arm: Her:* ventail, aventaile (of helmet).

ventaison [vɑ̃tɛzɔ̃], *s.f. Agr:* windburn.

vente [vɑ̃ːt], *s.f.* **1.** sale; selling; **v. d'un immeuble,** sale of a house, of premises; property sale; **v. d'une terre,** sale of an estate; **v. aux enchères,** sale by auction; **salle des ventes (aux enchères publiques),** auction rooms; **salle de v.,** saleroom; **v. de charité,** charity bazaar; **v. judiciaire,** sale by order of the court; **v. de gré à gré, à l'amiable,** sale by private treaty, contract, agreement; *Com:* **v. directe au(x) consommateur(s),** personal selling; **v. par correspondance, v. sur catalogue,** mail-order selling, business; **v. contre remboursement,** cash-on-delivery selling; **v. par distributeur(s) automatique(s),** automatic vending; **v. forcée,** forced sale; **v. (de) liquidation,** winding-up sale; **v. totale (des stocks),** selling off, out (of stocks); clearance sale; **v. publique,** public sale, auction (sale); **v. promotionnelle,** promotion sale; **v. réclame,** bargain sale; **v. rapide,** ready sale; quick returns; **ventes manquées,** lost sales; *St.Exch:* **v. de consolidation,** funding sale; **v. de liquidation,** clearing sale; **contrat de v.,** sale contract; **bureau de v.,** selling agency, sales agency; **campagne de v.,** selling campaign, drive; **promotion de v.,** sales promotion; **en v.,** for sale, on sale; **en v. chez . . .,** on sale at . . ., to be had from . . .; **point de v.,** shop where a particular article is stocked; stockist; **mettre, offrir, (qch.) en v.,** to put (sth.) up for sale; to offer (sth.) for sale; *Publ:* to publish (a book); **mise en v. (de qch.),** offering (of sth.) for sale; *Publ:* publishing, publication (of book); *War Adm:* **en v. libre,** (for sale) unrationed; **(re)mise en v. libre,** derationing; **hors de v.,** (i) no longer on sale; (ii) unsaleable, *F:* dud (stock); **retirer de la v.,** to withdraw from sale; **(livre) retiré de la v.,** (book) withdrawn from sale; (copies) recalled; **de v. facile, difficile,** easy, difficult, to place, to sell; **article de (bonne) v.,** article that sells well; (*of book*) **avoir rencontré la, fait une, forte v.,** to be a best seller; **nous n'en avons pas la v.,** we have no sale for it; *s.a.* ACTE 2, CHANDELLE 1, DÉCOUVERT 3, EXTINCTION 1. **2.** timber felled; felling (of timber); **jeune(s) vente(s),** new undergrowth. **3.** *A:* meeting, conventicle (of carbonari, etc., representing themselves as meeting for a charcoal sale).

venté [vɑ̃te], *a.* **1.** wind-driven (tide). **2. arbre (faux) v.,** windbent tree; wind-shaken tree; **plaine ventée,** windswept, windblown, plain.

venteaux [vɑ̃to], *s.m.pl.* air holes, valves (of bellows).

ventelle [vɑ̃tɛl], *s.f. Hyd.E:* sluice valve, paddle.

venter [vɑ̃te], *v.i.* **1.** *impers.* to blow, to be windy; **il vente fort,** it is blowing fresh, hard; it is very windy; (*with cogn.acc.*) **il ventait tempête,** it was blowing a gale, a gale was blowing; it was blowing great guns. **2.** (*a*) **on ne peut empêcher le vent de v.,** one cannot keep the wind from blowing; (*b*) *v.tr.* **la brise vente la marée,** the wind is driving the tide; (*c*) *v.tr.* **v. des grains,** to winnow grain.

venteux, -euse [vɑ̃tø, -øːz], *a.* **1.** (*a*) windy (weather, season); windswept (country); (*b*) (food) causing flatulence; *F:* windy (food). **2.** blistered (casting).

ventilateur [vɑ̃tilatœːr], *s.m.* ventilator. **1.** ventilating aperture or pipe; **v. de fosse d'aisance,** blow-off pipe (of a cesspool). **2. v. rotatif,** fan; **v. à ailes, v. soufflant,** fan(ner), blower; **v. négatif, v. aspirant,** suction fan; **v. électrique,** electric fan; **v. de plafond,** ceiling fan; *Metall:* **v. sous grille,** under-grate blower. **3.** *Av: F:* helicopter, *F:* whirlybird, chopper.

ventilation[1] [vɑ̃tilasjɔ̃], *s.f.* ventilation; **v. artificielle,** artificial ventilation; **puits de v.,** ventilating shaft.

ventilation[2], *s.f.* (*a*) *Jur:* separate valuation (of chattels or parts of estate); (*b*) *Book-k:* apportionment, analysis, breakdown (of prices, expenses, etc.); **v. des prix de revient,** cost distribution; (*c*) *Elcs:* (*computers*) dispersion; **v./regroupement,** scatter/gather.

ventiler[1] [vɑ̃tile], *v.tr.* to ventilate, air (room, mine, etc.); **mal ventilé,** stuffy; **machine à v.,** ventilating engine; **toute la question demande à être ventilée,** the whole question requires to be aired, ventilated.

ventiler[2], *v.tr. Jur:* to value separately (chattels or parts of estate); *Book-k:* to apportion; *Elcs:* (*computers*) to disperse, to explode, to scatter.

ventileuse [vɑ̃tiløːz], *s.f. Ap:* fanner bee.

ventis [vɑ̃ti], *s.m.pl.* trees blown down by the wind.

ventôse [vɑ̃toːz], *s.m. Hist:* sixth month of the Fr. Republican calendar (Feb.-March).

ventosité [vɑ̃tozite], *s.f. Med: Vet: A:* flatulence.

ventousaire [vɑ̃tuzɛːr], *a. Biol:* **organe v.,** suctorial organ, sucker.

ventouse [vɑ̃tuːz], *s.f.* **1.** (*a*) *Med:* cupping glass; **v. scarifiée,** wet cup; **v. sèche,** dry cup; **appliquer, faire, des ventouses à qn,** to cup s.o.; **application des ventouses,** cupping; **faire v.,** to adhere by suction; (*b*) *Z:* sucker (of leech); **v. postérieure,** acetabulum; **v. (d'un gecko),** suction lamella; (*c*) nozzle (of vacuum cleaner); (*d*) suction cup, disc; **cendrier à v.,** suction-grip ashtray; (*e*) *Plumb:* **(déboucheur à) v.,** (rubber) plunger, force cup; *Obst:* **v. obstétricale,** vacuum extractor; (*f*) *attrib. F:* **voiture v.,** car that seems to be parked permanently (on a spot); (*g*) *P:* (*pers.*) leech, limpet, (crashing) bore. **2.** (*a*) airhole, ventilator, vent(hole); *Mch:* air valve (of furnace door); *Nau:* air scuttle; (*b*) *Hyd.E:* air chamber (of water conduit).

ventouser [vɑ̃tuze], *v.tr. Med:* to cup (patient).

ventouseur, -euse [vɑ̃tuzœːr, -øːz], *s. Med:* cupper.

ventrailles [vɑ̃trɑːj], *s.f.pl. F:* entrails, guts.

ventral, -ale, -aux [vɑ̃tral, -o]. **1.** *a.* (*a*) *Anat: Bot: etc:* ventral; *Ich:* **nageoires ventrales,** ventral fins; *Med:* **hernie ventrale,** ventral rupture; (*b*) **parachute v.,** lap pack (parachute). **2.** *s.f. Ich:* **ventrale,** ventral fin.

ventralement [vɑ̃tralmɑ̃], *adv. Nat.Hist:* ventrally.

ventre [vɑ̃ːtr̥], *s.m.* **1.** (*a*) abdomen, belly; **se coucher à plat v.,** to lie flat on one's stomach; **tomber, se jeter, à plat v.,** to fall flat (on one's face); **se mettre à plat v. devant qn,** to grovel before s.o.; to cringe to s.o. (*of horse*) **v. à terre,** at full speed; (*of cavalry*) **passer sur le v. à l'ennemi,** to ride the enemy down; **avoir mal au v.,** to have stomach ache, bellyache; *Med:* **v. aigu chirurgical,** acute abdomen; **avoir le v. libre,** to have one's bowels properly cleared; **avoir le v. serré,** to be constipated; **avoir du v.,** to be stout, *F:* to be pot-bellied; **prendre du v.,** to grow stout; *F:* to develop a corporation; **se serrer le v.,** to tighten, pull in, one's belt; to be on short commons; *F:* **faire rentrer les paroles dans le v. à qn,** to make s.o. eat his words; *Farr:* **cheval qui n'a pas de v.,** horse too thin in the belly; **cheval qui a du v.,** horse too full in the belly; **poutre en v. de poisson,** fish-bellied girder; *a.inv.* **v. de biche,** fawn-bellied (in colour); (*b*) stomach; **reconnaissance du v.,** cupboard love; **avoir le v. creux,** to have an empty stomach; **être porté sur son v., faire un dieu de son v.,** to make a god of one's belly; *F:* **tout fait v.,** everything helps to make a meal; **n'avoir rien dans le v.,** (i) to be starving; (ii) *F:* to have no guts; *F:* **je savais bien qu'il avait quelque chose dans le v.,** I was sure there was something in him; *A:* **il n'a pas un an dans le v.,** he hasn't a year to live; *Prov:* **v. affamé n'a point d'oreilles,** it's no use reasoning with a hungry man; (*c*) **porter un enfant dans son v.,** to bear a child in one's womb; (*d*) *Hist: Iron:* The Centre Party (in Parliament); (*e*) *Fr.C:* **v. de bœuf,** pothole (in road); (*f*) *int. A:* **v. saint-Georges! v. saint gris!** gadzooks! **2.** *Tchn:* (*a*) bulge, paunch, swell (of vase, bottle, girder); belly, sag (of sail); belly (of ship, aircraft); belly, body (of blast furnace); **faire v.,** (i) to bulge out, to belly out; (ii) to sag; **mur qui fait v.,** bulging wall; *Pol.Ec:* **le v. (de la courbe),** the bulge; (*b*) *Ph:* antinode loop (of wave, vibrating segment); ventral segment (of vibrating medium); *El:* **v. d'intensité,** current antinode, loop; **v. de tension,** tension antinode, loop; **v. de potentiel,** antinode, loop, of potential.

ventrebleu [vɑ̃trəblø], *int. A:* (*attenuated form of* **ventre-Dieu**) gadzooks!

ventrée [vɑ̃tre], *s.f.* **1.** litter, fall (of lambs, etc.). **2.** *F:* bellyful.

ventriculaire [vɑ̃trikylɛːr], *a. Anat:* ventricular.

ventricule [vɑ̃trikyl], *s.m. Anat:* ventricle (of the heart, of the brain).

ventriculitidés [vɑ̃trikylitide], *s.m.pl. Paleont:* Ventriculitidae.

ventriculo-aortique [vɑ̃trikyloaɔrtik], *a. Anat:* ventriculo-bulbous; *pl. ventriculo-aortiques.*

ventriculogramme [vɑ̃trikylɔgram], *s.m. Med:* ventriculogram.

ventriculographie [vɑ̃trikylɔgrafi], *s.f. Med:* ventriculography.

ventrière [vɑ̃trijɛːr], *s.f.* **1.** (*a*) *Harn:* = SOUS-VENTRIÈRE; (*b*) sling (for hoisting horse); (*c*) *Med:* abdominal belt; binder. **2.** (*a*) *N.Arch:* bilge block (for launch); (*b*) *Const:* purlin; cross-tie.

ventriloque [vɑ̃trilɔk]. **1.** *a.* ventriloquous. **2.** *s.m. & f.* ventriloquist.

ventriloquie [vɑ̃trilɔki], *s.f.* ventriloquy, ventriloquism.

ventripotent [vɑ̃tripɔtɑ̃], *a. F:* ventripotent, big-bellied.

ventrouiller (se) [səvɑ̃truje], *v.pr.* to wallow in the mud; (*of fish*) to lie on the bottom (of stream, etc.).

ventru [vɑ̃try], *a.* **1.** corpulent, portly, *F:* pot-bellied (person); big-bellied (bottle, etc.). **2.** (*of cover, diaphragm, etc.*) dished, bulging. **3.** *s.m. Hist: Iron:* member of the Centre Party, supporter of the Government.

venturi [vɑ̃tyri], *s.m. I.C.E:* venturi; choke (of a carburettor).

venturon [vɑ̃tyrɔ̃], *s.m. Orn:* **v. alpin, montagnard,** citril finch.

venu, -ue[1] [v(ə)ny]. **1.** *a.* (*with adv., esp.* **bien, mal**) (*a*) **plante bien venue,** sturdy, healthy, plant; **enfant mal v.,** sickly, stunted, child; (*b*) **bien v.,** pleasing; appropriate; **mal v.,** displeasing; inappropriate; **il serait mal v. d'insister,** it would be unbecoming, ill-mannered, to insist. **2.** *s.* (*with* **premier, dernier, nouveau**) **le premier v.,** (i) the first arrival; (ii) anybody; **le premier v. vous dira cela,** anybody will tell you that; **confier ses secrets au premier v.,** to tell one's secrets to all and sundry; **le dernier v.,** (i) the latest arrival; (ii) *Pej:* a mere nobody; **ce n'est pas le premier, le dernier, v.,** he's somebody, he's not just anybody; **les nouveaux venus, les nouvelles venues,** the newcomers; **un tard v.,** a child (i) born a long time after his brothers or sisters, (ii) born of middle-aged parents.

venue[2] [v(ə)ny], *s.f.* **1.** coming, arrival (of s.o., etc.); advent, approach (of spring, etc.); rush, irruption, inflow (of water); penetration (of gas, etc.); **des allées et venues,** comings and goings; **lors de ma v. au monde,** when I was born; *Phot:* **surveiller la v. des détails,** to watch for the appearance, for the coming out, for the coming up, of detail. **2.** growth (of tree, etc.); **d'une belle v.,** well-grown; **tout d'une v.,** (i) (*of legs, figure, etc.*) straight up and down; shapeless; (ii) (*of character*) straightforward, uncomplicated.

vénule [venyl], *s.f. A:* = VEINULE.

Vénus [venys], *Pr.n.f. Myth: Astr: Moll:* Venus; *F:* **ce n'est pas une V., mais elle est bonne fille,** she isn't a Venus, she's no beauty, but she's a real good sort; *Bot:* **cheveu de V.,** maidenhair fern, venushair, Venus's hair fern; *Geol:* **cheveux de V.,** Venus('s) hair stone(s); *Bot: F:* **V. attrape-mouches,** Venus's flytrap; *P:* **V. de carrefour,** prostitute, tart; *Med: P:* **coup de pied de V.,** V.D.

vénusien, -ienne [venyzjɛ̃, -jɛn], *a.* Venusian.

vénuste [venyst], *a. Lit:* beautiful, graceful, charming, Venus-like.

vénusté [venyste], *s.f. Lit:* charm, grace.

vêpre [vɛpr̥]. **1.** *s.m. A:* evening; *A:* **je vous donne le bon v.,** I wish you good evening. **2.** *s.f.pl. Ecc:* vespers; evensong; **je le verrai avant vêpres, après vêpres,** I shall see him before, after, vespers; **chanter les vêpres,** to sing vespers; *Hist:* **les Vêpres Siciliennes,** the Sicilian Vespers.

vêprée [vɛpre], *s.f. A:* eventide.

ver [vɛːr], *s.m.* **1.** (*a*) **v. (de terre),** (earth)worm; **v. de sable, v. des pêcheurs, v. rouge,** lobworm; **pêcher des anguilles avec un paquet de vers,** to bob for eels; *Pej: O:* **c'est un v.,** he's a (mere) worm; *F:* **nu comme un v.,** stark naked; (*b*) *Med:* **v. solitaire,** tapeworm; *F:* **tuer le v.,** to drink a glass of spirits on an empty stomach; *F:* **tirer les vers du nez à qn,** to pump s.o., to worm secrets out of s.o.; *F:* **vers des enfants,** ascarids, nematode worms; **cet enfant a des vers,** this child has worms; **poudre à vers,** worm powder; **v. de Médine, de Guinée,** Guinea worm, hair worm; *Vet:* **v. rouge, fourchu,** gapeworm; (*c*) *Bot: F:* **herbe aux vers,** tansy. **2.** (*a*) larva, grub; maggot; **v. blanc,** cockchafer grub; **v. gris, v. des moissons,** cutworm; **v. militaire,** army worm; **v. des fruits,** apple worm; *F:* maggot; **fruits pleins de vers,** maggotty fruit; **v. de viande,** maggot; **v. de farine,** mealworm; **v. de fromage,** cheese mite, *esp. U.S:* cheese hopper, maggot, skipper; **v. du bois,** woodworm; **rongé, piqué, des vers,** wormeaten; **mangé aux vers,** motheaten; **v. à soie,** silkworm; **v. rongeur,** (i) canker(worm); (ii) (worm of) remorse; (iii) constant drain on the resources; **rose rongée de vers,** cankered rose; *F:* **être la proie des vers,** to be food for worms; (*b*) **v. luisant,** glow-worm; (*c*) **v. de mer,** teredo, shipworm.

vérace [veras], *a.* veracious.

véracité [verasite], *s.f.* **1.** veracity, truthfulness. **2.** veracity (of a fact); truth (of a statement).

véraison [verɛzɔ̃], *s.f.* ripening (of grapes, etc.).

véranda [verɑ̃da], *s.f.* veranda(h), *U.S:* porch.

vérascope [veraskɔp], *s.m. Phot:* verascope.

vératre [veratr̥], *s.m. Bot: Pharm:* veratrum; white hellebore, false hellebore.

vératrine [veratrin], *s.f. Ch:* veratrine; cevadine.

vératrique [veratrik], *a. Ch:* veratric (acid).

vératrol(e) [veratrɔl], *s.m. Ch: Med:* veratrol.

verbal, -aux [vɛrbal, -o], *a.* **1.** (*of promise, order, etc.*) verbal, by word of mouth; **convention verbale,** verbal agreement; *Jur:* simple contract; *Dipl:* **note verbale,** verbal note. **2.** *Gram:* verbal (adjective, etc.).

verbalement [vɛrbalmɑ̃], *adv.* verbally, by word of mouth.

verbalisateur [vɛrbalizatœːr], *a. & s.m.* (agent) v., policeman who took down the particulars (of motoring offence, etc.).

verbalisation [vɛrbalizasjɔ̃], *s.f.* **1.** *Jur:* entry of charge (by policeman, etc. for minor offence); *F:* taking of (s.o.'s) name and address. **2.** *Psy:* verbalization.

verbaliser [vɛrbalize], *Jur:* **1.** *v.i.* (*a*) (*of policeman*) **v. contre un automobiliste,** to take a motorist's name, and full particulars of the offence; to charge a motorist; (*b*) to draw up an official report (of an offence, etc.); to make a formal statement. **2.** *v.tr.* to certify (copy, etc.) in writing. **3.** *v.tr. Psy:* to verbalize (experience), to express (sth.) in words.

verbalisme [vɛrbalism], *s.m. Phil:* verbalism.

verbe [vɛrb], *s.m.* **1.** tone of voice; speech; **avoir le v. haut,** (i) to have a high-pitched voice; (ii) to be dictatorial. **2.** *Theol:* **le Verbe,** the Word; Logos; **le V. s'est fait chair,** the Word was made flesh. **3.** *Gram:* verb; **transformer un mot en v.,** to verbalize a word.

verbénacé [vɛrbenase], *Bot:* **1.** *a.* verbenaceous. **2.** *s.f.pl.* **verbénacées,** Verbenaceae.

verbeusement [vɛrbøzmɑ̃], *adv.* verbosely.

verbeux, -euse [vɛrbø, -øːz], *a.* verbose, long-winded, prosy (orator, etc.); wordy (epistle, etc.).

verbiage [vɛrbjaːʒ], *s.m.* (*a*) verbosity, verbiage; wordiness; mere words; (*b*) wording.

verbomanie [vɛrbɔmani], *s.f.* (*a*) *Psy:* verbomania; (*b*) *F:* verbal diarrhoea.

verboquet [vɛrbɔkɛ], *s.m. Const: Civ.E:* guy, guide rope.

verbosité [vɛrbozite], *s.f.* verbosity, wordiness, prosiness.

Verceil [vɛrsɛːj], *Pr.n. Geog:* Vercelli.

ver-coquin [vɛrkɔkɛ̃], *s.m.* **1.** vine grub. **2.** (*a*) *Vet:* (i) stagger-worm (of sheep); hydatid; (ii) staggers; blind staggers; (*b*) *F: A:* whim, fancy; *pl. vers-coquins.*

verdage [vɛrdaːʒ], *s.m. Agr:* manure crop.

verdal [vɛrdal], *s.m. Const:* pavement glass; basement light; *pl. verdals.*

verdâtre [vɛrdɑːtr], *a.* greenish.

verdée [vɛrde], *s.f. Vit:* verdea (Tuscan white grape or wine).

verdelet, -ette [vɛrdəlɛ, -ɛt], *a.* **1.** *A:* greenish, verging on green. **2.** (*of wine*) tart, slightly acid. **3.** (*of old people*) hale and hearty, enjoying a green old age.

verdereau, -eaux [vɛrdro], *s.m.*, **verderet** [vɛrdrɛ], *s.m. F:* green lizard.

verderolle [vɛrdrɔl], *s.f. Orn:* (**rousserolle**) **v.,** marsh warbler.

verdet [vɛrdɛ], *s.m.* **1.** *Dy: A:* verdigris. **2.** *Ven:* young stag in rut.

verdeur [vɛrdœːr], *s.f.* **1.** (*a*) greenness (of immaturity); (*b*) sap (in wood); greenness (of wood). **2.** tartness, acidity (of fruit, wine, speech); **la v. de sa réplique,** the crudeness of his reply. **3.** vigour, vitality (of old people); **la v. de l'âge,** the greenness of old age.

verdiau [vɛrdjo], *s.m. Bot: F:* purple willow.

verdict [vɛrdikt], *s.m. Jur:* finding of the jury; verdict; **prononcer, rendre, un v.,** to return a verdict; to bring in a verdict, a finding (**en faveur de,** for; **contre,** against); to find (for or against s.o.); **v. d'acquittement,** verdict of not guilty; **le v. de l'opinion publique,** the verdict of public opinion.

verdier [vɛrdje], *s.m.* **1.** *Orn:* greenfinch; **v. des oiseleurs,** yellowhammer, yellow bunting. **2.** *Hist:* verderer.

verdir [vɛrdiːr]. **1.** *v.tr.* to make (sth.) green; to paint (sth.) green; **la mousse verdit les vieux murs,** the moss forms a green mantle on the old walls. **2.** *v.i.* (*a*) (*of vegetation*) to grow, become, turn, green; (*b*) (*of copper*) to become covered with verdigris; **verdi,** verdigrised.

verdissage [vɛrdisaːʒ], *s.m.* dyeing, colouring, (sth.) green.

verdissant [vɛrdisɑ̃], *a.* growing green; verdant.

verdissement [vɛrdismɑ̃], *s.m.* growing, becoming, green; greening (of oyster); *Bot:* appearance of chlorophyll (in young plants).

verdoiement [vɛrdwamɑ̃], *s.m.* turning, becoming, green.

verdoyant [vɛrdwajɑ̃], *a.* (*a*) green, *Lit:* verdant (meadow, etc.); (*b*) (*of colour*) greenish.

verdoyer [vɛrdwaje], *v.i.* (**il verdoie; il verdoiera**) (*of field, etc.*) to take on a green colour, to become green; to look green.

verdunisation [vɛrdynizasjɔ̃], *s.f. A:* light chlorination (of water).

verduniser [vɛrdynize], *v.tr. Hyg: A:* to chlorinate (water) lightly.

verdunois, -oise [vɛrdynwa, -waːz], *a. & s. Geog:* (native, inhabitant) of Verdun.

verdure [vɛrdyːr], *s.f.* **1.** (*a*) greenness; (*b*) verdure, greenery; **salle, cabinet, de v.,** green arbour; **tapis de v.,** greensward; green; **théâtre de v.,** open-air theatre; **v. pour bouquets,** foil. **2.** *Cu:* salad vegetables; pot herbs. **3.** *A:* verdure; (*a*) tapestry representing trees or foliage; (*b*) *pl.* flowered borders (in tapestry, etc.).

verdurier, -ière [vɛrdyrje, -jɛːr], *s. A:* greengrocer.

vérécondieux, -ieuse [verekɔ̃djø, -jøːz], *a. Lit:* reserved; discreet.

vérétille [veretiːj], *s.f. or m. Coel:* veretillum.

véreux, -euse [verø, -øːz], *a.* **1.** wormy, maggoty (fruit). **2.** *F:* of dubious character, *F:* fishy; **financier v.,** shady financier; **maison véreuse,** unsafe firm; **compagnie véreuse,** bogus company; **affaire véreuse,** bubble scheme; fishy business; **dettes véreuses,** bad debts; **son cas est v.,** his case is very dubious.

verge [vɛrʒ], *s.f.* **1.** (*a*) rod; wand; cane; *B:* **la v. d'Aaron,** Aaron's rod; **v. de fer,** iron rod; *Lit:* **gouverner avec une v. de fer,** to rule with a rod of iron; *Lit:* **être sous la verge de qn,** to be ruled by s.o.; to be under s.o.'s thumb; *B:* **battu de verges,** beaten with rods; **vous lui donnez des verges pour vous fouetter,** you are making a rod for your own back; *Mil: A:* **passer par les verges,** to run the gauntlet; *Com:* **fer, étain, en verges,** bar iron, tin; **v. d'huissier,** usher's wand; *A:* **huissier à v.,** tipstaff; **v. de bedeau,** (verger's) verge; **v. de charpentier,** foot rule; **v. d'arpenteur,** surveyor's rod; (*b*) (**poignée de**) **verges,** birch rod; **frapper, battre, de verges un enfant,** to birch a child; (*c*) shank (of anchor); rod (of pendulum); beam (of balance); cross arm (of fly press); spindle pin (of weather vane, etc.); spear (of pump); stick (of rocket); *A:* **v. de piston,** piston rod; **compas à v.,** beam compass; (*d*) *Bot: F:* **v. d'or,** golden rod, Aaron's rod; **v. à pasteur,** shepherd's rod, staff. **2.** *Anat:* (*a*) penis; (*b*) verge (of invertebrate). **3.** *Meas:* (*a*) *A:* **v. carrée** = VERGÉE; (*b*) *Fr.C:* yard.

vergé [vɛrʒe], *a.* **1.** *Tex:* (*a*) badly dyed, streaky; (*b*) corded. **2.** laid (paper); *s.m.* **v. blanc,** cream-laid paper. **3.** wormeaten (wood).

vergée [vɛrʒe], *s.f. A.Meas: approx.* = $1\frac{1}{4}$ rood.

vergence [vɛrʒɑ̃ːs], *s.f. Opt:* vergency.

vergeoise [vɛrʒwaːz], *s.f.* (low-grade) brown sugar.

verger[1] [vɛrʒe], *s.m.* orchard.

verger[2], *v.tr.* (**je vergeai(s); n. vergeons**) *A:* to measure (land) with a rod.

vergerette [vɛrʒərɛt], *s.f. Bot:* fleabane.

vergeté [vɛrʒəte], *a.* **1.** streaky (complexion, etc.). **2.** *Her:* paly.

vergeter [vɛrʒəte], *v.tr.* (**je vergette, n. vergetons; je vergetterai**) *A:* **1.** to beat, dust, brush, whisk, switch (clothes). **2.** to streak.

vergette [vɛrʒɛt], *s.f.* **1.** (*a*) small cane, switch; (*b*) *Her:* pallet. **2.** *pl.* clothes whisk. **3.** hoop (of drum); **v. de roulage,** flesh hoop.

vergeture [vɛrʒətyːr], *s.f.* (*a*) weal, red mark (caused by lash of whip, overtight garment, etc.); (*b*) *Obst:* vibex.

vergeur [vɛrʒœːr], *s.m. Paperm:* dandy roll.

vergeure [vɛrʒyːr], *s.f.* **1.** *Paperm:* (*a*) (laid) wires (of the mould for laid paper); (*b*) wire mark (on laid paper). **2.** streakiness (of textile).

verglaçant [vɛrglasɑ̃], *a.* **pluie verglaçante,** freezing rain (that makes the roads icy).

verglacé [vɛrglase], *a.* **route verglacée,** icy road.

verglacer [vɛrglase], *v.impers.* **il verglace,** it is icy underfoot; the roads are icy.

verglas [vɛrgla], *s.m.* ice crust ((i) on snow, (ii) on rock surface); (*on roads, etc.*) black ice, glazed frost, glazed ice, *U.S:* glaze; freezing rain; **il fait du v.,** it's slippery, icy, underfoot; **plaque de v.** (**sur la route**), patch of ice, icy patch (on the road); **il tombe, il y a, du v.,** there's sleet (coming down).

vergne[1] [vɛrɲ], *s.m. Bot:* alder (tree).

vergne[2], *s.f.* (river) embankment facing (built with stakes and fascines).

vergner [vɛrɲe], *v.tr.* to face (river bank, etc.) (with stakes and fascines).

vergogne [vɛrgɔɲ], *s.f. A:* shame; *still used in:* **sans v.,** shameless(ly).

vergogneux, -euse [vɛrgɔɲø, -øːz], *a. A:* ashamed; shameful; lowly.

vergue [vɛrg], *s.f. Nau:* yard; **grande v.,** main yard; **v. de misaine,** foreyard; **v. barrée,** cross-jack (yard); **v. de grand cacatois,** main royal yard; **v. de petit cacatois,** fore royal yard; **v. de hunier,** topsail yard; **v. de perroquet,** topgallant yard; **basses vergues,** lower yards; **bout de v.,** yardarm; **vergues de signaux, à signaux,** signal yards; **avoir (le) vent sous v., être vent sous v.,** to scud before the wind; **être v. à v.,** to be yardarm to yardarm; to be yard and yard.

véricle [verikl], *s.m. Lap:* imitation (precious) stone; paste stone.

véridicité [veridisite], *s.f. Lit:* **1.** veracity, truthfulness (of person). **2.** veracity (of fact).

véridique [veridik], *a.* **1.** veracious, truthful, trustworthy (person). **2.** veracious (account); in accord with the facts.

véridiquement [veridikmɑ̃], *adv.* veraciously, truthfully.

vérifiabilité [verifjabilite], *s.f.* verifiability, verifiableness.

vérifiable [verifjabl], *a.* verifiable (statement, etc.).

vérificateur, -trice [verifikatœːr, -tris]. **1.** *s.* (*pers.*) verifier, inspector, examiner, checker, tester; *Adm:* **v. des poids et mesures,** inspector of weights and measures; **v. de comptes, v. comptable,** auditor. **2.** *a. & s.m.* **appareil v.,** testing machine; (**instrument**) **v.,** gauge, calipers. **3.** *s.f. Elcs:* (*computers*) (*machine*) **vérificatrice,** verifier.

vérificatif, -ive [verifikatif, -iːv], *a.* verificatory (experiment, etc.).

vérification [verifikasjɔ̃], *s.f.* (*a*) verification (of statements, etc.); inspection, examination, checking, testing (of work, measures, etc.); *Aut: etc:* **v. sur place,** spot check; *Adm:* **v. des suffrages,** scrutiny of the votes; **v. en douane,** customs examination (of goods); *Adm: Com:* **v. de comptes, vérifications comptables,** audit(ing) of accounts; **balance de v.,** trial balance; *Jur:* **v. d'un testament,** probate; **soumis à v.,** under examination; (*b*) *Elcs:* (*computers*) verifying, checking; checkout; **caractère de v.,** check character; **total mêlé de v.,** hash total, gibberish total.

vérifier [verifje], *v.tr.* (*p.d. & pr.sub.* **n. vérifiions, v. vérifiiez**) **1.** to verify (notes, etc.); to inspect, examine, check, test (work, measures, etc.); to overhaul (machinery, connections, etc.); *Com:* to audit (accounts); **vérifié et revérifié,** checked, double-checked and cross-checked; *Adm:* **v. les suffrages,** to scrutinize the votes cast; **v. si tout est prêt,** to make sure that everything is ready; **v. des références,** to take up references; **v. la tension artérielle,** to test blood pressure; **v. un chronomètre,** to rate a chronometer; *Elcs:* (*computers*) **v.** (**les perforations de cartes**), to key-verify; **v. visuellement** (**des cartes perforées**), to sight-check (punched cards); **v. le codage,** to code check. **2.** to verify, prove, confirm (statement, etc.); **sa prédiction s'est vérifiée,** his prediction proved correct, came true.

vérifieur, -euse [verifjœːr, -øːz], *Elcs:* (*computers*) **1.** *s.* verifier operator. **2.** *s.f.* **vérifieuse,** verifier.

vérin [verɛ̃], *s.m.* (*a*) *Tchn:* jack; **v. à vis,** screw jack; **v. de calage,** stabilizing jack; **v. hydraulique,** hydraulic jack; **v. à huile,** oil jack; **v. à galet,** roller jack; **v. de levage,** lifting jack; **v. de serrage,** strut jack; *Min:* tool jack; **mise sur v.,** jacking (up); (*b*) *Av:* **v. électrique,** electric actuator; **v. de commande de la profondeur,** elevator control; **v. d'escamotage, de rentrée,** (**du train d'atterrissage**), retraction actuator; (landing-gear) retracting mechanism; **v. d'aileron,** aileron control; **v. de volet,** flap control; **v. de commande des volets d'atterrissage,** retraction actuator; **vérins actionnant la tuyère à section variable,** jacks actuating the variable-area nozzle; (*c*) *Nau:* **v. de chasse, v. de poussée,** starting ram (on launching ways); **v. de retenue,** launching pawl, trigger.

vérine [verin], *s.f. Nau:* **1.** hook rope (for handling anchor chains); tripping line. **2.** *Nau:* (*a*) *A:* binnacle lamp; (*b*) glazed-in light; lantern.

vérisme [verism], *s.m. Art: etc:* verism.

vériste [verist], *a. & s.m. & f. Art: etc:* verist.

véritable [veritabl], *a.* **1.** (*a*) true (religion, story, etc.); **cela est pourtant v. que j'ai cinquante ans!** yes, I'm fifty, right enough! (*b*) *A:* veracious (historian). **2.** real, genuine, veritable; **bénéfice v.,** actual profit; **verres de v. cristal,** genuine, real, crystal glasses; **le v. prix des choses,** the real, true, value of things; **des larmes véritables,** genuine tears; **un v. ami,** a real, true, friend; **il s'est montré un v. ami,** he proved a good friend; **c'est un v. coquin,** he's a regular, downright, absolute, rogue; **c'est un v. épouvantail,** she's a perfect fright; **ce fut un v. déluge,** we had a real downpour; **ce fut une v. explosion de cris de joie,** they literally screamed with delight; **ce fut une v. surprise,** it was a real surprise.

véritablement [veritabləmɑ̃], *adv.* **1.** truly, truthfully, veritably. **2.** really, indeed.

vérité [verite], *s.f.* **1.** truth, verity (of statement, etc.); **la simple v., la v. pure et simple,** the (pure and) simple truth; the plain, honest, unvarnished, truth; **la v. toute nue,** the naked truth; **dire la v.,** to speak the truth; **être près de la v.,** to be near the mark; **loin de la v.,** wide of the mark; **rester au-dessous de la v.,** to remain within the truth; **être en dessous de la v.,** to fall short of the truth; **et je suis en dessous de la v.,** and this is a conservative estimate; **outrepasser les bornes de la v.,** to overstep the truth; to stretch veracity too far; **la v. finit toujours par se découvrir,** truth will out; murder will out; *adv.phr.* **à la v.,** to tell the truth; as a matter of fact; **en vérité,** really, actually; *B:* **car je vous dis en v.,** for verily I say unto you. **2.** fact, truth; *Jur:* **la v., toute la v., rien que la v.,** the truth, the whole truth, and nothing but the truth; **les vérités scientifiques,** scientific truths, facts; **c'est la v.,** it is a fact; *F:* **c'est la v. vraie,** it's an actual fact; it's the honest truth; **dire à qn (toutes) ses vérités, ses quatre vérités,** to tell s.o. a few home truths; **toutes les vérités ne sont pas bonnes à dire, toute v. n'est pas bonne à dire,** not all truths are suitable for telling; **il n'y a que la v. qui blesse,** nothing hurts like the truth. **3.** *(a)* sincerity, truthfulness; **parler avec un air de v.,** to speak with a show, an air, of sincerity; *(b) Lit: Art:* truthfulness to life.

verjus [vɛrʒy], *s.m.* **1.** verjuice; **ce vin n'est que du v.,** this wine is far too sour; **caractère aigre comme v.,** sour, tart, disposition. **2.** verjuice grape.

verjuté [vɛrʒyte], *a.* verjuiced; acid, sour (sauce, wine); tart, acid (reply etc.).

vermandois, -oise [vɛrmɑ̃dwa, -wa:z], *Geog:* **1.** *a. & s.* (native, inhabitant) of Vermand. **2.** *Pr.n.m.* (the) Vermandois (region).

vermée [vɛrme], *s.f. Fish:* worms (used as bait); **pêcher à la v.,** to fish with worms.

vermeil, -eille [vɛrmɛ:j]. **1.** *a.* *(a)* vermilion, bright red; red (lips); rosy (cheeks); *(b) (of fruit)* mellow; *(c) Geog:* **la Côte vermeille,** the coast of Roussillon. **2.** *s.m.* *(a)* silver-gilt, vermeil; *(b)* vermeil varnish.

vermet [vɛrmɛ], *s.m. Moll:* vermetid, worm shell.

vermi- [vɛrmi], *comb.fm.* vermi-.

vermicelle [vɛrmisɛ:l], *s.m.* **1.** *Cu:* vermicelli. **2.** *Phot:* **vermicelles noirs sur un cliché,** black streaks, vermiculations, on a negative.

vermicellé [vɛrmisɛle], *a.* vermiculated; *(of pottery, etc.)* **avec des ornements vermicellés,** with a vermicelli design.

vermicellerie [vɛrmisɛlri], *s.f.* *(a)* manufacture of vermicelli; *(b)* vermicelli factory.

vermicellier, -ière [vɛrmisɛlje, -jɛ:r], *s.* manufacturer, maker, of vermicelli, of pasta.

vermicide [vɛrmisid], *Pharm:* **1.** *a.* vermicidal (drug). **2.** *s.m.* vermicide.

vermiculaire [vɛrmikylɛ:r]. **1.** *a.* *(a)* vermicular, worm-shaped; *Anat:* **appendice v.,** vermiform appendix; *Mil:* **tranchées au tracé v.,** sinuous line of trenches; *(b) Physiol:* vermicular (motion of bowels). **2.** *s.f. Bot:* **v. âcre,** biting yellow stonecrop.

vermiculation [vɛrmikylasjɔ̃], *s.f.* vermiculation, vermicular marking.

vermiculé [vɛrmikyle], *a.* **1.** *Arch:* vermiculated (stonework, column, etc.). **2.** engine-turned (watch case, etc.). **3.** *Nat.Hist:* vermiculate (markings).

vermiculer [vɛrmikyle], *v.i. Metall:* to be vermiculated.

vermiculite [vɛrmikylit], *s.f. Min:* vermiculite.

vermiculure [vɛrmikyly:r], *s.f. Arch: Metall:* vermiculation, vermicular marking.

vermidiens [vɛrmidjɛ̃], *s.m.pl. Z:* Phoronid(e)a.

vermien, -ienne [vɛrmjɛ̃, -jɛn], *a. Anat:* vermian.

vermiforme [vɛrmifɔrm], *a.* vermiform, vermicular; *Anat:* **appendice v.,** vermiform appendix; **éminences vermiformes du cervelet,** vermiform processes of the cerebellum.

vermifuge [vɛrmify:ʒ], *a. & s.m. Med: Pharm:* vermifuge, anthelmintic; **poudre v.,** worm powder.

vermigrade [vɛrmigrad], *a.* vermigrade.

vermilingue [vɛrmilɛ̃:g], *Rept:* **1.** *a.* vermilingual. **2.** *s.m.pl.* **vermilingues,** Vermilinguia, Vermilingues.

vermille [vɛrmi:j], *s.f. Fish:* ground line.

vermiller [vɛrmije], *v.i.* *(of boar, etc.)* *(a)* to worm; *(b)* to root, to rout.

vermillon [vɛrmijɔ̃], *s.m.* **1.** vermilion; cinnabar. **2.** vermilion (colour); bright red; **j'admirais le v. de ses joues,** I admired her red, rosy, cheeks; *a.inv.* **des rubans vermillon,** bright red ribbons.

vermillonnement [vɛrmijɔnmɑ̃], *s.m.* vermilioning (of sth.); painting (of sth.) bright red.

vermillonner¹ [vɛrmijɔne], *v.tr.* to vermilion (sth.); to paint (sth.) bright red; to rouge (one's cheeks).

vermillonner², *v.i.* *(of badger)* to burrow, grub (for edible roots).

vermination [vɛrminasjɔ̃], *s.f. Med:* vermination; infestation with worms.

vermine [vɛrmin], *s.f.* **1.** vermin *(usu. restricted in meaning to body parasites, esp. lice, fleas and bugs: occ. extended to rats and mice)* **couvert de v.,** *F:* **grouillant de v.,** verminous (beggar, etc.). **2.** *F:* *(pers.)* good-for-nothing; *pl.* vermin, rabble.

vermineux, -euse [vɛrminø, -ø:z], *a.* **1.** *Med: O:* **maladies vermineuses,** verminosis, diseases caused by, due to, worms. **2.** verminous, infested with vermine.

vermis [vɛrmis], *s.m. Anat:* vermis (of the cerebellum).

vermisseau, -eaux [vɛrmiso], *s.m.* small (earth) worm.

vermivore [vɛrmivɔ:r], *a. Z:* vermivorous.

vermouler (se) [səvɛrmule], *v.pr.* *(of wood, etc.)* to become wormeaten.

vermoulu [vɛrmuly], *a.* *(a)* wormeaten (wood, etc.); *(b)* decrepit.

vermoulure [vɛrmuly:r], *s.f.* **1.** wormhole (in wood, etc.). **2.** worm dust (from wormhole). **3.** wormeaten state (of wood, etc.).

vermout(h) [vɛrmut], *s.m.* vermouth.

vernaculaire [vɛrnakylɛ:r], *a. & s.m.* vernacular.

vernaille [vɛrna:j], *s.f. Miner:* corundum.

vernal, -aux [vɛrnal, -o], *a.* vernal *(Bot:* plant; *Astr:* point, equinox, etc.); *Astr:* **les signes vernaux,** the vernal signs.

vernalisation [vɛrnalizasjɔ̃], *s.f. Agr:* vernalization.

vernation [vɛrnasjɔ̃], *s.f. Bot:* vernation, prefoliation.

verne [vɛrn], *s.m. Bot:* alder (tree).

verni [vɛrni], *a.* *(a)* varnished; French polished; **cuir v.,** patent leather; **souliers vernis,** *s.m.pl.* **vernis,** patent(-leather) shoes; *F:* **être v.,** to be lucky; to have a charmed life; *(b)* **tuile en grès v.,** vitrified drain tile.

vernier [vɛrnje], *s.m. Astr: Mth: Surv:* vernier; sliding gauge.

vernir [vɛrni:r], *v.tr.* **1.** to varnish (picture, etc.); to (French-)polish (mahogany, etc.); to japan (iron, leather); **v. un meuble au tampon,** to French-polish a piece of furniture. **2.** *Cer:* (= VERNISSER) to glaze.

vernis [vɛrni], *s.m.* **1.** *(a)* varnish, polish, glaze, gloss; *attrib.* **peinture v.,** gloss paint; **v. gras,** oil varnish; **v. à l'alcool,** spirit varnish; **v. à l'essence,** turpentine varnish; **v. au copal,** copal varnish; **v. cellulosique,** cellulose varnish; **v. japonais,** japan; **v. au tampon,** French polish; *Cer:* **v. luisant,** glaze; **v. de plomb,** lead glaze; **v. à ongles,** nail varnish; *(b)* **v. de politesse,** veneer of politeness, of good manners; **couvrir ses actions sous un v. de légalité,** to give a varnish, a gloss, of legality to one's actions; **il a pris le v. de la société,** he has acquired polish. **2.** *Bot:* **v. du Japon,** varnish tree, lacquer tree, tree of heaven. **3.** *Moll:* (type of) clam.

vernis-émail [vɛrniema:j], *s.m.* japan enamel; *pl. vernis-émaux.*

vernis-émulsion [vɛrniemylsjɔ̃], *s.m.* emulsion paint; *pl. vernis-émulsions.*

vernissage [vɛrnisa:ʒ], *s.m.* **1.** *(a)* varnishing; glazing; japanning; **v. au tampon,** French-polishing; *(b)* private view, varnishing day (at an exhibition). **2.** varnish; glaze.

vernissé [vɛrnise], *a.* *(a)* glazed; *(b)* glossy; **feuilles vernissées,** glossy leaves; *Lit:* **joues vernissées,** shiny cheeks.

vernisser [vɛrnise], *v.tr.* to glaze (pottery).

vernisseur, -euse [vɛrnisœ:r, -ø:z], *s.* *(pers.)* **1.** varnisher; japanner; **v. au tampon,** French polisher. **2.** *Cer:* glazer.

vernissure [vɛrnisy:r], *s.f.* **1.** *(a)* varnishing; *(b) Cer:* glazing. **2.** *(a)* varnish; *(b) Cer:* glaze.

vernonais, -aise [vɛrnɔnɛ, -ɛ:z], *a. & s. Geog:* (native, inhabitant) of Vernon.

vérole [verɔl], *s.f. Med:* **1.** *P:* syphilis, pox. **2. petite** v., smallpox. **3.** *P:* **flanquer, foutre, la v.,** to create a disturbance, an upheaval; **quelle v.!** what a (bloody) nuisance!

vérolé [verɔle], *a.* **1.** *P:* syphilitic, poxed. **2. tuile vérolée,** pitted tile.

vérolique [verɔlik], *a. Med: A:* syphilitic.

véron [verɔ̃], *s.m. Ich:* minnow.

véronais, -aise [verɔnɛ, -ɛ:z], *a. & s. Geog:* Veronese.

véronal [verɔnal], *s.m. Pharm:* veronal; barbitone; **v. sodique,** medinal.

Vérone [verɔn], *Pr.n.f. Geog:* Verona.

Véronèse [verɔnɛ:z], *Pr.n.m. Hist. of Art:* Veronese.

Véronique [verɔnik]. **1.** *Pr.n.f.* Veronica. **2.** *s.f.* *(a) Ecc:* veronica, *A:* vernicle; *(b) Bot:* speedwell, veronica; **v. mâle,** common speedwell; **v. fausse-pâquerette,** daisy-leaved speedwell; **v. cressonnée,** brooklime; **v. à feuilles de lierre,** ivy-leaved speedwell; **v. petit-chêne,** germander speedwell; **v. femelle,** fluellen; **v. des jardiniers, v. amourette,** ragged robin; *(c) (bull-fighting)* veronica.

véroter [verɔte], *v.i.* to search for worms.

vérotis [verɔti], *s.m. Fish:* brandling.

verraille [vɛra:j], *s.f. A:* (small) glassware.

verrat [vɛra], *s.m. Breed:* boar.

verre [vɛ:r], *s.m.* **1.** *(a)* glass; **v. de plomb,** lead glass, flint glass; **v. à base de soude,** soda glass; **v. quartzeux,** quartz glass; **v. de Bohême, à gobeleterie,** Bohemian glass; **v. blanc,** white glass; **v. à bouteilles,** bottle glass; **v. d'optique,** optical glass; **v. à vitres,** sheet glass; window glass; **v. moulé,** pressed glass; **v. laminé, cylindré, à glaces,** plate glass; **v. armé, v. grillagé,** wire(d) glass, gauze glass; **v. de couleur,** coloured glass; stained glass; **v. fumé,** smoked glass; **v. de sûreté,** safety glass; **v. trempé,** tempered glass, toughened glass; **v. cellulaire,** foam glass; **v. double,** flashed glass; **v. triplex,** three-ply flashed glass; **v. de riz, d'albâtre,** rice-stone glass; **v. dépoli,** frosted glass, ground glass; **v. fêlé,** spun glass; **articles de v.,** glassware; **œil de v.,** glass eye; **peintre sur verre,** artist in stained glass; **sous v.,** under glass; in a glass case; **il est à mettre sous v.,** he ought to be kept in a glass case; **maison de v.,** house where nothing can be kept secret; *(b)* **v. organique,** synthetic glass; transparent plastic; **laine de v.,** glass wool; **fibre de v.,** glass fibre, *R.t.m:* Fibreglass; **coton de v., fil de v.,** spun glass; **papier de v.,** glass paper, sandpaper. **2.** *(object made of glass)* **v. de lunettes,** lens; **il porte des verres,** he wears glasses; *(on driving licence)* **doit porter des verres,** requires spectacles for driving; **verres de contact,** contact lenses; **v. grossissant,** magnifying glass; **v. ardent,** burning glass; **v. de champ,** field lens (of surveying instrument); **v. de montre,** watch glass; *F:* **se casser le v. de montre,** to land on one's backside, on one's rear; **v. de lampe,** lamp glass; **v. de pile électrique,** battery jar; **v. coloré,** coloured shade (of sextant, etc.); *Nau:* **v. de hublot,** bull's eye; *Const:* **v. dormant,** fixed light; window that cannot be opened; **verres dalles,** pavement lights. **3.** *(a)* **v. (à boire),** (drinking) glass; **v. gobelet,** tumbler; **v. à pied, v. à vin,** stemmed glass, wineglass; *coll.* **verres à pied,** stemware; **v. à Bordeaux,** claret glass; **v. à madère,** sherry glass; **v. à liqueur,** liqueur glass; **v. à eau,** tumbler; **v. gradué,** graduated measure; medicine glass; **v. à dents,** tooth glass; *Prov:* **qui casse les verres les paye,** the culprit must pay for the damage; *(b)* glass(ful); **v. de vin,** glass of wine; **boire un petit v.,** to have a drop of spirits, to have a dram; **prendre un v. de trop,** to have one too many, a drop too much; **tempête dans un v. d'eau,** storm in a teacup; *(c) Com:* **on ne reprend pas les verres,** empties are not returnable. **4. v. soluble,** waterglass. **5.** *Ch:* **v. d'antimoine,** glass of antimony; *Miner:* **v. volcanique,** volcanic glass, obsidian.

verré [vɛre], *a. A:* **1.** coated with powdered glass; **papier v.,** glasspaper; sandpaper. **2. cuve verrée,** glass-lined tank.

verrée [vɛre], *s.f. A:* glassful.

verrerie [vɛr(ə)ri], *s.f.* **1.** glassmaking. **2.** glass works. **3.** glassware; **magasin de v. et porcelaine,** glass and china shop; **v. allant au four,** oven (-proof) glass.

verrier [vɛrje], *s.m.* **1.** glassmaker, glass blower; *a.* **peintre v.,** artist in stained glass. **2.** glass rack, stand.

verrière [vɛrjɛ:r], *s.f.* **1.** glass casing (to protect shrine, picture, etc.). **2.** stained glass window. **3.** glass roof (of railway station, etc.); *Av:* **v. d'habitacle,** pilot's canopy.

verrine [vɛrin], *s.f.* **1.** glass casing. **2.** *Hort:* bell glass. **3.** *Nau:* *(a)* hook rope, tripping line; *(b)* (i) *A:* binnacle lamp; (ii) glazed-in light; lantern. **4.** barometer glass.

Verrines [vɛrrin], *s.f.pl. Lt.Lit:* (Cicero's) Verrine Orations.

verroterie [vɛrɔtri], *s.f.* small glassware; glass trinkets; glass beads.

verrou [vɛru], *s.m.* **1.** (*a*) bolt, bar; **v. glissant,** sliding bolt; **v. à platine,** slip bolt; **v. à ressort,** spring bolt, spring stud; **fermer une porte à, au, v.,** to bolt a door; **s'enfermer au v.,** to bolt oneself in; **pousser le v., mettre les verrous,** to shoot the bolt(s), to bolt the door; **tirer, ouvrir, le(s) verrou(s) d'une porte,** to unbolt a door; **être sous les verrous,** to be under lock and key, locked up, in safe custody; to be in jail; *A:* **porter l'épée en v.,** to wear the sword horizontal; (*b*) *Elcs:* **v. électromagnétique,** scrubber. **2.** (*a*) *Sm.a:* breech bolt (of shotgun); (*b*) *Rail:* **v. de blocage,** switch lock, control lock. **3.** (*a*) *Geog:* **v. glaciaire,** glacial threshold; (*b*) key point, position. **4.** *Mil:* *Sp:* **mouvement, jeu, de v.,** defensive movement, game.

verrouillable [vɛrujabl̩], *a.* lockable, boltable (door, etc.).

verrouillage [vɛrujaːʒ], *s.m.* **1.** bolting, locking; *Av:* **v. (du train),** (i) up-locking, (ii) down-locking (of undercarriage). **2.** locking apparatus, mechanism. **3.** *Elcs:* (*computers*) lock-out; **v. de clavier, d'écriture,** keyboard lock-out, write lock-out.

verrouiller [vɛruje], *v.tr.* (*a*) to bolt (door, window); **v. qn,** to bolt s.o. in; to lock s.o. up; **se v.,** to bolt oneself in; *Mec.E:* **le levier se trouve verrouillé,** the lever has become locked; **v. le chariot sur la coulisse,** to lock the saddle to the (lathe) bed; to block the saddle; *Sm.a:* **v. la culasse,** to lock the breech; (*b*) *Elcs:* (*computers*) to interlock.

verrucaire [vɛrykɛːr], *s.f.* *Moss:* verrucaria, wartwort.

verrucosité [vɛrykozite], *s.f.* *Med:* verrucosity; warty swelling.

verrue [vɛry], *s.f.* (*a*) *Med:* verruca, wart; **v. plantaire,** plantar wart; **ce bâtiment, hideuse v. à la face de Paris,** this building that stands out like a hideous wart on the face of Paris; (*b*) *Bot:* *F:* **herbe aux verrues,** (i) *Moss:* verrucaria; (ii) wartwort.

verruqueux, -euse [vɛrykø, -øːz], *a.* warty (hand); verrucous, verrucose (condition, etc.); *Bot:* verrucose, warted (branch, etc.).

verruga [vɛryga], *s.f.* *Med:* **v. du Pérou,** verruga peruana.

vers[1] [vɛːr], *s.m.* (*a*) verse, line (of poetry); **v. alexandrins,** alexandrines; **v. blancs,** blank verse; **v. libres,** free verse; (*b*) **écrire des v.,** to write verse, poetry.

vers[2], *prep.* **1.** (*of place*) (*a*) toward(s), to; **v. la ville,** towards the town; **il me conduisit v. la fenêtre,** he led me over to the window; *P.N:* (*at marine station*) **v. les bateaux,** to the boats; **je l'ai envoyé v. vous,** I sent him to you; **il vint v. moi,** he came towards me; **cligner de l'œil v. qn,** to wink at s.o.; **façade qui regarde v. la forêt,** façade facing the forest; (*b*) (*abstract*) **le scepticisme est le premier pas v. la vérité,** scepticism is the first step towards truth; (*c*) (*with no idea of movement*) **v. le nord,** towards the north; **situé vers la droite,** situated on, towards, the right; **v. Pau,** in the neighbourhood of Pau; (*d*) *Av:* **naviguer v. sept cents mètres,** to fly out about seven hundred metres; (*e*) *A:* (= ENVERS) **comment pourrai-je m'acquitter v. vous?** how can I repay you? **2.** (*of time*) (*a*) towards; **v. la fin du siècle,** towards the end of the century; **v. le milieu de sa vie,** towards the middle of his life; (*b*) about; **venez v. les trois heures,** come at about three (o'clock); **v. 1840,** in about 1840; **v. trente ans,** about thirty (years old).

versable [vɛrsabl̩], *a.* that can easily be (i) overturned, (ii) spilt; that is easy to pour.

versage [vɛrsaːʒ], *s.m.* **1.** *Min:* tipping, emptying (of truck). **2.** *Agr:* first ploughing (of land).

versaillais, -aise [vɛrsajɛ, -ɛːz], *a.* & *s.* **1.** *Geog:* (native, inhabitant) of Versailles. **2.** *s.m.pl.* *Hist:* the regular troops (during the Commune, 1871).

versant [vɛrsɑ̃], *s.m.* (*a*) slope, side, versant (of mountain); bank (of canal, etc.); **le v. nord (d'une montagne),** the north face (of a mountain); **v. de colline,** hillside; **à cinquante ans on est sur l'autre v.,** at fifty a man is past his prime; (*b*) slope (of a roof).

versatile [vɛrsatil], *a.* **1.** changeable, fickle, inconstant, unstable, volatile (disposition, etc.); fond of change. **2.** *Bot:* *Orn:* versatile (anther, toe).

versatilité [vɛrsatilite], *s.f.* **1.** variableness, inconstancy, fickleness. **2.** versatility (of anther, of bird's toe).

verse[1] [vɛrs], *s.f.* **1.** lodging, laying, beating down (of corn, etc., by wind, etc.). **2.** *adv.phr.* **à v.,** in torrents; **il pleut à v.,** it's pouring; *F:* it's raining cats and dogs, raining in buckets. **3.** *F:* (*in café*) **la v.!** one expresso, one!

verse[2], *a.* *Geom:* **sinus v.,** versed sine; versine.

versé [vɛrse], *a.* **1.** versed, experienced, practised, well up (**dans, en,** in); conversant (with); **homme v. dans les arts,** man (well) versed in the arts; **il était v. dans la magie,** he was an adept in magic. **2.** *Her:* reversed, renversé.

Verseau (le) [ləvɛrso], *Pr.n.m.* *Astr:* Aquarius, the Water-bearer.

versement [vɛrs(ə)mɑ̃], *s.m.* **1.** pouring (out, forth) (of liquid, etc.). **2.** *Fin:* payment, paying in, deposit; **v. partiel,** instalment; **en plusieurs versements, par versements échelonnés,** by instalments; **premier v.,** down payment; *Bank:* **bulletin de v.,** paying-in slip, *U.S:* deposit slip; **carnet de v.,** paying-in book. **3.** *Mil:* issue (of stores).

verser [vɛrse]. **1.** *v.tr.* (*a*) to overturn, upset (vehicle, passengers); (*of wind, etc.*) to lodge, lay, beat down (crops); *Min:* to tip (trucks); **il trouva son malade à demi versé hors du lit,** he found his patient half thrown out of bed; *Agr:* **les endroits versés (dans un champ),** the laid places in a field; *F:* (= RENVERSER) **v. du vin sur sa robe,** to spill wine on one's dress; (*b*) to pour (out) (liquid, etc.); **v. à boire à qn,** to pour out a drink for s.o.; **se v. à boire,** to pour oneself a drink; **versons à boire à . . .,** shall we, let us, drink to . . .; **v. le thé, le café,** to pour out the tea, the coffee; **rivière qui se verse dans un lac,** river that flows, empties itself, into a lake; **v. du blé dans un sac,** to pour corn into a sack; *A:* **v. des décombres,** to shoot rubbish; **v. l'or à pleines mains,** to throw one's money about; **v. le ridicule sur qn,** to pour ridicule on s.o.; *Lit:* **verser ses chagrins dans le cœur de qn,** to pour out one's troubles to s.o.; (*c*) to shed (tears, blood); **je n'ai jamais versé le sang d'un homme qu'à mon corps défendant,** I have never killed a man, shed blood, except in self defence; **v. son sang,** (i) to be wounded, (ii) to die (for one's country, a cause); **la lampe versait une douce lumière,** the lamp shed a soft light; (*d*) *Fin:* to pay (in), deposit (money); **v. des fonds dans une affaire,** to invest capital, put money, in an undertaking; **capitaux versés,** paid-up capital; *abs.* **v. (au) comptant,** to pay in cash; **v. des arrhes,** to pay a deposit; *Jur:* **v. la somme à laquelle ils ont été condamnés,** to remit the sum awarded against them; (*e*) **v. un document au dossier,** to add a document to the file; (*f*) *Mil:* to draft (**dans,** into); **v. des hommes à un régiment, dans une arme,** to draft, to assign, to transfer, men to a regiment, to an arm; (*g*) *Mil:* to issue (stores); (*h*) *Agr:* **v. un champ,** to turn over, to plough, a field; *abs.* **charrue qui verse à droite, à gauche,** plough that throws over to the right, to the left. **2.** *v.i.* (*a*) *A:* (*of vehicle*) to turn over (on its side); to overturn; (*of crops*) to be lodged, beaten down, blown over, laid flat; **v. en beau chemin,** to come to grief when all was going well; (*b*) **v. dans . . .,** to fall into . . .; to drift into . . .; **v. dans l'ivrognerie,** to drift into drunkenness; **son drame verse dans le mélo,** his play degenerates into melodrama.

verset [vɛrsɛ], *s.m.* **1.** *Ecc:* verse (of Bible, Koran, etc.). **2.** *Typ:* versicle.

verseur, -euse [vɛrsœːr, -øːz]. **1.** (*a*) *s.* pourer (of liquids); waiter, waitress (who serves drinks); (*b*) *s.m.* *Min:* tipper (of trucks). **2.** *s.f.* **verseuse,** coffee pot. **3.** *a.* **bec v.,** spout; **casserole verseuse,** saucepan with a lip.

versicolore [vɛrsikɔlɔːr], *a.* **1.** versicolour(ed), particoloured, variegated (ribbon, etc.). **2.** versicolour, chameleon-like; changeable in colour.

versicule [vɛrsikyl], *s.m.*, **versiculet** [vɛrsikylɛ], *s.m.* versicle, little verse.

versificateur, -trice [vɛrsifikatœːr, -tris], *s.* versifier.

versification [vɛrsifikasjɔ̃], *s.f.* versification.

versifier [vɛrsifje], *v.* (*p.d.* & *pr.sub.* **n. versifiions, v. versifiiez**) **1.** *v.i.* to versify, to write poetry, verse. **2.** *v.tr.* to versify; to put (prose) into verse; to write (sth.) in verse.

version [vɛrsjɔ̃], *s.f.* **1.** (*a*) version, translation; *B:* **la v. des Septante,** the Septuagint, the Alexandrian version; (*b*) *Sch:* translation; unseen; **v. latine,** Latin unseen; *Cin:* **film en v. originale,** film in the original language, undubbed (foreign) film; **film américain en v. française,** American film dubbed in French. **2.** (*a*) version, account (of event, etc.); (*b*) version (of car, etc.); **la v. militaire de cet avion,** the military version of this aircraft. **3.** *Obst:* version.

vers-librisme [vɛrlibrism], *s.m.* *no pl.* the writing of free verse, vers libres.

vers-libriste [vɛrlibrist], *s.m.* writer of free verse; vers-librist; *pl. vers-libristes.*

verso [vɛrso], *s.m.* verso, back, reverse (of sheet of paper); left-hand page (in book); *Bookb:* off side, off board; **voir au v.,** see overleaf; **la solution se trouve au v.,** the answer is on the back; (*computers*) **v. d'une carte,** card back; *Fin:* **effets comme au v.,** bills as per back; *pl. versos.*

versoir [vɛrswaːr], *s.m.* *Agr:* mould board (of plough).

verste [vɛrst], *s.f.* *Russian Meas:* verst.

vert, verte [vɛːr, vɛrt]. **1.** *a.* (*a*) green; *Her:* vert; *Aut: etc:* **feu v.,** green light; **donner le feu v. à qn,** to give s.o. the green light, the signal to go ahead; **v. comme pré,** as green as grass; **légumes verts,** green vegetables, *F:* greens; *Husb:* **mettre un cheval au régime v.,** to soil a horse; **régime v.,** soiling; (*b*) **bois v.,** green wood; **employer le v. et le sec,** to leave no stone unturned; **plantes vertes,** evergreens; **chêne v.,** holm oak, ilex; **haricots verts,** French beans; **feuilles encore vertes,** unturned leaves, leaves that are still green; **fruits verts,** unripe fruit; *Prov:* **ils sont trop verts,** sour grapes; **vin v.,** hard, sharp, wine; young wine; **café v.,** unroasted coffee; **cuir v.,** raw hide, green hide; **pierre verte,** stone fresh from the quarry; **c'est la verte jeunesse,** that's just like young people; *P:* **je suis v.,** I've been had (for a mug); (*c*) **verte vieillesse,** green old age; **un vieillard encore v.,** a spry old man; an old man who is still hale and hearty; (*d*) sharp, tart (reprimand, etc.); **on leur a fait une verte semonce,** they got a good dressing down; (*e*) *F:* spicy, risqué, blue (story, etc.); **il en a raconté des vertes,** it would have made a sailor blush; **en dire des vertes et des pas mûres,** not to mince one's words; **il en a vu des vertes et des pas mûres,** he's been through a lot; (*f*) **langue verte,** slang; (*g*) **fonte v.,** brass; gunmetal; *Miner:* **cendre verte,** malachite; (*h*) *Geog:* **le cap V.,** Cape Verde. **2.** *s.m.* (*a*) (the colour) green; *Her:* vert; **des rubans v. bouteille, v. chou, v. olive, v. cendré,** bottle-green, cabbage-green, olive-green, sage-green, ribbons; **v. de mer, v. d'eau,** sea green; **v. pomme,** apple green; (*b*) *Ch:* *Miner:* **green; v. minéral,** mineral green; **v. de terre,** verditer; **v. antique,** verd antique; ophicalcite; **v. de cuivre, de montagne,** malachite; *Metall:* **couler à v.,** to cast in green sand; (*c*) green grass; fresh vegetation; **mettre un cheval au v.,** to turn a horse out to grass; *F:* **se mettre au v.,** (i) to go into the country to recuperate; (ii) to settle down to a quiet (reformed) life; to turn over a new leaf; *A:* (*from the old practice of wearing a green leaf throughout the month of May*) **prendre qn sans v.,** to catch s.o. napping; (*d*) *Golf:* (putting) green; (*e*) hardness, sharpness (of wine). **3.** *s.f.* **verte:** (*a*) *Dial:* grass snake; (*b*) *F:* *A:* **une verte,** an absinthe; (*c*) *F:* **la grande verte,** the sea.

vert-de-gris [vɛrdəgri], *s.m.inv.* verdigris.

vert-de-grisé [vɛrdəgrize], *a.* verdigrised, coated with verdigris; *pl. vert-de-grisé(e)s.*

vert-de-griser (se) [səvɛrdəgrize], *v.pr.* to become coated with verdigris.

vertébral, -aux [vɛrtebral, -o], *a.* *Anat:* vertebral; **colonne vertébrale,** vertebral column, spine, backbone.

vertèbre [vɛrtɛbr̩], *s.f.* *Anat:* vertebra.

vertébré [vɛrtebre], *a.* & *s.m.* *Z:* vertebrate; *s.m.pl.* **vertébrés,** vertebrates, Vertebrata.

vertébro-iliaque [vɛrtebrɔiljak], *a.* *Anat:* vertebro-iliac; *pl. vertébro-iliaques.*

vertébrothérapeute [vɛrtebrɔterapøt], *s.m.* & *f.* specialist in spinal manipulation; manipulator; chiropractor.

vertébrothérapie [vɛrtebrɔterapi], *s.f.* *Med:* manipulation of the vertebral column, of the vertebrae; spinal manipulation.

vertement [vɛrtəmɑ̃], *adv.* sharply, smartly, roughly; **répondre v.,** to reply sharply; **il le réprimanda v.,** he reprimanded him severely.

verterelle [vɛrtərɛl], *s.f.*, **vertevelle** [vɛrtəvɛl], *s.f.* (bolt) staple.

vertex [vɛrtɛks], *s.m.* **1.** *Anat:* *Z:* vertex; top of the head (of vertebrates). **2.** *Astr:* vertex, zenith.

vertical, -ale, -aux [vɛrtikal, -o]. **1.** *a.* vertical; perpendicular; plumb; upright; **ligne verticale,** vertical line; **position verticale,** upright position; **éclairage v.,** overhead light(ing); *Pol.Ec:* **concentration verticale, ascendante et descendante,** vertical combination, integration; **l'écriture chinoise est verticale,** Chinese is written vertically; *Elcs: (computers)* **alimentation verticale,** vertical feed; **espacement v.,** line space. **2.** *a. & s.m. Astr:* **(cercle) v.,** vertical circle. **3.** *s.f.* **verticale,** vertical; vertical position; **déviation de la verticale,** deviation from the vertical; **les verticales du gothique anglais perpendiculaire,** the vertical lines of English perpendicular gothic; **à la verticale,** straight up; **falaise à la verticale,** sheer cliff.

verticalement [vɛrtikalmɑ̃], *adv.* vertically; *(in crossword puzzles)* down; **la pluie tombe v.,** the rain's coming straight down.

verticalité [vɛrtikalite], *s.f.* verticality, perpendicularity, uprightness.

verticille [vɛrtisil], *s.m. Bot:* verticil, whorl.

verticillé [vɛrtisil(l)e], *a. Bot:* verticillate, whorled.

verticité [vɛrtisite], *s.f. Ph:* verticity.

vertige [vɛrtiːʒ], *s.m.* **1.** *(a)* dizziness, swimming of the head, giddiness; *Med:* **v. apoplectique, ténébreux,** vertigo; **être pris de v.,** to become dizzy; **cela me donne le v.,** it makes me feel dizzy, giddy, makes my head swim; **avoir le v.,** to feel dizzy, giddy; **avoir des vertiges, être sujet à des vertiges,** to have fits of giddiness, dizzy spells; **le fait d'être élu maire lui a donné le v.,** his election as mayor has gone to his head; **souffrir du v. du pouvoir,** to be drunk, dizzy, with power; *(b) A:* bewilderment. **2.** fear of heights; **avoir facilement le v.,** to have a bad head for heights.

vertigineusement [vɛrtiʒinøzmɑ̃], *adv.* vertiginously, dizzily, in a whirl.

vertigineux, -euse [vɛrtiʒinø, -øːz], *a.* **1.** vertiginous; dizzy, giddy (height, etc.); **vitesse vertigineuse,** vertiginous, breakneck, speed; **hausse vertigineuse des prix,** staggering rise in prices. **2.** *(a) Med:* **accès v.,** fit of dizziness, of vertigo; *(b) Vet:* causing staggers.

vertigo [vɛrtigo], *s.m.* **1.** *Vet:* staggers, blind staggers. **2.** *F: A:* whim, caprice, **3.** *Moll:* vertigo.

vertouin, -ine [vɛrtwɛ̃, -in], *a. & s. Geog:* (native, inhabitant) of Vertou.

vertu [vɛrty], *s.f.* **1.** *A:* courage, valour; **n'avoir ni force ni v.,** to have neither strength nor courage. **2.** virtue; **vertus chrétiennes,** Christian virtues; **les trois vertus théologales,** the three theological virtues; **les quatre vertus cardinales,** the four cardinal virtues; **vivre dans la v.,** to lead a good life; **faire de nécessité v.,** to make a virtue of necessity. **3.** *(a)* chastity; **femme de petite v.,** woman of easy virtue; *(b) F:* virtuous woman; **épouser une v.,** to marry a puritan; *F:* **ce n'est pas une v.,** she's no saint, she's no better than she should be. **4.** quality, property (of remedy, etc.); **plantes qui ont la v. de guérir,** plants that have healing virtues, healing properties; *prep.phr.* **en v. de,** by virtue of; *Jur:* in pursuance of; **en v. de cet arrangement,** under this agreement; **en v. d'un traité,** under the terms of a treaty; **il était rentré en v. d'une amnistie,** he had returned under an amnesty. **5.** *Theol:* **les Vertus,** the Virtues (order of angels).

vertubleu [vɛrtyblø], **vertuchou** [vɛrtyʃu], *int. A: (attenuated forms of* **vertu Dieu**) oddsbodikins!

vertueusement [vɛrtɥøzmɑ̃], *adv.* virtuously; **suivre v. les modes les plus absurdes,** to follow religiously the most absurd fashions.

vertueux, -euse [vɛrtɥø, -øːz], *a.* **1.** *A:* courageous. **2.** virtuous. **3.** *(of woman)* chaste.

vertugadin [vɛrtygadɛ̃], *s.m. A.Cost:* farthingale.

vérumontanum [verymɔ̃tanɔm], *s.m. Anat:* verumontanum.

verve [vɛrv], *s.f.* animation, life, (good) spirits, zest, verve; **v. endiablée,** irrepressible spirits; **v. d'un discours,** verve, liveliness, of a speech; **être en v.,** to be in the best of form; **plein de v.,** full of life; lively, spirited; *(of speech)* lively, inspired; **jouer avec v.,** to give a spirited performance; to play, act, with verve.

verveine [vɛrvɛn], *s.f. Bot:* vervain, verbena; **v. officinale,** common vervain.

vervelle [vɛrvɛl], *s.f. A.Ven:* varvel, vervel.

vervet [vɛrvɛ], *s.m. Z:* vervet (monkey).

verveux[1], **-euse** [vɛrvø, -øːz], *a.* animated, lively, spirited; **tout v.,** full of animation; in the best of spirits.

verveux[2], *s.m.* **1.** pannier. **2.** *Fish:* hoop net.

verviétois, -oise [vɛrvjetwa, -waːz], *a. & s. Geog:* (native, inhabitant) of Verviers.

vervinois, -oise [vɛrvinwa, -waːz], *a. & s. Geog:* (native, inhabitant) of Vervins.

Vésale [vezal], *Pr.n.m. Med.Hist:* Vesalius.

vésanie [vezani], *s.f.* vesania, insanity; **la guerre, cette monstrueuse v.,** war, this monstrous insanity, incredible madness.

vesce [vɛs], *s.f. Bot:* vetch, tare.

vésical, -aux [vezikal, -o], *a. Anat:* vesical; **artères vésicales,** vesical arteries; **plexus v.,** vesical plexus; *Med:* **calculs vésicaux,** vesical calculus, *F:* stones in the bladder.

vésicant [vezikɑ̃], *a. & s.m. Med: Pharm:* blistering (plaster); vesicant, vesicatory.

vésicateur [vezikatœːr], *s.m. Med:* vesicatory.

vésication [vezikasjɔ̃], *s.f.* vesication, blistering.

vésicatoire [vezikatwaːr], *Med: Pharm:* **1.** *a.* vesicatory. **2.** *s.m.* blister, vesicatory; **appliquer un v. à qn,** to blister s.o.

vésico- [veziko], *comb.fm.* vesico-.

vésico-intestinal, -aux [vezikoɛ̃tɛstinal, -o], *a. Anat:* vesicointestinal.

vésico-pustule [vezikopystyl], *s.f. Med:* vesicular pustule; *pl. vésico-pustules.*

vésico-rectal, -aux [vezikorɛktal, -o], *a. Anat:* vesicorectal.

vésico-utérin [vezikoyterɛ̃], *a. Anat:* vesicouterine; *pl. vésico-utérin(e)s.*

vésico-vaginal, -aux [vezikovaʒinal, -o], *a. Anat:* vesicovaginal.

vésiculaire [vezikylɛːr], *a.* **1.** *Nat.Hist:* vesicular; bladder-like. **2.** *Med:* **murmure v. de la respiration,** normal vesicular murmur of the respiration.

vésiculation [vezikylasjɔ̃], *s.f. Med:* vesiculation.

vésicule [vezikyl], *s.f.* **1.** *Anat: Nat.Hist:* vesicle; *Bot:* air cell; *Anat:* **v. biliaire,** gall bladder; **v. du fiel,** bile cyst; *Med:* **v. variolique,** smallpox vesicle; **groupe de vésicules,** cluster of vesicles; *Ich:* **v. aérienne,** air bladder; sound; *Nat.Hist:* **v. à venin,** poison bag. **2.** *Metall:* blister (in casting).

vésiculectomie [vezikylɛktɔmi], *s.f. Surg:* vesiculectomy.

vésiculeux, -euse [vezikylø, -øːz], *a.* vesiculose, vesiculate; *Med:* **maladie vésiculeuse,** pemphigus.

vésiculite [vezikylit], *s.f. Med:* vesiculitis.

vesou [vəzu], *s.m. Sug.-R:* cane juice.

Vespasien [vɛspazjɛ̃], *Pr.n.m. Rom.Hist:* Vespasian.

vespasienne [vɛspazjɛn], *s.f.* street urinal.

Vesper [vɛspɛːr], *Pr.n.m. Astr:* Vesper, Hesper; the evening star.

vespéral, -aux [vɛsperal, -o]. **1.** *a.* evening; *Astr: Nat.Hist:* vespertine; **clarté vespérale,** evening light. **2.** *s.m. Ecc:* vesperal.

vespère [vɛspɛːr], *s.m. Ent:* longhorn beetle; *(genus)* Vesperus.

vespertilio [vɛspɛrtiljo], *s.m.*, **vespertilion** [vɛspɛrtiljɔ̃], *s.m. Z:* vespertilio (bat); **v. de Daubenton,** Daubenton's bat.

vespertilionidés [vɛspɛrtiljɔnide], *s.m.pl. Z:* Vespertilionidae.

vespidés [vɛspide], *s.m.pl. Ent:* Vespidae, the wasp family.

vespiforme [vɛspifɔrm], *a.* vespiform, wasp-like.

Vespuce [vɛspys], *Pr.n.* **Améric V.,** Amerigo Vespucci.

vessard, -arde [vɛsaːr, -ard], *P: A:* **1.** *a.* funky. **2.** *s.* funk.

vesse [vɛs], *s.f.* **1.** *P: (not used in polite conversation)* silent (and odoriferous) fart. **2.** *(a) P:* blue funk; *(b) int: Sch: A:* look out! cave!

vesse-de-loup [vɛsdəlu], *s.f. Fung: F:* puffball; *pl. vesses-de-loup.*

vesser [vɛse], *v.i. P: (not used in polite conversation)* to give a silent (and odoriferous) fart; *A:* **v. du bec,** to have bad breath.

vesseron [vɛsrɔ̃], *s.m. Bot: F:* everlasting pea.

vesseur, -euse [vɛsœːr, -øːz], *a. & s. P:* = VESSARD, -ARDE.

vessie [vesi], *s.f. (a) Anat: etc:* bladder; *Ich:* **v. natatoire,** air bladder; sound; *F:* **prendre des vessies pour des lanternes,** to believe that the moon is made of green cheese; **il vous ferait prendre des vessies pour des lanternes,** he would talk black into white; **je ne prends pas des vessies pour des lanternes,** I know chalk from cheese; *(b) Fb:* **v. de ballon,** football bladder; *Med:* **v. à glace,** ice bag.

vessigon [vɛsigɔ̃], *s.m. Vet:* wind gall; **v. chevillé,** thoroughpin; **v. du grasset,** stifle.

Vesta [vɛsta], *Pr.n.f. Rom.Myth: Astr:* Vesta.

vestale [vɛstal], *s.f. Rom.Ant:* vestal (virgin).

veste [vɛst], *s.f. (a) Cost:* (short) jacket; *F:* **tomber la v.,** to get into one's shirtsleeves, to take off one's jacket; *F:* **retourner sa v.,** to change one's mind, one's party; to be a turncoat; *(b) F:* abysmal failure; **prendre, ramasser, remporter, une v.,** to come a cropper.

vestiaire [vɛstjɛːr]. **1.** *s.m. (a) (esp. in factory etc.)* locker (for keeping clothes, etc.); *(b)* hat-and-coat rack; *(c)* cloakroom, locker room (of school, factory, etc.); *Sp: etc:* changing room, dressing room; *Jur: etc:* robing room (for judges, etc.); *(c)* cloakroom, *U.S:* checkroom (in theatre, etc.); **dame de v., préposé(e) au v.,** cloakroom attendant; *F:* **v. monsieur?** would you like to leave your things, sir? *esp. U.S:* check your coat, sir? *F:* **mon v., s'il vous plaît!** my hat and coat, my things, please! *Th: F: (to poor actors)* **au v.!** go and get changed! *(d)* collecting centre (for clothing for distressed areas, etc.). **2.** *a. A:* vestiary; relating to clothes, to vestments.

vestibulaire [vɛstibylɛːr], *a. Anat:* vestibular; **face v. de l'incisive,** vestibular face of the incisor; *Med:* **syndrome v.,** vestibular syndrome.

vestibule [vɛstibyl], *s.m.* **1.** vestibule, (entrance) hall, lobby. **2.** *Anat:* vestibule (of ear).

vestige [vɛstiːʒ], *s.m.* **1.** *A:* mark, trace, footprint (of man, animal etc.). **2.** vestige, remains, trace (of former habitations, etc.); **derniers vestiges de . . .,** last remnants of . . .; **vestiges du passé,** relics of the past.

vestimentaire [vɛstimɑ̃tɛːr], *a.* vestimentary; **dépenses vestimentaires,** expenditure, money spent, on clothes; **l'industrie v.,** the clothing trade.

vestiture [vɛstityːr], *s.f. Nat.Hist:* vestiture.

veston [vɛstɔ̃], *s.m. Cost:* (man's) jacket; *Mil:* short overcoat; *Nau:* monkey jacket; **v. droit, croisé,** single-breasted, double-breasted, jacket; **v. court,** round jacket; **v. d'intérieur,** smoking jacket; **complet v.,** lounge suit; **il était en v.,** he was wearing a lounge suit.

vestonné [vɛstɔne], *a.* wearing a jacket, jacketed.

vésulien, -ienne [vezyljɛ̃, -jɛn], *(a) a. & s. Geog:* (native, inhabitant) of Vesoul; *(b) a. & s.m. Geol:* Vesulian.

Vésuve [vezyːv], *Pr.n.m. Geog:* Vesuvius.

vésuvianite [vezyvjanit], *s.f. Miner:* vesuvianite.

vésuvien, -ienne [vezyvjɛ̃, -jɛn], *a.* Vesuvian.

veszélyite [vezeliit], *s.f. Miner:* veszelyite.

vêtement [vɛtmɑ̃], *s.m.* garment, *pl.* clothes, clothing, dress; **la nourriture et le v.,** food and clothing; **industrie du v.,** clothing trade; **tissus pour vêtements,** dress materials; **v. d'hiver, d'été,** winter, summer, garment; **serrer ses vêtements d'hiver,** to put away one's winter clothes, *F:* one's winter things; **vêtements de dessous,** underwear, underclothing; **vêtements de travail,** working clothes; **vêtements de sport,** sportswear; **vêtements de plage,** beachwear; **vêtements de pluie,** rainwear; *F:* **je vais chercher un v. et je sors avec vous,** I'll just get a coat and then I'll come out with you; *Ecc:* **vêtements sacerdotaux,** (church) vestments.

vétéran [veterɑ̃], *s.m.* **1.** *Mil: etc:* veteran; old campaigner; *Nau:* old hand; *Pol: F:* **les vétérans (de la politique),** the Elder Statesmen. **2.** *Sch: O:* student, pupil who repeats a course.

vétérance [veterɑ̃ːs], *s.f. A:* veteran standing.

vétérinaire [veterinɛːr]. **1.** *a.* veterinary (medicine, etc.). **2.** *s.m. & f.* veterinary surgeon, *F:* vet, *U.S:* veterinary.

vétillard, -arde [vetijaːr, -ard], *Pej: (a) a.* quibbling, hair-splitting (person); *(b) s.* quibbler, caviller.

vétille [vetiːj], *s.f.* **1.** bagatelle, trifle, *F:* fleabite; **s'arrêter à des vétilles,** to make a fuss about trifles; to stick at trifles; **punir un enfant pour une v.,** to punish a child for a mere trifle, for next to nothing. **2.** *Pyr:* squib.

vétiller [vetije], *v.i.* to make a fuss about trifles; to split hairs; to niggle; to quibble.

vétillerie [vetijri], *s.f.* quibbling, hair-splitting, captiousness.

vétilleur, -euse[1] [vetijœːr, -øːz], *s. O:* = VÉTILLARD.

vétilleux, -euse[2] [vetijø, -øːz], *a.* **1.** delicate, ticklish, finicky (business, etc.). **2.** finicky, fussy, fastidious (person).

vêtir [vetiːr], *v.tr. (pr.p.* **vêtant;** *p.p.* **vêtu;** *pr.ind.* **je vêts,** n. **vêtons;** *p.d.* **je vêtais;** *p.h.* **je vêtis;** *fu.* **je vêtirai.** *The forms* **vêtissant, vêtissons, vêtissais,** *etc., are also met with)* **1.** to clothe; to dress (s.o.) **(de,** in); **v. un enfant,** to dress a child; **v. un singe d'un habit rouge,** to dress a monkey in a red coat; **chaudement vêtu,** warmly dressed; **à moitié vêtu,** half-dressed; **elle est vêtue d'une robe de soie,** she is wearing a silk dress; **professeurs vêtus de leur toges,** professors wearing, in, their gowns; **tout de noir vêtu,** clad all in black; *F:* **vêtu comme un oignon,** all wrapped up in layer upon layer of clothing. **2.** *A:* (= REVÊTIR) to put on, don (garment); **elle avait vêtu une robe noire,** she had put on a black dress.

se vêtir, to dress; **donnez-moi le temps de me v.,** give me time to dress, to put on my clothes; **elle s'était vêtue d'une robe noire,** she had put on a black dress; **elle ne gagne pas de quoi se v.,** she doesn't earn enough to clothe herself.

vétiver [vetivɛːr], *s.m. Bot:* vetiver, cuscus (grass, root).

veto [veto], *s.m.* veto; **avoir le v.,** to have the power of veto; **mettre son v. à qch.,** to veto sth.; **droit de v.,** right of veto; **v. absolu,** absolute veto; **v. suspensif,** suspensory veto.

véto [veto], *s.m. F:* (= VÉTÉRINAIRE) vet.

vêture [vetyːr], *s.f.* **1.** *Ecc:* taking of the habit, of the veil; entering religion. **2.** *Adm: A:* providing of clothing (for the necessitous); **être chargé de la v. des enfants assistés,** to look after the clothing of waifs and strays.

vétuste [vetyst], *a.* decayed, decrepit.

vétusté [vetyste], *s.f.* decay, decrepitude; **la maison tombe de v.,** the house is falling to pieces with age; *Ins:* **clause de v.,** obsolescence clause.

vétyver [vetivɛːr], *s.m.* = VÉTIVER.

veuf, veuve [vœf, vœːv]. **1.** *a.* widowed (man, woman); **elle resta veuve à trente ans,** she was left a widow at thirty; **elle resta veuve,** she remained a widow; **un piédestal v. de sa statue,** a pedestal bare of its statue, bereft of its statue, minus its statue. **2.** *s.* widower, *f.* widow; *F:* **veuve à titre temporaire, demi-veuve,** grass widow; *F:* **la Veuve,** the guillotine; *A:* **épouser la Veuve,** to be guillotined. **3.** *s.f.* **veuve:** (*a*) *Orn:* widow bird, whydah (bird); **veuve de Jackson,** Jackson's whydah; **veuve parasite,** parasite whydah; (*b*) *Arach:* **v. noire,** black widow spider; (*c*) *Bot:* **(fleur de) veuve,** sweet scabious, purple scabious, mourning bride.

veule [vøːl], *a.* weak, feeble, flabby (person, etc.); (person) with no backbone; **sourire v.,** feeble smile; **bouche v.,** slack mouth; *A:* **plante v.,** sickly plant; **terre v.,** poor soil.

veulement [vølmɑ̃], *adv.* weakly, feebly; in a cowardly manner, out of cowardice.

veulerie [vølri], *s.f.* (*a*) *A:* inertia, listlessness; (*b*) cowardice; lack of backbone.

veuvage [vœvaːʒ], *s.m.* (i) widowhood; (ii) widowerhood.

veveysan, -ane [vəvɛzɑ̃, -an], *a. & s. Geog:* (native, inhabitant) of Vevey.

vexant [vɛksɑ̃], *a.* vexing, provoking, annoying.

vexateur, -trice [vɛksatœːr, -tris]. **1.** *a.* vexatious, oppressive. **2.** *s. A: & Lit:* vexer.

vexation [vɛksasjɔ̃], *s.f.* **1.** *O:* (*a*) vexation, harassing; persecuting; (*b*) vexatious, oppressive, measure; infliction. **2.** mortification; **essuyer des vexations,** to meet with rebuffs.

vexatoire [vɛksatwaːr], *a.* vexatious, oppressive (measures, etc.).

vexer [vɛkse], *v.tr.* **1.** *A:* to harass, to persecute (s.o.). **2.** to annoy, offend, hurt (s.o.); **v. qn par une réflexion,** to hurt, upset, s.o. by a remark; **cela me vexe d'apprendre que . . .,** I am sorry to hear that . . ..

se vexer de qch., to be upset, irritated, offended, annoyed, about sth.; **il se vexe d'un rien,** he gets offended over trifles.

vexillaire [vɛksil(l)ɛːr]. **1.** *a.* (*a*) vexillary (soldier); (*b*) *Bot:* vexillar. **2.** *s.m. Rom.Ant:* vexillary; standard bearer.

vexille [vɛksil], *s.m. Rom.Ant:* vexillum.

vexillé [vɛksil(l)e], *a. Bot:* vexillate.

vézélien, -ienne [vezeljɛ̃, -jɛn], *a. & s. Geog:* (native, inhabitant) of Vézelay.

vi [vi], *adv.* (= OUI) *Iron:* yeah? you're telling me!

via [vja], *prep.* via, by way of (Cherbourg, etc.).

viabilisation [vjabilizasjɔ̃], *s.f. Adm:* development (of a building site).

viabilisé [vjabilize], *a. Adm:* **terrain v.,** building site on which roads have been made (and public services connected).

viabiliser [vjabilize], *v.tr. Adm:* **v. un terrain,** to develop a building site.

viabilité[1] [vjabilite], *s.f.* (*a*) viability, capacity for living (of newborn child, etc.); (*b*) viability, workability (of a system).

viabilité[2], *s.f.* **1.** practicability, traffic condition (of road); **état de v.,** condition of the road; **mettre une route en état de v.,** to make a road fit for traffic; to recondition a road; **route de v. douteuse,** impracticable road; road in a poor condition. **2.** *Const:* development (of site ready for building).

viable[1] [vjabl̥], *a.* (*a*) viable (infant); capable of living; (*b*) (*of plan, government, etc.*) that has some prospect of survival; viable; **politique non v.,** policy that cannot hope to survive.

viable[2], *a.* (road) fit for traffic.

viaduc [vjadyk], *s.m.* viaduct.

viager, -ère [vjaʒe, -ɛːr]. **1.** *a.* for life, during one's lifetime; **bien v.,** life estate; **rente viagère,** life annuity, life interest; **rentier v.,** annuitant; **acheter, vendre, une maison en v.,** to buy, sell, a house on an instalment system to provide the seller with a life annuity. **2.** *s.m.* life interest; **placer son argent en v.,** to invest one's money at life interest, in a life annuity; to buy an annuity.

viagèrement [vjaʒɛrmɑ̃], *adv.* for life, during one's lifetime; **jouir v. d'une maison,** to have the life tenancy of a house.

viagraphe [vjagraf], *s.m. Civ.E:* viagraph.

viande [vjɑ̃ːd], *s.f.* meat. **1.** *A:* food, viands; *Prov:* **il n'est viande que d'appétit,** hunger is the best sauce. **2.** flesh; meat; **v. de boucherie,** *A:* **grosse v.,** butcher's meat; *A:* **menue v.,** fowls and small game; **v. fraîche,** fresh meat; **v. frigorifiée,** frozen, chilled, meat; **v. rouge,** red meat; **v. blanche,** white meat; **v. noire,** brown meat; **v. de cheval,** horseflesh; (*on menu*) **viandes froides,** cold buffet; **abstinence des viandes,** abstention from meat. **3.** *P:* human body, carcass; **amène ta v.,** come along.

viander [vjɑ̃de], *v.i.* (*of deer*) to graze, feed.

se viander, *Mount: P:* to fall.

viandis [vjɑ̃di], *s.m.* pasture, grazing (for deer).

viatique [vjatik], *s.m.* viaticum. **1.** (*a*) *Ecc. & O:* money, provisions, resources, for a journey; (*b*) *F:* fare home (given to gamblers at Monte Carlo who have lost everything). **2.** *Ecc:* last sacrament; **mourir sans v.,** to die without receiving the last sacraments.

vibice [vibis], *s.f. Med:* vibex.

vibor(d) [viboːr], *s.m. N.Arch:* sheer strake (of ship).

vibraculaire [vibrakylɛːr], *s.m. Z:* vibraculum, vibracularium.

vibrage [vibraːʒ], *s.m. Tchn:* vibrating; **v. du béton,** vibrating of concrete.

vibrance [vibrɑ̃ːs], *s.f.* vibrancy.

vibrant [vibrɑ̃], *a.* **1.** vibrating, vibrant (cord, pulse, etc.); throbbing (pulse); **le public se montra v. et réceptif,** the public was eager and receptive. **2.** (*a*) resonant; **d'une voix vibrante,** in ringing tones; **voix vibrante d'émotion,** voice vibrating, ringing, quivering, with emotion; (*b*) rousing, stirring (speech). **3.** *Ling:* **consonne vibrante,** *s.f.* **vibrante,** lingual, uvular, rolled, consonant. **4.** *Ent: F:* **mouche vibrante,** ichneumon fly.

vibraphone [vibrafɔn], *s.m. Mus:* vibraphone.

vibraphoniste [vibrafɔnist], *s.m. & f. Mus:* vibraphonist.

vibrateur [vibratœːr], *s.m. Elcs: etc:* vibrator; *Civ.E: etc:* (concrete) vibrator.

vibratile [vibratil], *a. Biol:* vibratile (cilium, etc.).

vibration [vibrasjɔ̃], *s.f.* **1.** vibration; *Av: Ac:* flutter; **v. d'un moteur,** vibration of an engine. **2.** resonance (of voice).

vibratoire [vibratwaːr], *a. Ph: etc:* vibratory, vibrating; *W.Tel:* **circuit v.,** oscillatory circuit; *Med:* **massage v.,** vibro-massage.

vibré [vibre], *a. Const:* **béton v.,** vibrated concrete.

vibrer [vibre], *v.i.* to vibrate; **faire v. qch.,** to make sth. vibrate; to vibrate sth.; **faire v. le cœur de qn,** to stir s.o., s.o.'s heart; *El:* **appel vibré,** buzzer call (apparatus).

vibreur [vibrœːr], *s.m. El:* trembler, vibrator, make-and-break (of trembler coil); buzzer (of buzzer apparatus); **v. de départ,** magneto booster coil; **v. (pour vérification des induits),** armature tester; *Tchn:* **crayon v.,** (electric) engraving tool, pen.

vibrion [vibrijɔ̃], *s.m. Bac: Med:* vibrio; **v. septique,** gas bacillus; **v. cholérique,** cholera vibrio.

vibrionien, -ienne [vibrijɔnjɛ̃, -jɛn], *a. Bac: Med:* vibrionic.

vibriose [vibrijoːz], *s.f. Vet:* vibrionic abortion, vibriosis.

vibrisse [vibris], *s.f. Anat: Z:* vibrissa.

vibrographe [vibrɔgraf], *s.m.* vibrograph.

vibro(-)massage [vibrɔmasaːʒ], *s.m.* vibro-massage.

vibromasseur [vibrɔmasœːr], *s.m.* (electric) vibrator (for massage).

vibromètre [vibrɔmɛtr], *s.m.* vibrometer.

vibroscope [vibrɔskɔp], *s.m.* vibroscope.

vicaire [vikɛːr]. **1.** *s.m.* (*a*) *A:* deputy, substitute (of official, etc.); (*b*) *Ecc:* **v. apostolique,** vicar apostolic; **grand v., v. général,** vicar-general; **le v. de Jésus-Christ,** the Vicar of Jesus Christ, the Pope; (*c*) *Ecc:* curate (of parish); *R.C.Ch:* assistant priest. **2.** *a. Theol:* vicarious (satisfaction).

vicairie [vikɛri], *s.f. Ecc:* chapel of ease served by a curate, by an assistant priest.

vicarial, -iaux [vikarjal, -jo], *a.* **1.** vicarial. **2.** *Ecc:* (duties, etc.) of a curate, an assistant priest.

vicariance [vikarjɑ̃ːs], *s.f. Physiol:* vicariousness.

vicariant [vikarjɑ̃], *a. Physiol:* vicarious (organ, etc.).

vicariat [vikarja], *s.m. Ecc:* **1.** vicariate. **2.** curacy, assistant priestship. **3.** = VICAIRIE.

vice [vis], *s.m.* **1.** (*a*) vice, depravity, corruption; **vivre dans le v.,** to live in vice; *Lit:* **bourbier du v.,** sink of iniquity; (*b*) vice, moral failing; **il a tous les vices,** he has all the vices. **2.** fault, defect, blemish, flaw, imperfection; **v. de construction,** faulty construction; **v. caché,** latent defect; *Vet: etc:* **v. de conformation,** defect in shape, in build; physical defect, malformation; **v. de prononciation,** faulty pronunciation; **v. d'écriture,** mistake in copying; **v. du sang,** impurity in the blood; *Jur:* **v. de forme,** vice of form; flaw (in a deed, etc.); faulty drafting (of a deed, etc.); **v. propre,** inherent defect (in goods); unseaworthiness (of ship). **3.** (*a*) **cheval qui a du v.,** restive horse; (*b*) *F:* **il a du v., il ne manque pas de v.,** (i) he's a sly customer; (ii) he's impudent, cheeky.

vice- [vis], *pref.* vice-; deputy.

vice-amiral [visamiral], *s.m.* **1.** vice-admiral; **v.-a. d'escadre,** admiral. **2.** vice-admiral's flagship; *pl. vice-amiraux.*

vice-amirauté [visamirote], *s.f.* vice-admiralty, vice-admiralship; *pl. vice-amirautés.*

vice-chambellan [visʃɑ̃bɛlɑ̃], *s.m.* vice-chamberlain; *pl. vice-chambellans.*

vice-chancelier [visʃɑ̃səlje], *s.m.* vice-chancellor; *pl. vice-chanceliers.*

vice-consul [viskɔ̃syl], *s.m.* (*a*) vice-consul; (*b*) pro-consul; *pl. vice-consuls.*

vice-consulat [viskɔ̃syla], *s.m.* **1.** vice-consulship. **2.** vice-consulate; *pl. vice-consulats.*

vice-gérance [visʒerɑ̃ːs], *s.f.* vice-managership; *pl. vice-gérances.*

vice-gérant [visʒerɑ̃], *s.m.* deputy-manager, vice-manager; acting manager; *pl. vice-gérants.*

vice-gérent [visʒerɑ̃], *s.m. Ecc: A:* vicegerent; *pl. vice-gérents.*

vicelard, -arde [vislaːr, -ard], *P:* **1.** *a.* (*a*) cunning, sly; (*b*) vicious, depraved. **2.** *s.* cunning, sly, person.

vice-légat [vislega], *s.m. Ecc:* vice-legate; *pl. vice-légats.*

vice-légation [vislegasjɔ̃], *s.f. Ecc:* vice-legateship; *pl. vice-légations.*

Vicence [visɑ̃ːs], *Pr.n. Geog:* Vicenza.

vicennal, -aux [visen(n)al, -o], *a.* vicennial.

vicentin, -ine [visɑ̃tɛ̃, -in], *a. & s. Geog:* (native, inhabitant) of Vicenza.

vice-présidence [visprezidɑ̃ːs], *s.f.* (*a*) vice-presidency, vice-presidentship; (*b*) vice-chairmanship; *pl. vice-présidences.*

vice-président [visprezidɑ̃], *s.m.* (*a*) vice-president; (*b*) vice-chairman; *pl. vice-présidents.*

vice-recteur [visrɛktœːr], *s.m.* vice-rector, sub-rector; pro-rector (of university, college, etc.); *pl. vice-recteurs.*

vice-reine [visrɛn], *s.f.* vice-reine; *pl. vice-reines.*

vice-roi [visrwa], *s.m.* **1.** *Hist:* viceroy. **2.** *Ent:* viceroy (butterfly); *pl. vice-rois.*

vice-royal, -aux [visrwajal, -o], *a.* viceregal.

vice-royaume [visrwajoːm], *s.m. Hist:* **le v.-r. espagnol de Mexico,** the Spanish viceroyalty of Mexico; *pl. vice-royaumes.*

vice-royauté [visrwajote], *s.f.* viceroyalty; *pl. vice-royautés.*

vicésimal, -aux [visezimal, -o], *a. Mth:* vigesimal; vicenary (notation).

vice versa [visevɛrsa], *Lt.adv.phr.* vice versa; conversely.

Vichnou [viʃnu], *Pr.n.m. Rel:* Vishnu.

Vichnouisme [viʃnuism], *s.m. Rel:* Vishnuism.

Vichy [viʃi]. **1.** *Pr.n. Geog:* Vichy; *Hist:* **le gouvernement de V.,** the Vichy government; **eau de V.,** Vichy (water); **pastille de V.,** Vichy tablet, digestive tablet. **2.** *s.m. Tex:* = gingham.

vichysme [viʃism], *s.m. Hist:* Vichyism.

vichyssois, -oise [viʃiswa, -waːz], *a. & s.* (*a*) *Geog:* (native, inhabitant) of Vichy; (*b*) *Pol: Hist:* governmental (referring to the Vichy Government); (*c*) *s.f. Cu:* **vichyssoise,** Vichyssoise (soup).

vichyste [viʃist], *a. Hist:* Vichyist.

viciable [visjabl̩], *a.* **1.** corruptible. **2.** (document, deed) that can be invalidated, vitiated.

viciateur, -trice [visjatœːr, -tris], *a.* vitiating, contaminating.

viciation [visjasjɔ̃], *s.f.* **1.** vitiation; corruption (of morals, tastes, etc.); contamination (of the air, etc.); poverty (of blood). **2.** *Jur:* vitiation (of deed, contract, etc.).

vicié [visje], *a.* vitiated, corrupt (taste, etc.); spoilt, tainted (food, etc.); poor, thin (blood); **air v.,** (i) polluted, (ii) stale, air.

vicier [visje], *v.tr.* (*p.d. & pr.sub.* **n. viciions, v. viciiez**) **1.** to vitiate, corrupt, spoil (s.o., sth.); **v. l'air,** to pollute, contaminate, the air; to make the air foul. **2.** *Jur:* to vitiate, invalidate (deed, contract).

vicieusement [visjøzmɑ̃], *adv.* faultily, imperfectly; **parler v.,** to speak incorrectly.

vicieux, -ieuse [visjø, -jøːz], *a.* **1.** depraved, corrupt (person). **2.** defective, faulty, imperfect (formation, etc.); **raisonnement v.,** vicious reasoning; **cercle v.,** vicious circle; **locution vicieuse,** faulty, incorrect, expression; **usage v. d'une locution,** wrong use of a phrase. **3.** tricky, restive, bad-tempered (horse, etc.); **nature vicieuse,** vice, viciousness, restiveness (of horse).

vicinal, -aux [visinal, -o]. **1.** *a.* **chemin v.,** local road (maintained by the *commune*). **2.** *s.m. Belg:* tramway (serving a series of villages).

vicinalité [visinalite], *s.f.* **1.** local status, vicinal status (of road); **chemin de grande v.,** important local road. **2.** (system of) local roads, local communication.

vicissitude [visisityd], *s.f.* vicissitude, mutability (of fortune, fashion, etc.); **les vicissitudes de la vie,** the vicissitudes, the ups and downs, of life.

vicomtal, -aux [vikɔ̃tal, -o], *a.* of, pertaining to, a viscount; *A:* viscontal.

vicomte [vikɔ̃ːt], *s.m.* viscount.

vicomté [vikɔ̃te], *s.f.* **1.** viscountcy, viscountship. **2.** viscounty.

vicomtesse [vikɔ̃tɛs], *s.f.* viscountess.

victime [viktim], *s.f.* **1.** victim (of sacrifice). **2.** victim, sufferer; **être la v. de qn,** to be the victim of s.o.; **j'ai été la v. d'un escroc,** I have been cheated, *F:* had, by a swindler; **être (la) v. de son héroïsme,** to be the victim of one's heroism; **les victimes du désastre,** the victims of the disaster; the casualties; **mourir, périr, v. de la petite vérole,** to die a victim to smallpox; **être la v. d'une illusion,** to labour under a delusion; **j'ai été v. de la grippe,** I have been down with influenza, with flu; *F:* **je ne suis pas v. de votre histoire,** you're not taking me in with that story.

victimer [viktime], *v.tr. A:* to victimize (s.o.).

victoire [viktwaːr]. **1.** *s.f.* (*a*) victory; **remporter la v.,** to gain a, the, victory (**sur,** over); to carry, win, the day; **la v. est à nous,** the victory is ours; **la v. n'est pas aux forts,** the battle is not to the strong; **chanter, crier, v.,** to crow, to triumph; **v. à l'arraché,** hard-won victory; **v. à la Pyrrhus,** Pyrrhic victory; (*b*) *Art:* (statue of) victory; **la v. de Samothrace,** the Winged Victory of Samothrace. **2.** *Pr.n.f.* Victoria.

Victor [viktɔːr], *Pr.n.m.* Victor.

Victoria [viktɔrja]. **1.** *Pr.n.f.* Victoria. **2.** *s.f.* (*a*) *Veh:* Victoria; (*b*) *Bot:* water platter; **v. regia,** victoria (regia), royal waterlily.

victorien, -ienne [viktɔrjɛ̃, -jɛn], *a.* Victorian (era, etc.).

victorieusement [viktɔrjøzmɑ̃], *adv.* victoriously.

victorieux, -ieuse [viktɔrjø, -jøːz], *a.* victorious; **être v.,** to win the day; to gain the victory; **être v. de qn,** to be victorious over s.o.; **avoir un air v.,** to have a triumphant air; **sortir v. du scrutin,** to be successful at the polls.

victorin [viktɔrɛ̃], *s.m. Ecc:* Victorine, canon regular of the Order of St Victor.

victuailles [viktɥɑːj], *s.f.pl.* victuals, eatables, food; **emporter des v.,** to take some food, sth. to eat, with one.

vidage [vidaːʒ], *s.m.* **1.** (*a*) emptying (of vessel, etc.); gutting, cleaning (of fish); drawing (of fowl); *Metalw:* expulsion (of metal during welding); *Elcs:* (*computers*) **v. (de) mémoire,** core, memory, store, dump; memory print-out; **v. sur incident grave,** disaster dump; (*b*) *F:* chucking out (from pub, etc.). **2.** *Civ.E:* earth thrown up (during excavation); parapet, embankment, bank (of canal).

vidame [vidam], *s.m. Fr.Hist:* vidame (secular deputy of bishop).

vidamé [vidame], *s.m. Fr.Hist:* vidameship.

vidamesse [vidamɛs], *s.f. Fr.Hist:* daughter, wife, of a vidame.

vidamie [vidami], *s.f.* = VIDAMÉ.

vidange [vidɑ̃ːʒ], *s.f.* **1.** (*a*) draining, emptying (of cesspools, ditches, etc.); **matières de v.,** night soil; (*b*) draining, emptying (of sump, etc.); blowing off (of boiler); *Aut:* oil change; **faire la v.,** to change the oil; **bouchon de v.,** *Mch:* (i) drain cock; (ii) blow-off cock; *I.C.E:* (i) sump plug; (ii) draining plug, draw-off plug (of radiator); **tuyau de v.,** (i) *Mch:* blow-off pipe; (ii) *I.C.E:* drain; **robinet de v.,** (i) *I.C.E:* drain-cock; (ii) *Mch:* blow-off; *Mch:* **trou de v.,** mud-hole (of boiler); **tonneau, vin, en v.,** broached cask, wine; tapped cask, cask in tap; (*c*) clearing, removing (of felled timber from forest). **2.** *usu. pl.* (*a*) night-soil; (*b*) sediment, sludge (in boiler); (*c*) *Obst: A:* lochia; (*d*) felled timber (to be removed). **3.** road ditch, drain.

vidanger [vidɑ̃ʒe], *v.tr.* (**je vidangeai(s); n. vidangeons**) to clean out; to empty (cesspool, radiator, etc.); to drain (engine sump, etc.); to blow off (boiler).

vidangeur [vidɑ̃ʒœːr], *s.m.* cesspool clearer; **voiture de v.,** cesspit emptier.

vidard, vidart [vidaːr], *a. Vet:* (horse) subject to diarrhoea.

vide [vid]. **1.** *a.* empty (room, purse, heart, etc.); blank (space in document, etc.); unoccupied (seat); **bouteilles vides,** empty bottles, *Com:* empties; **revenir les mains vides,** to return empty-handed; *F:* **avoir la tête v.,** to be empty-headed; **avoir le cerveau v.,** to feel light-headed (through hunger, etc.); **v. de sens,** void of meaning, devoid of meaning; meaningless; **phrases vides,** empty words; *F:* **un tas de discours vides,** a lot of hot air; *Th:* **la scène reste v.,** the stage remains empty; *Breed:* **jument v.,** unimpregnated mare; barren mare. **2.** *s.m.* (*a*) empty space; gap; cavity; void; interstice (between bars); blank (in document); **sa mort laisse un v. dans la famille,** his death leaves a gap, a blank, in the family circle; **combler les vides,** to fill up the gaps; *Mil:* to make good the casualties; **remplir les vides de sa journée,** to fill the unoccupied moments of one's day; **il y a encore du v. dans la malle,** there is still room in the trunk; **fût où il y a du v.,** ullaged cask; (*b*) *Ph:* vacuum; **faire le v. dans un espace,** to create a vacuum in a space; to exhaust a space; **casser le v.,** to break the vacuum; **pompe à v.,** vacuum pump; **nettoyage par le v.,** vacuum cleaning; *Ind:* **chaudière de concentration par le v.,** vacuum pan; *Elcs:* **tube à v.,** vacuum tube; *El:* **lampe à v.,** vacuum lamp; **v. très poussé,** very high vacuum; *W.Tel:* **valve à v. très poussé,** hard valve; *Ch:* **fiole à v.,** suction flask; *Rail:* **frein à v.,** vacuum brake; *Ind:* **emballage, sertissage, sous v.,** vacuum packing; **emballé, serti, sous v.,** vacuum-packed; *F:* **faire le v. autour de qn,** to isolate s.o., to drive all his friends away; **région où la disette a fait le v.,** region depopulated through lack of food; (*c*) emptiness; **taper dans le v.,** to (hit out and) miss the mark; to beat the (empty) air; **regarder dans le v.,** to stare into space; **le v. de l'esprit,** empty-headedness; **le v. des grandeurs humaines,** the hollowness, the nothingness, vanity, of human greatness; (*d*) *adv.phr.* **à v.,** empty; **camion revenant à v.,** lorry returning empty; **poids à v.,** unladen weight; (*of machine*) **marcher à v.,** to run on no load, to run light; *I.C.E:* (*of engine*) **tourner à v.,** to run in neutral (gear); **emballer le moteur à v.,** to race the engine (without a load); **démarrage à v.,** loadless starting; *El:* **courant à v.,** no-load current; **accu à v.,** discharged, run-down, battery; *Mus:* **corde à v.,** open string; *F:* **passage à v.,** bad patch; blank period; **frapper à v.,** to hit the air, to miss the mark (with hammer, etc.).

vidé [vide], *a.* **1.** (*a*) **poulet plumé et v.,** chicken that has been plucked and drawn; **hareng v.,** gutted herring; (*b*) emptied, exhausted; **c'est un homme v.,** he's played out. **2. jarrets vidés,** clean hocks (of horse).

vide-bouteille(s) [vidbutɛːj], *s.m.inv.* **1.** *A:* week-end cottage. **2.** siphon.

vide-cave [vidkaːv], *s.m.inv.* hydraulic pump (for emptying flooded buildings).

vide-chargé [vidʃarʒe], *a.m. Rail:* **freinage v.-c.,** adjustable braking (that can be regulated according to whether the wagon is full or empty).

vide-citron [vidsitrɔ̃], *s.m. O:* lemon-squeezer; *pl. vide-citrons.*

videcoq [vidkɔk], *s.m. Ven: F:* woodcock.

vide-gousset [vidgusɛ], *s.m.* **1.** *A:* = VIDE-POCHE(S) 1. **2.** pickpocket; *pl. vide-goussets.*

videlle [vidɛl], *s.f.* **1.** *Nau:* darn (in sail). **2.** fruit stoner, corer (used by confectioners). **3.** *Cu:* jagger, jagging iron.

videment [vidmɑ̃], *s.m. O:* emptying (of box, sack, etc.); draining (of cask, glass); clearing (of forest).

vidéo [video], *a. & s.m.inv. Elcs: T.V:* video; **bande v.,** video tape; **tube v.,** video tube; **v. radar,** radar display; **amplificateur v.,** video amplifier.

vidéofréquence [videɔfrekɑ̃ːs], *s.f. T.V:* video frequency.

vidéophone [videɔfɔn], *s.m.* videophone.

vide-ordures [vidɔrdyːr], *s.m.inv.* (*a*) rubbish chute; (*b*) sewage-disposal unit.

vide-poche(s) [vidpɔʃ], *s.m.inv.* **1.** *A: Furn:* (*a*) (dressing-table) tidy; pin tray; (*b*) pouch table. **2.** *Aut:* cubbyhole; glove compartment, box.

vide-pomme [vidpɔm], *s.m.* apple corer; *pl. vide-pommes.*

vider [vide], *v.tr.* **1.** to empty; to clear out (room, drawer); to clear (forest); to drain (cask, one's glass, etc.); to drain off (pond); to exhaust (mind, brain); to run down, blow off (boilers); to blow (an egg); *Elcs:* (*computers*) to dump; **v. un baril de son contenu,** to empty a barrel (of its contents); **le baril commence à se v.,** the barrel is beginning to (get) empty; **v. une bouteille ensemble,** *F:* to crack a bottle together; **videz vos verres! drink up! v. une embarcation, v. l'eau d'une embarcation,** to bail (out) a boat; **v. les lieux,** to vacate the premises, *F:* to clear out; *F:* **v. les lieux, le plancher,** to quit; to make oneself scarce; **v. le pays,** to clear out of the country; **le juge ordonna de faire v. la salle,** the judge ordered the court to be cleared; **v. une prison,** to clear a prison; *Jur:* **v. ses mains,** to hand over money in hand to someone appointed by the court; *P:* **v. qn,** (i) to dismiss, sack, s.o.; (ii) to reduce s.o. to a rag, to wear s.o. out; (iii) to suck s.o. dry; (iv) to ruin s.o., to clean s.o. out, to squeeze s.o. dry; **v. sa bourse,** to empty one's purse; to spend all one's money; **v. son sac,** (i) *P:* to empty one's bowels; (ii) *F:* to get sth. off one's chest; *Equit:* **v. les arçons, les étriers,** to be thrown (from one's horse); **se faire v.,** (i) *Equit:* to be thrown; (ii) *P:* to be sent out (of the room); to be chucked out (of school, bar, etc.); *Av:* **il fut vidé (de l'appareil),** he was thrown clear. **2.** *A:* to void (matter, stools). **3.** (*a*) to eviscerate (carcass); to gut, clean (fish); to draw (fowl); to core (apple); to stone (fruit); (*b*) to bore, hollow out (key, gun barrel); to cut out (comb); to pink out (leather, etc.). **4.** to settle (question, dispute); to set (question) at rest; **v. une querelle,** (i) to adjust, settle, a difference; (ii) to fight it out; to have it out; **v. ses comptes,** to make up one's accounts; *Jur:* (*of judges*) **v. un délibéré,** to give a verdict after consultation.

vide-tasses [vidtɑːs], *s.m.inv.* slop basin.

vide-tourie [vidturi], *s.m.inv. Ind:* carboy filter.

videur, -euse [vidœːr, -øːz], *s.* (*pers.*) (*a*) emptier; drawer (of chicken, etc.); gutter (of fish); **v. de poches,** pickpocket; *F:* **v. de pots,** (great) drinker, boozer; (*b*) *F:* chucker-out, *U.S:* bouncer.

vide-vite [vidvit], *s.m.inv. Av:* fuel jettison, fuel dump valve.

vidicon [vidikɔ̃], *s.m. T.V:* vidicon.

vidien, -ienne [vidjɛ̃, -jɛn], *a. Anat:* vidian (canal, artery, etc.).

vidimer [vidime], *v.tr. Jur:* to attest, to authenticate (a copy of a document).

vidimus [vidimys], *s.m. Jur:* vidimus, attested copy (of a document).

vidoir [vidwaːr], *s.m.* mouth (of rubbish chute, etc.).

vidual, -aux [vidɥal, -o], *a.* vidual; of a widow, a widower.

viduité [vidɥite], *s.f.* viduity, viduage, widowhood.

vidure [vidyːr], *s.f.* **1.** (*a*) entrails (of poultry, etc.); guts (of fish); **vidures pour le chat,** offal for the cat; (*b*) **vidures de poubelle,** rubbish for the dustbin. **2.** *Needlew: Leath:* openwork, pinking.

vie [vi], *s.f.* life. **1. v. végétative, animale,** vegetable, animal, life; **tout ce qui a v.,** everything that has life; **être en v.,** to be alive; **il est encore en v.,** he is still alive; **donner la v. à un enfant,** to give birth to a child; **avoir la v. dure,** to be hard to kill; to die hard; **il est entre la v. et la mort,** he is hovering between life and death; **question de v. ou de mort,** question of life and death; **il y va de la v.,** it's a case of life and death; **je le ferai ou j'y perdrai la v.,** I shall do it or perish in the attempt; **accorder la v. à**

qn, to grant s.o. his life; to spare s.o.; **demander la v.**, to beg for one's life; **sauver la v. à qn**, to save s.o.'s life; **rappeler qn à la v.**, to bring s.o. to life again; to bring s.o. back to life; **maintenir qn en v., conserver qn à la v.**, to keep s.o. alive; **tant qu'il y a de la v. il y a de l'espoir**, while there's life there's hope; *F: O:* **sur ma v.!** as I live! upon my life! **sans v.**, lifeless; **elle déborde de v.**, she is bubbling over with vitality; **portrait qui a de la v.**, living portrait; **musique pleine de v.**, lively, animated, music; *Bot:* **arbre de v.**, arbor vitae. **2.** (*a*) lifetime; **passer sa v. à voyager**, to spend one's life travelling; **toute une v. de bonheur**, a lifetime of happiness; **pour la v.**, for life; till death; **entre eux c'est à la v. à la mort; ils sont amis à la v. à la mort**, they are sworn friends; **une fois dans la v.**, once in a lifetime; **plus tard dans la v.**, later in life; **de toute ma v. je n'ai jamais entendu chose pareille!** I've never heard such a thing in all my life! **jamais de la v.!** never! **pension à v., la v. durant**, life pension; **nommé à v.**, appointed for life; *Ins:* **v. moyenne, probable**, expectation of life; (*b*) biography; **écrire la v. de qn**, to write s.o.'s life; **les vies de Plutarque**, Plutarch's lives. **3.** existence, mode of life, way of living; **ainsi va la v.! c'est la v.!** such is life! **je connais la v.**, I've seen something of life; **conformer sa v. à ses préceptes**, to live up to one's principles; **v. d'hermite**, hermit's life; *A:* **v. de cabinet**, sedentary life; **mener une v. tranquille**, to lead a quiet existence; *A:* **faire v. qui dure**, to husband one's resources; **mener joyeuse v.**, to lead a gay life; **mener la grande v.**, to lead a riotous life, to live it up; **ça, c'est la vraie v.!** that's the life! **changer de v.**, to mend one's ways, to turn over a new leaf; **il lui rendait la v. dure**, he made her life a burden, a misery; he made life hard for her, gave her a hard time; **la v. américaine**, the American way of life; **la v. nocturne**, night life; **mauvaise v.**, loose living; **femme de mauvaise v.**, loose woman; *F:* **faire la v.**, to kick up a row; **faire la v. à qn**, to make s.o.'s life a misery. **4.** living, livelihood; **niveau de v.**, standard of living; **le coût de la v.**, the cost of living; **prime de v. chère, indemnité de cherté de v.**, cost-of-living bonus; **la v. est chère à Paris**, the cost of living is high in Paris; **gagner sa v.**, to earn one's living; **comment gagne-t-il sa v.?** what does he do for a living? **être réduit à mendier sa v.**, to be reduced to begging.

viédase, viédaze [vjedaːʒ], *s.m. Dial:* (*S. of Fr.*) (*a*) aubergine; (*b*) *P:* (i) fool, idiot, clot; (ii) stroller (in the streets), gaper, *U.S:* rubberneck; (iii) *F:* (*form of address*) you old so-and-so!

vieillard [vjɛjaːr], *s.m.* (*f. usu.* **vieille**, *q.v. under* VIEUX, *but occ. Pej:* **vieillarde**) **1.** old man; **les vieillards**, old people; the elderly. **2.** *Z:* macaque (monkey), wanderoo.

vieillarder [vjɛjarde], *v.i.* (*of wine*) to assume (artificially) the quality of age.

vieillement [vjɛjmɑ̃], *adv.* in an elderly fashion, manner; **s'habiller plus v. que son âge**, to dress too old for one's age.

vieillerie [vjɛjri], *s.f.* (*a*) (*used esp. in pl.*) old things; old fashioned, out-of-date, things; outworn ideas; **théâtre qui ne joue que des vieilleries**, theatre that puts on nothing but outmoded plays; (*b*) *F:* **c'est la v.!** oh, that's old age!

vieillesse [vjɛjɛs], *s.f.* (*a*) old age; **atteindre la v.**, to reach old age, to become old; **dans leur v.**, in their old age; **c'est la v. qui vient!** it's old age creeping up! it's anno domini! **si v. pouvait**, if old age only could; **bâton de v.**, support, prop, of old age; (*b*) age (of building, custom); **la maison tombe de v.**, the house is falling to pieces with age; the house is so old that it's tumbling down; (*c*) *Geog:* (*in cycle of erosion*) **stade de v.**, old age; (*d*) *coll.* old people.

vieilli [vjeji], *a.* (*a*) grown old; marked by age; **visage v.**, age-worn face; (*b*) obsolescent (word, expression, etc.); old-fashioned, out-of-date (style, etc.).

vieillir [vjejiːr]. **1.** *v.i.* (*a*) to grow old; **il avait vieilli dans un emploi subalterne**, he had grown old in a subordinate position; (*b*) to age (in appearance); **il a vieilli, il est vieilli**, he looks older; (*c*) (*of custom, word, etc.*) to become obsolete, antiquated, out of date; **ce mot a vieilli**, this word is obsolescent; (*d*) (*of wine, cheese, etc.*) to mature; **laisser v. du vin**, to leave wine to mature. **2.** *v.tr.* (*a*) to age (s.o.); to make (s.o.) look older; **ce chapeau la vieillit**, this hat ages her, makes her look old; **sa maladie l'a vieilli**, his illness has aged him; **je ne porte jamais le noir, car je n'ai aucune envie de me vieillir**, I never wear black as I've no desire to look older than I am; (*b*) to make (s.o.) out to be older than he is; **il prend un plaisir étrange à se v.**, he takes a strange pleasure in pretending to be older than he is; (*c*) to age (wine, cheese); *Cer:* to mature (clay); to distress (furniture).

vieillissant [vjejisɑ̃], *a.* growing old; ageing.

vieillissement [vjejismɑ̃], *s.m.* **1.** (*a*) ageing, growing old; **signes de v.**, signs of ageing; **le v. de la population**, the ageing, rise in the average age, of the population; (*b*) becoming obsolete; obsolescence; **le prompt v. des modes**, the speed with which fashions become out of date; (*c*) *Metall:* age hardening. **2.** making old; **v. artificiel des vins, des meubles**, artificial ageing of wines, of furniture.

vieillot, -otte [vjɛjo, -ɔt], *a.* **1.** oldish; *s.* **petit(e) vieillot(te)**, little old man, little old woman. **2.** antiquated, oldfashioned. **3.** *A:* wizened (face, etc.).

vielle [vjɛl], *s.f. A.Mus:* vielle, hurdy-gurdy.

vieller [vjɛle], *v.i. A.Mus:* to play the vielle, the hurdy-gurdy.

vielleur, -euse [vjɛlœːr, -øːz], *s.*, **vielleux** [vjɛlø], *s.m. A.Mus:* hurdy-gurdyist.

Vienne [vjɛn], *Pr.n.f. Geog:* **1.** Vienna (in Austria). **2.** Vienne (in France).

viennois, -oise [vjɛnwa, -waːz], *a. & s. Geog:* **1.** Viennese. **2.** *Hist:* **le dauphin du Viennois**, (full title of) the Dauphin. **3.** (native, inhabitant), (i) of Vienna (in Austria), (ii) of Vienne (in France).

viennoiserie [vjɛnwazri], *s.f. Bak:* Viennese bread.

vierge [vjɛrʒ]. **1.** *s.f.* (*a*) virgin; **la (Sainte) V.**, the Blessed Virgin (Mary); **chapelle de la V.**, Lady chapel; *A:* **se coiffer à la V.**, to wear one's hair Madonna-braided; *B:* **les vierges folles**, the foolish virgins; **épouser une v.**, to marry a virgin; (*b*) *Astr:* **la V.**, Virgo. **2.** *a.* (*a*) virgin, virginal; **fille v., homme v.**, virgin; **terre v.**, virgin soil; *Agr:* unbroken ground; *Mount:* **montagne v.**, unscaled mountain; **forêt v.**, virgin forest; *Comest:* **huile v.**, virgin oil; **vigne v.**, Virginia creeper; (*b*) **page v.**, blank page; **couleur v.**, pure colour; **atmosphère v. de fumée**, atmosphere unpolluted by smoke; *Phot:* **plaque v.**, unexposed plate; *Rec:* **disque v.**, blank record, disc; **réputation v.**, untarnished reputation; (*c*) *Elcs:* (*computers*) **bande v.**, blank tape, virgin tape; **carte v.**, blank card; **support v.**, blank, empty, virgin, medium; **zone v.**, clear area.

vierzonnais, -aise [vjɛrzɔnɛ, -ɛːz], *a. & s. Geog:* (native, inhabitant) of Vierzon.

viet [vjɛt], *s.m. F:* Vietnamese soldier (of the Viet-Minh).

Vietnam(le) [ləvjɛtnam], *Pr.n.m. Geog:* Vietnam.

vietnamien, -ienne [vjɛtnamjɛ̃, -ɛn], *a. & s. Geog:* Vietnamese.

vieux, vieil, *f.* **vieille** [vjø, vjɛːj], *a.* (*the form* **vieil** *is used before masc. nouns beginning with a vowel or* **h** "*mute*," *but* **vieux** *also occurs in this position:* **un vieil homme**, *occ. A:* **un vieux homme; mon vieil ami**, *occ. A:* **mon vieux ami**) **1.** (*of pers.*) old; (*a*) (*in years*) **devenir v.**, to grow old; **se faire v.**, (i) to be getting old, to be getting on in years; (ii) to make oneself out older than one is; *F:* **voilà deux heures que je vous attends, je commençais à me faire v.**, I've been waiting for you for two hours and was beginning to get worried, to flap like an old woman; **v. de corps, jeune d'esprit**, old in body, young in mind; **vivre v., vieille**, to live to an old age, to a good age; to live to be old; **prendre un coup de v.**, to grow old overnight; *s.* **un v., une vieille**, an old man, an old woman; **un v. du volant**, a veteran motorist; *F:* **mes vieux**, my (old) parents, *F:* the old people; *F:* (*with no sense of old age*) **eh bien, mon v.!** well (what about it), old chap! **viens, ma vieille!** come on, old girl! *adv.* **elle s'habille plus v. que son âge**, she dresses too old for her age; (*b*) (*in service, office, etc.*) **un vieil ami**, an old friend, a friend of long standing; **il est v. dans ce métier**, he is an old hand at this job; *Prov:* **il n'est chasse que de v. chien**, the old horse for the hard road; **une vieille fille**, an old maid; *s. F:* **un v. de la vieille** (*i.e.* **de la vieille garde de Napoléon**), one of the old guard, of the old stalwarts; a veteran. **2.** (*of thgs*) (*a*) old, ancient (vase, building, custom, etc.); obsolete (term, etc.); stale (bread, news, etc.); worn, shabby (hat, etc.); **v. habits**, old, worn-out clothes; **v. papiers**, waste paper; **vieilles fontes**, foundry scrap; **v. comme le Pont-Neuf, comme les rues, comme Hérode**, as old as Adam, as the hills; **le bon v. temps**, the good old days; **cela sent son v. temps**, it smacks of the old days; **c'est une vieille histoire**, it's an old story; *adj.phr.inv.* **v. jeu**, old fashioned; **idées v. jeu**, old fashioned, antiquated, ideas; **être v. jeu**, to be a back number, *F:* a square; *Chr:* **le v. calendrier**, the old-style calendar; (*b*) (*of friendship, service, etc.*) of long standing; (*c*) *inv.* **des rubans vieil or**, old-gold ribbons. **3.** *s.f. Ich:* **vieille**, wrasse, sea wife; **vieille (des coraux)**, pudding wife.

vif, vive[1] [vif, viːv]. **1.** *a.* (*a*) alive, living; **chair vive**, living flesh; **être brûlé v.**, to be burnt alive; **plus mort que v.**, more dead than alive; **de vive force**, by main force; **de vive voix**, by word of mouth; viva voce; **haie vive**, quickset hedge; **eau vive**, running water, spring water, *B:* living water; **vives eaux** [vivzo], spring tide; **roc v.**, live, living, rock; solid rock; **le plus v. de nos intérêts**, our most vital interests; **chaux vive**, quicklime; **force vive, puissance vive**, kinetic energy; **acquérir de la force vive**, to gather momentum; (*of pers.*) **c'est une force vive**, he's a live wire; (*b*) lively, animated; fast, brisk (action, game, discussion, etc.); brisk, hot (fire), **enfant v.**, lively child; **vive allure, allure vive**, brisk pace; **avoir l'humeur un peu vive**, to be short-tempered, quick-tempered; **v. à répliquer**, quick to retort; **v. à répondre**, smart, alert, quick, in answering; **il y eut un échange de paroles vives**, words ran high; **il y avait entre eux de vives animosités**, animosity ran high between them; **avec mes plus vives félicitations**, with my warmest congratulations; **il intervint dans la discussion au moment où elle était le plus vive**, he plunged into the thick of the discussion; **cheval v.**, high-spirited horse; (*c*) sharp (wind, reprimand, etc.); **l'air est v.**, there is a tang in the air; **arête vive**, sharp edge; *adv.* **il gèle v.**, it's freezing hard; (*d*) keen, quick (wit, etc.); vivid (imagination, impression, etc.); **v. plaisir**, keen pleasure; **vive satisfaction**, great satisfaction; **v. à toutes les jouissances**, keen to enjoy life; (*e*) **couleurs vives**, bright, vivid, colours; **albums aux vives couleurs**, picture-books full of bright colours; **yeux d'un bleu très v.**, intensely blue eyes. **2.** *s.m. Jur:* living person; **disposition entre vifs**, donation inter vivos. **3.** *s.m.* (*a*) **peindre au v., sur le v.**, to paint from life; **scènes prises sur le v.**, scenes taken from life; **c'était lui pris sur le v.**, it was a lifelike picture of him, it was him to the life; (*b*) heart (of tree); shaft (of column); (*c*) living flesh, quick; **couper ses ongles jusqu'au v.**, to cut one's nails to the quick; **blessé, piqué, au v.**, stung to the quick; **cette parole l'atteignit au v.**, this remark touched him on the raw; **critique qui touche au v.**, cutting criticism; **avoir les nerfs à v.**, to have one's nerves on edge; **entrer dans le v. de la question, du sujet**, to come to the heart of the matter; (*d*) *Oc:* **v. de la marée, de l'eau**, spring tide; (*e*) **le v. du combat**, the thick of the battle, the heart of the combat; (*f*) **pêcher au v.**, to fish with live bait.

vif-argent [vifarʒɑ̃], *s.m.* (*a*) *O:* quicksilver, mercury; (*b*) **il a du v.-a. dans les veines**, he's never still for a minute; **c'est un v.-a.**, he's just like quicksilver.

vigésimal, -aux [viʒezimal, -o], *a. Mth:* vigesimal; vicenary (notation).

vigie [viʒi], *s.f. Nau:* **1.** (*a*) lookout; **être de v., en v.**, to be on the lookout; (*b*) lookout (man) (on ship or on coast); (*c*) watchtower; *Rail:* (observation) box (on van); **v. de signaux**, signal cabin; **v. de frein**, brake cabin. **2.** *Nau:* (*a*) (*on chart*) vigia; (*b*) danger buoy.

vigilamment [viʒilamɑ̃], *adv.* vigilantly, watchfully.

vigilance [viʒilɑ̃ːs], *s.f.* vigilance; **surprendre la v. de qn**, to catch s.o. napping; **endormir la v. de qn**, to put s.o. off his guard; **avec v.**, vigilantly.

vigilant [viʒilɑ̃]. **1.** *a.* vigilant, watchful, alert, on one's guard; **soins vigilants**, careful attention. **2.** *s.m.* night watchman.

vigile[1] [viʒil], *s.f. Ecc:* **1.** vigil (of feast day); **v. des Quatre-Temps**, ember-eve. **2. vigiles des morts**, vigils of the dead, office for the dead.

vigile[2], *s.m. Rom.Ant:* night watchman.

Vigile[3], *Pr.n.m. Ecc.Hist:* Vigilius.

vigne [viɲ], *s.f.* **1.** *Vit:* (*a*) vine; **feuille de v.**, vine-leaf; **serre à vignes**, vinery; (*b*) vineyard; *Lit:* **travailler à la vigne du Seigneur**, to work in the Lord's vineyard; *F:* **être dans les vignes, dans la v., du Seigneur**, to be in one's cups; **raisins de v.**, wine grapes; **pêches de v.**, (i) small peaches grown between rows of vines; (ii) late-ripening peaches. 2. *Bot:* **v. de Judée, de Judas,** bitter-sweet, woody nightshade; **v. de Salomon, v. blanche,** clematis, traveller's joy; **v. vierge,** Virginia creeper.

vigneau, -eaux [viɲo], *s.m. Moll:* periwinkle.

vigneron, -onne [viɲrɔ̃, -ɔn]. 1. *s.* vine grower; viticulturist. 2. *a.* (*a*) **charrue vigneronne,** vineyard plough; (*b*) **hélice vigneronne,** Burgundy snail.

vignetage [viɲta:ʒ], *s.m.* ornamentation (of book, page, etc.) with vignettes.

vigneter [viɲte], *v.tr.* (**je vignette, n. vignetons; je vignetterai**) to ornament (page, book, etc.) with vignettes.

vignette [viɲɛt], *s.f.* 1. (*a*) *Art: Engr: etc:* vignette; *Typ:* text illustration, cut; head-and-tail piece; ornamental border; **papier à vignettes,** fancy writing paper (ornamented with borders, heading, or design); (*b*) *Adm:* (stamped) revenue band (on packets of tobacco, matches, etc.); *Aut:* special tax label; (*c*) cigarette card. 2. *Bot: F:* (*a*) meadowsweet; (*b*) clematis; (*c*) mercury.

vignettiste [viɲetist], *s.m.* vignettist, vignette engraver.

vigneture [viɲəty:r], *s.f. Mediev.Art:* decorative border of vine leaves (in illuminated MSS).

vignoble [viɲɔbl̩]. 1. *s.m.* vineyard; **pays de vignobles,** wine district. 2. *a.* **région v.,** wine region.

vignon [viɲɔ̃], *s.m. Bot: F:* gorse, furze.

vignot [viɲo], *s.m. Moll:* periwinkle.

vigogne [vigɔɲ], *s.f.* (*a*) *Z:* vicuña, vicuna; (*b*) *Tex:* vicuña (wool, cloth); **manteau de v.,** lama coat.

vigoureusement [vigurøzmɑ̃], *adv.* vigorously.

vigoureux, -euse [vigurø, -ø:z], *a.* vigorous, strong, sturdy (child, horse, resistance, etc.); **secouer qn d'un bras v.,** to shake s.o. vigorously; **coup v.,** powerful blow; **faire une opposition vigoureuse à un projet,** to offer vigorous, firm, strenuous, opposition to a plan; *Art:* **trait, pinceau, v.,** strong, firm, line or touch; *Phot:* **cliché v.,** strong negative.

vigueur [vigœ:r], *s.f.* 1. vigour, strength; **donner, redonner, de la v. à qn,** to invigorate, re-invigorate, s.o.; to brace, *F:* buck, s.o. up; **reprendre (de la) v.,** to regain strength; **se sentir sans v.,** to feel exhausted, washed out; **style sans v.,** flat, lifeless, style; **s'exprimer avec v.,** to express oneself vigorously, forcibly; **v. intellectuelle,** strength of intellect; **dans la v. de l'âge,** in the prime of life; *Art:* **v. de coloris,** vigour, strength, of colouring; *pl.* **vigueurs,** strong lines; strength (of colour, design). 2. (*of decree, etc.*) **en v.,** in force; **les règlements en v.,** the regulations in force, the prevailing regulations; **entrer en v.,** to come into force, into effect; **cesser d'être en v.,** to lapse; **mettre un règlement en v.,** (i) to put a regulation into effect, into force; (ii) to enforce a regulation; **remettre un règlement en v.,** to revive a regulation; **mise en v. d'un traité,** putting into force, enforcing, enforcement, of a treaty.

viguier [vigje], *s.m. Jur: A:* provost (in S. of Fr.).

Viking [vikiŋ], *a. & s.m. Hist:* Viking.

vil [vil], *a.* 1. cheap (goods, etc.); **vendre qch. à v. prix,** to sell sth. dirt cheap, for a mere song. 2. (*a*) *A:* lowly (origin, condition, etc.); **le plus v. des métiers,** the lowest of trades; (*b*) base (metal, etc.). 3. *A: & Lit:* vile, base (person, motive, etc.); **âme vile,** base soul; **vile calomnie,** base, foul, vile, calumny; **v. calomniateur,** base calumniator.

vilain, -aine [vilɛ̃, -ɛn]. 1. *s.* (*a*) *Hist:* villein; (*b*) rogue; *Prov:* **à v. v. et demi,** set a thief to catch a thief; (*c*) *F:* **oh, le v.! la vilaine!** you naughty boy! you naughty girl! you little villain! (*d*) *A:* miser; *Prov:* **il n'est chère que de v.,** there's nothing like a miser's feast; (*e*) *F:* trouble; **ça va faire, il y aura, du v.,** there's going to be trouble; **il y a du v. dans l'air,** there are spots on the sun. 2. *a.* (*a*) nasty, bad, unpleasant (person, thoughts, weather, etc.); **c'est un v. monsieur,** *P:* **un v. coco,** he's a most objectionable person, a nasty piece of work; **ce sont de vilaines gens,** they're a bad lot; **un v. tour,** a mean, dirty, trick; **c'est une vilaine histoire,** it's not a nice story; it's an ugly story; **un v. mot,** an ugly word; a nasty word; **le v. côté de la vie,** the seamy side of life; **une vilaine blessure,** a nasty, ugly, wound; **une vilaine maladie,** an unpleasant, a nasty, disease; **il fait v.,** the weather's awful, it's filthy weather; (*b*) ugly (feature, house, etc.); ugly, shabby (hat, etc.); sordid, wretched (street, etc.); (*c*) *A:* avaricious, mean.

vilainage [vilɛna:z], *s.m. Hist:* villeinage.

vilainement [vilɛnmɑ̃], *adv.* in an ugly fashion, uglily; shabbily; badly; **manger v.,** to eat poorly; **parler v.,** to speak impolitely, in a coarse manner.

vilayet [vilajɛ], *s.m. Turkish Adm:* vilayet.

vilebrequin [vilbrəkɛ̃], *s.m.* 1. *Tls:* (*a*) (i) (bit) brace; (ii) brace and bit; **v. à cliquet,** ratchet brace; (*b*) **v. à engrenage,** geared ratchet brace; **v. à conscience,** breast drill. 2. (*a*) *Mch: I.C.E:* **(arbre à) v.,** crankshaft; **bras, flasque, de v.,** crank(shaft) web; **coude de v.,** crank throw; **butée de v.,** crankshaft ball thrust bearing; **palier, portée, de v.,** crankshaft (journal) bearing; **soie de v.,** crankpin; (*b*) crankpin (of Maxim gun).

vilement [vilmɑ̃], *adv.* vilely, basely; dishonestly.

vilenie [vilәni], *s.f.* 1. *A:* meanness, stinginess. 2. (*a*) mean, vile, low, action; **faire une v. à qn,** to play a lowdown trick on s.o.; **il médite quelque v.,** he is up to some mischief; (*b*) **dire des vilenies à qn,** to hurl abuse at s.o.; **on m'a raconté des vilenies sur votre compte,** they have been blackening your character; I have heard horrid things about you.

vileté [vilte], *s.f.* 1. (*a*) **v. de prix,** cheapness; low price; (*b*) worthlessness. 2. (*a*) vileness (of character, of language); (*b*) low action; mean action.

vilipender [vilipɑ̃de], *v.tr.* to vilify, abuse; to speak disparagingly of (s.o., sth.); to run (s.o.) down.

villa [vila], *s.f.* (*a*) *Rom.Ant: etc:* villa; (*b*) house (in a residential area); **petite v. de banlieue,** little house in the suburbs.

village [vila:ʒ], *s.m.* village; (*a*) **il est bien de son v.,** he's very countrified, awkward (in manner); you can tell that he comes from the back of beyond; **tout le v. en parlait,** the whole village was talking about it; (*b*) **v. de toile,** camping area, camp site, canvas town.

villageois, -oise [vilaʒwa, -wa:z]. 1. *s.* (*a*) villager, inhabitant of a village; (*b*) *O:* country bumpkin. 2. *a.* (*a*) country, village (customs, etc.); country (dances); (*b*) *O:* boorish (manners, etc.).

villanelle [vil(l)anɛl], *s.f. A:* 1. *Lit:* villanelle, pastoral poem. 2. *Danc: Mus:* villanella.

Villanoviens [vilanəvjɛ̃], *s.m.pl. Prehist:* Villanovans.

villarsia [vilarsja], *s.m. Bot:* floating heart.

ville [vil], *s.f.* town; city; **v. de province,** provincial town; country town; **grande v.,** city; **v. d'eaux,** spa; *Hist:* **v. franche,** free city; **la V. éternelle,** the Eternal City, Rome; **demeurer dans la, en, v.,** to live in the heart of the town (as opposed to the suburbs); **demeurer à la v.,** to live in town (as opposed to the country); **se rendre à la v.,** to go (in)to town; **être en v.,** to be in town; **dîner en v.,** to dine out; (*on letters*) **en v.,** local; **toilette de v.,** (woman's) town clothes; **tenue, costume, de v.,** (man's) lounge suit; **hôtel de v.,** town hall; city hall; *A:* **le corps de v.,** the municipal officers; **toute la v. en parle,** the whole town is talking about it; **aménagement des villes,** town planning.

ville(-)champignon [vilʃɑ̃piɲɔ̃], *s.f.* mushroom town; boom town; *pl. villes(-)champignons.*

ville-dortoir [vildɔrtwa:r], *s.f.* dormitory town; *pl. villes-dortoirs.*

villégiateur [vil(l)eʒjatœ:r], *s.m.* holiday maker; visitor (at a resort).

villégiature [vil(l)eʒjaty:r], *s.f.* (*a*) stay in the country; **être en v.,** to be staying in the country; (*b*) holiday (out of town); **en v.,** on holiday; **période de v.,** holiday season; (*c*) summer resort.

villégiaturer [vil(l)eʒjatyre], *v.i.* (*a*) to stay in the country; (*b*) to spend one's holiday (à, at).

villégiaturiste [vileʒjatyrist], *s.m. & f.* holiday-maker.

villeneuvois, -oise [vilnœvwa, -wa:z], *a. & s. Geog:* (native, inhabitant) of Villeneuve.

ville-ruban [vilrybɑ̃], *s.f.* town with ribbon development; *pl. villes-rubans.*

ville-satellite [vilsatɛlit], *s.f.* satellite town; *pl. villes-satellites.*

villeux, -euse [vil(l)ø, -ø:z], *a. Nat.Hist:* villous, villose, hairy.

villiaumite [viljomit], *s.f. Miner:* villiaumite.

villifère [vil(l)ifɛ:r], *a. Nat.Hist:* hairy, covered with hairs.

villiforme [vil(l)ifɔrm], *a.* villiform.

villosité [vil(l)ozite], *s.f.* (*a*) hairiness; (*b*) *Anat: etc:* villosity; villus (of small intestine, of chorion).

villotte [vilɔt], *s.f. Agr:* shock (of corn).

villus [villys], *s.m. Anat:* villus.

vimaire, vimère [vimɛ:r], *s.f. For: A:* storm damage.

vimonastérien, -ienne [vimɔnasterjɛ̃, -jɛn], *a. & s. Geog:* (native, inhabitant) of Vimoutiers.

vimynois, -oise [viminwa, -wa:z], *a. & s. Geog:* (native, inhabitant) of Vimy.

vin [vɛ̃], *s.m.* 1. wine; **les grands vins,** wines from the famous vineyards; vintage wines; **v. fin, v. de marque,** vintage wine; **v. ordinaire, v. de table,** dinner wine, beverage wine; **v. de Bordeaux,** claret; **v. du Rhin,** hock; **v. de Bourgogne,** burgundy; **v. rosé, v. gris,** rosé wine; **v. mousseux,** sparkling wine; **v. cuit,** aperitif wine; **v. doux naturel,** sweet aperitif wine; **v. de dessert,** dessert wine; **v. chaud,** mulled wine; **v. de messe,** communion wine; *Sw.Fr:* **v. ouvert,** carafe wine; **v. en cercles,** wine in the wood, in the cask; **distillation de v.,** brandy distilling; **tache de v.,** strawberry mark (on the skin); *s.a.* CRU^2, ENSEIGNE 1, PAILLE 1; **marchand de v.,** (i) *A:* = publican; (ii) retail wine merchant; **négociant en vins,** (wholesale) wine merchant; **le commerce des vins,** the wine trade; **offrir un v. d'honneur à qn,** to hold a reception in honour of s.o.; **être pris de v.,** to be the worse for drink; **cuver son v.,** to sleep it off; *F:* **un sac à v.,** a drunkard, a boozer; **avoir le v. gai, mauvais, triste,** to be merry, quarrelsome, maudlin, in one's cups; **entre deux vins,** (somewhat) drunk, tight; *Prov:* **le v. est tiré, il faut le boire,** the thing is done now and we must go through with it, we must face the consequences; it is too late to draw back now; the wine is drawn, it must be drunk; *Prov:* **v. versé n'est pas avalé,** there's many a slip 'twixt the cup and the lip; **mettre de l'eau dans son v.,** (i) to water one's wine; (ii) *F:* to moderate one's pretensions; to draw in one's horns; to cut down expenses. 2. *F: A:* **v. de pommes,** cider; **v. de palme,** palm wine; **v. de prunelles,** (i) sloe wine; (ii) *F: A:* tart wine, poor wine.

vinage [vina:ʒ], *s.m.* 1. fortifying (of wine, by adding alcohol); fortification. 2. *A.Jur:* vinage.

vinaigre [vinɛgr], *s.m.* 1. vinegar; (*a*) **v. de bière, de vin,** malt vinegar, wine vinegar; **v. à l'estragon,** tarragon vinegar; **v. de bois,** wood vinegar; **on ne prend pas les mouches avec du v.,** harsh treatment pays no dividends; (*b*) **v. de toilette, v. parfumé,** aromatic vinegar, toilet vinegar; **v. rosat,** rose vinegar; *A:* **v. des quatre voleurs,** Marseilles vinegar; **sels de vinaigre,** smelling salts. 2. *Games:* **donner du v.,** to turn (the skipping rope) quickly; *F:* **faire v.,** to hurry, to get a move on.

vinaigrer [vinegre], *v.tr.* 1. to season (sauce, salad) with vinegar; *A:* **v. sa louange,** to give an acid flavour to one's praise. 2. *A:* to disinfect (letters, etc.) with vinegar.

vinaigrerie [vinɛgrəri], *s.f.* 1. vinegar factory. 2. (*a*) vinegar making; (*b*) vinegar trade.

vinaigrette [vinɛgrɛt], *s.f.* 1. *Cu:* vinaigrette, oil and vinegar dressing; French dressing; **à la v.,** served with a vinaigrette sauce. 2. *A:* two-wheeled sedan; vinaigrette (of the 18th cent.). 3. *Bot:* (kind of) amaranth.

vinaigrier [vinɛgrije], *s.m.* 1. vinegar (i) manufacturer, (ii) merchant; **v. en gros,** wholesale vinegar merchant. 2. vinegar cruet. 3. *Bot:* tanner's, tanning, sumac. 4. *Ent: F:* carab beetle, ground beetle.

vinaire [vinɛ:r]. 1. *a. A:* relating to wine; **industrie v.,** wine trade. 2. *s.m. Ecc:* cellarer.

vinasse [vinas], *s.f.* 1. *Dist:* residuary liquor, wash. 2. *F:* poor-quality wine; **sentir, puer, la v.,** to smell of wine.

vinca [vɛ̃ka], *s.f. Bot:* periwinkle; (*genus*) Vinca.

vincennois, -oise [vɛ̃sɛnwa, -wa:z], *a. & s. Geog:* (native, inhabitant) of Vincennes.

Vincent [vɛ̃sɑ̃], *Pr.n.m.* Vincent; *Med:* **angine, bacille, de V.,** Vincent's angina, bacillus.

vincien, -ienne [vɛ̃sjɛ̃, -jɛn], *a. & s. Geog:* (native, inhabitant) of Venice.

vindas [vɛ̃dɑ(:s)], *s.m.,* **vindau, -aux** [vɛ̃do], *s.m.* 1. windlass, winch, (crab) capstan. 2. *Gym: O:* giant stride.

vindicatif, -ive [vɛ̃dikatif, -i:v], *a.* 1. vindictive, spiteful, revengeful. 2. **justice vindicative,** punitive, retributive, vindicatory, justice.

vindicativement [vɛ̃dikativmɑ̃], *adv.* vindictively, spitefully, revengefully.

vindicte [vɛ̃dikt], *s.f. Jur:* prosecution (of crime); **v. publique,** vindication of public morality.

vinée [vine], *s.f.* 1. fruit branch (of a vine). 2. vintage, wine crop. 3. *Wine-m:* fermenting sheds.

vinelle [vinɛl], *s.f.* wine with low alcoholic content.

viner [vine], *v.tr.* to fortify, add alcohol to (wine, must).
vinette [vinɛt], *s.m.* 1. *Bot:* (*a*) sorrel; (*b*) barberry. 2. *Orn:* warbler.
vinettier [vinɛtje], *s.m. Bot:* common barberry.
vineux, -euse [vinø, -øːz], *a.* 1. (*of wine*) full-bodied. 2. (*a*) vinous (flavour); wine-flavoured (peach, drink); (*b*) wine-coloured (horse, etc.); *F:* **nez v.**, ruby, winy, bibulous, nose. 3. (*of region, season*) rich in vintage; **année vineuse,** good vintage year.
vingeon [vɛ̃ʒɔ̃], *s.m. Orn:* widgeon.
vingt [vɛ̃], *num.a.inv. & s.m. inv.* twenty; **v. mille francs,** twenty thousand francs; **cinq heures moins v.**, twenty to five; **v. et un,** [vɛ̃teœ̃], twenty-one; *Cards:* vingt et un; **vingt-deux** [vɛ̃tdø], twenty-two; *P:* **v.-deux!** watch it! look out! **v.-deux (voilà) les flics!** beat it (here come) the cops! **le v. juin** [ləvɛ̃ʒɥɛ̃], (on) the twentieth of June; **numéro v.**, number twenty; **au chapitre v. de . . .**, in the twentieth chapter, in chapter twenty, of . . .; **les années v.**, the twenties (1920-1929); **il n'a pas encore v. ans,** he's not twenty yet, he's still in his teens; **les moins de v. ans,** the teenagers; **je n'ai plus mon appétit de v. ans,** I've lost my youthful appetite; I can't eat as I did when I was twenty, was young; **sommé de vider les lieux dans les vingt-quatre heures** [vɛ̃tkatrœːr], ordered to vacate the premises within twenty-four hours; *F:* **je vous l'ai dit v. fois,** I've told you so a hundred times, again and again, time and time again; **faire v. pas dans le jardin,** to take a stroll round the garden; NOTE; *as a card.a.* **vingt** *takes an s when multiplied: see* QUATRE-VINGTS, QUINZE-VINGTS, *etc.; thus also A. & Dial:* **six-vingts,** six score; **huit-vingt(s) mille francs,** eight score thousand francs.
vingtaine [vɛ̃tɛn], *s.f.* 1. (about) twenty; a score; twenty or so; **une v. de gens,** a score of people, some twenty people. 2. *Const:* (*a*) lashing (for scaffolds); (*b*) guy (rope).
vingt-huit [vɛ̃tɥi(t)], *num.a. & s.m.inv.* twenty-eight; *Mil:* (*of reservist*) **faire ses vingt-huit jours,** to put in a four weeks' extra training; *F:* **un vingt-huit jours,** a reservist.
vingtième [vɛ̃tjɛm]. 1. *num.a. & s.* twentieth. 2. *s.m.* twentieth (part).
vingtièmement [vɛ̃tjɛmmɑ̃], *adv.* in the twentieth place.
vingtuple [vɛ̃typl̥], *a. & s.m.* twentyfold; **cent est (le) v. de cinq,** a hundred is twenty times as much as five.
vingtupler [vɛ̃typle], *v.tr. & i.* to increase (one's fortune, etc.) twentyfold, to multiply (expenditure, etc.) by twenty.
vinhatico [vinatiko], *s.m. Bot:* vinhatico (wood).
vinicole [vinikɔl], *a.* wine (-growing), viticultural, vinicultural (district, etc.).
viniculture [vinikyltyːr], *s.f.* viniculture.
vinifère [vinifɛːr], *a.* viniferous, vine-bearing, wine-producing (soil, etc.).
vinificateur [vinifikatœːr], *s.m. Vit:* (*apparatus*) vinificator.
vinification [vinifikasjɔ̃], *s.f.* vinification.
vinique [vinik], *a. Ch:* vinic (alcohol, etc.).
vinomètre [vinɔmɛtr̥], *s.m.* vinometer, oenometer.
vinosité [vinozite], *s.f.* vinosity; flavour and strength (of a wine).
vinouse [vinuːz], *s.f. Vit:* fruiting branch (of vine).
Vintimille [vɛ̃timiːj], *Pr.n. Geog:* Ventimiglia.
vinylacétylène [vinilasetilɛn], *s.m. Ch:* vinylacetylene.
vinylbenzène [vinilbɛ̃zɛn], *s.m. Ch:* vinylbenzene.
vinyle [vinil], *s.m. Ch:* vinyl; **acétate de v.,** vinyl acetate.
vinylique [vinilik], *a. Ch:* (of) vinyl; **plastique v.,** vinyl plastic.
vinylogue [vinilɔg], *Ch:* 1. *a.* vinylogous. 2. *s.m.* vinylog.
vinylpyridine [vinilpiridin], *s.f. Ch:* vinylpyridine.
viol [vjɔl], *s.m.* 1. *Jur:* rape. 2. violation (of a sanctuary, etc.); **v. du secret professionnel,** abuse, violation, of professional secrecy.
violable [vjɔlabl̥], *a.* violable.
violacé [vjɔlase]. 1. *a.* violaceous; purplish-blue (colour); (*of pers.*) **prendre un teint v.**, to go blue; **visage v. par le froid,** face blue with cold. 2. *s.f.pl. Bot:* **violacées,** Violaceae.
violacer [vjɔlase], *v.tr.* (**n. violaçons, je violaçai**) to turn blue, purplish; **arbres qui se violaçaient dans la brume,** trees turning a purplish colour in the mist.
violane [vjɔlan], *s.f. Miner:* violan(e).
violanthrone [vjɔlɑ̃trɔn], *s.f. Ch: Dy:* violanthrone.
violariées [vjɔlarje], *s.f.pl. Bot:* Violaceae.
violateur, -trice [vjɔlatœːr, -tris], *s.* 1. (*a*) infringer, transgressor (of laws, etc.); **v. du repos dominical,** breaker, profaner, of the Sabbath; (*b*) violator (of a sanctuary, etc.). 2. *Jur:* rapist, raper.
violation [vjɔlasjɔ̃], *s.f.* violation, infringement, breach (of law, etc.); **agir en v. d'un traité,** to act in violation of a treaty; **v. des règles,** breaking of rules; **agir en v. d'une règle,** to act in contravention of a rule; **v. du repos dominical,** breaking of the Sabbath; **v. de foi,** breach of faith; *Jur:* **v. de clôture,** breach of close; **v. de domicile,** illegal entry; **v. de secret professionnel,** breach of professional secrecy; **v. de promesse de mariage,** breach of promise; **v. de sépulture,** desecration of a grave; **v. de frontière,** violation of a frontier; *Mil:* **v. d'arrêts,** breaking one's arrest.
violâtre [vjɔlɑːtr̥], *a.* purplish.
viole [vjɔl], *s.f.* 1. *A.Mus:* viol; **basse de v., v. de gambe,** bass viol, viol(a) da gamba; **v. d'amour,** viol(a) d'amore. 2. carpenter's jack screw.
violement [vjɔlmɑ̃], *s.m.* 1. *O:* = VIOLATION. 2. *A:* = VIOL.
violemment [vjɔlamɑ̃], *adv.* 1. violently; **attaquer, frapper, qn v.**, to lay violent hands on s.o. 2. **v. soupçonné de . . .**, strongly suspected of . . .
violence [vjɔlɑ̃ːs], *s.f.* violence, force; *Jur:* duress; **v. du temps,** stress of weather; **faire v. à qn,** to do violence to s.o.; **faire v. à une femme,** to violate a woman; **il l'a poignardée après lui avoir fait subir des violences,** he stabbed her after having raped, assaulted, her; **faire v. à ses principes,** to do violence to, act contrary to, one's principles; **faire v. à la loi,** to strain, stretch, the law; **se faire v.**, to do violence to one's feelings; **obtenir qch. par la v.**, to obtain sth. by violence, by force; **faire des scènes de v. à sa femme,** to bully one's wife; *F:* **se laisser faire une douce v.**, to allow oneself to be persuaded.
violent [vjɔlɑ̃], *a.* 1. violent (wind, person, pain, death, etc.); high, buffeting (wind); fierce (encounter); **déposer qch. d'un mouvement v.**, to slam, bang, sth. down; **attendre que le vent soit moins v.**, to wait until the wind abates; **mourir de mort violente,** to die a violent death; to die by violence; **poison v.**, violent poison; **un v. parfum de . . .**, a strong, pungent, smell of . . .; **la pluie tombait violente,** it was pouring (with rain); *F:* **c'est par trop v.!** it is really too bad! it's beyond a joke! it really is the limit! 2. **soupçon v.**, strong, grave, suspicion.
violenter [vjɔlɑ̃te], *v.tr.* 1. to offer, do, violence to (s.o.); **v. qn pour qu'il fasse qch., pour lui faire faire qch.**, to force, compel, s.o. to do sth.; to browbeat s.o. into doing sth.; **v. sa conscience,** to do violence to one's conscience. 2. to rape (a woman).
violer [vjɔle], *v.tr.* 1. to violate; to transgress (law); to break (law, treaty, faith); **v. les lois de la nature,** to fly in the face of nature; **v. le repos dominical,** to break the Sabbath; **v. un secret,** to violate a pledge of secrecy; **v. un serment,** to break an oath, one's promise; **v. une sépulture, un temple,** to desecrate a grave, a temple; to rifle, despoil a tomb; **v. le domicile de qn,** to break into s.o.'s house; **v. la neutralité d'un pays,** to violate the neutrality of a country; *Mil:* **v. ses arrêts,** to break one's arrest; *Nau:* **v. la quarantaine,** to break the quarantine regulations. 2. to rape (a woman).
violet, -ette[1] [vjɔlɛ, -ɛt], *a.* 1. violet, purple (-coloured); **il était violet de fureur,** he was purple with rage; **être v. de froid,** to be purple, blue, with cold; *Ph:* **rayons violets,** violet rays; *F:* **la promotion violette,** nominations to the order of the *Palmes académiques; inv. in compounds:* **tissus violet évêque,** materials of episcopal purple. 2. *s.m.* (the colour) violet. 3. *s.m. Z:* (*a*) *Dial:* (*S. of Fr.*) ascidian, *F:* sea squirt; (*b*) *F:* violet shell, violet snail.
violeter [vjɔlte], *v.tr.* (**je violette, n. violetons**) to dye (sth.) violet.
violette[2] [vjɔlɛt], *s.f.* 1. *Bot:* (*a*) violet; **v. de Parme,** Parma violet; **v. des blés,** corn violet; **v. des chiens,** dog violet; **parfum à la v.**, violet perfume, scent; **des yeux de v.**, violet(-coloured) eyes; *A:* **faire sa v.**, to play the shrinking violet; (*b*) **v. de Marie,** campanula, Canterbury bell. 2. *Com:* **bois de v.**, violet wood, kingwood.
violeur, -euse [vjɔlœːr, -øːz]. 1. *s.* violator (of laws, etc.). 2. *s.m.* raper (of women).
violier [vjɔlje], *s.m. Bot: F:* 1. stock. 2. **v. jaune,** wallflower.
violine [vjɔlin], *a.* violine, purple-violet (in colour).
violiste [vjɔlist], *s.m. Mus:* violist, performer on the viol, viol player.
violon [vjɔlɔ̃], *s.m.* 1. *Mus:* (*a*) violin; **c'est son v. d'Ingres,** it's his hobby; **l'architecture romane est mon v. d'Ingres,** I spend all my spare time studying romanesque architecture; romanesque architecture is my main interest (in life); *F:* **accordez vos violons,** make sure you all tell the same story; *F:* **c'est comme si on pissait dans un v.**, it's a waste of breath; it's like pouring water on a duck's back, talking to a brick wall; (*b*) violin (player); **premier v.**, (i) first violin; (ii) leader (of the orchestra); **second v.**, second violin; **jouer les seconds, les deuxièmes, violons,** to play second fiddle; **payer les violons,** (i) *A:* to give a ball (in honour of a beautiful young woman); (ii) *F:* to pay the piper; **il paie les violons et les autres dansent,** he pays the piper while the others call the tune. 2. *P:* **le v.**, the cells, the lockup; **au v.**, in the lockup. 3. (**poulie à**) **v.**, fiddle block, thick-and-thin (pulley) block. 4. *Nau:* (*a*) **violons de mer,** fiddles (for the tables); (*b*) **violons du beaupré,** bees of the bowsprit.
violoncelle [vjɔlɔ̃sɛl], *s.m. Mus:* (*a*) violoncello, 'cello; (*b*) 'cello (player), 'cellist.
violoncelliste [vjɔlɔ̃sɛlist], *s.* violoncellist, 'cellist.
violone [vjɔlɔn], *s.f. Mus:* violone.
violoner [vjɔlɔne], *v.i. F:* to fiddle.
violoneur [vjɔlɔnœːr], *s.m.*, **violoneux** [vjɔlɔnø], *s.m. F:* fiddler.
violoniste [vjɔlɔnist], *s.m. & f.* violinist.
violurique [vjɔlyrik], *a. Ch:* violuric.
viomycine [vjɔmisin], *s.f. Pharm:* viomycin.
viorne [vjɔrn], *s.f. Bot:* viburnum; **v. cotonneuse,** wayfaring tree; **v. des pauvres,** wild clematis; **v. obier,** guelder rose.
viorne-tin [vjɔrntɛ̃], *s.f. Bot:* laurustinus, laurustine; *pl. viornes-tin.*
vipère [vipɛːr], *s.f.* (*a*) viper, adder; **v. fer-de-lance, v. péliade,** (European) common viper, common adder; **v. à cornes,** horned viper; **v. aspic, v. avicenna,** *esp.* **v. clotho,** puff adder; **v. du sud-ouest de l'Afrique,** South-West African dwarf viper; **les vipères heurtantes,** the African puff adders; **v. arboricole d'Afrique,** African tree viper; **v. de la mort,** (Australian) death adder; **v. tigre,** tiger snake; **v. du Levant,** kufi; **v. du Gabon,** Gaboon viper; (*b*) *Ich: F:* **v. de mer,** pipefish; (*c*) *F:* (*of pers.*) snake; (**langue de**) **v.**, spiteful, viperish, venomous, tongue.
vipereau, -eaux [vipro], *s.m.* young viper.
vipère-flèche [vipɛrflɛʃ], *s.f. Rept:* (African) night adder; *pl. vipères-flèches.*
vipéridés [viperide], *s.m.pl. Rept:* Viperidae; the viper family.
vipérin, -ine [viperɛ̃, -in]. 1. *a.* viperine; *F:* **langue vipérine,** viperish, venomous, tongue. 2. *s.f.* **vipérine:** (*a*) *Bot:* viper's bugloss, blueweed, blue thistle; (*b*) *Rept:* viperine snake.
vipio [vipjo], *s.m. Ent:* ichneumon fly; (*genus*) Vipio.
virage [viraːʒ], *s.m.* 1. (*a*) turning, sweeping round, cornering (of car, cycle, aircraft, etc.); turning (round); slewing round, swinging round (of crane, etc.); *Nau:* tacking, going about; *Av:* **v. (incliné), v. sur l'aile,** bank(ing); **v. à pic, v. à la verticale,** vertical bank; **v. double,** double banking; **v. large,** gentle bank; **v. serré,** steep bank; **v. à droite, à gauche,** right, left, bank; **angle de v.**, angle of bank; **indicateur de v.**, bank angle; (*b*) *Ski:* turn; **v. de Christiania,** Christiania turn; **v. en chasse-neige,** snow-plough turn; **v. de télémark,** telemark turn; **v. en plaine,** kick turn; (*c*) *Med: Ch:* reversal. 2. (*a*) (sharp) turn, bend, corner (in road or track); **v. sans visibilité,** blind corner; **v. en épingle à cheveux,** hairpin bend; **v. à la corde,** sharp turn; *P.N:* **virages sur 5 km.**, bends for 5 kilometres; **prendre un v.**, to take a bend, to corner; **prendre un v. à toute vitesse,** to take a bend at speed; **voiture qui prend bien les virages,** car that corners well; (*b*) banked corner, bank (of racing track); (*c*) **idées qui prennent un v. dangereux,** ideas that are taking a dangerous twist, turn, direction. 3. (*a*) (*of coloured material*) changing of colour; **v. au rouge,** turning red; (*b*) *Phot:* toning (of proofs); **bain de v.**, toning bath; **v. bleu,** blue toning, iron toning.
virage-fixage [viraʒfiksaːʒ], *s.m. Phot:* combined toning and fixing; *pl. virages-fixages.*
virago [virago], *s.f.* virago, termagant; *F:* battle-axe.

virais, -aise [virɛ, -ɛːz], *a. & s. Geog:* (native, inhabitant) of Vire.

viral, -aux [viral, -o], *a. Med:* viral; viral, infectious (hepatitis); **maladie virale,** virus disease.

virant [virɑ̃], *a.* **bois v.,** cross-grained, spiral-grained, wood.

vire¹ [viːr], *s.f.* winding mountain track; traverse.

vire², *s.f. Med: F:* whitlow.

vire-andain [virɑ̃dɛ̃], *s.m. Agr:* (type of) mechanical tedder; *pl. vire-andains.*

virebouquet [virbukɛ], *s.m.* guy (rope).

virée [vire], *s.f.* **1.** (*a*) turning (about); **tournées et virées,** comings and goings; zigzagging; (*b*) *F:* trip, outing (in a car, etc.); *Av:* joyride; **faire des virées au bistro,** to go on a pub crawl. **2.** *For:* forest area on which a felling estimate is based.

virelai [virlɛ], *s.m. Lit: A:* virelay.

vire-lof [virlɔf], *s.m. Nau:* **v.-l. de la grande écoute,** horse of the main sheet.

virement [virmɑ̃], *s.m.* **1.** turning, sweeping round; slewing round; *Nau:* **v. de bord,** tacking, going about. **2.** *Nau:* **v. d'eau,** turn of the tide. **3.** (*a*) *Bank:* transfer; **mandat de v.,** order to transfer; **banque de v.,** clearing bank; **comptoir général de v.,** bankers' clearing house; **v. postal,** postal transfer; **v. télégraphique,** telegraphic transfer; (*b*) *Adm:* **v. de fonds,** transfer (often illegal) of funds from one article of the budget to another.

viréo [vireo], *s.m.*, **viréon** [vireɔ̃], *s.m. Orn:* vireo; **v. à œil rouge,** red-eyed vireo.

viréonidés [vireɔnide], *s.m.pl. Orn:* Vireonidae.

virer [vire]. **1.** *v.i.* to turn; to sweep round; (*a*) *Aut: etc:* to take a bend, a corner; to corner; **v. court,** to take a short turn; to corner sharply; **v. sur place,** to turn in one's own length; *F:* **v. sur la carrosserie,** to take a bend on two wheels; (*b*) *Av:* to bank; **v. à plat,** to under-bank; **v. trop penché,** to over-bank; (*c*) (*of crane, etc.*) to turn (round); to slew round, swing round; (*d*) *Nau:* **v. de bord,** (i) to tack, go about; (ii) (*of steamship*) to turn; (iii) *F:* to change sides; to rat; **v. court,** to go right about; **v. de bord cap,** to turn 16 points; **v. vent arrière,** to wear (ship); to veer; **v. vent devant, vent avant,** to go about in stays; to stay; **manquer à v.,** to miss stays; **bateau lent à v.,** ship slack in stays; **paré à v.!** ready about! (*of rocket*) **v. en s'éloignant de la direction prévue,** to veer off course; (*e*) *Nau:* **v. au cabestan,** to heave at the capstan; to heave; **v. à pic,** to heave short; **tiens bon v.!** avast heaving! (*f*) (*of coloured material*) to change colour; **encre qui vire au noir en séchant,** ink that turns black on drying, that dries black; (*g*) *Phot:* (*of print*) to tone. **2.** *v.tr.* (*a*) to turn (sth.) over; *F: A:* **tourner et v. qn,** to put s.o. through a searching examination; (*b*) *Bank:* (i) to transfer (a sum); (ii) to clear (cheques, etc.); (*c*) *Nau:* **v. un navire arrière,** to wear, veer, a ship; (*d*) *Nau:* **v. l'ancre, le câble,** to weigh anchor, to haul in the cable; **v. la chaîne,** to heave in the chain; (*e*) *Phot:* to tone (print); (*f*) *P:* to kick (s.o.) out; to chuck (s.o.) out.

virescence [virɛs(s)ɑ̃ːs], *s.f. Bot:* virescence.

vireton [virtɔ̃], *s.m.* (*archery*) vire; spirally-winged, grooved, quarrel.

vireur [virœːr], *s.m. I.C.E: Mch:* **1.** turning gear (to start engine, etc.). **2.** barring engine.

vireux, -euse [virø, -øːz], *a.* poisonous, noxious (plant, smell, etc.); malodorous.

virevau(t), vireveau, -eaux [virvo], *s.m.* (hand) winch, small windlass.

virevolte [virvɔlt], *s.f. Equit:* quick circling (of horse); **v. de la fortune,** sudden change of fortune.

virevoltant [virvɔltɑ̃], *a.* whirling, twirling.

virevolter [virvɔlte], *v.i.* (*a*) (*of horse*) to circle; (*b*) (*of pers.*) to spin round; **faire v. ses subordonnés,** to keep one's assistants on the go; to make one's assistants dance attendance on one; (*c*) **faire v. sa canne,** to twirl one's stick.

virga [virga], *s.f.* **1.** *Meteor:* virga. **2.** *A.Mus:* virga.

virgation [virgasjɔ̃], *s.f. Geol:* virgation.

Virgile [virʒil], *Pr.n.m. Lt.Lit:* Virgil, Vergil.

virgilien, -ienne [virʒiljɛ̃, -jɛn], *a.* Virgilian, Vergilian.

virginal, -ale, -aux [virʒinal, -o]. **1.** *a.* virginal; *Theol: Biol:* **naissance virginale,** virgin birth; **neige virginale,** virgin snow; *Bot:* **lis v.,** pure white lily; *Toil: O:* **lait v.,** benzoin skin lotion. **2.** *s.m. or f. A.Mus:* **virginale,** virginal; (pair of) virginals.

virginalement [virʒinalmɑ̃], *adv.* virginally.

Virginie [virʒini]. **1.** *Pr.n.f.* (*Christian name and geographical name*) Virginia. **2.** *s.m.* Virginia tobacco (or snuff).

virginien, -ienne [virʒinjɛ̃, -jɛn], *a. & s. Geog:* Virginian.

Virginie-Occidentale [virʒiniɔksidɑ̃tal], *Pr.n.f. Geog:* West Virginia.

virginipare [virʒinipaːr], *a. Ent:* virginoparous (insect).

virginité [virʒinite], *s.f.* virginity; maidenhood.

virgulaire [virgylɛːr], *s.f. Coel:* virgularian.

virgularidés [virgylaride], *s.m.pl. Coel:* Virgulariidae.

virgule [virgyl], *s.f.* **1.** (*a*) *Gram:* comma; **observer les points et les virgules,** to be very meticulous (in small matters); to dot one's i's and cross one's t's; *Med:* **bacille v.,** vibrio comma, comma bacillus, cholera vibrio; (*b*) *Mth:* = decimal point; **trois v. cinq** (3,5) = three point five (3·5); (*c*) *Elcs:* **v. flottante,** floating point; **v. réglable,** adjustable point; **emplacement de la v.,** radix point; **partie en v. fixe,** fixed-point part. **2.** *Clockm:* hook escapement.

virguler [virgyle], *v.tr.* to put the commas in (sentence); *A:* **un monsieur ponctué et virgulé,** a very punctilious, precise, gentleman.

viride [virid], *a.* verdant, green.

viridiflore [viridiflɔːr], *a. Bot:* bearing green flowers, green-flowered.

viridifolié [viridifɔlje], *a. Bot:* green-leaved.

viridine [viridin], *s.f. Ch: Dy:* viridine.

viridipenne [viridipɛn], *a. Nat.Hist:* green-winged.

viridite [viridit], *s.f. Miner:* viridite.

viridité [viridite], *s.f.* viridity, greenness.

viriel [virjɛl], *s.m. Ph:* virial.

virien, -ienne [virjɛ̃, -jɛn], *a.* viral, of a virus.

viril [viril], *a.* **1.** virile; (*a*) male (sex, attire, etc.); **toge virile,** toga virilis; *Anat:* **membre v.,** membrum virile; **parties viriles,** virilia, male genitals; (*b*) manly (action, soul); **l'âge v.,** man's estate; manhood. **2.** *Jur:* **portion virile,** lawful share (of succession).

virilement [virilmɑ̃], *adv.* like a man; in a manly fashion.

virilisant [virilizɑ̃], *a. Med:* **traitement v.,** virilizing treatment.

viriliser [virilize], *v.tr.* (*a*) *Med:* to virilize; (*b*) to instil manliness into; (*c*) (*of woman*) **se v.,** to make oneself like a man.

virilisme [virilism], *s.m.* virilism.

virilité [virilite], *s.f.* **1.** virility, manliness; manhood. **2.** masculine vigour. **3.** *pl.* virilia, male genitals.

virilocal, -aux [virilɔkal, -o], *a. Ethn:* virilocal.

viro-fixage [virɔfiksaːʒ], *s.m. Phot:* toning and fixing.

viro-fixateur [virɔfiksatœːr], *a. & s.m.* toning and fixing (bath); *pl. viro-fixateurs.*

virois, -oise [virwa, -waːz], *a. & s. Geog:* (native, inhabitant) of Vire.

virola [virɔla], *s.m. Com:* baboen (wood).

virolage [virɔlaːʒ], *s.m.* ferruling (of tool handles, boiler tubes).

virole [virɔl], *s.f.* **1.** ferrule (of walking stick, tool handle, boiler tube, etc.); joint; *Mec.E:* collar, hoop, sleeve; binding ring; thimble coupling; sleeve joint (connecting pipes); *Mil:* locking ring (of bayonet); **v. de raccordement,** coupling ring; *Mec.E:* **v. intérieure, extérieure,** inner, outer, shroud; **v. à air (d'un brûleur à gaz),** air clip (of gas burner). **2.** (*a*) *Num:* coining ferrule; ring die; collar; (*b*) *Her:* virole (surrounding bugle).

virolé [virɔle], *a. Her:* viroled (bugle, etc.).

viroler [virɔle], *v.tr.* to ferrule (tool handle, tubes of boiler, etc.); *Num:* to place (blanks) in the ring die.

virolet [virɔlɛ], *s.m. Ropem:* **1.** roller (of rope walk). **2.** spun-yarn winch.

virologie [virɔlɔʒi], *s.f.* virology.

virose [viroːz], *s.f. Med:* virus disease, virosis.

virtualité [virtɥalite], *s.f.* virtuality, potentiality.

virtuel, -elle [virtɥɛl], *a.* virtual (*Theol:* intention; *Opt:* image, focus; *Mec:* displacement).

virtuellement [virtɥɛlmɑ̃], *adv.* virtually; potentially; to all intents and purposes.

virtuose [virtɥoːz], *s.m. & f. Mus: etc:* virtuoso; *f. A:* virtuosa; **un v. du ski,** a brilliant skier.

virtuosité [virtɥozite], *s.f. Mus:* virtuosity; **il a fait montre d'une grande v.,** he gave a virtuoso performance.

virulence [virylɑ̃ːs], *s.f.* virulence (of poison, of satire, etc.); virulence, malignity (of disease, etc.).

virulent [virylɑ̃], *a.* (*a*) contagious (disease); (*b*) *O:* infected with a virus; virus (disease); (*c*) virulent (poison, disease, satire, etc.); **diatribe virulente,** scathing diatribe.

virulicide [virylisid], *a.* virulicidal, virucidal, viruscidal, viricidal.

virure [viryːr], *s.f. N.Arch:* strake; **v. de carreau,** sheerstrake; **v. de sous-carreau,** strake below sheerstrake; **v. d'hiloire,** tie plate; **v. bretonne,** spirketting.

virus [virys], *s.m.* (*a*) *Med:* virus; **v. filtrant,** filterable virus; **maladie à v.,** virus disease; (*b*) *F:* **avoir le v. de qch.,** to have a craze for sth.

vis¹ [vis], *s.f.* **1.** (*a*) screw, worm; **v. sans fin,** endless screw, worm (screw); *Mec.E:* **v. (sans fin) et secteur,** worm and segment; tangent screw and sector; **v. globique, globoïdale,** hour-glass screw; *Artil:* **v. culasse,** breech screw; **v. de pointage,** elevating screw; *Hyd.E:* **v. d'Archimède,** Archimedean screw; *Ind:* **v. de transport,** spiral conveyor, screw conveyor; creeper; *I.C.E: El: F:* **v. platinées,** contact points; (*b*) screw thread; **v. à droite, à gauche,** right-, left-handed screw or thread; **v. mâle,** male screw, external screw; **v. femelle,** female screw, screw nut; **v. imperdable,** captive screw; **tige à v.,** screwed, threaded, rod; **tabouret de piano, chaise, à v.,** swivel piano stool; swivel, revolving, chair; **serrer la v. à qn,** (i) *F:* to put the screw on s.o.; (ii) *P:* to garrotte s.o.; (*c*) **escalier à v.,** spiral staircase; **v. à jour,** open-newel stair. **2.** screw; **v. à bois,** wood screw; **v. à métaux,** metal screw; **v. à embase,** collar screw; **v. à épaulement,** shoulder bolt; **v. à tête carrée,** square-headed screw; **v. à tête cylindrique,** fillister head screw; **v. à tête cylindrique chanfreinée, à tête ronde plate,** cheese-headed screw; **v. à tête fendue,** slotted-head screw; **v. à tête fraisée, à tête noyée, à tête perdue,** countersunk (head) screw; **v. à tête fraisée bombée,** oval-headed screw; **v. à tête ronde,** round-headed screw; **v. à oreilles, à ailettes,** thumb screw, wing screw; **v. sans tête,** grub screw; **v. auto-taraudeuse, v. Parker,** self-tapping screw; **v. d'arrêt, de blocage,** lock(ing) screw, stop screw, clamping screw; **v. d'arrêt sans tête,** set screw; **v. de butée,** thrust screw, adjustment screw; **v. de réglage, de rappel,** adjusting screw; **v. de serrage, de pression,** press screw, binding screw, clamp(ing) screw, set screw; **v. d'assemblage, d'accouplement,** connecting screw; **v. de fixation,** fastening screw, hold-down screw, anchor screw; **v. de reliure,** interscrew; **fermer une boîte avec des v.,** to screw down (the lid of) a box.

vis², *s.m. Physiol:* **v. à tergo,** vis a tergo.

vis³, *s.f. Moll:* auger shell.

visa [viza], *s.m.* (*a*) visa (on passport); **apposer un v. à un passeport,** to stamp, visa, visé, a passport; (*b*) signature (on document, etc.); initials (of supervisor, etc., on bankslip, etc.); certification (of cheque); **payer sur le v. approbatif de qn,** to honour an order endorsed by s.o.; *Com: O:* **v., s'il vous plaît!** sign, please! (*c*) *Com:* **v. d'une lettre de change,** sighting of a bill; (*d*) *Rail:* stamping (of ticket, on break of journey); (*e*) *Cin:* **v. de censure, de contrôle,** censor's certificate; *pl. visas.*

visable [vizabl̩], *a.* that can be aimed at; (*of target*) within range.

visage [vizaːʒ], *s.m.* face; countenance; **homme au v. agréable,** pleasant-faced man; **vous avez toujours même v.,** you still look the same; **changer de v.,** to change countenance; **je n'ai jamais dit cela.—non, mais votre v. le dit,** I never said that.—no, but one can tell it from your expression; *F:* **épouser un v.,** to marry a pretty face; **se faire le v.,** to make (one's face) up; **frapper qn au v.,** to strike s.o. in the face; **donner à qn un démenti au v.,** to give s.o. the lie to his face; **à deux visages,** double-faced; **avoir bon v.,** to look well; **faire bon v.,** to look cheerful; **faire bon, mauvais, v. à qn,** to smile, frown, on s.o.; to behave in a friendly, an unfriendly, fashion towards s.o.; to give s.o. a warm, a cool, welcome; **sans v.,** faceless; **à v. découvert,** (i) with one's face uncovered; with the mask off; (ii) barefacedly; **voir les choses sous leur vrai v.,** to see things in their true light; *F:* **trouver v. de bois,** to find nobody at home; (*in language of N. American Indians*) **visages pâles,** Palefaces.

Visagiste [vizaʒist], *s.m. or f. R.t.m:* beautician (who specializes in the face).

vis-à-vis [vizavi]. **1.** (*a*) *adv.phr.* opposite; **la maison (qui est) v.-à-v.,** the house opposite; the house over the way; **ils étaient assis**

v.-à-v., they were sitting face to face; **places en v.-à-v.**, seats facing each other; (*b*) *prep.phr.* **Tain v.-à-v. Tournon,** Tain opposite, over against, Tournon (on the Rhône). **2.** *prep.phr.* **v.-à-v. de (qn, qch.)**: (*a*) opposite, facing (s.o., sth.); **v.-à-v. l'un de l'autre, l'un v.-à-v. de l'autre,** opposite one another; facing one another; (*b*) towards, with respect to, with regard to, in relation to (s.o., sth.); **ses sentiments v.-à-v. de moi,** his feelings towards me; **être sincère v.-à-v. de soi-même,** to be sincere with oneself; **la France v.-à-v. des échanges internationaux,** the attitude of France towards foreign exchanges; **neutralité d'un gaz v.-à-v. d'un métal,** neutrality of a gas in regard to a metal; *Med:* **sujets tolérants v.-à-v. de la lumière,** subjects tolerant of light. **3.** *s.m.* person opposite (at table, etc.); vis-à-vis; *Cards:* partner; **faire v.-à-v. à qn,** to be, stand, sit, opposite s.o.; to face s.o. **4.** *s.m.* (*a*) *Furn:* vis-à-vis; S-shaped couch; (*b*) *A.Veh:* vis-à-vis.

visbreaking [vizbrɛkiŋ], *s.m. Petroleum Ind:* visbreaking, viscosity breaking.

vis-butoir [visbytwaːr], *s.f.* stop screw (of clutch pedal, etc.); *pl. vis-butoirs.*

viscache [viskaʃ], *s.f.*, **viscaque** [viskak], *s.f. Z:* (plains) viscacha, vizcacha; vizcachon.

viscachère [viskaʃɛːr], *s.f. Z:* vizcachera, burrow of the plains vizcacha.

viscaire [viskɛːr], *s.f.*, **viscaria** [viskarja], *s.m. Bot:* viscaria, rock lychnis.

viscéral, -aux [vis(s)eral, -o], *a.* **1.** *Anat: Z:* visceral; **arc v.,** visceral arch; **ganglion v.,** visceral ganglion. **2.** *Jur: A:* essential (condition, clause). **3.** deep-seated; innermost; **haine viscérale,** deep-seated hatred; **les profondeurs viscérales de l'être humain,** man's innermost depths.

viscéralgie [vis(s)eralʒi], *s.f. Med:* visceralgia.

viscère [vis(s)ɛːr], *s.m.* (*rare in sg.*) *Anat:* viscus; internal organ; **les viscères,** the viscera.

viscéroptôse [vis(s)eroptoːz], *s.f. Med:* visceroptosis.

viscine [vis(s)in], *s.f. Ch:* viscin.

viscose [viskoːz], *s.f. Ch: Ind:* viscose.

visco(si)mètre [visko(zi)mɛtr̥], *s.m. Ph: Ind:* visco(si)meter.

visco(si)métrie [visko(zi)metri], *s.f. Ph: Ind:* visco(si)metry.

visco(si)métrique [visko(zi)metrik], *a. Ph:* visco(si)metric.

viscosité [viskozite], *s.f.* viscosity, viscidity; stickiness; **coefficient de v.,** coefficient of viscosity; **indice de v.,** viscosity index; **fluide à v. constante,** Newtonian fluid; *Pol.Ec:* **v. de la main-d'œuvre,** lack of fluidity of labour.

visé [vize], *s.m.* aimed shot.

visée [vize], *s.f.* **1.** aim; pointing (of telescope); *Mil: Surv:* aiming, sighting; **erreur systématique de v.,** aim(ing) bias; **prendre sa v.,** to take aim; **prendre sa v. trop haut, trop bas,** to aim too high, too low; **ligne de v.,** line of sight; **point de v.,** point aimed at; (i) *Ball:* **angle de v.,** angle of sight; (ii) (*for bombs*) dropping angle; *Artil:* (*anti-aircraft*) **(angle de) v. en avant,** the lead; **demi-angle de v. en avant,** half lead; *Aer:* **navigation par v. astronomique,** celestial navigation; **appareil de v.,** (i) sight, sighting (gear); (ii) director (of torpedo). **2.** *usu. pl.* aims, designs; **avoir de hautes visées,** to have high aims, great ambitions; to aim high; **changer de v.,** to alter one's mind, one's plan; to aim at something else; **avoir des visées belliqueuses,** to have warlike aims, intentions; **homme à grandes visées,** ambitious man.

viser¹ [vize]. **1.** *v.i.* to aim (**à, at**); **v. à une chaire, à l'effet,** to aim at a professorial chair, at effect; **je vise au solide, aux grands résultats,** I'm (all) out for sth. substantial, for big results; **v. à faire qch.,** to aim at doing sth., to do sth.; **à quoi vise tout cela?** what is the end in view? what is the object of it all? **2.** *v.tr.* (*a*) to aim, take aim, at (s.o., sth.); **v. droit, juste,** to aim straight; **v. haut,** to aim high ((i) with gun, (ii) = to be ambitious); **v. plus haut,** to set one's sights higher; **v. moins haut,** to lower one's sights; *F:* **pas mal visé pour un borgne,** it's better than one might have expected; **si je pouvais mieux v.,** if I had a better aim; **v. qn à la tête,** to aim at s.o.'s head; *Golf:* **v. la balle,** to address the ball; (*b*) *Surv:* to sight; to take a sight on (sth.); (*c*) to have (sth.) in view; to relate to (sth.); **négociations visant une alliance,** negotiations with a view to, relative to, an alliance; **accusation visant qn,** accusation directed against s.o.; **cette inculpation vise des faits graves,** the charge relates to serious acts; **les États visés dans l'article,** the States referred to in the article; **les denrées alimentaires ne sont pas visées par ce décret,** articles of food are not affected by this order; (*d*) to allude to (s.o.); **je ne vise personne,** I am not alluding to anybody in particular. **3.** *v.tr. P:* to look at; **vise-moi ça!** just look at that! *P:* get a load of that!

viser², *v.tr. Adm: Com: etc:* to visa, visé (passport); to countersign, initial (document); to certify (cheque); *Rail:* **v. un billet,** to stamp a ticket (on passenger's breaking journey).

viseur, -euse [vizœːr, -øːz]. **1.** *s.* aimer. **2.** *s.m.* (*a*) *Phot:* viewfinder; **v. clair,** brilliant viewfinder; **v. obscur,** reflecting viewfinder; **v. à cadre (sans lentille), v. direct, v. iconométrique,** direct(-vision) finder; (*b*) (*of surveying instrument, etc.*) sighting tube, sighting piece, eyepiece; sight vane (of compass); **v. à prisme,** prismatic sight; **v. optique,** telescopic sight; **v. de compte-gouttes,** (glass) sight of drip feed (of oil pump, etc.); *Av:* **v. de lancement,** bomb sights.

vishnuisme [viʃnyism], *s.m. Rel:* Vishnuism.

visibilité [vizibilite], *s.f.* (*a*) visibility; **champ de v.,** field of vision; **distance de v.,** visual distance; **v. nulle,** nil visibility; *Av: Nau: etc:* **v. vers le haut, vers le bas,** upward, downward, visibility; **v. vers l'avant,** forward vision; **v. latérale,** horizontal vision; *Av:* **vol sans v., vol en pilotage sans v. (P.S.V.),** blind, instrument, flying; (*b*) conspicuousness.

visible [vizibl̩], *a.* **1.** (*a*) visible, perceptible; **le monde v.,** the visible world; **il n'y avait personne de v.,** there was nobody about; (*b*) obvious, manifest, evident (sign, falsehood, etc.); **très v.,** conspicuous. **2.** (*a*) ready to receive company; **Madame D. est-elle v.?** is Mrs D. at home? **je ne suis v. à personne,** I am not at home to anyone; I can't see anyone; (*b*) disengaged; **je ne serai pas v. avant trois heures,** I shall be engaged until three o'clock; I can't see anybody before three o'clock; (*c*) **cette collection n'est pas v.,** this collection is not accessible, open, to the public.

visiblement [vizibləmɑ̃], *adv.* **1.** visibly, perceptibly, noticeably. **2.** obviously, evidently; conspicuously.

visière [vizjɛːr], *s.f.* **1.** (*a*) *Arm:* visor, vizor (of helmet); **à v. baissée,** vizored; **rompre en v. à, avec, qn,** (i) to quarrel openly with s.o.; (ii) to take up a diametrically opposite view to that of s.o.; (*b*) peak (of cap); (*c*) eye shade; (*d*) *Aut:* (headlight) visor. **2.** *Artil: Sm.a:* sight (of gun); **v. à charnière, à clapet,** folding sight. **3.** *Ind:* sighting aperture, inspection hole (of kiln, etc.).

Visigoth [vizigo], *s.m. Hist:* Visigoth.

vision [vizjɔ̃], *s.f.* **1.** vision; (*a*) (eye)sight; **l'organe de la v. est l'œil,** the organ of vision is the eye; (*b*) seeing; sight, view; **entre deux nuages j'eus une v. très nette de l'avion,** between two clouds I got a very clear view of the aircraft; **v. momentanée de qch.,** glimpse of sth.; (*c*) *Cin:* preview; **en première v.** = first showing. **2.** (mental) vision; imagination; **les visions d'un poète,** a poet's visions. **3.** fantasy; phantom.

visionnaire [vizjɔnɛːr], *a. & s.m. & f.* (= *given to seeing visions*) visionary; dreamer.

visionnement [vizjɔnmɑ̃], *s.m.* viewing.

visionner [vizjɔne], *v.tr.* to view; *Cin:* (*a*) to look at (film) on a viewer; (*b*) to see a preview of (a film), *U.S:* to preview.

visionneuse [vizjɔnøːz], *s.f. Cin: Phot:* viewer.

visiotéléphonie [vizjɔtelefɔni], *s.f. T.V:* videophone system.

visir [viziːr], *s.m. A:* vizier.

visitable [vizitabl̩], *a. F:* that can be visited; worth visiting.

visitandine [vizitɑ̃din], *s.f. R.C.Ch:* nun of the Order of the Visitation; Visitant, Visitandine.

visitation [vizitasjɔ̃], *s.f.* **1.** *A:* visit (of inspection). **2.** *Ecc:* visitation (of the Virgin to St Elisabeth); **ordre de la V.,** order (of nuns) of the Visitation of Our Lady.

visitatrice [vizitatris], *s.f. Ecc:* visitator.

visite [vizit], *s.f.* **1.** (*a*) visit; (social) call; **faire une v., rendre v., faire v., à qn,** to visit s.o.; to call on s.o.; **rendre une v. à qn,** to return s.o.'s visit, s.o.'s call; **il nous fait une petite v. tous les soirs,** he drops in on us every evening; **recevoir de la v., des visites,** to have visitors; **être en v. chez qn,** to be on a visit to s.o.; **v. de politesse,** duty call; **v. de cérémonie,** formal visit; **v. officielle,** official visit; *O:* **v. de digestion,** formal call (after a dinner party); **carte de v.,** visiting card; *A:* **sonnette de visites,** visitors' bell; *A:* **carnet de visites,** visiting book (for social engagements); *Com:* **recevoir les visites d'un représentant,** to be called on by a representative, a traveller; *Sp:* **équipe en v.,** visiting team, side; (*at hospital, boarding school, etc.*) **heures de v.,** visiting hours; (*b*) visitor; caller; **nous attendons des visites,** we are expecting visitors; (*c*) *Med:* **visites à domicile,** (doctor's) visits (to patients); **tournée de visites,** round (of visits); (*d*) *Jur:* **droit de v. aux enfants,** right of access to the children (by estranged, divorced, wife or husband). **2.** (*a*) inspection, examination, survey (of building by an architect, etc.); survey (of ship); overhauling (of rifle, machinery, etc.); (medical) examination; **v. périodique,** periodic inspection; **v. de surveillance,** inspection visit; **faire la v.,** to go on a round of inspection; *Nau:* **faire la v. des canots de sauvetage,** to overhaul the lifeboats; **passer (à) une v. médicale,** to undergo a medical examination; *Mil: etc:* **passer la v.,** to come before the medical officer, the medical board; *Ecc:* **v. pastorale, v. de l'évêque,** pastoral visit, visitation (by bishop); *Mch: etc:* **porte, panneau, de v.,** inspection door, panel; *El:* **boîte de v. (de canalisation),** inspection box; **trou de v.,** manhole (of sewer, etc.); (*b*) search (of house, ship, etc.); *Jur:* **v. domiciliaire,** domicilary visit; **v. des lieux,** search of the premises; *Nau:* **droit de v.,** right of search, of visit, of visitation; *Cust:* **v. de douane,** customs examination; (*c*) visit (to place of interest); **v. dirigée,** conducted tour (of a museum, etc.).

visiter [vizite], *v.tr.* **1.** (*a*) (i) *A:* to visit (s.o.); (ii) **v. la maison d'un ami,** to visit a friend's house; (*b*) (*of doctor*) to visit (a patient); *Com:* to call on (a client); (*c*) **v. les prisonniers, les malades,** to visit prisoners, the sick. **2.** (*a*) to inspect, examine (building, machinery, etc.); to overhaul (rifle, engine, etc.); to survey (ship); **j'ai visité toutes les pièces,** I have been into, examined, every room; **permis de v.,** (house agent's) order to view (house, etc.); *Sp:* **v. le terrain avant un match,** to inspect the ground before a match; (*b*) (*of police, etc.*) to visit, search (house, etc.); **v. les poches de qn,** to search s.o.'s pockets; **v. des malles (à la douane),** to examine trunks (at the customs); (*c*) to visit (as a tourist); **v. la Grèce, Paris,** to visit Greece, Paris; **v. une cathédrale,** to visit, go over, a cathedral; **v. les musées,** to visit, go round, the museums; **on nous a fait v. l'usine,** we were shown round, over, the factory.

visiteur, -euse [vizitœːr, -øːz]. **1.** *s.* (*a*) visitor; caller; **les femmes sont grandes visiteuses,** women like visiting, going to see each other, people; **v. de marque,** important visitor, *F:* V.I.P.; *Sp:* **les visiteurs,** the visitors, the visiting team; *Com:* **v. en soies, etc.,** representative, traveller, in silks, etc.; **v. médical, visiteuse médicale,** representative in pharmaceutical products (who calls personally on doctors); *F:* **l'appartement a eu des visiteurs,** our flat's been broken into, we've had burglars; (*b*) inspector; *Cust:* searcher; *Nau:* surveyor (of ship); (*c*) visitor (to a museum, etc.); tourist; **les visiteurs sont priés de ne pas toucher aux objets exposés,** visitors are requested not to touch the exhibits. **2.** *attrib. a.* visiting; **infirmière visiteuse** = district nurse; *A:* **dame visiteuse** = district visitor; (*freemasonry*) **(frère) v.,** brother visitor, visiting brother.

vis-mère [vismɛːr], *s.f. Mec.E:* lead(ing) screw, guide screw (of lathe, screw cutter); *pl. vis-mères.*

vismie [vismi], *s.f. Bot:* vismia, wax tree.

visnage [visnaːʒ], *s.m.*, **visnague** [visnag], *s.m. Bot:* bishop's weed.

vison [vizɔ̃], *s.m.* **1.** *Z:* vison, American mink. **2.** *Com:* (*a*) mink; (*b*) *F:* mink coat.

visonnette [vizɔnɛt], *s.f. Com:* simulated mink.

visonnière [vizɔnjɛːr], *s.f.* mink farm, minkery.

vison-visu [vizɔ̃vizy], *adv. F: A:* face to face, facing each other.

visorium [vizɔrjɔm], *s.m. Typ: O:* copy holder.

visqueux, -euse [viskø, -øːz], *a.* viscous, gluey, sticky; tacky (rubber solution, etc.); thick (oil); slimy (secretion, etc.).

vissage [visaːʒ], *s.m.* (*a*) screwing; (*b*) *F:* putting the screw on (s.o.).

visser [vise], *v.tr.* **1.** to screw, screw on, screw in, screw down, screw up (sth.); **v. à fond,** to screw home; *P:* **être mal vissé,** to be in a filthy temper; **boucles d'oreilles vissées,** screw-on ear-rings; *F:* **être vissé sur sa chaise,** to sit tight on one's chair; to be glued, screwed, to one's chair; **il y semble vissé,** there's no shifting him; *F:* **il a le**

chapeau vissé sur la tête, he never takes his hat off to anyone, never says good morning to anyone. **2.** *F:* (*a*) to treat (s.o.) severely; to put the screw on (s.o.); (*b*) *Mil: A:* to put (man) in clink.

visserie [visri], *s.f.* **1.** *coll.* screws, bolts. **2.** screw-cutting industry, shop.

vistadôme [vistado:m], *s.m. Rail:* (vista) dome, dome car.

Vistule (la) [lavistyl], *Pr.n.f. Geog:* the (River) Vistula.

visualisation [vizɥalizasjɔ̃], *s.f.* visualization; *Elcs: etc:* **unité de v.,** display unit.

visualiser [vizɥalize], *v.tr.* to visualize; to make (sth.) visible to the eye.

visuel, -elle [vizɥɛl]. **1.** *a.* visual (perception, nerve, point, angle); **champ, angle, v.,** field, angle, of vision; *Nau:* **garder le contact v.,** to keep within visual range; **mémoire, imagination, visuelle,** visual memory, imagination; **écrivain du type v.,** writer of the visual type, who is a visualizer. **2.** *s.m.* bull's eye (of target).

visuellement [vizɥɛlmɑ̃], *adv.* visually.

vit [vi], *P: A:* membrum virile.

vitacées [vitase], *s.f.pl. Bot:* Vitaceae.

vital, -aux [vital, -o], *a.* **1.** *Physiol: Biol: etc:* vital; **force vitale,** vital force; **parties vitales,** vitals. **2.** vital (**pour,** to); **question vitale,** vital question.

vitalement [vitalmɑ̃], *adv.* vitally.

vitalisation [vitalizasjɔ̃], *s.f.* vitalization.

vitaliser [vitalize], *v.tr.* to vitalize.

vitalisme [vitalism], *s.m. Biol:* vitalism.

vitaliste [vitalist], *Biol:* **1.** *a.* vitalistic, vitalist (doctrine, etc.). **2.** *s.* vitalist.

vitalité [vitalite], *s.f.* vitality.

vitamine [vitamin], *s.f. Bio-Ch:* vitamin.

vitaminé [vitamine], *a.* vitaminized, enriched with vitamins.

vitaminique [vitaminik], *a. Med:* **carence v.,** vitamin deficiency.

vitaminisation [vitaminizasjɔ̃], *s.f.* vitaminizing.

vitaminologie [vitaminɔlɔʒi], *s.f. Med:* vitaminology.

vitaminothérapie [vitaminɔterapi], *s.f. Med:* vitamin therapy.

vite [vit]. **1.** *a.* (*usually only in sporting context: other adjectival uses A:*) swift, rapid, speedy; **voitures légères et vites,** light speedy cars; **cheval v.,** fleet horse; *Fb:* **avants vites,** speedy forwards. **2.** *adv.* quickly, fast, rapidly, speedily; *Nau:* **"plus v.!"** "increase speed!" **le temps passe v.,** time passes swiftly; **aller v.,** to walk, run, ride, drive, fast; **vous marchez v.,** you are a fast walker; **vous allez trop v.,** (i) you are going too fast; (ii) you take too much for granted; **pour aller plus v., nous nous dispenserons de . . .,** for the sake of speed, to save time, we shall dispense with . . .; **vous allez v. en besogne,** you aren't long about it; you're a quick worker; that's smart work; **ça ne va pas v.,** it's slow work; **vous serez v. guéri,** you'll soon be better; **faites v.!** make haste! hurry up! be quick (about it)! **un peu v.!** quickly! get a move on! buck up! look alive! **allons, et plus v. que cela!** now then, be quick about it! **au plus v.,** as quickly as possible; **s'en retourner au plus v.,** to get home as quickly as possible; **avoir v. fait de faire qch.,** to be quick about doing sth.; **il eut v. fait de s'habiller,** he was dressed in no time; **on a v. fait de dire . . .,** it's easy to say . . ..

vitées [vite], *s.f.pl. Bot:* Vitaceae.

vitellifère [vitɛlifɛ:r], *a. Biol:* vitelliferous.

vitellin [vitɛlɛ̃], *a. Biol:* vitelline; **membrane vitelline,** vitelline membrane, yolk bag, yolk sac; **cellule vitelline,** vitelligenous cell.

vitelline [vitɛlin], *s.f. Ch:* vitellin.

vitellogène [vitɛlɔʒɛn], *a. Biol:* **glande v.,** vitelline gland; vitellarium, vitellogen(e).

vitellogénèse [vitɛlɔʒenɛ:z], *s.f. Biol:* vitellogenesis.

vitellus [vitɛlys], *s.m.* **1.** *Biol:* vitellus, yolk; **v. formatif,** formative yolk; **v. nutritif,** nutritive food, yolk. **2.** *Bot:* vitellus.

vitelotte [vitlɔt], *s.f.* kidney potato.

vitement [vitmɑ̃], *adv. A:* quickly, speedily.

Viterbe [vitɛrb], *Pr.n. Geog:* Viterbo.

viterbien, -ienne [vitɛrbjɛ̃, -jɛn], *a. & s. Geog:* (native, inhabitant) of Viterbo.

vitesse [vitɛs], *s.f.* **1.** (*absolute sense*) speed; rapidity; **la v. de décision est une condition du succès,** rapidity of decision is an essential for success; speedy decision is necessary if one is to succeed; **faire de la v.,** to move, go, quickly, at (a high) speed; to speed; *Aut: etc:* **excès de v.,** exceeding the speed limit; *F:* **en v.,** quickly, at speed; **partir en v.,** to rush away, to rush off; **un petit mot en v. pour vous dire . . .,** just a quick line to let you know . . .; **à une v. vertigineuse,** at a dizzy, headlong, breakneck, speed; **le temps fuit avec v.,** time flies at an incredible speed; **forcer la v.,** to force the pace; **lutter de v. avec qn,** to race s.o., to run a race with s.o.; **gagner, prendre, qn de v.,** (i) to outrun, outstrip, s.o.; *Rac:* to overtake, pass, sprint past, s.o.; (ii) to forestall s.o.; to steal a march on s.o.; **gagner en v., prendre de la v.,** to pick up speed, gather speed, increase speed; **perte de v.,** slowing down; *Av:* stall; **perdre la v., être en perte de v.,** (i) to lose speed, to slow down; *Av:* to stall; (ii) (*of production, etc.*) to slow down; to be losing ground; *Pol:* **ce parti est en perte de v.,** this party is losing ground, losing popularity; *Pol.Ec:* **stimuler une économie en perte de v.,** to stimulate a flagging economy; **conserver sa v.,** to maintain one's speed; to keep up one's pace. **2.** (*speed measured against time, distance*) (*a*) *Trans: etc:* speed (of ship, car, aircraft, etc.); **machine à grande, petite, v.,** high-speed, low-speed, engine; **v. régime (d'une machine),** normal running speed (of an engine); *Aut: etc:* **indicateur de v.,** speedometer; **v. maximum,** maximum, top, speed; **aller à toute v.,** to go at full, top, speed; *F:* to go all out; **la voiture passa à toute v.,** the car rushed by at top speed; **expédier un travail à toute v.,** to rush a job through; *Nau:* **en avant à toute v., à v. maximum,** full speed ahead; **porter la v. à 20 nœuds,** to increase the speed to 20 knots; **v. de route,** normal speed; *Nau:* sea-going speed, sea speed; **v. économique, v. de croisière,** cruising speed (of ship, aircraft, car); *Av:* **v. au sol,** ground speed; **v. propre,** (true) air speed; **v. indiquée,** indicated air speed; **v. de décrochage,** (i) escape velocity; (ii) stalling speed; **v. ascensionnelle,** rate of climb; **v. de plafond,** holding-off speed; **v. minimum de sustentation critique,** stalling speed; **ralentir un appareil au-dessous de la v. critique,** to stall a machine; **v. sonique,** sonic speed; **v. subsonique,** subsonic speed; **dépasser la v. du son,** to exceed the velocity of sound; (*b*) *Rail: A:* **grande v., petite v.,** fast, slow, goods service; (*c*) *Elcs:* (*computers*) **v. de défilement,** traverse speed; **v. de perforation,** punching rate; **v. de perforation (de bande),** perforation rate; **v. télégraphique,** telegraph speed, modulation rate; (*d*) *Med:* **v. de circulation, v. circulatoire,** circulation time; (*e*) *Cin:* **appareil grande v.,** super-speed camera; (*f*) *Pol.Ec:* **v. de transformation des capitaux ou de la monnaie en revenu,** income velocity of capital or money. **3.** (*a*) velocity; **v. relative,** relative velocity; **v. initiale,** (i) *Mec:* initial velocity; (ii) *Ball:* muzzle speed, velocity; *Ball:* **v. restante,** velocity on impact; *Mec:* **v. accélérée,** accelerated velocity; **v. uniformément accélérée,** uniform acceleration, uniformly accelerated velocity; **v. retardée,** retarded velocity, retardation; **v. angulaire,** angular speed, velocity; **v. acquise,** impetus; momentum; **mobile animé d'une v. de . . .,** body moving at a speed, a velocity, of . . .; (*b*) *Aut:* **changement de v.,** (i) change of gear; (ii) change-speed gear; **boîte de vitesses,** gearbox; **passer les vitesses,** to go through the gears; **je n'arrive pas à passer la v.,** I can't get (the car) into gear; **première vitesse,** first, bottom, gear; **démarrer en deuxième v.,** to start in second (gear); **filer en quatrième v.,** (i) to drive in top (gear); (ii) *F:* to disappear at top speed.

vitex [vitɛks], *s.m. Bot:* agnus castus, chaste tree; (*genus*) Vitex.

Viti [viti], *Pr.n. Geog: A:* **les îles V.,** the Fiji Islands.

viticole [vitikɔl], *a.* viticultural; wine (industry); **problèmes viticoles,** problems of the wine industry.

viticulteur [vitikyltœ:r], *s.m.* vine grower, viticulturist.

viticulture [vitikylty:r], *s.f.* vine growing, viticulture.

vitifère [vitifɛ:r], *a.* vine-producing.

vitiligo [vitiligo], *s.m. Med:* vitiligo, leucoderma.

vitonnière [vitɔnjɛ:r], *s.f. Nau:* pintle (of rudder).

vitrage [vitra:ʒ], *s.m.* **1.** glazing (of greenhouse, etc.); *Const:* **double v.,** double glazing. **2.** (*a*) windows (of church, etc.); (*b*) glass partition, door. **3.** *Furn:* vitrage net, curtain (of window).

vitrail, -aux [vitra:j, -o], *s.m.* leaded glass window; *esp.* stained glass (church) window; **fenêtre à vitraux sertis de plomb,** latticed window; **vitraux sertis de plomb,** cathedral glass.

vitrain [vitrɛ̃], *s.m. Min:* vitrain.

vitre [vitr̥], *s.f.* pane (of glass); window pane; **garnir une fenêtre de vitres,** to glaze a window; *F:* **casser les vitres,** to kick up a shindy.

vitré [vitre], *a.* **1.** glazed (door, partition, etc.) **2.** vitreous, glassy (substance, etc.); *esp.* **humeur vitrée, corps v.,** vitreous humour, vitreous body (of the eye). **3. électricité vitrée,** vitreous electricity.

vitréais, -aise [vitreɛ, -ɛ:z], **vitréen, -enne** [vitreɛ̃, -ɛn], *a. & s. Geog:* (native, inhabitant) of Vitré.

vitrer [vitre], *v.tr.* to glaze (window, greenhouse, etc.).

vitrerie [vitrəri], *s.f.* glaziery.

vitrescibilité [vitres(s)ibilite], *s.f.* vitrescibility, vitrifiability.

vitrescible [vitrɛs(s)ibl̥], *a.* vitrescible, vitrifiable.

vitreux, -euse [vitrø, -ø:z], *a.* vitreous (mass, fracture); glassy (appearance, etc.); **yeux v.,** glassy, glazed, eyes (of corpse, etc.); **porcelaine vitreuse,** vitreous china; *A:* **électricité vitreuse,** vitreous, positive, electricity; *Geol:* **roches vitreuses,** vitreous rocks; *Med:* **dégénérescence vitreuse,** vitreous degeneration.

vitrier [vitri(j)e], *s.m.* **1.** maker of glass (for windows, etc.); *F:* **ton père n'était pas v.,** you make a better door than a window. **2.** glazier. **3.** *pl. Mil: F: A:* **les vitriers,** the *chasseurs à pied,* the light infantry

vitrière [vitri(j)ɛ:r], *s.f. Com:* metal framing (for windows).

vitrifiabilité [vitrifjabilite], *s.f.* vitrifiability

vitrifiable [vitrifjabl̥], *a.* vitrifiable.

vitrificateur, -trice [vitrifikatœ:r, -tris], **vitrificatif, -ive** [vitrifikatif, -i:v], *a.* vitrifying.

vitrification [vitrifikasjɔ̃], *s.f.* **1.** vitrification; vitrifaction; **v. (de l'émail) par fusion,** fusing. **2.** vitrified body. **3.** glazing.

vitrifier [vitrifje], *v.tr.* (*p.d. & pr.sub.* **n. vitrifiions, v. vitrifiiez**) **1.** to vitrify (sand, etc.); **brique vitrifiée,** glazed brick; **v. (l'émail) par fusion,** to fuse. **2.** to coat (parquet, etc.) with transparent plastic.

vitrine [vitrin], *s.f.* **1.** (*a*) shop window; **v. réfrigérée,** refrigerated window; **local aux vitrines spacieuses,** premises with extensive window space; **faire une v.,** to dress a window; **étalagiste qui fait des vitrines,** window dresser; **articles en v.,** articles (on show) in the window; **article qui a fait de la v.,** article that has been in the window; shop-soiled article; **regarder, lécher, les vitrines,** to go window-shopping; (*b*) goods displayed in a shop window. **2.** glass case, cabinet; display cabinet; showcase; **articles exposés sous v., dans des vitrines,** articles exhibited under glass.

vitriol [vitri(j)ɔl], *s.m.* vitriol; (*a*) *Com: A:* **v. bleu,** blue vitriol, copper sulphate; **v. vert,** green vitriol, ferrous sulphate; **v. blanc,** white vitriol, zinc sulphate; (*b*) **(huile de) v.,** oil of vitriol, concentrated sulphuric acid (of commerce). **critique au v.,** vitriolic criticism.

vitriolage [vitri(j)ɔla:ʒ], *s.m.* **1.** *Tex:* souring (of material). **2.** vitriol throwing.

vitriolé, -ée [vitri(j)ɔle]. **1.** *a.* vitriolized (mineral, etc.). **2.** *s.* victim of vitriol-throwing.

vitrioler [vitri(j)ɔle], *v.tr.* **1.** *Tex:* to sour (material). **2.** to throw vitriol at (s.o.); to vitriolize, to vitriol (s.o.).

vitriolerie [vitri(j)ɔlri], *s.f. A:* **1.** the sulphuric acid industry. **2.** oil of vitriol manufactory, sulphuric-acid works.

vitrioleur, -euse [vitri(j)ɔlœ:r, -ø:z], *s.* vitriol thrower.

vitriolique [vitri(j)ɔlik], *a.* vitriolic.

vitriolisation [vitri(j)ɔlizasjɔ̃], *s.f. Miner:* vitriolization.

vitripenne [vitripɛn], *a. Ent:* transparent-winged.

vitrophyre [vitrɔfi:r], *s.m. Geol:* vitrophyre.

vitrosité [vitrozite], *s.f.* vitrescence, vitreousness.

Vitruve [vitry:v], *Pr.n.m. Rom.Hist:* Vitruvius.

vitryat, -ate [vitri(j)a, -at], *a. & s. Geog:* (native, inhabitant) of Vitry-le-François.

vitta [vita], *s.f. Rom.Ant: Bot:* vitta.

Vittel [vitɛl]. **1.** *Pr.n. Geog:* Vittel. **2.** *s.m.* Vittel water.

vittelois, -oise [vitɛlwa, -wa:z]. **1.** *a. & s. Geog:* (native, inhabitant) of Vittel. **2.** *s.f.* **vitteloise,** Vittel water.

vittigère [vitiʒɛ:r], *a. Nat.Hist:* vittate.

vitulaire [vitylɛ:r], *a. Vet:* vitular; **fièvre v.,** puerperal fever, milk fever (in cows).

vitupérateur, -trice [vityperatœ:r, -tris]. **1.** *a.* vituperative. **2.** *s.* vituperator.

vitupération [vityperasjɔ̃], *s.f.* vituperation; abuse.

vitupérer [vitypere] (je vitupère, n. vitupérons; je vitupérerai) (a) v.tr. Lit: to vituperate, abuse (s.o., sth.); (b) v.i. to vituperate, protest, storm (contre qn, qch., against s.o., sth.).

vivable [vivabḷ], a. F: (a) livable(-in); construire pour de bon un monde v., to make once and for all a world fit to live in; (b) il n'est pas v., he's just impossible.

vivace[1] [vivas], a. (a) long-lived; (b) Nat.Hist: F: hardy; robust; (c) Bot: perennial; pois v., everlasting pea; (d) haine v., undying, inveterate, hatred; préjugé v., inveterate, deeply rooted, deep-rooted, long-lived, prejudice; souvenirs encore vivaces, memories still green; remords v., enduring remorse.

vivace[2] [vivatʃe], a.inv. & adv. Mus: vivace.

vivacité [vivasite], s.f. 1. promptness, alertness; v. à agir, promptness to act. 2. (a) hastiness (of temper); petulance; avec v., hastily; brusquely; sharply; (b) hasty utterance; outburst of temper; pardonnez quelques vivacités, you must excuse what was said in the heat of the moment. 3. (a) acuteness (of feeling); heat (of a discussion); fire, intensity (of a passion); dans la v. du combat, in the heat of the fight; (b) vividness, brilliancy (of colour, light); v. du teint, high colour. 4. vivacity, vivaciousness, animation, sprightliness, liveliness; v. d'un discours, vivaciousness, spirited delivery, of a speech; v. d'esprit, readiness of mind, of wit; quick-wittedness; sparkling wit; avoir de la v., to be vivacious, animated, sprightly, full of life; avec v., vivaciously.

vivandier, -ière [vivɑ̃dje, -jɛːr], s. A: sutler, canteen-keeper; f. vivandière.

vivant [vivɑ̃]. 1. a. (a) alive, living; il est encore v., he is still alive; être enterré v., to be buried alive; F: s'ensevelir v., to bury oneself alive; nous les avons trouvés vivants, we found them alive; être v., living creature; un poisson v., a live fish; pas une âme vivante, not a living soul; il n'y a homme v. qui s'en souvienne, there is not a man alive who remembers it; portrait v., life-like portrait; être le portrait v. de qn, to be the living image of s.o.; rendre vivante une expression morte, to revive a dead phrase; langue vivante, modern language; F: c'est une bibliothèque vivante, he's a walking encyclopaedia; Th: tableau v., tableau vivant; Bot: herbe vivante, sensitive plant; (b) lively, animated (street, scene, etc.); (c) vivid, live (narrative); image vivante de . . ., vivid picture of . . .; pièce bien vivante, thoroughly live play; (d) gens bien vivants, mal vivants, people who live good lives, evil lives. 2. s.m. (a) living being; les vivants et les morts, the living and the dead; (b) bon v., bon vivant; man who enjoys (the pleasures of) life (esp. good food and wine). 3. s.m. (a) de son v., during his lifetime, in his day; du v. de votre père, when your father was alive; in your father's lifetime; du v. de la reine Anne, in the days of Queen Anne; (b) A: portrait fait sur le v., portrait from life.

vivarais, -aise [vivarɛ, -ɛːz], Geog: 1. a. & s. (native, inhabitant) of the Vivarais. 2. s.m. le V., the Vivarais.

vivarium [vivarjɔm], s.m. vivarium; pl. vivariums.

vivarois, -oise [vivarwa, -waːz], a. & s. Geog: (native, inhabitant) of Viviers.

vivat [viva(t)]. 1. int. O: hurrah! occ. vivat! 2. s.m.pl. les vivats des spectateurs, the cheers of the audience, the spectators.

vive[2] [viːv], s.f. Ich: weever, sting fish; petite v., v. vipère, lesser weever; grande v., greater weever.

vive-eau [vivo], s.f. Oc: spring tide; pl. vives-eaux.

vive-la-joie [vivlaʒwa], s.m.inv. F: A: cheerful type; man who enjoys life; bon vivant.

vivement [vivmɑ̃], adv. 1. (a) briskly, sharply; smartly; suddenly; poursuivre qn v., to hurry after s.o.; sortir v., to dart, dash, out; il se tourna v., he turned sharply round; ramasser qch. v., to snatch sth. up; v. contesté, strongly contested; (b) int. v.! il n'est que temps! quickly! there isn't much time! F: v. les vacances! roll on the holidays! F. v. le soleil! oh for some sun! (c) réprimander v. qn, to give s.o. a sharp reprimand; répondre v., to answer sharply, brusquely; excusez-moi si j'ai répondu v., forgive me if I replied brusquely. 2. (a) keenly; deeply; acutely; s'intéresser v. à qch., to take a keen interest in sth.; v. affecté, touché, par . . ., deeply affected by . . .; regretter v. qch., to be extremely sorry about sth.; cette nouvelle m'afflige v., I am terribly upset by the news; (b) remercier qn v., to thank s.o. warmly; (c) v. recommandé, highly recommended.

viverricula [vivɛrikyla], s.f., **viverricule** [vivɛrikyl], s.f. Z: small civet (cat); (genus) Viverricula.

viverridés [vivɛride], s.m.pl. Z: Viverridae.

viverrin [vivɛrɛ̃], a. Z: chat v., viverrine cat, fishing cat.

viveur, O: **-euse** [vivœːr, -øːz], s. Pej: pleasure seeker; les viveurs, the fast set; joyeux v., gay Lothario.

Viviane [vivjan], Pr.n.f. Lit: Vivian, Vivien.

vivianite [vivjanit], s.f. Miner: vivianite.

vividité [vividite], s.f. Psy: vividness.

Vivien [vivjɛ̃], Pr.n.m. Vivian.

Vivienne [vivjɛn], Pr.n.f. Vivienne, Vivien.

vivier [vivje], s.m. (a) fish pond (for preserving fish); fish preserve; (b) Fish: keep net; (c) (in boat) fish well; (d) breeding ground (de, for).

vivifiant [vivifjɑ̃], **vivificateur, -trice** [vivifikatœːr, -tris], a. vivifying, quickening; enlivening; (of air, etc.) invigorating, bracing; critique vivifiante, healthy criticism.

vivification [vivifikasjɔ̃], s.f., **vivifiement** [vivifimɑ̃], s.m. vivification, quickening; reviving.

vivifier [vivifje], v.tr. (p.d. & pr.sub. n. vivifiions, v. vivifiiez) to vivify, quicken; to vitalize; to endue (sth.) with life; (of air, etc.) to invigorate; v. l'industrie d'un pays, to revive, give fresh life to, a country's industry; v. une entreprise, to infuse new blood into an undertaking.

vivifique [vivifik], a. A: vivifying; reviving.

vivipare [vivipaːr], a. Bot: Z: viviparous; Ich: poisson v., live bearer.

viviparement [viviparmɑ̃], adv. viviparously.

viviparidés [vivipariḍe], s.m.pl. Moll: Viviparidae.

viviparité [viviparite], s.f., A: **viviparie** [vivipari], s.f., O: **viviparisme** [viviparism], s.m. viviparity, viviparousness.

vivisecteur [vivisɛktœːr], s.m. vivisector, vivisectionist.

vivisection [vivisɛksjɔ̃], s.f. vivisection; pratiquer des vivisections sur des animaux, to vivisect animals.

vivoir [vivwaːr], s.m. Fr.C: living room.

vivoter [vivɔte], v.i. (a) to live sparely; to keep body and soul together; v. d'une maigre rente, to rub along on a slender income, on a small pension; (b) usine qui vivote, factory that can just manage to keep going.

vivre[1] [viːvr]. I. v. (pr.p. vivant; p.p. vécu; pr.ind. je vis, il vit, n. vivons, ils vivent; pr.sub. je vive; p.d. je vivais; p.h. je vécus; fu. je vivrai) to live. 1. v.i. (a) to be alive; v. longtemps, to live long; les perroquets vivent longtemps, parrots are long-lived; les papillons ne vivent pas longtemps, butterflies are short-lived; le meilleur homme qui ait jamais vécu, the best man that ever lived; les soixante-douze ans qu'il avait vécu, the seventy-two years of his life; cesser de v., to die; Lit: il a vécu, he is dead; le Front populaire a vécu, the Popular Front has had its day, is finished, F: has had it; être las de v., to be tired of life; vive le roi! long live the King! vive l'armée! three cheers for the army! vive(nt) les vacances! hurray for the holidays! vive la joie! let us be merry! Mil: etc: qui vive? who goes there? ne rencontrer âme qui vive, to meet no one, not a living soul; Prov: qui vivra verra, live and learn; time will show; (b) to survive, endure; il vécut vieux, he lived to an old age; s'il vit encore deux jours . . ., if he lives for another two days . . .; ouvrage qui vivra, work that will live, that will endure; traditions qui vivent encore, traditions that are still alive. 2. v.i. to spend one's life; les poissons vivent dans l'eau, fish live in water; v. à Paris, to live in Paris; il a beaucoup vécu, he has seen life; vivant de la vie des paysans, sharing in the life of farming people, living side by side with country people; v. saintement, to live a godly life; v. content, to live a contented life; v. dans la terreur, to live in a state of terror; v. avec qn, (i) to live, keep house, with s.o.; (ii) to have relations, dealings, with s.o.; (iii) to cohabit with s.o.; être aisé à v., commode à v., to be easy to get on with; v. en bons, en mauvais, termes avec ses voisins, to be on friendly, unfriendly, terms with one's neighbours; savoir v., to know how to behave; to be well-bred; apprendre, montrer, à v. à qn, to teach s.o. (good, better) manners; Mil: etc: A: certificat de bien v., certificate of good behaviour; v. et laisser v., to live and let live; se laisser v., to take life easily; F: to take life easy, to take it easy; il fait bon v. ici, life is pleasant here. 3. v.i. to live; to subsist; il faut que tout le monde vive, everyone must live; v. bien juste, to be just able to make do; on vivait bien juste, we could just manage, just rub along; v. bien, to live in comfort; to eat well; A: v. de ménage, to live sparingly; A: v. à un hôtel, to take one's meals at a hotel; travailler pour v., to work for one's living; il fait cher v. ici, life is expensive here; faire v. sa famille, to support, keep, one's family; v. au jour le jour, to live from hand to mouth; v. de poisson, to live on fish; v. de régime, to be on a diet; v. de ses rentes, to have a private income; to be independent; v. de sa plume, to live by one's pen; v. sur, de, sa réputation, to live on one's reputation; v. d'espérance, to live on hope; Lit: v. d'industrie, to live by one's wits; v. de privations, to lead a life of privation; de quoi vit-il? (i) what does he live on? (ii) what does he do for a living? avoir de quoi v., to have enough to live on; avoir tout juste de quoi v., to have only just enough to live on, to have just enough to keep body and soul together; v. sur son capital, to live on one's capital; v. avec trois mille francs par mois, to live on three thousand francs a month. 4. v.tr. (a) (with cogn.acc.) v. sa vie, to live one's own life; v. une vie de privations, to live a life of privation; il vécut noblement sa vie, he lived a noble life; (b) to experience; les événements que nous avons vécu(s), the events we lived through; vous n'avez pas vécu ce problème, you have had no personal experience of this problem; v. son art, to live one's art.

II. vivre, s.m. (a) A: living; le v. devient tous les jours plus cher, living is getting dearer every day; (b) food; le v. et le couvert, board and lodging; (c) pl. provisions, supplies; Mil: rations; vivres de conserve, canned, tinned, foods; faire des vivres, to lay in a store of provisions; couper les vivres à qn, (i) to cut off s.o.'s supplies; (ii) to stop s.o.'s allowance; Mil: administration des vivres, commissariat department; aller aux vivres, to go and draw rations; vivres de réserve, iron rations; petits vivres, groceries; vivres du jour, day's rations; vivres d'ordinaire, mess rations; vivres en nature, rations in kind.

vivre[2], s.f. Her: serpent devouring, vorant, a child.

vivré [vivre], a. Her: (of fess, etc.) dancetté, dancetty.

vivrier, -ère [vivri(j)e, -ɛːr]. 1. a. cultures vivrières, food crops; bâtiment v., ship that carries food products. 2. s.m. Mil: commissary of provisions.

viza [viza], s.m. Ich: viza (sturgeon).

vizillois, -oise [vizilwa, -waːz], a. & s. Geog: (native, inhabitant) of Vizille.

vizir [viziːr], s.m. vizier.

vlan, v'lan [vlɑ̃], int. slap(-bang)! whack! wham! F: tomber v.! en plein milieu, to fall bang in the middle; il l'a fait v.! he did it straight off, as slick as anything; à la v., in a slap-up manner.

vobulateur [vɔbylatœːr], s.m. Elcs: wobbulator, wobbler.

vocable [vɔkabḷ], s.m. 1. vocable, word. 2. Ecc: name patronage (of saint); église sous le v. de saint Pierre, church dedicated to, under the invocation of Saint Peter.

vocabulaire [vɔkabylɛːr], s.m. 1. vocabulary; word list; livre édité avec un v. français-anglais, book, text, published with a French-English vocabulary. 2. (a person's) vocabulary; enrichir son v., to enlarge one's vocabulary; le v. de Balzac est très riche, Balzac had a very wide vocabulary; Pej: quel v.! what an expression! what a way of expressing yourself! le v. de la chimie, chemical vocabulary, terms.

vocal, -aux [vɔkal, -o], a. 1. (a) vocal (promise, music, prayer, Anat: cords); l'appareil v., the vocal organs; (b) Elcs: fréquence vocale, voice frequency; à commande par fréquence vocale, voice-operated; voie à fréquence vocale, voice grade channel. 2. s.pl. Ecc: A: vocaux, vocales, vocals (entitled to vote at certain elections).

vocalement [vɔkalmɑ̃], adv. vocally, by word of mouth; Ecc: (to pray) vocally, out loud.

vocalique [vɔkalik], a. Ling: vocalic, vowel (change, etc.); son v., vocalic sound; voiced sound; vowel sound.

vocalisateur, -trice [vɔkalizatœːr, -tris], s. vocalizer; s.f. vocalisatrice, coloratura soprano.

vocalisation [vɔkalizasjɔ̃], s.f. Ling: Mus: vocalization.

vocalise [vɔkaliːz], s.f. Mus: exercise in vocalization.

vocaliser [vɔkalize], v.tr. 1. Mus: to vocalize (a melody, etc.); abs. to vocalize. 2. Ling: to vocalize (a consonant). 3. v.i. F: to talk (loudly and emphatically).

vocalisme [vɔkalism], *s.m. Ling: Mus:* vocalism.

vocatif [vɔkatif], *s.m. Gram:* vocative (case); nominative of address; **au v.**, in the vocative (case).

vocation [vɔkasjɔ̃], *s.f.* **1.** vocation, (divine) call; **la v. des Gentils**, the vocation of the Gentiles; **la v. d'Abraham**, the call of Abraham; **je ne me sens pas la v. de la prêtrise**, I feel no call to the Church, no calling for the Church. **2.** vocation, calling, bent, inclination; **avoir la v. du commerce**, to have an aptitude for business; **avoir la v. du professorat**, to be cut out for a teacher; **manquer sa v.**, to miss one's vocation; **ne pas avoir la v. des armes**, not to be cut out for a soldier; **un médecin par v.**, a dedicated doctor. **3.** *Elcs:* (*computers*) **à v. de gestion**, business-oriented; **à v. scientifique**, scientific-oriented.

voceratrice [vɔtʃeratritʃe], *s.f.*, **vocératrice** [vɔseratris], *s.f.* (*in Corsica*) *vocero* singer.

vocero [vɔtʃero], *s.m.*, **vocéro** [vɔsero], *s.m.* Corsican funeral chant; *pl. voceri.*

vociférant [vɔsiferɑ̃], *a.* vociferous, clamorous, vociferant.

vociférateur, -trice [vɔsiferatœːr, -tris], *s.* vociferator; noisy clamourer.

vocifération [vɔsiferasjɔ̃], *s.f.* vociferation; outcry; *pl.* shouts; yells; **pousser des vociférations**, to shout (out); to vociferate.

vociférer [vɔsifere], *v.i.* (**je vocifère, n. vociférons; je vociférerai**) to vociferate (**contre**, against); to shout, yell; (*with cogn.acc.*) **v. des injures**, to shout insults (**contre**, at).

vodka [vɔdka], *s.f.* vodka.

vœu, -x [vø], *s.m.* **1.** vow; **faire v. de faire qch.**, to make, take, a vow to do sth.; **faire v. de pauvreté**, to take a vow of poverty; **accomplir un v.**, to fulfil a vow; **rester fidèle à un v.**, to remain faithful to a vow; to keep a vow; **violer un v.**, to break a vow; *Ecc:* **les trois vœux, les vœux monastiques**, the three vows, the monastic vows; **prononcer ses vœux**, to take one's vows; **les vœux de baptême**, the baptismal vows; **faire v. de se venger sur qn**, to vow vengeance on s.o. **2.** wish; **émettre un v.**, to express a wish; **être au comble de ses vœux**, to have reached the height of one's desires; **appeler qch. de tous ses vœux**, to pray for (the coming of) sth.; **v. pieux**, wishful thinking; **je fais des vœux pour qu'il ne pleuve pas dimanche**, I'm praying it won't rain on Sunday; **vite, fais un v.**, quick, (make a) wish; **faire un v. lorsqu'on aperçoit une, à la vue d'une, étoile filante**, to wish on a shooting star; **ton v. se réalisera**, your wish will come true; **exaucer les vœux de qn**, to grant s.o.'s wishes, desires; **tous mes vœux! avec mes, nos, meilleurs vœux**, with all good wishes; **vœux de bonne, de nouvelle, année**, New Year greetings; **carte de vœux**, greetings card; **les vœux de la population**, the wishes of the population; **le comité a adopté des vœux demandant que . . .**, the committee has adopted a resolution in favour of . . .; **nous exprimons le v. que** + *sub.*, we trust that . . .; **je fais des vœux pour que vous réussissiez**, I wish you every success, I do hope you'll succeed. **3.** *A:* votive offering.

voglite [vɔglit], *s.f. Miner:* voglite.

Vogoul(e)s [vɔgul], *s.m.pl. Ethn:* Voguls.

vogue [vɔg], *s.f.* **1.** *A:* speed, way (of a row-boat). **2.** fashion, vogue; **mettre qch. en v.**, to bring sth. into vogue; **avoir de la v., avoir une v., être en v.**, to be popular, in fashion, in vogue; *Com:* (*of article*) to be in request, popular; **entrer en v.**, to come into vogue, into fashion; **cette mode entre en v.**, this fashion is coming in; **v. de quelques mois**, few months' run; **avoir une longue v., rester longtemps en v.**, to have a long run; **la v. du diabolo ne dura pas**, the diabolo craze did not last long; **la mode en v.**, the prevailing fashion; **c'est la grande v. actuellement**, it's all the rage at present. **3.** *Dial:* (*in S. of Fr.*) patronal festival; village fête.

voguer [vɔge], *v.i. Nau:* **1.** *A:* (*a*) (*of galley, etc.*) to be rowed; **vogue la galère!** let's chance it! (*b*) to row. **2.** to sail; to proceed under sail; **le navire voguait vent arrière**, the ship was scudding before the wind; **les nuages voguant dans le ciel**, the clouds sailing by; the drifting clouds; **v. à pleines voiles**, to forge ahead; to advance from success to success. **3.** (*felt-making*) **faire v. l'étoffe**, to bow the fur.

voici [vwasi], *prep.* **1.** here is, are, etc.; **v. Henri**, here's Henry; **me v., les v.**, here I am, here they are; **nous v. arrivés!** this is the end of our journey; here we are! **v. l'heure, it's time** (to go, etc.); **du pain? en v.**, bread? here's some, here you are; **en v. bien d'une autre!** here's something new! this is another kettle of fish! **la v. qui vient**, here she comes; **v. venir Jeanne**, here comes Jeanne; **les v. venir**, here they come; **mon ami que v. vous le dira**, my friend here will tell you; **ma maison que v.**, my house that you see here; **v. que ces quelques jours m'avaient troublé**, those last few days had really upset me; **v. que là on a le sentiment que . . .**, and now you have the feeling there that . . .; **v. ce dont il s'agit**, this is what it's all about; **v. ce qu'il m'a dit**, this is what he told me; **v. qui pourra vous édifier**, here's something to edify you; **v. qu'éclate la fanfare**, now the band is striking up; **la petite histoire que v.**, the following little story; **je le ferai et v. comment**, I shall do it in the following manner; **v. pourquoi**, for this reason, this is why; **v. l'automne, les feuilles tombent**, autumn is coming, the leaves are falling; **v. Noël!** Christmas is here! **v.!** here are the facts! **2.** (= *il y a*) **je l'ai vu v. trois ans**, I saw him three years ago; **v. trois mois que j'habite ici**, I have been living here for the last three months.

voie [vwa], *s.f.* **1.** (*a*) way, road, route, track; *Adm: Aut:* traffic lane; **v. publique**, public thoroughfare; highway; *Rom.Ant:* **la v. Appienne**, the Appian Way; **v. sacrée**, via sacra; *Astr:* **la V. lactée**, the Milky Way; **être toujours par v. et par chemin**, to be always on the move; **v. de communication**, line of communication; road, thoroughfare; **grande v. de communication**, main artery, arterial road; **voies pour piétons**, pedestrian facilities; *P.N:* **v. sans issue**, no through road; **v. fluviale, v. navigable**, waterway; **la v. maritime du Saint-Laurent**, the St. Lawrence Seaway; **par v. de terre**, by land; overland; **par v. de mer**, by sea; *Av:* **v. aérienne**, air route; **par la v. des airs**, by air; *Post: A:* **par (la) v. de Londres, v. Londres**, via London; **robinet, pompe, à deux voies**, two-way cock, pump; *Min:* **v. d'aérage**, airway, windgate; **v. d'extraction**, ore-way; *Av:* **v. de départ**, runway; (*b*) *Ven:* (*often pl.*) tracks (of game); slot (of deer, etc.); **venir à bout de v.**, to come to a check; **mettre les chiens sur la v.**, to put the dogs on the scent; **mettre qn sur la v.**, to give s.o. a clue, a hint; to put s.o. on the right track; **être dans la bonne v., sur la v.**, to be on the right track; (*c*) *Rail:* **v. ferrée**, (i) railway track, permanent way, *U.S:* railroad; (ii) railway (line); **envoi par v. ferrée**, dispatch by rail; **v. principale**, main track; **v. accessoire**, side track; **v. de service, de garage**, siding; side track; *F:* **mettre un projet sur une v. de garage**, to shelve a scheme; **v. de passage, de jonction**, crossover; **changement de v.**, points; **v. impaire, v. descendante**, down line; **v. paire, v. montante**, up line; **ligne à une v., à deux voies**, single-track, double-track, line; **v. banalisée**, track signalled for two-way working; **largeur de v.**, gauge; **v. étroite**, narrow-gauge line; (*on train ferry*) **pont des voies**, train deck; **demander la v.**, to whistle for the road; **v. libre**, line clear; **obstacle sur la v.**, obstacle on the line; **la v. est endommagée**, the permanent way is damaged; **sur quelle v. arrive le train?** on which platform does the train come in? (*d*) *Elcs:* (*computers*) **v. d'entrée**, input channel; **v. d'information**, code track; **v. primaire**, primary route; **v. principale**, highway; **v. de transmission de données**, data link; (*e*) *El:* circuit; **v. dérivée**, shunt circuit; (*f*) *Tp: W.Tel: etc:* channel; **v. de transmission**, transmission channel; **v. téléphonique, télégraphique**, telephone, telegraph, channel; *Tp:* **v. de trafic**, traffic channel, *U.S:* traffic route; *Elcs:* **v. d'image**, picture channel; (*g*) (i) gauge (of wheels of vehicle); (ii) tracks (of vehicle); (*h*) (i) kerf clearance (of a tool); (ii) set (of a saw); **donner de la v. à une scie**, to set a saw; (*i*) *Nau:* **v. d'eau**, leak; **faire une v. d'eau**, to spring a leak; **boucher une v. d'eau**, to stop a leak; **aveugler une v. d'eau**, to stop a leak temporarily; (*j*) *Anat:* passage, duct; **les voies urinaires**, the urinary passages; **les voies digestives, respiratoires**, the digestive, respiratory, tract(s); **les voies biliaires**, the bile ducts. **2.** *A:* (carriageable) load (of wood, etc.); sack (of coal); **v. d'eau**, load of water (*usu.* two bucketfuls). **3.** (*a*) way; **les voies de Dieu**, the ways of God; **la v. étroite**, the narrow way; the strait way; **la v. du salut**, the way of salvation; **voies et moyens**, ways and means; **préparer les voies**, to prepare the way; **obtenir qch. par la v. de la persuasion**, to obtain sth. by (means of) persuasion; **la v. des armes nous est ouverte**, recourse to arms is open to us; **régler une affaire par v. diplomatique**, to settle a matter through the (ordinary) channels of diplomacy; **suivre la v. de l'honneur**, to take the honourable course; **vous vous engagez dans une v. dangereuse**, you are embarking on a dangerous course; **c'est la seule v. que je puisse suivre**, it is the only course open to me; **il a trouvé sa v.**, he's found his feet; **affaire en bonne v.**, business that is going, shaping, well; **en v. d'achèvement**, nearing completion; **en v. de formation, de développement, d'extension**, in process of formation, of development, of extension; **pays en v. de développement**, developing countries; **en v. de réparation**, under repair; **il est en v. de guérison**, he is on the mend; **son commerce est en v. de relèvement**, his business is improving, is picking up again; **être en v. de faire qch.**, to be (well) on the way to doing sth.; **être en (bonne) v. de réussir**, to be on the way, road, to success; *Jur:* **voies de droit**, recourse to legal proceedings; **v. de fait**, taking the law into one's own hands; **voies de fait**, acts of violence; assault and battery; **en venir aux voies de fait**, to come to blows, to exchange blows; **se porter à des voies de fait**, to commit an assault; **être tenu à s'abstenir de voies de fait contre qn**, to be bound over to keep the peace; **voies d'accommodement**, measures of conciliation; **l'affaire est en v. d'accommodement**, the matter is in process of settlement out of court; **voies de recours**, grounds for appeal (to a superior court); (*b*) *Ch: etc:* process, method, way; **v. sèche, humide**, dry, wet, process; **essai par la v. sèche**, dry test.

voilà [vwala], *prep.* **1.** (*a*) there is, are, etc.; **v. Henri**, there's Henry; **le v., les v.**, there he is, there they are; **la pendule que v.**, that clock (over there); **v. où il demeure**, that is where he lives; **en v. assez!** that's enough (of it)! that will do! **en v. une idée!** what an idea! **en v. de la reconnaissance!** there's gratitude for you! **en v. un qui fera son chemin!** there's a man who will get on! that man will get on! **v. tout**, that's all; **le v. qui entre, v. qu'il entre**, there he is coming in; **vous v. donc de retour!** so you're back (again)! **v. ce qui s'appelle danser aujourd'hui**, that's what we call dancing today, nowadays; **v. qui s'appelle danser!** that's something like dancing! **v. qui est curieux!** that's curious; **v. qui ne se concevait même pas**, that was something that couldn't even be imagined; **v. pour nos projets actuels**, so much for our present plans; **v. ce que c'est que de mentir**, that's what you get for telling lies; **v. qu'hier il me téléphone**, only yesterday he rang me up; **v. ce qu'il m'a dit**, that's what he told me; **v. mes ordres**, those are, were, my orders; **v. comme elle est; la v. bien!** that's just like her; **comme le v. sale!** how dirty he is! **v. qu'on frappe**, somebody's knocking at the door; **v. qu'il se remarie**, and now he's getting married again; *F:* **(ne) v.-t-il pas qu'il pleut!** there now! if it isn't raining! **ne v.-t-il pas qu'il devient amoureux!** lo and behold he goes and falls in love! **ne v.-t-il pas que j'ai perdu ma montre!** well, if I haven't lost my watch! **v.-t-il pas qu'il veut m'accompagner**, I'm blest if he doesn't want to come with me; *Dial:* **en v.-t-il!** what a lot! *abs.* **v.!** there you are! **et v.!** and that's that! (*in restaurants*) **v., monsieur!** coming, sir! (*b*) (= VOICI) **me v.!** here I am! **le v.!** here he comes; **nous v. seuls**, now we are alone; **que v. un livre original!** now here's an original book for you! **que nous v. loin de tout cela!** how far we are from all that! **vous v. ici!** so here you are! **m'y v.! nous y v.!** now I've, we've, done it! I've, we've, made it! this is it! **v. qu'arrive . . .**, along comes . . .. **2.** (= *il y a*) **il est mort en juin v. trois ans**, he died in June three years ago; **v. dix ans que je le connais**, I've known him for ten years.

voilage [vwalaːʒ], *s.m.* **1.** (*a*) net (on hat, etc.); transparent overskirt; (*b*) *pl.* net curtains, curtaining. **2.** *Mec.E:* buckling (of wheel, etc.).

voile [vwal]. **I.** *s.f. Nau:* **1.** sail; **grande v.**, mainsail; **v. carrée**, square sail; **v. aurique**, fore-and-aft sail; **voiles hautes**, light sails, upper sails; **voiles basses, basses voiles**, lower sails; courses; **voiles de l'avant**, head sails; **voiles de l'arrière**, after sails; **voiles de cape**, storm sails, storm canvas; **v. barrée**, jigger, cross jack; **v. à corne**, gaff sail; **v. de flèche, en cul**, gaff-topsail; **déferler les voiles**, to unfurl, set, the sails; **déployer, établir, une v.**, to set a sail; **mettre le vent dans les voiles**, to fill the sails; **bateau à voiles**, sailing boat; **bateaux sans voiles**, dumb craft; **aller à la v.**, to sail; **entrer dans un port à la v.**, to sail into a port; **vaisseau sous voile(s)**, ship under sail; **il se dirigeait sur nous à toutes voiles**, he bore down on us (at) full sail; **faire v., mettre à la v.,** to set sail (**pour,** for); to get under sail; **faire de la v.,** (i) to set more sail; (ii) to go sailing; to do some sailing; **faire force de voiles,** to crowd on, cram on, all sail; **sous v.,** under canvas; **toutes voiles dehors,** (i) in full sail, all sail(s) set, with every stitch of canvas spread; (ii) F: (of woman) dressed to kill; F: **avoir du vent dans les voiles,** to be tight, three sheets in the wind; P: **mettre, lever, les voiles,** to scram, do a bunk. 2. **une flotte de trente voiles,** a fleet of thirty sail.

II. **voile,** s.m. 1. (a) veil; **v. de casque,** puggaree; Ecc: **prendre le v.,** to take the veil, to become a nun; **prise de v.,** taking of the veil; **faire qch. sous le v. de la religion,** to do sth. under the cloak, mask, of religion; **les voiles de la nuit,** the shades of night; **avoir un v. devant les yeux,** to have a mist before one's eyes, to be blinded; Med: F: **v. noir,** blackout; **v. de larmes,** blur of tears; Furn: v. de fauteuil, antimacassar; Phot: **v. noir de mise au point,** focusing cloth; (b) pl. Lit: raiment; (c) Tex: voile; (d) Anat: **v. du palais,** soft palate, velum; **v. (de cornée),** grey film (on the cornea); (e) Bot: velamen; (f) Phot: fog; **v. faible,** veil; **plaque avec une grande résistance au v.,** non-fogging plate; (g) Rail: **v. de roue,** wheel centre; Aut: **roue à v.,** disc wheel. 2. Mec.E: buckle (of wheel, etc.); warping; displacement, eccentricity.

voilé [vwale], a. 1. (a) veiled, dim (light); dim (eyes); veiled, obscure (meaning); muffled (drum); **voix voilée,** husky voice; Mus: veiled voice; **des yeux voilés de larmes,** eyes dimmed, blurred, with tears; **visage v. d'un nuage de tristesse,** face clouded with sadness; **allusion peu voilée,** broad hint; **en termes peu voilés,** in thinly veiled, no uncertain, terms; (b) fogged (plate, print). 2. (of wheel, rod, etc.) buckled, bent; out of true; out of alignment.

voiler[1] [vwale], v.tr. Nau: to rig (ship) with sails; **navire bien voilé,** trim ship.

voiler[2], v.tr. 1. (a) to veil (face, sanctuary, etc.); **se v. la face,** (i) to veil one's face; (ii) to put up one's hands to one's face; to hide one's face in horror; **v. ses pensées, ses desseins,** to cloak, conceal, one's thoughts, plans; (b) to veil, obscure, dim, cloud (light, etc.); to muffle (sound, drum, etc.); to shade (light); **des nuages voilaient le soleil,** clouds obscured the sun; (c) Phot: to fog (plate, print). 2. to buckle, warp, bend (wheel, etc.).

se voiler. 1. (of sky, etc.) to become overcast, to cloud over; **le ciel se voile de nuages,** the sky is clouding over. 2. (of wheel, etc.) to become buckled, warped; to buckle.

voilerie [vwalri], s.f. Nau: 1. sail loft. 2. sail making.

voilette [vwalɛt], s.f. Cost: (hat) veil.

voilier, -ière [vwalje, -jɛːr]. 1. a. (a) Nau: sailing (qualities, etc.); **bâtiment bon v., mauvais v.,** good, bad, sailer; (b) Aer: **qualités voilières,** flying qualities; Orn: **oiseau v.,** long-flight bird. 2. s.m. sailing ship, sailing boat, sailer; windjammer. 3. s.m. sail maker; **le maître v.,** F: "sails." 4. s.m. (a) Ich: sailfish; (b) Moll: argonaut, paper nautilus.

voilure[1] [vwalyːr], s.f. (a) sails (of ship); **une v. neuve,** a new suit of sails; **réduire la v.,** to shorten sail; **yacht avec la v. d'une goélette,** schooner-rigged yacht; (b) Av: wing(s), flying surface, wing unit, aerofoil, U.S: airfoil; **v. basse, semi-basse, haute,** low, semi-low, high, wing; **avion à grande v.,** aircraft with large control surfaces, a large spread of wings; **appareil à v. fixe,** fixed-wing aircraft; **appareil à v. tournante,** rotary-wing aircraft; **avion à v. variable,** variable-wing aircraft; **avion à v. basculante,** tilt-wing aircraft; (c) Ph: aerodynamic surface.

voilure[2], s.f. buckling, bending (of wheel, etc.); warping (of board).

voir [vwaːr], v.tr. (pr.p. voyant; p.p. vu; pr.ind. je vois, il voit, n. voyons, ils voient; pr.sub. je voie; p.d. je voyais; p.h. je vis; fu. je verrai) 1. (a) to see; to set eyes on (s.o., sth.); to sight (ship); **voyez un peu cette étoile,** just look at that star; **v. voyez, page 300,** see page 300; **j'ai vu dans Tite-Live que . . .,** I read in Livy that . . .; **hôtel vu de face,** front view of the hotel; **(détail) vu de près,** close-up (detail); Chess: **mener une partie sans v.,** to play blindfold chess; F: **on aura tout vu!** wonders will never cease! **il ne voit pas plus loin que le bout de son nez,** he can't see further than the end of his nose; **cela vaut la peine d'être vu,** it's (a sight) worth seeing; **il faut le v. pour le croire,** it must be seen to be believed; **v. c'est croire,** seeing is believing; **je**

l'ai vu de mes propres yeux; je l'ai vu, de mes yeux vu, I saw it with my own eyes; **il n'y a rien à v.,** there is nothing to be seen; **que voyez-vous?** what do you see? **je le vois qui arrive,** I see him coming; **je la verrai toujours tombant à la renverse,** I shall never forget seeing her fall over backwards; **je lui ai vu beaucoup d'argent entre les mains,** I have seen a great deal of money in his hands; **on lui voit beaucoup d'amis,** he appears to have a lot of friends; **à le v. on dirait . . .,** by the look of him, to judge by his looks, one would say . . .; **avoir vu bien des batailles,** to have seen many a battle; **il n'avait encore jamais vu le feu,** he had never yet been under fire; **monument qui se voit de loin,** monument that can be seen from afar; **on voit son jupon,** her petticoat is showing; abs. **je n'y vois plus,** I can't see any more; **on n'y voit pas ici,** you can't see a thing here (it's so dark); (adverbial complement) **v. rouge,** to see red; **v. trouble,** to see things through a mist; to be dim-sighted; **regarder qch. sans v.,** to gaze vacantly at sth.; **regarder qn sans le v.,** to look through s.o.; **voyez vous-même!** see for yourself! Lit: **que vois-je?** what is this (that I see)? Iron: **voyez un peu!** just look at him (at it)! **il faut y aller v.,** we must go and see; A: **allez-y v.!** get away with you! **était-il coupable ou non, allez-y v.!** was he guilty or not, who can tell? **faire v., laisser v., qch. à qn,** to show sth. to s.o.; to let s.o. see sth.; **il fit v. sa blessure au chirurgien,** he showed the surgeon his wound; **faire v. un enfant au médecin,** to take a child to the doctor's; **il a laissé v. son ressentiment,** he showed his resentment; **laisser v. son ignorance,** to reveal, betray, one's ignorance; **faites v. un peu votre ouvrage,** just show me your work; let me look at your work; **il aime à se faire v.,** he likes to show himself; he likes to be seen; **faites v.! let me see it!** F: **allez vous faire v.!** get lost! F: **en faire v. (de toutes les couleurs) à qn,** to lead s.o. a dance; **voyons v.,** (i) let us see, let me see, let me consider; (ii) show it to me; **montrez v.,** just let me, us, see it; **dites v.,** let us hear it; **écoutez v.,** just listen; **essayez v.,** just have a try; **essayez v. si ça va,** try and see if it's all right; (b) Com: to sight (a bill of exchange); (c) (of building, etc.) **v. sur . . .,** to look out on . . ., to face . . . 2. **voir + infin.** (a) **v. venir qn,** to see s.o. coming; F: **il faut v. venir les choses,** we must wait and see; **je le vis tomber,** I saw him fall; **on le vit tomber,** he was seen to fall; **on ne l'avait jamais vu rire,** he had never been known to laugh; (b) **v. qn. faire qch.,** to see s.o. do sth.; **quels acteurs avez-vous vus jouer ce rôle?** what actors have you seen in this part? **que je le voie encore faire cela!** just let me catch him at it again! (c) (in very limited use) **v. faire qch. à qn,** to see s.o. do sth.; **il avait vu faire le même geste à X,** he had seen X make the same gesture; (d) (with the subject of the infin. unexpressed, in quasi passive constructions) **quelles pièces avez-vous vu jouer?** what plays have you seen (acted)? **les propositions que je désirerais v. étudier,** the proposals that I should like to have considered; **je m'attendais à le v. huer,** I expected he would be booed; **il se voyait refuser les fournitures les plus urgentes,** he was refused the most urgent supplies; **je me vois reprocher les bévues de mes collègues,** I am taken to task for my colleagues' mistakes. 3. (as aux. of the passive voice) **je me vis forcé de partir,** I was compelled to leave; **nous aurions tout sacrifié plutôt que de vous v. déshonoré,** we would have sacrificed everything rather than that you should suffer disgrace, rather than see you disgraced. 4. (a) to visit (s.o., sth.); **aller v. qn,** to go to see s.o.; to go and see s.o.; to look s.o. up; **venez me v. quand vous serez à Paris,** look me up, come and see me, when you are in Paris; **v. un malade,** to visit a patient; **nous avons vu les musées,** we visited the museums; **v. du pays,** to travel; (b) **v. qn,** to receive a visit; **il ne voit personne,** he sees no one; he is not at home to anyone; **nous le voyons beaucoup,** we see a great deal of him; **nous le voyons moins en hiver,** we see less of him in winter; **j'ai eu de nombreuses occasions de v. M. X,** I have frequently had occasion to meet Mr X; **on ne vous voit plus!** you are quite a stranger! **nous ne les voyons plus,** (i) we no longer see them; (ii) we have dropped them; A: **v. bonne compagnie,** to frequent, to keep, good company; **nous nous voyons souvent,** we often meet, see each other; **ils ne se voient pas,** they are not on visiting terms; F: **on ne voit que lui,** he's always there; there's no getting away from him. 5. (a) to

understand; **ne pas v. le sens d'un mot,** not to understand the meaning of a word; **je vois où vous voulez en venir,** I see, understand, what you are driving at; **comme on le verra bientôt,** as we shall soon see; **v. de loin, v. bien loin,** to be far-sighted; F: **ni vu, ni connu,** without anyone knowing anything about it, being the wiser for it; (b) to notice, observe (sth.); **tout le monde ne sait pas v.,** not everybody is observant; **il la voyait moins attentive,** he noticed she was less attentive; **je vois que vous avez compris,** I see you have understood; **on verra de quel bois je me chauffe,** I'll show them what stuff I am made of; **à ce que je vois,** from what I can see; **cela se voit,** that is obvious; **je ne vois pas que cela puisse vous intéresser,** I do not see that it can be of interest to you; **vous voyez ça d'ici,** you can imagine what it was (is, would be) like. 6. (a) to examine, to look after, to look into, to see to, to see about (sth.); **v. une affaire à fond,** to look into, to examine, a matter thoroughly; **faire qch. seulement pour v.,** to do sth. just as an experiment; just to see what would happen; **eh bien, je verrai,** well, I'll see about it; **c'est ce que nous verrons!** we shall see! that remains to be seen; F: **va-t'en v. si j'y suis!** (i) I'll see you further first! (ii) clear out! scram! A: **va-t'en v. s'ils viennent!** tell me another! rats! **il n'a rien à v. là-dedans,** it is nothing to do with him; it is no business of his; **vous n'avez rien à y v.,** you have nothing to do with it; it is no concern of yours; **cela n'a rien à v. à l'affaire,** that is beside the point, has no connection, nothing to do, with the matter; **ceci est à v., c'est à v.,** it remains to be seen; **vous allez v. ce que vous allez v.,** just wait and see; (b) **v. + inf. il va v. à nous loger,** he will see that we have somewhere to stay, to live; **v. + sub. c'est à vous de v. que rien ne nous fasse défaut,** it is up to you to see that we have everything we need; (c) int. **voyons!** (i) let's see; (ii) come, now! **vous ne croyez pas cela, voyons!** you surely don't believe that! 7. to consider, regard (sth. in a particular way); **sa façon de v. les choses,** his way of looking at things; his outlook; **sa manière de v. au sujet de . . .,** his views on . . .; **chacun a sa façon de v.,** everyone has his own way of looking at things; **v. mal les choses,** to see things in the worst possible light; **elle ne voit pas les choses comme moi,** she does not see eye to eye with me; **il se voyait déjà perdu,** he already imagined himself lost; **se faire bien v. de qn,** to gain s.o.'s favour; to get into s.o.'s good books; **se faire mal v. de qn,** to get into s.o.'s bad books; **être bien vu de tous,** to be highly esteemed, well thought of, by all; **mal vu,** poorly considered; held in suspicion; disliked; **je ne le vois pas marié,** I can't imagine him married. 8. F: **je ne peux pas le v.,** I can't stand the sight of him, can't stand him at any price.

voire [vwaːr], adv. 1. A: in truth. 2. indeed; **v. (même),** and even; or even; indeed even; **de longs mois, v. des années,** long months, indeed years; **j'en suis ahuri, v. révolté,** I'm astounded, indeed, even, disgusted; **ce remède est inutile, v. même dangereux,** this medicine is useless, not to say dangerous; **il est malade, v. même en danger de mort,** he is ill, and indeed, even, at death's door.

voirie [vwari], s.f. 1. (a) system of roads; **la grande v.,** the high roads; (b) **(la petite) v.,** administration of public thoroughfares; **le service de v.,** the highways department; **alignement de v.,** street line; **travaux de v.,** road works; **travailleur, employé, de la v.,** street sweeper. 2. refuse dump; **jeter les ordures à la v.,** to dump the refuse.

voironnais, -aise [vwarɔnɛ, -ɛːz], a. & s. Geog: (native, inhabitant) of Voiron.

voisement [vwazmɑ̃], s.m. Ling: voicing.

voiser [vwaze], v.tr. Ling: to voice; **voyelle voisée,** voiced vowel.

voisin, -ine [vwazɛ̃, -in]. 1. a. neighbouring, adjoining; **la chambre voisine,** the next room; **l'auberge la plus voisine,** the nearest inn; **deux maisons voisines,** two houses next to each other; two adjoining houses; **il habite dans la maison voisine,** he lives next door; Nat.Hist: **espèces voisines,** nearly allied species; closely related species; **être v. de qn, de qch.,** to be next to, near, s.o., sth.; **émotion voisine de la terreur,** A: **voisine à la terreur,** emotion akin to terror, bordering on terror; **v. de la mort,** at death's door; **plus d'une fois, j'ai été, je me suis trouvé, très v. de la mort,** it has been touch and go with me more than once; I have often been near to death; *Lit:* Noël était tout v., Christmas was (close) at hand. 2. *s.* neighbour; v. d'à côté, de porte à porte, next-door neighbour; mon v. de droite, de gauche, my right-hand, left-hand, neighbour; mon v. de table, my neighbour at table; agir en bon v., to act in a neighbourly way; *Prov:* bon avocat, mauvais v., a good lawyer makes a bad neighbour.

voisinage [vwazinaːʒ], *s.m.* 1. proximity, vicinity, nearness; les maisons dans le v. des montagnes, the houses near the mountains; le v. de la gare est un avantage, proximity to the station is an advantage. 2. neighbourhood, surrounding district; (*a*) demeurer dans le v., to live in the neighbourhood; il n'y avait personne dans le v., there was nobody about; (*b*) tout le v. en parle, all the neighbours are talking about it; the whole neighbourhood is talking about it. 3. neighbourly intercourse; relations de bon v., neighbourliness.

voisiner [vwazine], *v.i.* 1. (*a*) to visit one's neighbours; nous voisinons, we call on each other; we are neighbourly; nous voisinons avec les nouveaux locataires, we are on friendly terms with the new tenants; nous ne voisinons pas, (i) we keep ourselves to ourselves; (ii) we don't see anything of each other; à Paris on voisine peu, in Paris one doesn't see much of one's neighbours; (*b*) je voisinais à table avec un avocat, I was sitting next to a barrister at table. 2. (*of thgs*) to be placed side by side; to adjoin.

voiturage [vwatyraːʒ], *s.m.* cartage, carriage, conveyance (of goods, etc.).

voiture [vwatyːr], *s.f.* 1. (*a*) *A:* conveyance, transport; (*still so used in*) *Com:* lettre de v., waybill, consignment note; (*b*) carriage, cost of conveyance; *A:* payer sa v., to pay one's fare. 2. conveyance, vehicle; v. publique, public conveyance; *P.N:* attention aux voitures! beware of the traffic! (*a*) (horse-drawn) vehicle; carriage; cart; *A:* v. de maître, private carriage; v. découverte, open carriage; v. fermée, closed carriage; v. de gala, state coach; *O:* v. de remise, livery-stable carriage; v. à deux, à quatre chevaux, carriage and pair, carriage and four; *A:* v. de place, hackney carriage, cab; v. à âne, donkey cart; *A:* v. de roulier, waggon; *A:* entrepreneur de voitures publiques, carrier; transport par v., cartage; emporter qch. en v., to cart sth. away; *F:* nous avons pris la v. des cordeliers, des capucins, we came on Shanks's pony, mare; (*b*) v. (automobile), (motor) car, *U.S:* automobile; v. de tourisme, private car; v. de sport, sports car; v. de livraison, delivery van; v. de laitier, milk float; v. d'arrosage, water cart; v. école, driving-school car; v. cellulaire, prison van; avoir sa v. à soi, to keep a car, to have a car of one's own; nous sommes venus en v., we came by car; we drove here; (*c*) *Rail:* v. (de chemin de fer), railway coach, carriage; *U.S:* (railroad) car; v. à voyageurs, passenger coach; v. à marchandises, goods truck, wagon; *U.S:* freight car; en v.! take your seats! *U.S:* all aboard! v. de tramway, tramcar; (*d*) v. d'enfant, de bébé, perambulator, *F:* pram; *U.S:* baby carriage; v. de malade, *F:* petite v., invalid carriage; *O:* v. de promenade, Bath chair; v. à bras, barrow, hand cart; (*e*) *Mil:* *A:* v. atelier, travelling workshop; v. cuisine, travelling kitchen; v. porte-mitrailleuse, machine-gun waggon; *Artil:* v. canon, gun and limber; v. observatoire, wheeled observatory.

voiture-bar [vwatyrbaːr], *s.f.*, **voiture-buffet** [vwatyrbyfɛ], *s.f.* *Rail:* buffet car, refreshment car; *pl. voitures-bars, -buffets.*

voiturée [vwatyre], *s.f.* carriageful (of people); cartload (of goods, etc.).

voiture-lit [vwatyrli], *s.f.* *Rail:* sleeping car, *F:* sleeper; *pl. voitures-lits.*

voiture-pie [vwatyrpi], *s.f.* *F:* police patrol car; = panda car; *pl. voitures-pie.*

voiturer [vwatyre], *v.tr.* to convey, transport, carry, cart (goods, etc.); v. par eau, to convey by water; nuages voiturés par le vent, wind-driven clouds.

voiture-radio [vwatyrradjo], *s.f.* radio car; *pl. voitures-radio.*

voiture-restaurant [vwatyrrɛstɔrɑ̃], *s.f.* *Rail:* restaurant car, dining car; *pl. voitures-restaurants.*

voiture-salon [vwatyrsalɔ̃], *s.f.* *Rail:* saloon carriage, coach; *U.S:* parlour car; *pl. voitures-salons.*

voiturette [vwatyrɛt], *s.f.* trap, small spring-cart; *Aut:* minicar; baby car; *A:* v. à remorque latérale, sidecar; *Mil:* v. porte-mitrailleuse, machine-gun carrier; v. porte-mortier, mortar carrier; v. porte-munitions, ammunition carrier.

voiturier, -ière [vwatyrje, -jɛːr], *A:* 1. *a.* (*a*) carriageable; avenue voiturière, carriage drive; (*b*) l'industrie voiturière, the carrying trade. 2. *s.m.* (i) driver, coachman; (ii) drayman; v. public, common carrier; v. par eau, (i) carrier by water; (ii) raftsman.

voiturin [vwatyrɛ̃], *s.m.* *A:* 1. cabman. 2. cab; hired carriage.

voïvodat [vɔivɔda], *s.m.* *Hist:* voivodeship; office of voivode.

voïvode [vɔivɔd], *s.m.* *Hist:* voivode, vaivode.

voïvodie [vɔivɔdi], *s.f.* voivodeship, district governed by a voivode.

voix [vwa], *s.f.* 1. (*a*) voice; parler à v. haute, à haute v., (i) to speak in a loud voice; (ii) to speak aloud; parler à v. basse, à demi-v., à mi-v., to speak in a low voice, under one's breath, in a subdued voice, in an undertone; prendre, faire, la grosse v., (i) to speak in a severe tone; (ii) to take on a hectoring tone; v. de bronze, deep ringing voice; répondre d'une v. douce, to answer in a gentle voice; crier de toute la force de sa v., to shout at the top of one's voice; élever la v., to speak up; to raise one's voice; à portée de (la) v., within earshot, within call, within hail, within hailing distance; hors de portée de la v., out of hearing, out of earshot; (*of dogs*) donner de la v., to bark, to give tongue, to bay; *Mus:* v. de basse, de ténor, de soprano, bass voice, tenor voice, soprano voice; chanter d'une v. de basse, to sing in a bass voice; v. de poitrine, chest voice; v. de tête, head voice; v. de fausset, falsetto; v. fêlée, cracked voice; chanter à plusieurs v., to sing in parts; mise de v., (i) voice production; (ii) swell (on sustained note); je ne suis pas en v., I am not in voice; v. humaine, vox humana (stop of organ); la v. de l'orage, the voice of the storm; (*b*) v. d'une pièce de monnaie, v. de monnayage, ring of a coin. 2. (*a*) speech, word; demeurer sans v., to remain speechless; de vive v., by word of mouth, viva voce; la v. de la conscience, the voice, the dictates, of conscience; la v. de la nature, the call of nature; *Nau:* faites passer la v.! give the word there! (*b*) voice, opinion; la v. du peuple, vox populi, public opinion; d'une commune v., by common consent; (*c*) (individual) vote; donner sa v. à qn, to vote for s.o.; chaque délégation a une v., each delegation is allowed one vote; mettre une question aux v., to put a question to the vote, to the meeting; to take a vote on a question; mettre aux v. une résolution, to move a resolution; la Chambre alla aux v., the House divided; avoir v. au chapitre, to be entitled to give one's opinion, to have a say in the matter. 3. *Gram:* voice (of the verb); à la v. active, passive, moyenne, in the active voice, in the passive (voice), in the middle voice.

vol[1] [vɔl], *s.m.* 1. (*a*) flying, flight (of birds, arrow, etc.); prendre son v., (i) (*of bird*) to take wing; (ii) *Av:* to take off; au v., on the wing; tirer un oiseau au v., to shoot at a bird on the wing; saisir l'occasion au v., to seize, grasp, the opportunity; to leap at the opportunity; à v. d'oiseau, as the crow flies; vue à v. d'oiseau, bird's-eye view; vue de la plage à v. d'oiseau, the beach seen from the air, aerial view of the beach; à v. d'abeille, in a beeline; oiseau de haut v., high-flying bird; *Lit:* âme de haut v., lofty soul; escroc de haut v., high-class crook; (*b*) *Av:* flight; *Mil.Av:* sortie; contrôleur de v., flight indicator; v. "A" pour Bruxelles, flight "A" for Brussels; v. d'affrètement, charter flight; premier v., initial flight, maiden flight; v. de transition, transition (flight) (of VTOL aircraft); v. à vue, visual flight; règles de v. à vue, visual flight rules; v. radioguidé, v. sans visibilité, blind flying; v. d'entraînement, training flight; heures de v., flying time; avion en v., aircraft in flight; v. de nuit, night flying; v. isobare, pressure-pattern flying; v. cabré, steep attitude; v. stationnaire, hovering; v. à voile, gliding; faire du v. à voile, to glide; v. libre, coasting, free glide; v. de virtuosité, stunt flying, stunting; (*c*) *Space:* v. inertiel, v. sur la lancée (du projectile, du véhicule), coasting flight (of projectile, spacecraft); effectuer un v. inertiel, un v. sur lancée, to coast. 2. (*a*) (distance of) flight (of bird, etc.); flight (of imagination); (*b*) (= ENVERGURE) spread of (bird's) wings. 3. (*a*) flock, flight (of birds flying together); skein (of wild geese, etc.); covey (of game birds); un v. de sauterelles, a swarm of locusts; (*b*) *Ven:* cast (of hawks). 4. (chasse au) v., hawking.

vol[2], *s.m.* 1. (*a*) theft, larceny; thieving, stealing, robbery; *Jur:* v. qualifié, aggravated theft; robbery; v. avec effraction, housebreaking; v. de nuit avec effraction, burglary; v. insignifiant, minime, petty larceny; v. à la tire, pocket picking, purse snatching; v. à l'étalage, shop-lifting; v. à l'américaine, confidence trick; v. de grand chemin, highway robbery; v. à main armée, robbery under arms, armed robbery; v. avec violences, avec agression, robbery with violence; *F:* v. au poivrier, robbing, *U.S:* rolling, of drunken men; v. public, peculation; *F:* c'est du v. manifeste! it's (sheer) daylight robbery! (*b*) (act of) theft, robbery, burglary; commettre un v., plusieurs vols, to commit a theft, several thefts. 2. *A:* stolen goods; stolen object.

volable [vɔlabl̩], *a.* 1. worth stealing. 2. (*man*) easy to rob.

volage [vɔlaːʒ], *a.* (*a*) fickle, inconstant, flighty; d'humeur v., fickle-minded; (*b*) *Nau:* embarcation v., crank, cranky, topheavy, boat; compas v., unsteady compass.

volagement [vɔlaʒmɑ̃], *adv.* in a fickle manner; flightily.

volaille [vɔlɑːj], *s.f.* 1. poultry, fowls; marchand de v., poulterer. 2. *Cu:* poultry, *esp.* chicken; manger une v., to eat a chicken; foies de v., chicken livers. 3. *coll.* *P:* the cops, the fuzz.

volailler, -ère [vɔlɑje, -ɛːr], *s.* 1. *s.* poulterer. 2. *s.m.* poultry yard; poultry farm.

volailleur, -euse [vɔlɑjœːr, -øːz], *s.* poulterer.

volant [vɔlɑ̃]. I. *a.* 1. flying; *Nat.Hist:* volant (insect, etc.); fluttering (ribbons, tresses, etc.); light, floating (drapery); objet v. non identifié, unidentified flying object; *F:* soucoupe volante, flying saucer; *Her:* aigle v., eagle volant; *Ich:* poisson v., flying fish; *Navy:* escadre volante, flying squadron; *Pyr:* fusée volante, sky rocket. 2. loose (cable, etc.); movable (partition, stairs, etc.); feuille volante, loose leaf, detachable slip (of paper); chaise volante, light, easily moved, chair; table volante, occasional table; *Nau:* cabestan v., portable winch; lest v., shifting ballast; pont v., (i) spar deck; (ii) *Civ.E:* flying bridge; *Civ.E:* échafaud(age) v., flying scaffold, hanging stage, travelling cradle; *El:* fiche volante, wander plug; *A:* assiettes volantes, side-dishes.

II. volant, *s.m.* 1. *Games:* (*a*) shuttlecock; *F:* on se renvoie ces lettres de plainte comme des volants, these letters of complaints are bandied backwards and forwards; (*b*) jeu de v., (game of) battledore and shuttlecock; v. au filet, badminton. 2. (*a*) sail (of windmill); (*b*) *Nau:* upper topsail. 3. (*a*) flywheel (of engine); fly (in clockwork); former v., to act as a flywheel; v. porte-lame, band-saw pulley; *Mec.E:* v. régulateur, balance wheel; (*b*) (i) head of steam; (ii) steadying force or factor; reserve supply; store of energy (for smooth working); stocks qui constituent le v. nécessaire à la production, stocks forming the reserves necessary for steadiness of output. 4. handwheel (of engine, lathe, etc.); *Aut:* v. (de direction), steering wheel; tenir le v., to drive; il tient bien le v., he drives well; he is a good driver; allez-vous prendre le v.? are you going to drive? se mettre au v., to take the wheel; être tué au v., to be killed at the wheel, driving; *Artil:* v. de pointage en hauteur, elevating wheel; v. de pointage en direction, training wheel; *Av:* v. (de commande), control wheel. 5. talon et v., counterfoil and leaf. 6. *Dressm:* (i) flounce; (ii) shaped panel; volants froncés, gathered flounces. 7. *Const:* *etc:* span (of beam). 8. *Tex:* spindle whorl.

volapük [vɔlapyk], *s.m.* *Ling:* *A:* Volapuk.

volatil [vɔlatil], *a.* *Ch:* *etc:* volatile; *A.Ch:* alcali v., volatile alkali; ammonia; esprit v., volatile mind.

volatile [vɔlatil]. 1. *a.* *O:* winged. 2. *s.m.* winged creature, bird, *esp.* farmyard bird.

volatilisable [vɔlatilizabl̩], *a.* volatilizable.

volatilisation [vɔlatilizasjɔ̃], *s.f.* volatilization; *Atom.Ph:* *etc:* burn(-)up.

volatiliser [vɔlatilize], *v.tr.* (*a*) *Ch:* to volatilize; (*b*) *P:* on lui avait volatilisé sa montre, he'd had his watch stolen, s.o. had pinched his watch.

se volatiliser, (*of ideas, impressions, etc.*) to dissipate, fade away, vanish into thin air.

volatilité [vɔlatilite], *s.f.* volatility.

vol-au-vent [vɔlovɑ̃], *s.m.inv.* *Cu:* vol-au-vent.

volcan [vɔlkɑ̃], *s.m.* volcano; v. actif, dormant, éteint, active, dormant, extinct, volcano; v. hawaïen, v. bouclier, shield volcano; v. péléen, plug volcano; *Miner:* pierre des volcans, obsidian, volcanic glass; danser sur un v., to dance over a volcano; **être sur un v.**, to be on the edge of a volcano; **son imagination est un v.**, he has a vivid, fiery, imagination; **cet homme est un vrai v.**, this man has a volcanic temperament, is fiery, impetuous.

volcanique [vɔlkanik], *a.* volcanic (rock, etc.); fiery, ardent (passion); vivid (imagination).

volcaniquement [vɔlkanikmɑ̃], *adv.* volcanically; by volcanic action.

volcaniser [vɔlkanize], *v.i.* to become volcanic.

volcanisme [vɔlkanism], *s.m. Geol:* vulcanism, vulcanicity, volcanicity; *Geog:* volcanic features.

volcaniste [vɔlkanist], *s.m.* volcanist.

volcanologie [vɔlkanɔlɔʒi], *s.f.* volcanology, vulcanology.

volcanologue [vɔlkanɔlɔg], *s.m. & f.* volcanologist, vulcanologist.

Volces [vɔls], *s.m.pl. A.Hist:* Volcae.

vole [vɔl], *s.f.* (*in some card games*) vole, all the tricks; slam; **faire la v.**, to vole; to make a slam.

volée [vɔle], *s.f.* **1.** (*a*) flight (of bird, projectile, etc.); **prendre sa v.**, (*of small birds*) to take wing; to leave the nest; **tirer à toute v.**, to fire (a gun) (i) at maximum elevation, (ii) at random; **lancer qch., à toute v.**, to send sth. flying, to hurl sth.; *Cr:* **balle à pleine v.**, full-pitched ball; full toss; *Fb:* **coup de v.**, punt; **signifier un arrêt de v.**, to make a mark; *Ten:* **reprendre une balle de v.**, **relancer une balle à la v.**, to volley a return; **v. haute**, smash; **v. basse**, low volley; **v. amortie**, stop volley; drop volley; **prendre une balle entre bond et v.**, to half-volley a ball; **de bond ou de v.**, somehow or other; (*b*) *adv.phr.* **à la volée:** (i) flying, in the air; **tirer un oiseau à la v.**, to shoot a bird on the wing; **saisir une allusion à la v.**, to catch an allusion promptly, instantly; *Agr:* **semer à la v.**, to broadcast; (ii) at random, without thinking; **il nous a lâché cela à la v.**, he blurted it out; (*computers*) **imprimante à la v.**, hit-on-the-fly, on-the-fly, printer. **2.** (*a*) flock, flight (of crows, sparrows, etc.); covey (of partridges); bevy (of quails, larks); brood (of pigeons); band, company (of students, etc.); bevy (of girls, etc.); (*b*) rank, high standing; **une danseuse de la première v.**, a dancer of the first rank; **joueur de la première v.**, crack player, first-class player; **scientifique de première v.**, top-flight scientist. **3.** (*a*) volley (of missiles); (*b*) **v. de coups de bâton**, shower of blows; **une v. de coups de canne**, a caning, a thrashing; **recevoir une bonne v.**, to get a sound thrashing; (*c*) **v. de cloches**, full peal of bells; **sonner à toute v.**, (i) to set all the bells ringing; (ii) (*of bells*) to ring a full peal, to be in full peal. **4.** (*a*) revolution (of sails of windmill); **les ailes du moulin tournent à toute v.**, the sails of the mill revolve merrily; (*b*) *Mch:* throw (of piston); (*c*) *Metall:* rise (of steam hammer). **5.** *Const:* **v. d'escalier**, flight of stairs. **6.** (*a*) splinter-bar, trace-block, swingle-tree (of vehicle); (*b*) **cheval de v.**, leader, lead horse. **7.** jib (of crane); **transborder la charge par la v.**, to luff the load. **8.** chase (of gun). **9. cuisson des briques à la v.**, clamp firing (of bricks).

voler[1] [vɔle]. **1.** *v.i.* to fly; (*a*) **v. bas**, to fly low; **v. de ses propres ailes**, to fend for oneself; to find one's feet; **on aurait entendu v. une mouche**, you could have heard a pin drop; **le vent fait v. les feuilles**, the wind whirls the leaves about; **v. en éclats**, to shiver, to fly into pieces; to burst in pieces; **faire v. un cerf-volant**, to fly a kite; *F:* **faire v. la tête de qn**, to strike off s.o.'s head; **il fit v. l'assiette par la fenêtre**, he sent the plate flying out of the window; (*b*) *Av:* to fly; **je n'ai pas encore volé**, I haven't flown yet; **v. la tête en bas**, to fly upside down; (*c*) (*of the mind*) to soar; (*d*) to travel fast; to move with speed; **le temps vole**, time flies; **v. aux armes**, to fly, spring, to arms; **il vola revoir ses amis**, he rushed back, sped back, to his friends; **faire v. une nouvelle**, to spread a piece of news. **2.** *v.tr.* (*a*) (*of hawk, etc.*) to chase, to fly at (the quarry); (*b*) to fly (a hawk, etc.).

voler[2], *v.tr.* **1.** to steal (money, etc.); **v. un titre**, to usurp a title; **v. qch. à qn**, to steal sth. from s.o.; to rob s.o. of sth.; **on lui a volé sa montre**, he has been robbed of his watch; **la lettre avait été volée dans la sacoche**, the letter had been abstracted, taken, from the bag; **v. de l'argent dans la caisse**, to steal money from the till; *Sp: etc:* **v. le départ**, to jump the gun; *F:* **il ne l'a pas volé**, he richly deserves it; it serves him right. **2.** (*a*) to rob (s.o.), to steal from (s.o.); *abs.* **v. sur les grands chemins**, to commit highway robbery; (*b*) *F:* to swindle, cheat, do (s.o.); **on m'a volé, je me suis fait v., je suis volé**, I've been had.

volerie[1] [vɔlri], *s.f.* hawking; flying (of hawks); **haute v.**, flying of long-winged hawks, of hawks of the lure, of noble hawks; **basse v.**, flying of short-winged hawks, of hawks of the fist, of ignoble hawks.

volerie[2], *s.f. F:* thieving, robbery.

volet [vɔlɛ], *s.m.* **1.** (*a*) sorting board (for seeds, etc.); *F:* **trié sur le v.**, hand-picked; (*b*) float-board, paddle (of water wheel); (*c*) **v. de plate-forme**, chess (of pontoon bridge). **2.** (*a*) (i) inside shutter (of window); (ii) (= CONTREVENT) outside shutter; (iii) shop shutter; **volets roulants**, rolling shutters; **ouvrir, fermer, les volets**, to open, close, the shutters; **mettre les volets**, to put up the shutters; **enlever les volets**, to take down the shutters; **volets d'un triptyque**, volets of a triptych; (*b*) *Phot:* shutter (of plate holder); **v. à charnière**, hinged back (of printing frame); *Aut:* **volets thermo-régulateurs, volets thermiques**, radiator shutters; **radiateur à volets**, shuttered radiator; (*c*) *I.C.E:* throttle valve, butterfly valve (of carburettor); (*d*) *A:* (i) trap door (of dovecot, pigeon-house); (ii) dovecot, pigeon house; (iii) ledge (of dovecot); (*e*) *El:* **indicateur à volets**, drop indicator (of annunciator board, etc.); *Tp:* **v. d'appel**, call indicator, disc, drop; **v. de fin de conversation**, ring-off indicator; (*f*) (*computers*) **carte à v.**, stub card; (*g*) *Av:* flap; trimming tab; **v. d'atterrissage**, wing flap; **v. de courbure**, camber-changing flap; **v. d'intrados**, split flap; **v. hypersustentateur**, high-lift flap; **v. sorti, v. ouvert**, flap down, extended flap; **sortir les volets**, to lower flaps; **v. rentré**, flap raised, flap up, retraced flap; **rentrer les volets**, to raise flaps; **braquer les volets de décollage de 20°**, to set the take-off flaps at 20°; **indicateur de position des volets**, flap (position) indicator; *Ph:* **volets aérodynamiques**, aerodynamic surfaces; (*h*) *Mec.E: etc:* **v. de ventilation**, air louvre. **3.** *Ecc:* chalice cover. **4.** *A:* boat compass. **5.** *Bot: F:* **v. des étangs**, water lily.

volètement [vɔlɛtmɑ̃], *s.m.* = VOLETTEMENT.

voleter [vɔlte], *v.i.* (**il volette; il voletera**) (*a*) (*of young bird*) to flutter; (*b*) (*of bird*) **v. d'arbre en arbre**, to flit from tree to tree; (*c*) **v. de sujet en sujet**, to skip from subject to subject.

volette [vɔlɛt], *s.f.* **1.** *Agr:* wattle (for draining cheese, for picking wool); *Cu:* pastry stand. **2.** fly net (for horses).

volettement [vɔlɛtmɑ̃], *s.m.* (*a*) fluttering, flutter (of wings, of flag); (*b*) flitting (hither and thither).

voleur[1] [vɔlœːr], *Ven:* **1.** *a.* **faucon haut v.**, high-flying, noble hawk; **faucon bas v.**, low-flying, ignoble, hawk. **2.** *s.m.* **haut, bas, v.**, high, low, flier.

voleur[2], **-euse** [vɔlœːr, -øːz]. **1.** *s.* (*a*) thief; robber; burglar; **v. de grand(s) chemin(s)**, footpad, highwayman; **v. à la tire**, pickpocket; **v. à l'américaine**, confidence trickster, *F:* con man; **v., voleuse, à l'étalage**, shoplifter; **v. d'enfants**, kidnapper; (*in Austr.*) **v. des bois, de la brousse**, bush ranger; **au v.!** stop thief! *F:* **ce commerçant est un v.**, this shopkeeper cheats you left and right, is a daylight robber; *F:* **être fait comme un v.**, (i) *A:* to look like a tramp; (ii) to be caught out; (*b*) stealer (of sth. specified); **v. d'idées**, stealer of ideas; **v. de moutons**, sheep stealer. **2.** *a.* thieving, thievish (gipsy, etc.); fleecing, rapacious (tradesman, etc.); pilfering (child).

Volhynie [vɔlini], *Pr.n.f. Geog:* Volhynia.

volhynien, -ienne [vɔlinjɛ̃, -jɛn], *a. & s. Geog:* Volhynian.

volière [vɔljɛːr], *s.f.* (*a*) aviary; (large) birdcage; (*b*) pigeon run; pheasant mew; (*c*) *P:* brothel.

volige [vɔliːʒ], *s.f. Const:* (*a*) scantling, batten; **caisse en voliges**, crate; (*b*) slate lath, roofing strip.

voligeage [vɔliʒaːʒ], *s.m. Const:* (*a*) battening; (*b*) lathing.

voliger [vɔliʒe], *v.tr.* (**je voligeai(s); n. voligeons**) *Const:* (*a*) to batten; (*b*) to lath.

volis [vɔli], *s.m. For:* (*a*) windbreak; (*b*) broken tree top.

volitif, -ive [vɔlitif, -iːv], *a.* volitional, volitive.

volition [vɔlisjɔ̃], *s.f.* volition.

volitionnel, -elle [vɔlisjɔnɛl], *a.* volitional.

volley-ball [vɔlɛbɔl], *s.m. Sp:* volley ball.

volleyeur, -euse [vɔlɛjœːr, -øːz], *s.* **1.** volley-ball player. **2.** *Ten:* volleyer.

volnaisien, -ienne [vɔlnezjɛ̃, -jɛn], *a. & s. Geog:* (native, inhabitant) of Volnay.

volnay [vɔlnɛ], *s.m.* Volnay (wine).

volontaire [vɔlɔ̃tɛːr], *a.* **1.** voluntary; (*a*) **acte v.**, voluntary act, spontaneous act; **homicide v.**, voluntary homicide; **mutilation v.**, self-mutilation; *Mil:* **engagé v.**, voluntarily enlisted man; volunteer; (*b*) *Anat:* **muscle v.**, voluntary muscle. **2.** self-willed, wilful, wayward, headstrong, obstinate; **menton v.**, firm, determined, chin; **il est v.**, he has a will of his own. **3.** *s.m. Mil:* volunteer; **en v.**, as a volunteer; **s'engager comme v.**, to enlist.

volontairement [vɔlɔ̃tɛrmɑ̃], *adv.* **1.** voluntarily, spontaneously, willingly; **se proposer v. pour faire qch.**, to volunteer to do sth. **2.** deliberately, intentionally.

volontariat [vɔlɔ̃tarja], *s.m. Mil: A:* period of service shortened to one year in consideration of a monetary payment; voluntariate.

volontarisme [vɔlɔ̃tarism], *s.m. Phil:* voluntarism.

volontariste [vɔlɔ̃tarist], *a. & s.m. & f. Phil:* voluntarist.

volonté [vɔlɔ̃te], *s.f.* **1.** will; (*a*) **la v. de vaincre**, the will to victory; **v. de fer**, will of iron, iron will; **femme de forte v.**, strong-willed woman; **cause indépendante de la v. de qn**, cause beyond s.o.'s control; **par un effort de la v.**, by an effort of will; **faire appel à toute sa v.**, to exercise all one's willpower; **manque de v.**, lack of will; **ne pas avoir de v.**, to have no will of one's own; **la grande v. des troupes**, the high morale of the troops; the great spirit of the troops; **avec la meilleure v. du monde**, with the best will in the world; (*b*) **bonne v.**, goodwill; willingness; **mauvaise v.**, ill will; unwillingness; **montrer, faire preuve, de bonne, de mauvaise, v.**, to do sth. willingly, unwillingly; to do sth. with a good, a bad, grace; *F:* **il montre toujours de la bonne v.**, he always shows willing; **travailler de bonne v.**, to work with a will; **faire qch. de bonne v.**, (i) to do sth. of one's own free will, spontaneously; to volunteer to do sth.; (ii) to do sth. with a good grace; **homme de bonne v.**, volunteer (for dangerous enterprise, etc.); *Prov:* **à bonne v. ne faut faculté**, where there's a will there's a way; (*c*) *Ecc:* **que ta v. soit faite**, Thy will be done; *A:* **telle est la v. du roi**, the King wills it so; **suivre sa v.; en faire à sa v.**, to have one's own way; **il n'en fait qu'à sa v.**, he will not listen to reason; *adj. & adv.phr.* **à v.**, at will, at pleasure; ad lib; (*in restaurant*) **vin à v.** = drink as much wine as you like; **changer de visage à v.**, to change one's face at will; **billet payable à v.**, promissory note payable on demand; *A:* **voiture à v.**, carriage for hire; *Mil:* **feu à v.**, independent firing; fire at will; **armes à v.**, marching easy; **de sa propre v.**, of one's own accord; spontaneously; **agir contre, à l'encontre de, la v. de qn**, to act against s.o.'s wishes. **2.** (*a*) **acte de dernière v. (de qn), les dernières volontés (de qn)**, (s.o.'s) last will and testament; **ses dernières volontés**, his last wishes; (*b*) *pl.* whims, caprices; **elle fait ses quatre volontés**, she does just what she pleases; **il faut faire ses quatre volontés**, his every whim must be satisfied; **elle lui fait faire ses quatre volontés**, she makes him do everything she wants; she can twist him round her little finger.

volontiers [vɔlɔ̃tje], *adv.* (*a*) willingly, gladly, with pleasure; **très v.**, I'd love to; **il le fera v.**, he will be very pleased to do it; he won't mind doing it; **il consentit v.**, he readily consented; **je serais v. un père pour vos enfants**, I should like to be a father to your children; **je prendrais v. un verre de vin**, I could do with a glass of wine; **il cause, plaisante, v.**, he is fond of talking, of a joke; (*b*) easily, readily; **on croit v. que . . .**, we are apt to think that . . .; **le goût de ces oiseaux rappelle v. celui du poisson**, the taste of these birds rather recalls that of fish.

volsque [vɔlsk], *a. & s. A.Hist:* Volscian.

volt [vɔlt], *s.m. El.Meas:* volt.

voltage [vɔltaːʒ], *s.m. El:* voltage; **v. nul**, zero voltage.

voltaïque [vɔltaik], *a. El:* voltaic (cell, pile).

voltaire [vɔltɛːr], *s.m. A.Furn:* (**fauteuil**) **v.**, Voltaire (arm)chair (with low seat and high back).

voltairianisme [vɔltɛrjanism], *s.m.* Voltair(ian)-ism; *esp.* sceptical attitude towards religion.

voltairien, -ienne [vɔltɛrjɛ̃, -jɛn], *a. & s.* Voltairian.

voltaïte [vɔltait], *s.f. Miner:* voltaite.

voltamètre [vɔltamɛtr̥], *s.m. El:* voltameter.

voltampère [vɔltɑ̃pɛːr], *s.m. El.Meas:* voltampere; watt.

voltampèremètre [vɔltɑ̃pɛrmɛtr̥], *s.m.* wattmeter, voltammeter.

volte [vɔlt], *s.f.* 1. (*a*) *Equit: Fenc:* volt; (*b*) = VOLTE-FACE; (*c*) *Nau:* turn (to alter course). 2. *Gym:* **(exercices de) v.**, vaulting.

volte-face [vɔltəfas], *s.f.inv.* 1. turning round; volte-face; *A:* right-about turn, face; **faire v.-f.**, to volt-face, to face about; to turn right about (to meet pursuing enemy, etc.); *Pol: etc:* to reverse one's opinions, one's policy; to change sides; **des v.-f. de conduite**, complete changes of front, of policy. 2. (*bayonet fencing*) double turn-about re-establishing position two paces back.

volter [vɔlte], *v.i.* (*a*) *Fenc:* to make a volt; (*b*) *Equit:* **faire v. un cheval**, to make a horse circle; (*c*) *Nau:* to turn (to alter course).

voltige [vɔltiːʒ], *s.f.* 1. *Equit:* mounted gymnastics; **haute v.**, trick riding, balancing tricks; **saut en v.**, flying leap into the saddle. 2. (*a*) slack rope, leaping rope; (*b*) slack-rope gymnastics; leaping rope exercises; (*c*) flying-trapeze exercises; (*d*) *Av:* aerobatics; **pilote de v.**, stunt pilot; **école de v.**, stunt-flying school.

voltigeant [vɔltiʒɑ̃], *a.* fluttering (bird, insect).

voltigement [vɔltiʒmɑ̃], *s.m.* fluttering, flitting (of bird, insect); *A:* flapping (of curtain, etc.).

voltiger [vɔltiʒe], *v.i.* (**je voltigeai(s); n. voltigeons**) 1. *Equit: Gym: etc:* to perform on horseback, on the slack rope, on the flying trapeze; **il l'envoya v. en l'air**, he tossed him well up into the air. 2. (*of bird, insect*) to fly about; to flit, to hover; (*of curtain, flag, etc.*) to flutter, flap; **v. de fleur en fleur**, to flit from flower to flower; **parfois une fine ironie voltige à travers son récit**, at times a subtle irony streaks his narrative.

voltigeur, -euse [vɔltiʒœːr, -øːz], *s.* 1. *Equit: Gym:* performer on horseback, on the slack rope, on the flying trapeze. 2. *s.m. Mil: A:* light infantryman; rifleman. 3. *s.m. R.t.m:* kind of cigar. 4. *s.m. Z: F:* flying phalanger; *Austr:* flying squirrel.

voltinisme [vɔltinism], *s.m. Ent:* voltinism.

voltmètre [vɔltmɛtr̥], *s.m. El:* voltmeter; **v. thermique, à fil chaud**, hot-wire voltmeter; **v. apériodique**, dead-beat voltmeter; **v. enregistreur**, voltage recorder; **v. à cadre mobile**, galvanometer; **v. à lampe**, vacuum-tube voltmeter.

voltzine [vɔltzin], *s.f.*, **voltzite** [vɔltzit], *s.f. Miner:* voltzine, voltzite.

volubile [vɔlybil], *a.* (*a*) *Bot:* voluble, volubile, volubilate, twining (stalk); (*b*) (*of pers.*) voluble.

volubilis [vɔlybilis], *s.m. Bot:* convolvulus; **v. des jardins**, morning glory.

volubilisme [vɔlybilism], *s.m. Bot:* twining property of (plants).

volubilité [vɔlybilite], *s.f.* volubility; **parler avec v.**, to be a voluble talker, to talk volubly, glibly.

volucelle [vɔlysɛl], *s.m. Ent:* volucella; syrphid fly, syrphus fly, flower fly.

volucompteur [vɔlykɔ̃tœːr], *s.m. Tchn:* petrol pump indicator.

volue [vɔly], *s.f. Tex:* bobbin (of shuttle).

volume [vɔlym], *s.m.* 1. volume, tome; **ouvrage en six volumes**, work in six volumes; six volume(d) work; **il faudrait des volumes pour raconter . . .**, it would take volumes to relate . . .. 2. (*a*) volume, bulk, mass (of solid or fluid); **densités à v. égal**, densities for equal volumes; **le v. excessif de ces paquets**, the bulkiness of these parcels; *Nau:* **chargé en v.**, laden in bulk; *F:* **faire du v.**, to swank; to throw one's weight about; (*b*) volume (of sound, of the voice) *W.Tel: etc:* **diminuer, baisser, le v.**, to turn down the volume, **augmenter le v.**, to turn up the volume; (*c*) capacity (of bunkers, etc.).

voluménomètre [vɔlymenɔmɛtr̥], *s.m. Ph:* volumenometer.

volumètre [vɔlymɛtr̥], *s.m. Ph:* volumeter.

volumétrie [vɔlymetri], *s.f.* volumetry.

volumétrique [vɔlymetrik], *a.* volumetric(al); **pompe v.**, displacement meter.

volumétriquement [vɔlymetrikmɑ̃], *adv.* volumetrically.

volumineux, -euse [vɔlyminø, -øːz], *a.* 1. voluminous, bulky, large; **colis v.**, bulky parcel. 2. voluminous (writer); (author) of many volumes.

volumique [vɔlymik], *a. Ph:* voluminal (mass).

Volumnia [vɔlymnja], **Volumnie** [vɔlymni], *Pr.n.f. Rom.Hist:* Volumnia.

volupté [vɔlypte], *s.f.* (sensual) pleasure, delight; **toutes les voluptés**, every pleasurable sensation; **faire qch. avec v.**, to revel in, to take a sensual pleasure in, doing sth.

voluptuaire [vɔlyptɥɛːr], *a. Jur:* (*of expenses*) for embellishment; **améliorations voluptuaires**, embellishments.

voluptueusement [vɔlyptɥøzmɑ̃], *adv.* voluptuously.

voluptueux, -euse [vɔlyptɥø, -øːz]. 1. *a.* voluptuous. 2. *s.* voluptuary, sensualist.

voluptuosité [vɔlyptɥozite], *s.f.* voluptuousness.

volute [vɔlyt], *s.f.* (*a*) *Arch: etc:* volute, helix, scroll; **v. d'un violon**, scroll of a violin; **ressort en v.**, volute spring; helical spring; **v. d'une lame**, curl of a wave; **v. de fumée**, spiral curl of smoke; twirl, wreath, of smoke; (*b*) *Conch:* volute, whorl; (*c*) *Moll:* volute; (*genus*) Voluta; (*d*) *Mec.E: etc:* **v. d'admission**, inlet casing, volute; **v. de refoulement**, delivery, outlet, volute, casing (of a pump).

voluté [vɔlyte], *a. Arch: etc:* voluted, volute; scrolled; whorled.

volutidés [vɔlytide], *s.m.pl. Moll:* Volutidae.

volva [vɔlva], *s.f.*, **volve** [vɔlv], *s.f. Fung:* volva.

volvation [vɔlvasjɔ̃], *s.f. Z:* rolling into a ball (of hedgehog, etc.).

volvé [vɔlve], *a. Fung:* volvate.

volvocacées [vɔlvɔkase], *s.f.pl. Algae:* Volvocaceae.

volvocales [vɔlvɔkal], *s.f.pl. Algae:* Volvocales.

volvoce [vɔlvɔs], **volvox** [vɔlvɔks], *s.m. Prot:* volvox; **v. globuleux**, globe animalcule.

volvocidés [vɔlvɔside], *s.m.pl. Prot:* Volvocidae.

volvulose [vɔlvyloːz], *s.f. Med:* onchocercosis.

volvulus [vɔlvylys], *s.m. Med:* volvulus.

vombat [vɔ̃ba], *s.m. Z:* wombat.

vombatidés [vɔ̃batide], *s.m.pl. Z:* Vombatidae, the wombats.

vomer [vɔmɛːr], *s.m.* 1. *Anat:* vomer; ploughshare bone. 2. *Ich:* moonfish.

vomérien, -ienne [vɔmerjɛ̃, -jɛn], *a. Anat:* vomerine.

vomi [vɔmi], *s.m.* vomit; **sentir le v.**, to smell of vomit.

vomicine [vɔmisin], *s.f. Ch:* vomicine.

vomi-purgatif, -ive [vɔmipyrgatif, -iːv], *a. & s.m. Med:* emetocathartic (drug, etc.); *pl. vomi-purgatifs, -ives.*

vomique [vɔmik]. 1. *a. Bot: Pharm:* **noix v.**, nux vomica, vomit nut. 2. *s.f. Med:* vomica (abscess cavity or expectorated pus).

vomiquier [vɔmikje], *s.m. Bot:* nux vomica tree.

vomir [vɔmiːr], *v.tr.* (*a*) to vomit; to bring up, spew up (food); *abs.* to vomit, to be sick; **v. du sang**, to vomit blood; **envie de v.**, squeamish feeling; nausea; **avoir, se sentir, envie de v.**, to feel sick; *P:* **v. tripes et boyaux**, to be dreadfully sick; **faire des efforts pour v.**, to retch, to heave; **effort pour v.**, heave (of the stomach); **c'est à (faire) v.**, it's enough to make one sick; it's disgusting; (*b*) (*of chimney, volcano, etc.*) to vomit, belch (smoke, flames, etc.); **v. feu et flamme contre qn**, to make fiery, impassioned, speeches against s.o.

vomissement [vɔmismɑ̃], *s.m.* 1. vomiting; *Tchn:* vomition; **il fut pris de vomissements**, he began to vomit, to be sick. 2. vomit; *B:* **le chien retourne à son v.**, the dog returneth to his vomit.

vomisseur, -euse [vɔmisœːr, -øːz], *s.* vomiter.

vomissure [vɔmisyːr], *s.f.* vomit.

vomitif, -ive [vɔmitif, -iːv], *a. & s.m. Med:* emetic; vomitory; vomitive.

vomitoire [vɔmitwaːr]. 1. *s.m. Rom.Ant:* vomitorium; vomitory. 2. *a. & s.m. A:* = VOMITIF.

vomito (negro) [vɔmito(negro)], *s.m. Med:* vomito (negro), true yellow fever, black vomit.

vomiturition [vɔmityrisjɔ̃], *s.f. Med:* vomiturition.

voquer [vɔke], *v.tr.* to knead, pug (clay).

vorace [vɔras], *a.* voracious (animal, appetite, reader); ravenous (animal, pers.); (plant) that exhausts the soil.

voracement [vɔrasmɑ̃], *adv.* voraciously.

voracer [vɔrase], *v.tr. P:* to steal, pinch, knock off.

voracité [vɔrasite], *s.f.* voracity, voraciousness; **avec v.**, voraciously.

voran [vɔrɑ̃], *s.m. Ann: F:* horse leech.

vorge [vɔrʒ], *s.f. Bot: F:* darnel, cockle.

vorgine [vɔrʒin], *s.f. Agr:* area infested with cockle.

vortex [vɔrtɛks], *s.m.* 1. *Ph: Meteor: etc:* vortex. 2. *Ann:* vortex.

vorticelle [vɔrtisɛl], *s.f. Prot:* vorticel(la), vorticellid, bell animalcule.

vorticellidés [vɔrtisɛlide], *s.m.pl.* Vorticellidae.

vorticisme [vɔrtisism], *s.m. Art:* vorticism.

vorticiste [vɔrtisist], *s.m. & f. Art:* vorticist.

Vosges (les) [levoːʒ], *Pr.n.f.pl. Geog:* The Vosges (Mountains).

vosgien, -ienne [voʒjɛ̃, -jɛn], *a. & s.* Vosgian, Vosgean; (native, inhabitant) of the Vosges (Mountains, Department).

votant, -ante [vɔtɑ̃, -ɑ̃ːt]. 1. *a.* having a vote; voting (assembly, member). 2. *s.* voter; **liste des votants**, (parliamentary) register.

votation [vɔtasjɔ̃], *s.f.* voting; **mode de v.**, manner of voting; **v. par tête**, poll; *Sw.Fr:* **v. populaire**, referendum.

vote [vɔt], *s.m.* 1. (*a*) vote; (*b*) voting, ballot(ing), poll; **droit de v.**, franchise; **accorder le droit de v. aux femmes**, to enfranchise women, to give women the vote; **prendre part au v.**, to go to the poll; to vote; **participation au v.**, voting; **v. au scrutin secret**, ballot; **donner son v. à qch.**, to vote for sth.; **déclarer le résultat du v.**, to declare the poll, the result of the voting; **bulletin de v.**, voting paper, ballot paper; **section de v.**, polling district, station. 2. *Pol:* (*a*) **v. d'une loi**, passing of a bill; **loi en cours de v.**, bill before the House; (*b*) **provoquer un v.**, to challenge a division; (*c*) **v. de confiance**, vote of confidence; **se voir accorder un v. de confiance**, to receive a vote of confidence; (*d*) result of the voting; decision; **le v. est pour, contre**, the ayes, the noes, have it.

voter [vɔte]. 1. *v.i.* to vote; (*in Parliament*) to come to a division; to divide; **v. par appel nominatif**, to take a vote by calling over the names of the members; **v. à main levée**, to vote by (a) show of hands; **v. blanc**, to return a blank voting paper; **v. pour, contre, un projet de loi**, to vote for, against, a bill; **v. communiste**, to vote communist; **v. Thomas!** vote for Thomas! 2. *v.tr.* (*a*) to pass, carry (a bill); **si le projet de loi est voté**, if the bill passes; (*b*) to vote (money, etc.); **v. des remerciements à qn**, to pass a vote of thanks to s.o.; **v. 100.000 fr. pour les sinistrés**, to vote 100,000 fr. for the victims of the disaster.

voteur, -euse [vɔtœːr, -øːz], *a.* voting, having the right to vote.

votif, -ive [vɔtif, -iːv], *a.* votive (offering, mass).

votre, *pl.* **vos** [vɔtr̥, vo], *poss.a.* (*may refer to one pers. or several*) your; **v. fils et v. fille**, your son and (your) daughter; **un de vos amis**, a friend of yours; **à v. santé, Philippe!** your health, Philip! **c'est v. affaire à vous**, that's your business; **vos père et mère**, your father and mother; **il est v. meilleur ami**, he is your best friend; **c'est v. livre le plus récent?** is this your latest book?

vôtre [voːtr̥], (*may refer to one pers. or several*) 1. *occ. poss.a.* yours; **je suis tout v.**, I am entirely at your service; **nous tenons ces sentiments comme vôtres**, we take it that these are your feelings. 2. **le v., la v., les vôtres**; (*a*) *poss.pron.* yours, your own; **sa mère et la v.**, his mother and yours; **mes enfants ressemblent plutôt aux vôtres**, my children are more like yours; *Com: A:* **j'ai reçu la v. du 6 mai**, I am in receipt of yours of May the 6th; *P:* **à la v.!** cheers! *A. & Lit:* **quelle audace est la v.!** what audacity on your part! (*as letter ending*) *A:* **je suis bien le v.**, yours ever; (*b*) *s.m.* (i) your own (property, etc.); **il faut y mettre du v.**, you must put some of your own energy into it; you must do your share; (ii) *pl.* your own (friends, etc.); your own folk; **je bois à vous et aux vôtres**, I drink to you and yours; **je suis des vôtres**, I'm on your side, with you; **je serai des vôtres ce soir**, (α) I'll join you, your party, (β) I'll be thinking of you, tonight; (iii) *F:* **vous avez encore fait des vôtres**, you've been up to some of your tricks again.

vouède [vɥɛd], *s.f. Bot: F:* woad.

vouer [vwe], *v.tr.* to vow, dedicate, consecrate; **v. un temple à un dieu**, to vow, dedicate, a temple to a god; **v. une enfant au blanc et au bleu**, to dedicate a child to wear white and blue (in honour of the Virgin); **v. obéissance au roi**, to pledge one's allegiance to the king; **v. à qn une haine implacable**, to vow an implacable hatred to s.o.; **v. sa plume à la vérité**, to dedicate one's pen to the truth; **se v. au service de Dieu, des pauvres**, to dedicate one's life to the service of God, of the poor; **se v. au culte des Muses**, to devote oneself to the Muses; **v. sa vie, se v., à l'étude**, to devote, give up, one's life to study; *F:* **il ne sait (pas) à quel saint se v.**, he is at his wits' end, he doesn't know which way to turn; **poème voué à l'oubli**, poem doomed to oblivion, deservedly forgotten; **petites gens voués à un individualisme étroit**, petty people wrapped in narrow individualism.

vouge [vuːʒ], *s.m.* 1. *A.Mil:* vouge, voulge. 2. *Agr:* billhook. 3. *Ven:* boar spear.

vougier [vuʒje], *s.m. A.Mil:* soldier armed with a vouge.

voui [vwi], *adv.* (*as an idiosyncrasy of some people, also Dial: & Hum:*) (= OUI) yes; well . . . yes (I suppose so).

vouivre [vuivr̥], *s.f. Her:* serpent vorant a child.

vouloir [vulwaːr]. I. *v.tr.* (*pr.p.* **voulant**; *p.p.* **voulu**; *pr.ind.* **je veux, il veut, n. voulons, ils veulent**; *pr.sub.* **je veuille, n. voulions, ils veuillent**; *imp.* **veuille, veuillez,** *in* **1.** only **voulez**; *p.d.* **je voulais**; *p.h.* **je voulus**; *fu.* **je voudrai**) **1.** to will (sth.); to be determined on (sth.); **ceux qui ont voulu la guerre,** those who willed the war; **ceux qui voulaient la guerre,** those who wanted war; **le fait d'avoir voulu un crime est aussi coupable que de l'avoir exécuté,** willing a crime is as culpable as committing it; **je veux un succès complet,** I must have complete success; **ce que Dieu veut,** the will of God; **Dieu le veuille!** please God! **homme qui ne sait pas v.,** man who has no will-power, who cannot make up his mind; *Prov:* **v., c'est pouvoir,** where there's a will there's a way; **voulez et vous pourrez,** if you want to do it, you can; **il ne faut que v.,** the will is everything; **vous l'avez voulu!** you have only yourself to blame! **2.** (*a*) to want, to wish (for), to desire (sth.); **il sait ce qu'il veut,** he knows what he wants, he knows his own mind; he has a will of his own; **il ne sait pas ce qu'il veut,** he doesn't know his own mind; **faites comme vous voudrez,** do as you please; **c'est comme vous voudrez,** just as you like; as you choose, as you please; **vous le ferez, je le veux!** you *shall* do it; **qu'il le veuille ou non,** whether he chooses or not; willy-nilly; **je ne le veux pas!** I will not have it! **que voulez-vous? qu'est-ce que vous voulez?** what do you want? **que voulez-vous que j'y fasse?** how can I help it? **que voulez-vous! j'ai fait de mon mieux,** sorry! I did my best; **que voulez-vous!** well, what do, did, you expect? **que voudriez-vous de plus?** what more can you wish for? **est-ce tout ce que vous voulez?** is that all you want? **tant que vous voudrez,** as much as you like; **v. qch. de qn,** to want sth. from s.o.; **que voulez-vous de moi?** what do you want from me? what do you want of me? **que lui voulez-vous?** what is your business with him? what do you want of him? **quel prix voulez-vous de votre maison?** what price do you want for your house? **combien en voulez-vous?** how much are you asking for it? **prenez un verre de bière; ou voulez-vous du thé?** have a glass of beer; or would you like tea? would you prefer tea? (*partitive construction*) **v. de qch.,** to want (some of) sth.; **voulez-vous de ma compagnie?** would you like my company? shall I stay (or go) with you? **je ne veux point d'un trône,** I do not want a throne; **je ne veux pas de cela,** I'll have none of that; **ils ne veulent pas de moi,** they won't have me; **en voulez-vous?** do you want any? will you have some? would you like some? *adv.phr.* **en veux-tu, en voilà,** as much as you like; **il a de l'argent en veux-tu,** he has money galore; **s'embrasser à bouche que veux-tu,** to kiss passionately; *O:* **il y en avait à bouche que veux-tu,** there was any amount; there was enough and to spare; (*b*) **v. qn pour roi,** to want s.o. for a king, as king; **voulez-vous de moi pour compagnon?** would you like me to go with you? **je vous voudrais plus attentif,** I wish you were more attentive; **je te veux heureuse,** I want you to be happy; (*c*) **s'il avait le courage que je lui voudrais,** if he had the courage I should like to see in him; **v. du bien, du mal, à qn,** to wish s.o. well, harm; **je ne lui veux pas de mal,** I mean him no harm; do not intend him any harm; **en v. à qn,** (i) to bear s.o. a grudge; (ii) *A:* to have designs on s.o.; **ne m'en veuillez pas,** don't be cross with me; **en v. à qn de qch., d'avoir fait qch.,** to owe s.o. a grudge for sth., for doing sth.; **à qui en voulez-vous?** what's the trouble now? **s'en v.,** to be angry, annoyed, with oneself; **il s'en voulait de sa stupidité,** he could have kicked himself for being so stupid; **je m'en veux de ne pas être venu,** I'm furious, angry, with myself for not coming; **il m'en veut à mort,** he's furious, mad, with me; **je crois qu'il en veut à mon argent, à ma fille,** I think he has designs on, is after, my money, my daughter. **3. vouloir** + *inf.* (expressed or understood); **v. que** + *sub.:* (*a*) to will, to require, to demand; **si Dieu veut que je meure,** if God wills that I should die; **le sort voulut qu'il mourût,** fate willed (it) that he should die; **le mauvais sort voulut qu'il arrivât trop tard,** as ill luck would have it he arrived too late; **je veux être obéi,** I intend, mean, to be obeyed; **je veux que vous m'obéissiez,** you are going to obey me; I insist on being obeyed; I will be obeyed; **je veux réussir,** I mean to succeed; **v. absolument, à toute force, faire qch.,** to insist upon doing sth.; to be determined to do sth.; **je veux absolument que vous veniez,** I insist on your coming; **il voulut à toute force me faire entrer,** he would have me come in; **il voulut être payé sur le champ,** he insisted on being paid immediately; **la simple prudence veut que . . .,** elementary prudence demands that . . .; **je veux que cela soit,** I wish it to be so; **le moteur ne veut pas démarrer,** the engine won't start; **comment voulez-vous qu'ils comprennent?** how do you expect them to understand? how should they understand? (*b*) to want, wish; **il voulait me frapper,** he wanted to hit me; **si le Danemark veut rester le premier producteur de . . .,** if Denmark is to remain the leading producer of . . .; **il ne voulait pas s'en aller,** he didn't want to go; **je fais de lui ce que je veux,** I can do as I like with him, I can twist him round my little finger; **j'aurais tant voulu le voir,** I should so much like to have seen him; **j'aurais voulu y rester toujours,** I would, could, have stayed there for ever; **il aurait voulu être mort,** he wished himself dead; **j'aurais bien voulu rester à la maison,** I would rather have stayed at home; **je voudrais bien être à votre place,** I wish I were in your place; **je voudrais bien vous voir à ma place,** I'd like to see you in my place; **je voudrais (bien) avoir une bague,** I should like to have a ring; I wish I had a ring; **je voudrais vous voir plus attentif,** I wish you were more attentive; **je veux que vous sachiez que . . .,** I will, would, have you know that . . .; **j'aurais voulu qu'il le sache,** I wish he had been told; **je voudrais le voir me parler sur ce ton,** I'd like to see him speaking to me in that tone of voice; **je veux que vous soyez heureux,** I want you to be happy; **que voulez-vous que je fasse?** what would you have me do? what do you expect me to do? **comment voulez-vous que j'agisse?** how would you have me act? **rentrons, voulez-vous?** let's go in, shall we? (*c*) to try to (do sth.); **quand je voulus ouvrir la porte,** when I tried to open the door; **il voulut arrêter le coup,** he made an effort to stop the blow; **il voulut me frapper,** he made as if to strike me; **quand j'ai voulu l'embrasser,** when I tried to kiss her; (*d*) to mean, intend; **nous n'avons jamais su ce qu'il voulait faire,** we never knew what he meant to do; **il fit un geste qui voulait être un refus poli,** he made a gesture that was intended to indicate polite refusal; **il voulait me rendre service,** he meant to do me a service; **je voulais écrire un livre sur ce sujet,** I meant to write a book on the subject; **faire qch. sans le v.,** to do sth. unintentionally, without meaning it; **il ne s'agit pas de vous, je veux parler de Jean,** I am not talking of you, I mean John; (*e*) **v. (bien) faire qch.,** to consent, be willing, to do sth.; **le roi voulut bien accepter,** the king was pleased to accept; **je veux bien que vous veniez,** I'd like you to come; **voulez-vous bien me le donner?** will you kindly, be so kind as to, give it to me? **si vous voulez vous joindre à nous . . .,** if you would care to join us . . .; **voulez-vous bien que je fume une pipe?** do you mind, do you object to, my smoking a pipe? **je vous prie de v. bien** + *inf.*, will you kindly + *inf.*; will you be good enough to + *inf.*; **voulez-vous bien attendre un instant,** would you please wait a moment? **veuillez (bien) vous asseoir,** (i) will you please sit down; (ii) do (please) sit down; won't you sit down? **veuillez bien me dire l'heure,** please tell me the time; **je veux bien attendre,** I am willing to wait; **venez-vous avec nous?—je veux bien,** are you coming with us?—I'd love to; by all means; **je n'ai pas voulu répondre,** I did not choose to answer; **il aurait pu le faire s'il avait voulu,** he could have done it if he had chosen; **si vous voulez,** if you like, if you wish; *Iron:* **il est intelligent—si (l')on veut!** he's clever—I suppose so! **je viens quand je veux,** I come when I choose, when I like, when I please; **si vous (le) voulez bien,** if you don't mind; if you have no objection; **Dieu veuille que . . .,** God send, grant, that . . .; *Com.Corr:* **une liste que nous vous prions de bien v. examiner,** a list for your consideration; (*f*) (**bien** *used as an intensive*) **voulez-vous bien vous taire!** (i) *will* you be quiet! (ii) *F:* do shut up! **veux-tu bien ne pas te pencher dehors, Jean!** John! don't lean out! **4.** (*a*) to admit, allow (sth. for the sake of argument); **je veux bien que vous ayez raison,** you may be right; **je veux qu'il en soit ainsi,** (i) admitting that it is so; (ii) supposing that it is so; **vous n'avez rien à vous reprocher, je le veux bien, mais . . .,** you are in no way to blame, I am ready to admit, but . . .; (*b*) to be convinced, to maintain; **il veut absolument que je me sois trompé, qu'elle soit morte empoisonnée,** he insists that I was mistaken, that she died of poison; (*c*) **la légende veut que** + *ind. or sub.*, legend has it that . . .. **5.** (*of thg*) to require. need, demand (sth.); **la vigne veut un terrain crayeux,** the vine requires a chalky soil; **ce verbe veut l'accusatif,** this verb takes the accusative; **affaire qui veut être conduite avec soin,** matter that needs, wants, careful handling; **l'honneur veut que vous obteniez une réparation,** honour demands that you should obtain satisfaction.

II. **vouloir,** *s.m.* will; (*a*) *A:* **le v. de Dieu,** the will of God; **un homme d'audace et de v.,** an audacious, strong-willed, man; (*b*) **bon, mauvais, v.,** goodwill, ill will (**pour, envers,** towards); (*c*) **faire qch. de son bon v.,** to do sth. of one's own accord.

se vouloir. 1. je ne me voudrais pas à votre place, I shouldn't like to be in your shoes; **il s'était voulu prêtre de campagne,** he had chosen to become a country priest; **son rire se voulait sardonique,** his laugh was meant to be sardonic; **son œuvre se veut historique,** his work claims, professes, to be historical. **2.** *Lit:* **il se voulut, s'est voulu, défendre** (= **il voulut, a voulu, se défendre**), he endeavoured to defend himself.

voulu [vuly], *a.* **1.** required, requisite (formalities, etc.); **couper qch. à la longueur voulue,** to cut sth. to the required length; **cela se fera à l'heure voulue,** it will be done in due time; **j'agirai au moment v., en temps v.,** I shall take action at the proper moment. **2.** deliberate, intentional (action, omission, etc.); **négligence, impertinence, voulue,** studied carelessness, impertinence.

vous [vu], *pers.pron. sg. & pl.* **1.** (*unstressed*) (*a*) (*subject*) you; **v. y allez tout seul?** are you going (all) by yourself? **v. serez punis tous deux,** you shall both be punished; **l'avez-v. vu?** did you see him? *B:* **cherchez et v. trouverez,** seek and ye shall find; (*b*) (*object*) you; (*indirect*) to you; **il ne v. a jamais aimé(s),** he never liked you; **il v. a vus tous les quatre,** he saw all four of you; **il v. en parlera,** he will speak to you about it; **je v. en prêterai,** I will lend you some . . .; *F:* (*ethic dative*) **la mule v. lui détacha un coup de sabot,** the mule let fly a kick at him; (*c*) (*refl.*) **v. v. tuerez si v. ne prenez pas garde,** you will kill yourself, yourselves, if you are not careful; **v. v. êtes donné bien de la peine,** you have given yourself, yourselves, a lot of trouble; **taisez-v.,** be quiet, hold your tongue; (*with many verbs* vous *is not rendered into English: see* S'EN ALLER, SE BATTRE, SE DÉPÊCHER, *etc.*) (*d*) (*reciprocal*) **v. v. connaissez,** you know one another; (*e*) (*as object case of* **on**) **cette joie qui v. saisit quand on rencontre un ami,** the joy you feel when you meet a friend; **la solitude, on dit que ça v. change,** they say that solitude changes a man. **2.** (*stressed*) (*a*) (*subject*) you; **v. deux, v. tous,** you two, the two of you; you all, all of you; **v. et votre femme,** you and your wife; **v. seul êtes à blâmer,** you alone are to blame; **c'est vous qui êtes arrivé(s) le(s) premier(s),** it was you who arrived first; **v. autres Anglais, v. ne nous ressemblez pas,** you English are not like us; **je suis aussi riche que v.,** I am as rich as you (are); **faites-le v.-même,** do it yourself; (*b*) (*complement*) **je compte rester deux jours chez v.,** I hope to spend two days with you; **c'est à v. que je parle,** it's you I'm speaking to; **ces gants sont à v.,** these gloves are yours, belong to you; **c'est un ami à v.,** he is a friend of yours; **c'est à v. de jouer,** it is your turn to play; **de v. à moi il n'est pas si fâché qu'il en a l'air,** between ourselves, he isn't so angry as he pretends; **cela c'est pour v. deux,** that's for you two, for the two of you; **je voudrais v. parler à v. tous,** I should like to speak to you all, to all of you; **je voudrais bien lire qch. de v.,** I should like to read sth. of yours, sth. you have written; **si j'étais que de v.,** if I were in your place, in your shoes.

vous-même(s) [vumɛm], *pers.pron. See* VOUS 2, *and* MÊME 1 (*c*).

voussé [vuse], *a.* vaulted (roof, etc.); arched (entrance, etc.).

vousseau, -eaux [vuso], *s.m.* voussoir, arch stone.

voussoiement [vuswamɑ̃], *s.m.* = VOUVOIEMENT.

voussoir [vuswaːr], *s.m.* voussoir.

voussoyer [vuswaje], *v.tr.* = VOUVOYER.

voussure [vusyːr], *s.f. Arch: Const:* curve, bend (of arch); arching, coving (of ceiling bay, etc.); arch moulding.

voûte [vut], *s.f.* vault, arch; (*a*) *Arch:* vault; vaulting; **v. d'arête,** groined vault; **v. en berceau,** barrel vault; **v. d'ogives,** ribbed vault; **v. en arc de cloître,** domical vault; **v. à plein cintre,** semicircular vault; **v. en anse de panier,** basket-handle vault; **v. surhaussée,** surmounted vault; **v. surbaissée,** surbased vault; **voûte(s) en éventail,** fan vaulting; **v. oblique,** skew arch; **v. maîtresse,** centre arch; **on entre sous une v.,** you go in under an archway; *N.Arch:* **v. d'arcasse, v. arrière,** counter; (*b*) **branches en v.,** branches that form a canopy; *Lit:* **la v. céleste,** the vault, canopy, of heaven; **v. d'un fourneau,** vault, arch, crown, dome, of a furnace; *Anat:* **v. du crâne,** dome of the skull; **v. du palais,** roof of the mouth; (*c*) *Geol:* anticline.

voûté [vute], *a.* (*a*) vaulted, arched (roof, etc.); (*b*) stooping, bent, round-shouldered (person); **dos v.,** bent back; round shoulders; **il a le dos v.,** he has a stoop.

voûtelette [vutlɛt], *s.f.* small arch.

voûter [vute], *v.tr.* (*a*) to arch, to vault, to vault over (roof, etc.); to bend (horseshoe, etc.); (*b*) **l'âge voûte la taille,** age bows the back, brings on a stoop.

se voûter, (*a*) to arch, to vault; (*b*) (*of pers.*) to become bent, bowed; to begin to stoop.

voûtin [vutɛ̃], *s.m.* small arch, counter-arch.

voûture [vutyːr], *s.f. Med:* fracture of the skull.

vouvoiement [vuvwamɑ̃], *s.m.* use of the conventional **vous** in conversation (instead of the familiar **tu**).

vouvoyer [vuvwaje], *v.tr.* (**je vouvoie, n. vouvoyons; je vouvoierai**) to address (s.o.) as vous (instead of **tu**).

vouvray [vuvrɛ], *s.m.* Vouvray (wine).

vouvrillon, -onne [vuvrijɔ̃, -ɔn], *a.* & *s. Geog:* (native, inhabitant) of Vouvray.

vouzinois, -oise [vuzinwa, -waːz], *a.* & *s. Geog:* (native, inhabitant) of Vouziers.

voyable [vwajabl̩], *a. F:* (*a*) **je ne suis pas v.,** I'm not fit to be seen; (*b*) **ces gens-là ne sont pas voyables,** these are not people one wants to know.

voyage [vwajaːʒ], *s.m.* journey; trip; tour; **v. touristique accompagné,** conducted tour; **v. d'information,** fact-finding tour; **v. d'affaires,** business trip; **aimer les voyages,** to be fond of travel; **les voyages lui apprendront beaucoup de choses,** travelling will teach him a great deal; **les Voyages de Gulliver,** Gulliver's Travels; **v. en chemin de fer,** rail(way) journey; **v. (sur mer),** voyage; **faire un v.,** to go on a journey, on a voyage; **v. d'essai,** trial trip (of ship, etc.); **premier v.,** ship's maiden voyage; **petit v. d'agrément,** pleasure trip; **v. de vacances,** holiday trip; **v. de noces,** honeymoon; **v. autour du monde,** world tour; **aller, partir, en v., faire un v.,** to go on a journey, to leave home; **se mettre en v. pour l'Australie,** to set out for Australia; **je l'ai rencontré en v.,** I met him on my travels; **il est en v.,** he is travelling; **est-il toujours en v.?** is he still away, still on his travels? **il revient d'un v.,** he has just come back from a journey; **faire un v. à Paris,** to go to Paris, to take a trip to Paris; **je n'ai jamais fait le v. de Venise,** I have never been to Venice; **son esprit semblait toujours en v.,** his mind was always wool-gathering; **costume de v.,** travelling clothes; *Com:* travel wear; **frais de v.,** travelling expenses; **compagnon de v.,** (i) travelling companion; (ii) fellow passenger; **bon v.!** pleasant journey! bon voyage! have a good trip! *Lit:* **faire le grand v., le v. de l'autre monde,** to go on one's last journey.

voyager [vwajaʒe], *v.i.* (**je voyageai(s); n. voyageons**) **1.** (*a*) to travel; to make a journey, a trip; **v. sur mer, par mer,** to travel by sea; **v. d'un lieu à un autre,** to travel from one place to another; **il a beaucoup voyagé,** he has been a great traveller; he has travelled widely; **personne qui a beaucoup voyagé,** much-travelled, well-travelled, person; **ceux qui n'ont jamais voyagé,** people who have never travelled; **avec une voiture on voyage vite,** with a car you can get about quickly; **il voyage beaucoup,** he travels, gets about, a great deal; **faire v. des troupeaux,** to travel herds; (*b*) *Com:* to travel; *F:* to be on the road; **v. pour les vins,** to travel in wine; **v. pour une maison,** to travel for a firm; (*c*) (*of birds*) to migrate. **2.** (*of goods, etc.*) to be transported; **vin qui ne peut pas v.,** wine that does not travel.

voyageur, -euse [vwajaʒœːr, -øːz]. **1.** *s.* (*a*) traveller; (*in train, on boat, etc.*) passenger; (*in taxi*) fare; (*on bus*) **les voyageurs de l'intérieur,** the inside passengers; **les voyageurs de l'impériale,** the upper deck, *A:* outside, passengers; **voyageurs debout,** straphangers; **train de voyageurs,** passenger train; (*b*) *esp. Hist:* voyager, explorer; (*c*) **v. (de commerce),** (commercial) traveller; **le v. de MM. X et Cie,** the traveller for Messrs X and Co. **2.** *a.* (*a*) travelling; **commis v.,** commercial traveller; (*b*) **oiseau v.,** migratory bird; **pigeon v.,** carrier pigeon. **3.** *s.m. Bot:* (*a*) *F:* dandelion clock, blow ball; puffball; (*d*) **arbre du v.,** traveller's tree, ravenala.

voyance [vwajɑ̃ːs], *s.f. Psychics:* second sight, clairvoyance.

voyant, -ante [vwajɑ̃, -ɑ̃ːt]. **1.** *See* VOIR. **2.** *a.* & *s.* (*a*) seeing (person); seer (as opposed to blind); (*b*) clairvoyant; (*c*) *A:* seer, prophet. **3.** (*a*) *a.* gaudy, loud, garish (colour); showy, conspicuous (monument, etc.); conspicuous (landmark or seamark); (*b*) *s.m.* conspicuousness (of uniform, etc.). **4.** *s.m.* (*a*) mark, signal; *Surv: etc:* sighting board, slide vane, sight, target (of levelling rod); boning rod; *Nau:* sphere (of lightship); **v. (de bouée),** top mark; (*b*) sighting slit, aperture (of scientific instrument); **v. de visite,** inspection port; (*c*) signal light, pilot light, indicator light; warning light; **v. lumineux,** signal lamp, telltale lamp, control lamp, visual indicator; **v. d'appel d'ascenseur,** (i) lift coming, (ii) lift occupied, signal.

voye [vwa], *s.f. Fish:* buoy fixed to bottom nets.

voyelle [vwajɛl], *s.f. Ling:* vowel; **v. ouverte, fermée,** open, closed, vowel; **v. d'arrière, postérieure, vélaire,** back, velar, vowel.

voyer[1] [vwaje], *s.m. A:* (**agent**) **v.,** road surveyor, inspector.

voyer[2], *v.tr.* (**je voie, n. voyons; je voierai**) *Laundry:* to pour on (the lye); *Dy:* to run off (the lye).

voyette[1] [vwajɛt], *s.f. Laund:* hand bowl, bailer.

voyette[2], *s.f.* (straight) path (through a wood).

voyeur, -euse [vwajœːr, -øːz], *s.* **1.** voyeur, voyeuse; *F:* Peeping Tom. **2.** *s.f. A.Furn:* **voyeuse,** cock-fighting chair.

voyeurisme [vwajœrism], *s.m. Psy:* voyeurism.

voyou, -oute [vwaju, -ut]. **1.** *s. F:* (*a*) (cheeky) street urchin, guttersnipe; (*b*) (young) loafer, layabout; hooligan, yob. **2.** *a.* **langage v.,** language of the gutter; **verve voyoute,** gutter wit.

voyoucratie [vwajukrasi], *s.f. F:* **1.** the mob, the riff-raff; **le triomphe de la v.,** hooligan rule. **2.** customs, code, observed by the mob. **3.** mob rule.

voyouterie [vwajutri], *s.f. P:* **1.** (*a*) gutter wit; (*b*) gutter witticism. **2.** hooliganism.

vrac [vrak], *s.m. A:* rubbish, refuse; (*now used only in*) **en v.,** loose, in bulk; **charger en v.,** to lade in bulk; **marchandises en v.,** loose goods (not packed); **poissons en v.,** fish loosely packed (in barrels); **acheter des livres en v.,** to buy a job lot of books; **outils jetés en v. sur le plancher,** tools thrown higgledy-piggledy on the floor; **faire le v., transporter le v.,** to transport goods in bulk.

vrai [vrɛ]. **1.** *a.* (*a*) true, truthful, truth-telling; **une assertion vraie,** a true statement; a correct statement; **un ami v.,** a sincere, candid, friend; **un style v.,** a realistic, accurate, style; *Art:* **chairs vraies,** lifelike flesh; *O:* **c'est v. comme l'Évangile,** it's (the) gospel truth; **aussi v. que je m'appelle Georges,** as sure as my name is George; **c'est (bien) v.!** sure enough! true! **c'est ma foi v.!** quite true! so it is! you're quite right! **il est v. de dire que . . ., il est v. que . . .,** it is true that . . .; **c'est parfaitement v.,** it is quite true; **serait-ce v.?** can it be true? *adv.phr. F:* **pour de v.,** really, seriously; **c'est pour de v.,** I'm serious; I (really) mean it; **est-il parti pour de v.?** has he really gone? has he gone for good? **vous me dites cela pour de v.?** do you really mean it? (*b*) true, real, genuine; **le v. Dieu,** the true God; **un v. loup de mer,** a true sea dog; a real old salt; **un v. ami,** a true, real friend; **un v. Anglais d'Angleterre,** a real Englishman; an Englishman born and bred; **un v. diamant,** a real, genuine, diamond; **le v. théâtre,** the legitimate theatre, stage; **voilà sa vraie place,** that is its right place; **en vrais garçons ils avaient . . .,** being boys, they had . . .; as boys will, they had . . .; **les garçons grimpent comme de vrais singes,** boys climb like so many monkeys; *F:* **un v. de v.,** one of the lads; *Astr:* **temps v.,** true time, *Nau:* **longitude vraie,** true longitude; (*c*) downright, regular; **c'est une vraie attrape,** it's a downright swindle. **2.** *adv.* truly, really, indeed; **dire v.,** to tell the truth; **à v. dire, à dire v.,** if the truth must be told; strictly speaking; as a matter of fact; **faire v.,** to write, paint, etc., realistically; *F:* **eh bien v., celle-là est bonne!** well, really, that's a good one! **tu m'aimes, (pas) v.?** you *do* love me? you love me, don't you? **v. de v.!** really and truly! **vous m'écrirez, pas v.?** you *will* write to me, won't you? **pas v.?** I'm right, aren't I? *A:* & *Lit:* **de v.,** truly; indeed, in truth. **3.** *s.m.* (rational) truth (*as op. to* VÉRITÉ = truth to fact); **distinguer le v. du faux,** to distinguish truth from falsehood; **le v. de l'affaire, c'est que . . .,** the truth of the matter is that . . .; **le v. des choses,** the world of reality; **être dans le v.,** to be right; **il y a du v. dans ce bruit,** there is some truth in the rumour; **voici au v. ce qui s'est passé,** here is the truth about what happened.

vraic [vrɛk], *s.m. Dial:* (*in Normandy*) seaweed.

vraiment [vrɛmɑ̃], *adv.* (*a*) really, truly, in truth; **vous êtes v. trop bon,** you are really too kind; **cette nouvelle est v. surprenante,** the news is indeed surprising; **v.?** indeed? is that so? **ils voyagent beaucoup.—v.?** they travel a great deal.—do they? **je ne vais jamais au théâtre—v.?** I never go to the theatre.—don't you? **oui v.,** yes indeed; (*b*) **pour la première fois, je me suis vu v.,** for the first time, I saw myself in my true light, for what I really am.

vraisemblable [vrɛsɑ̃blabl̩]. **1.** *a.* probable, likely; credible; conceivable; **le vrai peut quelquefois n'être pas v.,** truth is sometimes stranger than fiction; **il est v. que** + *ind.*, it is probable, it is to be expected, that . . .; **il n'est pas v. que** + *sub.*, it is (i) hardly credible, (ii) hardly to be expected, that . . .; **excuse peu v.,** unconvincing excuse; **rendre une histoire v.,** to give credibility to a story; **l'histoire est v.,** the story is conceivably true. **2.** *s.m.* what is probable, likely; **au delà du v.,** beyond the bounds of probability.

vraisemblablement [vrɛsɑ̃blabləmɑ̃], *adv.* probably, very likely; conceivably; **je ne le verrai v. plus,** it is not likely that I shall see him again.

vraisemblance [vrɛsɑ̃blɑ̃ːs], *s.f.* (*a*) probability, likelihood, verisimilitude; **selon toute v.,** in all probability; **donner un peu de v. au récit,** to give a touch of verisimilitude to the story; **v. dramatique,** dramatic probability; (*b*) *Elcs:* (*computers*) **contrôle de v.,** absurdity, credibility, reasonableness, plausibility, limit, check.

vrbaïte [vrbait], *s.f. Miner:* vrbaite.

vrillage [vrijaːʒ], *s.m.* (*a*) *Tex:* kinking, kink (due to excessive twisting of thread); snarl; (*b*) *Av:* **v. aérodynamique,** aerodynamic twist; **v. d'aube,** twist angle (of a blade).

vrille [vriːj], *s.f.* **1.** *Bot:* tendril, clasper, cirrus. **2.** *Tls:* gimlet, borer, piercer; **v. en cuiller, à gouge,** shell gimlet; **yeux percés en v., yeux en trou de v.,** gimlet eyes, beady eyes. **3.** *Av:* spin; **descente en v.,** spinning dive; **faire la v., se mettre en v., tomber en v.,** to spin; to get into a spin; **monter en v.,** to corkscrew; **v. à plat,** flat spin; **v. serrée,** steep spin; **v. sur le dos,** inverted spin. **4.** *Bot: F:* bindweed. **5.** *Tex:* kink, snarl.

vrillé [vrije], *a.* **1.** (*a*) spiral, curled; twisted, kinked (thread, rope); (*b*) *Bot:* with tendrils; tendrilled, claspered. **2.** bored (with a gimlet).

vrillée [vrije], *s.f. Bot: F:* bindweed; **v. bâtarde,** black bindweed.

vriller [vrije]. **1.** *v.tr.* (*a*) to bore (with a gimlet); to gimlet; (*b*) *F:* **ne me vrillez pas les oreilles!** don't deafen me! **2.** *v.i.* (*a*) (*of rocket, etc.*) to whirl; to ascend in a spiral; (*b*) (*of thread, rope*) to twist, kink; to curl up, to corkscrew; *Tex:* to snarl.

vrillerie [vrijri], *s.f.* **1.** auger smithery. **2.** set of (carpenter's, armourer's) boring and piercing tools.

vrillette [vrijɛt], *s.f. Ent:* deathwatch (beetle); wood-fretter; **v. domestique,** furniture beetle; **v. du pain,** weevil.

vrillier [vrijje], *s.m.* auger smith.

vrillifère [vrijifɛːr], *a. Bot:* tendrilled.

vrillon [vrijɔ̃], *s.m. Tls:* small (i) screw auger, (ii) twist drill.

vrillonner [vrijɔne], *v.i.* (*a*) (*of rope, etc.*) to twist, kink; to corkscrew; (*b*) *Bot:* to form tendrils.

vrombir [vrɔ̃biːr], *v.i.* (*of flies, etc.*) to buzz; (*of top, aircraft*) to hum; (*of engine*) to throb, to purr, to hum.

vrombissant [vrɔ̃bisɑ̃], *a.* humming (top); throbbing, purring, humming (engine).

vrombissement [vrɔ̃bismɑ̃], *s.m.* buzzing (of insects); hum, humming (of top, aircraft); throbbing (of engine); purring (of motor).

vroncelle [vrɔ̃sɛl], *s.f. Bot: F:* bindweed.

vu, vue¹ [vy]. **1.** *s.* **être le bien vu, la bien vue, de qn,** to be in high favour with s.o.; to be s.o.'s favourite. **2.** *s.m.* (*a*) sight, inspection, examination; **au vu de tous,** openly, publicly, within sight of all; **au vu et au su de tous,** to everybody's knowledge, as everyone knows; **sur le vu de la facture,** upon presentation of the invoice; **cela fait l'effet du déjà vu,** it strikes one as familiar; *F:* **ça, c'est du déjà v.,** that's nothing new; (*b*) *Jur:* **le vu d'un arrêt,** the preamble of a decree. **3.** *prep.* considering, seeing; **vu la chaleur je voyagerai de nuit,** in view of the heat, owing to the heat, I shall travel by night; *Jur:* **vu la loi de 1929 sur les sociétés,** in the matter of the Companies Act 1929; *conj.phr.* **vu que +** *ind.,* seeing that . . ., considering that . . ., since . . .; (*in legal preambles*) whereas . . .

vu-arriver [vyarive], *s.m.inv. Com:* certificate of delivery.

vue² [vy], *s.f.* **1.** (*a*) sight; **avoir très bonne v.,** to have good eyesight; **perdre la v.,** to lose one's (eye)sight; **avoir la v. courte, basse,** to be short-sighted; **avoir la v. longue,** to be long-sighted; **se gâter la v.,** to spoil one's eyesight; to strain one's eyes; **le soleil me donne dans la v.,** I have the sun in my eyes; *F:* **toilette qui donne dans la v.,** dress that strikes, catches, the eye; **conspicuous dress; en mettre plein la v. (à qn),** to try to impress (s.o.); to shoot a line; *F:* **s'en mettre plein la v.,** to get an eyeful; **jeter la v. sur qch.,** to take a look at sth.; **tourner la v. du côté de la maison,** to look towards the house; **connaître qn de v.,** to know s.o. by sight; **garder qn de v., (i)** to keep s.o. in sight; (ii) to keep a close watch on s.o.; **perdre qn de v., (i)** to lose sight of s.o.; (ii) to lose touch with s.o.; **ne le perdez pas de v., (i)** keep him in sight; (ii) keep in touch with him; **vous perdez de v. que . . .,** you are losing sight of the fact that . . .; **la terre se perdit de v.,** the land faded out of sight; **à perte de v.,** as far as the eye can reach; **discourir à perte de v.,** to talk endlessly; to keep on talking; **personnes les plus en v.,** people most in the public eye, most to the fore; **un des acteurs les plus en v.,** a front-rank actor; **une personnalité en v.,** a prominent, conspicuous, personality; **mettre des marchandises bien en v.,** to display goods prominently; **faire qch. à la v. de tous,** to do sth. in sight of everybody; **se tenir hors de v.,** to keep out of sight; **à v. de nez,** at a rough estimate; **à v. d'œil, (i)** at a rough estimate; (ii) visibly; (iii) rapidly; **dépérir à v. d'œil,** to be visibly fading away; **mesurer, apprécier, les distances à la v.,** to judge distances by eye; *Av: Nau:* **navigation à v.,** visual navigation; *Av:* **vol à v.,** visual flight; (*b*) *Psychics:* **seconde v.,** second sight. **2.** (*a*) view; **échange de vues,** exchange of views; **avoir des vues saines sur une question,** to have sound views on a question; (*b*) *O:* view, survey, inspection; **la v. n'en coûte rien,** it costs nothing to look at it; **v. du passé,** review of the past; **porter sa v. bien loin dans l'avenir,** to look far ahead; **tout d'une v.,** with a comprehensive glance; **dessin à v.,** freehand drawing. **3.** aspect, sight; **à la v. de qn, de qch.,** at the sight of s.o., of sth.; **il s'arrêta à la v. de ce tableau,** he stopped at the sight of this picture; **à première v.,** at first sight; offhand; *Mus:* **lecture à v.,** reading at sight; **jouer un morceau à v.,** to play a piece at sight; **à v., en v., de terre,** (with)in sight of land; in view of land; **signalé en v.,** reported in sight; **navire en v.!** sail ho! *O:* **marcher à v. de pays,** to follow the lie of the land (in walking); *Com:* **payable à v.,** payable at sight; **à sept jours de v.,** seven days after sight; **traite à v.,** demand bill. **4.** view; (*a*) prospect, outlook; **chambre qui a v., qui prend v., sur le jardin,** room that looks out on the garden; **hôtel avec v. sur la mer,** hotel with sea view; **v. de face, de côté,** front view, side view; **v. en coupe, (i)** sectional drawing, cross-section; (ii) cut-away view; **v. en plan,** bird's eye view; **vues de Paris,** views of Paris; **examiner qch. à, de, plus d'un point de v.,** to examine sth. from more than one point of view, from more than one standpoint; **voir qch. sous un autre point de v.,** to see sth. in another light; **échappée de v.,** vista; (*b*) window, light (of house); **v. dérobée,** hidden light; **v. de terre,** pavement light; *Jur:* **droit de vues (et de jours),** ancient lights; **condamner les vues,** to block up the windows; (*c*) intention, purpose, design; **entrer dans les vues de qn,** to agree with s.o.'s views; **avoir qch. en v.,** to have sth. in view, in mind; **avez-vous quelque chose en v. pour demain?** have you anything in view for tomorrow? are you doing anything to-morrow? **avoir des vues pour qn,** to have sth. in view for s.o.; to have plans for s.o.'s future; **avoir des vues sur qn, sur qch.,** to have designs on s.o., on sth.; *prep.phr.* **en v. de,** with a view to; **poursuivre les négociations en v. d'une rapide conclusion,** to pursue the negotiations with a view to a speedy conclusion; **travailler en v. de l'avenir,** to work with an eye to the future; **épouser qn en v. de sa fortune,** to marry s.o. with an eye to her fortune; **en v. de plaire,** with a view to pleasing, in order to please; **prêt en v. d'améliorations,** loan for the purpose of improvements; **en v. d'un objet spécial,** with a special object in view; **faire un voyage en v. de sa santé,** to travel for the good of one's health. **5.** (*a*) **v.** (*pour projections*), (lantern)slide; **vues fondantes,** dissolving views; (*b*) *Cin:* **prendre les vues,** to shoot a film; **prise de vues,** shooting of a film; **preneur de vues,** camera man; (*c*) **vues stéréoscopiques,** stereoscopic views.

Vulcain [vylkɛ̃]. **1.** *Pr.n.m. Myth: Astr:* Vulcan. **2.** *s.m. Ent:* red admiral (butterfly).

vulcanal, -aux [vylkanal, -o], *a. Myth:* Vulcanian.

vulcanicité [vylkanisite], *s.f. Geol:* vulcanism, volcanism, vulcanicity, volcanicity; volcanic activity.

vulcanien, -ienne [vylkanjɛ̃, -jen], *a.* **1.** *Myth:* Vulcanian. **2.** *Geol:* Plutonic, Plutonian, Vulcanian (hypothesis, etc.).

vulcanique [vylkanik], *a.* volcanic.

vulcanisateur [vylkanizatœr], *s.m. Aut: Cy:* vulcanizer.

vulcanisation [vylkanizasjɔ̃], *s.f. Ind:* (*a*) vulcanization, cure, (of rubber); (*b*) haskinization (of wood).

vulcanisé [vylkanize], *a. Ind:* vulcanized.

vulcaniser [vylkanize], *v.tr. Ind:* (*a*) to vulcanize, to cure (rubber); (*b*) to haskinize (wood).

vulcanisme [vylkanism], *s.m. Geol:* Plutonic, Plutonian, Vulcanian, theory (of the formation of the earth).

vulcanite [vylkanit], *s.f.* (*a*) vulcanite, ebonite; (*b*) accelerator (of vulcanization).

vulcanologie [vylkanɔlɔʒi], *s.f.* vulcanology, volcanology.

vulcanologiste [vylkanɔlɔʒist], *s.m. & f.,* **vulcanologue** [vylkanɔlɔg], *s.m. & f.* vulcanologist, volcanologist.

vulgaire [vylgɛ:r]. **1.** *a.* vulgar; (*a*) common, everyday (custom, etc.); **l'opinion v.,** the common, general, opinion; **langue v.,** vernacular; **l'arabe v.,** vernacular Arabic; **le latin v.,** vulgar Latin; **nom v. (d'une plante),** common name (of a plant); (*b*) low, unrefined, coarse; **expression v.,** vulgarism; (*c*) (*placed before noun*) **vous avez pris cela pour du diamant, mais c'est du v. cristal de roche,** you mistook this for diamond but it's just ordinary rock crystal. **2.** *s.m.* (*a*) **le v.,** the common people; (*b*) **donner dans le v.,** to lapse into vulgarity.

vulgairement [vylgɛrmɑ̃], *adv.* vulgarly. **1.** generally, commonly; **pour parler v.,** to use the common phrase, *Lit:* to adopt the common parlance; *Th:* **l'amphithéâtre suprême, v. dit le poulailler,** the top gallery, commonly called the gods. **2.** with (a) lack of refinement; **s'exprimer v.,** to have a vulgar way of speaking.

vulgarisateur, -trice [vylgarizatœ:r, -tris], *s.* popularizer (of knowledge).

vulgarisation [vylgarizasjɔ̃], *s.f.* popularization (of knowledge); **ouvrage de v.,** popular work, popular treatise; **haute v.,** popularization at a high level; **services de v.,** advisory services, *U.S:* extension services.

vulgariser [vylgarize], *v.tr.* **1.** to popularize (knowledge). **2.** to coarsen, vulgarize.

se vulgariser, to grow vulgar.

vulgarisme [vylgarism], *s.m.* vulgarism.

vulgariste [vylgarist], *a. & s.* (*in Greece*) partisan of demotic Greek.

vulgarité [vylgarite], *s.f.* vulgarity; **v. criarde,** blatancy; **dire des vulgarités,** to make vulgar remarks.

Vulgate (la) [lavylgat], *s.f.* the Vulgate (version of the Bible).

vulgo [vylgo], *Lt.adv. Lit:* vulgarly, in common parlance.

vulgum pecus [vylgɔmpekys], *s.m.pl. F:* = hoi polloi, common herd.

vulnérabilité [vylnerabilite], *s.f.* vulnerability.

vulnérable [vylnerabl]; *a.* vulnerable.

vulnéraire [vylnerɛ:r]. **1.** *Pharm:* (*a*) *a.* vulnerary, healing (plant, remedy); **eau v.,** lotion for wounds; (*b*) *s.m.* vulnerary; *A:* **marchand de vulnéraires,** quack doctor. **2.** *s.f. Bot:* kidney vetch, lady's finger, woundwort.

vulnérant [vylnerɑ̃], *a.* wounding.

vulnération [vylnerasjɔ̃], *s.f. Surg:* (accidental) incision.

vulpin [vylpɛ̃], *s.m. Bot:* foxtail (grass); **v. des prés,** meadow foxtail.

vulpine [vylpin], *s.f. Bot: F:* meadow foxtail.

vulpinite [vylpinit], *s.f. Miner:* vulpinite.

vultueux, -euse [vyltɥø, -ø:z], *a.* (*of the face*) red and puffy; bloated; purply.

vultuosité [vyltɥozite], *s.f.* puffiness (of the face).

vulturidés [vyltyride], *s.m.pl.,* **vulturniens** [vyltyrnjɛ̃], *s.m.pl. Orn:* Vulturidae.

vulturin [vyltyrɛ̃], *a. Orn:* vulturine.

vulvaire [vylvɛ:r]. **1.** *a. Anat:* vulvar, vulval. **2.** *s.f. Bot:* stinking goosefoot.

vulve [vylv], *s.f. Anat:* vulva.

vulvectomie [vylvɛktɔmi], *s.f. Surg:* vulvectomy.

vulvite [vylvit], *s.f. Med:* vulvitis.

vulvo-vaginal, -aux [vylvɔvaʒinal, -o], *a. Anat: Med:* vulvovaginal.

vulvo-vaginite [vylvɔvaʒinit], *s.f. Med:* vulvovaginitis.

vumètre [vymɛtʒ], *s.m. Elcs:* modulation meter, monitor.

W

W, w (double v) [dubləve], *s.m.* (the letter) W, w; *Tp:* W comme William, W for William; *Biol:* chromosome W, W chromosome; *Av:* moteur en W, arrow engine, W engine.

wacke [wak], *s.f. Geol:* wacke.

wad [wad], *s.m. Miner:* wad, bog manganese, asbolite.

waders [weidɛrs], *s.m.pl. Fish:* waders.

wading [weidiŋ], *s.m. Fish:* wading.

wagage [waga:ʒ], *s.m.* river mud, slime (used as a fertilizer).

wagnérien, -ienne [vagnerjɛ̃, -jɛn], *a. & s. Mus:* Wagnerian.

wagnérisme [vagnerism], *s.m.* Wagner(ian)ism.

wagnériste [vagnerist], *a. & s.m. & f.* = WAGNÉRIEN.

wagnérite [vagnerit], *s.f. Miner:* wagnerite.

wagon [vagɔ̃], *s.m.* **1.** *Rail:* carriage, (passenger) coach, *U.S:* car; (goods) truck, wagon; w. à couloir central, w. (de) type américain, central-corridor coach, saloon coach; w. à couloir (latéral), w. à compartiments, (lateral-) corridor coach; w. de première, de deuxième (classe), first-class, second-class, coach; monter en w., to get into the train, *U.S:* to board the train; descendre de w., to get out of the train, to alight; accrocher, atteler, un w. à un train, to couple a coach, a truck, on to a train; ajouter un w. à un train, to put a coach, a truck, on to a train; décrocher, détacher, dételer, un w., to uncouple a coach, a truck; détacher, dételer, un w. en marche, to slip a coach; w. détaché (en marche), slip coach; w. de marchandises, goods truck, wagon, *U.S:* freight car; w. frigorifique, refrigerated van; w. couvert, fermé, covered truck, box wagon; w. découvert, ouvert, open truck, *U.S:* gondola (car); w. découvert, bâché, non bâché, sheeted, unsheeted, open truck; w. à haussettes, low-sided truck; w. plate-forme, flat (goods) truck, *U.S:* flat car; w. à bascule, dump wagon, tip truck; w. à benne, tipping truck, mine tub; w. de terrassement, ballast truck; w. à trémie, hopper wagon; w. railroute, roadrailer; w. à bagages, luggage van, *U.S:* baggage car; w. à bestiaux, cattle truck, *U.S:* stock car; w. à chevaux, horse van, horse box, *U.S:* horse car; w. à longs bois, timber truck; w. à minerai, ore wagon; w. de choc, w. de tête, front van; w. de queue, tail coach, van; w. de secours, breakdown van; w. particulier, private owner's wagon; *Com:* franco w., free on rail; prix sur w., price on rail; w. complet (de marchandises), truckload; marchandises expédiées par w. complet, goods consigned, forwarded, in truckloads; prix par w. complet, price per truckload; w. incomplet, part truckload; w. de groupage, through wagon, through coach. **2.** *Const:* chimney breast.

wagon-bar [vagɔ̃ba:r], *s.m. Rail:* buffet car; *pl. wagons-bars.*

wagon-citerne [vagɔ̃sitɛrn], *s.m. Rail:* tank car, tank wagon; *pl. wagons-citernes.*

wagon-couloir [vagɔ̃kulwa:r], *s.m. Rail:* corridor carriage, coach; *pl. wagons-couloirs.*

wagon-écurie [vagɔ̃ekyri], *s.m.* horse box, *U.S:* horse car; *pl. wagons-écuries.*

wagon-foudre [vagɔ̃fudr], *s.m. Rail:* tank car, tank wagon; *pl. wagons-foudres.*

wagon-frein [vagɔ̃frɛ̃], *s.m. Rail:* brake van; *pl. wagons-freins.*

wagon-lit [vagɔ̃li], *s.m. Rail:* sleeping car; *F:* sleeper; *pl. wagons-lits.*

wagonnage [vagona:ʒ], *s.m. Rail:* transport-(ation) by wagon.

wagonnée [vagone], *s.f. Rail: etc:* wagon load, truck load.

wagon(n)et [vagonɛ], *s.m.* tip truck, tip wagon; *Min: etc:* w. culbuteur, furnace charging carriage.

wagonnier [vagonje], *s.m. Rail:* truck shunter.

wagon-poste [vagɔ̃pɔst], *s.m. Rail:* mail van; *pl. wagons-poste.*

wagon-réservoir [vagɔ̃rezɛrvwa:r], *s.m.* = WAGON-CITERNE; *pl. wagons-réservoirs.*

wagon-restaurant [vagɔ̃rɛstɔrɑ̃], *s.m. Rail:* restaurant car; dining car; *pl. wagons-restaurants.*

wagon-salon [vagɔ̃salɔ̃], *s.m. Rail:* saloon (carriage, coach), *U.S:* parlor car; *pl. wagons-salons.*

wagon-tombereau [vagɔ̃tɔ̃bro], *s.m.* open goods wagon; flat truck, *U.S:* flat car; *pl. wagons-tombereaux.*

wagon-trémie [vagɔ̃tremi], *s.m. Rail:* hopper wagon, *U.S:* hopper car; *pl. wagons-trémies.*

walaba [walaba], *s.m.* wallaba (wood).

walchia [valkja], *s.m. Paleont:* walchia.

Walhalla (le) [ləvalala], *s.m. Myth:* Valhalla, Walhalla.

walkie-talkie [wɔkitɔki, walkitalki], *s.m. Telecom:* walkie-talkie; *pl. walkies-talkies.*

walk-over [walkɔvɛ:r], *s.m. Sp:* walkover; *pl. walk-overs.*

Walkyrie [valkiri], *s.f. Myth:* Valkyrie, Walkyrie.

wallaby [walabi], *s.m. Z:* wallaby; *pl. wallabies.*

wallace [valas, wa-], *s.f. F:* (also fontaine W.) drinking fountain.

wallérienne [valerjen], *a.f. Physiol:* dégénérescence w., Wallerian degeneration.

wallingant [valɛ̃gɑ̃], *s.m. Belg:* Walloon autonomist, nationalist.

Wallis [walis], *Pr.n. Geog:* les îles W., the Wallis Archipelago.

wallisien, -ienne [walizjɛ̃, -jɛn], *a. & s. Geog:* (native, inhabitant) of the Wallis Archipelago.

wallon, -onne [valɔ̃, -ɔn; wa-]. **1.** *a. & s. Geog:* Walloon. **2.** *s.m. Ling:* Walloon.

wallonner [valone, wa-], *v.i.* to speak Walloon.

Wallonie [valoni], *Pr.n.f. Geog:* Wallonia.

wallonisme [valonism], *s.m. Ling:* Walloon expression.

wallonniste [valonist], *s.m. & f. Ling:* expert on Walloon.

walpurgine [valpyrʒin], *s.f. Miner:* walpurgite.

walthérite [valterit], *s.f. Miner:* waltherite.

wampum [wampɔm], *s.m.* wampum belt (of N. American Indians).

wapiti [wapiti], *s.m. Z:* wapiti, American elk.

wardite [wardit], *s.f. Miner:* wardite.

warfarine [warfarin], *s.f. Pharm:* warfarin.

warpage [warpa:ʒ], *s.m. Tex:* warping.

warpeur [warpœ:r], *s.m. Tex:* warper.

warrant [warɑ̃:t, va-], *s.m. Com: Jur:* (a) (warehouse or dock) warrant; w. en marchandises, produce warrant; (b) w. hôtelier, bill of exchange signed by an hotel proprietor giving lien on his chattels.

warrantage [warɑ̃ta:ʒ, va-], *s.m. Com:* issuing of a warehouse warrant (for goods).

warranter [warɑ̃te, va-], *v.tr. Com:* to issue a warehouse warrant for (goods); marchandises warrantées, goods covered by a warehouse warrant.

Warren [warɛn], *Pr.n. Const:* poutre W., Warren girder, truss.

warwickite [wɔrwikit], *s.f. Miner:* warwickite.

washingtonia [waʃɛ̃gtonja], *s.m. Bot:* washingtonia.

wash-primer [wɔʃprimɛ:r], *s.m.inv. Ch:* wash primer.

wassingue [wasɛ̃:g, va-], *s.f.* (in N. of Fr. and Belg.) *Dom.Ec:* swab, floorcloth.

water-ballast [watɛrbalast], *s.m. Nau:* water ballast tank; *pl. water-ballasts.*

water-closet [watɛrklɔzɛt], *s.m.* lavatory, toilet; *pl. water-closets.*

watergang [watɛrgɑ̃:g], *s.m. Civ.E:* (in the Netherlands) water gang.

wateringue [watɛrɛ̃:g], *s.f.* (in N. of Fr. & the Low Countries) **1.** drainage works. **2.** draining syndicate.

water-polo [watɛrpolo], *s.m.* water polo.

waterproof [watɛrpruf], *s.m. O:* waterproof (coat); mackintosh.

waters [watɛ:r, *P:* vatɛ:r], *s.m.pl. F:* lavatory, loo, toilet, *U.S:* john.

watsonia [watsonja], *s.m. Bot:* watsonia.

watt [wat], *s.m. El.Meas:* watt, ampere-volt.

wattage [wata:ʒ], *s.m. El.Meas:* wattage.

watté [wate], *a.* (used incorrectly for actif) *El:* wattful, active; composante wattée, watt component (of alternating current).

watt-heure [watœ:r], *s.m. El.Meas:* watt-hour; *pl. watts-heures.*

watt-heuremètre [watœrmɛtr], *s.m. El.Meas:* watt-hour meter; *pl. watt-heuremètres.*

wattle [watɛl], *s.m. Bot:* black wattle (tree).

wattman [watman], *s.m. A:* driver (of electric tram or train); motor-man; *pl. wattmen* [watmɛn].

wattmètre [watmɛtr], *s.m. El.Meas:* watt-hour meter; wattmeter.

wavellite [wavɛlit], *s.f. Miner:* wavellite.

wealdien, -ienne [wildjɛ̃, -jɛn], *a. & s.m. Geol:* Wealden.

weber [vebɛ:r], *s.m. El.Meas:* weber (= 10[8] maxwells).

webstérite [wɛbsterit], *s.f. Miner:* websterite, aluminite.

week-end [wikɛnd], *s.m.* weekend; w. prolongé, long weekend; partir en w., to go away for the weekend; *pl. week-ends.*

weekendard [wikendar], *s.m. F:* weekend holidaymaker, weekender.

wehrlite [vɛrlit], *s.f. Miner:* wehrlite.

weinmannia [vɛjnmanja], *s.m. Bot:* weinmannia.

weinschenkite [vɛjnʃɛnkit], *s.f. Miner:* weinschenkite.

welche [vɛlʃ]. **1.** *a. & s. A:* barbarian. **2.** *a.* French-speaking (districts of the Vosges).

well-deck [wɛldɛk], *s.m. Nau:* well-decked ship, well decker; *pl. well-decks.*

wellingtonia [weliŋtonja], *s.m. Bot:* wellingtonia, *U.S:* washingtonia; sequoia.

wellsite [wɛlzit], *s.f. Miner:* wellsite.

welsh-springer [wɛlʃspriŋɛ:r], *s.m.* Welsh springer spaniel; *pl. welsh-springers.*

welsh-terrier [wɛlʃtɛrje], *s.m.* Welsh terrier; *pl. welsh-terriers.*

welter [vɛltɛ:r], *a. & s.m. Box:* welter, welterweight.

Wendes [vɑ̃:d], *s.m.pl. Hist:* Wends.

wergeld [wɛrgɛld], *s.m. Hist:* wergild, wergeld, weregild.

wernérite [vɛrnerit], s.f. Miner: wernerite.
werthérisme [vɛrterism], s.m. Lit.Hist: Wertherism; the morbid sentimentality of Goethe's Werther.
wesleyan, -enne [wɛslejɛ̃, -ɛn], a. & s. Rel.H: Wesleyan; méthodisme w., Wesleyanism, Wesleyan Methodism.
westerlies [wɛstɛrlis], s.m.pl. Meteor: westerlies.
western [wɛstɛrn], s.m. F: Cin: western.
Westphalie [vɛs(t)fali], Pr.n.f. Geog: Westphalia; Hist: les traités de W., the Peace of Westphalia.
westphalien, -ienne [vɛs(t)faljɛ̃, -jɛn], a. & s. Geog: Westphalian.
weymouth [wɛmut], s.m. Bot: Weymouth pine.
wharf [warf], s.m. wharf.
whewellite [wɛwelit], s.f. Miner: whewellite.
whiggisme [wigism], s.m. Pol.Hist: 1. Whiggery, Whiggism. 2. the Whig party.
whipcord [wipkɔrd], s.m. Tex: whipcord.
whisky [wiski], s.m. whisky; pl. whiskys.
whist [wist], s.m. whist; w. à trois avec un mort, dummy whist; petit w., short whist; grand w., long whist; w. de Gand, solo whist.
whisteur, -euse [wistœːr, -øːz], s. whist player.
whitneyite [witnejit], s.f. Miner: whitneyite.
wigwam [wigwam], s.m. wigwam.

wildcat [waildkat], s.m. Petroleum Ind: wildcat (oil, gas, well).
williamsite [wiljamzit], s.f. Miner: williamsite.
willow [wilou], s.m. Tex: willow.
wiltonien, -ienne [wiltɔnjɛ̃, -jɛn], a. Prehist: Wilton.
winch [wintʃ], s.m. Y: winch; pl. winch(e)s.
wintergreen [wintergrin], s.m. Pharm: wintergreen (oil), gaultheria oil.
wintérisation [winterizasjɔ̃], s.f. Ch: winterization.
wisigoth, -othe [vizigo, -ɔt], Hist: 1. a. Visigothic. 2. s. Visigoth.
wisigothique [visigɔtik], a. Hist: Visigothic.
wiski [wiski], s.m. A.Veh: whisky.
wistaria [vistarja], s.m., **wistarie** [vistari], s.f., **wisteria** [vistɛrja], s.f. Bot: wistaria.
withamite [vitamit], s.f. Miner: withamite.
withérite [viterit], s.f. Miner: witherite.
witloof [witlɔf], s.m. Bot: witloof (large-rooted Brussels chicory).
wittichénite [vitiʃenit], **wittichite** [vitiʃit], s.f. Miner: wittichenite.
wobbulateur [vɔbylatœːr], s.m. El.E: wobbulator, wobbler.
wohlfahrtia [vɔlfarsja], s.f. Z: wohlfahrtia.

wolfachite [vɔlfakit], s.f. Miner: wolfachite.
wolffia [vɔlfja], s.m. Bot: wolffia.
wolfram [vɔlfram], s.m. Miner: wolfram, tungsten.
wolframine [vɔlframin], s.f. Miner: wolframine.
wolframite [vɔlframit], s.f. Miner: wolframite; (in Cornwall) cal.
wolframocre [vɔlframɔkr], s.m. Miner: wolframine.
wolfsbergite [vɔlfsbɛrʒit], s.f. Miner: wolfsbergite, chalcostibite.
wollastonite [vɔlastɔnit], s.f. Miner: wollastonite, tabular spar.
wombat [vɔ̃ba], s.m. Z: wombat.
woodwardia [wudwardja], s.m. Bot: woodwardia.
wootz [vuts], s.m. Metall: A: wootz (steel); India steel.
worabée [vɔrabe], s.m. Orn: Napoleon weaver.
wormien [wɔrmjɛ̃], a.m. Anat: wormian (bone).
wulfénite [vylfenit], s.f. Miner: wulfenite.
würmien, -ienne [vyrmjɛ̃, -jɛn], a. Geol: Würmian.
wurtembergeois, -oise [vyrtɛ̃berʒwa, -waːz], Geog: 1. a. of Würtemberg. 2. s. Würtemberger.
Wurtzbourg [vyrtsbuːr], Pr.n. Geog: Würzburg.
wurtzite [vyrtsit], s.f. Miner: wurtzite.
wyandotte [vjɑ̃dɔt], a. & s.f. Husb: Wyandotte.

X

X, x [iks], *s.m.* the letter X, x; *Jur:* = person or persons unknown; *Tp:* **X comme Xavier** [gzavje], X for Xmas; **rayons X,** X-rays; *Biol:* **chromosome X,** X chromosome; (*computers*) **perforation X,** X punch; **tabouret en X,** cross-legged stool; *F: O:* **avoir les jambes en** *x,* to be knock-kneed; *Sch: F:* **l'X,** the *École polytechnique:* **un X,** a student at the *École polytechnique: F: O:* **fort en** *x,* good at maths; *F:* **je vous l'ai dit** *x* **fois,** I've told you a thousand times.

xancus [gzãkys], *s.f. Moll:* xancus.

Xante [gzã:t], *Pr.n. Geog:* Zante.

xanth(o)- [gzãt(ɔ)], *comb.fm.* xanth(o)-.

xantharsénite [gzãtarsenit], *s.m.* xanthoarsenite.

xanthate [gzãtat], *s.m. Ch:* xanthate.

Xanthe¹ (le) [ləgzã:t], *Pr.n.m. A.Geog:* the (river) Xanthus.

xanthe², *s.m. Crust:* xantho.

xanthéine [gzãtein], *s.f. Ch:* xanthein.

xanthélasma [gzãtelasma], *s.m. Med:* xanthelasma.

xanthène [gzãtɛn], *s.m. Ch:* xanthene.

xanthine [gzãtin], *s.f. Ch:* xanthin(e).

Xanthippe [gzãtip], *Gr.Hist:* **1.** *Pr.n.m.* Xanthippus. **2.** *Pr.n.f.* Xanthippe.

xanthique [gzãtik], *a. Ch:* xanthic.

xanthium [gzãtjɔm], *s.m. Bot:* xanthium.

xanthocarpe [gzãtɔkarp], *a.* xanthocarpous.

xanthochromie [gzãtɔkrɔmi], *s.f. Med:* xanthochromia.

xanthoconite [gzãtɔkɔnit], *s.f. Miner:* xanthoconite.

xanthoderme [gzãtɔdɛrm], *a. Anthr:* xanthoderm.

xanthogénate [gzãtɔʒenat], *s.m. Ch:* xanthogenate.

xanthogénique [gzãtɔʒenik], *a. Ch:* xanthogenic.

xanthoma [gzãtɔma], *s.m.,* **xanthome** [gzãtɔ:m], *s.m. Med:* xanthoma.

xanthomatose [gzãtɔmatoːz], *s.f. Med:* xanthomatosis.

xanthone [gzãtɔn], *s.f. Ch:* xanthone.

xanthophycées [gzãtɔfise], *s.m.pl. Nat.Hist:* Xanthophyceae.

xanthophylle [gzãtɔfil], *s.f. Bio-Ch: Bot:* xanthophyll.

xanthophyllite [gzãtɔfilit], *s.f. Miner:* xanthophyllite.

xanthopicrine [gzãtɔpikrin], *s.f.* xanthopicrin.

xanthoprotéique [gzãtɔprɔteik], *a. Ch:* xanthoproteic.

xanthopsie [gzãtɔpsi], *s.f. Med:* xanthopsia.

xanthoria [gzãtɔrja], *s.m. Moss:* parmelia.

xanthorrhée [gzãtɔre], *s.f. Bot:* xanthorrhoea, grass tree.

xanthorrhize [gzãtɔriːz], *s.f. Bot:* xanthorrhiza; **x. (à feuilles de persil),** yellow root.

xanthosoma [gzãtɔzɔma], *s.m. Bot:* xanthosoma.

xanthoura [gzãtura], *s.m. Orn:* xanthoura.

xanthoxyline [gzãtɔksilin], *s.f. Ch:* xanthoxylin.

xanthoxylum [gzãtɔksilɔm], *s.m. Bot:* xanthoxylum.

xanthydrol [gzãtidrɔl], *s.m. Ch:* xanthydrol.

xantusiidés [gzãtyziide], *s.m.pl. Rept:* Xantusiidae.

Xavier [gzavje], *Pr.n.m.* Xavier.

xén(o)- [ksen(ɔ)], *comb.fm.* xen(o)-.

xénarthres [ksenartr̥], *s.m.pl. Z:* Xenarthra.

xénie [kseni], *s.f. Bot:* xenia.

Xénocrate [gzenɔkrat], *Pr.n.m. Gr.Phil:* Xenocrates.

xénodiagnostic [ksenɔdjagnɔstik], *s.m. Med:* xenodiagnosis.

xénogame [ksenɔgam], *a. Bot:* xenogamous.

xénogamie [ksenɔgami], *s.f. Biol:* xenogamy.

xénogénèse [ksenɔʒenɛːz], *s.f. Biol:* xenogenesis.

xénoglossie [ksenɔglɔsi], *s.f.* xenoglossy.

xénolite [ksenɔlit], *s.f. Miner:* xenolite.

xénomorphe [ksenɔmɔrf], *a. Geol:* xenomorphic.

xénon [ksenɔ̃], *s.m. Ch:* xenon.

xénoparasitisme [ksenɔparazitism], *s.m.* xenoparasitism.

xénopeltidés [ksenɔpɛltide], *s.m.pl. Rept:* Xenopeltidae.

Xénophane [gzenɔfan], *Pr.n.m. Gr.Phil:* Xenophanes.

xénophile [ksenɔfil]. **1.** *a.* xenophilous. **2.** *s.m. & f.* xenophile.

xénophilie [ksenɔfili], *s.f.* xenophilism.

xénophobe [ksenɔfɔb], *a. & s.m. & f.* xenophobe.

xénophobie [ksenɔfɔbi], *s.f.* xenophobia.

Xénophon [gzenɔfɔ̃], *Pr.n.m. Gr.Lit:* Xenophon.

xénophore [ksenɔfɔːr], *s.m. Moll:* xenophoran.

xénophoridés [ksenɔfɔride], *s.m.pl. Moll:* Xenophoridae.

xénoplastique [ksenɔplastik], *a. Biol:* xenoplastic.

xénopsylla [ksenɔpsila], *s.f. Ent:* rat flea; (*genus*) Xenopsylla.

xénopus [ksenɔpys], *s.m. Amph:* West African clawed toad; (*genus*) Xenopus.

xénos [ksenɔs], *s.m. Ent:* xenos.

xénosauridés [ksenɔsɔride], *s.m.pl. Rept:* Xenosauridae.

xénotime [ksenɔtim], *s.m. Miner:* xenotime.

xér(o)- [kser(ɔ)], *comb.fm.* xer(o)-.

xéranthème [kserãtɛm], *s.m. Bot:* xeranthemum.

xérasie [kserazi], *s.f. Med:* xerasia.

Xérès [kserɛs, gzerɛs]. **1.** *Pr.n. Geog:* Jerez. **2.** *s.m.* (*also* vin de X.), sherry.

xérodermie [kserɔdɛrmi], *s.f. Med:* xeroderm(i)a.

xérographie [kserɔgrafi], *s.f.* xerography.

xérographique [kserɔgrafik], *a.* xerographic.

xérophagie [kserɔfaʒi], *s.f.* **1.** *Rel.H:* xerophagy. **2.** *Med: A:* dry diet.

xérophile [kserɔfil], *a. Bot:* xerophilous.

xérophtalmie [kserɔftalmi], *s.f. Med:* xerophthalmia.

xérophyte [kserɔfit], *Bot:* **1.** *a.* xerophytic. **2.** *s.f.* xerophyte.

xérophytique [kserɔfitik], *a. Bot:* xerophytic.

xérose [kseroːz], *s.f. Med:* xerosis.

xérosis [kserɔsis], *s.f. Med:* (*ophthalmology*) xerosis.

xérostomie [kserɔstɔmi], *s.f. Physiol: Med:* xerostomia.

xérothermique [kserɔtɛrmik], *a. Nat.Hist:* xerothermic.

xérus [kserys], *s.m. Z:* palm squirrel; (*genus*) Xerus.

Xerxès [gzɛrsɛs], *Pr.n.m. A.Hist:* Xerxes.

xi [ksi], *s.m. Gr.Alph:* xi.

ximénie [ksimeni], *s.f. Bot:* ximenia; *F:* sour plum.

xiph(o)- [ksif(ɔ)], *pref.* xiph(o)-.

xiphias [ksifjaːs], *s.m. Ich:* xiphias, swordfish.

xipho [ksifo], *s.m. Ich:* sword-tail.

xiphodon [ksifɔdʒ̃], *s.m. Paleont:* xiphodon.

xiphoïde [ksifɔid], *a. Anat:* xiphoid, ensiform, sword-shaped; **l'appendice x.,** the xiphoid appendage, cartilage, process; the processus xiphoideus; the xiphisternum.

xiphoïdien, -ienne [ksifɔidjɛ̃, -jɛn], *a. Anat:* xiphoidian, xiphisternal.

xiphopage [ksifɔpaːʒ], *a. Ter:* **monstre x.,** xiphopagus.

xiphophore [ksifɔfɔːr], *s.m. Ich:* xiphophorous; *F:* sword-tail.

xiphosures [ksifɔzyːr], *s.m.pl. Ent:* Xiphosura.

xoanon [gzɔanɔ̃], *s.m. A.Sculp:* xoanon.

xonotlite [gzɔnɔtlit], *s.f. Miner:* xonotlite.

xyl(o)- [ksil(ɔ)], *comb.fm.* xyl(o)-.

xylane [ksilan], *s.m. Bot:* xylan.

xylène [ksilɛn], *s.m. Ch:* xylene.

xylénol [ksilenɔl], *s.m. Ch:* xylenol.

xylidine [ksilidin], *s.m. Ch:* xylidine.

xylique [ksilik], *a.* xylic.

xylite [ksilit], *s.f.* **xylitol** [ksilitɔl], *s.m. Ch:* xylitol.

xylocarpe [ksilɔkarp], *a.* xylocarpous.

xylocope [ksilɔkɔp], *s.m. Ent:* xylocopa; carpenter bee.

xyloglyphie [ksilɔglifi], *s.f.,* **xyloglyptique** [ksilɔgliptik], *s.f.* xyloglyphy.

xylographe [ksilɔgraf], *s.m.* wood engraver.

xylographie [ksilɔgrafi], *s.f.* **1.** xylography, wood engraving. **2.** xylograph, woodcut.

xylographique [ksilɔgrafik], *a.* xylographic.

xylol [ksilɔl], *s.m. Ind: Ch:* xylol, raw commercial xylene.

xylologie [ksilɔlɔʒi], *s.f.* xylology.

xylophage [ksilɔfaːʒ], *Ent:* **1.** *a.* xylophagous, wood-eating (insect). **2.** *s.m.* xylophagan.

xylophone [ksilɔfon, gz-], *s.m. Mus:* xylophone.

xylopia [ksilɔpja], *s.m. Bot:* xylopia.

xylose [ksiloːz], *s.m. Ch:* xylose.

xylotome [ksilɔtom], *a. Ent:* xylotomous.

xyridacées [ksiridase], *s.f.pl. Bot:* Xyridaceae.

xyste [ksist], *s.m. Gr.Ant:* xystus, xyst.

Y

Y, y¹ (i grec) [igrɛk], *s.m.* (the letter) Y, y; *Tp:* Y comme Yvonne, Y for yellow; *Biol:* chromosome Y, Y chromosome; *Tchn:* raccord en Y, tubulure en Y, Siamese connection, joint; *El:* montage en Y, Y connection; *(computers)* perforation Y, Y punch.

y² [i], *unstressed adv. & pron.* **1.** *adv.* (= LÀ, *or stands for noun governed by* à, dans, en, sous, *etc.*) there; here; **est-il à Paris?—oui, il y est,** is he in Paris? Yes, he is (there); **allez-vous à Paris?—oui, j'y vais,** are you going to Paris? Yes, I am; **j'y suis, j'y reste!** here I am and here I stay! **Madame X y est-elle?** is Mrs X at home? **je n'y suis pour personne,** I am not at home to anybody; **j'y suis toujours pour vous,** I am always at home to you; **en quittant la table j'y laissai ma lettre,** when I got up from the table I left my letter on it; **il s'était senti sous le charme, il y était encore,** he had felt the charm and still felt it; *F:* **ah, j'y suis!** ah, now I understand! I've got it! I'm with you! **vous y êtes!** you've got it! you've hit the nail on the head! **y êtes-vous?** (i) *F:* do you get it? (ii) are you ready? **vous n'y êtes pas du tout,** you're not with it; you're wide of the mark; **je n'y suis plus,** I don't follow, I don't get you, I'm all at sea, I'm not with you; *F:* **il n'y est plus,** he's not all there; **pendant que vous y êtes,** while you are about, at, it; *F:* **je voudrais (bien) t'y voir!** I'd like to see you at it, in my position, make a better job of it if you can! **2.** *pron.inv.* (a) *(standing for thgs)* **j'y pense sans cesse,** I am always thinking of it; **et mon gâteau, y avez-vous goûté?** and what about my cake, have you tasted it? **mieux vaut n'y plus penser, ne plus y penser,** it is best to forget all about it; **j'y gagnerai,** I shall gain by it, I shall get sth out of it; **je m'y attendais,** I expected as much; (b) *(standing for clause governed by* à) **il me fallait tuer des lapins; je ne pouvais m'y décider,** I had to kill some rabbits; I couldn't bring myself to do it; **venez nous voir.—je n'y manquerai pas,** come and see us.—I shan't fail to do so, I most certainly shall; (c) *(standing for person just mentioned)* **pensez-vous à lui?—oui j'y pense,** do you think of him?—yes, I do; **cet homme-là, ne vous y fiez pas,** don't (you) trust that man; **les femmes? je n'y comprends rien,** women? I can't understand them; (d) *P: Dial:* (= LUI) **dites-y que je suis venu,** tell him I've come; **demandez-y s'il en a,** ask him if he has got any. **3.** *(indeterminate uses)* **je vous y prends!** I have caught you (at it, in the act)! **rien n'y faisait,** nothing availed, it was all in vain; **ça y est** [sajɛ]! (i) it's done! that's it! (ii) all right! done! (iii) that's done it! I knew it! **le compte y est,** the account, number, is right; **j'y suis pour un tiers,** I'm in for a third share; **il y est pour quelque chose,** he's got a hand in it; he's got something to do with it; he's got a finger in the pie; **je n'y suis pour rien,** I had no part in it, nothing to do with it; **je n'y suis plus pour rien,** I wash my hands of it; I'll have nothing more to do with it; *s.a.* ALLER 6, 7, AVOIR 8,

FAIRE IV. 2, VOIR 1. **4.** *(before a p.p. or adj.* la boîte et les clichés y contenus, the box and the negatives contained in it; **prix, y compris le port,** price, including carriage; **mon envoi et la facture y relative,** my consignment and the invoice relating to it. **5.** *(in stressed position after imperative)* **vas-y** [vazi], (i) go there; (ii) go ahead! get on with it! (iii) come on! **penses-y** [pɑ̃szi], think of it.

y³, *pers.pron. P:* = IL(s).

***yachmak** [jakmak], *s.m.* (Moslem woman's) yashmak.

***yacht** [jɔt, jat], *s.m. Nau:* yacht; y. à voiles, à vapeur, sailing yacht, steam yacht; y. de course, racing yacht; y. de plaisance, pleasure yacht; croisière en y., yachting cruise.

***yacht-club** [jɔtklyb; jat-; -klœb], *s.m.* yacht-club; *pl. yacht-clubs.*

***yachteur** [jɔtœːr, jatœːr], *s.m. O:* yachtsman.

***yachting** [jɔtiŋ, jatiŋ], *s.m.* yachting; y. sur glace, ice sailing.

***yacht(s)man,** ***yacht(s)woman** [jɔt(s)man, -wuman], *s. (the f. form is O:)* yachtsman, yachtswoman; *pl. yacht(s)men, -women.*

***ya(c)k** [jak], *s.m. Z:* yak.

***yahourt** [jaurt], *s.m. Comest:* yogh(o)urt.

Yahvé [jave], *Pr.n. Rel:* Yahweh, Jahweh.

yahviste [javist], *Rel:* **1.** *a.* Yahwist(ic). **2.** *s.* Yahwist.

Yakoutes [jakut], *s.m.pl. Ethn:* Yakuts.

Yakoutsk [jakutsk], *Pr.n. Geog:* Yakutsk.

Yalou (le) [lǝjalu], *Pr.n.m. Geog:* the (river) Yalu.

Yang-tsé-kiang (le) [lǝjɑ̃gtsekjɑ̃ːg], **Yang-tseu (-kiang)** [jɑ̃gtsø(kjɑ̃g)], *Pr.n.m. Geog:* the (river) Yangt(s)ze(-Kiang).

***yankee** [jɑ̃ki]. **1.** *s.m.* Yankee. **2.** *a.* la littérature yankee, American literature.

***yaourt** [jaurt], *s.m. Comest:* yogh(o)urt, yogurt, yaourt; *F: A:* pot de y., bubble car.

***yaourtière** [jaurtjɛːr], *s.f. Dom.Ec:* yog(o)urt-making machine.

***yapo(c)k** [japɔk], *s.m. Z:* oyapok, water opussum.

***yardang** [jardɑŋ], *s.m. Geog:* yardang.

***yatagan** [jatagɑ̃], *s.m.* yataghan.

***yawl** [jɔl], *s.m. Nau:* yawl.

***yearling** [jɛrliŋ], *s.m. Turf:* yearling (colt).

yèble [jebl], *s.f. Bot:* dwarf elder.

Yémen [jemɛn], *s.m. Geog:* le Y., (the) Yemen.

yéménique [jemenik], *a. Geog:* Yemeni(te).

***yéménite** [jemenit], *Geog:* **1.** *a.* Yemeni. **2.** *s.m. & f.* Yemeni, Yementite.

***yeti** [jeti], *s.m.* yeti.

yeuse [jøːz], *s.f. Bot:* ilex, holm oak, holly oak.

yeux [jø], *s.m.pl.* See ŒIL.

***yé-yé** [jeje]. **1.** *a.inv.* pop; chanteur, -euse, yé-yé, pop singer; chanson yé-yé, pop song. **2.** (a) *s.m.* pop music; (b) *s.* pop-mad teenager.

y-grec [igrɛk], *s.m.* (the letter) y.

yiddis(c)h [jidiʃ], *a. & s.* Yiddish.

ylang-ylang [ilɑ̃(g)ilɑ̃(ːg)], *s.m. Bot: Toil:* ylang-ylang.

ylem [ilɛm], *s.m.* ylem, primordial matter.

***yod** [jɔd], *s.m. Ling:* yod.

yodler [jɔdle], *v.i. Mus:* to yodel.

***yodleur, -euse** [jɔdlœːr, -øːz], *s.* yodler, yodeller.

***yoga** [jɔga], *s.m.* yoga.

***yog(h)ourt** [jogurt], *s.m. O:* yogh(o)urt.

***yogi** [jɔgi], *s.m.* yogi, (Indian) ascetic.

***yohimbehe** [jɔimbee], *s.m. Bot:* yohimbe, yohimbi.

***yohimbine** [jɔimbin], *s.f. Pharm:* yohimbine.

***yoldia** [jɔldja], *s.f. Moll:* yoldia.

***yole** [jɔl], *s.f. Nau:* gig, skiff, yawl; y. d'amiral, galley.

***yoleur** [jɔlœːr], *s.m. Nau:* gigsman.

yonnais, -aise [jɔnɛ, -ɛːz], *a. & s. Geog:* (native, inhabitant) of (i) the department of Yonne, (ii) La Roche-sur-Yon.

***youdi** [judi], *s.m. Pej:* (in N. Africa) Jew.

***yougoslave** [jugoslaːv], *a. & s. Geog:* Yugoslav, Jugoslav, Yugoslavian.

Yougoslavie (la) [lajugoslavi], *Pr.n.f. Geog:* Yugoslavia.

***youpin, -ine** [jupɛ̃, -in], **youtre** [jutr̥]. **1.** *s.m. & f. Pej:* Jew, sheeny; *f.* Jewess. **2.** *a.* Jewish.

***yourte** [jurt], *s.f. Geog:* yourt, yurt.

***youtrerie** [jutrǝri], *s.f. O: Pej:* **1.** sheenyism. **2.** the sheeny world. **3.** stinginess, meanness.

***youyou** [juju], *s.m. Nau:* dinghy.

***yo-yo** [jojo], *s.m. R.t.m: Toys:* yo-yo.

yoyoter [jojote], *v.i.* to play with a yo-yo; *P:* y. de la mansarde, to talk nonsense, to talk through one's hat.

ypérite [iperit], *s.f. Ch:* yperite; mustard gas.

ypérité [iperite], *a.* gassed.

yponomeute [ipɔnɔmøːt], *s.m. Ent:* ermine moth.

yponomeutidés [ipɔnɔmøtide], *s.m.pl. Ent:* Yponomeutidae.

ypréau, -aux [ipreo], *s.m. Bot:* **1.** broad-leaved elm; wych elm. **2.** white poplar; abele.

yprois, -oise [iprwa, -waːz], *a. & s. Geog:* (native, inhabitant) of Ypres [ipr̥].

Yseu(l)t [izø], *Pr.n.f. Lit:* Iseult, Isolde.

ysopet [izɔpɛ], *s.m. A:* collection of fables.

ytterbine [iterbin], *s.f. Ch:* ytterbium oxide.

ytterbium [iterbjɔm], *s.m. Ch:* ytterbium.

yttria [itrija], *s.m. Ch:* yttria.

yttrialite [itrjalit], *s.f. Miner:* yttrialite.

yttrifère [itrifɛːr], *a. Miner:* yttriferous.

yttrique [itrik], *a. Ch:* yttric; groupe y., yttrium group.

yttrium [itri(j)ɔm], *s.m. Ch:* yttrium.

yttrocalcite [itrɔkalsit], **yttrocérite** [itrɔserit], *s.f. Ch:* yttrocerite.

yttrocolumbite [itrɔkɔlœbit], *s.f. Miner:* yttrocolumbite.

yttrocrasite [itrɔkrasit], *s.f. Miner:* yttrocrasite.

yttrofluorite [itrɔflyɔrit], *s.f. Miner:* yttrofluorite.

yucatèque [jykatɛk], *Geog:* **1.** *a.* Yucatecan. **2.** *s.m. & f.* Yucatec, native, inhabitant, of Yucatan.

***yucca** [juka], *s.m. Bot:* yucca, Spanish bayonet, Adam's needle; *Ent:* papillon du y., yucca moth.

yvetotais, -aise [ivtɔtɛ, -ɛːz], *a. & s. Geog:* (native, inhabitant) of Yvetot.

Z

Z, z [zɛd], *s.m.* (the letter) Z, z; *Tp:* **Z comme Zoé**, Z for zebra; **barre, fer, en Z, Z-bar, zed-bar;** *F:* **O: être fait comme un Z,** to be deformed; *Mil:* **matériel Z,** antigas devices; **officier Z,** officer in charge of gas warfare.

zabre [zɑːbr̩], *s.m. Ent:* zabrus; caraboid beetle.

Zabulon [zabylɔ̃], *Pr.n.m. B.Hist:* Zebulun, Zebulon.

Zacharie [zakari], *Pr.n.m.* **1.** *B.Hist:* (a) (the prophet) Zechariah; (b) (the priest) Zacharias, Zechariah. **2.** *Ecc.Hist:* (Pope) Zacharias, Zachary.

Zachée [zaʃe], *Pr.n.m. B.Hist:* Zacchaeus.

zagaie [sagɛ], *s.f. A:* assegai.

zain [zɛ̃], *a.m.* zain, whole-coloured (horse, dog, with no white hairs).

zalophe [zalɔf], *s.m. Z:* sea lion; (*genus*) Zalophus.

Zambèze (le) [ləzɑ̃bɛːz], *Pr.n.m. Geog:* the Zambezi (river).

Zambie [zãbi], *Pr.n.f. Geog:* Zambia.

zambo [zãbo], *s.m. Ethn:* sambo, zambo.

zamenis [zamenis], *s.m. Rept:* zamenis.

zamia [zamja], *s.m. Bot:* zamia.

zamier [zamje], *s.m. Bot:* zamia (tree).

zancle [zɑ̃kl̩], *s.m. Ich:* zanclus; **z. cornu,** moorish idol.

zan(n)i [zani], *s.m.inv. A.Th:* zany; buffoon, merry-andrew (in old Italian comedy).

zannichellia [zanikɛlja], *s.m.,* **zannichellie** [zanikɛli], *s.f. Bot:* zannichellia.

zantedeschia [zɑ̃tedɛʃja], *s.m. Bot:* zantedeschia.

Zanzibar [zɑ̃zibaːr]. **1.** *Pr.n.m. Geog:* Zanzibar. **2.** *s.m.* (*P:* **zanzi** [zɑ̃zi]) throwing dice (for drinks).

zanzibarite [zɑ̃zibarit], *a. & s.m. & f. Geog:* (native, inhabitant) of Zanzibar.

zapatéado [zapateado], *s.m. Danc:* zapateado.

zapatero [zapatero], *s.m. Bot:* zapatero.

zaphrentis [zafrɑ̃tis], *s.m. Paleont:* zaphrentid; (*genus*) Zaphrentis.

zapode [zapɔd], **zapus** [zapys], *s.m. Z:* jumping mouse; (*genus*) Zapus.

zapodidés [zapɔdide], *s.m.pl. Z:* Zapodidae, the jumping mice.

zapotèque [zapɔtɛk], *a. & s.m. & f. Geog:* Zapotec.

zaratite [zaratit], *s.f. Miner:* zaratite.

zarétin, -ine [zaretɛ̃, -in], *a. & s. Geog:* (native, inhabitant) of Zadar, Zara.

Zébédée [zebede], *Pr.n.m. B.Hist:* Zebedee.

zébi(e) [zebi], *s.f. P:* **peau de z.,** (i) trash, rubbish; (ii) nothing, damn all; *U.S:* nix.

zèbre [zɛbr̩], *s.m.* **1.** zebra; *F:* **courir comme un z.,** to run like a hare. **2.** *F:* individual, type; **qu'est-ce que c'est que ces zèbres-là?** who are those types? **faire le z.,** to play the fool.

zébré [zebre], *a.* striped (de, with); stripy.

zébrer [zebre], *v.tr.* (je zèbre, n. zébrons; je zébrerai) to mask (sth.) with stripes; to streak; **le soleil zébrait le plancher,** the sun cast streaks of light on the floor.

zébrule [zebryl], *s.m. Z:* zebrula, zebrule, zebroid.

zébrure [zebryːr], *s.f.* **1.** stripe. **2.** (series of) stripes; zebra markings.

zébu [zeby], *s.m. Z:* zebu.

zédoaire [zedoɛːr], *s.f. Bot: A.Pharm:* zedoary; **z. longue,** long zedoary; **z. ronde,** round zedoary.

zef [zɛf], *s.m. Av: Nau: F:* (= ZÉPHIR) wind.

zéine [zein], *s.f. Ch:* zein.

zélandais, -aise [zelɑ̃dɛ, -ɛːz], *a. & s. Geog:* (native, inhabitant) of Zealand; *s.* Zealander.

Zélande [zelɑ̃ːd], *Pr.n.f. Geog:* Zealand (of the Netherlands).

zélateur, -trice [zelatœːr, -tris], *s.* (a) zealot; **z. d'une cause,** enthusiastic worker for a cause; (b) *B.Hist:* Zealot.

zèle [zɛl], *s.m.* zeal, ardour (**pour,** for); **avec z.,** zealously; **il y met du z.,** he puts his heart and soul into it; **z. à faire qch.,** anxiety, enthusiasm, eagerness, to do sth.; **brûler de z. pour qch.,** to be fired with enthusiasm for sth.; **stimuler le z. de qn,** to put s.o. on his mettle; **faux z.,** misguided zeal; *Ind:* **grève du z.,** work to rule (strike); *F:* **faire du z.,** (i) to make a show of zeal; (ii) to go beyond one's orders; **pas de z.!** don't overdo it!

zélé, -ée [zele], *a. & s.* zealous (person); **un partisan z. des arts,** a votary of art; **trop z.,** overzealous; **peu z.,** slack, remiss.

zélote [zelɔt], *s.m. B.Hist:* Zealot.

zélotisme [zelɔtism], *s.m.* zealotry.

zémindar [zemɛ̃daːr], *s.m.* (in India) zemindar, zamindar.

zemmi [zemi], *s.m. Z:* zemmi.

zen [zɛn], *a. & s.m. Rel:* Zen.

zénaïde [zenaid], *s.f. Orn:* zenaida.

zénana [zenana], *s.m.* **1.** (in India) zenana. **2.** *Tex:* zenana (cloth).

zend [zɛ̃d], *a. & s.m. Ling:* Zend.

zénith [zenit], *s.m.* zenith; **parvenu au z. de sa gloire,** having reached the zenith of his fame; having reached his zenith.

zénithal, -aux [zenital, -o], *a.* zenithal; **distance zénithale,** zenith distance.

Zénobie [zenɔbi], *Pr.n.f. A.Hist:* Zenobia.

Zénon [zenɔ̃], *Pr.n.m. Gr.Phil:* Zeno.

zénonique [zenɔnik], *a. Gr.Phil:* Zenonic, Zenonian (doctrine, etc.).

zénonisme [zenɔnism], *s.m. Gr.Phil:* Zenonism.

zénoniste [zenɔnist], *s.m. Gr.Phil:* (a) Zenonian, Zenonic; (b) stoic.

zéolite [zeɔlit], *s.f.,* **zéolithe** [zeɔlit], *s.m. Miner:* zeolite.

zéolit(h)ique [zeɔlitik], *a. Miner:* zeolitic.

zéolitisation [zeɔlitizasjɔ̃], *s.f. Geol:* zeolitization.

zéoscope [zeɔskɔp], *s.m. Ph:* zeoscope, ebullioscope.

zéphir [zefiːr]. **1.** *s.m.* (a) *Myth:* Zephyr, the West Wind; (b) balmy breeze; zephyr; (c) *P: A:* soldier of the African Disciplinary Companies. **2.** *a.inv. Tex:* **laine z.,** babywool; **tissu z.,** *s.m.* **z.,** zephyr cotton.

zéphyrantes [zefirɑ̃tɛs], *s.m. Bot:* zephyranthes.

zéphyrien, -ienne [zefirjɛ̃, -jɛn], *a. Lit:* soft, light, as a breeze, zephyrean, zephyreous, zephyrian; *Husb:* **œuf z.,** egg without a germ.

zeppelin [zɛplɛ̃], *s.m. Aer:* zeppelin.

zérène [zerɛn], *s.f. Ent:* **z. du groseillier,** currant moth.

zéro [zero], *s.m.* **1.** cipher, nought; *Tp:* 0 [ou]; *Com:* **trois cent vingt-six (francs) z. cinq** = 326 francs 05 centimes; *F:* **fortune réduite à z.,** fortune reduced to nothing, fortune wiped out; **c'est un z. (en chiffre),** he's a mere cipher, a nonentity, a nobody; *Sch:* **z. pointé,** absolute failure; **c'est un pur z. (dans l'équipe),** he's just a passenger (in the team); *Ten:* **trois à z.,** three love; **z. partout,** love all; *Biol:* **groupe z.,** O (blood) group. **2.** (a) starting point, zero (of various scales); **point z.,** zero point; **le thermomètre est à z.,** the thermometer is at zero (centigrade), at freezing point; *s.a.* ABSOLU 1; **correction du z., mise au point z.,** index correction, initial adjustment (of surveying instrument, etc.); *El:* **"zéro," "off"** (on electric stove, etc.); **interrupteur à z.,** no-load release; *Nau:* **z. des cartes,** low-water standard; **z. (la barre)!** helm amidships! *Mch:* **ligne z.,** base line (of diagram); *F:* **être à z., avoir le moral à z.,** to be in a low state; *P:* **les avoir à z.,** to be in a blue funk; (b) *El: Elcs:* null point; **méthode de z.,** null method; **indicateur de z.,** null indicator; *s.a.* PARTIR 2, REPARTIR 1. **3.** *a.:* **z. faute,** no mistakes; **z. degré,** 0 (nought) degrees; **z. heure,** 24.00 (twenty-four hundred) hours; **z. heure cinq,** 00.05 (double 0 0 five), five past twelve at night.

zérotage [zerɔtaːʒ], *s.m.* calibration (of thermometers, etc.); determination of the zero point.

zérovalent [zerɔvalɑ̃], *a. Ch:* zero-valent.

zérumbet [zerɔ̃bɛt], *s.m. Bot:* zerumbet.

zervanite [zɛrvanit], *s.m. & f. Rel:* Zervanite, Zarvanite.

zest [zɛst]. **1.** *int.* (a) *A:* pish! tush! (b) *O:* whizz!, hey presto! **2.** *s.m.* **être entre le zist et le z.,** to be neither one thing nor the other; to be betwixt and between; to hesitate between two courses of action.

zeste [zɛst], *s.m.* (a) *Cu:* outer skin, zest (of orange, lemon, etc.); **z. confit, z. d'Italie,** candied peel; (b) partition quartering the kernel (of walnut); *F: O:* **cela ne vaut pas un z.,** it's not worth a straw.

zester [zɛste], *v.tr.* to peel the zest, outer skin, off (lemon, orange).

zesteuse [zɛstøːz], *s.f.* orange peeler; lemon peeler.

zêta [zeta], *s.m. Gr.Alph:* zeta.

zététique [zetetik], *Phil:* **1.** *a. & s.m. & f.* zetetic. **2.** *s.f.* zetetics.

zeuglodon [zøglɔdɔ̃], *s.m. Paleont:* zeuglodon(t).

zeuglodontidés [zøglɔdɔ̃tide], *s.m.pl. Paleont:* Zeuglodontidae.

zeugme [zøːgm̩], **zeugma** [zøgma], *s.m. Gram: Rh:* zeugma.

zeunérite [zønerit], *s.f. Miner:* zeunerite.

Zeus [zøːs], *Pr.n.m. Myth:* Zeus.

zézaiement [zezɛmɑ̃], *s.m.* lisping, lisp.

zézayant [zezejɑ̃], *a.* **parler d'une voix zézayante,** to speak with a lisp, to lisp.

zézayer [zezeje], *v.i. & tr.* (je zézaie, je zézaye, n. zézayons; je zézaierai, je zézayerai) to lisp.

zeuzère [zøzɛːr], *s.f. Ent:* zeuzera, leopard moth.

zibeline [ziblin], *s.f.* **1.** *Z:* (martre) z., sable. **2.** *Cost:* sable (fur); zibel(l)ine.

zibeth [zibɛt], *s.m. Z:* zibet(h), Indian civet.

zieuter [zjøte], *v.tr. P:* = ZYEUTER.

zig [zig], *s.m. P:* fellow, chap; *esp.* **un bon z.,** a decent type, a good sort.

ziggourat [zigura], *s.f. Archeol:* ziggurat.

zigoteau, -eaux, zigoto [zigɔto], *s.m. P:* **c'est un drôle de z.,** he's a queer customer; **faire le z.,** to play the fool; to show off.

zigouiller [ziguje], *v.tr. P:* (a) to knife (s.o.); to cut (s.o.'s throat); (b) to kill, murder, massacre; **toute la bande a été zigouillée,** the whole band of them was wiped out.

zigue [zig], *s.m. P:* = ZIG.

zigzag [zigzag], *s.m.* **1.** (a) zigzag; **éclair en z.,** forked lightning; **tranchée en z.,** zigzag trenches; **barreaux de grille en z.,** interlocking grate bars; **faire des zigzags,** to stagger along (when drunk); to zigzag along; to move in zigzags; *P: A:* **être z.,** to be staggering drunk; *Nau:* **faire route en**

z., faire des zigzags, to zigzag; to steer a zigzag course; la route fait des zigzags, the road zigzags; *Mec.E:* disposés en z., staggered (rivets, etc.); *Com:* étiquettes pliées en z., gang labels; (*b*) *Arch:* zigzags, chevron moulding. 2. lazy tongs. 3. *Ent: F:* gipsy moth.

zigzaguer [zigzage], *v.i.* to zigzag; (*of bat, etc.*) to flit about; *Aut: etc:* to drive erratically; *Nau:* faire route en zigzagant, to zigzag; to steer a zigzag course.

zinc [zɛ̃:g], *s.m.* 1. zinc; *Com:* spelter; poussière de z., zinc powder; *Metall:* fleurs de z., zinc dust, zinc powder; *Metalw:* z. à souder, spelter solder; galvanisation au gris de z., sherardizing; *Com:* z. électrolytique, electrolytic spelter; *Pharm:* pommade à l'oxyde de z., zinc ointment; *s.a.* BLANC II. 4. 2. *F:* (zinc) counter (of public house); bar; prendre un verre sur le z., to have a glass at the counter, the bar. 3. *Phot.Engr:* (*a*) report sur z., transfer on to zinc; gravure sur z., zincograph; (*b*) *F:* zinc block, *F:* zinco. 4. *Av: F:* plane, *F:* crate.

zincage [zɛ̃ka:ʒ], *s.m.* = ZINGAGE.

zinc-alcoyle [zɛ̃kalkɔil], *s.m. Ch:* zinc alkyl; *pl.* zincs-alcoyles.

zincaluminite [zɛ̃kalyminit], *s.f. Miner:* zinc-aluminite.

zincate [zɛ̃kat], *s.m. Ch:* zincate.

zinc-éthyle [zɛ̃ketil], *s.m. Ch:* zinc diethyl.

zincide [zɛ̃sid], *a. Ch:* zinc-like, zincoid; *s.m.pl.* zincides, zinc and its compounds.

zincifère [zɛ̃sifɛ:r], *a.* zinciferous, zinc-bearing.

zincique [zɛ̃sik], *a. Ch:* zincic.

zincite [zɛ̃sit], *s.f. Miner:* zincite, red zinc ore.

zinckénite [zɛ̃kenit], *s.f. Miner:* zinckenite.

zinc-méthyle [zɛ̃kmetil], *s.m. Ch:* zinc dimethyl.

zincographe [zɛ̃kɔgraf], *s.m. Phot.Engr:* zincographer.

zincographie [zɛ̃kɔgrafi], *s.f.* zincography.

zincographier [zɛ̃kɔgrafje], *v.tr.* (*p.d. & pr.sub. n.* zincographiions, *v.* zincographiiez) to zincograph; to reproduce (a design, etc.) by zincography.

zincograveur [zɛ̃kɔgravœ:r], *s.m.* zincographer.

zincogravure [zɛ̃kɔgravy:r], *s.f. Phot.Engr:* 1. zincography. 2. (*a*) zincograph, zincotype; (*b*) zinc block, *F:* zinco.

zincosite [zɛ̃kɔzit], *s.f. Miner:* zincosite.

zingage [zɛ̃ga:ʒ], *s.m.* 1. covering (of roof, etc.) with zinc. 2. *Metall:* coating with zinc; zincing; z. au trempé, galvanizing (of iron).

zingana [zɛ̃gana], *s.m. Bot:* zingana, zebra-wood.

zingaro [dzingaro], *s.m. O:* gipsy, zingaro; *pl.* zingari.

zingibéracées [zɛ̃ʒiberase], *s.f.pl. Bot:* Zingiberaceae.

zingibérène [zɛ̃ʒiberɛn], *s.m. Ch:* zingiberene.

zinguer [zɛ̃ge], *v.tr.* 1. to cover (roof, etc.) with zinc. 2. (*a*) *Metall:* to coat with zinc; to zinc; to galvanize (iron); fer zingué, galvanized iron; (*b*) *A:* lumières zinguées d'un tableau, crude, harsh, lights of a painting.

zinguerie [zɛ̃gri], *s.f.* 1. zinc works. 2. zinc trade. 3. zincware.

zingueur [zɛ̃gœ:r], *s.m.* (*a*) zinc worker; (*b*) *Const:* zinc roofer.

zinjanthrope [zɛ̃ʒãtrɔp], *s.m. Prehist:* zinjanthropus.

zinnia [zinja], *s.m. Bot:* zinnia.

zinnwaldite [zinvaldit], *s.f. Miner:* zinnwaldite.

zinzin [zɛ̃zɛ̃], 1. *s.m. P: A:* (*a*) shell; cannon; (*b*) buzz (of insect, etc.). 2. *s.m. F:* what's its name, contraption. 3. *F:* (*a*) a cracked, bats; (*b*) *s.m.* c'est un z., he's bats, loopy.

zinzinuler [zɛ̃zinyle], *v.i.* (*of warblers and tits*) to sing.

zinzolin, -ine [zɛ̃zɔlɛ̃, -in], *a. & s.m.* reddish purple (colour).

zinzoliner [zɛ̃zɔline], *v.tr. O:* to dye (sth.) a reddish purple.

ziphiinés [zifiine], *s.m.pl. Z:* Ziphiinae.

zippéite [zipeit], *s.f. Miner:* zippeite.

zircon [zirkɔ̃], *s.m. Miner:* zircon.

zirconate [zirkɔnat], *s.m. Ch:* zirconate.

zircone [zirkɔn], *s.f. Ch: Ind:* zirconia.

zirconifluorure [zirkɔniflyɔry:r], *s.m. Ch:* zirconifluoride.

zirconique [zirkɔnik], *a. Ch:* zirconic.

zirconite [zirkɔnit], *s.f. Miner:* zirconite.

zirconium [zirkɔnjɔm], *s.m. Ch:* zirconium.

zirconyle [zirkɔnil], *s.m. Ch:* zirconyl.

zist [zist], *s.m. See* ZEST.

zizanie [zizani], *s.f.* 1. (*a*) *B:* tare; (*b*) discord; semer la z. entre les familles, to sow discord between families; perpétuellement en z., perpetually quarrelling, bickering, at loggerheads (avec,

---

with). 2. *Bot:* zizania, Canadian wild rice, Indian rice.

zizi [zizi], *s.m.* 1. *Orn:* (bruant) z., cirl bunting. 2. *P:* penis, *V:* cock.

ziziphus [zizifys], *s.m. Bot:* ziziphus.

zloty [zlɔti], *s.m. Num:* zloty (of Poland).

zoanthaire [zɔɑ̃tɛ:r], *a. & s.m. Coel:* zoantharian; *s.m.pl.* zoanthaires, Zoantharia.

zoanthides [zɔɑ̃tid], *s.m.pl. Coel:* Zoanthidae.

zoanthodème [zɔɑ̃tɔdɛm], *s.m. Coel:* zoanthodeme.

zoanthropie [zɔɑ̃trɔpi], *s.f. Med:* zoanthropy.

zoarcès [zɔarsɛs], *s.m. Ich:* (*genus*) Zoarces; z. vivipare, viviparous blenny.

zodiacal, -aux [zɔdjakal, -o], *a. Astr:* zodiacal (star, etc.); lumière zodiacale, zodiacal light.

zodiaque [zɔdjak], *s.m.* le z., the zodiac.

zoé¹ [zɔe], *s.f. Crust:* zoea.

Zoé², *Pr.n.f.* Zoe.

Zoïle [zɔil], *Pr.n.m. Lit:* (*a*) Zoilus (severe critic of Homeric poems, 4th cent. B.C.); *hence* (*b*) *s.m.* ill-natured critic, criticaster.

zoïque [zɔik], *a.* zoic.

zoïsite [zɔizit], *s.f. Miner:* zoisite.

zombi [zɔ̃bi], *s.m.* zombi(e).

zon [zɔ̃], *int.* (*sound of violin, etc.*) boom!

zona [zɔna], *s.m. Med:* shingles, zona.

zonage [zɔna:ʒ], *s.m. Town P: etc:* zoning; *Geog:* zonation; arrangement by zones.

zonaire [zɔnɛ:r], 1. *a.* zoned (alabaster, etc.). 2. (*a*) *s.f. Algae:* zonaria; (*b*) *s.m. Ent:* erotylus, fungus beetle.

zonal, -aux [zɔnal, -o], *a.* zonal.

zonalité [zɔnalite], *s.f. Geog:* zonality.

zone [zo:n], *s.f.* 1. *A.Cost: Lit:* zone, girdle. 2. zone; (*a*) *Mth:* z. sphérique, spherical zone; *Astr:* la z. du zodiaque, (the belt of) the zodiac; *Miner:* les zones de l'onyx, the zones, bands, of onyx; (*b*) *Geog:* z. glaciale, tempérée, torride, frigid, temperate, torrid, zone; z. des alizés, trade-wind belt; z. des calmes, doldrums; z. des calmes tropicaux, horse latitudes; z. désertique, desert belt; z. forestière, forest belt; (*in coastal waters*) z. subterrestre, splash zone; *Geol:* z. de fracture, zone of fracture; z. de plissement, zone of folds; z. houillère, coal belt; z. gazéifère, natural gas(-producing) area; z. d'altération, zone of weathering; *Meteor:* z. de dépression, trough (of low pressure); z. de haute pression, high pressure area; *Vit:* champagne de deuxième, de seconde z., non-vintage champagne; champagne from the outlying vineyards; *F:* écrivain de seconde z., second-rate writer; citoyen de seconde z., second-class citizen; (*c*) *Adm:* z. suburbaine, suburban area; z. verte, green belt; *Aut:* z. bleue = pink zone; parking-meter zone; z. postale, postal area; z. de desserte, service area; z. à urbaniser en priorité, area designated for immediate residential development; z. à aménagement différé, area designated for future development; z. frontière, frontier zone; *Geog:* Z. du Canal, Canal Zone; la Z., (i) *Hist:* the unbuilt area outside the line of the Paris fortifications, (ii) slum area, shanty town (on the outskirts of any large town); *F:* chez eux c'est la z., they're wretchedly poor; *Fr.Hist:* (*1939-45 war*) z. occupée, z. libre, occupied, unoccupied, France; (*d*) *Pol.Ec:* z. franche, free zone; z. de libre échange, free-trade area; z. monétaire, monetary area; z. dollar, franc, sterling, dollar, franc, sterling, area; (*e*) *Elcs:* (*computers*) z. de carte, card field; z. de mémoire, storage area; (*f*) *Mil:* z. de l'avant, z. avancée, forward area. z. logistique avancée, forward maintenance area; z. (de l') arrière, rear area; z. logistique arrière, rear maintenance area; z. des armées, zone of operations; z. de l'intérieur, zone of the interior; z. de communications, communications zone; z. de concentration, concentration area; z. de stationnement, lying up area, *U.S:* assembly area; z. de combat, fighting area, *U.S:* combat area, zone; z. dangereuse, danger zone, dangerous area; z. à séjour réglementé, regulated-stay area; z. interdite, prohibited, restricted, area; *Artil: Mil.Av:* bombardement sur z., area bombing; (*g*) *W.Tel:* z. de brouillage, interference area, nuisance area; z. de silence radio, skip zone, silent zone; étendue de la z. de silence radio, skip distance; *Nau: etc:* z. de veille radio, area of radio watch; (*h*) *Metall:* zone (of cementation, fusion, oxydation, etc.); z. fondue, fusion zone.

zoné [zone], *a. Bot: Z: Miner:* zoned, zonate.

zonier, -ière [zonje, -jɛ:r], 1. *s. A:* (*a*) dweller in the military zone round Paris; (*b*) *F:* dregs of the population about Paris (because in the military zone only hutments and shanties were permitted). 2. *a.* relating to a frontier zone.

---

zoniforme [zɔnifɔrm], *a.* belt-shaped.

zoning [zoniŋ], *s.m. Town P:* žoning.

zonitidés [zonitide], *s.m.pl. Moll:* Zonitidae.

zonulaire [zonylɛ:r], *a. Anat:* zonular.

zonule [zonyl], *s.f. Anat:* zonule of Zinn.

zonure [zony:r], *s.m. Rept:* zonure; girdle-tailed lizard.

zonuridés [zonyride], *s.m.pl. Rept:* Zonuridae.

zonzonner [zɔ̃zɔne], *v.i.* (*of violin*) to whine.

zoo [zo, zoo], *s.m. F:* zoo.

zoo- [zoɔ], *comb.fm.* zoo-.

zoobiologie [zoobjolɔʒi], *s.f.* zoobiology.

zoobiologique [zoobjolɔʒik], *a.* zoobiological.

zoocécidie [zoosesidi], *s.f. Bot:* zoocecidium.

zoochimie [zooʃimi], *s.f.* zoochemistry.

zoochimique [zooʃimik], *a.* zoochemical.

zoochlorelle [zooklɔrɛl], *s.f. Algae:* zoochlorella.

zoochore [zookɔ:r], *a. & s.f. Bot:* (plante) z., zoochore.

zoogène [zooʒɛn], **zoogénique** [zooʒenik], *a. Paleont: Geol:* zoogenic.

zoogéographe [zooʒeɔgraf], *s.m. & f.* zoogeographer.

zoogéographie [zooʒeɔgrafi], *s.f.* zoogeography.

zooglée [zoogle], *s.f. Biol:* zoogloea.

zoographe [zoograf], *s.m.* zoographer.

zoographie [zoografi], *s.f.* zoography; descriptive zoology.

zoographique [zoografik], *a.* zoographic(al).

zooïde [zooid], 1. *a.* zooid(al). 2. *s.m.* zooid.

zoolâtre [zoolɑtr], 1. *a.* zoolatrous. 2. *s.m. & f.* animal worshipper, zoolater.

zoolâtrie [zoolɑtri], *s.f.* zoolatry.

zoolit(h)e [zoolit], *s.m.* zoolite.

zoologie [zoolɔʒi], *s.f.* zoology.

zoologique [zoolɔʒik], *a.* zoological; jardin z., zoological garden(s), zoo.

zoologiquement [zoolɔʒikmã], *adv.* zoologically.

zoologiste [zoolɔʒist], **zoologue** [zoolɔg], *s.m. & f.* zoologist.

zoom [zum], *s.m. Cin: F:* zoom.

zoomagnétisme [zoomaɲetism], *s.m.* zoomagnetism.

zoométrie [zoometri], *s.f.* zoometry.

zoomorphe [zoomɔrf], **zoomorphique** [zoomɔrfik], *a.* zoomorphic.

zoomorphie [zoomɔrfi], *s.f.* zoomorphy.

zoomorphisme [zoomɔrfism], *s.m.* zoomorphism.

zoonomie [zoonɔmi], *s.f.* zoonomy.

zoonose [zoono:z], *s.f. Biol:* zoonosis.

zoonosologie [zoonozolɔʒi], *s.f. O:* zoonosology.

zooparasite [zooparazit], *s.m.* zooparasite.

zoopathologie [zoopatolɔʒi], *s.f.* zoopathology.

zoophage [zoofa:ʒ], 1. *a.* zoophagous, carnivorous. 2. *s.m.* zoophagan; *pl.* les zoophages, the Zoophaga.

zoophilie [zoofili], *s.f. Psy:* zoophilia; z. érotique, zooerasty.

zoophobie [zoofɔbi], *s.f. Psy:* zoophobia.

zoophore [zoofɔ:r], *s.m. Gr.Ant:* zophoros.

zoophytes [zoofit], *s.m.pl. Biol:* zoophytes, Zoophyta; Phytozoa.

zoophytique [zoofitik], *a.* zoophytal, zoophytic(al).

zoophytologie [zoofitolɔʒi], *s.f.* zoophytology.

zooplancton [zooplãktɔ̃], *s.m. Biol:* zooplankton.

zoopsie [zoopsi], *s.f. Med:* zoopsia.

zoosperme [zoospɛrm], *s.m. Physiol:* zoosperm, spermatozoon.

zoosporange [zoosporã:ʒ], *s.m. Bot:* zoosporangium, zoosporange.

zoospore [zoospɔ:r], *s.f. Biol:* zoospore, swarm spore.

zoosporé [zoospore], *a. Biol:* zoosporic, zoosporous.

zootaxie [zootaksi], *s.f.* zootaxy.

zootechnicien, -ienne [zooteknisjɛ̃, -jɛn]. 1. *a.* zootechnical. 2. *s.* zootechnician.

zootechnie [zootekni], *s.f.* zootechny.

zootechnique [zooteknik], *a.* zootechnic.

zoothérapie [zooterapi], *s.f. Vet:* zootherapy.

zootomie [zootomi], *s.f.* zootomy; comparative anatomy.

zootomique [zootomik], *a.* zootomic(al).

zootomiste [zootomist], *s.m. & f.* zootomist; comparative anatomist.

zootrope [zootrop], *s.m. Toys:* zootrope, zoetrope; wheel of life.

zooxanthelles [zoogzɑ̃tɛl], *s.f.pl. Algae:* Zooxanthellae.

zoraptères [zoraptɛ:r], *s.m.pl. Ent:* Zoraptera.

zorilla [zɔrija], *s.f., zorille* [zɔri:j], *s.f. Z:* zoril, zorillo; African, Cape, polecat.

Zoroastre [zɔrɔastr], *Pr.n.m. Rel.H:* Zoroaster.

zoroastrien, -enne [zɔrɔastriɛ̃, -ɛn], *a. & s. Rel.H:* Zoroastrian, Zarathustrian.

zoroastrisme [zɔrɔastrism], *s.m. Rel.H:* Zoroastrianism.

Zorobabel [zərɔbabɛl], *Pr.n.m. B.Hist:* Zerubbabel.

zorrino [zɔrino], *s.m.* zoril (fur).

Zosime [zɔzim], *Pr.n.m. Gr.Hist:* Zosimus.

zostère [zɔstɛːr], *s.f. Bot:* grass wrack, sea wrack, sea grass; zostera, eel grass.

zostéricole [zɔsterikɔl], *a. Bot:* living on zostera.

zostérien, -ienne [zɔsterjɛ̃, -jɛn], *Med:* **1.** *a.* relating to shingles. **2.** *s.* shingles patient.

zostéropidés [zɔsterɔpide], *s.m.pl. Orn:* Zosteropidae.

zouave [zwaːv], *s.m. Mil:* Zouave; *F:* **faire le z.**, to act the goat, the fool.

zoulou [zulu], *a. & s. usu. inv. in f.* Zulu; *pl. zoulous.*

Zoulouland [zululã(ːd)], *Pr.n. Geog:* Zululand.

zoum [zum], *s.m. F: Cin:* zoom.

zouzou [zuzu], *s.m. Mil: P: A:* Zouave; *pl. zouzous.*

zozo [zozo], *s.m. F:* **1.** sucker, mug. **2.** idiot, clot.

zozoter [zɔzɔte], *v.i. F:* to lisp.

zozotte [zɔzɔt], *s.f. P: O:* my dear; darling.

zugois, -oise [zygwa, -waːz], *a. & s. Geog:* (native, inhabitant) of Zug.

Zuiderzee (le) [ləzɥidɛrze], *Pr.n.m. Geog:* the Zuider Zee.

zunyite [zyniit], *s.f. Miner:* zunyite.

zurichois, -oise [zyrikwa, -waːz], *a. & s. Geog:* (native, inhabitant) of Zurich.

zut [zyt], *int. F:* (a) (of disappointment, anger) damn! hang it all! dash (it)! (b) (of contempt) rubbish! shut up! **z. pour vous!** go to blazes! **avoir un œil qui dit z. à l'autre,** to squint; (c) I can't be bothered!

Zuyderzée (le) [ləzɥidɛrze], *Pr.n.m.* = ZUIDERZEE.

Zwingle [zvɛ̃ːgl], *Pr.n.m. Rel.H:* Zwingli.

zwinglianisme [zvɛ̃gljanism], *s.m. Rel.H:* Zwinglianism.

zwinglien, -ienne [zvɛ̃gljɛ̃, -jɛn], *a. & s. Rel.H:* Zwinglian.

zyeuter [zjøte], *v.tr. P:* (a) to stare at, to look fixedly at (sth.); (b) to have a look, a squint, at (sth.); **zyeute-moi ça!** just look at that!

zygaénides [zigaenid], **zygénides** [ziʒenid], **zygénidés** [ziʒenide], *s.m.pl. Ent:* Zygaenidae.

zygène [ziʒɛn], *s.f. Ent:* burnet moth; zygaenid.

zygnéma [zignema], *s.m. Algae:* zygnema.

zygnémales [zignemal], *s.f.pl. Algae:* Zygnemales, Zygnematales.

zygo- [zigɔ], *comb.fm.* zygo-.

zygobranche [zigɔbrã:ʃ], *a.* zygobranchiate.

zygodactyle [zigɔdaktil], *Orn:* **1.** *a.* zygodactylous, zygodactyl. **2.** *s.m.* zygodactyl.

zygodonté [zigɔdɔ̃te], *a.* zygodont.

zygoma [zigɔma], *s.m. Anat:* zygoma; cheekbone.

zygomatique [zigɔmatik], *a. Anat:* zygomatic; **l'arcade z.,** the zygomatic arch.

zygomorphe [zigɔmɔrf], *a. Bot:* zygomorphous, zygomorphic.

zygomorphie [zigɔmɔrfi], *s.f. Bot:* zygomorphism, zygomorphy.

zygomycètes [zigɔmisɛt], *s.m.pl. Fung:* Zygomycetes, Zygomycetidae.

zygophyllacé [zigɔfilase], *Bot:* **1.** *a.* zygophyllaceous. **2.** *s.f.pl.* zygophyllacées, Zygophyllaceae.

zygophylle [zigɔfil], *s.f. Bot:* zygophyllum.

zygoptères [zigɔptɛːr], *s.m.pl. Ent:* Zygoptera.

zygose [zigoːz], *s.f. Biol:* zygosis, conjugation.

zygospore [zigɔspɔːr], *s.m. Bot:* zygospore.

zygote [zigɔt], *s.m. Biol:* zygote.

zygotène [zigɔtɛn], *a. Biol:* **stade z.,** zigotene.

zym(o)- [zim(ɔ)], *pref.* zim(o)-.

zymase [zimaːz], *s.f. Ch:* zymase.

zymogène [zimɔʒɛn], *s.m. Biol: Ch:* zymogen(e).

zymohydrolyse [zimɔidrɔliːz], *s.f.* zymohydrolysis; hydrolysis by fermentation.

zymologie [zimɔlɔʒi], *s.f.* zymology.

zymosimètre [zimɔzimɛtr̩], *s.m. Brew: etc:* zymometer; zymosimeter.

zymotechnie [zimɔtɛkni], *s.f.* zymotechnics.

zymotique [zimɔtik], *a. Med:* zymotic.

zython [zitɔ̃], **zythum** [zitɔm], *s.m. Ant:* zithum, zythum.

Common Abbreviations

Abbreviations read as initials unless the phonetic spelling is shown. The English translations and abbreviations have been given wherever appropriate, but the French expression has not been translated where there is no real equivalent in English.

A., 1. *Altesse*, Highness. 2. *austral*, south(ern), S. 3. *Clockm: avancer*, fast. 4. *association*, association, ass(oc)., fellowship. 5. *Ph: masse atomique*, atomic mass. 6. *El: ampère*, ampere, amp. 7. *Fin: Com:* (*a*) *argent*, cash; (*b*) *acheter*, buy.

a., 1. *assuré*, insured. 2. *Fin:* (*a*) *action*, share, shr.; (*b*) (*on bill*) *accepté*, accepted, acc. 3. *Meas: are*, 100 square metres. 4. *Mec: accélération*, acceleration, a.

aa, *Pharm: ana*, of each the same quantity, aa.

ab., *St.Exch: abandonné*, relinquished (right, etc.).

a.b.s., *Post: O: aux bons soins* (*de*), care of, c/o.

ac., *Com: acompte*, payment on account.

A.C., *Action catholique.*

a.c., *Com:* (*a*) *argent comptant*, ready money; (*b*) *avaries communes*, general average, gen.av.

acc., *Com: Fin: acceptation*, acceptance (of bill), acc.

A.C.F., *Automobile Club de France.*

A.C.P.G., *Anciens Combattants et Prisonniers de Guerre.*

act., *Fin: action*, share, shr.

A.C.T.H., *Biol: adréno-cortico-trophic-hormone*, adrenocorticotrophic hormone, A.C.T.H.

A.D., *anno Domini*, A.D.

A.D.A.C. [adak], *Av: avion à décollage et atterrissage courts*, short take-off and landing (aircraft), STOL.

A.D.A.V. [adav], *Av: avion à décollage et atterrissage verticaux*, vertical take-off and landing (aircraft), VTOL.

add., *Pharm: addatur*, add.

A.D.N., *acide désoxyribonucléique*, desoxyribonucleic acid, D.N.A.

ad(r)., *adresse*, address; *adr. tél.*, *adresse télégraphique*, telegraphic address, T.A.

A.d.S., *Académie des Sciences*, Academy of Science, A.S.

A.E.C., *Association des Écrivains combattants*, association of writers who served in the war.

A.E.F., *Hist: Afrique Équatoriale Française*, French Equatorial Africa.

A.E.L.E., *Association européenne de libre-échange*, European Free Trade Association, E.F.T.A.

A. & M., *Arts et Métiers.*

A.F., 1. *Pol: Action française.* 2. *allocations familiales*, = family allowance. 3. *Elcs: audiofréquence*, audio-frequency, a.f.

A.F.A.T. [afat], *auxiliaire féminine de l'armée de terre* = Women's Royal Army Corps, W.R.A.C.

aff., *Geog: affluent*, tributary.

A.F.M., *association française de marketing.*

A.F.N., *Hist: Afrique française du Nord.*

A.F.N.O.R., *association française de normalisation* = B.S.I. (British Standards Institution); *U.S:* A.N.S.I. (American National Standards Institute).

A.F.P., *Agence France-Presse.*

agr., *agriculture*, agriculture, agr(ic).

Ah, *El: ampère(s)-heure*, ampere-hour(s), a.h.

A.I., *Altesse Impériale*, Imperial Highness.

A.I.D., *Association internationale de développement.*

A.I.E.A., *Agence internationale de l'énergie atomique*, International Atomic Energy Association, I.A.E.A.

A.I.S.S., *Association internationale de la sécurité sociale.*

A.I.T.A., *Association internationale des transports aériens*, International Air Transport Association, I.A.T.A.

A.L.A.T. [alat], *Mil: aviation légère de l'armée de terre.*

a.m., *ante meridiem*, a.m.

A.M., 1. *Arts et Métiers.* 2. *assurance mutuelle*, mutual assurance. 3. *âge mental.*

A.-M., *Alpes-Maritimes.*

A.M.D.G., *Ecc: ad majorem Dei gloriam*, to the greater glory of God.

Abréviations courantes

Les abréviations se lisent comme lettres initiales à moins que la prononciation phonétique ne soit donnée. La traduction et les abréviations anglaises sont données dans la mesure du possible, mais l'expression française n'a pas été traduite quand il n'y a pas d'équivalent véritable en anglias.

A.M.E., *Accord monétaire européen.*

am(ort)., *Fin:* (i) *amortissable*, redeemable, red.; (ii) *amortissement*, redemption (of stock).

amp., *El: ampère*, ampere, amp.

anc., *ancien*, old.

anme, *Com:* (*société*) *anonyme*, limited (-liability) company, Ltd.

ant., *Ecc: antienne*, antiphon.

A.O.C., *appellation d'origine contrôlée.*

A.O.F., *Hist: Afrique Occidentale Française*, French West Africa.

ap., *apud, chez,*, in (book, author, etc.).

A.P., 1. *Com: à protester*, to be queried. 2. *Mil: avant-poste(s)*, outpost(s). 3. *A: Adm: assistance publique.*

a.p., *Com: avaries particulières*, particular average, p.a.

A.P.E.L. [apɛl], *Association des parents d'élèves de l'école libre.*

A.P.G., *ancien prisonnier de guerre*, ex-Prisoner-of-War, ex-P.O.W.

appt, 1. *Nau: etc: approvisionnement*, provisioning. 2. *appartement*, flat.

ap(r).J.-C., *après Jésus-Christ*, anno Domini, A.D.

AR., 1. *Mec: arrière*, rear. 2. *accusé de réception.*

A.R., 1. *Altesse Royale*, Royal Highness, R.H. 2. *Rail: aller et retour*, return ticket. 3. *anno regni*, in the year of the reign, a.r.

a.r., *Astr:* (*ascensio recta*) *ascension droite*, right ascension, r.a.

A.R.N., *acide ribonucléique*, ribonucleic acid, R.N.A.

ar(r).-g., *Mil: arrière-garde*, rear-guard.

arr., *Adm: arrondissement*, district, dist.

art., 1. *Mil: artillerie*, artillery, art(y). 2. *article*, article, art.

A.S., 1. *Altesse Sérénissime*, Most Serene Highness. 2. *Association sportive*, Sports Club. 3. *Adm: assurances sociales*, social insurance.

A.S.L.V., *assurance sur la vie*, life assurance.

A.S.P., *Com: accepté sans protêt*, accepted without protest.

A.S.P.P.C., *accepté sous protêt pour compté.*

asse, *assurance*, insurance, ins.

A.S.S.E.D.I.C. [asɛdik, asdik], *Association pour l'emploi dans l'industrie et le commerce.*

ass.extr., *assemblée extraordinaire.*

A.S.S.U.L. [asyl], *Sp: association sportive scolaire et universitaire laïque.*

A.S.V., *Av: atterrissage sans visibilité*, blind landing.

A.T., 1. *Ancien Testament*, Old Testament. 2. *assurance contre les accidents du travail*, employers' liability insurance; *U.S:* workmen's compensation insurance.

a.-t., *El: ampère-tours*, ampere-turns, ats.

atm., *Ph: atmosphère*, atmosphere, atm.

à t.p., *Com: Fin: à tout prix*, at any cost.

A.T.P., *Fin: autorisation de transferts préalables.*

at(t)., *St.Exch:* (*of coupon, etc.*) *attaché*, attached.

auj., *aujourd'hui*, to-day.

A.V., *Mec: avant*, front.

Av, *Book-k: avoir*, credit, cr.

av., *avenue*, Avenue, Av.

avdp., *Meas: avoirdupois*, avoirdupois, avoir., avdp.

av.dt., *avec droit*, with rights, W.R.

av.-g., *Mil: avant-garde*, vanguard.

av. J.-C., *avant Jésus-Christ*, before Christ, B.C.

av.-p., *Mil: avant-poste*, outpost.

A.V.P., *Tp: avec avis d'appel.*

B., 1. *baron*, Baron, B. 2. *boréal*, northern, N. 3. *Ecc: bienheureux*, blessed. 4. *P: bougre !* hell !

b., 1. *Com: balle*, bale. 2. *Fin:* (*a*) *billet*, bill; (*b*) *bénéfice*, profit; (*c*) *bonification*, backwardation. 3. *Ph: bougie*, candle-power, c.p.

B/, *Fin: billet à ordre*, promissory note, P.N., p.n.

B.A., 1. (*Boy Scouts*) *bonne action*, good deed; *F: faire sa B.A. quotidienne*, to do one's good deed for the day. 2. *Meteor: bulletin annuel.*

b.a., *Pharm: balneum arenae,* sand-bath.

B.-A., *Basses-Alpes.*

B.A.A., *Sch: Brevet d'apprentissage agricole.*

bacc., *Sch:* baccalauréat.

balce, *Book-k: balance,* balance, bal.

Banq., *Fin: banque,* bank, Bk.

b. à. p., *Com: billet à payer,* bill payable, b.p.

b. à. r., *Com: billet à recevoir,* bill receivable, b.r.

barr., *Com: barrique,* barrel, bar.

bat., *Mil: bataillon,* battalion, bat(t)., bn, btn.

batt., *Mil: batterie,* battery, bat(t).

bce, *Book-k: balance,* balance, bal.

B.C.G., *(vaccin) bilié (de) Calmette et Guérin,* B.C.G. (vaccine).

bco, *Fin: banco,* banco.

bd, *boulevard,* Boulevard, Boul.

bde, *Mil: brigade,* brigade, Brig.

B.-du-R., *Bouches-du-Rhône.*

B.E., *Sch: A: Brevet élémentaire, q.v.* under BREVET.

B.E.A., 1. *s.m. Sch: Brevet d'enseignement agricole.* 2. *s.f.* British European Airways, B.E.A.

beau, *Com: bordereau,* memorandum, invoice.

B.E.C., *Sch: Brevet d'enseignement commercial.*

B.E.H., *Sch: Brevet d'enseignement hôtelier.*

B.E.I., 1. *Banque européenne d'investissement,* European Investments Bank, E.I.B. 2. *Sch: Brevet d'enseignement industriel.*

B.E.M.S., *Mil: Brevet d'enseignement militaire supérieur.*

B.E.P.C., *Sch: Brevet d'études du premier cycle du second degré.*

B.E.S., *Sch: Brevet d'enseignement social.*

B.E.S.A., *Sch: Brevet élémentaire des sports aériens.*

B.F., *banque de France,* Bank of France.

B.H., *(Boy Scouts) bonne humeur,* good humour.

B.I., *Sch: Brevet industriel.*

Bib., 1. *Bible,* Bible, Bib. 2. *bibliothèque,* library, lib.

bie, *Mil: batterie,* battery, bat(t).

B.I.H., *Bureau international de l'heure,* International Time Bureau, I.T.B.

B.I.R.D., *Banque internationale pour la reconstruction et le développement,* = International Bank for Reconstruction and Development, I.B.R.D.

B.I.T., *Bureau international du travail,* International Labour Office, I.L.O.

biv., *Mil: bivouac,* bivouac.

bl, *Com: baril,* barrel, bar.

bld, *boulevard,* Boulevard, Boul.

blle, *Com: bouteille,* bottle.

B.L.U., *W.Tel: bande latérale unique.*

b.m., *Pharm: balneum mariae,* water bath.

B.M., 1. *Ecc: Beata Maria,* the Blessed Virgin. 2. *bibliothèque municipale =* public library. 3. *Meteor: bulletin mensuel,* monthly bulletin.

B.N., *Bibliothèque Nationale.*

b/n, *Fin: brut pour net,* weight for net.

B.N.C., *bénéfices non commerciaux.*

B.N.C.I., *O: Banque nationale pour le commerce et l'industrie.*

B.N.P., *Banque nationale de Paris.*

B.O., *Bulletin Officiel.*

B.O.F., *s.m. P: beurre-œufs-fromages,* spiv, black market teer.

bon, *Mil: bataillon,* battalion, bat(t)., bn, btn.

Bon, *Baron,* Baron, Bn.

Bonne, *Baronne,* Baroness, Bnss.

bot, *Com: ballot,* bale.

boul., *boulevard,* Boulevard, Boul.

B.P., *A: Brevet professionnel.*

b.p., *Ph: basse pression,* low pressure, l.p.

B.-P., *Basses-Pyrénées.*

B.P.F., *Fin: bon pour francs,* value in francs.

B.P.N.F., *Fin: bon pour nouveaux francs,* value in new francs.

B.Q.E., *Meteor: Bulletin quotidien d'études.*

B.Q.R., *Meteor: Bulletin quotidien de renseignements.*

Bque, *Fin: banque,* bank, bk.

bque, 1. *Com: barrique,* barrel, bar. 2. *Nau: barque,* bark, barque, bque.

br., 1. *Publ: broché,* sewn. 2. *Mil: breveté =* passed Staff College.

B.-Rh., *Bas-Rhin.*

brig., *Mil: brigade,* brigade, brig.

B.S., *Sch: A: Brevet supérieur, q.v. under* BREVET 2.

B.S.E.C., *Sch: Brevet supérieur d'études commerciales.*

B.S.G.D.G., *breveté sans garantie du Gouvernement,* patent without Government warranty (of quality).

B.S.P., *Brevet sportif populaire.*

bt, 1. *Com: brut,* gross. 2. *Fin: billet,* bill.

B.T., 1. *Brevet de technicien.* 2. *El: basse tension,* low voltage, l.v.

B.T.A., *Brevet de technicien agricole.*

B.T.E., *Bureau des temps élémentaires.*

bté, *breveté,* patent.

btn, *Mil: bataillon,* battalion, bat(t)., bn, btn.

B.T.S., *Brevet de technicien supérieur.*

b.v., *Pharm: balneum vaporis,* steam bath.

Bx-A., *Beaux-Arts.*

C., 1. *Hist: Commandeur,* Commander (of order of chivalry). 2. *Ph:* (a) *grande calorie,* kilogramme, large, great calory, Cal. (b) *Celsius,* Celsius, C. 3. *El: coulomb,* coulomb, C.

c., 1. *cent,* hundred, c., ct., cent. 2. *Adm: canton,* canton. 3. *Corr: courant,* instant, inst. 4. *Com: compte,* account, A/C. 5. *Num: centime,* centime, c. 6. *Ph:* (a) *centigrade,* centigrade, C.; (b) *petite calorie,* gramme calory, lesser calory, small calory, cal.; (c) *chaleur spécifique,* specific heat, sp.ht. 7. *El: capacité,* capacity. 8. *St.Exch:* (a) *coupon,* coupon, c.; (b) *coupure,* denomination; (c) *cours,* quotation; c. 1er, first quotation. 9. *Jur: contre,* versus, v.

c/, *Book-k: contre,* contra.

ca., *Meas: centiare,* centiare, ca.

C.A., 1. *Mil: corps d'armée,* army corps. 2. *chiffre d'affaires,* turnover.

c.a., *El: courant alternatif,* alternating current, A.C.

C.A.D., *Comité d'aide au développement.*

c.-à-d., *c'est-à-dire,* that is to say, i.e.

C.A.F., 1. *Com: coût, assurance, fret,* cost, insurance, and freight, C.I.F. 2. [kaf], *Club alpin français.*

cage, *Fin: courtage,* brokerage, Bkge.

caire, *commissionnaire,* agent, Agt.

Cal., *Ph: grande calorie,* (large, great) calory, Cal.

cal., 1. *Mil: calibre,* calibre. 2. *Ph: petite calorie,* gramme-calory, lesser calory, small calory, cal.

cant., *Mil: cantonnement,* cantonnement.

Cap., *Mil: capitaine,* captain, Capt.

cap., 1. *Fin: capital,* capital, cap. 2. *Geog: capitale,* capital, cap.

C.A.P., *Sch:* (a) *Certificat d'aptitude pédagogique (enseignement primaire)* = Teacher's diploma; (b) *Certificat d'aptitude professionnelle.*

C.A.P.E.S. [kapes], *Certificat d'aptitude au professorat de l'enseignement secondaire* = Diploma of Education, Dip.Ed.

C.A.P.E.T. [kapɛt], *Certificat d'aptitude au professorat de l'enseignement technique.*

car(t)., *Publ: cartonné,* bound in boards.

c.at(t), *St.Exch: coupon attaché,* cum dividend, c.d., cum coupon.

cav., *Mil: cavalerie,* cavalry, Cav.

cc., *centimètre(s) cube(s),* cubic centimetre(s), cc., c.c.

C.C., 1. *Mil: corps de cavalerie,* cavalry corps. 2. *Pharm: corne de cerf,* hartshorn. 3. *Sch: cours complémentaire.* 4. *Fin: compte courant,* current account, C.A.

c.c., 1. *El: courant continu,* direct current, D.C. 2. *Fin: cours de compensation,* making-up price, M/U.

c/c., 1. *Fin: compte courant,* current account, C.A. 2. *St.Exch: cours de compensation,* making-up price, M/U.

C.C.I., *Chambre de Commerce internationale,* International Chamber of Commerce.

C.C.P., *compte courant postal, compte chèque postal,* Giro account.

cd, *Ph: candela, nouvelle bougie,* candela, (new) candle, Cd.

c. de g., *Ph: centre de gravité,* centre of gravity.

c. de f., *chemin de fer,* railway, rly.

C.D.M., *T.V: centre de distribution de modulations.*

C.D.R., *Commission des Réparations,* Reparation(s) Commission.

Cdt, *Mil: commandant,* Commandant, Cdt, Cmdt.; Major, Maj.

C.-du-N., *Côtes-du-Nord.*

Ce, *Com: compagnie,* company, Co.

C.E., *Conseil de l'Europe,* Council of Europe.

C.E.A., 1. *Commissariat à l'énergie atomique.* 2. *Confédération européenne de l'agriculture.*

C.E.C.A. [seka], *Communauté européenne du charbon et de l'acier,* European Coal and Steel Community, E.C.S.C.

C.E.D., *Communauté européenne de défense,* European Defence Community, E.D.C.

C.E.E., 1. *Communauté économique européenne,* the European Economic Community, E.E.C. 2. *Commission économique (des Nations Unies) pour l'Europe.*

C.E.E.A., *Communauté européenne de l'énergie atomique,* Euratom.

C.E.G., *Sch: collège d'enseignement général.*

C.E.I., *Commission électrotechnique internationale,* International Electrotechnical Commission, I.E.C.

C.E.N., *centre d'études nucléaires.*

cent., 1. *centime,* centime, cent. 2. *centième,* hundredth. 3. *Meas: centiare,* centiare, cent.

C.E.P., *Sch: Certificat d'études primaires.*

C.E.R.N. [sɛrn], *Centre européen pour la recherche nucléaire.*

certif., *Sch: certificat,* certificate, cert.

C.E.S., *Sch: collège d'enseignement secondaire.*

C.E.T., *Sch: collège d'enseignement technique.*

C.E.T.A., *Sch: centre d'études techniques agricoles.*

cf., *confer,* cf.

C.F., *Com: coût et fret,* cost and freight, c. & f.

C.F.A., 1. *chemins de fer algériens.* 2. *Fin: O: Comptoir français d'Afrique, Communauté financière d'Afrique.* 3. *Sp: club de football amateur.*

C.F.D.T., *Confédération française démocratique du travail.*

C.F.F., *chemins de fer fédéraux suisses.*

C.F.L., *Société nationale des chemins de fer luxembourgeois.*

C.F.L.N., *Hist: Comité français de libération nationale.*

C.F.M., *Chemins de fer du Maroc.*

C.F.P., *Compagnie française des pétroles.*

C.F.T.C., *Confédération française des travailleurs chrétiens.*

cg., *Meas: centigramme,* centigramme, cg.

C.G., *Consul Général,* Consul General, C.G.

C.G.A., 1. *Confédération générale de l'agriculture.* 2. *Confédération générale artisanale.*

C.G.A.F., *Confédération générale de l'artisanat français.*

C.G.C., *Confédération générale des Cadres.*

C.G.E., *Compagnie générale d'électricité.*

cgr, 1. *Mth: centigrade,* hundredth part of a grade. 2. *Meas: centigramme,* centigramme, c.g.

C.G.S., *Ph: centimètre-gramme-seconde,* centimetre-gramme-second, C.G.S.

C.G.T., 1. *Confédération Générale du Travail,* General Confederation of Labour. 2. *Compagnie générale transatlantique,* French Line.

C.G.T.-F.O., *Confédération générale du travail-force ouvrière.*

ch., 1. *Lit: chant,* canto, can. 2. *Mec: cheval,* horse-power, h.p. **ch.eff.,** *chevaux effectifs,* effective horse-power, e.h.p. 3. *Mth: cosinus hyperbolique,* hyperbolic cosine.

ch(ap)., *chapitre,* chapter, ch(ap).

ch. d'aff., *chargé d'affaires.*

ch. de f., *chemin de fer,* railway, rly.

Ch(ev)., *Chevalier,* Knight, K.

ch. f., *Fin: change fixe,* fixed exchange.

chh., *Ph: cheval-heure,* horse-power-hour, h.p.-hr.

ch.-l., *chef-lieu* = country town.

C.H.R., *Mil: Compagnie hors rang,* Headquarters Company.

C.H.U., *centre hospitalier universitaire* = teaching hospital.

ch.v(ap)., *Mec: cheval-vapeur,* horse-power, h.p.

chx, *Mec: chevaux,* horse-power, h.p.

C.I., *certificat d'importation.*

Ci, *Ph: curie,* curie, C.

C.I.C.R., *Comité international de la Croix-Rouge.*

Cie, *Com: Compagnie,* Company, Co.

C.I.I. [sedøzi], *Compagnie internationale pour l'Informatique.*

cion, *Com: commission,* commission, com(m)., Com.

C.I.R., *Comité intergouvernemental pour les réfugiés.*

C.I.R.C., *Med: Centre international de recherche sur le cancer.*

C.I.S.C., *Confédération internationale des syndicats chrétiens.*

C.I.S.L., *Confédération internationale des syndicats libres,* International Confederation of Free Trade Unions.

c/j., *Fin: courts jours,* short-dated (bills).

C.J.M., *Code de justice militaire.*

C.J.P., *Centre des jeunes patrons.*

cl., *Meas: centilitre,* centilitre, cl.

C.L., *Fin: Crédit Lyonnais.*

cm., *Meas:* (a) *centimètre,* centimetre, cm.; cm², *centimètre(s) carré(s),* square centimetre(s), cm²; cm³, *centimètre(s) cube(s),* cubic centimetre(s), cm³. **cm/s.** *Rec: centimètres par seconde* = inches per second, i.p.s. **cm/s/s.,** *Ph: centimètres par seconde par seconde.* (b) *centimilli-,* one hundred thousandth.

Cm, *Ph: coefficient de moment,* moment coefficient.

C.M., 1. *Mil:* (a) *compagnie de mitrailleurs.* (b) *centre mobilisateur.* 2. *Sch: cours moyen.*

c/m., *St.Exch: cours moyen,* average quotation.

c/n., 1. *Book-k: compte nouveau,* new account. 2. *St.Exch: cours nul,* no dealings.

C.N.E., *Comptoir National d'Escompte.*

C.N.E.P., *O: Comptoir National d'Escompte de Paris.*

C.N.E.S., *Centre national d'études spatiales.*

C.N.P.F., *Conseil national du patronat français.*

C.N.R., (1939–45) *Conseil National de la Résistance.*

C.N.R.S., *Centre national de la recherche scientifique.*

C.N.S., *Comité national des sports.*

C.N.T., *Confédération nationale du travail.*

Co, *Com: Compagnie,* Company, Co.

C.O., C/o. c/o., *Com: compte ouvert,* open account.

cochl., *Pharm: cochleare,* spoonful, coch(l).

cochleat., *Pharm: cochleatim,* by spoonfuls.

C.O.D.E.R., [kɔdɛ:r] *Commission de développement économique régional.*

C.O.I., *comité olympique international,* International Olympic Committee, I.O.C.

Col., *Mil: colonel,* Colonel, Col.

colat., *Pharm: colature,* colature, colat.

com., *Com: commission,* commission, com(m).

COMECON, [kɔmɛkɔ̃] *Conseil pour l'aide économique mutuelle.*

Comm., 1. *Commandeur,* Commander, Com. 2. *Mil: Commandant,* Commandant, Cdt., Cmdt.; Major, Maj.

compt., *Com:* 1. *comptant,* ready (money). 2. *comptabilité,* book-keeping.

Comptes Rend., *Comptes Rendus de l'Académie des Sciences,* Proceedings of the Academy of Science.

Comt, *Mil: Commandant,* Commandant, Cdt., Comdt.; Major, Maj.

con, *Com: commission,* commission, com(m).

conf., *conferatur,* compare, conf., c.f.

confl., *Geog: confluent,* tributary, trib.

connt, *Com: connaissement,* bill of lading, B/L.

conv., *Fin: converti,* converted, convd.

coq., *Pharm: coquatur,* cook.

cor., *Geom: corollaire,* corollary, coroll.

cort., *Pharm: cortex,* bark, cort.

cos., *Trig: cosinus,* cosine, cos.

coséc., *Trig: cosécante,* cosecant, cosec.

cot(g)., *Trig: cotangente,* cotangent, cot.

coul., *El: coulomb,* coulomb, C.

coup., 1. *St.Exch: coupon,* coupon, cp. 2. *Fin: coupure,* denomination, denom.

cour., *Corr: courant,* instant, inst.

court., *Com: courtage,* brokerage.

C.P.E.M., *Sch: Certificat préparatoire aux études médicales.*

C.P.J.I., *Cour permanente de justice internationale,* Permanent Court of International Justice.

cpt, *Com: comptant,* ready (money).

cpte, *Com: compte,* account, acc.

C.Q.F.D., *Geom: ce qu'il fallait démontrer,* quod erat demonstrandum, Q.E.D.

cr., *Book-k: crédit,* credit, cr.

C.R., 1. *Hist: Calendrier Républicain,* Republican Calendar. 2. *compte rendu.*

C.R.E.D.I.F. [kredif], *Centre de recherche et d'étude pour la diffusion du français.*

C.R.F., *Croix-Rouge française,* French Red-Cross.

C.R.S., *Compagnies républicaines de sécurité,* (in France) State security police, riot police; *un C.R.S.,* a member of the C.R.S.

cs, *St.Exch: cours,* quotation, quot.

Cslt, *Consulat,* Consulate.

csse, *Com: caisse,* case, C/.

ct, *Corr: courant,* instant, inst.

C.T., *cabine téléphonique,* telephone box.

C.T.A., *Tg: communiquer à toutes adresses,* to be circulated to all addresses.

Cte, *comte,* count, Ct.

Ctesse, *comtesse,* countess.

ctg., 1. *Com: courtage,* brokerage. 2. *Trig: cotangente,* cotangent, cot.

cts, *Num: centimes,* centimes.

C.U., *charge utile,* useful load.

c.u., *St.Exch: cours unique,* sole quotation.

cub., *cube, cubique,* cube, cubic, c(ub).

cuill., *Pharm: cuillerée,* spoonful.

cum., *St.Exch: cumulatif,* cumulative, cum.

C.V., *curriculum vitae.*

c.v., 1. *Com.Corr: A: cette ville,* this town. 2. *Mec: cheval-vapeur,* horse-power, h.p.

Cx, *Ph: coefficient de traînée,* drag coefficient.

cyat., *Pharm: cyathus,* cupful, glassful, cyath.

Cz, *Ph: coefficient de portance,* lift coefficient.

D., 1. *Don,* Don. 2. *Ecc: Dom,* Dom. 3. *Rel: Dame,* Lady. 4. (route) *départementale* = B road. 5. *Com:* (a) *doit, débit,* debit, d.; (b) *départ,* starting date; (c) *déport,* backwardation, back.

d., 1. *droit,* right, r. 2. *Astr: déclinaison,* declination, d. 3. *Com: demande,* demand, dem. 4. *Ph: densité,* density, d. 5. *Pharm: dose,* dose, d. 6. *jours,* days.

do, *dito,* ditto, do.

D.A., 1. *Mil: directeur de l'arrière.* 2. *Com: documents contre acceptation,* documents against acceptance.

dag., *Meas: décagramme,* decagramme, dag.

dal., *Meas: décalitre,* decalitre, dal.

dam., *Meas: décamètre,* decametre, dam.

D.A.T., *Mil: défense antiaérienne du territoire.*

dB., *décibel,* decibel, db, dB.

D.B., *Mil: division blindée,* armoured division.

D.C., *Mus: da capo,* D.C.

D.C.A., *Mil: défense contre avions,* anti-aircraft defence.

d.d., *Pharm: donné dans,* given in.

D.D.P., *El: différence de potentiel,* potential difference, p.d.

D.D.T., *Ch: dichloro-diphényl-trichlorethane,* D.D.T.

deb., *Book-k: débit,* debit, d(eb).

débit., *débiteur,* debtor.

dec., *Pharm: decoctio,* decoction, decoct.

déc., 1. *décédé,* deceased, died, dec(d). 2. *décembre,* December, Dec.

decil., *décilitre,* decilitre, dl.

déclin., *Astr: déclinaison,* declination, d(ec).

del., *Engr: delineavit,* del(t).

délég., *St.Exch: délégation,* delegation, del.

delt., *Engr: delineavit,* del(t).

dem., *demain,* to-morrow.

dem. réd., *Com: demandes réduites.*

dép., *Adm: département.*

der(r), *Corr: dernier,* ultimo, ult.

D.E.S., *diplôme d'études supérieures.*

dét., *St.Exch:* (of coupon) *détaché,* detached.

dètt, *Mil: détachement,* detachment, det.

dg., *Meas: décigramme,* decigramme.

D.G., *Ecc: Dei gratia,* by the grace of God.

dgr, *Mth: décigrade,* one tenth of a grade.

D.I., *division d'infanterie,* infantry division.

dif., *St.Exch: différé,* deferred (stock), def.

dig., *Pharm: faites digérer,* digest, dig.

dil., *Pharm: faites diluer,* dilute, dil.

dist., *Pharm: distillez,* distil.

div., 1. *St.Exch: dividende,* dividend, div. 2. *Mil: division,* division, div.

dl., *Meas: décilitre,* decilitre, dl.

DM, *Deutsche Mark.*

dm., 1. *dimanche,* Sunday, Sun. 2. *Meas: décimètre,* decimetre, dm. **dm²,** *décimètre carré,* square decimetre, dm². **dm³,** *décimètre cube,* cubic decimetre, dm³.

D.M., *docteur en médecine,* Doctor of Medicine, M.D.

D.M.A., *Délégation ministérielle pour l'armement.*

D.M.P., *docteur en médecine de la Faculté de Paris.*

dne, *douane,* customs.

do, do, *dito,* ditto, do.

dol., *Mus: dolce,* dol.

dol(l)., *dollar,* dollar, dol.

D.O.M., 1. *Deo optimo maximo,* (dedicatory formula for churches, etc.). 2. *départements d'outre-mer.*

don, *Com: direction,* management.

D.O.T., *défense opérationnelle du territoire.*

douz., *douzaine,* dozen, doz.

D.P., 1. *Ecc: de profundis.* 2. *défense passive,* Civil Defence, C.D. 3. *personne déplacée,* displaced person, D.P. 4. *Com: documents contre payement,* documents against payment, D.A.P.

d.p., *décret parlementaire,* parliamentary enactment.

D.P.L.G., *diplômé par le gouvernement.*

D.Q., *Astr: dernier quartier,* last quarter.

Dr, *docteur,* Doctor, Dr.

dr, 1. *Book-k: débiteur,* debtor, dr. 2. *Jur: droit de souscription,* application right.

dr c., *St.Exch: dernier cours,* last quotation.

D.S.L., *Oc: (couche diffusante profonde),* deep scattering layer.

Dsse, *Duchesse,* Duchess.

D.S.T., *Direction de la surveillance du territoire* = Home Security Branch.

dt, 1. *St.Exch: dont, q.v.* 2. *Book-k: doit,* debit, deb.

d.u.e.l. [dyɛl], *Diplôme universitaire d'études littéraires.*

d.u.e.s. [dyɛs], *Diplôme universitaire d'études scientifiques.*

dz., *Com: douzaine,* dozen, doz.

D.Z., *Mil: Av: dropping zone.*

E., 1. *est,* east, E. 2. *(a) Éminence,* Eminence. *(b) Excellence,* Excellency, E(xc). 3. *Ph: équivalent mécanique de la chaleur,* mechanical equivalent of heat.

e., *El.E: force électromotrice,* electromotive force, e.m.f.

e. à p., *Fin: effet à payer,* bill payable, b.p.

e. à r., *Fin: effet à recevoir,* bill receivable, b.r.

E.B.R., 1. *Mil: engin blindé de reconnaissance,* reconnaissance armoured car. 2. *Bio-Ch: efficacité biologique relative.*

E.C.G., *électrocardiogramme,* electrocardiogram, E.C.G.

E.C.M., *Établissement central météorologique.*

E.C.P., *École Centrale des Arts et Manufactures de Paris.*

ECS, *échantillons commerciaux,* commercial samples.

éd., *édition,* edition, ed(it).

E.D.F. [ødeɛf, edeɛf], *Électricité de France.*

éd(it)., *édition,* edition, ed.

E.e., *envoyé extraordinaire,* Envoy Extraordinary, E.E.

E.e. & M.pl., *envoyé extraordinaire et ministre plénipotentiaire,* Envoy Extraordinary and Minister Plenipotentiary, E.E. & M.P.

E.E.G., *électroencéphalogramme,* electroencephalogram, E.E.G.

E.-et-L., *Eure-et-Loir.*

E.G.F., *Électricité et Gaz de France.*

E.H.M., *Mil: École militaire de haute montagne.*

E.L.O., *École des Langues Orientales,* School of Oriental Languages.

Em., *Éminence,* Eminence.

E.-M., *Mil: état-major,* headquarters, H.Q.

E.-M.A., *Mil: état-major d'armée,* army headquarters, A.H.Q.

E.-M.G., *Mil: état-major général,* general headquarters, G.H.Q.

E.N., *Sch: (a) École normale; (b) Éducation nationale.*

E.N.A., 1. *École nationale d'administration.* 2. *École nationale d'agriculture.*

E.-N.-E., *est-nord-est,* east-north-east, ENE, E.N.E.

ens., *ensemble,* together.

E.N.S., *École normale supérieure.*

E.N.S.E.T., *École normale supérieure de l'enseignement technique.*

env., *environ,* about.

e.o.o.e., e. & o.e., *Com: erreur ou omission exceptée,* errors and omissions excepted, E. & O.E.

E.O.R. [eɔɛr], *Mil: élève officier de réserve,* cadet.

E.P.S., *école primaire supérieure,* higher elementary school.

esc., *Mil: escadron,* squadron, sq.

E.S.C., *École supérieure de commerce.*

esca., *escadrille, Av:* flight, *Navy:* flotilla.

esc(te), *Com: escompte,* discount, dis(c), disct.

E.-S.-E., *est-sud-est,* east-south-east, ESE, E.S.E.

est., *St.Exch: estampillé,* stamped.

&, *et commercial,* ampersand.

établ., établt, *établissement,* establishment, est.

etc., *et cætera,* etcetera, etc.

E.T.P., *École spéciale des travaux publics, du bâtiment et de l'industrie.*

Ets., *établissements,* establishments.

E.-U., *États-Unis,* United States, U.S.

Euratom [œratɔm], *Communauté européenne de l'énergie atomique,* Euratom.

eV, *Ph: électron-volt,* electron-volt, eV.

E.V., *Post: en ville,* local.

ex., 1. *exemple,* example, ex. 2. *Book-k: exercice,* year's trading; *St.Exch: ex. att., exercice attaché,* cum dividend, c.d.

ex-bon, *St.Exch: ex-bonification,* ex-bonus.

Exc., *Excellence,* Excellency, Exc.

ex-c(oup)., *St.Exch: ex coupon,* ex coupon, ex cp; **ex-c. div.,** *ex-coupon de dividende,* ex dividend-coupon; **ex-c. int.,** *ex-coupon d'intérêt,* ex interest-coupon.

ex-d., *St.Exch: ex-dividende,* ex dividend, ex div.

ex-dr., *St.Exch: ex-droits,* ex rights.

exempl., *exemplaire,* copy.

E.X.I.M., *exportation-importation.*

expn, *expédition,* dispatching.

ex. rep., *ex-répartition,* ex-bonus.

F., 1. *Ecc: Frère,* Brother, Br. 2. *Ph: (a) force,* force, f. *(b) Fahrenheit,* Fahrenheit, F. 3. *Phot: distance focale,* focal length, f. 4. *El: farad,* farad, f.

f., 1. *franc(s),* franc(s). 2. *féminin,* feminine, fem. 3. *Ph: fréquence,* frequency, f.

F1, F2, F3, F4, F5, *appartement comprenant 1, 2, 3, 4, 5, pièces principales,* flat including 1, 2, 3, 4, 5, main rooms.

f. à b., *Com: franco à bord,* free on board, f.o.b.

fab., *Com: fabrication,* make.

fac. [fak], *Sch: F: faculté.*

F.A.C., *Adm: fonds d'aide et de coopération.*

f.a.c., *Nau.Ins: franc d'avarie commune,* free of general average, f.g.a.

F.A.F.L., *Fr.Hist: Forces aériennes de la France Libre,* Free French Air Force.

F.A.I., *Fédération aéronautique internationale.*

f.a.p., *Nau.Ins: franc d'avarie particulière,* free of particular average, f.p.a.

fasc., 1. *Pharm: fasciculus,* bundle. 2. *Publ: fascicule,* number.

faub., *faubourg,* suburb, sub.

F.B., *franc belge,* Belgian franc.

F.C., *football club.*

f.c., *Com: fin courant,* at the end of this month.

f.c.é.m., *El.E: force contre-électromotrice,* back electromotive force, back e.m.f.

F.C.F.A., *Fin: franc de la communauté financière d'Afrique, O: franc comptoirs français d'Afrique.*

F.D.F.P., *Fin: franc de la communauté financière du Pacifique, O: franc comptoirs français du Pacifique.*

f.c(t)., *Corr: fin courant,* at the end of this month.

fco, *Com: franco,* free of charge, f.o.c., carriage paid, C.P.

F.D., *Fin: franc Djibouti.*

F.D.E.S., *Fonds de développement économique et social.*

f.é.m., *El: force électromotrice,* electromotive force, e.m.f.

fév., *février,* February, Feb.

FF, *franc français.*

F.F.C., *Hist: Forces françaises combattantes.*

F.F.I., *Hist: Forces françaises de l'intérieur,* French Forces of the Interior.

F.F.L., *Hist: Forces françaises libres,* Free French Forces.

fg, *Ph: frigorie,* negative calorie.

F.G., *Fin: frais généraux,* overheads.

F.G.D.S., *Pol: Fédération de la gauche démocrate et socialiste.*

F.G.S., *Fédération gymnastique et sportive.*

F.G.T.B., *Fédération générale du travail de Belgique.*

F.I.A., *(a) Fédération internationale d'astronautique; (b) Fédération internationale de l'automobile,* International Automobile Federation, I.A.F.

F.I.A.P., *Fédération internationale de l'art photographique.*

F.I.A.T., *Fonds d'intervention pour l'aménagement du territoire.*

F.I.D.E.S. [fidɛs], *Fonds d'investissements pour le développement économique et social.*

F.I.D.O. [fido], *Aer:* Fog Investigation Dispersal Operation, FIDO.

fig., 1. *figure,* illustration, figure, fig. 2. *figuré,* figurative, fig.

F.I.L., *Fédération internationale de laiterie.*

filt., *Pharm: filtrez,* filter, filt.

F.I.S.E., 1. *Fédération internationale syndicale de l'enseignement.* 2. *Fonds international de secours à l'enfance.*

fl., 1. *florin,* florin, fl. 2. *fleuve,* river, riv. 3. *Pharm: fleurs,* flowers, fl.

F.L., *Fin: franc luxembourgeois.*

F.L.N., *Hist: Front de libération nationale.*

F.M., 1. *fusil mitrailleur,* Bren-gun. **2.** *Post: franchise militaire* = on active service, O.A.S. **3.** *W.Tel: frequency modulation,* F.M.

F.M.I., *Fonds monétaire international,* International Monetary Fund, I.M.F.

f.m.m., *El: force magnétomotrice,* magnetic potential.

F.N., *Pharm: formulaire des médicaments nouveaux.*

F.N.E.F. [fnɛf], *Fédération nationale des étudiants de France.*

fᵒ, *folio,* folio, fo(l).

F.O., *Pol: Force ouvrière.*

fol., *Pharm: folia,* leaves.

follic., *Pharm: follicules,* follicules.

fond., *Fin: part de fondateur* = founder's share.

f.p., *Corr: fin prochain,* at the end of next month.

F.P.A., *Formation professionnelle des adultes,* further education for adults.

fque, *Com: fabrique,* make.

Fr., 1. *Ecc: Frère,* Brother, Br. **2.** *Geog: France,* France.

fr(s)., *franc(s),* franc(s).

f.r., *St.Exch: faire reporter,* carry over.

fre, *Com: facture,* invoice, inv.

fro, *franco,* free of charge, carriage paid, f.o.c., C.P.

fruct., *Pharm: fructus,* fruit.

fs, *florins,* florins.

F.S., 1. *franc suisse,* Swiss franc. **2.** *Post: faire suivre,* please forward.

F.S.A., *Pharm: fac secundum artem,* prepare according to formula.

F.S.H., *Biol: folliculino-stimuline hypophysaire,* follicle-stimulating hormone, F.S.H.

F.S.I., *Fédération syndicale internationale,* International Federation of Trade Unions, I.F.T.U.

F.S.M., *Fédération syndicale mondiale,* World Federation of Trade Unions, W.F.T.U.

F.T.A., *Forces terrestres antiaériennes,* (i) anti-aircraft defence; (ii) *U.S:* (N.A.T.O.) anti-aircraft defence forces.

F.T.P.(F)., *Hist: francs-tireurs et partisans (français).*

G., *Grâce, Grandeur,* Highness. **S.G.,** *Sa Grâce, Sa Grandeur,* His Highness, H.H.; **V.G.,** *Votre Grâce, Votre Grandeur,* Your Highness.

g., 1. *gauche,* left, 1. **2.** *Meas: gramme(s),* gramme(s), gr. **3.** *Ph: gravité,* gravity, gr.

G.A., *Mil: groupe d'armée,* army group.

G.A.C., *Mil: groupe d'armées du centre,* army group of the centre.

Gal, *Mil: Général,* General, Gen.

gal, *général,* general, gen.

Gar., *Garonne.*

Gaux, *Généraux,* Generals.

G.B., *Grande Bretagne,* Great Britain, G.B.

G.C., 1. *Grand'croix,* Grand Cross (of the Legion of Honour), G.C. **2.** *A: (route de) grande communication* = B road.

G.D.F., *Gaz de France.*

gén., *Mil: génie,* (the) engineers.

gend., *Mil: gendarmerie.*

GeV., *El: gigaélectron-volt,* gigaelectron volt, GeV.

gf., *Ph: gramme-force,* gram weight.

g.g., *grand'garde,* outpost.

G.I.C., *grand infirme civil.*

G.I.G., *grand invalide de guerre.*

Gir., *Gironde.*

g.l., *Book-k: grand livre,* ledger, led.

G.-M., *Freemasonry: Grand-Maître,* Grand Master, G.M.

G.M.T., *Hor: Greenwich mean time,* G.M.T.

G.O., 1. *W.Tel: grandes ondes,* long wave, L.W. **2.** *see* G(r),O.

G.Q.G., *Mil: grand quartier général,* General Headquarters, G.H.Q.

gr., 1. *Meas: gramme(s),* gramme(s), gr. **2.** *Pharm: graines,* seeds.

Gr.C., *Grand'Croix,* Grand Cross (of the Legion of Honour), G.C.

gr.coup., *St.Exch: grosses coupures,* large denominations.

G(r).O., *Grand Officier,* Grand Officer (of the Legion of Honour), G.O.

G.V., *grande vitesse.*

H., *Ph: henry,* henry, H.

h., 1. *heure,* hour, h. **2.** *hypothèque,* mortgage, mortg. **3.** *St.Exch: hier,* yesterday. **4.** *Ph: constante de Planck,* Planck constant, h.

ha., *Meas: hectare,* hectare.

H.-A., *Hautes-Alpes.*

H.B.M., *A: habitation à bon marché.*

H.C., 1. *hors concours,* not competing. **2.** *Mil: hors cadre,* not on the strength. **3.** *hors classe,* unclassified.

H.C.H., *Ch: hexachlorocyclohexane.*

h.cn., *St. Exch: hier, cours nul,* no dealings yesterday.

H.E.C., *(école des) hautes études commerciales.*

hectom., *Meas: hectomètre,* hectometre, hm.

H.F., *haute fréquence,* high frequency, *H.F.*

hg., *Meas: hectogramme,* hectogramme, hectog.

H.-G., *Haute-Garonne.*

hl., *Meas: hectolitre,* hectolitre, hect.

H.-L., *Haute-Loire.*

H.L.M., *habitation à loyer modéré.*

hm., *Meas: hectomètre,* hectometre, hm.

H.-M., *Haute-Marne.*

hon., *Corr: honorée,* letter.

h.p., *haute pression,* high pressure, h.p.

H.-P., *Hautes-Pyrénées.*

H.P.C., *hautes parties contractantes,* high contracting parties.

H.-Rh., *Haut-Rhin.*

H.S., *Mil: hors de service,* unfit for service.

H.-Sav., *Haute-Savoie.*

H.T., 1. *Elcs: haute tension,* high voltage, H.V. **2.** *hors taxe.*

H.-V., *Haute-Vienne.*

hW, *El: hectowatt.*

hyp(oth)., *hypothèque,* mortgage, mortg.

Hz, *El.E:* hertz, cycles per second, c.p.s.

I., 1. *El: intensité,* intensity. **2.** *Mec: moment d'inertie,* moment of inertia.

Ibid., *ibidem,* ibidem, ibid.

I.C., *Jésus-Christ,* Jesus Christ, I.C.

I.C.N., *in Christi nomine,* in the name of Christ.

id., *idem,* idem.

I.D., *Tp: indication de durée; appel avec I.D.,* advise duration and charge call, A.D.C.

I.D.A., *immortalis Dei auspicio,* with the help of God.

I.D.H.E.C. [idɛk], *Institut des hautes études cinématographiques,* (the university of the film industry).

I.-et-L., *Indre-et-Loire.*

I.-et-V., *Ille-et-Vilaine.*

I.F.O.P. [ifɔp], *Institut français d'opinion publique.*

I.F.R.B., *Comité international d'enregistrement des fréquences,* International Frequency Registration Board, I.F.R.B.

I.G.A.M.E. [igam], *Inspecteur général de l'administration en mission extra-ordinaire.*

I.G.N., *Institut géographique national.*

I.H.S., *Jesus* (from Greek ΙΗΣΟΥΣ).

I.I.P., *Institut international de la presse,* International Press Institute.

I.M.A.O., *Ch: inhibiteur de la monoamine-oxydase.*

I.M.E.X., *importation-exportation.*

imp., *Com: impayé,* dishonoured bill.

I.M.P., *Sch: internat médico-pédagogique.*

I.N.A., *Institut national agronomique.*

ind., *industrie,* industry, ind.

inéd., *inédit,* unpublished, unpub.

I.N.E.D., *Institut national d'études démographiques.*

inf., 1. *Mil: infanterie,* infantry, inf. **2.** *Pharm: faites infuser,* infuse.

in-f(o)., in-fol., *Publ: in-folio,* folio, fo(l).

ing(én)., *ingénieur,* engineer, eng(r).

I.N.H., *Ch: isonicotinique-hydrazide.*

inj., *Pharm: injection,* injection, inj.

in-pl., *Publ: in-plano,* broadsheet.

I.N.R.I., *Ecc: Jesus Nazarenus Rex Judæorum,* Jesus of Nazareth, King of the Jews.

I.N.S.E.E., *Institut national des statistiques et des études économiques.*

INSERM [insɛrm], *Institut national de la santé et de la recherche médicale.*

Insp. gén., *inspecteur général,* Inspector General.

I.N.S.T., *Ecc: In nomine sanctæ Trinitatis,* in the name of the Holy Trinity.

int(er)., *Fin: intérêt,* interest, int.

inv., *invenit,* (he) designed (it), inv.

I.P.E.S. [ipɛs], *Institut de préparation aux enseignements du second degré.*

i.p.i., *Ecc: in partibus infidelium,* on a mission to the heathen.

I.P.P., *Adm: impôt sur le revenu des personnes physiques.*

I.P.S.A., *infirmières parachutables secouristes de l'air.*

I.U.T., *Institut universitaire de technologie.*

J., j. 1. *Mil: jour* = zero day. **2.** *El: joule,* joule, j.

J.A.C. [ʒak], *jeunesse agricole catholique.*

janv., *janvier,* January, Jan.

J.-B., *Jean-Baptiste.*

J.-C., *Jésus-Christ,* Jesus Christ, J.C.

jce, *Fin: jouissance* = cum dividend, c.d.

j/d., *Com: jours de date,* days after date, d.d., D/D.

Je, *jeune,* junior, jr., jnr., jun.

J.E.C. [ʒɛk], *jeunesse étudiante catholique.*

J.I.C. [ʒik], *jeunesse indépendante chrétienne.*

J.-J., *Jean-Jacques.*

jl, *Book-k: journal,* day-book, d.b.

J.M.F., *Jeunesses Musicales de France.*

Jne, *jeune,* junior, jr., jnr., jun.

J.O., 1. *Journal Officiel.* **2.** *Jeux Olympiques,* Olympic Games.

J.O.C. [ʒɔk], *jeunesse ouvrière catholique.*

jou., *St.Exch: jouissance* = cum dividend, c.d.

jr, *jour,* day, d.

juil., *juillet,* July, Jul.

j/v., *Com: jours de vue,* days after sight, d.s.

K., *Ph: (échelle de) Kelvin,* Kelvin scale, K.
k., *kilo,* kilo, k.
kA., *El: kiloampère,* kiloampere, kA.
kC, *El: kilocoulomb.*
kc., *El: kilocycle,* kilocycle, kc.
kcal, *Ph: kilocalorie,* kilocalory, kcal, kcl.
kg(r)., *Meas: kilogramme,* kilogramme, kg.
kgf., *Ph: kilogramme-force.*
kgm., *Mec: kilogrammètre,* kilogrammeter, kgm.
kg/m³, *Ph: kilogramme par mètre cube,* kilogramme per cubic metre, kg/m³.
kgp, *Ph: kilogramme-poids,* kilogramme-weight.
kHz, *El: kilohertz,* kilocycle, kc.
kilo, *Meas: kilogramme,* kilogramme, kilo.
kJ, *El: kilojoule,* kilojoule, kJ.
kl., *Meas: kilolitre,* kilolitre, kl.
km., *Meas: kilomètre(s),* kilometre(s), km; **km²,** *kilomètre(s) carré(s),* square kilometre(s), km²; **km³,** *kilomètre(s) cube(s),* cubic kilometre(s), km³; **km/h.,** *kilomètres (à l')heure,* kilometres per hour, km.p.h.
k.o., *Box: knock-out,* knock out; *il a été mis k.o.,* he was knocked out, he was K.O'd.
kt, *kilotonne,* kiloton.
kV, *El: kilovolt,* kilovolt, kv, kV.
kVA, *El: kilovoltampère,* kilovolt-ampere(s), kva.
kVAh, *El: kilovoltampèreheure.*
kvar, *Elcs: kilovar,* kilovar, kvar.
kvarh, *Elcs: kilovarheure,* kilovar-hour, kvarh.
kW., *El: kilowatt,* kilowatt, kw.
kWh., *El: kilowatt(s)-heure,* kilowatt-hour(s), kwhr.

L, *livre sterling,* pound sterling, £.
l., **1.** *Meas: (a) litre,* litre, l.; *(b) lieue,* league, l. **2.** *Com: A: liquidation,* liquidation, liq.; *en l., en liquidation,* in liquidation.
l.a., *Pharm: lege artis,* as directed, l.a.
larg., *largeur,* width, w.
lat., **1.** *Geog: latitude,* latitude, lat. **2.** *latin,* Latin, L(at).
lb., *Meas: livre,* pound, lb.
l.c., **1.** *loco citato,* at the place cited, loc. cit. **2.** *Meas: A: lieue carrée,* square league.
l/c., *leur compte,* their account.
l/cr., *lettre de crédit,* letter of credit, l.c.
leg., *légation,* legation.
L.-et-C., *Loir-et-Cher.*
L.-et-G., *Lot-et-Garonne.*
lib., *Fin: libéré,* fully paid, f.p.
Lieut, *Mil: lieutenant,* Lieutenant, Lt, Lieut.
Lieut-Col, *Mil: lieutenant-colonel,* Lieutenant-Colonel, Lieut.-Col.
lin., *Pharm: liniment,* liniment, lin.
liq., **1.** *Pharm: liqueur,* solution, liq. **2.** *St.Exch: liquidation,* settlement; **liq. cte,** *liquidation courante,* current account; **liq. pro.,** *liquidation prochaine,* next account.
liv(r)., *Com: livraison,* delivery, dely.
liv. st., *livre sterling,* pound sterling, £.
l.l., *loco laudato,* at the place indicated, l.l.
LL.AA., *Leurs Altesses,* Their Highnesses, T.H.
LL.AA.II., *Leurs Altesses Impériales,* Their Imperial Highnesses, T.I.H.
LL.AA.RR., *Leurs Altesses Royales,* Their Royal Highnesses, T.R.H.
LL.EE(M)., *Leurs Éminences,* Their Eminences.
LL.EE(xc)., *Leurs Excellences,* Their Excellencies.
LL.MM., *Leurs Majestés,* Their Majesties.
lm, *El: lumen,* lumen, l.
l/o, *Com: leur ordre,* their order.
loc.cit., *loco citato,* at the place cited, loc.cit.
log., *Mth: logarithme,* logarithm, log.
long., **1.** *longueur,* length, l., lgth. **2.** *Geog: longitude,* longitude, long.
L.Q., *Sch: lege quæso,* please read.
l.s., **1.** *loco sigilli,* where signed, l.s. **2.** *livre sterling,* pound sterling, £.
L.S.D., *Pharm: lysergique synthétique diéthylamine,* lysergic acid diethylamide, L.S.D.
Lt, *Mil: lieutenant,* Lieutenant, Lt.
Ltée, *Fr.C: limitée,* Limited (company), Ltd.
lu., *El: lumen,* lumen, l.
l.v., *Mus: læva manu.*
lx, *Ph: Meas: lux,* lux, lx.

M., **1.** *Monsieur,* Mr. **2.** *Majesté,* Majesty, M. **3.** *mars,* March, Mar. **4.** *mardi,* Tuesday, Tu. **5.** *mercredi,* Wednesday, Wed. **6.** *Astr: midi,* midday, m. **7.** *mille,* one thousand. **8.** *Ph: (a) Maxwell,* Maxwell, Max.; *(b) méga-,* mega-.
m., **1.** *mort,* died, deceased, d. **2.** *mon,* my. **3.** *masculin,* masculine, m. **4.** *Ch: méta.* **5.** *Meas: mètre,* metre, m.; **m²,** *mètre carré,* square metre, m²; **m³,** *mètre cube,* cubic metre, m³. **6.** *Pharm: misce,* mix, m. **7.** *Turf: manches,* sleeves. **8.** *mois,* month, m.
mA., *milliampère,* milliampere, m.amp., mA.
ma, *myria,* myria.
M.A., **1.** *Hist: moyen âge,* Middle Ages, M.A. **2.** *mérite agricole.*

Maj., *Mil: Major,* Major, Maj.
Mal, *Maréchal,* Marshal.
m. à m., *mot à mot,* word for word.
man., *Pharm: manipulus,* handful.
MAS [mas], *Mil: Manufacture d'armes de Saint-Étienne*
MAT [mat], *Mil: Manufacture d'armes de Tulle.*
mat, *mandat,* power of attorney, p.a.
mat.méd., *matière médicale,* materia medica.
max., *maximum,* maximum, max.
mb., *Meteor: millibar,* millibar, mb.
m/b., *Com: mon billet,* my bill.
Mc., *W.Tel: mégacycle,* megacycle, Mc.
m/c., *Com: mon compte,* my account, m/a.
md, *marchand,* merchant, mcht.
m.d., *Mus: main droite,* right hand, r.h.
m/d., *Com: mois de date,* month's date, m.d., M/D.
mde, *marchande,* merchant, mcht.
Me., *mercredi,* Wednesday, Wed.
Me, *Jur: Maître,* q.v.
mEq, *Ch: milliéquivalent,* milliequivalent, meq.
M.-et-L., *Maine-et-Loire.*
M.-et-M., *Meurthe-et-Moselle.*
MeV, *méga-electron-volt,* mega-electron-volt, mev, MeV.
mg., *Meas: milligramme,* milligramme, mg.
M.G., *Med: médecin de médecine générale,* general practitioner, G.P.
m.g., *Mus: main gauche,* left hand, l.h.
mgal, *Ph: milligal,* milligal, mGal.
M.G.P., *Sch: Certificat de mathématiques générales et physique.*
Mgr, *Ecc: Monseigneur,* Monsignor, Mgr.
mgr., *Meas: milligrade,* milligrade.
Mgrs, *Ecc: Messeigneurs,* Monsignori.
M.H.D., *Ph: magnétohydrodynamique,* magnetohydrodynamics.
M.I.C., *W.Tel: modulation par impulsions codées,* pulse code modulation, P.C.M.
mic.pan., *Pharm: mica panis,* breadcrumbs.
mill., *Num: millième,* millieme.
Min., *Adm: Ministre,* Minister.
min., *minimum,* minimum, min.
Mis, *Marquis,* Marquis.
MJ., *mégajoule.*
Mise, *Marquise,* Marchioness.
mise, *Com: marchandise,* goods, g.
M.J.C., *maison des jeunes et de la culture.*
m.kgf, *Ph: mètre-kilogramme-force.*
M.K.S.A., *Ph: mètre-kilogramme-seconde-ampère.*
ml., *Meas: millilitre,* millilitre, ml.
mle., *Mil: etc: modèle,* pattern, pat.
Mlle, *mademoiselle,* Miss.
Mlles, *mesdemoiselles,* the Misses.
MM., *Messieurs,* Messrs.
mm., *Meas:* **1.** *millimètre(s),* millimetre(s), mm.; **mm²,** *millimètre(s) carré(s),* square millimetre(s), mm²; **mm³,** *millimètre (s) cube(s),* cubic millimetre(s), mm³. **2.** *mégamètre,* megametre.
M.M., **1.** *messageries maritimes,* shipping companies. **2.** *marine marchande.*
m/m, *Fin: moi-même,* myself.
Mme, *Madame,* Mrs.
Mmes, *Mesdames,* Mesdames.
M.M.P., *Sch: Certificat de méthodes mathématiques de la physique.*
mN, *Ph: mètre-newton.*
M.N., *marine nationale.*
mn., *minute,* minute, m.
m/o, *Fin: mon ordre,* my order, m/o.
mol., *Ch: molécule,* molecule, mol.
Mon, *Com: maison,* firm.
M.-P., *mandat-poste,* postal order, P.O.
M.P.C., *Sch: Certificat de mathématique, physique et chimie.*
Mqs, *Marquis,* Marquis.
Mqse, *Marquise,* Marchioness.
Mr, *Monsieur,* Mr., Esq.
M.R.P., *Pol: Mouvement républicain populaire.*
Mrs, *Messieurs,* Messrs.
M.R.U., *Ministère de la reconstruction et de l'urbanisme.*
MS., *manuscrit,* manuscript, MS.; **MSS.,** *manuscrits,* manuscripts, MSS.
ms, *moins,* less.
m/s, *mètre par seconde,* metre(s) per second, m/s, m.p.s.
m/s², *mètre par seconde par seconde,* metre(s) per second per second, m. per sec².
M.S.A., *Mutualité sociale agricole.*
M.S.B.S., *Mil: Atom.Ph: (missile) mer-sol-balistique-stratégique =* underwater-to-land ballistic (missile).
msin, *magasin,* store.
M.T., *Rail: Service du matériel et de la traction.*
M.T.C.F., *Ecc: Mes très chers frères,* dearly beloved brethren.
mth, *Ph: millithermie,* kilogram(me) calorie.
M.T.S., *Mec: mètre-tonne-seconde,* metre-ton-second.

m/v., *Fin: mois de vue*, month's sight, m.s., M/S.

mx, *St.Exch: au mieux*, at best.

myg., *Meas: myriagramme*, myriagramme, myg.

myriam., *Meas: myriamètre*, myriametre, mym.

N., 1. *nord*, north, N. **2.** *nom*, name, n. **3.** *(route) nationale* = A Road. **4.** *M., Mme, Mlle, N.* = Mr, Mrs, Miss, X. **5.** *Fin: nominal*, nominal, n. **6.** *Ph:* (a) *Newton*, Newton; (b) *nombre d'Avogadro*, Avogadro number.

n., 1. *notre*, our. **2.** *neutre*, neuter, n. **3.** *Meas: nano-*, nano-.

Na, N.(B.), *nota bene*, N.B.

N.B.C., *Mil: nucléaire, biologique, chimique*.

N.C., *notable commerçant*.

n/c., *Com: notre compte*, our account.

N.-D., *Notre-Dame*, Our Lady.

N.D.E., *note de l'éditeur*.

N.D.L.R., *note de la rédaction*, editor's note.

N. du T., *note du traducteur*, translator's note.

N.-E., *nord-est*, north-east, NE, N.E.

nég., *Fin: négociable*, negotiable; **nég. ch. fixe**, *négociable au change fixe*, negotiable at fixed exchange.

nég(t)., *négociant*, wholesaler.

N.E.M.I., *Psy: nouvelle échelle métrique de l'intelligence*.

n. est., *St.Exch: non estampillé*, unstamped.

N.F., 1. *nouveau franc.* **2.** (a) *normalisation française*; (b) *normes françaises* = British standards.

N.F.C., *Fin: nouvelle feuille de coupon*, new sheet of coupons.

N.L., 1. *Astr: nouvelle lune*, new moon. **2.** *Rom.Jur: non liquet*.

N.-N.-E., *nord-nord-est*, north-north-east, NNE, N.N.E.

N.-N.-O., *nord-nord-ouest*, north-north-west, NNW, N.N.W.

NN.SS., *Nosseigneurs*, Monsignori.

NN.TT.CC.FF., *Ecc: nos très chers frères*, dearly beloved brethren.

No, Nº, nº, *numéro*, number, No., no.

N.-O., *nord-ouest*, north-west, NW, N.W.

nom., *Fin: nominatif*, registered (security).

nov, *novembre*, November, Nov.

Np., *Ph: neper*, neper, Np.

N.R.F., *Nouvelle Revue française*.

N.S., *Chr: nouveau style*, new style, N.S.

N.-S. (J.-C.), *Ecc: Notre-Seigneur (Jésus-Christ)*, our Lord (and Saviour) (Jesus Christ).

N.S.-P., *Notre Saint-Père*, our Holy Father.

n/sr, *Com: notre sieur . . .*, our Mr . . ..

nt, *négociant*, wholesaler.

N.T., *Nouveau Testament*, New Testament, N.T.

N.T.C.F., *Ecc: notre très cher frère*, beloved brother.

nte, *négociante*, wholesaler.

n/v., *Com: notre ville*, our town.

N.-W., *Nau: nord-ouest*, north-west, NW, N.W.

O., 1. *ouest*, west, W. **2.** *officiel*, official, off. **3.** *officier*, officer, off.; **O.A.**, *Officier d'Académie·* **O.I.**, *O: Officier de l'Instruction publique*.

o, *Ch: ortho*, ortho, o.

o/. . ., *Fin: à l'ordre de . . .*, to the order of . . ..

O.A.A., *Organisation pour l'alimentation et l'agriculture*, Food and Agriculture Organization, F.A.O.

O.A.C.I., *Organisation de l'aviation civile internationale*.

O.A.S., *Hist: organisation de l'Armée secrète*.

ob(l)., ob(lig)., *Fin: obligation*, debenture.

O.C., *W.Tel: ondes courtes*, short wave, S.W.

O.C.D.E., *Organisation de coopération et de développement économique*, Organization for Economic Co-operation and Development, O.E.C.D.

O.C.E., *Organisation de coopération commerciale*.

oct., *octobre*, October, Oct.

O.E.A., *Organisation des États américains*, Organization of American States, O.A.S.

O.E.C.E., *Organisation européenne de coopération économique*, Organization for European Economic Co-operation, O.E.E.C.

off., 1. *officier*, officer, off. **2.** *offert*, offered.

off.réd., *St.Exch: offres réduites*.

O.I.C., *Organisation internationale du commerce*.

O.I.P.C., *Organisation internationale de police criminelle*, Interpol.

O.I.R., *Organisation internationale pour les réfugiés*, International Refugee Organization, I.R.O.

O.I.T., *Organisation internationale du travail*, International Labour Organization, I.L.O.

O.J.D., *Adm: Office de justification de la diffusion*.

ol., *Pharm: oleum*, oil.

o/m/m., *Fin: à l'ordre de moi-même*, to our own order.

O.M.S., *Organisation mondiale de la santé*, World Health Organization, W.H.O.

O.N.E.R.A., *Office national d'études et de recherches aéronautiques*.

O.N.F., *Fr.C: Office national du film*.

O.N.M., *Office national météorologique* = Central Forecasting Office.

O.-N.-O., *ouest-nord-ouest*, west-north-west, WNW, W.N.W.

O.N.U. [ony], *Organisation des Nations Unies*, United Nations Organization, U.N.O.

op., *Mus: opus*, op.

O.P., 1. *ouvrier professionnel.* **2.** *orientation professionnelle*.

O.P.A. [opa], *Fin: offre publique d'achat*, takeover bid.

op.cit., *opere citato*, in the work quoted, op.cit.

O.P.E., *offre publique d'échange*.

O.P.E.P., *Organisation des pays exportateurs de pétrole*.

O.R., *officier de réserve*, reserve officer.

ord., *ordinaire*, ordinary, ord.

O.R.G.A.N.I.C. [ɔrganik], *caisse de compensation de l'organisation autonome nationale de l'industrie et du commerce*.

O.R.L., *Med: oto-rhino-laryngologie*.

O.R.S.E.C. [ɔrsek], *organisation des secours*.

O.R.T.F., *Office de la radiodiffusion et télévision françaises*.

O.S., *ouvrier spécialisé*, semi-skilled worker.

O.S.B., *Ecc: Ordre de Saint-Benoît*.

O.-S.-O., *ouest-sud-ouest*, west-south-west, WSW, W.S.W.

O.T.A.N. [ɔtɑ̃, ɔtan], *Organisation du traité de l'Atlantique nord*, North Atlantic Treaty Organization, N.A.T.O.

O.T.A.S.E. [ɔtaz], *Organisation du traité de l'Asie du sud-est*, South-East Asia Treaty Organization, S.E.A.T.O.

ouv., *ouverture*, opening.

ov., *Pharm: ovum*, egg.

O.V.N.I. [ovni, ɔvni], *objet volant non identifié*, unidentified flying object, U.F.O.

P., 1. *Ecc: Père*, Father. **2.** *Com: Fin: protesté, protêt*, protested, protest.

P1, P2, P3, . . . *(ouvrier) professionnel (de) premier. deuxième, troisième, échelon*, skilled worker grade 1, 2, 3 . . ..

p., 1. *page*, page, p. **2.** *par*, per, p.; **p. an**, *par an*, per annum, p.a. **3.** *pour*, per; **p. %**, *pour cent*, per cent. **4.** *Meas:* (a) *pied*, foot, ft.; (b) *pouce*, inch, in. **5.** *Fin: papier*, paper. **6.** *Med: pouls*, pulse. **7.** *Ph:* (a) *puissance*, power; (b) *poids*, weight, wt.; (c) *pression*, pressure. **8.** *Pharm: prenez*, take. **9.** *St.Exch: pair*, par. **10.** *Ch: para*, para. **11.** *Mus: piano*, piano, p. **12.** *Fin: prime*, premium, p.

P.A., 1. *propriété assurée*, insured property. **2.** *Com: pour ampliation*, true copy. **3.** *Sm.a: pistolet automatique*, automatic pistol.

P.A.B., *Bio-Ch: acide para-amino-benzoïque*, para-aminobenzoic acid, PABA.

pable, *Com: payable*, payable.

p.æ, *Pharm: partes æquales*, equal parts.

pain, *Corr: prochain*, next (month); proximo, prox.

P.A.S., *Bio-Ch: acide para-amino-salicylique*, para-aminosalicylic acid, P.A.S.

pass., *passim*, in various places.

p.at., *Ch: poids atomique*, atomic weight, at.wt.

P.A.V., *Tp: avec préavis*.

P.-B., *Pays-Bas*, Netherlands.

P.C., 1. *Mil: poste de commandement*, fighting post of headquarters. **2.** *Navy: poste central de conduite de tir*, transmitting station, T.S. **3.** *Pol: parti communiste.* **4.** *Sch: physique et chimie*.

p.c., 1. *pour cent*, per cent. **2.** *pas coté*, unlisted.

p/c., *pour compte*, on account.

P.C.B., *Sch: Certificat d'études physiques, chimiques et biologiques* = the medical preliminary examination.

P.C.C., *pour copie conforme*, true copy.

P.C.F., *Pol: parti communiste français*.

p.cp., *Fin: petites coupures*, small denominations.

P.C.V., *Tp: payable à l'arrivée*; *faire une communication en P.C.V.*, to reverse the charges.

pd, *Meas: pied*, foot, ft.

p.d., *Com: port dû*, carriage forward.

P.D.A., *pour dire adieu*, to say good-bye.

P.D.G., *président directeur général*, chairman.

P.-de-C., *Pas-de-Calais*.

P.-de-D., *Puy-de-Dôme*.

p.é., *Pharm: parts égales*, equal parts.

pel., *Mil: peloton*, squad.

per, *premier*, first.

perp(ét)., *St.Exch: perpétuel*, irredeemable.

P. et C., *Adm: Civ.E: ponts et chaussées*, highway department.

p. et m., *poids et mesures*, weights and measures.

P.E.T. [peete], *Postes et Télécommunications*.

p. ex., *par exemple*, for example, e.g.

P.F., *pour féliciter*, to offer congratulations.

P.F.A.T. [pefat], *Mil: personnel féminin de l'armée de terre* = Women's Royal Army Corps, W.R.A.C.

P.F.S.A., *pour faire ses adieux*, to say good-bye.

P.F.V., *pour faire visite*, to pay a call.

P.G., *prisonnier de guerre*, prisoner of war, P.O.W.

p.g., 1. *Post:* (on telegram) *pour garder*, to be called for; *poste restante.* **2.** *Med: paralysie générale*, general paralysis, G.P.

p.g.c.d., *Ar: plus grand commun diviseur*, highest common factor, H.C.F.

p.g.r., *Post: pour garder recommandée*, registered poste restante.

pH, *Ch: Biol: potentiel hydrogène*, log of reciprocal of hydrogen ion concentration, pH.
ph, *Ph: phot*, ph.
pil., *Pharm: pilule*, pill.
pinx., *Art: pinxit*, (he) painted (it), pinx.
P.J., *police judiciaire* = Criminal Investigation Department, C.I.D.
pl., *planche*, full-page illustration.
P.L., *Astr: pleine lune*, full moon.
P.L.M., *Rail: A: Paris-Lyon-Méditerranée*.
pl. ou m., *plus ou moins*, more or less.
P.M., *Sm.a: pistolet-mitrailleur*, machine pistol.
p.m., 1. *post meridiem*, p.m. 2. *poids mort*, dead weight, d.w.
P.M.(E.), *préparation militaire (élémentaire)* = Combined Cadet Force, C.C.F.
P.M.E., *Confédération générale des petites et moyennes entreprises*.
P.M.F.A.A., *personnel militaire féminin de l'armée de l'air* = Women's Royal Air Force, W.R.A.F.
p. mol., *Ch: poids moléculaire*, molecular weight, mol.wt.
P.M.S., *préparation militaire supérieure* = Senior Training Corps.
P.M.U., *pari mutuel urbain*.
P.N., *Rail: passage à niveau*, level crossing.
P.N.B., *produit national brut*.
Po, *Ph.Meas: poise*, poise.
po., *Meas: pouce*, inch, in.
P.O., 1. *par ordre*, by order. 2. *W.Tel: petites ondes*, medium wave, M.W. 3. *Rail: A: chemin de fer de Paris à Orléans*.
P.-O., *Pyrénées-Orientales*.
pp., *pages*, pages, pp.
P.P., 1. *profits et pertes*. 2. *Ecc: Pères*, Fathers.
p.p., *port payé*, carriage paid, C.P.
P.P.C., *pour prendre congé*, to take leave.
p.p.c.m., *Ar: plus petit commun multiple*, lowest common multiple, L.C.M.
P.P.L., *Ecc: priez pour lui*, pray for him.
P.P.N., *Ecc: priez pour nous*, pray for us.
ppo., *Meas: pouces*, inches, ins.
p. pon, *Com: par procuration*, per procuration, per pro.
p.p.s., *El.E: périodes par seconde*, cycles per second, c.p.s.
P.Q., *Astr: premier quartier*, first quarter.
Pr., *Prince*, Prince, Pr.
pr., 1. *pour*, per, for. 2. *Corr: prochain*, next (month), prox(imo). 3. *Fin: prime*, premium, prm.
P.R., *poste restante*, poste restante.
P.R.A., *Rail: poste tous relais automatiques*.
préc., *précédent*, preceding, prec.
préf., 1. *préfecture*, prefecture. 2. *Fin: préférence*, preference, pref.
priv(il)., *Fin: privilégié*, preferential (share).
prov., 1. *province*, province. 2. *proverbe*, proverb, prov.
P.R.S., *Rail: poste tous relais à transit souple*.
Ps., *Ecc: psaume*, psalm, Ps(a).
P.S., *post scriptum*, postscript, P.S.
p.s., 1. *Ph: poids spécifique*, specific gravity, s.g. 2. *Breed: pur sang*, thoroughbred.
Psse, *Princesse*, Princess.
P.S.U., *Pol: parti socialiste unifié*.
P.S.V., *Av: pilotage sans visibilité*, blind flying.
pte, 1. *Book-k: perte*, loss. 2. *Geog: pointe*, point.
pts, *parts*, parts, pts.
P.T.T., *O: postes, télégraphes et téléphones* = the Post Office, *F:* the G.P.O.
pug., *Pharm: pugillus*, pinch.
pulv., *Pharm: pulvis*, powder.
P.V., 1. *procès-verbal*. 2. *Rail: A: petite vitesse*, per goods train.
pvt, *par voie télégraphique*, by telegraph.

q., 1. *A: carré*, square, sq.; **mmq.**, *millimètre carré*, square millimetre, sq. mm. 2. *quai*, quay. 3. *quantité*, quantity, qnty. 4. *Meas: quintal*, quintal, q.
Q.D., *Psy: quotient de développement*, developmental quotient.
Q.E.D., *Geom: quod erat demonstrandum*, which was to be proved, Q.E.D.
qer, *quartier*, district, dist.
Q.G., *Mil: quartier général*, headquarters, H.Q.
Q.G.A., *Mil: quartier général d'armée*, army headquarters, army H.Q.
Q.G.C.A., *Mil: quartier général de corps d'armée*, army corps headquarters, army corps H.Q.
Q.I., *quotient d'intelligence, intellectuel*, intelligence quotient, I.Q.
qn, *quelqu'un*, someone, s.o.
q.p., *Pharm: quantum placet*, as desired, q.p.
qq., *quelques*, some.
qqf., *quelquefois*, sometimes.
Q.S., *Pharm: quantité suffisante, quod sufficit*, sufficient quantity, q.s., quant. suff.
qt., *Meas: quintal*, quintal, q.
qtaux, *Meas: quintaux*, quintals.
q.v., 1. *Pharm: quantum vis*, as much as desired, q.v. 2. *quod vide*, which see, q.v.
qx, *Meas: quintaux*, quintals.

R., 1. *Clockm: retarder*, slow. 2. *Ecc: répons*, response. 3. *Ph:* (a) *Réaumur*, Reaumur; (b) *röntgen*, röntgen, r. 4. *Fin: report*, report, rep.
r., 1. *rue*, road, Rd. 2. *Com: Fin: reçu*, received, recd. 3. *El: résistance*, resistance. 4. *Med: respiration*, breathing. 5. *Pharm: recipe*, take, t. 6. *Post: recommandé*, registered, regd.
R.A., *Rail: régime accéléré*, by fast goods service.
rac., *Pharm: racine*, root.
R.A.P., *règlement d'administration publique*.
R.Arg., *République Argentine*, Argentine Republic, Arg.Rep.
R.A.T.P., *Régie autonome des transports parisiens*, Paris transport authority.
R.A.U., *République arabe unie*, United Arab Republic, U.A.R.
rb., *Num: rouble*, rouble.
R.C., 1. *registre du commerce*, register of trade. 2. *Sp:* racing-club.
R.C.P., *Mil: régiment de chasseurs parachutistes*.
Rd, *Ecc: Révérend*, Reverend, Rev.
rd, *Mth: radian*, radian.
R.D., *route départementale*.
r.d., *rive droite*, right bank.
R.D.A., *République démocratique allemande*, German Democratic Republic, G.D.R.
R. (du) C., *registre du commerce*, register of trade.
rd.-vs, *rendez-vous*, meeting-place.
Réf., *référence*, reference, ref.
rég., *Mil: régiment*, regiment, Rgt.
rel., *Publ: relié*, bound, bd.
remb., *Fin:* 1. *remboursable*, redeemable, red. 2. *remboursement*, redemption.
rep., *St.Exch: report*, contango.
rép., *Fin: répartition*, allotment.
R.E.P., *Mil: régiment étranger parachutiste*.
R.E.R., *Rail: réseau express régional*.
résid., *résident*, resident.
Revd, *Révérend*, Reverend, Rev.
rev.var., *Com: revenu variable*, income from variable yield investments.
R.F., *République française*, (the) French Republic.
R.F.A., *République fédérale allemande*, Federal Republic of Germany.
R.G., *renseignements généraux*.
r.g., *rive gauche*, left bank.
Rh., *Med: rhésus*, rhesus, Rh.
rH, *Ch:* (*réduction hydrogène*); *potentiel d'oxydoréduction*.
R.I., *Mil: régiment d'infanterie*, infantry regiment.
R.I.P., *requiescat in pace*, may he, she, rest in peace, R.I.P.
R.I.T., *Mil: régiment d'infanterie territoriale*, territorial infantry regiment.
R.M.N., *Ph: résonance magnétique nucléaire*.
R.N., *route nationale*.
Ro, Ro, ro, *recto, recto*, ro.
R.O., *Rail: régime ordinaire*, by goods train.
roy., *royaume*, kingdom.
R.P., 1. *Révérend Père*, Reverend Father; **RR. PP.**, *Révérends Pères*, Reverend Fathers. 2. *Pol: représentation proportionnelle*, proportional representation, P.R. 3. *Post: recette principale*.
r.p., *réponse payée*, reply paid, R.P.
R.P.E., *Ph: résonance paramagnétique électronique*.
R.P.F., *Pol: A: Rassemblement du peuple français*, Rally of the French People.
R.P.I.Ma., *Mil: régiment parachutiste d'infanterie de marine*.
rse, *remise*, discount.
R.S.F.S.R., *République soviétique fédérative socialiste de Russie*, Russian Socialist Federated Soviet Republic, R.S.F.S.R.
R.S.L.P., *réponse s'il leur, lui, plaît*, the favour of their, his answer is requested.
R.S.V.P., *réponse s'il vous plaît*, the favour of an answer is requested, R.S.V.P.
R.-T., *radio-téléphonie*, radio-telephony, r.t.
R.T.F., *A: Radiodiffusion-télévision française*.

S., 1. *sud*, south, S. 2. *Ecc: Saint*, Saint, St. 3. *signum*.
s., 1. *son*, his, her. 2. *signé*, signed. 3. *seconde*, second, sec. 4. *soir*, evening. 5. *Com: sac*, sack. 6. *Geom: surface*, surface. 7. *Meas: stère*, cubic metre, stere, s.
s/, *sur*, on.
S.A., 1. *Com: société anonyme*, limited company. 2. *Son Altesse*, His, Her, Highness, H.H. 3. *German Hist:* (*Sturm Abteilung*) *section d'assaut*, storm troops, S.A.
s.a., *Pharm: secundum artem*, s.a.
S.A.B.E.N.A. [sabena], *Société anonyme belge d'exploitation de la navigation aérienne*.
S.A.E., *Son Altesse Électorale*, His Electoral Highness.
S.A.E(m)., *Son Altesse Éminentissime*, His Most Eminent Highness.
S.A.F.E.R. [safer], *Société d'aménagement foncier et d'équipement rural*.
s.-affl., *sous-affluent*, sub-tributary.
S.A.I., *Son Altesse Impériale*, His Imperial Highness, H.I.H.
S.A.R., *Son Altesse Royale*, His, Her, Royal Highness, H.R.H.
S.A.R.L., *société à responsabilité limitée* = limited liability company.
S.A.S., *Son Altesse Sérénissime*, His Most Serene Highness.
s/b., *Com: son billet*, his bill.

s.b.f., *Bank: sauf bonne fin*, under usual reserve.
sc., 1. *scène*, scene. 2. *sculpsit*, (he) carved (it), sc.
s.c., *St.Exch: seul cours*, sole quotation.
s/c., 1. *Com: son compte*, his account. 2. *Corr: sous le couvert*, under cover.
S.C.C., *Tp: (communication) sur compte courant*, (call) on credit card system.
sd, *Mth: stéradian*.
s.d., *sans date*, no date.
S.D.E.C.E., *Service de documentation étrangère et de contre-espionnage*, French Intelligence and counter-Intelligence Branch.
S.D.N., *Hist: Société des Nations*, League of Nations.
S.E., *Son Excellence*, His Excellency, H.E.
S.-E., *sud-est*, south-east, SE, S.E.
s.e. & o., **s.e. ou o.**, *Com: sauf erreur ou omission*, errors and omissions excepted, E. & O.E.
sec., *seconde*, second (of time), sec.
séc., *Trig: sécante*, secant, sec.
SECAM [sekam], *TV: séquentiel à mémoire*.
sec(t)., *section*, section, sec(t).
S.E.I.T.A. [seita, sɛːta], *Service et exploitation industrielle des tabacs et allumettes*.
S.E(m)., *Son Éminence*, His Eminence, H.E.
sem., *Pharm: semence*, seed.
sept., 1. *septembre*, September, Sept. 2. *septentrional*, northern.
S.-et-L., *Saône-et-Loire*.
S.-et-M., *Seine-et-Marne*.
S.-et-O., *Seine-et-Oise*.
S.E(xc)., *Son Excellence*, His, Her, Excellency, H.E.
sf., *Mus: sforzando*, sfz.
S.F., 1. *Com: sans frais*, no expenses. 2. *Mec.E: système français*, French system (of screw-threads).
S.F.F., *Services féminins de la Flotte* = Women's Royal Naval Service, W.R.N.S.
S.F.I.O., *Pol: section française de l'Internationale ouvrière*.
S.G., 1. *Sa Grâce*, His, Her, Grace, H.G. 2. *Sa Grandeur*, His, Her, Highness, H.H.
S.G.D.G., *sans garantie du gouvernement*, (patent) without government guarantee (of quality).
S.G.D.L., *Société des gens de Lettres*, association of men of letters.
sgt, *Mil: sergent*, sergeant, Serg(t), Sgt.
S.H., 1. *Sa Hautesse*, His, Her, Highness. 2. *Son Honneur*, His, Her, Honour.
S.H.A.P.E. [ʃep], *Pr.n.m.* Supreme Headquarters Allied Powers (Europe).
SI, *système d'unités international*, International System of Units.
S.I., 1. *syndicat d'initiative*, tourist office. 2. *système international (des poids et mesures)*.
S.I.C.A.V. [sikav], *Société d'investissement à capital variable*.
s.i., *St.Exch: sans intérêt*, ex-dividend, ex div.
SIDELOR [sidəlɔr], *Union sidérurgique lorraine*.
S.I.M., *Société internationale de musique*.
S.I.M.C.A. [simka], *Société industrielle de mécanique et carrosserie automobiles*.
sin., *Trig: sinus*, sine, sin.
s.-ing., *sous-ingénieur*, sub-engineer.
sir., *Pharm: sirop*, syrup, syr.
S.J., *Ecc: Societatis Jesu*, of the Society of Jesus, S.J.
s.l., *sauf livraison*, against delivery.
S.L.F., *Pharm: selon la formule*, according to formula.
s.l.n.d., *sans lieu ni date*, of no address and no date.
S.-lt, *Mil: sous-lieutenant*, sub-lieutenant.
S.M., *Sa Majesté*, His, Her, Majesty, H.M.
S.M.A.C., *salaire minimum agricole de croissance*.
S.M.A.G. [smag], *O: salaire minimum agricole garanti*.
S.M.B., *Sa Majesté Britannique*, His, Her, Britannic Majesty, H.B.M.
S.M.C., *Sa Majesté Catholique*, His, Her, Catholic Majesty, H.C.M.
S.M.I., *Sa Majesté Impériale*, His, Her, Imperial Majesty, H.I.M.
S.M.A.C., *salaire minimum interprofessionnel de croissance*.
S.M.I.G. [smig], *O: salaire minimum interprofessionnel garanti* = guaranteed minimum wage.
S.M.R., *Sa Majesté Royale*, His, Her, Royal Majesty.
S.M.S., *Sa Majesté Suédoise*, His, Her, Swedish Majesty.
S.M.T.C., *Sa Majesté Très Chrétienne*, His, Her, Most Christian Majesty.
S.M.T.F., *Sa Majesté Très Fidèle*, His, Her, Most Faithful Majesty.
S.N.C.A. [snɛka], *Société nationale de constructions aéronautiques*.
S.N.C.B., *Société nationale des chemins de fer belges*.
S.N.C.F., *Société nationale des chemins de fer français*.
S.N.E.C.M.A. [snɛkma], *Société nationale d'étude et de construction de moteurs d'avions*.
S.N.E.P., *Société nationale des entreprises de presse*.
S.N.P.A., *Société nationale des pétroles d'Aquitaine*.
S.N.P., *Ch: thiophosphate de diéthyle et de paranitrophényle*, parathion.
s.o., 1. *service officiel*, on official service; = On His, Her, Majesty's Service, O.H.M.S. 2. *sauf omission*, omissions excepted, o.e.
S.-O., *sud-ouest*, south-west, SW, S.W.
s/o., *Com: son ordre*, his order.

S.O.L., *Mil: service d'ordre légionnaire*.
solv., *Pharm: dissolvez*, dissolve, solv.
S.O.S., *W.Tel: Nau: S.O.S.*
S.P., 1. *sapeurs-pompiers*, fire brigade. 2. *service de presse*, publicity department.
S.-P., *Ecc: Saint-Père*, Holy Father, H.F.
S.P.A., *Société protectrice des animaux* = (Royal) Society for the Prevention of Cruelty to Animals, (R.)S.P.C.A.
S.P.C.N., *Sch: Certificat de sciences naturelles, physique et chimie*.
s.-pref., *sous-préfecture*, sub-prefecture.
sq, *sequentia*, following, sq. **sqq.**, *sequentiaque*, and the following.
s.q., *sufficiens quantitas*.
sr, *Com:* 1. *Sieur*, Mr. 2. *successeur*, successor. 3. *Mth: stéradian*.
SS., *Ecc: Saints*, Saints, SS.
ss., 1. *sequentia*, following, sq. 2. *steamer*, steamship, s.s.
S.S., 1. *Sa Seigneurie*, His Lordship. 2. *Sa Sainteté*, His Holiness, H.H. 3. *Ecc: Saint Sacrement*, Holy Sacrament. 4. *Adm: Sécurité Sociale*, National Health Service, N.H.S. 5. *Hist: Schutzstaffel*, S.S.
S.S.B.M., *Mil: Société française de secours aux blessés militaires*.
S.S.B.S., *Mil: sol-sol balistique stratégique*.
S.-S.-E., *sud-sud-est*, south-south-east, SSE, S.S.E.
S.-S.-O., *sud-sud-ouest*, south-south-west, SSW, S.S.W.
S.S.P., *sous seing privé*, under private seal.
SS.PP., *les saints Pères*, the Holy Fathers.
ssq., *sequentia*, following, sqq.
St, 1. *Saint*, Saint, St. 2. *Meas: stokes*, stoke.
st., *stère*, cubic metre, stere, s.
S.T.C.R.P., *A: Société des transports en commun de la région parisienne* = Paris Transport Authority.
Ste, *Sainte*, Saint, St.
Sté, *Com: Société*, Company, Co.
S.T.G.M., *Sa Très Gracieuse Majesté*, His, Her, Most Gracious Majesty.
S.T.O., *Hist: service du travail obligatoire*.
succ., *successeur*, successor, succ.
succle, *succursale*, branch, br.
suiv., *suivant*, following, fol.
sum., *Pharm: summitates*, tops (of plants).
surv., *surveillant*, overseer.
s.v., *St.Exch: sans valeur*, worthless.
S.V.P., *s'il vous plaît*, (if you) please.
svt, *suivant*, following, fol.
S.-W., *Nau: sud-ouest*, SW, S.W.
syr., *Pharm: sirop*, syrup, syr.

T, 1. *Fr.Hist: (Republican calendar) tridi*. 2. *Meas:* (a) *tesla*, tesla, T.; (b) *téra-*. 3. *Com: tare*, tare, t.
t., 1. *tour*, [turn, revolution, rev. **t/mn**. *tours par minute*, revolutions per minute, r.p.m., rpm. 2. *tonneau*, barrel, bar. 3. *tome*, volume, vol. 4. *Fin: titre*, security, stock, stk. 5. *Meas: tonne*, metric ton. 6. *Ph:* (a) *température*, temperature, temp.; (b) *temps*, time. 7. *Turf: toque*, cap.
T/, *Com: traite*, draft, dft.
T.A., *Astr: temps atomique*, atomic time.
T.A.B.D.T., *Med: (vaccins) antityphoparatyphoïdique, diphtérique et tétanique*.
tang., *Trig: tangente*, tangent, tan(g).
t. à v., *Corr: tout à vous*, yours ever.
TBF, *Elcs: très basse fréquence*, very low frequency, VLF.
T.C., *Mil: train de combat*, first line transport, *U.S: combat train*.
t.c., 1. *Post: télégramme collationné*, repetition paid (telegram). 2. *toutes coupures*, all denominations (of bank notes).
T.C.F., 1. *Touring Club de France*. 2. *Ecc: très cher frère*, beloved brother.
T.E., *Astr: temps des éphémérides*, ephemeris time.
TEC, *Meas: tonne-équivalent-charbon*.
T.E.C., *W.Tel: transistor à effet de champ*, Field Effect Transistor, F.E.T.
tel., 1. *télégraphique*, telegraphic. 2. *téléphone*, telephone, tel.
T.E.M., *Mil: train des équipages militaires*, approx. = Royal Corps of Transport, R.C.T.
T.E.P., *Théâtre de l'Est parisien*.
T.-et-G., *Tarn-et-Garonne*.
t.f., *travaux forcés*, hard labour.
tg., *Trig: tangente*, tangent, tan(g).
th., 1. *Geom: théorème*, theorem, theor. 2. *Ph: thermie*, therm.
T.H.T., *Elcs: très haute tension*, very high voltage.
tinct., *Pharm: tincture*, tincture, tinct.
tit., *Fin: titre*, security, stock, stk.
T.I.V., *Tchn: tableau indicateur de vitesse*, speedometer.
t.m., *Post: télégramme multiple*, multiple-address telegram.
TMG, *Astr: temps moyen de Greenwich*, Greenwich mean time, GMT.
T.M.P., *Sch: Certificat de techniques mathématiques de la physique*.
T.N.P., *Théâtre national populaire*.
T.N.T., *Exp: trinitrotoluène*, trinitrotoluene, T.N.T.
T.O.E., *Mil: théâtre d'opérations extérieures*.
tom., *tome*, volume, vol.
T.O.S., *W.Tel: taux d'ondes stationnaires*.
tp, *Meas: tonne-poids*.

T.P., 1. *Sch: travaux pratiques*, practical (work). **2.** *travaux publics*, = Civil engineering.

t.p., *Com: Fin: tout payé*, all expenses paid.

t.-p., *timbre-poste*, stamp.

T.P.E., *travaux publics de l'État*.

t.p.m., *Mec.E: tours par minute*, revolutions per minute, rpm, r.p.m.

T.P.S.F., *O: téléphonie sans fil*, wireless telephony, W.T.

tr., 1. *Fin: traite*, draft, dft. **2.** *tour*, revolution, rev.

t.r., *Bookb: tranches rognées*, with cut edges.

tra, *Pharm: tinctura*, tincture, tinct.

trav.pub., *travaux publics*, public works.

trs, *Fin: traites*, drafts.

T.S., *tarif spécial*, special rate.

T.S.F., *téléphonie sans fil; F: la T.S.F.*, the wireless; *F: une T.S.F.*, a wireless set; *F: O: un T.S.F.*, a radio operator.

T.S.S., *Ecc: Très Saint Sacrement*, Most Holy Sacrament.

T.S.V.P., *tournez s'il vous plaît*, please turn over, P.T.O.

t.t., *St.Exch: transfert télégraphique*, transfer by telegraph, T.T.

t.t.c., *toutes taxes comprises*.

T.T.D., *Ch: tétra-éthyle thiurane disulfure*, tetraethylthiuran disulphide.

T.U., *Hor: temps universel*, Greenwich mean time, GMT.

T.V., *télévision*, television, T.V.

T.V.A., *taxe à, sur, la valeur ajoutée*, value added tax, V.A.T.

tx, *Com: tonneaux*, barrels.

u., *unité*, unit.

U.C.I., *union cycliste internationale*.

U.C.P.A., *Union des centres de plein air*.

U.D.S.R., *Union démocratique et socialiste de la résistance*.

U.D.T., *Union démocratique du travail*.

U.E.O., *Union de l'Europe occidentale*, Western European Union, W.E.U.

U.E.P., *Union européenne des paiements*, European Payments Union, E.P.U.

U.E.R., *Union européenne de radiodiffusion*, European Broadcasting Union, E.B.U.

U.I.C., *Union internationale des chemins de fer*, International Union of Railways, I.U.R.

U.I.T., *Union internationale des télécommunications*, International Telecommunication Union, I.T.U.

un., *unité*, unit.

U.N.C., *Union nationale des anciens combattants*, National Union of Ex-service-men.

U.N.E.F. [ynɛf], *Union nationale des étudiants de France*.

U.N.E.S.C.O. [ynɛsko], *Organisation des Nations Unies pour l'éducation, la science et la culture*, United Nations Educational, Scientific and Cultural Organization, U.N.E.S.C.O., UNESCO.

ung., *Pharm: unguentum*, ointment, ung(t).

U.N.I.C.A. [ynika], *Union internationale de cinéma amateur*.

U.N.I.C.E.F., United Nations international children's emergency fund.

U.N.R., *Pol:* **1.** *Union nationale de la résistance*. **2.** *Union pour la nouvelle république*.

U.N.R.R.A. [ynra, unra], *Administration des Nations Unies pour la reconstruction et l'assistance*, the United Nations Relief and Rehabilitation Administration, U.N.R.R.A., UNRRA.

U.P., *Union postale*, Postal Union.

U.P.U., *Union postale universelle*, Universal Postal Union, U.P.U.

U.R.F., *Rail: Union des services routiers des chemins de fer européens*.

U.R.S.S. [yrs], *Union des républiques socialistes soviétiques*, Union of Soviet Socialist Republics, U.S.S.R.

U.R.S.S.A.F. [yrsaf], *Union pour le recouvrement des cotisations de Sécurité Sociale et d'allocations familiales*.

U.S.A., *(les), États-Unis*, (the) United States, U.S.A.

U.S.F.S.A., *Union des Sociétés Françaises de Sports Athlétiques*.

U.T., *Rail: unité technique des chemins de fer*.

U.T.A., *Av: Union des transports aériens*.

U.V., *ultraviolet*, ultraviolet, U.V.

V., *El: volt*, volt, v.

v., 1. *voyez, voir*, see. **2.** *votre*, your, yr. **3.** *Ecc: verset*, verse, v. **4.** *Mec: vitesse*, speed, sp. **5.** *Ph: volume*, volume, vol. **6.** *St.Exch: vendez*, sell; *vendeurs*, sellers. **7.** *Mus:* (a) *violon*, violin, v.; (b) *volti*, turn.

VA, *volt-ampère*, volt-ampere, va; *Votre Altesse*, Your Highness.

v/., val., *Fin: valeur*, security, stock, stk.

val.déc., *Cust: etc: valeur déclarée*, declared value.

vap., *vapeur* (i) steam, (ii) steamer, s.

V.B., *Rail: Service de la voie et des bâtiments*.

V.-C., *Vice-Consul*, Vice-Consul, V.C.

v/c., *Com: Fin: votre compte*, your account.

V.-C.G., *Vice-Consul Général*, Vice-Consul General.

Vcte, *Vicomte*, Viscount, Vis(c).

Vctesse, *Vicomtesse*, Viscountess, Vis(c).

V.D.Q.S., *vin délimité de qualité supérieure*.

Ve, *veuve*, widow.

V.É(m)., *Votre Éminence*, Your Eminence.

vend., *vendredi*, Friday, Fri.

V.E(xc)., *Votre Excellence*, Your Excellency.

V.G., 1. *Votre Grâce*, Your Grace. **2.** *Votre Grandeur*, Your Highness.

vg(e), *village*, village.

V.H., 1. *Votre Honneur*, Your Honour. **2.** *Votre Hautesse*, Your Highness.

v.h., *Corr: votre honorée*, your letter.

virt, *Fin: virement*, transfer, tfr.

V.M., *Votre Majesté*, Your Majesty.

vo, *verso*, back of the page, vo.

vol., *volume*, volume, vol.

V.R.D., *Const: voirie, réseaux divers*.

V.R.P., *Com: voyageur, représentant, placier*.

V.S., 1. *Votre Sainteté*, Your Holiness. **2.** *Votre Seigneurie*, Your Lordship. **3.** *Chr: vieux style*, old style.

V.T., *O: Navy: vedette torpilleur*, coastal motor boat, C.M.B.

Vte, *Vicomte*, Viscount, Vis(c).

vte, *vente*, sale.

Vtesse, *Vicomtesse*, Viscountess, Vis(c).

V.T.T., *Mil: véhicule transport de troupes*, troop carrier.

v/v., *Com: votre ville*, your town.

Vve, *veuve*, widow.

VV.MM., *Vos Majestés*, Your Majesties.

VV.NN.PP., *Vos Nobles Puissances*, Your Noble Powers.

W., 1. *El: watt*, watt, w. **2.** *Nau: ouest*, west, W.

wb, *Ph: weber*, weber, wb.

W.C., w.c. [vese], *water-closet*, water-closet, W.C.

wh., *El: watt(s)-heure*, watt-hour(s), wh.

W.L., *Rail: wagons-lits*, sleeping-cars.

W.R., *Rail: wagons-restaurants*, dining-cars.

wtt, *El: watt*, watt, w.

X., *nom*, name.

x.bon., *St.Exch: ex-bonification*, ex bonus.

Xbre, *décembre*, December, Dec.

x.c(oup)., *St.Exch: ex-coupon*, ex coupon, x.c.

x.d., *St.Exch: ex-dividende*, ex dividend, x.d.

x.dr., *St.Exch: ex-droits*, ex rights.

X.P., *Post: exprès payé*, express paid.

Z.A.D., *Adm: zone à aménagement différé*.

Z.I., *zone industrielle*, industrial area.

Z.U.P., *Adm: zone à urbaniser en priorité*.

%, *pour cent*, per cent, %.

°/oo, *pour mille*, per thousand, °/oo.

7bre, *A: septembre*, September.

8bre, *A: octobre*, October.

9bre, *A: novembre*, November.

Xbre, *A: décembre*, December.